BIOGRAPHICAL MAP

Shown here are some interesting biographical events in the histories of the fifty states. The events are not necessarily the most important . . . but they suggest the greatness and diversity of America's historic "who's."

STANDARD
AMERICAN
SELECTIVE
BIOGRAPHICAL
REFERENCE
THE A. N. MARQUIS COMPANY
FOUNDED 1897

WHO'S WHO IN AMERICAN HISTORY

®

CONSISTING OF:

I WHO WAS WHO IN AMERICA

THE HISTORICAL VOLUME (1607-1896)

Now again available in the Revised Edition (1967)
702 pages; 13,450 biographies
(Consisting of originally researched data)

THE FIRST VOLUME (1897-1942)

Now again available in the Sixth Printing (1966)
1,408 pages; 27,458 biographies
(Drawing from Vols. 1-21, inclusive, of "Who's Who")

THE SECOND VOLUME (1943-1950)

Now again available in the Fifth Printing (1966)
614 pages; 8,500 biographies
(Drawing from Vols. 22-26, inclusive, of "Who's Who")

THE THIRD VOLUME (1951-1960)

Now again Available in the Third Printing (1966)
959 pages; 12,828 biographies
(Drawing from Vols. 26-31, inclusive, of "Who's Who")

II WHO'S WHO IN AMERICA

THE CONTEMPORARY VOLUME

MARQUIS—WHO'S WHO
INCORPORATED

WHO WAS WHO
®
IN AMERICA

HISTORICAL VOLUME
1607—1896

Revised Edition, 1967

A COMPONENT VOLUME OF
WHO'S WHO IN AMERICAN HISTORY

A compilation of sketches of individuals, both of the United States of America and other countries, who have made contribution to, or whose activity was in some manner related to, the history of the United States, from the founding of Jamestown Colony to the year of continuation by VOLUME I of WHO WAS WHO.

MARQUIS WHO'S WHO
INCORPORATED
(The A. N. Marquis Company—Founded 1897)
Marquis Publications Building
CHICAGO, ILLINOIS 60611

Library of Congress Catalogue Card Number 43-3789

HISTORICAL VOLUME
(1607-1896)

Manufactured in The United States of America
by the Von Hoffmann Press, Inc., St. Louis, Missouri

TABLE OF CONTENTS

ACKNOWLEDGEMENTS

Grateful acknowledgement is accorded the many persons and groups who offered suggestions and nominated listees—most notably the following sponsors of the HISTORICAL VOLUME: Arkansas Historical Society; State of Colorado, Division of State Archieves and Public Records; State of Delaware Public Archieves Commission; Idaho Historical Society; Kansas State Historical Society; State Historical Society of Missouri; Historical Society of Montana; Nebraska State Historical Society; Pennsylvania Federation of Historical Societies; Clifford P. Monahon, Director, Rhode Island Historical Society; William T. Alderson, State Librarian and Archivist, Tennessee State Library and Archives; James L. Hupp, State Historian and Archivist; West Virginia Department of Archives and History; and the State Historical Society of Wisconsin; and Benjamin F. Goldstein of Chicago, for his steadfast encouragement and valuable advice.

Without the enthusiastic devotion of the Marquis—Who's Who staff, the idea of this book and the objectives of its compilation could not have been realized. Effort beyond the call of duty was required and freely given . . . to achieve the wide coverage and accuracy warranted by the subject. Everyone at Marquis contributed, but without the following there would have been no HISTORICAL VOLUME: David Martindell, whose conception it was; D. B. T. Freeman, Director of Research; his assistants, Mary P. Sliepka and Suzanne K. Thomas; his historical staff consisting of Wallace F. Tangwall, Chief Historian; George H. Davis, Assistant Chief Historian, and Historians Lester Lee Balick, Richard Becker, Peter Fiore, Albert J. Kearney, James E. Klodzinski, Robert Horace Richheimer, Howard Rosen, and Boyd Keith Swigger; Oscar B. Treiman, Director of Production; Diane Merring Seidler, Director of Sketch Writing, and her staff composed of Jean Bassan, Ann Lewis, Frances Sheldon, and Jean Smith; Barbara Wardell Galgoul, Chief Editor, and her assistants Juanita Wilson and Rose Konya; Lucille Lewis, head of the Order Department, who made available valuable material on eminent Negro Americans; Elizabeth Pedersen, Administrative Assistant; Betty Cahill, Director of Compilation; Madelynn Corbett and Jacqueline Strazzabosco. The project was under the general direction of Kenneth N. Anglemire, Executive Vice President of Marquis—Who's Who.

Our thanks go, too, to the university, public and historical librarians who obligingly and efficiently assisted in our procurement of obscure books, theses and maps.

The Publisher

THE COURSE OF HISTORY

Time-Line Chart

The chronological chart — extending from Leif Ericsson's time to 1963 — is intended both for ready reference and for historical-biographical perspective. For each period except 1100 to 1449, a representative individual in American history is named at the far left; the thumbnail facts below his name are only for the specific period. In adjoining panels are listed other principal names, events and accomplishments of the era or decade . . . in America and abroad, and in all fields of endeavor. The factual order in each panel is not necessarily by importance or date. Names in the Arts and Thought, Science and Invention generally are mentioned only once; an exception is made with individuals who distinguished themselves both in the sciences and humanities, like Leonardo da Vinci or Blaise Pascal.

THE COURSE OF HISTORY

KEY NAME AND ERA	HISTORICAL AND GENERAL EVENTS: AMERICAN	HISTORICAL AND GENERAL EVENTS: FOREIGN	THE ARTS AND THOUGHT	SCIENCE AND INVENTION
950-1099 A. D. LEIF ERICSSON Trip to Norway from Greenland home, conversion to Christianity, circa 999. Three voyages to N. Am., perhaps to spread faith; "Vinland" landing on 3d trip.	**The Indian:** tribal life, classified social structures, intertribal strife, agrarian pursuits, ceremonies, crafts. **Cliff Dweller** civilization in S. W.—community housing on cliffs (for protection), ceremonial chambers ("kivas"), irrigation, pottery, trade.	**Holy Roman Empire,** based on feudalism; papal crowning of Otto the Great as 1st emperor, 962. **Voyages:** Greenland settlement by Eric the Red (father of Leif Ericsson) in 980's after exile from Norway; Thorfinn Karlsefni landing at Baffin Is., 1004. **Norway:** Olaf Tryggvason seizure of crown, circa 995, and effort to spread Christianity. **England:** rule by Danish King Canute, 1017; by Wm. of Normandy after Battle of Hastings, 1066. **France:** struggle by Capetian dynasty to control robber barons, develop commerce. **Spain:** conquests by Al-Mansur for Omayyad caliphs. First Crusade against Islam, 1095-99.	**Foreign:** Philosophy: scholasticism (St. Anselm). Literature: manuscript of Beowulf, Eng. epic, circa 1000; Song of Roland, Fr. epic; Lady Murasaki's "Tale of Genji" (Jap. novel); Rubaiyat verses (attrib. to Persian mathematician Omar Khayyam). Music: Guido d'Arezzo's notation system. Architecture: Byzantine (St. Mark's cath., Venice); Romanesque (Pisa cath.).	**Foreign:** Arabian strides: Medicine (Avicenna's Canon of Med.; Abu'l-Qasim). Astronomy (Al-Biruni, Ibn Yunus). Trigonometry (Abu'l-Wafa). Optics (Ibn al-Haytham). Christian Europe: Gerbert (later Pope Sylvester II): introduction Arabic numerals, astrolabe. Med. sch., Montpellier, France (probable Jewish participation).
1100-1449	**S. W. Indians:** end Cliff Dweller period, circa 1300, after drought, Navaho and Apache invasions; succession by Pueblo villages (inc. Zuni "Seven Cities of Cibola").	**Scandinavia:** civil strife; econ. aggression by Hanseatic League (Ger. towns). **England:** Slaying of St. Thomas a Becket, Arch. Canterbury, by King Henry II partisans, 1170; King John's signing of Magna Carta, assuring baronial privileges, 1215; Scot. independence (Robt. Bruce), 14th cent. **Italy:** civil strife, Guelphs vs. Ghibellines. **Spain:** gradual Christian subdual of Moors (victory at Navas de Tolosa, 1212). **Crusades:** 2d thru 9th, 1147-1272, kindling Western interest in Near East; disastrous Children's Crusade, 1212. **Hundred Years War,** England vs. France, from 1337. (Joan of Arc burning at stake, 1431.) **Plague:** "Black Death" of 1/4 to 3/4 of Europe, from 1347. **Feudalism:** on wane in W. Europe at end of 14th cent. as towns, trade, centralized power grow. **Voyages:** Marco Polo in China, India, 13th cent.; Prince Henry of Portugal explorations into Africa, early	**Foreign:** Philosophy, theology: 12th cent. scholastics (Abelard vs. St. Bernard of Clairvaux; Peter Lombard's "Sentences") . . . Maimonides on Jewish law, metaphysics . . . Ibn Khaldun on social history . . . Aristotelian study by Averroes, Span. Arab . . . scholastic reconciliation Aristotle, Christianity (Grosseteste, St. Albertus Magnus; St. Thomas Aquinas' "Summa Theologica," 1267-73) . . . anti-Thomism (St. Bonaventure, Duns Scotus, Wm. of Occam) . . . growth of Franciscans, Spirituals. N. Eur. litt: Nibelungenlied, Ger. epic, circa 1160; Wolfram's Parzival . . . Mid. Eng. poetry ("Piers Plowman;" Chaucer's "Canterbury Tales") . . . Wycliffe Bible. Universities: founding, 13th cent., of Oxford, Cambridge, Sorbonne, Padua. Forerunners, Ital. Renaissance: Dante ("Commedia," 1302-21); humanist writers Petrarch, Boccaccio; painters Cimabue, Giotto. Early Renaissance, chiefly in Florence: painters—Angelico frescoes; Uccello, Masaccio perspective; sculptors—Ghiberti portals, Donatello vitality; architect Brunelleschi (Florence cath. dome); humanist critic Valla. Visual arts elsewhere: Gothic arch. (Notre Dame cath., Paris, 1163-1345); Moorish (Alhambra, Spain, comp. 1354) . . . Flem. sch. painting (the Van Eycks). Music: minnesingers, troubadours . . . religious plays with music . . . "Ars Nova" refinements (de Vitry, Machaut) . . . pioneer counterpoint (Leonin, Perotin, Dufay, Dunstable). Jap. Noh plays: Motokiyo et al., 15th cent.	**Foreign:** Ibn Ezra ("Rabbi Ben Ezra"): math., astronomy. Fibonacci: improvements, math. notation. Peregrinus: magnetism, primitive compass. Roger Bacon: experimental medicine, optics; gunpowder formula, 1249. Bradwardine: application math. to physics. Oresme: ballistics laws, 1382. Buridan: inertial theory of motion. Nicholas of Cusa: invention hygrometer (moisture measurer), bathometer (water-depth measurer), 1440. Other inventions: small guns (used at Battle of Crecy, 1346); modern ship rudder.

1450-1499 CHRISTOPHER COLUMBUS

Support from Span. throne for Atlantic voyage to "East." Sighting of New World, 1492.

Indian population north of Mexico an est. 1,000,000 in 1492 (will shrink to 300,000 by 1870). John Cabot arrival, Cape Breton Is., N. S., 1497; claim for Eng. King Henry VII.

Constantinople: siege, conquest by Mohammed II, Turks, 1453.
Spain: Marriage, Ferdinand of Aragon, Isabella of Castile, 1469; seizure Granada from Moors; start of Span. Inquisition; division New World, Africa, Asia with Portugal in Treaty of Tordesillas, 1494.
England: end War of the Roses (Lancaster vs. York noble houses) with Henry VII coronation, 1485 (Tudor dynasty).
France: emergence as nat. state under Louis XI.
Florence, Italy: virtual rule, art patronage, by Medici merchant princes; hanging of Savonarola, 1498, after his assaults on vice, authority.
Portugal: Vasco de Gama sea route to India via Cape of Good Hope, 1498.

Foreign:
Early to High Renaissance: painters—Piero della Francesca, Mantegna, Gio. Bellini, Verrocchio, Perugino, Ghirlandaio, Botticelli's flowing contours, Leonardo da Vinci ("Last Supper" comp. 1498); writers—Alberti on Roman architecture, Pico della Mirandola on philosophy. England: Morality plays ("Everyman"). France: Villon's poetic anguish . . . Fouquet's paintings. Spain: Encina's dramas, songs. Polyphonic music: Netherlands, Flem. schs. (Okeghem, Obrecht).

Foreign:
Movement Byzantine scientists, from Constantinople to Italy. Regiomentanus: planetary motion tables, comet study. Gutenberg: printing from movable type (Mazarin Bible, circa 1456). Math. advances: trigonometry (Puerbach); comml. arithmetic (Chiarino); algebra (Chuquet, Widman); Pacioli's "Summa," pub. 1494. Enlarged cannon: use in Constantinople siege.

1500-1549 HERNANDO DE SOTO

Gov. Cuba, 1537-42. Fla. landing, 1539. Discovery Mississippi River, 1541; burial in it, 1542.

Columbus' 4th voyage, W. Indies, 1502.
Other New World explorers, conquistadors: Amerigo Vespucci; Balboa (discoverer Pac. Ocean); Magellan; Cortez (conqueror Aztecs, Mex.); Pizzaro (conqueror Incas, Peru); Cartier (disc. St. Lawrence R.).
Discoveries, future U. S.: Fla. by Ponce de Leon; Southwest by Fray Marcos, Coronado; Grand Canyon by Cardenas; San Diego Bay by Cabrillo.

Reformation: Luther's posting 95 theses, Wittenberg, 1517; Zwingli's 67 theses, Zurich; Calvin's teachings, Geneva.
Catholic Reform: founding Soc. of Jesus (St. Ignatius of Loyola), 1534-41; Council of Trent on doctrine, from 1545.
England: Henry VIII kingship, 1509-47; estab. Ch. of Eng., 1530's; fighting with Scotland, France.
Spain, Holy Roman Empire: domain "where sun never set" under Chas. V; victories vs. France in Ital. Wars.
Germany: suppression peasant revolt, prolongation serfdom.
Portugal: commercial rise.
Sweden: modern emergence under Gustavus I.

Foreign:
High Renaissance: Art—Michelangelo power in "Last Judgment;" Giorgione, Raphael tenderness; Sarto, Correggio. Arch.—Bramante designs, St. Peter's Rome; Sansovino classicism in Venice. Writing—Castiglione social comment, Machiavelli polit. realism ("The Prince"), Guicciardini history. Philosophy: humanism (Erasmus' "Praise of Folly;" Bude; More's "Utopia"), Thomism (Cajetan). N. Eur. art: mystic intensity (Bosch, Durer, Grunewald); portraits (Holbein). France: Fontainebleau Palace; Lescot's designs for Louvre . . . Rabelais' serious ribaldry ("Gargantua and Pantagruel"). Music: madrigals . . . Sachs mastersongs . . . polyphonic enrichment (Josquin des Pres) . . . Lutheran chorales.

Foreign:
Renaissance versatility: da Vinci work on hydrostatics, diffraction, capillarity, flying machines. Copernicus, "Scientific Revolution": heliocentricity, earth revolution around sun. Tartaglia: application math. to artillery. Nunes: angle-measurement instrument. Agricola: classification, minerals. Paracelsus: new medicines. Fuchs: list of edible, medicinal plants. Vesalius: accurate anatomy.

1550-1599 SIR FRANCIS DRAKE

Marauding expeditions against Span. Amer. (St. Augustine, Fla., 1586). Exploration Pacific coast—likely San Francisco Bay.

Founding St. Augustine, oldest U. S. city, by Menendez, 1565.
Raleigh expeditions to Roanoke Is., N. C.; 2d (1587) "the lost colony."

Religious controversy: England—Queen Mary I effort to restore Cath. authority; succession by Eliz. I, Anglican. Scotland—Knox leadership of Reformation, Presbyterianism. France—St. Bartholomew's Day massacre of Huguenots, 1572; Edict of Nantes granting religious freedom, 1598.
Battle of Lepanto, 1571: Papal, Span., Venetian victory against Turk. naval threat to Mediterranean.
Portugal: absorption by Spain, 1580.
Span. Armada (130 ships) vs. Eng., 1588: destruction by Drake (and storms).

Foreign:
Late Renaissance:
Venice: Painting—Titian, Tintoretto, Veronese splendor. Music—Gabrielis' sumptuousness; Zarlino treatises on counterpoint, harmony. Arch.—Palladio. Rome: Painting—Caravaggio naturalism. Music—Palestrina demonstration of contrapuntal dignity (Pope Marcellus Mass). Florence: Cellini autobiography. Opera—true beginnings by "camerata" group at Count Bardi house (Peri's "Dafne," 1597). Spain: El Greco dynamism in art. Escorial, built 1563-84. England: Spenser allegorical verse ("Faerie Queen") . . . Lyly, Marlowe plays . . . Francis Bacon essays . . . Tallis, Byrd ch. music. France: Montaigne essays . . . Ronsard, Pleiade group, in poetry . . . Bodin on sovereignty. Flanders: Art—Brueghel the Elder folk realism. Music—Lassus polyphony.

Foreign:
Brahe: positions of planets, stars. Gilbert: magnetism; coinage term, "electrics." Viete: symbolic algebra. Mercator: cylindrical projection of maps.

1600-1634 WILLIAM BRADFORD

Plymouth Rock landing with other Separatists, 1620. Gov. Plymouth Colony, from 1621. Promoter of prosperity, friendship with Indians.

Footholds of rival Eur. powers:
England: Gosnold visit New Eng., 1602. London Co. party (inc. John Smith) to Jamestown, Va., 1607 (1st continuing Eng. settlement). Mass. Bay Colony (Salem, 1628). Md. settlement, 1633.
Netherlands: Hudson's voyage up Hudson R. for Dutch East India Co., 1609. Minuit purchase, Manhattan Is., from Indians, 1626.
Spain: Peralta's founding Santa Fe, N. M., 1609.
France: Champlain's discovery of lake bearing his name, 1609; rout of Iroquois nr. Crown Point, N. Y.
Negro slaves: 1st shipload, Va., 1619. 1st legislature: Ho. Burgesses, Va., 1619.

National, religious, social-class struggles in Europe.
Eng., Scotland: James I king of both lands; infuriation of Catholics, Puritans; dissolution of Puritan-inclined Parliament, 1611.
Thirty Years War, from 1618: petty Ger. princes, Sweden, France, Eng., Denmark vs. Holy Roman Empire, Hapsburgs.
France: Richelieu absolutism.
Russia: fall of Boris Godunov, 1605; Romanov dynasty, from 1613.

Foreign:
England: King James Bible, comp. 1611. Drama—Shakespeare's "Hamlet;" Jonson, Dekker, Ford, Beaumont & Fletcher; Webster, Tourneur "tragedies in blood." "Metaphysical poetry"—Donne, Herbert. Philosophy—Burton's "Anatomy of Melancholy." Arch.—Inigo Jones. Music: Monteverdi's mus., dramatic enhancement of opera ("Orfeo," 1607). Ger. oratorio (Schutz). Art: Ital. baroque (Guido Reni). Flem. vigor in human portrayal (Rubens, Van Dyck). Spain: Cervantes' "Don Quixote;" Lope de Vega dramatic verve. Rome: Inquisition burning of Bruno, infinity theorist, 1600.

Foreign:
Big thrust toward modernism in understanding of universe.
Kepler: ellipse, planetary motion laws, refraction. Galileo: astronomical telescope; Jupiter satellite, sun spot findings; confimation Copernicus on heliocentricity. Francis Bacon: inductive sci. method ("Novum Organum," 1620). Harvey: blood circulation. Napier: logarithm tables. Gunter: quadrant anticipating slide rule. Van Helmont: carbon dioxide; "gas" definition.

KEY NAME AND ERA	HISTORICAL AND GENERAL EVENTS AMERICAN	 FOREIGN	THE ARTS AND THOUGHT	SCIENCE AND INVENTION
1635-1669 ROGER WILLIAMS Banishment from Mass. Bay Colony, 1635, after challenging civil authority over religion. Founder Providence, R. I., 1636.	Religious intolerance: Anne Hutchinson banishment from Mass. Bay Colony, 1637. Boston deportation of Quaker immigrants, 1656. Massacre of Pequot Indians, 1637, after murder of Eng. trader. New Eng. Confed., 1643—1st federal experiment in Amer. New Netherland: Stuyvesant, Dutch surrender to Brit. Col. Nicolls.	Eng., Scotland: Civil war—defeat of Chas. I by Puritan, Parliament forces, 1644-45. Commonwealth govt. (Cromwell, Lord protector, 1653-58). Chas. II kingship, from 1660. Great Plague, London, 1665. End, Thirty Years War (Peace of Westphalia, 1648): wider domain to Louis XIV's France, Sweden; breakup of Holy Roman Empire; setback to Ger. economy, growth. Portuguese independence from Spain, 1640.	American: First coll.—Harvard—1636. Moral verse: Anne Bradstreet, Wigglesworth. Eliot's Indian Bible, 1663. Foreign: Thought: Hobbes plea for responsible absolute monarchy. Descartes on dualism of mind, physical world. Spinoza pantheism. Rise of Jansenist theology; Pascal's "Pensees." Browne on faith, death. Milton's "Paradise Lost," 1667. French classicism: Corneille tragedies. Moliere comedy. Poussin, Claude Lorrain paintings. La Rochefoucauld maxims. Fran. Mansard architecture. Dutch art: Rembrandt's self-expression. Vermeer, Hals, Steen sense of burgher life. Spain: Valazquez realism in court painting. Murillo religious art. Calderon philos. drama. Baroque adornment, Rome: Bernini sculpture, fountains.	Foreign: Descartes: combined algebra, geom. concepts (prelude to calculus). Torricelli: atmospheric pressure proof, barometer. Pascal: calculating machine, theory of probabilities, pressure principle. Fermat: theory of numbers. Redi: evidence against spontaneous generation. Huygens: astronomical findings; clock pendulum. Malphigi: blood vessel, respiration studies. Hevelius: moon's surface, phases of Mercury. Swammerdam: discovery red-blood corpuscles. Guericke: air pump, evacuated spheres, elec. charge. Boyle: chem. element-compound distinction; gas pressure, volume law.
1670-1699 WILLIAM PENN Creation of havens for Quakers. Provision of civil, religious liberty for W. Jersey colony, 1677, Pa., 1682. "Love and regard" for Indians.	French exploration, Miss R: Marquette, Joliet; La Salle claim, lower Miss. val. for Louis XIV, 1682. Nat. Bacon, yeomen's futile revolt against Va. Gov. Berkeley, aristocracy, 1676. King Philip's War: Indians vs. New Eng. colonists, 1675-76. King William's War, 1689-97: French-incited Indian attacks on New Eng., Schenectady. Witchcraft hysteria, Salem, Mass., 1692: 19 hangings.	Eng., Scotland: overthrow James II. Wm. and Mary accession; acceptance of Bill of Rights (giving Parliament supremacy). France: Louis XIV absolute rule. Successes, reverses in W. Eur. conflicts caused partly by colonial, trade rivalry. Renewed persecution of Huguenots. Vienna: repulse (with Polish aid) of Turkish siege, 1683. Russia: Peter the Great's Westernization, expansion program.	American: Arch: colonial style (Williamsburg, Va.), Wren influence. Writings: Cotton Mather's witchcraft "evidence." Edw. Taylor metaphysical poetry. Foreign: England: Phil.—Locke's foundations of empiricism, belief in constl. monarchy. Lit.—laureate Dryden's dominance; Bunyan's "Pilgrim's Progress." Opera—Purcell's "Dido and Aeneas." Arch.—Wren (St. Paul's Cath., London). French classicism in full flower: Racine tragedies. Mme. de la Fayette psychological novel. La Fontaine fables. Fenelon philosophy. Malebranche occasionalism. Fr. Baroque arch: J. H. Mansard's Paris planning. Perrault. Continental music: Lully dominance, Fr. opera. Corelli's developments in solo sonata, concerto grosso; Torelli's in solo concerto. Dutch landscape painting: Ruisdael, Hobbema.	Foreign: Newton (culmination Sci. Revolution): "Principia Mathematica," 1787; laws motion, gravitation. Calculus development, independently, by Newton, Leibniz. Roemer: speed of light. Cassini: parallax of Mars, distance of sun. Sydenham: epidemiology, clinical med. Leeuwenhoek: discoveries of protozoa, bacteria.
1700-1734 JAMES EDWARD OGLETHORPE Mem. Brit. Ho. Commons, from 1722. Founder Ga. colony (Savannah, 1733) as asylum for debtors, defense against Spanish.	Queen Anne's War, 1702-13: attacks by S. Carolinians on Span. St. Augustine, by New Eng. troops on Fr. Can. Deerfield (Mass.) Massacre, 1704, by Fr. soldiers, Indians. First regular newspaper: Postmaster Campbell's Boston News-Letter, 1704. Slave revolt, N. Y. C., 1712; 21 executions. Molasses Act, 1733: duty on non-Brit. sugar, circumvention by smuggling.	Britain: Gain of Gibraltar from Spain, 1704. Relative peace between Geo. I (king from 1714), Louis XV's France. Evolution of prime ministry under Robt. Walpole, Whigs. Prussia: emergence as kingdom, 1701 (Fred. I). Russia: Peter the Great's conquests in Baltic area, defeats in south. Colonial speculation failures: South Sea Bubble, Miss. Bubble.	American: Writings—Calef vs. Mather, witchcraft; Eben. Cook satire. Arch.—Independence Hall, Phila. (And. Hamilton). Foreign: Baroque music peak: "opera seria" development (Alex. Scarlatti); Couperin harpsichord suites; Vivaldi 3-part concertos; Bach passions ("St. Matthew," 1729); Handel operas, oratorios; Pergolesi's "opera buffa;" Rameau tone colors. Philosophy: Berkeley's subjective idealism. Leibniz monadology. Vico on hist. cycles. Theology: Methodism (Wesley bros., Whitefield). Brit. satire: Congreve, Pope, Addison & Steele, Swift ("Gulliver's Travels," 1726), Gay's "Beggar's Opera." Chronicles, seminal Eng. novel: Defoe. Fr. baroque art: Watteau; sculptor Girardon.	Foreign: Bernoulli bros.: theory of probability, applied calculus. Halley: comet-reappearance prediction. Newcomen, Calley: steam engine for mine use. Fahrenheit: accurate thermometer. Du Fay, Nollet: positive, negative electricity. De Moivre: probability tables.
1735-1769 BENJAMIN FRANKLIN Pub. Poor Richard's Almanack. Lightning experiment, 1752. Inventions. Dep. postmaster gen. of colonies, from	Freedom of press milestone: Zenger acquittal, 1735. Alaska discovery: Bering, 1741. King George's War, 1744-48: colonist victory vs. French at Louisburg, N. S. French & Indian War: Geo.	Britain: King Geo. III, from 1760; Tory prime ministers. Empire: Clive victory at Plassey, India, 1757. France: Dangerous undercurrents from Louis XV's court ex-	American: "Great Awakening" in religion: Tennent, Jon. Edwards, Davies; Whitefield's visit. Emerging native art: Copley. Foreign: Liberal French "Enlightenment": Encyclopedia ed. by Diderot; Montesquieu on types of govt.; Voltaire's "Candide," 1759; Rousseau's "Social Contract," 1762. Ger. Enlightenment: Lessing, M. Mendelssohn. Other thought: Hume skep-	American: Rittenhouse: astron. calculations. Foreign: "Industrial Revolution" inventions, Brit.: spinning jenny, circa 1765; Watts' steam enigne, Arkwright's

	da, Amer. Midwest, in 1763 treaty. Mason-Dixon line, S. Pa. boundary, 1763-69. Brit. levies: Sugar, Stamp, Townshend Acts, 1764-67. Protest: N. Y. Dec. of Rights, Pat. Henry in Va., formation Sons of Liberty (Sam. Adams, Revere).	ministration. Prussia: emergence as major mil. power after Fred. the Great triumph in Seven Years War. Great earthquake, 1755: Lisbon destruction.	("Tom Jones," 1749), Smollett, Sterne ("Tristram Shandy," 1759-67), Goldsmith, Hor. Walpole. Saml. Johnson's Dictionary, 1755. Music: Gluck's opera reforms ("Orfeo ed Euridice," 1762). Dom. Scarlatti's steps toward solo sonata form. Budding of symphony (Bach sons, Mannheim sch.). Art: Eng.—Hogarth satire; Reynolds, Gainsborough portraits. Ital. rococo—Tiepolo, Canaletto, Guardi. Fr. genre—Chardin. Light on antiquity: Winckelmann studies. Pompeii rediscovery. Blackstone on law.	driven carriage, Paris, 1769. Linnaeus: plant, mammal classifications. D'Alembert: differential equations, astronomy. Euler: lunar theories, calculus of variations. Reaumur: chem. nature of digestion. Buffon: pioneer evolutionary concepts on earth, man.
1770-1799 GEORGE WASHINGTON Comdr.-in-chief Continental Army, 1775-83. Pres. U. S. Constl. Conv., 1787. First Pres. U. S., 1789-97. Farewell Address, 1796.	Prelude to Revolution: Boston Massacre, 1770. Boston Tea Party, 1773. Intolerable Acts, 1774. Continental Congresses, from 1774. Revolution: Lexington, Concord, 1775. Dec. of Inde., 1776. Yorktown victory, 1781. Treaty of Paris, 1783. Growth fed. union: Articles of Confed., 1781. Adoption U. S. Constitution, 1788; its Bill of Rights, 1791. Rebellions: Shay's in Mass., 1787; W. Pennsylvanians over whisky tax, 1794. Westward planning: N. W. Ordinance, 1787; Wayne victory vs. Indians, Fallen Timbers; Jay's Treaty with Eng., 1794. Formation political parties: Rep. (later Dem.), Federalist. Pres. John Adams adm.: near-war with France over ship seizures, XYZ affair, 1798. Alien and Sedition Acts aimed at pro-French Republicans. Rep. answer in Ky. & Va. Resolutions (states' rights doctrine).	Britain: Replacement of king-dominated prime ministers by Wm. Pitt, 1783. Polish partition by Russia, Prussia, Austria, 1772. Russian annexation of Crimea, 1783. Australian settlement by Brit., 1788. French Revolution: Estab. Nat. Assembly, 1789; Dec. of Rights of Man; Reign of Terror, 1793-94; Napoleon's coup d'etat, 1799. French Revolutionary Wars: invasion by Austria, Prussia, 1792; grave peril from coalitions, 1799.	American: Writings: Patriotic (Paine, Jefferson, Freneau). Woolman's Quaker compassion ("Journal," 1774). Franklin's Autobiography. Federalist Papers, 1788. Chas. B. Brown's novels. Arch.: "Fed. City" (L'Enfant, Ellicott, Thornton). New Eng. styles (Bulfinch, McIntire, Benjamin). Roman influence (Jefferson's Monticello and Va. Capitol). Painting: West's historical, Stuart portraits. Music: Billings fuguing tunes; Hopkinson, Hewitt; Moravians (Antes, Peter). Foreign: Philosophy: Kant's phenomena, noumena. Econ., poli. thought: Condorcet on hist. progress. Adam Smith, free trade. Bentham utilitarianism. Malthus on population vs. subsistence. Babeuf, econ. equality. Burke conservatism. Gibbon on Rome's decline. Musical classicism: Haydn development symphony, string quartet; Mozart balanced emotion. Lit.: Satirical comedy (Sheridan, Beaumarchais). Early romanticism (Herder's "sturm und drang;") Schiller, Cowper, Burns, Blake, Coleridge, Klopstock; Holderlin's subjectivity; Novalis, Wieland, Richter. Boswell's Life of Johnson, 1791. Bourbon art twilight: Fragonard; Houdon's sculpture. Georgian arch: Adam bros. row houses.	American: Rumsey, Fitch: steamboats. Evans: mechanized flour mill. Whitney: cotton gin, 1793. Foreign: Cavendish: experiments on heat, air, earth density. Priestley: "dephlogisticated air" (oxygen). Lavoisier: explanation of oxygen, combustion. Herschel: Uranus discovery, 1781. Pinel: humane psychiatric treatment. Jenner: smallpox vaccination, 1796. Rumford: explanation heat vs. particle motion. Lagrange: astron. theory of perturbations. Coulomb: laws of electrostatics, magnetism. Cartwright: power loom, 1785. Murdock: coal-gas light. Galvani: electrical experiments. Laplace: nebular hypothesis. Geology: Hutton's uniformism vs. Bonnet's catastrophism. Sci. expeditions: Capt. Cook, Humboldt.
1800-1809 THOMAS JEFFERSON Pres. 1801-09. La. Purchase, 1803. Lewis & Clark Expdn., 1804-06.	Tripolitan war vs. U. S. over piracy tribute, 1801-05: Decatur exploits. Court power to review legislation: Marbury vs. Madison, 1803. Alex. Hamilton death in duel with Burr. Pike exploration, Rockies, 1806. Impact of Eur. wars: Embargo Acts, 1807. Nonintercourse (with Eng., France) Acts, 1809. Brit. impressment U. S. seamen. Slaves: Cong. ban on importation, 1808; defiance by smuggling. Madison inauguration as Pres., 1809.	Napoleon I: civil-law code, 1800-04. Coronation as emperor, 1804. Rout of Austrians, Prussians; defeat by Brit. at sea. Final dissolution, Holy Roman Empire. Ireland: union with Brit., 1800. Emmet uprising, 1803.	American: Noah Webster's Dictionary, 1806. Furniture styling: Duncan Phyfe. Foreign: Romantic emphasis on individual: Beethoven's "Eroica" Symphony (acme of sonata form), 1804. Goethe's "Faust," Part I, 1808. Wordsworth's "Prelude." Chateaubriand writings. Philosophy: Fichte's ethical idealism. Fourier formula for social org. (phalanxes). Art: Fr. Empire spirit (David; sculptor Canova). Goya's anti-tyrannical realism. Social irony: Kleist fiction. Ednl. method: Pestalozzi.	American: Fulton: steamboat ("Clermont" launching, 1807). Hare: blowpipe. McDowell: ovariotomy, 1809. Foreign: Volta: electric battery. Appert: food canning. Young: eye structure, vision; wave-nature-of-light applications. Davy: electrochemistry; isolation of potassium, sodium, calcium; hydrogen study. Gauss: fundamental theories of numbers. Dalton: atomic theory, gas pressure. Gay-Lussac: kinetic theory of gasses. Wollaston: palladium, rhodium. Lamarck: modification and "invertebrate" concepts of evolution.
1810-1819 JOHN MARSHALL Chief Justice, U. S. Milestone opinions, 1819: McCulloch vs. Md. (implied Constl., Congl. powers); Dartmouth Coll. vs. Woodward (safeguard of corp. contracts against state legislatures).	Westward expansion: fear of Indian, Brit. resistance in Midwest (Tippecanoe clash with Indians, 1811). Astoria, Ore., founding, 1811. Turnpikes: Cumberland Rd., 1818. War of 1812: Detroit surrender, recovery, 1812-13; lake victories; burning of Wash., D. C.; Treaty of Ghent, 1814; New Orleans victory, 1815. Hartford Conv., 1814-15: New Eng. objections to war, fgn. trade loss, western expansion. Econ. developments: Early mfg. (Waltham, Mass., cotton mill, 1814). Bank of U. S. charter. Protective tariff, 1816. Monroe inauguration as Pres., 1817: "Era of Good Feeling."	Napoleon I: invasion of Russia, retreat, 1812; loss of Paris to allies, exile, 1814; "100 days" return, Waterloo, 1815. Anti-liberal reaction: Cong. of Vienna for remaking Eur. (Metternich presiding), 1814-15. Holy Alliance. Quintuple Alliance. Ger. Confed. formation, 1815. South Amer. revolutions: Bolivar, San Martin, O'Higgins.	American: Nature poems: Bryant. Historical painting: Trumbull. Classic influence, arch: Latrobe churches. Foreign: Thought: Hegel's absolute idealism. Schopenhauer's philosophic pessimism. Ricardo's labor theory of value, "sound" currency. Brit. romanticism: Byron, Keats, Shelley poems. Novels—Austen social comedy, Peacock eccentiricity, Mary W. Shelley fantasy, Scott. Art—Lawrence portraits. Continental litt: Mme. de Stael romanticism; Constant's introspection; E. T. A. Hoffmann psychol. fantasy. Music: Rossini comic opera.	American: Rush: book on mental disease, 1812. Silliman: founding sci. journal, 1818. Foreign: Courtois: discovery iodine. Avogadro: molecular weight. Prout: atomic weight. Fraunhofer: solar spectrum's dark lines. Cuvier: comparative anatomy. Stephenson: steam locomotive. Biot: polarized-light concepts. Fourier: trigonometric series.

KEY NAME AND ERA	HISTORICAL AND GENERAL EVENTS: AMERICAN	HISTORICAL AND GENERAL EVENTS: FOREIGN	THE ARTS AND THOUGHT	SCIENCE AND INVENTION
1820-1829 JOHN JAMES AUDUBON Bird-drawing trip, Miss. and Ohio Rivers, 1820. Election Royal Soc. Edinburgh, 1827. First edit., Birds of Amer., 1827.	Slavery: Mo. Compromise on slave terr. (H. Clay), 1820-21. Lundy's anti-slavery jour., Ohio, 1821. Settlement free Negroes, Liberia, from 1822. Abolition by N. Y. state, 1827. Monroe Doctrine, 1823. Westward development: trade, Santa Fe Trail; founding Rocky Mountain Fur Co., 1822; 1st boats, Erie Canal, 1825; Jed. Smith, Thos. Fitzpatrick overland expdn., Cal.; ground-breaking, B&O RR., 1828. J. Q. Adams: election as Pres. by Ho. Reps. decision, 1825; rebuffal of his internal-improvements program. Anti-Masonic Party founding, 1826. Jackson as Pres., from 1829: common-man image; "Kitchen Cabinet" of advisors; spoils system.	Anti-liberalism: King Chas. X, France; Prime Min. Wellington, Brit.; Austrian domination, Cent. Euro. Greek War of Independece, 1821-27. Mexican independence, 1821; republic, 1823. Catholic Emancipation Act (R. Peel sponsorship), Brit., 1829.	American: Romantic lit: Irving, Cooper. Social-philos. experiment: Owen's New Harmony, Ind. Capitol, Wash., D. C., completion: Bulfinch. Minstrel shows: Rice's "Jim Crow." Foreign: Romanticism: Music—Schubert song cycles; Weber operas ("Der Freischutz," 1820). Painting—Gericault, Delacroix, Turner fervor; Constable landscapes. Lamartine, Heine, Vigny poems; Manzoni fiction; Grillparzer drama. Classicist persistence, art: Ingres. Eng. essay: Lamb, Hazlitt, DeQuincey. Regency arch: Nash. Social philos: Saint-Simon, Cobbett.	American: Cooper: "Tom Thumb" steam locomotive, 1829. Foreign: Niepce: 1st photograph. Carnot: thermodynamics, "motive power of fire." Ampere: electrodynamics. Berzelius: atomic weights, chem. notation. Ohm: elec. current, resistance laws. Lobachevsky: non-Euclidean geometry. Wohler: synthesis organic compounds.
1830-1839 ANDREW JACKSON Pres. to 1837. Fed. power vs. states' rights. Veto Bank of U. S. rechartering, 1832.	States' rights issue: Webster-Hayne debate, 1830; Calhoun objections to tariffs; nullification ordinance, S. C., 1832; Force Bill aimed at S. C., 1833. Slavery issue: Nat Turner slave revolt, 1831. Abolitionism (Garrison's "Liberator;" Lovejoy murder, Alton, Ill., 1837; Wen. Phillips speeches). Anti-Catholic bigotry: convent burning, Mass., 1834. Tex. independence from Mex.: Alamo, San Jacinto, 1936. Panic of 1837. Van Buren inauguration as Pres., 1837. Trans-Atlantic steam travel: "Great Western," 1838.	Brit: middle-class franchise, 1832; slavery ban, colonies, 1833; Chartist worker-class movement; formation Liberal Party (Russell). Accession Queen Victoria, 1837. France: "July Revolution," 1830; accession Louis Philippe. Russian Poland: futile revolt, 1830-31. Ger. Zollverein (customs union) formation, 1834: step to nat. unity. Belgium, Neth. separation, 1839.	American: Jos. Smith's "Book of Mormon," 1830. Art: Hudson R. sch. (Doughty, Cole); Hicks' fantasy. Sculptural beginnings (Greenough). Classic, Gothic-inspired arch: Davis. Popular romances: Simms, Bird. Rise quality mags. Edn. "McGuffey Eclectic Readers." Foreign: Social consciousness: Novels—Dickens ("Oliver Twist," 1837-39); Stendhal's psychol. approach; Balzac's "human comedy;" Hugo. Philos. satire—Carlyle. Drama—Buchner. Cartoons—Daumier. Analysis: Comte's sociology, positivism. Tocqueville's "Democracy in Am.," 1835. Oxford movement in religion (Newman, et al.) Musical romanticism: Berlioz narrative, dramatic symphonies; Mendelssohn, Chopin; operas by Donizetti, Bellini, Meyerbeer, Marschner. Emergence, Russ. culture: Glinka nat. opera, Pushkin writings. Heroism themes: Rude sculpture, Bulwer-Lytton fiction. Landscape painting: Barbizon sch. (T. Rousseau, Corot).	American: Henry: electromagnetic findings, inductance. Gray: botany. Hussey, McCormick: harvester. Deere, Andrus: steel plow. Colt: revolver. Wilkes: sci. expdn. Antarctic. Foreign: Faraday: elec. generator, electrolysis. Daguerre: photog. process. Bessel: star-distance measurement. Lyell: uniformism in geology. Payen: "diastase" organic catalyst. Quetelet: human-statistics systems. Schwann: cell theory. Fizeau: light's velocity in air. Thomsen: archeol.-age classification.
1840-1849 HENRY DAVID THOREAU Transcendentalism. Solitude, Walden Pond, 1845-47. Abhorence of slavery. "Civil Disobedience" essay, 1848.	Presidents: Harrison, 1841; Tyler, 1841; Polk, 1845; Taylor, 1849. Western growth: Ore. Trail (Bidwell, 1841; Bridger). Tex. annexation, 1845. Mormon arrival, Salt Lake val., 1847. Fremont explorations, Cal. Gold Rush, Cal., 1849. Mexican War: Rio Grande fighting, 1846; entry Mex. City, 1847; Treaty Guadalupe Hidalgo, S. W. land gains, 1848. Ore.-Canada boundary settlement, 1846. Slavery controversy: Repeal "gag rule" on debate, 1844; defeat Wilmot Proviso, 1846; growth Undeground Railroad; formation Free Soil Party, 1847-48; Fred. Douglass' jour.	Brit: settlement Opium War, control of Hong Kong, 1842. Corn Laws repeal, 1846. Ireland: potato blight, famine — 1,000,000 deaths, 1,600,000 emigrations, by 1854. Germany: depression, potato-crop failure—1,550,-000 emigrations 1841-60. Revolt, 1848. France: "Feb. Revolution," 1848 — overthrow Louis Philippe, election Louis Napoleon as Pres. Austria 1848 Revolution: downfall Metternich, accession absolutist Emperor Franz Josef. Other 1848 revolts: Hungary (Kossuth), Bohemia, Italy.	American: Transcendentalism — B. Alcott, Emerson (Essays, 1841, 1844), Fuller, Parker, poet Very; Brook Farm, 1841-47. Other writing—Longfellow, Jas. Russ. Lowell, Poe short stories, Dana on sailor hardship. New World history—Prescott, Parkman. Genre, portrait painting—Inman, Mount, Bingham, Durand. Gothic revival, arch: Upjohn's Trinity Ch., N.Y.C. Music: N. Y. Philharmonic, 1842. Fry native opera. Ednl. reform: Horace Mann. Foreign: Opinion: Kierkegaard foundations, existentialism. Proudhon criticism pvt. prop., strong govt. List's econ. nationalism. Communist Manifesto (Marx, Engels), 1848. Brit: Novels—Bronte sisters, Thackeray, Disraeli, Gaskell. Ruskin's moral aesthetic. Pre-Raphaelite brotherhood (D. G. Rossetti, Hunt, Millais), from 1848. Continental romanticism: Schumann poetic ardor in music. Sand, Stifter, Dumas fiction; Musset poems. Rethel's macabre art. Emerging realism, continent: Art—Courbet. Litt.—Merimee, Hebbel, Lermontov, Gogol.	American: Agassiz: Ice Age concept. Long, Morton: ether anesthesia. Morse: telegraph, 1844. Howe: sewing machine. Goodyear: rubber vulcanization. Dix: specialized treatment, insane. Smithsonian Institution, 1846. Foreign: Doppler: wave-motion principle. Adams, Leverrier: Neptune discovery by Newtonian calculation. Helmholtz: conservation of energy theory. Joule: "mech. equivalent of heat." Semmelweis: antisepsis. Kelvin: absolute scale of temperature. Stokes: viscous-fluids theory. Liebig: agricultural chem.

1850-1859 WALT WHITMAN Editor, carpenter, Bklyn., to 1859. First edit., "Leaves of Grass," 1855.	Presidents: Fillmore, 1850; Pierce, 1853; Buchanan, 1857. Sectional controversy: Compromise of 1850 (inc. Fugitive Slave Act). Kan.-Neb. Act, 1854. Anti-abolitionist "sack of Lawrence," Kan., 1856. Dred Scott decision, 1857. John Brown raid, Harper's Ferry, 1859. Gadsden Purchase, S. W. land, 1854. Trade treaty, Japan (Perry), 1854. Republican Party: formation, 1854; 1st Pres. nominee (Fremont), 1856; Lincoln vs. Douglas for Sen., 1858. Northern econ. development: growth iron, anthracite, textile industries; fed. land grants for railroads; 1st railroad across Miss. R.; 1st oil well, Titusville, Pa., 1859; Comstock Lode, Nev.; agri. shift west. Eur. immigration: 2,600,000 from 1851-60. Nativist reaction (Know-Nothings).	France: repression workers' uprising. Designation Louis Napoleon as Emperor Nap. III; absolute dictatorship. Crimean War, 1853-56: Turkey, Brit., France, Sardinia vs. Russia; check on Russ. influence in Europe. Sepoy Rebellion, India, 1857-58. Italy: Sardinia, with France, vs. Austria.	American: Classics: Melville's "Moby Dick," 1851; Hawthorne novels; Thoreau's "Walden," 1854. Anti-slavery writings: Stowe's "Uncle Tom's Cabin," 1851-52; Helper on South's "Impending Crisis." Women's rights: Stanton, Anthony. Art: Mills' equestrian sculpture. Currier, Ives prints. Music: Gottschalk local color, Foster songs. Arch.: Howard's "Belle Grove" manse, La., 1857; Renwick's St. Pat. Cath. (Gothic revival), N. Y. C. Rise native acting: Edwin Booth, Jos. Jefferson. Foreign: Opinion: Mill's humane utilitarianism. Lassalle's state socialism. Gobineau racism. Nihilism, Russia. Music: Liszt, symphonic poem. Wagner's music drama "of the future," leitmotifs ("Rheingold," 1854). Verdi, Gounod. Growth of realism: Flaubert's "Madame Bovary," 1857; Keller autobiog. novel; Goncharov's "Oblomov." Millet paintings. French poetry: Baudelaire subjective imagery. Brit. lit.: Tennyson's "In Memoriam." Meredith unconventionality. The Brownings, Trollope, Macaulay.	American: Otis: passenger elevator. Field: 1st Atlantic Cable, 1858. Foreign: Evolution theory, natural selection—Wallace's animal geography; Darwin's "Origin of Species," 1859. Huxley: disproof, vertebrate theory of skull: Owen: parathyroid glands. Foucault: experimental pendulum, gyroscope. Flor. Nightingale: sanitary reform. Bunsen: gas-air burner. Boole: symbolic logic. Virchow: cellular pathology. Bernard: glycogen, body chem. balance. Pflucker: cathode rays. Perkin: analine dye.
1860-1869 ABRAHAM LINCOLN Pres., 1861-65. Emancipation Proclamation, 1863. 2d Inaug. Address ("With malice toward none . . ."), 1865. Assassination, 1865.	Civil War: Ft. Sumter, 1st Bull Run battle, 1861; Davis inaug., Confed. pres., 1862; decisive Gettysburg, 1863; Atlanta campaign, 1864; surrender, Lee to Grant, Johnston to Sherman, 1865. War protest: Copperheads in North. N. Y. C. draft riots, 1863. "Poor man" desertions in Confed. Nat. development: Morrill (land-grant coll.) Act, Homestead Act, 1862; trans-cont. railroad, 1869. And. Johnson Presidency, 1865-69; impeachment, 1868. Reconstruction: Freedmen's Bureau; Civil Rights Act, 1866; ratification, 13th to 15th Amendments, Constitution, 1865-70; "reconstruction acts," mil. dists. in South, from 1867. Ku-Klux Klan. Rise small farm, share cropping, in South. Alaska purchase, 1867. Grant presidency, from 1869. Financial panic: "Black Friday," 1869.	Russia: emancipation, serfs, by Alex. II, 1861. Brit.: U. S. Civil War neutrality (cotton surplus, need for Northern wheat). Reform Bill (urban working-class franchise), 1867. Ital.: Risorgimento: Garibaldi conquest Sicily, Naples, 1860; church-state struggles. Mexico: French-backed Maximilian empire, 1864-67; Juarez victory, reforms. Bismarck, Ger. unification: Prussian-Austrian victory, Schleswig-Holstein, 1864; Prus. victory vs. Aus., 1866; North Ger. Confed., 1867. France: "Liberal Empire"—material progress, imperialism. Canada: dominion status, 1867. Suez Canal completion, 1869.	American: Lit.: Poetry—Em. Dickinson's modernism; Whitman's Lincoln elegies; Tuckerman symbolism. Alcott fiction. Orchestral tours: T. Thomas. Heroic sculpture: Ball, Rimmer. Arch.: Ruskin-influenced Venetian Gothic. Foreign: Lit.: Ibsen's modern ideological drama. Fiction—Tolstoy's epic "War and Peace;" Dostoyevsky's existential anguish; Geo. Eliot, Turgenev romantic realism; Collins mysteries; Lew. Carroll's "Alice;" Lautreamont surrealism. Poetic melancholy—Arnold's "Dover Beach," Swinburne. Econ. thought: Marx' dialectical materialism ("Kapital," Vol. I, 1867); Bakunin anarchism. History: Burckhardt on Rome, Renan on Jesus. Musical nationalism: Smetana, Moussorgsky, Grieg. Paris reconstruction: Haussmann. Parnassian poets, France: Sully-Prudhomme. Early Fr. impressionism, art: Manet, Boudin.	American: Ericsson: iron-clad ship ("Monitor," 1861). Westinghouse: air brake. Hyatt: celluloid. Foreign: Pasteur: germ theory of disease. Lenoir: internal combustion engine, circa 1860. Mendel: laws of heredity. Nobel: dynamite. Charcot: pathology, hysteria, senility. Kekule: molecular structure of benzene. Riemann: non-Euclidean geometry. Galton: eugenics. Lister: antiseptic surgery. Gramme: practical dynamo. Evolutionary theory: Spencer naturalism, Haeckel recapitulation.
1870-1879 THOMAS ALVA EDISON Menlo Park, N. J., lab., from 1876. Invention phonograph, 1877; incandescent lamp, 1879.	Econ. setbacks: Chgo. fire, 1871; Panic of 1873. Polit. scandals: Secy. War Belknap; Tammany "Boss" Tweed. Treaty of Wash. with Brit. (on Ala. Claims, etc.), 1871. Polit. developments: Greeley, Liberal Rep. Party, 1872; Greenback Party (farmer unrest); Hayes-Tilden disputed election, 1876; commn. decision for Hayes as Pres. Sioux outbreak: Custer's "last stand," 1876. Labor movement: breakup "Molly Maguires" (miners); railroad strike, 1877. End Reconstruction in South: troop withdrawal, home rule.	Germany: growth Social Dem. Party. Victory Franco-Prus. War, 1870-71; gain of Alsace, Lorraine. Proclamation Wm. I as emperor. Brit.: Disraeli domestic reforms, Empire expansion. France: formation 3d Republic, 1871; suppression left-wing Paris Commune. Italy: seizure French-backed Papal States, 1870. Bosnia, Hercegovina: anti-Turk. uprising, 1875. Russo-Turk. War, 1877-78: Turk. terr. losses, Balkans. Cong. Berlin, 1878: Bosnia, Hercegovina to Aus.-Hung.; Cyprus to Brit.	American: Philosophy: Peirce's "synechism," pragmatism. Sectional lit.: Harte, Joaq. Miller (West); Eggleston (Midwest); Lanier, Cable (South). Religion: Eddy "Sci. and Health," 1875. Painting: Ryder mysticism; Bierstadt, Inness landscapes. Arch.: Richardson's free Romanesque (Trinity Ch., Boston). Drama production: Aug. Daly. Econ. thought: George's "Progress and Poverty," 1879. Foreign: Art: Rodin's imaginative realism in sculpture. Impressionism (formal launching, 1874)—Monet, Sisley, Pissarro. New patterns, romantic symphony: Brahms, Bruckner. French lit.: Poetry—Mallarme, Verlaine, Rimbaud symbolism. Fiction—Daudet irony. Operetta: Gilbert & Sullivan; J. Strauss Jr.	American: Bell: telephone, 1876. Gibbs: dynamics of chem. reactions. Foreign: Mendeleev: periodic table of elements, 1871. Schliemann: excavation, Troy site. Plante: successful storage battery. Crookes: vacuum tube. Van't Hoff: asymmetry of molecules. Maxwell: electromagnetic theory of light. Golgi: nerve cell detection. Cantor: transfinite numbers.

KEY NAME AND ERA	HISTORICAL AND GENERAL EVENTS AMERICAN	FOREIGN	THE ARTS AND THOUGHT	SCIENCE AND INVENTION
1880-1889 SAMUEL LANGHORNE CLEMENS "MARK TWAIN" Wistful satirist. Author: "Life on the Mississippi," 1883; "Huckleberry Finn," 1885; "Connecticut Yankee," 1889.	Presidents: Garfield (assassination, 1881); Arthur, 1881; Cleveland, 1885; B. Harrison, 1889. Civil service reform: Pendleton Act, 1883. Indsl. development: Anaconda copper mines, Mesabi iron range, aluminum. Trusts (oil, whisky, sugar, match). Anti-Monopoly Party. Interstate Commerce Act, 1887. Labor movement: growth, decline, Knights of Labor; 8-hr.-day demonstrations; Haymarket Riot, Chgo., 1886; organization Amer. Fed. Labor (craft unions), 1886. Top immigration decade: over 5,000,000. Statue Liberty unveiling, 1886.	Empire expansion: Germans in Africa, Pacific; Brit. in Egypt, Rhodesia. Russia: assassination Alex. II, 1881; reign of terror, pogroms. Triple Alliance, 1882: Germany, Aus.-Hung., Italy. France: Boulanger's conservative nationalism, 1886-87. Social reform: Gladstone's Reform Bill of 1884 (full manhood suffrage), Brit.; health, old age insurance, Ger. "Kulturkampf": Bismarck abandonment, 1887, of struggle with Cath. Ch.	American: Lit. realism: Novels—Henry James psychol. penetration, Howells social portrayal, Howe's "country town." Drama B. Howard social barbs. Art: realism (Eakins, Homer); portraits (Whistler, Sargent); impressionism (Cassatt). Polit. cartoons (Nast). Arch: Jenney's steel-skeleton skyscraper, Chgo. Music: opening Met. Opera House, N.Y.C., 1883. Social theory: Ward sociology. Bellamy's utopia. Foreign: Philosophy: Nietzche's "superman" doctrines. Mach's positivism. Lit: Fiction—Zola naturalism; Huysmans symbolism; Hardy fatalism; Maupassant, Machado de Assis psychol. irony; Verga "verismo;" Bourget moralism; Stevenson, Doyle adventure. Drama—Strindberg's psychol. sombreness. Poetry — Hopkins mysticism, Thomson despair. Music: Franck's cyclic form; Dvorak, Borodin, Tchaikovsky. Art: Degas realism. Renoir's rainbow palette. H. Rousseau primitivism Redon symbolism. Polit. thought: Bryce's "Am. Commonwealth," 1888. Fabian socialism, Brit. Cultural outlook: Goncourt Journals.	American: Michelson, Morley: disproof of aether. Eastman: photog. film. Tesla: alternating current transmission. Foreign: Arrhenius: ionization. Koch: discovery TB bacillus. Benz, Daimler: automobile. Dunlop: pneumatic tire. Hertz: photoelectric effect. Koller: local anesthesia.
1890-1899 LOUIS SULLIVAN Modern functional architecture, individualized ornamentation. Transp. Bldg., World's Columbian Expn., Chgo., 1893.	Presidents: Cleveland, 1893; McKinley, 1897. Legislation: Sherman Anti-trust, 1890. Tariff hike, 1890. Panic of 1893. Farm unrest: mortgage debts; rise Populists (Weaver), Silver Dems. (Bryan). Labor scene: Pullman strike, 1894; Coxey's march, unemployed, 1894; formation Social Dem. Party (Debs). Erdman Act (railroad arbitration). Growing internationalism: intervention Venezuela-Brit. Guiana boundary dispute, 1896. Open-Door program, China. Span.-Am. War, 1898: "Maine" sinking; capture Santiago de Cuba; Treaty of Paris; acquisition Puerto Rico, Guam, Philippines, freedom of Cuba. Philippine revolt vs. U. S. (Aguinaldo), 1899.	Cuban Revolution, 1895. Germany: Wm. II dismissal of Bismarck; naval buildup, isolationism. Dual Entente: France, Russia. France: liberal vs. "ancien regime" rivalry; Dreyfus case. Greek-Turk. war over Crete, 1896-97. South Africa: Boer War, from 1899. China: war with Japan, Formosa loss, 1894-95; Boxer anti-foreign rebellion, 1899. Zionism: 1st world congress, 1897.	American: Ideas: Wm. James' pragmatism, "radical empiricism." Brooks Adams' law of civilization, decay. Dewey's "The Sch. and Society," 1899. Veblen on leisure class. Turner on receding frontier. Mahan on U. S. growth outward. Music: Ives' modern idiom; MacDowell, Parker romanticism. Jazz—Buddy Bolden band, New Orleans. Lit.: Fiction—Garland, Frederic realism; Crane, Norris ("McTeague," 1899) naturalism; Jewett local color; Bierce horror. Drama—Fitch's psychol. romance. Polit. satire—Dunne's "Mr. Dooley." Art: Sculpture—Saint-Gaudens' "Grief," 1891; Lorado Taft. Impressionism—Theo. Robinson, Hassam. Civic design—Burnham, McKim, Chgo.; White's Wash. Arch, N.Y.C. Foreign: Pope Leo XIII's "Rerum Novarum" on social justice. Musical transition to modernism: Mahler's symphonic palette. Faure, Debussy suggestiveness. D'Indy, Chausson cyclic form. Wolf songs. Puccini, Mascagni operatic realism. Brit. trends: Fiction—Conrad, individual dilemma; George Moore, Gissing naturalism; Wells sci. fantasy. Social comedy—Wilde. Pessimism, verse — Housman. Decadence — Dowson poems, Beardsley art. Imperialist lit.—Kipling. Continental lit.: Symbolism—Stefan George, Maeterlinck. Realism—Hauptmann. Pre-expressionism — Wedekind. Neo-romanticism — Rostand, Loti, D'Annunzio. Russia—Chekhov dramas of individual isolation; subjective acting (Stanislavsky, Moscow Art Theatre, from 1898). Art: Post-impressionism—Van Gogh, Gauguin color richness; Seurat, Signac pointillism; Cezanne vibrancy. Naturalism—Toulouse-Lautrec. Seeds Ger. expressionism—Munch. "Nabis" boldness—Denis, Bonnard. Fantasy—Ensor mask figures. "Ars Nouveau" design—Horta, van de Velde. Econ. thought: Wicksell on planned balances.	American: Steinmetz: alternating current. Lowell, Pickering, Barnard, Keeler: astron. findings. Acheson: discovery carborundum. Pupin: long-distance telephony. Foreign: Behring: diphtheria, tetanus antitoxins. Lippmann: color photography. Lorentz: electron mass, velocity equation. Roentgen: X-ray discovery. Marconi: the wireless. Thomson: electron discovery. Ostwald: catalysis. Finsen: light-ray therapy. Becquerel: uranium natural radioactivity. Diesel: diesel engine. The Curies: radium discovery, 1898. Durkheim: suicide analysis. Kraepelin: schizophrenia, manic depression. Le Bon: "crowd" psychology. Evans: archeol. excavations, Crete. Petrie: archeol. systematization.
1900-1909 THEODORE ROOSEVELT Pres., 1901-09. "Square Deal" policy, "trust busting." Conservationism (Pinchot appointment). Dollar diplomacy, Panama Canal.	Assassination, Pres. McKinley, 1901. Anti-saloon raids: Carry Nation. Legislation: Reclamation Act, 1902; Elkins Act (railroad rates), 1903; Hepburn Act (interstate commerce), 1906; pure food, drug laws, 1906. San Francisco earthquake, fire, 1906. Labor: anthracite strike (Roosevelt intercession), 1902. Formation I. W. W. (Wobblies), 1905. Danbury Hatters' Case. Panic	Brit.: accession Edw. VII, 1901. Prime Min. Asquith. Old-age pensions. France: victory, Dreyfus supporters. Clemenceau. Russia: defeat by Japan, 1904-05 (Roosevelt mediation). Revolution, 1905; establish-	American: "Muckrakers"—Tarbell, Baker, Steffens, Lawson, Phillips. Fiction trends: Naturalism—Dreiser's "Sister Carrie," 1900. Social realism—Sinclair. Social irony—Wharton. Modernity—Ger. Stein's "Three Lives." Adventure—London. Short story—O. Henry. Poetry, drama: Moody. "Ashcan Sch.," art—Henri, Glackens, Sloan, Luks. Music: Loeffler impressionism. Herbert operettas. Theory: Royce's idealism. Henry Adams on hist. forces. Santayana's "The Life of Reason." Sumner's "Folkways," 1907. Foreign: Art: Fauvism (Matisse, Derain, Vlaminck, Dufy). Cubism (Braque, Picasso). Expressionist "Die Brucke" (Kirchner,	American: Wright bros: the airplane, 1903. Sperry: gyrocompass. H. Ford: assembly-line auto mfg. De Forest: 3-electrode vacuum tube (basis of electronics). Cook, Peary: North Pole discovery. Foreign: Planck: quantum theory (discontinuous energy emission). Einstein: special

	of 1907. Pres. Taft, from 1907: sponsorship Constitutional amendments (direct election Senators, income tax). Tariff increase. Dismissal Pinchot.	ment Duma (parliament). Pan-Slavism. Alliances: Brit., French Entente Cordiale. Triple Entente (Brit., France, Russia). Bosnian crisis, 1908-09.	Nolde, Schmidt-Rottluff, Heckel). Poetry: Rilke, Blok emotional symbolism. Fiction, drama: Realism—Gorki, Andreyev, Reymont, Bennett. Idealism—Merezhkovsky, Rolland. Irony—Butler, Shaw, A. France, Chesterton, Barrie, Forster. Romanticism—Hudson. Abbey Theatre, Ireland (Yeats, Gregory, Synge). Galsworthy. Philosophy: Husserl's phenomenology. Social theory: Sorel's syndicalism. Jaures' pacifism. Simmel's interaction concepts. Music: Ravel sensuousness; Satie simplicity; Sibelius' evolving themes; Rachmaninoff, Elgar romanticism. Arch: Gaudi's sculptured effects.	theory of relativity. Freud: psychoanalysis; dynamic subconscious. Landsteiner: blood types; transfusions. Wasserman: syphillis test. Rutherford: nuclear atom, radioactive disintegration of elements. Einthoven: string galvanometer. Binet, Simon: intelligence test.
1910-1919 WOODROW WILSON Pres. from 1913. "New Freedom" reforms. Fourteen Points (for peace), 1918. League of Nations advocacy. Health breakdown, 1919.	Econ. laws: Fed. Reserve, 1913; Clayton Antitrust; Fed. Trade Commn.; La Follette Seamen's; Adamson (8-hr. day, railways); Fed. Farm Loan, 1916. Mil. expdns., riot-torn Latin Am: Haiti, 1915; Dominican Repub., 1916; Pershing vs. Mex., 1916-17; Cuba, 1917. U. S. in World War I: Protests, Ger. submarine warfare (Lusitania sinking, 1915); war declarations, 1917; offensives, Cantigny to Meuse-Argonne, 1918. Disasters: dynamiting, L. A. Times, 1910. Titanic wreck, iceberg (loss 1,517 U. S. lives), 1912. Bomb blast, San Fran. Preparedness Day Parade, 1916. Explosion, Jersey City munitions docks, 1916. Flu epidemic, 1918. Anti-liberalism: rebirth Ku Klux Klan, 1915. Imprisonment pacifist Debs, 1918. Atty. Gen. Palmer "Red scare" raids, deportations. Prohibition: 18th Amend. to Constn., 1919. Supreme Court: Holmes on bounds of free speech, 1919.	Brit.: breakup House of Lords power; Prime Min. Lloyd George; almost universal suffrage. War buildup: Italy vs. Turk. over Tripoli, 1911-12; Balkan Wars, "Greater Serbia" movement, 1913-14. World War I: Assassination Aus. Archduke Francis Ferd. by Serbian nationalist, 1914; Russ. mobilization; Ger. invasion Belgium, victory vs. Russ., 1914; Marne turning point, 1918. Versailles Treaty (inc. League of Nations Covenant), 1919; Ger. loss colonies, Alsace-Lorraine, Danzig. France: Clemenceau's "Sacred Union" polit. coalition, from 1917. Russian Revolution, 1917: overthrow of Czar Nich. II, then of moderate Kerensky; Lenin, Bolsheviki "dictatorship of proletariat." Austria-Hung.: establishment as independent repubs., 1918; Bela Kun's short-lived leftist dictatorship, Hung., 1919. Berlin: Spartacist uprising, suppression. China: Sun Yat-sen republican revolution, 1911-12. India: rise Gandhi non-violent independence movement.	American: Poetry: Frost's symbolic realism. Imagists (Amy Lowell, Pound, Fletcher). Sandburg's "Chicago." Lindsay jazz cadence. Masters. Fiction: Sher. Anderson subjectivity. Cabell fantasy. Hergesheimer sophistication. Cather prairie realism. Lardner satire. Nonfiction: Brooks, Bourne on Am. culture. Mencken's "Am. Lang." Beard econ. focus on Am. history. Muir on nature. Babbitt, More "new humanism." Hocking philos. idealism. Art: realism (Bellows). Romanticism (Davies). Modernism (Feininger; Armory Show, 1913, featuring Duchamp). Arch.: Wright's structural innovations (Imperial Hotel, Tokyo), environmental relationships (prairie houses). Gilbert's 60-story Woolworth Bldg., N.Y.C. Music: Griffes impressionism, modernity. "Blues" development ("Ma" Rainey). Ragtime craze. Little Theater movement: Provincetown, Mass. Cinema technique: D. W. Griffith. Foreign: Philos: Bergsons' "elan vital." Croce's idealism. Spengler's "Decline of the West," 1918. Music: Schoenberg atonality, 12-tone experiment. Stravinsky, Bartok rhythmic, harmonic boldness. Rich. Strauss post-Wagnerian realistic opera. Vaughan Williams, Delius impressionism. Nielsen, Busoni modern classicism. Janacek dynamics. Bloch romantic expressionism. Lit.: Psychol. dimension (Proust's "Remembrance of Things Past"). Spiritual quest—Jimenez, Valery, Alain-Fournier, Schnitzler, Peguy, Unamuno, Wassermann. Symbolism—Hofmannsthal plays. Surrealism—Apollinaire poems. Realistic novels—D. H. Lawrence, Maugham, Andersen Nexo, Hamsun. War's grimness—Owen, Sassoon, Brooke poems; Barbusse fiction. Satire—Beerbohm, Saki, Biely. Art: Dadaism (Tzara, Ball, Arp). Expressionist Blaue Reiter (Klee's psychic improvisation, Kandinsky's non-objectivity, Marc, Macke). Orphism (Delaunay). Cubist influence (Gris, Leger). Ital. Futurism (Balla, Boccioni). Modigliani's anguished distortion.	American: Bingham: disc. Machu Picchu ruins, Peru, 1911. Millikan: particulate nature of electricity. Morgan: chromosome findings. Richards: atomic weight determinations. Kettering: auto self-starter. Rous: tumor-inducing virus. Boas: race-culture anthropology. Adams: Sirius "hot star" analysis. Watson: Behaviorism. Foreign: Pavlov: conditioned reflex. Russell, Whitehead: "Principia Mathematica." Ehrlich: salvarsan spirochete-killer. Schick: diphtheria test. Moseley: atomic numbers of elements. Soddy: radioactive isotopes. Bohr: atomic structure, electron orbits. Psychoanalysis: Jung's personal and collective unconscious; Adler's "inferiority complex." Sikorsky: multimotor airplane. Amundsen: South Pole discovery, 1911. Wertheimer, Kohler: Gestalt psychology.
1920-1929 HENRY LOUIS MENCKEN Mag. editor. Attacker shams and hypocrisies. Author, "Notes on Democracy," 1926; "Prejudices" series.	Presidents: Harding, 1921; Coolidge, 1923; Hoover, 1929. Fgn. affairs: Sen. rejection Versailles Treaty (inc. League Nations), 1920; internat. conf., arms limitation, 1921-22; Dawes Plan, Ger. reparations, 1924; Marine landings, strife-torn China, Nicaragua. "Normalcy": Fordney-McCumber Tariff, 1922; tax cuts; immigration restrictions, 1924. Legal controversies: Sacco-Vanzetti case. Scopes evolution-instrn. trial (attys. Darrow, Bryan), 1925. Women suffrage: 19th Amend., Constn., 1920. "Teapot Dome" scandal over 1922 Naval Oil Res. leases.	Russia: Bolshevik (Communist) victory, civil war; U.S.S.R. constn., 1922; Lenin death, 1924; Stalin dictatorship, Trotsky expulsion, 1927; 1st Five-Year Plan (farm collectivization, indsl. growth), 1928. Germany: inflation, unemployment; Kapp's monarchist putsch, Berlin, 1920; Hitler's "beer hall" putsch, Munich, 1923; Hindenburg conservative presidency, from 1925. Italy: Mussolini "march on Rome," appointment as	American: Whitehead's philos. of organism ("Process and Reason," 1929). Fiction: Crisis of man's spirit—Hemingway's "Sun Also Rises," Faulkner's "Sound and the Fury," Fitzgerald's "Great Gatsby," Wolfe's "Look Homeward, Angel;" Con. Aiken. Social irony—Sinc. Lewis, Glasgow. Regionalism—Eliz. Madox Roberts, Rolvaag. Poetry: Emotional irony (Millay, Wylie, Cummings); disillusion (Jeffers, Leonard, Robinson); idealism (S. V. Benet). Drama: Psychol.—O'Neill expressionism; Kelly, Gale. Social—Rice. Music: Varese's instrumental (later electronic) adventurousness. Jazz—Chgo. verve (Beiderbecke, Teschemacher, Trumbauer); Armstrong "Hot Five;" Morton; Henderson band. Bes. Smith blues. Gershwin hits. Art: Abstract trends—Weber, Marin, Demuth, Kuhn, Sheeler, O'Keeffe. Lachaise's robust sculpture. Cinema: Chaplin "tramp" comedies. Flaherty documentaries. Modern dance: Ruth St. Denis, Shawn. Foreign: Fiction: Modern man's dilemna—Joyce's kaleidoscopic methods ("Ulysses," 1922); Va. Woolf stream-of-consciousness; Thos. Mann symbolism ("Magic Mountain"); Kafka's "trilogy of loneliness;" F. M. Ford, Svevo, Gide, Hesse, Duhamel, Babel, Mauriac; Aldous Huxley satire. Wit—Firbank. Hist.—Undset, Dinesen. Philos.: Heidegger existentialism. Karl Barth dialectical theology. Expressionism: Kokoschka, Beckmann art; Grosz caricature; Kaiser, Brecht drama; Mendelsohn, Klint architecture. Surrealism: Breton "Manifestoes," art (Miro, Ernst, de Chirico, Masson, Dali); Reverdy poetry. Abstract trends: Mondrian goemetric paintings. Sculpture—Gabo constructivism, Epstein massiveness, Brancusi symbolism. Music: Serial—	American: Compton: wavelength of scattered X-rays. Theiler: yellow-fever vaccine. Jas. Sumner: crystalline enzymes. Muller: X-ray-increased biol. mutations. Bush: analog computer. Foreign: Heisenberg: quantum theories, "uncertainty" principle. Banting, Best (Amer.), McCleod: insulin. Fleming: penicillin.

Continued on Next Page

KEY NAME AND ERA	HISTORICAL AND GENERAL EVENTS AMERICAN	FOREIGN	THE ARTS AND THOUGHT	SCIENCE AND INVENTION
	Agriculture: price declines; veto McNary-Haugen price-support bill. Labor unrest: coal, railway strikes, 1922; "open shop" drive by employers; A. F. L. endorsement, La Follette Progressive ticket, 1924. Stock market: Crash of '29. Crime: bootlegging; gang rivalry (St. Valentine's Day Massacre, Chgo., 1929).	premier, 1922; Fascist dictatorship. Lateran Treaty with Holy See, 1929. Brit.: gen. strike, 1926. Irish Free State. Turkey: Ataturk, Repub., 1923. World-wide depression, 1929.	Berg's "Wozzeck," 1925; Webern compression. Elemental force—Prokofief, Kodaly. Arch.: Bauhaus steel-glass simplicity, spatial freedom (Gropius, Mies van der Rohe). Le Corbusier cubic (later free-form) creativity. Drama: O'Casey ideological lyricism; Pirandello, Ghelerode on human identity; Capek satire. Poetry: T. S. Eliot disillusion ("Waste Land," 1922); Mayakovsky anguish; St.-John Perse's eternal spirit. Cinema: Eisenstein hist. epic. Social theory: Max Weber plurality of causes.	Rank: "birth trauma" psychoanalysis. Reich: "orgone" concept, biology. de Broglie: wave-mechanics theory. Schroedinger, Dirac: quantum theory. Eddington: astrophysics, relativity.
1930-1939 FRANKLIN DELANO ROOSEVELT Pres. from 1933. "New Deal" social, econ. reforms. Growing opposition to belligerent nations.	"Great Depression": unemployment over 14% labor force, 1931-40. Reconstruction Fin. Corp., 1932. "New Deal" legislation: Nat. Recovery Adm., 1933-36; public works (inc., T. V. A. dams); farmer subsidies, credit; Wagner Act on collective bargaining; Social Security; Hatch Act on polit. campaign expenditure; minimum wages, 1938. Supreme court nullification of part of New Deal program; Roosevelt court-"packing" failure, 1937. F. D. R. fgn. policies: reciprocal trade agreements; Latin-Am. "good neighbor" policy; Philippine independence, 1934 (eff. 1945); neutrality, Span. Civil War; call for moral quarantine of belligerent nations, 1937. Repeal Prohibition: 21st Amend., Constn., 1933. Labor organization, mass industries: John L. Lewis, formation C. I. O., 1935.	Japan: Manchuria occupation, 1931; acceleration China war, 1937. Nazi control, Germany: Hitler appointment as chancellor, 1st concentration camps, 1933; anti-Semitic laws; remilitarization Rhineland, 1936; seizure Austria, 1938, much of Czechoslovakia, (after Munich pact), 1938-39; "Axis" pacts with Italy, Japan; nonaggression pact with U.S.S.R., 1939. Spain: creation republic, 1931. Mil., conservative uprising, 1936, and victory (with Nazi, Ital. aid), 1939; Franco's establishment, corporate state. Italy: invasion Ethiopia, 1935-36; seizure Albania, 1939. World War II: Nazi invasion Poland, 1939; Brit., French declarations against Nazis; fall of Poland. U. S. S. R.: Great Purge, 1937-38; invasion E. Poland, Finland, 1939. Mexico: Cardenas' land reform, nationalization fgn. oil.	American: Prose: Social ills, the "forgotten man"—Farrell's "Studs Lonigan," Dos Passos' "U. S. A.," Steinbeck's "Grapes of Wrath;" M. Gold, Caldwell, Rich. Wright; Odets, Kingsley plays; Agee "documentary." Man's private turmoil—Henry Roth, Djuna Barnes, Kath. Anne Porter stories; (plays) Wilder's "Our Town," Hellman. Barbs at materialism—Marquand suavity, Hen. Miller ribaldry. Humor—Thurber. Hist. escapism—Mgt. Mitchell, K. Roberts. Poetry: MacLeish social idealism, Stevens reverie, Hart Crane mysticism; Max. Anderson play, "Winterset." Art: Regional—Benton, Curry, Bohrod, Speicher. Urban scenes—Hopper loneliness, Burchfield mystery, Marsh mockery. Calder mobiles, stabiles. Archipenko rhythmic sculpture. Music: Growth modernity (Harris, Thomson, Copland's "Piano Variations," Riegger's individualized 12-tone, Ruggles). "Swing" (Goodman, Ellington). Philos: Langer's symbolic logic. Cinema: Technicolor. Lorentz social documentaries. W. C. Fields comedy. Full-length carton (Disney). W. P. A. art, lit. projects. Foreign: Theory: Keynes on large-scale econ. planning. Ortega y Gasset on mass rule. Jaspers, Maritain existential philos. Berdyaev spirituality. Human concern in lit: Garcia Lorca, Giraudoux plays. Malraux, Romains, Broch, Silone, H. H. Richardson, Musil, Sholokhov fiction. Auden, Spender, MacNeice, Montale poems. Other lit. themes: Dylan Thomas poetic introspection. Celine misanthropy. Waugh satire. Robt. Graves hist. Art: Expressionist influence (Soutine; Roualt's spirituality). Zadkine's cubist romanticism. Rivera, Orozco, Siqueiros social protest. Music: Walton, Shostakovich vigor. Haba's quarter-tones. Orff medieval inspiration. Latin-Am. folk color (Villa-Lobos, Chavez). Cinema: Cocteau's surrealism.	American: Zworykin: TV camera, electron microscope. Lawrence: cyclotron. Urey: deuterium (heavy hydrogen). Oppenheimer: nuclear-fission explanation. Stanley: virus crystallization. Rabi: measurement magnetic properties of atoms. Pauling: chem.-bonding theory. Anderson: positron. Lewis: heavy water. Sullivan: soc. sci. relation to psychiatry. Huggins: hormonal treatment of cancer. Armstrong: frequency modulation. Foreign: Watson-Watt: radar. Chadwick: neutron discovery. F. and I. Joliot-Curie: artificial radioactivity. Zernicke: phase-contrast microscope. Whittle: air craft jet propulsion. Domagk: use Prontonsil (sulfa forerunner). Hahn, Meitner: uranium fission. Yukawa: meson prediction. Pauli: postulate on future neutrino. Mueller: DDT application. Szent-Gyorgyi: vitamins, biol. combustion.
1940-1949 ENRICO FERMI "Italian navigator" of the atomic age. Supervision 1st self-sustaining nuclear-chain reaction, Chgo., 1942.	1941 eve of war involvement: Lend-lease aid to Brit., Atlantic Charter (Roosevelt, Churchill); occupation Greenland, Iceland; loss destroyer Reuben James; protests of Japan's Indo-China, Thailand aggression. World War II: Jap. bombings Pearl Harbor, Manila, 1941. Land campaigns—Philippines, 1941, to Okinawa, 1945; North Africa, 1942, to Italy; French coast (D-day, 1944) to east of Rhine, 1945. First atomic bombing, Hiroshima, Japan, 1945. U. S. as "arsenal of democ-	World War II: Nazi conquests Denmark, Norway, Low Countries, France, 1940; "battle of Brit.;" Ital. invasions N. Africa, Greece; Nazi attack on U. S. S. R., 1941 (defeat at Volgograd, 1943); "Bulge" battle, Nazi surrender, 1945; U. S. S. R. vs. Japan, 1945. United Nations founding conf., San Francisco, 1945. Post-war Germany: division into 4-power occupation zones (as agreed at Yalta, Potsdam confs.). Pro-West Adenauer as chancellor, W. Ger., from 1949.	American: Men in war: Mailer, Burns, Cozzens novels. Shapiro poems. Ernie Pyle. Mauldin cartoons. Hersey's "Hiroshima." The social dilemma: Art. Miller's "Death of a Salesman," 1949. Warren's "All the King's Men." Algren, Motley novels on derelicts. Myrdal's "Am. Dilemma." 1944. The inner quest in lit.: Tenn. Williams, McCullers, Welty, Capote . . . Thos. Merton . . . Tate, Wm. Carlos Williams, Ransom, Robt. Lowell. Lit. criticism: Edmund Wilson. Art: abstract expressionism (Pollock, Hofmann, A. Gorky, Motherwell). Shahn's social concern. Tobey's orientalism. Lipchitz rhythmic sculpture. Ossorio assemblages. Jazz: "bop" dissonance, rhythmic freedom (Parker, Gillespie). "Progressive" (Kenton). Entertainment: Rodgers-Hammerstein musicals. Comml. TV. Foreign: Existential outlook: Sartre, Jaspers, Marcel, Camus. Man vs. despotism: Orwell, Paton, Koestler, Carlo Levi, Berto, Pratolini novels. Cassirer philos. on "the myth of the state."	American: Seaborg: plutonium identification. Wiener: cybernetics. Beadle, Tatum: gene function in heredity. Szilard: with Fermi on nuclear reactor. Enders: polio-virus growth. Kinsey: sexual behavior analysis. Waksman: antibiotics. Foreign:

	racy: 300,000 mil. planes, 71,000 naval vessels, 86,000 tanks, 1940-45. Roosevelt death, 1945; Truman succession. Fgn. aid: Truman Doctrine (aid to Greece, Turkey vs. Communism); Marshall Plan (Eur. recovery), 1947; Point Four program. Labor relations: coal strikes. Taft-Hartley Act passage (over Truman veto), 1947.	Post-war U. S. S. R.: expansion of Eur., Asia influence. Blockade W. Berlin (countered by Allied "airlift" of supplies), 1948-49. Post-war Japan: Allied occupation (MacArthur cmdr.); democratic constn., 1946. Organizations: Org. Am. States charter signing, 1948. NATO, 1949. Nat. independence: India, 1947. Israel, 1948. China: Communist control, mainland. Nationalist flight to Formosa, 1949.	C. P. Snow, Cary fiction. Ital. films. Avant garde lit. styles: Beckett's "theatre of the absurd" ("Waiting for Godot," 1948). Lowry's novel of alienation ("Under the Volcano," 1947). Sarraute "anti-novels." Genet symbolic decadence. Art: Sculpture—Moore's space-mass relation; Giocometti elongations. Painting—abstract expressionism (Dubuffet); surrealism (Magritte, Delvaux, Balthus); expressionist idiom (Chagall series on persecution). Music: Honegger, Britten, Dallapiccola, Henze sense of tragedy. Poulenc esprit. Messiaen exoticism. Jolivet boldness. Blacher's rhythmic progressions.	olism cycle. Appleton: ionosphere investigations.
1950-1959 (THE EISENHOWER ERA) JONAS EDWARD SALK, ALBERT B. SABIN Polio breakthroughs. Salk serum announcement, 1953. Sabin's 1st tests, oral vaccine, 1955.	Korean War: U. S., U. N. check of N. Korean invasion, S. Korea, 1950; repulse, Chinese "volunteer" counter-attack, 1951; Truman dismissal of Gen. MacArthur as cmdr. in escalation dispute, 1951; armistice, 1953 (after Eisenhower accession as Pres.). Subversion fears: Rosenberg conspiracy. Hiss perjury convictions. Sen. Jos. McCarthy investigations; "condemnation" of him by Sen., 1954. Fgn. affairs: Secy. State Dulles "containment" (of Communism) policies; Summit Confs.; Eisenhower Doctrine (offer econ., mil. aid to Mid. East); econ. aid, mil. "advisors," S. Vietnam. Civil rights: Supreme Court decisions against pub. sch. segregation, 1954-55. Negro bus boycott (Rev. Martin Luth. King), Montgomery, Ala., 1955-56. U. S. troops to Little Rock, Ark., in sch.-segregation row, 1957. Also: Sen. Kefauver hearings on crime, 1950-51; on drug prices, 1959. Puerto Rico commonwealth status (1952), econ. development. Offshore-oil legislation. A.F.L.-C.I.O. merger, 1955. St. Lawrence Seaway opening, 1959. Statehood votes (Alaska, 1958; Hawaii, 1959).	U. S. S. R.: Stalin death, 1953; Khrushchev dominance; suppression revolts Poland, Hungary, 1956. West. Eur.: Churchill retirement as prime min., Brit., 1955. Creation Eur. Econ. Community (Common Market), 1957. France—de Gaulle return to power, constn., election as Pres., 1958, after civil-war threat. Near East Africa: nationalist terrorism (Algeria, Kenya). Civil strife, Cyprus, from 1954. Egyptian seizure, Suez Canal; Israeli-French-Brit. attack on Egypt, cease-fire, U. N. patrol, 1956. Growth ind. states, Africa, from 1956. "Apartheid" (rigid racial segregation), South Africa. Far East: formation SEATO, 1954. French-Vietminh div. of strife-torn Vietnam, followed by Fr. withdrawal; Ngo Dinh Diem regime, S. Vietnam. Latin Am.: Venezuela—Betancourt non-Red, econ. reform program. Argentine—mil. overthrow of Peron, 1954. Cuba—Castro ouster of Batista, 1959.	American: Man's alienation in lit.: Salinger's "Catcher in the Rye," 1951; Styron, Bellow, Flan. O'Connor, W. Morris, Malamud; Nabokov, Cheever irony; Ellison, Baldwin on race; Roethke, Jarrell poetry; Inge, Robt. Anderson, Gelber drama; the Beatniks (Kerouac, Ginsberg). Ideas on man's plight: Tillich's "new being" theology. Fromm psychoanalysis. Riesman on "the lonely crowd." Arendt on totalitarianism. Music: Carter's "metrical modulation;" Sessions' partial 12-tone; psychol. opera (Weisgall, Menotti, Floyd); electronic (Luening, Ussachevsky). Jazz-classical fusion (Schuller, Lewis); "cool jazz" (Monk, Davis, Coleman). Art: Sculptural inventiveness in metal (Lippold, Roszak, Smith). Abstract expressionism (de Kooning, Kline). Social satire (Levine, Rivers). Arch.: Saarinen's domical innovation. Stone's ornamental motifs. Plaza-oriented skyscrapers. Modern ballet: Balanchine-Graham "Episodes," 1959. Dramatic prodn.: rise of Method acting (Strasberg). Growth "off-Broadway" (Quintero). Foreign: Man vs. society: Golding, Lagerkvist, Boll novels; Amis, Powell satire. Ionesco's theatre-of-the-absurd; Osborne, Duerenmatt, Wesker, Behan plays. Parkinson analysis, over-institutionalization. Man's spirit and identity: Existentialism (Buber's "I and thou" theology; Beauvoir, Colin Wilson writings). Teilhard's sci., religious approach. Toynbee's "A Study of History." Durrell, Kazantzakis, Pasternak novels, verse. Mishima, Borges fiction; Robbe-Grillet "objective" style. Seferis, Quasimodo, Bachmann poems. Ingmar Bergman films. Dramatic fantasy: Anouilh. Fry's blank verse. Music: Serial (Nono, Boulez). Electronic (Stockhausen, Badings). Art: Bacon, Buffet, Pignon social outcry. Colorists (Nay). Abstract vigor (Mathieu). Abstract concrete (Veysset). Arch.: Niemeyer's linear concepts (Brasilia, Brazil). Nervi's aesthetic engring. (Olympic bldgs., Rome).	American: Townes: the maser. Calvin: chem. steps of photosynthesis. Du Vigneaud: protein hormone synthesis. Woodward: synthesis cholesterol, cortisone. Mossbauer: recoil-free gamma ray measurement. Glaser: "bubble chamber" for sub-atomic study. Van Allen: radiation belts around earth. Segre, Chamberlain: anti-protons. Teller: hydrogen bomb. Rickover: atomic submarine. von Braun: Explorer I satellite, 1958. Foreign: Oort: spiral structure of galaxy. Watson, Crick, Wilkins: structure of DNA. U.S.S.R.'s Sputnik I satellite, 1957. Ventris: deciphering Minoan Linear B script.
1960-1963 JOHN FITZGERALD KENNEDY Inauguration as Pres., 1961. "New Frontier" peace, domestic program. Assassination, Dallas, 1963.	Internat. good-will effort: Alliance for Progress with Latin Am., Peace Corps, 1961. Limited nuclear-test ban, 1963. Fgn. crises: Failure of "Bay of Pigs" invasion, Cuba, by U. S.-backed anti-Castro exiles, 1961. Blockade, successful protest, against Soviet missiles in Cuba, 1962. Limited direct mil. aid, S. Vietnam. Civil rights: Lunch-counter "sit-ins," "Freedom Riders," 1960-61. Submission 24th Amend., Constn. (poll-tax ban), 1962. Enrollment Jas. Meredith, Negro, at U. Miss., 1962. Kennedy proposal for broad civil-rights law. Rights rally, Wash., D. C., 1963. Inflation fight: cancellation steel-price hike after Kennedy protest. Lyndon Johnson oath as Pres., 1963.	Africa: South Africa withdrawal from Brit. Commonwealth, 1960. Congo independence (1960), factional war (air-crash death of U. S. Secy.-Gen. Hammarskjold on peace mission). Algerian independence, 1961. Berlin: East Ger. border closing, wall, to stop exodus to West, 1961. Roman Catholicism: 21st Ecumenical Council, from 1962; papal call for interchurch ties. Death Pope John XXIII, 1963; succession by Paul VI. Israel: execution former Nazi leader Eichmann, 1962. S. Vietnam: rebel guerrilla gains; mil. coup, death Pres. Ngo Dinh Diem, 1963. Dominican Repub.: assassination dictator Trujillo, 1961.	American: Fiction: Satire—Barth's "Sot-Weed Factor," 1960; Mary McCarthy, Auchincloss . . . Phil. Roth, Heller, Kesey, Friedman. Individual dilemma—Hawkes, Updike. Drama: Albee's symbolic shock ("Who's Afraid of Va. Woolf?," 1962). Kopit's theatre-of-the-absurd. "Action" poetry: Ashbery, Frank O'Hara. Art: Impersonality (Johns). "Pop" style—Rauschenberg, Warhol, Oldenburg. Arch.: aesthetic values (Mayan Temple-like Boston City Hall). Music: Serial (Babbitt, Perle). Aleatory (Cage). "Jazz Revolution" (Coltrane, Ayler). Folk, protest songs (Seeger). Foreign: Roman Cath. social encyclical: Pope John XXIII "Mater et Magistra," 1961. Social outcry in lit.: younger Russia (Yevtushenko, Voznesensky); Grass, Lind. Individual dilemma—D. Lessing, Pat. White; Pinter drama. Arch.: Couelle's cave-inspired homes. Sculpture: abstract vigor (Stahly, Martin); machine construction (Tinguely, Caro). Serial music: Ginastera, Berio. Cinema: Surrealism (Resnais, Fellini). "New Wave" (Godard). Naturalism (Richardson).	American: Hofstadter: size, shape, of atomic nucleus. Gell-Mann: "Eightfold Way" nuclear-particle classification. Glenn: 1st American in space orbit, 1962. Foreign: Leakey: prehistoric-man excavation. Gagarin: 1st Soviet space traveler, 1961.

PREFACE

Appearance of this HISTORICAL VOLUME of WHO WAS WHO IN AMERICA was inevitable because of its appropriateness to four other Marquis—Who's Who biographical directories and because of its virtual necessity to reference users.

Together with Volumes I, II and III of WHO WAS WHO (covering the period from 1897 to 1960) and *Who's Who in America* (the Contemporary Volume), this new publication furnishes a chronologically complete WHO'S WHO IN AMERICAN HISTORY . . . by delving back from 1896 to the founding of the Jamestown, Virginia, Colony (our country's first permanent English-speaking settlement) in 1607. WHO WAS WHO Volumes I, II and III contain the sketches of deceased *Who's Who in America* listees, and began with 1897 because that was the first year embraced by the latter book's earlier edition.

To David Martindell of New York City fell the distinction of proposing the HISTORICAL VOLUME. Immediately and zealously, the Editors of Marquis—Who's Who proceeded with the herculean task of researching data and preparing sketches on some 13,000 memorable names—not only Americans but foreigners who made a contribution to or had some relationship to our nation in her first 289 years.

This is the first Marquis book actually researched and completely written by the firm's Editors, since data for *Who's Who in America* and our other publications are—and were—supplied by the biographees themselves. These data are then converted to our time-honored biography-in-brief format.

The "start-from-scratch" circumstances of the HISTORICAL VOLUME entailed the development of a unique data-research procedure. This drew upon (1) the permanent research staff of Marquis—Who's Who, (2) a fervent group of professional historians and students sifted by written and oral examination from various universities, and organized on the basis of specialties as well as a general knowledge of American history, and (3) historical societies which enthusiastically agreed to act as sponsors and suggested regionally significant names which might otherwise have been overlooked. The data prepared by these forces were put into sketch form by a staff of sketch writers, who necessarily were specially trained for the task.

Thorny problems were steadily encountered, such as questions of accuracy in the books and treatises consulted, and contradictions between these materials . . . the extent to which secondary but interesting facts and narrative should be used . . . difficulties in finding many vital statistics traditionally essential to Marquis biographical directories. The historical staff and sketch writers met these challenges with painstaking dedication, uncanny resourcefulness . . . and impeccable teamwork. A further substantial diminution of error resulted from careful proofreading and factual checking of the printers' galleys—a job performed by a volunteer task force recruited from all departments of the organization.

To assure the HISTORICAL VOLUME of a representative and balanced coverage, every field of American history was exhaustively researched for significant and interesting individuals, including the leading spirits in all the arts and sciences, hundreds of businessmen, key national, regional and local figures in public affairs, explorers, military heroes, educators, theologians.

This coverage, embracing approximately 13,250 names, provides the most comprehensive biographical reference material available under one cover for America's first three centuries. And the five-volume WHO'S WHO IN AMERICAN HISTORY of which this book is a component has a matchlessly comprehensive 115,000 names!

Following the main biographical section of the HISTORICAL VOLUME is an invaluable addendum starting on page 677 and containing:

(1) Supplemental biographical sketches researched too late for inclusion in the main

section, (2) sketches of persons omitted from Volumes I, II and III of WHO WAS WHO but who now are considered highly reference-worthy and who died after 1905—terminal date for listing in the main section of the HISTORICAL VOLUME, and (3) additional significant data on individuals sketched in other volumes of WHO WAS WHO, with reference to the number of the volume containing the basic sketch.

Although the "cut-off" date in the subtitle of the HISTORICAL VOLUME is 1896, the Editors deemed it advisable—to assure coverage of individuals who were still living in that year, but who had not previously been listed in WHO WAS WHO—to include decedents between that year and 1905 in the main biographical section. Also, while the subtitled starting date is 1607, more than a score of notables who died earlier have been included in that section.

With the thought that the reference value of such a book would be enhanced by *lists* of Americans who have held pre-eminent positions in our national, state and city governments, statistical and historical particulars on our principal cities, and some "firsts" and other major events in our country's evolution, the Addendum has been extended to provide such information under the title "Facts at Your Fingertips."

Books as manifold as the HISTORICAL VOLUME—and WHO'S WHO IN AMERICAN HISTORY as a whole—obviously serve many uses: 1) Reference and research by historical and biographical scholars, journalists, public speakers, college, secondary and elementary school students, both for general knowledge and specialties; 2) home use—not only for reference to names occurring in the course of one's reading of books and periodicals, but for casual browsing through sketches that pique attention (as observed by several members of our staff in looking over galley proofs). Educationally, the HISTORICAL VOLUME will serve pupil and home reader by exposing them to an important research methodology—the use of the widely-accepted abbreviations used in the sketches and explained in the Table on page 77.

That WHO WAS WHO and therefore the completed WHO'S WHO IN AMERICAN HISTORY fill an urgent reference need is decisively demonstrated by the fact that Volume I is in its fifth printing, Volume II in its fourth printing, and Volume III (published as recently as 1960) is already in its second . . . and by the widespread commendation these books have received and continue to receive.

This rounding out of WHO'S WHO IN AMERICAN HISTORY through the publication of the HISTORICAL VOLUME is a logical culmination of the undertaking which the first Marquis biographical compilation initiated 65 years ago. It recalls the following statement that appeared in the Preface of the first edition of *Who's Who in America*—a statement equally applicable to the HISTORICAL VOLUME: "Without claiming infallibility or inerrancy, it is believed that this publication will be a welcome addition to the list of handy helps that make up the library of indispensable books."

Certainly nothing in the form of dedicated care, persistent effort or financial expenditure has been spared in making the HISTORICAL VOLUME OF WHO WAS WHO fulfill the purposes of its compilation . . . its furtherance of American biographical/historical knowledge.

Jackson Martindell
Publisher

Chicago, Illinois
July 16, 1963

PREFACE TO THE REVISED EDITION

Publication of this revised edition of the HISTORICAL VOLUME, WHO WAS WHO IN AMERICA: 1607-1896, has been obligatory for two outstanding reasons.

First, the success of the original edition of 1963 has been so notable that the press run, albeit substantial, is exhausted. Both as a matchlessly informative individual volume and as an integral unit of *Who's Who in American History* (1607 to today), the book was eagerly greeted. It is in standard use in schools and colleges . . . libraries and other reference centers . . . by historians, researchers, journalists, laymen.

Second, the House of Marquis always has felt that success entails additional obligations rather than self-satisfaction. Accordingly this revision incorporates splendid new features, new biographical sketches, and meticulous additions and amendments in some earlier sketches and in the "Facts at Your Finger Tips" indexes.

These refinements lift the HISTORICAL VOLUME to an even higher peak of educational and reference value, stimulation and interest.

The new features—the Biographical Map inside the front and rear covers, the Course of History Time Line Chart—are fully explained in the "How to Use It" article starting on page 19.

Most of the approximately 200 additional sketches fall into the following categories:

1. Historic individuals who—while generally absent from other reference publications—deserve national reference recognition because of their role in the development of their vocation, their region or our way of life. For example, we have added some worthy transitional figures in the arts, philosophy, science, civic affairs, government. Also, we have amplified the number of Western explorers—including men identified (in primary source materials) with historic trails, settlements and present-day scenic glories. Although the volume's subtitle dates are 1607 to 1896, its main body covers American residents or influencers living between the 11th Century and 1905.

2. Further listings of post-1905 decedents in the Addendum Section. These generally are of persons who never were sketched in *Who's Who in America*" (and thus are not included in WHO WAS WHO VOLS. I, II and III) but have attained eminence since their death. Some of them had to await the judgment of time because they were unusual contributors in relatively new fields . . . fields like the cinema, jazz, the behavioral sciences. And several were foreigners or refugees whose influence on American science, art and thought has grown in recent years.

All these new sketches augment the unique comprehensiveness and balance not only of the HISTORICAL VOLUME but the entire AMERICAN HISTORY set.

All names appearing in the original edition have been retained.

Marquis editors have been gratified by the many attestations of authoritativeness in the original edition . . . by the warm comments of readers and reference users, who only rarely have raised factual questions. Nevertheless, for this revision, our researchers made an exhaustive review of the original edition. They resolved inevitable discrepancies among the excellent source materials that had been used. They took cognizance of new biographical scholarship that superseded earlier accounts.

Thus the amendments and additions to original sketches reflect our insistence on the latest and best information.

The revisions in the Facts at Your Finger Tips indexes—now shifted to the front of the book for your convenience—include a new section on state-name origins; the addition of 10 cities in the section on urban data, and the extension of the "Some Major Events" chronology to 1963.

This revision embraces the valuable suggestions offered by institutions and individuals . . . including historical societies that previously had been helpful in the original compilation. To all of these kindly correspondents we extend our profound gratitude . . . in behalf not only of the House of Marquis but the countless thousands who turn to these pages for instant and continuing knowledge, for fascinating lore, for the warm personal image of America's past.

THE HISTORICAL VOLUME —HOW TO USE IT

This HISTORICAL VOLUME of WHO WAS WHO IN AMERICA is your guide to the basic lives of 13,450 shining names of our country's past—but it is far more than that. With its Course of History chart, its Facts at Your Finger Tips tables, its end maps and other educational aids, it is like a school with many rooms. Each of the many features—like a classroom or assembly hall—is important in itself. Yet each is related to the others; like a school, they form a unit. They provide a broad, thorough service . . . for researcher, teacher and student alike . . . in biography, history, civics, geography and other social studies.

While the biographical section of this HISTORICAL VOLUME is devoted chiefly to the 1607-1896 period, the special instructional aids cover all periods. So if important individuals you meet in these aids lived after 1896, you would find their biographies in other volumes of WHO WAS WHO IN AMERICA or in WHO'S WHO IN AMERICA. Volume I of WHO WAS WHO contains the sketches of former "Who's Who in America" subjects who died between 1897 and 1942; Volume II does the same for 1943 to 1950, and Volume III for 1951 to 1960. The current edition of "Who's Who in America" sketches living notables. All of these books combine to form a set called WHO'S WHO IN AMERICAN HISTORY.

Exceptions should be borne in mind. Some individuals who never appeared in "Who's Who in America," but gained eminence after their death, are sketched in this HISTORICAL VOLUME (see details below). If the death of a "Who's Who" subject was learned too late for the appropriate WHO WAS WHO volume, his sketch was deferred to the next volume of WHO WAS WHO.

When WHO WAS WHO Volume IV (1961-1968) is published in January, 1968, it will have an index to the biographies in the HISTORICAL VOLUME and all other WHO WAS WHO'S, giving the volume and page where each sketch may be found. Thus, without knowing an individual's date of death, you instantly will learn where to find his biography.

AND NOW . . . let us take up—one by one—the many valuable features of this HISTORICAL VOLUME.

I BIOGRAPHICAL AND ADDENDUM SECTIONS . . . ABBREVIATIONS: Each sketch in the HISTORICAL VOLUME has a personality of its own . . . is a story of an interesting figure of the colorful past. Yet every sketch—as in the entire WHO'S WHO IN AMERICAN HISTORY set—presents each type of data in the same general order. As soon as you learn this arrangement, you promptly and easily will find the data you need in any sketch in any of the volumes. The order is as follows:

- Full name, with last name first
- Basic occupation
- Place and date of birth
- Parentage
- Education
- Marriage, children
- Chronological summary of career
- Other activities, memberships, awards
- Books, paintings, musical compositions or other specific projects
- Full addresses (except in HISTORICAL VOLUME)
- If dead: place and date of death, final resting place

Of course, not all of these types of information are pertinent or available for every sketch. Also, there are occasional departures from the arrangement to allow for exceptionally interesting or colorful facts.

To illustrate the basic order, let us consider the sketch of Thomas Jefferson:

(1) To find his sketch, you will flip through the alphabetically-arranged biographical section to the letter "J"—because all individuals are listed with last name first. Thus you will see "JEFFERSON, Thomas."

(2) After the name comes the basic vocation that identifies a man. While Jefferson was a versatile genius, the brief identification you find—"3rd Pres. U.S."—is enough to distinguish him from any other Jeffersons. (Vocational title is particularly important after a name like William Bradford—because six William Bradfords are listed in the HISTORICAL VOLUME!)

The abbreviations, "3rd Pres. U.S.," are easy to interpret—and so are most of those used in the sketches. A student should try to master them without help—because they are logical, standard abbreviations that he will meet progressively in other printed materials. In case of doubt, however, reference should be made to the Table of Abbreviations on Page 77. The abbreviations are important in making the biographies concise and direct; they will help the student absorb many details at a glance. When he spells out the abbreviations and supplies any omitted parts of speech (like "the" and "was"), the sentences will take on complete narrative form . . . and the sketch as a whole will become a formal but lively composition that he can copy in his notebook.

(3) The third item in Jefferson's sketch is his birth place and date. After the abbreviation "b." (for "born"), you will see "'Old Shadwell,'" Goochland (now Albemarle County), Va., Apr. 13, 1743." Old Shadwell was the name of the plantation and Goochland was the original name of Albemarle County.

The April 13 birth date follows the Gregorian or New Style calendar, which the volume generally uses for persons living in or after 1752, when England adopted that calendar. Jefferson's birth date according to the Old Style calendar was April 2.

(4) Parentage comes next. After an "s." (meaning "son" of), you will see "Peter and Jane (Randolph) J." Thus Jane Randolph was the mother's maiden name; the "J." signifies there was no difference in spelling between the parents' names and the son's. (In a sketch like that of pioneer philosopher Henry C. Brokmeyer, the father's last name is spelled out because it was "Brockmeyer.")

(5) Next, education. You will see that Thomas Jefferson attended the College of William and Mary but was not graduated (grad.), and then studied law under George Wythe.

(6) Marriage and children. We see that Jefferson married ("m.") Martha Wayles Skelton on January 1, 1772, and that they had six children, only two of whom, Martha and Marie, reached maturity.

(7) Career summary. Most of the sketch is devoted to a listing of the highlights of Jefferson's career, in chronological order, with dates. From his service as County Lt. (lieutenant) in 1770 through his two terms as President (1801-09), you will find a complete listing of his full-time positions and basic accomplishments, with brief elaboration where necessary. Once a scene of activity is given, you should regard his further activities as taking place there until another scene is indicated; thus his positions were in Albemarle County until he served in the Virginia House of Burgesses, and all his listed work was in Virginia until he served in the Continental Congress. You will notice that while his first two positions preceded his marriage, his entire career is kept together. Such separation will be a big help to you in organizing your study or research.

(8) Other activities, etc. After the career summary, you will find activities of Jefferson that were important but not related to his basic career in government and law. You will see, for instance, that he was founder, rector and architectural designer of the University of Virginia, and that he was president of the American Philosophical Society. An interesting project on the outside activities of great men can be developed simply by referring to this portion of their sketches.

(9) Authorship. Toward the end of Jefferson's sketch you will find a description or title of his writings. The Declaration of Independence and Kentucky Resolutions are not included here because they necessarily were mentioned in his career summary.

(10) You will see that Jefferson died at his home, Monticello, in Albemarle County, on the Fourth of July, 1826, and that he was buried at Monticello. Had he died in a city, its name rather than the county's would have been used. The name of the state is not given here because the sketch earlier had placed Albemarle County in Virginia.

Although the starting date in the subtitle of the HISTORICAL VOLUME is 1607, more than a score of notables who died earlier are sketched—in the interest of complete historical coverage. The year 1607 was selected because our nation's birthplace—the first permanent English colony at Jamestown, Virginia—was settled then.

And while the "cut-off" date in the subtitle is 1896, the main body of the book includes some individuals who died *as late as 1905*. These are persons who never were listed in "Who's Who in America" (and thus not in WHO WAS WHO Volumes I to III) but who have won prominence since their death.

The SUPPLEMENTAL BIOGRAPHIES section sketches such individuals who died *after 1905*. It also contains (1) listings researched too late for inclusion in the main biographical section, and (2) additional data on individuals sketched in other WHO WAS WHO volumes, with references to the volume number.

All sketches in the HISTORICAL VOLUME were prepared by Marquis researchers and scholars. Sketches in the other volumes of WHO'S WHO IN AMERICAN HISTORY—except those with an asterisk (*) at the end—were based on material supplied by the biographical subject.

II BIOGRAPHICAL MAP: The lively map —in front and rear inside covers—shows the 50 states and some thumbnail facts about the great personages who lived in each one . . . from 1513 to today. By seeing these names in their geographical setting, you will know more about their influence . . . and about the lore of each state. The men were not necessarily born where the map places them, and some (like Mark

Twain) were often on the move. You will enjoy referring from the map to the biographical section, and seeing how the items on the map relate to the men's entire lives. The map omits identification of locales to help you familiarize yourself with them.

III THE COURSE OF HISTORY Chart: This dynamic chart lets you see, all at once, the rise and development of American civilization. In chronologically arranged panels, it presents outstanding men, events and achievements of each era . . . including foreign activities that sooner or later influenced our country. For each principal period from Leif Ericsson's explorations to George Washington's Presidency and for each decade since, a "key name" in American history appears in the left-hand column. He is a man who expressed, and helped mold, the spirit of his period; a few of his chief activities of the period are given beneath his name. To suggest the variety that enriches American civilization, the key names were chosen from different fields—the arts and sciences as well as exploration and government. Other principal individuals and happenings of each period are described in adjoining columns, under their proper heading—Historical and General Events, American and Foreign . . . the Arts and Thought . . . Science and Invention.

For the 1860-69 decade, for example, you will notice that Abraham Lincoln is the key name. Beneath his name are basic facts that relate him to his decade—such as his tenure as President and the Emancipation Proclamation. In the second panel, you will find general American events of that decade, including the Homestead Act, the first transcontinental railroad and Reconstruction as well as some fundamental highlights of the Civil War. In the third panel, you will find general foreign developments like German unification and completion of the Suez Canal. The fourth panel—the Arts and Thought—includes Walt Whitman's authorship of the beloved elegies for Lincoln, and (as a foreign entry) Tolstoy's novel, "War and Peace." The last panel—Science and Invention—includes John Ericsson's iron-clad vessel, the Monitor, and (under "foreign") Mendel's laws of heredity. It should be noted that while Lincoln was lost to the county in 1865, the factual coverage in the panels is for the entire 1860-69 period.

Used along with the biographical section, the COURSE OF HISTORY chart clarifies the relations between different periods . . . between achievements in different fields . . . between our country and the world . . . between present and past.

IV FACTS AT YOUR FINGER TIPS: This series of indexes is a genuine almanac of historical and statistical information. Like the special features outlined above, it contributes to a *general* understanding of American biography and history; but its primary purpose is to give detailed *specific* information in many categories. The categories can be broken down as follows:

- THE FEDERAL GOVERNMENT. A listing (with terms of office or years of appointment) of all our Presidents, Vice Presidents, Cabinet Officers, Justices of the United States Supreme Court (with Chief Justices indicated in bold-face type), Speakers of the U.S. House of Representatives and Presidents Pro Tempore of the U.S. Senate. The listings for the Cabinet show the changes in its structure since Washington's administration, when it had only four members.
- THE STATES. You will find the name and term of office of the first Governor of each state; the year in which each state was admitted to the Union, and the origins of state names. You will see from these tables that the first 13 states in the War for Independence were the first to ratify the Constitution and enter the Union. State names, you will notice, were derived not only from the Indian languages, but from French, Spanish, Latin, Eskimo—and English.
- THE CITIES. For almost 150 principal American cities, you will find their county; years of founding and incorporation; source of name, and population change through 1960—beginning with the 1790 census (America's first) for the oldest cities. The section includes all state capitals and all cities with at least 175,000 inhabitants in 1960, plus several towns (like Plymouth and Salem, Mass.) chosen for historical interest.
- SOME MAJOR EVENTS, INCLUDING "FIRSTS", IN UNITED STATES HISTORY. This chronology gives you important (or interesting) events of every memorable year . . . from 1007 A.D. (when the first child of European parents was born in America) to 1963. The month and day, if significant to the event, are shown. While stressing the noteworthy, the entries also aim to suggest the spirit of the time. For example, the 1892 entries include not only Presidential nominations, the end of the Homestead Strike and a discovery in astronomy—but the birth of the tune, "Bicycle Built for Two", and the invention of the Ferris wheel. Similarly, the "firsts" for the various years range in

seriousness from the first graduated income-tax law to the first circus. A special theme of the chronology is the rise in the status of women—from the publication of the first book by a woman (Anne Bradstreet in 1640) to the appointment of the first woman Cabinet officer (Frances Perkins in 1933). Valuable for cross-reference with biographies and for ready reference, the chronology also is a delight for browsing. Flip the pages and you will find that popcorn, introduced to the colonists in 1630, had to wait until 1902 for its ideal mate—the motion picture theatre.

PRACTICAL APPLICATIONS FOR THIS VOLUME

With its wonderful wealth of life stories and special features, with its compact, orderly presentation, this book is ideal for many practical uses . . . by researcher, teacher and student . . . in classroom, library and home. For example, it is widely used to:

- Supplement textbook use in history, civics, biography, geography and other social studies . . . provide biographical background in studying the arts and sciences.
- Aid the teacher in organizing classroom discussions, projects, lectures . . . help the student prepare for recitations, themes and tests.
- Serve as a guide in special research projects at the library.
- Clarify or expand material found in histories, newspapers, magazines.
- Demonstrate concise expression and help the student organize his learning.
- Train the student in research techniques—as represented by the alphabetical and abbreviations system, biographical compilation, special features.
- Stimulate the student's interest in U.S. history, customs, culture . . . in great lives that can inspire him as a career-builder and citizen.
- Provide constructive enjoyment. Simply by browsing . . . by letting the eye lead the mind . . . the user of the HISTORICAL VOLUME absorbs important knowledge.

FACTS AT YOUR FINGER TIPS

PRESIDENTS AND VICE PRESIDENTS OF THE UNITED STATES

	President		Vice President	Service
1	George Washington	1	John Adams	Apr. 30, 1789—Mar. 3, 1797
2	John Adams	2	Thomas Jefferson	Mar. 4, 1797—Mar. 3, 1801
3	Thomas Jefferson	3	Aaron Burr	Mar. 4, 1801—Mar. 3, 1805
	*do	4	George Clinton	Mar. 4, 1805—Mar. 3, 1809
4	James Madison		do	Mar. 4, 1809—Mar. 3, 1813
	do	5	Elbridge Gerry	Mar. 4, 1813—Mar. 3, 1817
5	James Monroe	6	Daniel D. Tompkins	Mar. 4, 1817—Mar. 3, 1825
6	John Quincy Adams	7	John C. Calhoun	Mar. 4, 1825—Mar. 3, 1829
7	Andrew Jackson		do	Mar. 4, 1829—Mar. 3, 1833
	do	8	Martin Van Buren	Mar. 4, 1833—Mar. 3, 1837
8	Martin Van Buren	9	Richard M. Johnson	Mar. 4, 1837—Mar. 3, 1841
9	William Henry Harrison	10	John Tyler	Mar. 4, 1841—Apr. 4, 1841
10	John Tyler			Apr. 6, 1841—Mar. 3, 1845
11	James K. Polk	11	George M. Dallas	Mar. 4, 1845—Mar. 3, 1849
12	Zachary Taylor	12	Millard Fillmore	Mar. 5, 1849—July 9, 1850
13	Millard Fillmore			July 10, 1850—Mar. 3, 1853
14	Franklin Pierce	13	William R. King	Mar. 4, 1853—Mar. 3, 1857
15	James Buchanan	14	John C. Breckinridge	Mar. 4, 1857—Mar. 3, 1861
16	Abraham Lincoln	15	Hannibal Hamlin	Mar. 4, 1861—Mar. 3, 1865
	do	16	Andrew Johnson	Mar. 4, 1865—Apr. 15, 1865
17	Andrew Johnson			Apr. 15, 1865—Mar. 3, 1869
18	Ulysses S. Grant	17	Schuyler Colfax	Mar. 4, 1869—Mar. 3, 1873
	do	18	Henry Wilson	Mar. 4, 1873—Mar. 3, 1877
19	Rutherford B. Hayes	19	William A. Wheeler	Mar. 4, 1877—Mar. 3, 1881
20	James A. Garfield	20	Chester A. Arthur	Mar. 4, 1881—Sept. 19, 1881
21	Chester A. Arthur			Sept. 20, 1881—Mar. 3, 1885
22	Grover Cleveland	21	Thomas A. Hendricks	Mar. 4, 1885—Mar. 3, 1889
23	Benjamin Harrison	22	Levi P. Morton	Mar. 4, 1889—Mar. 3, 1893
24	Grover Cleveland	23	Adlai E. Stevenson	Mar. 4, 1893—Mar. 3, 1897
25	William McKinley	24	Garret A. Hobart	Mar. 4, 1897—Mar. 3, 1901
	do	25	Theodore Roosevelt	Mar. 4, 1901—Sept. 14, 1901
26	Theodore Roosevelt			Mar. 14, 1901—Mar. 3, 1905
	do	26	Charles W. Fairbanks	Sept. 4, 1905—Mar. 3, 1909
27	William H. Taft	27	James S. Sherman	Mar. 4, 1909—Mar. 3, 1913
28	Woodrow Wilson	28	Thomas R. Marshall	Mar. 4, 1913—Mar. 3, 1921
29	Warren G. Harding	29	Calvin Coolidge	Mar. 4, 1921—Aug. 2, 1923
30	Calvin Coolidge			Aug. 3, 1923—Mar. 3, 1925
	do	30	Charles G. Dawes	Mar. 4, 1925—Mar. 3, 1929
31	Herbert C. Hoover	31	Charles Curtis	Mar. 4, 1929—Mar. 3, 1933
32	Franklin D. Roosevelt	32	John N. Garner	Mar. 4, 1933—Jan. 20, 1941
	do	33	Henry A. Wallace	Jan. 20, 1941—Jan. 20, 1945
	do	34	Harry S Truman	Jan. 20, 1945—Apr. 12, 1945
33	Harry S Truman			Apr. 12, 1945—Jan. 20, 1949
	do	35	Alben W. Barkley	Jan. 20, 1949—Jan. 20, 1953
34	Dwight D. Eisenhower	36	Richard M. Nixon	Jan. 20, 1953—Jan. 20, 1957
	do		do	Jan. 20, 1957—Jan. 20, 1961
35	John F. Kennedy	37	Lyndon B. Johnson	Jan. 20, 1961—Nov. 22, 1963
36	Lyndon B. Johnson			Nov. 22, 1963—Jan. 20, 1965
	do	38	Hubert H. Humphrey	Jan. 20, 1965—

* do signifies ditto

CABINET OFFICERS OF THE UNITED STATES

Secretaries of State

	Apptd.
Thomas Jefferson	1789
Edmund Randolph	1794
Timothy Pickering	1795
do	1797
John Marshall	1800
James Madison	1801
Robert Smith	1809
James Monroe	1811
John Quincy Adams	1817
Henry Clay	1825
Martin Van Buren	1829
Edward Livingston	1831
Louis McLane	1833
John Forsyth	1834
do	1837
Daniel Webster	1841
do	1841
Hugh S. Legare	1843
Apel P. Upshur	1843
John C. Calhoun	1844
James Buchanan	1845
John M. Clayton	1849
Daniel Webster	1850
Edward Everett	1852
William L. Marcy	1853
Lewis Cass	1857
Jeremiah S. Black	1860
William H. Seward	1861
do	1865
Elihu B. Washburne	1869
Hamilton Fish	1869
William M. Evarts	1877
James G. Blaine	1881
F. T. Frelinghuysen	1881
Thomas F. Bayard	1885
James G. Blaine	1889
John W. Foster	1892
Walter Q. Gresham	1893
Richard Olney	1895
John Sherman	1897
William R. Day	1898
John Hay	1898
do	1901
Elihu Root	1905
Robert Bacon	1909
Philander C. Knox	1909
William J. Bryan	1913
Robert Lansing	1915
Bainbridge Colby	1920
Charles E. Hughes	1921
do	1923
Frank B. Kellogg	1925
Henry L. Stimson	1929
Cordell Hull	1933
Edward R. Stettinius, Jr.	1944
James F. Byrnes	1945
George C. Marshall	1947
Dean G. Acheson	1949
John Foster Dulles	1953
Christian A. Herter	1959
Dean Rusk	1961

Secretaries of the Treasury

	Apptd.
Alexander Hamilton	1789
Oliver Wolcott	1795
do	1797
Samuel Dexter	1801
do	1801
Albert Gallatin	1801
do	1809
George W. Campbell	1814
Alexander J. Dallas	1814
William H. Crawford	1816
do	1817
Richard Rush	1825
Samuel D. Ingham	1829
Louis McLane	1831
William J. Duane	1833
Roger B. Taney	1833
Levi Woodbury	1834
do	1837
Thomas Ewing	1841
do	1841
Walter Forward	1841
John C. Spencer	1843
George M. Bibb	1844
Robert J. Walker	1845
William M. Meredith	1849
Thomas Corwin	1850
James Guthrie	1853
Howell Cobb	1857
Philip F. Thomas	1860
John A. Dix	1861
Salmon P. Chase	1861
William P. Fessenden	1864
Hugh McCulloch	1865
do	1865
George S. Boutwell	1869
William A. Richardson	1873
Benjamin H. Bristow	1874
Lot M. Morrill	1876
John Sherman	1877
William Windom	1881
Charles J. Folger	1881
Walter Q. Gresham	1884
Hugh McCulloch	1884
Daniel Manning	1885
Charles S. Fairchild	1887
William Windom	1889
Charles Foster	1891
John G. Carlisle	1893
Lyman J. Gage	1897
do	1901
Leslie M. Shaw	1902
George B. Cortelyou	1907
Franklin MacVeagh	1909
William G. McAdoo	1913
Carter Glass	1919
David F. Houston	1920
Andrew W. Mellon	1921
do	1923
do	1929
Ogden L. Mills	1932
William H. Woodin	1933
Henry Morgenthau, Jr.	1934
Fred M. Vinson	1945
John W. Snyder	1946
George M. Humphrey	1953
Robert B. Anderson	1957
C. Douglas Dillon	1961

Secretaries of Defense

	Apptd.		Apptd.
James V. Forrestal	1947	Charles E. Wilson	1953
Louis A. Johnson	1949	Neil H. McElroy	1957
George C. Marshall	1950	Thomas S. Gates, Jr.	1959
Robert A. Lovett	1951	Robert S. McNamara	1961

Secretaries of War

	Apptd.		Apptd.
Henry Knox	1789	Edwin M. Stanton	1865
Timothy Pickering	1795	U. S. Grant	1867
James McHenry	1796	Lorenzo Thomas	1868
do	1797	John M. Schofield	1868
John Marshall	1800	John A. Rawlins	1869
Samuel Dexter	1800	William T. Sherman	1869
Roger Griswold	1801	William W. Belknap	1869
Henry Dearborn	1801	Alphonso Taft	1876
William Eustis	1809	James Don. Cameron	1876
John Armstrong	1813	George W. McCrary	1877
James Monroe	1814	Alexander Ramsey	1879
William H. Crawford	1815	Robert T. Lincoln	1881
Isaac Shelby	1817	do	1881
Geo. Graham	1817	William C. Endicott	1885
John C. Calhoun	1817	Redfield Proctor	1889
James Barbour	1825	Stephen B. Elkins	1891
Peter B. Porter	1828	Daniel S. Lamont	1893
John H. Eaton	1829	Russel A. Alger	1897
Lewis Cass	1831	Elihu Root	1899
Benjamin F. Butler	1837	do	1901
Joel R. Poinsett	1837	William H. Taft	1904
John Bell	1841	Luke E. Wright	1908
do	1841	Jacob M. Dickinson	1909
John McLean	1841	Henry L. Stimson	1911
John C. Spencer	1841	Lindley M. Garrison	1913
James M. Porter	1843	Newton D. Baker	1916
William Wilkins	1844	John W. Weeks	1921
William L. Marcy	1845	do	1923
George W. Crawford	1849	Dwight F. Davis	1925
Edward Bates	1850	James W. Good	1929
Charles M. Conrad	1850	Patrick J. Hurley	1929
Jefferson Davis	1853	George H. Dern	1933
John B. Floyd	1857	Harry H. Woodring	1936
Joseph Holt	1861	Henry L. Stimson	1940
Simon Cameron	1861	Robert P. Patterson	1945
Edwin M. Stanton	1862	Kenneth C. Royall	1947

Secretaries of the Navy

	Apptd.		Apptd.
Benjamin Stoddert	1798	John Y. Mason	1846
do	1801	William B. Preston	1849
Robert Smith	1801	William A. Graham	1850
Jacob Crowninshield	1805	John P. Kennedy	1852
Paul Hamilton	1809	James C. Dobbin	1853
William Jones	1813	Isaac Toucey	1857
Benjamin Williams Crowninshield	1814	Gideon Welles	1861
do	1817	do	1865
Smith Thompson	1818	Adolph E. Borie	1869
Samuel L. Southard	1823	George M. Robeson	1869
do	1825	Richard W. Thompson	1877
John Branch	1829	Nathan Goff, Jr.	1881
Levi Woodbury	1831	William H. Hunt	1881
Mahlon Dickerson	1834	William E. Chandler	1882
do	1837	William C. Whitney	1885
James K. Paulding	1838	Benjamin F. Tracy	1889
George E. Badger	1841	Hilary A. Herbert	1893
do	1841	John D. Long	1897
Abel P. Upshur	1841	do	1901
David Henshaw	1843	William H. Moody	1902
Thomas W. Gilmer	1844	Paul Morton	1904
John Y. Mason	1844		

Secretaries of the Navy — Continued

	Apptd.		Apptd.
Charles J. Bonaparte	1905	Curtis D. Wilbur	1924
Victor H. Metcalf	1906	Charles Francis Adams	1929
Truman H. Newberry	1908	Claude A. Swanson	1933
George von L. Meyer	1909	Charles Edison	1940
Josephus Daniels	1913	Frank Knox	1940
Edwin Denby	1921	James V. Forrestal	1944
do	1923	do	1945

Attorneys General

	Apptd.		Apptd.
Edmund Randolph	1789	William M. Evarts	1868
William Bradford	1794	Ebenezer R. Hoar	1869
Charles Lee	1795	Amos T. Akerman	1870
do	1797	George H. Williams	1871
Theophilus Parsons	1801	Edwards Pierrepont	1875
Levi Lincoln	1801	Alphonso Taft	1876
Robert Smith	1805	Charles Devens	1877
John Breckenridge	1805	Wayne MacVeagh	1881
Caesar A. Rodney	1807	Benjamin H. Brewster	1881
do	1809	Augustus Garland	1885
William Pinkney	1811	William H. H. Miller	1889
Richard Rush	1814	Richard Olney	1893
do	1817	Judson Harmon	1895
William Wirt	1817	Joseph McKenna	1897
do	1825	John W. Griggs	1898
John McP. Berrien	1829	Philander C. Knox	1901
Roger B. Taney	1831	do	1901
Benjamin F. Butler	1833	William H. Moody	1904
do	1837	Charles J. Bonaparte	1906
Felix Grundy	1838	George W. Wickersham	1909
Henry D. Gilpin	1840	J. C. McReynolds	1913
John J. Crittenden	1841	Thomas W. Gregory	1914
do	1841	A. Mitchell Palmer	1919
Hugh S. Legare	1841	Harry M. Daugherty	1921
John Nelson	1843	do	1923
John Y. Mason	1845	Harlan F. Stone	1924
Nathan Clifford	1846	John G. Sargent	1925
Isaac Toucey	1848	William D. Mitchell	1929
Reverdy Johnson	1849	Homer S. Cummings	1933
John J. Crittenden	1850	Frank Murphy	1939
Caleb Cushing	1853	Robert H. Jackson	1940
Jeremiah S. Black	1857	Francis Biddle	1941
Edwin M. Stanton	1860	Tom C. Clark	1945
Edward Bates	1861	J. Howard McGrath	1949
Titian J. Coffey	1863	J. P. McGranery	1952
James Speed	1864	H. Brownell, Jr.	1953
do	1865	William P. Rogers	1957
Henry Stanbery	1866	Robert F. Kennedy	1961

Postmasters General (Became Cabinet Post in 1829)

	Apptd.		Apptd.
Samuel Osgood	1789	John M. Niles	1840
Timothy Pickering	1791	Francis Granger	1841
Joseph Habersham	1795	do	1841
do	1797	Charles A. Wickliff	1841
do	1801	Cave Johnson	1845
Gideon Granger	1801	Jacob Collamer	1849
do	1809	Nathan K. Hall	1850
Return J. Meigs Jr.	1814	Samuel D. Hubbard	1852
do	1817	James Campbell	1853
John McLean	1823	Aaron V. Brown	1857
do	1825	Joseph Holt	1859
William T. Barry	1829	Horatio King	1861
Amos Kendall	1835	Montgomery Blair	1861
do	1837	William Dennison	1864
		do	1865

Postmasters General — Continued

	Apptd.		Apptd.
Alex. W. Randall	1866	Henry C. Payne	1902
John A. J. Creswell	1869	Robert J. Wynne	1904
James W. Marshall	1874	George B. Cortelyou	1905
Marshall Jewell	1874	George von L. Meyer	1907
James N. Tyner	1876	Frank H. Hitchcock	1909
David McK. Key	1877	Albert S. Burleson	1913
Horace Maynard	1880	Will H. Hays	1921
Thomas L. James	1881	Hubert Work	1922
Timothy O. Howe	1881	Harry S. New	1923
Walter Q. Gresham	1883	do	1923
Frank Hatton	1884	Walter F. Brown	1929
William F. Vilas	1885	James A. Farley	1933
Don M. Dickinson	1888	Frank C. Walker	1940
John Wanamaker	1889	Robt. E. Hannegan	1945
Wilson S. Bissel	1893	Jesse M. Donaldson	1947
William L. Wilson	1895	A. E. Summerfield	1953
James A. Gary	1897	J. Edward Day	1961
Charles E. Smith	1898		
do	1901		

Secretaries of the Interior

	Apptd.		Apptd.
Thomas Ewing	1849	David R. Francis	1896
James A. Pearce	1850	Cornelius N. Bliss	1897
Thoms M. T. McKennan	1850	Ethan A. Hitchcock	1899
Alex. H. H. Stuart	1850	do	1901
Robert McClelland	1853	James R. Garfield	1907
Jacob Thompson	1857	Richard A. Ballinger	1909
Caleb B. Smith	1861	Walter L. Fisher	1911
John P. Usher	1863	Franklin K. Lane	1913
do	1865	John B. Payne	1920
James Harlan	1865	Albert B. Fall	1921
Orville H. Browning	1866	Hubert Work	1923
Jacob D. Cox	1869	do	1923
Columbus Delano	1870	Roy O. West	1928
Zachariah Chandler	1875	Ray Lyman Wilbur	1929
Carl Schurz	1877	**Cabinet Officers**	**Apptd.**
Sam. J. Kirkwood	1881	Harold L. Ickes	1933
Henry M. Teller	1882	do	1945
Lucius Q. C. Lamar	1885	Julius A. Krug	1946
William F. Vilas	1888	Oscar L. Chapman	1949
John W. Noble	1889	Douglas McKay	1953
		Fred A. Seaton	1956
Hoke Smith	1893	Stewart L. Udall	1961

Secretaries of Agriculture

	Apptd.		Apptd.
Norman J. Colman	1889	Howard M. Gore	1924
Jeremiah M. Rusk	1889	W. M. Jardine	1925
J. Sterling Morton	1893	Arthur M. Hyde	1929
James Wilson	1897	Henry A. Wallace	1933
do	1901	Claude R. Wickard	1940
do	1909	Clinton P. Anderson	1945
David F. Houston	1913	Charles F. Brannan	1948
Edward T. Meredith	1920	Ezra Taft Benson	1953
Henry C. Wallace	1921	Orville L. Freeman	1961

Secretaries of Commerce and Labor

	Apptd.		Apptd.
Secretaries of Commerce and Labor		James J. Davis	1921
Geo. B. Cortelyou	1903	do	1923
Victor H. Metcalf	1904	do	1929
Oscar S. Straus	1906	William N. Doak	1930
Charles Nagel	1909	Frances Perkins	1933
Secretaries of Labor		L. B. Schwellenbach	1945
William B. Wilson	1913	Maurice J. Tobin	1948

Secretaries of Commerce and Labor — Continued

	Apptd.		Apptd.
Martin P. Durkin	1953	Roy D. Chapin	1932
James P. Mitchell	1953	Daniel C. Roper	1933
Arthur J. Goldberg	1961	Harry L. Hopkins	1939
C. W. Willard Wirtz	1962	Jesse Jones	1940
Secretaries of Commerce		Henry A. Wallace	1945
		do	1945
William C. Redfield	1913	W. Averell Harriman	1946
Josh W. Alexander	1919	Charles Sawyer	1948
Herbert C. Hoover	1921	Sinclair Weeks	1953
do	1923	Lewis R. Strauss	1958
William F. Whiting	1928	Frederick H. Mueller	1959
Robert P. Lamont	1929	Luther H. Hodges	1961

Secretaries of Health, Education and Welfare

	Apptd.		Apptd.
Oveta Culp Hobby	1953	Arthur S. Flemming	1958
Marion B. Folsom	1955	Abraham A. Ribicoff	1961
		Anthony Celebrezze	1962

Secretaries of the United States Air Force, Army and Navy

(Not Members of the President's Cabinet)

Secretaries of the Air Force	Appointed		Apptd.
W. Stuart Symington	Sept. 18, 1947	Robert T. Stevens	Feb. 4, 1953
Thomas K. Finletter	Apr. 24, 1950	Wilber M. Brucker	July 21, 1955
Harold E. Talbott	Feb. 4, 1953	Elvis T. Stahr, Jr.	Jan. 23, 1961
Donald A. Quarles	Aug. 12, 1955	**Secretaries of the Navy**	**Appointed**
James H. Douglas	Mar. 26, 1957	John L. Sullivan	Sept. 18, 1947
Dudley C. Sharpe	Dec. 10, 1959	Francis P. Matthews	May 25, 1949
Eugene M. Zuckert	Jan. 23, 1961	Dan A. Kimball	July 31, 1951
Secretaries of the Army	**Appointed**	Robert B. Anderson	Feb. 4, 1953
Kenneth C. Royall	Sept. 18, 1947	Charles S. Thomas	May 3, 1954
Gordon Gray	June 20, 1949	Thomas S. Gates, Jr.	Apr. 1, 1957
Frank Pace, Jr.	Apr. 12, 1950	William B. Franke	June 1, 1958
Earl D. Johnson (Acting)	Jan. 20, 1953	John B. Connally, Jr.	Jan. 23, 1961

JUSTICES OF THE UNITED STATES SUPREME COURT

Name and residence Chief Justices in Bold Face	Service Term	Yrs	Born	Died
John Jay, N.Y.	1789-1795	5	1745	1829
John Rutledge, S.C.	1789-1791	1	1739	1800
William Cushing, Mass.	1789-1810	20	1732	1810
James Wilson, Pa.	1789-1798	8	1742	1798
John Blair, Va.	1789-1796	6	1732	1800
Robert H. Harrison, Md.	1789-1790	...	1745	1790
James Iredell, N.C.	1790-1799	9	1751	1799
Thomas Johnson, Md.	1791-1793	1	1732	1819
William Paterson, N.J.	1793-1806	13	1745	1806
John Rutledge, S.C.	1795-(a)	...	1739	1800
Samuel Chase, Md.	1796-1811	15	1741	1811
Oliver Ellsworth, Conn.	1796-1799	4	1745	1807
Bushrod Washington, Va.	1798-1829	31	1762	1829
Alfred Moore, N.C.	1799-1804	4	1755	1810
John Marshall, Va.	1801-1835	34	1755	1835
William Johnson, S.C.	1804-1834	30	1771	1834
Brockholst Livingston, N.Y.	1806-1823	16	1757	1823
Thomas Todd, Ky.	1807-1826	18	1765	1826
Joseph Story, Mass.	1811-1845	33	1779	1845
Gabriel Duval, Md.	1812-1835	22	1752	1844
Smith Thompson, N.Y.	1823-1843	20	1768	1843
Robert Trimble, Ky.	1826-1828	2	1777	1828
John McLean, Ohio	1829-1861	32	1785	1861
Henry Baldwin, Pa.	1830-1844	14	1780	1844
James M. Wayne, Ga.	1835-1867	32	1790	1867
Roger B. Taney, Md.	1836-1864	28	1777	1864
Philip P. Barbour, Va.	1836-1841	4	1783	1841
John Catron, Tenn.	1837-1865	28	1786	1865
John McKinley, Ala.	1837-1852	15	1780	1852
Peter V. Daniel, Va.	1841-1860	19	1784	1860
Samuel Nelson, N.Y.	1845-1872	27	1792	1873
Levi Woodbury, N.H.	1845-1851	5	1789	1851
Robert C. Grier, Pa.	1846-1870	23	1794	1870
Benj. R. Curtis, Mass.	1851-1857	6	1809	1874
John A. Campbell, Ala.	1853-1861	8	1811	1889
Nathan Clifford, Me.	1858-1881	23	1803	1881
Noah H. Swayne, Ohio	1862-1881	18	1804	1884
Samuel F. Miller, Iowa	1862-1890	28	1816	1890
David Davis, Ill.	1862-1877	14	1815	1886
Stephen J. Field, Cal.	1863-1897	34	1816	1899
Salmon P. Chase, Ohio	1864-1873	8	1808	1873
William Strong, Pa.	1870-1880	10	1808	1895
Joseph P. Bradley, N.J.	1870-1892	21	1813	1892
Ward Hunt, N.Y.	1873-1882	9	1810	1886
Morrison R. Waite, Ohio	1874-1888	14	1816	1888
John M. Harlan, Ky.	1877-1911	34	1833	1911
William B. Woods, Ga.	1881-1887	6	1824	1887
Stanley Matthews, Ohio	1881-1889	7	1824	1889
Horace Gray, Mass.	1882-1902	20	1828	1902
Samuel Blatchford, N.Y.	1882-1893	11	1820	1893
Lucius Q. C. Lamar, Miss.	1888-1893	5	1825	1893
Melville W. Fuller, Ill.	1888-1910	21	1833	1910

JUSTICES OF THE UNITED STATES SUPREME COURT – Continued

ame and residence hief Justices in Bold Face	Service Term	Yrs	Born	Died
avid J. Brewer, Kan.	1890-1910	20	1837	1910
Ienry B. Brown, Mich.	1891-1906	15	1836	1913
eorge Shiras, Jr., Pa.	1892-1903	10	1832	1924
Iowell E. Jackson, Tenn.	1893-1895	2	1832	1895
dward D. White, La.	1894-1910	16	1845	1921
ufus W. Peckham, N.Y.	1896-1909	13	1838	1909
oseph McKenna, Cal.	1898-1925	26	1843	1926
liver W. Holmes, Mass.	1902-1932	29	1841	1935
Villiam R. Day, Ohio	1903-1922	19	1849	1923
Villiam H. Moody, Mass.	1906-1910	3	1853	1917
Iorace H. Lurton, Tenn.	1910-1914	4	1844	1914
harles E. Hughes, N.Y.	1910-1916	5	1862	1948
Villis Van Devanter, Wyo.	1911-1937	26	1859	1941
oseph R. Lamar, Ga.	1911-1916	5	1857	1916
dward D. White, La.	1910-1921	10	1845	1921
Iahlon Pitney, N.J.	1912-1922	10	1858	1924
as. C. McReynolds, Tenn.	1914-1941	26	1862	1946
ouis D. Brandeis, Mass.	1916-1939	22	1856	1941
ohn H. Clarke, Ohio	1916-1922	5	1857	1945
Villiam H. Taft, Conn.	1921-1930	8	1857	1930
eorge Sutherland, Utah	1922-1938	15	1862	1942
ierce Butler, Minn.	1922-1939	16	1866	1939
dward T. Sanford, Tenn.	1923-1930	7	1865	1930
Iarlan F. Stone, N.Y.	1925-1941	16	1872	1946

Name and residence Chief Justices in Bold Face	Service Term	Yrs	Born	Died
Charles E. Hughes, N.Y.	1930-1941	11	1862	1948
Owen J. Roberts, Pa.	1930-1945	15	1875	1955
Benjamin N. Cardozo, N.Y.	1932-1938	6	1870	1938
Hugo L. Black, Ala.	1937-		1886	
Stanley F. Reed, Ky.	1938-1957	19	1884	
Felix Frankfurter, Mass.	1939-1962	23	1882	
William O. Douglas, Conn.	1939-		1898	
Frank Murphy, Mich.	1940-1949	9	1890	1949
Harlan F. Stone, N.Y.	1941-1946	5	1872	1946
James F. Byrnes, S.C.	1941-1942	1	1879	
Robert H. Jackson, N.Y.	1941-1954	12	1892	1954
Wiley B. Rutledge, Iowa	1943-1949	6	1894	1949
Harold H. Burton, Ohio	1945-1958	13	1888	
Fred M. Vinson, Ky.	1946-1953	7	1890	1953
Tom C. Clark, Texas	1949-		1899	
Sherman Minton, Ind.	1949-1956	7	1890	
Earl Warren, Cal.	1953-		1891	
John Marshall Harlan, N.Y.	1955-		1899	
William J. Brennan, Jr., N.J.	1956-		1906	
Charles E. Whittaker, Mo.	1957-1962	5	1901	
Potter Stewart, Ohio	1958-		1915	
Byron R. White, Colo.	1962-		1917	
Arthur J. Goldberg, Ill.	1962-		1908	

(a) Appointment not confirmed by Senate

SPEAKERS OF THE UNITED STATES HOUSE OF REPRESENTATIVES

Party designations: A, American; D, Democratic; DR, Democratic Republican; F, Federalist; R, Republican; W, Whig

Name	Party, State	Term
rederick A. C. Muhlenberg	F, Pa.	1789-1791
onathan Trumbull	F, Conn.	1791-1793
rederick A. C. Muhlenberg	F, Pa.	1793-1795
onathan Dayton	F, N.J.	1795-1799
heodore Sedgwick	F, Mass.	1799-1801
Iathaniel Macon	DR, N.C.	1801-1807
oseph B. Varnum	DR, Mass.	1807-1811
Ienry Clay	DR, Ky.	1811-1814
angdon Cheves	DR, S.C.	1814-1815
Ienry Clay	DR, Ky.	1815-1820
ohn W. Taylor	DR, N.Y.	1820-1821
hilip P. Barbour	DR, Va.	1821-1823
Ienry Clay	DR, Ky.	1823-1825
ohn W. Taylor	D, N.Y.	1825-1827
ndrew Stevenson	D, Va.	1827-1834
ohn Bell	D, Tenn.	1834-1835
ames K. Polk	D, Tenn.	1835-1839
obert M. T. Hunter	D, Va.	1839-1841
ohn White	W, Ky.	1841-1843
ohn W. Jones	D, Va.	1843-1845
ohn W. Davis	D, Ind.	1845-1847
obert C. Winthrop	W, Mass.	1847-1849
Iowell Cobb	D, Ga.	1849-1851
inn Boyd	D, Ky.	1851-1855
Iathaniel P. Banks	A, Mass.	1856-1857
ames L. Orr	D, S.C.	1857-1859
William Pennington	R, N.J.	1860-1861
Galusha A. Grow	R, Pa.	1861-1863
Schuyler Colfax	R, Ind.	1863-1869
James G. Blaine	R, Me.	1869-1875
Michael C. Kerr	D, Ind.	1875-1876
Samuel J. Randall	D, Pa.	1876-1881
Joseph W. Keifer	R, Ohio	1881-1883
John G. Carlisle	D, Ky.	1883-1889
Thomas B. Reed	R, Me.	1889-1891
Charles F. Crisp	D, Ga.	1891-1895
Thomas B. Reed	R, Me.	1895-1899
David B. Henderson	R, Iowa	1899-1903
Joseph G. Cannon	R, Ill.	1903-1911
Champ Clark	D, Mo.	1911-1919
Frederick H. Gillett	R, Mass.	1919-1925
Nicholas Longworth	R, Ohio	1925-1931
John N. Garner	D, Tex.	1931-1933
Henry T. Rainey	D, Ill.	1933-1935
Joseph W. Byrns	D, Tenn.	1935-1936
William B. Bankhead	D, Ala.	1936-1940
Sam Rayburn	D, Tex.	1940-1947
Joseph W. Martin, Jr.	R, Mass.	1947-1949
Sam Rayburn	D, Tex.	1949-1953
Joseph W. Martin, Jr.	R, Mass.	1953-1955
Sam Rayburn	D, Tex.	1955-1961
John W. McCormack	D, Mass.	1961-

PRESIDENTS PRO TEMPORE OF THE UNITED STATES SENATE

Congress	President pro tempore
1st Congress (1789-91)	John Langdon
2nd Congress (1791-93)	Richard Henry Lee John Langdon
3rd Congress (1793-95)	Ralph Izard Henry Tazewell
4th Congress (1795-97)	Henry Tazewell Samuel Livermore
5th Congress (1797-99)	William Bradford Jacob Read Theodore Sedgwick John Laurance James Ross

PRESIDENTS PRO TEMPORE OF THE UNITED STATES SENATE—Continued

Congress	Years	President Pro Tempore
6th Congress	(1799-1801)	Samuel Livermore
		Uriah Tracy
		John E. Howard
		James Hillhouse
7th Congress	(1801-03)	Abraham Baldwin
		Stephen R. Bradley
8th Congress	(1803-05)	John Brown
		Jesse Franklin
		Joseph Anderson
9th Congress	(1805-07)	Samuel Smith
10th Congress	(1807-09)	Samuel Smith
		Stephen R. Bradley
		John Milledge
11th Congress	(1809-11)	Andrew Gregg
		John Gaillard
		John Pope
12th Congress	(1811-13)	William H. Crawford
13th Congress	(1813-15)	Joseph B. Varnum
		John Gaillard
14th Congress	(1815-17)	John Gaillard
15th Congress	(1817-19)	John Gaillard
		James Barbour
16th Congress	(1819-21)	James Barbour
		John Gaillard
17th Congress	(1821-23)	John Gaillard
18th Congress	(1823-25)	John Gaillard
19th Congress	(1825-27)	John Gaillard
		Nathaniel Macon
20th Congress	(1827-29)	Samuel Smith
21st Congress	(1829-31)	Samuel Smith
22nd Congress	(1831-33)	Littleton W. Tazewell
		Hugh L. White
23rd Congress	(1833-35)	Hugh L. White
		George Poindexter
		John Tyler
24th Congress	(1835-37)	William R. King
25th Congress	(1837-39)	William R. King
26th Congress	(1839-41)	William R. King
27th Congress	(1841-43)	William R. King
		Samuel L. Southard
		Willie P. Mangum
28th Congress	(1843-45)	Willie P. Mangum
29th Congress	(1845-47)	Ambrose H. Sevier
		David R. Atchison
30th Congress	(1847-49)	David R. Atchison
31st Congress	(1849-51)	David R. Atchison
		William R. King
32nd Congress	(1851-53)	William R. King
		David R. Atchison
33rd Congress	(1853-55)	David R. Atchison
		Lewis Cass
		Jesse D. Bright
34th Congress	(1855-57)	Jesse D. Bright
		Charles E. Stuart
		James Mason
35th Congress	(1857-59)	James Mason
		Thomas J. Rusk
		Benjamin Fitzpatrick
36th Congress	(1859-61)	Benjamin Fitzpatrick
		Jesse D. Bright
		Solomon Foot
37th Congress	(1861-63)	Solomon Foot
38th Congress	(1863-65)	Solomon Foot
		Daniel Clark
39th Congress	(1865-67)	Lafayette S. Foster
		Benjamin F. Wade
40th Congress	(1867-69)	Benjamin F. Wade
41st Congress	(1869-71)	Henry B. Anthony
42nd Congress	(1871-73)	Henry B. Anthony
43rd Congress	(1873-75)	Matthew H. Carpenter
		Henry B. Anthony
44th Congress	(1875-77)	Thomas W. Ferry
45th Congress	(1877-79)	Thomas W. Ferry
46th Congress	(1879-81)	Allen G. Thurman
47th Congress	(1881-83)	Thomas F. Bayard
		David Davis
		George F. Edmunds
48th Congress	(1883-85)	George F. Edmunds
49th Congress	(1885-87)	John Sherman
		John J. Ingalls
50th Congress	(1887-89)	John J. Ingalls
51st Congress	(1889-91)	John J. Ingalls
		Charles F. Manderson
52nd Congress	(1891-93)	Charles F. Manderson
53rd Congress	(1893-95)	Charles F. Manderson
		Isham G. Harris
		Matt W. Ransom
54th Congress	(1895-97)	William P. Frye
55th Congress	(1897-99)	William P. Frye
56th Congress	(1899-1901)	William P. Frye
57th Congress	(1901-03)	William P. Frye
58th Congress	(1903-05)	William P. Frye
59th Congress	(1905-07)	William P. Frye
60th Congress	(1907-09)	William P. Frye
61st Congress	(1909-11)	William P. Frye
62nd Congress	(1911-13)	William P. Frye
		Charles Curtis
		Augustus O. Bacon
		Jacob H. Gallinger
		Henry Cabot Lodge
		Frank B. Brandegee
63rd Congress	(1913-15)	James P. Clarke
64th Congress	(1915-17)	James P. Clarke
		Willard Saulsbury
65th Congress	(1917-19)	Willard Saulsbury
66th Congress	(1919-21)	Albert B. Cummins
67th Congress	(1921-23)	Albert B. Cummins
68th Congress	(1923-25)	Albert B. Cummins
69th Congress	(1925-27)	Albert B. Cummins
		George H. Moses
70th Congress	(1927-29)	George H. Moses
71st Congress	(1929-31)	George H. Moses
72nd Congress	(1931-33)	George H. Moses
73rd Congress	(1933-35)	Key Pittman
74th Congress	(1935-37)	Key Pittman
75th Congress	(1937-39)	Key Pittman
76th Congress	(1939-41)	Key Pittman
		William H. King
77th Congress	(1941-43)	Pat Harrison
		Carter Glass
78th Congress	(1943-45)	Carter Glass
79th Congress	(1945-47)	Kenneth D. McKellar
80th Congress	(1947-49)	Arthur H. Vandenberg
81st Congress	(1949-51)	Kenneth D. McKellar
82nd Congress	(1951-53)	Kenneth D. McKellar
83rd Congress	(1953-55)	Styles Bridges
84th Congress	(1955-57)	Walter F. George
85th Congress	(1957-59)	Carl Hayden
86th Congress	(1959-61)	Carl Hayden
87th Congress	(1961-63)	Carl Hayden

THE FIRST GOVERNORS AND YEARS OF ADMISSION OF THE SEVERAL STATES

State	Governor	Term of Office	Year Admitted to Union
Ala.	William Wyatt Bibb	Nov. 1819-July 1820	1819
Alaska	William Egan	1959-	1959
Ariz.	George P. W. Hunt	1911-1919	1912
Ark.	James S. Conway	1836-1840	1836
Cal.	Peter H. Burnett	1849-1851	1850
Colo.	John L. Routt	1876-1878	1876
Conn.	Jonathan Trumbull	1769-1784*	1788
Del.	John McKinley	1776-1777*	1787
Fla.	William D. Mosely	1845-1849	1845
Ga.	Archibald Bulloch	1776-1777*	1788
Hawaii	William A. Quinn	1959-1963	1959
Idaho	George L. Shoup	1890	1890
Ill.	Shadrach Bond	1818-1822	1818
Ind.	Jonathan Jennings	1816-1822	1816
Ia.	Ansell Briggs	1846-1850	1846
Kansas	Charles Robinson	1861-1862	1861
Ky.	Isaac Shelby	1792-1796	1792
La.	William C. C. Claiborne	1812-1816	1812
Me.	William King	1820-1821	1820
Md.	Thomas Johnson	1777-1779*	1788
Mass.	John Hancock	1780-1785*	1788
Mich.	Steven T. Mason	1836-1840	1837
Minn.	Henry H. Sibley	1857-1859	1858
Miss.	David Holmes	1817-1819	1817
Mo.	Alexander McNair	1820-1824	1821
Mont.	Joseph K. Toole	1889-1893	1889
Neb.	David Butler	1867-1871	1867
Nev.	Henry G. Blasdel	1864-1871	1864
N.H.	Mesheck Weare	1775-1785*	1788
N.J.	William Livingston	1776-1790*	1787
N.M.	W. C. McDonald	1912-1916	1912
N.Y.	George Clinton	1777-1795*	1788
N.C.	Richard Caswell	1776-1779*	1789
N.D.	John Miller	1889-1891	1889
Ohio	Edward Tiffin	1803-1807	1803
Okla.	Charles N. Haskell	1907-1911	1907
Ore.	John Whitacre	1859-1862	1859
Pa.	Thomas Mifflin	1790-1799*	1787
R.I.	Nicholas Cooke	1775-1778*	1790
S.C.	John Rutledge	1776-1778*	1788
S.D.	Arthur C. Mellette	1889-1893	1889
Tenn.	John Sevier	1796-1801	1796
Texas	J. Pinckney Henderson	1846-1847	1845
Utah	Heber M. Wells	1896-1905	1896
Vt.	Thomas Chittenden	1777-1789*	1791
Va.	Patrick Henry	1776-1779*	1788
Wash.	Elisha P. Ferry	1889-1893	1889
W.Va.	Arthur I. Boreman	1863-1869	1863
Wis.	Nelson Dewey	1848-1852	1848
Wyo.	F. E. Warren	1890-1892	1890

* First chief executive of state to serve after July 4, 1776, when the Thirteen Colonies declared their independence, joined by Vermont in 1777.

ORIGINS OF THE NAMES OF THE STATES

Alabama—"I make a clearing" (Choctaw)
Alaska—from Aleutian (Eskimo) name for the area
Arizona—"place of little springs" (Pima Indian)
Arkansas—French adaptation of Algonquin place name
California—name of Spanish fictional paradise
Colorado—"red" (Spanish), 1st applied to Colo. R.
Connecticut—"long river place" (Mohican)
Delaware—for Lord De La Warre, 1st governor of Va. Company
District of Columbia—for Columbus
Florida—"flowery" (Spanish)
Georgia—for George II of England
Hawaii—from native word meaning, perhaps, "homeland"
Idaho—"light on the mountains" (Shoshone)
Illinois—French adaptation of Algonquin word meaning "accomplished men," also name of a local tribe
Indiana—for the Indians
Iowa—Indian word for "sleepy people"
Kansas—plural of Kansa, a member of Sioux tribe, "wind people"
Kentucky—Cherokee place name meaning "dark, bloody ground"
Louisiana—for Louis XIV of France
Maine—for French province of Maine
Maryland—for Queen Henrietta Maria of England
Massachusetts—"large hill place" (Indian)
Michigan—"large expanse" (Chippewa)
Minnesota—"sky-colored water" (Dakota)
Mississippi—"large river" (Indian)
Missouri—"canoe people" (Indian)
Montana—"mountainous"
Nebraska—"flat river" (Indian)
Nevada—"snow-covered" (Spanish)
New Hampshire—for Hampshire Co., England
New Jersey—for Isle of Jersey
New Mexico—for Mexico
New York—for Duke of York
North Carolina—for Charles I of England
North Dakota—"allies" (Sioux), also name of a Sioux tribe
Ohio—"great, beautiful" (Indian), originally name of the river
Oklahoma—"red man" (Choctaw)
Oregon—from the Shoshoni meaning "undulating waters," 1st applied to the river
Pennsylvania—"Penn-woodland", for Adm. Wm. Penn
Rhode Island—"red island" and for Isle of Rhodes
South Carolina—for Charles I of England
South Dakota—"allies" (Sioux), also name of a Sioux tribe
Tennessee—from name of local Indian town
Texas—"allies" (Indian and Spanish usage)
Utah—for Ute Indians
Vermont—"green mountain" (from the French)
Virginia—for Elizabeth I of England, the Virgin Queen
Washington—for George Washington
West Virginia—former western counties of Va.
Wisconsin—"place of the beaver hole" (Ojibway)
Wyoming—"upon the great plains" (Indian)
Puerto Rico—"rich port" (Spanish)

SOME STATISTICAL AND HISTORICAL DATA O[N]

Cities	State	County	Date of Founding	Incorp.	Source of Name
Akron	Ohio	Summit	1825	1836	Greek "Akros" (high place)
*Albany	N. Y.	Albany	1652	1686	Duke of York & Albany
Albuquerque	N. M.	Bernalillo	1706	1890	Duke of Albuquerque, Viceroy
Allentown	Pa.	Lehigh	1762	1811	William Allen (founder)
Amarillo	Texas	Potter	1887	1892	Spanish for yellow
Anaheim	Cal.	Orange	1857	1878	Santa Ana River
*Annapolis	Md.	Anne Arundel	1649	1794	Anne Arundel
*Atlanta	Ga.	Fulton	1837	1847	Western & Atlanta Railroad
*Augusta	Me.	Kennebec	1754	1797	Augusta Dearborn
*Austin	Texas	Travis	1838	1839	Stephen F. Austin
Baltimore	Md.	Baltimore	1729	1745	Lord Baltimore
*Baton Rouge	La.	E. Baton Rouge	1699	1817	French for "Red Post"
Beaumont	Texas	Jefferson	1836	1881	Jefferson Beaumont
Berkeley	Cal.	Alameda	1864	1878	Anglican Bishop George Berkeley
Birmingham	Ala.	Jefferson	1871	1871	Birmingham, England
*Bismarck	N.D.	Burleigh	1871	1909	Prince Otto von Bismarck
*Boise	Idaho	Ada	1863	1864	French for "wooded"
*Boston	Mass.	Suffolk	1630	1630	Boston, England
Bridgeport	Conn.	Fairfield	1639	1821	Site of Stratfield-Newfield bridge
Buffalo	N. Y.	Erie	1804	1816	Buffalo Creek
Cambridge	Mass.	Middlesex	1630	1636	Cambridge, England
Camden	N. J.	Camden	1773	1828	(1st) Earl of Camden
Canton	Ohio	Stark	1805	1822	Canton, China
*Carson City	Nev.	Ormsby	1858	1861	Kit (Christopher) Carson
Charleston	S. C.	Charleston	1670	1783	Charles II (of England)
*Charleston	W. Va.	Kanawha	1794	1870	Charles Washington
Charlotte	N. C.	Mecklenburg	1750	1768	Queen Charlotte of England
Chattanooga	Tenn.	Hamilton	1835	1839	Indian name for Lookout Mt.
*Cheyenne	Wyo.	Laramie	1867	1869	Cheyenne tribe of Algonquin Indians
Chicago	Ill.	Cook	1830	1833	Indian "Checagou" meaning strong
Cincinnati	Ohio	Hamilton	1788	1802	Society of the Cincinnati
Cleveland	Ohio	Cuyahoga	1796	1814	Moses Cleaveland (founder)
*Columbia	S. C.	Richland	1786	1805	Christopher Columbus
*Columbus	Ohio	Franklin	1797	1816	Christopher Columbus
Columbus	Ga.	Muscogee	1828	1828	Christopher Columbus
*Concord	N. H.	Merrimack	1659	1733	N. H. legislature
Corpus Christi	Tex.	Neuces	1839	1852	Corpus Christi Bay
Dallas	Texas	Dallas	1846	1856	(Vice-President) Geo. M. Dallas
Dayton	Ohio	Montgomery	1796	1805	Gen. Jonathan Dayton
Dearborn	Mich.	Wayne	1833	1909	Gen. Henry Dearborn
*Denver	Col.	Denver	1859	1861	Gen. James W. Denver
*Des Moines	Ia.	Polk	1845	1851	Indian name "moingana" (name of Desmoines river)
Detroit	Mich.	Wayne	1701	1805	French word for strait
*Dover	Del.	Kent	1683	1829	Dover, England
Duluth	Minn.	St. Louis	1856	1870	Sieur Duluth (French explorer & settler)
Elizabeth	N. J.	Union	1664	1740	Elizabeth Carteret (wife of Englis[h] cabinet minister)
El Paso	Texas	El Paso	1827	1850	Spanish "El Paso del Norte" or Pas[s] of the North
Erie	Pa.	Erie	1795	1805	Lake Erie
Evansville	Ind.	Vanderburg	1812	1818	Gen. Robt. M. Evans
Flint	Mich.	Genessee	1819	1855	Flint River
Ft. Worth	Texas	Tarrant	1849	1873	Gen. William J. Worth
*Frankfort	Ky.	Franklin	1786	1786	Stephen Frank (early settler)
Fresno	Cal.	Fresno	1874	1884	Spanish for ash
Gary	Ind.	Lake	1906	1906	(Judge) Elbert H. Gary
Glendale	Cal.	Los Angeles	1884	1887	Residents of town selected by ballot
Grand Rapids	Mich.	Kent	1826	1838	Grand River rapids
Greensboro	N. C.	Guilford	1772	1808	Gen. Nathaniel Greene
Hammond	Ind.	Lake	1851	1884	George H. Hammond
Hampton	Va.		1610	1849	Hampton, England
*Harrisburg	Pa.	Dauphin	1786	1791	John Harris (founder)
*Hartford	Conn.	Hartford	1635	1662	Hertford, England

*Denotes state capitol c.—circa Blank spaces above indicate data unavailable

150 PRINCIPAL CITIES OF THE UNITED STATES

Pop. 1790	Pop. 1830	Pop. 1870	Pop. 1910	Pop. 1950	Pop. 1960
—	—	10,000	69,000	274,000	290,000
3,500	24,000	69,000	100,000	143,000	129,000
—	—	1,300	11,000	97,000	201,000
—	—	—	52,000	107,000	108,000
—	—	—	10,000	74,000	137,000
—	—	800	2,600	14,000	104,000
—	2,600	5,800	8,600	10,000	23,000
—	c. 8,000	22,000	154,000	330,000	490,000
—	4,000	7,000	13,000	20,000	21,000
—	—	—	30,000	130,000	190,000
13,000	80,000	270,000	560,000	950,000	940,000
—	—	6,500	15,000	125,000	150,000
—	—	—	20,000	95,000	120,000
—	—	—	40,000	113,000	111,000
—	—	c. 1,000	130,000	325,000	340,000
—	—	—	5,400	18,000	27,000
—	—	900	17,000	34,000	34,000
18,000	60,000	250,000	670,000	800,000	697,000
100	2,800	20,000	100,000	158,000	156,000
—	8,600	117,000	423,000	580,000	530,000
2,100	6,000	39,000	105,000	120,000	107,000
—	c. 6,000	20,000	94,000	124,000	117,000
—	1,300	8,500	50,000	117,000	113,000
	—	3,000	2,400	3,000	5,100
16,000	30,000	49,000	58,000	70,000	76,000
—	—	3,800	22,000	73,000	85,000
—	—	4,400	34,000	134,000	201,000
—	—	6,000	44,000	131,000	130,000
—	—	1,400	11,000	32,000	43,000
—	50	30,000	2,200,000	3,600,000	3,500,000
—	25,000	216,000	360,000	504,000	502,500
—	1,000	92,000	560,000	915,000	876,000
—	3,300	9,200	26,000	87,000	97,000
—	—	20,000	104,000	79,000	116,000
—	2,400	31,000	181,000	376,000	470,000
—	3,700	12,000	21,000	27,000	28,000
—	—	2,100	8,200	108,000	167,000
—	—	3,000	92,000	434,000	679,000
—	—	30,000	116,000	243,000	262,000
—	—	—	1,000	95,000	112,000
—	—	4,700	213,000	415,000	494,000
—	—	5,200	83,000	178,000	209,000
—	2,300	79,000	465,000	1,800,000	1,600,000
—	—	1,900	3,700	6,000	7,000
—	—	3,000	78,000	104,000	106,000
1,000	3,500	21,000	73,000	113,000	107,000
—	—	—	39,000	130,000	275,000
—	—	19,000	66,000	130,000	138,000
—	6,000	22,000	69,000	128,000	140,000
—	—	5,300	38,000	163,000	197,000
—	—	c. 1,000	73,000	278,000	356,000
—	—	5,400	10,000	12,000	18,000
—	—	c. 3,000	90,000	91,000	134,000
—	—	—	17,000	134,000	178,000
—	—	—	2,700	95,000	119,000
—	—	16,000	71,000	176,000	177,000
—	—	—	16,000	74,000	119,000
—	—	—	21,000	87,000	111,000
—	—		5,500	5,900	89,000
900	4,000	23,000	64,000	89,000	79,000
4,000	7,000	37,000	99,000	177,000	162,000

SOME STATISTICAL AND HISTORICAL DATA OI

Cities	State	County	Date of Founding	Incorp.	Source of Name
*Helena	Mont.	Lewis & Clark	1864	1881	Helena, Minn.
*Honolulu	Hawaii	Honolulu	1816	1909	Hawaiian for "sheltered harbor"
Houston	Texas	Harris	1836	1837	Sam Houston
*Indianapolis	Ind.	Marion	1820	1836	Name of state
*Jackson	Miss.	Hinds	1821	1833	Andrew Jackson
Jacksonville	Fla.	Duval	1825	1830	Andrew Jackson
*Jefferson City	Mo.	Cole	1821	1826	Thomas Jefferson
Jersey City	N. J.	Hudson	1630	1804	Isle of Jersey (England)
*Juneau	Alaska	Juneau	1880	c. 1925	Mt. Juneau
Kansas City	Kan.	Wyandotte	1886	1889	Name of state
Kansas City	Mo.	Jackson	1838	1850	Kansas (territory)
Knoxville	Tenn.	Knox	1786	1816	Gen. Henry Knox
*Lansing	Mich.	Ingham	1843	1859	Lansing, N. Y.
Lexington	Ky.	Fayette	1775	1782	Battle of Lexington
*Lincoln	Neb.	Lancaster	1859	1869	Abraham Lincoln
*Little Rock	Ark.	Pulaski	1820	1831	French name originally le Petite Roc
Long Beach	Cal.	Los Angeles	1840	1897	Seven mile strip of beach (alo Pacific)
Los Angeles	Cal.	Los Angeles	1781	1850	Father Felipe de Neve
Louisville	Ky.	Jefferson	1778	1779	Louis XVI of France
Lubbock	Texas	Lubbock	1891	1909	Thomas S. Lubbock
*Madison	Wis.	Dane	1836	1837	James Madison
Memphis	Tenn.	Shelby	1819	1826	Memphis, Egypt
Miami	Fla.	Dade	1895	1896	Algonquin Indian tribe called Miami
Milwaukee	Wis.	Milwaukee	1818	1839	Indian word for "beautiful land"
Minneapolis	Minn.	Hennepin	1852	1856	Sioux Indian word "minne" meani water
Mobile	Ala.	Mobile	1711	1819	French for a local Indian tribe
*Montgomery	Ala.	Montgomery	1819	1819	Gen. Richard Montgomery
*Montpelier	Vt.	Washington	1780	1828	Montpellier, France
*Nashville	Tenn.	Davidson	1780	1784	Gen. Francis Nash
Newark	N. J.	Essex	1666	1836	New-on-Trent, England
New Bedford	Mass.	Bristol	1760	1787	Bedford, England
Newburyport	Mass.	Essex	1635	1635	Newbury, England
New Haven	Conn.	New Haven	1637	1784	Newhaven, England
New Orleans	La.	New Orleans	1718	1805	Orleans, France
Newport News	Va.	Warwick	1882	1896	Newport News, England
New York City	N. Y.	N. Y.	1626	1656	Duke of York (& Albany)
Norfolk	Va.	Norfolk	1682	1805	Duke of Norfolk
Oakland	Cal.	Alameda	1850	1852	Moses Chase (Founder)
*Oklahoma City	Okla.	Oklahoma	1889	1890	Name of state
*Olympia	Wash.	Thurston	1851	1859	Mt. Olympus
Omaha	Neb.	Douglas	1854	1857	Omaha Indian tribe
Pasadena	Cal.	Los Angeles	1874	1886	Chippewa Indian word for "valley"
Paterson	N. J.	Passaic	1791	1831	William Paterson (founder)
Peoria	Ill.	Peoria	1819	1835	Peoria Indian tribe
Phila.	Pa.	Phila.	1682	1701	Greek for city of brotherly love
*Phoenix	Ariz.	Maricopa	1867	1881	Darrell Duppa (founder)
*Pierre	S. D.	Hughes	1880	1883	Pierre Chouteau
Pittsburgh	Pa.	Allegheny	1754	1794	William Pitt
Plymouth	Mass.	Plymouth	1620	1620	Plymouth, England
Portland	Me.	Cumberland	1632	1786	seaport location
Portland	Ore.	Multnomah	c. 1842	1851	Portland, Me.
Portsmouth	Va.	Norfolk	1750	1752	Portsmouth, England
*Providence	R. I.	Providence	1636	1644	Roger Williams (founder)
*Raleigh	N. C.	Wake	1792	1795	Sir Walter Raleigh
*Richmond	Va.	Henrico	1737	1742	Richmond, England
Rochester	N. Y.	Monroe	1811	1817	Col. Nathaniel Rochester
Rockford	Ill.	Winnebago	1834	1839	Ford near city
*Sacramento	Cal.	Sacramento	1849	1850	Sacramento River
St. Augustine	Fla.	St. John's	1565	c. 1900	St. Augustine
St. Louis	Mo.	St. Louis	1764	1809	St. Louis, King Louis IX of Franc
*St. Paul	Minn.	Ramsey	1840	1849	St. Paul
St. Petersburg	Fla.	Pinellas	1876	1903	Saint Peter
Salem	Mass.	Essex	1626	1629	Salem, England

***Denotes state capitol**
c.—circa
Blank spaces above indicate data unavailable

150 PRINCIPAL CITIES OF THE UNITED STATES – Continued

Pop. 1790	Pop. 1830	Pop. 1870	Pop. 1910	Pop. 1950	Pop. 1960
—	—	3,000	11,000	12,000	20,000
—	—	—	52,000	248,000	294,000
—	—	9,000	79,000	600,000	940,000
—	—	48,000	233,000	427,000	476,000
—	c. 2,000	4,200	21,000	98,000	144,000
—	—	6,800	7,000	204,000	201,000
—	—	4,400	12,000	25,000	28,000
—	c. 10,000	82,000	267,000	300,000	276,000
—	—	—	2,000	5,900	6,700
—	—	—	82,000	129,000	122,000
—	—	32,000	248,000	455,000	475,000
—	c. 1,000	8,000	36,000	124,000	111,000
—	—	5,200	31,000	92,000	107,000
—	—	15,000	35,000	55,000	63,000
—	—	12,400	44,000	99,000	128,000
—	2,000	12,000	46,000	102,000	107,000
—	—	—	18,000	250,000	344,000
—	—	5,700	320,000	1,900,000	2,400,000
200	10,000	100,000	224,000	369,000	390,000
—	—	—	1,900	70,000	128,000
—	—	9,000	25,000	96,000	126,000
—	c. 4,000	40,000	130,000	396,000	497,000
—	—	—	6,000	250,000	290,000
—	—	71,000	374,000	637,000	740,000
—	—	13,000	300,000	520,000	480,000
—	3,200	32,000	51,000	129,000	200,000
—	1,200	10,000	38,000	106,000	134,000
—	1,800	3,000	5,000	8,500	8,700
500	5,500	26,000	110,000	174,000	171,000
1,000	11,000	105,000	147,000	438,000	405,000
3,300	7,600	20,000	96,000	110,000	100,000
4,400	6,300	12,000	15,000	14,000	14,000
4,500	10,700	51,000	133,000	164,000	152,000
—	30,000	190,000	340,000	570,000	627,000
—	c. 500	700	20,000	42,000	113,000
32,000	197,000	942,000	4,700,000	7,800,000	7,700,000
—	10,000	19,000	67,000	213,000	305,000
—	—	10,000	150,000	384,000	367,000
—	—	—	64,000	243,000	324,000
—	—	1,200	6,900	15,000	18,000
—	—	16,000	124,000	251,000	302,000
—	—	—	30,000	104,000	116,000
500	c. 8,000	33,000	125,000	139,000	143,000
—	—	23,000	66,000	111,000	103,000
28,000	80,000	674,000	1,500,000	2,070,000	2,000,000
—	—	—	11,000	106,000	439,000
—	—	—	c. 1,000	5,000	10,000
400	12,000	86,000	534,000	676,000	604,000
3,000	4,700	6,200	12,000	10,000	6,000
2,200	12,000	31,000	58,000	77,000	72,000
—	—	8,300	207,000	373,000	372,000
1,800	3,000	10,000	33,000	80,000	114,000
6,300	17,000	69,000	224,000	248,000	207,000
—	1,000	7,800	25,000	65,000	94,000
3,700	6,000	51,000	127,000	230,000	220,000
1,600	6,000	62,000	220,000	332,000	318,000
—	—	11,000	45,000	93,000	126,000
—	—	—	44,000	137,000	191,000
c. 1,000	1,700	1,700	5,400	13,000	14,000
—	—	310,000	687,000	856,000	750,000
—	—	20,000	214,000	311,000	313,000
—	—	—	4,000	97,000	181,000
8,000	13,000	24,000	43,000	41,000	39,000

SOME STATISTICAL AND HISTORICAL DATA O

Cities	State	County	Date of Founding	Incorp.	Source of Name
*Salem	Ore.	Marion	1848	1860	Salem, Mass.
*Salt Lake City	Utah	Salt Lake	1847	1851	Salt Lake
San Antonio	Tex.	Bexar	1718	1837	Saint Anthony
San Diego	Cal.	San Diego	1769	1850	Saint Didacus de Alcala
San Francisco	Cal.	San Francisco	1835	1850	St. Francis
San Jose	Cal.	Santa Clara	1777	1850	St. John
Santa Ana	Cal.	Orange	1869	1886	Santa Ana Valley
*Santa Fe	N. M.	Santa Fe	1610	1851	Spanish for "holy faith"
Savannah	Ga.	Chatham	1733	1789	Savannah River
Scranton	Pa.	Lackawanna	1840	1856	George W. Scranton (founder)
Seattle	Wash.	King	1851	1869	Chief of Duwamish Indians
Shreveport	La.	Caddo	1834	1839	Henry M. Shreve
South Bend	Ind.	St. Joseph	1823	1835	Alexis Coquillard (founder)
Spokane	Wash.	Spokane	1872	1881	Indian for "children of the sun"
*Springfield	Ill.	Sangamon	1818	1832	Spring Creek
Springfield	Mass.	Hampden	1636	1641	William Pynchon (founder)
Syracuse	N. Y.	Onondaga	1796	1825	Syracuse, Greece
Tacoma	Wash.	Pierce	1868	1883	Indian for Mt. Ranier
Tampa	Fla.	Hillsborough	1823	1855	Indian for "close to it"
*Tallahassee	Fla.	Leon	1824	1825	Indian for "town"
Toledo	Ohio	Lucas	1835	1837	Toledo, Spain
*Topeka	Kan.	Shawnee	1854	1857	Indian for "smoky hill"
*Trenton	N. J.	Mercer	1714	1745	William Trent (founder)
Tucson	Ariz.	Pima	ca. 1776	1877	Maybe Piman for "dark spring"
Tulsa	Okla.	Tulsa & Osage	1882	1898	Talsi Indians
Utica	N. Y.	Oneida	1797	1832	Utica, Africa (Carthage)
Washington	D. C.		1790	1871	George Washington
Wichita	Kan.	Sedgewick	1869	1870	Wichita Indians
Worcester	Mass.	Worcester	1668	1848	Worcester, England
Yonkers	N. Y.	Westchester	1788	1855	De Jonkheer Van Der Donck (origin Dutch name)
Youngstown	Ohio	Mahoning	1797	1848	John Young (founder)

***Denotes state capitol**
c.—circa
Blank spaces above indicate data unavailable

Pop. 1790	Pop. 1830	Pop. 1870	Pop. 1910	Pop. 1950	Pop. 1960
—	—	1,100	14,000	43,000	49,000
—	—	13,000	92,000	182,000	189,000
—	—	12,000	97,000	408,000	588,000
—	—	2,300	40,000	334,000	573,000
—	—	149,000	417,000	775,000	740,000
—	—	9,000	29,000	95,000	204,000
—	—	1,400	10,000	45,000	100,000
—	—	4,700	8,000	27,000	34,000
2,300	c. 7,000	28,000	65,000	120,000	150,000
—	—	35,000	130,000	125,000	111,400
—	—	1,100	237,000	467,000	557,000
—	—	4,600	28,000	127,000	164,000
—	—	—	53,000	116,000	132,000
—	—	—	104,000	161,000	181,000
—	—	17,000	51,000	81,000	83,000
1,500	6,800	26,000	89,000	162,000	174,000
—	—	43,000	137,000	220,500	216,000
—	—	100	83,000	143,000	148,000
—	—	800	38,000	125,000	275,000
—	c. 1,000	4,800	7,000	27,000	48,000
—	—	31,000	168,000	303,000	318,000
—	—	5,800	43,000	78,000	119,000
1,900	4,000	23,000	96,000	128,000	114,000
—	—	3,200	13,000	45,000	213,000
—	—	—	18,000	182,000	260,000
—	8,300	28,000	74,000	100,000	100,000
—	40,000	132,000	330,000	800,000	760,000
—	—	1,000	52,000	168,000	254,000
—	6,000	41,000	146,000	203,000	187,000
—	1,700	18,000	79,000	152,000	190,000
—	1,400	8,000	79,000	168,000	166,000

SOME MAJOR EVENTS, INCLUDING "FIRSTS", IN UNITED STATES HISTORY

1007 Snorri, 1st child born of European parents on American soil (either Maine or Nova Scotia). Parents: Thorfinn and Gudrid Karlsefni.

1492 Christopher Columbus discovered America.

1497 John Cabot discovered Newfoundland.

1507 Martin H. Waldseemuller, 1st to use the word America as a geographical designation, in his Cosmographiae Introductio.

1513 April 2 Juan Ponce de Leon discovered Florida, claiming it for King of Spain.

1526 Fathers Antonio Montesino and Anthony de Cervantes, celebrated 1st Catholic Mass, in Virginia.

1540 Francisco Vasquez de Coronado, seeking storied treasurers of Cibola, explored Southwest. His aide, Garcia Lopez de Cardenas, discovered Grand Canyon.

1541 Hernando de Soto discovered the Mississippi River.

1542 Juan R. Cabrillo discovered land on what is now Pacific coast of U.S.

1564 Jacques Le Moyne de Morgues, 1st artist to come to America.

1565 Don Pedro Menendez founded the 1st permanent white settlement in North America at St. Augustine, Florida.

1579 Sir Francis Drake, exploring California coast, claimed area for Queen Elizabeth.

1587 Aug. 18 Virginia Dare, 1st English child born in America.

1602 Capt. Bartholomew Gosnold, 1st Englishman to land in New England. He named Cape Cod.

1603 Juan Cabezas de Altamirano, 1st Catholic bishop to visit America.

1604 Earliest French colony in North America planted at Neutral Island in St. Croix River, Me.

1606 Nov. 14 One of the earliest theatrical performances, La Theatre de Neptune en La Nouvelle France in Port Royal, Arcadia.

1607 May 13 First permanent English colony established at Jamestown, Va.

George Kendall led 1st known act of rebellion, against the Council of Jamestown and was shot.

John Robinson sued Edward Wingfield; 1st slander proceedings instituted, at Jamestown. Rev. Richard Seymour led 1st Thanksgiving Day service, Phippsburg, Me.

1608 A True Relation of Such Occurences and Accidents of Noate as Hath Hapened in Virginia since the First Planting of that Collony, written by John Smith.

1609 Henry Hudson sailed up Hudson River from New York Bay to Albany.

Don Pedro de Peralta built the oldest surviving, non-Indian building in America—the Governor's Palace at Santa Fe, N.M.

1610 Lawrence Bohune, 1st doctor in Virginia.

William Starchey wrote first-hand account of New England settlements: A True Reportory of the Wrack and Redemption of Sir Thomas Gates, Knight Upon and From the Islands of the Bermudas, his Coming to Virginia and the Estate of the Colony then and after the Government of the Lord La Ware.

Rev. Alexander Whitaker, founder, pastor, of the 1st Presbyterian church in America, in Virginia.

1612 John Rolfe, 1st to cultivate tobacco.

1613 Samuel Argall led 1st colonial naval expedition against French in Nova Scotia.

Pocahontas became converted to Christianity.

1614 First large-scale fishing expedition in America, led by Capt. John Smith.

1616 Smallpox among Indians relieved pressure of their attacks upon the New England colonies.

1619 July 30 First Legislative Assembly in America convened. The House of Burgesses at Old Church in Jamestown, Va.

Aug. A Dutch ship brought 20 Negroes to Jamestown to be sold as slaves. The first to appear in America.

1620 Estimated population of the various colonies: 2,499.

Nov. 2 Mayflower Compact signed by 41 adult males.

Dec. 21 Pilgrims reached Plymouth, Mass., aboard Mayflower after trip of 63 days.

Congregational Church founded in Plymouth, Mass., by 102 Pilgrim Separatists led by William Brewster, William Bradford and Edward Winslow. Ralph Smith was the 1st pastor.

1621 One of the earliest peace treaties between whites and Indians was concluded between the Wampanoags and Pilgrims. Signed at Plymouth, Mass.

Edward Leister v. Edward Doty: 1st duel, at Plymouth, Mass.

Robert Cushman, 1st exporter of furs.

1622 Mar. 22 Indian raid led by Powhaten's brother virtually wiped out the settlements outside Jamestown, Va.

Aug. 10 Province of Maine (land between the Merrimac and Kennebec rivers) given to John Mason and Ferdinando Gorges.

1623 First colonists sent by the Dutch West India Company settled along the Hudson River.

Rev. Greville Pooley sued Cicely (Sysley) Jordan in the 1st breach of promise suit.

Experience Miller, 1st leather tanner.

1624 Edward Winslow imported the 1st cows.

1626 Peter Minuit, First Director General of New Netherland, bought Manhattan Island for 60 guilders ($24).

1627 Francois Dollier de Casson and Rene de Brehant de Galinee discovered 1st oil spring, at Cuba, N.Y.

1628 Sept. 6 John Endecott entered Salem (Mass.) harbor.
Thomas Morton was the 1st person deported from America.
Thomas Beard was the first shoe manufacturer.

1629 Sept. 30 John Billington 1st person executed for a crime.

1630 Estimated colonial population: 5,700.
Boston founded by John Winthrop.
John Harvey established the first salt works.
Quadequina (Indian) introduced popcorn to the colonists.

1631 Feb. 5 Roger Williams arrived in Boston.
May 18 Restrictive Suffrage Act passed by the Mass. Bay General Court. Limited citizen privileges to church members.

1632 June 20 2d Lord Baltimore received charter for the settlement of Maryland.
Dixie Bull, 1st pirate, started his career.

1633 Adam Rollantsen, 1st schoolmaster in America, established 1st school in American colonies.
Boston Latin School founded, 1st secondary school in America.

1634 Mar. 4 Samuel Cole opened 1st tavern, in Boston.
Anne Hutchinson arrived in America.
Benjamin Syms established 1st educational endowment.
Sir John Harvey, 1st person tried for treason.
First Roman Catholic Church built in English colonies, at St. Mary's City, Md.

1635 Aug. 17 Richard Mather arrived in Boston.

1636 Roger Williams founded Rhode Island.
William Pynchon established 1st meat packing plant.
Oct. 28 Harvard College founded. First in America. Henry Dunster chosen as 1st president.

1637 Nov. 7 Anne Hutchinson fled to R.I. after being condemned in Mass. for preaching Antinomianism.
Pequot War, 500 Indians killed.

1638 Mar. 1 First Swedish settlers land at Ft. Christina, Del.
John Pearson established the 1st cloth mill.
First Almanac: An Almanak for the Year of Our Lord, 1639, Calculated for New England, written by William Pierce.
First printing press set up at Cambridge, Mass.
First Baptist Church in America, founded in Providence, R.I.
Swedish settlers introduced log cabin to the New World.

1639 Hezekiah Usher, 1st important bookseller, opened shop in Boston.
Thomas Lechford was the 1st lawyer to be disbarred.
Edward Rawson established the 1st gunpowder mill at Pecoit, Mass.
First document printed in English in America —Oath of a Free Man; printed at Cambridge, Mass., by Stephen Daye.
Elizabeth Pole, 1st woman to found a town—Taunton, Mass.
First postoffice authorized in America, in Mass. Bay colony.

1640 Anne Bradstreet, 1st woman author, published.
Rev. Reorus Torkillus, 1st Lutheran minister, arrived in America.
The Whole Booke of Psalmes Faithfully translated into English Metre; known as the Bay Psalm Book, was the 1st book published in America.

1641 John Cotton published 1st children's book, Milk for Babes.
Samuel Winslow received 1st patent granted by the colonies.
John Pride, 1st potter, began work.

1643 Francis de Florentia, 1st native Catholic priest, ordained.
Roger Williams published 1st English-Indian language dictionary.
John Winthrop, Jr. constructed 1st successful iron works near Lynn, Mass.

1645 Joseph Jencks opened 1st brass and iron foundry.

1647 William Berkely imported rice.
Achsah Young, 1st woman executed as a witch.
Margaret Brent, 1st advocate of woman suffrage.

1648 First labor organization in America authorized by Mass. Bay Colony.

1650 Capt. Abe Wood led the 1st expedition across the Allegheny Mountains.
Sam Hutchinson was the 1st to export iron.

1652 June 10 First mint established in Boston, Mass. John Hull was 1st mint-master.
Negro slaves imported into New Netherland.

1653 Migration began into what is now North Carolina.

1654 Mar. 25 Warfare between Catholics and Puritans ended in Maryland.
July 8 Jacob Barsimson, 1st Jew, arrived in New Netherland.
Joseph Jencks built 1st fire engine in Lynn, Mass.

1655 Saul Brown established 1st Jewish congregation in America, N.Y.C.

1656 July The 1st Quakers, Anne Austin and Mary Fisher, arrived in America.
Oct. 14 First legislation against Quakers enacted in Mass.

1658 Aug. 12 First police force established, in New Amsterdam.
Oct. 27 First Quakers hung in America (for violating the Mass. law of 1656).

1660 John Eliot founded 1st Indian church, at Natick, Mass.

1661 Mar. 14 William Leddra, last Quaker hung in Mass.
John Eliot published the 1st Bible printed in an Indian language.
First divorce case heard—in Del.

1662 May 3 Charter for the governing of Conn. drawn up.

Thomas Hackelton, 1st lime manufacturer, at Providence, R.I.

1664 New Netherland surrendered to the British. New Amsterdam became N.Y.C., Ft. Orange became Albany.

1665 Richard Nichols established 1st horse racing on a regular basis at Hempstead Plains, L.I.

1666 John Eliot published 1st grammar of an Indian language.

1667 July 21 Peace of Breda which concluded 2d Anglo-Dutch War signed.

1670 Estimated colonial population: 114,500.
April Charlestown (Charleston), S.C., founded.

Hiacoomes, 1st Indian preacher, ordained.

1671 Stephen Mumford organized 1st Seventh Day Baptist church at Newport, R.I.

1672 May Mass. General Court enacted first copyright law in America.

1673 Aug. 8-Feb. 4, 1674 Dutch again held New York.

Louis Hennepin discovered coal near (now) LaSalle, Ill.

1674 Dec. 4 Father Marquette built 1st building in what is now Chicago.

1675 June 24-Aug. 12, 1676: King Philip's War in progress.

1676 Nathaniel Bacon and yeomen rebelled against Gov. Berkeley at Jamestown, Va.

1677 William Penn framed 1st charter guaranteeing separation of church and state in American colonies, at West Jersey.

1680 Estimated colonial population: 155,600.

Sept. N.H. separated from Mass. by Royal Decree.

Thomas Brattle calculated the orbit of a comet.

1681 Mar 10 William Penn received charter from Charles II making him proprietor of Pa.

1682 Aug. 24 Delaware awarded to William Penn by the Duke of York.

La Salle took lower Mississippi River valley for King Louis XIV, naming it Louisiana.

1683 Oct. 6 First German settlers arrived in America.

John Reid, 1st landscape architect, arrived in America.

J. Shilders and P. Vorstman established 1st Labadist community, at Bohemia Manor, Md.

1684 Oct. 3 Mass. Charter revoked by Charles II.

1685 Nicholas More, chief justice of Phila., was 1st official to be impeached.

1686 Charter Oak incident in Conn. in which the colonists hid the charter of the colony from the royal authorities.

1687 William Phips, 1st native American to be knighted.

William Penn wrote the 1st law book in the colonies.

1689 Aug. 1 Protestant revolt in Maryland ended. First public school started in Phila. by William Penn.

1690 Estimated colonial population: 213,500.

Sept. 25 First issue of the 1st newspaper in the colonies, Public Occurences, published by Benjamin Harris in Boston.

William Rittenhouse built 1st paper mill, at Phila.

1691 Jacob Leisler, 1st colonist hanged for treason.

1692 Andrew Hamilton appointed 1st colonial postmaster-general.

Witchcraft trials and hangings at Salem, Mass.

1695 John Cornish built 1st worsted mill, at Boston. Capt. William Kidd was the 1st employer to enter into a workingmen's compensation agreement with his employees.

1696 Dinah Nuthead became the 1st woman printer.

1697 Sept. 30 Treaty of Ryswick ended King William's War.

1698 Settlement of Louisiana began.

John Tulley printed 1st road map for general use.

1699 Benjamin Hanks, 1st to manufacture chimes and bells.

1701 Oct. 16 Yale founded in Killingworth, Conn. Capt. William Kidd hanged for piracy and murder.

1703 John Hill published 1st business manual, Young Secretary's Guide.

1704 Apr. 24 America's first regularly published newspaper, Boston News-Letter, established by John Campbell, postmaster.

1707 Henrietta Johnston, 1st woman painter.

1711 Tuscarora War broke out in North Carolina.

1712 George Leason and Thomas Webber built 1st calico printery, in Boston.

1713 Mar. 31 Treaty of Utrecht signed.

Cotton Mather prepared 1st paleontology report in colonies.

1716 Capt. Arthur Savage exhibited 1st lion in America, at Boston.

1718 William Levingston built 1st theater, Williamsburg, Va.

1720 Estimated colonial population: 474,388.

Period of French expansion was getting underway.

Sir Robert Boyle established 1st permanent Indian school.

1721 Dr. Zabdiel Boylston gave 1st inoculations against smallpox, in Boston.

John Copson was the 1st fire insurance agent in America.

1722 The Albany treaty created the Indian confederation of the League of the Six Nations.

Gustavus Hesselius, 1st artist commissioned to do a public work.

1723 Hugh Jones wrote 1st English grammar by an American.

1724 Paul Dudley published 1st horticultural work in America.

1725 William Bradford founded 1st newspaper in N.Y., The Gazette.

1727 Mother Marie Tranchepaine founded 1st permanent convent, at New Orleans.
Benjamin Franklin organized the Junto, an association which opposed slavery.

1728 John Bartram established 1st botanical garden in America, at Philadelphia.
Peter Pelham, 1st mezzotint engraver to be published.
Johann Conrad Beissel published 1st German-language book in America.

1729 Isaac Greenwood published 1st American arithmetic book.
Sister St. Stanislaus Hachard, 1st nun ordained in America.
Daniel DeFoe wrote 1st newspaper serial story, which appeared in the Pennsylvania Gazette.
Royal control established in S.C.
Samuel Higley, 1st to manufacture steel, at Simsbury, Conn.

1730 Estimated population: 654,950.
Thomas Godfrey invented the quadrant.
Baltimore, Md., founded.

1731 Benjamin Franklin founded the 1st circulating library, in Phila.

1732 Feb. 22 George Washington, 1st Pres. U.S., born in Va.
George Farquhar produced the 1st play acted by professional players, at N.Y.C.
First stage line established, between Burlington and Amboy, N.J.
First number of Poor Richard's Almanac appeared, published by Benjamin Franklin.

1733 Feb. 12 Savannah, 1st settlement in Ga., founded by James Oglethorpe.
May 17 Molasses Act passed by Parliament.
Nov. 5 John Peter Zenger founded the New York Weekly Journal.
Johann Conrad Beissel founded the 1st communistic type society, at Lancaster, Pa.
First serious outbreak of influenza in America, in Phila. and N.Y.C.

1734 John Peter Zenger arrested for libel; successfully defended by Andrew Hamilton.
Jonathan Edwards led the "Great Awakening" in American revivalism.
George Boehnisch, 1st Moravian to arrive in America.
William Bull, 1st American to be graduated from a medical school (Univ. of Leiden).

1735 Feb. 8 First opera produced in the colonies, performed at Charleston, S.C. It was Flora, written by Colley Cibber.
Mar. 17 First celebration of St. Patrick's Day in America, held in Boston.
Oct. 30 John Adams, 2d Pres., born in Braintree, Mass.
Dec. 10 John Wesley arrived in Ga. at invitation of Oglethorpe.
First European settlers in Indiana—eight French families founded Vincennes.
William Brattle published 1st book on logic, the Compendium Logicae.
First Moravian community established in Savannah, Ga.
First copper coinage in colonies minted by John Higley, at Simsbury, Conn.

1736 John Wesley and Charles Delamotte founded the 1st Sunday school, at Savannah, Ga.

1737 Andrew Faneuil built 1st greenhouse.

1738 Dr. John Lining made 1st systematic weather records.

1739 John Winthrop, 1st important American astronomer, began observations.
Joseph Mallinson made 1st iron casting.
Plunket Fleeson, 1st to manufacture wallpaper.

1740 Estimated colonial population: 889,000.
Jan. Oglethorpe's forces raided Spanish-controlled Florida.
War of the Austrian Succession started (known in America as King's George's War).
George Whitefield founded the 1st permanent orphanage, in Georgia.

1741 Feb. 13 First publication of an American magazine; Andrew Bradford's American Magazine, or a Monthly View of the Political State of the British Colonies.
July 16 Vitus Bering sighted Mt. Elias volcano, Alaska.

1742 William Parks wrote the 1st American cookbook.
Countess Benigna Von Zinzendorf established the 1st school for Protestant girls.
Benjamin Franklin invented a stove for heating.

1743 Apr. 13 Thomas Jefferson, 3d Pres. U.S., born in Va.
Rev. Rector Clapp constructed 1st planetarium in America.
Samuel Kneeland and Timothy Green published 1st American religious journal, The Christian History.
Benjamin Franklin founded the American Philosophical Society, 1st scientific society in America.

1744 Certain territories north of the Ohio river ceded by the Iroquois League to the British in treaty signed at Lancaster, Pa.

1745 June 16 French stronghold, Ft. Louisbourg, captured by New England colonial troops and British forces during King George's War.
Benjamin Mecom did 1st sterotype printing.

1746 Oct. 22 Princeton College founded.

1747 New York Bar Association founded.
Abraham Redwood founded 1st public library in America, at Newport, R.I.

1748 Oct. 18 Treaty of Aix-la-Chapelle ended King George's War.
Benjamin Crabb established 1st candle factory.

1749 Oct. 26 Negro slavery extended into Georgia by permission of the proprietors.

Nov. 13 Benjamin Franklin founded the Academy and College of Phila., the forerunner of the Univ. of Pa.

Franklin invented the lightning rod.

Franklin was the 1st to cook with electricity.

James Wyatt opened the 1st wax works museum.

Thomas Kean and Walter Murray produced the 1st Shakespearean play, N.Y.C.

1750 Estimated colonial population: 1,207,000.

Ohio Land Company formed.

Jacob Yoder invented the flatboat.

1751 Mar. 16 James Madison, 4th Pres. U.S., born in Va.

Benjamin Franklin wrote Observations Concerning the Increase of Mankind.

Edward Willet exhibited the 1st trained monkey in America.

Thomas Bacon opened 1st manual training school.

1752 June Benjamin Franklin experimented with kite and key to prove lightning was a manifestation of electricity.

Liberty Bell cast in England and delivered to colonies.

Benjamin Franklin and Dr. Thomas Bond founded the 1st hospital, the Pennsylvania Hospital.

1753 Capt. Charles Swaine led expedition to discover Northwest Passage.

John Schuyler imported the 1st steam engine.

1754 May 28 George Washington led colonial troops in opening action of the French and Indian War.

June 19 Benjamin Franklin introduced Albany Plan of Union for colonial government.

July 3 Washington yielded Ft. Necessity to French forces.

Oct. 31 King's College (now Columbia Univ.) chartered, N.Y.C.

Benjamin Franklin drew 1st newspaper cartoon.

Jonathan Roberts opened 1st druggist's shop.

1755 June 16 First non-sectarian college in America chartered; the Univ. of Pa.

July 9 Gen. Braddock's forces defeated by French during French and Indian War and he was mortally wounded.

Hans Christiansen constructed first municipal water pumping plant, at Bethlehem, Pa.

Dr. Richard Shuckburg wrote "Yankee Doodle."

1756 Thomas Lord Fairfax established 1st public spa, at Bath, Va.

Oldest continuing newspaper in America, New Hampshire Gazette began publication in Portsmouth.

1757 Jan. 11 Alexander Hamilton born on island of Nevis, West Indies.

Benjamin Franklin established the 1st street cleaning service, at Phila.

1758 July 8 British and colonial troops beaten by French under Montcalm at Ft. Ticonderoga.

Aug. 27 British captured Ft. Frontenac.

Aug. First Indian reservation established, by New Jersey Assembly.

Nov. 25 British forces drove French from Ft. Duquesne and renamed it Pittsburg.

James Monroe, 5th Pres. U.S., born in Va.

A school for Negroes established in Phila.

Jane Colden, 1st American woman botanist, completed her work.

Two Penny Act passed by Virginia colonial assembly.

1759 July 26 French abandoned Ft. Ticonderoga.

Sept. 18 French defeated at Battle of Quebec.

Enoch Noyes established 1st comb factory.

Robert Cross founded 1st life insurance company.

Francis Hopkinson composed 1st American secular song, "My Days Have Been So Wondrous Free."

1760 Aug. 8 Cherokee Indians massacred garrison at Ft. Loudoun, Tenn.

Sept. 8 French surrendered to Gen. Amherst at Montreal.

Nov. 29 French surrendered Detroit to Maj. Robert Rogers.

Benjamin Franklin invented the rocking chair.

Conestoga wagon developed in Pennsylvania.

1761 John Winthrop led 1st scientific expedition, to Nova Scotia, for astronomical purposes.

1762 Bill Richmond became the 1st American prizefighter of distinction.

Ann Franklin was the 1st woman newspaper editor.

1763 Feb. 10 Treaty of Paris ended the French and Indian War.

William Henry built the 1st sternwheel steamboat in U.S.

1765 Mar. 22 Stamp Act passed by Parliament.

May 29 Patrick Henry attacked Stamp Act in famous speech in Va. colonial assembly.

Oct. 7 Stamp Act Congress met at Phila.

Oct. 19 Stamp Act Congress adopted 13 resolutions against the Stamp Act.

Drs. William Shippen Jr. and John Morgan established the 1st medical college; now the Univ. of Pa. School of Medicine.

1766 John Henry, 1st matinee idol, made his debut.

Martin Boehm and Phillip W. Otterbein founded the 1st Church of the United Brethren of Christ.

Abel Buell invented a gem cutting machine.

First Methodist society formed in America, by Phillip Embury, N.Y.C.

Nov. 10 Queen's College (now Rutgers Univ.) chartered in Brunswick, N.J.

1767 Mar. 15 Andrew Jackson, 7th Pres. U.S., born.

July 11 John Quincy Adams, 6th Pres. U.S., born in Braintree, Mass.

1768 Benjamin Franklin was 1st advocate of spelling reform.

John Archer, 1st doctor to receive a M.D.

John Sellers made 1st sieve.

1770 Estimated colonial population: 2,205,000.

Mar. 5 Seven colonists killed during the "Boston Massacre."

Apr. 12 Townshend Acts repealed by Parliament.

College of Charleston established.

1771 Benjamin Franklin began writing his Autobiography.

1773 Feb. 9 William Henry Harrison, 9th Pres. U.S., born at Berkeley, Va.

Apr. 27 Tea Act passed by Parliament.

Dec. 16 Boston Tea Party.

First Negro Baptist Church established at Silver Bluff, S.C.

John Winthrop received 1st honorary doctor of laws degree, from Harvard.

1774 Mar. 31 First of the Intolerable Acts passed by Parliament.

May 17 First call for intercolonial Congress issued in Rhode Island.

June 22 Quebec Act passed.

Sept. 5 First Continental Congress met in Phila. Peyton Randolph was elected president.

Oct. 14 Declaration of Rights adopted by the 1st Continental Congress.

Dec. 14 First military encounter of the Revolution occurred in which Maj. John Sullivan led a group of militia in seizing arms and stores from Ft. William & Mary.

Ann Lee was the leader of the 1st conscientious objectors in America.

Capt. Robert Keayne organized 1st anti-British military organization.

1775 Jan. 11 Francis Salvador became 1st Jew to hold elective office when he won a seat in the South Carolina Provincial Assembly.

Apr. 19 Battle of Lexington.

May 10 Ethan Allen captured Ticonderoga.

May 16 Provincial Congress of Mass. adopted a constitution.

June 15 George Washington selected supreme commander of the Continental Army.

June 17 Battle of Bunker Hill.

July 3 George Washington took command of colonial troops beseiging Boston.

July 25 Benjamin Church became 1st surgeon-general of Continental Army.

July 26 Postal system established by 2d Continental Congress. Benjamin Franklin appointed postmaster-general.

Sept. 2 Continental Navy established.

Nov. 10 U.S. Marine Corps established by Congress.

Dec. Esek Hopkins appointed 1st commander-in-chief of Continental Navy.

Michael Hillegas appointed 1st treasurer of U.S.

John Baldwin organized 1st abolition society.

First American novel, Adventures of Alonso, written by Thomas A. Digges.

1776 Jan. 1 Norfolk, Va., burned by British.

Jan. 10 Thomas Paine's Common Sense appeared.

Mar. 17 Gen. Howe evacuated Boston.

June 27 Thomas Hickey, who conspired against Washington, was 1st American soldier to be executed, on order of a military court martial.

July 2 New Jersey was 1st state to grant limited women suffrage.

July 4 Continental Congress adopted the Declaration of Independence.

Aug. 2 Declaration of Independence officially signed.

Sept. 2 Benjamin Franklin chosen to represent U.S. in France.

Sept. 9 Continental Congress adopted words "United States" in place of "United Colonies."

Sept. 22 Nathan Hale hanged by British as spy.

Dec. 19 First number of the pamphlets known as The Crisis, by Thomas Paine appeared.

Dec. 26 Washington surprised the enemy at Trenton, N.J.

Silas Deane was 1st to use invisible ink in U.S. diplomatic correspondence.

William Demont was the 1st traitor to the American cause.

David Bushnell built the 1st submarine for war purposes.

Phi Beta Kappa scholastic fraternity founded.

1777 July Vermont was 1st colony to abolish slavery and adopt universal male suffrage.

Sept. 27 British took possession of Phila.

Oct. 17 Gen. John Burgoyne surrendered to Gen. Gates at Saratoga.

Nov. 15 Articles of Confederation adopted by the Continental Congress.

Dec. 17 Washington retired to Valley Forge for the winter.

Timothy Pickering appointed 1st adjutant-general of the Army.

1778 May 4 Continental Congress ratified Treaty of Alliance with France.

June Secret Service organized under Aaron Burr.

July Conrad Alexander Gerard was 1st diplomatic representative accredited to U.S. (from France).

1779 Sept. 23 Bonhomme Richard, commanded by John Paul Jones, defeated the British ship Serapis.

Rev. John Murray organized the 1st Universalist church in America.

1780 Estimated population: 2,781,000.

Mar. 1 Pennsylvania was 1st state to abolish slavery.

Oct. 2 Maj. John Andre hanged as a British spy.

Oct. 7 British and Tory troops defeated at Battle of King's Mountain.

Zadoc Benedict established the 1st hat factory.

Marm Bett was the 1st slave to be emancipated.

1781 Sept. 5 French fleet under de Grasse defeated British on Chesapeake Bay.

Sept. 8 New London, Conn., seized by British under Benedict Arnold.

Oct. 19 Cornwallis surrendered at Yorktown, Va.

Dec. 31 Continental Congress established the Bank of North America.

1782 Aug. 7 The medal Purple Heart authorized.

Dec. 5 Martin Van Buren, 8th Pres. U.S., born at Kinderhook, N.Y. Was first Pres. to be U.S. citizen at birth.

William Barton designed the great seal of the U.S.

1783 Sept. 3 Peace Treaty with Great Britain signed.

Dec. 24 Washington resigned as commander-in-chief of Army.

1784 Edward Warren made the 1st balloon flight.

Tapping Reeve established the 1st law school, the Litchfield (Conn.) Law School.

Francis Asbury, the 1st Methodist bishop in America.

James Rumsey invented the motor boat.

David C. Claypole and John Dunlap began publication of the 1st daily newspaper, the Pennsylvania Packet and Daily Advertiser.

Samuel Seabury was the 1st Protestant Episcopal bishop.

1785 Mar. 10 Thomas Jefferson appointed minister to France and John Adams to England.

July 6 Thomas Jefferson proposed the establishment of a coinage system.

George Washington imported the 1st mule.

John Fitch began invention of first steamboat.

Benjamin Franklin invented bifocal eyeglasses.

John Marrant was ordained as the 1st Negro missionary.

First American Epic poem, Conquest of Canaan, (Timothy Dwight), published.

1786 Daniel Shays led rebellion in Mass.

Ice cream manufactured commercially for the 1st time.

Slavery was outlawed in New Jersey.

1787 May U.S. Constitutional Conv. held in Phila.

Dec. 7 Delaware was 1st state to ratify U.S. Constitution.

Northwest Ordinance adopted by Continental Congress.

Levi Hutchins invented alarm clock.

1788 June 21 New Hampshire ratified Constitution. Constitution became effective on this date as the minimum number of states had now ratified.

William Perry published 1st dictionary in America.

Isaac Briggs patented steamboat.

1789 Jan. 23 Georgetown College, 1st Catholic college in America founded.

Mar. 4 1st session of the U.S. Congress began.

Apr. 6 First Congress formally organized.

Apr. 30 George Washington inaugurated as 1st Pres. U.S.

June 1 Pres. Washington signed 1st legislation enacted by Congress.

Aug. 7 Henry Knox appointed 1st U.S. sec. of war.

Sept. 2 Alexander Hamilton appointed 1st U.S. sec. of treasury.

Sept. 26 John Jay confirmed as 1st chief justice of U.S. Supreme Court.

Sept. 26 Samuel Osgood appointed 1st postmaster general of U.S.

Sept. 26 Edmund J. Randolph appointed as 1st attorney-general.

Frederick A. C. Muhlenberg, 1st speaker of U.S. Ho. of Reps.

Tench Coxe, 1st U.S. commissioner of the revenue.

John Fenno started publication of the Gazette of the United States.

Barzillai Hudson and George Goodwin published 1st children's magazine.

Robert Gray completed 1st circumnavigation of the globe by an American (1787-90).

Richard Allison appointed as 1st surgeon in Legion of U.S.

1790 Population: 3,929,625.

Feb. Thomas Jefferson appointed as 1st U.S. sec. of state.

Mar. 1 Congress authorized the 1st U.S. Census.

Mar. 29 John Tyler, 10th Pres. U.S., born in Va.

Apr. 17 Benjamin Franklin died.

Richard Harrison, Thomas Hartley and Elias Boudinot were 1st lawyers to be admitted before the bar of U.S. Supreme Court.

James Derham, the 1st Negro doctor, practiced in Phila.

Samuel Hopkins received the 1st patent granted by the U.S.

1791 Mar. Thomas Paine wrote The Rights of Man.

Mar. 4 Vermont joined the Union.

Apr. 23 James Buchanan, 15th Pres. U.S., born in Pa.

Rev. John Hurt appointed 1st chaplain of U.S. Army.

Philip Ginter discovered anthracite coal in Pa.

Antonio Mendez opened the 1st sugar refinery, in New Orleans.

1792 Apr. 2 Congress authorized 1st U.S. Mint. David Rittenhouse chosen as the 1st director.

May 8 Congress passed 1st National Conscription Act.

May 17 New York Stock Exchange organized.

June 1 Kentucky became the 15th State in the Union.

Dec. 15 Bill of Rights amendments to U.S. Constitution went into effect when Va. provided the necessary ratification.

John Bill Ricketts established the 1st circus, at Phila.

Dr. Hugh Smith wrote the 1st maternity book.

1793 Mar. 4 Washington inaugurated as Pres. for his 2d term.

Apr. 22 Washington issued neutrality proclamation.

Eli Whitney invented the cotton gin.

John and Arthur Schofield built 1st wool carding machine, at Newburyport, Mass.

Merino sheep smuggled into the country.

1794 Apr. 22 Pennsylvania eliminated capital punishment except for first degree murder.

Aug. 7 Washington ordered the militia to put down the Whiskey Rebellion.

Aug. 20 Gen. Anthony Wayne defeated Miami Indians in Ohio.

Nov. 19 John Jay concluded treaty between U.S. and England.

Richard Allen, a former slave, founded the 1st Independent Methodist Church for Negroes.

Dr. Jesse Bennett performed the 1st successful caesarean operation, at Edom, Va.

1795 Feb. 25 Union College founded in Schenectady, N.Y.

Nov. 2 James K. Polk, 11th Pres. U.S., born in N.C.

Oliver Evans developed 1st practical steam engine, at Phila.

Sarah Waldrake and Rachel Summers were the 1st women employed by the federal govt.

1796 June 1 Tennessee became the 16th State in the Union.

Sept. 17 Washington delivered his Farewell Address.

James Finley designed the 1st suspension bridge, Westmoreland County, Pa.

The Monitor of Phila. was 1st newspaper to appear on a Sunday.

Amelia Simmons was the 1st American to write a cookbook.

Francis M. Barrere received the 1st passport issued by the U.S.

1797 Mar. 4 John Adams inaugurated as 2d Pres. of U.S.

Nathaniel Briggs patented the 1st washing machine.

1798 Jan. 8 11th Amendment adopted.

Apr. 3 XYZ Affair reported to Congress by Pres. Adams.

June 18 Amendments to the Naturalization Act of 1795 passed.

June 25 The Alien Act passed.

July 6 Alien Enemies Act passed.

Nov. 16 Kentucky Resolutions issued.

Benjamin Stoddert appointed 1st U.S. sec. of navy.

David Wilkinson patented the 1st nut and bolt machine.

John James Dufour established the 1st successful vineyard, Lexington, Ky.

1799 Nov. 22 Virginia Resolutions issued.

Dec. 14 George Washington died at Mt. Vernon, Va.

Jonathan Grout devised 1st semaphore telegraph system.

William Woodbridge founded 1st local educational association, at Middletown, Conn.

1800 Population: 5,308,483.

Jan. 7 Millard Fillmore, 13th Pres. U.S., born in N.Y.

Apr. 4 First Federal Bankruptcy Law enacted.

May 7 Indiana Territory created by act of Congress.

Nov. 17 Congress convened for the 1st time in Washington.

John Adams was the 1st Pres. U.S. to reside in Washington.

Jacob Albright founded the 1st Evangelical Church.

1801 Jan. 20 John Marshall appointed chief justice U.S. Supreme Court.

Feb. 17 Because of tie in Electoral College, Ho. of Reps. elected Thomas Jefferson as 3d Pres. U.S.

Mar. 4 Thomas Jefferson inaugurated as 3d Pres. U.S.; 1st to be inaugurated in Washington.

May 14 Start of war with Tripoli.

1802 Jan. 29 John Beckley designated as 1st librarian of Congress.

Jan. 29 Judiciary Act of 1801 repealed.

Mar. 16 U.S. Mil. Acad. founded at West Point, N.Y.

1803 Feb. 19 Ohio became the 17th state in the Union. First state in which slavery was forbidden from the beginning.

Feb. 24 Marbury v. Madison decided by Supreme Court.

Apr. 30 Louisiana purchased from France.

John James Audubon was the 1st person to band birds in America.

Thomas Moore invented a refrigerator.

1804 May 14 Lewis and Clark expedition started out from St. Louis to explore the Louisiana Territory.

July 11 Alexander Hamilton fatally wounded in duel with Aaron Burr.

Sept. 25 12th Amendment to the Constitution adopted.

Nov. 23 Franklin Pierce, 14th Pres. U.S., born in N.H.

Elizabeth Marshall was the 1st woman pharmacist.

1805 Mar. 4 Thomas Jefferson inaugurated for his 2d term.

June 14 Peace Treaty signed with Tripoli.

Oliver Evans invented the 1st steam operated amphibious vehicle.

1806 July 5 Zebulon M. Pike began his explorations in southwest U.S.

Aaron Burr arrested and tried for treason.

James Madison Randolph was the 1st child born in the White House.

David Melville installed the 1st gas street lights, at Newport, R.I.

1807 Jan. 1 Congress passed act forbidding the African slave trade and importation of slaves into America.

Feb. 27 Henry Wadsworth Longfellow born in Me.

June 22 The Chesapeake-Leopard Affair.

Dec. 22 Embargo Act signed by Thomas Jefferson.

John Stafford gave 1st instruction to the deaf, at N.Y.C.

Robert Fulton designed and built the first steamboat to make regular trips, between N.Y.C. and Albany.

Townsend Speakman prepared the 1st soda water, at Phila.

1808 Apr. 17 Napoleon issued the Bayonne Decree ordering the seizure of all American vessels in French ports.

Dec. 7 James Madison elected 4th Pres. U.S.

Dec. 29 Andrew Johnson, 17th Pres. U.S., born in N.C.

Jesse Fell burned 1st anthracite coal experimentally, at Wilkes-Barre, Pa.

Billy James Clark organized the 1st temperance society, at Saratoga Springs, N.Y.

First recorded duel between Congressmen occurred; George Campbell and Barent Gardenier.

1809 Feb. 12 Abraham Lincoln, 16th Pres. U.S., born in Ky.

Mar. 1 Embargo Act repealed.

Mar. 1 Non-Intercourse Act passed.

1810 Population: 7,239,881.

May 1 Macon's Bill Number 2 passed, designed to replace the Non-Intercourse Act.

Oct. 27 West Florida annexed by Pres. Madison.

Simeon Viets established the first important cigar factory, at West Suffield, Conn.

Johann Christian Gottlieb Graupner founded the 1st symphony orchestra, at Boston.

Thomas Brown invented the mail box.

Rodney H. Hanks established the 1st silk mill, at Mansfield, O.

Fletcher vs. Peck decided by the Supreme Court.

1811 Jan-Feb. Debate in Congress over the extension of the charter of the 1st Bank of the U.S.

Jan. 15 Secret act passed authorizing Pres. Madison to take possession of Florida.

Feb. 11 Pres. Madison prohibited trade with Gt. Britain under authority of the Macon bill.

Apr. 12 First permanent colony in Pacific northwest founded by a group of New York settlers.

May The Little Belt Affair, when U.S. frigate President fought H.M.S Little Belt.

Nov. 7 William H. Harrison defeated Indians at Tippecanoe River in Indiana.

Nov. Pro-war feeling swept many "War Hawks" into Congress.

Thomas Campbell founded 1st Church of the Disciples of Christ, at Brush Run, Pa.

William Monroe established the 1st pencil factory, at Concord, Mass.

George Clinton was the 1st vice-pres. U.S. to die in office.

1812 Mar. 3 First foreign aid bill, authorized $50,000 in relief to victims of a Venezuela earthquake.

Apr. 8 Louisiana entered union.

May 14 West Florida annexed to Miss. Territory.

June 18 War declared against Gt. Britain.

Aug. 16 Gen. Hull surrendered to British at Detroit.

Dec. 2 James Madison elected to his 2d term as Pres. U.S.

1813 Mar. 4 James Madison inaugurated for his 2d term.

Oct. 5 Gen. Harrison defeated the British at Battle of the Thames.

John Scott published 1st religious newspaper, The Religious Rembrancer, Phila.

1814 Mar. 29 Gen. Andrew Jackson defeated Creek Indians to end the Creek war.

Apr. 13 Francis Scott Key wrote the words of the national anthem.

July 25 Battle of Lundy's Lane.

Aug. 24 British captured and burned Washington, D.C.

Sept. 11 Thomas MacDonough defeated the British on Lake Champlain.

Dec. 15-Jan. 4, 1815 Hartford Conv. held.

Dec. 24 Peace Treaty ending War of 1812 signed at Ghent, Belgium.

Middlebury (Vt.) Seminary, 1st college for women, founded by Emma Hart Willard.

Benjamin Cummins produced the 1st circular saw.

1815 Jan. 8 Andrew Jackson defeated the British at Battle of New Orleans.

Mar. 3 U.S. declared war against Algiers.

June 17-19 Stephen Decatur engaged in naval battles against Algiers.

July 3 Peace treaty with Algiers signed.

1816 Mar. 16 James Monroe nominated for Presidency by Congressional Republican (Democratic) caucus.

Mar. 20 Supreme Court case Martin vs. Hunter's Lessee decided.

Apr. 11 Rev. Richard Allen established, appointed 1st bishop, of 1st African Methodist Episcopal Church in America, at Phila.

Dec. 4 James Monroe elected Pres. U.S., defeating Rufus King; Daniel D. Tompkins elected vice-pres.

Ferdinand R. Hassler appointed 1st U.S. coast survey superintendent.

Indiana admitted as 19th state.

1817 Jan. 7 Second Bank of the United States opened in Phila.

Mar. 1 Congress established office of Supreme Court reporter.

Mar. 3 Alabama Territory formed.

Mar. 4 James Monroe inaugurated as 5th Pres. U.S.

Apr. 28-29 Rush-Bagot Agreement between England and U.S., limiting naval power on Great Lakes to police force.

July 4 Construction of Erie Canal begun.

Dec. 10 Mississippi admitted as 20th state.

Charles Osborn published 1st abolition newspaper, the Philanthropist, at Mt. Pleasant, O.

Thomas Gallaudet helped found 1st free Amer. school for deaf, Hartford, Conn.

1818 Apr. Thirteen stripes on U.S. flag made constant by law.

May 27 Fall of Pensacola, Fla., to Gen. Andrew Jackson ended 1st Seminole War.

Dec. 3 Illinois admitted as 21st state.

Albert and John W. Picket edited and published 1st successful educational magazine, the Academician, N.Y.C.

E. B. Gardette grew 1st melons and cantaloupes, Germantown, Pa.

Martin Beaty drilled 1st flowing oil well, Monticello, Va.

Congress passed laws extending suffrage.

1819 Feb. 13 Talmadge amendment added to bill for Missouri statehood.

Feb. 22 Adams-Onis Treaty, by which Spain ceded Florida to U.S., signed.

Mar. 2 Congress enacted 1st immigration law.

Mar. 6 Supreme Court case McCulloch vs. Maryland decided.

May 26 Moses Rogers commanded the Savannah, 1st American steamboat to cross Atlantic; arrived Liverpool 25 days later.

Dec. 14 Alabama admitted as 22d state.

Thomas Jefferson founded Univ. of Va.

Washington Irving published Sketch Book.

John Stuart Skinner published 1st important agricultural journal, the American Farmer, Balt.

Charles Guille made 1st parachute jump, from a balloon.

William K. Clarkson received 1st bicycle patent.

Samuel Leonard produced 1st rolled angle iron, Pitts.

Thomas Blanchard patented 1st lathe.

Seth Boyden tanned 1st patent leather, Newark, N.J.

Bass Otis published 1st lithograph, "A Water Mill," Phila.

Capt. Alden Partridge founded 1st civilian-type military school, Norwich, Vt.

Thomas Wildey established 1st Odd Fellows Lodge, Balt.

Rodney and Horatio Hanks manufactured 1st silk thread, Mansfield, Conn.

1820 Population of U.S.: 9,638,453.

Feb. 6 Group of 86 Negroes sailed from N.Y.C. to Sierra Leone in 1st organized emigration from U.S. to Africa.

Mar. 3 Missouri Compromise passed.

Mar. 15 Maine admitted as 23d state.

May 15 African Slave Trade Act passed, making importation of slaves to U.S. illegal, punishable by death.

Dec. 6 James Monroe defeated John Quincy Adams in presidential election.

Capt. Henry Hall, 1st to cultivate cranberries, Dennis, Mass.

Capt. Nathaniel B. Palmer discovered Antarctica.

Elihu Embree published 1st anti-slavery magazine, the Emancipator, Jonesborough, Ark.

1821 Mar. 5 James Monroe inaugurated Pres. U.S. for 2d term. First Pres. to be inaugurated Mar. 5.

May 31 First Catholic Cathedral in U.S. dedicated, Cathedral of the Assumption of the Blessed Virgin Mary, Balt.

Aug. 10 Missouri admitted as 24th state.

Sept. Treaty signed by which Seminole Indians were to move to center of Fla.

Dec. 18 Univ. of Ala. chartered as state university.

James Boyd patented 1st rubber-lined cotton web fire hose.

James Fenimore Cooper wrote The Spy.

William Becknell pioneered the Santa Fe Trail.

Emma H. Willard founded 1st girls' high school, Troy, N.Y.

1822 Mar. 8 President Monroe, in a message to Congress, urged recognition of the new South American republics.

Apr. 27 Ulysses S. Grant, 18th Pres. U.S., born in Point Pleasant, O.

May 4 Pres. Monroe vetoed bill appropriating money for repair of Cumberland Road and authorizing toll charges.

May 30 Denmark Vesey slave plot uncovered and suppressed in Charleston, S.C., 37 participants executed.

Oct. 4 Rutherford B. Hayes, 19th Pres. U.S., born in Delaware, O.

Charles M. Graham received 1st patent for artificial teeth.

Daniel Treadwell manufactured 1st power printing press, Boston.

John Farr and Abraham Kunzi manufactured 1st quinine, Phila.

1823 May 8 "Home Sweet Home" 1st sung, in opera Clari, lyrics by John Howard Payne, music by Henry Bishop.

Dec. 2 Pres. Monroe announced Monroe Doctrine.

Edwin Forrest, 1st blackface minstrel, appeared as Negro Ruban in Tailor in Distress, by Sol Smith.

Samuel Read Hall founded 1st normal school devoted entirely to preparation of teachers, Concord (Vt.) Academy.

Charles June became 1st ice skating champion.

1824 Jan. 24 Kenyon College chartered, Gambier, O.

Feb. 14 Last Congressional nominating caucus convened and named William H. Crawford of Ga. as its candidate for president.

Mar. 2 Supreme Court decision in case of Gibbons vs. Ogden, which established federal control over interstate commerce.

Apr. 17 U.S.-Russian treaty signed. Russia abandoned some of her claims in the Southern Pacific area.

Aug. First nominating conv. held at Utica, N.Y. First time electors of nominees for offices were popularly elected.

Aug. 2 State of Illinois outlawed slavery.

Dec. 1 No candidate received sufficient majority of electoral votes in presidential election.

John Stevens built 1st American-made locomotive to pull a train (was never used).

First recorded strike in U.S. involving women employees, Pawtucket, R.I.

1825 Jan. 3 Robert Owen established 1st secular utopian society, New Harmony, Ind.

Feb. 12 Creek Indian Treaty signed. Creeks agreed to turn all of their lands in Ga. over to federal government and move further west.

Feb. 21 Amherst College chartered in Mass.

Feb. 28 John Quincy Adams chosen Pres. U.S. by Ho. of Reps.

Mar. 4 John Quincy Adams inaugurated as 6th Pres. U.S.

Mar. 7 Joel R. Poinsett appointed 1st U.S. minister to Mexico.

Mar. 24 First American settlers allowed in Mexican state of Texas; settled at Coahuila.

Oct. 26 Erie Canal officially opened, at Buffalo, N.Y.

Elie M. Durand, 1st bottler of mineral water, Phila.

Henry Wadsworth Longfellow published his 1st poems.

Hannah Lord Montague made 1st detachable collar.

First significant strike in U.S. for ten-hour day, called in Boston by carpenters.

1826 Jan. 24 Treaty of Washington signed, allowing Creek Indians to stay on their lands until 1827.

Feb. 7 Western Reserve College chartered, Hudson, O.

Apr. 8 Henry Clay and John Randolph fought duel over the Panama Congress controversy. Neither harmed.

July 4 Thomas Jefferson and John Adams died.

Aug. 22 Jedediah Smith organized expedition to explore Southwest; led 1st overland expedition to California.

Frances Wright founded Nashoba, a community of Negroes to colonize Africa.

James Kent published 1st volume of Commentaries on American Law.

Samuel Morey patented 1st internal combustion engine.

John Brown Russworm, 1st Negro college graduate, Bowdoin College, Brunswick, Me.

Henry Ogle invented 1st successful reaper.

Amasa Holcomb manufactured 1st reflecting telescope in U.S.

1827 Feb. 2 Supreme Court decision in case Martin vs. Mott, giving Pres. U.S. final authority to call out militia.

Aug. 6 Treaty between U.S. and Britain establishing joint occupation of Ore.

Nov. 15 Creek Indians ceded remaining lands in Ga. to U.S.

First state high school law passed, in Mass.

Madame Francisquy Hutin, star of 1st ballet presented in U.S., at N.Y.C.

John Hill Hewitt wrote 1st secular song hit, "The Minstrel's Return."

John Brown Russwurm and Samuel E. Cornish published 1st Negro newspaper, Freedom's Journal, N.Y.C.

New York State abolished slavery.

Harrison Gray Dyar constructed 1st telegraph.

1828 Jan. 24 Indiana Univ. chartered by state.

May 19 President Adams signed Tariff of Abominations.

July 4 Construction of Baltimore & Ohio R.R. begun.

Dec. 3 Andrew Jackson elected Pres. U.S.

National Republican Party formed.

Democratic Party formed.

Thomas Dartmouth Rice first sang "Jim Crow," America's 1st international song hit.

Joseph Henry invented 1st electric magnet.

James Gordon Bennett, 1st important Washington correspondent, reporting for N.Y.C. Enquirer.

Elias Boudinot, editor 1st Indian newspaper, the Cherokee Phoenix, New Echota, Ga.

1829 Mar. 4 Andrew Jackson inaugurated as 7th Pres. of U.S.

Oct. 17 Delaware and Chesepeake Canal formally opened.

Workingman's Party organized, N.Y.C. and Phila.

Dr. John Dix Fisher founded 1st school for the blind, in Boston. (Perkins Sch.)

Samuel L. Knapp published 1st history of American literature, Lectures on American Literature.

James Carrington patented 1st coffee mill.

Francis Lieber edited 1st American encyclopedia, Encyclopedia Americana.

John Gill made 1st revolving gun.

Chang and Eng (Bunker), 1st Siamese twins arrived.

John Stuart Skinner published 1st sports magazine, the American Turf Register, Balt.

William Austin Burt patented 1st typewriter.

1830 Population: 12,866,020.

Jan. 19-27 Webster-Hayne debates in Congress.

Apr. 6 Mexico forbade further colonization of Texas by American citizens.

Joseph Smith founded Church of Jesus Christ of the Latter Day Saints (Mormon Church), Fayette, N.Y.

May 28 President Jackson signed Indian Removal Act, calling for general move of Indians to west of Mississippi River.

July 15 Territory of Sac and Fox Indians ceded to U.S.

Oct. 5 Chester A. Arthur, 21st Pres. U.S., born in Fairfield, Vt.

Dec. 16 Mississippi College chartered in Clinton, Miss.

First covered wagons made trek from Missouri River to Rocky Mountains.

William Bryan organized 1st consumers cooperative society.

D. Hyde patented 1st fountain pen.

Samuel Colt invented 1st pistol with a revolving barrel.

R. L. Stevens invented "T" shaped railroad rails.

Charles C. Grice opened 1st veterinary hospital, N.Y.C.

1831 Jan. 1 William Lloyd Garrison published 1st issue of The Liberator.

Apr. Eaton Affair in President Jackson's Cabinet.

James Monroe died.

Aug. Nat Turner led Negro insurrection in Va.

William Driver, 1st to use term "Old Glory" to designate U.S. flag.

John Quincy Adams, 1st congressman who had been a Pres. U.S., took seat.

Moody Adams Pillsbury imported 1st Guernsey cattle.

Phineas Davis built 1st American coal-burning locomotive.

Robert Hoe made important improvements on cylinder printing press.

Cyrus Hall McCormick invented 1st practical reaper.

Joseph Henry invented the electric bell.

1832 Jan. 21 Senator William Learned Marcy of N.Y. originated expression, "To the victor belong the spoils."

Apr. 6-Aug. 27 Black Hawk War.

Oct. 22 Extraordinary session of S.C. Legislature to consider nullification acts.

Dec. 28 St. Louis Univ. chartered, St. Louis, Mo. First Catholic Univ. west of Alleghanies.

John Stephenson began 1st street car service, N.Y.C.

Elbert Herring appointed first U.S. commissioner of Indian affairs.

John C. Calhoun, 1st vice pres. U.S. to resign.

Excavation begun for Wabash & Erie Canal.

Words of "America" written by Dr. Samuel Francis Smith.

1833 Sept. 3 Beginning of mass journalism in U.S. with publication of 1st issue of N.Y. Sun.

Massachusetts last state to disestablish its church, completing legal separation of church and state in America.

Henry Perrine grew 1st avocado.

Jacob Ebert patented soda fountain.

1834 Feb. 17 Van Ness Conv. signed, settling territorial dispute between Spain and U.S.

June 28 Second Coinage Act passed, authorizing a 16 to 1 ratio between silver and gold.

Oct. 28 Seminole Indians ordered to evacuate Florida.

Bob Farrell composed "Turkey in the Straw."

Whig Party organized.

Thomas Davenport built electric motor.

Leonard Norcross patented 1st practical underwater diving suit.

Daniel M. Chapin manufactured 1st friction matches, at Springfield, Mass.

Jacob Perkins invented 1st ice-making machine.

Cyrus Alger made 1st rifled gun.

John Caut built 1st iron ship, the John Randolph.

1835 Jan. 30 Andrew Jackson attacked in 1st attempt to assassinate a Pres. U.S., by Richard Lawrence.

July 8 Liberty Bell cracked while tolling for death of Chief Justice John Marshall.

Nov. Second Seminole War began.

Nov. 24 Texas Rangers authorized by Texas Provisional Government.

Trustees of Oberlin Collegiate Institute (Oberlin Coll.) voted to admit students "irrespective of color."

J. G. Bennett founded N.Y. Herald.

Alexis de Tocqueville published Democracy in America, in Belgium.

Samuel F. B. Morse invented telegraph.

James Bowie invented Bowie knife.

William Firmstone 1st used coke commercially as fuel for a blast furnace.

Hiram Powers, 1st American sculptor.

Solyman Merrick patented wrench.

1836 Mar. 6 The Alamo captured by General Santa Anna.

Apr. 21 Santa Anna defeated by Texas army under Gen. Sam Houston at Battle of San Jacinto.

May 31 Astor Hotel opened in N.Y.C.

June 15 Arkansas admitted as 25th state.

Oct. 22 Sam Houston inaugurated 1st pres. of Republic of Texas.

Martin Van Buren elected Pres. U.S.; Richard M. Johnson chosen vice pres. 1st vice pres. chosen by Senate.

Construction of Washington Monument, designed by Robert Mills, begun.

Ralph Waldo Emerson published Nature and established Transcendental Club.

Conn. passed 1st general incorporation law.

Lt. Charles Wilkes commanded 1st scientific expedition financed by U.S. Govt.

Roswell Willson Haskins, 1st school superintendent of a city (Buffalo, N.Y.).

1837 Jan. 26 Michigan admitted as 26th state.

Mar. 3 Supreme Court membership increased from seven to nine by Congress.

Mar. 18 Univ. of Mich. chartered at Ann Arbor.

May 10 Panic of 1837 began.

Dec. Caroline Affair increased Anglo-American tensions.

First book of Charles Dickens published in America, The Pickwick Papers.

Washington Irving coined phrase "The Almighty Dollar" in his book The Creole Village.

Erastus Brigham Bigelow patented carpet loom.

Charles Goodyear received 1st important rubber patent.

John and Hiram Pitts patented 1st steam threshing machine.

Mt. Holyoke Seminary, 1st women's college, opened.

1838 Apr. 23 First transatlantic steamship service established.

Dec. 26 Wake Forest (N.C.) College chartered.

Pierre Maspero gave 1st free lunch, New Orleans.

William S. Otis invented steam shovel.

1839 Feb. 11 Univ. of Mo. chartered at Columbus.

Feb. 20 Dueling prohibited in District of Columbia.

Apr. 11 U.S. citizens granted arbitration rights in claims against Mexico.

Nov. 13 Anti-slavery forces founded the Liberty Party, with James G. Birney as Presidential nominee.

Sept. 25 France became 1st European nation to recognize Texas independence.

Samuel F. B. Morse brought 1st photographic equipment to U.S., from Paris.

Abner Doubleday invented game of baseball.

Joseph A. Adams produced 1st electrotype.

J. W. Draper made 1st celestial photograph, of the moon.

1840 Population: 17,069,453.

Jan. 8 Resolution passed making it a standard rule of Ho. of Reps. that no petition or resolution concerning the abolition of slavery "shall be received by this House, or entertained in any way whatever."

Jan. 19 Capt. Charles Wilkes claimed Antarctica for U.S.

Mar. 4 Univ. of Richmond (Va.) chartered as Richmond College.

Mar. 31 Ten-hour day established by executive order for all federal employes engaged in public works.

Dec. 2 William Henry Harrison elected Pres. U.S.; John Tyler elected vice pres.

First presidential campaign in which hats, buttons, etc., used.

Expression "O.K." originated; referred to "Old Kinderhook," Martin Van Buren's birthplace; also name of a Democratic club in N.Y.C.

Washingtonian Temperance Society formed, a forerunner of Alcoholics Anonymous.

James Fenimore Cooper published The Pathfinder.

Edgar Allan Poe 1st published, Lalu.

Richard Henry Dana, Jr. published Two Years Before the Mast; book influential in having flogging aboard ships outlawed.

Dr. Willard Parker opened 1st clinic in an American college, College of Physicians and Surgeons, N.Y.C.

Henry H. Hayden and Chapin A. Harris founded American Society of Dental Surgeons.

John Wagner brewed 1st lager beer, Phila.

Earl Trumbull built 1st cast iron girder bridge, over Erie Canal.

Nehemiah Kenison, 1st chiropodist, practised at Boston.

Micah Rugg and Martin Barnes established 1st nut and bolt factory.

Joseph Henry made 1st wireless radio impulse transmission.

1841 Mar. 4 William Henry Harrison, 9th Pres. U.S., inaugurated.

Apr. 4 William Henry Harrison, 1st Pres. to die in office.

John Tyler, first vice pres. to become Pres. automatically.

Aug. 19 Uniform bankruptcy systems made law by Congress.

Sept. 11 President Tyler's entire cabinet, with the exception of Sec. of State Daniel Webster, resigned in protest to Tyler's veto of bank bill.

First covered wagon arrived in Cal. via the Oregon Trail, Humboldt River, and Sierra Mountains.

Ralph Waldo Emerson published Essays.

Oberlin Coll. 1st in America to confer A. B. degree on women.

Samuel M. Kier, 1st to use oil commercially, as a patent medicine.

Dorothea Dix began career to secure reforms in care of paupers and insane.

Horace Greeley founded N.Y. Tribune.

Volney B. Palmer established 1st advertising agency, at Phila.

Orlando Jones patented cornstarch.

Edgar Allan Poe wrote 1st popular detective story, Murders in the Rue Morgue.

Joseph Nason and James J. Walworth installed first steam heating system, N.Y.C.

George Evans, 1st known senator to receive a mileage allowance for a trip he did not make.

Samuel Colt invented 1st underwater torpedo operated by electricity.

Adrien Delcambre and James H. Young patented typesetting machine.

1842 Mar. 3 Mass. enacted 1st legislation regulating working hours for children.

Mar. 30 Dr. Crawford W. Long, 1st to use anaesthesia in surgery, at Jefferson, Ga.

June 25 Reapportionment Act passed.

Aug. 9 Webster-Ashburton Treaty signed by U.S. and Britain, settling northeast boundary U.S.

Aug. 30 Tariff Act passed.

Mass. Supreme Court decision in case of Commonwealth vs. Hunt upheld legality of labor unions and right of workers to strike.

New York Philharmonic Society founded; Ureli C. Hill 1st president.

First American publication of poems by Alfred Tennyson.

Charles Dickens visited America.

John Fremont made 1st expedition to explore route to Oregon.

Samuel F. B. Morse laid underwater cable, N.Y. Harbor.

Daniel Decatur Emmett organized 1st minstrel show troupe.

Benjamin H. Day and Nathaniel P. Willis published 1st illustrated weekly, Brother Jonathan, N.Y.C.

John James Greenough patented sewing machine.

Mutual Life Insurance Co. of N.Y. chartered, the 1st mutual insurance company.

1843 June American Republican Party formed, N.Y.C.

July 12 Joseph Smith, Mormon leader, announced that divine revelation sanctioned polygamy.

Aug. 23 Pres. Santa Anna of Mexico warned U.S. that annexation of Texas would be considered a declaration of war.

Aug. 31 Liberty Party nominated James G. Birney for Pres. at national conv., Buffalo, N.Y.

George Brown appointed 1st diplomatic representative to Hawaii.

William Hickling Prescott published The Conquest of Mexico.

Millet's Music Saloon, N.Y.C., patented song "Old Dan Tucker."

N. E. Guerin patented incubator for eggs.

Charles Thurber patented 1st workable typewriter.

1844 Jan. 15 Univ. of Notre Dame (Ind.) chartered.

Feb. 24 Univ. of Miss. chartered at Oxford.

Mar. 6 John C. Calhoun appointed U.S. sec. of state.

Apr. 12 Texas annexation treaty signed by U.S. and Texas.

May 1 Henry Clay nominated for Pres. by Whig Nat. Conv., Balt.

May 27 James K. Polk, 1st "dark horse" candidate to receive nomination for Pres. at Dem. Nat. Conv., Balt.

June 8 Senate rejected Texas annexation treaty.

June 15 Charles Goodyear patented vulcanization of rubber.

June 27 Joseph Smith, founder of Mormonism, murdered at Carthage, Ill.

Sept. 19 Mesabi iron range discovered, near Lake Superior.

Dec. 3 Gag rule lifted by Ho. of Reps.

Dec. 4 James K. Polk elected Pres. U.S.

Moses Yale Beach published 1st practical guide book of credit standings and marriage possibilities, The Wealth and Biography of the Wealthy Citizens of N.Y.C.

Sarah Margaret Fuller published Woman in the Nineteenth Century.

Ralph Waldo Emerson published Essays, Second Series.

First American publication of The Three Musketeers by Alexandre Dumas.

Stephen Foster published 1st song, "Open Thy Lattice, Love."

George Esterly patented 1st successful American harvester.

Stuart Perry patented gas engine.

Richard Hoe manufactured 1st cylinder and flat bed combination printing press.

John Tyler, 1st Pres. U.S. to be married while in office.

First private bath in an American hotel installed in the New York Hotel.

First bridal suite, Irving House, N.Y.C.

1845 Jan. 23 Congress enacted law establishing a uniform election day for presidential elections.

Mar. 1 Joint resolution of Congress agreed to annexation of Texas.

Mar. 3 Florida admitted as 27th state.

Mar. 4 James K. Polk inaugurated as 11th Pres. of U.S.

Mar. 28 Mexico broke diplomatic relations with U.S.

June 15 Texas assured of U.S. protection if she agreed to annexation.

Oct. 10 Official opening of U.S. Naval Academy, Annapolis, Md.

Dec. 29 Texas admitted as 28th state.

Industrial Congress of the U.S. organized, N.Y.C.

Edgar Allan Poe published The Raven and Other Poems.

William Henry Fry, 1st native American composer to have an opera publicly performed (Leonora).

Macon B. Allen, 1st Negro lawyer admitted to bar (Mass.).

Ezra Cornell laid 1st practical submarine telegraph cable.

Alexander Joy Cartwright organized 1st professional baseball team.

Benjamin Talbert Babbitt, 1st to package soap powder.

1846 Apr. 13 Pennsylvania Railroad chartered.

Apr. 27 Virginia Minstrels of Edwin P. Christy made 1st appearance, N.Y.C.

Apr. 30-May 1 Mexican army crossed Rio Grande River.

May 4 Mich. Legislature enacted 1st law abolishing capital punishment.

May 8-9 Battle of Palo Alto.

May 9 Battle of Resaca de la Palma.

May 13 U.S. declared war on Mexico.

June 14 Bear Flag revolt began in California.

June 15 Oregon Treaty signed, establishing 49th parallel as boundary between U.S. and British Northwest Territory.

Aug. 8 Wilmot Proviso introduced by David Wilmot of Pa., providing that no slavery should be allowed in territory won from Mexico.

Sept. 25 General Zachary Taylor captured Monterey, Mexico.

Oct. 16 First public demonstration of anesthesia by William G. Morton, Boston.

Dec. 28 Iowa admitted as 29th state.

American Association for the Advancement of Science established.

Smithsonian Institution authorized by Congress.

First professional baseball game played, Hoboken, N.J.

James Renwick finished Grace Church, N.Y.C., 1st to employ Gothic Revival style architecture.

Herman Melville published 1st novel, Typee.

Exodus of Mormons from Nauvoo, Ill.

Benjamin F. Palmer patented 1st artificial leg.

John Dwight and Austin Church, 1st to manufacture baking soda, at N.Y.C.

Erastus B. Bigelow established 1st gingham factory.

R. E. House patented 1st telegraph ticker to print letters.

Sarah G. Bagley, 1st woman telegrapher.

1847 Feb. 25 State Univ. of Iowa chartered, Iowa City.

Feb. 22-23 Gen. Zachary Taylor defeated Gen. Santa Anna in Battle of Buena Vista.

Feb.-Mar. Donner Party tragedy.

Mar. 9 Gen. Winfield Scott landed at Vera Cruz.

May 7 American Medical Association organized, at Phila.

July 1 Post Office Dept. issued its 1st adhesive postage stamps.

July 24 Mormon leader Brigham Young, sighting Salt Lake Valley, Utah, said, "This is the right place."

Aug. 20 Gen. Winfield Scott defeated Mexican army at Battle of Churubusco.

Sept. Native American Party Nat. Conv. nominated Zachary Taylor for Pres.

Sept. 11 "Susanna" by Stephen Foster 1st sung, at Eagle Saloon, Pitts.

Sept. 14 Gen. Winfield Scott entered Mexico City.

Henry Wadsworth Longfellow published Evangeline.

J. J. Mapes developed 1st artificial fertilizer.

R. W. Thomson patented rubber tire.

William, Asa, and Simeon Rogers established 1st successful silver plating factory.

Dr. Frank Hastings Hamilton performed 1st skin grafting operation.

1848 Jan. 24 Gold discovered, Sutter's Mill, near Sacramento, Cal.

Feb. 2 Treaty of Guadalupe-Hidalgo signed ending Mexican War.

May 22-26 Dem. Nat. Conv., Balt., nominated Lewis Cass for Pres. and William D. Butler for vice-pres.

May 29 Wisconsin admitted as 30th state.

June 2 Liberty League Nat. Conv., Rochester, N.Y., nominated Gerrit Smith for Pres. and Charles E. Foote for vice-pres.

June 3 U.S. received travel rights across Isthmus of Panama by treaty with New Granada (now Colombia).

June 7-9 Whig Nat. Conv., Phila., nominated Gen. Zachary Taylor for Pres. and Millard Fillmore for vice-pres.

June 22 The Barnburners, a splinter group of Dem. party, held convention at Utica, N.Y., nominated Martin Van Buren for Pres.

June 27 First air conditioning installed in a theater, Broadway Theater, N.Y.C.

July 19 First convention in world convened for purpose of discussing rights of women, Seneca Falls, N.Y.

July 26 Univ. of Wis. chartered at Madison.

Aug. Free Soil Party organized; nominated Martin Van Buren for Pres. and Charles F. Adams for vice-pres. in nat. conv. at Buffalo, N.Y.

Nov. 1 Samuel Gregory founded 1st women's medical school, Boston Female Medical School.

Nov. 7 Gen. Zachary Taylor elected 12th Pres. U.S.

First Chinese immigrants landed at San Francisco.

Associated Press organized, N.Y.C.

Brussels Peace Congress, organized by Elihu Barritt, opened in Belgium.

John Humphrey Noyes established Perfectionist Community, Oneida, N.Y.

Jacob L. Martin, 1st representative to Vatican.

Charles Burton manufactured 1st baby carriage.

Elizabeth Smith Miller designed and introduced 1st bloomers.

James Bogardus designed 1st building constructed entirely of cast iron.

John Curtis manufactured 1st chewing gum.

M. Waldo Hanchett patented 1st dental chair.

Samuel Gridley Howe founded 1st school for feeble-minded, the Mass. School for the Idiotic, Boston.

William G. Young patented ice cream freezer.

Antoine Zerega established 1st macaroni factory, at Brooklyn, N.Y.

Oliver Fisher Winchester opened 1st shirt factory, Boston.

James Russell Lowell wrote Vision of Sir Launfal, 1st Biglow Papers.

1849 Mar. 3 U.S. Dept. of the Interior created; Thomas Ewing appointed 1st sec.

Mar. 3 Minnesota established as a territory.

Great Chinese Museum opened, N.Y.C.

Henry David Thoreau published Civil Disobedience.

C. Austin patented melodeon.

Lewis Phectic Hasler patented 1st gas mask.

Benjamin Chambers patented breech loading cannon.

Walter Hunt patented safety pin.

Elizabeth Blackwell 1st woman in U.S. to receive medical degree.

1850 Population: 23,191,876.

Jan. 29 Sen. Henry Clay introduced resolution from which Compromise of 1850 evolved.

Mar. 4 John Calhoun's last formal oration in Senate.

July 9 Millard Fillmore became 13th Pres. U.S. on death of Zachary Taylor.

July 25 Gold discovered in Rogue River, Ore.

Sept. 9 California admitted as 31st state.

Sept. 9 Texas and New Mexico Act passed.

Sept. 9 Edwin Booth made N.Y.C. debut, at National Theater.

Sept. 11 Jenny Lind made American singing debut at Castle Garden Theater, N.Y.C.

Sept. 18 Fugitive Slave Law passed.

Sept. 20 Slave trade abolished in District of Columbia.

Sept. 28 Flogging outlawed in Navy and Merchant Marine.

Oct. 23-24 First nat. conv. of women advocating women suffrage, Worcester, Mass.

Harper's Magazine founded, N.Y.C.

Nathaniel Hawthorne published The Scarlet Letter.

Herman Melville published White-Jacket.

Emanuel Leutze painted Washington Crossing the Delaware.

Thomas U. Walter completed final design of U.S. Capitol.

John E. Heath invented 1st American agricultural binder.

Cholera epidemic in Midwest.

First girls hired as clerks, in Phila. department store.

Du Boid D. Parmelee patented adding machine with depressible keys.

Nicholas Pike imported 1st sparrows.

Abner Cutler invented roll top desk.

Henry Waterman installed 1st platform elevator.

James Henry Knapp manufactured 1st derby hat.

F. Langenheim patented 1st glass plate magic lantern slides.

1851 Feb. 13 Univ. of Minn. established.

Mar. 3 Congress authorized coinage of 3c pieces.

July 23 Sioux Indians ceded all their lands in Iowa and Minn. to U.S.

Aug. 22 Schooner-yacht America defeated 14 British vessels in 60 mile yacht race around Isle of Wight. Trophy became known as "The American Cup."

Sept. 14 James Fenimore Cooper died.

Dec. 1 Charles Sumner appointed to fill seat vacated by Daniel Webster.

Dec. 24 Two-thirds of the collection of the Library of Congress destroyed by fire.

N.Y. Times founded; H. J. Raymond 1st editor.

Nathaniel Hawthorne published The House of the Seven Gables.

Herman Melville published Moby Dick.

Stephen Foster composed "Old Folks at Home."

John B. L. Soule originated phrase "Go West, young man, go West," used by Greeley.

First American chapter of Young Men's Christian Association organized, Boston.

John Wise 1st to suggest bombing from an airship.

Jesse Williams established 1st important cheese factory, at Rome, N.Y.

Elisha Kent Kane completed 1st Arctic expedition.

Gail Borden produced 1st commercial condensed milk.

Dr. John Gorrie patented 1st mechanical refrigerator.

Isaac Merritt Singer, 1st sewing machine manufacturer.

Bryan Mullanphy established 1st Travelers' Aid, St. Louis, Mo.

Eugenia Tucker Fitzgerald founded 1st woman's secret society, the Adelphian Soc., Wesleyan Coll., Macon, Ga.

1852 May 9 First Plenary Council of all Roman Catholic bishops and arch-bishops in U.S., Baltimore.

June 1-6 Dem. Nat. Conv., Balt., nominated Franklin Pierce for Pres. and William R. King for vice-pres.

June 16-21 Whig Nat. Conv., Balt., nominated Winfield Scott for Pres. and William A. Graham for vice-pres.

Aug. 3 Yale and Harvard met in 1st intercollegiate rowing race, Lake Winnepesauchee, N.H.

Aug. 11 Free Soil Nat. Conv., Pitts., nominated John P. Hale for Pres. and George W. Julian for vice-pres.

Oct. 6 American Pharmaceutical Association founded, Phila.

Nov. 2 Franklin Pierce elected Pres. U.S.

Nov. 5 American Society of Civil Engineers founded, N.Y.C.

Young America movement at peak of influence.

Stephen Foster composed "Massa's in de Cold Ground."

Harriet Beecher Stowe published Uncle Tom's Cabin.

Mass. enacted 1st effective school attendance law.

Word lingerie came into general use.

Frank Henry Temple Bellew published 1st Uncle Sam cartoon.

First Jewish hospital in U.S. established, N.Y.C.

Rebecca Mann Pennell became 1st woman college professor.

1853 Mar. 3 Transcontinental railroad survey authorized by Congress.

Mar. 4 Franklin Pierce inaugurated as 14th Pres. U.S.

July. Commodore Matthew C. Perry visits Japan with U.S. proposal on trade and safety of Amer. seamen.

Sept. 15 First national librarians' convention, N.Y.C.

Gadsden Purchase negotiated.

Native America, or Know Nothing Party formed.

Crystal Palace Exhibition of the Industry of All Nations, N.Y.C.

Antoinette Brown Blackwell, 1st woman ordained minister.

1854 Mar. 31 Commercial treaty with Japan signed by Commodore Perry.

May 26 Kansas-Nebraska Act passed.

July Federal land office opened in Kansas.

Oct. 2 Academy of Music opened in N.Y.C.

Anthony Faas patented the accordion.

J. R. Haskell invented 1st steel breech loading rifled cannon.

Henry B. Myer patented the sleeping car.

Republican Party organized in meetings at Ripon, Wis. and Jackson, Mich.

Walden published by Henry D. Thoreau.

Astor Library opened in N.Y.C.

Daniel B. Wesson patented the metal cartridge.

1855 Feb. 10 U.S. citizenship law changed to provide that all people born of American parents abroad were citizens.

Feb. 24 U.S. Court of Claims created.

June 5 The National Council of the Native American Party changed its name to the American Party.

John Bartlett compiled Familiar Quotations.

Walt Whitman wrote Leaves of Grass.

Henry W. Longfellow wrote "The Song of Hiawatha."

Henry Barnard began publication of the American Journal of Education.

Railway completed across the Isthmus of Panama.

Joshua C. Stoddard patented the calliope.

Dr. Emeline R. Jones became the 1st woman dentist.

Isaac M. Singer patented the 1st sewing machine motor.

Rev. Arthur Otto Brickman organized the 1st German Swedenborgian Society, at Balt.

Stephen Foster composed "Come Where My Love Lies Dreaming."

1856 Jan. 8 Borax discovered in California by Dr John Veatch.

Feb. 22 Millard Fillmore nominated for Pres in Phila., by the Know-Nothing Party.

Apr. 21 First railroad bridge over the Mississippi River built at Davenport, Ia.

May 22 Senator Charles Sumner beaten with a cane by Rep. Preston Brooks of S.C. on the Senate floor.

June 2-5 Dem. Party nominated James Buchanan for Pres. at Cincinnati, O.

June 17-19 John C. Fremont nominated for Pres. by the Republican Conv. at Phila.

Nov. 4 James Buchanan elected Pres. U.S.

John G. Whittier published The Panorama and Other Poems.

John L. Motley wrote The Rise of the Dutch Republic.

Illinois Central R.R. completed.

John Rider invented 1st self-cocking revolver.

1857 Mar. 3 Subsidy voted to aid in construction of transatlantic cable by Cyrus W. Field.

Mar. 4 James Buchanan inaugurated as 15th Pres. U.S.

Mar. 6 Dred Scott decision delivered by the Supreme Court which declared the Missouri Compromise unconstitutional.

May 1 Mass. required literacy test as a voting requirement.

June 23 Patent awarded to William Kelly for his process of converting pig iron to steel.

Oct. Exhibition of pre-Raphelite paintings exhibited in N.Y.C.

Oct. 6 American Chess Association organized.

Oct. 19 Lecompton Constitutional Conv. met in Kansas.

Atlantic Monthly founded in Boston by James Russell Lowell.

Hinton Rowan Helper wrote The Impending Crisis of the South: How to Meet It.

Harper's Weekly founded with George W. Curtis as editor.

Frederick L. Olmsted and Albert Vaux laid out Central Park, in N.Y.C.

Charity balls came into prominence.

Paul Charles Morphey became the 1st American chess champion.

Wagon train attacked, 120 killed, at Mountain Meadows, Utah.

Timothy Alden patented typesetting machine.

The oil lamp was developed.

1858 Apr. 12 First American billiards championship game played in Detroit.

May 11 Minnesota admitted as 32d state.

Aug. 16 First cable message sent across the Atlantic.

Oct. 25 Phrase "irrepressible conflict" 1st used in a speech by William H. Seward at Rochester, N.Y.

Construction of St. Patrick's Cathedral in N.Y.C. begun.

Oliver Wendell Holmes wrote The Autocrat of the Breakfast Table.

Phrase "Pike's Peak or Bust" came into use among the gold-rushers.

Edwin Holmes installed 1st burglar alarm, at Boston.

Richard Esterbrook produced 1st commercial steel pens, at Camden, N.J.

Hyman L. Lipman patented pencil with attached eraser.

Hamilton E. Smith patented rotary washing machine.

1859 Feb. 14 Oregon admitted as 33d state.

Mar. 7 Supreme Court decision in case of Ableman vs. Booth declared Fugitive Slave Law constitutional.

July 5 Kansas constitutional conv. convened, Wyandotte, Kan.

Oct. 16 John Brown seized the arsenal at Harper's Ferry, W.Va.

Comstock Lode discovered in Nevada.

Dan Emmett composed "Dixie."

Mass. Institute of Technology established, Cambridge.

John Wise made 1st balloon flight carrying mail.

Prof. M. G. Farmer installed 1st electric light for home illumination.

Jean Francois Gravelet, 1st man to cross Niagara Falls on a tight-rope.

E. D. Bowditch and Edwin L. Drake discovered 1st commercially productive oil well, Titusville, Pa.

William Goodale patented paper bag manufacturing machine.

Andrew Lanergan patented 1st rocket.

1860 Population: 31,443,321.

Feb. 2 Jefferson Davis offered a series of pro-slavery resolutions in U.S. Senate.

Feb. 22 Shoemakers struck for higher wages and recognition of union, Lynn, Mass.

Apr. 3 First relay on Pony Express mail service left St. Joseph, Mo.

Apr. 23 Dem. Nat. Conv. met at Charleston, S.C.

May 9 Constitutional Union Party Nat. Conv., Balt., nominated John Bell for Pres. and Edward Everett for vice-pres.

May 16-18 Rep. Nat. Conv., Chicago, nominated Abraham Lincoln for Pres. and Hannibal Hamlin for vice-pres.

June 18-23 Democrats reassembled at Baltimore, nominated Stephen A. Douglas for Pres. and Herschel V. Johnson for vice-pres.

June 23 Congress passed bill to establish government printing office.

June 28 Dem. seceders met at Charleston, S.C., nominated John C. Breckinridge for Pres.

Nov. 6 Abraham Lincoln elected Pres. U.S.

Dec. 20 South Carolina 1st state to secede from Union.

First Beadle Dime Novel appeared.

Ralph Waldo Emerson published The Conduct of Life.

John Greenleaf Whittier published Home Ballads.

Stephen Foster wrote "Old Black Joe."

Charles Darwin's Origin of Species 1st published in U.S.

John Dean Caton established 1st game preserve.

William Barnsdall and William H. Abbott established 1st commercial oil refinery, at Oil Creek Valley, Pa.

Oliver F. Winchester produced 1st repeating rifle.

J. W. Black and Samuel A. King made 1st aerial photograph.

1861 Jan. 9 Mississippi 2d state to secede from Union.

Jan. 10 Florida 3d state to secede from Union.

Jan. 11 Alabama 4th state to secede from Union.

Jan. 18 Vassar College chartered, Poughkeepsie, N.Y.

Jan. 19 Georgia 5th state to secede from Union.

Jan. 29 Kansas admitted as 34th state of Union.

Feb. 4 Confederate States of America formed at Montgomery, Ala.

Feb. 18 Jefferson Davis inaugurated Pres. Confederate States America.

Feb. 23 Texas 6th state to secede from Union.

Mar. 2 Creation of Nevada and Dakota territories.

Mar. 4 Abraham Lincoln inaugurated as 16th Pres. U.S.

Mar. 4 Confederate Conv., Montgomery, Ala., chose "Stars and Bars" as official flag.

Mar. 11 Confederate Congress adopted a constitution.

Apr. 12 Confederate troops under Gen. Beauregard fired on Fort Sumter, Charleston, S.C.

Apr. 13 Major Anderson surrendered Fort Sumter.

Apr. 15 Pres. Lincoln declared existence of an insurrection and issued 1st call for volunteer troops.

Apr. 17 Virginia 7th state to secede from Union.

Apr. 19 Pres. Lincoln ordered blockade of Southern ports.

May 6 Arkansas 8th state to secede from Union.

May 20 North Carolina 9th state to secede from Union.

May 21 Richmond, Va., chosen as Confederate capital.

June 8 Tennessee 10th state to secede from Union.

June 10 Dorothea Dix appointed superintendent of woman nurses.

July 21 First Battle of Bull Run.

July 25 Use of volunteer troops sanctioned by U.S. Congress.

Aug. 5 First income tax law passed by U.S. Congress.

Aug. 10 Battle of Wilson's Creek.

Sept. 13 First naval engagement; Union raid on Pensacola, Fla.

Oct. 4 U.S. Congress authorized construction of Monitor.

Oct. 21 Battle of Ball's Bluff, Leesburg, Va.

Oct. 24 Pres. Abraham Lincoln, in Washington, D.C. received 1st transcontinental telegram, from Sacramento, Cal.

Nov. 1 Gen. Winfield Scott succeeded by Gen. George McClellan as commander-in-chief of Union armies.

Yale Univ. 1st school to offer graduate courses for degree of Doctor of Philosophy.

Frederick Wm. Gunn established 1st camp for boys, at Milford, Conn.

Samuel D. Goodale patented 1st peep show machine.

Coleman Sellers made 1st attempt to take motion pictures.

1862 Feb. 8 Union forces captured Roanoke Island.

Mar. 8 Confederate ship Merrimac sank two Union frigates, Hampton Roads, Va.

Mar. 9 Monitor vs. Merrimac: 1st battle between ironclad ships.

Apr. 6-7 Battle of Shiloh.

May 1 Admiral David Farragut captured New Orleans.

May 15 U.S. Dept. of Agriculture established; Isaac Newton appointed 1st commissioner.

May 20 Homestead Act became law.

May 31-June 1 Battle of Seven Pines (Fair Oaks).

June 1 Gen. Robert E. Lee appointed Confederate commander of armies of Northern Va. and N.C.

July 1 U.S. Congress enacted anti-polygamy legislation.

July 1 Seven Days' Battle ended with Battle of Malvern Hill.

July 11 Maj. Gen. Halleck appointed commander-in-chief of all U.S. land forces.

July 12 Congress authorized Medal of Honor.

July 30 First use of term "Copperhead."

Aug. 18 Chief Little Crow led Sioux uprising in Minn.

Aug. 30 Second Battle of Bull Run.

Sept. 15 Harper's Ferry, W.Va., captured by Union forces.

Sept. 17 Battle of Antietam.

Nov. 5 Gen. Ambrose E. Burnside succeeded Gen. Geo. McClellan as chief Union general.

Dec. 13 Battle of Fredericksburg.

Pres. Lincoln signed "Morrill Act" offering public lands to the states for endowment of agricultural and mechanical arts colleges.

"Molly Maguires," secret labor organization founded.

Gerritt Smith Miller organized 1st football club, the Oneida in Boston.

Richard Jordan Gatling patented rapid fire machinegun.

William Bruce Mumford, 1st U.S. citizen to be executed for treason.

1863 Jan. 1 Emancipation Proclamation issued.

Mar. 3 First national conscription act issue

Mar. 3 National Academy of Sciences cha tered, Washington, D.C.

May 2 Battle of Chancellorsville.

June 20 West Virginia admitted as 35t state.

July 1-3 Battle of Gettysburg.

July 4 Gen. U. S. Grant captured Vicksbur

July 13-16 Anti-draft riots broke out, N.Y.

Sept. 19-20 Battle of Chickamauga.

Oct. 3 Thanksgiving Day made a nation holiday.

Nov. 19 Pres. Lincoln delivered Gettysbur Address.

Nov. 23-25 Battle of Chattanooga.

Dec. Edward Everett Hale published Ma Without a Country.

Eddie Cuthbert made 1st attempt to "steal a base, Phila.

Charles H. Shepard opened 1st Turkish bat N.Y.C.

Hugh McCulloch, 1st U.S. comptroller of th currency.

Alanson Crane patented fire extinguisher.

Daniel Freeman awarded 1st homestead, a Beatrice, Neb.

James Goodwin Batterson founded 1st acc dent insurance company, Travelers Insuranc Co., Hartford, Conn.

1864 May 5-6 Battle of Wilderness near Char cellorsville, Va.

May 10 U. S. Grant named commander i chief of Union forces.

May 26 Territory of Montana formed.

June 7 Union Party (Republican Party) Na Conv. at Balt. nominated Abraham Lincoln fo Pres. and Andrew Johnson for vice-pres.

June 19 Confederate cruiser Alabama sun by U.S.S. Kearsarge off of Cherbourg, Franc

Aug. 5 Phrase "Damn the torpedoes! G ahead," uttered by Adm. David Farragut a Mobile Bay.

Aug. 29 Dem. Nat. Conv., Chicago, nomi nated Gen. George McClellan for Pres. an George H. Pendleton for vice-pres.

Sept. 2 Gen. Sherman occupied Atlanta, Ga.

Oct. 31 Nevada admitted as 36th state.

Nov. 8 Abraham Lincoln re-elected Pres.

Dec. Salmon P. Chase appointed chief jus tice of U.S. Supreme Court.

Dec. 22 Gen. Sherman captured Savannah Ga.

Motto "In God We Trust" 1st appeared o U.S. coin.

George Huntington Hartford founded 1st chai store organization, the Great American Te Co.

Thomas Doughty invented periscope.

U. of Kansas established at Lawrence.

1865 Feb. 6 Gen. Robert E. Lee named General i chief of Confederate Army.

Mar. 3 Freedmen's Bureau founded.

Apr. 9 Gen. Lee surrendered to Gen. Grant.

Apr. 14 Abraham Lincoln assassinated.

Apr. 15 Andrew Johnson inaugurated at 17th Pres. U.S.

Aug. 14 Mississippi conv. passed ordinances voiding the secession ordinance.

Dec. 18 13th Amendment adopted.

Dec. 24 Ku Klux Klan founded at Pulaski, Tenn.

Mark Twain pub. "The Celebrated Jumping Frog of Calaveras County."

Walt Whitman pub. Drum Taps.

Francis Parkman pub. Pioneers of France in the New World.

San Francisco Examiner est. by William Moses.

Peace and Plenty painted by George Inness.

Purdue U., West Lafayette, Ind., chartered.

The Nation founded by James Miller McKim.

Union Stockyards, Chicago, opened.

James H. Nason patented coffee percolator.

Benjamin Talbert Babbitt, 1st to give premiums with merchandise.

1866 Feb. 12 First formal observance of Lincoln's Birthday.

Feb. 19 New Freedmen's Bureau Bill passed by Congress.

Apr. 2 Insurrection declared ended by Presidential proclamation.

Apr. 9 Civil Rights Act passed.

May 16 Congress authorized five cent piece.

Aug. 20 First National Labor Congress, Balt.

John Greenleaf Whittier wrote "Snow-Bound."

U. of New Hampshire, Durham, founded.

First Y.W.C.A. in U.S. opened in Boston.

Henry Bergh founded 1st humane society, the American Soc. for the Prevention of Cruelty to Animals, N.Y.C.

James Gordon Bennett's schooner Henrietta won 1st Transoceanic yacht race.

H. Ressegue, 1st to raise fur bearing animals commercially.

Ulysses S. Grant, 1st General of the U.S. Army.

Henry A. House invented 1st steam automobile.

Arthur Cummings pitched 1st curve ball.

J. Osterhoudt patented tin can with a key opener.

Edson P. Clark patented indelible pencil.

Charles M. Barras wrote 1st important burlesque show, "Black Crook."

Frank Sparks and John and Simeon Reno committed 1st railroad train robbery.

Charles E. Hires manufactured 1st root beer.

James L. Plimpton opened 1st public roller skating rink, at Newport, R.I.

1867 Mar. 1 Nebraska admitted as 37th state.

Mar. 2 First Reconstruction Act passed.

Mar. 2 Tenure of Office Act passed.

Mar. 7 Order of the Knights of St. Crispin founded.

Mar. 23 Second Reconstruction Act passed.

Mar. 30 U.S. agreed to purchase Alaska.

Credit Mobilier scandal broke open.

Sidney Lanier's Tiger Lilies published.

Bret Harte pub. The Lost Galleon and Other Tales.

Horatio Alger's Ragged Dick published.

James Redpath established a central booking office.

Eight-hour day enacted in Ill., N.Y. and Mo.

W.Va. U., Morgantown, U. of Ill., Urbana, Johns Hopkins U., Balt., founded.

Horse, Ruthless won 1st annual Belmont Stakes.

Oliver H. Kelley organized 1st important national agricultural society the National Grange of the Patrons of Husbandry.

Wm. E. Lincoln patented machine to show animated pictures, the Zoetrope.

1868 Feb. 21 Edwin M. Stanton resigned from office.

Feb. 24 Covode Resolution carried in House, impeached Pres. Johnson on 11 charges.

Mar. 13 Pres. Andrew Johnson's impeachment trial began.

Mar. 16 Johnson acquitted of impeachment.

Mar. 23 U. of Cal., Berkeley, chartered.

May 20-21 Republican Nat. Conv., Chicago, nominated Gen. Ulysses S. Grant for Pres. and Schuyler Colfax for vice-pres.

May 30 Decoration Day celebrated nationally for 1st time.

June 25 Congress provided eight-hour day for government employees.

June 25 Congressional representation granted to N.C., S.C., La., Ga., Ala., Fla.

July 4-9 Democratic National Conv. at N.Y.C. nominated Horatio Seymour for Pres. and Francis P. Blain for vice-pres.

July 28 14th Amendment adopted.

Oct. 21 San Francisco rocked by earthquake.

Nov. 3 Gen. U. S. Grant elected Pres. U.S.

Nov. 11 First amateur track and field meet (indoors) N.Y.C.

Dec. 3 Treason trial of Jefferson Davis began, Richmond, Va.

Dec. 25 Unqualified amnesty granted to all who had acted in "insurrection or rebellion" against U.S. by presidential proclamation.

Dec. 25 Benevolent Protective Order of Elks founded, in N.Y.C.

The Revolution founded by Susan B. Anthony.

Open hearth steel process introduced in America.

U. of Minn., Minneapolis, chartered.

Louisville (Ky.) Courier-Journal, established.

Brigham Young established the 1st department store, Salt Lake City, Utah.

Atlanta Constitution started by W. A. Hemphill.

Christopher Latham Sholes patented the 1st practical typewriter.

Louisa May Alcott published Little Women.

1869 Mar. 4 Ulysses S. Grant inaugurated as 18th Pres. U.S.

May 10 Transcontinental Railroad completed at Promontory Point, Utah.

Sept. 1 Prohibition Party organized in Chicago.

Sept. 24 "Black Friday"—Wall Street scandal.

Nov. 6 First intercollegiate football game at New Brunswick between Rutgers and Princeton.

Dec. 1 First national Negro labor union, Colored National Labor Convention, met in Washington, D.C.

First professional baseball team organized—The Cincinnati Red Stockings.

George Westinghouse patented the air brake.

William F. Semple patented chewing gum.

Henry J. Heinz, 1st food stuffs producer.

Mass. chartered the 1st state board of health.

Major John Wesley Powell led the 1st exploratory expedition of the Grand Canyon of the Colorado River.

Mass. organized the 1st state board of labor.

Henry Tibbe, 1st to commercially manufacture corncob pipe.

Ives W. McGaffey, patented 1st suction-type vacuum cleaner.

Cornelius Swarthout patented 1st waffle iron.

Harvard Univ. offered 1st summer courses.

Thomas Alva Edison patented 1st electric vote recorder.

1870 Population: 39,818,449.

Jan. 2 Construction of Brooklyn Bridge began.

Jan. 26 Virginia granted readmission to U.S. Congress.

Feb. 23 Miss. granted readmission to U.S. Congress.

Feb. 29 U.S. Weather Bureau established by Congress.

Mar. 30 Texas granted readmission to U.S. Congress.

Mar. 30 Fifteenth Admendment adopted.

July 15 Ga. granted readmission to U.S. Congress.

Oct. 4 Benjamin Helm Bristow, 1st U.S. solicitor general.

Dec. Gov. William Wood Holden of N.C., 1st governor impeached.

Thomas Nast drew 1st cartoon using Donkey as Dem. Party emblem.

Thomas Loftin Johnson invented coin box for street cars.

A. H. Kepley, 1st woman lawyer graduated from a law school.

Edward Joseph De Smedt patented sheet asphalt pavement.

Benjamin Chew Tilgham patented sand blasting process.

Scribner's Monthly founded.

Thomas B. Aldrich published The Story of a Bad Boy.

Corcoran Art Gallery incorporated by an Act of Congress.

Bret Harte's Luck of Roaring Camp published.

Atlantic City (N.J) boardwalk completed.

Standard Oil Company organized.

Ohio State Univ., Columbus, chartered.

1871 Feb. 21 District of Columbia provided with a territorial government.

Mar. 3 Indian Appropriation Act passed.

Mar. 4 Pres. Grant established 1st Civil Service Commission.

Mar. 27 Univ. of Arkansas founded at Fayetteville.

May 1 Legal Tender Act declared constitutional.

May 8 Treaty of Washington signed between Great Britain and U.S.

Oct. 8-11 Chicago fire.

Edward Eggleston published The Hoosier Schoolmaster.

Passage To India by Walt Whitman published.

Whistler's Mother painted.

Grand Central Station opened in N.Y.C.

National Association of Ballplayers organized (forerunner of National League).

Benjamin T. Babbitt, 1st to use band wagon for advertising purposes.

Wilhelm Schneider patented the carousel.

David O. Saylor patented process for making cement.

Univ. of Ill. started 1st college newspaper.

Thomas Alva Edison received 1st important radio patent.

Henry M. Stanley, sent by N.Y.C. newspaper found Dr. David Livingstone in Africa.

Augustus Saint Gaudens sculpted his 1st figure "Hiawatha," while in Rome.

Frances Elizabeth Willard, 1st woman college president.

1872 Feb. 22 Prohibition Party Nat. Conv. at Columbus, O., nominated James Black for Pres and Rev. John Russell for vice-pres.

Apr. 10 Arbor Day inaugurated in Nebraska.

May 1 Liberal Republican Party Nat. Conv at Cincinnati, O., nominated Horace Greeley for Pres. and P. Gratz Brown for vice-pres.

May 23 Workingman's Nat. Conv. at N.Y.C nominated Ulysses S. Grant for Pres. and Henry Wilson for vice-pres.

July 9 Dem. Nat. Conv. nominated Horace Greeley for Pres. and P. Gratz Brown for vice-pres.

Nov. 5 Ulysses S. Grant re-elected Pres. U.S.

National Labor Reform Party organized.

Mark Twain's Roughing It published.

Susan B. Anthony tested the 14th Amendment by organizing a group of women to cast ballots in the Presidential election.

Yellowstone Park Timberland Reserve established.

Edmund D. Barbour patented 1st adding machine to print totals and sub-totals.

Popular Science Monthly founded by Edward Livingston Youmans.

Albert H. Hook invented cigarette manufacturing machine.

Silas Noble and James P. Cooley patented toothpick manufacturing machine.

1873 Mar. 3 "Salary Grab Act" passed by Congress.

Mar. 3 Act passed prohibiting the sending of obscene literature through the mails.

Aug. 18 Mt. Whitney climbed.

Sept. 18 Panic of 1873 began.

Sept. 20 New York Stock Exchange closed.

Oct. 19 Yale, Princeton, Columbia and Rutgers drafted 1st code of rules for football, N.Y.C.

Nov. 19 William "Boss" Tweed convicted on 204 charges of fraud.

Longfellow completed Tales of a Wayside Inn.

Sidney Lanier composed Field-larks and Blackbirds, Swamp Robin, both for flute.

Albert Pinkham Ryder began annual exhibits of his art at Nat. Acad., N.Y.C.

Union of American Hebrew Congregations organized.

Epidemics of yellow fever, cholera and smallpox swept through Southern cities.

Cable street car invented by Andrew Smith Hallidie installed.

Bookmakers 1st appeared at U.S. race tracks.

Joseph Farwell Glidden manufactured barbed wire.

First penny post cards issued.

Survivor won 1st annual Preakness Stakes, Pimlico, Md.

Chester Greenwood invented earmuffs.

Eli Hamilton Jannet patented railroad coupler.

1874 May 16 Ashfield dam collapsed above Williamsburg, Mass.

June 20 Territorial government abolished in District of Columbia and replaced by a commission.

Nov. 25 Greenback Party formed, at Indianapolis, Ind., and nominated Peter Cooper for Pres.

The Gilded Age by Mark Twain and Charles Dudley Warner published.

Francis Parkman completed The Old Regime in Canada.

Henry Wadsworth Longfellow published The Hanging of the Crane.

University of Nevada, Reno, established.

Outlines of Cosmic Philosophy by John Friske published.

Woman's Christian Temperance Union established Cleveland, O.

Thomas Nast drew 1st Rep. cartoon using elephant emblem.

John H. Vincent and Lewis Miller organized 1st Chautaugua organization.

Charles Brewster Ross, 1st person kidnapped and held for ransom.

Mary E. Outerbridge, introduced lawn tennis.

David Kalakaua, 1st reigning king of Hawaii to visit U.S.

1875 Jan. 14 Special Resumption Act passed by Congress.

Jan. 30 Hawaiian Reciprocity Treaty signed.

Mar. 1 Civil Rights Acts passed by Congress.

May 1 Whiskey Ring conspiracy.

May 17 First Kentucky Derby, Churchill Downs, won by Aristides.

Sept. 10 American Forestry Association founded, Chicago.

Nov. 17 Theosophical Society of America founded, N.Y.C.

Nov. 23 National Railroad Conv. held, St. Louis, Mo.

"Boss" W. M. Tweed sentenced in civil action, fled to Spain.

A Passionate Pilgrim and Other Tales by Henry James published.

Luther Burbank set up nursery, Santa Rosa, Cal.

Baseball glove introduced by Charles G. Waite.

David Brown patented cash carrier system.

John McCloskey, 1st Am. Catholic priest to become a cardinal.

1876 Mar. 2 Impeachment proceedings recommended by Ho. of Reps. against Sec. of War William W. Belknap.

Apr. 2 First official National League baseball game; Boston vs. Phila.

May 17 Prohibition Party National Conv., held Cleveland O., nominated Green Clay Smith for Pres. and Gideon T. Stewart for vice-pres.

May 18 Greenback Party National Conv. held at Indianapolis, Ind., nominated Peter Cooper for Pres. and Samuel F. Perry for vice-pres.

June 6 Imperial Council of the Ancient Arabic Order of Nobles of the Mystic Shrine organized.

June 14-16 Republican National Conv. held, nominated Rutherford B. Hayes for Pres. and William A. Wheeler for vice-pres.

June 25 Gen. George A. Custer and his forces massacred at Battle of Little Big Horn in Mont.

June 27-29 Dem. National Conv. held, nominated Samuel J. Tilden for Pres. and Thomas A. Hendricks for vice-pres.

Aug. 1 Colorado admitted as 38th state.

Aug. 2 Wild Bill Hickok shot dead by Jack McCall at Deadwood, S.D.

Oct. 6 American Library Association established, Phila.

Nov. 7 Tilden seemed elected, however votes in Florida, Louisiana, South Carolina and Oregon were in dispute.

The Adventures of Tom Sawyer by Mark Twain published.

Roderick Hudson by Henry James published.

Chicago Daily News founded by Melville E. Stone and William Dougherty.

Winslow Homer painted Breezing Up.

American Chemical Society founded.

Lampoon published at Harvard University, 1st undergraduate humor magazine in America.

Central Park, N.Y.C., completed.

Dewey Decimal System originated by Melvil Dewey.

National Baseball League formed.

Intercollegiate Association of Amateur Athletes of America founded at Saratoga, N.Y.

George Washington Bradley pitched 1st no-hit baseball game; St. Louis defeated Hartford 2-0.

G. H. Coates manufactured 1st clipper for cutting hair.

Thomas A. Edison patented mimeograph.

James Gordon Bennett introduced polo.

John Knowles Paine, 1st American to write a symphonic work.

Alexander Graham Bell patented telephone.

Hollis Hunnewell introduced court tennis.

Daniel C. Stillson patented 1st practical pipe wrench.

1877 Jan. 2 Carpetbag government ended in Florida.

Jan. 29 Electoral Count Act passed by Congress.

Mar. 2 Rutherford B. Hayes declared 19th Pres. U.S.

Apr. 10 Carpetbag government rule ended in South Carolina.

Apr. 24 Carpetbag government ended in Louisiana.

June 1 Society of American Artists founded.

June 14 Flag Day celebrated nationally for 1st time in U.S.

Aug. 29 Death of Brigham Young.

Dec. 26 Socialist Labor Party organized, Newark, N.J.

Anti-Chinese riots broke out in California.

Harrigan and Hart introduced the "cakewalk" dance on N.Y. stage.

The American by Henry James published.

Thomas Edison patented the phonograph.

Asaph Hall discovered two satellites of Mars.

Albert Augustus Pope established 1st bicycle factory in U.S.

Helen Mcgill (Mrs. Andrew D. White) 1st woman to receive a Ph.D., Boston U.

Charles Williams, Jr. 1st to install a home telephone.

1878 Jan. 1 Knights of Labor established.

Jan. 14 Supreme Court decision declared unconstitutional any state law requiring a railroad to provide equal accommodations for all passengers regardless of race or color.

Jan. 17 Commercial treaty signed with Samoa.

Feb. 22 Greenback Labor Party formed, Toledo, O.; nominated James B. Weaver for Pres. and B. J. Chambers for vice-pres.

Feb. 28 Bland-Allison Act passed by Congress.

Aug. 21 American Bar Association founded, Saratoga, N.Y.

Oct. 27 $3,000,000 robbery of Manhattan Savings Institution, N.Y.C.

Dec. 17 Greenbacks reached par value on Wall Street exchange.

Yellow fever epidemic, New Orleans.

The Leavenworth Case by Anna Katharine Green published.

St. Louis Post-Dispatch formed by Joseph Pulitzer.

The Europeans by Henry James published.

A Book of Stories for Children by Sarah Or[illegible] Jewett published.

On a Method of Measuring the Velocity [illegible] Light by Albert A. Michelson published.

Report on the Lands of the Arid Region of th U.S. by John Wesley Powell published.

Frederick Winthrop Thayer patented 1s catcher's mask.

Paul Hines, 1st baseball player to make a unassisted triple play.

Auguste Renouard wrote 1st embalming book the Undertakers Manual.

Rear Admiral Daniel Ammen brought 1st gol[illegible] fish to U.S.

1879 Jan. 1 Government resumed specie paymen[illegible]

Jan. 13 Cycle of Mulligan plays began wit The Mulligan Guard Ball by Edward Harring ton.

Feb. 15 Women attorneys won right to argu cases before U.S. Supreme Court.

Sept. Progress and Poverty by Henry Georg published.

Daisy Miller by Henry James published.

Archaeological Institute of America founde[illegible] Boston.

Radcliffe College established, Cambridg[illegible] Mass.

Frank W. Woolworth established 1st success ful 5 & 10 cent store, Lancaster, Pa.

Phrase "The public be damned" uttered b William H. Vanderbilt.

George B. Selden filed first automobile paten[illegible]

James J. Ritty patented 1st cash register.

Mary Baker Eddy founded 1st Christian Sci ence Chapter.

R. S. Rhodes patented 1st important hearin aid.

Thomas A. Edison invented 1st practical elec tric lamp.

Thomas L. Rankin built 1st indoor ice skatin rink.

1880 Population: 50,155,783.

Mar. 1 Excluding Negroes from jury dut was held unconstitutional by Supreme Cour[illegible]

Apr. National Farmer's Alliance organize[illegible] Chicago.

June 5 Sentence "He will hew to the line o right, let the chips fall where they may," ut tered by Sen. Roscoe Conkling.

June 8 James A. Garfield nominated fo Pres. and Chester A. Arthur for vice-pres. a Republican national conv.

June 9 Nominating conv. of the Greenbac Labor Party held at Chicago; nominate James B. Weaver for Pres. and B. J. Chamber for vice-pres.

June 17 Nominating conv. of Prohibitio Party held at Cleveland, O.; nominated Nea Dow for Pres. and H. A. Thompson for vice pres.

June 22-24 Nominating conv. of Dem. Part held at Cincinnati, O., chose Gen. Winfield S Hancock for Pres. and William H. English fo vice-pres.

Oct. 4 Univ. of Southern Cal. founded, Lo Angeles.

Nov. 8 Sarah Bernhardt made U.S. debut, Booth's Theatre, N.Y.C.

Nov. 17 Chinese Exclusion Treaty signed.

Metropoliton Museum of Art opened, N.Y.C.

Five Little Peppers and How They Grew by Margaret Sidney (Harriet Lothrop) published.

Ben Hur by Lew Wallace published.

Democracy by Henry Adams published.

Uncle Remus, His Songs and His Sayings by Joel Chandler Harris published.

American Society of Mechanical Engineers founded.

American branch of the Salvation Army organized, Pennsylvania.

Illiteracy in America estimated at 17% of population.

Bryn Mawr (Pa.) College established.

First major gold strike in Alaska.

"Gold Brick" swindle, N.Y.C.

Kampfe brothers made 1st safety razor.

George Ligowosky patented 1st clay pigeon target for trapshooting.

1881 Jan. 24 Supreme Court declared Federal Income Tax Law of 1862 constitutional in decision Springer vs. U.S.

Mar. 4 James A. Garfield inaugurated as 20th Pres. U.S.

June 1 The Professor by William Gillette opened on N.Y.C. stage.

July 2 Pres. Garfield shot, Washington, D.C.

Sept. 20 Chester A. Arthur inaugurated as 21st Pres. U.S.

Oct. 15 American Angler published, Phila.

Nov. 22 Pan-American movement began.

The Portrait of a Lady by Henry James published.

University of Conn. established, Storrs.

American National Red Cross organized by Clara Barton, Washington, D.C.

Louise Blanchard Bethume, 1st woman architect.

David Henderson Houston patented roll film for cameras.

James A. Garfield, 1st presidential candidate to make campaign speeches in a foreign language.

1882 Jan. 2 Standard Oil Trust organized.

Feb. 2 Knights of Columbus founded, New Haven, Conn.

Feb. 7 John L. Sullivan won American Heavyweight championship.

Aug. 3 Congress approved 1st act to restrict immigration.

Sept. 25 First major league baseball doubleheader played.

A Modern Instance by William Dean Howells published.

The Prince and the Pauper by Mark Twain published.

New York Morning Journal started by Albert Pulitzer.

American Forestry Association founded.

Sarah Warren Keeler, 1st to give lip reading instruction for the deaf.

Schuyler Skaats Wheeler invented electric fan.

William Horlick invented malted milk.

1883 Jan. 16 Pendleton Act passed by Congress.

Feb. 23 Univ. of N.D., Grand Forks, chartered.

May 24 Brooklyn Bridge opened, N.Y.C.

Nov. 18 Standard time established.

Dec. 4 Sons of the American Revolution organized, N.Y.C.

Ladies' Home Journal established by Cyrus H. K. Curtis.

Life on the Mississippi by Mark Twain published.

The Old Swimmin' Hole and 'Leven More Poems by James Whitcomb Riley published.

Dynamic Sociology by Lester Frank Ward published.

Modern Language Association formed.

Oscar Hammerstein patented cigar rolling machine.

Benjamin J. Keith presented 1st vaudeville show.

William F. Cody presented 1st wild west show.

1884 May 14 Anti-Monopoly Organization of the United States founded, Chicago, nominated Benjamin F. Butler for Pres. U.S.

May 28 Nominating conv. of Republican Party held at Chicago, chose James G. Blaine for Pres. and John A. Logan for vice-pres.

July 8-11 Nominating conv. of Democratic Party held in Chicago, chose Grover Cleveland for Pres. and Thomas A. Hendricks for vice-pres.

July 23 Nominating conv. of Prohibition Party held in Pitts., chose John P. St. John for Pres. and William Daniel for vice-pres.

July 30 Nominating conv. of Labor Party held in Chicago; supported Democratic nominations.

Aug. 5 Cornerstone laid of the Statue of Liberty.

Oct. 6 Naval War College established, Newport, R.I.

Nov. 8 First newspaper syndicate in U.S., McClure's Syndicate, founded.

Equal Rights Party nominated Mrs. Belva A. Lockwood for Pres.

Montcalm and Wolfe by Francis Parkman published.

The Adventures of Huckleberry Finn by Mark Twain published.

American Historical Association formed, Saratoga, N.Y.

Greyhound racing introduced, Phila.

Lewis Edson Waterman invented 1st practical fountain pen.

John Joseph Montgomery made 1st glider flight.

1885 Jan. 24 New Orleans Exposition began.

Feb. 21 Washington Monument dedicated.

Mar. 3 U.S. Post Office established special delivery service.

Mar. 4 Grover Cleveland inaugurated 22d Pres. U.S.

Mar. 12 Univ. of Ariz. chartered.

Nov. 11 Stanford Univ., Palo Alto, Cal., chartered.

The Rise of Silas Lapham by William Dean Howells published.

Memoirs of Ulysses S. Grant published.

American Economic Association organized, Saratoga, N.Y.

William Le Baron Jenney finished 1st building known as a skyscraper, Chicago.

Sylvanus F. Bowser manufactured 1st gasoline pump.

Dr. William West Grant performed 1st appendectomy.

1886 Jan. 1 First Tournament of Roses parade held, Pasadena, Cal.

Jan. 19 Presidential Succession Act passed.

Mar. 4 Univ. of Wyo. chartered, Laramie.

May 4 Haymarket riot, Haymarket Square, Chicago.

May 10 Supreme Court decision Yick Wo vs. Hopkins defined the term Alien.

June 2 Pres. Grover Cleveland and Miss Frances Folsom married.

Oct. 28 Statue of Liberty unveiled.

Dec. 8 American Federation of Labor organized, Columbus, O.

Henry James' The Bostonians and The Princess Casamassima published.

"Whisky Trust" formed.

Charles Martin Hall invented process for making aluminum.

Griswold Lorillard introduced tuxedo coat.

George K. Anderson patented typewriter ribbon.

1887 Jan. 20 Pearl Harbor leased from Hawaii.

Feb. 3 Electoral Count Act passed by Congress.

Feb. 4 Interstate Commerce Act passed by Congress.

Mar. 2 Hatch Act passed by Congress.

Mar. 3 American Protective Association formed.

Apr. 19 Catholic Univ. of America, Washington, D.C., chartered.

Sept. 5 Labor Day 1st observed as a legal Holiday in U.S.

Marine Biological Laboratory founded, Wood Hole, Mass.

"Sugar Trust" formed.

Bertillon System of identifying criminals introduced.

Susanna Medora Salter, 1st woman mayor, Argonia, Kan.

1888 Feb. 19 Mount Vernon, Ill., destroyed by cyclone.

Feb. 22 Nominating conv. of Industrial Reform Party held at Washington, D.C., chose Albert E. Redstone for Pres. and John Colvin for vice-pres.

Mar. 12 Thirty-six hour blizzard struck N.Y.C.

May First public recitation by De Wolf Hopper of "Casey at the Bat," N.Y.C.

May 15 Nominating conv. of Equal Right Party held at Des Moines, Ia., chose Belv Lockwood for Pres. and Alfred Love for vic pres.

May 16 Nominating conv. of Union Lab Party held at Cincinnati, O., chose Robert Cowdery for Pres. and W. H. T. Wakefield fo vice-pres.

May 31 Nominating conv. of Prohibition Pa ty held at Indianapolis, chose John A. Broo for Pres. and Gen. Clinton B. Fiske for vic pres.

June 4 Electrocution replaced death by hang ing as capital punishment in N.Y. state.

June 5 Nominating conv. of Democratic Pa ty held at St. Louis, chose Grover Clevelan for Pres. and Allen G. Thurman for vice-pre

June 15 Dept. of Labor established.

June 25 Nominating conv. of Republican Pa ty held at Chicago, chose Benjamin Harriso for Pres. and Levi P. Morton for vice-pres.

Nov. 6 Benjamin Harrison elected Pres.

Australian secret ballot introduced into U.S in local election in Louisville, Ky.

Looking Backward 2000—1887 by Edward Be lamy, published.

The Wreck of the Hesperus by Arthur Foot presented, Boston.

Robert Elsmere by Mrs. Humphry Ward pub lished.

American Commonwealth by James Bryce pub lished.

George Eastman patented a roll film camer

Dr. William C. Deming constructed 1st incu bator for infants.

Charles Conn manufactured 1st saxophone.

Marvin Chester Stone patented drinkin straws.

Willard L. Bundy patented employee's time re corder.

1889 Jan. 24 $500,000 robbery of Connecticut Mu tual Life Insurance Company.

Jan. 30 Univ. of Ida. chartered, Moscow.

Mar. 2 First antitrust law passed Kansa state legislature.

Mar. 4 Benjamin Harrison inaugurated 23 Pres. U.S.

Apr. 22 Official opening of Oklahoma lan rush.

May 31 Johnstown (Pa.) Flood.

Nov. 2 North and South Dakota admitted a 39th and 40th states.

Nov. 8 Montana admitted as 41st state.

Nov. 11 First Congress of the Roman Cath olic laity held, Balt.

Nov. 11 Washington admitted as 42d state.

Dec. American Academy of Political and So cial Science founded, Phila.

A Connecticut Yankee at King Arthur's Cour by Mark Twain published.

Hull House established in Chicago.

University of N.M. established, Albuquerqu

I. M. Singer manufactured 1st electric sewin machine.

Elizabeth Cochrane (Nellie Bly), 1st woma to make tour of world unattended.

1890 Population: 62,947,714.

Feb. 24 Chicago chosen as site for World's Columbian Exposition.

May 19 Play Beau Brummell by Clyde Fitch, produced in N.Y.C.

May 21 Oklahoma territory established.

May 24 George Francis Train went around the world in 67 days, 31 hours, 3 minutes, and 3 seconds.

June 9 Robin Hood, a comic opera by Reginald De Koven, produced, Chicago.

July 2 Sherman Anti-Trust Act passed by Congress.

July 3 Idaho admitted as 43d state.

July 10 Wyoming admitted as 44th state.

Oct. 1 McKinley Tariff Act passed by Congress.

Oct. 6 Mormon Church, Salt Lake City, discontinued its sanction of polygamy.

Nov. 1 Mississippi adopted new constitution, became 1st state to restrict Negro suffrage.

Nov. 29 First Army-Navy football game played, West Point, N.Y.

The Influence of Sea Power upon History, 1660-1783 by Alfred Thayer Mahan published.

Poems by Emily Dickinson published.

How the Other Half Lives by Jacob A. Riis published.

Political Science and Comparative Constitutional Law by John W. Burgess published.

Sequoia and Yosemite National Parks established.

American Tobacco Company formed.

Estimated 1% of the people possessed more wealth than the other 99% in the U.S.

Two step dance became popular.

Charles Brady King invented pneumatic hammer.

1891 Mar. 3 Circuit Court of Appeals created by Congress.

Mar. 4 International copyright act passed by Congress.

May 5 Carnegie Hall opened, N.Y.C.

May 19 People's or Populist Party formed, Cincinnati, O.

Oct. 16 First correspondence school in U.S. opened by Thomas Jefferson Foster.

Oct. 18 First international 6-day bicycle race in U.S., N.Y.C.

Sculpture "Grief" created by Augustus Saint-Gaudens.

Tales of Soldiers and Civilians by Ambrose Bierce published.

University of Chicago chartered.

Basketball invented by Dr. James A. Naismith.

Marcellus Fleming Berry devised 1st travelers' checks.

Thomas Alexander Sperry originated the trading stamp.

1892 June 7-11 Republican Nat. Conv. held Minneapolis; nominated Benjamin Harrison for Pres. and Whitelaw Reid for vice-pres.

June 21-23 Nominating conv. of Democratic Party chose Grover Cleveland for Pres. and Adlai Ewing Stevenson for vice-pres.

June 29-July 1 Nominating conv. of Prohibition Party held at Cincinnati, O., chose John Bidwell for Pres. and James B. Cranfill for vice-pres.

July 4-5 Nominating conv. of Peoples (Populist) Party held at Omaha, Neb., chose James B. Weaver for Pres. and James G. Field for vice-pres.

Aug. 28 Socialist Labor Party Conv., N.Y.C., nominated Simon Wing for Pres. and Charles H. Matchett for vice-pres.

Oct. 28 Great fire in Milwaukee, Wis.

Nov. 8 Grover Cleveland elected Pres.

Nov. 20 Homestead Strike ended.

Dec. 19 University of Oklahoma, Norman, opened.

Composer Antonin Dvorak became the dir., Nat. Conservatory of Music, N.Y.C.

Song "Bicycle Built for Two" written.

Reliance Brass Band, New Orleans, founded by Jack "Papa" Laine.

"After the Ball Is Over" composed by Charles K. Harris.

Green Fields and Running Brooks by James Whitcomb Riley published.

Heresy trial of Prof. Charles A. Briggs took place.

Boll weevil 1st seen in U.S.

E. E. Barnard discovered 5th satellite of Jupiter.

American Psychological Association formed.

William Painter invented cork bottle cap.

George Washington Ferris invented the Ferris Wheel.

Joshua Pusey patented, manufactured book matches.

Thomas A. Edison built first moving picture studio.

1893 Feb. 1 U.S. established a protectorate in Hawaii.

Mar. 1 Diplomatic Appropriation Act passed by Congress.

May 1-Oct. 30 World's Columbian Expn., Chgo.; 28,000,000 visitors.

June 9 Ford's Theater bldg., Washington, D.C., collapsed; 22 dead.

June 26 Panic of 1893 began.

Sept. 16 Cherokee Strip land rush began.

Oct. 2 Cyclone raged along Gulf coast of Louisiana killing 2,000.

Frank Lloyd Wright's 1st independent commission was Winslow house, Chicago.

Premiere of Anton Dvorak's New World Symphony, N.Y.C.

Maggie: A Girl of the Streets by Stephen Crane published.

Luther Burbank published catalog, New Creations in Fruits and Flowers, listing 100 hybrids.

Ice hockey introduced by Yale and Johns Hopkins universities.

Anti-Saloon League organized, Oberlin, O.

William H. Ford and Henry D. Perky patented shredded wheat biscuits for breakfast food.

Charles B. McDonald designed and constructed 1st eighteen hole golf course, at Wheaton, Ill.

1894 Apr. 30 136,000 coal miners struck at Columbus, O.

May 11 The Pullman strike began in Chicago.

July 10 Eugene Debs indicted for criminal conspiracy and contempt of court.

June 21 Democratic Silver Conv. held at Omaha, Neb.

Aug. 18 Congress created Bureau of Immigration.

Aug. 27 First graduated income tax law passed Congress.

Dec. 22 United States Golf Association formed.

Anthony Hope published The Prisoner of Zenda.

"The Sidewalks of New York" was composed and written by Charles Lawler.

Henry Demarest Lloyd wrote Wealth Against Commonwealth.

Rose Hawthorne Lathrop established the 1st free cancer home for incurables, in N.Y.C.

1895 June 22 National Association of Manufacturers was founded.

Aug. 31 First professional football game was played at Latrobe, Pa.

Stephen Crane wrote The Red Badge of Courage.

William A. White purchased the Emporia Gazette.

The "Gibson Girl" began to come into vogue.

James F. Duryea won the 1st automobile race, at Chicago.

Charles E. Duryea manufactured the 1st automobiles for regular sale.

Lewis B. Halsey was the 1st to pasteurize milk commercially.

K. C. Gillette invented the 1st successful safety razor.

John P. Holland contracted for the 1st submarine for the U.S. Navy.

George Morgan invented the game of volley ball.

1896 Jan. 4 Utah admitted as the 45th state.

May 18 Jim Crow Car Law of La. declared constitutional by the U.S. Supreme Court in Plessy vs. Ferguson.

June 18 Republican Party at St. Louis nominated William McKinley for Pres. and Garret A. Hobart for vice-pres.

July 4-9 Socialist Labor Party in N.Y.C. nominated Charles H. Matchett for Pres.

July 7 William J. Bryan delivered his famous "Cross of Gold" speech.

July 11 William J. Bryan nominated by the Dem. Party for Pres. and Arthur Sewall for vice-pres. in Chicago.

Aug. 15 Phrase "What's the Matter with Kansas" appeared in editorial by William A. White in the Emporia Gazette.

Sept. 2-3 National Democratic Party nominated John M. Palmer for Pres. in Indianapolis.

Nov. 3 William McKinley elected Pres. U.S.

Song "There'll be a Hot Time in the Old Town Tonight" was written.

Dorothy Dix started 1st popular advice to the lovelorn column in a U.S. newspaper.

The 1st automobile accident in America occurred, in N.Y.C.

Elizabeth Lyon gave birth to 1st quintuplets in America.

Harvey Hubbell invented electric light socket with a pull chain.

Dr. Henry L. Smith took the 1st x-ray photograph.

1897 Jan. 12 National Monetary Conference held at Indianapolis.

Feb. 17 National Congress of Mothers held in Washington, D.C.

Mar. 4 William McKinley inaugurated as 25th Pres. U.S.

Charles William Post introduced cereal breakfast foods.

Martha H. Cannon, 1st woman state senator (Utah).

1898 Feb. 15 Battleship Maine blown up in Havana harbor.

Apr. 22 U.S. instituted a blockade of Cuba.

Apr. 22 Theodore Roosevelt organized the "Rough Riders."

Apr. 24 Spain declared war on the U.S.

Apr. 25 U.S. declared that a state of war with Spain had been in existence since Apr. 21.

May 1 Com. George Dewey won the Battle of Manila Bay.

June 11 600 Marines landed at Guantanomo, Cuba.

July 1 Federal Bankruptcy Act passed.

July 1-2 Battle of San Juan.

Dec. 10 Treaty ending the Spanish-American War signed.

Charles Ives completed 1st of 4 pioneeringly modern symphonies.

Royal Page Davidson designed the first armored car.

1899 Feb. 4 Philippine insurrection started.

Clyde Jay Coleman invented the 1st automobile electric self-starter.

George F. Grant patented the golf tee.

Humphrey O'Sullivan patented the rubber heel.

John T. Dorrance introduced canned soup.

John S. Thurman patented motor driven vacuum cleaner.

John Dewey published The School and Society.

1900 Population: 75,994,575.

Jan. 29 American Baseball League organized in Chicago.

Mar. 5 "Hall of Fame" founded in N.Y.C. to commemorate great Americans.

Mar. 6-7 Social Democratic Party Nat. Conv. in Indianapolis nominated Eugene V. Debs for Pres.

Mar. 14 Gold Standard Act made gold the single currency standard of the U.S.

Mar. 24 Carnegie Steel Corporation incorporated with a capitalization of $166 million, in N.J.

Apr. 15 First organized auto race held at Springfield, L.I., N.Y. A. L. Riher won in an electric car, going 50 miles in 2 hours, 3 minutes.

Apr. 12 Foraker Act established civil government in Puerto Rico, effective May 1, 1900.

May 10 Populist (Fusion) Nat. Conv. at Sious Falls, S.D., nominated William J. Bryan for Pres.

May 10 Populist (Middle-of-the-road) Conv. at Cincinnati, O., nominated Wharton Baker for Pres.

May 14 Sanford Dole appointed as 1st territorial governor of Hawaii.

June 2-8 Socialist Labor Party Nat. Conv. in N.Y.C. nominated Joseph P. Maloney for Pres.

June 21 Rep. Nat. Conv. in Phila. nominated Willliam McKinley for Pres. and Theodore Roosevelt for vice-pres.

June 21 Gen. Arthur MacArthur issued an amnesty proclamation for Philippine rebels.

June 27-28 Prohibition Party Nat. Conv. in Chicago nominated John G. Woolley for Pres.

July 3 Secretary of State John Hay issued a circular letter elaborating his "Open door" policy with regard to China.

July 5 Dem. Nat. Conv. in Kansas City, Mo., nominated William J. Bryan for Pres. and Adlai Stevenson for vice-pres.

Aug. 14 International expedition including U.S. troops relieved Peking, China, from the Boxer siege.

Sept. 18 First direct primary election in U.S. on a local level, held in Minneapolis, Minn.

Nov. 6 William McKinley re-elected Pres.

Carry Nation began her famous anti-liquor crusades by leading a group of women on saloon smashing expeditions through Kansas.

Theodore Dreiser's Sister Carrie appeared.

1901 Jan. 10 First great oil strike in Texas opened the great oil period in the history of the Southwest.

Feb. 2 Army Nurse Corps organized as a branch of the U.S. Army.

Mar. 2 Platt Amendment adopted by Congress. A series of provisions to which Cuba had to agree before the U.S. would withdraw its troops.

Mar. 4 William McKinley inaugurated as Pres. of the U.S., for his 2d term.

Mar. 12 Andrew Carnegie donated $5,200,000 to N.Y.C. for the establishment of a public library.

Mar. 23 Emilio Aguinaldo, Philippine rebel leader, captured.

May 27 Supreme Court decisions in "Insular Cases" important in establishing a tariff policy toward Puerto Rico and the Philippines.

June 21 Military government in the Philippines terminated, effective July 4, 1901.

Sept. 6 Pres. William McKinley shot while in Buffalo, N.Y.

Sept. 14 Pres. McKinley died, Theodore Roosevelt took the oath of office, as 26th Pres. of the U.S.

Nov. 18 Hay-Pauncefote Treaty abrogating the Clayton-Bulwer Treaty, gave British consent to the U.S. control of the Isthmus of Panama.

Nov. 27 Army War College opened.

Nov. 27 Mercury vapor lamp patented by Peter Cooper Hewitt.

Nov. 27 Anna Edison Taylor, 1st woman to go over Niagara Falls in a barrel.

1902 Jan. 1 First postseason football game (Rose Bowl). Univ. Mich. defeated Stanford 49-0.

Mar. 10 Pres. Roosevelt instructed attorney-general Knox to file suit for the dissolution of the Northern Securities Co.

June 2 Oregon, 1st state to adopt the initiative and referendum on a general scale.

June 17 National Reclamation Act (Newlands Act) passed.

July 1 Philippine Government Act made the islands an unorganized territory of the U.S. Rayon patented by W. H. Walker, Dr. A. D. Little and H. S. Mork.

First cancer research fund established by Mrs. Collis P. Huntington.

Thomas L. Tally opened 1st moving picture theatre, Los Angeles.

1903 Jan. 22 Hay-Herran Conv. ratified by the Senate, gave the U.S. a 99 yr. lease over a 6 mile wide canal zone in Panama.

Feb. 14 Department of Labor and Commerce established by Congress.

Nov. 18 Hay-Bunau-Varilla Treaty gave the U.S. control of a 10 mile strip of land in Panama in return for $10,000,000 in gold plus $250,000 a year.

Dec. 17 First successful flight of a large heavier-than-air machine by Orville and Wilbur Wright at Kitty Hawk, N.C.

Dec. 30 Fire in the Iroquois Theatre in Chicago killed 602 people.

Dec. 30 Henry James published The Ambassadors.

Dec. 30 Call of the Wild by Jack London published.

Dec. 30 First motion picture with a plot, "The Great Train Robbery," directed by Edwin S. Porter.

Dec. 30 Henry Ford organized the Ford Motor Co.

Dec. 30 Wisconsin was the first state to adopt direct primary election.

Dec. 30 First wildlife refuge established at Pelican Island, Fla.

Dec. Max Aronson (Broncho Billy) became 1st moving picture star.

1904 Feb. 29 Panama Canal Commission appointed by Pres. Roosevelt.

Mar. 14 Supreme Court ordered the dissolution of the Northern Securities Co.

May 5 Socialist Party Nat. Conv. in Chicago nominated Eugene V. Debs for Pres. and Benjamin Hanford for vice-pres.

June 16 The steamship "General Slocum" burned in N.Y. harbor killing 1,030.

June 21-23 Rep. Party Nat. Conv. in Chicago nominated Theodore Roosevelt for Pres. and Charles W. Fairbanks for vice-pres.

June 29-30 Prohibition Party Nat. Conv. in Indianapolis nominated Dr. Silas C. Swallow for Pres. and George W. Carroll for vice-pres.

July 2-8 Socialist Labor Party Nat. Conv. in N.Y.C. nominated Charles H. Corregan for Pres. and William W. Cox for vice-pres.

July 4 Peoples (Populist) Party Nat. Conv. in Springfield, Ill., nominated Thomas E. Watson for Pres. and Thomas H. Tibbles for vice-pres.

July 6-9 Dem. Party Nat. Conv. in St. Louis nominated Alton B. Parker for Pres. and Henry G. Davis for vice-pres.

July 25 Strike of 25,000 textile workers in Fall River, Mass.

Oct. 19 American Tobacco Co. formed by the merger of the Consolidated and the American & Continental Tobacco Companies.

Oct. 27 First rapid transit subway in the world began operation in N.Y.C.

Nov. 8 Theodore Roosevelt elected Pres. U.S.

Dec. 10 Bethlehem Steel Corp. founded in N.J.

Lincoln Steffens published The Shame of the Cities.

1905 Mar. 4 Theodore Roosevelt inaugurated Pres. U.S. for his 2d term.

June 8 President Roosevelt sent notes to Russia and Japan urging them to cease hostilities.

July 7 The International Workers of the World (Wobblies) established in Chicago.

Sept. 5 Treaty of Portsmouth (N.H.) signed by Japan and Russia ending the war.

First Rotary Club founded in Chicago by Paul Percy Harris.

1906 Apr. 18 San Francisco fire and earthquake killed an estimated 450.

June 29 Hepburn Act to regulate railroad rates in interstate commerce passed.

June 30 Pure Food and Drug Act prohibited the sale of adulterated foods and drugs.

June 30 Meat Inspection Act set standards for sanitation in the meat-packing industry.

Sept. 22 18 Negroes and 3 whites killed in race riot in Atlanta, Ga.

Sept. 29 U.S. took military control of Cuba, under the provisions of the Platt Amendment.

Nov. 9-26 President Roosevelt inspected the Panama Canal, the first Pres. who left the country while in office.

Dec. 12 Oscar S. Straus appointed secretary of commerce and industry, the first Jewish member of the Cabinet.

Upton Sinclair wrote The Jungle.

O. Henry (William Sidney Porter) published The Four Million, a collection of short stories.

Theodore Roosevelt awarded the Nobel Peace Prize, the first Nobel Prize awarded to an American.

Reginald Aubrey Fessenden made the first radio program broadcast.

1907 Jan. 26 Law prohibiting corporations from contributing to candidates for national office passed by Congress.

Feb. 26 General Appropriations Act increased the salaries of cabinet members, the speaker of the House, the vice-pres., and congressmen.

Mar. 14 Japanese Exclusion Act issued by Pres. Roosevelt.

Mar. 14 Inland Waterways Commission formed.

Mar. 21 U.S. marines landed in Honduras.

Oct. 21 Currency panic began with a run on the Knickerbocker Trust Co. of N.Y.C. which was forced to fold. Many other banks had to close before J. P. Morgan and others imported 100 million dollars in gold to end the panic.

Nov. 19 Oklahoma admitted to the Union as the 46th state.

Dec. 6 Mine explosion in Monongah, W.Va. killed 361.

Dec. 19 Mine disaster in Jacobs Creek, Pa., killed 239.

William Graham Sumner's "Folkways" published.

William D. "Big Bill" Haywood, president of the Western Miners Union, acquitted in the murder trial of ex-Governor of Idaho Frank Steunenberg. Clarence Darrow was defense counsel, William E. Borah was prosecuting attorney.

First Nobel Prize in physics awarded to an American won by A. A. Michelson, head of the Department of Physics at the U. of Chicago, for his studies of the speed of light.

The Robie House, designed by Frank Lloyd Wright, built in Chicago.

Anna Jarvis suggested the 1st Mother's Day.

Florence Lawrence became the 1st female moving picture star.

Emily P. Bissell designed the 1st modern Christmas seals.

1908 Apr. 2-3 People's Party Nat. Conv. in St. Louis nominated Thomas E. Watson for Pres. and Samuel Williams for vice-pres.

May 10-17 Socialist Party Nat. Conv. in Chicago nominated Eugene V. Debs for Pres. and Benjamin Hanford for vice-pres.

May 28 Congress passed a bill regulating the use of child labor in the District of Columbia.

May 30 Aldrich-Vreeland Act established a national Monetary Commission and authorized emergency monetary measures.

June 8 National Commission for the Conservation of Natural Resources appointed by Pres. Roosevelt.

June 16-20 Rep. Party Nat. Conv. nominated William H. Taft for Pres. and James S. Sherman for vice-pres.

June 24 Grover Cleveland died.

July 4 Socialist Labor Party Nat. Conv. nominated August Gilhaus for Pres. and Donald L. Munro for vice-pres.

July 7-10 Dem. Party Nat. Conv. nominated William J. Bryan for Pres. and John W. Kern for vice-pres.

July 15-16 Prohibition Party Nat. Conv. at Columbus, O., nominated Eugene W. Chafin for Pres. and Aaron S. Watkins for vice-pres.

July 27 Independence Party Nat. Conv. in Chicago nominated Thomas L. Hisgen for Pres. and John T. Graves for vice-pres.

Sept. 17 Lt. Thomas W. Selfridge 1st to be killed in an airplane accident.

Oct. 1 Model-T Ford introduced.

Nov. 3 William H. Taft elected Pres. of the U.S.

Forty-seven-story Singer building built in N.Y.C.

1909 Feb. 21 American fleet completed round-the-world cruise.

Mar. 4 William H. Taft inaugurated as 27th Pres. U.S.

Apr. 6 Robert E. Peary discovered the North Pole.

July 12 Sixteenth Amendment (income tax) submitted to the states for ratification.

Aug. 5 Payne-Aldrich Tariff, highly protectionist, enacted.

Aug. 7 Lincoln penny, designed by Victor D. Brenner, put into circulation, replacing the Indian-head penny.

Nov. 13 Mine explosion at Cherry, Ill., killed 259.

Nov. 18 U.S. troops sent to Nicaragua.

First wireless message sent from N.Y.C. to Chicago.

Boy Scouts of America chartered.

Campfire Girls organized.

Merkel Landis originated 1st Christmas savings club in a bank.

Outboard motor developed by Ole Evinrude.

1910 Population: 91,972,266.

June 18 Mann-Elkins Act placed telephone, telegraph, and cable companies under the jurisdiction of the ICC.

June 25 Congress enacted the Postal Savings Bank System.

June 25 White Slave Traffic Act (Mann Act) prohibited interstate transportation of women for immoral purposes.

Aug. 31 Theodore Roosevelt delivered his "New Nationalism" speech at Osawatomie, Kan., in which he proclaimed his "square deal," splitting with the conservatism of Taft.

Nov. 8 Democrats gained control of the House; Victor L. Berger, 1st Socialist elected to Congress.

Frederick W. Taylor advocated the scientific management of industry and labor, which became known as "Taylorization."

Glenn Hammond Curtiss made 1st experimental airplane bombing.

Eugene Ely made 1st airplane flight from a ship.

Mrs. John Bruce Dodd originated Father's Day.

Alva J. Fisher patented complete self-contained electric washing machine.

1911 Jan. 21 Nat. Progressive Republican League formed in Washington, D.C., under the leadership of Robert M. LaFollette.

May 15 Supreme Court ordered the dissolution of the Standard Oil Company.

May 19 The American Tobacco Company ordered dissolved as a monopoly in violation of the Sherman Anti-Trust Act.

Aug. 22 Pres. Taft vetoed Arizona statehood because its constitution permitted the recall of judges.

Sept. 17-Nov. 5 First cross-country flight made by Calbraith P. Rodgers.

Nov. 10 Andrew Carnegie established the Carnegie Corporation with an endowment of $125,000,000.

First electric self-starter demonstrated.

Earl Lewis Ovington, 1st air mail pilot.

First radio license issued to George Hill Lewis.

1912 Jan. 6 New Mexico admitted to the Union as the 47th state.

Jan. 12-Mar. Violent textile workers strike at Lawrence, Mass.

Feb. 14 Arizona admitted to the Union as the 48th state.

Apr. 14-15 "Titanic" sank with an estimated loss of 1,502 people.

May 17 Nat. Conv. of the Socialist Party in Indianapolis nominated Eugene V. Debs for Pres. and Emil Seidel for vice-pres.

June 5 U.S. marines landed in Cuba to protect American interests.

June 5-July 2 Nat. Conv. of Dem. Party at Balt. nominated Woodrow Wilson for Pres. and Thomas R. Marshall for vice-pres.

June 18 Nat. Conv. of the Rep. Party in Chicago nominated William H. Taft for Pres. This caused a split in the party and led to the formation by Theodore Roosevelt of the Progressive (Bull Moose) party.

July 10-12 Nat. Conv. of Prohibition Party at Atlantic City nominated Eugene W. Chafin for Pres. and Aaron S. Watkins for vice-pres.

Aug. 5 Nat. Conv. of Progressive Party nominated Theodore Roosevelt for Pres. and Hiram Johnson for vice-pres.

Oct. 10 Alexis Carrel awarded the 1st Nobel Prize in medicine and physiology to be given to an American.

Oct. 14 Theodore Roosevelt shot in Milwaukee, before giving a speech but insisted on giving it before going to the hospital.

Nov. 5 Woodrow Wilson elected Pres. U.S.

Theodore Dreiser's The Financier published.

James Thorpe won both the decathalon and pentathalon at the Olympics in Stockholm.

Juliette Gordon Low organized the Girl Scouts.

Isabella Goodwin appointed 1st woman detective.

1913 Jan. 1 Parcel Post went into service.

Feb. 14 Pres. Taft vetoed the Immigration Bill requiring literacy tests.

Feb. 17 International Exhibition of Modern Art, the "Armory Show," opened in N.Y.C. Featured many post-impressionists, including the controversial "Nude Descending A Staircase" by Marcel Duchamp.

Feb. 25-Apr. Silk workers strike in Paterson, N.J., led by the I.W.W.

Feb. 25 Sixteenth Amendment (income tax) adopted.

Mar. 1 Webb-Kenyon Interstate Liquor Act prohibited the shipment of liquor into states where illegal, passed over Pres. Taft's veto.

Mar. 4 Woodrow Wilson inaugurated as 28th Pres. of U.S.

Apr. 8 Pres. Wilson personally read his message on tariff revision to Congress, the first Pres. to do so since John Adams in 1800.

May 14 John D. Rockefeller donated $100 million to the Rockefeller Foundation.

May 19 Webb Alien Land-Holding Bill effectively excluded Japanese from land ownership, made law in Cal.

May 31 Seventeenth Amendment adopted, provided for the popular election of U.S. senators.

Oct. 3 Underwood-Simmons Tariff Act reversed the protectionism of previous tariffs, reduced duties on many articles.

Dec. 10 Nobel Peace Prize awarded to Elihu Root.

Dec. 23 Glass-Owen Bill established the Federal Reserve System.

Henry Ford set up his 1st assembly line for the mass production of Model-T's.

Dr. Herman Adolph De Vry invented portable moving picture projector.

1914 Feb. 13 The American Society of Composers, Authors and Publishers (ASCAP) organized in N.Y.C.

Apr. 16 Second "Coxey's Army" of unemployed workers organized at Massillon, O.

May 8 Smith-Lever Act provided federal funds for state agricultural colleges.

Aug. 4 U.S. issued formal neutrality proclamation.

Aug. 15 Official opening of Panama Canal.

Sept. 26 Federal Trade Commission established to regulate monopolies and ensure fair competition.

Oct. 15 Clayton Anti-Trust Act strengthened and supplemented the Sherman Anti-Trust Act.

Edgar Rice Burroughs published the 1st "Tarzan" book, Tarzan of the Apes.

Theodore William Richards, 1st American to receive the Nobel Prize in chemistry.

John Randolph Bray patented moving picture animation technique.

Mrs. Dolly Spencer, 1st woman chief of police, at Milford, O.

Corporal Bouligny, 1st American combatant casualty in World War I.

1915 Jan. 25 First transcontinental telephone call, made by Alexander Graham Bell and Dr. Thomas A. Watson, the two men who had the original telephone conversation in 1876.

Jan. 28 U.S. Coast Guard established.

Feb. 8 D. W. Griffith's "Birth of a Nation" premiered in Los Angeles.

May 7 The "Lusitania" sunk by a German submarine off Ireland, 1,198 killed, including 114 Americans.

May 13 U.S. sent the 1st Lusitania note to Germany.

July 2 U.S. Senate reception room destroyed by a bomb, placed there by a German teacher at Cornell U.

Sept. 1 German ambassador assured the safety of passenger liners and neutrals.

Sept. 16 Haiti became a U.S. protectorate.

Dec. 4 Henry Ford's "Peace Ship" sailed from Hoboken, N.J.

Carl Gebhard Muench patented 1st sound absorbing material.

1916 Jan. 1 First permanent Rose Bowl football game.

Feb. 15 Germany accepted responsibility for the sinking of the Lusitania and offered reparations.

Mar. 9 Francisco (Pancho) Villa raided Columbus, N.M., killing 17 Americans. General Pershing sent to Mexico to try to capture Villa.

Apr. 23 Nat. Conv. of Socialist Labor Party in N.Y.C. nominated Arthur E. Reimer for Pres. and Caleb Harrison for vice-pres.

May U.S. marines occupied Santo Domingo.

June 3 National Defense Act passed, increased the size of the standing army.

June 10 Nat. Conv. of Rep. Party nominated Charles Evans Hughes for Pres. and Charles Warren Fairbanks for vice-pres.

June 10 Nat. Conv. of Progressive Party at Chicago nominated Theodore Roosevelt for Pres. and John M. Parker for vice-pres. Roosevelt declined in favor of Charles Evans Hughes.

June 14-16 Nat. Conv. of Dem. Party in St. Louis nominated Woodrow Wilson for Pres. and Thomas R. Marshall for vice-pres.

June 15 Boy Scouts of America incorporated.

July 17 Federal Farm Loan Act provided long term credit facilities for farmers.

July 19-21 Nat. Conv. of Prohibition Party in St. Paul, Minn., nominated Frank Hanly for Pres. and Ira D. Landrith for vice-pres.

Aug. 4 U.S.-Danish Treaty signed for the sale of the Danish West Indies (Virgin Islands) to the U.S. for $25 million.

Aug. 29 Council of National Defense established to coordinate industry and resources for national security.

Aug. 29 Jones Act promised Philippine independence when ability for self government would be demonstrated.

Sept. 7 Shipping Act authorized the formation of the U.S. Shipping Board.

Nov. 7 Woodrow Wilson elected Pres. U.S.

Carl Sandburg published Chicago Poems.

First birth control clinic, opened in N.Y.C. by Margaret Sanger, Fania Mindell, and Ethel Byrne.

John Taliaferro Thompson invented the submachine gun.

1917 Jan. 22 Pres. Wilson made his "Peace without victory" speech, formulating his famous ten points.

Feb. 3 U.S. broke diplomatic relations with Germany.

Feb. 5 Immigration Act passed over Pres. Wilson's veto, excluded Asiatic laborers.

Feb. 23 Smith-Hughes Act established a Federal Board for Vocational Education.

Feb. 24 The "Zimmerman Note" revealed that Germany had offered Mexico part of the U.S. if it would ally with Germany if a war broke out.

Mar. 2 Jones Act made Puerto Rico a U.S. territory, and Puerto Ricans became U.S. citizens.

Mar. 5 Woodrow Wilson inaugurated Pres. of the U.S. for his 2d term.

Mar. 8 Cloture rule, terminating debate adopted by the Senate.

Mar. 22 U.S. 1st to recognize the new Russian government.

Apr. 2 Pres. Wilson delivered his war message to Congress.

Apr. 2 Jeanette Rankin 1st woman member of the Ho. of Reps.

Apr. 6 Pres. Wilson signed the resolution for claiming a state of war between the U.S. and Germany.

Apr. 14 Committee on Public Information formed to control censorship of news and propaganda.

Apr. 17 The destroyer "Smith" attacked by a German submarine, 1st military action in the war.

Apr. 24 Liberty Loan Act passed to help finance the war.

May 18 Selective Service Act required all men between 21 and 30 to register for the draft.

June 15 Espionage Act provided severe penalties for treasonable activity.

July 4 First U.S. troops arrived in San Nazaire, France.

July 28 War Industries Board created.

Aug. 10 Lever Food and Fuel Control Act authorized the Pres. to fix prices and control the distribution of food and fuels for the war effort.

Oct. 3 War Revenue Act provided tax revenue to finance the war.

Dec. 18 Eighteenth Amendment (Prohibition) approved by Congress.

First Pulitzer prize for a play awarded to J. L. Williams for his "Why Marry?"

1918 Jan. 8 Pres. Wilson, in an address to Congress, listed his Fourteen Points for the conclusion of a "just peace."

Apr. 5 War Finance Corporation founded to finance war industries.

Apr. 8 National War Labor Board for labor disputes appointed by Pres. Wilson.

Apr. 14 Lt. Douglas Campbell became 1st American-trained flyer to shoot down a German plane.

May 15 First Regular air mail service instituted, between N.Y.C. and Washington, D.C.

May 16 Sedition Act provided heavy penalties for false statements obstructing the war effort.

May 28 American Railroad Express Co. organized.

Sept. 14 Eugene V. Debs sentenced to 10 years in prison under terms of the Sedition Act.

Nov. 5 Republican Party obtained a majority in both houses of Congress.

Nov. 11 Armistice with Germany signed.

Annette Abbott Adams appointed 1st woman district attorney of the U.S.

1919 Jan. 18 Opening of peace negotiations in Paris.

Jan. 29 Eighteenth Amendment (Prohibition) ratified.

Feb. 14 Covenant of the League of Nations completed.

May 15 American Legion formed in Paris.

June 28 Treaty of Versailles signed.

Aug. 31 Communist Labor Party of America founded in Chicago.

Sept. 26 Pres. Wilson suffered a stroke while on a speaking tour to gather support for the Treaty of Versailles and the League of Nations.

Nov. 19 Senate refused to ratify the Versailles treaty.

Nov. 20 First municipal airport in U.S. opened near Tucson, Ariz.

Henry Adams posthumously won Pulitzer prize for The Education of Henry Adams.

J. B. Watson expounded his theories of behavorial psychology.

John J. Pershing appointed 1st General of the Armies of the U.S.

1920 Population: 105,710,620.

May Arrest of Sacco and Vanzetti.

May 5-10 Nat. Conv. of Socialist Labor Party, N.Y.C. nominated W. W. Cox for Pres. and August Gillhaus for vice-pres.

May 8-14 Nat. Conv. of Socialist Party, N.Y.C. nominated Eugene V. Debs for Pres. and Seymour Stedman for vice-pres.

June 8-12 Nat. Conv. of Republican Party, Chicago, nominated Warren G. Harding for Pres. and Calvin Coolidge for vice-pres.

June 10 Water Power Act established the Federal Power Commission.

June 28-July 5 Dem. Nat. Conv. nominated James M. Cox for Pres. and Franklin D. Roosevelt for vice-pres.

July 20 Air mail service begun between N.Y.C. and San Francisco.

Aug. 26 Nineteenth Amendment, providing women's suffrage, was ratified.

Nov. 2 Warren G. Harding elected Pres. U.S.

Nov. 2 First regular radio broadcasting begun by station KDKA, in East Pittsburgh, Pa.

Dec. 10 Woodrow Wilson received Nobel Peace Prize.

Sinclair Lewis published Main Street.

Eugene O'Neill wrote Emperor Jones.

Attorney General A. Mitchell Palmer made mass arrests and deportations of political and labor agitators, known as the "Palmer Raids."
Walter Johannes Damrosch conducted Symphonic Society of N.Y.C. on 1st European tour made by an American orchestra.

Owen D. Smith opened 1st dog race track using artificial rabbit.

1921 Mar. 4 Warren G. Harding inaugurated as 29th Pres. U.S.

May 19 Quota system applied to immigration.

June 10 Budget and Accounting Act authorized the Office of Comptroller General and created a Budget Bureau in the Treasury Dept. John Raymond McCarl appointed 1st comptroller general.

Oct. 5 First play-by-play broadcast of a World Series game, on station WUZ, Newark, N.J.

Nov. 2 American Birth Control League founded in N.Y.C.

Nov. 12 Washington Disarmament Conference opened.

Dec. 23 Pres. Harding commuted the sentence of Eugene V. Debs and 23 others convicted under the Espionage Act.

William Howard Taft, 1st president to become chief justice of U.S.

Alice Mary Robertson, 1st congresswoman to preside over Ho. of Reps.

1922 Feb. 6 Nine Power Treaty signed to respect the territorial integrity of China.

May 26 Federal Narcotics Control Board created.

June 14 Pres. Harding made 1st radio broadcast by a Pres. U.S.

Oct. 3 Rebecca Latimore Felton became 1st U.S. woman senator.

Nov. 15 Dr. Alexis Carrel announced the discovery of leucocytes.

Dr. Herbert M. Evans discovered Vitamin E.

First successful use of technicolor.

Henry Adler Berliner made 1st helicopter flight.

Sinclair Lewis wrote Babbitt.

Florence Ellinwood Allen, 1st woman associate justice of a state supreme court.

1923 Mar. 4 Intermediate Credit Act facilitated loans for crop financing.

Mar. 5 First old age pension grants in the U.S. enacted by Montana and Nevada.

Aug. 2 Pres. Harding died in San Francisco.

Aug. 3 Calvin Coolidge sworn in as 30th Pres. U.S.

Sept. 15 Oklahoma placed under martial law due to terrorist activities of the Ku Klux Klan.

Oct. 25 First Senate meeting in the investigation of the "Teapot Dome" scandal.

Nov. 6 Col. Jacob Schick received patent for 1st electric shaver.

Du Pont Corporation produced 1st cellophane.

Robert A. Millikan, Univ. of Chicago, won Nobel Prize in physics.

Dr. Lee De Forest made 1st sound on moving picture film.

E. E. Cummings published his 1st volume of poetry.

1924 Feb. 3 Woodrow Wilson died.

Mar. 18 Tornado struck Ill., Ind., Tenn., Ky., and Mo. killing 800.

May 11-13 Socialist Labor Party Nat. Conv., N.Y.C., nominated F. T. Johns for Pres. and Verne L. Reynolds for vice-pres.

June 5 Prohibition Party Nat. Conv., Columbus, O., nominated H. P. Faris for Pres. and Marie C. Brehm for vice-pres.

June 12 Rep. Nat. Conv. nominated Calvin Coolidge for Pres. and Charles G. Dawes for vice-pres.

June 19 Farmer-Labor Progressive Party Nat. Conv. nominated Duncan MacDonald for Pres. and William Bouck for vice-pres. Ticket later changed to William Z. Foster and Benjamin Gitlow.

June 30 Henry Sinclair and Edward Doheny indicted on charges of conspiracy and bribery in hearings of "Teapot Dome."

July 4 Nat. Conv. of the Conference for Progressive Political Action nominated Robert M. LaFollette for Pres. and Burton K. Wheeler for vice-pres.

July 9 Dem. Nat. Conv., N.Y.C. nominated John W. Davis for Pres. and Charles W. Bryan for vice-pres.

Nov. 4 Calvin Coolidge elected Pres. U.S.

Eugene O'Neill wrote Desire Under the Elms.

George Gershwin's Rhapsody in Blue 1st performed.

Sigmund Romberg's Student Prince 1st presented.

H. L. Mencken began editing caustic magazine, The American Mercury.

Gee Jon, victim of 1st lethal gas execution, in Nev.

1925 Jan. 5 Mrs. William B. (Nellie Tayloe) Ross inaugurated as 1st woman governor of a state (Wyo.).

Mar. 4 Calvin Coolidge inaugurated 30th Pres. U.S.

July 10-21 John T. Scopes tried for teaching evolution in public school, Dayton, Tenn., with Clarence Darrow as counsel for the defense and William Jennings Bryan as prosecutor.

Oct. 28-Dec. 17 Court martial of Gen. William (Billy) Mitchell.

Charles G. Dawes won Nobel Peace Prize.

Sinclair Lewis wrote Arrowsmith.

John Dos Passos wrote Manhattan Transfer.

F. Scott Fitzgerald wrote The Great Gatsby.

Florence Rena Sabin, 1st woman to become a member of National Academy of Science.

Robert Andrews Millikan discovered cosmic rays.

1926 Mar. 7 First successful transatlantic telephone conversation held between N.Y.C. and London.

May 9 Adm. Richard Byrd and Floyd Bennett made the 1st successful flight over the North Pole.

May 10-June 5 U.S. Marines were landed in Nicaragua.

July 2 U.S. Army Air Corps was created.

Gertrude Ederle was the 1st woman to swim the English Channel.

Dreiser's An American Tragedy published; Hemingway's The Sun Also Rises.

1927 Apr. 7 First successful demonstration of television.

July 29 Philip Drinker and Louis Agassiz Shaw first put the iron lung into use.

Aug. 2 President Calvin Coolidge announced that he would not be a candidate for reelection.

Aug. 23 Sacco and Vanzetti executed.

Nov. 13 Holland Tunnel between N.Y. and N.J. opened. First underwater tunnel for traffic in the U.S.

Oct. 6 "The Jazz Singer" released. First talking picture.

Charles A. Lindbergh flew solo across the Atlantic Ocean and was awarded the distinguished flying cross.

Thornton Wilder wrote The Bridge of San Luis Rey.

Arthur H. Compton was awarded the Nobel prize in physics.

1928 Apr. 13-18 Socialist Party Conv. in N.Y.C. nominated Norman Thomas for Pres.

May Pres. Coolidge vetoed the McNary-Haugen Farm Relief Bill.

May 22 Merchant Marine Act passed.

May 25 Amelia Earhart was the 1st woman to fly the Atlantic.

May 27 Nat. Conv. of the Workers' Party nominated William Z. Foster for Pres.

June 12-15 Republican Party Nat. Conv. nominated Herbert Hoover for Pres. and Charles Curtis for vice-pres.

June 26-29 Democratic Nat. Conv. nominated Alfred E. Smith for Pres. and Joseph T. Robinson for vice-pres.

July 30 First exhibition of colored movies made by George Eastman.

Aug. 27 Kellog-Briand Peace Pact signed.

Nov. 6 Herbert Hoover elected Pres. U.S.

Station WGY in Schenectady, N.Y., began 1st program of scheduled television broadcasts.

Herbert G. Dorsey invented the fathometer.

1929 Mar. 4 Herbert Hoover inaugurated as 31st Pres. U.S.

June 15 Agricultural Marketing Act established a Federal Farm Board to promote the sale of farm goods.

Oct. 3-29 Stock Market decline and crash, the forerunner of the Depression years.

Nov. 29 Richard E. Byrd made the 1st flight over the South Pole.

Emil Jannings and Janet Gaynor won the 1st movie "Oscars."

Thomas Wolfe wrote Look Homeward, Angel.

Albert B. Fall was the 1st cabinet member to be convicted of a crime.

1930 Population: 122,775,046.

Feb. 3 Charles Evans Hughes appointed chief justice U.S. Supreme Court.

May 11 Adler Planetarium, donated by Max Adler, the 1st planetarium in U.S.

June 17 The Hawley-Smoot Tariff bill passed.

July 3 Veterans Administration Act passed.

Nov. 5 Sinclair Lewis was the 1st American to receive the Nobel prize for literature.

Clyde William Tombaugh discovered the planet Pluto.

Dr. Karl Landsteiner won the Nobel prize for medicine and physiology.

Dievdonne Coste and Maurice Bellonte made the 1st transatlantic flight from Europe to America.

Albert H. Taylor and Leo C. Young 1st detected airplanes by radar.

Painter Grant Wood exhibited satirical American Gothic in Chicago.

1931 Jan. 19 The Wickersham Report advocated revision but not repeal of the 18th (Prohibition) Amendment.

Oct. 5 Hugh Herndon and Clyde Pangborn made the 1st non-stop flight across the Pacific.

Oct. 26 Eugene O'Neill's Mourning Becomes Electra produced.

George Kenneth End was the 1st to can and sell rattlesnake meat.

1932 Feb. 2 The Reconstruction Finance Corporation was established.

Mar. 23 Passage of the Norris-La Guardia Act which restricted the use of injunctions in labor disputes.

Apr. 30-May 2 Socialist Labor Party nominated Verne L. Reynolds for Pres.

May 20 Amelia Earhart was the 1st woman to make a transatlantic solo flight.

May 22-24 Socialist Party nominated Norman Thomas for Pres.

May 28 The Communist Party nominated William Z. Foster for Pres.

May 29-July 28 The "Bonus Army" was in Washington, D.C.

June 14-16 Rep. Party nominated Herbert Hoover for Pres. and Charles Curtis for vice-pres.

June 27-July 2 Dem. Party nominated Franklin D. Roosevelt for Pres. and John Nance Garner for vice-pres.

July 22 Federal Home Loan Bank Act passed.

Nov. 8 Franklin D. Roosevelt elected Pres. U.S.

Irving Langmuir won the Nobel prize in chemistry.

The 1st polaroid glass was produced.

William Nelson Goodwin patented the camera exposure meter.

Herbert Hoover was the 1st Pres. to invite the Pres.-elect to the White House to discuss governmental problems.

William Faulkner's Light in August published.

The number of unemployed had reached 13 million.

1933 Feb. 6 Twentieth Amendment adopted.

Feb. 15 Attempted assassination of Pres.-elect Roosevelt.

Mar. 1 Bank Holidays declared in six states.

Mar. 4 Franklin D. Roosevelt inaugurated as 32d Pres. U.S.

Mar. 5 Roosevelt declared a national bank holiday.

Mar. 9 Emergency Banking Relief Act passed.

Mar. 12 Roosevelt made 1st of his numerous "fireside chats."

Mar. 31 Civilian Conservation Corps Reforestation Act.

Apr. 19 U.S. officially went off the Gold standard.

May 12 Agricultural Adjustment Act passed.

May 18 Tennessee Valley Act created the Tennessee Valley Authority.

May 27 Federal Securities Act passed.

June 16 The Glass-Steagall Act created the Federal Bank Deposit Insurance Corp.

June 16 National Industrial Recovery Act passed.

Nov. 8 Civil Works Administration established.

Dec. 5 Twenty-first Amendment ratified.

Dr. Earl W. Flosdorf and Dr. Stuard Mudd established the 1st blood bank.

Frances Perkins, 1st woman appointed to the cabinet (sec. of labor).

Ruth Bryant Owen, 1st woman diplomat (minister to Denmark and Iceland).

First drive-in theater was opened.

"Ranger," the 1st U.S. aircraft carrier, launched.

1934 Jan. 30 Gold Reserve Act passed.

June 6 Securities Exchange Act established the Securities and Exchange Commission.

June 19 Federal Communications System established.

June 28 The Federal Housing Administration created.

Ernest O. Lawrence developed the cyclotron.

Carl D. Anderson discovered the positron.

F. Scott Fitzgerald published Tender is the Night.

Harold C. Urey won the Nobel prize in chemistry.

G. R. Minot, W. P. Murphey and G. H. Whipple shared the Nobel prize in medicine and physiology.

1935 Apr. 8 Works Progress Administration created.

May 11 Rural Electrification Administration established.

May 27 Supreme Court declared the Nat. Reconstruction Administration unconstitutional.

June 10 Alcoholics Anonymous organized in N.Y.C.

July 5 National Labor Relations Board created.

Aug. 14 Social Security Act passed.

Sept. 8 Huey Long assassinated.

Oct. 10 "Porgy and Bess" by George Gershwin opened in N.Y.C.

Nov. 10 Congress of Industrial Organizations (CIO) organized by John L. Lewis.

James T. Farrell wrote Studs Lonigan.

Maxwell Anderson wrote Winterset.

Leonard Keeler invented the lie detector.

1936 Apr. 25-28 Socialist Labor Party nominated John W. Aiken for Pres.

May 25 Socialist Party nominated Norman Thomas for Pres.

June 9-12 Rep. Party nominated Alfred Landon for Pres. at Cleveland.

June 23-27 Democratic Party at Phila. nominated Franklin D. Roosevelt for Pres.

June 26 U.S. Maritime Commission established.

Nov. 3 Franklin Roosevelt elected Pres. U.S. for 2d term.

Margaret Mitchell's Gone with the Wind was published.

Eugene O'Neill awarded the Nobel prize for literature, Carl D. Anderson for physics.

Vladimir K. Zworykin invented the electron tube.

Jesse Owens was 1st American to win 4 1st place prizes at the Olympic Games.

1937 Jan. 20 Franklin D. Roosevelt, 1st Pres. to be inaugurated on this date.

Feb.-July 22 Roosevelt tried unsuccessfully to increase the members of the U.S. Supreme Court.

May 1 The Neutrality Act passed.

May 6 The 1st coast-to-coast radio program made by Herbert Morrison in describing the landing and explosion of the dirigible "Hindenberg."

May 12 First world-wide radio program heard in the U.S. in the broadcast of the coronation of George VI of England.

July 22 The Bankhead-Jones Act established the Farm Security Administration.

The Golden Gate bridge was opened in San Francisco.

Clinton Davisson won the Nobel prize in physics.

John Steinbeck published Of Mice and Men.

John Dos Passos completed U.S.A.

Mrs. Wallis Warfield Simpson married Edward, the former King of England.

Charles Willis Howard opened the 1st Santa Claus school.

1938 Jan. 28 Pres. Roosevelt asked Congress for appropriations to build up the Armed Forces.

Feb. 16 Pres. Roosevelt signed the Second Agricultural Adjustment Act.

May 26 Formation of House Committee to investigate Un-American Activities.

Sept. 30 Munich Agreement signed.

William Faulkner published The Unvanquished.

Ernest Hemingway wrote The Fifth Column.

John Dewey published Experience and Education.

Florescent lamps introduced in the U.S.

Pearl Buck, novelist, became first American woman to win Nobel Prize.

Thornton Wilder's Our Town produced.

Fiberglass perfected.

1939 Jan. 12 Pres. Roosevelt recommended a $535 million defense program for the next two years, to Congress.

July 1 Pres. Roosevelt established the Federal Works Agency.

Sept. 1 Germany invaded Poland.

Sept. 3 British ship, Athenia, with 30 Americans aboard sunk by German submarine.

Oct. 18 Presidential Order closed all U.S. ports and waters to belligerent submarines.

Nov. 4 Neutrality Act of 1939 passed.

Kateri Tekakwitha, first American Indian to be canonized by Roman Catholic Church.

First regular transatlantic flights.

Discovery of the RH factor.

1940 Population: 131,669,275.

Apr. 17 Socialist Party nominated Norman Thomas for Pres.

May 15 First successful helicopter flight in U.S.

June 28 Alien Registration Act passed (Smith Act).

Sept. 3 U.S. exchanged fifty destroyers with Great Britain for military bases leases.

Sept. 16 Congress enacted 1st peacetime Selective Service Act.

Oct. 24 Forty hour week, part of the Fair Labor Standards Act, went into effect.

Nov. 5 Franklin D. Roosevelt elected Pres. U.S., 1st Pres. to be elected to a 3d term.

Richard Wright wrote Native Son.

You Can't Go Home Again published by Thomas Wolfe.

First fission of Plutonium.

First U.S. antibiotic, antinomycin, developed.

1941 Feb. 3 U.S. Supreme Court upheld the Federal Wage and Hours Law unanimously.

Mar. 11 Pres. Roosevelt signed the Lend-Lease Bill.

June 14 Pres. Roosevelt ordered the freezing of all German and Italian assets in the U.S.

July 25 Pres. Roosevelt ordered an embargo on all shipments of scrap iron and oil to Japan.

Aug. 9-12 Atlantic Charter formulated by Winston Churchill and Pres. Roosevelt in a secret meeting off New Foundland.

Dec. 7 Pearl Harbor, Hawaii, attacked by Japanese Naval and Air Forces.

Dec. 8 U.S. delcared war against Japan.

Dec. 10 Japanese invaded the Philippines at Luzon.

Dec. 11 Germany and Italy declared war against the U.S.

Dec. 22 Wake Island fell to the Japanese.

Penicillin developed.

Grand Coulee Dam began operation.

1942 Jan. 2 MacArthur's forces in Manila forced to withdraw to Bataan.

Jan. 12 National War Labor Board created by executive order.

Mar. 17 Gen. MacArthur named Commander-in-Chief of the Southwest Pacific.

Apr. 10 Bataan Death March began at dawn —American and Philippine prisoners forced to march 85 miles in six days. More than 5,200 men lost their lives.

Apr. 18 Tokyo bombed by bomber group led by Maj. Gen. Doolittle—1st offensive blow in the Pacific.

May 4-8 Americans inflicted heavy losses on the Japanese fleet in the Battle of the Coral Sea.

May 6 Gen. Wainwright surrendered Corregidor to the Japanese.

June 4-6 American forces defeated Japanese forces at the Battle of Midway.

June 28 First land attack upon the Japanese when a contingent of commandos assaulted Salamaua, New Guinea.

July 30 Waves organized as Women's Reserve Unit of the U.S. Naval Reserve.

Aug. 7 U.S. Marines occupied Guadalcanal, Solomon Islands.

Nov. 7 American forces began landing in North Africa with the support of British Naval and Air Units.

First American jet plane—Bell-P-59.

First continuous nuclear reaction, at the Univ. of Chicago.

1943 Jan. 14 Pres. Roosevelt arrived in Casablanca for a conference with Winston Churchill.

Mar. 2-4 Battle of the Bismarck Sea—impressive victory for the Americans.

May 12 North African Campaign ended with the capture of Gen. von Arnim.

July 10 Sicily invaded by Gen. Patton's 7th Army, Montgomery's 8th and Canadian and French forces.

July 19 Rome bombed.

July 25 Mussolini resigned upon the insistence of King Victor Emmanuel.

Aug. 17 Sicily conquered.

Sept. 8 Italy surrendered unconditionally to the United Nations.

Sept. 11 Salamaua, New Guinea fell to the Americans under Gen. MacArthur.

Nov. 2 Japan suffered its worst naval defeat at Rabaul.

Nov. 22 Pres. Roosevelt met at Cairo with Prime Minister Churchill and Generalissimo Chiang Kai-Shek.

Nov. 28-Dec. 1 Roosevelt, Churchill and Stalin met at Teheran.

Dec. 24 Gen. Eisenhower named Supreme Commander of European Invasion Forces.

Wendell L. Willkie published One World.

The Human Comedy written by William Saroyan.

1944 Jan. 22 British and American forces landed at Anzio and Nettuno, Italy.

Mar. 6 Berlin attacked by flying fortresses.

May 18 Cassino evacuated by Germans.

June 6 D. Day: Allies invade Europe.

Aug. 9 Guam fell to the Americans.

Aug. 15 Southern France invaded by American 7th Army under Lt. Gen. Patch.

Aug. 21 Dumbarton Oaks Conference opened at Washington, D.C.—laid plans for establishing the United Nations.

Oct. 23-26 Japanese fleet suffered heavy losses at Leyte Gulf.

Nov. 7 Pres. Roosevelt elected for his 4th term.

Dec. 15 Four Generals—Henry Arnold, Dwight Eisenhower, MacArthur and George C. Marshall —elevated to new rank of General Of the Army ("Five Star" Generals).

Tennessee Williams' The Glass Menagerie produced.

1945 Feb. 7 Gen. MacArthur entered Manila.

Feb. 9 U.S. Marines established a beachead on Iwo Jima.

Mar. 7 1st U.S. Army crossed the Rhine.

Mar. 16 Iwo Jima fell to U.S. Marines.

Apr. 1 U.S. troops invaded Okinawa.

Apr. 12 Pres. Franklin D. Roosevelt died in Warm Springs, Ga.

Apr. 12 Harry S. Truman inaugurated as 33d Pres. U.S.

Apr. 24 United Nations Conference opened at San Francisco with delegates from fifty nations attending.

May 7 Germany unconditionally surrendered to the Allies.

June 21 Japanese surrendered at Okinawa.

July 5 Gen. MacArthur reported the liberation of the Philippines.

July 16 First atomic bomb exploded at Alamogordo, New Mexico.

July 28 U.S. Senate ratified the U.N. Charter by a vote of 89-2.

Aug. 6 First atomic bomb dropped on Hiroshima, Japan.

Aug. 9 Atomic bomb dropped on Nagasaki, Japan.

Aug. 14 Unconditional surrender of Japan announced by Pres. Truman.

Sept. 2 Surrender document signed aboard the U.S.S. Missouri in Tokyo Bay by Japanese Premier and Allies.

1946 July 4 Independence of Philippines proclaimed by Pres. Truman.

July 5 First mail delivery by helicopter.

July 7 Mother Frances Xavier Cabrini canonized by Roman Catholic Church—1st naturalized American to be canonized.

Dec. 31 State of hostilities officially ended by Pres. Truman.

Cortisone synthesized.

First electronic digital computer—ENIAC—used by U.S. Army.

1947 Apr. 11 Jackie Robinson became 1st Negro baseball player in the major leagues.

May 22 Pres. Truman signed Greek-Turkish Aid Bill—known as the Truman Doctrine.

June 2 Marshall Plan proposed at a Harvard commencement by Sec. of State George C. Marshall.

June 14 U.S. Senate ratified peace treaties with Italy, Rumania, Bulgaria, and Hungary.

Sept. 17 National Defense Department formed.

Oct. 5 Harry S. Truman made 1st Presidential address on television.

Oct. 14 First airplane to break sound barrier piloted by Charles E. Yeager at Muroc, Calif.

1948 Mar. 22 A.B.C. made 1st simultaneous AM-FM radio broadcast.

Apr. 1 First commercial electronically operated elevators installed, N.Y.C.

June 24 Thomas Dewey chosen as candidate for Pres. by Rep. Nat. Conv. in Phila.

June 24 Pres. Truman signed Selective Service Act.

Nov. 2 Harry S. Truman elected Pres. U.S.

Oct. 24 Bernard M. Baruch termed phrase "Cold War" before a Senate War Investigating Committee.

Production of aureomycin begun.

Transistor invented.

First U.S. built electric locomotive with gas turbine.

1949 Jan. 20 Harry Truman inaugurated as Pres. U.S.

Mar. 2 First non-stop round-the-world airplane flight completed at Fort Worth, Texas.

Apr. 4 North Atlantic Treaty signed at Washington, D.C.

Oct. 14 Eleven top communists found guilty by Judge Harold Medina. of conspiring to advocate the overthrow of the government.

Oct. 24 United Nations dedicated at N.Y.

Arthur Miller wrote Death of a Salesman.

Nobel Prize for literature awarded to William Faulkner.

1950 Population: 150,697,361.

Jan. 21 Alger Hiss found guilty of perjury on two counts.

Jan. 31 Pres. Truman ordered development of hydrogen bomb.

May 20 First Armed Forces Day.

June 25 North Korean troops attacked the Republic of South Korea.

June 25 Pres. Truman ordered U.S. troops to the aid of S. Korea.

June 27 First military support of U.N.

Sept. 23 Internal Security Act of 1950 became law over Presidential veto.

Sept. 26 Seoul recaptured by American troops.

Oct. 7 U.S. forces invaded North Korea by crossing 38th parallel.

Nov. 20 U.S. troops reached the Manchurian border on Yalu River.

Nov. 29 U.S. forces retreated under heavy attack from Chinese Communist Units.

Dec. 16 State of emergency declared by Pres. Truman.

Dec. 19 Gen. Dwight D. Eisenhower appointed Supreme Commander of the Western Europe Defense forces by the North Atlantic Council.

1951 Jan. 1 Chinese Communist troops broke through defense perimeter around Seoul.

Feb. 1 U.N. formally accused Communist China of aggression in Korea.

Feb. 22 Twenty-second Amendment adopted.

Mar. 14 Seoul recaptured by U.N. forces.

Apr. 4 SHAPE (Supreme Headquarters Allied Powers in Europe) established at Paris.

Apr. 11 General Douglas MacArthur relieved of command by Pres. Truman.

July 10 First Korean truce talks held between U.N. and Communists at Kaesong.

Sept. 8 Japanese Peace treaty signed. 1 at San

Oct. 10 Mutual Security Act of 1951 signed by Pres. Truman.

Oct. 24 State of war with Germany officially ended.

J. D. Salinger's The Catcher in the Rye published.

1952 Jan. 24 Peace negotiations in Korea deadlocked.

July 25 Puerto Rico became 1st commonwealth of U.S.

Nov. 4 Gen. Dwight D. Eisenhower elected Pres. U.S. defeating Ill. Gov. Adlai C. Stevenson.

1953 U.S. armed forces casualties in Korea totaled 131,051.

Jan. 20 Gen. Dwight D. Eisenhower inaugurated as 34th Pres. U.S.

Apr. 25 Sen. Wayne Morse spoke 22 hours 26 minutes, opposing controversial offshore oil reserves bill.

July 27 Korean Armistice signed at Panmunjon by U.N. and Communist delegates.

Aug. 7 Refugee Relief Act of 1953 signed.

1954 Mar. 1 Five Congressmen shot on the floor of the Ho. of Reps. by Puerto Rican Nationalists.

Apr. 1 U.S. Air Force Academy authorized.

May 17 U.S. Supreme Court ruled racial segregation in public schools unconstitutional.

Oct. 25 First public and televised cabinet meeting held.

1955 Jan. 1 Financial aid to South Vietnam, Cambodia and Laos begun by the U.S.

Jan. 17 U.S. submarine Nautilus went to sea under atomic power.

Jan. 19 First filmed Presidential Press Conference.

Apr. 12 Announcement was made of the successful development of an antipolio vaccine.

July 18 Geneva Conference held with heads of state from U.S., U.S.S.R., Gt. Britain and France.

Nov. 25 Racial segregation on interstate trains and buses banned by Interstate Commerce Commission.

Dec. 5 A.F.L. and the C.I.O. formally merged.

1956 May 21 U.S. made first aerial H-bomb test over Namu I, Bikini Atoll.

June 30 Two commercial airliners collided over Grand Canyon; 128 dead.

July 22 Panama Declaration outlining principles of Organization of American States signed by Pres. Eisenhower and heads of 18 other lands.

Oct. 27 Pres. Eisenhower sent peace plea prior to Israeli-British-French military action against Egypt. U.N. later achieved cease-fire.

Nov. 6 Dwight D. Eisenhower re-elected Pres. U.S.

1957 Jan. 5 Pres. Eisenhower asked Congress for authority to use armed forces to protect Middle East from Communist aggression—the Eisenhower Doctrine.

Aug. 28 Sen. Strom Thurmond of South Carolina took floor for a record 24 hours, 28 minutes, in "educational debate" against civil-rights bill.

Sept. 25 Pres. Eisenhower sent federal troops to Little Rock, Ark., to prevent interference with court-ordered school desegregation.

James Gould Cozzens' novel, By Love Possessed, published.

1958 Jan. 31 Army launched Explorer I, first U.S. earth satellite to go into orbit.

Mar. 8 Last U.S. battleship, the Wisconsin, joined mothball fleet at Bayonne, N.J.

July 15 Pres. Eisenhower sent U.S. Marines into revolution-threatened Lebanon at request of Pres. Chamoun. Troops began leaving Aug. 12 after calm returned.

Dec. 10 First domestic jet passenger service in U.S. opened by national Airlines between New York and Miami.

James Agee awarded Pulitzer Prize for posthumously published A Death in the Family.

New York's Edgard Varese composed Poeme Electronique for Brussels Exposition.

1959 Jan. 3 Alaska officially became 49th state by Presidential proclamation.

Apr. 25 St. Lawrence Seaway opened, permitting ocean ships to reach Great Lakes cities.

July 21 World's first atomic-powered merchant ship, the Savannah, launched at Camden, N.J.

Aug. 21 Hawaii proclaimed 50th state.

Sept. 14 Pres. Eisenhower signed into law a bill ending import duty on "modern" art.

Sept. 15-27 Soviet Premier Khrushchev made unprecedented tour of U.S., conferred with Pres. Eisenhower.

Nobel Prizes awarded to Emilio Segre and Owen Chamberlain in physics, Severo Ochoa and Arthur Kornberg in medicine and physiology.

1960 Population: 179,323,175.

May 1 U.S. reconnaissance plane, a U-2 flown by Francis Gary Powers, shot down in Soviet Union, prompting a controversy.

July-Aug. Pres. Eisenhower virtually eliminated sugar imports from Cuba, where Fidel Castro had attained power in 1959. Cuba confiscated more property of U.S. companies.

July 13 Sen. John Fitzgerald Kennedy, 43, of Massachusetts, nominated for Pres. by Democratic Nat. Convention in Los Angeles.

July 27 Richard Milhous Nixon, 47, two-term Vice Pres. under Eisenhower, nominated for Pres. by Republican Nat. Convention in Chicago.

Nov. 8 John F. Kennedy elected Pres. of the U.S., narrowly defeating Richard M. Nixon, 34,227,096 to 34,108,546.

Dec. 16 Two commercial airliners collided in fog over New York City and crashed in 2 boroughs; 134 killed in air and on ground.

Nobel Prizes awarded to Donald A. Glaser in physics, Willard F. Libby in chemistry.

William Styron's novel, Set This House on Fire, published.

1961 Jan. 3 U.S. severed diplomatic relations with Cuba.

Mar. 1 Pres. Kennedy announced establishment of Peace Corps to teach skills to people in underdeveloped countries.

Mar. 13 Pres. Kennedy proposed that Latin American republics join U.S. in 10-year program to raise hemisphere's living standards—the Alliance for Progress.

Apr. 17 "Bay of Pigs" invasion of Cuba by some 1,200 anti-Castro exiles, backed by U.S.; instantly crushed.

May 5 First U.S. spaceman, Navy Cmdr. Alan B. Shepard, Jr., was rocketed 116.5 miles above the earth in Mercury capsule.

July 2 Ernest Hemingway, Nobel Prize novelist, died in Ketchum, Ida.

July 21 Second American astronaut, Capt. Virgil I. Grissom, made 118-mile-high, 303-mile-long rocket flight over Atlantic.

Sept. 25 Pres. Kennedy told U.N. the West was prepared to fight over Berlin, where East Germans built wall dividing city; he added that he preferred "peace race" to "arms race."

Nobel Prizes awarded Robert Hofstadter in physics, Melvin Calvin in chemistry, George von Bekesy in medicine and physiology.

1962 Feb. 20 Lt. Col. John H. Glenn, Jr., became first American in orbit earth—3 times in 4 hours, 56 minutes, in Mercury capsule Friendship 7.

Mar. 26 U.S. Supreme Court ruled that federal courts had right and duty to try cases involving distribution of state legislative seats.

May 24 Lt. Cmdr. M. Scott Carpenter made 3-orbit flight in Mercury capsule Aurora.

June 25 U.S. Supreme Court ruled unconstitutional the New York State official prayer in public schools.

Aug. 14 Gang took $1,551,277 in holdup of U.S. mail truck near Plymouth, Mass.

Sept. 14 Twenty-fourth Amendment to the Constitution, barring the poll tax in federal elections, submitted to State legislatures after Congressional approval; ratification completed in 1964.

Sept. 23 Philharmonic Hall—first unit of Lincoln Center for the Performing Arts, New York—opened with concert that included commissioned work by Aaron Copland.

Oct. 1 James H. Meredith, escorted by U.S. marshals, enrolled at University of Mississippi in defiance of segregationist opposition.

Oct. 22 Pres. Kennedy revealed Soviet missiles buildup in Cuba and imposed blockade; agreement reached with Soviet Premier Khrushchev Oct. 28, and missile bases were dismantled.

Nov. 7 Mrs. Eleanor Roosevelt, widow of Pres. Franklin D. Roosevelt, died at her New York City home.

Nov. 21 Pres. Kennedy lifted blockade of Cuba.

Dec. 24 Cuba released 1,113 prisoners of 1961 invasion attempt.

Nobel Prizes awarded to James D. Watson in medicine and physiology, John Steinbeck in literature, and Linus D. Pauling (1954 chemistry winner) in peace.

Katherine Anne Porter's novel, The Ship of Fools, published.

1963 May 15-16 U.S. Air Force Maj. Leroy Gordon Cooper orbited earth 22 times.

June 19 Pres. Kennedy proposed broad civil rights law covering public accommodations, school-desegregation litigation, community relations, etc.

June 20 U.S. and U.S.S.R. agreed to set up "hot line" teletype intercommunication to curb risk of accidental war.

July 25 U.S., British and U.S.S.R. representatives initialed a treaty prohibiting nuclear-weapons tests in earth's atmosphere, in outer space and under water.

Aug. 28 More than 200,000 Negroes and Whites held civil-rights rally in Washington, D.C., parading to Lincoln Memorial.

Nov. 1-2 Pres. Ngo Dinh Diem of U.S.-aided South Vietnam was ousted and died in coup by armed forces.

Nov. 21 Pres. Kennedy asked Congress for $95,701,235 in appropriations for medical and research facilities, student loans, training of teachers of handicapped, expansion of maternal and child-health care programs, U.N. peace-keeping costs in Middle East, and research on possible pesticide dangers.

Nov. 22 John F. Kennedy, 35th President of the United States, was fatally shot while riding in motorcade in Dallas, Tex.

TABLE OF ABBREVIATIONS

The Following Abbreviations and Symbols are Frequently Used in This Compilation

A.A., Associate in Arts.
A.A.A., Agricultural Adjustment Administration; Anti-Aircraft Artillery.
A.A.A.S., American Association for the Advancement of Science.
AAC, Army Air Corps.
A. and M., Agricultural and Mechanical.
AAF, Army Air Force.
A.A.H.P.E.R., American Association for Health, Physical Education, and Recreation.
A.A.O.N.M.S., Ancient Arabic Order of the Nobles of the Mystic Shrine.
A.A.S.R., Ancient Accepted Scottish Rite (Masonic).
A.B., Bachelor of Arts.
ABC, American Broadcasting Company.
A.B.C.F.M., American Board of Commissioners for Foreign Missions (Congregational).
A.,B.&C.R.R., Atlanta, Birmingham & Coast R.R.
AC, Air Corps.
acad., academy; academic.
A.C.L. R.R., Atlantic Coast Line R.R.
A.C.P., American College of Physicians.
A.C.S., American College of Surgeons.
a.d.c., aide-de-camp.
adj., adjutant; adjunct.
adm., admiral.
adminstr., administrator.
adminstrn., administration.
adminstrv., administrative.
adv., advocate; advisory.
advt., advertising.
A.E., Agricultural Engineer.
A.E. and P., Ambassador Extraordinary and Plenipotentiary.
AEC, Atomic Energy Commission.
AEF, American Expeditionary Forces.
aero., aeronautical, aeronautic.
AFB, Air Force Base.
A.F.D., Doctor of Fine Arts.
A.F. and A.M., Ancient Free and Accepted Masons.
AFL (or A.F. of L), American Federation of Labor.
A.F.T.R.A., American Federation TV and Radio Artists.
agr., agriculture.
agrl., agricultural.
agt., agent.
agy., agency.
A.I.A., American Institute of Architects.
AID, Agency for International Development.
A.I.M., American Institute of Management.
A.L.A., American Library Association.
Alta., Alberta.
Am., American, America.
A.M., Master of Arts.
A.M.A., American Medical Association.
A.M.E., African Methodist Episcopal.
Am. Inst. E.E., American Institute of Electrical Engineers.
Am. Soc. C.E., American Society of Civil Engineers.
Am. Soc. M.E., American Society of Mechanical Engineers.
A.N.A., Associate National Academician.
anat., anatomical.
ann., annual.
ANTA, American National Theatre and Academy.
anthrop., anthropological.
A.P., Associated Press.
apptd., appointed.
apt., apartment.
A.R.C., American Red Cross.
archeol., archeological.
archtl., architectural.
Arts.D., Doctor of Arts.
arty., artillery.
AS, Air Service.
A.S.C.A.P., American Society of Composers, Authors and Publishers.
ASF, Air Service Force.
assn., association.
asso., associate; associated.
asst., assistant.
astron., astronomical.
astrophys., astrophysical.
ATSC, Air Technical Service Command.
A.,T.& S.F. Ry., Atchison, Topeka & Santa Fe Ry.
atty., attorney.
AUS, Army of the United States.
Aux., Auxiliary
Av., Avenue.

b., born.
B., Bachelor.
B.A., Bachelor of Arts.
B.Agr., Bachelor of Agriculture.
Balt., Baltimore.
Bapt., Baptist.
B.Arch., Bachelor of Architecture.
B.&A. R.R., Boston & Albany R. R.
B.A.S., Bachelor of Agricultural Science.
Batn., Battalion.
B.B.A., Bachelor of Business Administration.
BBC, British Broadcasting Corp.
B.C., British Columbia.
B.C.E., Bachelor of Civil Engineering.
B.Chir., Bachelor of Surgery.
B.C.L., Bachelor of Civil Law.
B.C.S., Bachelor of Commercial Science.
bd., board.
B.D., Bachelor of Divinity.
B.Di., Bachelor of Didactics.
B.E., Bachelor of Education.
B.E.E., Bachelor of Electrical Engineering.
BEF, British Expeditionary Force.
B.F.A., Bachelor of Fine Arts.
bibl., biblical.
bibliog., bibliographical.
biog., biographical.
biol., biological.
B.J., Bachelor of Journalism.
Bklyn., Brooklyn.
B.L., Bachelor of Letters.
bldg., building.
B.L.S., Bachelor of Library Science.
Blvd., Boulevard.
B.& M. R.R., Boston & Maine R.R.
Bn., Battalion.
B.O., Bachelor of Oratory.
B.& O. R.R., Baltimore & Ohio R.R.
bot., botanical.
B.P., Bachelor of Painting.
B.P.E., Bachelor of Physical Education.
B.P.O.E., Benevolent and Protective Order of Elks.
B.Pd., Bachelor of Pedagogy.
B.Py., Bachelor of Pedagogy.
br., branch.
B.R.E., Bachelor of Religious Education.
brig.gen., brigadier general.
Brit., British; Britannica.
Bro., Brother.
B.S., Bachelor of Science.
B.S.A., Bachelor of Agricultural Science.
B.S.D., Bachelor of Didactic Science.
B.S.T., Bachelor of Sacred Theology.
B.Th., Bachelor of Theology.
bull., bulletin.
bur., bureau.
bus., business.
B.W.I., British West Indies.

C.Am., Central America.
CAA, Civil Aeronautics Adminstrn.
CAB, Civil Aeronautics Board.
CAC, Coast Artillery Corps.
Can., Canada.
Cantab., Of or pertaining to Cambridge University, England.
capt., captain.
Cath., Catholic.
cav., cavalry.
CBI, China, Burma, India Theatre of Operations.
C.,B.& Q. R.R., Chicago, Burlington & Quincy R.R. Co.
CBS, Columbia Broadcasting System.
CCC, Commodity Credit Corporation.
C.,C.,C.& St.L. Ry., Cleveland, Cincinnati, Chicago & St. Louis Ry.
C.E., Civil Engineer, Corps of Engineers.
CEF, Canadian Expeditionary Force.
C.&E.I. R.R., Chicago & Eastern Illinois R.R.
C.G.W. R.R., Chicago Great Western Ry.
ch., church.
Ch.D., Doctor of Chemistry.
chem., chemical.
Chem.E., Chemical Engineer.
Chgo., Chicago.
Chirurg., Chirurgical.
chmn., chairman.
chpt., chapter.
Cia. (Spanish), Company.
CIA, Central Intelligence Agency.
CIC, Counter Intelligence Corps.
C.,I. &L. Ry., Chicago, Indianapolis & Louisville Ry.
Cin., Cincinnati.
CIO, Congress of Industrial Organizations.
Cleve., Cleveland.
climatol., climatological.
clin., clinical.
clk., clerk.
C.L.U., Chartered Life Underwriter.
C.M., Master in Surgery.
C.,M.,St.P.&P.R.R., Chicago, Milwaukee, St. Paul & Pacific R.R. Co.
C.&N.-W.Ry., Chicago & Northwestern Ry.
Co., Company, County.
C. of C., Chamber of Commerce.
C.O.F., Catholic Order of Foresters.
C. of Ga. Ry., Central of Georgia Ry.
col., colonel.
coll., college.
com., committee.
comd., commanded.
comdg., commanding.
comdr., commander.
comdt., commandant.
commd., commissioned.
comml., commercial.
commn., commission.
commr., commissioner.
condr., conductor.
conf., conference.
Congl., Congregational; Congressional.
Conglist., Congregationalist.
cons., consulting, consultant.
consol., consolidated.
constl., constitutional.
constn., constitution.
constrn., construction.
contbd., contributed.
contbg., contributing.
contbn., contribution.
contbr., contributor.
conv., convention.
coop. (or **co-op.**), cooperative.
corp., corporation.
corpl., corporal.
corr., correspondent; corresponding; correspondence.
C.&O.Ry., Chesapeake & Ohio Ry. Co.
C.P.A., Certified Public Accountant.
C.P.C.U., Chartered Property and Casualty Underwriter.
C.P.H., Certificate of Public Health.
cpl., corporal.
C.P. Ry., Canadian Pacific Ry. Co.
C.,R.I.&P. Ry., Chicago, Rock Island & Pacific Ry. Co.
C.R.R. of N.J., Central Railroad Co. of New Jersey.
C.S., Christian Science.
C.S.B., Bachelor of Christian Science.
C.S.D., Doctor of Christian Science.
C.& S. Ry. Co., Colorado & Southern Ry. Co.
C.,St.P.,M.&O. Ry., Chicago, St. Paul, Minneapolis & Omaha Ry. Co.
ct., court.
C.T., Candidate in Theology.
C.Vt. Ry., Central Vermont Ry.
C.& W.I. R.R., Chicago & Western Indiana R.R. Co.
CWS, Chemical Warfare Service.
cyclo., cyclopedia.
C.Z., Canal Zone.

d., daughter.
D.Agr., Doctor of Agriculture.
D.A.R., Daughters of the American Revolution.
dau., daughter.
D.C., District of Columbia.
D.C.L., Doctor of Civil Law.
D.C.S., Doctor of Commercial Science.
D.D., Doctor of Divinity.
D.D.S., Doctor of Dental Surgery.
dec., deceased.
Def., Defense.
del., delegate.
Dem., Democratic; Democrat.
D.Eng., Doctor of Engineering.
denom., denominational.
dep., deputy.
dept., department.
dermatol., dermatological.
desc., descendant.
devel., development.
D.F.C., Distinguished Flying Cross.
D.H.L., Doctor of Hebrew Literature.
D.&H.R.R., Delaware & Hudson R.R. Co.
dir., director.
disch., discharged.
dist., district.
distbg., distributing.
distbn., distribution.
distbr., distributor.
div., division; divinity; divorce proceedings.
D.Litt., Doctor of Literature.
D.,L& W.R.R., Delaware, Lackawanna & Western R.R. Co.
D.M.D., Doctor of Medical Dentistry.
D.M.S., Doctor of Medical Science.
D.O., Doctor of Osteopathy.
DPA, Defense Production Administration.
D.P.H., Diploma in Public Health.
Dr., Doctor, Drive.
D.R., Daughters of the Revolution.
D.R.E., Doctor of Religious Education.
D.& R.G.W. R.R. Co., Denver & Rio Grande Western R.R. Co.
Dr.P.H., Doctor of Public Health; Doctor of Public Hygiene.
D.Sc., Doctor of Science.
D.S.C., Distinguished Service Cross.
D.S.M., Distinguished Service Medal.
D.S.T., Doctor of Sacred Theology.
D.T.M., Doctor of Tropical Medicine.
D.V.M., Doctor of Veterinary Medicine.
D.V.S., Doctor of Veterinary Surgery.

E., East.
E. and P., Extraordinary and Plenipotentiary.
ECA, Economic Cooperation Administration.
eccles., ecclesiastical.
ecol., ecological.
econ., economic.
ECOSOC, Economic and Social Council (of the UN).
ed., educated.
E.D., Doctor of Engineering.
Ed.B., Bachelor of Education.
Ed.D., Doctor of Education.
edit., edition.
Ed.M., Master of Education.
edn., education.
ednl., educational.
E.E., Electrical Engineer.
E.E. and M.P., Envoy Extraordinary and Minister Plenipotentiary.
Egyptol., Egyptological.
elec., electrical.
electrochem., electrochemical.
electrophys., electrophysical.
E. M., Engineer of Mines.
ency., encyclopaedia.
Eng., England.
engr., engineer.
engring., engineering.
entomol., entomological.
ethnol., ethnological.
ETO, European Theater of Operations.
Evang., Evangelical.
exam., examination; examining.
exec., executive.
exhbn., exhibition.
expdn., expedition.
expn., exposition.
expt., experiment.
exptl., experimental.

F., Fellow.
F.A., Field Artillery.
FAA, Federal Aviation Agency.
FAO, Food and Agriculture Organization (of the UN).
FBI, Federal Bureau of Investigation.
FCA, Farm Credit Administration.
FCC, Federal Communications Commission.
FCDA, Federal Civil Defense Administration.
FDA, Food and Drug Administration.

FDIA, Federal Deposit Insurance Administration.
F.E., Forest Engineer.
Fed., Federal.
Fedn., Federation.
Fgn., Foreign.
FHA, Federal Housing Administration.
FOA, Foreign Operations Administration.
Found., Foundation.
frat., fraternity.
F.R.C.P., Fellow Royal College of Physicians (England).
F.R.C.S., Fellow Royal College of Surgeons (England).
FSA, Federal Security Agency.
Ft., Fort.
FTC, Federal Trade Commission; Federal Tariff Commission.

G.-1 (or other number), Division of General Staff.
gastroent., gastroenterological.
GATT, General Agreement on Tariffs and Trade.
G.,C.& S.F. Ry., Gulf, Colorado & Santa Fe Ry. Co.
G.D., Graduate in Divinity.
gen., general.
geneal., genealogical.
geod., geodetic.
geog., geographical; geographic.
geol., geological.
geophys., geophysical.
G.H.Q., General Headquarters.
G.,M.& N. R.R., Gulf, Mobile & Northern R.R. Co.
G.,M.& O. R.R., Gulf, Mobile & Ohio R.R. Co.
G.N. Ry., Great Northern Ry. Co.
gov., governor.
govt., government.
govtl., governmental
grad., graduated; graduate.
Gt., Great.
G.T. Ry., Grand Trunk Ry. System.
G.W. Ry. of Can., Great Western Ry. of Canada.
gynecol., gynecological.

Hdqrs., Headquarters.
H.H.D., Doctor of Humanities.
HHFA, Housing and Home Finance Agency.
H.I., Hawaiian Islands.
H.M., Master of Humanics.
hist., historical.
HOLC, Home Owners Loan Corporation.
homeo., homeopathic.
hon., honorary; honorable.
Ho. of Dels., House of Delegates.
Ho. of Reps., House of Representatives.
hort., horticultural.
hosp., hospital.
H.T., Territory of Hawaii.
Hwy., Highway.
hydrog., hydrographic.

IAEA, International Atomic Energy Agency.
IBM, International Business Machines Corp.
ICA, International Cooperation Administration.
ICC, Interstate Commerce Commn.
I.C.R.R., Illinois Central R.R. System.
I.E.E.E., Institute of Electrical and Electronics Engineers.
IFC, International Finance Corp.
I.G.N. R.R., International - Great Northern R.R.
IGY, International Geophysical Year.
illus., illustrated.
ILO, International Labor Orgn.
IMF, International Monetary Fund.
Inc., Incorporated.
ind., independent.
Indpls., Indianapolis.
Indsl., industrial.
inf., infantry.
ins., insurance.
insp., inspector.
inst., institute.
instl., institutional.
instn., institution.
instr., instructor.
instrn., instruction.
internat., international.
intro., introduction.

I.O.O.F., Independent Order of Odd Fellows.
I.R.E., Institute of Radio Engineers.
J.B., Jurum Baccalaureus.
J.C.B., Juris Canonici Bachelor.
J.C.L., Juris Canonici Lector.
J.D., Doctor of Jurisprudence.
j.g., junior grade.
jour., journal.
jr., junior.
J.S.D., Doctor of Juristic Science.
jud., judicial.
J.U.D., Juris Utriusque Doctor: Doctor of Both (Canon and Civil) Laws.

K.C., Knight of Columbus.
K.C.C.H., Knight Commander of Court of Honor.
K.P., Knight of Pythias.
K.C.S. Ry., Kansas City Southern Ry.
K.T., Knight Templar.

lab., laboratory.
lang., language.
laryngol., laryngological.
lectr., lecturer.
L.H.D., Doctor of Humane Letters.
L.I., Long Island.
lieut., lieutenant.
L.I.R.R., Long Island R.R. Co.
lit., literary: literature.
Litt.B., Bachelor of Letters.
Litt.D., Doctor of Letters.
LL.B., Bachelor of Laws.
LL.D., Doctor of Laws.
LL.M., Master of Laws.
L.& N. R.R., Louisville & Nashville R.R.
L.O.M., Loyal Order of Moose.
L.R.C.P., Licentiate Royal Coll. Physicians.
L.R.C.S., Licentiate Royal Coll. Surgeons.
L.S., Library Science.
lt., lieutenant.
Ltd., Limited.
Luth., Lutheran.
L.V. R.R., Lehigh Valley R.R. Co.

m., marriage ceremony
M., Master.
M.A., Master of Arts.
mag., magazine.
M.Agr., Master of Agriculture.
maj., major.
Man., Manitoba.
M.Arch., Master in Architecture.
math., mathematical.
M.B., Bachelor of Medicine.
M.B.A., Master of Business Administration.
MBS, Mutual Broadcasting System.
M.C., Medical Corps.
M.C.E., Master of Civil Engineering.
M.C.S., Master of Commercial Science.
mcht., merchant.
M.C.R.R., Michigan Central R.R.
M.D., Doctor of Medicine.
M.Di., Master of Didactics.
M.Dip., Master in Diplomacy.
mdse., merchandise.
M.D.V., Doctor of Veterinary Medicine.
M.E., Mechanical Engineer.
mech., mechanical.
M.E. Ch., Methodist Episcopal Church.
M.Ed., Master of Education.
med., medical.
Med. O.R.C., Medical Officers' Reserve Corps.
Med. R.C., Medical Reserve Corps.
M.E.E., Master of Electrical Engineering.
mem., member.
Meml., Memorial.
merc., mercantile.
met., metropolitan.
metall., metallurgical.
Met.E., Metallurgical Engineer.
meteorol., meteorological.
Meth., Methodist.
metrol., metrological.
M.F., Master of Forestry.
M.F.A., Master of Fine Arts (carries title of Dr.).
mfg., manufacturing.
mfr., manufacturer.
mgmt., management.
mgr., manager.
M.H.A., Master of Hospital Administration.
M.I., Military Intelligence.

micros., microscopical.
mil., military.
Milw., Milwaukee.
mineral., mineralogical.
M.-K.-T. R.R., Missouri-Kansas-Texas R.R. Co.
M.L., Master of Laws.
M.L.D., Magister Legnum Diplomatic.
M.Litt., Master of Literature.
Mlle., Mademoiselle
M.L.S., Master of Library Science.
Mme., Madame
M.M.E., Master of Mechanical Engineering.
mng., managing.
Moblzn., Mobilization.
M.P., Member of Parliament.
M.Pd., Master of Pedagogy.
M.P.E., Master of Physical Education.
M.P.H., Master of Public Health.
M.P.L., Master of Patent Law.
Mpls., Minneapolis.
M.P. R.R., Missouri Pacific R.R.
M.R.E., Master of Religious Education.
M.S., Master of Science.
M.Sc., Master of Science.
M.S.F., Master of Science of Forestry.
M.S.T., Master of Sacred Theology.
M.& St. L. R.R., Minneapolis & St. Louis R.R. Co.
M.,St.P.& S.S.M. Ry., Minneapolis, St. Paul & Sault Ste. Marie Ry.
M.S.W., Master of Social Work.
Mt., Mount.
MTO, Mediterranean Theater of Operations.
mus., museum; musical.
Mus.B., Bachelor of Music.
Mus.D., Doctor of Music.
Mus. M., Master of Music.
Mut., Mutual.
M.W.A., Modern Woodmen of America.
mycol., mycological.

N., North.
N.A., National Academician; National Army.
N.A.A.C.P., National Association for the Advancement of Colored People.
NACA, National Advisory Committee for Aeronautics.
N.A.D., National Academy of Design.
N.Am., North America.
N.A.M., National Association of Manufacturers.
NASA, National Aeronautics and Space Administration.
nat., national.
NATO, North Atlantic Treaty Organization.
NATOUSA, Northern African Theater of Operations, U.S. Army.
nav., navigation.
N.B., New Brunswick.
NBC, National Broadcasting Company.
N.,C.& St.L. Ry., Nashville, Chattanooga & St. Louis Ry.
NDRC, National Defense Research Committee.
N.E., Northeast.
N.E.A., National Education Association.
neurol., neurological.
New Eng., New England.
N.G., National Guard.
NIH, National Institutes of Health.
NLRB, National Labor Relations Bd.
No., Northern.
NPA, National Production Authority.
N.P. Ry., Northern Pacific Ry.
nr., near.
NRA, National Recovery Administrn.
NRC, National Research Council.
N.S., Nova Scotia.
NSC, National Security Council.
NSF, National Science Foundation.
NSRB, National Security Resources Board.
N.T., New Testament.
numis., numismatic.
N.W., Northwest.
N.& W. Ry., Norfolk & Western Ry.
N.Y.C., New York City.
N.Y.C. RR., New York Central R.R. Co.
N.Y.,C.& St.L. R.R., New York, Chicago & St. Louis R.R. Co.
N.Y.,N.H.& H. R.R., New York, New Haven & Hartford R.R. Co.
N.Y.,O.& W. Ry., New York, Ontario & Western Ry.

OAS, Organization of American States.
O.B., Bachelor of Oratory.
obs., observatory.
obstet., obstetrical.
OCDM, Office of Civil and Defense Mobilization.
ODM, Office of Defense Mobilization.
OECD, Organization European Cooperation and Development.
OEEC, Organization European Economic Cooperation.
O.E.S., Order of the Eastern Star.
ofcl., official.
Ont., Ontario.
OPA, Office of Price Administration.
ophthal., ophthalmological.
OPM, Office of Production Management.
OPS, Office of Price Stabilization.
O.Q.M.G., Office of Quartermaster General.
O.R.C., Officers' Reserve Corps.
orch., orchestra.
orgn., organization.
ornithol., ornithological.
O.S.L. R.R., Oregon Short Line R.R.
OSRD, Office of Scientific Research and Development.
OSS, Office of Strategic Services.
osteo., osteopathic.
O.T., Old Testament.
O.T.C., Officers' Training Camp.
otol., otological.
otolaryn., otolaryngological.
O.T.S., Officers' Training School.
O.U.A.M., Order United American Mechanics.
OWI, Office of War Information.
O.-W.R.R.&N. Co., Oregon-Washington R.R. & Navigation Co.
Oxon., Of or pertaining to Oxford University, Eng.

paleontol., paleontological.
Pa. R.R., Pennsylvania R.R.
path., pathological.
Pd.B., Bachelor of Pedagogy.
Pd.D., Doctor of Pedagogy.
Pd.M., Master of Pedagogy.
P.E., Protestant Episcopal.
Pe.B., Bachelor of Pediatrics.
P.E.I., Prince Edward Island.
P.E.N., Poets, Playwrights, Editors, Essayists and Novelists (Internat. Assn.).
penol., penological.
pfc., private first class.
PHA, Public Housing Administration.
pharm., pharmaceutical.
Pharm.D., Doctor of Pharmacy.
Pharm.M., Master of Pharmacy.
Ph.B., Bachelor of Philosophy.
Ph.C., Pharmaceutical Chemist.
Ph.D., Doctor of Philosophy.
Ph.G., Graduate in Pharmacy.
Phila., Philadelphia.
philol., philological.
philos., philosophical.
photog., photographic.
phys., physical.
Phys. and Surg., Physicians and Surgeons (College at Columbia U.).
physiol., physiological.
P.I., Philippine Islands.
Pitts., Pittsburgh.
Pkwy., Parkway.
Pl., Place.
P.& L.E. R.R., Pittsburgh & Lake Erie R.R.
P.M. R.R., Pere Marquette R.R. Co.
P.O., Post Office.
polit., political.
poly., polytechnic; polytechnical.
pomol., pomological.
P.Q., Province of Quebec.
P.R., Puerto Rico.
prep., preparatory.
pres., president.
Presbyn., Presbyterian.
presdl., presidential.
prin., principal.
proc., proceedings.
prod., produced (play production).
prodn., production.
prof., professor.
profl. professional.
prog., progressive.
propr., proprietor.
pros. atty., prosecuting attorney.
pro tem, pro tempore (for the time being).
psychiat., psychiatric.

TABLE OF ABBREVIATIONS

psychol., psychological.
P.T.A., Parent-Teacher Association.
PTO, Pacific Theater of Operations.
pub., public; publisher; publishing; published.
publ., publication.
pvt., private.
PWA, Public Works Administration.

q.m., quartermaster.
Q.M.C., Quartermaster Corps.
Q.M.O.R.C., Quartermaster Officers' Reserve Corps.
quar., quarterly.
Que., Quebec (province).
radiol., radiological.
RAF, Royal Air Force.
R.A.M., Royal Arch Mason.
R.C., Roman Catholic; Reserve Corps.
RCA, Radio Corporation of America.
RCAF, Royal Canadian Air Force.
Rd., Road.
R.D., Rural Delivery.
R.E., Reformed Episcopal.
rec., recording.
ref., reformed.
regt., regiment.
regtl., regimental.
rehab., rehabilitation.
Rep., Republican.
rep., representative.
Res., Reserve.
ret., retired.
Rev., Reverend.
rev., review, revised.
RFC, Reconstruction Finance Corp.
R.F.D., Rural Free Delivery.
rhinol., rhinological.
R.N., Registered Nurse.
röntgenol., röntgenological
R.O.S.C., Reserve Officers' Sanitary Corps.
R.O.T.C., Reserve Officers' Training Corps.
R.P., Reformed Presbyterian.
R.R., Railroad.
R.T.C., Reserve Training Corps.
Ry., Railway.

s., son.
S., South.
S.A., (Spanish) Sociedad Anonima; (French) Societe Anonyme.
SAC, Strategic Air Command.
S.A.L. Ry., Seaboard Air Line Ry.
S.Am., South America.
san., sanitary.
S.A.R., Sons of the Am. Revolution.
Sask., Saskatchewan.
S.A.T.C., Student's Army Training Corps.
Sat.Eve.Post, Saturday Evening Post.
savs., savings.
S.B., Bachelor of Science.
SCAP, Supreme Command Allies Pacific.
Sc.B., Bachelor of Science.
Sc.D., Doctor of Science.
S.C.D., Doctor of Commercial Science.
sch., school.
sci., science; scientific.
S.C.V., Sons of Confederate Veterans.
S.E., Southeast.
SEATO, Southeast Asia Treaty Organization.
SEC, Securities and Exchange Commn.
sec., secretary.
sect., section.
seismol., seismological.
sem., seminary.
sgt. (or **sergt.**), sergeant.
SHAEF, Supreme Headquarters, Allied Expeditionary Forces.
SHAPE, Supreme Headquarters Allied Powers in Europe.
S.I., Staten Island.
S.J., Society of Jesus (Jesuit).
S.J.D., Doctor Juristic Science.
S.M., Master of Science.
So., Southern.
soc., society.
sociol., sociological.
SOS, Services of Supply.
S.P. Co., Southern Pacific Co.
spl., special.
splty., specialty.
Sq., Square.
sr., senior.
S.R., Sons of the Revolution.
S.S., Steamship.
SSS, Selective Service System.
St., Saint; Street.
sta., station.
statis., statistical.
S.T.B., Bachelor of Sacred Theology.
Stblzn., Stabilization.
S.T.D., Doctor of Sacred Theology.
S.T.L., Licentiate in Sacred Theology; Lector of Sacred Theology.
St.L.-S.F. R.R., St. Louis-San Francisco Ry. Co.
supr., supervisor.
supt., superintendent.
surg., surgical.
S.W., Southwest.

T.A.P.P.I., Technical Association Pulp and Paper Industry.
Tb (or **TB**), Tuberculosis.
tchr., teacher.
tech., technical; technology.
technol., technological.
Tel.&Tel., Telephone and Telegraph
temp., temporary.
Ter., Territory.
T.H., Territory of Hawaii.
Th.D., Doctor of Theology.
Th.M., Master of Theology.
theol., theological.
tng., training.
topog., topographical.
T.&P. Ry., Texas & Pacific Ry. Co.
trans., transactions; transferred.
transl., translation.
transp., transportation.
treas., treasurer.
TV, Television.
TVA, Tennessee Valley Authority.
Twp., Township.
Ty., Territory.
typog., typographical.

U., University.
UAR, United Arab Republic.
U.A.W., International Union United Automobile, Aircraft, and Agricultural Implement Workers of America-AFL-CIO.
U.B., United Brethren in Christ.
U.D.C., United Daughters of the Confederacy.
U.K., United Kingdom.
UN, United Nations.
UNESCO, United Nations Educational, Scientific and Cultural Organization.
UNICEF, United Nations International Childrens Emergency Fund.
univ., university.
UNRRA, United Nations Relief and Rehabilitation Administration.
U.P., United Presbyterian.
U.P.I., United Press International.
U.P. R.R., Union Pacific R.R.
urol., urological.
U.S., United States.
U.S.A., United States of America.
USAAF, United States Army Air Force.
USAC, United States Air Corps.
USAF, United States Air Force.
USCG, United States Coast Guard.
USES, United States Employment Service.
USIA, United States Information Agency.
USIS, United States Information Service.
USMC, United States Marine Corps.
USMHS, United States Marine Hospital Service.
USN, United States Navy.
U.S.N.A., United States National Army.
U.S.N.G., United States National Guard.
USNR, United States Naval Reserve.
USNRF, United States Naval Reserve Force.
U.S.O., United Service Organizations.
USOM, United States Operations Mission.
USPHS, United States Public Health Service.
U.S.S., United States Ship.
USSR, Union of Soviet Socialist Republics.
U.S.V., United States Volunteers.

VA, Veterans Administration.
vet., veteran; veterinary.
V.F.W., Veterans of Foreign Wars.
V.I., Virgin Islands.
vice pres., vice president.
vis., visiting.
vol., volunteer; volume.
v.p., vice president.
vs., versus.

W., West.
WAC, Women's Army Corps.
Wash., Washington (state).
WAVES, Womens Reserve, U.S. Naval Reserve.
W.C.T.U., Women's Christian Temperance Union.
WHO, World Health Organization (of the UN).
W.I., West Indies.
W.& L.E. Ry., Wheeling & Lake Erie Ry. Co.
WPA, Works Progress Administration.
WPB, War Production Board.
W.P. R.R. Co., Western Pacific R.R. Co.
WSB, Wage Stabilization Board.

YMCA, Young Men's Christian Assn.
YMHA, Young Men's Hebrew Assn.
YM and YWHA, Young Men's and Young Women's Hebrew Assn.
Y.&M.V. R.R., Yazoo & Mississippi Valley R.R.
YWCA, Young Women's Christian Assn.

zoöl., zoölogical.

WHO WAS WHO IN AMERICA

HISTORICAL VOLUME

1607—1896

BIOGRAPHIES

ABBETT, Leon, gov. N.J.; b. Phila., Oct. 8, 836; s. Ezekiel and Sarah (Howell) A.; ed. Central ligh Sch., Phila.; m. Mary Briggs, Oct. 8, 1862. admitted to Phila. bar, 1858; corp. atty., Hoboken, J., 1863; elected to N.J. Assembly, 1864-66, 69, 0; mem. N.J. Senate from Hudson County, 1874-7, pres. Senate, 1877; gov. N..J, 1883-85, 89-93; pptd. judge N.J. Supreme Ct. by Gov. Werts, 1893. ied Jersey City, N.J., Dec. 4, 1894.

ABBEY, Henry Eugene, impressario; b. Akron, O., une 27, 1846; s. Henry Stephen and Elizabeth Smith) A.; m. Kate Kingsley, 1876, 2 children; n. 2d, Florence Gerard, 1886. Acquired Acad. Muic, Buffalo, N.Y., 1876; introduced Sarah Bernhardt o Am., 1880; mgr. Met. Opera House, N.Y.C., 1883-4, 91-96; mgr. Am. tours of Adelina Patti and The ondon Gaity, 1889-90; opened Abbey's Theatre, 893; one of 1st theatrical mgrs. to present exensive entertainment outside of large cities. Died .Y.C., Oct. 17, 1896.

ABBOT, Abiel, clergyman; b. Andover, Mass., Aug. 7, 1770; s. John and Abigail Abbot; grad. Harvard, 791; m. Eunice Wales, 1796. Preached at ch., laverhill Mass., 1793-95, pastor, 1795-1803; astor, Beverly, Mass., 1803-28; traveled to Cuba o recover health, 1828. Author: Letters from Cuba, 829. Died of yellow fever on trip home from Cuba, une 7, 1828.

ABBOT, Benjamin, educator; b. Andover, Mass., ept. 17, 1762; s. John Abbot; B.A., Harvard, 1788; n. Hannah Tracy Emery, Nov. 1, 1791; m. 2d, Mary erkins, 1798; 4 children. Prin., Phillips Exeter (Mass.) Acad., 1788-1838, taught Latin, Greek, nathematics (his pupils included Lewis Cass, Daniel Webster, Edward Everett, Jared Sparks, Francis Bowen); received tribute (given by Webster) at his etirement. Died Exeter, Oct. 25, 1849.

ABBOT, Ezra, Bibl. scholar; b. Jackson, Me., Apr. 8, 1819; s. Ezra and Phoebe A.; grad. Bowdoin Coll., 1840, M.A., 1843; LL.D., Yale, 1869; D.D., Harvard, 1872. Taught high sch., Cambridgeport, Mass., 1847; mem. Am. Oriental Soc., 1852, reording sec., 1853; mem. library staff Boston Athenaeum; mem. library staff Harvard, asst. librarian, 1856; mem. Am. Acad. Arts and Scis., 1861; ectr. on textual criticism of New Testament, Harvard, 1871, Bussey prof. Divinity Sch., 1872; mem. New Testament Com. for Revision of English Bible, 1871. Editor: Critical History of the Doctrine of a Future Life, 1864; Church of the First Three Centuries, 1865. Died Cambridge, Mass., Mar. 21, 1884.

ABBOT, Gorham Dummer, clergyman, educator;). Brunswick, Me., Sept. 3, 1807; s. Jacob and Betsey (Abbot) Abbot; grad. Bowdoin Coll., 1826; attended Andover Theol. Sem.; m. Rebecca S. Leach, Feb. 11, 1834. Helped conduct Mt. Vernon Sch. for Girls (with brother Jacob), Boston, 1831-33; ordained to ministry Presbyn. Ch., 1837; pastor Presbyn. Ch., New Rochelle, N.Y., 1837-41; helped in movement to supply schs. with textbooks, libraries and ednl. journals; with literary dept. Am. Tract Soc., 1841-43; a founder girls sch., N.Y.C., 1843; later took 40 of his pupils and established Spingler Inst. for Girls, N.Y., heavily endowed by Americans and Europeans until 1870; influenced Matthew Vassar in education of women; ret. to South Natick, Mass., 1870. Author: The Family at Home; or, Familiar Illustrations of the Various Domestic Duties, 1834; Mexico and the United States, Their Mutual Relations and Common Interests, 1869. Died South Natick, Aug. 3, 1874.

ABBOT, Joel, naval officer; b. Westford, Mass., Jan. 18, 1793; s. Joel and Lydia (Cummings) A.; m. Mary Wood, Jan. 1820; m. 2d, Laura Wheaton, Nov. 29, 1825; 10 children. Apptd. midshipman U.S. Navy, 1812; served under Commodore John Rodgers in frigate President, 1812; captured by English while acting officer of ship, 1813, exchanged; served in Commodore Thomas Macdonough's squadron on Lake Champlain; on spl. mission disguised as Brit. officer destroyed large supply ships' parts; took part in Battle of Lake Champlain, 1814, received sword of honor from Congress for his service there; commd. lt., 1818; discovered frauds against U.S. Govt. while on duty at Charleston (S.C.) Navy Yard, 1822, preferred charges on his commandant Capt. Isaac Hull, offered no proof, court martialed and suspended 2 years; commd. capt., 1850; picked by Commodore M.C. Perry to command frigate Macedonian in fleet in expdn. to Japan, 1852, visited Japanese, Bonin, Philippine, Formosa islands; made comdg. officer of fleet on his return to U.S. Died Hongkong, China, Dec. 14, 1855.

ABBOTT, Amos, congressman; b. Andover, Mass., Sept. 10, 1786; attended Bradford Acad. Became a mcht.; hwy. surveyor, 1812, 14, 16; town clk., 1822, 26, 28; town treas., 1824-29; mem. sch. com., 1828-29, 30; a founder Boston Portland R.R. (now Boston & Me. R.R.), 1833, dir., 1833-41; mem. Mass. Ho. of Reps., 1835, 36, 37, 43, mem. Mass. Senate, 1840-42; mem. U.S. Ho. of Reps. (Whig) from Mass., 28th-30th congresses, 1843-49. Died Andover, Nov. 2, 1868; buried South Parish Cemetery.

ABBOTT, Austin, lawyer; b. Boston, Dec. 18, 1831; s. Jacob Abbott; grad. N.Y. U., 1851; LL.D. (hon.), U. City N.Y., 1887; m. Ella E.D. Gilman, 1854; m. 2d, Mrs. Anna Rowe Worth, 1879. Admitted to bar, N.Y.C., 1852; partner firm Abbott Bros., 1852-70; assisted commrs. in preparing codes of N.Y., 1865; govt. counsel in prosecution of Charles J. Guiteau, assassinator of Pres. James A. Garfield, 1881; dean law sch. U. N.Y., also prof. pleading, equity and evidence, 1891-96. Author: (fiction) Come Cut Corners; the Experiences of a Conservative Family in Fanatical Times, 1855; (with bro. Benjamin) Reports of Practice Cases Determined in the Courts of the State of New York, 1st vol., 1855; (fiction, in collaboration with bros., under pseudonym Benauly) Matthew Caraby, 1859; Reports of Decisions of the Court of Appeals of New York, 1850-69, 4 vols. 1873-74; New Cases, Courts of the State of New York, 31 vols. covering 1876-94; Abbott's Digest of New York Statutes and Reports (new edit.), 6 vols., 1873; Official Report of the Trial of Henry Ward Beecher, 2 vols., 1875; also numerous briefs and other legal writings, 1875-95. Died N.Y.C., Apr. 19, 1896.

ABBOTT, Benjamin, evangelist; b. Pa., 1732; s. Benjamin and Mrs. (Burroughs) A. Hatter's apprentice, Phila.; worked on his brother's farm, N.J.; addicted to card-playing, cock-fighting, drinking, brawling; converted to Methodism by preaching of Abraham Whitworth, 1772; became local preacher; ordained deacon, 1790, elder and circuit preacher, 1793; attacked Calvinism, preached Methodism as only means of salvation; converted much of Southern N.J. to Methodism. Died Salem, N.J., Aug. 14, 1796.

ABBOTT, Benjamin Vaughan, lawyer; b. Boston, June 4, 1830; son of Jacob Abbott; grad. U. N.Y., 1850; attended Harvard Law Sch., 1851; m. Elizabeth Litcomb, 1853. Admitted to N.Y. bar, 1852, practiced in partnership with brother Austin; sec. N.Y. Code Commn., 1864, drew up penal code (basis for law now existing); a commr. to revise statutes of U.S., 1870-72. Author: (fiction, with his brothers) Come Cut Corners; the Experiences of a Conservative Family in Fanatical Times, 1855, Matthew Caraby (under pseudonym Benauly), 1859; (with Austin Abbott) Abbott's Reports of Practice Cases in the Courts of the State of New York, 1855, Reports of cases in Admiralty, United States District Court for Southern New York, 1847-50, published 1857, A Collection of Forms of Pleadings in Actions, 1858; Digest of New York Statutes and Reports, 5 vols., 1860; A Collector of Forms of Practice and Pleading in Actions, 1864; The Clerk's and Conveyancer's Assistant, 1866; Digest of the Reports of the United States Courts and Acts of Congress, 4 vols., 1867; General Digest of the Law of Corporations, 1869; Digest of Reports of Indiana to the Year 1871; Reports of Decisions Rendered in the Circuit and District Courts of the United States, 1863-71, 2 vols., 1870-71; United States Digest, 14 vols., 1879; Dictionary of Terms and Phrases used in American or English Jurisprudence, 1879; General Digest of English and American Cases on the Law of Corporations, 1868-78, published 1879; National Digest, 4 vols. (U.S. ct. decisions of year 1884, supplement published 1889), 1884; The Patent Laws of All Nations, 2 vols., 1886; Decisions on the Law of Patents for Inventions, English Cases, 1662-1843, 3 vols., 1887. Died Bklyn., Feb. 17, 1890.

ABBOTT, Emma, soprano; b. Chgo., Dec. 9, 1850 d. Seth and Almira (Palmer) Abbott; studied under Achille Errani, N.Y.C., circa 1870, later under Sangiovanni, Milan, Italy, under Delle Sedie, Paris, France; m. Eugene Wetherell, 1878. Made debut as guitar player and singer, Peoria, Ill., 1859; met Clara Louise Kellogg, Toledo, O., 1867, encouraged by her to go to N.Y.C.; became soprano at Ch. of Divine Paternity, circa 1870; appeared as Marie in Daughter of the Regiment, Convent Garden, London, Eng., 1876; returned to N.Y.C., formed Abbott English Opera Co., managed by Eugene Wetherell, toured the country; became popular for the "Abbott kiss"; played leading roles in operas including La Traviata, Romeo and Juliette, Paul and Virginia, H.M.S. Pinafore, Martha, Sonnambula. Died Salt Lake City, Utah, Jan. 5, 1891.

ABBOTT, Frank, dentist, educator; b. Shapleigh, Me., Sept. 5, 1836; studied dentistry with Dr. J.E.

Ostrander, Onedia, N.Y., 1855; M.D., U. City N.Y., 1871; m. Catharine Ann Cuyler, 3 children. Practised dentistry, Johnstown, N.Y., 1858; served as 1st lt. 115th N.Y. Volunteer Inf., U.S. Army, Civil War, captured at Harper's Ferry, 1862, exchanged, returned to practice dentsitry; moved to N.Y.C., 1863; became clin. lectr. N.Y. Coll. of Dentistry, 1866, prof. operative dentistry, 1868, dean, 1869-97, failed in attempts to establish chairs of pathology and bacteriology (with his son as incumbent) and substitution of new charter for the act of incorporation of U. State N.Y., 1894-95; pres. Am. Dental Assn., 1888; pres. Nat. Assn. Dental Faculties, 1895. Author: Dental Pathology and Practice (textbook), 1896. Died Apr. 20, 1897.

ABBOTT, Horace, iron mfr.; b. Sudbury, Mass., July 29, 1806; s. Alpheus and Lydia (Fay) A.: m. Charlotte Hapgood, 1830, 7 children. Owner Canton Iron Works, Balt., specialized in prodn. wrought iron shafts, cranks, axles and other equipment for steamboats, railroads; constructed a rolling-mill capable of turning out the largest rolled plate in the U.S., 1850, other mills erected 1857, 59, 61; made armor plates for the Monitor and for nearly all vessels of Monitor class constructed on the Atlantic Coast; elected pres. Abbott Iron Co., 1865; a founder Balt. 1st Nat. Bank; dir. 2d Nat. Bank, Balt. Copper Co., Union R.R. of Balt. Died Aug. 8, 1887.

ABBOTT, Jacob, educator, writer; b. Hallowell, Me., Nov. 14, 1803; s. Jacob II and Betsey Abbot; grad. Bowdoin Coll., 1820; studied theology Andover (Me.) Sem., 1821-22,24; m. Harriet Vaughan, May 18, 1829; m. 2d, Mrs. Mary Dana Woodbury, 1853; at least 1 son, Edward. Tchr., Portland (Me. Acad. (Henry Wadsworth Longfellow was one of his pupils), 1820-21; tchr., Beverly, Mass., 1823; tutor Amherst Coll., 1824-25, prof. mathematics and natural philosophy, 1825; licensed to preach by Hampshire Assn., Congregationalist Ch., 1826; moved to Bsoton, 1828; founder, prin. Mt. Vernon Sch. (one of earliest schs. for young women, largely self-governing), 1828-33; minister Eliot Congregational Ch., Roxbury, Mass., 1834-35; founder (with his brothers) Abbott's Instn., N.Y.C., 1843-51, Mt. Vernon Sch. for Boys, 1845-48; sole author of 180 volumes, joint author of 31 vols.; books include: The Young Christian (1st important work), 1832; The Corner Stone (became subject of controversy because of emphasis on Unitarianism, changed wording in later edits. to clarify meanings), 1834; Rollo series (stories for elementary instrn. of children), 28 vols., begun 1834. Died Farmington, Me., Oct. 31, 1879.

ABBOTT, Joel, congressman; b. Fairfield, Conn., Mar. 17, 1776; studied medicine under father in Fairfield. Began practice medicine in Washington, Ga., 1794; held several local offices; mem. Ga. Ho. of Reps., 1809, twice re-elected; mem. U.S. Ho. of Reps. (Democrat) from Ga., 15th-18th congresses, 1817-25; del. to conv. in Phila. which met to prepare 1st Nat. Pharmacopoeia, 1820. Died Washington, Ga., Nov. 19, 1826; buried Rest Haven Cemetery.

ABBOTT, John Stevens Cabot, author, clergyman; b. Brunswick, Me., Sept. 18, 1805; s. Jacob and Betsey Abbot; grad. Bowdoin Coll., 1825, Andover Theol. Sem., 1829; m. Jane Williams Bourne, Aug. 17, 1830, 1 child. Ordained to ministry Congregational Ch., Worcester, Mass., 1830; pastor Central Calvinistic Ch., Worcester, 1829-34, Eliot Congregational Ch., Roxbury, Mass., 1835-41, First Congl. Ch., Nantucket, Mass.; taught at Abbott's Instn., N.Y.C., 1843-53; made trips to France in 1859, 67, became friends with Emperor Louis Napoleon; pastor Howe Street Ch., New Haven, Conn., 1861-66, Second Ch., Fair Haven, Conn., 1870-74. Author: The Mother at Home, or the Principles of Maternal Duty Familiarly Illustrated (his 1st work), 1833; The History of Napoleon Bonaparte, 1855; The Empire of Austria, 1859; The Empire of Russia, 1860; Italy, 1860; Practical Christianity, 1862; Civil War in America, 2 vols., 1863, 66; History of Frederick the Great, 1871; Pioneers and Patriots of America (last work), circa 1872. Died Fair Haven, June 17, 1877.

ABBOTT, Joseph Carter, journalist, senator, govt. ofcl.; b. Concord, N.H., July 15, 1825; s. Aaron and Nancy (Badger) A.; grad. Phillips Acad., Andover, Mass. Admitted to N.H. bar, 1852; adj. gen. N.H., 1860; owner, editor Manchester Daily American, 1852-57; editor Boston Atlas and Bee, 1859-61; among the 1st to offer troops to Pres. Lincoln, 1861; commd. lt. col. 7th Regt., N.H. Volunteers, later col.; brevetted brig. gen., 1865; mem. N.C. Constl. Conv., 1868; mem. U.S. Senate from N.C., 1868-71; lumber mfr, Wilmington, N.C.; editor Wilmington Post, 1871-81; collector Port of Wilmington under Pres. Grant; U.S. insp. of ports under Pres. Hayes. Died Wilmington, Oct. 8, 1882.

ABBOTT, Josiah Gardner, congressman, lawyer; b. Chelmsford, Middlesex County, Mass., Nov. 1, 1814; grad. Harvard, 1832; studied law. Sch. tchr.; admitted to Mass. bar, 1835, began practice law, Lowell, Mass., 1837; mem. Mass. Ho. of Reps., 1836, Mass. Senate, 1841, 42; mem. staff of Gov. Morton, 1843; master in chancery, 1850-55; mem. Mass. Constl. Conv., 1853; justice superior ct. of Suffolk County, 1855-58; overseer of Harvard, 1859-65; declined appointment to Supreme Ct., 1860; moved to Boston, 1861; mem. U.S. Ho. of Reps. (Democrat, contested election) from Mass., 44th Congress, July 28, 1876-77; apptd. mem. Electoral Commn. to decide contests in various states in presdl. election of 1876, 1877; held mfg. and other interests in addition to practice law. Died Wellesley Hills (nr. Boston), June 2, 1891; buried St. Mary's Cemetery, Newton Lower Falls, Mass.

ABBOTT, Nehemiah, congressman, lawyer; b. Sidney, Me., Mar. 29, 1804; studied law at Litchfield (Conn.) Law Sch. Admitted to bar, 1836, began practice in Calais, Me.; moved to Columbus, Miss., 1839; returned to Me., 1840; began practice law, Belfast, Me., 1840; mem. Me. Ho. of Reps., 1842, 43, 45; mem. U.S. Ho. of Reps. (Republican) from Me., 35th Congress, 1857-59; city mayor, 1865-66. Died Belfast, July 26, 1877; buried Grove Cemetery.

ABBOTT, William, theatrical mgr. With Haymarket Theatre, London, Eng.; became mgr. New Charleston Theater, Charleston, S.C., 1837-41, brought distinguished stars including Ellen Tree, Booth, Cooper, Vandenhoff, to Charleston, maintained excellent resident company.

ABBOTT, William Hawkins, oil producer; b. Middlebury, Conn., Oct. 27, 1819; s. David and Hannah (Hawkins) A.; m. Jane Wheeler, Sept. 1845. Clk., gen. store, Watertown, Conn., circa 1837-44; moved to Newton Falls, O., entered gen. merc. bus., 1845; partner in store Bronson & Abbott, 1846-47, sole owner, 1848-62, also in real estate bus., 1848-62; became interested in oil (discovered in Pa. circa 1860), leased farm where well was being drilled; went to N.Y. (after well produced oil), sold 200 barrels oil at 35¢ per gallon to Schieffelin Bros. (marked beginning of oil trade); a builder of 1st refinery at Titusville, Pa., 1861; moved to Titusville, 1862, brought in coal for domestic use (1st retail coal bus.); engaged in coal mining, 1865; organized co., built Titusville and Pitt-Hole plank road at cost of $200,000, 1865; formed (with Henery Harley) Pa. Transp. Co. (1st oil pipe-line consolidation), 1867; helped revive interest in Union & Titusville R.R. Co., 1870 (opened 1871); pres. Citizens Bank of Titusville. Died Jan. 8, 1901.

ABEEL, David, missionary; b. New Brunswick, N.J., June 12, 1804; s. Capt. David and Jane (Hassert) A.; grad. New Brunswick Sem., 1826. Began study of medicine, changed to religion; ordained minister Dutch Reformed Ch., Athens, N.Y., 1826, pastor, 1826-28; went to island of St. John, West Indies to recover health, winter 1828-29; apptd. chaplain Seamen's Friend Soc.; left N.Y. on ship Roman 1829, arrived Canton, China, 1830; joined Am. Bd. Commrs. for Fgn. Missions, 1831, visited Java, Malacca, Siam, Singapore; visited Eng., Switzerland, France, Germany, Holland, 1833-34; founded Soc. for Promoting Female Edn. in China and the East, in Eng.; returned to Am. to secure Dutch Reformed missionaries, 1835-38; visited Malay Archipelago, 1839; established mission station, Amoy, China, 1841. Author: To the Bachelors of India, by a Bachelor, 1833; A Narrative of Residence in China, 1834; The Claims of the World to the Gospel, 1838. Died Albany, N.Y., Sept. 4, 1846.

ABELL, Arunah Shepherdson, journalist; b. East Providence, R.I., Aug. 10, 1806; s. Caleb and Elona (Shepherdson) A.; m. Mary Fox, 1838, 8 children. Apprenticed by his father to Providence Patriot, 1822; started Public Ledger, Phila., 1836; issued 1st number Balt. Sun, 1837, continued as sole propr., 1868; established daily pony express from New Orleans, 1847; 1st to use telegraphy to transmit news, 1st to buy Hoe cylinder press. Died Balt., Apr. 19, 1888.

ABERCROMBIE, James, congressman; b. Hancock County, Ga., 1795; studied law. Moved to Monroe (now Dallas) County, Ala., 1812, to Montgomery County, Ala., 1819; served as cpl. Maj. F. Freeman's Squadron, Ga. Cav., War of 1812; mem. Ala. Ho. of Reps., 1820-22, 24, 38, 39; capt. Ala. Militia, commanded cavalry at reception for Gen. Lafayette, 1825; mem. Ala. Senate, 1825-33, 47-50; moved to Russell County, 1834; mem. U.S. Ho. of Reps. (Union Whig) from Ala., 32d-33d congresses, 1851-55; moved to Fla., 1856; became govt. brick contractor. Died Pensacola, Fla., July 2, 1861; buried Linwood Cemetery, Columbus, Ga.

ABERCROMBY, James, army officer; b. Glassaugh, Banffshire, Scotland, 1706; s. Alexander and Helen (Meldrum) A.; m. Mary Duff, 1 son, James. Mem. Parliament for Banff, 1734-54; King's painter in Scotland; dep. gov. Stirling Castle; lt. col. 1st Battalion Royal Scots, 1746; 2d in command Brit. Army in Am., commd. maj. gen., 1756; supreme comdr. all Brit. forces in Am., col.-in-chief Royal Am. Regt., 1758; ordered attack on Ft. Ticonderoga, N.Y., July 8, 1758, defeated; recalled to Eng 1758; commd. lt. gen., 1759 gen., 1772. Died Sti ling, Scotland, Apr. 23, 1781.

ABERNETHY, George, mcht., 1st provisional go Ore.; b. N.Y.C., Oct. 7, 1807; m. Anne Cope, Ja 21, 1830. Mcht., bought wheat, traded supplie considered most important Am. businessman of Paci ic N.W., for many years; established 1st newspap in Ore.; established comml. connections with Hawai Cal., Atlantic coast ports; 1st provisional gov. Ore 1845-48. Died Portland, Ore., May 2, 1877.

ABERT, James William, topog. artist; b. Nov. 1 1820, Mt. Holly, N.J.; grad. U.S. Mil. Acad., 184 Served with Topog. Engrs. Corps, U.S. Army; ma several expdns. into West, illustrated reports expdns. with sketches; asst. in drawing U.S. Mi Acad., 1848-50; engaged in improvement of Weste rivers, circa 1850-60; served with Union Army durir Civil War, wounded, ret. as col., 1864; became pro mathematics and drawing U. Mo. after Civil Wa his original watercolors are now privately owne Died 1871.

ABERT, John James, topog. engr.; b. Shepherds town, Va., Sept. 17, 1788; s. John and Margari (Meng) A.; grad. U.S. Mil. Acad., 1811; m. Elle Matlack Stretch, Jan. 5, 1812, 6 children includir James William, Silvanus Thayer, William Stretc Asst. to chief clk. War Office, 1811-14; admitted t D.C. bar, 1813; volunteer in D.C. Militia, 1814 served in battle of Bladensburg; apptd. maj. Topog Engrs., U.S. Army, 1814; assisted in geodetic su veys Atlantic coast, 1816-18; made topog. survey for river and harbor improvements, canals and de fense; brevetted lt. col., 1824; in charge of Topog Bur., War Dept., 1829-31, chief Topog. Bur. (aft its creation as separate br. of War Dept.), 1831, 34 61; commr. for Indian affairs, 1832-34; promote to col. when Topog. Engrs. became a staff corps army, 1838; founder, dir. Nat. Inst. Sci., Washing ton, D.C.; mem. Geog. Soc. of Paris; mem. bd. vis itors U.S. Mil. Acad., 1842. Died Washington, Jar 27, 1863.

ACCAU (ACCAULT), Michel, see Aco, Michel.

ACO, Michel, explorer; b. Potiers, France; m Mary (Christian name of dau. Indian chief Rou ensa), 1693, at least 2 children, Pierre, Michel With Robert La Salle in expdn. in Mississipp Valley, 1679-80, knew language Illinois and Iro quois tribes, able to communicate with Iowa, Ot Chippewa and Kickapoo tribes; sent by La Sall with 2 others to explore Upper Mississippi, 1680 captured by Sioux near St. Anthony Falls, Minn. rescued by Daniel Du Shut (French explorer and brought to mouth Wisconsin River; fron there went up Wisconsin River to Fox River, dow that to Green Bay and Machinac; went to Mon treal, 1681, traded furs collected on journey; i Misssissippi Valley again as business partn with 2 friends, 1693; connected in trade wit fort in Ill. on Lake Peoria. Flourished 1680-1702

ACRELIUS, Israel, clergyman; b. Oster-Aker Sweden, Dec. 4, 1714; s. Johan and Sara Acrelius attended U. Upsala (Sweden), 1727-43; m. Katarina Elisabet Strangh, 1759. Ordained to ministr Lutheran Ch., 1743; pastor, Riala, Kulla, Norr Ljustero, Sweden, 1745; pastor, Christina (no Wilmington, Del.), 1749-56; provost Swedish congregations in New Sweden (now Del.), 1749-56 learned English lang., aided German Lutherans i Pa.; made zool., bot. and geol. collections; returned to Sweden, 1756; pastor, Fellingsboro Sweden, 1758. Author: History of New Swede (treats of eccles. matters, gen. history of area unde Swedish, Dutch and English control), 1759. Die Apr. 25, 1800.

ADAIR, James, Indian trader, author; b. County Antrim, Ireland, circa 1709. Came to Am., circa 1735; traded with Catawba and Cherokee Indians 1735-44, with Choctaw Indians, 1744-51; moved t dist. 96, Laurens County, S.C., 1751; commande band of Chickasaws as capt. during Indian War 1760-61. Author: The History of the America Indians (maintaining Indians are descendants c ancient Jews), 1775. Died N.C., circa 1783.

ADAIR, John, senator, gov. Ky.; b. Chester County, S. C., Jan. 9, 1757; s. Baron William Adair. Settled in Mercer County, Ky., 1786; commd. lt. col Ky. Militia, 1792, later brig. gen.; mem. Ky. Ho. o Reps. from Mercer County, 1793-95, 98, 1800-03 17, speaker, 1801-03; mem. U.S. Senate from Ky. 1805-06, resigned 1806; aide to Gov. Shelby during War of 1812; fought at battles of Thames and New Orleans; gov. Ky., 1820-24; mem. U.S. Ho. of Reps from Ky., 22d Congress, 1831-33, mem. com. or mil. affairs; Adair County (Ky.) named in his honor Died Harrisburg, Ky., May 19, 1840; buried Frankfort, Ky.

ADAMS, Abigail, first lady; b. Weymouth, Mass., Nov. 23, 1744; d. Rev. William and Elizabeth (Quincy) Smith; m. John Adams (2d Pres. U.S.) Oct. 25, 1764, children—John Quincy (6th Pres U.S.), Thomas, Charles, Abby. Two volumes of he ıtters published by her grandson Charles Francis ıdams under titles Letters of Mrs. Adams, the 'ife of John Adams; Familiar Letters of John Adams ıd his wife during the Revolution; letters give ıluable background material of era during wartime, ılso original background of European society; opposing polit. contemporaries argued that she asserted undue polit. influence over her husband. ome: Braintree (now Quincy), Mass. Died of typhoid fever Quincy, Oct. 28, 1818; buried Quincy.

ADAMS, Abijah, journalist; b. Boston, circa 1754; . Lucy Ballard, July 11, 1790, stepson, David C. allard. Trained as a tailor; became clk., bookkeeper ıdependent Chronicle (Jeffersonian jour. controlled y his brother Thomas), Boston, 1799, indicted for bel in controversy over stand taken by paper on lien and Sedition Acts, 1799, escaped with short il sentence, became edtior (with Ebenezer Rhodes), 800; convicted of libel due to offensive comments n jud. conduct of Theophilus Parsons, chief justice lass. Supreme Ct., 1811, pardoned. Died May 18, 816.

ADAMS, Alvin, express co. exec.; b. Andover, Vt., ıne 16, 1804; s. Jonas and Phebe (Hoar) A.; m. ın Rebecca Bridge, Nov. 10, 1831, 1 child. Pioneer ı express bus.; established (with Ephraim Farnsworth) Adams Express Co., 1840, incorporated (with 10,000,000 capital) and became pres., 1854; ought Norwich Route to Boston, 1841, extended gencies to Phila., 1842, later to Balt., Washington (D.C.), Pitts., Cincinnati, Louisville (Ky.), St. ouis; entered Cal. field, 1849, within year opened 5 offices in towns and mining camps; started br. gencies, banking houses, Melbourne and Sydney Australia), 1852. Died Watertown, Mass., Sept. 1, 877.

ADAMS, Andrew, Continental congressman, jurist; . Stratford, Conn., Dec. 11, 1736; s. Samuel and lary (Fairchild) A.; B.A., Yale Coll., 1760, LL.D. hon.), 1796; m. Eunice Canfield. Admitted to onn. bar, 1763; mem. upper house Conn. Gen. Assembly, 1776-77, 82-89; mem. Conn. Council of afety; commd. maj., later col. Conn. Militia; apptd. el. to Continental Congress, 1777; signer Articles f Confederation; asso. judge Conn. Superior Ct., 789, chief justice, 1793-97. Died Litchfield, onn., Nov. 26, 1797.

ADAMS, Benjamin, congressman; b. Mendon, lass., Dec. 16, 1764; grad. Brown U., 1788; tudied law. Admitted to bar, began practice law in xbridge, Mass.; mem. Mass. Ho. of Reps., 1809-4, Mass. Senate, 1814, 15, 22-25; mem. U.S. Ho. f Reps. (Federalist, filled vacancy) from Mass., 4th-16th congresses, Dec. 2, 1816-21. Died Uxbridge, Mar. 28, 1837; buried Prospect Hill emetery.

ADAMS, Charles, diplomat; b. Pomerania, Germany, Dec. 19, 1845; s. Karl Heinrich and Maria . (Markman) Schwanbeck (dropped last name circa 870); m. Margaret Thompson Phelps, circa 1870. 'ought in Civil War; apptd. brig. gen. Colo. Militia, 870; Ute Indian agt. until 1874; post office insp., 874, 82-85; U.S. minister to Bolivia, 1880-82; .S. arbitrator for Bolivia and Chile War confs., rica, Bolivia. Engaged in glass manufacture, mining, mineral water devel. Died Denver, Colo., Aug. 9, 1895.

ADAMS, Charles Baker, naturalist; b. Dorchester, lass., Jan. 11, 1814; s. Charles J. Adams; grad. mherst, 1834; m. Mary Holmes, Feb. 1839. Asst. n Geol. Survey of N.Y., 1836; tutor, lectr. geology mherst, 1837, prof. natural history, astronomy, 847-53; prof. chemistry, natural history Middlebury (Vt.) Coll., 1838-47; state geologist Vt., 845-48. Died Jan. 18, 1853.

ADAMS, Charles Francis, congressman, diplomat;). Boston, Aug. 18, 1807; s. John Quincy (6th Pres. U.S.) and Louisa Catherine (Johnson) A.; grad. Harvard, 1825; m. Abigail Brown, Sept. 5, 1829, children including Henry, Charles Francis. Admitted to Mass. bar, 1829; member of Mass. Senate, 1835-40; founder The Boston Whig, 1846; candidate for vice pres. on Free Soil ticket with Martin Van Buren, 1848; mem. U.S. Ho. of Reps. (Republican) from Mass., 36th-37th congresses, 1859-61; U.S. minister to Eng., 1861-68, an effective diplomat, prevented land rams, two blockade-breaking, armor-plated ships from going to confederacy from Eng.; U.S. arbitrator at Geneva Tribunal to settle Ala. claims under Treaty of Washington, 1871-72. Author: A Whig of the Old School (essay), 1835; Conservatism and Reform, 1860; editor Works of John Adams, 10 vols., 1850-56. Died Boston, Nov. 21, 1886; buried Quincy, Mass.

ADAMS, Charles R., opera singer; b. Charlestown, Mass., Feb. 9, 1834; s. Charles and Eliza Ann (Runey) A.; learned music from Edwin Bruce, Mme. Arnault and R. Mulder, all of Boston. Sang tenor in The Creation with Handel and Haydn Soc., Boston, 1856; toured country and West Indies, 1856-61; sang tenor in Vienna Opera in La Sonnambula; toured Russia and Holland; with Royal Opera, Berlin, Germany for 3 years; prin. tenor Imperial Opera (Hofoper), Vienna, 1867-76; sang opera 2 seasons in Covent Garden, London, 1 season at Royal Opera, Madrid, Spain, 1 season at La Scala, Milan, Italy; with Strakosch Co. in America, 1877-78; in German opera with Mme. Poppenheim and Italian opera with Clara Louise Kellogg, Maria Litta and Annie Louise Cary; sang in 1st Am. performance of Rienzi; greatest roles Manrico, Lohengrin, Rienzi, and Tannhauser; lived in Boston, 1879-1900; taught school, 1880-1900, pupils included Grace Hiltz, Nellie Melba and Emma Eames. Died West Harwich, Cape Cod, Mass., July 4, 1900.

ADAMS, Daniel, physician, author; b. Townsend, Mass., Sept. 29, 1773; s. Daniel and Lydia (Taylor) A.; grad. Dartmouth, 1797, B.M., 1799, M.D., 1799; m. Nancy Mulliken, Aug. 17, 1800. Practiced medicine, Leominster, Mass.; delivered eulogy for George Washington at meml. service in Leominster, 1800; published with Salmon Wilder weekly newspaper Telescope, Mass., 1800-02; moved to Boston, circa 1805, taught at pvt. sch.; edited Med. and Agrl. Register (monthly periodical); moved to Mt. Vernon, N.H., 1813, again practiced medicine; mem. N.H. Senate, 1838-40; moved to Keene, N.H., 1846. Author: The Scholar's Arithmetic, 1801; The Understanding Reader of Knowledge before Oratory, 1805; Geography, or a Description of the World, 1814, 2d edit., 1816; The Monitorial Reader, 1841; Primary Arithmetic, 1848; Bookkeeping, 1849. Died Keene, June 8, 1864.

ADAMS, Daniel Weissiger, lawyer, army officer; b. Lynchburg, Va., 1820; s. George and Anna (Weissiger) A.; ed. U. Va. Began practice law in La., 1842; apptd. mem. mil. bd. to organize La. for war, 1861; apptd. lt. col. inf. Confederate Army, advanced through grades to brig. gen., 1862; comdr. cavalry brigade; comdr. Dist. of Central Ala., 1864; comdr. State of Ala., North of Gulf Dept., 1865; participated in defense of Selma, 1865, in battle at Columbus (Ga.), 1865; resumed law practice, New Orleans, 1865-72. Died New Orleans, June 13, 1872.

ADAMS, Dudley, W., horticulturist, granger; b. Winchendon, Mass., Nov. 30, 1831; s. Joseph Boynton and Hannah (Whitney) A. Tchr. in Mass.; one of 1st settlers of Waukon, Ia., 1852; county assessor, Ia., 1852-62; established Iron Clad Nursery, 1856, one of best tree nurseries in that area; mem. Nat. Grange of Patrons of Husbandry, master, 1873; father of 1st attempt to pass railroad freight legislation; aided in framing proposals for forbidding discrimination in fixing rates introduced into Congress 1873-74, called unconstl. at that time, but passed as constl. in Ia., stimulated nat. and state railroad regulation; moved to Fla., 1875, promoted horticulture; organized and pres. Fla. Hort. Soc. Died Feb. 13, 1897.

ADAMS, Ebenezer, educator; b. Oct. 22, 1765; s. Ephraim and Rebecca (Locke) A.; grad. Dartmouth, 1791; m. Alice Frink, July 9, 1795, 5 children; m. 2d, Beulah Minot, May 17, 1807, 2 children. Became preceptor acad., Leicester, Mass., 1792; 1st prof. mathematics and natural philosophy Phillips Exeter Acad.; prof. langs. Dartmouth, 1809-33; pres. Bible Soc. of N.H. Died Aug 15, 1841.

ADAMS, Edwin, actor; b. Medford, Mass., Feb. 3, 1834. Began stage career with appearance in The Hunchback, Nat. Theatre, Boston, 1853; appeared (with Kate Bateman) in Hamlet, 1860; other roles include appearances in The Serf, 1865, The Dead Heart, Wild Oats, The Lady of Lyons, Narcisse, The Marble Heart; last appearance at Cal. Theatre, San Francisco, May 27, 1876; considered one of America's best light comedians. Died Phila., Oct. 28, 1877.

ADAMS, Eliphalet, clergyman; b. Dedham, Mass., Mar. 26, 1677; s. Rev. William and Mary (Manning) A.; grad. Harvard, 1694; m. Lydia Pygan, Dec. 15, 1709; m. 2d, Elizabeth Wass, Sept. 21, 1751; 6 children. Asst. to Rev. Benjamin Colman at Brattle Street Ch., Boston, 1701-03; ordained, 1709; pastor at New London, Mass., 1709-52; prepared many boys for ministry in his home; missionary to Pequot, Mohegan and Niantic Indians; trustee Yale, 1720-38. Died New London, Oct. 4, 1753.

ADAMS, Frederick W., physician; b. Pawlet, Vt., 1786; grad. Dartmouth, 1822; married twice; at least 1 child. Practiced medicine in vicinity of Barton, Vt., 1822-36; attended med. lectures, Phila., 1835-36; practiced medicine, Montpelier, Vt., 1836-58; made violins as an avocation. Author works on theology including: Theological Criticism; or, Hints of the Philosophy of Man and Nature, 1843. Died Montpelier, Dec. 17, 1858.

ADAMS, Green, congressman; b. Barbourville, Ky., Aug. 20, 1812; studied law. Admitted to bar, practiced law; mem. Ky. Ho. of Reps., 1839; Whig presdl. elector, 1844; mem. U.S. Ho. of Reps. (Whig) from Ky., 30th Congress, 1847-49, (Am. Party) 36th Congress, 1859-61; judge Circuit Ct. of Ky., 1851-56; 6th auditor Treasury Dept., 1861-64; practiced law in Phila.; chief clk. U.S. Ho. of Reps., 44th-46th congresses, 1875-81. Died Phila., Jan. 18, 1884; buried West Laurel Hill Cemetery.

ADAMS, Hannah, author; b. Medfield, Mass., Oct. 2, 1755; d. Thomas and Elizabeth (Clark) Adams. First native Am. female profl. author, wrote: Alphabetical Compendium of the Various Sects Which Have Appeared from the Beginning of the Christian Era to the Present Day, 1784; A Summary History of New England, 1799; The Truth and Excellence of the Christian Religion, 1804; History of the Jews, 1812; Letters on the Gospels, 1826. Died Boston, Dec. 15, 1831; buried Mt. Auburn Cemetery, Cambridge, Mass.

ADAMS, Isaac, inventor, mfr.; b. Rochester, N.H Aug. 16, 1802; s. Benjamin and Elizabeth (Horne) A. Invented Adams Power Press the leading machine used in book binding, 1836-1900), 1827; formed firm I. & S. Adams, 1836. Died July 19, 1883.

ADAMS, James Hopkins, gov. S.C.; b. S.C., Mar. 15, 1812; s. Henry Walker and Mary (Goodwyn) A.; grad. Yale, 1831; m. Jane Margaret Scott, Apr. 1832. Joined S.C. States Rights Party, 1832; mem. S.C. Ho. of Reps., 1834-37, 40-41, 48-49, S.C. Senate, 1850-53; served as brig. gen. S.C. Militia; gov. S.C., 1854-56; elected one of commrs. to U.S. Govt. to negotiate transfer of U.S. property in S.C. to the state govt., Washington, D.C. Died Columbia, S.C., July 13, 1861.

ADAMS, Jasper, clergyman, coll. pres.; b. East Medway, Mass., Aug. 27, 1793; s. Maj. Jasper and Emma (Rounds) A.; grad. Brown U., 1815; m. Mercy D. Wheeler, May 16, 1820; m. 2d, Miss Mayrant. Tchr. Phillips Acad., Andover, Mass., 3 years; prof. mathematics and natural philosophy Brown U., 1819; ordained priest Episcopal Ch., 1820; pres. Charleston Coll., 1824-26, 28-36; 1st pres. Geneva (now Hobart) Coll., N.Y., 1826-28; chaplain, prof. geography, history and ethics U.S. Mil. Acad., 1838-40. Author: Elements of Moral Philosophy, 1837. Died Pendleton, S.C., Oct. 25, 1841.

ADAMS, John, clergyman, author; b. probably Nova Scotia, 1704; son of John Adams; graduated from Harvard, 1721. Ordained to ministry Congregational Ch., Newport, R.I., 1728; preached for a few years, then devoted himself to literature; knew 9 langs. Author works including: A Collection of Poems by Several Hands, 1744; Poems on Several Occasions, Original and Translated, by the late Rev. John Adams, M.A., 1745. Died Cambridge, Mass., Jan. 22, 1740.

ADAMS, John, 2d Pres. U.S.; b. Braintree (now Quincy), Mass., Oct. 30, 1735; s. John and Susanna (Boylston) A.; grad. Harvard, 1755; m. Abigail Smith, Oct. 25, 1764; children—John Quincy (6th Pres. U.S.), Thomas, Charles, Abby. Admitted to Boston bar, 1758; entered politics as opponent of Stamp Act; rep. from Boston to Mass. Gen. Ct., 1770; one of Mass. dels. to 1st Continental Congress, 1774; apptd. chief justice Superior Ct. of Mass., 1775; mem. drafting com. and signer Declaration of Independence, 1776, proposed Washington for gen. Continental Army; resigned office of chief justice Superior Ct. to become mem. newly-created Bd. of War, 1777; elected commr. to France, 1777; worked to negotiate fgn. aid from Netherlands, securing loan, 1782; with Jay and Jefferson negotiated treaty of Paris with Gt. Britain, 1783; 1st U.S. minister to Gt. Britain, 1785-88; elected 1st vice pres. U.S., 1788, reelected, 1792; elected 2d Pres. U.S., 1796, served as buffer between Hamilton and Jefferson (inclined more toward Hamilton and Federalists), signed Alien and Sedition Acts, resisted pressure to declare war on France, 1798, one of last acts was to appoint John Marshall as chief justice U.S. Supreme Ct., defeated for 2d term by Thomas Jefferson, 1800, ret. to Quincy, 1801; conducted memorable corr. with Jefferson. Author numerous published works, including: Thoughts on Government, 1776; Defense of the Constitutions of the Government of the United States of America, 1787; Novanglus and Massachusettensis, 1819. Died Quincy, July 4, 1826; buried under old 1st Congregational Ch., Boston.

ADAMS, John, educator; b. Canterbury, Conn., Sept. 18, 1772; s. Capt. John and Mary (Parker A.; grad. Yale, 1795, LL.D. (hon.), 1854; m. Elizabeth Ripley, 1798, 10 children including William; m. 2d, Mrs. Mabel Burritt, 1829. Tchr., Plainfield (N.J.) Acad., 1800-03; prin. Bacon Acad., Colchester, Conn., 1803-10, Phillips Acad., Andover, Mass., 1810-32; prin. acad., Elbridge, N.Y.; pres. female sem., Jacksonville, Ill.; agt. for middle west region Am. Sunday Sch. Union, organized several hundred Sunday Schs. Died Jacksonville, Apr. 24, 1863; buried Jacksonville.

ADAMS, John, congressman; b. Oak Hill, Greene County, N.Y., Aug. 26, 1778; studied law. Taught sch. in Durham, N.Y.; admitted to bar, 1805, began practice in Durham; apptd. surrogate of Greene County, 1810; mem. N.Y. State Assembly 1812, 13; mem. U.S. Ho. of Reps. from N.Y., (Democrat, contested election) 14th Congress, Mar.-Dec. 1815, (Jackson Democrat) 23d Congress, 1833-35; became dir. Catskill-Canajoharie R.R. in 1835. Died Catskill, N.Y., Sept. 25, 1854; buried Thomson Street Cemetery.

ADAMS, John, army officer; b. Nashville, Tenn., July 1, 1825; grad. U.S. Mil. Acad., 1846; m. Georgia McDougal, 1852. Commd. 2d lt., 1st Dragoons, U.S. Army, Mexican War, served at Rayado, Las Vegas, N.M., 1850-51, promoted 1st lt.; lt. col., aide-de-camp to gov. Minn., 1853; capt. Dragoons, 1856; resigned commn., 1861; commd. col. Confederate Army, 1862, brig. gen., 1862. Killed at Battle of Franklin (Tenn.), Nov. 30, 1864.

ADAMS, John Quincy, 6th Pres. U.S.; b. Braintree (name now Quincy), Massachusetts, July 11, 1767; son of John (2d Pres. U.S.) and Abigail (Smith) A.; graduate of Harvard, 1787; m. Louisa Johnson, July 26, 1797, 4 children including Charles Francis. Admitted to Mass. bar, 1790; apptd. U.S. minister to Netherlands by Pres. Washington, 1794; elected to Mass. Senate, 1802; mem. U.S. Senate from Mass., 1803-08, resigned, 1808; U.S. minister to Ct. of St. Petersburg (Russia), 1809-11; nominated to U.S. Supreme Ct., 1811, declined; one of negotiators of peace after War of 1812; U.S. minister to Gt. Britain, 1815; U.S. sec. of state, 1817-25, considered prin. author of Monrore Doctrine drawn up during his term; 6th Pres. U.S., 1825-29, defeated for 2d term by Andrew Jackson, 1828; mem. U.S. Ho. of Reps. from Mass., 22d-30th congresses, 1831-48, leading opponent of slavery, gag rule efforts of So. reps., also instrumental in getting favorable vote for establishment of Smithsonian Instn., 1846. Author: Memoirs (edited by Charles Francis Adams), 12 vols., 1874-77; Writings (edited by W. C. Ford), 7 vols., 1913. Died Washington, D.C., Feb. 23, 1848; buried Quincy.

ADAMS, Joseph Alexander, engraver; b. New Germantown, N.J., 1803. Apprentice in printing bus.; work had appeared in Treasury of Knowledge, Cottage Bible, by 1833; engraved "Last Arrow" for N.Y. Mirror, 1837; engraved sixteen hundred illustrations for Harper's Illuminated Bible, published 1843, said to have been 1st electrotyper in Am., made improvements in process. Died N.J., Sept. 11, 1880.

ADAMS, Nehemiah, clergyman; b. Salem, Mass., Feb. 19, 1806; s. Nehemiah and Mehitable (Torrey) A.; grad. Harvard, 1826, Andover Theol. Sem., 1829; D.D. (hon.), Amherst Coll., 1847; m. Martha Hooper, Jan. 11, 1832; m. 2d, Sarah Brackett, May 15, 1850; 9 children. Ordained to ministry as co-pastor First Congregational Ch., Cambridge, Mass., 1829, pastor, 1831-34; pastor Union Congregational Ch., Boston, 1834-78; visited South, 1854, wrote A South-side View of Slavery, 1854, attacked by abolitionists because of its moderation; answered abolitionists in The Sable Cloud, 1861; mem. Am. Tract Soc., Am. Bd. Fgn. Missions. Author: Remarks on the Unitarian Belief, 1832; The Life of John Eliot, 1847. Died Oct. 6, 1878.

ADAMS, Parmenio, congressman; b. Hartford, Conn., Sept. 9, 1776; attended common schs. Moved to Phelps Corners, Batavia, Genesee County (now Attica, Wyoming County), N.Y., 1806; served with N.Y. Militia, 1806-16, as lt. light inf., capt. Grenadiers, 2d and 1st maj., div. insp. Inf.; served as maj. and commandant N.Y. Volunteers, in War of 1812; sheriff of Genesee County, 1815-16, 18-21; engaged in agrl. pursuits, also as constrn. contractor on Erie Canal; mem. U.S. Ho. of Reps. from N.Y. (contested election), 18th, 19th congresses, Jan. 7, 1824-27. Died Alexander, N.Y., Feb. 19, 1832.

ADAMS, Robert Huntington, senator, lawyer; b. Rockbridge County, Va., 1792; grad. Washington Coll. (now Washington and Lee U.), 1806; studied law. Began as apprentice in cooper's trade; admitted to the bar, began practice law, Knoxville Tenn.; moved to Natchez, Miss., 1819; mem. Miss. Ho. of Reps., 1828; mem. U.S. Senate (Jackson Democrat, filled vacancy) from Miss., Jan. 6, 1830-July 2, 1832. Died Natchez, July 2, 1832; buried Natchez City Cemetery.

ADAMS, Samuel, gov. Mass., Continental congressman; b. Boston, Sept. 27, 1722; grad. Harvard, 1740, M.A., 1743; m. Elizabeth Checkley, 1749; m. 2d, Elizabeth Wells, 1764; 2 children. Apptd. tax collector Boston, 1756; drafted instrns. given by Town of Boston opposing Stamp Act of 1764; leading spirit behind Boston Tea Party; organizer (with John Hancock) Sons of Liberty, 1765; mem. Mass. Gen Ct., 1765-74; mem. Continental Congress, 1774-82; signer Declaration of Independence; opposed adoption U.S. Constn., 1788; lt. gov. Mass., 1789-94, gov. 1794-97. Writings of Samuel Adams, 4 vols., published 1904-08. Died Oct. 2, 1803; buried Granary Burial Ground, Boston.

ADAMS, Silas, congressman, lawyer; b. Pulaski County, Ky., Feb. 9, 1839; attended Ky. U. at Harrodsburg, Transylvania U., Lexington Law Sch. Served with Union Army, Civil War, from 1st lt. to col., 1st Regt., Ky. Volunteer Cavalry; admitted to bar, practiced law; county atty., 2 terms; mem. Ky. Ho. of Reps., 1889-92; mem. U.S. Ho. of Reps. (Republican) from Ky., 53d Congress, 1893-95. Died Liberty, Casey County, Ky., May 5, 1896; buried Brown Cemetery, Humphrey, Ky.

ADAMS, Stephen, senator, congressman, jurist; b. Pendleton Dist., S.C., Oct. 17, 1807; studied law. Admitted to Tenn. bar, 1829; mem. Tenn. Senate, 1833-34; moved to Aberdeen, Miss., began practice law, 1834; circuit ct. judge, 1837-45, 48; mem. U.S. Ho. of Reps. (Democrat) from Miss., 29th Congress, 1845-47; mem. Miss. Ho. of Reps., 1850; mem. Miss. Constl. Conv., 1851; mem. U.S. Senate (Union Democrat, filled vacancy caused by resignation of Jefferson Davis) from Miss., Mar. 17, 1852-57; moved to Memphis, Tenn. Died Memphis, May 11 1857; buried Elmwood Cemetery.

ADAMS, Thomas, Continental congressman; b. New Kent County, Va., 1730; attended common schs. Clk. of Henrico County; went to Eng. to look after his extensive bus. interests, 1762-74; mem. Va. Ho. of Burgesses, signed Articles of Association, 1774; chmn. New Kent County Com. of Safety, 1774; mem. Continental Congress from Va., 1778-80; a signer Articles of Confederation; moved to Augusta County, Va., 1780; mem. Va. Senate, 1783-86. Died on his estate "Cowpasture," Augusta County, Aug. 1788.

ADAMS, William, clergyman, coll. pres.; b. Colchester, Conn., Jan. 25, 1807; s. John and Elizabeth (Ripley) A.; grad. Yale, 1827; grad. Andover Theol. Sem., 1830; m. Susan P. Magoun, July 1831; m. 2d, Martha B. Magoun, Aug. 1835. Pastor Congregational Ch., Brighton, Mass., 1831, Central Presbyn. Ch., N.Y.C., 1832; mem. group founders Union Theol. Sem., 1836, pres., 1874; moderator gen. assembly New Sch. Party, 1852; chmn. New Sch. Com. of Confs., 1866; corporate mem. Am. Bd. Fgn. Missions; pres. Presbyn. Fgn. Bd. Died Aug. 31, 1880.

ADAMS, William Taylor (Oliver Optic), author; b. Bellingham, Mass., July 30, 1822; s. Capt. Laban and Catherine (Johnson) A.; m. Sarah Jenkins, 1846, 2 children. Tchr. Boston schs., 1845-65; mem. Sch. Com. of Dorchester (now part of Boston), Mass., 14 years; mem. Mass. Legislature, 1869; author fiction for boys under name Oliver Optic: Hatchie, the Guardian Slave, 1853; Indoors and Out, 1855; The Boat Club, 1855; others. Died Dorchester, Mar. 27, 1897.

ADAMS, William Wirt, army officer; b. Frankfort, Ky., Mar. 22, 1819; s. Judge George and Anna (Weissiger) A.; grad. Bardstown (Ky.) Coll., 1839; m. Sallie Mayrant, 1850. Served as pvt. under Col. Burleson's command Republic of Tex. Army, 1839; mem. Miss Legislature, 1858, 60; assisted in securing withdrawal of La. from the Union, 1861; commd. brig. gen. Confederate States Army, 1863; surrendered Ala., 1865; revenue agt. Miss., 1880-85; apptd. postmaster of Jackson (Miss.) by Pres. Cleveland, 1885. Died in street duel with John Martin, Vicksburg, Miss., May 1, 1888.

ADDAMS, William, congressman; b. Lancaster County, Pa., Apr. 11, 1777. Moved to Berks County, Pa., nr. Reading, served as auditor, 1813, 14; commr. Berks County, 1814-17; mem. Pa. Ho. of Reps., 1822-24; mem. U.S. Ho. of Reps. (Democrat) from Pa., 19th, 20th congresses, 1825-29; mem. com. Deaf and Dumb. Instn. for the States of N.Y. and Ohio; asso. judge Berks County, 1839-42; capt. Reading City Troop; farming interests. Died Spring Twp., Pa., May 30, 1858; buried St. John's Ch. Cemetery, Sinking Springs, Pa.

ADGATE, Andrew, musician. Founder, Instn. for Encouragement of Church Music, Phila., 1784 (became Free Sch. for Spreading the Knowledge of Vocal Music 1785); directed choral concerts, Phila., 1785-93, performed both Am. and European works; founded Uranian Acad., 1787. Author: Rudiments of Music; Philadelphia Harmony; Selection of Sacred Harmony. Died 1793.

ADGATE, Asa, congressman, mfr.; b. Canaan, N.Y., Nov. 17, 1767. Iron mfr., farmer, Adgates Falls, Clinton County (now Ausable Chasm, Essex County), N.Y., from 1793; clk. Town of Peru, N.Y., 1793-95, supr., 1795, assessor, 1796, 97, commr. schs., 1798; mem. N.Y. State Assembly from Clinton County, 1798; served as lt., inf., N.Y. Militia, 1798, 99; mem. 1st commn. of peace for Essex County as a judge ct. of common pleas, 1799, several years; mem. U.S. Ho. of Reps. (Democrat, filled vacancy) from N.Y., 14th Congress, June 7, 1815-17; mem. N.Y. State Gen. Assembly from Essex County, 1823. Died Ausable Chasm, Feb. 15, 1832; buried Ausable Chasm Cemetery, Clinton County.

ADLER, George J., philologist; b. Leipzig, Germany, 1821; s. John J. Adler; grad. N.Y.U., 1844. Came to U.S., 1833. Prof. modern langs. N.Y.U., 1846-53; Compiler: Dictionary of German and English Languages, 1849 (marked him as one of great philologians of his period); went insane from stra of publishing the dictionary, semi-permanent res dent of Bloomingdale (N.Y.) Asylum, 1853-6. Died Bloomingdale, Aug. 24, 1868; buried S Michael's Episcopal Ch., Bloomingdale.

ADLER, Samuel, clergyman; b. Worms, German Dec. 3, 1809; s. Isaac Adler; attended U. Bor (Germany), 1831; Ph.D., U. Giessen (Germany) 1836; m. Henrietta Frankfurter, 1843; 3 childre including Felix, Isaac. Rabbi, Worms, circa 183 42; chief rabbi, Alzey, Germany, 1842-57; mem rabbinical reform confs., Brunswick, German 1844, Frankfort-on-the-Main, Germany, 1845, Bre lau, Germany, 1846; rabbi Emanu-El Congregatio N.Y.C., 1857-74, rabbi emeritus, 1874-91; c founder Hebrew Orphan Asylum, N.Y.C. Author: Th Day of Atonement According to the Bible—I Origin and Meaning; A Biblio-Critical Study of th Passover; The Levitical Tithe; Karaitic Question Phariseeism and Sadduceeism. Died June 9, 1891

ADLUM, John, viticulturist; b. York, Pa., Ap 29, 1759; m. Margaret Adlum, 1813. Commd. ma Provisional Army; brig. gen. Pa. Militia; asso. judg Lycoming County (Pa.), 1795-98; establishe exptl. farm and nursery, Georgetown, D.C., studie about 30 native varieties of grapes, also wine-makir processes; introduced and propagated Catawba grap among 1st to urge fed. aid to agrl. research; climbir fumitory plant Adlumia named in his honor. Autho A Memoir on the Cultivation of the Vine in Americ and the Best Mode of Making Wine, 1823; Adlu on Making Wine, 1826. Died "Vineyard" nr. George town, Mar. 1, 1836.

ADRAIN, Garnett Bowditch, congressman; b N.Y.C., Dec. 15, 1815; grad. Rutgers Coll., Ne Brunswick, N.J., 1833; studied law in brother' law office. Licensed as atty., 1836, as a counselo 1839, began practice law, New Brunswick; mem U.S. Ho. of Reps. (Democrat) from N.J., 35th-36t congresses, 1857-61. Died New Brunswick, Aug 17, 1878; buried Van Liew Cemetery.

ADRAIN, Robert, mathematician, educator; b Carrickfergus, Ireland, Sept. 30, 1775; m. An Pollock, 1 child. Came to Am., 1789; prof. natur philosophy and mathematics Queens Coll. (now Rut gers U.), New Brunswick, N.J., 1809-12, 26; pro Columbia, N.Y.C., 1813-25; prof. mathematics U Pa., 1827-34, vice provost, 1828-34; considered or of most brilliant mathematicians of his time in Am. founder journals Analyst, or Mathematical Com panion, 1808, The Mathematical Diary, 1825-33 Died New Brunswick, Aug. 10, 1843.

AGASSIZ, Jean Louis Rodolphe, zoologist; b Motier-en-Vuly, Canton Fribourg, Switzerland, Ma 28, 1807; attended Coll. Lausanne (France) 1822-24, U. Zurich (Germany), 1824-26, U. Heide berg (Germany), 1826-27; M.D., U. Munich (Ge many); 1827; Ph. D., U. Erlangen (Germany) 1829; m. Cecile Braun, Oct. 1833; children—Alex ander, Ida, Pauline; m. 2d, Elizabeth Cabot Cary 1850. Conducted zool. research under Fren naturalist Cuvier, Paris, 1831-32; prof. natura history U. Neuchatel (Switzerland), 1832-46; es tablished Hotel des Neuchatelois for glaci study; came to Am., 1846, toured East Coast deli vering lectures in comparative embryology; wen on scientific cruise along Mass. coast, 1847; pro zoology and geology Lawrence Scientific Sch. Harvard, 1848-73; made exploration cruise Fla. coral reefs, 1851; curator of mus. of compara tive zoology, Cambridge, Mass., 1859-73; becam naturalized Am. citizen. 1861; collected specimen for Cambridge Mus. in Brazil, 1863; non-residen prof. natural history Cornell U., Ithaca, N.Y. 1868; made scientific voyage around Cape Hor aboard Hassler, 1871-72; established Anderso Sch. of Natural History, Penikese Island, Buz zard's Bay, 1873. Author: The Fishes of Brazil 1829; Recherches sur les Poissons (foundation o our present knowledge of fish), 1833-44; Histor of the Fresh Water Fishes of Central Europe, 1839 42; Etudes sur les Glaciers, 1840; Etudes Critique sur les Mollusque fossilin, 1840-45; Nomenclato Zoologicus, 1842-46; Monograph on the Fossi Fishes of the Old Red or Devonian of the Britis Isles, 1844-45; Systeme Glaciare, 1846; Nouvelle etudes et experiences sur les Glaciers actuels 1847; Contributions to the Natural History of th United States (contained Essay on Classification) 1857. Died Cambridge, Mass., Dec. 14, 1873; burie Mt. Auburn Cemetery, Cambridge.

AGATE, Alfred T., painter; b. Sparta, N.Y., Feb 14, 1812; s. Thomas and Hannah Agate; m. Eliza beth Hill Kennedy. Painted primarily miniatures asso., Nat. Acad. Design, 1832-40, hon. mem. 1840-46, exhibited painting Cocoanut Grove N.A.D., Washington, D.C., 1840; botanical artis of scientific corps on Charles Wilkes Explorin Expdn. to N.W. Am. coast, Pacific islands an Antarctica, 1838-42. Died Washington, Jan. 5 1846.

AGATE, Frederick Styles, painter; b. Shipley Eng., Jan. 29, 1803; s. Thomas and Hannah Agate studied painting under John Rubens Smith N.Y.C., 1818-25. Painted under S.F.B. Morse cad. of Fine Arts, 1825; a founder Nat. Acad. ' Design, N.Y.C.; hist. and portrait painter, .Y.C., 1827-44; most famous works: Ugolino, ld Oaken Bucket (exhibited Nat. Acad. Art xhbn. 1834); went to Paris and Florence, 1834-5. Died Sparta, N.Y., May 1, 1844.

AGNEW, Cornelius Rea, ophthalmologist, med. rganizer; b. N.Y.C., Aug. 8, 1830; s. William and lizabeth (Thompson) A.; grad. Columbia, 1849, .D., 1852; m. Mary Nash, 1856. Began practice ' medicine, 1854; surgeon Eye and Ear Infirmary, .Y.C., 1855-64; surgeon gen. N.Y. Militia, 1858; ed. dir. N.Y. State Hosp. for Volunteers during ivil War; an organizer U.S. Sanitary Comm.; rganizer Sch. of Mines, Columbia, 1864, an ophalmic clinic at Coll. Physicians and Surgeons (of olumbia), Bklyn. Eye and Ear Hosp., Manhattan ye and Ear Hosp.; prof. diseases of the eye and ar Coll. Physicians and Surgeons, 1869-88. Died .Y.C., Apr. 18, 1888.

AGNEW, David Hayes, surgeon, educator; b. Lanaster County, Pa., Nov. 24, 1818; s. Robert and Irs. (Henderson) A.; grad. med. dept. U. Pa., 838; m. Margaret Irwin, 1841. A founder Irwin Agnew Iron Foundry, 1846; bought, revived Phila. ch. Anatomy, 1852-62; surgeon Phila. Hosp., 854, Wills Eye Hosp., 1863, Pa. Hosp., 1865, rthopedic Hosp., 1867; became asst. prof. surgery . Pa., 1854, prof. clin. surgery, 1870; prof. surery, 1871-89, prof. emeritus, 1889; pres. Phila. oll. of Physicians, 1889; chief cons. to Pres. Gareld when he was shot by Guiteau, 1881; one of his lasses painted by Thomas Eakins. Author: Treatise n the Principles and Practice of Surgery, 3 vols., 878-83. Died Phila., Mar. 22, 1892.

AGNEW, Eliza, missionary; b. N.Y.C., Feb. 2, 807; d. James and Jane Agnew. Joined Orange treet Presbyn. Ch., N.Y.C., 1823; applied to Am. d. of Boston for missionary post in Ceylon, 1839; rrived Jaffna, Ceylon, 1840; conducted female oarding sch., Oodooville, Ceylon, 1842-79. Died lanepay, Ceylon, June 14, 1883; buried Oodooille.

AHL, John Alexander, congressman, physician; . Strasburg, Pa., Aug. 16, 1813; grad. in mediine U. Md., 1832. Practiced medicine, Centerille, Pa., until 1856; began in real estate bus., perated paper mill, Newville, Pa., 1856; del. emocratic Nat. Conv., Cincinnati, 1856; mem. .S. Ho. of Reps. (Democrat) from Pa., 35th ongress, 1857-59; mfr. paper, operator iron urnace, Antietam, Md.; surgeon State Militia; lanner, major builder Harrisburg & Potomac R.R. ied Newville, Apr. 25, 1882; buried Big Spring resbyn. Cemetery.

AIKEN, Charles Augustus, clergyman, coll. pres.; . Manchester, Vt., Oct. 30, 1827; S. John and larriet (Adams) A.; grad. Dartmouth, 1846, Andver Theol Sem., 1853; m. Sarah Noyes, Oct. 17, .854. Ordained pastor Congregational Ch., Yarnouth, Me., 1854; prof. Latin lang. and lit. Dartnouth, 1859-66, Coll. of N.J. (now Princeton), 866-69; pres. Union Coll., Schenectady, N.Y., 869-71; 1st Archibald Alexander prof. of Christian thics and apologetics at Princeton Theol. Sem., 871-92. Died Jan. 14, 1892.

AIKEN, David Wyatt, army officer, agrl. editor, ongressman; b. Winnsboro, S.C., Mar. 17, 1828; s. William and Nancy (Kerr) A.; grad. S.C. Coll., 849; m. Mattie Gaillard; m. 2d, Virginia Smith, 852. Served as adj. 7th S.C. Regt. of Volunteers, ommd. col., 1862; mem. S.C. Ho. of Reps. from Abbeville Dist., 1864-66; co-owner Rural Carolinan, 1870-75, sole owner, editor, 1876; dep.-at-large Nat. Grange, 1872; organizer, sec., master S.C. Grange, 1875-77; mem. U.S. Ho. of Reps. from S.C., 45th-49th congresses, 1877-87. Died Cokesbury, S.C., Apr. 6, 1887; buried Magnolia Cemetery, Greenwood, S.C.

AIKEN, George L., actor; b. Boston, Dec. 19, 1830. Made debut as Ferdinand in The Six Degrees of Crime, Providence, R.I., 1848; adapted Orion, the Gold Beater, produced play at Nat. Theater, N.Y.C., 1851; wrote, acted in stage version of Uncle Tom's Cabin; opened Troy (N.Y.) Musuem, 1852, played 100 nights; gave 325 performances at Purdy's Nat. Theater, N.Y.C., 1853; dramatized novel The Old Homestead (Ann S. Stephen), opened 1856; opened The Doom of Deville; or, The Maiden's Vow, Barnum's Museum, N.Y.C., 1859, house dramatist, 1859, 61; acted at Phila. Arch Street Theatre, 1860; asso. mgr. Troy Theater, 1863; ret. from stage, 1867. Died Jersey City, N.J., Apr. 27, 1876.

AIKEN, William, gov. S.C., congressman; b. Charleston, S.C., Jan. 28, 1806; s. William and Henrietta (Wyatt) A.; grad. S.C. Coll., 1825; m. Harriet Lowndes, Feb. 3, 1831. Mem. lower house S.C. Legislature, 1838-42. S.C. Senate, 1842; gov. S.C., 1844-46; mem. U.S. Ho of Reps. from S.C., 32d-34th congresses, 1851-57; trustee Peabody Endl. Fund. Died Flat Rock, N.C., Sept. 6, 1887; buried Magnolia Cemetery, Charleston.

AIME, Valcour, sugar planter; b. St. Charles Parish, La., 1798; s. Francois and Miss (Fortier) A.; m. Josephine Roman. Owner St. James Plantation (9,500 acres), contained 1st sugar refinery in U.S.; a leader in agrl. and mech. improvements in sugar prodn. for over 50 years; contbr. to chs. of his parish, also New Orleans; contbr. to Jefferson Coll. Died St. James Plantation, La.; Dec. 31, 1867; buried Little Grave Yard, St. James Ch.

AINSLIE, Hew, poet; b. Ayrshire, Scotland, Apr. 5, 1792; s. George Ainslie; m. Janet Ainslie (cousin), 1812. Came to U.S., 1822; mem. New Harmony (Ind.) Colony, 1826. Author: Scottish Songs, Ballads and Poems, 1855. Died Louisville, Ky., Mar. 11, 1878.

AITKEN, Robert, printer, publisher, engraver; b. Dalkeith, Scotland, 1734. Bookseller, Phila., 1769, 71; publisher The Pennsylvania Magazine, 1775-76; published New Testament, 1777, 1778, 1779, 1781; printed 1st Am. Bible, 1782. Died Phila., July 15, 1802.

AKERMAN, Amos Tappan, atty. gen.; b. Portsmouth, N.H., Feb. 23, 1821; s. Benjamin and Olive (Meloon) A.; grad. Dartmouth, 1842; m. Martha Galloway. Admitted to Ga. bar, 1844; mem. Ga. Constl. Conv., 1868; U.S. dist. atty., 1869; apptd. atty. gen. U.S. by Pres. Grant, 1870, resigned, 1871. Died Cartersville, Ga., Dec. 21, 1880.

AKERS, Benjamin Paul, sculptor; b. Saccarappa, Me., July 10, 1825; m. Mrs. Elizabeth (Chase) Taylor, Aug. 1860. Worked as printer, Portland, Me.; went to Boston, 1849, learned plaster-casting from Joseph Carew; opened own studio, Portland; made busts of Henry W. Longfellow, Samuel Appleton, John Neal; spent 2 years in Florence, Italy, produced 2 bas-reliefs Night and Morning; his 1st statue was Benjamin in Egypt; while in Washington (D.C.) made busts of Franklin Pierce, Linn Boyd, Gerritt Smith, Edward Everett, John McLean, also medallion head of Sam Houston; produced his best works in Rome including: Una and the Lion; St. Elizabeth of Hungary; Dead Pearl Diver; and head of John Milton; last work was bust of John Frothingham. Died Phila., May 21, 1861.

AKERS, Thomas Peter, congressman; b. Knox County, O., Oct. 4, 1828; grad. from an Ohio coll.; studied law. Admitted to the bar; sch. tchr., Ky.; moved to Lexington, Mo., 1853; prof. mathematics, moral philosophy Masonic Coll., Lexington, Mo., 1855, 56; pastor local Methodist Ch.; mem. U.S. Ho. of Reps. (Am. Party, filled vacancy) from Mo., 34th Congress, Aug. 18, 1856-57; moved to N.Y.C., 1861, became v.p. gold bd.; moved to Utah because of ill health; returned to Lexington. Died Lexington, Apr. 3, 1877; buried Machpelah Cemetery.

ALARCON, Hernando, see De Alarcon, Hernando.

ALBERT, William Julian, congressman, businessman; b. Balt., Aug. 4, 1816; grad. Mt. St. Mary's Coll., nr. Emmittsburg, Md., 1833. In hardware bus., until 1855, then in banking bus.; pres. Md. Electoral Coll., 1864, voted for Lincoln; prominent Union leader in Md., helped prevent secession of state; offered entire personal fortune, if needed, to help depleted fed. finances, 1860; a founder, dir. First Nat. Bank of Md.; dir. several savs. banks, mfg. cos., ins. cos.; mem. U.S. Ho. of Reps. (Republican) from Md., 43d Congress, 1873-75. Died Balt., Mar. 29, 1879; buried Greenmount Cemetery.

ALBERTSON, Nathaniel, congressman, businessman; b. Fairfax, Va., June 10, 1800. Moved to Salem, Ind., engaged in agrl. pursuits; mem. Ind. Ho. of Reps., 1838-40; farmer in Greenville, nr. New Albany, Ind., 1835-53; mem. U.S. Ho. of Reps. (Democrat) from Ind., 31st Congress, 1849-51; moved to Keokuk, Ia., 1853, became a mcht.; mcht. Boonville, Mo., 1856-60; in hotel bus., had mining interests, Central City, Colo., 1860-63. Died Central City, Dec. 16, 1863; buried Central City Graveyard.

ALBRIGHT, Charles, congressman, army officer, lawyer; b. Bucks County, Pa., Dec. 13, 1830; attended Dickinson Coll.; studied law. Admitted to Pa. bar, 1852, practiced law in Mauch Chunk, Pa.; moved to Territory of Kan., 1854-56; resumed practice law, Mauch Chunk, 1856; del. Republican Nat. Conv., Chgo., 1860; promoted to maj. 132d Regt., Pa. Volunteer Inf., 1862, lt. col., 1862, col., 1863; commd. col. 34th Pa. Militia, 1863; commd. col. 202d Regt., Pa. Vol. Inf., 1864, brevetted brig. gen. Volunteers, 1865; resumed practice law, Mauch Chunk, 1865; del. Rep. Nat. Conv., Phila., 1872; mem. U.S. Ho. of Reps. (Rep.) from Pa., 43d Congress, 1873-75. Died Mauch Chunk, Sept. 28, 1880; buried Mauch Chunk Cemetery.

ALBRIGHT, Charles Jefferson, congressman; b. Carlisle, Pa., May 9, 1816. Employed in harness shop, later clk. in rural store; apprenticed as a printer; became farmer in Guernsey County, nr. Cambridge, O., 1832; owner, publisher Guernsey Times, 1840-45, 48-55; sec. Guernsey County Bd. Sch. Examiners, 1841-44; mem. U.S. Ho. of Reps. (Republican) from Ohio, 34th Congress, 1855-57; v.p. Rep. State Conv., 1855; del. 1st, 2d Rep. nat. convs., Phila., 1856, Chgo., 1860, chmn. Guernsey County Mil. Com., during Civil War; internal revenue collector 16th Ohio dist., 1862-69; mem. Ohio bd. of charities, 1875; pres. bd. sch. examiners Cambridge Union Sch., 1881-83. Died Cambridge, O., Oct. 21, 1883; buried South Cemetery.

ALBRIGHT, Jacob, clergyman; b. Pottstown, Pa., May 1, 1759; s. Johann Albrecht; m. Catherine Cape. Became preacher Methodist Ch., 1796; preached throughout Eastern Pa., Md. and Va.; founded 1st Evangelical Ch., 1800; elected minister by his followers, 1803; elected bishop The Newly Formed Meth. Conf., 1807. Died May 18, 1808.

ALCORN, James Lusk, senator, gov. Miss.; b. Golconda, Ill., Nov. 4, 1816; s. James and Louisa (Lusk) A.; ed. Cumberland Coll.; m. Mary C. Stewart, 1839; m. 2d, Amelia Walton Glover, 1850. Dep. sheriff, Livingston, Ky., 1839; mem. Ky. Legislature, 1843; admitted to Ky. bar, 1843; mem. Miss. Ho. of Reps., 1846, 56, 65, Miss. Senate, 1848-56; served as brig. gen. Miss. Militia during Civil War; pres. Miss. Levee Bd.; elected to U.S. Senate, 1865, not permitted to take seat; gov. Miss., 1869-71; mem. U.S. Senate from Miss., 1871-77; defeated as Independent candidate for gov. Miss., 1873. Died "Eagle Nest," Coahoma County, Miss., Dec. 20, 1894; buried "Eagle Nest."

ALCOTT, Amos Bronson, educator, author; b. Wolcott, Conn., Nov. 29, 1799; s. Joseph Chatfield and Anna (Bronson) Alcox; m. Abigail May, May 23, 1830, children—Louisa May, Abby May, Anna, Elizabeth. Taught sch., Cheshire, Mass., 1823-27, Boston, 1828-30, Germantown,Pa., 1831-33, Temple Sch., Boston, 1834-39; as sch. master tried to reform conditions and methods of ednl. system; described experience with Platonic dialogue method and innovations in The Record of A School Exemplifying the General Principles of Spiritual Culture, 1835, Conversations with Children on the Gospels, 1836, 37; visited sch. based on his theories in Eng., 1842; a founder Fruitlands, (a Utopian, vegetarian community), 1843-45; backer of extreme transcendentalist, anti-slavery societies, temperence movements, lectr. on these topics; supt. schs. Concord (Mass.), 1859, introduced singing, dancing, parent-tchrs. club; founder Concord Summer Sch. of Philosophy and Literature, 1879. Author: Observations on the Principles and Methods of Infant Instruction, 1830; The Doctrine and Discipline of Human Culture, 1836; Concord Days, 1872; Table Talk, 1877; New Connecticut, 1881. Died Mar. 4, 1888.

ALCOTT, Louisa May, author; b. Germantown, Pa., Nov. 29, 1832; d. Amos Bronson and Abigail (May) A.; studied under Thoreau, Emerson, Theodore Parker. Work published in Atlantic Monthly, 1860; nurse Union Hosp., Georgetown, D.C., 1861-63; editor Merry's Museum, (a mag. for children), 1867; author: Little Women, 2 vols., 1868-69; An Old Fashioned Girl, 1870; Little Men, 1871; Eight Cousins, 1875; A Modern Mephistopheles, 1877; Under the Lilacs, 1878; Jo's Boys, 1886; A Garland for Girls, 1888; others. Died Boston, Mar. 6, 1888.

ALCOTT, William Andrus, educator; b. Wolcott, Conn., Aug. 6, 1798; attended Yale Med. m. Phebe Bronson, 1836, 2 children. Taught sch., Litchfield and Hartford counties, Conn., 1816-20; in charge of Central Sch., Bristol, Conn., 1824-25; taught sch. privately most of his life; editor Juvenile Rambler, 1832-33, Parley's Mag., 1833-37. Author 108 volumes on gen. edn., phys. edn., health, other subjects, including: Confessions of a Schoolmaster, 1829; Lectures for the Fireside, 1852; The Home Book of Life and Health, 1856; Forty Years in the Wilderness of Pills and Powders, 1859. Died Newton, Mass., Mar. 29, 1859; buried Newton.

ALDEN, Ebenezer, physician; b. Randolph, Mass., May 17, 1788; s. Dr. Ebenezer and Sarah (Bass) A.; grad. Harvard, 1808; M.B., Dartmouth Med. Sch., 1811; M.D., U. Pa., 1812; m. Anne Kimball, 1818, 6 children. Practiced medicine, Randolph, 70 years; mem. Mass. Med. Soc. Author: Historical Sketch of the Origin and Progress of the Massachusetts Medical Society, 1838; The Early History of the Medical Profession in the Country of Norfolk, Mass., 1853; Memorial of the Descendants of the Hon. John Alden, 1867; The Medical Uses of Alcohol (read before Mass. Temperance Assn.), 1868. Died Randolph, Jan. 26, 1881.

ALDEN, Ichabod, army officer; b. Duxbury, Mass., Aug. 11, 1739. Commd. lt. col. Continental Army, 1775; in command of 25th Continental Inf., then col. 7th Mass. Regt., 1776. Killed in attack by raiding party of Indians, Tories and British, Cherry Valley, N.Y., Nov. 11, 1778; buried Ft. Schuyler, N.Y.

ALDEN, James, naval officer; b. Portland, Me., Mar. 31, 1810; s. James and Elizabeth (Tate) A. Commd. midshipman U.S. Navy, served on ship Concord, 1828; served as lt. in Wilkes' South Sea Exploring Expdn., 1838-42; served at battles of Veracruz and Tabasco in Mexican War; commd. comdr., 1855; commanded ship Richmond in battles of New Orleans and Vicksburg; promoted capt., 1863; commanded ship Brooklyn at Battle of Mobile Bay; commd. commodore, 1866; ret. as rear adm. Died San Francisco, Feb. 6, 1877.

ALDEN, John, pilgrim, colonial ofcl.; b. England, 1599; m. Priscilla Mullens, 1623, 11 children. Came to Am., 1620; a signer Mayflower Compact; one of 8 bondsmen assuming colonial debt, 1627; gov.'s assistant Colony of Mass., 1632-33, 40-41, 50-86, treas., 1656-58, dep. gov., 1664-65, 77; agt. trading post on Kennebec River, 1634; surveyor hwys.; dep. from Duxbury to Mass. Gen. Ct., 1641-49; mem. Duxbury Council of War, 1675, Mass. Council of War, 1646, 53, 58, 67. Died Duxbury, Sept. 12, 1687; buried South Duxbury, Mass.

ALDEN, Joseph, clergyman, coll. pres.; b. Cairo, N.Y., Jan. 4, 1807; s. Eliab and Mary (Hathaway) A.; grad. Union Coll., 1829, D.D., 1839; LL.D., Columbia, 1857; m. Isabella Livingston, 1834, 1 son, William Livignston; m. 2d, Amelia Daly, 1882. Ordained pastor Congl. Ch., Williamstown, Mass., 1834; prof. Williams Coll., 1835-52; prof. moral philosophy Lafayette Coll., 1852-57; pres. Jefferson Coll., 1857-62; prin. State Normal Sch., Albany, N.Y., 1867-82. Author over 70 published writings. Died N.Y.C., Aug. 30, 1885.

ALDEN, Timothy, clergyman, coll. pres., antiquarian; b. Yarmouth, Mass. (now Me.), Aug. 28, 1771; s. Timothy and Sarah (Weld) A.; grad. Harvard, 1794; m. Elizabeth Wormsted; m. 2d., Sophia Mulcock, 1822. Ordained to ministry Congregational Ch.; pastor South Congl. Ch., Portsmouth, N.H., 1799-1805; pres., prof. Allegheny Coll., 1817-31; assisted in organ. Am. Antiquarian Soc.; librarian Mass. Hist. Soc.; prepared library catalogue of N.Y. Hist. Soc. Author: Missions Among the Senecas, 1827. Died Pitts., July 5, 1839.

ALDRICH, Anne Reeve, author; b. N.Y.C., Apr. 25, 1866; dau. of James Aldrich. Began writing verse, circa 1881; published 1st poem in Lippincott's Mag., 1883; contbd. to several mags., N.Y.C. Author works including: The Rose of Flame and Other Poems of Love, 1889; The Feet of Love, 1890. Died N.Y.C., June 29, 1892.

ALDRICH, Cyrus, congressman; b. Smithfield, R.I., June 18, 1808; attended common schs. Was sailor, boatman, farmer, contractor on public works, mail contractor; moved to Alton, Ill., 1837; mem. Ill. Ho. of Reps., 1845-47; register of deeds Jo Daviess County, Ill., 1847-49; receiver U.S. land office, Dixon, Ill., 1849-53; moved to Minneapolis, Minn., 1855, engaged in lumber bus.; mem. Minn. Constl. Conv., 1857; mem. U.S. Ho. of Reps. (Republican) from Minn., 36th, 37th congresses, 1859-63; mem. Minn. Ho. of Reps., 1865; chmn. bd. suprs. Town of Minneapolis, 1865; mem. commn. to examine claims for indemnity of those who had suffered in Sioux War of 1862, apptd. 1863; postmaster Minneapolis, 1867-71. Died Minneapolis, Oct. 5, 1871; buried Lakewood Cemetery.

ALDRICH, James, poet; b. Mattituck, N.Y., July 14, 1810; at least 1 child, Anne Reeve Aldrich. Engaged in merc. pursuits until journalism became his main activity; established Literary Gazette, N.Y.C., 1840, contbd. to it regularly; best known poem: "A Death-Bed." Died N.Y.C., Sept. 9, 1866.

ALDRICH, Louis, actor; b. Ohio, Oct. 1, 1843; attended White Water Coll., Wayne County, Ind., 1857; m. Clara Shropshire. Toured country as child star playing Richard III, Macbeth and Shylock, before 1857; mem. juvenile March Players, St. Louis, 1858-63; with Maguire's Opera House Co., San Francisco, 1863-66; played in Leah the Forsaken, Boston, 1867; leading man of Mrs. John Drew's co., Arch Street Theater, Phila., 1873-74; player Parson in McKee Ranker's adaptation of The Danites, 1877; played Joe Saunders in Bartley Campbell's My Partner, 1879-85; pres. Actors' Fund of Am., 1897-1901. Died Kennebunkport, Me., June 17, 1901.

ALDRICH, William, congressman, businessman; b. Greenfield Center, N.Y., Jan. 19, 1820; attended common schs.; at least 1 son, James Franklin. Sch. tchr., until 1846; moved to Jackson, Mich., 1846, became a mcht.; moved to Two Rivers, Wis., 1851, mcht., also mfr. lumber, woodenware, furniture; supt. schs., 1855, 56; chmn. county bd. suprs., 1857, 58; mem. Wis. Ho. of Reps., 1859; moved to Chgo., 1861, became wholesale grocer; mem. Chgo. City Council, chmn. 1876; mem. U.S. Ho. of Reps. (Republican) from Ill., 45th-47th congresses, 1877-83; resumed bus. interests, Chgo., milling bus., Fond du Lac, Wis. Died Fond du Lac, Dec. 3, 1885; buried Rosehill Cemetery, Chgo.

ALDRIDGE, Ira Frederick, tragedian; b. N.Y.C., circa 1805; s. Joshua Aldridge. Negro tragedian; engaged in London, 1826-65; leading roles include Othello, King Lear, Macbeth. Decorated Grand Cross of Leopold by Emperor of Austria; recipient Medal of Merit at Berne (Switzerland); mem. Imperial and Archducal Order of Our Lady of the Manger (Austria); hon. mem. Imperial Acad. of Beaux Arts in St. Petersburg. Died Lodz, Poland, Aug. 10, 1867.

ALEMANY, Jose Sadoc, missionary; b. Catalonia, Spain, July 13, 1814. Joined Dominican Order; ordained priest Roman Catholic Ch., 1837; missionary to Western states of Am., 1841; bishop of Monterey, 1850; became 1st archbishop of San Francisco, 1853; Old St. Mary's Ch. dedicated as seat of archdiocese, Christmas Eve 1854; retired to Valencia, Spain, 1884. Author: Life of St. Dominick. Died Valencia, Apr. 14, 1888.

ALEXANDER, Abraham, legislator; b. 1717. Justice of peace Mecklenburg County, N.C., 1762; a commr. for establishing town of Charlotte, N.C., 1766; mem. N.C. Assembly from Mecklenburg County, 1769-70; mem. Mecklenburg County Com. of Safety. Trustee Queen's Mus., Liberty Hall Mus., 1777. Elder Presbyn. Ch. Died Apr. 23, 1786.

ALEXANDER, Adam Rankin, congressman; b. Rockbridge County, Va. Became a surveyor; moved to Blount County, Tenn., 1801; moved to Madison County, Tenn., circa 1806, established Town of Alexandria (named for him); mem. Tenn. Senate, 1817; register land office for 10th surveyors' dist.; mem. 1st Madison County Ct., 1821; mem. U.S. Ho. of Reps. (Federalist) from Tenn., 18th-19th congresses, 1823-27; moved to Shelby County, Tenn.; county rep. Tenn. abolitionist conv., 1834; mem. Tenn. Ho. of Reps., 1841, 43. Died Jackson, Tenn.

ALEXANDER, Adam, clergyman, also educator; b. Rockbridge County, Va.; Apr. 17, 1772; s. William and Ann (Reid) A.; ed. Liberty Hall (later Washington Coll.); m. Janetta Waddel, Apr. 5, 1802, 7 children including James W., Joseph A., Samuel D. Licensed to preach by Lexington (Va.) Presbytery, 1791; spent months in missionary tour of Va. and N.C.; ordained pastor chs. of Briery, Cub Creek (Charlotte County, N.C.), 1794; pres. Hampden-Sydney Coll., 1796-1801; pastor Pine St. Ch., Phila., 1807; a founder Princeton Theol. Sem., became 1st prof., 1812-51. Died Princeton, N.J., Oct. 22, 1851.

ALEXANDER, Armstead Milton, congressman, lawyer; b. Winchester, Ky., May 26, 1834; grad. Bethany (Va., now W. Va.) Coll., 1853; studied law. Worked as blacksmith, nr. Paris, Mo.; 1848; gold miner in Cal., 1849; in bus., Paris, Mo.; served with Confederate Army during Civil War; admitted to Mo. bar, 1870, began practice law in Paris (but did not sign record there until 1881); pros. atty. Monroe County, Mo., 1872-76; del. Mo. Constl. Conv., 1875; mem. U.S. Ho. of Reps. (Democrat) from Mo., 48th Congress, 1883-85. Died Paris, Mo., Nov. 7, 1892; buried Walnut Grove Cemetery.

ALEXANDER, Barton Stone, army officer; b. Nicholas County, Ky., Sept. 4, 1819; s. John and Margaret (Davidson) A.; grad. U.S. Mil. Acad., 1842. Joined Corps Engrs., U.S. Army, 1842, advanced through grades to lt. col., brevetted brig. gen., 1865; took part in 1st Battle of Bull Run, Peninsular campaign, during Civil War; designed Ft. McPherson. Died San Francisco, Dec. 15, 1878.

ALEXANDER, Cosmo, artist; b. Scotland, circa 1724. Portrait painter, Edinburgh, Scotland; exhibited at London Soc. of Artists, 1765; came to Am., circa 1768, painted in N.Y.C., 1768, Burlington, N.J., 1768-69, Newport, R.I., 1769-70, in the South, 1770-71, Phila., 1770-71; instr. of Gilbert Stuart, Newport; returned to Edinburgh with Stuart, circa 1771; name also appears as Cosmo John, Cosmos. Died Edinburgh, Aug. 25, 1772.

ALEXANDER, Evan Shelby, congressman, Mecklenburg County, N.C., circa 1767; grad. Princeton, 1787; studied law. Admitted to N.C. bar, began practice law, Salisbury, N.C.; mem. N.C., House of Commons, 1796-1803; trustee U. N.C., 1799-1809; mem. U.S. Ho. of Reps. (filled vacancy) from N.C., 9th-10th congresses, Feb. 24, 1806-09. Died Oct. 28, 1809.

ALEXANDER, Francis, portrait painter, lithographer; b. Killingly, Conn., Feb. 3, 1800; ed. Acad. Fine Arts, 1820; m. Lucia Gray Swett. Portraits include Daniel Webster (1835), Benjamin R. Curtis, Mrs. Daniel Webster, Charles Dickens. Died Florence, Italy, circa 1881.

ALEXANDER, Henry Porteous, congressman, businessman; b. Little Falls, N.Y., Sept. 13, 1801; attended public schs. Mcht. and banker, Little Falls; pres. Village of Little Falls, 1834, 35; pres. Herkimer County Bank, Little Falls, 1839-67; mem. U.S. Ho. of Reps. (Whig) from N.Y., 31st Congress, 1849-51. Died Little Falls, Feb. 22, 1867; buried Church Street Cemetery.

ALEXANDER, James, lawyer; b. Scotland, 1691; m. Mrs. Provoost, 5 children including William. Fought in Rebellion of 1715 (resulted in exile of Stuarts from Eng.); surveyor gen. Province of N.J., 1715; recorder of Perth Amboy (N.J.) 1718; mem. Council of N.Y., 1721-32; admitted t N.J. provincial bar, 1723; mem. Council of N.J. 1723-35; atty. gen. N.J., 1723-27; temporaril disbarred because of serving as co-defense lawy for John Peter Zenger (charged with treasono editorials, 1734). Died Albany, N.Y., Apr. 2, 175

ALEXANDER, James, Jr., congressman, bus nessman; b. nr. Delta, Pa., Oct. 17, 1789. Move to Northwest Territory with father, 1799, engag in farming, St. Clairsville, O., also river trans on Ohio and Mississippi rivers, later became mcht. St. Clairsville; mem. Ohio Ho. of Reps., 1830, 3 34; asso. judge Ct. of Common Pleas, 1831 mem. U.S. Ho. of Reps. (Democrat) from Ohi 25th Congress, 1837-39; purchased large tract c land and moved to Wheeling, Va. (now W. Va.) 1843; owner extensive farm land in Ill. Died Mc Nabb, Ill., Sept. 5, 1846; buried Scotch Rid Cemetery, nr. St. Clairsville.

ALEXANDER, James Waddel, clergyman, educa tor; b. Louisa County, Va., Mar. 13, 1804; son c Archibald Alexander; grad. Princeton, 1820; studie theology at Princeton Sem.; at least 1 son William Cowper. Tutor, Princeton, 1824-25, prof rhetoric and belles lettres, 1833-44, prof. eccles history and ch. govt. Princeton Theol. Sem., 1849-51 licensed to preach by Presbytery of New Bruns wick, N.J., 1824; pastor of ch., Charlotte County Va., 1825-28, 1st Presbyn. Ch., Trenton, N.J., 1828 32; editor The Presbyn., Phila., 1932-33; pasto Duane Street Presbyn. Ch., N.Y.C., 1844-49, Fift Avenue Presbyn. Ch., N.Y.C., 1851-59. Author work including: The American Mechanic and Workingma (essays); Discourses on Christian Faith and Practice 1858. Died Virginia Springs, Va., July 31, 1859

ALEXANDER, John, congressman, lawyer; b Crowsville, Spartanburg Dist., S.C., Apr. 16, 1777 studied law. Moved to Ohio, 1803; admitted to Ohi bar, began practice law, 1804; began practice law Xenia, O., 1805, also practiced in Columbus, Chil licothe (O.), and before U.S. Supreme Ct.; pros atty., 1808-33; mem. U.S. Ho. of Reps. (Democrat, from Ohio, 13th-14th congresses, 1813-1817; mem Ohio Senate, 1822, 23; served 2 terms in Ohio Ho of Reps.; ret. from law practice, 1834. Died Xenia June 28, 1848; buried Woodlawn Cemetery

ALEXANDER, John Henry, scientist; b. Anna polis, Md., June 26, 1812; s. William and Mary (Stockett) A.; ed. St. John's Coll., 1826; m. Margaret Hammer, 1836, 6 children. Apptd. stat topog. engr. Md., 1834; a founder Georges Creek Coal & Iron Co., pres., 1836-45; published A Universal Dictionary of Weights and Measures Ancient and Modern, 1850; incorporator Nat. Acad Sci. Died Balt., Mar. 2, 1867.

ALEXANDER, Joseph Addison, educator; b. Phila., Apr. 24, 1809; s. Archibald and Janetta (Waddel) A.; grad. Princeton, 1826; D.D. (hon.), Rutgers Coll., 1844. Prof. ancient langs. and lit. Princeton, 1830-33; instr. Princeton Theol. Sem., 1834, asso. prof., 1838, prof. oriental and bibl. lit., 1840-51, prof. bibl. and eccles. history, 1851. Author: The Psalms, 2 vols., 1850; Isaiah, 2 vols., 1846-47; Acts, 2 vol., 1857; Mark, 1858. Died Princeton, N.J., Jan. 28, 1860.

ALEXANDER, Mark, congressman; b. nr. Boydton, Mecklenburg County, Va., Feb. 7, 1792; grad. U. N.C., 1811; studied law. Admitted to the bar, began practice law, Boydton; mem. Va. Ho. of Dels., 1817-19; mem. U.S. Ho. of Reps. (State Rights Democrat) from Va., 16th-22d congresses, 1819-33; del. State Constl. Conv., 1829; ret. from polit. life to manage large estate. Died Scotland Neck, N.C., Oct. 7, 1883; buried cemetery of the old Episcopal Ch.

ALEXANDER, Nathaniel, state gov., congressman; b. nr. Concord, Mecklenburg County, N.C., Mar. 5, 1756; grad. Princeton, 1776; studied medicine and surgery. Served as surgeon during Revolutionary War, 1778-82; practiced medicine, High Hills of Santee, S.C., after war; continued practice later in Charlotte, N.C.; mem. N.C. House of Commons, 1797, N.C. Senate, 1801, 02; mem. U.S. Ho. of Reps. from N.C., 8th-9th congresses, 1803-Nov. 1805; resigned to become gov. N.C., 1805-07. Died Salisbury, N.C., Mar. 7, 1808; buried Old Cemetery, Charlotte.

ALEXANDER, Robert, Continental congressman; b. Cecil County, Md.; studied law. Admitted to the bar, practiced law; mem. Md. Provincial Conv., 1774, 75, 76; sec. Balt. com. of observation, mem. council of safety, 1775; mem. Continental Congress from Md., 1775, 76; fled from Md. (after Declaration of Independence carried out), joined Brit. Fleet, became mem. Associated Loyalists of Am., sailed for London, Eng., 1782; found guilty of high treason, property confiscated, 1780. Died London, Eng.

ALEXANDER, Samuel Davies, clergyman; b. Princeton, N.J., May 3, 1819; s. Archibald and anetta (Waddel) A.; grad. Coll. of N.J. (now Princeton), 1838; attended Princeton Theol. Sem., 1844-47. Ordained to ministry by 2d Presbytery of Phila., 1847; pastor Richmond Ch., Phila., 1847-49, Presbyn. Ch., Freehold, N.J., 1851-56; in charge of 15th Street Ch. (later known as Phillips Ch.), N.Y.C., 1856-89, pastor emeritus, 1889-94. Author: Life Sketches from Scottish History, 1855; Princeton College during the Eighteenth Century, 1872; The Presbytery of New York 1738 to 1888. Died Oct. 26, 1894.

ALEXANDER, Stephen, astronomer; b. Schenectady, N.Y., Sept. 1, 1806; s. Alexander and Maria ...; grad. Union Coll., 1824; attended Princeton Theol. Sem., 1832. LL.D. (hon.), Columbia, 1852; m. Louisa Meads, Oct. 3, 1826; m. 2d, Caroline Foreman, Jan. 2, 1850; 5 children. Tutor in mathematics Coll. of N.J. (now Princeton), 1832, prof. astronomy, 1840, prof. mathematics, 1845-54, prof. astronomy, mechanics, 1855-78; head expdn. to observe solar eclipse, Labrador, 1860. An original mem. Nat. Acad. Scis., 1862; mem. Am. Philos. Soc., Am. Acad. Arts and Scis., A.A.A.S. (pres. 1859). Died June 25, 1883.

ALEXANDER, William (known as Lord Stirling), army officer; b. N.Y.C., 1726; s. James Alexander; m. sister of Gov. Livingston of N.J. Surveyor gen. N.J.; attempted to establish claim to title 6th earl Stirling, 1756, claim rejected by English Ho. of Lords, 1762; mem. N.J. Common Council, asst. to gov. N.J.; fought in French and Indian War; commd. col. 1st N.J. Regt., 1775, brig. gen. Continental Army, 1776; comdr.-in-chief N.Y.C., 1776, built fts. Lee and Washington for defense of city, also Ft. Stirling (named for him), Brooklyn Heights, N.Y., 1777; head right wing Continental Army at Battle of L.I., 1776; fought at Battle of Trenton, promoted maj. gen., 1777; led div. Battle of Brandywine, commanded reserves Battle of Germantown, left wing Battle of Monmouth; served on ct. inquiry at trial of Benedict Arnold, 1780; an early gov. King's Coll. (now Columbia). Died Albany, N.Y., Jan. 15, 1783.

ALFONCE (Alfonse), Jean, see Allefonsce, Jean.

ALFORD, Julius Caesar, congressman; b. Greensboro, Ga., May 10, 1799; studied law. Admitted to Ga. bar, practiced law, also planter, LaGrange, Ga.; mem. Ga. Ho. of Reps.; commanded a co. in Creek War of 1836; mem. U.S. Ho. of Reps. from Ga. (State Rights Whig, filled vacancy), 24th Congress, Jan. 2-Mar. 3, 1837, (Harrison Whig) 26th-27th congresses, 1839-Oct. 1, 1841, resigned; moved to Tuskegee, Ala., then nr. Montgomery, Ala.; del. Union Conv., Montgomery, 1852; practiced law. Died on plantation nr. Montgomery, Jan. 1, 1863; buried family cemetery on his estate nr. Montgomery.

ALGER, Cyrus, iron-master, inventor; b. West Bridgewater, Mass., Nov. 11, 1781; s. Abiezer and Hepsibah (Keith) A.; m. Lucy Willis, 1804, 7 children; m. 2d, Mary Pillsbury, 1833. Established iron foundry, 1809; designed 1st cylinder stoves 1822; contbr. rapid devel. of South Boston; alderman South Boston, 1824-27; formed So. Boston Iron Co., 1827; his shop turned out 1st gun ever rifled, 1834; Cyrus Alger Primary Sch. named after him, 1881; considered one of outstanding metallurgists of his time. Died Boston, Feb. 4, 1856.

ALISON, Francis, clergyman, coll. ofcl.; b. County Donegal, Ireland, 1705; attneded U. Glasgow (Scotland), D.D. (hon.), 1758; A.M. (hon.), Yale, 1755, Princeton, 1755; m. Hannah Armitage, at least 2 children including Dr. Francis, Came to Am. 1735, went to Md., then New London, Pa.; tutor in home of Samuel Dickinson, Md.; licensed to preach by Presbyn. Ch., circa 1737; opened Coll. of Phila., 1743, subsidized by Synod of Phila., became vice provost, 1755; asst. pastor 1st Presbyn. Ch. of Phila; founded Presbyn. Soc. for Relief of Ministers and their Widows. Died Phila., Nov. 28, 1779.

ALLAIRE, James Peter, master mechanic, steam engine builder; b. 1785; m. Frances Roe; m. 2d, Calicia Tompkins. Began as brass founder, N.Y.C., 1813; founder Allaire Works (1st steam engine works in N.Y.), 1815, Howell Works, 1831; built 1st compound-type engine for marine purposes; built 1st house designed as tenement, N.Y.C., 1833. Died May 20, 1858.

ALLAN, Chilton, congressman, lawyer; b. Albemarle County, Va., Apr. 6, 1786; attended common schs., studied law. Served as an apprentice to a wheelwright, 3 years; admitted to Ky. bar, 1808, began practice law, Winchester, Ky.; mem. Ky. Ho. of Reps., 1811, 15, 22, 30, 42; mem. Ky. Senate, 1823-27; mem. U.S. Ho. of Reps. (Clay Democrat) from Ky., 22d-24th congresses, 1831-37; pres. Ky. Bd. Internal Improvements, 1837-39. Died Winchester, Sept. 3, 1858; buried Winchester Cemetery.

ALLAN, John, army officer; b. Edinburgh Castle, Scotland, Jan. 3, 1747; s. William and Isabella (Maywell) A.; m. Mary Patton, Oct. 10, 1767, 5 children. Came with family to Nova Scotia, Can., 1749; justice of peace, clk. of sessions, clk. Supreme Ct., (all at Halifax, N.S.), engaged in argl. and merc. bus.; mem. N.S. Provincial Assembly, 1770-76; came to Mass. to fight in Am. Revolution, 1776; leader St. John Expdn. of 1777; apptd. col. Mass. Militia, 1777; apptd. agt. to Eastern Indians by Continental Congress, 1777-83, kept Indians from joining the British; became leader Am. sympathizers in N.S. after Am. Revolution; engaged in merc. bus., Passamaquoddy Bay, Me., 1784-86. Died Allan's Island, Passamaquoddy Bay, Feb. 7, 1805.

ALLEFONSCE, Jean, explorer; b. Saintonge, France, circa 1482. Chief pilot for Roberval on journey to Am., Apr.-June 1542; explored for Western Passage along St. Lawrence River; made maps of coasts which appeared in Cosmographie, 1545. Author: Voyages Avantureux, published posthumously, 1559. Died reef of Rochelle, Bay of Biscay, France, circa 1557.

ALLEN, Andrew, Continental congressman, Loyalist; b. Phila., June 1740; s. William and Margaret (Hamilton) A.; grad. U. Pa., 1759; m. Sally Coxe, Apr. 21, 1768. Admitted to practice Pa. Supreme Ct., 1765; became atty. gen. Province of Pa., 1769; recorder city of Phila., 1774; mem. Pa. Com. of Safety, 1775; mem. Continental Congress, from Pa., 1776-77, renounced allegiance to Congress, took oaths of allegiance to the king, returned to Eng. Died London, Eng., Mar. 7, 1825.

ALLEN, Andrew Jackson, actor; b. N.Y.C., Dec. 1776. Appeared in Romeo and Juliet, John Street Theatre, N.Y.C., 1787, in extravagant prodn. The Battle of Lake Champlain, Bernard's Green Street Theater, Albany, N.Y., 1815; character actor, in gen. played villains and clowns in pantomimes; fled because of debts to Pensacola, Fla., 1820, managed theater in Pensacola; toured Ohio and Va. sending up balloons, 1822; became costumer, followed Edwin Forrest throughout U.S. and to Europe, then established himself in N.Y.C. Died N.Y.C., Oct. 29, 1853.

ALLEN, Anthony Benezet, farmer; b. Hampshire County, Mass., June 24, 1802; s. Samuel and Ruth (Falley) A; m. Mary E. Butterworth, 1852. Moved to Buffalo (N.Y.) to farm and breed livestock, 1833; visited Eng. to study livestock, 1841; founder, co-editor (with brother Richard L.) Am. Agriculturist, 1842-56; formed (with Richard) farm machinery bus. A.B. Allen & Co., 1847; toured Europe studying farming methods, 1867; purchased farm on Toms River, Ocean County, N.J., 1870. Died Jan. 12, 1892.

ALLEN, Charles, congressman, jurist; b. Worcester, Mass., Aug. 9, 1797; grandson of Samuel Adams; attended Leicester Acad., 1809-11, Yale, 1811, 12; studied law. Admitted to Mass. bar, 1818, practiced New Braintree, Mass.; began practice law, Worcester, 1824; mem. Mass. Ho. of Reps., 1830, 33, 35, 40; mem. Mass. Senate, 1836, 37; mem. Northeastern Boundary Commn., 1842; judge Ct. of Common Pleas, 1842-45; del. Whig Nat. Conv., Phila., 1848; mem. U.S. Ho. of Reps. (Free Soil Party) from Mass., 31st-32d congresses, 1849-53; mem. Mass. Constl. Conv., 1853; chief justice Suffolk County Superior Ct., 1859-67; del. to Washington (D.C.) Peace Conv., 1861. Died Worcester, Aug. 6, 1869; buried Rural Cemetery.

ALLEN, David Oliver, missionary; b. Barre, Mass., Sept. 14, 1799; s. Moses and Mehitable (Oliver) A.; grad. Amherst Coll., 1823, Andover Theol. Sem., 1827; m. Myra Wood, 1827; m. 2d, Orpah Graves, Feb. 22, 1838; m. 3d, Azuba Condit, Dec. 12, 1843; m. 4th, Mrs. Mary S. Barnes, May 3, 1858; 1 son, Myron Wood. Ordained to ministry Congregational Ch., Westminster, Mass., ordained to Fgn. Missionary Service, 1827; sec. Bombay Tract and Book Soc., 1827-32; sec. Brit. and Fgn. Bible Soc., 1832-52; active Seaman's Friend Soc., Bombay Edn. Soc., Bombay Dist. Benevolent Soc.; mem. Royal Soc., Am. Oriental Soc.; translated part, published whole of Bible into Marathi Indian lang. Author: India, Ancient and Modern, 1856; editor The Temperance Advocate. Died Lowell, Mass., July 19, 1863.

ALLEN, Elisha Hunt, congressman, diplomat; b. New Salem, Mass., Jan. 28, 1804; s. Samuel Clessen and Mary (Hunt) A.; grad. Williams Coll., 1823; m. Sarah Fessenden; m. 2d, Mary Hobbs; children include son, Frederick. Admitted to Mass. bar, 1826; mem. Me. Ho. of Reps., 1835-40; mem. U.S. Ho. of Reps. (Whig) from Me., 27th Congress, 1841-43; mem. Mass. Legislature from Boston, 1849; U.S. Consul to Hawaii, 1850-57; minister of finance in Hawaii, 1857; chancellor, chief justice of Hawaii, 1857-76; Hawaiian minister, Washington, D.C., 1876-83. Died suddenly at Pres. Arthur's New Years reception, Washington, Jan. 1, 1883; buried Mt. Auburn Cemetery, Cambridge, Mass.

ALLEN, Ethan, army officer; born in Litchfield, Conn., Jan. 21, 1738; s. Joseph and Mary (Baker) A.; m. Mary Bronson, 1762; m. 2d, Mrs. Frances (Montresor) Buchanan, 1784; 8 children including Fanny, Hannibal, Ethan. Served in French and Indian War, 1757; lived in N.H. Grants (area over which control was disputed by N.Y. and N.H.), 1769; became col. comdt. Green Mountain Boys (group formed for purpose of making N.H. Grants into the separate province of Vt.). 1770; his activities caused gov. of N.Y. to offer reward of 20 pounds for his capture, 1771 (increased to 100 pounds, 1774); apptd. (with others) at Westminster meeting to prepare petition to King, 1775; his efforts to make Vt. a separate state were interrupted by Battle of Lexington; captured Ft. Ticonderoga (on instructions from Conn.), 1775; captured while serving in expdn. against Canada, 1775, exchanged for Col. Archibald Campbell, 1778; brevetted col. Continental Army by Gen. George Washington; presented Vt. claims to Continental Congress (with no success), 1778; promoted maj. gen. Vt. Militia; corresponded with comdr. of Brit. forces in Canada (not known whether Allen actually wanted Vt. to become Brit. province, or used correspondence to pressure Congress into making Vt. a separate state), 1780; moved to Burlington, Vt., 1787. Author: An Animadversory Address to the Inhabitants of the State of Vermont, 1778; A Narrative of Col. Ethan Allen's Captivity (does not mention Benedict Arnold's aid in capturing Ft. Ticonderoga), 1779; Reason the Only Oracle of Man; or, A Compendious System of Natural Religion, Bennington, 1784. Died Burlington, Feb. 2, 1789; buried with mil. honors in a valley nr. Winooski, Vt.

ALLEN, Frances, nun; b. Sunderland, Vt., Nov. 13, 1784; d. Gen. Ethan Allen. Went to Montreal, Can., at age 21, studied under Sisters of Congregation of Notre Dame; became convert to Roman Catholic Ch.; made religious profession at Hotel Dieu, 1810. Died Montreal, Sept. 10, 1819.

ALLEN, Frederic De Forest, philologist; b. Oberlin, O., May 25, 1844; s. George N. and Mary (Rudd) A.; grad. Oberlin Coll., 1863; Ph.D. in Philosophy, U. Leipzig (Germany), 1870; A.M. (hon.), Yale, 1879; m. Emmeline Laighton, Dec. 26, 1878, 1 child. Prof. Greek and Latin, U. East Tenn., Knoxville, 1866-68, 70-73; tutor in Greek, Harvard, 1873, prof. classical philology, 1880; prof. Greek, Yale, 1879; pres. Am. Philol. Assn., 1881-82; dir. Am. Sch. Classical Studies, Athens, Greece, 1885-86. Author: Remnants of Early Latin, 1880; revised Hadley's Greek Grammar, 1884. Died Cambridge, Mass., Aug. 4, 1897.

ALLEN, George, educator; b. Milton, Vt., Dec. 17, 1808; s. Heman and Sarah (Prentiss) A.; grad. U. Vt., 1827; m. Mary Hancock Withington, July 7, 1831, 4 children. Prof. langs. U. Vt., 1828-1830; admitted to Vt. bar, 1831; tchr. Vt. Episcopal Inst.; ordained minister Episcopal Ch., 1834; prof. langs. Del. Coll., 1837-45; prof. Latin and Greek U. Pa., 1845; became Roman Catholic, 1847; counsel for Pope Pius IX, Phila.; mem. Shakespeare Soc. of Phila. Author: Chapters on Chess in Philadelphia, 1859; The Life of Philidor, 1863. Died Worcester, Mass., May 28, 1876; buried Cathedral Cemetery, Phila.

ALLEN, Harrison, anatomist, physician; b. Phila., Apr. 17, 1841; s. Samuel and Elizabeth (Thomas) A.; M.D., U. Pa., 1861; m. Julia A. Colton, Dec. 1869. Asst. surgeon U.S. Army, 1862, brevetted maj., 1865; prof. zoology, comparative anatomy Auxiliary Faculty Medicine, U. Pa., 1865-97; prof. anatomy and surgery Pa. Dental Coll., 1866-78. Fellow Coll. Physicians of Phila.; mem. Path. Soc., Am. Laryngol. Assn. (a founder). Author: Monograph of the Bats of North America, 1864; System of Anatomy, 1884. Died Phila., Nov. 14, 1897.

ALLEN, Heman (of Milton, Vt.), congressman; b. Ashfield (now Deerfield), Mass., June 14, 1777; attended acad., Chesterfield, N.H.; studied law. Admitted to Vt. bar, 1803, began practice law, Milton, Vt.; mem. Vt. Ho. of Reps., 1810-14, 16, 17, 22, 24-26; began practice law, Burlington, Vt., 1828; mem. U.S. Ho. of Reps. (Whig) from Vt., 22d-25th congresses, 1831-39. Died Burlington, Dec. 11, 1844; buried Elmwood Av. Cemetery.

ALLEN, Heman, (of Colchester), congressman; b. Poultney, Vt., Feb. 23, 1779; grad. Dartmouth, 1795; m. Elizabeth Hart, circa 1823. Admitted to Vt. bar, 1801; practiced in Colchester, Vt.; sheriff Chittenden County (Vt.), 1808-09, chief justice county court, 1811-14; mem. Vt. Ho. of Reps., 1812-17; mem. U.S. Ho. of Reps. (Democrat) from Vt., 15th Congress, 1817-Apr. 20, 1818; U.S. marshal for dist. of Vt., 1818-22; U.S. minister to Chile, 1823-27; pres. Burlington (Vt.) br. U.S. Bank, 1830-36; moved to Highgate, Vt., resumed law practice. Died Highgate, Apr. 7, 1852; buried Allen Cemetery, Burlington.

ALLEN, Henry Watkins, army officer, gov. La.; b. Prince Edward County, Va., Apr. 29, 1820; s.

Dr. Thomas and Ann (Watkins) A.; attended Marion Coll. (Mo.), 1835-37; m. Salome Crane. Elected to La. Legislature, 1853; commd. col. 4th La. Regt., Confederate Army, 1862, brig. gen., 1863; gov. La., 1864-65. Author: The Travels of a Sugar Planter, 1861. Died Mexico City, Mexico, Apr. 22, 1866.

ALLEN, Horatio, civil engr., inventor; b. Schenectady, N.Y., May 10, 1802; s. Dr. Benjamin and Mary (Benedict) A.; A.B., Columbia, 1823; m. Mary Moncrief Simons, 1834, 4 children. Chief engr. S.C. R.R. Co., 1829; asst. prin. engr. Croton Aqueduct, 1838; cons. engr. N.Y. & Erie R.R. Co.; a propr. Novelty Iron Works, 1842; pres. Erie R.R., 1843; cons. engr. constrn. Bklyn. Bridge, also Panama R.R., 1870. An organizer N.Y Gallery Art; pres. Am. Soc. C.E., 1872; a founder Union League Club, N.Y.C. Died South Orange, N.J., Dec. 31, 1899.

ALLEN, Ira, pioneer, army officer; b. Cornwall, Conn., May 1, 1751; s. Joseph and Mary (Baker) A.; m. Jerusha Enos, circa 1789, 3 children including Ira H. Lived in N.H. Grants (now Vt.) with brothers Ethan, Herman, Heber and Levi, 1772, mem. Green Mountain Boys; represented Colchester in Dorset Conv. (Vt.), 1776; mem. Constl. Com. of Windsor Conv. (Vt.), 1777, wrote preamble to constn. sec. Council of Safety; mem. V.t Gov.'s Council, 1777; 1st treas. Vt., 1778; involved in plot with Gt. Britain to make Vt. a province of England, 1780-81, apparently hoped to force Continental Congress to recognize independence of Vt.; negotiated comml. treaties with Quebec; gave land valued at 4,000 pounds to build U. Vt.; in England to secure arms for Vt. Militia (of which he was maj. gen.), 1795, obtained them in France instead, captured by British while sailing home in ship Olive Branch, 1796, Brit. courts decided in his favor; returned to U.S., 1801, found that his land had been seized, thrown into prison released by Vt. Legislature, granted immunity from arrest for 1 year; fled to Phila. Author: Natural and Political History of the State of Vermont, 1798; Particulars of the Capture of the Ship Olive Branch, 1798; also pamphlets listed in M.D. Gilman's Bibliography of Vermont, 1897. Died Phila., Jan. 15, 1814.

ALLEN, Jeremiah Mervin, engr.; b. Enfield, Conn., May 18, 1833; s. Jeremiah V. and Emily (Pease) A.; m. Harriet S. Griswold, 1856. Taught sch., Longmeadow, Mass., 1861-65; with ins. co., Hartford, Conn., 1865-67; pres. of firm which insured against damage to steam-boilers, 1867-1903; trustee Hartford Theol. Sem.; pres. YMCA, 1 term. Died Dec. 29, 1903.

ALLEN, John, congressman, lawyer; b. Great Barrington, Mass., June 12, 1763; attended Litchfield (Conn.) Law Sch. Admitted to Conn. bar, 1786, began practice of law, Litchfield; mem. Conn. Ho. of Reps., 1793-96, clk., 1796; mem. U.S. Ho. of Reps. (Federalist) from Conn., 5th Congress, 1797-99; mem. Conn. Council, also Supreme Ct. of Errors, 1800-06. Died July 31, 1812; buried East Cemetery.

ALLEN, John, dentist, inventor; b. Broome County, N.Y., Nov. 4, 1810; s. Nirum Allen. M.D., Cincinnati Med. Coll.; studied dentistry under Dr. James Harris, Chillicothe, O.; m. Charlotte Dana, 1835, 1 son, Charles; m. 2d, Mrs. Cornelia Reeder, 1 dau. Practiced dentistry primarily in N.Y.C.; devised new denture; recipient gold medal from Am. Soc. Dental Surgeons for devising method of restoring facial contours which fell in due to previous denture practices, 1845; granted patent for new denture method, 1851; made false teeth of porcelain with platinum base instead of gold (enabled him to devise continous gum to prevent oral fluids from entering into crevices of teeth); involved in much litigation over invention with Dr. William Hunter. Mem. Am. Soc. Dental Surgeons; a founder Ohio Coll. Dental Surgery, 1845, N.Y. Coll. Dentistry, 1865. Died Plainfield, N.J., Mar. 8, 1892.

ALLEN, John F., inventor; b. Eng., 1829. Came to Am., 1841; engr. aboard ship Curlew in Long Island Sound, invented new form of high speed valve motion; became engr. for Henry A. Burr, felt-hat body mfr., N.Y.C., 1860; formed (with Charles Porter, inventor of engine governor) Porter-Allen Co., produced Porter-Allen engine (pioneer high-speed steam engine); invented inclined tube vertical water-tube boiler; opened his own shop, Mott Haven, N.Y.; inventor of 2 pneumatic riveting systems (1 by percussion, 1 by pressure). Died N.Y.C., Oct. 4, 1900.

ALLEN, John James, jurist; b. Woodstock, Va., Sept. 25, 1797; s. James and Jean (Steele) A.; attended Washington Coll. (Va.), Dickinson Coll. (Pa.); married, 1824. Admitted to Va. bar, 1818; mem. Va. Senate, 1827-30; mem. U.S. Ho. of Reps. from Va., 23d Congress, 1833-35; commonwealth atty. for counties of Harrison, Lewis and Preston (Va.), 1834; judge 17th Circuit Ct. Va., 1836-40; judge Va. Supreme Ct. of Appeals, 1840-65, presiding justice 1852-65. Died Botetourt County, Va., Sept. 18, 1871.

ALLEN, John William, congressman, businessman; b. Litchfield, Conn., Aug. 1802; studied law, Chenango County, N.Y. and Cleve. O. Admitted to Ohio bar, 1826, began practice law, Cleve.; pres. Village of Cleve., 1831-35; a dir. Comml. Bank of Lake Erie, from 1832; an incorporator Cleve., Newburg R.R. Co., 1834; an organizer Ohio R.R. Co., 1836; mem. Ohio Senate, 1836, 37; mem. U.S. Ho. of Reps. (Whig) from Ohio, 25th-26th congresses, 1837-41; elected mayor Cleve., 1841; became pres. Cleve., Columbus & Cincinnati R.R., 1845; del. to 1st conv. on river and harbor improvement, Chgo., 1847; postmaster Cleve., 1870-75; one of 1st bank commrs. of Ohio. Died Cleve., Oct. 5, 1887; buried Erie St. Cemetery.

ALLEN, Joseph, congressman; b. Boston, Sept. 2, 1749; grad. Harvard, 1774. In bus., Leicester, Mass., moved to Worcester, Mass., 1776; mem. Mass. Constl. Conv., 1788; Federalist presdl. elector, 1797; clk. of the cts., until 1810; mem. U.S. Ho. of Reps. (filled vacancy) from Mass., 11th Congress, Oct. 8, 1810-11; state councilor, 1815-18. Died Worcester, Sept. 2, 1827; buried Mechanic Street Burying Ground.

ALLEN, Joseph Henry, clergyman; b. Northboro, Mass., Aug. 21, 1820; s. Joseph and Mrs. (Ware) A.; grad. Harvard, 1840, divinity dept., 1843; m. Anna Minot Weld, May 22, 1845, 3 sons, 3 daus. Ordained to ministry 1st Congregational Soc. of Jamaica Plain,, Mass., 1843; in charge of Unitarian Ch., Washington, D.C., 1847; minister, Bangor, Me., 1850; taught in Jamaica Plain, Northboro and West Newton, 1857-60; asso. editor Christian Examiner, 1863-65; lectr. eccles. history Harvard, 1878-82; editor Unitarian Review, 1887-91. Author: Manual Latin Grammar, 1868; Latin Primer, 1870. Died Cambridge, Mass., Mar. 20, 1898.

ALLEN, Judson, congressman, businessman; b. Plymouth, Conn., Apr. 3, 1797; attended public schs. In lumber bus.; moved to Harpursville, N.Y.; apptd. postmaster Harpursville, 1830-39; judge Broome County (N.Y.) Ct., 8 years; mem. N.Y. State Assembly, 1836-37; mem. U.S. Ho. of Reps. (Democrat) from N.Y., 26th Congress, 1839-41; moved to St. Louis, Mo., engaged in produce, lumber, marble, grocery bus. Died St. Louis, Aug. 6, 1880; buried Bellefontaine Cemetery.

ALLEN, Lewis Falley, stock breeder; b. Westfield, Mass., Jan. 1, 1800; s. Samuel and Ruth (Falley) A.; m. Margaret Cleveland, 1825. Prominent resident of Buffalo, N.Y., 1836-90; editor Am. Shorthorn Herdbook; mem. N.Y. Legislature; pres. N.Y. State Agrl. Soc. Author: American Cattle, 1868; History of the Shorthorn Cattle, 1872. Died May 2, 1890.

ALLEN, Nathan, physician; b. Princeton, Mass., Apr. 25, 1813; s. Moses and Mehitable (Oliver) A.; grad. Amherst Coll., 1836; M.D., U. Pa., 1841; m. Sarah H. Spaulding, Sept. 24, 1841; m. 2d, Annie A. Waters, May 20, 1857. Editor, Am. Phrenol. Journal and Miscellany, 1839-42; practiced medicine, Lowell, Mass., 1841-89. Author: The Intermarriage of Relations, 1869; Physical Degeneracy, 1870; The Treatment of the Insane, 1876. Died Lowell, Jan. 1, 1889.

ALLEN, Nathaniel, congressman; b. East Bloomfield, N.Y., 1780; attended common schs. Worked as blacksmith, Canandaigua, N.Y.; started blacksmith shop at Richmond, nr. Allens Hill, N.Y., 1796; served as officer in militia; apptd. postmaster Honeoye Falls, N.Y., 1811; commr. and paymaster on Niagara frontier, 1812; mem. N.Y. State Assembly, 1812; sheriff Ontario County, N.Y., 1815-19; mem. U.S. Ho. of Reps. from N.Y., 16th Congress, 1819-21; supr. Town of Richmond, 1824-26; prosecuted claims for money due in connection with constrn. Louisville & Portland Canal. Died Gault House, Louisville, Ky., Dec. 22, 1832; buried churchyard Episcopal Ch., Allens Hill, Ontario County, N.Y.

ALLEN, Paul, editor, author; b. Providence, R.I., Feb. 15, 1775; s. Paul and Polly (Cooke) A.; grad. R.I. Coll. (now Brown U.), 1793. Delivered oration at college on death of classmate Roger Williams Howell (his 1st published work), 1792; published at least 6 other published orations still in existence, 1796-1806; moved to Phila., contbr. to U.S. Gazette and Port Folio, supervised printing of History of the Expedition, Under the Command of Captains Lewis and Clark, 1814; Portico, Balt., 1814-26; edited Fed. Republican and Balt. Telegraph, Journal of the Times, Balt., Morning Chronicle, Balt., 1818-24, Saturday Evening Herald 1824; published Morning Post. Author: Original Poems, Serious and Entertaining, 1801; Noah, 1821. Died Balt., Aug. 18, 1826.

ALLEN, Philip, mfr., senator, gov. R.I.; b. Providence, R.I., Sept. 1, 1785; s. Capt. Zachariah and Nancy (Crawford) A.; grad. R.I. Coll. (now Brown U.), 1803; m. Phoebe Aborn, Jan. 1814, 11 children. Constructed 1st steam engine ev built in Providence; mem. R.I. Ho. of Reps. fro Providence, 1819-21; pres. R.I. br. U.S. Ban 1827-36; gov. R.I (Democrat), 1851-53; mer U.S. Senate from R.I., 1853-59, chmn com. agr. Died Providence, Dec. 16, 1865; buried Nor Burial Ground Providence.

ALLEN, Richard, clergyman; b. Phila., Feb. 1 1760. Ordained minister at 1st conf. of Methodi Ch., Balt., 1784; preacher St. George Methodi Ch., Phila., 1786; influenced majority of mems. Free African Soc. to organize as an independe Methodist ch., 1794, ordained deacon of new formed ch., 1799, elder, 1816; 1st bishop Afric Methodist Episcopal Ch. (formed by union wi other Negro congregations of N.Y., N.J., Del. ar Md. 1816), 1816-31. Died Mar. 26, 1831.

ALLEN, Richard Lamb, argiculturist; b. Wes field, Mass., Oct. 20, 1803; s. Samuel and Ru (Falley) A.; m. Sally O. Lyman, Dec. 30, 183 Owner (with brother Anthony B.) farm, Buffal N.Y.; founded Am. Agriculturist, N.Y.C., 184 co-editor, 1849-56; formed (with brother) A. Allen & Co., farm machinery bus. Author: A Bri Compend of American Agriculture, 1846. Di Stockholm, Sweden, Sept. 22, 1869.

ALLEN, Robert, congressman; b. August County, Va., June 19, 1778; attended Coll. Willia and Mary; studied law. Practiced law; moved Carthage, Tenn., 1804, became a mcht.; becam clk. of Smith County; served as col., commande regt. Tenn. Volunteers under Gen. Andrew Jack son, War of 1812; mem. U.S. Ho. of Reps. (Demo crat) from Tenn., 16th-19th congresses, 1819-2 del. Tenn. Conv., 1834. Died Carthage, Aug. 1 1844; buried Greenwood Cemetery, Lebanon, Tenn

ALLEN, Robert, congressman, lawyer; b. Wood stock, Shenandoah County, Va., July 30, 1794; at tended Dickinson Coll., Carlisle, Pa., 1811-12; grad Washington Coll. (now Washington and Lee U.) 1815; studied law. Farmed in Shenandoah County admitted to Va. bar, began practice law in Woodstock pros. atty. Shenandoah County; mem. Va. Senate 1821-26; mem. U.S. Ho. of Reps. (Democrat from Va., 20th-22d congresses, 1827-33; moved Bedford County, farmed. Died Mount Prospect Va., Dec. 30, 1859; buried Longwood Cemetery Liberty (now Bedford City), Va.

ALLEN, Robert, army officer; b. Ohio, July 1812; grad. U.S. Mil. Acad., 1836. Commd. 2 lt. 2d Arty., U.S. Army, served in Seminole War commd. capt., 1846; served as q.m. under Gen Zachary Taylor during Mexican War; treas., chie q.m. Mil. Govt. of Cal.; promoted maj., becam q.m. Dept. of Mo., U.S. Army (under Gen. Joh Fremont), 1861; held temporary rank col. U.S Army, 1862; commd. brig. gen. U.S. Volunteers 1863; chief q.m. various Union campaigns in Wes against Confederacy; commd. col., 1866; ret. 1878. Died Geneva, Switzerland, Aug. 5, 1886

ALLEN, Samuel Clesson, congressman, clergy man; b. Bernardston, Mass., Jan. 5, 1772; grad Dartmouth, 1794; studied theology, law. Ordaine as minister; pastor Congregational Ch., North field, 1795-98; admitted to Mass. bar, 1800, prac ticed law in New Salem; mem. Mass. Ho. of Reps. 1806-10, Mass. Senate, 1812-15, 31; mem. U.S. Ho of Reps. from Mass., 15th-20th congresses, 1817 29; mem. Mass. Gov.'s Exec. Council, 1829-30; lectr. trustee, Amherst Coll.; trustee U. Vt. Died North field, Mass., Feb. 8, 1842; buried Village Cemetery Bernardston, Mass.

ALLEN, Thomas, railroad builder, congressman b. Pittsfield, Mass., Aug. 29, 1813; s. Jonatha and Eunice (Larned) A.; grad. Union Coll., 1832 m. Ann Russell, 1842. Admitted to N.Y. bar, 1835 started The Madisonian (a Democratic paper) Washington, D.C., 1837; printer to U.S. Ho. o Reps., 1837-39; moved to St. Louis, 1842; mem Mo. Senate, 1850-54; pres. Pacific R.R., 1851 organizer banking house Allen, Copp & Nisbet, 1858; mem. U.S. Ho. of Reps. from Mo., 47t Congress, 1881-82. Died Washington, D.C., Apr 8, 1882; buried Pittsfield (Mass.) Cemetery.

ALLEN, Thomas M., clergyman; b. Shenandoa (now Warren County) Va., Oct. 21, 1797; studie law Transylvania U.; m. Rebecca Russell, 1819. Ordained to ministry, Disciples of Christ Ch., Ol Union Ch., Fayette County, Ky.; moved to Boon County, Mo., 1836; prominent in establishin Disciples of Christ in Mo.; pres. bd. curators U. Mo., 1839, 41, 64. Died Oct. 10, 1871.

ALLEN, William, jurist, mayor Phila.; b. Phila., Aug. 5, 1704; s. William Allen; m. Margaret Hamilton, Feb. 5, 1733. Entered Phila. Council, 1727, mem. Pa. Assembly, 1731-39; elected grand maste Freemasons, 1732; mayor Phila.; 1735; recorde City of Phila., 1741; chief justice Pa., 1750-74 mem. Md.-Pa. Boundary Commn., 1750-51; lai out community of Allentown, Pa. (named in hi honor), 1765; mem. bd. trustees U. Pa.; mem., officer Am. Philos. Soc. Died Eng., Sept. 6, 1780.

ALLEN, William, clergyman, coll. pres.; b. Pitts-eld, Mass., Jan. 2, 1784; s. Rev. Thomas and lizabeth (Lee) A.; grad. Harvard Coll., 1802; m. Iaria Wheelock, Jan. 28, 1813, 8 children; m. 1, Sarah Breed, Dec. 2, 1831. Licensed to preach y Berkshire Assn., 1804; asst. librarian Harvard, 805-10; compiler The American Biographical and Iistorical Dictionary, 1809; pastor 1st Congrega-onal Ch., Pittsfield, 1810-17; pres. Dartmouth, 817-19; pres. Bowdoin Coll., 1819-31, 33-38, ounder Med. Sch. of Me. at Bowdoin. Died North-ampton, Mass., July 16, 1868.

ALLEN, William, senator, gov. Ohio; b. Edenton, .C., Dec. 18, 1803; s. Nathaniel and Sarah Colburn) A.; m. Effie Coons, 1842. Admitted to hio bar 1824; mem. U.S. Ho. of Reps. from Ohio, 3d Congress, 1833-35; mem. U.S. Senate from hio, 1837-49; gov. Ohio, 1874-76; originated olit. slogan "Fifty-four forty or fight!" (referring) Ore. boundary question), 1844; known as Earthquake Allen." Died Chillicothe, O., July 1, 1879; buried Grand View Cemetery, Chillicothe.

ALLEN, William, congressman, lawyer; b. nr. Iamilton, O., Aug. 13, 1827; studied law. Sch. chr.; admitted to Ohio bar, 1849, began practice aw, Greenville, O., 1850; pros. atty. Darke County, 850-54; mem. U.S. Ho. of Reps. (Democrat) 36th-7th congresses, 1859-63; became Republican at lose of Civil War; apptd. judge ct. of common pleas, d Jud. Dist., 1865; had banking interests. Died reenville, July 6, 1881; buried Greenville Ceme-ery.

ALLEN, William Francis, classical scholar, ed-cator; b. Northboro, Mass., Sept. 5, 1830; s. oseph and Lucy (Ware) A.; grad. Harvard, 1851; 1. Mary Lambert, July 2, 1862; m. 2d, Margaret oring Andrews, June 30, 1868; 4 children in-luding Katherine. Asso. prin. English and Class-cal Sch., West Newton, Mass., 1856-63; agt. San-tary Commn., Helena, Ark., 1864; became prof. ncient langs. and history U. Wis., 1867. Author: hort History of the Roman People, (published osthumously), 1890. Co-editor widely-used sch. eries of Latin manuals. Died Madison, Wis., Dec. , 1889.

ALLEN, William Henry, naval officer; b. Provi-ence, R.I., Oct. 21, 1784; s. Gen. William and arah (Jones) A. Became midshipman U.S. Navy, 800, served aboard frigate George Washington nder Capt. William Brainbridge; promoted 3d lt. board frigate Chesapeake, commanded gun div. hen Chesapeake attacked by Brit. ship Leopard, 807; successfully petitioned (with 6 officers) to ave Commodore James Barron removed from ommand of Chesapeake (after Barron surrendered ithout engaging Leopard in action); 1st lt. in rigate United States under commodore De-atur, 1809; took part in capture of Brit. frigate Iacedonian, 1812; took command of Macedonian ith rank of master-comdt., 1812, then given com-nand of ship Argus; sailed (with Crawford, Am. ninister to France, aboard) for France, 1813, after anding Crawford at l'Orient, harried Brit. commerce n Irish Channel. Mortally wounded when Argus was aptured by British brig Pelican, Aug. 14, 1813, ied Mills Prison hosp., Aug. 18, 1813.

ALLEN, William Henry, coll. pres.; b. Read-ield (now Manchester), Me., Mar. 27, 1808; s. onathan and Thankful (Longley) A.; grad. Bowdoin Coll. 1833; m. Martha Richardson; 2d, Ellen onora; 3d, Mary Frances Quincy; 4th, Anna Gam-ill. Prof. chemistry and natural history Dickinsor Coll., 1836-46, prof. philosophy and English lit., 846-49; pres. Girard Coll., 1849-62, 67-82, Pa. Agrl. Coll., 1865-67. Pres. Am. Bible Soc., 1872. ied Phila., Aug. 29, 1882.

ALLEN, Willis, congressman, lawyer; b. nr. Ro-anoke, Va., Dec. 15, 1806; studied law. Taught ch.; moved to Wilson County, Tenn.; moved to Franklin (now Williamson) County, Ill., 1830, armed; admitted to Ill. bar, began practice law, Marion, Ill.; sheriff Franklin County, 1834-38; nem. Ill. Ho. of Reps., 1838-40; pros. atty. 1st Jud. Circuit, 1841; Democratic presdl. elector, 1844; mem. Ill. Senate, 1844-47; mem. Ill. Con-stl. Conv. 1847, 48; mem. U.S. Ho. of Reps. (Democrat) from Ill., 32d-33d congresses, 1851-55; elected judge 26th Circuit Ct. of Ill., 1859. Died Harrisburg, Ill., Apr. 15, 1859; buried Marion Cemetery.

ALLEN, Zachariah, scientist, inventor; b. Prov-idence, R.I., Sept. 15, 1795; s. Zachariah and Anne (Crawford) A.; grad. Brown U., 1813; m. Eliza Arnold, 1817. Admitted to R.I. bar, 1815; constructed 1st central furnace system for heating houses by hot air, 1821; mem. Town Council of Providence, 1822; inventor automatic steam-engine cut off, 1834; founder Mfrs. Mut. Fire Ins. Co., 1835. Died Providence, Mar. 17, 1882.

ALLERTON, Isaac, colonial ofcl.; b. circa 1586; m. Mary Norris, 1611, 3 children including Mary; m. 2d, Fear Brewster, circa 1623-27; m. 3d wife, before 1644. Joined congregation at Ley-den, S. Holland, Netherlands, 1608; a buyer and equipper of ship Speedwell, later transferred to Mayflower at Eng., sailed for Am., 1620; asst. gov. Plymouth Colony, 1621-24; went to Eng. to settle with mchts. for supplying Plymouth Colony, 1626; returned to Eng. to borrow money to pur-chase supplies and cattle to end proverty at Ply-mouth, also to arrange for rest of Leyden congre-gation to come to Plymouth, 1629; secured patent of 1630 (gave Pilgrims title to lands and property); became a trader, 1630; renounced as Plymouth's trading agt. for exceeding his authority, 1631; left Plymouth, 1631, began trading with Dutch at Manhattan, also with Delaware Bay, Va., and W.I.; mem. New Amsterdam Council, 1643. Died New Haven, Conn., Feb. 1659.

ALLEY, John Bassett, congressman, business-man; b. Lynn, Mass., Jan. 7, 1817; attended common schs. Apprenticed to shoemaker, 1831-36; moved to Cincinnati, 1836, freighted mdse. up and down Mississippi River; entered shoe mfg. bus., Lynn, Mass., 1838; established hide and leather house, Boston, 1847; mem. 1st bd. alderman, Lynn, 1850; mem. Gov.'s Council, 1847-51; mem. Mass. Senate, 1852; mem. Mass. Constl. Conv., 1853; mem. U.S. Ho. of Reps. (Republican) from Mass., 36th-39th congresses, 1859-67; became connected with Union Pacific R.R.; ret. from bus., 1886; took European trip. Died West Newton, Mass., Jan. 19, 1896; buried Pine Grove Cemetery, Lynn.

ALLIBOXE, Samuel Austin, lexicographer; b. Phila., Apr. 17, 1816; m. Mary Henry. Worked for Ins. Co. of N.Am., Phila.; editor, corr. sec. Am. Sunday Sch. Union, 1867-73, 77-79; librarian Lenox Library, N.Y.C., 1879-88; contbr. articles on George Bancroft, Alexander H. Everett and others to Appleton's Cyclopaedia of American Bibiography; went to Euorpe, 1888; works include: A Review by a Layman of a Work Entitled "New Themes for the Protestant Clergy." 1852; A Crit-ical Dictionary of English Literature and British and American Authors; An Alphabetical Index to the New Testament, 1868; The Divine Origin of the Holy Scriptures, 1869; Prose Quotations from Socrates to Macaulay, 1876; Contributions to a Catalogue of the Lenox Library. Died Lucerne, Switzerland, Sept. 2, 1889.

ALLINE, Henry, clergyman; b. Newport, R.I., June 14, 1748; s. William and Rebecca (Clerk) A. Moved to Nova Scotia, 1760; became a follower of New Light Revivalist movement headed by George Whitefield; became itinerant preacher (re-vivalist) throughout N.S., 1775; ordained minister by lay reps. from chs. he helped establish, 1779; brought New Light movement to N.S. Author: Hymns and Spiritual Songs, 1802; Two Mites Cast Into the Offering of God for the Benefit of Man-kind, 1804; Life and Journal, 1806. Died New Hampton, N.H., Feb. 2, 1784.

ALLIS, Edward Phelps, mfr.; b. Cazenovia, N.Y., May 12, 1824; s. Jere and Mary (White) A.; grad. Union Coll., Schenectady, N.Y., 1845; m. Margaret Watson, 1848, 12 children. Built and operated tanneries, Two Rivers, Wis., 1846-54; banker and realtor, 1854-61; established Reliance Iron Works, Milw., 1861, expanded to largest indsl. plant in Midwest, produced machinery for flour mill roller process, also Corliss engine; unsuccessful candidate for gov. Wis., 1877. Died Milw., Apr. 1, 1889.

ALLISON, James, Jr., congressman, lawyer; b. nr. Elkton, Md., Oct. 4, 1772; attended David Johnson's Sch., Beaver, Pa.; studied law; at least 1 son, John. Served in Indian war at Yellow Creek, Pa., admitted to Pa. bar, 1796; began practice law in Washington, Pa; practiced law, Beaver, 1803-22; pros. atty. Beaver County, 1803-09; mem. U.S. Ho. of Reps. (Whig) from Pa., 18th-19th congresses, 1823-25, resigned before 19th Con-gress assembled; ret. from law practice, 1848. Died Beaver, June 17, 1854; buried Old Cemetery.

ALLISON, John, congressman, lawyer, mfr.; b. Beaver, Pa., Aug. 5, 1812; s. of James Allison, Jr.; studied law. Admitted to the bar, engaged in limited law practice; manufactured hats, operated a tan-nery; mem. Pa. Ho. of Reps., 1846, 47, 49; mem. U.S. Ho. of Reps. (Whig) from Pa., 32d, 34th congresses, 1851-53, 55-57; del. Republican Nat. Conv., Phila., 1856, nominated Abraham Lincoln as vice pres. U.S.; del. Rep. Nat. Conv., Chgo., 1860; register of the treasury, Washington, D.C., 1869-78. Died Washington, Mar. 23, 1878; buried Beaver Cemetery.

ALLISON, Richard, army med. officer; b. nr. Goshen, Orange County, N.Y., 1757. Surgeon's mate 5th Pa. Regiment, Continental Army, 1778-83; transferred to 1st Pa. Regiment, 1783; sur-geon's mate 1st Inf. Regt., U.S. Army, 1784-88, promoted regtl. surgeon, 1788; stationed at Ft. Bibiography; went to Europe, 1888; works include: campaigns under Gen. Josiah Harmar and Gen. Arthur St. Clair; apptd. surgeon to Legion of U.S., 1792, honorably discharged when Legion dissolved, 1796; practiced medicine, Cincinnati, 1796-1816. Died Cincinnati, Mar. 22, 1816; buried Wesleyan Cemetery, Cumminsville, O.

ALLISON, Robert, congressman, lawyer; b. Greencastle, Pa., Mar. 10, 1777; studied law. Clk. in brother's office, Huntingdon, Pa.; admitted to Pa. bar, 1798, began practice law in Huntingdon; served as capt. Huntingdon Volunteers, War of 1812; burgess of Huntingdon, 1815, 17, 19, 21-24, 26; mem. U.S. Ho. of Reps. (Whig) from Pa., 22d Congress, 1831-33. Died Huntingdon, Dec. 2, 1840; buried River View Cemetery.

ALLOUEZ, Claude Jean, missionary; b. Saint-Didier, Haute Loire, France, June 6, 1622; grad. Coll. of Le Puy (France), 1639. Entered novitiate Soc. of Jesus, Toulouse, France, 1639; ordained priest Roman Catholic Ch., 1655; came to Quebec, Can., 1658; missionary among Indian tribes along St. Lawrence River, 3 years; became vicar gen. of all natives and traders in Northwest, 1663; made missionary tour to Western missions, 1667-69; missionary among Potawatomi Indians, nr. Green Bay, Wis., 1669; missionary to Outagami tribe, 1670, established St. Mark's Mission, 1670; founded mission of St. James among Miami and Mascouten Indians, 1670; returned to Green Bay missions, 1670; prin. speaker at ceremony which formally declared N.W. Territory subject to King of France, held at Sault St. Marie, 1671; estab-lished Mission of Rapides des Peres (now De Pere, Wis.) on Fox River, 1671; ordered to continue Marquette's work among Ill. Indians, arrived at Kaskaskia, 1677; worked among Ill. Indians, 1678-89. Died nr. present site of Niles, Mich., Aug. 22, 1689; buried Niles.

ALLSTON, Robert Francis Withers, planter, gov. S.C.; b. All Saints Parish, S.C., Apr. 21, 1801; s. Benjamin and Charlotte Anne (Allston) A.; grad. U.S. Mil. Acad., 1821; m. Adele Petigru, 1832. Planter, All Saints Parish; surveyor gen. S.C., 1823-77; elected to lower house S.C. Gen. Assembly, 1826-32; del. to Nashville Conv., 1850; mem. S.C. Senate, 1834-56, speaker, 1847-56; gov. S.C., 1856-58. Author: Introduction and Planting of Rice in South Carolina, 1843. Died Georgetown, S.C., Apr. 7, 1864.

ALLSTON, Washington, painter, author; b. Brook Green Domain, S.C., Nov. 5, 1779; s. Capt. Wil-liam and Rachel (Moore) A.; grad. Harvard, 1800; m. Ann Channing, 1809; m. 2d, Martha R. Dana, 1830. Painted in Charleston, S.C., after 1800; sailed for London to study art with Benjamin West, 1801; went to Paris, France, influenced by Ren-aissance artists; called "The American Titian"; returned to U.S., 1809; in Eng., 1811-18; paint-ed in Boston, 1818-43; paintings include: Portrait of Coleridge, Dead Man Revived by Touching the Bones of the Prophet Elijah, The Death of King John, Spalatro's Vision of the Bloody Hand, Rosalie, Belshazzar's Feast (unfinished). Author: The Sylphs of the Seasons, 1813; Monaldi, 1841; Lec-tures on Art and Peoms, published posthumously, 1850. Died July 9, 1843.

ALLYN, Robert, coll. pres.; b. Ledyard, Conn., Jan. 25, 1817; grad. Wesleyan U., Conn., 1841; m. Emeline Denison, Nov. 18, 1841, 2 children; m. 2d, Mary Budington, June 22, 1845, 3 chil-dren. Prin. Wesleyan Acad., 1846, Providence Conf. Sem., East Greenwich, R.I., 1848; commr. R.I. pub. schs., 1854-57; prof. ancient langs. Ohio State U., 1857-61; pres. Wesleyan Female Acad., Cincinnati, 1861-63, McKendree Coll., Lebanon, Ill., 1863; 1st pres. So. Ill. State Normal U., Carbondale, 1874-92. Died Carbondale, Jan. 7, 1894.

ALMY, John Jay, naval officer; b. Newport, R.I., Apr. 24, 1815; s. Samuel Almy. Became midshipman U.S. Navy, 1829; served on brig Con-cord in Mediterranean Sea, 1830-32; served in Mexican War; promoted lt., 1846; served on block-ading duty off Confederate coast during Civil War; captured or destroyed over $1,000,000 in Confed-erate blockade runners in 1864 alone; commd. rear adm. (ret.), 1877, had served longest period of active duty of any officer up to that time. Died May 16, 1895.

ALSOP George, author; b. Eng., 1638. Came to Am., 1658. Author: A Character of the Province of Mary-Land, wherein is Described in four distinct Parts, (Viz.) I. The Scituation, and plenty of the Province. II. The Laws, Customs, and natural Demeanor of the Inhabitant. III. The worst and best Usage of a Mary-Land Servant, opened in view. IV. The Traffique and vendable Commodities of the Country. Also a small Treatise on the wilde and naked Indians (of Susquehanokes) of Mary-Land, their Customs, Manners, Absurdities & Religion. Together with a Collection of Historical Letters, 1666.

ALSOP, John, Continental congressman; b. New Windsor, Orange County, N.Y., 1724; completed prep. edn. Moved to N.Y.C., became a mcht. and importer; N.Y.C. rep. in colonial legislature; an incorporator N.Y. Hosp., gov. hosp., 1770-84; mem. Continental Congress from N.Y., 1774, 75; mem. com. of 100 apptd. to govern N.Y.C. until conv. assembled, 1775; pres. N.Y. C. of C., 1784,

85. Died Newtown, L.I., N.Y., Nov. 22, 1794; buried Trinity Ch. Cemetery, N.Y.C.

ALSOP, Richard satirist; b. Middletown, Conn., Jan. 23, 1761; s. Richard and Mary (Wright) A.; attended Yale, circa 1778, M.A., 1798. Wrote The Conquest of Scandinavia (one of writings influenced by his study of European culture); wrote satirical works including "The Echo." in Am. Mercury mag., 1791-1805; one of group known as "Hartford Wits;" contbr. to Monthly Mag. and Am. Review; other writings include: the Political Greenhouse; American Poems, 1793; A Poem: Sacred to the Memory of George Washington, 1800; Narrative of the Adventures and Sufferings of John R. Jewitt, Only Survivor of the Ship Boston, During a Captivity of Nearly Three Years among the Savages of Nootka Sound, 1815. Died Flatbush, L.I., N.Y., Aug. 20, 1815.

ALSTON, Joseph, lawyer, gov. S.C.; b. All Saints Parish, S.C., 1779; s. Col. William and Mary (Ashe) A.; attended Coll. of N.J. (now Princeton), 1794; read law under Edward Rutledge; m. Theodosia Burr, Feb. 2, 1801. Admitted to S.C. bar; mem. lower house S.C. Legislature, 1802-03, 05-12; gov. S.C., 1812-14; implicated in plots of Aaron Burr (as son-in-law). Died Sept. 10, 1816.

ALSTON, Lemuel James, congressman, lawyer; b. eastern part of Granville (now Warren) County, N.C., 1760; studied law. Moved to Greens Mill (now Greenville), S.C. after Revolutionary War; admitted to S.C. bar, began practice law in Greenville; mem. U.S. Ho. of Reps. from S.C., 10th-11th congresses, 1807-11; moved to Grove Hill, Clarke County, Ala., 1816; presided over orphans' ct., also county ct., 1816-21. Died "Alston Place," Clarke County, 1836.

ALSTON, William Jeffreys, congressman, lawyer; b. Milledgeville, Ga., Dec. 31, 1800; attended pvt. sch. in S.C.; studied law. Moved to Marengo County, Ala., taught sch.; admitted to Ala. bar, began practice law in Linden, 1821; judge Marengo County Ct.; mem. Ala. Ho. of Reps., 1837-55; mem. Ala. Senate, 1839-42; mem. U.S. Ho. of Reps. (Whig) from Ala., 31st Congress, 1849-51. Died Magnolia, Ala., June 10, 1876; buried Magnolia Cemetery.

ALSTON, Willis, congressman; b. nr. Littleton, Halifax County, N.C., 1769; attended Princeton. Farmed on plantation, Halifax County; mem. N.C. House of Commons, 1790-92, 1820-24; mem. N.C. Senate, 1794-96; mem. U.S. Ho. of Reps. from N.C. (War Democrat), 6th-13th congresses, 1799-1815, 19th-21st congresses, 1825-31, mem. ways and means com. during War of 1812. Died Halifax, N.C., Apr. 10, 1837; buried at plantation "Butternut," nr. Littleton.

ALTER, David, inventor; b. Westmoreland County, Pa., Dec. 3, 1807; s. John and Eleanor (Sheetz) A.; grad. Reformed Med. Coll., N.Y.C., 1831; m. Laura Rowley, 1832; m. 2d, Elizabeth A. Rowley, 1844; 11 children. Invented an electric clock, model of electric locomotive; invented elec. telegraph, 1836; discovered method of purifying bromine, method of obtaining coal oil from coal, 2d law of spectrum analysis (various elemental gases have spectra peculiar to themselves). Died Sept. 18, 1881.

ALTHAM, John, missionary; b. Warwickshire, Eng., 1589. Sailed for Am. as Jesuit with Lord Calvert, 1633, arrived Chesapeake Bay, 1634; did missionary work among Indians, Kent Island, Va., 1634-40. Died St. Mary's, Md., Nov. 5, 1640.

ALVARADO, Juan Bautista, gov. Mexican Cal.; b. Monterey, Cal., Feb. 14, 1809; s. José and Maria Josefa (Vallejo) A.; m. Martina Castro, 1839, at least 5 children. Sec. of Cal. territorial "disputacion", 1827-34; with José Castro led rebellion which usurped Cal. territorial governorship from Gutierrez, Nov. 1836; gov. of independent Cal., 1836-38, sanctioned Mexican gov. Cal. territory, 1838-42; commd. col. Mexican Army, 1842; with José Castro led revolt against Gov. Manuel Micheltorena, 1844-45; elected to Mexican Congress, 1848, lacked funds to travel to Mexico to take seat. Died July 13, 1882.

ALVORD, Benjamin, army officer; b. Rutland, Vt., Aug. 18, 1813; s. William and Lucy (Claghorn) A.; grad. U.S. Mil. Acad., 1833; m. Emily Louise Mussey, 1846, 6 children. Commd. in 4th Inf., U.S. Army, 1833; served in Seminole War, 1835-37, chief paymaster in Mexican War, 1846-48, and in Ore. 1854-62; commd. brig. gen. U.S. Volunteers, 1862; paymaster gen. U.S. Army, 1872-80. Author numerous articles on mathematics and geography. Died Oct. 16, 1884.

ALVORD, Corydon Alexis, printer; b. Winchester, Conn., May 12, 1813; s. John and Experience (Webb) A.; m. Mary Ann Buckland, Sept. 6, 1836, 10 children. Printing apprentice, Hartford, Conn., then opened own shop, N.Y.C., 1845, specialized in unusual and illustration printing, such as facsimiles of old books and newspapers; printed Thomas Daring's Recollection of the Jersey Prison-Ship, 1865, James Parton's Life and Times of Benjamin Franklin, 1865, Greene Halleck's Fanny: A Poem, 1866; moved to Hartford, 1867, continued bus. in N.Y.C.; merged with other printing firms to form N.Y. Printing Co., 1871, City of N.Y. confiscated co. for associations with "Tweed Ring," 1871. Author: Genealogy of the Descendants of Alexander Alvord, published posthumously, 1908. Died Hartford, Nov. 28, 1874.

ALVORD, James Church, congressman, lawyer; b. Greenwich, Mass., Apr. 14, 1808; grad. Dartmouth, 1827; studied law. Admitted to Mass. bar, 1830, began practice law in Greenfield; mem. Mass. Ho. of Reps., 1837, Mass. Senate, 1838; mem. U.S. Ho. of Reps. (Whig) from Mass., 26th Congress, Mar. 4-Sept. 27, 1839. Died Greenfield, Sept 27, 1839; buried Federal St. Cemetery.

AMADAS, Phillip, naval officer; flourished 1584-85. A comdr. in Walter Raleigh's fleet, sent out by Queen Elizabeth to discover new lands; left Eng., Apr. 1584, went 1st to Canary Islands, then to W.I., reached coast of N.C., July 1584, discovered Wokokon isle nr. Pamlico Sound; visited Ohanoak (Roanoke) Island; took 2 Indians back to Eng. on return trip, Sept. 1584; went with Sir Richard Grenville to colonize new colony (named Va. by Queen Elizabeth), 1585.

AMAT, Thaddeus, clergyman; b. Barcelona, Spain, Dec. 31, 1810. Ordained a Lazarist, Paris, France, 1838; sent to La., 1838; master of novices in Lazarist houses, Mo. and Pa.; consecrated bishop of Monterey, Cal., 1854 (see transferred to Los Angeles, 1859); opened St. Vincent's Coll., Los Angeles, brought in Franciscans for work in parochial schs., also Sisters of Charity and Sisters of Immaculate Heart of Mary. Died Los Angeles, May 12, 1878.

AMBLER, James Markham Marshall, mil. surgeon; b. Fauquier County, Va., Dec. 30, 1848; s. Dr. Richard Cary and Susan (Marshall) A.; attended Washington Coll., U. Md. Enlisted in Confederate Army, 1864; an asst. surgeon U.S. Navy, 1874; surgeon in Arctic exploring ship The Jeannette, 1879 (ship frozen in Arctic). Died while attempting to get back to civilization, Oct. 30, 1881.

AMELIA, see Welby, Amelia Ball Coppuck.

AMERMAN, Lemuel, congressman, lawyer; b. nr. Danville, Pa., Oct. 29, 1846; attended Danville Acad.; grad. Bucknell U., 1869; studied law. Taught sch.; admitted to Pa. bar, 1873, practiced law in Phila, 1873-76; began practice law in Scranton, Pa., 1876, also in banking bus.; solicitor Lackawana County, Pa., 1879, 80; mem. Pa. Ho. of Reps., 1881-84; city comptroller City of Scranton, 1885, 86; reporter decisions Supreme Ct. of Pa., 1886, 87; mem. U.S. Ho. of Reps. (Democrat) from Pa., 52d Congress, 1891-93. Died Blossburg, Pa., Oct. 7, 1897; buried Forest Hill Cemetery, Scranton.

AMES, Edward Raymond, bishop; b. Adams County, O., May 20, 1806; s. Sylvanus and Nabby (Johnson) A.; attended Ohio U., 2 or 3 years. Opened a sem. at Lebanon Coll. (later McKendree Coll.), 1828; joined Ill. Methodist Conf., became an itinerant minister, 1830; corr. sec. Missionary Soc. of South and West, travelled 25,000 miles systematizing missionary work, obtaining land grants for ednl. work among Indians, taking inventory of the property, 1840-44; became bishop of Indpls., 1852; only Meth. bishop serving as chaplain in Union Army during Civil War; commr. (with Hamilton Fish) to visit prisoners at Richmond, Va., 1862, commn. refused entrance into Richmond by Confederate Govt. Died Balt., Apr. 25, 1879.

AMES, Ezra, artist; b. Framingham, Mass., May 5, 1768; s. Jesse and Bette (Bent) Ames or Emes; m. Zipporah Wood, Oct. 6, 1794. Painter of carriages, furniture, Worcester, Mass., 1790, also painted miniatures, sold 25 (no longer extant), 1790-98; engraved rings, spoons, Masonic emblems, 1797-98; oil paintings included portraits of a Mr. Glen, (1st and best-known) 1812, Gov. DeWitt Clinton (exhibited at Pa. Acad. Fine Arts), Solomon Allen, Clarkson Crolius, Charles Genet, Leonard Gansevoort, Alan Melville, James King, also a self-portrait. Died Feb. 23, 1836.

AMES, Fisher, congressman; b. Dedham, Mass., Apr. 9, 1758; s. Nathaniel and Deborah (Fisher) A.; grad. Harvard, 1774; m. Frances Worthington, July 15, 1792. Admitted to Suffolk (Mass.) bar, 1781; mem. Mass. Conv. which ratified U.S. Constn., 1787, leader in its support; Dedham rep. Mass. Gen. Ct., 1788; mem. U.S. Ho. of Reps. (Federalist) from Mass., 1st-4th congresses, 1789-97; gave speech in support of Jay Treaty (said to have secured its passage), 1796; mem. Mass. Gov's Council, 1799-1801; declined presidency of Harvard Coll., 1805. Writings collected in Works of Fisher Ames, also Speeches of Fisher Ames in Congress. Died Dedham, July 4, 1808; buried Old 1st Pari Cemetery, Dedham.

AMES, Frederick Lothrop, realtor, philanthr pist, state senator; b. North Easton, Mass., Ju 8, 1835; s. Oliver and Sarah (Lothrop) A.; e Harvard, 1854; m. Rebecca Blair, June 7, 186 6 children. A fellow of Harvard Coll.; owner exte sive realty holdings, Boston; pres. Home for Incu ables; contbr. to Unitarian Soc., Mass. Sch. for t Blind, Perkins Inst., McLean Insane Asylum, Chi drens Hosp.; elected to Mass. Senate, 1872. Di Sept. 13, 1893.

AMES, James Tyler, mfr.; b. Lowell, Mass., M 13, 1810; s. Nathan Peabody and Phoebe (Tyle A.; M.A. (hon.), Amherst Coll., 1863; m. Ell Huse, 1838, 3 children. Mechanic in his father factory, Lowell, before 1829; moved (with enti family) to Chicopee Falls, Mass., 1829; form (with brother Nathan P. Ames, Jr.) Ames Mf Co., specializing in cutlery and tools, 1834, e panded into mfg. of brass cannon, then became 1 sword co. in U.S.; became head of co. after dea of brother, 1847-74, expanded co.'s operation began manufacture of cotton-machinery, lathe planes, turbine water wheels, 1849; manufacture Eldredge Sewing Machine and 1st Victor a Eagle bicycles; expanded operations to inclu bronze castings, before Civil War; casted Crawfo Doors on East wing U.S. Capitol Bldg., statue Washington in Boston Public Gardens, Minu Man at Concord, Mass., Lincoln Monument Springfield, Ill.; manufactured munitions (1 North's largest factories) during Civil War; man factured sabers for Turkey during Russo-Turki War, for France during Franco-Prussian War; i vented (with Gen. James of Providence, R.I.) ca non-ball which necessitated rifled cannon, als invented machinery for manufacture of rifled ca non. Died Feb. 16, 1883.

AMES, Joseph Alexander, artist; b. Roxbu (now part of Boston), 1816; married, at least child (dau.). Gained reputation as portrait paint in Boston area, before 1848; sailed to Rome, Ital to further art studies, 1848; painted portrait Pope Pius IX; returned to Boston; painted portra of Daniel Webster, 1852; moved for health reaso to Balt., 1870, then to N.Y.C., 1870; mem N.A.D.; portraits include: William Conway Felto Rufus Choate, William H. Seward, Ralph Wald Emerson; other works include: Maud Miller, Th Old Stone Pitcher, The Last Days of Daniel Web ster at Marshfield. Died N.Y.C., Oct. 30, 187 buried N.Y.C.

AMES, Nathan Peabody, mfr.; b. Chelmsfor Mass., Sept. 1, 1803; s. Nathan Peabody an Phoebe (Tyler) A.; m. Mary Bailey, no childre Learned mechanic's trade in father's cutlery sho Chelmsford, before 1829, inherited bus., 182 (with brother) moved factory to Dwight Mi Bldg., Chicopee Falls, Mass., 1829-33; contbd half of his savings to aid building of 3d Co gregational Ch. of Chicopee, Mass., 1834; organiz Ames Mfg. Co., Chicopee, 1834, specialized i cutlery and tools; began manufacture of brass can non, leather belting, bells, turbine water-wheels 1836; with boom of textile industry in New Eng. produced every type of cotton machinery; invent rotary bell-clapper; commd. by U.S. Ordnanc Dept. to study arsenals and gun factories in Europ 1840. Died Chicopee, Apr. 3, 1847.

AMES, Nathaniel, publisher, physician; b Bridgewater, Mass., July 22, 1708; s. Nathanie and Susannah (Howard) A.; m. Mary Fisher, Sept 14, 1735; m. 2d, Deborah Fisher, 1740, 5 chil dren including Nathaniel. Published 1st annua almanac (became standard New Eng. almanac fo 50 years), 1725; moved to Dedham, Mass., 173 after wife's death (1737), claimed inheritance o wife's residuary interest in certain property und Provincial Law; successfully brought suit agains others who claimed the inheritance under Com mon Law (thereby establishing an exception to th rule of inheritance in Mass.); local physician Dedham, Mass.; propr. Sun tavern, Dedham, 1750 Died Dedham, July 11, 1764; buried Dedham

AMES, Oakes, manufacturer, congressman; bo Easton, Massachusetts, on January 10, 180 son of Oliver and Susannah (Angier) Ames; m Evelyn Gilmore. Controlled Oliver Ames & Sons shovel co., 1844; dir. Emigrant Aid Co. during Kan troubles, 1858; mem. Exec. Council Mass., 186 mem. U.S. Ho. of Reps. from Mass., 38th-42d con gresses, 1863-73; partially controlled Credit Mobil ier Co., 1865; sold shares to congressmen to fore stall investigation of doubtful affairs of constr of Union Pacific R.R., 1867-68; exposed 187 publicly censured by vote of U.S. Congress, 187 Died North Easton, Mass., May 8, 1873; buri Unity Cemetery, North Easton.

AMES, Oliver, mfr.; b. West Bridgewater, Mass. Apr. 11, 1779; s. Capt. John and Susanna (How ard) A.; m. Susannah Angier, 2 daus., 6 son including Oakes, Oliver. Apprentice gunmaker un der his brother David (1st supt. of Springfield Mass. armory); took over father's shovel-makin ıs., moved co. to North Easton, Mass., 1803, ɛcame very successful due to embargo and War of ß12, developed lighter but less durable shovels; ıilt shops at Braintree, Mass., 1823, Canton, ɪass., 1844; turned bus. Oliver Ames & Sons over sons Oliver and Oakes, circa 1844. Died Sept. 1, 1863.

AMES, Oliver, mfr., railroad ofcl.; b. Plymouth, ɪass., Nov. 5, 1807; s. Oliver and Susannah (Angier) .; ed. Franklin Acad. of North Andover; m. ɪarah Lothrop, children—Helen, Frederick L. Mem. ɪass. Senate, 1852-54, 58-60; engaged in building

ɪaston Branch R.R., 1855; acting pres. Union ɪacific R.R., 1866-68, pres., 1868-71; not involved ı scandals of Credit Mobilier (which financed ɪnion Pacific R.R.); trustee Taunton Insane Asy-ɪm; dir. Atlantic & Pacific R.R., Kansas Pacific ɪ.R., Denver Pacific R.R., v.p. Mass. Total Abstin-ɪnce Soc. Died Mar. 9, 1877.

AMES, Oliver, financier, gov. Mass.; b. North ɪaston, Mass., Feb. 4, 1831; s. Oakes and Evelyn Gilmore) A.; ed. Brown U.; m. Anna Ray, 1860, children. Pres. Union Pacific R.R.; elected to ɪass. Senate, 1880; lt. gov. Mass. (Republican) nder Benjamin Butler, 1882-86, gov., 1887-90; ɪwner Booth's Theater, N.Y.C.; pres. Boston Art ɪlub, Boston Merchants' Club; built Oakes Ames ɪeml. Hall. Died Oct. 22, 1895.

AMES, Samuel, jurist; b. Providence, R.I., ɪept. 6, 1806; s. Samuel and Anne (Chichele) A.; ɪrad. Brown U., 1823; m. Mary Dorr, June 27, ɪ839. Admitted to R.I. bar, 1826; mem. R.I. Gen. ɪssembly from Providence, 1841; q.m. gen. R.I. ɪilitia, 1842; state rep. to adjust boundary be-ɪween R.I. and Mass., 1853; chief justice Supreme t. R.I., 1856. Died Providence, Dec. 20, 1865.

AMHERST, Jeffery (1st baron Amherst), army ɪfficer, colonial gov.; b. Kent County Eng., Jan. 9, 1717; s. Jeffery and Elizabeth (Kerril) A. ɪommd. lt. col. Brit. Army, 1745; aide-de-camp ɪo Duke of Cumberland, 1747; commd. maj. gen., 1758; commanded army which captured Louisbourg, ɪuly 27, 1758; comdr.-in-chief Brit. Army in N. ɪm., 1759; captured Ticonderoga, Crown Point, 1759, Montreal, 1760; gov. Va. (apptd. by King ɪeorge II), 1760-68; comdr.-in-chief all Brit. ɪorces in Eng., 1778; field marshall, 1796; created ɪnight of the Bath, 1761, granted title Baron ɪmherst, 1776; towns in Mass. and N.H., Amherst ɪounty (Va.) named for him. Died Kent County, ɪug. 3, 1797.

AMMEN, Daniel, naval officer; b. Ohio, May 16, 1819; s. David and Sally (Houtz) A.; m. Mary Jack-ɪon; m. 2d, Zoe Atocha, Apr. 11, 1866; 5 ɪhildren. Commd. midshipman U.S. Navy, advanced ɪhrough grades to rear adm.; in charge of Bur. ɪards and Docks, Bur. Navigation; sec. Isthmian ɪanal Commn., 1872-76; fought in battles of Port ɪoyal (1861), Ft. McAllister (1863), Ft. Fisher 1864); ret. as rear adm., 1878. Author: The ɪtlantic Coast, 1883: The Old Navy and the New, 1891. Died July 11, 1898.

AMMEN, Jacob, educator, army officer; b. Fin-ɪastle, Va., Jan. 7, 1807; s. David and Sally (Houtz) ɪ.; grad. U.S. Mil. Acad., 1831; m. Caroline L. ɪierce; m.2d, Martha Beasley. Prof. mathematics ɪacon Coll. (now Transylvania U.), 1837, 48-55, ɪefferson (Mo.) Coll., 1839-40, 43-48, U. Ind., ɪloomington, 1840-43; civil engr., Ripley, O., 1855-ɪ1; commd. capt. 12th Ohio Volunteers, later lt. ɪol., 1861; commd. brig. gen. U.S. Volunteers, 1862, resigned commn., 1865. Died Lockland, O., ɪeb. 6, 1894.

AMORY, Thomas, mcht.; b. Limerick, Ireland, May 1682; m. Rebecca Holmes, May 9, 1721. In-dentured to French mcht., Nicolas Oursel, London, Eng., 1699-1706; became mcht., Terceira, Azores, 1706, traded with Portugal, Eng., Holland, Am.; made unsuccessful attempt to establish merc. co., Charleston, S.C., 1712-19; invested in ship build-ing, mcht. bus., Boston, 1720-28. Died June 20, 1728.

ANAGNOS, Julia Romana Howe, educator; b. Rome, Italy, Mar. 12, 1844; d. Dr. Samuel G. and Julia (Ward) Howe; m. Michael Anagnos, Dec. 1870. Instr. (worked with her father) Perkins Inst. for Blind, helped establish kindergarten tng. at the inst.; a founder, pres. Boston Methaphysical Club. Author works including: Stray Chords, 1883; Philosophiae Quaestor, 1885. Died Boston, Mar. 10, 1886.

ANDERLEDY, Anthony Maria, clergyman; b. Berisal, Switzerland, June 3, 1819. Joined Soc. of Jesus, 1839; taught at Freiburg until Soc. was expelled, 1848; came to St. Louis, ordained priest Roman Catholic Ch.; pastor, Green Bay, Wis., 2 years; returned to Germany, directed Jesuit studies at Cologne and Paderborn; became provincial, 1859; purchased mediaeval abbey of Maria-Laach, tchr. moral theology there, 1865-70; became vicar gen. Soc. of Jesus, 1887. Died Fiesole, Italy, Jan. 18, 1892.

ANDERS, John Daniel, clergyman; b. Germany, Aug. 9, 1771; grad. Moravian Coll., Germany; grad. theol. sem., Herrnhut, Saxony. Prof. theol. sem. in charge of Moravian Ch., Berlin, Germany; in charge of No. dist. Am. Moravian Ch., 1827-36; consecrated bishop, 1827; attended gen. synod Moravian Ch., Germany, 1836, elected to supervise exec. bd. of Unitas Fratrum, did not return to U.S. Died Herrnhut, Nov. 6, 1847.

ANDERSON, Alexander, engraver; b. N.Y.C., Apr. 21, 1775; s. John and Mary A.; medical degree, 1796; m. Ann Van Vleck, Apr. 1797. Became 1st wood engraver in Am., 1794; produced wood and copper plate engravings for leading mags. and book publishers, 1794-1868; mem. Acad. Fine Arts, N.A.D. Died Jersey City, N.J., Jan. 17, 1870.

ANDERSON, Alexander Outlaw, senator, lawyer; b. "Soldiers Rest," Jefferson County, Tenn., Nov. 10, 1794; s. of Joseph Anderson; grad. Washington Coll., Greeneville, Tenn.; studied law, Washington, D.C. Served under Gen. Andrew Jackson at Battle of New Orleans, War of 1812; admitted to bar, Dandridge, Tenn., 1814, began practice of law, Dandridge; moved to Knoxville, Tenn.; supt. U.S. land office in Ala., 1836; govt. agt. for removing Indians from Ala. and Fla., 1838; mem. U.S. Senate (Democrat, filled vacancy) from Tenn., Feb. 26, 1840-41; leader of overland co. to Cal., 1849; mem. State Senate, 1850, 51; supreme ct. judge of Cal., 1851-53; returned to Tenn., 1853; later practiced law in Washington, D.C. before Ct. of Claims, U.S. Supreme Ct.; during Civil War moved to Ala., practiced law in Mobile and Camden, Ala. Died Knoxville, May 23, 1869; buried Old Gray Cemetery.

ANDERSON, George Alburtus, congressman, lawyer; b. Botetourt County, Va., Mar. 11, 1853; grad. Carthage (Ill.) Coll., 1876; studied law in Lincoln, Neb. and Sedalia, Mo. Admitted to the bar, 1878, began practice of law, Quincy, Ill., 1880; city atty. City of Quincy, 1884, 85; mem. U.S. Ho. of Reps. (Democrat) from Ill., 50th Congress, 1887-89. Died Quincy, Jan. 31, 1896; buried Woodlawn Cemetery.

ANDERSON, George Thomas, army officer; b. Ga., Mar. 3, 1824; s. Joseph Stewart and Lucy (Cunningham) A. Served as 2d lt. Ga. Mounted Volunteers, 1847-48; capt. 1st Cavalry, 1855-58; commd. col. 11th Ga. Regt., 1861; commanded brigade during Seven Days' conflicts in Peninsular Campaign, 1862, wounded at 2d Battle of Manassas, 1862; commd. brig. gen., 1862; served in battle for Round Top Hill, wounded at Devil's Den during Battle of Gettysburg, 1863; joined Gen. Longstreet in siege of Knoxville; served under Gen. Robert E. Lee until surrender at Appomattox; chief of police Atlanta (Ga.). Died Anniston, Ala., Apr. 4, 1901.

ANDERSON, Henry Hill, lawyer; b. Boston, Nov. 9, 1827; s. Rufus and Eliza (Hill) A.; A.B., Williams Coll., 1848, A.M., 1851; studied law under Judge Henry Ebenezer Davies; m. Sarah Ann Gilbert, Aug. 23, 1853; m. 2d, Sarah Bostwick Burrall, Dec. 26, 1861; 5 children including Henry Burrall, William Burrall, Chandler Parsons. Admitted to bar, 1849; asst. corp. counsel N.Y.C., 1849-52, 59-63; became partner (with A.T. Willard and Peter B. Sweeny) in law firm, N.Y.C., 1852; pvt. practice, N.Y.C., 1863-92; a reorganizer University Club, N.Y.C., pres. 10 years. Died York Harbor, Me., Sept. 17, 1896.

ANDERSON, Henry James, educator; b. N.Y.C., Feb. 6, 1799; grad. Columbia, 1818; grad. Coll. Physicians and Surgeons, N.Y.C., 1823. Prof. Mathematics and astronomy Columbia, 1825-50, became trustee, 1851, prof. emeritus mathematics and astronomy, 1866; went to Europe, circa 1850, converted to Catholicism, geologist for Dead Sea expdn. while travelling in Holy Land; one of pilgrims who travelled to Lourdes (France), received by Pope Pius IX, 1874; mem. Am. scientific expdn. to observe patterns of planet Venus; served as pres. St. Vincent de Paul Soc., N.Y.C.; an originator Catholic Union, N.Y.C.; a founder Cath. Protectory, Westchester, N.Y.; visited India, stricken with fatal disease. Died Lahore, Northern Hindustan, India, Oct. 19, 1875.

ANDERSON, Henry Tompkins, clergyman; b. Caroline County, Va., Jan. 27, 1812; s. John Burbage and Martha (Tompkins) A.; m. Henriette Ducker. Ordained elder Ch. of Disciples of Christ, 1833; pastor, Hopkinsville, Ky. Translator: New Testament, translated from the original Greek, 1864; Codex Sinaiticus (Tischendorf), published 1918. Died Washington, D.C., Sept. 19, 1872.

ANDERSON, Hugh Johnston, congressman, gov. Me.; b. Wiscasset, Me., May 10, 1801; studied law. Clk. in uncle's merc. bus., Belfast, Me., 1815; clk. Waldo County cts., 1824-36; mem. U.S. Ho. of Reps. (Democrat) from Me., 25th-26th congresses, 1837-41; gov. Me., 1844-47; Democratic presdl. elector, 1848; commr. of customs U.S. Treasury Dept., Washington, D.C., 1853-58; head of commn. for reorganization U.S. Mint, San Francisco, 1857; auditor of the treasury, Washington, 1866-69; moved to Portland, Ore., 1880. Died Portland, May 31, 1881; buried Grove Cemetery, Belfast, Me.

ANDERSON, Isaac, congressman; b. nr. Valley Forge, Pa., Nov. 23, 1760. Carried dispatches between Gen. Washington's hdqrs. at Valley Forge and Congress, in session at York, Pa., during Revolutionary War, also served with Continental Army; became ensign 5th Battalion, Chester County Militia; commd. 1st lt., 5th Battalion, 6th Co., 1779; justice of peace Charlestown Twp.; mem. Pa. Ho. of Reps., 1801; mem. U.S. Ho. of Reps. (Jefferson Democrat) from Pa., 8th-9th congresses, 1803-07; farmer, operator of sawmill; Democratic presdl. elector, 1816. Died "Anderson Place," Charlestown Twp., Pa., Oct. 27, 1838; buried family burying ground nr. Valley Forge, Pa.

ANDERSON, James Patton, army officer; b. Franklin County, Tenn., Feb. 12, 1822. Raised battalion of Miss. Militia in Mexican War; elected to Miss. Legislature, 1850; apptd. U.S. marshal for Territory of Wash., 1853; del. from Territory of Wash. to U.S. Congress, 1855; commd. col. in Fla. Militia, 1861; commd. brig. gen., 1862, fought at battles of Shiloh, Perryville, Murfreesboro, Chickamauga; commd. maj. gen. Confederate Army, 1864; comdr. Dist. of Fla.; surrendered at Greensboro, N.C.; editor of agrl. paper, Memphis, Tenn., after Civil War. Died Memphis, Sept. 1, 1873.

ANDERSON, James R., actor; b. Eng. Tragedian, made 1st stage appearance in A Winter's Tale, Covent Garden Theatre, London, Eng., 1836; made Am. debut as Othello, Park Theatre, N.Y.C., 1844; returned to Am. as Othello, Broadway Theatre, N.Y.C., 1848; appeared with Agnes Ellsworthy, Wallack's Theatre, on last visit to Am., 1856.

ANDERSON, John, congressman; b. Windham, Me., July 30, 1792; grad. Bowdoin Coll., 1813; studied law. Admitted to Me. bar, 1816, began practice law in Portland, Me.; mem. Me. Senate, 1823; mem. U.S. Ho. of Reps. (Jefferson Democrat) from Me., 19th-22d congresses, 1825-33; mayor Portland, 1833-36, 42; U.S. atty. for dist. of Me., 1833-36; collector of customs Port of Portland, 1837-41, 43-48; resumed practice of law. Died Portland, Aug. 21, 1853; buried Town Cemetery, Windham.

ANDERSON, John Alexander, coll. pres., congressman; b. Washington County, Pa., June 26, 1834; son of Reverend William C. Anderson; grad. Miami U., Oxford, O., 1853; m. Nannie Foote, 1864. Ordained to ministry Presbyn. Ch., 1857; trustee Insane Asylum of Cal., 1860; chaplain 3d Regt., Cal. Volunteer Inf., 1862; Cal. corr., agt. U.S. Sanitary Commn., 1863-67; supt. transp. U.S. Army in Wilderness Campaign, 1864; editor Sanitary Bulletin, Phila.; minister 1st Presbyn. Ch., Junction City, Kan., 1868-72; pres. Kan. State Agrl. Coll., 1873-79; mem. U.S. Ho. of Reps. from Kan., 46th-51st congresses, 1879-91; U.S. consul gen. at Cairo, Egypt, 1891. Died Liverpool, Eng., May 18, 1892; buried Highland Cemetery, Junction City, Kan.

ANDERSON, Joseph, senator, jurist; b. nr. Phila Nov. 5, 1757; s. William and Elizabeth (Inslee) A: m. Only Patience Outlaw, 1797, 7 children. Commd. 2d lt. Us army, 1776, capt., 1777, maj., 1783; admitted to bar; apptd. U.S. judge of Territory South of the Ohio River, 1791-96; mem. U.S. Senate from Tenn., 1797-1815; 1st comptroller U.S. Treasury, 1815-36; trustee Blount Coll., Washington Coll. (Tenn.); charter mem. Del. chpt. Soc. of the Cincinnati; Anderson County (Tenn.) named for him. Died Washington, D.C., Apr. 17, 1837; buried Congressional Cemetery, Washington.

ANDERSON, Joseph Halstead, congressman; b. Harrison, nr. White Plains, N.Y., Aug. 25, 1800; attended common schs. Farmer nr. White Plains; mem. N.Y. State Assembly, 1833, 34; sheriff Westchester County (N.Y.), 1835-38; mem. U.S. Ho. of Reps. (Democrat) from N.Y., 28th-29th congresses, 1843-47. Died White Plains, June 23, 1870; buried "Anderson Hill," nr. White Plains.

ANDERSON, Joseph Reid, iron mfr.; b. Fincastle, Va., Feb. 6, 1813; s. William and Anna (Thomas) A.; grad. U.S. Mil. Acad. 1836; m. Sally Archer, 1837, 5 children; m. 2d Mary Pegram. Chief engr. Valley Turnpike Co. (Va.), 1838-41; became owner Tredegar Iron Co., 1848, shop produced majority of shot, rails and iron products of South during Civil War; mem. Va. Ho. of Dels., 1852-55; commd. brig. gen. Confederate States Army, 1861; fought in Peninsula Campaign, 1862; elected pres. Richmond (Va.) C. of C., 1874; mem. Common Council of Richmond. Died Isles of Shoals, N.H., Sept. 7, 1892.

ANDERSON, Josiah McNair, congressman, lawyer; b. nr. Pikeville, Tenn., Nov. 29, 1807; studied law. Admitted to the bar, began practice law, Jasper, Tenn.; mem. Tenn. Ho. of Reps., 1833-37, speaker; mem. Tenn. Senate, 1843-45, presiding officer; mem. U.S. Ho. of Reps. (Whig) from Tenn., 31st Congress, 1849-51; del. to Washington (D.C.) Peace Conv., 1861; col. Tenn. Militia, 1861; was killed after making secession speech. Died

Looneys Creek, nr. present town of Whitwell, Tenn, Nov. 8, 1861; buried on a farm nr. Dunlap, Tenn.

ANDERSON, Martin Brewer, clergyman, coll. pres.; b. Brunswick, Me., Feb. 12, 1815; s. Martin and Jane (Brewer) A.; grad. Waterville Coll., 1840; attended Newton (Mass.) Theol. Instn., 1840; m. Elizabeth Gilbert, Jan. 1848. Ordained to ministry Baptist Ch.; instr. Greek, Latin, mathematics Waterville Coll. (now Colby Coll.), 1841, prof. rhetoric, 1843-50; editor, propr. N.Y. Recorder, 1850; 1st pres. U. Rochester (N.Y.), 1853-88; pres. Am. Bapt. Missionary Union. Died Lake Helen, Fla., Feb. 22, 1890.

ANDERSON, Richard Clough, army officer, pioneer; b. Hanover County, Va., Jan. 12, 1750; s. Robert and Elizabeth (Clough) A.; m. Elizabeth Clark, 1785; m. 2d, Sarah Marshall, 1797; at least 6 children, Richard Clough, Larz, Robert, William Marshall, John, Charles. In Boston during Boston Tea Party, 1773; capt. Hanover County Company in Revolutionary War; capt. 5th Va. Regt., Continental Army, almost ruined George Washington's plans at Trenton by alarming Hessians on the night before battle; served in battles of Germantown, Brandywine and Monmouth; commd. maj., 1778; aided in attempt to capture Savannah, 1779, wounded there; stationed at Charleston (S.C.), captured, prisoner 9 months, released and joined Gen. Daniel Morgan; acted as messenger for Marquis de Lafayette; sent to organize Va. Militia; commd. lt. col. nr. end of war; surveyor-gen. to divide lands in West reserved by Va. for her Continental troops, 1783; settled nr. Louisville, Ky.; mem. Ky. Constl. Conv., 1788. Died Louisville, Oct. 16, 1826.

ANDERSON, Richard Clough, Jr., congressman, diplomat; b. "Soldiers' Retreat" nr. Louisville, Ky. Aug. 4, 1788; s. Richard and Elizabeth (Clark) A.; grad. Coll. William and Mary, 1804. Admitted to bar, practiced law in Louisville; mem. Ky. Ho. of Reps., 1812, 14, 15, 21, 22, speaker, 1822; mem. U.S. Ho. of Reps. from Ky., 15th-16th congresses, 1817-21, chmn. com. pub. lands; became 1st U.S. minister to Republic of Colombia, 1823, negotiated 1st treaty between U.S. and a S.Am. republic, 1824; commd. E.E. and M.P. to Panama Congress of Nations, 1823; Anderson County (Ky.) named after him. Died en route to Panama Congress of Nations, Turbaco, Colombia, July 24, 1826; buried "Soldiers Retreat."

ANDERSON, Richard Heron, army officer; b. Statesburg, S.C., Oct. 7, 1821; s. Dr. William Wallace and Mary (MacKenzie) A.; grad. U.S. Mil. Acad., 1842; m. Sarah Gibson, 1850, 2 children; m. 2d, Martha Mellette, 1874. Served with U.S. Army during Mexican War, also on Western Frontier; brevetted 1st lt. for services during Battle of Vera Cruz, 1848 resigned commn., 1861; commd. col. 1st S.C. Inf. Regt., 1861, brig. gen. Confederate Army, 1861; brigade comdr. Army of No. Va., 1862; commd. maj. gen., 1862, div. comdr.; served in battles of Seven Pines, Seven Days, 2d Bull Run, Manassas, Harper's Ferry, Chancellorsville, Crampton's Gap, Fredericksburg, Gettysburg, Spotsylvania Court House, Cold Harbor; one of 3 famous div. comdrs. of Robert E. Lee; held temporary rank of lt. gen., 1864; employed by S.C. R.R. Co. after Civil War; state insp. phosphates S.C. Died Beaufort, S.C., June 26, 1879.

ANDERSON, Robert, army officer; b. Louisville, Ky., June 14, 1805; s. Richard and Sarah (Marshall) A.; grad. U.S. Mil. Acad., 1825. Commd. capt. U.S. Army, 1847; served in Black Hawk, Seminole and Mexican Wars; promoted maj. U.S. Army, 1857; in command of Ft. Sumter during Confederate attack, 1861; commd. brig. gen., 1861 (due largely to service at Fort Sumter); largely inactive during Civil War because of illness; brevetted maj. gen., 1865. Died Nice, France, Oct. 26, 1871.

ANDERSON, Rufus, clergyman; b. North Yarmouth, Me., Aug. 17, 1796; s. Rufus and Hannah (Parsons) A.; grad. Bowdoin Coll., 1818, LL.D. (hon.) 1866; grad. Andover Theol. Sem., 1822; D.D. (hon.), Dartmouth, 1836; m. Eliza Hill, Jan. 8, 1827; children—Henry Hill, Edward, Sarah, Mary, William Porter. Editor, Missionary Herald (organ of Am. Bd. Fgn. Missions), 1822, later editor-in-chief for a time; asst. to sec. Am. Bd. Fgn. Missions, 1822-24, asst. sec., 1824-32, corr. sec., 1832-66; lectr. Andover Theol. Sem., 1867-69; a founder Mt. Holyoke Sem., 1837; a founder Am. Oriental Soc., 1842; an organizer Hanover Street Ch., Boston. Author: Irish Missions in the Early Ages, 1839; Missions in the Levant, 1860; A History of the Missions of the American Board of Foreign Missions, 5 vols., 1872. Died Boston, May 30, 1880.

ANDERSON, Samuel, congressman, physician; b. Middletown, Pa., 1773; studied medicine. Began practice medicine, 1796; became asst. surgeon U.S. Navy, 1799, promoted surgeon, 1800-01; began practice medicine, Chester, Pa., 1801; raised a co. volunteers known as Mifflin Guards, War of 1812; commd. capt. Pa. Militia, 1814, promoted lt. col. 100th Regt., 2d Brigade, 3d Div., 1821; mem. Pa. Ho. of Reps., 1815-18, 23-25, 29-35, speaker, 1833; sheriff Delaware County, 1819-23; reentered naval service as spl. physician to Adm. David Porter (comdr. W. Indian Squadron), 1823, resigned because of ill health; mem. U.S. Ho. of Reps. from Pa., 20th Congress, 1827-29; apptd. insp. customs, 1841; justice of peace, 1846-50. Died Chester, Jan. 17, 1850; buried Middletown Presbyn. Cemetery, nr. Media, Pa.

ANDERSON, Simeon H., congressman, lawyer; b. nr. Lancaster, Ky., Mar. 2, 1802; studied law; at least 1 son, William Clayton. Admitted to the bar, 1823, began practice of law, Lancaster, Ky.; mem. Ky. Ho. of Reps., 1828, 29, 32, 36-38; mem. U.S. Ho. of Reps. (Whig) from Ky., 26th Congress, 1839. Died nr. Lancaster Aug. 11, 1840; buried family cemetery.

ANDERSON, Sophie, artist; dau. Charles A.C. Gengembre; m. Walter Anderson. Came with parents to Am., 1849, settled in Cincinnati; painted portraits; contbd. 5 illustrations to Henry Howe's Historical Collections of the Great West, 1851; moved with family to Manchester, Pa.; lived in Europe with husband, many years, primarily on Isle of Capri, and London, Eng.; frequent exhibitor, London, 1856-90; returned to Am., 1860, exhibited at N.A.D.; said to have painted portraits of many of early citizens of Pitts.

ANDERSON, Thomas Lilbourne, congressman, lawyer; b. nr. Bowling Green, Ky., Dec. 8, 1808; studied law. Admitted to Ky. bar, 1828, began practice law, Franklin, Ky.; practiced law, Palmyra, Mo., from 1830; mem. Mo. Ho. of Reps., 1840-44; Whig presdl. elector, 1844, 48, 52, 56; mem. Mo. Constl. Conv., 1845; mem. U.S. Ho. of Reps. from Mo., (American Party) 35th Congress, 1857-59, (Independent Democrat) 36th Congress, 1859-61. Died Palmyra, Mar. 6, 1885; buried City Cemetery.

ANDERSON, Walter, artist; m. Sophie Gengembre. Lived in Europe, chiefly on Isle of Capri and in London, Eng., many years; exhibited frequently, London, 1856-86; returned to U.S., 1860, exhibited at N.A.D.; specialized in landscape painting. Died circa 1886.

ANDERSON, William, congressman; b. Accomack County, Va., Dec. 1762; m. Elizabeth Dixon, 3 children including Evelina. Mem. Lafayette's staff, 1777; admitted to Phila. bar, 1785; mem. U.S. Ho. of Reps. from Pa., 11th-13th, 15th congresses, 1809-15, 17-19; judge Delaware County (Pa.) Ct., 1826-29; U.S. collector of customs, Chester, Pa. 1829. Died Chester, Dec. 15, 1829; buried Old St. Paul's Cemetery, Chester.

ANDERSON, William Clayton, congressman, lawyer; b. Lancaster, Ky., Dec. 26, 1826; son of Simeon H. Anderson; grad. Centre Coll., Danville, Ky., 1845; studied law. Admitted to Ky. bar, practiced law in Lancaster; began practice in Danville, 1847; mem. Ky. Ho. of Reps., 1851-53; Am. Party presdl. elector, 1856; mem. U.S. Ho. of Reps. (Am. Party) from Ky., 36th Congress, 1859-61; elected as Unionist to Ky. Ho. of Reps., 1861. Died Frankfort, Ky., Dec. 23, 1861; buried Bell View Cemetery, Danville.

ANDERSON, William Wallace, physician, naturalist; b. S.C. Capt., Med. Corps, U.S. Army; collected birds in Tex. and N.M.; discovered Virginia's warbler (named for his wife), 1858.

ANDRE, John, army officer; b. London, Eng., 1751; never married. Served as officer Brit. Army; taken prisoner by Gen. Richard Montgomery at St. John's, 1775; later served on staffs Gen. Gray and Sir Henry Clinton; apptd. adj. gen. Brit. Army in Am. 1779; under name John Anderson conspired with Benedict Arnold in surrender of West Point, 1780, met Arnold and received plans of defenses at West Point, captured before mission completed; tried by 6 maj. gens. and 8 brig. gens., found guilty, condemned to death as spy. Hanged nr. Tappan Village, N.Y., Oct. 2, 1780; reinterred Westminster Abbey, London, Eng., 1821.

ANDRE, Louis, clergyman; b. St. Remy, France, May 28, 1631/32. Ordained priest Soc. of Jesus; came to Can., 1669; assisted in formal ceremony declaring the N.W. Territory for Louis XIV of France; served 1st missionary duty among Indians around Lake Huron; built (with Allouez) De Pere Mission of St. Francis Xavier, Wis.; missionary among Menominee, Potawatomi, Winnegabo Indian tribes around Green Bay, Wis.; at Mackinac, 1682-83; taught at Jesuit Coll., Quebec, Can., several years; missionary on lower St. Lawrence River, 1691-92. Died Quebec, Sept. 19, 1715.

ANDREW, James Osgood, clergyman; b. Wilkes County, Ga., May 3, 1794; s. Rev. John and Mary (Cosby) A.; m. Ann McFarlane, 1816; m. 2d, Mrs. Leonora Greenwood, 1844; m. 3d, Mrs. Emily Sims Childers; 4 children. Licensed to preach, 1812; elected bishop Methodist Episcopal Ch., 1832; 1st bishop Meth. Episcopal Ch. South (led Southern ministers in split of church over slavery issue), 184 Died Mobile, Ala., Mar. 2, 1871.

ANDREW, John Albion, gov. Mass.; b. Windhar Me., May 31, 1818; s. Jonathan and Nancy (Pierc A.; grad. Bowdoin Coll., 1837; m. Eliza Herse 1848. Admitted to Mass. bar, 1840; mem. low house Mass. Legislature, 1858; gov. Mass., 1860-6 chmn. Mass. delegation to Republican Nat. Conv 1860; a founder Free Soil Party in Mass.; an o ganizer 1st Colored Regt., U.S. Army, 1863; rais money for defense of John Brown. Died Boston, Oc 30, 1867.

ANDREW, John Forrester, congressman, la yer; b. Hingham, Mass., Nov. 26, 1850; grad. Harvar 1872, Harvard Law Sch., 1875. Admitted to Su folk bar, 1875, began practice law in Boston; men Mass. Ho. of Reps., 1880-82, Mass. Senate, 188 85; commr. parks City of Boston, 1885-90, 94; u successful candidate for gov. Mass., 1886; mem. U. Ho. of Reps. (Democrat) from Mass., 51st-52 congresses, 1889-93. Died Boston, May 30, 189 buried Mt. Auburn Cemetery, Cambridge, Mas

ANDREW, Samuel, clergyman; b. Cambridg Mass., Jan. 29, 1656; s. Samuel and Elizabe (White) A.; grad. Harvard, 1675; m. Abigail Trea Tutor, Harvard, 1675-84; pastor Congregational Ch Milford, Conn., 1685-1738; a founder Yale Coll trustee, 1701-38, rector pro tem, 1707-19; men Saybrook Synod of 1708. Died Jan. 24, 1738.

ANDREWS, Ambrose, artist, Itinerant portrai miniature and landscape painter; painted in Schuy lerville, N.Y., 1824, Troy, N.Y., 1829-31, Stock bridge, Mass., 1836, New Haven, Conn., 1837, Ne Orleans, 1841-42, N.Y.C., 1847-53; exhibited sev eral views of Montreal, Vt. and Conn. at Am. Art Union, 1847-53; painted in Buffalo, 1856-59, St Louis; exhibited portrait of Henry Clay at Am Inst., 1856; exhibited at Royal Acad., 1859, Nat. Pa. acads.; painted watercolor portrait of Phili Schuyler and family (owned by N.Y. Hist. Soc.) Flourished, 1824-59.

ANDREWS, Charles, congressman, lawyer; b Paris, Me., Feb. 11, 1814; grad. Hebron (Me. Acad.; studied law. Admitted to Me. bar, 183 began practice law in Turner, Me.; returned Paris; mem. Me. Ho. of Reps., 1839-43, speake 1842; clk. of the cts. for Oxford County, Me. 1845-48; del. Democratic Nat. Conv., Balt., 1848 mem. U.S. Ho. of Reps. (Democrat) from Me. 32d Congress, 1851-52. Died Paris, Apr. 30 1852; buried Hillside Cemetery.

ANDREWS, Chauncey Hummason, railroad builder mine promoter; b. Vienna, O., Dec. 2, 1823; s Norman and Julia (Hummason) A.; m. Louisa Bald win, July 1, 1857. Opened a coal mine, 1857; buil Mahoning Coal R.R., 1871; organizer P. & L.E. R.R a developer Pitts., Youngstown & Chgo. R.R., Pitts. Chgo .& Toledo R.R.; pres. Wood Mower & Reape Mfg. Co., Youngstown, O.; organizer Imperial Coa Co.; del. Nat. Republican Conv., 1884. Died Dec 25, 1893.

ANDREWS, George Leonard, army officer, engr. educator; b. Bridgewater, Mass., Aug. 31, 1828; s Manasseh and Harriet (Leonard) A.; grad. U.S. Mil. Acad., 1851. Assisted in constrn. of fortifications in Boston Harbor, 1851-54; instr. civil anc mil. engring. U.S. Mil. Acad., 1854-55; civil engr. in pvt. practice 1855-61; engr. Amoskeag Mfg. Co. Mfg. Co., Youngstown, O.; organizer Imperila Coa Manchester, N.H., 1855-57; commd. lt. col. 2 Mass. Inf., 1861; in command of a regt. at battle of Winchester and Cedar Mountain 1861-62; commd col., 1862; commd. brig. gen. U.S. Volunteers 1862; chief-of-staff of Gen. Banks, 1863; brigade comdr. Red River expdn., 1863; comdr. Corps d Afrique (later known as U.S. Colored Troops) 1864; provost marshal gen. Army of Gulf, 1865 chief-of-staff to Gen. Canby, 1865; U.S. marshal for Mass., 1867-71; prof. French, U.S. Mil. Acad. 1871-82, prof. modern langs., 1882-92; ret. fron active duty, 1892. Died Brookline, Mass., Apr. 4, 1899.

ANDREWS, George Rex, congressman, lawyer b. Ticonderoga, N.Y., Sept. 21, 1808; grad. Alban Law Sch. Admitted to N.Y. bar, 1836, began prac tice law in Ticonderoga; mem. U.S. Ho. of Reps (Whig) from N.Y., 31st Congress, 1849-51; move to Oshkosh, Wis., 1852, engaged in timber an lumber bus. Died Oshkosh, Dec. 5, 1873; burie Riverside Cemetery.

ANDREWS, Israel DeWolf, diplomat; s. Israel anc Elizabeth Andrews; M.A. (hon.), Yale, 1858; neve married. U.S. consul at New Brunswick, Can., 1849 apptd. spl. agt. to gather information concernin Brit. commerce in N.Am. 1849; prepared reports fo U.S. on Canadian trade and commerce on St. Joh River, 1851-52; lobbied in Canada and U.S. for re ciprocal trade agreements, openly bought votes o U.S. senators and N.S. and N.B. legislators and succeeded in establishing Canadian-Am. trade reciprocal treaty (opened U.S. markets to Canadian products in exchange for fishing privileges in water around N.S. and N.B.), unsuccessful in attempts t in reimbursement for his expenses in this project; prisoned for debt, several times. Died of chronic coholism, Boston, Feb. 17, 1871.

ANDREWS, Israel Ward, coll. pres.; b. Danbury, nn., Jan. 3, 1815; s. Rev. William and Sarah Parkhill) A.; grad. Williams Coll., 1837, D.D. on.), 1856; LL.D., (hon.), Ia. Coll., 1874, Wash Coll., 1876; m. Sarah Clarke, Aug. 8, 1839; m. l, Marianne Clarke, 1842. Instr. mathematics Maetta (O.) Coll., 1838, prof. mathematics and naral philosophy, 1839-55, pres., prof. moral, intelctual and polit. philosophy, 1855-85, pres. emeris, prof. polit. philosophy, 1855-88; trustee Lane neol. Sem.; pres. Ohio Edn. Assn.; mem. Nat. hrs. Assn.; asso. editor Ohio Jour. of Edn. Author: anual of the Constitution, 1874. Died Hartford, nn., Apr. 18, 1888.

ANDREWS, John, clergyman; b. Cecil County, d., Apr. 4, 1746; s. Moses and Letitia A.; grad. oll. of Phila. (now U. Pa.), 1764; D.D. (hon.), ashington Coll., 1785; m. Elizabeth Callender, 772, 10 children. Taught grammar sch., Phila.; in arge of classical sch., Lancaster, Pa., studied eology under Rev. Thomas Barton; ordained to inistry Anglican Ch., London, Eng., 1767, sent missionary to Lewes (Del.) by Soc. for Propagatg Gospel in Fgn. Parts, 1767-70; moved to York, a.; rector St. John's Ch., Queen Anne's County, d., went back to York, started classical school, et Maj. John Andre; returned to Md., rector St. homas's Ch., Baltimore County, 1782; mem. conv. hich separated from Brit. rule and organized Protstant Episcopal Ch. of Md., 1784; later urged union Episcopalians and Methodists; head P.E. Acad., hila., 1785; vice provost U. Pa., 1791-1810. Auor textbooks: A Compend of Logick, 1801; Eleents of Rhetorick and Belles Lettres, 1813. Died ar. 29, 1813.

ANDREWS, John Tuttle, congressman, mcht.; nr. Schoharie Creek, Greene County, N.Y., May , 1803; attended dist. sch., Dundee, N.Y. Taught h.; became a mcht. in Irelandville and Watkins, .Y.; justice of peace Steuben County, 1836, 37; em. U.S. Ho. of Reps. (Democrat) from N.Y., 5th Congress, 1837-39; mcht. in Dundee, 1866-77. ied Dundee, June 11, 1894; buried Hillside Cemery, Dundee.

ANDREWS, Joseph, engraver; b. Hingham, ass., circa 1805; s. Ephraim and Lucy (Lane) .; married twice. Apprenticed to engraver Abel owen, Boston, 1821; mem. Carter, Andrews Co., Lancaster, Mass., 1827; studied under Joeph Goodyear, London, Eng., 1835; went to Paris, rance, engraved head of Benjamin Franklin for Jorks of Franklin (edited by Jared Sparks); isited Europe, 1840-42; engraved 6 plates for alerie Historique de Versailles under patronage Louis Philippe, Paris; began engraving of Duke Urbino (Titian), Florence, Italy; returned to aris, 1853; engraved Plymouth Rock 1620 (after ainting by Peter Frederick Rothermael); other orks include; portrait of George Washington from painting by Gilbert Stuart), Oliver Wolcott, ohn Quincy Adams, Zachary Taylor, Jared Sparks from portrait by Gilbert Stuart), Crossing the ord (after painting by Alvan Fisher), The Panther cene (after painting by George Loring Brow), argaining for a Horse (after painting by William . Mount). Died Hingham, May 7, 1873.

ANDREWS, Landaff Watson, congressman, awyer; b. Flemingsburg, Ky., Feb. 12, 1803; grad. aw dept. Transylvania U., Lexington, Ky., 1826. dmitted to Ky. bar, 1826, began practice law in lemingsburg; pros. atty. Fleming County, 1829-9; mem. Ky. Ho. of Reps., 1834-38, 61-62; mem. .S. Ho. of Reps. (Whig) from Ky., 26th, 27th ongresses, 1839-43; Whig presdl. elector, 1845; em. Ky. Senate, 1857; judge circuit ct., 1862-68. ied Flemingsburg, Dec. 23, 1887; buried Fleming ounty Cemetery.

ANDREWS, Lorin, coll. pres.; b. Ashland, O., Apr. 1, 1819; s. Alanson and Sally (Needham) A.; ttended Kenyon Coll., 1838-40; m. Sarah Gates, ct. 30, 1843; 3 children. Supt. Union Sch., Masslon, O.; a founder Ohio State Tchrs. Assn., 1847; res. Kenyon Coll., Gambier, O., 1853-61; col. 4th hio Volunteers, 1861. Died Gambier, Sept. 18, 861; buried Kenyon Coll. Cemetery.

ANDREWS, Lorrin, missionary, jurist, educator; East Windsor, Conn., Apr. 29, 1795; grad. Jefferson Coll.; grad. Princeton Theol. Sem., 1825; m. Mary Wilson, 1827. Ordained to ministry Congregational Ch., 1827; mem. Hwiaian Islands Mission, 1827, rin. mission high sch., 1831-41; published 1st Hawaiian newspaper, 1834; translated entire Bible nto Hwaiian lang.; judge govt. Ct., Hawaii, 1845; mem. Superior Ct. of Law and Equity of Hawaii, 1848; 1st asso. justice Supreme Ct. of Hawaii, 1852-55; judge Hawaiian Ct. Probate and Divorce, 1855-59; published a Hawaiian dictionary, 1865. Died Honolulu, Hawaii, Sept. 29, 1868.

ANDREWS, Samuel George, congressman, busiessman; b. Derby, Conn., Oct. 16, 1796; atended classical acad., Chester, Conn. Moved to Rochester, N.Y., 1815, became a mcht.; clk. N.Y. State Assembly, 1831, 32; clk. Monroe County, 1834-37; mem. bd. of aldermen, 1838; sec. N.Y. Senate, 1840, 41; clk. ct. of errors, 2 years; postmaster of Rochester, 1842-45; mayor Rochester, 1846, 50; mem. U.S. Ho. of Reps. (Republican) from N.Y., 35th Congress, 1857-59; engaged in milling bus. Died Rochester, June 11, 1863; buried Mt. Hope Cemetery.

ANDREWS, Sherlock James, congressman; b. Wallingford, Conn., Nov. 17, 1801; s. Dr. John Andrews; grad. Union Coll., 1821; m. Ursula McCurdy 1828. First pres. Cleve. City Council, Pub. Library Bd. of Cleve.; promoter Cleve. & Pitts. Ry; mem. U.S. Ho. of Reps. from Ohio, 27th Congress, 1841-May 1842; apptd. judge Superior Ct. Cleve., 1848-50; del. Ohio Constl. Conv., 1850,-73; 1st pres. Cleve. Bar Assn., 1873. Died Cleve., Feb. 11, 1880; buried Lakeview Cemetery, Cleve.

ANDREWS, Sidney, journalist; b. Sheffield, Mass., Oct. 7, 1835; s. Charles Henry and Nancy (Noble) A.; attended U. Mich., 1856-59; m. Hila Marie Breeze, Nov. 1866; m. 2d, Sarah Lucretia Washburn, Nov. 1873. Moved to Dixon, Ill., 1846; asst. editor, then editor Daily Courier, Alton, Ill.; followed gold rush to Colo.; attendant in U.S. Senate, during Civil War; spl. correspondent for Chgo. Tribune and Boston Advertiser, 1864-69, visited Carolinas and Ga., wrote newspaper articles published as The South Since the War, 1866; moved to Boston, 1869; mem. staff of publ. Every Saturday, 1871; pvt. sec. to Mass. Gov. William Washburn, 1872; sec. Mass. Bd. of State Charities, 1874-79. Author: The St. Thomas Treaty—A Series of Letters to the Boston Advertiser, 1869; contbr. Wo Lee and His Kinsfolk to Atlantic Monthly, 1870. Died Apr. 10, 1880.

ANDREWS, Stephen Pearl, reformer, linguist; b. Templeton, Mass., Mar. 22, 1812; s. Rev. Elisha and Wealthy Ann (Lathrop) A.; attended Amherst Coll.; m. Mary Ann Gordon, 1835, at least 1 child. Joined brother Thomas to study law, New Orleans, 1831; admitted to La. bar; moved to Houston, Tex., 1839; abolitionst, forced to flee from home, went to England; tried to obtain loan from Gt. Britain to purchase slaves and then to free them, failed; learned short-hand system from Isaac Pitman; returned to Boston, opened school of phonography; moved to N.Y., 1847, interested in spelling reform, edited 2 mags. with printing in phonetic type, Anglo-Saxon and Propagandist; linguist, master some 32 langs. devised internat. lang. Alwato, forerunner Esperanto and Volapiik; greatest achievement was establishment Universology, deductive science of universe; thought ideal society was Pantarch, semi-anarchy; started colloquium (soc. for free discussion), N.Y.C., 1882; mem. Manhattan Liberal Club, N.Y., Am. Acad. Arts and Scis., Am. Ethnol. Soc. Author: (with Augustus F. Boyle) The Comprehensive Phonographic Class-Book, 1845, The Phonographic Reader, 1845; Discoveries in Chinese . . . A Practical Aid in the Acquisition of the Chinese Language, 1854; Primary Grammar of Alwato, 1877; The Basic Outline of Universology, 1877; Ideological Etymology, 1881; The Church and Religion of the Future, 1886. Died N.Y.C., May 21, 1886.

ANDREWS, Timothy Patrick, army officer; b. Ireland, 1794. Served in U.S. Navy in War of 1812; paymaster in army, 1822-47; commanded regt. of volunteers during Mexican War, 1847; served in Battle of Molino del Rey; brevetted brig. gen. for gallant conduct in Battle of Chapultepec; dep. paymaster gen. 1851; paymaster gen. with rank of col. U.S. Army, circa 1861-64. Died Washington, D.C., Mar. 11, 1868.

ANDREWS, William Watson, clergyman; b. Windham, Conn., Feb. 26, 1810; s. William and Sarah (Purkhill) A.; grad. Yale, 1831; m. Mary A. Given, July 24, 1833; m. 2d, Elizabeth Byrne Williams, July 1858. Ordained to ministry Congregational Ch., 1834; pastor, Kent, Conn., 1834-49; joined Catholic Apostolic Ch. (whose followers were known as Irvingites), pastor, Potsdam, N.Y., 8 years; evangelist throughout U.S. and Can., approximately 30 years; wrote over 30 religious tracts in support of movement. Died Oct. 17, 1897.

ANDRIEU, Mathuren Arthur, artist; b. France; studied at French Royal Acad. Came to U.S.; employed in New Orleans, circa 1840; exhibited series of dissolving views of London, the Crystal Palace, and New Orleans at Charleston, S.C., 1851; exhibited panoramas of St. Louis and "Southern Life", St. Louis, 1853; worked in Macon, Ga., 1855; settled in Providence, R.I., 1862; painted portraits, landscapes, scenery, and panoramas. Died Providence, 1896.

ANDROS, Sir Edmund, colonial gov.; b. London, Eng., Dec. 6, 1637. Served as Maj. Prince Rupert's Dragoons, 1672; bailiff of Guernsey, Eng., 1674; gov. Province of N.Y., 1674-81; knighted, 1681; appt. col. Princess of Denmark's Regt., 1685; gov. Dominion of New Eng., 1686-89, with English Revolution of 1689, was deposed and imprisoned by citizens of Boston; colonial gov. Va., 1692-98 a founder Coll. William and Mary, 1692; promoted mfg. and agr.; recalled to Eng., 1698; lt. gov. Guernsey, 1704-06. Died London, Feb. 24, 1714; buried St. Anne's, Soho, Eng.

ANGEL, Benjamin Franklin, diplomat; b. Burlinton, Otsego County, N.Y., Nov 28, 1815; s. Benjamin and Abigail (Stickney) A.; studied law, Hudson, N.Y., 1834; married twice, at least 3 children. Surrogate, Livingston County (N.Y.), 1836-40, 44-46; admitted to N.Y. bar, 1837; master of chancery, commr. Supreme Ct., 1848; U.S. consul, Honolulu, Hawaii, 1853-54; envoy of Pres. Pierce to China, 1855, successfully settled dispute between Am. mchts. and Chinese custom ofcls. over exaction of import duties; unsuccessful candidate from N.Y. for U.S. Ho. of Reps.; U.S. minister to Norway and Sweden, 1857-61; pres. N.Y. Agrl. Soc., 1873-74. Died Genesee, N.Y., Sept. 11, 1894.

ANGEL, William G., congressman, lawyer; b. New Shoreham, Block Island, R.I., July 17, 1790; attended common schs., Litchfield, N.Y.; began study of medicine, 1807; studied law. Admitted to N.Y. bar, began practice law in Burlington, N.Y., 1817; mem. U.S. Ho. of Reps. from N.Y., (John Quincy Adams Democrat) 19th Congress, 1825-27, (Jackson Democrat) 21st-22d congresses, 1829-33; practiced law, Hammondsport, N.Y.; mem. N.Y. State Constl. Conv., 1846; became judge Allegany County, N.Y., 1847. Died Angelica, Allegany County, Aug. 13, 1858; buried Until the Day Dawn Cemetery.

ANGELA, Mother, (christened Eliza Maria Gillespie), educator; b. nr. Brownsville, Pa., Feb. 21, 1824; d. John Purcell and Mary Madelein (Niers) Gillespie; grad. Visitation Convent sch., Georgetown, D.C., 1842. Tchr., Episcopalian sem., St. Mary's County, Md.; organized Catholic sch., Lancaster, Md.; joined Sisters of Holy Cross, 1853, novitiate in France, returned to Acad., Bertrand, Mich.; took name Mother Mary of St. Angela; superior of Sisters of Holy Cross in U.S., 30 years; established St. Mary's Acad., La Salle Portage, nr. Notre Dame U. in Ind.; founded (with Father Edward Sorin) Catholic mag. Ave Maria; supervised work of her order in U.S. Army hosps. during Civil War. Died Mar. 4, 1887.

ANGELL, Israel, army officer; b. Providence, R.I., Aug. 24, 1740; s. Oliver and Naomi (Smith) A.; m. Martha Angell; m. 2d, Susanne Wright; m 3d, Sarah Wood; 17 children. Commd. maj. R.I. Volunteers at beginning of Revolutionary War; commd. maj. 11th Continental Inf., 1776; lt. col., then col. 2d R.I. Regt., 1777; served in siege of Boston, 1775-76, battles of Brandywine, Red Bank, 1777, Monmouth, 1778, Springfield, 1780; ret., 1781. Died Smithfield, R.I., May 4, 1832.

ANGELL, Joseph Kinnicutt, lawyer; b. Providence, R.I., Apr. 30, 1794; s. Nathan and Amey (Kinnicutt) A.; grad. Brown U., 1813; attended Litchfield (Conn.) Law Sch. Admitted to R.I. bar, 1816; went to Eng. to settle estate of William Angell, 1819; returned to U.S., 1822, devoted himself to legal writing; reporter R.I. Supreme Ct., 1847-49. Author: The Common Law in Relation to Watercourses, 1824; The Right of Property in Tide Waters, 1826; Adverse Possession, 1827; The Limitation of Actions, 1829; (with Samuel Ames) The Law of Private Corporations Aggregate, 1832; Law of Assignment, 1835; The Law of Carriers, 1849; The Law of Insurance, 1854. Editor 1st vol. The United States Law Intelligencer and Reviews, 1824. Died Boston, May 1, 1857.

ANGELL, William Gorham, inventor; b. Povidence, R.I., Nov. 21, 1811; s. Enos and Catherine (Gorham) A.; m. Ann R. Stewart, 2 children including Edwin. Partner in reed-making firm, circa 1832; experimented in making iron screws for woodwork; agt., mgr. Eagle Screw Co., 1838; invented screw superior to that of English models which were flooding Am. market; became pres., mgr. Am. Screw Co. (merger of Eagle Screw Co. and New Eng. Co.), 1858; also draftsman, architect and builder. Died May 13, 1870.

ANSCHÜTZ, Karl, musician; b. Koblenz, Germany, Feb. 1815; studied under Friedrich Schneider. Dir. music sch. founded by his father, 1844-48; went to London, Eng., 1848, conducted Wednesday Concerts; came to U.S., 1857; became conductor Strakosch & Ullmann's opera-troupe, N.Y.C., 1857; conducted Arion Singing Soc., 1860-62; opened a season of German opera, 1862. Published compositions consist of a few piano pieces. Died N.Y.C., Dec. 30, 1870.

ANTES, Henry, religious leader; b. Germany, 1701; s. Philip Frederick and Anna Antes; m. Christina Elizabeth De Wees, 1726, 11 children including Philip Frederick, Ann Margaret. Came to Am. with family, circa 1720; settled in Frederick, Pa.; mem. Reformed Ch., Falkner Swamp, Pa., became lay preacher; in the interest of religious unity, formed (with other Germans) "Associated Brethren of Shippack," which met until 1740; called for and presided at Meeting of Christians at Germantown, Pa., 1742, also presided at following confs. which failed in their purpose of uniting the various religious denominations of area; left Reformed Ch. 1740, became agt. of Moravian Ch. in 1741, bought 500 acre tract of land along Lehigh River for 400 pounds (became center of town of Bethlehem, Pa.), moved to Bethlehem, 1745; bus. mgr. for Moravians, 1748, also justice of peace of Bethlehem and investigator of grievances with Indians; became friends with famous religious leaders including Nicholas Zinzendorf, Augustus Spangenberg, George Whitefield and Henry Muhlenberg; left Bethlehem and Moravian Ch. because of various disagreements, 1750, returned to Frederick; with others made trip to N.C., 1752-53, purchased 100,000 acres of land near Yadkin River (became Moravian colony of Wachovia); justice of peace Philadelphia County (Pa.), 1752. Died Fredericktown, Pa., July 20, 1755.

ANTES, John, musician, missionary; b. Montgomery County, Pa., Mar. 24, 1740; ed. Moravian boys' sch., Bethlehem, Pa. Made perhaps the 1st violin, viola and cello in Am.; went to Europe to serve Moravian Ch., also working as watchmaker in Germany; later ordained to Moravian ministry, became 1st Am. missionary in Egypt, was tortured and imprisoned by Turkish bey; composed 3 string trios while recovering in Cairo; settled in Eng., pub. trios there between 1783 and 1790, giving authorship as Giovanni A-T-S, Dillettante (sic) Americano; also composed anthems, motets, chorales, arias; devised mechanism for better violin tuning, improvements for violin bow and keyboard hammer, machine to turn pages of mus. scores. Regarded as 1st important Am. composer of chamber music; influenced primarily by Haydn, also by Handel, Graun, Hasse. Died Bristol, Eng., Dec. 17, 1811.

ANTHON, Charles, educator, author; b. N.Y.C., Nov. 19, 1797; s. Dr. George Christian and Genevieve (Jadot) A.; grad. Columbia, 1815; studied law in office of brother John, 1815-19. Admitted to N.Y. bar, 1819, never practiced; adjunct prof. Greek and Latin, Columbia, 1820-30, in charge of Grammar Sch. of Columbia, also Jay prof. Greek lang. and literature, 1830-67, called "Bull" by grammar sch. pupils because of teaching methods; 1st Am. to introduce into U.S. an exegetical and critical edition of a classical work (probably greatest single influence in U.S. of study of classics). Author: Horatii Poemata, 1830; A System of Latin Prosody and Metre, 1838; A System of Ancient and Mediaeval Geography for the Use of Schools and Colleges, 1850; several text books and revised and edited dictionaries. Died N.Y.C., July 29, 1867.

ANTHON, Charles Edward, educator, numismatist; b. N.Y.C., Dec. 6, 1822; s. John and Judith (Hone) A.; grad. Columbia, 1839. Prof. history St. Johns Coll., Annapolis, Md., after return from trip to Europe; prof. history and belles-lettres N.Y. Free Acad. (now Coll. City N.Y.), 1852-83; became interested in numismatics, circa 1865, gathered large collection including several rare coins; editor Am. Jour. Numismatics, 1867-70; pres. Am. Numismatic Soc., Archael. Soc. of N.Y., 1869-83. Author: A Pilgrimage to Treves, through the Valley of the Meuse and the Forest of Ardennes in the Year 1844, 1845; The Son of the Wilderness, 1848; The Gloria Regni (Gloriam Regni Tui Dicent 1670) or Silver Louis of 15 Sous, and of 5 Sous, Struck for Circulation in French America, 1877. Died N.Y.C., June 7, 1883.

ANTHON, John, lawyer, author; b. Detroit, Mich., May 14, 1784; s. Dr. George Christian and Genevieve (Jadot) A.; grad. Columbia, 1801; m. Judith Hone, 1810, at least 3 children including William Henry, Charles Edward. Moved with family to N.Y.C., 1786; admitted to N.Y. bar, 1805, began law practice, N.Y.C., circa 1807, worked primarily for mayor's ct., drafted act which merged mayor's ct. with N.Y. Ct. of Common Pleas; a founder N.Y. Law Inst. (inc. 1830), 2d v.p., 1839-52, pres., 1852-63; studied Italian, Greek, Latin classics and horticulture. Author: American Precedents and Declarations, 1810; Digested Index to the Reported Decisions of the United States Court, 1813; The Law of Nisi Prius, 1820. Died N.Y.C., Mar. 5, 1863.

ANTHONY, George Tobey, gov. Kan.; b. Fulton County, N.Y., June 9, 1824; s. Benjamin and Anna (Odell) A.; m. Rosa A. Lyon, 1852. Editor Daily Bulletin, Daily Conservative (both Leavenworth, Kan.), 1865-67; editor Kan. Farmer; asst. assessor internal revenue U.S., 1867, collector of internal revenue, 1868; pres. Kan. Bd. Agr., 1874-76, bd. mgrs. Centennial Expn.; gov. Kan., 1876; apptd. gen. Supt. Mexican Ry., 1881; Leavenworth County rep. Kan. Legislature, 1885; mem. Kan. Bd. Railroad Commrs., 1889. Died Leavenworth, Aug. 5, 1896.

ANTHONY, Henry Bowen, senator, gov. of R.I.; b. Coventry, R.I., Apr. 1, 1815; s. William and Eliza (Greene) A.; grad. Brown U., 1833; m. Sarah Aborn, Oct. 16, 1837. Editor Providence (R.I.) Jour., 1838-59; gov. R.I., 1849-51; mem. U.S. Senate from R.I.,1859-84, mem. com. naval affairs, 1863-84, pres. pro tem, 1869-70, 71, mem. coms. mines and mining, post offices, chmn. com. pub. printing; bequeathed 6,000 vols. to Brown U. (known as Harris Collection of Am. Poetry). Died Providence, Sept. 2, 1884; buried Swan Point Cemetery, Providence.

ANTHONY, John Gould, zoologist; b. Providence, R.I., May 17, 1804; s. Joseph and Mary (Gould) A.; m. Anna W. Rhodes, Oct. 16, 1832. Moved with parents to Cincinnati, 1816, engaged in bus., until 1851; became interested in natural history, collected mollusks in Ohio River; corresponded with mollusk collectors and students in East and Europe, including Louis Agassiz and S.S. Holderman, from 1835; toured Ky., Tenn., Ga. for health reasons, also to collect mollusks, 1853; apptd. by Agassiz in charge of mollusk collection Mus. of Comparative Zoology, Cambridge, Mass., 1863; mem. scientific staff on expdn. to Brazil, 1865; spent later years in classifying and arranging collections at Cambridge, also gathering data on family history. Author papers: "Two Species of Fossil Asterias in the Blue Limestone of Cincinnati", 1846, "Descriptions of New Species of American Fluviate Gasteropods," 1861, "Description of a New Species of Shells," 1865. Died Cambridge, Oct. 16, 1877.

ANTHONY, Joseph Biles, congressman, jurist; b. Phila., June 19, 1795; studied law. Admitted to the bar, practiced law; mem. Pa. Senate, 1830-33; mem. U.S. Ho. of Reps. (Democrat) from Pa., 23d-24th congresses, 1833-37; apptd. judge of "Nichelson Ct.", engaged in sale of titles to large tracts of land in Pa.; elected pres. judge 8th Dist., 1844-51. Died Williamsport, Pa. Jan. 10, 1851; buried Williamsport Cemetery.

ANTHONY, Sister (born Mary O'Connell), nun; b. Limerick, Ireland, 1814; d. William and Catherine (Murphy) O'Connell; attended Ursuline Academy, Charlestown, Mass. Novitiate of Am. Sisters of Charity in St. Joseph's Valley, 1835-37; in Cincinnati, 1837-82; placed in charge of St. John's Hotel for Invalids (new hosp.), 1852; served as nurse on battlefields of Camp Dennison, Winchester, Va., Cumberland, Tenn., Richmond, Va., Nashville, Tenn., Gallipolis, O., Culpeper Court House, Va., Murfreesboro, Tenn., Pittsburg Landing, Miss., Lynchburg, Va., Stone River, Tenn., during Civil War; in recognition of her services 2 non-Catholic citizens of Cincinnati purchased U.S. Marine Hosp. for her under direction of her order, property given to her to be used as maternity hosp., 1873; received recognition for work in yellow fever epidemic, 1877; ret. from active service, 1880. Known as "the angel of the battlefield" and "the Florence Nightingale of America." Died Dec. 8, 1897.

ANTOINE, Pére (Francisco Ildefonse Mareno), clergyman; b. Sedella, Spain, Nov. 18, 1748; s. Pedro and Ana (of Arze) Moreno. Ordained priest Roman Catholic Ch. by bishop of Guadex in convent of Capuchins, Granada, Spain, 1771; came to La., 1780; curé Parish of St. Louis, New Orleans, 1785-87; auxiliary vicar La. Territory; requested by Bishop Cyril of La. to leave for Spain because suspected of trying to install Inquisition in La., 1790; refused to leave after Gov. Estaban Miro made arrangements for his departure, 1790; produced royal order making him Supreme Officer of Holy Inquisition of Cartagena in La., demanded that gov. supply troops to put orders into effect; as result, bound in irons and returned to Spain; returned to La. as honorary preacher to His Majesty, 1795, reinstated in his parish of New Orleans by royal order; his character questioned by U.S. Sec. of State James Madison and Archbishop John Carroll of Md. (during transfer of La. from France to U.S.); suspended from his duties after dispute with Rev. Patrick Walsh, vicar-gen. of La. (who designated Convent of Ursuline Nuns as only place where sacraments could be administered), 1805; defied the suspension, stating that church was property of citizens of New Orleans; retained his position (after Catholics of city held meeting, elected body of wardens who chose him as their parish priest); also supported by Spanish king; secret polit. agt. for Spanish govt., 1813-16, acted against revolts in Mexico; established confraternity to instruct Negroes in Cath. faith, 1816; declined bishopric of New Orleans; administered to sick during yellow fever epidemic, 1819; at his funeral the courts and both houses of La. Legislature adjourned for day to assist at interment, and mems. of New Orleans City Council wore crepe for 30 days; datepalm tree near his house became famous landmark. Died New Orleans, Jan. 19, 1829.

ANZA, Juan Bautista de, see de Anza, Juan Bautista.

APES, William, missionary, author; b. Colrai Mass., Jan. 31, 1798; married. Ran away fro home, enlisted in U.S. Army, 1813, took part campaigns at Montreal and Lake Champlain; o dained to ministry Methodist Ch., 1829; visited Ma shpec Indians on Cape Cod, 1833, found them need of aid, became mem. of tribe; as their spokes man initiated tribal laws forbidding whites to c wood on their plantation, arrested for forceful unloading a wagonload of wood belonging to a M Sampson, tried for inciting riot, sentenced to 3 days in jail; after release persuaded Mass. legislatu to adopt laws aiding his tribe. Author: A Son the Forest, 1829; The Experiences of Five Chris ian Indians: or the Indian's Looking-Glass for th White Man, 1833.

APPENZELLER, Henry Gerhard, missionary; b Suderton, Pa., Feb. 6, 1858; s. Gideon and Mar (Gerhard) A.; grad. Franklin and Marshall Coll. Lancaster, Pa., 1882; attended Drew Theol. Sem Madison, N.J.; m. Ella Dodge, Dec. 17, 1884, children including Alice R. (1st white child born i Korea). Licensed to preach by Methodist Ch., Lar caster, 1879; apptd. missionary to Korea; ordaine to ministry, San Francisco, 1885, arrived Chemulpo Korea, 1885, settled in Seoul, translated parts Scripture into Korean; co-editor Korean Repositor (name changed to Korean Review), became editor established Pai Chai School for Boys, 1886; buil Methodist Ch., Seoul, 1895; received injurie in scuffle with Japanese railroad workers, delaye departure for the South, 1902; set sail on Kumagawa which collided with the Kisawaga, 1902. Died a sea, June 11, 1902.

APPLE, Thomas Gilmore, clergyman, coll. pres. b. Easton, Pa., Nov. 14, 1829; s. Andrew and Elizabeth (Gilmore) A.; grad. Marshall Coll., 185 Ph.D. (hon.), Lafayette Coll., 1866; D.D. (hon.) Franklin and Marshall Coll., 1868; m. Emma Miller Aug. 27, 1851, 11 children. Ordained to ministr German Reformed Ch., 1852; pres. Mercersburg Coll. 1865-71; editor Mercersburg Review (later becam Reformed Church Quarterly Review), 1868-98; pro Theol. Sem., Lancaster, Pa., 1871-77; pres. Franklin and Marshall Coll., Lancaster, 1877-89. Die Washington, D.C., Sept. 17, 1898.

APPLEGATE, Jesse, surveyor, legislator; b. Ky. July 5, 1811; s. Daniel and Rachel (Lindsey) A. attended Rock Spring Sem. (later Shurtleff Coll.) Shiloh, Ill., 1827-28; m. Cynthia Parker, 1832. Dep surveyor-gen. Mo.; moved to Ore. territory, 1843 organized opening of southern road into Ore., 1845 mem. legislative com. Ore. Provisional Govt., 1845 secured polit. unity and govt. which lasted unti Ore. became U.S. territory, 1849; mem. Ore. Constl Conv., 1857. Author: A Day with the Cow-Column 1843. Died Apr. 22, 1888.

APPLESEED, Johnny, see Chapman, John.

APPLETON, Daniel, publisher; b. Haverhill, Mass. Dec. 10, 1785; s. Daniel and Lydia (Ela) A.; m Hannah Adams, May 4, 1813; 8 children includin William Henry. Established House of Appleton and began publishing in 1831, became D. Appleton & Co., 1838; among the 1st to print children's books. Died N.Y.C., Mar. 27, 1849.

APPLETON, James, reformer; b. Ipswich, Mass., Feb. 14, 1785; s. Samuel and Mary (White) A.; m. Sarah Fuller; 10 children. Commd. lt. col. Gloucester (Mass.) Regt., brig. gen. 1st brigade, 1812 represented Gloucester in Gen. Ct., Mass. 1813-14 1st to propose state prohibition of manufacture and sale of liquor, 1832; mem. Me. Gen. Assembly from Portland, 1836-37; unsuccessful Liberty Party candidate for gov. Me., 1842, 43, 44; known as father of Prohibition. Advocated pub. edn., state aid to poor, abolition of slavery. Died Aug. 25, 1862.

APPLETON, Jesse, clergyman, coll. pres.; b. New Ipswich, N.H., Nov. 17, 1772; s. Francis and Elizabeth (Hubbard) A.; grad. Dartmouth, 1792; m. Elizabeth Means, 1800, 6 children including Jane Means (wife of Pres. Franklin Pierce). Ordained to ministry Congregational Ch., Hampton, N.H., 1797; minister Congregational Ch., Hampton, 1797-1807; pres. Bowdoin Coll., 1807-19; mem. Acad. Arts and Scis.; trustee Phillips Exeter Acad. Author: The Works of Jesse Appleton, D.D., 1836, 3 editions. Died Brunswick, Me., Nov. 12, 1819.

APPLETON, John, jurist; b. New Ipswich, N.H., July 12, 1804; s. John and Elizabeth (Peabody) A.; grad. Bowdoin Coll., 1822; m. Sarah N. Allen, 1834; m. 2d, Annie Greely, Mar. 30, 1876. Admitted to Me. bar, 1826; wrote law reforming Me. judiciary system, 1852; asso. justice Me. Supreme Judicial Ct., 1852-62, chief justice, 1862-83. Author: Reports of the Supreme Judicial Court of Maine, 2 vols., 1841; The Rules of Evidence, 1860. Died Feb. 7, 1891.

APPLETON, John congressman, diplomat; b. Beverly, Mass., Feb. 11, 1815; s. John W. and Sophia (Williams) A.; grad. Bowdoin Coll., 1834; m. Susan Dodge, Nov. 27, 1840. Admitted to Cumberland County (Me.) bar, 1837; edited Eastern Argus,

39-44; chief clk. Navy Dept., 1845-48, Dept. ate, 1848; charge d'affaires, Bolivia, 1848-49; m. U.S. Ho. of Reps. (Democrat) from Me., 32d ngress, 1851-53; U.S. sec. legation in London, g. under Ambassador (later Pres.) Buchanan, 55-56; asst. sec. of state U.S., 1857-60; minister Russia, 1860-61. Died Portland, Me., Aug. 22, 64; buried Evergreen Cemetery, Portland.

APPLETON, Nathan, cotton mfr., congressman; b. w Ipswich, N.H., Oct. 6, 1779; s. Rev. Isaac and ary (Adams) A.; m. Maria Gold, 1806, m. 2d, rriet Sumner, 1833; 7 children including Frances izabeth. A founder Waltham Cotton Factory lass.), operating 1st loom used in U.S., 1813; de-oped cotton producing centers Waltham and Law-nce, Mass., also Manchester, N.H.; a founder city Lowell (Mass.); mem. Mass. legislature, 1815, 16, , 23, 24, 27; mem. U.S. Ho. of Reps. from Mass., d, 27th congresses, 1831-33, 42; active Mass. st. Soc.; an organizer Boston Athenaeum; mem. ad. Arts and Scis. Author: Remarks on Currency and nking, 1841. Died Boston, July 14, 1861; ried Mt. Auburn Cemetery, Cambridge, Mass.

APPLETON, Nathaniel Walker, physician, med. iter; b. Boston, June 14, 1755; s. Nathaniel d Mary (Walker) A.; A.B., Harvard, 1773, A.M., 76; studied medicine under Edward Holyoke, lem, Mass.; m. Sarah Greenleaf, May 24, 1780, children. A founder, incorporator Mass. Med. Soc., '81, recording sec., 1781-91, kept careful reports every meeting of soc.; chmn. com. which pro-ced 1st vol. of Medical Communications, 1790, ntbr. papers "An Account of the Successful eatment of Paralysis of the Lower Limbs, Oc-sioned by a Curvature of the Spine," "History of emorrhage from a Rupture of the Inside of the ft Labium Pudendi." Died Apr. 15, 1795.

APPLETON, Samuel, mcht., philanthropist; b. w Ipswich, N.H., June 22, 1766; s. Isaac and ary (Adams) A.; m. Mary Gore, 1819. Engaged cotton manufacturing, real estate, railroads, altham and Lowell, Mass.; mem. Mass. Legislature, 28-31; trustee Mass. Gen. Hosp.; contbr. to Bos-n Female Asylum, New Ipswich Acad., Dartmouth, arvard; patron Boston Athenaeum, Mass. Hist. c.; bequeathed $200,000 for scientific, literary, ligious, and charitable purposes. Died Boston, ly 12, 1853.

APPLETON, Thomas Gold, author; b. Boston, ar. 31, 1812; s. Nathan and Maria Theresa Gold) A.; grad. Harvard, 1831. Mem. Saturday ub; trustee Boston Athenaeum, Boston Public brary, Boston Museum of Fine Arts. Author: ded Leaves, 1872; Fresh Leaves, 1874; A Sheaf Papers, 1875; A Nile Journal, 1876; Syrian nshine, 1877; Windfalls, 1878; Chequer Work, 79. Died Apr. 17, 1884.

APPLETON, William, congressman; b. Brook-eld, Mass., Nov. 16, 1786; attended schs. in New swich and Francestown, N.H., also Tyngsboro, ass. Worked in country store in Temple, N.H., 801; moved to Boston, 1807, became a mcht.; es. Boston br. U.S. Bank, 1832-36; mem. U.S. Ho. Reps. (Whig) from Mass., 32, 33d, 37th con-esses, 1851-55, Mar.-Sept. 27, 1861, resigned ecause of failing health. Died Longwood (Brook-ne), Mass., Feb. 15, 1862; buried Mount Auburn emetery, Cambridge, Mass.

APPLETON, William Henry, publisher; b. Haver-ll, Mass., Jan. 27, 1814; s. Daniel and Hannah Adams) A.; m. Mary Worthen, Apr. 16, 1844, 4 ildren including William Worthen. Formed partner-ip with father under name D. Appleton & Co., 338, brothers replaced father in bus., 1848; spe-alized in text-books, scientific publs.; published t Appleton's Cyclopedia of Biography, 1865; pub-shed travel guides, also numerous memoirs by Civil ar notables; pres. Am. Publishers Copyright eague, 1887; endowed Appleton Ch. Died N.Y.C., ct. 19, 1899.

ARBUCKLE, Matthew, musician; b. 1828. Noted rnet-player and band master. Author: Complete rnet Method. Died N.Y.C., May 23, 1883.

ARCHDALE, John, colonial gov. b. Buckingham-ire County, Eng., Mar. 5, 1642; s. Thomas and ary (Nevill) A.; m. Ann Dobson, Dec. 1663, 4 ildren. Commr. to gov. Mass., 1664; emissary for ing Charles II in Mass.-Me. boundary dispute, 664; col. Me. Militia, 1665; gov. Carolinas, 1694-8; mem. English Parliament, 1698. Author: His-ry and Description of Carolina, 1707. Died Chip-ng Wycombe, Buckinghamshire, July 4, 1717.

ARCHER, Branch Tanner, Texan revolutionist; Va., 1790; s. Maj. Peter Field and Frances Tanner) A. Moved to Tex., 1831; mem. Tex. onv. which adopted provisional constn. and titioned Mexican Congress for admission as co-ate into Mexican Confedn., 1833; chmn. Tex. nsultation of 1835 which favored independence; mmr. to U.S. to seek aid necessary for War of x. Independence, 1836; mem. Republic of Tex. o. of Reps., 1st, 2d congresses, 1836-39, speaker, 838-39; sec. of war under Pres. Lamar of Repub-ic of Tex. Died Brazoria County, Tex., Sept. 22, 1856.

ARCHER, James J., army officer; b. Stafford, Hartford County, Md., Dec. 19, 1817; attended Princeton, also Bacon Coll., Georgetown, Ky. Served in Mexican War; brevetted maj. U.S. Army for gallantry at battle of Chapultepec; dis-charged 1848; reentered U.S. Army as capt., 1855; entered Confederate Army, 1861; commd. brig. gen., 1862; led Archer's brigade in battles of Seven Days, Cedar Mountain, Second Manassas, Antietam, Fredericksburg, Chancellorsville, and Gettysburg; captured at Battle of Gettysburg, held prisoner for over year; died soon after re-lease. Died Oct. 24, 1864.

ARCHER, John, physician, congressman, army officer; b. Harford County, Md., May 5, 1741; B.A., Princeton, 1760; A.M., 1763, B.M., Phila. Coll. Medicine, 1768 (1st med. degree awarded in Am.); m. Catherine Harris, 10 children (5 became doc-tors), including Stevenson. Commd. maj. Continental Army, 1776; mem. conv. which framed Md. Constn. and Bill of Rights, 1776; a founder, exec. mem. Med. and Chirurg. Faculty Md., 1799; presdl. elec-tor; mem. U.S. Ho. of Reps. from Md., 7th-9th congresses, 1801-07; introduced Senega in treatment croup; contbd. to Med. Repository N.Y. Died Har-ford County, Sept. 28, 1810; buried Presbyn. Ceme-tery, Churchville, Md.

ARCHER, Stevenson, congressman, jurist; b. Harford County, Md., Oct. 11, 1786; s. John and Catherine (Harris) A.; grad. Princeton, 1805; m. Pamelia Hays, 1811. Mem. Md. Legislature, 1809, 10, U.S. Ho. of Reps. from Md., 12th-14th, 16th congresses, 1811-17, 19-21; judge Mississippi Terri-tory, 1817-19; chief justice Baltimore and Harford counties. 1824: chief judge Md. Ct. Appeals, 1844. Died Harford, Md., June 26, 1848; buried Presbyn. Cemetery, Churchville, Md.

ARCHER, Stevenson, congressman, lawyer; b. nr. Churchville, Hartford County, Md., Feb. 28, 1827; s. Stevenson Archer; attended Bel Air (Md.) Acad.; grad. Princeton, 1848; studied law. Ad-mitted to bar, 1850, began practice law, 1850; mem. Md. Ho of Dels., 1854; mem. U.S. Ho. of Reps. (Democrat) from Md., 40th-43d congresses, 1867-75; practiced law, Bel Air, 1875-98. Died Aug. 2, 1898; buried Presbyn. Cemetery, Church-ville.

ARCHER, William Segar, senator; b. Amelia Coun-ty, Va., Mar. 5, 1789; s. Maj. John and Elizabeth (Eggleston) A.; grad. Coll. William and Mary, 1806. Admitted to bar; mem. Va. Ho. of Dels., 1812-19; mem. U.S. Ho. of Reps. (Whig) from Va., 16th-23d congresses, Jan. 1820-Mar. 1835; mem. U.S. Senate (Whig) from Va., 1841-47, chmn. com. fgn. affairs. Died "The Lodge," Amelia County, Mar. 28, 1855; buried "The Lodge."

ARGALL, Samuel, maritime explorer, colonial gov.; b. Bristol, Eng., 1572. Discovered shortest Northern route from Eng. to Va., 1609; captured Pocahontas and brought her to Jamestown, 1612; regained French settled coast of Me. and Nova Scotia for Eng., destroyed French settlements St. Croix and Port Royal, 1613; dep. gov. Va., 1617-19; captained expdn. against Algerines, 1620; adm. Brit. Naval Force in Cecil's expdn. against Spain, 1625; knighted by King James I, 1626; mem. New Eng. Royal Council. Died 1639.

ARGUELLO, Jose Dario, colonial gov. A Mexi-can noble; acting gov. Cal., 1814-15; acting gov. Lower Cal., until 1822, succeeded by son, Luis.

ARGUELLO, Luis Antonio, colonial gov.; b. San Francisco, 1784; son of Jose Dario Arguello. Became commandant of Cal., 1806; led expdn. to Columbia River, 1821; gov. Cal. (1st native of area to hold post), 1822-25. Died 1830.

ARMISTEAD, George, army officer; b. New Mar-ket, Va., Apr. 10, 1780; s. John and Lucy (Baylor) A.; m. Louisa Hughes, Oct. 26, 1810. Commd. 2d lt. U.S. Army, 1799, 1st lt., 1799, capt., 1806, maj. 3d Arty., 1813; played prominent part in cap-ture of Ft. George (N.Y.) from British, 1813; brevetted lt. col., 1814; comdr. Ft. McHenry where his defense prevented Brit. assault on Balt. and inspired Francis Scott Key's writing "Star Spangled Banner." Died Balt., Apr. 25, 1818.

ARMISTEAD, Lewis Addison, army officer; b. Newbern, N.C., Feb. 18, 1817; s. Gen. Walker Keith and Elizabeth (Stanley) A.; m. Cecelia Lee Love. Commd. 2d lt. 6th Inf., U.S. Army, 1839, 1st lt., 1844; served in Mexican War at battles of Contreras, Churubusco and Molina del Rey, 1846-47; commd. capt., 1855; comdr. detachment which defeated Indians from Ft. Mohave (Colo.), 1859; apptd. col. 57th Va. Regt., Confederate States Army, 1861, brig. gen., 1862; served at Battle of Antietam, 1862; in charge of brigade in Gen. George Pick-ett's Div. at Battle of Gettysburg (Pa.), 1863. Killed at Battle of Gettysburg, July 3, 1863.

ARMSTRONG, David Hartley, senator; b. N.S., Can., Oct. 21, 1812; attended Me. Wesleyan Sem. Sch. tchr., New Bedford, Mass., 1833-37; moved to St. Louis, Mo., 1837; then tchr. McKendree Coll., Lebanon, Ill.; returned to Mo. as prin. pub. sch., Benton, 1838-47; comptroller of St. Louis, 1847-50; postmaster of St. Louis, 1854-58; mem. bd. police commrs., St. Louis, 1873-76; mem. bd. free holders which framed present St. Louis city charter, 1876; mem. U.S. Senate (Democrat, apptd. to fill vacancy) from Mo., Sept. 29, 1877-Jan. 26, 1879. Died St. Louis, Mar. 18, 1893; buried Bellefontaine Cemetery.

ARMSTRONG, George Buchanan, govt. ofcl.; b. County Armagh, Ireland, Oct. 27, 1822; m. Julia H. W. McKee, circa 1846. Clk., U.S. Post Office Dept., Washington, D.C., 1852, transferred to Chgo., 1854; unsuccessfully engaged in business, 1856-58; asst. postmaster, Chgo., 1858; col. Ill. Volunteers during Civil War; proposed reforms of mail service to U.S. Post Office Dept., 1864, main suggestion was to abandon mail distributing offices and sort mail on trains, received permis-sion from Postmaster Gen. Blair to experiment with this system on any railroad which would grant him the privilege, made 1st trial on C. & N.-W. Ry., 1864 (system regarded as success by end of year); spl. agt. U.S. Post Office to organize "traveling post office" system, 1864; Congress rec-ognized system and authorized its full devel. under postmaster gen., 1865; apptd. spl. agt. for this system in West; gen. supt. Bur. Ry. Mail Service, 1869-71. Died Chgo., May 5, 1871.

ARMSTRONG, George Dod, clergyman; b. Mend-ham, Morris County, N.J., Sept. 15, 1813; s. Rev. Amzi and Polly (Dod) A.; grad. Princeton, 1832; attended Union Theol. Sem., Prince Edward Coun-ty, Va., 1836; married, at least 4 children. Prof. chemistry and mechanics Washington (now Wash-ington and Lee U.) Coll., Lexington, Va., 1838-51; pastor First Presbyn. Ch., Norfolk, Va., 1851-99. Author: The Summer of the Pestilence, 1856; The Christian Doctrine of Slavery, 1857; A Doctrine of Baptism, 1857; A Discussion on Slaveholding. . ., 1858; The Two Books of Nature and Revelation Collated, 1886. Died May 11, 1899.

ARMSTRONG, George Washington, express co., railroad exec.; b. Boston, Aug. 11, 1836; s. David and Mahalia (Lovering) A.; m. Louisa Marston, 1868; m. 2d, Flora E. Greene, 1882; 4 children. Partner in restaurant concession at Boston terminal of Boston and Albany R.R., 1863, sole owner, 1871; established Armstrong Transfer Co., 1865, (1st of its type in U.S., transporting baggage and freight on New Eng. railroads); owned restaurant and news concessions on Boston and Albany, Old Colony, Boston, Revere and Lynn, and Boston and Me. railroads; dir. Worcester, Nashua & Roches-ter R.R., Manchester and Lawrence R.R., U.S. Trust Co. Died Brookline, Mass., June 30, 1901.

ARMSTRONG, James, congressman, physician; b. Carlisle, Pa., Aug. 29, 1748; attended Phila. Acad., Coll. of N.J. (now Princeton); studied medi-cine Dr. John Morgan's Sch., Phila.; grad. U. Pa., 1769. Began practice medicine, Winchester, Va.; med. officer, Revolutionary War; studied medi-cine, London, Eng., 1785-88; returned to Carlisle, 1788, then moved to Mifflin County, Pa., practiced there for 12 years; apptd. an asso. justice, repelled riot at courthouse by use of firearms, 1791; mem. U.S. Ho. of Reps. (Federalist) from Pa., 3d Con-gress, 1793-95; asso. judge Cumberland County Ct., 1808-28. Died Carlisle, May 6, 1828; buried Old Carlisle Cemetery.

ARMSTRONG, John, army officer, Continental congressman; b. County Fermanagh, Ireland, Oct. 13, 1717; s. James Armstrong; m. Rebecca Lyon; children—John, James. Surveyor, laid out Town of Carlisle (Pa.); commd. capt. Pa. Militia, 1756, lt. col., 1756; fought in French and Indian War, led successful night attack on Delaware Indians at Kittanning, 1756 (called Hero of Kittanning); commd. brig. gen. Continental Army, 1776, maj. gen., 1777; mem. Continental Congress, 1778-80, 87-88. Died Carlisle, Mar. 9, 1795; buried Old Carlisle Cemetery.

ARMSTRONG, John army officer, explorer; b. N.J., Apr. 20, 1755; s. Thomas and Jane (Hamil-ton) A.; married a dau. of Judge William Goforth; 1 son, William Goforth. Served as officer Pa. Mili-tia, 1777-84, Continental Army, 1784-93; com-mandant Ft. Pitt, 1875-86, Ft. Hamilton, 1791; explored Wabash River to Lake Erie, 1790; served in Gen. Josiah Harmar's unsuccessful expdn. against Indians in what is now Ind., 1790, unsuccessful expdn. of Arthur St. Clair against same Indians, 1791; treas. Northwest Territory; founder Arm-strong's Station on the Ohio River, 1796. Died Armstrong's Station, Feb. 4, 1816.

ARMSTRONG, John, army officer, sec. of war, diplomat; b. Carlisle, Pa., Nov. 25, 1758; s. John and Rebecca (Lyon) A.; attended Princeton, 1775; m. Alida Livingston, 1789. Aide-de-camp under John Frances Mercer and Horatio Gates in Revolu-tionary War; author Newburgh Letters threatening army action if Congress refused to pay arrears in soldiers' salaries, 1783; after war became sec. of state, adj.-gen. Pa.; del. Continental Congress, 1787; mem. U.S. Senate from N.Y., 1800-02, 03-04; U.S. minister to France, 1804-10; believed to have contbd. to outbreak of French-British War, 1812; commd. brig. gen. in command N.Y.C., 1812; sec. of war U.S., 1813-14; considered responsible for failure of Montreal and Plattsburg campaigns and Brit. capture of Washington, D.C., 1814. Died Red Hook, N.Y., Apr. 1, 1843; buried Rhinebeck (N.Y.) Cemetery.

ARMSTRONG, Robert, army officer; b. Abingdon, Va., Sept. 28, 1792; s. Trooper Armstrong; m. Margaret Nichol, June 1814. Served to sgt. U.S. Army in War of 1812; served as lt. arty. under Andrew Jackson during Creek Indian campaign; wounded at battle of Enotochapho, 1814; mem. Jackson's staff at Battle of New Orleans; postmaster Nashville (Tenn.), 1829-35; commd. brig. gen. during Second Seminole War, 1836-37; engaged in Battle of Wahoo Swamp; unsuccessful candidate for gov. Tenn., 1837; consul at Liverpool, 1845-49; propr. Washington (D.C.) Union, 1851-54. Died Washington, Feb. 23, 1854.

ARMSTRONG, Samuel Chapman, army officer, educator; b. Hawaiian Islands, Jan. 30, 1839; s. Rev. Richard and Clarissa A.; grad. Williams Coll., 1862; m. Emma Walker, 1869; m. 2d, Mary Ford, 1890. Commd. capt. 125th N.Y. Volunteer Regt., 1862, commd. 9th Colored Regt., U.S. Colored Troops (in this capacity developed interest in the Negro); brig. gen., 1865; agt. Freedmen's Bur., 1866; founder Hampton (Va.) Normal and Indsl. Inst. for Negroes, 1868. Died Hampton, May 11, 1893.

ARMSTRONG, Samuel Turell, publisher, gov. Mass.; b. Dorchester, Mass., Apr. 29, 1784; s. John and Elizabeth A. Printed Panoplist and Missionary Magazine United, a Charlestown (Mass.) monthly, 1808; printed religious works, Boston; deacon Old South Ch.; discovered 3d volume of original manuscript of History of New England (John Winthrop), 1816; mem. Am. Bd. Commrs. for Fgn. Missions; Boston rep. to Mass. Gen. Ct., 1822,23, 28, 29; lt. gov. Mass., 1833-35, gov., 1835; leading subscriber in successful effort to save Plymouth Rock, 1835; mayor Boston, 1836; mem. Mass. Senate, 1839. Died Boston, Mar. 26, 1850.

ARMSTRONG, William, congressman; b. Lisburn, County Antrim, Ireland, Dec. 23, 1782; studied law, Winchester, Va. Came to U.S., 1792, settled in Va.; U.S. tax collector, 1818, 19; mem. Va. Ho. of Dels., 1822, 23; Democratic presdl. elector, 1820, 24; mem. U.S. Ho. of Reps. from Va., 19th-22d congresses, 1825-33; in tavern bus., Romney, W.Va., until 1862. Died Keyser, W. Va., May 10, 1865; buried Indian Mound Cemetery, Romney.

ARNOLD, Aza, inventor, patent atty.; b. Smithfield, R.I., Oct. 4, 1788; s. Benjamin and Isabel (Greene) A.; m. Abigail Dennis, July 28, 1815. As youth learned carpenter's and machinist's trades; worked in mfg. plant of Samuel Slater, Pawtucket, R.I., 1808; operated (with Larned Pritcher and P. Hovey) machine shop, Pawtucket until 1819; opened cotton mill, Great Falls, N.H., 1819; went back to R.I. few years later (North Providence), made machine for mfg. textile machinery; obtained patent for roving machine for spinning cotton, 1823, introduced into England, 1825, brought law suits because of infringement of patent rights (new code of patent laws passed largely because of his suits, 1836, however he received no compensation); operated Mulhausen Print Works, Phila., 1838-50; patent atty., Washington, D.C., circa 1850-65; invented self-raking and self-setting saw for sawing machines (his last invention, patented 1856). Died 1865.

ARNOLD, Benedict, army officer; b. Norwich, Conn., Jan. 14, 1741; s. Benedict and Hannah (Waterman) A.; m. Margaret Mansfield, Feb. 22, 1767; m. 2d, Margaret Shippen, Apr. 1779; 8 children including Benedict, Richard, Henry. Commd. capt. Conn. Militia, then col., 1775; captured Ft. Ticonderoga from British, 1775; defeated in attack on Quebec, 1775; commd. brig. gen., 1776; twice stopped British in their attempted expdn. down Lake Champlain, 1776; promoted maj. gen., 1777, played major role in defeat and surrender of Burgoyne at Battle of Saratoga; mil. comdr. of Phila., 1778; commanded Am. post at West Point (N.Y.), 1780; started correspondence with Sir Henry Clinton, Brit. comdr.-in-chief in N.Am. (after a court martial, congressional slights and opposition to the French Alliance); correspondence culminated in his arrangement with Maj. John André of Clinton's staff to betray West Point, 1780; fled to British after discovery of his treason, became brig. gen. Brit. Army, 1780; led raids on Va., 1780, on Conn., 1781; granted land in Canada, 1797. Died London, Eng., June 14, 1801.

ARNOLD, Benedict, congressman; b. Amsterdam, N.Y., Oct. 5, 1780; attended common schs. Mcht., landowner, philanthropist; supr. of Amsterdam, 1813-16; mem. N.Y. State Assembly, 1816, 17; mem. U.S. Ho. of Reps. from N.Y., 21st Congress, 1829-31; pres. bd. trustees Village of Amsterdam, 1832. Died Amsterdam, Mar. 3, 1849; buried Green Hill Cemetery.

ARNOLD, George, author; b. N.Y.C., June 24, 1834. Enjoyed greatest success with series of papers under pseudonym "McArone" in Vanity Fair, 1860, Leader, and Weekly Rev., 1865; contbr. to Cahill's Parlor Theatricals, 1859; most famous poem: Jolly Old Pedagogue; served mil. duty on Governor's Island during Civil War. Author: Life and Adventures of Jeff Davis (humor), 1865; The Poems of George Arnold, Complete Edition, 1886. Died Strawberry Farms, N.J., Nov. 9, 1865; buried Greenwood Cemetery, Srawberry Farms.

ARNOLD, Isaac Newton, congressman, historian; b. Hartwick, N.Y., Nov. 30, 1815; s. Dr. George and Sophia (Mason) A.; m. Catherine Dorrance; m. 2d, Harriet Dorrance; 10 children. Admitted to bar, 1835; city clk. Chgo., 1837; mem. Ill. Legislature, 1842-45, 56, chmn. house com. finance; mem. U.S. Ho. of Reps. from Ill., 37th-38th congresses, 1861-65; auditor of Treasury for Post Office Dept., 1865-66; a founder Chgo. Hist. Soc., pres., 1876-84. Author: Life of Abraham Lincoln, 1885; Life of Benedict Arnold, 1880. Died Chgo., Apr. 24, 1884; buried Graceland Cemetery, Chgo.

ARNOLD, John, Jr., congressman; b. Elmira, N.Y., Mar. 11, 1831; attended Yale, did not graduate. After death of father became banker in Elmira; pres. Village of Elmira, 1859-64, pres. bd. village trustees, 1859, 60, 64; served as paymaster with rank of maj., U.S. Army, stationed in Elmira, during Civil War; mayor Elmira (after it was chartered as a city), 1864, 70, 74; mem. U.S. Ho. of Reps. (Democrat) from N.Y., 48th, 49th congresses, 1883-Nov. 20, 1886. Died Elmira, Nov. 20, 1886; buried Woodlawn Cemetery.

ARNOLD, Jonathan, physician, legislator; b. Providence, R.I. Dec. 3, 1741; s. Josiah and Amy (Phillips) A.; m. Molly Burr; m. 2d, Alice Crawford; m. 3d, Cynthia Hastings; 9 children. Mem. R.I. Gen. Assembly, 1776, author of act repealing laws for oath of allegiance to England, 1776; organized Revolutionary Hosp. of R.I., 1776, surgeon, 1776-81; del. from R.I. to Continental Congress, 1782-84; founder St. Johnsbury, Vt.; judge Orange County Ct., 1782-93; attended Vt. Gen. Assembly which voted to accept U.S. Constn., 1791; trustee U. Vt. Died St. Johnsbury, Feb. 2, 1793; buried Mt. Pleasant Cemetery, St. Johnsbury.

ARNOLD, Lauren Briggs, dairy farmer; b. Fairfield, N.Y., Aug. 14, 1814; s. George and Elizabeth (Grimes) A.; grad. Union Coll., Schenectady, N.Y., 1843; m. Melissa Bishop, 1852; m. 2d, Mrs. Elizabeth Woodward; 2 children. Taught school, did mech. work in N.Y., 1833; after college took over father's farm, Fairfield; became greatly interested in dairying, spent rest of life in discovery of new and better methods; built model cheese factory and dairy lab. on his farm, 1867 (results brought improvements in mfg. cheese, adopted by Canada, U.S. and Scotland); formed Little Fall Farmer's Club; because of bad health moved to smaller farm nr. Rochester, N.Y., 1874; expert judge in dairy section Centennial Expn., Phila., 1876; del. from U.S. to conf. in London by invitation of Brit. Dairymen's Assn., 1885; contbr. articles to papers. Author: American Dairying, 1876. Died Mar. 7, 1888.

ARNOLD, Lemuel Hastings, gov. of R.I., congressman, lawyer; b. St. Johnsbury, Vt., Jan. 29, 1792; son of Jonathan Arnold; grad. Dartmouth, 1811; studied law. Admitted to bar, 1814, began practice law in Providence, R.I.; in mfg., merc. pursuits, 1821; mem. R.I. Ho. of Reps., 1826-31 gov. R.I., 1831, 32; mem. exec. council during Dorr Rebellion, 1842, 43; mem. U.S. Ho. of Reps. (Liberation Whig) from R.I., 29th Congress, 1845-47; practiced law in South Kingston, R.I., 1847-52. Died June 27, 1852; buried Swan Point Cemetery, Providence.

ARNOLD, Lewis Golding, army officer; b. N.J., Jan. 15, 1817; grad. U.S. Mil. Acad., 1837. Served with 2d Arty., U.S. Army in Seminole War, 1837-38; commd. 1st lt., 1838; served at siege of Vera-cruz in Mexican War; brevetted capt. and maj., 1847; served with 2d Arty. in Fla. War, 1853-56; commd. maj. 1st Arty., 1861; brevetted lt. col., 1861; served at Santa Rosa Island (Fla.), 1861, Ft. Pickens, 1861-62; brig. gen. U.S. Volunteers, New Orleans, 1862; commanded Dept. of Fla., 1862; lt. col. U.S. Army, 1863; lt. col. 2d Arty., 1863; ret. 1864. Died Boston, Sept. 22, 1871.

ARNOLD, Peleg, Continental congressman; b. Smithfield, R.I., June 10, 1751; attended Brown U.; studied law. Admitted to the bar, practiced law; elected dep. to R.I. Gen. Assembly, 1777-78, 82-83, 1817-19; col. 2d Regt., Providence County Militia, 1787-89; keeper "Peleg Arnold Tavern," Smithfield; asst. gov. of R.I., 1790; incorporator Providence Soc. for the Abolition of Slavery, 1790; chief justice R.I. Supreme Ct., 1795-1809, 10-12; pres. Smithfield Union Bank, 1803; pres. Smithfield Acad., 1810. Died Smithfield, Feb. 13, 18[illegible] buried Union Cemetery, Union Village, nr. Wo[illegible] socket, R.I.

ARNOLD, Richard, army officer; b. Providen[illegible] R.I., Apr. 12, 1828; s. Lemuel Hastings and Sa[illegible] (Lyman) A.; grad. U.S. Mil. Acad., 1850. Comn[illegible] in U.S. Arty., 1850, served in Fla. and Cal.; [illegible] gaged in road building and exploration in Nor[illegible] west for 2 years; promoted 1st lt., 1854; a.d.c. [illegible] Gen. John E. Wool, 1855-61; promoted capt. 5[illegible] U.S. Arty., 1861; participated in 1st Battle of B[illegible] Run; chief of arty. in Gen. William Franklin's [illegible] vision, 1862; spent most of Peninsular Campaign [illegible] staff 6th Corps, served at battles of Savage S[illegible] tion, Glendale, Malvern Hill (Battle of Sev[illegible] Days) (all Va.); brevetted maj. U.S. Volunte[illegible] for services at Malvern Hill; chief of arty. Dept. [illegible] Gulf, 1862; brig. gen. U.S. Volunteers, 1862, w[illegible] to New Orleans; participated in seige of Port H[illegible] son, La., 1863, commander of cavalry at Red Ri[illegible] Expdn., 1864; his field service ended with capture [illegible] Ft. Morgan, Ala.; promoted maj. 5th Arty., 18[illegible] Died Governor's Island, N.Y. Harbor, Nov. 8, 18[illegible]

ARNOLD, Richard Dennis, physician, city of[illegible] b. Savannah, Ga., Aug. 19, 1808; s. Capt. Jos[illegible] and Eliza (Dennis) A.; grad. Princeton, 1826, [illegible] Pa. Med. Sch., 1830; m. Margaret Stirk, 18[illegible] Resident physician Blockly Hosp., Phila., 1830-[illegible] owner, editor Savannah Georgian; mem. Ga. Ho. [illegible] Reps. from Chatham County, 1839; elected to [illegible] Senate, 1842; city health officer, chmn. bd. ald[illegible] men, chmn. bd. edn., Savannah; mayor Savann[illegible] (during his term of office Savannah was surrende[illegible] to No. Armies, Dec. 1864); dir. Municipal Hos[illegible] pres. local med. soc.; established Savannah M[illegible] Coll.; a founder, 1st sec. A.M.A., 1846, v.p., 18[illegible] Died Savannah, July 10, 1876.

ARNOLD, Samuel, congressman; b. Hadda[illegible] Conn., June 1, 1806; attended acad., Plainfie[illegible] Conn., also Westfield Acad., Mass. Farmer, ow[illegible] controlling interest in stone quarry, owner [illegible] of schooners operating between N.Y. and Phil[illegible] pres. Bank of East Haddam; mem. Conn. Ho. [illegible] Reps., 1839, 42, 44, 51; mem. U.S. Ho. of Re[illegible] (Democrat) from Conn., 35th Congress, 1857-[illegible] Died Haddam, May 5, 1869; buried in a mausole[illegible] on his estate nr. Haddam.

ARNOLD, Samuel Greene, senator, historian; Providence, R.I., Apr. 12, 1821; s. Samuel Gre[illegible] and Frances (Rogers) A.; grad. Brown U., 18[illegible] LL.B., Harvard, 1845. After graduation visited [illegible] Petersburg, Russia; admitted to R.I. bar, 18[illegible] spent much time travelling in S.Am., Eng., Fran[illegible] Egypt, Syria, elsewhere; lt. gov. R.I., 1852, 61-[illegible] mem. U.S. Senate (Republican) from R.I., Dec. [illegible] 1862-Mar. 3, 1863; commanded battery of infant[illegible] a.d.c. to Gov. William Sprague of R.I. during C[illegible] War; trustee R.I. Reform Sch., Butler Hosp.; pre[illegible] contbr. to Charitable Baptist Soc.; pres., spea[illegible] R.I. Hist. Soc. Author: History of Rhode Isla[illegible] and Providence Plantation, 1859; Memorial Pap[illegible] on A. C. Greene, William Staples, and Usher P[illegible] sons; Historical Sketches of Middletown, 1880. D[illegible] Providence, Feb. 13, 1880; buried Swan Point Ce[illegible] etery, Providence.

ARNOLD, Thomas Dickens, congressman, la[illegible] yer; b. Spotsylvania County, Va., May 3, 17[illegible] studied law. Enlisted as drummer boy in War [illegible] 1812; sch. tchr., Knox and Grainger count[illegible] Tenn.; admitted to Tenn. bar, 1820, began pr[illegible] tice law in Knoxville, Tenn.; mem. U.S. Ho. [illegible] Reps. (Whig) from Tenn., 22d Congress, 1831-[illegible] (attempt was made to assassinate him on Cap[illegible] steps, Apr. 1833), mem. 27th Congress, 1841-[illegible] made brig. gen. Tenn. Militia, 1836; moved [illegible] Greeneville, Tenn.; Whig presdl. elector, 18[illegible] Died while attending ct., Jonesboro, Tenn., [illegible] 26, 1870; buried Oak Grove Cemetery, Gree[illegible] ville.

ARRICITIVA, Juan, clergyman. A Mexi[illegible] Franciscan of 18th century; prefect of Coll. [illegible] Propaganda at Queretaro. Author: 2d volume [illegible] Chronicles of Queretaro (on mission work [illegible] Ariz. and Cal.).

ARRINGTON, Alfred W. (pseudonym Cha[illegible] Summerfield), lawyer, author; b. Iredell Coun[illegible] N.C., Sept. 17, 1810; s. H. Archibald and M[illegible] (Moore) A. Moved with father to Ark., 1819; Me[illegible] odist itinerant preacher in Ark., Ind. and Mo., 18[illegible] 33; admitted to Mo. bar, 1835; returned to Ar[illegible] 1835/36, practiced law; mem. Ark. Legislatu[illegible] visited N.Y. and Tex. writing articles for news[illegible] pers, 1847-49; went to Tex., 1849; elected U[illegible] judge 12th Jud. Dist., 1850-55; moved to N.[illegible] 1856, to Chgo., 1857; met great success as law[illegible] Author: (under pseudonym) The Desperadoes of [illegible] Southwest, 1847, The Rangers and Regulators [illegible] the Tanaka, 1856; (under name Arrington) Sketc[illegible] of the South and South West; The Mathemati[illegible] Harmonies of the Universe; Poems by Alfred W. [illegible] rington, 1869. Died Chgo., Dec. 31, 1867.

ARRINGTON, Archibald Hunter, congre[illegible] man; b. nr. Nashville, N.C., Nov. 13, 1809;

ended Louisburg (N.C.) Coll.; studied law. Large landowner engaged in extensive planting; mem. U.S. Ho. of Reps. (Democrat) from N.C., 27th-28th congresses,, 1841-45; supporter of Confederacy, mem. of secession conv., 1861; mem. 1st Confederate Congress from N.C., 1861; del. Union Nat. Conv., Phila., 1866; chmn. ct. of common pleas and quarter sessions, Nash County, N.C., 1866, 67; commr: Nash County, 1868. Died nr. Nashville, Nash County, N.C., July 20, 1872; buried family graveyard on his plantation.

ARTHUR, Chester Alan, 21st Pres. U.S.; b. Fairfield, Vt., Oct. 5, 1830; s. Rev. William and Malvina (Stone) A.; grad. Union Coll., 1848; m. Ellen Herndon, Oct. 29, 1859, children—Chester Alan, Ellen, William Lewis Herndon. Admitted to N.Y.C. bar, 1851; began practice of law, 1851; engr.-in-chief, insp. gen., q.m. gen. N.Y. State Militia, 1861-63; collector Port of N.Y., 1871-78; became vice pres. U.S., Mar. 4, 1880; became Pres. U.S. after assassination of Pres. Garfield, Sept. 20, 1882, as Pres. supported Pendleton Civil Service Reform Bill (important because he had been noted supporter and symbol of spoils system in fight over N.Y.C. Port Authority), approved laws modernizing U.S. Navy, vetoed Chinese Extension Bill, Rivers and Harbours Bill (as too expensive), left office, Mar. 3, 1885, not renominated. Died N.Y.C., Nov. 18, 1886; buried Royal Cemetery, Albany, N.Y.

ARTHUR, Timothy Shay, editor, author; b. Newburgh, N.Y., June 6, 1809; m. Ellen Alden, 1836, 7 children. Moved to Balt. with family, 1817, became watchmaker's apprentice; became mem. 1st temperance league of Md.; Western agt. for a Balt. bank, 1833; mem. young literary group of Balt. with Dr. Nathan C. Brooks, Rufus Dawes, W. H. Carpenter), met and was influenced by Edgar Allen Poe; edited Balt. Athenaeum, Balt. Saturday Visitor; co-editor Balt. Book and Balt. Literary Mag., 1838-39; editor Balt. Mcht., 1840; became writer for Saturday Courier, Graham's Mag., and Godey's Lady's Book, Phila., 1841; established monthly Arthur's Ladies' Mag., 1845; founder, publisher weekly papers Arthur's Home Gazette, 1850-85 (became monthly Arthur's Home Mag., 1853); published juvenile periodical Children's Hour, 1867; published mag. Once A Month, 1869; followed this with The Workingman (monthly journal for farmers and mechanics); leading member Swedenborgian Ch., Phila.; mem. exec. com. Centennial Exhbn., 1876. Author: Six Nights with the Washingtonians: A Series of Original Temperance Tales, 1842; Married and Single: or Marriage and Celibacy Contrasted, 1845; The Lady at Home, 1847; The Maiden, 1848; Ten Nights in a Barroom and What I Saw There, 1854 (2d in sales only to Uncle Tom's Cabin); Cast Adrift, 1873; Woman to the Rescue, 1874. Died Phila., Mar. 6, 1885.

ARTHUR, William, clergyman; b. Balleymina, Ireland, Dec. 5, 1797; s. Alan and Eliza (McHarg) A.; grad. Queen's Coll., Belfast, Ireland, 1815; studied law with Cornelius P. Van Ness, Burlington, Vt.; m. Malvina Stone, Apr. 12, 1821, 7 children including Chester Alan. Came to Vt.; became Baptist preacher in Fairfield, Vt.; preached in Pownal, Waterville, Willistown, Jericho, Burlington, Hinesburgh, Richford (Vt.), 1835; then preached in York, Greenwich, Perry, Lansingburgh, Hoosic, West Troy, Schenectady (all N.Y.); pastor State Street Bapt. Ch., Albany, N.Y., 1857-64; published 4 vol. mag. The Antiquarian, and General Review: Comprising Whatever Is Useful and Instructive in Ecclesiastical or Historical Antiquities; Serving as a Book of Useful Reference, on Subjects of Research and Curiosity. Author: An Etymological Dictionary of Family and Christian Names, With an Essay on Their Derivation and Import, 1857. Died Newtonville, N.Y., Oct. 27, 1875.

ARTHUR, William Evans, congressman, lawyer; b. Cincinnati, Mar. 3, 1825; attended pvt. schs.; studied law. Admitted to Ky. bar, 1850, began practice law, Covington, Ky.; commonwealth atty. 9th Jud. Dist. of Ky. 1856-62; Democratic presdl. elector, 1880; judge 9th Jud. Circuit, Ky., 1866-68, resigned; mem. U.S. Ho. of Reps. (Democrat) from Ky., 42d-43d congresses, 1871-75; judge 12th Jud. Circuit, Ky., 1886-93, resigned; practiced law, Covington, 1893-97. Died Covington, May 18, 1897; buried Linden Grove Cemetery.

ARY, Henry, artist; b. R.I., 1802, or Hudson, N.Y., 1807. Advertised as portrait painter, Albany, N.Y., 1831-32; moved to Catskill, N.Y.; returned to Hudson, 1844, painted mainly Hudson River landscapes; exhibited at N.A.D., 1845, 53, 58, Am. Art-Union, 1846-53. Died Jan. 28 or Feb., 1859.

ASBOTH, Alexander Sandor, army officer; b. Keszthely, Hungary, Dec. 18, 1811. Mem. Austrian army; fought under Louis Kossuth in Hungarian revolt, 1848-49, came with Kossuth to U.S.; became Am. citizen and officer in U.S. Army; on staff Gen. John Frémont, 1861; commanded division under Gen. Samuel Curtis in campaign in Ark. and Mo., winter 1861; wounded at Battle of Pea Ridge (Ark.), 1862; commd. brig. gen. U.S. Volunteers, 1862, later in command in Columbus, Ky., and Ft. Pickens, Fla.; wounded in Marianna, Fla., 1864; left army with rank of brevetted maj. gen., 1865; U.S. minister to Uruguay and Argentina, 1866-68. Died Buenos Aires, Argentina, Jan. 21, 1868.

ASBURY, Francis, clergyman; b. Straffordshire, Eng., Aug. 20, 1745; s. Joseph and Elizabeth (Rogers) A. Local and itinerant preacher in Eng.; admitted to Methodist Wesleyan Conf., 1766; came to Phila. as missionary of Methodism in colonies, 1771, a founder Meth. Episcopal Ch. in U.S.; apptd. John Wesley's gen. supt. in colonies, 1772; attended 3d conf. in Phila., refused to take oath of allegiance required by State of Md., forced to take refuge in Del., 1777-78, became citizen of Del.; became 1st bishop of Meth. Ch. in U.S., consecrated at Balt. Conf., 1784, assumed title of bishop, 1785, governed Meth. Ch. in U.S. until 1816; a talented organizer, sent preachers to remote parts of states and frontiers of Ky. and Ohio. Asbury Park (N.J.) named in his honor. Died Spotsylvania, Va., Mar. 31, 1816; buried Eutau Meth. Episcopal Ch., Balt.

ASCH, Morris Joseph, physician, army officer; b. Phila., July 4, 1833; s. Joseph M. and Clara (Ulman) A.; grad. Jefferson Med. Coll., 1852, M.D., 1855. Clin. asst. to Dr. Samuel Gross, Jefferson Med. Coll.; asst. surgeon U.S. Army in Civil War, worked in surgeon gen.'s office, 1861-62; surgeon-in-chief to arty. reserve of Army of Potomac; med. insp. Army of Potomac, med. dir. 24th Army Corps, med. insp. Army of the James and staff surgeon to Gen. Philip H. Sheridan, 1865-73, served at battles of Chancellorsville, Mine Run, Gettysburg and Appomatox Ct. House; brevetted maj. for Civil War services, 1865; while on Sheridan's staff active in cholera epidemic of 1866 and yellow fever epidemic of 1867; with Sheridan in Chgo. until 1873; practiced medicine, N.Y.C., specialized in laryngology; a founder Am. Laryngol. Assn.; surgeon to throat dept. N.Y. Eye and Ear Infirmary, Manhattan Eye and Ear Hosp. Author articles including "A New Operation for Deviation of the Nasal Septum," (known as Asch operation). Died Oct. 5, 1902.

ASH, Michael Woolston, congressman, lawyer; b. Phila., Mar. 5, 1789; studied law. Admitted to Pa. bar, 1811, began practice law in Phila.; served as 1st lt. and lt. col. First Regular Pa. Volunteers, War of 1812; became law partner of James Buchanan (15th Pres. of U.S.), Phila., after War of 1812; mem. U.S. Ho. of Reps. from Pa., 24th Congress, 1835-37. Died Phila., Dec. 14, 1858; buried Christ Ch. Burial Ground, Phila.

ASHBURNER, Charles Albert, geologist; b. Phila., Feb. 9, 1854; s. Algernon Eyre and Sarah (Bakiston) A.; grad. U. Pa., 1874; m. Roberta M. John, 1881, 2 children. As undergraduate took part in raft survey of Delaware River between Easton and Trenton, N.J.; an organizer Engrs. Club, Phila., 1873; influenced to study geology by J. P. Lesley; asst. to Lesley in 2d Geol. Survey of Pa., wrote report on Aughwick Valley and East Broad Top Coal-Basin in Report F, 1878; commd. to survey important oil counties (McKean, Elk, Cameron, Forest) of Pa., 1876-78; placed in charge of survey anthracite field, 1880-86; scientific expert with Westinghouse firm, Pitts., 1886-89; mem. Am. Philos. Soc., Am. Inst. Mining Engrs., Phila. Acad. Natural Sciences, Franklin Inst., others. Died Pitts., Dec. 24, 1889.

ASHBURTON, 1st baron, see Baring, Alexander.

ASHBY, Turner, army officer; b. Plantation Rose Bank, Fauquier County, Va., Oct. 23, 1828; s. Turner and Dorothy (Green) A. Collected a band of men which merged with 7th Va. Cavalry at outbreak of Civil War; served as scout; commd. lt. col. Va. Militia, 1861, promoted col., 1862; fought with Stonewall Jackson in Shenandoah Valley; commd. brig. gen. Confederate Army, 1862. Killed in battle, Harrisonburg, Va., June 6, 1862.

ASHE, John, colonial legislator, army officer; b. Grovely, N.C., 1720; s. John Baptista and Elizabeth (Swann) A.; m. Rebecca Moore. Speaker, N.C. Colonial Assembly, 1762-65; mem. Com. of Correspondence, Com. of Safety, Provincial Congress (all N.C.); commd. col. N.C. Militia 1775, brig. gen., 1778; defeated at Brier Creek by Gen. Prevost, 1779 (gave British control of Ga., and made communication possible between Ga. and the Carolinas and the Indians), censured for cowardice by mil. tribunal, 1779; Asheville and Ashe County (N.C.) named for him. Died Sampson County, N.C., Oct. 24, 1781.

ASHE, John Baptista, congressman; b. Rocky Point, N.C., 1748; s. Samuel and Mary (Porter) A.; m. Eliza Montfort, children include Samuel. Command. capt. Continental Army, 1776, later lt. col.; mem. N.C. Ho. of Commons, 1784-86; speaker, 1786; mem. Continental Congress, 1787-88; mem. N.C. Senate, 1789; mem. N.C. Conv. to ratify U.S. Constn.; mem. U.S. Ho. of Reps. (Federalist) from N.C,. 1st-2d congresses, 1789-93; elected gov. N.C., 1802, died before inauguration. Died Halifax, N.C., Nov. 27, 1802; buried Churchyard Cemetery, Halifax.

ASHE, John Baptista, congressman, lawyer; b. Rocky Point, N.C., 1810; attended Fayetteville Acad.; grad. Trinity Coll., Hartford, Conn., 1830; studied law. Admitted to the bar, 1832; moved to Tenn., began practice law in Brownsville, Tenn.; mem. U.S. Ho. of Reps. (Whig) from Tenn., 28th Congress, 1843-45; moved to Galveston, Tex., practiced law. Died Galveston, Dec. 29, 1857; buried in a cemetery nr. Galveston.

ASHE, Samuel, gov. N.C.; b. nr. Beaufort, N.C., 1725; s. John Baptista Ashe; ed. Harvard; m. Mary Porter; m. 2d, Elizabeth Merrick; 2 children (youngest son Samuel became a Federalist, campaigned against Republicans led by his father, early 1800's). Pres. N.C. Council of Safety, 1774-76; speaker N.C. Senate; mem. N.C. Constl. Conv., 1776; chief justice 1st N.C. Supreme Ct., 1776-95; gov. N.C., 1795-98: pres. bd. trustees U. N.C. Died Rocky Point, N.C., Feb. 3, 1813.

ASHE, Thomas Samuel, congressman; b. Orange County, N.C., July 19, 1812; s. Pasquale and Elizabeth (Strudwick) A.; grad. U. N.C., 1832; m. Caroline Burgwin, 1837. Elected to N.C. Ho. of Commons, 1842; mem. N.C. Senate, 1854; mem. Confederate Congress, 1861-64; elected to Confederate Senate, 1864 (did not serve due to termination of Civil War); mem. U.S. Ho. of Reps. from N.C., 43d-44th congresses, 1873-77; asso. justice Supreme Ct. N.C., 1878-87. Trustee U. N.C. Died Wadesboro, N.C., Feb. 4, 1887; buried East View Cemetery, Wadesboro.

ASHE, William Shepperd, congressman, railroad exec.; b. Rocky Point, N.C., Sept. 14, 1814; s. Samuel and Elizabeth (Shepperd) A.; ed. Trinity Coll. (now Duke); m. Sarah Greene, Jan., 1836. Admitted to N.C. bar, 1836; mem. N.C. Senate, 1846-48, 58-60; mem. U.S. Ho. of Reps. from N.C., 31st-33d congresses, 1849-55; pres. Wilmington & Weldon R.R., 1854; commd. col. Confederate Army, 1861. Died Rocky Point, Sept. 1862; buried Ashton, N.C.

ASHLEY, Chester, senator, lawyer; b. Westfield, Mass., June 1, 1790; grad. Williams Coll., Litchfield (Conn.) Law Sch. Admitted to the bar, 1817, began practice law, Hudson, N.Y.; moved to Edwardsville, Ill., 1818, to St. Louis, Mo., 1819; to Little Rock, Ark., 1820; practiced law in Little Rock; mem. U.S. Senate (Democrat, fiilled vacancy) from Ark., Nov. 4, 1844-Apr. 29, 1848. Died Washington, D.C., Apr. 29, 1848; buried Congressional Cemetery.

ASHLEY, Delos Rodeyn, congressman; b. The Post, Ark., Feb. 19, 1828; academic edn., studied law. Admitted to the bar, 1849, practiced law; moved to Cal., 1849, practiced law in Monterey, 1850; dist. atty., 1851-53; mem. Cal. Ho. of Reps., 1854, 55; mem. Cal. Senate, 1856, 57; state of Cal., 1862, 63; began practice law in Virginia City, Nev., 1864; mem. U.S. Ho. of Reps. (Republican) from Nev., 39th, 40th congresses, 1865-69; practiced law in Pioche, Nev., 1871-72; moved to San Francisco, 1872. Died San Francisco, Cal., July 18, 1873; buried Calvary Cemetery.

ASHLEY, Henry, congressman, mfr.; b. Winchester, N.H., Feb. 19, 1778; attended common schs. Clk., Village of Winchester, 1811; justice of the peace, 1817; leather mfr., Catskill, N.Y.; chmn. tanners' assn., 1825; mem. U.S. Ho. of Reps. from N.Y., 19th Congress, 1825-27; pres. bd. of trustees Village of Catskill, 1828; trustee Apprentices' Library, 1828. Died Catskill, Jan. 14, 1829; buried Thomson St. Cemetery.

ASHLEY, James Mitchell, territorial gov., congressman; b. Allegheny County, Pa., Nov. 14, 1824; s. John and Mary (Kilpatrick) A.; m. Emma Smith, 1851; children—James M., Henry W., Charles S., Mary. Editor Democrat, Portsmouth, O., 1848; admitted to bar, 1849; mem. U.S. Ho. of Reps. from Ohio, 36th-40th congresses, 1859-69, drew up bill to abolish slavery in D.C., 1862, introduced 1st proposition for constl. amendment to abolish slavery, 1863; initiated impeachment proceedings against Pres. Andrew Johnson, 1867; territorial gov. Mont., 1869-70; pres. Toledo, Ann Arbor & No. Mich. R.R., 1877-93. Died Sept. 16, 1896; buried Woodlawn Cemetery, Toledo, O.

ASHLEY, William Henry, fur trader, explorer, congressman; b. Powhatan County, Va., 1778; m. Mary Able, m. 2d, Eliza Christy, Oct. 26, 1825, m. 3d, Mrs. Elizabeth Wilcox, Oct. 1832. Commd. brig. gen. Upper La. Militia, 1808; trustee Potosi Acad.; gen. Mo. Territorial Militia, 1820; lt. gov. Mo. (newly formed), 1820; sent fur trading parties up Missouri River to the Yellowstone, 1822-23, into Wyo., 1823-24; explored Green River, Wyoming Region, 1824-25, Gt. Salt Lake Region, 1826; mem. U.S. Ho. of Reps. from Mo., 22d-24th congresses, 1831-37. Died Boonesville, Mo., Mar. 26, 1838.

ASHMEAD, Isaac, printer; b. Germantown, Pa., Dec. 22, 1790; s. Jacob and Mary (Noglee) A.; m. Belina Farren, 1828. Served in War of 1812; apprentice to printer William Bradford, Phila.; founded Sunday and Adult Sch. Union (later Am. Sunday Sch. Union), 1819, printer for the Union; established printing business in Phila., 1821, 1st to introduce composition roller and hydraulic press for smooth-pressing wet sheets; 1st in Phila. to use power printing press; mgr. Phila. Inst. for Apprentices. Died Phila., Mar. 1, 1870.

ASHMORE, John Durant, congressman; b. Greenville, Dist., S.C., Aug. 18, 1819; attended common schs.; studied law. Admitted to the bar, never practiced law; engaged in agrl. pursuits; mem S. C. Ho. of Reps., 1848-52; comptroller gen. State of S.C., 1853-57; mem. U.S. Ho. of Reps. (Democrat) from S.C., 36th Congress, 1859-Dec. 21, 1860, resigned; col. 4th S.C. Regt., resigned before regt. called into service; mcht. in Greenville. Died Sardis, Miss. Dec. 5, 1871; buried Black Jack Cemetery, nr. Sardis.

ASHMUN, Eli Porter, senator; b. Blandford, Mass., June 24, 1770; grad. Middlebury Coll., 1807; studied law; at least 1 son, George. Mem. Mass. Ho. of Reps., 1803, 04; admitted to Mass. bar, 1807, began practice in Blandford, 1807; moved to Northampton, Mass., 1807, continued practice law; mem. Mass. Ho. of Reps. for several years; mem. Mass. Senate, 1808-10, 13; mem. gov.'s council, 1816; mem. U.S. Senate (filled vacancy) from Mass., June 12, 1816-May 10, 1818, resigned. Died Northampton, May 10, 1819; buried Bridge St. Cemetery.

ASHMUN, George, congressman; b. Blandford, Mass., Dec. 25, 1804; s. Eli Ashmun; grad. Yale, 1823; m. Martha Hall, 1828. Began Practice of law, Mass., 1828; mem. Mass. Legislature (4 terms in Ho. of Reps., 2 terms in Senate), 1833-41, speaker house, 1841; mem. U.S. Ho. of Reps. from Mass., 29th-31st congresses, 1845-51, voted against army supply bill during Mexican War, 1846; chmn. Republican Nat. Conv., Chgo., 1860; dir. Union Pacific R.R. Died Springfield, Mass., July 17, 1870; buried Springfield Cemetery.

ASHMUN, Jehudi, govt. ofcl.; b. Champlain, N.Y., Apr. 21, 1794; son of Samuel Ashmun; attended Middlebury (Vt.) Coll. 3 years; grad. U. Vt., 1816; m. C. L. Gray, Oct. 7, 1818. Ordained to ministry Congregational Ch.; organizer, prin. Me. Charity Sch., Hampden, resigned 1818; edited Theol. Repertory (monthly periodical of Episcopal Ch.), Washington, D.C.; supported Am. Colonization Soc., apptd. by U.S. Govt. as rep. to Liberia; put in charge of brig Strong sailing to new colony of Liberia, landed there, 1822, found colony in state of sickness and upheaval by native chiefs; helped colony fight off 2 native attacks; replaced by new agent (who stirred up colonists to revolt, then caught fever and returned to Am.), 1823; after investigation (which ended in his praise), 1824, became fully authorized agent until 1828; went to West Indies to recover health, 1828. Author: History of the American Colony in Liberia from December 1821 to 1823, published 1826. Died Boston, Aug. 25, 1828.

ASHTON, John, clergyman; b. Ireland, 1742. Became a Jesuit, 1759; missionary in Yorkshire; one of 1st priests to Balt., arrived between 1776-84, served congregation of 40 members (mostly Acadian refugees); chosen to begin building Georgetown U., 1788. Died Md., circa 1814.

ASPER, Joel Funk, congressman, lawyer; b. Adams County, Pa., Apr. 20, 1822; attended local coll. in Warren, O.; studied law. Admitted to Ohio bar, 1844, began practice law in Warren; justice of the peace, 1846; pros. atty. Geauga County, 1847; del. Free-Soil Conv., Buffalo, N.Y., 1848; editor Western Reserve Chronicle, 1849; moved to Ia., 1850; publisher Chardon (Ia.) Democrat; raised a co., served as capt., 1861, during Civil War; wounded in Battle of Winchester, promoted to lt. col., 1862, mustered out of service because of wounds, 1863; moved to Chillicothe, Mo., 1864, practiced law; founded the Spectator, 1866; del. Republican Nat. Conv., Chgo., 1868; mem. U.S. Ho. of Reps. (Radical Republican) from Mo., 41st Congress, 1869-71. Died Chillicothe, Oct. 1, 1872; buried Edgewood Cemetery.

ASPINWALL, William, physician; b. Brookline, Mass., June 4, 1743; s. Thomas and Joanna (Gardner) A.; grad. Harvard, 1764; m. Susanna Gardner, 1776, 7 children. Served as volunteer in Battle of Lexington, 1775; brigade surgeon in Continental Army, served as deputy dir. army hosp., Jamaica Plain, Mass., 1776-81; established inoculation hosp. for smallpox, Brookline; practiced medicine, Brookline until 1823; mem. Mass. Gen. Ct., Mass. Senate, Gov.'s Council. Died Apr. 16, 1823.

ASPINWALL, William Henry, mcht., railroad promoter; b. N.Y.C., Dec. 16, 1807; s. John and Susan (Howland) A.; m. Anna Breck; 5 children. Admitted as partner G.G & S. Howell (leading shipping firm in N.Y.C., renamed Howland & Aspinwall 1837), 1832; founder Pacific Mail S.S. Co., 1848; joined Pacific R.R. and Panama S.S. Co., 1849-51; head of group which financed bldg. of Panama R.R., 1850-55, resigned presidency of corp., 1856; secret Union emissary to Gt. Britain to persuade British to stop supplying iron-clads to Confederacy; trustee Lenox Library; charter mem. Soc. for Prevention Cruelty to Animals, 1866; leader in N.Y.C. C. of C.; a founder Union League Club (N.Y.C.). Died N.Y.C., Jan. 18. 1875

ASTON, Anthony, actor; b. Eng. Strolling player in Jamaica, 1701; actor in Charles-Town (now Charleston), S.C., for short time, 1703; went to N.Y.C., 1703-04, returned to Eng., 1704; thought to be 1st profl. actor in Am. Author: The Fool's Opera; or, the Taste of the Age (under name Mat Medley), 1730.

ASTOR, John Jacob, fur trader; b. Waldorf, Germany, July 17, 1763; s. Jacob Astor; m. Sarah Todd, 1785; 1 son, William Backhorse. Came to U.S., 1784; established shop dealing in furs, musical instruments, N.Y.C., 1786; made frequent fur-buying expdns. to West N.Y. and Can.; incorporated Am. Fur Co., 1808; formed Pacific Fur Co., 1810; founded Astoria, Ore., 1811; purchased much Manhattan real estate; made profitable loans to govt., 1814; monopolized fur trade in Mississippi Valley, 1816, in Missouri region, 1821; became the leading mcht. in trade with China; established a Western dept. Am. Fur Co., 1822; bought City Hotel, N.Y.C., 1828; sold all fur interests 1834; built Park Hotel (later Astor House), N.Y.C. 1834-36; founder Astor Library of N.Y.; sponsored the writing of Astoria (Washington Irving), published 1836; at his death was wealthiest man in Am. Died N.Y.C., Mar. 29, 1848.

ASTOR, John Jacob, financier, philanthropist; b. N.Y.C., June 10, 1822; s. William Backhouse and Margaret (Armstrong) A.; grad. Columbia Coll., 1839, Harvard Law Sch., 1842; m. Charlotte Gibbes, 1842, 1 son, William Waldorf. Employed in adminstrn. of father's estate, 1843-61, 65-75; served as col. on staff Gen. George B. McClellan, U.S. Army, 1861-65; inherited half of his father's estate, 1875; owned large amounts of real estate, N.Y.C., devoted his financial efforts to increasing these holdings; dir. Western Union, several N.Y.C. banks; treas. Astor Library, N.Y.C.; contbd. large sums to Astor Library, Met. Museum, N.Y. Cancer Hosp., St. Luke's Hosp., Trinity Ch., Children's Aid Soc. (all N.Y.C.). Died Feb. 22, 1890.

ASTOR, William Backhouse, businessman; b. N.Y. C., Sept. 19, 1792; s. John Jacob and Sarah (Todd) A.; m. Margaret Armstrong, 1818; children—John Jacob, William. Joined father's firm John Jacob Astor & Son, as head Am. Fur Co. div., 1815; inherited bulk of father's estate, 1848; continued father's policy of buying N.Y.C. real estate, became commonly known as "landlord of New York;" one of richest men in U.S. in his time, left estate of approximately $47,000,000. Died N.Y.C., Nov. 24, 1875.

ATCHISON, David Rice, senator; b. Frogtown, Ky., Aug. 11, 1807; s. William and Catherine (Allen) A.; grad. Transylvania U., 1828. Admitted to Ky. bar, 1830; mem. Mo. Ho. of Reps., 1834, 38; mem. U.S. Senate from Mo., Oct. 14, 1843-Mar. 3, 1855; elected pres. pro tem., 1846-49, 52-54; maj. gen. Mo. Militia; Atchison County (Mo.), City of Atchison (Kan.) named after him. Died Gower, Clinton County, Mo., Jan. 26, 1886; buried Greenlawn Cemetery, Plattsburg, Mo.

ATHERTON, Charles Gordon, senator, congressman; b. Amherst, N.H., July 4, 1804; s. Charles and Mary Ann (Toppan) A.; grad. Harvard, 1822; m. Ann Clark, 1828. Admitted to N.H.bar, 1825; mem. N.H. Legislature, 1830; clk N.H. Senate, 1831-32; mem. N.H. Ho. of Reps., 1833-36; mem. U.S. Ho. of Reps. (Democrat) from N.H., 25th-27th congresses, 1837-43, on Dec. 11, 1838 he introduced gag resolutions which held that Congress has no jurisdiction over the institution of slavery in the several states of the Confederacy (in effect to 1845); mem. U.S. Senate from N.H., 1843-49, mem. ways and means com.; chmn. finance com. N.H. Constl. Conv. of 1850. Died Manchester, N.H., Nov. 15, 1853; buried Nashua (N.H.) Cemetery.

ATHERTON, Charles Humphrey, congressman, lawyer; b. Amherst, N.H., Aug. 14, 1773; grad. Harvard, 1794; studied law; at least 1 son, Charles Gordon. Admitted to bar, 1797; practiced in Amherst; register of probate, 1798-1807; mem. U.S. Ho. of Reps. (Federalist) from N.H., 14th Congress, 1815-17; mem. N.H. Ho. of Reps., 1823-39. Died Amherst, Jan. 8, 1853; buried Old Cemetery.

ATHERTON, Gibson, congressman, lawyer; b. nr. Newark, Licking County, O., Jan. 19, 1831; attended Denison U., Granville, O.; grad. Miami U., Oxford, O., 1853; studied law. Prin. acad., Osceola, Mo., 1853-54; admitted to bar,, 1855; practiced in Newark, O.; pres. Newark Bd. Edn. 15 years; elected pros. atty. Licking County, 1857, 59, 61; mayor of Newark, 1860-64; mem. Newark C[illegible] Council 2 years; del. Nat. Democratic Conv., S[illegible] Louis, 1876; mem. U.S. Ho. of Reps. (Dem.) fr[illegible] Ohio, 46th-47th congresses, 1879-1883; appt[illegible] judge Ohio Supreme Ct., 1882, served 6 montl[illegible] Died Newark, Nov. 10, 1887; buried Cedar H[illegible] Cemetery.

ATHERTON, Joshua, lawyer; b. Harvard, Mass June 20, 1737; s. Peter and Experience (Wright) A grad. Harvard, 1762; m. Abigail Goss, 1765. Pra[illegible] ticed law, Litchfield, Conn., and Merriman, Mass 1765-73; register of probate County of Hillsborou[illegible] (Mass.), 1773; Loyalist during Revolutionary W[illegible] arrested, 1777, held prisoner until 1778; took oa[illegible] of allegiance to State of N.H., 1779; mem. N.[illegible] constl. convs., 1784, 92; mem. N.H. Senate, 179[illegible] 93; atty. gen. State of N.H., 1793-1801. Died A[illegible] 3, 1809.

ATKINS, Jearum, inventor; b. Vt., flourish[illegible] 1840-80. Millwright, nr. Chgo., circa 1840; invent[illegible] of the self-rake which was added to the reaper a[illegible] imitated motion of human arms, patented 185[illegible] reaper with his attachment manufactured by J. [illegible] Wright, Chgo., 1853-56.

ATKINSON, Archibald, congressman, lawyer; [illegible] Isle of Wight County, Va., Sept. 15, 1792; a[illegible] tended law dept. Coll. William and Mary, William[illegible] burg, Va. Served in War of 1812; Admitted to ba[illegible] practiced in Smithfield, Isle of Wight Count[illegible] mem. Va. Ho. of Dels., 1815-17, 28-31; me[illegible] Va. Senate, 1839-43; mem. U.S. Ho. of Rep[illegible] (Democrat) from Va., 28th-30th congresse[illegible] 1843-49; pros. atty. Isle of Wight County. Di[illegible] Smithfield, Jan. 7, 1872; buried graveyard of O[illegible] St. Luke's Ch., nr. Smithfield.

ATKINSON, George Henry, clergyman; b. Ne[illegible] bury (now Newburyport), Mass., May 10, 1819; William and Anna (Little) A.; grad. Dartmou[illegible] Coll., 1843, Andover Theol. Sem., 1846; m. Nan[illegible] Bates, 1846. Ordained to ministry Congregation[illegible] Ch., circa 1846; went to Pacific N.W. as rep. [illegible] Am.; Home Missionary Soc., 1848; organized o[illegible] of 1st Conglist. chs. in Ore., remained as its pasto[illegible] 15 years; pastor 1st Conglist. Ch., Portland, unt[illegible] 1872; organized Tualatin Acad. (now Pacific U.[illegible] Died Feb. 25, 1889.

ATKINSON, Henry, army officer; b. N.C., 178[illegible] m. Mary Ann Bullitt, Jan. 16, 1826; 1 son, Edwar[illegible] Commd. capt. 3d Inf., U.S. Army, 1808, col. 45 Inf., 1814, col. 6th Inf., 1815; commanded Yello[illegible] stone Expdn. instituted by Sec. of War John [illegible] Calhoun, fought against the Indians and Brit. f[illegible] traders; brig. gen. in charge of Western Dept., 182[illegible] reappt. col. 6th Inf. after a revision of army ra[illegible] ings, 1821; commanded expdn. to Upper Mo. Rive[illegible] 1825; appt. commr. to make treaties with Indian[illegible] selected site for Jefferson Barracks, Mo., 1826; di[illegible] patched mission which resulted in the establishme[illegible] of Ft. Leavenworth, 1827; served in Black Hawk Wa[illegible] 1832; supr. removal of Winnebago Indians from Wi[illegible] to Neutral Ground, Ia. Died Jefferson Barrack[illegible] Mo., June 14, 1842.

ATKINSON, John, clergyman; b. Deerfield, N.Y Dec. 6, 1835; m. Catharine O'Hanlon, 1856. Join[illegible] N.J. Conf., Methodist Episcopal Ch., 1853; pasto[illegible] Chgo., Bay City, Mich., Newark, N.J., Jersey Cit[illegible] N.J., Haverstraw, N.Y. Author: The Living Wa[illegible] 1856; Memorials of Methodism in N.J., 1860; al[illegible] hymn Shall We Meet Beyond the River. Died De[illegible] 8, 1897.

ATKINSON, Thomas, clergyman; b. Mansfiel[illegible] Va., Aug. 6, 1807; s. Thomas and Mary (Tob[illegible] A.; grad. Hampden-Sydney Coll., 1825; D.[illegible] (hon.), Trinity Coll., 1846; LL.D. (hon.), U. N.C 1862, Cambridge (Eng.), U., 1867; m. Joseph[illegible] Wilder, 1828, 3 children. Licensed to practice la[illegible] 1828; ordained deacon Protestant Episcopal Ch 1836, priest, 1837; rector St. Paul's Ch., Norfol[illegible] Va., 1837-43, St. Peter's Ch., Balt., 1843-5[illegible] built Grace Ch., Balt., soon after 1850; elect[illegible] bishop Protestant Episcopal Ch. in N.C., 1853; founder U. of South, Sewanee, Tenn.; instrument[illegible] in re-uniting No. and So. branches Protesta[illegible] Episcopal Ch. (split during Civil War). Died Wi[illegible] mington, N.C., Jan. 4, 1881; buried St. Jam[illegible] Ch., Wilmington.

ATKINSON, William Yates, gov. Ga.; b. Oak[illegible] land, Ga., Nov. 11, 1854; s. John P. and Theodo[illegible] (Ellis) A.; grad. U. Ga., 1877; m. Susie Milto[illegible] Feb. 23, 1880. Mem. Ga. Ho. of Reps., 1888-9[illegible] pres. Ga. Democratic Conv., also chmn. Ga. Dem[illegible] Exec. Com., 1890; gov. Ga., 1894-98; trust[illegible] U. Ga.; pres. bd. trustees Ga. Normal and Inds[illegible] Coll for Girls. Died Newman, Ga., Aug. 8, 1899.

ATLEE, John Light, surgeon; b. Lancaster, Pa Nov. 2, 1799; s. Col. William Pitt and Sarah (Light A.; M.D., U. Pa., 1820; m. Sarah Franklin, Ma[illegible] 12, 1822, 3 children. First doctor to remove su[illegible] cessfully both ovaries in 1 operation, 1843; a found[illegible] er, pres. Lancaster County Med. Soc., 1844; founder Pa. Med. Soc., 1848, pres., 1857; a organizer A.M.A., Phila., v.p., 1865, pres., 1882;

omoter of Franklin and Marshall Coll., Lancaster, of. anatomy until 1869; mem. Pa. Pub. Sch. Bd.; ıstee Pa. State Lunatic Asylum; hon. fellow Am. ʼnecol. Soc. Died Lancaster, Oct. 1, 1885.

ATLEE, Samuel John, Continental congressman, my officer; b. Trenton, N.J., 1739; studied law. command company of provincial service from ıncaster County (Pa.) during French and Indian ar; commd. ensign in Col. William Clapham's ugusta Regt., 1756, promoted lt., 1757; served Forbes campaign; in battle nr. Ft. Duquesne, 758; commd. capt., 1759; apptd. col. Pa. Mustry Battalion, 1776; captured by British at attle of L.I. in Revolutionary War, 1776, exanged, 1778; mem. Continental Congress from ı., 1778-82; mem. Pa. Gen. Assembly, 1782, 85, ; elected supreme exec. councilor for Lancaster ounty, 1783; apptd. mem. bd. commrs. to deal ith Indians from Pa. unpurchased lands, 1784; arter mem. Soc. of Cincinnati. Died Phila., Nov. 5, 1786; buried Christ Churchyard.

ATLEE, Washington Lemuel, surgeon; b. Lanster, Pa., Feb. 12, 1808; s. William Pitt and ırah (Light) A.; began study medicine with broth-, John L. Atlee, 1824; grad. Jefferson Med. Coll., 329; m. Ann Eliza Hoff, 10 children. Mem. staff ancaster Hosp.; treas. commrs. of Lancaster Coun-, 1837; founder Lancaster Conservatory of Arts nd Scis.; founder Lancaster County Med. Soc., 1844; rof. med. chemistry Med. Coll. of Phila., 1844-52; ioneer of ovariotomy operation; pres. Pa. State Med. oc., 1874, v.p. nat. soc., 1875. Died Sept. 6, 378.

ATTUCKS, Crispus, insurrectionist; b. circa 1723. ed a group of 50 or 60 men from Dock Sq. to tate St., Boston, Mar. 5, 1770, began conflict with rit. troops under Capt. Preston, killed when British red on crowd (incident became known as Boston lassacre).

ATWATER, Caleb, pioneer; b. North Adams, lass., Dec. 25, 1778; s. Ebenezer and Rachel (Park-) A.; B.A., Williams Coll., 1804; m. Diana Lawence; m. 2d, Belinda Butler, Apr. 3, 1811. Adıitted to N.Y. bar, circa 1805; moved to Circleville, ., 1821; unsuccessful candidate for U.S. ongress, 1822; mem. Circleville Sch. Bd., 1823; ounder Ohio Sch. System; U.S. commr. to Winneago Indians, nr. Prairie du Chien, Wis., 1829. Auhor: The Writings of Caleb Atwater, 1833; A History the State of Ohio, Natural and Civil, 1838; An ssay on Education, 1841. Died Circleville, Mar. 3, 1867.

ATWATER, Lyman Hotchkiss, clergyman, educaor; b. Cedar Hill (now part of New Haven), Conn., eb. 3, 1813; s. Lyman and Clarissa (Hotchkiss) .; grad. Yale, 1831, Yale Divinity Sch., 1835; m. usan Sanford, Oct. 7, 1835. Tchr., Mt. Hope em., Balt., 1831-32; ordained to ministry Conregational Ch., 1835; pastor 1st Congregational h., Fairfield, Conn., 1835-54; prof. philosophy, ater prof. moral and polit. sci. Coll. of N.J. (now rinceton), 1854-83; a strong advocate of old line alvinist thought; opposed Darwinian ideas of Herert Spencer; adhered to traditional views in ednl. heory and polit. issues, opposed women's rights iovement. Author: Manual of Elementary Logic, 867; contbr. numerous articles to Princeton Reew. Died Princeton, N.J., Feb. 17, 1883; buried rinceton.

ATWOOD, Charles B., architect; b. Charlestown, lass., May 18, 1849; s. David and Lucy (Bowles) .; attended Lawrence Scientific Sch., Harvard, 868-70. Mem. archtl. firm Ware and Van Brunt, oston, 1870-72; pvt. practice architecture, Boson, 1872-75; went to N.Y.C. to supervise archtl. vork of Herter Bros., 1875, designed twin Vanderilt houses, N.Y.C.; later entered pvt. practice, N.Y.C., designed Twombly and Webb houses; chief rchitect Chgo. World's Fair, 1893, designed more han 60 bldgs., including combination of Music lall, Peristyle and Casino, Art Bldg. Died Dec. 19, 1895.

ATWOOD, David, congressman, editor; born the city of Bedford, New Hampshire, December 5, 1815; s. David and Mary (Bell) A.; m. Mary weeney, Aug. 23, 1849. Partner in jour. Express later known as Wis. Express), 1848; established Wis. State Journal, 1852; mem. lower house Wis. egislature from Madison dist., 1861; U.S. internal evenue assessor 2d Congl. Dist., 1861-65; mem. J.S. Ho. of Reps. (Republican) from Wis., 41st ongress, Feb. 23, 1870-1871; pres. Madison Mut. ns. Co., Madison Gas Light & Coke Co. Died Dec. 1, 1889; buried Forest Hill Cemetery, Madison, Vis.

ATWOOD, Jesse, artist; b. N.H., circa 1802; n. Anna, at least 2 children including George, Mary. Itinerant portrait painter, circa 1828-54; ived in R.I., later moved to Pa., circa 1830; ainted in Deerfield, Mass., 1832, Richmond, Va., 1841, Phila., 1841, 43, 49-54; in Monterey, Mexico, 1847 (during Mexican War), painted portrait of Gen. Zachary Taylor (now owned by Hist. Soc. Pa.). Died circa 1854.

AUCHMUTY, Richard Tylden, philanthropist; b. N.Y.C., July 15, 1831; s. Richard Tylden and Mary (Allen) A.; attended Columbia, 1847-49; studied architecture with James Renwick, N.Y.C., circa 1852; m. Ellen Schermerhorn. Became partner (with James Renwick) in archtl. firm, circa 1856; commd. capt. 5th Corps, U.S. Army, 1861; served at Battle of Gettysburg, 1863, brevetted col.; helped prepare defenses of Washington, D.C. against Early's expdn., 1864; returned to practice of architecture, N.Y.C., after Civil War; active in affairs of Lenox, Mass. (where he owned summer home), from circa 1866; founded N.Y. Trade Sch. (for young men to learn trades without spending excessive apprenticeship terms), 1881, maintained sch. until 1892, when endowment received from J.P. Morgan; active in Trinity (Episcopal) Ch., N.Y.C., served as vestryman. Died Lenox, July 18, 1893.

AUCHMUTY, Robert, jurist; b. Scotland; admitted to Middle Temple, London, Eng., 1705, studied law. Called to bar in Eng., 1711; came to Am., circa 1720, began practice of law, Boston; judge Admiralty Ct., Mass., 1733-41; resided in Roxbury, Mass., from 1733; went to Eng. as agt. for Mass. in boundary dispute with R.I., 1741; wrote pamphlet urging mil. movement to take Louisbourg, published 1744. Died Roxbury, 1750.

AUCHMUTY, Robert, Loyalist; b. Boston; s. Robert Auchmuty; ed. by pvt. tutors. Practiced law, Boston, circa 1760; judge of vice-admiralty for Mass. and N.H., 1767; served (with John Adams) as atty. for Capt. Preston in Boston Massacre Case of 1770; his home in Roxbury a well-known rendezvous for Tories in Boston area; quartered Brit. officers at his home, 1775-76; wrote letters to friends in Eng. (who were sympapthetic to Am. cause), letters sent by Frankliin to Boston, 1773, published there; went to Eng., 1776, became mem. New Eng. Club of Loyalists; property in Boston confiscated, 1779, granted pension by Brit. Govt. after Revolutionary War. Died Eng., Nov. 1788.

AUCHMUTY, Samuel, clergyman, Loyalist; b. Boston, Jan. 26, 1722; grad. Harvard, 1742; S.T.D., Oxford (Eng.) U., 1766, King's Coll. (now Columbia), 1767; m. Mrs. Tucker, Dec. 1749. Ordained priest Anglican Ch., London, Eng., 1747; became asst. to rector Trinity (Anglican) Ch., N.Y.C., 1748, rector, 1764-77 (during his rectorship St. Paul's Chapel built and put into use, 1766); revealed loyalist sympathies in pamphlets and sermons at outbreak of Am. Revolution. Died N.Y.C., Mar. 4, 1777; buried N.Y.C.

AUDUBON, John James, artist, ornithologist; b. Les Cayes, Santo Domingo (now Haiti), Apr. 26, 1785; illegitimate son of Jean Audubon and a Creole woman known as Mademoiselle Rabin, legalized by adoption (1794) as son of Jean and Anne (Moynet) A.; m. Lucy Bakewell, June 1808; children—Victor, John W. Went with father to live in France, 1789, baptized Jean Jacques Fougère Audubon, 1800; came to U.S., 1803, settled on father's estate "Mill Grove," nr. Phila., 1804; began studies of Am. birds, made 1st bird-banding expt., 1804; engaged in various bus. activities, N.Y.C. and Louisville, Ky.; jailed for debt, 1819; taxidermist Western Museum, Cincinnati, 1819-20; began trip down Mississippi and Ohio rivers to observe birds, 1820, paid expenses by painting portraits; tutor, drawing tchr., street sign painter, New Orleans; made unsuccessful trip to Phila. to find a publisher for his bird drawings, 1824; taught music and drawing (to wife's pupils), St. Francisville, La., 1825; took drawings to Europe, 1826, met with favorable reception; elected to Royal Soc. Edinburgh (Scotland), 1827; paid expenses by painting birds; engaged in preparing drawings and texts for his 1st book, Edinburgh, returned several times to continue work; returned to Am. with reputation as foremost American naturalist, 1831; elected fellow Am. Acad., 1830; settled on estate "Minnie's Land" (now Audubon Park), N.Y.C., 1841; subject of much controversy during his life; responsible for drawings and literature for his books (most of scientific identification and nomenclature supplied by others). Author: Birds of America, 4 vols., 1827-38; Ornithological Biography, 5 vols., 1831-38; Synopsis of the Birds of North America, 1839; Viviparous Quadrupeds of North America (completed by his sons), colored plates pub. in 2 vols., 1842-45, text in 3 vols., 1846-54. Died N.Y.C., Jan. 27, 1851.

AUDUBON, John Woodhouse, painter; b. Ky., 1812; son of John James Audubon; studied painting under his father. Accompanied his father in search of specimens, Labrador and Fla., circa 1831; Mississippi steamboat clk., circa 1832; rejoined his father, 1833; went to Europe, continued study of art, 1834; aided father in engraving plates and writing text for Quadrupeds of North America, circa 1839; collected animal specimens in Tex., 1845; painted in Zool. Gardens, London, 1846-47; went to Cal. in search of gold and animal specimens, 1849. Died N.Y.C., 1862.

AUDUBON, Victor Gifford, artist; b. Louisville, Ky., June 12 or 29, 1809; s. John James Audubon; studied painting with his father; m. Mary Eliza Bachman, circa 1839. Worked as clk. in a comml. house, Louisville; went to Eng. as sec. and agt. for his father to arrange for publication of Birds of America, 1832; exhibited at Royal Acad. in Eng., several times; returned to Am., 1839, settled in N.Y.C., 1840; exhibited at N.A.D., Apollo Assn., Am. Art-Union; became mem. N.A.D.; collaborated with his brother on new editions of their father's works; painted miniatures, including one of his father exhibited at Carolina Art Assn., 1936; mem. N.A.D. Died Manhattan Island, N.Y., Aug. 17/18, 1860.

AUGUR, Christopher Columbus, army officer; b. Kendall, N.Y., July 10, 1821; s. Ammon and Annis (Wellman) A.; grad. U.S. Mil. Acad., 1843; m. Jane Arnold, 1844. Served as aide-de-camp to Brig. Gen. Hopping and Gen. Caleb Cushing during Mexican War, 1846-47; commd. capt., 1852; served in campaigns against Indians in Ore. and Wash. territories, 1852-56; promoted maj., 1861; comdt. cadets U.S. Mil. Acad., 1861; commd. brig. gen. U.S. Volunteers at start of Civil War, 1861; brevetted maj. gen. U.S. Volunteers, col. U.S. Army for services in Battle of Cedar Mountain, 1862; commanded action at Port Hudson Plains, 1863, Dept. of Washington, Oct. 1863-Aug. 1866; promoted brig. gen. for service at Port Hudson, 1865, commanded Dept. of the Platte, 1867; commd. brig. gen. U.S. Army, 1869, brig. gen. Dept. of Tex., 1869-75, of the Gulf, 1875-78, of Dept. of the South and Mo., 1878-85; ret., 1885. Died Georgetown, D.C., Jan. 16, 1898.

AUGUR, Hezekiah, sculptor; b. New Haven, Conn., Feb. 21, 1791; s. Hezekiah and Lydia (Atwater) A.; apprentice apothecary, circa 1806-07; M.A. (hon.), Yale, 1833. Partner in dry goods bus., New Haven, 1813-17 (went bankrupt); established wood carving bus., specializing in carved mirrors, circa 1818; began to carve in marble, 1820's, made head of Apollo Belvedere, 1823; commd. to execute bust of Oliver Ellsworth (in Supreme Ct. room of Capitol Bldg.); did bust of Prof. Alexander Fisher of Yale, 1827; best known work: Jephthah and His Daughter, purchased by Trumbull Gallery at Yale, 1837; created bronze medals commemorating 200th anniversary of founding of New Haven, 1838; invented carving machine, worsted lace machine, bracket saw. Died in financial difficulties partly owing to the early bankruptcy, New Haven, Jan. 10, 1858; buried New Haven.

AUGUSTUS, John, philanthropist; b. Boston, 1785. Shoemaker in Boston, until 1846; became interested in helping arrange bail for persons before Boston Police Ct. and assisting them in rehabilitation, 1841; retired from bus. to devote full time to philanthropic activities, 1846; provided bail for approximately 2,000 people in Boston, 1842-59, received no compensation for activities, represented no orgn. or group in his endeavors; received only small pvt. contbns. Died Boston, June 21, 1859.

AUSTELL, Alfred, financier; b. Dandridge, Tenn., Jan. 14, 1814; s. William and Jane (Wilkins) A.; m. Francina Cameron, 1853. Organizer, 1st pres. Atlanta Nat. Bank (Ga.) (1st So. instn. chartered under Nat. Banking Act of 1863), 1865; chmn. bd. Atlanta & Charlotte Air Line R.R.; organizer cotton firm Austell & Inman, which became Inman, Swann & Co. (largest cotton brokerage in world in that period). Died Atlanta, Dec. 7, 1881.

AUSTEN, Benjamin, mfr., state legislator; b. Boston, Nov. 18, 1752; s. Benjamin and Elizabeth (Waldo) A.; m. Jane Ivers, 1785, 1 son, Charles. Engaged in rope-making bus., Boston, 1780's-1820; attracted attention as author of series of pamphlets advocating legal reform, particularly abolition of lawyers (with court apptd. referees) and simplification of legal code, 1786; mem. Mass. Senate from Boston, 1787, 89-94, 96; became leader of mob in local politics; an extreme anti-Federalist; mgr. Harvard Coll. lotteries; a leader Boston Constl. Club (encouraged popular riots and aroused bitter opposition of Federalists), 1794; lost influence in local politics after 1796; published many newspaper articles supporting Republican cause; apptd. fed. loan commr. by Pres. Jefferson, 1803. Died Boston, May 4, 1820; buried Boston.

AUSTIN, Archibald, congressman, lawyer; b. nr. Buckingham, Va., Aug. 11, 1772; studied law. Admitted to bar; practiced in Buckingham County; mem. Va. Ho. of Dels., 1815, 16, 35-37; mem. U.S. Ho. of Reps. (Democrat) from Va., 15th Congress, 1817-19; Dem. presdl. elector, 1832, 36. Died nr. Buckingham Court House, Va., Oct. 16, 1837; buried family cemetery on his estate.

AUSTIN, David, clergyman; b. New Haven, Conn., Mar. 19, 1759; s. David and Mary (Mix) A.;

grad. Yale, 1779; studied theology under Dr. Joseph Bellamy, Bethlehem, Conn.; m. Lydia Lathrop, June 5, 1783. Licensed to preach by New Haven Assn. of Congregational Ministers, 1780; traveled in Europe, 1781, then preached in several chs., Conn.; ordained to ministry Presbyn. Ch., 1788, became pastor Presbyn. Ch., Elizabeth, N.J.; editor the Christian's, Scholar's and Farmer's Mag. (bi-monthly), Elizabeth, from 1789; published Am. Preacher, mag., 1791-93; interested in prophecy, became convinced that 2d coming of Christ was near, 1791, reinforced in this belief by a case of scarlet fever, 1795, predicted the event for May 15, 1796; was asked to leave the Ch., 1797; spent fortune building homes and warehouses for Jews in New Haven (believed they would gather there enroute to Holy Land to await the Messiah); pastor Bozrah (Conn.) Congregational Ch., 1815-31. Author: The Voice of God to the People of these United States, 1796; A Prophetic Leaf, 1798; The Millennial Door Thrown Open, 1799; The Dawn of Day, 1800; Republican Festival, 1803. Died Bozrah, Feb. 5, 1831.

AUSTIN, Henry, architect; b. Mt. Carmel, Conn., Dec. 4, 1804; s. Daniel and Adah (Dorman) A.; studied architecture in office of Ithiel Town, New Haven, Conn., until circa 1836; married twice. Became a carpenter, Conn., 1819; opened archtl. office, New Haven, 1836, trained many architects, thus gained title "Father of Architects"; commd. to design library for Yale Coll., 1842 (aided by Henry Flockton) produced best designed bldg. on Yale campus; designed gateway of Grove Street Cemetery, New Haven, 1845-48, monument to Nathan Hale, Coventry, Conn., 1846, ch. with spire 210 feet high, Danbury, Conn., 1857; commd. to design New Haven City Hall, 1861; other works include: Cutler and Hoadlery bldgs., Eaton Sch., Trinity Ch. Home (all New Haven). Died Dec. 17, 1891.

AUSTIN, James Trecothick, state ofcl.; b. Boston, Jan. 10, 1784; s. Jonathan Loring and Hannah (Ivers) A.; grad. Harvard, 1802; m. Cathrine Gerry, Oct. 3, 1806. Admitted to Mass., bar, 1805; editor Boston Emerald, 1806; county atty. Suffolk County (Mass.), 1807, 1812-32; town advocate Boston, 1809; mem. Mass. Constl. Conv., 1826; mem. Mass. Senate; atty. gen. Mass., 1832-43; opponent of anti-slavery movement; mem. bd. overseers Harvard; pres. Suffolk County Bar Assn., 1835. Author: A Life of Elbridge Gerry. Died Boston, May 8, 1870.

AUSTIN, Jane Goodwin, author; b. Worcester, Mass., Feb. 25, 1831; d. Isaac and Elizabeth (Hammatt) Goodwin; m. Loring Henry Austin, 1850, 3 children. Lived most of her life in Boston area; friend of Ralph Waldo Emerson, Louisa May Alcott, Hawthorne family; contbd. stories to Atlantic Monthly, Harper's Mag., Putnam's Mag., Emerson's Mag., Galaxy, from circa 1863. Author: Fairy Dreams, 1859; The Novice, 1865; The Tailor Boy, 1865; Outpost, 1867; Queen Tempest, 1892; The Twelve Great Diamonds; also Pilgrim book series covering U.S. history of period 1607-1775, published 1889-91. Died Boston, Mar. 30, 1894.

AUSTIN, Jonathan Loring, commonwealth ofcl.; b. Boston, Jan. 2, 1748; s. Hon. Benjamin and Elizabeth (Waldo) A.; grad. Harvard, 1766; m. Hannah Ivers, 1781, 1 son, James T. Served as maj. in volunteer N.H. Regt., 1775; sec. Mass. Bd. War, circa 1775-76; sent to Paris (France) to advise Benjamin Franklin of Gen. Burgoyne's surrender at Battle of Saratoga, 1777, pvt. sec. to Franklin in Paris, 1777-79; mem. Mass. Senate from Boston, 1801, Mass. Ho. of Reps. from Cambridge, 1803-06; sec. Commonwealth of Mass., 1806-08, treas., 1811-12. Died Boston, May 10, 1826.

AUSTIN, Moses, businessman; b. Durham, Conn., Oct. 4, 1761; s. Elias and Eunice Austin; m. Martha Brown, 1784, 3 children including Stephen F. Leadminer, Middletown, Conn., during Revolutionary War; joined importing firm Manning, Merrill & Co., Phila., 1783, reorganized and expanded firm (with his brother Stephen), 1784, established branch Moses Austin & Co., Richmond, Va.; became owner Chiswell lead mines in S.W. Va., 1789; surveyed lead mines of S.E. Mo., 1796-97, received land grant in area, established town of Potosi, Mo.; organized (with others) Bank of St. Louis, 1816 (bank failed); went to San Antonio, Tex., successfully applied to Spanish govt. for permit to bring some 300 families into Tex., died before plans could be fully arranged. Died La., June 10, 1821.

AUSTIN, Samuel, clergyman; b. New Haven, Conn., Oct. 7, 1760; s. Samuel and Lydia (Wolcott) A.; grad. Yale, 1783; m. Jerusha Hopkins, Sept. 14, 1788. Ordained pastor Fair Haven Congregational Ch., New Haven, 1786; pastor First Congregational Ch., Worcester, Mass., 1790-1815; pres. U. Vt., 1815-21; pastor Congregational Ch., Newport, R.I., 1821-25; organizer Gen. Assn. Mass. Ministers and Mass. Missionary Soc.; edited The Works of President Edwards, 1808. Author: The Apology of Patriots, 1812; Dissertations upon Several Fundamental Aticles of Christian Theology, 1826. Died Dec. 4, 1830.

AUSTIN, Stephen Fuller, founder of Tex.; b. Wythe County, Va., Nov. 3, 1793; s. Moses and Maria (Brown) A.; grad. Transylvania U., 1810; never married. Mem. Mo. Territorial Legislature, 1814-20; apptd. judge 1st Jud. Circuit of Ark., 1820; went to San Antonio (Tex.) to obtain Spanish governor's permission to establish colony of 300 Anglo-Americans on land which had been granted to his father; founded Colony of San Felipe de Austin, 1822, governed it until Tex. combined with Coahuila and organized as Mexican state, 1828; mem. Coahuila and Tex. Legislature, 1831-32; commr. to Mexico City to petition for establishment of Tex. as separate Mexican state, 1833; imprisoned on charge of attempting to revolutionize Tex., until 1835; comdr.-in-chief Tex. Revolutionary Army, 1835; commr. to U.S. to obtain aid for Texans in struggle with Mexico and to obtain recognition of Tex. as independent nation, 1835; defeated by Sam Houston in election for presidency of Tex., 1836; sec. of state Republic of Tex., 1836; advocated independence from U.S. and continuation of slave trade; Mexican citizen, at 1st opposed delaration of Texan independence; Austin (capitol of Tex.) named in his honor. Died Dec. 27, 1836.

AUSTIN, William, legislator, author; b. Charlestown, Mass., Mar. 2, 1778; s. Nathaniel and Margaret (Rand) A.; grad. Harvard, 1798; m. Charlotte Williams, June 17, 1806; m. 2d, Lucy Jones, Oct. 3, 1822; 14 children. Admitted to bar, 1803; rep. from Charlestown to Mass. Gen. Ct., 1811-12, 16, 27, 34; del. Mass. Constl. Conv., 1820; mem. Mass. Senate from Middlesex County, 1821-23. Author: Oration on the Battle of Bunker Hill, 1801; Letters from London (illustrated attitude of New Eng. Republican to English customs), 1804; An Essay on the Human Character of Jesus Christ (vol. of Unitarian views), 1807; Peter Rugg, the Missing Man (significant in development of Am. fiction), 1824; The Sufferings of a County Schoolmaster, 1825; The Late Joseph Natterstrom, 1831; The Man with the Cloaks: a Vermont Legend; Martha Gardner; or Moral Reaction, 1837. Died Charlestown, June 27, 1841.

AVERELL, William Woods, army officer, inventor; b. Cameron, N.Y., Nov. 5, 1832; s. Hiram and Huldah (Hemenway) A.; grad. U.S. Mil. Acad., 1855; attended Cavalry Sch. for Practice, Carlisle, Pa., 1857; m. Kezia Hayward, Sept. 24, 1885. Drug clk., Bath, N.Y., until circa 1851; commd. brevet 2d lt. of mounted rifles U.S. Army, circa 1855; stationed Jefferson Barracks, Mo., 1855-56, ordered to frontier in N.M., 1857; received leave of absence due to wounds, 1859; became asst. adj. gen. on Gen. Andrew Porter's staff, 1861, served in 1st Battle of Bull Run; apptd. col. 3d Pa. Cavalry, U.S. Volunteers, Aug. 1861; lead charge with his brigade in Battle of 2d Manassas, Mar. 1862; served at Yorktown, Williamsburg, Fair Oaks, Malvern Hill, White Oak Swamp (all Va.), 1862; commd. capt. U.S. Army, apptd. brig. gen. U.S. Volunteers, 1862; made raids in Va., Dec. 1862; in command of 2d Cavalry Div. at Battle of Kelly's Ford (Va.), 1863, brevetted maj. U.S. Army for this action; served in Stoneman's Raid, Richmond, Va., May 1863, then transferred to W.Va.; brevetted lt. col. after Battle of Droop Mountain, 1863; took part in raids in Tenn., brevetted col. U.S. Army; commanded 2d Cavalry Div. in several battles under Gen. Philip Henry Sheridan, 1864; brevetted brig. gen. and maj. gen. U.S. Army, 1865, resigned 1865; apptd. U.S. consul gen. for Brit. N.Am. at Montreal, 1865-68; had interests in mfg. and engring.; invented and patented asphalt paving, 1879, insulating conduits for wires and conductors, 1884-85; insp. gen. Soldiers' Home, Bath, N.Y., 1880-98; awarded $700,000 in patent infringement suit against Barbour Asphalt Paving Co., 1898. Died Bath, Feb. 3, 1900.

AVERETT, Thomas Hamlet, congressman, physician; b. nr. Halifax, Va., July 10, 1800; grad. Jefferson Med. Coll., Phila. Drummer boy in War of 1812; practiced medicine, Halifax and adjacent counties; mem. Va. Senate, 1848, 49; mem. U.S. Ho. of Reps. (Democrat) from Va., 31st-32d congresses, 1849-53. Died nr. Halifax Court House, Va., June 30, 1855; buried family burial ground nr. Halifax Court House.

AVERILL, John Thomas, congressman, mcht.; b. Alna, Lincoln County, Me., Mar. 1, 1825; grad. Me. Wesleyan Sem., Readfield, 1846. Sch. tchr. short time; lumberman for 1 year; moved to Winthrop, Me., merchant 3 years; moved to Northern Pa., 1852, lumberman until 1857; moved to Lake City, Minn., became mcht., in grain business; mem. Minn. Senate, 1858-60; served in Union Army during Civil War; commd. lt. col. 6th Regiment, Minn. Volunteer Inf., 1862, promoted col., 1864; mustered out, 1865; brevetted brig. gen. Volunteers for meritorious service in recruitment of Army of U.S., 1865; moved to St. Paul, Minn 1866, in wholesale paper and stationery busines mem. Republican Nat. Com., 1868-80; mem. U. Ho. of Reps. (Rep.) from Minn., 42d-43d co gresses, 1871-75. Died St. Paul, Oct. 3, 188 buried Oakland Cemetery.

AVERY, Benjamin Parke, journalist, diploma b. N.Y.C., Nov. 11, 1828; s. Samuel Putnam a Hannah (Parke) A.; m. Mary A. Fuller, 186 Established weekly Hydraulic Press, North San Jua Cal., 1856; editor, part owner Marysville (Cal. Appeal (1st daily newspaper in Cal. outside Sa Francisco), 1860; elected state printer Cal., 186 editor San Francisco Bulletin, 1863-73; organiz San Francisco Art Assn., 1872; editor San Fra cisco Overland Monthly, 1874; U.S. minister t China, 1874-75. Died Peking, China, Nov. 8, 187 buried San Francisco.

AVERY, Daniel, congressman; b. Groton, Conn Sept. 18, 1766; attended common schs. Appt ensign 6th Co., 8th Regt., Conn. Militia, serve as lt. and capt. until 1794; moved to Aurora, N.Y 1795, became owner large tract of land farmed b tenants; mem. U.S. Ho. of Reps. (Democra filled vacancy) from N.Y., 12th-13th, 14th co gresses, 1811-15, Sept. 30, 1816-17; connecte with land office, Albany, N.Y., 20 years. Die Aurora, Jan. 30, 1842; buried Oak Glen Cemetery

AVERY, Henry Ogden, architect; b. Bklyn., Ja 31, 1852; s. Samuel P. and Mary A. Avery; a tended Ecole des Beaux Arts, Paris, France, 1872 79. Opened office, N.Y.C., 1883; mem. Archt League, N.Y. chpt. A.I.A., N.Y. Soc. of Archaeo ogical Inst. of Am.; designer Union Prisoners War monument, Washington, D.C. (design selecte after his death). Died N.Y.C., Apr. 30, 1890.

AVERY, Isaac Wheeler, journalist; b. St. Augus tine, Fla., May 2, 1837; s. Isaac and Mary (King A.; grad. Oglethorpe U., 1854; m. Emma Bivings Jan. 1, 1868. Admitted to Savannah (Ga.) bar 1860; col. enlisted as pvt. 8th Ga. Inf., serve in capture of Ft. Pulaski, 1861; rose to rank c col. of cavalry Confederate Army, commanded brigad 1863; editor-in-chief Atlanta (Ga.) Constitution 1869; del. Nat. Democratic Conv., 1872; owne Atlanta Herald, 1875; sec. Ga. Exec. Dept., 1877 83; chief public div. U.S. Treasury, 1887-89 U.S. appraiser, 1890. Author: Digest of the Georgia Supreme Court Reports, 1866; History of the State of Georgia from 1850-1881, published 1881 asso. editor for Ga. National Cyclopedia of American Biography. Died Atlanta, Sept. 8, 1897.

AVERY, John, educator; b. Conway, Mass., Sept 18, 1837; s. Joseph and Sylvia (Clary) A.; grad Amherst Coll., 1861; studied philogy Yale, 1863-67; studied Sanskrit and Zend, Berlin and Tübinegen, Germany, 1867-68; m. Cornelia M. Curtiss, Aug. 21, 1866, 1 child. Taught at Leicester (Mass.) Acad., 1861; tutor at Amherst, 1862; tutor physics Sheffield Scientific Sch., 1865-67; became mem. Am. Oriental Soc., 1870; asst. editor Am. Antiquarian and Oriental Journal, 1875-87; 1st American admitted to Royal Asiatic Soc. of London; master of some 15 langs.; specialized in studies of N. India; prof. Latin, Ia. Coll., Grinell, 1870-71, prof. Greek, 1871-77; prof. Greek, Bowdoin Coll., Brunswick, Me., 1877-87. Died North Bridgeton, Me., Sept. 1, 1887.

AVERY, William Tecumsah, congressman, lawyer; b. Hardeman County, Tenn., Nov. 11, 1819; grad. Jackson Coll., nr. Columbia, Maury County, Tenn.; studied law. Admitted to bar; moved to Memphis, Tenn., 1840, practiced law; mem. Tenn. Ho. of Reps., 1843; mem. U.S. Ho. of Reps. (Democrat) from Tenn., 35th-36th congresses, 1857-61; served as lt. col. Confederate Army in Civil War; clk. criminal court, Shelby County, 1870-74. Drowned in Ten Mile Bayou, Crittenden County, Ark. (opposite Memphis), May 22, 1880; buried Elmwood Cemetery, Memphis.

AVERY, William Waightstill, Confederate congressman; b. Burke County, N.C., May 25, 1816; s. Isaac and Harriet (Erwin) A.; grad. U. N.C., 1837; m. Corrina Mary Morehead, 1846, 5 children. Admitted to N.C. bar, 1839; mem. N.C. Legislature, 1850, 52, N.C. Senate, 1856, 60; head N.C. delegation to Nat. Democratic Conv., 1856, 60; mem. Confederate Provisional Congress, 1861, chmn. com. mil. affairs. Died Morganton, N.C., July 3, 1864.

AWL, William Maclay, physician; b. Harrisburg, Pa., May 24, 1799; s. Samuel and Mary (Maclay) A.; studied medicine, Harrisburg, circa 1817; attended U. Pa. Med. Sch., 1819; m. Rebecca Loughey, Jan. 28, 1830. Began practice medicine, Harrisburg; practiced in Lancaster, O., 1826, Columbus, O., 1833-76; 1st surgeon West of Alleghanies to tie left common carotid artery; became interested in mental diseases, believed he could control any mentally unbalanced person by merely gazing into his eyes; mem. Ohio Legislature; advocated bill to place insane under state care (became law 1835);

ecame supt. State Hosp. when it opened, 1838; res. Assn. of Supts. and Asylums for Insane of J.S. and Can., 1838-51; drew up bill for founding dnl. schs. for blind and feeble-minded in Ohio; a ounder Ohio Med. Soc., 1846. Died Columbus, Nov. 19, 1876.

AXEL, Hans (count von Fersen), army officer; b. Stockholm, Sweden, Sept. 4, 1755; s. Field Marshal Fredrik Axel and Countess Hedvig de la Gardie. Col. of a French regt., 1778; aide-de-camp to Count of Rochambeau, rendered distinguished service to America, left with expeditionary force at Brest, 1780; frequent bearer dispatches between Gen. Washington and Count of Rochambeau; successfully eluded 2 Brit. frigates to hasten embarkation of French siege arty.; attempted to rescue French royal family, 1791; statesman and diplomat to King Gustavus III; imperial marshal Rikmarskalk, 1801. Died at hands of a mob Stockholm, June 20, 1810.

AXTELL, Samuel Beach, senator, territorial gov.; b. Fanklyn County, O., Oct. 14, 1819; s. Samuel Loree and Nancy (Sanders) A.; grad. Western Res. Coll., 1844; m. Adaline Williams, Sept. 20, 1840. Became 1st dist. atty. Amador County, Cal., 1854, served 3 successive terms; mem. U.S. Ho. of Reps. from Cal., 40th-41st congresses, 1867-71; gov. Utah, 1874-June 1875, N.M., 1875-78; chief justice Supreme Ct. N.M., 1882-85; chmn. territorial Republican com. N.M., 1890. Died Morristown, N.J., Aug. 6, 1891; buried 1st Presbyn. Ch. Cemetery, Morristown.

AYALA, Juan Manuel de, see De Ayala, Juan Manuel.

AYCRIGG, John Bancker, congressman, physician; b. N.Y.C., July 9, 1798; grad. Coll. Physicians and Surgeons (now med. dept. Columbia U.), N.Y.C., 1818. Moved to Paramus, N.J., practiced medicine there; mem. U.S. Ho. of Reps. (Whig) from N.J., 25th Congress, 27th Congress, 1837-39, 41-43. Died Passaic, N.J., Nov. 8, 1856; buried Paramus Ch. Cemetery, Ridgewood, N.J.

AYER, James Cook, businessman; b. Ledyard, Conn., May 5, 1818; s. Frederick and Persis (Cook) A.; studied medicine under Dr. Samuel L. Dana; M.D., U. Pa.; m. Josephine Mellen Southwick, Nov. 14, 1850. Learned mechanics trade in his grandfather's factory, Preston, Conn.; worked in apothecary shop of Jacob Robbins, Lowell, Mass., became owner, 1841; became dealer in patent medicines, including sugar-coated pills (1854), sarsaparilla extract (1855), Ayer's Hair Vigor; invested in textile mills, became involved in controversy with Richard S. Fay over collapsing of companies at Lowell and Lawrence, Mass., furnished material exposing co. officers in investigations; obtained patents for ore-reducing processes, 1865; financed Lake Superior Ship Canal & R.R. & Iron Co.; purchased timber country, built sawmills in Fla.; after trip to Europe presented Victory monument to Town of Lowell; Town of Groton Junction (Mass.) renamed for him, 1871, donated Ayer Town Hall; built Lowell & Andover R.R., 1874; proposed project to build interocean canal between Panama and Tehuantepec. Author: Some of the Usages and Abuses in the Management of Our Manufacturing Corporations. Died Winchendon, Mass., July 3, 1878; buried Lowell Cemetery.

AYER, Richard Small, congressman; b. Montville, Waldo County, Me., Oct. 9, 1829; attended common schs. Agriculturist and mcht. many years; enlisted as pvt. in Co. A., 4th Regiment, Me. Volunteer Inf., Union Army in Civil War, 1861, promoted to 1st lt., mustered out as capt., for disability, 1863; moved to Va., 1865, lived nr. Warsaw; del. Va. Constl. Conv., 1867; mem. U.S. Ho. of Reps. (Republican) from Va., 41st Congress, Jan. 31, 1870-71; moved back to Montville; mem. Me. Ho. of Reps., 1888. Died Liberty, Waldo County, Dec. 14, 1896; buried Mt. Repose Cemetery, Montville.

AYETA, Francisco de, clergyman. Franciscan visitor of Province of N.M. and area South to Yucatan; issued unheeded warnings to Madrid that Pueblo Indians were ready for war, as early as 1678; cared for more than 2,000 refugees at El Paso when Indians invaded the area, 1680 (subsequently occupied area for 14 years); wrote number of defenses of Franciscan Order, published circa 1690.

AYLLON, Lucas Vasquez De, see De Ayllon, Lucas Vasquez.

AYLWIN, John Cushing, naval officer; b. Que., Can., circa 1780; s. Thomas and Lucy (Cushing) A. Worked on Brit. naval vessel, although he disliked practice of impressment, promoted to mate of his ship, 1795; kidnapped by his capt. after a dispute, forced to sail on gun-brig. for 6 years; never joined Brit. Navy; allowed to rejoin his parents in Boston, after his health failed; later became capt. of several Boston mcht. vessels; served as lt. in frigate Constitution, U.S. Navy, 1812, aided in capture of Brit. frigate Guerriere, and saw capture of ship Java before dying in battle. Died at sea, Jan. 28, 1813.

AYRES, Anne, Protestant sister; b. London, Eng., Jan. 3, 1816; d. Robert Ayres. Came to U.S., 1836; worked with Dr. William Augustus Muhlenberg; consecrated sister of Holy Communion, N.Y.C., 1845 (1st woman in Am. to become a Protestant sister). Author: The Life and Work of William Augustus Muhlenberg, 1880. Died Feb. 9, 1896.

AYRES, Romeyn Beck, army officer; b. Montgomery County, Dec. 20, 1825; grad. U.S. Mil. Acad., 1847. Served with U.S. Army at various posts throughout U.S., promoted capt., 1861; participated in 1st Battle of Bull Run; served with Army of Potomac throughout Civil War; capt., chief arty. for a div., later a corps; promoted brig. gen. U.S. Volunteers, 1862; commd. lt. col. U.S. Army, 1866; col 2d U.S. Arty., 1879. Died (still on active duty) Port Hamilton, N.Y., Dec. 4, 1888.

AYRES, Thomas A., artist; b. N.J. Went West, 1849; spent 7 years in Cal.; accompanied 1st party to visit Yosemite Valley, sketched earliest known views; painted panorama which appeared at McNulty's Hall, Sacramento, Cal.; returned to East, 1857; exhibited in N.Y.C.; engaged to write series of articles on Cal. for Harpers mag., 1857; made sketching tour in So. Cal., 1858. Drowned in sinking of ship Laura Bevan on his way back to San Francisco, Apr. 26, 1858.

AZARIAS, Brother, see Mullany, Patrick Francis.

B

BABBITT, Benjamin Talbot, inventor, mfr.; b. Westmoreland, N.Y., 1809; s. Nathaniel and Betsey (Holman) B.; m. Rebecca McDuffie, 2 daus. Established machine shop, Little Falls, N.Y., 1831, manufactured pumps, engines, farm machinery; developed new, cheaper way to make baking soda, 1843; manufactured various brands of soap; obtained 1st patent for pump and fire engine, 1842; patented brush trimming machine, 1846; patented over 100 devices, including car ventilator, automatic boiler feeder, steam generator cleaning apparatus, rotary engine, balance valve, air pump, air compressor, wind motors, pneumatic propulsion, air blasts for forges; 1st to use samples free for advt. Died Oct. 20, 1889.

BABBITT, Elijah, congressman, lawyer; b. Providence, R.I., July 29, 1795; studied law. Admitted to bar, 1824; practiced in Milton, Pa., 1824-26; Erie, Pa., 1826; atty. for borough, later City of Erie; pros. atty. Erie County, 1833; dep. atty. gen. State of Pa., 1834, 35; mem. Pa. Ho. of Reps., 1836, 37; mem. Pa. Senate, 1843-46; mem. U.S. Ho. of Reps. (Unionist) from Pa., 36th Congress, (Republican), 37th Congress, 1859-63. Died Erie, Jan. 9, 1887; buried Erie Cemetery.

BABBITT, Isaac, inventor; b. Taunton, Mass., July 26, 1799; s. Zeba and Bathsheba (Luscombe) B.; m. Sally Leonard; m. 2d, Eliza Barney; 9 children. Made 1st Brittania-ware manufactured in U.S., 1831, 1st brass cannon cast in U.S., 1834; patented journal-box lined with alloy known as "Babbitt metal," (an anti-friction bearing metal used in all railroad car axle-boxes), 1839; awarded Gold medal by Mass. Mechanics Assn., 1841, also granted $20,000 by U.S. Congress for this invention. Died Somerville, Mass., May 26, 1862.

BABCOCK, Alfred, congressman, physician; b. Hamilton, Madison County, N.Y., Apr. 15, 1805; attended Gaines (N.Y.) Acad.; studied medicine. Practiced medicine, Gaines; elected trustee Village of Gaines, 1839; mem. U.S. Ho. of Reps. (Whig) from N.Y., 27th Congress, 1841-43; moved to Ill., 1850, practiced medicine in Galesburg, Ill. Died Galesburg, May 16, 1871; buried Hope Cemetery.

BABCOCK, George Herman, inventor, mfr.; b. Unadilla Forks, N.Y., June 17, 1832; s. Asher M. and Mary (Stillman) B.; married 4 times. Chief draftsman Hope Iron Works, Providence, R.I.; inventor Babcock & Wilcox high pressure boiler; co-inventor 1st polychromatic printing press; pres. Babcock, Wilcox & Co., boiler mfrs., 1881-93; pres. bd. trustees Alfred U.; pres. Plainfield (N.J.) Bd. Ed. Plainfield Pub. Library; pres. Am. Soc. M.E., 1887. Died Plainfield, Dec. 16, 1893.

BABCOCK, James Francis, chemist; b. Boston, Feb. 23, 1844; s. Archibald D. and Fannie F. (Richards) B.; attended Lawrence Scientific Sch. of Harvard U., 1862; m. Mary Crosby, Mar. 28, 1869; m. 2d, Marion Alden, Aug. 24, 1892; 5 children. Prof. chemistry Mass. Coll. Pharmacy, 1869-74, Boston U., 1874-80; state assayer Mass., 1875-85, introduced 3 percent limit as defining intoxicating liquor; insp. milk Boston, 1885; inventor Babcock fire extinguisher; pres. Druggists' Assn. Boston, 1894. Died Dorchester, Mass., July 19, 1897.

BABCOCK, Leander, congressman, lawyer; b. Paris, Oneida County, N.Y., Mar. 1, 1811; grad. Union Coll., Schenectady, N.Y., 1830; studied law. Admitted to bar, 1834; moved to Oswego, N.Y., practiced law; dist. atty. Oswego County, 1841-43; mayor of Oswego, 1850, 51; mem. U.S. Ho. of Reps. (Democrat) from N.Y., 32d Congress, 1851-53; pres. bd. edn., 1853-55. Died Richfield Springs, N.Y., Aug. 18, 1864; buried Riverside Cemetery, Oswego.

BABCOCK, Maltbie Davenport, clergyman; b. Syracuse, N.Y., Aug. 3, 1858; s. Henry and Emily Maria (Maltbie) B.; grad. Syracuse U., 1879, Auburn Theol. Sem., 1882; m. Katherine Eliot Tallman, Oct. 4, 1882. Ordained to ministry Presbyn. Ch., 1882, pastor 1st Presbyn. Ch., Lockport, N.Y., Brown Meml. Ch., Balt., 1887-99, Brick Presbyn. Ch., N.Y.C., 1899-1901; took a trip to the Holy Land, stricken with a fever, Naples, Italy, 1901. Committed suicide by cutting arteries of his wrists and drinking corrosive sublimate as a result of 2d attack of acute melancholia, Naples, Italy, May 18, 1901.

BABCOCK, Orville Elias, engr., army officer; b. Franklin, Vt., Dec. 25, 1835; s. Elias and Clara (Olmstead) B.; grad. U.S. Mil. Acad., 1861; m. Annie Eliza Campbell, Nov. 8, 1866. Assigned to Corps Engrs., U.S. Army as 2d lt., 1861, then ordered to Army of Potomac; mem. staff of Gen. W. B. Franklin, 1862; apptd. acting chief engr. Dept. of Ohio, 1864, in charge of positions, defenses, bridges, etc.; promoted to lt. col, 1864; a.d.c. to Gen. Ulysses S. Grant, 1864-68; served in Battle of Wilderness, subsequent battles of Army of Potomac; breveted brig. gen. U.S. Volunteers, 1865; promoted to col. U.S. Army; served as Pres. Grant's pvt. sec., 1868-71; appt. supt. engr. of pub. bldgs. and grounds, 1871; indicted by grand jury of St. Louis because of connections with John McDonald (one of the known leaders of the Whiskey Ring), 1875, acquitted through Pres. Grant's intercession; returned to duties at White House, ret. shortly afterwards. Drowned in Mosquito Inlet, Fla., June 2, 1884.

BABCOCK, William, congressman, mcht.; b. Hinsdale, Westmoreland County, N.H., 1785. Moved to Penn Yan, Yates County, N.Y., 1813, became merchant; apptd. by gov. as 1st treas. Yates County; mem. U.S. Ho. of Reps. from N.Y., 22d Congress, 1831-33; hotel keeper. Died Penn Yan Oct. 20, 1838; buried City Hill Cemetery, nr. Penn Yan.

BACHE, Alexander Dallas, physicist, coll. pres.; b., Phila., July 19, 1806; s. Richard and Sophia (Dallas) B.; grad. U.S. Mil. Acad., 1825; LL.D., N.Y.U., 1836; U. Pa., 1837; Harvard U., 1851; m. Nancy Fowler, 1829, Commd Engrs. Corps, U.S. Army, in constrn. Ft. Adams, Newport, R.I., 1825-29; prof. natural philosophy and chemistry U. Pa., 1828-41; 1st pres. Girard Coll., Phila., 1836-circa 1848; supt. U.S. Coast Survey, 1843-67; a founder A.A.A.S.; an incorporator, regent Smithsonian Instn., 1846; a founder, 1st pres. Nat. Acad. Scis.; pres. Am. Philos. Soc., 1855; adviser to the Pres. U.S., also v.p. Sanitary Commn. during Civil War; Hon. mem. Royal Soc. London, Royal Acad. Turin, Imperial Geog. Soc. Vienna, Inst. of France. Author: Observations at the Observatory of Girard College, 3 vols, 1840-45. Died Providence, R.I., Feb. 17, 1867.

BACHE, Benjamin Franklin, journalist; b. Phila., Aug. 12, 1769; s. Richard and Sarah (Franklin) B.; ed. Coll. Phila. (now U. Pa.), 1785; m. Margaret Hartman Markoe, Nov. 17, 1791; at least one child, Franklin. Accompanied Benjamin Franklin (his grandfather) to Europe as a boy; established Gen. Advertiser (better known as Aurora), Phila., 1790; succeeded Philip Freneau's paper the Nat. Gazette (suspended after epidemic of yellow fever) as mouthpiece for the Republicans; notorious for vicious personal abuse in his editorials (a feature for which that decade of journalism was famous); printed substance of Jay Treaty before contents were publicly known, 1795, published full treaty in pamphlet form (having received a copy of the treaty from Sen. Stevens Thompson Mason); denounced the Pres. and all Federalist policies on the occasion of Pres. George Washington's retirement from office, 1797; accused of being in the employ of the French Directory during the adminstrn. of John Adams, denied charge; arrested on charge of libelling Pres. John Adams, released on parole, 1798; circulation of jour. fell off during the XYZ affair. Died of yellow fever, Phila., Sept. 10, 1798.

BACHE, Franklin, physician, educator; b. Phila., Oct. 25, 1797; s. Benjamin Franklin and Margaret (Markoe) B.; grad. U. Pa., 1810, M.D., 1814; m. Aglae Dabadie, 1818. Entered U.S. Army as asst. surgeon, 1813, promoted to full surgeon, 1814, served until 1816; practiced medicine, Phila., 1816-24; physician to Walnut Street Prison, Phila., 1824-36; prof. chemistry Franklin Inst., Phila., 1826-32; an editor N.Am. Med. and Surg. Jour., 1826-31; fellow Coll. Physicians and Surgeons, Phila., 1829; prof. chemistry Phila. Coll. Pharmacy, 1831-41, Jefferson

Med. Coll., Phila., 1841-64; pres. Am. Philos. Soc., 1853-55. Author: System of Chemistry for the Use of Students in Medicine, 1819; Dispensatory of the United States of America, 1833. Died Phila., Mar. 19, 1864.

BACHE, Richard, businessman, postmaster gen.; b. Settle, Eng., Sept. 12, 1737; s. William and Mary (Blyckenden) B.; m. Sarah Franklin (only dau. of Benjamin Franklin), Oct. 3, 1767. Came to N.Y. C. with his brother Theophylact, 1765; moved to Phila., 1766, made acquaintance of Benjamin Franklin; went into bus. with his brother, underwrote marine ins. risks, Phila.; pres. Republican Soc. of Phila. at beginning of Revolutionary War; mem. Pa. Com. of Correspondence; mem. bd. war; apptd. by Benjamin Franklin as sec., comptroller, registrar gen. of Pa., 1775-76; succeeded Franklin as postmaster gen. Am. colonies under Articles of Confedn., 1776-82. Died Berks County, Pa., July 29, 1811.

BACHE, Theophylact, mcht.; b. Yorkshire, Eng., Jan. 17, 1735; s. William and Mary (Blyckenden) B.; m. Ann Barclay, Oct. 16, 1760, 15 children. Came to Am., 1751; Inherited uncle's business during 1750's; partner (with brother Richard) firm trading wth West Indies and Newfoundland, also agts. for trans-Atlantic packets; royal incorporator Marine Soc. of N.Y., 1770; pres. N.Y.C. C. of C., 1773-74; gov., pres. bd. N.Y. Hosp.; pres. St. George's Soc., 1788-99. Died N.Y.C., Oct. 30, 1807; buried Trinity Ch., N.Y.C.

BACHE, William, artist; b. Broomsgrove, Worcestershire, Eng., Dec. 22, 1771. Came to Am.; painted in Phila., circa 1793, 1812, Richmond (Va.), 1804, Salem (Mass.), Hartford and New Haven (Conn.), 1810, thought to have painted in La. and West Indies; moved to Wellsboro, Pa., 1812; lost right arm, became propr. gen. store; postmaster of Wellsboro, 1822-45; represented in collections at Conn., R.I. hist. socs. Died 1845.

BACHELDER, John Badger, artist, historian; b. Gilmanton, N.H., Sept. 1825. Painted view of Manchester (N.H.), 1854, view of N.J. from Lycoming County (Pa.) side of Delaware River, circa 1854; thought to have painted at Providence (R.I.) and N.Y.C., 1858; painted picture of firemen's muster at Manchester, 1859; print publisher, Boston, 1863-65; painted The Death of Lincoln in oil, 1865 (now at Brown U.); painted views of Haverhill, Salem and Worcester (Mass.), also Providence; name also appears as Batchelder. Died Hyde Park, Mass., Dec. 22, 1894.

BACHMAN, John, clergyman, naturalist; b. Rhinebeck, N.Y., Feb. 4, 1790; s. Jacob Bachman; ed. Williams Coll.; Ph.D. (hon.), U. Berlin (Germany), 1838; m. Harriet Martin, 1816. Sec. to Johannes Knickerbocker in an exploring expdn. and embassy to Oneida Indians; taught sch., Ellwood, Pa., later in Phila.; licensed to preach in Lutheran Ch., Phila., 1813, ordained to ministry, 1814, served at St. John's Ch., Charleston, S.C.; founder S.C.'s Luth. Theol. Sem.; made collection of Southern animals and studied their habits and habitats, led to assn. with John Audubon (who used Bachman's work in his book on ornithology, 1830-35; a founder S.C. Hort. Soc., 1833; travelled in Europe with Audubon, 1838; tried to reconcile scripture with science during evolution controversey of 1850's; devoted minister to sick and the dying during Civil War; collaborated with Audubon on The Viviparous Quadrupeds of North America, published in 3 volumes, 1845-59; The Unity of the Human Race, 1850. Died Columbia, S.C., Feb. 24, 1874.

BACKUS, Azel, clergyman, coll. pres.; b. nr. Norwich, Conn., Oct. 13, 1765; s. Jabez and Deborah (Fanning) B.; grad. Yale, 1787; D.D., Coll. of N.J. (now Princeton), 1810; m. Melicent Deming, Feb. 7, 1791. Licensed to preach, 1789; pastor 1st Congl. Ch., Bethlehem, Conn., 1791; 1st pres. Hamilton Coll., 1812-16. Author: Absalom's Conspiracy (Federalist attack on Thomas Jefferson, consequently charged with, but not convicted of, libeling a U.S. Pres.), 1798. Died Clinton, N.Y., Dec. 28, 1816.

BACKUS, Isaac, clergyman; b. Norwich, Conn., Jan. 9, 1724; s. Samuel and Elizabeth (Winslow) B.; ed. by a local clergyman; m. Susannah Mason, Nov. 29, 1749. Ordained to ministry Separatist (New Light) Congregational Ch., Middleborough, Mass., 1748; withdrew from New Light connection over question of infant baptism; established Baptist Ch., Middleborough, 1756-circa 1802; gained fame as itinerant preacher to other Bapt. settlements in New Eng., made nearly 1,000 trips away from home to preach; agt. Warren Assn. (governing body of Bapt. Ch. in New Eng.); advocate of religious liberty in Mass., vigorously opposed establishment of Congregational Ch. in state; sent to speak for religious liberty in Mass. to 1st Continental Congress, 1774; an organizer Baptist chs. in Va., 1788; mem. Mass. Conv. to ratify U.S. Constn., 1789. Author: A History of New England, with Particular Reference to the Denomination called Baptists, 3 vols., 1777, 84, 96. Died Middleborough, Nov. 20, 1806.

BACON, David, clergyman; b. Woodstock, Conn., Sept. 4, 1771; s. Joseph and Abigail (Holmes) B.; studied theology under Rev. Levi Hart; m. Alice Parks, 1 son, Leonard B. Commd. to expt. with missionary work among the Indian tribes beyond Lake Erie by Conn. Missionary Soc., 1800; missionary on Mackinac Island, worked among Ojibwa Indians, 1801-05; returned to Conn., circa 1805, contracted with Benjamin Tallmadge to establish a community in Western Reserve area, built log cabins, surveyed and plotted Town of Tallmadge (O.), 1807; had set up a church by 1809, forced by financial difficulties to return to Conn. Died Hartford, Conn., Aug. 27, 1817.

BACON, David William, clergyman; b. N.Y.C., Sept. 15, 1813; studied at Montreal, also Mt. St. Mary's, Md. Ordained priest Roman Catholic Ch., Balt., 1838; pastor in upper N.Y. State; pastor of parish, Bklyn., 1841-55; became 1st Roman Cath. bishop of Portland (Me.), 1855, built diocese from 8 parishes in 1855 to 63 parishes by 1874. Died N.Y., Nov. 5, 1874.

BACON, Delia Salter, author; b. Tallmadge, O., Feb. 2, 1811; d. Rev. David and Alice (Parks) Bacon; attended Catharine Beecher's sch., Hartford, Conn., 1817-26. With an elder sister tried unsuccessfully to establish schs. in Southington, Conn., Perth Amboy, N.J., Jamaica, N.Y., for 4 years; began writing books and delivering lectures; became convinced that William Shakespeare's plays were written by a literary group (Francis Bacon, Walter Raleigh, Edmund Spenser) to further their polit. philosophies, 1852; went to Eng. to study this theory, encouraged by Ralph Waldo Emerson; lived in shabby surroundings in London, Eng., for 3 years; made friends with Nathaniel Hawthorne, London; borrowed money from Hawthorne to publish a book, but her mind began to fail; felt that proof of her theory could be found in Shakespeare's tomb, made plans to have tomb opened, 1856; also believed proof might be found in tombs of Bacon, Spenser or Raleigh; became insane, was taken home by her nephew, George Bacon, 1858; 1st to try to discredit the writings of Shakespeare. Author: Tales of the Puritans, 1831; The Bride of Fort Edward, 1839; Philosophy of the Plays of Shakspere Unfolded, Apr. 1857. Died Sept. 2, 1859.

BACON, Ezekiel, congressman, jurist; b. Boston, Sept. 1, 1776; s. John Bacon; grad. Yale, 1794; attended Litchfield Law Sch.; studied law with Nathan Dane, Beverly, Mass.; at least 1 son, William Johnson. Admitted to bar, 1800; practiced in Stockbridge, Mass.; mem. Mass. Ho. of Reps., 1805, 06; mem. U.S. Ho. of Reps. (Democrat, filled vacancy) from Mass., 10th-12th congresses, Sept. 16, 1807-13; chief justice Ct. of Common Pleas, for Western Dist. of Mass., 1811-14; 1st comptroller U.S. Treasury, 1814-15, resigned; moved to Utica, N.Y., 1816; apptd. asso. justice Ct. of Common Pleas, 1818; mem. N.Y. State Assembly, 1819; del. N.Y. State Constl. Conv., 1821. Died Utica, Oct. 18, 1870; buried Forest Hill Cemetery.

BACON, John, congressman, jurist; b. Canterbury, Conn., Apr. 5, 1738; s. John and Ruth (Spaulding) B.; grad. Princeton, 1765; m. Elizabeth Goldthwaite. Pastor Old South (Congregationalist) Ch., Boston, 1771-75; mem. Com. of Correspondence, Inspection and Safety, 1777; mem. Mass. Constl. Conv., 1799-80; asst. judge Ct. of Common Pleas. of Berkshire Country (Mass.) 1779-1807., presiding judge, 1807-11; mem. Mass. Ho. of Reps., 1780, 83, 84, 86, 89-91, 93, removed many discriminatory provisions from Mass. Constn.; mem. Mass. Senate, 1781, 82, 94-96, 98, 1803-06, pres., 1806; mem. U.S. Ho. of Reps. from Mass., 7th Congress, 1801-03; presdl. elector, 1804; chief justice Mass. Supreme Ct., 1809. Died Stockbridge, Mass., Oct. 25, 1820; buried Stockbridge Cemetery.

BACON, Leonard, clergyman; b. Detroit, Feb. 19, 1802; s. David and Alice (Parks) B.; grad. Yale, 1820, Andover Theol. Sem., 1823; m. Lucy Johnson, July 1825; m. 2d, Catherine Terry, June 1847; 14 children. Ordained to ministry Congregational Ch., Hartford, Conn., 1824; minister 1st Congregational Ch., New Haven, Conn., 1825-66; an editor Christian Spectator, 1826-38, called attention to values and heritage of New Eng. Congregationalism; played leading role in resolving differences within ch., especially Taylor-Tyler dispute (circa 1840), Bushnell controversy (1849); anti-slavery advocate, but opposed extreme abolitionism; became an editor of Independent (pro-free-soil publ.), 1848; prof. theology and ch. history Yale Divinity Sch., 1866-81. Author: Thirteen Historical Discourses, 1839; The Genesis of the New England Churches, 1874. Died New Haven, Dec. 24, 1881; buried New Haven.

BACON, Nathaniel, leader rebellion; b. Suffolk, Eng., Jan. 2, 1647; son of Thomas Bacon; attended Cambridge (Eng.) U.; studied law Gray's Inn; m. Elizabeth Duke. Came to Va., circa 1670, engage in agr., became mem. Gov.'s Council; raised arme force to subdue Indians when govt. of colony fail to protect frontier areas, 1676; used this opportuni to demand sweeping reforms of laws which favor large planters over small farmers; forced summonir of spl. session of assembly to enact reforms; con ducted successful expdn. against Pamunky Indians hostile to Va. Gov. Berkeley for his lack of energ against Indians and his refusal to commn. Bac officer in charge of Va. troops; burned Jamestow Va., when Berkeley (who had fled upon Bacon' rise) returned and threatened reprisals; obtain recognition of his supremacy in govt. from citizer of colony, but died before any further steps we taken, rebellion collapsed. Died Gloucester County Va., Oct. 1676.

BACON, Thomas, clergyman; b. Isle of Man Eng., circa 1700; m. Elizabeth Bozman, 1757. Ordained priest Ch. of Eng., 1745; came to Talbo County, Md., 1745, became chaplain to Proprietar of Colony, also rector St. Peter's Ch., Oxford, Md. moved to Dover, Md., 1747, devoted himself t edn. of Negro population; founded charity sch. providing manual tng. for boys and girls of both races 1750; became reader All Saints Ch., Frederick, Md. 1759, rector, 1762, continued his efforts in fiel of popular edn. Author: Laws of Maryland, 1765 Died Frederick, May 24, 1768.

BACON, William Johnson, congressman, lawyer; b. Williamstown, Mass., Feb. 18, 1803; s Ezekiel Bacon; grad. Hamilton Coll., 1822; grad Litchfield Law Sch., 1824. Admitted to bar, 1824 practiced in Utica, N.Y.; apptd. atty. City c Utica, 1837; mem. N.Y. State Assembly, 1850 elected trustee Hamilton Coll., 1851; elected judg N.Y. State Supreme Ct. of 5th Dist., 1854-70 pres. Utica Cemetery Assn., 1874; mem. U.S. Ho of Reps. (Republican) from N.Y., 45th Congress 1877-79. Died Utica July 3, 1889; buried Fores Hill Cemetery.

BADEAU, Adam, army officer, diplomat; b. N.Y C., Dec. 29, 1831; s. Nicholas Badeau. Commd aide-de-camp U.S. Volunteers, 1862; commd. lt col., served as mil. sec. to Gen Grant, 1864-69; ret as brevet brig gen U.S. Army, 1869; sec. U.S legation, London, Eng., 1869-70; U.S. consul gen at London, 1870-81, Havana, 1882-84; known a "court historian" of Grant administrn. Author The Vagabond, 1859; Military History of Ulysses S Grant, 3 vols, 1868, 81, Grant in Peace (a study o Grant's activities), 1887; Conspiracy, a Cuban Ro mance, 1885. Died Ridgewood, N.J., Mar. 19, 189

BADGER, George Edmund, senator; b. Newbern N..C., Apr. 17, 1795; s. Thomas and Lydia (Cogdell) B.; attended Yale, 1810-11, A.M., 1925, LL.D (hon.), 1848; m. Rebecca Turner; m. 2d, Mary Polk; m. 3d, Delia (Haywood) Williams. Admitte to N.C. bar 1814; mem. N.C. Ho. of Commons 1816; judge Superior Ct. N.C., 1820-25; apptd. U.S sec. of navy by Pres. Harrison. 1841; mem. U.S Senate from N.C., Nov. 25, 1846-55; organize Constl. Union party during secession crisis; del. t Secession Conv. 1861; regent Smithsonian Instn Died Raleigh, N.C., May 11, 1866; buried Oakwood Cemetery, Raleigh.

BADGER, Joseph, artist; b. Charlestown, Mass., Mar. 14, 1708; s. Stephen and Mary (Kettell) B. m. Katherine Felch, June 2, 1731. Prin. portrait painter, Boston, 1748-60; did not sign his work, charged very low prices for his services; painted portraits of Timothy Orne and his wife, received 5 pounds a portrait, 1758; received 12 pounds for 5 pictures from George Bray; conjectured to have beer tchr. of John Singleton Copley; notable portraits include James Bowdoin (now at Bowdoin Coll.), Rev. William Cooper (Mass. Hist. Soc.). Died 1765.

BADGER, Joseph, clergyman; b. Wilbraham, Mass., Feb. 28, 1757; s. Henry and Mary (Langdon) B.; grad. Yale, 1785; m. Lois Noble, Oct. 1784; m. 2d, Abigail Ely, Apr. 1819; 6 children. Served in Am. Revolution; ordained to ministry Congregational Ch., 1787; pastor Congregational Ch., Blandford, Mass., 1787-1800; apptd. missionary to territory of Western Reserve by Missionary Soc. of Conn., 1800; founded 1st ch. in Western Reserve, Austinburg, O., 1800; missionary in Ohio Region until 1827; pastor Congregational Ch., Gustavus, O., 1827-35 (ret.). Died Perrysburg, O., Apr. 5, 1846; buried Perrysburg.

BADGER, Luther, congressman, lawyer; b. Partridgefield (now Peru), Mass., Apr. 10, 1785; attended Hamilton Coll., 1807; studied law. Admitted to bar, 1812; practiced in Jamesville, Onondaga County, N.Y.; served as judge advocate 27th Brigade, N.Y. Militia, 1819-27; mem. U.S. Ho. of Reps. from N.Y., 19th Congress, 1825-27; moved to Broome County, N.Y., 1832; examiner in chancery, 1833-47; apptd. commr. of U.S. loans, 1840-43; dist. atty. Broome County, 1847-49; practiced law, Jordan, Onondaga County. Died Jordan, 1869; buried Jordan Cemetery.

BADIN, Stephen Theodore, clergyman; b. Orleans, rance, July 17, 1768; ed. Coll. Montaigu Paris, ulpician Sem., Orleans. Ordained priest Roman atholic Ch. (1st Roman Cath. priest ordianed in .S.), Balt., 1793; vicar gen. Ky., 1797; pubished Principles of Catholics, (1st Cath. work rinted in the West), 1805; erected Ch. of St. eter, Lexington, Ky., 1812; obtained land on hich U. Notre Dame now stands, 1832. Died incinnati, Apr. 19, 1853; buried South Bend, Ind.

BAER, George, Jr., congressman, mcht.; b. rederick, Md., 1763; s. George Baer; attended ommon schs. Became merchant; mem. Md. Ho. f Dels., 1794, 1808, 09; mem. U.S. Ho. of Reps. Federalist) from Md., 5th-6th, 14th congresses, 797-1801, 15-17; judge Orphans' Ct., Frederick ounty (Md.), 1813; mayor of Frederick, 1820. ied Frederick, Apr. 3, 1834; buried Mt. Olivet emetery.

BAGBY, Arthur Pendleton, senator, gov. Ala.; b. ouisa County, Va., 1794; s. Capt. James and Mary Jones) B.; m. Emily Steele; m. 2d, Anne Elizabeth onnell, 1828; children—Arthur Pendleton, Lt. S.C. agby. Admitted to Ala. bar, 1819; mem. lower ouse Ala. Legislature, 1821-22, 24, 34-36, chosen peaker, 1822, 36; mem. Ala. Senate, 1825; gov. la., (Democrat), 1837-41; mem. U.S. Senate Democrat) from Ala., Nov. 24, 1841-June 16, 848; U.S. minister to Russia, 1848-49; mem. ommn. to codify state laws of Ala., 1852. Died Mobile, Ala., Sept. 21, 1858; buried Magnolia emetery, Mobile.

BAGBY, George William, editor; b. Buckingham County, Va., Aug. 13, 1828; s. George and Virginia Evans) B.; attended Edgehill Sch., Princteon, .J.; attended Del. Coll., 1845-47; grad. U. Pa., 849; m. Lucy Chamberlayne, 1863, 10 children. racticed medicine, Lynchburg, Va., 1849-circa 853; became asst. editor Lynchburg Virginian, irca 1852; partner in newspaper Express, Lynchurg, circa 1855-58; correspondent, Washington, .C., circa 1858-60; editor Southern Literary Mesenger, newspaper, Richmond, Va., 1860-61, 62-64; erved with Confederate Army, 1861-62, discharged ecause of ill health; served as correspondent for arious So. newspapers until end of Civil War; beame popular lectr., 1865; editor Native Virginian, range, Va., 1867-83, became well known for humrous portrayal of rural life in Va. Author: Selecions from the Miscellaneous Writings of Dr. eorge Bagby (includes lectures The Old Virginia entleman, Canal Reminiscences), printed privately, 884. Died Richmond, Va., Nov. 29, 1883; buried ichmond.

BAGBY, John Courts, congressman, lawyer; b. lasgow, Ky., Jan. 24, 1819; grad. as civil engr. acon Coll., Harrodsburg, Ky., 1840; studied law. dmitted to bar, 1845; practiced in Rushville, chuyler County, Ill., 1846; mem. U.S. Ho. of eps. (Democrat) from Ill., 44th Congress, 1875-7; judge Schuyler County, 1822-85; judge 6th d. Circuit Ct. of Ill., 1885-91. Died Rushville, pr. 4, 1896; buried Rushville Cemetery.

BAGOT, Sir Charles, diplomat; b. Rugeley, Stafordshire, Eng., Sept. 23, 1781; son William Bagot; .A., Christ Ch., Oxford (Eng.) U., 1804. Member arliament, 1807; undersec. fgn. affairs until 1814; inister to France, 1814, to U.S., 1815-20; negoated agreement with Richard Rush limiting naval orces on Great Lakes, 1817; created knight, 1820; mbassador to Russia, 1820-24, to Netherlands, 824-41; gov. gen. of Can., 1841-43. Died Kingson, Can., May 18, 1843.

BAILEY, Alexander Hamilton, congressman, awyer; b. Minisink, N.Y., Aug. 14, 1817; grad. rinceton, 1837; studied law. Admitted to bar, bean practice of law; examiner in chancery Greene County, 1840-42; justice of peace Catskill, N.Y. years; mem. N.Y. State Assembly, 1849; judge reene County, 1851-55; moved to Rome, Oneida ounty, 1840-42; justice of peace, Catskill, N.Y. tate Senate, 1861-64; mem. U.S. Ho. of Reps. Republican, filled vacancy) from N.Y., 40th-41st ongresses, Nov. 30, 1867-71; elected judge Oneida County Ct., 1871-74. Died Rome, Apr. 20, 1874; uried Rome Cemetery.

BAILEY, Ann, frontier woman; b. Liverpool, Eng., 742; dau. of Mr. Hennis; m. Richard Trotter, circa 762; m. 2d, John Bailey, circa 1776; 1 son. Came o Am., 1761; became scout, skilled in frontier life, fter death of her 1st husband (killed in war gainst Indians at Point Pleasant, Va., 1774); nown as White Squaw of the Kanawha; when Ft. ee (nr. present Charleston, W.Va.) was under Inian siege, she rode 100 miles to Ft. Lewisburg to et gunpowder, 1791; after death of 2d husband lived ith her son in Gallia County, O. Died Gallia Couny, Nov. 22, 1825.

BAILEY, Anna Warner; b. Groton, Conn., Oct. 758; m. Capt. Elijah Bailey, circa 1782. An orhan, lived with her uncle, Edward Mills, Groton, rom early childhood; made her way to battlefield uring Battle of Groton Heights (Sept. 6, 1781) and brought home her mortally wounded uncle (event later celebrated in poetry and legend); gained name "Mother Bailey" during War of 1812 when she gave her flannel petticoat to Groton soldiers to use in making cartridges, 1813; local chpt. D.A.R. named in her honor. Died Groton, Jan. 10, 1851; buried Groton.

BAILEY, David Jackson, congressman, lawyer; b. Lexington, Ga., Mar. 11, 1812; studied law. Admitted to bar, 1831, practiced law, Jackson, Butts County, Ga.; served as capt. of co. in Seminole and Creek Wars; mem. Ga. Ho. of Reps., 1835, 47; mem. Ga. Senate, 1838, 49-50, 55-56, sec., 1839-41, pres., 1855-56; del. Democratic county convs., 1838, 50; mem. U.S. Ho. of Reps. (State Rights Dem.) from Ga., 32d-33d congresses, 1851-55; mem. Ga. Secession Conv., 1861; served with Confederate Army, became col. 30th Regt., Ga. Inf.; moved to Griffin, Spalding County, Ga., 1861. Died Griffin, June 14, 1897; buried Oak Hill Cemetery.

BAILEY, Ebenezer, educator; probably born in Conn. June 25, 1795; s. Paul and Emma (Carr) B.; grad. Yale, 1817; m. Adeline Dodge, 1825. Operated pvt. sch., New Haven, Conn., 1817-18; tutor in home of Col. Carter, Va., 1818-19; conducted pvt. girls' sch., Newburyport, Mass., 1819-23; headmaster Franklin Grammar Sch. (for boys), Boston, 1826-27; conducted pvt. Young Ladies High Sch., Boston, 1827-37 (failed in panic of 1837); ran pvt. sch. for boys, Roxbury, Mass., 1838, moved sch. to Lynn, Mass., 1839; founder Am. Inst. Instrn.; mem. Boston Common Council. Author: First Lessons in Algebra, 1833; The Young Ladies Class Book, 1833. Died Lynn, Aug. 5, 1839; buried Lynn.

BAILEY, Francis, printer, journalist; b. Lancaster County, Pa., circa 1735; s. Robert and Margaret (McDill) B.; married, at least 1 son, Robert. Publisher Lancaster Almanac, 1771-96; owner printing shop, Lancaster, after 1772, published many fgn. (chiefly German) materials, also 4th edit. of Common Sense (Thomas Paine), 1776; coroner Lancaster County, 1777; served as brigade maj. Pa. Militia at Valley Forge, 1778; published U.S. Mag., Phila., 1778-79; became ofcl. printer Continental Congress, also State of Pa., Phila., 1781; became editor Freeman's Journal or the N. Am. Intelligencer, weekly which opened columns to all polit. factions, 1781 (contbrs. included Philip Freneau, James Wilson, George Osborne); established printing office, Sadsbury, Pa., 1797, continued as state printer; gradually turned business over to son, after 1800. Died Octoraro, nr. Phila., 1815.

BAILEY, Gamaliel, journalist; b. Mt. Holly, N.J., Dec. 3, 1807; s. Gamaliel Bailey; grad. Jefferson Med. Coll., Phila., 1827; m. Margaret Shands, 1833. Served as ship's surgeon on voyage to China, 1827-28; became editor Methodist Protestant, Balt., circa 1828; physician in charge of charity hosp., Cincinnati, 1831-circa 1836; became interested in anti-slavery cause, circa 1834; coeditor (with J. G. Birney) Cincinnati Philanthropist (anti-slavery weekly newspaper), 1836, became editor, owner, 1837, his paper was mobbed 3 times, equipment totally destroyed on 1 occasion; published Herald (anti-slavery daily), Cincinnati, 1843-47; editor Nat. Era (weekly organ of Am. and Fgn. Anti-Slavery Soc.), Washington, D. C., 1847-59, printed works of contbrs. including John Greenleaf Whittier, Harriet B. Stowe, Theodore Parker; known for fairness as editor and as opponent of Know-Nothing movement. Died at sea, June 5, 1859; buried Washington.

BAILEY, Goldsmith Fox, congressman, lawyer; b. Westmoreland, Cheshire County, N.H., July 17, 1823; attended pub. schs., Fitchburg, Mass.; studied law. Editor, publisher Bellows Falls (Vt.) Gazette, 1844; admitted to bar, 1848; practiced in Fitchburg; mem. Fitchburg Sch. Com., 1849-54; apptd. postmaster, Fitchburg, 1851-53; mem. Mass. Ho. of Reps., 1857, Mass. Senate, 1858-60; mem. U.S. Ho. of Reps. (Republican) from Mass., 37th Congress, 1861-62. Died Fitchburg, May 8, 1862; buried Laurel Hill Cemetery.

BAILEY, Jacob, clergyman, Loyalist; b. Rowley, Mass., 1731; s. David and Mary (Hodgkins) B.; grad. Harvard, 1755; m. Sally Weeks, Aug. 1761. Taught sch., Kingston, N.H., also Gloucester, 1755-58; ordained to ministry by Congregational Assn., N.H., 1758; became adherent Anglican Ch., ordained in Eng., 1760; apptd. missionary to eastern Mass. frontier by Soc. for Promoting Gospel in Fgn. Parts, 1760; lived at Ft. Shirley; later built St. John's Ch., Pownalborough, Mass.; refused to support Am. cause in Revolutionary War, was permitted to leave Mass., 1776; settled in Annapolis, Nova Scotia, 1776; rector Anglican Ch., Annapolis, 1776-1818. Contbr. Observations on the Antiquities of America. . .to Collections of Mass. Hist. Soc. for 1795. Died Annapolis, Mar. 22, 1818; buried Annapolis.

BAILEY, Jacob Whitman, educator; b. Auburn, Mass., Apr. 29, 1811; s. Isaac and Jane (Whitman) B.; grad. U.S. Mil. Acad., 1832; m. Maria Slaughter, Jan. 23, 1835, 1 son, 1 dau. Commd. 2d lt., arty. U. S. Army, 1832; became asst. prof. chemistry U.S. Mil. Acad., 1834, prof. chemistry and geology, 1838-57; did valuable research in botany (his field of greatest interest, specializing in minor algae, crystals of plant tissue); wrote many scientific papers on botany, chemistry and geology. Died West Point, N.Y., Feb. 27, 1857.

BAILEY, James Edmund, senator, lawyer; b. Montgomery County, Tenn., Aug. 15, 1822; attended Clarksville Acad., U. Nashville; studied law. Admitted to bar, 1843; practiced in Clarksville, Montgomery County; Whig mem. Tenn. Ho. of Reps., 1853; served as col. 49th Tenn. Regiment, Confederate Army in Civil War; apptd. mem. court of arbitration by Tenn. gov., 1874; mem. U.S. Senate (Democrat, filled vacancy) from Tenn., Jan. 19, 1877-81. Died Clarksville, Dec. 29, 1885; buried Greenwood Cemetery.

BAILEY, James Montgomery, journalist; b. Albany, N.Y., Sept. 25, 1841; s. James and Sarah (Magee) B.; m. Catherine Stewart, 1866. Carpenter, Danbury, Conn., 1860-62; served with Conn. 17th Volunteers, U.S. Inf., 1862-65; contbd. humorous articles on army life to a Danbury newspaper during war; became partner Danbury Times (Democratic newspaper), 1866; began publication of Danbury News, weekly which gained nat. popularity because of his humorous articles on commonplace situations, 1870; began publication Danbury Evening News, daily newspaper, 1878; a founder Danbury Hosp.; pres. Danbury Relief Soc. Author: Life in Danbury, 1873; They All Do It, 1877; The Danbury Boom, 1880. Died Danbury, Mar. 4, 1894; buried Danbury.

BAILEY, Jeremiah, congressman, lawyer; b. Little Compton, R.I., May 1, 1773; grad. Brown U., 1794; studied law. Admitted to bar; practiced in Wiscasset, Mass. (now Me.), 1798; Federalist presdl. elector, 1808; mem. Gen. Ct., 1811-14; judge of probate, 1816-34; mem. U.S. Ho. of Reps. (Whig) from Me., 24th Congress, 1835-37; collector of customs Wiscasset, 1849-53. Died Wiscasset, July 6, 1853; buried Evergreen Cemetery.

BAILEY, John, congressman; b. Stoughton (later Canton), Norfolk County, Mass., 1786; grad. Brown U., 1807. Tutor, librarian, Providence, R.I., 1807-14; mem. Mass. Ho. of Reps., 1814-17; clk. Dept. of State, Washington, D.C., 1817-23; mem. U.S. Ho. of Reps. from Mass., 18th-21st congresses, Dec. 13, 1824-31; mem. Mass. Senate, 1831, 34; unsuccessful Anti-Masonic candidate for gov. Mass., 1834. Died Dorchester, Mass., June 26, 1835; buried Oak Grove Cemetery.

BAILEY, Joseph, congressman; b. Pennsbury Twp., Chester County, Pa., Mar. 18, 1810; attended common schs.; studied law. Learned hatter's trade, Parkersville, Pa.; mem. Pa. Ho. of Reps., 1840; mem. Pa. Senate, 1843, 51-53; treas. of Pa., 1854; admitted to bar, 1860; mem. U.S. Ho. of Reps. (Democrat) from Pa., 37th-38th congresses, 1861-65; mem. Pa. Constl. Conv., 1872. Died Bailey Station, Perry County, Pa., Aug. 26, 1885; buried Bloomfield Cemetery, New Bloomfield, Pa.

BAILEY, Joseph, army officer; b. Pennsville, O., May 6, 1825; studied engring., Ill.; m. Mary Spaulding, 1846. In lumber business and engring. constrn., Kilbourn City, Wis., 1847-61; organized company in 4th Wis. Volunteer Regt., 1861, had rank of capt., became maj., 1863, lt. col., 1863, col., 1864, brig. gen., 1864, brevetted maj. gen., 1865; served in Point Hudson, New Orleans, also on Red River expdn. (built dams for withdrawal of Banks' army); moved to Vernon County, Mo., 1865; sheriff Vernon County, 1866. Murdered by 2 criminals he had placed under arrest, Nevada, Mo., Mar. 21, 1867.

BAILEY, Joseph T., jeweler; b. Poughkeepsie, N.Y., Dec. 16, 1806; apprenticed to silversmith Peter Hages, Poughkeepsie, 1822-27. With jewelry firm Thibault & Bros., Phila., 1827-32; founder firm Bailey & Kitchen, Jewelers, Phila. (later Bailey & Co., became 1 of largest jewelry firms in U.S.), 1832-54. Died Matanzas, Cuba, Mar. 12, 1854.

BAILEY, Lydia R., printer; b. Phila., Feb. 1, 1779; no formal edn.; m. Robert Bailey, 1798, 4 children including Robert William. Took over printing bus. following death of husband, Phila., 1808; did much printing for govt. of Pa., circa 1800-20; printed 3d edition of Poems (Philip Freneau), 1809; city printer of Phila., 1830-50; trained many famous printers of Phila.; ret., 1861; contbd. 1st gift to endowment fund of 3d Presbyn. Ch., Phila. Died Phila., Feb. 21, 1869; buried 3d Presbyn. Ch. Cemetery.

BAILEY, Rufus William, clergyman, coll. pres.; b. North Yarmouth, Me., Apr. 13, 1793; s. Lebbeus and Sarah (Myrick) B.; grad. Dartmouth, 1813; attended Andover Theol. Sem., circa 1815; m. Lucy

Hatch, 1820; m. 2d, Mrs. Mariette Lloyd. Ordained pastor Congregational Ch., Norwich, Vt., after 1818; editor The Patriarch, 1841; prof. langs. Austin (Tex.) Coll., 1854 pres., 1858-63. Author: The Issue; The Mother's Request; The Family Preacher; A Primary Grammar; The Scholar's Companion (popular textbook). Died Huntsville, Tex., Apr. 25, 1863.

BAILEY, Theodorus, senator, congressman, lawyer; b. nr. Fishkill, Dutchess County, N.Y., Oct. 12, 1758; attended rural schs.; studied law. Admitted to bar, 1778; practiced in Poughkeepsie, N.Y.; adjutant in Col. Freer's Regt., N.Y. Militia, later in Col. Morris Graham's Regt., in Revolutionary War; maj. N.Y. State Militia, 1786, lt. col., 1797, brig. gen., 1801-05; mem. U.S. Ho. of Reps. (Democrat) from N.Y., 3d-4th, 6th, (filled vacancy) 7th congresses, 1793-97, 99-1801, Oct. 6, 1801-03; mem. N.Y. State Assembly, 1802; mem. U.S. Senate from N.Y., 1803-Jan. 16, 1804; postmaster City of N.Y., 1804-28. Died N.Y.C., Sept. 6, 1828; buried Dutch Burying Ground, reinterred Rural Cemetery, Poughkeepsie, N.Y., Jan. 8, 1864.

BAILEY, Theodorus, naval officer; b. Chateaugay, N.Y., Apr. 12, 1805; s. William and Phoebe (Platt) B.; m. Sarah Ann Platt, June 23, 1830. Apptd. midshipman U.S. Navy, 1818; served on coast of Africa, then transferred to Pacific, 1818-20; 1st command was store-ship Lexington, 1846; served in Lower Cal. during Mexican War; promoted to comdr., 1849, capt., 1855; comd. St. Mary's in the Pacific, 1853-56, frigate Colo. in blockade of Fla., 1861; 2d in command under Admiral David Farragut in attack on New Orleans, La., 1862, led Union fleet up Mississippi River and accepted surrender of New Orleans; comd. East Gulf blockading squadron, 1862-64, Portsmouth Navy Yard, 1864-66; promoted to rear adm., 1866, ret., 1866. Died Washington, D.C., Feb. 10, 1877.

BAILLY, Joseph Alexis, sculptor; b. Paris, France, Jan. 21, 1825; s. Joseph Bailly; studied under Baron Bozio at French Inst., Paris, circa 1845; m. Louisa David, 1850. Came to Am., 1849; settled in Phila., circa 1850; became well known for his busts and statues; became mem. Pa. Acad., 1856, instr. in sculpture, 1876-77; better known works include busts of Gen. Grant and Gen. Meade, a statue of Benjamin Franklin, equestrian statue of Pres. Blanco of Venezuela, 2 groups known as The Expulsion, The First Prayer (now in Pa. Acad.). Died Phila., June 15, 1883; buried Mt. Peace Cemetery, Phila.

BAIN, George Luke Scobie, businessman; b. Stirling, Scotland, May 5, 1836; s. Robert Scobie and Charlotte (Brown) B.; m. Clara Mather, Nov. 5, 1857. Came to Can., 1851; accountant, Montreal, Can., 1851-54; with Mackintosh & Co., flour firm, Portland, Me., 1854; organized Bain & Clarke, grain commn. house, Chgo., 1857, George Bain & Co., grain bus., St. Louis, 1865; became part owner Atlantic Mills, flour mfg. firm, 1871, initiated direct shipment of flour from St. Louis to fgn. countries, 1871-90; pres. Millers' Nat. Assn., 1876-83. Died St. Louis, Oct. 22, 1891; buried St. Louis.

BAINBRIDGE, William, naval officer; b. Princeton, N.J., May 7, 1774; s. Dr. Absolom and Miss (Taylor) B.; m. Susan Hyleger, 1798, 5 children. Commd. lt. comdt. U.S. Navy, 1798, given command ship Retaliation; commd. master comdt., given command consort Norfolk; promoted capt. (at that time highest rank in navy), 1800, given command frigate George Washington; comdr. frigate Philadelphia, 1803, ran aground in harbor of Tripoli, taken prisoner, ship later burned by Stephen Decatur (so it would not be used against Am. fleet); received command ship President, 1808; comdt. Charlestown (Mass.) Navy Yard, 1812, obtained command flag ship Constitution; supt. constrn. war ship Independence, 1813; established 1st U.S. naval sch. at Boston Navy Yard, 1815, presided over 1st bd. examiners, 1819; commanded battleship New Columbus, 1820; commanded Phila. Navy Yard, 1821, Charlestown Navy Yard, 1823; U.S. naval commr., 1823. Died Phila., July 27, 1833.

BAIRD, Charles Washington, clergyman; b. Princeton, N.J., Aug. 28, 1828; s. Robert and Fermine (DuBuisson) B.; grad. U. City N.Y., 1848, Union Theol. Sem., 1852; m. Margaret Eliza Strang, circa 1862. Chaplain under auspices Am. and Fgn. Christian Union, Am. Chapel, Rome, 1852-54; engaged in literary and hist. studies, 1854-59; pastor Reformed Dutch Ch., South Brooklyn, N.Y., 1859-61, Presbyn. Ch., Rye, N.Y., 1861-87. Author: Eutaxia or the Presbyterian Liturgies, 1855; A Book of Public Prayer, 1856; A History of Rye, 1660-1870, published 1871; The History of the Huguenot Emigration to America, 2 vols., 1885. Died probably Rye, Feb. 10, 1887.

BAIRD, Matthew, locomotive mfr.; b. Londonderry, Ireland, 1817; attended common schs., Phila. Came with family to Am., 1821, settled in Phila.; apprentice New Castle Mfg. Co. (Del.), 1834-37; supt. New Castle railroad shops, 1837-38; supt. boiler div. Baldwin Locomotive Co., Phila., 1838-50, became partner, 1854, sole propr., 1866, reorganized co. as Baldwin Locomotive Works, M. Baird & Co., Proprs., ret., 1873; in marble bus., Phila., 1850-54; known for inventiveness in mfg. processes; a founder Am. S.S. Co.; active in many philanthropies, Phila. Died Phila., May 19, 1877; buried Phila.

BAIRD, Robert, clergyman; b. Pitts., Oct. 6, 1798; s. Robert and Elizabeth (Reeves) B.; attended acad., Uniontown, Pa., 1813-circa 1815; attended Washington, Jefferson colls., circa 1815-19; grad. Princeton Theol. Sem., 1822; m. Fermine DuBuisson, Aug. 24, 1824. Prin., Princeton (N.J.) Acad., 1822-27; lobbyist for passage of common sch. legislation in N.J. Legislature, 1820's; gen. agt. Am. Sunday Sch. Union, 1829-34, travelled widely, founding Sunday schs. in all parts of U.S.; agt. for French Assn. (group for assisting Protestants in France), lived in Paris for several years; became active in popularizing temperance movement in Europe; later agt. for Am. and Fgn. Christian Union (outgrowth of French Assn.). Author: History of Temperance Societies in the United States, 1836; Visit to Northern Europe, 1841; Religion in the U.S.A., 1843; Sketches of Protestantism in Italy Past and Present, 1845. Died Mar. 15, 1863.

BAIRD, Samuel John, clergyman; b. Newark, O., Sept. 17, 1817; s. Rev. Thomas Dickson and Esther (Thompson) B.; attended Jefferson Coll., circa 1837-38; grad. Centre Coll., Danville, Ky., circa 1841, Ind. Theol. Sem., New Albany, 1843; m. Jane Wilson, 1840. Preached in Balt., also Ky., 1844-54; ordained to ministry, Cedar Rapids, Ia., 1854; became pastor Presbyn. Ch., Muscatine, Ia., 1854; pastor ch., Woodbury, N.J., 1857-65; agt. Am. Bible Soc., 1865-75; pastor 3d Presbyn. Ch., Woodbury, 1875-84; pastor, Ronceverte, W.Va., 1884-88; ret., Blacksburg, Va., 1888. Author: (works in fields of ch. govt., ch. history) The Church of Christ, its Constitution and Order, 1864; The Assembly's Digest (compilation of decisions of Gen. Assembly of Presbyn. Ch.), 1854; History of the New School, 1868; The Great Baptiser; A Bible History Of Baptism, 1882. Died West Clinton Forge, Va., Apr. 10, 1893.

BAIRD, Spencer Fullerton, naturalist; b. Reading, Pa., Feb. 3, 1823; s. Samuel and Lydia (Biddle) B.; A.B., Dickinson Coll., 1841, M.A., 1843, Ph.D. (hon.), 1856; M.D. (hon), Phila. Med. Coll., 1848; LL.D. (hon.), Columbia, 1875; m. Mary Helen Churchill, 1846; 1 dau., Lucy Hunter. Prin. founder Marine Lab., Wood's Hole, Mass.; prof. natural history Dickinson Coll., 1845; inaugurated the method of field study of botany and zoology in Am.; made explorations for U.S. Govt. in Wyo. Territory, 1850-60; sec. A.A.A.S., 1850-51; mem. Nat. Acad. Sci., 1864; 1st U.S. commr. Fish and Fisheries, 1871; elected asst. sec. Smithsonian Instn., 1850, sec., 1878. Author: Catalogue of North American Mammals, 1857; Catalogue of North American Birds, 1858; Review of American birds, 1864-66; editor Iconographic Ency., 1849; The Annual Record of Science and Industry, 1871-77; The Annual Reports of Smithsonian Instn., 1878-87; prepared Smithsonian Instn.'s Instructions to Collectors. Died Wood's Hole, Aug. 19, 1887; buried Oak Hill Cemetery, Washington, D.C.

BAIRD, Thomas H., jurist; b. Washington, Pa., Nov. 15, 1787; s. Dr. Absalom and Susan (Brown) B.; studied law with Joseph Pentecost. Admitted to bar, 1808; pres. judge 14th Dist. of Pa., 1818-37, impeached by Pa. Legislature for removing a majority of the attys. from roll in Fayette County, 1835, acquitted; moved to Pitts., 1837, admitted to Pitts. bar, 1838. Died Nov. 22, 1866; buried Washington, Pa.

BAKER, Abijah Richardson, clergyman; b. Franklin, Mass., Aug. 30, 1805; s. Capt. David and Jemima (Richardson) B.; grad. Amherst Coll., 1830; grad. Andover Theol. Sem., 1835; D.D. (hon.), Austin (Tex.) Coll.; m. Harriette Newell Woods, Oct. 1, 1835, 6 children. Tchr. English, Phillip's Acad., Andover, Mass., 1835-38; pastor Congregational Ch., Medford, Mass., 1838-51; founder Congregational Ch., Lynn, Mass., 1851, pastor, 1851-55; pastor Congregational Ch., Wellesley, Mass., 1855-63; pastor E Street Ch., South Boston, 1863-66. Author: The Catechism Tested by the Bible (translated into 6 langs.). Died Dorchester, Mass.. Apr. 30, 1876.

BAKER, Benjamin Franklin, musician; b. Wenham, Mass., July 10, 1811; son of John and Sally Baker; m. Sabra Heywood, Nov. 21, 1841. Taught voice, also active in choirs, Boston, 1831; went into business, Bangor, Me., 1833; returned to Boston, 1837; sang at Chauncey Place Ch.; in charge of music at ch. of William E. Channing, 1839-47; instr. music in Boston schs., 1841-50; organized music instrn., Lowell (Mass.) schs., 1850's; organizer, prin., voice tchr. Boston Music Sch 1857-68; editor Boston Music Journal, 1870's; pre Boston Mus. Edn. Soc.; published (with L.H. Sout ard) Haydn Collection of Church Music, 1850. Aut or: (textbooks) Theory of Harmony, 1847, Th oretical and Practical Harmony, 1870. Compose (vocal quartet) Death of Osceola, 1846; (cantatas Storm King, 1856, The Burning Ship, 1865. Di Boston, Mar. 11, 1889; buried Boston.

BAKER, Caleb, congressman; b. Providenc R.I., 1762; studied law. Moved to N.Y., 1790, liv in Chemung, Ashland, Newton (Tioga County 1790-1836; admitted to bar; assessor Town Chemung, 1791; taught school at site of prese Baptist Graveyard, Wellsburg, Chemung Count 1803, 04; apptd. surrogate Tioga County, 1806, 2 29; apptd. judge of common pleas, 1810; mer N.Y. State Assembly, 1814, 15, 29; justice of peac Chemung, 1816; mem. U.S. Ho. of Reps. from N.Y 16th Congress, 1819-21; foreman 1st grand ju of Chemung County, 1836. Died Southport (nc part of Elmira), Chemung County, June 26, 184 buried Fitzsimmons Cemetery.

BAKER, Charles Henry, businessman; b. Phila Feb. 20, 1793; s. John R. Baker. Entered countir house Eyre & Massey after graduation from hi sch., made bus. trips to Canton, China, 1811-1 partner (with his father) in firm importing Fren and German goods, 1814-29; interested in bankin 1829-32; dir. Phila. Marine Ins. Co., 1832-3 pres., 1836-45. Died Sept. 21, 1872.

BAKER, Daniel, clergyman, coll. pres.; b. Mi way, Ga., Aug. 17, 1791; attended Hampden-Sydn (Va.) Coll., 1811-13; grad. Princeton, 1815; n Elizabeth McRobert, 1816. Pastor, Presbyn. chs Harrisonburg, Va., Washington, D.C., Savannah, Ga Tuscaloosa, Ala., 1816-40; evang. missionary Pre byn. Ch. to Republic of Tex., 1840, an organizer 1st presbytery in Tex.; pastor ch., Holly Spring Miss., 1841-48; organized Austin (Tex.) Coll., 184 gen. agt. for coll., obtained funds for its endo ment, pres. coll., 1853-57; instrumental in passa of public sch. act by Tex. Legislature, 1854; Dani Baker Coll. (Brownwood, Tex.) named in his hon Died Austin, Dec. 10, 1857.

BAKER, David Jewett, senator, lawyer; b. E Haddam, Conn., Sept. 7, 1792; grad. Hamilton Col 1816; studied law. Admitted to bar, 1819; pra ticed in Kaskaskia, Ill.; probate judge Randol County, Ill., 1827-30; mem. U.S. Senate (Dem crat, filled vacancy) from Ill., Nov. 12-Dec. 1 1830; U.S. dist. atty. for Dist. of Ill., 1833-4 Died Alton, Madison County, Ill., Aug. 6, 186 buried City Cemetery.

BAKER, Edward Dickinson, senator; b. Londo Eng., Feb. 24, 1811; m. Mary A. Lee, Apr. 27, 183 Came to U.S., 1825, moved to Springfield, Ill 1830; admitted to Ill. bar, 1830; mem. Ill. Ge Assembly from Sangamon County, 1837-40; mer Ill. Senate, 1840-44; mem. U.S. Ho. of Reps. fro Ill. as Whig (defeated Lincoln), 29th Congres 1845-Dec. 30, 1846, as Republican, 31st Congres 1849-51; raised a co. of volunteers, 1846, col. Mexican War, participated in siege of Veracru commanded brigade at Battle of Cerro Gordo; mer U.S. Senate from Ore., Oct. 2, 1860-Oct. 21, 186 col. 71st Regt., Pa. Volunteer Inf., in charge of brigade, 1861; commd. col., then maj. gen. U. Volunteers, 1861. Killed in Battle of Ball's Bl (Va.), Oct. 22, 1861; buried Lone Mountain Cem tery, San Francisco.

BAKER, Ezra, congressman; b. Tuckerton, N.J studied medicine. Practiced medicine; moved Absecon, N.J., 1799; collector of customs Port Great Egg Harbor, N.J., 1813-15; mem. U.S. H of Reps. from N.J., 14th Congress, 1815-17; move to "Wabash country" with his sons, 1818, gre castor beans for New Orleans market. Died "W bash country."

BAKER, Francis Asbury, clergyman; b. Balt Mar. 30, 1820; s. Sam Baker; grad. Princeto 1839. Became a minister Episcopalian Ch., serve 2 chs. in Balt.; influenced by Oxford Movemen became convert to Roman Catholic Ch., 185 ordained priest, 1856; joined Redemptorist mi sion group, then left (with Hecker, others) to e tablish Paulists. Died N.Y.C., Apr. 4, 1865.

BAKER, George Augustus, painter; b. N.Y.C Mar. 1821; son of George Baker; studied at N.A.D 1837-44, in Europe, 1844-46. Became miniatu painter, working in oils, N.Y.C., 1846; elected me Nat. Acad. Arts, 1851; built his reputation o portrait painting; exhibited at Paris Expn. of 186 lived in Darien, Conn., 1867-80. Best known wor include: Wild Flowers, Faith, portrait of John Ke sett (now in Met. Mus., N.Y.C.). Died probab Darien, Apr. 2, 1880.

BAKER, Harriette Newell Woods, author; Andover, Mass., Aug. 19, 1815; d. Dr. Leona and Abby (Wheeler) Woods; attended Abbott F male Sem.; m. Abijah Richardson Baker, Oc 1, 1835, 6 children. Contbd. short stories to mag hile still in her 'teens; wrote over 200 prose pieces some translated into German and French). Works nclude: The Courtesies of Wedded Life, 2d edit., 869; Tim: The Scissors Grinder. Died Bklyn., Apr. 6, 1893.

BAKER, James, trapper, frontiersman; b. Belleille, Ill., Dec. 19, 1818; married 6 Indian wives. Iem. James Bridger's fur trapping expdn. for Am. 'ur Co., 1839-40; engaged in trapping, Wyo. and 'olo., 1840's-50's; scout for Gen. Harney at Ft. aramie, 1855; guide for U.S. Army expdn. against Iormons, 1857; engaged in trapping and trading 'ith Indians, nr. what is now Denver, 1858; ret. to ome in valley of Little Snake River, Wyo., 1873.)ied nr. Savery, Wyo., May 15, 1898; buried nr. avery.

BAKER, John, congressman, lawyer; b. Fredrick County, Md.; attended Washington Coll. now Washington and Lee U.), Lexington, Va. 3 ears; studied law. Admitted to bar; practiced in 'erkeley County, Va. (now Jefferson County, /. Va.); mem. Va. Ho. of Dels., 1798-99; a lawyer 'ho defended Aaron Burr when he was tried for reason; mem. U.S. Ho. of Reps. (Federalist) rom Va., 12th Congress, 1811-13; Commonwealth tty. for Jefferson County. Died Shepherdstown, efferson County, Aug. 18, 1823; buried Old Episopal Ch. Cemetery.

BAKER, La Fayette Curry, chief U.S. Secret ervice; b. Stafford, N.Y., Oct. 13, 1826; s. Rememer Baker; m. Jennie Curry, Dec. 24, 1852. Itinerant iechanic, 1848-60; mem. San Francisco Vigilance 'om., 1856; spl. provost marshall War Dept., 1862; ommd. brig. gen. U.S. Army, 1865; chief U.S. ecret Service, 1862-circa 1867, directed capture of ohn Wilkes Booth and D.C. Herold; dismissed by 'res. Johnson for continuing espionage activities t Washington (D.C.) after Civil War; chief witness gave false testimony) against Johnson in impeachient proceedings. Author: History of the United tates Secret Service, 1867. Died Phila., July 3, 868.

BAKER, Lewis, actor, theater mgr.; b. Phila.; i. Alexina Fisher, May 3, 1851. Visited Galveston, ex., 1844, influenced building of a theater there; iade debut at Arch Street Theatre, Phila., 1849; ppeared at the 2d Jenny Lind Theater, San rancisco, 1852; managed Adelphi Theater, San rancisco, 1852-53, made $30,000 profit for mgmt. most prosperous season in history of Cal. theater) that time); mgr. Am. Theater, San Francisco, 853-54; leased Nat. Theatre, Cincinnati, 1857.

BAKER, Osmon Cleander, clergyman; b. Marlow, .H., July 30, 1812; s. Dr. Isaac and Abigail (Kider) B.; attended Wesleyan U., 1827-30, A.M., 837, D.D., 1852; m. Mehitabel Perley, 1833. rdained to ministry Methodist Ch., 1829; rin. of acad., Newbury, Vt., 1838-44; oranized Theol. Soc. of Newbury Sem., 1840; prof. Ieth. Gen. Bibl. Inst., Concord, N.H., 1847-0; presiding elder N.H. dist. Meth. Ch., 1847; lected bishop by Gen. Conf., 1852; Author: Guide ook in the Administration of the Discipline of he Methodist Episcopal Church, 1855. Died Conord, Dec. 20, 1871.

BAKER, Osmyn, congressman, lawyer; b. Amerst, Mass., May 18, 1800; attended Amherst cad.; grad. Yale, 1822; studied law. Admitted to ar, 1825; practiced in Amherst, 1825; mem. Mass. Io. of Reps., 1833, 34, 36, 37; commr. Hampshire ounty, 1834-37; mem. U.S. Ho. of Reps. (Whig, lled vacancy) from Mass., 26th-28th congresses, n. 14, 1840-45; practiced in Northampton, Mass., 845; 1st pres. Smith Charities, 1860-70. Died orthampton, Feb. 9, 1875; buried Bridge Street emetery.

BAKER, Peter Carpenter, publisher; b. North Iampstead, N.Y., Mar. 22, 1822; s. John and Iargaret (Boyce) B.; attended Harlem Acad., N.Y. , circa 1830-33; apprenticed to printer, from 834; m. Malvina Lockwood, 3 children. Supt., ohn F. Trow's printing firm, N.Y.C., circa 1838-0; became partner (with Daniel Godwin) in rinting bus., N.Y.C., 1850, became nationally known or craftsmanship; asso. with Baker, Voorhis & Co., i field of law publishing, from 1866; an organizer 'ypothetae (profl. printers' soc. for maintaining igh standards), N.Y.C.; active exponent of temerance movement; benefactor Hahnemann Hosp., I.Y.C. Died N.Y.C., May 19, 1889; buried N.Y.C.

BAKER, Remember, army officer; b. Woodbury, 'onn., June 1737; s. Remember and Tamar (Warer) B.; m. Desire Hurlbut, Apr. 3, 1760, 1 son, zi. Served in French and Indian War, 1757—circa 760; settled in Arlington (in what now is Vt.), 764; became involved in controversy between N.Y. nd N.H. over control of territory that is now State f Vt.; joined Green Mountain Boys under Ethan llen to enforce claims to grants made by N.H. govt.) settlers in territory, 1770-74. Killed in encounter 'ith Indians while serving in Gen. Schuyler's scoutng expdn. up Lake Champlain, at St. John's, N.Y., ug. 1775.

BAKER, Stephen, congressman; b. N.Y.C., Aug. 12, 1819; attended common schs. Importer and jobber in woolen goods; moved to Poughkeepsie, N.Y., 1850; mem. U.S. Ho. of Reps. (Republican) from N.Y., 37th Congress, 1861-63. Died (on train en route to Cal. for his health) nr. Ogden, Utah, June 9, 1875; buried Rural Cemetery, Poughkeepsie.

BAKER, William Mumford, clergyman; b. Washington, D.C., June 5, 1825; s. Daniel and Elizabeth (McRobert) B.; grad. Princeton, 1846, attended Sem., 1847-48; m. Susan Hartman, Jan. 5, 1850. Licensed to preach by N.J. Presbytery, 1848; ordained to ministry Presbyn. Ch., Little Rock, Ark., 1850; pastor First Presbyn. Ch., Austin, Tex., 1850-65; Unionist during Civil War; pastor at Zanesville, O., 1866-72, Newburyport, Mass., 1872-74, South Boston, 1874-76, South Ch., Phila., 1881-83; wrote several books, 1876-81. Author: Inside: A Chronicle of Secession (record of his life in South during Civil War), 1866; Oak Mot, 1878; The Ten Theophanies, 1883. Died Boston, Aug. 20, 1883; buried Boston.

BALATKA, Hans, musician; b. Hoffnungsthal, Moravia, Mar. 5, 1827; studied music, Vienna, Austria. Conducted Academical Singing Socs., Vienna, 1846-48; came to Am., 1849; founder Milw. Musikverein, 1851, condr., 1851-60; became condr. Chgo. Philharmonic Soc., 1860, Musical Union, 1862; gave independent symphony concerts, 1867; condr. Germania Männerchor, 1867; made concert tours with Mme. Pappenheim, 1870; organized Liederkranz, also Mozart Club, Chgo., after 1873; condr. Symphony Soc., Chgo. Composer: The Power of Song, 1856; Festival Cantata, 1869; also numerous choruses and quartets, songs, other pieces. Died Chgo., Apr. 17, 1899.

BALBOA, Vasco Nuñez de, explorer; b. Jerez de los Caballeros, Estremodura, Spain, circa 1475. Sailed with Rodrigo de Bastidas, 1501, probably went to Hispaniola; fled from creditors in Spain on Martin Fernandez de Enciseo's vessel to San Sebastian, Panama, 1510; proposed they go to Darien, founded new town St. Maria de la Antigua del Darien, took over leadership from Encisco, sent him back to Spain as prisoner; heard that Encisco had complained to king and sentence was being issued condemning him and ordering him back to Spain; decided that some great enterprise would win back his freedom; set out with expdn. to find Great Sea to West, 1513; 1st sighted Pacific Ocean, 1513, reached and claimed ocean and all shores it washed for Spain; visited Pearl Islands, returned with booty which he sent to Spanish crown; granted as reward title "adelantado of South Sea (or Admiral of Pacific) and gov. of Panama"; built 2 small brigantines and took possession of Pearl Islands for Spain; (meanwhile Pedro Arias de Avilla had been sent to replace him); lured to Aela, Panama, by Pedros Arias (who had him thrown into prison and forced judge to condemn him). Beheaded in public square, Aela, 1517.

BALD, J. Dorsey, banknote engraver; b. circa 1826; s. Robert Bald. Began career as lawyer, circa 1849; took charge of family engraving interests, 1854; sr. partner engraving firm Bald, Cousland & Co., Phila. and N.Y.C.; an organizer Am. Bank Note Co., 1858. Died circa 1878.

BALDWIN, Abraham, senator, univ. pres.; b. North Gilford, Conn., Nov. 22, 1754; s. Michael and Lucy (Dudley) B.; grad. Yale, 1772. Licensed minister; tutor Yale, 1775-79; chaplain 2d Conn. Brigade, Continental Army, 1779-83; admitted to Fairfield County (Conn.) bar, 1783, Ga. bar, 1784; mem. Ga. Ho. of Assembly from Wilkes County, 1785; mem. Continental Congress, 1785-88; founder U. Ga., 1785, 1st pres., 1786-1800, pres. bd. trustees, 1800-07; mem. U.S. Constl. Conv., 1787; mem. U.S. Ho. of Reps. (Federalist) from Ga., 1st-5th congresses, 1789-99; mem. U.S. Senate from Ga., 1799-1807, pres. pro tem, 1801; U.S. commr. to treat regarding ceding of Ga. lands to U.S. Govt., 1802; an original mem. Conn. br. Soc. of Cincinnati; Baldwin counties (Ga. and Ala.) named for him. Died Washington, D.C., Mar. 4, 1807; buried Rock Creek Cemetery, Washington.

BALDWIN, Edward J., financier, hotel-theater owner. Opened (with Thomas Maguire) Baldwin's Hotel-Theater, San Francisco, 1876.

BALDWIN, Elihu Whittlesey, clergyman, coll. pres.; b. Durham, Green County, N.Y., Dec. 25, 1789; s. Deacon Jonathan and Submit (Christopher) B.; grad. Yale, 1812, Andover Theol. Sem., 1817; D.D., Inc. U., Bloomington, 1839; m. Julia Baldwin, May 12, 1819. Ordained to ministry Presbyn. Ch.; 1st pres. Wabash Coll., Crawfordsville, Ind., 1835-20; established 7th Presbyn. Ch., N.Y.C., installed pastor, 1820. Died Oct. 15, 1840.

BALDWIN, Henry, asso. justice U.S. Supreme Ct.; b. New Haven, Conn., Jan. 14, 1780; s. Michael and Theodora (Wolcott) B.; grad. Yale, 1797, LL.D., 1830. Admitted to bar in Phila., 1798; began practice of law, also engaged in iron mfg.; mem. U.S. Ho. of Reps. (Federalist) from Pa., 15th-17th congresses, 1817-22, chmn. com. on domestic manufactures; asso. justice U.S. Supreme Ct., 1830-44, opposed John Marshall's liberal interpretation of Constn. Author: A General View of the Origin and Nature of the Constitution and Government of the United States, 1837. Died Phila., Apr. 21, 1844; buried Greendale Cemetery, Meadville, Pa.

BALDWIN, Henry Porter, senator, gov. Mich.; b. Coventry, R.I., Feb. 22, 1814; s. John and Margaret (Williams) B.; m. Harriet M. Day, 1835; m. 2d, Sibyle Lambard, Nov. 21, 1866. Elected to Mich. Senate, 1861-62; pres. 2d Detroit Nat. Bank, 1863-87; gov. Mich., 1868-73; mem. U.S. Senate from Mich., Nov. 17, 1879-Mar. 3, 1881. Died Dec. 31, 1892; buried Elmwood Cemetery, Detroit.

BALDWIN, James Fowler, mcht., educator; b. Charlestown, Mass., Aug. 8, 1818; s. Thomas and Sophia (Kendal) B.; attended Harvard, 1834-35; m. Eunice Hooper, Nov. 9, 1843; m. 2d, Martha Johnson, Oct. 4, 1848. Engaged in merc. bus., Honolulu, Hawaii, 1838-59; spl. envoy of Hawaiian king to secure guarantee of Hawaiian independence from Gt. Britain, 1843; mem. Hawaiian Legislature, advocated temperance measures; served as paymaster gen. Mass. troops, also agt. Mass. Sanitary Commn., 1861-65; trustee, treas., instr. Hampton Inst., Va., 1870-84. Died Weston, Mass., May 6, 1891; buried Weston.

BALDWIN, John, congressman, lawyer; b. Mansfield, Conn., Apr. 5, 1772; grad. Brown U., 1797; studied law. Admitted to bar, 1800; practiced in Windham, Conn.; probate judge Windham County (Conn.), 1818-24; mem. U.S. Ho. of Reps. from Conn., 19th-20th congresses, 1825-29; affiliated with Whig Party after its formation. Died Windham, Mar. 27, 1850; buried Windham Cemetery.

BALDWIN, John, grindstone mfr., philanthropist; b. North Branford, Conn., Oct. 13, 1799; s. Joseph and Rosanna (Meloy) B.; m. Mary Chappel, Jan. 31, 1828. Founder, Berea Grindstone Industry (O.), 1842; donated land and bldgs. to No. Ohio Conf., Methodist Ch. for establishment Berea Inst. (now Baldwin-Wallace Coll.), 1845; founder Baldwin U., 1846, Baker U., 1859, high sch. for boys, another for girls, Bangalore, India, 1880. Died Baldwin, La., Dec. 28, 1884.

BALDWIN, John Brown, lawyer; b. Jan. 11, 1820; s. Briscoe and Martha (Steele) B.; attended Staunton (Va.) Acad., U. Va., 1836-39; m. Susan Peyton, Sept. 20, 1842. Admitted to Staunton bar, 1841, practiced law; elected as Whig to Va. Ho. of Dels., 1846, served 1 term; opposed secession of Va. as mem. Va. Conv., 1861; col. 52d Va. Infantry, 1861-62; mem. 1st, 2d Confederate Congresses, 1862-65; active in public life following end of war; speaker Va. Ho. of Dels., 1865-66. Died probably Staunton, Sept. 30, 1873.

BALDWIN, John Denison, congressman, journalist; b. North Stonington, Conn.; s. Daniel and Hannah (Stanton) B.; attended Yale, 1826-27, grad. Divinity Sch., 1834; m. Lemira Hathaway, 1832. Ordained to ministry Congregational Ch.; pastor West Woodstock, Conn., 1834-37. North Killingly, Conn., 1837-49; editor newspaper Charter Oak (organ of Free-Soil party) Hartford, Conn.; editor Commonwealth, Boston, until 1859; owner, editor Worcester (Mass.) Spy (newspaper he made into Republican organ), 1859-83; mem. U.S. Ho. of Reps. (Rep.) from Mass., 38th-40th congresses, 1863-69. Author: The Story of Raymond Hill and Other Poems, 1847; Ancient America, 1872. Died Worcester, July 8, 1883; buried Worcester.

BALDWIN, Joseph Glover, judge, author; b. Winchester, Va., Jan. 1815; s. Joseph Clarke and Eliza (Baldwin) B.; no formal edn.; m. Sidney White, 1839. Practiced law, De Kalb, Miss., 1836; settled in Gainesville, Ala., 1839; Whig mem. Ala. Legislature, 1844-49; moved to Mobile, Ala., 1853, to San Francisco, 1853, practiced law there; instrumental in establishing system of justice in San Francisco; asso. justice Cal. Supreme Ct., 1858-62. Author: The Flush Times of Alabama and Mississippi, 1853; Party Leaders, 1855. Died Sept. 30, 1864.

BALDWIN, Loammi, civil engr.; b. North Woburn, Mass., Jan. 21, 1745; s. James and Ruth (Richardson) B.; m. Mary Fowle, 1772; m. 2d, Margery Fowle, 1791; 2 sons, George, Loammi. Apprenticed in cabinet making; engaged in surveying and engring., Woburn, Mass., circa 1765; apptd. lt. col. 38th Infantry Regt. in Continental Army, 1775; served with Washington's army in attack on Trenton, N.J., 1776; discharged due to ill health, 1777; represented Woburn in Mass. Gen. Ct., 1778-79, 1800-04; sheriff Middlesex County (Mass.), 1780-circa 1785; chief engr. Middlesex Canal (connecting Charles and Merrimac rivers), 1793-1803; discovered strain of apple known as Baldwin in later years; mem. Am. Acad. Arts and Scis. Died Woburn, Oct. 20, 1807; buried Woburn.

BALDWIN, Loammi, Jr., civil engr., lawyer; b. North Woburn, Mass., May 16, 1780; s. Loammi and Mary (Fowle) B.; grad. Harvard, 1800; m. Ann Williams; m. 2d, Catherine Beckford, Admitted to Mass. bar, 1804; helped construct Ft. Strong, Boston Harbor, 1814; engr. of improvements City of Boston, 1819; engr. Union Canal, 1821; mem. com. for erection Bunker Hill Monument, 1825. designed and built dry docks at Charlestown (Mass.), Norfolk (Va.) navy yards, 1833; mem. Mass State Exec. Com., 1835; presdl. elector, 1836. Author: Thoughts on the Study of Political Economy as Connected with the Population, Industry and Paper Currency of the United States (pamphlet), 1809; Report on the Subject of Introducing Pure Water into the City of Boston, 1834. Died Charlestown, June 30, 1838.

BALDWIN, Matthias William, mfr., philanthropist; b. Elizabethtown, N.J., Dec. 10, 1795; s. William Baldwin; m. Sarah Baldwin (cousin), 1827, 3 children. Devised and patented process for gold plating; constructed Old Ironsides (one of 1st Am. locomotives used in transp.); a founder Franklin Inst. for Betterment of Labor, 1824; manufactured stationary engines, 1827, locomotives, 1831; mem. Pa. Constl. Conv., 1837; founded sch. for Negro children, 1835; founder M.W. Baldwin (now Baldwin Locomotive Works); donated money for 7 chs. and chapels in Phila.; mem. Pa. Legislature, 1854; mem. Am. Philos. Soc., Am. Hort. Soc., Pa. Acad. Fine Arts, Music Fund Soc. Died Phila., Sept. 7, 1866.

BALDWIN, Noyes, army officer, mcht.; b. Woodbridge, Conn., Sept. 8, 1826; at least 1 son. Went to Cal., 1849; served as capt. 1st Nev. Volunteers at Ft. Churchill, 1861-63, transferred to Ft. Bridger; promoted maj., transferred to Camp Douglas, Utah, then to Post Provo, 1864; commander Ft. Bridger, 1865; engaged in trading and merchandising, Wyo., 1869-89; del. Wyo. Constl. Conv., 1889, did not sign constn. Died Lander, Wyo., Jan. 12, 1893.

BALDWIN, Roger Sherman, senator, gov. Conn.; b. New Haven, Conn., Jan. 4, 1793; s. Simeon and Rebecca (Sherman) B.; grad. Yale, 1811, LL.D. (hon.), 1845; attended Litchfield (Conn.) Law Sch.; LL.D. (hon.), Trinity Coll., 1844; m. Emily Perkins 1820, 9 children. Admitted to Conn. bar, 1814; alderman, mem. Common Council, New Haven; mem. Conn. Senate, 1837, 38; noted for defense and securement of liberty (in assn. with John Quincy Adams) for mutinied slaves on the Cuban-owned ship Armistad, 1839; mem. Conn. Gen. Assembly 1840, 41; gov. Conn. (1st gov. under universal manhood sufferage), 1844-46; mem. U.S. Senate (Whig) from Conn., 1847-51; Republican presdl. elector, 1860; del. from Conn. to Nat. Peace Conf., Washington, D.C., 1861, mem. resolutions com. Died New Haven, Feb. 19, 1863; buried Grove Street Cemetery, New Haven.

BALDWIN, Simeon, congressman, jurist; b. Norwich, Conn., Dec. 14, 1761; s. Ebenezer and Bethiah (Barker) B.; grad. Yale, 1781; m. Rebecca Sherman, July 29, 1787; m. 2d, Mrs. Elizabeth Burr; 9 children, including Roger S. Baldwin. Admitted to New Haven (Conn.) bar, 1786; clerk of the U.S. Dist. and Circuit Cts. for Conn., 1789-1806; collector revenue, city alderman New Haven; mem. U.S. Ho. of Reps. from Conn., 8th Congress, 1803-05; judge Superior Ct. Conn., 1806, Conn. Supreme Ct. of Errors, 1808-18; mayor New Haven, 1826. Died May 26, 1851; buried Grove Street Cemetery New Haven.

BALDWIN, Sylvanus, architect; b. probably between 1787-92. Credited with design of 1st State house, Montpelier, Vt. (erected between 1809 and 1836).

BALDWIN, Theron, missionary; b. Goshen, Conn., July 21, 1801; s. Elisha and Clarissa (Judd) B.; grad. Yale, 1827, Divinity Sch., 1829; m. Caroline Wilder, 1831. Went to Ill. as one of Ill. Assn. from Yale dedicated to spreading religion and edn. in that state, 1829; became preacher, Vandalia, Ill.; helped found Ill. Coll., 1835; 1st prin. Monticello Sem. (sch. for girls), Godfrey, Ill., 1838-43; sec. Soc. for Promotion Collegiate and Theol. Edn. in West, N.Y.C., 1843-70, instrumental in establishment many instns. of higher learning including Western Res. U., Oberlin, Marietta, Grinnell, Beloit colls. Died Orange, N.J., Apr. 10, 1870.

BALDWIN, William, physician, botanist; b. Newlin, Pa., Mar. 29, 1779; s. Thomas and Elizabeth (Garretson) B.; M.D., U. Pa., 1807; m. Hannah M. Webster, 1808. Practiced medicine, Wilmington, Del., 1808-12; naval surgeon, St. Mary's, Ga., 1812-16; made bot. surveys of Del. and Ga., lived, collected specimens among Creek Indians in Ga. for several months; travelled to S.Am., 1816-17; apptd. botanist on expdn. to Rocky Mountains under command of Maj. Stephen H. Long, 1819. Died Franklin, Mo., Aug. 31, 1819.

BALESTIER, Charles Wolcott, publisher, author; b. Rochester, N.Y., Dec. 13, 1861; s. Henry and Anna (Smith) B.; attended Cornell U., 1881-82. Travelled in West and South, 1882-83; in charge of patent library Astor Library, N.Y.C., 1884; wrote 1st novel, 1884; editor Tid-bits (weekly mag.), 1885-86, Times (weekly humor publ.), 1886-89; partner Heinemann & Balestier, publishers English and Am. books in Europe, London, Eng., 1889-91. Author: (novels) A Potent Philtre, 1884, Benefits Forgot, 1894; (short stories) The Average Woman, 1892. Died Dresden, Germany, Dec. 6, 1891; buried Dresden.

BALL, Edward, congressman, lawyer; b. nr. Falls Church, Fairfax County, Va. Nov. 6, 1811; studied law. Moved to Ohio, farmed nr. Zanesville; dep. sheriff Muskingum County, 1837, 38, sheriff, 1839-43; mem. Ohio Ho. of Reps., 1845-49, 68-70; editor Zanesville Courier, 1849; mem. U.S. Ho. of Reps. (Whig) from Ohio, 33d-34th congresses, 1853-57; admitted to bar, 1860, practiced in Zanesville; del. Republican Nat. Conv., Chgo., 1860; Rep. presdl. elector, 1860; sergeant at arms of U.S. Ho. of Reps. in 37th Congress, 1861-63. Killed by railroad train nr. Zanesville, Nov. 22, 1872; buried Greenwood Cemetery.

BALL, Ephraim, inventor; b. Lake Twp., O., Aug. 12, 1812; m. Lavina Babbs, circa 1835. Carpenter, Stark County, O., circa 1832; built threshing machine (with brother), circa 1838, built factory for mfg. parts, Greentown, O., 1840, manufactured Blue Plough and Hussey Reaper during 1840's, reorganized firm with new partners, 1851; developed Ohio Mower (1st of 2-wheeled flexible mowers), patented, 1857, produced mower in his factory from 1859. Died Jan. 1, 1872.

BALL, William Lee congressman; b. Lancaster County, Va., Jan. 2, 1781; had liberal edn. Served as paymaster in War of 1812, with 92d Va. Regiment; mem. U.S. Ho. of Reps. (Democrat) from Va., 15th-18th congresses, 1817-Feb. 28, 1824. Died Washington, D.C., Feb. 28, 1824; buried Congressional Cemetery.

BALLARD, Bland Williams, frontiersman; b. Fredericksburg, Va., Oct. 16, 1759; s. Bland Ballard; no formal edn.; m. Elizabeth Williamson, 1783; m. 2d, Diana Matthews, Aug. 17, 1835; m. 3d, Mrs. Elizabeth Garrett, Oct. 28, 1841. In Ky., 1779-80, active in war against Indians; with Gen. George Rogers Clark, 1781-82; in war in Pickaway towns in Ohio; with Gen. Clark in expdn. against Indians on Wabash River, 1787; survived Indian attack on homestead in Shelbyville, Ky., 1787; participated in Battle of Fallen Timbers, 1793; became farmer in Shelbyville; mem. Ky. Legislature for 5 terms between 1703-1810; participated in Battle of Tippecanoe, 1811; served with Col. John Allen's Regt. in War of 1812, at Battle of Raisin River, 1813. Died Shelbyville, Sept. 5, 1853; buried State Cemetery, Frankfort, Ky.

BALLOU, Adin Augustus, reformer; b. Cumberland County, R.I., Apr. 23, 1803; s. Ariel and Edilda (Tower) B.; m. Abigail Sayles, 1822; m. 2d, Lucy Hunt, 1830; children—Abigail (Ballou) Heywood, Adin Augustus. A founder Mass. Assn. Universalist Restorationists, 1831; editor Independent Messenger, 1831-39, The Practical Christian; founder, pres. Hopedale Community, Milford, Mass., (19th century Christian Utopian colony), 1841; opposed to slavery, war and intemperance. Author: Memoirs of Adin Augustus Ballou, 1853; Practical Christian Socialism, 1854; Primitive Christianity and its Corruptions, 1870; History of the Hopedale Community, 1897. Died Hopedale (part of Milford), Aug. 5, 1890.

BALLOU, Hosea, clergyman; b. Richmond, N.H., Apr. 30, 1771; s. Maturin and Lydia (Harris) B.; attended acad., Richmond, N.H., 1790; m. Ruth Washburn, Sept. 11, 1796, 1 son, Maturin. Became mem. Universalist Ch., 1791; taught sch., R.I., also Mass., 1791-94; ordained to ministry Universalist Ch., 1794; circuit preacher based from Dana, Mass., 1796-1803, Barnard, Vt., 1803-09; pastor in Portsmouth, N.H., 1809-15; founder Gospel Visitant (1st Universalist quarterly), Portsmouth, 1811; pastor in Salem, Mass., 1815-18, 2d Universalist Ch., Boston, 1818-52; editor Universalist Mag., 1819-28, Universalist Expositor, 1830-52; popular exponent of developing Unitarian theology as distinct from orthodox Calvinism. Author: Treatise on the Doctrine of the Atonement, 1805; Examination of the Doctrine of Future Retribution, 1834. Died Boston, June 7, 1852; buried Mt. Auburn Cemetery, Cambridge, Mass.

BALLOU, Hosea II, clergyman, coll. pres.; b. Guilford, Vt., Oct. 18, 1796; s. Asahel and Martha (Starr) B.; D.D. (hon.), Harvard, 1845; m. Clarissa Hatch, Jan. 26, 1820, 5 children. Ordained to ministry Universalist Ch., 1817; pastor, Stafford, Conn., 1817-21, New Universalist Ch., Roxbury, Mass., 1821-38; editor Universalist Mag., 1822, Universalist Expositor, 1830-40; bd. overseers Harvard, 1843-58; incorporated Tufts U., 1852, 1st pres., 1854-61; mem. Mass. Bd. Edn., 1854; editor Universalist Quar. and Gen. Review, 1844-56. Author: Ancient History of Universalism, 1829. Died Somerville, Mass., May 27, 1861.

BALLOU, Maturin Murray, author; b. Bosto Apr. 14, 1820; s. Rev. Hosea and Ruth (Wasl burn) B.; attended English High Sch., Boston; r Mary Anne Roberts, Sept. 15, 1839. Clk., Bosto Post Office, 1839; travelled widely in U.S. ar abroad during 1840's and 1850's, gathered materi for books and mag. articles; dep. naval agt. Bo ton Customs House, circa 1845; founded what b came Ballou's Pictorial (one of 1st illustrate newspapers in U.S.), circa 1850; 1st editor Bostc Daily Globe, 1872-74. Author: The Naval Office 1845; The History of Cuba, 1854; Due West; Round the World in Ten Months, 1884; Under tl Southern Cross; or Travels in Australia, Ta mania, New Zealand, Samoa, and other Pacif Islands, 1888. Died Boston, Mar. 27, 1895; burie Boston.

BALTES, Peter Joseph, clergyman; b. Enshein Bavaria, Apr. 7, 1820; brought to Oswego, N.Y circa 1826; attended Holy Cross Coll. Ordaine priest Roman Catholic Ch., Montreal, 185 worked in parishes in Ill.; became vicar gen theologian to Bishop Juncker at 2d Plenary Cou cil at Balt., 1866; consecrated bishop of Alton, Il at Belleville Cathedral (which he had built), 187 active in exactness of liturgical ceremony, eccle discipline, ch. property law. Died Alton, Feb. 1 1886.

BALTIMORE, 1st baron, see Calvert, George.

BALTIMORE, 3d baron, see Calvert, Charles.

BALTIMORE, 1st lord, see Calvert, Leonard.

BALTIMORE, 2d lord, see Calvert, Cecil.

BAMBOROUGH, William, artist; b. Durham Eng., 1792; m. Lucy, at least 1 child, Mary. Cam to U.S., settled in Columbus, O., 1819; travele with John James Audubon in South between 182 and 1832; worked at Shippenport, O., 1830, Louis ville, Ky., 1832, at Columbus, O., 1850; painte portraits. Died 1860.

BANCROFT, Aaron, clergyman; b. Reading Mass., Nov. 10, 1755; s. Samuel and Lydia (Parl er) B.; grad. Lucretia Chandler, 13 children i cluding George, Mary. Licensed to preach Congregational Ch., 1780, preacher in N.S., 178 83; went to Worcester, 1783, served interim pa torate but rejected for permanent post because his Arminian views in theology; became past voluntary religious soc. in Worcester (1st paris in Central Mass. to break from Congl. Ch. f doctrinal reasons); following schism in Cong Ch. (1815) betwen Unitarians and Calvinists, le his church to Unitarian side; contbr. to Christia Register; 1st pres. Am. Unitarian Assn., 1825-3 Author: Life of Washington, 1807; Sermons o Christian Doctrine, 1822. Died Worcester, Au 19, 1839; buried Worcester.

BANCROFT, Edward, inventor, Brit. agt.; b Westfield, Mass., Jan. 9, 1744; no formal ed Went to England, circa 1770, became contb articles on Am. to Monthly Review; acquainte with Benjamin Franklin, London; served as ag for Franklin in London, at outbreak of An Revolution; agt. for Silas Deane (Am. commr.) France while under pay Brit. govt., until 1783 gave to Brit. govt. information regarding treati and movements of troops and ships from Franc to Am. during Revolution; lived in Eng. aft 1783; invented dyes for use in textile mfg.; mem Royal Soc. Author: Essay on the Natural Histor of Guiana, 1769; Experimental Researches Con cerning the Philosophy of Permanent Colors, 1794 Died Margate, Eng., Sept. 8, 1821; buried Mar gate.

BANCROFT, George, historian, sec. of navy, dip lomat; b. Worcester, Mass., Oct. 3, 1800; s. Aaro and Lucretia (Chandler) B.; grad. Harvard, 1817 Ph.D., M.A., U. Gottingen (Germany), 1820 D.C.L. (hon.), Oxford (Eng.) U., 1849; m. Sarah H Dwight, Mar. 1, 1827; m. 2d, Mrs. Elizabeth (Dav is) Bliss; 3 children. A founder Round Hill Sch. Northampton, Mass., 1823; wrote series on "Ger man Literature," published in Am. Quarterly Re view, 1827-28 (1st comprehensive treatment German literature and philosophy to appear i Am.); collector Port of Boston, 1838; a Mass. de to Democratic Nat. Conv., 1844; U.S. sec. of navy 1845-46, established U.S. Naval Acad., Annapolis Md., 1845; U.S. minister to Gt. Britain, 1846-49 to Prussia, 1867-71, to German Empire, 1871-74 correspondent Inst. of France; pres. Am. Geog Soc.; devoted most of his time and energies t writing of History of the United States in whic he expounded his democratic theories. Autho History of the United States, 10 vols., 1834-74 Literary and Historical Miscellanies, 1855; Histor of the Formulation of the Constitution of th United States, 1886; Martin Van Buren to th End of his Public Career, 1889. Died Washington D.C., Jan. 17, 1891.

BANGS, Francis Nehemiah, lawyer; b. N.Y.C. Feb. 23, 1828; s. Rev. Nathan and Mary (Bolton B.; grad. Coll. City N.Y., 1845; attended Yale La

Sch., 1845-circa 1848; m. Frances Bull, Mar. 12, 1855; m. 2d, Mary Batcheller; 1 son, John Kendrick. Admitted to N.Y.C. bar, 1850; specialist in comml. and bankruptcy law; prominent in investigation of Tweed Ring, 1871, 72; instrumental in removal several corrupt judges on N.Y. State and N.Y.C. bench; later active in railway and corp. cases; pres. N.Y.C. Bar Assn., 1882-83; a founder Union League Club, N.Y.C. Died Ocala, Fla., Nov. 30, 1885.

BANGS, Nathan, clergyman; b. Stratford, Conn., May 2, 1778; s. Lemuel and Rebecca (Keeler) B.; ed. common schs.; m. Mary Bloton, Apr. 23, 1806, 1 son, Francis Nehemiah. Licensed to preach in Methodist Ch., 1801; itinerant preacher, Upper Canada, 1801; admitted to Meth. Conf. as elder, 1804; built substantial Meth. community in Que., Can., 1804-12; presiding Meth. elder in N.Y. State, 1812-20; worked for separation church and state in Conn.; agt. Book Concern (publisher Meth. literature), N.Y., 1820-36; editor Methodist Mag. and Methodist Quarterly Review in 1820's; founder Meth. Missionary Soc., circa 1830; acting pres. Wesleyan U., Middletown, Conn., 1841. Author: Errors of Hopkinsianism, 1815; Vindication of Methodist Episcopacy, 1820; History of the Methodist Episcopal Church, 4 vols., 1838-40. Died May 3, 1862.

BANISTER, John, botanist; b. Twigwoth, Eng., 1650; s. John Bannister; grad. Magdalen Coll., Oxford (Eng.) U., 1671, M.A., 1674; m. 1688. Came to Charles City County, Va., 1678, owned land on Appomattox River and acted as minister to Bristol Parish; engaged in studies local flora and fauna from his arrival, corresponded about his studies with other scientists including Compton, Sloane and Ray; trustee Coll. William and Mary, from circa 1690; part of his herbarium now in collection Brit. Museum; many of his scientific articles published posthumously in Philosophical Transactions of Royal Acad. Died nr. Roanoke River, Va., May 1692.

BANISTER, John, Continental congressman, army officer; b. Bristol Parish, Va., Dec. 26, 1734; s. John and Willmuth (or Wilmet, or Wilmette) Banister; m. Patsy Bland; m. 2d, Anne Blair. Mem. Middle Temple, 1753; mem. Va. Conv., 1776; mem. Va. Ho. of Burgesses, 1777; mem. Continental Congress from Va., 1778-79, a framer and signer Articles of Confederation, lt. col. Va. Cavalry in Revolutionary War, 1778-81. Died Sept. 30, 1788; buried on family estate Hatcher's Run, nr. Petersburg, Va.

BANISTER, Zilpah Grant, educator; b. Norfolk, Conn., May 30, 1794; d. Joel and Zilpah (Cowles) Grant; attended common schs., Norfolk; seminary, Byfield, Mass., 1823-24; m. William B. Banister, Sept. 7, 1841. Began to teach in dist. schs., East Norfolk, Conn., 1809; taught in Winchester, Conn., 1809-11, Norfolk, 1811-23; prin. Adams Female Acad., Derry, N.J., 1824-28; prin. own sch. for girls, Ipswich, Mass., 1828-39, her teaching stressed study English, Bible and scis.; retired from teaching following her marriage. Died probably Newburyport, Mass., Dec. 3, 1874.

BANKS, John, congressman, lawyer; b. nr. Lewisburg, Juniata County, Pa., Oct. 17, 1793; studied law. Admitted to bar, 1819; practiced in Juniata County, 1819, Mercer County, Pa.; mem. U.S. Ho. of Reps. (Whig) from Pa., 22d-24th congresses, 1831-36, resigned; judge Berks Jud. Dist., 1836, resigned to accept state position; treas. of Pa., 1847; practiced in Reading, Pa. Died Reading, Apr. 3, 1864; buried Charles Evans Cemetery.

BANKS, Linn, congressman; b. Madison (then Culpeper) County, Va., Jan. 23, 1784; studied law. Admitted to Madison County bar, 1809; mem. Va. Ho. of Dels., 1812-38, speaker 20 successive years; mem. U.S. Ho. of Reps. (Democrat, filled vacancy, contested election) from Va., 25th-27th congresses, Apr. 28, 1838-Dec. 6, 1841, practiced law; served as col. in Va. Militia. Drowned while attempting to ford Conway River nr. Wolftown, Va., Jan. 13, 1842; buried family burying ground on his estate nr. Graves Mill, Madison County.

BANKS, Nathanial Prentiss, gov. Mass., congressman; b. Waltham, Mass., Jan. 30, 1816; s. Nathanial P. and Rebecca (Greenwood) B.; m. Mary Palmer, Mar. 1847, 3 children, including Maude, Admitted to Mass. bar, 1839; mem. lower house Mass. Legislature, 1849, speaker, 1851; pres. Mass. Constl. Conv., 1853; mem. U.S. Ho. of Reps. from Mass., 33d-34th, 39th-42d, 44th-45th, 51st congresses, 1853-57, 65-73, 75-79, 89-91, speaker, 1856-57; governor of Mass., 1858-60; served with U.S. Volunteers during Civil War, from 1861, comdr. 5th Corps, Dept. of Shenandoah, U.S. Army Upper Potomac, 1861, Shenandoah Valley, 1862, led unsuccessful attack at Cedar Mountain, 1862, captured Port Hudson, 1863; apptd. U.S. marshall for Mass., 1879-88; called the Bobbin Boy. Died Waltham, Sept. 1, 1894; buried Grove Hill Cemetery, Waltham.

BANNEKER, Benjamin, mathematician, abolitionist; b. Ellicott's Mills, Md., Nov. 9, 1731; s. Robert and Mary B.; ed. at home; attended integrated neighborhood sch. for a time. Inherited his father's farm; showed unusual mechanical ability, constructed a wooden clock with no previous training; took part in gentlemen's game of exchanging difficult math. problems; began making astron. calculations for almanacs, circa 1773; accurately calculated an eclipse, 1789, soon after sold his farm, concentrated on study of mathematics and astronomy; named to Capitol Commn. (1st presdl. appointment granted a Negro); assisted L'Enfant in survey of D.C., 1790; published in almanac, 1792, wrote dissertation on bees; did study of locust plague cycles; wrote famous letter to Jefferson on segregationist trends in Am. Died Balt., Oct. 1806.

BANNER, Peter, architect; b. England; flourished 1794-1828. 1 son, Peter. Arrived Boston, 1794, carpenter, 1795-98; became interested in architecture, circa 1806; designed Park Street Ch., Boston (noted for its New Eng. spire); designed Old South Parsonage House, Boston, 1809; designed 1st building which housed Am. Antiquarian Soc., Worcester, Mass., 1819.

BANNING, Henry Blackstone, congressman, lawyer; b. Bannings Mills, O., Nov. 10, 1836; attended Mt. Vernon (O.) Acad., also Kenyon Coll., Gambier, O.; studied law. Admitted to bar, 1857; practiced in Mt. Vernon; enlisted as pvt. Union Army in Civil War, 1861; commd. capt. 4th Regt., Ohio Volunteer Inf., 1861, col. 87th Regt., 1862, commd. lt. col. 125th Regt., 1863, later transferred to 121st Regt., 1863, col., 1863; brevetted brig. gen. and maj. gen. Volunteers for gallant and meritorious services during Civil War, 1865; resigned from Army, 1865; mem. Ohio Ho. of Reps., 1866, 67; moved to Cincinnati, 1869, practiced law; mem. U.S. Ho. of Reps. (Democrat) from Ohio, 43d-45th congresses, 1873-79. Died Cincinnati, Dec. 10, 1881; buried Spring Grove Cemetery.

BANNISTER, Nathaniel Harrington, playwright; b. either Del. or Balt., Jan. 13, 1813; m. Amelia (Greene) Stone, 1835. Made debut as actor at Front Street Theatre, Balt., 1830; his 1st play Rathanemus opened at Camp Street Theatre, Phila., 1835; his early plays followed hist. and contemporary themes such as Life in Philadelphia; or, the Unfortunate Author (produced at Walnut Street Theatre, Phila., 1838), The Syracusan (Franklin Theatre, N.Y.C., 1838); his most successful play was Putnam (Bowery Theatre, N.Y.C., 1844). Author: (published plays) Gaulantus, 1836; England's Iron Days, 1837; The Three Brothers, 1840. Died N.Y.C., Nov. 2, 1847.

BANVARD, John, painter, author; b. N.Y.C., Nov. 15, 1815; s. Daniel Banvard; married, had children. Began profl. career by touring Wabash River with floating art gallery; later exhibited paintings in New Orleans, Natchez, Louisville and Cincinnati; operated museum, St. Louis; began touring Mississippi River by skiff to make sketches for panorama of the river, spring 1840 (completed Panorama of the Mississippi covered ½ mile of canvas, was exhibited throughout U.S., also London); toured Europe, Africa, Asia; painted Panorama of the Nile; painted The Orison (from which 1st Am. chromo was taken). Author: A Description of the Mississippi River, 1849; A Pilgrimage to the Holy Land, 1852; Carrina, 1875; The Tradition of the Temple, 1876. Died Watertown, S.D., May 16, 1891.

BANVARD, Joseph, clergyman; b. N.Y.C., May 9, 1810; s. Daniel Banvard; grad. Newton Theol. Sem., 1835. Pastor, Second Baptist Ch., Salem, Mass. for 11 years, later in Boston, West Cambridge, Mass., Pawtucket, R.I., Worcester, Mass., and N.Y.; pres. Nat. Theol. Inst., Washington, D.C., 1866. Author: The Christian Melodist; A Collection of Hymns, 1850; Novelties of the New World, 1852; The American Statesman; or Illustrations of the Life and Character of Daniel Webster, 1853; Old Grips and Little Tidd, 1873; Soldiers and Patriots of the Revolution, 1876. Died Neponset, Mass., Sept. 28, 1887.

BAPST, John, missionary, coll. rector; b. La Roche, Fribourg, Switzerland, Dec. 17, 1815; grad. Coll. of St. Michel, La Roche, 1846. Joined Soc. of Jesus; ordained priest Roman Catholic Ch., 1846; came to U.S., circa 1847; missionary among Abnaki Indians, Oldtown, Me.; later became parish priest in Protestant town of Ellsworth, Me., tarred, feathered and driven out of Ellsworth because of his protests to sch. council which required Cath. children to participate in Protestant religious exercises; 1st rector Boston Coll., 1862-69; built St. Joseph Ch., Providence, R.I., 1877. Died Woodstock, Me., Nov. 2, 1887.

BARANOV, Alexander Andrevich, fur trader; b. 1746. Mcht., Kargopol, Russia; moved to Siberia, 1780; took over trading companies of G.I. Shelekhov, Alaska, 1790, organized companies into Russian Am. Co., Alaska, 1799; traded primarily in sea-otter skins, left Alaska, 1818. Died aboard ship Kutuzov, Apr. 27, 1819.

BARAZA, Frederic, missionary; b. Dobernig, Germany, June 29, 1797; s. Johann and Maria Katherin (Josefa) B.; grad. U. Vienna. Ordained as priest Roman Catholic Ch., 1823; administered to various parishes in Germany, 1823-30; arrived in Cincinnati, 1831; began missionary work among Ottawa Indians, Arbre Croche (now Harbor Springs), Mich., 1831; operated mission near present site of Grand Rapids, Mich., 1833-35; missionary at La Pointe, Madeline Island, 1835-38; went to Europe to raise funds, 1838; returned to N.W. to continue his work, 1839; bishop of Upper Mich., 1853-68. Compiler: Theoretical and Practical Grammar of the Otchepive Language, 1850; Dictionary of the Otchepive Language, 1853. Died Marquette, Mich., Jan. 19, 1868.

BARBEE, William Randolph, sculptor; b. nr. Luray, Va., Jan. 17, 1818; studied law. Admitted to Va. bar, 1843, practiced in Luray, 10 years; gave up law for sculpture; worked with Hart and Powers in Italy; exhibited his prin. works The Coquette and The Fisher Girl in Richmond (Va.), Balt. and N.Y.C., 1858-59; failed to secure commn. for work on U.S. Capitol, 1857; obtained ofcl. patronage and had studio in Capitol before and after Civil War; executed plaster bust of Speaker of House Orr, exhibited at Pa. Acad., 1859-60. Died "Barbee Bower" nr. Luray, June 16, 1868.

BARBELIN, Felix Joseph, clergyman, coll. pres.; b. Luneville, Lorraine, May 30, 1808; ed. French schs. and sems. Joined Soc. of Jesus in Md., 1831; taught at Georgetown U.; became pastor St. Joseph's, Phila., 1838; built a hosp.; active in care of the young; became 1st pres. St. Joseph's Coll., 1852. Died Phila., June 8, 1869.

BARBER, Daniel, clergyman; b. Simsbury, Conn., Oct. 2, 1756. Served in Am. Revolution; became a minister Episcopalian Ch., at age 30; preached in Schenectady, N.Y., Claremont, N.H.; converted to Roman Catholic Ch., 1819. Author: Catholic Worships and Piety Explained, 1821; History of My Own Times, 1827. Died St. Inigoes, Md., 1834.

BARBER, Francis, army officer; b. Princeton, N.J., 1751; grad. Princeton, 1767; m. Mary Ogden; m. 2d, Anne Ogden. Rector of academy, Elizabethtown, N.J., circa 1769-76; maj. 3d N.J. Regt., 1776, lt. col., 1776; took part in Princeton campaign, battles of Brandywine and Germantown; asst. insp. gen. to Gen. von Steuben, Valley Forge; wounded at Battle of Monmouth; transferred to 1st N.J. Regt., 1781; quelled mutiny of underpaid soldiers from Pa. and N.J., thereby winning commendation of Gen. Washington; commanded battallion of light infantry under Lafayette at Battle of Green Spring. Killed by falling tree while army was stationed at Newburgh, N.Y., Feb. 11, 1783.

BARBER, Joel Allen, congressman, lawyer; b. Georgia, nr. St. Albans, Franklin County, Vt., Jan. 17, 1809; attended Georgia Acad., U. Vt.; studied law. Admitted to Prince Georges County (Md.) bar, 1834; taught sch., Prince Georges County; practiced law, Fairfield, Vt.; moved to Wis., 1837, lived in Lancaster, Grant County, practiced law; clk. Grant County, 4 years, dist. atty., 3 terms; mem. Wis. 1st Constl. Conv., 1846; mem. Wis. Assembly, 1852-53, 63-64, speaker, 1864; mem. Wis. Senate, 1856, 57; founder Lancaster Acad.; mem. U.S. Ho. of Reps. (Republican) from Wis., 42d-43d congresses, 1871-75. Died Lancaster, June 17, 1881; buried Hillside Cemetery.

BARBER, John Warner, engraver, historian; b. East Windsor, Conn., Feb. 2, 1798; s. Elijah and Mary (Warner) B.; m. Harriet Lines; m. 2d, Ruth Green; 4 children. Apprentice engraver under Abner Reed, East Windsor, 1814-21; operated own engraving business, New Haven, Conn., 1823; primarily interested in writing hist. and religious works (for which he engraved illustrations). Author: Historical Sciences in the United States, 1827; Our Whole Country, or the Past and Present of the United States, Historical and Descriptive, 1861; Religious Allegories, 1866. Died New Haven, June 22, 1885.

BARBER, Levi, congressman; b. Simsbury, Hartford County, Conn., Oct. 16, 1777. Moved to Ohio; surveyor for Fed. Govt.; mem. Ohio Ho. of Reps., 1806; commd. receiver U.S. land office, Marietta, O., 1807; aide to Gov. Meigs during War of 1812; mem. U.S. Ho. of Reps. from Ohio, 15th, 17th congresses, 1817-19, 21-23; clk. Ct. Common Pleas and Ct. of Washington County; justice of peace; pres. Bank of Marietta. Died Harmar (now part of Marietta), O., Apr. 23, 1833; buried Harmar Cemetery.

BARBER, Noyes, congressman, mcht.; b. Groton, Conn., Apr. 28, 1781; attended common schs. Became merchant; maj. 8th Conn. Regt. in War of 1812, detailed to defend coast towns during blockade by Brit. fleet; mem. Conn. Ho. of Reps., 1818;

mem. U.S. Ho. of Reps. (Democrat) from Conn., 17th-23d congresses, 1821-35; mem. Conn. Whig convs., from 1836. Died Groton, Jan. 3, 1844; buried Starr Cemetery.

BARBER, Virgil, clergyman; b. Claremont, N.H., May 9, 1782; son of Daniel Barber; married, 4 daus., 1 son. An Episcopalian minister; prin. Fairfield Acad., nr. Utica, N.Y.; converted (with wife and children) to Roman Catholic Ch.; joined Soc. of Jesus, served Indian missions in Me., taught at Georgetown U. (wife became Visitation nun, daus. Ursulines, son a Jesuit). Died Georgetown, Mar. 25, 1847.

BARBOT, Louis J., architect; ed. Charleston, S.C.; began study of architecture in office of Edward C. Jones, 1849; possibly father of Decimus C. Barbot. Practiced as architect, Charleston, until 1887; asso. with John H. Seyle (a builder).

BARBOUR, James, senator, sec. of war; b. Barboursville, Va., June 10, 1775; s. Col. Thomas and Mary (Thomas) B.; D.C.L. (hon.), Oxford (Eng.) U., 1829; m. Lucy Johnson, 1792, 5 children. Admitted to Va. bar, 1794; supported Va. resolutions of 1798; mem. Va. Ho. of Dels., 1798-1812, speaker. 1809, drew up bill which established Va. Literary Fund, 1810; gov. Va., 1812-15; mem. U.S. Senate (Democrat) from Va., 1815-25, chmn. coms. mil. affairs, fgn. relations; U.S. sec. of war, 1825-28; apptd. U.S. minister to Gt. Britain, 1828-29; pres. Va. Agrl. Soc. Died Orange County, Va., June 7, 1842.

BARBOUR, John Strode, congressman, lawyer; b. Fleetwood, nr. Brandy Station, Culpeper County, Va., Aug. 8, 1790; grad. Coll. William and Mary, 1808; studied law. Admitted to bar, 1811; practiced in Culpeper, Va.; a.d.c. to Gen. Madison in War of 1812; mem. Va. Ho. of Dels., 1813-16, 20-23, 33, 34; mem. U.S. Ho. of Reps. (State Rights Democrat) from Va., 18th-22d congresses, 1823-33; mem. Va. Constl. Convs., 1828, 30; chmn. Nat. Dem. Conv., Balt., 1852. Died Fleetwood, Jan. 12, 1855; buried family burying ground on his estate.

BARBOUR, John Strode, Jr., railroad exec., congressman; b. Culpeper County, Va., Dec. 29, 1820; s. John S. and Eliza A (Byrne) B.; B.L., U. Va., 1842; m. Susan Daingerfield, 1865. Mem. Va. Ho. of Dels., 1847-51; dir. Orange & Alexandria R.R. Co., became pres., 1852; mem. U.S. Ho. of Reps. from Va., 47th-49th congresses, 1881-87; mem. Nat. Democratic Com., 1884-92; mem. U.S. Senate from Va., 1889-92. Died Culpeper County, May 14, 1892; buried "Poplar Hill," Prince Georges County, Md.

BARBOUR, Lucien, congressman, lawyer; b. Canton, Hartford County, Conn., Mar. 4, 1811; grad. Amherst (Mass.) Coll., 1837; studied law. Moved to Ind., 1837, lived in Madison, Jefferson County; admitted to bar, 1838, practiced in Indpls., 1839; arbitrator between State of Ind. and pvt. corps., numerous times; apptd. by Pres. Polk as U.S. dist. atty. for Dist. of Ind.; mem. commn. to codify laws of Ind., 1852; mem. U.S. Ho. of Reps., (Free Soil, Temperance, Know Nothing parties) from Ind., 34th Congress, 1855-57; affiliated with Republican Party from 1860. Died Indpls., July 19, 1880; buried Crown Hill Cemetery.

BARBOUR, Oliver Lorenzo, lawyer, author; b. Cambridge, N.Y., July 12, 1811; s. Oliver and Rosamond (Walworth) B.; m. Elizabeth Berry, Nov. 19, 1832. Admitted to N.Y. bar, 1832; confidential clk. to Judge Reuben Hyde Walworth, Saratoga Springs, N.Y.; gave up law practice for legal writing. Author: Analytical Digest of Equity Cases, 1837; Magistrates Criminal Law, 1841; A Treatise on the Practice of the Court of Chancery, 1843; Reports on Cases in Law and Equity in the Supreme Court of the State of New York, 1848-78; A Treatise on the Rights of Persons and the Rights of Property, 1890. Died Saratoga Springs, N.Y, Dec. 17, 1889.

BARBOUR, Philip Pendleton, asso. justice U.S. Supreme Ct.; b. Orange County, Va., May 25, 1783; s. Col. Thomas and Mary (Thomas) B.; ed. Coll. William and Mary; m. Frances Johnson, 1804, 7 children. Mem. Va. Ho. of Dels. from Orange County. 1812-14; mem. U.S. Ho. of Reps. from Va., 13th-18th, 20th-21st congresses, 1814-25, 1827-30, speaker, 1821-23; mem. Va. Constl. Conv., 1829-30; judge U.S. Dist. Ct. of Eastern Va., 1830-36; candidate for vice pres. U.S., running against Van Buren, 1832; asso. justice U.S. Supreme Ct., 1836-41. Died Washington, D.C., Feb. 25, 1841; buried Congressional Cemetery, Washington.

BARCLAY, David, congressman, lawyer; b. Punxsutawney, Jefferson County, Pa., 1823; attended Washington (now Washington and Jefferson) Coll.; studied law, Pitts. Admitted to bar; practiced in Punxsutawney, also Brookville, Kittanning, Pa.; an editor and publisher Pittsburgh Union and Legal Journal, 1850-55; mem. U.S. Ho. of Reps. (Democrat) from Pa., 34th Congress, 1855-57. Died Freeport, Armstrong County, Pa., Sept. 10, 1889; buried Freeport Cemetery.

BARCLAY, Thomas, Loyalist, diplomat; b. N.Y.C. Oct. 12, 1753; s. Henry and Mary (Rutgers) B.; ed. Columbia; m. Susanna De Lancey, Oct. 2, 1775. Commd. maj. Loyalist forces in N.Y., 1777, fled to Can. at end of Am. Revolution; held office under Brit. govt. in N.S., circa 1781-circa 1811, also speaker of assembly, adj. gen. N.S. militia, commissary for prisoners; commr. to carry out terms of Jay Treaty, 1795; consul gen. N.Y., 1799-1830; commr. under 4th and 5th articles Treaty of Ghent; consul of Gt. Britain for Northern and Eastern states in U.S., 1802-12. Died N.Y.C., Apr. 21, 1830.

BARD, David, congressman, clergyman; b. Carroll's Delight, Adams County, Pa., 1744; grad. Princeton, 1773; studied theology. Licensed to preach by Donegal Presbytery, 1777; ordained to ministry Presbyn. Ch., at Lower Conotheague, 1779; missionary in Va. and West of Allegheny Mountains; pastor at Bedford, Pa., 1786-89, Frankstown (now Hollidaysburg), Blair County, Pa.; mem. U.S. Ho. of Reps. from Pa., 4th-5th, 8th-14th congresses, 1795-99, 1803-15. Died Alexandria, Huntingdon County, Pa., Mar. 12, 1815; buried Sinking Valley Cemetery, nr. Arch Spring, Blair County.

BARD, John, physician; b. Burlington, N.J., Feb. 1, 1716; s. Peter Bard; m. Miss Valleau, 1 son, Samuel. One of 1st to conduct dissections for ednl. purposes; 1st to record extra-uterine pregnancy, 1759; apptd. health officer N.Y.C., 1759; 1st pres. Med. Soc. State N.Y., 1795. Died Hyde Park, N.Y., Mar. 30, 1799.

BARD, Samuel, physician, educator; b. Phila., Apr. 1, 1742; s. John and Mrs. (Valleau) B.; grad. King's Coll. (now Columbia), 1760; M.D., U. Edinburgh (Scotland), 1765; LL.D. (hon.), Princeton, 1816; m. Mary Bard, 1770, 10 children, including William. Prof. medicine Knig's Coll., 1769-89, dean faculty, trustee, prof. theory and practice of physics, 1792, pres. Coll. Phys. and Surg., N.Y.C., 1811-21; personal physician to George Washington in N.Y.C. after Am. Revolution; a founder City Library, N.Y. Dispensary; pres. Agrl. Soc. of Dutchess County, Hyde Park, N.Y.; founder Protestant Episcopal Ch., Hyde Park. Author: The Shepherd's Guide; De Viribus Opii, 1765; The Use of Cold In Hemorrhage, 1807. Died Hyde Park, May 24, 1821.

BARD, William, life ins. exec.; b. N.Y.C., Apr. 4, 1778; s. Dr. Samuel and Mary Bard; grad. Columbia. 1797; m. Catherine Cruger, Oct. 7, 1802. Organizer, became pres., actuary N.Y. Life Ins. & Trust Co. (1st company to specialize in life ins.), 1830; published booklet replying to criticism of life ins. and predicting its rapid devel., 1832. Died Staten Island N.Y., Oct. 17, 1853.

BARING, Alexander, (1st baron Ashburton), diplomat; b. Eng., Oct. 27, 1774; s. Sir Francis and Harriet (Herring) B.; D.C.L., Oxford (Eng.) U.; m. Anne Bingham, 1798, several children. Spent early years in his father's banking house, Eng.; sent to Am. by his father, formed close ties with several U.S. banking houses; returned to Eng., became head of firm, 1810; mem. Parliament for Taunton, 1806-26, for Callington, 1826-31, Thetford, 1831-32, North Essex, 1832-35; strong antagonist of reform; chancellor of exchequer, 1832; pres. bd. trade and master of mint, 1834; created 1st baron of Ashburton, 1835; sent to U.S. to conclude Webster-Ashburton Treaty (provided compromise settling N.E boundary of Me., extradition regulations, mut. suppression of slave-trade off African coast), 1842; disapproved free-trade projects of Robert Peel, opposed Charter Act of 1844; trustee Brit. Museum, Nat. Gallery. Author: An Enquiry into the Causes and Consequences of the Orders in Council, 1808; The Financial and Commercial Crisis Considered, 1847. Died Bath, Eng., May 13, 1848.

BARK, John Daly, playwright, historian; b. Ireland, circa 1775; attended Trinity Coll., Dublin. Came to U.S., 1796; founder unsuccessful paper, Polar Star and Boston Daily Advertiser, 1796; produced play Bunker Hill, or the Death of General Warren, 1797; moved to N.Y.C., 1797, unsuccesfully published Time Piece; produced Female Patriotism, or the Death of Joan D'Arc, 1798; moved to Petersburg, Va. Author: A History of the Late War in Ireland, 1799; (plays) Innkeeper of Abbeville; The Death of General Montgomery in Storming the City of Quebec, 1797; Bethlem Gabor, Lord of Transylvania. Killed in duel, Apr. 11, 1808.

BARKER, Benjamin Fordyce, physician; b. Wilton, Me., May 2, 1818; s. Dr. John and Phoebe (Abbott) B.; grad. Bowdoin Coll., 1837, M.D., 1841; m. Elizabeth Dwight, Sept. 14, 1843. Prof. obstetrics Bowdoin Med. Coll., 1844; pres. Conn. Med. Soc., 1848; an incorporator, prof. obstetrics N.Y. Med. Coll., 1849; pres. N.Y. State Med. Soc., 1856; prof. obstetrics and diseases of women Bellvue Hosp. Med. Sch., N.Y.C., 1861; founded, 1st pres. Am. Gynecol. Soc.; pres. N.Y. Acad Medicine, 1882; 1st Am. physician to use hypodermic syringe. Author: Puerperal Diseases (translated into 6 langs.), 1874. Died N.Y.C., May 30, 1891.

BARKER, David, Jr., congressman, lawyer; b. Stratham, N.H., Jan. 8, 1797; attended Phillips Exeter (N.H.) Acad.; grad. Harvard, 1815; studied law. Admitted to bar, 1819; practiced in Rochester, N.H.; mem. N.H. Ho. of Reps., 1823, 25, 26; mem. U.S. Ho. of reps. from N.H., 20th Congress, 1827-29; an original mem. N.H. Hist. Soc. Died Rochester, Apr. 1, 1834; buried Old Rochester Cemetery.

BARKER, David R., artist; b. Westchester County, N.Y., 1806. Employed as grocery clk. and penmanship instr.; became portrait painter; painted in N.Y.C., 1836-48, exhibited at N.A.D., Apollo Assn.; painted portraits and miniatures, Charleston, S.C., 1848-49; returned to N.Y.C., 1849, exhibited at Am. Inst., N.A.D.; maintained auction house, N.Y.C., 1856-71. Died N.Y.C., Mar. 14/15, 1881.

BARKER, Jacob, banker, legislator; b. Swan Island, Me., Dec. 17, 1779; s. Robert and Sarah (Folger) B.; m. Elizabeth Hazard, 1801, 12 children. A founder Soc. of Tammany Hall; founder Exchange Bank, Wall St., N.Y.C., 1815; founder newspaper Union in support of Gov. Clinton; dir. Life & Fire Ins. Co., N.Y.C. (failed in depression of 1826); helped carry Gilbert Stuart portrait from burning White House under direction of Dolly Madison, 1814; mem. N.Y. Senate, 1816; admitted to New Orleans bar, 1834; pres. Bank of Commerce, New Orleans, until 1869. Died Phila., Dec. 26, 1871.

BARKER, James Nelson, dramatist, mayor Phila.; b. Phila., June 17, 1784; s. Gen. John Barker; m. Mary Rogers, June 1811. Commd. capt. 2d U.S. Arty., 1812; commd. maj., asst. adj. gen. U.S. Army 1814-17; alderman Phila., 1817, mayor, 1819; collector Port of Phila., 1829-38; comtroller U.S. Dept. Treasury, 1838-58. Author and producer plays: Tears and Smiles (comedy on Phila. manners), 1807; The Indian Princess (operatic melodrama, 1st play written about Indians, 1st story about Pocahontas, 1st Indian play acted in Eng.), 1808; Superstition, 1824; also The Sisters, Little Red Riding Hood. Died Washington, D.C., Mar. 9, 1858.

BARKER, James William, mcht., politician; b. White Plains, N.Y., Dec. 5, 1815. Clk. in merc. house, 1828, later started own business; mem. N.Y. Grand Council, 1853; unsuccessful Know-Nothing Party candidate for mayor N.Y.C., 1854; founder Order of Star Spangled Banner (secret soc. aiming for nonparticipation of fgn.-born citizens in politics); established dry goods house, Pitts., 1860; pres. Eclectic Life Ins. Co. of N.Y., 1867-69. Died Rahway, N.J., June 26, 1869.

BARKER, Jeremiah, physician; b. Scituate, Mass., Mar. 31, 1752; s. Samuel and Patience (Howland) B.; studied medicine under Dr. Bela Lincoln; m. 5 times. Ship's surgeon during Revolutionary War, served in privateer, then in Penobscot expdn.; after war practiced medicine in Gorham, Me.; mem. Mass., Me. med. socs. Author: Vade Mecum; A Book of Anatomy. Died Oct. 4, 1835.

BARKER, Joseph, congressman, clergyman; b. Branford, Conn., Oct. 19, 1751; attended Harvard 2 years; grad. Yale, 1771; studied theology. Licensed to preach, 1775; ordained to ministry Congregatonal Ch., 1781; pastor Middleboro, Plymouth County, Mass., 1781-1815; mem. U.S. Ho. of Reps. (Democrat) from Mass., 9th-10th congresses, 1895-09; mem. Mass. Ho. of Reps., 1812, 13. Died Middleboro, July 5, 1815; buried Green Cemetery.

BARKER, Josiah, ship builder; b. Marshfield, Mass.; s. Ebenezer and Priscilla (Loring) B.; m. Penelope Hatch, Dec. 9, 1787. Learned ship building trade on North River, Pembroke, Mass.; constructed his 1st ships at St. Andrews and St. Johns, N.B., Can., 1786-87; opened shipyard, Charlestown, Mass., 1795; during War of 1812 built Frolic and was master carpenter for Independence (1st U.S. Navy ship of line); U.S. Naval constructor, 1826-46; built ships Vermont, Virginia and Cumberland; rebuilt Constitution, 1834; designed and built Portsmouth, 1843. Died Charlestown, Sept. 23, 1847.

BARKSDALE, Ethelbert, congressman, journalist; b. Smyrna, Rutherford County, Tenn., Jan. 4, 1824. Moved to Jackson, Miss., became journalist; editor Miss. ofcl. state journal, 1854-61, 76-83; mem. Confederate Congress, 1861-65; del. Nat. Democratic convs., 1860, 68, 72, 80; Dem. presdl. elector, 1876, also pres. Miss. Electoral Coll.; chmn. Miss. Dem. Exec. Com., 1877-79; mem. U.S. Ho. of Reps. (Democrat) from Miss., 48th-49th congresses, 1883-87; farmer, Yazoo County, Miss.

Died Yazoo City, Miss., Feb. 17, 1893; buried Greenwood Cemetery, Jackson.

BARKSDALE, William, congressman, army officer; b. Rutherford County, Tenn., Aug. 21, 1821; attended U. Nashville. Admitted to Miss. bar, 1839; editor Columbus (Miss.) Democrat, 1840; served as capt. U.S. Volunteers in Mexican War, 1847-48; del. Nat. Democratic Conv., 1852; mem. U.S. Ho. of Reps. (States' Rights Democrat) from Miss., 33d-36th congresses, 1853-61; commd. col. 13th Miss. Regt., 1861; commd. brig. gen. Confederate States Army, 1862; served in battles of Bull Run, Antietam, Fredericksburg, Chancellorsville. Killed in Battle of Gettysburg (Pa.), July 3, 1863; buried Greenwood Cemetery, Jackson, Miss.

BARLOW, Bradley, congressman, mcht.; b. Fairfield, Franklin County, Vt., May 12, 1814; attended common schs. Mcht., Phila. until 1858; moved to St. Albans, Vt., 1858; del. Vt. constl. convs., 1843, 50, 57, asst. sec., 1843; mem. Vt. Ho. of Reps., 1845, 50-52, 64-65; banker railroad exec., 1860-83; chmn. St. Albans Sch. Com.; pres. village corp.; treas. Franklin County, 1860-67; mem. Vt. Senate, 1866-68; mem. U.S. Ho. of Reps. (Nat. Republican) from Vt., 46th Congress, 1879-81. Died Denver, Nov. 6, 1889; buried Greenwood Cemetery, St. Albans.

BARLOW, Francis Channing, army officer, lawyer; b. Bklyn., Oct. 19, 1834; s. Rev. David Hatch and Almira (Penniman) B.; grad. Harvard, 1855; studied law under William Curtis Noyes, N.Y.C.; m. Arabella Wharton Griffith, Apr. 20, 1861; m. 2d, Ellen Shaw, 1867. Raised in Brookline, Mass.; moved to N.Y.C., circa 1856; admitted to N.Y. bar, 1858; law partner George Bliss, Jr., 1859-61, 66; enlisted 12th N.Y. Infantry, 1861; apptd. 1st lt. U.S. Army, 1861, mustered out, 1861; reentered U.S. Army as lt. col. 61st N.Y. Infantry, 1861, promoted col.; served in Peninsular Campaign; commanded 2d Brigade, 2d Div. under Gen. Howard at Battle of Antietam, wounded; brig. gen. U.S. Volunteers, 1862; commanded brigade in Chancellorsville Champaign; wounded at Battle of Gettysburg, 1863; in command of 1st Div. under Hancock, 1864, served in Wilderness Campaign; led attack at Spottsylvania, 1864; took leave of absence and toured Europe for health reasons, returned 1865; brevetted maj. gen. for highly meritorious conduct at Spotsylvania; promoted maj. gen., 1865; in service against Lee near end of war; entered politics after Civil war; sec. of state N.Y. State, 1865-67, 69-70; U.S. marshal for So. Dist. N.Y. State, 1869; apptd. by Pres. Grant to stop movement for independence in Cuba, 1869; atty. gen. N.Y. State, 1871-73, began prosecution of Tweed Ring, 1871; founder N.Y. Bar Assn.; had private law practice, 1874-76; a commr. to investigate Hayes-Tilden election in Fla., 1876. Died N.Y.C., Jan. 11, 1896; buried Brookline.

BARLOW, Joel, poet, diplomat; b. Reading, Conn., Mar. 24, 1754; s. Samuel and Esther (Hull) B.; grad. Yale, 1778; m. Ruth Baldwin, 1781. Founder (with Elisha Babcock) American Mercury, 1784; in Am. Revolution; went to Eng., 1791-93; mem. Constitutional Soc.; U.S. consul to Algiers, 1795, effected treaties with Tunis, Algiers and Tripoli, closing one phase of war, although Barbary Pirates continued at different periods; U.S. minister to France, 1811; mem. U.S. Mil. Philos. Soc., Am. Philos. Soc.; dir. Bank of Washington (D.C.); leading light of so-called Hartford Wits; U.S. negotiator with Napoleon, Zarnavica, Poland, 1812. Author: The Vision of Columbus, 1787; Letter to National Convention of France on the Defects in the Constitution of 1791 (for which he received French citizenship), 1791; Advice to the Privileged Orders, 1792; The Conspiracy of Kings, 1792; Hasty Pudding, 1796; The Columbiad, 1807. Died from cold and privation, Zarnavica, Dec. 14, 1812.

BARLOW, Samuel Kimbrough, pioneer; capt. Ore. emigrant party, 1845; pioneered land route south of Mt. Hood, thus discovering alternate route to Wash., avoiding the Dalles and dangerous Columbia Gorge, winter 1845; his party had to be aided by rescue team from Ft. Vancouver due to severe weather, but was successful; built (with Philip Foster) toll road over his route, spring-summer 1846.

BARLOW, Samuel Latham Mitchill, lawyer; b. Granville, Mass., June 5, 1826; s. Samuel Bancroft and Mrs. (Brillot-Savarin) B.; m. Mary Townsend. Worked in law office Willett & Greig, N.Y.C.; admitted to N.Y. bar, 1849; formed law firm Bowdoin, Larocque & Barlow, 1852, (became Shipman, Barlow, Larocque & Choate, 1881); dealt primarily in corporation law; settled dispute between Commodore Vanderbilt and William H. Aspinwall as representative of group of Pacific Mail Co. shareholders; settled case arising from contract between Commodore Garrison to procure arms for Gambetta (rep. of French Govt. during Franco-German War); successfully represented English Shareholders' Assn. by straightening out affairs of Erie R.R. and procuring $9.000,-000 settlement from Jay Gould in their behalf, 1872. Died Glen Cove, N.Y., July 10, 1889.

BARLOW, Stephen, congressman, lawyer; b. Redding, Fairfield County, Conn., June 13, 1779; attended Yale; studied law. Moved to Meadville, Crawford County, Pa., 1816. Admitted to bar, 1821; practiced in Meadville; mem. U.S. Ho. of Reps. (Democrat) from Pa., 20th Congress, 1827-29; mem. Pa. Ho. of Reps., 1828-31; apptd. asso. judge Crawford County, 1831-45. Died Meadville, Aug. 24, 1845; buried Greendale Cemetery.

BARNARD, Charles Francis, clergyman; b. Boston, Apr. 17, 1808; s. Charles and Sarah (Bent) B.; grad. Harvard, 1828, attended Divinity Sch.; m. Adeline M. Russell, May 1834; m. 2d, Sarah Holmes, Jan. 1837; 6 children. Ordained to ministry Unitarian Ch., 1834; founder Warren Street Chapel (sch. and ch. for children), Boston, 1836; financed greenhouse which eventually became Boston's Public Gardens; during Civil War his church used as recruiting center for Union Army; centered the attention of his ch. on underprivileged children in Boston, tried to feed and educate them. Died Somerville, Mass., Nov. 8, 1884.

BARNARD, Daniel Dewey, congressman, diplomat; b. Sheffield, Mass., July 16, 1797; s. Timothy and Phebe (Dewey) B.; grad. Williams Coll., 1818; m. Sara Livingstone, 1825; m. 2d, Catherine Walsh, 1832. Admitted to N.Y. bar, 1821; elected pros. atty.Monroe County (N.Y.), 1825, dist. atty., 1826; mem. U.S. Ho. of Reps. (Whig) from N.Y., 20th Congress, 1827-29, 26th-28th congresses, 1839-45, chmn. judiciary com., 1844-45; mem. N.Y. State Assembly, 1838; U.S. minister to Prussia, 1850-53. Died Albany, N.Y., Apr. 24, 1861; buried Albany Rural Cemetery.

BARNARD, Frederick Augustus Porter, coll. pres.; b. Sheffield, Mass., May 5, 1809; s. Robert and Augusta (Porter) B.; grad. Yale, 1828, LL.D. (hon.), 1859; LL.D. (hon.), Jefferson Coll., 1855; D.D. (hon.), U. Miss., 1861; m. Margaret McMurray, Dec. 27, 1847. Prof. mathematics and natural history U. Ala.; prof. mathematics and natural philosophy U. Miss., 1854-56, pres., 1856-58; published Letter to the President of the United States by a Refugee, 1863; pres. Columbia, 1864-89, founder Law Sch., Sch. Polit. Scis., Sch. Mines, Barnard Coll.; U.S. commr. Universal Exposition, Paris, France, 1867; asst. U.S. commr. gen. Paris Exposition, 1878; mem. U.S. Coast Survey; originator system of teaching deaf and dumb; mem. bd. Am. Bur. Mines; pres. Am. Meteorol. Soc., 1874-80; a founder, pres. A.A.A.S.; a founder Nat. Acad. Scis. Author: (principal works) Treatise on Arithmetic, 1830; Analytical Grammar, 1836; A History of the United States Coast Survey; Recent Progress of Science, 1859; The Metric System, 1871. Editor: Johnston's Cyclopedia. Died N.Y.C., Apr. 27, 1889; buried Sheffield.

BARNARD, Henry, coll. pres.; b. Hartford, Conn., Jan. 24, 1811; s. Chauncey and Elizabeth (Andrus) B.; grad. Yale, 1830, attended Yale Law Sch., 1833-34; m. Josephine Desnoyers, Sept. 1, 1847, 5 children. Del., Whig Nat. Conv., 1831; admitted to Conn. bar, circa 1834; toured Europe, 1835-36; mem. Conn. Gen. Assembly, 1837, 38, 39; sec. Conn. Sch. Bd. Commrs., 1838-42; founder editor Conn. Common Sch. Jour.; initiated reforms, especially the need for trained tchrs., better sch. houses; agt. R.I. sch. system to introduce reforms, 1843-49; a founder R.I. Inst. of Instrn., 1845; prin. the normal sch., New Britain, Conn., also supt. Conn. common schs., 1849-55; del. Internat. Expn. of Ednl. Methods, London, 1854; published Am. Jour. Edn., 1855-82; chancellor U. Wis., 1858-60; pres. St. John's Coll., Annapolis, Md., 1866-67; 1st U.S. commr. of edn., 1867-70. Author: History of the Legislation of Connecticut Respecting Common Schools Down to 1838, published 1853; School Architecture, or Contributions to the Improvement of Schoolhouses in the United States, 1854; Library of Education, 52 vols. Died Hartford, Conn., July 5, 1900; buried Hartford.

BARNARD, Isaac Dutton, senator, lawyer; b. Aston Twp., Delaware County, Pa., July 18, 1791; attended pub. schs.; studied law. Apptd. capt. and maj. 14th Regt., U.S. Inf., 1812, served in War of 1812; admitted to bar, 1816; practiced in West Chester, Chester County, Pa.; dep. atty. gen. Chester County, 1817-21; mem. Pa. Senate, 1820-26; sec. state, 1826; mem. U.S. Senate (Federalist) from Pa., 1827-Dec. 6, 1831, resigned. Died West Chester, Feb. 28, 1834; buried Oakland's Cemetery, nr. West Chester.

BARNARD, John, clergyman; b. Boston, Nov. 6, 1681; s. John and Esther Barnard; grad. Harvard, 1700; m. Anna Woodbridge, 1718. Chaplain of Mass. Army in expdn. to capture Port Royal and Acadia, 1707; chaplain aboard ship bound for London, Eng., 1709, remained in Eng. for 1 year, returned to New Eng., 1710; ordained to ministry Congregational Ch., Marblehead, Mass., 1716, remained there until 1770. Author: Ashton's Memorial, an History of the Strange Adventures and Signal Deliverances of Mr. Philip Ashton, 1725; A New Version of the Psalms of David, 1752. Died Jan. 24, 1770.

BARNARD, John Gross, army officer, engr.; b. Sheffield, Mass., May 19, 1815; s. Robert Foster and Augusta (Porter) B.; grad. U.S. Mil. Acad.; m. Jane Brand, circa 1840; m. 2d, Mrs. Anna Boyd, 1860. Commd. lt. in Corps Engrs., U.S. Army, assigned to coastal defenses, 1833; supervising engr. fortifications several ports including N.Y., Portland and Mobile during 1840's; supervised fortifications at base of Tampico during Mexican War; brevetted maj. for services; conducted survey for railroad across isthmus of Panama for Tehuantepec R.R. Co. of New Orleans, 1850; supt. U.S. Mil. Acad., 1855-56; planned defenses of Washington (D.C.) following beginning of Civil War, 1861; commd. brig. gen. of Volunteers, 1861, brevetted maj. gen., 1864; chief engr. for Gen. McClellan during Peninsular campaign, 1862; chief engr. all field armies on Gen. Grant's staff, 1864; chmn. adv. bd. on improvements of mouth Mississippi River, 1871; retired from army, 1881; pres. Permanent Bd. Engs. for Fortifications and River and Harbor Improvements, 1881; author many articles including A Report on the Defenses of Washington, 1871, The Phenomena of the Gyroscope Analytically Examined, 1858. Died May 14, 1882.

BARNES, Albert, clergyman, author; b. Rome, N.Y., Dec. 1, 1798; s. Rufus and Anna Barnes; grad. Hamilton Coll., 1820, Princeton Theol. Sem., 1824; m. Abby Smith. Pastor Presbyn. Ch., Morristown, N.J., 1824-30, First Presbyn. Ch., Phila., 1830-70; became center of controversy when he denied doctrine of original sin in sermons, suspended from ministry by Synod, 1836-37, restored to pastorate after vindication by Synod under control of New Sch. Presbyns. (at time of nat. split between Old and New Sch. Presbyns.); active in causes of abolition, prohibition, Sunday Sch. establishment, during following decades; worked to achieve reconciliation 2 factions of Presbyns. in 1869; trustee Union Theol. Sem. Author: Notes, Explanatory and Practical (commentaries on New Testament), 11 vols., 1832-53; Lectures on the Evidences of Christianity, 1868. Died Phila., Dec. 24, 1870; buried Phila.

BARNES, Charlotte Mary Sanford, actress, playwright; b. N.Y.C., 1818; d. John and Mary (Greenhill) Barnes; no formal edn.; m. Edmon S. Conner, 1847. Made 1st appearance on N.Y. stage, 1834; specialized in tragic roles; played in Hamlet in England, 1842; wrote and starred in Octavia Bragaldi; or the Confession, N.Y.C., 1837; following marriage starred in husband's acting company; wrote and played role of Pocahontas in The Forest Princess, Phila., 1848; adapted play A Night of Expectations from the French, played leading role in N.Y.C., 1850. Author: Plays, Prose, and Poetry, 1848. Died N.Y.C., Apr. 14, 1863.

BARNES, Demas, congressman; b. Gorham Twp., Ontario County, N.Y., Apr. 4, 1827; attended pub. schs. Became merchant; moved to N.Y.C., 1849, in drug business; crossed U.S. in wagon and studied mineral resources of Colo., Nev., Cal., returned to N.Y.C., wrote articles and published works about his experiences; mem. U.S. Ho. of Reps. (Democrat) from N.Y., 40th Congress, 1867-69; founder, editor Brooklyn Argus, 1873; in real estate business; mem. bd. edn.; an original trustee Bklyn. Bridge (when it was pvt. enterprise). Died N.Y.C., May 1, 1888; buried Greenwood Cemetery.

BARNES, James, army officer, engr.; b. Boston, Dec. 28, 1801; s. William Barnes; grad. U.S. Mil. Acad., 1829; Assigned to Arty., U.S. Army, commd. 1st lt., 1836, resigned 1836; became railroad engr. and supt., also engaged in railroad constrn.; col. 18th Mass. Volunteers, 1861; took part in battles of Mechanicsville, Antietam; commd. brig. gen. U.S. Volunteers, 1862; brevetted maj. gen. 1864; wounded at Battle of Gettysburg. Died Springfield, Mass., Feb. 12, 1869.

BARNES, Mrs. John, actress; b. Eng.; m. John Barnes. Arrived in N.Y.C. from Theater Royal, Drury Lane, London, Eng., 1816, appeared at Park Theater, N.Y.C., for next 5 seasons.

BARNES, Joseph K., army officer, surgeon; b. Phila., July 21, 1817; s. Judge Joseph Barnes; M.D U. Pa., 1838; m. Mary Fauntleroy. Apptd. asst. surgeon U.S. Mil. Acad., 1840; served in Seminole War, 1840-43; served under gens. Zachary Taylor and Winfield Scott in Mexican War; attending surgeon, Washington, D.C., 1862; apptd. surgeon-gen., chief Med. Dept., U.S. Army, 1864; attended deathbed of Pres. Lincoln, personal physician to Sec. of State William H. Seward after attempted assassination, attended Pres. James Garfield after he was shot; hon. mem. royal med. socs. of London, Eng., Paris, France and Moscow, Russia. Died Washington, D.C., Apr. 5, 1883; buried Oak Hill Cemetery, Washington.

ABBREVIATIONS PAGE 77

BARNES, Mary Downing Sheldon, educator; b. Oswego, N.Y., Sept. 15, 1850; d. Edward A. and Frances (Stiles) Sheldon; grad. U. Mich., 1874; m. Earl Barnes, 1884. Tchr., Oswego Normal Sch., 1874-76, 82-84; prof. history Wellesley Coll., 1876-80; tchr. history Leland Stanford U. (1st woman mem. faculty), 1891-96; a pioneer in use of Pestalozzian methods in teaching history. Author: Studies in General History, 1885; Studies in Historical Method, 1896; (with Earl Barnes) Studies in American History, 1891, Sheldon's General History. Died Aug. 27, 1898.

BARNETT, William, congressman, physician; b. Amherst County, Va., Mar. 4, 1761; studied medicine. Moved to Ga. with his father; returned to Va. at outbreak of Revolutionary War; joined military company from Amherst County under Marquis de Lafayette, present at surrender of Cornwallis at Yorktown; returned to Ga. at end of war, settled on Broad River, Elbert County; practiced medicine, Elbert County; sheriff Elbert County, 1780; mem. Ga. Senate, also pres.; mem. U.S. Ho. of Reps. (State Rights Democrat, filled vacancy) from Ga., 12th-13th congresses, Oct. 5, 1812-15; apptd. commr. to establish boundaries of Creek Indian Reservation, 1815; moved to Montgomery County, Ala. Died Montgomery County, Oct. 25, 1834; buried Smyrna Churchyard, nr. Washington, Wilkes County, Ga.

BARNEY, John, congressman; b. Balt., Jan. 18, 1785. Apptd. capt., asst. dist. q.m. gen. U.S. Army, 1814, discharged, 1815; mem. U..S Ho. of Reps. (Federalist) from Md., 19th-20th congresses, 1825-29; engaged in literary pursuits until 1857. Died Washington, D.C., Jan. 26, 1857; buried Greenmount Cemetery, Balt.

BARNEY, Joshua, naval officer; b. Balt., July 6, 1759; s. William and Frances (Holland) B.; m. Anne Bedford, Mar. 1780; 1 child. Commd. lt. U.S. Navy, 1776; taken prisoner by British, exchanged, 1777; lt. in ship Virginia, 1777, took several Brit. ships as prizes; commanded several armed mcht. ships, 1778-80, captured by British, 1780, imprisoned in Eng., escaped, 1781; commanded armed merchantman Hyder-Alley, 1782, by brilliant maneuvering captured larger Brit. ship General Monk, received sword from Pa. for services in engagement; declined appointment as 1 of 6 capts. U.S. Navy, 1794; served as commodore French Navy, 1796-1802; commanded privateers during War of 1812; commanded spl. force to defend Washington, D.C., 1814, fought with distinction nr. Bladensburg; served as naval officer at Balt., 1815. Died Pitts., Dec. 1, 1818.

BARNITZ, Charles Augustus, congressman, lawyer; b. York, Pa., Sept. 11, 1780; attended York County (Pa.) Acad.; studied law. Admitted to bar, 1811; practiced in York; mem. Pa. Senate, 1815-19; agt. of heirs of William Penn for their interests in Springettsbury Manor (now center of York), 1820-50; mem. U.S. Ho. of Reps. (Whig) from Pa., 23d Congress, 1833-35; pres. York Bank; mem. Pa. Constl. Conv., 1838; del. Nat. Whig Conv., Harrisburg, Pa., 1840, Balt., 1844. Died York, Jan. 8, 1850; buried First Presbyn. Churchyard.

BARNUM, Henry A., army officer; b. Jamesville N.Y., Sept. 24, 1833; s. Alanson Levi and Beersheba (Pixley) B.; grad. Syracuse Inst.; m. Lavinia King; m. 2d, Josephine Reynolds; 3 children. Commd. capt. 1st Co., 12th N.Y. Volunteers, 1861, served Battle of Bull Run and Battle of Blackburn's Ford; promoted maj., 1861, served in Peninsula Campaign; wounded and captured at Battle of Malvern Hill, July 1, exchanged, July 18, 1862; recruiter and col. 149th N.Y. Volunteers, 1862, served at battles of Gettysburg and Lookout Mountain, also in Gen. William Sherman's campaign in Ga., led Union forces which occupied Savannah, Ga.; brevetted brig. gen., then maj. gen., 1865, resigned, 1866; insp. of prisons N.Y., 1865-69; dep. tax. commr. N.Y.C., 1869-72, harbor master, port warden, 1888-92; mem. N.Y. Legislature, 1885; recipient medal of Honor, U.S. War Dept., 1889, Gold medal U.S. Congress, 1889. Died N.Y.C., Jan. 29, 1892.

BARNUM, Phineas Taylor, showman; b. Bethel, Conn., July 5, 1810; s. Philo F. and Irena (Taylor) B.; m. Charity Hallet, 1829; m. 2d, Nancy Fish, 1874. Bought Scudder's Am. Museum and Peale's Museum, opened a new Am. Museum, 1842; brought Jenny Lind to U.S. for concert tour, 1850; exploited midget Tom Thumb, pioneered freak shows, devoted entire life to circus; mem. Conn. Legislature, circa 1867-69; mayor Bridgeport (Conn.), laid out and built eastern part of city; opened The Greatest Show on Earth, Apr., 1871; founder (with rival James A. Bailey) Barnum and Bailey Circus, N.Y., 1881; sold over 82 million tickets for Barnum exhbns., 1875-91; much philanthropic work during life; contbd. money to build natural history mus. at Tufts Coll.; provided funds for parks, cemeteries and streets, Bridgeport; financed bldgs. for Fairfield County (Conn.) Hist. Soc., Bridgeport Scientific Soc., Fairfield County Med. Soc. Author: Life of P.T. Barnum Written by Himself, 1st edit., 1855, final edit., 1922; Humbugs of the World, 1865. Died Bridgeport, Apr. 7, 1891.

BARNUM, Samuel Weed, clergyman, editor; b. North Salem, N.Y., June 4, 1820; s. Horace and Cynthia (Weed) B.; grad. Yale, 1841, Yale Divinity Sch., 1844; m. Charlotte Betts, Apr. 16, 1849, 2 sons, 2 daus. Minister in Congregational chs., Granby, Conn., also Chesterfield, Phillipston (both Mass.), 1844-65; lived in New Haven, Conn., from 1865; helped revise Webster's Dictionary, 1845-46; pronunciation editor for Webster's Internat. Dictionary. Editor: Smith's Comprehensive Dictionary of the Bible, 1868; Romanism As It Is, 1871; Vocabulary of English Rhymes, 1876. Died New Haven, Nov. 18, 1891; buried New Haven.

BARNUM, William Henry, senator, congressman, mfr.; b. Boston Corner, Columbia County, N.Y., Sept. 17, 1818; attended common schs. Apprenticed to iron founder; became partner (with father) in iron business, Lime Rock, Litchfield County, Conn.; mem. Conn. Ho. of Reps., 1851, 52; mem. U.S. Ho. of Reps. (Democrat) from Conn., 40th-44th congresses, 1867-May 18, 1876 (resigned); mem. U.S. Senate, (Democrat, filled vacancy) from Conn., May 18, 1876-79; del. Nat. dem. convs., 1868, 72, 76, 80, 84, 88; chmn. Dem. Nat. Com., 1876-79. Died Lime Rock, Apr. 30, 1889; buried Lime Rock Cemetery.

BARNUM, Zenus, telegraph exec.; b. Wilkes-Barre, Pa., Dec. 9, 1810; s. Richard and Roseanna (Jemison) B.; studied civil engring.; m. Annie McLaughlin, Mar. 9, 1848. Went to Balt., 1840, in partnership with uncle in mgmt. of Barnum's Hotel, became famous as place of nat. polit. convs. during 1830's and 1840's; organizer, pres. Bain Line telegraph system from Washington (D.C.) to N.Y., 1848, merged with Samuel Morse's co., 1852; pres. Balt. Central R.R., circa 1855-circa 1859; pres. Am. Telegraph Co., 1859-65; known for philanthropies in Balt. Died Balt., Apr. 5, 1865; buried Balt.

BARNWELL, John, colonial ofcl.; b. Ireland, circa 1671; m. Anne Berners. Came to S.C., 1701; served as volunteer in Queen Anne's War; dep. sec., clk. of Provincial Council, circa 1710; led a force which defeated Indians nr. Neuse River during Tuscorora Indian uprising against white settlers in N.C., 1712; agt. for Colony of S.C. in London, Eng., 1720, was consulted on new form of govt. for S.C. after proprietary regime had been overthrown; built Ft. George on Altamaha River, S.C., 1721. Died S.C., June 1724.

BARNWELL, Robert, Continental congressman; b. Beaufort, S.C., Dec. 21, 1761; ed. common schs., pvt. tutors; at least 1 son, Robert Woodward. Volunteered in Revolutionary War at age 16; received 17 wounds in Battle on Johns Island, S.C., recovered, served as lt. with his company at siege of Charleston, 1780, when Charleston fell became prisoner aboard ship Pack Horse, released in gen. exchange prisoners, 1781; pres. bd. trustees Beaufort Coll. many years; mem. Continental Congress from S.C., 1788, 89; mem. S.C. Conv. to ratify U.S. Constn., 1788; mem. U.S. Ho. of Reps. (Federalist) from S.C., 2d Congress, 1791-93; mem. S.C. Ho. of Reps., 1795-97, speaker, 1795; mem. S.C. Senate, 1805, 06, pres., 1805. Died Beaufort, Oct. 24, 1814; buried St. Helena's Churchyard.

BARNWELL, Robert Woodward, senator, congressman, coll. pres.; b. Beaufort, S.C., Aug. 10, 1801; s. Robert and Elizabeth (Hayne) B.; grad. Harvard, 1821; m. Eliza Barnwell, Aug. 9, 1827. Mem. S.C. Ho. of Reps., 1826-29; mem. U.S. Ho. of Reps. from S.C., 21st-22d congresses, 1829-33; signer S.C. Nullification Ordinance, 1832; pres. S.C. Coll. (now U. S.C.), 1835-41 (adminstrn. marked by expansion), dean faculty, 1865-73, librarian, 1877-82; mgr. plantations in S.C., 1841-61; mem. U.S. Senate (filled vacancy) from S.C., 1850; mem. S.C. Conv. which passed secession ordinance, 1860; temporary chmn. Confederate Provisional Congress, Montgomery, Ala., 1861; mem. Confederate Senate from S.C., 1861-65; operator girls sch., Columbia, S.C., 1873-77. Died Columbia, Nov. 5, 1882.

BARR, Thomas Jefferson, congressman; b. N.Y.C., 1812; attended pub. schs. Moved to Scotch Plains, N.J., 1835, ran roadhouse; returned to N.Y.C., 1842; asst. alderman 6th ward, 1849, 50, alderman, 1852, 53; mem. N.Y. State Senate 1854, 55; mem. U.S. Ho. of Reps., (as Democrat, filled vacancy) from N.Y., 35th (as Independent Democrat) 36th congresses, Jan. 17, 1859-61; police commr. N.Y.C., 1870-73; with custom house, after 1873. Died N.Y.C., Mar. 27, 1881; buried Calvary Cemetery, L.I., N.Y.

BARRADALL, Edward, lawyer; b. England, 1704; s. Henry and Catherine (Blumfield) B.; studied law; m. Sarah Fitzhugh, Jan. 17, 1736. Called t Inner Temple, London, Eng.; came to Colony of Va., circa 1730, practiced in Williamsburg; legal asst. to Lord Fairfax, 1734; atty. gen. Colony of Va., 1737-43; del. from Coll. William and Mary to Va. Provincial Assembly, 1737-42; judge Ct. of Vice-Admiralty, circa 1736-43. Author: Cases Adjudged in the General Court of Virginia (valuable for reports of cases dealing with wide variety of litigation including land titles and wills), 1733-41. Died Williamsburg, June 19, 1743.

BARRALET, John James, artist, engraver; b. Dublin, Ireland, circa 1747. Successful painter of portraits and landscapes, book illustrator, drawing master, Dublin and London, Eng.; came to U.S., 1795, settled in Phila.; employed as book illustrator, worked in assn. with engraver Alexander Lawson; invented ruling machine for use of engravers made improvements in ink used in copperplate print ing; exhibited numerous paintings at Soc. Artists, Pa. Acad. Died Phila., Jan. 16, 1815.

BARRERE, Granville, congressman, lawyer; b New Market, nr. Hillsboro, Highland County, O. July 11, 1829; attended Augusta (Ky.) Coll. grad. Marietta (O.) Coll.; studied law. Admitted to Chillicothe (Ross County), O. bar, 1853; practiced in Marion, Crittenden County, Ark.; moved to Bloomington, McLean County, Ill., 1855, then to Canton, Fulton County, Ill., 1855, practiced law there; mem. Canton Bd. Edn.; mem. Canton Bd. Suprs.; mem. U.S. Ho. of Reps. (Republican) from Ill., 43d Congress, 1873-75. Died Canton Jan. 13, 1889; buried Greenwood Cemetery.

BARRERE, Nelson, congressman, lawyer; b New Market, nr. Hillsboro, Highland County, O. Apr. 1, 1808; grad. Augusta (Ky.) Coll., 1830 studied law. Admitted to bar, 1833; practiced in Hillsboro; moved to West Union, Adams County O., 1834, practiced law; returned to Hillsboro 1846; mem. Ohio Ho. of Reps., 1837, 38,; mem U.S. Ho. of Reps. (Whig) from Ohio, 32 Congress 1851-53. Died Hillsboro, Aug. 20, 1883; buried Presbyn. Cemetery, New Market.

BARRETT, Benjamin Fiske, clergyman, author; b. Dresden, Me., June 24, 1808; s. Oliver and Elizabeth (Carleton) B.; grad. Bowdoin Coll., 1832; grad. Harvard Div. Sch., 1838; m. Elizabeth Allen, 1840. Became adherent of religious doctrines of Swedenborg early in life; ordained to ministry New Ch. Soc., N.Y.C., 1840, minister, 1840-48; in charge of New Ch. congregation, Cincinnati, 1848-50; engaged in bus., probably Cincinnati, 1850-54; engaged in preaching to New Ch. congregations and writing, 1854-64; editor Swedenborgian periodical New Christianity, Phila., 1870's. Author: Life of Emmanuel Swedenborg, 1841; Binding and Loosing, 1857; Swedenborg and Channing, 1877; Footprints of the New Age, 1884; The True Catholicism, 1886; Autobiography, 1890. Died Germantown, Pa., Aug. 6, 1892; buried Germantown.

BARRETT, George Horton, actor; b. Exeter, Eng., June 9, 1794; s. Giles Barrett; no formal edn.; m. Mrs. Anne Henry, June 24, 1825, 1 dau., Georgiana. Made 1st appearance in N.Y.C. in role of Young Norval, 1806; had reputation for roles as light comedian in such plays as The West Indian, 1822, Rule of a Wife; mgr. Bowery Theater, N.Y.C., 1828-29; appeared in all parts of U.S. and England in comedy roles, 1837; mgr. Broadway Theater, N.Y.C., 1847; made notable appearance in The School for Scandal, N.Y.C., 1848; theater mgr., Charleston, S.C., 1852-53; actor in N.Y.C. before retirement from stage, 1855; tchr. elocution, N.Y.C., 1855-60. Died N.Y.C., Sept. 5, 1860; buried N.Y.C.

BARRETT, Lawrence, actor; b. Paterson, N.J., Apr. 4, 1838; s. Thomas Barrett; no formal edn. Made 1st appearance in N.Y.C. in The Hunchback, 1857; mem. Boston Museum Co., 1858-61; served as capt. 28th Mass. Volunteer Regt., 1861-62; often acted at Winter Garden Theatre, N.Y.C. during 1860's, toured other major U.S. cities; played opposite Edwin Booth at Booth's Theater, N.Y.C., 1870-71; famed throughout nation for Shakespearian roles (particularly Richard III, King Lear, Romeo, Hamlet); produced many new works on Am. stage including Harebell from the German, 1871, A Counterfeit Presentment (W. D. Howells), 1877, Ganelon (William Young), 1889; toured nation in partnership with Edwin Booth with extensive Shakespearian repertory, 1886-91. Died N.Y.C., Mar. 20, 1891; buried Cohasset, Mass.

BARRIERE, Hippolite, ice cream magnate, theater owner. Opened Pavilion Theatre, Chatham Garden (outdoor, canvas theatre in which summer concerts, variety shows and operas were given), N.Y.C., 1823; opened permanent Chatham Theatre, N.Y.C., 1824, presented new actors to the public very frequently, including Mrs. Barrett, Mr. and Mrs. Wallack, Mr. and Mrs. Durang, Joseph Jefferson.

BARRINGER, Daniel Laurens, congressman, lawyer; b. Poplar Grove, Cabarrus County, N.C., Oct. 1, 1788; studied law. Admitted to bar; practiced in Raleigh, N.C.; mem. N.C. Ho. of Commons, 1813, 14, 19-22; mem. U.S. Ho. of Reps. (Democrat, filled vacancy) from N.C., 19th-23d congresses, Dec. 4, 1826-35; moved to Bedford County, Tenn., circa 1830, settled in Shelbyville, practiced law; mem., speaker Tenn. Ho. of Reps., 1843-45; Whig presdl. elector, 1844. Died Shelbyville, Oct. 16, 1852; buried Willow Mount Cemetery.

BARRINGER, Daniel Moreau, congressman, diplomat; b. Concord, N.C., July 30, 1806; s. Gen. Paul and Elizabeth (Brandon) B.; grad. U. N.C., 1826; m. Elizabeth Wethered. Admitted to N.C. bar 1829; mem. N.C. Ho. of Commons from Cabarrus County, 1829; del. N.C. Constl. Conv., 1835; mem. U.S. Ho. of Reps. from N.C. 28th-30th congresses, 1843-49; apptd. U.S. minister to Spain by Pres. Zachary Taylor, 1849; del. from N.C. to Peace Conf., Washington, D.C., Feb. 1861; del. Nat. Union Conv., 1866; del. Nat. Democratic Conv., 1872. Died White Sulphur Springs, Va., Sept. 1, 1873; buried Greenmount Cemetery, Balt.

BARRINGER, Rufus, army officer; b. Cabarrus County, N.C., Dec. 2, 1821; s. Paul Barringer; grad. U. N.C., 1842; m. 1st, Eugenia Morrison, 1854; m. 2d, Rosalie Chunn; m. 3d, Margaret Long. Admitted to N.C. bar, practiced in Concord, 1845; mem. N.C. Assembly (Whig), 1848, apptd. capt. 1st N.C. Cavalry, 1861, served in Confederate Army of No. Va.; participated in battles of Peninsular campaign, 2d Bull Run, Antietam, Fredericksburg and Chancellorsville; promoted maj., 1863, also lt. col.; promoted col., brig. gen., 1864; led brigade in Gen. W.H.F. Lee's cavalry div. 1864-65; assisted in Lee's retreat from Richmond, 1865; practiced in Charlotte, N.C., 1865-84; joined Republican Party in N.C., active in politics; del. N.C. Constl. Conv., 1875; unsuccessful candidate for lt. gov. N.C., 1880. Died Charlotte, Feb. 3, 1895; buried Charlotte.

BARRON, James, naval officer; b. probably Norfolk, Va., Sept. 15, 1768; s. James and Jane (Cowper) B.; no formal edn. Commd. lt. U.S. Navy, 1798, capt., 1799; commanded ship President in Mediterranean fleet, 1800-05; surrendered Chesapeake to Brit. warship which demanded alleged deserters, nr. Norfolk, 1807, court martialed, 1808; served in French Navy while under suspension from U.S. Navy, 1808-13; fought duel with Commodore Stephen Decatur (leader of group of officers opposed to his restoration to active duty), 1820, subsequently never restored to active service. Died Norfolk, Apr. 21, 1851; buried Norfolk.

BARRON, Samuel, naval officer; b. Hampton, Va., Nov. 28, 1809; s. Samuel and Jane (Sawyer) B.; no formal edn.; m. Imogen Wright, Oct. 31, 1832, 3 sons, 3 daus. Apptd. midshipman U.S. Navy at age 3 (as a tribute to his father, Commodore Barron), 1812; made 1st voyage in Brandywine which took Lafayette to France, 1825; comdr. ship John Adams off coast of Africa, 1849-53; promoted capt., 1855; resigned to join Confederate Navy, 1861; chief Bur. Orders and Detail, Confederate Navy, 1861; commanded Ft. Hatteras, imprisoned after its capture, 1861-62, comdr. naval forces in Va., 1862-63; went to Eng. to secure delivery of 2 ironclad rams, 1863; comdr. Confederate naval forces in Europe, supervised operations of the raiders Stonewall and Georgia, 1863-65; resigned 1865. Died "Malvern" nr. Loretto, Va., Feb. 26, 1888; buried Essex County, Va.

BARROW, Alexander, senator, lawyer, planter; b. nr. Nashville, Tenn., Mar. 27, 1801; attended U.S. Mil. Acad., 1816-18; studied law. Admitted to bar, 1822; practiced in Nashville; moved to La., settled in Feliciana Parish, practiced law for awhile; became planter; mem. La. Ho. of Reps. several terms; mem. U.S. Senate (Whig) from La., 1841-Dec. 29, 1840. Died Balt., Dec. 29, 1846; buried pvt. cemetery at Alton Villa Plantation, nr. Bayou Sara, La.

BARROW, Frances Elizabeth Mease, author; b. Charleston, S.C., Feb. 22, 1822; d. Charles Benton and Sarah (Graham) Mease; m. James Barrow, Jr., Dec. 7, 1841. Began writing juvenile literature (which came to have wide circulation in U.S. and Eng.) under pseudonym Aunt Fanny, 1855. Author works including: The Letter G. (a periodical story), 1864; Little Pet Books, 3 vols., 1860; Good Little Hearts, 4 vols., 1864; The Six Mitten Books, 6 vols. Died N.Y.C., May 7, 1894.

BARROW, Washington, congressman editor; b. Davidson County, Tenn., Oct. 5, 1817; attended Davidson Acad. Admitted to Tenn. bar, circa 1837, practiced in Nashville, Tenn.; active in Tenn. politics as Jacksonian, later as Whig; chargé d'affaires at Lisbon, Spain (reward for polit. activity), 1841-44; editor Nashville Republican Banner (organ of Whig Party), 1844-47; mem. U.S. Ho. of Reps. (Whig) from Tenn., 30th Congress, 1847-49; pres. Nashville Gas Co., 1848; mem. Tenn. Senate, 1858-61; a commr. from Tenn. during formation of Tenn. alliance with Confederacy, 1861; publisher Republican Banner, 1862-65. Died St. Louis, Oct. 19, 1866; buried East Nashville, Tenn.

BARRY, Henry W., congressman, lawyer; b. Schoharie County, N.Y., Apr. 1840; grad. law dept. Columbian Coll. (now George Washington U.), 1867. Prin., Locust Grove Acad., Ky.; enlisted in Union Army in Civil War; organized regt. Colored troops in Ky.; commd. 1st lt. 10th Regt. Ky. Volunteer Inf., 1861; col. 8th U.S. Colored Artillery, 1864; brevetted brig. gen. Volunteers for faithful and meritorious services, 1865; admitted to bar, 1867; practiced in Columbus, Lowndes County, Miss.; del. Miss. Constl. Conv., 1867; mem. Miss. Senate 1868; mem. U.S. Ho. of Reps. (Republican) from Miss., 41st-43d congresses, Feb. 23, 1870-75. Died Washington, D.C., June 7, 1875; buried Oak Hill Cemetery.

BARRY, John, navy officer; b. County Wexford, Ireland, 1745; s. John and Catherine B.; no formal edn.; m. Mary Burns; m. 2d, Sarah Austin, July 7, 1777. Commanded ship Lexington in U.S. Navy, 1776; promoted capt., given command of Effingham, 1777; comdr. Raleigh, captured many Brit. ships, 1778-81; in command of Alliance, captured Brit. ships Atalanta and Trepassy, 1781; ret. from Navy, 1783; appt. sr. capt. in command of the ship United States during Algerine conflict, 1794, in command of U.S. naval forces in West Indies, 1798; commanded U.S. naval sta. at Guadaloupe, 1800-01. Died Sept. 13, 1803.

BARRY, John, clergyman; b. Oylegate, Wexford, Ireland, 1790. Ordained priest Roman Catholic Ch., Charleston, S.C., 1825; worked in Ga., founded 1st Catholic sch. in Savannah; vicar gen. Charleston; superior of seminary, Charleston, 1844; consecrated bishop at Balt., 1857. Died while travelling in Europe for health reasons, Paris, France, Nov. 19, 1859.

BARRY, John Stewart, gov. Mich.; b. Amherst, N.H., Jan. 29, 1802; s. John and Ellen (Stewart) B.; m. Mary Kidder. Mem. Mich. Constl. Conv., 1835; mem. Mich. Senate, 1836, 40; gov. Mich., 1841-46, 48-52; mem. Democratic Nat. Conv., 1864; presdl. elector, twice. Died Constantine, Mich., Jan. 14, 1870.

BARRY, Patrick, horticulturist; b. Belfast, Ireland, May 24, 1816; m. Harriet Huestis, 1847, 8 children including William C. Came to N.Y., 1837; a founder Mt. Hope Nurseries (became largest nursery in country, did much importing), Rochester, N.Y., 1840; hort. editor Genessee Farmer, 1845-53; editor The Horticulturist, until 1855; founder Fruit Growers' Soc. Western N.Y., 1855; chmn. exec. com.; mem. 1st bd. of control N.Y. Agrl. Expt. Sta., Geneva; organizer, pres: Flour City Nat. Bank, 1956; organizer, pres. Mechanics Savs. Bank, Rochester City R.R. Co., Powers Hotel Co.; pres. N.Y. State Agrl. Soc., 1877; pres. Western N.Y. Hort. Soc., 30 years. Author: The Fruit Garden, 1851; Catalogue of the American Pomological Society (guide for Am. fruit growers). Died June 23, 1890.

BARRY, William Farquhar, army officer; b. N.Y.C., Aug. 18, 1818; grad. N.Y.C. High Sch., 1831, U.S. Mil. Acad., 1838; m. Kate McNight, 1840. Began service with 2d Arty. Corps, U.S. Army, 1838; participated in Mexican War as adjutant gen. at Veracruz; served in Seminole Indian War in Fla., 1857-58; in charge of arty. under Gen. McDowell at Battle of Bull Run, 1861; promoted capt., 1852, maj., 1861; commd. brig. gen. U.S. Volunteers, 1862; brevetted col. U.S. Army and maj. gen. volunteers, 1864, brig. gen. and maj. gen. U.S. Army, 1865; commd. col. U.S. Army, 1865; served as head of arty. Army of Potomac, 1862; insp. arty. Armies of the U.S., Washington, D.C., 1862-64; chief of arty. for Gen. Grant, 1864, for W. T. Sherman, 1864-65; commanded 2d Arty. U.S. Army in service on No. border during Fenian conflicts, 1866; organized, headed U.S. Army Arty. Sch., Ft. Monroe, Va., 1867-77. Died Ft. McHenry, Balt., July 18, 1879; buried Ft. McHenry.

BARRY, William Taylor, senator, postmaster gen.; b. Lunenburg, Va., Feb. 5, 1785; s. John and Susannah (Dozier) B.; grad. Coll. William and Mary, 1803; m. Lucy Overton; m. 2d, Catherine Mason. Admitted to bar, 1805; mem. Ky. Ho. of Reps., 1809 14, speaker, 1814; mem. U.S. Ho. of Reps. (Democrat) from Ky., 11th Congress, Aug. 1810-11; sec. and aide-de-camp to Gen. Isaac Shelby during War of 1812, served in Battle of the Thames, 1813; mem. U.S. Senate (Democrat) from Ky., 1814-16; judge 11th Circuit Ct. of Ky., 1816-17; mem. Ky. Senate, 1817-21; lt. gov. Ky., 1820; tried to establish an effective system of pub. edn.; prof. law, politics Transylvania U., 1822-24; sec. of state Ky., 1824; chief justice Ky. Ct. of Appeals, 1825; postmaster-gen. U.S., 1829-35; apptd. U.S. minister to Spain, 1835, died before serving. Died Liverpool, Eng., Aug. 30, 1835; buried Frankfort (Ky.) Cemetery.

BARRY, William Taylor Sullivan, congressman, army officer; b. Columbus, Miss., Dec. 10, 1821; s. Richard and Mary (Sullivan) B.; grad. Yale, 1841; m. Sally Fearn, Dec. 20, 1851. Admitted to Miss. bar, practiced in Columbus, circa 1844; mem. Miss. Legislature, 1849, 50; mem. U.S. Ho. of Reps. from Miss., 33d Congress, 1853-55; mem., speaker Miss. Lower House, 1855-61; became leader of states' rights secessionist branch of Democratic Party during 1850's; pres. Miss. Conv. which passed secession ordinance, 1861; del. to Montgomery (Ala.) Conv. which organized Confederate Govt., 1861; mem. Confederate Provisional Congress from Miss., 1861-62; organizer, col. 35th Miss. Inf. Regt., Confederate Army, 1862; participated in Corinth and Vicksburg campaigns; captured at Mobile, Ala., 1865; practiced law in Columbus, 1866-68. Died Columbus, Jan. 29, 1868; buried Columbus.

BARRYMORE, Georgiana Emma Drew, actress; b. Phila., 1856; d. John and Louisa (Lane) Drew; no formal edn.; m. Maurice Barrymore, Dec. 31, 1876, 3 children, Ethel, Lionel, John. Made debut at Arch Street Theater, Phila., 1872; played roles in As You Like It, The School for Scandal and The Princess Royal during 1870's; mem. Palmer's Stock Co., circa 1880, acted with Edwin Booth, Lawrence Barrett and John McCullough; played roles in Diplomacy, The Wages of Sin and Mr. Wilkinson's Widow during 1880's; made last appearance in The Sportsman, Boston, 1892. Died Santa Barbara, Cal., July 2, 1893.

BARSTOW, Gamaliel Henry, congressman, physician; b. Sharon, Litchfield County, Conn., July 20, 1784; studied medicine, Barrington, Mass. Moved to Tioga County, N.Y., 1812, worked on his father's farm, also taught school; practiced medicine; mem. N.Y. State Assembly, 1815-19, 23-36; apptd. 1st judge Tioga County Ct., 1818-23; mem. N.Y. State Senate, 1819-22; treas. N.Y. State, 1830; mem. U.S. Ho. of Reps. (Nat. Republican) from N.Y., 22d Congress, 1831-33; practiced medicine, also farmed, Nichols, N.Y. Died Nichols, Mar. 30, 1865; buried Ashbury Cemetery, nr. Nichols.

BARSTOW, Gideon, congressman; b. Mattapoisett, Plymouth County, Mass., Sept. 7, 1783; attended Brown U., 1799-1801; studied medicine. Practiced medicine, Salem, Mass.; mem. Mass. Constl. Conv., 1820; mem. U.S. Ho. of Reps. (Democrat) from Mass., 17th Congress, 1821-23; mem. Mass. Ho. of Reps., 1823, 29, 33, 37; mem. Mass. Senate, 1827, 34; Whig presdl. elector, 1832; moved to St. Augustine (Fla.) because of ill health, became merchant. Died St. Augustine, Mar. 26, 1852; buried Huguenot Cemetery.

BARSTOW, William Augustus, gov. Wis.; b. Plainfield, Conn., Sept. 13, 1813; s. William A. Barstow; m. Maria Quarles, Apr. 1844. Sec. of state Wis., 1850; pres. St. Croix & Lake Superior R.R. Co., 1855; elected gov. Wis. (Democrat) 1854, re-elected, 1856 (election contested by Republicans, and Wis. Supreme Ct., for 1st time in history of any Am. state, removed gov. from office after installation); commd. col. U.S. Army, 1861; provost-marshal gen. Kan., 1862; brevetted brig. gen. U.S. Volunteers, 1865. Died Leavenworth, Kan., Dec. 14, 1865.

BARTHBERGER, Charles, architect; b. Baden, Germany, 1823; grad. Poly. Inst., Carlsruhe, Germany, 1843. Came to U.S., 1845, settled in Pitts.; became a leading architect, Pitts.; designed numerous bldgs. in Western Pa. and Eastern Ohio; asso. in partnership with Ernest C. Diedrich, after 1885, specialized in ecclesiastical work; churches built by firm include St. Paul's Cathedral, 18th Street Presbyn. Ch., St. Philomon's Ch., Episcopal Ch. of St. Matthew; architect bank bldg. on 5th St., also Odd Fellow's Hall (later occupied by Opera House), Pitts.; practiced with son (C. M. Barthberger) in later years. Died Pitts., Aug. 19, 1896.

BARTHOLOMEW, Edward Sheffield, sculptor; b. Colchester, Conn., July 8, 1822; s. Abdial and Sarah (Gustin) B.; attended Bacon Acad., Colchester, circa 1832-36, N.A.D., N.Y.C., circa 1839-40; studied anatomy in N.Y.C., 1848; Curator, Wadsworth Gallery, Hartford, Conn., circa 1842, became interested in sculpture; settled in Italy, 1850; executed many portraits, relied on Bibl. and classical subjects; executed statue Eve Repentant (gained reknown in Italy); other works include Sappho, Diana, Ganymede. Died Naples, Italy, May 1858.

BARTHOLOMEW, Truman C., artist; b. Vershire, Vt., Dec. 15, 1809; s. Erastus Bartholomew. Painted in Boston, circa 1830-67; painted theater scenery and panoramic views; asso. with Minard Lewis, 1838-41; collaborated with Lewis on scenery for play based on Kane's Arctic voyages; painted view of Jerusalem shown in Charleston (S.C.), 1847. Died Melrose, Mass., Dec. 7, 1867.

BARTHOLOMEW, William Newton, artist; b. Boston, Feb. 13, 1822; s. Erastus Bartholomew. Trained and practiced as cabinetmaker; became artist; went to Cal. with J. Wesley Jones, 1850; introduced systematic instrn. in drawing to several Boston schs., 1852, later in charge of drawing instrn. in all Boston High Schs., until 1871; published series of popular drawing books. Died Newton Centre, Mass., 1898.

BARTLESON, John, pioneer guide; capt. of Bidwell's (became Bartleson's) party from Jackson County, Mo. to Cal. (1st Am. land-route migrating party to reach Cal.), 1841; left train briefly, Oct. 7-12, 1841.

BARTLET, William, mcht., philanthropist; b. Newburyport, Mass., Jan. 31, 1748; s. Edmund and Hannah (Hall) B.; no formal edn.; m. Elizabeth Lascomb, 1774. Engaged in merc. activities during and after Am. Revolution; established one of 1st textile factories in New Eng., Newburyport, in 1780's; benefactor Andover (Mass.) Theol. Sem. (established 1808), Bartlet Chapel (1818), Bartlet Hall (1821) named for him, bequeathed $50,000 to Sem. Died Newburyport, Feb. 8, 1841; buried Newburyport.

BARTLETT, Bailey, congressman; b. Haverhill, Essex County, Mass., Jan. 29, 1750; attended common schs. Merchant until 1789; mem. Mass. Ho. of Reps., 1781-84, 88; mem. Mass. Conv. to ratify U.S. Constn., 1788; mem. Mass. Senate, 1789; high sheriff Essex County, 1789-11, 1812-30; mem. U.S. Ho. of Reps. (Federalist, filled vacancy) from Mass., 5th-6th congresses, Nov. 27, 1797-1801; treas. Essex County, 1812; del. Mass. Constl. Conv., 1820. Died Haverhill,, Sept. 9, 1830; buried Pentucket Cemetery.

BARTLETT, Elisha, physician, educator; b. Smithfield, R.I., Oct. 6, 1804; s. Otis and Waite (Buffum) B.; grad. in medicine Brown U., 1826; m. Elizabeth Slater, 1829. Settled in Lowell, Mass., 1827, practiced medicine; prof. anatomy Berkshire Med. Instn., Pittsfield, Mass., 1832-40; an editor Med. Mag., Boston, 1832-35; prof. medicine Transylvania U., Lexington, Ky., 1841, 46, U. Md., Balt., 1844-45, U. Louisville (Ky.), 1849-50, N.Y.U., 1850-52, Coll. Physicians and Surgeons, N.Y.C., 1852-55. Author treatises: The Fevers in the United States, 1842; History, Diagnosis, and Treatment of Edematous Laryngitis, 1850. Died Smithfield, July 19, 1855; buried Smithfield.

BARTLETT, Ichabod, congressman; b. Salisbury, July 24, 1786; s. Dr. Joseph and Hannah (Colcord) B.; grad. Dartmouth, 1808. Admitted to N.H. bar, 1811; clk. N.H. Senate, 1817-18; appeared in Superior Ct. as counsel for Woodward in Dartmouth Coll. Case, 1817; state solicitor for Rockingham County, 1818-21; mem. N.H. Ho. of Reps. from Portsmouth, 1819-21, 30, 38, 51, 52, speaker, 1821; mem. U.S. Ho. of Reps. (Anti-Democrat) from N.H., 18th-20th congresses, 1823-29; mem. N.H. Constl. Conv., 1850; a founder N.H. Hist. Soc., pres., 1826-30. Died Portsmouth, Oct. 19, 1853; buried Harmony Grove Cemetery, Portsmouth.

BARTLETT, John Russell, state ofcl., bibliographer; b. Providence, R.I., Oct. 23, 1805; s. Smith and Nancy (Russell) B.; m. Eliza Ann Rhodes, May 15, 1831; m. 2d, Ellen Eddy, Nov. 12, 1863; children. Mem. Franklin Soc.; mem. R.I. Hist. Soc., 1831; corr. sec. N.Y. Hist. Soc.; apptd. by Pres. Taylor U.S. commr. to establish boundary between U.S. and Mexico, 1850; explored extensively in Tex., N.M., Cal., also Chihuaha and Sonora (Mexico); sec. of state R.I., 1855-72; founder (with Albert Gallatin) Am. Ethnol. Soc. Author: Records of the Colony of Rhode Island, 1636-1792, 10 vols.; The Process of Ethnology, 1847; Dictionary of Americanisms, 1848; Naval History of Rhode Island, 1880; John Carter Brown Catalogue (bibliography of early Americana), 1882. Died Providence, May 28, 1886.

BARTLETT, John Sherren, editor; b. Dorsetshire, Eng., 1790; s. Thomas Bartlett. Apptd. asst. surgeon Brit. Navy, 1812; editor English polit. newspaper in U.S., The Albion, N.Y.C., 1822-48; introduced Indian corn into Eng.; publisher The European (paper with latest news from Europe, printed in Liverpool, Eng., then shipped via Cunard to Am.) 1840-42; pres. St. George's Soc. N.Y., 1847; founder, editor Anglo-Saxon, Boston, 1855; apptd. temporary Brit. consul, Balt., 1857. Died Middletown Point, N.J., Aug. 23, 1863.

BARTLETT, Joseph, author, lawyer; b. Plymouth, Mass., June 10, 1762; s. Sylvanus and Martha (Wait) B.; grad. Harvard, 1782; m. Anna Wetherell, Nov. 15, 1745. Wrote play, acted in another, Edinburgh, Scotland, 1783; admitted to Mass. bar, circa 1785, practiced in Woburn; moved to Cambridge, Mass., circa 1795; represented Cambridge in Mass. Gen. Ct., 1798-1801; moved to Saco, Mass. (now Me.), 1803, practiced law; mem. Mass. Senate (Jeffersonian Democrat), 1804; editor Freeman's Friend (Jeffersonian newspaper), Saco, 1805-06; moved to Portsmouth, N.H., circa 1809, to Boston, 1822. Author: The New Vicar of Bray, 1823; Physiognomy, 1810. Died Boston, Oct. 20, 1827; buried Boston.

BARTLETT, Josiah, gov. N.H.; b. Amesbury, Mass., Nov. 21, 1729; s. Stephen and Hannah (Webster) B.; studied medicine privately, 1745-50; M.D. (hon.), Dartmouth, 1790; m. Mary Bartlett, Jan. 15, 1754, 12 children. Began practice medicine, Kingston, N.H., 1750; mem. N.H. Provincial Assembly from Kingston, 1765-75; justice of peace, Kingston, 1767; col., regt. N.H. Militia, 1767; del. to Continental Congress, 1775, 76, 78; signer Declaration of Independence, 1776, Articles of Confedn., 1779; chief justice N.H. Ct. Common Pleas, 1779-82; asso. justice N.H. Superior Ct., 1784-88, chief justice, 1788-89; mem. Constl. Conv., Phila., 1787; pres. State of N.H., 1790-93; secured charter for N.H. Med. Soc., 1791, 1st pres.; 1st gov. N.H., 1793-94. Died Kingston, May 19, 1795; buried Kingston.

BARTLETT, Josiah, Jr., congressman, physician; b. Kingston, N.H., Aug. 29, 1768; s. Josiah Bartlett; grad. Exeter (N.H.) Acad.; studied medicine. Practiced medicine, Stratham, Rockingham County, N.H.; mem. N.H. Senate, 1809, 10, 24, pres., 1824; mem. U.S. Ho. of Reps. from N.H., 12th Congress, 1811-13; treas. Rockingham County; presdl. elector, 1824, supported John Quincy Adams. Died Stratham, Apr. 16, 1838; buried Old Congregational Cemetery.

BARTLETT, Samuel Colcord, clergyman, coll. pres.; b. Salisbury, N.H., Nov. 25, 1817; s. Samuel C. and Eleanor (Pettengill) B.; grad. Dartmouth, 1836, LL.D. (hon.), D.D. (hon.); grad. Andover Theol. Sem., 1842; LL.d. (hon.) Harvard, Princeton m. Laura Bradlee, Aug. 1843; m. 2d, Mary Learned, May 12, 1846; children—Edwin Julius, Alice Stimson, William Alfred, Samuel Colcord. Ordained to ministry Congregational Ch., 1843; pastor Congregational Ch., Monson, Mass., 1843-46; prof. intellectual philosophy and rhetoric Western Res. Coll., Cleve., O., 1846-52; pastor Franklin Street Ch., Manchester, N.Y., 1852-57, New Eng. Ch., Chgo., 1857-59; prof. Bibl. lit. Chgo. Theol. Sem., 1858-77; pres. N.H. Home Missionary Soc., 15 years; corporate mem. Am. Bd. Commrs. for Fgn. Missions; pres. Dartmouth, Hanover, N.Y., 1877-92. Author: Life and Death Eternal, a Refutation of the Doctrine of Annihilation, 1866; Sketches of the Missions of the American Board of Commissioners for Foreign Missions, 1872; Future Punishment, 1875. Died Hanover, Nov. 16, 1898.

BARTLETT, Thomas, Jr., congressman, lawyer; b. Sutton, Caledonia County, Vt., June 18, 1808; attended common schs.; studied law. Admitted to bar, 1833; practiced in Groton, Vt.; moved to Lyndon, Vt., 1836, practiced law; state's atty. for Caledonia county, 1839-42; mem. Vt. Senate, 1841, 42; mem. Vt. Ho. of Reps., 1849, 50, 54, 55; del. Vt. Constl. Convs., 1850, 57; mem. U.S. Ho. of Reps. (Democrat) from Vt., 32d Congress, 1851-53. Died Lyndon, Sept. 12, 1876; buried Lyndon Town Cemetery, Lyndon Center, Vt.

BARTLETT, William Henry, artist; b. Kentishtown, London, Eng., Mar. 26, 1809. Made 4 visits to U.S. between 1836 and 1852; published series of views as American Scenery, circa 1840; engravings based on his views were used in History of the United States of North America, published posthumously, circa 1856; diorama Jerusalem and the Holy Land (based on drawings made by Bartlett on several visits to Near East) exhibited in London and Boston, 1856. Died on board ship returning from voyage to Orient, Sept. 13, 1854.

BARTLEY, Mordecai, gov. Ohio, congressman; b. Fayette County, Pa., Dec. 16, 1783; s. Elijah and Rachel (Pearshall) B.; m. Miss Welles, 1804. Adj. with rank of capt. under Gen. Harrison in Northwest during War of 1812; mem. Ohio Senate, 1817; register Ohio Land Office, 1818-23; mem. U.S. Ho. of Reps. from Ohio, 18th-21st congresses, 1823-31; gov. Ohio, 1844-46. Died Mansfield, O., Oct. 10, 1870; buried Mansfield Cemetery.

BARTOL, Cyrus Augustus, clergyman; b. Freeport, Me., Apr. 30, 1813; s. George and Ann (Given) B.; grad. Bowdoin Coll., 1832; attended Harvard Divinity Sch., D.D. (hon.), 1859; m. Elizabeth Howard, Feb. 7, 1838, 1 child. Pastor, West Unitarian Ch., Boston, 1837-89; a follower of Ralph Waldo Emerson's ideas, home became central meeting place for transcendental thinkers in Boston. Author: Discourses on the Christian Spirit and Life, 1850; Pictures of Europe Framed in Ideas, 1855; Radical Problems, 1873; The Rising Faith, 1874. Died Boston, Dec. 16, 1900.

BARTON, Andrew (perhaps pen name for Col. Thomas Forrest), librettist. Wrote The Disappointment: or, The Force of Credulity (1st opera libretto written in Am., comic opera statirizing search for treasures of Blackbeard the Pirate), scheduled for stage presentation in Phila., Apr. 20, 1767, however on Apr. 16 Pennsylvania Gazette carried notice of withdrawal of opera supposedly because it disparaged famous Philadelphians.

BARTON, Benjamin Smith, physician, botanist; b. Lancaster, Pa., Feb. 10, 1766; s. Thomas and Esther (Rittenhouse) B.; attended York Acad., Lancaster; M.D., U. Göttingen (Germany); studied medicine in England, 1786; m. Mary Pennington, 1792, 2 children including Thomas P. Became mem. Royal Med. Soc.; practiced medicine, Phila., 1789; prof. botany U. Pa., 1790-1813, prof. medicine, 1813-15; editor Phila. Med. and Phys. Jour., 1805-08. Author: Elements of Botany (1st elementary botany text by an American), 1803; Collections for an Essay Towards a Materia Medica of the United States (description of medicinal plants), 1804. Died Phila., Dec. 19, 1815; buried Phila.

BARTON, David, senator; b. Greeneville, Tenn., Dec. 14, 1783; s. Isaac and Keziah (Murphy) B. Dep. atty. gen. Mo. Territory, 1813-15; volunteer Mo. ranger, 1814; circuit judge Howard County (Mo.), 1815-16, presiding judge, 1816-17; speaker Mo. Territorial Legislature, 1818, helped draw up petition for statehood; pres. Mo. Constl. Conv., 1820; mem. U.S. Senate from Mo., 1821-31, chmn. com. on public lands, 1823-30; mem. Mo. Senate, 1834; circuit judge Cooper County (Mo.), 1835-37; judged insane, 1837. Died Boonville, Mo., Sept. 28, 1837; buried City Cemetery, Boonville, reinterred Walnut Grove Cemetery, Boonville, 1858.

BARTON, James, actor, stage mgr.; b. Eng. Appeared at Park Theatre, N.Y.C., 1832; appeared as Hamlet at Arch Street Theatre, Phila., 1833; 1 of 1st stars to appear at Emanuel Street Theatre, Mobile, Ala.; stage mgr. St. Charles Theatre, New Orleans, for several seasons. Died 1848.

BARTON, John Rhea, surgeon; b. Lancaster, Pa., Apr. 1794; s. William and Elizabeth (Rhea) B.; M.D., U. Pa., 1818; m. Susan Ridgeway. Practiced medicine, Phila., 1818-40; surgeon Phila. Hosp., 1920-22, Pa. Hosp., Phila., 1823; performed pioneer operation in case of anchylosis of hip joint, 1826; known for knowledge and treatment of bone fractures; author paper "A New Treatment in a Case of Anchylosis," 1837; chair in his honor established by his widow at U. Pa. Med. Sch. Died Phila., Jan. 1, 1871; buried Phila.

BARTON, Richard Walker, congressman, lawyer; b. Shady Oak, nr. Winchester, Frederick County, Va., 1800; studied law. Admitted to bar; practiced in Winchester; mem. Va. Assembly, 1823, 24, 32, 35, 39; mem. U.S. Ho. of Reps. (Whig) from Va., 27th Congress, 1841-43. Died on his estate Springdale, nr. Winchester, Mar. 15, 1859; buried family burying ground at Springdale.

BARTON, Samuel, congressman; b. New Dorp, Richmond County, N.Y., July 27, 1785; attended common schs. Agt. for Commodore Vanderbilt's steamship lines; maj. in N.Y. State Militia, 1818, col., 1833; mem. N.Y. State Assembly, 1821, 22; served on Andrew Jackson reception committee, 1833; mem. U.S. Ho. of Reps. (Jacksonian Democrat) from N.Y., 24th Congress, 1835-37; in steamship business; dir. Tompkinsville Lyceum, 1842. Died New Dorp, Jan. 29, 1858; buried Moravian Cemetery.

BARTON, Thomas Pennant, diplomat; b. Phila., 1803; s. Benjamin Smith and Mary (Pennington) B.; m. Cora Livingston, Apr. 1833. Lived in France, 1815-circa 1830; sec. U.S. legation, Paris, France, 1833-36, U.S. chargé d'affaires during negotiations of French spoliation claims, 1835-36; lived on estate nr. Barrytown, N.Y., 1836-69; acquired one of largest collections of rare books in nation (contained over 16,000 volumes), specialized in early editions of Shakespeare and other Elizabethan authors, also many areas of French literature; collection purchased after his death by Boston Pub. Library. Died N.Y.C., Apr. 5, 1869.

BARTON, William, army officer; b. Warren, R.I., May 26, 1748; s. Benjamin and Lydia B.; m. Rhoda Carver, 1770. Hatter in R.I., 1770; became R.I. Militia capt., 1775, maj., 1776, lt. col., 1777; conceived and executed capture of Brig. Gen. Prescott by R. I. Militia, 1777, during occupation of R.I. by Brit., received sword from Congress in recognition of exploit; mem. R.I. Conv. to ratify U.S. Constn., 1790. Died Providence, R.I., Oct. 22, 1831; buried Providence.

BARTON, William Paul Crillon, naval surgeon, botanist; b. Phila., Nov. 17, 1786; s. William and Elizabeth (Rhea) B.; grad. Princeton, 1805; studied medicine under uncle B.S. Barton, 1805-08; m. Esther Sergeant, Sept. 1814. Apptd. surgeon USN, 1809, served in hosps. in Phila., Norfolk, Pensacola; prof. botany U. Pa. (though still on Navy active list), 1815-18; charges brought by fellow Navy surgeons that he had criticized marine hosps. unjustifiably were dismissed, 1818; prof. medicine Jefferson Med. Sch., circa 1825; 1st chief Bur. Medicine and Surgery, USN, 1842-44; as mem. inactive Navy list served as pres. Bd. Med. Examiners, 1852. Author: Vegetable Materia Medica of United States, 1817-19 (description medicinal plants). Died Phila., Feb. 29, 1856; buried Phila.

BARTRAM, John, botanist; b. nr. Darby, Pa., Mar. 23, 1699; s. John and Elizabeth (Hunt) B.; m. Mary Morris, Jan. 1723; m. 2d, Ann Mendenhall, Sept. 1729; 11 children including John, William.

First native Am. botanist; founded 1st bot. garden in U.S., Kingsessing, Pa., 1728; apptd. Am. botanist to King George III, 1765; made bot. and sci. journeys adding new descriptions of plants and zool. specimens; conducted 1st experiments in hybridization in N. Am, 1728; name commemorated in Bartramia genus of mosses; designated by Linnaeus as greatest contemporary "natural botanist". Author: Observations on the Inhabitants, Climate, Soil, etc. made by John Bartram in His Travels from Pennsylvania to Lake Ontario, 1751; Descriptions of East Florida, 1769. Died Kingsessing, Sept. 22, 1777.

BARTRAM, William, naturalist; b. Phila., Feb. 9, 1739; s. John and Ann (Mendenhall) B.; Apprenticed to mcht., 1757-61; in business as trader, Cape Fear, N.C., 1761; explored St. John's River with father, 1765-66; engaged in extensive travels through Southern part of nation gathering specimens and seeds along with drawings for Dr. John Fothergill of London, 1773-78; partner with brother John in operating botanic garden founded by father on bank of Schuylkill River, nr. Phila., 1777-1812; elected mem. Am. Philos. Soc., 1786; name commemorated in genus Bartramia of upland plovers, also in Bartram's sandpiper; compiled list of 215 native birds (most complete in existence until Wilson's American Ornithology). Author: Travels (description of natural life in South of high literary quality), 1791; article "Account of the Species, Hybrids, and Other Varieties of the Vine in North America," 1804. Died Kingsessing, Pa., July 2, 1823; buried Phila.

BARZYNSKI, Vincent, clergyman; b. Sandomierz, Poland, Sept. 20, 1838; s. Joseph and Mary (Sroczynska) B.; grad. Sem. of Lublin (Poland), 1861. Ordained priest Roman Catholic Ch., Poland, 1861; came to U.S., 1866; did missionary work among Polish immigrants, Galveston, Tex., 1866-74; in charge of St. Stanislaus Parish in Polish area of Chgo., 1874-99, responsible for founding many new parishes among Polish population of Chgo., instrumental in establishment of parochial edn. and charity instns. in Polish community of Chgo. Died Chgo., May 2, 1899; buried St. Adalbert Cemetery, Chgo.

BASCOM, Henry Bidleman, clergyman, coll. pres.; b. Hancock, N.Y., May 27, 1796; s. Alpheus and Hannah (Houk) B.; m. Miss Van Antwerp, Mar. 7, 1839, 2 children. Licensed to preach by Ohio Annual Conf. of Methodist Ch., 1813; chaplain U.S. Congress, 1824-26; 1st pres. Madison Coll., Uniontown, Pa., 1827-29; agt. Am. Colonization Soc., 1829-31; pres. Transylvania U., Lexington, Ky., 1842-49; mem. Louisville (Ky.) Conv. which organized Methodist Ch. South, 1845; editor Southern Meth. Quarterly Rev., 1846; Methodist bishop of St. Louis, 1850. Author: Methodism and Slavery, 1847; Sermons, 1849. Died Louisville, Sept. 8, 1850.

BASHFORD, Coles, gov. Wis.; b. nr. Cold Spring, N.Y., Jan. 24, 1816; attended Wesleyan Sem., (now Genesee Coll.), Lima, N.Y.; m. Frances Foreman, Oct. 12, 1847. Admitted to N.Y. bar, 1841; dist. atty. Wayne County (N.Y.), 1847-50; mem. Wis. Senate, 1852-55; gov. Wis., 1855-58; atty. gen., councillor, pres. legislative council Territory of Ariz., 1864-67; del. from Territory of Ariz. to U.S. Congress, 40th Congress, 1867-69; sec. of state Territory of Ariz., 1871-76, compiled session laws of Ariz., 1871-76. Died Prescott, Ariz., Apr. 25, 1878; buried Mountain View Cemetery, Oakland, Cal.

BASS, Edward, clergyman; b. Dorchester, Mass., Nov. 23, 1726; s. Joseph and Elizabeth (Breck) B.; grad. Harvard, 1744; m. Sarah Beck, 1754; m. 2d, Mercy Phillips, 1789. Ordained to ministry Ch. of England, London, 1752; rector St. Paul's Episcopal Ch., Newburyport, Mass., 1752-1803; elected 1st bishop of Mass., 1796, consecrated, 1797, served until 1803, diocese extended during his service to include Episcopal churches of R.I. and N.H. Died probably Newburyport, Sept. 10, 1803; buried Newburyport.

BASS, Lyman Kidder, congressman, lawyer; b. Alden, Erie County, N.Y., Nov. 13, 1836; grad. Union Coll., Schenectady, N.Y., 1856; studied law. Admitted to bar, 1858; practiced in Buffalo, N.Y.; dist. atty. Erie County, 1865-72; mem. U.S. Ho. of Reps. (Democrat) from N.J., 43d-44th congresses, 1873-77; moved to Colorado Springs, Colo., 1877, practiced law; gen. counsel Denver & Rio Grande R.R. Co., 1878-84. Died N.Y.C., May 11, 1889; buried Forest Lawn Cemetery, Buffalo.

BASS, Sam, outlaw; b. Mitchell, Ind., July 21, 1851; s. Daniel and Elizabeth (Sheeks) B. Employed in mill, Rosedale, Miss., 1870-71; worked in hotel, Denton County, Tex., 1871, dep. sheriff Denton County, 1873-75; engaged in driving cattle to Kan., 1875; robbed stage coaches with 4 companions, Deadwood, S.D., 1876; robbed Union Pacific train with gang, Big Springs, Neb., 1877; robbed banks in Tex., 1878. Killed during gun battle in attempted bank robbery, Round Rock, Tex., July 21, 1878; buried Round Rock.

BASS, William Capers, coll. pres.; b. Augusta, Ga., Jan. 13, 1831; s. Rev. Henry and Amelia (Love) B.; grad. Emory Coll., 1852, D.D. (hon.), 1892; m. Octavia Nickelson, 1854. Prof. natural science Wesleyan Female Coll., Macon, Ga., 1859-74, pres., 1874-94, also taught philosophy; licensed to preach by Gen. Conf., Methodist Ch., 1867. Died Macon, Nov. 15, 1894.

BASSE, Jeremiah, colonial gov. In his early life was an Anabaptist minister; agt. of West Jersey Soc., 1692; gov. N.J., 1697-99, (discontent with his adminstrn. was main cause for making N.J. a royal colony, 1702); secured royal patent as sec. Royal Govt. in N.J., 1702; mem. N.J. Assembly, circa 1715; named atty. gen., 1719. Died 1725.

BASSETT, Burwell, congressman; b. New Kent County, Va., Mar. 18, 1764; attended William and Mary Coll. Mem. Va. Ho. of Dels., 1787-89, 1819-21; mem. Va. Senate, 1793-1805; mem. U.S. Ho. of Reps. (Democrat) from Va., 9th-12th, 14th-15th, 17th-20th congresses, 1805-13, 15-19, 21-29. Died New Kent County, Feb. 26, 1841.

BASSETT, Richard, senator; b. Cecil County, Md., Apr. 2, 1745; s. Michael and Judith (Thompson) B.; m. Ann Ennals; m. 2d, Miss Bruff; children—Mary, Ann; adopted dau., Rachel. Mem. Del. Council of Safety, 1776; mem. Del. Gov.'s Council, circa 1776-86; served as capt. Dover Light Horse in Revolutionary War, 1777; mem. Del. constl. convs., 1776, 92; mem. Del. Senate, 1782, Del. Ho. of Reps., 1786; del. to U.S. Constl. Conv., 1787, mem. Del. Conv. which ratified U.S. Constn., 1787; mem. U.S. Senate (Federalist) from Del., 1789-93; chief justice Del. Ct. of Common Pleas, 1793-99; Federalist presdl. elector, 1797; gov. Del., 1798-1801; judge U.S. Circuit Ct. for 3d Dist., 1801-15. Died Bohemia Manor, Del., Sept. 15, 1815; buried Brandywine Cemetery, Wilmington, Del.

BATCHELDER, John Putnam, physician; b. Wilton, N.H., Aug. 6, 1784; s. Archelaus and Betty (Putnam) Batchelor; grad. Harvard. Licensed to practice medicine by N.H. Med. Soc.; settled in N.Y. C., lectr. anatomy and surgery, Castleton, Vt., also Berkshire (Mass.) Inst.; considered 1st Am. physician to perform operation to remove head of thigh bone; invented one-handed craniotome (instrument used in opening skull). Died N.Y.C., Apr. 8, 1868.

BATCHELDER, Samuel, mfr., inventor; b. Jaffrey, N.H., June 8, 1784; s. Samuel and Elizabeth (Woodberry) B.; m. Mary Montgomery, 1810, 6 children. Mgr., Hamilton Mfg. Co., Lowell, Mass., 1824-31, pres., 1859-70, treas., 1869-71; mem. 1st Bd. Selectmen, East Chelmsford, Mass., 1825; inventor stop-motion for drawing frame, 1832; perfected dynamometer (force-measurer), 1837; mem. Mass. Legislature, 1847; treas. Everett Mills, 1859-70; pres. Essex Co., 1867-70. Author: Responsibilities of the North in Relation to Slavery, 1856; Early Progress of Cotton Manufacture in United States, 1863, also newspaper articles. Died Cambridge, Mass., Feb. 5, 1879.

BATEMAN, Ephraim, senator, congressman; b. Cedarville, N.J., July 9, 1780; attended Nathaniel Ogden's Latin Sch.; studied medicine with Dr. Jonathan Elmer, 1801, U. Pa., 1802, 03. Apprenticed as tailor, 1796; taught sch., 1799-1801; practiced medicine Cedarville; mem. N.J. Ho. of Assembly, 1808, 09, 11, 13, speaker, 1813; mem. U.S. Ho. of Reps. (Democrat) from N.J., 14th-17th congresses, 1815-23; mem. N.J. Council, 1826, pres., cast vote which elected him rather than Theodore Frelinghuysen to U.S. Senate (filled vacancy) from N.J., Nov. 10, 1826-Jan. 12, 1829, resigned because of health. Died Cedarville, Jan. 28, 1829; buried Old Stone Ch. Cemetery, Fairfield Twp., N.J.

BATEMAN, Newton, ednl. adminstr., coll. pres.; b. Fairtown, N.J., July 27, 1822; s. Bergen and Ruth (Bower) B.; grad. Ill. Coll., 1843; m. Sarah Dayton, 1850; m. 2d, Annie W. Tyler. County supt. schs., Jackson, Ill., 1859; supt. pub. instrn. Ill., 1859-63, 65-75; editor The Ill. Tchr.; mem. com. which drafted bill creating U.S. Bur. Edn.; mem. Ill. Bd. Health, 1877-91; pres. Knox Coll., Galesburg, Ill., 1874-92, then pres. emeritus; editor Historical Encyclopedia of Illinois. Died Galesburg, Oct. 21, 1897.

BATEMAN, Sidney Frances Cowell, playwright, actress, b. either N.Y.C. or N.J., Mar. 29, 1823; d. Joseph and Frances (Sheppard) Cowell; m. Hezekiah Linthicum Bateman, Nov. 10, 1839, 3 daus., Kate, Ellen, Isabella. Began acting career, New Orleans, circa 1837; wrote comedy Self which opened at Bateman's St. Louis Theatre, 1856; wrote romantic play Geraldine, or Love's Victory which opened at Wallack's Theatre, N.Y.C., 1859, dramatization of Longfellow's poem Evangeline, opened 1862; moved to England, 1863; mgr. Lyceum Theatre, London, Eng., 1871-78, Sadler's Wells Theatre, London; produced Joaquin Miller's The Danites, 1st Am. play performed by entirely Am. company in Eng., 1880. Died London, Jan. 13, 1881.

BATES, Barnabas, postal reformer; b. Edmonton, Eng., 1785. Came to R.I. with parents when a child; pastor Baptist Ch., Bristol, N.J., 1814; collector Port of Bristol (R.I.); moved to N.Y.C., 1824; began weekly jour. The Christian Inquirer, 1825; asst. postmaster N.Y.C., circa 1835; organized 1st public meeting for postal reform, N.Y.C., 1843, successfully petitioned Congress to charge flat postal rate of 5 cents per ounce regardless of distance; corr. sec. N.Y. Cheap Postage Assn., 1848. Died Boston, Oct. 11, 1853.

BATES, Daniel Moore, jurist; b. Laurel, Del., Jan. 28, 1821; s. Rev. Jacob and Mary (Jones) Moore; adopted by Martin Waltham Bates after death of parents; grad. Dickinson Coll., 1839, A.M. (hon.), 1842; m. Margaret Handy, Nov. 1844. Admitted to Del. bar, 1842; sec. of state Del., 1847-51; commr. for revision state laws Del. Gen. Assembly, 1849; U.S. dist. atty. for Del., 1852-61 del. from Del. to Washington (D.C.) Peace Conf., 1861; chancellor Del., 1865-73; pres. Hist. Soc. Del. Died Richmond, Va., Mar. 28, 1879.

BATES, David Stanhope, civil engr.; b. Morristown, N.J., June 10, 1777; s. David and Sarah (Tappan) B.; m. Sarah Johnson, 1799; children—John, Timothy, David. Land surveyor, Oneida County, N.Y., 1810-11; mgr. iron factory, Rotterdam, N.Y., 1811-17; asst. engr. on mid-section Erie Canal, 1817-18, division engr., 1818-24; designed and built aqueduct over Genesee River at Rochester, N.Y., 1823; built system of locks at Lockport; cons. engr. for Ohio Canal Commrs., 1824-29, surveyed 800 miles of canal sites; chief engr. Louisville & Portland Canal Co., 1825-28; chief engr. Niagara River Hydraulic Co., 1828-34. Died Rochester, Nov. 28, 1839; buried Rochester.

BATES, Edward, atty. gen., congressman; b. Belmont, Va., Sept. 4, 1793; s. Thomas Fleming and Caroline (Woodson) B.; m. Julia Davenport Coalter, May 29, 1823, 17 children. Moved to St. Louis, 1814; admitted to Mo. bar, 1816; atty. gen. Mo., 1820-22; mem. Mo. Constl. Conv., 1820; U.S. dist. atty., 1821-26; mem. Mo. Ho. of Reps., 1822, 34; mem. U.S. Ho. of Reps. (Whig) from Mo., 20th Congress, 1827-29; mem. Mo. Senate, 1830-34; pres. River and Harbor Improvement Conv., Chgo., 1847; declined appointment as U.S. sec. of war, 1850; pres. Whig. Nat. Conv., Balt., 1856; nominated for Pres. U.S. at Republican Conv., 1860; U.S. atty. gen. under Lincoln, 1861-64 (1st cabinet mem. from region West of Mississippi River); suggested establishment of naval fleet on Mississippi River; opposed admission of W.Va. as state. Died St. Louis, Mar. 25, 1869; buried Bellefontaine Cemetery, St. Louis.

BATES, Frederick, gov. Mo.; b. Belmont, Va., June 23, 1777; s. Thomas Fleming and Caroline (Woodson) B.; m. Nancy Ball, Mar. 4, 1819, 4 children. Asso. judge Mich. Territory, 1805; sec. La. Territory, 1806; responsible for revision Code of La. Territory, 1808; acting gov. La. Territory, 1807; published compilation of laws of Louisiana (1st book to be printed in Mo.), 1808; mem. Mo. Constl. Conv., 1820; gov. Mo., 1824-25. Died Chesterfield, Mo., Aug. 4, 1825.

BATES, Harriet Leonora Vose, author; b. Quincy, Ill., July 30, 1856; dau. of Prof. George L. Vose; m. Arlo Bates. Began to write under pseudonym Eleanor Putnam in her youth, contbd. to various periodicals; contbr. to Atlantic Monthly, 1885-86; wrote mostly of life in Salem, Mass. Died Boston, Mar. 1886.

BATES, Isaac Chapman, senator, congressman, lawyer; b. Granville, Mass., Jan. 23, 1779; grad. Yale, 1802. Admitted to bar, 1808; practiced in Northampton, Mass., 1808; mem. Mass. Ho. of Reps., 1808, 09; mem. U.S. Ho. of Reps. (Anti-Jackson candidate) from Mass., 20th-23d congresses, 1827-35; Whig presdl. elector, 1836, 40; mem. U.S. Senate (Whig, filled vacancy) from Mass., Jan. 13, 1841-45. Died Washington, D.C., Mar. 16, 1845; buried Bridge Street Cemetery, Northampton.

BATES, James, physician, congressman; b. Greene, Me., Sept. 24, 1789; s. Solomon and Mary (Macomber) B.; ed. Harvard Med. Sch.; m. Mary Jones, July 27, 1815. Served with med. dept. U.S. Army, 1813; mem. U.S. Ho. of Reps. from Me., 22d Congress, 1831-33; supt. Insane Asylum, Augusta, Me., 1845. Died Yarmouth, Me., Feb. 25, 1882; buried Old Oak Cemetery, Norridgewock, Me.

BATES, James Woodson, congressman; b. Goochland County, Va., Aug. 25, 1788; attended Yale; grad. Princeton, 1807; studied law. Admitted to bar; practiced in Va.; moved to St. Louis, 1816, to Post of Ark., 1819; mem. U.S. Congress from Ark. Territory, 16th-17th congresses, Dec. 21, 1819-23; practiced law, Batesville, Ark.; judge 4th Jud. Circuit of Ark. Territory, 1824-28; judge Ark. Superior Ct., 1828-32; del. Ark. Constl. Conv., 1835; judge probate Ct. of Crawford County, 1836; register land office, Clarksville, 1841-45. Died Van Buren, Crawford County, Ark., Dec. 26, 1846; buried family burying ground at Moores Rock, Crawford (now Sebastian) County, Ark.

BATES, John, industrialist, theatre owner. Purchased theater, Louisville, Ky., 1846; opened theater on Pine Street between 3d and 4th streets, St. Louis, Mo., 1851, promoted appearances by stars W.J. Florence and the Barney Williamses, 1851-53, all leading visiting stars, after 1853; sold Bates Theater to Ben de Bar (who renamed it St. Louis Theater), 1856.

BATES, Joshua, financier; b. Weymouth, Mass., Oct. 10, 1788; s. Col. Joshua and Tirzah (Pratt) B.; m. Lucretia Augustus Sturgis, 1 son, 1 dau. Apprentice in William R. Gray's counting house, Boston, 1802; entered partnership (with Capt. Beckford) in firm Beckford & Bates, Boston, firm collapsed, 1812; European agt. for William Gray, 1816-36; entered bus. partnership with John Baring, England, 1826-28, firm merged with accounting house of Baring Bros. & Co., Eng., 1828, became full partner; handled claims dispute between U.S. and Eng., 1854; founder Boston Public Library, 1855. Died Sept. 24, 1864.

BATES, Walter, loyalist; b. Stamford (now Darien), Conn., Mar. 14, 1760; s. John and Sarah (Bostwick) B.; married. Held in stockade for alleged allegiance to British, 1775; joined Tories in L.I. after his release; settled in Nova Scotia, 1783; 1st man to be married in N.S.; sheriff King's County (N.S.). Author: The Mysterious Stranger, 1816; Kingston and the Loyalists of the "Spring Fleet" of 1783, published posthumously, 1889. Died Feb. 11, 1842.

BATTEY, Robert, surgeon; b. Augusta, Ga., Nov. 26, 1828; s. Cephas and Mary (Magruder) B.; attended Phila. Coll. Pharmacy, 1856; M.D., Jefferson Med. Coll., 1857; m. Martha Smith, Dec. 20, 1849, 14 children including Dr. Henry H. Performed successful operation for vesico-vaginal fistula, 1858; served as surgeon 19th Ga. Volunteers, Confederate Army, Civil War, established hosp., Macon, Ga., 1864; editor Atlanta Med. and Surg. Jour., 1872-76; founder Martha Battey Hosp., Rome Ga.; performed Battey's Operation (removal of normal human ovaries to establish menopause), 1872; prof. obstetrics Atlanta (Ga.) Med. Coll., 1873-75; pres. Ga. Med. Assn., 1876; introduced iodized phenol in gynecol. work, 1877; mem. Atlanta Acad. Medicine, Am. Gynecol. Soc., A.M.A. Died Rome, Ga., Nov. 8, 1895.

BATTLE, William Horn, jurist; b. Edgecombe County, N.C., Oct. 17, 1802; s. Joel and Mary (Johnson) B.; grad. U. N.C., 1820, LL.D. (hon.), 1833; m. Lucy M. Plummer, June 1825, 8 children including Kemp P. Admitted to N.C. bar, 1825; mem. N.C. Ho. of Commons. 1833-34; one of 3 appointees to compile Revised Statutes of N.C., 1833; reporter N.C. Supreme Ct., 1834-40; del. Whig Nat. Conv., 1839; judge Superior Ct. N.C., 1840; prof. law U. N.C., 1845-68; asso. justice N.C. Supreme Ct., 1852-68; pres. Raleigh Nat. Bank; mem. commn. which revised statutes of N.C. Died Chapel Hill, N.C., Mar. 14, 1879; buried Raleigh.

BAUDOIN, Michael, clergyman; b. Quebec, Can., Mar. 8, 1692. Joined Soc. of Jesus in France, at age 21; returned to N.Am. to serve among Choctaw Indians; superior gen. La. mission, 1749-63; allowed (because of his age) to remain in La. after dispersal of Jesuits, 1763, lived with a friendly planter until death. Died New Orleans, circa 1768.

BAUER, Augustus, architect; b. Germany, 1827; grad. Poly. Sch., Darmstadt, Germany. Came to U.S., 1850; employed as archtl. draftsman in office of Jonathan Snook, N.Y.C.; asso. firm Carstensen & Gildemeister (architects of Crystal Palace), until 1853; moved to Chgo., 1853, practiced in partnership with Asher Carter, until 1866; practiced alone, 1871-81; mem. firm Bauer & Hill, Chgo., 1881-94; designed numerous bus. and comml. bldgs. (most of which are now demolished); mem. Chgo. Bd. Edn., after 1874, designed many city schs.; pres. Chgo. chpt. A.I.A., 1879-86. Died Chgo., 1894.

BAUGHER, Henry Louis, clergyman, coll. pres.; b. Abbotstown, Pa., July 18, 1804; s. Christian Frederick and Ann; grad. Dickinson Coll., 1826; attended Princeton Theol. Sem.; m. Clara Brooks, Oct. 29, 1829. Licensed to preach by W. Pa. Synod of Lutheran Ch., 1828; pastor, Boonesboro, Md., 1829-31; In charge of Boonesboro Classical Sch., 1830; prof. Greek and rhetoric Pa. Coll. (now Gettysburg Coll.), 1832-50, pres., 1850-68. Died Gettysburg, Apr. 14, 1868.

BAUMAN, Edward, architect; b. Danzig, Germany, 1828; grad. Poly. Sch., Gradentz. Came to U.S., 1850; settled in Chgo.; employed by Edward Burling, 10 years; began practice as architect; moved to Memphis, Tenn., returned to Chgo. after Civil War; practiced in assn. with Harris W. Huehl. Died Berlin, Germany, Feb. 2, 1889.

BAXLEY, Henry Willis, surgeon; b. Balt., June 1803; s. George and Mary (Merryman) B.; attended St. Mary's Coll.; grad. U. Md., 1824. Attending physician Balt. Gen. Dispensary, 1826-29; physician Md. Penitentiary, 1831-32; co-founder Coll. Dental Surgery, Balt. (1st instn. of kind in U.S.), 1839, prof. anatomy, 1839-46; prof. surgery Washington Med. Coll., Balt., 1846-47; physician Balt. Alms House, 1849-50; prof. anatomy and surgery Med. Coll. of Ohio, Cincinnati, 1850-54; insp. hosps. U.S. Govt., 1865; Baxley Med. Professorship of Johns Hopkins Med Sch. named after him. Author: Spain, Art Remains and Art Realities, Painters, Priests and Princes, 1875. Died Mar. 13, 1876.

BAXTER, Elisha, gov. Ark.; b. Rutherford County, N.C., Sept. 1, 1827; s. William and Catherine (Lee) B.; m. Harriet Patton, 1849, 6 children. Moved to Ark., 1852; operator gen. store, Batesville, Ark., 1853-55; mem. Ark. Legislature, 1854, 58; pros. atty. of Ark. under Confederate Govt.; joined Union cause when Gen. S. R. Curtis came to Batesville; moved to Mo.; brought back to Little Rock (Ark.), convicted for treason, escaped from prison, raised 4th Ark. Mounted Inf., U.S. Army; mem. Ark. Supreme Ct., 1864, resigned to become mem. U.S. Senate, not admitted to Senate seat; judge Ark. 3d Circuit Ct., 1868; gov. Ark., 1873-74, gave up office after election was successfully contested by Joseph Brooks, returned to office after Ark. Legislature nullified Brooks' claim. Died May 31, 1899.

BAXTER, Henry, army officer, diplomat; b. Sidney Plains, N.Y., Sept. 8, 1821; s. Levi and Lois (Johnson) B.; m. Elvira E. George, 1854. Commd. capt. U.S. Army, 1861, col., 1862, brig. gen. U.S. Volunteers, 1863; commanded brigade at battles of Fredericksburg and Gettysburg; wounded in battles of Antietam and Fredericksburg; served in Battle of Five Forks; mustered out, 1865; brevetted maj. gen. U.S. Volunteers, 1865; U.S. minister to Honduras, 1866-69, to Holland, 1869-72. Died Jonesville, Mich., Dec. 30, 1873.

BAXTER, John, editor, jurist; b. N.C., Mar. 5, 1819; s. William and Catherine (Lee) B.; m. Orra Alexander, June 26, 1842. Mem. N.C. Legislature, speaker lower house; Whig; leader neutral forces in Unionist Conv., Greenville, Tenn., 1861; editor newspaper Daily Chronicle (pro-Union), Knoxville, Tenn., 1862-67; mem. Tenn Constl. Conv., 1870, chmn. judiciary com.; U.S. circuit judge, 1877-86. Died Apr. 2, 1886.

BAXTER, Portus, congressman; b. Brownington, Orleans County, Vt., Dec. 4, 1806; attended Norwich Mil. Acad., U. Vt. Moved to Derby Line, Orleans County, 1828; Whig presdl. elector, 1852; Republican presdl. elector, 1856; mem. U.S. Ho. of Reps. (Rep.) from Vt., 37th-39th congresses, 1861-67. Died Washington, D.C., Mar. 4, 1868; buried Strafford (Va.) Cemetery.

BAXTER, William, clergyman, coll. pres.; b. Leeds, Yorkshire, Eng., July 6, 1820; s. Henry and Mary B.; grad. Bethany Coll., 1845; m. Mrs. Fidelia (Pico) Vail, Mar. 7, 1854. Came to Allegheny City, Pa., 1828; pastor, Port Gibson, Miss., Baton Rouge, La.; prof. belles lettres Newton (Miss.) Coll.; pres. Ark. Coll., Fayetteville, 1860-63; pastor Christian Ch., Lisbon, O., 1865-75. Author: Pea Ridge and Prairie Grove, or Scenes and Incidents of the War in Arkansas, 1864; Life of Elder Walter Scott, 1874. Died New Castle, Pa., Feb. 11, 1880.

BAY, William Van Ness, congressman, lawyer; b. Hudson, N.Y., Nov. 23, 1818; attended pub. schs.; studied law. Admitted to bar; moved to Union, Franklin County, Mo., 1836, practiced law; mem. Mo. Ho. of Reps., 1844-48; mem. U.S. Ho. of Reps. (Democrat) from Mo., 31st Congress, 1849-51; judge Mo. Supreme Ct., 1863-65; moved to St. Louis, practiced law, retired, 1886; moved to Eureka, Mo. Died Eureka, Feb. 10, 1894; buried Oak Hill Cemetery, Kirkwood, St. Louis County, Mo.

BAYARD, James Asheton, senator, diplomat; b. Phila., July 28, 1767; s. James Asheton and Agnes (Hodge) B.; grad. Princeton, 1784; m. Ann Bassett, Feb. 11, 1795, children—James Asheton, Richard Henry. Admitted to Pa. bar, 1787; mem. U.S. Ho. of Reps. from Del., 5th-7th congresses, 1797-1803, liason for Jefferson, securing consequential presdl. election; mem. U.S. Senate from Del., 1805-13; apptd. by Pres. Madison to represent U.S. at Ghent, 1813-14, Treaty of Ghent. Died Wilmington, Del., Aug. 6, 1815; buried Wilmington (Del.) and Brandywine Cemetery.

BAYARD, James Asheton, lawyer, senator; b. Wilmington, Del., Nov. 15, 1799; s. James Asheton and Ann (Bassett) B.; ed. Princeton, Union Coll. (grad. 1818); m. Ann Francis, July 8, 1823; son, Thomas Francis. Admitted to Del. bar, 1822; a dir. U.S. Bank, 1834; U.S. dist. atty. for Del., 1837-41; mem. U.S. Senate from Del., 1851-63, 67-69; delegate to Del. Constl. Conv., 1852-53. Died Wilmington, June 13, 1880; buried Old Swedes Burial Ground, Wilmington, Del.

BAYARD, John Bubenheim, mcht., Continental congressman; b. Cecil County, Md., Aug. 11, 1738; s. James and Mary (Ashton) B.; ed. Nottingham Instn.; m. Margaret Hodge; m. 2d, Mrs. Mary Hodgden; m. 3d, Johannah White, 1787. Mem. merc. firm John Rhea, Phila., 1756-1807; signer Non-Importation Agreement of 1765; mem. Pa. Provincial Congress, July 1774; mem. Phila. Council o Safety, 1776; participated in battles of Brandywine, Germantown, Princeton, 1776-77; speaker Pa Assembly, 1777-78; mem. Bd. of War; maj. 2 Battalion of Phila. Associators (volunteers with Continental Army), col., 1777; mem. Supreme Exec Council Pa., 1781; del. Continental Congress from Pa., 1785-87; mayor New Brunswick (N.J.), 1790 Died New Brunswick, Jan. 7, 1807; buried First Presbyn. Churchyard, New Brunswick.

BAYARD, Nicholas, colonial ofcl., mayor N.Y.C.; b. Alphen, Holland, 1644; s. Samuel and Anna (Stuyvesant) B.; m. Judith Varlet, May 22, 1666, 1 son, Samuel. Came to Am., 1647; clk. N.Y. Common Council, 1664; sec. Province of N.Y., 1664; pvt. sec. to Gov. Stuyvesant of N.Y., 1665; continued as provincial sec. N.Y. under Dutch occupation, 1672, commd. receiver gen., 1672; lt. Dutch Militia, 1672 given power of atty. to collect debts for Dutch Govt.; commd. mayor N.Y.C., 1685-87; mem. N.Y. Gov.'s Council; comdr.-in-chief N.Y. Militia, 1688. Died N.Y.C., 1707.

BAYARD, Richard Henry, senator, diplomat; b. Wilmington, Del., Sept. 23, 1796; s. James Asheton and Ann (Bassett) B.; grad. Princeton, 1814; m. Mary Caroll, Feb. 28, 1815. Mayor, Wilmington, 1832; mem. U.S. Senate from Del., 1836-39, 40-45; chief justice Del., 1839; U.S. charge d'affaires, Brussels, 1850-53. Died Phila., Mar. 4, 1868; buried Wilmington (Del.) and Brandywine Cemetery.

BAYARD, Samuel, lawyer; b. Phila., Jan. 11, 1767; s. John and Margaret (Hodge) B.; grad. Coll. of N.J. (now Princeton), 1784; studied law under William Bradford; m. Margaret Pintard, Aug. 1790, 1 son, Lewis Pintard. Clk., U.S. Supreme Ct., 1791; agt. of U.S. to England to prosecute U.S. claims before English Admiralty Cts., 1794-98; judge Westerfield County (N.Y.), 1798-1803; practiced law, N.Y.C., 1803; trustee, treas. Princeton; a founder Princeton Theol. Sem., 1812; judge Ct. Common Pleas of Somerset County (N.J.); mem. N.J. Legislature. Author: A Digest of American Cases on the Law of Evidence, Intended as Notes to Peake's Compendium, 1810; Letters on the Sacrament of the Lord's Supper, 1825. Died May 11, 1840.

BAYARD, Thomas Francis, senator; b. Wilmington, Del., Oct. 29, 1828; s. James Asheton and Ann (Francis) B.; m. Louisa Lee, Oct. 1856; m. 2d, Mary W. Clymer, Nov. 7, 1889. Admitted to Del. bar, 1851; U.S. dist. atty. for Del., 1853-54; mem. U.S. Senate (Democrat) from Del., 1869-85, pres. pro tem, 1881; mem. Electoral Commn., 1876, 80, 84; U.S. presdl. candidate, 1880, 84, advocated sound currency, low tariffs, civil service reform, limitation of the power and activity of fed. govt; U.S. sec. state under Pres. Cleveland, 1885-89; apptd. ambassador to Gt. Britain (the 1st to hold that diplomatic rank), 1893-97. Died Dedham, Mass., Sept. 28, 1898; buried Swedes Cemetery, Wilmington.

BAYARD, William, mcht.; b. Greenwich, N.Y., 1761; s. Col. William and Catherine (McEvers) B.; m. Elizabeth Cornell, 1783, 2 sons, William, Robert. Formed partnership with H. LeRoy, 1786, firm later became LeRoy, Bayard & McEvers (foremost comml. house in N.Y.C.); pres. Bank of America, N.Y. State C. of C., others; chmn. meeting of mchts. to protest high tariff, Phila., 1824. Died Sept. 18, 1826.

BAYLEY, James Roosevelt, clergyman, historian; b. Rye, N.Y., Aug. 23, 1814; s. Guy Carleton and Grace (Roosevelt) B.; attended Trinity Coll., Hartford, Conn., Sem. of St. Sulpice, Paris, France. Ordained to ministry Episcopal Ch., 1835; rector St. Peter's Ch., Harlem, N.Y.; went to Europe and investigated Catholicism because of theol. controversy in Anglican Ch. and influence of John Henry Newman's Tract 90, 1841; became Roman Catholic, 1842; ordained priest Roman Cath. Ch., N.Y.C., 1844; v.p. St. John's Coll., N.Y.C., 1844-48; sec. to Bishop Hughes of N.Y.C., 1848-53; bishop Diocese of Newark, N.J., 1853-72, Diocese of Balt., 1872-77. Author: A Brief Sketch of Early History of the Catholic Church on the Island of New York, 1853, 74; Memoirs of the Rt. Rev. Simon William Gabriel Bruté, First Bishop of Vincennes, 1855, 76. Died Newark, N.J., Oct. 3, 1877; buried St. Joseph's Convent, Emmitsburg, Md.

BAYLEY, Richard, physician; b. Fairfield, Conn., 1745; studied medicine under John Charlton, N.Y.C.; studied anatomy under William Hunter, London, Eng., 1769-71; m. Miss Charlton. Went to London, 1769-71; during croup epidemic made study of disease's causes and treatment which cut mortality rate in half, 1774; in England, 1775-76; surgeon Brit. Army under Gen. Howe, Newport, R.I., 1776-77; practiced medicine, N.Y.C., 1777; prof. anatomy and surgery Columbia, 1792; 1st physician in Am. to amputate arm at shoulder-joint; health physician Port of N.Y., 1795. Author: An Account of the Epidemic Fever which Prevailed in the City of New York during Part of the Summer and Fall of 1795, published 1796; Letters from the Health Office Submitted to the New York Common Council. Died Aug. 17, 1801.

BAYLIES, Francis, congressman, historian; b. Taunton, Mass., Oct. 16, 1784; s. Dr. William Baylies; m. Mrs. Elizabeth Deming, 1823. Admitted to Mass. bar, 1811; register of probate Bristol County, 1812-20; mem. U.S. Ho. of Reps. from Mass., 17th-19th congresses, 1821-27; mem. Mass. Legislature, 1827-32; minister to Buenos Aires, 1832. Author: An Historical Memoir of the Colony of New Plymouth, 1830; A History of the Plymouth Colony, 1866. Died Taunton, Oct. 28, 1852; buried Old Plain Cemetery, Taunton.

BAYLIES, William, congressman, lawyer; b. Dighton, Mass., Sept. 15, 1776; grad. Brown U., 1795; studied law. Admitted to bar, 1799; practiced in Bridgewater (West Parish), Mass., 1799; mem. Mass. Ho. of Reps., 1808-09, 12-13, 20-21; mem. Mass. Senate, 1825-26, 30-31; mem. U.S. Ho. of Reps. (War Democrat, contested election) from Mass., 11th, 13th-14th, 23d congresses, Mar. 4-June 28, 1809, 13-17, 33-35. Died Taunton, Bristol County, Mass., Sept. 27, 1865; buried Old Cemetery, Dighton.

BAYLOR, George, army officer; b. Newmarket, Va., Jan. 12, 1752; s. Col. John and Fanny (Walker) B.; m. Lucy Page. Mil. aide to Gen. Washington during Am. Revolution; promoted col. for his service in Battle of Trenton; comdr. regt. of cavalry, wounded when his regt. was attacked by English troops under Gen. Grey while encamped after Battle of Monmouth, 1778. Died Bridgetown, Barbados, Mar. 1784.

BAYLOR, Robert Emmett Bledsoe, congressman, jurist; b. Lincoln County, Ky., May 10, 1793; s. Walker and Jane (Bledsoe) B. Elected to Ky. Legislature, 1819, Ala. Legislature, 1824; mem. U.S. Ho. of Reps. from Ala., 21st Congress, 1829-31; apptd. judge 3d dist. Tex., 1841; asso. justice Tex. Supreme Ct.; 1st dist. judge under Constn. of 1845; pres. Baptist Edn. Soc. in Tex., 1843; projected plan for 1st Bapt. Coll. in Tex., 1845; Baylor County, also Baylor Coll. (chmn. bd. trustees) named after him; moderator Tex. Bapt. Union Assn.; pres. Bapt. State Conv. Died Washington County, Tex., Dec. 30, 1873; buried Baylor Coll., Belton, Tex.

BAYLY, Thomas, congressman, lawyer; b. Wellington, nr. Quantico, Somerset (now Wicomico) County, Md., Sept. 13, 1775; grad. Princeton, 1797; studied law. Admitted to bar; practiced in Somerset and Worcester counties, Md.; mem. Md. Ho. of Dels., 1804-14; mem. U.S. Ho. of Reps. (Democrat) from Md., 15th-17th congresses, 1817-23. Died Wellington, 1829; buried family cemetery at Wellington.

BAYLY, Thomas Henry, congressman, jurist; b. Mt. Custis, Va., Dec. 11, 1810; s. Thomas M. and Margaret (Cropper) B.; m. Evelyn H. May. Mem. Va. Ho. of Dels., 1836-42; apptd. judge of a dist. circuit ct. Va., 1842; mem. U.S. Ho. of Reps. from Va. 29th-34th congresses, May 6, 1844-June 22, 1856; commd. brig. gen. Va. Militia. Died June 22, 1856.

BAYLY, Thomas Monteagle, congressman, lawyer, planter; b. Hills Farm, nr. Drummondtown, Accomac County, Va., Mar. 26, 1775; attended Washington Acad., Md.; grad. Princeton, 1794; studied law; at least 1 son, Thomas Henry. Admitted to bar, circa 1796; practiced in Accomac County; became planter; mem. Va. Ho. of Dels., 1798-1801, 19, 20, 28-31; mem. Va. Senate, 1801-09; col. of militia during War of 1812; mem. U.S. Ho. of Reps. (Democrat) from Va., 13th Congress, 1813-15; del. Va. constl. convs., 1829, 30. Died on his plantation Mt. Custis, nr. Accomac, Va., Jan. 7, 1834; buried family cemetery at Mt. Custis.

BAYMA, Joseph, clergyman, mathematician; b. Cirie, France, Nov. 9, 1816; attended Royal Acad., Turin, France. Entered Jesuit novitiate, Chieti, France, 1832, ordained Jesuit priest, 1847; missionary to Algiers, 1847; asst. to astronomer Angelo Secchi and later dir. Osservatorio del Collegio Romano, Rome, Italy; rector Episcopal Sem., Bertinoro, Italy, 1852-58; prof. philosophy Stonyhurst Coll., Eng., 1858-69; pres. St. Ignatius Coll., San Francisco, 1869-72, prof. higher mathematics, 1872-80; retired to Santa Clara (Cal.) Coll. because of ill health, 1880. Author: (with Enrico Vasco) Il Ratio Studiorum adattato ai tempi presenti; De studio religiosae perfectionis excitando, 1852; Philosophia Realis, 1861; Elements of Molecular Mechanics, 1866. Died Santa Clara Coll., Feb. 7, 1892.

BAYNE, Thomas McKee, congressman, lawyer; b. Bellevue, Allegheny County, Pa., June 14, 1836; attended Westminster Coll., New Wilmington, Pa.; studied law. Served as col. 136th Regt., Pa. Volunteer Inf., Union Army, in Civil War, 1862; in battles of Fredericksburg and Chancellorsville; admitted to Allegheny County bar, 1866; elected dist. atty. Allegheny County, 1870-74; mem. U.S. Ho. of Reps. (Republican) from Pa., 45th-51st congresses, 1877-91; retired from public life and business activities. Died Washington, D.C., June 16, 1894; buried Uniondale Cemetery, Pitts.

BAYNHAM, William, surgeon; b. probably S.C., Dec. 7, 1749; s. John Baynham; studied surgery under Dr. Walker, probably S.C., 1764-69, St. Thomas Hosp., London, Eng., 1769-72. Prepared anatomical demonstrations and instructed in dissection for med. students at Cambridge (Eng.) U., 1772-81; practiced surgery, London, 1781-85; returned to U.S., 1785; practiced medicine specializing in surgery, Essex, Va., 1785-1814; gained reputation as surgeon in operations for stone, cataracts and extra-uterine pregnancy; descriptions of some of his operations in Vol. I of New York Med. and Surg. Jour. Died Essex, Dec. 8, 1814.

BAZIN, John Stephen, clergyman; b. Duerne, France, Oct. 15, 1796. Ordained priest Roman Catholic Ch., Lyons, France, 1822; came to U.S., 1830, served in Mobile (Ala.) area, 17 years, became vicar gen. of diocese; visited France and brought back Jesuits for Spring Hill Coll., also Bros. of Christian Schs. for an orphanage; became bishop Vincennes, Ind., 1847. Died Vincennes, Apr. 23, 1848.

BEACH, Alfred Ely, publisher, inventor; b. Springfield, Mass., Sept. 1, 1826; s. Moses Yale and Nancy (Day) B.; m. Harriet Eliza Holbrook, June 30, 1847. Founder (with Orson D. Munn) firm Munn & Co., publishers, 1846; editor Scientific America; patentee typewriter, 1847, typewriter for blind, 1857, cable railways and tunneling shield, 1864; inventor pneumatic carrier system now used in mail tubes; recipient Gold medal for work on typewriter from Am. Inst., 1856. Died N.Y.C., Jan. 1, 1896.

BEACH, Lewis, congressman; b. N.Y.C., Mar. 30, 1835; grad. Yale Law Sch., 1856. Admitted to bar, 1856; practiced in N.Y.; moved to Orange County, N.Y., 1861; mem., treas. N.Y. State Democratic Central Com., 1877-79; mem. U.S. Ho. of Reps. (Democrat) from N.Y., 47th-49th congresses, 1881-Aug. 10, 1886. Died Knoll View, Cornwall, Orange County, Aug. 10, 1886; buried Greenwood Cemetery, Bklyn.

BEACH, Moses Sperry, publisher, inventor; b. Springfield, Mass., Oct. 5, 1822; s. Moses Yale and Nancy (Day) B.; m. Chloe Buckingham, 1845. Apprentice printer on N.Y. Sun, 1834, circa 1840; co-owner Boston Daily Times, 1845; operated N.Y. Sun (with brother and father), 1845-52, sole owner, 1852-60, 62-68 (newspaper controlled by syndicate interested in religious affairs, 1860-62), designed Sun around tastes of working men, reprinting popular fiction liberally in its columns, expounded Democratic editorial policy, supported Buchanan and Douglas during 1850's; devised new method for feeding paper to presses and pioneered printing both sides of sheet at once; retired to estate in Peekskill, N.Y., following sale of Sun to group represented by Charles A. Dana, 1868; travelled widely abroad. Died Peekskill, July 25, 1892; buried Peekskill.

BEACH, Moses Yale, publisher, inventor; b. Wallingford, Conn., Jan. 15, 1800; s. Moses Sperry and Lucretia (Stanley) B.; m. Nancy Day, Nov. 19, 1819; children—Moses Sperry, Alfred Ely. Apprentice cabinet maker, Hartford, Conn., 1814-18; developed engine using power of gunpowder explosions, 1819; partner in cabinet mfg. bus., 1819-circa 1828; invented rag cutting machine, circa 1826; part owner paper mill, Saugerties, N.Y., 1829-34; part owner N.Y. Sun (a leading "penny paper" in N.Y. C.), 1834-38, owner, publisher, 1838-48, increased circulation to 38,000 in 1843 by such devices as "Balloon Hoax" (1844), quick reporting of news through such methods as ship news service, spl. trains and horse expresses; established N.Y. Asso. Press (with other N.Y.C. newspaper publishers) to gather news in all major cities in nation during Mexican War; apptd. by Pres. Polk as spl. emissary to Mexico, 1846; 1st publisher to use syndicated newspaper articles (1841), to publish fgn. edition (1848); publisher Weekly Sun (for farmers), Illustrated Sun and Monthly Literary Journal; lived in retirement, Wallingford, 1848-68. Died Wallingford, July 19, 1868; buried Wallingford.

BEACH, William Augustus, lawyer; b. Saratoga Springs, N.Y., Dec. 9, 1809; s. Miles and Cynthia (Warren) B.; attended Partridge's Mil. Inst., Norwich, Vt.; studied law with uncle. Admitted to N.Y. bar, 1833, practiced in Saratoga Springs; dist. atty. Saratoga County (N.Y.), 1843-47; moved to Troy, N.Y., 1851, practiced until 1870; gained reputation for defense of Col. North in Washington, D.C., 1865; moved to N.Y.C., 1870, had extensive law practice; employed by Vanderbilt in Erie R.R. litigation, served as counsel for Judge Barnard, 1872; appeared for plaintiff in Tilton vs. Beecher; appeared as defense counsel in many criminal cases in N.Y.C. Died N.Y.C., June 21, 1884; buried N.Y.C.

BEACH, Wooster, physician, writer; b. Trumbull, Conn., 1794; attended Coll. Physicians and Surgeons, N.Y.C., 1825-29; m. Eliza de Grove, 1823, 2 sons. Author numerous articles and treatises on med. subjects often strongly critical of traditional med. opinion and practice, from 1825; established U.S. Infirmary (clinic where he treated patients many years), 1828; instrumental in orgn. of univ. med. dept., Worthington, O., 1830; elected mem. N.Y. County Med. Soc., 1832; established Eclectic Med. Jour., 1836; pres. Nat. Eclectic Med. Assn., 1855; also published Telescope and Ishmaelite (2 sheets expressing views on a variety of subjects). Author: The American Practice of Medicine (one of 1st med. textbooks dealing with relation between pathology and disease), 3 vols., 1833, later edits., 1846, 51; An Improved System of Midwifery (a treatise), 1851; Treatise on Pulmonary Consumption, 1840. Died N.Y.C., Jan. 28, 1868; buried N.Y.C.

BEADLE, Erastus Flavel, publisher; b. Stewart's Patent (now Pierstown), N.Y., Sept. 11, 1821; s. Flavel and Polly (Turner) B.; m. Mary Ann Pennington, Apr. 22, 1846, 3 children, Irwin, Walter, Sophie. Established (with brother Irwin) firm Beadle & Bros., steryotypers, Buffalo, N.Y., 1852, name changed to Beadle & Adams and firm moved to N.Y.C., 1858; published mag. Youth's Casket, 1852-57; published Home, a Fireside Monthly, 1856-60, published under title Beadle's Home Monthly, 1860-89; published Dime Song Book (his 1st paperbacked book), 1858; published 1st dime novel Malaeska, the Indian Wife of the White Hunter, 1860, success of this book led him to publish several series of dime paperbacks, sales greatly increased during Civil War because of book's portability; concentrated on Western stories after Civil War, until 1875, then crime stories, 1875-89; ret. 1889. Died Cooperstown, N.Y., Dec. 18, 1894; buried Lakewood Cemetery, Cooperstown.

BEALE, Edward Fitzgerald, surveyor, explorer; b. Washington, D.C., Feb. 4, 1822; s. George and Emily (Truxton) B.; attended Georgetown Coll., circa 1837-38; grad. U.S. Naval Acad., 1842; m. Mary Edwards, June 27, 1849. Made 6 trips between Washington and Pacific Coast relaying mil. information during Mexican War; promoted lt. U.S. Navy, 1850, resigned, 1850; involved in mining enterprises in Cal., 1850-52; supt. for Cal. and Nev. Indian affairs, 1852-56; led railroad survey in Southern Cal. and Utah, 1853; apptd. by Pres. Buchanan to lead surveying expdn. for road from Ft. Defiance (N.M.) to Colorado River, 1857; active in politics as Republican after 1856; served as surveyor gen. of Cal. and Nev., 1861-65; retired to ranch nr. Bakersfield, Cal., 1865, lived half of each year in Washington; apptd. U.S. minister to Austria-Hungary (apptd. by Pres. Grant), 1876-77. Died Washington, Apr. 22, 1893.

BEALE, James Madison Hite, congressman; b. Mt. Airy, Shenandoah County, Va., Feb. 7, 1786; ed. in preparatory studies. Farmer; mem. U.S. Ho. of Reps. (Democrat) from Va., 23d-24th, 31st-32d congresses, 1833-37, 49-53. Died Putnam County, W.Va., Aug. 2, 1866; buried Beale Cemetery, nr. Gallipolis Ferry, Mason County, W.Va.

BEALE, Richard Lee Turberville, army officer, congressman; b. Hickory Hill, Va., May 22, 1819; s. Robert and Martha (Turberville) B.; grad. U. Va., 1839. Admitted to Va. bar, 1839; mem. U.S. Ho. of Reps. (Democrat) from Va., 30th Congress, 1847-49; del. Va. Constl. Conv., 1851; mem. Va. Senate, 1858-60; commd. 1st lt. Lee's Legion, Confederate Army, 1861; maj., 1862; col., comdr. brigade, 1864, brig. gen., 1865; mem. U.S. Ho. of Reps. from Va., 46th Congress, 1879-81. Died Apr. 21, 1893.

BEALL, John Yates, army officer; b. Jefferson County, Va., Jan. 1, 1835; s. George and Miss (Yates) B.; attended U. Va., circa 1855-59; studied law. Served in Stonewall Brigade, Confederate Army, 1861; apptd. acting master Confederate Navy, 1862, sabotaged Union ships in Chesapeake Bay area, 1862-63; captured several Fed. vessels including Alliance; attempted from base in Canada to capture Union warship on Lake Erie and to free some Confederate prisoners, 1864, plan failed because of mutiny; arrested following attempts to derail trains in N.Y., tried, 1864, convicted of espionage, executed despite pleas for clemency by Gov. Andrew of Mass. and Thaddeus Stevens. Executed Ft. Lafayette, N.Y., Feb. 24, 1865.

BEALL, Reasin, congressman; b. Montgomery County, Me. Dec. 3, 1769; limited schooling. Served as officer under Gen. Harmer, 1790; apptd. ensign U.S. Army, 1792, battalion q.m., 1793; served under Gen. Wayne in campaign against Indians; moved to New Lisbon, O., 1803; commd. brig. gen. Volunteers, 1812; moved to Wooster, O., 1815; mem. U.S. Ho. of Reps. (Whig, filled vacancy) from Ohio, 13th Congress, Apr. 20, 1813-June 7, 1814, resigned; register land offices, Canton, Wooster, O., 1814-24; presided over Whig Conv., Columbus, O., 1840; Whig presdl. elector,

1840. Died Wooster, Feb. 20, 1843; buried Wooster Cemetery.

BEALL, Samuel Wootton, polit. leader; b. Montgomery County, Md., Sept. 26, 1807; s. Lewis and Eliza B.; grad. Union Coll., Schenectady, N.Y., 1827; m. Elizabeth Cooper, 1827. Apptd. receiver of public land sales in N.W., Green Bay, Wis., 1827-34, Cooperstown, N.Y., 1834-40; moved to Wis., settled in Fond du Lac County, 1840, became farmer; advocated statehood for Wis. Territory; del. Wis. Constl. Conv., 1846, 47; drafted constn. for new state, Madison, Wis.; lt. gov. Wis., 1851-53; Indian agt. for Wis. tribes, 1853-59; led expdn. to Pike's Peak, Colo., 1859; a founder Denver (Colo.), helped obtain charter for Denver in Washington, D.C., 1860; returned to Wis., 1861; served as lt. col. 18th Wis. Inf. Regt. during Civil War, 1862-65; participated in campaigns of Shiloh and Vicksburg; moved to Helena, Mont., 1866. Killed in newspaper office in Helena in controversy with editor George Pinney of Montana Post, Sept. 26, 1868; buried Helena.

BEAMAN, Fernando Cortez, congressman, lawyer; b. Chester, Vt., June 28, 1814; attended Malone (N.Y.) Acad.; studied law. Taught school; moved to Rochester, N.Y., 1836, Manchester, Mich., 1838; admitted to bar, 1839; practiced law; moved to Tecumseh, Mich., 1841, practiced law, also in Clinton, Mich.; moved to Adrian, Lenawee County, Mich., 1843; apptd. pros. atty. Lenawee County, 1843-50; atty. City of Adrian; mem. conv. that organized Republican Party, Jackson, Mich., 1854; del. 1st Nat. Rep. Conv., Phila., 1856; Rep. presdl. elector, 1856; mayor Adrian, 1856; judge Lenawee County Probate Ct., 1856-60; mem. U.S. Ho. of Reps. (Rep.) from Mich., 37th-41st congresses, 1861-71; apptd. judge of probate Lenawee County, 1871, elected, 1872, 76; apptd. to U.S. Senate, 1879, declined, also declined appointments to Mich. Supreme Ct., and as U.S. commr. Indian Affairs. Died Adrian, Sept. 27, 1882; buried Oakwood Cemetery.

BEAN, Benning Moulton, congressman; b. Moultonboro, Carroll County, N.H., Jan. 9, 1782; attended public schs., Moultonboro, also pvt. tutors. Educator, farmer; selectman, Moultonboro, 1811-29, 32-38; justice of peace, 1816; trustee Sandwich Acad., 1824; mem. N.H. Ho. of Reps., 1815-23, 27; mem. N.H. Senate, 1824-26, 31, 32, pres., 1832; mem. N.H. Gov.'s Council, 1829; mem. U.S. Ho. of Reps. (Democrat) from N.H., 23d-24th congresses, 1833-37. Died Moultonboro, Feb. 6, 1866; buried Bean Cemetery.

BEARD, George Miller, physician; b. Montville, Conn., May 8, 1839; s. Spencer and Lucy (Leonard) B.; attended Phillips Acad., Andover, Mass., 1854-58; grad. Yale, 1862, Coll. Physicians and Surgeons, N.Y.C., 1866; m. Elizabeth Alden, Dec. 25, 1866. Began research in med. use of electricity, 1866, published 1st works in this field; lectr. diseases of nerves N.Y.U., 1868; mem. staff Demilt Dispensary, N.Y.C., from circa 1870; founded mag. Archives of Electrology and Neurology, 1874; del. Internat. Med. Congress, London, Eng., 1881; one of 1st neurologists in U.S.; 1st to formulate causes and treatment of seasickness, also pioneer in reforms for care of insane. Author: Medical and Surgical Uses of Electricity, 1871; Hay Fever, 1876; The Scientific Basis of Delusions, 1877; Nervous Exhaustion, 1880; numerous other publs. Died N.Y.C., Jan. 23, 1883; buried N.Y.C.

BEARD, James Henry, artist; b. Buffalo, N.Y., May 20, 1812; s. Capt. James and Harriet (Wolcott) B.; m. Mary Carter, Aug. 28, 1833, 6 children including James Carter, Harry, Thomas, Francis, Danile Carter. Portraits include: Henry Clay, John Quincy Adams, Gen. Harrison, Gen. Taylor; charter mem. Century Club; hon. mem. N.A.D., 1848, elected academician, 1872; painted portrait Gen. Sherman, 1887; best known works include: Peep at Growing Danger, 1871; The Widow, 1872; Mutual Friend, 1875; Patson's Pets, 1875; Attorney and Clients; Out all Night; There's Many a Slip, 1876. Died Flushing, N.Y., Apr. 4, 1893.

BEARD, Richard, clergyman, coll. pres.; b. Sumner County, Tenn.; grad. Cumberland Coll., Princeton, Ky., circa 1833; m. Cynthia Castleman, Jan. 21, 1834. Licensed to preach as circuit rider in Tenn., 1820; taught at Cumberland Coll., 1833-38, pres., 1843-54; head Sharon Acad., Miss., 1838-43; prof. theology Cumberland U., Lebanon, Tenn., 1854; moderator Presbyn. Ch. after Civil War, worked for reunion of ch. Author: Lectures on Theology, 3 vols., 1860, 64, 70; Miscellaneous Sermons, Reviews, and Essays, 1875. Died probably Lebanon, Dec. 2, 1880.

BEARDSLEY, Eben Edwards, clergyman; b. Stepney, Conn., Jan. 8, 1808; s. Elihu and Ruth (Edwards) B.; grad. Trinity Coll., 1832, D.D. (hon.), 1854; LL.D. (hon.), Columbia, 1874; m. Jane Matthews, Oct. 11, 1842. Ordained deacon Episcopal Ch., 1835, priest, 1836; in charge of St. Peter's Ch., Cheshire, Conn., also Episcopal Acad. of Conn., South Norwalk, 1835-48; rector Parish of St. Thomas's Ch., New Haven, Conn., 1848-91; pres. Conn. Ho. of Deputies, 2 times; trustee Episcopal Acad. Conn., St. Margaret's Sch. for Girls, Trinity Coll.; a founder New Haven Colony Hist. Soc., pres., 1873-74. Author: The History of the Episcopal Church in Connecticut from the Settlement of the Colony to the Death of Bishop Brownwell in 1865, 2 vols., N.Y., 1865; The Life and Correspondence of Samuel Johnson, 1874; Addresses and Discourses, 1892. Died New Haven, Dec. 21, 1891.

BEARDSLEY, Samuel, congressman, jurist; b. Rensselaer County, N.Y., Feb. 6, 1790; s. Obadiah and Eunice (Moore) B.; LL.D. (hon.), Hamilton Coll., 1849. Admitted to N.Y. bar, 1815; commd. capt. N.Y. Militia, 1815, brigade judge advocate, 1818; dist. atty. Oneida County, N.Y., 1821; mem. N.Y. State Senate from 5th dist. (Democrat), 1822; mem. N.Y. State Senate from 5th dist. (Democrat), 1822; U.S. atty. for No. N.Y., 1823; mem. U.S. Ho. of Reps. from N.Y., 21st, 25th congresses, 1830-31, 36; atty. gen. State of N.Y., 1836; asso. judge N.Y. Supreme Ct., 1844, chief justice, 1847. Died Utica, N.Y., May 6, 1860.

BEASLEY, Frederick, clergyman, educator; b. Edenton, N.C., 1777; s. John and Mary (Blount) B.; grad. Coll. of N.J. (now Princeton), 1797; m. Susan Dayton, Aug. 22, 1803, 1 child; m. 2d, Maria Williamson, Nov. 27, 1804, 9 children. Ordained to ministry Episcopal Ch., 1802; rector St. John's Ch., Elizabethtown (now Elizabeth), N.J., St. Peter's Ch., Albany, N.Y., 1803-09, St. Paul's Ch., Balt., 1809-13, St. Michael's Ch., Trenton, N.J., 1829-36; provost, prof. philosophy U. Pa., 1813-28; theol. writings characterized by conservatism and opposition to idealist thinkers. Author: A Search of Truth in the Science of the Human Mind, 1822; A Vindication of the Fundamental Principles of Truth. . .from the Allegations of the Reverend William E. Channing, 1830; An Examination of No. 90 of the Tracts for the Times, 1842. Died Elizabethtown, Nov. 1, 1845; buried Elizabethtown.

BEASLEY, Mercer, jurist; b. Phila., Mar. 27, 1815; attended Princeton, 1833-34; studied law with Samuel Southard, Trenton, N.J., 1834-35; m. Frances Higbee, circa 1847; m. 2d, Catherine Haven, Oct. 16, 1854. Admitted to bar, 1835, practiced in Trenton; Whig, became Democrat, circa 1850; apptd. chief justice of N.J., 1864-97, noted for fairness in cases involving polit. controversy and integrity in cases of state's rights regarding riparian lands. Died Trenton, Feb. 19, 1897.

BEATTY, Adam, lawyer; b. Hagerstown, Md., May 10, 1777; s. William and Mary (Grosh) B.; m. Sally Green, 1804. Practiced law, Washington, Mason County, Ky., 1802; Ky. circuit judge, 1811; mem. Ky. Legislature, at various times, 1809-circa 1820; mem. Ky. Senate, 1836-39; v.p. Ky. Agrl. Soc., 1838. Author: Essays in Practical Agriculture, 1844. Died Mason County, June 9, 1858.

BEATTY, Charles Clinton, clergyman; b. Antrim County, Ireland, circa 1715; s. John and Christiana (Clinton) B.; attended "Log Coll.," Neshaminy, Pa.; m. Anne Reading, June 24, 1746. Licensed to preach, 1742; assisted in William Tennent's ch., Neshaminy, 1743, pastor, 1743; missionary in Va. and N.C., 1754; chaplain Pa. troops engaged in fighting in Indian wars, 1755; active in organizing relief funds for ministers' widows and in conversion of Indians; moderator Presbyn. Synod of N.B. (Can.), 1764; became trustee Coll. of N.J. (now Princeton), 1763. Author: Journal of a Two Months Tour among the Frontier Inhabitants of Pennsylvania, 1768. Died Barbados, W.I., Aug. 13, 1772; buried Barbados.

BEATTY, John, congressman; b. Neshaminy, Pa., Dec. 19, 1749; s. Rev. Charles and Anne (Reading) B.; grad. Princeton, 1769; m. Mary Longstreet, Mar. 22, 1774; m. 2d, Mrs. Kitty Lalor, 1818. Began practice of medicine, Hartsville, Pa., 1772; commd. capt. Pa. Batallion, 1776; maj. 6th Pa. Militia, 1776; mem. N.J. Legislature; del. Continental Congress, 1784;85; mem. N.J. Conv. which ratified Fed. Constn., 1787; mem. U.S. Ho. of Reps. from N.J., 3d Congress, 1793-95; sec. of state N.J., 1795-1805; pres. Trenton Banking Co. (N.J.), 1815-26; pres. Del. Bridge Co. Died Trenton, Apr. 30, 1826.

BEATTY, William, congressman; b. Stewartstown, County Tyrone, Ireland, 1787. Came to U.S., 1807, settled in Butler, Pa.; sgt. in Capt. Thompson's Company in War of 1812; sheriff Butler County (Pa.), 1823-26; mem. U.S. Ho. of Reps. (Van Buren Democrat) from Pa., 25th-26th congresses, 1837-41; mem. Pa. Ho. of Reps., 1840-42; apptd. dep. sheriff Butler County. Died Butler, Apr. 12, 1851; buried Old Butler Cemetery.

BEATY, Martin, congressman; b. Abingdon, Va. Operated iron furnace; moved to Wayne County, Ky., 1817, became driller of wells for brine, manufactured salt, Saltville, Ky.; mem. Ky. Senate, 1824-28, 32; Whig presdl. elector, 1832, 36; mem. U.S. Ho. of Reps. (Whig) from Ky., 23d Congress, 1833-35; mem. Ky. Ho. of Reps., 1848; moved to farm nr. Belmont, Tex., 1856, became farmer, raised cattle. Died Southfork, Owsley County, Ky.; buried Belmont Cemetery.

BEAU JONATHAN, see Hazard, Jonathan J.

BEAUCHAMP, William, clergyman; b. Kent County, Del., Apr., 26, 1772; s. William Beauchamp; m. Frances Russell, June 7, 1801. Itinerant circuit rider in Pa., 1794; ordained to ministry Methodist Ch. on Pitts. circuit, 1796; served in Pitts., N.Y.C., Boston, 1796-1800, Nantucket Island, Mass., 1800-07, Wood County, Va., 1807-15; led revivals in Southern Ohio, 1815-17; a founder Mt. Carmel, Ill., 1817; editor Western Christian Monitor, Chilicothe, O., 1816; del. Meth. Gen. Conf., Balt., 1823; presiding elder Meth. Ch. in Ind., 1824. Author: Letters on the Call and Qualifications of Ministers, 1849. Died Paoli, Ind., Oct. 7, 1824; buried Orange County, Ind.

BEAUJOLAIS, Louis Charles D'Orleans (comte de Beaujolais), artist; b. 1779. Came to U.S. with brother Louis Philippe, 1797; travelled in U.S., made drawings and paintings from nature, including an oil painting of Genesee Falls, N.Y. (now at N.Y. Hist. Soc.); returned to Europe, 1800. Died Malta, 1808.

BEAUMONT, Andrew, congressman; b. Lebanon, New London County, Conn., Jan. 24, 1790; studied law. Moved to Pa., 1808; never practiced law; collector of revenue, 1814; prothontary and clk. of courts Luzerne County, Pa., 1816-19; mem. Pa. Ho. of Reps., 1821, 22, 26, 49; mem. U.S. Ho. of Reps. (Democrat) from Pa., 23d-24th congresses, 1833-37; commr. public buildings, Washington, D.C., 1846-47. Died Wilkes-Barre, Pa., Sept. 30, 1853; buried Hollenback Cemetery.

BEAUMONT, John Colt, naval officer; b. Wilkes-Barre, Pa., Aug. 27, 1821; s. Andrew and Julia (Colt) B.; m. Fanny Dorrance, Oct. 27, 1852; m. 2d, Fannie King, 1874. Commd. midshipman U.S. Navy, 1838, lt., 1852; ship comdr. during Civil War; played leading part in capture of Ft. Wagner, July 1863; commanded Miantonomah (1st monitor to cross Atlantic Ocean); commd. capt., 1867; commandant Portsmouth Navy Yard, 1882; ret. as rear adm., 1882. Died Durham, N.H., Aug. 2, 1882; buried Arlington (Va.) Nat. Cemetery.

BEAUMONT, William, surgeon; b. Conn., Nov. 21, 1785; s. Samuel and Luctetia (Abel) B.; m. Mrs. Deborah Platt, 1821, 1 son, 2 daus. Apprenticed to physician, St. Albans, Vt., 1810-13; licensed to practice medicine by 3d Med. Soc. of Vt., 1812; surgeon 6th Inf., Plattsburg, N.Y., 1812-15; practiced medicine, Plattsburg, 1815-20; post surgeon Ft. Mackinac, Mich., 1820-25; treated patient with stomach wound and made important discoveries regarding digestive processes, 1822, conducted expts. with patient (Alexis St. Martin) until 1834 while stationed as post surgeon at Ft. Niagara, 1825-26, Ft. Howard, 1826-28, Ft. Crawford, 1828-34, corresponded with leading scientists about gastric fluids in digestion; served in St. Louis, 1834-39; resigned from Army Med. Corps, 1839; practiced medicine, St. Louis, until 1853. Author: Experiments and Observations on the Gastric Juice and the Physiology of Digestion (pioneer studies on digestion including over 200 expts.), 1833, 2d edit., 1847. Died St. Louis, Apr. 25, 1853; buried Bellefontaine Cemetery, St. Louis.

BEAUREGARD, Pierre Gustave Toutant, army officer, state ofcl.; born in St. Bernard Parish, Louisiana, May 28, 1815; the son of Jacques and Helene (de Reggio) B.; grad. U.S. Mil. Acad., 1838; m. Laure Villere, Sept. 1841; m. 2d, Caroline Deslonde, 1860. Served in Corps Engrs., U.S. Army, La., 1838-46; mem. staff Gen. Scott as engr. during Mexican War, 1846-47; received brevets for conduct at battles of Cerro Gordo and Contreras; promoted capt., 1853, served in Corps Engrs.; apptd. supt. U.S. Mil. Acad., 1860, resigned to join Confederate Army, 1861; commd. brig. gen. Confederate Army, 1861, maj. gen., 1861; 2d in command at 1st Battle of Bull Run, 1861; in command Confederate Army at Battle of Shiloh, 1862; retreated from Corinth (Miss.) after fortifying it; in charge of coastal defense of Ga. and S.C., 1863; served in Va. theater, defeated Gen. Butler, fought at Battle of Petersburg, 1864; 2d in command to Gen. J. E. Johnston in Carolinas, circa 1865; pres. New Orleans, Jackson & Miss. R.R., circa 1866-71; served as adjutant gen. of La. for many years after war. Author: Principles and Maxims of the Art of War, 1863; A Commentary on the Campaign of Manassas, 1891. Died New Orleans, Feb. 20, 1893.

BECK, Charles, classical scholar; b. Heidelberg, Germany, Aug. 19, 1798; Ph.D., U. Tubingen (Germany), 1823; m. Louisa Henshaw, 1827; m. 2d, Mrs. Theresa Phillips, 1831. Ordained to ministry

Lutheran Ch., Heidelberg, 1822; came to U.S., 1824; taught at Round Hill Sch., Northampton, Mass., 1824-30; conducted sch., Phillipstown, N.Y., 1830-32; prof. Latin, Harvard, 1832-50; elected mem. Am. Acad. Arts and Scis., 1845; influential in introduction of German scholarship in U.S. Author: Introduction to the Metres of Horace, 1835. Editor: Seneca's Medea, 1834, Hercules Furens, 1845, manuscripts of Satyricon of Petronius Arbiter, 1863. Died Cambridge, Mass., Mar. 19, 1866.

BECK, George, artist; b. Ellford, Eng., 1748 or 50; m. Mary, 1786. Exhibited in London, Eng.; came to Am., 1795; worked primarily in Balt., circa 1795-97, Phila., 1798-1807; toured Western part of U.S., 1804, painted view of Niagara Falls; thought to have worked in Pitts., 1804-06, painted view of town, 1806; painted view of Wright's Ferry on Susquehanna River in Pa., 1808; exhibited at Soc. of Artists, Phila., 1811-14. Died Lexington, Ky., Dec. 14, 1812.

BECK, James Burnie, senator, congressman; b. Dumfriesshire, Scotland, Feb. 13, 1822; grad. Transylvania U., Lexington, Ky., 1846. Came to U.S., 1838, settled in Wyoming County, N.Y.; moved to Lexington, 1843; admitted to bar; practiced in Lexington; del. Nat. Democratic Conv., Charleston, Balt., 1860; mem. U.S. Ho. of Reps. (Dem.) from Ky., 40th-43d congresses, 1867-75; apptd. mem. commn. to define boundary line between Md. and Va., 1876; mem. U.S. Senate from Ky., 1877-May 3, 1890. Died Washington, D.C., May 3, 1890; buried Lexington Cemetery.

BECK, Lewis Caleb, chemist, educator; b. Schenectady, N.Y., Oct. 4, 1798; s. Caleb and Catherine (Romeyn) B.; grad. Union Coll., Schenectady, 1817; attended Coll. Physicians and Surgeons, N.Y.C., 1816; m. Hannah Smith, Oct. 17, 1825. Licensed to practice medicine in N.Y., 1818; lived in various parts of U.S., 1818-24, began bot. collection; prof. botany Berkshire Med. Inst., 1824; prof. chemistry and botany Vt. Med. Acad., 1826; prof. chemistry Rutgers U., 1830, N.Y.U., 1836; prof. chemistry and pharmacy Albany (N.Y.) Med. Coll., 1840-53. Author: Botany of the Northern and Middle States, 1833; Minerology of New York, 1842. Died Albany, Apr. 20, 1853.

BECK, Mary, tchr., artist; m. George Beck, 1786. Came to Am., 1795; conducted schs. for girls, Balt. and Phila., Cincinnati and Lexington (Ky.), after 1808; painted landscapes. Died 1833.

BECK, Theodric Romeyn, physician, educator; b. Schenectady, N.Y., Aug. 11, 1791; s. Caleb and Catherine (Romeyn) B.; grad. Union Coll., Schenectady, N.Y., 1807; grad. Coll. Physicians and Surgeons, N.Y.C., 1811; m. Harriet Caldwell, 1814, 2 daus. Practiced medicine, Albany, N.Y., 1811-17; prin. Albany Acad., 1817-53; prof. medicine Western Coll. Physicians and Surgeons, Fairfield, N.Y., 1815-40, Albany Med. Coll., 1840-43; sec. N.Y. Bd. Regents, 1841-54; pres. N.Y. State Med. Soc., 3 terms; founder N.Y. State Library, N.Y. State Insane Asylum. Author: Elements of Medical Jurisprudence, 1823. Died Albany, Nov. 19, 1855.

BECKNELL, William, trader, explorer; b. Amherst County, Va., 1796. Led trading party to Taos and Santa Fe (N.M.) following fall of Spanish regime in Mexico, 1821; led another trading expdn. which took route to San Miguel by way of Cimarron and forks of Canadian River and across mountain pass, 1822, route became famed Santa Fe trail used by pioneers and traders. Died Apr. 30, 1865.

BECKWOURTH, James P., frontiersman; b. Va., Apr. 26, 1798; no formal edn.; m. several Indian women. Mem. W.H. Ashley's trading expdns. to St. Louis, 1823, to Rocky Mountain area, 1824-25; lived among Crow Indians, 1825-33; lived in Cal., 1833-44; mem. Gen. Stephen Kearny's forces in Cal., 1844-47; lived in both Cal. and Mo., 1847-59, moved to Colo., 1858; participated in Cheyenne War of 1864. Life and Adventures of James P. Beckwourth, Mountaineer, Scout, and Pioneer and Chief of the Crow Nation by T. D. Bonner, largely autobiographical, 1856, reissued, 1892. Died Denver, circa 1867; buried Denver.

BEDELL, Gregory Thurston, clergyman; b. Hudson, N.Y., Aug. 27, 1817; s. Rev. Gregory and Penelope (Thurston) B.; grad. Bristol (Pa.) Coll., 1836, Episcopal Theol. Sem., Alexandria, Va., 1840. Ordained deacon Episcopal Ch., Phila., 1840, priest, 1841; pastor Trinity Ch., West Chester, Pa., 1840-43, Ch. of Ascension, N.Y.C., 1843-59; consecrated asst. bishop Diocese of Ohio, 1859-73, bishop, 1873-75; bishop Northern part of Diocese of Ohio (after diocese split), 1875-89; del. (chosen by Ho. of Bishops) to Soc. for Propagation of Gospel in Fgn. Parts, London, Eng., 1884. Author works including: Notiae Parochiales; Parish Statistics, 1860; The Pastor: A Manual of Pastoral Theology, 1880; Memorial of Stephen H. Tyng, 1886. Died N.Y.C., Mar. 11, 1892.

BEDELL, Gregory Townshend, clergyman; b. Fresh Kill, S.I., N.Y., Oct. 28, 1793; s. Israel and Mrs. (Moore) B.; grad. Columbia, 1811; D.D. (hon.), Dickinson Coll.; m. Penelope Thurston, 1 son, Gregory Thurston. Ordained to ministry Episcopal Ch., 1814; pastor of ch., Hudson, N.Y., 1814-17, Fayetteville, N.C., 1818-22; a founder St. Andrews Ch., Phila., circa 1822. Author works including: Bible Studies, 1829; Ezekiel's Vision; It Is Well. Died Balt., Aug. 30, 1834.

BEDFORD, Gunning, governor of Delaware; born in Phila., Apr. 7, 1742; s. William Bedford; m. Mary Read, 1796. Served as maj. Continental Army, 1775, then q.m. gen.; promoted to lt. col. of a Del. regt., 1776, became muster-master gen., 1776; served in Battle of White Plains, 1776; prothonotary, 1779; delegate to the Delaware Congress, 1783-85; mem. Del. Privy Council, 1783-90; mem. Del. Legislature from New Castle County, 1784-86; mem. Del. Conv. which ratified U.S. Constn., 1787; mem. Del. Senate 1788; presdl. elector, 1789; register of wills New Castle County, 1788, justice of peace, 1789; gov. Del., 1796-97; leader in devel. Del. Pub. Sch. System. Died New Castle, Sept. 30, 1797.

BEDFORD, Gunning, Continental congressman, jurist; b. Phila., 1747; s. Gunning and Susannah (Jacquett) B.; grad. Coll. of N.J. (now Priceton), 1771; m. Jane Parker. Admitted to Del. bar, 1772; aide-de-camp to George Washington during Revolutionary War; mem. Del. Legislature, Del. Council; del. to Continental Congress, 1783-86; atty. gen. Del., 1784; del. Annapolis Conv., 1786, U.S. Constl. Conv., 1787 (proposed equal representation of the states, short presdl. terms, powerful legislative br.), Del. Constl. Conv.; mem. Del. Senate, 1788; apptd. by Washington 1st judge U.S. Dist. Ct. for Del. 1789; presdl. elector, 1789, 93; pres. trustees Wilmington (Del.) Acad. Died Wilmington, Mar. 30, 1812; buried 1st Presbyn. Churchyard, Wilmington.

BEDFORD, Gunning S., physician; b. Balt., 1806; grad. St. Mary's Coll., Md., 1825; med. degree, Rutgers; postgrad. abroad. Apptd. prof. obstetrics at med. coll., Charleston, S.C., 1833; also taught in Albany, N.Y., N.Y.C.; founded 1st obstet. clinic for charity patients in N.Y.C., also Univ. Med. Coll., 1840. Author: 2 med. textbooks. Died Sept. 5, 1870.

BEDINGER, George Michael, army officer, congressman; b. Va., Dec. 10, 1756; s. Henry and Magdalene (von Schlegel) B.; m. Nancy Keane; m. 2d, Henrietta Clay; 9 children. Commanded a battalion in St. Clair's expdn., 1791; commd. maj. inf., U.S. Army, 1792-93; mem. Ky. Legislature from Bourbon County, 1792, 94; mem. U.S. Ho. of Reps. from Ky., 8th-9th congresses, 1803-07. Died Blue Licks, Ky., Dec. 8, 1843; buried cemetery at Licking River, Ky.

BEDINGER, Henry, congressman, diplomat; b. nr. Shepherdstown, Jefferson County, Va. (now W. Va.), Feb. 3, 1812; attended common schs.; studied law. Admitted to bar, 1832; practiced in Shepherdstown; moved to Charlestown, Va., practiced law; mem. U.S. Ho. of Reps. (Democrat) from Va., 19th-30th congresses, 1845-49; apptd. charge d'affaires to Denmark, 1853, minister resident, 1854-58, Died Shepherdstown, Nov. 26, 1858; buried Elmwood Cemetery.

BEDLE, Joseph Dorsett, gov. N.J., jurist; b. Middletown Point, N.J., Jan. 5, 1821; s. Thomas I. and Hannah (Dorsett) B.; studied law under William Dayton, Trenton, N.J.; LL.D. (hon.), Princeton, 1875; m. Althea F. Randolph; children—Bennington F., Joseph D., Thomas F., Randolph, Althea. Admitted to N.J. bar, 1853; practiced law, Middletown Point, 1853-55; Freehold, N.J., 1855-65; justice N.J. Supreme Ct., 1865-75; gov. N.J., 1875-78; practiced law, 1878-94. Died N.Y.C., Oct. 21, 1894.

BEE, Barnard Elliott, army officer; b. Charleston, S.C., Mar. 1824; s. Barnard E. Bee; grad. U.S. Mil. Acad., 1845. Commd. 2d lt. 3d Inf., U.S. Army, 1845; brevetted for meritorious conduct at Battle of Chapultepec; promoted 1st lt., 1851; served as capt. on Utah expdn. against Mormons, 1855, commd. maj. inf. Confederate Army, then Brig. gen., 1861; gave Thomas J. Jackson the nickname "Stonewall." Killed at Battle of Bull Run, July 21, 1861.

BEE, Hamilton Prioleau, army officer; b. Charleston, S.C., July 22, 1822; s. Barnard E. Bee; m. Mildred Taruer, 1854. Sec., U.S.-Tex. Boundary Commn., 1839; sec. Tex. Senate, 1846; served as lt. Tex. Rangers, Mexican War; mem. Tex. Ho. of Reps., speaker for 1 term; commd. brig. gen. Tex. Militia, 1861; brig. gen. Confederate Army, 1862, primarily occupied with adminstrv. work concerning importing munitions from Europe through Mexico; served at Battle of Sabine Cross Roads, 1864; promoted maj. gen., 1865. Died San Antonio, Tex., Oct. 2, 1897.

BEE, Thomas, Continental congressman; b. Charleston, S.C., 1725; educated in Charleston, also Oxford (Eng.) U.; studied law. Admitted to Charleston bar, 1761; practiced in Charleston; became planter; mem. Commons House, Province of S.C. for St. Pauls, 1762-64, for St. Peters, 1765, for St. Andrews, 1772-76; justice of peace, 1775; del. 1st and 2d Provincial Congresses, 1775, 76; mem. S.C. Ho. of Reps., 1776-79, 82, speaker, 1777-79; played active part in Revolutionary War; mem. council of safety, 1775, 76; law judge, 1776-78; mem. S.C. Legislative Council, 1776-78; lt. gov. S.C., 1779, 80; mem. Continental Congress from S.C., 1780-82; apptd. judge U.S. Ct. for Dist. of S.C. by Pres. Washington, 1790; published reports of dist. ct. of S.C., 1810. Died Pendleton, S.C., Feb. 18, 1812; buried Woodstock Cemetery, Goose Creek, S.C.

BEECHER, Amariah Dwight, artist; b. Avon Springs, N.Y., 1839; studied law; studied art under Colby Kimble, Rochester, N.Y., 1854-57. Had studio, Avon Springs; opened studio in Rochester, 1865; moved to Chgo., 1870, suffered heavy losses in Chgo. fire, 1871; moved to Geneva, Ill., later to N.Y.C.; returned to Chgo., 1877, gained local reputation as portrait and genre painter; exhibited at N.A.D., circa 1860.

BEECHER, Catharine Esther, educator, reformer; b. East Hampton, L.I., N.Y., Sept. 6, 1800 dau. Rev Lyman and Roxana (Foote) B. Organizer girls sch., Hartford, Conn., 1824-32, Western Female Inst., Cincinnati, 1832-37, Ladies' Soc. for Promoting Edn. in West, Boston, also 3 female colls.; an early leader higher edn. for women; a determined opponent of woman suffrage; Author: An Essay on Slavery and Abolitionism, with Reference to the Duty of American Females, 1837; A Treatise on Domestic Economy for the Use of Young Ladies at Home and at School, 1841; The Duty of American Women to their Country, 1845; The Evils Suffered by American Women and American Children: the Causes and the Remedy, 1846; Woman Suffrage and Woman's Profession, 1871. Died May 12, 1878.

BEECHER, Edward, clergyman, coll. pres.; b. East Hampton, L.I., N.Y., Aug. 27, 1803; s. Rev. Lyman and Roxana (Foote) B.; grad. Yale, 1822; attended Andover Theol. Sem.; D.D. (hon.), Marietta Coll., 1841; m. Isabelle P. Jones, 11 children. Pastor, Park Street Congregational Ch., Boston, 1825-30; 1st pres. Ill. Coll. Jacksonville, 1830-44; pastor Salem Street Ch., Boston, 1844-55; editor-in-chief The Congregationalist, 1849-53; 1st pastor First Congregational Ch., Galesburg, Ill., 1855-70. Author numerous religious works including: The Papal Conspiracy Exposed, 1855; Narrative of the Alton Riots; The Concord of Ages, 1860; History of Opinions; or, The Scriptural Doctrine of Retribution, 1878; contbr. to Christian Union. Died July 28, 1895.

BEECHER, Eunice White Bullard, author; b. West Sutton, Mass., Aug. 26, 1812; dau. of Dr. Artemas Bullard; m. Henry Ward Beecher, Aug. 3, 1837. Author: From Dawn to Daylight: A Simple Story of a Western Home, 1859; Motherly Talks with Young Housekeepers, 1875; Letters from Florida, 1878; Home, 1883. Died 1897.

BEECHER, Henry Ward, clergyman; b. Litchfield, Conn., June 24, 1813; s. Lyman and Roxana (Foote) B.; attended Mt. Pleasant Classical Inst., Amherst, Mass., 1826-30; grad. Amherst Coll., 1834, Lane Theol. Sem., Cincinnati, 1837; m. Eunice Bullard, Aug., 3, 1837, 10 children. Ordained by New Sch. Presbytery of Cincinnati, 1838; pastor ch., Lawrenceburg, Ind. until 1839, 2d Presbyn. Ch., Indpls., 1839-47, Plymouth Congregational Ch., Bklyn., 1847-87; gained nat. fame for emotional and florid sermons, his theology never orthodox; outspoken advocate of reform; anti-slavery leader, opposed Compromise of 1850, advocated Northern colonization of Kan.; campaigned for Frémont and Lincoln, 1856, 60; editor Christian Union, 1861-64, 70-81; contbr. to Independent and New York Ledger in 1860's and 1870's; became object of nat. attention as defendent in Tilton vs. Beecher law suit (charged with adultery with Mrs. Tilton), 1874, publicly cleared by com. of Plymouth Ch. Author: Seven Lectures to Young Men, 1844; Life of Jesus Christ, 1st vol., 1871, last vol., 1891; Evolution and Religion, 1885; also numerous sermons published in pamphlet form. Died Bklyn., Mar. 8, 1887; buried Greenwood Cemetery, Bklyn.

BEECHER, Laban S., figurehead carver; b. circa 1805. Went to Boston, 1822, became prominent carver; commd. to carve Andrew Jackson figurehead for ship Constitution, 1834; gave up carving, circa 1839, went into leather bus.; went West, circa 1843, became prosperous landowner, nr. Sharon, Wis.

BEECHER, Lyman, clergyman; b. New Haven, Conn., Oct. 12, 1775; s. David and Esther (Lyman) B.; grad. Yale, 1797; m. Roxana Foote, Sept. 19,

1799; m. 2d, Harriet Porter, Nov. 1817; m. 3d, Mrs. Lydia (Beals) Jackson, July 7, 1835; 13 children including Henry Ward Beecher, Catharine, and Harriet (Beecher) Stowe. Ordained to the ministry Presbyn. Ch., East Hampton, L.I., N.Y., 1799; pastor Presbyn. Ch., Litchfield, Conn.; a founder Domestic Missionary Soc.; established Am. Bible Soc.; founder, contbr. to Conn. Observer; 1st pres., prof. theology Lane Theol. Sem., Cincinnati, also pastor 2d Presbyn. Ch. of Cincinnati, 1832-50. Died Bklyn., Jan. 10, 1863.

BEECHER, Philemon, congressman, lawyer; b. Kent, Litchfield County, Conn., 1775; classical edn.; studied law. Admitted to bar, practiced law; moved to Lancaster, O., 1801, practiced law; mem. Ohio Ho. of Reps., 1803, 05-07, speaker, 1807; maj. gen. Ohio Militia; mem. U.S. Ho. of Reps. (Federalist) from Ohio, 15th-16th, 18th-20th congresses, 1817-21, 23-29. Died Lancaster, Nov. 30, 1839; buried Elmwood Cemetery.

BEEKMAN, John K., theater owner. Purchased (with John Jacob Astor) the Park Theatre, for $50,000, N.Y.C., 1806; financed building of new Park Theatre, N.Y.C., 1821.

BEEKMAN, Thomas, congressman; b. Wayne County, N.Y. Town clk., Smithfield, N.Y., 1824; mem. U.S. Ho. of Reps. from N.Y., 21st Congress, 1829-31. Died Peterboro, N.Y.

BEERS, Cyrus, congressman, mcht.; b. Newtown, Conn., June 21, 1786; had limited edn. in public schools. Became merchant, also in lumber business; moved to Ithaca, N.Y., 1821, merchant; del. N.Y. State Dem. Conv., Herkimer, 1830; apptd. commr. of deeds, Ithaca, 1837; mem. U.S. Ho. of Reps. (Democrat, filled vacancy) from N.Y., 25th Congress, Dec. 3, 1838-39; del. N.Y. and Erie R.R. Conv., Ithaca, 1839. Died Ithaca, June 5, 1850; buried City Cemetery.

BEERS, Ethel Lynn, poet; b. Goshen, N.Y., Jan. 13, 1827; d. Horace William and Keziah (Westcott) Eliot; m. William H. Beers, Mar. 5, 1846. Contbd. to magazines at early age; contbr. to New York Ledger; wrote poem The Picket Guard (known for its opening words "All Quiet Along the Potomac") published in Harper's Mag., 1861; works include: General Frankie: A Story for Little Folks, 1863; All Quiet Along the Potomac, and Other Poems, 1879. Died Oct. 11, 1879.

BEESON, Henry White, congressman, farmer; b. Uniontown, Fayette County, Pa., Sept. 14, 1791; attended public schools. Became farmer; served as col. Fayette County Militia; mem. U.S. Ho. of Reps. (Democrat, filled vacancy) from Pa., 27th Congress, May 31, 1841-43. Died North Union Twp., nr. Uniontown, Oct. 28, 1863; buried Oak Hill Cemetery.

BEEST, Albert Van, artist; b. Rotterdam, Holland, June 11, 1820. Served in Dutch Navy; came to U.S., circa 1855; worked in New Bedford (Mass.), 1855, 57, N.Y.C., 1856, 58-60; shared studio with his pupil William Bradford, New Bedford, 1857; exhibited at Boston Athenaeum, 1857, posthumously 1861. Died N.Y.C., Oct. 8, 1860.

BEGOLE, Josiah Williams, gov. Mich., congressman; b. Groveland, Livingston County, N.Y., Jan. 20, 1815; attended public schs., Mt. Morris, Temple Hill Acad., Geneseo, N.Y. Moved to Flint, Genesee County, Mich., 1836; taught school, 1837, 38; farmer, 1839-56; school inspector; justice of peace and twp. treas.; treas. Genesee County, 1856-64; in lumber business, 1863; mem. Mich. Senate, 1870, 71; mem. Flint City Council 3 years; del. Nat. Republican Conv., Phila., 1872; mem. U.S. Ho. of Reps. (Rep.) from Mich., 43d Congress, 1873-75; resumed lumber business, later manufactured wagons, also engaged in banking; gov. Mich., 1883-85. Died Flint, June 5, 1896; buried Glenwood Cemetery.

BEHRENS, Henry, clergyman; b. Munstadt, Hanover, Germany, Dec. 10, 1815. Began novitiate in Soc. of Jesus, Stäffis (Estrayer), Switzerland; ordained Jesuit priest, circa 1842; prof. Coll. of Freiburg (Switzerland), until 1847; came to U.S. to found instn., circa 1847, upon his arrival learned instn. could not be started because of death of bishop who had brought him to U.S., returned to Germany; provincial of German province for 3 years; superior Jesuit chaplains and nurses during Franco-Prussian War; expelled from Germany because of his polit. beliefs; came to Buffalo, N.Y., 1872; superior Buffalo Mission, 1872-78, 86-92; established St. Ignatius Coll. (now John Carroll U.), Cleve., 1886, St. Francis and Holy Rosary missions, S.D. Died Oct. 17, 1895.

BEIRNE, Andrew, congressman, mcht.; b. Dangan, County Roscommon, Ireland, 1771; grad. Trinity U., Dublin, Ireland. Came to U.S., 1793, settled in Union, Monroe County, Va. (now W. Va.), became merchant and farmer; mem. Va. Ho. of Dels., 1807, 08; served as capt. of rifle company and as col. Monroe County Militia in War of 1812; del. Va. Constl. Conv., 1829, 30; mem. Va. Senate, 1831-36; Democratic presdl. elector, 1836; mem. U.S. Ho. of Reps. (Van Buren Dem.) from Va., 25th-26th congresses, 1837-41. Died Gainesville, Sumter County, Ala., Mar. 16, 1845; buried family burying ground, Union.

BEISSEL, Johann Conrad, clergyman, composer; b. Eberbach on the Neckar, Palatinate, Apr. 1690. Came to Am., 1720; asso. with Ch. of Brethren, Germantown, Pa.; organized ascetic religious community, Lebanon County, Pa., 1721; began monastic community (known as sect of Solitary Brethren of the Community of Seventh Day Baptists) at Ephrata (Pa.) which became a religious and artistic center, 1735; wrote over 1,000 hymns (some published by Benjamin Franklin), composed tunes for his hymns, harmonized them according to his own rules (collections of his hymns now in Library of Congress and Library of Hist. Soc. of Pa.). Author: Turtel Taube, 1747. Died Ephrata, July 6, 1768; buried Ephrata.

BELCHER, Hiram, congressman, lawyer; b. Hallowell, Me., Feb. 23, 1790; attended local academy, Hallowell, 1805-07; studied law. Admitted to Bar, 1812; practiced in Farmington, Kennebec County, Me., 1812; elected town clk., Farmington, 1814-19; mem. Me. Ho. of Reps., 1822, 29, 32; mem. Me. Senate, 1838, 39; mem. U.S. Ho.of Reps. (Whig) from Me., 30th Congress, 1847-49. Died Farmington, May 6, 1857; buried Center Meeting House Cemetery.

BELCHER, Jonathan, colonial gov.; b. Cambridge, Mass., Jan. 8, 1682; s. Andrew and Sarah (Gilbert) B.; grad. Harvard, 1699; m. Mary Partridge, 1705; m. 2d, Mary Teal, Sept. 9, 1748. Mem. Mass. Council,1718-20, 22-23, 26-27, 29; gov. Mass. and N.H., 1730-41; gov. N.J., 1746-57; a founder Coll. of N.J. (now Princeton), 1746-48, donated his library, 1757. Died Elizabethtown, N.J., Aug. 31, 1757.

BELCHER, Nathan, congressman; b. Preston (now part of Griswold), Conn., June 23, 1813; grad. Amherst (Mass.) Coll., 1832; studied Cambridge Law Sch. Admitted to bar, 1836; practiced in Clinton, Conn.; moved to New London, Conn., 1841, manufactured tools, hardware and kitchen utensils; mem. Conn. Ho. of Reps., 1846, 47; mem. Conn. Senate, 1850; Democratic presdl. elector, 1852; mem. U.S. Ho. of Reps. (Dem.) from Conn., 33d Congress, 1853-55; became banker along with mfg. activities. Died New London, June 2, 1891; buried Cedar Grove Cemetery.

BELCHER, Supply, composer, violinist; b. Stoughton, Mass., Mar. 29, 1751; m. Margaret More, Mar. 2, 1775; 10 children. Tavernkeeper in Stoughton, then moved to Hallowell, Me., 1785, to Farmington, Me., 1791, there became magistrate, state legislator, tchr., town's 1st choir leader; called The Handel of Maine. Composer: The Harmony of Maine (collection psalms, hymns, fuguing pieces, anthems), 1794. Died Farmington, June 9, 1836.

BELCOURT, George Antoine, missionary; b. Bay du Febvre, Apr. 22, 1803; s. Antoine and Josephte (Lemire) B.; grad. Nicolet (Que., Can.) Coll., 1803. Ordained as priest Roman Catholic Ch., 1827; assigned as missionary in Western Canada, stationed in Winnipeg among Chippewa Indians, 1831; built mission at Baie St. Paul, nr. Winnipeg, 1834, ministered to needs of Indians (often as physician), until 1847, accompanied Indians on Buffalo hunt, 1845, rendered great service pacifying dispute between mchts. of Hudson's Bay Co. and Indians, 1846; missionary at Pembina in Minn. Territory, 1847-50, St. Joseph in Minn. Territory, 1850-58; rector ch. at Rustico, Prince Edward Island, N.B., Can., 1858-68. Author: Principles of the Language of the Saulteux Indians, 1839. Died Shediac, N.B., May 31, 1874; buried Shediac.

BELDEN, George Oglivie, congressman; b. Norwalk, Conn., Mar. 28, 1797; attended public schools; studied law with Charles Baker, Bloomingburg, N.Y. Admitted to bar; practiced in Monticello, Sullivan County, N.Y.; mem. U.S. Ho. of Reps. (Democrat) from N.Y., 20th Congress, 1827-29; served as gen. 23d Brigade, N.Y. State Infantry, 1831. Died Monticello, Oct. 9, 1833; buried Old Cemetery on St. John Street.

BELDEN, Josiah, pioneer, entrepreneur; b. Cromwell, Conn., May 4, 1815; s. Josiah and Ruth (McKee) B.; attended common schs.; m. Sarah M. Jones, 1849. Apprenticed to jeweler, Albany, N.Y., 1830-35; jeweler, Phila., 1836; mem. Bartleson-Bidwell expdn. to Pacific Coast from Independence (Mo.), 1841; operated store, Santa Cruz, Cal., 1842-44; purchased ranch in Sacramento Valley, 1844; mgr. Mellus & Howard store, San Jose, Cal., 1849; elected 1st mayor of San Jose, 1850; became owner extensive San Francisco real estate holdings in 1850's; supported Republican Party in Cal., 1860; active in Sanitary Fund during Civil War; moved to N.Y.C., 1881; mem. Union League Club, N.Y.C.; dir. Erie R.R. Died N.Y.C., Apr. 23, 1892; buried N.Y.C.

BELKNAP, Daniel, composer, singing master; b. Framingham, Mass., 1771; m. Mary Parker, 1800; [illegible] children. Worked as farmer, mechanic and singing master, Framingham; moved to Pawtucket, R.I., 1812. Published The Harmonist's Companion, 1797, The Evangelical Harmony, 1800; The Village Compilation of Sacred Music, 1806; best known for hymn Concord. Died Pawtucket, 1815.

BELKNAP, Jeremy, clergyman; b. Boston, June 4, 1744; s. Joseph and Sarah (Byles) B.; grad. Harvard, 1762; m. Ruth Eliot, 1767. Taught sch., Milton, Mass., Greenland, N.H., 1762-66; ordained to ministry Congregational Ch., 1766; pastor, Dover, N.H., 1766-86, Federal Street Ch., Boston, 1787-98; chaplain to Am. troops, Cambridge, Mass., 1775; engaged in writing history of N.H., 1767; a founder Antiquarian Soc., Boston, 1791, became Mass. Hist. Soc., 1794, sec. until 1798. Author: History of New Hampshire, 1st vol., 1784; 2d vol., 1791, 3d vol., 1792; The Foresters, 1787; American Biography, 1st vol., 1794, 2d vol., 1798; Dissertations on the Character, Death, and Resurrection of Jesus Christ, and the Evidence of His Gospel, 1795. Died Boston, June 20, 1798; buried Boston.

BELKNAP, William Worth, army officer, sec. of war; b. Newburgh, N.Y., Sept. 22, 1829; s. Gen. William G. and Ann (Clark) B.; grad. Princeton, 1852; m. Cora LeRoy; m. 2d, Carrie Thompson; m. 3d, Mrs. John Bower. Admitted to D.C. bar, 1851; mem. Ia. Legislature (Democrat), 1857-58; commd. maj. 15th Ia. Inf., U.S. Army, 1861, served at battles of Shiloh, Corinth and Vicksburg; commd. brig. gen. U.S. Volunteers, 1864, served under Gen. William Sherman in Ga. campaign; commanded 14th div. 17th Army Corps; collector internal revenue in Ia., 1865; U.S. sec. of war under Pres. Grant, 1869-76, impeached for accepting bribes from John Evans in return for appointing Evans post-trader at Ft. Sill, allowed (by Grant) to resign before his trial, found not guilty (but most of senators who voted in his favor did so because they believed him no longer under their jurisdiction). Died Washington, D.C., Oct. 13, 1890.

BELL, Charles Henry, senator, gov. N.H.; b. Chester, N.H., Nov. 18, 1823; s. John and Persis (Thom) B.; attended Phillips Exeter Acad., 1836-40; grad. Dartmouth, 1844; m. Sarah Gilman, May 6, 1847; m. 2d, Mrs. Mary Gilman, June 3, 1857. Admitted to bar, circa 1847, practiced in Chester, N.H., Somersworth, N.H. until 1854; settled in Exeter, N.H., 1854, practiced law, 1854-68; solicitor Rockingham County (N.H.), 1856-66; mem. N.H. Legislature, 1858-60, 72-73, speaker, 1860; mem. N.H. Senate, 1863-64; mem. U.S. Senate (filled vacancy) from N.H., 1879-80; Republican gov. N.H., 1881-83; pres. N.H. Constl. Conv., 1889; prominent mem. N.H. Hist. Soc. Author: John Wheelwright, 1876; History of the Town of Exeter, New Hampshire, 1888; The Bench and Bar of New Hampshire, 1894. Died Exeter, Nov. 11, 1893; buried Exeter.

BELL, Henry Haywood, naval officer; b. N.C., Apr. 13, 1808; Commd. midshipman U.S. Navy, 1823, lt., 1831; served on ship Grampus against pirates in Cuban waters, 1828-29; commd. comdr., 1854; commanded San Jacinto in East India Squadron, 1856; promoted to commodore, 1862; fleet-capt. West Gulf Squadron, 1862; served in battles of Ft. Jackson, St. Philip in opening Mississippi River; commanded East India Squadron, 1865; commd. rear-adm., 1866, ret., 1867. Died Osaka, Japan, Jan. 11, 1868; buried Hiogo, Japan.

BELL, Hiram, congressman, lawyer; b. Salem, Vt., Apr. 22, 1808; ed. pub. schs., Salem; studied law. Admitted to bar, 1829; practiced in Greenville, Darke County, O.; auditor Darke County, 1829, 34; mem. Ohio Ho. of Reps., 1836, 37, 40; mem. U.S. Ho. of Reps. (Whig) from Ohio, 32d Congress, 1851-53. Died Greenville, Dec. 21, 1885; buried Greenville Cemetery.

BELL, Isaac, mcht.; b. N.Y.C., Nov. 6, 1846; s. Isaac Bell; student pvt. schs., N.Y.C.; m. Jeanette Gordon Bennett, 1878. Asso. with Brown Bros. & Co., N.Y.C., circa 1864, interested in cotton speculation; established cotton brokerage firm, Savannah, Ga., circa 1870, some after became partner Barnwell & Co., cotton brokers, Charleston, S.C.; established firm Isaac Bell & Co., cotton brokerage house, N.Y.C., New Orleans, circa 1873; retired, 1877, moved to Newport, R.I.; active in R.I. politics as Democrat; U.S. minister to The Hague (apptd. by Pres. Cleveland) 1885-88; del. Nat. Dem. Conv., 1888. Died probably Newport, Jan. 29, 1889.

BELL, Jacob, ship builder; b. Darien, Conn., Dec. 17, 1792; s. John and Deborah (Clock) B.; no formal edn.; m. Mary Clock, May 10, 1821. Partner with David Brown in shipyard on East River, N.Y.C., 1820-48, ran business on his own after Brown's death, 1848; launched 1st ships William Tell and Orbit, 1821, built sailing vessels and steamships; in assn. with Edward K. Collins built N.Y. Marine Dry Dock Co., 1834, built several packet ships for 'ollins Line; launched the Lion and Eagle (1st teamships in N.Y.) 1840; built clippers Oriental, 849, White Squall, 1850, steamships Pacific and altic (both for Collins Line). Died N.Y.C., July 1, 1852; buried N.Y.C.

BELL, James, senator, lawyer; b. Francistown, Hillsboro County, N.H., Nov. 13, 1804; s. Samuel 'ell; attended Phillips Acad., Andover, Mass.; rad. Bowdoin Coll., 1822; studied law Litchield (Conn.) Law Sch. Admitted to bar, 1825; racticed in Gilmanton, N.H.; moved to Exeter, .H., 1831, Gilford, N.H., 1846; mem. N.H. Ho. of eps., 1846, 50; del. N.H. Constl. Conv., 1850; unuccessful candidate for gov. N.H., 1854, 55; mem. U.S. Senate (Whig) from N.H., July 0, 1855-May 26, 1857. Died Laconia, Belknap ounty, N.H., May 26, 1857; buried Exeter Cemeery.

BELL, James Madison, abolitionist, poet; b. Gallipolis, O., Apr. 3, 1826; m. Louisiana Sanderline, 848, several children. Plasterer's apprentice in outh; lived in Can., 1854-60; friend of abolitionist ohn Brown, helped recruit men for raid on Harper's 'erry, 1859; went to Cal., wrote poetry, 1860; ectured to freedmen in various Eastern cities after ivil War; del. Ohio Republican Conv., 1868; del. rom Ohio to Rep. Nat. Conv.; most noteworthy poems nclude: The Day and the War, The Progress of Liberty. Died 1902.

BELL, James Martin, congressman, lawyer; b. untingdon County, Pa., Oct. 16, 1796; ed. public chs.; studied law, Steubenville, O. Admitted to ar, 1817; practiced in Cambridge, O.; served s maj. gen. 15th Div., Ohio Militia; pros. atty. uernsey County (O.), 1818-32; mem. Ohio Ho. f Reps., 1826-31, speaker, 1830, 31; master ommr., 1827; justice of peace, 1830; county sch. caminer, 1830; mem. U.S. Ho. of Reps. (Demorat) from Ohio, 23d Congress, 1833-35; mayor f Cambridge, 1838-40. Died Cambridge, Apr. 4, 849; buried Founders' Burial Ground.

BELL, John, congressman; b. Pennsboro, Lyoming County, Pa., June 19, 1796. Moved to ower Sandusky, O., 1823; mayor Lower Sanusky, 1830; probate judge Sandusky County (O.) everal terms; commd. maj. gen. Ohio Militia, 834; commanded Ohio forces in Toledo War, 835; postmaster, Lower Sandusky, 1838-41; mem. hio Ho. of Reps., 1844, 45; mayor Fremont (O.), 845, 46; mem. U.S. Ho. of Reps. (Whig, filled acancy) from Ohio, 31st Congress, Jan. 7, 1851-Mar. 3, 1851; probate judge, 1852-55, 58-63. Died remont, May 4, 1869; buried Oakwood Cemetery.

BELL, John, senator, sec. of war; b. Nashville, enn., Feb. 15, 1797; s. Samuel and Margaret Edmiston) B.; grad. Cumberland Coll., Nashville, 817; m. Sally Dickinson; m. 2d, Jane Yeatman. dmitted to bar, 1817, began practice law in Frankn, Tenn.; moved to Nashville, practiced law, circa 819; mem. U.S. Ho. of Reps. from Tenn., 20th-6th congresses, 1827-41, opposed Jackson's bank olicy and nomination of Van Buren, 1836; became Whig in late 1830's; U.S. sec. of war under Pres. Harrison, 1841; mem. U.S. Senate from Tenn., 1847-9, opposed Kan.-Neb. Act and LeCompton Constn. n Kan.; became mem. Am. Party, late 1850's; dvocated moderation on slave issue; Constl. Union arty candidate for Pres. U.S., 1860; favored comromise to save Union, but after Ft. Sumter adsed Tenn. to join Confederacy; lived in Confederacy uring Civil War. Died Stewart County, Tenn., Sept. 0, 1869; buried Stewart County.

BELL, Joshua Fry, congressman, lawyer; b. anville, Boyle County, Ky., Nov. 26, 1811; grad. entre Coll., Danville, 1828; studied law, Lexingn, Ky. Traveled in Europe several years; admited to bar; practiced law, Danville; mem. U.S. o. of Reps. (Whig) from Ky., 29th Congress, 845-47; sec. state of Ky., 1849; Whig presdl. ector, 1852; del. Washington (D.C.) Peace Conv., 861; del. Border State Conv., 1861; mem. Ky. o. of Reps., 1862-67. Died Danville, Aug. 17, 870; buried Bellevue Cemetery.

BELL, Luther Vose, physician, politician; b. rancestown, N.H., Dec. 20, 1806; s. Samuel and Mehitabel (Dana) B.; grad. Bowdoin Coll., 1823; M.D., Dartmouth, 1836; m. Frances Pinkerton, 1834. Began practice of medicine, Chester, N.H., 1837; mem. N.H. Legislature, 1835-36, instrumental in btaining public support for a state hosp. for inane; mem. Whig Party; popular lyceum lectr. on cientific subjects; supt. McLean Hosp. for Insane, harlestown, Mass., 1836-56; an exec. councillor of Mass., 1850; del. Whig Conv., 1852; served as sureon 11th Mass. Regt., U.S. Volunteers, 1861-62. Died Budd's Ferry, Mo., Feb. 11, 1862.

BELL, Peter Hansborough, army officer, gov. Tex.; Fredericksburg, Va., Mar. 11, 1810; s. James and lizabeth (Hansborough) B.; m. Ella Eaton, 1857. Moved to Tex., 1836; asst. adj. gen. (apptd. by Sam Houston, pres. Republic of Tex.), 1837-39; asst. adj. gen., insp. gen., 1839-40; commd. capt. Tex. Rangers, 1845; commd. lt. col. U.S. Volunteers, 1846; gov. Tex, 1849-53; mem. U.S. Ho. of Reps. from Tex., 33d-34th congresses, 1853-57. Died Littleton, N.C., Apr. 20, 1898; buried City Cemetery, Littleton.

BELL, Robert, publisher; b. Glasgow, Scotland, circa 1732; apprentice bookbinder; married, circa 1766, 2 children. Came to Am., 1766; established as bookseller, auctioneer, 1770; published an edit. of The History of the Reign of Charles the Fifth, Emperor of Germany (Robertson), 1770, Blackstone's Commentaries, 1771, 1st edit. of Common Sense (Thomas Paine), 1776; opposed restrictions on selling books by auction passed by Pa. Assembly, 1784, wrote pamphlet Bell's Address to Every Free Man to defend his view. Died Richmond, Va., Sept. 23, 1784; buried Richmond.

BELL, Samuel, senator, gov. N.H.; b. Londonberry, N.H., Feb. 8, 1770; s. John and Mary (Gilmore) B.; grad. Dartmouth, 1793; LL.D., Bowdoin Coll., 1821; m. Mehitable Dana, Nov. 26, 1797; m. 2d, Lucy Smith, July 4, 1828. Admitted to N.H. bar, 1796; mem. N.H. Legislature from Francetown, 1804-06; pres. N.H. Senate, 1807-08; mem. N.H. Exec. Council, 1809; asso. justice N. H. Superior Ct., 1816; gov. N.H., 1819-23; mem. U.S. Senate from N.H., 1823-35. Died Chester, N.H., Dec. 23, 1850; buried Chester Cemetery.

BELL, Samuel Newell, congressman, lawyer; b. Chester, Rockingham County, N.H., Mar. 25, 1829; attended Phillips Acad., Andover, Mass.; grad. Dartmouth, 1847; studied law. Admitted to bar, 1849; practiced in Meredith, Belknap County, N.H.; mem. U.S. Ho. of Reps. (Democrat) from N.H., 42d, 44th congresses, 1871-73, 75-77; had large real estate holdings; pres. several railroads; v.p. N.H. Fire Ins. Co.; declined appointment as chief justice N.H. Superior Ct. Died North Woodstock, Grafton County, N.H., Feb. 8, 1889; buried Valley Cemetery, Manchester, N.H.

BELL, Solomon, see Snelling, William Joseph.

BELLAMY, Edward, author; b. Chicopee Falls, Mass., Mar. 26, 1850; s. Rufus and Maria (Putnam) B.; attended Union Coll., Schenectady, N.Y., circa 1867-68; m. Emma Sanderson, 1882. Admitted to Mass. bar, circa 1877, began practice in Springfield; editorial writer N.Y. Evening Post, 1878; founder (with brother) Springfield Daily News, 1880; advocated nationalization of industry in his published works; devoted career to writing and propagation of socialist ideas, after 1885; founder New Nation, (weekly devoted to utopian socialism), Boston, 1891. Author: Dr. Heidenhoff's Process, 1880; Mrs. Ludington's Sister, 1884; Looking Backward (most famous novel, outlined his utopian econ. thinking), 1888; Equality, 1897; The Blind Man's World and Other Stories (collection short stories), 1898. Died Chicopee Falls, May 22, 1898; buried Chicopee Falls.

BELLAMY, Joseph, theologian; b. Cheshire, Conn., Feb. 20, 1719; s. Matthew and Sarah (Wood) B.; grad. Yale, 1735; studied theology with Jonathan Edwards, 1735-37; m. Frances Sherman, Apr. 27, 1744; m. 2d, Abiah Burbank, 1786. Pastor, Congregational Ch., Bethlehem, Conn., 1738-90; a powerful advocate in sermons of New Light theology of Great Awakening, became well-known as preacher in So. New Eng., 1740's, 50's; published works dealing with sin and theory of atonement, aroused controversy in Congregational ministry. Author: True Religion Delineated, 1750; The Wisdom of God in the Permission of Sin, 1758. Died Bethlehem, Conn., Mar. 6, 1790; buried Bethlehem.

BELLEW, Frank Henry Temple, cartoonist; b. Cawnpore, India, Apr. 18, 1828; married, at least 1 son, Frank. Came to Am., 1850, settled in N.Y.C.; became comic illustrator for Harper's Mag., The Illustrated Am. News (N.Y.C.), for books (especially children's books); some of most famous caricature work appeared in Fifth Avenue Jour., 1872; a founder such comic sheets as Nick-Nax, The Lantern, Vanity Fair. Author and illustrator: The Art of Amusing, 1866. Died N.Y.C., June 29, 1888; buried N.Y.C.

BELLINGER, Joseph, congressman; born in S.C. Democratic presdl. elector, 1808; mem. U.S. Ho. of Reps. from S.C., 15th Congress, 1817-19.

BELLINGHAM, Richard, colonial gov.; b. Lincolnshire, Eng., circa 1592; s. Frances Amcotts (mother); received legal tng. in Eng.; m. Elizabeth Backhouse; m. 2d, Penelope Pelham, 1641. Came to Am., 1634, resided in Boston; dep. gov. colony of Mass., 1635, 40, 53, 55-65, treas., 1637-40, gov., 1641, 54, 65-72; asst. in Mass. Gen. Ct., 1636-40, 42-53; known as legal expert in colony, took popular side in disputes in opposition to Gov. Winthrop; denied authority of Royal Commn. sent from Eng. to investigate colony's govt., 1665. Died Boston, Dec. 7, 1672; buried Boston.

BELLOMONT, 1st earl, see Coote, Richard.

BELLOWS, Albert Fitch, landscape painter; b. Milford, Mass., Nov. 29, 1829; s. Albert and Pamela (Fitch) B.; studied at Royal Acad. of Antwerp, Belgium, 1856-58; m. Candace J. Brown, Aug. 5, 1851. Noted painter in Boston; prin. New Eng. Sch. of Design, Boston, 1850-56; water color painter, N.Y.C., 1858-67; mem. N.A.D., 1861; painted in Europe, 1867-72, N.Y.C., 1872-83; an original member Am. Soc. Painters in Water Color; exhibited at Paris Expn., 1878. Author: Water Color Painting, 1868. Died N.Y.C., Nov. 24, 1883; buried N.Y.C.

BELLOWS, Henry Whitney, clergyman; b. Walpole, N.H., June 11, 1814; s. John and Betsy (Eames) B.; grad. Harvard, 1832, Harvard Divinity Sch., 1837; m. Eliza Townsend, Aug. 13, 1839; m. 2d, Anna Peabody, June 30, 1874. Minister, Unitarian Ch., Mobile, Ala., 1837-39, 1st Unitarian Ch., N.Y.C., 1839-82; editor Christian Register, circa 1855; deeply interested in many types of reform movements during career; a founder, head U.S. San. Commn. during Civil War; a founder Nat. Conf. Unitarian Chs., 1865; a founder Antioch Coll., Yellow Springs, O.; editor Christian Examiner, 1866-77; advocate of civil sevice reform, circa 1880. Author: The Treatment of Social Diseases, 1857; Restatements of Christian Doctrine, 1860; The Old World and Its New Face, 1868-69. Died N.Y.C., Jan. 30, 1882; buried N.Y.C.

BELMONT, August, banker, diplomat; b. Alzei, Rhenish Palatinate, Dec. 2, 1816; s. Simon and Frederika (Elsaas) B.; m. Caroline Slidell Perry, 1849. Came to Am., 1837; established banking firm in N.Y.C. (became August Belmont & Co.), 1837, served as U.S. agt. for Rothschild banking interests; active in Democratic politics in N.Y., from 1840's; amassador to The Hague (apptd. by Pres. Pierce), 1853-57; adherent of Douglas faction Dem. Party, until 1860; Unionist during Civil War; visited Europe to obtain support for No. cause; ret. from politics, 1872; pres. Am. Jockey Club; owned one of finest art collections of era. Died N.Y.C., Nov. 24, 1890; buried N.Y.C.

BELSER, James Edwin, congressman, lawyer; b. Charleston, S.C., Dec. 22, 1805; ed. public schs., pvt. tutors; studied law. Moved to Ala., 1825, settled in Montgomery; admitted to bar; practiced law, Montgomery; elected clk. county ct.; mem. Ala. Ho. of Reps., 1828, 53, 57; editor Planters Gazette several years; apptd. solicitor Montgomery County, 1828, later elected; apptd. by gov. as Ala. commr. to procure settlement claims against U.S. Govt. for money advanced in Indian War of 1836, 1842; mem. U.S. Ho. of Reps. (Democrat) from Ala., 28th Congress, 1843-45; affiliated with Whig Party, 1848. Died Montgomery, Jan. 16, 1859; buried Oakwood Cemetery.

BEMAN, Nathan Sidney Smith, clergyman; b. New Lebanon, N.Y., Nov. 26, 1785; s. Samuel and Silence (Douglass) B.; grad. Middlebury Coll., 1807. Tchr., Newcastle, Me. and Middlebury, Vt., 1807-10; pastor 1st Presbyn. Ch., Portland, Me., 1810-12; head sch., Mt. Zion, Ga., 1812-23; pastor 1st Presbyn. Ch., Troy, N.Y., 1823-63; v.p. Rensselaer Poly. Inst., Troy, 1842-45, pres., 1845-65, also prof. philosophy; aroused theol. controversy in Presbyn. Ch. through advocacy of revivals, during 1820's, 30's, became leader New Sch. faction Presbyn. clergy, played important role in separation of ch., 1838. Author: Four Sermons on the Doctrine of Atonement, 1825; Letters to Rev. John Hughes, 1851. Died probably Troy, Aug. 6, 1871.

BEMENT, Caleb N., agrl. writer, inventor; b. N.Y. State, 1790. Engaged as printer in N.Y., circa 1820; bought "Three Hills Farm" nr. Albany, N.Y., 1834, began agrl. experimentation; developed Bement's corn cultivator, Bement's turnip drill; breeder imported live stock; an editor monthly agrl. jour. Central N.Y. Farmer, 1844; mgr. Am. Hotel, Albany, 1844-circa 1850; propr., editor Am. Quarterly Jour. of Agr. and Science, 1848 (failed after 1 year); owner Albany Steam Mills producing substitute for yeast, 1853-55; farmer, Dutchess County, N.Y., 1855-67. Author: American Poulterer's Companion, 1844; The Rabbit Fancier, 1855; contbr. numerous articles to agrl. jours. Died Poughkeepsie, N.Y., Dec. 22, 1868; buried Poughkeepsie.

BEMIS, George, legal publicist; b. Waltham, Mass., Oct. 13, 1816; s. Seth and Sarah (Wheeler) B.; grad. Harvard, 1835, Harvard Law Sch., 1839. Admitted to bar, 1839; practiced in Boston, 1839; achieved prominence in cases Commonwealth vs. Rogers, 1844, trial of Dr. Webster, 1850; recognized as expert in criminal law and penology; discontinued practice, 1858; advised U.S. Govt. in Ala. claims case, 1868-72; wrote pamphlets and treatises on internal law dealing with status of neutrals during wartime. Author: American Neutrality, Its Honorable Past, Its Expedient Future, 1866; The Alabama Negotiations, Their Just Repudiation by the United States Senate, 1869. Died Nice, France, Jan. 5, 1878.

BENADE, James Arthur, artist; b. Bethlehem, Pa., 1823; s. Bishop Andrew Benade; studied with Gustavus Grunewald. Exhibited at Artists' Fund Soc., Phila., 1838; exhibited 2 landscapes at Pa. Acad., 1848; collaborated with his pupil F.D. Devlan on Landscape and Cattle, exhibited at Pa. Acad., 1853. Died Reading, Pa., Feb. 2, 1853.

BENBRIDGE, Henry, artist; b. Phila., May 20, 1744; s. James and Mary (Clark) B.; no formal edn.; studied with Batoni and Raphael Mengs, Italy, 1765; m. Miss Sage, 1771. Painted portrait of Pascal Paoli for James Boswell, Corsica, 1769; exhibited in England, 1769, became acquainted with Benjamin West; returned to Am., 1770, painted portraits; lived in Phila., 1771-72; mem. Am. Philos. Soc., 1771; portrait painter, Charleston, S.C., 1772, Norfolk, Va., 1800-12; instructed Thomsas Sully in oil painting. Died Norfolk, Feb. 1812; buried Norfolk.

BENDIRE, Charles E., physician, naturalist; maj. Med. Corps, U.S. Army; collector animals and plants; Bendire's thrasher named in his honor.

BENEDICT, David, clergyman, historian; b. Norwalk, Conn., Oct. 10, 1779; s. Thomas and Martha (Scudder) B.; grad. Brown U., 1806; m. Margaret Gano, May 5, 1808, 12 children. Pastor, First Baptist Ch., Pawtucket, R.I., 1806-29; became trustee Brown U., 1818; resigned pastorate to give full time to study of Bapt. history, 1829; postmaster Pawtucket, during 1830's and 40's; travelled widely in U.S. gathering hist. material; active in founding Sunday schs., Blackstone Valley, R.I.; mem. corp. Brown U., 1859-74. Author: History of All Religions, 1824; A General History of the Baptist Denomination in America and Other Parts of the World, 1848; Fifty Years Among the Baptists, 1860. Died Pawtucket, Dec. 5, 1874; buried Pawtucket.

BENEDICT, Erastus Cornelius, lawyer, univ. chancellor; b. Branford, Conn., Mar. 19, 1800; s. Rev. Joel T. and Currance (Wheeler) B.; grad. Williams Coll., 1821; LL.D. (hon.), Rutgers Coll., 1865; m. Caroline Bloodgood, May 7, 1833. Admitted to N.Y. bar, 1824, soon became one of most distinguished admiralty lawyers of the time; dep. clk. U.S. Dist. Ct. for So. N.Y., 1824; mem. NY.C. Common Council, 1840; pub. sch. trustee, N.Y.C., 1842; mem. N.Y. State Legislature, 1848; mem. N.Y.C. Bd. Edn., 1850-63, pres.; trustee Williams Coll., 1855; regent Univ. State N.Y., 1855-80, chancellor, 1878-80; a founder Coll. City N.Y.; mem. N.Y. State Senate, 1872; bd. govs. N.Y. State Woman's Hosp.; mem. N.Y. Hist. Soc. Author: American Admiralty, 1850; A Run Through Europe, 1860; Medieval Hymns, 1861. Died N.Y.C., Oct. 22, 1880.

BENEZET, Anthony, philanthropist, author; b. San Quentin, France, Jan. 31, 1713; s. Jean Etienne Benezet; no formal edn.; m. Joyce Marriott, May 1736. Came to Am. with family, 1731, settled in Phila., became mcht.; taught at Germantown Acad., circa 1736-42, Friends' English Sch., Phila., 1742-55; conducted girls' sch., Phila., 1755-66; began writing on slavery and treatment of Indians, during 1740's a leader in helping French immigrants from Acadia in Phila., 1756. Author: A Caution and Warning to Britain and Her Colonies on the Calamitous State of Enslaved Negroes, 1766; Historical Account of Guinea, 1771; Short Account of the People Called Quakers, 1780; Observations on the Situation . . . of the Indian Natives of this Continent, 1784. Died Phila., May 3, 1784; buried Phila.

BENHAM, Henry Washington, army officer, engr.; b. Quebec, Montreal, Can., Apr. 8, 1813; s. Jared and Rebecca (Hill) B.; grad. U.S. Mil. Acad., 1837; m. Elizabeth McNeill, Oct. 3, 1843; 3 children. Moved to Conn. when mother remarried; entered U.S. Army, brevetted 2d lt. engrs., 1837, commd. 1st lt., 1838; served in Mexican War; brevetted captain for services at Battle of Buena Vista, 1847; capt. engrs., 1848; in charge of repairs for defenses of N.Y. Harbor, 1848-53; built Boston Lighthouse; asst. in U.S. Coast Survey Office, 1853-56; chief engr. Dept. of Ohio, U.S. Army, 1861; commd. maj. engrs. U.S. Army, 1861; brevetted col.; commd. brig. gen. U.S. Volunteers; charged with violation of orders during Battle of Secessionville (S.C.), 1862, appointment of brig. gen. revoked, revocation cancelled by Pres. Lincoln, 1863; commanded engr. brigade Army of the Potomac, 1863; commd. lt. col. engrs., Army, 1863; brevetted brig. gen., also maj. gen. U.S. Army, brevetted maj. gen. U.S. Volunteers, 1865; commd. col. engrs., 1867; in charge defense of Boston, N.Y. harbors 1865-82. Died N.Y.C., June 1, 1884.

BENJAMIN, Asher, architect, author; b. Greenfield, Mass., June 15, 1773; m. Achsah Hitchcock, Nov. 30, 1797; m. 2d, Nancy Bryant, July 24, 1805. Lived in Greenfield, Mass., 1790's, practiced as architect in area; began archtl. practice, Windsor, Vt., circa 1800, Boston, circa 1805; designed Old South Meeting House (Windsor), First Congl. Ch. (Bennington, Vt.), West Ch. (Boston), Carew house (Springfield, Mass.), Hollister house (Greenfield); wrote numerous works on bldg. styles (popularized Greek Revival architecture), including: The Country Builder's Assistant, 1797; The American Builder's Companion, 1806; The Rudiments of Architecture, 1814; The Practical House Carpenter, 1830. Died Springfield, July 26, 1845; buried Springfield.

BENJAMIN, John Forbes, congressman, lawyer; b. Cicero, Onondaga County, N.Y., Jan. 23, 1817; attended public schs.; studied law. Moved to Tex., 1845, to Mo., 1848; admitted to bar, 1848; practiced in Shelbyville, Shelby County, Mo., 1848; mem. Mo. Ho. of Reps., 1850-52; Democratic presdl. elector, 1856; entered U.S. Army as pvt., 1861, promoted to capt., maj., lt. col., brig. gen.; provost marshal 8th Dist. of Mo., 1863, 64; del. Nat. Republican Conv., Balt., 1864; mem. U.S. Ho. of Reps. (Radical Rep.) from Mo., 39th-41st congresses, 1865-71; moved to Washington, D.C.,, 1874, became banker. Died Washington, Mar. 8, 1877; buried pvt. cemetery, Shelbina, Shelby County.

BENJAMIN, Judah Philip, senator, Confederate cabinet officer; b. St. Croix, B.W.I., Aug. 6, 1811; s. Philip and Rebecca (de Mendes) B.; attended Yale, 1825-27; m. Natalie St. Martin, 1833. Admitted to La. bar, 1832; became mem. La. Legislature, 1842; del. La. Constl. Conv., 1844-45; Whig presdl. elector, 1848; prin. organizer Jackson R.R. (now I.C. R.R.), 1852; mem. U.S. Senate (Whig) from La., 1853-61; apptd. atty. gen. Provisional Govt. of Confederate States Am., Feb. 1861; acting sec. of war Confederate States Am., Sept.-Nov. 1861, sec. of war (censured severely and unjustly for Confederate losses of Roanoke Island, Forts Henry and Donelson), Nov. 1861-Mar. 1862, resigned during Confederate Congress investigation of Roanoke Island affair; apptd. sec. of state by Jefferson Davis, was highly unpopular with Southern people, but possessed Davis' firm confidence; advocated arming of slaves and providing for ultimate emancipation, winter 1864-65 (plan rejected by Confederate Congress); promoted Hampton Roads Conf., Feb. 1865, believed in viability of Confederate regime until the end, but with Davis refused to make essential concessions in negotiations with U.S. Govt. in 1865; escaped to Eng. following collapse of Confederacy, Apr. 1865; admitted to bar at Lincoln's Inn, June 1866; practiced law before English courts, 1866-83, revealed logical capacities of highest order, specialized in appeal and chancery cases; argued important cases involving principles of criminal jurisdiction over foreigners, constl. issues, corporation law; ret. to residence in Paris, France, 1883. Author: Treatise on the Law of Sale of Personal Property, 1868. Died Paris, May 8, 1884.

BENJAMIN, Nathan, missionary; b. Catskill, N.Y., Dec. 14, 1811; s. Nathan and Ruth (Seymour) B.; grad. Williams Coll., 1831, Andover Theol. Sem., 1834; m. Mary Wheeler, Apr. 25, 1836. Ordained to ministry, 1836; went to Greece under auspices of Am. Bd. Commrs. for Fgn. Missions, 1836, served in Argos, later Athens, 1837-45; translated Bibl. lit. into Greek, preached in both Greek and English; in U.S., 1845-47, in Smyrna, 1847-52, Constantinople, 1852-55; supplied Armenians with Christian literature in vernacular, Constantinople; established Morning Star (1st Armenian newspaper), Smyrna. Died Constantinople, Jan. 27, 1855; buried Constantinople.

BENJAMIN, Park, editor, poet; b. Demerara, Brit. Guiana, Aug. 14, 1809; s. Parke and Mary (Gall) B.; grad. Trinity Coll., Hartford, Conn., 1829; attended Harvard Law Sch., 1830-32. Editor, New Eng. Mag., Boston, 1834-35; co-editor Am. Monthly Mag., N.Y.C., 1835-38; literary editor New Yorker mag., 1838-39; founded Evening Signal and New World (weekly lit. periodicals), N.Y.C., 1839, latter publ. survived until 1845, relied on reprints from Brit. novels; his publishing efforts characterized by sensationalism; active as Lyceum lectr. and literary agt. in 1840's and 1850's; contbr. to The Harbinger (collection of verse), Boston, 1833. Died N.Y.C., Sept. 12, 1864; buried N.Y.C.

BENNER, Philip, mcht., mfr.; b. Chester County, Pa., May 19, 1762; s. Henry and Dinah (Thomas) B.; no formal edn.; m. Ruth Roberts, circa 1785, 8 children. Served as pvt. under Gen. Anthony Wayne during Revolutionary War; engaged in iron mfg., Coventry, Pa., 1783; in business with sawmill in addition to iron forge, Rock Forge, Centre County, Pa., 1792, built another forge and nail-mill, 1800; sold iron products in both East and West; a founder Bellefonte (Pa.), circa 1805; 1st pres. Center & Kishacoquillas Turnpike Co., 1821; began mfg. at Logan's Branch Woolen Factory, Centre County, 1824; Jacksonian Democrat; founded Centre Democrat (pro-Jackson newspaper), 1827. Died Centre County, July 27, 1832.

BENNET, A. A., architect; b. Schoharie, N.Y., 1825. Apprenticed to carpenter-builder, Schoharie; studied architecture and bldg. under Orson Phelps (his brother-in-law); Went to Ala., 1846, worked in Montgomery and other cities in Ala., 2 years; embarked from New Orleans on S.S. Galveston for Cal., 1849; began archtl. practice, San Francisco, practiced until 1876; apptd. state architecture State of Cal., 1876, moved office to Sacramento; in charge of work on State Capitol, Gov.'s Mansion, Sacramento, bldgs. at prison in San Quentin, br. bldgs. in Folsom; architect Mechanics Art Coll., Berkeley, Cal., ct. houses in Yolo, Stanislaus, Merced, Tulare and Kern counties (Cal.); resumed practice in San Francisco, 1883, asso. with John M. Curtis; designed ct. houses, including those for Sonoma County (Santa Rosa, Cal.) and Humboldt County (Eureka, Cal.); architect several pub. bldgs., San Francisco. Died San Francisco, Dec. 1890.

BENNET, Benjamin, congressman, clergyman; b. Bucks County, Pa., Oct. 31, 1764; attended common schs.; studied theology. Ordained to ministry Baptist Ch., Middletown, Monmouth County, N.J., 1793, pastor there; became farmer, nr. Middletown; mem. U.S. Ho. of Reps. from N.J., 14th-15th congresses, 1815-19. Died on his farm nr. Middletown, Oct. 8, 1840; buried Baptist Cemetery, Holmdel, N.J.

BENNET, Sanford Fillmore, physician, songwriter; b. Eden, N.Y., June 21, 1836; s. Robert and Sally (Kent) B.; attended U. Mich., 1858-circa 1861; M.D., Rush Med. Coll., Chgo., 1874; m. Gertrude Crosby Johonnatt. Moved to Ill. with family, 1842; taught sch., Wauconda, Ill., 1854; in charge of public schs., Richmond, Ill.; owner, editor with Frank Leland of Elkhorn (Wis.) Independent, circa 1864; 2d lt. 40th Inf. Regt., Wis. Volunteers, 1864; propr. drug store, began study medicine after Civil War, Elkhorn; wrote songs as hobby, most popular being "The Sweet By and By" (translated into many langs.); editor, publisher Richmond Gazette. Author: (with J. P. Webster) The Signet Ring (anthology of songs) 1871; The Pioneer, an Idyll of the Middle West, 1898. Died June 11, 1898.

BENNETT, Caleb Prew, gov. Del.; b. Chester County, Pa., Nov. 11, 1758; s. Joseph and Elizabeth (Prew) Wiley B.; m. Catherine Britton, Apr. 5, 1792. Joined Continental Army, 1775, sgt., 1777, served at Valley Forge, winter 1777-78; commd. 2d lt., 1778, served at battles of Brandywine and Germantown; commd. 1st lt., 1780; treas. New Castle County (Del.), 1807-33; maj. arty. Del. Militia, 1813; in command Port of New Castle during War of 1812; 1st Democratic gov. Del., 1833-36. Died Wilmington, Del., May 9, 1836; buried Friends Meeting House Cemetery, Wilmington.

BENNETT, David Smith, congressman; b. nr. Camillus, Onondaga County, N.Y., May 3, 1811 attended common schs., local acad., Onondaga Farmer; moved to Syracuse, N.Y.; in produce business, extended business to N.Y.C.; moved to Buffalo, N.Y., 1853, built and operated several grain elevators, purchased original Dart grain elevator; mem. N.Y. State Senate, 1865; mem. U.S. Ho. of Reps. (Republican) from N.Y., 41st Congress, 1869-71. Died Buffalo, Nov. 6, 1894 buried Oakwood Cemetery, Syracuse.

BENNETT, De Robigne Mortimer, freethinker; b. nr. Otsego Lake, N.Y., Dec. 23, 1818; m. Mary Wicks, Oct. 12, 1846. Mem. Shaker Soc. (religious sect), New Lebanon, N.Y., 1832; practiced medicine of roots, barks and herbs, became physician of New Lebanon; left New Lebanon, 1846, lived itinerant life for 27 years; sold "Dr. Bennett's Quick Cure Golden Liniment, Worm Lozenges, and Root and Plant Pills," Cincinnati; editor, publisher Truth seeker (freethinker's organ), Paris, Ill., 1873-79 convicted for sending indecent matter through mails 1879, in prison, 1879-80; del. to Congress of Free thinkers, Brussels, Belgium; travelled around world 1881-82. Died Dec. 6, 1882.

BENNETT, Edmund Hatch, jurist; b. Manchester Vt., Apr. 6, 1824; s. Miles Lyman and Adalin (Hatch) B.; grad. U. Vt., 1843; m. Sally Crocker at least 2 children including Samuel C. Admitted to Vt. bar, 1847, Suffolk County (Mass.) bar, 1848 practiced law, Taunton, Mass., 1848-98; judge of probate and insolvency Bristol County (Mass.) 1858-83; 1st mayor of Taunton, 1865-68; lectr. Dane Sch. Law, Harvard, 1870-72; dean Boston U Law Sch., 1876-98; chmn. bd. commrs. for the Promotion of Uniformity of Legislation in the U.S. 1891; chmn. com. to revise statutes of Mass., 1896 Author: Selection of Leading Cases in Criminal Law 1856; Mass. Digest 1804-57, 1862, Mass. Digest 1857-69, 1872, Mass. Digest 1869-79, 1881; Fire Insurance Cases, 1872; Farm Law, 1880. Died Jan 2, 1898.

BENNETT, Hendley Stone, congressman, lawyer; b. nr. Franklin, Williamson County, Tenn. Apr. 7, 1807; attended public schs., West Point Miss.; studied law. Admitted to bar, 1830; practiced in Columbus, Miss.; judge circuit ct., 1846-54; mem. U.S. Ho. of Reps. (Democrat) from Miss., 34th Congress, 1855-57; moved to Paris Tex., 1859, practiced law; served as capt. Co. G

2d Regt. Tex. Cavalry, Confederate States Army, 861-62; returned to Tenn., 1886, settled in Frankin, practiced law. Died Franklin, Dec. 15, 1891; uried Oakwood Cemetery, Syracuse.

BENNETT, Henry, congressman, lawyer; b. New Lisbon, Otsego County, N.Y., Sept. 29, 1808; ttended public schs.; studied law. Admitted to ar, 1832; practiced in New Berlin, Chenango County, N.Y.; clk. New Berlin, 1846; mem. U.S. Io. of Reps. (as Whig) from N.Y., 31st, (as Republican) 32d-35th congresses, 1849-59. Died New Berlin, May 10, 1868.

BENNETT, James Gordon, newspaper editor; b. Keith, Scotland, Sept. 1, 1795; m. Henreitta Crean, 1840, 3 children including James Gordon. Came to Halifax, N.S., Can., 1819, to N.Y.C., 1822; worked or Charleston (S.C.) Courier, 1823; asso. editor N.Y. Enquirer, 1827-28, N.Y. Courier and Enquirer, 1829-32; issued 1st number of N.Y. Globe, 1832; ounder N.Y. Herald, 1835, editor, 1835-67 (paper grew to circulation of 90,000 copies a day, had horough coverage of Europe, employed 63 war corespondents during Civil War, of great polit. importance from 1840's onward, relatively independent n polit. affiliation); refused appointment by Linoln as U.S. minister to France, 1864. Died Bklyn., June 1, 1872; buried Greenwood Cemetery, Bklyn.

BENNETT, Louis, see Deerfoot.

BENNETT, Nathaniel, jurist; b. Clinton, N.Y., June 27, 1818; attended Hamilton Coll. and Yale; never married. Admitted to N.Y. bar, 1840, admitted as counselor, 1843; practiced law, Buffalo, N.Y., 1840-49; made fortune as gold miner, Cal., 1849; practiced law, San Francisco, 1849-86; mem. Cal. Senate, 1849-50; asso. justice 1st Supreme Ct. of Cal., 1850-51; chmn. 1st Cal. State Republican State Conv., Sacramento, 1857. Died San Francisco, Apr. 20, 1886.

BENNETT, Thomas Warren, congressman; b. Union County, Ind., Feb. 16, 1831; grad. law dept. Ind. Asbury (now DePauw) U., 1854. Admitted o bar, 1855; practiced in Liberty, Union County; lected mem. Ind. Senate, 1858, resigned, 1861, 4-67; commd. capt. 15th Regt., Ind. Volunteer Inf., 1861; became maj. 36th Regiment, 1861, ol. 69th Regt., 1862, apptd. brig. gen., 1865; returned to Richmond, Ind.; mayor Richmond, 1869, 0, 77-83, 85-87; gov. Territory of Ida. (apptd. by Pres. Grant), 1871-75; mem. U.S. Congress (Independent, contested election) from Ida. Territory, 1875-June 23, 1876; practiced in Richmond. Died Richmond, Feb. 2, 1893; buried Earlham Cemetery.

BENNETT, William James, artist; b. Eng., 1787. Exhibited in London (Eng.) galleries, 1808-25; came to Am., 1826, settled in N.Y.C.; painted and engraved view of Bowling Green; moved to Nyack, N.Y., 1843; made several sketching trips through U.S., to Boston, Balt., and West Point (N.Y.), 1830, to Buffalo (N.Y.), and Detroit, 1834-35; mem. N.A.D. Died N.Y.C., May 1844.

BENNING, Henry Lewis, lawyer, army officer; b. Columbia County, Ga., Apr. 2, 1814; s. Pleasant Moon and Matilda (White) B.; grad. Franklin Coll. (now U. Ga.), 1834; m. Mary Howard Jones, Sept. 12, 1839, 10 children. Admitted to Ga. bar, 1835, practiced law, Columbus, Ga., 1835-75; mem. Ga. Gen. Assembly; secessionist del. to Nashville Conf. of 1850 which met to consider fed. legislation on expansion of slavery; asso. justice Ga. Supreme Ct., 1853-59; del. Nat. Democratic Conv., Charleston, S.C., 1860; v.p. Nat Dem. Conv., Balt., 1860; del. Ga. Secession Conv., 1861; Ga. commr. to Va. conv. to consider Ordinance of Secession, 1861; served as brig. gen. Confederate Army, participated in battles of Sharpsburg, Antietam, Chickamauga, Gettysburg, The Wilderness. Died Columbus, Ga., July 10, 1875.

BENSEL, James Berry, author; b. N.Y.C., Aug. 2, 1856. Began writing career, circa 1873. Author: King Cophetua's Wife, 1883; In the King's Garden, 1886. Died N.Y.C., Feb. 3, 1886.

BENSON, Carl, see Bristed, Charles Astor.

BENSON, Egbert, congressman, jurist; b. N.Y.C., June 21, 1746; s. Robert and Cathrine (Van Borsum) B.; grad. King's Coll. (now Columbia), 1765; LL.D. (hon.), Union Coll., 1779, Harvard, 1808, Dartmouth, 1811. Admitted to N.Y. bar, 1769; atty. gen. N.Y. State, 1771-87; mem. 1st N.Y. State Legislative Assembly, 1777; N.Y. del. Anapolis Conv., 1786; mem. U.S. Ho. of Reps., 1st-2d congresses, 1789-93; justice N.Y. Supreme Ct.; chief judge 2d U.S. Circuit Ct., 1794-1802; mem. U.S. Ho. of Reps. from N.Y., 13th Congress, 1813-15; regent Univ. State of N.Y., 1787-1802; trustee Columbia, 1804-15; a founder N.Y. Hist. Soc., 1st pres., 1805-15. Author: Vindication of the Captors of Major Andre, 1817. Died Jamaica, N.Y., Aug. 24, 1833.

BENSON, Samuel Page, congressman, lawyer; b. Winthrop, Me., Nov. 28, 1804; attended Monmouth (Me.) Acad.; grad. Bowdoin Coll., 1825; studied law. Admitted to Kennebec County (Me.) bar, 1828; practiced in Unity, Me., returned to Winthrop, practiced until 1850; railroad builder; sec. Androscoggin & Kennebec (now Me. Central) R.R.; mem. Me. Ho. of Reps., 1833, 34; mem. Me. Senate, 1836, 37; sec. state, 1838-41; overseer Bowdoin Coll., 1838-76, pres. of bd. 16 years; chmn. bd. selectmen, 1844-48; mem. U.S. Ho. of Reps. from Me. (as Whig) 33d, (as Republican) 34th congresses, 1853-57. Died Yarmouth, Cumberland County, Me., Aug. 12, 1876; buried Maple Cemetery, Winthrop.

BENT, Charles, fur trader; b. Charles Town, Va. (now W.Va.), Nov. 11, 1799; s. Silas and Martha (Kerr) B.; m. Maria Ignacia Jaramillo, 1835. Began trapping as agt. Am. Fur. Co. in Sioux Indian Country, 1823; trapper (with his 3 bros. and Ceran St. Vrain) in Colo., N.M., 1824-28; founded fur trading co. Bent & St. Vrain, 1828; built Bent's Fort nr. what is now La Junta, Colo., 1828-32; led trading caravans from U.S. to Santa Fe, 1829, 32, 33; civil gov. of N.M. after U.S. conquest, 1846-47. Killed in Mexican and Indian revolt, Taos, N.M., Jan. 19, 1847.

BENT, Josiah, mfr.; b. Milton, Mass., Apr. 26, 1771; s. John and Hannah (Coller) B.; m. Susanna Tucker, Mar. 28, 1794; 8 children. First to manufacture water crackers in U.S., 1801-30, these crackers became almost a necessity in New Eng. homes (known as common crackers); mem. Mass. Legislature, 1832-33. Died Apr. 26, 1836.

BENT, Silas, naval officer; b. St. Louis, Oct. 10, 1820; s. Silas and Martha (Kerr) B.; m. Ann Eliza Tyler, 1857. Apptd. midshipman U.S. Navy, 1836, promoted lt.; flag lt. aboard ship Mississippi in Japan Expdn. led by Commodore Matthew Perry, made extensive hydrographic surveys of seas around Japan, studied Kuro Siwo current (similar to Gulf Stream); assigned to Hydrographic div. of Coast Survey, 1860; resigned because of So. sympathies, 1861. Died Shelter Island, L.I., N.Y., Aug. 26, 1887; buried Louisville, Ky.

BENT, William, fur trader; b. St. Louis, May 23, 1809; s. Silas and Martha (Kerr) B.; m. Owl Woman, 1835; m. 2d, Yellow Woman, 1849; m. 3d, Adalina, 1867; 4 children. Began trapping with his brother and Ceran St. Vrain on Colo. frontier, 1824; mem. Bent & St. Vrain Fur Co., established 1828, gen. dir., co. handled dealings with traders, Indians, became sole owner, 1848; supr. constrn. of Bent's Fort, nr. what is now LaJunta, Colo., 1828-32; destroyed Bent's Fort after death of 1st wife and 3 bros., 1849; built fort on Colorado River, 1849, sold it to U.S. Govt., 1859 (became Fort Lyon); Indian agt. in Colo., 1859; built stockade on Purgatoire River (later Boggsville, Colo., now Las Animas, Colo.); became rancher, 1859. Died Boggsville, May 19, 1869.

BENTLEY, William, clergyman; b. Boston, June 22, 1759; s. Joshua and Elizabeth (Paine) B.; grad. Harvard, 1777; never married. Tutor in Greek and Latin, Harvard, 1780-83; ordained to ministry Congregational Ch., 1783; pastor East Congregational Ch., Salem, Mass., 1783-1819; mem. Mass. Hist. Soc.; a leader of liberal theologians in New Eng.; kept diary published by Essex Inst. as Diary of William Bentley, 1784-1819, 4 vols., 1905-14. Died Salem, Dec. 29, 1819.

BENTON, Charles Swan, congressman, journalist; b. Fryeburg, Oxford County, Me., July 12, 1810; attended Lowville (N.Y.) Acad.; studied law.; learned tanner's trade. Editor Mohawk Courier and Little Falls (N.Y.) Gazette, 1830-32; admitted to bar, 1835; practiced in Little Falls; surrogate Herkimer County, 1837; judge adv. N.Y. State Militia; mem. U.S. Ho. of Reps. (Democrat) from N.Y., 28th-29th congresses, 1843-47; clk. Ct. of Appeals, 1847-49; moved to Milw., 1855, became editor Milw. News; register U.S. Land office (apptd. by Pres. Pierce), La Crosse, Wis., 1856-61; became farmer, West Salem, Wis., at Galesburg, Ill., 1865; returned to La Crosse, 1869; judge La Crosse County, 1874-81. Died La Crosse, May 4, 1882; buried Oak Grove Cemetery.

BENTON, Jacob, congressman, lawyer; b. Waterford, Caledonia County, Vt., Aug. 19, 1814; grad. Burr and Burton Sem., Manchester, 1839; studied law. Tchr. several years; moved to Lancaster, Coos County, N.H., 1842; admitted to bar, 1843; practiced in Lancaster; mem. N.H. Ho. of Reps., 1854-56; del. Nat. Republican Conv. Chgo., 1860; brig. gen., commanded N.H. Volunteers; mem. U.S. Ho. of Reps. (Rep.) from N.H., 40th-41st congresses, 1867-71. Died Lancaster, Sept. 29, 1892; buried Summer Street Cemetery.

BENTON, James Gilchrist, army officer; b. Lebanon, N.H., Sept. 15, 1820; s. Calvin and Mary (Gilchrist) B.; grad. U.S. Mil. Acad., 1842; m. Catherine Webb, Aug. 17, 1859. Brevetted 2d lt. U.S. Ordnance Corps, 1842, commd. 2d lt., 1847, 1st lt., 1848, capt., 1856; instr. ordnance and gunnery U.S. Mil. Acad., 1857-61; prin. asst. to chief of ordnance, 1861-63; commanded Washington Arsenal, 1863-66,; maj., 1863, brevetted lt. col. and col., 1865; commanded Nat. Armory, Springfield, Mass., 1866-81; promoted lt. col., 1874, col., 1875; inventor electro-ballistic chronograph for determining velocity of shells, a velocimeter, a spring dynamometer, a cap-filling machine, made improvements on Springfield rifle. Died Springfield, Aug. 23, 1881.

BENTON, Lemuel, congressman, farmer; b. Granville County, N.C., 1754; Moved to Cheraw Dist. (now Darlington County, S.C.), became planter, large landowner; elected maj. Cheraw Regt., 1777, served throughout Revolutionary War; promoted to col., 1781, resigned commn., 1794; mem. S.C. Ho. of Reps., 1781-84, 87; county court justice Darlington County, 1785, 91; escheator Cheraw Dist. (now Chesterfield, Darlington and Marlboro counties), 1787; del. S.C. Conv. to ratify U.S. Constn., 1788; sheriff Cheraw Dist., 1789, 91; del. S.C. Constl. Conv., Columbia, 1790; mem. U.S. Ho. of Reps. (Democrat) from S.C., 3d-5th congresses, 1793-99. Died Darlington, S.C., May 18, 1818; buried on his estate Stony Hill, nr. Darlington.

BENTON, Thomas Hart, senator; b. Hillsboro, N.C., Mar. 14, 1782; s. Col. Jesse and Ann (Gooch) B.; m. Elizabeth McDowell, 1821, 4 children, including Jessie (Benton) Fremont. Mem. Tenn. Senate, 1809; admitted to Nashville (Tenn.) bar, 1811; editor Mo. Enquirer, 1815; mem. U.S. Senate (Democrat) from Mo., 1821-51, supported sound money, (called "Old Bullion"), Jackson's position in Nat. Bank dispute, strong spokesman for Western expansion; his stand against the Compromise of 1850 (he felt Compromise gave too much to the slave states) led to his senatorial defeat in 1850; unsuccessful candidate for gov., 1856; mem. U.S. Ho. of Reps. from Mo., 33d Congress, 1853-55; Author: Thirty Years View (autobiography), 1854-56. Died Washington, D.C., Apr. 10, 1858.

BENTON, Thomas Hart, educator; b. Williamson County, Tenn., Sept. 5, 1816; s. Samuel Benton; attended Marion (Mo.) Coll.; m. Susan Culbertson, 1851. Conducted 1st classical sch. in Ia., 1838-39; mem. 1st Ia. Senate, 1846-48, chmn. com. on schs.; supt. pub. instrn. State of Ia., 1848-54; exec. sec. Ia. Bd. Edn., 1858-62; commd. col. 29th Ia. Inf., U.S. Volunteers, 1862, brevetted brig. gen., 1865; collector U.S. revenue for 6th Dist. of Ia., 1866-69. Died St. Louis, Apr. 10, 1879; buried Marshalltown, Ia.

BERESFORD, Richard, Continental congressman; b. nr. Charleston, S.C., 1755; ed. S.C. and Eng.; studied law, Middle Temple, London, Eng. Admitted to bar, 1773; practiced in Charleston; became planter, had extensive estates in Berkeley and Colleton counties, S.C., also in Eng.; took active part in Revolutionary War; served under Gen. Huger in Ga. campaign, 1778; captured at fall of Charleston, 1780, prisoner at St. Augustine until 1781, exchanged; mem. S.C. Ho. of Reps., 1781; elected mem. privy council by S.C. Gen. Assembly, 1782; elected lt. gov. S.C., 1783, resigned short time later; mem. Continental Congress from S.C., 1783-84. Author: Vigil, 1798. Died Charleston, Feb. 6, 1803.

BERG, Joseph Frederic, clergyman; b. Antigua, B.W.I., June 3, 1812; s. Christian Frederic and Hannah (Tempest) B.; M.D., Jefferson Med. Coll., Phila.; m. Eleonora Pomp, Feb. 4, 1835, at least 1 child. Licensed to preach in German Reformed Ch., 1831, ordained, 1835; pastor, Harrisburg, Pa., 1835-37, Race Street Ch., Phila., 1837-52; withdrew from German Reformed Ch. because he thought it was drifting towards Romanism, 1852; pastor 2d Dutch Reformed Ch., Phila., 1852-61; prof. didactic and polemic theology Theol. Sem., New Brunswick, N.J., 1861-71; prof. evidences of Christianity, Rutgers Coll., 1862-67. Author: Lectures on Romanism, 1840; Papal Rome, 1841; The Inquisition; Church and State; or, Rome's Influence upon the Civil and Religious Institutions of our Country, 1851. Died July 20, 1871.

BERGEN, John Teunis, congressman; b. Gowanus, Bklyn., 1786; completed prep. studies. Apptd. lt. N.Y. State Militia, 1812, promoted capt., 1815; served in War of 1812; sheriff Kings County (N.Y.), 1821-25, 28-31; purchased L.I. (N.Y.) Patriot, 1829, became Bklyn. Advocate, later Bklyn. Daily Eagle; mem. U.S. Ho. of Reps. (Democrat) from N.Y., 22d Congress, 1831-33; became farmer, nr. Bay Ridge, New Utrecht, N.Y.; moved to Bklyn., in grocery business; conducted planing mill with his sons, N.Y.C., 1837; moved to Genesee County, N.Y., became farmer. Died Batavia, Genesee County, Mar. 9, 1855; buried Batavia Cemetery.

BERGEN, Teunis Garret, congressman; b. Bklyn., Oct. 6, 1806; attended Erasmus Hall Acad., Flatbush, N.Y. Farmer, surveyor; supr. New Utrecht, Kings County, N.Y., 1836-59; mem. N.Y. State Constl. Convs., 1846, 67, 68; del. Nat. Democratic convs., Balt., Charleston, 1860; mem. U.S. Ho. of Reps. (Dem.) from N.Y., 39th Congress, 1865-67; farmer, surveyor, nr. New Utrecht, also in literary and historical activities; served as ensign, capt., adjutant, lt. col., col. 241st Regt. (known as Kings County Troop) N.Y. State Militia. Died Bklyn., Apr. 24, 1881; buried Greenwood Cemetery.

BERGH, Christian, shipbuilder; b. Duchess County, N.Y., Apr. 30, 1763; s. Christian II and Catrina (Van Benschoten) B.; m. Elizabeth Ivers, 2 children, including Henry. Built U.S. frigate President; built war vessels for U.S. on Lake Ontario, 1812-15; his ships were unsurpassed in design and constrn. until 1837. Died June 24, 1843.

BERGH, Henry, social reformer; b. N.Y.C., Aug. 29, 1811; s. Christian and Elizabeth (Ivers) B.; attended Columbia; m. Catherine Taylor, 1836 sec. of U.S. legation, St. Petersburg, Russia, 1863-64; founder, Am. Soc. for Prevention of Cruelty to Animals, 1866, 1st pres., 1866-88; a founder Soc. for Prevention of Cruelty to Children, 1875. Author: Streets of New York; (drama) Love's Alternative. Died N.Y.C., Mar. 12, 1888.

BERGMANN, Carl, orch. conductor; b. Ebersbach, Saxony, Apr. 11, 1821. Came to Am., 1849; condr. Germania Orch., N.Y.C., 1849-52; condr. Handel and Haydn Soc., Boston, 1853-54, Männergesangverein Arion,, N.Y.C., 1854-58; condr. N.Y. Philharmonic Soc., 1858-59, 65-76, alternate condr., 1859-65; conducted 1st Am. performance of Beethoven's Fidelio, 1856, Wagner's Tannhäuser, 1859; condr. N.Y. Harmonic Soc., Mendelssohn Union. Died Aug. 10, 1876.

BERING, Vitus Jonassen, navigator, explorer; b. Horsens, Denmark, 1680. Joined Russian Navy, 1703, served in Russian-Swedish war, 1721; interested in plan of Peter the Great to explore North coast of Asia, travelled to Kamchatka (Siberia); sent by Russian govt. overland to Okhotsk, 1725, crossed by ship to Kamchatka where he built ship Gabriel, sailed North until no more land could be seen either North or East, 1728, returned to St. Petersburg, having failed to find new lands, 1730; commd. again by Russia; established settlement Petropavlosk in Kamchatka; built 2 ships St. Peter and St. Paul by 1740, sailed towards America, 1741, storm separated ships but his ship sighted Southern coast of Alaska and landed at Kayak Island; forced to quick return, discovered some of Aleutian Islands on way back; taken ill with scurvy, relinquished command of ships at island (now Bering Island) in S.W. Bering Sea (also named for him). Died (with many of his crew) Bering Island, Dec. 19, 1741.

BERKELEY, John, ironmaster; b. Eng.; m. Mary Snell, 10 children including Maurice. Came to Am. to establish ironworks for Va. Council, 1621; 1st ironmaster in Am.; set up machinery on Fall Creek, nr. what is now Richmond, Va.; 1st in Am. to smelt iron; Indians destroyed his machinery, 1622, ironmaking not reestablished in Am. until 1710. Killed by Indians led by Opechancanough, Mar. 22, 1622.

BERKELEY, Norborne (1st baron Botetourt), colonial gov.; b. Eng., 1718; s. John Berkeley. Col., North Gloucestershire Militia, 1761; member Parliament, 1764; created peer, 1764; gov. Va., 1768-70, dissolved Ho. of Burgesses for passing resolutions condemning parliamentary taxation, 1769, colonists established embargo against all goods taxed by Parliament; tried unsuccessfully to restore friendly relations between Eng. and colonists; statue in his honor at Coll. of William and Mary until Civil War, now located at Williamsburg (Va.) Insane Asylum; Botetourt County (Va.) named for him. Died Williamsburg, Va., Oct. 15, 1770.

BERKELEY, Sir William, colonial gov. Va.; b. Bruton Eng., 1608; s. Maurice Berkeley; attended Queen's Coll., Oxford (Eng.) U., 1623; B.A., St. Edmund Hall, 1624; M.A., Merton Coll., 1629. Knighted by King Charles I at Berwick, 1639; apptd. commr. Canadian affairs (his 1st colonial office); colonial gov. Va., 1642-52, 60-77; his policies caused Bacon's Rebellion, 1676. Died Twichenham, Eng., July 13, 1677.

BERKENMEYER, Wilhelm Christoph, clergyman; b. Bodenteich, Lüneburg (now Holland), 1686; m. Benigna Sibylla von Kocherthal, Oct. 25, 1727. Ordained to ministry Lutheran Ch., 1725; came to Am., 1725, only ordained Luth. pastor in N.Y.C., until 1743; consecrated Trinity Ch., N.Y.C., 1731; preached in Dutch, German and English; travelled in N.J. and N.Y., 1725-31, upper N.Y., 1731-51. Died 1751; buried Athens, N.Y.

BERMUDEZ, Edouard Edmund, jurist; b. New Orleans, La., Jan. 19, 1832; s. Joachim and Emma (Troxler) B.; B.A., Spring Hill Coll., Mobile, Ala., 1851; law degree U. La. (now Tulane U.), 1852; studied law under Thomas B. Monroe; m. Amanda Elizabeth Maupassant, Jan. 1853. Admitted to La. bar, 1852, practiced law, New Orleans, 1852-61, 67-80; del. La. Conv. of 1860, opposed secession; lt. 1st La. Brigade, Confederate Army, 1861, served as judge advocate, adjutant, provost-marshal-gen., commandant at Mobile; asst. city atty. of New Orleans, 1865-67; asso. justice La. Supreme Ct., 1880-92. Died New Orleans, Aug. 22, 1892.

BERNARD, Sir Francis, colonial gov.; b. Nettleham, Eng., July 1712; s. Rev. Francis and Margery (Winlowe) B.; scholar St. Peter's Coll., Westminster, 1725; grad. Oxford (Eng.) U., 1736, D.C.L. (hon.), 1772; m. Amelia Offley, 1741, 8 children. Admitted to Middle Temple, 1733, called to bar, 1737; provincial counsel, Lincoln, Eng., 1737-58; gov. N.J. 1758-60, Mass., 1760-69, removed from office because of poor adminstrv. abilities and harsh policies, returned to Eng.; created baronet, Sir Francis Bernard of Nettlebaum, 1769. Died Aylesbury, Eng., June 16, 1779.

BERNARD, John, actor; b. Portsmouth, Eng., 1756; s. John and Ann Bernard; m. Miss Cooper, 1775; m. 2d, Miss Fisher; m. 3d, Miss Wright. Toured Eng. as comedian and actor, 1774-97; came to Am., 1797; made Am. debut as Goldfinch in The Road to Ruin, N.Y.C., 1797; appeared in Phila., 1797-1803, Boston, 1803-11, 16-19; mgr. Federal St. Theater, Boston, 1806-11; mgr. 1st theatre in Albany, N.Y., 1813-16; returned to Eng., 1819. Died Nov. 29, 1828.

BERNARD, Simon, mil. engr.; b. Dole, France, Apr. 22, 1779; grad. Ecole Polytechnique; m. Marie de Lerchenfeld, Mar. 10, 1809. Commd. of engrs. French Army, 1797; charge of design and constrn. fortifications at Antwerp, served in Army of Rhine; commd. capt., 1800, col., aide-de-camp to Napoleon, 1813; marechal de camp (brig. gen.) Army of Restoration, 1814; came to U.S. after Napoleonic Wars; brig. gen. U.S. Army on bd. for planning Atlantic coast defenses, 1814-31; greatest achievement was planning of Ft. Monroe in Va.; returned to French Army as lt. gen., 1831; aide-de-camp to King Louis Philippe; insp. gen. of engrs.; French minister of war, 1834, 36-39; created baron, 1839. Died Paris, France, Nov. 5, 1839.

BERNARD, William Bayle, dramatist; b. Boston, Nov. 27, 1807; s. John and Mrs. (Wright) B. Settled in Eng., 1819; became clk. Army Accounts Office, London, Eng., also began writing plays; wrote one of earliest dramatic prodns. of Rip Van Winkle, 1832, presented at Park Theatre, N.Y.C., 1833; wrote many comedies including The Kentuckian, His Last Legs (1839); popularizer of the eccentric rural American on the stage; compiled (from his father's papers) Early Days of the American Theatre, serialized in Tallis's Dramatic Mag., 1850-51. Author: Retrospections of the Stage, by the late John Bernard, Manager of the American Theatre and formerly Secretary of the Beefsteak Club, 1830. Died Aug. 5, 1875.

BERNHISEL, John Milton, congressman, physician; b. Sandy Hill, Tyrone Twp., nr. Harrisburg, Pa., July 23, 1799; attended common schs.; grad. med. dept. U. Pa. Practiced medicine, N.Y.C.; moved to Nauvoo, Hancock County, Ill., 1843; moved to Territory of Utah, settled in Salt Lake City, 1848, practiced medicine; mem. U.S. Congress (Whig) from Utah Territory, 32d-35th, 37th congresses, 1851-59, 61-63; regent U. Utah. Died Salt Lake City, Sept. 28, 1881; buried Salt Lake City Cemetery.

BEROUJON, Claude, architect. Practiced architecture in Mobile, Alabama; credited with designing and/or bldg. Cathedral of Immaculate Conception, Mobile (erected between 1830-50), also main bldg. Spring Hill Coll. (in assn. with James Freret). Flourished mid-19th Century.

BERRIEN, John Macpherson, senator, atty. gen.; b. N.J., Aug. 23, 1781; s. John and Margaret (MacPherson) B.; grad. Princeton, 1796. Admitted to Ga. bar, 1799; judge Eastern Circuit Ct., Ga., 1810-21; mem. Ga. Senate, 1822-23; mem. U.S Senate from Ga. as Democrat, 1824-29, as Whig 1841-45, 45-52; atty. gen. U.S. in Pres. Jackson's cabinet, 1829-31; considered ablest constl. lawyer of his time in U.S. Died Savannah, Ga., Jan. 1, 1856; buried Laurel Grove Cemetery, Savannah.

BERRY, Hiram Gregory, army officer; b. Rockland, Me., Aug. 27, 1824; s. Jeremiah and Frances (Gregory) B.; m. Almira Merriman, Mar. 23, 1845. Mem. Me. Legislature, 1852; mayor Rockland, 1856; commd. col. 4th Me. Regt. during Civil War; commd. brig. gen. then maj. gen. U.S. Volunteers, 1862; distinguished at battles of Williamsburg and Fair Oaks; gen. of div. 3d Corps. Killed at Battle of Chancellorsville (Va.), May 3, 1863.

BERRY, John, congressman, lawyer; b. n Carey, Crawford (now Wyandot) County, O Apr. 26, 1833; attended Ohio Wesleyan U.; gra law dept. Cincinnati Coll., 1857. Admitted to ba 1857; practiced in Upper Sandusky, O.; electe pros. atty. Wyandot County, 1862, 64; may Upper Sandusky, 1864; mem. U.S. Ho. of Reps (Democrat) from Ohio, 43d Congress, 1873-7 Died Upper Sandusky, May 18, 1879; burie Oak Hill Cemetery, nr. Upper Sandusky.

BERRY, Nathaniel Springer, gov. N.H.: b. Bat Me., Sept. 1, 1796; s. Abner and Betsey (Springer B.; m. Ruth Smith, Jan. 26, 1821; m. 2d, Mrs Louise Farley, Jan. 1860; 2 children. Mem. N.H Legislature from Bristol, 1828, 33, 34, 37, fro Hebron, 1854; mem. N.H. Senate from 11th dist 1835-36; probate judge Grafton County, N.H. del. Nat. Democratic Conv., Balt., 1840; ass justice N.H. Ct. Common Pleas, 1841-56; go N.H. (Republican), 1861-63. Died Bristol, Ap 27, 1894.

BERTRAM, John, sea capt., mcht.; b. Jerse Island, Feb. 11, 1796; s. John and Mary (Perchard B.; m. Mary G. Smith, 1823; m. 2d, Mrs. Clariss Millett, 1838; m. 3d, Mary Ann Ropes, 1848. Move with family to Am., 1807; cabin boy in merchant man Hazard, 1812, later served in privateers Mon key and Herald; held prisoner (after Herald wa captured by English) until end of War of 1812 became mate, 1821, held 1st command in shi General Brewer; entered mcht. business b gathering hides from Patagonia coast; mad last voyage as capt. aboard Black Warrior, 1830 32; began full-scale mcht. business, 1832; sent 1s ship from U.S. to Cal. during gold rush; founde Bertram Home for Aged Men, Salem Fuel Fund Died Mar. 22, 1882.

BETHUNE, George Washington, clergyman; b N.Y.C., Mar. 18, 1805; s. Divie and Joanna (gra ham) B.; grad. Dickinson Coll., 1823; studie theology Princeton, 1823-25; m. Mary Williams Nov. 4, 1825; Ordained by 2d Presbytery of N.Y. 1827, entered Dutch Reformed Ch.; pastor Rhine beck, N.Y., 1827-30, Utica, N.Y., 1830-34, 1st 3d churches, Phila., 1834-49, Brooklyn Heights N.Y., 1850-59, 21st Street Ch., N.Y.C., 1859-62 prominent mem. Am. Colonization Soc.; Democrat Author: Lays of Love and Faith (volume of poetry) 1848. Editor: The British Female Poets with Bio graphical and Critical Notices, 1848; 1st Am. edit Complete Angler (Walton); also author well-know hymns. Died Florence, Italy, Apr. 28, 1862.

BETHUNE, Lauchlin, congressman, farmer; b. nr. Fayetteville, Cumberland County, N.C., Apr 15, 1785; attended pvt. schs., Lumberton (N.C.) Male Acad. Became farmer, nr. Fayetteville; mem. N.C. Senate, 1817, 18, 22-25, 27; mem. U.S. Ho. of Reps. (Jacksonian Democrat) from N.C., 22 Congress, 1831-33. Died on his plantation, nr. Fayetteville, Oct. 10, 1874; buried Presbyn. Cemetery, Aberdeen, Moore County, N.C.

BETHUNE, Marion, congressman, lawyer; b. nr. Greensboro, Greene County, Ga., Apr. 8, 1816; attended pvt. schs., De Hagan's Acad.; studied law. Became mcht., Talbotton, Talbot County, Ga.; admitted to bar, 1842; practiced at Talbotton; probate judge Talbot County, 1852-68; mem. Ga. Constl. Conv. at time of repeal of ordinance of secession; mem. Ga. Ho. of Reps., 1867-71; mem. U.S. Ho. of Reps. (Republican, filled vacancy) from Ga., 41st Congress, Dec. 22, 1870-71; U.S. census supr., 1890. Died Talbotton, Feb. 20, 1895; buried Oakhill Cemetery.

BETTON, Silas, congressman, lawyer; b. Londonderry, N.H., Aug. 26, 1768; grad. Dartmouth, 1787; studied law. Admitted to bar, 1790; practiced in Salem, Rockingham County, N.H., 1790; mem. N.H. Ho. of Reps., 1797-99, 1810, 11; mem. N.H. Senate, 1801-03; mem. U.S. Ho. of Reps. from N.H., 8th-9th congresses, 1803-07; high sheriff Rockingham County, 1813-18. Died Salem, Jan. 22, 1822; buried Old Parish Cemetery, Center Village, Salem.

BETTS, Samuel Rossiter, congressman, jurist; b. Richmond, Mass., June 8, 1787; s. Uriah and Sarah (Rossiter) B.; grad. Williams Coll., 1806; m. Caroline Dewey, Nov. 4, 1816. Admitted to bar, 1809; judge adv. U.S. Volunteers during War of 1812; mem. U.S. Ho. of Reps. from N.Y., 14th Congress, 1815-17; circuit judge N.Y. Supreme Ct., 1823; judge U.S. Dist. Ct. for So. N.Y. (apptd. by John Quincy Adams), 1826-27; mem. council N.Y. U., 1830-35; noted for restatement of maritime law. Died New Haven, Conn., Nov. 3, 1868; buried Woodlawn Cemetery, N.Y.C.

BETTS, Thaddeus, senator; b. Norwalk, Conn., Feb. 4, 1789; grad. Yale, 1807; studied law. Admitted to bar, 1810; practiced in Norwalk; mem. Conn. Ho. of Reps., 1815, 30; mem. Conn. Senate, 1831; elected lt. gov. Conn., 1832, 36; mem. U.S. Senate (Whig) from Conn., 1839-Apr. 7, 1840. Died Washington, D.C., Apr. 7, 1840; buried Union Cemetery, Norwalk.

BEVERLY, Robert, historian; b. Middlesex County, Va., circa 1673; s. Robert and Miss (Keeble) B.; m. Ursula Byrd, 1681; at least 1 child, William. Clk., Va. Gen. Ct., also Va. Gen. Assembly, 1696; mem. Va. Ho. of Burgesses, 1699, 1700-02, 05-06; planter, King and Queen County, Va., 1705-22. Author: History and Present State of Virginia (described Va. society of period), 1705; The Abridgement of the Public Laws of Virginia, 1722. Died "Beverly Park," King and Queen County, Va., 1722.

BEWLEY, Anthony, clergyman; b. Tenn., May 22, 1804; married. Methodist preacher in Tenn. Conf., 1829-37; moved to Mo., 1837; mem. Mo. Meth. Conf., from 1843; refused adherence to So. Meth. Episcopal Ch., 1845; joined Mo. Conf. of No. Meth. Episcopal Ch., assigned to Washington Mission, Ark., 1848-58; missionary, Johnson County, Tex., 1858-60; fled Tex. after publication of letter allegedly implicating him in abolitionist activities, 1860. Captured by mob and murdered, Fort Worth, Tex., Sept. 13, 1860.

BIARD, Pierre, missionary; b. Grenoble, France, circa 1567. Mem. Soc. of Jesus; came to Am. as head of Jesuit mission at Acadia, 1611; converted Indians, ministered to their physical needs from base at Port Royal, 1611-13; founder settlement of St. Saussaye (now Bar Harbor, Me.), 1613, captured when post was attacked by British, 1613, later returned to France; prof. theology, Lyons, France, 1616-22. Died Avignon, France, Nov. 17, 1622; buried Avignon.

BIBB, George Motier, senator, jurist; b. Prince Edward County, Va., Oct. 30, 1772; s. Richard and Lucy (Booker) B.; grad. Hampden-Sydney Coll., 1792; Coll. William and Mary, 1792; married twice, 17 children. Apptd. to bench Ky. Ct. Appeals, 1808, 27-28, chief justice, 1809-10, mem. Ky. Ho. of Reps., 1810-17; mem. U.S. Senate from Ky., Mar. 4, 1811-Aug. 23, 1814, 1829-35, chancellor Louisville Ct. Chancery, 1835-44; U.S. sec. of treasury, 1844-45. Died Georgetown, D.C., Apr. 14, 1859; buried State Cemetery, Frankfort, Ky.

BIBB, William Wyatt, senator, gov. Ala.; b. Amelia County, Va., Oct. 2, 1781; s. William and Sally (Wyatt) B.; grad. in medicine U. Pa., 1801; m. Mary Freeman, 1803, 2 children. Mem. Ga. Ho. of Reps., Ga. Senate; mem. U.S. Ho. of Rps. from Ga., 9th-13th congresses, Jan. 26, 1805- Nov. 6, 1813; mem. U.S. Senate from Ga., Dec.6, 1813-Nov. 9, 1816; gov. Territory of Ala. (apptd. by Pres. Monroe), 1817-19; 1st gov. state of Ala. 1819-20. Died Autauga County, Ala., July 10, 1820; buried family cemetery, Coosada Station, Ala.

BIBIGHAUS, Thomas Marshal, congressman, lawyer; b. Phila., Mar. 17, 1817; attended common schs.; studied law. Admitted to bar, 1839; practiced in Lebanon, Pa.; mem. U.S. Ho. of Reps. (Whig) from Pa., 32d Congress, 1851-53. Died Lebanon, June 18, 1853; buried Mt. Lebanon Cemetery.

BICKERDYKE, Mary Ann Ball, nurse; b. Knox County, O., July 19, 1817; d. Hiram and Anna (Rodgers) Ball; attended Oberlin Coll., 1833-37; studied nursing, Cincinnati; m. Robert Bickerdyke, Apr. 27, 1847 (died 1858). Lived in Galesburg (Ill.) at start of Civil War; began nursing in hosps., Cairo, Ill.; nurse in 19 battles during Civil War, also acted as agt. U.S. San. Comm.; spl. attaché Gen. Sherman's Corps, 1863-65, began establishment of army laundries; pension atty. after Civil War; housekeeper Chgo. Home for the Friendless; ran hotel, Salina, Kan., then did missionary work in N.Y.; monument erected to her, Galesburg, 1903. Died Bunker Hill, Kan., Nov. 8, 1901; buried Galesburg.

BICKNELL, Bennet, congressman; b. Mansfield, Conn., Nov. 14, 1781; attended public schools. Moved to Morrisville, Madison County, N.Y., 1808; served in War of 1812; mem. N.Y. State Assembly, 1812; mem. N.Y. State Senate, 1814-18; clk. Madison County, N.Y., 1821-25; editor Madison Observer; mem. U.S. Ho. of Reps. (Democrat) from N.Y., 25th Congress, 1837-39. Died Morrisville, Sept. 15, 1841; buried Morrisville Rural Cemetery.

BICKNELL, George Augustus, congressman, jurist; b. Phila., Feb. 6, 1815; grad. U. Pa., 1831; attended Yale Law Sch., 1 year; completed law studies. Admitted to bar, 1836; practiced in N.Y.C.; moved to Lexington, Scott County, Ind., 1846; elected pros. atty. Scott County, 1848; circuit prosecutor, 1850; moved to New Albany, Floyd County, Ind., 1851; judge 2d Jud. Circuit of Ind., 1852-76; prof. law U. Ind., 1861-70; mem. U.S. Ho. of Reps. (Democrat) from Ind., 45th-46th congresses, 1877-81; apptd. commr. of appeals Ind. Supreme Ct., 1881-85; elected judge Circuit Ct. of Ind., 1889-91. Died New Albany, Apr. 11, 1891; buried Fairview Cemetery.

BIDDLE, Charles John, congressman, lawyer; b. Phila., Apr. 30, 1819; grad. Princeton, 1837; studied law. Admitted to bar, 1840; practiced in Phila., 1840; served in Mexican War, brevetted maj.; entered Union Army as col. regt. of Pa. Reserve Corps, 1861; mem. U.S. Ho. of Reps. (Democrat, filled vacancy) from Pa., 37th Congress, July 2, 1861-63; chmn. Pa. Dem. Central Com., 1863; a propr., editor-in-chief Phila. Age until 1873. Died Phila., Sept. 28, 1873; buried Old St. Peter's Ch. Cemetery.

BIDDLE, Clement, army officer, mcht.; b. Phila., May 10, 1740; s. John and Sarah (Owen) B.; m. Mary Richardson; m. 2d, Rebekah Cornell; 13 children, including Clement Cornell. Signed Phila. Non-Importation Agreement, 1765; partner father's shipping house, 1771; apptd. q.m. gen. with rank of col. for militias of Pa. and N.J., by 2d Continental Congress, 1776; participated in battles of Trenton, Princeton, Brandywine and Portsmouth; aide-de-camp to Gen. Greene, 1776; commissary gen. of forage, 1777; q.m. gen. (col.) Pa. Militia, 1781; justice Pa. Ct. Common Pleas, 1788; apptd. U.S. marshall Pa. by Pres. Washington, 1789; Gen. Washington's factor (purchasing agt., seller produce of Mt. Vernon), 1780's-1790's. Died Phila., July 14, 1814.

BIDDLE, Edward, Continental congressman; b. Phila., 1738; studied law. Entered provincial army as ensign, 1754, promoted lt., capt., served until 1763, resigned; admitted to bar; practiced in Reading, Pa.; mem. Pa. Assembly, 1767-75, 78, speaker, 1774; mem. Provincial Conv., Phila., 1775; mem. Continental Congress, 1774-76, 78, 79. Died at Chatsworth, nr. Balt., Sept. 5, 1779; buried St. Paul's Churchyard, Balt.

BIDDLE, James, naval officer; b. Phila., Feb. 18, 1783; s. Charles and Hannah (Shepard) B.; attended U. Pa., circa 1798-1800. Apptd. midshipman U.S. Navy, 1800, served in Tripolitan War, 1802-03; promoted to lt., 1803, master-commandant, 1813, capt., 1814, commodore, 1822; commanded sloop-of-war Syren, 1810; 1st lt. on Wasp which captured Brit. brig Frolic, 1812; commanded Hornet, 1813-15, captured Brit. Penguin; sailed to Columbia River to take possession of Ore. Territory, 1817; commodore of West India station, 1822; on duty in S.Am. and Mediterranean seas, 1826-32; pres. Naval Asylum, Phila., 1838-42; commodore East Indian Squadron, signed 1st treaty between China and U.S., 1846; commanded Pacific Coast Squadron during Mexican War. Died Phila., Oct. 1, 1848; buried Phila.

BIDDLE, John, congressman; b. Phila., Mar. 2, 1792; attended Princeton. Enlisted in War of 1812; apptd. 2d lt. 3d Arty., 1812, 1st lt., 1813, capt. 42d Inf., 1813; asst. insp. gen. with rank of maj., 1817-21; with Gen. Scott's staff on Niagara frontier; paymaster, Indian agt., Green Bay, Wis., 1821, 22; register land office, Detroit, Mich. Territory, 1823-37; commr. for determining ancient land claims at Detroit, Mackinaw, Sault Ste. Marie, Green Bay, Prairie du Chien; mayor Detroit, 1827, 28; mem. U.S. Congress (Whig) from Mich. Territory, 21st Congress, 1829-Feb. 21, 1831 (resigned); pres. Mich. Constl. Conv., 1835; pres. Mich. Central R.R. Co., 1835; unsuccessful candidate for gov. Mich.; mem. Mich. Ho. of Reps., 1841, speaker; lived on his farm, nr. Wyandotte, Mich.; spent much time on his estate, nr. St. Louis, Gratiot County, Mich. Died White Sulphur Springs, Va., Aug. 25, 1859; buried Elmwood Cemetery, Detroit.

BIDDLE, Nicholas, naval officer; b. Phila., Sept. 10, 1750; s. William and Mary (Scull) B. Given command of privateer Franklin with rank of lt. by Continental Congress, 1775; commd. capt., given command of Andrea Doria, 1775; captured numerous ships in N. Atlantic, 1775-76; comdr. ship Randolph, assigned to West Indies, 1776, captured ships including British vessel Triton, 1777. Killed in explosion of Randolph during engagement with Brit. ship Yarmouth nr. Charleston, S.C., Mar. 7, 1778.

BIDDLE, Nicholas, banker; b. Phila., Jan 8, 1786; s. Charles and Hannah (Shepard) B.; grad. (valedictorian) Coll. of N.J. (now Princeton), 1801; m. Jane Craig, Oct. 4, 1811. Sec. to Gen. John Armstrong (minister to France), 1804; sec. legation, London, Eng., 1806; an editor literary mag. Portfolio, 1806-12; admitted to Pa. bar, 1809; mem. Pa. Ho. of Reps., 1810-11, Pa. Senate, 1814-18; dir. 2d Bank of U.S., 1819; pres. Bank of U.S., 1823-36; leading advocate of rechartering of the bank (became major issue of 1832 presdl. election); became president U.S. Bank of Pa. (successor to Bank of U.S. after President Jackson's veto of rechartering), 1836-39; pres. bd. trustees Girard Coll., also U. Pa.; pres. agrl. and hort. socs. Author: History of the Expedition of Captains Lewis and Clark, 1814. Died Phila., Feb. 27, 1844.

BIDDLE, Richard, congressman, lawyer; b. Phila., Mar. 25, 1796; grad. U. Pa., 1811; studied law. Volunteer in Washington Guards in War of 1812; admitted to Phila. bar, 1817; practiced in Pitts., 1817; went to Eng., 1827, stayed for 3 years; published works on Am. discovery and travel; mem. U.S. Ho. of Reps. (Whig) from Pa., 25th-26th congresses, 1837-40 (resigned). Died Pitts., July 6, 1847; buried Allegheny Cemetery.

BIDLACK, Benjamin Alden, diplomat; b. Paris, N.Y., Sept. 8, 1804; s. Benjamin and Lydia (Alden) B.; m. Fanny Stewart, circa 1827; m. 2d, Margaret Wallace, Sept. 8, 1829. Admitted to bar, practiced law in Luzerne County, Pa., circa 1830; co-owner newspaper Republican Farmer, Luzerne County, 1833; editor newspaper No. Eagle, 1st in Pike County, Pa., 1834-41; mem. Pa. Assembly, 1835-36; mem. U.S. Ho. of Reps. (Democrat) from Pa., 32d-33d Congresses, 1841-45; U.S. chargé d'affaires in New Granada, S.Am., 1845-49, responsible for negotiation of treaty with New Granada providing for abolition of differential duties and right of U.S. to cross Isthmus of Panama, 1846. Died Bogota, Colombia, S.Am., Feb. 6, 1849.

BIDWELL, Barnabas, congressman; b. Tyringham, Mass., Aug. 23, 1763; s. Adonijah and Jemimah B.; grad. Yale, 1785 M.A. (hon.); M.A. (hon.), Williams Coll.; LL.D. (hon.), Brown U.; m. Mary Gray, 1793. Treas., Berkshire County, 1791; mem. U.S. Ho. of Reps. from Mass., 9th-10th congresses, 1805-July 13, 1807; apptd. atty. gen. Mass., 1807. Author: The Mercenary Match. Died Kingston, Ont., Can., July 27, 1833; buried Kingston Cemetery.

BIDWELL, John, congressman; b. Chautauqua County, N.Y., Aug. 5, 1819; s. Abram and Clarissa (Griggs) B.; m. Annie Kennedy, 1868. Prin., Kingsville Acad., Ashtabula, O., 1836-38; lived for a time in Mo., went to Cal. as part of 1st immigrant train from Mo., 1841; worked at Ft. Sutter, Cal., 1841-45; naturalized by Mexico as citizen of Cal., 1844; mem. com. which drew up proclamation of independence from Mexico, 1846; 2d lt. Cal. Battalion in revolt against Mexico, 1846; discovered gold during Cal. Gold Rush, 1849, bought 22,000 acres of land north of Sacramento; mem. Cal. Senate, 1849; mem. Cal. Democratic convs., 1854, 60; brig. gen. Cal. Militia, 1863; mem. Union Party Conv., Balt., 1864; mem. U.S. Ho. of Reps. (Unionist) from Cal., 39th Congress, 1865-67; presdl. candidate Prohibition Party, 1892. Died Chico, Cal., Apr. 4, 1900; buried Chico Cemetery.

BIDWELL, Marshall Spring, lawyer, politician; b. Stockbridge, Mass., Feb. 16, 1799; s. Richard and Mary (Gray) B.; m. Clara Willcox, 1820. Admitted to bar, 1820, began practice of law, Kingston, Upper Canada; an adherent of Reform Party in Canadian politics; mem. Legislature of Upper Can., 1825-36, speaker, 1829, 35; involved in polit. turmoil, threatened with treason charges, came to N.Y.C., 1837; practiced law, N.Y.C., specializing in law of trusts and wills, 1837-72; gained renown for defense in case of James Fenimore Cooper vs. W.L. Stone (editor N.Y. Comml. Advertiser). Died N.Y.C., Oct. 24, 1872; buried N.Y.C.

BIDWELL, Walter Hilliard, publisher, editor; b. Farmington, Conn., June 21, 1798; s. William and Mary (Pelton) B.; grad. Yale, 1827; grad. Yale Divinity Sch., 1833; m. Susan Duryea, circa 1828. Ordained to ministry Congregational Ch., 1833, pastor Congregational Ch., Medfield, Mass., 1833-37; went to Phila., 1838; editor Nat. Preacher and Village Pulpit (monthly mag.), 1841-60; owner editor N.Y. Evangelist, 1843-55, Bibl. Repository and Classical Review, 1846-49; editor Eclectic Mag., 1846-68; publisher, 1868-81; publisher Am. Theol. Review, 1860-62; served as spl. U.S. commr. to Egypt, Greece and the Levant, 1867. Died Saratoga Springs, N.Y., Sept. 11, 1881.

BIENVILLE, sieur de, see Le Moyne, Jean Baptiste.

BIGELOW, Abijah, congressman, lawyer; b. Westminster, Mass., Dec. 5, 1775; attended Leicester (Mass.) Acad., also acad., New Ipswich, N.H.; grad. Dartmouth, 1795; studied law, Groton, Mass. Admitted to bar, 1798; practiced in Leominster, Mass., 1798; town clk. Leominster, 1803-09; mem. Mass. Ho. of Reps., 1807-09; justice of peace, 1809-60; justice of quorum, 1812-60; mem. U.S. Ho. of Reps. (Federalist, filled vacancy) from Mass., 11th-13th congresses, Oct. 8, 1810-15; moved to Worcester, Mass., 1817; clk. courts of Worcester County, 1817-33; practiced in Worcester; trustee Leicester Acad., 1819, 20, treas., 1820-53; apptd. master in chancery, 1838. Died Worcester, Apr. 5, 1860; buried Rural Cemetery.

BIGELOW Erastus Brigham, inventor, economist; b. West Boylston, Mass., Apr. 2, 1814; s. Ephraim and Mary (Brigham) B.; m. Susan King; m. 2d, Eliza Means; 1 child. Inventor power loom for prodn. of coach lace, 1837, power loom for prodn. Brussels, Wilton tapestry and velvet carpetings, 1839; chartered Clinton Co., nr. Lancaster, Mass., to build and operate looms, 1841, built plants, Lowell, Mass., and Derby, Conn.;mem. com. founding Mass. Inst. Tech., 1861; an organizer Nat. Assn. Wool Mfrs. Author: The Tariff Question Considered in Regard to the Policy of England and the Interests of the United States, 1862; The Tariff Policy of England and the United States Contrasted, 1872. Died Boston, Dec. 6, 1879.

BIGELOW, Henry Jacob, surgeon, educator; b. Boston, Mar. 11, 1818; s. Jacob and Mary (Scollay) B.; grad. Harvard, 1837, M.D., 1841; m. Susan Sturgis, May 8, 1847, 1 son, William Sturgis. Tchr. surgery Tremont Street Med. Sch., Boston, 1845-49; surgeon Mass. Gen. Hosp., 1846-86; published 1st account of use of ether in surg. operation; asso. with discovery of surg. anaethesia, 1846; prof. surgery Harvard Med. Sch., 1849-84; did research and experiments on anatomy of hip-joint and removal of bladder stones, circa 1852; 1st Am. surgeon to excise hip-joint, 1852; inventor operating chair. Author: Manual of Orthopedic Surgery (Boylston prize essay), 1844; Medical Education in America, 1871; writings collected in Works of Henry Jacob Bigelow (edited by William Sturgis Bigelow), 3 vols., 1900. Died Newtown Creek, Mass., Oct. 30, 1890.

BIGELOW, Jacob, physician, botanist; b. Sudbury, Mass., Feb. 27, 1787; s. Jacob and Elizabeth (Wells) B.; grad. Harvard, 1806; M.D., U. Pa., 1810. Began practice medicine, Boston, 1811; gave 1st lectures on botany at Harvard, 1812, active next decade collecting bot. specimens in New Eng.; prof. medicine Harvard Med. Sch., 1815-35; Rumford prof. applied science Harvard, 1816-27; founded Mt. Auburn Cemetery, Cambridge, Mass., as public health project, 1831; pres. Am. Acad. Arts and Scis., 1847-63. Author: Florula Bostoniensis, 1814; American Medical Botany, 3 vols., 1817, 18, 20; Treatise on Materia Medica, 1822; Discourse on Self Limited Diseases, 1835; Elements of Technology, 1829; Brief Expositions of Rational Medicine, 1858. Died Boston, Jan. 10, 1879; buried Mt. Auburn Cemetery.

BIGELOW, Lewis, congressman, lawyer; b. Petersham, Worcester County, Mass., Aug. 18, 1785; grad. Williams Coll., 1803; studied law. Admitted to bar; practiced in Petersham; mem. Mass. Senate, 1819-21; editor 1st 17 volumes Massachusetts Reports, also digest of 6 volumes of Pickering's Reports; mem. U.S. Ho. of Reps. from Mass., 17th Congress, 1821-23; moved to Peoria, Ill., 1831, practiced law; became interested in real estate business and operation ferry boats; justice of peace; apptd. clk. Circuit Ct. of Peoria County, 1835-38. Died Peoria, Oct. 2, 1838; buried presumably in Old Centre Cemetery, Petersham.

BIGGS, Asa, senator, jurist; b. Martin County, N.C., Feb. 4, 1811; s. Joseph and Chloe (Daniel) B.; attended Williamston Acad., Martin County, circa 1821-26; m. Martha Andrews, 1832, 10 children. Admitted to bar, began practice in Martin County, N.C., 1831; active in Democratic politics; mem. N.C. Constl. Conv., 1835; mem. N.C. Ho. of Commons, 1840, 42, N.C. Senate, 1844, 54; mem. U.S. Ho. of Reps. from N.C., 29th Congress, 1845-47; joint codifier N.C. laws, 1851-55; mem. U.S. Senate from N.C., 1855-May 5, 1858, mem. finance com.; U.S. dist. judge for N.C., 1858-61; dist. judge for N.C., Confederate States of Am., 1861-65; practiced law Norfolk, Va., 1868-78. Co-author: Moore and Biggs's Code of N.C. Laws, 1855. Died Norfolk, Mar. 6, 1878; buried Norfolk.

BIGGS, Benjamin Thomas, gov. Del., congressman; b. nr. Summit Bridge, New Castle County, Del., Oct. 1, 1821; attended public schs., Pennington Sem., N.H.; attended Wesleyan U., Middletown, Conn. Tchr. short time; became farmer; mem. Del. Constl. Conv., 1853; dir. Kent & Queen Annes R.R.; mem. U.S. Ho. of Reps. (Democrat) from Del., 41st-42d congresses, 1869-73; del. Nat. Dem. Conv., Balt., 1872; elected gov. Del., 1887-91. Died Middletown, New Castle County, Del., Dec. 25, 1893; buried Bethel Cemetery, nr. Chesapeake City, Cecil County, Md.

BIGLER, Henry William, diarist; b. Shinnstown, W.Va., Aug. 15, 1815; s. Jacob and Elizabeth (Harvey) B.; m. Cynthia Jane Whipple, Nov. 18, 1855 (dec. 1874); m. 2d, Eleanor Emmett, 1878. Became a Mormon, 1837; moved to Mo., 1938, to Quincy, Ill., 1839; became elder in Mormon Ch., preached in Ill., Mo., Va. until 1846; traveled to Cal. with Mormons prior to their settlement of Salt Lake City; kept diary which provides only eyewitness account of discovery of gold at Sutter's Mill, Jan. 4, 1848; settled in Salt Lake City. Died Nov. 24, 1900.

BIGLER, John, gov. Cal., diplomat; b. Carlisle, Pa., Jan 8, 1805; s. Jacob and Susan (Dock) B.; 1 child. Editor, Centre County (Pa.) Democrat, 1827-32; mem. 1st Cal. Assembly, 1849-51, twice speaker; gov. Cal., (Dem.), 1852-56; U.S. minister to Chile (apptd. by Pres. Buchanan), 1857-61. Died Nov. 29, 1871.

BIGLER, William, senator, gov. Pa.; b. Shermansburg, Pa., Jan. 1, 1814; s. Jacob and Susan (Dock) B.; m. Maria Reed, Mar. 23, 1836. Founder, editor Democrat, Clearfield, Pa., 1834; mem. Pa. Senate, 1841-47, pres., 1843-44; gov. Pa., 1851; pres. Phila. & Erie R.R. Co., 1855; mem. U.S. Senate (Democrat) from Pa., Jan. 14, 1856-Mar. 3, 1861; del. Dem. Nat. Conv., Chgo., 1864, N.Y., 1868; del. Union Nat. Conv., Phila., 1866; mem. Pa. Constl. Conv., 1872, rep. Pa. on bd. finance Centennial Expn., 1876. Died Aug. 9, 1880; buried Hillcrest Cemetery, Clearfield.

BILLINGHURST, Charles, congressman, lawyer; b. Brighton, Franklin County, N.Y., July 27, 1818; attended common schs.; studied law. Admitted to bar, 1847; practiced in Rochester, N.Y.; moved to Wis., 1847, settled in Juneau, Dodge County, practiced law; elected mem. 1st Wis. Legislature, 1848; Democratic presdl. elector, 1852; mem. U.S. Ho. of Reps. (Republican) from Wis., 34th-35th congresses, 1855-59. Died Juneau, Aug. 18, 1865; buried Juneau Cemetery.

BILLINGS, Frederick, railroad exec.; b. Royalton, Vt., Sept. 27, 1823; s. Oel and Sophia (Wetherbe) B.; grad. U. Vt., 1844; m. Julia Parmly, Mar. 31, 1862. Admitted to bar, circa 1846; began practice of law, San Francisco, during Gold Rush; atty. gen. Cal., atty. for Gen. John Fremont; original stockholder and pres. N.P. R.R., 1879-81; active promoter Nicaraguan Canal project; philanthrapies include constrn. of chapel for Congregational Ch., Woodstock, constrn. and endowment of library U. Vt., gifts to Amherst Coll. and Moody's Sch., Northfield, Mass.; Billings (Mont.) named for him. Died Sept. 30, 1890.

BILLINGS, Josh, see Shaw, Henry Wheeler.

BILLINGS, William, choir master, composer; b. Boston, Oct. 7, 1746; s. William and Elizabeth (Clark) B.; no formal edn.; m. Mary Leonard, Dec. 13, 1764; m. 2d, Lucy Swan, July 26, 1774. Began musical career as voice tchr., circa 1767, later choir master Brattle St. Ch., Cambridge, Mass., Old South Ch., Boston; founder singing sch., Stoughton, Mass., 1774, became Stoughton Musical Soc., 1786; pioneered use of pitch pipe and the violincello to help ch. choirs maintain pitch in absence of instrumental accompaniment. Author: New England Palm-Singer; or American Chorister, 1770; The Singing Master's Assistant, 1778; Music in Miniature, 1779; The Suffolk Harmony, 1786; The Continental Harmony, 1794. Died Boston, Sept. 26, 1800; buried Boston.

BILLY the KID, see Bonney, William H.

BIMELER, Joseph Michael, founder religious community; b. Württemberg, Germany, circa 1778; no formal edn.; married. Came to U.S., 1817, leader of a group of Separatists from So. Germany; founded community of Zoar on tract in Tuscarawas County (O.), 1817-18; all property in settlement held communally, no marriage permitted in early years of colony's existence; supervised establishment of community brewery, mill, textile factory, foundry; acted as religious as well as civil leader until his death. Died Zoar, O., Aug. 27, 1853; buried Zoar.

BINES, Thomas, congressman; b. Trenton, N.H.; attended common schs. Apptd. coroner Salem County, N.J., 1802; elected sheriff Salem County, 1808-10; mem. U.S. Ho. of Reps. (Democrat, filled vacancy) from N.J., 13th Congress, Nov. 2, 1814-15; elected justice of peace, Lower Penns Neck Twp., Salem County, 1822-26. Died Lower Penns Neck Twp., Apr. 9, 1826.

BINGHAM, Anne Willing, society leader; b. Phila., Aug. 1, 1764; d. Thomas and Anne (McCall) Willing; m. William Bingham, Oct. 26, 1780. Travelled in European capitals including London, The Hague, Paris (presented to Louis XVI), 1783-88; dominated society in Phila., 1790's, known for Federalist preferences, aristocratic manners and tastes; "Mansion House" (her home in Phila.) copied from Duke of Manchester's home in England. Died Bermuda Islands, May 11, 1801; buried Phila.

BINGHAM, Caleb, author; b. Salisbury, Conn., Apr. 15, 1757; s. Daniel and Hannah (Conant) B.; grad. Dartmouth, 1782; m. Hannah Kemble, 2 daus. Head Moor's Indian Charity Sch., Dartmouth Coll., 1782-84; conducted pvt. sch. for girls, Boston, 1784-89; began writing textbooks in grammar, spelling, reading; publisher, bookseller, Boston, 1796-1817; politically active as Republican; strong advocate of free public edn. in Mass.; dir. Mass. State Prison 1810-circa 1816. Author: The Young Lady's Accidence, 1785; The Child's Companion, 1792; The American Preceptor, 1794; Astronomical and Geographical Catechism, 1803. Died Boston, Apr. 6, 1817; buried Boston.

BINGHAM, George Caleb, painter; b. Augusta County, Va., Mar. 20, 1811; s. Henry and Mary (Amend) B.; attended Pa. Acad. Fine Arts, 1837; m. Elizabeth Hutchison, 1836; m. 2d, Eliza Thomas 1847; m. 3d, Mrs. Mattie Lykins, 1878. Opene studio, Mo., circa 1834, lived most of life in Mo. had studios in Jefferson City, St. Louis, Kansa City (all Mo.) at various times; lived in Washingtor D.C., 1840-44; known especially for portraits an paintings depicting polit. events; mem. Mo. Legis lature (Whig), 1848; in Europe, 1856-58; treas State of Mo., 1862-65, adj. gen., 1875. Noteworth paintings include: Emigration of Daniel Boone 1851; Verdict of the People, 1854; General Lyo and General Blair Starting for Camp Jackson, 1862 Died Kansas City, July 7, 1879; buried Kansa City.

BINGHAM, Harry, lawyer, state legislator; b Concord, Vt., Mar. 30, 1821; s. Warner and Luc (Wheeler) B.; grad. Dartmouth, 1843; studied la in Bath, N.H. Admitted to N.H. bar, 1846, bega practice law in Littleton, N.H.; mem. N.H. Ho. c Reps., 1861-83, 87-91; mem. N.H. Senate, 1883-87 chmn. judiciary com. at various times; mem. Demo cratic nat. convs., 1868, 72, 80, 84, 90; mem. N.H Constl. Conv., 1876; U.S. Treasury agt. in N.H for a time; leading N.H. lawyer of his time. Die Sept. 12, 1900.

BINGHAM, Hiram, missionary; b. Bennington Vt., Oct. 30, 1789; s. Calvin and Lydia (Denton B.; grad. Middlebury Coll., 1816, Andover Theol Sem., 1819; m. Sybil Moseley, Oct. 11, 1819; m 2d, Naomi Morse, Aug. 24, 1854. Mem. Conglist mission in Hawaii under auspices of Am. Bd Commrs. Fgn. Missions, 1820; built ch. in Honolulu 1821; with other mems. of mission formed Hawaiia Clerical Assn., 1823; toured islands preaching, in strumental in spreading literacy among natives; com pleted (with other missionaries) translation of Bibl into Hawaiian language, 1839; returned to U.S. 1840, devoted remainer of career to writing an preaching in Easthampton, Mass. and New Haven Conn. Author: First Book for Children, 1831; Scrip ture Catechism, 1831; Residence of Twenty-On Years in the Sandwich Island, 1863. Died Nev Haven, Nov. 11, 1869; buried New Haven.

BINGHAM, John Armor, congressman, diplomat b. Mercer, Pa., Jan. 21, 1815; son of Hugh Bing ham; attended Franklin Coll., 2 years; m. Amand Bingham (cousin), 3 children. Admitted to Ohi bar, 1840; dist. atty. Tuscarawas County, O., 1846 49; mem. U.S. Ho. of Reps. (Republican) fror Ohio, 33d-37th, 39th-42d congresses, 1855-63, 65 73; served as maj., judge advocate U.S. Army, 1864 helped frame 14th Amendment to U.S. Constn. U.S. minister to Japan, 1873-85. Died Cadiz, O. Mar. 19, 1900; buried Cadiz Cemetery.

BINGHAM, Kinsley Scott, senator, gov. Mich. congressman; b. Camillus, Onodaga County, N.Y. Dec. 16, 1808; attended common schs.; studied law Syracuse, N.Y. Moved to Green Oak, Livingstor County, Mich., 1833; admitted to bar; practicec law; farmer; held number local offices includin justice of peace, postmaster, 1st judge probate o Livingston County; mem. 1st Mich. Ho. of Reps. 1837, reelected 4 times, speaker 3 terms; mem U.S. Ho. of Reps. (Democrat) from Mich., 30th-31st congresses, 1847-51; elected Republican gov Mich., 1854, 56; instrumental in establishmen Mich. Agrl. Coll., also other ednl. instns; mem U.S. Senate (Rep.) from Mich., 1859-Oct. 5, 1861 Died Green Oak, Oct. 5, 1859; buried Old Village Cemetery, Brighton, Livingston County, Mich.

BINGHAM, William, banker, senator; b. Phila. Mar. 8, 1752; s. William and Marry (Stamper B.; grad. U. Pa., 1768; m. Anne Willing, Oct. 26 1780, 2 children. Apptd. Brit. consul St. Pierre Martinique, 1770; founder, dir. Pa. Bank, 178 (chartered as Bank of N.Am., 1781); mem. Con tinental Congress from Pa., 1786-89; mem. Pa Assembly, 1790-95; mem. U.S. Senate from Pa. 1795-1801; founder Binghamton (N.Y.); 1st pres Phila. and Lancaster Turnpike Corp.; v.p. Soc. fo Polit. Inquiries; trustee U. Pa. Author: A Lette from an American on the Subject of the Restrainin Proclamation 1784; Description of Certain Tract of Land in the District of Maine, 1793. Died Bath Eng., Feb. 7, 1804; buried Paris Ch., Bath.

BINGHAM, William, educator; b. Mt. Repose, N C., July 7, 1835; s. William Bingham; grad. U. N.C. 1856; m. Owen White, Dec. 1856. Head Bingham Sch. in partnership with relatives, Mt. Repose, 1856-64, moved sch. to Orange County, N.C., 1864, converted it into mil. boarding sch., became sole owner 1865; known for successful teaching methods. Author A Grammar of the Latin Language, 1863; Caesar's Commentaries on the Gallic Wars, 1864; A Grammar of the English Language, 1868; A Latin Reader 1869. Died Mebane, N.C., Feb. 18, 1873; buriec Orange County.

BINNEY, Amos, naturalist; b. Boston, Oct. 18 1803; s. Col. Amos and Hannah (Dolliver) B. grad. Brown U., 1821; M.D., Harvard, 1826; m Mary Ann Binney, Dec. 20, 1827, 5 children including William Greene. A founder Boston Soc

Natural History, 1830, curator, 1830-32, treas., 1832-34, corr. sec., 1834-37, v.p., 1837-43, pres. 1843-47; a founder Am. Assn. Geologists and Naturalists; mem. Mass. Legislature, 1836-37. Author: Terrestial Air-Breathing Moilusks of the United States and Adjacent Territories of North America. Died Rome, Italy, Feb. 18, 1847.

BINNEY, Horace, lawyer, congressman; b. Phila., Jan. 4, 1780; s. Dr. Barnabas and Mary (Woodrow) B.; grad. Harvard, 1797; m. Esther Cox, Apr. 3, 1804, 7 children. Admitted to Phila. bar, 1800; mem. Pa. Legislature, 1806-07; dir. 1st U.S. Bank, 1808; mem. Phila. Common Council, 1810, Phila. Select Council, 1816-19; leader in Pa. Bar, expert on land titles, won Girard Tust Case, 1844, also Lyle vs. Richards case; mem. U.S. Ho. of Reps. (Whig) from Pa. 23d Congress, Dec. 2, 1833-1835; author case reports and biographies. Died Phila., Aug. 12, 1875; buried St. James the Less Cemetery, Phila.

BINNS, John, editor; b. Dublin, Ireland, Dec. 22, 1772; s. John and Mary (Pemberton) B.; m. Mary Anne Byster, 1801, 10 children. Came to U.S., 1801 founder and editor Democratic paper Republican Argus, Northumberland, Pa., 1802-07; founder Democratic Press (leading paper in Pa.), Phila., 1807-29; alderman Phila., 1822-44. Author: Binns' Justice (a manual of Pa. law), 1850. Died Phila., June 16,1860.

BINNS, John Alexander, farmer; b. Loudoun County, Va., 1761; s. Charles and Ann (Alexander) B. Introduced use of gypsum as fertilizer, 1784; started Loudoun System of soil treatment; incorporated ideas on agrl. improvement in A Treatise on Practical Farming, 1803; turned exhausted fields back into production in Va. Died 1813.

BINSSE, Louis Francis de Paul, artist; b. France, 1774; m. Victoria, at least 1 son, Lewis B. Held ofcl. position in Haiti under Vicomte de Rochambeau, settled in N.Y.C., circa 1805; painted portraits and miniatures, 1806-09; a signed miniature now at N.Y. Hist. Soc. Died N.Y.C., Dec. 24, 1844.

BIRCH, Thomas, painter; b. England, July 26, 1779; s. William Birch; no formal edn.; m. Ann Goodwin, June 1, 1802. Came to U.S., 1794, lived in Phila.; painted views of homes in vicinity of Phila. published by William Birch & Son, circa 1805; began to paint seascapes, 1807; exhibitor at 1st showing of Soc. of Artists at Pa. Acad. Fine Arts, 1811; designed several coins for U.S. Mint, circa 1807; became known for depiction of battles at sea during War of 1812; painted Engagement of the Constitution and the Guerriere (now at U.S. Naval Acad.), 1813, The United States and the Macedonian; made designs for many pictures in Naval Monument, 1816. Died probably Phila., Jan. 14, 1851.

BIRCH, William Russell, painter, engraver; b. Warwickshire, Eng., Apr. 9, 1755; received profl. tng., London, Eng.; married, 1 son, Thomas. Exhibited miniatures at Soc. of Artists, London, 1775; exhibited miniature and painting at Royal Acad., 1781; came to U.S., 1794; engraved scenes of Phila.; obtained fame for portraits in miniature, made miniature of Washington from life, 1796; published engravings Delices de la Grande, Eng., 1789, Views of Philadelphia, 1798-1800. Died Phila., Aug. 7, 1834.

BIRD, John, congressman, lawyer; b. Litchfield, Conn., Nov. 22, 1768; grad. Yale, 1786; studied law. Admitted to bar; practiced in Litchfield; moved to Troy, N.Y., 1793, practiced law; mem. N.Y. State Assembly, 1796-98; mem. U.S. Ho. of Reps. (Democrat) from N.Y., 6th-7th congresses, 1799-July 25, 1801 (resigned). Died Troy, Feb. 2, 1806; buried Mt. Ida Cemetery.

BIRD, Robert Montgomery, playwright, editor; b. New Castle County, Del., Feb. 5, 1806; s. John and Elizabeth (von Leuvenigh) B.; M.D., U. Pa., 1827; m. Mary Mayer, 1837; 1 son, Rev. Frederick Mayer. Practiced medicine for short time; prof. medicine, materia medica Pa. Med. Coll., 1841, lectr., 1841-43; mainly interested in writing; his early plays include: The Cowled Lover, The City Looking Glass, The Gladiator (1st performed 1831, became standard in repertoire of Edwin Forrest), The Broker of Bogota (considered his best play), 1834; hon. mem. English Dramatic Authors' Soc. (elected for The Gladiator); paid very little for plays (many not published until 1917); became an editor Phila. North American. 1847; suffered several breakdowns due to financial and writing difficulties. Author: (novels including) Calavar; or the Knight of the Conquest, 1834; The Infidel; or The Fall of Mexico, 1835. Died Phila., Jan. 23, 1854; buried Laurel Hill Cemetery, Phila.

BIRDSALL, James, congressman, lawyer; b. N.Y., 1783; studied law. Admitted to bar, 1806; 1st lawyer to practice in Norwich, Chenango County, N.Y.; surrogate Chenango County, 1811; mem. U.S. Ho. of Reps. (Democrat) from N.Y., 14th Congress, 1815-17; mem. N.Y. State Assembly, 1827; an incorporator Bank of Chenango; moved to Fenton, Genesee County, Mich., 1839, later to Flint, Mich. Died Flint, July 20, 1856; buried Glenwood Cemetery.

BIRDSALL, Samuel, congressman, lawyer; b. Hillsdale, Columbia County, N.Y., May 14, 1791; attended common schs.; studied law in office Martin Van Buren. Admitted to bar, 1812; practiced in Cooperstown, N.Y.; master in chancery, 1815; moved to Waterloo, Seneca County, N.Y., 1817; division judge adv. with rank of col., 1819; counselor in Supreme Ct. and solicitor in chancery, 1823; surrogate Seneca County, 1827-37; bank commr., 1832; mem. U.S. Ho. of Reps. (Democrat) from N.Y., 25th Congress, 1837-39; admitted to U.S. Supreme Ct. bar, 1838; dist. atty. Seneca County, 1846; postmaster, Waterloo, 1853-63. Died Waterloo, Feb. 8, 1872; buried Maple Grove Cemetery.

BIRDSEYE, Victory, congressman, lawyer; b. Cornwall, Conn., Dec. 25, 1782; grad. Williams Coll., 1804; studied law. Admitted to bar, 1807; practiced in Pompey Hill, Onondaga County, N.Y.; mem. U.S. Ho. of Reps. from N.Y., 14th, (Whig) 27th congresses, 1815-17, 41-43; postmaster, Pompey Hill, 1817-38; master of chancery Onondaga County, 1818-22; del. N.Y. State Constl. Conv., 1821; mem. N.Y. State Assembly, 1823, 38-40; mem. N.Y. State Senate, 1827. Died Pompey, N.Y., Sept. 16, 1853; buried Pompey Hill Cemetery.

BIRGE, Henry Warner, army officer; b. Hartford, Conn., Aug. 25, 1825. Mcht., Norwich, Conn., before Civil War; commd. maj. 4th Inf. Conn. Volunteers, 1861, col. 13th Inf., 1862, promoted brig. gen., 1863; participated in expdn. to take New Orleans, 1862; mem. picked force to storm Port Hudson before its surrender, 1863; commanded brigade under Gen. Banks in Red River campaign, 1864; served with Schofield's army in N.C., 1865, commanded dist. of Savannah; resigned from army, 1865; engaged in cotton and lumber enterprises in Ga. after Civil War. Died N.Y.C., June 1, 1888; buried N.Y.C.

BIRKBECK, Morris, pioneer, state ofcl.; b. Settle, Eng., Jan. 23, 1764; s. Morris and Hannah (Bradford) B.; m. Prudence Bush, Apr. 24, 1794. Came to U.S., 1814; obtained tract and founded settlement in Edwards County, Ill.; instrumental in attracting settlers to Ill. through writings published in U.S. and abroad; prominent as anti-slavery leader in Ill. politics; sec. of state Ill., 1824. Author: Notes on a Journey in America from the Coast of Virginia to the Territory of Illinois, 1817; Letters from Illinois, 1818. Died nr. Fox River, Ind., June 4, 1825.

BIRNEY, David Bell, army officer; b. Huntsville, Ala., May 29, 1825; s. James Gillespie and Agatha (McDowell) B.; 6 children. Family moved to Cincinnati, 1833; admitted to Mich. bar, 1848; moved to Phila., 1848; commd. lt. col. Pa. Militia, 1860; commd. lt. col. 23d Pa. Volunteers, 1861; col., then brig. gen. U.S. Volunteers, 1862; div. comdr. Army of the Potomac, 1862-63; brevetted maj. gen. volunteers for service at Battle of Chancellorsville, 1863; took part in Battle of Gettysburg. Died from fever contracted during army service, Phila., Oct. 18, 1864.

BIRNEY, James, gov. Mich., diplomat; b. Danville, Ky., June 7, 1817; s. James Gillespie and Agatha (McDowell) B.; grad. Miami U., Oxford, O., 1836; LL.D., Yale; m. Amanda Moulton, June 1, 1841, 2 children. Trustee, Saginaw Bay Co., 1857; mem. Mich. Senate (Republican), 1859; lt. gov. Mich., 1860; judge 18th Jud. Circuit, 1861-65; acting war gov. Mich., 1861-63; mem. Mich. Constl. Conv., 1867; founder Bay City (Mich.) Chronicle, 1871; commr. from Mich. to Centennial Exposition, Phila., 1876; minister resident The Hague (Netherlands), 1876-82; pres. Bay City Bd. Edn., 1886-88. Died Bay City, May 8, 1888.

BIRNEY, James Gillespie, reformer, legislator; b. Danville, Ky., Feb. 4, 1792; s. James Birney; grad. Coll. of N.J. (now Princeton), 1810; m. Agatha McDowell, February 1, 1816; m. 2d, Miss Fitzhugh, 1841; children include Dion, David, and Fitzhugh. Admitted to bar, 1814; elected mem. lower house Ky. Legislature, 1816; rep. 1st Gen. Assembly Ala., 1819; agt. Am. Colonization Soc., 1832; exec. sec. Am. Anti-Slavery Soc., 1837; v. p. World Anti-Slavery Conv., 1840; Liberty Party candidate for U.S. Pres., 1840, 44; advocated abolition by polit. action. Author: The American Churches the Bulwarks of American Slavery, 1840. Died Perth Amboy, N.J., Nov. 25, 1857.

BISHOP, Abraham, politician; b. New Haven, Conn., Feb. 5, 1763; s. Samuel and Mehetabel (Bassett) B.; grad. Yale, 1778; m. Nancy Dexter, Mar. 11, 1792; m. 2d, Betsey Law, 1802; m. 3d, Mrs. Elizabeth Lynde, Jan. 3, 1819. Admitted to Conn. bar, 1785; in Europe, 1787-88; taught sch., Conn., 1788-96; clk. New Haven County Ct., 1795, New Haven Probate Ct., 1796, New Haven Superior Ct., 1798-1800; active as Jeffersonian Republican in Conn. politics, circa 1794-1801; became known as polit. orator in New Eng.; collector Port of New Haven, 1801-29. Author addresses: An Oration of the Extent and Power of Political Delusion, 1800, Proofs of a Conspiracy, Against Christianity, and the United States Government, 1802. Died probably New Haven, Apr. 28, 1844.

BISHOP, James, congressman, mcht.; b. New Brunswick, N.J., May 11, 1816; attended Spaulding Sch., Rutgers Coll. Prep. Sch., New Brunswick. Became mcht., New Brunswick; mem. N.J. Ho. of Assembly, 1849, 50; mem. U.S. Ho. of Reps. (Whig) from N.J., 34th Congress, 1855-57; prominent in rubber trade, N.Y.C.; chief Bur. Labor Statistics of N.J., 1878-93; lived in Trenton, N.J. Died Kemble Hall, nr. Morristown, Morris County, N.J., May 10, 1895; buried Elmwood Cemetery, New Brunswick.

BISHOP, Joel Prentiss, legal writer; b. Volney, N.Y., Mar. 10, 1814; s. Amos and Fanny (Prentiss) B. Taught sch. for a time; editor The Friend of Man (organ of N.Y. Anti-Slavery Soc.); admitted to Mass. bar, 1844, began specializing in legal writing. Author: Commentaries on the Law of Marriage and Divorce, and Evidence in Matrimonial Suits, 1852; Commentaries on the Criminal Law, 2 vols., 1856-58; Thoughts for the Times, 1863; Secession and Slavery, 1863; Prosecution and Defense, 1885; Commentaries on the Law of Contracts, 1887. Died Cambridge, Mass., Nov. 4, 1901.

BISHOP, Nathan, educator, philanthropist; b. Vernon, N.Y., Aug. 12, 1808; s. Elnathan and Statira (Sperry) B.; grad. Brown U., 1837; m. Caroline Caulwell Bleecker, 1858. Tutor, Brown U., 1837-38; supt. schs., Providence, R.I., 1839-51, Boston, 1851-57; active in raising money for Brown U., 1849-50, became trustee, 1842; moved to N.Y.C., 1857; became prominent in N.Y. Sabbath Com., 1859; chmn. U.S. Christian Com. during Civil War; trustee Am. Bible Soc., 1865; active Am. wing of Evang. Alliance, 1866; mem. Bd. State Commrs. for Public Charities, 1867; an original trustee Vassar Coll. Died N.Y.C., Aug. 7, 1880; buried N.Y.C.

BISHOP, Phanuel, congressman; b. Rehoboth, Mass., Sept. 3, 1739; attended common schs. Innkeeper; mem. Mass. Senate, 1787-91; mem. Mass. Ho. of Reps., 1792, 93, 97, 98; mem. U.S. Ho. of Reps. from Mass., 6th-9th congresses. 1799-1807. Died Rehoboth, Jan. 6, 1812; buried Old Cemetery, Rumford, East Providence, R.I.

BISHOP, Robert Hamilton, clergyman, coll. pres., b. Whitburn County, Scotland, July 26, 1771; s. William and Margaret (Hamilton) B.; grad. U. Edinburgh (Scotland), 1798; attended Theol. Sem., Selkirk, Scotland, 1898-1902; m. Ann Ireland, Aug. 26, 1802, children—William Wallace, Mary Ann, George Brown, Ebenezer Brown, Robert Hamilton, Catherine Wallace, John Mason, Jane Ridgely. Licensed by Presbytery of Perth (Scotland), 1802; sailed for Am. in service of Asso. Reformed C. of North Am. in Ohio Valley, fall 1802; prof. philosophy Transylvania U., 1804124; pres. Miami U., Oxford, O., 1824-41, held an exptl. professorship of history and philosophy of social relations (one of earliest modern courses in sociology), 1833, resigned, 1841; continued courses in social philosophy at an acad. (became Farmers' Coll. 1846, now Ohio Mil. Inst.), Pleasant Hill, O. 1845-55; began to establish Sunday schs. for Negroes, 1815; joined Presbyn. Ch., 1819, attempted to prevent its division, organized group of ministers who advocated continued union of the ch., 1838, assisted in publishing Western Peace-Maker and Monthly Religious Jour. (mag. of the group), 1839-40; editor, publisher Evang. Record and Western Review, 1812-13. Author: Sermons on Plain and Practical Subjects, 1809; An Outline of the History of the Church in the State of Kentucky, 1824; A Manual of Logic, 1830 republished as Elements of Logic, 1833; A Plea for United Christian Action, 1833; Sketches of the Philosophy of the Bible, 1833; Elements of the Science of Government, 1839. Died Coffe Hill, Ohio, Apr. 29, 1855; buried campus of Farmer's Coll., Pleasant Hill.

BISSELL, Edwin Cone, clergyman; b. Schoharie, N.Y., Mar. 2, 1832; s. George and Elizabeth (White) B.; grad. Amherst Coll., 1855, Union Theol. Sem., 1859; studied in Germany, 1878-80; m. Emily Pomeroy, 1859. Ordained to ministry Congregational Ch., 1859; pastor, West Hampton, Mass., until 1864; organized, served with Company K, 52d Mass. Inf. Volunteers, 1862-63; pastor Green Street Congregational Ch., San Francisco, 1864-69; pastor, Winchester, Mass., 1870-73; missionary in Austria, 1873-78; prof. Hebrew, Hartford Theol. Sem., 1881-92, McCormick Theol. Sem., Chgo., 1892-94. Author: The Historic Origin of the Bible, 1873; The Apocrypha of the Old Testament (translation), 1880; The Pentateuch, Its Origin and Structure; Biblical Antiquities, 1888. Died Chgo., Apr. 10, 1894; buried Chgo.

BISSELL, George Henry, petroleum exec.; b. Hanover, N.H., Nov. 8, 1821; s. Isaac and Nina (Wempe) B.; grad. Dartmouth, 1845; LL.B., Jefferson Coll., 1846; m. Ophie Griffin, 1855. Admitted to N.Y. bar, 1853, organizer Pa. Rock Oil Co. (1st U.S. oil co. to develop Pa. oil lands), 1854; pioneer in technique of obtaining petroleum through drilled wells. Died Nov. 19, 1884.

BISSELL, William Henry, gov. Ill., congressman; b. Hartwick, N.Y., Apr. 25, 1811; s. Luther and Hannah Bissell; grad. Jefferson Med. Coll., 1835; attended Lexington (Ky.) Law Sch.; m. Emily James Oct. 1840; m. 2d, Elizabeth Kane, 1852; 2 children. M. Ill. Legislature, 1840; admitted to Ill. bar, 1843; pros. atty. St. Claire County (Ill.), 1844; commd. col. 2d Ill. Volunteers during Mexican War, served in Battle of Buena Vista, 1847; mem. U.S. Ho. of Reps. (Democrat) from Ill., 30th-33th congresses, 1849-54; gov. Ill., 1857-60. Died Springfield, Ill., Mar. 18, 1860; buried Oak Ridge Cemetery, Springfield.

BISSOT, Francois Marie (sieur de Vincennes), pioneer; b. Montreal, Can., June 27, 1700; s. Jean Baptiste and Marguerite (Forestier) B. Commanded at Ke-ki-onga, Miami Indian Village on site of Ft. Wayne (Ind.); commd. ensign Continental Army, 1722; complied with requests of gov. La., built ft. on present site of Vincennes, Ind., circa 1732; assisted La. in struggle with Indians (especially Chickasaw) to save Mississippi Valley for France, built post on Wabash River. Killed by Chickasaw Indians, nr. present site of Memphis, Tenn., Mar. 25, 1736.

BISSOT, Jean Baptiste (sieur de Vincennes), Indian trader; b. Jan. 19, 1668; s. François and Marie (Couillard) Bissot; m. Marguerite Forestier, 1696, 1 son, François M. Commd. ensign French Army, 1687; sent by Gov. Frontenac to command Indians in Miami (O.) area, 1696-1705; explored (with Henry de Tonty) areas of West, 1698; suspended from command among Miami Indians for liquor trading, 1705; had large trading post at present site of Ft. Wayne (Ind.); kept Miami Indians as allies of French as long as he lived; aided in defense of Ft. Detroit, 1712. Died 1719.

BIXBY, Anna Pierce Hobbs, physician; b. probably Phila., circa 1808; m. Jefferson Hobbs; m. 2d, Eson Bixby. Traveled westward with family, 1824, settled in Rock Creek, Ill.; distressed by pioneer health conditions, returned to take med. tng. in Phila.; returned to Rock Creek, 1828, remained only health practitioner in area until death; concerned with milksick disease that plagued men and cattle; with assistance of Shawnee squaw, determined its cause to be white snakeroot plant. Died Rock Creek, 1869

BLACK, Edward Junius, congressman, lawyer; b. Beaufort, S.C., Oct. 30, 1806; grad. Richmond Acad., Augusta, Ga.; studied law; at least 1 son, George Robinson. Admitted to bar, 1827; practiced in Augusta, Ga.; mem. Ga. Ho. of Reps., 1829-31; moved to Screven County, Ga., 1832; mem. U.S. Ho. of Reps. (State Rights Whig) from Ga., 26th, (Democrat, filled vacancies) 27th-28th congresses, 1839-41, Jan. 3, 1842-45. Died Millettville, Barnwell Dist., S.C., Sept. 1. 1846; buried family burying ground, nr. Millettville.

BLACK, George Robison, congressman; b. nr. Jacksonboro, Screven County, Ga., Mar. 24, 1835; s. Edward Junius Black; attended U. Ga. at Athens, U. S.C. at Columbia; studied law. Admitted to bar, 1857; practiced in Savannah, Ga.; served as 1st lt. Phoenix Rifleman, Confederate Army; promoted lt. col. 63d Ga. Regt.; del. Ga. Constl. Conv., 1865; del. Nat. Democratic Conv., Balt., 1872; mem. Ga. Senate, 1874-77; v.p. Ga. Agrl. Soc.; mem. U.S. Ho. of Reps. (Democrat) from Ga., 47th Congress, 1881-83. Died Sylvania, Screven County, Nov. 3, 1886; buried Sylvania Cemetery.

BLACK, Henry, congressman; b. nr. borough of Somerset, Pa., Feb. 25, 1783; attended common schs. Farmer; mem. Pa. Ho. of Reps., 1816-18; justice of peace; asso. judge Somerset County (Pa.), 1820-40; mem. U.S. Ho. of Reps. (Whig, filled vacancy) from Pa., 27th Congress, June 28, 1824-Nov. 28, 1841. Died Somerset, Nov. 28, 1841; buried family cemetery, Stony Creek Twp., Somerset County.

BLACK, James, congressman; b. Newport, Perry County, Pa., Mar. 6, 1793; attended common schs. Became mcht.; mem. Pa. Ho. of Reps., 1830, 31; mem. U.S. Ho. of Reps. (Democrat, filled vacancy) from Pa., 24th, 28th-29th congresses, Dec. 5, 1836-37, 43-47; asso. judge Perry County, 1842, 43; Pa. collector of tools on Juniata Canal. Died New Bloomfield, Perry County, June 21, 1872; buried New Bloomfield Cemetery.

BLACK, James, lawyer, a founder Nat. Prohibition Party; b. Lewisburg, Pa., Sept. 23, 1823; s. John and Jane (Egbert) B.; attended Lewisburg Acad., 1840-43; m. Eliza Murray, 1845. Joined Washington Temperance Soc., 1840; admitted to Lancaster County (Pa.) bar, 1846; right grand worthy councilor Lancaster Lodge Good Templars, 1864; secured conv. of Sons of Temperance and Good Templars in Harrisburg for Pa. polit. action, 1867; a founder Nat. Prohibition Party, 1869, elected 1st pres., 1872; owned most extensive temperance library in world. Author: Cider Tract, 1864; Is There a Necessity for a Prohibition Party, 1876; A History of the Prohibition Party, 1880; The Prohibition Party, 1885. Died Lancaster, Pa., Dec. Dec 16, 1893.

BLACK, James Augustus, congressman; b. Ninety Six Dist., nr. Abbeville, S.C., 1793; attended common schs. on father's plantation. Apptd. 2d lt. 8th Inf. in War of 1812, promoted 1st lt., 1813-15; mined iron ore at present site of Cherokee Falls, S.C.; moved to Ga., settled in Savannah, became cotton dealer; tax collector Chatham County, Ga.; returned to S.C., settled in Columbia; br. cashier State bank; mem. U.S. Ho. of Reps. (Calhoun Democrat) from S.C., 28th-30th congresses, 1843-Apr. 3, 1848. Died Washington, D.C., Apr. 3, 1848; buried graveyard First Presbyn. Ch., Columbia.

BLACK, Jeremiah Sullivan, cabinet officer; b. Somerset Cunty, Pa., Jan. 10, 1810; s. Henry and Mary (Sullivan) B.; m. Mary Forward, 1836. Admitted to a. bar, 1831; dep. atty. gen. Somerset County, 1831; apptd. president judge Pa. Ct. Common Pleas, 1842; chief justice Supreme Ct. Pa., 1851-54; U.S. atty. gen. under Buchanan, 1857-60, sec. of state, 1860-61; exposed Cal. land grant scandals; counsel for Andrew Johnson at impeachment trial, for Samuel J. Tilden, also Vanderbilt Will Case, Miliken Case. Died York, Pa., Aug. 19, 1833.

BLACK, John, senator, lawyer; b. Mass.; studied law. Tchr. for few years; practiced law in La.; moved to Miss.; elected judge 4th Circuit and Supreme Ct., 1826-32; mem. U.S. Senate (filled vacancies) from Miss., Nov. 12, 1832-33, Nov. 22, 1833-Jan. 22, 1838 (resigned); affiliated with Whig Party after its formation; practiced in Winchester, Va. Died Winchester, Aug. 29, 1854; buried Mt. Hebron Cemetery.

BLACKBEARD, see Teach, Edward.

BLACKBURN, Gideon, clergyman, educator; b. Augusta County, Va., Aug. 27, 1772; s. Robert Blackburn; attended Martin Acad., East Tenn.; m. Grizzel Blackburn, Oct. 3, 1793. Licensed to preach in East Tenn., 1792; founded New Providence Ch., East Tenn., 1793; became active in missionary work among Cherokee Indians, 1793; obtained support of Gen. Assembly for his work, 1803; founder, conductor sch. for Cherokee children, 1804-10; pres. Harpeth Acad., 1810-33; pastor Presbyn. chs., Louisville, Versailles, Ky.; fund raiser for Ill. Coll., 1833-35; raised funds for instn., 1836-38, opened as Blackburn Theol. Sem., 1857, later Blackburn Coll. Died possibly Carlinville, Ill., Aug. 23, 1838.

BLACKBURN, Joseph, portrait painter; b. England, circa 1700; received tng. in England. Came to Am., circa 1750; probably lived in Boston and Portsmouth during 1750's and 1760's; painted portraits in Bermuda, 1753, Jamaica, 1763; did portraits of many prominent colonial families and individuals including Jeffery Amherst, Mrs. Joshua Babcock, Sir Alexander Grant, Mrs. Thomas Hancock, James Otis, Joshua Winslow.

BLACKBURN, Luke Pryor, physician, gov. Ky.; b. Woodford County, Ky., June 16, 1816; s. Edward M.and Lavina (Bell) B: M.D., Transylvania U., 1834: m. Ella Boswell, Nov. 24, 1835; m. 2d, Julia Churchill, Nov 17, 1857. Organized control of cholera epidemic at Versailles, Ky., 1835; mem. Ky. Legislature, 1843; assumed gen. control yellow fever epidemic in lower Mississippi Valley, 1848-54, in L.I., N.Y., 1856, Memphis, Tenn., 1875, Hickman, Ky. 1878; surgeon to Gen. Sterling Price's staff Conferderate Army during Civil War, set up Marine Hosp., Natchez, Miss., obtained fed. control for future marine hosps.; gov. Ky., 1879-83, instituted prison reforms. Died Frankfort, Ky., Sept. 14, 1887.

BLACK HAWK (Indian name Ma-ka-tai-me-she-kia-kiak), Indian chief; b. Sac (also Sauk) Village (now Rock Island, Ill.,) 1767. Mem. Sauk tribe; opposed Treaty of 1804 by which Sauk and Fox Indians ceded all their lands East of Mississippi River to U.S.; fought with British under command of Shawneee Indian chief Tecumseh in War of 1812; sought to form Indian confederacy (with medicine man named White Cloud) to resist Am. expansion; promised aid by Potawatomies, Winnebagoes, and Mascoutins, then led his tribe into Ill. in effort to repossess Indian lands, 1832; began Black Hawk War (Apr.-Aug. 1832) when forces commanded by Gen. Henry Atkinson attacked Indian envoys sent by Black Hawk to talk with Americans; defeated at Battle of Bad Axe River in Wis. taken Prisoner; taken to Washington (D.C.) to meet Pres. Andrew Jackson, 1833; returned to Ia. Died village on Des Moines River, Ia., Oct. 3, 1838.

BLACK KETTLE, Indian chief; b. in what is n S.D., circa 1803. Mem. Southern nation of Cheyen Indians, became head chief, sometime after 185 1 of Plains chiefs who negotiated treaty at F Wise, Colo., 1861; chief leader of Cheyenne India in war against whites, conducted mainly in Col 1864; sued for peace, Sept. 1864, but would r accede to unconditional surrender; escaped affair Sand Creek, Nov. 1864; signed new treaty with U. Govt., Oct. 1865, also Treaty of Medicine Lodg Oct. 1867; killed at Battle of Cheyenne Camp, Was ita Valley, Indian Territory (now Okla.), 1868 (af er many Cheyenne Indians had raided settlers a working parties of transcontinental railroads, 186 68); may have been responsible for Cheyenne ta tics of fighting in summer, then attempting to si favorable treaty for winter, which would be brok again in following year. Died Nov. 27, 1868.

BLACKLEDGE, William, congressman; b. Crav County, N.C.; at least 1 son, William Salter. Me N.C. Ho. of Commons, 1797-99, 1809; mem. U. Ho. of Reps. (Democrat) from N.C., 8th-10t 12th congresses, 1803-03, 11-13, a mgr. apptd. conduct impeachment proceedings against Jo Pickering (judge U.S. Dist. Ct. for N.H.), 180 Died Spring Hill, Craven County, Oct. 19, 182

BLACKLEDGE, William Salter, congressma b. Pitt County, N.C., 1793; s. William Blackledg grad. U. N.C., 1813. Moved to Craven County, N.C settled in New Bern. Mem. N.C. Ho. of Commor 1820; mem. U.S. Ho. of Reps. (Democrat, fill vacancy) from N.C., 16th-17th congresses, Fe 7, 1821-23. Died New Bern, Mar. 21, 1857; buri New Bern Cemetery.

BLACKMAR, Esbon, congressman, mcht.; Freehold, Greene County, N.Y., June 19, 180 grad. high sch. In gen. mdse. business; mem. N.Y State Senate, 1838, 41; mem. U.S. Ho. of Rep (Whig, filled vacancy) from N.Y., 30th Congres Dec. 4, 1848-49. Died Newark, Wayne Count N.Y., Nov. 19, 1857; buried Willow Avenue Cem etery.

BLACKSTONE, William, colonist; b. Salisbury Eng., 1595; grad. Cambridge (Eng.) U., 161 M.A., 1621; m. Sarah Stevenson, 1659, 1 son Joh Came to Am., 1623, settled at Boston, did not ge along with Puritan settlers in region; settled n Pawtucket, R.I., 1634; maintained friendly relatio with Indians; planted 1st orchards in Mass. Die Cumberland, R.I., May 1675; probably buried Cum berland.

BLACKWELL, Julius W., congressman; b. Va. attended public schools. Moved to Tenn., settle in Athens, McMinn County; mem. U.S. Ho. of Rep (Van Buren Democrat) from Tenn., 26th, 28t congresses, 1839-41, 43-45.

BLADEN, William, publisher, colonial ofcl.; b Yorkshire, Eng., Feb. 27, 1673; s. Nathaniel an Isabella (Fairfax) B.; m. Anne Van Swearinge 1696, 1 son Thomas. Came to Am., 1690, settle in Md.; transcribed public laws which were sent t England; clk. Md. Assembly, 1695; clk. Md. Gov.' Council, 1698; began operation of printing press 1700, printed ofcl. and state legal documents; col lector Port of Annapolis (Md.); atty. gen. of Md Died Annapolis, circa Aug. 7, 1718.

BLAINE, James Gillespie, senator, sec. of state b. West Brownsville, Pa., Jan. 31, 1830; s. Ephrain and Maria (Gillespie) B.; grad. Washington Coll. 1847; m. Harriet Stonwood, June 30, 1850, 7 children. Tchr., Pa. Instn. for Blind, Phila., 1852-54 mem. editorial staff Portland Advertiser, also edito Kennebec Journal, 1854-60; a founder Republica Party in Me., 1854; mem. Me. Ho. of Reps., 1858 62, speaker, 1860-62; chmn. Rep. State Com. 1859; mem. U.S. Ho. of Reps. from Me., 38th-44th congresses, 1863-July 10, 1876, speaker, 1869-75 became leader Half-Breed wing Rep. Party; mem. U.S. Senate from Me., July 10, 1876-1881; U.S. sec. of state under Pres. Garfield, Mar.-Dec. 1881 unsuccessful candidate for Pres. U.S., 1884, los election when Rep. Party split into Mugwumps wing because of graft accusations connecting Blair with railroad bonds (accusations revived and enlarged from those previously made in "Mulligan Letters" which had probably lost him Rep. nomination in 1876); lost State of N.Y. by 600 votes largely due to Irish vote influenced by Democratic press (capitalizing on Rev. S.D. Burchard's description of Dem. Party as party of "rum, Romanism and rebellion," 1880); U.S. sec. of state under Pres. Harrison, 1889-92, organized and presided over 1st Pan-Am. Congress, promoted thoery of reciprocal tariffs, secured treaty concerning Pacific seal hunting with Gt. Britain; known as Plumed Knight. Author: Twenty Years of Congress, 2 vols., 1884, 86; Political Discussions (collection of speeches), 1887. Died Washington, D.C., Jan. 27, 1893; buried Blaine Meml. Park, Augusta, Me.

BLAIR, Austin, gov. Mich., congressman; b. Caroline, Tompkins County, N.Y., Feb. 8, 1818; s.

eorge and Rhoda (Blackman) B.; grad. Union Coll., 837; m. Sarah Ford, Feb. 1849, 1 son, Charles A. dmitted to Tioga County (Mich.) bar, 1841; mem. ich. Ho. of Reps., 1845-49; mem. Free Soil Party, 854, participated in orgn. Republican Party mem., epublican leader Mich. Senate, 1855; leader Mich. braham Lincoln, 1860; mem. U.S. Ho. of Reps, elegation in Rep. Nat. Conv. which nominated Republican) from Mich., 40th-42d congresses 867-73; regent U. Mich., 1882-90; gov. Mich., 861-65. Died Jacksonville, Mich., Aug. 6, 1894.

BLAIR, Bernard, congressman, lawyer; b. Wilamstown, Mass., May 24, 1801; grad. Williams oll., 1825; studied law. Moved to Salem, Washgton County, N.Y., 1825; admitted to bar, 828; practiced in Salem; admitted as counselor d solicitor in chancery; mem. U.S. Ho. of Reps. Whig) from N.Y., 27th Congress, 1841-43; beame active in business. Died Salem, May 7, 1880; uried Evergreen Cemetery.

BLAIR, Francis Preston, politician, journalist; b. bingdon, Va., Apr. 12, 1791; s. James Blair; grad. ransylvania U., 1811; m. Eliza Gist, 2 sons, Montomery, Francis P. Contbr. to reformist newspaper rgus of Western America, Frankfort, Ky., circa 818; supported Andrew Jackson in Ky. politics om 1825; founded Democratic newspaper Globe at vitation of Pres. Jackson, Washington, D.C., 1830-5; mem. Jackson's "Kitchen Cabinet;" used newsaper to oppose nullification, Am. System, and ank of U.S.; adherent of Free-Soil Party, 1848; pposed Southern domination of Dem. Party, suported Republican Party, 1856; supporter, adviser to res. Lincoln during Civil War; returned to Dem. arty because of Radical Reconstrn., 1868, 72. ied Silver Spring, Md., Oct. 18, 1876.

BLAIR, Francis Preston, Jr., senator, congressan; b. Lexington, Ky., Feb. 19, 1821; s. Francis reston Blair; grad. Princeton, 1841; postgrad. in aw Translyvania U.; m. Appolene Alexander, Sept. , 1847. Admitted to Ky. bar, 1843; served in Mexcan War; mem. Mo. Ho. of Reps., 1852-56, 70; nem. U.S. Ho. of Reps. (as Free-Soiler) from Mo., 5th-36th congresses, 1857-60 (resigned), 37th Congress, 1860-61 (resigned), (as Republican, conested election), 38th Congress, 1863-64, chmn. om. on mil. def., 1861; commd. col. U. S. Army, 861, promoted maj. gen., 1862; defender Linoln's reconstrn. plan, 1864; unsuccessful Democratc nominee for vice pres. U.S., 1868; mem. U.S. Senate from Mo., 1871-73; helped secure Horace Greeley's nomination for pres. U.S., 1872; state upt. life ins. Mo., 1874. Author: Life and Public Service of General William O. Butler, 1848. Died July 9, 1875; buried Bellefontaine Cemetery, St. Louis.

BLAIR, James, clergyman, coll. pres.; b. Scotland, 1655; M.A., U. Edinburgh (Scotland), 1673; m. Sarah Harrison, June 2, 1687. Ordained to ministry Ch. of Eng., circa 1673; sent as missionary to Va. (unofcl. dep. of Bishop of London), 1685; most important founder Coll. William and Mary, 1693, 1st pres., 1693-1743; pres. Va. Council, acting gov. Colony of Va., 1740-41; minister Jamestown (Va.) Ch., 1694; rector Bruton Parish, Williamsburg, Va. Author: Our Saviour's Divine Sermon on the Mount (sermon). Died Va., Apr. 18, 1743.

BLAIR, James, congressman; b. Waxhaw settlenent, Lancaster County, S.C., circa 1790. Became planter; sheriff Lancaster Dist.; mem. U.S. Ho. of Reps. (Democrat) from S.C., 17th, (Union Dem.) 21st, (Dem.) 22d-23d congresses, 1821-May 8, 1822, 29-Apr. 1, 1834, resigned in 1822. Died Washington, D.C., Apr. 1, 1834; buried Congressional Cemetery.

BLAIR, John, colonial ofcl.; b. Va., 1687; s. Archibald Blair; grad. Coll. William and Mary, circa 1707; m. Mary Monro, 10 children. Dep. auditorgen. of Va., 1728-71; mem. Va. Ho. of Burgesses, 1734-40; mem. Va. Gov.'s Council, 1745-70, served as pres., acting gov. during vacancy of governorship, 1758, 68, favored religious toleration toward Baptists, 1768; owned land tracts in Western Va.; mem. com. for revision of colony's laws, 1746. Died Va., 1771.

BLAIR, John, asso. justice U.S. Supreme Ct.; b. Williamsburg, Va., 1732; s. John and Mary (Monro) B.; m. Jean Balfour. Admitted to Middle Temple, London, Eng., 1755; mem. Va. Ho. of Burgesses, 1766-1770; clk. Va. Council, 1770-75; mem. Va. Constl. Conv., 1776, Va. Privy Council, 1776; judge Va. Gen. Ct., 1778-80. judge 1st Ct. Appeals of Va., 1780-89, during which time the case of Commonwealth of Va. vs. Caton arose, establishing precedent of judiciary review of state legislation; del. U.S. Constl. Conv., 1786; firm believer in the constn. and strong fed. govt.; asso. justice U.S. Supreme Ct. (apptd. by Pres. Washington), 1789-96. Died Williamsburg, Aug. 31, 1800.

BLAIR, John, congressman, lawyer; b. Blairs Mill, nr. Jonesborough (now Jonesboro), Washington County, Tenn., Sept. 13, 1790; attended Martain Acad.; grad. Washington (Tenn.) Coll., 1809; studied law. Admitted to bar, 1813; practiced law; mem. Tenn. Ho. of Reps., 1815-17, 49, 50; mem. Tenn. Senate, 1817-21; mem. U.S. Ho. of Reps. (Democrat) from Tenn., 18th-23d congresses, 1823-35. Died Jonesboro, July 9, 1863; buried Old Cemetery.

BLAIR, Montgomery, postmaster-gen.; b. Franklin County, Ky., May 10, 1813; s. Francis P. and Eliza (Gist); grad. U.S. Mil. Acad., 1835; m. Miss Buckner; m. 2d, Miss Woodbury. Commd. lt. U.S. Army, 1835; admitted to bar, 1839; apptd. U.S. dist. atty. for Mo. 1839; mayor St. Louis, 1842-43; judge St. Louis Ct. of Common Pleas, 1845-49; del. Democratic Nat. Conv., 1844, 48, 52; moved to Md., 1852; 1st solicitor U.S. Ct. of Claims, 1855, a counsel for Dred Scott; pres. Md. Republican Conv. 1860; postmaster-gen. U.S. under Lincoln, 1861-64; Tilden's counsel before Electoral Commn., 1876; mem. Md. Ho. of Dels., 1878; unsuccessful candidate for U.S. Congress, 1882. Died Silver Spring, Md., July 27, 1883.

BLAIR, Samuel, clergyman; b. Ulster, Ireland, June 14, 1712; s. William Blair; attended "Log Coll.," Neshaminy, Pa., 1729-33. Ordained to ministry Presbyn. Ch., 1733; pastor in Middletown and Shrewsbury, N.J., 1733-39; a founder Presbytery of New Brunswick, N.J., 1738; became a leading preacher in region in 1730's; pastor, New Londonderry, Pa., 1739-51; strong supporter of Whitefield in 1740's; adherent of New Side (revivalist) wing of Presbyn. Ch. Died New Londonderry, July 5, 1751; buried Chester County, Pa.

BLAIR, Samuel Steel, congressman, lawyer; b. Indiana, Indiana County, Pa., Dec. 5, 1821; grad. Jefferson Coll., Canonsburg, Pa., 1838; studied law. Admitted to bar, 1845; practiced in Hollidaysburg, Blair County, Pa., 1846; del. to several Pa. convs.; del. Nat. Republican Conv., Phila., 1856; mem. U.S. Ho. of Reps. (Rep.) from Pa., 36th-37th congresses, 1859-63. Died Hollidaysburg, Dec. 8, 1890; buried Presbyn. Cemetery.

BLAISDELL, Daniel, congressman, jurist; b. Amesbury, Mass., Jan. 22, 1762; attended public schs.; had some legal knowledge. Served in Revolutionary War, 1776-77; moved to Canaan, N.H., 1780; taught sch.; became farmer; held several local offices; mem. N.H. Ho. of Reps., 1793, 95, 99, 1812, 13, 24, 25, mem. exec. council, 1803-08; moderator of Canaan, 1808, 09, 12, 22, 24, 26, 30; mem. U.S. Ho. of Reps. (Federalist) from N.H., 11th Congress, 1809-11; served in War of 1812; selectman Canaan, 1813, 15, 18; mem. N.H. Senate, 1814, 15; chief justice Ct. of Sessions, 1822. Died Canaan, N.H., Jan. 10, 1833; buried Wells Cemetery.

BLAKE, Eli Whitney, inventor, mgr.; b. Westborough, Mass., Jan. 27, 1795; s. Elihu and Elizabeth (Whitney) B.; grad. Yale, 1816; m. Eliza O'Brien, July 8, 1822, 6 sons, 6 daus. Partner firearms business with uncle Eli Whitney, New Haven, 1817-25, continued bus. with brother after uncle's death, 1825-36; propr. hardware factory, Westville, Conn., 1836-71; received patents for door lock, bedstead castors, stone crusher; a founder Conn. Acad. Scis.; contbr. to Am. Jour. of Science. Author: Original Solution of Several Problems in Aerodynamics, 1882. Died New Haven, Conn., Aug. 18, 1886; buried New Haven.

BLAKE, Harrison Gray Otis, congressman, lawyer; b. Newfane, Windham County, Vt., May 17, 1818; attended public schs.; studied medicine, Seville for 1 year; studied law. Moved to Medina, O., 1836, became mcht.; admitted to bar; practiced in Medina; mem. Ohio Ho. of Reps., 1846, 47; mem. Ohio Senate, 1848, 49, pres.; mem. U.S. Ho. of Reps. (Republican, filled vacancy) from Ohio, 36th-37th congresses, Oct. 11, 1859-63; col. 166th Regt., Union Army, 1864; declined appointment gov. Ida. Territory; in banking and merc. activities; del. Loyalist Conv., Phila., 1866. Died Medina, Apr. 16, 1876; buried Spring Grove Cemetery.

BLAKE, Homer Crane, naval officer; b. Dutchess County, N.Y., Feb. 1, 1822; s. Elisha and Marilla (Crane) B.; m. Mary Flanagan, 2 children. Apptd. midshipman U.S. Navy, 1842, commd. lt., 1855, lt. comdr., 1862, comdr., 1866, capt., 1871, commodore, 1879; commanded Hatteras, 1862, destroyed by Confederate raider Alabama; later commanded Eutaw in North Atlantic Squadron. Died Jan. 21, 1880.

BLAKE, John, Jr., congressman; b. Ulster County, N.Y., Dec. 5, 1762; attended public schs. Served in N.Y. State Militia in Revolutionary War; apptd. dep. sheriff Ulster County, 1793; mem. N.Y. State Assembly, 1798-1800, 12, 13, 19; sheriff Orange County, N.Y., 1803-05; mem. U.S. Ho. of Reps. from N.Y., 9th-10th congresses, 1805-09; judge Orange County Ct. of Common Pleas, 1815-18; supr. Town of Montgomery, Orange County, 15 terms. Died Montgomery, Jan. 13, 1826; buried Berea Churchyard, nr. Newburgh, N.Y.

BLAKE, John Lauris, clergyman; b. Northwood, N.H., Dec. 21, 1788; s. Jonathan and Mary (Dow) B.; grad. Brown U., 1812; m. Louisa Richmond, June 25, 1814; m. 2d, Mary Howe, Dec. 6, 1816. Ordained to ministry Episcopal Ch., 1815; founder, rector St. Paul's Parish, Pawtucket, R.I. until 1820; conducted girls sch., Concord, N.H., 1820-22, Boston, 1822-30; rector St. Matthews Ch., Boston, 1824-32; editor Gospel Advocate, Boston, 1824-27; wrote textbooks and religious books in N.Y.C. and N.J., 1832-57. Author: General Biographical Dictionary, 1st edit., 1835; A Family Encyclopedia of Useful Knowledge, 1852; A Family Textbook for the Country, 1853. Died Orange, N.J., July 6, 1857; buried Orange.

BLAKE, Lyman Reed, inventor, shoe mfr.; b. South Abington, Mass., Aug. 24, 1835; s. Samuel and Susannah (Bates) B.; m. Susie Hollis, Nov. 27, 1855. Joined shoemaking firm Gurney & Mears (became Gurney, Mears & Blake), 1856, ret. before 1861; inventor form of shoe that could be sewed, 1857, also machine for sewing soles to uppers (essentially the modern process). Died Oct. 5, 1883.

BLAKE, Thomas Holdsworth, congressman, lawyer; b. Calvert County, Md., June 14, 1792; attended public schs.; studied law, Washington, D.C. Mem. D.C. Militia which took part in Battle of Bladensburg, 1814; moved to Ky., later to Ind.; admitted to bar; practiced in Terre Haute, Ind.; pros. atty. and judge circuit court; discontinued law practice, became businessman; mem. Ind. Ho. of Reps.; mem. U.S. Ho. of Reps. (Adams Republican) from Ind., 20th Congress, 1827-29; apptd. commr. Gen. Land Office by Pres. Tyler, 1842-45; chosen pres. Erie & Wabash Canal Co.; visited Eng. as financial agt. of State of Ind., died while returning home. Died Cincinnati, Nov. 28, 1849; buried Woodlawn Cemetery, Terre Haute.

BLAKE, William Rufus, actor; b. Halifax, N.S., Can., 1805; no formal edn.; m. Caroline Placide Waring, Aug. 26, 1826. Made 1st appearance in U.S. in comedy Poor Gentleman, N.Y.C., 1824; mgr. Tremont Theater, Boston, 1827-29, Walnut Street Theater, Phila., 1829, Mitchell's Olympic Theater, N.Y.C., 1837; specialized in comedy roles; noted for his performance of Dornton in The Road to Ruin; stage mgr. Broadway Theater, N.Y.C., 1848; mem. Burton's and Wallack's stock companies in 1840's and 1850's; ret., 1863. Died probably N.Y.C., Apr. 22, 1863.

BLAKELY, Johnston, naval officer; b. Seaford, Ireland, Oct. 1781; s. John Blakely; attended U. N.C., 1797; m. Jane Hoope, Dec. 1813, 1 child. Apptd. midshipman U.S. Navy, 1800, promoted lt., 1807, master comdt., 1813, capt., 1814; participated in Tripolitan War; commanded in Enterprise, 1811-13, Wasp, 1813-14; destroyed Brit. ship Reindeer, 1814, captured Atalanta, 1814; received gold medal and thanks of Congress for triumph over Reindeer, 1814. Died at sea, Oct. 1814.

BLANC, Antoine, clergyman; b. Sury, France, Oct. 11, 1792. Ordained priest Roman Catholic Ch., 1816; apptd. vicar-gen., 1831; consecrated bishop of Diocese which included states La. and Miss., 1835, later included Tex., 1838; 1st archbishop of New Orleans, 1851-60; one of Am. dels to Rome when dogma of Immaculate Conception was proclaimed, 1855; founder Sisters of Holy Family (1st Negro sisterhood in U.S.). Died New Orleans, June 20, 1860; buried St. Louis Cathedral.

BLANCHARD, John, congressman, lawyer; b. Peacham Twp., Caledonia County, Vt., Sept. 30, 1787; grad. Dartmouth, 1812; studied law. Moved to Pa., settled in York, York County, 1812; taught sch.; admitted to bar, 1815; practiced in Lewistown, Mifflin County, Pa.; moved to Bellefonte, Pa., 1815, practiced law; mem. U.S. Ho. of Reps. (Whig) from Pa., 29th-30th congresses, 1845-49. Died Columbia, Lancaster County, Pa., Mar. 9, 1849; buried Union Cemetery, Bellefonte.

BLANCHARD, Jonathan, Continental congressman; b. Dunstable, N.H., Sept. 18, 1738; attended public schs. Chosen mem. Council of 12, 1775; del. 5th Provincial Congress, 1775; served in 1st N.H. Ho. of Reps., 1776; apptd. N.H. atty. gen. 1777; mem. Com. of Safety, 1777, 78; a commr. from N.H. to conv. at New Haven (Conn.) to regulate prices, 1778; mem. Continental Congress from N.H., 1783, 84, 87; 1st gen. of Militia, 1784-88. Died Dunstable, July 16, 1788; buried Old South Burying Ground, Dunstable (now merged into Nashua, N.H.).

BLANCHARD, Jonathan, clergyman, coll. pres.; b. Rockingham, Vt., Jan. 19, 1811; s. Jonathan and Maryy (Lovel) B.; grad Middlebury Coll., 1832; m. Mary Bent, 1838, 12 children including Charles Albert. Ordained pastor Sixth Presbyn. Ch., Cincinnati,

1838; attended World Anti-Slavery Conv., London, Eng.; 1843; founder, editor church newspaper Herald and Presbyter; pres. Knox Coll., Galesburg, Ill., 1845-57; founder, editor Christian Era, 1858; pres. Wheaton (Ill.) Coll., 1860-82, pres. emeritus, 1882-92. Died Wheaton, May 14, 1892.

BLANCHARD, Thomas, inventor; b. Sutton, Mass., June 24, 1788; s. Samuel and Susanna (Tenney) B. Invented machine that could produce 500 tacks per minute, 1806; devised a lathe which performed 2 different operations (turned rifle barrels externally and when breech was reached, cut both flat and oval portions); with Springfield (Mass.) Arsenal, 5 years; patented machine which could produce various irregular forms from a single pattern, 1820; invented steam-wagon, 1825; unsuccessfully promoted co. to build railroads, 1826; patented steamboat which was able to ascend rivers against strong currents and rapids, 1831; developed heavy timber-bending process, 1851. Died Boston, Apr. 16, 1864.

BLANCHET, Francois Norbert, clergyman; b. Que., Can., Sept. 3, 1795; s. Pierre and Rosalie Blanchet; attended Sulpician Major Sem., 1816-19. Missionary among Acadians and Micmac Indians, N.B., Can., 1821-28; rector of parish The Cedars, Can., 1829; vicar gen. Ore. Territory, 1838; vicar apostolic and titular bishop Ore. Territory, 1843-81; 1st archbishop See of Oregon City, 1846-81; del. 1st U.S. Plenary Council, Balt.; visited S. Am. to raise funds, 1856; del. Ecumenical Council, Rome, 1870; built St. Michael's Coll., 1871; known as Apostle of Ore. Author: Fiftieth Jubilee Sermon, 1869; Letters on Catholic Indian Missions Together with Reply of Secretary of Interior, 1871; Historical Sketches of the Catholic Church in Oregon, 1878, 1910; Historical Notes and Reminiscences, 1883. Died June 18, 1883.

BLAND, Richard, continental congressman; b. Williamsburg, Va., May 6, 1710; s. Richard and and Elizabeth (Randolph) B.; grad. Coll. William and Mary, 1730; attended U. Edinburgh (Scotland); m. Anne Poythress; m. 2d, Martha Macon; m. 3d, Elizabeth Blair; 12 children. Mem. Va. Ho. of Burgesses from Prince George County, 1745-75, mem. com. to remonstrate with Parliament concerning taxation. leader, 1748; signer Non-Importation Agreement 1769; me., Va. Com. of Correspondence, 1773; del. from Va. to Continental Congress, 1774, 75. Author: Inquiry Into the Rights of British Colonies (1st published work stating colonial position on taxation), 1766. Died Williamsburg, Oct. 26, 1776, buried Jordan Point Plantation on James River, Va.

BLAND, Theodorick, army officer, congressman; b. Prince George County, Va., Mar. 21, 1742; s. Theodorick and Frances (Bolling) B.; M.D., U. Edinburgh (Scotland), 1763; m. Martha Dangerfield. Commd. capt. 1st troop Va. Cavalry 1776; commd. col. 1st Continental Dragoons, 1779; del. to Continental Congress from Va. 1780-83; mem. Va. Ho. of Dels., 1786-88; unsuccessful candidate for gov. Va., 1786; mem. Va. Conv. to ratify U.S. Constn., 1788, voted against ratification; mem. U.S. Ho. of Reps. from Va., 1st Congress, 1789-90. Died N.Y.C., June 1, 1790; buried Trinity Churchyard, N.Y.C.

BLAND, Thomas, naturalist; b. Newark, Eng., Oct. 4, 1809; s. Dr. Thomas and Mrs. (Shepard) B. Practiced law, London; moved to Barbados, 1842; moved to Jamaica, began study of fauna of W.I., 1849; supt. of gold mine, Marmato, New Granada (now Columbia), 1850; moved to N.Y.C., 1852; wrote 72 papers on Mollusca of U.S. and Antilles; fellow Royal Geol. Soc. of London; mem. Am. Philos. Soc. Author: (with William G. Binney) Land and Fresh Water Shells of North America, 1869. Died Aug. 20, 1885.

BLASDEL, Henry Goode, gov. Nev.; b. Dearborn County, Ind., Jan. 20, 1825; s. Jacob and Elizabeth Blasdel; m. Sarah Jane Cox, Dec. 9, 1845. Moved to Aurora, Ind., 1847; a produce mcht., also engaged in steamboat business, Aurora; in produce bus., San Francisco, then moved to Virginia City, Utah Territory, 1860; built Empire and Hoosier State Mills, Virginia City; 1st supt. Potosi mine; gov. Nev., 1864-70; resumed mining bus., after 1870. Died July 26, 1900; buried Mountain View Cemetery, Oakland, Nev.

BLATCHFORD, Richard Milford, laywer; diplomat; b. Stratford, Conn., Apr. 23, 1798; s. Samuel and Alicia (Windeatt) B.; grad. Union Coll., 1815; m. Julia Ann Munford, May 17, 1819; m. 2d, Angelica Hamilton, Nov. 8, 1860; m. 3d, Katherine Hone, Jan. 18, 1870; 1 son, Samuel. Admitted to N.Y. bar, 1820; apptd. counsel and financial agt. Bank of Eng. in U.S., 1826; elected mem. N.Y. Assembly, 1855; apptd. U.S. minister to States of the Ch., Rome, 1862; became commr. pub. parks N.Y.C., 1872. Died Newport, R.I., Sept. 4, 1875.

BLATCHFORD, Samuel, asso. justice U.S. Supreme Ct.; b. N.Y.C., Mar. 9, 1820; s. Richard and Julia (Mumford) B.; grad. Columbia, 1837; LL.D. (hon.), 1867; m. Caroline Appleton, Dec. 17, 1844. Pvt. sec. to William Seward (gov. N.Y.), 1837-41, mil. sec. on Seward's staff, 1841-43; admitted to bar, 1842; resident minister to States of Ch. of Rome, 1862-63; trustee Columbia, 1867-93; apptd. dist. judge dist. N.Y. by Pres. Grant, 1867; circuit judge 2d U.S. Jud. Dist., 1872; asso. justice U.S. Supreme Ct. (apptd. by Pres. Arthur), 1882-93. Died Newport, R.I., July 7, 1893.

BLAVATSKY, Helena Petrovna Hahn, leader philos. orgn.; b. Ekaterinoslav, Russia, July 30, 1831; d. Col. Peter and Helena Pavlovna (Fadeev) Hahn; m. Gen. Nikifor Vasilevich Blavatsky, July 7, 1848; m. 2d, M. C. Betanelly. Became spiritualist, Paris, France, 1858; practiced spiritualism, Cairo, Egypt, 1871; came to N.Y.C., 1873; founded Theosophical Soc. for purpose of studying Egyptian occultism, N.Y.C., 1875; went to India to spread theosophical movement, 1879-80; published the Theosophist; spread theosophism to Ceylon, 1880; established permanent hdqrs., Adyar, India, 1882; movement hindered by stories of trickery, 1883, movement investigated by Brit. Soc. for Phys. Research, 1884; sailed for Europe, 1884; founder Blavatsky Lodge, London, Eng., 1887; head European Theosophical Orgn., 1890. Author: Isis Unveiled, 1877; The Secret Doctrine, 1888; Voice of Silence, 1889; The Key to Theosophy, 1889; Nightmare Tales, 1892. Died May 8, 1891.

BLEDSOE, Albert Taylor, lawyer, journalist, educator. b. Frankfort, Ky., Nov. 9, 1809; s. Moses Ousley and Sophia (Taylor) B.; grad. U.S. Mil. Acad., 1830; m. Harriet Coxe, 1836, several children including Sophia (Bledsoe) Herrick. Adjunct prof. mathematics, instr. French, Kenyon Coll., Gambier, O., 1833-34; prof. mathematics Miami U., Oxford, O., 1835-36, U. Miss., 1848-54, U. Va., 1854-61; practiced law, Springfield, Ill., 1838-48; commd. col. Confederate States Army, 1861; apptd. asst. sec. war Confederacy, 1861; Confederate agt., London, Eng., 1861-65; founder, editor Southern Review, Balt., 1867-77, used magazine to try to keep lost cause of South alive; opposed reconciliation and all forms of Northern influence. Author: Examination of President Edwards' "Inquiry into the Freedom of the Will," 1845; A Theodicy; or Vindication of the Divine Glory, 1853; Essay on Liberty and Slavery, 1856; Is Davis a Traitor?; or Was Secession a Constitutional Right Previous to the War of 1861?, 1866. Died Alexandria, Va., Dec. 8, 1877.

BLEDSOE, Jesse, senator; b. Culpeper County, Va., Apr. 6, 1776; attended Transylvania Sem., Transylvania U., Lexington, Ky.; studied law, Lexinton. Admitted to bar, circa 1800; practiced law; apptd. sec. state under Gov. Charles Scott, 1808; mem. Ky. Ho. of Reps., 1812; mem. U.S. Senate from Ky., 1813-Dec. 24, 1814, resigned; mem. Ky. Senate, 1817-20; Democratic presdl. elector, 1820; judge Lexington circuit, 1822; settled in Lexington; prof. law Transylvania U.; minister Disciples Ch.; moved to Miss., 1833, to Tex., 1835; collector hist. material. Died nr. Nacogodoches, Tex., June 25, 1836.

BLEECKER, Ann Eliza, poet; b. N.Y.C., Oct. 1752; d. Brandt and Margareta (Van Wyck) Schuyler; m. John J. Bleecker, Mar. 29, 1769, at least 3 children including Margaretta V. Faugeres. Lived in frontier village of Tomhanick, N.Y.; often forced to flee home because of Indian attacks; poems appeared in N.Y. Mag.; poems published as The Posthumous Works of Ann Eliza Bleecker (collected by Margaretta Bleecker Faugeres), 1793. Died Tomhanick, Nov. 23, 1783.

BLEECKER, Harmanus, congressman, lawyer; b. Albany, N.Y., Oct. 9, 1779; studied law. Admitted to bar, 1801; practiced in Albany; mem. U.S. Ho. of Reps. (Federalist) from N..Y, 12th Congress, 1811-13; mem. N.Y. State Assembly, 1814, 15; regent U. State of N.Y., 1822-34; charge d'affaires to Netherlands, 1837-42. Died Albany, July 19, 1849; buried Rural Cemetery.

BLENKINSOP, Peter, educator; b. Dublin, Apr. 19, 1818; son of Peter Blenkinsop; brought to U.S. (Balt.), 1826; studied at Georgetown. Joined Soc. of Jesus, 1834; ordained priest Roman Catholic Ch., 1846; pres. Holy Cross Coll., 1854-57; taught at Georgetown, also St. Joseph's, Phila. Died Phila., Nov. 5, 1896.

BLENNERHASSETT, Harman, planter; b. Hampshire, Eng., Oct. 8, 1765; s. Conway and Miss (Lacy) B.; grad. Trinity Coll., Dublin, Ireland; m. Margaret Agnew, 1796. Admitted to Irish bar, 1790; came to U.S., 1796; owned estate on island in Ohio River, nr. Parkersburg, Va. (now O.), home became hdqrs. for Aaron Burr and his followers who planned to colonize Western lands and invade Mexico; island captured by Wood County (Va.) Militia, 1806; arrested after escape to Ky., charges dropped after Burr was found innocent, 1807; estate ruir by militia invasion, fire and floods; became cot planter in Miss.; practiced law, Montreal, Que., Ca 1819-22; returned to England, 1822. Died Gue sey, Eng., Feb. 2, 1831.

BLISS, Edwin Elisha, missionary; b. Putn Vt., Apr. 12, 1817; s. Henry and Abigail (Grou B.; grad. Amherst Coll., 1837; grad. Andover The Sem., 1842; m. Isabella Holmes Porter, Feb. 2 1843. Taught at Amherst Acad., 1838-40; (dained to ministry Congregational Ch., 18 sailed in ship Emma Isadora to Smyrna, Turk 1843; missionary, Trebizond, Turkey, 1843-5 Marsovan, Turkey, 1851-56; lived in Constantino 1856-92; editor Avedaper, Constantinople, 18 92. Author: Bible Handbook. Died Dec. 20, 18

BLISS, George, congressman; b. Jericho, V Jan. 1, 1813; attended Granville Coll.; studied la Admitted to bar, 1841; practiced in Akron, O apptd. presiding judge 8th Jud. Dist., 1850, serv until office discontinued, mem. U.S. Ho. of Re (Democrat) from Ohio, 33d, 38th congresse 1853-55, 63-65; moved to Wooster, O., practic law; del. Union Nat. Conv., Phila., 1866. Di Wooster, Oct. 24, 1868; buried Oak Hill Cemeter

BLISS, George, mcht., banker; b. Northampto Mass., Apr. 21, 1816; s. William and Martha (Pa sons) B.; m Catherine Sanford, 1840; m. 2d, A gusta H. Smith, July 22, 1868. Began as cl Harvey Sanford's dry-goods store, New Haven, 183 became partner, 1837; formed dry-goods fi Phelps, Chittenden & Bliss, N.Y.C., 1844, b came head of firm, changed name to Geor Bliss & Co., 1853; formed banking firm Morto Bliss & Co:, 1869. Died N.Y.C., Feb. 2, 189

BLISS, George, lawyer; b. Springfield, Mass May 3, 1830; s. George and Mary (Dwight) B grad. Harvard, 1851; m. Catherine Van Rennsele Dwight, Oct. 22, 1856; m. 2d, Anais Casey, M 25, 1887. Admitted to N.Y. bar, 1857; pvt. se to Gov. E.D. Morgan of N.Y. State, 1859; co paymaster N.Y. Militia, 1862; commd. capt. 4 N.Y. Heavy Arty.; atty. Bd. of Health and Met. B of Excise, N.Y.C., 1866-72; apptd. U.S. atty. f So. Dist. N.Y., 1872; drafted N.Y.C. Charter 1873; mem. of commn. drafting The Special a Local Laws Affecting Public Interests in the Ci of New York, 1879-80; helped draft New York Ci Consolidation Act, 1881. Died Wakefield, R. Sept. 2, 1897.

BLISS, Jonathan, jurist; b. Springfield, Mass. Oct. 1, 1742; s. Luke and Mercy (Ely) B.; gra Harvard, 1763; read law in office of Lt. Go William Hutchinson. Began law career in Bosto mem. Mass. Gen. Ct., 1768; supported Brit. poi of view during pre-revolutionary period; went Eng. because of Loyalist stand, 1775; atty. ge Province of New Brunswick, 1785; mem. N.B Assembly, 1785; chief justice N.B., 1809-22 Died Oct. 1, 1822.

BLISS, Philemon, congressman, jurist; b North Canton, Conn., July 28, 1814; s. Asahel an Lydia (Griswold) B.; m. Martha Sharp, 184 Admitted to Ohio bar, 1840; judge 14th Jud. Dist of Ohio, 1849-52; mem. U.S. Ho. of Reps. (Repub lican) from Ohio, 34th-35th congresses, 1855-5 chief justice Dakota Territory (helped organize th cts.), 1861; Mo. probate judge, 1864; mem. Bu chanan County (Mo.) Ct.; asso. justice Mo. Su preme Ct., 1868-72; prof. law Mo. State U., 1872 89, a founder Mo. State U. Law Sch., 1873, dean 1873-89: Died St. Paul, Minn., Aug. 24, 1889 buried Columbia, Mo.

BLISS, Phillip Paul, evangelist, song writer; b Clearfield County, Pa., July 9, 1838; s. Isaac an Lydia (Doolittle) B.; studied music at acad., Geneso N.Y.; m. Lucy J. Young, June 1, 1859. Worked o farms, in lumber camps and taught sch. durin youth; became mem. music publishing firm Root an Cady, Chgo., circa 1865; conducted musica convs., gave concerts throughout Ill.; became chor ister of 1st Congregational Ch. of Chgo.; evangelis (with D. W. Whittle) throughout West and South 1874-76; Author: (song books) The Charm, 1871 The Song Tree, 1872; The Sunshine, 1872; Th Joy, 1873; co-author: Gospel Songs, 1874. Die in train wreck, Dec. 29, 1876.

BLISS, Porter Cornelius, journalist; b. N.Y. Dec. 28, 1838; s. Rev. Asher and Cassandr (Hooker) B.; B.A., Hamilton Coll. Interested i Indian life, began working for a Boston soc. to in vestigate conditions of Indians in Me., N.B. an N.S.; clk. in Interior Dept., 1861; sec. to Jame Watson Webb, minister to Brazil, 1861-62; worke for Argentine govt., explored Grand Chaco region 1862-63, also edited River Plate Mag., Bueno Aires; pvt. sec. to Charles A. Washburn, ministe to Paraguay, 1866; commd. by Pres. Lopez t write history of Paraguay, 1866; arrested by Para guay on suspicions of his loyalty (after Paragua declared war on Brazil, Uruguay, Argentina) eventually released on demand of U.S. Govt.; becam translator for U.S. State Dept.; sec. to U.S.

gation in Mexico, 1870-74; became mem. Mexican Geog. and Statis. Soc., also sec. archeol. com.; editor Johnson's New Universal Cyclopedia, 1874-77; editor N.Y. Herald, 1878, S. Am. corr., 1879; participated in unsuccessful gold hunting expdn. to Mexico, 1881; editor New Haven Morning News, for a time. Author: (with L.P. Brockett) The Conquest of Turkey, 1878. Died Feb. , 1885.

BLITZ, Antonio, magician; b. England, June 21, 1810; m. Marie Blitz. Supposed to have learned magic tricks from Gypsies; made 1st profl. appearance in Hamburg, Germany, 1823; toured Europe, 1823-25; also learned ventriloquism; came to U.S., 1834; played N.Y.C., also toured U.S., Can. and West Indies; settled permanently in Phila.; had at least 13 imitators (who even used his name); became noted bird trainer. Author: Fifty Years in the Magic Circle (autobiography; most of records of his life taken from this), 1871. Died Phila., Jan. 28, 1877.

BLOCK, Adriaen, mariner, explorer. Made trip to Hudson River, 1610; in charge of Dutch exploring expdn. which went up Hudson River, 1614; explored N.Y. bay region, L.I. Sound, New Haven Harbor, Connecticut River, went to Buzzard's Bay, Cape Cod, as far North as Nahant Bay (gave all these places Dutch names), then returned to Holland; trip resulted in 1st detailed map of Southern New Eng. coast; engaged in whaling, 1615-24.

BLODGETT, Samuel, mcht., mfr.; b. Woburn, Mass., Apr. 1, 1724; s. Caleb and Sarah (Weyman) B.; m. Hannah White, 1748, 1 son Samuel. Served in French and Indian War; engaged in farming; became gen. mcht., Boston; later started mfg. potash and pearl-ash, extended operations to other Mass. towns; expanded into lumber business; 1st justice Inferior Ct. of Hillsborough County (Mass.); a sutler to Continental Army during Revolutionary War; engaged in constrn. of canal from Amoskeag Falls to Merrimac River, 1794-1806, completed with help of Mass. Legislature. Died Derryfield, Mass., Sept. 1, 1807.

BLODGETT, Samuel, mcht., speculator, architect; b. Goffstown, N.H., Aug. 28, 1757; s. Samuel and Hannah (White) B.; m. Rebecca Smith, 1792. Served as capt. N.H. Militia, 1775-77; became wealthy as East India mcht.; moved to Phila., 1789; dir. Ins. Co. of N.Am., 1792; designed bldg. for 1st Bank of U.S.; became interested in Washington (D.C.) real estate; supt. bldgs. under commrs. of Washington; engaged in lotteries in effort to promote devel. of city, caused him financial ruin; imprisoned for debt. Died Balt., Apr. 11, 1814.

BLONDEL, Jacob D., artist; b. N.Y.C., 1817; studied with William Paige, N.Y.C. Exhibited at Apollo Assn., 1839-41; frequent exhibitor at Am. Art-Union, N.A.D., Boston Athenaeum, Washington (D.C.) Art Assn.; resided in Washington, 1847-48; asso. N.A.D.; spent last years in poverty; name also spelled Blondell. Said to have starved to death in his studio, N.Y.C., 1877.

BLOODWORTH, Timothy, senator, Continental congressman; born in New Hanover County, North Carolina, 1736. Member New Hanover County Com. of Safety, 1775; mem. N.C. Legislature, 1779-84; mem. Continental Congress from N.C., 1784-87; opposed adoption of U.S. Constn.; mem. U.S. Senate from N.C., 1795-1801; collector of customs Port of Wilmington, 1807-14. Died Washington, D.C., Aug. 24, 1814.

BLOOM, Issac, congressman; b. Jamaica, N.Y., circa 1716. Moved to Dutchess County, N.Y., circa 1740; capt. minutemen of Charlotte precinct, Dutchess County, 1775; became mcht., 1784; mem. N.Y. State Assembly, 1788-92; del. N.Y. State Conv., 1801; mem. N.Y. State Senate, 1800-02; mem. U.S. Ho. of Reps. from N.Y., 8th Congress, Mar. 4-Apr. 26, 1803. Died Clinton, Dutchess County, Apr. 26, 1803; buried probably in Jamaica.

BLOOMER, Amelia Jenks, reformer; b. Homer, N.Y., May 27, 1818; d. Augustus and Lucy (Webb) Jenks; m. Dexter Bloomer, 1840. Started women's paper the Lily (1st paper of its kind published by a woman), 1849; wrote articles on edn., marriage laws, women's suffrage; known for style of dress reform for women, trousers of which became known as Bloomers. Died Council Bluffs, Ia., Dec. 30, 1894.

BLOOMFIELD, Joseph, gov. N.J., congressman; b. Woodbridge, N.J., Oct. 18, 1753; s. Dr. Moses and Sarah (Ogden) B.; m. Mary McIlvaine, Dec. 17, 1778; m. 2d, Isabella. Admitted to N.J. bar, 1774; commd. capt. Col. Elias Dayton's Regt., 1775; served as maj., judge adv. Northern Dept., Continental Army during Revolutionary War, 1776; clk. N.J. Assembly; register N.J. Ct. of Admiralty; atty. gen. N.J., 1783-88; presdl. elector, 1792; mayor Burlington (N.J.), 1795-1800; gov. N.J., 1801, 1805-12; Bloomfield Compilation of N.J. Laws named in his honor, 1811; apptd. brig. gen. U.S. Army by Pres. Madison, 1812; mem. U.S. Ho. of Reps. from N.J., 15th-16th congresses, 1817-21. Died Burlington, Oct. 3, 1823; buried Episcopal Churchyard, Bloomington.

BLOUNT, Thomas, congressman; b. Edgecombe County, N.C., May 10, 1759; s. Jacob and Barbara (Gray) B.; m. Jacky Sullivan Sumner. Enlisted in 5th N.C. Regt., Continental Army, 1776; taken prisoner by British, 1777, imprisoned in England until 1781; mem. N.C. Conv. to ratify U.S. Constn.; mem. N.C. Legislature, 1789-93; mcht., Tarboro, N.C.; mem. U.S. Ho. of Reps. (Democrat) from N.C., 3d-5th, 9th-10th, 12th congresses, 1793-99, 1805-09, 11-12. Died Washington, D.C., Feb. 7, 1812; buried Congressional Cemetery, Washington.

BLOUNT, William, senator; b. Bertie County, N.C., Mar. 26, 1749; s. Jacob and Barbara (Gray) B.; m. Mary Grainger, Feb. 12, 1778, 2 children. Paymaster N.C. Militia, 1777; mem. N.C. Ho. of Commons, 1780-84; mem. N.C. Senate, 1788-90; del. to Continental Congress, 1786-87; mem. U.S. Constl. Conv., 1787; signer U.S. Constn., 1787; mem. N.C. Conv. which ratified U.S. Constn., 1789; apptd. gov. (by Pres. Washington) territory south of Ohio River (Tenn.), 1790-95; supt. Indian Affairs, 1790-96; chmn. 1st Tenn. Constl. Conv., 1796; 1st mem. U.S. Senate from Tenn., Aug. 2, 1796-July 8, 1797, expelled for plotting with British to attack Spanish Fla. and La.; elected to Tenn. Legislature, 1798; pres. Tenn. Senate; Blount County (Tenn.) named after him. Died Knoxville, Tenn., Mar. 21, 1800; buried First Presbyn. Ch. Cemetery, Knoxville.

BLOUNT, William Grainger, congressman, lawyer; b. nr. New Bern, Craven County, N.C., 1784; s. William Blount; attended New Bern Acad.; studied law. Admitted to bar, 1805; practiced in Knoxville, Tenn., also became mcht.; mem. Tenn. Ho. of Reps., 1811; sec. state Tenn., 1811-15; mem. U.S. Ho. of Reps. (Democrat, filled vacancy) from Tenn., 14th-15th congresses, Dec. 8, 1815-19; moved to Paris, Henry County, Tenn., 1826, practiced law. Died Paris, May 21, 1827; buried City Cemetery.

BLOUNT, Willie, gov. Tenn., jurist; b. Bertie County, N.C., Apr. 18, 1768; s. Jacob and Hannah (Baker) B.; ed. Princeton and Columbia; m. Lucinda Baker, 1809. Represented Montgomery County in Tenn. provincial assemblies, 1794-95; judge Tenn. Superior Ct., 1796; mem. Tenn. Legislature, 1807-09; gov. Tenn., 1809-15; unsuccessful candidate for gov. against Sam Houston, 1827; del. Tenn. Constl. Conv., 1834; trustee Blount and Cumberland colls.; monument erected to him at Clarksville (Tenn.). Died Clarksville, Sept. 10, 1835.

BLOW, Henry Taylor, mfr., congressman, diplomat; b. Southampton County, Va., July 15, 1817; s. Peter and Elizabeth (Taylor) B.; grad. St. Louis U., 1835; m. Minerva Grimsley, 12 children. Pioneer in lead and lead products bus., St. Louis; instrumental in opening of large lead mines of Southwestern Mo.; pres. Iron Mountain R.R.; Whig; mem. Mo. Senate, 1854-58; del. to Republican Nat. Conv., 1860; apptd. U.S. minister to Venezuela by Pres. Lincoln, 1861; mem. U.S. Ho. of Reps. (Republican) from Mo., 38th-39th congresses, 1863-67; U.S. minister to Brazil, 1869-71; mem. bd. commrs. of D.C., 1874-75. Died Saratoga, N.Y., Sept. 11, 1875; buried Bellefontaine Cemetery, St. Louis.

BLOWERS, Sampson Salter, jurist, Loyalist; b. Boston, Mar. 10, 1742; s. John and Sarah (Salter) B.; grad. Harvard, 1763; studied law under Lt. Gov. William Hutchinson; m. Sarah Kent, 1774. Admitted to Mass. bar, 1766, practiced in Boston; one of 3 defense attys. in trial of Brit. soldiers in aftermath of Boston Massacre; supported royal govt., went to England, 1774; returned to Boston, 1778, arrested because of his Loyalist stand; in Nova Scotia (Can.) after release from prison, 1778-79; apptd. judge R.I. Ct. of Vice Admiralty, Newport, 1779; went to England on Brit. evacuation of Newport, 1779; solicitor gen. for N.Y., 1779-83; forced to flee to N.S., 1783; atty. gen. N.S., 1784; speaker N.S. Ho. of Reps., 1785-88; mem. N.S. Legislative Council, 1788-97; chief justice N.S., 1797-1833. Died Halifax, N.S., Oct. 25, 1842.

BLUNT, Edmund March, hydrographer; b. Portsmouth, N.H., June 20, 1770; s. William and Elizabeth (March) B.; m. Sally Ross, 1793, 2 children George William, Edmund. Co-publisher Impartial Herald, Newburyport, Mass., 1793-96, also owned bookstore during same period; published L. Furlon's The American Coast Pilot, 1796, editor all subsequent editions, from this time on published only nautical works including charts and maps made in his office; later continued business in N.Y.C. Died Sing Sing (now Ossining), N.Y., Jan. 4, 1862.

BLUNT, George William, hydrographer; b. Newburyport, Mass., Mar. 11, 1802; s. Edmund March and Sally (Ross) B.; m. Martha Garsett, 1821. Ran away from home to serve on mcht. ships, 1816-21; started publishing business with his brother E. & G. W. Blunt, N.Y.C., 1821, specialized in nautical works, edited many of publications, firm became large producer of charts; U.S. Hydrographic Office started mainly with purchases from his firm; served on Am. Bd. Pilot Commrs. for long period; U.S. commr. of immigration, 1852-54. Died N.Y.C., Apr. 19, 1878.

BLUNT, James Gillpatrick, physician, army officer; b. Trenton, Me., July 21, 1826; M.D., Starling Med. Coll., Columbus, O., 1849; m. Nancy Carson Putnam. Served in various mcht. ships, 1841-46; practiced medicine, New Madison, O., 1849-56; moved to Kan., 1856, practiced medicine, also became involved in anti-slavery movement; a friend of John Brown, helped slaves escape to Canada; mem. anti-slavery conv. which drew up Kan. Constn., 1859, chmn. militia com.; lt. col. 3d Kan. Volunteers, U.S. Army, 1861; promoted brig. gen. U.S. Volunteers with command of Dept. of Kan., 1862; took command Army of Frontier after defeating Confederates with their Indian allies at Battle of Old Ft. Wayne (Mo.); promoted maj. gen., 1862; fought on Ark.-Kan.-Mo. frontier throughout war, helped to keep Kan. and Mo. from being captured by Confederate forces; left U.S. Army, 1865, practiced medicine, Leavenworth, Kan.; solicitor of claims, Washington, D.C., 1869-71; indicted by U.S. Govt. as member of a conspiracy to defraud govt. and band of Cherokee Indians, 1873, charges dismissed by U.S. Dist. Ct., 1875. Died July 25, 1881.

BLUNT, John S., artist; b. probably Portsmouth, N.H., 1798; married. Painted landscapes, marine, paintings, portraits and miniatures, Portsmouth; probably visited N.Y.C., circa 1823, painted Picknick on Long Island; exhibited at Boston Athenaeum, 1829, 31; worked in Boston, 1830. Died on board ship traveling between New Orleans and Boston, 1835.

BLYTHE, David Gilmour, artist; b. nr. East Liverpool, O., May 9 ,1815. Apprenticed to a wood carver, Pitts., 1832-35; wood carver, carpenter, house painter, Pitts., 1835-36; went to New Orleans, 1836; served as ship's carpenter U.S. Navy, 1837-40; became itinerant portrait painter in Western Pa. and Eastern Ohio, 1841-45; settled in Uniontown, Pa., 1846-51; toured with a panorama to Cumberland (Md.) and Balt., Pitts., Cincinnati, East Liverpool; carved statue of Lafayette for county courthouse, Uniontown; painted portraits in Western Pa., 1852-55; visited Ind., 1853; spent last years in Pitts., 1855-65. Died Passavant Hospital, Pitts., May 15, 1865; buried East Liverpool.

BOARDMAN, Elijah, senator; b. New Milford, Conn., Mar. 7, 1760; ed. pvt. tutors; at least 1 son, William Whiting. Served in Col. Charles Webb's Regt. in Revolutionary War; clk. in merc. establishment; became mcht., 1781-1812; mem. Conn. Ho. of Reps., 1803-05, 16; mem. N.Y. State Upper House, 1817, 18; mem. N.Y. State Senate, 1819-21; mem. U.S. Senate (Democrat) from Conn., 1821-Oct. 8, 1823. Died Boardman, O., Oct. 8, 1823; buried Center Cemetery, Mew Milford.

BOARDMAN, Henry Augustus, clergyman; b. Troy, New York., Jan. 9, 1808; grad. Yale, 1829; attended Princeton Theol. Sem., 1830-33. Licensed to preach by N.Y. Presbytery, 1833; ordained to ministry Presbyn. Ch., 1833; pastor 10th Presbyn. Ch., Phila., 1833-76, pastor emeritus, 1876-80; bd. dirs. Princeton Sem., 1835-80. Author works including: The Scripture Doctrine of Original Sin, 1839; The Bible in the Family, 1851; The Book, 1861; A Handful of Corn, 1885. Died Phila., June 15, 1880.

BOARDMAN, Thomas Danforth, pewterer; b. Litchfield, Conn., Jan. 21, 1784; s. Oliver and Sarah (Danforth) B.; m. Elizabeth Bidwell Lewis, May 28, 1812. Apprenticed to pewterer, Hartford, Conn.; began pewter craft, Hartford, circa 1807; later entered into partnership with his brother; among his works still in existence is flagon 13½" high. Died Sept. 10, 1873.

BOARDMAN, William Whiting, congressman, lawyer; b. New Milford, Conn., Oct. 10, 1794; s. Elijah Boardman; attended Bacon Acad., Colchester, Conn.; grad. Yale, 1812; studied law, Cambridge, Litchfield law schs. Practiced law, New Haven, Conn., 1819; clk. Conn. Senate, 1820; judge of probate; mem. Conn. Ho. of Reps., 1836-39, 45, 49, 51, speaker, 1836, 39, 45; mem. U.S. Ho. of Reps. (Whig, filled vacancy) from Conn., 26th-27th congresses, Dec. 7, 1840-43. Died New Haven, Aug. 27, 1871; buried Grove Street Cemetery.

BOCKEE, Abraham, congressman, lawyer; b. Shekomeko, Dutchess County, N.Y., Feb. 3, 1784; grad. Union Coll., Schenectady, N.Y., 1803; studied law, Poughkeepsie, N.Y. Admitted to bar, 1806; practiced in Poughkeepsie until 1815; returned to Shekomeko, became farmer; mem. N.Y.

State Assembly, 1820, 40-44; mem. U.S. Ho. of Reps. (Jackson Democrat) from N.Y., 21st, 23d-24th congresses, 1829-31, 33-37; elected judge Ct. of Errors, 1843; 1st judge Dutchess County Ct., 1846. Died Shekomeko, June 1, 1865; buried on his estate nr. Shekomeko.

BOCOCK, Thomas S., congressman; b. Buckingham County, Va., May 18, 1815; s. John Thomas and Mary (Flood) B.; grad. Hampden-Sydney Coll., 1838; m. Sarah Flood; m. 2d, Annie Faulkner; 1 child. Mem. Va. Gen. Assembly, 1842-45; pros. atty. Appomattox County (Va.), 1845-46; mem. U.S. Ho. of Reps. from Va. 30th-36th congresses, 1847-61; Va. del. to Provisional Congress, Confederate States Am., 1861; speaker Confederate Ho. of Reps., 1st, 2nd congresses; mem. Va. Gen. Assembly, 1869-70; del. to Democratic Nat. Conv., 1868, 76, 80, presiding officer Va. convs.; atty. for 3 railroads; collected one of largest pvt. libraries in Va. Died Appomattox County, Aug. 20, 1891.

BODEN, Andrew, congressman; b. Carlisle, Cumberland County, Pa.; attended public schs.; studied law. Admitted to bar; practiced law, also engaged in real estate business; mem. U.S. Ho. of Reps. from Pa., 15th-16th congresses, 1817-21. Died Carlisle, Dec. 20, 1835.

BODLE, Charles, congressman; b. nr. Poughkeepsie, N.Y., 1787. Became wagon maker; justice of peace; held several polit. offices in Bloomingburg, Sullivan County, N.Y., 1833-35; mem. U.S. Ho. of Reps. from N.Y., 23d Congress, 1833-35. Died N.Y.C., Oct. 31, 1835; buried Bloomingburg Cemetery.

BODMER, Karl, artist, engraver; born Riesbach, Switzerland, Feb. 6, 1809. Accompanied Maximilian (Prince of Wied-Neuvied) on a tour of U.S., 1832-34; made sketches of landscapes, views of towns, portraits, studies of equipment, numerous Indian studies (formed basis for plates in Maximilian's Travels). Died Barbizon, France, Oct. 30, 1893.

BOEHLER, Peter, clergyman; b. Frankfurt-am-Main, Germany, Dec. 31, 1712; s. John Conrad and Antonetta Elizabetha (Hanf) B.; attended U. Jena (Germany); m. Elizabeth Hobson, Feb. 20, 1742. Magister legens U. Jena, 1736; converted to Moravian Ch.; became Moravian missionary to Am., 1738; went to Ga., 1738, went to Pa. with group of Moravians, 1739; returned to Europe to organize another group of Moravian settlers, 1741; preached in Am., made another trip to Europe; consecrated bishop English Moravian Ch., 1748; leader Bethlehem Moravian community, 1753-64; recognized leader Am. br. of Moravian Ch. Died Eng., Apr. 27, 1775; buried Moravian Cemetery, Chelsea, Eng.

BOEHM, Henry, clergyman; b. Lancaster County, Pa., June 8, 1775; s. Martin and Eve (Steiner) B. Became itinerant preacher of Methodist Ch.; preached in both German and English; held no ofcl. church offices, preferred to be traveling preacher in Am. frontier communities. Died Dec. 28, 1875.

BOEHM, John Philip, clergyman; b. Hochstadt, Germany, 1683; s. Philip Ludwig and Maria B.; m. Anna Maria Stehler; m. 2d, Anna Maria Scherer. Schoolmaster of German Reformed congregation, Worms, 1708-15, Lambsheim, 1715-20; came to Pa.; founded German Reformed Ch. in Pa.; Rev. George Micheal Weiss attempted to take over his duties because he had not yet been ordained; ordained on appeal to Europe, 1729; elected pres. The Coetus of Pa., 1747. Author: Getreuer Warnungsbrief an die Hochteutsche Evangelisch Reformirten Gemeinden und alle deren Glieder in Pennsylvanien (an effort to prevent his Church from being joined to Moravian Ch.), 1742. Died Hellertown, Pa., Apr. 29, 1749.

BOEHM, Martin, clergyman; b. Lancaster County, Pa., Nov. 30, 1725; s. Jacob Boehm; m. Eve Steiner, 1753; 1 son, Henry. Chosen Mennonite preacher, 1756; bishop of Mennonite Ch.; 1759, later excluded from Mennonite communion on grounds of his liberalism and unorthodox point of view; founder (with William Otterbein) Ch. of United Brethren in Christ, 1800, chosen bishop (with Otterbein) at 1st ann. conf., 1800; became affiliated with Methodist Ch. (without leaving Ch. of United Brethren in Christ), 1802. Died Mar. 23, 1812.

BOELEN, Jacob, silversmith; b. Netherlands, circa 1654; m. Catharine Klock, May 21, 1679, at least 1 son, Henricus. Came to Am. with parents, circa 1659; engaged as silversmith, had shop with his brother, later his son in N.Y.C.; became freeman of N.Y.C., 1698, a city assessor, 1685-94, alderman, 1695-1701; known mainly for quality of his work, many pieces survive today. Died 1729.

BOERUM, Simon, Continental congressman; b. New Lots (now Bklyn.), L.I., N.Y., Feb. 29, 1724; grad. Dutch sch., Flatbush, N.Y. Became farmer and miller; apptd. clk. Kings County by Gov. Clinton, 1750-75, also clk. bd. suprs. until 1775; mem. Colonial Assembly, 1761-75; dep. provincial Conv., 1775; mem. Continental Congress from N.Y., 1775. Died Bklyn., July 11, 1775; buried Glenwood Cemetery.

BOGARDUS, Everardus, clergyman; b. Woerden, Netherlands, 1607; s. Willem Bogardus; attended U. Leyden (Holland), 1626-30; m. Anneke Jans, 1638. Ordained to ministry Dutch Reformed Ch., 1632; apptd. minister to New Netherland colony, 1632; involved in conflict with colony's public prosecutor and dir. gen. Wouter van Twiller; succeeded in having public prosecutor Lubbert van Dincklagen excommunicated, 1640, also criticized policies of new dir. gen. Kieft; set sail with Kieft for Amsterdam to present their respective cases to classis of Amsterdam, ship wrecked off Southern coast of Wales. Died at sea, Sept. 27, 1647.

BOGARDUS, James, inventor; b. Catskill, N.Y., Mar. 14, 1800; s. James and Martha (Spencer) B.; m. Margaret Maclay, Feb. 12, 1831. Awarded gold medals Am. Inst. N.Y. for 8-day, 3-wheeled chronometer clock, 1828, for invention of dry gas meter, 1835; won award for engraving machine and new method of making postage stamps, 1839; introduced cast-iron usage for frames, floors and all bldg. supports; built Bogardus Bldg. (1st all cast iron bldg. in world), 1850; designer Balt. Sun Bldg., Birch Bldg. Chgo., Pub. Ledger Bldg., Phila.; made numerous improvement in manufacture of tools and machinery. Died N.Y.C., Apr. 13, 1874.

BOGART, William Henry, author; b. Albany, N.Y., Nov. 28, 1810; s. Gerrit and Margaret (Nexun) B. Admitted to N.Y. bar, 1832; mem. N.Y. Legislature, 1840. Author works including: Life of Daniel Boone, 1856; Who Goes There?, 1866. Died Aurora, N.Y., Aug. 21, 1888.

BOGGS, Charles Stuart, naval officer; b. New Brunswick, N.J., Jan. 28, 1811; s. Robert Morris and Mary (Lawrence) B.; m. Sophia Dore, Dec. 4, 1832; m. 2d, Henrietta (Molt) Bull, Apr. 8, 1875. Apptd. midshipman U.S. Navy, 1826; served against North African Pirates passed midshipman, 1832; master ship-of-line North Carolina, 1836; became acting lt., 1836, lt., 1837; served on sloop Saratoga against African slave trade; participated in Mexican War; promoted comdr., 1855; participated in capture of New Orleans under David Farragut, 1862; promoted capt. for bravery; commanded steamer Connecticut, 1866; promoted rear adm., 1870; commanded European fleet, 1871-72; ret., 1872. Died Apr. 22, 1888.

BOGGS, Lillburn W., gov. Mo.; b. Lexington, Ky., Dec. 14, 1792; s. John M. and Martha (Oliver) B.; m. Julia Bent, circa 1816; m. 2d, Panthea Grant Boone, 1823. Went to St. Louis, 1816; bank cashier and store keeper, later became trapper and Indian trader; mem. Mo. Senate, 1826-32, 42-46; lt. gov. Mo., 1833-37, gov., 1837-41, adminstrn. noted for charter of bank of Mo., 1st state sch. law, new state capitol bldg., expulsion of Mormons from Mo.; moved to Cal., 1846; mil. alcalde in Cal. after Am. conquest. Died Napa Valley, Cal., Mar. 14, 1860.

BOGGS, William Brenton, artist; b. New Brunswick, N.J., July 2, 1809; attended Capt. Partridge's Mil. Sch., Middletown, Conn.; m. Eleanor Carter, 1842. Employed by Phoenix Bank, N.Y.C.; exhibited landscapes of N.Y., N.J. and N.H. at N.A.D., 1839-41, 44; asso. N.A.D., 1842-45; became civilian clk. Navy Dept., Washington, D.C.; commd. purser U.S. Navy, 1852, served on ship Vincennes with Pacific Surveying Expdn., 1852-56; on spl. duty, Washington, 1856; with ship Plymouth, 1857-59, Wyoming, 1859-61; with Bur. of Provisions, 1862; purchasing pay master with spl. duty Miss. Squadron, Western Flotilla, 1862-64; injured while rescuing books and papers from a fire on board ship Mound City, 1864; stationed in Washington, 1864-73, became pay dir., 1871; exhibited at 1st Annual Exhbn., Washington Art Assn., 1857, N.A.D.; asso. N.A.D.; represented at Corcoran Gallery, Washington. Died Georgetown, D.C., Mar. 11, 1875.

BOGLE, James, artist; b. Georgetown, S.C., circa 1817. Painted in Charleston, 1840-41, 43, Balt., 1842, N.Y.C., 1843-73; exhibited at N.A.D., became mem., 1861; exhibited at Washington (D.C.) Art Assn. Died Bklyn., Oct. 12, 1873.

BOGY, Lewis Vital, senator; b. Ste. Genevieve, Mo., Apr. 9, 1813; s. Joseph and Marie (Beauvois) B.; grad. Transylvania U., Lexington, Ky., 1835; m. Pelagie Pratte. Practiced law, St. Louis, 1836-61; mem. St. Louis Bd. Aldermen, 1838; mem. Mo. Ho. of Reps., 1840, 41, 54, 55; U.S. commr. of Indian affairs, 1867-68; pres. St. Louis City Council, 1872; acting pres. St. Louis and Iron Mountain Ry.; mem. U.S. Senate (Democrat) from Mo., 1873-Sept. 20, 1877. Died St. Louis, Sept. 20, 1877; buried Calvary Cemetery, St. Louis.

BOHLEN, Diedrich A., architect; children include Oscar. Settled in Indpls., 1851, began archtl. career in office of Francis Costigan; helped design original Asylum for the Blind (now site of War Meml. Indpls.; opened office, practiced independent until 1884, established firm D.A. Bohlen & So 1884, sr. partner; architect numerous pub. bldgs Indpls., including Tomilson Hall and Market, St. Vi cent's Hosp. (original bldg.; now known as Trans Bldg.), Convent of Little Sisters of the Poor; d signed bldgs. at Oldenburg Acad., Convent a Chapel of St. Mary-of-the-Woods, (both Ohio Died Apr. 15, 1890.

BOHUNE, Lawrence, physician. First physici gen. of London Co. in Va., 1620-22; imported fru trees and seed to Va.; partner of James Smith transporting colonists to Va. Killed in sea batt with Spanish in West Indies, Mar. 30, 1622.

BOKEE, David Alexander, congressman, mcht b. N.Y.C, Oct. 6, 1805; attended public schs studied law. Admitted to bar, practiced law; pre Bklyn. Bd. Alderman, 1840-43, 45-48; men N.Y. State Senate, 1846-49; trustee N.Y. Li Ins. Co., 1848-60; mem. U.S. Ho. of Reps. (Whig from N.Y., 31st Congress, 1849-51; naval offic of customs (apptd. by Pres. Fillmore) Port of N.Y 1851-53; became shipping mcht. Died Washingtor D.C., Mar. 15, 1860; buried Greenwood Cemetery Bklyn.

BOKER, George Henry, author, diplomat; b Phila., Oct. 6, 1823; son of Charles Boker; grad Coll. of N.J. (now Princeton), 1842; m. Julia Mar deville Riggs, 1844, at least 1 son, George. Poet playwright, Phila.; a founder Union League of Phila. 1862, sec., 1862-71, pres., 1878; U.S. minister t Turkey, 1871-75; E.E. and M.P. to Russia, 1875-78 pres. Philadelphia Club, 1878, Fairmount Par Commn., 1886-90. Author: (plays) Calaynos, 1848 Anne Boleyn, 1850, The Betrothal, 1850, Th World a Mask, 1851, The Widow's Marriage, Leono de Guzman, 1853, Francesca da Rimini, 1855, Ny dia, 1885, Glaucus, 1886; (poems) A Lesson c Life, 1848, Plays and Poems, 1856, Poems of th War, 1864, Königsmark, The Legend of th Hounds, and Other Poems, 1869. Died Phila., Jan 2, 1890.

BOLIVAR, Simón, liberator; b. Caracas, Venezuela, July 24, 1783; s. Juan Vicente and Mari Concepcion (Palacios y Sojo) Bolivar y Ponte; ed in Europe; m. Miss Toro, 1801. Visited U.S., 1809 saw for 1st time workings of free instns.; on returr home became asso. with independence movement anc fought successfully for liberation of Colombia, Peru, Bolivia; pres. Colombia, 1821-27, 28-30; perpetual protector of Bolivia, 1825-26, pres., 1826; statue erected to him in Bogota, Colombia, 1846, Lima, Peru, 1858, N.Y.C., 1884. Died San Pedro, Colombia, Dec. 17, 1830; buried San Pedro; reinterred Caracas, 1842.

BOLL, Jacob, geologist, naturalist; b. Bremgarten, Canton Aargau, Switzerland, May 29, 1828; s. Henry and Magdalena (Peier) B.; attended U. Jena; m. Henriette Humbel, 1854. Owned pharmacy, Bremgarten, 1854-74; studied natural history of Canton Aargau; visited Tex., 1869-70, collected specimens for Louis Agassiz; studied geology and natural history of Tex., 1874-80; collected fossils and reptiles in North and N.W. Tex.; employed by U.S. Entomol. Commn. for study of Rocky Mountain locust, 1877-80; commd. by Canton Aargau to collect specimens of Colo. potato beetle, seeds of woody plants, fresh water and marine mollusks of Tex. Died Wilbarger County, Tex., Sept. 29, 1880.

BOLLAN, William, lawyer, colonial agt.; b. England, 1710; studied law under Robert Auchmutz; m. Frances Shirley, Sept. 19, 1743, 1 dau., Frances Shirley. Practiced law, Boston, circa 1732-45; advocate gen. of Mass., 1743-45; Mass. agt. to London (Eng.) to secure remuneration for expenses of Louisburg expdn., 1745-62; London agt. for Mass. Council, 1762-69; opposed attempt to alter Mass. charter, 1749, order against erecting slitting mills, 1750, and act forbidding issue paper money, 1751, proposed conciliatory measures, 1775. Died London, May 24, 1782.

BOLLES, Frank, univ. ofcl., nature writer; b. Winchester, Mass., Oct. 31, 1856; s. John A. and Catherine (Dix) B.; grad. Harvard Law Sch., 1882; m. Elizabeth Quincy Swan, Oct. 1884, 4 children. Founder, 1st pres. Harvard Coop. Soc.; mem. editorial staff Boston Advertiser; sec. to Pres. Charles Eliot of Harvard, 1886-87, univ. sec., 1887-94; founder Harvard Grads. Mag.; established univ. loans and employment agy. for needy students; studied nature on his farm in N.H. Author: The Land of the Lingering Snow, 1891; At the North of Bearcamp Water, 1893; From Blomidon to Smoky, and Other Papers, 1894; Chocorua's Tenants, 1895. Died Boston, Jan. 10, 1894.

BOLLMAN, Justus Erich, adventurer; b. Hoya, Hanover, Germany, 1769; studied medicine, U. Göttingen (Germany). Attempted to rescue Maruis de Lafayette from Austrian prison, 1792, imprisoned, later released on condition that he leave Austria; came to U.S., 1796; served as U.S. consul at Rotterdam, comml. agt. at Santo Domingo, Indian agt., Natchitoches, La.; became agt. of Aaron Burr, 1805; attempted to promote settlement of Bastrop land grant; arrested at New Orleans, 1806, freed by decision of Chief Justice John Marshall, 1807; testified as witness for defense at Burr's treason trial, 1807; went to England, 1816. Died Jamaica, B.W.I., Dec. 9, 1821.

BOLOTOV, Ivan Il'ich, missionary; b. Strazhkoo, Russia, on February 4, 1761; s. Il'ia Bolotov; attended Tver and Yaroslav sems. Became Russian Orthodox monk, 1786; chief of mission with rank of archimandrite, Kodiak Island, 1793; ordained bishop of Kodiak at Irkutsk, 1799; his efforts were 1st towards Christianizing Alaska and Aleutians. Drowned en route to Kodiak, Nov. 1799.

BOLTON, Abby, artist; b. Henley-on-Thames, Eng., Feb. 3, 1827; d. Rev. Robert Bolton. Came to Am. with family, 1836; lived at Pelham, N.Y., 1839-49; exhibited a flower painting at N.A.D., 1845. Died Pelham, June 16, 1849.

BOLTON, John, architect, clergyman; b. Bath, Eng., Feb. 7, 1818; s. Rev. Robert Bolton; at least 1 dau., Abby. Came to Am. with family, 1836; became an architect; ordained priest Protestant Episcopal Ch., 1862; rector Ch. of Holy Trinity, West Chester, Pa., 1864-91; dean of Chester, 1891-98; collaborated with brother William Jay Bolton in stained glass and wood carvings, examples of which are now in Christ Ch. and Pelham (N.Y.) Priory, Ch. of Holy Trinity, Bklyn. Died 1898.

BOLTON, Sarah Tittle Barrett, poet; b. Newport, Ky., Dec. 18, 1814; d. Jonathan Belcher and Esther (Pendleton) Barrett; m. Nathaniel Bolton, Oct. 1831; m. 2d, Addison Reese, Sept. 15, 1863; 2 children including Adah (Bolton) Mann. Contbd. poems to newspapers in Madison, Ind., and Cincinnati; operated dairy for 1st husband nr. Indpls.; writings include: Paddle Your Own Canoe; Poems, 1865; The Life and Poems of Sarah T. Bolton, 1880; Songs of a Life Time, 1892. Died Indpls., Aug. 4, 1893.

BOLTON, William Jay, artist, clergyman; b. Bath, Eng., Aug. 31, 1816; s. Rev. John Robert Bolton; attended Cambridge (Eng.) U. Came to Am. with family, 1836; studied painting at N.A.D.; Became asso. N.A.D.; designed and made stained glass; examples of work now in Christ Ch. and Pelham (N.Y.) Priory, Ch. of Holy Trinity, Bklyn.; went to Eng., circa 1845, opened glass-staining studio, Cambridge; ordained to ministry Anglican Ch., circa 1853; vicar of Stratford East, London, Eng., 1866-81, St. James' Ch., Bath, 1881-84. Died Bath, 1884.

BOLTZIUS, Johann Martin, clergyman; b. Dec. 26, 1703; grad. U. Halle (Germany); m. Miss Kroher, 3 children. Ordained pastor Lutheran Ch., 1733; led (with Israel Christian Gronau) party of Protestant refugees from Duchy of Salzburg to Ga., 1734; founded Town of Ebenezer (Ga.), 1734, chief pastor, 1734-65; founded Ebenezer Orphanage. Died Ebenezer, Nov. 19, 1765.

BOMBERGER, John Henry Augustus, clergyman, coll. pres.; b. Lancaster, Pa., Jan. 13, 1817; s. George and Mary (Hoffmeir) B.; grad. Marshlal Coll., 1837, Mercersburg Theol. Sem., 1838; m. Marian Huston, 1839; m. 2d, Julia Wight, 1863. Ordained to ministry German Reformed Ch., 1838; pastor Race Street Ch., Phila., 1854-70; a founder, founder, editor Reformed Ch. Monthly, 1868-76; 1st pres. Ursinus Coll., 1869-90; mem. Am. Tract Soc., Am. Bible Sco., Am. Sunday Sch. Union. Author: The Protestant Theological and Ecclesiastical Encyclopedia, 1858-60, Kurtz's Textbook of Church History, 2 vols., 1860-62. Died Collegeville, Pa., Aug. 19, 1890.

BOMFORD, George, army officer; b. N.Y.C., 1782; m. Miss Barlow. Apptd. cadet U.S. Army, 1804; commd. 2d lt. engrs., 1805; worked on fortifications in N.Y. Harbor and Chesapeake Bay, 1805-12; promoted 1st lt., 1806, capt., 1808, maj., 1812; assigned to ordnance dept., 1813; invented howitzer; lt. col. ordnance, 1815, col., 1832; chief ordnance U.S. Army, 1832-48; owned large estate "Kalorama" (famous meeting place of diplomats and govt. ofcls.), Washington, D.C.; lost fortune when cotton mill he owned failed. Died Boston, Mar. 25, 1848.

BONAPARTE, Charles Lucien, ornithologist; b. Paris, France, May 24, 1803; son of Lucien Bonaparte; nephew of Napoleon Bonaparte; ed. in Italy; married Zenaide (his cousin). Came to U.S. (Phila.), 1822; completed Wilson's Ornithology, (listing at least 100 species of birds he discovered), 1825-33; contbr. articles on ornithology to sci. journals; returned to Italy to continue studies, 1828; became prince of Canino and Musignano (upon death of his father), 1840; entered Italian politics, joined anti-papal faction, served as v.p. of republican assembly; fled Italy, 1848, settled in France, 1850; became dir. Jardin des Plantes, 1854. Author: Geographical and Comparative List of Birds of Europe and North America, 1838; several other studies, published 1827-58. Died Paris, July 29, 1857.

BONAPARTE, Charlotte Julie (comtesse de Survilliers), artist; d. Joseph Bonaparte (comte de Survilliers, ex-King of Spain). Lived with father on estate nr. Bordentown, N.J., 1819-28; exhibited at Pa. Acad., 1822, 23, 24; said to have designed 11 views which appeared in Joubert's Picturesque Views of American Scenery; painted portrait of Cora Monges, 1822 (now owned by Hist. Soc. Pa.). Died 1839.

BONAPARTE, Elizabeth Patterson, b. Balt., Feb. 6, 1785; d. William and Dorcas (Spear) Patterson; m. Jerome Napoleon Bonaparte (brother of Emperor Napoleon), Dec. 24, 1803 (divorced 1815), 1 son Jerome Napoleon. Marriage to Jerome not recognized by Emperor Napoleon, Jerome ordered to return to France alone; went to Europe with Jerome, 1805, banned from European soil, left Jerome at Lisbon to go to Eng. while Jerome went on to France where he was unsuccessful in influencing Napoleon to favor the marriage; Pope Pius VII would not annul their marriage, annulled by French council of state (Jerome then married Princess Catharine of Wüttemberg, became King of Westphalia); granted annual pension of 60,000 francs from Napoleon as long as she remained in Am. and gave up Bonaparte name; resided in Balt. until 1815; divorced from Jerome by act of Md. Legislature, 1815; lived in European society, 1815-40; returned to Balt., 1861. Died Balt., Apr. 4, 1879.

BONAPARTE, Jerome Napoleon, army officer; b. Balt., Nov. 5, 1830; s. Jerome Napoleon and Susan (Williams) B.; attended Harvard; grad. U.S. Mil. Acad., 1852; m. Caroline LeRoy (Appleton) Edgar. Served as 2d lt. Mounted Riflemen (now 3d Cavalry), U.S. Army, 1852-54; resigned commn., became 2d lt. French Army after outbreak of Crimean War, 1854, served in battles of Balaklava, Inkermann, 1854; decorated Legion of Honor; commd. capt. French Army, 1859, maj., 1865, lt. col., 1870; commanded a regt. Franco-Prussian War, 1870-71; lived in Am. after downfall of Napoleon III. Died Pride's Crossing, Mass., Sept. 3, 1893.

BONAPARTE, Louis Napoleon, emperor of France; b. Paris, France, Apr. 20, 1808; s. Louis and Hortense (de Beauharnais) B.; m. Eugénie de Montijo, Jan. 30, 1853, 1 son, Eugenè Louis Jean Joseph. Escaped to U.S. after unsuccessful revolt at Strassburg, Germany, 1837, returned to Europe, 1837; pres. 2d French Republic, 1848-52; emperor of France, 1852-70; established Catholic, Latin empire in Mexico after France, Eng. and Spain had intervened in Mexico in collection of debts, 1863, placed Maximillian (archduke of Austria) on throne; U.S. unable to concern itself deeply in this affair because of Civil War, applied Monroe Doctrine in 1865, forced France out of Mexico, 1867. Died Jan. 9, 1873.

BONAPARTE, Napoleon, French emperor; b. Ajaccio, Corsica, Aug. 15, 1769; s. Carlo Maria and Letizia (or Laetitia) (Romolino) de Buonaparte; m. Josephine de Beauharnais, Dec. 1, 1804; m. 2d, Maria Louise, Apr. 2, 1810, 1 son, Napoleon Francis Joseph Charles (Napoleon II); 1 illegitimate son, Comte Alexandre Walewski. First consul of France, 1800-04; emperor of France, 1804-14; relinquished idea of building colonial empire in Am. after having been unsuccessful in squelching native revolt in Santo Domingo (which he had hoped to make center of overseas colonies), 1803; sold La. to U.S. for 60 million francs, 1803; exiled to Elba, 1815, escaped, returned to Paris; defeated by Continental forces at Waterloo, Belgium, Mar. 17, 1815, exiled to St. Helena, 1815-21. Died St. Helena, May 5, 1821.

BONARD, Louis, benefactor; b. Rouen, France, 1809. Left France, circa 1849; mcht. in S.Am. and Cal.; became real estate dealer, N.Y.C.; bequeathed $150,000 to Am. Soc. for Prevention of Cruelty to Animals, will was unsuccessfully contested by 2 possible heirs in France who claimed Bonard was insane. Died N.Y.C., Feb. 21, 1871; buried Greenwood Cemetery, Bklyn.

BOND, George Phillips, astronomer; b. Dorchester, Mass. May 20, 1825; s. William C. and Selina (Cranch) B.; grad. Harvard, 1845; m. Harriet Harris, Jan. 27, 1853, at least 3 children. Asst. observer Harvard Observatory, 1845-59, dir., 1859-65, Phillips prof. astronomy, 1859-65; credited with discovery of Hyperion (8th satellite of Saturn) and of crape ring, 1850; founder photographic astronomy; received gold medal from Royal Astron. Soc. of London; papers include "Cometary Calculations," "The Method of Mechanical Quadratures." Died Cambridge, Mass., Feb. 17, 1865.

BOND, Hugh Lenox, jurist; b. Balt., Dec. 16, 1828; s. Dr. Thomas E. and Christian (Birckhead) B.; grad. U. City N.Y., 1848; m. Ann Penniman, 1856; children—Nicholas P., Hugh L., Summerfield. Admitted to Balt. bar, 1851; apptd. judge Md. Criminal Ct., 1860-68; apptd. judge 4th U.S. Circuit Ct. (including Md., Va., W. Va., the Carolinas), 1870, chief justice 1876-93; broke power of Ku Klux Klan in S.C. by imposing harsh sentences. Died Balt., Oct. 24, 1893.

BOND, Richard, architect. Practicing architect, by 1848; planned and-or built numerous important bldgs. in Boston and vicinity, including Gore Hall, Harvard, Bowdoin Sq. Baptist Ch., Boston (now site of Telephone Bldg.), old Tremont Bank, Boston; asso. with Charles E. Parker on other bldgs. in Boston; supposed to have been architect Ct. House at Salem; attended meeting of U.S. architects to discuss formation of Nat. Soc. of Architects (superseded by A.I.A., 1857), 1838. Flourished mid-19th Century.

BOND, Shadrach, gov. Ill.; b. Baltimore County Md., 1773; s. Nicodemus and Rachel (Stevenson) B.; m. Achsad Bond, 1810. Elected mem. Ill., Territorial Legislature, 1806; presiding judge St. Clair County Ct. of Common Pleas, 1808; first delegate to U.S. Ho. of Reps. from Ill., 12th-13th congresses, 1812-14; 1st gov. Ill., 1818-22. Died Kaskaskia, Ill., Apr. 13, 1832; buried Evergreen Cemetery, Chester, Ill.

BOND, Thomas, physician; b. Calvert County, Md., 1712; s. Richard and Elizabeth (Chew) B.; studied medicine under Dr. Alexander Hamilton, Annapolis, Md.; studied medicine in Paris; m. Sarah Roberts, 7 children. Began practice of medicine, Phila., circa 1734; founder Pa. Hosp., Phila., oldest hosp. in U.S., 1752; delivered 1st course in clin. lectures in U.S., 1766; mem. original bd. trustees Coll. of Phila. (now U. Pa.); a founder Am. Philos. Soc., 1768; mem. Phila. Com. of Safety, 1776; pres. Humane Soc. of Phila., 1780. Author: "An Account of Worm Bred in the Liver;" "A Letter to Doctor Fothergill on the Use of the Peruvian Bark in Scrofula;" "Essay on the Utility of Clinical Lectures." Died Mar. 26, 1784.

BOND, William Cranch, astronomer; b. Portland, Me., Sept. 9, 1789; s. William and Hannah (Cranch) B.; A.M. (hon.), Harvard, 1842; m. Selina Cranch, July 18, 1819; m. 2d, Mary Roope Cranch, 1831; 6 children including William Cranch, George P. Independent discoverer Comet of 1811; did pioneer work on rates of chronometers, meteorology and magnetism, 1831-39; dir. Harvard Observatory, 1839-59, did intensive studies of planets, also Orion and Andromeda nebulae; constructed 1st sea-going chronometer made in Am.; discovered 8th satellite of Saturn, 1848; mem. Am. Acad. Arts and Scis., Am. Philos. Soc., Royal Astron. Soc. (Eng.). Died Cambridge, Mass., Jan. 29, 1859.

BOND, William Key, congressman, lawyer; b. St. Marys County, Md., Oct. 2, 1792; attended Litchfield Law Sch. Moved to Chillicothe, O., 1812; admitted to bar, 1813; practiced in Chillicothe; mem. U.S. Ho. of Reps. (Whig) from Ohio, 24th-26th congresses, 1835-41; moved to Cincinnati, 1841, practiced law; surveyor Port of Cincinnati (apptd. by Pres. Fillmore), 1849-53; became interested in devel. railroads in West. Died Cincinnati, Feb. 17, 1864; buried Spring Grove Cemetery.

BONFIELD, George R., artist; b. Portsmouth, Eng., 1802. Came to Am., circa 1836, settled in Phila.; resided briefly in Beverly, Bordentown and Burlington (all N.J.), during 1850's; frequent exhibitor at Artists' Fund Soc., 1836-45, Pa. Acad., 1847-67, N.A.D., 1837-44, Apollo Assn., Am. Art-Union, 1838-49, Md. Hist. Soc., 1848; hon mem. N.A.D. Died Phila., 1898.

BONHAM, Milledge Luke, gov. S.C., congressman, b. Red Bank, Mass., Dec. 25, 1813; s. James and Sophie (Smith) B.; grad. S.C. Coll., 1834; m Ann Griffin, Nov. 13, 1845. Mem. S.C. Legislature, 1840-44; commd. col. 12th Inf., U.S. Army, 1846; elected solicitor So. dist. S.C., 1848-57; mem. U.S. Ho. of Reps. from S.C. (states rights Democrat), 35th-36th congresses, 1857-60; commd. brig. gen. Confederate Army, reapptd. brig. gen. cavalry, 1865; confederate gov. S.C., 1862; apptd. S.C. railroad commr. to reorganize wrecked railroad system, 1878. Died White Sulphur Springs, Va., Aug. 27, 1890.

BONNER, John, mariner, mapmaker; probably born in London, Eng. circa 1643; m. Rebecca Greene; m. 2d, Mary Clark; m. 3d, Persis Wanton, Sept. 28, 1699; m. 4th, Susannah Stilson, June 2, 1709. Came to Boston, circa 1670; owner of the Recovery, sailed to Va., Barbados, Eng., Ireland, Boston, 1671-72; owner vessels Amity, Speedwell, Crown, Mary, Two Brothers, Three Friends, Hope; mem. com. to build galley for Province of Mass., 1693; chief pilot Adm. Walker's expdn., 1711; charted the Canada

River, circa 1711; published "A Curious ingraven map of the town of Boston," 1722. Died Feb. 10, 1726.

BONNER, Sherwood, see MacDowell, Katherine Sherwood Bonner.

BONNEVILLE, Benjamin Louis Eulalie de, see de Bonneville, Benjamin Louis Eulalie.

BONNEY, William H. (known as Billy the Kid), desperado; b. N.Y.C., Nov. 23, 1859; s. William H. and Kathleen B. Moved from Kan. to N.M., 1868; at age 16 killed 3 peaceful Indians for furs nr. Ft. Bowie, Ariz.; held supposed record of 12 killings, 1877; one of party of 6 that killed Sheriff James Brady and deputy, 1878; Pat Garrett accepted nomination for sheriff to break up the Kid's band, 1880; forced to surrender shortly after fight at Ft. Sumner, convicted of killing Sheriff Brady and sentenced to hang on May 13, 1880; escaped by killing 2 dep. guards, Apr. 28, 1880. Trapped and shot to death by Sheriff Garrett, Ft. Sumner, July 15, 1881.

BOODY, Azariah, congressman, businessman; b. Stanstead County, Que., Can., Apr. 21, 1815; attended common schs. Moved to Rochester, N.Y., 1850, became farmer; donated portion of his farm to U. Rochester, 1853, trustee, 1853-65; mem. U.S. Ho. of Reps. (Whig) from N.Y., 33d Congress, Mar. 4-Oct. 1853 (resigned); moved to N.Y.C., 1855, active in constrn. railroads, canals, bridges; pres. Wabash R.R. Co.; retired from business, 1875. Died N.Y.C., Nov. 18, 1885; buried Mt. Hope Cemetery, Rochester.

BOOKER, George William, congressman, lawyer; b. nr. Stuart, Patrick County, Va., Dec. 5, 1821; attended public schs.; studied law. Taught sch.; admitted to bar, 1846; practiced in Patrick County; elected justice of peace, Henry County, Va.; mem. and presiding justice county court, 1856-68; mem. Va. Ho. of Dels., 1865, 73; elected Republican atty. gen. of Va., 1868, resigned, 1869; mem. U.S. Ho. of Reps. (Conservative) from Va., 41st Congress, Jan. 26, 1870-71; practiced in Martinsville, Henry County. Died Martinsville, June 4, 1883; buried family cemetery.

BOON, Ratliff, gov. Ind., congressman; b. Franklin County, N.C., Jan 18, 1781; attended public schs. Moved to Danville, Ky., learned gunsmith's trade; moved to what is now Boon Twp., Warrick County, Ind., 1809; apptd. 1st treas. of Warrick County at its orgn., 1813; mem. Ind. Ho. of Reps., 1816, 17; mem. Ind. Senate, 1818; elected lt. gov. Ind., 1819, became gov. when gov. resigned, 1822, reelected lt. gov., 1822-24; mem. U.S. Ho. of Reps. (Jacksonian Democrat) from Ind., 19th, 21st-25th congresses, 1825-27, 29-39; moved to Pike County, Mo., 1839. Died Louisiana, Mo., Nov. 20, 1844; buried Riverview Cemetery.

BOONE, Andrew Rechmond, congressman, lawyer; b. Davidson County, Tenn., Apr. 4, 1831; attended public schs.; studied law. Admitted to bar, 1852; Practiced in Mayfield, Graves County, Ky.; elected judge Graves County Ct., 1854, 58-61, resigned; mem. Ky. Ho. of Reps., 1861; circuit judge 1st Jud. Dist. of Ky., 1868-74; mem. U.S. Ho. of Reps. (Democrat) from Ky., 44th-45th congresses, 1875-79; chmn. Ky. R.R. Commn., 1882-86. Died Mayfield, Jan. 26, 1886; buried Mayfield Cemetery.

BOONE, Daniel, Indian fighter, scout; b. Bucks County, Pa., Feb. 11, 1735; s. Squire and Sarah (Morgan) B.; m. Rebeccah Bryan, Aug. 14, 1756, 9 children. Moved to N.C., 1750; served as wagoner in Braddock's unsuccessful expdn. to Ft. Duquesne, 1755; served under Gen. John Forbes in successful expdn. to Ft. Duquesne, 1758; visited Ky. for 1st time on hunting trip, 1767, returned for more thorough expdn. (accompanied by brother), 1769-71, twice captured by Indians; made 1st colonizing attempt, 1773, failed because of heavy Indian attacks; returned to Ky. with group of men, 1775, established Wilderness Trail over Cumberland Gap through Alleghany Mountains, and founded Boonesborough (or Boonesboro) on Kentucky River; became capt. Va. Militia, 1776; captured by Shawnee Indians, 1778, adopted by tribe; escaped, warned Boonesbroough of impending attack and aided in its defense, 1778; charged by some with disloyalty during this period, acquitted and returned to N.C.; returned to Ky., 1779, founded Boone's Station; mem. Va. Legislature, 1780, 83; sheriff, county lt., dep. surveyor, Fayette County, Va. (now Ky.), 1782; influential in extending Am. settlement and in defense of Revolutionary frontier; went to Mo., 1799; had trouble with land titles in both Ky. and Mo., part of Mo. acreage restored by Congressional intercession. Died La Charette, Mo., Sept. 26, 1820; buried Frankfort, Ky.

BOONE, Thomas, colonial gov.; flourished 1759-64. Lived in S.C., owned an estate there; gov. N.J., 1760-61; became gov. S.C., 1761, gained unfavorable reputation by becoming sole judge of all elections, resulting in controversy with Assembly; sailed for Eng. with controversy still not settled, 1764.

BOORMAN, James, railroad exec., philanthropist; b. Kent, Eng., 1783; s. John and Mary (Colgate) B.; m. Mary Wells Davenport, Nov. 10, 1810, 1 adopted dau. Joined merc. house Boorman & Johnston, N.Y.C., 1813; originator, pres. Hudson River R.R.; major stockholder Troy & Schenectady R.R.; founder Bank of Commerce; contbr. to Instn. for Blind, Protestant Half-Orphan Asylum, Southern Aid Soc., Union Theol. Sem., Trinity Ch. Died N.Y.C., Jan. 24, 1866.

BOOTH, Edwin Thomas, actor; b. nr. Bel Air, Md., Nov. 13, 1833; s. Junius Brutus and Mary Anne (Holmes) B.; m. Mary Devlin, July 7, 1860; m. 2d, Mary McVicker, June 7, 1869; 1 child. First appeared in Richard III at Boston Museum, 1849; 1st major role as Richard III in Nat. Theatre, N.Y.C., 1851; accompanied father to Cal., 1852, performed at Jenny Lind Theatre, San Francisco (then managed by brother Junius Brutus); after unsuccessful engagement in Nev. returned to San Francisco, appeared in roles including Hamlet, Macbeth, Richard III, later joined troupe at newly-opened Met. Theatre; made unsuccessful tour of Australia (with Laura Keene and D. C. Anderson), 1854; returned to West Coast, performed with Mrs. Catherine Forrest Sinclair, Met., Forrest, other theaters; played King Lear in his final appearance at Sacramento Theatre, 1856; went East, 1857, opened at Front Street Theatre, Balt.; toured South, then opened in Boston as Sir Giles Overreach; enjoyed successful engagement at Burton's Met. Theatre, N.Y.C.; toured Eng. appearing as Shylock, Sir Giles and Cardinal Richelieu (most famous role), London and Manchester, 1861; appeared at Winter Garden, N.Y.C., 1862-63, purchased the theater, 1863; played 100 nights as Hamlet, season 1864-65; after burning of Winter Garden (1867), opened Booth Theatre with performance Romeo and Juliet, 1869, there reached heights of his career performing his most famous roles including Antony, Brutus, Cassius, seasons 1869-74; went bankrupt as result of Panic of 1873-74; worked as traveling actor, 1874-82, acting ability declined; toured Brit. Isles and Europe, 1882; played continuously with Lawrence Barrett, 1887-91; gave last performance in Hamlet at Acad. of Music, Bklyn., 1891; retired to Gramercy Park, N.Y.C. Editor: Edwin Booth's Prompt Book, 1878. Died N.Y.C., June 7, 1893; buried N.Y.C.

BOOTH, James Curtis, chemist; b. Phila., July 28, 1810; s. George and Ann (Bolton) B.; A.B., U. Pa., 1829; LL.D. (hon.), Lewisburg U. (now Bucknell U.), 1867; Ph.D. (hon.), Rensselaer Poly. Inst., 1884; m. Margaret Cardoza, Nov. 17, 1853. Prof. chemistry Franklin Inst., 1836-45; melter and refiner Phila. Mint, 1849-88; prof. chemistry U. Pa., 1851-55; mem. 1st Geol. Survey of Pa.; state geologist Del. mem. Am. Philos. Soc., Acad. Natural Scis., Md. Inst. for Promotion Mechanic Arts, Phila. Soc. for Promotion of Agr., Hist. Soc. Pa.; pres. Am. Chem. Soc., 1883-85. Died Haverford, Pa., Mar. 21, 1888.

BOOTH, John Wilkes, actor; b. nr. Bel Air, Md., 1838; s. Junius Brutus and Mary Ann (Holmes) B. Mem. famous acting families of Am.; noted for his Shakespearian roles; appeared in major U.S. theatres opposite his brother Edwin Booth, 1860-63; ardent Confederate sympathizer (unlike rest of his family); mem. unit of Va. Militia at Harpers Ferry during capture of John Brown, 1859; organized scheme to abduct Pres. Abraham Lincoln which failed because Lincoln did not appear at the spot at which Booth and his accomplices were waiting, 1864; assassinated Lincoln at Ford's Theater, Apr. 14, 1865; either was shot or killed himself during escape. Died Apr. 26, 1865; buried in unmarked grave, Greenmount Cemetery, Balt.

BOOTH, Junius Brutus, actor; b. London, Eng., May 1, 1796; s. Richard Booth; m. Marie Christine Adelaide Delancy, May 8, 1815; m. 2d, Mary Anne Holmes, Jan. 13, 1821; children include Junius Brutus, Edwin, John Wilkes, Asia Frigga. Made 1st appearance in London, 1813; toured in Belgium and Holland in comedy troupe, 1814-15; became known as leading actor of English stage following performance of Richard III at Covent Garden (London), 1817; toured in Brit. Isles in such roles as King Lear, Iago, Cassius, Othello, 1817-21; came to U.S., 1821, settled in Harford County, Md.; toured in major cities of East and South; best known in roles of Shakespearean villains; played role of Pescara (written for him) in Apostage at Park Theater, N.Y.C., 1827; mgr. Camp Street Theater, New Orleans, 1828, Adelphi Theater, Balt., 1831; toured Eng., 1825-26, 36-37; made last tour with sons Junius Brutus and Edwin in Cal., 1852, last appearance in New Orleans, 1852. Died on board ship nr. Cincinnati, Nov. 30, 1852; buried Greenmount Cemetery, Balt.

BOOTH, Mary Louise, editor; b. Yaphank, L.I., N.Y., Apr. 19, 1831; d. William Chatfield Booth. Editor, Harper's Bazaar, 1867-88; Author: History of the City of New York, 1859; translated (from French) The Marble-Workers' Manual, 1856, Th Uprising of a Great People (Count Agenor de Gas parin), 1861, Results of Slavery (Augustin Cochin) 1863, Results of Emancipation, 1863. Died Mar. 5 1889.

BOOTH, Newton, senator, gov. Cal.; b. Salem Ind., Dec. 25, 1825; s. Beebe and Hannah (Pitts B.; grad. DePauw U., 1846; m. Mrs. J. T. Glover Feb. 29, 1892. Admitted to Ind. bar, 1849; mem Cal. Senate from Sacramento, 1863; gov. Cal., 1871 75; mem. U.S. Senate from Cal., 1875-81, mem coms. on pub. lands, patents, manufactures, ap propriations. Died Sacramento, July 14, 1892 buried City Cemetery, Sacramento.

BOOTH, Walter, congressman, mfr.; b. Wood bridge, Conn., Dec. 8, 1791; attended public schs Settled in Meriden, New Haven County, Conn. became mfr.; col. 10th Regt., 2d Battalion c Militia, 1825-27, brig. gen., 1827, 28, maj gen. 1st Div., 1831-34; judge county court, 1834 mem. Conn. Ho. of Reps., 1838; mem. U.S Ho. of Reps. (Free-Soiler) from Conn., 31s Congress, 1849-51. Died Meriden, Apr. 30, 1870 buried East Cemetery.

BOOTT, Kirk, mfr.; b. Boston, Oct. 20, 1790 s. Kirk and Mary (Love) B.; attended Harvard m. Ann Haden, circa 1813. Went to Eng., serve under Duke of Wellington in Peninsular War, commanded a force at siege of San Sebastian; returne to Boston, 1817; agt. Merrimack Mfg. Co., 1821 Pawtucket Canal enlarged under his direction; begar machine-shop, manufactured 1st locomotives in Am. built a village where his employees lived (became Lowell, Mass., 1826). Died Lowell, Apr. 11, 1837.

BORDEN, Gail, surveyor, inventor; b. Norwich N.Y., Nov. 9, 1801; s. Gail and Philadelphia (Wheeler) B.; m. Penelope Mercer, 1828; m. 2d, Mrs. A. F. Stearns; m. 3d, Mrs. Emeline Eunice (Eno) Church, 1860; several children. Moved with family to Covington, Ky., 1815, to Ind. Territory, 1816; sch. tchr. Ind. Ty., 1820-22; moved to Amite County, Miss., 1822; county surveyor, U.S. dep. surveyor Amite County, 1822-circa 1829; moved to Tex., circa 1829; supt. ofcl. surveys of Tex. colonies; del. San Felipe (Tex.) Conv., 1833; made 1st topog. map and planned layout of Galveston, Tex.; land agt. Galveston City Corp., 1839-51; became interested in concentrated foods, invented "meat biscuit" exhibited at London Fair, 1851; developed a form of condensed milk, Lebanon, N.Y., patented it, 1856; began mfg. condensed milk, Wassaic, N.Y., 1861; moved to Borden, Tex., after Civil War; continued research into concentration of foods, patented process of concentrated juices and fruit, 1862. Died Tex., Jan. 11, 1874.

BORDEN, Nathaniel Briggs, congressman, businessman; b. Fall River, Bristol County, Mass., Apr. 15, 1801; attended dist. sch., Plainfield (Conn.) Acad. Organizer Pocasset Mfg. Co., Fall River; mem. Mass. Ho. of Reps., 1831, 34, 51, 64; mem. U.S. Ho. of Reps. (Van Buren Democrat) from Mass., 24th-25th, (Whig) 27th congresses, 1835-39, 41-43; mem. Mass. Senate, 1845-48; elected mayor Fall River, 1856, 57; became banker; pres. Fall River Savs. Bank, Fall River Union Bank, Fall River R.R. Co. Died Fall River, Apr. 10, 1865; buried Oak Grove Cemetery.

BORDEN, Richard, mfr.; b. Fall River, Mass., Apr. 12, 1795; s. Thomas and Mary (Hathaway) B.; m. Abbey Durfee, Feb. 22, 1828, 7 children. A founder Fall River Iron Works, 1821; owner, pres. Watuppe Reservoir Co.; owner, pres., dir. Am. Print Works, 1834, Troy Cotton and Woolen Manufactory; owner Fall River Manufactory; owner, dir. Annawan Mill, 1825, Metacomet Mill, 1846; pres., dir. Am. Linen Co., Richard Borden Mill Co., Mt. Hope Mill Co.; pres. Fall River Nat. Bank. Died Feb. 25, 1874.

BORDEN, Simeon, civil engr.; b. Fall River, Mass., Jan. 29, 1798; s. Simeon and Amy (Briggs) B. Moved with family to Tiverton, R.I., 1806; began work in machine shop, 1826, supt., 1828; constructed base bar used for measuring base line in trigonometrical map survey of Boston (most accurate map in its time in U.S.), 1830; mem. Mass. Legislature, 1832-33, 44-45, 49; chief surveyor Boston Map Survey, 1834-41; chief surveyor railroads in Me., N.H., Mass., Conn., 1841-51; surveyed railroad line between R.I. and Mass. Died Oct. 28, 1856.

BORDLEY, John Beale, agriculturist; b. Annapolis, Md., Feb. 11, 1727; s. Thomas and Ariana (Frisby) B.; m. Margaret Chew, 1750; m. 2d, Mrs. Sarah Mifflin, Oct. 8, 1776. Prothonotary, Baltimore County, Md., 1753-62; judge Md. Provincial Ct., 1766, Ct. of Admiralty, 1767; commr. for settlement of Md.-Del. boundary, 1768; engaged in agrl. experimentation with new machinery, seeds, crop rotation on extensive lands at mouth Wye River and Pool's Island, Md. from 1770; a founder Phila. Soc. for Promoting Agr., 1785, v.p., 1785-1804. Author ssays: A Summary View of the Courses of Crops the Husbandry of England and Maryland, 1784, Money, Coins, Weights, and Measures, 1789; Essays nd Notes on Husbandry and Rural Affairs, 1801. ied on farm nr. Joppa, Md., Jan. 26, 1804.

BORDLEY, John Beale, artist; b. "Wye Island," albot County, Md., 1800; studied law, Phila. Painted portraits, Balt., circa 1834-51; exhibited at Pa. Acad., 1832, N.A.D., 1843; ret. to farm, Harford ounty, Md., 1851, continued to paint; moved to Bel Air, Md., then to Balt.; name also appears as eale Boardley, Peale Boardley. Died Balt., 1882.

BORE, Jean Etienne, planter, mayor New Orleans; . France, Dec. 27, 1741; s. Jean and Celeste (Carere) B.; m. Marguerite Destrehans. Mem. household guard of king of France, circa 1760-70; came o Am., circa 1770, settled nr. New Orleans on lantation raising indigo; planted sugar because of rop blights in 1790's; became 1st planter in La. o successfully produce granulated sugar, 1795; mayor of New Orleans (apptd. by French), 1803-04; apptd. to 1st Legislative Council in La. (under Am. control), refused to serve. Died nr. New Orleans, Feb. 2, 1820.

BOREMAN, Arthur Ingram, senator, gov. W. Va.; . Waynesburg, Pa., July 24, 1823; s. Kenner and Sarah (Ingram) B.; m. Laurane Bullock, Nov. 30, 1864. Admitted to Va. bar, 1843; mem. Va. Ho. f Dels. from Wood County, 1855-61; judge Va. Circuit Ct., 1861; 1st gov. W. Va., 1863-69; mem. U.S. Senate from W. Va. 1869-75, mem. coms. on manufactures, claims, chmn. com. on polit. disabilities and territories; judge W. Va. Circuit Ct., 1888-96. Died Parkersburg, W. Va., Apr. 19, 1896, buried Odd Fellows Cemetery, Parkersburg.

BORGESS, Caspar Henry, clergyman; b. Kloppenburg, Hanover, Germany, Aug. 1, 1824; came o U.S., studied at seminaries, Cincinnati, Phila. Ordained priest Roman Catholic Ch., 1848; served at Columbus, 10 years; pastor, Cincinnati, 1859; apptd. titular bishop of Calydon, 1870; became coadjutor Detroit, 1870, bishop, 1870-88; apptd. titular bishop of Phacusa, 1888. Died Kalamazoo, Mich., May 3, 1890.

BORIE, Adolph Edward, sec. of navy; b. Phila., Nov. 25, 1809; s. John Joseph and Sophia (Beauveau) B.; grad. U. Pa., 1825; m. Elizabeth Dundas McKean, 1839. Became partner in father's mercantile business, 1828, engaged primarily in silk and tea trade with Far East; consul to Belgium, 1843; pres. Bank of Commerce of Phila., 1848-60; apptd. U.S. sec. of navy by Pres. Grant, 1869; apptd. U.S. sec. of navy by Pres. Grant, 1869; accompanied Grant on his world tour, 1878-79. Died Phila., Feb. 5, 1880.

BORLAND, Charles, Jr., congressman, lawyer; b. Miniskink, Orange County, N.Y., June 29, 1786; grad. Union Coll., Schenectady, N.Y., 1811; studied law. Admitted to bar, practiced law; pres. bd. trustees of Montgomery, N.Y., for 10 years; mem. N.Y. State Assembly, 1820, 21, 36; mem. U.S. Ho. of Reps. (filled vacancy) from N.Y., 17th Congress, Nov. 8, 1821-23; dist. atty. Orange County, 1835-41. Died Wardsbridge, N.Y., Feb. 23, 1852; buried Riverside Cemetery, Montgomery.

BORLAND, Solon, diplomat, senator, army officer; b. Suffolk, Va., Sept. 21, 1808; studied medicine, N.C.; m. Mrs. Huldah Wright; m. 2d, Mrs. Hunt; m. 3d, Mary Melbourne; 3 sons, 2 daus. Practiced medicine, Little Rock, Ark., circa 1832-46, 54-61; served as volunteer in Mexican War, 1846-47; mem. U.S. Senate (Democrat) from Ark., Mar. 30, 1848-Apr. 3, 1853; U.S. minister to Nicaragua and C. Am., including Honduras, 1853-54, involved in controversy in Greytown (Nicaragua) over right of Nicaragua to arrest Am. citizen, resulted in U.S. bombardment of Greytown because of insults to him as U.S. rep.; organized, col. 3d Ark. Calvary, Confederate Army, 1861; served in campaigns in Miss. and in Battle of Port Hudson; promoted brig. gen. Confederate Army. Died nr. Houston, Tex., Jan. 1, 1864; buried City Cemetery, Houston.

BORST, Peter I., congressman; b. Middleburg, Schoharie County, N.Y. Apr. 24, 1797; attended common schs. Served as officer N.Y. State troops, on staff Gov. William C. Bouck; held various local positions; mem. U.S. Ho. of Reps. (Jackson Democrat) from N.Y., 21st Congress, 1829-31; mem. com. apptd. by county bd. suprs. to oversee building of 1st county almshouse, 1838. Died Middleburg, Nov. 14, 1848; buried family burying ground on his estate The Hook, Schoharie County.

BORTHWICK, John David, artist; b. Edinburgh, Scotland; ed. Edinburgh. Came to Am., after 1840; went to Cal., 1851, gold seeker, artist, 1851-54; went to Australia, 1854; recorded Cal. experiences in Three Years in California. . .with Eight Illustrations by the Author, 1857, also in drawings published in Illustrated London News; returned to Eng., 1860, exhibited at English galleries including Royal Acad.

BOSS, John Linscom, Jr., congressman, lawyer; b. Charleston, S.C., Sept. 7, 1780; studied law. Admitted to bar; practiced in Newport, R.I.; held many important local offices; mem. R.I. Ho. of Reps., 1806-15; mem. U.S. Ho. of Reps. from R.I., 14th-15th congresses, 1815-19. Died Newport, Aug. 1, 1819; buried Common Burial Ground.

BOSSIER, Pierre Evariste John Baptiste, congressman; b. Natchitoches, La., Mar. 22, 1797; had classical edn. Became sugar and cotton planter; mem. La. Senate, 1833-43; mem. U.S. Ho. of Reps. (Calhoun Democrat) from La., 28th Congress, 1843-Apr. 24, 1844. Died Washington, D.C., Apr. 24, 1844; buried Congressional Cemetery, Washington; reinterred Catholic Cemetery, Natchitoches.

BOTELER, Alexander Robinson, congressman; b. Shepherdstown, Va. (now W. Va.), May 16, 1815; s. Dr. Henry and Priscilla (Robinson) B.; grad. Princeton, 1835; m. Helen Stockton, 1836. Mem. U.S. Ho. of Reps. from Va., 36th Congress, 1859-61; rep. from Va. to Confederate Provisional Congress, 1861, Confederate Congress, 1862-64; mem. Tariff Commn., 1881; asst. atty. U.S. Dept. Justice, 1882-83. Died Shepherdstown, May 8, 1892; buried Elmwood Cemetery, Shepherdstown.

BOTETOURT, 1st baron, see Berkeley, Norborne.

BOTTA, Anne Lynch, author; b. Bennington, Vt., Nov. 11, 1815; d. Patrick and Charlotte (Gray) Lynch; grad. Albany Female Acad., 1834; m. Vincenzo Botta, 1855. Conducted sch. for girls, Providence, R.I., 1835-45; taught at Bklyn. Acad. for Women, 1845-50; travelled in Europe, 1853; home became gathering place for writers and artists, N.Y.C., during 1850's and 1860's, entertained Bryant, Emerson, Greeley, Willis, Poe. Author: Collected Poems, 1st edit., 1849; A Handbook of Universal Literature, 1860; contbd. frequently to Democratic Review. Died N.Y.C., Mar. 23, 1891; buried N.Y.C.

BOTTA, Vincenzo, educator; b. Piedmont, Italy, Nov. 11, 1818; grad. U. Turin, circa 1838, Ph.D., circa 1846; m. Anne Lynch, 1855. Mem. Sardinian Parliament, 1849-50; came to Am. to study ednl. practices, 1853, became Am. citizen; prof. Italian literature U. City N.Y. (now N.Y. U.), 1854-circa-1890; Unionist during Civil War; named comdr. Order of Crown of Italy, 1871. Author: Public Instruction in Sardinia, 1858; Discourse on the Life of Count Cavour, 1862; Dante as a Philosopher, Patriot, and Poet, 1867; Introduction to the Study of Dante, 1886. Died N.Y.C., Oct. 5, 1894; buried N.Y.C.

BOTTINEAU, Pierre, guide; b. Bear Point, at mouth of Turtle River, circa 1817; son of Joseph Bottineau and Clear Sky (Indian woman). Guide for Dickson expdn. from Selkirk to Ft. Snelling, 1837; employed by Henry Sibley of Am. Fur Co., 1837-40; established claim in Minn. Territory at present site of St. Paul, 1841; guide for various expdns. into Northwest, 1850's-60's; guide for Pacific R.R. party of Gov. Stevens, 1853, Fiske expdn. to Mont., 1862, Gen. Sibley's mil. expdn. against Sioux Indians to Missouri River, 1863; led dirs. of N.P.Ry. on survey of railroad route, 1869; lived in No. Minn., from 1870. Died Red Lake, Minn., July 26, 1895.

BOTTS, Charles Tyler, editor; b. Fredericksburg, Va., 1809; s. Benjamin and Jane (Tyler) B.; studied law, Richmond, Va., circa 1826-29; m. Margaret Marshal. Engaged in agr. in Va., from circa 1829; mem. Henrico County (Va.) Agrl. Soc., investigated problem of soil exhaustion; founded and conducted Southern Planter (agrl. mag., achieved wide circulation through low prices), 1841-46; moved to Cal., 1848; mem. Cal. Constl. Conv., 1849; admitted to Cal. bar, 1849, began practice of law, San Francisco; publisher Sacramento Standard (newspaper), 1856-61; state printer Cal., 1861-65; practiced law, Oakland, Cal., 1870's. Died Oakland, 1884; buried Oakland.

BOTTS, John Minor, congressman, lawyer, author; b. Dunfries, Va., Sept. 16, 1802; s. Benjamin and Jane (Tyler) B.; m. Mary Blair. Admitted to Va. bar, 1820; mem. Va. Legislature, 1833-39; mem. U.S. Ho. of Reps. Va., 26th-27th, 30th congresses, 1839-43, 47-49; antisecessionist; del. to So. Loyalist Conv., Phila., 1866; signed Jefferson Davis' $100,000 bail bond. Author: The Great Rebellion, Its Secret History, 1866. Died Culpeper, Va., Jan. 7, 1869.

BOUCHER, Jonathan, clergyman; b. Cumberland, Eng., Mar. 24, 1738; s. James and Ann (Barnes) B.; attended schs. at Bromfield and Wigton, Eng.; m. Eleanor Addison, 1773. Ordained to ministry Ch. of Eng., 1762; rector St. Mary's Ch., Caroline County, Va., 1762-70, St. Anne's, Annapolis, Md., 1770-73, Queen Anne's parish, Prince Georges County, Md., 1773-75; chaplain lower house Md. Legislature, 1772-75; advocate of Anglican Episcopate in Am.; a Loyalist, preached doctrine of religious obligation of subjects to obey king; left Am., 1775; served parishes in Paddington and Epsom, Eng., 1775-1804. Author: A View of the Causes and Consequences of the American Revolution, 1797. Died Epsom, Apr. 27, 1804; buried Epsom.

BOUCICAULT, Dion, playwright, actor; b. Dublin, Ireland, Dec. 26 1820; probably illegitimate son of Dionysius Lardner and Anne (Darley) Boursiquot; attended U. London (Eng.), circa 1836; m. Agnes Robertson, circa 1853; m. 2d, Louise Thorndyke, 1885. Came to Am., 1853; wrote numerous plays for Am. stage, 1853-62, including The Young Actress, 1853, The Poor of New York, 1857, The Octoroon, 1859; owned theater, Washington, D.C., 1858; mgr. Winter Garden Theater, N.Y.C., 1859; acted with Laura Keene in several Irish comedies including The Collegians, 1860-62; lived in Eng., 1862-72; wrote and produced The O'Dowd (1873), The Shaughraun (1874) in which he toured U.S.; wrote or adapted over 130 plays during career as mgr. and actor. Died N.Y.C., Sept. 18, 1890; buried N.Y.C.

BOUCK, Joseph, congressman; b. Bouck's Island, nr. Fultonham, Schoharie County, N.Y., July 22, 1788; attended rural schs., Schoharie County. Farmer, Schoharie County many years; insp. turnpike roads Schoharie County, 1828; mem. U.S. Ho. of Reps. (Democrat) from N.Y., 22d Congress, 1831-33; moved to Middleburgh, N.Y. Died Middleburgh, Mar. 30, 1858; buried Middleburgh Cemetery.

BOUCK, William C., gov. N.Y.; b. Schoharie County, N.Y., Jan. 7, 1786; s. Christian and Margaret (Borst) B.; m. Catherine Lawyer, 1807, 11 children. Town clk., supr., sheriff Schoharie County, before 1820; mem. N.Y. State Senate, 1820; commr. superintending constrn. Erie Canal, 1821-40; gov. N.Y., 1842-44; del. to N.Y. State Constl. Conv., 1846; fed. asst. treas. in N.Y.C. (apptd by Pres. Polk.), 1846-49. Died Schoharie County, Apr. 19, 1859.

BOUDE, Thomas, congressman, lumber exec.; b. Lancaster, Pa., May 17, 1752; attended pvt. schs. Served as lt. under Gen. Anthony Wayne with 2d, 4th, 5th Pa. battalions in Revolutionary War, 1776-83; promoted capt., brevetted maj.; lumber dealer, Columbia, Pa.; mem., an organizer Soc. of Cincinnati; mem. Pa. Ho. of Reps., 1794-96; mem. U.S. Ho. of Reps. (Federalist) from Pa., 7th Congress, 1801-03. Died Columbia, Oct. 24, 1822; buried Brick Graveyard of Mt. Bethel Cemetery.

BOUDET, Dominic W., artist; s. Nicholas Vincent Boudet. Worked with father, 1805-20; dancing master, Richmond, Va., 1805; worked in Balt., 1807-08, Washington, D.C., 1810; copied portraits by John Hesselius on estate of John Mason, Va., 1811; worked in Phila., 1814; worked with father on painting Battle of North Point for City of Balt., 1819-20; worked in Charleston, S.C., 1820, N.Y.C., 1825, 27-28, 30-33, 37; exhibited at N.A.D., 1831; exhibited The Raising of Lazarus at Frederick (Md.) City Hall, 1833, La Belle Nature at New Orleans, 1833; worked as portrait and miniature painter, Charleston, 1838. Died Balt., Oct. 29, 1845.

BOUDET, Nicholas Vincent, artist; 1 son, Dominic W., 1 dau. Painted in Phila., 1793, Charleston, S.C., 1803, Richmond, Va., 1805, Balt., 1807-08, Washington and Balt., 1810; collaborated with son on painting Battle of North Point for City of Balt., 1819, brought near bankruptcy by project, 1820.

BOUDINOT, Elias, Continental congressman; b. Phila., May 2, 1740; s. Elias III and Catherine (Williams) B.; LL.D., Yale, 1790; m. Hannah Stockton, Apr. 21, 1762. Licensed counselor and atty. at law, 1760; sgt. at law, 1770; trustee Coll. of N.J. (now Princeton), 1772-1821; mem. N.J. Com. of Safety, 1775; commissary gen. of prisoners Continental Army, 1776-79; mem. N.J. Provincial Congress; del. from N.J. to Continental Congress, 1777-84, pres., 1782-83, signed peace treaty with Gt. Britain, alliance treaty with France, sec. fgn. affairs com., 1783-84; dir. U.S. Mint, 1795-1805; mem. N.J. Conv. which ratified U.S. Constn.; mem. U.S. Ho. of Reps. from N.J., 1st-3d congresses, 1789-95; 1st pres. Am. Bible Assn., 1816-21. Died Burlington, N.J., Oct. 24, 1821.

BOUDINOT, Elias, editor; b. Ga., circa 1803; son of Cherokee Indian parents, took name of founder of sch. he attended in Cornwall, Conn., 1818; m. Harriet Ruggles Gold, 1826; m. 2d, Delight Sargent, 1836; 6 children. Became editor weekly newspaper Cherokee Phoenix (established by Nat. Cherokee Council, 1824), 1828, printed paper largely in English with some portions in Cherokee, 1828-35 (paper suppressed by Ga. govt. after criticism of ofcl. policies); signatory of treaty with state govt. providing for removal of Cherokees from Ga., 1835. Author: Poor Sarah or the Indian Woman, published by United Brethren's Missionary Soc., 1833. Murdered for role in making 1835 treaty, on Indian reservation, Ga., June 22, 1839.

BOUDINOT, Elias Cornelius, lawyer; b. Rome, Ga., Aug. 1, 1835; s. Elias and Harriet (Gold) B. (of Cherokee Indian descent); studied law, Fayetteville, Ark., 1853-56; m. Clara Minear, 1885. Admitted to Ark. bar, began practice of law, Fayetteville, 1856; wrote editorials for Arkansian (newspaper), 1857-60; state chmn. Ark. Democratic Party, 1860; sec. Ark. conv. which enacted secession ordinance, 1861; served as lt. col. Indian regt., Confederate Army, 1861-63; mem. Confederate Congress from Ark. Indian Territory, 1863-65; owner tobacco factory, 1865-68; practiced law, Ft. Smith, Ark. Indian Territory, 1868-90. Died Ft. Smith, Sept. 27, 1890; buried Ft. Smith.

BOUGHTON, George Henry, artist; b. Norwich, Eng., Dec. 4, 1833. Came to Am., 1838; landscape painter, Albany, N.Y., 1852-58; visited Scotland, 1856; worked in N.Y.C., 1859-60; went to Paris, France, 1861; settled in London, Eng.; exhibited at N.A.D., 1856-76, hon. profl. mem., 1859-60, mem., 1871-1905; elected asso. Royal Acad., 1879, mem., 1896; exhibited at Am. Art-Union, 1852, Washington (D.C.) Art Assn., 1857, Md. Hist. Soc., 1868; known for subject-pictures, including Pilgrims Going to Church (now at N.Y. Hist. Soc.). Died London, Jan. 19, 1905.

BOULDIN, James Wood, congressman, lawyer; b. Charlotte County, Va., 1792; attended common schs.; studied law. Admitted to bar, 1813; practiced at Charlotte Court House, Va.; mem. U.S. Ho. of Reps. (Jacksonian Democrat, filled vacancy) from Va., 23th-25th congresses, Mar. 15, 1834-39; farmer, Charlotte County. Died at his country home Forest Hill, Charlotte County, Mar. 30, 1854; buried pvt. burial ground on his estate.

BOULDIN, Thomas Tyler, congressman, lawyer; b. nr. Charlotte Court House, Charlotte County, Va., 1781; attended country schs.; studied law. Admitted to bar, 1802; practiced at Charlotte Court House; apptd. judge circuit court; mem. U. S. Ho. of Reps. (Democrat, filled vacancy) from Va., 21st-23d congresses, 1829-33, Aug. 26, 1833-Feb. 11, 1834. Died Washington, D.C., Feb. 11, 1834; buried pvt. cemetery on his farm Golden Hills, nr. Drakes Branch, Charlotte County.

BOULIGNY, Dominique, senator; b. New Orleans, circa 1771; s. Francisco and Marie (D'Auverville) B.; m. Arthemise Le Blanc, 6 sons, 6 daus. Mem. 1st Legislature of Territory of Orleans from Parish of Orleans, 1805; subscribed money for defense of New Orleans during War of 1812; mem. com. of 9 to maintain loyalty of New Orleans to U.S., 1814; mem. U.S. Senate from La., 1824-29. Died New Orleans, Mar. 5, 1833; buried New Orleans.

BOULIGNY, John Edward, congressman, lawyer; b. New Orleans, Feb. 5, 1824; attended public schools; studied law. Admitted to bar; practiced in New Orleans; held several local offices; mem. U.S. Ho. of Reps. (Am. Party) from La., 36th Congress, 1859-61, strongly opposed to secession, only La. mem. to retain seat after La. seceded from Union in Jan. 1861; retired to pvt. life, remained in North after Civil War. Died Washington, D.C. Feb. 20, 1864; buried Congressional Cemetery.

BOUNETHEAU, Henry Brintell, painter; b. Charleston, S.C., Dec. 14, 1797; s. Peter Bounetheau; m. Julia Dupre, 1 son, Henry. With merc. firm Dart & Spear, Charleston, 1813-circa 1822; became partner Hamilton, Son & Co., Charleston, circa 1825; head accountant C.N. Hubert Co., Charleston, 1830's-1877; became known as painter of miniature portraits, from 1820's, painted subjects including Charles C. Pinckney, Nathanael Greene, William Ravenel, Charles A. Pringle. Died Charleston, Jan. 31, 1877; buried Charleston.

BOUQUET, Henry, Army officer; b. Rolle, Switzerland, 1719. Lt. col. 1st battalion Royal Am. Regt., 1755; came to Am., 1756; center of Phila. quartering dispute, 1756; served as col. on Ft. Duquesne expdn., 1758; naturalized by Md., also by Supreme Ct. of Pa., 1762; served in French and Indian Wars, 1756-63; leader Bouquet's Expdn., 1763-65, ordered to relief of Ft. Pitt, defeated Indian attack, 1763, returned to Muskingum River, 1765, negotiated peace treaty with Shawnee and Delaware Indians, thus ending Indian rebellion. on Pa. border; commd. brig. Brit. Army, 1765 contbd. to crushing of Pontiac Indian rebellion. Died Pensacola, Fla., Sept. 2, 1765.

BOURGMONT, sieur de (Etienne Venyard), explorer; b. Normandy, France, circa 1680; son of Charles de Venyard. In command of French forces at Detroit, 1705-06; lived among Indian tribes on Missouri River in La., 1707-17; sent to France to report on colony, 1719, given permission to build Ft. Orleans on Missouri River above Grand River, 1723; popular with the Indians; explored in present state of Kan., 1724; returned to France with Chicagou, chief of Michigami. Author: La Description (article tracing course of Missouri River), 1717. Died France, circa 1730.

BOURKE, John Gregory, army officer, ethnologist; b. Phila., June 23, 1846; s. Edward and Anna (Morton) B.; grad. U.S. Mil. Acad., 1869. Served with 15th Regt., Pa. Volunteer Cavalry in Civil War, 1862-65; served with 3d U.S. Cavalry stationed in S.W., 1869-96; made intensive study of Indian life while on mil. duty. Author: (papers) The Snake Dance of the Moquis of Arizona, 1884; On the Border with Crook, 1891; The Medicine Men of the Apache, 1892; Scatalogic Rites of all Nations, 1892. Died June 8, 1896.

BOURNE, Benjamin, congressman, jurist; b. Bristol, R.I., Dec. 9, 1755; s. Shearjashub and Ruth (Bosworth) Church B.; A.B., Harvard, 1775, A.M. (hon.), 1778; m. Hope (Child) Diman, 4 children. Quarter master of a company R.I. Regt., 1776; mem. R.I. Council of War, 1780; elected to R.I. Legislaturer from Bristol, 1780; mem. R.I. Gen. Assembly, 1787-90; mem. U.S. Ho. of Reps. from R.I., 1st-4th congresses, 1790-96; judge U.S. Dist. Ct. for R.I., 1801; influential in persuading R.I. to ratify U.S. Constn. (last state to do so). Died Bristol, Sept. 17, 1808; buried Juniper Hill Cemetery, Bristol.

BOURNE, George, clergyman, abolitionist; b. Westbury, Eng., June 13, 1780; grad. Homerton Sem., London, Eng. Came to U.S., circa 1813; pastor Presbyn. Ch., South River, Va., 1814-18, agitated against slavery; pastor Presbyn. Ch., also prin. acad., Sing Sing, N.Y., circa 1819-23; minister, Quebec, Can., 1825-28; editor The Protestant (religious anti-slavery journal), N.Y.C., 1831-33; pastor Houston Street Dutch Reformed Ch., N.Y.C., 1833-39; engaged in writing books and tracts against slavery, N.Y.C., 1839-45. Author: The Book and Slavery Irreconcilable, 1816; Picture of Slavery in the U.S.A., 1834; Slavery Illustrated and Its Effects upon Woman and Domestic Society, 1837; A Condensed Anti-Slavery Bible Argument, 1845. Died N.Y.C., Nov. 20, 1845; buried N.Y.C.

BOURNE, Nehemiah, ship builder, naval officer; b. London, Eng., circa 1611; s. Robert and Mary Bourne. Came to Am., 1638, settled in Charlestown, Mass.; later engaged in shipbuilding, merc. pursuits, Boston; constructed ship Trial for Gov. Winthrop (1st ship built in Boston), 1641; returned to Eng., circa 1645, became rear adm. in Parliamentary Navy, supervised fitting out and supplying of ships of Parliamentary fleet. Died Eng., Feb. 1691; buried Bunhill Fields, Eng.

BOURNE, Shearjashub, congressman, lawyer; b. Barnstable, Mass., June 14, 1746; grad. Harvard, 1764, studied law. Admitted to bar; practiced in Boston; mem. Mass. Ho. of Reps., 1782-85, 88-90; mem. Mass. Conv. to ratify U.S. Constn., 1788; mem. U.S. Ho. of Reps. from Mass., 2d-3d congresses, 1791-95; justice Suffolk County Ct. Common Pleas, 1799-1806. Died Boston, Mar. 11, 1806.

BOUTELLE, De Witt Clinton, artist; b. Troy, N.Y., Apr. 6, 1820; at least 1 son, Edward C. Worked in N.Y.C., 1846, 51-55, Baskingridge, N.J., 1848, Phila., 1855-57, Bethlehem, Pa., 1858-84; exhibited at N.A.D., 1846-74, became asso., 1851; exhibited at Pa. Acad., 1854-69, Boston Athenaeum, 1854-61, Washington (D.C.) Art Assn., 1857-59, Am. Art-Union, 1845-52; represented in Karolik Collection, also in Moravian Archives, Bethlehem. Died Bethlehem, Nov. 5, 1884.

BOUTON, John Bell, journalist, author; b. Concord, N.H., Mar. 15, 1830; s. Rev. Nathaniel and Mary Anne Persis (Bell) B.; grad. Dartmouth, 1849; m. Eliza Nesmith, Dec. 4, 1873. Editor, Cleve. Plain-Dealer, 1851-57; moved to N.Y.C., 1857; owner editor N.Y. Jour. of Commerce; editor Appleton's Annual Cyclopedia. Author: Loved and Lost, 1857; Round the Block, an American Novel, 1864; Uncle Sam's Church: His Creed, Bible and Hymn-book, 1895. Died Nov. 18, 1902.

BOUTON, Nathaniel, clergyman, historian; b. Norwalk, Conn., June 29, 1799; s. William and Sarah (Benedict) B.; grad. Yale, 1821, Andover Theol. Sem., 1824; m. Harriet Sherman, June 11, 1825; m. 2d, Mary Ann Bell, June 8, 1829; m. 3d, Elizabeth Cilley, Feb. 18, 1840; at least 1 son, John. Pastor, 1st Congregational Ch., Concord, N.H., 1824-66; engaged in study of N.H. history from 1840's; mem. N.H. Hist. Soc.; state historian N.H., 1866-76. Author: History of Concord, 1856; Documentary History of New Hampshire, 10 vols., 1867-77. Editor: Vols. VII, VIII of N.H. Hist. Soc. Collections, 1850. Died Concord, June 6, 1878; buried Concord.

BOUVIER, John, jurist; b. Condognan, France, 1787; s. John and Marie (Benezet) B. Came to Am., 1801, settled in Phila.; published weekly newspaper Am. Telegraph, Brownsville, Pa., during War of 1812; admitted to bar, 1818, began practice of law, Uniontown, Pa.; engaged in compilation of legal dictionary, 1830's; elected recorder of Phila., 1836; judge criminal ct., Phila., 1838-51. Author: A Law Dictionary. . ., 1839, Institutes of American Law, 1851. Editor: Abridgement of the Law (Matthew Bacon), 1841-45. Died Phila., Nov. 18, 1851; buried Phila.

BOVEE, Matthias Jacob, congressman; b. Amsterdam, Montgomery County, N.Y., July 24, 1793; attended rural schs. Tchr. sch. in winter, farmer in summer; became mcht., 1815; chmn. Town of Amsterdam; mem. county bd. suprs.; elected mem. N.Y. State Assembly, 1826; trustee Village of Amsterdam, 1831; mem. U.S. Ho. of Reps. (Jacksonia Democrat) from N.Y., 24th Congress, 1835-37; moved to Milw., 1843, settled nr. Eagle, Waukesha County, became farmer; justice of peace for 1 years. Died Eagle, Sept. 12, 1872; buried Oak Ridge Cemetery.

BOWDEN, John, clergyman, educator; b. Ireland, Jan. 7, 1751; grad. King's Coll. (now Columbia) 1772. Ordained in Ch. of Eng., London, Eng., 1774; asst. minister Trinity Ch. (Anglican), N.Y.C., 1774; rector St. Paul's Episcopal Ch., Norwalk, Conn. 1784-89, Anglican Ch., St. Croix, W.I., 1789-91; conducted sch., Stratford, Conn., 1791-96; declined election as Episcopal bishop of Conn., 1796; prin. Episcopal Acad. of Conn., Chesire, 1796-1802; prof. philosophy Columbia Coll., N.Y.C., 1803-17. Author A Full Length Portrait of Calvinism, 1809. Died Ballston Spa, N.Y., July 31, 1817; buried Ballston Spa.

BOWDEN, Lemuel Jackson, senator, lawyer; b. Williamsburg, James City County, Va., Jan. 16, 1815; grad. Coll. William and Mary; studied law. Admitted to bar, 1838; practiced in Williamsburg, mem. Va. Ho. of Dels., 1841-46; del. Va. constl. convs., 1849, 51; Constl. Union presdl. elector, 1860; mem. U.S. Senate (Republican) from Va., 1863-Jan. 2, 1864. Died Jan. 2, 1864; buried Congressional Cemetery.

BOWDITCH, Henry Ingersoll, physician; b. Salem, Mass., Aug. 9, 1808; s. Nathaniel and Mary (Ingersoll) B.; attended Boston Latin Sch., 1823-25; grad. Harvard, 1828, M.D., 1832; studied medicine, Paris, France, 1832-34; m. Olivia Yardley, 1838. Mem. Staff Mass. Gen. Hosp., Boston, 1831-32, 38-92; practiced medicine, Boston, from 1834; abolitionist leader from 1830's, friend of William L. Garrison; active in case of runaway slave George Latimer, 1842-43; became expert on diseases of chest, especially tuberculosis; pioneer in performing operations for pleural effusions with suction pump; prof. Harvard Med. Sch., 1859-67; an original mem. Mass. Bd. Health, 1869-79; noted for work in fields preventive medicine and public sanitation; fellow Am. Acad. Arts and Scis. Author: The Young Stethoscope, 1846; Public Hygiene in America, 1877. Died Boston, Jan. 14, 1892.

BOWDITCH, Nathaniel, astronomer, mathematician, ins. exec.; b. Salem, Mass., Mar. 26, 1773; s. Habbakkuk and Mary (Ingersoll) B.; A.M. (hon.), Harvard, 1802; m. Mary Boardman, Mar. 25, 1798; m. 2d, Mary Ingersoll (cousin), Oct. 28, 1800; 8 children including Jonathan Ingersoll, Henry Ingersoll. Prepared 1st Am. edit. The Practical Navigator (J.H. Moore), 1799, revised and enlarged under title The New American Practical Navigator, 1802, 9 edit. published during his lifetime, 56 reprints or edits. published since his death; portions of the work reprinted under title Bowditch's Useful Tables, 1844; his skill in mathematics led to positions as pres. Essex Fire & Marine Ins. Co., 1804, actuary Mass. Hosp. Life Ins. Co., 1823-38; made survey of Salem harbors, 1804-06; published 23 papers on nautical and astron. subjects in Memoirs of Am. Acad. of Arts and Scis., 1804-20; published translation with commentary of 1st 4 vols. of Mechanique Celeste (LaPlace) (most important sci. work); best known papers include one concerning meteor which exploded over Weston, Conn., 1807, another discussing the motion of a pendulum; mem. Am. Acad. Arts and Scis., 1799, pres., 1829-38. Died Boston Mar. 17, 1838; buried Mt. Auburn Cemetery, Cambridge, Mass.

BOWDOIN, James, colonial gov.; b. Boston, Aug. 7, 1726; s. James and Hannah (Pordage) B.; grad. Harvard, 1745; LL.D., Edinburgh U.; m. Elizabeth Erving, Sept. 15, 1748. Elected to Mass. Gen. Ct., 1753-56; mem. Mass. Council, 1757; pres. Mass. Provincial Congress, 1775, Mass. Constl. Conv., 1779; gov. Mass., 1785-87; suppressed Shay's Rebellion, 1786; mem. Mass. Conv. to ratify U.S. Constn., 1788; 1st pres. Am. Acad. Arts and Scis.; fellow Harvard, 1779; fellow royal socs. of London and Edinburgh; Bowdoin Coll. named in his honor. Died Boston, Nov. 6, 1790.

BOWDOIN, James, mcht., diplomat; b. Boston, Sept. 23, 1752; s. James Bowdoin; grad. Harvard, 1771; m. Sarah Bowdoin, May 18, 1781. In merc. pursuits, Boston, 1771-circa 1786; rep. Mass. Gen. Ct. from Dorchester, 1786-90; mem. Mass. Conv. to ratify U.S. Constn., 1788, supported ratification; mem. Mass. Senate, 1794, 1801; mem. Mass. Gov.'s Council, 1796; supported Jeffersonians politically; U.S. minister to Spain, 1804-08, spent most of time abroad in Paris negotiating with Napoleon concerning Am. acquisition of Fla. territory; bequeathed his library, collection of European paintings, also land and cash to Bowdoin Coll. (named for his father). Author: (pamphlet) Opinions Respecting the Commercial Intercourse between the U.S.A. and the Dominions of Britain, 1797. Died Buzzard's Bay, Mass., Oct. 11, 1811.

BOWDON, Franklin Welsh, congressman, lawyer; b. Chester Dist., S.C., Feb. 17, 1817; grad. U. Ala., 1836; studied law. Admitted to bar; practiced in Talladega, Ala.; mem. Ala. Ho. of Reps., 1844, 45; mem. U.S. Ho. of Reps. (Democrat, filled vacancy) from Ala., 29th-31st congresses, Dec. 7, 1846-51; moved to Henderson, Rusk County, Tex., 1852, practiced law; Dem. presdl. elector, 1856. Died Henderson, June 8, 1857; buried City Cemetery.

BOWEN, Abel, engraver; b. Greenbush, N.Y., Dec. 3, 1790; s. Abel and Delia (Mason) B.; m. Eliza Healy, 10 children. Moved to Boston, 1811, became printer and wood engraver; published many volumes illustrated with copperplates and woodcuts during 1820's and 1830's; an organizer Boston Bewick Co., (profl. group Boston wood engravers), circa 1833, instrumental in planning engravings in Am. Mag. of Useful and Entertaining Arts, published in Boston, 1834-circa 1838; influenced work of engravers including George Loring Brown, Hammat Billings; executed engravings and woodcuts for History of Boston (by Caleb Snow), 1825; Picture of Boston, 1828; The Young Ladies Book, 1830. Died Boston, Mar. 11, 1850; buried Boston.

BOWEN, Christopher Columbus, congressman, lawyer; b. Providence, R.I., Jan. 5, 1832; attended public schs.; studied law. Moved to Ga., 1850; became farmer; admitted to bar, 1862; practiced in Charleston, S.C.; enlisted in Confederate Army, served as capt. in Coast Guard throughout War; mem. S.C. Republican Conv., Charleston, 1867; 1st chmn. S.C. Rep. Central Com.; del. S.C. Constl. Conv., 1867; mem. U.S. Ho. of Reps. (Rep.) from S.C, 40th-41st congresses, July 20, 1868-71; elected sheriff Charleston, 1872: Died N.Y.C.. June 23, 1880; buried St. Laurence Cemetery, Charleston.

BOWEN, Daniel, artist, showman; b. circa 1760. Modeled wax portraits of Franklin and Washington; one of 1st Am. museum proprs.; advertised museum and waxworks, N.Y.C., 1789, 94, Phila., 1790, 93-94, Boston, 1791; opened Columbian Museum, Boston, 1795, propr. until museum burned down, 1807; exhibited panorama of New Haven in Phila., 1818. Died Phila., Feb. 29, 1856.

BOWEN, Francis, educator, philosopher b. Charlestown, Mass., Sept. 8, 1811; s. Dijah and Elizabeth (Flint) B.; attended Phillips Exeter Acad.; grad. Harvard, 1833; m. Arabella Stuart. Taught at Exeter Acad., 1833-35; tutor philosophy, Harvard, 1837-39, Alvord prof. philosophy, 1853-89; studied in Europe, 1839-41; editor N.Am. Rev., 1843-52; achieved prominence during campaign for criticism of height of tariffs; minimized differences between philosophy and Christianity in his philos. writings; critical of concept of evolution. Author: Life of Baron Steuben, 1838; Life of Benjamin Lincoln, 1847; Principles of Political Economy, 1856; Treatise on Logic, 1864; Modern Philosophy from Descartes to Schopenhauer and Hartmann, 1877; A Layman's Study of the English Bible, 1885. Died Boston, Jan. 21, 1890.

BOWEN, George, missionary; b. Middlebury, Vt., Apr. 30, 1816; attended Union Theol. Sem., N.Y., 1844-47. Toured Europe, 1836-40; missionary in India, 1848-88; asso. editor Bombay Guardian, 1851-54, editor, 1854-88; joined Methodist Ch., 1873; known as "white saint of India." Died Feb. 5, 1888.

BOWEN, Henry Chandler, mcht., editor; b. Woodstock, Conn., Sept. 11, 1813; s. Griffith and Lydia Wolcott (Eaton) B.; m. Lucy Maria Tappan, June 6, 1844, 7 sons, 3 daus.; m. 2d, Ellen Holt, Dec. 25, 1865, 1 son. Established firm Bowen & McNamee, silk traders, 1838; founder Independent (Conglist. newspaper), 1848; owner Bklyn. Union. Died Bklyn., Feb. 24, 1896.

BOWEN, John Henry, congressman, lawyer; b. Washington County, Va., Sept. 1780; attended schs., Lexington, Ky.; studied law. Admitted to bar; practiced in Gallatin, Tenn.; mem. U.S. Ho. of Reps. (Democrat) from Tenn., 13th Congress, 1813-15. Died Gallatin, Sept. 25, 1822.

BOWEN, Rees Tate, congressman, farmer; b. Maiden Springs, nr. Tazewell, Va., Jan. 10, 1809; attended Abingdon Acad., Va. Farmer; apptd. brig. gen. Va. Militia; mem. Va. Ho. of Dels., 1863, 64; magistrate Tazewell County for several years prior to Civil War; presiding justice Tazewell County Ct.; mem. U.S. Ho. of Reps. (Conservative) from Va., 43d Congress, 1873-75. Died Maiden Springs, Aug. 29, 1879; buried family burying ground Maiden Springs.

BOWER, Gustavus Miller, congressman, physician; b. nr. Culpeper, Va., Dec. 12, 1790; attended public schs.; studied medicine, Phila. Moved to Ky. before 1812, lived nr. Nicholasville; enlisted as surgeon dresser in War of 1812, one of few survivors of massacre at Frenchtown, nr. Detroit, 1813; moved to Monroe County, Mo., 1833, settled near Paris; practiced medicine, became farmer; mem. U.S. Ho. of Reps. (Democrat) from Mo., 28th Congress, 1843-45. Died nr. Paris, Nov. 17, 1864; buried family burying ground nr. Paris.

BOWERS, Elizabeth Crocker, actress; b. Ridgefield, Conn., Mar. 12, 1830; d. Rev. William Crocker; m. David P. Bowers, Mar. 4, 1847; m. 2d, Dr. Brown; m. 3d, James C. McCollum, Jan. 20, 1883. Made dramatic debut in Child of Nature, 1846; appeared as Donna Victoria in A Bold Stoke for a Husband, Walnut Street Theatre, Phila., 1847; mem. stock company of Arch Street Theatre, Phila., 1853-57; mgr. People's Theatre (formerly Walnut Street Theatre), Phila., 1857-59; went to Eng., 1861-63; appeared in The Hunchback, England; played in Lady Audley's Secret, Winter Garden, N.Y.C.; toured Eastern U.S., 1864-66; retired temporarily from stage after her 3d marriage; returned to stage, 1892. Died Washington, D.C., Nov. 6, 1895.

BOWERS, John Myer, congressman, lawyer; b. Boston, Sept. 25, 1772; grad. Columbia Coll., N. Y.C.; studied law. Admitted to bar, 1802; practiced in Cooperstown, N.Y.; moved to his country home Lakelands, nr. Cooperstown, 1805; mem. U.S. Ho. of Reps. (filled vacancy, contested election) from N.Y., 13th Congress, May 26-Dec. 20, 1813. Died Cooperstown, Feb. 24, 1846; buried Lakewood Cemetery.

BOWERS, Theodore Shelton, army officer; b. Hummelstown, Pa.; s. George and Ann Maria. Editor, Register, Mt. Carmel, Ill.; served as pvt. 48th Ill. Inf., 1861, commd. 1st lt., 1862, capt., 1862, maj. 1863, promoted lt. col. after Battle of Vicksburg, 1863; clk. in hdqrs. of Gen. U.S. Grant, 1862, also aide; served in Va. campaigns of 1863-65; capt. Q.M. Dept., U.S. Army, 1864. Died after falling under train wheels while trying to board train, Garrison, N.Y., Mar. 6, 1866; buried West Point, N.Y.

BOWIE, James, soldier, pioneer; b. Burke County, Ga., 1796; s. Rezin and Alvina (Jones) B.; m. Maria Ursula, Apr. 25, 1831, 2 children. Moved to Texas, 1828; became Mexican citizen, 1830; developed "Bowie knife" as an effective weapon in close-in fighting; fought in Battle of Nacogdoches, 1832; favored Texas resistance to Mexico early after arrival in Tex.; served as col. Tex. Army, 1835-36; killed at The Alamo, San Antonio, Tex., Mar. 6, 1836.

BOWIE, Oden, gov. Md.; b. Prince George's County, Md., Nov. 10, 1826; s. William D. and Mary Eliza (Oden) B.; grad. St. Mary's Coll., 1845; m. Alice Carter, 1851, 7 children. Entered Md. Ho. of Dels., 1849; pres. Balt. and Potomac R.R., 1860 elected gov. Md., 1867-72; an organizer, pres. Md. Jockey club. Died "Fairview," Prince George's County, Dec. 4, 1894.

BOWIE, Richard Johns, congressman; b. Georgetown, D.C., June 23, 1807; s. Col. Washington and Margaret (Johns) B.; grad. Georgetown U. Law Sch., 1826; m. Catherine L. Williams, 1833. Admitted to D.C. bar, 1826, to U.S. Supreme Ct., 1829; moved to Rockville, Md., 1829; mem. Md. Ho. of Reps., 1835-37, Md. Senate, 1837-41; state's atty. for Montgomery County, Md., 1844-49; mem. U.S. Ho. of Reps. from Md., 31st-32d congresses, 1849-53; chief judge Md. Ct. of Appeals, 1861-67, asso. judge, 1871-81; chief judge 6th Jud. Circuit, 1871-88. Died Rockville, Md., Mar. 12, 1881; buried Rockville Cemetery.

BOWIE, Robert, gov. Md.; b. Prince George's County, Md., Mar. 1750; s. Capt. William and Margaret (Sprigg) B.; m. Pricilla Mackall, 1770. Commd. capt. 2d bn. Md. Flying Arty., 1776; mem. Md. Ho. of Dels., 1785-90, Md. Legislature, 1801-03; gov. Md., 1803-07, 11; presdl. elector, 1809; dir. 1st state bank incorporated in Annapolis, Md. 1810. Died Nottingham, Md., Jan. 8, 1818; buried Mattapoui Cemetery, Prince George's County.

BOWIE, Thomas Fielder, congressman, lawyer; b. Queen Anne, Prince Georges County, Md., Apr. 7, 1808; attended Princeton; grad. Union Coll., Schenectady, N.Y., 1827; studied law. Admitted to bar, 1829; practiced in Upper Marlboro, Md.; dep. atty. gen. for Prince Georges County, 1833-42 mem. Md. Ho. of Dels., 1842-46; unsuccessful candidate for gov. Md., 1843; mem. Md. Constl. Conv., 1851; Whig presdl. elector, 1852; mem. U.S. Ho. of Reps. (Democrat) from Md., 34th-35th congresses, 1855-59. Died Upper Marlboro, Oct. 30, 1869; buried Waring family burying ground, Mt. Pleasant, nr. Upper Marlboro.

BOWIE, Walter, congressman; b. Mattoponi, nr. Nottingham, Prince Georges County, Md., 1748; attended Rev. John Eversfield's Sch., nr. Nottingham, Craddock's Sch., nr. Balt. Farmer, large landowner; interested in shipping; mem. Md. Constl. Conv., 1776; capt., later maj. Prince Georges County Co. during Revolutionary War; mem. Md. Ho. of Dels., 1780-1800; mem. Md. Senate, 1800-02; mem. U.S. Ho. of Reps. (Democrat, filled vacancy) from Md., 7th-8th congresses, Mar. 24, 1802-05. Died nr. Collington, Prince Georges County, Nov. 9, 1810; buried family burying ground on his estate.

BOWLER, Metcalf, jurist; b. London, Eng., 1726; s. Charles Bowler; m. Anne Fairchild, 11 children including Bathsheba. Came to Am., circa 1743, settled in Newport, R.I.; mem. R.I. Gen. Assembly, 1767-76; asst. judge R.I. Supreme Ct., 1768, chief justice, 1776; signer R.I. Declaration of Independence, May 4, 1776. Author: Treatise on Agriculture and Practical Husbandry, 1786. Died Sept. 24, 1789.

BOWLES, Samuel, journalist; b. Hartford, Conn., June 8, 1797; m. Huldah Deming, Feb. 12, 1822, 1 son, Samuel. Publisher, Hartford Times, 1819-23; founder, editor, publisher weekly Springfield (Mass.) Republican, 1824-51, founder daily edit., 1844. Died Springfield, Sept. 8, 1851.

BOWLES, Samuel II, journalist; b. Springfield, Mass., Feb. 9, 1826; s. Samuel and Huldah (Deming) B.; m. Mary Schermerhorn, Sept. 6, 1848, 10 children. Editor daily edit. Springfield Republican, 1844-78, held nat. audience and led nat. pubopinion for 30 years; pioneer of independent journalism, devoted to valid reporting of polit. issues; high journalistic policies and editorial standards made Springfield Republican an outstanding paper of is time, noted for originality of views; trustee Amherst Coll. Author: Across the Continent, 1865; The Switzerland of America, 1865; Our New West, 1869. Died Springfield, Jan. 16, 1878.

BOWLES, William Augustus, adventurer; b. Frederick County, Md., Oct. 22, 1763; s. Thomas and Eleanor Bowles; m. dau. of Creek Indian chief, many children including Chief Bowles. Ensign in Md. Loyalist Corps, 1778, dismissed in disgrace, reinstated, 1781, put on half pay, 1783; after wandering around Southern states came into contact with former gov. of Va. (Lord Dunmore) and John Miller who put him in charge of trading company to deal with Creek Indians; made unsuccessful attempt, to supplant Panton, Leslie & Co.; made invasions of Fla. attacking Panton's storehouse, 1790, 99, once took Ft. St. Marks, but captured each time; taken to Spain, escaped; finally captured, 1803. Died Spain, Dec. 23, 1805.

BOWLIN, Jamer Butler, congressman, lawyer; b. Fredericksburg, Spotsylvania County, Va., Jan. 16, 1804; studied law. Moved to Lewisburg, Greenbrier County, Va., 1825; admitted to bar, 1826; practiced in Greenbrier County; moved to St. Louis 1833, practiced law; established Farmers and Mechanics' Advocate; chief clk. Mo. Ho. of Reps., 1836; mem. Mo. Ho. of Reps., 1836, 37; apptd. dist. atty. for St. Louis, 1837; elected judge criminal court, 1839-42, resigned; mem. U.S. Ho. of Reps. (Democrat) from Mo., 28th-31st congresses, 1843-51; apptd. minister resident to New Granada by Pres. Pierce, 1854; apptd. commr. to Paraguay by Pres. Buchanan, 1858-59. Died St. Louis, July 19, 1874; buried Bellefontaine Cemetery.

BOWMAN, James, artist; b. Alleghany County, Pa., 1793; m. Julia M. Chew, 1836. Employed as itinerant portraitist in Pitts., Phila., Washington, D.C., smaller towns, until 1822; went to Europe, 1822; returned to Am., opened gallery in Pitts., 1829; painted portrait of Gov. Henry Dodge of Wis. Territory 1836 (now at Wis. Hist. Soc.); opened studio, Rochester, N.Y., 1841; work included portraits of Lafayette and his daus., James Fenimore Cooper, Altbert Thorwaldsen, Justice Henry Baldwin (all have disappeared). Died Rochester, May 18, 1842.

BOWMAN, John Bryan, univ. founder; b. Mercer County, Ky., Oct. 16, 1824; s. John and Mary (Mitchum) B.; grad. Bacon Coll., 1842; m. Mary Williams, 1845. Founded and chartered Ky. U. (now U. Ky.), 1858, regent, incorporator, 1865-78; regent, incorporator Transylvania U., 1865-78; participated in founding Hocker (now Hamilton) Coll., Comml. Coll., Coll. of the Bible. Died Harrodsburg, Ky., Sept. 29, 1891.

BOWNE, John, religious leader; b. Matlock, Eng., Mar. 12, 1628; s. Thomas Bowne; m. Hannah Feake, 1656; m. 2d, Hannah Bickerstaff; m. 3d, Mary Cook. Came to Am., 1651, settled in Boston, moved to Flushing, L.I., N.Y., 1653; arrested as leader of Quakers, 1663, after 4 months imprisonment deported to Ireland, then went to Amsterdam, Holland, 1663; appeared before bd. dirs. West India Co., secured passport, returned to L.I., became a farmer; treas. Queens County (N.Y.), 1683; mem. N.Y. Gen. Assembly from Queens County, 1691, not seated because of refusal to take prescribed oaths; continued as Quaker leader after return to Am. Died Oct. 10, 1695.

BOWNE, Obadiah, congressman; b. nr. Richmond, Staten Island, N.Y., May 19, 1822; attended Princeton, 1838-40. Held several local offices;

mem. U.S. Ho. of Reps. (Whig) from N.Y., 32d Congress, 1851-53; quarantine commr., 1857-59; Republican presdl. elector, 1864. Died Richmond Village, S.I., Apr. 27, 1874; buried St. Andrew's Cemetery.

BOWNE, Samuel Smith, congressman, lawyer; b. New Rochelle, N.Y., Apr. 11, 1800; attended common schs.; studied law. Engaged in agriculture; moved to Laurens, N.Y., 1825; admitted to bar, 1832, began practice of law, Laurens; mem. N.Y. State Assembly, 1834; mem. U.S. Ho. of Reps. (Van Buren Democrat) from N.Y., 27th Congress, 1841-43; moved to Rochester, N.Y., 1846, continued practice of law; judge Otsego County (N.Y.), 1851-55. Died on his farm nr. Morris, N.Y., July 9, 1865; buried Friends Burying Ground.

BOYCE, James Petigru, clergyman, educator; b. nr. Charleston, S.C., Jan. 11, 1827; s. Ker and Amanda Jane Caroline (Johnson) b.; grad. Brown U., 1847; attended Princeton Theol. Sem.; m. Lizzie Llewellyn Ficklen, Dec. 20, 1858. Pastor, Baptist Ch., Columbia, S.C., 1851; prof. theology Furman U., Greenville, S.C., 1855; an organizer, head So. Bapt. Theol. Sem., Greenville, 1859-61, closed sem. at outbreak of Civil War, reopened sem. at Louisville, Ky., after war; served as chaplain of a S.C. regt. during Civil War; spent last years of life in Europe because of poor health. Died Pau, France, Dec. 28, 1888.

BOYCE, John, clergyman, author; b. Donegal, Ireland, 1810; studied at Navan and Maynooth. Ordained priest Roman Catholic Ch., 1837; missioner to Eastport, Me., 1845; transferred to Worcester, Mass., 1847-64. Author: (popular novels) Shandy Maguire or Tricks upon Travellers, 1848; The Spaewife or the Queen's Secret, 1853; Mary Lee or the Yankee in Ireland, 1859; also contbr. to Boston Pilot and mags. Died Worcester, Jan. 2, 1864.

BOYCE, William Waters, congressman, lawyer; b. Charleston, S.C., Oct. 24, 1818; attended S.C. Coll. (now U. S.C.) at Columbia, also U. Va. at Charlottesville; studied law. Admitted to bar, 1839, practiced law, Winnsboro, S.C.; mem. S.C. Ho. of Reps.; mem. U.S. Ho. of Reps. (State Rights Democrat) from S.C., 33d-36th congresses, 1853-Dec. 21, 1860 (ret.); apptd. del. for S.C. to Confederate Provisional Congress, 1861; mem. 1st, 2d Confederate congresses, 1862-64; moved to Washington, D.C., 1866, continued practice of law. Died at his country home "Ashland," Fairfax County, Va., Feb. 3, 1890; buried Episcopal Cemetery, Winnsboro.

BOYD, Adam, congressman, jurist; b. Mendham, N.J., Mar. 21, 1746. Moved to Bergen County, circa 1770, later to Hackensack, N.J.; mem. bd. freeholders and justices, 1773, 84, 91, 94, 98; sheriff Bergen County, 1778-81, 89; mem. N.J. Ho. of Assembly, 1782-83, 87, 94-95; judge Bergen County Ct. of Common Pleas, 1803-05, 13-33; mem. U.S. Ho. of Reps. (Democrat) from N.J., 8th, 10th-12th congresses, 1803-05, Mar. 8, 1808-13. Died Hackensack, Aug. 15, 1835; buried 1st Reformed Ch. Cemetery.

BOYD, Alexander, congressman; b. Albany, N.Y., Sept. 14, 1764. Engaged in agriculture, Schoharie County, N.Y.; mem. U.S. Ho. of Reps. (Whig) from N.Y., 13th Congress, 1813-15. Died Esperence, N.Y., Apr. 8, 1857; buried Schoharie (N.Y.) Cemetery.

BOYD, Belle, Confederate spy, actress; b. Martinsburg, Va., May 9, 1843; attended Mt. Washington Coll., 1855-59; m. Lt. Sam W. Hardinge, Aug. 1864; m. 2d, John Hammond, 1869; m. 3d, Nathaniel High, 1885. During Civil War obtained valuable information for Gen. Stonewall Jackson when Federals under Gen. James Shields held war councils at her aunt's house, Martinsburg; twice arrested, released due to lack of evidence; sailed to Eng. with letters from Jefferson Davis, 1864; made debut on English stage in Lady of Lyons at Theatre Royal, Manchester; after successful career in Eng., made Am. debut at Ben De Bar's Theatre, St. Louis; joined Miles and Bates stock co. of Cincinnati, 1868. Died Kilbourne, Wis., June 11, 1900.

BOYD, David French, army officer, coll. pres.; b. Wytheville, Va., Oct. 5, 1834; s. Thomas Jefferson and Minerva Anne (French) B.; grad. U. Va., 1856; m. Esther Gertrude Wright, Oct. 5, 1865, 8 children. Sch. tchr., Homer and Rocky Mount, La., 1857-60; prof. ancient langs. and English, La. State Sem. of Learning, Pineville, 1860-61; enlisted as pvt. Co. B., 9th La. Volunteers, 1861, sent to Va., rose to maj. in Stonewall Jackson's corps by 1862, transferred to Trans-Miss. Dept. construeted Fort DeRussy on Red River, 1863, captured nr. Black River, La., 1864, imprisoned in New Orleans, 1864; an instigator of law stating that every parish in La. should have 1 or more public schs., one for Negroes, 1 for whites, 1869; supt. La. State Sem., 1865-70, became pres. when sem. was renamed La. State U., 1870, instrumental in merger of La. State U. and La. Agrl. and Mech. Coll., 1874; removed from presidency by La. Legislature, 1880, reinstated, 1884, attempted to expand univ. without operating through bd. of suprs., resigned as a result, 1885, prof. mathematics 1886-88, prof. philosophy, civics, 1897-99; supt. Ky. Mil. Inst., Farmingdale, Ky., 1888-93; tchr. Ohio Mil. Acad., Germantown, 1893-94; prof. Mich. Mil. Acad., Orchard Lake, 1894-97. Died Baton Rouge, La., May 27, 1899.

BOYD, John Huggins, congressman; b. Salem, N.Y., July 31, 1799; grad. Washington Acad., Salem, 1818; studied law. Admitted to bar, 1823, began practice of law, Salem; moved to Whitehall, N.Y.; justice of peace, many years from 1828; mem. N.Y. State Assembly, 1840; supr. Whitehall, 1845, 48, 49; mem. U.S. Ho. of Reps. (Whig) from N.Y., 32d Congress, 1851-53; spl. surrogate Washington County (N.Y.), 1857-59; pres. of village. Died Whitehall, July 2, 1868; buried Evergreen Cemetery, Salem.

BOYD, John Parker, adventurer, army officer; b. Newburyport, Mass., Dec. 21, 1764; s. James and Susanna Boyd. Commd. ensign U.S. Navy, 1784, advanced to rank of lt.; went to India to seek fortune, 1789, sold his services successively to French, British, Mohammedans (all seeking to control country); returned to U.S., 1799; commd. col. 4th Inf., U.S. Army, 1808, fought under William Henry Harrison at Tippecanoe, 1811; commd. brig. gen. at outbreak of War of 1812, served on Canadian border; led a brigade at battles of Ft. George, Chrystler's Farm; discharged from army, 1815; naval officer for port of Boston in later life Died Oct. 4, 1830.

BOYD, Lynn, congressman; b. Nashville, Tenn., Nov. 22, 1800; s. Abraham Boyd; m. Alice Bennett, 1832; m. 2d, Mrs. Anna L. Dixon, 1850. Assisted in securing what is known as Jackson Purchase from Chickasaw Indians (Ky. lands west of Tennessee River), 1819; mem. Ky. Ho. of Reps. from Calloway County, 1827-32; mem. U.S. Ho. of Reps. (Democrat) from Ky., 24th, 26th-33d congresses, 1835-37, 39-55, speaker, 1851-55, staunch supporter of Andrew Jackson, led joint movement for resolution annexing Tex., chmn. com. on mil. affairs during Mexican War, chmn. com. on territories; elected lt. gov. of Ky., 1859, died before taking office. Died Paducah, Ky., Dec. 17, 1859; buried Oak Grove Cemetery, Paducah.

BOYD, Sempronius Hamilton, congressman, lawyer, b. nr. Nashville, Tenn., May 28, 1828; studied law. Moved to Mo., 1840, to Cal., 1849; prospected for gold, taught sch.; returned to Mo., 1854; clk. Greene County Ct., 1854-56; admitted to bar, 1856, began practice of law, Springfield, Mo.; mayor Springfield, 1856; mem. U.S. Ho. of Reps. (Emancipationist) from Mo., 38th Congress, 1863-65, (Republican), 41st Congress, 1869-71; raised 24th Mo. Inf. during Civil War, served as col.; judge 14th Jud. Dist., 1865; mem. Republican Nat. Com., 1864-68; del. Rep. Nat. Conv., Balt., 1864; a builder and operator S.W. Pacific R.R., 1867-74; operator wagon factory, 1874-76; minister resident and consul gen. to Siam (apptd. by Pres. Harrison), 1890-92. Died Springfield, June 22, 1894; buried Hazelwood Cemetery.

BOYD, Thomas Alexander, congressman, lawyer; b. nr. Bedford, Pa., June 25, 1830; grad. Marshall Coll., Mercersburg, Pa., 1848; studied law, Chambersburg, Pa. Admitted to bar, began practice of law, Bedford; practiced law, Lewistown, Ill., 1856-61; commd. capt. 17th Regt., Ill. Inf., during Civil War; mem. Ill. Senate, 1866, 70; mem. U.S. Ho. of Reps. (Republican) from Ill., 45th-46th congresses, 1877-81; resumed practice of law. Died Lewistown, May 28, 1897; buried Oak Hill Cemetery.

BOYDEN, Elbridge, architect; b. 1819. Moved to Worcester, Mass., circa 1844; architect numerous churches, hotels, pvt. homes; pres. Worcester chpt. A.I.A. (later inc. with Boston Soc. Architects). Died Jan. 25, 1896.

BOYDEN, Nathaniel, congressman, lawyer; b. Conway, Mass., Aug. 16, 1796; grad. Union Coll., Schenectady, N.Y., 1821; studied law. Served in War of 1812; moved to Stokes County, N.C., 1822, taught sch. for several years; admitted to bar, practiced law; mem. N.C. Ho. of Commons, 1838, 40; moved to Salisbury, N.C., 1842; mem. N.C. Senate, 1844; mem. U.S. Ho. of Reps. from N.C. (as Whig), 30th Congress, 1847-49, (as Republican), 40th Congress, July 13, 1868-69; mem. N.C. Constl. Conv., 1865; asso. justice N.C. Supreme Ct., 1872-73. Died Salisbury, Nov. 20, 1873; buried Lutheran Cemetery.

BOYDEN, Seth, inventor, mfr.; b. Foxborough, Mass., Nov. 17, 1788; s. Seth and Susanna (Atherton) B.; m. Abigail Sherman; children—Susan, for making patent leather, 1819, malleable iron, Obadiah, Matilda, George, Seth. Inventor process for making patent leather, 1819, malleable iron, 1826; manufactured stationery steam engines; developed forerunner of "Am. Process" furnace grate bar, 1847, an inexpensive process for manufacturing sheet-iron, a hat-forming machine; made 1st Am. daguerreo-type; originated machines for manufacturing nails and cutting files; described by Thomas Edison as one of America's greatest inventors. Died Hilton, N.J., Mar. 31, 1870.

BOYDEN, Uriah Atherton, engr., inventor; b. Foxborough, Mass., Feb. 17, 1804; s. Seth and Susanna (Atherton) B. Worked with brother Seth, a mfr., Newark, N.J., 1825; took part in 1st survey Boston and Providence R.R., worked on constrn. other railroads; opened engring. office, Boston, 1833; supr. constrn. Nashua and Lowell R.R., 1836-38; as engr. Amoskeag Mfg. Co. designed hydraulic works, Manchester, N.H.; designed turbine water-wheel for Appleton Cotton Mills, Lowell, Mass., 1844, designed three 190 horsepower turbines for same co.; best-known for developing the spiral approach which has advantage of admitting water to the turbine at uniform velocity; left most of his money to Bd. Trustees, Foxborough, Mass. for constrn. of observatories. Died Oct. 17, 1879.

BOYER, Benjamin Markley, congressman; b. Pottstown, Pa., Jan. 22, 1823; grad. U. Pa. at Phila., 1841; studied law. Admitted to bar, 1844, practiced law; dep. atty. gen. Montgomery County (Pa.), 1848-50; mem. U.S. Ho. of Reps. (Democrat) from Pa., 39th-40th congresses, 1865-69; judge Montgomery County Ct., 1882-87. Died Norristown, Pa., Aug. 16, 1887; buried West Laurel Hill Cemetery, Phila.

BOYESEN, Hjalmar Hjorth, author, educator; b. Frederiksuarn, Norway, Sept. 23, 1848; Ph.D., U. Christiania, Norway, 1868; studied philosophy and linguistics at U. Leipsig; m. Elizabeth Keen, 1874. Came to Am., settled in Chgo., 1869; became editor Norwegian weekly Fremad; Greek and Latin tutor Urbana U., Ohio; wrote novel Gunnar, published serially in Atlantic (through his acquaintance with William Dean Howells), 1873; prof. German, Cornell U., 1874-80; mem. German dept. Columbia, 1880-95, became Gebhard prof. German, 1882, prof. Germanic langs. and lits., 1890. Author: Goethe and Schiller, 1879; Idyls of Norway, 1886; The Modern Vikings, 1887; also 21 other volumes of novels, short stories, critical essays, books for boys. Died Oct. 4, 1895.

BOYLE, Charles Edmund, congressman; b. Uniontown, Pa., Feb. 4, 1836; attended Waynesburg (Pa.) Coll.; studied law. Admitted to bar, 1861, practiced law; dist atty. Fayette County (Pa.), 1862; mem. Pa. Ho. of Reps., 1865-66; pres. Pa. Democratic Conv., 1867, 71; del. Dem. Nat. Conv., 1876, 80; mem. U.S. Ho. of Reps. (Democrat) from Pa., 48th-49th congresses, 1883-87; judge Wash. Territory, 1888. Died Seattle, Wash., Dec. 15, 1888; buried Oak Grove Cemetery, Uniontown.

BOYLE, Jeremiah Tilford, railroad exec.; s. John and Elizabeth (Tilford) B.; studied law under Gov. William Owsley, Transylvania, Ky.; m. Elizabeth Owsley Anderson, 1842, 12 children. Practiced law, Danville, Ky., until 1861; a slave owner, but supported Union at outbreak of Civil War; commd. brig. gen. of co. of volunteers, 1861; apptd. by Edwin Stanton as mil. comdr. of Ky. after Battle of Shiloh, removed from post because of mil. ineptitude, 1864; organizer, pres. Louisville City R.R. Co.; pres. Evansville, Henderson & Nashville R.R., 1866. Died July 28, 1871.

BOYLE, John, congressman, jurist; b. "Castle Woods," nr. Clinch River, Va., Oct. 28, 1774; son of John Boyle; studied law under Thomas Davis; m. Elizabeth Tilford, 1797. Admitted to Ky. bar, 1797, began practice of law, Lancaster, Ky.; mem. Ky. Ho. of Reps., 1800; mem. U.S. Ho. of Reps. (Democrat) from Ky., 8th-10th congresses, 1803-09, mem. congl. bd. that conducted impeachment proceedings against judges John Pickering and Samuel Chase; judge Ky. Ct. of Appeals, 1809-10, chief justice, 1810-26; U.S. dist. judge for Ky., 1826-35. Died nr. Danville, Ky., Jan. 28, 1835; buried Bellevue Cemetery, Ky.

BOYLE, Thomas, privateersman; probably born Marblehead, Mass., circa June 29, 1776. In command of schooner Comet during War of 1812, took a total of 27 prizes and sum of over half-million dollars in spoils; given command of ship Chasseur, 1814, captured 18 prizes on ship's 1st cruise, captured Brit. schooner St. Lawrence off Cape Cod during Chasseur's final cruise, 1815; established war record of 80 prizes and over $1,000,000 in spoils (equals record of James Chever); returned to mcht. trade after war. Died at sea, circa Oct. 12, 1825.

BOYLSTON, Zabdiel, physician; b. Brookline, Mass., Mar. 9, 1679; s. Dr. Thomas and Mary (Gardner) B.; m. Jerusha Minot, Jan. 18, 1705, 8 children. First physician to introduce small pox inoculation into Am. during Boston epidemic, 1721, for which he was persecuted and his life frequently threatened; wrote books in defense of inoculation, including The Little Treatise on the Small pox, 1721; An Historical Account of the Small pox Inocculated in New England, 1726; fellow Royal Soc. Died

Brookline, Mar. 1, 1766; buried Old Cemetery, Brookline.

BOYNTON, Charles Brandon, clergyman; b. West Stockbridge, Mass., June 12, 1806; s. Henry and Mary (Meacham) B.; attended Williams Coll., 1824-26; m. Maria Van Buskirk, Nov. 5, 1834, 7 children. Ordained to ministry by Columbia Presbytery, 1840; in charge of Presbyn. Ch., Housatonic, Mass., 1840-45, Lansingburg, N.Y., 1845-46; minister 6th Presbyn. Ch., Cincinnati, 1846-56, 58-65, 73-77; chaplain U.S. Ho. of Reps., 1865-69. Author: A Journey Through Kansas, 1855; The Russian Empire: Its Resources, Government and Policy, 1856; English and French Neutrality and the Anglo-French Alliance, in their Relations to the United States and Russia, 1864; History of the Navy during the Rebellion, 1867-68. Died Cincinnati, Apr. 27, 1883.

BOYNTON, Edward Carlisle, army officer, educator; b. Windsor, Vt., Feb. 1, 1824; s. Thomas and Sophia (Cabot) B.; grad. U.S. Mil. Acad., 1846; m. Mary J. Hubbard. Commd. in Arty., served under Gen. Zachery Taylor in Mexican War; later served in battles of Vera Cruz, Cerro Gordo and Contreras under Gen. Winfield Scott; taught at U.S. Mil. Acad., 1849-56; prof. chemistry, mineralogy and geology U. Miss., 1856-61; allowed to leave Miss. at outbreak of Civil War after he took pledge not to take field against Confederacy; as result of pledge declined colonelcy of Vt. regt.; capt. 11th Inf., assigned as adjutant and q.m. of U.S. Mil. Acad., 1861-71; retired to Newburgh, N.Y., 1871; supt. water works for 8 years. Author: History of West Point, and Its Military Importance during the American Revolution; and the Origin and Progress of the United States Military Academy. Died May 13, 1893.

BOZEMAN, John M., pioneer; b. Ga., 1835; never married. Went to gold fields, Cripple Creek, Colo., 1861, then traveled to Virginia City, Mont., 1862; opened trail across Rocky Mountains from Virginia City to Julesburg, Colo. (now called Bozeman Pass), 1863-65; founded Town of Bozeman in Southwestern Mont. Killed by Blackfoot Indians while crossing Yellowstone River, Mont., Apr. 20, 1867.

BOZMAN, John Leeds, lawyer, historian; b. Oxford Neck, Md., Aug. 25, 1757; s. John and Lucretia (Leeds) B.; grad. Pa. Coll. (now U. Pa.), circa 1776; studied law under Judge Robert Greensborough, also Middle Temple, London, Eng. Admitted to Md. bar on his return from Eng.; dep. atty. gen. Md., 1789-1807; later retired to farm in Md. to devote himself to writing. Author: Observations on the Statute of 21 Jac. I. Ch. 16 in Application to Estates Tail, 1794; An Essay on the Late Institution of American Society for Colonizing the Free People of Color of the United States, 1820; The History of Maryland, from its First Settlement . . . To The Restoration, 2 vols., 1837. Died Apr. 20, 1823.

BRABSON, Reese Bowen, congressman, lawyer; b. Brabsons Ferry, nr. Knoxville, Tenn., Sept. 16, 1817; attended Dandridge (Tenn.) Acad.; grad. Maryville (Tenn.) Coll., 1840; studied law. Admitted to bar, 1848, began practice of law, Chattanooga, Tenn.; also engaged in agriculture; mem. Tenn. Ho. of Reps., 1851-52; mem. U.S. Ho. of Reps. (Democrat) from Tenn., 36th Congress, 1859-61. Died Chattanooga, Aug. 16, 1863; buried Citizens Cemetery.

BRACE, Charles Loring, author; b. Litchfield, Conn., June 19, 1826; s. John and Lucy (Porter) B.; grad. Yale, 1846; attended Yale Divinity Sch., 1847-49; m. Letitia Neill, circa 1854. Taught sch. in Ellington and Winchendon, Conn., 1846; took walking trips in Ireland, Eng. and Rhine Country, 1850, spent winter in Berlin; went to Hungary, spring 1851, imprisoned for being Kossuth sympathizer; founded Children's Aid Soc. (did work among immigrants), N.Y.C., 1853; became friend of Ralph Waldo Emerson, Charles Darwin, John Stuart Mill, during last years of his life; made final trip to Europe for health reasons, circa 1889. Author works including: Hungary in 1851; published 1852; Home Life in Germany, 1853; The Best Method of Disposing of our Pauper and Vagrant Children, 1859. Died Aug. 11, 1890.

BRACE, John Pierce, educator, editor; b. Litchfield, Conn., Feb. 10, 1793; s. James and Susan (Pierce) B.; grad. Williams (Mass.) Coll., 1812; attended Litchfield Law Sch.; m. Lucy Porter; m. 2d, Louisa Moreau. Head tchr., then asso. prin. of Miss Sarah Pierce's Sch., 1814-32, expanded curriculum by adding botany, astronomy and chemistry; prin. Hartford Female Sem., 1832-47; taught in acad., New Milford, Conn., 1847-49; editor Hartford (Conn.) Courant, 1849-63. Author: (novels) Tales of the Devils, 1847; The Fawn of the Pale Faces or, Two Centuries Ago, 1853. Died Litchfield, Oct. 18, 1872; buried Hartford.

BRACE, Jonathan, congressman, jurist; b. Harwinton, Conn., Nov. 12, 1754; grad. Yale, 1779; studied law. Admitted to bar, Bennington, Vt., 1779, began practice of law, Pawlet, Vt.; moved to Manchester, Vt., 1782; mem. council of censors to revise constn.; pros. atty. Bennington County, 1784-85; moved to Glastonbury, Conn., 1786; admitted to Conn. bar, 1790; mem. Conn. Gen. Assembly, 1788, 91-94, asst., 1798; moved to Hartford, Conn., 1794; judge City Ct., 1797-1815 (except for 2 years); mem. U.S. Ho. of Reps. (Federalist, filled vacancy) from Conn., 5th-6th congresses, Dec. 3, 1798-1800 (resigned); pros. atty. Hartford County, 1807-09; judge county ct., 1809-21; judge probate, 1809-24; mayor Hartford, 1815-24; mem. Conn. Senate, 1819-20. Died Hartford, Aug. 26, 1837; buried Old North Cemetery.

BRACKENRIDGE, Henry Marie, congressman, author; b. Pitts., May 11, 1786; s. Hugh Henry Brackenridge; studied law, Pitts., admiralty law, Balt., Spanish law, New Orleans; m. Caroline Marie Brackenridge, 1827. Admitted to Pa. bar, 1806; practiced in Carlisle, Somerset (both Pa.), also Mo. and La., 1810-14, Balt., 1814-17; contbr. articles to Mo. Gazette; dep. atty. gen., later dist. judge for La., mem. Md. Legislature, 1814-17, 19-21, supported bill to admit Jews to public office; sec., translator for Fla. Gov. Andrew Jackson, 1821-32, later became judge Fla. Territory (removed by Jackson); mem. U.S. Ho. of Reps. (Whig) from Pa., 26th Congress, Oct. 13, 1840-41; mem. commn. that provided for Mexican Treaty, 1839; ret. to Tarentum, Pa., devoted rest of life to literary activities. Author: Views of Louisiana, 1814; History of the Late War, 1816; The Voyage to South America, 1819; Letters to the Public, 1832; History of the Western Insurrection in Western Pennsylvania, 1859. Died Pitts., Jan. 18, 1871; buried Prospect Cemetery, Brackenridge, Pa.

BRACKENRIDGE, Hugh Henry, jurist, author; b. Campbeltown, Scotland, 1748; grad. Princeton, 1771, M.A., 1774; studied law under Samuel Chase, Annapolis, Md.; married twice; m. 2d, Sabina Wolfe, 1792; at least 1 son, Henry Marie. Came to York County, Pa., 1753; took charge acad., Md., 1763; collaborated with Philip Freneau on poem The Rising Glory of America, 1771; editor United States Mag., Phila., 1799; moved to Pitts., 1781; a founder Pitts. Gazette (1st newspaper in Pitts.), 1786, established Pitts. Acad., 1787, 1st bookstore in Pitts., 1789; mem. Pa. Assembly, 1793-94; took part in Whiskey Rebellion, 1793-94, exonerated by Alexander Hamilton; justice Pa. Supreme Ct., 1799-1816. Author: (plays) The Battle of Bunker Hill, 1776, The Death of General Montgomery (performed by Harvard students), 1777; Modern Chivalry, 1792-1815; The Standard of Liberty, 1804; Law Miscellanies, 1814. Died June 25, 1816.

BRACKENRIDGE, William D., botanist; b. Ayr, Scotland, June 10, 1810; studied under Friedrick Otto, Berlin, Germany. Head gardener of Dr. Patrick Neill's Grounds, Edinburgh, Scotland; came to Phila. in service of Robert Buist, 1837; mem. U.S. Govt. expdn. to explore Pacific, 1838-42 (collected 10,000 species of plants representing 40,000 specimens; findings formed core of Nat. Herbarium); in charge of greenhouse, Washington, D.C., entrusted with care of living plants and preparation of report on ferns of expdn., 1842-55; ret. to Balt., 1855, purchased 30-acre farm; hort. editor Am. Farmer for some years. Author: Filices, Including Lycopodiaceae and Hydropterides, Vol. XVI, 1854. Died Balt., Feb. 3, 1893.

BRADBURY, George, congressman, lawyer; b. Falmouth, Mass., Oct. 10, 1770; grad. Harvard, 1789; studied law. Admitted to bar, began practice of law, Portland, Mass. (now Me.); mem. Mass. Ho. of Reps., 1806-10, 11-12; mem. U.S. Ho. of Reps. (Federalist) from Mass., 13th-14th congresses, 1813-17; asso. clk. Portland Ct., 1817-20; mem. State Senate, 1820; charter mem. Me. Hist. Soc. Died Portland, Nov. 7, 1823; buried Eastern Cemetery.

BRADBURY, James Ware, senator, lawyer; b. Parsonfield, Me., June 10, 1802; s. Dr. James and Ann (Moulton) B.; grad. Bowdoin Coll., 1825; studied law in Me.; m. Eliza Ann Smith, Nov. 25, 1834. Prin., Hallowell Acad., 1829; founder 1st normal sch. in New Eng., at Effingham, N.H.; admitted to Me. bar, 1830, began practice of law, Augusta, Me.; editor Me. Patriot, Augusta, 1830; pros. atty. Me., 1834-38; presdl. elector for James Polk, 1844; mem. U.S. Senate (Democrat) from Me., 1847-53, supported Compromise of 1850, prepared bill which eventually led to creation of U.S. Ct. of Claims; elected overseer Bowdoin Coll., 1850, later trustee; pres. Me. Hist. Soc., 1873-89; practiced law, Augusta, until 1876. Died Augusta, Jan. 6, 1901; buried Forest Grove Cemetery, Me.

BRADBURY, Theophilus, congressman, jurist; b. Newbury, Mass., Nov. 13, 1739; s. Theophilus and Ann (Woodman) B.; grad. Harvard, 1757; m. Sarah Jones, 1762. Taught sch., Falmouth (now Portland, Me.); licensed to practice law before Me. Ct. of Common Pleas, 1762, began practice of law, Falmouth; apptd. collector of excise for Me. Dist. of Mass., 1763; admitted to bar of Superior Ct., Me. Dist. of Mass., 1765; state atty. Me. Dist. of Mass., 1777-79; moved to Newburyport, Mass., 1779; mem. Mass. Senate, 1791-94; mem. U.S. Ho. of Reps. (Federalist) from Mass., 4th-5th congresses, 1795-July 24, 1797 (resigned); judge Mass. Supreme Ct., 1797-1803. Died Newburyport, Sept. 6, 1803; buried Newburyport Cemetery.

BRADBURY, William Batchelder, music tchr., author; b. York, Me., Oct. 6, 1816; s. David and Sophia (Chase) B.; studied harmony under Sumner Hill, Boston, singing under Lowell Mason, Boston; studied under Boehme and Hauptmann, Leipsig, Germany, 1847-49. Taught singing, Machias, Me., 1836; organist Bklyn. Ch., 1840, 1st Baptist Ch., N.Y.C., 1841; initiated free singing classes, N.Y.C.; established (with brother Edward G.) Lighte, Newton & Bradbury Piano Co., 1854, later became Bradbury Piano Co. Author: The Young Choir, 1841; Mendelssohn Collection, 1849; The Shawm, 1853, also 47 other books on singing. Died Montclair, N.J., Jan. 7, 1868.

BRADDOCK, Edward, army officer; b. Perthshire, Scotland, 1695; s. Edward Braddock. Commd. maj. gen. Brit. Army, 1754; noted for his continental European mil. experience and stern mil. discipline; came to Hampton (Va.) as comdr.-in-chief of all His Majesty's forces in Am., 1755; built 1st road across Alleghanies in preparation for attack on Ft. Duquesne; victim of primitive Indian "guerrilla style" warfare (as opposed to continental column formation) at Battle of Ft. Duquesne; had horse shot from under him before he himself was killed; only the Indians' propensity for scalping dead and familiarity of colonial troops (under Washington) with Indian fighting, allowed fair number of defeated troops to escape safely to rear guard, thence to Ft. Cumberland. Died Great Meadows, Pa., July 13, 1755; buried Great Meadows.

BRADFORD, Alexander Warfield, lawyer; b. Albany, N.Y., Feb. 23 ,1815; s. Rev. John M. and Mary (Lush) B.; grad. Union Coll., Schenectady, N.Y., 1832. Admitted to N.Y. bar, 1837, began practice of law, N.Y.C.; corporation counsel to N.Y.C., 1843; surrogate for N.Y.C., 1848-58; mem. com. to reduce N.Y. State laws to systematic code, 1857-65. Author: American Antiquities and Researches into the Origin and History of the Red Race, 1841; Reports of Cases Argued and Determined in the Surrogate's Court of the County of New York, 4 vols., 1851-57. Died N.Y.C., Nov. 5, 1867.

BRADFORD, Allen, editor; b. Duxbury, Mass., Nov. 19, 1765; s. Col. Gamaliel and Sarah (Alden) B.; grad. Harvard, 1786; studied for ministry under Samuel West; m. Margaret Stevenson, 1795. Taught Sch., Milton, Mass., 1787; licensed to preach, 1790; tutor in Greek, Harvard, 1790-93; became pastor Congregational Ch., Wiscasset, Me., 1793, served until contracting tuberculosis; clk. of ct. for Lincoln County, Mass., until 1811; sec. Commonwealth of Mass., 1812-24; became editor Boston Gazette, 1824. Author: History of Massachusetts to 1820, published 1822-29; Life of Jonathan Mayhew, 1838; also 38 other books. Died Oct. 26, 1843.

BRADFORD, Allen Alexander, congressman; b. Friendship, Me., July 23, 1815; studied law, Mo. Admitted to bar, practiced law; clk. circuit ct. Atchison County (Mo.), 1845-51; moved to Ia.; judge 6th Jud. Dist., 1852-55; moved to Neb. Territory; mem. Neb. Territorial Ho. of Reps., 1856-58; moved to Colo. Territory, 1860; apptd. judge Supreme Ct. Colo. Territory by Pres. Lincoln, 1862; mem. U.S. Congress (Republican) from Colo. Territory, 39th, 41st congresses, 1865-67, 69-71; practiced law, Pueblo, Colo., until 1888. Died Pueblo, Mar. 12, 1888; buried City Cemetery.

BRADFORD, Andrew, publisher; b. 1686; s. William and Elizabeth (Sowle) B.; m. Miss Dorcas; m. 2d, Cornelia Smith; at least 1 child, William (adopted son). Went to N.Y.C. with his father, 1693, learned printing trade; moved to Phila., 1712, printed The Laws of the Province of Pennsylvania, 1714; later became ofcl. printer for Province of Pa., also imported books from Eng.; began publishing Am. Weekly Mercury (1st newspaper in Phila.), 1719; councilman of Phila.; vestryman Christ's Ch., Phila., 1726-37; postmaster Phila., 1728-38; began publishing Am. Mag. (1st Am. mag.), 1741. Died Nov. 24, 1742.

BRADFORD, Augustus Williamson, gov. Md.; b. Belair, Md., Jan. 9, 1806; s. Samuel and Jane (Bond) B.; grad. St. Mary's Coll., 1824; m. Elizabeth Kele, 1835, 7 children. Admitted to bar, 1827; Clk. Baltimore County (Md.), 1845; rep. from Md. to Washington (D.C.) Peace Conf., 1861; became gov. Md., 1861; surveyor Port of Balt., 1867-69. Died Balt., Mar. 1, 1881.

BRADFORD, Edward Green, jurist; b. Bohemia Manor, Md., July 17, 1819; s. Moses and Phoebe

(George) B.; attended Del. Coll., 1839; studied law under Edward Woodward Gilpin in Del. Admitted to Del. bar, 1842; dep. atty. gen. Del., 1842-50; mem. Del. Legislature, 1849; dist. atty. Del. (apptd. by Pres. Abraham Lincoln), 1861-66, resigned, returned to law practice; apptd. U.S. dist. ct. judge for Del. by Pres. U.S. Grant, 1871; dir. Wilmington Farmers' Bank (Del.), 30 years. Died Jan. 16, 1884.

BRADFORD, John, printer; b. Prince William, Va., June 6, 1749; s. Daniel and Alice Bradford; m. Eliza James, 1771, at least 1 son, Daniel. Moved to Ky., 1779, took part in survey Kentucky County (Va.) under George May; apptd. by 3d conv. for statehood of Ky. to publish Kentucke Gazette (spelling changed to Kentucky 1789), 1787; published Kentucke Almanac, 1788, Acts of First Session of Ky. Legislature (1st book printed in Ky.), 1792; served as dep. under Col. Thomas Marshall, 1st surveyor Fayette County (Ky.); clk. bd. Transylvania Sem. until 1795; founder Transylvania U., 1799, 1st chmn. bd.; helped found Lexington (Ky.) Library; mem. Ky. Ho. of Reps., 1797, 1802; published "Notes of Kentucky" in Ky. Gazette, 1826-29. Died Mar. 30, 1830.

BRADFORD, Joseph, (christened William Randolph Hunter), journalist, actor, playwright; b. nr. Nashville, Tenn., Oct. 24, 1843; attended U.S. Naval Acad., 1860-61. Enlisted as acting master's mate in North Atlantic Blockading Squadron, U.S. Navy, 1862, served in U.S.S. Minnesota and U.S.S. Putnam (this caused break with family); after Civil War went on stage under name Joseph Bradford in Balt.; later toured with stock co. along Eastern seaboard; wrote articles for Boston Courier signed Jay Bee. Author: (4 plays with F. Stinson including) New German, 1872, Law in New York, 1873; also, Out of Bondage, 1876; Our Bachelors, 1877; 10 other plays. Died Apr. 13, 1886.

BRADFORD, Taul, congressman, lawyer; b. Talladega, Ala., Jan. 20, 1835; grad. U. Ala. at Tuscaloosa, 1854; studied law. Admitted to bar, 1855, began practice of law, Talladega; served as maj. 10th Regt. Ala. Inf., then as lt. col. 13th Regt., Confederate Army during Civil War; mem. Ala. Ho. of Reps., 1871-72; mem. U.S. Ho. of Reps. (Democrat) from Ala., 44th Congress, 1875-77. Died Talladega, Oct. 28, 1883; buried Oak Hill Cemetery, Talladega.

BRADFORD, Thomas, publisher; b. May 4, 1745; s. William and Rachel (Budd) B.; attended U. Pa.; m. Mary Fisher, 1768, 6 children including Samuel, William, Thomas. Began working under his father on Pa. Journal and Weekly Advertiser, 1762, became full partner, 1766; took active part in resisting Stamp Act; his press temporarily suspended during Brit. occupation of Phila., 1777; served as capt. Pa. Militia, also lt. col. Continental Army, during Revolutionary War; started paper Mchts.' Daily Advertiser (specialized in news of business world), 1797, changed name to True American, 1798, added literary supplement; charter mem. Am. Philos. Soc. Died May 7, 1838.

BRADFORD, William, colonial gov.; b. Austerfield, Yorkshire, Eng., Mar. 1589; s. William and Alice (Hanson) B.; m. Dorothy May, Dec. 10, 1613; 1 son, John; m. 2d, Alice Carpenter, Aug. 14, 1623; 3 children, including William, Joseph. Mem. Separatists who settled in Leyden (Holland), 1609; defined his religious position as Calvinist in theology, Congregational in polity; a leader Pilgrim expdn. to N. Am., 1620; signer Mayflower Compact; one of those who landed at Plymouth Rock, Dec. 1620; mem. Miles Standish's 1st exploratory expdn. in N. Am., 1620; gov. Plymouth Colony, 1621-32, 35, 37, 39-43, 45-56, as gov. acted as prin. judge and treas. (no distinction then existed between exec., judicial and legislative authority), until 1637; possessed proprietary rights over colony under Warwick Patent of 1630; mem. com. which drafted 1st govtl. laws of Plymouth colony; one of 12 "undertakers" responsible for colony's debts, 1627, hampered by corruption among London mchts.; believed that econ. success depended on each resident having a financial interest in colony's prosperity; maintained attitude of religious toleration; friendly toward Mass. Bay Colony, co-operated in Pequot War, 1637, New Eng. Confedn., 1643; attempted to secure public support for ministry and public schs. Author: History of Plymouth Plantation, written, 1630-31, 46-50, 1st published, 1856. Died Plymouth, Mass., May 19, 1657.

BRADFORD, William, printer; b. Leicestershire, Eng., May 20, 1663; s. William Bradford; m. Elizabeth Sowle, Apr. 28, 1685; m. 2d, Cornelia Smith. Came to Phila., 1685; asso. founder 1st colonial paper mill, 1690; printer to King William and Queen Mary, N.Y., 1693-1742; printed Votes (proceedings of N.Y. Assembly, 1st Am. printed legislative proceedings); printed 1st N.Y. paper currency, 1709, 1st Am. Book of Common Prayer, 1710, 1st colonial written drama, 1714, 1st history of N.Y., 1727, 1st copperplate plan of N.Y., 1730; ofcl. printer N.J., 1703-33; founder, publisher N.Y. Gazette (1st newspaper in N.Y.C.), Nov. 8, 1725. Died N.Y.C., May 23, 1752.

BRADFORD, William, printer, patriot; b. N.Y.C., Jan. 19, 1722; s. William and Sytji (Santvoort) B.; m. Rachel Budd, Aug. 15, 1742, 6 children. Founder, editor Weekly Advertiser or Pa. Journal, 1742-93, became most widely circulated Am. newspaper of its time, successful rival to Benjamin Franklin's Pa. Gazette, editorial commentaries significantly influenced and directed pre-revolutionary pub. opinion, active supporter of colonist cause, dedicated opponent to Stamp Act of 1765; mem. Sons of Liberty; signer Non-Importation Resolutions of 1765; originator journalistic slogan "Unite or Die," 1774-75; printer 1st Continental Congress, 1775; served in Pa. Militia, 1776-78; chmn. Pa. Navy Bd., 1778. Died Phila., Sept. 25, 1791; buried Trinity Churchyard, N.Y.C.

BRADFORD, William, senator, lawyer; b. Plympton, Mass., Nov. 4, 1729; studied medicine, Hingham, Mass.; studied law. Practiced medicine, Warren, R.I.; admitted to bar, 1767, began practice of law, Bristol, R.I.; mem. R.I. Ho. of Reps., 1764-65, served as speaker; mem. R.I. Com. of Correspondence, 1773; dep. gov. R.I., 1775-78; elected del. to Continental Congress, did not serve; mem. U.S. Senate from R.I., 1793-Oct. 1797 (resigned), pres. pro tem, 1797. Died Bristol, July 6, 1808; buried East Burial Ground.

BRADFORD, William, lawyer, jurist; b. Phila., Sept. 14, 1755; s. William and Rachel (Budd) B.; A.B., Princeton, 1772, A.M., 1775; studied law under Edward Shippen; m. Susan Vergereau Boudinot. Served from pvt. to col., Continental Army, 1776-79, served at Valley Forge, White Plains, Fredericksborough and Raritan; admitted to Pa. bar, practiced in Yorktown, Pa.; atty. gen. of Pa., 1780-91; justice Pa. Supreme Ct., 1791-94; 2d atty. gen. U.S. under Pres. George Washington, 1794-95; on intimate terms with Washington circle (so-called "Republican Court"); indirectly responsible for Pa. Senate removing capitol punishment (except for 1st degree murder) from statute books. Died Aug. 23, 1795; buried St. Mary's Churchyard, Burlington, N.J.

BRADFORD, William, painter; b. Fairhaven, Mass., Apr. 30, 1823; s. Melvin and Hannah (Kempton) B.; m. Mary Breed, 1846. Began painting pictures of ships in Lynn Harbor, Mass., after his business failed, 1854, later painted landscapes; shared studio with Albert Van Beest, 2 years; made trip to Arctic with Dr. Hayes, also several trips to Labrador to paint icebergs and ice-floats; exhibited in most major cities of U.S., especially in Providence, R.I.; his painting "Steamer Panther Among Icebergs and Field-Ice in Melville Bay, Under the Light of the Midnight Sun" purchased by Queen Victoria and exhibited at Royal Acad., London, Eng., 1875; his work known for its exactness and realism. Died Apr. 25, 1892.

BRADISH, Alvah, artist; b. Sherburne, N.Y., Sept. 4, 1806. Worked in Rochester, N.Y., 1837-47; made several trips West; exhibited at N.A.D., 1846-47, 51; moved to Detroit, circa 1847; prof. art U. Mich, 1852-63; one of most successful portrait painters in Detroit for many years. Died Detroit, Apr. 2, 1901.

BRADISH, Luther, lawyer; b. Cummington, Mass., Sept. 15, 1783; s. Col. John and Hannah (Warner) B.; grad. Williams (Mass.) Coll., 1804; m. Helen Elizabeth Gibbs, 1814; m. 2d, Mary Eliza Hart, 1839; 2 children. Admitted to N.Y. bar; served as volunteer in War of 1812; sent by Sec. of State John Q. Adams to Turkey to seek out possibilities of a trade treaty (treaty delayed by Greek revolt), 1820; visited many European countries, returned to U.S., 1826; mem. N.Y. Assembly, 1827-30, 35-38, speaker, 1838; lt. gov. N.Y., 1838-42; asst. U.S. treas. for N.Y., 1842-44; pres. N.Y. Hist. Soc., 1849-63; pres. Am. Bible Soc. Died Newport, R.I., Aug. 30, 1863.

BRADLEE, Caleb Davis, clergyman; b. Boston, Feb. 24, 1831; s. Samuel and Elizabeth (Williams) B.; grad. Harvard, 1852; D.D. (hon.), Galesville U., 1888, Ph.D., 1889; D.D. (hon.), Tufts Coll., 1891; m. Caroline Gay, June 7, 1855. Ordained to ministry Congregational Ch., circa 1853; pastor ch., Cambridge, Mass., 1854-57, East Boston, Mass., 1861-64, various chs., Boston, 1864-93; moderator Boston Assn. of Ministers, 1892; hon. mem. Royal Soc. of No. Antiquaries (Copenhagen), Royal Acad. of Heraldry (Pisa, Italy), Soc. of Science, Letters and Art (London, Eng.). Author works including: Sermons for All Sects, 1882. Died Boston, 1897.

BRADLEE, Nathaniel J., architect; b. Boston; ed. Chauncey Hall Sch., Boston. Draftsman, in office of George M. Dexter, over 10 years, succeeded to Dexter's practice; became well known as architect of comml. bldgs. in Boston (perhaps as many as 500), including New Eng. Mut. Life Ins. Bldg. in Post Office Sq. (razed 1946), Boston & Me. R.R. Station in Haymarket Sq., Rialto Bldg., Hemenway Bldg., Commonwealth Bank Bldg.; employed by City of Boston to superintend removal of Hotel Pelham, 1868; architect numerous pub. bldgs., including State Insane Asylum, Danvers, Mass.; credited with design of Gray's Hall, Harvard (begun 1858); asso. with firm Winslow & Bigelow. Died on a train en route to Bellows Falls, Vt., Dec. 17, 1888.

BRADLEY, Charles William, diplomat; b. New Haven, Conn., June 27, 1807; s. Luther and Mary (Atwater) B.; attended Washington (now Trinity) Coll., Hartford, Conn., 1825, M.A. (hon.); grad. Gen. Theol. Sem., N.Y.C., 1830; M.A. (hon.), Yale; LL.D. (hon.), Hobart Coll., Geneva, N.Y., 1846. Rector several parishes in Conn., 1830-40; sec. of state Conn., 1846-47; U.S. consul at Amoy, 1849-54, at Singapore, 1854-57, Ningpo, 1857-60 (all China); negotiated Am.-Siamese treaty, 1857; mem. Pei-ho expdn. to China, 1858; sr. mem. Commn. on Am. Claims against Chinese Govt., 1859-60; asst. Imperial Chinese Customs Office, Hankow, 1860-63. Author: Patronomatology, 1842; The Connecticut Register: Being an Official State Calendar of Public Officers and Institutions in Connecticut for 1847, published 1848. Died New Haven, Mar. 8, 1865.

BRADLEY, Edward, congressman, lawyer; b. East Bloomfield, N.Y., Apr. 1808; attended acad., Canadaigua; studied law. Asso. judge Ontario County (N.Y.) Ct. of Common Pleas, 1836; moved to Detroit, 1839; admitted to bar, 1841, began practice of law, Marshall, Mich.; pros. atty. Calhoun County (Mich.), 1842; mem. Mich. Senate, 1842-43; mem. U.S. Ho. of Reps. (Democrat) from Mich., 30th Congress, 1847. Died in N.Y.C., en-route to Washington, D.C., Aug. 5, 1847; buried Congressional Cemetery, Washington.

BRADLEY, Frank Howe, geologist; b. New Haven, Conn., Sept. 20, 1838; grad. Yale, 1863; m. Sarah M. Bolles, 1867, 2 children. Discovered new species of trilobite in Potsdam sandstone of N.Y., 1857; after graduation spent over year in Panama collecting coral and other zool. materials; asst. geologist in survey of Ill., 1867, of Ind., 1869; prof. geology and mineralogy U. Tenn., 1869-75; mem. Nat. Survey, 1872, assigned to Snake River area of Ida.; contbr. article On the Silurian Age of the Southern Appalachians to Am. Jour. Sci., 1876. Killed (while engaged in pvt. mining venture) in cave-in nr. Nacooche, Ga., Mar. 27, 1879.

BRADLEY, Guy M., conservationist; b. 1870; s. E. R. Bradley; married, 2 sons. Lived in Flamingo, Fla.; apptd. ofcl. game warden (sponsored by Nat. Com. of Audubon Socs.) Monroe County (Fla.), 1902, in charge of rookeries in Cape Sable area, engaged in protecting the snowy egret from extinction due to demand for plumage by the millinery trade; attempted to arrest Tom Smith for poaching, 1905, shot by his father Capt. Walter Smith; Smith was arrested, prosecuted by attys. engaged by Nat. Assn. of Audubon Socs., but released after trial due to insufficient evidence; irate citizens of Flamingo burned Smith's house; Bradley's death spurred movement which ultimately resulted in founding of Everglades Nat. Park (Fla.), and preservation of several species of rare and beautiful birds; meml. marker placed at Cape Sable by Fla. Audubon Soc. Killed Oyster Keys, Fla., July 8, 1905; buried Everglades Nat. Park.

BRADLEY, Joseph P., asso. justice U.S. Supreme Ct.; b. Berne, N.Y., Mar. 14, 1813; s. Philo and Mercy (Gardiner) B.; grad. Rutgers Coll., 1836; LL.D. (hon.), Lafayette Coll., 1859; m. Mary Hornblower, 1844. Asso. Justice U.S. Supreme Ct. (apptd. by Pres. Grant), 1868-92, cast decisive vote in Knox vs. Lee Legal Tender Act, 1869, also Hayes-Tildon Electoral Commn., 1877; author opinions influential in U.S. constl. law; assigned to 3rd Circuit (including Pa., N.J. and Del.), 1880. Died Washington, D.C., Jan. 22, 1892.

BRADLEY, Lucas, architect; b. London, Eng. Came to U.S., settled in St. Louis; practiced architecture, St. Louis; designed 2d Presbyn. Ch., St. Louis (built 1840); 1st Presbyn. Ch., Racine, Wis., built from his plans, 1851. Flourished mid-19th Century.

BRADLEY, Stephen Row, senator; b. Wallingford (later Cheshire), Conn., Feb. 20, 1754; s. Moses and Mary (Row) B.; grad. Yale, 1775; studied law under Tapping Reeve, Litchfield, Conn.; m. Merab Atwater, at least 1 son, William Czar; m. 2d, Thankful Taylor; m. 3d, Belinda Willard. Commd. capt. volunteers Continental Army, 1776, resigned as col. at end of Revolutionary War; admitted to Vt. bar, 1779; state's atty. for Cumberland County, Vt., 1780; register probate for Westminister, Vt., 1782; judge Windham County, Vt., 1783; speaker Vt. Ho. of Reps., 1785; asso. justice Vt. Superior Vt., 1788; mem. Westminster City Council, 1798; mem. U.S. Senate from Vt., Oct. 17, 1791-95, Oct. 15, 1801-13, pres. pro tem, 1802-03, 08, introduced bill to establish nat. flag of 15 stripes and 15 stars, used from 1795-1814 (sometimes called Bradley flag). Died Walpole, N.H., Dec. 9, 1830; buried Old Cemetery, Westminster, Vt.

BRADLEY, Warren Ives, author; b. Bristol, Conn., Mar. 27, 1847. Author: Boys at Dr. Murray's,

1866; Uncle Donnie's Home, 1866; Gay Cottage, 1867; After Years, 1868; Mr. Pendleton's Cup, 1869; other works. Died Bristol, June 15, 1868.

BRADLEY, William Czar, congressman; b. Westminster, Vt., Mar. 23, 1782; s. Stephen Row and Merab (Atwater) B.; attended Yale, 1 year; studied law under Judge Simeon Strong, under Mr. Ashmun, Mass.; m. Sarah Richards, 1802, at least 1 child. After being expelled from Yale father presented him with dung fork and set him to work at manure heap; sec. of commr. of bankruptcy of Westminster, 1800; admitted to Vt. bar, 1802; pros. atty. Windham County, Vt., 1804-11; mem. Vt. Ho. of Reps., 1806-07, 50; mem. Vt. Gov.'s Council, 1812; mem. U.S. Ho. of Reps. (Democrat) from Vt., 13th, 18th-19th congresses, 1813-15, 23-27; U.S. agt. under Treaty of Ghent with Eng. to fix Me.-Can. border, 1815-20; mem. Vt. Constl. Conv., 1857. Died Westminster, Mar. 3, 1867; buried Old Cemetery, Westminster.

BRADSHAW, Samuel Carey, congressman, physician; b. Plumstead, Pa., June 10, 1809; grad. Pa. Med. Coll., 1833. Practiced medicine, Quakertown, Bucks County, Pa.; mem. U.S. Ho. of Reps. (Whig) from Pa., 34th Congress, 1855-57. Died Quakertown, June 9, 1872; buried Friends Burial Ground.

BRADSTREET, Anne Dudley, poetess; b. Northampton, Eng., circa 1612; d. Thomas and Dorothy Dudley; m. Simon Bradstreet, 1628, 8 children. Came to Mass. Bay with her husband and family in party of John Winthrop, 1630; moved to North Andover, Mass., 1644, began writing her 1st book of poems (1st woman to write poetry in Am.); wrote mostly didactic and religious (but anti-ritualistic) verse, in 7-line stanzas closing with an alexandrine (in tradition of Sidney and Spenser); most famous poems: "Elements," "Ages," "Seasons," "The Four Monarchyes." Author: The Tenth Muse, published in Eng., 1650. Died Sept. 16, 1672.

BRADSTREET, John, army officer; b. Horbling, Eng., 1711. Sent as young Brit. officer to Am., 1745; served as lt. col. Pepperell's Regt. in expdn. against Louisburg, Me.; made capt., 1745; lt. gov. St. John's, Newfoundland, 1746-55; adjutant gen. to Gov. Shirley, Boston, 1755-57; lt. col. 60th Regt. Royal Americans, 1757-58; participated in attack on Ft. Ticonderoga; served under Lord Jeffery Amherst, 1759; served in Pontiac's War, negotiated Peace Treaty in Detroit, 1764. Died N.Y.C., Sept. 25, 1774.

BRADSTREET, Simon, colonial gov.; b. Lincolnshire, Eng., Mar. 1603; A.B., Emmanuel Coll., Cambridge (Eng.) U., 1620, A.M., 1624; m. Anne Dudley (poet), 1628, 8 children; m. 2d, Anne (Downing) Gardner. Came to Mass., 1630; assistant to Mass. Bay Co., 1630-78; sec. Mass. Bay Colony, 1630-36; mem. commn. to deal with other New Eng. colonies (resulted in founding of New Eng. Confederation), 1643; mem. New Eng. Confederation, 1644-77; gov. Mass., 1679-86, 89-92. Died Salem, Mass., Mar. 27, 1697.

BRADWELL, Myra Colby, lawyer; born in Manchester, Vt., Feb. 12, 1831; d. Eben and Abigail (Willey) Colby; m. Judge B. Bradwell, 1852, 4 children. Sch. tchr.; established a pvt. sch. with husband, Memphis, Tenn.; went to Chgo., 1854; husband admitted to Ill. bar, 1855; studied law independently and under her husband; founded Chgo. Legal News, 1868, acted as editor, also bus. mgr.; passed Ill. bar exam, 1869, refused admission to bar because she was a married woman under disability, refused again on re-argument because she was a woman, U.S. Supreme Ct. upheld decision of state ct., 1873; largely responsible for passage by Ill. Legislature of law granting freedom of choosing a profession to all persons, 1884; I[illegible] Supreme Ct. directed that she be given a license [illegible]practice, 1885; admitted to practice before U.S. Supreme Ct., 1892; 1st woman mem. Ill. State Bar Assn., Ill. Press Assn.; summoned 1st woman's suffrage conv., Chgo., 1869. Died Chgo., Feb. 14, 1894.

BRADY, James Topham, lawyer; b. N.Y.C., Apr. 9, 1815; s. Thomas Brady. Admitted to N.Y. bar, 1836; apptd. dist. atty. N.Y., 1843; counsel in 52 murder trails (failed in only one); Democratic candidate for gov. N.Y., 1860; refused Tammany mayorship of N.Y.C., 1861; considered one of most brilliant of all members N.Y. bar. Died N.Y.C., Feb. 9, 1869.

BRADY, Jasper Ewing, congressman, lawyer; b. Sunbury, Pa., Mar. 4, 1797; attended common schs.; studied law. Learned hatter's trade; taught sch., Franklin County, Pa.; admitted to bar, 1827, began practice of law, Chambersburg, Pa.; treas. Franklin County, 3 years; mem. Pa. Ho. of Reps., 1844-45; mem. U.S. Ho. of Reps. (Whig) from Pa., 30th Congress, 1847-49; moved to Pitts., 1849, resumed practice of law; clk. Office of Paymaster Gen., War Dept., Washington, D.C., 1861-69. Died Washington, Jan. 26, 1871; buried City Cemetery, Sunbury; reinterred Rock Creek Cemetery, Washington, 1893.

BRADY, Matthew B., photographer; b. Warren County, N.Y., 1823; m. Julia Handy, 1860. Established portrait studio, N.Y.C., circa 1842, br. studio Washington, D.C., 1858; exhibited ann. exhbns. Am. Inst., 1844-48 (recipient silver medal in each); recipient 1st gold medal ever awarded for daguerreotypes, 1849; held exhbn. called Gallery of Illustrious Americans, 1850; converted to actual photography, 1855; Civil War photographer; his collections form the basis of photographic histories of Civil War; suffered financially from Civil War, Panic of 1873. Died N.Y.C., Jan. 15, 1896.

BRAGG, Braxton, army officer; b. Warren County, N.C., Mar. 22, 1817; s. Thomas and Margaret (Crossland) B.; grad. U.S. Mil. Acad., N.Y., 1837; m. Elisa Ellis, 1849. Brevetted capt. U.S. Army, 1846; served with distinction under Zachary Taylor during Mexican War; served as lt. col. at Battle of Buena Vista, 1847; served as col., maj. gen. La. Militia, 1861; commd. brig. gen. Confederate States Army, 1861, maj. gen., 1862, gen., 1862; fought against Gen. Don Carlos Buell at Battle of Perryville (Ky.), Oct. 8, 1862, forced to retreat into Tenn., battle marked end of Confederate invasion of Ky.; most famous for victory at Battle of Chickamauga, 1863; later defeated by U.S. Grant at Battle of Chattanooga, forced to retreat into Ga.; comdr.-in-chief Confederate Army, also mil. adviser to Pres. Davis, 1864; supt. New Orleans Water Works, 1869; chief engr. Gulf, Colorado and Santa Fe. R.R., 1874. Died Galveston, Tex., Sept. 27, 1876.

BRAGG, John, congressman, lawyer; b. nr. Warrenton, N.C., Jan. 14, 1806; grad. U. N.C. at Chapel Hill, 1824; studied law. Admitted to bar, 1830, began practice of law, Warrenton; mem. N.C. Ho. of Commons, 1830-34; moved to Mobile, Ala., 1836, continued practice of law; apptd. judge 10th Jud. Circuit, 1842; mem. Ala. Ho. of Reps.; mem. U.S. Ho. of Reps. (State Rights Democrat) from Ala., 32d Congress, 1851-53; del. from Mobile to Ala. Constl. Conv., 1861. Died Mobile, Aug. 10, 1878; buried Magnolia Cemetery.

BRAGG, Thomas, senator, gov. N.C., Confederate ofcl.; b. Warrentown, N.C., Nov. 9, 1810; s. Thomas and Margaret (Crossland) B.; m. Isabella Cuthbert, Oct. 4, 1837. Mem. N.C. Legislature, 1842-43; gov. N.C., 1854-58; mem. U.S. Senate from N.C., 1859-July 1861; atty. gen. Confederacy, 1861-62; resumed practice of law after Civil War. Died Raleigh, N.C., Jan. 21, 1872.

BRAINARD, Daniel, surgeon, educator; b. N.Y., May 15, 1812; s. Jeptha and Catherine (Comstock) B., Jr.; studied medicine under Dr. R. S. Sykes, Whitesboro, N.Y., Dr. Harold H. Hope, Rome, N.Y.; attended Fairfield Med. Coll., N.Y.; M.D., Jefferson Med. Coll., 1834; m. Evelyn Slight, Feb. 6, 1845. Practiced medicine, Chgo., 1836; went to Paris, France, 1839-41, influenced by French sch. of surgery; prof. anatomy and surgery Rush Med. Coll., Chgo., 1843-66; a founder Ill. Med. and Surg. Jour., 1844; also contbr.; corr. mem. Societé de Chirurgie, 1853; pres. Ill. Med. Soc., 1854. Author papers including The Venom of Rattlesnakes; The Effects of the Venom, and the Means of Neutralizing its Absorption, 1853. Died Chgo., Oct. 10, 1866.

BRAINARD, John Gardiner Calkins, poet; b. Conn., Oct. 21, 1796; s. Jeremiah G. and Sarah (Gardiner) B.; grad. Yale, 1815; studied law under William F. Brainard in Conn. Admitted to Conn. bar, 1819, practiced law in Conn. for a short time; editor Conn. Mirror, 1822-27. Author: Occasional Pieces of Poetry, 1825; Fort Braddock Letters, 1827. Died New London, Conn., Sept. 26, 1828.

BRAINERD, David, missionary; b. Haddam, Conn., Apr. 20, 1718; s. Hezekiah and Dorothy (Hobart) B.; attended Yale, 1742; studied theology under Rev. Jedediah Mills, Ripton, Conn. Licensed to preach by Assn. of Ministers, Danbury, Conn., 1742; apptd. an Indian missionary by Correspondents of the Soc. in Scotland for the Propagation of Christian Knowledge, 1742; worked among Indians at Kaunaumeek, N.Y., 1743; ordained by Presbytery of N.Y. at Newark, N.J., 1744, did missionary work among Indians around what is now Easton, Pa. Died Oct. 9, 1747.

BRAINERD, John, missionary; b. Haddam, Conn., Feb. 28, 1720; s. Hezkiah and Dorothy Hobart (Mason) B.; grad. Yale, 1746; m. Experience Lyon, Nov. 1752; m. 2d, Mrs. Price. Licensed to preach by N.Y. Presbytery, 1747; apptd. Indian missionary by Correspondents of Soc. in Scotland for Propagation of Faith, 1747, dismissed for his inability to care for the Indians, 1755; given charge of ch., Newark, N.J.; trustee Coll. of N.J., 1754; made several unsuccessful attempts at missionary work; his last post was pastor of ch., Deerfield, N.J. Died Deerfield, Mar. 18, 1781; buried under Presbyn. Ch., Deerfield.

BRAINERD, Lawrence, businessman, senator; b. East Hartford, Conn., Mar. 16, 1794; s. Ezra and Mabel (Porter) B.; m. Fidelia B. Gadcomb, 1819, 12 children. Established merc. bus., 1814; dir., later pres. Bank of St. Albans (Vt.), 1826; engaged in railroad bldg. in Can.; mem. Vt. Legislature, 1834; mem. U.S. Senate from Vt. Oct. 14, 1854-Mar. 3, 1855 (filled vacancy); presided over 1st Nat. Republican Conv., Phila., 1856. Died St. Albans, May 9, 1870; buried Greenwood Cemetery, St. Albans.

BRAINERD, Thomas, clergyman; b. Leyden, N.Y., June 17, 1804; s. Jesse and Mary (Thomas) B.; grad. Andover Theol. Sem., 1831; m. Sarah J. Langstroth, Oct. 20, 1831; m. 2d, Mrs. Mary Whiting, Oct. 29, 1836. Ordained to ministry Presbyn. Ch., in N.Y., 1831, accepted commn. to take over ch. nr. Cincinnati, 1831-33; asso. pastor 2d Ch. of Cincinnati, 1833-37; editor of several mags., Cincinnati, 1833-37; pastor 3d Ch. of Phila., 1837-66; moderator New Sch. Gen. Assembly of Pa., 1864-66. Author works including: The Life of John Brainerd, 1865. Died Scranton, Pa., Aug. 21, 1866.

BRAMLETTE, Thomas E., gov. Ky.; b. Cumberland County, Ky., Jan. 3, 1817; m. Sallie Travis, 1837, m. 2d, Mrs. Mary E. Adams, 1874. Admitted to Ky. bar, 1837; states atty. Ky., 1848; judge 6th Jud. Dist. Ky., 1856; U.S. dist. atty., 1862; commd. maj. gen. U.S. Army, 1863; gov. Ky. (Union Democrat), 1863-67; declined Dem. vice presdl. nomination, 1864. Died Louisville, Ky., Jan. 12, 1875.

BRANCH, John, senator, gov. N.C.; b. Halifax County, N.C., Nov. 4, 1782; s. Col. John and Mary (Bradford) B.; grad. U. N.C., 1801; m. Elizabeth Fort, m. 2d, Eliza Jordan, 9 children. Mem. N.C. Senate, 1811, 13-17, 22, 34, speaker, 1815-17; gov. N.C., 1817-20; mem. N.C. br. Am. Colonization Soc., 1819; mem. U.S. Senate from N.C., 1823-29; U.S. sec. of navy, 1829-31; mem. U.S. Ho. of Reps. from N.C., 22d Congress, 1831-33; mem. N. C. Constl. Conv., 1835; gov. Territory of Fla., 1843-45. Died Enfield, N.C., Jan. 4, 1863.

BRANCH, Lawrence O'Bryan, army officer; congressman, b. Enfield, N.C., July 7, 1820; s. John and Susan (O'Bryan) B.; grad. Princeton, 1838; m. Nancy Blount, 1844. Pres., Raleigh & Gaston R.R. Co., (N.C.) 1852-55; mem. U.S. Ho. of Reps. from N.C., 34th-36th congresses, Dec. 3, 1855-61; commd. brig. gen. Confederate Army, 1862. Died Battle of Antietam, Sept. 17, 1862.

BRANDEIS, Frederic (Friedrich), musician; b. Vienna, Austria, July 5, 1835; studied music. Came to U.S., 1849; made debut as pianist, N.Y.C., 1851; toured U.S. with various troupes, including Vincent Wallace's concert-company, appeared as solo pianist and condr.; organist for several churches, N.Y.C. Composer numerous works for piano, also songs. Died N.Y.C., May 14, 1899.

BRANDON, Gerard Chittocque, gov. Miss.; b. Natchez, Miss., Sept. 15, 1788; s. Col. Gerard and Dorothy (Nugent) B.; grad. Coll. William and Mary, 1808; m. Margaret Chambers, 1816; m. 2d, Elizabeth Stanton, 1824; 10 children including Gerard, John C.; Elected to Mississippi Territory Legislature, 1815; mem. Miss. Constl. Conv., 1817; 32; lt. gov. Miss., 1825-26, gov., 1827-31; declined U.S. senatorship, 1832. Died Wilkinson County, Miss., Mar. 28, 1850.

BRANDT, Carl Ludwig, artist; b. Hamburg, Germany, Sept. 22, 1831. Came to Am., 1852, settled in N.Y.C.; exhibited at N.A.D., 1855, 60, 1862-84, elected mem., 1872; dir. Telfair Acad., Savannah, Ga. Died Savannah, Jan. 20, 1905.

BRANN, William Cowper, editor; b. Humboldt, Ill., Jan. 4, 1855; m. Carrie Martin, Mar. 3, 1877, at least 2 children, Grace Gertrude, William Carlyle. Reporter, St. Louis Globe-Democrat, circa 1875-87, 92; editorial writer Houston (Tex.) Post, 1887-91; founded, edited monthly journal Iconoclast, Austin, Tex., 1891; editor San Antonio (Tex.) Express, 1892-94; established newspaper Iconoclast, Waco, Tex., 1894-98, editorials caused much public resentment because of their fanatical calls for reform and vituperative language; started violent quarrel with Baylor U., Baptist school in Waco. Killed in gunfight with T. E. Davis (patron of Baylor who was angered by Brann's attacks on the univ.), Waco, Apr. 2, 1898.

BRANNAN, John Milton, army officer; b. D.C., July 1, 1819; grad. U.S. Mil. Acad., 1841. Brevetted 2d lt. arty. U.S. Army, 1841, stationed at Plattsburg, N.Y. until 1842; commd. 2d lt., 1842; promoted 1st lt. arty. at outbreak Mexican War, 1846, adjutant 1st Arty., 1847; served in battles of Vera Cruz, Contreras and Churubusco; brevetted capt. for bravery, 1847; wounded in assault on Chapultepc, served in occupation of city; promoted capt., 1854; engaged in battle with Seminole Indians in Fla., 1856-58; apptd. brig. gen. U.S. Volunteers in charge of Key West, Fla., also operations on St. John's River, at beginning of Civil War; brevetted lt. col. U.S. Army for bravery at Jacksonville, 1862; promoted maj., 1863; brevetted col. for bravery at Chickamauga, 1863; served at Battle of Missionary Ridge, 1863; commanded arty. at siege of Atlanta; brevetted brig. gen. U.S. Army for bravery at Atlanta, 1865; commanded garrison at Ogdensburg, N.Y.; promoted lt. col. 4th Arty., 1877, col., 1881; ret., 1882. Died Dec. 16, 1892.

BRANNAN, Samuel, businessman; b. Saco, Me., Mar. 2, 1819. Learned printing trade, Ohio, 1836; converted to Ch. of Jesus Christ of Latter Day Saints, 1842; moved to N.Y.C.; published N.Y. Messenger, 1842; elder Mormon Ch., chosen to lead expdn. to Mexican Cal., 1845; sailed in ship Brooklyn with 238 persons; arrived in Cal. (1st Anglo Am. settlers in Cal. after its capture by U.S. during Mexican War), 1846; published Cal. Star (1st paper in San Francisco), 1847-48; moved to Sutter's Ft., 1848-49, left for San Francisco when gold rush made San Francisco more prosperous; mem. 1st city council of San Francisco, circa 1849; an organizer Soc. Cal. Pioneers; 1st pres. San Francisco Com. of Vigilance, 1851; promoter and investor in agr., railroads, telegraph, banks, became one of wealthiest men in Cal. Died in poverty (mainly due to excessive drinking), Escondido, Cal., May 5, 1889.

BRANT, Joseph (Indian name: Thayendanegea), Indian chief; b. Ohio River Banks, 1742; ed. Moor's Charity Sch., Lebanon, Conn. Chief, Mohawk Indians; became Anglican convert; sec. to supt. Indian affairs, 1774; served as capt. Brit. Army during Am. Revolution; directed Cherry Valley Massacre of 1778; painted by Romney in Mohawk regalia; presented at Ct. in Eng., 1785; built 1st Episcopal Ch. erected in upper Can., 1786; King of Eng. gave him an estate at head of Lake Ont. Died Wellington Sq., Can., Nov. 24, 1807.

BRATTLE, Thomas, mcht.; b. Boston, June 20, 1658; s. Thomas and Elizabeth (Tyng) B., grad. Harvard, 1676; never married. Inherited father's estate and business, 1683; treas., Harvard, 1693-1713; chief organizer Brattle St. Ch., 1698; involved in controversy with the Mathers over orgn. of Harvard corp., also in intense religious dispute with the Mathers, condemned Salem witchcraft proceedings, 1692. Died Boston, May 18, 1713.

BRATTLE, William, clergyman; b. Boston, Nov. 22, 1662; s. Thomas and Elizabeth (Tyng) B.; grad. Harvard, 1680; m. Elizabeth Hayman; m. 2d, Elizabeth Gerrish; at least 1 son, William. Tutor, Harvard, 1680-96; fellow Harvard Corp., 1696-1700, gained title "Father of the College" for his heroic work during smallpox epidemic; ordained to ministry Congregational Ch., became pastor of ch. in Cambridge, Mass., 1696. Author works including: Compendium Logicae Secundum Principia D. Renati Cartesii (1st Am. textbook on logic used at Harvard). Died Feb. 26, 1717.

BRATTON, John, physician, state legislator; b. Winnsboro, S.C., Mar. 7, 1831; s. Dr. William, Jr. and Isabella (Means) B.; grad. S.C. Coll., 1850; M.D., S.C. Med. Coll., 1853; m. Elizabeth DuBose, 1859. Practiced medicine, Fairfield County, S.C., until Civil War; served with 6th Regt., S.C. Volunteers during Civil War, promoted capt., 1861, col., 1862, brig. gen., 1864, known as "Old Reliable"; mem. S.C. Constl. Conv., 1865, S.C. Senate, 1865-66, S.C. Ho. of Reps., 1884-85. Died Winnsboro, Jan. 12, 1898.

BRATTON, Robert Franklin, congressman, lawyer; b. Barren Creek Springs, Somerset (now Wicomico) County, Md., May 13, 1845; grad. Washington Coll., Chestertown, Md., 1864. Dep. register of wills Somerset County; admitted to bar, 1867; mem. Md. Conv. of 1865 (which sent dels. to peace conv., Phila., 1866); mem. Md. Ho. of Reps., 1869; mem. Md. Senate, 1873, 79, 87, 90, pres., 1890; practiced law, Princess Anne, Md.; mem. U.S. Ho. of Reps. (Democrat) from Md., 53d Congress, 1893-94. Died Princess Anne, May 10, 1894; buried St. Andrew's Cemetery.

BRAXTON, Carter, Continental congressman; b. Newington, Va., Sept. 10, 1736; s. George and Mary (Carter) B.; ed. Coll. William and Mary; m. Judith Robinson, 1755; m. 2d, Elizabeth Corbin, May 1761; 16 children. Mem. Va. Ho. of Burgesses, 1761-75; signer Resolutions, 1769, Non-importation Agreement, 1769; rep. Va. Revolutionary convs., 1774, 75, 76; mem. Continental Congress, 1776; signer Declaration of Independence; mem. Continental Congress, 1775-76, 77-83, 1785; mem. Council State of Va., 1786-94. Died Richmond, Va., Oct. 10, 1797.

BRAXTON, Elliott Muse, congressman, lawyer; b. Matthews, Va., Oct. 8, 1823; attended common schs.; studied law. Admitted to bar, 1849, began practice of law, Richmond, Va.; moved to Richmond County; mem. Va. Senate, 1851-55; moved to Fredericksburg, Va., 1860, continued practice of law; raised company for Confederate Army, elected its capt., during Civil War; commd. maj., served on staff of Gen. J. R. Cooke; mem. Fredericksburg Common Council, 1866; mem. U.S. Ho. of Reps. (Democrat) from Va., 42d Congress, 1871-73. Died Fredericksburg, Oct. 2, 1891; buried Confederate Cemetery.

BRAY, Thomas, clergyman; b. Marton, Eng., 1656; grad. All Souls Coll., Oxford (Eng.) U., 1678. Apptd. commissary of Ch. of Eng. to Md., 1696; influential in furnishing Md. with library collections; organizer Soc. for Promoting Christian Knowledge, 1699; a promoter of founding Soc. for Propagation of Gospel, 1701; rector St. Botolph's Without, Aldgate, Md., 1706-30. Author: Missionalia, 1727. Died Feb. 26, 1730.

BRAYMAN, Mason, gov. Ida.; b. Buffalo, N.Y., May 23, 1813; s. Daniel and Anna (English) B.; m. Mary Williams. Admitted to N.Y. bar, 1836; city atty. Monroe, Mich., 1838; revised, published Statutes of Illinois, 1844-45; atty. I.C. R.R., 1851; promoter railroad enterprises in Mo., Ark. and S.W.; editor Ill. State Jour., 1872-73; gov. Territory of Ida., 1876-80. Died Kansas City, Mo., Feb. 27, 1895.

BRAYTON, William Daniel, congressman; b. Warwick, R.I., Nov. 6, 1815; attended Kent Acad., East Greenwich, also Kingston Acad.; attended Brown U., 2 years. Engaged in business; served as maj. 4th Regt. R.I. Militia in Dorr Rebellion; town clk. Warwick, 1844, mem. town council; mem. R.I. Ho. of Reps., 1841, 51, R.I. Senate, 1848, 53; Republican presdl. elector, 1856; mem. U.S. Ho. of Reps. (Rep.) from R.I., 35th-36th congresses, 1857-61; collector internal revenue for 2d Dist. R.I., 1862-71; del. Rep. Nat. Conv., Phila., 1872; in charge of money-order div. Providence (R.I.) Post Office, several years. Died Providence, June 30, 1887; buried Brayton Cemetery, Apponaug, R.I.

BRAZER, John, clergyman; b. Worcester, Mass., Sept. 21, 1789; s. Samuel and Betsey Brazer; grad. Harvard, 1813, D.D. (hon.), 1836; m. Anne Warren Sever, Apr. 19, 1821. Prof. Latin, Harvard, 1817-20; ordained to ministry Unitarian Ch., 1820; pastor North Ch., Salem, Mass., 1820-46; contbr. to N. Am. Review, Christian Examiner; a forerunner of Transcendentalism in U.S. Died Charleston, S.C., Feb. 25, 1846.

BREARLEY, David, jurist; b. Spring Grove, N.J., June 11, 1745; s. David and Mary (Clark) B.; m. Elizabeth Mullen, circa 1767; m. 2d, Elizabeth Higbee, Apr. 17, 1783. Commd. lt. col. 4th N.J. Regt., Continental Army, 1776, 1st N.J. Regt., 1777; mem. N.J. Constl. Conv., 1779; chief justice Supreme Ct. of N.J., 1779; N.J. del. to U.S. Constl. Conv., 1787; chmn. N.J. Conv. to ratify U.S. Constn., 1788; U.S. dist. judge, 1789-90; v.p. N.J. Soc. of Cincinnati; del to Episcopal Gen. Conv., 1786. Died Trenton, N.J., Aug. 16, 1790.

BRECK, Daniel, congressman, lawyer; b. Topsfield, Mass., Feb. 12, 1788; grad. Dartmouth, 1812; studied law. Taught sch.; admitted to bar, 1814, began practice of law, Richmond, Ky.; judge Richmond County Ct.; mem. Ky. Ho. of Reps., 1824-27, 34; Whig presdl. elector, 1841; pres. Richmond br. State Bank of Ky., 1835-43; asso. justice Ky. Supreme Ct., 1843-49; mem. U.S. Ho. of Reps. (Whig) from Ky., 31st Congress, 1849-51. Died Richmond, Feb. 4, 1871; buried Richmond Cemetery.

BRECK, James Lloyd, clergyman; b. nr. Phila., June 27, 1818; s. George and Catherine D. (Israell) B.; grad. U. Pa., 1838; attended Gen. Theol. Sem., N.Y.C.; m. Jane Maria Mills, 1855; m. 2d, Sarah Styles, 1864. Travelled to Nashotah, Wis., 1841, Episcopalian missionary among settlers, 1842-50, a founder Nashotah Theol. Sem. (a revival of disciplined religious community life); attempted to found strict religious order in St. Paul, Minn., missionary among Chippewa Indians, 1855-59; opened ednl., agrl. and mission centers at Crow Wing and Leech Lake; missionary, Faribault, Minn., 1859-67; founder St. Augustine Coll., St. Mary's Sch. for girls, Benicia, Cal., 1867-76. Died Mar. 30, 1876. Leech Lake; missionary, Faribault, Minn., 1859-67; founder St. Augustine Coll., St. Mary's Sch. for girls, Benicia, Cal., 1867-76. Died Mar. 30, 1876.

BRECK, Samuel, congressman; b. Boston, July 17, 1771; s. Samuel and Hannah (Andrews) B.; attended Royal Mil. Sch., Soreze, France; m. Jean Ross, Dec. 24, 1795. Returned to Boston after French edn., 1787; visited Eng. and France, 1790, soon after received gift of $10,000 from father to start a business; became mcht., set up firm on Long Wharf, Boston; moved to Phila., 1792; a founder Soc. of Sons of New Eng.; mem. Pa. Senate, 1817-21, introduced emanicipation bill for Negroes still enslaved in Pa., 1821; mem. U.S. Ho. of Reps. (Federalist) from Pa., 18th Congress, 1823-25. Author: (essay) Continental Paper Money; (book) Recollections (includes parts from diary started 1800), published 1877. Died Phila., Aug. 31, 1862; buried St. Peter's Churchyard, Phila.

BRECKENRIDGE, James, army officer, congressman; b. Fincastle, Va., Mar. 7, 1763; s. Robert and Letitia (Preston) B.; grad. Coll. William and Mary, 1785; m. Anne Selden, Jan. 1, 1791. Mem. Va. Ho. of Dels. from Botetourt County, 13 sessions between 1780-1824; admitted to the bar, circa 1787, practiced law, 1787-89; commd. maj. gen. Va. Militia during War of 1812; unsuccessful candidate for gov. Va.; mem. U.S. Ho. of Reps. from Va., 11th-14th congresses, 1809-17; leader Federal party in Va.; a founder, mem. bd. visitors U. Va.; promoter Chesapeake & Ohio Canal. Died Fincastle, May 13, 1833.

BRECKENRIDGE, John, clergyman, coll. pres.; b. Cabell's Dale, Ky., July 4, 1797; s. John and Mary (Cabell) B.; grad. Coll. of N.J. (now Princeton), 1818, attended Princeton Theol. Sem., 1820-21; m. Margaret Miller, Jan. 1823; m. 2d, Mary Babcock, 1840. Licensed to preach by Presbytery of New Brunswick, 1822; chaplain, U.S. Congress, 1822-23; ordained by Presbytery of West Lexington (Ky.), 1823; sec., gen. agt. Bd. Edn. of Presbyn. Ch., 1831; prof. pastoral theology Princeton Theol. Sem., 1836-38; sec., gen. agt. Am. Bd. Fgn. Missions, 1838-40; pres. Oglethorpe (Ga.) U., 1841; noted for controversialist religious debates with Rev. John Hughes (archbishop of N.Y.). Died Cabell's Dale, Aug. 4, 1841.

BRECKINRIDGE, James Douglas, congressman, lawyer; b. Woodville, nr. Louisville, Ky.; attended Washington Coll., (now Washington and Lee U.), 1800-03; studied law. Admitted to bar, began practice of law, Louisville; mem. Ky. Ho. of Reps., 1809-11; mem. U.S. Ho. of Reps. (filled vacancy) from Ky., 17th Congress, Nov. 21, 1821-23. Died Louisville, May 6, 1849; buried St. John's Cemetery; reinterred St. Louis Catholic Cemetery, Louisville, 1867.

BRECKINRIDGE, Jefferson, clergyman, educator; b. Cabell's Dale, Ky., Mar. 8, 1800; s. John and Mary Hopkins (Cabell) B.; attended Jefferson Coll., 1816-18, Yale; grad. Union Coll., Schenectady, N.Y., 1819; m. Ann Sophronisba Preston, Mar. 11, 1823; m. 2d, Mrs. Virginia Shelby, 1847; m. 3d, Margret White, 1859; several children including William Campbell Preston, Joseph Campbell. Studied law, managed mother's estate, Lexington, Ky., 1819-24; practiced law, 1824; mem. Ky. Legislature from Fayette County, 1825-28; death of 2 of his sons and his own severe illness caused him to join Presbyn. Ch.; defeated for Ky. Legislature on platform of opposition to slavery, 1831; del. from West Lexington Presbytery to Gen. Assembly, Cincinnati, 1831; licensed to preach, 1832; studied at Princeton to prepare for ministry, 1832; pastor 2d Presbyn. Ch., Balt., 1832-45; an author "Act and Testimony" which came to divide Church into Old and New School groups by 1837; went to Europe for health and as rep. of Gen. Assembly, 1836; opposed slavery in heated polemic, Glasgow, Scotland; pres. Jefferson Coll., 1845-47; apptd. supt. public instrn. and pastor 1st Presbyn. Ch., Lexington, 1847; increased public school enrollment ten-fold, 1847-52; prof. Danville Theol. Sem., 1853-69; supported Union cause; Lincoln's chief adviser and counsellor in Ky.; headed Ky. contingent to Balt. Union Party Conv., 1864, presided over conv. Author: The Knowledge of God, Objectively Considered, 1858; also several books and pamphlets; edited Literary and Religious Magazine, Balt.; edited Danville Quarterly Review, 1861-65. Died Nov. 27, 1871.

BRECKINRIDGE, John, senator, atty. gen.; b. Staunton, Va., Dec. 2, 1760; s. Robert and Letitia (Preston) B.; attended Coll. William and Mary, 1778-80; m. Mary Cabell, 1785, 9 children. Elected to Va. Ho. of Burgesses, 1780, not allowed to take seat because of age; admitted to Va. bar, 1785; atty. gen. Ky., 1795-97; mem. lower house Ky. Legislature from Fayette County, 1797-1801, speaker, 1799-1801; mem. U.S. Senate (Democrat) from Ky., 1801-05; atty. gen. U.S., 1805-06. Died Lexington, Ky., Dec. 14, 1806; buried Lexington Cemetery.

BRECKINRIDGE, John Cabell, vice pres. U.S., senator; b. Lexington, Ky., Jan. 21, 1821; s. Joseph and Mary (Smith) B.; grad. Centre Coll., 1839; attended Transylvania U., Lexington, 1840; m. Mary Burch, Dec. 1843. Mem. Ky. Legislature, 1849; mem. U.S. Ho. of Reps. from Ky., 32d-33d congresses, 1851-55; vice pres. U.S. (Democrat), 1857-61; presdl. candidate of pro-slavery branch Democratic Party, 1860, ran 3d in election after Lincoln and Douglas; mem. U.S. Senate from Ky., Mar 4-Dec. 2, 1861; commd. brig. gen. Confederate Army, 1861, maj. gen., 1862; sec. of state Confederate States Am., 1865; v.p. Elizabethtown, Lexington & Big Sandy R.R., circa 1870. Died Lexington, May 17, 1875; buried Lexington.

BREED, Ebenezer, shoe mcht.; b. Lynn, Mass., May 12, 1766; s. Benjamin and Ruth (Allen) B. Wholesale shoe mcht., Phila.; gave dinner for mems. of 1st Congress, 1789; pleaded cause of tariff protection for infant shoe industry; traveled to England and France, 1792-93; in Lynn Poor House, 1800; occasionally worked as cobbler. Died Dec. 23, 1839; buried at public expense, Lynn.

BREEN, Patrick, pioneer; b. Ireland; m. Margaret, at least 7 children including Eliza. Came to U.S., 1828; went West with family, 1846; joined Donner party (group of 81 pioneers), Independence, Mo., left for Cal.; snowbound at Truckee (now Donner) Lake, Sierra Mountains, Cal. (36 mems. of group died), winter 1846-47; kept diary which recorded hopelessness, fear and privation of group; survived (with his entire family), settled in San Benito County, Cal. Died Dec. 21, 1868.

BREESE, Randolph Kidder, naval officer; b. Phila., Apr. 14, 1831. Apptd. midshipman U.S. Navy, 1846, assigned to ship Saratoga for duty in Mexican War, 1847; served in ship St. Mary's, 1848, Brandywine, until 1850; sailed in ship St. Lawrence to Eng., 1851; prepared for midshipman's exam., 1851-52; reported to ship Mississippi, commanded by M.C. Perry for voyage to Japan, 1852; ordered to Preble for S. Am. trip, 1858-59; assigned to duty in Portsmouth on African coast, 1860, then stationed in ship San Jacinto until 1861; assigned to command mortar flotilla to help open Mississippi River, 1861; promoted lt. comdr., 1862, joined Adm. Porter's Mississippi Fleet; commanded flagship Black Hawk; fleet-capt. to Adm. Porter's N. Atlantic Squadron, 1864-65; promoted comdr., 1866; asst. supt. U.S. Naval Acad.; insp. of ordnance Washington Naval Yard; in command of Plymouth on European Station, 1870; stationed Bur. of Ordnance, Navy Dept., 1872; commandant of midshipmen U.S. Naval Acad., 1873; commd. capt., 1874; commanded ship Pensacola, 1878; ordered home on sick leave, 1880. Died Sept. 13, 1881.

BREESE, Sidney, senator, jurist; b. Whitesboro, N.Y., July 15, 1800; s. Arthur and Catherine (Livingston) B.; grad. Union Coll., Schnectady, N.Y., 1818. Admitted to Ill. bar, 1820; postmaster, Kaskaskia, Ill., 1821; pros. atty. 3d Ill. Jud. Circuit, 1822-26, U.S. dist. atty. for Ill., 1827-29; served in Black Hawk War, 1832; judge 2d Ill., Circuit Ct., 1835-41; mem. U.S. Senate from Ill., 1843-49; regent Smithsonian Instn., 1845-49; mem. Ill. Ho. of Reps., 1850; justice Ill. Supreme Ct., 1841-42, 57-78, became chief justice, 1873, gave decision upholding state power to regulate grain elevators in famous Munn v. Illinois case, 1877; dir. B.&O. R.R. Author: Breese's Reports (reported decisions of Ill. Supreme Ct. 1820-31), 1831; Origin and History of the Pacific Railroad, 1869. Died Pinckneyville, Ill., June 27, 1878; buried Carlyle (Ill.) Cemetery.

BREHAN, Marquise de, see de Brehan, Marquise.

BREITUNG, Edward, congressman, businessman; b. Schalkau, Duchy of Saxe-Meiningen, Germany, Nov. 10, 1831; attended Coll. of Mining, Meiningen, 1849. Came to U.S., settled in Kalamazoo County, Mich.; moved to Detroit, 1851, became clk. in merc. house; moved to Marquette, Mich., engaged in merc. activities until 1859; moved to Negaunee, Mich., 1859; became operator of iron mines, 1864, located several profitable mines in Marquette and Menominee counties, 1864-67; later engaged in gold and silver mining in Colo.; mem. Mich. Ho. of Reps., 1873-74, Mich. Senate, 1877-78; mayor Negaunee, 1879-80, 82; mem. U.S. Ho. of Reps. (Republican) from Mich., 48th Congress, 1883-85. Died Negaunee, Mar. 3, 1887; buried Park Cemetery, Marquette.

BRENGLE, Francis, congressman; b. Frederick, Md., Nov. 26, 1807; studied law. Admitted to bar, practiced law, Frederick; mem. Md. Ho. of Dels., 1832, 34, 36; mem. U.S. Ho. of Reps. (Whig) from Md., 28th Congress, 1843-45. Died Frederick, Dec. 10, 1846; buried Mt. Olivet Cemetery.

BRENT, Henry Johnson, author; b. Washington, D.C., 1811. Acquired early reputation as painter and writer; contbd. articles and sketches (signed Stirrup) to Porter's Spirit of the Times; a founder Knickerbocker Mag. Author: (works include) Was It a Ghost? By J.B. (1868); Life Almost Alone. Died N.Y.C., Aug. 3, 1880.

BRENT, Margaret, landowner; b. Gloucester, Eng., 1600; d. Richard and Elizabeth (Reed) Brent. Came to St. Mary's, Md., 1638, received land in her own name due to family connections; raised band of armed volunteers to aid Gov. Calvert in suppression of Claiborne Rebellion, 1646; apptd. executrix to Gov. Leonard Calvert; apptd. atty. for Lord Baltimore by Md. Provincial Ct., thus was involved in more lawsuits than any one in colony; established another home in Westmoreland County, Va., 1650; held annual court leets for her slaves, tenants and employees; 1st advocate of women's rights. Died 1670/71.

BRENT, Richard, senator, congressman; b. "Richland," Stafford County, Va., 1757; studied law. Admitted to bar, practiced law; mem. Va. Ho. of Dels., 1788, 93-94, 1800-01; mem. U.S. Ho. of Reps. from Va., 4th-5th, 7th congresses, 1795-99, 1801-03; mem. Va. Senate, 1808-10; mem. U.S. Senate from Va., 1809-14. Died Washington, D.C., Dec. 30, 1814; buried family burial ground "Richland."

BRENT, William Leigh, congressman; b. Port Tobacco, Md., Feb. 20, 1784; studied law. Admitted to bar, began practice of law, La., circa 1809; apptd. dep. atty. gen. Western Dist. Territory of Orleans by Pres. Madison; mem. U.S. Ho. of Reps. from La., 18th-20th congresses, 1823-29; became a Whig upon formation of the party; practiced law, La., also Washington, D.C. Died St. Martinsville, La., July 7, 1848; buried St. Martin's Catholic Cemetery.

BRENTANO, Lorenz, journalist, congressman; b. Mannheim, Baden, Germany, Nov. 4, 1813; s. Peter Paul and Helene (Haeger) Bartholomeus; attended U. Heidelberg, U. Freiburg, U. Giessen (all Germany); m. Caroline Aberle. Active in govt. in Germany; participated in revolt of 1848-49, forced to flee; came to U.S., 1850; editor Der Leuchtturm (anti-slavery German weekly), Pottsville, Pa., 1850-51; farmer nr. Kalamazoo, Mich., 1851-59; settled in Chgo., 1859; practiced law, Chgo.; began writing for Ill. Staatszeitung, 1860, bought half interest, 1862; elected to Ill. Legislature, 1862; presdl. elector for Grant-Colfax, 1868; pres. Chgo. Bd. Edn., 5 years; visited Germany, 1869; U.S. consul at Dresden, 1872-76; mem. U.S. Ho. of Reps. (Republican) from Ill., 45th Congress, 1877-79; ret., wrote history and legal treatises; supported Grover Cleveland for Pres., 1884. Died Sept. 17, 1891.

BRENTON, Samuel, congressman, clergyman; b. Gallatin County, Ky., Nov. 22, 1810; attended public schs. Ordained to ministry Methodist Ch., 1830; moved (for health reasons) to Danville, Ind., 1834; mem. Ind. Ho. of Reps., 1838-41; minister, Crawfordsville, Perryville, Lafayette, Ft. Wayne, Ind., 1841-48; register land office, Ft. Wayne, 1849-51; mem. U.S. Ho. of Reps. from Ind. (as Whig), 32d Congress, 1851-53, (as Republican), 34th-35th congresses, 1855-57. Died Ft. Wayne, Mar. 29, 1857; buried Lindenwood Cemetery.

BRESCHARD, equestrian, circus mgr. Promoted constrn. of circus bldg. at corner 9th and Walnut streets, Phila., 1809, promoted expansion of circus bldg. into Olympic Theatre, Phila., 1811; erected circus bldg. in Vaux-Hall Garden, Charleston, S.C., 1812.

BREVARD, Joseph, congressman, lawyer; b. Iredell, N.C., July 19, 1766; studied law. Joined Continental Army while still a boy; commd. lt. N.C. Militia, 1782, served throughout Revolutionary War; moved to Camden, S.C.; sheriff Camden Dist., 1789-91; commr. in equity, 1791; admitted to bar, 1792, began practice of law, Camden; compiled law report which bears his name, 1793-1815; judge S.C. Supreme Ct., 1801-15; mem. U.S. Ho. of Reps. (Whig) from S.C., 16th Congress, 1819-21. Died Camden, Oct. 11, 1821; buried Quaker Cemetery.

BREVOORT, James Carson, civil engr.; b. N.Y.C., July 10, 1818; son of Henry Brevoort; diploma in civil engring., Central Sch. of Arts and Manufactures, Paris, France; LL.D. (hon.), Williams Coll., 1863; m. dau. of Leffert Lefferts, 1845. Asst. to his uncle on Northeastern boundary survey, 1837-38; pvt. sec. to Washington Irving, 1838-40; toured Europe, 1840-45; lived in Bklyn., 1845-87; pres. L.I. Hist. Soc., 1863-73; regent U. State N.Y., 1861-87; contbr. to Am. Journal of Numismatics, Hist. Mag. Author: Verrazano the Navigator; or, Notes on Giovanni de Verrazano, and on a Planisphre of 1529, Illustrating His American Voyage in 1524, published 1874. Died Bklyn., Dec. 7, 1887.

BREWER, Charles, sea capt.; b. Boston, Mar. 27, 1804; s. Moses and Abigail (May) B.; m. Martha Turner, 1840/41. Apprenticed to a Boston mcht., 1818-21; made voyages to Calcutta, India, East Indies, England, 1821-24; capt. brig. Chinchilla trading between Honolulu (Hawaii), N. Am. and China, 1825-29; master of brig. Ivanhoe, 1829-31; capt. schooner trading directly from Hawaii to mainland, 1831-33; capt. schooner Unity, 1833; continued to trade from Honolulu to Siberian coast, 1834-35; formed partnership with Henry A. Peirce, 1836, used Hawaii as home base; returned to Boston, 1839-41; company became C. Brewer & Co. (after withdrawal of Peirce), 1843; sold most of business, 1845, returned to Boston; made business trip to Honolulu, 1847-49, continued in Far Eastern and Hawaiian trade until 1884; contbr. to Honolulu charities, brought night-blooming cereus to islands. Died Oct. 11, 1885.

BREWER, Francis Beattie, congressman, physician; b. Keene, N.H., Oct. 8, 1820; attended Newbury (Vt.) Sem., Kimball Union Acad., Meriden, N.H.; grad. Dartmouth, 1843, med. dept., 1846. Practiced medicine, Barnet, Vt., Plymouth, Mass., then Titusville, Pa., 1849-61; pioneer oil operator, lumberman, Titusville; moved to Westfield, N.Y., 1861, engaged in banking, mfg., agriculture; state mil. agt. with rank of maj. during Civil War; mem. bd. suprs. Chautauqua County (N.Y.), 1868-79; del. Republican Nat. Conv., Phila., 1872; mem. N.Y. State Assembly, 1873-74; govt. dir. Union Pacific R.R., 4 years; apptd. mgr. state insane asylum, Buffalo, N.Y., 1881; mem. U.S. Ho. of Reps. (Rep.) from N.Y., 48th Congress, 1883-85. Died Westfield, N.Y., July 29, 1892; buried Allegheny Cemetery, Pitts.

BREWER, George St. P., artist; b. Eng., Mar. 1814; married, children include George, Georgiann, George R. Came to Am., circa 1830; exhibited panorama of Mammoth Cave (his most popular work) in Louisville, Ky., Phila., New Orleans, Cincinnati, Boston, 1848-51; painted panorama Grand View of the Torrid, Temperate and Figid Zones (exhibited posthumously until 1859). Died St. Louis, Dec. 26, 1852.

BREWER, Thomas Mayo, publisher, ornithologist; b. Boston, Nov. 21, 1814; s. James Brewer; grad. Harvard, 1835, Harvard Med. Sch., 1838; m. Sally R. Coffin, 1849. Practiced medicine; gave up practice to write for Boston Atlas, later became editor; asso. with publishing firm Swan & Tileston (later Brewer & Tileston), until 1875; mem. Boston Soc. Natural History, 1835-80; published Supplement to Prof. Hitchcock's Catalogue of the Birds of Massachusetts, 1837, Wilson's Ornithology, 1840, North American Oology, 1857; mem. Boston Sch. Com., 1844-80; compiled (with Baird and Ridgeway), History of North American Birds, 1875. Died Jan. 23, 1880.

BREWSTER, Benjamin Harris, atty. gen. U.S.; b. Salem County, N.J., Oct. 13, 1816; s. Francis E. and Maria (Hampton) B.; grad. Princeton, 1834, LL.D. (hon.), 1867; LL.D. (hon.), Dickinson Coll.; m. Elizabeth von Myerbach de Reinfeldts, 1857; m. 2d, Mary Walker, 1870; 1 child. Admitted to Phila. bar, 1835; commr. to settle Cherokee Indian claims, 1846; atty. gen. Pa., 1867-68; atty. gen. U.S., 1881-85; chief prosecutor at Star Route trials. Died Phila., Apr. 4, 1888.

BREWSTER, David P., congressman, lawyer; b. Cairo, N.Y., June 15, 1801; grad. Union Coll., Schenectady, N.Y., 1823; studied law. Admitted to bar, began practice of law, Oswego, N.Y.; trustee Village of Oswego, 1828, 36, 45; pros. atty. Oswego County, 1829-33; treas. Village of Oswego, 1832-34, pres., 1837; judge Ct. of Common Pleas, 1833-41; mem. U.S. Ho. of Reps. (Democrat) from N.Y., 26th-27th congresses, 1839-43; postmaster Oswego, 1845-49; mem. excise bd. commn., pres., 1870-73; engaged in agriculture. Died Oswego, Feb. 20, 1876; buried Riverside Cemetery.

BREWSTER, Frederick Carroll, lawyer, state ofcl.; b. Phila., May 15, 1825; s. Francis Enoch and Maria (Hampton) B.; grad. U. Pa., 1841; m. Emma Barton, 1850. Admitted to Phila. bar, 1844; attained prominence as lawyer as result of victory in 3 important criminal cases; won acquittal for pres. of Bank of Pa. (charged with conspiracy to defraud bank of $250,000); city solicitor Phila., 1862-66; counsel in Schollemberger-Brinton case which established constitutionality of Legal Tender Act of 1862; judge Ct. of Common Pleas of City and County of Phila., 1866-69; atty. gen. Pa., 1869-72. Author: A Treatise on Practice in the Courts of Pennsylvania, 1891; A Treatise on Equity Practice in Pennsylvania, 1895. Died Dec. 30, 1898.

BREWSTER, James, wagon mfr.; b. Preston, New London County, Conn. Aug. 6, 1788; s. Joseph and Hannah (Tucker) B.; m. Mary Hequembourg, 1810. Apprenticed to wagon-maker, Northampton, Mass., 1804-09; moved to N.Y.C., 1809; opened wagon shop, New Haven, Conn., 1810; became known for quality in all types of horse drawn transp.; opened warehouse and repair shop, N.Y.C., 1827; helped finance New Haven & Hartford R.R. (1st Conn. railroad), pres., 1834-38; contbr. to an orphan asylum, almshouse, street improvement, temperance movements, other philanthropic interests. Died Nov. 22, 1866.

BREWSTER, Osmyn, printer; b. Worthington, Mass., Aug. 2, 1797; s. Moses and Lucy (Watts) B.; m. Mary Jones, Jan. 15, 1824, 2 sons, 7 daus. Apprentice to a Boston printer, 1811-18, became partner, 1818 (firm name changed to Crocker & Brewster, 1825); printed primarily religious books, only Boston publishing firm to survive panic of 1837; elected to Mass. Ho. of Reps. from Boston, 1848, served 5 terms; mem. Mass. Senate, 1853; del. from Boston to Mass. Constl. Conv., 1853; mem. bd. aldermen Boston, 1856-58; pres. Franklin Savs. Bank, 1881-87; treas. Mass. Charitable Mechanic Assn., 25 years; sold printing business to Houghton & Co., 1876. Died July 15, 1889.

BREWSTER, William, Pilgrim father; b. Nottinghamshire, Eng., 1567; ed. Peterhouse, Cambridge U.; m. Mary, 1591, 6 children. Holland emigre, 1608; elder New Puritan Ch., Leyden, 1609; sailed to New World on Mayflower, 1620; sole ch. officer Plymouth (Mass.) Colony, 1621-29; one of undertakers who assumed indebtedness of the Plymouth Colony to the company in Eng., 1627; major influence in the affairs of Plymouth Colony. Died Plymouth, Apr. 10, 1644.

BRICE, Calvin Stewart, railroad builder, senator; b. Denmark, O., Sept. 17, 1845; s. William and Elizabeth (Stewart) B.; grad. Miami U., Oxford, O., 1863; m. Catherine Meily, 1870, 6 children. Commd. lt. col. U.S. Army, 1865; admitted to Cincinnati bar, 1866; presdl. elector, 1876; pres. Lake Erie & Western R.R., 1887; ofcl., investor 10 other railroads; dir. So. Trust Co.; chmn. Democratic Nat. Com., 1889; mem. U.S. Senate (Democrat) from Ohio, 1891-97, chmn. Pacific R.R. com., mem. select com. on dist. corps. Mem. Ohio Soc., Am. Geog. Soc., Ardsley Casino, Met. Mus. Art, Am. Fine Arts Soc., Delta Kappa Epsilon. Clubs: Metropolitan, Manhattan, Lawyer's, Riding, Democratic, Whist, Atlantic Yacht (all N.Y.C.). Died N.Y.C., Dec. 15, 1898; buried Woodlawn Cemetery, Lima, O.

BRIDGER, James, fur trader, frontier scout; b. Richmond, Va., Mar. 17, 1804; s. James and Chloe Bridger; m. 3 Indian wives, at least 4 children. Fur trader most familiar with Midwestern territory in 1st half of 19th century; 1st white man to visit Gt. Salt Lake, 1824; built (with partner Louis Vasquez) Ft. Bridger on Ore. Trail at Black's Fork, Wyo., 1843, driven out by Mormons, 1853; discovered Bridger's Pass in Wyo.; guide for U.S. Govt., 1857-68, for Albert Sidney Johnston's troops in Utah Campaign, 1857-58; guide for Powder River expdns., 1865-66; became farmer nr. Kansas City, Mo., 1868. Died Washington, Mo., June 17, 1881.

BRIDGERS, Robert Rufus, Confederate congressman, railroad exec.; b. Edgecombe County, N.C., Nov. 28, 1819; s. John and Elizabeth (Routh) B.; grad. U. N.C., 1841; m. Margaret Johnston, 1849. Admitted to N.C. bar, 1841; mem. N.C. Assembly from Edgecombe County, 1844-46, 56-61; organizer bank, Tarboro, N.C., pres., 1851; mem. N.C. Ho. of Reps., chmn. judiciary com., 1856-61; dir. Wilmington & Weldon R.R. (became base line of Atlantic Coast Line R.R.), 1860-88, pres., 1865-88; mem. Confederate Congress, circa 1861-65. Died Columbia, S.C., Dec. 10, 1888; buried St. James's Churchyard, Wilmington, N.C.

BRIDGES, George Washington, congressman, lawyer; b. Charleston, Tenn., Oct. 9, 1825; attended E. Tenn. U. at Knoxville; studied law. Admitted to bar, 1848, began practice of law, Athens, Tenn.; also engaged in agriculture; atty. gen. Tenn., 1849-60; raised 10th Regt., Tenn. Cavalry for U.S. Army, during Civil War, served from capt. to col.; elected mem. U.S. Ho. of Reps. (Unionist) from Tenn., 37th Congress, arrested enroute to Washington, D.C., held prisoner in Tenn. for more than a year, escaped and served in U.S. Congress, Feb. 25-Mar. 3, 1863; circuit judge 4th Jud. Dist. of Tenn., 1866. Died Athens, Mar. 16, 1873; buried Cedar Grove Cemetery.

BRIDGES, Robert, colonial mfr.; b. Eng.; m. Mary Woodcock. Came to Mass., 1641; became freeman; mem. Ancient and Honorable Arty. Co.; served as capt. Mass. Colonial Militia; organized Co. of Undertakers for Iron Works which began working bog iron deposits, nr. Lynn, Mass., 1643; rep. to Mass. Gen. Ct., Boston, 1644; apptd. mem. Quarterly Ct., Salem, Mass.; commr. to investigate differences between French govs. LaTour and D'Aulnay who claimed jurisdiction over Acadia and caused trouble to some Plymouth traders, 1646. Died 1656.

BRIDGES, Robert, physician; b. Phila., Mar. 5, 1806; s. Culpepper and Sarah (Clifton) B.; grad. Dickinson Coll., Carlisle, Pa., 1824; M.A., U. Pa., 1828. Became tchr. chemistry Phila. Coll. Pharmacy, 1831, trustee, 1839, prof. gen. and pharm. chemistry, 1842, prof. emeritus, 1879; vaccine physician, several years; apptd. dist. physician during cholera epidemic, 1832; prof. chemistry Franklin Med. Coll., 1846-48; became mem. Acad. Natural Scis., 1835, presented index of genera in its Herbarium (with Dr. Paul B. Goddard), 1835, revised index, 1843, pres. acad., 1864; became fellow Coll. Physicians of Phila., 1842, librarian, 1867-79, catalogued Urinary Calculi in Mutter Mus.; became mem. Franklin Inst. of Phila., 1836, Am. Philos. Soc., 1844; asso. editor Am. Jour. Pharmacy, 1839-46, mem. com. for revision of pharmacopoeia, 1840, 70; editor Am. editions of Elementary Chemistry (George Fownes), Elements of Chemistry (Thomas Graham). Died Feb. 20, 1882.

BRIDGES Samuel Augustus, congressman, lawyer; b. Colchester, Conn., Jan. 27, 1802; grad. Williams Coll., Willamstown, Mass., 1826; studied law. Admitted to bar, 1829, began practice of law, Doylestown, Pa.; moved to Allentown, Pa., 1830; town clk., 1837-42; dep. atty. gen. for Lehigh County (Pa.), 1837-44; del. Democratic State Conv., 1841; mem. U.S. Ho. of Reps. (Democrat, filled vacancy) from Pa., 30th, 33d, 45th congresses, Mar. 6, 1848-49, 53-55, 77-79. Died Allentown, Jan. 14, 1884; buried Union Cemetery.

BRIDGMAN, Elijah Coleman, missionary; b. Belchertown, Mass., Apr. 22, 1801; s. Theodore and Lucretia (Warner) B.; grad. Amherst Coll., 1826, Andover Theol. Sem., 1829; m. Eliza Jane Gillett, June 28, 1845. Became missionary in China, 1829; joint sec. Soc. for Diffusion of Useful Knowledge, 1834; a founder Morision Edn. Soc., Med. Missionary Soc.; mem. N. China br. Royal Asiatic Soc., editor of its journal; published Chinese Repository, 1832-47, Chinese Christomathy, 1841. Died Nov. 2, 1861.

BRIDGMAN, Laura Dewey, subject of ednl. expt.; b. Hanover, N.H., Dec. 21, 1829; d. Daniel and Harmony B. Left blind, deaf and mute after an attack of scarlet fever at age 1½; put under care of Samuel Gridley Howe at Perkins Inst., Boston, 1837, responded to systematic edn., spoke with signs and learned to write; returned home, 1852, returned to Perkins Inst., remained for rest of life. Died May 24, 1889.

BRIDPORT, Hugh, artist; b. London, Eng., 1794. Exhibited miniatures at Royal Acad., Eng., 1813; came to Am., circa 1816, settled in Phila.; conducted drawing acad. (with brother George), Phila., 1816-17; visited Mass., 1820, Troy, N.Y., 1822; exhibited frequently at Pa. Acad., 1817-43, Artists' Fund Soc., 1844-45. Died Phila., circa 1868.

BRIERTON, John, clergyman; b. Norwich, Eng., 1572; s. Cuthbert and Joan (Howse) B.; attended Gonville and Caius Coll., Cambridge (Eng.) U., 1589-93, M.A., 1596. Ordained deacon Protestant Episcopal Ch., 1596, priest, Norwich, 1598; curate, Lawshall, Suffolk, Eng.; sailed to New Eng. in ship Concord (with Bartholomew Gosnold), 1602; saw Me. and Cape Cod, traded and inspected coast; published A Briefe and True Relation of the Discouerie of the North Part of Virginia, 1602; returned to Lawshall, 1604; rector, Brightwell, Suffolk, by 1619. Died circa 1619.

BRIGGS, Charles Frederick, journalist, author; b. Nantucket Island, Mass., Dec. 30, 1804; s. Jonathan C. and Sally Coffin (Barrett) B.; married, at least 1 dau. Went to sea as youth; mcht., N.Y.C.; published novels The Adventures of Henry Franco: A Tale of the Great Panic, 1839, The Haunted Merchant, 1843; founder Broadway Journal, 1844; published Working a Passage, 1847; an editor Putnam's Mag., 1853-56, 66, N.Y. Times; with N.Y. Custom House; financial editor Bklyn. Union, 1870-73, editor for short time; mem. editorial staff N.Y. Independent, until 1877; mem. 1st bd. commrs. Central Park, N.Y.C. Died June 20, 1877.

BRIGGS, George, congressman; b. nr. Broadalbin, N.Y., May 6, 1805; attended public schs., Vt. Became a hardware dealer; mem. Vt. Ho. of Reps., 1837; moved to N.Y.C., 1838, continued in hardware bus.; mem. U.S. Ho. of Reps. (Whig) from N.Y., 31st-32d congresses, 1849-53, (Am. Party candidate), 36th Congress, 1859-61; del. Union Nat. Conv., Phila., 1866. Died at summer home "Woodlawn," Saratoga Springs, N.Y., June 1, 1869; buried Greenwood Cemetery, N.Y.C.

BRIGGS, George Nixon, gov. Mass., congressman; b. Adams, Mass., Apr. 12, 1796; s. Allen and Nancy (Brown) B.; read law with Luther Washburn, Lanesboro, Mass.; m. Harriet Hall, May 1818. Admitted to Mass. bar, 1818; elected town clk. Lanesboro, 1824; registrar of deeds Berkshire County (Mass.), 1824-31, chmn. bd. commrs. of hwys., 1826; mem. U.S. Ho of Reps. from Mass., 22d-27th congresses, 1831-43; gov. Mass. (Whig), 1844-51; judge Mass. Ct. Common Pleas, 1853-58; mem. Mass. Constl. Conv., 1853; pres. Am. Temperance Union, 1856; pres. Baptist Missionary Union; trustee Williams Coll.; a founder Republican Party in Mass.; U.S. commr. to adjust differences between New Granada and U.S., 1861 (accidentally shot before leaving for S. Am.). Died Pittsfield, Mass., Sept. 11, 1861; buried Pittsfield Cemetery.

BRIGHAM, Amariah, physician; b. New Marlboro, Mass., Dec. 26, 1798; s. John Brigham; trained in offices of Drs. E.C. Peet (New Marlboro) and Plumb (Canaan, Conn.); m. Susan C. Root, Jan. 23, 1833. Practiced medicine, Enfield, Mass., 1820-22, Greenfield, Mass., 1822-29, Hartford, Conn., 1830-37; prof. anatomy and surgery Coll. Physicians and Surgeons, N.Y.C.; physician, supt. Retreat of Insane, Hartford, 1840, N.Y. State Lunatic Asylum, 1842-49; founder Am. Jour. of Insanity. Author: Remarks on the Influence of Mental Cultivation on Health, 1832; Observations on the Influence of Religion on the Health of Mankind, 1835. Died Sept. 8, 1849.

BRIGHAM, Elijah, congressman; b. Westboro (now Northboro), Mass., July 7, 1751; grad. Dartmouth, 1778; studied law. Engaged in business, Westboro; mem. Mass. Ho. of Reps., 1791-93; justice Ct. of Common Pleas, 1795-1811; mem. Mass. Senate, 1796, 98, 1801-05, 07-10; state councilor, 1799-1800, 06; mem. U.S. Ho. of Reps. (Federalist) from Mass., 12th-14th congresses, 1811-16. Died Washington, D.C., Feb. 22, 1816; buried Congressional Cemetery.

BRIGHAM, Lewis Alexander, congressman; b. New York Mills, Oneida County, N.Y., Jan. 2, 1831; attended Whitestown Sem., Whitesboro, N.Y.; grad. Hamilton Coll., Clinton, N.Y., 1849; studies law. Admitted to bar, 1855, began practice of law, N.Y.C.; supt. public schs., Bergen, N.J., 1866-70; mem. bd. police commrs. Jersey City, N.J., 1874-76; mem. N.J. Ho. of Assembly, 1877; mem. U.S. Ho. of Reps. (Republican) from N.J., 46th Congress, 1879-81; resumed practice of law, N.Y.C. Died Jersey City, Feb. 19, 1885; buried Old Bergen Ch. Cemetery.

BRIGHAM, Mary Ann, educator; b. Westboro, Mass., Dec. 6, 1829; d. Dexter and Mary Ann (Gould) Brigham; grad. Mt. Holyoke Sem. Taught pvt. sch. in her father's home; instr. Mt. Holyoke Sem., 1844-58; prin. Ingham U., Leroy, N.Y., 1858-63; asst. prin. Bklyn. Heights Sem., 1863-89; apptd. 1st pres. Mt. Holyoke Coll., killed in railroad wreck before taking office. Died June 29, 1889.

BRIGHT, Edward, clergyman; b. Kington, Herefordshire, Eng., Oct. 6, 1808; s. Edward Bright; m. Adeline Osborn; m. 2d, Anna Leslie Reid. Apprenticed to printer; became partner firm Bennet & Bright; licensed to preach Baptist Ch., 1839, ordained to ministry, 1840; became pastor Bleeker St. Baptist Ch., Utica, N.Y.; elected fgn. sec. Am. Bapt. Missionary Union Hdqrs., Boston; edited Bapt. Missionary Mag.; purchased Register (Baptist newspaper), N.Y., 1855, changed name to Examiner; trustee U. Rochester, Vassar Coll.; concerned with Bapt. mission work, edn. and all denominational matters. Died May 17, 1894.

BRIGHT, Jesse David, senator; b. Norwich, Chenago Cuunty, N.Y., Dec. 18, 1812; s. David Graham and Rachel (Graham) B.; m. Mary E. Turpin, 1840. Moved with family to Madison, Ind., 1820; admitted to Ind. bar, 1831; probate judge Jefferson County (Ind.), 1834-39; mem. Ind. Ho. of Reps., 1836; apptd. U.S. marshal Ind. Dist., 1840; lt. gov. Ind., 1843-45; mem. U.S. Senate (Democrat) from Ind., 1845-62, pres. pro tem, 1854, 56, 60, expelled for recognizing (in letter) Jefferson Davis as legitimate pres. Confederate States Am.; unsuccessful candidate for reelection to U.S. Senate, 1863; ret. to farm he owned in Ky.; mem. Ky. Ho. of Reps., 1866; pres. Raymond City Coal Co., 1871; moved to Balt., 1874. Died Balt., May 20, 1875; buried Balt., Greenmount Cemetery.

BRIGHT EYES, see La Flesche, Susette.

BRIGHTLY, Frederick Charles, lawyer; b. Bungay, Suffolk, Eng., Aug. 26, 1812; s. Henry A. Brightly; m. Sarah Corfield, 1835. Went to sea as midshipman in E. Indian trade; studied navigation, London, Eng., 1829; came to U.S., settled in Phila., 1831; established large consultative practice; retired from practice to devote full energies to writing, 1868; collected notable library of early Pa. history. Author: The Law of Costs of Pennsylvania, 1847; The Equitable Jurisdiction of the Courts of Pennsylvania, 1855; The Bankrupt Law of the United States, 1869; The Constitution of Pennsylvania as Amended in 1874, published 1874. Died Jan. 24, 1888.

BRINCKE, William Draper, physician, pomologist; b. Kent County, Del., Feb. 9, 1798; s. John and Elizabeth (Gordon) B.; grad. Princeton, 1816; M.D., U. Pa., 1819; m. Sarah T. Physick, 1821; m. 2d, Elizabeth Bispham Reeves, 1832. Began practice of medicine, Wilmington, 1819, Phila., 1825; physician concerned with contagious diseases City Hosp., 1827-39; active in control of Asiatic cholera epidemic, 1832; a pomologist, developed numerous fruit varieties, worked primarily with small fruits and pears; published findings of strawberry expt. in Farmer's Cabinet, 1846; frequent contbr. to Horticulturist; a founder Am. Pomol. Soc.; retired from med. practice due to ill health, 1859. Died Dec. 16, 1862.

BRINKERHOFF, Henry Roelif, congressman; b. Adams County, Pa., Sept. 23, 1787; attended country schs., Cayuga County, N.Y. Commanded militia company in War of 1812, distinguished himself in Battle of Queenstown Heights; engaged in agriculture; mem. N.Y. State Assembly, 1828-29; sr. maj. gen. N.Y. State Militia, 1824, commanded mil. escort for Gen. Lafayette's tour of N.Y.; moved to Huron County, O., 1837; mem. U.S. Ho. of Reps. (Democrat) from Ohio, 28th Congress, 1843-44. Died Huron County, Apr. 30, 1844; buried Pioneer Cemetery, Plymouth, O.

BRINKERHOFF, Jacob, congressman; b. Niles, N.Y., Aug. 31, 1810; s. Henry I. and Rachel (Bevier) B.; read law, Bath, N.Y., 2 years; m. Caroline Campbell; m. 2d, Marion Titus. Began practice of law, Mansfield, O., 1836; prosecutor Richland County (O.), 1839-43; mem. U.S. Ho. of Reps. (Democrat) from Ohio, 28th-29th congresses, 1843-47; became affiliated (because of strong anti-slavery sentiments) with Free-Soil Party, later with Republican Party; asso. justice Ohio

Supreme Ct., 1856-71; supported liberal Republicans, 1872. Died July 19, 1880; buried Mansfield Cemetery.

BRISBANE, Albert, reformer; b. Batavia, N.Y., Aug. 22, 1809; s. James and Mary (Stevens) B.; studied under tutors, N.Y.C., 1824-26; studied in Europe, 1827-34, with cousin and Guizot in Paris, with Hegel in Berlin; m. Sarah White, 3 children; m. 2d, Redelia Bates. Journeyed to Constantinople to study Turkish Empire, returned to Paris, 1830; influenced by Charles Fourier's Traite de L'association Domestique-Agricole; studied with Fourier, 2 years, returned to U.S., 1834; organized Fourier Soc., 1839; began proselytizing Fourier's philosophy, gained interest of Horace Greeley (who gave him use of N.Y. Tribune); editor of Chronicle; writer for Plebeian, Dial; editor (with Osborne MacDaniel) Phalanx, 1843-45. Author: Social Destiny of Man, 1840; Association, 1843; General Introduction to Social Sciences, 1876. Died May 1, 1890.

BRISBIN, James S., army officer; b. Boalsburg, Pa., May 23, 1837; studied law, Bellefonte, Pa. Editor, Centre Democrat, Bellefonte; admitted to Pa. bar; entered U.S. Army as pvt., 1861, commd. 2d lt. soon after; wounded at 1st Battle of Bull Run, 1861; later promoted capt. 6th U.S. Cavalry; served with Army of Potomac in Peninsular Campaign, 1862; brevetted maj. U.S. Army for services at Battle of Malvern Hill, 1863; commanded Pa. regt. at Battle of Gettysburg, 1863; commd. col. 5th U.S. Colored Cavalry, 1864; brevetted brig. gen., maj. gen. U.S. Volunteers, 1865; brevetted col. U.S. Army, 1865; capt. 6th U.S. Cavalry, 1866-68; commd. maj. 2d Cavalry, 1868, lt. col. 9th Cavalry, 1885, col. 1st Cavalry, 1889; stationed mostly on the frontier, 1868-89, took part in most of Indian battles in Northwest.

BRISBIN, John, congressman, lawyer; b. Sherburne, N.Y., July 13, 1818; studied law. Taught sch.; admitted to bar, began practice of law, Tunkhannock, Wyoming County, Pa., circa 1843; mem. U.S. Ho. of Reps. (Whig, filled vacancy) from Pa., 31st Congress, Jan. 13-Mar. 3, 1851; pres. Del., Lackawanna & Western Ry. Co., 1863-67, mem. bd. mgrs., gen. counsel, 1867-80. Died Newark, N.J., Feb. 3, 1880; buried Evergreen Cemetery, Elizabeth, N.J.

BRISTED, Charles Astor, author; b. N.Y.C., Oct. 6, 1820; s. Rev. John and Magdalen (Astor) B.; B.A., Yale, 1839; grad. Trinity Coll., Cambridge (Eng.) U., 1845; m. Laura Brevoort, Jan. 14, 1847; m. 2d, Grace Sedgwick, 1867. Traveled in Europe, then returned to U.S.; wrote under pen name Carl Benson for some years; contbr. to various journals. Author: Selections from Catullus for School Use, 1849; The Upper Ten Thousand, 1852; Five Years in an English University, 1852; No Surrender, 1863; Anacreontics, 1872; Some Exaggerations in Comparative Philology, 1873. Died Jan. 14, 1874.

BRISTED, John, clergyman; b. Sherborne, Dorset, Eng., Oct. 17, 1778; attended Winchester Coll.; studied medicine at Edinburgh; studied law under Joseph Chitty (editor of Blackstone's Commentaries); studied under Episcopal Bishop Griswold, Bristol, R.I., also under Bishop Smith of Ct.; m. Magdalen Astor, Mar. 8, 1820, 1 son, Charles Astor. Practiced medicine for short time; admitted to Inner Temple; arrived in N.Y.C., 1806; practiced law, lectured and wrote; editor Monthly Register, 1807; became asst. to Bishop Griswold, 1828, succeeded Griswold as rector Bristol Ch., 1829-43 (resigned because of poor health). Author: The Advisor, 1802; A Pedestrian Tour Through Part of Scottish Highlands in 1801, published 1804; Edward and Anna, 1806; The Resources of the British Empire, 1811. Died Feb. 23, 1855.

BRISTOW, Benjamin Helm, sec. of treasury; b. Elkton, Ky., June 20, 1832; s. Francis and Emily (Helm) B.; grad. Jefferson Coll., 1851; m. Abbie Briscoe, Nov. 21, 1854. Admitted to Ky. bar, 1853; commd. lt. col. 25th Ky. Inf., U.S. Volunteers, 1861, col. 8th Ky. Cavalry, 1863; served at battles of Ft. Henry, Ft. Donelson, Shiloh; mem. Ky. Senate, 1863-65; U.S. atty. for Ky., 1866-70; U.S. solicitor gen., 1870-72; U.S. sec. of treasury (apptd. by Pres. Grant), 1874-76, collected evidence resulted in conviction of Whiskey Ring, 1875; Republican nominee U.S. Pres., 1876, lost nomination to James G. Blaine, 1876; opened law firm, N.Y.C., 1878; 2d v.p. Am. Bar Assn., 1879; v.p. Civil Service Reform Assn.; mem. Metropolitan Union, Union League clubs, N.Y.C. Died N.Y.C., June 22, 1896.

BRISTOW, Francis Marion, congressman, lawyer; b. Clark County, Ky., Aug. 11, 1804; studied law. Admitted to bar, began practice of law, Elkton, Ky.; mem. Ky. Ho. of Reps., 1831-33, Ky. Senate, 1846; del. Ky. constl. conv., 1849; mem. U.S. Ho. of Reps. (Whig, filled vacancy) from Ky., 33d, 36th congresses, Dec. 4, 1854-55, 59-61; mem. Washington (D.C.) Peace Conv., 1861. Died Elkton, June 10, 1864; buried family burying ground.

BRISTOW, George Frederick, composer; b. Bklyn., Dec. 19, 1825; son of William Richard Bristow; studied violin, piano, organ and composition under his father, also Henry C. Timm, G.A. MacFarren; m. Louise Westervelt Holden. Violinist in orchestra of Olympic Theatre, N.Y.C., 1836, N.Y. Philharmonic Soc., 1842; conducted Harmonic Soc., 1851-62; pianist at 1st Am. concert of Theodore Thomas; protested (with group of fellow mems. N.Y. Philharmonic) policy of favoring fgn. composers over Americans, 1854; connected with musical programs in N.Y.C. public schs., 1854-98. Composer works including: Concert Overture, Opus 3; (cantata) Eleutheria; (operas) Rip Van Winkle, Columbus (incomplete); (oratorios) Praise to God, Daniel; 1st Symphony in E flat, 2d Symphony in D minor, 3d Symphony in F sharp minor, 4th (Arcadian) Symphony in E minor, 5th (Niagara) Symphony. Died Dec. 13, 1898.

BRITTAN, Belle, see Fuller, Hiram.

BROADHEAD, James Overton, congressman; b. Charlottesville, Va., May 29, 1819; s. Achilles and Mary Winston (Carr) B.; attended U. Va., 1835-36; m. Mary S. Dorsey, May 13, 1847; studied law, St. Louis. Tutor, family of Edward Bates, St. Louis, 1837; licensed and began practice law, Bowling Green, Mo., 1842; del. Mo. Constl. Conv., 1845; mem. Mo. Ho. of Reps. (Whig), 1846-47, Mo. Senate, 1850-53; became partner (with Fidelio C. Sharp) in New firm, St. Louis, 1859; an organizer Com. of Safety to resist pro-Southern forces in St. Louis; mem. Mo. Constl. Conv. which declared provisional govt. favorable to Union, 1861; apptd. provost-marshal gen. of dist. including Mo., So. Ia., Kan., Indian Territory and Ark., 1861; mem. Mo. State Constl. Conv., 1875; govt. counsel for Whiskey Ring cases, 1876; pres. Am. Bar Assn., 1878; mem. U.S. Ho. of Reps. from Mo., 48th Congress, 1883-85, mem. judiciary com.; apptd. by Pres. Cleveland spl. commr. to France to investigate govt. archives in relation to French spoliation claims; minister to Switzerland, 1893-97. Died Aug. 7, 1898; buried Bellefontaine Cemetery, St. Louis.

BROADUS, John Albert, clergyman; b. Blue Ridge County, Va., Jan. 24, 1827; s. Edmund and Nancy (Sims) B.; grad. U. Va.; m. Maria Harrison, Nov. 13, 1850; m. 2d, Charlotte Eleanor Sinclair, Jan. 4, 1859. Converted to Baptist Ch. at revival during coll. years, began to preach; became minister Bapt. Ch., Charlottesville, Va., also taught ancient langs. U. Va.; prof. New Testament and homiletics Bapt. Theol. Sem., Greenville, N.C., 1858; preached in Confederate Army camps during Civil War; corr. sec. Bapt. Sunday-Sch. Bd., 1862-64; aide-de-camp to gov. N.C., 1865; made trip to Europe, 1870; mem. Internat. Lesson Com., 1878-95; began revival of Theol. Sem. now located Louisville, Ky., pres., 1889; delivered Lyman Beecher lectures on preaching at Yale, 1889; occasional contbr. to Religious Herald. Died Mar. 16, 1895.

BROCKENBROUGH, William Henry, congressman; b. Va., Feb. 23, 1812; studied law. Admitted to bar; moved to Tallahassee, Fla.; mem. Fla. Ho. of Reps., 1837, Fla. Senate, 1840-44, pres., 1842; U.S. dist. atty., 1841-43; mem. U.S. Ho. of Reps. (Democrat, contested election) from Fla., 29th Congress, Jan. 24, 1846-47. Died Tallahassee, Jan. 28, 1850; buried Episcopal Cemetery.

BROCKETT, Linus Pierpont, author; b. Canton, Conn., Oct. 16, 1820; s. Rev. Pierpont and Sarah (Sage) B.; attended Conn. Literary Inst., Suffield, also Brown U.; grad. Yale Med. Sch., 1843; m. Lucy Maria Thacher, 1846, at least 1 child. Practiced medicine briefly; prof. physiology and anatomy, Georgetown (Ky.) Coll., 1844-45; with Hartford (Conn.) publishing house, various times, 1847-57; apptd. commr. to investigate idiocy in Conn., 1854, published findings, 1856; moved to Bklyn., 1860; editor Bklyn. Monthly, Bklyn. Advance; intense Union supporter; author approximately 50 books including: The History and Progress of Education, 1860; The Life and Times of Abraham Lincoln, 1865; Women's Work in the Civil War, 1867. Died Jan. 13, 1893.

BROCKLESBY, John, educator; b. West Bromwich, Eng., Oct. 8, 1811; grad. Yale, 1835; LL.D. (hon.), Hobart Coll., 1868. Came with family to Am., 1820 tutor mathematics Yale, 1839-40; admitted to Conn. bar, 1840, practiced law, Hartford, Conn.; prof. mathematics and natural philosophy Trinity Coll., Hartford, 1842-73, prof. astronomy and natural philosophy, 1873-82, prof. emeritus, from 1882, acting pres. of coll., 1860, 64, 66-67, 74. Author: Elements of Meteorology, 1848; Views on Microscopic World, 1850; Elements of Astronomy, 1855. Died Hartford, June 21, 1889.

BROCKWAY, John Hall, congressman; b. Ellington, Conn., Jan. 31, 1801; grad. Yale, 1820; studied law. Taught sch.; admitted to bar, 1823, began practice of law, Ellington; mem. Conn. Ho. of Reps., 1832-38, Conn. Senate, 1834; mem. U.S. Ho. of Reps. (Whig) from Conn., 26th-27th congresses, 1829-43; pros. atty. Tolland County (Conn.), 1849-67. Died Ellington, July 29, 1870; buried Ellington Center Cemetery.

BRODERICK, David Colbreth, senator; b. Washington, D.C., Feb. 4, 1820; s. Miss Copway. Moved to N.Y.C. with family, 1834, became head of family upon father's death, 1837; with an engine co., 1840; active in Tammany Hall ward politics, became important politically; saloon owner; mem. City Charter Conv., 1846; unsuccessful candidate for U.S. Congress, 1846; sold business, took Panama route to Cal., 1849; went into bus. coining short weight gold pieces, then entered town real estate bus.; del. Cal. Constl. Conv., 1849; elected to fill seat in Cal. Senate (Democrat), 1850, pres. Senate, 1851; boss Cal. Dem. Party, 1851-54; mem. U.S. Senate (Democrat) from Cal., 1857-59. Killed in duel with David S. Terry (chief justice Cal. Supreme Ct.), Sept. 16, 1859; buried Lone Mountain Cemetery, San Francisco.

BRODHEAD, Daniel, army officer; b. Albany, N.Y., Sept. 17, 1736; s. Daniel II and Hester (Wyngart) B.; m. Elizabeth Dupui; m. 2d, Rebecca Mifflin. Brught up on large family holdings in Bucks County, Pa.) dep. surveyor-gen., Reading, Pa., 1773; raised co. of riflemen to join Washington; promoted lt. col. after Battle of L.I., 1776, col., 1777; given command of regt. at Pitts., 1779; raided and terrorized Delaware Indians, 1779-81; acquitted in court martial resulting from complaints from officers and civilians; brevetted brig. gen. by Gen. Washington; strong mil. disciplinarian; served as surveyor gen. Pa. Died Nov. 15, 1809.

BRODHEAD, John, congressman, clergyman; b. Lower Smithfield, Pa., Oct. 5, 1770; attended Stroudsburg (Pa.) Acad.; studied theology. Ordained to ministry, active as a minister, 44 years; became supr. Methodist socs. in Conn. Valley, 1796; settled in Canaan, N.H., 1801; moved to Newfields Village, Newmarket, N.H., 1809; mem. N.H. Senate, 1817-27; chaplain N.H. Ho. of Reps., 1825; mem. U.S. Ho. of Reps. (Democrat) from N.H., 21st-22d congresses, 1829-33. Died Newfields, Apr. 7, 1838; buried Locust Cemetery.

BRODHEAD, John Curtis, congressman; b. Modena, Ulster County, N.Y., Oct. 27, 1780; attended dist. schs. Engaged in business and agriculture; sheriff Ulster County, 1825-28; mem. U.S. Ho. of Reps. (Democrat) from N.Y., 22d, 25th congresses, 1831-33, 37-39. Died Modena, Jan. 2, 1859; buried Modena Rural Cemetery.

BRODHEAD, John Romeyn, historian; b. Jan. 2, 1814; s. Rev. Jacob and Elizabeth (Bleecker) B.; grad. with honors Rutgers Coll., 1831; read law in Hugh Maxwell's office, 1831-35; m. Eugenia Bloodgood, 1856. Admitted to N.Y. bar, 1835; practiced law, 1835-37; attaché to Harmanus Bleecker at The Hague, 1837-41; apptd. by Gov. Seward as agt. to procure hist. material to fill gaps in N.Y. State archives, 1841; collected materials (edited by E.B. O'Callaghan and B. Fernow as Documents Relating to The Colonial History of New York, published by State of N.Y., 1856-86), published his own report, 1845; sec. of legation under George Bancroft, London, Eng., 1846-49; apptd. naval officer Port of N.Y., 1853; trustee Astor Library, 1867-71; mem. N.Y. Hist. Soc., St. Nicolas Soc.; active alumnus Rutgers Coll., helped establish Brodhead Prize for excellence in the classics. Author: History of the State of New York, 2 vols., 1853, 71. Died May 6, 1873; buried Trinity Cemetery, N.Y.C.

BRODHEAD, Richard, senator; b. Lehman Twp., Pike County, Pa., Jan. 5, 1811; studied law. Moved to Easton, Pa., 1830; admitted to bar, 1836, began practice of law, Easton; mem. Pa. Ho. of Reps., 1837-39; apptd. treas. Northampton County, 1841; mem. U.S. Ho. of Reps. (Democrat) from Pa., 28th-30th congresses, 1843-49; mem. U.S. Senate from Pa., 1851-57. Died Easton, Sept. 16, 1863; buried Easton Cemetery.

BROMFIELD, John, mcht.; b. Newburyport, Mass., Apr. 11, 1779; s. John and Ann (Roberts) B. Apprentice to 2 merc. firms, Charlestown, 1792-99; agt. for various investors around the world, 1800-13; made profits which were basis of future wealth, China, 1809; investor in China trade, Boston, from 1813; left estate of $200,000, bequests to Mass. Gen. Hosp., McLean Asylum, Mass. Eye and Ear Infirmary, Boston Female Asylum, Asylum for Indigent Boys, Farm Sch. at Thompson's Island, Asylum for Blind, Seaman's Aid Soc. of Newburyport. Died Dec. 9, 1849.

BRONLEM, Isaac Hill, journalist; b. Norwich, Conn., Mar. 6, 1833; s. Isaac and Mary (Hill) B.; attended Yale, 1849-53, B.A., 1868; read law in office of L. F. B. Foster, Norwich, Conn.; m. Adelaide Emma Roath, Dec. 25, 1855. Admitted to Conn. bar, 1854; asst. clk. Conn. Ho. of Reps., 1856, clk., 1857; clk. Conn. Senate, 1858; began publishing Norwich (Conn.) Bulletin, 1858; served as capt. 18th Conn. Volunteers, 1862-64; mem. Conn. Gen. Assembly, 1866; editor Evening Post, Hartford, 1868-72; traveled to Far West, gave lectures after return to East; contbr. to N.Y. Tribune, 1873-82; apptd. a govt. dir. U.P. R.R. by Pres. Arthur, 1882, became asst. to pres. railroad 1884-89; wrote for Comml. Advertiser, Evening Telegram (both N.Y.C.), also Post-Express, Rochester; editor N.Y. Tribune, 1891-98. Died Aug. 11, 1898.

BRONSON, David, congressman, lawyer; b. Suffield, Conn., Feb. 8, 1800; grad. Dartmouth, 1819; studied law. Admitted to bar, 1823, began practice of law, North Anson, Me.; mem. Me. Ho. of Reps., 1832, 34; justice of peace; mem. U.S. Ho. of Reps. (Whig, filled vacancy) from Me., 27th Congress, May 31, 1841-43; moved to Augusta, Me., 1843; mem. Me. Senate, 1846; collector of customs, Bath, Me., 1850-53; judge of probate Sagadahoc County, 1854-57. Died St. Michaels, Talbot County, Md., Nov. 20, 1863; buried Episcopal Cemetery, St. Michael's Parish.

BRONSON, Henry, physician; b. Waterbury, Conn., Jan. 30, 1804; s. Judge Bennet and Anna (Smith) B.; M.D., Yale, 1827; m. Sarah Miles Lathrop, 1831. Settled in West Springfield, Mass., then moved to Albany, N.Y., developed large med. practice; sent by mayor as ofcl. observer to Montreal cholera epidemic; traveled in Europe; prof. materia medica and therapeutics Yale Med. Sch., 1842-60; became pres. New Haven Bank (Conn.), 1860; mem. New Haven Bd. Edn., 1865-66; pres. Conn. Med. Soc., 1869; contbr. to Yale, New Haven and Waterbury hosps. Author: History of Waterbury, 1858. Died Nov. 26, 1893.

BRONSON, Isaac Hopkins, congressman, jurist; b. Rutland, N.Y., Oct. 16, 1802; attended public schs.; studied law. Admitted to bar, 1822, began practice of law, Watertown, N.Y.; mem. U.S. Ho. of Reps. (Democrat) from N.Y., 25th Congress, 1837-39; apptd. judge 5th Jud. Dist. N.Y., 1838; moved to St. Augustine, Fla., later to Palatka, Fla.; apptd. U.S. judge for Eastern Dist. Fla., 1840, judge of Eastern Circuit, 1845; apptd. U.S. judge for Dist. of Fla., 1846, then U.S. judge No. Dist. Fla., until 1855. Died Palatka, Aug. 13, 1855; buried Episcopal Ch. Cemetery.

BROOKE, Francis Taliaferro, jurist; b. Smithfield, Va., Aug. 27, 1763; s. Richard and Elizabeth (Taliaferro) B.; studied medicine with brother Lawrence; read law with brother Robert; m. Mary Randolph Spotswood, Oct. 1791; m. 2d, Mary Champe Carter, 1804; children include Francis Jr. Commd. lt. Continental Army, 1780; served under Lafayette, 1781, later under Gen. Green; admitted to Va. bar, 1788, practiced law, Monongahela and Harrison counties; apptd. atty. Va. Dist. Ct.; mem. Va. Ho. of Dels., 1794-95; commd. maj. Va. Militia, 1796; moved to Fredericksburg, Va., 1796; commd. brig. gen. Va. Militia, 1802; elected mem. Va. Senate, 1800, speaker, 1804; judge Va. Gen. Ct., 1804-11; judge Va. Supreme Ct. of Appeals, 1811-51, pres., 1824-30; v.p. Soc. of Cincinnati. Died Mar. 3, 1851.

BROOKE, Walter, senator, lawyer; b. nr. Winchester, Va., Dec. 25, 1813; grad. U. Va. at Charlottesville, 1835; studied law. Admitted to bar, 1838, began practice of law, Lexington, Miss.; mem. Miss. Ho. of Reps., 1848, Miss. Senate, 1850, 52; mem. U.S. Senate (Whig, filled vacancy) from Miss., Feb. 18, 1852-53; moved to Vicksburg, Miss., 1857, continued practice of law; del. Miss. Constl. Conv., 1861; became a Democrat, 1861; mem. Provisional Confederate Congress from Miss., 1861; apptd. mem. permanent mil. ct. Confederate States Am. Died Vicksburg, Feb. 18, 1869; buried Vicksburg Cemetery.

BROOKES, Samuel Marsdon, artist; b. Newington Green, Middlesex, Eng., Apr. 8, 1816. Came to Am., 1832, settled in Chgo. with praents; began painting, 1841; moved to Milw., 1842; sold paintings by lottery; returned to Eng., 1845; returned to Am., 1847; worked in Milw., 1847-62, in assn. with Thomas H. Stevenson, after 1855; settled in San Francisco, 1862; a founder San Francisco Art Assn., Bohemian Club; best known as painter of fish; painted portraits and Indian studies (preserved in Wis.). Died San Francisco, Jan. 31, 1892.

BROOKS, Arthur, clergyman; b. Boston, June 11, 1845; s. William Gray and Mary Ann (Phillips) B.; grad. Harvard, 1867; attended Andover Theol. Sem., 1868, Phila. Divinity Sch., 1868-70; D.D. (hon.) U. City N.Y.; S.T.D. (hon.) Princeton; m. Elizabeth Mather Willard, Oct. 17, 1872. Ordained deacon Episcopal Ch., 1870, priest, 1870; pastor Trinity Ch., Williamsport, Pa., 1871, St. James' Ch., Chgo., 1871-74, Ch. of the Incarnation, N.Y.C., 1874-95; a founder Barnard Coll. for women, N.Y., chmn. bd. trustees, 1889 (when it was incorporated into Columbia); mem. N.Y. Sons of Revolution. Author works including: The Life of Christ in the World, 1886; Christ for To-day. Died at sea, July 10, 1895.

BROOKS, Charles, clergyman, educator; b. Medford, Mass., Oct. 30, 1795; s. Jonathan and Elizabeth (Albree) B.; grad. Harvard, 1816, M.A. in Theology, 1819; m. Cecilia Williams, 1827, 1 son, 1 dau.; m. 2d, Mrs. Charlotte Ann Haven Lord, 1839. Pastor 3d Congregational (Unitarian) Ch., Hingham, Mass., 1821-39; became impressed with Prussian ednl. system while traveling in Europe 1833-34; began campaign to improve Conn. state sch. system, 1835; instrumental in formation of state bd. of edn. and state normal schs., 1838; spoke in favor of ednl. reform to legislatures of N.H., Vt., Me., N.J.; prof. natural history U. City N.Y., 1838-43; traveled in Europe, 1839-43. Author: Family Prayer Book, 1821; Remarks on Europe, Relating to Education, Peace, Labor, and Their Reference to the United States, 1846. Died July 7, 1872.

BROOKS, Charles Timothy, clergyman; b. Salem, Mass., June 20, 1813; s. Timothy and Mary King (Mason) B.; attended Harvard, 1828-32, Harvard Divinity Sch., 1832-35; m. Harriet Lyman Hazard, Oct. 18, 1837. Pastor, Unitarian Congregational Ch., Newport, R.I., 1837-71; took charge of Unitarian Ch., Mobile, Ala., while wintering there for health, 1842, 51; spent year in India for health, 1853-54; traveled in Europe, 1865-66. Translator (from German): William Tell, 1837, Homage of the Arts (both Schiller), 1853; German Lyric Poetry, 1842; 1st part of Faust, 1856; Titan, 1862, Hesperus (both J.P. Richter), 1864; Layman's Breviary (Leopold Schefer), 1867, The Wisdom of the Brahmin (F. Ruckert), 1882. Died June 14, 1883.

BROOKS, David, congressman; b. Phila., 1756; attended public schs.; studied law. Commd. lt. Pa. Battalion of Flying Camp, Continental Army, during Revolutionary War, 1776; captured at Ft. Washington, 1776, exchanged, 1780; apptd. asst. clothier gen.; admitted to bar, practiced law; settled in New York County, N.Y.; mem. N.Y. State Assembly, 1787-88, 94-96, 1810; judge Dutchess County (N.Y.), 1795-1807; mem. U.S. Ho. of Reps. from N.Y., 5th Congress, 1797-99; apptd. commr. to negotiate treaty with Seneca Indians; clk. Dutchess County, 1807-09, 10-11, 13-15; apptd. an officer U.S. Customs Service; an original mem. Soc. of Cincinnati. Died Poughkeepsie, N.Y., Aug. 30, 1838; probably buried Old Rural Cemetery.

BROOKS, Erastus, journalist, state legislator; b. Portland, Me., Jan. 13, 1815; s. James and Elizabeth (Folsom) B.; attended Brown U.; m. Margaret Dawes. Left coll. to begin newspaper Yankee, Wiscasset, Me.; taught sch., Haverhill, Mass., for short time; editor, owner Haverhill Gazette; reporter Portland Advertiser; moved to Washington, D.C., 1835; contbr. articles N.Y. Daily Advertiser, Boston Transcript, Balt. Am., St. Louis Republican, others; became editor Portland Advertiser, 1840; traveled from So. tip of Africa to Moscow, Russia, sent back regular reports, 1843; editor (with his brother James) N.Y. Express, until 1877, actively opposed Catholic exemption from tax; became mem. N.Y. State Senate (Know-Nothing Party), 1853; unsuccessful Know-Nothing candidate for gov. N.Y., 1856; mem. Know-Nothing Nominating Conv., 1856; mem. Constl.-Union Party Conv. that hominated Bell and Everett, 1860; mem. N.Y. State Constl. Conv., 1866-67; mem. Constl. Commn., 1872-73; mem. N.Y. Assembly from Richmond County, 5 terms. Died Nov. 25, 1886.

BROOKS, George Merrick, congressman, jurist; b. Concord, Mass., July 26, 1824; grad. Harvard, 1844; studied law. Admitted to bar, 1847, began practice of law, Concord; mem. Mass. Ho. of Reps., 1858, Mass. Senate, 1859; mem. joint com. of Mass Senate and Ho. of Reps. to revise statutes of Mass., 1859; mem. U.S. Ho. of Reps. (Republican, filled vacancy) from Mass., 41st-42d congresses, Nov. 2, 1869-May 14, 1872 (resigned); judge of probate for Middlesex County, 1872-93. Died Concord, Sept. 22, 1893; buried Sleepy Hollow Cemetery.

BROOKS, George Washington, jurist; b. Elizabeth City, N.C., Mar. 16, 1821; s. William C. and Catherine (Davis) B.; m. Margaret Costin, June 20, 1850, 3 sons, 2 daus. Licensed to practice law N.C. County Cts., 1844; admitted to practice before Superior Cts. N.C., 1846; mem. N.C. Ho. of Commons (Whig), 1852, 65-66; U.S. judge Dist. N.C., 1865-82. Died Jan. 6, 1882.

BROOKS, James, congressman, editor; b. Portland, Me., Nov. 10, 1810; attended acad., Monmouth, Me.; grad. Waterville (Me.) Coll., 1831; studied law. Taught sch. at 16 years of age; edited Portland Advertiser, Washington correspondent, 1832; mem. Me. Ho. of Reps., 1835; founded N.Y. Daily Express, N.Y.C., circa 1836, editor until 1873; mem. N.Y. State Assembly, 1847; mem. U.S. Ho. of Reps. (Whig) from N.Y., 31st-32d congresses, 1849-53, (Democrat), 38th-39th, 40th-43d congresses, 1863-65, Mar. 4, 1865-Apr. 7, 1866, 1867-73; mem. N.Y. State Constl. Conv., 1867; apptd. a govt. dir. U.P. R.R., 1867. Died Washington, D.C., Apr. 30, 1873; buried Greenwood Cemetery, Bklyn.

BROOKS, James Gordon, journalist; b. Red Hook N.Y., Sept. 3, 1801; s. David Brooks; grad. Union Coll., Schenectady, N.Y., 1818; studied law, Poughkeepsie, N.Y.; m. Mary Elizabeth Aiken, 1828. Began writing under pen name Florio, 1819; literary editor Mag. Minerva (merged with Literary Gazette then purchased by Am. Athenaeum), 1823-27 editor N.Y. Morning Courier (merged to Courier and Enquirer), 1827-30; editor Winchester (Va.) Republican, 1830-38, Albany (N.Y.) Advertiser, 1838-39 moved to N.Y.C., 1839; editor New Era, for short time. Author: The Rivals of Este, and Other Poems 1829. Died Albany, Feb. 20, 1841.

BROOKS, John, army officer; gov. Mass.; b. Medford, Mass., May, 1752; s. Caleb and Ruth (Albree) B.; grad. Dr. Tufts' med. sch., 1773; A.M. (hon.) Harvard, 1787, M.D., 1810, LL.D., 1817; m. Lucy Smith, 1774, 2 children. Served as capt. Reading Co. of Minute Men, fought at Concord; commd. capt. Continental Army, 1776; served as lt. col. 8th Mass. Regt.; mem. Mass. Gen. Ct., 1785-86; commd. maj. gen. Middlesex (Mass.) Militia, 1786; mem. Mass. Conv. to ratify U.S. Constn., 1788; U.S. marshal for Mass. dist., 1791; mem. Mass. Senate from Middlesex County, 1791; served as brig. gen. U.S. Army 1792-96; adj. gen. Mass., 1812-16; gov., 1816-22 pres. Mass. Med. Soc., Mass. Soc. of Cincinnati Washington Monument Soc.; bd. overseers Harvard 1815. Died Medford, Mar. 1, 1825.

BROOKS, Maria Gowen, poet; b. Medford, Mass. 1794; d. William and Eleanor (Cutter) Gowen; m. John Brooks, Aug. 26, 1810; children—Horace Edgar. At age 15 married widower nearly 50 years old, moved to Portland, Me.; did not like narrow provincial life, found solace in writing poetry; after death of husband (1823), moved with her brother to coffee plantation in Cuba; twice attempted suicide because of disappointments in love; made short visit to Boston, then returned to Cuba where she inherited property; moved with son Horace to Hanover, N.H., 1829; became acquainted with Marquis de Lafayette (who procured West Point appointment for Horace) while visiting Europe; returned to U.S., 1833, to Cuba, 1843-45. Author: Judith, Esther and Other Poems, By a Lover of Fine Arts, 1820; Zophiël, 1825; Idomen, 1838. Died Cuba, Nov. 11, 1845; buried Limonal, nr. Matanzas, Cuba.

BROOKS, Micah, congressman; b. Brooksvale, nr. Cheshire, Conn., May 14, 1775. One of earliest surveyors of Western N.Y.; justice of peace, 1806, mem. N.Y. State Assembly, 1808-09; served as col. on frontier, also at Ft. Erie, 1812-14; served as maj. gen. N.Y. State Inf., 1828-30; mem. U.S. Ho. of Reps. from N.Y., 14th Congress, 1815-17; engaged in agriculture; del. from Ontario County to N.Y. State Constl. Conv., 1821; presdl. elector on Adams ticket, 1824. Died Fillmore, N.Y., July 7, 1857; buried Nunda (N.Y.) Cemetery.

BROOKS, Peter Chardon, businessman; b. North Yarmouth, Me., Jan. 11, 1767; s. Rev. Edward and Abigail (Brown) B.; m. Nancy Gorham, 1792, 13 children. Apprenticed to mcht., Boston, 1781; opened insurance brokerage in Bunch of Grapes Tavern, 1789, made huge profits, retired, 1803; built mansion at Medford; returned to business for short time as pres. New Eng. Marine Ins. Co., 1806; mem. Mass. Senate (Federalist), 1806-14, 20-22; mem. Mass. Council, 1817-19; mem. Mass. Ho. of Reps., 1819, 21, 23; del. Mass. Constl. Conv., 1820; continued to invest money in mortgages and loans, reputed to be richest man in New Eng. at time of death. Died Jan. 1, 1849.

BROOKS, Phillips, clergyman; b. Boston, Dec. 13, 1835; s. William G. and Mary A. (Phillips) B.; grad. Harvard, 1855; studied Episcopal Sem., Alexandria, Va. Ordained deacon Episcopal Ch., Alexandria, 1859; clergyman, Ch. of Advent, Phila., 1859-62, Holy Trinity, Phila., 1862-69, Trinity Ch., Boston, 1869-91; excelled in spiritual oratory and leadership; 1st American to preach before a mem. English royal family (Queen Victoria), 1880; bishop of Mass., 1891-93; most famous Episcopal minister of his time. Author: The Influence of Jesus, 1879; The Candle of the Lord, 1881; The Light of the World, 1890; New Starts in Life, 1896; others; also verses to Redner's O Little Town of Bethlehem, 1865. Died Boston, Jan. 23, 1893; buried Mt. Auburn Cemetery, Cambridge, Mass.

BROOKS, Preston Smith, congressman; b. Edgefield, S.C., Aug. 6, 1819; s. Whitefield and Mary P. (Carroll) B.; grad. S.C. Coll. (now U.S.C.), 1839; m. Caroline Means, 1841; m. 2d, Martha Means, 1843. Admitted to S.C. bar, 1843; elected to S.C. Legislature, 1844; mem. U.S. Ho. of Reps. from S.C., 33d-34th congresses, 1853-57; remembered for his physical attack on Senator Charles Sumner (which left Sumner permanently disabled) in Senate chambers, May 22, 1856. Died Washington, D.C., Jan. 27, 1857; buried Edgefield.

BROOKS, William Thomas Harbaugh, army of-cer; b. New Lisbon, O., Jan. 28, 1821; grad. U.S. il. Acad., 1841. Served with 3d Inf., U.S. Army, 841, against Seminole Indians in Fla., 1842-43; erved under Gen. Taylor, 1846, fought in battles ' Palo Alto, Resaca de la Palma; promoted 1st lt., 846; brevetted capt. and maj. after battles of onterey, Vera Cruz and Cerro Gordo, 1846; aide-e-camp to Gen. Twigg, 1848-51; commd. capt. .S. Army, 1851; became brig. gen. U.S. Volunteers, 861; promoted maj. U.S. Army, 1862; served in attles of Yorktown, Savage Station, Glendale, An-etam; in command of a div., 1862-63; commanded ept. of Monongahela, 1863; continued as div. comdr., 863-64; resigned because of ill health, 1864; farmer, untsville, Ala., 1864-70. Died July 19, 1870.

BROOM, Jacob, congressman, lawyer; b. Balt., uly 25, 1808; s. James Madison Broom; studied w. Admitted to bar, began practice of law, hila.; apptd. dep. auditor Pa., 1840; clk. Phila. rphans' Ct., 1848-52; Native Am. Party nominee r Pres. of U.S., 1852; mem. U.S. Ho. of Reps. Am. Whig) from Pa., 34th Congress, 1855-57. ied Washington, D.C., Nov. 28, 1864; buried Con-essional Cemetery, Washington.

BROOM, James Madison, congressman, lawyer; . nr. Wilmington, Del., 1776; grad. Princeton, 794; studied law. Admitted to bar, 1801, prac-ced law, New Castle and Wilmington, also Balt.; em. U.S. Ho. of Reps. (Federalist) from Del., th-10th congresses, 1805-07 (resigned); moved Phila., 1819; mem. Pa. Ho. of Reps., 1824. Died hila., Jan. 15, 1850; buried St. Mary's Church-rd, Hamilton Village (now part of Phila.).

BROOMALL, John Martin, congressman, law-er; b. Delaware County, Pa., Jan. 19, 1816; at-nded pvt. schs.; studied law. Taught sch. for veral years; admitted to the bar, 1840, began actice of law, Chester, Pa.; mem. Pa. Ho. of eps., 1851-52, Pa. Revenue Bd., 1854; del. Re-ublican Nat. Conv., Chgo., 1860; Rep. presdl. ector, 1860, 72; moved to Media, Pa., 1860, con-nued practice of law; served as capt. Co. C,)th Regt., Pa. Emergency Men, during Civil 'ar; mem. U.S. Ho. of Reps. (Rep.) from Pa., 8th-40th congresses, 1863-69; judge Delaware ounty Cts., 1874-75. Died Phila., June 3, 1894; uried Media Cemetery.

BROSS, William, journalist, state ofcl.; b. Sussex ounty, N.J., Nov. 4, 1813; son of Deacon Moses ross; grad. with honors Williams Coll., Williams-own, Mass., 1838; m. Miss Jansen, 1839. Prin., idgebury Acad., 1838-43; tchr. Chester Acad., 1843-8; partner Briggs, Bross & Co., bookselling house, hgo., 1848-49; conducted (with Rev. J.A. Wight) ligious weekly newspaper Prairie Herald, 1849-52; ormed (with John L. Scripps) Democratic Press, 852 (became Republican Party organ 1854, com-ined with Tribune to become Press Tribune due to anic of 1857); early advocate of Lincoln's nomina-on for Pres. U.S.; became lt. gov. Ill., 1864; elped solicit aid from neighboring cities after Chgo. ire, 1871. Author: History of Chicago, 1876; Tom uick (biog. sketch), 1887. Died Jan. 27, 1890.

BROUGH, John, gov. Ohio; b. Marietta, O., Sept. 7, 1811; s. John and Jane (Garnet) B.; attended hio U., Athens; m. Achsa Pruden, 1832, 1 son, dau.; m. 2d, Caroline A. Nelson, 1843, 2 sons, daus. Published Western Republican (Democratic aper), Marietta; became owner Ohio Eagle, Lan-aster, 1833; clk. Ohio Senate, 1835-37; mem. Ohio o. of Reps. (Democrat), 1837; auditor State of hio, 1839-45, improved state credit, reorganized ccount system, added about 1 million acres to ate tax list; trustee Ohio U., 1840-43; became wner and editor Cincinnati Advertiser, 1844, re-amed paper Cincinnati Enquirer; practiced law; en-aged in railroading, 1848-63; pres. Madison & ndpls., Bellefontaine Line, Indpls., Pitts. & Cleve. .R.; retained Lincoln's confidence during Civil War; ov. Ohio (defeated Clement Vallandigham), 1863-5, conducted adminstrn. characterized by reform nd honesty; advocated senority system in army which made many enemies); withdrew as gubernator-al candidate, 1865. Died Aug. 29, 1865; buried Voodland Cemetery, Cleve.

BROUGHAM, John, actor, playwright; b. Dublin, reland, May 9, 1810; ed. Trinity Coll., Peter Street Hosp.; m. Emma Williams; m. 2d, Mrs. Annette elson Hodges. Went to London, Eng., 1830; be-ame mem. Mme. Vestris' co. at Olympic Theatre, 831, later at Covent Garden; became mgr. London yceum, 1840, wrote several plays for repertoire; egan Am. career in play His Last Legs, Park heatre, N.Y.C., 1842; actor and playwright with urton's Chambers Street Theatre, N.Y.C.; opened rougham's Lyceum, N.Y.C., 1850 (venture failed); evived play King John at Bowery Theatre; joined Vallack's co., continued to write plays prolifically; eturned to Eng., 1860-65; came back to U.S., 865; opened Brougham's Theatre, 1869 (house aken from him by Jim Fisk, Jr.); received some 10,000 raised at testimonial benefit, 1878. Author pproximately 75 plays including a dramatization of Bleak House, Pocahontas, Columbus, The Duke's Mot-to, Better Late Than Never, The Dramatic Review for 1868. Died June 7, 1880.

BROUGHTON, William R., Brit. navy officer; first to explore Columbia River, under orders from Brit. Navy Capt. George Vancouver, 1792; ascended river for 120 miles, landing his boat at Chatham Point Vancouver (several miles above present site Vancouver, Wash.); named Baker's Bay, Barings River, Puget Island.

BROWERE, Albertus D.O., artist; b. Tarrytown, N.Y., Mar. 17, 1814; s. John Henri Isaac Browere. Exhibited at N.A.D., 1831; moved to Catskill, N.Y., 1834, clk. drug store; sailed for Cal., 1852, returned to Catskill, 1856; went to Cal., 1858, remained in San Francisco, until 1861; settled in Catskill, 1861; noted as painter of genre pictures of Am. life; ex-hibited at Am. Acad., Apollo Assn., Am. Art-Union. Died Catskill, Feb. 17, 1887.

BROWERE, John Henri Isaac, sculptor; b. N.Y.C., 1792; s. Jacob and Ann Catherine (Gen-don) B.; attended King's Coll. (now Columbia); studied art with Archibald Robertson; m. Eliza Derrick, 1810, at least 8 children including Albur-tis. Traveled in Europe, 2 years, made pedestrian tour of Italy, Austria, Greece, Switzerland, France and Eng., studied art; developed superior molding material for life masks; gained fame with bust of Lafayette; other busts include: A. Hamilton, John Adams, John Q. Adams, Charles F. Adams, Jefferson, Madison, Van Buren, De Witt Clinton, Henry Clay; busts exhibited at Phila. Centennial, 1876; also a painter and poet. Died Sept. 10, 1834; buried Carmine St. Churchyard, N.Y.C.

BROWN, A. Page, architect; b. 1859; grad. Cor-nell U. With office of McKim, Mead & White; toured Europe; returned to N.Y.C., 1885, opened office; practiced architecture, N.Y.C., several years; designed Clio and Whig halls, Mus. of Historic Art, Princeton; moved to San Francisco, 1889, began practice as architect; recognized as one of most progressive architects in San Francisco; archi-tect numerous pub. and bus. structures, including Crocker Office Bldg., Sharon Office Bldg., 1892, Ferry Bldg., So. Pacific Depot (begun 1893, finished by Willis Polk, 1903), Donajue Office Bldg., Trinity Ch.; architect Cal. Bldg. erected at World's Co-lumbian Expn., Chgo., 1893. Died Jan. 20, 1896.

BROWN, Aaron Venable, gov. Tenn., U.S. post-master gen.; b. Brunswick County, Va., Aug. 15, 1795; s. Rev. Aaron and Elizabeth (Melton) B.; grad. U. N.C., 1814; m. Sarah Burruss; m. 2d, Mrs. Cynthia Saunders, 1845; 5 children. Ad-mitted to bar, 1816; partner (with James K. Polk) in law firm, for a time; mem. Tenn. Senate, 1821-25, Tenn. Ho. of Reps., 1831-33; mem. U.S. Ho. of Reps. (Democrat) from Tenn., 26th-28th con-gresses, 1839-45; gov. Tenn., 1845-47; U.S. post-master-gen., 1857-59. Died Washington, D.C., Mar. 8, 1859; buried Mt. Olivet Cemetery, Nash-ville, Tenn.

BROWN, Albert Gallatin, senator; gov. Miss.; b. Chester Dist., S.C., May 31, 1813; s. Joseph Brown; attended Miss. Coll., 1829-32; m. Eliza-beth Taliaferro, Oct. 1835; m. 2d, Roberta Young, Jan. 12, 1841; children—Robert Y., Joseph A. Elected col. Copiah County (Miss.) Militia, 1832, commd. brig. gen., 1834; admitted to Miss. bar, 1834; mem. Miss. Ho. of Reps., 1835-39; mem. U.S. Ho. of Reps. from Miss., 26th, 30th-32d con-gresses, 1839-41, Jan. 1848-53; circuit judge, 1841-43; gov. Miss. 1844-48; mem. U.S. Senate from Miss., 1854-60 mem. Confederate Senate from Miss., 1862-65; capt. Brown's Rebels. Died nr. Terry, Hinds County, Miss., June 12, 1880; buried Greenwood Cemetery, Jackson, Miss.

BROWN, Alexander, banker; b. Ballymena, Ireland, Nov. 17, 1764; s. William and Margaretta (Davison) B.; m. Grace Davison; children—Wil-liam, George, John, James. Came to Am., 1800; started bus. career as importer Irish linen, de-veloped firm into financial instn., Alexander Brown and Sons (internat. banking and import-export firm, oldest of its type in Am.), admitted sons as partners (who started branches in various cities of world); an organizer B. & O. R.R.; one of 1st Am. millionaires. Died Balt., Apr. 3, 1834; buried Balt.

BROWN, Anson, congressman, lawyer; b. Charlton, N.Y., 1800; grad. Union Coll., Schenec-tady, N.Y., 1819; studied law. Admitted to bar, began practice of law, Ballston Spa, N.Y.; an original dir. Ballston Spa State Bank (organ-ized 1830, later called Ballston Spa Nat. Bank); mem. U.S. Ho. of Reps. (Whig) from N.Y., 26th Congress, 1839-40. Died Ballston Spa, June 14, 1840; buried Ballston Spa Cemetery Assn. Ceme-tery.

BROWN, Bedford, senator; b. Caswell County, N.C., June 6, 1795; s. Jethro B. and Lucy (Wil-liamson) B.; attended U. N.C.; m. Mary L. Glenn, at least 1 son, Bedford. Mem. N.C. Ho. of Reps. from Caswell County, 1815-18, 23; mem. N.C. Sen-ate, 1828-29, 58-63; mem. U.S. Senate from N.C. (filled seat vacated when John Branch became mem. Jackson's cabinet), 1829-40, supported Jackson on nullification and bank issues, resigned from Senate rather than follow instrns. from N.C. Legislature to condemn Jackson policy; unsuccessful candidate for reelection to U.S. Senate, 1842; moved to Mo., 1843, spent short time in Va., then returned to N.C., 1852; advocated states-rights (assured by constl. amendment) within the Union; supported Buchanan at Nat. Dem. Conv., 1856; opposed secession, 1860; elected to U.S. Congress, 1865, not allowed to take seat; elected to N.C. Constl. Conv., 1867, denied his seat. Died Dec. 6, 1870; buried "Rose Hill" family plot, Caswell County.

BROWN, Benjamin, congressman, physician; b. Swansea, Mass., Sept. 23, 1756; studied medicine. Began practice of medicine, Waldoboro, Mass. (now Me.); served as surgeon in Am. frigate Bos-ton (Commanded by Commodore Tucker), which conveyed John Adams as Am. commr. to France, 1778; captured (with Commander Tucker) in Am. warship Thorne at mouth of St. Lawrence River, imprisoned on Prince Edward Island; es-caped to Boston; mem. Mass. Ho. of Reps., 180-11-12, 19; mem. U.S. Ho. of Reps. from Mass., 14th Congress, 1815--17. Died Waldoboro, Sept. 17, 1831; buried Waldoboro Cemetery.

BROWN, Benjamin Gratz, senator, gov. Mo.; b. Lexington, Ky., May 28, 1826; s. Mason and Judith (Bledsoe) B.; attended Transylvania U.; grad. Yale, 1847. Admitted to Ky. bar, 1849; mem. Ky. Legislature, 1852-59; significant figure in forma-tion of Nat. and Mo. Republican parties; commd. col. 4th regt. Mo. Volunteers; mem. U.S. Senate from Mo., Dec. 14, 1863-67; gov. Mo., 1871-73; nominated for vice pres. U.S. on Liberal Republi-can ticket, 1872. Died St. Louis, Dec. 13, 1885; buried Oak Hill Cemetery, Kirkwood, Mo.

BROWN, Charles, congressman; b. Phila., Sept. 23, 1797; ed. in public schs. and privately. Served as officer N.J. Militia, 1817-19; town clk. Dover Twp., 1819; sch. tchr., Dividing Creek, 1820-21; entered cordwood bus., Phila., 1823; apptd. a dir. Phila. Public Schs., 1828; mem. Phila. City Coun-cil, 1830-31; mem. Pa. Ho. of Reps., 1830-33; del. Pa. Constl. Conv., 1834-38; mem. U.S. Ho. of Reps. (Democrat) from Pa., 27th, 30th congresses, 1841-43, 47-49; pres. State Conv. to nominate candi-dates for bd. canal commrs., 1843; mem. bd. commrs. No. Liberties Twp., 1843; mem. bd. in-sps. Eastern State Penitentiary, 1851-53; collec-tor of customs Port of Phila., 1853-57; mem. bd. guardians of poor of Phila., 1860; engaged in agriculture, Dover, Del., 1861; town commr. Do-ver, 1864-65; del. Union Nat. Conv., Phila., 1866; pres. bd. trustees Dover Public Schs., 1871-78. Died Dover, Sept. 4, 1883; buried Laurel Hill Cemetery, Phila.

BROWN, Charles Brockden, novelist, journalist; b. Phila., Jan. 17, 1771; s. Elijah and Mary (Arm-itt) B.; m. Elizabeth Linn, Nov. 1804. Edited Lit-erary Mag. and Am. Register, 1803-07, Am. Register or Gen. Repository of History, Politics and Science, 1807-10. Called father of Am. novel; 1st Am. profl. author, 1st Am. author to gain internat. reputation. Author: Arthur Mervyn, published in 2 parts, 1799-1800; Wieland, 1798; Ormond, 1799; Edgar Huntly, 1799; others. Died Phila., Feb. 22, 1810.

BROWN, Charlotte Emerson, club organizer; b. Andover, Mass., Apr. 21, 1838; d. Ralph E. and Eliza (Rockwell) Emerson; studied music and lang. abroad; attended comml. course, Chgo.; m. Rev. William B. Brown, July 27, 1880. Taught sch., Montreal, Can., 1 year; became personal sec. to her brother Ralph; organized musical, French clubs, Rockford; founder Rockford Conservatory of Music; taught modern langs. Rockford Sem.; traveled in Europe, 1880-83, returned to East Orange, N.J.; elected pres. Women's Club; became pres. Gen. Fedn. Women's Clubs, 1890, greatly increased its member-ship; supported Congregational mission work, mem. Women's Bd. of Missions. Died Feb. 5, 1895.

BROWN, David Paul, lawyer; b. Salem, N.J., Sept. 28, 1795; s. Paul and Rhoda (Thackara) B.; studied medicine under Benjamin Rush, Phila., 1812-13; began study law under William Rawle, Phila., 1813; m. Emmeline Catherine Handy, Dec. 24, 1826, at least 1 son, Robert Eden. Admitted to Phila. bar, 1816, soon after to Pa. Supreme, Dist., Circuit Ct. bars and U.S. Supreme Ct. bar; de-livered welcome address to Marquis de Lafayette, 1824; enhanced reputation with successful de-fense of Judge Robert Porter (impeached by Pa. Legislature); became a leading lawyer of Phila.; wrote light poetry. Author: (reminiscences) The Forum, 2 vols., 1856; (plays) Sertorius, The Pro-phet of St. Paul's, The Trail, Love and Honor. Died July 11, 1872.

BROWN, Ebenezer, clergyman, mfr.; b. Ches-terfield, Mass., 1795. Became minister Methodist Ch., 1818; missionary to French in New Orleans

(1st missionary attempt of Am. Methodism), 1819-21; pastor, Middlebury, Vt., 1821, Hartford, Conn., 1822, N.Y.C., 1823-24; retired from ministry due to ill health, 1825; became dry goods mcht., Troy, N.Y., 1827; manufactured 1st detachable shirt collars, 1829-34; founded commn. house, E. Brown & Co., N.Y.C., 1834. Died Balt., Jan. 3, 1889; buried Woodlawn Cemetery, Phila.

BROWN, Elias, congressman; b. nr. Balt., May 9, 1793; attended common schs. Democratic presdl. elector, 1820; Whig presdl. elector, 1828, 36; mem. U.S. Ho. of Reps. (Whig) from Md., 21st Congress, 1829-31; mem. Md. Ho. of Reps., 1834-35, Md. Senate, 1836-38; del. Md. Constl. Conv., 1836. Died nr. Balt., July 7, 1857; buried pvt. cemetery nr. Eldersburg, Md.

BROWN, Eliphalet M., Jr., artist; b. Newburyport, Mass., 1816; m. 1875. Drew lithograph of "Boz" after D. Lawrence for Currier & Ives, published 1839; exhibited at N.A.D., 1841; worked with firms E. & J. Brown, 1846, 48, Brown & Severyn, 1851; accompanied Commodore Perry's expdn. to Japan as daguerreotypist and artist, published sketches of landing in Japan; served with U.S. Navy, 1855-75, as master and ensign during Civil War, later sec. to adm. Mediterranean Squadron; work represented in Library of Congress, N.Y. Pub. Library, Museum of City N.Y. Died N.Y.C., Jan. 23, 1886.

BROWN, Ethan Allen, senator, gov. Ohio; b. Darien, Conn., July 4, 1766; s. Roger Brown; studied law under Alexander Hamilton. Admitted to bar, 1802; apptd. by legislature as judge Ohio Supreme Ct., 1810-18; gov. Ohio, 1818-22; mem. U.S. Senate (Democrat) from Ohio, 1822-25, chmn. com. on roads and canals; canal commr. Ohio, 1825-30; U.S. minister to Brazil, 1830-34; commr. Gen. Land Office, Washington, D.C., 1835-36; mem. Ind. Ho. of Reps., 1842. Died Indpls., Nov. 24, 1852; buried City Cemetery, Rising Sun, Ind.

BROWN, Francis, coll. pres.; b. Chester, N.H., Jan. 11, 1784; s. Benjamin and Prudence (Kelly) B.; grad. Dartmouth, 1805, studied theology, 1806-09; D.D. (hon.), Williams Coll., Hamilton Coll.; m. Elizabeth Gilman, Feb. 4, 1811, at least 1 son, Samuel Gilman. Tutor at Dartmouth, 1806-09; pres., 1815-19; ordained to ministry Congregational Ch.; pastor Congregational Ch., North Yarmouth, Me., 1810-15; overseer Bowdoin Coll., 1810-14, trustee, 1814-15. Died July 27, 1820.

BROWN, George, financier; b. Ballymena, Antrim County, Ireland, Aug. 17, 1787; s. Alexander and Grace (Davidson) B.; m. Isabella McLanahan, 1818. Came to Balt., 1802; joined father's firm Alexander Brown & Sons; a founder B. & O. R.R. (1st passenger steam railroad in U.S.), 1827, became treas., 1827, supervised (with father) laying of road, 1828; connected with Ross Winan's devel. of 8-wheeled railroad car, 1831-32; became head of Brown Clan upon death of father, 1834; directed investments toward nat. (rather than internat.) banking; active in civic affairs, Balt.; contbd. portions of fortune to House of Refuge, Peabody Inst., other charities. Died Aug. 26, 1859.

BROWN, George, physician; b. Wilton, N.H., Oct. 11, 1823; s. Ephriam and Sarah (King) B.; attended U. Vt., Jefferson Med. Coll., Phila.; M.D., U. City N.Y.; m. Catherine Wood, Nov. 28, 1850, at least 1 son, Dr. Robert A. Began practice medicine, Barre, Mass., 1850; became interested in Elm Hill Sch. for Feeble-Minded Children, became supt., 1851, expanded sch. into largest pvt. instn. of its kind in U.S., (with wife) devoted his life to sch.; mem. Barre Sch. Bd.; a founder Barre Library Assn. Died May 6, 1892.

BROWN, George Houston, congressman, lawyer; b. Lawrenceville, N.J., Feb. 12, 1810; attended Lawrenceville Acad.; grad. Princeton, 1828; studied law Yale, 1 year, also in law office, Somerville, N.J. Tchr., Lawrenceville Acad., 1828-30; admitted to bar, 1835, began practice of law, Somerville; mem. N.J. Council, 1842-45; del. N.J. Constl. Conv., 1844; mem. U.S. Ho. of Reps. (Whig) from N.J., 32d Congress, 1851-53; asso. justice N.J. Supreme Ct., 1861-65. Died Somerville, Aug. 1, 1865; buried Old Cemetery.

BROWN, George Loring, painter; b. Boston, Feb. 2, 1814; studied wood engraving under Alonzo Hartwell. Illustrator for some of Peter Parley's natural history books; went to Europe to study, became disheartened in Belgium, went instead to London; returned to Boston, 1832; went to Paris to study, 1840, returned to U.S., 1860. Paintings include: Palermo, Bay of Naples, Capri, Bay of New York. Died Malden, Mass., June 25, 1889.

BROWN, George William, jurist; b. Balt., Oct. 13, 1812; s. George John and Esther (Allison) B.; attended Dartmouth; grad. with highest honors Rutgers, 1831; m. Miss Brune. Became partner (with Fred. W. Brune) in law firm, 1839; mayor Balt. (Independent) 1859, helped protect 6th Mass. Regt. when it retreated through Balt.; arrested (along with many other Md. polit. figures) by Gen. Dix, 1861, imprisoned 15 months; judge Balt. Supreme Ct., 1872-88; a founder, trustee U. Md.; trustee Johns Hopkins, Peabody Inst., St. Johns Coll., Enoch Pratt Free Library. Author: Baltimore and the 19th of April, 1861, a Study of the War, published 1887. Died Sept. 5, 1890.

BROWN, Goold, educator; b. Providence, R.I., Mar. 7, 1791; s. Smith and Lydia (Gould) B.; married, 2 daus. Taught sch. nr. Providence, R.I.; apptd. to staff of Nine Partners Boarding Sch., Mechanic, Dutchess County, N.Y., 1811; tchr. John Grisom's Sch., N.Y.C., 1813; opened pvt. acad., N.Y.C.; mem. N.Y. Soc. of Friends, mem. joint com. of N.Y. and Phila. Yearly Meetings, 1830; moved to Lynn, Mass. Author: Child's First Book, 1822; Catechism of English Grammar, 1827; Grammar of English Grammars, 1851. Died Mar. 31, 1857.

BROWN, Henry Kirke, sculptor; b. Leyden, Mass., Feb. 24, 1814; s. Elijah and Rhoda (Childs) B.; apprenticed to portrait painter Chester Harding, Boston, 1832; m. Lydia Louise Udall, 1839. Went to Cincinnati, sculpted his 1st head in clay, 1836-37; sculptor in Troy and Albany (N.Y.), 1839-42, Rome, Italy, 1842-46; maintained studio, N.Y.C., 1846-50; built his own bronze foundry; moved studio to Bklyn., 1850; became full mem. Nat. Acad. Design, 1851; his Union Square group unveiled, N.Y.C., 1856; became officer U.S. San. Commn.; mem. Art Commn. apptd. by Pres. Buchanan, 1859-60; lived in Newburgh, N.Y., 1861-86; best known for large equestrian statues, including that of Pres. Washington; 4 of his figures stand in Statuary Hall, Washington, D.C. Died July 10, 1886.

BROWN, Isaac Van Arsdale, clergyman; b. Duckemin, N.J., Nov. 4, 1784; s. Abraham R. and Margaret Brown; grad. Coll. of N.J. (now Princeton), 1802; D.D., Lafayette Coll., Easton, Mass., 1858; m. Mary Wright Houston, 1807. Tutor, Coll. of N.J., 1805-06; licensed and ordained to ministry by New Brunswick Presbytery, 1807; pastor Maidenhead (later Lawrenceville) Presbyn. Ch., 1807-42; established Maidenhead Acad. (later Lawrenceville Classical and Comml. Sch.), 1810, prin., until 1833; trustee Coll. of N.J., 1816-61, Princeton Sem., 1822-61; organized Presbyn. Ch., Mt. Holly, N.J., 1842; a founder Am. Colonization Soc.; an original mem. Am. Bible Soc. Author: Memories of Robert Finley, 1819; Slavery Irreconcilable with Christianity and Sound Reason, 1858. Died Apr. 16, 1861.

BROWN, Jacob Jennings, army officer; b. Bucks County, Pa., May 9, 1775; s. Samuel and Abi (White) B.; m. Pamelia Williams, 1802. Surveyor, U.S. Govt. in Ohio, 1796-98; judge Jefferson County (N.Y.), 1806; in command of a regt. N.Y. Militia, 1809, commd. brig. gen., 1811; defended Sackett's Harbor, Lake Ontario during War of 1812, 1813; commd. brig. gen. U.S. Army, 1813; won battles of Chippewa, Lundy's Lane, Ft. Erie, 1814; in command Battle of Niagara, 1814; sr. officer U.S. Army, 1815, comdr.-in-chief, 1821-28. Died Washington, D.C., Feb. 24, 1828.

BROWN, James, senator, diplomat; b. Staunton, Va., Sept. 11, 1766; s. Rev. John and Margaret (Preston) B.; grad. Coll. William and Mary, 1786; m. Miss Hart, 1791. Admitted to Ky. bar, 1787; sec. of state Ky., 1792; sec. Territory of Orleans, 1804, later dist. atty.; mem. U.S. Senate from La., 1813-17, 19-23; U.S. minister to France, 1823-29. Died Phila., Apr. 7, 1835.

BROWN, James, banker; b. Ireland, Feb. 4, 1791; s. Alexander and Grace (Davison) B.; m. Louisa Kirkland Benedict, 1817; m. 2d, Eliza Maria Coe, 1831. Came to U.S., 1802; joined family banking house Alexander Brown & Sons, Balt.; established branch, Brown Bros. and Co. N.Y.C., 1825 (became one of N.Y.'s wealthiest firms); mem. N.Y. C. of C.; trustee N.Y. Life Ins. Co., Bank for Savings; a founder Assn. for Improving the Condition of the Poor, also Presbyn. Hosp.; trustee Union Coll., N.Y. Orthopedic Dispensary and Hosp., Union Theol. Sem. Died Nov. 1, 1877.

BROWN, James, publisher; b. Acton, Mass., May 19, 1800; s. Capt. Joseph and Abigail (Putnam) B.; m. Mary Anne Perry, May 1825; m. 2d, Mary Derby Hobbs, Apr. 1846. Servant to Levi Hedge (Harvard prof.), 1815-18; worked for publisher-bookseller William Hilliard, Cambridge, Mass., 1818-37; partner (with Charles Little) in publishing firm (became Little, Brown & Co.), Boston, 1837-55; made 5 trips to Europe to select titles, 1842-53; patron Boston Athenaeum, Natural History Soc.; mem. Agr. Soc.; willed $5,000 to Harvard Library. Died Mar. 10, 1855.

BROWN, James Salisbury, mfr., inventor; b. Pawtucket, R.I., Dec. 23, 1802; s. Sylvanus and Ruth (Salisbury) B.; m. Sarah Phillips Gridley, 1829, 2 daus., 1 son James. Pattern maker for David Wilkinson, Pawtucket, 1817-19; joined Pitcher & Ga cotton machinery mfrs., 1819, became partner, 18 gained control of firm, 1842, changed name Brown Machine Works, continually expanded fir patented improvement for lathe slide-rest (1st vented by his father), 1820; designed cutter cutting bevel gears, 1830; patented spl. drill machine, 1838; produced guns and gun making m chines during Civil War, returned to mfg. cott machinery after war. Died Dec. 29, 1879.

BROWN, James Sproat, congressman, lawy b. Hampden, Me., Feb. 1, 1824; attended pul schs.; studied law. Admitted to bar, 1843, be practice of law, Milw., 1844; apptd. pros. at Milwaukee County, 1846; atty. gen. Wis., 1848-mayor Milw., 1861; mem. U.S. Ho. of Reps. (De ocrat) from Wis., 39th Congress, 1863-65; w to Europe to recover health, 1865, returned U.S., 1873. Died Chgo., Apr. 15, 1878; bur Forest Home Cemetery, Milw.

BROWN, Jeremiah, congressman; b. Lanc ter County, Pa., Apr. 14, 1785. Engaged in mi ing and agriculture; mem. Pa. Ho. of Reps., 18 del. Pa. Constl. Conv., 1836; mem. U.S. Ho. Reps. (Whig) from Pa., 27th-28th congress 1841-45; 1st asso. judge for Lancaster, 1851-5 Died Lancaster County, Pa., Mar. 2, 1858; bur. cemetery adjoining Penn Hill Quaker Meet House, Little Britain (later Fulton) Twp., Pa.

BROWN, John, mcht., congressman; b. Jan. 1736; s. James and Hope (Power) B.; m. Sa Smith, Nov. 27, 1760, 6 children. Mem. fam merc. firm N. Brown & Co., Providence, ur 1770; spoke against Stamp Act while in R.I. A sembly, 1765; formed own merc. house, 1770; aid in bringing R.I. Coll. (now Brown U.) to Providen 1770, trustee, 1774-1803; led party which boar and burned H.M.S. Gaspee for her attempts to h smuggling, 1772; supporter of Continental Ass 1775; profited greatly by supplying Continental Ar and Navy and building own privateers, during A Revolution; mem. R.I. Assembly; elected to Con nental Congress, 1784-85, did not serve; entered up profitable trading ventures with the East, after w mem. U.S. Ho. of Reps. (Federalist) from R. 6th Congress, 1799-1801. Died Providence, Se 20, 1803; buried North Burial Ground, Providen

BROWN, John, army officer; b. Haverhill, Mas Oct. 19, 1744; s. Daniel and Mehitabel (Sanfor B.; grad. Yale, 1771; read law with brother-in-l Oliver Arnold, Providence, R.I.; m. Huldah K bourne. Admitted to Tryon County (R.I.) bar; beg practice law, Johnstown, N.Y.; moved to Pittsfie Mass., 1773; mem. Pittsfield Com. of Corresponden 1774; mem. Provincial Congress from Pittsfield, 17 75; went to Montreal (Can.), to discover streng and nature of revolutionary sentiment there, 177 commd. maj. Continental Army, 1775, served battles at Lake Champlain, Montreal, Ft. Chamb served under Gen. Montgomery in unsuccessful a tempt to take Que. (Can.), 1776, was clearly subordinate in this action; resigned commn., 17 published handbill attacking Benedict Arnold; ele ted col. Berkshire Militia, 1777, captured Ft. Geor returned to law practice; mem. Mass. Gen. C 1778; judge county ct. of common pleas, 17 Ambushed and killed while leading group of Ma Militia, Oct. 19, 1780.

BROWN, John, congressman. Mem. Md. Ho. Dels., 1807-08; mem. U.S. Ho. of Reps. (Dem crat) from Md., 11th-12th congresses, 1809- (resignd); clk. Queen Annes County (Md.) C 1810-15. Died Centerville, Md., Dec. 13, 18 buried Chesterfield Cemetery.

BROWN, John, senator, Continental congre man; b. Staunton, Va., Sept. 12, 1757; s. John a Margaret (Preston) B.; ed. Princeton, Coll. W liam and Mary; studied law under Thomas J ferson; m. Margaretta Mason, 1799. Fought Am. Revolution; admitted to Va. bar, 1782; re resented Ky. in Va. Legislature, 1784-88; d Continental Congress, 1787-88; mem. Ky. Cons Conv., 1788; mem. Va. Conv. to ratify U. Constn., 1789, voted against ratification; me U.S. Ho. of Reps. from Va., 1st-2d congress 1789-92; mem. U.S. Senate from Ky., 1792-180 pres. pro tem, 1803-04; his home "Liberty Hall, Frankfort, Ky., designed by Thomas Jeffers Died Frankfort, Aug. 29, 1837; buried Frankfo Cemetery.

BROWN, John, congressman; b. Kishacoquill Valley, nr. Lewistown, Pa., Aug. 2, 1772; a tended common schs. Engaged in grist-mill a sawmill operation, Lewiston; mem. Pa. Ho. Reps., 1809-13; mem. U.S. Ho. of Reps. fr Pa., 17th-18th congresses, 1821-25; became far er and realtor, Limestone, N.C., circa 1827. Di nr. Skyland, N.C., Oct. 12, 1845; buried Riversi Cemetery, Asheville, N.C.

BROWN, John, abolitionist; b. Torrington, Con May 9, 1800; s. Owen and Ruth (Mills) B.; Dianthe Lusk, 1820; m. 2d, Mary Anne Day, 183

) children. Ardent abolitionist, favored use of vionce; kept sta. of Underground Ry. for escaping aves, located at Richmond, Virignia, led free ›il forces of Pennsylvania at the Potawatomie iver massacre in Mo., 1856; claimed to be an inrument of God, also influenced by sack of Ft. awrence, Kan., by pro-slavery forces; conceived plan ' slave refuge base in Md. or Va., polit. basis of hich would be a constl. state govt. set up to beat 'f all attacks (state or fed.), also to promote slave surrection; captured Harper's Ferry, Va., also U.S. rmory, 1859; captured by Robert E. Lee at Harper's erry, Oct. 16, 1859; convicted of treason by State Va. (although not citizen that state), hanged ec. 2, 1859; regarded by abolitionists as martyr; ther portions of No. population looked favorably 1 his sincerity, calm conduct during trial; subject ' song John Brown's Body; called "Old Brown of awatomie." Executed Charles Town, Va., Dec. 2, 859.

BROWN, John A., banker; b. Ireland, May 21, 788; s. Alexander and Grace (Davison) B.; m. abella Patrick, 1813; m. 2d, Grace Brown, 1823. ame to Am., 1802; joined family firm Alexander rown & Sons, Balt.; established branch, John . Brown & Co., Phila., 1818, retired after profitbly expanding business, 1837; contbd. to Caly Presbyn. Ch., Am. Sunday Sch. Union, resbyn. Hosp. Died Dec. 31, 1872.

BROWN, John Calvin, gov. Tenn.; b. Giles County, enn., Jan. 6, 1827; s. Duncan and Margaret Smith) B.; grad. Jackson Coll., Columbia, Tenn., 846; m. Ann Pointer; m. 2d, Elizabeth Childress, 864; 4 children. Admitted to bar, Pulaski, Tenn., 848; col. 3d Tenn. Inf., Confederate Army, 1861, ig. gen., 1862, maj. gen., 1864; mem. Tenn. Legisture, 1869; gov. Tenn. (Democrat), 1870-74; es. Nashville Ry.; v.p. T. & P. Ry., 1876, receiver, 885, pres., 1888; gen. solicitor of the 6 Gould ailroads West of the Mississippi, 1881; pres. Tenn. oal, Iron & R.R. Co., 1889. Died Red Boiling prings, Tenn., Aug. 17, 1889.

BROWN, John Carter, mcht., book collector; . Providence, R.I., Aug. 28, 1797; s. Nicholas nd Ann (Carter) B.; grad. R.I. Coll. (now Brown .), 1816; m. Sophia Augusta Brown, June 23, 859, at least 1 son, John Nicholas. Joined large amily merc. firm, Providence, circa 1816; trus e R.I. Coll., 1828-42, fellow, 1842-74; accumu ted large book collection with emphasis on Vestern Hemisphere from the discovery to 1800 collection eventually contbd. to Brown U.); mem. .I. Legislature, 1 term. Died June 10, 1874.

BROWN, John Henry, artist; b. Lancaster, Pa., ug. 21, 1818; studied painting under Arthur rmstrong. Clk., Recorder's Office, Lancaster; beame profl. portrait painter, Lancaster, 1839, painted nly miniatures, after 1844; moved to Phila., 1845; ainted a miniature of Lincoln at Springfield (Ill.), 860; frequent exhibitor at Pa. Acad., 1844-64; xhibited at N.A.D., 1875. Died Phila., Apr. 3, 891.

BROWN, John Mifflin, clergyman; b. Odessa, Del., ept. 8, 1817; ed. Wesleyan Acad., 1838-40; D.D. nd D.C.L. (hon.), Howard U.; m. Mary Louise ewis, Feb. 13, 1872, 11 children. Born a mulatto; ounded 1st sch. for Negro children in Detroit, 1844; ecame prin. Union Sem. (founded by African Methdist Episcopal Conf. 1844), 1847; editor Christian Recorder (oldest negro newspaper in U.S.), 1864; rdained bishop African Methodist Ch., presiding ver S.C., Ga., Ala., Fla., 1868-72, La., Tex., Ark., Tenn., 1872-76, Md., Va., N.C., S.C., 1876-80, Pa., N.J., N.Y. and New Eng., 1880-84, Mo., Kan., Ill., Ia. and Cal., 1884-88; established Payne Inst. (now Allen U.), Columbia, S.C.; founder Paul Quinn Coll., Waco, Tex.; trustee Howard U. Died Washington, D.C., Mar. 16, 1893.

BROWN, John Newton, clergyman; b. New London, Conn., June 29, 1803; s. Charles and Hester (Darrow) B.; grad. Madison Coll. (now Colgate), 1823. Ordained to ministry Baptist Ch., 1824; preached in Buffalo, N.Y., 1824-25; pastor, Malden, Mass., 1827-29, Exeter, N.H., 1829-38; prof. theology and ch. history Academical and Theol. Inst. of New Hampton, N.H., 1838-45; pastor Lexington, Va., 1845-49; ednl. sec. Am. Bapt. Publ. Soc., also editor Christian Chronicle, Nat. Baptist, 1849. Author: New Hampshire Confession of Faith, 1833; Emily and Other Poems, 1840. Died May 14, 1868.

BROWN, John Porter, diplomat, Orientalist; b. Chillicothe, O., Aug. 17, 1814; married. Joined his uncle Commodore David Porter, minister resident at Constantinople, 1832; studied Turkish and Arabic langs.; asst. dragoman, 1833, consul, 1835, dragoman, 1836; arranged 1st Turkish mission to U.S., 1850; his bravado almost involved U.S. in an internat. incident with Austria over Koszta Affair, 1853; became consul-gen., 1857, sec. of legation, 1858-72. Translator: Conquest of Persia by the Arabs (al-Tabori), On the Tesavaf, or Spiritual Life of the Soffus (Muhammad Misri); Wonders of Remarkable Incidents and Rareties of Ancedotes (Ahmad bin Hamdan Suahili). Died Apr. 28, 1872.

BROWN, John W., congressman, lawyer; b. Dundee, Scotland, Oct. 11, 1796; came to U.S., 1802; attended public schs., N.Y.; studied law. Admitted to bar, 1818, began practice of law, Newburgh, N.Y.; elected justice of peace, 1820; mem. U.S. Ho. of Reps. (Democrat) from N.Y., 23d-24th congresses, 1833-37; judge Supreme Ct. for 2d Jud. Dist. N.Y., 1849-65. Died Newburgh, Sept. 6, 1875; buried Cedar Hill Cemetery.

BROWN, Joseph, mfr.; b. Providence, R.I., Dec. 3, 1733; s. James and Hope (Power) B.; M.A. (hon.), R.I. Coll. (now Brown U.), 1770; m. Elizabeth Power, Sept. 30, 1759. Joined family merc. firm, Providence, R.I.; engaged in scientific investigation, observed transit of Venus, 1769; trustee R.I. Coll., 1769-85, became prof. natural philosophy, 1784; partner, sometimes tech. adviser to iron mfg. firm Furnace Hope (controlled by Brown interests); mem. R.I. Assembly, several years. Died Dec. 3, 1785.

BROWN, Joseph Emerson, senator, gov. Ga.; b. Pickens Dist., S.C., Apr. 15, 1821; s. Mackey and Sally (Rice) B.; grad. Yale Law Sch., 1846; m. Elizabeth Grisham, 1847. Admitted to Ga. bar, 1845; mem. Ga. Senate, 1849; Franklin Pierce presdl. elector, 1852; judge Blue Ridge Circuit, 1855; gov. Ga. (Democrat), 1857-65, extreme states rights advocate, often quarrelled with Jefferson Davis over powers of central govt., opposed conscription and suspension of habeas corpus; imprisoned for short time, 1865, pardoned by Pres. Andrew Jackson; became a Republican, urged compliance with Congressional reconstrn. rule; chief justice Supreme Ct. Ga., 1868-70; pres. Western & Atlantic R.R., 1870-94; mem. U.S. Senate (Democrat) from Ga., 1881-91. Died Atlanta, Ga., Nov. 30, 1894.

BROWN, Joseph Rogers, inventor, mfr.; b. Warren, R.I., Jan. 26, 1810; s. David and Patience (Rogers) B.; m. Caroline B. Niles, Sept. 18, 1837, 1 child. Perfected and built linear dividing engine, 1850; perfected vernier caliper reading to thousandths of an inch, 1851, applied vernier to protractors, 1852; became partner (with Lucian Sharpe) in firm J. R. Brown & Sharpe, 1853, incorporated as Brown & Sharpe Mfg. Co., 1868; micrometer caliper, 1867; invented precision gear cutter to make clock gears and to supply his jobbing customers with gears, 1855; greatest achievement was invention of universal grinding machine, patent issued, 1877 (after his death). Died Isles of Shoals, N.H., July 23, 1876.

BROWN, Mather, painter; b. Eng., Oct. 7, 1761; s. Gawen and Elizabeth (Byles) B.; studied under Gilbert Stuart; never married. Painted miniatures; exhibited 4 pictures Royal Acad. Exhbn., 1783, later exhibited there regularly; painted portraits of George IV (now at Buckingham Palace), 1784; portraits of Pres. John Adams, Pres. Thomas Jefferson, Charles Bulfinch, Sir William Pepperell, Thomas Paine; invited (with others) to contribute paintings for Boydell Shakespeare Gallery; represented in the royal collections, Nat. Portrait Gallery, London, also in several Am. collections. Died London, May 25, 1831; buried St. John's Wood, Marylebone, Eng.

BROWN, Milton, congressman, lawyer; b. Lebanon, O., Feb. 28, 1804; studied law. Admitted to bar, practiced law, Paris, then Jackson, Tenn.; judge Chancery Ct. of W. Tenn., 1835-41; mem. U.S. Ho. of Reps. (Whig) from Tenn., 27th-29th congresses, 1841-47; a founder Southwestern U. (later Union U.), Lambuth Coll. (both in Jackson); pres. Miss. Central & Tenn. R.R. Co., 1854-56, Mobile & Ohio R.R. Co., 1856-71. Died Jackson, May 15, 1883; buried Riverside Cemetery.

BROWN, Morris, clergyman; b. Charleston, S.C., Feb. 12, 1770; born a free Negro (probably of white father); obtained good informal edn. Ordained deacon African Methodist Episcopal Ch., 1817, elder, 1818; began preaching, 1818; forced to flee to Phila. following Denmark Vesey insurrection, 1822; elevated to episcopate, 1828, became bishop, 1831; influential in expanding membership of church. Died May 9, 1849.

BROWN, Moses, mfr., philanthropist; b. Providence, R.I., Sept. 23, 1738; s. James and Hope (Power) B.; m. Anna Brown, 1764; m. 2d, Mary Olney, 1779; m. 3d, Phoebe Lockwood, 1799; 3 children including Sarah, Obadiah. Admitted to firm Nicholas Brown & Co., 1763, ret., 1773; an organizer R.I. Abolition Soc., 1774; started plan to move R.I. Coll. (later renamed Brown U. because of family benefactions), from Warren to Providence, 1770, gave $1,000 to endowment, 1771; treas. Friends' Sch. (now Moses Brown Sch.), 1784; mem. R.I. Gen. Assembly, 1764-71; a founder many socs., including Providence Athenaeum Library, R.I. Bible Soc., R.I. Peace Soc.; mem. R.I. Hist. Soc. Died Providence, Sept. 7, 1836.

BROWN, Moses, mcht., philanthropist; b. Newbury, Mass., Oct. 2, 1742; s. Joseph and Abigail (Pearson) B.; apprenticed to chaise-maker, Mass.; m. Mary Hall, 1772; m. 2d, Mary White, 1886; 1 dau., Mrs. William B. Bannister. Became carriage mfr. in Mass., then mcht. in sugar and molasses trade with W.I.; increased his investments, became owner several warehouses, distilleries and wharves, Newburyport, Mass.; made contbns. to Andover Theol. Sem. including $10,000 to Assn. Found. (1808), $1,000 for library, $25,000 to establish professorship eccles. history (1819); willed $6,000 (to be kept at interest until reaching $15,000) to people of Newburyport for constrn. and support of grammar sch. Died Feb. 9, 1827.

BROWN, Neill Smith, gov. Tenn., diplomat; b. Pulaski, Tenn., Apr. 18, 1810; s. Duncan and Margaret (Smith) B.; studied law with Chancellor Bramlett; m. Mary Ann Trimble, 1839, 8 children. Admitted to Tenn. bar, 1834, began practice law, Pulaski; served in Robert Armstrong's brigade Tenn. Militia during Seminole War, 1836-43; mem. Tenn. Legislature, 1837, 53, speaker, 1853; gov. Tenn., 1847; U.S. minister to Russia, 1850; mem. Tenn. Mil. and Financial Bd., 1861; imprisoned by Gov. Andrew Johnson, 1862; a founder Peabody Coll., Nashville, Tenn.; del. Tenn. Constl. Conv., 1870. Died Jan. 30, 1886.

BROWN, Nicholas, mcht.; b. Providence, R.I., Aug. 8, 1729; s. James and Hope (Power) B.; m. Rhoda Jenckes, May 2, 1762; m. 2d, Avis Binney, Sept. 9, 1785; 10 children including Nicholas, Hope. Became asst., then partner (with his uncle and 3 brothers) in firm Obadiah Brown & Co., changed firm name to Nicholas Brown & Co. (upon death of uncle), 1762, extended trade from W.I. to Marseilles and Nantes (France), Copenhagen, Hamburg and London; brought about change in candle manufacture (from home to factory prodn.), nr. Providence; leading figure (with his brothers) in United Co., spermaceticandle mfrs., Providence and Newport (earliest monopoly in Am.), 1763; established Furnace Hope, iron mfg. plant, Scituate, R.I., 1764; engaged in secret importation for Continental Congress during Am. Revolution; influenced building of R.I. Coll. (now Brown U.) Providence; benefactor Bapt. Soc. of Providence. Died May 29, 1791.

BROWN, Nicholas, mcht., philanthropist; b. Providence, R.I., Apr. 4, 1769; s. Nicholas and Rhoda (Jenckes) B.; grad. R.I. Coll. (now Brown U.), 1786; m. Ann Carter, Nov. 3, 1791; m. 2d, Mary Bowen Stelle, July 22, 1801; 4 children including John Carter. Became partner in firm Brown & Benson, 1791 (name changed to Brown and Ives 1796), became important in East India and China trade; also cotton mfr., speculator in Ohio lands; Trustee R.I. Coll., 1791, treas., 1796-1825, gave $5,000 to endow chair of oratory and belles lettres, 1804, (gift resulted in change of name to Brown U.); built (with nephews) Hope Coll., 1823; built Manning Hall, 1834; mem. R.I. Gen. Assembly; a founder Providence Athenaeum; contbr. to Baptist Soc., resulted in establishment Butler Hosp. for Insane. Died Providence, Sept. 27, 1841.

BROWN, Obadiah, mcht., philanthropist; b. Providence, R.I., July 15, 1771; s. Moses and Anna B.; m. Dorcas Hadwen, 1798. Became partner firm Brown & Almy (produced 1st pure cotton goods made in U.S.), Pawtucket, R.I., 1792; donated land to reestablish Friends' Yearly Meeting Sch. which he had attended in youth (now Moses Brown Sch.), Providence, 1814, donated $2,000 for constrn. of sch., $500 for furnishings, $1,000 to be given annually for 5 years maintenance, 1815; donated (with Almy) about $3,750 to finish sch., 1817 (sch. opened 1819); presented book to each grad., mem. sch. com., willed $100,000, also library of maps and books to sch. Died Providence, Oct. 15, 1822.

BROWN, Phoebe Hinsdale, hymn writer; b. Canaan, N.Y., May 1, 1783; d. George and Phoebe (Allen) Hinsdale; m. Timothy Hill Brown, June 1, 1805, 4 children including Samuel Robbins. Lived in East Windsor, Conn., 1805-13, Ellington, Conn., 1813-18, Monson, Mass., 1818-53; wrote hymn I Love to Steal Awhile Away, published in Village Hymns (Asahel Nettleton), 1824; other hymns published in Spiritual Songs (Thomas Hasting), 1831, Mother's Hymn Book, 1834, Select Hymns, 1836, Parish Hymns, 1843. Author: (prose works) The Tree and Its Fruits, 1836; The Village School, 1836. Died Henry, Ill., Aug. 10, 1861.

BROWN, Robert, congressman; b. Weaversville, Pa., Dec. 25, 1744; attended common schs. Apprenticed to a blacksmith; commd. 1st lt. Pa. Flying Camp at beginning of Revolutionary War, captured at surrender of Ft. Washington, 1776; held prisoner in prison ship Judith, later in old City Hall, N.Y.C.; paroled on board ship, 1777; mem. Pa. Senate, 1783-87; mem. U.S. Ho. of Reps. (Democrat, filled vacancy) from Pa., 5th-13th congresses,

Dec. 4, 1798-1815. Died nr. Weaversville, Feb. 26, 1823; buried East Allen Presbyn. Churchyard.

BROWN, Samuel, surgeon; b. Augusta County, Va., Jan. 30, 1769; s. Rev. John and Margaret (Preston) B.; B.A., Dickinson Coll., 1789; med. degree U. Aberdeen (Scotland); m. Catherine Perry, 1809, 2 children. Introduced smallpox vaccination at Lexington, Ky., 1802; prof. theory and practice of medicine Transylvania U., 1819-25; started North Am. Med. and Surg. Jour., 1825; founder Kappa Lambda Soc. of Hippocrates (soc. of men pledged to profl. ideals). Died Huntsville, Ala., Jan. 12, 1830.

BROWN, Samuel Gilman, clergyman, coll. pres.; b. North Yarmouth, Me., Jan. 4, 1813; s. Francis and Elizabeth (Gilman) B.; grad. Dartmouth, 1831, LL.D. (hon.), 1868; grad. Andover Theol. Sem., 1837; D.D. (hon.), Columbia, 1852; m. Sarah Savage, Feb. 10, 1846, 7 children. Mem. faculty Dartmouth, 1840-67, lectr., 1882-83; ordained to ministry Congl. Ch., 1852; pres. Hamilton Coll., 1867, also trustee; trustee Auburn Theol. Sem., 1872-84. Author: The Works of Rufus Choate, with a Memoir of His Life, 1862. Died Utica, N.Y., Nov. 4, 1885.

BROWN, Samuel Robbins, clergyman, missionary; b. East Windsor, Conn., June 16, 1810; s. Timothy and Phoebe (Hinsdale) B.; grad. Yale, 1832; m. Elizabeth Bartlett, Oct. 10, 1838. Ordained to ministry Presbyn. Ch. by 3d Presbytery N.Y., 1838; missionary to China, 1839-47, Japan, 1859-79; founder, pres. Asiatic Soc. of Japan; founder com. which translated New Testament into Japanese; prepared Canton Colloquial portion for James Legge's Lexilogus; conducted sch. at Rome, N.Y., 1848-51; a founder, dir. Elmira (N.Y.) Coll. while pastor Reformed Dutch Ch., 1851-59. Author: Colloquial Japanese, 1863; Prendergast's Mastery System Adapted to the Japanese, 1875. Died Monson, Mass., June 20, 1880.

BROWN, Simon, editor, publisher; b. Newburyport, Mass., Nov. 29, 1802; s. Nathaniel and Mary (Sleeper) B.; m. Ann Caroline French, 1828. Apprentice in printing shop, Concord, N.H., 1818; settled in Hingham, Mass., 1826 (after having toured South studying agr. and relationship between slave and master); publisher paper Hingham Gazette, 1826-29; opened printing office, Chester, N.H., 1829, published N.H. Law Reports; owner (with brother-in-law) paper N.H. Spectator, Newport, 1830-35; employed in office of clk. U.S. Ho. of Reps., Washington, D.C., 1838; librarian U.S. Ho. of Reps. until 1848; published Concord (Mass.) Freeman, 1 year; lt. gov. Mass., 1855; editor New Eng. Farmer, Boston, 1858; mem. Mass. Bd. Agr. Died Feb. 26, 1873.

BROWN, Solyman, dentist, clergyman, poet; b. Litchfield, Conn., Nov. 17, 1790; s. Nathaniel and Thankful (Woodruff) B.; grad. Yale, 1812, A.M., 1817; D.D.S. (hon.), Balt. Coll. Dental Surgery, 1842; m. Elizabeth Butler, Dec. 23, 1834, 8 children including E. Parmly. Licensed minister Congregational Ch., 1813, failed to obtain renewal of license; went to N.Y.C., 1820; began preaching in New Jerusalem Ch. (Swedenborgian), 1822; studied dentistry; practiced with Samuel Avery, 1834; contbd. to N.Y. Mirror; an organizer (with Eleazer Parmly) Soc. of Surgeon Dentists of City and State of N.Y.; asso. with brother Augustus Woodruff, 1837-44; practiced dentistry; major contbr., editor Am. Journal of Dental Science; dentist, teacher, preacher in Fourier community, Leraysville, Pa., 1844; preached at Swedenborgian churches in Upper N.Y., 1846-50; opened dental supply house, N.Y.C., 1850; edited Semi-Annual Dental Expositor, 1852-54; minister, Danby, N.Y., 1862-70; retired to Minn., 1870. Author: An Address to the People of Litchfield County (written as result his failure to obtain renewal of license), 1818; An Essay on American Poetry, 1818; Sermons, 1829; Dental Hygeia, 1838; Llewellen's Dog; a Ballad, 1840; Cholera King, and other Poems; Union of Extremes: A Discourse on Liberty and Slavery, 1859; Dentologia (poem on dentistry, best known work), 1858. Died Dodge Center, Minn., Feb. 13, 1876.

BROWN, Sylvanus, millwright, inventor; b. Valley Falls, R.I., June 4, 1747; s. Philip and Priscilla (Carpenter) B.; m. Ruth Salisbury, 1 son, James Salisbury. Learned millwright trade; served aboard Continental Navy vessel Alfred, at beginning of Am. Revolution; worked for State of R.I. arsenal; supervised constr. several grist and saw mills, New Brunswick; made short trip to Europe, returned to Pawtucket, R.I., reestablished machine shop; assisted Samuel Slater in constructing Am.'s 1st practical power spinning wheel, 1790, credited with crucial part in turning Slater's memories of English spinning machines into working model; developed many machines essential to profitable constn. of textile machinery; possibly 1st to use slide-crest lathe; superintended furnaces in cannon factory, Scituate, R.I., 1796-1801. Died Pawtucket, July 30, 1824.

BROWN, Titus, congressman; b. Alstead, N.H., Feb. 11, 1786; grad. Middlebury (Vt.) Coll., 1811; studied law. Admitted to bar, began practice of law, Reading, Vt., 1814; moved to Francestown, N.H., 1817; mem. N.H. Ho. of Reps., 1820-25; solicitor Hillsborough County, 1823-25, 29-34; mem. U.S. Ho. of Reps. from N.H., 19th-20th congresses, 1825-29; mem. N.H. Senate, pres., 1842; chmn. bds. of bank and railroad commrs. Died Francestown, Jan. 29, 1849; buried Mill Village Cemetery.

BROWN, Vandyke, see Cook, Marc.

BROWN, William, physician; b. Haddingtonshire, Scotland, 1752; s. Richard and Helen (Bailey) B.; M.D., U. Edinburgh (Scotland), 1770; m. Catherine Scott, several children including Gustavus Alexander. Apptd. surgeon 2d Va. Regt., Revolutionary War, 1776, surgeon gen. army hosp. of middle dept. Continental Army, 1777-78, physician gen., 1778-80; wrote 1st U.S. published pharmocopeia, 1778; chmn. trustees Alexandria (Va.) Acad. Died Jan. 11, 1792; buried Old Pohick Ch., Alexandria.

BROWN, William, congressman; b. Frederick County, Va., Apr. 19, 1779; attended common schs.; studied law. Admitted to bar, practiced law; served as col. in War of 1812; mem. Ky. Ho. of Reps.; mem. U.S. Ho. of Reps. from Ky., 16th Congress, 1819-21; moved to Jacksonville, Ill., 1832. Died Jacksonville, Oct. 6, 1833.

BROWN, William Garl, Jr., artist; b. Eng., Oct. 1823; s. William Garl Brown; m. Mary McFeely, 1876. Came to Am., 1837; exhibited portrait at N.A.D., 1840; went to Va., established himself as portrait painter, Richmond; made trip to Mexico to paint portraits of Zachary Taylor and other heroes of Mexican War, exhibited in Richmond and Phila., 1847; traveled in South, during 1850's; lived in N.Y.C., 1856-65; visited South after Civil War, painted portraits of many people in N.C. and Va.; name also spelled Browne. Died Buffalo, N.Y., July 28, 1894.

BROWN, William Gay, congressman, lawyer; b. Kingwood, Va. (now W.Va.), Sept. 25, 1800; attended public schs.; studied law. Admitted to bar, 1823, began practice of law, Kingwood; mem. Va. Ho. of Dels., 1832, 40-43; mem. U.S. Ho. of Reps. (as Democrat) from Va., 29th-30th congresses, 1845-49, (as Unionist) 37th Congress, 1861-63, from W.Va., 38th Congress, Dec. 7, 1863-65; del. Va. constl. convs., 1850, 61; del. Democratic nat. convs., Charleston and Balt., 1860. Died Kingwood, Apr. 19, 1884; buried Maplewood Cemetery.

BROWN, William Henry, artist; b. Charleston, S.C., May 22, 1808; m. Emmaline, at least 2 sons. Employed as engr., Phila.; sillhouettist, circa 1830-59; worked in New Eng., travelled in South; published collection of sillhouettes as Portrait Gallery of Distinguished Americans (his best known work), 1846; engr. in Pa., after 1859, later returned to Charleston. Died Charleston, Sept. 16, 1883.

BROWN, William Hill, author; b. Boston, 1765; s. Gowen and Elizabeth (Hill) B. Contbr. poetry to Massachusetts Mag., Boston, 1789-93, a series of patriotic essays to newspaper Columbia Centinel, Boston, 1790; active in lobbying for legislation permitting opening of theatre in Mass.; author plays: Andre (based on execution Maj. John Andre); West Point Preserved, or the Treason of Arnold; Penelope (all produced in Boston); novels include: The Power of Sympathy, or The Triumph of Nature (his 1st novel), 1789; Ira and Isabella, or the Natural Children. Died Murfreesborough, N.C., Sept. 2, 1793.

BROWN, William Hughey, coal operator; b. North Huntington Twp., Pa., Jan. 15, 1815; s. James and Sarah Brown; m. Mary Smith, Sept. 3, 1840, at least 1 son, Samuel S.B. Worked at a variety of jobs in youth; began selling coal in wagons during 1840's, profited and expanded bus.; began towing coal barges with steam boats on Ohio River, 1858; bought interests in steel, steamboats, mines; increased bus. due to Civil War contracts; ret., 1873. Died Phila., Oct. 12, 1875.

BROWN, William John, congressman, lawyer; b. nr. Washington, Ky., Aug. 15, 1805; attended Franklin Acad., Clermont County, O.; studied law. Admitted to bar, 1826, began practice of law, Rushville, Ind.; mem. Ind. Ho. of Reps., 1829-32, 41-43; pros. atty., 1831-35; sec. of state Ind., 1836-40; moved to Indpls., 1837; mem. U.S. Ho. of Reps. (Democrat) from Ky., 28th, 31st congresses, 1843-45, 49-51; 2d asst. postmaster gen. (apptd. by Pres. Polk), 1845-49; chief editor Indpls. Sentinel, 1850-55; chmn. Dem. Central Com. of Ind., many times; spl. agt. Post Office Dept. for Ind. and Ill. (apptd. by Pres. Pierce), 1853-57. Died nr. Indpls., Mar. 18, 1857; buried Crown Hill Cemetery.

BROWN, William Wells, reformer, writer; b. Lexington, Ky., circa 1816; s. George Higgins and a Negro slave belonging to Higgins; m. 1834, 2 daus. Escaped from slavery into Ohio and took last name of man who befriended him, 1834; worked on Lake Erie steamboats; occasional lectr. for Western N.Y. a Mass. anti-slavery socs., 1843-49; involved also temperance, prison reform, women's rights movemen asso. in work with William Lloyd Garrison and We dell Phillips; traveled in Europe, 1849-54, also stu ied medicine abroad. Author: Narrative of Willi W. Brown, A Fugitive Slave, 1847; Three Years Europe, 1852; Clotel, or the President's Daught A Narrative of Slave Life in the U.S., 1853; T Dough Face, The Escape or a Leap for Freed (plays); The Black Man, His Antecedents, His Ge us and His Achievements, 1863, The Negro in T American Rebellion: His Heroism and His Fideli 1867, The Rising Son: or, The Antecedents and Advancement of the Colored Race, 1874. Died Ch sea, Mass., Nov. 6, 1884.

BROWNE, Benjamin Frederick, druggist, private b. Salem, Mass., July 14, 1793; s. Benjamin and El abeth (Andrew) B.; m. Sally Bott, Jan. 23, 182 Apprenticed to apothecary, 1807-12; shipped abo privateer Alfred during War of 1812; captain's cl purser on privateer Frolic, 1813-14; captured crew of H.M.S. Heron, sent to Eng. as prison 1814, released, 1815, returned to Salem, owner dr store, 1815-60; rep. to Mass. Gen. Ct., 1831; me Mass. Senate, 1843; postmaster of Salem, 1845-4 Author: Papers of an Old Dartmoor Prisoner (edit by Nathaniel Hawthorne), 1846. Died Salem, N 23, 1873.

BROWNE, Charles Farrar (pseudonym Artem Ward), humorist; b. nr. Waterford, Me., Apr. 2 1834; s. Levi and Caroline (Farrar) Brown. Receiv early tng. on various New Eng. country newspape in Boston printing trade, 3 years; with Clevela Plain Dealer; contbd. to Vanity Fair, later st writer, N.Y.C., 1859-61; became a lectr., 186 lectured in Washington, D.C., 1862, West Coa 1863, N.Y.C. and Can., 1864, London, Eng., 186 67; gained reputation as humorist. Author: Artem Ward: His Book, 1862; Artemus Ward: His Trave 1865; contbr. to Punch and Carpet Bag mags. Di Southampton, Eng., Mar. 6, 1867.

BROWNE, Daniel Jay, agrl. writer; b. Fremon N.H., Dec. 4, 1804; s. Isaac and Mary B.; attend Harvard. Engaged in farming; founder The Naturalis 1830; traveled to W.I., Europe, S.Am., 1833-35; i volved in various engring. projects, N.Y.C. a Cuba, 1836-42; 1st corr. sec. Am. Agrl. Assn.; me bd. agr. Am. Inst., N.Y.C.; with R. L. Allen & Co an editor Am. Agriculturalist mag., 1845-51; wi U.S. Census Office, 1852-53, U.S. Patent Offic 1853-59, sent to Europe to collect information a seeds, 1854-55, sent to Europe to investigate cult vation and manufacture of flax, 1861 chiefly respons ble for numerous reports, 1853-61. Author: Trees America, 1846; American Poultry Yard, 1850; Ame ican Muck Book, 1851.

BROWNE, George Huntington, congressma lawyer; b. Gloucester, R.I., Jan. 6, 1811; gra Brown U., 1840; studied law. Admitted to ba 1843, began practice of law, Providence, R.I elected rep. to "Charter" Gen. Assembly of R.I 1842; attended "Suffrage" legislature, 1842; me R.I. Gen. Assembly under constn., 1849-52; U. dist. atty., 1852-61; del. Dem. nat. convs., Charle ton and Balt., 1860; del. Washington (D.C.) Pea Conv., 1861; em. U.S. Ho. of Reps. (Democrat from R.I., 37th Congress, 1861-63; declined a pointment as gov. Ariz. Territory, 1861; serve as col. 12th Regt., R.I. Volunteer Inf., throug out Civil War; mem. R.I. Senate, 1872-73; d clined office of chief justice R.I. Supreme Ct., 187 Died Providence, Sept. 26, 1885; buried Swa Point Cemetery.

BROWNE, Irving, lawyer; b. Marshall, N.Y., Sept 14, 1835; s. Lewis C. and Harriet (Hand) B.; rea law, Hudson, N.Y., 1853; grad. Albany Law Sch. 1857; m. Miss Clark, 1858; m. 2d, Lizzie B. Ferri 1894. Admitted to N.Y. State bar, 1857; practice law, Troy, N.Y., 1857-78; editor Albany Law Jour. 1879-93; prof. criminal law and law of domesti relations Albany Law Sch., 1879-93; tchr. Buffal Law Sch., 1893-96; lectr. Cornell U., also in Bosto librarian N.Y. Supreme Ct., Buffalo, 1896. Autho Humorous Phases of the Law, 1876; National Ban Cases, Federal and State Courts, 1878-80; Element of Criminal Law, 1892; In the Track of the Book worm (collection of verse), 1897; Short Studie in Evidence, 1897; translator Racine's Les Plaideur 1871; editor New York Reports, volumes 16-100 Ruling Cases; American Reports: Decisions Courts o Last Resort of the Several States, volumes 28-60 Died Feb. 6, 1899.

BROWNE, John, colonial ofcl.; b. Eng.; m. Doro thy, at least 3 children. Arrived in Plymouth Colony 1634, assistant to gov., 1635-45, 47-54; moved t Cohasset (now Taunton), Mass., 1639; apptd. (wit Edward Winslow) to purchase land from Mass. Ba Colony, 1641; an incorporator of Rehoboth, Mass. 1643; mem. council of war Plymouth Bay Colony 1642, 46, 53; a commr. New Eng. Confedn., 1644-56; friendly towards Antinomians, close friend o Sir Henry Vane; returned to Eng., 1656-60; lived o is plantation on Naragansett Bay, 1660-62. Died pr. 10, 1662.

BROWNE, John Ross, diplomat, author; b. Dublin, reland, Feb. 11, 1817; s. Thomas and Elana (Buck) B.; m. Lucy Mitchell, 1844, 10 children. Reporter, .S. Senate, 1841; travelled throughout world, 1842-7; U.S. minister to China, 1868-69; ofcl. reporter st Cal. Constl. Conv. Author: Etchings of a Whaling ruise with Notes of a Sojourn on the Island of anzibar, 1846; Yusef, or the Journey of the Fragi; Crusade in the East, 1853; Adventures in the pache Country, 1869; Resources of the Pacific lope, 1869; Crusoe's Island, with Sketches of Adentures in California and Washoe, 1864; The Land f Thor, 1866; The Adventures of an American Family n Germany. Died Oakland, Cal., Dec. 9, 1875.

BROWNE, Junius Henri, journalist; b. Seneca alls, N.Y., Oct. 14, 1833; attended St. Xavier oll., Cincinnati. War correspondent N.Y. Tribune uring Civil War, reported campaigns in S.W. and ctivities on Mississippi River, 1861-63; captured y Confederate Army while on expdn. against Vicksurg, 1863, escaped after about a year and a half n various Confederate prisons; continued writing for .Y. Tribune, also N.Y. Times, after Civil War; orrespondent for other papers throughout country. uthor: Four Years in Secession, 1865; The Great etropolis; a Mirror of New York, 1869; Sights and ensations in Europe, 1871. Died N.Y.C., Apr. 2, 902.

BROWNE, Thomas, army officer, Loyalist. Lived n Augusta, Ga., 1775; tarred and feathered beause of strong loyalist views, desire for vengeance uided his war career, began raiding patriot positions, 776, aided Brit. attack on Fort McIntosh, Ga., 777, formed regt. called King's Rangers, 1778, beame lt. col.; repulsed but never defeated in numerus raids, 1778-80; irregularly held Augusta, 1780-1; captured with 300 of his men, 1781, exchanged, ngaged in last conflict, 1782; known for his sadism nd brutality; his S.C. and Ga. estates confiscated fter war; lived in Bahamas, 1783-1809; lived on nd granted him by British on St. Vincent, B.W.I., 809-25. Died St. Vincent, Aug. 3, 1825.

BROWNE, Thomas Henry Bayly, congressman; . Accomac Court House, Va., Feb. 8, 1844; atended Hanover and Bloomfield acads., Va.; grad. aw dept. U. Va. at Charlottesville, 1867. Served s pvt. Co. F, 39th Regt., Va. Volunteer Inf., Conederate Army, in Civil War, later as pvt. Chew's attery of Stuart Horse Arty.; surrendered with rmy of No. Va., 1865; admitted to bar, 1868, bean practice of law, Accomac, Va.; elected pros. tty. Accomac County, 1873; Republican presdl. lector, 1884; mem. U.S. Ho. of Reps. (Rep.) from a., 50th-51st congresses, 1887-91. Died Accomac, ug. 27, 1892; buried Mt. Curtis Cemetery.

BROWNE, Thomas McLelland, congressman, awyer; b. New Paris, O., Apr. 19, 1829; attended ommon schs., Ind.; studied law. Admitted to bar, 849, began practice of law, Winchester, Ind.; lected pros. atty. 13th Jud. Circuit, 1855, relected, 1857, 59; sec. Ind. Senate, 1861, mem., 863; an organizer, capt. 7th Regt., Ind. Volnteer Cavalry, U.S. Army, 1863, commd. lt. ol., 1863, col., 1865; brevetted brig. gen., 1865; .S. atty. for Dist. Ind., 1869-72; unsuccessful canidate for gov. Ind., 1872; del. Republican Nat. onv., Cincinnati, 1876; mem. U.S. Ho. of Reps. Rep.) from Ind., 45th-51st congresses, 1877-91. ied Winchester, July 17, 1891; buried Fountain ark Cemetery.

BROWNE, William, gov. Bermuda, jurist; b. alem, Mass., Mar. 5, 1737; s. Samuel and Catherne (Winthrop) B.; grad. Harvard, 1755; m. Ruth anton. Elected to Mass. Assembly, 1762; colector Port of Salem, 1764, dismissed for criticism f Parliament, 1766; judge Essex County (Mass.) t. Common Pleas, 1770; commd. col. Essex Miliia, 1771; judge Mass. Superior Ct., 1774; evacuated oston with Lord Howe, fled to Eng., 1776; ermanently banished from Mass. by Mass. Legisature, 1778, property confiscated by state, 1779; ov. Bermuda, 1781-88. Died London, Eng., Feb. 3, 1802.

BROWNELL, Henry Howard, poet; b. Providence, R.I., Feb. 6, 1820; s. Dr. Pardon and Lucia (de Wolf) B.; grad. Washington (now Trinity) Coll., Hartford, Conn., 1841. Tchr., Mobile, Ala.; admitted to bar, 1844; published 1st poems, 1847; published rhymed version of Adm. Farragut's "General Orders," 1862, resulted in appointment as personal sec. to Farragut aboard steam sloop Hartford, sec. until 1868; works include: Poems, 1847; The People's Book of Ancient and Modern History, 1851; The Discoveries, Pioneers, and Settlers of North and South America, 1853; Ephemerson, 1855; Lyrics of a Day, or Newspaper-Poetry by a Volunteer in the U.S. Service, 1864. Died Oct. 31, 1872.

BROWNELL, Thomas Church, clergyman, coll. pres.; b. Westport, Mass., Oct. 19, 1779; s. Sylvester and Nancy (Church) B.; attended Coll. of R.I. (now Brown U.), 1800-02; grad. Union Coll. 1804; m. Charlotte Dickinson, Aug. 1811. Prof. belles lettres and moral philosophy Union Coll., Schenectady, N.Y., 1807, prof. chemistry and mineralogy, 1809; ordained deacon Protestant Episcopal Ch., 1816, priest, 1816; bishop Diocese of Conn., 1819-65; 1st pres. Trinity Coll., Hartford, Conn., 1823-31, chancellor, 1831-65. Died Hartford, Jan. 13, 1865; buried Hartford.

BROWNING, Orville Hickman, cabinet officer; b. Harrison County, Ky., Feb. 10, 1806; s. Micaijah and Sally (Brown) B.; ed. Augusta Coll.; m. Eliza Caldwell, 1836. Admitted to Ky. bar, 1831; served in Black Hawk War, 1832; mem. Ill. Senate (Whig), 1836, Ill. Gen. Assembly, 1842; mem. U.S. Senate (Republican, filling unexpired term of Stephen A. Douglas) from Ill., 1861-62, spokesman of Lincoln's Border State policy; U.S. sec. of interior under Andrew Johnson, 1866-69, concurrently U.S. atty. gen., brief period, 1868; mem. Ill. Constl. Conv., 1869-70. Died Quincy, Ill., Aug. 10, 1881.

BROWNLEE, William Craig, clergyman; b. Scotland, 1784; s. James B. and Margaret (Craig) B.; M.A., U. Glasgow, D.D., 1824; m. Maria McDougall, 1807. Licensed to ministry Presbyn. Ch. by Presbytery of Sterling, 1808; came to U.S., 1808; pastor associate Scotch Ch., Mt. Pleasant, Pa., 1808-13, Phila., 1813-16; head Queen's Coll. (now Rutgers) Acad., New Brunswick, N.J., 1816-19; pastor Presbyn. Ch., Basking Ridge, N.J., 1818-25; prof. languages Rutgers, 1826-43; asso. pastor Collegiate Ch., N.Y.C., 1826-43; became paralyzed, 1843. Author: Inquiry into the Principles of the Quakers, 1824; Letters in the Roman Catholic Controversy, 1834; Popery an Enemy to Civil and Religious Liberty, 1836; The Whigs of Scotland, a Romance. Died Feb. 10, 1860.

BROWNLOW, William Gannaway, editor, senator, gov. Tenn.; b. Wythe County, Va., Aug. 29, 1805; s. Joseph and Catherine (Gannaway) B.; m. Eliza O'Brien. Called fighting parson; itinerant Methodist minister, 1826-36; editor Tenn. Whig, Elizabethton, 1838-61, Jonesboro, 1839-49, Knoxville, 1849- (closed by Confederate troops); mem. Tenn. River Commn., 1850; leader Union sympathizers in Tenn.; del. Tenn. Constl. Conv., 1864; gov. Tenn., 1865-69; mem. U.S. Senate (Republican) from Tenn., 1869-75; owner, editor Knoxville Whig, 1875-77. Author: Helps to the Study of Presbyterianism, 1834; Sketches of the Rise, Progress and Decline of Secession, 1862. Died Knoxville, Apr. 29, 1877; buried Old Grey Cemetery, Knoxville.

BROWNSON, Nathan, gov. Ga., Continental congressman; b. Woodbury, Conn., May 14, 1742; grad. Yale, 1761; studied medicine. Practiced medicine, Woodbury; moved to Liberty County, Ga., circa 1764; mem. Provincial Congress, 1775; served as surgeon in Revolutionary Army; mem. Continental Congress from Ga., 1776-78; mem., speaker Ga. Ho. of Reps., 1781, 88; gov. Ga., 1782; del. Ga. Conv. to ratify U.S. Constn., 1788, Ga. Constl. Conv., 1789; mem. Ga. Senate, 1789-91, served as pres. Died on his plantation nr. Riceboro, Ga., Nov. 6, 1796; buried Old Midway Burial Ground.

BROWNSON, Orestes Augustus, clergyman, journalist; b. Stockbridge, Vt., Sept. 16, 1803; s. Sylvester Augustus and Relief (Metcalf) B.; m. Sally Elbridge, June 19, 1827, at least 2 sons, Henry F., Orestes. Presbyn., 1822-24; joined Universalist Ch., 1824; ordained to ministry Universalist Ch., 1826; preached in New Eng., 1826-29; editor Auburn (N.Y.) Gospel Advocate, 1829; corr. editor progressive Free Enquirer; early organizer Workingmen's Party; after brief excursion into area of social and polit. action returned to Church; Unitarian minister, Walpole, N.H., 1832-34, Canton, Mass., 1834-36; formed his own church, Soc. for Christian Union and Progress (attractive to Boston laboring class), 1836; edited Boston Quarterly Review (Democratic, merged with N.Y. Dem. Review, 1842) 1838-43; resumed his own publ. Brownson's Quarterly Review, 1844-65; his polit. and literary friends included Thoreau, Channing and J.C. Calhoun; converted to Catholicism, 1844. Author: New Views of Christianity, Society and the Church, 1836; Charles Elwood, or, The Infidel Converted, 1840; The Mediatorial Life of Jesus, 1842; The Spirit-Rapper, An Autobiography, 1854; The Convert; or, Leaves from My Experience, 1857. Died Detroit, Apr. 17, 1876.

BRUCE, Archibald, physician, educator, mineralogist; b. N.Y.C., Feb. 1777; s. William and Judith (Bayard) B.; A.B., Med. Faculty of Columbia, 1797; M.D., U. Edinburgh (Scotland), 1800; m. 1803. Secured charter Coll. of Physicians and Surgeons, N.Y.C., 1807, mem. faculty (1st Am. prof. materia medica and mineralogy), 1807-11; founder Am. Mineralogy Jour., 1810; mem. faculty Queens Coll., 1812-18; mem. most leading scientific socs.; an original mem. N.Y. Hist. Soc.; bructie metal was named for him, (a magnesium hydroxide which he discovered in N.J.); discovered deposits of zinc oxide, Sussex County, N.J. Died N.Y.C., Feb. 22, 1818.

BRUCE, Blanche Kelso, senator; b. Farmville, Prince Edward County, Va., Mar. 1, 1841; attended Oberlin Coll., 1866-68; m. Josephine Wilson, June 24, 1878. A slave until he fled North at beginning of Civil War; sgt.-at-arms Miss. Senate, 1870; apptd. assessor Bolivar County, Miss., 1871, sheriff, 1872; mem. Bd. Levee Commrs. of Mississippi River, 1872; mem. U.S. Senate from Miss. (Republican), 1874-81; register U.S. Treasury Dept., 1881-85, 95-98; recorder of deeds, Washington, D.C., 1889-95; reputed wealthiest Am. Negro of his period. Died Washington, D.C., Mar. 17, 1898; buried Woodlawn Cemetery, Washington.

BRUCE, George, type-founder; b. Edinburgh, Scotland, June 26, 1781; m. Margaret Watson, Jan. 1, 1803; m. 2d, Catherine Wolfe, 1811. Came to Phila., 1795; apprenticed to bookbinder, then to printer; with brother David traveled to Albany, N.Y., 1798, then began work in N.Y.C.; foreman N.Y. Daily Advertiser, 1803, also printer, publisher of paper for owner, 1803-06; opened book-printing office with David, N.Y.C., 1806-16, improved English stereotyping process; co-owner type foundry, 1816-22, concentrated on type-founding after partnership ended, developed successful type-casting machine with nephew; pres. Mechanics Inst. of N.Y.; officer Gen. Soc. of Mechanics and Tradesmen; patron N.Y. Typog. Soc., Printers' Library; mem. N.Y. Hist. Soc. Died N.Y.C., July 5, 1866.

BRUCE, Phineas, lawyer; b. Mendon, Mass., June 7, 1762; grad. Yale, 1786; studied law. Admitted to bar, 1790, began practice of law, Machias, Mass. (now Me.); mem. Mass. Ho. of Reps., 1791-98, 1800; elected mem. U.S. Ho. of Reps. from Mass., 8th Congress, 1803-05, did not serve because of illness. Died Uxbridge, Mass., Oct. 4, 1809; buried Old Burying Ground; reinterred Prospect Hill Cemetery.

BRUCE, Robert, clergyman, ednl. adminstr.; b. Scone, Perthshire, Scotland, Feb. 20, 1778. Licensed to preach by Presbytery of Perth (Scotland) Asso. Ch., 1806, ordained, 1808; pastor Asso. Ch., Pitts., 1808-46; moderator Pa. Synod, 1810; founder, 1st prin. Western U. of Pa., 1819-43; published discourses on Christian doctrine and practice, 1829; a founder Duquesne Coll., 1843, chartered, 1844. Died June 14, 1846.

BRUFF, Joseph Goldsborough, draftsman, diarist; b. Washington, Oct. 2, 1804; s. Thomas and Mary (Oliver) B.; entered U.S. Mil. Acad., 1820, forced to resign after fighting duel, 1822; married, 5 children. Served with U.S. Navy, 3 years; draftsman in Washington, 1827-49; organized and led Washington City Co. expdn. to Cal. via S. Pass of Rocky Mountains, 1849, brought party safely through treacherous Lassen Trail; kept copious, illustrated jour. of westtrn travels, recording daily events, personalities, local topography, geology, zoology and anthropology (pub. as Gold Rush, edited by Read and Gaines, 1949); draftsman U.S. Treasury Dept., Washington, 1853-78. Mem. Cal. Mining Assn. (pres.), Oldest Inhabitants' Assn., Washington Monument Soc. Mason (charter mem. Fed. lodge). Home: 1009 24th St., Washington. Died Washington, Apr. 14, 1889; buried Congl. Cemetery.

BRÜHL, Gustav, physician, author; b. Herdorf, Prussia, May 31, 1826; attended univs. Siegen, Münster-Eifel, Trier; studied philosophy, medicine at univs. Munich, Halle, Berlin (all Germany); m. Margarete Reis, 3 children. Came to U.S., 1848; began practice medicine, Cincinnati; practising physician St. Mary's Hosp., Cincinnati, several years; lectr. Miami Med. Coll., Cincinnati; active mem. various scientific socs.; a founder, 1st pres. Peter Claver Soc. for edn. Negro children; mem. council U. Cincinnati; interested in archaeology, travelled in Central and South Am., Mexico, Western U.S.; editor Der Deutsche Pioneer, monthly, Cincinnati, 1869-70, also contbr. poems including In den Anden, Tupac-Amaru, Das Feuerschiff, Regina, Steuben, De Kalb, 1869-87. Author: (poetry) Poesiendes Urwalds, 1871; (archeol. works) Die Culturvolker Alt-Amerikas, 1875-87, Zwischen Alaska and Feuerland Bilder aus der Neune Welt, 1896. Died Feb. 16, 1903.

BRULÉ, Étienne, explorer; b. Champigny, France, circa 1592. Came with Samuel de Champlain to New France (now Can.), 1608; helped build settlement at Quebec; lived with Algonquin Indians, 1610-11, became interpreter for Champlain; possibly 1st white man to see Great Lakes (while living with Huron Indians), 1612; accompanied Champlain on voyage to Huronia, around Lake Superior region, 1615; sent on mission to Andastes tribe on headwaters of Susquehanna River (N.Y.), also explored Susquehanna to its outlet in Chesapeake Bay; related his adventures (including capture by Iroquois Indians and rescue by a storm) to Champlain, 1618; lived rest of life with Huron Indians; explored, visited copper mines of Lake Superior, 1622; committed treason by selling his services to English during English occupation, 1629-32; killed and eaten in resultant quarrel with Hurons (Champlain refused to revenge his death because of his traitorous acts). Died 1632.

BRUMBY, Richard Trapier, educator; b. nr. Sumter, S.C., Aug. 4, 1804; s. Thomas B. and Susannah (Greening) B.; grad. S.C. Coll., 1824; read law in office of Stephan D. Miller and William C. Preston; m. Mary Isabelle Brevard, Apr. 22, 1828, at least 5 sons. Admitted to S.C. bar, 1825; partner William C. Preston, 1825-27; traveled, 1827-28; practiced law in Lincolnton, N.C., 1828-31; moved to Montgomery, Ala., 1831; editor The Expositer, Tuscaloosa, Ala., 1832-34, strong advocate of nullification; prof. chemistry, mineralogy and geology U. Ala., 1834-49, addd physiology, conchology, agrl. chemistry to his. dept.; published 1st systematic report of Ala. mineral resources, 1839; prof. S.C. Coll., 1849-55; ret. to Marietta, Ga. Died Marietta, Oct. 6, 1875.

BRUMIDI, Constantino, painter; b. Rome, Italy, July 26, 1805; ed. Acad. Fine Arts, Rome, also Academia di San Lucca; m. 3d, Lola Germon. One of 3 Roman artists commd. to restore Raphael frescoes in Vatican Loggia; painted portrait of Pope Pius IX; exiled to Am. because of polit. activities, 1852; naturalized, 1852; painted frescoes Capitol Bldg., Washington, D.C., 1855-80; pianted 1st Am. frescoe Cincinnatus at the Plough in agrl. com. room Capitol Bldg., 1855; began Capitol Rotunda (his most ambitious undertaking; never completed) 1870. Died Washington, D.C., Feb. 19, 1880.

BRUNNER, Nicholaus Joseph, clergyman; b. Mumliswil, Switzerland, Jan. 10, 1795. Joined the Benedictines, Maria Stein, 1812; ordained priest Roman Catholic Ch., 1819, transferred to Trappists at Oehlemberg (until house suppressed by govt.); founded sch. for boys at Lowenberg; joined Congregation of the Most Precious Blood, 1838; after tng. at Albano, Italy, returned to Germany to develop a province, met continuing govt. hostility; came to U.S., established (with 8 priests) 1st Am. house of Congregation of Most Precious Blood, Norwalk, O. Died (while seeking funds for his missions in Europe), Lichtenstein, Dec. 29, 1859

BRUSH, Henry, congressman; b. Dutchess County, N.Y., June 1778; studied law. Admitted to bar, 1803, began practice of law, Chillicothe, O.; mem. Ohio Ho. of Reps., 1810, Ohio Senate, 1814; moved to London, O.; mem. U.S. Ho. of Reps. from Ohio, 16th Congress, 1819-21; judge Ohio Supreme Ct., 1828. Died on his farm, nr. London, O., Jan. 19, 1855; buried Oak Hill Cemetery.

BRUTÉ de RÉMUR, Simon William Gabriel, clergyman; b. Rennes, France, Mar. 20, 1779; s. Simon Gabriel and Jeanne Renée (Le Saulnier) B. de R.; attended U. Rennes; grad. Faculté de Medicine, U. Paris, 1803. Ordained priest Roman Catholic Ch., 1808; joined Sulpicians; travelled to U.S., circa 1810; tchr. St. Mary's Sem., Balt., 2 years; apptd. tchr. moral philosophy, science and scripture St. Mary's Coll., Emmittsburg, Md.; returned to France, 1815; apptd. rector Balt. Sem., transported his library of 5000 vols. to U.S.; tchr., Emmittsburg, 1818-34, also spiritual dir. Sisters of Charity; became bishop of Vincennes (Ind.), 1834. Died June 26, 1839.

BRUYN, Andrew De Witt, congressman, lawyer; b. Warwarsing, Ulster County, N.Y., Nov. 18, 1790; attended Kingston (N.Y.) Acad.; grad. Princeton, 1810; studied law. Admitted to bar, 1814, began practice of law, Ithaca, N.Y.; justice of peace, 1817; 1st surrogate Tompkins County (N.Y.), 1817-21; mem. N.Y. State Assembly, 1818; trustee Village of Ithaca, 1821, pres., 1822, treas., 1826-28; county supr., 1825; judge Ct. of Common Pleas, 1826-36; dir. Ithaca & Owego R.R., 1828; also a banker; Democratic presdl. elector, 1828; mem. U.S. Ho. of Reps. (Democrat) from N.Y., 25th Congress, 1837-38. Died Ithaca, July 27, 1838; buried Ithaca City Cemetery.

BRYAN, George, colonial ofcl., jurist; b. Dublin, Ireland, Aug. 11, 1731; s. Samuel and Sarah (Dennis) B.; m. Elizabeth Smith, Apr. 21, 1757. Came to Am., 1752; partner (with James Wallace) in mcht. bus., 1752-55; commr. Phila. Harbor, 1762; elected with Thomas Willing (defeating Benjamin Franklin and Joseph Galloway) to Pa. Assembly, 1764; judge Pa. Orphans Ct., Pa. Ct. Common Pleas, 1764; del. Stamp Act Congress, 1765; naval officer Port of Phila., 1776; mem. Supreme Exec. Council of Pa., 1776; acting pres. Pa., 1777-79; mem. Pa.-Va. Boundary Line Commn., 1779; mem. Pa. Assembly, 1779, probable author of Pa. law abolishing slavery; judge Supreme Ct. of Pa., 1780-91; mem. Pa. Council of Censors, 1784; trustee Univ. State of Pa. Died Phila., Jan. 27, 1791.

BRYAN, Henry H., congressman; b. Martin County, N.C.; attended grammar and high schs. Moved to Tenn., held several local offices; mem. U.S. Ho. of Reps. from Tenn., 16th Congress, 1819-21. Died Montgomery County, Tenn., May 7, 1835.

BRYAN, John Heritage, congressman, lawyer; b. New Bern, N.C., Nov. 4, 1798; attended New Bern Acad.; grad. U. N.C., 1815; studied law. Admitted to bar, 1819, began practice of law, New Bern; mem. N.C. Senate, 1823-24; trustee U. N.C. at Chapel Hill, 1823-68; mem. U.S. Ho. of Reps. (Whig) from N.C., 19th-20th congresses, 1825-29; moved to Raleigh, N.C., 1839, continued practice of law. Died Raleigh, May 19, 1870; buried Oakwood Cemetery.

BRYAN, Joseph, congressman, planter; b. Savannah, Ga., Aug. 18, 1773; attended Oxford (Eng.) U. Traveled in France, during Revolutionary War; engaged in agriculture, Wilmington Island, Ga.; mem. U.S. Ho. of Reps. (Democrat) from Ga., 8th-9th congresses, 1803-06 (resigned). Died on his estate "Nonchalance," Wilminton Island, Sept. 12, 1812; buried family burial ground at "Nonchalance."

BRYAN, Joseph Hunter, congressman; b. Windsor, Bertie County, N.C. Mem. N.C. Ho. of Commons, 1804-05, 07-09; trustee U. N.C. at Chapel Hill, 1809-17; mem. U.S. Ho. of Reps. from N.C., 14th-15th congresses, 1815-19.

BRYAN, Nathan, congressman; b. Craven (now Jones) County, N.C., 1748. Mem. N.C. Ho. of Commons, 1787, 91-94; mem. U.S. Ho. of Reps. from N.C., 4th-5th congresses, 1795-98. Died Phila., June 4, 1798; buried Baptist burial ground on 2d Street; reinterred at unknown location.

BRYANT, Gridley, civil engr., inventor; b. Scituate, Mass., Aug. 26, 1789; s. Zina and Eunice (Wade) B.; m. Maria Fox, Dec. 3, 1815, 10 children. Contractor for U.S. Govt.; built Boston br. U.S. Bank, 1823; inventor portable derrick, 1823; supervising engr. Quincy (Mass.) R.R., 1826; inventor 8-wheeled railroad car; one of earliest railroad builders. Died Scituate, June 13, 1867.

BRYANT, Henry, artist; b. Manchester Green, East Hartford, Conn., Dec. 7, 1881. Apprenticed to engraver; became itinerant portrait painter, circa 1832; painted in Albany, N.Y., 1834-35, N.Y.C., 1835-40; exhibited at N.A.D., 1837-40, 52-54, became asso., 1837; exhibited at Apollo Assn., N.Y.C., 1838-39; one of 1st artists to take up daguereotyping, practiced in Va., 1844-46; began to specialize in landscapes, circa 1850; returned to East Hartford, circa 1850. Died East Hartford, Dec. 8, 1881.

BRYANT, William Cullen, journalist, poet; b. Cummington, Mass., Nov. 3, 1794; s. Dr. Peter and Sarah (Snell) B.; attended Williams Coll., 1810-11; studied law under Mr. Howe, Worthington, Mass., 1811-14; m. Frances Fairchild, June 11, 1821, 2 children. Published an attack on Pres. Jefferson called The Embargo, 1808; admitted to Mass. bar, 1815; practiced law, Great Barrington, Mass., 1816-25; published collection of poems responsible for his fame, including Thanatopsis (1817), To a Waterfowl (1818), The Ages (1821), 1821; editor N.Y. Review and Athenaeum Mag., 1825; asst. editor N.Y. Evening Post, 1826-29, editor, 1829-78; politically powerful as editor, backed free-trade, anti-slavery ideas, supported Democrats, 1848, gradually shifted to Republican Party; editor one of most powerful papers in U.S. during Civil War, said to have influenced Abraham Lincoln in issuance of Emancipation Proclamation; called "First Citizen of the Republic"; author poetical works including: Poems, 1821; Poems, 1832; The Fountain and Other Poems,. 1842; The White-Footed Doe, and other Poems, 1844; published Tales of the Glauber Spa (short stories), 1832; Letters of A Traveller (travelog), 1850; translator The Iliad, 1870, The Odyssey, 1872. Died N.Y.C., June 12, 1878; buried Roslyn (L.I., N.Y.) Cemetery.

BUCHANAN, Andrew, congressman, lawyer; b. Chester County, Pa., Apr. 8, 1780; grad. Dickinson Coll., Carlisle, Pa.; studied law. Admitted to bar, 1798, began practice of law, York, Pa.; moved to Waynesburg, Pa., 1803; mem. Pa. Ho. of Reps., Pa. Senate; mem. U.S. Ho. of Reps. (Democrat) from Pa., 24th-25th congresses, 1835-39. Died Waynesburg, Dec. 2, 1848; buried Greene Mount Cemetery.

BUCHANAN, Franklin, naval officer; b. Balt., Sept. 17, 1800; s. Dr. George and Loetitia (McKean) B.; m. Ann Catherine Lloyd, Feb. 19, 1835. By command of U.S. sec. of navy Bancroft, submitted plan for new naval sch. at Annapolis, Md., 1845; 1st supt. U.S. Naval Acad., Annapolis, 1845-47, initiator high standards of naval discipline and efficiency; in command Susquehanna, flagship of Commodore Oliver Perry's squadron to Japan, 1852; comdr. Washington (D.C.) Navy Yard, 1859; commd. capt. Confederate Navy, 1861, Adm., 1862; commanded Chesapeake Bay Squadron; comdr. Merrimac; comdr. Battle of Mobile Bay, 1864; taken prisoner of war, 1864, released, 1865. Died Talbot County, Md., May 11, 1874.

BUCHANAN, Hugh, congressman; b. Argyleshire, Scotland, Sept. 15, 1823; came to U.S., settled in Vt.; attended public schs.; studied law. Admitted to bar, 1845, began practice of law, Newnan, Ga., 1846; mem. Ga. Senate, 1855, 57; del. Democratic nat. convs., 1856, 68; Dem. presdl. elector, 186 served with Confederate Army throughout Civil W judge Superior Ct. of Coweta Circuit, 1872-8 del. Ga. Constl. Conv., 1877; mem. U.S. Ho. Reps. (Democrat) from Ga., 47th-48th congress 1881-85. Died Newnan, June 11, 1890; buried O Hill Cemetery.

BUCHANAN, James, 15th Pres. U.S.; b. Merce burg, Pa., Apr. 23, 1791; s. James and Elizab (Speer) B.; grad. Dickinson Coll., 1809; never ma ried. Admitted to Pa. bar, 1812; served as volunte in War of 1812; mem. Pa. Ho. Reps., 1814; me U.S. Ho. of Reps. from Pa., 17th-21st congress 1821-31; U.S. minister to Russia, 1831-34; me U.S. Senate from Pa., 1834-45; sec. of state U.S 1844-49; U.S. minister to Gt. Britain, 1852-5 helped to draft Ostend Manifesto (which stated th if Spain refused to sell Cuba, U.S. was entitled take it by force; helped ensure success as presc candidate, later proved a source of embarrassme to U.S.), 1854; 15th Pres. U.S. (Democrat), 185 61; adhered strictly to constructionist viewpoir favored entrance of Kansas as slave state, failed prevent secession of S.C. (touching off Civil War Died June 1, 1868, Lancaster, Pa.; buried La caster.

BUCHANAN, John, jurist; b. Prince George County, Md., 1772; s. Thomas and Mary (Cook) B m. Sophia Williams, Oct. 4, 1808, 2 children. Me lower house Md. Legislature, 1797-99; apptd. chi judge 5th Jud. Dist., 1806; asso. justice Md. C Appeals; chief justice Appellate Ct., 1824; we to Eng. on behalf of Md. to negotiate sale $8,000,000 of state-secured railroad and can stocks to build Chesapeake and Ohio Canal, 183 Died Nov. 6, 1844; buried Williamsport, Md.

BUCHANAN, Joseph, educator, journalist, inve tor; b. Washington County, Va., Aug. 24, 1785; Andrew and Joanna B.; attended Transylvania U Lexington, Ky.; m. Nancy Rodes Garth; 1 so Joseph Rodes. Apptd. prfo. insts. of medicine Tra sylvania U., 1809; went to Phila. to study Pestalo zian ednl. methods, returned to Lexington, teste methods in his classes; studied law, then lecture in pvt. law sch.; with Lexington Reporter, Fran fort (Ky.) Palladium, Western Spy and Litera Gazette; editor Louisville (Ky.) Focus, 1826-2 developed spiral boiler, applied boiler to wago 1825. Author: Philosophy of Human Nature, 1812 A Practical Grammar of the English Language, 182 Died Sept. 29, 1829.

BUCHANAN, Robert Christie, army officer; b Balt., Mar. 1, 1811; s. Andrew and Carolina (John son) B.; grad. U.S. Mil. Acad., 1829; m. Mis Windsor, circa 1847. Commd. 2d lt. 4th Inf., U.S Army, 1830; served in Black Hawk War, 1832; ad of his regt., 1835-38; commd. 1st lt., 1836; serve in Seminole War; commd. capt., 1838; brevette maj. during Mexican War, 1846, lt. col., 1847 commd. maj. U.S. Army, 1855, lt. col., 1861; bre vetted col. for action at Battle of Gaine's Mil commd. brig. gen. U.S. Volunteers, 1862, col. 1863; brevetted brig. gen., 1865; fought at battle of Antietam, 2d Bull Run, Fredericksburg during Civ War; mem. Ia. Claims Commn., 1867; asst. commr Freedman's Bur., 1868; comdr. Dept. of La., 1868 Died Washington, D.C., Nov. 29, 1878.

BUCHANAN, Thomas, mcht.; b. Glasgow, Scot land, Dec. 24, 1744; s. George and Jean (Lowden) B.; attended U. Glasgow; m. Almy Townsend, Mar 17, 1766, at least 1 son, George. Came to N.Y.C. 1763; partner (with his relative Walter Buchanan) in shipping firm W.J.T. Buchanan, 1763-72; signe original non-importation agreement, 1766; electe mem. N.Y.C. C. of C., 1768, v.p., 1780-83, electe pres., 1783, declined to serve for fear being to closely asso. with rebels; mem. local Com. of On Hundred, 1775; shifted toward Loyalist side, signe Loyalists' pledge to Gen. Howe, 1776; continued i fgn. trade throughout Am. Revolution without an tagonizing either patriot or Loyalist side; mem 1st Presbyn. Ch., N.Y.C.; dir. United Ins. Co. Died N.Y.C., Nov. 10, 1815.

BUCHER, John Conrad, soldier, clergyman; b. Neunkirch, Switzerland, June 10, 1730; s. Hans Jacob and Anna Dorothea (Burgauer) B.; attended U. Marburg (Germany), 1752-55; m. Mary Magdalena Hoke, Feb. 26, 1760, 6 children. Arrived in U.S., 1755; commd. ensign 1st Battalion, Pa. Militia, 1758, commanded garrison at Carlisle, Pa., 1759-60, promoted to lt. 2d Pa. Battalion, 1760, then to adj. and capt., 1760; began preaching, 1763; ordained to ministry German Reformed Ch., 1767, made occasional missionary trips West; 1st minister to preach in German lang. beyond Allegheny Mountains; chaplain "German Regt." under Baron Von Arnt, 1775-77. Died Annville, Pa., Aug. 15, 1780; buried Lebanon, Pa.

BUCHER, John Conrad, congressman, lawyer; b. Harrisburg, Pa., Dec. 28, 1792; attended public schs.; studied law. Admitted to bar, began practice of law, Harrisburg; clk. land dept. of Pa., 1813; nem. borough council Harrisburg; mem. bd. sch. lirs.; mem. U.S. Ho. of Reps. from Pa., 22d Congress, 1831-33; trustee Harrisburg Acad., Franklin Coll., Marshall Coll.; asso. judge Dauphin County, 1839-51. Died Harrisburg, Oct. 15, 1851; buried City Cemetery.

BUCHSER, Frank (Franz), painter; b. nr. Solothurn, Switzerland, 1828; traveled extensively in Europe, 1950-53, in Eng., 1861-63; Spanish battle painter in Moroccan campaign, 1857; came to Am., 1866, painted numerous portraits; traveled with Gen. Sherman in West, summer 1866, did numerous oil studies and sketches; traveled on Great Lakes, summer 1868; returned to Europe, 1871, continued travels in Italy, Dalmatia, Greece, 1870's-80's; founder Swiss Artists Assn.; promoted Swiss Salon. Died Solothurn, 1890.

BUCHTEL, John Richards, businessman; b. Green Twp., O., Jan. 18, 1820; s. John and Catherine (Richards) B.; m. Elizabeth Davidson, 1844. Became mower and reaper salesman Ball, Aultman & Co., 1854, later 1st pres. Akron (O.) br. factory; with other investors began devel. of mineral resources of Hocking Valley (O.), 1877; trustee Ohio State Agrl. Coll.; trustee U. Akron, 1870-92, donated about ½ million dollars; paralysis ended bus. activities, 1887. Died Akron, May 23, 1892.

BUCK, Daniel, congressman, state ofcl.; b. Hebron, Conn., Nov. 9, 1753; s. Thomas and Jane Buck; m. Content Ashley, Sept. 22, 1786, 11 children including Daniel. Fought in Am. Revolution; one of Vt.'s earliest settlers, 1780; admitted to Vt. bar, 1783; pros. atty. Orange County (Vt.), 1783-85; clk. Orange County Ct., 1783-84; del. to Vt. Conv. which ratified U.S. Constn., 1791; speaker Vt. Assembly, 1793-94; mem. Vt. Council Censors, 1792; atty. gen. Vt., 1794, 1814; mem. U.S. Ho. of Reps. (Federalist) from Vt., 4th Congress, 1795-97; states atty. Windsor County (Vt.), 1802-03. Died Chelsea, Vt., Aug. 16, 1816; buried Old Cemetery, Chelsea.

BUCK, Daniel Azro Ashley, congressman; b. Norwich, Vt., Apr. 19, 1789; s. Daniel Buck; grad. Middlebury Coll., 1807, U.S. Mil. Acad., 1808; studied law. Commd. lt. Engr. Corps, U.S. Army, 1808, resigned, 1811; apptd. 2d lt. 3d Arty., 1811; raised and served with volunteer co. of rangers, 1813-15; promoted capt. 31st Inf., 1813; admitted to bar, 1814, began practice of law, Chelsea, Vt.; mem. Vt. Ho. of Reps., 1816-26, 28-30, 33-35, speaker, 1820-22, 25-26, 29; state atty. Orange County, 1819-22, 30-34; Democratic presdl. elector, 1820; mem. U.S. Ho. of Reps. (Democrat) from Vt., 18th, 20th congresses, 1823-25, 27-29; clk. War Dept., 1835-39, Treasury Dept., 1840. Died Washington, D.C., Dec. 24, 1841; buried Congressional Cemetery, Washington.

BUCK, Gurdon, surgeon; b. N.Y.C., May 4, 1807; s. Gurdon and Susannah (Manwaring) B.; M.D., Coll. Physicians and Surgeons, N.Y.C., 1830; studied in Paris (France), Berlin (Germany), Vienna (Austria), 1832-34; m. Henriette Wolff, July 27, 1836, 1 son, Albert H. Vis. surgeon N.Y. Hosp., 1837, St. Luke's Hosp., 1846; asso. with N.Y. Eye and Ear Infirmary, 1852-62; vis. surgeon Presbyn. Hosp., 1872; among chief contbns. was Buck's extension (a treatment of thigh fractures by weights and pulleys); pioneer in plastic face surgery. Author: Description of an Improved Extension Apparatus for the Treatment of Fracture of the Thigh, 1867; Contributions to Reparative Surgery, 1876. Died N.Y.C., Mar. 6, 1877.

BUCKELEY, Peter, clergyman; b. Bedfordshire, Eng., Jan. 31, 1583; s. Edward and Olyff (Irby) B.; M.A., St. Johns Coll., Cambridge, 1608; m. Jane Allen; m. 2d, Grace Chetwode; 12 children. Came to Am., 1636; founder, 1st minister Puritan Ch., Concord, Mass., 1635; prominent in New Eng. theocracy. Died Concord, Mar. 9, 1659; buried Concord.

BUCKHOUT, Isaac Craig, civil engr.; b. Morrisania (now Eastchester), N.Y., Nov. 7, 1830; s. Jacob and Charlotte Eveline (DeVal) B.; studied under a Prof. Davies. Engr., supt. water works Paterson, N.J.; surveyor N.Y.C., 1853; constructed aqueduct over Harlem flats, also bridge over Harlem River, circa 1853; designed and supervised work on Grand Central Depot, 4th St. Ry., N.Y.C.; drew plans for underground railroad from Grand Central to City Hall; designed subways in Bklyn.; mem. N.Y.C. Com. on Rapid Transit. Died White Plains, N.Y., Sept. 27, 1874.

BUCKINGHAM, Joseph Tinker, editor; b. Windham, Conn., Dec. 21, 1779; s. Nehemiah and Mary (Huntington) Tinker (baptized name for maternal grandmother). Editor, Polyanthos, 1806-07, 12-14, The Ordeal, 1809, New Eng. Galaxy and Masonic Mag., 1817-28; founder, editor Boston Courier, 1824-48; editor New Eng. Mag., 1831-34; mem. Mass. Gen. Ct., 7 years; mem. Mass. Senate, 4 years. Author: Specimens of Newspaper Literature, with Personal Memoirs, Anecdotes and Reminiscences, 1850; Personal Memoirs and Recollections of Editorial Life, 1852. Died Cambridge, Mass., Apr. 11, 1861.

BUCKINGHAM, William Alfred, senator, gov. Conn.; b. Lebanon, Conn., May 29, 1804; s. Samuel and Joanna (Matson) B.; m. Eliza Ripley, Sept. 27, 1830, 2 children. Began dry goods bus., Norwich, Conn., 1826; treas. Hayward Rubber Co.; mayor Norwich, 1849-50, 56-57; gov. Conn., 1858-66; mem. U.S. Senate from Conn., 1869-75; a founder Norwich Free Acad., 1856; pres. Am. Temperance Union. Died Norwich, Feb. 5, 1875; buried Yantic Cemetery, Norwich.

BUCKLAND, Cyrus, inventor; b. Manchester, Conn., Aug. 10, 1799; s. George and Elizabeth B.; m. Mary Locke, May 18, 1824, 3 children. Instrumental in manufacture of eccentric bit and auger used in cutting lock, guard plate, side plate, breech plate, rod spring and barrels to gunstocks; designed and patented rifling machine to cut groove of regularly decreasing depth from breech to muzzle (sec. of war paid $10,000 for U.S. Govt. rights to invention). Died Springfield, Mass., Feb. 26, 1891.

BUCKLAND, Ralph Pomeroy, army officer, congressman; b. Leyden, Mass., Jan. 20, 1812; s. Ralph and Anna (Kent) B.; attended Kenyon Coll.; m. Charlotte Boughton, Jan. 1838; 8 children. Admitted to Ohio bar, 1837; mayor Fremont (O.), 1843-45; mem. Ohio Senate, 1855-59; organizer 72d Regt., Ohio Volunteer Inf., 1861; commanded 4th brigade of Sherman's div. at Battle of Shiloh; brevetted brig. gen. U.S. Volunteers, 1862; comdr. Dist. of Memphis, 1864; brevetted maj. gen. U.S. Volunteers, 1865; mem. U.S. Ho. of Reps. Reupublican from Ohio, 39th-40th congresses, 1865-69; pres. Ohio Soldier and Sailor's Home, 1870; govt. dir. Union Pacific R.R., 1878-80. Died Fremont, May 27, 1892; buried Oakwood Cemetery, Fremont.

BUCKLAND, William, architect; b. Eng.; ed. Oxford (Eng.) U. Came to Am. under indenture, 1754, settled in Phila.; moved to Annapolis, Md., practice as architect before Am. Revolution; designed mansion known as Hammon-Harwood house (built from his plans, 1770-74), remains as one of city's landmarks; designed several other homes, including Chase house, Brice mansion, Doctor Scott house, so-called Paca House (Carvel Hall Hotel), Rideout house.

BUCKLER, Thomas Hepburn, physician; b. "Evergreen," Balt., Jan. 4, 1812; s. William and Anne (Hepburn) B.; attended St. Mary's Coll., Balt.; M.D., U. Md., 1835; studied in clinics, Paris, France, 1836; m. Anne Fuller, 1861; m. 2d, Eliza Ridgely, Nov. 21, 1865. Physician of Balt. City and County Almshouse, several years; physician to public figures including Chief Justice Roger B. Taney, Pres. James Buchanan, Gen. Robert E. Lee, 1850-55; Southern sympathizer during Civil War; lived in Paris, practiced medicine under license of French Govt., 1866-90; advocated use of ammonium phosphate in treating rheumatism, laparotomy for intestinal obstruction, and rest and open-air treatment for Tb. Author: A History of Epidemic Cholera, as it appeared at the Baltimore City and County Almshouse, in the Summer of 1849, with Some Remarks on the Medical Topography and Diseases of this Region, 1851; On the Etiology, Pathology and Treatment of Fibro-bronchitis and Rheumatic Pneumonia, 1853. Died Apr. 20, 1901.

BUCKLEY, Samuel Botsford, physician, naturalist; b. Torrey, N.Y., May 9, 1809; grad. Wesleyan U., Middletown, Conn., 1836; studied medicine Coll. Physicians and Surgeons, N.Y.C., 1842-43; Ph.D. (hon.), Waco (Tex.) U., 1872; m. Charlotte Sullivan, 1852; m. 2d, Sarah Porter, 1855; m. 3d, Libbie Myers, 1864. Collected plants in Ala., Tenn., N.C., S.C., 1842, collected in Fla., 1843; asst. geologist and naturalist Tex. Geol. Survey, 1860-61; state geologist Tex., 1865-67, 74-77, supervised 2d Tex. Geol. Survey; agrl. editor State Gazette, Austin, Tex., 1871-72; a class of squirrels, a shrub and Buckley's Peak (Tenn.) are all named for him. Died Austin, Feb. 18, 1883.

BUCKLIN, James C., architect; b. 1801. Apprenticed to John Holden Greene, Providence, R.I.; later worked with William Tallman (builder and lumber mcht.); designed (with Russell Warren) Arcade Bldg., Providence (built 1828), Westminster Congregational Ch. (built 1829); designed numerous comml. and pub. bldgs. in Providence, including Benefit St. Sch., circa 1832, Library (1834) and R.I. Hall (1838) at Brown U., City High Sch., 1843, Washington Bldg., 1843, "cabinet" of R.I. Hist. Soc., 1844, Butler Hosp., 1845, Phenix Bldg., circa 1860, alterations to Providence Athenaeum,, 1867, Reynolds Block, circa 1870, Howard Bldg., 1870; architect several pvt. homes, including Thomas Davies house, 1869, S.S. Sprague residence, circa 1870, old Hoppin homestead, circa 1875. Died 1880.

BUCKMINSTER, Joseph Stevens, clergyman; b. Portsmouth, N.H., May 26, 1784; s. Rev. Joseph and Sarah (Stevens) B.; grad. Harvard, 1800. Tchr., Phillips Exeter (N.H.) Acad., 1801-02; tutor for family of Theodore Lyman, Boston; candidate for ministry Unitarian Ch., preached 1st sermon, York, Me., 1804; ordained to ministry Unitarian Ch., at Brattle Street Ch., Boston, 1805; went for health reasons to Europe, 1806-07, returned with library of some 3,000 books; largely responsible for introduction of Bibl. scholarship into U.S.; founder Boston Athenaeum, 1807; published Am. edit. Griesbach's Greek Testament, 2 vols., 1809; delivered Phi Beta Kappa oration Harvard, 1809; mem. Anthology Club of Boston; 1st Dexter lectr. on Bibl. criticism Harvard. Died Boston, June 9, 1812.

BUCKNELL, William, speculator; b. Delaware County, Pa., Apr. 1, 1811; s. William and Sarah (Walker) B.; m. Harriet Ashton, 1836; m. 2d, Margaret Crozer, 1839; m. 3d, Emma Ward. Following brief career as wood carver turned to land speculation, moved to Phila. where he enlarged bus. to include speculation in securities and real estate; trustee U. Lewisburg (Pa.) (name of univ. changed to Bucknell U. because of his numerous contbns., 1887); donated $1,000,000 to charity, including ½ million to Baptist chs. and charities. Died Mar. 5, 1890.

BUCKNER, Alexander, senator, lawyer; b. Jefferson County, Ky., 1785; studied law. Moved to Charleston, Ind., 1812, to Jackson, Mo., 1818; practiced law, also engaged in agriculture; apptd. circuit atty. Cape Girardeau (Mo.) Dist.; pres. Mo. Constl. Conv., 1820; mem. Mo. Senate, 1822-26; mem. U.S. Senate from Mo., 1831-33. Died Cape Girardeau County, June 6, 1833; buried on his farm, Cape Girardeau County; reinterred City Cemetery, Cape Girardeau, 1897.

BUCKNER, Aylette, congressman, lawyer; b. Greensburg, Ky., July 21, 1806; s. Richard Aylett Buckner; attended New Athens Sem.; studied law. Admitted to bar, began practice of law, Greensburg; mem. Ky. Ho. of Reps., 1842-43; mem. U.S. Ho. of Reps. (Whig) from Ky., 30th Congress, 1847-49. Died Lexington, Ky., July 3, 1869; buried Lexington Cemetery.

BUCKNER, Aylett Hawes, congressman; b. Fredericksburg, Va., Dec. 14, 1816; attended Georgetown Coll., Washington, D.C., U. Va. at Charlottesville; studied law. A tchr. for several years; moved to Palmyra, Mo., 1837, became dep. sheriff; admitted to bar, 1838, began practice of law, Bowling Green, Mo.; became editor Salt River Journal; elected clk. Pike County Ct., 1841; practiced law, St. Louis, 1850-55; atty. for Bank of State of Mo., 1852; commr. of public works, 1854-55; settled on a farm nr. Bowling Green, circa 1855; elected judge 3d Jud. Circuit, 1857; del. Washington (D.C.) Peace Conv., 1861; moved to St. Charles, Mo., 1862; became tobacco mfr., also engaged in merc. activities; moved to Mexico, Mo.; mem. Democratic Central Com., 1868; del. Dem. Nat. Conv., Balt., 1872; mem. U.S. Ho. of Reps. (Democrat) from Mo., 43d-48th congresses, 1873-85. Died Mexico, Mo., Feb. 5, 1894; buried Elmwood Cemetery.

BUCKNER, Richard Aylett, congressman; b. Fauquier County, Va., July 16, 1763; studied law. Admitted to bar, practiced law; taught sch.; moved to Greensburg, Ky., 1803; county atty., Commonwealth's atty. Green County; mem. Ky. Ho. of Reps., 1813, 15, 37-39; mem. U.S. Ho. of Reps. (Anti-Democrat) from Ky., 18th-20th congresses, 1823-29; asso. judge Ct. of Appeals, 1831; unsuccessful Whig candidate for gov. Ky., 1832; presdl. elector on Harrison tickets, 1836, 40; circuit judge, 1845; judge Ky. Ct. of Appeals. Died Greensburg, Dec. 8, 1847; buried family graveyard at "Buckner's Hill."

BUCKSTONE, John B., comedian, playwright; b. 1802. Made Am. debut as Peter Pinkey in his own comedy Single Life, Park Theatre, N.Y.C., 1840; appeared as guest star New Nat. Theater, N.Y.C., 1840; appeared at St. Charles Theatre, New Orleans, 1841; performed with Fanny Fitzwilliam at Poydras Street American, New Orleans; wrote over 100 plays, many of which were produced. Died 1879.

BUEL, Alexander Woodruff, congressman, lawyer; b. Castleton, Vt., Dec. 13, 1813; grad. Middlebury Coll., Vt., 1830; studied law. Taught sch.; moved to Detroit, 1834; admitted to bar, 1835, began practice of law, Detroit; city atty., 1837; mem. Mich. Ho. of Reps., 1838, 48, 59-60, speaker, 1848; pros. atty. Wayne County, 1843-46; mem. U.S. Ho. of Reps. (Democrat) from Mich., 31st Congress, 1849-51; postmaster Detroit, 1860-61. Died Detroit, Apr. 19, 1868; buried Elmwood Cemetery.

BUEL, Jesse, journalist, agriculturist; b. Coventry, Conn., Jan. 4, 1778; s. Elias Buel; m. Susan Pierce, 1801. Apprenticed to printer, Rutland, Vt., 1792-96; journeyman printer, 1796-97; began (with various assos.) 3 weekly newspapers; ran Kingston Plebeian, 1803-13; sometime judge Ulster County Ct.; moved to Albany, N.Y., 1813; published Albany Argus, 1813-19; printer to N.Y. State, 1814-19; developed interest in farming; purchased small farm nr. Albany to which he applied his scientific agrl. concepts, 1821; rec. sec. N.Y. State Bd. Agr., 1822; often mem. N.Y. State Assembly, 1823-36, became leading spokesman for farming interests; established Farm Journal Cultivator, 1834; presided over state agrl. conv., 1836; unsuccessful Whig candidate for gov. N.Y., 1836. Author: The Farmer's Companion, 1839; The Farmer's Instructor, 1839. Editor: A Treatise in Agriculture (John Armstrong). Died Oct. 6, 1839.

BUELL, Abel, inventor, engraver, silversmith; b. Killingworth, Conn., Feb. 1742; son of John Buell; m. Mary Parker, 1762; m. 2d, Aletta Devoe, 1771; m. 3d, Mrs. Rebecca Parkman, 1779; m. 4th, Sarah. Apprenticed to silversmith Ebenezer Chittenden, Killingworth; opened own shop, 1762; 1st signs of his ability were some Conn. 5 shilling bank notes which he artfully improved to 5 pound notes (this indiscretion cost him some months in jail plus branding and confiscation of property); upon release from prison, constructed lapidary machine for cutting and finishing precious stones; learned craft of typefounding, produced 1st known example of Am. typefounding, 1769; granted 100 pounds by Conn. Assembly to aid in establishing type-foundry at New Haven, 1769; began copperplate engraving, 1770; produced map of territories of U.S. according to Peace of 1783 (his chief engraving work), 1784; remained in New Haven where his business operations extended to operating packet boats; developed marble quarry; owned 2 privateersmen; fashioned silver; cast type; practiced engraving; a diffuse and rarely profitable businessman; constructed money coining machine, 1785; traveled to England, 1789; worked at N.Y. cotton mfg. plant, 1793; returned to Hartford (Conn.) and continued silversmithing and engraving, 1799; silversmith in Stockbridge, Mass., 1805; a believer in Thomas Paine's doctrines until 1813 when he embraced Christianity. Died in New Haven Alms House, Mar. 10, 1822.

BUELL, Alexander Hamilton, congressman, mcht.; b. Fairfield, N.Y., July 14, 1801; attended Fairfield Acad. Became a mcht., Fairfield, also maintained gen. stores in other cities; mem. N.Y. State Assembly, 1845; mem. U.S. Ho. of Reps. (Democrat) from N.Y., 32d Congress, 1851-53. Died Washington, D.C., Jan. 29, 1853; buried Episcopal Cemetery, Fairfield.

BUELL, Don Carlos, army officer; b. nr. Marietta, O., Mar. 23, 1818; s. Salmon D. and Eliza (Buell) B.; grad. U.S. Mli. Acad., 1841; m. Margaret Hunter. Commd. 2d lt. 3d Inf., U.S. Army, 1841; fought in Seminole War; served as 1st lt. at battles of Monterey, Churubusco during Mexican War; brevetted capt., 1846; adj. gen. of his regt., 1847; commd. lt. col. Adj. Gen.'s Dept., 1860; commd. brig. gen. U.S. Volunteers, 1861; an organizer Army of Potomac; comdr. Army of Ohio, 1861; commd. maj. gen. U.S. Volunteers, 1862; fought at battles of Shiloh, Perryville; relieved of command for failure to pursue Confederate Army after Battle of Perry ville; resigned commn., 1864; pres. Green River Iron Works, 1865. Died Rockport, Ky., Nov. 19, 1898.

BUFFINGTON, Joseph, congressman, jurist; b. West Chester, Pa., Nov. 27, 1803; attended Western U., Pitts.; studied law. Edited weekly newspaper, Butler County, Pa.; admitted to bar, 1826, began practice of law, Butler, Pa.; moved to Kittanning, Pa., 1827; mem. U.S. Ho. of Reps. (Whig) from Pa., 28th-29th congresses, 1843-47; apptd. pres. judge 18th Dist., 1849-51; declined appointment by Pres. Fillmore as chief justice Utah Territory, 1852; judge 10th Dist. Pa., 1855-71. Died Kittanning, Feb. 3, 1872; buried Kittanning. Cemetery.

BUFFIN(G)TON, James, congressman; b. Fall River, Mass., Mar. 16, 1817; attended Friends Coll., Providence, R.I.; studied medicine. Engaged in merc. activities, Fall River; mayor Fall River, 1854-55; mem. U.S. Ho. of Reps. (Republican) from Mass., 34th-37th, 41st-44th congresses, 1855-63, 69-75; spl. agt. U.S. Treasury, also internal revenue collector for Dist. of Mass., 1867-69. Died Fall River, Mar. 7, 1875; buried Oak Grove Cemetery.

BUFFORD, John H., lithographer, publisher. Worked in N.Y.C., 1835-39, Boston, 1839-71; asso. with B.W. Thayer & Co., Boston, 1841-44; head firm J.H. Bufford & Co., Boston, 1845-52, J.H. Bufford & Sons, after 1852; known work includes view of Princeton U. in 1836, numerous town views in New Eng. and N.Y. Died circa 1871.

BUFFUM, Arnold, reformer; b. Smithfield, R.I., Dec. 13, 1782; s. William and Lydia (Arnold) B.; m. Rebecca Gould, 1803; children—Elizabeth, Edward. Pres., New Eng. Anti-Slavery Soc., 1832; a founder Am. Anti-Slavery Soc., 1833; lectr. for both socs. editor Protectionist (moderate mag. advocating emancipation), 1840-41; repudiated leadership of W.L. Garrison and Wendell Phillips in 1840's, became moderate on slavery question; adherent of Liberty, Free-Soil and Republican parties, 1840's-50's. Died Perth Amboy, N.J., Mar. 13, 1859.

BUFFUM, Joseph, Jr., congressman; b. Fitchburg, Mass., Sept. 23, 1784; grad. Dartmouth, 1806; studied law. Practiced law, Westmoreland and Keene, N.H.; mem. U. S. Ho. of Reps. (Democrat) from N.H., 16th Congress, 1819-21; apptd. judge Ct. of Common Pleas, 1825; engaged in agriculture. Died Westmoreland, Feb. 24, 1874; buried South Village Cemetery.

BUFORD, Abraham, army officer; b. Culpeper County, Va., July 31, 1749; s. John and Judith Beauford; m. Martha McDowell, Oct. 1788. Raised company of minutemen who helped in expulsion of Gov. Dunmore of Va., 1774; commd. maj. 14th Va. Regt., 1776; promoted to lt. col. 5th Va. Regt., 1777, col. in command 11th Va. Regt., 1778-81; comdr. 3d Va. Regt., Continental Army, 1781; became large landowner after Am. Revolution; moved to Ky. Died Georgetown, Ky., June 30, 1833.

BUFORD, Abraham, army officer, stock raiser; b. Woodford County, Ky., Jan. 18, 1820; s. William B. and Frances (Kirtley) B.; grad. U.S. Mli. Acad., 1841; m. Amanda Harris, 1845, 1 son, William. Commd. 1st lt. U.S. Army during Mexican War, 1846, capt., 1853; stock raiser, specializing in horses and short horn cattle, Ky., 1854-61; commd. brig. gen. Confederate Army, 1862; returned to stock raising after war, also bred race horses. Died Danville, Ind., June 9, 1884.

BUFORD, John, army officer; b. Woodford County, Ky., Mar. 4, 1826; s. John and Anne (Bannister) Watson B.; grad. U.S. Mil. Acad., 1848; m. Martha McDonald Duke, May 9, 1854. Brevetted to 2d lt. U.S. Army, 1848, commd. 2d lt., 1849, 1st lt., 1853, regimental g.m., 1855; frontier duty, Tex., N.M., Kan.; took part in Sioux Expdn., 1855; commd. brig. gen. U.S. Volunteers, 1862, assigned to cavalry; wounded at Battle of Centerville, 1862; chief cavalry Army of Potomac, 1862; served in battles of Antietam, Fredericksburg, Gettysburg; promoted maj. gen. volunteers shortly before death. Died on sick leave, Washington, D.C., Dec. 16, 1863; buried U.S. Mil. Acad., West Point, N.Y.

BUFORD, Napoleon Bonaparte, army officer; b. Woodford County, Ky., Jan. 13, 1807; s. John and Mary (Hickman) B.; grad. U.S. Mil. Acad., 1827; m. Sarah Childs; m. 2d, Nancy Anne Greenwood. Commd. lt. arty. U.S. Army 1827; asst. prof. natural and exptl. philosophy U.S. Mil. Acad., 1834-35, sec. bd. visitors, 1850; commd. col. 27th Ill. Volunteers, 1861, participating in operations in Ky., Tenn. and Miss., 1861; commd. brig. gen. U.S. Volunteer, 1862, maj. gen., 1865; supt. Fed. Union Mining Co., Colo., 1866; U.S. commr. Indian affairs, 1867; a founder Chgo. Soc. Sons of Va. Died Chgo., Mar. 28, 1883; buried Rock Island, Ill.

BUGG, Robert Malone, congressman; b. Boydton, Va., Jan. 20, 1805; attended public schs. Taught sch., Williamson County, Tenn., several years; moved to Giles County, Tenn., engaged in agriculture; justice of peace, 1840; mem. Tenn. Ho. of Reps., 1851-52; mem. U.S. Ho. of Reps. (Whig) from Tenn., 33d Congress, 1853-55; mem. Tenn. Senate, 1871-72. Died Lynnville, Tenn., Feb. 18, 1887; buried McLaurine Cemetery, nr. Lynnville.

BULFINCH, Charles, architect; b. Boston, Aug. 8, 1763; s. Thomas and Susan (Apthorp) B.; grad. Harvard, 1781; m. Hannah Apthorp, Nov. 20, 1788, 11 children including author Thomas Bulfinch. Designed Old Hollis St. Ch., Boston, 1788; a designer Boston Theatre; designed Beacon Monument, 1789; selectman City of Boston, 1791-1817, chmn. bd., 1799-1817; designed Boston State House, 1800; architect India Wharf, Cathedral of Holy Cross, New South Ch., Conn. State House, Me. State Capitol; successor to Benjamin Latrobe as architect Capitol Bldg., Washington, D.C., 1817-30; considered one of best early Am. architects. Died Boston, Apr. 15, 1844.

BULFINCH, Thomas, author; b. Newton, Mass., July 15, 1796; s. Charles and Hannah (Aphtorp); grad. Harvard, 1814; never married. Clk. Mchts. Bank of Boston, 1837-67; sec. Boston Soc. Natural History, 6 years; best writings concerned with mythology and legend; works include: Hebrew Lyrical History, 1853; The Age of Fable (best known work), 1855; The Age of Chivalry, 1858; The Boy Inventor, 1860; Legends of Charlemagne, 1863; Poetry of the Age of Fable, 1863; Shakespeare Adapted for Reading Classes, 1865; Oregon and Eldorado, 1866. Died Boston, May 27, 1867.

BULKLEY, John Williams, educator; b. Fairfield, Conn., Nov. 3, 1802; grad. Hamilton Coll., Clinton, N.Y. Took sea voyage to restore health; tchr., Fairfield, 1825-31; tchr., adminstr., Troy, N.Y., 1831-38; organizer Troy Tchrs. Soc.; tchr. new pub. sch. Albany, N.Y., 1838-40; a founder N.Y. State Tchrs Assn., 1845, pres., 1845, 51; became supt. Williamsburg, Brunswick and Brooklyn (N.Y.) Sch System, 1850, asst. supt., 1873-85; a founder Nat Tchrs. Assn. (now N.E.A.), 1st sec., 4th pres Died June 19, 1888.

BULL, Ephraim Wales, horticulturist, legislator b. Boston, Mar. 4, 1806; s. Epaphras and Esthe (Wales) B.; m. Mary Walker, Sept. 10, 1826. Developed and exhibited Concord grape, 1853; mem Mass. Ho. of Reps., 1855, chmn. com. on agr. chmn. agr. Mass. Senate, 1856; mem. Mass. Bd Agr., 1856-58. Died Sept. 26, 1895.

BULL, John, Continental congressman; b. Princ William's Parish, S.C., circa 1740. Justice o peace, Greenville County; mem. Provincial Ho of Commons, 1772; dep. sec. of Province, 1772 del. 1st, 2d provincial congresses, 1775, 76; mem 1st Gen. Assembly, 1776; mem. S.C. Ho. of Reps. 1778-81, 84; mem. Continental Congress fror S.C., 1784-87; mem. S.C. Senate, 1798. Died S.C. 1802; buried Prince William's Parish Churchyard Beaufort County, S.C.

BULL, John, congressman, physician, clergy man; b. Va., 1803; studied medicine, Balt.; studie theology. Practiced medicine, nr. Glasgow, Mo. ordained to ministry Methodist Ch., becam pastor in Glasgow vicinity; unsuccessful candidat for gov. Mo.; Democratic presdl. elector, 1828 mem. U.S. Ho. of Reps. (Whig) from Mo., 23 Congress, 1833-35; resumed ministerial and med ical duties. Died nr. Rothville, Mo., Feb. 1863 buried Hutcheson Cemetery, nr. Rothville.

BULL, William, colonial ofcl.; b. 1683; s. Stephen Bull; m. Mary Quintyne, at least 1 son William. Mem. S.C. Commons House, 1706-19 served as capt. militia during Tuscarora and Yemassee Indian wars; apptd. lord protector's dep. 1719; mem. gov.'s council, 1721-37; a commr. to manage Indian trade, 1721; an adviser to Jame Oglethorpe in locating Ga.'s 1st settlement, 1733 acting gov. S.C., 1737-38, lt. gov., 1738-55, mad 3 significant constl. changes during his adminstrn. gov. excluded from council of legislative sessions house gained control of financial legislation, hous won right to elect treas. independent of gov. o council. Died Mar. 21, 1755.

BULL, William, colonial gov.; b. Ashley Hall S.C., Sept. 24, 1710; s. William and Mary (Quintyne) B.; M.D., U. Leyden (Holland); m. Hanna Beale, Aug. 17, 1746. Mem. S.C. Ho. of Commons 1736-49, speaker, 1740-42, 44-49; mem. S.C Gov.'s Council, 1748-59; lt. gov. S.C., 1759, actin gov., 60-61, 64-66, 68, 69-71, 73-75, his plan fo free pub. schs. for S.C. was set aside because o approaching Revolutionary War, 1770; Loyalist, departed with Brit. troops, 1782; 1st native America to receive M.D. degree; contributed 150 pounds t Coll. of Phila. (now U. Pa.). Died London, Eng. July 4, 1791.

BULLARD, Henry Adams, congressman, jurist, b. Pepperell, Mass., Sept. 9, 1788; s. John and Elizabeth (Adams) B.; B.A., Harvard, 1807, M.A., 1836; m. Sara Kaiser, Oct. 24, 1816. Mem. band of Mexican revolutionaries, 1812-13; began practice of law, New Orleans, 1813; dist. judge La., 1822-30; mem. U.S. Ho. of Reps. (Whig) from La., 22d-23d, 31st congresses, 1831-34, 50-51; asso. justice La. Supreme Ct., 1834-46; sec. of state La., 1839, prof. civil law U. La. (now Tulane U.), 1847-50 mem. La. Ho. of Reps., 1850; a founder La. Hist. Soc., pres., 1846-51; corr. mem. Mass. Hist. Soc. Died New Orleans, Apr. 17, 1851; buried Girod Street Cemetery, New Orleans.

BULLARD, Otis A., artist; b. Howard, N.Y., Feb. 25, 1816; received instrn. in portrait painting from Philip Hewins; m. dau. of Philip Hewins. Apprenticed to sign and wagon painter; painted portraits of family of Emily Dickinson, Amherst, Mass., 1840; settled in N.Y.C., 1842; exhibited at N.A.D., Am. Art-Union; chief work was panorama of N.Y.C., painted between 1846 and 1850, exhibited throughout N.Y State, shown posthumously in Balt., Cincinnati, Davenport, Ia.; said to have painted over 900 portraits of which only 8 are known. Died N.Y.C., Oct 18, 1853.

BULLITT, Alexander Scott, state ofcl.; b. Dumfreis, Va., 1761; s. Cuthbert and Helen (Scott) B. m. Priscilla Christian, Oct. 1785; m. 2d, Mary Churchill Prather. Mem. Va. Ho. of Dels., 1783 county lt. Jefferson County, Ky., 1786; truste City of Louisville (Ky.), 1787; mem. Ky. Constl Conv., 1792; mem. Ky. Senate, 1792-1800, 04-08 pres. 2d Ky. Constl. Conv., 1799; 1st lt. gov. Ky. 1800-08; Bullitt County (Ky.) named for him Died Apr. 13, 1816.

BULLITT, Henry Massie, med. educator; b Shelby County, Ky., Feb. 28, 1817; s. Cuthber and Harriet (Willit) B.; grad. U. Pa., 1838; m ulia Anderson, May 26, 1841, 7 children; m. 2d, Irs. Sarah Crow Paradise, Sept. 14, 1854, 1 son, daus. Practiced medicine, Louisville, Ky., 1838-5; studied medicine in Europe, 1845-46; lectured n practice of medicine St. Louis Med. Coll., 846-48; prof. materia medica Transylvania U., exington, Ky., 1849-50; founded, operated Ky. ch. Medicine, Louisville, 1850-66; prof. principles nd practice medicine U. Louisville, 1866-68, prof. hysiology, 1867-68; founded, directed Louisville Ied. Coll., 1868-80; contbd. articles to St. Louis Ied. Journal, Translylvania Medical Record, Iedical Examiner, Phila. Died Feb. 5, 1880.

BULLOCH, Archibald, acting gov. Ga.; b. Charleston, S.C., 1729-30; s. James and Jean (Stobo) B.; m. Mary de Veaux, Oct. 9, 1764. Elected to Ga. Ho. of Commons, 1768-73; 1st pres. Ga. Provincial Congress, 1775-77 (as pres. congress was acting gov. and comdr.-in-chief Ga.); led party of Ga. Militia and Indians against Brit. base on Tybee Island, 1777. Died Savannah, Ga., Feb. 22, 1777.

BULLOCH, William Bellinger, senator, banker; avannah, Ga., 1777; s. Archibald Bulloch; tudied law. Admitted to bar, began practice of aw, Savannah, 1797; apptd. U.S. dist. atty., 1804; mayor Savannah, 1812, aldermen, 1814; served ith Savannah Heavy Arty. during War of 1812; olicitor gen. Ga.; a founder State Bank of Ga., res., 1816-43; 2d v.p. Ga. Hist. Soc., 1829; ollector of customs, 1849-50; mem. Ga. Ho. of eps., Ga. Senate; mem. U.S. Senate (Democrat, lled vacancy) from Ga., Apr. 8, 1813-Nov. 6, 813. Died Savannah, May 6, 1852; buried Laurel Grove Cemetery.

BULLOCK, Alexander Hamilton, gov, Mass.; b. Royalston, Mass., Mar. 2, 1816; s. Rufus Bullock; grad. Amherst Coll., 1836; LL.D. (hon.), Harvard, 1866; m. Elvira Hazard, 1 son, 2 daus. Admitted to Mass. bar, 1841; mem. Mass. Legislature, 1845-49, 62-64, Mass. Senate, 1849; editor Aegis, Worcester, Mass., 1850; mayor Worcester, 858; gov. Mass., 1866-78. Died Worcester, Jan. 7, 1882.

BULLOCK, James Dunwoody, naval officer; b. avannah, Ga., June 25, 1823; s. Maj. James Stephens and Hester (Elliott) B.; attended U.S. Naval Sch., Phila., 1844-45; m. Elizabeth Euphemia Caskie, Nov. 19, 1851; m. 2d, Mrs. Harriott Cross Foster, Jan. 1857. Became midshipman U.S. Navy, 839, served in ship United States, then in sloop f war Decatur, stationed in Brazil area; served in attleship Delaware in Mediterranean Sea, 1842; erved in Pacific Coast survey, 1849-51; succeeded t. D.D. Porter in command of mail steamer Georgia, ater retired from navy; entered pvt. business, N.Y.; ecame fgn. naval agt. to secure vessels in Eng. or Confederacy during Civil War; made 1st trip to London, 1861, secured aid of Fraser, Trenholm & Co. in building Confederate vessels, responsible for onstrn. and equipment of all Confederate blockade-unners except the Georgia; returned to Eng., 1862, ecured constrn. of ships Florida and Alabama, forced to leave by English pressure and stricter enforcement of Fgn. Enlistment Act; went to Paris, secured French promise of non-intervention in building Confederate ships in French ports; engaged in cotton us., Liverpool, Eng., after Civil War. Author: The Secret Service of the Confederate States in Europe history of his secret service during Civil War), vols., 1884. Died Jan. 7, 1901.

BULLOCK, Stephen, congressman; b. Rehoboth, Mass., Oct. 10, 1735; attended common schs. aught sch.; served as capt. 6th Co., Col. Thomas Carpenter's Regt., during Revolutionary War, erved in Battle of R.I., 1778; del. 1st Mass. Constl. Conv., 1780; mem. Mass. Ho. of Reps., 783, 85-86, 95-96; mem. U.S. Ho. of Reps. (Federalist) from Mass., 5th Congress, 1797-99; judge Bristol County (Mass.) Ct. of Common Pleas; mem. Mass. Gov.'s Council, 1803-05. Died Rehoboth, Feb. 2, 1816; buried Burial Place Hill.

BULLOCK, William A., inventor; b. Greenville, N.Y., 1813; 1 dau. Apprentice to iron founder nd machinist, Catskill, N.Y., 1821-34; owner achine shop (developed shingle-cutting machine), Prattsville, N.Y., 1836-38; established unsuccessful shingle mfg. firm, Savannah, Ga.; then opened hop making hay and cotton presses of his own esign, also artifical legs, N.Y.C.; opened patent gy., machine shop (3 original designs came rom this shop, grain drill, seed planter, lath itting machine), Phila., 1849; printed daily newspaper The Banner of The Union, 1849-53, became nterested in printing machinery, devoted rest of fe to devel. and eventual patenting of Bullock ress which revolutionized printing by printing n both sides of the paper, printing from continuous roll of paper and cutting newsprint either efore of after printing, 1863. Died Apr. 12, 1867.

BULLOCK, Wingfield, congressman; b. Spotsylvania, Va.; studied law. Moved to Ky.; mem. Ky. Senate, 1812-14; mem. U.S. Ho. of Reps. om Ky., 17th Congress, Mar. 4-Oct. 13, 1821. Died Shelbyville, Ky., Oct. 13, 1821; buried old arying ground nr. Shelbyville.

BUMSTEAD, Freeman Josiah, surgeon; b. Boston, Apr. 21, 1826; s. Josiah Freeman and Lucy Douglas (Willis) B.; grad. Williams Coll., 1847; attended Tremont Med. Sch.; M.D., Harvard, 1851; m. Mary Josephine White, 1861. Took trip to Europe, 1851-52; began practice of medicine in N.Y.C., 1852; surgeon No. Dispensary, N.Y.C., 1853-55, N.Y. Eye and Ear Infirmary, 1857-62; apptd. surgeon to venereal wards Charity Hosp., 1860, decided to devote life work to venereal diseases; prof. venereal disease Coll. Physicians and Surgeons, Columbia, 1867-71; traveled abroad for reasons of health, 1871-73. Translator and editor Treatise on the V.D. (John Hunter), 1853, Pathology and Treatment of V.D., 1861. Died N.Y.C., Nov. 28, 1879.

BUNCE, Oliver Bell, author, publisher; b. N.Y.C., Feb. 8, 1825; 4 children. Clk. in bookstore; wrote 1st play The Morning of Life, produced at Bowery Theatre, 1848, founded Bunce & Brother, publishers, 1853; mgr. James C. Gregory, publishers; literary mgr. Harper & Bros.; literary mgr. D. Appleton & Co., editor Appleton's Jour., conceived idea successful Picturesque Am. etc. series; novels include: The Romance of The Revolution, 1852; Bensley, 1863; The Opinions and Disputations of Bachelor Bluff, 1881; The Adventures of Timian Terrystone, 1885; plays include: Marco Bozzaris, 1850; Love in '76, 1857. Died May 15, 1890.

BUNCH, Samuel, congressman; b. Grainger County, Tenn., Dec. 4, 1786; attended public schs. Engaged in agriculture; served as capt. co. of mounted riflemen under Gen. Jackson during Creek War, participated in attack on Hillibeetown, 1813; sheriff Grainger County, several years; mem. U.S. Ho. of Reps. (Whig) from Tenn., 23d-24th congresses, 1833-37. Died on his farm nr. Rutledge, Tenn., Sept. 5, 1849; buried on his farm.

BUNDY, Hezekiah Sanford, congressman, lawyer; b. Marietta, O., Aug. 15, 1817; attended public schs., studied law. Engaged in agriculture; admitted to bar, 1850, practiced law, 1850-60; entered iron bus., 1860; mem. Ohio Ho. of Reps., 1848, 50, Ohio Senate, 1855; Republican presdl. elector, 1860; mem. U.S. Ho. of Reps. (Rep.) from Ohio, 39th, 43d, 53d congresses, 1865-67, 73-75, Dec. 4, 1893-95; moved to Wellston, O., 1887, resumed practice of law. Died Wellston, Dec. 12, 1895; buried City Cemetery.

BUNDY, Jonas Mills, journalist; b. Coldbrook, N.H., Apr. 17, 1835; grad. Beloit Coll., 1853. Reporter for Milw. Daily Wisconsin; commd. maj. 3rd regt. U.S. Volunteer Inf., 1861-65; drama critic N.Y. Evening Post, 1865-68; a founder, editor-in--chief N.Y. Evening Mail, 1868-81, N.Y. Evening Mail and Express, 1881-91. chosen by James A. Garfield to write his campaign biography, 1880. Died Paris, France, Sept. 8, 1891.

BUNDY, Solomon, congressman, lawyer; b. Oxford, N.Y., May 22, 1823; attended Oxford Acad.; studied law. Taught sch. for several years; became a mcht.; admitted to bar, 1859, began practice of law, Oxford; justice of peace, also clk. bd. suprs. Chenango County (N.Y.); dist. atty. Chenango County, 1862-65; mem. U.S. Ho. of Reps. (Republican) from N.Y., 45th Congress, 1877-79. Died Oxford, Jan. 13, 1889; buried Riverview Cemetery.

BUNNER, Henry Cuyler, journalist; b. Oswego, N.Y., Aug. 3, 1855; s. Rudolph and Ruth (Tuckerman) B.; m. Alice Learned, 1886, 3 children. Created Am. cartoon of Blaine as the "Tattoed Man," 1884; editor Am. comic weekly Puck, 1877-96. Author: Airs from Arcady and Elsewhere (1st poems), 1884; The Midge, 1886; The Story of a New York House, 1887; The Runaway Browns, 1892; In Partnership: Studies in Storytelling, 1884; Short Sixes, 1890; Zodoc Pines, 1891; More Short Sixes, 1894; Made in France, 1893. Died Nutley, N.J., May 11, 1896.

BUNNER, Rudolph, congressman; b. Savannah, N.Y., Aug. 17, 1779; grad. Columbia, 1798; studied law. Admitted to bar, practiced law, Newburgh, N.Y., 1819-22; moved to Oswego, N.Y., 1822; became a mfr., also an extensive landowner; dir. Oswego Cloth & Carpet Mfg. Co.; mem. 1st bd. dirs. Oswego Canal Co.; mem. U.S. Ho. of Reps. (Adams Democrat) from N.Y., 20th Congress, 1827-29. Died Oswego, July 16, 1837; buried Riverside Cemetery.

BUNTLINE, Ned, see Judson, Edward Zane Carroll.

BURBRIDGE, Stephen Gano, army officer; b. Scott County, Ky., Aug. 1, 1831; s. Capt. Robert and Eliza Ann (Barnes) B.; attended Georgetown (Ky.) Coll., Ky. Mil. Inst.; m. Lizzie Goff, 1, dau., Sara R. Studied law; farmed in Logan County, Ky.; commd. col. 26th Ky. Inf. in U.S. Army, 1861; served with Army of Ohio at battle of Shiloh; promoted brig. gen. U.S. Volunteers, 1862; active at Vicksburg campaign; given temporary command of Dist. of Ky., 1864, successful in his mil. operation, his civilian responsibilities; but antagonized moderate Union faction with his civilian policies; accused of using extra legal methods in Ky. in order to assure Lincoln's reelection, 1864; suppressed Ky. Home Guards, disbanded state troops raised to resist guerrillas; called "murderer" for his brutal suppression of guerrilla forces; relieved of command, 1865; his methods earned such general hatred from populace that he did not feel safe to live in Ky. Died Bklyn., Dec. 2, 1894.

BURCH, John Chilton, congressman; b. Boone County, Mo., Feb. 1, 1826; attended Bonne Femme Acad., Kemper Coll.; studied law, Jefferson City. Admitted to bar, practiced law; dep. clk. Cole County; asst. adj. gen. Mo.; moved to Cal., 1850, worked in mines until 1851; clk. Trinity County; apptd. dist. atty., 1843; mem. Cal. Assembly, 1856, Cal. Senate, 1857-59; mem. U.S. Ho. of Reps. (Democrat) from Cal., 36th Congress, 1859-61; resumed practice of law, San Francisco; code commr., 4 years. Died San Francisco, Aug. 31, 1885; buried City Cemetery, Sacramento, Cal.

BURCHARD, Samuel Dickinson, clergyman; b. Steuben, N.Y., Sept. 6, 1812; s. Jabez and Lucina (Brton) B.; grad. Centre Coll., 1836. Licensed to preach, 1838; pastor Houston St. Presbyn. Ch., N.Y.C., 1839-79; chancellor Ingham U., 1866-74; pastor Murray Hill Presbyn. Ch., N.Y.C., 1779-85; pres. Rutgers Femal Acad.; gave speech supporting Republican James Blaine during presdl. election of 1884, in which he identified Blaine with opposition to "rum, Romanism, and rebellion", resulted in accusations of anti-Catholic sentiments against Blaine which may have cost him the votes of N.Y. State (whose electoral votes decided the outcome of the election). Died Saratoga, N.Y., Sept. 25, 1891.

BURD, George, congressman; b. 1793; studied law. Admitted bar, Carlisle, Pa., 1810, practiced law; mem. U.S. Ho. of Reps. from Pa., 22d-23d congresses, 1831-35; moved to Mercer County, 1843. Died Bedford, Pa., Jan. 13, 1844; buried Bedford Cemetery.

BURDEN, Henry, ironmaster, inventor; b. Dunblane, Scotland, Apr. 20, 1791; s. Peter and Elizabeth (Abercrombie) B.; m. Helen McQuat, Jan. 17, 1821. Came to Am., 1819; patented machine for making wrought iron spikes, 1825; 1st patented horseshoe machine (his most widely known invention), 1835. Died Troy, N.Y., Jan., 19, 1871; buried family vault, Albany (N.Y.) Rural Cemetery.

BURDETT, Herbert C., architect; b. Boston, 1855; grad. Harvard. Received early archtl. tng. with firm Hartwell & Richardson, Boston; moved to Buffalo, circa 1880, practiced as architect under firm name Burling & Burdett; designed numerous bldgs., including Saturn Club (best known), also several pvt. homes in Buffalo and suburbs. Died Apr. 19, 1891.

BURGES, Dempsey, congressman; b. Shiloh, Camden County, N.C., 1751. Mem. Provincial Congress, 1775-76; served as maj. Pasquotank Minutemen, later as lt. col. Gregory's Continental Regt. during Revolutionary War; mem. U.S. Ho. of Reps. from N.C., 4th-5th congresses, 1795-99. Died Camden County, Jan. 13, 1800; buried Shiloh Baptist Churchyard.

BURGES, Tristam, congressman; b. Rochester, Mass., Feb. 26, 1770; studied medicine, Wrentham; grad. R.I. Coll. (now Brown U.), 1796; studied law. Admitted to bar, 1799, began practice of law, Providence, R.I.; mem. R.I. Ho. of Reps., 1811; prominent mem. Federal Party; apptd. chief justice R.I. Supreme Ct., 1815; prof. oratory Brown U.; mem. U.S. Ho. of Reps. from R.I., 19th-23d congresses, 1825-35; unsuccessful Whig candidate for gov. R.I., 1836. Died "Watchmoket Farm" (now part of East Providence, R.I.), Oct. 13, 1853; buried North Burial Ground, Providence.

BURGESS, Edward, entomologist, yacht designer; b. West Sandwich, Mass., June 30, 1848; s. Benjamin and Cordelia (Ellis) B.; A.B., Harvard, 1871; m. Caroline Sullivant, 2 children. Sec. Nat. History Soc. Boston, 1872; instr. entomology Harvard, 1879-82; mem. U.S. Naval Bd., 1887; permanent chmn. U.S. Life Saving Service, 1888; designed yachts Puritan, Mayflower and Volunteer (winners of Internat. Yacht Race). Died Boston, July 12, 1891.

BURGESS, George, clergyman; b. Providence, R.I., Oct. 31, 1809; s. Thomas B. and Mary (Mackie) B.; grad. Brown U., 1826, studied theology, 1829-31; read law in father's office, Providence; m. Sophia Kip, Oct. 26, 1846. Tutor, Brown U., 1829-31; travelled in Europe, attended lectures at univs. of Berlin, Bonn, Göttingen (Germany), 1831-33; ordained priest Episcopal Ch., 1834; rector Christ Ch., Hartford, Conn., 1834-37; bishop of Me. Diocese, 1847-66; moved to Gardiner, Me. Author: Poems of the Rt. Rev. George Burgess, 1868; The Last Enemy, Conquering and Conquered, 1850. Died on ship off coast of Haiti, Apr. 23, 1866; buried Christ Ch. Cemetery, Gardiner.

BURGEVINE, Henry Andrea, fgn. mercenary officer, b. probably Chapel Hill, N.C., 1836; s. Gen. Andrea and Julia (Gillette) B. Fought in Crimean War; next heard of in China; became mercenary officer for Fred Townsend Ward who was attempting to capture Sungkiang (China) from Taiping rebels, 1860, left 3d in command of army (about 4000 men) after Ward's death, 1862, soon came to command entire force; enlisted his army on side of imperial rulers (directly subordinated to Gov. Li Hung Chang); dismissed by gov. for uncontrollable, insubordinate and mutinous conduct; formed small army of 100 and eventually joined remains of Ward's old army and was captured; following his release was delivered to U.S. consul at Shanghai; set free upon his parole to leave China; returned to Fukien on route to join last of Taiping rebels, captured by imperialist forces. Drowned (while being conveyed with other prisoners in small boat which capsized), June 26, 1865.

BURGIS, William, engraver; b. Eng.; m. Mrs. Mehitable Selby, Oct. 1, 1728. Came to N.Y.C., 1718, moved to Boston; partner in engraving business with William Price and Thomas Selby; following Selby's sudden death married his widow, exhausted most of wife's inheritance and disappeared, 1731; known engravings include: A South Prospect of Ye Flourishing City of New York; A South East View of the Great Town of Boston; A Prospect of the Colleges in Cambridge in New England; Boston Light.

BURGOYNE, John, army officer, dramatist; b. Sutton Park, Bedfordshire, Eng., 1722; s. Capt. John Burgoyne; attended Westminster Sch.; m. Lady Charlotte Stanley, 1743; 4 illegitimate children (by Susan Caulfield) including Sir John Fox. Cornet, 13th Brit. Light Dragoons, 1740, purchased lt.'s commn., 1741, captaincy, 1743; sold his commn. and went to France, 1746; made capt. 11th Dragoons at start of Seven Years War, 1756; lt. col. Coldstream Guards, 1758; mem. Parliament for Midhurst, 1761, for Preston, 1768-74; served as brig. gen. in Portugese Army, 1762; maj. gen. Brit. Army, 1772; went to Am. to reinforce Gen. Gage, 1774; turned Faneuil Hall (Boston) into playhouse for performances by soldiers, 1775; made 2d in command to Sir Guy Carleton in Canada, 1775; drew up plan for invasion of Northern Am. states to join up with Gen. Sir William Howe at Albany; promoted lt. gen., 1777; surrendered after unsuccessful campaign to Gen. Gates at Saratoga, 1777. Author: The Maid of Oaks, 1774; Blocade of Boston (farce), 1775; The Heiress, 1786 (all plays); The Lord of the Manor, 1780 (comic opera). Died Mayfair, London, Eng., 1792; buried Westminster Abbey, London.

BURKE, Aedanus, congressman, jurist; b. Galway, Ireland, June 16, 1743; studied theology St. Omer, France; studied law, Stafford County, Va., 1769; never married. Visited West Indies; came to Am., settled in S.C.; resigned commn. as lt. 2d S.C. Continental Regt., 1778; judge S.C. Supreme Ct., 1778-80, 85-1802; served as capt. Continental Army, 1780-82; mem. S.C. Ho. of Reps., 1781, 82, 84-89, favored leniency toward Loyalists; a commr. to prepare digest of S.C. laws, 1785; mem. S.C. Conv. to ratify U.S. Constn., 1788, opposed ratification unless amendment added restricting Pres. to 1 term; mem. U.S. Ho. of Reps. from S.C., 1st Congress, 1789-91, opposed U.S. Bank and excise tax, favored U.S. assumption of state debts and slavery; chancellor S.C. Ct. of Equity, 1799-1802. Author: (pamphlets including) An Address to the Freemen of South Carolina, 1783; Considerations on the Order of the Cincinnati (translated into French, German), 1783. Died Charleston, S.C., Mar. 30, 1802; buried "Burnt Church," nr. Jacksonboro, S.C.

BURKE, Charles St. Thomas, actor; b. Mar. 27, 1822; s. Thomas and Cornelia (Thomas) B.; m. Margaret Murcoyne; m. 2d, Mrs. Sutherland; 1 stepdau. Appeared as Prince of Wales in Richard III, Nat. Theatre, N.Y.C., 1836, also as Prince John in Henry IV and as Irus in Ion, 1836; began singing comic songs which added to popularity; traveled as actor through West and South, 1837; returned to East, 1847, spent rest of life acting in theatres of Phila. and N.Y.; portrayed Paul Pry in comedy The Spectre Bridgegroom (John Poole), Ichabod Crane, Sir Andrew Aguecheek, Caleb Plummer, Touchstone, Solon Shingle, Bob Acres, Rip Van Winkle; famous for line "Are we so soon forgot when we are gone?" Died N.Y., Nov. 10, 1854.

BURKE, Edmund, polit. philosopher; b. Dublin, Ireland, Jan. 12, 1729; s. Richard and Mrs. (Nagle) B.; grad. Trinity Coll., U. Dublin, 1748, LL.D. (hon.), 1780; studied law Middle Temple, London, Eng.; m. Jane Nugent, 1756; children—Richard, Christopher. Aided in rewriting book An Account of the European Settlements in America (published under his name), 1757; mem. Brit. Ho. of Commons, 1766-94; his 1st speech was for reception and consideration of petitions from Am. colonies against Stamp Tax; opposed most of Brit. colonial legislation for Am. on grounds of practicality (it would be unpopular and cause trouble), urged compromise of issues between colonies and mother country; apptd. colonial agt. for N.Y., 1771, worked with Benjamin Franklin (colonial agt. for Pa., other states) against colonial taxation; gave speech "On American Taxation" calling for compromise (made him 1 of most popular Englishmen with Americans, as they felt he was on colonial side), 1774; spoke in opposition to Boston Port Acts (legislative punishment for Boston Tea Party), 1775, tried in vain to compromise the issues which were to cause Am. Revolution; offered 13 Resolutions for Conciliation (basing position on humanity, reason and justice, rather than on Am. position of natural rights), 1775; opposed use of Indians against Am. states, 1778, led attacks on conduct of war under misguided belief that issues could still be compromised; elected lord rector Glasgow (Scotland) U., 1784; as a polit. philosopher, stated what are now the traditional conservative theories in his speeches and books on French Revolution. Author: Thoughts on the Causes of the Present Discontent, 1770; Reflections on the French Revolution, 1790. Died Beaconsfield, Eng., July 7, 1797; buried Parish Ch., Beaconsfield.

BURKE, Edmund, congressman; b. Westminster, Vt., Jan. 23, 1809; attended public schs.; studied law. Admitted to bar, 1826, began practice of law, Colebrook, N.H.; moved to Claremont, N.H., 1833; editor N.H. Argus (merged with Spectator, Newport, N.H., 1834), several years; commd. adj. N.H. Militia, 1837, brigade insp., 1838; mem. U.S. Ho. of Reps. (Democrat) from N.H., 26th-28th congresses, 1839-45; commr. of patents (apptd. by Pres. Polk), 1846-50; del. Democratic nat. convs., Balt., 1844, 52; presiding officer N.H. Dem. Conv., 1867; mem. N.H. Bd. of Agr., 1871. Died Newport, Jan. 25, 1882; buried Maple Grove Cemetery.

BURKE, Thomas, gov. N.C.; b. County Galway, Ireland, 1747; s. Ulrick and Letitia (Ould) B.; ed. Dublin (Ireland) U.; m. Mary Freeman, 1770, 1 dau., Mary. Licensed to practice law by Superior Ct. Orange County (N.C.), 1772; mem. 3d N.C. Provincial Congress, 1774-75, mem. 13 coms.; mem. Continental Congress from N.C., 1776-78; gov. N.C. 1781-82 (so successful in organizing N.C. mil. forces that Torys made a raid on Hillsboro for the express purpose of capturing him, 1781, he escaped 1782); Burke County, N.C. named after him. Died Hillsboro, N.C., Dec. 2, 1783.

BURLEIGH, Charles Calistus, abolitionist; b. Plainfield, Conn., Nov. 3, 1810; s. Rixaldo and Lydia (Bradford) B.; m. Gertrude Kimber, Oct. 2, 1842, 3 children. Editor, Unionist (an abolitionist newspaper), Brooklyn, Conn., 1833-35; admitted to the bar, 1835; agt., lectr. Middlesex Anti-Slavery Soc., 1835-38; editor Pa. Freeman, 1838; mem. bus. com. Am. Anti-Slavery Sc., corr. sec., 1859; opposed capital punishment; supported temperance and female suffrage movements. Author: Thoughts on the Death Penalty, 1845; The Anti-Slavery History of the John Brown Year, 1861; Slavery and the North, 1855. Died Northampton, Mass., June 13, 1878.

BURLEIGH, John Holmes, congressman, businessman; b. South Berwick, Me., Oct. 9, 1822; s. William Burleigh; attended local acad. Became a sailor at 16 years of age, commanded ship, 1846-53; became woolen mfr., South Berwick, 1853, also engaged in banking; mem. Me. Ho. of Reps., 1862, 64, 66, 72; del. Republican Nat. Conv., Balt., 1864; mem. U.S. Ho. of Reps. (Rep.) from Me., 43d-44th congresses, 1873-77. Died South Berwick, Dec. 5, 1877; buried Portland Street Cemetery.

BURLEIGH, Walter Atwood, congressman; b. Waterville, Me., Oct. 25, 1820; attended public schs.; studied medicine, Burlington, Vt., also N.Y.C.; studied law. Served as pvt. in Aroostook War, 1839; practiced medicine, Richmond, Me., then Kittanning, Pa.; Indian agt., Greenwood, Dakota Territory, 1861-65; mem. U.S. Congress (Republican) from Dakota Territory, 39th-40th congresses, 1865-69; mem. Dakota Territorial Council, 1877; a contractor and farmer; moved to Miles City, Mont., 1879, practiced law; mem. spl. session Mont. Territorial Council, 1887; del. Mont. Constl. Conv., 1889; mem. 1st Mont. Ho. of Reps.; pros. atty. Custer County, 1889-90; returned to S.D., 1893; mem. S.D. Senate, 1893. Died Yankton, S.D., Mar. 7, 1896; buried Yankton Cemetery.

BURLEIGH, William, congressman; b. Northwood, N.H., Oct. 24, 1785; attended common schs.; studied law; at least 1 son, John Holmes Burleigh. Taught sch. for several years; admitted to bar, 1815, began practice of law, South Berwick, Me.; mem. U.S. Ho. of Reps. (Adams Democrat) from Me., 18th-20th congresses, 1823-27. Died South Berwick, July 2, 1827; buried Portland Street Cemetery.

BURLEIGH, William Henry, journalist, reformc b. Woodstock, Conn., Feb. 2, 1812; s. Rinaldo a Lydia (Bradford) B.; m. Harriet Adelia Frink; r 2d, Celia Burr, 1865; 7 children. Journeyma printer Stonington (Conn.) Phoenix, 1830-3 printer, reporter Schenectady (N.Y.) Cabinet, 183 asst. editor Unionist, Brooklyn, Conn., 1833-3 lectr. for Am. Anti-Slavery Soc., 1836-43; edit Literary Journal, Schenectady, 1836-37, Christi Freeman (newspaper of Am. Anti-Slavery Soc. Hartford, Conn., 1843-49, Prohibitionist (paper Albany, N.Y., 1849-55; lectr. for N.Y. Sta Temperance Soc., 1849-55; harbor master Port N.Y., 1855-70. Author: Poems, 1841; The Ru Fiend and Other Poems, 1871. Died Bklyn., Ma 18, 1871.

BURLESON, Edward, army officer, legislato b. Buncombe County, N.C., Dec. 15, 1798; s. Jam and Elizabeth (Shipman) B.; m. Sarah Owen, 181 Commd. capt. Mo. Militia, 1816, later col.; comm col. Tenn. Militia, 1823; moved to Tex., 183 settled on Colorado River at extreme edge of wh was then the frontier; local leader against Indi raids; commd. lt. col. Tex. Army, 1832; participa ed in Tex. Revolution against Mexico, command Tex. Army besieging Mexican Gen. Cos, San Antoni 1835, participated in Battle of San Jacinto; me 1st Senate of Republic of Tex., 1836; commd. co Tex. Army, 1838, served in Cherokee War, 183 Comanche War, 1840; v.p. Republic of Tex., 184 defeated for presidency, 1844; mem. Tex. Sta Senate, 1849-51. Died Austin, Tex., Dec. 26, 185

BURLING, Edward, architect; b. Newburgh, N.Y 1819. Carpenter's apprentice; engaged as carpente until 1843; went to Chgo., 1843; began as builde later established archtl. office; 2d profl. archite to practice in Chgo.; planned many bldgs. prior Chgo. Fire of 1871, including Marine Bank Bldg 1852-55, St. James Episcopal Ch., 1857, 1st Na Bank Bldg., 1860, Chamber of Commerce (consic ered his most noteworthy bldg.), Tribune Bldg 1868, Garrett Bldg., Portland Block, commd. to re build all these bldgs. (except C. of C.) after the fir supervised erection Custom House, U.S. Post Offic asso. with Dankmar Adler, 1871-78, work includir Methodist Ch. block; asso. with Francis M. Whit house under firm name Burling & Whitehouse, de signed 1st Nat. Bank, Chgo., 1882, Epiphany Epis copal Ch., Chgo., 1885, Yerkes House (Hotel) Trinity Ch., St. Louis, 1888. Died Mar. 1892.

BURLINGAME, Anson, congressman, diploma b. New Berlin, N.Y., Nov. 14, 1820; s. Joel a Freelove (Angell) B.; grad. U. Mich., 1841, Ha vard Law Sch., 1846; m. Jane Livermore, June 1847, 3 children including Edward Livermore. Ac mitted to Mass. bar, 1847; elected to Mass. Senat 1852; mem. Mass. Constl. Conv., 1853; mem. U.S Ho. of Reps. from Mass., 34th-36th congresse 1855-61; U.S. minister to China, 1861-67; sp minister to fgn. powers for Chinese Govt., 186 70, negotiated Burlingame Treaty (establishing fr immigration between U.S. and China), 1868; tour Europe in an effort to obtain similar treaties. Di St. Petersburg, Russia, Feb. 23, 1870; buried M Auburn Cemetery, Cambridge, Mass.

BURNAP, George Washington, clergyman; Merrimack, N.H., Nov. 30, 1802; s. Jacob a Elizabeth (Brooks) B.; grad. Harvard, 1824; n Nancy Williams, July 18, 1831. Ordained past Unitarian Ch., Baltl., 1828; regent U. Md.; a original trustee Peabody Inst.; a founder Md. His Soc. Author: Lectures on the Doctrines of Chri tianity in Controversy between Unitarians and oth Denominations of Christians, 1835; Lectures Young Men, 1840; Lectures on the Sphere and Du of Woman, 1840; Lectures on the History of Chris ianity, 1842; Expository Lectures on the Princip Passages of the Scriptures which Relate to t Doctrine of the Trinity, 1845; Popular Objectio to Unitarian Christianity Considered and Answere 1848; Discourses on the Rectitude of Human Natur 1850; Christianity, Its Essence and Evidence, 185 Died Balt., Sept. 8, 1859.

BURNELL, Barker, congressman; b. Nantucke Mass., Jan. 30, 1798. Mem. Mass. Ho. of Reps 1819, Mass. Constl. Conv., 1820, Mass. Senat 1824-25; del. Whig Nat. Conv., Harrisburg, Pa 1840; mem. U.S. Ho. of Reps. (Whig) fro Mass., 27th-28th congresses, 1841-43. Died Was ington, D.C., June 15, 1843; buried Congression Cemetery; reinterred Prospect Hill Cemetery, Na tucket, 1844.

BURNES, James Nelson, congressman, busines man; b. Marion County, Ind., Aug. 22, 1827; gra Harvard Law Sch., 1853. Admitted to bar, bega practice of law, Mo.; atty. Dist. of Mo., 185 Democratic presdl. elector, 1856; judge Ct. Common Pleas, 1868-72; a banker and railro exec.; pres. Mo. Valley R.R. Co.; prin. owne pres. St. Joseph Waterworks Co.; mem. U.S. H of Reps. (Democrat) from Mo, 48th-50th co gresses, 1883-89. Died Washington, D.C., Jan. 2 1889; buried Mt. Mora Cemetery, St. Joseph, Mo.

BURNET, David Gouverneur, 1st pres. Texas; b. Newark, N.J., Apr. 4, 1788; s. William and Gertrude (Gouverneur) B.; m. Miss Estis, 1831. Commd. . of Francisco de Miranda's expdn. which attempted to free Venezuela from Spain, 1806; apptd. one of 1st 3 dist. judges of Tex., 1834; mem. gen. Consultation which issued Declaration of Independence for Tex., Washington on the Brazos, Tex., 1836; pres. ad interim (1st pres.) Republic of Texas, 1836, v.p., 1840-42; sec. of state Tex., 1846-47; elected to U.S. Senate by 1st Reconstrn. Legislature, 1866, was not seated; del. to Nat. Democratic Conv., 1868; presdl. elector. Died Galveston, Tex., Dec. 5, 1870

BURNET, Jacob, senator, coll. pres.; b. Newark, N.J., Feb. 22, 1770; s. Dr. William and Mary (Camp) B.; grad. Princeton, 1791, LL.D. (hon.); LL.D. (hon.), U. Lexington; m. Rebecca Wallace, Jan. 2, 1800, 11 children. Admitted to N.J. bar, 1796; mem. Territorial Councils of Ohio, 1799-1802; mem. Ohio Legislature, 1812-16; a leader in passage of Nat. Land Act. of 1820; judge Ohio Supreme Ct., 1821-28; mem. U.S. Senate (Federalist) from Ohio, 1828-31; mem. commn. apptd. by Va. and Ky. to settle controversy over statute of limitation passed by Ky., 1831; pres. Cincinnati br. U.S.Bank; gave presdl. nomination speech for William Henry Harrison, 1839; pres. Cincinnati Astron. Soc.; 1st pres. Cincinnati Colonization Soc.; a founder, 1st pres. Cincinnati Coll.; pres. Med. Coll. of Ohio. Author: Notes on the Northwest Territory, 1847. Died Cincinnati, May 10, 1853; buried Spring Grove Cemetery, Cincinnati.

BURNET, William, colonial gov.; b. The Hague, Holland, Mar. 1688; s. Gilbert and Mary (Scott) B.; attended Trinity Coll., Cambridge (Eng.) U., 1701; m. Anna Van Horne. Came to Am., 1720; provincial gov. N.Y. and N.J., 1720-28; gov. Mass., 1725-29. Died Boston, Sept. 7, 1729.

BURNET, William, Continental congressman, surgeon-gen.; b. Elizabeth, N.J., Dec. 13, 1730; s. Dr. Ichabod and Hannah B.; grad. Coll of N.J. (now Princeton), 1749; m. Mary Camp; m.2d, Gertrude Gouverneur; fourteen children including Jacob Burnet. Chairman of the Newark (N.J.) Com. Pub. Safety, 1775; chmn. Essex County (N.J.) Com. Safety; mem. Continental Congress, 1776-77, 80-81; presiding judge Essex County Cts., 1776; apptd. presiding judge N.J. Ct. Common Pleas; elected surgeon-gen. Eastern dist. U.S. Army, 1777; a founder, pres. N.J. Med. Soc. Died Oct. , 1791.

BURNETT, Charles Henry, otologist; b. Phila., May 28, 1842; s. Eli Seal and Hannah (Mustin) B.; grad. Yale, 1864; M.D., U. Pa., 1867; studied otology in Europe, 1870-72; m. Anna Davis, June 18, 1874. Practiced medicine specializing in otology, Phila., 1872-1902; prof. otology Phila. Polyclinic; mem. Coll. Physicians of Phila.; pres. Am. Otol. Soc.; developed operation for relief of progressive deafness and vertigo by performing tympanotomy and removing incus. Author: The Ear; Its Anatomy, Physiology, and Diseases, 1877; Hearing and How to Keep It, 1879. Editor: System of Diseases of the Ear, Nose, and Throat, 1893; Textbook of Diseases of the Ear, Nose and Throat, 1901. Died Bryn Mawr, Pa., Jan. 30, 1902.

BURNETT, Henry Cornelius, congressman, lawyer; b. Essex County, Va., Oct. 5, 1825; attended acad. at Hopkinsville, Ky.; studied law. Admitted to bar, 1847, began practice of law, Cadiz, Ky.; clk. Trigg County (Ky.) Circuit Ct., 1851-53; mem. U.S. Ho. of Reps. (Democrat) from Ky., 34th-37th congresses, 1855-Dec. 3, 1861 (expelled); served as col. 8th Regt., Ky. Inf., Confederate Army, during Civil War; pres. Ky. So. Conf., Russellville, 1861; pres. Sovereignty Conv. (passed ordinance of secession, organized state govt.), Russellville, 1861; rep. from Ky. to Provisional Confederate Congress, 1861-62; senator from Ky. to 1st, 2d Confederate Congresses, 1862-65. Died Hopkinsville, Oct. 1, 1866; buried East End Cemetery, Cadiz.

BURNETT, Joseph, mfr., philanthropist; b. Southborough, Mass., Nov. 11, 1820; s. Charles and Keziah (Pond) B.; m. Josephine Cutter, 1847. Partner (with Theodore Metcalf) in perfumery mfg., Southborough, 1837-54; established own firm Joseph Burnett & Co., Southborough, 1854, pres., 1854-94; owned Deerfoot Farm, nr. Southborough, 1847-94, one of 1st in New Eng. to raise high bred stock; built 1st Episcopal Ch. in Southborough, 1860; founded St. Mark's Sch., Southborough, 1865; mem. Southborough Sch. Bd.; mem. Mass. Prison Commn. Died Aug. 11, 1894.

BURNETT, Peter Hardeman, gov. Cal.; b. Nashville, Tenn., Nov. 15, 1807; s. George and Dorothy (Hardeman) Burnet; m. Harriet Rogers, Aug. 20, 1828. Pros. atty., Liberty, Mo., 1840-42; mem. wagon train from Independence (Mo.) to Ore., 1843; mem. Legislative Com. of Ore., 1844; judge Ore. Supreme Ct., 1845; mem. Ore. Territorial Legislature, 1848; moved to Cal., 1848; judge Cal. Supreme Ct., 1849, 57-58; 1st gov. Cal. 1849-51, resigned before news of granting statehood reached Cal.; founder, pres. Pacific Bank, San Francisco. Died San Francisco, May 17, 1895.

BURNHAM, Alfred Avery, congressman; b. Windham, Conn., Mar. 8, 1819; attended coll. 1 year; studied law. Admitted to bar, 1843, began practice of law, Windham; mem. Conn. Ho. of Reps., 1844-45, 50, 58, 70, speaker, 1858, 70; clk. Conn. Senate, 1847; lt. gov., 1857; mem. U.S. Ho. of Reps. (Republican) from Conn., 36th-37th congresses, 1859-63. Died Windham, Apr. 11, 1879; buried Windham Cemetery.

BURNS, Anthony, slave; b. Stafford County, Va., May 31, 1834; attended Oberlin Coll., 1857-62. Escaped from Va., 1854, fled to Boston, arrested, 1854, sent back to Va. (after abolitionists in Boston stormed Ct. House in unsuccessful attempt to free him); Boston abolitionists bought his freedom, 1854; pastor Negro Baptist Ch., Indpls., 1860, St. Catharines, Can., 1862. Died St. Catharines, July 27, 1862.

BURNS, Joseph, congressman; b. Waynesboro, Va., Mar. 11, 1800; attended rural schs., Ohio. Engaged in agriculture, Coshocton County, O.; auditor Coshocton County, 1821-38; mem. Ohio Ho. of Reps., 1838-40; county clk., 1843-51; served as maj. gen. Ohio Militia; mem. U.S. Ho. of Reps. (Democrat) from Ohio, 35th Congress, 1857-59; entered drug bus., Coshocton; probate judge Coshocton County. Died Coshocton, May 12, 1875; buried Oak Ridge Cemetery.

BURNS, Otway, shipbuilder; b. Onslow County, N.C., 1775; son of Otway Burns; m. Miss Grant; m. 2d, Jane Hall, 1814; m. 3d, Jane Smith, 1842. Commanded privateer Snapdragon in service of U.S., 1812-15, preyed on Brit. commerce full length of Americas' Atlantic seaboard; captured or destroyed $2.5 million worth of Brit. commerce in period of 3 months in 1813; shipbuilder, New Bern, N.C., 1815-35; mem. N.C. Gen. Assembly, 1821-35; lost his fortune through investments in Dismal Swamp Canal; keeper Brant Island Schoal Light, 1835-40. Died Oct. 25, 1850.

BURNS, Robert, congressman, physician; b. Hudson, Hillsboro County, N.H., Dec. 12, 1792; studied medicine, Warren; attended Dartmouth Med. Sch., 1815. Taught sch.; began practice of medicine, Warren; practiced medicine, Hebron, N.H., 1818-35; fellow N.H. Med. Soc., 1824; mem. N.H. Senate, 1831; mem. U.S. Ho. of Reps. (Democrat) from N.H., 23d-24th congresses, 1833-37; practiced medicine, Plymouth, N.H., until 1866. Died Plymouth, June 26, 1866; buried Trinity Churchyard, Holderness, N.H.

BURNSIDE, Ambrose Everett, army officer, senator, gov. R.I.; b. Liberty, Ind., May 23, 1824; s. Edghill and Pamelia (Brown) B.; grad. U.S. Mil. Acad., 1847; m. Mary Bishop, Apr. 27, 1852. Invented a breech-loading rifle; maj. gen. R.I. Militia; organized 1st R.I. Regt., 1861; commd. brig. gen., 1861, maj. gen., Mar. 18, 1862; comdr. Army of Potomac, 1862; relieved of his command upon failure of Fredericksburg campaign; served under Grant at Petersburg, failed to force way through after mine explosion, resigned from U.S. Army upon ct. of inquiry's assertion of blame, 1865; gov. R.I., 1866-69; mem. U.S. Senate from R.I., 1875-81. Died Bristol, R.I., Sept. 13, 1881.

BURNSIDE, Thomas, congressman, jurist; b. nr. Newton Stewart, County Tyrone, Ireland, July 28, 1782; came to U.S., settled in Norristown, Pa., 1793; studied law. Admitted to bar, 1804, began practice of law, Bellefonte, Pa.; apptd. dep. atty. gen., 1809; mem. Pa. Senate, 1811-12, 23, presiding officer, 1823; mem. U.S. Ho. of Reps. (filled vacancy), 14th Congress, Oct. 10, 1815-Apr. 1816 (resigned); pres. judge Luzerne Dist. Cts., 1815-19; pres. judge 4th Jud. Dist., 1826-41, later pres. judge 7th Jud. Dist.; asso. justice Pa. Supreme Ct., 1845-51. Died Germantown, Pa., Mar. 25, 1851; buried Union Cemetery, Bellefonte.

BURR, Aaron, clergyman, coll. pres.; b. Jan. 4, 1716; s. Daniel and Elizabeth B.; grad. Yale, 1735; m. Esther Edwards, June 29, 1752, 2 children, including Aaron Burr. Ordained to the ministry of the Presbyterian Church in 1736; trustee Coll. of N.J. (now Princeton), acting pres., 1747-48, pres., 1748-57. Died Princeton, N.J., Sept. 24, 1757; buried Princeton Cemetery.

BURR, Aaron, senator, vice pres. U.S.; b. Newark, N.J., Feb. 6, 1756; s. Aaron and Esther (Edwards) B.; grad. Coll. N.J. (now Princeton), 1772; m. Mrs. Theodosia Prevost, July 1782, 1 dau., Theodosia; m. 2d, Mrs. Stephen Jumel, 1833; Served in Revolutionary War, 1777-79, commd. lt. col. Continental Army, 1777; served in battles of L.I., Monmouth; admitted to N.Y. bar, 1782; practiced law, N.Y.C., 1783; atty. gen. N.Y. State, 1789-91; mem. U.S. Senate from N.Y., 1791-97; mem. N.Y. State Assembly, 1797; tied with Jefferson for U.S. presidency in election of 1800, Jefferson became Pres. on 36th ballot in U.S. Ho. of Reps., Burr became vice pres. U.S. (Republican), 1801-05 (this situation produced 12th amendment); mortally wounded Alexander Hamilton, a polit. enemy, in duel, Weehawken, N.J., 1804; formulated conspiracy to seize S.W. Territory from Spanish America in order to set up a new republic; arrested 1807, tried for treason before Chief Justice Marshall of U.S. Circuit Ct. in Va., May 22, 1807, acquitted, Sept. 1, 1807; journeyed abroad, attempted to interest France and Eng. in his schemes, 1807, failed, returned home, 1812, resumed law practice, N.Y.C. Died S.I., N.Y., Sept. 14, 1836; buried Princeton, N.J.

BURR, Albert George, congressman; b. nr. Batavia, N.Y., Nov. 8, 1829; studied law. Taught sch., Vandalia, Ill., several years; moved to Winchester, 1850, engaged in merc. pursuits; admitted to bar, 1856, began practice of law, Winchester; mem. Ill. Ho. of Reps., 1861-64; moved to Carrollton, Ill., 1868, continued practice of law; mem. Ill. Constl. Conv., 1870; mem. U.S. Ho. of Reps. (Democrat) from Ill., 40th-41st congresses, 1867-71; circuit judge 7th Jud. Circuit, 1877-82. Died Carrollton, June 10, 1882; buried Carrollton Cemetery.

BURR, Alfred Edmund, journalist; b. Mar. 27, 1815; s. James and Lucretia (Olcott) B.; m. Sarah Booth, Apr. 1841, at least 1 son, Willie Olcott. Partner, Hartford (Conn.) Weekly Times, 1839-41, owner, editor, 1841-1900, changed paper to Daily Times, 1841, supported Democratic Party, opposed Civil War; mem. Conn. Ho. of Reps., 1853, 66; del. to all Dem. nat. convs., 1844-98; chmn. commn. to build Conn. capitol building. Died Hartford, Jan. 8, 1900.

BURR, Theodosia, adventurer; b. N.Y.C., June 21, 1783; d. Aaron and Theodosia (Bartow) Burr; educated in Greek and Latin; m. Joseph Alston, Feb. 2, 1801, 1 son, Aaron Burr Alston. Took over social responsibilities for her father at her mother's death, 1794; planned with father to establish Burr dynasty in Mexico, her son to succeed her father as emperor; with her father during his trial for treason in Richmond, Va., 1807; acted as financial agt. in U.S. for father, 1808-12. Died in wreck of ship Patriot off coast of N.C. while on the way to visit her father in N.Y.C., Jan. 1813.

BURRALL, William Porter, lawyer, railroad exec.; b. Canaan, Conn., Sept. 18, 1806; s. Hon. William M. and Abigail (Stoddard) B.; grad. Yale, 1826; m. Harriet Holley, May 1831. Admitted to Litchfield County bar, 1829; practiced in Conn., 1831-39; v.p. Hartford and New Haven R.R. Co., 1856-67, pres., 1867-72; v.p. N.Y., N.H. and H. RR., 1872; treas. I.C. R.R., 1852, pres., 1853-55; mem. Conn. Gen. Assembly from Salisbury, 1861; mem. Conn. Senate. Died Hartford, Conn., Mar. 3, 1874.

BURRILL, Alexander Mansfield, lawyer, author; b. N.Y.C., June 19, 1807; s. Ebenezer and Phebe (Cahoone) B.; grad. Columbia Coll., 1824. Admitted to N.Y. bar, 1828; practiced in N.Y.C. for short time, then devoted himself to writing. Author: Practice of the Supreme Court of the State of New York in Personal Actions, 2 vols., 1840; New Law Dictionary and Glossary, 1850-51; Law and Practice of Voluntary Assignments for the Benefit of Creditors, 1853; The Nature, Principles and Rules of Circumstantial Evidence, Especially that of the Presumptive Kind, in Criminal Cases, 1856. Died Kearney, N.J., Feb. 7, 1869.

BURRILL, James, senator; b. Providence, R.I., Apr. 25, 1772; s. James and Elizabeth (Rawson) B.; grad. R.I. Coll. (now Brown U.), 1788; m. Sally Arnold, Oct. 8, 1797. Admitted to bar, 1791; atty. gen. R.I.., 1797-1813; trustee Brown U.; mem. R.I. Ho. of Reps., 1813-16, speaker, 1814-16; elected chief justice Supreme Jud. Ct., R.I., 1816; mem. U.S. Senate from R.I., 1817-20. Died Washington, D.C., Dec. 25, 1820.

BURRINGTON, George, colonial gov.; b. Devonshire, Eng., 1680. Commd. capt. Brit. Army; sent to Am. as gov. N.C., 1724, gov., 1724-29, 31-34. Mysteriously murdered in London, Eng., Feb. 22, 1759.

BURRITT, Elihu, reformer; b. New Britain, Conn., Dec. 8, 1810; never married. Worked as blacksmith, Worcester, Mass., 1828-39; published The Literary Gemini (periodical in French), Worcester, 1839-40; published Christian Citizen, Worcester, 1844-45; edited Peace Advocate, Worcester, 1849-51; in England, 1846-49; founded League of Universal Brotherhood to further cause of world peace, London, 1846; organized Brussels Peace Congress of 1848; advocated world peace congress and international court; opposed Civil War; U.S. consul at Birmingham, Eng., 1863-70. Author: Sparks from the Anvil, 1848; Olive Leaves, 1853; Hand-Book of the Nations, 1856; The Mission of Great Sufferings, 1867; Walks in the Black Country, 1868. Died New Britain, Mar. 6, 1879.

BURROUGHS, John Curtis, clergyman, univ. pres.; b. Stamford, N.Y., Dec. 2, 1818; grad. Yale, 1842, Madison Theol. Sem., 1846; D.D. (hon.) U. Rochester, 1858; LL.D. (hon.) Madison U., 1869; m. Elvira Fields, 1843. Ordained to ministry Baptist Ch., circa 1846; pastor 1st Bapt. Ch., Chgo., 1852; 1st pres. U. Chgo., 1857-73; mem. Chgo. Bd. Edn. with spl. supervision over high schs., 1880-83; asst. supt. pub. schs. Chgo., 1885-92. Died Chgo., Apr. 21, 1892.

BURROUGHS, Silas Mainville, congressman, lawyer; b. Ovid, N.Y., July 16, 1810; studied saw. Village clk. Medina, Orleans County, N.Y., 1835, village trustee, 1836, 39-43, 45-47; admitted to N.Y. State bar in Orleans County, 1840, began practice law in Medina; village atty., 1845-47; brig. gen. N.Y. State Militia, 1848-58; mem. N.Y. Assembly, 1837, 50-51, 53; mem. U.S. Ho. of Reps. (Republican) from N.Y., 35th-36th congresses, 1857-60. Died Medina, June 3, 1860; buried Boxwood Cemetery.

BURROUGHS, William Seward, inventor; b. Auburn, N.Y., Jan. 28, 1855; s. Edmund and Ellen Burroughs; m. Ida Selover, 1879, 4 children, Jennie, Horace, Mortimer, Helen. Worker in father's shop making models for castings and new inventions, St. Louis, 1881; employed by Future Great Mfg. Co., St. Louis, 1881-84; invented machine to solve arithmetical problems, 1844-85, (not commercially practical); organized Am. Arithmometer Co. to produce machines for solving arithmetical problems, St. Louis, 1885; granted patent for 1st practical machine, 1892; awarded John Scott medal of Franklin Inst. for his invention, 1897. Died Citronelle, Ala., Sept. 15, 1898.

BURROWES, Thomas Henry, state ofcl.; b. Strasburg,Pa., Nov. 16, 1805; s. Thomas Bredin and Anne (Smith) B.; grad. Yale; m. Salome Carpenter, Apr. 6, 1837, 15 children. Admitted to Pa. bar, 1829; mem. Pa. Ho. of Reps., 1831-32; sec. Commonwealth of Pa., 1835-38; supt. schs. of Pa., 1835-38, 60-63; founder, editor Pa. Sch. Jour., 1852-70; organized Soldiers' Orphans' Schs. in Pa.; pres. Pa. Agrl. Coll., 1871. Died Feb. 25, 1871.

BURROWS, Daniel, congressman; b. Ft. Hill, Groton, Conn., Oct. 26, 1766; prep. edn. studied theology. Mfr. carriages, wagons, New London, Conn.; ordained to the ministry Methodist Ch.; mem. Conn. Ho. of Reps., 1816-20, 26; del. Conn. Constl. Conv., 1818; a commr. to establish boundary between Conn. and Mass.; mem. U.S. Ho. of Reps. (Democrat) from Conn., 17th Congress, 1821-23; resident Middletown, Conn., 1823-54; surveyor and insp. customs Port of Middletown, 1823-47. Died Mystic, Conn., Jan. 23, 1858; buried Elm Grove Cemetery.

BURROWS, Lorenzo, congressman; b. Groton, Conn., Mar. 15, 1805; attended acads., Plainfield, Conn., Westerly, R.I. Moved to Albion, Orleans County, N.Y., 1824; clk., till 1826, then became a mcht.; a founder Bank of Albion, 1839, became cashier; treas. Orleans County, 1840, assignee in bankruptcy Orleans County, 1841; Whig presdl. elector, 1844; supr. Town of Barre, 1845; mem. U.S. Ho. of Reps. (Whig) from N.Y., 31st-32d congresses, 1849-53; comptroller State of N.Y., 1855-57; dir., pres. Niagara Falls Internat. Bridge Co.; regent U. of N.Y., 1858-85; a commr. Mt. Albion Cemetery, 1862-85. Died Albion, Mar. 6, 1885; buried Mt. Albion Cemetery.

BURROWS, William, naval officer; b. Kinderton, Pa., Oct. 6, 1785; s. W. W. Burrows; never married. Apptd. midshipman U.S. Navy, 1799, served on ship Portsmouth 1799-1803; acting lt., 1803; served on ship Constitution in Tripolitan War, 1803-08; promoted to 1st lt., 1809; during furlough went on mcht. voyage to China, 1810-11; given command of Enterprise, 1813; mortally wounded in victory over Brit. brig Boxer. Died at sea nr. Portland, Me., Sept. 5, 1813.

BURT, Armistead, congressman, lawyer; b. Clouds Creek, nr. Edgefield, S.C., Nov. 13, 1802; studied law. Admitted to S.C. bar, 1823, practiced law, Pendleton, S.C., 1823-28; became lawyer, farmer, Abbeville, S.C., 1828; mem. U.S. Ho. of Reps. (Democrat) from S.C., 28th-32d congresses, 1843-53, speaker pro tem., 1848; del. Dem. Nat. Conv., N.Y.C., 1868. Died Abbeville, Oct. 30, 1883; buried Episcopal Cemetery.

BURT, Charles Kennedy, artist; b. Edinburgh, Scotland, Nov. 8, 1823. Came to Am.; worked in N.Y.C.; executed head of Queen Victoria to be used by Canadian govt. for a postage stamp (rated as outstanding stamp by philatelists); engraved portraits, hist. scenes, landscapes. Died Bklyn., Mar. 25, 1892.

BURT, John, inventor, mfr.; b. Wales, N.Y., Apr. 18 1814; s. William and Phoebe (Coles) B.: m. Julia Calkins, Dec. 3, 1835, 3 children. Dep. surveyor Mich., 1841; began constrn. railroad from Marquette to Lake Superior, completed in 1857; 1st supt. Saulte St. Marie Canal; devised number of improvements for manufacture of pig and wrought iron, involving methods of carbonization (patented 1869); Patented type of canal lock 1867, put into use, 1881; Republican elector-at-large, 1868; pres. Lake Superior & Peninsula Iron Co., Burt Freestone Co. Died Detroit Aug. 16, 1886.

BURT, William Austin, inventor, surveyor; b. Worcester, Mass., June 13, 1792; s. Alvin and Wealthy (Austin) B.; m. Phoebe Cole 1813; 5 children, including John. Served as justice of peace, postmaster, county surveyor Detroit; invented the typographer (predecessor of typewriter), patented, 1829; elected surveyor Macomb County, 1841; apptd. dist. surveyor in Mich; asso. judge Mich. Circuit Ct., 1833; postmaster Mt.Vernon (Mich.); apptd. U.S. dep. surveyor Washington D.C. by Gen. Land Office, constructed solar compass, patented, 1836, equatorial sextant, patented, 1856; mem. Mich., Territorial Legislative Council 1826-27; mem. Mich. Legislature, 1853, chmn. com. internal improvements. Recipient Scott medal Franklin Inst., 1840. Died Detroit, Aug. 18, 1858.

BURTON, Asa, clergyman; b. Stonington, Conn., Aug. 25, 1752; s. Jacob and Rachel Burton grad. Dartmouth, 1777; D.D. (hon.) Middlebury Coll., 1804; m. Mercy Burton, 1778; m. 2d. Polly Child, 1801; m. 3d, Mrs. Rhoda White, 1809. Ordained to ministry Congregational Ch., 1779; founder Thetford Acad., Kimball Union Acad.; a founder, trustee U. Vt; mem. corp. Middlebury Coll. Died Thetford, Vt., May 1, 1836.

BURTON, Hutchings Gordon, governor N.C., congressman; b. N.C., 1784; s. John and Mary (Gordon) B.; student U. N.C., 1795-98; m. Sarah Jones, 2 children. Elected to N.C. Ho. of Commons, 1809-17; atty. gen. N.C., 1810-16 mem. U.S. Ho. of Reps. from N.C. 16th-18th congresses, 1819-24; gov. N.C. 1824-27 Died Iredell County, N.C., Apr. 21, 1836; buried Unity Churchyard, Beattie's Ford, N.C.

BURTON, Nathaniel Judson, clergyman; b. Trumbull, Conn., Dec. 17, 1824; s. Henry and Betsy (Porter) B.; grad. Wesleyan U., 1850, Yale Divinity Sch., 1854; m. Rachel Chase, Sept. 14, 1853. Ordained to ministry Congregational Ch., 1853; pastor 2d Congregational Ch., Fairhaven, Conn. (now Pilgrim Ch., New Haven, Conn.), 1853-57, Park Ch., Hartford, Conn., 1870-87; mem. corp. Yale, 1882-87, Lyman Beecher lectr., 1884, lectr. Divinity Sch., 1885-87. Lectures at Yale collected in In Pulpit and Parish, 1925. Died Oct. 13, 1887.

BURTON, Robert, Continental congressman; b. nr. Chase City, Mecklenburg County, Va., Oct. 20, 1747; attended pvt. schs. Became a planter in Granville County, N.C., 1775; served to col. as a q.m. gen. in Revolutionary Army; mem. gov.'s council, 1783, 84; mem. Continental Congress from N.C., 1787-88; mem. commn. to establish boundary line between N.C., S.C., Ga., 1801. Died Granville (now Vance) County, N.C., May 31, 1825; buried on his estate "Montpelier," Williamsboro (now Henderson), N.C.

BURTON, Warren, clergyman; b. Wilton, N.H., Nov. 23, 1800; s. Jonathan and Persis (Warren) B.; grad. Harvard, 1821; grad. Harvard Theol. Sch., 1829; m. Sarah Flint, 1828; m. 2d, Mary Merritt, 1845. Ordained to ministry Congregational Ch., 1828; pastor Congregational Ch., East Cambridge, Mass., 1828-39, South Hingham, Mass., 1833-35, Waltham, Mass., 1835-37, Boston, 1844-48; chaplain Worester (Mass.) Prison, 1849, Mass. Senate, 1852, Mass. Constl. Conv., 1853, Mass. Ho. of Reps., 1853-60; became a Swedenborgian, circa 1844; participant Brooke Farm Expt., 1841-44. Author: My Religious Experience at my Native Home, 1829; Cheering Views of Man and Providence, 1832; The District School as It Was, 1833; Helps to Education in the Homes of Our Country, 1863. Died Salem, Mass., June 6, 1866.

BURTON, William, physician, gov. Del.; b. Milford, Del., Oct. 16, 1789; s. John and Mary (Vaughan) B.: M.D., U. Pa.; m. Mrs. Eliza Wolcott; m. 2d, Ann Hill, 1830; 1 child. Sheriff, Kent County, 1830, unsuccessful candidate for gov. Del., 1854, gov. Del. 1859-63. Died Milford, Aug. 5, 1866.

BURTON, William Evans, actor, author; b. London, Eng., Sept. 24, 1804; s. William George Burton; married, Apr. 10, 1823; m. 2d, Caroline Glessing, July 18, 1834; 3 children. Joined acting co., Eng., 1825; came to U.S., 1834; appeared in Phila., 1834-38; performances include Wormwood in The Lottery Ticket, also Dr. Ollapod in The Poor Gentleman; publisher Gentleman's Mag., Phila., 1837-40 (with Edgar Allan Poe as editor); travelled in the East, 1838-41; managed theaters, 2 in Phila., one each in Balt. and Washington, D.C., 1841-48; managed and appeared at Burton's Theater, N.Y.C., 1848-58. Author: Waggaries & Varg ries (a collection of sketches), 1848; Ellen Warehai 1833; The Toodles, 1837 (both plays); editor T Cyclopaedia of Wit and Humor, 1858. Died N.Y.C Feb. 10, 1860; buried Greenwood Cemetery, Bkly

BURWELL, William Armisted, congressma b. nr. Boydton, Mecklenburg County, Va., Ma 15, 1780; grad. Coll. William and Mary. Moved Franklin County, Va., 1802; mem. Va. Ho. of Del pvt. sec. to Pres. Thomas Jefferson; mem. U. Ho. of Reps. from Va. (filled vacancy) 9th, 10t 16th congresses, Dec. 1, 1806-21. Died Washir ton, D.C., Feb. 16, 1821; buried Congressio Cemetery.

BUSBY, George Henry, congressman; b. Dav town, Pa., June 10, 1794; attended pub. schs. Mov to Royaltown, Fairfield County, O., 1810, becar a mcht.; maj. of militia War of 1812; a found Town of Marion (O.), 1823; became a mch clk, Marion County (O.) cts., clk. supreme c 1824-28, recorder of deeds, 1831-35; mem. U.S. H of Reps. (Democrat) from Ohio, 32d Congre 1851-53; mem. Ohio Senate, 1853-55; prob judge Marion County, 1866-69. Died Marion, Au 22, 1869; buried Marion Cemetery.

BUSH, George, clergyman, educator; b. Norwic Vt., June 12, 1796; s. John and Abigail (Marvi B.; grad. Dartmouth, 1818; m. Miss Condi 1825; m. 2d, Mary Fisher, Jan. 4, 1849 Ordained Salem (Ind.) Presbytery, 1825; prof. Hebrew lar and lit. N.Y. U., 1831-47; instr. sacred lit. Uni Theol. Sem., 1836-37; editor: New Church Repo tory and Monthly Review, 1848. Author: The L of Mohammed (1st important work), 1830; A Tr tise on the Millennium, 1832; A Grammar of t Hebrew Language, 1835. Died Rochester, N.Y Sept. 19, 1859.

BUSHNELL, David; inventor; b. Saybrook, Con 1742; grad. Yale, 1775. Completed man-propell submarine boat, 1775; originator modern submari warfare; capt.-lt. Continental Army, 1779, cap 1781. Died Warrenton, Ga. 1824.

BUSHNELL, Horace, clergyman; b. Banta Conn., Apr. 14, 1802; s. Ensign and Dotha (Bisho B. grad. Yale, 1827, attended Yale Divinity Sc 1832-33, LL.D. (hon.), 1871; D.D. (hon.), Wesle an U., 1842, Harvard, 1852; m. Mary Aptho Sept. 13, 1833. Literary editor Jour. Commer N.Y.C., 1827-28; tutor Yale, 1829-31; ordain to ministry Congregational Ch., 1833; pastor Nor Ch., Hartford, Conn., 1833-59; travelled in Euro 1845-46; contended that human language was capable of expressing nature of God in his bo God in Christ, 1849, tried for heresy for this bel by Gen. Assn. Conglist. Ministers, 1850, char dropped. Author: The True Wealth and Weal of N tions, 1837; Christian Nurture, 1847; Christ Theology, 1851; The Age of Homespun, 1851; Pop lar Government by Divine Right, 1864; Work a Play, 1864; The Vicarious Sacrifice, 1866; Mo Uses of Dark Things, 1868; Forgiveness and La 1874. Died Hartford, Feb. 17, 1876.

BUTLER, Andrew Pickens, senator; jurist; Edgefield, S.C., Nov. 18, 1796; s. William a Behethland (Moore) B.: grad. S.C.Coll., 1817; Susan Anne Simkins; m. 2d, Harriet Hayne, 18 1 child. Admitted to S.C. bar, 1819; elected to S. Legislature, 1824 trustee S.C. Coll., 18 circuit judge S.C., 1833; became judge S.C. Appeals; mem. U.S. Senate from S.C. Dec. 18 May 25, 1857, chmn. judiciary com., 1849. D Edgefield, May 25, 1857.

BUTLER, Benjamin Franklin, cabinet officer; Columbia County, N.Y., Dec. 17, 1795; s. Med and Hannah (Tylee) B.; M. Harriet Allen, 18 a son, William Allen. Admitted to Albany (N.Y bar, 1817; dist. atty. Albany County. (N.Y.),18 24; mem. N.Y. State Legislature. 1827-33; U atty. gen., 1833-38; U.S. sec. of way, 1836-3 U.S. atty for So. dist. N.Y., 1838-41, 45-48; orga ized dept. law U. City N.Y., 1838; head electo Coll. N.Y., 1845. Died Paris, France, Nov. 8, 18

BUTLER, Benjamin Franklin, army offic gov. Mass., congressman; b. Deerfield, N.H. N 5, 1818; s. John and Charlotte (Ellison) B.: gr Waterbury Coll. (now Colby U.), 1838; m. Sa Hildreth May 16, 1844, 1 dau., Blanche. Admit to Mass. bar, 1840; mem. Mass. Ho. of Reps., 18 Mass. Senate, 1859; commd. brig. gen. Mass. litia at beginning of Civil War; occupied Bal 1861; comdr. in capture of New Orleans, 1862, m gov. New Orleans, 1862; controversial politics a regulatory tactics led to charges of corruption a graft; in command Eastern Va. and N.C. dist 1863; sent to N.Y. to preserve order during el tion, 1864; mem. U.S. Ho. of Reps. from Ma 40th-43d, 45th congresses, 1867-75, 77-79; g Mass., 1882; U.S. presidential nominee of An Monopoly Party 1884, Greenback Party, 1884. A thor: Butler's Book (autobiography), 1892. D Washington, D.C., Jan. 11, 1893.

BUTLER, Charles, lawyer, sem. pres.; b. Kind hook Landing, N.Y., Jan. 15, 1802; s. Medad lannah (Tylee) B.; LL.D. (hon.) Wabash Coll., 853; m. Eliza Ogden, Oct. 10, 1825. Dep. clk. state Senate, 1822; admitted to N.Y. bar, 1824; a ounder Hobart Coll.; asst. dist. atty. Albany Coun-y; a founder Union Theol. Sem., 1836, mem. 1st d. dirs., pres. Sem., 1870-97; mem. council Univ. ity N.Y., 1836. Died N.Y.C., Dec. 13, 1897.

BUTLER, Chester Pierce, congressman; b. Vilkes-Barre, Pa., Mar. 21, 1798; attended Wilkes-arre Acad.; grad. Princeton, 1817; studied law itchfield Law Sch. Trustee Wilkes-Barre Acad., 818-38, sec. bd.; admitted to Pa. bar, 1820, began ractice of law, Wilkes-Barre; register and ecorder Luzerne County, Pa., 1821-24; mem. Pa. Io. of Reps., 1832, 38-39, 43; mem. U.S. Ho. of eps. (Whig) from Pa., 30th-31st congresses, 847-50. Died Phila., Oct. 5, 1850; buried Hollen-eck Cemetery, Wilkes-Barre.

BUTLER, Clement Moore, clergyman, educator; . Troy, N.Y., Oct. 16, 1810; grad. Trinity Coll., lartford, Conn., 1836; attended Gen. Theol. Sem., I.Y., 1836-37. Ordained to ministry Protestant piscopal Ch., 1837; pastor St. Paul's Ch., Syracuse, .Y., 1838-40; rector Zion Ch., Palmyra, N.Y., hen asst. rector Christ Ch., Balt., later rector St. ohn's Ch., Georgetown, D.C.; pastor Grace Ch., oston, 1846-49; rector Trinity Ch., Washington, .C., 1849-61, Grace Ch., Rome, Italy, 1861-64; rof. eccles. history Divinity Sch. of P.E. Ch., Phila., 864-84; delivered funeral sermons of John C. Cal-oun, Henry Clay. Author: The Book of Common rayer Interpreted by its History, 2d edit., 1849; ectures on the Revelation of St. John, 1850; Man-al of Ecclesiastical History from the First to the ineteenth Century, 2 vols., 1868, 72; History of he Reformation in Sweden, 1883. Died Phila., Nov. 2, 1890.

BUTLER, Ezra, gov. Vt., congressman; b. Lan-aster, Mass., Sept. 24, 1763; s. Asaph and Jane McAllister) B.; m. Thyphena Diggins. Fought in m. Revolution; admitted to Vt. bar 1786; town k., Waterbury, Vt., 1790; mem. Vt. Legislature om Waterbury, 1794-97, 99-1804, 07-08; or-ained to ministry Baptist Ch., 1801; judge Chit-enden County (Vt.); Ct., 1803-06, chief justice, efferson County (Vt.) Ct., 1812-13, 15-27; mem. .S. Ho. of Reps. (Republican) from Vt., 13th ongress, 1813-15; mem. Vt. Constitutional Conv., 822; gov. Vt., 1826-28. Died Waterbury, July 12, 838; buried Waterbury Cemetery.

BUTLER, John, army officer; b. New London, onn., 1728; s. Walter and Deborah B.; m. Catharine, t least 3 children including Walter. Served as capt. .Y. Militia in expdn. against Crown Point, 1755; ommanded Indian forces in Niagara expdn., 1759, in Iontreal expdn., 1775-80; Loyalist during Am. evolution; commd. maj. Brit. Army, 1777, lt. col., 780; led mixed force of Indians and Loyalists known as Butler's Rangers) in campaigns of Mo-awk and Wyoming valleys; served at battles of riskany and Forty Fort; led forces which perpe-rated the Wyoming Massacre, 1778; fled to Can., 780; property confiscated by State of N.Y.; loyal ommr. Indian Affairs, Niagara, Can., 1780-96. ied Niagara, May 1796.

BUTLER, John Jay, clergyman, educator; b. Ber-ick, Me., Apr. 9, 1814; grad. Bowdoin Coll., 1837, .D. (hon.), 1860; grad. Andover Theol. Sem., 1844; .M. (hon.), Hamilton Coll., 1849. Sch. tchr., Par-nsfield and Farmington, Me., 1838-39; prin. Clin-n Sem. (N.Y.), 1841-42; prof. systematic theology hitestown Sem. (N.Y.), 1844-54; ordained to min-try Free Baptist Ch., 1846; prof. systematic theol-gy New Hampton Theol. Inst. (N.H.), 1854-70; rof. theology Bates Coll., Me., 1870-73, Hillsdale Mich.) Coll., 1873-83; editor Morning Star (organ Free Bapt. Ch.) for number of years from 1834. uthor: Natural and Revealed Theology, 1861; Com-entary on the Gospels, 1870. Died 1891.

BUTLER, Josiah, congressman, lawyer; b. Pel-am, N.H., Dec. 4, 1779; grad. Harvard, 1803; udied law. Taught sch., Va., 3 years; admitted Va. bar, 1807; returned to Pelham, began actice of law, 1807; moved to Deerfield, N.H., 809; sheriff Rockingham County, N.H., 1810-13; k. ct. of common pleas; mem. N.H. Ho. of Reps., 815-16; mem. U.S. Ho. of Reps. (Democrat) from .H., 15th-17th congresses, 1817-23; asso. justice .H. Ct. of Common Pleas, 1825-35. Died Deer-eld, Oct. 27, 1854; buried Granite Cemetery, outh Deerfield, N.H.

BUTLER, Pierce, senator; b. County Carlow, Ireland ily, 11, 1744; s. Sir Richard and Henrietta (Percy) ; m. Mary Middleton, Jan. 10, 1771. Commd. maj. er Majesty's 9th Regt.; rep. S.C. Legislature, 1778-9; 84-89; adj.gen. S.C., 1779; elected to fix S.C. oundaries, 1786; del. from S.C. to Congress of onfederation, 1787; del. U.S. Consti. Conv., 1787, rote fugitive slave clause, advocated strong central ovt. with property as one of main bases for represen-ation; mem. U.S. Senate (Federalist) Senate from .C., 1789-96, 1802-04; dir. 1st and 2d U.S. anks. Died Phila., Feb. 15, 1822.

BUTLER, Pierce Mason, gov. S.C., army officer; b. Mt. Willing, S.C., Apr. 11, 1798; s. William and Behethland (Moore) B.; m. Miranda Duval. Commd. U.S. Army 1818, capt., 1825; trustee S.C. Coll., 1833; gov. S.C., 1836-38; apptd. agt. for Cherokees Indians by Pres. Van Buren, 1836-46; organizer and col. Palmetto regt. in Mexican War, 1846 distinguished for bravery at battles of Cerro Gordo, and Churubusco. Killed in action Battle of Churubusco, Aug. 20, 1847; buried Edgefield, S.C.

BUTLER, Richard, army officer, Indian agt.; b. St. Bridget's, Dublin, Ireland, Apr. 1, 1743; s. Thomas and Eleanor (Parker) B.; m. Mary Smith. Indian agt., 1775; commd. maj. 8th Pa. Regt., 1776; served as lt. col. with Morgan's Rifles, 1777; brevetted brig. gen., 1783, Indian commr. under Articles of Confederation; supt. Indian affairs for No. Dist. 1786; mem. Pa. Senate judge Ct. Common Pleas; pres. Ct. Inquiry invetigating Gen. Josiah Harmar, 1790, maj. gen. U.S. Army, 2d in command under Gen. Arthur St. Clair, 1791. Died during St. Clair expdn. against Ohio Indians, Nov. 4, 1791.

BUTLER, Sampson Hale, congressman, lawyer; b. nr. Ninety Six, S.C., Jan. 3, 1803; attended S.C. Coll. (now U. S.C.); studied law. Admitted to S.C. bar, 1825, began practice law, Edgefield, S.C., continued practice in Barnwell, S.C.; sheriff Barnwell County, 1832-39; mem. S.C. Ho. of Reps., 1836-39; mem. U.S. Ho. of Reps. (Democrat) from S.C., 26th-27th congresses, 1839-Sept. 27, 1842 (resigned); moved to Fla. Died Tallahassee, Fla., Mar. 16, 1848; buried Tallahassee.

BUTLER, Simeon, publisher; b. Wethersfield, Conn., circa Mar. 25, 1770; s. Josiah and Martha (Ranney) B.; m. Mary Hunt, 1795; m. 2d, Charlotte McNeill, 1833; 10 children. Moved to Northampton, Mass., became bookbinder, bookseller, circa 1790; established 1st publishing house in Western Mass., Northampton, 1792; partner with cousin William Butler as publishers of Hampshire Gazette, 1793; engaged for a time in papermaking with brother Asa, Suffield, Conn., believed to have produced 1st Am. letter paper used in U.S. Senate; postmaster of Northampton, 1800-06; his bookstore still in existence under name of Bridgman & Lyman (one of 2 or 3 oldest bookstores in U.S.). Died Northampton, Nov. 7, 1847.

BUTLER, Thomas, congressman, lawyer; b. nr. Carlisle, Pa., Apr. 14, 1785; attended coll. in Pitts.; studied law. Admitted to Pa. bar, 1806, practiced law, Pitts., 1806-07; moved to Miss. Territory, circa 1807, admitted to territory bar, 1808; capt. cavalry troop Miss. Territory Militia, 1810; purchased land, settled in parish of Feliciana, Orleans Territory, 1811; apptd. parish judge, 1812; apptd. judge of 3d Dist. by gov. of La., 1813; mem. U.S. Ho. of Reps. from La. (filled vacancy), 15th-16th congresses, Nov. 16, 1818-21; apptd. spl. judge 3d Jud. Dist., 1822, 40; mem. Whig Party, later mem. Am. Party; owner sugar, cotton plantations; pres. bd. trustees La. Coll., Jackson; mem. Pa. Soc. of the Cincinnati. Died St. Louis, Aug. 7, 1847; buried on his plantation "The Cottage," nr. Francisville, La.

BUTLER, Thomas Belden, Congressman, jurist; b. Wethersfield Conn., Aug. 22, 1806; s. Frederick and Mary (Belden) B.; grad. Yale Med. Sch., 1828; m. Mary Crosby, Mar. 14, 1831. Mem. Conn. Legislature from Norwalk 1832-45; admitted to Fairfield County bar, 1837; mem. Conn. Senate 1847-48; mem. U.S. Ho. of Reps. (Whig) from Conn., 31st Congress 1849-51, apptd. judge Conn. Superior Ct. by Gen. Assembly, 1855; asso. justice Conn. 1861-70; chief justice 1870-73. Died Norwalk, Conn., June 8, 1873.

BUTLER, Walter N., Loyalist; b. Johnstown, N.Y., s. Lt.-Col. John and Catherine Butler; studied law, Albany, N.Y. Fled to Can. with father and other Loyalist leaders from Western N.Y., 1776; mem. Gen. Barry S. Leger's expdn. down Mohawk Valley, 1777; captured by Continental soldiers, 1777, escaped; leader Loyalists and Indians in Cherry Valley Massacre in which over 40 people were murdered, Nov. 11, 1778; killed in Loyalist raid on Mohawk Valley, 1781. Died Oct. 30, 1781.

BUTLER, William army officer, congressman; b. Prince William County, Va., Dec. 17, 1759; s. James and Mary (Simpson) B.; M.D., S.C. Coll., 1778; m. Behethland Moore, June 3, 1784; children James, Andrew, George William Frank, Pierce, Emmala, Leontine. Commd. S.C. Militia, 1781; mem. S.C. Ho. of Reps., 1876; del. S.C. Conv. to ratify U.S. Constn., 1787, voted against Constn.; sheriff 96th Dist., 1791; commd. brig. gen. S.C. Militia, 1794, then maj. gen.; mem. U.S. Ho. of Reps. from S.C., 7th-12th congresses, 1801-13. Died Columbia, S.C., Sept. 23, 1821.

BUTLER, William, congressman, physician; b. Edgefield Dist., S.C., Feb. 1, 1790; s. of William Butler; grad. S.C. Coll. (now U. S.C.), 1810; studied medicine; at least 1 son, Matthew Calbraith. Licensed to practice medicine; served as surgeon Battle of New Orleans, War of 1812, served with U.S. Navy until 1820; mem. U.S. Ho. of Reps. (Whig) from S.C., 27th Congress, 1841-43; agt. of Cherokee Indians, 1849-50. Died Fort Gibson, Indian Territory (now Okla.), Sept. 25, 1850; buried nr. Van Buren, Ark.

BUTLER, William, missionary; b. Dublin, Ireland, Jan. 30, 1818; grad. Hardwick Street Mission Sem., Dublin; grad. Didsbury Coll., Manchester, Eng., 1844; m. Clementina Rowe, Nov. 23, 1854; 4 children including Clementina. Ordained to ministry Methodist Ch.; preached in Ireland, 1844-50; came to Am. with family, 1850; admitted to N.Y. East Conf., Meth. Ch., 1851, served in various parishes; pastor, Lynn, Mass.; accepted post as missionary to India, 1856, set sail with wife and 2 sons, 1857, set up mission Bareilly, India, held 1st ofcl. meeting, 1858, missions consisted of girls' orphanage, Bareilly, boys' orphanage, Lucknow; returned to U.S. because of illness, 1864, pastor Chelsea, Mass., Dorchester Street Ch., Boston; sec. Am. and Fgn. Christian Union; missionary to Mexico, 1873-79.

BUTLER, William Orlando, army officer, congressman; b. Jessamine County, Ky., Apr. 19, 1791; s. Percival and Mildred (Hawkins) B.; grad. Transylvania U., 1812. Commd. capt. U.S. Army, served under Andrew Jackson, 1813, brevetted a maj., 1816; mem. Ky. Legislature from Gallatin County, 1817-18; mem. U.S. Ho. of Reps. from Ky., 26th-27th congresses, 1839-43; served as maj. gen. during Mexican War, 1846, present at capture of Mexico City, succeeded Gen. Scott in command of Army in Mexico, voted a sword by U.S. Congress, also by Ky. for bravery in Battle of Monterey; Democratic nominee for vice pres. U.S. 1848; declined appointment by Pres. Pierce as gov. Neb., 1855. Author: The Boatman's Horn and other Poems. Died Carrollton, Ky., Aug. 6, 1880.

BUTLER, Zebulon, naval, army officer; b. Lyme, Conn., Jan. 23, 1731; s. John and Hannah (Perkins) B.; m. Anna Lord, Dec. 23, 1760; m. 2d, Lydia Johnston, Aug. 1775; m. 3d, Phebe Haight, Nov. 1781. Served as Ensign during French and Indian Wars, 1757, lt. and q.m., 1759, capt., 1760; led band of Conn. settlers to Wyoming Valley (now Luzerne County, Pa.), 1769; dir. Susquehanna Co.; mem. Conn. Assembly from Wyoming, 1774-76; commd. lt. col. Continental Army, 1776, col., 1778. Died Wilkes-Barre, Pa., July 28, 1795.

BUTMAN, Samuel, congressman; b. Worcester, Mass., 1788. Moved to Me., 1804, became a farmer in Dixmont, Penobscot County; served as capt. in War of 1812; mem. Me. Constl. Conv., 1820; mem. Me. Ho. of Reps., 1822, 26-27; mem. U.S. Ho. of Reps. from Me., 20th-21st congresses, 1827-31; commr. Penobscot County, 1846; pres. Me. Senate, 1853. Died Plymouth, Me., Oct. 9, 1864.

BUTTERFIELD, Daniel, army officer; b. Utica, N.Y., Oct. 31, 1831; s. John and Melinda (Baker) B.; B.A., Union Coll., 1849; m. 1st wife, Feb. 12, 1857; m. 2d, Mrs. Julia L. James, Sept. 21, 1886. Commd. capt. 71st Regt., N.Y. Militia; commd. col. 12th Regt. (1st Union forces to enter Va., crossing Long Bridge May 24, 1861), 1861; promoted brig. gen. U.S. Volunteers, 1861; decorated Congressional Medal of Honor (1892) for service at Gaines's Mill during Gen. George McClellan's Peninsular Campaign of 1862; commd. maj. gen., in command 5th Army Corps, served at Battle of Fredericksburg, 1862; became chief of staff under Gen. Thomas Hooker, 1863, also at Battle of Lookout Mountain, 1863; served at Battle of Chancellorsville, under Gen. George Meade at Battle of Gettysburg; commanded 3d Div., 20th Army Corps in Gen. William Sherman's march through Ga.; commd. col. U.S. Army, 1863; brevetted maj. gen., 1865, resigned, 1870; apptd. asst. U.S. treas., N.Y.C., 1870; constructed railroad in Guatemala; pres. Albany and Troy Steamboat Co.; owner Bklyn. Annex Steamships; dir. Mechanics & Tracers Bank N.Y.C.; grand marshall of parade during Washington Centennial. Celebration, N.Y.C., 1899; pres. Soc. of Army of Potomac; mem. Grand Army of Republic. Died Cold Spring, N.Y., July 17, 1901.

BUTTERFIELD, John, express co. exec.; b. Berne, N.Y., Nov. 18, 1801; s. Daniel Butterfield; m. Malinda Baker, Feb. 1822 , 9 children including Daniel. Originated street ry. of Utica (N.Y.); established N.Y., Albany and Buffalo Telegraph Co.; formed express firm Butterfield, Wasson & Co., 1849, effected consolidation with 2 other firms to form Am. Express Co., 1850; pres. Overland Mail Co., longest stagecoach line in U.S. (nearly 2800 miles); dir. Utica City Nat. Bank; builder Butterfield House, Butterfield Block; mayor Utica, 1865. Died Utica, Nov. 14, 1869.

BUTTERFIELD, Martin, congressman; b. Westmoreland, N.H., Dec. 8, 1790; attended common schs. Moved to Palmyra, N.Y., 1828, in hardware bus., also mfr. rope and cordage; Whig presdl. elector, 1848; mem. U.S. Ho. of Reps. (Republican) from N.Y., 36th Congress, 1859-61. Died Palmyra, Aug. 6, 1866; buried Village Cemetery.

BUTTERICK, Ebenezer, inventor; b. Sterling, Mass., May 29, 1826; s. Francis and Ruhamah (Buss) B.; m. Ellen. Became tailor and shirt-maker, Sterling; idea conceived (by him or his wife) for method of unlimited reproduction of shirts with set of graded shirt patterns, circa 1859; placed 1st patterns on market, 1863, moved to larger town of Fitchburg, Mass., because of success, 1863; upon wife's suggestion made patterns for boys' suits ("Garibaldi" suits modeled from uniform of internat. hero Guiseppe Garibaldi); opened office on Broadway, N.Y.C., 1864, extended patterns to women's garments; formed (with J. W. Wilder and A. W. Pollard) E. Butterick & Co., 1867, opened branches in London, Paris, Berlin and Vienna, by 1876; reorganized firm as Butterick Publishing Co., Ltd., 1881, served as sec., 1881-94. Died Mar. 31, 1903.

BUTTERWORTH, Benjamin, congressman; b. Warren County, O., Oct. 22, 1837; s. William and Elizabeth (Linton) B.; grad. Ohio U., Cincinnati Law Sch.; m. Mary Seiler, Nov. 2, 1863. Admitted to Ohio bar, 1861 ; U.S.dist. atty. for So. Ohio, 1870; mem. Ohio Senate from Butler and Warren counties, 1873-75; mem. U.S. Ho. of Reps. from Ohio, 46th-47th, 49th-51st congresses, 1879-83, 85-90; retained by U.S. atty. gen. as spl. counsel in S.C. election cases; U.S. commr. patents, 1883; 97; commr. to investigate certain phases of N.P. Ry., 1883; opened law office, Washington, D.C., 1890. Died Thomasville, Ga., Jan. 16, 1898; buried Rock Creek Cemetery, Wahington, D.C.

BUTTON, Stephen D., architect; b. Preston, Conn., 1803. Apprenticed in office of George Purvis, N.Y.C.; designed original State House, Montgomery, Ala., 1847 (his 1st important work), in charge of constrn. to replace bldg. after it was destroyed by fire; returned to Phila., 1849, practiced in partnership with J. C. Hoxie (his brother-in-law), 1849; designed several comml. bldgs., Phila., also several residence in Rittenhouse Sq.; designed City Hall, several chs., 13 schs., Camden, N.J.; an organizer Pa. Inst. Architects, 1861, became Phila. chpt. A.I.A., 1869; Died Jan. 17, 1897.

BUTTRE, John Chester, artist, publisher; b. Auburn, N.Y., June 10, 1821. Worked as engraver, N.Y.C., circa 1847; partner firm Rice & Buttre, N.Y.C., 1848-50; best known as publisher of The American Portrait Gallery, 3 vols., 1880-81. Died Ridgewood, N.J., Dec. 2, 1893.

BUTTS, Isaac, newspaper editor; b. Dutchess county, N.Y., Jan. 11, 1816; s. Nicholas and Elizabeth (DeWitt) B.; m. Mary Smyles, 1844, 5 children. Became owner Daily Advertiser (oldest daily paper West of Albany, N.Y.), 1844; owner Rochester (N.Y.) Daily Union, 1852; an early investor Western Union Telegraph Co. Author: Brief Reasons for Repudiation, Applicable to the War Debts of All Countries, 1869; Protection and Free Trade: An Inquiry Whether Protective Tariffs can Benefit the Interests of a Country in the Aggregate, 1875. Died Rochester, Nov. 20, 1874.

BYFORD, William Heath, gynecologist, educator; b. Eaton, O., Mar. 20, 1817; s. Henry T. and Hannah B.; M.D., Ohio Med. Coll., 1845; m. Mary Ann Holland, Oct. 3, 1840; m. 2d, Lina Flersheim, 1873. Apptd. prof. anatomy Evansville Med. Coll., 1850; prof. obstetrics and diseases of women and children Rush Med. Coll., Chgo., 1857; head gynecology, 1879; a founder Chgo. Med. Coll., 1859. Author med. works including Treatise on the Theory and Practice of Obstetrics, 1870. Died Chgo., May 21, 1890.

BYINGTON, Cyrus, missionary; b. Stockbridge, Mass., Mar. 11, 1793; s. Capt. Asahel and Lucy (Peck) B.; learned Latin and Greek from Joseph Woodbridge; grad. Andover (Mass.) Theol. Sem., 1819. Admitted to Mass. bar, practiced law in Stockbridge and Sheffield; ordained to ministry Congregational Ch., 1819, preached in Mass.; missionary to Choctaw Indians in Miss., 1820-68; prepared a grammar and dictionary of the Choctaw tongue, in 7th revision at time of death, edtied by Daniel G. Brinton in Proceedings of the American Philosophical Soc., 1871, XII, 317-67, edited by J. R. Swanton and H. S. Holbert in Bull. 46, Bur. of Am. Ethnology, 1915. Died Belpre, O., Dec. 31, 1868.

BYLES, Mather, clergyman, author; b. Boston, Mar. 26, 1707; s. Josiah (or Josias) and Elizabeth (Mather) Greenough B.; A.B., Harvard, 1725, A.M., 1728; S.T.D. (hon.), U. Aberdeen (Scotland); m. Mrs. Anna Gale, 1733; m. 2d, Rebecca Tailer, 1747; 9 children including Mather. Ordained to ministry Congregational Ch. 1732, minister Hollis Street Congregational Ch., Boston, 1732-76; Tory during Revolutionary War, let Brit. troops use his ch.; dismissed from pulpit by local patriots after evacuation of British; tried and banished from pulpit, banishment not enforced. Author: The Flourish of the Annual Spring, 1741; Poems on Several Occasions, 1744; The Conflagration Applied to that Grand Period or Catastrophe of Our World, When the Face of Nature Is To Be Changed by a Deluge of Fire, As Formerly it Was by That of Water, The God of Tempest and Earthquakes, 1755. Died Boston, July 5, 1788.

BYNNER, Edwin Lassetter, lawyer, author; b. Bklyn., Aug. 5, 1842; s. Edwin and Caroline (Edgarton) B.; LL.B., Harvard, 1865. Admitted to Mass., Mo., N.Y. bars, 1865, practiced law in each state for a time, then devoted career to writing; contbr. to various mags. Author: Nimport, 1877; Damen's Ghost, 1881; The Begum's Daughter, 1889. Died Boston, Aug. 5, 1893.

BYNUM, Jesse Atherton, congressman, lawyer; b. Halifax County, N.C., May 23, 1797; attended Princeton, 1818-19; studied law. Admitted to the bar, began practice of law, Halifax, N.C.; mem. N.C. House of Commons, 1823-24, 27-30; mem. U.S. Ho. of Reps. (Democrat) from N.C., 23d-26th congresses, 1833-41; moved to Alexandria, La., became a farmer. Died Alexandria, Sept. 23, 1868; buried Rapides Cemetery, Pineville, La.

BYRD, William, planter, mcht., colonial legislator; b. London, Eng., 1652; s. John and Grace (Stegg) B.; m. Mary Horsmanden, 1673; 1 son, William. Engaged in tobacco trade with Eng. and West Indies; fur trader, land speculator; owner plantation nr. what is now Richmond, Va. imported, used, sold numerous slaves; comdr. Henrico County (Va.) Militia; mem. Va. Ho. of Burgesses, 1677-82, mem. Va. Council of State, 1683-1704, pres., 1703-04; mem. Albany Conv. to treat with Indians, 1685; auditor gen. Va., 1688. Author: A History of the Dividing Line; A Progress to the Mines; also recently published diaries. Died Westover, Va., Dec. 4, 1704.

BYRD, William, colonial ofcl.; b. Westover, Va., Apr. 8, 1674; s. William and Mary (Horsmanden) B.; attended Middle Temple, London, Eng., 1692; m. Lucy Parke, 1706; m. 2d, Marion Taylor; at least 2 children, William, Evelyn. Mem. Va. Ho. of Burgesses, 1693; agt. for Va. in Eng., 1697-1704, 10-20; mem. Va. Council of State, 1709-44, pres., 1743-44; commr. to determine boundary line between Va. and N.C., 1728; owned largest library in Va.; founder Richmond (Va.), 1737; fellow Royal Soc. Died Westover, Sept. 6, 1744.

BYRNE, Andrew, clergyman; b. Navan, Ireland, Dec. 5, 1802. Ordained priest Roman Catholic Ch., 1827; came to N.Y., 1836, served as asst. Cathedral of St. James and Ch. of Nativity; apptd. 1st. Roman Catholic bishop Diocese of Little Rock (comprising Akr. and Indian Territory), 1844; pioneer in establishment Catholicism in U.S., introduced order Sister of Mercy; attended 6th Provincial Council, Balt., 1846, 1st Provincial Council of New Orleans, 1856. Died Little Rock, Ark., June 10, 1862.

BYRNE, Edward, clergyman; b. Navan, Meath, Ireland, Dec. 5, 1802; studied at diocesan sem., Navan. Came to U.S., ordained priest Roman Catholic Ch., Charleston, S.C., 1827; asst., vicar gen. to Bishop John England, served as England's theologian at 2d Provincial Council, Balt.; moved to N.Y., 1836, pastor several chs.; apptd. 1st bishop of Little Rock, Ark., 1843, developed missionaries for the Indians, brought in priests and nuns from Ireland, encouraged immigration to Southwest. Died Helena, Ark., June 10, 1862.

BYRNE, John, physician; b. Kilkeel, Ireland, Oct. 13, 1825; s. Stephen and Elizabeth (Sloane) B.; M.D., U. Edinburgh (Scotland), 1846; grad. N.Y. Med. Coll., 1853. Came to Am., 1848; practiced medicine, Bklyn., 1848-1902; mem. exec. bd., also clin. prof. uterine surgery L.I. Coll. Hosp.; surgeon-in-chief St. Mary's Hosp., N.Y.C., 1858-1902; devised means of using electric cautery-knife in surgery of malignant disease of uterus. Author: Clinical Notes on the Electric Cautery in Uterine Surgery, 1872. Died Montreux, Switzerland, Oct. 1, 1902.

BYRNE, Richard, army officer; b. Cavan County, Ireland, 1832. Came to U.S., 1844; joined U.S. Army, 1849; served with 2d Cavalry against Indians in Fla. and Ore.; commd. lt. at beginning of Civil War, commd. col. 28th Mass. Volunteers, 1862; served with Army of Potomac at Fredericksburg, Chancellorsville and Gettysburg; recruited replacements, given command of Irish Brigade, 1864; mortally wounded at Cold Harbor, Va. Died Washington, D.C., June 10, 1864.

BYRNE, William, clergyman; b. Wicklow County, Ireland, 1780; came to U.S. at age 25; studied at Georgetown and Mt. St. Mary's, Emmitsburg, Md., also St. Thomas' Sem., Bardstown, Ky. Ordained priest Roman Catholic Ch., 1819; in charge of missions nr. Louisville; opened St. Mary's Coll., nr. Bardstown, 1821, twice rebuilt it after destruction by fire, later turned sch. over to Jesuits. Died during cholera epidemic, Bardstown, June 5, 1833.

C

CABELL, Edward Carrington, congressman; b. Richmond, Va., Feb. 5, 1816; attended Washington Coll. (now Washington and Lee U.), 1832-3 Reynold's Classical Acad., 1833-34; grad. U. Va 1836. Moved to Fla., 1837, became a farmer, r Tallahassee; del. Fla. Constl. Conv., 1838; r turned to Va. to study law, admitted to Va. ba 1840; returned to Tallahassee; mem. U.S. Ho. Reps. from Fla., 29th Congress (election co tested), Oct. 6, 1845-Jan. 24, 1846, (Whig) 30t 32d congresses, 1847-53; moved to St. Louis, 185 served at lt. col. Confederate Army, Civil War; pra ticed law, N.Y.C., 1868-72, later in St. Lou mem. Mo. Senate, 1878-82. Died St. Louis, Fe 28, 1896; buried Bellefontaine Cemetery.

CABELL, James Lawrence, physician, educato b. Nelson County, Va., Aug. 26, 1813; s. D George and Susanne (Wyatt) C.; M.A., U. Va 1833; M.D., U. Md., 1834; LL.D. (hon.), Ham den-Sydney Coll., 1873; m. Margaret Gibbons, Fe 5, 1839. Prof. anatomy, surgery and physiology Va., 1837-89, chmn. faculty, 1846-47; a leader early pub. health movement in U.S.; chief surge Confederate hosps., Charlottesville; pres. Med. So Va.; pres. Am. Pub. Health Assn., 1 year; pre Nat. Bd. Health, 1879-84. Author: Unity of Ma kind. 1858. Died Albemarle County, Va., Aug. 1 1889.

CABELL, Joseph Carrington, legislator, car co. exec.; b. Nelson County, Va., Dec. 28, 177 s. Col. Nicholas and Hannah (Carrington) C.; gra Coll. William and Mary, 1798; m. Mary Cart Jan. 1, 1807. Mem. Va. Ho. of Dels., 1809, 31-3 instrumental in establishing Literary Fund; me Va. Senate, 1810-29; secured legislative sancti and obtained financial appropriations for U. V (prin. coadjutor of Thomas Jefferson in founding called DeWitt Clinton of Va. for services as pionee pres. James River & Kanawha Canal Co. Died Fe 5, 1856.

CABELL, Nathaniel Francis, author; b. Nels County, Va., July 23, 1807; s. Nicholas and Ma garet (Venable) C.; grad. Hampden-Sydney Coll 1825; grad. Harvard Law Sch., 1827; m. An Blaws Cocke, Sept. 14, 1831; m. 2d, Mary Kelle at least 1 child. Mrs. R. Kenna Campbell. Own large estate "Liberty Hall." Nelson County, Va 1832-91; devoted time to writing; contbr. to r ligious and agrl. periodicals; became a Swedenbo gian, 1842; writings include: Reply to Rev. D Pond's "Swedenborgianism Reviewed," 1848; A Le ter on the Trinal Order for the Ministry of the N Church, 1848; The Progress of Literature duri the Preceding Century When Viewed from a R ligious Standpoint, 1868; editor: Early History the University of Virginia as Contained in Lette of Thomas Jefferson and Joseph C. Cabell, 185 Died Bedford City, Va., Sept. 1, 1891; buri "Liberty Hall."

CABELL, Samuel Jordan, congressman; b. A herst County, Va., Dec. 15, 1756; s. Col. Willi and Margaret (Jordan) C.; m. Sally Syme, 178 Commd. maj. 6th Va. Regt., 1775, served at Vall Forge and in Washington's campaigns of 177 commd. lt. col., 1779; lt. Amherst County (Va Militia, 1784; mem. Va. Legislature, 1785-86; me U.S. Ho. of Reps. from Va., 4th-7th congress 1795-1803; an original mem. Va. Soc. of Cinci nati. Died Nelson County, Va., Aug. 4, 1818; buri family burial grounds "Soldiers' Joy" farm, N wood, Va.

CABELL, William, planter, public ofcl.; b. Gooc land County, Va., Mar. 24, 1730; s. William a Elizabeth (Burks) C.; m. Margaret Jordan, 17 7 children including Samuel Jordan. Sheriff of Alb marle County (Va.), 1751; granted large esta in Amherst County (Va.) by King George III, 17 mem. Va. Ho. of Burgesses, 1757-75; 1st presidi magistrate, 1st lt., 1st surveyor, 1st coroner A herst County; del. Stamp Act Congress, 1765; sig Articles of Association, Williamsburg, Va., 17 mem. Va. Com. of Safety; mem. Va. Senate, 177 81, Va. Ho. of Reps., 1781-83, 87-88; del. V Conv. to ratify U.S. Constn., 1788, voted agai ratification; presdl. elector, 1789; trustee Ham den-Sydney Coll., 1789-98. Died Union Hill; Va Mar. 23, 1798.

CABELL, William H., gov. Va.; b. Cumberla County, Va., Dec. 16, 1772; s. Col. Nicholas a Hannah (Carrington) C.; received law degree Co William and Mary, 1793; m. Elizabeth Cabell, A 9, 1795; m. 2d, Agnes Gamble, Mar. 11, 180 Licensed to practice law, 1794; mem. Va. Legis ture from Amherst County, 1796-1805; presdl. el tor, 1800, 04; elected gov. Va., 1805-08; trus Hampden-Sydney Coll., 1809-30; judge Va. Ge Ct. 1808-11; judge Va. Ct. Appeals, Apr., 1811, apptd., 1830, pres., 1842; mem. bd. commrs. app by Va. Legislature to select site for U. Va., 18 Died Richmond, Va., Jan. 12, 1853; buried Sho hoe Cemetery, Richmond.

CABET, Etienne, Utopian reformer; b. Dijo France, Jan. 1, 1788; Dr. Law, U. Dijon, 1812; Delphine Lesage. Participant in July 1830 Revol tion; founder newspaper Le Populaire, 1833; pol exile, 1834-39; leader expdn. to Nauvoo, Ill.

ound Utopian settlement Icaria, 1849, pres., 849-56; became Am. citizen, 1854. Died St. Louis, Nov. 8, 1856.

CABLE, Joseph, congressman, newspaper publisher; b. Jefferson County (then Territory North-West of Ohio River) now Ohio, Apr. 17, 1801; studied law. Admitted to bar, began practice law in Jefferson County; founder, publisher Jeffersonian and Democrat, Steubenville, O., 1831, later of the Ohio Patriot, New Lisbon, O.; mem. U.S. Ho. of Reps. (Democrat) from Ohio, 31st-32d congresses, 1849-53; began publishing Daily Sandusky (O.) Mirror, 1853; established the American, later the Bulletin, Van Wert, O., 1857; moved to Wauseon, O., established Wauseon Republican; later moved to Paulding, O., published Polit. Review. Died Paulding, May 1, 1880; buried Live Oak Cemetery.

CABOT, Edward Clarke, architect; b. Boston, Apr. 17, 1818; s. Samuel and Eliza (Perkins) C.; m. Martha Robinson, July 7, 1842; m. 2d, Louisa Sewall, Oct. 13, 1873; 8 children. Architect, Boston, 1845-88; practiced in partnership with brother James, 1849-58, 62-65, Frank Chandler, 1875-78; mem. archtl. firm Cabot, Everett & Meade, 1878-88; commd. lt. col. 44th Mass. Inf., U.S. Volunteers, 1861; designer Boston Theatre, 1852, Johns Hopkins U. Hosp., 1889. Died Jan. 5, 1901.

CABOT, George, senator, businessman; b. Salem, Mass., Dec. 3, 1751; s. Joseph and Elizabeth (Higginson) C.; ed. Harvard; m. Elizabeth Higginson, 1774. Mem. Mass. Provincial Congress, 1776; dir. Mass. Bank, 1784; mem. Mass. Conv. which adopted U.S. Constn., 1788; promoter Essex Bridge and Beverly Cotton Manufactory, 1788; mem. U.S. Senate from Mass., June 1791-May 1796, framed Act of 1792 granting bounties for codfishing; pres. Boston br. U.S. Bank, 1803; dir. Suffolk Ins. Co.; pres. Boston Marine Ins. Co., circa 1809. Died Boston, Apr. 18, 1823; buried Mt. Auburn Cemetery, Cambridge, Mass.

CABOT, John, explorer; b. Genoa, Italy, 1450; 3 sons—Lewes, Sebastian, Santius. Engaged in trading activities in early life; became interested in finding Western water route to Orient; moved with family to Bristol, Eng., circa 1484; calculated that he would try to reach island of Brazil or Seven Cities (of fable) and then continue to Asia; attempted trips for several years (all unsuccessful); when news of Columbus' discovery came (1493) he gave up idea of reaching islands, decided instead to push on to Asia; by ofcl. permission of King Henry VII (1496) finally set sail in ship Mathew with 18 men, 1497; sailed N.W. from Ireland and reached Cape Breton Island, 1497, claimed it for Henry VII, convinced he had reached Asia; sailed North, naming several more islands on his way back, reached Bristol, 1497; convinced Henry VII that another voyage could reach Japan and thus enrich throne; granted new patents by king, 1498; left Bristol with intentions to reach Greenland (or Asia as he thought) and follow coast South, 1498; reached Greenland in early June, named it Labrador's Land for 1 of his sailors, Joao Fernandes, (called Llavrador); sailed North encountering many icebergs; crew mutinied and refused to proceed further North, 1498; reached modern Baffin Land, in 66° latitude, thought it to be part of Asia and proceeded South; passed Newfoundland, N.S. and New Eng. still searching for Japan as far South as 38th parallel; finding no signs of civilization, returned to Eng. late 1498. Died 1498.

CABOT, Sebastian, explorer; probably born Venice, Italy, circa 1476; son of John Cabot. Came to N.Am. to search for N.W. passage, May 1498; discovered Newfoundland, sailed along coast as far South as Chesapeake Bay; apptd. mem. Council of the New Indies by Ferdinand V of Spain; pilot-major, W.I., 1518; tried to discover S.W. passage to India, 1526; discovered Plata River, 1527; went to Spain, 1530; summoned to Eng. by Edward VI to supervise exploratory expdns., 1548; became pres. of exploration co., 1556. Died London, Eng., circa 1557.

CABRILLO, Juan Rodriguez, explorer; b. Portugal, Went to Mexico, 1520; with Hernando de Cortés in capture of Mexico City, 1520; explored Cal. under commn. of King of Spain, 1542-43; discoverer of islands of Santo Tomás, Santa Cruz, San Miguel, San Bernardo, Asunción, San Esteban, Santa Catalina; discovered San Diego Bay, Santa Monica Bay, Santa Bárbera Channel, Monterey Bay, Santa Lucia Mountains. Author: Viaje y descubrimientos hasta el grado 43 de Latitud. Died San Miguel Island, Cal., Jan. 3, 1543.

CADILLAC, Sieur de, see de la Mothe, Antoine.

CADWALADER, John, army officer; b. Phila., Jan. 1742; s. Dr. Thomas and Hannah (Lambert) C.; ed. U. Pa.; m. Elizabeth Lloyd, Oct. 1768; m. 2d, Williamina Bond, Jan. 30, 1779. Commd. col. of a Phila. bn.; commd. brig. gen. Pa. Militia, 1776; participated in battles of Trenton, Brandywine, Princeton, Germantown; challenged and wounded Gen. Conway (of Conway Cabal, plot to undermine authority of George Washington as comdr.-in-chief) in a duel, winter 1777-78. Died Shrewsbury, Kent County, Md., Feb. 10, 1786; buried Shrewsbury Ch.

CADWALADER, John, jurist, congressman; b. Phila., Apr. 1, 1805; s. John and Mary (Biddle) C.; grad. U. Pa., 1821; m. Mary Binney, 1825; m. 2d, Henrietta Maria Bancker, 1833. Admitted to Pa. bar, 1825; counsel Bank of U.S., 1830; vice provost Law Acad. of Phila., 1833-53; mem. U.S. Ho. of Reps. from Pa., 34th Congress, 1855-57; judge U.S. Dist. Ct. of Eastern Pa., 1858-79. Died Phila., Jan. 26, 1879; buried Christ Churchyard, Phila.

CADWALADER, Lambert, army officer, congressman; b. Trenton, N.J., 1743; s. Dr. Thomas and Hannah (Lambert) C.; ed. U. Pa.; m. Mary McCall, 1793. Signer, Non-Importation Agreement of 1765; mem. Com. of Correspondence; mem. Pa. Provincial Conv., 1775, Pa. Constl. Conv., 1776; commd. lt. col. 3d Pa. Bn., 1776; mem. Continental Congress from N.J., 1784-87; mem. U.S. Ho. of Reps. from N.J., 1st, 3d congresses, 1789-91, 93-95. Died Trenton, Sept. 13, 1823; buried Friends Burying Ground, Trenton.

CADWALADER, Thomas, surgeon; b. Phila., 1708; s. John and Martha (Jones) C.; m. Hannah Lambert, 1738. A founder (with Benjamin Franklin) Phila. Library, 1731; performed earliest recorded autopsies in Am. 1742; subscribed to founding Pa. Hosp., 1751; trustee U. Pa., 1751; mem. Common Council of Phila., 1751-74, Provincial Council of Pa., 1755-76; signer Non-Importation Agreement of 1765; mem. Am. Philos. Soc.; one of most noted 18th century Am. physicians. Died Trenton, N.J., Nov. 14, 1799.

CADY, Daniel, congressman, jurist; b. Chatham, N.Y., Apr. 29, 1773; s. Eleazer and Tryphena (Beebe) C.; m. Margaret Livingston, July 8, 1801; children include Elizabeth (Cady) Stanton. Admitted to N.Y. bar, 1795; elected to N.Y. Legislature, 1808-09, 11-13; mem .U.S. Ho. of Reps. from N.Y., 14th Congress, 1815-1817; elected asso. judge Supreme Ct. N.Y., 1847, reelected, 1849-1854. Died Johnstown, N.Y., Oct. 31, 1859; buried Johnstown Cemetery.

CADY, John Watts, congressman, lawyer; b. Florida, N.Y., June 28, 1790; grad. Union Coll., Schenectady, N.Y., 1808; studied law. Admitted to N.Y. bar, began practice Law in Johnstown, N.Y.: town clk. Town of Johnstown, 1814, 16, 17; county supr., 1818-22, 26-29; mem. N.Y. State Assembly, 1822; mem. U.S. Ho. of Reps. (Whig) from N.Y., 18th Congress, 1823-25; dist. atty. Fulton County (N.Y.), 1840-46; justice of the peace Johnstown, 1853. Died Johnstown, Jan. 5, 1854; buried Johnstown Cemetery.

CAFFERTY, James H., artist; b. Albany, N.Y., 1819. Went to N.Y.C., circa 1840; frequent exhibitor at Am. Acad., exhibited at N.A.D., became asso., 1850, mem., 1853; exhibited at Boston Athenaeum, Washington (D.C.) Art Assn., Pa. Acad. Died N.Y.C., Sept. 7, 1869.

CAGE, Harry, congressman, lawyer; b. Cages Bend, Sumner County, Tenn.; studied law. Moved to Miss. in early youth; admitted to Miss. bar, began practice law in Woodville, Miss.; judge Supreme Ct. of Miss., 1829-32; mem. U.S. Ho. of Reps. from Miss., 23d Congress, 1833-35; ret. from practice law, settled on Woodlawn Plantation, nr. Houme, Terrebonne Parish, La. Died New Orleans, 1859; buried Stewart family cemetery, Wilkinson County, Miss.

CAHOON, William, congressman; b. Providence, R.I., Jan. 12, 1774; attended common schs. Moved to Lyndon, Vt., 1791, engaged in milling, agrl. pursuits; mem. Vt. Ho. of Reps., 1802-10; succeeded father as town clk., 1808; Democratic presdl. elector, 1808, messenger to deliver electoral vote of Vt.; county judge, 1811-19; apptd. maj. gen. Vt. Militia, 1808, served during War of 1812; del. Vt. constl. convs., 1814, 28; mem. exec. council, 1815-20; lt. gov. of Vt., 1820-21; mem. U.S. Ho. of Reps. (Anti-Masonic Party) from Vt., 21st-22d congresses, 1829-33. Died Lyndon, May 30, 1833; buried Lyndon Town Cemetery, Lyndon Center, Vt.

CAIN, Richard Harvey, clergyman, congressman, coll. pres.; b. Greenbrier County, Va., Apr. 12, 1825; ed. Wilberforce U., 1860, D.D. (hon.), 1873. Born of free Negro parents; ordained deacon African Methodist Episcopal Ch., 1859, elder, 1862; published newspaper Missionary Record, Washington, D.C.; mem. S.C. Constl. Conv. 1868; mem. S.C. Senate from Charleston dist., 1868-70; mem. U.S. Ho. of Reps. from S.C., 43d, 45th congresses, 1873-75, 77-79; bishop Diocese of La. and Tex., 1880; founder, pres. Paul Quinn Coll.; presiding bishop 1st Episcopal dist. A.M.E. Ch., including confs. of N.Y., N.J., and Phila. Died Washington, D.C., Jan. 18, 1887; buried Graceland Cemetery, Washington.

CAINES, George, lawyer; b. 1771. Practiced law, N.Y.C., 1802-04, 07-25; reporter N.Y. Supreme Ct. (1st in U.S. to hold such a post), 1804-07. Author: An Inquiry into the Law Merchant of the United States, 1802; N.Y. Term Reports of Cases Argued and Determined in the Supreme Court of that State, 3 vols., 1804-06; Cases in Error, 2 vols., 1805-07; Summary of Practice in the Supreme Court of the State of N.Y., 1808. Died Catskill, N.Y., July 10, 1825.

CALDWELL, Capt. Billy (The Sauganash), Indian chief; b. Can., 1780; s. William Caldwell and a Potawatomi Indian woman; m. a Potawatomi, 1 son. Saved prisoners of Chgo. Massacre, 1812; trained by Roman Cath. priests, Detroit; interpreter, and perhaps sec. for Tecumseh, 1807-13; held title of capt. of Indian Dept. under Brit. Govt.; made his residence at present site of Chgo. and avowed allegiance to U.S., circa 1820; justice of peace, Chgo., 1826; with two other negotiators, kept Winnebago Indian chief Big Foot at peace, 1827; his house (built for him by govt. 1828) thought to have been 1st frame structure erected in Chgo. region; chief of Ottawa and Potawatomi Indians, dissuaded Indians from joining Black Hawk's band, 1832. Died Council Bluffs, Ia., Sept. 28, 1841.

CALDWELL, Charles, surgeon; b. Caswell County, N.C., May 14, 1772; s. Lt. Charles and Miss (Murray) C.; M.D., U. Pa., 1796; m. Eliza Leaming, 1799. Prof. faculty phys. scis. U. Pa.; founder med. dept. Transylvania U., prof. insts. medicine and clin. practice, 1819-37; 1st prof. U. Louisville (Ky.) 1837-49; author more than 200 books and papers. Died Louisville, July 9, 1853.

CALDWELL, Charles Henry Bromedge, naval officer; b. Hingham, Mass., June 11, 1823; s. Charles H. and Susan (Blagge) C. Commd. midshipman U.S. Navy, 1838, promoted lt., 1852, comdr., 1862, capt., 1867; chief of staff N. Atlantic fleet, 1870; promoted commodore, 1847; acting rear adm. in command S. Pacific fleet, 1876, S. Atlantic fleet 1877. Died Waltham, Mass., Nov. 30, 1877; buried Waltham.

CALDWELL, David, clergyman; b. Lancaster County, Pa., Mar. 22, 1725; s. Andrew and Ann (Stewart) C.; grad. Coll. of N.J. (now Princeton), 1761; m. Rachel Craighead, 1766. Licensed to preach by New Brunswick (N.J.) Presbytery, 1763; ordained to ministry Presbyn. Ch., Trenton, N.J., 1765; became pastor in Province of N.C., 1768, preached, practiced medicine, conducted classical sch.; tried unsuccessfully to prevent Battle of Alamance, 1771; mem. N.C. Constl. Conv., 1776; forced to remain in hiding for awhile because Charles Cornwallis offered reward of 200 pounds for his capture; home plundered by British; mem. N.C. Conv. to ratify U.S. Constn. Died N.C., Aug. 25, 1824.

CALDWELL, George Alfred, congressman, lawyer; b. Columbia, Ky., Oct. 18, 1814; studied law. Admitted to Ky. bar, 1837, began practice law in Adair County; mem. Ky. Ho. of Reps., 1839-40; mem. U.S. Ho. of Reps. (Democrat) from Ky., 28th Congress, 1843-45, 31st Congress, 1849-51; commd. maj. and q.m. Volunteers, Mexican War, 1846, maj. inf., 1847, maj. of volunteers, 1847, brevetted lt. col., 1847 for gallant service in Battle of Chapultepec; del. Union Nat. Conv., Phila., 1866. Died Louisville, Ky., Sept. 17, 1866; buried Cave Hill Cemetery.

CALDWELL, Greene Washington, congressman, lawyer, physician; b. Belmont, Gaston County, N.C., Apr. 13, 1806; grad. med. dept. U. Pa., 1831; studied law. Practiced medicine; asst. surgeon U.S. Army, 1832; admitted to N.C. bar, began practice law in Charlotte; mem. N.C. House of Commons, 1836-41; mem. U.S. Ho. of Reps. (Democrat) from N.C., 27th Congress, 1841-43; apptd. supt. U.S. Mint at Charlotte, 1844; served as capt. of inf., Mexican War, commd. capt. Third Dragoons, 1847; mem. N.C. Senate, 1849; resumed practice of medicine. Died Charlotte, N.C., July 10, 1864; buried Old Cemetery.

CALDWELL, James, clergyman; b. Charlotte County, Va., Apr. 1734; s. John Caldwell; grad. Coll. of N.J. (now Princeton), 1759; m. Hannah Ogden, Mar. 14, 1763; 2 children, including John E. Ordained to ministry by Presbytery of New Brunswick, N.J., 1761; pastor First Presbyn. Ch., Elizabethtown, N.J., 1761-80; chaplain of Dayton's N.J. Brigade, 1776-81; his ch. used as a hosp. by Continental Army until it was burned by a Loyalist, 1780; active at Battle of Springfield, 1781. Killed by an Am. sentry (who was later hanged) in an argument over a package, Elizabethtown, N.J., Nov. 24, 1781.

CALDWELL, James, congressman; b. Balt., Nov. 30, 1770; ed. in Wheeling, Va. (now W.Va.). Moved to St. Clairsville, O., 1799, became a mcht., later a banker; del. 1st Ohio Constl. Conv.; clk. ct. of

Belmont County, O., 1806-10; capt. of an Ohio regt., War of 1812; mem. Ohio Senate, 1809-12; mem. U.S. Ho. of Reps. (Democrat) from Ohio, 13th, 14th congresses, 1813-17; Democratic presdl. elector, 1820, 24. Died Wheeling, May 1838; buried Episcopal Cemetery, St. Clairsville, O.

CALDWELL, James H., comedian; b. Eng., 1793. Brought to Charleston (S.C.) by Joseph G. Holman as new talent for Charleston Theatre, 1816; acted at St. Philippe Theatre, New Orleans, 1820, 21, at Petersburg, Va., summer season, 1821; promoted constrn. of Camp Street Theatre (1st gas lit bldg. in New Orleans), 1822; opened Salt House Theatre, St. Louis, 1827; built St. Charles Theatre, New Orleans, 1835; built theatre, Mobile, Ala., 1840; claimed bankruptcy and retired, 1843. Died 1863.

CALDWELL, Joseph, mathematician, coll. pres.; b. Lamington, N.J., Apr. 21, 1773; s. Joseph and Rachel (Harker) C.; grad. Princeton, 1791, LL.D. (hon.), 1816; A.M. (hon.), U. N.C., 1799, LL.D. (hon.), 1816; m. Susan Rowan, 1804; m. 2d, Helen Hogg, 1809. Tutor mathematics Princeton, 1795; prof. mathematics U. N.C., pres., 1804-12, 17-35; scientific expert in running boundary line between N.C. and S.C., 1813; erected astron. observatory 1830. Died Chapel Hill, N.C., Jan. 27, 1835.

CALDWELL, Joseph Pearson, congressman, lawyer; b. nr. Olin, N.C., Mar. 5, 1808; attended Bethany Acad., nr. Statesville, N.C.; studied law. Admitted to N.C. bar, began practice law in Statesville; mem. N.C. Senate, 1833-34; mem. N.C. House of Commons, 1838-44; mem. U.S. Ho. of Reps. (Whig) from N.C., 31st-32d congresses, 1849-53. Died Statesville, June 30, 1853; buried Old Statesville Cemetery.

CALDWELL, Patrick Calhoun, congressman, lawyer; b. nr. Newberry, S.C., Mar. 10, 1801; grad. S.C. Coll. (now U. S.C.), 1820); studied law. Admitted to S.C. bar, 1822, began practice law; mem. S.C. Ho. of Reps., 1836-38; mem. U.S. Ho. of Reps. (State Rights Democrat) from S.C., 27th Congress, 1841-43; mem. S.C. Senate, 1848. Died S.C., Nov. 22, 1855.

CALDWELL, Robert Porter, congressman, lawyer; b. Adair County, Ky., Dec. 16, 1821; attended public schs. in Troy and Lebanon, Tenn., studied law at Troy. Admitted to Tenn. bar, began practice law in Trenton, Tenn., 1845; mem. Tenn. Ho. of Reps., 1847-48, Tenn. Senate, 1855-56; atty. gen. for 16th Jud. Circuit of Tenn., 1858; served as maj. 12th Regt., Tenn. Inf., Confederate Army, Civil War; mem. U.S. Ho. of Reps. (Democrat) from Tenn., 42d Congress, 1871-73. Died Trenton, Mar. 12, 1885; buried Oakland Cemetery.

CALDWELL, Samuel Lunt, clergyman, coll. pres.; b. Newburyport, Mass., Nov. 13, 1820; grad. Waterville (Me.) Coll. (now Colby), 1839, D.D. (hon.), 1858; grad. Newton (Mass.) Theol. Sem., 1845; LL.D. (hon.), Brown U., 1884. Taught at various acads. after coll. graduation; ordained to ministry Baptist Ch., 1845; pastor Bapt. Ch., Alexandria, Va., 1845-46, 1st Bapt. Ch., Bangor, Me., 1846-50, 1st Bapt. Ch., Providence, R.I., 1858-73; prof. ch. history Newton Theol. Instn., 1873-78; pres. Vassar Coll., 1878-85. Compiler (hymn book) Service of Song. Editor: Publications of the Narragansett Club, Vols. III, IV, 1865. Died Providence, Sept. 10, 1889.

CALEF, Robert, mcht.; b. Eng., 1648; 8 children including Robert. Mcht., Boston, 1688-1719; started dispute with Mather family by accusing Cotton Mather of attempting to start "witch hunt" similar to one at Salem, Mass., 1693; believed that witches existed, but denied possibility of proving anyone to be a witch; expressed his views in More Wonders of the Invisible World, 1697, copy of book publicly burned in Harvard Square by Increase Mather. Died Roxbury, Mass., Apr. 13, 1719.

CALHOON, John, congressman, lawyer; b. Henry County, Ky., 1797; studied law. Admitted to the bar, practiced law; mem. Ky. Ho. of Reps., 1820-21, 29-30; elected to 20th Congress from Ky. to fill vacancy, 1827, resigned in order to avoid contest; mem. U.S. Ho. of Reps. (Whig) from Ky., 24th-25th congresses, 1835-39; moved to St. Louis, 1839, practiced law; returned to Ky.; apptd. judge 14th Jud. Circuit, Ky., 1842.

CALHOUN, John, legislator; b. Boston, Oct. 14, 1806; s. Andrew and Martha (Chamberlin) C.; m. Sarah Cutter, Dec. 29, 1831, 9 children. Elected to Ill. Legislature, 1838, clk. Ho. of Reps., 1839-40, 40-41; mayor Springfield (Ill.); surveyor gen. Kan., 1854; pres. Kan. Constl. Conv., 1857, blamed for pro-slavery constl. clause scandal in which vote was practically denied free-soil adherents. Died St. Joseph, Mo., Oct. 13, 1859.

CALHOUN, John Caldwell, vice pres. U.S., senator; b. Abbeville Dist., S.C., Mar. 18, 1782; s. Patrick and Martha (Caldwell) C.; grad. Yale, 1804, Litchfield (Conn.) Law Sch., 1806; m. Floride Bouneau, Jan. 1811, 9 children. Admitted to S.C. bar, 1807; mem. S.C. Legislature, 1808; mem. U.S. Ho. of Reps. from S.C., 12th-15th congresses, 1811-17, acting chmn. house com. on fgn. affairs, 1811, one of group called War Hawks, presented resolution recommending declaration of war on Eng., 1812; resigned U.S. Ho. of Reps. to become U.S. sec. of war, 1817-25; vice pres. U.S. under John Q. Adams, 1825-29, under Andrew Jackson, 1829-32 (resigned because of dispute with Jackson over states rights and nullification); leader and polit. theoretician of states rights point of view; formulated S.C.'s policy during nullification crisis, declaring that a state can nullify laws it considers unconstl., 1832-33; mem. U.S. Senate from S.C., 1832-43, 45-50, leading senatorial champion of slavery and the So. cause of states rights under his philosophy of "concurrent majorities" or mutual checks whereby each sect. of the country was to share equally in fed. power; U.S. sec. of state under Tyler, 1843-45. R.K. Crallé published compilation of Calhoun's works, 6 vols., 1851-55. Died Washington, D.C., Mar. 31, 1850; buried St. Philip's Churchyard, Charleston, S.C.

CALHOUN, Joseph, congressman; b. Staunton, Va., Oct. 22, 1750. Became a farmer nr. the present town of Abbeville, S.C.; mem. S.C. Ho. of Reps., 1804-05; col. S.C. Militia; mem. U.S. Ho. of Reps. (Democrat, filled vacancy) from S.C., 10th-11th congresses, June 2, 1807-11; returned to farming and milling. Died Calhoun Mills, Abbeville Dist. (now Mount Carmel, McCormick County), S.C., Apr. 14, 1817; buried family burying ground.

CALHOUN, William Barron, congressman; b. Boston, Dec. 29, 1796; s. Andrew and Martha (Chamberlain) C.; grad. Yale, 1814; (hon.) LL.D., Amherst Coll., 1858; m. Margaret Kingsbury, May 11, 1837. Admitted to Mass. bar, 1818; mem. Mass. Legislature, 1825-35, speaker house, 1828-33; trustee Amherst Coll., 1829-65; chmn. Am. Inst. Instrn., 1830, also v.p., pres.; mem. U.S. Ho. of Reps. from Mass., 24th-27th congresses, 1834-43; presdl. elector, 1844; mem. Mass. Senate, 1846; sec. Commonwealth of Mass., 1848-51; mayor Springfield (Mass.), 1859. Died Springfield, Nov. 8, 1865; buried Springfield Cemetery.

CALIFORNIA JOE, see Milner, Moses Embree.

CALKINS, Norman Allison, ednl. adminstr.; b. Gainesville, N.Y., Sept. 9, 1822; s. Elisha Remings and Abigail (Lockwood) C.; m. Mary Hoosier, 1854. Prin., Central Sch., Gainesville; supt. schs. Gainesville, 1845-46; editor The Student (monthly mag. for sch. age children), N.Y.C., 1846-56; asst. supt. schs. N.Y.C., 1862-95; prof. methods and principles of teaching at Saturday sessions of N.Y.C. Normal Coll.; pres. dept. elementary schs. N.E.A., 1873, pres. dept. sch. superintendence, 1883, treas., 1883-85, pres., 1886. Author: Primary Object Lessons for a Graduated Course of Development, 1861; Teaching Color, 1877; Manual of Object-Teaching, 1882; How to Teach Phonics, 1889. Died N.Y.C., Dec. 22, 1895.

CALKINS, William Henry, congressman, lawyer; b. Pike County, Ind., Feb. 18, 1842; studied law. Admitted to the bar, practiced law; served with Union Army, 1861-65, attached to 14th Ia. Inf., then 12th Ind. Cavalry; moved to LaPorte County, Ind.; state's atty. 9th Ind. Jud. Circuit, 1866-70; mem. Ind. Ho. of Reps., 1871; mem. U.S. Ho. of Reps. (Republican) from Ind., 45th-48th congresses, 1877-Oct. 20, 1884 (resigned); practiced law in Tacoma, Wash.; apptd. U.S. asso. judge for Territory of Wash. (until admitted as state), Apr.-Nov. 11, 1889. Died Tacoma, Jan. 29, 1894; buried Tacoma Cemetery.

CALL, Jacob, congressman, lawyer; b. in Ky.; grad. acad. in Ky.; studied law. Admitted to the bar, practiced law, Vincennes and Princeton, Ind.; judge Knox County Circuit Ct., 1817-18, 22-24; mem. U.S. Ho. of Reps. from Ind., (filled vacancy) 18th Congress, Dec. 24, 1824-25. Died Frankfort, Ky., Apr. 20, 1826.

CALL, Richard Keith, territorial gov.; b. Pittsfield, Va., 1791; s. William and Helen (Walker) C.; m. Mary Kirkham, 1824. Commd. 1st lt. 44th Inf., U.S. Army, 1814, capt. 1818; commd. brig. gen. W. Fla. Militia, 1823; territorial del. from Fla. to U.S. Congress, 1823; built 3d railroad in Am., from Tallahasse (Fla.) to St. Marks, Fla., 1832-34; gov. Territory of Fla., 1836-39, 41-44; commd. maj. gen. Fla. Militia, 1846. Died Tallahasse, Sept. 14, 1862.

CALLENDER, James Thomson, polit. writer; b. Scotland, 1758; 4 children. Came to Am. as polit. refugee, 1793; reporter Phila. Gazette, 1793-96; an excellent scandal monger, exposed Alexander Hamilton's illicit affair with a Mrs. Reynolds in History of the United States for 1796, published 1797; reporter Richmond (Va.) Examiner, 1799-1800, The Recorder, 1802-03; imprisoned under Sedition Law for remarks made about Pres. John Adams, 9 months, 1800; conducted slander campaigns against Thomas Jefferson because he was disappointed in his hopes for an important presdl. appointment, 1801-03. Drowned in James River while intoxicated, Richmond, Va., July 17, 1803.

CALLENDER, John, clergyman; b. Boston, 1706; s. John Callender; grad. Harvard, 1723; m. Elizabeth Hardin, 1730; 6 children. Licensed to preach by First Baptist Ch., Boston, 1727; pastor at Swansey, Mass., 1728-30, First Bapt. Ch., Newport, R.I., 1731-48. Author: Historical Discourse on the Civil and Religious Affairs of the Colony of Rhode Island and Providence Plantations (only written history of R.I. until 1840), 1739. Died Newport, Jan. 26, 1748.

CALLIÉRES BONNEVUE, Louis Hector de, see De Calliéres Bonnevue.

CALVERT, Cecil (lord of Maryland and Avalon, 2d lord Baltimore); b. 1606; eldest son of George Calvert; ed. Oxford (Eng.) U.; m. Anne Arundel, circa 1623. Inherited charter of Md. on his father's death, 1632; sent group of 20 colonists and 300 laborers to Md., under his brother Leonard's leadership, 1633 (group established settlement at St. Mary's); did not come to Md. himself, kept in Eng. by enemies who tried throughout his life to break the royal grant and gain Md. plantation for Va.; Anne Arundel County (Md.) named for his wife. Died 1675.

CALVERT, Charles (3d baron Baltimore), propr. province Md., proprietary gov.; b. London, Eng., Aug. 27, 1629; s. Cecilius (2d baron Baltimore) and Anne (Arundel) C.; married 4 times, 5 children. Proprietary gov. Md., 1661-75, proprietor of province, 1675-88 (title ended with Protestant Revolution). Died Epsom, Eng., Feb. 21, 1715.

CALVERT, Charles Benedict, congressman; b. Riverdale, Md., Aug. 23, 1808; s. George and Rosalie Eugenia (Stier) C.; grad. U. Va., 1827; m. Charlotte Norris, June 6, 1839. Founder, Md. Agrl. Coll.; mem. com. on agr. U.S. Agrl. Soc., 1853, lobbied in Congress for establishment U.S. Dept. of Agr.; mem. U.S. Ho. of Reps. from Md. (Republican), 37th Congress, 1861-63, mem. com. on agr., wrote bill establishing Bur. of Agr., 1862. Died Riverdale, Md., May 12, 1864.

CALVERT, George (1st baron Baltimore), founder Md.; b. Kipling, Eng., circa 1580; s. Leonard and Grace (Crossland) C.; grad. Trinity Coll., Oxford (Eng.) U., 1597, M.A. (hon.), 1605; m. Anne Mynne, 1604-05; m. 2d, Joan; 11 children, including Philip, Cecilius, Leonard, George. Clk. of the crown County Clare (Ireland), 1606; mem. Parliament for Boissiney, 1609, for Yorkshire, 1621-24, returned as mem. for Oxford U., 1624-25; member of the Virginia Co., 1609-20; clk. Privy Council, 1613; created knight, 1617; prin. sec. of state, 1619-25, resigned office when converted to Catholicism, 1625; created baron of Baltimore, 1625; mem. of the council New England Company, 1622; mem. Privy Council, 1619-32; purchased tract of land on portion of peninsula of Avalon, Southeast Newfoundland, 1620, received grant from King James for the whole of Newfoundland, 1622, on visit there found the climate too severe, 1627, appealed to crown for a tract in Va.; Va. settlers inhospitable to his Catholicism, received grant for what is now Md., 1632; wrote charter of Md., laid foundations for one of most successful govts. in colonies, died before sealing of charter, charter issued to son Cecilius, June 20, 1632. Died Apr. 15, 1632, London, Eng.

CALVERT, George Henry, mayor, author; b. Bladensburg, Md., June 2, 1803; s. George and Rosalie Eugenia (Stier) C.; grad. Harvard, 1823; m. Elizabeth Steuart, Mar. 8, 1829. Editor, Balt. American; chmn. Newport (R.I.) Sch. Com; Democratic mayor Newport, 1853-54; author over 30 vols. including: Illustrations of Phrenology, 1832; A Volume from the Life of Herbert Barclay, 1833; Don Carlos, 1836; Count Julian, 1840; Cabiro, 1840-64; Scenes and Thoughts in Europe, 1846-52; Poems, 1847; Comedies, 1856; Joan of Arc, 1860; The Gentleman, 1863; Anyta and Other Poems, 1863; Arnold and Andre, 1864; Ellen, 1869; Goethe, his Life and Works, 1872; Wordsworth, a Biographic, Aesthetic Study, 1875. Died Newport, May 24, 1889.

CALVERT, Leonard, colonial gov.; b. Eng., 1606; s. George (1st lord Baltimore) and Anne (Mynne) C.; m. Anne Brent; children—William, Anne. Came to Md., 1634, took possession for King of Eng.; established seat of govt., St. Mary's, Md.; commd. 1st gov. Md., also comdr.-in-chief armed forces, chief magistrate, chancellor and chief justice, 1637; lost Md. due to an insurrection, 1644, recovered possession, 1646; monument erected in his memory by State of Md., 1890. Died Md., June 9, 1647.

CALVIN, Samuel, congressman, lawyer; b. Washingtonville, Pa., July 30, 1811; attended Milton Acad.; studied law. Taught in Huntingdon Acad.;

admitted to Pa. bar, 1836, began practice law, Hollidaysburg, Pa.; mem. U.S. Ho. of Reps. (Whig) from Pa., 31st Congress, 1849-51; dir. Hollidaysburg Sch. Bd. for 30 years; mem. Pa. Revenue Bd.; mem. Pa. Constl. Conv., 1873. Died Hollidaysburg, Mar. 12, 1890; buried Presbyn. Cemetery.

CALYO, Nicolino, artist; b. Naples, Italy; studied at Naples Acad.; 2 sons, John A., Hannibal. Came to Am., circa 1830; worked in Balt., 1835; went to N.Y.C., painted great fire of Dec. 16 and 17, 1835; painted scenes from Mexican War, panorama of Connecticut River, exhibited in N.Y.C., Phila., Boston, New Orleans, 1847-52; worked in Spain, returned to Am., 1874. Died N.Y.C., Dec. 9, 1884.

CAMBRELENG, Churchill Caldom, congressman, diplomat; b. Washington, N.C., Oct. 24, 1786. Mem. U.S. Ho. of Reps. (Democrat) from N.Y., 17th-25th congresses, 1821-39; U.S. minister to Russia, 1840-41; represented Suffolk County, in N.Y. Constl. Conv., 1846, chmn. coms. on ways and means, commerce, fgn. affairs. Died West Neck, L.I., N.Y. Apr. 30, 1862; buried Greenwood Cemetery, Bklyn.

CAMERON, Alexander, architect; b. Halifax, N.S., Can., 1830; children include Robert A. Came to U.S., lived in New England., until 1859; practiced as architect, St. Louis; designed 4-story addition to Equitable Bldg., St. Louis; supervising architect for U.S. Govt. on old Custom House, St. Louis. Died Aug. 3, 1890.

CAMERON, Andrew Carr, labor leader, editor; b. Berwickon-Tweed, Eng., Sept. 28, 1836. Prominent mem. Typog. Union; editor Workingman's Advocate, 1864-80; leading labor editor of his time; pres. Chgo. Trades Assembly, Grand Eight Hour League, Ill. Labor Assn.; an organizer Nat. Labor Union; editor Inland Printer (leading typog. tech. jour.). Died Chgo., May 28, 1892.

CAMERON, Angus, senator, lawyer; b. Caledonia, N.Y., July 4, 1826; attended Genesee Wesleyan Sem., Lima, N.Y.; studied law, Buffalo, N.Y.; grad. Nat. Law Sch., Ballston Spa, N.Y., 1853. Admitted to N.Y. bar, 1853, began practice law in Buffalo, engaged in banking, one year; moved to LaCrosse, Wis., 1857, resumed practice law; mem. Wis. Senate, 1863-64, 71-72; mem. Wis. Assembly, 1866-67, speaker, 1867; del. Republican Nat. Conv., Balt., 1864; regent U. Wis., 1866-75; mem. U.S. Senate (Rep., filled vacancy) from Wis., 1875-81, Mar. 14, 1881-85. Died LaCrosse, Mar. 30, 1897; buried Oak Grove Cemetery.

CAMERON, Archibald, clergyman; b. Ken Loch in Lochaber, Scotland, circa 1771; s. John and Jannet (McDonald) C.; attended Transylvania Sem. Came to Am., 1774; licensed to preach, 1795; ordained to ministry Presbyn. Ch., 1796; frontier missionary in Ky.; mem. Ky. Synod of 1804. Author: The Faithful Steward, 1806; A Defense of the Doctrines of Grace, 1816; An Exposure of Falsehood and Folly, 1829. Died Dec. 4, 1836.

CAMERON, John, lithographer; b. Scotland, circa 1828. Came to Am.; lithographer with firm Currier & Ives, N.Y.C., 1848-62, specialized in horse prints, comics, caricatures; worked independently, did series of plates for Letts' Pictorial View of California, 1853; partner firms Lawrence & Cameron, Cameron & Walsh, 1859-60.

CAMERON, Robert Alexander, colonist, army officer; b. Bklyn., Feb. 22, 1828; s. Robert A. C.; grad. Ind. Med. Coll., 1849; m. Miss Flower. Owner Valparaiso (Ind.) Republican, 1857; served in Ind. Legislature, 1860; commd. capt. 9th Ind. Volunteres, 1861, lt. col. 19th volunteers, 1861, col. 34th volunteers, 1862; brig. gen. 3 divs. 13th Corps, U.S. Army, 1863; comd. Lafourche dist. Dept. of Gulf, 1864; brevetted Maj. gen., 1865; v.p. Union Colony which settled in Colo., 1869, pres., 1871; supt. Fountain Colony, founded Colorado Springs, 1871; founded Ft. Collins, 1873; warden of penitentiary, Canon City, Colo., 1885-87; immigration agt. Ft. Worth & Denver City R.R. Died Mar. 15, 1894.

CAMERON, Simon, senator, sec. of war, b. Lancaster County, Pa., Mar. 8, 1799; s. Charles and Martha (Pfoutz) C.; m. Margaret Brua; 5 children. Editor Bucks County (Pa.) Messenger, 1821; owner Harrisburg Republican, 1824; state printer Pa., circa 1825-27; adj. gen. Pa., 1826; constructed network of railroads in Pa. united into No. Central R.R.; founder Bank of Middleton, 1832; commr. for settling Winnebago Indian claims, 1838; mem. U.S. Senate from Pa., 1845-49, 57-61, 67-77 (radical Republican, 1867-77); leader Rep. Party in Pa., 1857-77, one of most successful machine politicians of his time, had strong support as Rep. presdl. nominee in conv., 1860; U.S. sec. of war, 1861-62; appt. U.S. minister to Russia, 1862. Died Lancaster County, Pa., June 26, 1889; buried Harrisburg, Pa.

CAMM, John, clergyman, coll. pres.; b. Eng., 1718; s. Thomas Camm; B.A., Trinity Coll., Cambridge; m. Betsy Hansford, 1769. Ordained to ministry Anglican Ch., Newport Parish, Va., 1745; successful in having Two Penny Acts of 1755 and 1758 disallowed by King in Council, 1759; prof. divinity Coll. William and Mary, 1749-56, 60-71, pres. 1771-77; rector Bruton Parish; commissary of Bishop of London; mem. Gov.'s Council, Va., Died Va., 1778.

CAMMERHOFF, John Christopher Frederick, missionary; b. Hillersleben, Germany, Aug. 8, 1721; grad. U. Jena (Germany), Moravian Theol. Sem., Marienborn, Germany, 1745; m. Anna von Pahlen, Aug. 3, 1746. Consecrated bishop of Moravian Ch., 1746; came to Am., 1746; asst. to Bishop A.G. Spangenberg, Pa., 1746-51; preached among Pa. Indians; adopted by Turtle tribe of Oneida Indians; attended Grand Council of Iroquois Confederacy, Onandaga, N.Y., 1750. Died Apr. 28, 1751.

CAMP, Hiram, clockmaker; b. Plymouth, Conn., Apr. 9, 1811; s. Samuel and Jeannette (Jerome) C.; m. Elvira Rockwell Skinner; m. 2d, Lucy Davis. Partner (with uncle Chauncey Jerome) in clockmaking shop, Bristol, Conn., 1829-53, opened branch, New Haven, Conn., 1843; founder New Haven Clock Co., 1853, pres., 1853-92, trustee, 1892-93, became largest clock mfr. in world; manufactured world's 1st "dollar watch"; selectman, councilman of New Haven; mem. Conn. Ho. of Reps., 1859; founded Mt. Hermon Boys' Sch., Northfield Sem. for Young Ladies. Died July 8, 1893.

CAMP, John Henry, congressman, lawyer; b. Ithaca, N.Y., Apr. 4, 1840; grad. Albany Law Sch., 1860. Admitted to N.Y. bar, 1860, began practice law in Lyons, N.Y.; clk. of surrogate ct., 1863; pros. atty. Wayne County, 1867-70; Republican presdl. elector, 1872, sec. of Electoral Coll.; mem. U.S. Ho. of Reps. (Rep.) from N.Y., 45th-47th congresses, 1877-83. Died Lyons, Oct. 12, 1892; buried Grove Cemetery, Trumansburg, N.Y.

CAMP, John Lafayette, army officer, territorial ofcl.; b. nr. Birmingham, Ala., Feb. 20, 1828; s. John L. and Elizabeth (Brown) C.; grad. U. Tenn., 1848; m. Mary Ward. Practiced law, Gilman, Tex., 1848-91; elected col. 14th Tex. Cavalry, 1865; elected to U.S. Congress from Tex. dist., 1866, not permitted to take seat; del. Tex. Constl. Conv., 1866; de. Nat. Democratic Conv., 1872; mem. Tex. Senate, 1874; judge Tex. Dist. Ct., 1878; registrar Ariz. Land Office, 1884-86; Camp County (Tex.) named after him. Died San Antonio, Tex., July 16, 1891.

CAMPANIUS, John, clergyman; b. Stockholm, Sweden, Aug. 26, 1601; s. Jonas Peter Campanius; attended U. Uppsala (Sweden). Ordained to ministry Lutheran Ch., 1633; came to Am., 1643, chaplain to Swedish gov. of Del., John Puntz; pastor at Ft. Christina (now Wilmington, Del.), 1643-48; missionary to Delaware Indians; pastor at Frosthult and Hernevi, Sweden, 1649-83. Died Sept. 28, 1683.

CAMPAU, Joseph, trader; b. Detroit, Feb. 25, 1769; s. Jacques and Catherine (Menard) C.; m. Adelaide Dequindre, May 12, 1808, 12 children. Owned many Indian trading posts, including those at Detroit, Saginaw, St. Clair (all Mich.) until 1843; invested in Detroit real estate; 1st millionaire in Mich.; largest landowner in Mich. by 1863; trustee, treas., assessor, and appraiser of Detroit, at various times; apptd. ensign Mich. Militia, 1796, later promoted maj. Died Detroit, July 23, 1863.

CAMPBELL, Albert H., civil engr., artist; b. Charlestown, Va. (now W.Va.), Oct. 23, 1836; grad. Brown U., 1847. Served as engr. and surveyor with several railroad surveys in S.W., circa 1850-60; chief Topographic Bur., Confederate States Army, during Civil War, made maps which were important to Confederate mil. tactics; chief engr. for several railroads in W.Va., after Civil War. Died Ravenswood, W.Va., Feb. 23, 1899.

CAMPBELL, Alexander, senator, physician; b. Frederick County, Va., 1779; ed. Pisgah Acad., Woodford County, Ky.; studied medicine Transylvania U. Began practice medicine, Cynthiana, Ky., 1801; mem. State Ho. of Reps. from Harrison County, 1803, from Adams County, 1807-09; speaker, 1808-09; practiced medicine, engaged in merc. pursuits, Adams County, Ky. (later set off to Brown County, O.), 1804-15; mem. U.S. Senate from Ohio (filled vacancy, Dec. 11, 1809-13; moved to Staunton (now Ripley), O., 1815, became 1st physician in town; mem. Ohio Ho. of Reps. from Clermont County, 1819, speaker pro tem, 1832-33; Democratic presdl. elector, 1820; Whig presdl. elector, 1836; mem. Ohio Senate, 1822-24; unsuccessful candidate for gov. Ohio, 1826; v.p. 1st gen. antislavery soc. ofOhio,1835; mayor Ripley, 1838-40. Died Ripley, Nov. 5, 1857; buried Maplewood Cemetery.

CAMPBELL, Alexander, a founder Disciples of Christ; b. County Antrim, Ireland, Sept. 12, 1786; s. Rev. Thomas and Jane (Corneigle) C.; attended U. Glasgow (Scotland), 1808; m. Margaret Brown, 1811. Came to Am. 1809; pastor Brush Run Ch.; started publ. Christian Baptist, 1823; with his father formed Disciples of Christ, 1827 (became known as Campbellites), membership numbered 350,000 by 1864; mem. Va. Constl. Conv., 1829; founder Bethany Coll., 1840, pres., 1840-66. Author: The Christian System, 1839; Memoirs of Elder Thomas Campbell, 1861. Died Bethany, W. Va., Mar. 4, 1866.

CAMPBELL, Allan, civil engr.; b. Albany, N.Y., Oct. 11, 1815; s. Archibald and Margaret (Adams) C.; m. Julia Cooper, 1843, 3 children, including Col. John Campbell. Civil engr. Erie Canal and Ohio River improvement, 1836-50; surveyed and constructed Copiapo to Caldera route, Chile (1st railroad operated in S. Am.), 1850-56; pres. Harlem R.R., 1856-62; engr. harbor defenses Port of N.Y., 1862-65; pres. Consolidation Coal Co.; commr. pub. works N.Y., 1876-80; comptroller N.Y., 1880; hon. mem. Am. Soc. C.E.; mem. N.Y. Hist. Soc., Century Club; vestryman Trinity Ch., N.Y.C. Died N.Y.C., Mar. 18, 1894.

CAMPBELL, Andrew, inventor, mfr.; b. Trenton, N.J., June 14, 1821; married, 1848, 4 children. Brushmaker, St. Louis, 1842-50; built 1st St. Louis omnibus; patented printing machine, 1858, began The Campbell Country Press; erected plant, Bklyn., 1866; developed 2 revolution picture press, 1867, large press for fine illustrations, 1868; made 1st press which printed, inserted, pasted, folded and cut in 1 continuous operation. Died Bklyn., Apr. 13, 1890.

CAMPBELL, Bartley, playwright, journalist; b. Pitts., Aug. 12, 1843; s. Bartley and Mary (Eckles) C. Editor, part owner Pitts. Leader, 1860; founder, editor So. Monthly Mag. New Orleans, 1869; mem. Bohemian Club, 1875; playwright, enjoyed fair internat. reputation, influential in establishing playwright profession in Am. Author plays: My Partner (most significant play), 1885; Fire, Peril, Fate, Risks, The Virginian (all 1872); Stan Vale, 1874; On The Rhine, The Big Bonanza (both 1875); A Heroine in Rags, 1876; How Women Love, Clio (both 1878), Fairfax, The Galley Slave (both 1879); Matrimony, 1880; Little Sunshine (only published play). Died Middletown, N.Y., July 30, 1888.

CAMPBELL, Brookins, congressman, lawyer; b. Washington County, Tenn., 1808; grad. Washington Coll. (now Washington and Lee U.); studied law. Admitted to the bar, practiced law; mem. Tenn. Ho. of Reps., 1835-39, 41-46, 51-53, speaker, 1845; served in Mexican War as asst. q.m. with rank of maj. U.S. Army, 1846; mem. U.S. Ho. of Reps. (Democrat) from Tenn., 33d Congress, 1853. Died Washington, D.C., Dec. 25, 1853; buried Providence Presbyn. Churchyard, Greene County, Tenn.

CAMPBELL, Charles, historian; b. Petersburg, Va., May 1, 1807; s. John Wilson Campbell; grad. Princeton, 1825. Wrote articles for So. Literary Messenger, 1837; founder, operator classical sch., Petersburg, 1842-55; prin. Anderson Acad., Petersburg, 1855-70; collector numerous hist. documents, manuscripts. Author: Bland Papers, 1840-43; An Introduction to the History of the Colony and Ancient Dominion of Virginia, 1847, 60; Genealogy of the Spotswood Family, 1868; published reprint and introduction of The History of Virginia (R. Beverley), 1855; author and editor Some Materials for a Memoir of John Daly Burk, 1868. Died Staunton, Va., July 11, 1876.

CAMPBELL, George Washington, senator, congressman; b. Sutherlandshire, Scotland, Feb. 8, 1769; s. Archibald and Elizabeth (Mackay) C.; grad. Princeton, 1794; m. Harriet Stoddert, 1812, 4 children. Came to Am. 1772; admitted to Tenn. bar, circa 1795; practiced in Knoxville, Tenn.; mem. U.S. Ho. of Reps. (Democrat) from Tenn., 8th-10th congresses, 1803-09; judge Tenn. Supreme Ct. of Errors and Appeals, 1809-11; mem. U.S. Senate from Tenn., Oct. 8, 1811-Feb. 11, 1814, Oct. 10, 1815-Apr. 20, 1818; U.S. sec. treasury, 1814; U.S. minister to Russia, 1818-21; mem. French Spoliation Claims Commn., 1831. Died Nashville, Tenn., Feb. 17, 1848; buried City Cemetery, Nashville.

CAMPBELL, George Washington, horticulturist; b. Cherry Valley, N.Y., Jan. 12, 1817; s. David Campbell; m. Elizabeth Little, Aug. 29, 1846. In mercantile business, Delaware, O., 1849-56; comml. horticulturist specializing in grapes, Delaware, 1856-98; rediscovered Delaware grape; discovered Campbell Early hybrid grape (named after him); U.S. commr. to Universal and Internat. Exhbn., Paris, France, 1878. Died July 15, 1898.

CAMPBELL, Henry Fraser, surgeon; educator; b. Augusta, Ga., Feb. 10, 1824; s. James and Mary (Eve) C.; M.D., Med Coll. Ga., 1842; m. Sarah (Sibley) Bosworth, June 17, 1844. Prof. comparative and microscopical anatomy Med. Coll. Ga., 1854-57; prof. anatomy, 1857-66, prof. orthopedic surgery and gynecology, 1868-91; recipient prize for investigation of excreto-secretory system by A.M.A., 1857; corrrespondent Acad. Natural Scis. Phila.; mem. Imperial Acad. Medicine St. Petersburg, 1860; served as surgeon Confederate Army, 1861, Bd. Med. Examiners; med. dir. Gen. Mil. Hosp. of Richmond (Va.); did original studies on nature of nervous system; pioneer in preventive medicine; pres. Ga. Med. Assn., 1871; mem. Ga. Bd. Health, 1875; a founder Am. Gynecol. Soc., 1876; pres. A.M.A., 1885; editor So. Med. and Surg. Jour., 1857-61. Died Augusta, Ga., Dec. 15, 1891.

CAMPBELL, Jacob Miller, congressman, businessman; b. "White Horse," nr. Somerset, Pa., Nov. 20, 1821; attended public schs. Learned printing trade in the office of the Somerset Whig; later connected with mag. publishing co., Pitts., newspapers in New Orleans; engaged in steamboating on lower Mississippi River, 1814-47, gold mining in Cal., 1851; aided in bldg. Cambria Iron Works, Johnstown, Pa., 1853, with co., 1853-61; del. 1st Republican Nat. Conv., Phila., 1856; served in Union Army as 1st lt. and q.m. Co. G, 3d Regt., Pa. Volunteer Inf., recruited the 54th Regt. of Inf., commd. as its col., 1862. brevetted brig. gen. for gallant service in Battle of Piedmont (Va.), 1865; surveyor gen. (later sec. internal affairs) of Pa., 1865-71; mech., indls. pursuits; mem. U.S. Ho. of Reps. (Rep.) from Pa., 45th, 47th-49th congresses, 1877-79, 81-87; financial interests in banking and steel mfg.; chmn. Pa. Rep. Conv., 1887. Died Johnstown, Sept. 27, 1888; buried Grand View Cemetery.

CAMPBELL, James, postmaster gen.; b. Phila., Sept. 1, 1812; s. Anthony and Catharine (McGarvey) C.; m. Emilie Chapron, Oct. 28, 1845, 3 children. Admitted to Phila. bar, 1833; sch. commr. Phila., 1840; judge Pa. Ct. Common Pleas, 1842-52; atty. gen. Pa., 1852; U.S. postmaster gen., 1853-57, lowered fgn. postal rates; unsuccessful candidate for U.S. Senate, 1863; trustee Girard Coll., Jefferson Med. Coll. Died Phila., Jan. 27, 1893.

CAMPBELL, James Hepburn, congressman, diplomat; b. Williamsport, Pa., Feb. 8, 1820; s. Francis and Jane (Hepburn) C.; grad. Dickinson Coll., 1841; LL.D., Carlisle (Pa.) Law Sch., 1841; m. Juliet Lewis, 1843. Admitted to Pa. bar, 1841; mem. U.S. Ho. of Reps. from Pa., 34th, 36th-37th congresses, 1855-57, 59-63, chmn. spl. com. on Pacific R.R.; served as lt. col. in command 39th Pa. Volunteers, 1863; apptd. U.S. minister to Sweden by Pres. Lincoln, 1864-67; declined appointment as U.S. minister to Bogota, Colombia, 1866. Died Wayne, Pa., Apr. 12, 1895, buried Woodlands Cemetery, Phila.

CAMPBELL, James Valentine, jurist; b. Buffalo, N.Y., Feb. 25, 1823; s. Henry M. and Lois (Bushnell) C.; grad. St. Paul's Coll., 1841; LL.D. (hon.), U. Mich., 1866; m. Cornelia Hotchkiss, Nov. 18, 1849. Admitted to Detroit bar, 1844; justice Mich. Supreme Ct., 1858-70, opinions recorded in Michigan Reports, 70 vols.; prof. law U. Mich., 1859-84. Author: Outlines of the Political History of Michigan, 1876. Died Detroit, Mar. 26, 1890.

CAMPBELL, John, journalist; b. Scotland, 1653; m. Mary Clarke; children—Sarah, Elizabeth. Came to Mass., 1695; postmaster, Boston, 1702-18; printed Boston Newsletter (1st established newspaper in Am., concerned chiefly with fgn. news), 1704-22; justice of peace, Boston. Died Boston, Mar. 15, 1727/28.

CAMPBELL, John (4th earl Loudoun), army officer; b. Scotland, May 5, 1705; s. Hugh (3d earl Loudoun) and Margaret (Dalrymple) C.; never married. Entered Scots Greys as cornet, 1727, rose to capt. with rank of lt. col. 3d Foot Guards, Brit. Army, by 1739; Scottish rep. in English Ho. of Lords (one of few Scottish peers allowed to sit), 1734; became gov. Stirling Castle, 1741; elected fellow Royal Soc., 1738; a.d.c. to King George II; adj. gen. to Sir John Cope during Jacobite rebellion, 1745; col. 30th Regt., Brit. Army, 1749, commd. maj. gen., 1755; comdr. in chief all forces in N.Am., col. in chief Royal Am. Regt., gov. gen. of Va., 1756-57; made improvements in tng. and transp. of troops in Am.; unsuccessful in attempt to take Louisbourg, recalled, 1757; commd. lt. gen., 1758; became gov. Edinburgh Castle, 1763; promoted gen., 1770, col. Scots Guards. Died Loudoun Castle, Scotland, Apr. 27, 1782.

CAMPBELL, John, congressman, lawyer; b. nr. Port Tobacco, Md., Sept. 11, 1765; studied law. Admitted to the bar, practiced law; held several local offices; mem. Md. Senate for several years; mem. U.S. Ho. of Reps. (Federalist) from Md., 7th-11th congresses, 1801-11; judge of orphans, ct., Charles County Md. Died "Charleston" farm, Charles County, June 23, 1828; buried pvt. burying ground on estate of Daniel Jenifer.

CAMPBELL, John, congressman, lawyer; b. nr. Brownsville, S.C.; grad. S.C. Coll. (now U. S.C.), 1819; studied law. Admitted to the bar, began practice law in Brownsville; moved to Parnassus, Marlboro Dist., S.C., continued law practice; mem. U.S. Ho. of Reps. from S.C., (States Rights Whig) 21st Congress, 1829-31, (State Rights Democrat) 25th-28th congresses, 1837-45. Died Parnassus (now Blenheim), S.C., May 19, 1845; buried pvt. cemetery nr. Blenheim.

CAMPBELL, John Allen, diplomat, gov. Wyo. Territory; b. Salem, Columbiana County, O., Oct. 8, 1835. Served as adj. gen. on Maj. Gen. Schofield's staff during Civil War; brevetted brig. gen., 1864; apptd. asst. sec. of war, 1868; 1st gov. Wyo. Territory, 1869-75; 3d asst. sec. of state, 1875-77; U.S. consul at Basel, Switzerland, 1877-80. Died Washington, D.C., July 14, 1880.

CAMPBELL, John Archibald, justice U.S. Supreme Ct.; b. Washington, Wilkes County, Ga., June 24, 1811; s. Duncan and Mary (Williamson) C.; grad. Franklin Coll. (now U. Ga.), 1825; attended U.S. Mil. Acad., 1825-28; m. Anna Goldthwaite. Admitted to Ga. bar, 1829; served 2 terms in Ala. Legislature; del. to Nashville Conv., 1850; asso. justice U.S. Supreme Ct., 1853-61; asst. sec. of war Confederate States Am., 1862-65; mem. Hampton Roads Peace Commn. that met with Lincoln, 1865. Died Balt., Mar. 12, 1889.

CAMPBELL, John Hull, congressman, lawyer; b. York, Pa., Oct. 10, 1800; studied law. Admitted to the bar in Phila., 1823, began practice law, Phila.; mem. Pa. Ho. of Reps., 1831; mem. U.S. Ho. of Reps. (Whig) from Pa., 29th Congress, 1845-47. Died Phila., Jan. 19, 1868; buried Monument Cemetery.

CAMPBELL, John Pierce, Jr., congressman, businessman; b. nr. Hopkinsville, Ky., Dec. 8, 1820; studied law. Admitted to Mo. bar, 1841, began practice law in Lexington, Mo.; mem. Mo. Ho. of Reps., 1848-52; returned to Hopkinsville, became a farmer; mem. U.S. Ho. of Reps. (Am. Party) from Ky., 34th Congress, 1855-57; pres. Henderson & Nashville R.R., 1870; organizer Mastodon Coal & Iron Co. (succeeded by St. Bernard Coal Co.); devoted later life to large land estates. Died Hopkinsville, Oct. 29, 1888; buried Riverside Cemetery.

CAMPBELL, John Wilson, congressman, jurist; b. Augusta County, Va., Feb. 23, 1782; s. William and Elizabeth (Wilson) C.; m. Eleanor Doak, 1811. Admitted to Ohio bar, 1808; mem. Ohio Legislature from Adams County, 1813-17; mem. U.S. Ho. of Reps. from Ohio, 15th-19th congresses, 1817-27; U.S. dist. judge for Ohio, 1828-33. Died Delaware, O., Sept. 24, 1833; buried Old North Cemetery, Columbus, O.

CAMPBELL, Lewis Davis, editor, congressman, diplomat; b. Franklin, Warren County, O., Aug. 9, 1811; s. Samuel and Mary (Small) G.; m. Jane Reily, 3 children. Admitted to Ohio bar, 1835; mem. U.S. Ho. of Reps. (Whig, later Democrat) from Ohio, 31st-35th, 42d congresses, 1849-59, 71-73, chmn. com. ways and means, 34th Congress; commd. col. 69th Regt., Ohio Volunteers, during Civil War; U.S. minister to Mexico, 1866-67. Died Hamilton, O., Nov. 26, 1882; buried Greenwood Cemetery, Hamilton.

CAMPBELL, Robert, fur trapper, banker; b. County Tyrone, Ireland, Mar. 1804; m. Virginia Kyle, 3 children. Came to U.S., 1824; fur trapper in Mo. and Western Mountains, 1824-35; pres. Bank of State of Mo., also Mchts.' Nat. Bank, 1842; col. on staff Gov. Edwards of Mo., 1846; apptd. (by Pres. Fillmore) Indian commr. Great Indian Conf., Ft. Laramie, 1851; reapptd. commr. by Pres. Grant, 1869. Died St. Louis, Oct. 16, 1879.

CAMPBELL, Robert Blair, congressman, diplomat; b. Marlboro County, S.C.; grad. S.C. Coll. (now U. S.C.), 1809. Became a farmer; commd. capt. S.C. Militia, 1814; mem. S.C. Senate, 1821-23, 30; mem. U.S. Ho. of Reps. from S.C., 18th Congress, 1823-25, (Nullifier, filled vacancy) 23d Congress, Feb. 27, 1834-35, (Whig) 24th Congress, 1835-37; during nullification movement, commd. gen. S.C. troops, 1833; moved to Lowndes County, Ala., circa 1840; mem. Ala. Ho. of Reps., 1840; consul at Havana, Cuba, 1842-50; moved to San Antonio, Tex.; apptd. a commr. for U.S. to aid in settlement of disputed boundary line between Tex. and Mexico, 1853; consul at London, Eng., 1854-61 (recalled). Died London, July 12, 1862; buried in the crypt of Kensington Ch.

CAMPBELL, Samuel, congressman; b. Mansfield, Conn., July 11, 1773; attended common schs. Became farmer in Columbus, N.Y.; supr. Town of Columbus, 1807-08, 21, 40; mem. N.Y. State Assembly, 1808-09, 12, 20; served on staff Maj. Gen. Nathaniel King as div. q.m., War of 1812; asso. judge Chenango County (N.Y.) Ct., 1814; justice of the peace, Columbus, 25 years; sheriff Chenango County, 1815-19; mem. U.S. Ho. of Reps. from N.Y., 17th Congress, 1821-23; became a Whig. Died Columbus, June 2, 1853; buried Lambs Corners Cemetery.

CAMPBELL, Thomas, clergyman; b. Scotland Feb. 1, 1763; s. Alexander Campbell; grad. U Glasgow (Scotland); at least 1 child, Alexander Became minister Secession Ch. (sect which ha broken away from Presbyn. Ch.); came to U.S. 1807; settled at Washington, Pa.; founded Christian Assn. of Washington (later known as Campbellites and Disciples of Christ); itinerant preache and schoolteacher in Pa. until becoming blind jus before death. Died Bethany, Va. (now W.Va.), Jan. 4, 1854.

CAMPBELL, Thomas Jefferson, congressman; b Rhea County, Tenn., 1786; attended public schs. Asst. insp. gen. to Maj. Gen. Cole's div. of East Tenn. Militia, 1813-14; clk. Tenn. Ho. of Reps., 1817-19, 21, 25-31, mem. Tenn. Ho. of Reps. 1833-37; Whig presdl. elector, 1840; mem. U.S. Ho. of Reps. (Whig) from Tenn., 27th Congress 1841-43; clk. U.S. Ho. of Reps., 30th-31st congresses, 1847-50. Died Washington, D.C., Apr. 13, 1850; buried Calhoun, McMinn County, Tenn.

CAMPBELL, Thompson, congressman; b. in Ireland, 1811; studied law in Pa. Admitted to bar in Pitts.; moved to Galena, Ill., engaged in mining; sec. of state State of Ill., 1843-46; del. Ill. Constl. Conv., 1847; mem. U.S. Ho. of Reps. (Democrat) from Ill., 32d Congress, 1851-53; del. Dem. Nat. Conv., Balt., 1852, Charleston, 1860; apptd. U.S. land commr. for Cal., 1853-55; returned to Ill.; nominated elector at large on Breckinridge and Lane ticket, 1860; returned to Cal.; mem. (Union Party) Cal. Ho. of Reps., 1863-64; del. Republican Nat. Conv., Balt., 1864. Died San Francisco, Cal., Dec. 6, 1868; buried Laurel Hill Cemetery.

CAMPBELL, William, army officer; b. Augusta County, Va., 1745; s. Charles and Miss (Buchanan) C.; m. Elizabeth Henry. Served as capt. Va. Militia; Indian fighter; justice Fincastle County (Va.), 1773; campaigned in Lord Dunmore's War, 1774; signed address from Fincastle County to Continental Congress declaring loyalty to Crown and willingness to fight for "constitutional rights," 1775; led his company to Williamsburg to help expel Gov. Dunmore, 1776; became boundary commr. between Va and Cherokees, 1778; became lt. col. and justice Washington County (Va.), 1777; del. to Va. Legislature; commd. col., 1780; led 400 men from Washington County to join Evan Shelby and John Sevier, fought Gen. Ferguson in Carolinas, 1780; led Va. Militia at Battle of Guilford, 1781, voted thanks, horse and sword by Continental Congress; elected to Va. Legislature, 1781; apptd. brig. gen. Va. Militia, 1781; fought under Lafayette in Battle of Jamestown. Died Rocky Mills, Va., Aug. 22, 1781.

CAMPBELL, William, colonial gov.; s. Archibald (4th duke Argyll) and Mary (Bellenden) C.; m. Sarah Izard, Apr. 7, 1763. Commd. capt., Brit. Navy, 1762; mem. Brit. Ho. of Commons, 1764; gov. Nova Scotia, 1766; last royal gov. S.C., 1775-77. Died Southampton, Eng., Sept. 5, 1778.

CAMPBELL, William Bowen, gov. Tenn., congressman; b. Sumner County, Tenn., Feb. 6, 1807; s. David and Catherine (Bowen) C.; m. Frances Owen, 1835. Admitted to Tenn. bar, 1829, mem. lower house Tenn. Legislature, 1835; served as capt. of co. in Seminole War, 1836; mem. U.S. Ho. of Reps. from Tenn., 25th-27th, 39th congresses, 1837-43, 66-67; elected to command 1st Regt. Tenn. Volunteers during Mexican War; last Whig gov. Tenn., 1851-53; circuit judge, 1857; commd. brig. gen. U.S. Volunteers, 1862. Died Lebanon, Tenn., Aug. 19, 1867; buried Cedar Grove Cemetery, Lebanon.

CAMPBELL, William Henry, clergyman, coll. pres.; b. Balt., Sept. 14, 1808; s. William and Ann (Ditchfield) C.; grad. Dickinson Coll., 1828; m. Katherine Schoonmaker, 1831. Licensed to preach by 2d Presbytery of N.Y., 1831; prin. Erasmus Hall, 1833-39; pastor, East N.Y., 1839-41, 3d Reformed Ch., Albany, 1841-48; prin. Albany Acad., 1848-51; prof. Oriental lit. Rutgers Coll., 1851-63, pres., 1863-82; established Suydam St. Ch., New Brunswick, N.J. Author: Subjects and Modes of Baptism, 1844, Influence of Christianity in Civil and Religious Liberty, 1873. Died New Brunswick, Dec. 7, 1890.

CAMPBELL, William W., congressman, jurist; b. Otsego County, N.Y., June 10, 1806; s. James and Sarah (Elderkin) C.; grad. Union Coll., 1827; LL.D. (hon.); m. Maria Starkweather, Aug. 13, 1833; m. 2d, Catherine Livingston, 1853. Admitted to N.Y. bar, 1831; master in chancery, 1841; mem. U.S. Ho.of Reps. from N.Y., 29th Congress, 1845-47; justice N.Y.C. Superior Ct., 1849-55; judge 6th Jud. dist. Supreme Ct. N.Y., 1857-65; presiding justice N.Y. State Supreme Ct., 1863; active mem. Native Am. Party. Author: Annals of Tyron County, 1831; Life of Mrs. Grant, Missionary to Persia, 1840; Life and Writings of DeWitt Clinton, 1849; Sketches of Robin Hood and Captain Kidd, 1853. Died Cherry Valley, N.Y., Sept. 7, 1881; buried Cherry Valley Cemetery.

CANARY, Martha Jane (Calamity Jane), frontierswoman; b. possibly Princeton, Mo., circa 1852; d. Robert and Charlotte Canary; m. at least once, Clinon Burke, circa 1885-95. Moved with parents to Virginia City, Mont. (where parents separated), circa 1863-65; grew up in rough mining and frontier communities, sometimes serving as nurse or midwife; usually wore men's clothing, swore and drank heavily; boasted of her skill and exploits as marksman and scout in Black Hills of S.D., with Pony Express, and with Custer's forces; known to have been in Deadwood, S.D., 1876, and to have toured West in burlesque show; appeared in Pan-Am. Expn., Buffalo; her nickname's origin is uncertain; capitalized on her fame by selling her autobiography and photographs of herself. Died in poverty, Aug. 1, 1903; buried beside her friend Wild Bill Hickock, on Mt. Moriah, Deadwood, S.D.

CANBY, Edward Richard Sprigg, army officer; b. Ky., Aug. 1817; s. Israel T. Canby; grad. U.S. Mil. Acad., 1839. Serverd as 2d lt. 2d Inf., U.S. Army, 1st lt., 1846; asst. adj. gen. with rank col., 1847-48; served in Mexican War, 1847; commd. maj. 10th Inf., 1855, col. 19th Inf., 1861; commanded Dept. of N.M., 1861-62; brig. gen. U.S. Volunteers, 1862; repelled Confederate Gen. Sibley in N.M.; maj. gen. U.S. Volunteers, 1864; comdr. La. Army and Mil. Div of West Mississippi, 1864; captured Mobile, Ala., 1865; commd. brig. gen. U.S. Army, 1866; assigned a command on Pacific Coast, 1870. Died Siskiyou County, Cal., Apr. 11, 1873.

CANBY, Richard Sprigg, congressman, lawyer; b. Lebanon, O., Sept. 30, 1808; attended Miami U., Oxford, O., 1826-28; studied law. Worked in merc. firm; admitted to the bar, circa 1840, began practice law, Bellefontaine, O.; mem. Ohio Ho. of Reps., 1845-46; mem. U.S. Ho. of Reps. (Whig) from Ohio, 30th Congress, 1847-49; became a Republican when party formed, 1856; moved to Olney, Ill., 1863, resumed practice law; elected judge 2d Jud. Circuit of Ill., 1867; ret. from law practice, 1882. Died Olney, July 27, 1895; buried Haven Hill Cemetery.

CANDEE, Leverett, mfr.; b. Oxford, Conn., June 1, 1795; s. Job and Sarah (Benham) C.; m. Jane Caroline Tomlinson, 1 child. Partner dry goods firm Candee, Dean & Cattee, New Haven, Conn., circa 1810-33; commission mcht. and mfr. of paper, New Haven, also Westville, Conn., 1833-42; mfr. rubber overshoes (using Charles Goodyear's vulcanization process), Hamden, Conn., 1842-63, organized firm as Candee & Co., 1852, pres., 1852-63. Died Nov. 27, 1863.

CANNING, George, Brit. prime minister; b. London, Eng., Apr. 11, 1770; s. George and Mary Anne (Costello) C.; attended Eton; grad. Oxford (Eng.) U., 1791; m. Joan Scott, June 1800. Mem. Brit. Parliament, from 1793; fgn. sec. Gt. Britain, 1807-09, 23-27; leader Ho. of Commons, 1823-27; became prime minister Gt. Britain, 1827; broke with European Holy Alliance, recognized independence of Spanish colonies in S.Am., 1823; proposed joint declaration with U.S. warning European nations against interference with new nations of S.Am., Aug. 1823, used phrase "called New World into existence to redress the balance of the Old"; his proposal resulted in enunciation of Monroe Doctrine by Pres. James Monroe in his Annual Message to Congress, Dec. 1823. Died London, Aug. 8, 1827.

CANNON, Charles James, author; b. N.Y.C., Nov. 4, 1800. Earned his living as clerk, N.Y.C. Author: (poems) Facts, Feelings and Fancies, 1835, The Crowning Hour and Other Poems, 1843, Poems, Dramatic and Miscellaneous, 1851; (plays) The Oath of Office, 1854, Dramas, 1857; (stories) Ravellings from the Web of Life, 1855, Mora Carmodi, 1844. Died Nov. 9, 1860.

CANNON, George Quayle, clergyman, congressman; b. Liverpool, Eng., Jan. 11, 1827; s. George and Ann (Quayle) C.; m. 5 times, including Elizabeth Hoagland. Came to U.S., 1842; settled with other Mormons in Salt Lake Valley, Utah, 1847; missionary for Ch. of Jesus Christ of Latter-day Saints, Sandwich Islands, 1850-53; editor Western Standard, San Francisco, 1856-58; apptd. mem. Council of Apostles, 1859; in charge of missionary work, also editor Mormon paper Millenial Star, Liverpool, Eng., 1860-64; published Juvenile Instructor, Salt Lake City, 1866-1901; editor Deseret News, Salt Lake City, 1867-70; mem. U.S. Ho. of Reps. from Utah, 43d-47th congresses, 1873-83; co-founder Utah Central R.R.; dir. U.P. R.R. Died Apr. 12, 1901.

CANNON, Harriet Starr, Protestant sister; b. Charleston, S.C., May 7, 1823; d. William and Sally (Hinman) C. Became full mem. Episcopal Sisterhood of Holy Communion, 1857; took charge House of Mercy (a reformatory), 1863, Sheltering Arms (for friendless children), 1864, St. Barnabas' House for Homeless Women; a founder, 1st mother superior Sisterhood of St. Mary (which was incorporated May 1865); founder St. Mary's Sch., St. Mary's Hosp. for Children. Died Peekskill, N.Y., Apr. 5, 1896.

CANNON, Newton, gov. Tenn. congressman; b. Guilford County, N.C., May 22, 1781; s. Minos and Letitia (Thompson) C.; m. Leah Perkins, Aug. 26, 1813; m. 2d, Rachel Wellborn, Aug. 27, 1818; 11 children. Mem. Tenn. Senate, 1811; served as col. Tenn. Mounted Rifles during War of 1812; served briefly as col. of a regt. mounted volunteers during Creek War, 1813; mem. U.S. Ho. of Reps. (Democrat) from Tenn., 13th-14th, 16th-17th congresses, 1814-17, 19-23; commr. to Chickasaw Indians, 1819; 1st Whig gov. Tenn., 1835-39. Died Harpeth, Tenn., Sept. 16, 1841; buried pvt. estate, Williamson County, Tenn.

CANNON, William, gov. Del.; b. Sussex County, Del., Mar. 15, 1809; s. Josiah and Nancy (Bowlin) C.; m. Margaret Laws. Mem. Del. Ho. of Reps., 1845-49; state treas. Del., 1851; mem. Del. delegation to Nat. Peace Conv., Washington, D.C., 1861; gov. Del. (Union Party), 1863-65. Died Bridgeville, Del., Mar. 1, 1865.

CANONCHET, Indian chief; son of Miantanomo. Chief sachem of Narragansett Indians; signed treaty with English whereby he agreed to fight against King Philip and his allies, 1675, broke treaty by giving aid to Wampanoags, New Eng. Confederation sent punitive expdn. against him, destroyed his camp and winter supplies, killed over 1000 Indians in Great Swamp Fight, 1675. Captured and executed while trying to get seed corn, near what is now Bristol, R.I., Apr. 1676.

CANONGE, Louis Placide, editor; b. New Orleans, June 29, 1822; s. J.F. and Amelie Mercier (Amelung) C.; ed. College Louis-le-Grand, Paris, France; m. Helene Halphern. Contbr. to L'Abeille, circa 1838-93; editor in chief Le Propagateur Catholique; contbr. series of essays under title Institutions Americaines to La Presse; editor La Lorgnette; wrote plays during 1840's and 1850's, including: L'Ambassador d'Autiche, 1850; Le Comte de Carmagnola, 1856; 3 librettos; mem. La. Legislature; supt. edn. New Orleans; prof. French, La. State U.; decorated twice by French Govt. for work in field of French letters. Died Jan. 22, 1893.

CANONICUS, Indian chief; b. circa 1565; a son, Meika. Chief Narragansett Indian tribe in Mass.; sent famous war challenge to Pilgrims upon their landing at Plymouth Rock, 1620; gave Roger Williams grant of R.I., 1636; noted for loyal friendship to English; signed treaty acknowledging Brit. sovereignty, 1644. Died June 4, 1647.

CANTER, Joshua, artist; b. Denmark; studied painting in Copenhagen, Denmark. Came to Am., circa 1788; advertised as portrait and landscape painter, Charleston, S.C.; an original dir. S.C. Acad. Fine Arts; moved to N.Y.C., after 1819. Died N.Y.C., Nov. 1, 1826.

CAPEN, Nahum, postmaster; b. Canton, Mass., Apr. 1, 1804; s. Andrew and Hannah (Richards) C.; m. Elizabeth More, Oct. 14, 1830. One of 1st to propose an internat. copyright to Congress; confidant and adviser to Johann Spurzheim, 1832; editor Mass. State Record, 1847-51; organizer, sec. Boston Phrenological Soc.; instrumental in establishing Mass. Bd. Edn.; postmaster Boston, 1857-61, introduced street letter boxes and free delivery system in U.S. Author: The Republic of the U.S., 1848; The History of Democracy in the United States, 1874; Reminiscences of Dr. Spurzheim and George Combe, 1881; A Review of the Science of Phrenology, 1881. Died Dorchester, Mass., Jan. 8, 1886.

CAPERS, William, clergyman; b. St. Thomas' Parish, S.C., Jan. 26, 1790; s. William and Mary (Singeltary) C.; attended S.C. Coll. at Union, 1807-08; m. Anna White, Jan. 13, 1813; m. 2d, Susan McGill, Oct. 31, 1816. Licensed to preach by Methodist Ch., 1808, ordained deacon, 1810, elder, 1812; held many pastorates in South; supt. of missions to Creek Indians, 1821-25; sec. So. Missionary Dept. of Meth. Ch., 1840-44; consecrated bishop of Meth. Ch. South, 1846; worked primarily among plantation slaves. Died nr. Anderson Court House, S.C., Jan. 29, 1855.

CAPERTON, Allen Taylor, senator, lawyer; b. nr. Union, Monroe County, Va. (now W.Va.), Nov. 21, 1810; s. of Hugh Caperton; attended U. Va.; grad. Yale, 1832; studied law in Staunton, Va. Admitted to the bar, practiced law; Mem. (Whig) Va. Ho. of Dels., 1841-42, 57-61; mem. Va. Senate, 1844-48; del. Whig Nat. Conv., Phila., 1848; del. Va. constl. convs., 1850, 61; mem. Confederate States Senate from Va., until 1865; mem. U.S. Senate (Democrat) from W.Va., 1875-76. Died Washington, D.C., July 26, 1876; buried Green Hill Cemetery, Union, W.Va.

CAPERTON, Hugh, congressman, planter, mcht.; b. Greenbrier County, Va. (now W.Va.), Apr. 17, 1781; at least 1 son, Allen Taylor. Planter and mcht.; moved to Monroe County, Va. (now W.Va.), became sheriff Monroe County, 1805; mem. Va. Ho. of Dels., 1810-18, 26-30; mem. U.S. Ho. of Reps. (Federalist) from Va., 13th Congress, 1813-15. Died on estate "Elmwood" nr. Union, Va. (now W.Va.), Feb. 9, 1847; buried Green Hill Cemetery, Union.

CAPRON, Horace, agriculturist; b. Attleboro, Mass., Aug. 31, 1804; s. Dr. Seth and Eunice (Mann) C.; m. Louisa V. Snowden, June 5, 1834; m. 2d, Margaret Baker, 1854. Owner, supt. cotton factory, Laurel, Md., 1836-51; nationally known for his progressive farming techniques; commd. lt. col. 14th Ill. Cavalry during Civil War, 1863, commd. brig. gen. U.S. Volunteers, 1865, U.S. Army, 1866; U.S. commr. of agriculture, 1867-71; agrl. commr., chief adviser Japanese Govt., 1871-75; his farming methods revolutionized Japanese system of agriculture. Died Washington, D.C., Feb. 22, 1885.

CAPTAIN JACK, Indian chief; b. 1837. Modoc Indian chief; escaped (with band of followers) from Klamath Reservation, Cal., 1872; set up stronghold in lava beds, Tule Lake, Cal.; killed peace commrs. sent to negotiate with him, 1873; finally captured by forces under Col. Jefferson C. Davis, 1873, tried, convicted, hanged for murder, 1873. Died Ft. Klamath, Cal., Oct. 3, 1873.

CARDELLI, Pietro, artist, sculptor; b. probably Italy. Worked in Paris, 1806-10, London, Eng., 1815-16; executed decorative carving for U.S. Capitol, Washington, D.C., 1818; sculpted portrait busts for several distinguished Americans, including Jefferson and Madison; went to New Orleans, 1820; prof. design at the "Establishment," New Orleans; architect of facade of City Hall, New Orleans. Died New Orleans, Oct. 1822.

CARDENAS, Garcia Lopez de, see de Cardenas, Garcia Lopez.

CARDOZO, Jacob Newton, editor; b. Savannah, Ga., June 17, 1786. Editor, Southern Patriot, Charleston, S.C., 1817-23, owner, editor, 1823-45; co-founder Charleston, C. of C., 1823; publisher, editor Evening News, Charleston, 1845-47, comml. editor, 1847-61; wrote for Savannah Morning News, 1865-73. Author: Notes on Political Economy, 1826; A Plan of Financial Relief Addressed to the Legislature of Georgia and Confederate States Congress, 1863. Died Savannah, Aug. 30, 1873.

CARDY, Samuel, architect. Practiced as architect, Charleston, S.C.; in charge of constrn. St. Michael's Ch., Charleston, 1762; architect 1st lighthouse at entrance to Charleston Harbor (erected 1767). Died 1764.

CAREY, Henry Charles, economist, publisher; b. Phila., Dec. 15, 1793; s. Matthew Carey. Leading partner Carey, Lea & Carey (important Am. publishing house, Am. publisher for Thomas Carlyle, Washington Irving, Sir Walter Scott); leader Am. nationalist sch. polit. economy; converted from laissez-faire to protectionist doctrine, 1844; critic English classical economists and socialist econ. thought; del. Pa. Constl. Conv., 1872. Author: The Rates of Wages (essay), 1835; Principles of Political Economy (internat. acclaimed; translated into Italian and Swedish), 3 vols., 1837-40; Commercial Associations in France and England, 1845; Past, Present and Future (announced attitude as foe of free trade system), 1848; Harmony of Interests: Manufacturing and Commercial, 1851; Slave Trade, Domestic and Foreign, 1853; Letters to the President, 1858; The Principles of Social Science, 3 vols., 1858-59; Unity of Law, 1872; most works translated into German, French, Italian, Russian, Spanish. Died Phila., Oct. 13, 1879.

CAREY, Mathew, publisher, economist; b. Dublin, Ireland, Jan. 28, 1760, s. Christopher Carey; m. Bridget Flahavan, 1791, 9 children including Henry. Editor, Freeman's Journal, Dublin, 1780-83, Volunteer's Journal, 1783-84; came to Am., 1784; founder, editor Pa. Herald, 1785, Columbian Magazine, 1786; published Am. Museum mag., 1789; dir. Bank of Pa., 1802; mem. Phila. Soc. for Promotion of Nat. Industry; founder Hibernian Soc. for relief of Irish immigrants; his writings constitute a major influence in hist. devel. and direction of Am. nationalist sch. of econ. thought. Author: Autobiographical Sketches, 1829; Miscellaneous Essays, 1830. Died Phila., Sept. 16, 1839.

CARLETON, Henry (original name Henry Carleton Cox), jurist, author; b. Va., circa 1785; grad. Yale, 1806; m. Aglae D'Avezac de Castera, May 29, 1815, a dau., Aglae Marie. m. 2d, Mrs. Maria (Vanderburgh) Wiltbank. Served as lt., inf. U.S. Army under Jackson defending New Orleans against British, 1814-15; U.S. dist. atty., 1832; asso. justice Supreme Ct. La., 1837-39; Author: Liberty and Necessity, 1857; Essay on the Will, 1863; translator (with Louis Moreau Lislet) Las Siete Partidas (the Spanish legal code in La.). Died Phila., Mar. 28, 1863.

CARLETON, Peter, congressman; b. Haverhill, Mass., Sept. 19, 1755; attended pub. schs. Engaged in farming; served with a Mass. regt. during Revolutionary War; moved to Landaff, N.H., circa 1789; mem. N.H. Constl. Conv., 1790; mem. N.H. Ho. of Reps., 1803-04; mem. N.H. Senate, 1806-07; mem. U.S. Ho. of Reps. (Democrat) from N.H., 10th Congress, 1807-09. Died Landaff, Apr. 29, 1828; buried City Cemetery.

CARLILE, John Snyder, senator; b. Winchester, Va., Dec. 16, 1817. Admited to Va. bar, 1840; mem. Va. Senate, 1847-51; mem. Va. Constl. Conv., 1850; mem. U.S. Ho. of Reps. from Va., 34th Congress, 1855-57, mem. com. accounts, 1856; embodied his ideas on secession in "Declaration of the People of Virginia," adopted by 2d Wheeling Conv., 1861; mem. U.S. Senate from Va. 1861-63 from W. Va., July 1863-65, mem. coms. public lands, territories. Died Clarksburg, W. Va., Oct. 24, 1878.

CARLIN, Andrew B., artist; b. Pa., circa 1816; m. Anna Maria, at least 5 children. Deaf-mute; worked as artist, Phila., 1839-60; became profl. photographer, 1860; exhibited paintings at Artists' Fund Soc., 1840; painted Sherman's March Through Georgia, 1864 (only extant painting), 1871.

CARLIN, Charles L., architect; b. Balt., 1847. Practiced as architect, Balt.; maintained large practice in South, during late 1880's; instr. dept. architecture Md. Inst. Design; mem. A.I.A.; architect numerous bldgs., Balt. Died Dec. 28, 1891.

CARLIN, John, artist, writer; b. Phila., June 15, 1813; attended Pa. Inst. for Deaf and Dumb, 1821-25; studied drawing under John Rubens Smith, portrait painting under John Neagle, 1833-34; married, several children. Exhibited at Artists' Fund Soc., 1835-38; went to Europe, studied at Brit. Museum, London, also with Paul Delaroche, Paris, France; returned to Am., settled in N.Y.C.; exhibited at N.A.D., Am. Inst., Am. Art-Union, Md. Hist. Soc., Pa. Acad.; specialized in miniatures, later in genre and landscape painting; wrote The Scratchside Family, 1861; wrote poem The Mute's Lament. Died N.Y.C., Apr. 23, 1891.

CARLIN, Thomas, gov. Ill.; b. Fayette County, Ky., July 18, 1789. Settled in Ill., 1811; served as pvt. in War of 1812, as capt. in Black Hawk War; settled in Greene County, Ill., 1818, became 1st sheriff; twice mem. Ill. Senate; register Quincy Land Office; elected gov. Ill. (Democrat), 1838. Died Carrollton, Ill., Feb. 14, 1852.

CARLIN, William Worth, architect; b. Chautauqua, N.Y.; studied architecture under James W. Smith, Jamestown, N.Y. Practiced as architect, Buffalo, N.Y.; became partner firm Carlin & Coxhead, 1890, sr. mem. firm, engaged in planning comml. bldgs.; pres. Western Assn. Architects; charter mem. Buffalo chpt. A.I.A., 1890. Died Mar. 21, 1894.

CARLISLE, James Mandeville, lawyer; b. Alexandria, Va., May 22, 1814; s. Christopher and Anne (Mandeville) C. Admitted to U.S. Supreme Ct. bar, 1837; practiced law, Washington, D.C., 1837-77; often represented foreign powers in U.S.; legal adviser to Brit. legation, 1852-77; counsel for Costa Rica, 1862, for Columbia, 1864, for Spain, 1871 (all in cases of claims of Am. citizens against these govts.). Died Washington, May 19, 1877.

CARMICHAEL, Richard Bennett, congressman, lawyer; b. Centerville, Md., Dec. 25, 1807; attended Dickinson Coll.; grad. Princeton, 1828; studied law. Admitted to the bar, 1830, began practice law in Centerville; mem. Md. Ho. of Dels., 1831, 41-66; mem. U.S. Ho. of Reps. (Jackson Democrat) from Md., 23d Congress, 1833-35; del. Democratic Nat. convs., 1856, 64, 68, 76; judge of the circuit ct., 1858-64; presiding judge Queen Annes County (Md.) Ct., 1861; mem., also pres. Md. Constl. Conv., 1867. Died "Wye" nr. Carmichael, Queen Annes County, Oct. 21, 1884; buried family burying ground at "Wye".

CARMICHAEL, William, diplomat, continental congressman; b. Queen Annes County, Md.; s. William Carmichael; ed., Edinburgh, Scotland; m. 2d, Antonia Reynon; 1 child. Sec. of commn. to enlist aid of France for colonies, 1775, responsible for Lafayette's coming to Am. sent to Berlin to propose treaty relations with Frederick the Great, 1776; mem. Continental Congress, 1778-79; sec. to Minister Plenipotentiary John Jay, to secure treaty with Spain, acting charge d'affaires, Spain legation. 1782-90, charge d'affaires, 1790-94. Died Madrid, Spain, Feb. 9, 1795; buried Madrid.

CARNAHAN, James, coll. pres.; b. Carlisle, Pa., Nov. 15, 1775; grad. with highest honors Coll. of N.J., (now Princeton), 1800, LL.D., 1854; S.T.D., Hamilton Coll., 1821, m. Mary Van Dyke. Licensed to preach by Presbytery of New Brunswick, 1804; pastor United Chs. Whitesborough and Utica, 1804-14; pres. Princeton, 1823-54; trustee, pres. bd. Princeton Theol. Sem. Died Newark, N.J., Mar. 3, 1859.

CARNES, Thomas Petters, congressman, lawyer; b. Md., 1762; studied law. Admitted to the bar, practiced law in Milledgeville, Ga.; mem. Ga. Ho. of Reps., 1786-87, 89, 97, 1807-08; solicitor gen. for Western Circuit of Ga.; atty. gen. State of Ga., 1789-92; mem. U.S. Ho. of Reps. from Ga., 3d Congress, 1793-95; judge Western Circuit Ct. of Ga., 1798-1803; 09-10; mem. Ga. Constl. Conv., 1798; a commr. to settle boundary disputes between Ga. and N.C., 1806. Died on his farm in Franklin (now Hart) County, Ga., May 5, 1822; buried on his estate.

CARNEY, Thomas, gov. Kan.; b. Delaware County, O., Aug. 20, 1827; s. James and Sarah Carney; m. Rebecca Canaday, 1851. Owner 2 wholesale houses, St. Louis; mem. Kan. Legislature, 1861; elected gov. Kan. (Republican), 1862-65, established state's penal, philanthropic and higher ednl. instns.; elected U.S. Senate from Kan., Feb. 1864, legality of election doubtful, did not claim seat. Died Leavenworth, Kan., July 28, 1888.

CARNOCHRAN, John Murray, surgeon; b. Savannah, Ga., July 4, 1817; s. John and Harriet (Putnam) A.; grad. U. Edinburgh (Scotland), 1834; M.D., Coll. Physicians and Surgeons, N.Y.C., 1836; studied medicine, Paris, France, 1836-42, London, Eng., 1842-47; m. Estelle Morris. Practiced medicine, N.Y.C., 1847-87; surgeon-in-chief N.Y. State Emigrant Hosp. Ward's Island, 1851; prof. surgery N.Y. Med. Coll., 1851-62; health officer port of N.Y., 1870-71; mem. N.Y. Medico-Legal Soc., 1871-87. Author: Etiology, Pathology, and Treatment of Congenital Dislocation of the Head of the Femur, 1850; Contributions to Operative Surgery and Surgical Pathology, 1858; Cerebral Localization in Relation to Insanity, 1884. Died Oct. 28, 1887.

CAROL, Kate, see Osgood, Frances Sargent Locke.

CARONDELET, Baron Francisco Luis Hector de, see de Carondelet.

CARPENTER, Cyrus Clay, gov. Ia.; b. Susquehanna County, Pa., Nov. 24, 1829; s. Asahel and Amanda (Thayer) C.; m. Susan Burkholder, 1864. Tchr. 1st sch. opened, Ft. Dodge, Ia., 1854; mem. Ia. Gen. Assembly, 1857, 1884; commissary of subsistance in U.S. Army under Gen. Sherman; brevetted col., 1865; register Land Office Ia., 1866; gov. Ia., 1871-75; comptroller of treasury U.S., 1875; mem. U.S. Ho. of Reps. from Ia., 46th-47th congresses, 1879-83; postmaster Ft. Dodge. Died Ft. Dodge, May 29, 1898; buried Oakland Cemetery, Ft. Dodge.

CARPENTER, Davis, congressman, lawyer, physician; b. Walpole, N.H., Dec. 25, 1799; grad. Middlebury (Vt.) Coll., 1824; studied medicine, also law. Admitted to the bar, began practice law in Brockport, N.Y.; mem. U.S. Ho. of Reps. (Whig, filled vacancy) from N.Y., 33d Congress, Nov. 8, 1853-55; practiced medicine in Brockport. Died Brockport, Oct. 22, 1878; buried High Street Cemetery.

CARPENTER, Decatur Merritt Hammond, see Carpenter, Matthew Hale.

CARPENTER, Levi D., congressman, lawyer; b. Waterville, N.Y., Aug. 21, 1802; studied law. Admitted to the bar, began practice law in Waterville; supr. Town of Sangerfield, 1855; mem. U.S. Ho. of Reps. (Democrat, filled vacancy) from N.Y., 28th Congress, Nov. 5, 1844-45. Died Waterville, Oct. 27, 1856; buried City Cemetery.

CARPENTER, Matthew Hale (real name Decatur Merritt Hammond Carpenter), senator; b. Moretown, Vt., Dec. 22, 1824; s. Ira and Esther (Luce) C.; attended U.S. Mil. Acad., 1843-45; m. Cardine Dillingham, 1855. Admitted to Vt. bar, 1847; settled in Wis., 1848; judge adv. gen. Wis., 1861; mem. U.S. Senate from Wis., 1869-75, 79-81; represented Sec. War Belknap in his impeachment trial; represented Tilden at electoral commn.'s inquiry into 1876 election. Died Washington, D.C., Feb. 24, 1881.

CARPENTER, Samuel H., engraver; b. N.J. or Pa., circa 1798-99; m. Ann; children—Emily, Joseph, Samuel H. Worked in Phila., 1846-60; partner banknote engraving firm Toppan, Carpenter & Co., merged with Am. Bank Note Co., 1858.

CARPENTER, Stephen Cullen, journalist; b. Ireland. Editor, Courier, Charleston, S.C., 1803-06, Monthly Register, Charleston, 1806; publisher, editor People's Friend, N.Y.C., 1806-07; publisher Mirror of Taste and Dramatic Censor, Phila., 1807-08. Died Washington, D.C., 1820.

CARPENTER, Stephen Haskins, educator; b. Little Falls, N.Y., Aug. 7, 1831; s. Calvin Carpenter; grad. U. Rochester, 1852; m. Frances Curtis, 1856. Editor, a publisher Daily Patriot, Western Fireside (both in Wis.); asst. supt. public instrn. Wis., 1858-60; prof. ancient langs. St. Pauls Coll., Palmyra, Mo., 1860-65; city clk. Madison (Wis.), 1864-68; prof. rhetoric and English lit. U. Wis., 1868; clk. Madison Bd. Edn., 1865-72. Author: English of the Fourteenth Century, 1872; An Introduction to the Study of the Anglo-Saxon Language (textbook), 1875; Elements of English Analysis (widely used as grammar text), 1877. Died Geneva, N.Y., Dec. 7, 1878.

CARR, Benjamin, composer; b. England, 1769. Came to U.S., 1793; operator 1st music store in Phila., 1793-1831; appeared as musician in Phila. founder Musical Fund Soc., 1820. Works include The Archers (opera), 1796; Masses, Vespers, and Litanies, 1805; Lessons in Vocal Music, 1811; A Collection of Chants, 1816; The Chorister, 1820. Died May 24, 1831.

CARR, Dabney, jurist; b. Richmond, Va., Apr. 27, 1773; s. Dabney and Martha (Jefferson) C.; attended Hampden-Sydney Coll.; m. Elizabeth Carr, 1800. Chancellor, Winchester Dist., Va., 1811-24; judge U.S. Ct. of Appeals in Va., 1824-37; wrote articles for William Wirt's Old Bachelor. Died Richmond, Jan. 8, 1837.

CARR, Dabney Smith, journalist, diplomat; b. Albemarle County, Va., Mar. 5, 1802; s. Peter and Hester (Smith) C.; m. Sidney Nichols, 7 children. Founder newspaper Balt. Republican and Comml. Advertiser, 1827; naval officer Port of Balt., 1829-43; U.S. minister to Turkey, 1843-50. Died Charlottesville, Va., Mar. 24, 1854; buried Monticello, Va.

CARR, Francis, congressman, businessman; b. Newbury, Mass., Dec. 6, 1751; attended common schs.; at least 1 son, James. In merc. bus.; mem. Mass. Ho. of Reps. from Haverhill, 1791-95, 1801-03, from Orrington (now Me.), 1806-08; mem. Mass. Senate, 1809-11; mem. U.S. Ho. of Reps. (Democrat, filled vacancy) from Mass., 12th Congress, Apr. 6, 1812-13. Died Bangor, Me., Oct. 6, 1821; buried Mt. Hope Cemetery, Bangor.

CARR, James, congressman; b. Bangor, Mass. (now Me.), Sept. 9, 1777; son of Francis Carr; attended Exeter and Byfield acads. Clk. on ship U.S.S. Crescent; sec. to U.S. consul at Algiers, 2 years; in merc. bus., Orrington, Mass. (now Me.); mem. Mass. Ho. of Reps., 1806-11; mem. U.S. Ho. of Reps. from Mass., 14th Congress, 1815-17. Drowned in Ohio River, Aug. 24, 1818; meml. headstone placed in Mt. Hope Cemetery, Bangor, Me.

CARR, John, congressman; b. Uniontown, Ind., Apr. 9, 1793; attended public schs. Fought in Battle of Tippecanoe; apptd. lt. in a co. of U.S. Rangers (authorized by Act of Congress for defense of western frontiers), 1812; brig. gen. and maj. gen. Ind. Militia until death; clk. Clark County (Ind.), 1824-30; Democratic presdl. elector, 1824; mem. U.S. Ho. of Reps. (Dem.) from Ind., 22d-24th, 26th congresses, 1831-37, 39-41. Died Charlestown, Ind., Jan. 20, 1845; buried Old Cemetery.

CARR, Joseph Bradford, army officer; b. Albany, N.Y., Aug. 16, 1828; s. William and Ann C. Commd. Col. N.Y. State Militia, 1849, col. of a militia regt., 1859, col. 2d N.Y. Inf., 1861, commanded a brigade in Peninsula Campaign and 2d Battle of Bull Run; commd. brig. gen. U.S. Volunteers, 1862, led troops at center of Union line at Battle of Gettysburg, 1863; apptd. maj. gen. N.Y. Militia, 1865; sec. of state N.Y. State, 1879, 81, 83; unsuccessful Republican nominee for lt. gov. N.Y., 1885; maj. gen. in command 3d Div. N.Y. Militia, 1893. Died Troy, N.Y., Feb. 24, 1895.

CARR, Nathan Tracy, congressman, lawyer; b. Corning, N.Y., Dec. 25, 1833; grad. Starkey Acad., 1851; studied law. Admitted to Midland County (Mich.) bar, 1858, began practice law, Vassar, Mich.; mem. Mich. Ho. of Reps., 1858-60; recorder Midland County, 1861-62; served as lt. 2d Regt., Mich. Volunteer Inf., 1862, during Civil War; moved to Columbus, Ind., 1867; pros. atty. for Bartholomew, Shelby, Jackson, Brown counties (Ind.), 1870; mem. U.S. Ho. of Reps. (Democrat, filled vacancy) from Ind., 44th Congress, Dec. 5, 1876-77; apptd. judge 9th Jud. Circuit Ct. of Ind., 1878. Died Columbus, May 28, 1885; buried City Cemetery.

CARR, Thomas Matthew, clergyman; b. Galway, Ireland, 1750; studied theology in Toulouse, France. Ordained as an Augustinian priest, Roman Catholic Ch., chosen to establish an Augustinian house in U.S., 1795; came to Am., 1796; assigned by Bishop John Carroll to St. Mary's, Phila., directed activities of missions in Wilmington, Del., New Castle, Del., Trenton, N.J., Burlington, N.J., South Jersey, N.J.; rector of St. Augustine's, Phila., 1802-20 (building completed 1802, George Washington a contbr. to ch.); opened new sch. St. Augustine's Acad., Phila., 1811, sch. closed 1815; delivered meml. address to George Washington at St. Mary's, Phila., 1800. Died Sept. 29, 1820.

CARRELL, George Aloysius, clergyman; b. Phila., June 13, 1803; studied at Mt. St. Mary's Md., also Georgetown. Ordained priest Roman Catholic Ch., 1827; pastor in Phila.; joined Soc. of Jesus, 1835, became rector St. Francis Xavier Ch., St. Louis; 1st bishop Covington, Ky., 1853-68. Died Sept. 25, 1868.

CARRICK, Samuel, clergyman, coll. pres.; b. York (now Adams) County, Pa., July 17, 1760; m. Elizabeth Moore; m. 2d, Annis McClellen, Jan. 1794. Licensed to preach in Presbyn. Ch., 1782; pastor at Rocky Spring, Va., 1783; became traveling missionary in Tenn.; pastor 1st church in Knoxville, Tenn., 1791-1809; pres. Blount Coll. (later East Tenn. Coll., now U. Tenn.), 1794-1809. Died Aug. 17, 1809.

CARRINGTON, Edward, Continental congressman; b. Goochland County, Va., Feb. 11, 1748. Mem. county com., 1755-76; served in Continental Army, commd. lt. col Arty., 1776, served as q.m. gen. on staff Gen. Greene, commanded Arty. at battle of Hobkirks Hill., 1781, also at Yorktown; mem. Continental Congress from Va., 1785-86; apptd. by Pres. Washington as marshal of Va., 1789; foreman of jury in Aaron Burr treason trial, 1807. Died Richmond, Va., Oct. 28, 1810; buried St. John's Cemetery.

CARRINGTON, Paul, jurist; b. Charlotte County, Va., Mar. 16, 1733; s. George and Ann (Mayo) G.; grad. Coll. William and Mary, 1753; m. Margaret Read, Oct. 1, 1755; m. 2d, Priscilla Sims, 1793. Became King's atty. for 4 counties, 1756; cmmd. maj. Va. Militia, 1761, col., 1764; mem. Va. Ho. of Burgesses, 1765-75; county lt. Charlotte County Militia; presiding justice Charlotte County, 1765; mem. Merc. Assn. of 1770; chmn. Revolutionary Com. of Charlotte County; mem. Va. Com. of Safety, 1775-76; Charlotte rep. Va. Senate, 1765-67; chief justice Va. Gen. Ct., 1780; judge Va. Ct. of Appeals, 1789-1807. Died Charlotte County, June 22, 1818.

CARROLL, Anna Ella, author; b. Somerset County, Md., Aug. 29, 1815; d. Thomas King and Juliana (Stevenson) Carroll. Wrote for various newspapers; wrote The Great American Battle, or Political Romanism, also The Star of the West, before Civil War; freed her slaves at outbreak of Civil War, used all her influence on side of Union element in Md.; wrote pamphlet War Powers of the Government, at request of U.S. Govt., 1861; later wrote Relation of Revolted Civizens to the National Government, also pamphlet titled Reconstruction, at request of Pres. Lincoln; adviser to U.S. War Dept. at various times during Civil War; a bill in U.S. Congress to give her a salary equivalent to that of maj. gen. for her war services was defeated, 1881. Died Washington, D.C., Feb. 19, 1894.

CARROLL, Charles, landowner; b. 1703; son of Charles Carroll; m. Elizabeth Brooke; at least 1 son, Charles Carroll of Carrollton. Held several important posts in Md.; opposed laws against Roman Catholics in the colony; became wealthy landowner. Died 1783.

CARROLL, Charles, Continental congressman, lawyer; b. Annapolis, Md., Mar. 22, 1723; s. of Dr. Charles Carroll; ed. English House, West Lisbon, Portugal, also Eaton, London, Eng., Cambridge (Eng.) U.; studied law Middle Temple, Garden Ct., Eng. Began practice law in Annapolis, 1746; mem. Md. Lower House of Assembly (filled vacancy caused by death of father), 1755; served on numerous important coms. in Md. convs., framed important state documents, including Declaration of Rights adopted by conv. of Md., 1776; became mem. Council of Safety, 1775; mem. Continental Congress from Md. (filled vacancy), Nov. 10, 1776-Feb. 15, 1777; mem. 1st Md. Senate, 1777, 1781-83. Died Mt. Clare, nr. Balt., Mar. 23, 1783.

CARROLL, Charles, Continental congressman, senator; b. Annapolis, Md., Sept. 19, 1737; s. Charles and Elizabeth (Brooke) C.; ed. College de St. Omer (French Flanders), College de Louis le Grand, Paris, France, 1757; m. Mary Darnall, June 5, 1768, 2 children. Mem. Annapolis Com. of Correspondence, 1774-75; mem. Md. Revolutionary Conv., 1775, 76; mem. Md. Com. of Correspondence, Com. of Safety; rep. from Md. to Continental Congress, 1776-78, mem. bd. war; signer Declaration of Independence, Aug. 2, 1776 (last surviving signer); mem. Md. Senate, 1778-88, 91-1801; mem. U.S Senate (Federalist) from Md., 1789-92; mem. 1st bd. dirs. B. & O. R.R.: known as Charles Carroll of Carrollton. Died Balt., Nov. 14, 1832; buried Doughoregan Manor, nr. Ellicott City, Howard County, Md.

CARROLL, Charles Hobart, congressman; b. Bellevue, Georgetown Heights, D.C., May 4, 1794; grad. St. Mary's Coll., Balt., 1812; studied law, never practiced. Became farmer, land agt. in N.Y.; supr. Groveland, Livingston County, N.Y., 1817, 18, 22, 39-40, 48; county judge, 1823-29; mem. N.Y. State Senate, 1827-28; mem. N.Y. State Assembly, 1836; mem. U.S. Ho. of Reps. (Clay Whig) from N.Y., 28th-29th congresses, 1843-47; managed large estate nr. Groveland; Am. Party presdl. elector, 1856. Died Groveland, June 8, 1865; buried Williamsburgh Cemetery.

CARROLL, Daniel, congressman, commr. D.C.; b. Prince George's County, Md., July 22, 1730; s. Kean and Eleanor (Darnall) C.; m. Elizabeth Carroll (a 2d cousin), 1750. Del. from Md. to Continental Congress, 1781-84, signed Articles of Confederation, 1781; del. to Md. Constl. Conv., 1787; mem. U.S. Ho. of Reps. from Md., 1789-91; mem. commn. to survey D.C. on banks of Potomac River, 1791. Died Rock Creek, Md., May 7, 1796.

CARROLL, James, congressman, businessman; b. Balt., Dec. 2, 1791; grad. old St. Mary's Coll., Balt., 1808; studied law, did not practice. Settled on farm on West River; returned to Balt., 1831; judge of orphans' ct., trustee of the poor; dir. B. & O. R.R. Co., Chesapeake & Ohio Canal Co.; mem. U.S. Ho. of Reps. (Democrat) from Md., 26th Congress, 1839-41; unsuccessful candidate for gov. Md., 1844; ret. from polit. life. Died Balt., Jan. 16, 1873; buried St. Paul's Burying Ground.

CARROLL, John, clergyman; b. Upper Marlboro, Md., Jan. 8, 1735; s. Kean and Eleanor (Darnall) C.; ed. St. Omer's Coll., France, 1753; LL.D. (hon.), St. Mary's Coll., 1793; Apptd. prof. St. Omer's Coll., 1759; took final vows as Jesuit, ordained, 1767; returned to America, 1773; named prefect-apostolic by Pope Pius VI, 1784-85; named 1st Roman Cath. bishop in U.S., 1789, consecrated, 1790; founded Georgetown Acad., 1789; became 1st archbishop Balt., 1808; a founder St. Mary's Coll., Annapolis, Md., 1792, St. Joseph Coll., Emmitsburg, Md., 1809. Died Georgetown, D.C., Dec. 3, 1815.

CARROLL, Samuel Sprigg, army officer; b. Washington, D.C., Sept. 21, 1832; s. William Thomas Carroll; grad. U.S. Mil. Acad., 1856. Quartermaster, U.S. Mil. Acad., 1860-61; commd. 1st lt. 10th Inf., U.S. Army, 1861, capt, 1861; commd. col. 8th Ohio Inf., 1861; commanded brigade in operations in central Va., 1862; participated in No. Va. Campaign and Battle Cedar Mountain; commanded brigade at battles of Fredricksburg, Chancellorsville and Gettysburg; commd. brig. gen. U.S. Volunteers, 1864; commd. lt. col. 21st Inf., 1867, maj. gen. (ret.), 1869. Died Washington, D.C., Jan. 28, 1893; buried Oak Hill Cemetery, Washington.

CARROLL, William, gov. Tenn.; b. Pitts., Mar. 3, 1788; s. Thomas and Mary (Montgomery) C.; m. Cecelia Bradford, circa 1813. Moved to Nashville, Tenn., 1810; commd. capt. Tenn. Militia, 1812, served as col. during Creek War, 1813, commd. maj. gen., 1814; gov. Tenn., 1821-27, 29-35, noted for reform policies. Died Nashville, Mar. 22, 1844.

CARSON, Charles L., architect; b. 1847. Practiced as architect, Balt.; asso. with Thomas Dixon in firm Dixon & Carson, designed branch of Enoch Pratt Free Library, Fireman's Fund Ins. Bldg., Eutaw Pl. Presbyn. Ch., all Balt.; taught at dept. architecture Md. Inst. Design. Died Dec. 24, 1891.

CARSON Christopher (Kit Carson), Indian agt., army officer; b. Madison County, Ky., Dec. 24, 1809; s. Lindsay and Rebecca (Robinson) C.; m. Alice (an Indian girl), 1836, 1 dau., Adaline; m. 2d, Maria Josepha Jaramillo, Feb. 6, 1843. Fur trapper in Far West, 1829-41; guide to Fremont's expdns., 1843-44, 45; apptd. lt. Mounted Riflemen by Pres. Polk, appointment rejected by U.S. Senate, 1847; Indian agt., 1853-61; an organizer 1st New Mexican Volunteer Inf., commd. lt. col., 1861, col., 1861; brevetted brig. gen. U.S. Volunteers for gallantry in Battle of Valverde and for distinguished services in N.M., 1865: led campaigns against S.W. Indians during Civil War; took command Ft. Garland in Colo., 1866; dictated account of his life to Lt. Col. DeWitt C. Peters, 1857-58, published as The Life and Adventures of Kit Carson, The Nestor of the Rocky Mountains, 1858. Died Ft. Lyon, Colo., May 23, 1868.

CARSON, Joseph, physician; b. Phila., Apr. 19, 1808; s. Joseph and Elizabeth (Lawrence) C.; grad. U. Pa., 1826, M.D., 1830; m. Mary Goodard, 1841; m. 2d, Sarah Hollingsworth, 1848; 4 children. Practiced medicine, Phila., 1832-76; mem. Acad. Natural Sciences of Phila., 1835-76; prof. materia medica Phila. Coll. Pharmacy, 1836; prof. materia medica and pharmacy U. Pa., 1850-76; physician lying-in dept. Pa. Hosp., 1849-54; editor Am. Journal of Pharmacy; mem. Coll. Physicians of Phila., Am. Philos. Soc. Author: Illustrations of Medical Botany, 1847; History of the Medical Department of the University of Pennsylvania, 1869. Died Dec. 30, 1876.

CARSON, Samuel Price, congressman; b. Pleasant Gardens, N.C., Jan. 22, 1798; ed. by pvt. tutors. Engaged in agrl. pursuits; mem. N.C. Senate, 1822-24, 34; mem. U.S. Ho. of Reps. (Democrat) from N.C., 19th-22d congresses, 1825-33; supported nullification doctrine of Calhoun (not re-elected to Congress because of this); del. N.C. Constl. Conv., 1865; moved to Tex., 1856; mem. conv. which adopted constn. of Tex. Republic, 1836; sec. of state Republic of Tex., 1836-38; sent as a commr. to Washington, D.C., to intercede for recognition of independence of Tex., 1836. Died Hot Springs, Ark., Nov. 2, 1838; buried Govt. Cemetery, Hot Springs.

CARTER, Asher, architect; b. Morris County, N.J., Jan. 24, 1805. Carpenter and millwright, Morristown, N.J.; became supt. constrn. of 2d Presbyn. Ch., Chgo., 1840; designed houses and other bldgs., Chgo.; entered partnership with Augustus Bauer in firm Carter & Bauer, Chgo., 1855-63, with William E. Drake, 1863, then with Peter B. Wight, firm later reorganized as Carter, Drake & Leobnitz; ret., 1873; dir. Mchts. Loan & Trust Co., Chgo. Died Jan. 14, 1877.

CARTER, Elias, architect; b. Ward, Mass., May 30, 1781; s. Timothy and Sarah (Walker) C.; m. Eudocia Lyon, May 25, 1807. Architect whose work showed strong "late colonial" influences, designed typical New Eng. churches, adapted Greek detail for New Eng. design of houses, Worcester, Mass.; prin. works include: Unitarian Ch., 1828, Insane Hosp., 1832 (both Worcester); Leicester (Mass.) Acad., 1832; Insane Asylum, Concord, N.H., 1842, mem. Mass. Gen. Ct., 1834; mem. Worcester town coms., 1834-37. Died Mar. 23, 1864.

CARTER, Henry Alpheus Pierce, businessman, diplomat; b. Honolulu, Hawaii, Aug. 7, 1837; s. Joseph Oliver and Hannah (Lord) C.; m. Sybil Augusta Judd, Feb. 27, 1862. Partner merc. firm C. Brewer & Co., Honolulu, 1852-91; dealt in whaling and sugar trades; privy counsellor to King Ralakaua, 1874-79, sent to U.S. to establish reciprocal trade treaties, to Europe to establish trade arrangements with Britain, France and Germany; Hawaiian minister of interior, 1880-82; Hawaiian minister to U.S., 1883-91. Died N.Y.C., Nov. 1, 1891.

CARTER, James Gordon, edn. reformer; b. Leominster, Mass., Sept. 7, 1795; s. Capt. James and Betsy (Hale) C.; grad. Harvard, 1820; m. Anne M. Packard, 1827, 1 child. Editor Literary Gazette, U.S. Gazette, 1824, N.Y. Review, 1826; wanted edn. to be based on scientific principles; helped found Am. Inst. Instrn., 1830; mem. Mass. Ho. of Reps., 1835-38, Mass. Senate, 1839, chmn. com. on edn.; 1st mem. apptd. to Mass. Bd. Edn. Author: Letters to the Hon. William Prescott on the Free Schools of New England, with Remarks on the Principles of Instruction, 1824; Essays upon Popular Principles of Instruction, 1824; Essays upon Popular Education with an Outline of an Institution for the Education of Teachers, 1826; Geography of Massachusetts, 1830; Geography of New Hampshire, 1831. Died Chgo., July 2, 1849.

CARTER, John, colonial legislator; b. Va., 1737; m. Elizabeth Taylor, 1758, 1 son, Landon. One of 1st settlers Watauga community, N.C.; chmn. Watauga Ct.; mem. N.C. Provincial Congress, 1776; mem. N.C. Senate from Washington dist., 1777, 81; public entry-taker. Died 1781.

CARTER, John, journalist; b. Phlia., July 21, 1745; s. John and Elizabeth (Spriggs) C.; m. Amey Crawford, May 14, 1769, 12 children. Apprenticed to Benjamin Franklin; owner, editor, printer Providence Gazette (an influence in R.I. affairs), 1768-1813; mem. Com. of Correspondence of Providence during Revolutionary War; postmaster Providence, 1772-92. Died Providence, Aug. 19, 1814.

CARTER, John, congressman, lawyer; b. on Black River, nr. Camden, S.C., Sept. 10, 1792; grad. S.C. Coll. (now U. S.C.), 1811; studied law. Admitted S.C. bar, 1814, began practice law in Camden; commr. in equity, 1814-20; mem. U.S. Ho. of Reps. from S.C., (filled vacancy) 18th-20th congresses, Dec. 11, 1822-29; practiced law in Camden, 1829-36; moved to Georgetown, D.C., 1836. Died Georgetown, June 20, 1850.

CARTER, Landon, pioneer, public ofcl.; b. Va., Jan. 29, 1760; s. John and Elizabeth (Taylor) C. m. Elizabeth Maclin, 1784. Served in Revolutionary War, 1780-83, as capt. in John Sevier's expdn. against the Cherokee Indians, 1780; apptd. maj. N.C. Militia, by N.C. legislature, 1788; lt. col., comdr. S.W. Territory) Militia, Washington Dist. 1790; served as col. during Indian campaign, 1792-93; from Washington County mem. N.C. Ho. of Commons, 1784, 89; sec. State of Franklin, 1784-89, Jonesborough Conv. of 1784, also speaker 1st Senate of Franklin, advocate of entry Franklin as state; treas. Washington dist. Govt. of S.W. Territory; elected by 1st Tenn. Legislature as treas. for dists. of Washington and Hamilton (Tenn.), 1796; trustee, incorporator Martin Acad.; trustee Greenville Coll.; Carter County (Tenn.) named after him; Elizabethton (Tenn.) named for his wife. Died June 5, 1800.

CARTER, Luther Cullen, congressman; businessman; b. Bethel, Me., Feb. 25, 1805. Moved to N.Y.C., became a mcht. mem. N.Y.C. Bd. of Edn., 1853; ret. from bus., moved to Long Island City, N.Y., became a farmer; mem. U.S. Ho. of Reps. (Union Republican) from N.Y., 36th Congress, 1859-61. Died N.Y.C., Jan. 3, 1875; buried Greenwood Cemetery, Bklyn.

CARTER, Robert, colonial ofcl.; b. Lancaster County, Va., 1663; s. John and Sarah (Ludlow) C.; m. Judith Armistead; m. 2d, Elizabeth Landon several children. Mem. Va. Ho. of Burgesses, 1691-92, 95-99, speaker, 1696, 99; mem. Gov.'s Council, 1699-1732, pres. of council, 1726-32; treas. of Va., 1699-1705; col. and comdr.-in-chief Lancaster County; agt. for proprietors of Northern Neck of Va., 1702-11, 22-32; one of wealthiest men in Va.; rector, trustee Coll. William and Mary: built Christ Ch., Lancaster County. Died Aug. 4, 1732.

CARTER, Robert, editor, author; b. Albany, N.Y., Feb. 5, 1819; ed. Jesuit Sch. at Chambly, Can.; m. Ann Gray, 1846; m. 2d Susan Nichols, 1864 Chief clk. Cambridge (Mass.) Post Office, 1845; pvt. sec. to William H. Prescott (historian); editor Boston Commonwealth (chief organ of the Free-Soilers), 1848-55; sec. Mass. Free Soil Com., 1854; editor Boston Telegraph, 1855, Daily Atlas, 1856; personally convoked Worcester Conv. 1854 which founded Republican Party by adoption of name he suggested and approval of his prepared platform; editor newspaper Democrat, Rochester, N.Y., 1863-68, Appleton's Jour., 1869-73; asso. editor Am. Cyclopedia, 1873, took part in revision. Author: The Hungarian Controversy, 1852; A Summer Cruise on the Atlantic Coast of New England, 1858. Died Cambridge, Feb. 15, 1879.

CARTER, Samuel Powhatan, naval and army officer; b. Elizabethtown, Tenn., Aug. 6, 1819; s. Alfred Moore and Evaline (Parry) C.; attended Washington Coll., Princeton; grad. U.S. Naval Acad., 1846; m. Carrie Potts. Commd. Midshipman U.S. Navy, 1846; asst. prof. mathematics U.S. Naval Acad,, 1850-53, asst. to exec. officer, 1857-60; detailed from U.S. Navy to spl. duty at War Dept., 1861; brig. gen. Tenn. Volunteers, defeated Morgan, 1862; commanded 1st important cavalry raid by U.S. Army at battles of Holsten, Carter's Station and Jonesville; commd. lt. comdr. U.S. Navy, 1863, comdr., 1865; comdr. steamer Monacacy, 1866; commd. capt., 1870; commandant U.S. Naval Acad, 1870-73; mem. Lighthouse Bd., 1877-80; commodore, 1878, rear adm. (ret.), 1882; only Am. officer to be both rear adm. U.S. Navy and maj. gen. U.S. Army. Died Washington, D.C., May 26, 1891; buried Oak Hill Cemetery, Washington.

CARTER, Timothy Jarvis, congressman; lawyer; b. Bethel, Mass. (now Me.); Aug. 18, 1800; studied law, Northampton, Mass. Admitted to the bar, 1826, began practice law in Rumford, Me.; moved to Paris, Me., 1827, continued practice law; sec. Me. Senate, 1833; atty. Oxford County (Me.), 1833-37; mem. U.S. Ho. of Reps. (Democrat) from Me., 25th Congress, Sept. 4, 1867-68. Died Washington, D.C., Mar. 14, 1838; buried Congressional Cemetery.

CARTER, William Blount, congressman; b. Elizabethton, Carter County, Tenn., Oct. 22, 1792; attended public schs. Served as col. in War of 1812; mem. Tenn. Ho. of Reps., also mem. Tenn. Senate; del., presiding officer Tenn. Constl. Conv., 1834; mem. U.S. Ho. of Reps. (Whig) from Tenn., 24th-26th congresses, 1835-41. Died Elizabethton, Apr. 17, 1848 buried Carter Cemetery.

CARTERET, Sir George, colonizer; b. St. Ouen, Eng., circa 1610; s. Helier de Carteret. Comptroller, English Navy, 1639-43; bailiff of Jersey (Eng.), 1643, lt. gov., 1643; commd. vice adm. of Jersey, 1644, engaged in privateering; created knight and baronet by the future Charles II (although Parliament considered him pirate), 1650; granted an island off coast of Va. (to be called New Jersey) by Charles, 1650, made no settlement on this grant; surrendered Jersey (Eng.) to Parliament forces, 1651, fled to France; returned to Eng. at Restoration; treas. of navy, 1661-67; dep. treas. Ireland, 1667; commd. to Bd. of Trade and Plantations; received grant to territory between Hudson and Delaware rivers (named N.J. in his honor), 1664. Died Jan. 1680.

CARTERET, Philip, colonial gov.; b. Jersey, Channel Islands, 1639; m. Miss Smith. First gov. Province of N.J., 1664-76, his policy of perpetual quit-rents led to N.J.-Elizabethtown Controversy; authority vested in him under Concessions and Agreements of the Proprietors defied by colonists' refusal to pay rents, 1668; gov. East Jersey, 1676-82, resigned as consequence of N.Y.-N.J. controversy regarding East Jersey's right to collect customs. Died 1682.

CARTIER, Jacques, explorer; b. St. Malo, Brittany, 1491. Sent as leader expdn. to discover N.W. passage to East, 1534; reached Newfoundland, 1534, named Brion Island off coast; mistook Magdalen and Prince Edward islands for main coast; stayed 10 days in Gaspé Harbour making friends with Huron-Iroquois Indians from Que.; returned to St. Malo, 1534; set out again, 1536, anchored in Pillage Bay (named it Bay of St. Lawrence); after reaching island of Orleans was told by Indians he was in Canada (Indian word for village); reached Indian village of Hochelaga (now site of Montreal), 1536; returned to St. Malo with 12 Indians as proof of his discovery of what he thought was Northern Mexico, 1537; set sail again, 1541, made his hdqrs. nr. Que. at Cap Rouge. Died St. Malo, Sept. 1, 1557.

CARTTER, David Kellogg, congressman, jurist; b. Jefferson County, N.Y., June 22, 1812; studied law in Rochester, N.Y. Admitted to N.Y. bar, 1832, began practice law in Rochester; moved to Akron, O., circa 1836, then Massillon, O., continued practice law; mem. U.S. Ho. of Reps. (Democrat) from Ohio, 31st-32d congresses, 1849-53; moved to Cleve., O., 1856, practiced law; del. Republican Nat. Conv., Chgo., 1860; U.S. minister to Bolivia, 1861-1862; chief justice Supreme Ct. of D.C., 1863-87. Died Washington, D.C.., Apr. 16, 1887; buried Lakeview Cemetery, Cleve.

CARTWRIGHT, Alexander Joy, baseball pioneer; b. N.Y.C., Apr. 17, 1820. Suggested to group of N.Y. baseball players that they organize, resulting in formation of Knickerbocker Base Ball Club, 1845 (this team played 1st profl. game); introduced new rules including 90 foot baselines, 9-man team, 9 inning game; pioneered game in West and Hawaii; his name entered in Baseball Hall of Fame as "builder of baseball," Cooperstown, N.Y., 1939. Died Honolulu, Hawaii, July 12, 1892.

CARTWRIGHT, Peter, clergyman; b. Amherst County, Va., Sept. 1, 1785; s. Justinian Cartwright; m. Frances Gaines, Aug. 18, 1808, 9 children. Ordained deacon Methodist Ch., 1806, elder, 1808; circuit rider in Ky. and Tenn.; elected to Gen. Conf., Meth. Ch., 12 times; twice mem. Ill. Legislature; ran for U.S. Congress against Abraham Lincoln, 1846, defeated. Died Pleasant Plains, Ill., Sept. 25, 1872.

CARUTHERS, Robert Looney, congressman, lawyer, educator; b. Smith County, Tenn., July 31, 1800; attended Woodward's Acad., nr. Columbia, Tenn., also Greenville Coll., 1820-21; studied law. In merc. bus., 1817-19; admitted to Tenn. bar, 1827; clk. Tenn. Ho. of Reps., 1824; clk. chancery ct. of Smith County, also editor Tenn. Republican; moved to Lebanon, Tenn., 1826; state's atty., 1827-32; mem. Tenn. Ho. of Reps., 1835; founder Cumberland U., Lebanon, 1842, founder its law dept., 1847, prof. law, from close of Civil War until 1882; Whig presdl. elector, 1844; mem. U.S. Ho. of Reps. (Whig) from Tenn., 27th Congress, 1841-43; judge Supreme Ct. of Tenn., 1852-until start of Civil War; mem. Washington (D.C.) Peace Conv., 1861; elected gov. Tenn., 1862, never assumed duties because of occupation of state by U.S. forces. Died Lebanon, Oct. 2, 1882; buried Cedar Grove Cemetery.

CARUTHERS, Samuel, congressman, lawyer; b. Madison County, Mo., Oct. 13, 1820 grad. Cumberland U., Lebanon, Tenn.; studied law. Admitted to the bar, began practice law in Fredericktown, Mo.; moved to Cape Girardeau, Mo., 1844, held several local offices; mem. U.S. Ho. of Reps. from Mo., (Whig) 33d-34th congresses, 1853-57, (Democrat) 35th Congress, 1857-59. Died Cape Girardeau, July 20, 1860.

CARUTHERS, William Alexander, author; b. Va., circa 1800; attended Washington Coll. (now Washingtin and Lee U.), 1819-20. Practiced medicine; author: The Kentuckian in New York, 1834; The Cavaliers of Virginia, 1837; The Knights of the Horseshoe, A Traditionary Tale of the Cocked Hat Gentry in the Old Dominion, 1845. Died Marietta, Ga., Aug. 29, 1846.

CARVALHO, Solomon Nunes, artist; b. Charleston, S.C., Apr. 27, 1815; s. David N. Carvalho; married; children—David, Jerrite, Jacob, Solomon. Began career as artist, Phila., circa 1838; exhibited at Pa. Acad., 1849; made profl. visits to Charleston and Washington, D.C.; moved to N.Y.C., 1860; artist and photographer, N.Y.C., 1860-80; pres. Carvalho Heating & Super-heating Co., N.Y.C., after 1880. Died N.Y.C., 1894.

CARVER, John, Pilgrim father, colonial gov.; b. Nottinghamshire or Derbyshire, Eng., circa 1576. Went to Holland, 1609; joined Leyden Pilgrims, circa 1610-11; agt. to Eng. to secure charter from Virginia Co.; responsible for Common Stock agreement under which Mayflower Pilgrims sailed for New World, hired Mayflower to go to New Eng.; 1st gov. Plymouth Colony 1620-21; obtained treaty with Indian chief Massasoit, 1621. Died Plymouth, Mass., Apr. 5, 1621.

CARVER, Jonathan, army officer; b. Weymouth, Mass., Apr. 24, 1710; s. David and Hannah (Dyer) C.; m. Abigail Robbins, Oct. 21, 1746; m. 2d, Mary Harris, 1774; at least 3 children. Sgt. in Brit. Army at siege of Ft. William Henry, 1757, promoted lt., 1759, capt., 1760; selectman of Montague, Mass., 1759; travelled West through Great Lakes region to Minn. and back, 1766-67; went to Eng., 1769, engaged in literary pursuits. Author: Travels in Interior Parts of America, 1778. Died England, Jan. 31, 1780.

CARY, Alice, poet; b. nr. Cincinnati, Apr. 26, 1820; d. Robert and Elizabeth (Jessup) Cary. Lived and wrote in N.Y.C. with her sister Phoebe; 1st pres. of 1st woman's club in Am. (now Sorosis). Author: Poems of Alice and Phoebe Cary, 1849 Clovernook Papers, 1852; Lyra and Other Poems 1852; Married, not Mated, 1856; Ballads, Lyric and Hymns, 1866; The Lover's Diary, 1868. Died N.Y.C., Feb. 12, 1871.

CARY, Archibald, planter, industrialist, b. Va. 1721; s. Henry and Anne (Edwards) C.; ed. Coll. William and Mary.; m. Mary Randolph, 1744. Mil operator, cattle raiser; justice of the peace, burgess vestryman Goochland and Cumberland counties, Va. 1747-50; Chesterfield County rep. to Va. Assembly 1756-87, chmn. pub. claims com., 1762, speaker until 1787; mem. Com. of Correspondence, 1773 chmn. com. of Whole, read Va.'s Resolution of Independence to conv. Died Va., Sept. 1787.

CARY, George, congressman, lawyer, newspaper man; b. nr. Allens Fresh, Charles County, Md. Aug. 7, 1789; studied law. Admitted to the bar began practice law in Frederick, Md., also farmed moved to Appling, Ga.; mem. Ga. Ho. of Reps. 1819-21, 34; mem. U.S. Ho. of Reps. from Ga., 18th-19th congresses, 1823-27; editor Hickory Nut newspaper. Died Thomaston, Ga., Sept. 10, 1843; buried Methodist Churchyard.

CARY, George Booth, congressman, planter; b. "Bonny Doon" nr. Courtland, Va., 1811; received a liberal edn. Engaged in planting; mem. U.S. Ho. of Reps. (Democrat) from Va., 27th Congress 1841-43. Died Bethlehem, Va., Mar. 5, 1850; buried on "Bonny Doon" estate nr. Courtland.

CARY, Jeremiah Eaton, congressman, lawyer; b. Coventry, R.I., Apr. 30, 1803; studied law. Moved to Cherry Valley, N.Y., 1820; admitted to N.Y. bar, 1829, began practice law in N.Y.C.; mem. U.S. Ho. of Reps. (Democrat) from N.Y., 28th Congress, 1843-45; resumed practice law in N.Y.C., moved to Plainfield, N.J., 1860; practiced law. Died Rockville Center, L.I., N.Y., June 1888; buried Grace Episcopal Ch. Cemetery, Plainfield.

CARY, Lott, missionary; b. Charles City County, Va., 1780; m. twice; 2 children. Purchased his freedom, 1813; licensed to preach by First Baptist Ch., Richmond, Va., 1813; an organizer Richmond African Bapt. Missionary Soc., 1815; went to Liberia, 1821; organized 1st Bapt. Ch. in Liberia, 1821; pastor at Cape Montserado, Liberia, 1822-28; vice agt. of Liberia, 1826. Died Nov. 10, 1828.

CARY, Phoebe, poet; b. nr. Cincinnati, Sept. 4, 1824; d. Robert and Elizabeth (Jessup) Cary. Lived with her sister Alice in N.Y.C. Author: Poems of Alice and Phoebe Cary, 1849; Poems and Parodies, 1854; Poems of Faith, Hope, and Love, 1868. Died July 31, 1871.

CARY, Shepard, congressman, businessman; b. New Salem, Mass., July 3, 1805; attended common schs. Moved to Houlton, Me., 1822; engaged in extensive lumber operations, agrl., merc. pursuits; mem. Me. Ho. of Reps., 1832-33, 39-42, 48, 49, 62; Democratic presdl. elector, 1836; mem. Me. Senate, 1843, 50-53; mem. U.S. Ho. of Reps. (Democrat) from Me., 28th Congress, May 10, 1844-45; Liberal Party candidate for gov. Me., 1854. Died Houlton, Aug. 9, 1866; buried Evergreen Cemetery.

CASE, Charles, congressman, lawyer; b. Austinburg, O., Dec. 21, 1817; studied law. Admitted to the bar, began practice law in Fort Wayne, Ind.; mem. U.S. Ho. of Reps. (Democrat, filled vacancy) from Ind., 35th-36th congresses, Dec. 7, 1857-61; served as 1st lt. and adjutant 44th Regt., Ind. Volunteer Inf., then maj. 3d Regt., Ind. Volunteer Cavalry, Civil War, 1861-62; practiced law in Washington, D.C. Died Brighton, Washington County, Ia., June 30, 1883; buried Congressional Cemetery, Washington, D.C.

CASE, Jerome Increase, mfr.; b. Williamstown, N.Y., Dec. 11, 1818; s. Caleb and Deborah (Jackson) C.; m. Lydia Bull, 1849, 4 children. Designed built, used combined thresher and separator, (eliminated the fanning mill), 1844; incorporated J. I. Case Threshing Machine Co., 1880; established Mfrs.' Nat. Bank of Racine (Wis.) and First Nat. Bank of Burlington (Wis.), 1871, pres. both banks; mem. bd. trustees Northwestern Mut. Life Ins. Co.; Republican mayor Racine, 1856, 59; mem. Wis. Senate; one of Wis. commrs. at Centennial Exposition, 1876; a founder Wis. Acad. Science, Art and Letters. Died Dec. 22, 1891.

CASE, Leonard, lawyer; b. Westmoreland County, Pa., July 29, 1786; s. Meshach and Magdalene (Eckstein) C.; m. Elizabeth Gaylord, 1817. Admitted to Ohio bar, 1814; cashier Comml. Bank of Lake Erie, Cleve., 1816-19; auditor Cuyahoga County (O.), 1820-24; pres. Cleve. Village, 1821-25; mem. Ohio Ho. of Reps., 1824; pros. atty. Cuyahoga County, 1826-30; mem. Cleve. City Council, 1838; dir. Cleve., Columbus & Cincinnati R.R., 1847-49; agt. for Conn. Land Co., 1827-55. Died Dec. 7, 1864.

CASE, Leonard, philanthropist; b. Cleve., June 27, 1820; s. Leonard and Elizabeth (Gaylord) C.; grad. Yale, 1842; attended Cincinnati Law Sch., 1842-44; never married. Admitted to Ohio bar, 1844, practiced in Cleve., 1842-45, intermittently thereafter; inherited father's fortune in Cleve. real estate, 1864; endowed Cleve. Library Assn. (now Case Library); benefactor Western Reserve Hist. Soc. bequeathed money for founding of Case sch. Applied Science (now Case Inst. Tech. Cleve., 1880. Died Jan. 6, 1880.

CASE, Walter, congressman, lawyer; b. Pleasant Valley, N.Y., 1776; attended Newburgh Acad.; grad. Union Coll., Schenectady, N.Y., 1799; studied law. Admitted to the bar, 1802, began practice law in Newburgh, N.Y.; mem. U.S. Ho. of Reps. from N.Y., 16th Congress, 1819-21; became affiliated with Whig party; practiced law in N.Y.C., 1844-48, ret. Died Fishkill, N.Y., Oct. 7, 1859; buried Fishkill Rural Cemetery.

CASEY, Joseph, jurist; b. Washington County, Md., Dce. 17, 1814; s. Joseph and Rebecca (McLaughlin) C.; m. Mary Krettle. Admitted to Pa. bar, 1838; mem. U.S. Ho. of Reps. (Whig) from Pa., 31st Congress, 1849-51; prepared, published Pennsylvania State Reports, 1856-61; apptd. commr. commr. to investigate and end Erie R.R. War, 1855; judge U.S. Ct. of Claims, 1861-63; 1st chief justice reorganized U.S. Ct. of Claims, 1863-70. Died Feb. 10, 1879.

CASEY, Levi, congressman; b. in S.C., circa 1752. Served with Continental Army. Revolutionary War; elected brig. gen. of militia; justice Newberry County Ct., 1785; mem. S.C. Ho. of Reps.; mem. U.S. Ho. of Reps. from S.C., 8th-9th congresses, 1803-07, reelected to 10th Congress. Died Washington, D.C., Feb. 3, 1807; buried Congressional Cemetery.

CASEY, Silas, army officer; b. East Greenwich, R.I., July 12, 1807; grad U.S. Mil Acad., 1826. Commd. 2d lt. inf., U.S. Army, 1826; fought in Seminole War in Fla., 1837-42; commd. capt., 1839; fought at battles of City of Mexico, Churubusco, Chapultepec, during Mexican War, 1847; prepared tactics manual adopted by Army, 1862; commd. lt. col. 9th Inf., 1855, col., 1861, brig. gen. U.S. Volunteers, 1861, maj. gen., 1862; ret. 1868. Died Bklyn., Jan. 22, 1882.

CASEY, Zadoc, congressman, lt. gov. of Ill.; b. Greene County, Ga., Mar. 7, 1796; attended common schs. Moved to nr. present site of Mount Vernon, Ill., 1819; mem. Ill. Ho. of Reps., 1822-26, 48-52, speaker 1852; mem. Ill. Senate, 1826-30, 60-62; elected lt. gov. of Ill., 1830; served as volunteer in Black Hawk War, 1832; mem. U.S. Ho. of Reps. (Jackson Democrat) from Ill., 23d-27th congresses, 1833-43; del. Ill. constl. convs., 1848, 60; ret. to farm "Elm Hill" nr. Mt. Vernon, 1862. Died Caseyville, Ill. (named for him), Sept. 4, 1862; buried old Union Cemetery, nr. Mt. Vernon.

CASILEAR, John William, artist; b. N.Y.C., June 25, 1811; s. John and Rebecca (Stevens) C.; m. Ellen Howard, 1867. Became an asso. N.A.D., 1835, full mem., 1851; made engraving designs for bank notes; made one of finest Am. engravings of period, a reproduction of Daniel Huntington's Sybil; mdm. Artists' Fund Soc.; works include: A Swiss Lake, 1868, Genesee Meadows, 1871, September Afternoon, 1874, A Scene in New Hampshire, 1877, View of the Rocky Mountains, 1881, Scene on Long Island, 1883, Genesee Valley, 1885, Early Summer, Long Island Sound, 1886, Genesee River, 1887, Rogers Slide, Lake George, 1891. Died Saratoga Springs, N.Y., Aug. 17, 1893.

CASKIE, John Samuels, congressman, lawyer; b. Richmond. Va., Nov. 8, 1821; grad. U. Va., 1842; studied law. Admitted to the bar. circa 1842; practiced law in Richmond; pros. atty. City of Richmond, 1842-46; judge Richmond and Henrico circuits, 1846-49; mem. U.S. Ho. of Reps. (Democrat) from Va., 32d-35th congresses, 1851-59. Died Richmond, Dec. 16, 1869; buried Hollywood Cemetery.

CASS, George Washington, engr., railroad exec.; b. Muskingum County, O., Mar. 12, 1810; s. George W. and Sophia (Lord) C.; grad. U.S. Mil. Acad., 1832. Detailed for duty with Corps Engrs., U.S. Army, as asst. to supt. in charge constrn. Cumberland Rd., 1832-36; erected 1st cast-iron tubular-arch bridge built in U.S., 1837; established Adams Express Co., 1849, effected consolidation of company lines between Boston and St. Louis and South to Richmond, Va., 1854, pres. co., 1855; became pres., dir. Ohio & Pa. R.R. Co. (later consol. und name Pitts., Ft. Wayne & Chgo. R.R.), 1856. Died Mar. 21, 1888.

CASS, Lewis, senator, territorial gov.; b. Exeter, N.H., Oct. 9, 1782; s. Jonathan and Mary (Gilman) G.; m. Elizabeth Spencer, 1806. Admitted to Ohio bar, 1802; mem. Ohio legislature, 1806; U.S. marshall for Ohio, 1807-12; apptd. col. 3d Ohio Regt., War of 1812; commd. col., brig. gen. U.S. Army, 1813; gov. Mich. territory, 1813-31; U.S. sec. of war under Pres. Jackson, 1831-36; apptd. U.S. minister to France, 1836; mem. U.S. Senate (Democrat) from Mich., 1845-48, 49-57; Democratic nominee for U.S. Pres., 1848, supported "squatter sovereignty", defeated by Zachary Taylor; U.S. sec. of state under Pres. Buchanan, 1857-60. Author: France, Its King, Court and Government, 1840; also articles on mil., western, Indian subjects. Died Detroit, June 17, 1866.

CASSEDY, George, congressman, lawyer; b. Hackensack, N.J., Sept. 16, 1783; studied law. Admitted to the bar, 1809, began practice law in Hackensack; postmaster Hackensack, 1805-06; mem. U.S. Ho. of Reps. (Democrat) from N.J., 17th-19th congresses, 1821-27. Died Hackensack, Dec. 31, 1842; buried in cemetery of First Reformed Ch.

CASSERLY, Eugene, senator, lawyer; b. Mullingar, County Westmeath. Ireland, Nov. 13, 1820; grad. Georgetown Coll.; studied law. Came to U.S., 1822; admitted to the bar, 1844, began practice law in N.Y.C.; editor Freeman's Jour., also contbr. to newspapers in other cities; corp. counsel City of N.Y., 1846, 47; moved to San Francisco, Cal., 1850; publisher Public Balance, the True Balance, the Standard; elected state printer State of Cal., 1851; ret. from journalism, resumed practice law; mem. U.S. Senate (Democrat) from Cal., 1869-Nov. 29, 1873, resigned; mem. Cal. Constl. Conv., 1878-79. Died San Francisco, June 14, 1883; buried Calvary Cemetery.

CASSIDY, George Williams, congressman, newspaper man; b. nr. Paris, Ky., Apr. 25, 1836; studied law but never practiced. Moved to Eureka, Nev., 1870, engaged in newspaper work; mem. Nev. Senate, 1872-79, pres., 1879; mem. U.S. Ho. of Reps. (Democrat) from Nev., 47th-48th congresses, 1881-85; nat. bank examiner for Nev., Utah, Cal., Colo., 1886-90; del. Democratic Nat. Conv., Chgo., 1892. Died Reno, Nev., June 24, 1892; buried Hillside Cemetery.

CASSIDY, William, journalist; b. Albany, N.Y., Aug. 12, 1815; s. John and Margaret C.; grad. Union Coll., 1833; m. Lucie Rochefort. Admitted to N.Y. bar, never practiced; writer for Plaindealer and Rough Hewer, Albany, 1840; state librarian N.Y., 1841-43; part owner, joint editor daily Atlas, Albany, 1843, became editor consol. newspaper Argus and Atlas, 1856, pres. Argus Co., 1865-73; mem. N.Y. State Constl. Conv 1867; sec. N.Y. State Democratic Com., 1868-73; mem. commn. on revision N.Y. State Constn., 1872. Died Albany, Jan. 23, 1873.

CASSIN, John, ornithologist; b. Delaware County, Pa., Sept. 6, 1813. Became mcht., Phila., 1834, later established engraving and lithographing bus.; mem. Acad. Natural Scis.; identified and arranged ornithol. specimens in collection of Dr. Thomas B. Wilson. (largest collection then in existence); studied taxonomy, synonomy and nomenclature of ornithology; contbr. papers to govt. and scientific publs. Author: Illustrations of the Birds of California, Texas, Oregon, British, and Russian America, 1856. Died Jan. 10, 1869.

CASTRO, Jose, govt. and mil. ofcl.; gov. Alta Cal., Sept. 1835-Jan. 1836, Nov.-Dec. 1836; mil. comdr. of area, Feb. 1845-Aug. 1846; antagonized Am. settlers of Sacramento Valley by deporting Isaac Graham and about 40 followers, 1840 (incident helped provoke Bear Flag Revolt of 1846; ordered Fremont out of Cal., Mar. 1846, gathered forces against him, using horses obtained through Gen. M.G. Vallejo (horses stolen by band led by Am. agt. Ezekial Merritt); driven out of area by Fremont, June-July 1846, retreated to Mexico.

CASWELL, Alexis, scientist, univ. pres.; b. Taunton, Mass., Jan. 29, 1799; s. Samuel and Polly (Seaver) C.; grad. Brown U., 1822, D.D. (hon.), 1841, LL.D. (hon.), 1865; m. Esther Thompson, 1830; m. 2d, Elizabeth Edmands, 1855; 6 children. Prof. ancient langs. Columbian U., Washington, D.C., 1825-27; entered ministry as pastor of a Baptist Ch., Halifax, N.S., Can., 1827; prof. mathematics and natural philosophy Brown U., 1828-63, pres., 1868-72, trustee, 1873-75; became asso. fellow Am. Acad. Arts and Scis., 1850; v.p. A.A.A.S., 1855; chosen by U.S. Govt. as one of 50 incorporators Nat. Acad. Scis., 1863; became pres. Nat. Exchange Bank, also Am. Screw Co. (both Providence, R.I.), 1863; pres. R.I. Hosp., 1875-77; dir., v.p. Providence Athenaeum. Author: Smithsonian Contributions to Knowledge, 1860; other works include: Lectures on Astronomy, 1858, Memoirs of John Barstow, 1864. Died Providence, Jan. 8, 1877.

CASWELL, Richard, army officer, gov. N.C., Continental congressman; b. Cecil County, Md., Aug. 3, 1729. Surveyor, Raleigh, N.C., dep. surveyor N.C., clk. Orange County (N.C.) mem. N.C. Assembly, 1754-71, speaker, 1770-71; presided over N.C. Provincial Congress during Am. Revolution; presided over N.C. Constl. Conv., 1776; N.C. del. to Continental Congress 1774-76; commd. col. N.C. Partisan Rangers, Continental Army, 1776-77; maj. gen. N.C. Militia, 1780-83; 1st gov. N.C., 1776-80, 5th gov., 1785-87; comptroller gen. N.C., 1782; pres. N.C. Senate, 1782-84, 89; presided over N.C. Conv. to ratify U.S. Constn., 1789. Died Fayetteville, N.C., Nov. 10, 1789; buried in family cemetery, Lenoir County, N.C.

CATESBY, Mark, naturalist; b. Sudbury, Suffolk, Eng., 1679; 2 children. Came to Am., 1712; studied floral and fauna in Va., 1712-19, S.C., Ga., Fla., 1722-25, Bahamas, 1726; mem. Royal Soc., 1733-49. Author: The Natural History of Carolina, Florida, and the Bahama Islands, Vol. 1, 1731, Vol. 2, 1743, appendix, 1748; Hortus Britanno-Americanus: or, A Curious Collection of Trees and Shrubs, 1763. Died London, Eng., Dec. 23, 1749.

CATHCART, Charles William, senator, congressman; b. Funchal, Island of Madeira (father U.S. consul), July 24, 1809; attended pvt. schs. Became a sailor, 1819; moved to Washington, D.C., 1830, clk. in Gen. Land Office; went with ammunition team to Ft. Dearborn (now Chgo.), Ill., 1832; joined a mil. co. under command of Capt. Finch; justice of the peace New Durham Twp., Ind., 1833; became a farmer, nr. La Porte, Ind., 1837; became U.S. land surveyor; mem. Ind. Senate, 1837-40; Democratic presdl. elector, 1844; mem. U.S. Ho. of Reps. (Democrat) from Ind., 29th-30th congresses, 1845-49; mem. U.S. Senate from Ind., (apptd. to fill vacancy), Dec. 6, 1852-53. Died on his farm, nr. La Porte, Aug. 22, 1888; buried Pine Lake Cemetery.

CATHCART, James Leander, diplomat; b, County of Westneath, Ireland, June 1, 1767; s. Malcolm and Miss (Humphreys) C.; m. Jane Bancker, June 5, 1798, 12 children. As seaman on schooner Maria of Boston, captured 1785, sold into slavery in Algiers; while prisoner became clk. of the Marine, 1787-88, also clk. Bagnio Gallera, clk. to prime minister, and in 1792 chief Christian secretary to the Dey and Regency of Algiers; sailed for Phila., 1796, carrrying letter from Dey to Pres. Washington; 1796 apptd. U.S. consul at Tripoli, 1797; spl. diplomatic agt. accompanying William Eaton to Tunis; apptd. consul at Tunis, 1803; consul at Maderia, Portugal, 1807-15, at Cadiz, Spain, 1815-17. Died Oct. 6, 1843.

CATLIN, George, artist, author; b. Wilkes-Barre, Pa., July 26, 1796; s. Putnam and Polly (Sutton) C.; m. Clara B. Gregory. Specialized in portrait painting in oil and miniature; visited Albany, N.Y. painted portrait of Gov. DeWitt Clinton, 1828; painted portrait of Dolly Madison, Washington, D.C.; painter 600 portraits of distinguished Indians, 1829-38 (collection now in U.S. Nat. Mus.). Author: Letters and Notes on the Manners, Customs and Conditions of the North American Indians, 1841; Life Among the Indians, 1867; Last Rambles Amongst the Indians of the Rocky Mountains and the Andes, 1867. Died Jersey City, N.J., Dec. 23, 1872.

CATLIN, George Smith, congressman, lawyer; b. Harwinton, Conn., Aug. 24, 1808; attended Amherst Coll., Litchfield (Conn.) Law Sch. Admitted to the bar, 1828, practiced law in Windham, Conn., 1829-31; mem. Conn. Ho. of Reps., 1831, 46; sec. to the gov. of Conn., 1831-33; pros. atty. Windham County, 1842, 43; mem. U.S. Ho. of Reps. (Democrat) from Conn., 28th Congress, 1843-45; unsuccessful Democratic candidate for gov. of Conn., 1848; mem. Conn. Senate, 1850; judge Windham County Ct., 1850-51. Died Windham, Dec. 26, 1851; buried Windham Cemetery.

CATON, John Dean, jurist; b. Monroe, N.Y., Mar. 19, 1812; s. Robert and Hannah (Dean) C.; LL.D. (hon.), Hamilton Coll., 1866; m. Laura Sherill, July 1835, Mem., sec. 1st polit. conv. held in Ill., 1834; justice of the peace, Ottawa; admitted to Ill. bar, 1835; asso. justice Supreme Ct. Ill., 1842-64, chief justice, 1855, 1857-64; pres. Ill. & Miss. Telegraphic Co., 1852-67. Author: A Summer in Norway, 1875; The Antelope and Deer of America, 1877; contbr. papers on nature subjects to Ottawa Acad. Science. Died Chgo., July 30, 1895.

CATRON, John, justice U.S. Supreme Ct.; b. Wythe County, Va., 1778. Admitted to Tenn. bar, 1815; elected to Tenn. Ct. of Last Resort, 1824; 1st chief justice Tenn., 1831-34; apptd. asso. justice U.S. Supreme Ct. by Pres. Jackson 1837. Died Nashville, Tenn., May 30, 1865.

CATTELL, Alexander Gilmore, banker, senator; b. Salem N.J., Feb. 12, 1816; s. Thomas and Keziah (Gilmore) C.; m. Eliza Gillmore. Mem. N.J. Legislature, 1841-42, clk. lower house; del. N.J. Constnl. Conv., 1844; mem. Phila. Common Council, 1848-54; dir. Mechanics Bank Phila.; pres. Corn Exchange Assn., 1857; organizer Corn Exchange Bank, Phila., 1858; mem. U.S. Senate from N.J., 1866-71; financial agt. U.S. Treasury, London, Eng.,

1873; asso. with Jay Cooke and George M. Robeson in some of the scandals of the Grant adminstrn. Died Jamstown NY., Apr. 8, 1894.

CATTELL, William Cassaday, clergyman, coll. pres.; b. Salem, N.J., Aug. 30, 1827; s. Thomas W. and Keziah (Gilmore) C.; grad. Coll. of N.J. (now Princeton), 1848, grad. Princeton Theol. Sem., 1852, D.D. (hon.); D.D. (hon.), Hanover Coll.; LL.D. (hon.), Wooster Coll.; m. Elizabeth McKeen, Aug. 4, 1859. Ordained to ministry Presbyn. Ch., 1856; prof. Latin, Lafayette Coll., Easton, Pa., 1855-63, trustee, 1861-63, pres., 1863-83; pastor Pine Street Presbyn. Ch., Harrisburg, Pa., 1860-83; corr. sec. Presbyn. Bd. Ministerial Relief, 1884-86; pres. Presbyn. Hist. Soc., 1890-98; bd. dirs. Princeton Theol. Sem., 1864-98; v.p. Am. Philol. Soc. Died Feb. 11, 1898.

CATTON, Charles, Jr., artist; b. London, Eng., Dec. 30, 1756; s. Charles Catton; studied painting with his father. Exhibited frequently at Royal Acad., 1776-1800; published set of 36 animals Drawn from Nature, and Engraved in Acquatinta, 1789; came to Am., circa 1802, settled on farm, New Paltz, N.Y.; work exhibited at Am. Acad., 1816, 18, 22, 27. Died New Paltz, Apr. 24, 1819.

CAULFIELD, Bernard Gregory, congressman, lawyer; b. Alexandria, Va., Oct. 18, 1828; grad. Georgetown Coll., 1848; grad. law dept. U. Pa., 1850. Admitted to the bar, 1850, began practice law in Lexington, Ky.; moved to Chgo., 1853, practiced law; mem. U.S. Ho. of Reps. (Democrat, filled vacancy) from Ill., 43d-44th congresses, Feb. 1, 1875-77; moved to Dakota Territory, 1878, practiced law, became a large landowner in Deadwood. Died Deadwood, Territory of Dakota (now S.D.), Dec. 19, 1887; buried Calvary Cemetery, St. Louis.

CAUSIN, John M.S., congressman, lawyer; b. St. Marys County, Md., 1811; studied law. Admitted to the bar in Prince Georges County, Md., circa 1836, began practice law in Leonardtown, St. Marys County; mem. Md. Ho. of Reps., 1837, 43; mem. U.S. Ho. of Reps. (Whig) from Md., 28th Congress, 1843-45; moved to Annapolis, Md.; del. Md. Constl. Conv.; Whig presdl. elector, 1848; moved to Chgo., 1858, practiced law. Died Cairo, Ill., Jan. 30, 1861; buried City Cemetery (now Lincoln Park), Chgo.

CAVANAUGH, James Michael, congressman, lawyer; b. Springfield, Mass., July 4, 1823; studied law. Engaged in newspaper work; admitted to the bar, 1854, began practice law in Davenport. Ia.; began practice law in Chatfield, Minn., 1854; mem. U.S. Ho. of Reps. (Democrat, elected when state entered union) from Minn., 35th Congress, May 11, 1858-59; moved to Colo., 1861, practiced law, engaged in mining; mem. Colo. Constl. Conv., 1865; moved to Mont., 1866; mem. U.S. Congress (Democrat) from Mont. Territory, 40th-41st congresses, 1867-71; practiced law in N.Y.C.; moved to Leadville, Colo., 1879. Died Leadville, Oct. 30, 1879; buried Greenwood Cemetery, N.Y.C.

CAVELIER, Robert, see La Salle, Sieur de.

CAZENOVE, Theophile, financier; b. Amsterdam, Holland, Oct. 24, 1740; s. Theophile and Marie (de Raspin-Thogras) C.; m. Margaretha Helena van Jever, 1763. In brokerage business, Amsterdam, 1763-88; purchasing agt. for Dutch speculators in Am. state and federal securities, 1788-1802, company adopted name Holland Land Co., 1796; came to U.S., 1790, became U.S. citizen, 1794; in addition to govt. securities invested his company's funds in real estate, canal and mfg. companies in U.S.; lived in Phila., 1790-99; returned to Europe, 1799. Died Paris, France, Mar. 6, 1811.

CELERON de BLAINVILLE, Pierre Joseph de, see de Céleron de Blainville.

CERACCHI, Guiseppe, sculptor; b. Rome, Italy, July 4, 1751; studied under Tomaso Righi. Went to Eng., 1775, soon became well known in London; sculptured bust of Sir Joshua Reynolds; came to Am., 1789; attempted a statue entitled Liberty, which U.S. Congress refused to back financially because of its expense; did various busts, including Washington, Hamilton, John Paul Jones, while in U.S.; discouraged by what he considered lack of appreciation, went to France; joined conspiracy against Napoleon Bonaparte, was captured and guillotined. Died Paris, Jan. 30, 1802.

CERRE, Jean Gabriel, mcht.; b. Montreal, Que., Can., Aug. 23, 1734; s. Joseph and Marie (Picard) C.; m. Catherine Giard, 1764, 4 children including Marie Therese (Cerre) Chouteau. Fur trader, Kaskaskia, Ill., 1755-79; sent 1st organized parties of hunters into Missouri River country; became one of richest men in Ill. area; gave money and provisions to George Rogers Clark and his men during Am. Revolution; moved to St. Louis, 1799; mem. 1st co. of St. Louis Militia, 1780; a founder New Madrid in Spanish La. (now Mo.), 1780. Died Apr. 4, 1805.

CESSNA, John, congressman, lawyer; b. nr. Bedford County, Pa., June 29, 1821; attended Hall's Mil. Acad., Bedford, Pa.; grad. Marshall Coll., Mercersburg, Pa., 1842; studied law. Admitted to the bar, 1845, began practice law in Bedford; mem. Pa. Ho. of Reps., 1850, 51, 62, 63, 92, speaker, 1850, 63; del. Democratic nat. convs., 1856, 60; became affiliated with Republican Party, 1863, chmn. Rep. State Conv., 1865, elected chmn. Rep. state central com., 1865, del. Rep. nat. convs., 1868, 76, 80; mem. U.S. Ho. of Reps. (Republican) from Pa., 41st 43d congresses, 1869-71, 73-75. Died Bedford, Dec. 13, 1893; buried Bedford Cemetery.

CHABRAT, Guy Ignatius, clergyman; b. Chambres, Cantal, France, Dec. 28, 1787; attended St. Fleur Sem.; came to U.S., 1809, attended St. Thomas' Sem., Ky. Joined Sulpicians, ordained priest Roman Catholic Ch., 1811; did missionary work, Ky.; superior Congregation of Sisters of Liretto, 1824-46; consecrated titular bishop of Bolina, coadjutor of Bardstown, 1834; caused to resign by blindness, 1847, returned to France. Died Mauriac, France, Nov. 21, 1868.

CHACE, Elizabeth Buffum, reformer; b. Providence, R.I., Dec. 9, 1806; d. Arnold and Rebecca (Gould) Buffum; m. Samuel Buffington Chace, June 1828, 10 children including Lillie (Chace, Wyman, Arnold B. Operated underground railroad station at her home in Valley Falls, R.I., in 1840's; R.I. agt. for New Eng. Anti-Slavery Soc.; promoted Woman's Rights Conv., Worcester, R.I., 1850; a founder R.I. Woman Suffrage Assn., 1868, pres., 1870-99; mem. Am. Woman Suffrage Assn. lobbied successfully for creation of bd. of women visitors to state penal instns. for women, 1870, mem. bd. for several years; del. Internat. Congress on Prevention and Repression of Crime, including Penal Reformatory Treatment, London, Eng., 1872; founder R.I. Home and Sch. for Dependent Children, 1884. Died Central Falls, Dec. 12, 1899.

CHADBOURNE, Paul Ansel, coll. pres.; b. North Berwick, Me., Oct. 21 1823: S. Isaiah and Pandora (Dennett) C.; grad. Williams Coll., 1848, LL.D., 1868; D.D., Amherst Coll., 1872. m. Elizabeth Page, Oct. 9, 1850. First prof. botan and chemistry Williams Coll., 1853; dean Me. Med. Sch., 1852-58; mem. Mass. Senate, 1865; 1st pres. Mass. Agrl. Coll. Amherstr, 1866-67, 1882-83; pres. U.. Wis., 1867-70, Williams Coll., 1872-81; mem. Mass. bd. Agr., 1874-83. Mem. Royal Soc. Northern Antiquaries of Copenhagen. Author: Lectures on Natural History, Its Relation to Intellect, Taste, Wealth and Religion (presented at Smithsonian Instn. 1859), 1860; Lectures on Natural Theology (Lowell Inst. lectures), 1867; Instinct in Animals and Men, 1872; Hope of the Righteous, 1877. Conducted exploring and scientific expdns. to Newfoundland, 1855, Fla., 1857, Greenland, 1861. Died N.Y.C.. Feb. 23, 1883.

CHAFFEE, Calvin Clifford, congressman, physician; b. Saratoga Springs, N.Y., Aug. 28, 1811; grad. med. sch. Middlebury (Vt.) Coll., 1835. Began practice medicine, Springfield, Mass.; mem. U.S. Ho. of Reps. (Am. Party) from Mass., 34th, 35th congresses, 1855-59; librarian U.S. Ho. of Reps., 1859-61; practiced medicine in Washington, D.C., until 1876; moved to Springfield, 1876; pres. Union Relief Assn., 1880-93; pres. Hampden County (Mass.) Children's Aid Assn. Died Springfield, Aug. 8, 1896; buried Springfield Cemetery.

CHAFFEE, Jerome Bunty, senator, banker; b. nr. Lockport, Niagara County, N.Y., Apr. 17, 1825; s. Warren and Elizabeth (Otto) C.; m. Miriam Comstock, 1848, 4 children, including Fannie Josephine (Mrs. U. S. Grant, Jr.). Mem. lower house Colo. Territorial legislature, 1861, speaker, 1864-65; founder, pres. 1st Nat. Bank of Denver, 1865-80; chosen U.S. senator when Colo. hoped to become a state, 1865, not permitted to take seat; del. to U.S. Congress from Colo. Territory, 1871-75; mem. U.S. Senate (Republican) from Colo., Nov. 15, 1876-79; chmn. Republican Nat. Exec. Com., 1884. Died Salem Center, Westchester County, N.Y., Mar. 9, 1886; buried Adrian (Mich.) cemetery.

CHALKLEY, Thomas, clergyman, mcht.; b. Southwark, Eng., May 3, 1675; s. George and Rebecca C.; m. Martha Betterton, 1699; m. 2d, Martha Brown, 1719. Came to Am. on preaching tour of Quaker churches, 1698; toured Md., Va., N.C., 1703, New Eng., 1704, later visited Western settlements and Indians; preached in England, 1707-10; capt. trading vessels between Phila., Bermuda, Barbados, and Eng. after 1701; owned plantation nr. Phila., 1723-41. Author: A Collection of the Works of Thomas Chalkley, published posthumously, 1749. Died Tortola, V.I., Nov. 4, 1741.

CHALMERS, James Ronald, army officer, congressman; b. Halifax County, Va., Jan. 11, 1831 s. Joseph Williams and Fannie (Henderson) C. grad. S.C. Coll., 1851; m. Rebecca Arthur, circa 1865, 1 daughter. Admitted to Miss. bar, 1853 dist. atty. Miss., 1858; chmn. com. on mil. affairs Miss. Secession Conv., 1861; commd. capt. Confederate Army, 1861, col., 1861, brig. gen., 1862; comdr. 1st div. Forrest's Cavalry Army Corps, 1865; mem. Miss. Senate, 1875, 76; mem. U.S. Ho. of Reps. from Miss., as Democrat, 45th-47th congresses, 1877-83, as Independent, 48th Congress, 1884-85; spl. asst. to U.S. dist. atty., 1883-84. Died Memphis, Tenn., Apr. 9, 1898; buried Elmwood Cemetery, Memphis.

CHALMERS, Joseph Williams, senator, lawyer, b. Halifax County, Va., Dec. 20, 1806; studied law U. Va., also in Richmond, Va.; at least 1 son, James Ronald. Admitted to the bar, practiced law; moved to Jackson, Tenn., 1835, to Holly Springs, Miss., 1839, continued practice law; vice chancellor No. Miss. Dist., 1842-43; mem. U.S. Senate (Democrat, apptd. to fill vacancy, then elected) from Miss., Nov. 3, 1845-47; Deomcratic presdl. elector, 1848. Died Holly Springs, June 16, 1853 buried Hill Crest Cemetery.

CHAMBERLAIN, Ebenzer Mattoon, congressman, lawyer; b. Orrington, Me., Aug. 20, 1805; studied law. Employed in father's shipyard; moved to Connersville, Ind.; admitted to Ind. bar, 1832, began practice law in Elkhart County, 1833; mem. Ind. Ho. of Reps., 1835-37; mem. Ind. Senate, 1839-42; pros. atty. 9th Jud. Circuit, 1842, pres. judge 9th Jud. Dist., 1843-52; del. Democratic Nat. Conv., Balt., 1844; mem. U.S. Ho. of Reps. (Democrat) from Ind., 33d Congress, 1853-55; practiced law in Goshen, Ind., 1855-61. Died Goshen, Mar. 14, 1861; buried Oak Ridge Cemetery.

CHAMBERLAIN, Jacob Payson, congressman, businessman; b. Dudley, Mass., Aug. 1, 1802; attended public schs. Moved to Seneca Falls, N.Y., 1807; operator flour mills, malt houses, woolen mills; organizer 1st savs. bank in Village of Seneca Falls; supr. of Seneca Falls, also mem. bd. edn.; mem. N.Y. State Assembly, 1859-61; mem. U.S. Ho. of Reps. (Republican) from N.Y., 37th Congress, 1861-63. Died Seneca Falls, Oct. 5, 1878; buried Restvale Cemetery.

CHAMBERLAIN, John Curtis, congressman, lawyer; b. Worcester, Mass., June 5, 1772; grad. Harvard, 1793; studied law. Admitted to the bar, 1796, began practice law in Alstead, N.H.; mem. N.H. Ho. of Reps., 1802-04, 18; moved to Charlestown, N.H., 1804; mem. U.S. Ho. of Reps (Federalist) from N.H., 11th Congress, 1809-11; moved to Honeoye Falls, N.Y., 1826, then to Utica, N.Y. Died Utica, Dec. 8, 1834.

CHAMBERLAIN, Nathan Henry, clergyman; b. Sandwich (now Bourne), Mass., Dec. 28, 1828; s. Artemis White and Lydia (Ellis) C.; grad. Harvard, 1853; attended Harvard Divinity Sch., U. Heidelburg (Germany); m. Hannah Simonds Tewkesbury, Feb. 19, 1855; m. 2d, Mariette Cleveland Hyde, Apr. 6, 1869. Ordained to ministry Unitarian Ch., 1857; pastor, Canton, Mass., later Balt.; changed beliefs, ordained priest Protestant Episcopal Ch., 1864; rector, Birmingham (now Derby), Conn., Morrisania, N.Y., Milw., East Boston, Mass.; retired from ministry, 1889. Author: The Autobiography of a New England Farm House, 1864; What's the Matter? or Our Tariff and Its Taxes, 1890; Samuel Sewall and the World He Lived In, 1897. Died Bourne, Apr. 1, 1901.

CHAMBERLAIN, William, congressman, lt. gov. of Vt.; b. Hopkinton, Mass., Apr. 27, 1755; attended common schs. Moved to Loudon, N.H., 1774; served as sgt., Revolutionary War; became land surveyor and farmer; moved to Peacham, Vt., 1780, clk. of the proprietors Town of Peacham, 1780, town clk., 1785-87, town rep., 12 years; mem. Vt. Ho. of Reps., 1785, 87-96, 1805, 08; justice of the peace, 1786-96; del. Vt. constl. convs., 1791, 1814; brig. gen. Vt. Militia, 1794, maj. gen., 1799; asst. judge Orange County, 1795; chief judge Caledonia County, 1796-1803; sec. bd. trustees Caledonia County Grammar Sch., 1795-1812, pres. 1813-28; state councilor State of Vt., 1796-1803; Federalist presdl. elector, 1800; mem. U.S. Ho. of Reps. (Federalist) from Vt., 8th, 11th congresses, 1803-05, 09-11; lt. gov. of Vt., 1813-15. Died Peacham, Sept. 27, 1828; buried Peacham Cemetery.

CHAMBERS, David, congressman; b. Allentown, Pa., Nov. 25, 1780; tutored by farther. Served as confidential express rider for Pres. Washington during Whiskey Insurrection, 1794; learned art of printing; moved to Zanesville, O., 1810, established a newspaper, became state printer of Ohio; volunteer a.d.c. to Gen. Cass, War of 1812; served as recorder and mayor of Zanesville; mem. Ohio Ho. of Reps., 1814, 28, 36-38, 41-42; clk. Ohio Senate, 1817; clk. Muskingum County (O.) Ct.

of Common Pleas, 1817-21; mem. U.S. Ho. of Reps. from Ohio, (filled vacancy) 17th Congress, Oct. 9, 1821-23; affiliated with Whig party after its formation; mem. Ohio Senate, 1843-44, pres., 1844; del. Ohio Constl. Conv., 1850; farmed until 1856. Died Zanesville, Aug. 8, 1864; buried Greenwood Cemetery.

CHAMBERS, Ezekiel Forman, senator, jurist; b. Kent County, Md., Feb. 28, 1788; s. Benjamin and Elizabeth (Forman) C.; attended Washington Coll., 1805. LL.D., Yale, 1833, LL.D., Delaware Coll., 1852. Admitted to Md. bar, 1808; advanced to brig. gen. Md. Militia, War of 1812; mem. Md. Senate, 1822; mem. U.S. Senate (Whig) from Md., 1826-34; apptd. chief judge 2d Jud. Dist., also judge Md. Ct. of Appeals, 1834-51; del. Md. Constnl. Conv., 1850; pres. bd. trustees Washington Coll. Died Chestertown Md., Jan. 30, 1867; buried Chester County, Chestertown.

CHAMBERS, George, congressman; b. Chambersburg, Pa., Feb. 24, 1786; s. Benjamin and Sarah (Brown) C.; grad. Princeton, 1804; m. Alice Lyon. Admitted to Cumberland County (Pa.) bar, 1807; mem. Chambersburg Town Council, 1821, town burgess, 1829-33; mem. U.S. Ho. of Reps. (Whig) from Pa., 23d-24th congresses, 1832-36; mem. Pa. Constl. Conv. from Franklin County 1837; asso. judge Supreme Ct. of Pa., 1851. Author: A Tribute to the Principles, Virtues, Habits and Public Usefulness of the Irish and Scotch Early Settlers of Pennsylvania, 1856. Died Chambersburg, Mar. 25, 1866, buried Falling Spring Presbyn. Churchyard, Chambersburg.

CHAMBERS, Henry H., senator, physician; b. nr. Kenbridge, Va., Oct. 1, 1790; grad. Coll. of William and Mary, 1808; grad. med. dept. U. Pa., 1811. Moved to Madison, Ala., 1812, practiced medicine; served in earlier Indian wars as surgeon on staff of Gen. Andrew Jackson; settled in Huntsville, Ala.; mem. Ala. Constl. Conv., 1819; mem. Ala. Ho. of Reps., 1820; unsuccessful candidate for gov. Ala., 1821, 23; Democratic presdl. elector, 1824; mem. U.S. Senate (Democrat) from Ala., 1825-26. Died nr. Kenbridge, Va. (while en route to Washington, D.C.), Feb. 24, 1826; buried family burial ground, nr. Kenbridge.

CHAMBERS, John, territorial gov., congressman; b. Somerset County, N.J., Occt. 6, 1780; s. Rowland and Phoebe (Mullican) C.; m. Margaret Taylor, June 16, 1803; m. 2d, Hannah Taylor, Oct. 29, 1807; 12 children. Served as aid-de-cacmp to Gen. William Henry Harrison during War of 1812; mem. Ky. Legislature, 1812, 15, 30, 32; mem. U.S. Ho. of Reps. from Ky., 21st, 24-25th congresses, 1829-31, 35-39; gov. Ia. Territory, 1841-46; U.S. commr. to negotiate treaty with Sioux Indians, 1849. Died Paris, Ky., Sept. 21, 1852.

CHAMBERS, Talbot Wilson, clergyman; b. Carlisle, Pa., Feb. 25, 1819; s. William C. and Mary (Ege) C.; grad. Rutgers, 1834; attended Princeton Theol. Sem., 1836-37; m. Louise Freylinghuysen, May 21, 1841, 11 children. Licensed to preach by Presbyn. Ch., 1838; withdrew, joined Dutch Reformed Ch., 1839; pastor 2d Reformed Ch. of Raritan, Somerville, N.J., 1840-49, Collegiate Reformed Ch., N.Y.C., 1849-96; mem. Old Testament Co. of Am. Com. on Revision of English Bible; pres. Gen. Synod of Reformed Ch., 1863; orgaized Alliance of Reformed Chs. Holding the Presbyn. System, chmn. Western sect., 1884-92, pres. of Alliance, 1892-96. Died N.Y.C., Feb. 3, 1896.

CHAMPION, Epaphroditus, congressman, businessman b. Westchester parish, Colchester, Conn., Apr. 6, 1756; attended common schs. Served in commissary and purchasing depts. Continental Army, Revolutionary War; moved to East Haddam, Conn., 1782; served as capt. 24th Regt., Conn. Militia, 1784-92, maj., 1793-94, lt. col., 1795-98, brig. gen. 7th Brigade, 1800-03; was a mcht., shipowner, exporter, importer; mem. Conn. Assembly, 1791-1806; mem. U.S. Ho. of Reps. (Federalist) from Conn., 10th-14th congresses, 1807-17. Died East Haddam, Dec. 22, 1834; buried Riverview Cemetery.

CHAMPLAIN, Samuel, see de Champlain Samuel.

CHAMPLIN, Christopher Grant, senator, congressman; b. Newport, R.I., Apr. 12, 1768; grad. Harvard, 1786; postgrad. Coll. of St. Omer, France. Mem. U.S. Ho. of Reps. from R.I., 5th-6th congresses, 1797-1801; was a mcht.; mem. U.S. Senate from R.I. (filled vacancy), June 26, 1809-Oct. 2, 1811 (resigned); pres. R.I. Bank. Died Newport, Mar. 18, 1840; buried Common Burial Ground.

CHAMPLIN, Stephen, naval officer; b. South Kingston, R.I., Nov. 17, 1789; s. Stephen and Elizabeth (Perry) C.; m. Minerva Pomeroy, Jan. 5, 1817, 5 children. Became sailing master U.S. Navy, 1812; participated in expdns. against York and Ft. George; fired 1st shot in Battle of Lake Erie; served in Battle of Mackinac; promoted lt., 1814; in command of Porcupine on survey of Canadian boundary, 1816-18; involved in little active service, 1818-45; in command of lake station ship Michigan, 1845-48 promoted capt., 1850; commd. commodore (ret.) 1867. Died Buffalo, N.Y., Feb. 20, 1870.

CHANCA, Diego Alvarez, physician, 15th century. Court physician to Ferdinand and Isabella of Spain; acompanied 2d expdn. of Columbus to Am., 1493, saved life of Columbus and others suffering malaria; selected site for 1st permanent settlement of Isabella, Haita. Author of detailed and accurate account of New World as he saw it during 3-month stay; also wrote study of treatment of pleurisy, published 1506, after his return to Spain.

CHANCHE, John Mary Joseph, clergyman, coll. pres.; b. Balt., Oct. 4, 1795; s. John and Catherine (Provost) C.; attended St. Mary's Coll., Balt., 1806. Ordained priest Roman Catholic Ch., Balt., 1819; prof., v.p., then pres. St. Mary's Coll., Balt., 1834-40; accepted diocese of Natchez, Miss., 1840, consecrated bishop in Balt., 1841, took over barren parish property and land lost to U.S. when U.S. took over area from Spain; went to Cuba to search for claims to this property, 1844, found proof, presented it to Congress, petitioned for indemnification of lands, petition never granted; used funds put aside for his parish in New Orleans in Propagation of Faith fund, obtained additional funds from Europe and from congregation, laid cornerstone for his cathedral in Natchez, 1842; brought in Sisters of Charity from Emmitsburg, Md., 1848, sisters opened orphanage in Natchez; built 11 chs., 17 missions in Miss. Died Frederick City, Md., July 22, 1852.

CHANDLER, Elizabeth Margaret, author; b. Centre, Del., Dec. 24, 1807; d. Thomas and Margaret (Evans) Chandler. Regular contbr. to Genius of Universal Emancipation, charge female dept., 1829, Author: (best known poem) The Slave Ship, The Brandywine, The Sunset Hour, Summer Morning; Essays, Philanthropic and Moral, 1836; works collected in Poetical Works of Elizabeth Margaret Chandler (published by Benjamin Lundy), 1836. Died Nov. 2, 1834.

CHANDLER, John, army officer, senator; b. Epping, New Hampshire, February 1, 1762; s. Capt. Joseph and Lydia (Eastman) C.; m. Mary Whittier (also spelled Whitcher), Aug. 28, 1783. Served with Continental Army, 1777, 80, Participated in Battle of Saratoga, mem. Mass. Senate, 1803, 04, 19; mem. U.S. Ho. of Reps. from Mass., 9th-10th congresses, 1805-09; sheriff Kennebec County, Mass. (now Me.), 1809-12; commd. brig. gen. U.S. Army during War of 1812; del. Me. Constl. Conv., 1819; pres. Me. Senate, 1820; mem. U.S. Senate from Me., dir U.S. Br. Bank, Portland, Me., 1829-30; founder Monmouth Acad.; trustee Bowdoin Coll., 1821-38; U.S. collector of customs Dist. of Portland and Falmouth, 1829-37. Died Augusta, Me., Sept. 25, 1841.

CHANDLER, John Greene, engraver; b. "Deer Farm," Petersham, Mass., Dec. 18, 1815; m. Sarah Ann Guild, 1850. Partner, wood engraving firm Chandler, Wright & Mallory, Boston, 1836-39; illustrated (and possibly wrote) The Remarkable Story of Chicken Little, published 1840; worked with brother as Chandler & Co., or Samuel W. Chandler & Co., Boston, 1854-55; moved to Lancaster, Mass., after 1857; manufactured paper dolls and cut-outs, a toy circus, games. Died Lancaster, Sept. 11, 1879.

CHANDLER, John Winthrop, congressman, lawyer; b. N.Y.C., Sept. 14, 1826; grad. Columbia Coll., N.Y.C., 1847; attended U. Heidelberg (Germany); studied law; at least 1 son, William Astor. Admitted to N.Y. bar, practiced law; mem. N.Y. Assembly, 1858-59; mem. U.S. Ho. of Reps. (Democrat) from N.Y., 38th-40th congresses, 1863-69. Died nr. Rhinebeck, Dutchess County, N.Y., Oct. 19, 1877; buried Trinity Cemetery, Red Hook, N.Y.

CHANDLER, Joseph Ripley, journalist, congressman; b. Kingston, Mass., Aug. 25, 1792; s. Joseph and Saba (Ripley) C.; ed. U. Pa. Editorial writer U.S. Gazette, 1822, became part owner, 1826, editor until 1847; editor Graham's Am. Monthly Mag. of Lit., Art and Fashion; pres. bd. dirs. Girard Coll., 1848; mem. U.S. Ho. of Reps. from Pa., 31st-33d congresses, Dec. 3, 1849-55; U.S. minister to the Two Sicilies, 1858-60; sent by Phila. Soc. for Alleviating Miseries of Public Prisons to Internat. Congress, London, Eng., 1872. Author: Outlines of Penology, Grammar of the English Language, 1848; The Beverly Family or Home Influence of Religion, 1875. Died Phila., July 10, 1880.

CHANDLER, Peleg Whitman, lawyer; b. New Gloucester, Me., Apr. 12, 1816; s. Peleg and Esther (Parsons) C.; grad. Bowdoin Coll., 1834; attended Dane Law Sch., Harvard; m. Martha Ann Bush, Nov. 30, 1837. Admitted to Mass. bar, 1837, practiced in Boston; publisher, editor monthly jour. Law Reporter, Boston, 1838-40; U.S. commr. in bankruptcy, Boston, 1842; mem. Boston Common Council, 1843-45, pres., 1844, 45; mem. Mass. Ho. of Reps., 1844-45, 2663-; solicitor City of Boston, 1846-53 revised Boston city ordinances, 1850. Author: Bankruptcy Laws of the United States, and the Outline of the System with Rules and Forms in Massachusetts, 1842; Observations on the Authority of the gospels, By a Layman, 1867; Memoir of Governor Andrew, with Personal Reminiscences, 1880. Died May 28, 1889.

CHANDLER, Thomas, congressman; b. Bedford, N.H., Aug. 10, 1772; attended public schs. Justice of peace, 1808; capt. N.H. Militia, 1815; mem. N.H. Ho. of Reps., 1818, 27; mem. U.S. Ho. of Reps. (Democrat) from N.H., 21st-22d congresses, 1829-33; innkeeper and farmer. Died Bedford, Jan. 28, 1866; buried Bedford Cemetery.

CHANDLER, Thomas Bradbury, clergyman; b. Woodstock, Conn., Apr. 26, 1726; s. Capt. William and Jemima (Bradbury) C.; grad. Yale, 1745; M.A., Oxford (Eng.) U., 1753, D.D., 1766; D.D., Columbia, 1767; m. Jane M. Emott, 1750, 6 children. Called to service St. John's Ch., Elizabethtown N.J., 1747; ordained to Anglican Ch., London, Eng., circa 1751; leading advocate of Am. episcopacy; Loyalist, attacked Continental Congress in pamphlet What Think Ye of Congress Now?, 1775; fled to Eng., 1775, returned to Elizabethtown, 1785. Author: An Appeal to the Public in Behalf of the Church of England in America, 1767. Died Elizabethtown, June 17, 1790; buried St. John's Ch.

CHANDLER, Zachariah, senator, sec. of interior; b. Bedford N.,H., Dec. 10, 1813; s. Samuel and Margaret (Orr) C.; m. Letitia Douglass, Dec. 10, 1844. Mayor, Detroit, 1851-52; del. to Republican Nat. Conv., Pitts., 1856, became mem. Nat. Rep. Com.; mem. U.S. Senate from Mich., 1857-75, 79, chmn. com. on commerce, 1861-75; boss Rep. Machine in Mich., asso. with radical wing Rep. Party; chmn. Rep. Congl. Com. during campaigns of 1868-76, Joint com. on Conduct War; sec. of interior U.S., 1875-77. Died Chgo., Nov. 1, 1879.

CHANEY, John, congressman; b. Washington County, Md., Jan. 12, 1790. Moved to Ohio, 1810, settled in Bloom Twp., Fairfield County, engaged in farming; justice of peace, 1821, 24, 27; trustee Bloom Twp. for 23 years; maj., col., paymaster Ohio State Militia; mem. Ohio Ho. of Reps., 1828-30, 42, 55, speaker, 1842 asso. judge Fairfield County, 1831; Democratic presdl. elector, 1832, on the Jackson ticket; mem. U.S. Ho. of Reps. (Jackson Democrat) from Ohio, 23d-25th congresses, 1833-39; settled in Canal Winchester, Franklin County, O.; mem. village council; mem. Ohio Senate, 1844-45; del. Ohio Constl. Conv., 1851. Died Canal Winchester, Apr. 10, 1881; buried Union Grove Cemetery.

CHANFRAU, Francis S., actor; b. N.Y.C., Feb. 22, 1824; s. Mehitable Trenchard; m. Henrietta Baker, July 23, 1858. Specialized in mimicry; established his reputation as an actor as Jeremiah Clip in The Widow's Victim; played part of Cedric in Ivanahoe at Palmo's Opera House, 1845; 1st success was as Mose in Glance at New York, 1848; last stage success was as Kit in Kit the Arkansas Traveler, which he played continuously for 13 years. Died Jersey City, N.J., Oct. 2 1884.

CHANG and **ENG** (adopted legal surname Bunker), Siamese twins; b. Meklong, Siam, May 1811; Chang m. Sarah Yates, Eng m. Adelaide Yates at dual ceremony, Apr. 1843; Chang had 10 children, Eng had 9 children. Siamese twins, connected at waist by cartilaginous structure; partners in duck and egg business, Siam, 1819-24; sold by parents to Brit. mcht., 1824; brought to U.S., 1829; subsequently made tours of U.S. and Britain, advertised as edнl. exhbn.; began collecting profits of teaching for themselves, 1832; too attached to each other to be surgically separated; because wives (sisters) could not get along they maintained separate homes at Wilkes, N.C., made alternate 3-day visits; partners in farm, Wilkes; Chang died of intemperance on voyage from Liverpool to N.Y.C., Eng died of fright few hours later. Died at sea, Jan. 17, 1874

CHANNING, Edward Tyrrell, educator; b. Newport, R.I., Dec. 12, 1790; s. William and Lucy (Ellery) C.; attended Harvard, 1803-07, A.M. (hon.), 1819; m. Henrietta Ellery, 1826. Admitted to bar, 1813; editor North American Review, 1818-20; Boylston prof. rhetoric and oratory Harvard, 1819-50, trained Emerson Holmes, Sumner, Lowell and others. Author: Lectures Read to the Seniors in Harvard College, published posthumously, 1856. Died Cambridge, Mass., Feb. 8, 1856.

CHANNING, Walter, physician, coll. dean; b. Newport, R.I.., Apr. 15, 1786; s. William and

Lucy (Ellery) C.; B.A., Harvard, 1808, M.D., 1812; M.D., U. Pa., 1809; m. Barbara Higginson Perkins, 1815; m. 2d, Elizabeth Wainwright, 1831. First prof. obstetrics and med. jurisprudence Harvard Med. Sch., 1815-circa 1844, dean, 1819-47; co-editor Boston Med. and Surg. Jour., 1828; librarian Mass. Med. Soc., 1822-25, treas., 1828-40; a founder Boston Lying-In Hosp., 1832; mem. Am. Acad. Arts and Scis.; 1st to use ether in childbirth cases. Died Boston, July 27, 1876.

CHANNING, William Ellery, clergyman b. Newport, R.I., Apr. 7, 1780; s. William and Lucy (Ellery) C.; grad. Cambridge (Eng.) U. 1798; m. Ruth Gibbs, 1814. Ordained to ministry, 1803; pastor Federal Street Ch., Boston, 1805-42; did not approve of denominational ties but became leader in Unitarin movement by his arguments against Calvinist doctrine; organized Berry Street conf. of liberal ministers, 1820, it in turn organized Am. Unitarian assn., 1825; interested in politics (Jeffersonian) and literature believed that literature (particularly Am. literature) could lead to intellectual and moral reformation of man; influenced writers such as Emerson and Thoreau; supported abolition, temperance and Peace. Soc. Author: Remarks on American Literature, 1830; Slavery, 1835; The Abolitionist, 1836; Duty of the Free States, 1842. Died Oct. 2, 1842.

CHANNING, William Francis, inventor; b. Boston, Feb. 22, 1820; s. William Ellery and Ruth (Gibbs) C.; M.D., U. Pa., 1844; m. Mary Jane Tarr. Asst., 1st geol. survey of N.H., 1841-42; asst. editor Latimer Jour., Boston, 1842; asst. on geol. survey of Lake Superior copper region, 1847; worked with Moses Farmer on devel. of fire-alarm telegraph, 1845-51, 1st used in Boston, 1851, patented and sold to Gamewell & Co., 1857; patented ship ry. for inter-oceanic transport of ships, 1865; invented portable electromagnetic telegraph, 1877. Died Mar. 19, 1901.

CHANNING, William Henry, clergyman, reformer, author; b. Boston, May 25, 1810; s. Francis Dana and Susan (Higginson) C.; grad. Harvard, 1829, Harvard Divinity Sch., 1833; m. Julia Allen, Dec. 1836. Ordained to ministry Unitarian Ch., 1839; editor Western Messenger (organ of Unitarianism in West), Cincinnati, 1839-41; editor The Present (Socialist organ), 1843-44; Transcendentalist; lived at Brook Farm, 1845; original mem., minister religious union of associationists, Boston, 1847-50; editor The Spirit of the Age, 1849; went to Eng.; succeeded James Martineau as minister Hope Street Unitarian Chapel Liverpool, Eng., 1857; returned to Am., 1861; pastor Unitarian Soc., Washington, D.C., 1861-63; chaplain U.S. Ho. of Reps., 1863-65; also served in various army camps, hosps. during Civil War; returned to Eng. 1866. Author: (translated) Jouffroy's Introduction to Ethics, 1841; The Gospel of Today, 1847; The Life of William Ellery Channing (his uncle), 3 vols., 1848; (with Ralph Waldo Emerson and J.F. Clarke) Memoirs of Margaret Fuller Ossoli, 2 vols. 1852; Lessons from the Life of Theodore Parker, 1860. Died London, Eng., Dec. 23, 1884.

CHAPIN, Aaron Lucius, clergyman, coll. pres.; b. Hartford, Conn., Feb. 4, 1817; s. Laertes and Laura (Colton) C.; grad. Yale, 1837, Union Theol. Sem., 1842; D.D., Williams Coll., 1853; LL.D., U. State N.Y., 1882; m. Martha Colton, Aug. 23, 1843; m. 2d, Fanny Coit, Aug. 26, 1861. Pastor 1st Presbyn. Ch., Milw., 1843; ordained to ministry Presbyn. Ch., 1844; 1st pres. Beloit, Wis. Coll., 1849-86; trustee Chgo. Theol. Sem., 1858-91, Rockford Sem., 1845-92; corporate mem. Am. Bd. for Fgn. Missions, 1851-89; dir. Am. Home Missionary Soc., 1850-83; pres. Wis. Inst. for Deaf and Dumb 1873-81; a founder Wis. Acad. Scis., 1870, pres., 1878-81; mem. Nat. Council Edn., 1881-88; asso. editor Johnson's Cyclopedia, 1875-78. Died Beloit, July 22, 1892.

CHAPIN, Calvin, clergyman; b. Chicopee, Mass., July 22, 1763; s. Edward and Eunice (Cotton) C.; grad. Yale, 1788; m. Jerusha Edwards, Feb. 2, 1795. Licensed to preach by Hartford North Assn. of Congregational Ch., 1791; tutor Yale. 1791-94; pastor Stepney parish, Wethersfield (now Rocky Hill), Conn., 1794-1851; trustee Missionary Soc. of Conn., 1805-31; co-founder Conn. Bible Soc., 1809; co-founder Am. Bd. Fgn. Missions, 1810, recording sec., 1810-42 co-founder Conn. Soc. for Promotion Good Morals, 1813; mem. bd. visitors Andover Theol Sem., 1816-51, clk. of bd., 1816-32; mem. corp. Yale, 1820-46. Died Mar. 16, 1851.

CHAPIN, Chester William, railroad promoter, congressman; b. Ludlow, Mass., Jan. 16, 1797; s. Ephraim and Mary (Smith) C. Owner (with Horatio Sargeant) Brattleboro & Hartford State Lines; owner steamship lines on Conn. River from Hartford, Sound and New Haven to N.Y.C.; pres. Conn. River R.R., 1850-54, Boston & Albany R. R., 1854-77; founder Chapin Bank, Agawam Bank; v.p. Hampden Savs. Bank; dir. Springfield Fire & Marine Ins. Co., Massasoit Ins. Co.; elected to Mass. Legislature (Democrat), 1844; mem. Mass. Constl. Conv., 1853; mem. U.S. Ho. of Reps. from Mass., 44th Congress, 1875-77. Died Springfield, Mass., June 10, 1883.

CHAPIN, Edwin Hubbell, clergyman; b. Union Village, N.Y., Dec. 29, 1814; s. Alpheus and Beulah (Hubbell) C.; m. Harriet Newland, 1838. Ordained to ministry Universalist Ch., 1838; pastor, Richmond, Va., later Charlestown, Mass. and Boston; pastor Fourth Universalist Soc., N.Y.C., 1848-80; founder Chapin Home for Indigent Men and Women, N.Y.C.; trustee Bellevue Coll. and Hosp., N.Y.C. Author: Duties of Young Men, 1840; The Philosophy of Reform, 1843; The Crown of Thorns, 1848; Duties of Young Women, 1848; Moral Aspects of City Life, 1853; Lessons of Faith and Life, 1877; The Church of the Living God, 1881. Died Dec. 26, 1880.

CHAPIN, Graham Hurd, congressman, lawyer b. Salisbury, Conn., Feb. 10, 1799; grad. Yale Coll., 1819; studied law. Moved to Lyons, Wayne County, N.Y., 1817; admitted to N.Y. bar, 1823, practiced law, Lyons; surrogate Wayne County, 1826-33; dist. atty. Wayne County, 1829, 30; moved to Rochester, N.Y., 1833, continued practice of law; mem. U.S. Ho. of Reps. (Democrat) from N.Y., 24th Congress, 1835-37. Died Mt. Morris, Livingston County, N.Y., Sept. 8, 1843.

CHAPIN, Mrs. Jane Catherine Louise Value, artist; b. Hartford, Conn., Sept. 10, 1814; attended sch., N.Y.C., 1826; painted on velvet, taught drawing and painting, drew views for engraving, colored photographs; painted miniatures and portraits, including a life portrait of Chief Justice John Marshall. Died Providence, Nov. 29, 1891.

CHAPLIN, Jeremiah, clergyman, coll. pres.; b. Rowley (now Georgetown), Mass., Jan. 2, 1776; s. Asa and Mary (Bailey) C.; grad. Brown U., 1799;; m. Marcia O'Brien, 10 children. Pastor, Baptist Ch., Danvers, Mass., 1802-18; prin., prof. theology Me. Lit. and Theol. Instn. (became Waterville Coll.), 1818; 1st pres. Waterville (Me.) Coll. (now Colby Coll.), 1821-33; pastor Bapt. chs., Rowley, Mass., Willington Conn., Hamilton, N.Y. Author: The Greatness of Redemption, 1808; The Evening of Life, 2d edit., 1859; The Memorial Hour, published posthumously, 1864. Died Hamilton, N.Y., May 7, 1841.

CHAPMAN, Alvan Wentworth, botanist, physician b. Southampton, Mass., Sept. 28, 1809; s. Paul and Ruth (Pomeroy) C.; A.B., Amherst Coll., 1830; m. Mary Ann (Simmons) Hancock, Nov. 1839. Practiced medicine, Quincy, Marianna and Apalachicola, Fla.; became leading botanist in South; friend and correspondent of Asa Gray; genus Chapmania named in his honor; helped Union soldiers escape from prison nr. his home at Apalachicola during Civil War. Author: Flora of the Southern States (only manual for Southern botany until after turn of century), 1860. Died Apalachicola, Apr. 6, 1899.

CHAPMAN, Andrew Grant, congressman, lawyer; b. La Plata, Md., Jan. 17, 1839; s. John Grant; attended Charlotte Hall Acad., St. Mary's County, Md.; grad. St. John's Coll., Annapolis, Md., 1858; grad. law dept. U. Va., Charlottesville, 1860. Moved to Balt., 1860; admitted to Md. bar, 1860, began practice of law, Balt.; moved to Port Tobacco, Md., 1864, continued law practice, also involved in farming; mem. Md. Ho. of Dels., 1867-68, 70, 72, 79, 85; apptd. aide and insp. with rank ofbrig. gen., 1874, Gov. Groome's staff, reapptd. by Gov. Carroll mem. U.S. Ho. of Reps. (Democrat) from Md., 47th Congress, 1881-83; apptd. dep. collector internal revenue, 1885, collector, 1888; del. Democratic Nat. Conv., St. Louis, 1888. Died at home Normandy, nr. La Plata, Md., Sept. 26, 1892; buried Mt. Rest Cemetery, La Plata.

CHAPMAN, Augustus Alexandria, congressman, lawyer; b. Union, Va. (now W. Va.), Mar. 9, 1803; studied law. Admitted to bar, 1825, began practice of law, Union; mem. Va. Asembly, 1841-43; mem. U.S. Ho. of Reps. (Van Buren Democrat) from Va., 28th-29th congresses, 1843-47; brig. gen. state militia at outbreak of Civil War, took field with his command, 1861, served Confederate Army in Kanawha Valley; resumed practice of law, Union, also involved in farming. Died Hinton, Summers County, W. Va., June 7, 1876, while on way to attend W. Va. Democratic Conv., Charleston; buried Green Hill Cemetery, Union.

CHAPMAN, Bird Beers, congressman, lawyer; b. Salisbury, Conn., Aug. 24, 1821; studied law. Admitted to bar, began practice of law, Elyria, Lorain County, O.; moved to Territory of Neb., settled in Omaha; editor Omaha Nebraskan, 1855-59; mem. U.S. Congress (Democrat) from Neb. Territory, 34th Congress, 1855-57. Died Put in Bay, O., Sept. 21, 1871; buried Ridgelawn Cemetery, Elyria.

CHAPMAN, Charles, congressman, lawyer; b Newtown, Conn., June 21, 1799; studied law Litch field (Conn.) Law Sch. Admitted to Conn. bar 1820; began practice of law, New Haven, Conn. 1827; moved to Hartford, 1832, became editor Ne Eng. Review; mem. Conn. Ho. of Reps. 1840, 47-48 62, 64; U.S. dist. atty. for Conn. Dist., 1841-48 mem. U.S. Ho. of Reps. (Whig) from Conn., 32 Congress, 1851-53; unsuccessful temperance can didate for gov. Conn., 1854. Died Hartford, Aug 7, 1869; buried Cedar Hill Cemetery.

CHAPMAN, Frederic A., artist; b. Conn., 1818 Painted hist. scenes of Boston, circa 1850; exhibite landscape and hist. paintings at Am. Art-Union 1850; settled in Bklyn., circa 1850; 1st pres. Bklyn Art Assn.; painted series of Civil War scenes in oil Died Jan. 26, 1891.

CHAPMAN, Henry, congressman, lawyer; b Newtown, Pa., Feb. 4, 1804; attended Doylestowr Acad., also Dr. Gummere's pvt. boys' schs., nr Burlington, N.J.; studied law. Admitted to Pa bar, 1825, began law practice, Doylestown, Pa., mem. Pa. Senate, 1843; judge 15th Jud. Dist., 1845-49 mem. U.S. Ho. of Reps. (Democrat) from Pa., 35th Congerss, 1857-59; judge Buck County Ct., 1861-71. Died at Frosterley, nr. Doylestown, Apr. 11, 1891; buried graveyarc Doylestown Presbyn. Ch.

CHAPMAN, J.H., architect; b. N.Y.C.; studiec architecture Yale, also in Germany. Began as draftsman in office of Ware & Van Brunt, Boston; became partner of Horace S. Fraser, 1892; designed numerous bldgs. in New Eng., including Mchts. Bank, New Bedford, Mass., State Armory, Nashua, N.H., High Sch., Concord, Mass., mumerous residences in Boston and suburbs. Died 1895.

CHAPMAN, John, congressman; b. Wrightstown Twp., Bucks County, Pa., Oct. 18, 1740; presumably studied medicine as he called himself a practitioner of physic. Commd. justice of peace, 1779; a justice commd. judge Ct. of Common Pleas of Buck County 1779; moved to Upper Makefield, Pa., prior to 1776, his home was hdqrs. of Col. Alexander Hamilton while Gen. Washington's Army was camped on west bank of the Delaware, just before the Battle of Trenton; mem. Pa. Assembly, 1787-96; mem. U.S. Ho. of Reps. (Federalist) from Pa., 5th Congress, 1797-99. Died Upper Makefield, Jan. 27, 1800; buried Friend's Burying Ground, Wrightstown, Pa.

CHAPMAN, John (known as Johnny Appleseed), pioneer, folk hero; b. Springfield, Mass., circa 1775. Said to have saved people of Mansfield (O.) from massacre at the hands of Indians by a nightlong journey through wilderness; scattered medicinal herbs throughout his travels; settled in Ohio River Valley, traveled throughout area planting and pruning apple trees, 1800-10; many folk legends concerning him have arisen; subject of numerous lit. works including Johnny Appleseed's Rhymes (Denton J. Snider); In Praise of Johnny Appleseed (Vachel Lindsay). Died Allen County, Ind., Mar. 11, 1847; buried Archer's Graveyard, nr. Ft. Wayne, Ind.

CHAPMAN, John Gadsby, artist; Alexandria, Va., Dec. 8, 1808. Studied Pa. Acad. Fine Arts, 1827; a founder Century Club; full mem. N.A.D. 1836; executed wood engravings and portrait paintings for Harper's Bible published 1846; one of America's 1st etchers; best known work was Baptism of Pocahontas, in rotunda of Capitol Bldg., Washington, D.C. Author: The American Drawing Book, 1847. Died Bklyn., Nov. 28, 1889.

CHAPMAN, John Grant, congressman; b. La Plata, Md., July 5, 1798; attended coll. in Pa., 1812-13; grad. Yale, 1817; studied law; at least 1 son, Andrew Grant. Admitted to Md. bar, 1819, began practice of law, Port Tobacco, Md.; also interested in farming; mem. Md. Ho. of Dels., 1824-32, 43-44, speaker, 1826-29, 44; mem. Md. Senate, 1832-36, pres., 1833-36; served in Md. Militia; unsuccessful candidate for gov. Md., 1844; mem. U.S. Ho. of Reps. (Whig) from Md., 29th 30th congresses, 1845-49; pres. Md. Constl. Conv., 1851; pres. Whig Nat. Conv., Balt., 1856. Died on sister's estate Waverly, Charles County, Md., Dec. 10, 1856; buried at family estate St. John's, reinterred Mt. Rest Cemetery, La Plata.

CHAPMAN, Maria Weston, reformer; b. Weymouth, Mass., July 25, 1806; d. Warren and Anne (Bates) Weston; m. Henry Grafton Chapman, 1830. Treas., Mass. Anti-Slavery Socl., 1834, edited its ann. reports Right and Wrong in Boston; an editor the Non-resistant; edited (with Edmund Quincy) the Liberator; mem. exec. com. Am. Anti-Savery Soc., 1840, del. world's conv., 1840; edited Liberty Bell (ann. devoted to abolition). Author: Songs of the Free and Hymns of Christian Freedom, 1836; How Can I Help to Abolish Slavery, 1855. Died Weymouth, July 12, 1885.

CHAPMAN, Nathaniel, physican; b. Fairfax County, Va., May 28, 1780; s. George and Amelia (Macrae) C.; grad. U. Pa. Med. Sch., 1800; M. D., U. Edingurgh (Scotland), 1804; m. Rebecca Biddle, 1808. Founder Med. Inst. Phila., 1817; editor Jour. Med. and Phys. Scis.; pres. Phila. Med. Soc.; 1st pres. A.M.A.; pres. Am. Philos. Soc. Author: Elements of Theraputics and Materia Medica, 1817; Lectures on the More Imoprtant Diseases of the Thoracic and Abdominal Viscera, 1844; Lectures on the More Important Eruptive Fevers, Hemorrhages and Dropsies and on Gout and Rheumatism, 1844; A Compendium of Lectures on the Theory and Practice of Medicine, 1846. Died Phila., July 1, 1853.

CHAPMAN, Reuben, gov. Ala.; b. Bowling Green, Va., July 15, 1799; s. Col. Reuben and Anne (Reynolds) C.; m. Felicia Pickett, Oct.17,1838, 6 children. Admitted to Ala. bar, 1825; mem. Ala. Senate, 1832-35; mem. U.S. Ho. of Reps. (Democrat) from Ala., 24th-29th congresses, 1835-47; gov. Ala., 1847-49; elected to lower house Ala. Legislature, 1855. Died Huntsville, Ala., May 16, 1882; buried Maple Hill Cemetery, Huntsville.

CHAPMAN, William Williams, congressman; b. Clarksburg, Va. (now W.Va.), Aug. 11, 1808; studied law while serving as clk. of ct. Admitted to bar, began law practice, Middleton; an original settler of Burlington, Ia. (then Mich. Territory), 1835; pros. atty. Mich. Territory, 1836; 1st dist. atty. when Wis. Territory was organized, 1836; mem. U.S. Congress (Democrat) from Ia. Territory, 25th-26th congresses, Sept. 1838-Oct. 1840; moved to Agency City (Indian village), Wapello County, Ia., 1843; elected del. from Wapello County to 1st constl. conv., Iowa City, 1844; started to cross plains to become a pioneer of Ore., 1847; went to Cal., 1848; returned to Ore.; mem. Ore. Ho. of Reps.; a founder of the Oregonian (1st newspaper established in Ore. Territory); surveyor gen.. 1858. Died Portland, Ore., Oct. 18, 1892; buried Lone Fir Cemetery.

CHAPPEL, Alonzo, artist; b. N.Y.C., Mar. 1, 1828; studied at N.A.D. Exhibited at Am. Inst. before age of 17; moved to Bklyn., painted, 1848-68; spent later years on Middle Island, L.I., N.Y., illustrated hist. books; work represented at N.Y., Chgo. hist. socs. Died Middle Island, Dec. 4, 1887.

CHAPPELL, Absalom Harris, railroad builder, congressman; b. Hancock County, Ga., Dec. 18, 1801; s. Joseph and Dorothy (Harris) C.; grad. U. Ga., 1820; m. Loretto Lamar, May 1842. Admitted to Ga. bar, 1821; an organizer Monroe Ry., Western & Atlantic Ry., 1836-37; trustee U. Ga., mem. both houses Ga. Legislature; mem. U.S. Ho. of Reps. from Ga., 28th Congress, 1843-44; mem. many public commns. in Ga. Author: Miscellanies of Georgia (hist. essays), 1874. Died Columbus, Ga., Dec. 11, 1878.

CHAPPELL, John Joel, congressman, lawyer; b. Little River, nr. Columbia, S.C., Jan. 19, 1782; grad. law dept. S.C. Coll. (now U. S.C.), Columbia. Admitted to S.C. bar, 1805, began practice of law, Columbia; apptd. adj. 33d S.C. Regt., 1805, elected capt., then col., 1808; apptd. trustee S.C. Coll., 1809; served in War of 1812; mem. U.S. Ho. of Reps. (States Rights War Democrat) from S.C., 13th-14th congresses, 1813-17; dir. Columbia br. State Bank S.C., 1830-58; moved to Lowndes County, Ala., became a cotton planter. Died Lowndes County, Ala., May 23, 1871; buried 1st Baptist Ch. Cemetery, Columbia.

CHARDON, Jean Baptiste, missionary; b. Bordeaux. France, Apr. 27, 1672. Joined Soc. of Jesus, 1687, sent to Can., 1699, missionary nr. Ottawa, 2 years, then worked with missions around Green Bay, Wis., until 1743. Died Quebec, Can., Apr. 11, 1743.

CHARLES, William, caricaturist; b. Edinburgh, Scotland, 1776; m. Mary Charles. Came to U.S., 1805; in caricaturist business, N.Y.C., 1805-14, Phila., 1814-20; illustrated Am. Mag. of Wit, 1808; etched set of caricatures of War of 1812; illustrated Pinkerton's Travels, 1810-12, The Tour of Doctor Syntax in Search of the Picturesque, The Vicar of Wakefield. Died Phila., Aug. 29, 1820; buried New Market Street Baptist Churchyard, Phila.

CHARLESS, Joseph, editor, printer; b. Westmeath, Ireland, July 16, 1772; m. Sarah (Jordan) McCloud, 1798. Arrived in N.Y.C., 1796; printer, editor Mo. Gazette, St. Louis, (a pioneer newspaper of West), 1808-34. Died July 28, 1834.

CHARLEVOIX, Pierre Francois Xavier de, see de Charlevoix, Pierre Francois Xavier.

CHARLTON, Robert Milledge, senator, lawyer; b. Savannah, Ga., Jan. 19, 1807; studied law. Admitted to Ga. bar, began practice of law Savannah; mem. Ga. Ho. of Reps.; U.S. dist. atty.; elected judge Superior Ct., 1832, resigned to devote himself to law; mem. U.S. Senate (filled vacancy) from Ga., 1852-53; mayor Savannah. Died Savannah, Jan. 18, 1854; buried Laurel Grove Cemetery.

CHARLTON, Thomas Usher Pulaski, jurist; b. Camden, S.C., Nov. 1779; s. Thomas and Lucy (Kenan) C.; ed. St. John's Coll., Annapolis, Md.; m. Emily Walter; m. 2d, Ellen Glasco; 2 children. admitted to Ga. bar, 1800; mem. Ga. Legislature, 1801; atty. gen. Ga., 1804; published biography of Gen. James Jackson, 1804; judge Eastern circuit, Ga., 1807-11; 21-22; chmn. Com. Pub. Safety during War of 1812; mayor Savannah (Ga.); compiled 1st vol. of Ga. court decisions Reports of Cases Argued and Determined in the Superior Courts of the Eastern District of the State of Georgia, 1824. Died Dec. 14, 1835.

CHASE, Dudley, senator, jurist; b. Cornish, N.H., Dec. 30, 1771; grad. Dartmouth, 1791; studied law. Admitted to bar, 1793, practiced law, Randolph, Vt.; pros. atty. Orange County, 1803-12; mem. Vt. Ho. of Reps., 1805-12, 23-24, speaker, 1808-12; del. Vt. constl. convs., 1814, 22; mem. U.S. Senate (Jeffersonian Democrat), 1813-17, 25-31; chief justice Vt. Supreme Ct., 1817-21; engaged in farming. Died Randolph Center, Orange County, Vt., Feb. 23, 1846; buried Randolph Cemetery.

CHASE, George William, congressman; b. Maryland, N.Y.; attended common schs. Engaged in farming; engaged in merc. and milling pursuits, Schenevus, Otsego County, N.Y.; mem. U.S. Ho. of Reps. (Whig) from N.Y., 33d Congress, 1853-55. Died Chaseville, N.Y., Apr. 17, 1867; buried in Chase vault, Schenevus Cemetery.

CHASE, Irah, clergyman, educator; b. Stratton, Vt., Oct. 5, 1793; s. Isaac and Sarah (Bond) C.; grad. Middlebury Coll., 1814, Andover Theol. Sem., 1817; m. Harriet Savage, Mar. 15, 1821; m. 2d, Martha Raymond, Oct. 13, 1835; 9 children. Ordained to ministry Baptist Ch., 1817; prof. theology Columbian Coll., Washington, D.C., 1818-25; prof. Newton Theol. Instn., 1825-45; advocate of scientific study of Bible; influenced raising of ednl. standards of Bapt. Ch. Died Nov. 1, 1864.

CHASE, Jeremiah Townley, Continental congressman; b. Balt., May 23, 1748. Mem. coms. observation and correspondence, 1774; del. Md. Constl. Conv., 1776; moved to Annapolis, Md., 1779; mem. Gov.'s Council, 1780-84, 86-88; mayor Annapolis, 1783; mem. Continental Congress from Md., 1783-84; anti-federalist mem. of conv. to ratify U.S. Constn., 1788; judge Gen. Ct., 1789, chief justice Ct. of Appeals until his resignation, 1824. Died Annapolis, May 11, 1828; buried City Cemetery.

CHASE, Lucien Bonaparte, congressman, lawyer; b. Derby Line, Vt., Dec. 5, 1817; studied law. Moved to Dover, Tenn., circa 1838, taught sch.; admitted to Tenn. bar, began law practice, Charlotte, Tenn.; moved to Clarksville, Tenn.; mem. U.S. Ho. of Reps. (Democrat) from Tenn., 29th-30th congresses, 1845-49; moved to N.Y.C., 1849. Died Derby Line, Dec. 4, 1864; buried Greenwood Cemetery, Bklyn.

CHASE, Philander, clergyman, coll. pres.; b. Cornish, N.H., Dec. 14, 1775; s. Dudley and Allace (Corbett) C.; grad. Dartmouth, 1796; m. Mary Fay, 1796; m. 2d, Sophia Ingraham, July 1819; 4 children. Ordained deacon Episcopal Ch., 1798, priest, 1799; 1st Episcopal bishop of Ohio, 1818-31; pres. Cincinnati Coll., 1821-22; founder Kenyon Coll., Gambier, O., 1824, 1st pres., 1824-31; became bishop Diocese of Ill., 1835-52; prin. founder Jubilee Coll., Ill. (now site Jubilee State College Park), 1838; presiding bishop of Episcopal Ch., 1843-52. Died Jubilee Coll., Sept. 20, 1852.

CHASE, Pliny Earle, educator, scientist; b. Worcester, Mass., Aug. 18, 1820; s. Anthony and Lydia (Earle) C.; grad. Harvard, 1839, M.A. (hon.), 1844; LL.D. (hon.), Haverford Coll., 1844; m. Elizabeth Brown Oliver, 1843, 6 children. Prof. natural sciences Haverford Coll., 1871, prof. philosophy and logic, 1875, acting pres., 1886; lectr. psychology and logic Bryn-Mawr Coll.; mem. Am. Philos. Soc. (v.p., sec., recipient Magellanic medal for paper "Numerical Relations between Gravity and Magnetism"); linguist; mgr. Franklin Inst.; fellow A.A.A.S., 1874. Author textbooks including: Elements of Arithmetic, 1844; The Common School Arithmetic, 1848; Elements of Meteorology for Schools and Households, 1884. Died Haverford, Pa., Dec. 17, 1886.

CHASE, Salmon Portland, chief justice U.S. Supreme Ct.; b. Cornish, N.H., Jan. 13, 1808; s. Ithamar and Janette (Ralston) C.; grad. Dartmouth, 1826; m. Katherine Garniss, Mar. 4, 1834; m. 2d, Eliza Smith, Sept. 26, 1839; m. 3d, Sarah Ludlow, Nov. 6, 1846; 6 children. Admitted to Ohio bar, 1829; published compilations as Statutes of Ohio, 3 vols., 1833-35; active in Free Soil Movement of 1848; defender of escaping slaves, known as atty. gen. for runaway negroes; mem. U.S. Senate from Ohio, 1849-55, 60; gov. Ohio, 1855-59; Ohio commr. to Washington Peace Conv., 1861; U.S. sec. of treasury in Lincoln's cabinet, 1861-64, nat. banking system originated during his term of office, 1863; his cabinet relations with Lincoln were strained as he considered Lincoln an incompetent adminstr.; proposed as Republican presdl. nominee in 1864, but Lincoln easily won nomination; chief justice U.S. Supreme Ct., 1864-73, presided at inconclusive trial of Jefferson Davis, at Senate impeachment trials of Pres. Johnson, also interpreter many pieces Reconstruction legislation, such as Mississippi vs. Johnson, Texas vs. White, Georgia vs. Stanton, Ex Parte Garland, court generally upheld this type legislation as constnl. Died N.Y.C., May 7, 1873.

CHASE, Samuel, congressman; b. Cooperstown, N.Y. Dist. atty. Otsego County (N.Y.), 1821-29; mem. U.S. Ho. of Reps. (Adams Democrat) from N.Y., 20th Congress, 1827-29. Died Richfield, N.Y., Aug. 3, 1838.

CHASE, Samuel, asso. justice U.S. Supreme Ct.; b. Somerset County, Md., Apr. 17, 1741; s. Rev. Thomas and Martha (Walker) C.; m. Ann Baldwin, May 21, 1762; m. 2d, Hannah Giles, Mar. 3, 1784; 4 children. Admitted to Md. bar, 1761; mem. Md. Assembly, 1764-84; del. Continental Congress, 1774-78, 84, 85; mem. Md. Com. of Correspondence, 1774; mem. Md. Conv., Md. Council of Safety, 1775; signer Declaration of Independence; served on 30 congressional coms., 1777-78; chief judge Balt. Criminal Ct., 1788; opponent of U.S. Constn., voted against ratification at Md. Constl. Conv., 1788; chief judge Md. Gen. Ct., 1791; asso. justice U.S. Supreme Ct., 1796-1811, impeached, 1804, acquitted, 1805 (accused of biased, underhanded trial conduct toward Jeffersonians in 1799). Died June 19, 1811.

CHASE, Thomas, coll. pres.; b. Worcester, Mass., June 16, 1827; s. Anthony and Lydia (Earle) C.; grad. Harvard, 1848, LL.D. (hon.), 1878; L.H.D. (hon.), Haverford Coll., 1880; m. Alice Cromwell, Feb. 8, 1860, 5 children. Prof. of Latin, Harvard, 1850; prof. philology Haverford Coll., 1855, pres., 1875; apptd. sr. editor Chase & Stuart series of Latin texts, 1871; mem. New Testament Co. of Am. Com. for Revision of Bible; published a Latin grammar, 1882. Author: The Early Days of Hellas, 1858; Hellas: Her Monuments and Scenery, 1862, Dr. Schliemann and the Archeological Value of his Discoveries, 1891. Died Providence, R.I., Oct. 5, 1892.

CHASTAIN, Elijah Webb, congressman; b. nr. Pickens, S.C., Sept. 25, 1813; studied law. Served as capt., then col. in Seminole Indian War; farmer, Union County, Ga.; mem. Ga. Senate, 1840-50; admitted to Ga. bar, 1849, practiced in Blairsville, Ga;. mem. U.S. Ho. of Reps. (Union Democrat) from Ga., 32d-33d congresses, 1851-55; del. Secession Conv., Milledgeville, Ga., 1860; served as lt. col. 1st Ga. Regt., Confederate Army during Civil War; state's atty. for Western & Atlantic R.R., 1860-61. Died nr. Dalton, Ga., Apr. 9, 1874; buried family cemetery nr. Morganton, Ga.

CHATHAM, 1st earl, see Pitt, William.

CHAUMONOT, Pierre Joseph Marie, missionary; b. Burgundy, France, Mar. 9, 1611. Received as novice in Soc. of Jesus, 1632; arrived in Que., Can., 1639; missionary to Huron Indians at Huronia on Georgian Bay, 1639-50; missionary to Iroquois Indians in what is now N.Y. State and in Can., 1655-58; priest to Huron Indians, Isle d'Orleans, Can., 1658-92; compiled a Huron grammar. Died Feb. 21, 1693.

CHAUNCEY, Isaac, naval officer; b. Black Rock, Conn., Feb. 20, 1772; s. Wolcott and Ann (Brown) C.; m. Catharine Sickles; children—Charles W., John S. Served in war with Tripoli, 1802-05; comdr. ships New York, John Adams; commd. capt. U.S. Navy, 1806; comdr. naval forces on lakes Ontario and Erie during War of 1812; transported Gen. Dearborn's Army to York (now Toronto), Ont., Can., 1813; established navy-yard, naval hosp., naval sch.; took command ship Washington, 1815; pres. Bd. Navy Commns., 1821-24, 32-40. Died Washington, D.C., Jan. 27, 1840; buried Congressional Cemetery, Washington.

CHAUNCY, Charles, clergyman, coll. pres.; b. Hertfordshire. Eng.. Nov. 1592: s. George and Agnes (Welch) C.; B.A., Trinity Coll., Cambridge (Eng.) U., 1613, M.A., 1617, B.D., 1624; m. Catharine Eyre, Mar. 17, 1630, 6 children. Fellow, Trinity Coll., 1614; vicar of St. Michael's, Cambridge, 1626; vicar of Ware, Hertfordshire, 1827-33; vicar of Marston St. Lawrence, 1633-37; eccles. reaction to his unorthodox views induced him to flee to Am., 1638; pres. Harvard, 1654-72. Author: The Document of Sacrament, 1642; The Plain Doctrine of the Justification of a Sinner in the Sight of God, 1659. Died Cambridge, Mass., Feb. 19, 1672.

CHAUNCY, Charles, clergyman; b. Boston, Jan. 12, 1706; s. Charles and Sarah (Walley) C.; grad. Harvard, 1721, A.M., 1724; m. Elizabeth Hirst, Feb. 14, 1727; m. 2d, Elizabeth Townsend, Jan. 8, 1738; m. 3d, Mary Stoddard, Jan. 15, 1760.

Pastor, First Ch., Boston, 1727-78; leader religious liberals of the time; objected to revivalism of Jonathan Edwards on grounds that emotions were poor guide to religion when compared to the intellect; opposed movements to reestablish close connection between church and provincial govt.; believed (contrary to Edwards and Calvin) that salvation is possible for all men. Author: Sermon on Enthusiasm, 1742; Seasonable Thoughts on the State of Religion in New England, 1743; Complete View of Episcopacy, 1771; Salvation for All Men Illustrated and Vindicated as a Scripture Doctrine, 1782; The Benevolence of the Deity, 1784. Died Feb. 10, 1787.

CHAUVENET, William, astronomer, mathematician, univ. chancellor; b. Milford, Pa., May 24, 1820; s. William Marc and Mary B. (Kerr) C.; grad. with high honors Yale, 1840; m. Catherine Hemple, 1842. Prof. mathematics in Naval Asylum, Phila., 1841, serving on U.S.S. Mississippi; influenced orgn. of U.S. Naval Acad., 1845, chmn. dept. mathematics and astronomy, 1853-55; prof. Washington U., St. Louis, 1855-69, chancellor, 1862-69; elected mem. Am. Philos. Soc., Am. Acad. Arts and Scis.; an incorporator Nat. Acad. Scis.; pres. A.A.A.S. Author: A Treatise on Plane and Spherical Trigonometry, 1850; A Manual of Spherical and Practical Astronomy, 1863; A Treatise on Elementary Geometry with Appendices Containing a Collection of Exercises for Students and an Introduction to Modern Geometry, 1870. Died St. Paul, Minn., Dec. 13, 1870; buried Bellefontaine Cemetery, St. Louis.

CHAVIS, John, clergyman, educator; b. West Indies, 1763; attended Coll. of N.J. (now Princeton), Washington Acad. (now part of Washington and Lee U.). Sent to college as expt. to see whether Negro was capable of learning in same way as White man (expt. successful); licensed to preach in Presbyn. Ch., 1801; minister to White people and slaves in N.C., 1809-32, pvt. tutor to children of wealthy White people in region. Author: The Extent of the Atonement, 1832. Died 1838.

CHEATHAM, Benjamin Franklin, army officer; b. Nashville, Tenn., Oct. 20, 1820; s. Leonard Pope and Elizabeth (Robertson) C.; m. Anna Bell Robertson, 1866. Served as capt. Tenn Volunteers during Mexican War, 1847; commd. brig. gen. Tenn. Militia, upon ordinance of secession, 1861; commanded div. in Polk's and Hardee's Corps; commd. maj. gen. Confederate Army, 1862; commanded one of Hood's Corps in Tenn. campaign, 1864; served in battles of Belmont, Shiloh, Chickamauga, Chattanooga, 1861-65; supt. Tenn. prisons, 4 years; apptd. postmaster Nashville by Pres. Cleveland, 1885. Died Sept. 4, 1886.

CHEATHAM, Richard, congressman; b. Springfield, Tenn., Feb. 20, 1799; pursued preparatory studies. Became a mcht., stock raiser, cotton gin operator; mem. Tenn. Ho. of Reps., 1833; mem. Tenn. Constl. Conv., Nashville, 1834; gen. Tenn. Militia; mem. U.S. Ho. of Reps. (Whig) from Tenn., 25th Congress, 1837-39. Died while visiting White's Creek Springs, nr. Springfield, Sept. 9, 1845; buried Old City Cemetery.

CHECKLEY, John, clergyman; b. Boston, 1680; attended Oxford (Eng.) U.; m. Rebecca Miller, May 28, 1713. Travelled and studied in Europe, 1695-1710; opened book and drug store, Boston, 1717; visited England, 1722, 27, 38; took holy orders in Anglican Ch., 1738; founder Boston Episcopal Charitable Soc., 1723; apptd. missionary by Soc. for Propgaation of Gospel; rector King's Ch., Providence, R.I., 1742-52. Author: Choice Dialogues between a Godly Minister and an Honest Countryman Concerning Election and Predestination, 1719; Modest Proof of the Order and Government Settled by Christ and His Apostles, 1723. Died Feb. 15, 1754.

CHEER, Miss, actress; m. Lord Rosehill, 1768. Made debut in comedy, A Wonder! A Woman Keeps a Secret, Charleston, S.C., 1764; performed with David Douglass and The Am. Company, Phila., also N.Y.C., 1764-68.

CHEESMAN, Forman, ship-builder; b. Dec. 11, 1763; s. Thomas and Elizabeth (Forman) C.; m. Ann Cummings, Feb. 16, 1786. Owner large shipyards, N.Y.C., influential in growth of ship-bldg. industry in N.Y.C., helping to make city a successful competitor with Phila. in the field; builder ships including Briganza, Draper, Ontario, Silenus, Triton, Illionis; most famous ship was frigate President, built 1800. Died Oct. 10, 1821.

CHEETHAM, James, journalist; b. Manchester, Eng., 1772. Came to Am., 1798; bought half interest in Greenleaf's Argus, edited, issued it under name Am. Citizen, 1801; published weekly Am. Watchman. Author: Life of Thomas Paine, 1809; A Narrative of the Suppression by Colonel Aaron Burr of the History of the Administration of John Adams, Written by John Wood, 1802; A View of the Political Conduct of Aaron Burr, Esq., Vice President of the United States, 1802; Antidote to John Wood's Poison, 1802; Nine Letters on Aaron Burr's Political Defection, 1803; Reply to Aristides, 1804; Peace or War? Or Thoughts on our Affairs with England, 1807. Died N.Y.C., Sept. 10, 1810.

CHEEVER, Ezekiel, educator; b. London, Eng., an. 25, 1615; s. William Cheever; m. Mary Cheever, 1638; m. 2d, Ellen Lathrop, 1652. Came to Am., 1637; master of public sch., New Haven, Mass., 1638-50; mem. Mass. Gen. Ct., 1646; taught sch., Ipswich, Mass., 1650-61, Charlestown, Mass., 1661-70, Boston Latin Sch., 1670-1708. Author: Scripture Prophecies Explained, 1757; Accidence, a Short Introduction to the Latin Tongue, 1758. Died Boston, Aug. 21, 1708.

CHEEVER, George Barrell, clergyman; b. Hallowell, Me., Feb. 6, 1814; s. Nathaniel and Charlotte (Barrell) C.; grad. Bowdoin Coll., 1825, Andover Sem., 1830; m. Elizabeth Wetmore, Nov. 21, 1845. Ordained to ministry Congregational Ch., 1833; pastor Howard Street Congl. Ch., Salem, Mass., 1833-38, Allen Street Presbyn. Ch., N.Y.C., 1838-44, Ch. of Puritans, N.Y.C., 1846-67; editor New York Evangelist, 1845. Author: Studies in Poetry, 1830; God's Hand in America, 1841; Lectures on the Pilgrim's Progress, 1844; A Defense of Capital Punishment, 1846; The Voices of Nature to Her Foster Child, The Soul fo Man, 1853; God Against Slavery, 1857; God's Time-Piece for Man's Eternity, 1888. Died Englewood, N.J., Oct. 1, 1890.

CHEEVER, Henry Theodore, clergyman; b. Hallowell, Me., Feb. 6, 1814; s. Nathaniel and Charlotte (Barrell) C.; grad. Bowdoin Coll., 1834, Bangor (Me.) Theol. Sem., 1839; m. Jane Tyler, 1857. Went to Hawaiian Islands for health, 1841; ordained to ministry Congregational Ch., 1847; pastor in N.J., N.Y.C., L.I., N.Y., and Conn.; had final pastorate, Worcester, Mass., 1863-72; editor New York Evangelist, 1849-52; sec. Ch. Anti-Slavery Soc., 1859-64. Author: The Whale and His Captors, 1849; Life in the Sandwich Islands, 1851; Correspondences of Faith and View of Madame Guyon, 1885; The Bible Eschatology, 1893. Died Worcester, Feb. 13, 1897.

CHENEY, Benjamin Pierce, express co. exec.; b. Hillsborough, N.H., Aug. 12, 1815; s. Jesse and Alice (Steele) C.; m. Elizabeth Clapp, June 6, 1865. Established Cheney & Co.'s Express between Boston and Montreal, 1842, with which he consol. Fisk & Rice's Express; further consolidations resulted in U.S. & Can. Express Co., as treas. and dir. merged this co. with Am. Express Co.; pioneer in promoting N.P.R.R.; active in A., T. & S.F. Ry. project; founder, dir. Market Nat. Bank Boston, Am. Loan & Trust Co. Died Wellesley, Mass., July 23, 1895.

CHENEY, John, engraver; b. South Manchester, Conn., Oct. 20, 1801; s. George and Electra (Woodbridge) C.; never married. Financially independent due to share in brothers silk mill; engraver for publishers at N.Y., Phila., Boston; travelled extensively in U.S. and Europe; works include: The Guardian Angels, The Young Princess, Lesbia, The Orphans. Died South Manchester, Aug. 20, 1885.

CHENEY, Seth Wells, artist; b. South Manchester, Conn., Nov. 26, 1810; s. George and Electra (Woodbridge) C.; m. Emily Pitkin, Sept. 1847; m. 2d, Edna Littlehole, 1853. Financially independent due to share in brother's silk mill; became portrait artist, concentrating primarily on heads of children done in crayon; works include Mother and Child (considered best work). Died Sept. 10, 1856.

CHENEY, Ward, silk mfr.; b. South Manchester, Conn., Feb. 23, 1813; s. George and Electa (Woodbridge) C.; m. Caroline Jackson, 3 children. With bros. leased farm at Burlington, N.J., 1836-41, operated nursery and cocoonery; organized Mt. Nebo Silk Mfg. Co., South Manchester, 1838, inc. as Cheney Bros. Silk Mfg. Co., 1854, pres., 1854-76; pres. Silk Assn. Am. Died Manchester, Conn., Mar. 22, 1876.

CHESEBROUGH, Caroline, author; b. Canandaigua, N.Y., Mar. 30, 1825; d. Nichols Goddard and Betsey (Kimball) Chesebrough; never married. Began writing for magazines, 1848; contbr. to Knickebocker, Putnam's and Harper's mags.; taught English composition Packer Collegiate Inst., Bklyn., 1865-73. Author: Dream-Land by Daylight, 1852; The Children of Light, 1853; The Beautiful Gate, and Other Tales, 1855; Peter Carradine, 1863; The Foe in the Household, 1871. Died Piermont, N.Y., Feb. 16, 1873.

CHESNUT, James, Jr., senator; b. Kershaw County, S.C., Jan. 18, 1815; s. James and Mary (Cox) C.; grad. Princeton, 1835; m. Mary Miller, Apr. 23, 1840. Admitted to S.C. bar, 1837; mem. lower house S.C. Gen. Assembly from Kershaw County, 1840-46, 47-48, 49-52; mem. S.C. Senate, 1852-58, pres., 56-58; mem. U.S. Senate from S.C., 1858-60; mem. drafting com. S.C. Ordinance of Secession, 1860; expelled from U.S. Senate upon his appointment to Confederate Provisional Congress, July 11, 1861; mem. Exec. Council S.C., 1861-62; col. cavalry Confederate Army on Pres. Davis' staff; commd. brig. gen. in command S.C. Res. Forces, 1864; del. Democratic Nat. Conv., 1868; chmn. exec. com. taxpayer's convs., S.C. 1871, 74; chmn. Kershaw County Dem. Conv., 1876. Died Saarsfield, nr. Camden, S.C., Feb. 1, 1885; buried Knights Hill Cemetery, nr. Camden.

CHESTER, Joseph Lemuel, genealogist; b. Norwich, Conn., Apr. 30, 1821; s. Joseph and Prudee (Tracy) C.; m. Catherine Henrickson Hubbard, June 26, 1839. Journalist for Phila. Inquirer and Daily Sun, 1852; mem. Phila. City Council, 1855; asst. clk. U.S. Ho. of Reps., 1856; mem. staff Gov. Pollock of Pa.; went to Eng., 1858; studied genealogy and history of early New Eng. settlers. Author: Greenwood Cemetery and Other Poems, 1843; Educational Laws in Virginia; . . . , 1854; John Rogers: the Compiler of the First Authorized English Bible; the Pioneer of the English Reformation; and its First Martyr, 1861. Died London, May 26, 1882.

CHETWOOD, William, congressman, lawyer; b. Elizabeth, N.J., June 17, 1771; grad. Princeton, 1792; studied law. Admitted to N.J. bar, 1796, began law practice, Elizabeth; served as prosecutor of pleas for Essex County; mem. State Council N.J.; maj. militia, served as aide-de-camp to Maj. Gen. Henry Lee in Whisky Rebellion of 1794; mem. U.S. Ho. of Reps. (Jacksonian Democrat, filled vacancy) from N.J., 24th Congress, Dec. 5, 1836-37. Died Elizabeth, Dec. 17, 1857; buried Evergreen Cemetery.

CHEVER, James W., sea capt.; b. Salem, Mass., Apr. 20, 1791; s. James and Sarah (Browne) C. Went to sea as cabin boy, 1804; 2d in command of ship Fame, 1810; in command of ship Belisarius, 1811; served as prizemaster during War of 1812; capt. of privateer America (owned by Crowninshields), 1813, took 25 ships as prizes, 1813-15; skipper Salem mcht. vessels for many years, retired, circa 1840; owned wharf, Salem. Died May 2, 1857.

CHEVERUS, Jean Louis Anne Magdelene Lefebre (or Lefebrye) de, see de Cheverus, Jean Louis Anne Magdelene Lefebvre.

CHEVES, Langdon, banker, congressman; b. Abbeville County, S.C., Sept. 17, 1776; s. Alexander and Mary (Langdon) Chivas; m. Mary Dullas, May 6, 1806. Admitted to S.C. bar, 1797; warden for city ward, Charleston, 1802-08; presdl. elector, 1809; mem. U.S. Ho. of Reps. from S.C., 11th-13th congresses, 1811-15, chmn. ways and means com., 1812-13, chmn. select com. on naval establishment, speaker, 1814; asso. judge S.C., 1816-19; pres. U.S. Bank, 1819-22, put bank in order, strengthened its resources; known as the Hercules of the U.S. Bank; an architect of some note. Died Columbia, S.C., June 26, 1857; buried Magnolia Cemetery, Charleston.

CHEW, Benjamin, jurist; b. West River, Md., Nov. 29, 1722; s. Dr. Samuel Chew; m. Mary Thomas; m. 2d, Elizabeth Oswald; at least 1 dau., Peggy. Admitted to Phila. bar, 1754; city recorder Phila., 1754-75; atty. gen. Pa., 1755-69; register gen. Pa., 1765-77; mem. Pa. Exec. Council, 1775-76; chief justice Pa. Supreme Ct., 1774 circa 1776; judge, pres. High Ct. Errors and Appeals of Pa., 1791-1808. Died Germantown, Pa., Jan. 20, 1810.

CHICKERING, Jonas, piano mfr.; b. Mason Village, N.H., Apr. 5, 1797; s. Abner and Eunice (Dakin) C.; m. Elizabeth Sumner Harraden, Nov. 30, 1823, 4 children. Mem. Handel and Haydn Soc., 1818, trustee, pres., 1843-50; with partner (James Stewart) began piano mfg. bus. Stewart & Chickering, 1823; founded, developed one of earliest and largest Am. piano mfg. houses, 1830; introduced many improvements; casted iron frame able to sustain great tension needed in good quality piano, 1837; pres. Mass. Charitable Mechanics Assn.; known as father of Am. piano-making. Died Boston, Dec. 8, 1853.

CHIEF JOSEPH (Indian name Hinmajon-Yalakit, meaning Thunder Coming From the Water), Indian chief; b. Wallowa Valley, Ore., circa 1840. Became chief of Nez Percé Indians upon death of his father, 1873; attacked a white settlement (as result of outrages by whites), 1876; 1 of greatest Indian tacticians; attempted to escape to Can., defeated U.S. Army at Battle of Big Hole River, 1877; cut off by Gen. Nelson Miles, forced to surrender, Oct. 1877; was settled on Colville Reservation, Wash.; recognized as 1 of most remarkable men of his race, visited Pres. Theodore Roosevelt and Gen. Miles, Washington, D.C., 1903. Died Nespelim, Wash., Sept. 21, 1904.

CHILCOTT, George Miles, congressman, senator; b. nr. Cassville, Pa., Jan. 2, 1828; studied medicine until 1850; studied law. Sheriff, Jefferson County (Ia.), 1853; moved to Territory of Neb., 1856; mem. Neb. Territorial Ho. of Reps., 1856;

moved to Territory of Colo., 1859; mem.Colo. Territorial Council, 1861-62, 72-74; admitted to bar, 1863; register U.S. Land Office, 1863-67; mem. U.S. Congress (Republican) from Colo-Territory, 40th Congress, 1867-69; mem. Colo. Ho. of Reps., 1878; mem. U.S. Senate (filled vacancy) from Colo., 1882-83. Died St. Louis, Mar. 6, 1891; buried Masconic Cemetery, Pueblo, Colo.

CHILD, David Lee, journalist; b. West Boylston, Mass., July 8, 1794; s. Zachariah and Lydia (Bigelow) C.; grad. Harvard, 1817; m. Lydia Maria Francis, Oct. 1828. Tchr., Boston Latin Sch., 1818-20; sec. of legation, Lisbon, Portugal, 1820; admitted to Mass. bar, 1828; mem. Mass. Legislature, 1828; editor Mass. Jour., 1828; abolitionist; trustee Noyes Acad., 1834, introduced racial integration; operator 1st beet-sugar plant in U.S., Northampton, Mass., 1836-44; editor (with wife) Nat. Anti-Slavery Standard, N.Y.C., 1843-44. Died Wayland, Mass., Sept. 18, 1874.

CHILD, Francis James, philologist; b. Boston, Feb. 1, 1825; s. Joseph and Mary (James) C.; grad. Harvard, 1846, LL.D. (hon.), 1884; studied at Gottingen and Berlin (Germany); Ph.D., (hon.) U. Gottingen, 1854; L.H.D. (hon.), Columbia, 1887; m. Elizabeth Sedgewick, Aug. 23, 1860. Tutor mathematics Harvard, 1846-48, tutor history and econs., 1848-49, prof. rhetoric and oratory, 1851-76, prof. English, 1876-96; noted English philologist. Editor: Poetical Works of Edmund Spenser; English and Scottish Ballads 8 vols., 1857-58. Author: Observations on the Language of Chaucer. Died Cambridge, Mass., Sept. 11, 1896.

CHILD, Lydia Maria Francis, author abolitionist; b. Medford, Mass., Feb. 11, 1802; d. Convers and Susannah (Rand) Francis; m. David Lee Child, Oct. 1828. Sch. tchr., Watertown, Mass., 1825-28; began publication bi-monthly mag. Juvenile Miscellany, 1826; joined abolitionist movement, 1828; editor Nat. Anti-Slavery Standard, 1841-49; believed that Negroes were emotionally and anthropologically the same as whites; after Harper's Ferry, asked permission to go to Va. to nurse John Brown in prison. Author: Hobomok (novel), 1824; The Rebels (novel), 1825; The First Settlers of New England, 1829; The Frugal Housewife, 1829; The Mother's Book, 1831; An Appeal in Favor of that Class of Americans Called Africans, 1833; Letters from New York, 2 vols., 1843, 45; Progress of Religious Ideas through Successive Ages, 3 vols., 1855; Age of Pericles; A Romance of the Republic, 1867. Died Wayland, Mass., Oct. 20, 1880.

CHILD, Thomas, Jr., congressman, lawyer; b. Bakerfield, nr. St. Albans, Vt., Mar. 22, 1818; entered U. Vt., Burlington, at age 14; studied law. Mem. Vt. Constl. Conv., 1838; admitted to Vt. bar, 1839, began law practice, East Berkshire, Vt.; justice of peace, 1840; moved to N.Y.C., circa 1848, active in distilling bus.; mem. U.S. Ho. of Reps. (Democrat) from N.Y., 34th Congress (never attended a session due to illness); moved to Port Richmond, Staten Island, N.Y., 1857, ret. from active bus.; supr. Town of Northfield, N.Y., 1865-66; mem. N.Y. Assembly, 1866. Died Port Richmond, Mar. 9, 1869; buried Greenwood Cemetery, Bklyn.

CHILDE, John, civil engr.; b. West Boylston, Mass., Aug. 30, 1802; s. Zachraiah and Lydia (Bigelow) C.; grad. U.S. Mil. Acad., 1827; m. Laura Dwight, 1832, at least 1 dau.; m. 2d, Ellen Healy, 1856. Served with Corps Engr., U.S. Army, 1827-35, resigned, 1835; cons. civil engr. to railroads in survey and location work, from 1835; became well-known in profession after locating route for Albany and W. Stockbridge R.R. through Green Mountains, 1844; became chief engr. Mobile R.R. Co., 1848, supervised constrn. of 500 miles of track through 4 states, obtained land grant from Congress, 1849, active in promotion of stock of co. until 1856; head of engring. corps which made survey regarding constrn. of new harbor facilities for Bd. Harbor Commrs., Montreal, Can., 1857. Died Springfield, Mass., Feb. 2, 1858; buried Springfield.

CHILDS, Cephas Grier, engraver, editor, publisher; b. Bucks County, Pa., Sept. 8, 1793; s. Cephas and Agnes (Grier) C. Enlisted in Washington Guards, 1813; commd. col. 128th regt. Pa. Militia, 1834; comml. lithography pioneer in U.S.; engraved, published periodical Childs Views in Phila., 1827-30; a founder lithographic firm Pendleton, Kearny & Childs, Phila., 1829, publishers of Phila. Comml. Herald (merged with North Am. mag. 1840); propr., editor mag. Comml. List and Phila. Price Current, 1835-52; pres. New Creek Coal Co., 1855-64; sec. bd. dirs. Phila. Bd. Trade, 1839-51; dir. Bank of Northern Liberties, Pa. Acad. Fine Arts. Died July 7, 1871.

CHILDS, George William, publisher, philanthropist; b. Balt., May 12, 1829; m. Emma Peterson. Started confectionery business George W. Childs & Co., 1848; founded Am. Publishers' Circular and Literary Gazette, 1863; bought Public Ledger, newspaper, 1864; joined R. E. Peterson, book-seller (became Childs and Peterson 1854), 1849; mem. firm J. B. Lippincott & Co., 1860-61; gave Shakespeare Meml. Fountain at Stratford-upon-Avon, Herbert meml. windows at Westminster Abbey, Milton meml. window in St. Margaret's Westminster, Eng., his manuscript collection to Drexel Inst. Author: Recollections of General Grant, 1885; Recollections by George W. Childs, 1890. Died Phila., Feb. 3, 1894; buried Laurel Hill Cemetery, Phila.

CHILDS, Thomas, army officer; b. Pittsfield, Mass., 1796; s. Dr. Timothy and Rachael (Easton) C.; grad. U.S. Mil. Acad., 1814; m. Ann Eliza Coryton, Jan. 5, 1819, 9 children. Served in Niagara campaign, 1814; commd. 1st lt. U.S. Army, 1818, capt., 1826; planned attack on Ft. Drane during Seminole War, 1836, for which he was brevetted maj. 1st Arty.; promoted lt. col., 1841; mil. gov. stationed at Jalapa in Mexican War, 1847; made brig. gen. for his defense of Puebla, 1847; in command of mil. operations East Fla., 1852-53. Died Ft. Brooke, Fla., Oct. 8, 1853.

CHILDS, Timothy, congressman; b. Pittsfield, Mass., 1785; grad. Williams Coll., Williamstown, Mass., 1811; studied law. Admitted to N.Y. bar, practiced in Rochester, N.Y.; pros. atty. Monroe County, 1821-31; mem. N.Y. Assembly, 1828, 33; mem. U.S. Ho. of Reps. from N.Y., 21st, 24th-25th, (as Whig) 27th congresses, 1829-31, 35-39, 41-43. Died Santa Cruz, N.M., Nov. 8, 1847.

CHILES, Joseph B. (Colonel), pioneer; b. Ky., 1810; m., 1830 (wife dec. 1837); 4 children. Farmed in Mo.; fought at battle of Lake Okeechokee in Seminole War; went west with Bartleson party (1st Am. land route migration party to reach Cal.), 1841; made 5 other trips to Cal., mostly from Mo., leading various groups and opening several new routes both eastward and westward, 1842, 43, 47, 48, 54.

CHILTON, Samuel, congressman, lawyer; b. nr. Warrenton, Va., Sept. 7, 1804; studied law. Admitted to Va. bar, 1826, practiced in Warrenton; mem. U.S. Ho. of Reps. (Whig) from Va., 28th Congress, 1843-45; resumed law practice in Warrenton and Washington, D.C.; del. Va. constl. convs., 1850-51; apptd. to defend John Brown at Harpers Ferry, but was dismissed by his client because he advocated that the defendant plead insanity. Died Warrenton, Jan. 14, 1867; buried Warrenton Cemetery.

CHILTON, Thomas, congressman, lawyer, clergyman; b. nr. Lancaster, Ky., July 30, 1798; studied law. Admitted to Ky. bar, began law practice, Owingsville, Ky.; mem. Ky. Ho. of Reps., 1819; moved to Elizabethtown, Ky.; mem. U.S. Ho. of Reps. from Ky., 20th (contested election), 21st, 23rd (Whig) congresses, Dec. 22, 1827-Mar. 3. 1831, 1833-35; presdl. elector voting for Clay and Sergeant, 1832; moved to Talladega, Ala., resumed practice of law; pastor a ch., Hopkinsville, Ky.; pres. Ala. Baptist State Conv., 1841, abandoned law practice, became gen. agt. of Ala. Conv.; continued ministerial duties, Montgomery, Greensboro, Newbern, Ala.; moved to Houston, Tex., 1851, served as pastor a Baptist ch. Died Montgomery, Tex., Aug. 15, 1854; buried Old Cemetery.

CHILTON, William Paris, jurist, legislator; b. Ky., Aug. 10, 1810; s. Thomas John and Margaret (Bledsoe) C.; m. Mary Morgan; m. 2d, Elvira Morgan. Moved to Ala., 1834; elected mem. Ala. Legislature (Whig) from Talladega County 1839; chief justice Ala. Supreme Ct., 1852-56; mem. Ala. Senate from Macon County, 1859; mem. Confederate Congress from Montgomery, Ala., 1859-65. Died Montgomery, Jan. 20, 1871.

CHINN, Joseph William, congressman; b. Epping Forrest, nr. Nuttsville, Lancaster County, Va., Nov. 16, 1798; grad. Union Coll., Schenectady, N.Y., 1819; studied law, Needham, Va. Admitted to Va. bar, 1821, practiced law in Lancaster County; mem. Va. Ho. of Dels., 1826-28; mem. Va. Senate, 1829-31; mem. U.S. Ho. of Reps. (Democrat) from Va., 22d-23d congresses, 1831-35; moved to Richmond, Va. Died on his estate Wilna, nr. Richmond, Va., Dec. 5, 1840; buried in the family burying ground, Wilna.

CHINN, Thomas Withers, congressman; b. nr. Cynthiana, Ky., Nov. 22, 1791; studied medicine and law. Served as pvt. 1st Rifles of Ky. Militia Volunteers in War of 1812; clerked in gen. store, Cynthiana, until 1813; moved to Woodville, Miss., became a mcht.; began practice of medicine, St. Francisville, West Feliciana Parish, La., circa 1817; admitted to bar, 1825, began law practice, St. Francisville; appt. judge West Feliciana Parish, 1826; moved to Cypress Hall Plantation, nr. Baton Rouge, La., 1831; continued practice of law also engaged in sugar-cane planting; mem. U.S. Ho. of Reps. (Whig) from La., 26th Congress, 1839-41; appt. by Pres. Taylor as minister to the Two Sicilies, 1849 (never assumed duties due to ill health). Died Cypress Hall Plantation, May 22, 1852; buried Gross Tete, nr. Rosedale, La.

CHIPMAN, Daniel, congressman; b. Salisbury, Conn., Oct. 22, 1763; s. Samuel and Hannah (Austin) C.; grad. Dartmouth, 1788; m. Elatheria Hedge, 1796. Admitted to Rutland County (Vt.) bar, 1790; mem. Vt. Constl. Conv., 1793, 1814, 36,43, 50; state atty. Addison County, Vt., 1797; mem. Vt. Gen. Assembly from Middlebury, 1798; prof. law Middlebury Coll., 1806-16; speaker Vt. Legislature, 1813-14; mem. U.S. Ho. of Reps. from Vt., 14th Congress, 1815-16, resigned, May 5, 1816; apptd. 1st reporter Vt. Supreme Ct., 1823. Died Ripton, Vt., Apr. 23, 1850; buried West Cemetery, Middlebury, Vt.

CHIPMAN, John Logan, congressman, lawyer; b. Detroit, June 5, 1830; student U. Mich., Ann Arbor, 1843-45. Explorer Lake Superior region Montreal Mining Co., 1846; asst. clk. Mich. Ho. of Reps., 1853; admitted to Mich. bar, 1854, practiced law in Lake Superior region; returned to Detroit; city atty. Detroit, 1857-60; mem. Mich. Ho. of Reps., 1865-66; atty. police bd. Detroit, 1867-79; elected judge Superior Ct. Detroit, 1879, reelected 1885, served until 1887; mem. U.S. Ho. of Reps. (Democrat) from Mich., 50th-54th congresses, 1887-93. Died Detroit, Aug. 17, 1893; buried Elmwood Cemetery, Detroit.

CHIPMAN, John Smith, congressman, lawyer; b. Shoreham, Addison County, Vt., Aug. 10, 1800; grad. Middlebury Coll., Vt., 1823; studied law. Admitted to Vt. bar, practiced law Addison County, also Essex County (N.Y.); moved to Centerville, Mich., 1838, held several local offices; mem. Mich. Ho. of Reps., 1842; mem. U.S. Ho. of Reps. (Democrat) from Mich., 29th Congress, 1845-47; moved to San Francisco, 1850, resumed law practice; moved to San Jose, Cal., 1869. Died July 27, 1869; buried Oak Hill Cemetery.

CHIPMAN, Nathaniel, jurist, senator; b. Salisbury, Conn., Nov. 15, 1752; s. Samuel and Hannah (Austin) C.; grad. in absentia Yale, 1777; m. Sarah Hill, 1781, 9 children. Served as lt. Continental Army at battles of Valley Forge, Monmouth, White Plains; admitted to Litchfield (Conn.) bar, 1779, also to Rutland County (Vt.) bar, June 1779; mem. Vt. Legislature, 1784; justice Vt. Supreme Ct., 1787-90, chief justice, 1790, 96-98, mem. N.Y.-Vt. Boundary Commn., 1789; helped negotiate admission of Vt. to Union; judge U.S. Ct. in Vt. dist., 1791-93; mem. U.S. Senate from Vt., 1799-1805; mem. Vt. Council of Censors, 1813; prof. law Middlebury (Vt.) Coll., 1816-43. Author: Sketches of the Principles of Government, 1793. Died Tinmouth, Vt., Feb. 15, 1843.

CHIPMAN, Ward, Loyalist; b. Marblehead, Mass., July 30, 1754; s. John and Elizabeth (Brown) C.; M.A., Harvard, 1770; m. Elizabeth Hazer, Oct. 24, 1786; 1 son, Ward. Went to Eng., 1776; returned to Am., 1777, served in civilian capacity for Brit. for remainder of Revolutionary War; came to Can. from Eng., 1784, established residence in St. John, New Brunswick; elected to 1st House Assembly of N.B. from St. John, 1785, 1802; apptd. agt. to determine St. Croix Treaty of 1783, 1796; mem. N.B. Council, 1806; judge Supreme Ct. N.B., 1809; agt. for Crown to locate N.W. angle of Nova Scotia, 1816; pres., comdr.-in-chief Province of N.B., 1823; advocated separation of N.B. from N.S. Died Fredericktown, N.B., Feb. 9, 1824.

CHIRSMEN, James Stone, congressman, lawyer; b. Monticello, Ky. Sept. 14, 1818; studied law. Engaged in farming; admitted to Ky. bar, 1849, began practice, Monticello; del. Ky. Constl. Conv., 1849; mem. U.S. Ho. of Reps. (Democrat) from Ky., 33d Congress, 1853-55; rep. from Ky. to 1st, 2d Confederate congresses, 1862-65; mem. Ky. Ho. of Reps., 1869-71. Died Monticello, July 29, 1881; buried pvt. cemetery on his farm.

CHIRSTIE, Gabriel, congressman; b. Perryman, Md., 1755; Mem. militia co. during Revolutionary War; mem. Md. Ho. of Dels.; apptd. a commr. by Gov. William Smallwood to "straighten and amend the post road from Havre de Grace to Baltimore town," 1787; mem. U.S. Ho. of Reps. from Md., 3d-4th, 6th congresses, 1793-97. 99-01; a commr. Havre de Grace, 1800-01, 06; appt. collector Port of Balt., served until 1808. Died Balt., Apr. 1, 1808; buried Spesutia Churchyard, Perryman.

CHISOLM, John Julian, surgeon, oculist; b. Charleston, S.C., Apr. 16, 1830; s. Robert Trail and Harriet Chisolm; M.D., Med. Coll. S.C., 1850; m. Mary Edings Chisolm, Feb. 3, 1852; m. 2d, Elizabeth Steel, Jan. 14, 1854. Practiced medicine, Charleston, 1852-61; conducted free hosp. for slaves, also 1 of 1st Am. summer schs. of medicine, 1853-58; prof. surgery Med. Coll. of S.C., 1858-61, dean, 1865-69; 1st commd. med. officer in Confederate Army, 1861; served as chief surgeon mil. hosp., Richmond, Va., later dir. plant for manufacture of medicines, Charleston; prof. eye and ear surgery U.

Md., 1869, dean, 1869-95, prof. emeritus, 1895-1903; founder Balt. Eye and Ear Inst., 1870; founder Presbyn. Eye and Ear Charity Hosp., Balt., 1877, chief surgeon, 1877-98; limited his practice to opthamology, after 1873; 1 of 1st to use cocain in eye surgery and to use chloroform anesthesia. Died Petersburg, Va., Nov. 2, 1903; buried Greenmount Cemetery, Balt.

CHISUM, John Simpson, rancher; b. Hardeman County, Tenn., Aug. 15, 1824; s. Claiborne and Lucy (Chisum) C. Moved (with family) to Tex., 1837; entered contracting bus., also became clk. Lamar County, Tex., 1840's; in cattle bus., Lamar County, 1854-57, Denton County, Tex., from 1857: became one of earliest Tex. ranchers to establish operations in N.M., 1866, drove herds from Tex. to N.M., thence for sale in Colo. and Wyo.; largest cattle owner in U.S., by 1870's; lived in South Springs, N.M., from 1873; played disputed role in "Lincoln County (N.M.) War," 1878-79, but took active part in establishing law and order in region (with appointment of new sheriff), 1880. Died Eureka Springs, Ark., Dec. 23, 1884.

CHITTENDEN, Martin, gov. Vt.; b. Salisbury, Conn., Mar. 12, 1769; s. Thomas and Elizabeth (Meigs) C.; grad. Dartmouth, 1789; m. Anna Bentley, 1796, 12 children. Mem. Vt. Gen. Assembly from Jericho, 1790-98, from Williston, 1798; del. from Jericho to Bennington (Vt.) Conv. to ratify U.S. Constn.; del. to Vt. Constl. Conv., Windsor, 1793; chief judge Chittenden County (Vt.) Ct.; mem. U.S. Ho. of Reps. from Vt., 8th-12th congresses, 1803-13; gov. Vt., 1813-15; judge Vt. Probate Ct., 1821-22. Died Williston, Sept. 5, 1840.

CHITTENDEN, Simeon Baldwin, congressman; b. Guilford, Conn., Mar. 29, 1814; s. Abel and Anna (Baldwin) C.; m. Mary Hartwell; m. 2d, Cornelia Coltons. Vice pres. N.Y.C. C. of C., 1867-69; dir. Continental Bank, D., L. & W. R.R.; founder daily newspaper Union; mem. U.S. Ho. of Reps. from N.Y., 43d-46th congresses, 1874-81; contbr. to Acad. of Music, Free Library, Poly. Inst., L.I. Hist. Soc.; gave $125,000 library bldg. to Yale. Died Bklyn., Apr. 14, 1889.

CHITTENDEN, Thomas, gov. Vt.; b. East Guilford, Conn., Jan. 6, 1730; s. Ebenezer and Mary (Johnson) C.; m. Elizabeth Meigs, Oct. 1750, 10 children including Martin, Noah, Giles, Truman, Mary. Represented Williston (Vt.) at Dorser Conv. to consider Vt.'s independence, 1776; pres. Vt. Council of Safety; helped draw up Vt. Constn., 1777; 1st gov. Vt., 1778-89, 3d gov., 1790-97; a monument erected in his memory by State of Vt., 1895. Died Williston, Aug. 25, 1797.

CHITTENDEN, Thomas Cotton, congressman, lawyer, banker; b. Stockbridge, Mass., Aug. 30, 1788; studied law. Admitted to N.Y. bar, 1813, began law practice, Adams, N.Y.; mem. U.S. Ho. of Reps. (Whig) from N.Y., 26th-27th congresses, 1839-43; apptd. judge Jefferson County, 1843, served for 5 years also engaged in banking. Died Watertown, N.Y., Aug. 22, 1866; buried Brookside Cemetery.

CHIVERS, Thomas Holley, poet; b. Washington, Ga., Oct. 18, 1809; s. Robert and Mrs. (Digby) C.; M.D., Translyvania U., 1830; married twice; m. 2d, Harriet Hunt, 4 children including Florence Allegra, Aster. Privately printed his 1st vol. of poems, The Path of Sorrow, 1832; lived in Springfield, Mass., 1834, N.Y.C., 1837; issued 3d book of poetry (1st commercially published edit.), N.Y.C., 1837; worked on play for prodn. in N.Y.C. (never actually produced), 1839; lived nr. Decatur, Ga., from circa 1840; contbd. poetry to Graham's Mag., other publs., from 1842; became friend of Edgar Allen Poe, 1845, corresponded with him until Poe's death, engaged in controversy with Poe over alleged plagiarism of each other's work (both appeared to be at fault), early 1850's; contbd. substantially to A. J. Davis' Univercoelum, 1848. Works include: Nacoochee (vol. poems), 1837; The Lost Pleiad and Other Poems, 1845; Eonchs of Ruby, A Gift of Love, 1850; Virginalia, or Songs of My Summer Nights (incorporated unusual experiments in meter), 1853; Atlanta, or the True Blessed Island of Poesy, 1853; The Sons of Usna: A Tragi-Apotheosis (play), 1858. Died Decatur, Dec. 18, 1858; buried Decatur.

CHIVINGTON, John Milton, clergyman, army officer; b. Warren County, O., Jan. 27, 1821; s. Isaac and Jane (Runyon) C.; m. Martha Rollason, 1840; m. 2d, Mrs. Isabella Arnzen, 1873; children—Thomas, Elizabeth Jane, Sarah. Worked with his brothers in family's small timber business, later became carpenter's apprentice; converted to Methodism, 1842; ordained to ministry Methodist Ch., 1844; became mem. Order of Masons, 1864; itinerant preacher in Ohio, 1844-48; itinerant preacher to both Whites and Indians on frontier, 1848-54; founded 1st Masonic order in Kan., 1854; anti-slavery advocate, supported Free-Soil group during Kan. Border Wars, 1854-56; became known as the Fighting Parson; apptd. maj. 1st Colo. Volunteers, 1861, promoted col., 1862, served in Colo. and N.M. campaigns against Confederacy; apptd. comdr. of mil. dist. of Colo., 1863; wanted policy of unconditional surrender from various Plains Indian tribes; led controversial attack on Indians at Sand Creek, Colo., Nov. 1864 (variously referred to as a battle or a massacre); 3 separate hearings were held on matter, but no ofcl. action of any type was instituted against him; he was personally castigated both at hearings and for years afterward; engaged in freighting bus., Neb., 1865-67; returned to Colo., 1883, engaged in newspaper work, held various public offices. Died of cancer, Denver, Colo., Oct. 4, 1894; buried Denver.

CHOATE, Rufus, senator; b. Ipswich, Mass., Oct. 1, 1799; s. David and Miriam (Foster) C.; grad. Dartmouth (valedictorian), 1819; m. Helen Olcott, 1825, 7 children. Admitted to practice Mass. Ct. Common Pleas, Sept. 1822, Mass. Supreme Ct., Nov. 1825; elected to lower house Mass. Gen. Ct., 1825; mem. Mass Senate, 1827; mem. U.S. Ho. of Reps., 22d-23d congresses, 1831-34, resigned, June 30, 1834; assisted in orgn. Whig Party in Mass.; mem. U.S. Senate from Mass., 1841-45; mem. Mass. Constl. Conv., 1853. Author: Discourse Commemorative of Daniel Webster. Died Halifax, N.S., Can. (en route to Europe), July 13, 1859; buried Mt. Auburn Cemetery, Cambridge, Mass.

CHORIS, Ludovik, artist; b. Russia, Mar. 22, 1795. Made drawings of bot. specimens for naturalist F. A. Marschall von Bieberstein in the Caucasus; joined South Sea expdn. of Otto von Kotzebue as ofcl. artist, visited Cal. with expdn., 1816, made water color sketches of Presidio at San Francisco, and of natives, published sketches in Voyages Pittoresque Autour du Monde, 1822; published Vues et Paysages des Regions Equinoxialles, 1826. Killed on visit to Western Hemisphere, Vera Cruz, Mexico, Mar. 22, 1828.

CHORPENNING, George, mail agt.; b. Somerset, Pa., June 1, 1820; s. George and Elizabeth (Flick) C.; m. Mary Pile, Jan. 19, 1841; m. 2d, Mrs. Carrie Dunlap. Mgr. of a store, Somerset, circa 1840; received (with Absolom Woodward) contract to carry U.S. mails from Salt Lake City to Cal., 1850; used Sierra route, 1852, forced to abandon route by Indians and weather difficulties, then adopted Mormon Trail; instituted a weekly schedule on Salt Lake-Los Angeles run (using coaches), 1858; used route across Nevada desert for 1st time in 1859, abandoned route when U.S. Post Office cancelled contract, 1860 (claims adjusted by Congress, 1870, but award of over $400,000 suspended because of charges of fraud raised by extortioners; claim never settled during his lifetime); commd. maj. 1st Md. Inf., 1861, organized 2 Union regts. in Md., but did not serve during Civil War. Died Apr. 3, 1894.

CHOULES, John Overton, clergyman; b. Bristol, Eng., Feb. 5, 1801; m. Martha T. Garland, 1829; m. 2d, Elizabeth G. Pope. Came to Am., 1824; prin. of an acad., Red Bank, N.Y., also part-time preacher, 1824-27; pastor 2d Baptist Ch., Newport, R.I., 1827-32, 44-56; held succession of pastorates, New Bedford, Mass., Buffalo, N.Y., N.Y.C.; pastor Bapt. ch., Jamaica Plain, Mass., 1843-44. Author: A History of Missions, 1832; The Christian Offering. Editor: (for a time) Boston Christian Times. Died Newport, Jan. 15, 1856.

CHOUTEAU, Jean Pierre, fur trader, Indian agt.; b. New Orleans, Oct. 10, 1758; s. Rene Auguste and Marie Therese (Bourgeois) C.; m. Pelagie Kiersereau, July 26, 1783; m. 2d, Brigitte Saucier, Feb. 17, 1794; 9 sons including Auguste Pierre, Jean Pierre. Stationed with Osage Indians as commandant of Ft. Carondele, 1794-1802; established 1st permanent White settlement in Okla. (now Salina), 1796; U.S. agt. for Osage Indians, 1803; a founder St. Louis Mo. Fur Co., 1809. Died nr. St. Louis, July 10, 1849.

CHOUTEAU, Pierre, mcht., fur trader; b. St. Louis, Jan. 19, 1789; s. Jean Pierre and Pelagie (Kiersereau) C.; m. Emilie Gratiot, Aug. 13, 1814, 5 children. In fur trade with father, 1809; formed Indian trade and gen. merchandising bus., 1813; del. from St. Louis County to Mo. Constl. Conv., 1820; joined firm Bernard Pratte & Co. (later Pratte, Chouteau & Co.), 1831; organized Pierre Chouteau, Jr. & Co., 1838; joined Am. Iron Co., St. Francois County, Mo., 1843; joined Chouteau, Harrison & Valle, operated rolling mill in North St. Louis, 1850; an original incorporator Ohio & Miss. R.R. of Ill., 1851. Died St. Louis, Sept. 6, 1865.

CHOUTEAU, Pierre Auguste, fur trader; b. St. Louis, May 9, 1786; s. Pierre and Pelagie (Kiersereau) C.; grad. U.S. Mil. Acad., 1806; m. Sophie Labbadie, Aug. 13, 1814, 1 son, 5 daus. Served as aide to Gen. James Wilkinson, 1807; mem. expdn. to restore Mandan chief, received commendation for role in battle with Arikaras; partner St. Louis (Mo.) Fur Co., 1808-11; served as capt. Territorial Militia, during War of 1812; apptd. judge Ct. of Common Pleas, St. Louis, 1813, did not serve; led trading expdn. to Upper Arkansas River, 1815, captured by Spanish, 1817, imprisoned in Santa Fe for 2 months; continued trading ventures in Kan. and Mo. region; established trading bus. in Ark. Osages country on Verdigris River in middle of settlements of many Indian tribes, 1823; maintained a feudal establishment with Indian servants and slaves nr. what is now Salina, Kan.; built new trading post on site of abandoned Camp Holmes, 1835; served as Indian emissary for U.S. Govt., 1837, helped pacify hostile tribes in Okla. and Kan. Died nr. Ft. Govson, Okla., Dec. 25, 1838; buried Ft. Gibson.

CHOUTEAU, Rene, trader; b. New Orleans, Sept. 7, 1749; m. Marie Cerre, Sept. 26, 1786. Accompanied expdn. of Pierre Laclede (his stepfather) in founding of St. Louis, 1763; asst. to Laclede in various trading enterprises, took over business after his death, 1778; obtained monopoly on Osage Indian trade, nr. Osage River in Mo., 1794; apptd. 1 of 1st justices Ct. of La. Territory, 1804; served as col. St. Louis Militia,1808;U.S. pension agt. for Mo. Territory, 1819-20; a trader, living in St. Louis, after 1808. Died St. Louis, Feb. 24, 1829; buried St. Louis.

CHOVET, Abraham, surgeon, anatomist; b. London, Eng., May 25, 1704; s. David Chovet. Chosen demonstrator of anatomy Surgeons' Hall, London, 1734; practiced surgery Kingston, Jamaica, 1759; came to Am., circa 1773; a founder Coll. Physicians of Phila., 1787. Died Pa., Mar. 24, 1790.

CHRISTIAN, William, army officer; b. Berkeley County, Va., 1732; s. Israel and Elizabeth (Stark) C.; m. Anne Henry. Commd. capt. Col. William Byrd's Regt., 1763; represented Fincastle County in lower house Va. Legislature, 1773-75, Fincastle and Botetourt counties in Va. Senate, 1776, 80-83; mem. Va. Com. of Safety, 1775; commd. col. Va. Militia by Va. Council Defense, 1776; one of 3 commrs. of Va. to negotiate Cherokee treaty signed at L.I., July 20, 1777. Killed nr. Jeffersonville, Ind. while leading pursuit party against marauding Wabash Indians, Apr. 9, 1782.

CHRISTIANCY, Isaac Peckham, senator, diplomat; b. Johnstown, N.Y., May 12, 1812; s. Thomas and Zilpha (Peckham) C.; m. Elizabeth McClusky, Nov. 1839; m. 2d, Lilly Lugenbeel; 7 children. Clk., U.S. Land Office, 1832; admitted to bar, 1838; pros. atty. Monroe County, N.Y., 1841-46; attended Free-Soil Party Conv., Buffalo, 1848; mem. Mich. Senate, 1850-52; del. to 1st Republican Nat. Conv., Phila., 1856; bought, edited Monroe Comml., 1856; mem. U.S. Senate from Mich., 1875-79; apptd. minister to Peru by Pres. Hayes, 1879-81. Died Lansing, Mich., Sept. 8, 1890.

CHRISTY, David, antislavery writer, geologist; b. 1802. Journalist, 1824-35; apptd. agt. Am. Colonization Soc. in Ohio, 1848; delivered messages before Ohio Ho. of Reps., 1849, 50, published as pamphlet "On the Present Relations of Free Labor to Slave in Tropical and Semi-Tropical Countries"; published The Republic of Liberia: Facts for Thinking Men, 1852, Cotton is King: Or the Economical Relations of Slavery (most important work) 1855, pamphlet "Ethiopia: Her Gloom and Glory," 1857; made geol. observations reported in series of letters 1st published in Cincinnati Gazette; geologist Nantahala & Tuckasege Land & Mineral Co. of N.C.; engaged in writing Geology Attesting Christianity, 1867. Died circa 1868.

CHRISTY, Edwin P., minstrel; b. 1815; at least 2 children, E. Byron, William A. Organized Christy Minstrels, Buffalo, N.Y., 1842, travelled through South and West with his troupe (including Lansing Durand, Zeke Backus, Enom Dickerson); made 1st appearance in N.Y.C. at Palmo's Opera House, 1846, continued performances in N.Y.C., until 1852; met with great success in London, Eng.; one of the earliest performers to produce type of show (with distinctive harmony and solos) which became known as ministrelsy; ret. from show bus., 1854, show carried on by sons. Killed when jumped from window of home during period of temporary insanity, N.Y.C., May 21, 1862; buried N.Y.C.

CHUBBUCK, Thomas, engraver; b. Boston. Moved to Brattleboro, Vt., engraved Brattleboro postmaster's provisional postage stamp of 1846 (now a rare and valuable stamp); moved to Springfield, Mass., 1849; drew and engraved a view of Mt. Holyoke Sem., South Hadley, Mass., 1860. Died Springfield, Jan. 10, 1888.

CHURCH, Alonzo, coll. pres.; b. Brattleboro, Vt., Apr. 9, 1793; s. Reuben and Elizabeth (Whipple) C.; grad. Middlebury Coll., 1816; m. Sarah J. Trippe, 1817. Headmaster of acad., Eatonton, Ga., 1817; apptd. prof. mathematics Ga. State U. at Athens, 1819, pres., 1829-59, successful in building up univ. and controlling faculty and trustees (though religious discord was apparnet between Presbyns. and Meth.-Bapt. faction); became involved in controversy with LeConte brothers (faculty mems.) over issue of modernization of univ.'s curriculum (resulted in reorgn. of faculty

1856); ordained to ministry Presbyn. Ch., 1824. Died Athens, Ga., May 18, 1862; buried Athens.

CHURCH, Benjamin, carpenter, army officer; b. Plymouth, Mass., 1639; s. Richard and Elizabeth (Warren) C.; m. Alice Southworth, Dec. 26, 1671. Engaged in carpenter's trade, Plymouth Colony, circa 1658; moved to Little Compton, R.I., by 1674; played prominent role in King Philip's War, 1675, organized English settlers' forces against Indian attacks, urged necessity for pursuing Indians after encounters; wounded in Great Swamp Fight, 1675, nr. South Kingston, R.I., took Indian leader Philip prisoner, 1676; lived in Plymouth Colony, 1676-88, served as selectman and magistrate; served as maj. Plymouth forces during King William's War, 1689-97, also Queen Anne's War, 1791-14; led expdn. against French town of Les Mines, 1704; resumed carpenter's trade, Little Compton, circa 1690. Died Little Compton, Jan. 17, 1718.

CHURCH, Benjamin, physician, Loyalist; b. Newport, R.I., Aug. 24, 1734; s. Benjamin Church.; attended Boston Latin Sch., 1745-50; grad. Harvard, 1754; m. Hannah Hill, circa 1758. Settled in Raynham, Mass., circa 1768, practiced medicine; published polit. essays supporting colonial cause, but also wrote replies advocating Tory position; probably wrote for Loyalist paper The Censor, 1773-75; mem. Com. of Correspondence, 1774, suspected of giving information to Tories; del. Mass. Provincial Congress, 1774; known to have consulted with Brit. Gen. Gage (while claming to have been taken prisoner), 1775; chief of 1st Continehtal Army Hosp., Cambridge, Mass., 1775; tried by court martial (presided over by Gen. Washington), Oct. 1775, found guilty of having sent secret letter to a Brit. officer at Newport during the preceding summer; paroled, left Boston for W.I., 1776. Died when ship was lost at sea, 1776.

CHURCH, Pharcellus, clergyman; b. Seneca, N.Y., Sept. 11, 1801; s. Willard and Sarah (Davis) C.; grad. Hamilton Literary and Theol. Inst. (now Colgate U.), 1824; m. Clara Emily Conant, 1828, at least 2 children, John Adams, William. Pastor, Poultney, Vt., 1825-28, Providence, R.I., 1828-34, 1st Bapt. Ch., Rochester, N.Y., 1835-48, Bowdoin Square, Boston, 1848-52, 2d Bapt. Ch., Bklyn., 1853-55. Author: Antioch: or, Increase of Moral Power in the Church, 1843; Seed-Truths, 1871; contbr. to Watchman and Reflector, Boston, also N.Y. Chronicle, circa 1848-55. Died June 5, 1886.

CHURCHMAN, William Henry, educator; b. Balt., Nov. 23, 1818; s. Micajah and Eliza Churchman; m. Mary Marshall. Became totally blind by age 18; entered sch. for blind, Phila., 1836; later taught music and mathematics in sch. for blind, Columbus, O.; in charge of sch. for blind, Nashville, Tenn., later at Indpls., then at Janesville, Wis.; planned and superintended policies of N.Y. State Instn. for Blind, 1866; influenced Ind. Legislature to recognize Ind. Instn. for Edn. of Blind (1st state to officially recognize instn. of this type as dept. of public edn.). Died May 18, 1882.

CHURCHWELL, William Montgomery, congressman, lawyer; b. nr. Knoxville, Tenn., Feb. 20, 1826; attended Emory and Henry Coll., Emory, Va., 1840-43; studied law. Admitted to Tenn. bar, began practice in Knoxville; a judge for Knox County; mem. U.S. Ho. of Reps. (Democrat) from Tenn., 32d-33d congresses, 1851-55; provost marshal dist. of East Tenn.; sent on secret mission to Mexico during Pres. Buchanan's adminstrn.; served as col. 4th Tenn. Regt., Confederate Army during Civil War. Died Knoxville, Aug. 18, 1862; buried Old Gray Cemetery.

CILLEY, Bradbury, congressman; b. Nottingham, N.H., Feb. 1, 1860; attended common schs. Involved in farming; U.S. marshal for dist. of N.H. (appt. by Pres. John Adams), 1798-1802; mem. U.S. Ho. of Reps. (Federalist) from N.H., 13th-14th congresses, 1813-17; col., aide Gov. Gillman's staff, 1814-16; retired from pub. life. Died Nottingham, Dec. 17, 1831; buried Gen. Joseph Cilley Burying Ground in Nottingham Square.

CILLEY, Joseph, army officer, legislator; b. Nottingham, N.H., 1735; s. Capt. Joseph and Alice (Rollins) C.; m. Sarah Longfellow, Nov. 4, 1756, 10 children. Mem. N.H. Provincial Congress; coast guard duty; took part in Siege of Boston, battles of L.I., Trenton, Princeton; commd. maj. 2d N.H. Inf., 1775, 8th Continental Inf., 1776; participated in Battle of Ticonderoga, 1777; commd. col. 1st N.H. Inf., 1777; promoted maj. gen. N.H. Militia, 1786; mem. N.H. Senate, 1790-91, N.H. Ho. of Reps., 1792; mem. N.H. Council, 1797-98. Died Nottingham, Aug. 25, 1799.

CILLEY, Joseph, senator; b. Nottingham, N.H. Jan. 4, 1791; grad. Atkinson Acad., N.H. Involved in farming; commd. ensign 18th N.H. Regt., 1811, also in 11th U.S. Inf., 1812; lt., 21st Inf., 1814; resigned at brevet capt., 1816; quartermaster N.H., 1817; div. insp., 1827; mem. U.S. Senate (Democrat, filled vacancy) from N.H., 1846-47. Died on his farm, Nottingham, Sept. 12, 1887; buried Gen. Joseph Cilley Burying Ground in Nottingham Square.

CIST, Charles, publisher, printer; b. St. Petersburg, Russia; s. Charles Jacob and Anna (Thomasson) Thiel; grad. U. Halle (Germany); m. Mary Weiss, June 7, 1781; children—Charles, Jacob. Came to Am., 1769, changed name from Thiel to Cist; settled in Phila.; translator for Henry Miller, Phila.; became partner in printing firm Styner & Cist, 1775, printed The American Crisis (Thomas Paine), 1776, Pharmacopoeia Simpliciorium (William Brown), 1778; published Am. Herald, 1786, Columbus Mag.; organized Lehigh Coal Co., 1792; public printer Washington, D.C., during John Adams' adminstrn. Died Bethlehem, Pa., Dec. 1, 1805; buried Moravian Cemetery, Bethlehem.

CIST, Charles, editor; b. Phila., Apr. 24, 1792; s. Charles and Mary (Weiss) C.; m. Janet White, Nov. 18, 1817, 13 children. Moved to Cincinnati, 1827, engaged in merc. bus., 1827-40; opened and managed 1st Sunday Sch. in Cincinnati; editor Western General, 1843-45; editor Cist's Advertizer, 1845-53. Author: Cincinnati in 1841, published 1841; Sketches and Statistics of Cincinnati in 1851, published 1851; Sketches and Statistics of Cincinnati in 1859, published 1859. Died College Hill, nr. Cincinnati, Sept. 5, 1868.

CIST, Jacob, naturalist, inventor; b. Phila., Mar. 13, 1782; s. Charles and Mary (Weiss) C.; m. Sarah Hollenback, Aug. 25, 1807, at least 2 daus. Postmaster, Wilkes-Barre, Pa.; mined anthracite coal, Mauch Chunk, Pa., 1815-21; collected fossil plants and flora, described coal formations, 1815-21; founder, corresponding sec. Luzerne County Agrl. Soc.; invented artist's paint mixing mill, 1803, printer's ink from anthracite coal, 1808, anthracite coal burning stove, 1817. Died Dec. 30, 1825.

CLAFLIN, Horace Brigham, mcht.; b. Milford, Mass., Dec. 18, 1811; s. John and Lydia (Mellen) C.; m. Agnes Sanger, Nov. 28, 1836, at least 2 sons. Became businessman, Worcester, Mass., 1834; entered wholesale dry-goods bus., N.Y.C., 1843; pioneer in combining mfg. with importing and distbn. of merchandise; trustee Plymouth Ch., Bklyn., 38 years. Died Nov. 14, 1885.

CLAGETT, Clifton, congressman, lawyer; b. Portsmouth, N.H., Dec. 3, 1762; studied law. Admitted to N.H. bar, began practice law, Litchfield, N.H., 1787; mem. U.S. Ho. of Reps. from N.H., 8th, 15th-16th congresses, 1803-05, 17-21; apptd. justice of peace and quorum, 1808; apptd. judge probate for Hillsborough County, 1810-12; moved to Amherst, N.H., 1812; apptd. judge supreme ct., 1812; mem. N.H. Ho. of Reps., 1816; judge probate, 1823-29. Died Amherst, Jan. 25, 1829.

CLAGETT, Wyseman, lawyer; b. Bristol, Eng., Aug. 1721; son of Wyseman Clagett; m. Lettice Mitchell, 1759. Admitted to Ct. of King's Bench; practiced law, Antigua, W.I., 1748-58; came to Portsmouth, N.H., 1758; King's atty. for N.H. Province, 1765-69; visited Eng., 1769-71; moved to Litchfield, N.H., 1771; mem. Council and Com. of Public Safety, N.H., 1776; spl. justice N.H. Superior Ct., 1778-81; solicitor-gen. N.H., 1781-84. Died Litchfield, Dec. 4, 1784.

CLAGHORN, George, army officer, shipbuilder; b. July 6, 1748; s. Shubael and Experience (Hawes) C.; m. Deborah Brownell, 4 sons, 4 daus. Served as 1st lt., then capt. 2d Bristol Regt., wounded in Battle of Bunker Hill, later commd. maj., then col.; shipbuilder, New Bedford, N.H., launched ship Rebecca, 1785; naval constructor of ship Constitution, 1794 (launched 1797). Died Seekonk, R.I., Feb. 3, 1824.

CLAIBORNE, John, congressman, physician; b. Brunswick County, Va., 1777; s. Thomas Claiborne; grad. med. dept. U. Pa., Phila., 1798; Practiced medicine; mem. U.S. Ho. of Reps. from Va., 9th-10th congresses, 1805-08. Died Brunswick County, Va., Oct. 9, 1808; buried family burying ground of Parson Jarratt, Dinwiddie, Va.

CLAIBORNE, John Francis Hamtramck, congressman, editor; b. Natchez, Miss., Apr. 24, 1809; s. Gen. Ferdinand Leigh and Magdalene (Hutchins) C.; LL.D., U. Miss., 1882; m. Martha Dunbar, Dec. 1828, at least one son, Willis Herbert. Elected to Miss. Legislature from Adams County, 1829-35; mem. U.S. Ho. of Reps. from Miss., 24th-25th congresses, 1835-38; editor Jeffersonian, New Orleans, 1844; editor Statesman, also La. Courier; U.S. timber agt. for La. and Miss., 1853. Author: Life and Correspondence of General John A. Quitman, 1860; Life and Times of General Samuel Dale, 1860; History of Mississippi as a Province, a Territory and a State, 1880. Died Natchez, May 17, 1884; buried Trinity Churchyard, Natchez.

CLAIBORNE, Nathaniel Herbert, congressman; b. Sussex County, Va., Nov. 14, 1777; s. Col. William and Mary (Leigh) C.; m. Elizabeth Binford, 1815, 11 children. Mem. Va. Ho. of Dels., 1810-12; mem. Va. Exec. Council during War of 1812; mem. Va. Senate, 1821-25; mem. U.S. Ho. of Reps. from Va., 19th-24th congresses, 1825-37. Author: Notes on the War in the South, 1819. Died Franklin County, Va., Aug. 15, 1859; buried family cemetery, nr. Rockymount, Franklin County.

CLAIBORNE, Thomas, congressman; b. Brunswick County, Va., Feb. 1, 1749; children—John, Thomas. Mem. Va. Ho. of Dels., 1783-88; col. in command of Brunswick County Militia, 1789; sheriff Brunswick County, 1789-92; mem. Va. Senate, 1790-92; mem. U.S. Ho. of Reps. from Va., 3d-5th, 7th-8th congresses, 1793-99, 1801-05. Died on estate in Brunswick County, Va., 1812.

CLAIBORNE, Thomas. congressman, lawyer; b. nr. Petersburg, Brunswick County, Va., May 17, 1780; s. Thomas Claiborne; studied law. Served as maj. on Gen. Andrew Jackson's staff in the Creek War; admitted to Tenn. bar, began law practice, Nashville, Tenn., 1807; mem. Tenn. Gen. Assembly; mem. U.S. Ho. of Reps. (Democrat) from Tenn., 15th Congress, 1817-18. Died Nashville, Jan. 7, 1856; buried Nashville City Cemetery.

CLAIBORNE, William, colonial ofcl.; b. Eng., circa 1587; s. Edmund and Grace (Bellingham) Cliburne. Came to Va. Colony as an apptd. surveyor, 1621; sec. of state Va. Colony, 1625-37, 52-60; led expdns. against Indians, 1629, 44; began trading settlement on Kent Island, Chesapeake Bay, 1631; became involved in controversy with Lord Baltimore over alleged support of Indian violence, 1634; refused to accept certain English policies, which resulted in Lord Baltimore's reducing Kent Island to submission, 1638; held control of Province of Va. after insurrection against Gov. Calvert, 1644-46. Died circa 1677.

CLAIBORNE, William Charles Coles, gov. La., congressman; b. Sussex County, Va., 1775; s. William and Mary (Leigh) C.; ed. Coll. William and Mary; m. Eliza Lewis, 1801; m. 2d, Clarissa Duralde; m. 3d, Suzette Bosque. Mem. Tenn. Constl. Conv., 1796; apptd. judge Supreme Ct. Tenn. by Gen. Sevier; mem. U.S. Ho. of Reps. from Tenn., 5th, 6th congresses, 1797-1801; gov. Miss. Territory, 1801; asso. with Gen. James Wilkinson as commr. to receive province of La. from French, sent to New Orleans as gov. La. Territory, 1803-12 took possession of dist. of Baton Rouge and Mobile in Madison's annexation of W. Fla. and incorporated both with La., 1810; 1st gov. La., 1812-16; mem. U.S. Senate (Democrat) from La., 1817-Nov. 23, 1817. Died New Orleans, Nov. 23, 1817; buried Metairie Cemetery, New Orleans.

CLAP, Nathaniel, clergyman; b. Dorchester, Mass., 1668; grad. Harvard, 1690. Minister, Congregational Ch., began preaching in Newport, R.I., 1695; founded 1st Congregational Ch. in R.I., 1695; pastor 1st Congregational Ch., Newport, 1720-45. Author: Advice to Children, 1691; The Lord's Voice Crying to the People in Some Extraordinary Dispensations (sermon), 1715. Died Newport, Oct. 30, 1745.

CLAP, Thoms, clergyman, coll. pres.; b. Scituate, Mass., June 26, 1703; s. Stephen and Temperance Clap; grad. Harvard, 1722; m. Mary Whiting, Nov. 23, 1727; m. 2d, Mary Haynes, Feb. 5, 1740. Called to Congregational Ch., Windham, Conn., 1726; ordained, 1726; elected rector Yale Coll., 1739, under his leadership coll. drafted more liberal charter (granted 1745), he drew up code of laws (approved 1745), served as pres. Yale, 1745-66. Author: Annals of Yale College, 1766. Died New Haven, Conn., Jan. 7, 1767.

CLAPP, Asa, shipmaster, mcht., legislator; b. Mansfield, Mass., Mar. 15, 1762; s. Abiel and Bathsheba (Pratt) C.; m. Eliza Quincy, 1787. Officer on Am. ship Charming Sally during Revolutionary War; in mcht. service West Indian trade until 1798; mcht., Portland, Me., 1798; mem. Council of Mass., 1811; supported govt., subscribing half his fortune to the nat. loan, War of 1812; largest subscriber in Me. and commr. to obtain subscriptions to capital stock of Bank of U.S., 1816; mem. Me. Constl. Conv., 1819; mem. Me. Ho. of Reps., 1820-23; wealthiest man in Me. at that time. Died Portland, Apr. 17, 1848.

CLAPP, Asa William Henry, congressman; b. Portland, Me., Mar. 6, 1805; grad. Norwich (Vt.) Mil. Acad., 1823. Merchant, Portland, involved in both domestic and foreign commerce; mem. U.S. Ho. of Reps. (Democrat) from Me., 30th Congresses, 1847-49; del. Dem. Nat. Conv., Balt., 1848; del. at large to conv. at Balt. where Franklin Pierce was nominated for U.S. Pres., 1852; dir. Me. Gen. Hosp., Portland Public Library. Died Portland, Mar. 22, 1891; buried Evergreen Cemetery.

CLAPP, William Warland, editor; b. Boston, Apr. 11, 1826; s. William Warland and Hannah (Lane)

C.; m. Caroline Dennie, 1850, 3 children. Owner and editor Saturday Evening Gazette, Boston, 1847-65; editor Boston Jour., 1865-91; Republican, polit. views reflected in his papers. Author: A Record of the Boston Stage, 1853; also several plays including La Fiaminna, John Gilbert and His Daughters, My Husband's Minor. Died Boston, Sept. 13, 1891.

CLARK, Abraham, congressman; b. Elizabethtown, N.J., Feb. 15, 1726; s. Thomas Clark; m. Sarah Hatfield, 1749, 10 children. High sheriff Essex County (N.J.), clk. N.J. Colonial Assembly; mem. N.J. Com. of Safety, 1774, later sec.; mem. N.J. Provincial Congress which drafted 1st N.J. Constn.; voted for and signed Declaration of Independence, 1776; mem. Continental Congress, 1779-83, 87-88; mem. N.J. Assembly, 1782-87; del. to Annapolis Conv., 1786; mem. U.S. Ho. of Reps. from N.J., 2d-3d congresses, 1791-94. Died Rahway, N.J., Sept. 15, 1794; buried Rahway Presbyn. Ch.

CLARK, Alvan, astronomer, lens maker; b. Ashfield, Mass., Mar. 8, 1804; s. Alvan and Mary (Bassett) C.; A.M. (hon.), Amherst Coll., Chgo. U., Princeton, Harvard; m. Maria Pease, Mar. 25, 1826, children include Alvan Graham, George Bassett. Started firm Alvan Clark & Sons, 1852, produced world's largest telescopes; produced lenses for Vienna Observatory, Wesleyan U., Middletown, Conn., Lick Obs., Cal., 18 inch lens for Dearborn Obs., Evanston, Ill., 23 inch for Princeton, 26 inch telescopes for Naval Observatory and U. Va., 30 inch telescope for Pulkova Observatory, Russia, 1879; made 36 inch lens for Lick telescope. Recipient Rumford medal Am. Acad. Arts and Scis. Died Cambridge, Mass., Aug. 19, 1887.

CLARK, Alvan Graham, astronomer, lens maker; b. Fall River, Mass., July 10, 1832; s. Alvan and Maria (Pease) C.; m. Mary Willard, Jan. 2, 1865. Discovered star Sirius for which he was awarded Lalande gold medal French Acad.; discovered 16 double stars; made 40 inch lenses of Yerkes telescope (then world's largest), at U. Chgo.; made 30 inch refractor for Imperial Observatory, St. Petersburg, Russia; mem. total eclipse expdn. to Spain, 1870, Wyo. Mission, 1878. Fellow Am. Acad. Arts and Scis., A.A.A.S. Died Cambridge, Mass., June 9, 1897.

CLARK, Ambrose Williams, congressman; b. nr. Cooperstown, N.Y., Feb. 19, 1810; attended public schs. Publisher Otsego Jour., 1831-36, No. Jour. Lewis County, 1836-44, No. N.Y. Jour., Watertown, 1844-60; surrogate, five years; mem. U.S. Ho. of Reps. (Republican) from N.Y., 37th-38th congresses, 1861-65; apptd. consul at Valparaiso by Pres. Abraham Lincoln, served 1865-69; acted as charge d'affaires, Chile, 1869. Died Watertown, N.Y., Oct. 13, 1887; buried Brookside Cemetery.

CLARK, Charles, gov. Miss.; b. Cincinnati, 1810; m. Ann Darden. Went to Miss., 1831; mem. Miss. Legislature (Whig), 1838-44, 56-61; served as col. in Mexican War; mem. state conv. to consider Miss. relations to Union, 1851; rep. Miss. Legislature, 1856-61; del. Nat. Democratic convs., Charleston and Balt., 1860; commd. brig. gen. Miss Militia, 1860, advanced to maj. gen.; commd. brig. gen. Confederate Army; gov. Miss., 1863-65; arrested and imprisoned by U.S. Army for governorship of unrecognized state; chancellor 4th dist. Miss., 1876. Died Dec. 18, 1877.

CLARK, Charles Benjamin, congressman; b. Theresa, Jefferson County, N.Y., Aug. 24, 1844; attended common schs. Served with Co. I, 21st Regt., Wis. Volunteer Inf. during Civil War; merchant, banker, mfr. of paper; mayor Neenah (Wis.), 1880-83; mem. city council Neenah, 1883-85; mem. Wis. Assembly, 1885; mem. U.S. Ho. of Reps. (Republican) from Wis., 50th-51st congresses, 1887-91. Died while visiting Watertown, N.Y., Sept. 10, 1891; buried Oak Hill Cemetery, Neenah.

CLARK, Christopher Henderson, congressman, lawyer; b. Albermarle County, Va., 1767; ed. Washington Coll. (now Washington and Lee U.), Lexington, Va.; studied law in the office of Patrick Henry. Admitted to Va. bar, 1788, began law practice in New London (now Bedford Springs), Va.; mem. Va. Ho. of Dels., 1790; mem. U.S. Ho. of Reps. (Jeffersonian Democrat, filled vacancy) from Va., 8th-9th congresses, Nov. 5, 1804-July 1, 1806 (resigned). Died nr. New London, Nov. 21, 1828; buried pvt. cemetery at Old Lawyers Station, nr. Lynchburg, Va.

CLARK, Daniel, congressman; b. Sligo, Ireland, circa 1766; ed. Eton, other schs., Eng. Came to U.S., 1786, settled in New Orleans; active in land speculation, banking; mem. U.S. Congress from Territory of Orleans, 9th-10th congresses, Dec. 1, 1806-09. Died New Orleans, Aug. 16, 1813; buried St. Louis Cemetery Number 1.

CLARK, Daniel, senator, jurist; b. Stratham, N.H., Oct. 24, 1809; s. Benjamin and Elizabeth (Wiggen) C.; grad. Dartmouth, 1834; m. Hannah Robbins, June 9, 1840; m. 2d, Anne Salter, May 13, 1846; 2 children. Admitted to N.H. bar, 1836; moved to Manchester, N.H., 1839, active in Manchester affairs, held several offices and trusteeships; mem. N.H. Legislature, 1842-55, in charge of bill for incorporation of Manchester, 1846; dir. Amoskeag Corp.; mem. U.S. Senate from N.H., 1857-67; prominent figure in Washington affairs for 9 years; apptd. U.S. judge for dist. N.H. by Pres. Johnson, 1866-91; pres. N.H. Constl. Conv., 1876. Died Manchester, Jan. 2, 1891; buried Valley Cemetery, Manchester.

CLARK, David Wasgate, clergyman; b. Mt. Desert, Me., Feb. 12, 1812; grad. Me. Wesleyan Sem., Readfield, 1833; grad. Wesleyan U., Middletown, Conn., 1836, D.D. (hon.), 1851; m. Mary J. Redman, 1839, 4 children. Prin., tchr. mathematics and moral philosophy Amenia Sem., N.Y., 1836-43; mem. N.Y. Methodist Episcopal Conf., 1843-53; editor Ladies' Repository, mag., Cincinnati, 1853-64; apptd. bishop Meth. Episcopal Ch., 1864. Author: Elements of Algebra; Man All Immortal. Died Cincinnati, May 23, 1871.

CLARK, Elijah, army officer; b. Edgecombe County, N.C., 1733; m. Hannah Harrington; 3 sons, including John, 6 daus. Commd. capt. Ga. Militia, 1776, later col., brig. gen., 1781; served at battles of Kettle Creek, Musgrove's Mill, Beattie's Mill and both sieges of Augusta (Ga.) in Revolutionary War; given estate in Wilkes County by State of Ga. for his mil. services; participated in battle with Indians at Jack's Creek, 1787; involved in French minister Edmond Genet's scheme to seize Spanish lands in Am., commd. maj. gen. French Army, 1793, plans failed when Genet was recalled; attempted to set up state in Creek Indian territory, 1794, established several forts but forced to give up venture by Ga. Militia. Died Richmond County, Ga., Dec. 15, 1799.

CLARK, Ezra, Jr., congressman; b. Brattleboro, Vt., Sept. 12, 1813; attended pub. schs. Iron merchant; mem. common council, bd. aldermen; pres. Nat. Screw Co. of Hartford (Conn.), later consolidated with Am. Screw Co. Providence (R.I.); dir. Exchange Bank; pres. Spring Grove Cemetery Assn.; judge municipal ct.; mem. U.S. Ho. of Reps. (Am. Party, Republican) from Conn., 34th-35th congresses, 1855-59; pres. Hartford Bd. Water Commrs., 1882-95; pres. Young Men's Inst. Hartford. Died Hartford, Sept. 16, 1896; buried Spring Grove Cemetery.

CLARK, Franklin, congressman; b. Wiscasset, Me., Aug. 2, 1801; attended common schs. Active in lumber and shipping bus., Wiscasset; mem. Me. Senate, 1847; mem. U.S. Ho. of Reps. (Democrat) from Me., 13th Congress, 1847-49; active in lumber mfg.; exec. councilor, 1855. Died Bklyn., Aug. 24, 1874; buried Greenwood Cemetery.

CLARK, George Rogers, army officer; b. nr. Charlottesville, Va., Nov. 19, 1752; s. John and Ann (Rogers) C. Minor exploring attempts on Ohio River, 1772; served as capt. Va. Militia in Dunmore's War, 1774; surveyor in Ky.; organizer, leader frontier defense against British-supported Indian raids, 1776-77; set out to conquer Ill., largely under auspices of Gov. Patrick Henry of Va., captured key points, Kaskaskia, Cahokia and Vincennes, thus assuring Colonial control Ky. and Ill. countries (Northwest); commd. brig. gen. Va. Militia, engaged in several battles and expdns. to protect Northwest region, 1779-83; mem. bd. commrs. which supervised allotment of lands in Ill. grant; served on commn. making a treaty with Indians of Northwest; set out on retaliatory expdn. against Wabash tribe, not wholly successful, 1786; polit. and econ. fortunes declined toward end of life. Author: Memoir, 1791. Meml. to him erected by U.S. Govt., Vincennes, Ind., 1928. Died Louisville, Ky., Feb. 13, 1818; buried Cave Hill Cemetery, Louisville.

CLARK, Henry James, educator; b. Easton, Mass., June 22, 1826; s. Rev. Henry Porter and Abigail (Orton) C.; grad. U. City N.Y., 1848, Lawrence Scientific Sch., 1854; m. Mary Young Holbrook, 1854, 8 children. Pvt. asst. to Louis Agassiz, 1854-65; asst. prof. zoology Scientific Sch. at Harvard, 1860-65; prof. botany, zoology and geology Pa. State Coll., 1866-69, U. Ky., 1869-72; prof. Mass. Agrl. Coll., 1872-73. Author: Mind in Nature; or the Origin of Life, and the Mode of Development of Animals, 1865. Died July 1, 1873.

CLARK, Henry Selby, congressman; b. nr. Leechville, N.C., Sept. 9, 1809; grad. U. N.C. at Chapel Hill, 1828; studied law. Admitted to N.C., began law practice, Washington, N.C.; mem. N.C. Ho. of Commons, 1834-36; solicitor for dist., 1842; mem. U.S. Ho. of Reps. (Democrat) from N.C., 29th Congress, 1845-47; moved to Greenville, N.C., and resumed law practice. Died Greenville, Jan. 8, 1869; buried at his country home nr. Leechville.

CLARK, Horace Francis, railroad exec., congressman; b. Southbury, Conn., Nov. 29, 1815; s. Rev. Daniel and Eliza (Barker) C.; grad. Williams Coll., 1833, LL.D. (hon.), 1868; m. Marie Louise Vanderbilt, Apr. 13, 1848. Admitted to N.Y. bar, 1837; mem. U.S. Ho. of Reps. from N.Y., 36th Congres 1857-59; dir. N.Y. & Harlem R.R., 1857; pres. Lak Shore, Mich. So. & No. Ind. R.R., U.P. R.R.; di 5 railroads, stockholder in others; railroad hol ings so large they influenced prices on N.Y. Stoc Exchange; mem. exec. com. Union Trust Co. N.Y. chmn. exec. com. Western Union Telegraph C Died N.Y.C., June 19, 1873; buried Woodlaw Cemetery, N.Y.C.

CLARK, James, gov. Ky., congressman; b. Bed ford County, Va., Jan. 16, 1779; s. Robert and Su san C.; m. Mrs. (Buckner) Thornton. Admitted t Ky. bar, 1797; mem. Ky. Ho. of Reps., 1807-09 judge Ky. Ct. Appeals, 1810-12; mem. U.S. Ho. Reps. from Ky., 13th-14th, 19th-21st congress 1813-16, 25-31; judge Circuit Ct. Ky., 1817-24 mem. Ky. Senate, 1832-36, speaker, 1835; gov. Ky. 1836-39. Died Frankfort, Ky., Sept. 27, 1839 buried Winchester, Ky.

CLARK, James West, congressman; b. Bert County, N.C., Oct. 15, 1779; grad. Princeton Coll. 1797. Mem. N.C. Ho. of Commons, 1802-03, 11 presdl. elector Madison ticket, 1812; mem. N.C Senate, 1812-14; mem. U.S. Ho. of Reps. (Demo crat) from N.C., 14th Congress, 1815-17; chie clk. Navy Dept. (apptd. by Sec. Branch), 1829-31 Died Tarboro, N.C., Dec. 20, 1843.

CLARK, John, gov. Ga.; b. Edgecombe County N.C., Feb. 28, 1766; s. Gen. Elijah Clark; m Nancy Williamson 1787. Commd. capt. Continenta Army, 1792; commd. maj. Ga. Militia, 1787, maj gen., 1811; received generous grant of bounty land after Revolution; presdl. elector, 1816; gov. Ga., 1819-23; apptd. Indian agt., Fla., 1827. Died o yellow fever at St. Andrew's Bay, Fla., Oct. 12, 1832.

CLARK, John Bullock, congressman, lawyer; b Madison County, Ky., Apr. 17, 1802; studied law Admitted to Mo. bar, 1824, began practice law Fayette, Mo.; clk. Howard County Cts., 1824-34 col. Mo. Mounted Volunteers, Black Hawk War 1832; maj. gen. militia, 1848; mem. Mo. Ho. o Reps., 1850-51; mem. U.S. Ho. of Reps. (Demo crat) from Mo. (filled vacancy) 35th-37th con gresses, Dec. 7, 1857-July 13, 1861 (expelled) mem. 1st Confederate Senate from Mo.; in 2 Confederate Congress; brig. gen. Mo. Confederat State Troops. Died Fayette, Oct. 29, 1885; burie Fayette Cemetery.

CLARK, John Chamberlain, congressman; b Pittsfield, Mass., Jan. 14, 1793; grad. William Coll., Williamstown, Mass., 1811. Admitted t N.Y. bar, began law practice Hamilton, N.Y. moved to Bainbridge, N.Y., circa 1818; dist. atty. 1823-27; mem. U.S. Ho. of Reps. from N.Y., (a Democrat) 20th, (elected as Democrat, change politics) 25th, (as Whig) 26th-27th congresses 1827-29, 37-43; 1st auditor of Treasury, 1849 moved to Chemung County, N.Y., entered lumbe bus. Died Elmira, N.Y., Oct. 25, 1852; burie St. Peter's Churchyard, Bainbridge, N.Y.

CLARK, Jonas, clergyman; b. Newton, Mass., Dec. 14, 1731; s. Thomas and Mary (Bowen) C.; grad. Harvard, 1752; m. Lucy Bowen, Sept. 27, 1757; 13 children including Polly, Betsey, Lucy, Liddy Patty, Sally, Thomas, Jonas, William, Peter, Bowen, Harry. Ordained to ministry Congregationalist Ch. 1755; pastor 1st Parish Ch., Lexington, Mass., 1755-1805; close friend and adviser John Hancock, Samuel Adams. Author: The Importance of Military Skill, Measures for Defense, and a Martial Spirit in a Time of Peace, 1768; The Fate of Blood Thirsty Oppressors and God's Tender Care of His Distressed People, 1776. Died Lexington, Nov. 15, 1805.

CLARK, Jonas Gilman, businessman, philanthropist; b. Hubbardston, Mass., Feb. 1, 1815; s. William Smith and Elizabeth Clark; m. Susan Wright. Apprenticed to carriage-maker, 1831-36; became owner carriage mfg. bus., 1836, later operated hardware stores, Lowell and Milford, Mass., until 1853; engaged in selling supplies to Cal. miners, after 1853; real estate investor, San Francisco, N.Y. C.; mem. San Francisco Vigilantes; founder Union League of Cal.; contbd. $1,000,000 to founding of Clark U., Worcester, Mass. (opened 1889). Died Mar. 23, 1900.

CLARK, Joseph Sylvester, clergyman; b. Monomet Ponds, South Plymouth, Mass., Dec. 19, 1800; s. Seth and Mary (Tupper) C.; grad. Amherst Coll., 1831; m. Harriet B. Bourne, Dec. 27, 1831. Ordained to ministry Congregational Ch., 1831; minister Congregational Ch., Sturbridge, Mass., 1831-38; sec. Mass. Missionary Soc., 1839-57; corresponding sec. Congregational Library Assn., 1855-61, financial agt., 1857-61; editor Congregational Quarterly, 1859. Author: Historical Sketch, 1838; A Historical Sketch of the Congregational Churches of Massachusetts from 1620-1858, published 1858. Died Aug. 17, 1861.

CLARK, Lewis Gaylord, editor; b. Otisco, N.Y., Oct. 5, 1808; s. Eliakin and Miss (Gaylord) C.; m. Ella Maria Curtis, Oct. 1834, 6 children. Editor, art-owner Knickerbocker Mag., N.Y.C., 1834-61, 3; became leading figure in N.Y.C. society; mem. t. Nicholas Soc., 1840-73; co-founder Century Club, 1846; contbr. articles to Harper's Magazine, 1863-73; clk. N.Y. Customs House. uthor: The Literary Remains of the Late Willis aylord Clark; The Knickerbocker Sketch-Book, 845; Knick-Knacks from an Editors' Table, 852; The Life, Eulogy, and Great Orations of aniel Webster, 1854. Died Piermont, N.Y., Nov. , 1873; buried Nyack Cemetery, Piermont.

CLARK, Lincoln, congressman, lawyer; b. Conway, Mass., Aug. 9, 1800; grad. Amherst (Mass.) oll., 1825; studied law. Admitted to bar, 1831, egan practice of law, Pickensville, Ala.; mem. la. Ho. of Reps., 1834-35, 45; moved to Tuscaoosa, Ala., 1836; elected gen. atty. by state legisature, 1839; apptd. circuit judge by Gov. Fitzatrick, 1846; moved to Dubuque, Ia., 1848; Demoratic presdl. elector 1852; mem. U.S. Ho. of Reps. Democrat) from Ia., 32d Congress, 1851-53; esumed law practice, Chgo.; apptd. U.S. register bankruptcy, 1866; ret., returned to Conway. ied Conway, Sept. 16, 1886; buried Howland emetery.

CLARK, Lot, congressman, lawyer; b. Hillsdale, olumbia County, N.Y., May 23, 1788; studied law. dmitted to bar, 1816, practiced law, Norwich, .Y.; dist. atty. Chenango County, 1822-23, 28-9; mem. U.S. Ho. of Reps. (Whig) from N.Y., 8th Congress, 1823-25; postmaster Norwich, 1825-8; continued practice of law, Lockport, N.Y., 1829; ecame pres. Lockport Bank, 1829; mem., agt. lbany Co. (owners of unsold lands in various .Y. counties); moved to Buffalo, N.Y., 1835; rojector of 1st wire-cable bridge over Niagara; res. Suspension Bridge Co., until 1862; mem. .Y. State Assembly, 1846. Died Buffalo, Dec. 8, 1862; buried Greenwood Cemetery, Bklyn.

CLARK, Meriweather Lewis, architect; flourished arly 19th century; b. St. Louis; s. Gen. William nd Julia (Hancock) C.; grad. U.S. Mil. Acad., 830; studied architecture. Served with U.S. Army, esigned; practiced as architect, St. Louis; deigned Ch. of St. Vincent de Paul (one of his best nown works; built 1844), Soulard mansion, St. ouis ("Shakespeare") Theatre (built 1837, detroyed by fire, 1855), all St. Louis.

CLARK, Myron Holley, gov. N.Y.; b. Naples, .Y., Oct. 23, 1806; s. Maj. Joseph and Mary (Suton) C.; m. Zelpha Watkins. Sheriff, Ontario ounty (N.Y.), 1837; pres. Canadaigua, N.Y., 850-51; went to N.Y. Senate to uphold prohibition ause, 1852, received chief credit for passage of a rohibition law by both houses, 1854 (vetoed by ov.); nominated for gov. N.Y. by Whigs, Free emocracy, Anti-Nebraska and Temperance parties, 1854, gov. N.Y., 1855-57; U.S. collector inernal revenue, 1862-68; Prohibitionist Party canlidate for gov. N.Y., 1874. Died Canadaigua, Aug. 3, 1892.

CLARK, Robert, congressman, b. Washington ounty, N.Y., June 12, 1777; studied medicine n brother's office. Practiced medicine, Galway, Vashington County, 1799; moved to Stamford, elaware County, later settled nr. Delhi, Delaware County, practiced medicine; mem. N.Y. State ssembly, 1812-15; mem. U.S. Ho. of Reps. (Demorat) from N.Y., 16th Congress, 1819-21; del. N.Y. tate Constl. Conv., 1821; moved to Monroe County, Mich., lived on farm nr. Monroe, practiced medicine, ecame interested in scientific cultivation of fruits nd grasses, drainage; apptd. register Land Office or 2d Dist. of Mich. Territory, 1823-31. Died Oct. 1, 1837.

CLARK, Rufus Wheelwright, clergyman; b. Newburyport, Mass., Dec. 17, 1813; grad. Yale, 1836; attended Andover Theol. Sem.; D.D. (hon.), N.Y. U., 1860; m. Eliza Walton, 1843, 6 children including Rufus Wheelwright, William Walton, Edward, Fletcher. Clk. in merc. store, N.Y.C., before entering oll.; ordained to ministry Congregational Ch., 1841; astor 2d Presbyn. Ch., Washington, D.C., 1841-42, North Congregational Ch., Portsmouth, N.H., 1842-2; East Boston Congregational Ch., 1852-57, South Congregational Ch., Bklyn., 1857-62, 1st Dutch Reformed Ch., Albany, N.Y., 1862-66; known as orceful preacher, often asked to take up new pastorates. Author approximately 130 works including: ectures to Young Men, Romanism in America. Died Nantucket, Mass., Aug. 9, 1866.

CLARK, Rush, congressman, lawyer; b. Schellsburg, Bedford County, Pa., Oct. 1, 1834; grad. efferson Coll., Canonsburg, Pa., 1853; studied aw. Admitted to bar, 1853, practiced in Iowa ity, Ia.; mem. Ia. Ho. of Reps., 1860-64, 76, speaker, 1863, 64; mem. Ia. gov.'s staff, 1861, 62; n organizer volunteer regt. from Ia. in Civil War; trustee Ia. U., 1862-66; mem. U.S. Ho. of Reps. (Republican) from Ia., 45th-46th congresses, 1877-Apr. 29, 1879. Died Washington, D.C., Apr. 29, 1879; buried Oakland Cemetery, Iowa City.

CLARK, Samuel, congressman, lawyer; b. Clarksville, Cayuga County, N.Y., Jan. 1800; attended Hamilton Coll., studied law, Auburn, N.Y. Admitted to bar; practiced in Waterloo, N.Y., 1826; mem. U.S. Ho. of Reps. (Democrat) from N.Y., 23d, (from Mich.) 33d congresses, 1833-35, 53-55; moved to Kalamazoo, Mich., 1842, practiced law; mem. Mich. Constl. Conv., 1850; aided in locating and inaugurating land office at Buchanan (at head Lake Superior); discontinued law practice, retired from polit. activities, became farmer. Died Kalamazoo, Oct. 2, 1870; buried Mountain Home Cemetery.

CLARK, Sheldon, philanthropist; b. Oxford, Conn., Jan. 31, 1785; attended Yale, 1811-12. Worked farm inherited from his grandfather, nr. Oxford, 1812-40; lived simply in order to save money to contribute to Yale, bought telescope, 1822, founded Sheldon Clark Professorship of Philosophy, 1823, estabilshed scholarship fund, 1824; mem. Conn. Gen. Assembly, 1825. Died Oxford, Apr. 10, 1840.

CLARK, William, explorer, territorial gov.; b. Caroline County, Va., Aug. 1, 1770; s. John and Ann (Rogers) C.; m. Julia Hancock, Jan. 1808; m. 2d, Harriett Kennerly, 1821; 5 children, including Meriwether Lewis, George Rogers Hancock, Jefferson Kennerly. Commd. lt. inf. U.S. Army, 1792, in charge of rifle corps, 1793, served under Gen. Anthony Wayne in Battle of Fallen Timbers, 1794, resigned commn., 1796; Meriwether Lewis proposed Clark should accompany him as joint leader expdn. which Pres. Jefferson was sending to explore continent, find route to Pacific Ocean, 1803, expdn. recruited in Ill., 1803-04, embarked up Missouri River, May 14, 1804, descended Columbia River, reached Pacific, returned to St. Louis, Sept. 23, 1806; apptd. brig. gen. La. Territorial Militia, 1807; gov. Mo. Territory, 1813-21, protected frontiers from Indian invasions during War of 1812, at war's end reconciled Western Indians by series of treaties; U.S. supt. Indian affairs, St. Louis, 1813-38; surveyor gen. for Ill., 1824-25; attempted to effect permanent peace with Indians in Treaty of Prairie du Chien, 1825; laid out Town of Paducah (Ky.), 1828; mapmaker, wildlife artist; diary of Lewis and Clark published as Expeditions Under the Commands of Captains Lewis and Clark, 1814. Died St. Louis, Sept. 1, 1838.

CLARK, William, sec. of treasury, congressman; b. Dauphin, Pa., Feb. 18, 1774. Capt. Dauphin County Militia, 1793, 95; moved to Crawford County, Pa.; asso. judge Crawford County, 1803-18; served in War of 1812; brigade insp. Western Dist. of Pa., 1800-17; served in flagship Lawrence in engagement with Brit. fleet on Lake Erie; sec. Pa. Land Office, 1818-21; treas. Pa., 1821-27; U.S. sec. of treasury, 1828-29; mem. U.S. Ho. of Reps. (Whig) from Pa., 23d-24th congresses, 1833-37; mem. Pa. Constl. Revision Commn., 1837; became farmer. Died nr. Dauphin, Mar. 28, 1851; buried English Presbyn. Cemetery.

CLARK, William Smith, army officer, scientist, coll. pres.; b. Ashfield, Mass., July 31, 1826; s. Dr. Atherton and Harriet (Smith) C.; grad. Amherst Coll., 1848; Ph.D., Gottingen U., 1852; m. Harrietta Richards, May 25, 1853, 11 children. Tchr. natural scis. Williston Sem., 1848-50; prof. chemistry Amherst (Mass.) Coll., 1852, prof. zoology, 1853, prof. botany, 1854; mem.-at-large Mass. State Bd. Agr., 1859-61; commd. maj. 21st Mass. Volunteers, 1861, lt. col., 1862, col., 1862; returned to Amherst; presdl. elector, sec. Electoral Coll., 1864; mem. Mass. Gen. Ct., 1864, 65, 67; pres., also prof. botany and horticulture Mass. Agrl. Coll., 1867-79; organizer, pres. Imperial Coll. of Agr. in Japan, 1867-77. Author: The Phenomena of Plant Life, 1875. Died Amherst, Mar. 9, 1886.

CLARK, Willis Gaylord, poet, editor; b. Otisco, N.Y., Oct. 5, 1808; s. Eliakim and Miss (Gaylord) C.; m. Ann Caldeleugh, 1836. Owner, editor Phila. Gazette; foremost Phila. poet of his day; most noteworthy poems include: The Spirit of Life, The Past and Present; 1st to advocate in print internat. copyright. Died Phila., June 12, 1841.

CLARKE, Archibald Smith, congressman; b. on plantation Prince Georges County, Md., 1788; attended grammar and high schs.; studied law. Admitted to bar; practiced law, Niagara County, N.Y.; surrogate Niagara County, 1808, 09; mem. N.Y. State Assembly, 1809-11, N.Y. Senate, 1813-16; county clk., 1815, 16; mem. U.S. Ho. of Reps. (filled vacancy) from N.Y., 14th Congress, Dec. 2, 1816-17. Died Clarence, Erie County, N.Y. Dec. 4, 1821.

CLARKE, Bayard, congressman; b. N.Y.C., Mar. 17, 1815; grad. Geneva Coll., 1835; attended Royal Cavalry Sch.; studied law. Admitted to bar; attache to Gen. Cass (U.S. minister to France), 1836-40; apptd. 2d lt. 8th Infantry, 1841; transferred to 2d Dragoons, 1841, resigned, 1843; lived in Westchester County, N.Y.; mem. U.S. Ho. of Reps. (Am. Whig) from N.Y., 34th Congress, 1855-57. Died Schroon Lake, Essex County, N.Y., June 20, 1884; buried Newtown, L.I., N.Y.

CLARKE, Beverly Leonidas, congressman, diplomat; b. Winterfield, Chesterfield County, Va., Feb. 11, 1809; attended common schs.; studied law, Franklin, Ky.; grad. Lexington Law Sch., 1831. Admitted to bar, 1833, practiced in Franklin; mem. Ky. Ho. of Reps., 1841-42; del. Ky. Constl. Conv., 1849; mem. U.S. Ho. of Reps. (Democrat) from Ky., 30th Congress, 1847-49; unsuccessful Dem. nominee for gov. Ky., 1855; apptd. by Pres. Buchanan minister to Guatemala (also accredited to Honduras), 1858-60. Died Guatemala, Mar. 17, 1860; buried State Cemetery, Frankfort, Ky.

CLARKE, Charles Ezra, congressman, lawyer; b. Saybrook, Conn., Apr. 8, 1790; grad. Yale, 1809; studied law. Admitted to bar, 1815, practiced in Watertown, N.Y.; moved to Great Bend, Jefferson County, N.Y., 1840; mem. N.Y. State Assembly, 1839, 40; mem. U.S. Ho. of Reps. (Whig) from N.Y., 31st Congress, 1849-51; built and operated gristmill, became farmer. Died Great Bend, Dec. 29, 1863; buried Brookside Cemetery, Watertown.

CLARKE, Elijah, army officer; b. Edgecombe County, S.C., 1733; m. Hannah Arrington, at least 1 son, John Clark. Commd. capt. Ga. Militia, 1776, later col., brig. gen., 1781; served at battles of Kettle Creek, Musgrove's Mill, Beattie's Mill and both sieges of Augusta (Ga.) in Revolutionary War; given estate in Wilkes County by State of Ga. for his mil. services; participated in battle with Indians at Jack's Creek, 1787; involved in French minister Edmond Genet's scheme to seize Spanish lands in Am., commd. maj. gen. French Army, 1793, plans failed when Genet was recalled; attempted to set up state in Creek Indian territory, 1794, established several forts but forced to give up venture by Ga. Militia. Died Wilkes County, Ga., Jan. 15, 1799.

CLARKE, Freeman, congressman, businessman; b. Troy, N.Y., Mar. 22, 1809; attended common schs. In business for himself at age 15; began financial career as cashier Bank of Orleans, Albion, N.Y.; moved to Rochester, N.Y., 1845; became dir. and pres. numerous banks, railroads, telegraph, trust companies, Rochester, N.Y.C.; del. Nat. Whig Conv., Balt., 1852; v.p. 1st N.Y. State Republican Conv., 1854; Rep. presdl. elector, 1856; apptd. comptroller of currency, 1865-67; del. N.Y. State Constl. Conv., 1867; mem. U.S. Ho. of Reps. (Rep.) from N.Y., 38th, 42d-43d congresses, 1863-65, 71-75. Died Rochester, June 24, 1887; buried Mt. Hope Cemetery.

CLARKE, George, colonial ofcl.; b. Eng. 1676; s. George Clarke; m. Ann Hyde, 1705. Sec., Province of N.Y., 1703; mem. Council of N.Y., 1716; commd. to run Conn. boundary line, 1718; dep. for N.Y. to Auditor Gen. of Plantations; amassed considerable fortune as result of extensive dealings in land; by 1736; lt. gov. N.Y., 1736-43; returned to Eng. 1745 Died Cheshire, Eng., Jan. 12, 1760; buried Chester Cathedral; Cheshire.

CLARKE, James Freeman, clergyman; b. Hanover, N.H., Apr. 4, 1810; s. Samuel and Rebecca (Hull) C.; grad. Harvard, 1829, Divinity Sch., 1833, D.D. (hon.), 1863; m. Anna Huidekoper, Aug. 1839. Ordained to ministry Unitarian Ch., Boston, 1833; minister, Louisville, Ky., 1833-40; editor Western Messenger, 1836-39; founded Ch. of the Disciples (new Unitarian ch.), Boston, 1841; minister Unitarian Ch., Meadville, Pa., 1850-54; mem. Mass. Bd. Edn., 1863-69; trustee Boston Public Library, 1879-88; non-resident prof. Harvard Divinity Sch., 1867-71, lectr. on ethic, 1867-77, bd. overseers Harvard Coll., 1863-72, 73-85, 86-88; active on behalf of temperance, anti-slavery, women's suffer-age. Author: The Christian Doctrine of Forgiveness of Sin, 1852; Orthodoxy, Its Truths and Errors, 1866; Ten Great Religions, 2 vols., 1870, 86; Essentials and Non-essentials in Religion, 1878; Self Culture, 1880; Anti-Slavery Days, 1883. Died Jamaica Plain, Mass., June 8, 1888.

CLARKE, John, clergyman, colonial ofcl.; b. Suffolk, Eng., Oct. 8, 1609; s. Thomas and Rose Kerrich C.; m. Elizabeth Harris; m. 2d, Jane Flecher, 1671; m. 3d, Sarah Davis. Came to Boston, 1637; driven from Mass. for religious beliefs, 1638, one of buyers of Aquidneck (R.I.) from Indians; an original settler Newport, R.I.; pastor Baptist Ch., practiced medicine, Newport; sent with Roger Williams to Eng. to protect interests of the colony, 1651, remained 10 years; mem. commn. which made Conn.-R.I. boundary agreement, Apr. 7, 1663; secured Royal Charter for R.I., 1663; mem. R.I. Gen. Assembly, 1664-69; dep. gov. R.I., 1669-72. Author: Ill News from New England, 1652. Died Newport, Apr. 28, 1676.

CLARKE, John Hopkins, senator, mfr.; b. Elizabeth, N.J., Apr. 1, 1789; grad. Brown U., 1809; studied law. Admitted to bar, practiced in Providence, R.I., 1812; clk. Providence County Supreme Ct., 1813; propr. distillery, Cranston, R.I. until 1824; became cotton mfr., Providence, Pontiac, Woonsocket, 1824; mem. R.I. Ho. of Reps., 1836-42, 45-47; mem. U.S. Senate (Whig) from R.I., 1847-53. Died Providence, Nov. 23, 1870; buried North Burial Ground.

CLARKE, Mary Bayard Devereux, author; b. Raleigh, N.C., May 13, 1827; d. Thomas Pollock and Katherine Anne (Johnson) Devereux; m. William J. Clarke, 1848, 4 children. Wrote under pseudonym Tenella; wrote patriotic verse for Southern newspapers during Civil War; editor Southern Field and Fireside, Raleigh, 1865. Author: Wood Notes, 1854; Mosses from a Rolling Stone or Idle Moments of a Busy Woman, 1866; Clytie and Zenobia, 1871; Miskodeed (libretto). Died New Bern, N.C., Mar. 30, 1886.

CLARKE, Mary Francis, nun; b. Dublin, Ireland, Mar. 2, 1803; d. Cornelius and Catherine (Hyland) Clarke. Came to U.S. with 4 other women, 1833, formed Order of Sister of Blessed Virgin Mary, consecrated at Phila., 1833, superior of order, Phila., 1833-43, Dubuque, Ia., 1843-87; papal decree of Final Approbation and Confirmation issued to Order, 1885. Died Dec. 4, 1887.

CLARKE, McDonald, poet; b. Bath, Me., June 18, 1798; m. Mary Brundage. Known as "Mad Poet" in N.Y.C. for his extreme sensitivity and eccentricity; travelled in high social circles (although always poor); became completely insane in later years, committed to asylum on Blackwell's Island, N.Y.; works include: The Elixir of Moonshine, 1822; Sketches, 1826; Afara, a Poem, 1829; Poems of McDonald Clarke, 1836; A Cross and a Coronet, 1841. Drowned in water running from open faucet, Blackwell's Island, Mar. 5, 1842.

CLARKE, Reader Wright, congressman; b. Bethel, O., May 18, 1812; studied law. Learned printing; admitted to bar, 1836, practiced in Batavia, O.; publisher Whig paper, Shawneetown, Ill. for few years; returned to Batavia; mem. Ohio. Ho. of Reps., 1840-42; Whig presdl. elector, 1844; clk. Clermont County Ct., 1846-52; mem. U.S. Ho. of Reps. (Republican) from Ohio, 39th-40th congresses, 1865-69; 2d auditor of Treasury, 1869-70; apptd. collector internal revenue in Ohio. Died Batavia, May 23, 1872; buried Union Cemetery.

CLARKE, Richard, mcht.; b. Boston, May 12, 1711; s. William and Hannah (Appleton) C.; grad. Harvard, 1729; m. Elizabeth Winslow, May 3, 1733, 6 children including Jonathan, Isaac, Susannah (Clarke) Copley. Operator firm Richard Clarke and Sons, mchts., Boston, became factors for East India Co., 1773; one of consignees of tea used in Boston Tea Party, 1773, attacked by mob of Sons of Liberty in his warehouse when he and other consignees refused to resign commns. as factors, forced by public pressure to sign Non-Importation Agreement; he and his sons attacked by mobs several times, 1773-75; went to Eng., 1775, joined Loyalist Club of London; some of his U.S. property confiscated by U.S. Govt. Died London, Feb. 27, 1795.

CLARKE, Staley Nichols, congressman; b. Prince Georges County, Md., May 24, 1794. Moved to Buffalo, N.Y., 1815; clk. Bank of Niagara; clk. Holland Land Co., Batavia, N.Y., 1819-22, agt. Cattaraugus County, Ellicottville, N.Y., 1822; treas. Cattaraugus County, 17 years; mem. U.S. Ho. of Reps. (Whig) from N.Y., 27th Congress, 1841-43. Died Ellicottville, Oct. 14, 1860; buried Jefferson Street Cemetery.

CLARKE, Walter, colonial gov.; b. Newport, R.I., circa 1638; s. Jeremiah and Frances (Latham) C.; m. Content Greenman, 1660, 3 children; m. 2d, Hannah Scott, Feb. 1667/8, 6 children; m. 3d, Freeborn Williams, Mar. 1682/83; m. 4th, Sarah Prior, Aug. 31, 1711. Dep., city of Newport, 1667, 70, 72, 73; dep. gov. R.I., 1679-86, 1700-14, gov. R.I., 1676-77, 86, 96-98; refused to serve as gov. when Royal Charter of R.I. was suspended, hid original charter until the fall of Sir Edmund Andros, 1689, then restored it to the people. Died Newport, May 23, 1714; buried Clifton Burial Ground, Newport.

CLARKSON, Coker Fifield, editor; b. Frankfort, Me., Jan. 21, 1811; s. Richard Perkinhohn and Mary (Simpon) C.; m. Elizabeth Goudie, Apr. 2, 1833; m. 2d, Elizabeth Colescott, 1849; 2 children, Richard, James. Publisher, editor Indiana American, Cincinnati, 1820-54; moved to Grundy County, Ia., bought large farm, 1854; del. from Ia. to Nat. Republican Conv., 1860; mem. Ia. Senate, 1863-67; publisher, agrl. editor Ia. State Register, Des Moines, 1870-90; an organizer Farmers Protective Assn. to oppose Barber Wire Syndicate (group of capitalists who were trying to establish monopoly of barbed wire), assn. began mfg. its own wire. Died May 7, 1890.

CLARKSON, Matthew, Continental congressman, mayor; b. N.Y..C, Apr. 1733. Moved to Phila.; justice Ct. Common Pleas, Quarter Sessions of Peace, Phila. Orphans' Ct., 1771, 72; mem. Continental Congress from Pa., 1785, may not have served; mem. bd. alderman, 1789; mayor Phila., 1792-96. Died Phila., Oct. 5, 1800; buried Christ Ch. Burying Grounds.

CLARKSON, Matthew, army officer, philanthropist; b. N.Y.C., Oct. 17, 1758; s. David and Elizabeth (French) C.; m. Mary Rutherfurd, May 24, 1785; m. 2d, Sarah Cornell, Feb. 14, 1792. Participated in Battle of L.I. as a volunteer and aide-de-camp to Benedict Arnold, 1778-79; attached to staff of Gen. Benjamin Lincoln, served with him until end of Revolutionary War, 1779-83, participated in siege of Savannah Ga., defense of Charleston, S.C., present at surrender of Yorktown, 1781; asst. to U.S. Sec. of War Benjamin Lincoln; commd. brig. gen., then maj. gen. N.Y. State Militia; regent State U. N.Y.; mem. N.Y. State Assembly, 1789-90; U.S. marshal, 1791-92; mem. N.Y. State Senate, 1794-96; one of commrs. apptd. by N.Y. State Legislature to build new prison, 1796; pres. N.Y. Hosp., 1799; pres. Bank of N.Y., 1804-25; Federalist candidate for U.S. Senate, 1802, defeated by DeWitt Clinton; supported numerous socs. and movements for pub. improvement. Died N.Y.C., Apr. 25, 1825.

CLAUSEN, Claus Lauritz, clergyman; b. Aero, Denmark, Nov. 3, 1820; s. Erik and Karen (Pedersen) C.; m. Martha Rasmussen; m. 2d, Bergette Hjort, 1847. Came to U.S., 1843; ordained to ministry Am. Lutheran Ch., 1843; pastor, Muskego, Wis., 1843-46, Luther Valley, Wis., 1846-53; travelled as missionary in Wis., Minn., Ia.; an organizer Norwegian Synod, 1853; pastor at St. Ansgar, Ia., 1853-72; immigrant commr. of Ia., 1856-59; chaplain 15th Wis. Regt., U.S. Volunteers, 1861-62; left Norwegian Synod after dispute over Sabbath observance, 1868; co-founder Norwegian-Danish Conf., 1870, pres., 1870; pastor at Phila., 1875-77, Blooming Prairie, Minn., 1877-85; an organizer United Norwegian Luth. Ch., 1890. Died Paulsbo, Wash., Feb. 20, 1892.

CLAWSON, Isaiah Dunn, congressman, physician; b. Woodstown, Salem County, N.J., Mar. 30, 1822; attended Delaware Coll., Newark, N.J., Lafayette Coll., Easton, Pa.; grad. Princeton, 1840; grad. mem. dept. U. Pa., 1843. Practiced medicine, Woodstown; mem. N.J. Ho. of Assembly, 1854; mem. U.S. Ho. of Reps. (Whig) from N.J., 34th-35th congresses, 1855-59. Died Woodstown, Oct. 9, 1879; buried Baptist Cemetery.

CLAY, Brutus Junius, congressman, farmer; b. Richmond, Madison County, Ky., July 1, 1808; grad. Centre Coll., Danville, Ky. Became farmer, stock raiser; moved to Bourbon County, 1837, mem. Ky. Ho. of Reps., 1840, 60; elected pres. Bourbon County Agrl. Assn., 1840, served 30 years; pres. Ky. Agrl. Assn., 1853-61; mem. U.S. Ho. of Reps. (Unionist) from Ky., 38th Congress, 1863-65. Died nr. Paris, Ky., Oct. 11, 1878; buried family burial ground Auvergne, nr. Paris.

CLAY, Clement Claiborne, senator, Confederate agt.; b. Huntsville, Ala., Dec. 13, 1816; s. Clement Comer and Susanna (Withers) C.; grad. U. Ala., 1835; law degree U. Va., 1839; m. Virginia Tunstall, Feb. 1, 1843. Pvt. sec. to Gov. Clay of Ala. (his father); editorial work Huntsville Democrat; mem. Ala. Legislature, 1842, 44, 45; judge Madison (Ala.) Ct., 1846-48; mem. U.S. Senate (Democrat) from Ala., 1853-61, withdrew from Senate with Ala.'s secession; mem. Confederate Senate (elected by Ala. Legislature), 1861-63; apptd. mem. secret and confidential mission to Can. by Jefferson Davis, 1864; accused (with Davis and others) of inciting and encouraging Lincoln's assassination, of conspiring (while in Can.) to release Confederate prisoners of war on Johnson's Island and of plotting raids from Can. against U.S. territory; surrendered to comdg. officer U.S. Army, taken to Fortress Monroe, kept in solitary confinement for about 1 year, released, 1866; returned to practice law, Huntsville. Died Huntsville, Jan. 3, 1882.

CLAY, Clement Comer, senator, gov. Ala.; b. Halifax County, Va., Dec. 17, 1789; s. William and Rebecca (Comer) C.; grad. U. Tenn., 1807; m. Susanna Withers, 1815, 3 children including Clement Claiborne. Admitted to Knoxville (Tenn.) bar, 1809; served as adj. of a battalion in Creek War of 1813; mem. Ala. Territorial Legislature, 1817-19; del. to 1st Ala., Constl. Conv. 1819; chief justice Tenn., 1820-23; elected mem. Ala. Legislature, 1827, served as speaker lower house; mem. U.S. Ho. of Reps. from Ala., 21st-23d congresses, 1829-35, instrumental in securing passage preemption laws for settlers and relief laws for purchasers of governmental lands in Ala.; supported Jackson's attacks on the U.S. Bank, also his opposition to nullification in S.C.; gov. Ala., 1835-37; mem. U.S. Senate from Ala. (elected to fill vacancy before gov.'s term expired), 1837-41, resigned, 1841; commd. by legislature to prepare digest of Ala. laws, completed, 1843; asso. justice Ala. Supreme Ct., 1843. Died Huntsville, Ala., Sept. 7, 1866; buried Maple Hill Cemetery, Huntsville.

CLAY, Edward Williams, artist; b. Phila., Apr. 19, 1799; s. Robert and Eliza (Williams) C. Etcher, engraver, Phila., 1825-36, N.Y., 1837-circa 1840, gave up art; register court of chancery, clk. Del. Orphans' Ct., 1854-56; etched and engraved for Phila. publishers, published several volumes of satiric caricatures. Author: Life in Philadelphi 1829; Sketches of Character, 1829. Died N.Y.C Dec. 31, 1857; buried Christ Ch. Burial Groun Phila.

CLAY, Green, army officer, legislator; b. Pov hatan County, Va., Aug. 14, 1757; s. Charles Cla m. Sally Lewis, 7 children including Cassius Ma cellus, Brutus J. Came to Ky. circa 1777; de surveyor Lincoln County (Ky.), 1781; amassed fortune by locating lands; settled in Madison Cour ty, Ky.; became trustee Town of Boonesboroug (Ky.), 1787; mem. Va. Legislature, 1788, 8 mem. lower house Ky. Legislature, from Madis County, 1793-94; mem. Ky. Senate, 1795-98, 180 represented Madison County at conv. to draft 2 constn. for Ky., 1799; commd. maj. gen. Ky. Mil tia, marched with 3000 state troops to relieve Ger Harrison at Ft. Meigs; Clay County (Ky.) named i his honor. Died Madison County, Oct. 31, 1826.

CLAY, Henry, senator; b. Hanover County, Va. Apr. 12, 1777; s. John and Elizabeth (Hudson) C. married Lucretia Hart, Apr. 1799, 11 children in cluding Thomas, James, and John. License in law, 1797; moved to Lexington, Ky., 1797; mem Ky. Legislature, 1803-06, mem., speaker, 1807-1 mem. U.S. Senate from Ky., 1806-07 (even thoug he was less than required 30 years of age), 181 11, 31-42, 49-52; opposed rechartering of U.S. Ban mem. U.S. Ho. of Reps. from Ky., 12th-16th, 18 congresses, 1811-21, 23-25, speaker, 1811-20, 2 25, a leader of the War Hawks during 12th Congres active supporter of Pres. James Madison and W of 1812, mem. Ghent Peace Commn., 1814, deve oped American System (program of nationalism in cluding internal improvements in transp., re-chart ering of nat. bank, tariff protection for Am. indus tries, a policy of nat. defense); achieved ba charter and protective tariff of 1816; organize campaign for recognition of South American state 1818; resigned as speaker to attack Andrew Jack son on floor of Ho. of Reps. for his invasion of Fla. 1819; earned title of Great Pacificator as result Missouri Compromise of 1820; secured passag highest protective tariff enacted to that tim 1824; presdl. nominee of Whig Party, 1824, thre his support to John Quincy Adams when defeat be came evident, accused of secret alliance (charge strengthened when Adams apptd. him to cabinet) U.S. sec. of state under Adams, 1825-29; resolve crisis caused by S.C.'s nullification of Tariff Act 1832 with Compromise of 1833; unsuccessful Wh presdl. candidate, 1832, 44; prin. author series o resolutions known as Compromise of 1850 (b which he sought to avoid civil war). Died Washing ton, D.C., June 29, 1852, buried Lexington (Ky. Cemetery.

CLAY, James Brown, congressman; b. Washing ton, D.C., Nov. 9, 1817; s. Henry Clay; attende Transylvania U., Lexington, Ky., Kenyon Coll. Gambier, O.; studied law Lexington Law Sch. Clk in countinghouse, Boston, 1832-34; admitted t bar; practiced with his father, Lexington; charg d'affaires to Portugal, 1849-50; lived in Mo. 1851, 52; returned to Lexington, 1852; mem U.S. Ho. of Reps. (Democrat) from Ky., 35t Congress, 1857-59; mem. Washington (D.C. Peace Conv., 1861; identified with Confedera in Civil War; went to Montreal, Can., for health Died Montreal, Jan. 26, 1864; buried Lexingto Cemetery.

CLAY, Joseph, mcht., Continental congressma b. Yorkshire, Eng., Oct. 16, 1741; s. Ralph an Elizabeth (Habersham) C.; m. Ann Legardere, Jan 2, 1763; children include Joseph. Rice planter mcht., asso. at various times with Joseph Clay Co. Seth John Cuthbert & Co., Clay, Talfair & Co. partner William Fox & Co.; mem. Ga. Revolution ary Com., 1774; participated in seizure 600 pound of powder from King's magazine, Savannah, Ga. May 11, 1775; mem. Ga. Council of Safety, 1775 mem. Provisional Congress, 1775; paymaster gen So. dept. Continental Army, 1777; mem. Continenta Congress, 1778-80; one of 25 rebel leaders indicte for treason by Royalist Assembly, 1780; state treas Ga., 1782; mem. bd. created by Ga. Gen. Assembl to establish instn. higher edn., thus became founder U. Ga. (1st state univ. chartered in Am.) Died Savannah, Nov. 15, 1804; buried Colonial Par Cemetery, Savannah.

CLAY, Joseph, jurist, clergyman; b. Savannah Ga., Aug. 16, 1764; s. Joseph and Ann (Legardere) C.; grad. Princeton, 1784; m. Mary Savage, Nov. 25 1789. Admitted to Ga. bar, 1790; influential mem Conv. of 1795 which revised Ga. Constn.; apptd U.S. dist. judge for Ga., 1796; U.S. judge for 5t Circuit Ga., 1801, legislated out of office, 1892 ordained to ministry Baptist Ch., 1804; mem. gen com. Ga. Bapt. Assn.; pastor 1st Bapt. Ch., Boston 1807. Died Boston, Jan. 11, 1811; buried Old Gran ary Burying Ground, Boston.

CLAY, Joseph, congressman; b. Phila., July 24 1769. Mem. U.S. Ho. of Reps. from Pa., 8th-10t congresses, 1803-08, resigned to become banker mgr. apptd. by House to conduct impeachment proceedings against John Pickering (judge U.S. Dist. Ct. for N.H.), 1804; cashier Farmers & Mechanics' Bank of Phila. Died Phila., Aug. 27, 1811; buried Christ Ch. Burying Ground.

CLAY, Matthew, congressman; b. Halifax, County, Va., Mar. 25, 1754; s. Charles and Martha (Green) C.; m. Polly Williams; m. 2d, Miss Saunders. Commd. ensign 9th Va. Regt., 1776, 2d lt., 1777, 1st lt., 1778; q.m. 1st Va. Regt., 1778-81; mem. Va. Ho. of Dels., 1790-94; mem. U.S. Ho. of Reps. from Va., 4th-12th, 14th congresses, 1795-1813, Mar. 4-May 27, 1815. Died Halifax Court House, Va., May 27, 1815; buried family burying ground Pittsylvania County, Va.

CLAYTON, Augustin Smith, congresman, jurist; b. Fredericksburg, Va., Nov. 27, 1783; s. Philip and Mildred (Dixon) C.; A.B., U. Ga., 1804, A.M., m. Julia Carnes, 1808. Admitted to Ga. bar, 1806; commd. by Ga. Legislature to compile Ga. laws from 1800-10, 1810, published, 1812; mem. Ga. Gen. Assembly, 1810-12; clk. Ga. Ho. of Reps., 1813-15; judge Superior Circuit Ct., Western Ga., 1819-25, 28-31, upheld Ga. jurisdiction over Cherokee Indians who attempted to set up separate state, 1828-31; mem. Ga. Senate, 1826, 27; presdl. elector, 1829; mem. U.S. Ho. of Reps. from Ga., 22d-23d congresses, 1821-35, supported nullification resolution, 1832, opposed rechartering Bank of U.S.; trustee U. Ga., 1816-39. Died Athens, Ga., June 21, 1839.

CLAYTON, Charles, congressman; b. Devonshire, Eng., Oct. 5, 1825; attended public schs. Came to U.S., 1842, settled in Wis.; went to Ore., 1847, San Francisco, 1848; alcalde of Santa Clara, 1849, 50; built Santa Clara flour mills, 1852; returned to San Francisco, 1853, in grain and flour business; mem. Cal. Assembly, 1863-66; mem. San Francisco Bd. Suprs., 1864-69; apptd. surveyor customs of port and dist. of San Francisco by Pres. Grant, 1870; mem. U.S. Ho. of Reps. (Republican) from Cal., 43d Congress. 1873-75; Cal. prison dir., 1881,, 82. Died Oakland, Cal., Oct. 4, 1885; buried Mountain View Cemetery.

CLAYTON, John, botanist; b. Fulham, Eng., 1685. Came to Am., 1705. Asst. clk. Gloucester County, Va., 1705-22, 1st clk., 1722-73; collected bot. specimens in Middle Tidewater dists. of Va.; his specimens identified and categorized in John Frederick Gronovius' book Flora Virginia, 1739, 43; part of his collection now in Nat. Herbarium in England, Died Dec. 15, 1773.

CLAYTON, John Middleton, senator, sec. of state; b. Dagsborough, Del., July 24, 1796; s. James and Sarah (Middleton) C.; grad. Yale, 1815; m. Sarah Fisher, 1822. Admitted to Del. bar, 1819; mem. Del. Legislature, 1824; sec. of state Del., 1826-28; mem. U.S. Senate (Nat. Republican) from Del., 1829-36, active supporter of Jackson in nullification crisis, contbd. to passage Clay Compromise tariff, 1833, conducted investigations of post office scandals, leading reform and reorgn., 1831, chmn. judiciary com., aided in settlement Mich.-Ohio boundary dispute; chief justice Del., 1837-39; mem. U.S. Senate (Whig) from Del., 1845-49, 53-56; U.S. sec of state, 1849-50; negotiator Clayton-Bulwer treaty with Gt. Britain for an Am. isthmian canal, 1850. Died Dover, Del., Nov. 9, 1856; buried Presbyn. Cemetery, Dover.

CLAYTON, Joshua, physician, gov. Del.; b. Dover, Del., Dec. 20, 1744; s. John and Grace Clayton; attended U. Pa., 1757-62; m. Rachael McCleary, 1776. Commd. maj., 2d in command Bohemia Bn. of Md., 1776; commd. col., apptd. mem. staff of Gen. Washington; elected mem. Del. Ho. of Assembly, 1785, 87; state treas. Del., 1786; pres. Del., 1789-92; 1st gov. Del., 1792-96; mem. U.S. Senate from Del., Jan. 19-Aug. 11, 1798. Died Bohemia Manor, Del., Aug. 11, 1798.

CLAYTON, Thomas, senator, jurist; b. Massey's Cross Roads, Md., Mar. 9, 1778; s. Joshua and Rachael (McCleary) C.; studied law, 3 years Dover, Del.; m. Jeanette Macomb. Admitted to Dover bar, 1799; clk. Del. Ho. of Reps., 1800, mem., 1802-06, 10, 12-13; mem. Del Senate, 1808, 21; sec. of state Del. under Gov. Truitt, 1808-10, atty. gen. Del., 1810-15; mem. U.S. Ho. of Reps. (Federalist) from del., 14th Congress 1815-17, U.S. Senate (Whig) from Del.; 1824-27, 37-47; chief justice Del. Ct. Common Pleas, 1828-32; chief justice Superior ct. Del., 1832-37; presiding judge Supreme Ct. Del., 1847-54. Died New Castle, Aug. 21, 1854.

CLEAVELAND, Moses, army officer, pioneer; b. Canterbury, Conn., Jan. 29, 1754; s. Col. Aaron and Thankful (Paine) C.; grad. Yale, 1777; m. Esther Champion, Mar. 21, 1794. Commd. ensign 2d Conn. regt. Continental Army, 1777, lt., 1777, served under Washington, 1777-81; mem. Conn. Soc. Cincinnati; commd. brig. gen. Conn. Militia; mem. Conn. Gen. Assembly from Canterbury, 1787-1806; mem. Conn Conv. which ratified U.S. Constn., 1788; dir. Conn. Land Co., 1795; led party to survey Western Res. Land Co. land purchase; founder Cleve., 1796; Died Canterbury, Nov. 16, 1806.

CLEAVELAND, Parker, educator, scientist; b. Byfield, Mass., Jan. 15, 1780; s. Parker and Elizabeth (Jackman) C.; grad. Harvard, 1799. Taught sch., York, Me., 1799-1802; tutor mathematics and natural philosophy Harvard, 1803-05; prof. mathematics and natural philosophy Bowdoin Coll., Brunswick, Me., 1805-58; prof. materia medica Med. Sch. of Me., Brunswick, 1820-58; mineral Cleavelandite named for him. Author: Elementary Treatise on Mineralogy and Geology (1st Am. work on subject), 1816; Agricultural Queries, 1827. Died Oct. 15, 1858.

CLEBURN, Patrick Ronayne, army officer; b. County Cork, Ireland, Mar. 17, 1828; s. Joseph and Mary Ann (Ronayne) C. Came to New Orleans, 1849; admitted to Ark. bar, 1856; served with Confederate Army in Tenn., also in battles of Shiloh, Richmond, Chattanooga, Atlanta, 1861-64; organized Confederate mil. co. called Yell Rifles, which seized Fed. Arsenal, Little Rock, Ark., promoted to brig. gen. in command 3d brigade Army of Miss., 1862; commd. maj. gen., 1862; known as Stonewall Jackson of the West for his stand at Battle of Missionary Ridge; composed letter recommending liberation of slaves and their enlistment into Confederate cause (considered inexpedient by Jefferson Davis). Died Battle of Franklin (Tenn.), Nov. 30, 1864; buried Helena, Ark.

CLEMENS, Jeremiah, senator, novelist; b. Huntsville, Ala., Dec. 28, 1814; s. James and Miss (Mills) C.; attended La. Grange Coll.; grad. U. Ala., 1833; studied law Transylvania U., Lexington, Ky.; m. Mary Read, Dec. 4, 1834. Admitted to Ala. bar, 1834; U.S. dist. atty. for No. Ala., 1838-39; mem. Ala. Ho. of Reps., 1838-41, 43-44; served as lt. col. Army of Tex. in Tex. War for independence, 1842; apptd. maj. 13th Inf. U.S. Army, 1847, lt. col., 1847; chief dept. civil and mil. purchases in Mexico, 1848; mem. U.S. Senate (Democrat) from Ala., Nov. 30, 1849-53; spent several years writing hist. novels; editor Memphis (Tenn.) Eagle and Enquirer, 1859; mem. Ala. Secession Conv., 1861; apptd. maj. gen. Ala. Militia, 1861, never saw active service; Unionist; lived in Phila., 1862-65. Author: Bernard Lile: An Historical Romance of the Texan Revolution and the Mexican War, 1856; Mustang Gray, 1858; The Rivals, 1860; Tobias Wilson: A Tale of the Great Rebellion, 1865. Died Huntsville, May 21, 1865; buried Maple Hill Cemetery, Huntsville.

CLEMENS, Sherrard, congressman, lawyer; b. Wheeling, Va. (now W.Va.), Apr. 28, 1820; attended U.S. Mil. Acad. 6 months; grad. in law Washington (Pa.) (now Washington and Jefferson) Coll. Admitted to bar, 1843; practiced in Wheeling; mem. U.S. Ho. of Reps. (Democrat, filled vacnacy) from Va., 32d, 35th-36th congresses, Dec. 6, 1852-53, 57-61, against secession; Dem. presdl. elector, 1856; moved to St. Louis, practiced law. Died St. Louis, June 30, 1881; buried Calvary Cemetery.

CLEMMER, Mary, author; b. Utica, N.Y., May 6, 1839; d. Abraham and Margaret (Kneale) Clemmer; m. Daniel Ames, 1855 (divorced 1874); m. 2d, Edmund Hudson, 1883. Did most of her writing in N.Y.C. and Washington, D.C.; wrote column "A Woman's Letters from Washington" for N.Y.C. Independent, 1869-84; wrote column for Brooklyn Daily Union. 1869-72; works include: Victoire, 1864; Eirene; or a Woman's Right, 1871; Memorial of Alice and Phoebe Cary, 1873; Outlines of Men, Women, and Things, 1873; His Two Wives, 1874; Ten Years in Washington, 1874; Poems of Life and Nature, 1882. Died Washington, Aug. 18, 1884; buried Rock Creek Cemetery, Washington.

CLEMSON, Thomas Green, diplomat; b. Phila., July 1, 1807; m. Anna Maria Calhoun, 1838. Cons. mining engr. in Paris, France, Phila., Washington, D.C., 1832-39; U.S. charge d'affaires in Belgium, 1844-51; a founder Md. Agrl. Coll., 1856; U.S. supt. agr., 1859-61; supr. mines and metal works Trans-Mississippi Dept., Confederate States Am., 1865; endowment in his will led to founding Clemson (S.C.) Agrl. Coll. Died Ft. Hill, S.C., Apr. 6, 1888.

CLENDENIN, David, congressman. Moved from Harford County, Md. to nr. Stuthers, Mahoning Valley, O., circa 1806; pioneer iron and steel industry, built 2d stack constructed in Ohio; lived in Trumbull County, O.; served as 1st lt. Capt. James Hazlep's co. of arty. attached to regt. of Ohio Militia in War of 1812; lt. paymaster 2d Regt., Ohio Militia, 1812-13; asst. dist. paymaster U.S. Army, 1814; mem. U.S. Ho. of Reps. (filled vacancy) from Ohio, 13th-14th congresses, Oct. 11, 1814-17.

CLERC, Laurent, educator b. La Balme, France, Dec. 26, 1785; s. Joseph and Marie (Candy) C.; m. Eliza Boardman, 1819. Was deaf and mute; asst. tchr. Paris Inst., 1805; came to U.S., 1816; opened Am. Sch. for the Deaf (1st permanent sch. for the deaf and dumb), Hartford, Conn., 1817, taught there, 1817-58. Died Hartford, July 18, 1869.

CLEVELAND, Aaron, clergyman; b. Cambridge, Mass., Oct. 29, 1715; s. Aaron and Abigail (Waters) C.; grad. Harvard, 1735; m. Susannah Porter, Aug. 4, 1739. Pastor, Strict Congregational Ch., Haddam, Conn., 1839-46, South Ch., Malden, Mass., 1747-50, Mather's Ch., Halifax, N.S., Can., 1750-54; changed beliefs, ordained to ministry Protestant Episcopal Ch. by Bishop of London, 1754; missionary Soc. for Propagation of Gospel, 1754-57; apptd. pastor at New Castle, Del., 1757, became ill, died before taking charge. Died Phila., Aug. 11, 1757.

CLEVELAND, Benjamin, army officer, legislator; b. Prince William County, Va., Mar. 26, 1738; s. John and Martha (Coffee) C.; m. Mary Graves. Justice Wilkes County Ct., N.C.; elected mem. N.C. Ho. of Commons, 1778; mem. N.C. Senate, 1780; commd. capt. 2d regt. N.C. Militia; hero Battle of King's Mountain (defeated the English in the South), 1780. Died Tugalo Valley, S.C., Oct. 1806.

CLEVELAND, Chauncey Fitch, gov. Conn.; b. Hampton, Conn., Feb. 16, 1799; s. Silas and Lois (Sharpe) C.; LL.D., Trinity Coll.; m. Diantha Hovey, Dec. 13, 1821; m. 2d, Helen Litchfeild, Jan. 27, 1869; 2 children. Admitted to Windham County (Conn.) bar, 1819; mem. Conn. Gen. Assembly, 1827-30, 33, 36-37, 39; probate judge Windham County, 1829, pros. atty., 1833; state bank commr. Conn., 1837; speaker Conn. Ho. of Reps., 1835-36, 63; gov. Conn., 1842-43; mem. U.S. Ho. of Reps. (Democrat) from Conn., 31st-32d congresses, 1849-53; v.p. Conn. Republican Conv., 1856, 60; Rep. presdl. elector, 1860; del. Peace Conv., Washington, D.C., 1861. Died Hampton, June 6, 1887.

CLEVELAND, Horace William Shaler, landscape architect; b. Lancaster, Mass., Dec. 16, 1814; s. Richard Jeffry and Dorcas (Hiller) C.; m. Maryann Dwinel, Sept. 4, 1842, 2 children. In partnership with R. Morris Copeland in landscape and ornamental gardening, Boston, 1854-69; worked in Chgo., 1869-86, 98-1900, Mpls., 1886-98; designed Mpls. Park System, Sleepy Hollow Cemetery, Concord, Mass., Washington Park, Chgo. Author: A Few Hints on Landscape Gardening in the West, 1871; Landscape Architecture as Applied to the Wants of the West, 1873; The Culture and Management of our Native Forests, 1886; Voyages of a Merchant Navigator, 1886. Died Hinsdale, Ill., Dec. 5, 1900; buried Mpls.

CLEVELAND, Jesse Franklin, congressman; b. Greenville, S.C., Oct. 25, 1804; attended local schs. Moved to Ga.; mem. Ga. Senate, 1831-34; mem. U.S. Ho. of Reps. (Union Democrat, filled vacancy) from Ga., 24th-35th congresses, Oct. 5, 1835-39; moved to Charleston, S.C., 1839, became mcht.; dir. Bank of S.C. until 1841. Died Charleston, June 22, 1841; buried St. Michael's Ch. Burial Ground.

CLEVELAND, Orestes, congressman, mfr.; b. Duanesburg, Schenectady County, N.Y., Mar. 2, 1829; attended common schs. Moved to Jersey City, N.J., 1845; with Joseph Dixon Crucible Co., mfrs. black lead, stove polish, pencils; mem. Jersey City Bd. Aldermen, 1861, 62, pres., 1862; mayor Jersey City, 1864-66, 86-91; mem. U.S. Ho. of Reps. (Democrat) from N.J., 41st Congress, 1869-71; with Forbes Fibre Co. of Jersey City; an organizer Jersey City Bd. Trade, 1888, 1st pres.; moved to Tenafly, 1892, to Englewood, N.J. later. Died Norwich, Windsor County, Vt., Mar. 30, 1896; buried Fairview Cemetery.

CLEVELAND, Richard Jeffry, mcht. navigator; b. Salem, Mass., Dec. 19, 1773; s. Stephen and Margaret (Jeffry) C.; m. Dorcas Hiller, Oct. 12, 1804, 1 son, Horace W.S. Mcht. capt., traded throughout world, 1797-1821; sailed twice around world while on trading ventures, 1797-1804; made large fortune, lost it through poor investments; U.S. vice consul at Havana, Cuba, 1828-33. Author: Narrative of Voyages and Commercial Enterprises, 2 vols., 1842. Died Danvers, Mass., Nov. 23, 1860.

CLEVENGER, Shobal Vail, sculptor; b. nr. Middletown, O., Oct. 22, 1812; s. Samuel C. Clevenger; m. Elizabeth Wright, Aug. 5, 1833, 3 children including Shobal Vail. Busts represented in collections Pa. Acad. Fine Arts, N.Y. Hist. Soc., Boston Athenaeum, Met. Mus., N.Y.; his bust of Webster on 15c stamp; completed "North American Indian" (called 1st distinctive Am. sculpture), Rome, Italy. Died on Atlantic Ocean, 1 day from Gibralter, Sept. 23, 1843.

CLEVER, Charles P., congressman; b. Cologne, Prussia Feb. 23, 1830; attended Gymnasium of Cologne, U. Bonn; studied law. Came to U.S.,

1848; settled in Santa Fe, N.M., 1850; in trade, 1855-62, apptd. U.S. marshal for N.M., 1857; an owner Santa Fe Weekly Gazette, paper published in English and Spanish, 1858; admitted to bar, 1861, practiced in Santa Fe; apptd. U.S. marshal and census enumerator, 1861; served as adjutant on staff Gen. Canby at Battle of Valverde in Civil War; adjutant gen. of N.M., 1861-65, 67, 68; atty. gen., 1862-67; mem. U.S. Congress (Democrat, contested election) from N.M. Territory, 40th Congress, Sept. 2, 1867-Feb. 20, 1869; apptd. an incorporator Centennial Expn., 1869; a commr. to revise and codify N.M. laws; practiced law in Tome, Valencia County, N.M. until 1874. Died Tome, July 8, 1874; buried Nat. Cemetery, Santa Fe.

CLIFFORD, John Henry, railroad pres., gov. Mass.; b. Providence, R.I., Jan. 16, 1809; s. Benjamin and Achsah (Wade) C.; grad. Brown U., 1827, LL.D. (hon.) 1849; LL.D. (hon.), Harvard, 1853, Amherst Coll. 1853; m. Sarah Allen, Jan. 16, 1832, 2 children. Admitted to Mass. bar, 1830; rep. Mass. Gen. Ct., 1835; dist. atty. for So. Mass., 1839-49; atty. gen. Mass., 1849, 54-58; gov. Mass., 1853; U.S. Commn. on Fisheries under arbitration treaty with Gt. Britain; pres. Boston & Providence R.R.; mem. Mass. Senate, 1862; mem. bd. overseers Harvard, 1854-59, 65-68, pres. bd., 1869-74; trustee Peabody Edn. Fund; mem. Am. Acad. Arts and Scis., Mass. Hist. Soc. Died New Bedford, Mass., Jan. 2, 1876.

CLIFFORD, Nathan, asso. justice U.S. Supreme Ct.; b. Rumney, N.H., Aug. 18, 1803; s. Nathaniel and Lydia (Simpson) C.; ed. Hampton Coll.; m. Hannah Ayer, after 1827. Admitted to bar, 1827; mem. Me. Legislature, 1830-34, speaker-1832-34; del. to Nat. Democratic Conv., 1832; atty. gen. Me., 1834-38; mem. U.S. Ho. of Reps. (Democrat) from Me., 26th-37th congresses, 1839-43; atty. gen. U.S. under Pres. James Polk, 1846-48; on peace mission to Mexico in connection with end of Mexican War, 1848-49, asso. justice U.S. Supreme Ct., 1858-81; headed spl. electoral commn. investigation of Hayes-Tilden election, 1877. Died Cornish, Me., July 25, 1881; buried Evergreen Cemetery, Portland, Me.

CLIFFTON, William, poet; b. Phila., 1772. Devoted life to literary and social activities due to delicate health; wrote many satiric polit. poems, also lyric poems; mem. Anchor Club, Phila. (advocated war with France); poems include Rhapsody on the Times, The Chimeriad, Soul of Columbia, Il Penseroso, The Flight of Fancy; collections of poetry include: The Group, 1796; Poems, Chiefly Occasional, 1800. Died Dec. 1799.

CLIFTON, Josephine, actress; b. N.Y.C., 1813; d. Mr. Miller; m. Robert Place, July 1846. Made debut as Belvedera in Venice Preserved, N.Y.C., 1831; toured U.S., 1833-34; went to London, Eng., 1834, 1st Am. actress to appear there in starring role; appeared in Bianca Visconti (tragedy written for her by Nathaniel P. Willis), N.Y.C., 1837; made few appearances after 1838. Died New Orleans, Nov. 21, 1847; buried Phila.

CLINCH, Charles Powell, playwright; b. N.Y.C., Oct. 20, 1797; s. James Clinch. Mem. N.Y. State Legislature, 1835; lost fortune in ins. business, 1835; insp., dep. collector, asst. collector N.Y. Custom House, 1838-76; mem. literary circle of Joseph R. Drake and Fitz-Green Halleck (known as Knickerbockers); wrote literary criticism for N.Y.C. papers; wrote and delivered public addresses; author plays The Spy, 1822, The Expelled Collegians, The First of May. Died N.Y.C., Dec. 16, 1880.

CLINCH, Duncan Lamont, congressman, army officer; b. Ard-Lamont, Edgecombe County, N.C., Apr. 6, 1787. First lt. 3d Infantry, U.S. Army, 1808, promoted capt., 1810; apptd. lt. col. 43d Regt., U.S. Infantry, 1813. apptd. col. 8th Regt., 1819; brig. gen., 1829; in command at Battle of Ouithlacoohee against Seminole Indians, 1835; resigned, 1836; settled on plantation nr. St. Marys, Ga.; mem. U.S. Ho. of Reps. (Whig, filled vacancy) from Ga., 28th Congress, Feb. 15, 1844-45. Died Macon, Ga., Nov. 27, 1849; buried Bonaventure Cemetery, Savannah, Ga.

CLINGAN, William, Continental congressman; probably born nr. Wagontown, West Colen Twp., Chester County, Pa. Justice of peace, 1757-86; mem. Continental Congress from Pa., 1777-79; one of 1st signers Articles of Confederation, 1778; pres. county cts., 1780-86. Died May 9, 1790; buried Upper Octorara Burial Grounds, Chester County.

CLINGMAN, Thomas Lanier, senator, army officer; b. Huntsville, N.C., July 27, 1812; s. Jacob and Jane (Poindexter) C.; grad. U. N.C., 1832. Admitted to N.C. bar, 1834; mem. N.C. Legislautre, 1835, N.C. Senate, 1840; mem. U.S. Ho. of Reps (Whig) from N.C., 28th Congress, 1843-45, 30th-35th congresses, 1847-58; determined highest peak in Smoky Mountains (Clingman's Peak), 1858; mem. U.S. Senate (Democrat) from N.C., Dec. 6, 1858-1861; del. Confederate States Conv., Montgomery, Ala., 1861; commd. col. 25th N.C. Volunteers, 1861; brig. gen. Confederate Army, 1862; del. Nat. Dem. Conv., N.Y.C., 1868; mem. N.C. Constl. Conv., 1875; made many contbns. to geology and mineralogy. Author: Follies of the Positive Philosophers, 1878. Died Morganton, N.C., Nov. 3, 1897; buried Riverside Cemetery, Asheville, N.C.

CLINTON, DeWitt, gov. N.Y.; b. Little Britain, N.Y., Mar. 2, 1769; s. James and Mary (DeWitt) C.; A.B., Columbia, 1786; m. Maria Franklin, Feb. 13, 1796 (dec. 1818), 10 children; m. 2d, Catherine Jones, May 8, 1819. Admitted to N.Y. bar, 1789; mem. N.Y. State Assembly, 1797, N.Y. State Senate, 1798-1802, 06-11; mem. U.S. Senate from N.Y., 1802-03; became leader Republican Party in N.Y. State, circa 1803; mayor of N.Y.C., 1803-07, 09-10, 11-15; mem. Council of Appointment, 1801; prin. organizer, 1st pres. Public Sch. Soc. of N.Y.C., 1805; chief patron N.Y. Orphan Asylum, N.Y. City Hosp.; canal commr., 1810-24, chief supporter of Erie Canal (finished during his governorship, 1825); lt. gov. N.Y., 1811-13, gov., 1817-21, 25-28; Peace Party candidate for U.S. Pres., 1812; a founder N.Y. Hist. Soc., elected pres., 1817; a founder Lit. and Philos. Soc., 1816; 2d pres. Am. Acad. Art; v.p. Am. Bible Soc., Edn. Soc. of Presbyn. Ch.; naturalist, discovered a native Am. wheat, also a new fish (Salma Otsego). Author: Introductory Discourse (concerning state of scientific knowledge in Am.), 1814; Memoir on the Antiquities of the Western Parts of the State of New York, 1820; also numerous scientific papers. Died Albany, N.Y., Feb. 11, 1828.

CLINTON, George, naval officer, colonial gov.; b. Eng., 1686; s. Francis and Susan (Penniston) C.; m. Anne Carle, 2 children including Henry. Joined Brit. Navy, 1708, commd. capt., 1716, commodore, comdr.-in-chief Mediterranean squadron, 1737, rear adm., 1743; gov. Newfoundland, 1732-41; gov. N.Y., 1743-53, allowed colonial assembly to take excessive control over civil affairs, contrary to his instructions; mem. Brit. Ho. of Commons from Saltash, 1754-60; returned to Eng., 1754, became adm. White Fleet, Brit. Navy. Died July 10, 1761.

CLINTON, George, vice pres. U.S., gov. N.Y.; b. Little Britain, Ulster (now Orange County), N.Y., July 26, 1739; s. Charles and Elizabeth (Denniston) C.; m. Cornelia Tappan, Feb 7, 1770, 6 children. Del. N.Y. Provincial Assembly, 1768; del. Continental Congress, 1775-76; commd. brig. gen. Continental Army, 1777; 1st gov. N.Y., 1777-95; 1801-04; pres. N.Y. State Conv. to ratify U.S. Constn., 1788, opposed ratification; his opposition resulted in writing of the Federalist (by Madison, Hamilton and Jay) to destroy his influence; vice pres. U.S. under Jefferson and Madison, 1805-13. Died Washington, D.C., Apr. 20, 1812; buried Congressional Cemetery, Washington.

CLINTON, George, congressman; b. N.Y.C., June 6, 1771; s. George Clinton. Del. N.Y. State Constl. Conv., 1801; mem. N.Y. State Assembly, 1804, 05; mem. U.S. Ho. of Reps. (Democrat, filled vacancy) from N.Y., 8th-10th congresses, Feb. 14, 1805-09. Died N.Y.C., Sept. 6, 1809.

CLINTON, Sir Henry, Brit. army officer; b. Colony of Newfoundland (father was colonial gov.), circa 1738; s. Adm. The Honorable George Clinton; m. Harriett Carter, 1767, 2 sons, Sir Henry, Sir William Henry. Lt. in Coldstream Guards, 1751; promoted capt. Grenadier Guards, 1758, col., 1762, maj. gen., 1772; sent to duty in Am. 1775; made 2d in command to Sir William Howe, 1776; took part in battles of Bunker Hill and L.I.; promoted lt. gen., 1776; created knight of Bath, 1777; made comdr.-in-chief in N.Am., 1778; mgr. Theater Royal, N.Y.C.. 1778-80, specialized in performances Richard Sheridan's The Rivals and School for Scandal; in command at time when Cornwallis surrendered at Yorktown, Va.; resigned his N.Am. command to Sir Guy Carleton and returned to Eng., 1781. Author: Narrative (defense of his mil. policy during Revolutionary War), 1783. Died Gibraltar (while serving as gov.), Dec. 23, 1795.

CLINTON, James, army officer; b. Orange County, N.Y., Aug. 9, 1733; s. Col. Charles and Elizabeth (Denniston); m. Mary DeWitt, 1764, 1 son, DeWitt; m. 2d, Mrs. Mary Gray. Commd. capt. N.Y. Militia, 1756; lt. col., 1775; elected dep. Provincial Congress N.Y., May 1775; commd. col. N.Y. State Militia, 1775; commd. brig. gen. Continental Army, 1776, in command of No. Dept., Albany, N.Y., 1780; N.Y. State commr. to adjust boundary line between Pa. and N.Y., 1785; mem. N.Y. State Conv. ratified U.S. Constn. Died Orange County, Dec. 22, 1812; buried Little Britain, Orange County.

CLINTON, James Graham, congressman, lawyer; b. Little Britain, Orange County, N.Y., Jan. 2, 1804; attended common schs., Newburgh (N.Y.) Acad.; studied law. Admitted to bar, 1823, practiced in Newburgh; master in chancery Oran County; judge Orange County Ct. Common Plea dir. Newburgh Whaling Co., Del. & Hudson R. project; col. N.Y. State Militia; mem. U.S. H of Reps. (Democrat) from N.Y., 27th-28th co gresses, 1841-45. Died N.Y.C., May 28, 184 buried family cemetery Little Britain.

CLONNEY, James Goodwyn, artist; b. Liverpo Eng., Jan. 28, 1812. Came to Am. as youth, esta lished himself as miniature painter, N.Y.C., 183 specialized in genre painting, after 1841; lived New Rochelle, N.Y., 1842-52, Cooperstown, N.Y after 1852; exhibited frequently at N.A.D., Apol Assn., Am. Art-Union, Pa. Acad.; asso. N.A. Died Binghamton, N.Y., Oct. 7, 1867.

CLOPTON, David, congressman, jurist; b. Pu nam County, Ga., Sept. 29, 1820; s. Dr. Alford a Sarah (Kendrick) C.; grad. Randolph-Macon Col 1840; m. Martha E. Ligon; m. 2d, Mrs. Mary Char bers; m. 3d, Mrs. Virginia Clay. Admitted to G bar, 1841; mem. U.S. Ho. of Reps. from Ala., 36 Congress, 1859-61; rep. from Ala. to 1st, 2d Co federate congresses, 1862-65; mem., speaker Al Ho. of Reps., 1878-79; apptd. asso. justice Al Supreme Ct. 1884-92. Died Montgomery, Ala., Fe 5, 1892.

CLOPTON, John, congressman; b. St. Peter Parish, New Kent County, Va., Feb. 7, 1756; William Clopton; grad. U. Pa., 1776; m. Sara Bacon. Mem. Va. Ho. of Dels., 1789-91; mem. U.S Ho. of Reps. from Va., 4th-5th, 7th-14th congresses 1795-99, 1801-16; mem. Privy Council Va., 179 Died at his plantation nr. Turnstall, New Ke County, Va., Sept. 11, 1816; buried on his planta tion.

CLORIVIÈRE, Joseph-Pierre Picot ed Limoëla de, see de Clorivière.

CLOUD, Noah Bartlett, planter; b. Edgefield, S.C Jan. 26, 1809; s. Noah and Margaret (Sweringen C.; studied medicine, Phila.; m. Mary Barton, 183 Owner cotton plantation, La Place, Macon Count Ala., 1846-75; mem. Chunnenugga Hort. Soc. Macon County; helped establish and edit America Cotton Planter (agrl. monthly), 1853-57, combine with Soil of the South, 1857, editor, until 1861 surgeon Confederate Army, 1861-65; supt. publ instrn. in Ala., 1868-70. Died Montgomery, Ala. Nov. 5, 1875.

CLOVER, Lewis P., Jr., artist; b. N.Y.C., Feb 20, 1819; Successful portrait, landscape and gen painter, N.Y.C. and Balt., during 1840's; exhibite at N.A.D., Am. Acad., Apollo Assn., Artists' Fun Soc., Boston Athenaeum; elected asso. N.A.D. 1840; ordained to ministry Episcopal Ch., 185 minister, Lexington, Va., Springfield, Ill.; painte portrait of Lincoln, 1860. Died N.Y.C., Nov. 9 1896.

CLOWNEY, William Kennedy, congressma lawyer; b. Union County, S.C., Mar. 21, 1797 grad. S.C. Coll., Columbia, 1818; studied la Tchr. Unionville Public Schs., U. S.C.; mem. S. Ho. of Reps.; admitted to bar; practiced in Unio commr. in equity of S.C., 1830-33; mem. U.S. H of Reps. (as Nullifier) from S.C., 23d, (as Stat Rights Democrat) 25th congresses, 1833-35, 37 39; mem. S.C. Senate, 1840; lt. gov. S.C. Di Union, Mar. 12, 1851; buried Fairforest Cemeter Union County.

CLYMAN, James, trapper, guide; b. Fauqui County, Va., Feb. 1, 1792; m. Hannah Mecombs Aug. 22, 1849. Served as mounted ranger in War o 1812; mem. William Ashley's 2d expdn. up Missou River, 1823, reached Green River, 1824, one of 1s white men to cross South Pass in Wyoming; wit 3 companions circumnavigated Gt. Salt Lake, 182 served in Black Hawk War, 1832-34; joined wago train from Independence (Mo.) to Oregon, 1844 went to Cal., 1847; guided wagon train from In dependence to Cal., where he settled, 1848; mad total of 5 trips to Cal., kept diary of trip east wit Hastings, 1846; renowned as mountaineer. Die Napa, Cal., Dec. 27, 1881.

CLYMER, George, mcht., Continental congress man; b. Phila., Mar. 16, 1739; s. Christopher an Deborah (Fitzwater) C.; m. Elizabeth Meredith 1765, 1 child. Established shipping firm Meredith & Clymer, Phila.; mem. Pa. Com. of Safety; del from Pa. to Continental Congress, 1776-78, 80-83 served on bds. war, treasury; a signer Declaratio of Independence, July 20, 1776, del. U.S. Constl Conv., 1787, signer U.S. Constn., 1788; mem. Pa Conv. which ratified U.S. Constn.; mem. U.S. Ho of Reps., 1st Congress, 1789-91; 1st pres. Phila Bank, Acad. Fine Arts; v.p. Phila. Agrl. Soc., 1805 13. Died Morrisville, Bucks County, Pa., Jan. 23 1813; buried Friends Graveyard, Trenton, N.J.

CLYMER, George E., inventor; b. Bucks County Pa., 1754; m. Margaret Backhouse, 3 daus. In vented The Columbian (an improved printing press 1st outstanding Am. invention in printing field) recipient gold medal for invention from King o Netherlands. Died London, Eng., Aug. 27, 1834.

CLYMER, Hiester, congressman; b. nr. Morgan-›wn, Caernarvon Twp., Berks County, Pa., Nov. , 1827; grad. Princeton, 1847; studied law. Ad-itted to Berks County bar, 1849; practiced in eading and Berks County until 1851; moved to ottsville, Schuylkill County, 1851, returned to eading, 1856; Berks County rep. Pa. Bd. Reve-ıe Commrs., 1860; del. nat. Democratic convs., harleston, Balt., 1860, N.Y., 1868; mem. Pa. enate, 1860-66, resigned; unsuccessful Dem. andidate for gov. Pa., 1866; mem. Pa. Bd. Chari-ies, 1870; pres. Pa. Dem. Conv., Reading, 1872; em. U.S. Ho. of Reps. (Dem.) from Pa., 43d-6th congresses, 1873-81; v.p. Union Trust Co., hila.; pres. Clymer Iron Co.; dir. Reading Fire ıs. Co.; trustee Charles Evans Cemetery. Died eading, June 12, 1884; buried Charles Evans emetery.

COAN, Titus, missionary; b. Killingworth, Conn., eb. 1, 1801; s. Gaylord and Tamza (Nettleton) .; attended Auburn Theol. Sem., 1831-33; m. idelia Church, Nov. 3, 1834; m. 2d, Lydia Bing-ım, 1873. Licensed as minister by Cayuga County resbytery, 1833; ordained missionary for Am. Bd. r Fgn. Missions, 1833; missionary to Patagonia, 833-34, Hilo, H.I., 1835-82; del. Hawaiian Mis-onary Soc., sent to Marquesas Islands to establish issions, 1860, 67. Author: Adventures in Pata-›nia, 1880; Life in Hawaii, 1882. Died Dec. 1, 882.

COATES, Samuel, mcht., philanthropist; b. hila., Aug. 24, 1748; s. Samuel and Mary (Lang-ale) C.; m. Lydia Saunders, 1775; m. 2d, Amy íornor, 1791. Mcht., 1st as partner firm Reynell Coates, later alone, 1760-1830; mgr. Pa. Hosp., 785-1826, pres. bd. dirs., 1812; helped organize, ıstain Overseers of Pub. Schs. (managed Quaker chs. of Phila.), 1786-1823; dir. 1st Bank of U.S., 800-12. Died Phila., June 4, 1830.

COBB, Clinton Levering, congressman, lawyer; Elizabeth City, Pasquotank County, N.C., Aug. 5, 1842; grad. U. N.C.; studied law. Admitted › bar, 1867; practiced in Elizabeth City; became ıcht.; mem. U.S. Ho. of Reps. (Republican) from .C., 41st-43d congresses, 1869-75. Died Elizabeth ity, Apr. 30, 1879; buried Episcopal Cemetery.

COBB, David, army officer, congressman, jurist; Attleborough, Mass., Sept. 14, 1748; Thomas and Lydia (Leonard) C.; grad. Harvard, 766. del. to Mass. Provincial Congress, 1775; ›mmd. lt. col. Mass. Militia, 1777, brevetted ·ig. gen., 1783, commd. maj. gen., 1786; judge ristol County (Mass.) Ct. of Common Pleas, 1784 ›6; speaker Mass. Ho.of Reps., 1789-93; mem. .S. Ho. of Reps. (Federalist), from Mass. 3d ongress, 1793-95; pres. Mass. Senate, 1802-05; . gov. Mass., 1809; chief justice Hancock County, Mass.), 1812; mem. Mass. Bd. of Mil. Defense, 812. Died Taunton, Mass., Apr. 17, 1830; buried lain Cemetery, Taunton.

COBB, Elijah, sea capt.; b. Harwich (now Brew-ter), Mass., July 4, 1768; s. Scottow and Mary Freeman) C.; m. Mary Cobb, 1793, 4 children. Vent to sea as cabin boy, 1783; became capt. ship ·ading with Cadiz, 1794; captured by French, re-ased after audience with Robespierre; began nuggling rum to Ireland; did not sail during War of 812; traded with Europe and Africa, 1814-20; etired from sea, 1820; town clk. of Brewster; mem. Iass. Senate, Mass. Ho. of Reps.; insp. gen. of Iass. Died Nov. 2, 1848.

COBB, George Thomas, congressman, business-ıan; b. Morristown, N.J., Oct. 13, 1813; had ttle schooling. Clk. in store, Denville, N.J. t early age; worked in iron works owned by Capt. Villiam Scott, Powerville, Boonton, N.J., trans-erred to N.Y.C.; engaged in fgn. trade; made for-une, retired from business, returned to N.J.; mem. .S. Ho. of Reps. (Democrat) from N.J., 37th ongress, 1861-63; affiliated with Republican arty, 1863; Rep. mem. N.J. Senate, 1865, 68: ıayor Morristown, 1865-69; trustee Drew Theol. em. 1868-70; pres. Sabbath Sch. Assn of Morris ounty. Killed in accident on Chesapeake & Ohio R.R., at Jerrys Run, nr. White Sulphur Springs, 'a., Aug. 12, 1870; buried Evergreen Cemetery, Iorristown.

COBB, Howell. congressman, farmer; b. Gran-ille County, N.C., Aug. 3, 1772. Moved to Ga., ettled nr. Louisville, Jefferson County, became armer; served as ensign and lt. 2d Sub Legion U.S. Army, capt. in Artillerists and Engrs., 1793-1806, esigned; mem. U.S. Ho. of Reps. from Ga. 10th-2th congresses, 1807-12, resigned. Died on his lantation Cherry Hill, nr. Louisville, Jefferson County, May 26, 1818; buried family cemetery on is estate.

COBB, Howell, senator, gov. Ga., b. Jefferson County, Ga., Sept. 7, 1815; s. John and Sarah Rootes) C..; grad. U. Ga., 1834; m. Mary Ann amar, 1834. Admitted to Ga. bar, 1836; state olicitor-gen. Western Circuit of Ga., 1837; mem. J.S. Ho. of Reps. from Ga., 28th-31st, 34th congresses, 1843-51, 55-57, parliamentary leader Democratic Party in Ho., 1848, speaker, 1849-51; gov. Ga., 1851-53; U.S. sec. of treasury under Buchanan, 1857-60; demanded Ga.'s immediate secession upon Lincoln's election; chmn. Montgomery Conv. which formed Confederacy, 1861; maj. gen. Confederate Army in command Ga. dist., 1863. Died N.Y.C., Oct. 9, 1868; buried Oconee Cemetery, Athens Ga.

COBB, Jonathan Holmes, lawyer, silk mfg.; b. Sharon, Mass., July 8, 1799; s. Jonathan and Sibbel (Holmes) C.; grad. Harvard, 1817; m. Sophia Doggett, Sept. 26, 1822. Admitted to Mass. bar, 1820; founder Dedham Inst. for Savs., treas., 1831-34; register of probate Norfolk County (Mass.), 1833-79; town clk. Dedham (Mass.), 1845-75; attempted to grow silk; opened silk factory, 1837. Author: A Manual Containing Information Respecting the Growth of the Mulberry Tree with Suitable Directions for the Culture of Silk, 1831. Died Mar. 12, 1882.

COBB, Lyman, ednl. writer; b. Lenox, Mass., Sept. 18, 1800; s. Elijah William and Sally (Whitney) C.; m. Harriet Chambers, 1822. Wrote widely-used textbooks and articles on philosophy of edn., including: Critical Review of Noah Webster's Spelling Book; The Juvenile Reader, Number 1, 1830; North American Reader, 1835; The New Sequel, or Fourth Reading Book, 1843; The Evil Tendencies of Corporal Punishment, 1847. Died Colesburg, Pa., Oct. 26, 1864; buried Colesburg.

COBB, Stephen Alonzo, congressman; b. Madison, Somerset County, Me., June 17, 1833; attended Beloit Coll. 2 years; grad. Brown U., 1858. Settled in Wyandotte, Kan., 1859, practiced law; entered Union Army, 1862; became capt. and commissary sgt. of Volunteers, 1864; brevetted maj., 1865; mayor Wyandotte, 1862, 68; mem. Kan. Senate, 1862, 69, 70; mem. Kan. Ho. of Reps., 1872, speaker; mem. U.S. Ho. of Reps. (Republican) from Kan., 43d Congress, 1873-75. Died Wyandotte (now part of Kansas City), Aug. 24, 1878; buried Oak Grove Cemetery, Kansas City, Kan.

COBB, Sylvanus, clergyman; b. Norway, Me., July 17, 1798; s. Ebenezer and Elizabeth (Cobb) C. (parents cousins); m. Eunice Hale Waite, Sept. 10, 1822, 9 children including Sylvanus. Ordained to ministry Universalist Ch., 1821; pastor in Winthrop and Waterville (Me.), 1821-28, Malden, Mass., 1828-39; one of 1st Universalist ministers in Me.; founder, editor The Christian Freeman and Family Visitor, Waltham, Mass., 1839-62; preached at chs. in Waltham and Boston; served in both Mass. and Me. legislatures. Author: Compend of Divinity, 1846; New Testament of Our Lord and Savior Jesus Christ with Explanatory Notes and Practical Observations, 1864. Died Boston, Oct. 31, 1866.

COBB, Sylvanus, journalist, author; b. Waterville, Me., June 5, 1823; s. Sylvanus and Eunice (Waite) C.; m. Jane Head, June 29, 1845. Served with U.S. Navy, publisher, editor Rechabite, Norway, Me., 1846-50; staff mem. Flag of Our Union and Pictorial Drawing Room, 1850-56; wrote for N.Y. Ledger, 1856-87; wrote hundreds of short stories, novelettes, pictorial essays, based much of his writings on material gathered while at sea. Died Hyde Park, Mass., July 20, 1887.

COBB, Thomas Reed, congressman, lawyer; b. Springville, Lawrence County, Ind., July 2, 1828; attended Ind. U.; studied law. Admitted to bar, 1851, practiced in Bedford, Ind.; commd. maj. Ind. Militia, 1852; moved to Vincennes, Ind., 1867; mem. Ind. Senate, 1858-66; Democratic presdl. elector, 1868; pres. Ind. Dem. Conv., 1876; del. Nat. Dem. Conv., St. Louis, 1876; mem. U.S. Ho. of Reps. (Democrat) from Ind., 45th-49th congresses, 1877-87; became farmer; retired from public life. Died Vincennes, June 23, 1892; buried Old Vincennes Cemetery.

COBB, Thomas Reed Rootes, army officer, Confederate Legislator; b. Jefferson County, Ga., Apr. 10, 1823; s. John H. and Sarah (Rootes) C.; grad. U. Ga., 1841; m. Marion Lumpkin, at least 3 children, Callendar, Belle, Marion. Admitted to Ga. bar, 1842; advocated Ga.'s immediate secession upon Lincoln's election to Presidency; mem. Ga. Secession Conv.; Ga. del. to Montgomery Conv. of Seceding states, 1861; prin. contributor to the Confederate Constn., mem. Confederate Provisional Congress, 1861; commd. brig. gen. Confederate Army, participated in Battle of Fredericksburg (Va.). Author: Digest of the Laws of Georgia, 1851; Inquiry into the Law of Negro Slavery in the U.S., 1858; Historial Sketch of Slavery, 1859. Killed in Battle of Fredricksburg, Dec. 13, 1862.

COBB, Thomas Willis, senator, congressman; b. Columbia County, Ga., 1784; had prep. studies; studied law. Admitted to bar, practiced in Lexington, Ga.; moved to Greensboro, Greene County, Ga.; mem. U.S. Ho. of Reps. from Ga., 15th-16th, 18th congresses, 1817-21, 23-Dec. 6, 1824 (resigned); mem. U.S. Senate (filled vacancy) from Ga., Dec. 6, 1824-28 (resigned); judge Ga. Superior Ct. Died Greensboro, Feb. 1, 1830.

COBB, Williamson Robert Winfield, congressman; b. Rhea County, Tenn., June 8, 1807; had limited edn. Clock peddler for short time; became mcht., Bellefontaine, Madison County, Ala.; mem. Ala. Ho. of Reps., 1845, 46; lived on plantation, Madison County, became cotton raiser; mem. U.S. Ho. of Reps. (Democrat) from Ala., 30th-36th congresses, 1847-Jan. 30, 1861 (withdrew); elected to Confederate Ho. of Reps., 1863, did not take his seat when new Congress met, his loyalty suspected, expelled by unanimous vote. Killed accidentally by his own pistol while putting up fence on his plantation, Bellefontaine, Nov. 1, 1864; buried on Cobb family estate, Madison County.

COBBETT, William, journalist; b. Farnham, Surrey, Eng., Mar. 9, 1763; s. George and Ann (Vincent) C.; m. Ann Reid. Came to U.S. as polit. refugee from England, 1792; settled at Phila. as English tchr.; became involved in polit. disputes, became one of founders of party journalism in America; defended Federalist viewpoint and engaged in pamphlet "wars" with Republicans; wrote under pseudonym Peter Porcupine; his writings were sarcastic and vicious, included personal attacks on many famous men; published Porcupine's Gazette and Daily Advertiser, 1797-98; attacked Dr. Benjamin Rush for his extensive and near-disastrous practice of bleeding patients during yellow fever epidemic of 1797, sued for libel by Rush, lost case; published Rush-Light, N.Y.C., 1798-1800; allowed to return to Eng., 1800, forced to flee back to U.S., 1817; settled on farm, L.I., N.Y.; returned to Eng., 1819. Author: Observations on the Emigration of Dr. Joseph Priestly, 1794; A Bone To Gnaw for the Democrats, 1795; A Little Plain English Addressed to the People of the United States, 1795; The Life and Adventures of Peter Porcupine, 1796; A Journal of a Year's Residence in the United States, part I, 1818, parts II and III, 1819. Died Eng., June 18, 1835.

COBERO, Pedro Rodriguez, Spanish gov.; b. Calatayvd, Spain, 1645. First to tour world from West to East and in part by land, 1670-79, published short account of voyage; apptd. Spanish gov. N.M., 1692, took office, 1697, gov. until 1703; made treaty with Acoma and Zuni Indians. Died Mexico, 1704.

COBURN, Abner, gov. Me.; b. Canaan, Me., Mar. 22, 1803; s. Eleazar and Mary (Weston) C. Reorganized his father's lumber firm A. & P. Coburn; mem. Me. Legislature, 1838, 40, 44; mem. Gov.'s Council Me., 1855, 57; a founder, mem. exec. council Me. Republican Party; gov. Me., 1863; presdl. elector, 1860, 84; pres. Me. Central R.R., 1870; pres. bd. mgrs. Me. State Coll.; trustee Colby U., 1845-85, pres. bd., 1874-85; left bequests of over $1,000,000 to various instns. Died Skowhegan, Me., Jan. 4, 1885.

COBURN, Stephen, congressman, lawyer; b. Bloomfield (now Skowhegan), Me., Nov. 11, 1817; attended Waterville (Me.) and China acads.; grad. Waterville (now Colby) Coll., 1839; attended Harvard Law Sch. Tchr. plantation sch., Tarboro, N.C., 1839-40; prin. Bloomfield Acad., 1840-44; admitted to bar, 1845, practiced in Skowhegan; mem. Me. Bd. Edn., 1849, 50; del. several Me. Republican convs.; mem. U.S. Ho. of Reps. (Rep., filled vacancy) from Me., 36th Congress, Jan. 2-Mar. 3, 1861; mem. Washington (D.C.) Peace Conv., 1861; postmaster Skowhegan, 1868-77. Drowned in Kennebec River, Skowhegan, July 4, 1882; buried South Cemetery, Skowhegan.

COCHISE, Indian chief. Apache chief of Chiricahua band in Ariz., from before 1860 until 1874; noted for his integrity, courage, mil. skill; made pact with T. J. Jeffords (who had contract to carry mail from Silver City to Yuma), 1860; signed peace treaty with Gen. O. O. Howard, rep. of Pres. Grant, 1872 (treaty was held until after Cochise's death). Died 1874.

COCHRAN, James, congressman, farmer; b. Person County, N.C., circa 1767; attended public schs. Became farmer, nr. Helena, N.C.; mem. N.C. Ho. of Commons, 1802-06: mem. N.C. Senate, 1807; mem. U.S. Ho. of Reps. (Democrat) from N.C., 11th-12th congresses, 1809-13. Died Roxboro, Person County, Apr. 7, 1813; buried burial ground at Leas Chapel, nr. Roxboro.

COCHRAN, James, congressman; b. Albany, N.Y., Feb. 11, 1769; grad. Columbia Coll., N.Y.C., 1788; studied law. Admitted to bar; commd. maj. by Pres. John Adams in U.S. Army; regent U. State of N.Y., 1796-1820; mem. U.S. Ho. of Reps. from N.Y., 5th Congress, 1797-99; mem. N.Y. State Senate, 1814-18; moved to Oswego, N.Y., 1826; postmaster Oswego, 1841-45; editor Oswego Democratic Gazette several years.

Died Oswego, Nov. 7, 1848; buried Riverside Cemetery.

COCHRAN, John, surgeon; b. Sudsbury, Pa., Sept. 1, 1730; s. James and Isabella; m. Mrs. Gertrude Schuyler, Dec. 4, 1760. A founder N.J. Med. Soc., pres., 1769; apptd. physician surgeon gen. Middle Dept. Continental Army, by George Washington, 1777, later chief physician and loans for N.Y., 1785. Died Palatine, N.Y., Apr. 6, 1807.

COCHRANE, Clark Betton, congressman, lawyer; b. New Boston, N.H., May 31, 1815; grad. Union Coll., Schenectady, N.Y., 1841; studied law. Admitted to bar, 1841; practiced in Amsterdam, Montgomery County, N.Y., 1841-51, Schenectady, 1851-55, Albany, N.Y., 1855-67; elected Democrat mem. N.Y. State Assembly, 1844, 66; trustee Union Coll., 1853-67; mem. U.S. Ho. of Reps. (Republican) from N.Y., 35th-36th congresses, 1857-61; del. Nat. Rep. Conv., Balt., 1864. Died Albany, Mar. 5, 1867; buried Green Hill Cemetery, Amsterdam.

COCHRANE, John congressman; b. Palatine, N.Y., Aug. 27, 1813; s. Walter Livingson and Cornelia (Smith) C.; grad. Hamilton Coll., 1831. Admitted to N.Y. bar, 1834; surveyor Port of N.Y., 1852; mem. U.S. Ho. of Reps. from N.Y., 35th-36th congresses, 1857-61; commd. brig. gen. U.S. Volunteers, 1862, participated in battles of Fair Oaks, Malvern Hill, Antietam, Williamsport, Fredericksburg, under Gen. Couch; atty. gen. N.Y., 1863-65; nominated vice pres. U.S. on ticket with John C. Fremont for Pres., 1864; U.S. collector Internal Revenue, 1869; mem. Soc. of Cincinnati, pres. until 1898; pres. Common Council, N.Y.C., 1872; chmn. N.Y. Delegation to Liberal Republican Nat. Conv., 1872. Died N.Y.C., Feb. 7, 1898; buried Rural Cemetery, Albany, N.Y.

COCHRANE, John C., architect; b. Hillsboro, N.H., Nov. 7, 1835; studied architecture and engring. in New Eng. Went to Chgo., 1854, unsuccessful in finding work; moved to Davenport, Ia., designed St. Luke's Ch. and other bldgs.; returned to Chgo. after Civil War; designed churches and homes, Chgo.; awarded 1st prize in design competition for Ill. State Capitol, 1867; formed partnership with Alfred H. Piquenard in firm Cochrance & Piquenard, 1867, firm engaged in constrn. of Capitol; architect Cook County Hosp., Michael Reese Hosp., Rush Med. Coll., Jefferson Park Presbyn. Ch., 1st Presbyn. Ch., all Chgo. Died Dec. 11, 1887.

COCKE, John, congressman; b. Brunswick, Nottoway County, Va., 1772; s. William Cocke; attended public schs. in Tenn.; studied law. Admitted to bar, 1793; practiced in Hawkins County; mem. Tenn. Ho. of Reps., 1796-97, 1807, 09, 12, 37, speaker, 1812, 37; mem. Tenn. Senate, 1799-1801, 43; served as maj. gen. Tenn. Volunteers in Creek War, 1813; served as col. regt. Tenn. riflemen under Gen. Andrew Jackson at New Orleans; mem. U.S. Ho. of Reps. from Tenn., 16th-19th congresses, 1819-27; became farmer; founded school for deaf-mutes, Knoxville, Tenn. Died Rutledge, Tenn., Feb. 16, 1854; buried Methodist Ch. Cemetery.

COCKE, John Hartwell, planter, army officer; b. Surry County, Va., Sept. 19, 1780; s. John Hartwell and Elizabeth (Kennon) C.; grad. Coll. William and Mary, 1798; m. Ann Barraud, Dec. 25, 1802, several children including Philip St. George. Promoted new agrl. methods, founded agrl. socs., promoted steam navigation, various other pub. improvements; commd. brig. gen., commander Va. Militia guarding Richmond in War of 1812, 1814-15; served on Am. Bd. Commrs. for Fgn. Missions; sr. v.p. Am. Colonization Soc. from its orgn. to his death, 1819-66; elected pres. U.S. Temperance Soc., 1836; a founder U. Va., mem. bd. visitors, 1819-52. Died Fluvanna County, Va., July 1, 1866.

COCKE, Philip St. George, planter, army officer; b. Fluvanna County, Va., Apr. 17, 1809; s. John Hartwell and Ann (Barraud) C.; grad. U.S. Mil. Acad., 1832; m. Sally Bowdoin, June 4, 1834; 11 children. Owner 7 plantations in Va. and Miss.; served as 2d lt., adj., 2d U.S. Arty., 1832-33; pres. Va. Agrl. Soc., 1853-56; served 9 years on bd. Va. Mil. Inst., founded there 1st sch. of sci. agr. in Va.; commd. brig. gen. Confederate Army, 1861, assigned command of mil. dist. along Potomac. Author: Plantation and Farm Instruction, 1852; Address to the Virginia Farmer's Assembly, 1856. Died Powhatan County, Va., Dec. 26, 1861.

COCKE, William, army officer, senator; b. Amelia County, Va., 1748; s. Abraham Cocke; m. Sarah Maclin; m. 2d, Mrs. Kissiah Sims. Fought in Revolutionary War; mem. Va. Assembly, 1777, N.C. Legislature, 1778; leader attempt to establish separate state of Franklin, 1784-88, brig. gen. Militia of State of Franklin, 1784-88; mem. Tenn. Constl. Conv., 1796; mem. U.S. Senate from Tenn., 1796-97, 1799-1805; judge 1st Tenn. Circuit Ct., 1809-12, impeached, removed from judgeship, 1812; fought in wars against Seminole and Creek Indians, 1812-15; Indian agt. Chickasaw Nation, 1814-15; mem. Miss. Legislature, 1822; a founder U. Tenn. Died Columbus, Miss., Aug. 22, 1828; buried Columbus.

COCKE, William Michael, congressman; b. Rutledge, Grainger County, Tenn., July 16, 1815; grad. East Tenn. Coll., Knoxville; studied law. Admitted to bar, practiced in Rutledge and Nashville, Tenn.; mem. Tenn. Ho. of Reps.; mem. U.S. Ho. of Reps. (Democrat) from Tenn., 29th-30th congresses, 1845-49; held many local and state offices. Died Nashville, Feb. 6, 1896; buried Mt. Olivet Cemetery.

COCKERILL, John Albert, journalist; b. Adams County, O., Dec. 4, 1845; s. Joseph Randolph and Ruth (Eylar) C. Bought, edited True Telegraph, Hamilton, O., 1865; editor Dayton Daily Ledger, 1868; mng. editor Cincinnati Enquirer, 1872, corr. in Russo-Turkish War, 1876; helped establish Washington Post, 1878; mng. editor Balt. Gazette, 1878; editor-in-chief N.Y. World, 1883-91; assigned to Far East as spl. corr. in China and Japan for N.Y. Herald, 1895; editor N.Y. Advertiser, 1891; decorated Third Order of Sacred Treasure by Emperor of Japan. Died Cairo, Egypt, Apr. 10, 1896.

COCKERILL, Joseph Randolph, congressman, lawyer, b. Loudoun County, Va., Jan. 2, 1818; attended public schs.; studied law. Moved to Scott Twp., Adams County, O., 1837, settled in Youngstown; taught sch.; county surveyor, 1840; admitted to bar, 1851, practiced in West Union, O.; clk. Ct. Common Pleas; mem. Ohio Ho. of Reps., 1853, 54, 68-71; mem. U.S. Ho. of Reps. (Democrat) from Ohio, 35th Congress, 1857-59; served as col. 70th Ohio Volunteer Inf. in Union Army during Civil War; brevetted brig. gen. of Volunteers, 1865. Died West Union, Oct. 23, 1875; buried West Union Cemetery.

CODDINGTON, William, colonial gov.; b. Boston, Eng., 1601; m. Mary Mosely; m. 2d, Mary Coddington; m. 3d, Anne Brinley; 13 children. Came to Am. as asst. dir. Mass. Bay Co., 1630; built 1st brick house in Boston; mem. com. on mil. affairs, 1635; treas. Mass. Bay Co., 1634-36; dep. of Boston, 1636-37; banished to Aquidneck Island (now R.I.) for Antinomian beliefs, 1638; founded Newport (R.I.), 1639; Newport united with Portsmouth (controlled by religious influences of Anne Hutchinson and Samuel Gorton) to form Colony of Aquidneck, 1640; Aquidneck was made part of Roger Williams' Colony of Providence Plantations by order of Parliament, 1644, this patent set aside, 1651, reinstated 1652; gov. Aquidneck Island (now R.I., 1640-56, title was meaningless in latter years; owned large estate and mcht. house, Newport; chief magistrate of R.I. and Providence Plantations, 1674, 75, 78. Died Nov. 1, 1678.

CODMAN, Charles, artist; b. Portland, Me., 1800; possibly son of William P. and Susan C. Employed as limner, Portland, 1823; recognized as landscape painter, after 1828; exhibited at Boston Athenaum, N.A.D., Apollo Gallery. Died probably Portland, 1842.

CODMAN, John, sea capt.; b. Dorchester, Mass., Oct. 16, 1814; s. John and Mary (Wheelwright) C.; attended Amherst Coll., 1832-34; m. Anna Day, Nov. 3, 1847. Went to sea on clipper trader, 1834; made trading trips to China, East Indies; transported troops for Turkey during Crimean War; capt. Quaker City transporting goods for Union during Civil War; owned ranch, Ida. Author: Sailors' Life and Sailors' Yarns, 1847; Ten Months in Brazil, 1867; The Round Trip, 1879; Winter Sketches from the Saddle, 1888; An American Transport in the Crimean War, 1896. Died Boston, Apr. 6, 1900.

COE, George Simmons, banker; b. Newport, R.I., Mar. 27, 1817; s. Adam Simmons and Ann (Pease) C.; m. Almira Stanley, June 15, 1843; m. 2d, Mary E. Bigelow. Vice pres. Am. Exchange Bank, 1854, pres., 1860-94; trustee or dir. several N.Y. corps.; helped originate clearing house system and certificates for banks; active mem. N.Y.C. C. of C., 37 years; pres. Am. Bankers Assn., 1881; mem. Presbyn. Bd. Fgn. Missions. Died Englewood, N.J., May 3, 1896.

COE, Israel, brass mfr.; b. Goshen, Conn., Dec. 14, 1794; s. Abijah and Sibyl (Baldwin) C.; m. Nancy Wetmore, Sept. 12, 1817, 7 children; m. 2d, Huldah DeForest, Oct. 16, 1839. Moved to Waterbury, Conn., 1821; active in local politics; mem. Conn. Ho. of Reps. from Waterbury, 1824, 25; directed Wolcottville Brass Co. (1st in country to make brass-ware by "battery" process), 1834-45; mem. Conn. Senate from Wolcottville dist., 1843; justice of peace Bloomfield (N.J.) commr. of deeds Essex County (N.J.); returned to Waterbury, 1887. Died Waterbury, Dec. 18, 1891.

COFER, Martin Hardin, army officer, jurist; b. Elizabethtown, Ky., Apr. 1, 1832; s. Thomas and Mary (Hardin) C.; m. Mary E. Bush, 1853. Admitted to Ill. bar, 1856; editor Elizabethtown Democra lt. col. 6th Ky. Inf., Confederate Army, 1861-6 made provost marshal Confederate Army of Tenn 1864; judge Circuit Ct., Ky., 1870-74; asso. justi Ky. Ct. Appeals, 1874-81, chief justice, 1881. A thor: A Supplemental Digest of Decisions of t Court of Appeals of Kentucky, 1853-67, publish 1867 (standard authority on judicial procedure Ky.). Died Frankfort, Mar. 22, 1881.

COFFEE, William J., sculptor, painter; b. cir 1774. Worked as sculptor, Derby and London, Eng 1795-1816, exhibited at Royal Acad.; came to Am 1816, settled in N.Y.C.; executed bust of Hugh W liamson (now at N.Y. Hist. Soc., 1816; exhibit 2 terra cotta animals, several paintings of anima and dead game at Am. Acad., 1817; executed bus of Thomas Jefferson, his dau. and granddau., 181 lived in Albany, N.Y., 1827-45, executed seve bas-reliefs for City Hall; exhibited at N.A.D., 183 Apollo Gallery, 1839. Died probably Albany, cir 1846.

COFFIN, Charles Dustin, congressman, lawy b. Newburyport, Mass., Sept. 9, 1805; attend public schs.; studied law. Admitted to bar, 182 practiced in New Lisbon, Columbiana County, O clk. Columbiana County cts., 1828; mem. U. Ho. of Reps. (Whig, filled vacancy) from Oh 25th Congress, Dec. 20, 1837-39; became banke pres. Columbiana Bank of New Lisbon; moved Cincinnati, 1842, practiced law; elected jud Superior Ct., 1845, served 7 years, apptd. to sar position by Gov. Denison, 1861. Died Cincinna Feb. 28, 1880; buried Spring Grove Cemete

COFFIN, Sir Isaac, naval officer; b. Bosto May 16, 1759; s. Nathaniel and Elizabeth (Barne C.; m. Elizabeth Greenly, Mar. 1811. Entered Roy Navy, 1773, lt., 1778, capt. ship Shrewsbury, 178 served under Lord Rodney in victory over Count Grasse, 1782; apptd. rear adm., 1804; creat baronet, 1804; commd. vice adm., 1808, full adm 1814; mem. Brit. Parliament, 1818; philanthrop efforts include founding Coffin Sch., Nantucke Mass., 1827. Died Cheltenham, Eng., July 23, 183

COFFIN, James Henry, mathematician, meteo ologist; b. Williamsburg, Mass., Sept. 6, 1806; Matthew and Betsy (Allen) C.; grad. Amherst Col 1828, M.A. (hon.), 1831; LL.D. (hon.), Rutger 1859; m. Aurelia Jennings, 1833; m. 2d, Ab Young, 1851. Opened pvt. sch. for boys, Greenfie Mass., 1829, added manual labor dept., 1830 (1 sch. of its kind in U.S., was beginning of Fellenbe Manual Labor Instn.); tutor Williams Coll., 184 43; prof. mathematics and natural philosophy L fayette Coll., 1846-73; collaborated in work Smithsonian Instn., published results of meteoro studies under auspices Smithsonian Instn. as: Win of the Northern Hemisphere, 1853; Psychrometric Tables, 1856; The Orbit and Phenomena of a M teoric Fire Ball, 1869; The Winds of the Globe, the Laws of the Atmospheric Circulation over t Surface of the Earth, published posthumously, 187 author textbooks Solar and Lunar Eclipses, 184 Analytical Geometry, 1849; Conic Sections, 185 Died Easton, Pa., Feb. 6, 1873.

COFFIN, John, Loyalist; b. Boston, 1756; Nathaniel and Elizabeth (Barnes) C.; m. An Mathews, 1 dau., Judith. Apptd. ensign Brit. Arm by Gen. Gage for gallantry at Battle of Bunk Hill, 1775; organized and commanded Orange Gran ers in battles of L.I. and Germantown; with N. Volunteers (Loyalist) at battles of San Luci Bryars Creek, 1778, 79, Camden, 1780, Hampto Hobkerks Hill, Eutaw Springs, 1781; commd. col 1797, maj. gen., 1803, gen., 1819; mem. Canadi Assembly; chief magistrate Kings County (N.B Can.); mem. Kings County Council. Died Kin County, June 12, 1838.

COFFIN, John Huntington Crane, mathematicia b. Wiscasset, Me., Sept. 14, 1815; grad. Bowdoi Coll., 1834, LL.D. (hon.), 1884; married, 5 chi dren. Prof. mathematics on various vessels, U. Navy, 1836-43; with U.S. Naval Observatory, Wash ington, D.C., 1843-53; prof. mathematics, astronom and navigation U.S. Naval Acad., 1853-66; chief e itor Nautical Almanac, 1866-77; mem. Am. Acad Scis., Am. Philos. Soc., Nat. Acad. Scis; wrote var ous math. papers. Died Washington, Jan. 8, 1890.

COFFIN, Levi, abolitionist; b. New Garden Cit N.C., Oct. 28, 1789; s. Levi and Prudence (Wi liams) C.; m. Catharine Stanton White, Oct. 2 1824, 4 sons, 2 daus. Operated store, Newpor Ind., 1826-47; abolitionist, home became a pri depot on Underground R.R., aiding runaway slav to escape to Can.; mem. Com. on Concerns of Pe ple of Color, in charg of ednl. activities; active temperance movement; opened wholesale free-lab goods store (sponsored by Quaker Conv. in Ind.) Cincinnati, 1847; organizer English Freedmen's A Soc. in Eng., 1864; del. Internat. Anti-Slave Conv., Paris, France, 1867. Died Avondale, Cinci nati, Sept. 16, 1877; buried Spring Grove Cemeter Cincinnati.

COFFIN, Peleg, Jr., congressman; b. Nan-ucket, Mass., Nov. 3, 1756; completed acad. tudies. Pres., New Eng. Marine Ins. Co.; mem. Mass. Ho. of Reps., 1783, 84, 89; mem. Mass. enate, 1785, 86, 90-92, 95, 96, 1802; mem. .S. Ho. of Reps. from Mass., 3d Congress, 1793-5; treas. Mass., 1797-1802. Died Boston, Mar. 6, 805; probably buried Friends Burial Grounds; einterred Mt. Auburn Cemetery, 1833.

COGDELL, John Stevens, lawyer, artist; b. harleston, S.C., Sept. 19, 1778; s. George and lizabeth (Stevens) C.; ed. Coll. Charleston; m. Maria Gilchrist, 1806. Admitted to S.C. bar, 1799; mem. S.C. Ho. of Reps., 1810, 14, 16, 18; comp-roller-gen. S.C., 1818; pres. Bank of S.C., 1832-7; acquired interest in painting while traveling in taly as young man, painted numerous portraits; lso sculptor, did several busts of friends and noted ersons. Died Feb. 25, 1847.

COGGESHALL, George, sea captain; b. Milford, onn., Nov. 2, 1784; s. William and Eunice (Mal-ett) C.; m. Sarah; m. 2d, Elizabeth. Received 1st ommand, 1809, sea capt., nearly 26 years; capt. rivateers David Porter and Lev, during War of 1812. uthor: Voyages to Various Parts of the World, 851; History of the American Privateers and Let-ers-of-Marque, 1856. Died Milford, Aug. 6, 1861.

COGGESHALL, William Turner, journalist, dip-omat; b. Lewistown, Pa., Sept. 6, 1824; s. William . and Eliza (Grotz) C.; m. Mary Carpenter, Oct. 8, 1845, 1 dau., Jessie. Editor, The Genius of the Vest, 1854-56; librarian Ohio State Library, Co-umbus, 1856-62; editor Ohio Edn. Monthly, 1858-9; editor Ohio State Jour., Columbus; owner, editor pringfield (O.) Republic, 1862-65; U.S. minister o Ecuador, 1866-67. Author: Signs of the Times, 851; Easy Warren and His Contemporaries, 1854; oets and Poetry of the West, 1860; Stories of rontier Adventure, 1863; The Journeys of A. Lin-oln as President Elect and as President Martyred also known as The Lincoln Memorial), 1865. Died r. Quito, Ecuador, Aug. 2, 1867; buried Columbus, .

COGHLAN, John Maxwell, congressman, lawyer; . Louisville, Ky., Dec. 8, 1835; studied law. Ad-itted to bar, practiced in Suisun City, Cal.; mem. al. Assembly, 1865, 66; mem. U.S. Ho. of Reps. Republican) from Cal., 42d Congress, 1871-73; racticed law in Oakland, Cal. until 1879. Died akland, Mar. 26, 1879; buried Mountain View emetery.

COGSWELL, Joseph Green, tchr., librarian; b. pswich, Mass., Sept. 27, 1786; s. Francis and nstis (Manning) C.; grad. Harvard, 1806, LL.D., 863; LL.D., Trinity Coll., 1842; m. Mary Gilman, pr. 17, 1812. Admitted to Mass. bar, 1812; at U. ottingen (Germany), (one of 1st group Am. cholars at a German univ.), 1817; librarian, also rof. mineralogy and chemistry Harvard, 1820-23; founder Round Hill Sch., Northampton, Mass., 823; edited N.Y. Review, 1837; organizer, supt. Astor Public Library, N.Y.C., 1848-61. Died Cam-ridge, Mass., Nov. 26, 1871; buried Ipswich.

COGSWELL, William, congressman, lawyer; b. Bradford, Mass., Aug. 23, 1838; attended Phillips cad., Andover, Mass., also Dartmouth; grad. ane Law Sch., Harvard, 1860. Admitted to bar, racticed in Salem, Mass.; served in Union Army n Civil War; commd. capt. 2d Regt., Mass. Volun-eer Inf., 1861, lt. col., 1862, col., 1863, bre-etted brig. gen. of Volunteers, 1864; mayor alem, 1867-69, 73, 74; mem. Mass. Ho. of Reps., 870, 71, 81-83; mem. Mass. Senate, 1885, 86; el. Nat. Republican Conv., Mpls., 1892; mem. .S. Ho. of Reps. (Rep.) from Mass., 50th-54th ongresses, 1887-95. Died Washington, D.C., May 2, 1895; buried Harmony Grove Cemetery, Salem.

COGSWELL, William F., artist; b. Sandusky, N.Y., uly 15, 1819. Worked in color factory, Buffalo, .Y.; worked as profl. artist, N.Y.C., during 1840's; xhibited at N.A.D., Am. Art-Union; went to Cal., 849, returned to N.Y.C.; painted portrait of Lin-oln (now in White House); moved to Cal., 1873. Died South Pasadena, Cal., Dec. 24, 1903.

COIT, Henry Augustus, clergyman; b. Wilming-on, Del., Jan. 20, 1830; s. Joseph Howland and Harriet Jane (Hard) C.; ed. U. Pa.; D.D. (hon.), rinity Coll., 1863; LL.D. (hon.), Yale; m. Mary Bowman Wheeler, Mar. 27, 1856. Ordained deacon Episcopal Ch., Lancaster, Pa., 1854; ordained priest, hila., 1854; 1st rector St. Paul's Sch., Concord, .H., 1856-95. Died Concord, Feb. 5, 1895, buried Concord.

COIT, Joshua, congressman; b. New London, Conn., Oct. 7, 1758; grad. Harvard, 1776; studied law. Admitted to bar, practiced in New London, 1779; mem. Conn. Ho. of Reps., 1784, 85, 89, 90, 92, 93, clk. several terms, speaker 1793; mem. U.S. Ho. of Reps. (Federalist) from Conn., 3d-5th congresses, 1793- Sept. 5, 1798. Died New London, Sept. 5, 1798; buried Cedar Grove Cemetery.

COIT, Thomas Winthrop, clergyman, educator; b. New London, Conn., June 28, 1803; s. Thomas and Mary Wanton (Saltonstall) C.; grad. Yale, 1821; attended Andover Theol. Sem., Princeton Sem.; m. Eleanor (Forrester) Carlile, June 28, 1828. Ordained deacon Episcopal Ch., New Briton, Conn., 1826, priest, Salem, Mass., 1827; pres. Transylvania U., Lexington, Ky., 1834-37; prof. ch. history Trinity Coll., Hartford, Conn., 1849-54; rector St. Paul's Ch., Troy, N.Y., 1854-72; Berkeley Divinity Sch., Middletown, Conn., 1872-85. Author: Remarks on Norton's Statement of Reasons, 1833; Paragraph Bible, 1834; Townsend's Bible, 2 vols., 1837-38; Puritanism, 1845. Died Middletown, June 21, 1885.

COKE, Richard, senator, gov. Tex., b. Williamsburg, Va., Mar. 13, 1829; s. John and Eliza (Hawkins) C.; grad. Coll. William and Mary, 1849; m. Mary Horne, 1852, 4 children. Admitted to Tex. bar, 1850; judge 19th Jud. Dist. Tex., 1865; asso. justice Tex. Supreme Ct., 1866-67; gov. Tex. (Democrat), 1874-76 (his adminstn. marked end of reconstrn.); mem. U.S. Senate from Tex., 1876-94. Died Waco, Tex., May 14, 1897; buried Oakwood Cemetery, Waco.

COKE, Richard, Jr., congressman; b. Williamsburg, Va., Nov. 16, 1790; grad. Coll. William and Mary; studied law. Admitted to bar, practiced in Gloucester County, Va.; mem. U.S. Ho. of Reps. (Jacksonian Democrat) from Va., 21st-22d congresses, 1829-33. Died on his plantation Abingdon Place, Gloucester County, Mar. 31, 1851; buried family burying ground on his estate.

COKE, Thomas, clergyman; b. Brecon, Wales, Sept. 20, 1747; s. Bartholomew and Anne (Phillips) C.; grad. Jesus Coll., Oxford, Eng., 1768. Became follower of John Wesley, 1776; came to U.S. as 1st supt. Methodist Ch. in Am., 1784; brought Wesley's instructions for orgn. of Am. Ch.; made preaching tour of Eastern seaboard, 1784; ordained Francis Asbury gen. supt. of Am. Ch. at conf. of Meth. ministers, Balt., 1784; made 9 trips to U.S., 1784-1803; founded Cokesbury Coll., Abingdon, Md., 1787; attempted to unite Meth. and Episcopal churches in Eng. and Am.; co-founder Meth. Missionary Com. in Eng., 1790, pres., 1804-14. Died May 3, 1814.

COLBURN, Dana Pond, educator; b. West Dedham, Mass., Sept. 29, 1823; s. Isaac and Mary Colburn; grad. Bridgewater (Mass.) Normal Sch., 1843. Asst. prin. Bridgewater Normal Sch., 1848-52; tchr. pvt. sch. (became R.I. Normal Sch.), Providence, 1852-54, prin., 1854-59. Author many textbooks emphasizing learning by rational rather than memorization methods, including: First Steps in Numbers, 1847; Decimal System, Interest and Discount Arithmetic and the Applications, 1855; Common School Arithmetic, 1858; Child's Book of Arithmetic, 1859; Intellectual Arithmetic, 1859. Died R.I., Dec. 15, 1859.

COLBURN, Warren, educator; b. Dedham, Mass., Mar. 1, 1793; s. Richard and Joanna (Eaton) C.; grad. Harvard, 1820; m. Temperance Horton, Aug. 28, 1823, 7 children. Conducted pvt. sch., Boston, 1820-23; supt. cotton mill of Merrimac Mfg. Co., Lowell, Mass., 1824-33; mem. 1st sch. bd of Lowell, 1826-29; co-founder Am. Inst. of Instrn., Boston; mem. Am. Acad. Arts and Scis.; mem. examining com. for mathematics Harvard. Author: First Lessons in Arithmetic, on the Plan of Pestalozzi, with Some Improvements, 1821-26; An Introduction to Algebra upon the Inductive Method of Instruction, 1825; Lessons in Reading and Grammar, 1830-33. Died Sept. 13, 1833.

COLBURN, Zerah, prodigy, clergyman; b. Cabot, Vt., Sept. 1, 1804; s. Abiah and Elizabeth (Hall C.; m. Mary Hoyt, Jan. 13, 1829, 6 children. As child was capable of solving any arithmetical problem mentally; taken to London by his father, 1812, earned small fortune by publicly displaying his ability; toured England and France, 1812-16; returned to U.S., 1824; itinerant Methodist preacher, 1826-35; prof. langs. Norwich (Vt.) U., 1835-39. Author: A Memoir of Zerah Colburn Written by Himself, 1833. Died Norwich, Mar. 2, 1839.

COLBY, Gardner, mcht., ry. exec., philanthropist; b. Bowdoinham, Me., Sept. 3, 1810; s. Josiah C. and Sarah (Davidson) C.; m. Mary Lou Roberts, 1836, 6 children including Charles Lewis, Rev. Henry Francis. Laid foundation for great wealth with Civil War contracts for manufacture of woolens; pres. Wis. Central R.R.; treas. Baptist Edn. Soc.; treas. Newton Theol. Inst., 1844-68; trustee Brown U.; Waterville Lit. Coll. renamed Colby Coll. in his honor, 1867; most conspicuous benefactions were to Brown U., Bapt. Missionary Union, Colby Coll., Newton Theol. Inst. Died Newton Centre, Mass., Apr. 2, 1879.

COLBY, Luther, spiritualist journalist; b. Amesbury, Mass., Oct. 12, 1814; s. William and Mary C. Employed by Boston Daily Post, 1836-56, rose from journeyman printer to night editor; became friend and follower of spiritualists such as Charles Crowell, Mrs. J. H. Conant and William Berry; with Berry established Banner of Light (weekly spiritualist paper), 1857, editor, 1857-94; believed that his paper would revolutionize world, spreading spiritual truth by printing spirit messages received by spiritualists such as Berry. Died Oct. 7, 1894.

COLCOCK, William Ferguson, congressman, lawyer; b. Beaufort S.C., Nov. 5, 1804; attended Hulburt's Sch., Charleston, S.C.; grad. S.C. Coll. (now U. S.C.), 1823; studied law. Admitted to bar, 1825, practiced in Coosawhatchie, Jasper County, S.C.; became planter; mem. S.C. Ho. of Reps., 1831-48, speaker, 1841-48; mem. U.S. Ho. of Reps. (Democrat) from S.C., 31st-32d congresses, 1849-53; regent Smithsonian Instn., 1850-53; collector Port of Charleston, 1853-65, under both U.S. and Confederate States govts.; del. Nat. Dem. Conv., Charleston, 1860. Died McPhersonville, Hampton County, S.C., June 13, 1889; buried Stoney Creek Cemetery, Beaufort County, S.C.

COLDEN, Cadwallader, Loyalist, colonial gov., scientist; b. Ireland, Feb. 17, 1688; s. Rev. Alexander Colden; A.B., U. Edinburgh, 1705; m. Alice Christie, Nov. 11, 1715, children—Jane, Elizabeth, David. Came to Am., 1710, N.Y.C., 1718; surveyor gen. N.Y., 1720; apptd. to N.Y. Gov.'s Council, 1721; lt. gov. colony N.Y., 1761-76; supported Britain in Revolutionary War; a noted botanist of his day, master of Linnaean system of plant classification; signed original charters for Marine Soc. of N.Y., N.Y. State C. of C.; 1st advocate of cooling regimen in treating fevers; proposed cure for cancer. Author: History of the Five Indian Nations Depending upon New York, 1727; An Explication of the First Causes of Action in Matter, and, of the Cause of Gravitation, 1745; Principles of Action in Matter, 1752. Died L.I., N.Y., Sept. 28, 1776.

COLDEN, Cadwallader David, lawyer, mayor N.Y.C.; b. Spring Hill, L.I., N.Y., Apr. 4, 1769; s. David and Ann (Willett) C.; m. Maria Provost, 1793. Admitted to N.Y. bar, 1791; dist. atty. N.Y.C., 1798, 1810; served as col. in War of 1812; commd. maj. gen. N.Y. Militia; mayor N.Y.C., 1818-20; mem. U.S. Ho. of Reps. from N.Y., 17th Congress, 1821-23; mem. N.Y. State Senate, 1825-27. Author: Life of Robert Fulton, 1817; Vindication of the Steamboat Rights Granted by the State of New York, 1819; Memoir of the Celebration of the Completion of the New York Canals, 1825. Died Jersey City, N.J., Feb. 7, 1834.

COLDEN, Jane, botanist; b. N.Y., Mar. 27, 1724; d. Cadwallader and Alice (Christie) Colden; m. Dr. William Farquhar, Mar. 12, 1759, 1 child. First woman in the New World to be distinguished as a botanist; author botannical publs. Died Mar. 10, 1766.

COLE, Joseph Foxcroft, painter; b. Jay, Me., Nov. 9, 1837; s. Samuel and Selinda (Allen) C.; m. Irma de Palgrom. Apprentice with Winslow Homer at Bufford Lithograph; went to Paris, France, 1860, exhibited Paris Salon of 1866, 73, 74, 75, Internat. Exposition of 1867; mem. Soc. Am. Artists; best known works: Coast of Normandy, The Aberjond, both in Winchester (Mass.) Library. Died May 2, 1892; buried Wildwood Cemetery, Winchester.

COLE, Thomas, painter; b. Bolton-le-Moor, Eng., Feb. 1, 1801; s. James and Mary Cole; m. Maria Bartow, Nov. 22, 1836. Worked with father in oil-cloth and wallpaper mfg. bus., 1819-24; went to N.Y.C., 1825, to Europe, 1829; a founder Hudson River sch. of painting, one of 1st painters to concentrate on Am. landscapes; exhibited at N.Y. Hist. Soc. Museum; prin. works include: The Course of Empire (5 paintings), Voyage of Life, Sicilian Landscape (1842), Mount Etna, The White Mountains, Expulsion from Paradise, Angels Appearing to the Shepherds, Dreams of Arcadia, Departure, View on the Thames, Cross in the Wilderness, L'Allegro, Il Penseroso, Mountain Ford, Vale of Segesta, Chocorua Peak, Catskill Creek. Died Catskill, N.Y., Feb. 11, 1848.

COLE, William Hinson, congressman; b. Balt., Jan. 11, 1837; attended pvt. sch.; studied medicine and law; grad. U. Louisville, 1860. Admitted to bar, practiced in Balt., 1857; moved to Kansas City, Kan., practiced law; mem. Kan. Territorial Ho. of Reps.; enlisted in Confederate Army, apptd. surgeon Bartow's 8th Ga. Regt.; served in Battle of Gettysburg, took charge of wounded in Longstreet's Corps; prisoner in Ft. McHenry, Balt., 6 months; returned to South, surgeon on staff Gen. Bradley Johnson of Md. until end of war; returned to Balt.; apptd. dep. register of Balt., 1870; chief clk. 1st br. Balt. Council; reading clk. Md. Ho. of Dels., 1874-78; reporter Balt. Evening Commercial, later propr.; later connected with Balt. Gazette and its successor The Day, until 1885; mem. U.S. Ho. of Reps. (Democrat) from Md., 49th Congress, 1885-86. Died Washington, D.C., July 8, 1886; buried Bonnie Brae Cemetery, Balt.

COLEMAN, Lyman, educator; b. Middlefield, Mass., June 14, 1796; s. Dr. William and Achsah (Lyman) C.; grad. Yale, 1817; M.A. (hon.), Middlebury Coll., 1833; LL.D. (hon.), Coll. N.J., 1847; m. Maria Flynt, Sept. 21, 1826; m. 2d, Marion B. Philleo, Oct. 1873. Prin., Latin Grammar Sch., Hartford, 1817-20; ordained to ministry Congl. Ch., Belchertown, Mass., 1825; prin. English dept. Phillips Acad., Andover, Mass., 1837-42; instr. classics Amherst Coll., 1843-46; prof. German, Coll. of N.J. (now Princeton), 1847-49; became prof. classics Lafayette Coll., Easton, Pa., 1861. Author: The Apostolic and Primitive Church, 1841; Historical Geography of the Bible, 1850; Ancient Christianity Exemplified, 1852; Prelacy and Ritualism, 1869; Lyman Genealogy. Died Easton, Mar. 16, 1882.

COLEMAN, Nicholas Daniel, congressman, lawyer; b. Cynthiana, Ky., Apr. 22, 1800; grad. Transylvania Coll., Lexington, Ky.; studied law. Admitted to bar, practiced law; mem. Ky. Ho. of Reps., 1824, 25; mem. U.S. Ho. of Reps. (Jacksonian Democrat) from Ky., 21st Congress, 1829-31; moved to Vicksburg, Miss., practiced law; postmaster Vicksburg, 1841-44. Died Vicksburg, May 11, 1874; buried Cedar Hill Cemetery.

COLEMAN, William, journalist; b. Boston, Feb. 14, 1766; m. Carrie M. Page, Aug. 1852, 2 sons. In law partnership with Aaron Burr, N.Y.C., 1797; mem. Mass. Ho. of Reps. 1795, 96; editor, owner Evening Post (leading Federalist jour.), N.Y.C., 1800-29. Died N.Y.C., July 14, 1829.

COLEMAN, William Tell, mcht., vigilante; b. Cynthiana, Ky., Feb. 29, 1824; s. Napoleon B. Coleman; attended St. Louis U., 1842-44; m. Carrie Page, Aug. 1852, 2 children. Went to Sutter's Mill (Cal.) 1849, became dealer in cattle and real estate; established mdse. firm William T. Coleman & Co., San Francisco, 1850; mem. exec. com. San Francisco Com. of Vigilance, 1851, also mem. Com. of Thirteen; established branch of firm, in N.Y.C., 1852-55; returned to San Francisco, 1856, decided that conditions warranted revival of Com. of Vigilance, pres. exec. com. hanged 4 criminals and chased many others out of city; organized Com. of Safety to preserve order during anti-Chinese riots of 1877; his business failed, 1886. Died San Francisco, Nov. 22, 1893.

COLES, Edward, gov. Ill.; b. Albemarle County, Va., Dec. 15, 1786; s. Col. John and Rebecca (Tucker) C.; attended Coll. William and Mary; m. Sally Roberts, Nov. 28, 1833, 1 son, Edward. Pvt. sec. to Pres. Madison, 1809-15; sent by Madison on diplomatic mission to Russia, 1816; an organizer 1st state agrl. soc. of Ill., 1819; gov. Ill., 1822-26; Coles County (Ill.) named in his honor. Died Phila., July 7, 1868.

COLES, Isaac, congressman; b. Richmond, Va., Mar. 2, 1747; attended Coll. William and Mary; at least 1 son, Walter. Served as col. of militia in Revolutionary War; mem. Va. Ho. of Dels., 1783-87; mem. Va. Conv. to ratify U.S. Constn., 1788; during polit. career lived on plantation on Staunton River, Coles Ferry, Halifax County; moved to Pittsylvania County, Va., 1798; mem. U.S. Ho. of Reps. from Va., 1st, 3d-4th congresses, 1789-91, 93-97. Died on his plantation Coles Hill, nr. Chatham, Va., June 3, 1813; buried family cemetery on his plantation.

COLES, Walter, congressman, farmer; b. Coles Ferry, Halifax County, Va., Dec. 8, 1790; s. Isaac Coles; attended Hampden-Sydney Coll., Washington Coll. (now Washington and Lee U.), Lexington, Va. Served as 2d lt. 2d Regt. of Light Dragoons in War of 1812; promoted to capt. of riflemen on Northern frontier, discharged, 1815; became farmer in Va.; justice of peace; mem. Va. Ho. of Dels., 1817-18, 33-34; mem. U.S. Ho. of Reps. (Democrat) from Va., 24th-28th congresses, 1835-45. Died Coles Hill, nr. Chatham, Va., Nov. 9, 1857; buried family burying ground at Coles Hill.

COLFAX, Schuyler, vice pres. U.S.; b. N.Y.C., Mar. 23, 1823; s. Schuyler and Hannah (Stryker) C.; m .Evelyn Clark, Oct. 10, 1844; m. 2d Ellen W. Wade, Nov. 18, 1868. Dep. auditor South Bend (Ind.), 1841-49; asst. enrolling clk. Indiana Senate, 1842-44; corr. Indiana State Journal; converted South Bend Free Press into one of Ind.'s leading Whig publs. under name St. Joseph Valley Register (part owner); mem. Ind. Constl. Conv. of 1850; mem. U.S. Ho. of Reps. (Republican) from Ind., 34th-40th congresses, Dec. 1855-69, speaker, 1863-69, chmn. com. on post offices and post rds., 1859-61; vice pres. U.S. under Grant, 1869-73, involved in Credit Mobilier scandals which ruined polit. career. Died Mankato, Minn., Jan. 13, 1885; buried South Bend.

COLGATE, William, soap mfr.; b. Kent, Eng., Jan. 25, 1783; s. Robert and Sarah (Bowles) C.; m. Mary Gilbert, 1811; 3 children—Samuel, Robert, James Boorman. Employed with Slidell & Co., largest tallow-chandlery in N.Y.C., 1804, became bus. mgr.; started own establishment mfg. laundry and toilet soap (direct predecessor of Colgate & Co.), 1806; gave at least a tenth of his net yearly earnings to charity; liberal supporter Madison U. (renamed Colgate U. in his honor); an organizer Am. Bible Soc., Am. and Fgn. Bible Soc. (treas. 13 years). Died N.Y.C., Mar. 25, 1857.

COLHOUN, John Ewing, senator; b. Staunton, Augusta County, Va., 1750; grad. Princeton, 1774; studied law. Mem. S.C. Ho. of Reps., 1778-1800; admitted to bar, 1783, practiced in Charleston, S.C.; returned to Ninety Six Dist., became farmer; elected mem. Privy Council, also commr. confiscated estates, 1785; mem. S.C. Senate, 1801; mem. com. to report modification of judiciary system of U.S.; mem. U.S. Senate (Democrat) from S.C., 1801-02. Died Pendleton, S.C., Oct. 26, 1802; buried Old Stone Churchyard.

COLLAMER, Jacob, senator, jurist; b. Troy, N.Y., Jan. 8, 1791; s. Samuel and Elizabeth (Van Ornum) C.; grad. U. Vt., 1810; m. Mary Stone, July 15, 1817. Admitted to Vt. bar, 1813; mem. Vt. Legislature from Royalton, 1821-22, 27-28; asst. judge Vt. Supreme Ct., 1833-42; mem. U.S. Ho. of Reps. (Whig) from Vt., 28th-30th congresses, 1843-49; postmaster gen. U.S. in Pres. Taylor's cabinet, 1849; judge Vt. Circuit Ct., 1850-54; mem. U.S. Senate (Republican) from Vt., 1855-65; pres. Vt. Med. Coll., 1855-62. Died Woodstock, Vt., Nov. 9, 1865; buried River Street Cemetery, Woodstock.

COLLENS, Thomas Wharton, jurist; b. New Orleans, June 23, 1812; s. John Wharton and Marie Louise (de Tabiteau) C.; m. Amenaide Milbrou, 8 children. Admitted to La. bar, 1833; clk., reporter La. Senate, 1834; chief dep. Fed. Circuit Ct., 1836-38; dist. atty. New Orleans, 1840-42; presiding judge City Ct. New Orleans, 1842-46; mem. La. Constl. Conv., 1852; judge 1st Dist. Ct. New Orleans, 1856, 7th Dist. Ct., 1867-73. Author plays: The Martyr Patriots, 1858; Humanics, 1836. Died New Orleans, Nov. 3, 1879.

COLLES, Christopher, engr.; b. Ireland, May 3, 1739; s. Richard and Henrietta (Taylor) C.; m. Anne Keugh, Jan. 14, 1764. Came to Am., 1765; lectr. pneumatics, Phila., 1772, on inland navigation, N.Y.C., 1773; devised plan (not used) for replacing N.Y.C.'s well and spring water system with system of reservoirs and pipes; instr. arty. of Continental Army, 1775-77; designed one of 1st Am. steam engines; suggested system of canals and river improvements to connect Great Lakes with Hudson River planned and surveyed roads between N.Y.C. and Phila.; mfr. small household utensils, N.Y.C., 1796, also traded in Indian goods and furs; built, operated semaphoric telegraph at Castle Clinton (N.Y.) during War of 1812; later employed in customs service, N.Y.C.; supt. Am. Acad. Fine Arts. Author: Syllabus of Lectures on Natural Philosophy, 1773; A Survey of the Roads of the United States of America, 1789; Proposals of a Design for Inland Communication of a New Construction, 1808; Description of the Universal Telegraph, 1813. Died N.Y.C., Oct. 4, 1816.

COLLIER, Daniel Lewis, lawyer; b. Litchfield, Conn., Jan. 19, 1796; s. Thomas Collier; studied law under John C. Wright, Steubenville, O.; m. Hattie Lorrimore, 1823. Admitted to Ohio bar, 1818; practiced law, Steubenville, 1818-57; moved to Phila., 1857; mem. bd. mgrs. Ho. of Refuge, Blind Asylum, Colonization Soc.; v.p. Presbyn. Bd. of Publ.; ruling elder West Spruce St. Presbyn. Ch. (all Phila.). Died Phila., Mar. 30, 1869.

COLLIER, Henry Watkins, gov. Ala., jurist; b. Lunenburg County, Va., Jan. 17, 1801; s. James and Elizabeth (Bouldin) C.; m. Mary Ann Battle, Apr. 26, 1826; children—Mary Williams, Evelyn Hewitt, James Wyatt, Sallie Bouldin. Admitted to Ala. bar, 1822; elected to Ala. Legislature, 1827; dist. judge, 1828-36; asso. justice Ala. Supreme Ct., 1836-37, chief justice, 1837-49; gov. Ala., 1849-53. Died Bailey Springs, Ala., Aug. 28, 1855; buried Tuscaloosa, Ala.

COLLIER, John Allen, congressman; b. Litchfield, Conn., Nov. 13, 1787; attended Yale, 1803; studied law Litchfield Law Sch. Admitted to Troy (N.Y.) bar, 1809; practiced in Binghampton, Broome County, N.Y.; dist. atty. Broome County, 1818-22; mem. U.S. Ho. of Reps. (Clay Democrat) from N.Y., 22d Congress, 1831-33; comptroller State of N.Y., 1841-42; apptd. commr. to revise statutes, 1847; Whig presdl. elector, 1848. Died Binghampton, Mar. 24, 1873; buried Spring Forest Cemetery.

COLLIER, Peter, educator, chemist; b. Chittenango, N.Y., Aug. 17, 1835; s. Jacob and Elizabeth Mary Collier; grad. Yale, 1861, Ph.D. in Chemistry, 1866; M.D. (hon.), U. Vt., 1870; m. Caroline Angell, Oct. 18, 1871; at least 1 child. Prof. chemistry, mineralogy and metallurgy U. Vt., 1867-77, prof. toxicology and chemistry, med. sch., de med. faculty, 1871-74; sec. Vt. Bd. Agr., Min and Manufacture, 1872-76; chief chemist U.S. De Agr., 1877-83; dir. N.Y. Agrl. Expt. Sta., Gene 1887. Author: Sorghum: Its Culture and Manuf ture Economically Considered, and as a Source Sugar Syrup and Fodder, 1884. Died Ann Arb Mich., June 29, 1896.

COLLIN, John Francis, congressman, farmer; Hillsdale, N.Y., Apr. 30, 1802; attended Le Acad. Became farmer; mem. N.Y. State Assemb 1834; supr. of Hillsdale; mem. U.S. Ho. of Re (Democrat) from N.Y., 29th Congress, 1845-4 Died Hillsdale, Sept. 16, 1889; buried Hillsd Rural Cemetery.

COLLINS, Edward Knight, ship owner; b. Tru Mass., Aug. 5, 1802; s. Capt. Israel Gross a Mary Ann (Knight) C.; m. Mary Ann Woodruff; 2d, Mrs. Sarah Browne; 5 children. Organizer U. Mail Steamship Co. (known as Collins Line; larg and best equipped ocean line in U.S.), began se ice when ship Atlantic sailed, 1850, added sh Pacific, Arctic and Baltic, 1850; set speed recor line received large $33,000 subsidy from U.S. Go for each round trip, failed after 2 ships sank, we out of business, by 1858. Died N.Y.C., Jan. 2 1878.

COLLINS, Ela, congressman, lawyer; b. Me den, Conn., Feb. 14, 1786; attended Clinton Aca studied law; at least 1 son, William. Admitted bar, practiced in Lowville, Lewis County, N.Y 1807; mem. N.Y. State Assembly, 1815; di atty. Lewis, Jefferson, St. Lawrence counti 1815-18, Lewis County, 1818-40; del. N. State Constl. Conv., 1821; mem. U.S. Ho. Reps. (Democrat) from N.Y., 18th Congre 1823-25. Died Lowville, Nov. 23, 1848; buri Jackson Street Cemetery.

COLLINS, Francis Dolan, congressman, lawy b. Saugerties, Ulster County, N.Y., Mar. 5, 18 attended St. Joseph's Coll., nr. Montrose, Susqu hanna County, Pa., Wyoming Sem., Kingston, P studied law. Admitted to bar, 1866; practic in Scranton, Pa.; elected dist. atty. Mayor's (Dist., 1869; mem. Pa. Senate, 1872-74; me U.S. Ho. of Reps. (Democrat) from Pa., 44th-45 congresses, 1875-79. Died Scranton, Nov. 2 1891; buried Cathedral Cemetery, Hyde Pa Scranton.

COLLINS, John, gov. R.I., Continental congres man; b. Newport, R.I., Nov. 1, 1717; s. Samu and Elizabeth C.; m. Mary Avery. Mem. Continent Congress from R.I., 1779-81, 82-83; signer Ar cles of Confederation; gov. R.I., 1786-90. Di Newport, Mar. 4, 1795

COLLINS, John Anderson, reformer; b. Manche ter, Vt.; attended Middlebury Coll., Andover Thec Sem. Sent to England to raise funds for Mass. Ant Slavery Soc.; editor Monthly Garland (abolitioni monthly), 1840-41; became Fourierist socialis bought farm nr. Skaneateles, N.Y., led expt. in s cialist living, 1843-46; went to Cal., 1849, attemp ed to make money by mining sands of Klama River, lost capital his backers had raised; lived Cal., 1879. Flourished 1810-79.

COLLINS, Joshua, frontier theater builder, mg Managed theatrical co. (with William Jones), Nas ville, Tenn., 1819; built (with Jones) Columb Street Theater, Cincinnati, 1820; managed (wi Jones) various Ohio Valley theatrical prodns.; r sponsible for bringing Edwin Forrest to West.

COLLINS, Napoleon, naval officer; b. Pa., Ma 4, 1814. Commd. lt. U.S. Navy, 1846; participate sieges of Tuspan and Tabasco on sloop Decatur du ing Mexican War, 1846-48; commanded ship An costa, Potomac fleet, 1861, gunboat Unadilla, S Atlantic squadron, 1861-62; Union comdr. Oct rara, West Indian squadron, 1862; captured sh Florida in harbor of Bahia, Brazil, 1864, towed h to U.S. authorities at Hampton Roads, Va.; wh Brazil demanded her return or rendition, Sec. S ward disavowed the act of Comdr. Collins, who wa tried by Navy ct.; commd. capt., 1866; comdr. sh Sacramento, 1867; commd. commodore, 187 lighthouse insp. until 1874; rear adm. in commar S. Pacific squadron, 1874. Died Callao, Peru, Au 9, 1875.

COLLINS, William, congressman, lawyer; l Lowville, Lewis County, N.Y., Feb. 22, 1818; Ela Collins; studied law. Admitted to bar, pra ticed in Lowville; dist. atty. Lewis County, 184 47; mem. U.S. Ho. of Reps. (Democrat) from N.Y 30th Congress, 1847-49; moved to Cleve., 185 practiced law; became banker; dir. Lake Sho R.R., East Cleveland R.R.; affiliated with Repu lican Party at its organization, 1856. Died Cleve. June 18, 1878; buried Lake View Cemetery.

COLMAN, Benjamin, clergyman; b. Boston, Oc 19, 1673; s. William and Elizabeth C.; grad. Harvard 1692, A.M., 1695; D.D. (hon.), U. Glasgow (Sco nd), 1731; m. Jane Clark, Oct. 5, 1700; m. 2d, arah (Crisp) Clark, May 6, 1732; m. 3d, Mary rost, Aug. 12, 1745. In England, 1695-99; ordained to ministry by London Presbytery, 1699; pastor Brattle Street Ch., Boston, 1699-1747; fellow Harvard, 1717-28, overseer, 1728-47; led liberal Presbyns. in conflict with Congregationalists over proper procedure of worship until conciliation between the factions in 1700. Died Aug. 29, 1747.

COLMAN, Henry, clergyman, farmer; b. Boston, Sept. 12, 1785; s. Dudley and Mary (Jones) C.; grad. Dartmouth, 1805; m. Mary Harris, Aug. 11, 1807. Ordained pastor Congregational Soc. (Unitarian), Hingham, Mass., 1807, pastor until 1820; taught sch., Boston, 1820-25; pastor Independent Congregational Ch., Salem, Mass., 1825-31; bought farm, Deerfield, Mass., 1833; commd. to make agrl. survey of Mass., 1837-41; studied agr. in England and Europe, 1843-48; went to England again, 1849. Author: Sermons on Various Occasions, 1820; Sermons on Various Subjects Preached at the Church in Boston Square, Salem, 1833; European Agriculture and Rural Economy from Personal Observations, 1844; European Life and Manners in Familiar Letters to Friends, 2 vols., 1849. Died Islington (now part of London), Eng., Aug. 17, 1849.

COLMAN, John, mcht.; b. London, Eng., Jan. 3, 1670; s. William and Elizabeth C.; m. Judith Hobby, July 19, 1694. Came to Am., 1671; selectman, justice of the peace Boston; favored limited paper money, expressed this view in pamphlet "The Distressed State of the Town of Boston" (caused controversy in which he was arrested), 1720; known for participation in currency disputes of 1720's; became partner Land Bank of 1739, Boston. Died circa 1753.

COLQUITT, Alfred Holt, senator, gov. Ga.; b. Walton County, Ga., Apr. 20, 1824; s. Walter T. and Nancy (Lane) C.; grad. Princeton, 1844; m. Dorothy Tarver, May 1848; m. 2d, Sarah Tarver. Admitted to Ga. bar, 1845; served as maj. U.S. Army during Mexican War, 1846-48; mem. U.S. Ho. of Reps. from Ga., 33d Congress, 1853-55; mem. Ga. Legislature, 1859; presdl. elector-at-large, 1860; del. to Ga. Secession Conv., 1861; commd. brig. gen., then maj. gen. Confederate Army during Civil War; pres. Ga. Democratic Conv., 1870; gov. Ga., 1876-82; mem. U.S. Senate from Ga., 1883-94. Died Washington, D.C., Mar. 26, 1894; buried Rose Hill Cemetery, Macon, Ga.

COLQUITT, Walter Terry, congressman, jurist; b. Halifax County, Va., Dec. 27, 1799; s. Henry and Nancy (Holt) C.; ed. Princeton; m. Nancy Lane, Feb. 3, 1823; m. 2d, Alphia Todd, 1841; m. 3d, Harriet Ross, 1842; 12 children, including Alfred Holt. Admitted to Ga. bar, 1820; judge Chattahoochee Superior Ct. Dist. (1st ct. ever held in Columbus, Ga.), 1826-32; mem. Ga. Senate, 1834-37; mem. U.S. Ho. of Reps. from Ga., 26th-27th Congress (Whig), 1839-43 mem. U.S. Senate from Ga., 1843-48. Died Macon, Ga., May 7, 1855.

COLSTON, Edward, congressman; b. estate Honeywood, nr. Martinsburg, Berkeley County, Va., (now W.Va.), Dec. 25, 1786; grad. Princeton, 1806; studied law. Admitted to bar, practiced law; served in War of 1812; mem. Va. Ho. of Dels., 1812-14, 16-17, 23-28, 33; high sheriff Berkeley County, 1844-45; mem. U.S. Ho. of Reps. (Federalist) from Va., 15th Congress, 1817-19. Died Honeywood, Apr. 23, 1852; buried family burying ground, Honeywood.

COLSTON, Raleigh Edward, army officer; b. Paris, France, Oct. 31, 1825; s. Dr. Raleigh Edward and Elizabeth (Marshall) C.; grad. Va. Mil. Inst., 1846; m. Louise Gardiner, 1846. Came to U.S., 1842; asst. prof. French, Va. Mil. Inst., 1846-54, prof., 1854-61; commd. brig. gen. Confederate Army, 1861; commanded div. at battles of Chancellorsville, Lynchburg; reinforced Gen. Magruder, engaging in battles of Yorktown, Williamsburg, Seven Pines, 1862; after Thomas (Stonewall) Jackson's death (1863) in command defenses St. Augustine River in Gen. Beauregard's dept.; established mil. sch., Wilmington, N.C.; served on mil. staff Khedive of Egypt, in Egypt, 1873-79, went on 2 expdns. exploring South country between Egypt and the Equator, 1873-74, 74-76; recipient firman, also decorated knight comdr. Turkish Imperial Order Osmanish by Sultan. Died Richmond, Va., June 29, 1896.

COLT, Samuel, inventor, firearms mfr.; b. Hartford, Conn., July 19, 1814; s. Christopher and Sarah (Caldwell) C.; m. Elizabeth H. Jarvis, June 5, 1856. Invented multi-shot firearm of revolving barrel type, constructed wooden model; constructed pistols, 1831, sent description to U.S. Patent Office, 1832, received 1st U.S. patent for 1st practical revolving firearm (widely used in opening of Am. West), 1836; introduced electricity as agt. for igniting gun powder; operated mfg. plant, Hartford. Died Hartford, Jan. 10, 1862.

COLTER, John, trapper, explorer; b. Staunton, Va., circa 1775; s. Joseph and Ellen (Shields) C. With Lewis and Clark's Expdn. Co., 1803; mem. Manuel Lisa's expdn. to Big Horn Country, undertook mission to Crow Indians (at Lisa's request) over Wind River and Teton Mountains and into Yellowstone area, perhaps 1st white man to see Yellowstone area; established Colter's Route of 1807; guided party sent by St. Louis Fur Co. to region of upper Missouri River, 1809. Died Dundee, Mo., Nov. 1813.

COLTON, A.M.F., architect; b. circa 1823; children include Samuel. Practiced as architect, Chgo., later joined in practice by his son; worked on numerous commns. for Cyrus McCormick (his best client), designed Chapel, Fowler and Ewing halls at McCormick Theol. Sem., McCormick family residences, remodelled McCormick Office Bldg., Reaper Block; designed numerous residences, including A. G. Tucker house, Wilbur C. Craig, Carrier and Johnson residences, Chgo., Congdon house, Evanston, Ill.; fellow A.I.A. Died Mar. 14, 1896.

COLTON, Calvin, journalist, author; b. Longmeadow, Mass., Sept. 14, 1789; s. Luther and Thankful (Woolworth) C.; grad. Yale, 1812; attended Andover Theol. Sem., 1812-14; m. Abby Raymound. Ordained to ministry Presbyn. Ch., Batavia, N.Y., 1815; became Episcopalian, 1836; rector Ch. of Messiah, N.Y.C., 1837-38; English corr. N.Y. Observer, 1832; became ofcl. biographer Henry Clay, 1844, edited Speeches of Henry Clay, 1857, Private Correspondence of Henry Clay, 1855; editor The True Whig (newspaper), Washington, D.C., 1842-43; prof. public economy Trinity Coll., Hartford, Conn., 1852-57; wrote many religious books including: Church and State in America, 1834; Protestant Jesuitism, 1836; The Genius and Mission of the Protestant Episcopal Church in the United States, 1853; wrote pamphlets "The Crisis of the Country" (supported Whig party), "Abolition and Sedition" (opposing abolition); strong advocate of high tariffs; other works include: A Manual for Emigrants to America, 1832; The Americans, 1833; Abolition a Sedition, 1839; Abolition and Colonization Contrasted, 1839; Public Economy in the United States, 1848. Died Savannah, Ga., Mar. 13, 1857.

COLTON, Gardner Quincy, dentist, inventor; b. Georgia, Vt., Feb. 7, 1814; s. Walter and Thankful (Cobb) C.; studied medicine under Dr. Willard Parker, N.Y.C., 1842. Gave exhbn. of effects of nitrous oxide (laughing gas) when inhaled, N.Y.C., 1844, toured other cities with laughing gas; invented an electric motor, 1847; participated in Cal. gold rush, 1849; justice of the peace San Francisco; reporter Boston Transcript, 1860; laughing gas became popular in dental anesthesia. Died Rotterdam, Holland, Aug. 9, 1898.

COLTON, Walter, journalist; b. Rutland County, Va., May 9, 1797; s. Deacon Walter and Thankful (Cobb) C.; grad. Yale, 1822, Andover Theol. Sem., 1825; m. Cornelia B. Colton, June 26, 1844. Became prof. moral philosophy and belles lettres Scientific and Mil. Acad., Middletown, Conn., 1825; editor The American Spectator, 1828-30; apptd. chaplain U.S. Navy; historiographer, chaplain South Sea Surveying and Exploring Squadron, 1837; chaplain Naval Sta., Phila., 1838; established The Californian (1st Cal. newspaper), 1846; built 1st sch. house in Cal., also pub. bldg. Colton Hall; responsible for pub. announcement in East (in a letter to the Phila. North American and U.S. Gazette) of discovery of gold in Sacramento Valley. Author: Ship and Shore in Madeira, Lisbon and the Mediterranean, 1835; A Visit to Athens and Constantinople, 1836; Three Years in California, 1850. Died Phila., Jan. 22, 1851.

COLUMBUS, Christopher, navigator, explorer; b. Genoa, Italy, circa 1449; s. Domenico and Suzanna (Fontanarossa) Columbo; studied at U. Pavia (Italy); m. Felipe Moñiz de Perestrello, circa 1478; 2 illegitimate sons (by Beatriz Enriquez), Diego, Ferdinand. Map and chart maker, Santo Porto (Madeira Islands), circa 1479; became convinced from this work that the East could be reached by sailing West; used 3 sources to determine this theory: Travels (Marco Polo), Imago Mundi (Pierre d'Ally), Cosmographia (Aeneas Sylvius Piccolomini, Pope Pius II); misjudged in his calculations the amount of land comprising the surface of earth and the distance to India; tried to gain help for venture from John II of Portugal, failed and went to Spain; received little attention at Spanish court; had friends plead his case in Eng. and France; happened to meet Father Juan Perez (Queen Isabella's confessor), which led to support by Spanish throne; prepared for his 1st voyage with 3 ships, Santa Maria, Pinta (commanded by Martin Pinzon), Niña (commanded by Vincente Yoñez); set sail, Aug. 3, 1492; put in at Teneriffe (Canary Islands) when Pinta lost its rudder 3 days after embarking; set sail again in 3 days; sighted New World (he believed it to be "Indies," as Asia was called, Oct. 12, 1492; discovered islands of Santa Maria de la Concepcion (Bahama Islands), Fernandina (Amelia Island), Isabella (Bahama Islands), Cuba, Hispaniola; built fort La Navidad on Santa Maria Island, left 44 men there; returned to Spain, Mar. 14, 1493, was received with great fanfare; set out on 2d voyage with 1500 men (including 12 missionaries) and 17 ships, Sept. 25, 1493; discovered islands of Dominica (Windward Islands), Marigalante, Guadalupe, Monserrat, Antigua (Leeward Islands), San Martin, Santa Cruz, Virgin Islands, Porto Rico; established mining camp in Central Hispaniola; shipped 1st slaves into New World on 2d voyage; started on 3d voyage, May 30, 1498, discovered island of Trinidad and coast of S.Am.; sailed as far South as Honduras, went to Jamaica; returned to Cuba, was arrested and put in chains by royal gov. Francisco de Bobadilla (had been sent by King Ferdinand, who never favored Columbus, to rule Columbus' discoveries and investigate charges of cruelty); released in Spain, made provisions for 4th voyage, leaving on May 9, 1502; still hoped to find passage to the East on this voyage; was refused entry into port of Santo Domingo; lost 2 ships in a gale and 2 others in wreck off Jamaica, where some of his men revolted and settled; managed to get supplies and repair his ships, returned to Spain, Sept. 12, 1504; his voyages must be observed as great navigational feats; his use of only basic navigational instruments may rate him as 1 of best navigators of all time. Died Vallodolid, Spain, May 20, 1506; buried Santa Maria de las Cuevas, Seville, Spain; reinterred Cathedral of San Domingo, Hispaniola; reinterred Havana, Cuba; reinterred Cathedral, Seville.

COLUMBUS, Diego, younger brother of Christopher Columbus. Accompanied brother on 2d voyage to Am. sent (with Christopher and Bartolommeo) back to Spain in chains, 1500; became a priest Roman Catholic Ch., returned to West Indies, 1509. Died circa 1510.

COLUMBUS, Fernando Colon; b. Cordova, Spain, Aug. 15, 1488; illegitimate son of Christopher Columbus and Beatriz Enriquez de Hrana. Became his father's favorite, accompanied him on last voyage to Am.; page to Queen Isabella, 1498; established Biblioteca Columbina, Seville, Spain. Author of travel description of Spain, also biography of his father. Died Seville, July 12, 1539.

COLVER, Nathaniel, clergyman; b. Orwell, Vt., May 10, 1794; s. Nathaniel and Esther (Dean) C.; m. Sally Clark, Aug. 27, 1815; m. 2d, Sarah Carter, Jan. 26, 1825. Ordained Baptist preacher, 1819; pastor small churches in Vt. and N.Y. until 1839; agt. for Am. Anti-Slavery Soc., 1839; pastor First Free Bapt. Ch., Boston, 1839-52; del. World Anti-Slavery Conv., London, 1840; later pastor at Detroit, Cincinnati, Chgo.; a founder Chgo. Bapt. Theol. Inst. (now Div. Sch. of U. Chgo.), 1865; founder Colver Inst. (now theol. dept. Va. Union U.) for tng. Negro ministers, Richmond, Va., 1867. Died Sept. 25, 1870.

COLVOCORESSES, George Musalas, naval officer; b. Chios, Greece, Oct. 22, 1816; s. Constantine and Franka (Grimaldi) C.; m. Eliza Halsey, May 17, 1846; m. 2d, Adeline Swasey, July 19, 1863; had four children including George Partridge. Came to U.S., 1822; apptd. midshipman U.S. Navy, 1832, passed midshipman, 1838; sailed with Wilkes Exploring Expdn. in Antarctic and South Pacific, 1838-42; commd. lt., 1843; served in Pacific Squadron during Mexican War, in Mediterranean, 1847-49, in East India Squadron, 1854-56; commd. comdr., 1861; commanded storeship Supply, 1861-63, Saratoga off Ga. coast, 1864, St. Mary's on Pacific coast off S.Am., 1865-66; ret. as capt., 1867. Author: Four Years in a Government Exploring Expedition, 1852. Killed by thieves in the street, Bridgeport, Conn., June 3, 1872.

COLWELL, Stephen, polit. economist; b. Brooke County, Va. (now W.Va.), Mar. 25, 1800; grad. Jefferson Coll. (Pa.), 1819. Admitted to Ohio bar, 1821; practiced law until 1836; became iron mfr.; trustee U. Pa., Princeton Theol. Sem.; helped establish chair of Christian ethics Princeton; dir. Camden and Atlantic, Reading and Pa. railroads; active mem. Am. Colonization Soc.; mem. U.S. Revenue Commn.; a founder Union League of Phila.; wrote and spoke for protective tariff and social responsibility of bus. leaders. Author: The Relative Position in our Industry of Foreign Commerce, Domestic Production and Internal Trade, 1850; New Themes for the Protestant Clergy, 1851; Politics for American Christians, 1852; Preface and Notes to Race for Riches, 1853; The Ways and Means of Commercial Payment, 1858. Died Phila., Jan. 15, 1871.

COLYER, Vincent, artist; b. Bloomingdale (now part of N.Y.C.), N.Y., Sept. 30, 1824; s. George Carmon and Cordelia (Webb) C.; attended N.A.D.; m. Mary Lydia Hancock; m. 2d, Louise Carolyn; 1 dau. Became mem. N.A.D., 1849, academician, 1866; opened studio in N.Y.C. before 1849; served in Civil War; mem. Union League Club; a founder Artists' Fund Soc. of N.Y.; Indian commr. in Alaska (under U.S. Grant). Paintings include: Columbia River, 1875; Spring Flowers, 1885; A French Waiter, 1886. Died Rowayton, Conn., July 12, 1888.

COMBS, Leslie, state legislator; b. Clark County, Ky., Nov. 29, 1793; s. Benjamin and Sarah (Richardson) C.; m. Margaret Trotter, 1819; m. 2d, Mary Brownell, 1849; 14 children. Dep. county clk. Jessamine County (Ky.), 1812; served as capt. in War of 1812; admitted to Ky. bar, 1818; mem. Ky. Legislature, 1827-29, 33, 45-47, 57-59, speaker ho. of reps., 1846; commd. col. Ky. Militia, 1836; clk. Ky. Ct. of Appeals, 1860-66. Died Lexington, Ky., Aug. 22, 1881.

COMBS, Moses Newell, mfr.; b. Morris County, N.J., 1753; m. Mary Haynes, 13 children including David, Isaac. Became tanner and shoemaker, Newark, N.J., circa 1781; 1st to export goods manufactured at Newark, 1790; treas. Springfield-Newark Turnpike Co., 1806; co-founder, dir. Newark Fire Ins. Co., conducted 1st night sch. in U.S. for his employees and apprentices (one of 1st free schs. in U.S.), 1794-1818. Died Apr. 12, 1834.

COMEGYS, Joseph Parsons, senator, jurist; b. Cherbourg, Kent County, nr. Dover, Del., Dec. 29, 1813; attended old acad., Dover; studied law. Admitted to bar, 1835, practiced in Dover; mem. Del. Ho. of Reps., 1842, 48; mem. commn. to revise Del. statutes, 1852; mem. U.S. Senate (Whig, filled vacancy) from Del., Nov. 19, 1856-Jan. 14, 1857; del. Nat. Constl. Union Conv., Balt., 1860, Nat. Union Conv., Phila., 1866; apptd. by Gov. Cochran chief justice Del. Supreme Ct., 1876-93. Died Dover, Feb. 1, 1893; buried Presbyn. Cemetery.

COMINGO, Abram, congressman; b. nr. Harrodsburg, Mercer County, Ky., Jan. 9, 1820; grad. Centre Coll., Danville, Ky.; studied law. Admitted to Harrodsburg bar, 1847; moved to Independence, Mo., 1848, practiced law; del. Mo. Conv., 1861; apptd. provost marshal 6th Dist. of Mo., 1863; elected recorder of deeds Jackson County, 1868; mem. U.S. Ho. of Reps. (Democrat) from Mo., 42d-43d congresses, 1871-75; apptd. by Pres. Grant mem. commn. to arbitrate with Sioux Indians for possession Sioux lands in Dakota bordering on Black Hills, 1876; moved to Kansas City, Mo., 1881, retired from public life. Died Kansas City, Nov. 10, 1889; buried Elmwood Cemetery.

COMINS, Linus Bacon, congressman; b. Charlton, Mass., Nov. 29, 1817; grad. Worcester County Manual Tng. High Sch. Became mfr., Roxbury, Mass.; mem. Roxbury City Council, 1846-48, pres., 1847-48; mayor Roxbury, 1854; mem. U.S. Ho. of Reps. (American Party) from Mass., 34th, (Republican) 35th congresses, 1855-59; del. Nat. Rep. Conv., Chgo., 1860. Died Jamaica Plain, Mass., Oct. 14, 1892; buried Forest Hills Cemetery, Boston.

COMSTOCK, Elizabeth L., clergywoman; b. Maidenhead, Berkshire, Eng., Oct. 30, 1815; d. William and Mary Rous; m. Leslie Wright, 1847, at least 1 dau. Caroline; m. 2d, John T. Comstock, 1858. Became minister Soc. of Friends, Belleville, Ont., Can., 1854; minister, Rollin, Mich., 1858-85; operated station for Underground R.R.; travelled extensively, spoke as Quaker minister, abolitionist and advocate of peace, temperance, prison reform and women's rights; worked at prison camps and hosps. during Civil War; visited Pres. Lincoln, 1864; largely responsible for relief program for Negro immigrants to Kan., 1879-80. Died Union Springs, N.Y., Aug. 3, 1891.

COMSTOCK, George Franklin, jurist; b. Williamstown, N.Y., Aug. 24, 1811; s. Serejah Comstock; grad. Union Coll., 1834, LL.D. (hon.), 1858; m. Cornelia Nixon, 1839. Admitted to N.Y. bar, 1837; 1st reporter N.Y. Ct. Appeals, 1847-51; solicitor gen. U.S., 1852-53; judge N.Y. Ct. Appeals, 1855-61, chief justice, 1860-61; del.-at-large N.Y. Constl. Conv., 1868; trustee Hobart Coll., 1870-77, Syracuse U., 1870-90; founder St. John's Sch. for Boys, Manlius, N.Y. Editor: Kent's Commentaries. Died Syracuse, N.Y., Sept. 27, 1892.

COMSTOCK, Henry Tompkins Paige, prospector; b. Trenton, Ont., Can., 1820; s. Noah and Catherine (Tompkins) C. Served in Black Hawk, Patriot and Mexican wars; prospector, active in Nev., 1856-62, discovered Comstock Lode, Virginia City, Nev. Died nr. Bozeman, Mont., Sept. 27, 1870; buried Bozeman.

COMSTOCK, Oliver Cromwell, congressman; b. Warwick, R.I., Mar. 1, 1780; studied medicine, theology. Practiced medicine, Trumansburg, N.Y.; mem. N.Y. State Assembly, 1810-12; 1st judge common pleas Seneca County, N.Y., 1812-15, Tompkins County, 1817, 18; mem. U.S. Ho. of Reps. (Democrat) from N.Y., 13th-15th congresses, 1813-19; licensed to preach, then ordained to ministry Bapt. Ch.; pastor First Bapt. Ch., Rochester, N.Y., 1825-34; elected Chaplain Nat. Ho. of Reps., 1836-37; moved to Mich.; minister in Detroit, 1839; regent U. Mich., 1841-43; Mich. supt. public instrn., 1843-45. Died Marshall, Calhoun County, Mich., Jan. 11, 1860; buried Oakridge Cemetery.

CONANT, Hannah O'Brien Chaplin, author, translator; b. Danvers, Mass., Sept. 5, 1809; d. Jeremiah and Marcia (O'Brien) Chaplin; studied Oriental langs., French, German under her father; m. Thomas Jefferson Conant, July 12, 1830, 10 children. Editor, Mother's Monthly Jour., Utica, N.Y., 1839-65; author: The Earnest Man; A Sketch of the Character and Labors of Dr. A. Judson, the First Missionary to Burma, 1855; The English Bible; A Popular History of the Translation of the Holy Scriptures into the English Tongue, 1856; translator (from German): Lea; or, the Baptism in Jordan (G.F.A. Strauss), 1844; Erna, the Forest Princess; or Pilgrimage of the Three Wise Men to Bethlehem (G. Nieritz), 1855; The New England Theocracy; A History of the Congregationalists in New England to the Revivals of 1740 (F. H. Uhden), 1859. Died Feb. 18, 1865.

CONANT, Hezekiah, mfr., inventor; b. Dudley, Mass., July 28, 1827; s. Hervey and Dolly (Healy) C.; m. Sarah Williams Learned, Oct. 4, 1853; m. 2d, Harriet Knight Learned, Nov. 1859; m. 3d, Mary Eaton Knight, Dec. 6, 1865; 2 children. Patented pair of lasting pinchers for use in shoe mfg., 1852; journeyman machinist, Boston, Worcester, Mass., 1852-55; employed at Colt Firearm Co., Hartford, Conn., 1855-circa 1859; invented gas check for breech loading firearms, 1856; invented machines for dressing sewing thread and winding thread on spools automatically, 1859, sold patent to Willimantic Linen Co. (Conn.), 1860, mech. expert, 1860-68; organized Conant Thread Co., Pawtucket, R.I., 1868, merged with J. & P. Coates Co. of Paisley, Scotland (largest thread mfrs. in Europe), 1869, name changed from Conant Thread Co. to J.& P. Coates Co., Ltd., 1893. Died Jan. 22, 1902; buried Dudley.

CONANT, Roger, colonist, colonial gov.; b. Devonshire, Eng., circa 1592; s. Richard and Agnes (Clarke) C.; m. Sarah Horton, Nov. 11, 1618, 9 children. Came to Plymouth (Mass.), 1623; organizer 1st Puritan ch. Cape Ann Settlement, Mass., 1624; mgr. (gov.) Cape Ann Settlement, 1625; a founder Salem (Mass.), gov., 1626; elected mem. Mass. Gen. Ct. from Salem, 1634; apptd. justice Quarterly Ct., Essex County, Mass., 1637. Died Beverly, Mass., Nov. 19, 1679.

CONANT, Thomas Jefferson, philologist; b. Brandon, Vt., Dec. 13, 1802; s. John and Charity (Broughton) C.; grad. Middlebury Coll., 1823; studied philosophy under Prof. R. B. Patton, N.Y.C., 1823-25; m. Hannah O'Brien Chaplin, July 12, 1830, 10 children. Tutor classics Columbian Coll., Washington, D.C., 1825-27; prof. langs. Colby Coll., Waterville, Me., 1827-33; ordained to ministry Baptist Ch., 1834; prof. Hebrew and Bibl. criticism Hamilton (N.Y.) Literary and Theol. Instn., 1835-41; travelled and studied langs., Europe, 1841-42; prof. Bibl. literature and criticism Rochester (N.Y.) Theol. Sem., 1850-57; mem. Am. Revision Com. to produce revised translation of Bible, 1873-81. Author: The Laws of Translation; translator: Hebrew Grammar (by Gesenius), 1839; The Book of Job, 1857; The Gospel of Matthew, 1860; The Entire New Testament, 1867; The Book of Genesis, 1868; The Book of Psalms, 1868; The Book of Proverbs, 1872; The First Thirteen Chapters of Isaiah, 1874; The Historical Books of the Old Testament, Joshua to II Kings, 1884. Died Bklyn., Apr. 30, 1891.

CONARD, John, congressman; b. Chester Valley, Chester County, Pa., Nov. 1773; attended Friends Sch.; studied law. Admitted to bar, practiced law; prof. mathematics local acad., Germantown, Pa.; mem. U.S. Ho. of Reps. (Democrat) from Pa., 13th Congress, 1813-15; mem. Soc. of Friends, earned title "Fighting Quaker" because of his sympathy for patriots and his desire to repel British during War of 1812; asso. judge dist. ct.; apptd. U.S. marshal for Eastern Dist. of Pa. by Pres. Monroe, reapptd. by Pres. Adams, served 2 years under Pres. Jackson; retired from public life, 1832; lived in Cecil County, nr. Port Deposit, Md., 1834-51; moved to Phila., 1851. Died Phila., May 9, 1857; buried St. Ann's Protestant Episcopal Churchyard, North East, Cecil County.

CONARROE, George W., artist; b. Del., 1803; m. Charlotte; children—George, Maria, Ellen. Resided in Salem, N.J., 1829-31, Phila., after 1831; exhibited frequently at Artists' Fund Soc., Pa. Acad., Boston Athenaeum, Apollo Gallery, Md. Hist. Soc., Washington (D.C.) Art Assn. Died Phila., 1882/84.

CONDICT, Lewis, congressman; b. Morristown, Morris County, N.J., Mar. 3, 1772; grad. med. dept. U. Pa., 1794. Practiced medicine in Morristown; sheriff Morris County, 1801-03; mem. commn. for adjusting boundary line between N. State and N.J., 1804; mem. N.J. Ho. of Assembl 1805-09, 37, 38 speaker various times; mem. U. Ho. of Reps. (Anti-Federalist) from N.J., 12t 14th, 17th-22d congresses, 1811-17, 21-33; pr N.J. Med. Soc., 1816, 19; elected trustee Coll. N.J. (now Princeton), 1827-61, resigned; an i corporator Morris & Essex R.R. Co., 1st pres 1835; Whig presdl. elector, 1840. Died Morristow May 26, 1862; buried Presbyn. Ch. cemetery.

CONDICT, Silas, Continental congressman; Morristown, Morris County, N.J., Mar. 7, 173 Large landholder in Morristown and vicinity; me N.J. Council, 1776-80; mem. Com. of Safety; me Continental Congress from N.J., 1781-84; mem. J. Gen. Assembly, 1791-94, 96-98, 1800, speake 1792-94, 97. Died Morristown, Sept. 6, 180 buried First Presbyn. Ch. cemetery.

CONDIT, John, surgeon, congressman; b. We Orange, N.J., July 8, 1755; s. Samuel and Ma (Smith) C.; m. Abigail Halsey, 1776; m. 2d, Rho Halsey, 1785; 8 children—including John S., Ab gail Smith, Jacob A., Silas. Served as surgeon Col. Van Cortland's battalion, Heard's briga during Revolutionary War, 1776; a founder Oran (N.J.) Acad., 1785; mem. N.J. Legislature, 178 89; mem. N.J. Council; mem. U.S. Ho. of Rep from N.J., 6th-7th, 16th congresses, 1799-180 19-20; mem. U.S. Senate from N.J., 1803-17; ass collector customs Port of N.Y.; hon. mem. N. Med. Soc., 1830. Died Orange Twp., N.J., May 1834; buried Old Graveyard, Orange, N.J.

CONDIT, Silas, congressman, mcht.; b. Orang N.J., Aug. 18, 1778; s. John Condit; grad. Princ ton, 1795. Became mcht., Orange; moved to Ne ark, N.J.; clk. Essex County, N.J., 1804-11, sheri 1813-16; mem. N.J. Gen. Assembly, 1812, 13, 1 mem. N.J. Council, 1819-22; pres. Newark Ban ing Co., 1820-42; mem. U.S. Ho. of Reps. (Cl Democrat) from N.J., 22d Congress, 1831-33; de N.J. Constl. Conv., 1844. Died Newark, Nov. 2 1861; buried First Presbyn. Ch. cemetery.

CONE, Spencer Houghton, clergyman; b. Princ ton, N.J., Apr. 30, 1785; s. Conant and Ali (Houghton) C.; ed. Coll. of N.J. (now Princeton) 1797-99, D.D. (hon.), 1832; m. Salley Morrel May 10, 1813. Treas., bookkeeper Balt. America 1812; chaplain U.S. Congress, 1815-16; past Baptist Ch., Alexandria, Va., 1816-23, 1st Bap Ch., N.Y.C., 1841-55; pres. Bapt. Gen. Conv 1832-41, Am. Bible Union, 1837-50. Died N.Y.C Aug. 28, 1855.

CONEY, Jabez, millwright, engr.; b. Dedha Mass., Oct. 21, 1804; s. Jabez and Irene (Gay) C m. Mary Whiting, Oct. 25, 1827, 3 children. B lieved to have built 1st iron vessel constructed New Eng.; built 1st large marine engine, 1st gra excavator; represented Ward 10 (South Bosto in Boston City Council, 1847, 50. Died Jan. 2 1872.

CONEY, John, silversmith; b. Boston, Jan. 1655; s. John and Elizabeth (Nash) Coney; n Sarah Coney; m. 2d, Mary Atwater; at least 2 chi dren. Apprenticed to silversmith Jeremiah Dumme Boston; owned large silver-work business, Bosto engraved plates for 1st paper money issued b Mass. Bay Colony; signed petition acknowledgi King Charles II's authority; served with Mas Militia. Died Aug. 20, 1722.

CONGDON, Charles Taber, journalist, author; b New Bedford, Mass., Apr. 7, 1821; s. Benjami Taler and Deborah (Hartt) C.; attended Bro U., 1837-40, A.M. (hon.), 1879; m. Charlot Bagliss, 1 dau., Alice B. Successively employe on Daily Register, Daily Bulletin and Daily Me cury, all New Bedford, 1840-54; editor Atlas, Bo ton, 1854-57; mem. editorial staff N.Y. Tribun 1857-82; N.Y.C. corr. for Boston Courier; contb to many mags. including Vanity Fair, Knickerbock Magazine, North American Review, also to Tribu Essays, 1869; wrote Flowers Plucked by a Travell on the Journey of Life (poems), 1840, The Warnin of War, 1862; Reminiscences of a Journalist, 188 Died N.Y.C., Jan. 18, 1891; buried New Bedford.

CONGER, Harmon Sweatland, congressman, la yer; b. Freeport, Cortland County, N.Y., Apr. 1816; attended local acad., Cortland, N.Y., 183 studied law. Admitted to bar, 1844; practiced i Cortland; editor, owner Cortland County Whig 1840-45; mem. U.S. Ho. of Reps. (Whig) from Y., 30th-31st congresses, 1847-51; moved to Jane ville, Rock County, Wis., 1855, practiced la elected judge Circuit Ct., 1870, reelected, 187 82. Died Janesville, Oct. 22, 1882; buried O Hill Cemetery.

CONGER, James Lockwood, congressman; Trenton, N.J., Feb. 18, 1805; attended Cananda gua (N.Y.) Acad.; studied medicine and law. Mov to Lancaster, O., 1822; taught sch. several year admitted to bar, 1825, practiced in Lancaste moved to Cleve., practiced law, 1826-37; moved lacomb County, Mich., 1837, laid out Town of elvidere; became banker, mcht. until 1850; moved) Mt. Clemens, Mich.; mem. U.S. Ho. of Reps. Free-Soil Whig) from Mich., 32d Congress, 1851-3; supported Greeley and Brown, 1872; retired om business activities because of ill health. Died t. Clair, Mich., Apr. 10, 1876; buried Green Lawn emetery, Columbus, O.

CONKLING, Alfred, congressman, judge, diplo-at; b. Amagansett, Suffolk County, L.I., N.Y., ct. 12, 1789; s. Benjamin and Esther (Hand) C.; rad. Union Coll., 1810, LL.D. (hon.), 1847; m. liza Cockburn, 1812, seven children including rederick and Roscoe. Admitted to the New York ır, 1812; dist. atty. Montgomery County (N.Y.) 813-18; mem. U.S. Ho. of Reps., 17th Congress, 821-23; U.S. judge for No. N.Y. dist., 1825-52; '.S. minister to Mexico, 1852-53. Author: The oung Citizens Manual, 1836; A Treatise on the rganization and Jurisdiction of the Supreme, Cir-uit and District Courts of the United States, 1842; ırisdiction, Law and Practice in Admiralty and laritime Causes, 1848; Powers of the Executive epartment of the United States, 1866. Died Uti-a, N.Y., Feb. 5, 1874.

CONKLING, Frederick Augustus, congressman, usinessman; b. Canajoharie, Montgomery County, .Y., Aug. 22, 1816; s. Alfred Conkling; attended lbany Acad. Mem. N.Y. State Assembly, 1854, 9-60; organized 84th Regt., N.Y. Volunteers in ivil War, 1861, became its col.; served through-ut Shenandoah campaign; served on provost-guard uty, Balt., 1863; an organizer West Side Savs. ank, N.Y.C., pres. many years; pres. Aetna Fire ns. Co., Hartford, Conn. until 1880; mem. U.S. o. of Reps. (Republican) from N.Y., 37th Con-ress, 1861-63; unsuccessful Rep. candidate for ayor N.Y.C., 1868; mem. N.Y. C. of C., N.Y. ist. Soc., N.Y. Geog. Soc.; oldest gov. N.Y. Iosp.; trustee Coll. Physicians and Surgeons. Au-nor numerous pamphlets on polit., comml. and sci. ubjects. Died N.Y.C., Sept. 18, 1891; buried reenwood Cemetery, Bklyn.

CONKLING, Roscoe, senator; b. Albany, N.Y., ct. 30, 1829; s. Alfred and Eliza (Cockburn) C.; ttended Mt. Washington Collegiate Inst., N.Y.C., 842-46; m. Julia Seymour, June 25, 1855. Ad-itted to N.Y. bar, 1850; dist. atty. Albany, 1850; ayor Utica, N.Y., 1858-59; mem. U.S. Ho. of eps. from N.Y., 35th-37th, 39th congresses, 1859-3, 65-67; mem. U.S. Senate from N.Y., 1867-81, pposed policies of Pres. Rutherford B. Hayes, olicies on civil service and awards system induced im to withdraw support of Hayes during Republi-an Nat. Conv., 1880, resigned from Senate in pro-est of Pres. Garfield's policies, 1881; closely af-liated with Ulysses S. Grant's N.Y. polit. machine. ied N.Y.C., Apr. 18., 1888.

CONNELLY, Cornelia, founder Soc. of Holy Child esus; b. Phila., Jan. 15, 1809; d. Ralph and Mary wope (Bowen) Peacock; m. Rev. Pierce Connelly, ec. 1, 1831, 5 children. Became Roman Catholic, 835; her husband ordained priest, 1845; left her hildren to join convent, 1845; founded Soc. of Ioly Child Jesus as an ednl. order in Eng., 1846, stablished 1st Am. convent, 1862. Died Apr. 18, 879.

CONNELLY, Henry, mcht., territorial gov.; b. Nelson (now Spencer) County, Ky., 1800; s. John nd Frances (Brent) C.; M.D., Transylvania U., 828; m. Dolores Perea Chavez, 1836, 6 children. eader mcht. and teamster bus. in N.M.; elected ov. by citizens of N.M., 1850, but U.S. Govt. nade N.M. a territory, and apptd. a different gov.; pptd. gov. Territory of N.M. by Pres. Lincoln, 861. Died Santa Fe, N.M., July 1866.

CONNELLY, Pierce Francis, sculptor; b. Grand oteau, La., Mar. 29, 1841; s. Pierce and Cornelia Peacock) C.; studied art, Paris, Rome. Went to urope as child; worked as sculptor in Florence, taly, and England; exhibited at Royal Acad. Exhbn., ondon, Eng., 1871; came to U.S. to exhibit at entennial Expn., Phila., 1876; went to New Zea-and, 1876, interested in painting, mountain climb-ng; returned to Florence, 1883 and 1900; sculp-ures include: Honor Arresting the Triumph of eath, 1869; Ophelia; St. Martin and the Beggar; hetis, 1874; Queen Philippa; Viola; The Thread f Life. Whereabouts unknown after 1900.

CONNER, David, navy officer; b. Harrisburg, Pa., 792; s. David and Abigail (Rhodes) C.; m. Miss 'hysick, June 25, 1828, 2 sons. Commd. midship-nan U.S. Navy, 1809; served as lt. on ship Hornet, 812-15; commd. capt., 1835; mem. bd. commrs. '.S. Navy, 1841-42; commodore West India and ome squadron, 1843; head Bur. Constrn., Equip-nent and Repair, until 1843; commanded Am. aval forces in Gulf and Caribbean, 1843-47, in harge of navy side of Scott's army's landing nr. era Cruz, Mexico, during Mexican War, put 10,000 en on beaches in 5 hours; comdt. Phila. Navy ard, 1849-50. Died Phila., Mar. 20, 1856.

CONNER, James, army officer, state ofcl.; b. harleston, S.C., Sept. 1, 1829; s. Henry and Juliana (Courtney) C.; grad. S.C. Coll., 1849; m. Sallie Enders, 1866. Admitted to S.C. bar, 1851; U.S. atty. for dist. S.C., 1856-60; commd. brig. gen. Confederate Army, 1864; solicitor S.C. R.R.; receiver Greenville & Columbia R.R. Co.; chmn. S.C. Democratic Exec. Com., 1876; atty. gen. S.C., 1861, 1876-77. Died Richmond, Va., June 26, 1883.

CONNER, John Coggswell, congressman; b. Noblesville, Hamilton County, Ind., Oct. 14, 1842; attended Wabash Coll., Crawfordsville, Ind., U. S. Naval Acad., 1861-62. Commd. 2d lt. 63d Regt., Ind. Volunteer Inf. during Civil War, 1862., 1st lt., 1862-64; served as capt. 41st Regt., U.S. Inf., 1866-69; mem. U.S. Ho. of Reps. (Democrat) from Tex., 41st-42d congresses, Mar. 31, 1870-73. Died Washington, D.C., Dec. 10, 1873; buried Old Ceme-tery, Noblesville.

CONNER, Samuel Shepard, congressman, lawyer; b. Exeter, N.H., circa 1783; attended Philips Exe-ter Acad., 1794; grad. Yale, 1806; studied law. Admitted to bar, practiced in Waterville, Me. (then dist. of Mass.), 1810; served as maj. 21st Inf. in War of 1812, lt. col. 13th Inf., 1813-14; mem. U.S. Ho. of Reps. from Mass., 14th Congress, 1815-17; apptd. surveyor gen. Ohio land dist., 1819. Died Covington, Ky., Dec. 17, 1820.

CONNOLLY, Daniel Ward, congressman; b. Co-checton, Sullivan County, N.Y., Apr. 24, 1847; attended public schs., Scranton, Pa.; studied law. Admitted to bar, 1870, practiced in Scranton; elected pres. judge Lackawanna County, 1878, did not serve because Pa. Supreme Ct. held there was no vacancy; mem. U.S. Ho. of Reps. (Democrat) from Pa., 48th Congress, 1883-85; apptd. post-master Scranton, 1885-89. Died Scranton, Dec. 4, 1894; buried Forest Hill Cemetery.

CONNOLLY, John, army officer; b. Wright's Fer-ry, Pa., 1743; s. John and Susanna (Howard) C.; m. Susanna Semple, before 1767; m. 2d, Margaret Wellington; 2 children. Med. officer Pa. Militia in Indian campaigns, 1762-64; studied Indian langs., Kaskaskia, 1767-70; practiced medicine, Pitts., 1770-72; received grant of land in Ky. from Lord Dunmore (gov. Va.), 1773; acted as Dunmore's agt. in land speculation; commd. capt. Va. Militia and apptd. magistrate for dist. of West Augusta, 1773; attempted to organize settlers in Western Pa. in Va. Militia, 1774, almost started civil war between Pa. and Va. traders when he stopped Pa. trade with Indians and imposed Va. fur tax on Pitts. traders; made treaty with Iroquois and Dela-ware Indians wherein they agreed to support British, 1775; commd. lt. col. Brit. Army, 1775; while en route West to lead Brit. and Indian forces captured by colonial forces, 1776, imprisoned, 1776-80; joined Lordr Cornwallis at Yorktown, 1781, again captured and imprisoned, 1781-82; went to Eng-land, 1782; sent to Detroit as lt. gov., 1788; at-tempted to persuade leaders in Ky. to shift allegi-ance to British, unsuccessful; dep. supt. of Indian affairs, 1799-1800. Died Jan. 30, 1813.

CONNOLLY, John, clergyman; b. Slane County, Ireland, 1750. Ordained priest Roman Catholic Ch., 1775; dir. Casanate Library; bishop Diocese of New York, Roman Catholic Ch., 1814 (diocese embraced all of N.Y. State and half of N.J.); established orphan asylum, introduced Sisters of Charity. Died N.Y.C., Feb. 6, 1825.

CONNOR, Henry William, congressman; b. nr. Amelia Court House, Prince George County, Va., Aug. 5, 1793; grad. S.C. Coll. (now U. S.C.), 1812. Served as a.d.c. to Brig. Gen. Joseph Graham with rank of maj. in expdn. against Creek Indians, 1814; settled in Falls Town, Iredell County, N.C.; became planter; mem. U.S. Ho. of Reps. (Democrat) from N.C., 17th-26th congresses, 1821-41; mem. N.C. Senate, 1848-50. Died Beatties Ford, Lincoln County, N.C., Jan. 6, 1866; buried Rehoboth Metho-dist Ch. Cemetery, nr. Sherrills Ford, N.C.

CONNOR, Patrick Edward, army officer, Indian fighter, pioneer; b. County Kerry, Ireland, Mar. 17, 1820; m. Johanna Connor, Aug. 1854. Commd. 1st lt. Tex. Volunteers, 1846, capt. under Albert Signey Johnston, 1847; commd. col. 3d Cal. Inf. during Civil War, commanded mil. dist. of Utah (including Nev.); brevetted maj. gen. U.S. Volunteers, 1865; organized 16,000 non-Mormons, founded community Camp Douglass, nr. Salt Lake City, Utah, 1866; located 1st silver mine in Utah Territory; wrote 1st mining law, placed 1st steamboat on Gt. Salt Lake, built 1st silver smelting works; founded Town of Stockton (Utah); established paper Union Vidette (Utah's 1st daily newspaper). Died Salt Lake City, Dec. 17, 1891.

CONOVER, Obediah Milton, lawyer, educator; b. Dayton, O., Oct. 8, 1825; s. Sarah Miller; grad. Coll. of N.J. (now Princeton), 1844, grad. Prince-ton Theol. Sem., 1849; m. Julia Darst, 1849; m. 2d, Mrs. Sarah Dean, 1882. Tchr., Latin and Greek, Lexington, Ky.; went to Wis., 1849; admitted to Dane County (Wis.) bar, 1859; editor North West-ern Jour.; prof. ancient langs. and lit. U. Wis., 1852-58, mem. bd. regents, 1859-65, also state librarian; asst. reporter Wis. Supreme Ct., 1861, reporter, 1864-84. Died London, Eng., Apr. 29, 1884.

CONRAD, Charles Magill, congressman, sec. of war; b. Winchester, Va., Dec. 24, 1804; s. Fred-erick and Frances (Thruston) C.; m. M.W. Angela Lewis. Admitted to La. bar, 1828; mem. La. Legis-lature, 1840; mem. U.S. Senate from La., Apr. 1842-Mar. 1843; mem. La. Constl. Conv., 1844; mem. U.S. Ho. of Reps. from La., 31st Congress, 1849-51; U.S. sec. of war under Pres. Fillmore, 1850-53; mem. Confederate Provisional Congress, 1861; represented La. in 1st, 2d Confederate con-gresses, 1862-64; commd. brig. gen. Confederate Army. Died New Orleans, Feb. 11, 1878; buried Girod St. Cemetery.

CONRAD, Frederick, congressman; b. Worcester Twp., Montgomery County, Pa., 1759; attended common schs. Elected to Pa. Assembly, 1798, 1800, 02; paymaster 51st Regt., Pa. Militia, 1804, 05; mem. U.S. Ho. of Reps. (Federalist) from Pa., 8th-9th congresses, 1803-07; apptd. justice of peace, 1807; apptd. prothonotary and clk. of cts., 1821, reapptd., 1824; lived nr. Center Point, Pa., became farmer; moved to Norristown, Pa. Died Norristown, Aug. 3, 1827; buried Wentz's Reformed Ch. Cemetery, Center Point.

CONRAD, Robert Taylor, journalist, jurist, dram-atist; b. Phila., June 10, 1810; s. John and Eliza Conrad. Admitted to Pa. bar, 1831; published Daily Comml. Intelligences, 1832; judge criminal sessions for City and County of Phila., 1838; asso. editor North American, 1845; 1st mayor Greater Phila., 1854-57; judge quarter session, 1856-57. Author: Alymere or the Bondman of Kent and other Poems; also plays Conrad of Naples, 1832; The Noble Yeoman, 1835; Jack Cade, 1841; Heretic, 1861. Died Phila., June 27, 1858.

CONRAD, Timothy Abbot, conchologist; b. nr. Trenton, N.J., June 21, 1803; son of Solomon White Conrad; studied natural history and science privately. Assisted his father in printing bus. until father's death, 1831; became especially interested in conchology; became mem. Phila. Acad. of Scis., 1831; state geologist and paleontologist of N.Y., 1837-42; mem. Am. Philos. Soc.; his work is not well known because of his opposition to Darwin's theory of evolution; contbr. articles to various journ-als; drew many of plates for his own works. Author: American Marine Conchology; or, Descriptions and Colored Figures of the Shells of the Atlantic Coast, 1831. Died Trenton, Aug. 9, 1877.

CONROY, John Joseph, clergyman; b. Clonaslee, Leix, Ireland, July 25, 1819; attended Sulpician Coll., Montreal, Can., also Mt. St. Mary's Coll., Md. and St. Joseph's Sem., Troy, N.Y. Ordained priest Roman Catholic Ch., 1842; v.p., then pres. St. John's Coll., Fordham, 1842-44; did parish work, N.Y. archdiocese, next 21 years; theologian, 1st Plenary Council of Balt., 1852; adminstr. N.Y. archdiocese, 1864-65; bishop of Albany, 1865-77; attended 2d Plenary Council of Balt., 1866, Vatican Council, 1870; apptd. titular bishop of Curium,, 1878. Died N.Y.C., Nov. 20, 1895.

CONSIDÉRANT, Victor Prosper, socialist; b. Salins, France, Oct. 12, 1808; s. Jean-Baptiste Considérant; attended École Polytechnique, Paris, École de Metz; m. 2d, Miss Vigoureux. Became capt. engring. div. of French Army; active in war against Algiers, 1830, resigned 1830; became Fourierist; published socialist monthly Le Phalan-stère, 1830-43, name changed to La Phalange, 1836; established Fourierist library, Paris, France, also daily paper La Democratic Pacifique, 1843; mem. French Constl. Assembly, 1848; went to Bel-gium as polit. refugee, 1849; came to U.S., 1852, travelled in Tex.; in Belgium, 1852-55; returned to Tex., 1855, founded Reunion (Fourierist col-ony); became disgusted after financial problems arose, moved to San Antonio, Tex.; returned to France, 1869; colony dissolved, 1875. Author: Des-tinée social, 3 vols., 1834-44; Manifeste de l'école societaire 1841; Exposition alrégée du system Phalansterien de Fourier, 1845; Principes du social-isme, 1847; Théorie du droit de propriété et du droit au travail, 1848; Socialisme devant le vieux monde, 1849; Au Texas, 1854; European Coloniza-tion in Texas, An Address to the American People, 1857. Died Paris, Dec. 27, 1893.

CONSTABLE, Albert, congressman; b. nr. Charles-town, Md., June 3, 1805; studied law. Admitted to bar, 1829, practiced in Bel Air, Harford County, Md.; moved to Balt., practiced law; later moved to Perryville, Cecil County, Md. mem. U.S. Ho. of Reps. (Democrat) from Md., 29th Congress, 1845-47; judge Md. Circuit Ct., 1851. Died Camden, N.J., Sept. 18, 1855.

CONTEE, Benjamin, Continental congressman, congressman, clergyman; b. Brookfield, nr. Notting-ham, Prince Georges County, Md., 1755; attended pvt. sch. Served as lt. and capt. 3d Md. Battalion in Revolutionary War; mem. Md. Ho. of Dels., 1785-87; mem. Continental Congress from Md.,

1787-88; mem. U.S. Ho. of Reps. from Md., 1st Congress, 1789-91; travelled various European countries, studied theology; ordained to ministry Episcopal Ch., 1803; pastor Episcopal ch., Port Tobacco, Charles County, Md.; presiding judge Charles County Orphans' Ct. until 1815. Died Charles County, Nov. 30, 1815; buried at Bromont (his former home), nr. Port Tobacco.

CONVERSE, Amasa R., businessman, territorial ofcl.; b. Hinsdale, Mass., Mar. 26, 1842. Engaged in merc. business, Cheyenne, Wyo., 1867-72; organizer, pres. 1st Nat. Bank of Cheyenne, 1871-85; territorial treas. Wyo., 1875-76, 77-79; mem. Wyo. Pioneer Assn.; Converse County (Wyo.) named for him. Died N.Y.C., June 9, 1885; buried Three Rivers, Mich.

CONVERSE, George Leroy, congressman, lawyer; b. Georgesville, Franklin County, O., June 4, 1827; attended Central Coll., O.; grad. Denison U., Granville, O., 1849; studied law. Admitted to bar, 1851; practiced in Columbus, O., 1852; pros. atty. Franklin County, 1857; mem. Ohio Ho. of Reps., 1860-63, 74-76, speaker, 1874; mem. Ohio Senate, 1864-65; mem. U.S. Ho. of Reps. (Democrat) from Ohio, 46th-48th congresses, 1879-85; chmn. Nicaraguan Canal Conv., 1892. Died Columbus, Mar. 30, 1897; buried Green Lawn Cemetery.

CONWAY, Elias Nelson, gov. Ark.; b. Greene County, Tenn., May 17, 1812; s. Thomas and Ann (Rector) C. Auditor, Ark. Territory, 1835-49; originated donation land laws of Ark., homestead laws of U.S.; introduced idea of donation of forfeited land to actual settlers, 1840 (adopted as nat. policy, 1862); gov. Ark., 1852-60. Burned to death in the fire of Little Rock, Ark., Feb. 28, 1894.

CONWAY, Frederick Bartlett, actor; b. Clifton, Eng., Feb. 10, 1819; s. William A. Conway; m. 2d, Sarah Crocker, 1852; at least 2 children Lillian, Minnie. Came to U.S., 1850; made Am. debut as Charles Surface in The School for Scandal, N.Y.C., 1850; toured U.S. with his 2d wife appearing primarily in N.Y.C., Boston, Phila.; held lease to Pike's Opera House, Cincinnati, 1859-61; leased Park Theatre, Bklyn., 1864, changed name to Conway's Theatre, appeared there after 1864; roles include: Iago in Othello, N.Y.C., 1851; Armand in Camille (1st to play this part in U.S.) 1853, Cardinal Richelieu in The Three Guardsmen, John Mildway in Still Waters Run Deep. Died Manchester, Mass., Sept. 7, 1874.

CONWAY, Henry Wharton, congressman; b. nr. Greeneville, Greene County, Tenn., Mar. 18, 1793; ed. pvt. tutors. Enlisted as ensign in War of 1812, promoted lt., 1813; clk. Treasury Dept., Washington D.C., 1817; moved to Mo. Territory, 1818, to Ark. Territory, 1820; receiver public moneys, 1820-21; mem. U.S. Congress (Democrat) from Ark. Territory, 18th-20th congresses, 1823-27. Died nr. Arkansas Post, Ark. (then territorial seat), Nov. 9, 1827; buried Arkansas Post Cemetery.

CONWAY, James Sevier, gov. Ark.; b. Greene County, Tenn., Dec. 9, 1798; s. Thomas and Ann (Rector) C.; m. Mary Bradley, Dec. 21, 1826, 2 children. Surveyor-gen. Ark. Territory, 1829-36; 1st gov. Ark., 1836-40. Died Walnut Hills, Lafayette County, Ark., Mar. 3, 1855.

CONWAY, Martin Franklin, congressman; b. Harford County, Md., Nov. 19, 1827; s. Dr. W.D. and Frances (Maulsby) C.; m. Emily Dykes, June 1851. A founder Typog. Union; admitted to the bar; mem. 1st Kan. Territorial Legislature; del. Leavenworth (Kan.) Constl. Conv., 1858, pres., 1859; chief justice Supreme Ct. under Topeka (Kan.) Constn.; mem. U.S. Ho. of Reps. from Kan., 36th-37th congrerses, Jan. 29, 1861-Mar. 3, 1863; U.S. consul at Marseilles, France, 1866. Died St. Elizabeth's Hosp. for the Insane, Washington, D.C., Feb. 15, 1882.

CONWAY, Thomas, army officer; b. Ireland, Feb. 27, 1735. Commd. brig. gen. Continental Army, May 13, 1777; recommended for promotion to maj. gen., promotion opposed by Washington, as result, Conway resigned; resignation not accepted, became maj. gen. and insp. gen., Dec. 14, 1777; served in battles of Germantown, Brandywine, 1777; organizer conspiracy Conway Cabal to replace Washington with Gen. Horatio Gates, 1778, badly wounded in duel with Gen. Cadwallader, July 4, 1778; gov. gen. French possessions in India, 1787; resigned from Continental Army, 1778; named comdr. Order St. Louis, 1787; called Count de Conway. Died 1800.

CONYNGHAM, Gustavus, naval officer; b. County Donegal, Ireland, 1744; s. Gastavus Conyngham; m. Ann Hockley, 1773. Came to Am., 1763; commd. capt. ship Surprise, Continental Navy, 1777, captured ships Joseph, Prince of Orange, 1777; took command ship Revenge; arrived at Phila. with 60 prizes, 1779; captured by British, shipped to Eng., escaped, 1779, re-captured, 1780, exchanged, 1781; became mcht., Phila.; mem. Phila. Common Council during War of 1812. Died Nov. 27, 1819; buried St. Peter's Churchyard, Phila.

COOK, Burton Chauncey, congressman, lawyer; b. Pittsford, Monroe County, N.Y., May 11, 1819; attended Collegiate Inst., Rochester, N.Y.; studied law. Moved to Ottawa, Ill., 1835; practiced law, 1840; state's atty. for 9th Jud. Dist., 1846-52; mem. Ill. Senate, 1852-60; del., seconded nomination of Lincoln for Pres., Nat. Republican Convs., Chgo., 1860, nominated Lincoln for Pres., Balt., 1864; mem. Washington (D.C.) Peace Conv., 1861; mem. U.S. Ho. of Reps. (Rep.) from Ill., 39th-42d congresses, 1865-Aug. 26, 1871 (resigned); practiced law, Evanston, Ill. Died Evanston, Aug. 18, 1894; buried Oakwood Cemetery, Chgo.

COOK, Clarence Chatham, art critic; b. Dorchester, Mass., Sept. 8, 1828; s. Zebedee and Caroline (Tuttle) C.; grad. Harvard, 1849; studied architecture, Newburg, N.Y.; m. Louisa (de Wendt) Whittemore, Sept. 1853. Wrote art column for N.Y. Tribune, 1863-66, spl. corr., Paris, France, 1869-70; his 1st important criticism was paintings at Sanitary Fair, N.Y., 1863; wrote critical pamphlet attacking Cypriote antiquities at Met. Mus. of Art, also Luigi Palma de Cesnola's character (refused to testify in lawsuit that ensued because he had no proof); editor mag. The Studio, 1884-92. Author: The New York Central Park, 1869 (pamphlet); Life of the Virgin, 1878; The House Beautiful, 1878; Art and Artists of our Time, 3 vols., 1888. Died June 2, 1900.

COOK, Daniel Pope, congressman; b. Scott County, Ky., 1794; attended common schs.; studied law. Admitted to bar, practiced in Kaskaskia, Ill., 1815; in newspaper work Edwardsville, Ill., 1816; editor Ill. Intelligencer; auditor public accounts, 1816; judge Western Circuit; apptd. 1st atty. gen. of Ill., 1819; mem. U.S. Ho. of Reps. from Ill., 16th-19th congresses, 1819-27; directed by Pres. Adams to report on polit. conditions in Cuba, 1827; Ill. county named in his honor. Died Scott County, Oct. 16, 1827.

COOK, Ebenezer, poet; b. presumably in Eng.; lived in Md.; satirized Md. in The Sot-Weed Factor, pub. 1708; also apparently wrote Sot-Weed Redivivus, or The Planter's Looking Glass, pub. Annapolis, Md., 1730.

COOK, George Hammell, geologist, educator; b. Hanover, N.J., Jan. 5, 1818; s. John and Sarah (Munn) C.; grad. Rensselaer Poly. Inst., 1839, B. Natural Scis., 1840, M.S., 1841; Ph.D. (hon.), U. City N.Y., 1875; LL.D. (hon.), Union Coll., 1866; m. Mary Thomas, Mar. 6, 1846. Prof. geology and civil engring. Rensselaer Poly. Inst., 1842, prof. mathematics and natural philosophy, 1848; prof. mathematics and natural philosophy, Albany Acad., 1848-52, prin., 1851; prof. chemistry and natural scis. Rutgers Coll., 1853-89; state geologist N.J., 1864-89; organizer N.J. State Coll. (for promotion agr. and mech. arts), attached to Rutgers, 1864; helped form, mem. exec. bd. N.J. Bd. Agr.; dir. agrl. expt. stas. in N.J., 1880; influential in promotion Act of Congress 1887 creating agrl. expt. stas. in all states; pres. New Brunswick (N.J.) Bd. Water Commrs.; mem. N.J. Bd. Health; chief dir. N.J. Weather Service, 1886. Died New Brunswick, Sept. 22, 1889.

COOK, Isaac, govt. ofcl., wine co. exec.; b. Long Branch, N.J., July 4, 1810; s. Stephen Cook; m. Harriet Norton, 3 children. Sheriff, treas. Cook County, Ill., 1848; instrumental in founding Chgo. Daily Times, 1854; apptd. postmaster Chgo., 1855, reapptd., 1858; asso. with founding Daily Chgo. Herald, 1858; asst. treas. Chgo., Rock Island & Pacific R.R.; pres. Am. Wine Co., St. Louis, 1859-86. Died Eureka Springs, Ark., June 23, 1886.

COOK, James, naval officer, explorer; b. Marton Village, Yorkshire, Eng., Oct. 28, 1728. Rose to importance in Brit. Navy by participating in seige of Quebec, 1759, and by charting St. Lawrence River below Que., also charting coast of Newfoundland and Labrador (published 1776-78); made 1st voyage of exploration, 1768-71, took group of observers to study planet Venus from Tahiti, charted New Zealand, surveyed entire coast of Australia; made 2d voyage, 1772-75, surveyed Antarctic regions, discovered island of New Georgia (Solomon Islands); made 3d voyage to survey Arctic regions, 1776-79, explored much of western coast of N.Am., discovered Hawaii; kidnapped Hawaiian king to hold as hostage after Hawaiian natives stole one of his vessels. Killed (with several of his crew) by the highly-insulted natives,, Kealakekua, Hawaii, Feb. 14, 1779.

COOK, James Merrill, politician, financier; b. Ballston Spa, N.Y., Nov. 19, 1807. Mem. N.Y. Constl. Conv., 1846; mem. N.Y. State Senate, 1848-51; treas. State of N.Y., 1851, comptroller, 1854-55; supt. N.Y. State Banking Dept., 1856-61; mem. N.Y. Senate, 1864-67; pres. Ballston Spa Bank. Died Saratoga Springs, N.Y., Apr. 12, 1868.

COOK, John Parsons, congressman, lawyer; Whitestown, Oneida County, N.Y., Aug. 31, 181 studied law. Admitted to bar, 1842, practic in Tipton, Cedar County, Ia.; mem. Ia. Territor Council, 1842-45; mem. Ia. Senate, 1848-5 moved to Davenport, Ia., 1851, practiced law; me U.S. Ho. of Reps. (Whig) from Ia., 33d Congre 1853-55; became banker, Davenport. Died Dave port, Apr. 17, 1872; buried Oakdale Cemete

COOK, Joseph Platt, Continental congressma b. Stratford (now Bridgeport), Conn., Jan. 4, 173 grad. Yale, 1750. Represented town in about sessions of Conn. Gen. Assembly, 1763-83; j tice of peace, 1764; apptd. col. 16th Regt. Militia, 1771; accompanied Gen. Wolcott's for to N.Y. in Revolutionary War, 1776; in comma Continental forces when British burned Danbu Conn., 1777; resigned as col., 1778; mem. Coun of Safety, 1778; mem. Conn. Ho. of Reps., 177 78, 80-82, 84; mem. Continental Congress fr Conn., 1784-88; judge Danbury dist. Probate C 1776-1813; mem. gov.'s council, 1803. Died Da bury, Feb. 3, 1816; buried Wooster Cemetery.

COOK, Marc, author; b. Providence, R.I., M 1, 1854; s. Theodore Dwight Cook; attended Ham ton Coll., N.Y., 1870-74. Wrote poem Prince Ta at age 12 (poem later published); worked on vario newspapers, Worcester, also N.Y.C., until circa 187 wrote poetry mainly under pseudonym Vandy Brown. Author: The Wilderness Cure; The Poe of Vandyke Brown, 1883. Died Utica, N.Y., 188

COOK, Martha Elizabeth Duncan Walker, autho translator; b. Northumberland, Pa., July 23, 180 d. Jonathan Hoge and Mary (Duncan) Walk m. Lt. William Cook, 1824. Moved with family Pitts., circa 1820; editor Continental Monthl 1863-64; sympathized with people of Poland a their cause of freedom. Translated works includi Life of Chopin (Franz Liszt), 1863; Life of Jo of Arc (Guido Goerres), series in Freeman's Jour from German; The Undivine Comedy and oth Poems (Court Sigismund Krasinki) from French a German, 1875. Author: Appeal to the Friends Poland in the United States of America, 187 Died Hoboken, N.J., Sept. 15, 1874.

COOK, Orchard, congressman; b. Salem, Mass Mar. 24, 1763; attended public schs. Became mch assessor Pownal Borough, 1786; town clk., Milfor dist. of Me., 1795-97; justice of peace; jud Lincoln County Ct. Common Pleas, 1799-181 apptd. asst. assessor 25th dist., 1798; overs Bowdoin Coll., 1800-05; mem. U.S. Ho. of Re from Mass., 9th-11th congresses, 1805-11; sher Lincoln County (Me.), 1811; postmaster W casset, Lincoln County, 1811-19. Died Wiscass Aug. 12, 1819; buried Evergreen Cemetery.

COOK, Philip, congressman, army officer; Twiggs County, Ga., July 30, 1817; s. Philip a Martha (Wooten) C.; grad. Ogelthorpe U., Milledg ville, Ga.; grad. U. Va. Law Sch., 1841; m. Sa Lumpkin, 1842, 1 son, Philip. Admitted to G bar, practiced in Ga. at various times until 18 mem. Ga. Senate, 1859-60, 63-64; volunteered pvt. in Confederate Army in Macon County Volu teers, assigned to 4th Ga. Regt., 1861, adjutar 1862; commd. lt. col. after Battle of Seven Day promoted col. after battles of Second Manassas a Sharpsburg (Antietam); promoted brig. gen., 186 wounded and captured at Battle of Petersburg, hosp. there until 1865; mem. Ga. Constl. Con 1865; mem. U.S. Ho. of Reps. (Democrat) fr Ga., 43d-47th congresses, 1873-83; mem. Ga. ca tal commrs. to select new site for capital, 1883-8 sec. state Ga., 1890-94. Died Atlanta, May 2 1894; buried Rose Hill Cemetery, Macon, G

COOK, Russell S., clergyman; b. New Marlbo Mass., Mar. 6, 1811; grad. Auburn (N,Y.) The Sem.; m. Ann Maria Mills, 1837; m. 2d, Harr Newell Rand, 1841; m. 3d, Harriet Ellsworth; 4th, Miss Malan. Ordained to ministry Congreg tional Ch.; pastor Congregational Ch., Lanesbo Mass., 1837-38 (forced to retire due to p throat); corresponding sec. Am. Tract Soc., 183 57; established mag. Am. Messenger, 1843, merg with Trust Mag. (resulting in greatly increas circulation), also published German lang. edi started The Child's Paper, 1852; made popu the system of "colportage," in which evang. studen travelled about selling books; visited Europe, 185 56, contracted lung disease in Switzerland, 185 was unable to continue his work. Died Pleasa Valley, N.Y., Sept. 4, 1864.

COOK, Zadock, congressman; b. Va., Feb. 1 1769; self-educated. Moved to Hancock Count Ga.; one of 1st settlers Clark County, Ga.; ensi in Washington County Militia, 1793; capt. 11 Co., Hancock County Militia, 1796; mem. Ga. H of Reps., 1806-07, 22; mem. Ga. Senate, 1810-1 23-24; mem. U.S. Ho. of Reps. (filled vacanc from Ga., 14th-15th congresses, Dec. 2, 1816-1 retired from public life, settled on his plantati nr. Watkinsville, Ga., became farmer. Died Aug. 1863; buried Jackson Cemetery, Clark (now Ocone County, Ga.

COOK, Zebedee, ins. exec., horticulturist; b. wburyport, Mass., Jan. 11, 1786; s. Zebedee and rah (Knight) C.; Pres., Eagle Ins. Co. of Boston, 22-27; founder Mass. Hort. Soc., 1829, v.p., 2d s.; mem. Mass. Ho. of Reps., 1835-38; pres. Mut. fety Ins. Co. of N.Y.C., Astor Ins. Co., N.Y.C. ed Framingham, Mass., June 24, 1858.

COOKE, Bates, congressman; b. Wallingford, nn., Dec. 23, 1787; attended public schs.; studied . Moved to Lewiston, N.Y.; admitted to bar, ca 1815, practiced in Lewiston; served in War of 12; supr. Town of Cambria, 1814; mem. U.S. of Reps. (Anti-Mason) from N.Y., 22d Congress, 31-33; elected comptroller State of N.Y., 1839; ved as bank commr., 1840-41. Died Lewiston, y 31, 1841; buried Oak Wood Cemetery.

COOKE, Ebenezer (last name sometimes spelled ok), poet; b. London, Eng., 1670; s. Andrew and ne (Bowyer) C. Dep. receiver-gen. Cecil County, ., 1721-23; admitted to Prince George's County d.) bar, 1728; wrote satirical poems primarily. thor: The Sot-Weed Factor, 1708; Sotweed Redi-us, 1830; The Maryland Muse, 1731. Died 1732.

COOKE, Edward Dean, congressman; b. Cascade, buque County, Ia., Oct. 17, 1849; studied law, buque; grad. law dept. Columbian (now George shington) U., 1873. Admitted to bar, 1873, cticed in Chgo.; mem. Ill. Ho. of Reps., 1883; m. U.S. Ho. of Reps. (Republican) from Ill., th-55th congresses, 1895-97. Died Washington, C., June 24, 1897; buried Rosehill Cemetery, go.

COOKE, Eleutheros, congressman, lawyer; b. anville, Washington County, N.Y., Dec. 25, 1787; ended country schs.; studied law. Admitted to , practiced in Granville; moved to Ind., 1817, Sandusky, O., 1819; mem. Ohio Ho. of Reps., 22-23, 25, 40; obtained 1st charter granted to lroad in U.S., Mad River & Lake Erie R.R. from io Legislature, 1826 (ground broken for it, 32); mem. U.S. Ho. of Reps. (Nat.-Republican) m Ohio, 22d Congress, 1831-33. Died Sandusky, c. 27, 1864; buried on his estate Ogontz, nr. ila.

COOKE, Elisha, colonial legislator; b. Boston, pt. 16, 1637; s. Richard and Elizabeth C.; grad. rvard, 1657; m. Elizabeth Leverett, June 1668, son, Elisha. Dep. from Boston to Mass. Gen. Ct., 81-84, speaker, 1682-84, mem. bd. assistants, 84; a leader in overthrow of Joseph Dudley res. New Eng.) and Sir Edmund Andros (gov. w Eng.), and re-establishing separate existence colonies; colonial agt. in London, Eng., 1690- ; councillor, 1694-1703; influential in ending crease Mather's efforts to set up new charter for rvard, also in forcing his resignation as pres. rvard, 1701. Died Boston, Oct. 31, 1715.

COOKE, Elisha, physician, jurist; b. Boston, Dec. , 1678; s. Elisha and Elizabeth (Leverett) C.; ad. Harvard, 1697; m. Jane Middlecott, 1703. em. Mass. Ho. of Reps., 1715-34, speaker, 1720; osen to Mass. Gov.'s Council, 1717, 18, 24-26, ; judge Ct. Common Pleas of Suffolk County lass.), 1731; upholder colonists rights of repre-ntation. Died Aug. 24, 1737.

COOKE, George, artist; b. St. Mary's County, l., Mar. 17, 1793; m. Mary Ann Heath, Mar. , 1816. Mcht., St. Mary's County, 1810; in ocery and china bus., Georgetown, D.C., 1812; led in bus., 1818, went West; began painting ofessionally, 1819-20; painted 130 portraits, be-re 1825; painted extensively in cities in East d South; gallery built by Daniel Pratt to display oke's paintings, Prattville, Ala.; exhibited at Bos-n Athenaeum, N.A.D., Pa., Am. acads., Apollo llery and Assn., Richmond, Va. Died New Orleans, ar. 26, 1849; buried Prattville.

COOKE, Henry David, journalist, businessman, gov. ashington, D.C.; b. Sandusky, O., Nov. 23, 1825; Eleutheros and Martha (Carswell) C.; grad. ansylvania U., 1844; m. Laura Humphreys. Fi-ncial editor U.S. Gazette; editor Register, San-sky; in Cal. at time of discovery of gold at Sac-mento River; obtained specimens, on return trip Valparaiso, deviated to Isthmus of Panama, ere he had Lt. Beale carry his gold nuggets to brother Jay Cooke, a Phila. banker (1st Cal. ld ever seen in East), in this way news of dis-very of Cal. gold 1st reached the East; editor io State Jour., 1856; in charge of Washington fice Jay Cooke & Co.; 1st pres. Georgetown St. . Co.; organizer 1st Nat. Bank of D.C., Nat. Life s. Co.; 1st gov. Washington, D.C., 1871-73, or-nized system of improved streets and hwys. in C. Died Georgetown, D.C., Feb. 29, 1881.

COOKE, John Esten, physician, educator; b. Ber-ida, Mar. 2, 1783; s. Dr. Stephen and Catherine sten) C.; M.D., U. Pa., 1805. Practiced medi-ne, Warrenton, Va., 1805-21; prof. theory and actice medicine Transylvania U. Med. Sch., Lexing-n, Ky., 1827-32; published (with C. W. Short) Transylvania Journal of Medicine and the Associate Sciences, 1828; prof. ch. history and polity Episcopalian Sem., 1832-37; co-founder Louisville (Ky.) Med. Inst. (later U. Louisville), 1837, prof. theory and practice medicine, 1837-44, dismissed for his radical med. practices. Author: Treatise on Pathology and Therapeutics, 1828 (earliest Am. systematic med. textbook); Essays on the Autumnal and Winter Epidemics, 1829; Essay on the Invalidity of Presbyterian Ordination, 1829. Died Oct. 19, 1853.

COOKE, John Esten, author; b. Winchester, Va., Nov. 3, 1830; s. John Rogers and Maria (Pendleton) C.; studied law with father; m. Mary Francis Page, Sept. 18, 1867, 3 children. Admitted to Va. bar, 1851, practiced in Richmond, 1 year; author: Leather Stocking and Silk, 1854; The Virginia Comedians, 1854; Henry St. John, 1859; served as capt. Confederate Army, 1861-65; author: Life of Stonewall Jackson, 1863; Surry of Eagle's Nest, 1866; Wearing of the Gray, 1867; Mohun, 1869; Hammer and Rapier, 1870, The Heir of Gaymount, 1870; A Life of General Robert E. Lee, 1871; Virginia, 1883; My Lady Pokahontas, 1885. Died "The Briars," Clarke County, Va., Sept. 27, 1886.

COOKE, John Rogers, state legislator; b. Bermuda, 1788; s. Stephen and Catherine (Esten) C.; attended Coll. William and Mary; m. Maria Pendleton, Nov. 18, 1813, at least 3 children including Philip Pendleton, John Esten. Admitted to Va. bar, 1812; practiced in Martinsburg, Va. (now W.Va.), 1812-16, Winchester, Va., 1816-40, Richmond, Va., 1840-54; mem. Va. Ho. of Dels. from Frederick County, 1814; mem. Va. Constl. Conv., 1829-30, mem. com. which drafted constn. Died Richmond, Dec. 15, 1854.

COOKE, Josiah Parsons, chemist, educator; b. Boston, Oct. 12, 1827; s. Josiah and Mary (Pratt) C.; grad. Harvard, 1848, LL.D. (hon.), 1889; LL.D. (hon.), Cambridge (Eng.) U., 1882; m. Mary Huntington, 1860. Erving prof. chemistry and mineralogy Harvard, 1850-94; 1st coll. instr. to use lab. in undergrad. course; noted for investigation of atomic weight of Antimony; Mem. Nat. Acad. Scis., Am. Acad. Arts and Scis. (corr. sec. 1873-92, pres. 1892-94). Author: Elements of Chemical Physics, 1860; First Principles of Chemical Philosophy, 1868; The New Chemistry, 1872, rev. edit., 1884; Chemical and Physical Researches, 1881. Died Cambridge, Mass., Sept. 3, 1894.

COOKE, Philip Pendleton, poet; b. Martinsburg, Va. (now W.Va.), Oct. 26, 1816; s. John Rogers and Maria (Pendleton) C.; grad. Princeton, 1834; m. Willie Anne Burwell, 1836. Admitted to Va. bar, 1836, practiced in Clarke County, Va., 1836-50; wrote poem "Florence Vane," 1840, short stories, "The Gregories of Hackwood," "The Two Country Houses," "John Carper, the Hunter of Lost River," "The Crime of Andrew Blair" (all between 1848-49); wrote Froissart Ballads and Other Poems, 1847. Died Jan. 20, 1850.

COOKE, Philip St. George, army officer; b. Leesburg, Va., June 13, 1809; s. Dr. Stephen and Catherine (Esten) C.; grad. U.S. Mil. Acad., 1827; m. Rachel Hertzog; children—John Rogers, Flora. Served as adj., 1st lt., capt. U.S. Army in Blackhawk War, 1831; served as 1st lt. in Tex., Ark., N.M., 1833; commd. capt., 1835; accompanied Col. Kearney through St. Pass, Rocky Mountains, thence to Ft. Leavenworth via the headwaters of Ark. River, 1845; commd. lt. col., 1846, ordered to make exploring expdn. to Cal., making a practical wagon road en route, 1846; reached San Diego Mission, 1847, here acquired for govt. 250,000 sq. miles of territory; commanded battalion Mo. Volunteers in Cal. during Mexican War, 1846-48; maj. 2d Dragoons, 1847; supt. cavalry barracks, Carlisle, Pa., 1848-52; commd. col., 1858; brig. gen. U.S. 1861; in command cavalry Army of Potomac at Siege of Yorktown, also battles of Gaines Mill, Frayser's Farm, Williamsburg, Glendale; gen. supt. recruiting for U.S. Army; ret., 1873. Died Detroit, Mar. 20, 1895.

COOKE, Rose Terry, author; b. nr. Hartford, Conn., Feb. 17, 1827; d. Henry Wadsworth and Anne (Harlbut) Terry; grad. Hartford Female Sem., 1843; m. Rollin H. Cooke, 1873. Taught sch., Hartford and Burlington, N.J.; became governess until able to support herself by writing, circa 1860; contbr. poems to N.Y. Tribune; writings include: Poems, 1860, Happy Dodd, or She Hath Done What she Could (collected short stories), 1878; Somebody's Neighbors, 1881; Root-Bound and Other Sketches, 1885; The Spinx's Children and Other People's, 1886; Steadfast (novel), 1889; poems include My Apple Tree, The Sheepfold, The River, The Snow-Filled Nest, Trailing Arbitus. Died Pittsfield, Mass., July 18, 1892.

COOKE, Thomas Burrage, congressman; b. Wallingford, Conn., Nov. 21, 1778. Moved to N.Y., circa 1802, settled in Catskill; became mcht.; mem. U.S. Ho. of Reps. (Democrat) from N.Y., 12th Congress, 1811-13; elected pres. of what is now Catskill Nat. Bank, 1813; justice of peace, 1818; in water freight business, 1823; an incorporator Catskill & Canajoharie Ry., 1830; mem. N.Y. State Assembly, 1838-39. Died Catskill, Nov. 20, 1853; buried Village Cemetery.

COOKMAN, Alfred, clergyman; b. Columbia, Pa., Jan. 4, 1828; s. George Grimston and Mary (Barton) C.; m. Annie E. Brunner, Mar. 6, 1851. Preached to sailors in youth; joined Phila. Conf. of Methodist Episcopal Ch., 1848; pastor various chs., Phila., N.Y.C., Newark, N.J., Wilmington, Del. Died Newark, Nov. 13, 1871.

COOLEY, Thomas MacIntyre, jurist, educator; b. Utica, N.Y., Jan. 6, 1824; s. Thomas and Rachel (Hubbard) C.; m. Mary Horton, Jan. 1846. Admitted to Mich. bar, 1846; ofcl. reporter Mich. Supreme Ct., 1858; Jay prof. law Dept. Law, U. Mich., 1859-84, sec., prof., dean Sch. Polit. Sci., 1859-98; justice Mich. Supreme Ct., 1864-78, chief justice, 1868-69; lectr. on constl. law Johns Hopkins, 1877-79; receiver Wabash R.R. System, 1885; chmn. U.S. Interstate Commerce Commn., 1887-91. Died Ann Arbor, Mich., Sept. 12, 1898.

COOLIDGE, Cornelius, architect; b. 1778, Engaged in merc. bus.; practiced as architect, Boston; designed and built numerous residences in Boston, including about 50 houses on Beacon Hill. Died circa 1843; buried Granary Burying Ground, Boston.

COOMBE, Thomas, clergyman; b. Phila., Nov. 1, 1747; grad. Coll. of Phila., 1766. Went to England, 1768; ordained to ministry Ch. of England, 1769; returned to Am., 1772; asst. minister Christ Ch. and St. Peter's Ch., Phila., 1772-78; friendly toward cause of colonies but ordination oath made it impossible for him to approve of Declaration of Independence; went to N.Y.C., 1778, to England, 1779; chaplain to Earl of Carlisle, later chaplain in ordinary to King George III; prebendary of Canterbury, 1800-08; rector 3 united London parishes, 1808-22. Author: The Harmony between the Old and New Testaments Respecting the Messiah, 1774, Influence of Christianity on the Condition of the World, 1790 (both sermons); The Peasant of Auburn; or the Emmigrant (poems), 1783. Died London, Aug. 15, 1822.

COOPER, Elias Samuel, surgeon; b. nr. Somerville, O., Nov. 25, 1820; s. Jacob and Elizabeth (Walls) C.; M.D., St. Louis U., 1841. An organizer Med. Soc. Cal.; founded 1st med. coll. on Pacific coast (became part of Stanford 1908), San Francisco, 1858; with med. dept. U. Pacific. Died San Francisco, Oct. 13, 1862.

COOPER, Ezekiel, clergyman; b. Caroline County, Md., Feb. 22, 1763; s. Richard and Ann Cooper. Admitted on trial to ministry Methodist Ch., 1785, ordained deacon, 1788; pastor at L.I., N.Y., East Jersey and Trenton, N.J., Balt., Annapolis, Md., Alexandria, Va., Boston, N.Y.C., Bklyn., Phila., Wilmington, Del.; agt. Meth. Book Concern, 1799-1808; wrote letters printed in Md. Gazette, Va. Gazette and Md. Jour. in which he advocated abolition of slavery, 1790-91. Author: A Funeral Discourse on the Death of that Eminent Man the Late John Dickins, 1799; The Substance of a Funeral Discourse . . . on the Death of the Reverend Francis Asbury, 1819. Died Feb. 21, 1847.

COOPER, George Bryan, congressman; b. Long Hill, Morris County, N.J., June 6, 1808; attended public schs. Moved to Ann Arbor, Mich., 1830, to Jackson, Mich., 1835, became mcht.; postmaster Jackson, 1836-46; mem. Mich. Senate, 1837-38; established iron foundry, Jackson, 1840; mem. Mich. Ho. of Reps., 1842; treas. Mich., 1846-50; became banker, Jackson, 1851; mem. U.S. Ho. of Reps. (Democrat, contested election) from Mich., 36th Congress, 1859-May 15, 1860; returned to N.J., lived in New Bedford, Monmouth County. Died Aug. 29, 1866; probably buried Shark River, N.J.

COOPER, George Victor, artist; b. Hanover, N.J., Jan. 12, 1878. Worked in N.Y.C., 1835-36; exhibited portraits at Apollo Assn., N.A.D., 1839; provided illustrations for California Illustrated (J. M. Lett), published 1853; worked in N.Y.C., 1851-78; painted portrait of Lincoln, 1865. Died N.Y.C., Nov. 12, 1878.

COOPER, Henry, senator, lawyer; b. Columbia, Maury County, Tenn., Aug. 22, 1827; attended Dixon Acad., Shelbyville, Tenn.; grad. Jackson (Tenn.) Coll., 1847; studied law. Admitted to bar, 1850, practiced in Shelbyville; mem. Tenn. Ho. of Reps., 1853-60; del. Nat. Democratic Conv., Balt., 1860; apptd. judge Tenn. 7th Jud. Circuit, 1862-66, resigned; prof. law sch., Lebanon, Tenn., 1866-67, resigned; moved to Nashville, Tenn., practiced law; mem. Tenn. Senate, 1869-70; mem. U.S. Senate (Democrat) from Tenn., 1871-77. Killed by bandits while engaged in mining operations, Tierra Blanca, Guadelupe y Calvo, Mexico, Feb. 3, 1884; buried where he was killed.

COOPER, James, senator; b. Frederick County, Md., May 8, 1810; grad. Washington Coll., 1832. Admitted to Pa. bar, 1834; mem. U.S. Ho. of Reps. from Pa., 26th-27th congresses, 1839-43; mem. Pa. Legislature, 1844-48, speaker Pa. Assembly, 1847; atty. gen. Pa., 1848-49; mem. U.S. Senate from Pa., 1849-55; commd. brig. gen. Md. Volunteers, 1861; in command of Camp Wallace, Columbus, O.; comdr. Camp Chase, nr. Columbus. Died Camp Chase, Mar. 28, 1863.

COOPER, James Fenimore, novelist; b. Burlington, N.J., Sept. 15, 1789; s. William and Elizabeth (Fenimore) C.; ed. Yale, 1803-05; M.A. (hon.), Columbia, 1824; m. Susan DeLancey, Jan. 1, 1811; children—Susan Augusta, Paul. Wrote The Spy, 1821, became largest selling Am. book up to that time, 3d edit. published 1822, dramatized, 1822, equally popular in Eng., translated into French, 1822, later into other European langs.); wrote at least 1 book per year, after 1824; apptd. U.S. consul at Lyons (France), 1826-29; welcomed in Europe as the outstanding Am. novelist, stayed until 1833; authored several books (circa 1838) expressing discontent with Am. way of life, resulting in loss of popularity; other works include: Precaution, 1820; The Pioneers, The Pilot, 1823; Lionel Lincoln, 1825; The Last of the Mohicans, 1826; The Prairie, The American Democrat, 1827; The Red Rover, Nations of the Americans, 1828; The Water Witch, 1830; The Bravo, 1831; The Headsman, 1833; The Monihins, 1835; Sketches of Switzerland, 1836; Homeward Bound, Home as Found, 1838; Gleamings in Europe, 1837-38; A History of the Navy of the U.S.A., 1839; The Pathfinder, 1840; The Deerslayer, 1841; The Redskins, 1846. Died Cooperstown, N.Y., Sept. 14, 1851; buried Cooperstown.

COOPER, James Graham, naturalist; b. N.Y.C., June 19, 1830; s. William and Frances (Graham) C.; grad. Coll. Physicians and Surgeons, N.Y.C., 1851; m. Rosa Wells, Jan. 9, 1866. Physician Pacific R.R. Survey Expdn., 1853-55; contract surgeon to U.S. Army; zoologist Geol. Survey of Cal.; became expert on geog. and biologic aspects of Pacific coast regions; one of 1st to collect materials and write about natural history of Cal. and Ore.; wrote chapter on zoology for Natural Wealth of California (T. F. Cronise), 1868; practiced medicine, Santa Cruz, Cal., 1866-71; lived in Ventura County, Cal., 1871-75, Oakland, Cal., 1871-1902. Cooper Ornithol. Soc. named in his honor. Died July 19, 1902.

COOPER, John, Continental congressman; b. nr. Woodbury, Gloucester County, N.J., Feb. 5, 1729; had liberal edn. Mem. Gloucester County Com. on Correspondence, 1774; mem. Provincial Congress, 1775-76, mem. com. that drafted 1st N.J. Constn.; apptd. by Provincial Congress as treas. Western div. of N.J., 1775-76; mem. N.J. Legislative Council from Gloucester County, 1776-80, 84; mem. Continental Congress from N.J., 1776; mem. N.J. Council of Safety, 1778; elected judge of pleas Gloucester County Cts., 1779, reelected, 1784-85. Died Woodbury, Apr. 1, 1785; buried Quaker Cemetery.

COOPER, Mark Anthony, congressman, businessman; b. Hancock County, Ga., Apr. 20, 1800; s. Thomas and Sallie C.; A.B., U. S.C., 1819; m. Mary Evalina Flournoy, 1821; m. 2d, Sophronia A.R. Randle, 1826; 10 children. Admitted to Eatonton (Ga.) bar, 1821; mem. Ga. Legislature, 1833; organized cotton mill, Eatonton, 1833; founder bank Columbus, Ga., 1835; shareholder nail factory, Etowah, Ga., organizer East & West R.R. in Northwest Ga.; mem. U.S. Ho. of Reps. from G., 26th-28th congresses, 1839-45. Died Etowah, Mar. 17, 1885.

COOPER, Myles, clergyman, coll. pres.; b. Eng., 1737; s. William and Elizabeth Cooper; B.A., Queen's Coll., Oxford (Eng.) U., 1756, M.A., 1760; LL.D., Oxford, 1768. Ordained to ministry Anglican Ch., 1761; came to Am., 1762; prof. moral philosophy, fellow King's Coll. (now Columbia), N.Y., 1762, pres. 1763-75, fled to Eng. because his Loyalist sentiments endangered life. Author: Poems on Several Occasions, 1761; The American Querist, 1774. Died Edinburgh, Scotland, May 20, 1785.

COOPER, Peter, mfr., inventor, philanthropist; b. N.Y.C., Feb. 12, 1791; s. John and Margaret (Campbell) C.; m. Sarah Beedell, Dec. 18, 1813, 6 children. Mfr. glue, N.Y.C., 1828; built Canton Iron Works, Balt., 1828; built 1st Am. steam locomotive, 1830; promoter, financial backer laying of Atlantic Cable; rolled 1st structural iron for fireproof bldgs. in his Trenton (N.J.) factory, for which he received Bessemer gold medal award Iron and Steel Inst. of Gt. Britain, 1870; pres. N.Y., Newfoundland & London Telegraph Co., N. Am. Telegraph Co.; founder Cooper Union Coll., N.Y.C., 1857-59; Greenback Party candidate for Pres. U.S., 1876; owner foundries at Ringwood, N.J., wire factory, Trenton, rolling mill, N.Y.C.; inventor washing machine, machine for using tides as source of power. Died N.Y.C., Apr. 4, 1883.

COOPER, Richard Matlack, congressman; b. Gloucester County, N.J., Feb. 29, 1768; completed prep. studies. Became banker; coroner, 1795-99; judge and justice Gloucester County Cts., 1803-23; mem. N.J. Gen. Assembly, 1807-10; pres. State Bank of N.J., Camden, 1813-42; mem. U.S. Ho. of Reps. from N.J., 21st-22d congresses, 1829-33. Died Camden, Mar. 10, 1843; buried Newton Burying Ground.

COOPER, Samuel, clergyman; b. Boston, Mar. 28, 1725; s. Rev. William and Judith (Sewall) C.; grad. Harvard, 1743; D.D., U. Edinburgh (Scotland), 1767; m. Judith Bulfinch, 2 daus. Ordained to ministry Congregational Ch., 1746; Asst. pastor Brattle Square Ch., Boston, 1743-47, pastor, 1747-83; a leader in pre-Revolutionary agitation in Boston; v.p. Mass. Acad. Arts and Scis.; 1780; mem. Soc. for the Promotion of the Gospel; mem. corp. Harvard., 1767-83. Died Dec. 23, 1783.

COOPER, Samuel army officer; b. Hackensack, N.J., June 12, 1798; s. Samuel and Mary (Horton) C.; grad. U.S. Mil. Acad., 1815. Aide to Gen. Alexander Macomb, 1828-36; chief-of-staff to Col. W. J. Worth during Seminole War, 1836-37; asst. adj. gen. with rank of maj., 1838; commd. lt., 1847; adj. gen. with rank of col. U.S. Army, 1852-61; adj. and insp. gen. Confederate Army during Civil War. Author: A Concise System of Instruction and Regulations for the Militia and Volunteers of the United States, 1836. Died Cameron, Va., Dec. 3, 1876.

COOPER, Sarah Brown Ingersoll, philanthropist; b. Cazenovia, N.Y., Dec. 12, 1836; d. Capt. Samuel and Laura (Case) Ingersoll; grad. Cazenovia Sem., 1853; m. Halsey Fenimore Cooper, Sept. 4, 1855, 1 dau., Harriet. Pres., Women's Press Assn.; treas. World Fedn. Women's Clubs; dir. Asso. Charities; elected to Pan-Republican Congress of Chgo. World's Fair; organizer Women's Congress in San Francisco, pres. 1894-96; organizer Golden Gate Kindergarten Assn., 1879; founder 44 free kindergartens in San Francisco; pres. Internat. Kindergarten Union (1st pres.), 1892. Died San Francisco, Dec. 11, 1896.

COOPER, Susan Fenimore, author; b. Mamaroneck, L.I., N.Y., Apr. 17, 1813; d. James Fenimore and Susan (De Lancey) Cooper. Travelling companion of her father until his death; editor Am. edition of County Rambles (John Leonard Knapp), 1853; founder Orphan House of Holy Saviour, Cooperstown, N.Y., 1873; wrote reminiscences of her father and accounts of rural life; works include: Rural Hours, 1850; Rhyme and Reason of Country Life, 1854; Rural Rambles, 1854; Mount Vernon, a Letter to the Children of America, 1859; Pages and Pictures from the Writings of James Fenimore Cooper, 1861; William West Skiles, a Sketch of Missionary Life in Valle Crucis in Western North Carolina, 1842-62, 1890. Died N.Y.C., Dec. 31, 1894.

COOPER, Thomas, scientist, coll. pres.; b. London, Eng., Oct. 22, 1759; s. Thomas Cooper; entered Oxford (Eng.) U., 1779; studied medicine London and Manchester; LL.D. (hon.), U.S.C., 1834, m. Alice Greenwood; m. 2d, Elizabeth Hemming, 1811; 8 children. Came to Am. in reaction to English conservative policies, 1794; convicted, sentenced and fined under Sedition Act, 1800; commr. in Luzerne County, Pa., 1801-04; state judge Pa., 1804-11; prof.chemistry Dickinson Coll., 1811-15; prof. applied chemistry and mineralogy U. Pa., 1816-19; prof. chemistry U. S.C., 1820, pres., 1821-34; influential in establishing 1st sch. medicine and 1st insane asylum in S.C., mem. Am. Philos. Soc. Author: On the Constitution, 1826; Lectures on Political Economy, 1826. Editor: Statutes at Large of South Carolina, 5 vols, 1836-39; Thomson System of Chemistry, 4 vols., 1818. Died Columbia, S.C., May 11, 1839; buried Trinity Churchyard, Columbia.

COOPER, Thomas, congressman, lawyer; b. Little Creek Hundred, Sussex County, Del., 1764; completed prep. studies; studied law. Mem. Del. Ho. of Reps., 1803-08; admitted to bar, 1805, practiced law; mem. Del. Senate, 1808; mem. U.S. Ho. of Reps. (Federalist) from Del., 13th-14th congresses, 1813-17; practiced in Georgetown, Del. Died Georgetown, 1829; buried Cooper family cemetery, nr. Laurel, Del.

COOPER, Thomas Abthorpe, actor, theatrical mgr.; b. Harrow-on-the-Hill, Eng., Dec. 16, 1776; s. Thomas and Mary Grace C.; m. Mary Fairlie, June 11, 1812, 7 children. Made Am. debut, Balt., 1796; recognized by N.Y. theater as unrivaled tragic actor in Am., 1798; made 1st appearance Drury Lane, London, Eng., 1803; lessee Park Theater, Boston, 1805-06; last appeared on N.Y. stage, 1835, ret., 1838; most conspicuous figure of his time on Am. stage, known to have acted in every state of Union prior to 1830, appeared in at least 164 different plays; his career an important step in evolution from stock to starring system; greatest roles includ Macbeth, also Roman characters. Died Bristc Pa., Apr. 21, 1849.

COOPER, Thomas Buchecker, congressman, ph sician; b. Coopersburg, Pa., Dec. 29, 1823; attend Pa. Coll., Gettysburg; grad. med. dept. U. Pa 1843. Practiced in Coopersburg; mem. U.S. H of Reps. (Democrat) from Pa., 37th Congres 1861-62. Died Coopersburg, Apr. 4, 1862; buri Woodland Cemetery.

COOPER, William, clergyman; b. Boston, 169 grad. Harvard, 1712. Ordained to ministry Co gregational Ch., 1716; pastor Brattle Street Co gregational Ch., Boston, 1716-43; declined presiden Harvard, 1737; staunch conservative in theol. view sided with Cotton Mather in defense of smallp innoculation. Died Boston, Dec. 13, 1743.

COOPER, William, jurist; b. Phila., Dec. 1754; s. James and Hanna (Hibbs) C.; Elizabeth Fenimore, Dec. 12, 1775; a so novelist James Fenimore Cooper, Founder, Coope town (N.Y.); erected a seminary, 1st jud Otsego County (N.Y., Ct. Common Pleas, 179 mem. U.S. Ho. of Reps. from N.Y., 4th, 6th co gresses, 1795-97, 99-1801. Died Albany, N.Y Dec. 22, 1809; buried Cooperstown.

COOPER, William, naturalist; b. N.Y., 179 Cooper's hawk (of which he collected type spec men in Hudson County, N.Y.) named in his hono 1828.

COOPER, William Raworth, congressman, farm b. nr. Bridgeport, Gloucester County, N.J., Fe 20, 1793; attended local schs. Became farm mem. N.J. Gen. Assembly, 1839-41; mem. U. Ho. of Reps. (Democrat) from N.J., 26th Congre 1839-41. Died nr. Bridgeport, Sept. 22, 185 buried Cooper family burying ground, nr. Bridgepo

COOPER-POUCHER, Matilda S., educator; Blauveltville, N.Y., Feb. 2, 1839; d. Mr. Coop grad. Albany (N.Y.) State Normal Sch., 185 m. Issac B. Poucher, Feb. 4, 1890. Tchr., Oswe (N.Y.) schs., 1856-65; critic tchr., later tc langs. and methods, perceptress Normal Boardi Hall at Oswego State Normal Sch., 1865-86; car for parents until their death, at home, Nyac N.Y., 1886-89; lived with husband (dean Oswe State Normal Sch.), 1890-1900; bd. dirs. Oswe Hosp.; mem. N.E.A. Died Apr. 5, 1900.

COOTE, Richard (1st earl Bellomont), colon gov.; b. 1636; s. Richard and Mary (St. Georg C.; m. Catherine Nanfan. Mem. Parliament f Droitwich, 1688-95; treas., receiver-gen. to Quee 1687; gov. N.Y., Mass. and N.H., 1697-1701; command Militia for R.I., Conn. and the Jerse during Queen Anne's War; commd. to deal wi colonial problem of illegal trade and pirac brought about arrest of Captain Kidd, 1699. Di N.Y.C., Mar. 5, 1701; buried N.Y.C.

COPE, Caleb, mcht., financier; b. Greer burg. Pa., July 18, 1797; s. William and Eliz beth (Rohrer) C.; m. Josephine Porter, De 1864. Founder firm Caleb Cope & Co., 182 became one of wealthiest men in country; founder Mchts. Hotel Co.; pres. Phila. Sa Fund Soc., 1864; dir. U.S. Bank; an origir trustee Lehigh Coal & Navigation Co.; mgr. F Hosp., Instn. for Instrn. for Blind. Died May 1 1888.

COPE, Edward Drinker, zoologist, paleonto gist; b. Phila., July 28, 1840; s. Alfred a Hanna (Edge) C.; ed. U. Pa., Phila. Aca Scis., Smithsonian Instn.; A.M. (hon.), Hav ford Coll., 1870; Ph.D. (hon.), Heidelberg (G many) U., 1885; m. Annie Pim, Aug. 14, 18 1 child. Prof. comparative zoology and bota Haverford Coll., 1864-67; mem. Phila. Aca Natural Scis., 1861, curator, 1865, mem. counc 1879; paleontologist U.S. Geol. Survey, 187 discovered about 1000 new species extir vertebrata; prof. geology and mineralogy U. Pa 1889-95, prof. zoology and comparative anaton 1895-97. mem. Nat. Acad. Scis., A.A.A. (pres. 1896). Author: Synopsis of the Extir Cetacea of the United States, 1867-68; Syster atic Arrangement of the Extinct Batrach Reptilia and Aves of North America, 1869-7 Relation of Man to Tertiary Mammalia, 187 Died Phila., Apr. 12, 1897.

COPE, Thomas Pym, mcht.; b. Lancaster, Pa Aug. 26, 1768; s. Caleb and Mary (Mendenhal C.; m. Mary Drinker. Established 1st regu line of packet ships between Phila. and Liverpo Eng., 1821; mem. Pa. Legislature, 1807; mer Pa. Constl. Conv., 1837; a founder, pres. f many years Merc. Library Co., an original mer Phila. Bd. Trade, pres., 1832-54; instrumen in completion Chesapeake & Delaware Canal; act in pioneering constrn. Pa. Central R.R.; bd. di Girard Coll. Died Phila., Nov. 22, 1854.

COPE, Walter, architect; b. Phila., Oct. 2 1860; s. Thomas P. and Elizabeth (Stokes) C tudied architecture in office of T. P. Chandler, Phila.; m. Eliza Middleton Kane, 1893. Partner with John Stewardson in archtl. firm, Phila., 1886-96; designed Radnor Hall, 1886, Pembroke, East, West, and Denbeigh halls (all at Bryn Mawr Coll.), Archeol. Museum, Law Sch. (both at U. Pa.), Blair Hall, 1896, Ivy Club, 1897; gymnasium, 1903 (all at Princeton), Lady Chapel of St. Mark's Ch., Phila., Municipal Bldg., Washington, D.C., Pa. Inst. for Instrn. of Blind, Overbrook; fellow A.I.A., 1893-1900; apptd. ofcl. architect U. Pa., 1900, lectr. Sch. Architecture, mgr. Stewardson Travelling scholarship in architecture; chmn. Com. to Restore Congress Hall, Phila.; a founder T-Square Club, Phila. Died Nov. 1, 1902.

COPELAND, Charles W., naval engr.; b. Coventry, Conn., 1815; s. Daniel Copeland; attended Columbia Coll. Designed the machinery of Fulton (1st steam war-vessel to be constructed under direct supervision of U.S. Navy Dept.); supt. Allaire Works, N.Y.C., 1850-60; constrn. engr. U.S. Lighthouse Bd., 1865-95. Died Bklyn., Feb. 6, 1895.

COPLEY, John Singleton, painter; b. Boston, 1738; s. Richard and Mary (Singleton) C.; m. Susannah Clarke, Nov. 16, 1769, 4 children. Largely self-taught, precocious as an artist, famous as painter of hist. subjects, a pioneer Am. pastellist; fellow Soc. Artists of Gt. Britain, 1766; went to Eng. because of Loyalist sympathies, 1775, given choice commns. by the nobility (which portraits he did not consider as good as earlier work in Am.); asso. mem. Royal Acad., 1775, full mem., 1783; works include: The Boy with the Squirrel, 1766, The Death of Lord Chatham, The Red Cross Knight, Abraham Offering Up Isaac, Hagar and Ishmael in the Wilderness, The Death of Major Pierson, The Arrest of Five Members of the Commons by Charles the First, The Siege of Gibralter, The Resurrerction; portraits include John Hancock, Samuel Adams, John Adams, John Quincy Adams, Mrs. Thomas Boylston, Lady Wentworth, Mrs. Robert Harper, Lord Cornwall, Earl of Mansfield. Died London, Eng., Sept. 9, 1815.

COPLEY, Lionel, colonial gov.; 3 children. Commd. capt. Royal Foot Guards, 1676; commd. 1st royal gov. Md., 1691, sworn in, 1692; instituted three separate treaties of peace with the Piscataway, Maltawoman, Choptico Indians, 1692. Died Sept. 9, 1693.

COPPEE, Henry, army officer, coll. pres.; b. Savannah, Ga., Oct. 13, 1821; s. Edward and Carolina (De Lavillate) C.; attended Yale; grad. U.S. Mil. Acad., 1845; A.M (hon.), U. Ga., 1848; LL.D. (hon.), U. Pa., 1866, Union Coll., 1866; m. Julia de Witt, 1848. Engaged in most of battles on Gen. Scott's march from Vera Cruz to Mexico City during Mexican War, 1846-48; brevetted capt. for distinguished service at battles of Contreras and Churubusco, 1847; asst. prof. French, U.S. Mil. Acad., 1848-49; held chair English lit. and history U. Pa., 1855-66; editor U.S. Service Mag., 1864-66; 1st pres. Lehigh U., 1866-75, also prof. history and lit., until 1874, acting pres., 1893-95; regent Smithsonian Instn., 1874-95. Author: Elements of Rhetoric, 1859; The Field Manual for Battalion Drill, 1862; The Field Manual of Evolution of the Line, 1862; Grant and His Campaigns, 1866; Songs of Praise in the Christian Centuries, 1866; English Literature Considered as an Interpreter to English History, 1873; History of the Conquest of Spain by the Arab Moors, 2 vols., 1881; The Classic and the Beautiful, 1888-92; General Thomas, 1893. Died Bethlehem, Pa., Mar. 21, 1895.

COPWAY, George (Indian name Kah-Ge-Ga-Gah-Bowh), Indian chief, missionary; b. Ont., Can., 1818; m. Elizabeth Howell, 1840. Hereditary chief Chippewa (Ojibway) Indians; converted to Methodism, 1830; sent to Lake Superior region as missionary's helper, 1834; missionary in Mich., Minn., Wis., Ia., and Ill.; visited Europe, attended Peace Congress, Frankfurt, Germany, 1850. Author: The Life, History, and Travels of Kah-Ge-Ga-Gah-Bowh, 1847; The Traditional History and Characteristic Sketches of the Ojibway Nation, 1850; The Ojibway Conquest, a Tale of the Northwest, 1850; Organization of a New Indian Territory East of the Missouri River, 1850; Running Sketches of Men and Places in England, France, Germany, Belgium, and Scotland, 1851. Died nr. Pontiac, Mich., 1863.

CORAM, Thomas, mcht.; b. Lyme Regis, Dorsetshire, Eng., 1668; m. Eunice Wayte, June 27, 1700. Came to Am. as head group of shipwrights, 1693; established shipyard, Taunton, Mass., 1697; attempted to extend Ch. of England in Am., caused physical and legal conflicts with his Puritan neighbors; returned to Eng., 1704, traded with colonies on behalf of Admiralty; advocated suppression of Am. industries which competed with English mfrs.; lobbied for Hat Act, 1732; devised various schemes for colonizing Am. with pensioners, convicts, unemployed, artisans (never materialized); mem. Ga. Trust Co. Died Mar. 29, 1751.

CORAM, Thomas, artist; b. Bristol, Eng., Apr. 25, 1757. Came to Charleston, S.C., 1769; took up engraving after 1770; engraved bills of credit for State of S.C. during Am. Revolution; advertised as drawing master, 1784. Died Charleston, May 2, 1811.

CORBIN, Austin, banker, railroad exec.; b. Newport, N.H., July 11, 1827; s. Austin and Mary (Chase) C.; grad. Harvard Law Sch., 1849; m. Hannah Wheeler, 1853, 2 children. Established banking house Maklot & Corbin, Davenport, Ia., 1854 (only banking house in Davenport to pass through panic of 1857); organizer 1st Nat. Bank of Davenport, 1863 (the 1st nat. bank to open for bus. in U.S.); developer Manhattan Beach Ry. to Coney Island; reorganizer L.I. R.R.; pres. Phila. & Reading R.R., Phila. & Reading Coal & Iron Co.; projected trans-Atlantic S.S. line from Ft. Pond Bay (L.I., N.Y.) to Europe. Died Newport, June 4, 1896.

CORBIN, Margaret, heroine; b. in what is now Franklin County, Pa., Nov. 12, 1751; d. Robert Cochran; m. John Corbin, 1772. Accompanied husband when he marched to war with 1st Co., Pa. Arty., Continental Army, 1776; took her husband's place when he was killed while defending a cannon against Hessians in Battle of Ft. Washington, 1776; fought until severely wounded, captured, but not held prisoner; went to Phila., granted lifetime pension by Continental Congress for her bravery. Died Westchester County, N.Y., Jan. 16, 1800.

CORBY, William, clergyman, coll. pres.; b. Detroit, Oct. 2, 1833; ed. U. Notre Dame, 1853-60. Apptd. prefect discipline U. Notre Dame, 1858, prof., dir. Manual Labor Sch., 1860, v.p., 1865, pres., 1866-72, 1877-81, rebuilt univ. during 2d term as pres., added new depts., raised standards; ordained priest Roman Catholic Ch., 1860; chaplain (commd. by gov. N.Y.) to N.Y. "Irish Brigade serving with Army of Potomac, 1861-64; pres. Sacred Heart Coll., Watertown, Wis., 1872-77 founder, comdr. Notre Dame Post 569, Grand Army Republic. Author: Chaplain Life: Three Years in the Army of the Potomac, 1894. Died Notre Dame, Ind., Dec. 28, 1897.

CORCORAN, Katherine, see Herne, Katherine Corcoran.

CORCORAN, Michael, army officer; b. Carrowkeel, Sligo, Ireland, Sept. 21, 1827. Served in Royal Irish Constabulary, 1846-49; came to N.Y., circa 1849; rose through ranks to col. 69th Regt., N.Y. Militia, 1859; up for trial for refusing to permit his men to parade in honor of Prince of Wales, 1860 (court-martial dropped when Civil War began); captured at Battle of Bull Run, imprisoned for 13 months; raised 4 regts. (called Irish Legion) in N.Y., served as brig. gen. of Legion in engagements in Va., 1 year. Died when thrown from his horse, Fairfax Court House, Va., Dec. 22, 1863.

CORCORAN, William Wilson, banker, philanthropist; b. Georgetown, D.C., Dec. 27, 1798; s. Thomas and Hannah (Lemmon) C.; attended Georgetown Coll.; m. Louise Morris Dec.23, 1835. Esablished dry-goods co., W.W. Corcoran, Washington, D.C., 1817; formed banking firm Corcoran & Biggs, Washington, 1840, financed major part of Mexican War bonds, 1848, ret., Louise Home, 1869; gave charitable donations totaling $5,000,000 to various instns., including Columbia U., Ascension Protestant Episcopal Ch., U. Va., Coll. William and Mary, Va. Mil. Inst., Washington and Lee U., Episcopal Theol. Sem., Protestant Orphan Asylum, Acad. of the Visitation of Washington. Died Washington, D.C., Feb. 24, 1888.

CORKER, Stephen Alfestus, congressman, lawyer; b. nr. Waynesboro, Burke County, Ga., May 7, 1830; attended common schs.; studied law. Admitted to bar, practiced in Waynesboro; became farmer; entered Confederate Army, 1861, served as capt. Co. A, 3d Ga. Regt.; mem. Ga. Ho. of Reps.; mem. U.S. Ho. of Reps. (Democrat, filled vacancy) from Ga., 41st Congress, Dec. 22, 1870-71. Died Waynesboro, Oct. 18, 1879; buried Old Cemetery, Waynesboro.

CORLETT, William Wellington, congressman; b. Concord, O., Apr. 10, 1842; grad. Willoughby (O.) Collegiate Inst., 1861; attended U. Mich. Law Sch.; grad. Union Law Coll., Cleve., 1866. Enlisted in Union Army, 1862; served in 28th Regt., Ohio Volunteer Inf. short time, transferred to 87th Regt.; captured with command at Harpers Ferry, 1862, paroled; returned to Ohio; sch. tchr., Kirkland, Painesville, O.; reentered Army with 25th Ohio Battery, later placed on detached service with 3d Ia. Battery, served until end of Civil War; returned to Ohio, 1865; admitted to bar, 1866; prof. elementary law State U. and Law Coll.; lectr. several comml. colls., Cleve.; settled in Cheyenne, Wyo., 1867; practiced law; postmaster Cheyenne, 1870; mem. Wyo. Territorial Senate, 1871; pros. atty. Laramie County, 1872-76; mem. U.S. Congress (Republican) from Wyo. Territory, 45th Congress, 1877-79; declined appointment as chief justice Wyo. Territory, 1879; mem. Wyo. Legislative Council, 1880-82. Died Cheyenne, July 22, 1890; buried Lakeview Cemetery.

CORLISS, George Henry, inventor, mfr.; b. Easton, N.Y., June 2 1817; s. Dr. Hiram and Susan (Sheldon) C.; attended Castleton Acad., 1835-38; m. Phoebe F. Frost, Jan. 1839; m. 2d, Emily A. Shaw, 1866. Invented machine for sewing boots (as a result of customer's complaints), patented 1842; joined firm Fairbanks, Bancroft & Co., 1844; invented improvements for steam engines, patented 1849; merged John Barstow and E.J. Nightingale Co. into Corliss, Nightingale & Co., 1849; incorporated, became pres. Corliss Engine Co., 1856; mem.. R.I. Legislature, 1868-70; built Corliss steam engine (1st to use rotary valves); patented gear cutting machine, an improved boiler with condensing apparatus, pump engine for water-works. Died Providence, R.I., Feb. 21, 1888.

CORNBURY, Viscount, see Hyde, Edward.

CORNÉ, Michel Felice, artist; b. Elba Island, Italy, circa 1752. Brought to Am. by mcht. Elias Hasket Derby, Jr., 1799; worked in Salem, Mass., 1799-1806; in assn. with Samuel McIntire, William King; lived in Boston, 1807-22, became known for paintings of ships and naval battles of War of 1812, some of which were engraved for Abel Bowen's The Naval Monument, 1816; lived in Newport, R.I., after, 1822, did wall paintings; introduced the tomato as an edible to Am. Died Newport, July 10, 1845.

CORNELL, Ezekiel, army officer, Continental congressman; b. Situate, R.I., Mar. 27, 1733; s. Richard and Content (Brownell) C.; m. Rachel Wood, 1790. Dep. adj. gen. 11th Continental Inf., 1776; commd. comdr. with rank brig. gen. R.I. Brigade, 1777; mem. Continental Congress, 1780-83; insp. Continental Army under Washington 1782. Died Milford, Mass., Apr. 25, 1800.

CORNELL, Ezra, telegraph magnate, philanthropist; b. Westchester, N.Y., Jan. 11, 1807; s. Elijah and Eunice (Barnard) C.; m. Mary Ann Wood, Mar. 19, 1831, 1 son, Alonzo B. Worked in flour and plaster mills of J. S. Beebe, Ithaca, N.Y., 1828-41, became gen. mgr.; with Samuel F. B. Morse devised means for insulating telegraph wires on poles and helped erect line from Balt. to Washington, D.C.; owned cos. bldg. lines between many major cities in East and Midwest, including Magnetic Telegraph Co., Erie & Mich. Telegraph Co., N.Y. & Erie Telegraph Co., merged with competing lines to form Western Union Telegraph Co., dir., 1855-74, largest stockholder until 1870; built free pub. library, Ithaca, 1863, model farm, nr. Ithaca; pres. N.Y. State Agrl. Soc., 1862; mem. N.Y. State Assembly, 1861-63, N.Y. State Senate, 1863-67; founded, endowed Cornell U., 1868, provided for edn. of women and poor students in liberal and mech. arts. Died Dec. 9, 1874.

CORNELL, Thomas, congressman; b. White Plains, N.Y., Jan. 27, 1814; attended public schs. In steamboat transp. business between Rondout and N.Y.C., 1843, also in railroad and banking activities; commd. maj. N.Y. Militia in Civil War; mem. U.S. Ho. of Reps. (Republican) from N.Y., 40th, 47th congresses, 1867-69, 81-83; in transp. and banking businses, Kingston, N.Y.; del. Nat. Rep. Conv., Chgo., 1884; Rep. presdl. elector, 1888. Died Kingston, Mar. 30, 1890; buried Montrepose Cemetery.

CORNING, Erastus, railroad exec., congressman; b. Norwich, Conn., Dec. 14, 1794; s. Bliss and Lucinda (Smith) C. Began iron mfg., Albany, N.Y., 1814; 1st pres. Utica and Schenectady R.R., 1833-53 (merged with N.Y. Central, 1853), pres. N.Y.C. R.R., 1853-64, dir., 1864-67; dir. Mich. Central R.R., Hudson River R.R., 1849-63; organized Corning Land Co. to establish comml. center on Chemung River, 1835, named village Corning in his honor; mayor Albany, 1834-37; mem. N.Y. State Senate, 1842-46; mem. U.S. Ho. of Reps. (Democrat) from N.Y., 35th, 37th-38th congresses, 1857-59, 61-Oct. 5, 1863; mem. Washington (D.C.) Peace Conv., 1861; mem. N.Y. State Constl. Conv., 1867; regent U. .N.Y., 1833-72. Died Albany, Apr. 9, 1872; buried Rural Cemetery, Albany.

CORNSTALK (Indian name Keigh-tugh-gua), Indian chief; b. Pa., 1720. Shawnee Indian chief; ally of French, made 1st attack on English settlers, Rockbridge County, Va., 1759; ally of Pontiac, 1763; taken hostage (with brother Silver Heels) and released on parole; remained at peace with settlers during border skirmishes, 1764-74; objected to authorities after his brother was maliciously shot and wounded; Lord Dunmore (gov. Va.) decided to settle matter by force (Lord Dunmore's War, 1764, ended by treaty of Camp Charlotte, 1774); taken hostage at Ft. Pitt (now Ohio) while on mission to warn settlers of impending Shawnee uprising, 1777. Murdered with other hostages after Indians killed a white soldier, Ft. Pitt, 1777.

CORNWALLIS, Charles (1st marquis and 2d earl of Cornwallis), army officer, gov.-gen. of India; b. Grosvenor Sq., London, Eng., Dec. 31, 1738; s. Charles Cornwallis (1st earl of Cornwallis); attended Eton, also Turin (Italy) Mil. Acad.; m. Jemima Tullikens, 1768, 1 son, Charles. Commd. ensign Grenadier Guards, 1756; promoted capt. 85th Regt., 1759; lt. col. 12th Regt., 1761; col. 33d Regt., 1766; joint vice treas. of Ireland, 1769-70; constable of Tower of London, 1770; promoted maj. gen. Brit. Army, 1775; sent to duty in Am., 1776; served in battles of S.I., L.I., Bklyn., also capture of N.Y.C.; won Battle of Brandywine and occupied Phila., 1777; made 2d in command in N.Am. to Sir Henry Clinton, 1778; drew up plans for invasion of Southern colonies took charge of these operations, 1779, captured Charleston, S.C., 1780; forced to surrender at Yorktown, Va. (after Gen. Washington cut him off from aid by Clinton), 1781, blamed Clinton's inactivity for the failure; gov.-gen. of India (rendered services considered invaluable to the Crown), 1785-93. Died Ghazipore, India (while gen.-in-chief in India), Oct. 5, 1805; buried Ghazipore.

CORONADO, Francisco Vázquez de, Spanish explorer; b. Salamanca, Spain, circa 1510; m. Beatriz de Estrada, 1537. Came to Mexico in retinue of Antonio de Mendoza (1st viceroy New Spain), 1535; acquired estate nr. Mexico City through marriage, 1537; helped suppress negro uprising in mines of Amatepeque; became gov. Nueva Galicia, 1538, did much to improve capital city, Guadalajara; assisted Fray Marcos de Niza in embarking upon his No. explorations, 1538 (from which he returned with reports of wealthy Seven Cities of Cibola); apptd. capt.-gen. of large expdn. (over 1,000 men) to find the Seven Cities, started on quest, Feb. 1540; conquered Zuni pueblos, but found no treasure, July 1540; sent out 3 lieuts. who did valuable exploration in arca (especially Garcia Lopez de Cárdenas, discoverer Grand Canyon of Colo.); learned from Plains Indian named Turk that rich country called Gran Quivira lay Northeast, set out to find it, Apr. 1451; traveled over mountains, down Pecos River, across Tex. Panhandle, and into Okla. and Kan., only to find Quivira an ordinary Indian (probably Wichita) settlement; his expdn. considered a failure; dismissed as gov. and fined after investigation of his ill treatment of natives, 1544; ret. to Mexico City, served as regidor in municipal adminstrn. until death; made last pub. appearance, Jan. 26, 1554. Died sometime before Nov. 12, 1554.

CORRE, Joseph, theatre mgr. Promoted building of Corre's Mt. Vernon Gardens, 1st of spl. summer theatres in N.Y. presenting standard plays with prominent actors as well as the usual concerts and variety acts (precursor of present-day "straw-hat" theatres), N.Y.C., 1800.

CORSE, John Murray, army officer; b. Pitts., Apr. 27, 1835; s. John T. and Sarah (Murray) C.; entered U.S. Mil. Acad., 1853; m. Ellen F. Prince, Dec., 1856; m. 2d Frances McNeil, 1882; 2 children. Commd. maj. 6th Ia. Inf., 1861, lt. col. U.S. Volunteers, 1862, col., 1863, brig. gen., 1863; insp. gen. U.S. Army under Gen. Sherman, 1864; collector internal revenue, Chgo., 1866 postmaster, Boston, 1885. Died Winchester, Mass., Apr. 27, 1893; buried Burlington, Ia.

CORSON, Juliet, home economist; b. Roxbury, Mass., Feb. 14, 1842; d. Peter R. and Mary Ann (Henderson) Corson. Librarian, Working Women's Library, N.Y.U., 1860-73; wrote weekly column for N.Y. Leader; conducted Free Tng. Sch. for Women, 1873-76, taught sewing, cooking and secretarial skills; conducted cooking sch. with tuition, 1876; began giving lectures and short schs. in cooking throughout U.S., also appeared in Canada and Europe; editor Household Monthly, 1890-91; won prize for scientific cooking and sanitary dietetics World's Columbian Expn., Chgo., 1893. Author: Fifteen Cent Dinners for Workingmen's Families, 1877; Cooking Manual, 1877; Family Living on $500 a Year, 1887. Died N.Y.C., June 18, 1897; buried Greenwood Cemetery, Bklyn.

CORTAMBERT, Louis Richard, author; b. Paris, France, 1808; m. Susan Chouteau. Editor, La Revue de l'Ouest (weekly French paper), St. Louis, 1855-58, Le Messager Franco-Américain (French daily), N.Y.C., 1864-81; abolitionist and follower philosophy of Thoreau; writings include: Voyage aux Pays des Osages, 1847; Les Trois Époques du Catholicisme, 1849; Le Catéchisme Rationaliste, 1855; L'Histoire de la Guerre Civile Américaine, 1867; Histoire Universelle Selon la Science Moderne, 1879; Religion du Progrés, 1884. Died Mar. 28, 1881.

CORTEZ, Hernando (Hernán Cortés), conquistador, explorer; b. Medellin, Estremadura, Spain, 1485; s. Martin and Catalina (Altamirano) C.; attended U. Salamanca, 1499-1501; m. Catalina Juarez, circa 1515. Soldier in San Domingo, 1504-11; accompanied Diego Valasquez in conquest of Cuba, 1511; became mayor of Santiago; given command of Spanish effort to explore and conquer Mexico, sailed with troops, 1519; founded town of Vera Cruz, 1519; heard reports of rich Kingdom of Aztecs; burned his fleet to cut off escape route, and so he could use the sailors as soldiers; marched on Mexico City; skillfully exploited Indian superstitions and internal malcontents of Aztec empire; admitted into Mexico City as relative of the Sun God, captured emperor Montezuma; Velasquez, who had tried to recall Cortez previously, sent troops under Narvaez to force his return to Cuba; Cortez left Mexico City, 1520, defeated Narvaez, returned to Mexico City and found armed natives blocking his way; defeated Aztec army, July 1520, recaptured Mexico City, 1521; created capt. gen. of Mexican Troops, also marques of Oaxaca by Spanish king; extended conquests in Mexico peninsula, 1521-26; visited Spain, 1828-30; discovered Lower Cal., 1536; returned to Spain, 1540; died in obscurity because of his failure to keep his power, property and positions in Spanish colonial Mexico. Died nr. Seville, Spain, Dec. 2, 1547.

CORWIN, Franklin, congressman, lawyer; b. Lebanon, O., Jan. 12, 1818; attended pvt. schs.; studied law. Admitted to bar, 1839, practiced in Wilmington, O.; mem. Ohio Ho. of Reps., 1846, 47; mem. Ohio Senate, 1847-49; moved to Peru, Ill., 1857; mem. Ill. Ho. of Reps., speaker; mem. U.S. Ho. of Reps. (Republican) from Ill., 43d Congress, 1873-75; practiced law, Peru. Died Peru, June 15, 1879.

CORWIN, Moses Biedso, congressman, lawyer; b. Bourbon County, Ky., Jan 5, 1790; attended rural schs.; studied law. Admitted to bar, 1812, practiced law. Urbana, Champaign County, O.; mem. Ohio Ho. of Reps., 1838, 39; mem. U.S. Ho. of Reps. (Whig) from Ohio, 31st, 33d congresses, 1849-51, 53-55. Died Urbana, Apr. 7, 1872; buried Oak Dale Cemetery.

CORWIN, Thomas, senator, gov. Ohio; b. Bourbon County, Ky., July 29, 1794; s. Matthias and Patience (Halleck) C.; m. Sarah Ross, 1822. Admitted to Ohio bar, 1817; practiced in Lebanon, O.; pros. atty. Warren County, O., 1818-28; mem. Ohio Ho. of Reps., 1822, 23, 29; mem. U.S. Ho. of Reps. from Ohio 22d-26th, 36-37th congresses, 1831-May 30, 1840, 59-Mar. 12, 1861; gov. Ohio, 1840-42; mem. U.S. Senate from Ohio, 1845-50; U.S. sec. treasury, 1850-53; U.S. minister to Mexico, 1861-64. Died Washington, D.C., Dec. 18, 1865; buried Lebanon Cemetery.

CORWINE, Aaron H., artist; b. nr. Maysville, Ky., Aug. 31, 1802; studied with Thomas Sully, Phila. Successful portrait painter, Cincinnati, 1820-29, subjects included Andrew Jackson, Lafayette; went to Eng., 1829, returned to Am., 1830. Died Phila., July 4, 1830.

COSBY, William, colonial gov.; b. 1690; m. Grace Montague, some children including William. Served as col. Brit. Army; gov. Minorca and Leeward Islands; gov. N.Y., 1731-36; became involved in law suit with former gov., Rip Van Dam, because of controversy over financial matters (suit later dropped by both parties); became unpopular by ignoring elective franchise and keeping same assembly intact for 6 years; received 22,000-acre grant known as Cosby's Manor from King Gorge II, 1734. Died Mar. 21, 1736.

COSDEN, Jeremiah, congressman; b. 1768. Mem. U.S. Ho. of Reps. (contested election) from Md., 17th Congress, 1821-Mar. 19, 1822. Died Balt., Dec. 5, 1824.

COSTANSÓ, Miguel, engr. Ensign Spanish Army on expdn. to Alta California under Gaspar de Portola, 1769-70, made astron. observations and maps of region; cons. engr. on proposed road from Sonora Mexico to Alta California 1772; cons. engr. in fortification of Mexican coast, 1794-95, in drainage of canals around Mexico City, in fortification of Veracruz and Guanajuato, 1811. Author: Diario histórico de los viages de mar y tierra hechos al norte de la California, 1770. Flourished 1769-1811.

COSTIGAN, Francis, architect; b. Washington, D.C., 1810. Employed as carpenter and builder, Balt.; moved to Madison, Ind., 1840, became known as architect of fine homes, including Lanier House (considered his masterpiece; now a state museum); designed Shrewsbury residence, old Madison Hotel (opened 1860, known as finest inn on Ohio River between Cincinnati and Louisville); moved to Indpls., practiced as architect; completed plans (begun by John Elder) for Inst. for Blind, Indpls. (now site of War Meml. Plaza); designed Odd Fellows Bdg., Inst. for Deaf and Dumb, Hosp. for Insane, all Indpls. Died 1865.

COTHRAN, James Sproull, congressman, lawyer; b. nr. Abbeville, S.C., Aug. 8, 1830; grad. U. Ga., 1852; studied law. Admitted to bar, 1853, practiced in Abbeville; served from pvt. to capt. Con federate Army, during Civil War; with his Compan at surrender Army of Northern Va. at Appomatto elected solicitor 8th Jud. Circuit, 1876, 80, appto judge 8th Jud. Circuit, 1881, elected by S.C Legislature to same office, 1882, 85; mem. U.S Ho. of Reps. (Democrat) from S.C., 50th-51st con gresses, 1887-91; practiced in Abbeville and Green ville, S.C. Died in sanitarium, N.Y.C., Dec. 5, 1897 buried Upper Long Cane Cemetery, Abbeville.

COTTING, John Ruggles, geologist; b. Acton Mass., 1783; attended Harvard, Dartmouth Med Sch. Ordained to ministry Congregational Ch., circ 1810; devoted most of his life to scientific pur suits; state geologist of Ga., 1835-37, made 1s geol. survey of state; gathered valuable collection c plants, minerals and fossils (divided among variou colls. at his death); a copy of his state geol report (1836) was requested by Czar of Russia fc Royal Library. Author: Introduction to Chemistry 1822; Synopsis of Lectures on Geology, 1825. Die Milledgeville, Ga., Oct. 13, 1867.

COTTMAN, Joseph Stewart, congressman, law yer; b. nr. Allen, Somerset (now Wicomico County, Md., Aug. 16, 1803; attended Princeton 1821, Yale, 1822-23; studied law. Admitted t bar, 1826, practiced in Princess Anne, Md.; mem Md. Ho. of Dels., 1831-32, 39; mem. Md. Senate 1837; presdl. elector on Taylor and Fillmor ticket, 1848; mem. U.S. Ho. of Reps. (Independen Whig) from Md., 32d Congress, 1851-53; becam farmer. Died on his farm Mortherton, nr. Allen Jan. 28, 1863; buried St. Andrew's Epsicopa Churchyard, Princess Anne.

COTTON, John, clergyman; b. Derby, Eng., Dec 4, 1584; s. Roland Cotton; A.B., Trinity Coll. Cambridge (Eng.) U., 1603, A.M., 1606, B.D. Emanuel Coll., 1613; m. Elizabeth Harrocks July 3, 1613; m. 2d, Sarah (Hawkridge) Story Apr. 25, 1632; 6 children including Maria, Seaborn rectr., dean Emanuel Coll., 1606-12; ordaine deacon, priest Ch. of Eng., 1610; vicar St. Bot olph's Ch., Lincolnshire, Eng., 1612-33 summoned to appear before High Ct. c Comm., 1632, fled to Boston, 1633; becam leader of Congregationalism in Am.; tchr. Puri tan Ch. of Boston; complied Moses, His Judicial (an abstract of laws of Moses); participated i banishment of Anne Hutchinson and Roge Williams, 1636, Author: The Keys of th Kingdom of Heaven, 1644; Spiritual Milk fc Babies (a standard New Eng. catechism), 1645 The Way of the Churches of Christ in New England 1645; The Way of the Congregational Churche Cleared, 1648. Died Boston, Dec. 23, 1652

COTTRELL, Calvert Byron, inventor, mfr.; b. West erley, R.I., Aug. 10, 1821; s. Lebbeus and Lydi (Maxson) C.; m. Lydia W. Perkins, May 4, 1849 5 children. Machinist and employing contractor fo Levalley, Lanphear & Co., Phoenix, R.I., 1840-55 in partnership (with Nathan Babocck) firm Cottre & Babcock, mfrs. printing presses, Westerley, 1855 80, name changed to C. B. Cottrell & Sons, 1880 invented air spring for reversing bed of press tapeless sheet delivery to drum cylinder, rotar color printing press, shifting tympan for a we perfecting press. Died Westerley, June 12, 1893

COTTRELL, James La Fayette, congressman b. King William County, Va., Aug. 25, 1808; com pleted prep. studies; studied law. Admitted t bar, 1830; practiced law, Hayneville, Ala.; mem Ala. Ho. of Reps., 1834, 36-37; mem. Ala. Sen ate, 1838-41, pres., 1840; mem. U.S. Ho. of Reps (Democrat, filled vacancy) from Ala., 29th Con gress, Dec. 7, 1846-47; moved to Fla., 1854; mem Fla. Senate, 1865-85; apptd. collector customs Cedar Keys, Levy County, Fla., served until 1885 Died Cedar Keys, Sept. 7, 1885; buried Old Tow (Fla.) Cemetery.

COUCH, Darius Nash, army officer; b. Southeast N.Y., July 23, 1822; s. Jonathan Couch; grad. U.S Mil. Acad., 1846; m. Mary Caroline Crocker Aug. 31, 1854. Served as 2d lt. 4th Arty., U.S Army at Battle of Buena Vista during Mexica War; commd. 1st lt., 1847; stationed on Atlanti coast, 1847-53, 55; on leave of absence to mak zool. expdn. to Northern Mexico, 1853-54; resigne commn., 1855; commd. col. 7th Mass. Inf., U.S Volunteers, 1861, promoted brig. gen., 1861, maj gen., 1862; served in Peninsular campaign; par ticipated in battles of Fair Oaks, Antietam, Fred ericksburg, Chancellorsville, Gettysburg, and Nash ville; in charge of ceremonies consecrating nat. cem etery at Gettysburg (Pa.) 1863; resigned commn 1865; collector Port of Boston; pres. of a mining an mfg. company; q.m. and adjutant gen. of Conn Died Norwalk, Conn., Feb. 12, 1897; buried Taun ton, Mass.

COULDOCK, Charles Walter, actor; b. London Eng., Apr. 26, 1815; at least 1 dau., Eliza. A leading actor in England before coming to U.S. 1849; made Am. debut in The Stranger, N.Y.C.

1849; leading man Walnut Street Theatre, Phila., 1849-53; toured with Laura Keene's company, 1858; active on Am. stage for almost 50 years; played Luke Fielding in The Willow Copse, 1853, Abel Murcott in Our American Cousin, 1858. Died N.Y. C., Nov. 17, 1898.

COULTER, Richard, congressman; b. Westmoreland County, Pa., Mar. 1788; attended Jefferson Coll.; studied law. Admitted to bar, 1811, practiced in Greensburg, Westmoreland County; mem. Pa. Ho. of Reps., 1816-20; mem. U.S. Ho. of Reps. (Independent) from Pa., 20th-21st, (Democrat) 22d-23d congresses, 1827-35; judge Pa. Supreme Ct., 1846-52. Died Greensburg, Apr. 21, 1852; buried St. Clair Cemetery.

COUPER, James Hamilton, planter; b. nr. Brunswick, Ga., Mar. 4, 1794; s. John and Rebecca (Maxwell) C.; grad. Yale, 1814; children include Hamilton, John. Owned half of "Hopeton" (a Ga. rice plantation), also rice plantation on Cannon's Point, St. Simon's Island, Ga.; supervised over 1800 slaves; 1st American to operate rice plantation scientifically, using diking and drainage system; built 1st cotton-seed oil mill in U.S., Natchez, Miss., 1834; one of 1st to grow Bermuda grass and olives in U.S.; plantations and fortune destroyed in Civil War. Died June 3, 1866; buried Frederika, St. Simon's Island.

COUTURIER, Hendrick, mcht., artist; b. probably Leyden, Holland; attended St. Luke's Guild Art Sch., Leyden, 1648; m., 1648. Moved to Amsterdam, Holland, 1649; came to Am., circa 1661, settled at New Amstel on Delaware River; trader and pub. ofcl.; obtained burgher right of City of New Amsterdam (now N.Y.C.) by painting portrait of Gov. Stuyvesant and making drawings of his sons; said to have moved to Eng., 1674; 1st European-trained artist to practice in Am. Died Eng., circa 1684.

COVINGTON, Leonard, congressman, army officer; b. Aquasco, Md., Oct. 30, 1768; had liberal schooling. Entered U.S. Army as cornet of Cavalry, 1792; commd. lt. of Dragoons by Gen. Washington, 1793, joined Army under Gen. Wayne; distinguished himself at Ft. Recovery and Battle of Miami; promoted capt., resigned, 1795; became farmer; mem. Md. Ho. of Dels. many years; mem. U.S. Ho. of Reps. (Democrat) from Md., 9th Congress, 1805-07; apptd. by Pres. Jefferson lt. col. of Light Dragoons, 1809, col., 1809; in command at Ft. Adams on Mississippi River, 1810; took possession of Baton Rouge and portion of West Fla.; ordered to Northern frontier, 1813; apptd. brig. gen. by Pres. Madison, 1813; mortally wounded at Battle of Chryslers Field, 1813. Died Frenchs Mills, N.Y., Nov. 14, 1813; remains removed to Sackets Harbor, Jefferson County, N.Y., Aug. 13, 1820; buried at Mt. Covington.

COVODE, John, congressman; b. Mar. 18, 1808; s. Jacob C. and Mrs. (Updegraff) C. Owned woolen-mill, Lockport, Pa.; invested in Pa. Canal, Pa. R.R. and Westmoreland Coal Co.; mem. Pa. Ho. of Reps.; mem. U.S. Ho. of Reps. from Pa., 34th-37th, 40-41st congresses, 1855-63, 67-71, chmn. Covode House Investigation Com. to investigate alleged use of improper influence by Pres. James Buchanan in attempts to secure passage Lecompton Bill (House ignored findings); mem. Republican Exec. Congl. Com. in presdl. campaign, 1860. Died Harrisburg, Pa., Jan. 11, 1871; buried Methodist Episcopal Cemetery, West Fairfield, Pa.

COWAN, Edgar, senator; b. Greensburg, Pa., Sept. 19, 1815; grad. Franklin Coll., Athens, O., 1839; m. Lucetta Oliver, 1842. Admitted to Pa. bar, 1839; practiced in Greensburg; presdl. elector, 1860; mem. U.S. Senate (Republican) from Pa., 1861-67; supported Pres. Andrew Johnson's reconstrn. programs; apptd. minister to Austria, 1867 (not confirmed by Senate). Died Greensburg, Aug. 31, 1885; buried St. Clair Cemetery, Greensburg.

COWAN, Jacob Pitzer, congressman, physician; b. Florence, Washington County, Pa., Mar. 20, 1823; attended common schs.; studied medicine; grad. Starling Med. Coll., Columbus, O., 1855. In woolen mfg. until 1843; moved to Ashland County, O.,, 1846, practiced medicine; mem. Ohio Ho. of Reps., 1855-57; mem. U.S. Ho. of Reps. (Democrat) from Ohio, 44th Congress, 1875-77. Died Ashland, O., July 9, 1895; buried Ashland Cemetery.

COWELL, Joseph Leathley, actor, artist; b. nr. Torquay, Eng., Aug. 7, 1792; at least 1 son, Joseph. Served with Brit. Navy during Napoleonic Wars; took up portrait painting; became actor, 1812, made debut in N.Y.C.; worked as actor and scene-painter, London and North Country (Eng.), until 1821; came to Am., 1821, played in low comedy in Charleston (S.C.), Phila., Wilmington (Del.), Boston, N.Y.C.; exhibited several English landscapes and marine views at Pa. Acad., 1828, N.A.D., 1829. Author: Thirty Years of Theatrical Life, 1844.

COWEN, Benjamin Sprague, congressman; b. Washington County, N.Y., Sept. 27, 1793; attended common schs.; studied medicine and law. Served as pvt. in War of 1812; moved to Moorefield, O., 1820, practiced medicine; admitted to bar, 1829, practiced law, St. Clairsville, O.; editor Belmont Chronicle, 1836-40; del. Nat. Whig Conv., Harrisburg, Pa., 1839; mem. U.S. Ho. of Reps. (Anti-slavery Whig) from Ohio, 27th Congress, 1841-43; mem. Ohio Ho. of Reps., 1845, 46; presiding judge Ct. Common Pleas, 1847. Died St. Clairsville, Sept. 27, 1860.

COWLES, Edwin, journalist; b. Austinburg, O., Sept. 19, 1825; s. Dr. Edwin W. and Almira (Foote) C.; m. Elizabeth C. Hutchinson, 1849, children—Alfred, Eugene. Partner (with T. H. Smead) printing bus., 1844-53; became partner Medill, Cowles & Co., publishers Cleve. Leader, 1853, became sole owner, editor, 1855; a founder Republican Party; postmaster, Cleve., 1861-66; v.p. Rep. Nat. Conv., 1884. Died Mar. 4, 1890.

COWLES, Henry Booth, congressman, lawyer; b. Hartford, Conn., Mar. 18, 1798; grad. Union Coll., Schenectady, N.Y., 1816; studied law. Admitted to bar, practiced in Putnam County; mem. N.Y. State Assembly, 1826-28; mem. U.S. Ho. of Reps. from N.Y., 21st Congress, 1829-31; moved to N.Y.C., 1834, practiced law until 1873. Died N.Y.C., May 17, 1873; buried Rhinebeck (N.Y.) Cemetery.

COX, Hannah Pierce, abolitionist; b. Longwood, Chester County, Pa., Nov. 12, 1797; d. Jacob and Hannah (Buffington) Pierce; m. J. Pennell, 1820/21; m. 2d, John Cox, 1823; 4 children. Operated station for Underground R.R. at Longwood; a friend of John Greenleaf Whittier, Thomas Garret, Lucrecia Mott and other abolitionists; organized her movement on behalf of Negroes as Progressive Friends of Longwood. Died Longwood, Apr. 15, 1876.

COX, Henry Hamilton, farmer, poet; b. Ireland, 1769; s. Joshua and Mary (Cox) Hamilton (took mother's last name as condition for inheriting grandfather's estate "Dunmanway," (County Cork, Ireland); m. Letita Elinor Cox, several children. Came to U.S., 1799; leased farm in Chester County, Pa., 1813-17; became mem. Soc. of Friends, circa 1813; returned to Ireland, 1817. Author: Metrical Sketches, By a Citizen of the World, 1817. Died 1821.

COX, Jacob, artist; b. Phila., Nov. 9, 1810. Went to Indpls., 1833, practiced tinsmith's trade; became portrait painter, circa 1840, painted in Indpls.; frequent exhibitor at Cincinnati Art Union; collaborated with Henry Waughh on temperance panorama, 1853-54. Died Indpls., Jan. 2, 1892.

COX, James, congressman; b. Monmouth, N.J., June 14, 1753; attended public schs. In command company of militia at battles of Germantown and Monmouth; attained rank brig. gen.; mem. N.J. Gen. Assembly, 1801-07, speaker, 1804-07; mem. U.S. Ho. of Reps. (Democrat) from N.J., 11th Congress, 1809-10. Died Monmouth, Sept. 12, 1810; buried Yellow Meeting House Cemetery, Upper Freehold Twp., N.J.

COX, Leander Martin, congressman, lawyer; b. Cumberland County, Va., May 7, 1812; completed academic studies; studied law. Admitted to bar, practiced law; moved to Flemingsburg, Ky.; mem. Ky. Ho. of Reps., 1843-45; capt. 3d Ky. Volunteers in Mexican War, 1847; Whig presdl. elector, 1852; mem. U.S. Ho. of Reps. from Ky., (as Whig) 33d, (as Am. Party candidate) 34th congresses, 1853-57. Died Flemingsburg, Mar. 19, 1865; buried Fleming County (Ky.) Cemetery.

COX, Lemuel, engr.; b. Boston, 1736; s. William and Thankful (Mandsley) C.; m. Susannah Hickling, 1763. Supervised constrn. of 1st bridge over Charles River, between Charlestown (Mass.) and Boston, 1785-86; architect, builder Essex Bridge from Salem to Beverly (Mass.); built bridge at Waterford, Ireland, 1793; received grant of land from Mass. for inventing 1st machine to cut card wire, 1796. Died Charlestown, Feb. 18, 1806.

COX, Rowland, lawyer; b. Phila., July 9, 1842; s. John Cooke and Ann (Johns) C.; grad. Princeton, 1863; m. Fanny Cummins Hill, Oct. 29, 1868. Served as maj. U.S. Volunteers in Civil War; participated in battles of Chickamauga and Atlanta; with Gen. W. T. Sherman in his march through Ga. and Carolinas; admitted to Ill. bar, 1868; practiced in Washington, D.C., 1868-75; specialized in patent law, N.Y.C., 1875-1900. Author: American Trade Mark Cases, 1871; Manual of Trade Mark Cases, 1881; editor: American Law Times Reports, vols. II-VI, 1869-75, vols. I-IV, 1874-77, vols. V, VI, 1878. Died Plainfield, N.J., May 13, 1900.

COX, Samuel Hanson, clergyman, coll. pres.; b. Rahway, N.J., Aug. 25, 1793; s. James and Elizabeth (Shepard) C.; D.D. (hon.), Williams Coll., 1823; LL.D. (hon.), Marietta Coll., 1855, S.C. Coll., 1863; m. Abia Hyde Cleveland, Apr. 7, 1817; m. 2d, Anna Fosdick Bacon, Nov. 16, 1869; 15 children including Arthur Cleveland. Licensed by N. Y. Presbytery, 1816; ordained to ministry Presbyn. Ch., 1817; pastor Spring St. Ch., N.Y.C., 1821, Laight Street Ch., 1825; a founder N.Y.U.; dir. Union Theol. Sem., 36 years; prof. sacred rhetoric and pastoral theology Auburn Sem., 1835-37; pres. Ingham U. (women), Le Roy, N.Y., 1856-63. Died Bronxville, N.Y., Oct. 2, 1880.

COX, Samuel Sullivan, congressman; b. Zanesville O., Sept. 30, 1824; s. Ezekiel Taylor; grad. Brown U., 1846; m. Julia Buckingham, 1849. Editor, chief owner Ohio Statesman, Columbus; sec. of legation in Eng., 1855; mem. U.S. Ho. of Reps. from Ohio, 35th-38th congresses, 1857-65, from N.Y., 41st-53d congresses, 1869-95; U.S. minister to Turkey, 1885-86; reform advocate on issues of tariff and civil service. Author: A Buckeye Abroad, 1852; Eight Years in Congress, 1865; Three Decades of Federal Legislation, 1880. Died N.Y.C., Sept. 10, 1889; buried Greenwood Cemetery, Bklyn.

COXE, Arthur Cleveland, clergyman; b. Mendham, N.J., May 10, 1818; s. Samuel Hanson Cox; grad. U. City of N.Y., 1838, Gen. Theol. Sem., N.Y.C., 1841; m. Katherine Hyde, Sept. 21, 1841. Ordained priest Protestant Episcopal Ch., 1842; rector St. John's Ch., Hartford, Conn., 1842-54, Grace Ch., Balt., 1854-63, Calvary Ch., N.Y.C., 1863-65; bishop Western N.Y., 1865-96. Author: Christian Ballads, 1840; Apology for the English Bible, 1857; Letter to Pius the Ninth, 1869; Apollos, or the Way of God, 1871; Holy Writ and Modern Thought, 1892. Died July 20, 1896.

COXE, Daniel, landowner, jurist; b. Aug. 1673; s. Daniel and Rebecca (Coldham) C.; m. Sarah Eckley, 1707, inherited father's titles to West Jersey, large part of the Carolinas, land beyond Mississippi River; asso. judge Supreme Ct. Province of N.J., 1706; elected to N.J. Assembly, 1714, 16, chosen speaker, 1716; apptd. 1st grand master Masons in Am., 1730; judge N.J. Supreme Ct., 1734-39. Died Apr. 25, 1739.

COXE, Eckley Brinton, mining engr., inventor; b. Phila., June 4, 1839; s. Charles Sidney and Ann (Brinton) C.; grad. U. Pa., 1858; studied mining in Europe, 1860-63; m. Sophia G. Fisher, June 27, 1868. Organized Coxe Bros. Co., 1865; pres. Cross Creek Co.; pres. Del., Susquehanna & Schuylkill R.R., 1890; a founder Am. Inst. Mining Engrs., pres., 1878-89; pres. Am. Soc. M.E., 1892-94; mem. Pa. Senate, 1880-84; an original trustee Lehigh U., invented automatic slate-picking machine, mech. stoker, gyrating screens, steel measuring tapes. Died May 13, 1895.

COXE, John Redman, physician; b. Trenton, N.J., Sept. 16, 1773; s. Daniel and Sarah (Redman) C.; M.D., U. Pa., 1794; m. Sarah Cox, 6 children. Introduced Jalap plant into U.S.; editor Medical Museum, 1805-11; prof. chemistry U. Pa., 1809-19, prof. materia medica and pharmacy Med. Dept., 1819-35. Died Phila., Mar. 22, 1864.

COXE, Richard Smith, lawyer; b. Burlington, N.J., Jan. 1792; s. William and Rachael (Smith) C.; grad. Coll. of N.J. (now Princeton), 1808; m. Susan Griffith, Jan. 23, 1816; m. 2d, Mrs. Susan Wheeler, 1840. Admitted to Pa. bar, 1812, N.J. bar, 1817, D.C. Circuit Ct. bar, 1822; practiced law in Phila.; compiled Reports of Cases Argued and Determined in the Supreme Court of New Jersey from April Term 1790 to November Term 1795 Both Inclusive; dep. atty. gen. Burlington County (N.J.), 1817-22; moved to Washington, D.C., had large practice before U.S. Supreme Ct.; prepared Digest of Decisions, Supreme, Circuit, and District Courts, United States, 1789-1829. Author: A New Critical Pronouncing Dictionary of the English Language Compiled by an American Gentleman, 1813; Review of the Relations Between the United States and Mexico, 1846; Present State of the African Slave-Trade, 1858. Died Washington, Apr. 28, 1865.

COXE, Tench, polit. economist, Continental congressman; b. Phila., May 22, 1755; s. William and Mary Francis C.; attended Coll. of Phila. (now U. Pa.); m. Catherine McCall; m. 2d, Rebecca Coxe. Del. Annapolis Conv., 1786; mem. Continental Congress, 1787-88; asst. sec. of treasury, U.S. 1789-92; U.S. commr. revenue, 1792-97; U.S. purveyor of public supplies, 1803-12; pres. Pa. Soc. Encouragement of Mfrs. and Useful Arts; one of 1st to urge cultivation of cotton as a staple in the South, also active in promotion of cotton manufacture. Author: An Examination of the Constitution of the United States, 1788; View of The United States, 1794. Died Phila., July 16, 1824; buried Christ Ch. Burying Ground, Phila.

COXE, William, congressman, pomologist; b. Phila., May 3, 1762; s. William and Mary

(Francis); C. m. Rachael Smith, 1789; at least 2 children, Richard Smith, Emily. Mem. N.J. Legislature, 1796-1804, 06-09, 16-17, speaker, 1798-1800, 02; mem. U.S. Ho. of Reps. Federalist from N.J., 13th Congress, 1813-15; authority on fruits; introduced Sekel pear into Eng. Died Burlington, N.J., Feb. 25, 1831; buried St. Mary's Churchyard, Burlington.

COXETTER, Louis Mitchell, privateer; b. N.S., Dec. 10, 1818; m. Antonica Geiger, 4 children, Before Civil War commanded schooner in trade between Charleston (S.C.) and St. Augustine (Fla.), commanded 1st line of steam packets operating between the 2 cities; commanded Confederate privateers and blockade runners Jefferson Davis, Theodora, Herald, Antonica, and Beauregard during Civil War; employed by Fraser, Trenholm and Co. (English agts. of Confederate States Am.), Liverpool, Eng.; resumed command of packet line after Civil War. Died Charleston, July 10, 1873; buried St. Laurence Cemetery, Charleston.

COZZENS, Frederick Swartwout, author, mcht.; b. N.Y.C., Mar. 11, 1818; s. Frederick Cozzens; m. Susan Meyers. Wine mcht., N.Y.C., 1839-68; an original mem. Century Club, N.Y.C.; editor Wine Press, trade monthly, 1854-61. Author. Yankee Doodle, 1847; Prismatics, 1853; Tike Sparrowgrass Papers, 1856; Acadia; or, a Month with the Bluenoses, 1859; The Sayings of Dr. Bushwacker and Other Learned Men, 1867. Died Dec. 23, 1869.

CRABB, George Whitfield, congressman; b. Botecourt County, Va., Feb. 22, 1804; attended public schs. Moved to Tuscaloosa, Ala.; elected asst. sec. state and comptroller public accounts, 1829; served in Fla. Indian War of 1836, lt. col. Ala. Volunteers; mem. Ala. Ho. of Reps., 1836-37, Ala. Senate, 1837-38; served as maj. gen. of militia; mem. U.S. Ho. of Reps. (Whig, filled vacancy) from Ala., 25th-26th congresses, Sept. 4, 1838-41; apptd. judge Mobile County Ct., 1846. Died Phila., Aug. 15, 1846; buried Greenwood Cemetery, Tuscaloosa.

CRABB, Jeremiah, congressman; b. Montgomery County, Md., 1760. Served as 2d lt., 1st Md. Regt. in Revolutionary War; promoted 1st lt., 1777-78, resigned because of ill health from winter at Valley Forge; extensive landowner, Montgomery County; served as gen. with Gen. Harry Lee in Pa. during Whisky Rebellion; mem. U.S. Ho. of Reps. (Democrat) from Md., 4th Congress, 1795-96 (resigned). Died nr. Rockville, Montgomery County, 1800; buried family burying ground nr. Derwood, Montgomery County.

CRACCHI, Guiseppe, see Ceracchi, Guiseppe.

CRADLEBAUGH, John, congressman; b. Circleville, Pickaway County, O., Feb. 22, 1819; attended Kenyon Coll., Gambier, O., Oxford (O.) U.; studied law. Admitted to bar, 1840; apptd. U.S. asso. justice for Dist. of Utah, 1858; moved to Carson City, Nev.; mem. U.S. Congress from Nev. Territory, 37th Congress, Dec. 2, 1861-63; served as col. 114th Regt., Ohio Volunteer Inf., Union Army during Civil War, 1862-63; wounded at Vicksburg; in mining business, Eureka, Nev. Died Eureka, Feb. 22, 1872; buried Forest Cemetery, Circleville.

CRAFTS, Samuel Chandler, senator, gov. Vt., b. Woodstock, Conn., Oct. 6, 1768; grad. Harvard, 1790. Moved to Vt. with his father who founded town of Craftsbury), 1791, town clk., 1799-1829; youngest del. Vt. Constl. Conv., 1793; mem. Vt. Ho. of Reps., 1796, 1800-03, 05, clk., 1798-99; register of probate, 1796-1815; asst. judge Orleans County (Vt.) Ct., 1800-10, 25-28; made extensive botanical reconnaissance of Mississippi Valley, 1802; mem. Vt. Council, 1809-13; chief judge Orleans County Ct., 1810-16; mem. U.S. Ho. of Reps. from Vt., 15th-18th congresses, 1817-25; Vt. councilor, 1825, 26; gov. Vt., 1828-31; mem. Vt. Constl. Conv., 1829, served as pres.; clk. Orleans County, 1836-39; Whig presdl. elector, 1840; mem. U.S. Senate (filled vacancy) from Vt., Apr. 23, 1842-43; retired to his farm, Craftsbury. Died Craftsbury, Orleans County, Nov. 19, 1853; buried North Craftsbury (Vt.) Cemetery.

CRAFTS, William, state legislator, author; b. Charleston, S.C., Jan. 24, 1787; s. William and Margaret (Tebout) C.; grad. Harvard, 1805, M.A., 1809; m. Caroline Crofts Homes, June 19, 1823. Admitted to S.C. bar, 1809, practiced in Charleston, 1809-26; mem. S.C. Ho. of Reps., 1810, 12, 13, S.C. Senate, 1820-26. Author: The Raciad, and Other Occasional Poems, 1810; The Sea Serpent: A Dramatic Jeu d'Esprit, 1819; Sullivan's Island, the Raciad, and Other Poems, 1820. Died Lebanon Springs, N.Y., Sept. 23, 1826; buried King's Chapel Churchyard, Boston.

CRAGHAN, George, Indian trader, agt.; b. nr. Dublin, Ireland; several children including Susannah. Came to Am., 1741; established Indian trading post, Carlisle, Pa., later established posts in Upper Ohio regions; agt. for Pa. in negotiations with Indians; dep. supt. Indian affairs, 1756-72; at capture of Ft. Duquesne, 1758, Detroit, 1760; opened Ill. country to English settlers by concluding peace treaty with Pontiac, 1765; owned much land in N.Y., Pa., Ind., Ill., Ohio; mem. Indiana Land Co., Grand Ohio Co.; mem. Com. of Corr., Pitts., 1775. Died Passyunk, Pa., Aug. 31, 1782.

CRAIG, Alexander Kerr, congressman, farmer; b. nr. Claysville, Washington County, Pa., Feb. 21, 1828; attended common schs.; had pvt. tutor; studied law. Taught sch. at age 16; became farmer, taught sch. in winter months; prin. Claysville Pub. Schs.; enlisted in 87th Regt., Pa. Volunteer Inf. in Civil War, 1865; present at surrender of Gen. Lee at Appomattox; sch. dir., justice of peace, Claysville; mem. U.S. Ho. of Reps. (Democrat, contested election) from Pa., 52d Congress, Feb. 26-July 29, 1892. Died Claysville, July 29, 1892; buried Claysville Cemetery.

CRAIG, Austin, clergyman, coll. pres.; b. Peapack, N.J., July 14, 1824; s. Moses and Rachel (Carhart) C.; ed. Lafayette Coll., Easton, Pa., 1840-43, M.A. (hon.), 1864; D.D. (hon.), Antioch Coll., 1857; m. Adelaide Churchill, Aug. 12, 1858; m. 2d, Sarah J. McCarn, M.D., June 24, 1879. Ordained to ministry Christian Ch., 1845; pastor Blooming Grove (N.Y.) Ch., 1849-56; prof. Greek, Antioch Coll., 1856, prof. logic and rhetoric, 1857, pres.; 1862-68; prof. Meadville (Pa.) Theol. Sem., 1864-67; pres. Christian Bibl. Inst., Stanfordville, N.Y., 1869-81. Died Stanfordville, N.Y., Aug. 27, 1881.

CRAIG, Daniel H., journalist; b. Rumney, N.H., circa 1814. Experimented with carrier pigeons to carry news; ind. news collector in Boston, 1844-48; started collecting news in Europe for sale in Am., 1848; joined Assoc. Press as Halifax rep., 1850, gen. agt., 1851, pres., 1861-66; aided Ezra Cornell in devel. of telegraphic lines. Author: Machine Telegraphy of Today, 1888. Died Jan. 5, 1895.

CRAIG, Hector, congressman; b. Paisley, Scotland, 1775. Came to U.S., settled in Orange County, N.Y., 1790, founded Town of Craigsville, built paper mill, grist mill, saw mill; mem. U.S. Ho. of Reps. (Jackson Democrat) from N.Y., 18th, 21st congresses, 1823-25., 29-July 12, 1830 (resigned); apptd. surveyor Port of N.Y. by Pres. Jackson, 1830; U.S. commr. of insolvency, 1832; surveyor of customs in N.Y., 1833-39. Died Craigsville, Jan. 31, 1842; buried pvt. cemetery on Caldwell estate, Blooming Grove, N.Y.

CRAIG, James, congressman; b. Washington County, Pa., Feb. 28, 1818; attended public schs.; studied law. Admitted to New Philadelphia (O.) bar, 1839; moved to St. Joseph, Mo., 1844, practiced law; capt. volunteer company in Mexican War, served until 1848; state's atty. for 12th Jud. Circuit, 1852-56; mem. Mo. Ho. of Reps., 1856, 57; mem. U.S. Ho. of Reps. (Democrat) from Mo., 35th-36th congresses, 1857-61; commd. brig. gen. Volunteers by Pres. Lincoln during Civil War, 1862; 1st pres. Hannibal & St. Joseph R.R.; 1st comptroller City of St. Joseph; negotiated Platt purchase comprising all N.W. Mo. Died St. Joseph, Oct. 22, 1888; buried Mt. Mora Cemetery.

CRAIG, Robert, congressman, planter; b. nr. Christiansburg, Va., 1792; attended Washington Coll. (now Washinton and Lee U.), Lexington, Va.; grad. Lewisburg Acad., Greenbrier County. Became a planter; mem. Va. Ho. of Dels., 1817-18, 25-29, 50-52; mem. va. Bd. Public Works, 1820-23; mem. U.S. Ho. of Reps. (Democrat) from Va., 21st-22d, 24th-26th congresses, 1829-33, 35-41. Died on estate "Green Hill," nr. Salem, Va., Nov. 25, 1852; buried family burying ground "Green Hill."

CRAIG, Thomas, mathematician; b. Ayrshire, Scotland, Dec. 20, 1855; s. Alexander and Mary (Hall) C.; grad. Lafayette Coll., 1875; Ph.D., Johns Hopkins, 1878; m. Louise Alvord, May 4, 1880. Lectr., Johns Hopkins, 1877-79, fellow, later asso. prof. mathematics, 1881-92, prof., 1892-1900; mathematician U.S. Coast and Geodetic Survey, 1879-81; editor Am. Jour. of Mathematics, 1894-99. Author: Elements of the Mathematical Theory of Fluid Motion, 1879; A Treatise on Projections, 1882; A Treatise on Linear Differential Equations, 1889. Died May 8, 1900.

CRAIGE, Francis Burton, congressman; b. nr. Salisbury, Rowan County, N.C., Mar. 13, 1811; grad. U. N.C. at Chapel Hill, 1829; studied law. Editor, propr. Western Carolinian, 1829-31; admitted to bar, 1832, began practice of law, Salisbury; mem. N.C. Ho. of Reps., 1832-34; mem. U.S. Ho. of Reps. (Democrat) from N.C., 33d-36th congresses, 1853-61; del. N.C. Secession Conv., 1861, introduced ordinance of secession (adopted); del. Provisional Congress of Confederate States Am., Richmond, Va., 1861. Died Concord, Cabarrus County, N.C., Dec. 30, 1875; buried old English Cemetery, Salisbury.

CRAIGIE, Andrew, financier, apothecary; b. Boston, June 18, 1743; s. Andrew and Elizabeth C.; m. Elizabeth Shaw. Continental apothecary gen., 1775-83; commd. lt. col. Continental Army, 1779; mem. Soc. of Cincinnati, 1783; speculation in govt. certificates and supplies earned him large fortune; dir. 1st U.S. Bank; owned much real estate in Boston and Cambridge (Mass.); owned mansion in Cambridge which became one of most important social centers in New Eng. Died Cambridge, Sept. 19, 1819.

CRAIK, James, physician; b. Arbigland, Scotland, 1730; studied medicine, U. Edinburgh (Scotland); m. Marianne Ewell, Nov. 13, 1760, at least 1 son, George W. Commd. surgeon Va. Militia, 1754, chief med. officer under Col. George Washington, 1755-63; asst. dir. gen. hosps. of middle dist., Continental Army, 1777-80; chief hosp. physician Continental Army, 1780-81, chief physician and surgeon, 1781-83; dir. gen. hosp. dept. U.S. Army, 1798, physician gen., 1798-1800; attended Pres. Washington during his final illness (with Dr. Elisha Cullen Dick), 1799; owned large plantation and practiced medicine, Port Tobacco, Charles County, Md. Died Alexandria, Va., Feb. 6, 1814.

CRAIK, William, congressman; b. nr. Port Tobacco, Md., Oct. 31, 1761; attended Delameve Sch., Frederick County; studied law. Admitted to bar, began practice of law, Port Tobacco and Leonardtown; moved to Balt.; chief justice 5th Jud. Dist. of Md., 1793-96, 1801-02; mem. U.S. Ho. of Reps. from Md., 4th-6th congresses, Dec. 5, 1796-1801. Died before 1814.

CRAIN, Willam Henry, congressman; b. Galveston, Tex., Nov. 25, 1848; grad. St. Francis Xavier's Coll., N.Y.C., 1867; studied law, Indianola, Tex. Lived on ranch, 2 years, then taught sch.; admitted to bar, 1871, began practice of law, Indianola; mem. Tex. Senate, 1876-78; dist. atty. 23d Jud. Dist. of Tex., 1872-76; mem. U.S. Ho. of Reps. (Democrat) from Tex., 49th-54th congresses, 1885-96. Died Washington, D.C., Feb. 10, 1896; buried Hillside Cemetery, Cuero, De Witt County, Tex.

CRAMER, John, congressman; b. Waterford, Saratoga County, N.Y., May 17, 1779; grad. Union Coll., Schenectady, N.Y., 1801; studied law. Admitted to bar, began practice of law, Waterford; presdl. elector on Democratic ticket, 1804; apptd. master in chancery, 1805; mem. N.Y. State Assembly, 1806, 11, 42, N.Y. Senate, 1823-25; del. N.Y. Constl. Conv., 1821; mem. U.S. Ho. of Reps. (Democrat) from N.Y., 23d-24th congresses, 1833-37. Died Waterford, June 1, 1870; buried Waterford Rural Cemetery.

CRAMER, Michael John, clergyman, diplomat; b. Schaffhausen, Switzerland, Feb. 6, 1835; s. John Jacob and Magdalene (Baumann) C.; grad. Ohio Wesleyan Coll., 1859, LL.D. (hon.), 1895; D.D. (hon.), Syracuse U., 1873; m. Mary Frances Grant, Oct. 27, 1863. Came to Am., 1845; joined on trial Cincinnati conf. Methodist Episcopal Ch., 1860, ordained circa 1860; pastor Pearl St. Ch., Cincinnati, 1860-64; reorganized Meth. chs., Nashville, Tenn. (disbanded after fall of Vicksburg), 1864; chaplain U.S. Army, Newport Barracks, Tenn., 1867; U.S. consul at Leipzig, 1867; minister to Denmark, 1871-81; resident U.S. minister, consul gen., Berne, Switzerland, 1881-85; prof. systematic theology Boston U. Sch. Theology; prof. ch. history Drew Theol. Sem., 1886-87; prof. philosophy Dickinson Coll. Mem. Victoria Inst., Soc. Bibl Exegesis, Am. Soc. Ch. History, Am. Inst. Christian Philosophy. Died Carlisle, Pa., Jan. 23, 1898.

CRAMP, William, shipbuilder b. Phila., Sept. 22, 1807; m. Sophia Miller, 1827, several children including Charles Henry. Established William Cramp Shipbldg. Co., Phila., 1830, pres., 1830-79, name changed to William Cramp & Sons' Ship and Engine Bldg. Co., 1872, one of 1st shipbuilders to make change from wood to iron and steel vessels; built ships for U.S., Russian and Venezuelan navies; built U.S.S. New Ironsides (largest ironclad used in Civil War), 1862. Died Atlantic City, N.J., July 6, 1879.

CRANCH, Christopher Pearse, artist; b. Alexandria, D.C. (now Va.), Mar. 8, 1813; s. William and Anna (Greenleaf) C.; grad. Columbian Coll., Washington, D.C., 1831; attended Harvard Divinity Sch.; m. Elizabeth De Windt, Oct. 10, 1843, at least 2 children, George, Caroline. Unitarian minister at Andover, Bangor and Portland (all Me.), Richmond, Va., also Washington, D.C., St. Louis, Cincinnati, Louisville (Ky.); editor Western Messenger, Louisville; pastor at Boston, 1840; devoted time to art after 1843; in Europe, 1846-48, 55-63; mem. N.A.D., 1864-92; paintings include October Afternoon, 1867, Washington Oak, 1868, Roman Citizen, 1870, Venice, 1870, Venetian Fishing-Boats, 1871. Author: (poems) Poems, 1844, Bird and Bell, with Other Poems, (children's stories) 1875; The Last of the Huggermuggers, 1856, Koboltozo, 1857; Satan, a Libretto, 1874. Died Cambridge, Mass., Jan. 20, 1892.

CRANCH, John, artist; b. Washington, D.C., Feb. 2, 1807. Worked in Italy, 1830-34, N.Y.C., 1838-39, 48-54 Cincinnati, 1839-44, Washington, 1857-78; exhibited at N.A.D., 1838-39, later became asso.; exhibited Apollo Assn., Boston Athenaeum, Am. Art-Union, Washington Art Assn. Died Urbana, O., Jan. 1, 1891.

CRANCH, William, jurist; b. Weymouth, Mass., July 17, 1769; s. Richard and Mary (Smith) C.; grad. Harvard 1787, LL.D. (hon.), 1829; m. Anna Greenleaf; 1 son Christopher Pearse (the artist). Admitted to Mass. bar, 1790; commr. pub. bldgs. D.C., 1800; jr. asst. judge U.S. Circuit Ct. of D.C., 1801; reporter U.S. Supreme Ct., 1802-17; chief justic U.S. District Ct. of D.C., 1805-55. Editor: Reports of Cases Argued and Adjudged in the Supreme Court of the United States, 1801-15, 9 vols., published 1804-17. Died Wahington, D.C., Sept. 1, 1855.

CRANDALL, Prudence, educator, reformer, b. Hopkinton, R.I., Sept. 3, 1803; d. Pardon and Esther Crandall; m. Rev. Calvin Philleo, Aug. 1834. Opened school for girls, Canterbury, Conn., admitted Negro girl, 1831; opened school for Negro girls, 1832, causing violent reaction throughout Conn.; imprisoned, prosecuted and tried under act hurriedly passed by Conn. Legislature forbidding Negro schs. unless approved by the local town, 1833; defendant in famous trial case in which entire country took sides, lost case in lower ct., but decision reversed by Conn. Supreme Ct., 1834. Died Elks Falls, Kan., Jan. 28, 1889.

CRANE, Anne Moncure, author; b. Balt., Jan. 7, 1838; d. William and Jean (Daniel) Crane; never married. Lived quiet life, N.Y.C.; contbd. to various mags. Author: Emily Chester, 1864; Opportunity, 1867; Reginald Archer, 1871. Died Stuttgart, Germany, Dec. 10, 1872.

CRANE, John, army officer; b. Braintree, Mass., Dec. 18, 1744; s. Abijah and Sarah (Beverly) C.; m. Mehitable Wheeler, 1767. Served with Mass. Militia during French and Indian War; mem. Sons of Liberty; participated in Boston Tea Party, 1773; commd. capt., later maj. R.I. Arty., 1775; col. 3d Arty., Continental Army, 1777; brevetted brig. gen., 1783; served in siege of Boston and at battles of Saratoga and Red Bank; granted estate in Me. by Mass. Legislature for mil. services; judge Mass. Ct. of Common Pleas, 1790-1805. Died Whiting, Me., Aug. 21, 1805.

CRANE, Jonathan Townley, clergyman; b. Union, N.J., June 18, 1819; s. William and Sarah (Townley) C.; grad. Princeton 1843; m. Mary Helen Peck, Jan. 8, 1848, 14 children including Stephen (author Red Badge of Courage). Licensed as Methodist preacher, 1844, admitted to ministry, 1845; published essay on Dancing, 1848; prin. N.J. Conf. Sem., Pennington, N.J., 1848-58; presiding elder Newark dist. Meth. Ch., 1868-72, Elizabeth dist., 1872-76. Author: The Right Way, 1853; Popular Amuseements, 1869; Methodism and Its Methods, 1875. Died Port Jervis, N.Y., Feb. 16, 1880.

CRANE, Joseph Halsey, congressman; b. Elizabethtown (now Elizabeth), N.J., Aug. 31, 1782; attended Princeton; studied law. Admitted to N.J. bar, 1802, began practice of law; moved to Dayton, O., 1804; mem. Ohio Ho. of Reps., 1809; pros. atty. Montgomery County (O.), 1813-16; became pres. judge Ct. of Common Pleas, 1817; mem. U.S. Ho. of Reps. (Whig) from Ohio, 21st-24th congresses, 1829-37; resumed practice law, Dayton, 1837; asso. justice Ohio Supreme ct. until 1851. Died Dayton, Nov. 13, 1851; buried Woodland Cemetery.

CRANE, Stephen, Continental congressman; b. Elizabethtown (now Elizabeth) N.J., July 1709. Sheriff, Essex County; chosen by Elizabethtown Assos. to present petition before King in Eng., 1743; mem. town com., 1750, chmn., 1776; judge Ct. of Common Pleas during Stamp Act controversy; mem. N.J. Gen. Assembly, 1766-73, speaker, 1771; mayor Elizabethtown, 1772-74; chmn. county com. of New Brunswick, 1774; mem. Continental Congress from N.J., 1774-76; mem. N.J. Council, 1776, 77, 79. Died Elizabeth, July 1, 1780; buried 1st Presbyn. Ch. Cemetery.

CRANE, William Montgomery, naval officer; b. Elizabeth, N.J., Feb. 1, 1784; s. Gen. William and Abigail (Miller) C.; m. Eliza King. Commd. midshipman U.S. Navy, 1799, lt., 1803; distinguished in 2d attack on Tripoli, 1804; commanded brig. Nautilus during War of 1812; commanded ship General Pike, Lake Ontario, 1814; commanded Mediterranean Squadron, 1827-29; commandant Portsmouth (N.H.), Navy Yard, 1832-40; navy commr., 1841-42; chief Bur. of Ordnance and Hydrography, 1842-46. Died Washington, D.C., Mar. 18, 1846; buried Congressional Cemetery, Washington.

CRANSTON, Henry Young, congressman; b. Newport, R.I., Oct. 9, 1789; ed. public schs. Mcht., New Bedford, Mass.; moved to Newport, 1810; employed in commn. bus., 1810-15; admitted to bar, 1819, began practice of law, Newport; clk. Ct. of Common Plans, 1818-33; mem. R.I. Ho. of Reps., 1827-43, 47-54, speaker 3 years; v.p. R.I. Constl. Conv., 1842; mem. U.S. Ho. of Reps. from R.I., 28th-29th congresses, 1843-47. Died Newport, Feb. 12, 1864; buried Island Cemetery.

CRANSTON, John, physcian, colonial gov.; b. Eng., 1625; s. Rev. James Cranston; m. Mary Clarke, June 3, 1658, 1 son, Samuel. Atty. gen. R.I., 1654-56; commr. R.I. Gen. Assembly from Newport, 1655-66; dep. gov. R.I., 1672-78; commd. maj. Mass. Militia during King Phillip's War, 1676; gov. R.I., 1678-80. Died R.I., Mar. 12, 1680; buried Cemetery on Farewell St., Newport.

CRANSTON, Robert Bennie, congressman; b. Newport, R.I., Jan. 14, 1791; ed. public schs. Collector of internal revenue, 1812-15; sheriff Newport County, 1818-27; postmaster Newport, 1827; mem. U.S. Ho. of Reps. (Whig) from R.I., 25th-27th, 30th congresses, 1837-43, 47-49; mem. R.I. Ho. of Reps., 1843-47, speaker 1 year; mem. R.I. Senate; refused election as 1st mayor Newport, 1853; presdl. elector on Republican ticket, 1864, Died Newport, Jan. 27, 1873; buried Common Burial Ground.

CRANSTON, Samuel, colonial gov. R.I.; b. Newport, R.I., Aug. 1659; s. John and Mary (Clarke) C.; m. Mary Williams Hart; m. 2d, Judith Parrot Cranston (former sister-in-law); 7 children. Colonial gov. of R.I., 1698-1727; largely responsible for preserving R.I.'s charter rights by defending colony against privateers; successfully resolved boundary disputes with Mass. and Conn. Died May 7, 1727.

CRARY, Isaac Edwin, congressman; b. Preston, Conn., Oct. 2, 1804; s. Elisha and Nabby (Avery) C.; grad. Trinity Coll., 1827; married twice. Admitted to Mich. bar, 1833; editor Marshall Expounder; territorial del. U.S. Congress from Mich., 1835; 1st mem. U.S. Ho. of Reps. from Mich., 25th-26th congresses, 1837-41; mem. Mich. Legislature, 1842-46, speaker house, 1846; a founder U. Mich., mem. bd. regents, 1837-44; mem. Mich. Bd. Edn., 1850-52. Died Marshall, Mich., May 8, 1854; buried Oakridge Cemetery, Marshall.

CRAVEN, Braxton, coll. pres.; b. Randolph County, N.C., Aug. 22, 1822; B.A., Randolph-Macon Coll., 1850, A.M. (hon.), 1852; D.D. (hon.), Andrew Coll.; LL.D. (hon.), U. Mo. First pres. Trinity Coll. (now Duke U.), Durham, N.C., 1849-82, except for a period during Civil War 1863-66). Author: Theory of Common Schools. Died Trinity Coll., Nov. 7, 1882.

CRAVEN, John Joseph, physician, inventor; b. Newark, N.J., Sept. 8, 1822; m. Catherine S. Tichenor. Devised gutta-percha insulation for cables which pointed way for later successful ocean cable; med. dir. Dept. of South, U.S. Army, 1862, 10th Corps, 1864; physician to Jefferson Davis while the latter was in prison at Ft. Monroe, Va. Author: The Prison Life of Jefferson Davis, 1866. Died Patchague, N.Y. Feb. 14, 1893.

CRAVEN, Thomas Tingey, naval officer; b. Washington, D.C., Dec. 20, 1808; s. Tunis and Hannah (Tingey) C.; m. Virginia Wingate; m. 2d, Emily Truxtun; 8 children. Commd. midshipman U.S. Navy, 1828, lt., 1830; comdt. of midshipmen U.S. Naval Acad., Annapolis, Md., 1850-55, 58-60, initiated practice of cruises (still feature of the course at Acad.); promoted comdr., 1852; commd. capt. while in command of Potomac flotilla, 1861, commodore, 1863, rear-adm., 1866; comdt. Mare Island Navy-yard; comdr. Pacific Squadron; ret., 1869; port adm., San Francisco, 1870. Died Boston, Aug. 23, 1887.

CRAVEN, Tunus Augustus Macdonough, naval officer; b. Portsmouth, N.H., Jan. 11, 1813; s. Tunus and Hannah (Tingey) C.; m. Mary Carter, 1838; m. 2d, Marie Stevenson. Served as lt. on ships Falmouth, 1841-43, North Carolina, 1843-46; chief editor U.S. Nautical Mag. (one of 1st periodicals devoted to interests of navy), 1845-46; comdr. ship Dale, in Pacific squadron, assisted in conquest of Cal., 1848; comdr. Atrato expdn. in survey for ship canal across Isthmus of Darien, 1857; comdr., Apr. 1861; comdr. monitor Tecumseh with Adm. Farragut's squadron in Mobile, Ala.; Tecumseh was destroyed by the Confederate ram Tennessee in Battle of Mobile Bay, Aug. 5, 1864, and Craven went down with his ship. Died Aug. 5, 1864.

CRAVENS, James Addison, congressman; b. Rockingham County, Va., Nov. 4, 1818; ed. public schs. Moved with family to Washington County, Ind., 1820; became farmer and stock raiser served as maj. 2d Ind. volunteers in Mexican War, 1846-47; mem. Ind. Ho. of Reps., 1848-49, Ind. Senate, 1850-53; commd. brig. gen. Ind. Militia, 1854; mem. U.S. Ho. of Reps. (Democrat) from Ind., 37th-38th congresses, 1861-65; del. Union Nat. Conv. of Conservatives, Phila., 1866, Dem. Nat. Conv., N.Y.C., 1868. Died Hardinsburg, Ind., June 20, 1893; buried Hardin Cemetery.

CRAVENS, James Harrison, congressman; b. Harrisonburg, Va., Aug. 2, 1802; studied law. Admitted to bar, 1823, began practice of law, Harrisonburg; moved to Franklin, Pa., 1823; became farmer, Madison, Ind., 1829; mem. Ind. Ho. of Reps., 1831-32; moved to Ripley County, Ind., 1833, practiced law, managed farm; mem. Ind. Senate, 1839; Whig presdl. elector, 1840 mem. U.S. Ho. of Reps. from Ind., 1841-43; unsuccessful Free-Soil Party candidate for gov. Ind., 1852; mem. Ind. Ho. of Reps., 1856; served as lt col. 83d Regt., Ind. Volunteer Ind. during Civil War, taken captive during Morgan's raid in Ind. Died Osgood, Ripley County, Dec. 4, 1876; buried Versailles (Ind.) Cemetery.

CRAWFORD, George Washington, gov. Ga., congressman b. Columbia County, Ga., Dec. 22, 1798; grad. Princeton, 1820; studied law. Admitted to bar, 1822, began practice of law, Augusta, Ga.; atty. gen. Ga., 1827-31; mem. Ga. Ho. of Reps., 1837-42 mem. U.S. Ho of Reps. from Ga. (elected as Whig to fill vacancy), Jan. 7-Mar. 3, 1843; gov. Ga., 1843-47; U.S. sec. of war under Pres. Taylor, 1849-50; presided over Ga. Secession Conv., 1861. Died "Bel Air," nr. Augusta, July 22, 1872; buried Summerville Cemetery.

CRAWFORD, Joel, congressman; b. Columbia County, Ga., June 15, 1783; attended Litchfield (Conn.) Law Sch. Admitted to bar, began practice of law, Sparta, Ga., 1808; moved to Milledgeville, Ga., 1811; served as 2d lt., aide-de-camp to Brig. Gen. Floyd in war against Creek Indians, 1813-14; mem. Ga. Ho. of Reps., 1814-17 mem. U.S. Ho. of Reps. (Democrat) from Ga, 15th-16th congresses, 1817-21; commr to run boundary line between Ala. and Ga., 1826; mem. Ga. Senate, 1827-28; unsuccessful candidate for gov. Ga., 1828, 31 del. Internat. Improvement Conv., 1831; state commr. to locate and construct Western & Atlantic R.R., 1837. Died nr. Blakely, Early County, Ga., Apr. 5, 1858; buried family burying ground on plantation, Early County.

CRAWFORD, John, physician; b. May 3, 1746; med. degree, U. Leyden (Holland). Set forth the theory of infection or contagion (his most useful contbn. to med. sci.); helped to found The Balt. Library, 1798, Soc. for the Promotion of Useful Knowledge, The Balt. Dispensary. Died Balt., May 9, 1813 buried Presbyn. Cemetery, Balt.

CRAWFORD, Martin Jenkins, congressman, jurist; b. Jasper County, Ga., Mar. 17, 1820; s. Hardy and Betsey (Jenkins). C.; m. Amanda Reese, 1842. Admitted to Ga. bar, 1838; mem. Ga. Legislature, 1845-47; del. Nashville Conv., 1850 judge superior cts. Chatahoochee Circuit, 1853-55; mem. U.S. Ho. of Reps. from Ga., 34th-36th congresses, 1855-61; del. Confederate Provisional Congress, 1861-62; served with Confederate Army; most important of the three mems. apptd. by Jefferson Davis to serve on a peace commn.; judge Chattahoochee Circuit, 1875; asso. justice Ga. Supreme Ct., 1880-83. Died Columbus, Ga., July 23, 1883; buried Linnwood Cemetery, Columbus.

CRAWFORD, Thomas, sculptor; b. N.Y.C., Mar. 22, 1813; s. Aaron and Mary (Gibson) C.; studied under the Dane, Thorvaldsen; m. Louisa Ward, 1844; 1 dau., Francis Marion. Commd. by Va. to execute a monument for Richmond, 1849, executed equestrian monument of Washington; executed sculptural decorations for U.S. Capitol, including marble pediment, bronze doors of Senate wing, bronze Armed Liberty; supervised History of Justice over Senate doors; other works include Orpheus (1st important group), Dancing Girl, 1844, Dying Indian Maiden, 1848, Flora, 1853 (all in Met. Mus. Art, N.Y.C.); Statue of Beethoven (in Boston Music Hall); Children in Wood (Lenox Library, N.Y.C.); Hebe and Ganymede (Boston Art Mus.); Died London, Eng., Oct. 10, 1857; buried Greenwood Cemetery, Bklyn.

CRAWFORD, Thomas Hartley, congressman, jurist; b. Chambersburg, Pa., Nov. 14, 1786; grad. Princeton, 1804 studied law. Admitted to bar, 1807; began practice of law, Chambersburg; mem. U.S. Ho. of Reps. (Jackson Democrat) from Pa., 21st-22d congresses, 1829-33; mem. Pa. Ho. of Reps., 1833-34; apptd. commr. to investigate alleged frauds in sale of Creek Indian Reservation, 1836; commr. Indian affairs (apptd. by Pres. Van Buren), 1838-45; judge D.C. Criminal Ct. 1845-61. Died Washington, D.C., Jan. 27, 1863; buried Congressional Cemetery, Washington.

CRAWFORD, William, army officer; b. Berkeley County, Va., 1732. Served in French and Indian War; capt., leader of scouts with Gen. Braddock in expdn. against Ft. Duquesne, 1755; served as capt. during Pontiac War, 1763-64; justice Pa. Ct. Quarter Sessions; commd. lt. col. 5th Regt., Va. Militia, 1776, col. 7th Regt., 1776; participated in battles of L.I., Trenton, Princeton, Brandywine, Germantown; in charge of Va. Frontier Militia, 1778; comdr. expdn. against Wyandote and Delaware Indians in Ohio. Captured and killed at "Battle Island," Wyandot County, O., June 11, 1782.

CRAWFORD, William, congressman, physician; b. Paisley, Scotland, 1760, degree in medicine U. Edinburgh (Scotland), 1781. Came to U.S., settled nr. Gettysburg, Pa.; physician, farm owner, 1785-1823; asso. judge for Adams County, 1801-08 mem. U.S. Ho. of Reps. (Democrat) from Pa., 11th-14th congresses, 1809-17. Died Adams County, Pa., Oct. 23, 1823; buried Evergreen Cemetery, Gettysburg.

CRAWFORD, William Harris, senator, cabinet officer; b. Nelson County, Va., Feb. 24, 1772; s. Joel and Fannie (Harris) C.; ed. privately in classical studies; student Richmond Acad., Augusta, Ga.; m. Susanna Girardin, 1804. Moved to Edgefield, S.C., 1779, to Columbia County, Ga., 1783; admitted to Ga. bar, 1799; mem. Ga. Senate, 1803-07; mem. U.S. Senate from Ga., 1807-13, pres. pro tem, 1812; minister to France, 1812-13; agt. for sale of land donated to U.S. govt. by Lafayette, 1815; U.S. sec. of war, 1815-16; U.S. sec. of treasury, 1816-25; Democratic candidate for Pres. U.S., 1824, paralytic stroke ruined chance in 1824. Died Oglethorpe County, Ga., Sept. 15, 1834; buried "Woodlawn," nr. Crawford, Oglethorpe County.

CRAZY HORSE, (Indian name: Tashunca-vitco), Indian chief; b. circa 1849; married a mem. of Cheyenne tribe. Chief of Sioux Confederacy; moved North with his bank of 1200 Oglalas and Cheyennes, joined large body under Sitting Bull, Valley of Little Big Horn, Wyo., 1876; led a force of Cheyennes in battle of Little Big Horn, June 25, 1876, surrounded Gen. Custer in flanking movements from the North and West, destroyed Custer's entire command; later surrendered. Killed while resisting imprisonment, Sept. 5, 1877.

CREAMER, David, govt. ofcl., hymnoligist; b. Balt., Nov. 20, 1812; s. Joshua and Margaret (Smith) C.; m. Eliza Ann Taylor, Nov. 27, 1834. Partner Joshua Creamer & Son, lumber co., Balt., 1832-38; publisher, co-editor Balt. Monument, 1836-38; recruiting officer of Md., 1862; assessor of internal revenue, 1863; clk. Post Office dept., Washington, D.C.; trustee Dickinson Coll., 1866-87. Author: Methodist Hymnology, 1848; Hymns for the Use of the Methodist Episcopal Church, 1849. Died Balt., Apr. 8, 1887.

CREATH, Jacob, clergyman b. Cumberland, N.S., Can., Feb. 22, 1777; s. Samuel and Susan (Moore) C.; m. Milly Carter, Jan. 24, 1799. Ordained to ministry baptist Ch., 1798; pastor in Matthews County, Va., 1798-1803; itinerant preacher Elkhorn Bapt. Assn. in Ky., 1803-30; dropped from Bapt. Assn. for Campbellite sentiments, 1830 travelling preacher, organizer churches of Disciples of Christ in Ky., 1830-54. Died Mar. 13, 1854.

CREATH, Jacob, clergyman; b. Mecklenburg County, Va., Jan. 17, 1799; s. William C. and Lucretia (Brame) C.; m. Susan Bedford, Sept. 1831; m. 2d, Prudence Rogers, Mar. 1842. Licensed to preach in Baptist Ch., 1818, ordained to ministry, 1820; mem. Elkhorn Bapt. Assn. in Ky., 1823-30 dropped from Bapt. Ch. for Campbellite sentiments, 1830; travelled and established Campbellite churches in South, particularly Mo., 1830-86; agt. to raise funds for Bible Revision Com., 1855-61. Died Jan. 8, 1886.

CREBS, John Montgomery, congressman; b. Middleburg, Loudoun County, Va., Apr. 9, 1830; ed. public schs.; studied law. Moved with family to White County, Ill., 1837 admitted to bar, 1852, began practice of law, White County; commd. lt. col. 87th Regt., Ill. Inf., 1862; served in Miss., Vicksburg and Ark. campaigns in Civil War; commanded cavalry brigade in Dept. of Gulf; mem. U.S. Ho. of Reps. (Democrat) from Ill., 41st-42d congresses, 1869-73; practiced law, 1873-90. Died Carmi, White County, June 26, 1890 buried Maple Ridge Cemetery.

CREESY, Josiah Perkins, sea capt.; b. Marblehead, Mass., Mar. 23, 1814; s. Josiah P. and Mary (Woolridge) C.; m. Eleanor Horton Prentiss, 1841. Commanded clipper ships in trade with China, 1837-65; set sailing record of 89 days from N.Y.C. to San Francisco in ship Flying Cloud; volunteer acting lt. in command of U.S.S. Ino, 1861-62. Died Salem, Mass., June 5, 1871; buried Marblehead.

CREIGHTON, Edward, banker, telegraph builder, philanthropist; b. Licking County, O., Aug. 31, 1820; s. James and Bridget (Hughes) C.; m. Mary Lucretia Wareham. Organizer, pres. 1st nat. bank in Neb.; engaged (with brother John Andrew Creighton and Hiram Sibley) in extending telegraph lines to Pacific Coast, 1860-61; bequeathed $100,000 to establish a univ.; this was carried out through his wife's will, resulted in founding of Creighton U., Omaha, Neb. Died Nov. 5, 1874.

CREIGHTON, William, congressman; b. Berkeley County, Va., Oct. 29, 1778; s. William Creighton; grad. Dickinson Coll., 1795; m. Elizabeth Meade, Sept. 5, 1805. Admitted to Ohio bar, 1799; 1st sec. of state Ohio, 1803-08; U.S. dist. atty., 1809-11; mem. U.S. Ho. of Reps. from Ohio, 13th-14th, 20th-22d congresses, 1813-17, 27-33. Died Chillicothe, O., Oct. 1, 1851; buried Grand View Cemetery, Chillicothe.

CRERAR, John, railroad exec., philanthropist; b. N.Y.C., Mar. 8, 1827; s. John and Agnes (Smeallie) C. Mfr. railroad supplies, contractors materials, Chgo., 1859; an incorporator, dir. Pullman Palace Car Co., 1867; dir. Il. Trust & Savs. Bank, Chgo. & Alton R.R. Co.; pres. Chgo. & Joliet Ry. Co.; part of estate went toward creation John Crerar Library, Chgo. Died Chgo., Oct. 19, 1889.

CRESAP, Michael, army officer; b. Alleghany County, Md., July 10, 1742; s. Thomas Cresap; m. Mary Whitehead. Precipitated Dunmore's War by leading Whites in Yellow Creek Massacre (in which several families of peaceful Indians were slaughtered), 1774; capt. Va. Militia which defeated Indians at Point Pleasant, 1774; commd. by Md. Assembly to recruit troops for Continental Army, 1775. Died N.Y.C., Oct. 18, 1775.

CRESAP, Thomas, pioneer; b. Skipton, Eng., circa 1702; m. Hannah Johnson, circa 1727, 1 son, Michael. Came to Md., 1717; one of most prominent men of the Appalachian border; served as capt. Md. Militia, 1734; Indian trader, translator; an organizer Ohio Co., 1749; fought in Am. Revolution. Died circa 1790.

CRESPI, Juan, missionary, explorer; b. 1721. Joined Portola expdn. for occupation San Diego, Cal. and Monterey, Cal.; one of first pioneers at San Diego, 1769; accomplished first European expdn. by land up Cal. coast; discovered San Francisco Bay with Portola, 1772; a founder Mission Carmel (Cal.). Died Carmel, Jan. 1, 1782.

CRESSON, Elliott, mcht., philanthropist; b. Phila., Mar. 2, 1796; s. John Elliot and Mary (Warder) C. Partner, Cresson, Wistar & Co., mchts.; an organizer Young Men's Colonization Soc. of Pa., 1834; bequests by his will include $50,000 to Am. Sunday Sch. Union, $10,000 to Phila. Sch. Design for Women, $10,000 to Hist. Soc. Pa., $10,000 for monument to William Penn. $5,000 to Pa. Hosp. for Insane, U. Pa., founding of a miner's sch. in Pa., Pa. Agrl. Soc. noted for attention to promotion of welfare of Indians and Negroes in U.S.; Quaker. Died Phila., Feb. 20, 1854.

CRESWELL, John Angel James, senator postmaster gen.; b. Port Deposit, Md., Nov. 18, 1828; s. John G. and Rebecca (Webb) C.; grad. Dickinson Coll., 1848; m. Hannah Richardson. Admitted to Md. bar, 1850 mem. Md. Ho. of Dels., 1862; adj. gen. Md., 1862-63; mem. U.S. Ho. of Reps. from Md., 38th Congress, 1863-65; mem. U.S. Senate from Md., Mar.-July, 1865; postmaster gen. U.S., 1869-74, introduced 1c postal cards; counsel for Ala. claims U..S Ct. Commrs., 1874-76; noted for improvements of U.S. Postal System. Died Elkton, Md., Dec. 23, 1891; buried Elkton Presbyn. Cemetery.

CRETIN, Joseph, clergyman; b. Lyons, France, Dec. 19, 1799; s. Joseph and Jane (Mery) C.; ed. Seminary, St. Sulpice, Paris, France. Ordained to Roman Catholic Ch., 1823; opened a preparatory coll., became pastor as Cure de Ferney arrived in Dubuque, Ia., 1839; made vicar-gen. diocese of over 30,000 Indians; apptd. by U.S. Govt. as missionary to Winnebagoes at Prairie du Chien, Wis., 1843; became 1st bishop of St. Paul (embracing the State of Minn.), Roman Cath. Ch., 1850, consecrated, 1851. Died St. Paul, Feb. 22, 1857.

CREVECOEUR, Michel-Guillaume Jean De, see de Crevecoeur.

CRISFIELD, John Woodland, congressman; b. nr. Chestertown, Kent County, Md., Nov. 8, 1806; attended Washington Coll., Chestertown; studied law. Admitted to bar, 1830, began practice of law, Princess Anne, Somerset County, Md.; mem. Md. Ho. of Reps., 1836; mem. U.S. Ho. of Reps. from Md. (as Whig), 30th Congress, 1847-49, (as Union Republican), 37th Congress, 1861-63; del. Md. Constl. Conv., 1850; mem. Washington (D.C.) Peace Conf., 1861; del. Union Nat. Conv., Phila., 1866; founder Town of Crisfield (Md.), 1866; a builder, pres. Eastern Shore R.R. Died Princess Anne, Jan. 12, 1897; buried Manokin Presbyn. Cemetery.

CRISP, Charles Frederick, congressman; b. Sheffield, Eng., Jan. 29, 1845; s. William and Elizabeth C.; m. Clara Belle Burton, 1867; 1 son, Charles R. Served as lt. Confederate Army during Civil War; admitted to Ga. bar, 1866; Ga. solicitor gen. Southwestern Jud. Dist., 1872-77, judge Ga. Superior Ct., 1877-82; mem. U.S. Ho. of Reps. from Ga., 48th-54th congresses, 1883-96, speaker, 1891-95. Died Atlanta, Ga., Oct. 23, 1896; buried Oak Grove Cemetery, Atlanta.

CRIST, Henry, congressman; b. Fredericksburg, Spotsylvania County, Va., Oct. 20, 1764; attended public schs., Pa. A surveyor in Ky.; moved to Bullitt County, Ky., 1788, became salt mfr.; mem. Ky. Ho. of Reps., 1795, 1806, Ky. Senate, 1800-04; mem. U.S. Ho. of Reps. from Ky., 11th Congress, 1809-11; became a Whig. Died nr. Shepherdsville, Bullitt County, Aug. 11, 1844; buried State Cemetery, Frankfort, Ky.

CRITTENDEN, George Bibb, army officer; b. Russellville, Ky., Mar. 20, 1812; s. John Jordan and Sally (Lee) C.; grad. U.S. Mil. Acad., 1832. Commd. capt. co. of mounted rifles during Mexican War; brevetted maj. for gallantry at battles of Contreras and Churubusco; commd. lt. col., 1856, brig. gen., 1857; commd. maj. gen. Confederate Army, 1861, comdr. S.E. Ky. and part of E. Tenn., 1861; state librarian Ky., 1867-74. Died Danville, Ky., Nov. 27, 1880; buried Frankfort (Ky.) Cemetery.

CRITTENDEN, John Jordan, senator, gov. Ky.; b. Versailles, Ky., Sept. 10, 1787; s. John and Judith (Harris) C.; grad. Coll. William and Mary, 1807; m. Sally Lee, 1811; m. 2d, Maria Innes, 1826; m. 3d, Mrs. Elizabeth Ashley, 1853; 9 children, including George Bibb, Thomas L. Atty. gen. Ill. Territory, 1809-10; mem. Ky. Legislature, 1811-17, 25, 29-32, speaker house, 1815-16, 29-32; mem. U.S. Senate from Ky., 1817-19 (filled vacancy), 1835-41, 1842-48, 55-61; U.S. dist. atty. for Ky., 1827-29; sec. of state Ky., 1834; atty. gen. U.S., 1841, 50-53; gov. Ky., 1849; mem. U.S. Ho. of Reps. from Ky., 37th Congress, 1861-63; unsuccessfully introduced Crittenden Compromise as measure of conciliation between North and South. Died Frankfort, Ky., July 26, 1863; buried State Cemetery, Frankfort.

CRITTENDEN, Thomas Leonidas, army officer, state ofcl.; b. Russellville, Ky., May 15, 1819; s. John Jordan and Sally (Lee) C.; m. Kittie Todd. Admitted to Ky. bar, 1840; commonwealth's atty. in Ky., 1842; U.S. consul, Liverpool, 1848-53; commd. maj. gen. Ky. Militia, 1860; commd. brig. gen. U.S. Army, 1861, promoted to maj. gen. (for distinguished service at Battle of Shiloh, 1862), 1862; commanded corps at battles of Stone River, 1862-63; investigated after his corps retreated at Battle of Chickamauga, 1863, acquitted; trans. to Army of Potomac, comdr. portion of 9th Corps throughout operations during 1864; apptd. state treas. Ky. 1866; brevetted brig. gen., 1867. Died Staten Island, N.Y., Oct. 23, 1893; buried Frankfort (Ky.) Cemetery.

CROCHERON, Henry, congressman; b. Staten Island, N.Y., Dec. 26, 1772; ed. common schs. Engaged in bus., Northfield; supr. Northfield, 1808-14; mem. U.S. Ho. of Reps. (Democrat) from N.Y., 14th Congress, 1815-17; commd. capt. Militia, 1818. Died New Springville, Richmond County, N.Y., Nov. 8, 1819; buried St. Andrews' Churchyard, S.I.

CROCHERON, Jacob, congressman; b. Staten Island, N.Y., Aug. 23, 1774. A farmer; sheriff Richmond County (N.Y.), 1802, 11, 21; mem. U.S. Ho. of Reps. (Jackson Democrat) from N.Y., 21st Congress, 1829-31; presdl. elector on Democratic ticket, 1836. Died S.I., Dec. 27, 1849; buried St. Andrew's Churchyard, S.I.

CROCKER, Alvah, industrialist, gov. Mass., congressman; b. Leominster, Mass., Oct. 14, 1801; s. Samuel and Comfort (Jones) C.; m. Abigail Fox, Aug. 14, 1829; m. 2d, Lucy Fay, Apr. 9, 1851; m. 3d, Minerva Cushing, Oct. 20, 1872. Mem. Mass. Legislature, 1835-38, 42-43, 61-65; mem. Mass. Gen. Ct., 1836; chiefly responsible for bldg. Fitchburg R.R. between Boston and Fitchburg, (Mass.), 1843-45; an organizer Fitchburg Mut. Fire Ins. Co., 1847; reorganized paper factory owned by Gardner Burbank as Crocker, Burbank & Co., 1850; trustee Fitchburg Savs. Bank, 1851-74; gov. Mass., 1872; mem. U.S. Ho. of Reps. from Mass., 42d-43d congresses, Jan. 2, 1872-Dec. 26, 1874; pres. Vt. & Mass. R.R. Died Fitchburg, Dec. 26, 1874.

CROCKER, Charles, mcht., railroad builder; b. Troy, N.Y., Sept. 16, 1822; s. Isaac and Eliza (Wright) C.; m. Mary Deming, Oct., 1852, 4 children. Opened store, Sacramento, Cal., 1852; mem. Sacramento City Council, 1855; mem. Cal. Legislature, 1860; in charge constrn. Central Pacific R.R., 1863-69; pres. Contract & Finance Co.; pres. So. Pacific R.R. of Cal., 1871; led in consolidation of Central and So. Pacific railroads, 1884. Died Monterey, Cal., Aug. 14, 1888.

CROCKER, Hannah Mather, reformer; b. Boston, June 27, 1752; d. Samuel and Hannah (Hutchinson) Mather; m. Joseph Crocker, Apr. 13, 1779, 10 children. Organized women's club based on Masonic principles, Boston; advocate of women's equality and temperance. Author: Series of Letters on Freemasonry, by a Lady of Boston, 1815; The School of Reform, or Seaman's Safe Pilot, to the Cape of Good Hope, 1816; Observations on the Real Rights of Women, with Their Appropriate Duties, Agreeable to Scripture, Reason, and Common Sense, 1818. Died Boston, July 11, 1829; buried Copp's Hill, Boston.

CROCKER, Samuel Leonard, mfr., congressman; b. Taunton, Mass., Mar. 31, 1804; grad. Brown U., Providence, R.I., 1822. Became a mfr.; mem. Mass. Exec. Council, 1849; mem. U.S. Ho. of Reps. (Whig) from Mass., 33d Congress, 1853-55; pres. Taunton Copper Mfg. Co. Died Boston, Feb. 10, 1883; buried Mt. Pleasant Cemetery, Taunton.

CROCKER, Sarah G., actress; b. Ridgefield, Conn., 1834; m. Frederick B. Conway, 1850. Mem. John E. Owens acting co., Balt., 1849, co. at Purdy's Nat. Theatre, Chatham Street, N.Y.C., 1850; mem. J. W. Wallack's Co., N.Y., 1852; toured U.S., 1853-64 co-mgr. Park Theatre, Bklyn., 1864. Died Bklyn., Apr. 28, 1874.

CROCKER, Uriel, publisher; b. Marblehead, Mass., Sept. 13, 1796; s. Uriel and Mary (James) C.; grad. acad. Marblehead, 1811; A.M. (hon.) Darthmouth, 1866; m. Sarah Kidder Haskell, Feb. 11, 1829, 3 children. Established Armstrong, Crocker and Brewster, printing house, 1819, became Crocker & Brewster (popular house of textbooks and religious publishing), 1825-76; Old Colony R.R. Co., 1844-50, 63-83; pres. Atlantic & Pacific R.R. Co., 1874; mem. Boston Dispensary, Old South Soc.; dir. Bunker Hill Monument Assn., 1833-69, v.p., 1869-87; dir. Northern (N.H.) R.R., Franklin Savs. Bank, U.S. Hotel Co., South Bay Improvement Co.; overseer Boston House of Correction; mem. Mass. Charitable Soc., Mass. Charitable Mechanics Assn.; trustee Mt. Auburn Cemetery; mem. Mass. Hort. Soc., New Eng. Historic Geneal. Soc., Bostonian Soc. Died Cohasset, Mass., July 19, 1887; buried Mt. Auburn Cemetery, Cambridge, Mass.

CROCKETT, David, frontiersman, congressman; b. Limestown, Tenn., Aug. 17, 1786; s. John and Rebecca (Hawkins) C.; m. Polly Findlay, 1809, 5 children including John Wesley. Known as Davy Crockett; served under Andrew Jackson in Creek War, 1813-14; frontiersman in Western Tenn.; mem. Tenn. Legislature, 1821-23; mem. U.S. Ho. of Reps. from Tenn., 20th-21st, 23d congresses, 1827-31, 33-35; served in Tex. Army during Tex. War of Independence, 1836. Perhaps author of books published under his name: A Narrative of the Life of David Crockett, 1834; An Account of Col. Crockett's Tour to the North and Down East, 1834; Col. Crockett's Exploits and Adventures in Texas, 1836. Killed at Battle of Alamo, Mar. 6, 1836.

CROCKETT, John Wesley, congressman; b. Trenton, Tenn., July 10, 1807; s. David Crockett; attended public schs.; studied law. Admitted to bar, began practice of law, Paris, Tenn.; held various local, state offices; mem. U.S. Ho. of Reps. (Whig) from Tenn., 25th-26th congresses, 1837-41; atty. gen. 9th Dist. Tenn., 1841-43; became commn. mcht., New Orleans, 1843; became editor of the National, 1848; established the Crescent, 1850; moved to Memphis, Tenn., 1852. Died Memphis, Nov. 24, 1852; buried Old City Cemetery, Paris, Tenn.

CROGHAN, George, army officer; b. Locust Grove, Ky., Nov. 15, 1791; s. William and Lucy (Clark) c.; grad. Coll. William and Mary, 1810; m. Serena Livingston, May 1816. Aide to Col. Boyd at Battle of Tippecanoe, War of 1812, 1811; aide-de-camp Gen. Harrison, 1813; commanded defense of Ft. Stephenson in No. Ohio, for which he was brevetted lt. col., 1813; postmaster New Orleans, 1824; insp. gen. with rank of col. U.S. Army, 1824; served under Gen. Taylor in Battle of Monterey during Mexican War. Died New Orleans, Jan. 8, 1849.

CROIX, Teodoro de, commandant gen. Provincias Internas of Mexico; b. Lille, Flanders, June 30, 1730. Commd. brig. gen. Spanish Army, 1770; commandant gen. Provincias Internas of Mexico, 1776-83, over what now comprises the states Cal., N.M., Tex. (U.S.), Sinaloo, Mexico; 1st commandant gen.; commd. lt. gen., 1783; viceroy of Peru, 1784-89. Died Madrid, Spain, circa 1792.

CROLY, David Goodman, journalist; b. N.Y.C., Nov. 3, 1829; s. Patrick and Elizabeth C; grad. Univ. City N.Y., 1854; m. Jane Cunningham, 1857, 1 son, Herbert. In charge of city intelligence dept. N.Y. Herald, 1855-58; founder, editor Daily News, Rockford, Ill., 1858-60; city editor World, N.Y.C., 1860-62, mng. editor 1862-67; noted for editorial prediction of financial crisis of 1873, also for naming Jay Cooke & Co. as 1st victim and No. & Pacific as 1st corp. to suffer, 1872; editor Daily Graphic, N.Y.C., 1873-78. Author. Seymour & Blair, 1868; A History of Reconstruction, 1868; Primer of Positivism, 1876. Died N.Y.C., Apr. 29, 1889.

CROMPTON, George, inventor, mfr.; b. Lancashire, Eng., Mar. 23, 1829; s. William and Sarah (Low) C.; m. Mary Pratt, Jan. 9, 1853; 9 children. Sole owner Crompton Loom Works (at the time one of Am.'s largest and best-known machine shops), 1859; Crompton looms in worldwide competition received 1st award at Paris Exposition; commn. pronounced them the best looms for fancy weaving at Centennial Exposition, 1876; a founder, 1st policy holder Hartford Steam Boiler Inspection & Ins. Co. (Conn.); a founder, pres. Crompton Carpet Co. Died Worcester, Mass., Dec. 29, 1886.

CROMPTON, William, inventor, mfr.; b. Preston, Eng., Sept. 10, 1806; s. Thomas and Mary (Dawson) C.; m. Sarah Low, May 26, 1828, 8 children including George. Came to Am., 1836; perfected a weaving loom, 1837; went to Eng. for patent, 1838; designed looms to produce patterned woolens at Middlesex Mills, Lowell, Mass., 1839; opened mill, Millbury, Mass. Died Windsor, Conn., May 1, 1891.

CROOK, George, army officer; b. nr. Dayton, O., Sept. 23, 1829; s. Thomas and Elizabeth (Mathers) C.; grad. U.S. Mil. Acad., 1852; m. Mary Dailey. Commd. 2d lt. U.S. Army, 1852, 1st lt. on frontier duty in N.W., 1852-61; col. 36th Ohio Inf., 1861, in command 3d brigade Army of W. Va., served in battles of Lewisburg, South Mountain, Antietam, 1861; brevetted maj. U.S. Army, 1862; commd. brig. gen. U.S. Volunteers, in command of calvalry div. Army of Cumberland, 1863; brevetted col., 1863, brig. gen., 1864; in command W.Va., also in personal command one of corps in Sheridan's Army of the Shenandoah; commd. maj. gen. U.S. Volunteers; commd. maj. gen. U.S. Army, served in battles of Winchester, Fisher's Hill, Cedar Creek, 1864, battles of Dinwiddie Court House, Sailor's Creek, Farmville, 1865; commd. lt. col. 23d Inf., U.S. Army, 1865, commanded Boise (Ida.) dist., 1865; commd. brig. gen. 1873; commanded Dept. of Platte, 1875, 86-88; participated in Gt. Sioux War, 1876; fought against Apache Indians, 1882-86; maj. gen. in command of Div. of Mo., 1888. Died Chgo., Mar. 21, 1890.

CROOKE, Philip Schuyler, congressman; b. Poughkeepsie, N.Y., Mar. 2, 1810; grad. Dutchess Acad., Poughkeepsie; studied law. Admitted to bar, 1831, began practice of law, Bklyn.; moved to Flatbush, N.Y., 1838; mem. bd. suprs. Kings County. (N.Y.) 1844-52, 58-70, chmn., 1861-62, 64-65; presdl. elector on Democratic ticket, 1852; mem. N.Y. State Gen. Assembly (Republican), 1863; mem. N.Y. State N.G., 40 years, served from pvt. to brig. gen., commanded 5th Brigade in Pa., 1863, during Civil War; mem. U.S. Ho. of Reps. (Rep.) from N.Y., 43d Congress, 1873-75. Died Flatbush, Mar. 17, 1881; buried Greenwood Cemetery, Bklyn.

CROOKS, Arthur, architect; b. England, circa 1838. Came to U.S. before Civil War; enlisted in Union Army, rose to col.; became draftsman in office of Richard Upjohn, N.Y.C., after Civil War, acquired tng. in church design; completed St. Thomas' Ch., N.Y.C. (begun by Upjohn); established archtl. office, designed over 100 churches in N.Y.C. and suburbs, also numerous residences and other bldgs. Died 1888.

CROOKS, George Richard, clergyman, educator; b. Phila., Feb. 3, 1822; grad. Dickinson Coll., 1840; m. Susan Emory, June 10, 1846. Ordained to ministry Methodist Episcopal Ch.; adjunct prof. Latin and Greek, Dickinson Coll., 1845; editor The Methodist, 1860-75; prof. hist. theology Drew Sem., 1880-97. Died Feb. 20, 1897.

CROOKS, Ramsay, fur trader; b. Greenock, Scotland, Jan. 2, 1787; s. William and Margaret (Ramsay) C.; m. Marianne Pratte, Mar. 10, 1825. Partner, gen. mgr. John Jacob Astor's Am. Fur Co., 1817-34, pres., 1834-59; 1st pres. Mohawk & Hudson R.R. Co.; trustee Astor Library. Died N.Y.C., June 6, 1859.

CROSBY, Alpheus, educator; b. Sandwich, N.H., Oct. 13, 1810; s. Dr. Asa and Abigail (Russell) C.; grad. Dartmouth, 1827; attended Andover Theol. Sem., 1831-33; m. Abigail Grant Jones Cutler, Aug. 27, 1834; m. 2d, Martha Kingman, Feb. 12, 1861. Preceptor, Moor's Charity Sch., Hanover, N.H., 1827-28; tutor Dartmouth, 1828-31, prof. Latin and Greek, 1833-37, prof. Greek, 1837-49, prof. emeritus, 1849-74; supt. public schs., Newburyport, Mass., 1849-54; agt. Mass. Bd. Edn., 1854-57; prin. Mass. State Normal Sch., Salem, 1857-65; editor Mass. Tchr. (Mag.), The Right Way (Abolitionist organ). Author: Greek Grammar; Essay on the Second Advent, 1850; First Lessons in Geometry, 1851; Explanatory Notes to the Anabasis, 1874. Died Salem, Apr. 17, 1874.

CROSBY, Howard, clergyman, educator; b. N.Y.C., Feb. 27, 1826; s. William Bedlow and Harriet (Ashton) C.; grad. Univ. City N.Y., 1844; D.D. (hon.), Harvard, 1859; LL.D. (hon.) Columbia, 1871; m. Margaret E. Givan; 1 son, Ernest Howard (1856-1902). Prof. of Greek, Univ. City N.Y., 1851-59; an organizer Young Men's Christain Soc., also 2d pres.; prof. Greek, Rutgers U., 1859; ordained to ministry Presbyn. Ch., 1861; minister 4th Av. Presbyn. Ch., 1863; mem. council Univ. City N.Y., 1864, chancellor, 1870-81; mem. New Testament Co. of Am. Revision Com., 1872-80; founder, pres. Soc. Prevention of Crime. Author: Jesus, His Life and Work, 1871; Expository Notes on the Book of Joshua, 1875; The Christian Preacher, 1880; Commentary on the New Testament, 1885. Died N.Y.C., Mar. 29, 1891.

CROSBY, Nathan, lawyer; b. Sandwich, N.H., Feb. 12, 1798; s. Dr. Asa and Betsy (Holt) C.; grad. Dartmouth, 1820, LL.D. (hon.), 1879; m. Rebecca Marquand Moody, Sept. 28, 1824, 1 son, Stephen Moody. Began practice of law, 1823; corp. counsel for Lowell Mfg. Corp., 1845-46; justice Lowell (Mass.) Police Ct., 1846-85. Author: First Half-Century of Dartmouth College, 1877. Died Lowell, Feb. 9, 1885.

CROSBY, Pierce, naval officer; b. Delaware County, Pa., Jan. 16, 1824; s. John P. and Catharine (Beale) C; m. Matilda Boyer, Oct. 16, 1850; m. 2d Julia Wells, Mar. 1861; m. 3d, Miriam Gratz, Feb. 15, 1870; m. 4th, Louise Audenried, June 24, 1880. commd. lt. U.S. Navy, 1853; served in Brazilian Squadron, 1857; in command tugs protecting trade in Chesapeake Bay, 1861; served spl. duty under Gen. Butler as harbor master at Hampton Roads, 1861; commanded tug Fanny in capture of Hatterus Inlet, 1861; took command steamer Pinola at Balt., joined Farragut below New Orleans, 1861, attempted to break barrier across river below New Orleans, 1862; fleet capt. N. Atlantic Blockading Squadron, 1862-63; commanded ships Florida, 1864, Keystone State (in same squadron), captured 9 blockade runners; served on ship Metacomet in Gulf Squadron, 1864-65; participated in later operations leading to capture of Mobile, Ala.; promoted capt., 1868; commd. commodore, 1874; became rear adm. comdg. S. Atlantic Squadron, 1882, Pacific Squadron, 1883; ret., 1883. Died June 15, 1889.

CROSS, Asa Beebe, architect; b. Camden, N.J., Dec. 9, 1826; received archtl. tng., St. Louis. Settled in Kansas City, Mo. (1st profl. architect in Kansas City), 1857; designed Pacific Hotel (destroyed by fire 1867, rebuilt 1868), 1st Kansas City Union Depot in assn. with William Taylor, 1878, hotel known as Blossom House, Keith & Perry Bldg., 1887, Jackson County Ct. House (2d bldg.), 1890, all Kansas City; designed Clay County Ct. House (probably 2d bldg.), Liberty, Mo., Union Depot, Denver, Colo.; ret., 1892. Died Aug. 18, 1894.

CROSS, Edward, jurist, congressman; b. Va., Nov. 11, 1798; s. Robert Cross; read law under Adam Huntsman, Monroe, Tenn.; m. Laura Elliott, Aug. 4, 1831. Admitted to Tenn. bar, 1822; justice Superior Ct. for Territory Ark., 1832; surveyor gen. pub. lands State of Ark., 1836-38; mem. U.S. Ho. of Reps. from Ark., 26th-28th congresses, 1839-45; spl. justice Supreme Ct. of Ark., 1852; a promoter Cairo & Fulton R.R., 1853, pres., 1855-62; atty. gen. Ark., 1874. Died "Marlbrook" nr. Washington, Hempstead County, Ark., Apr. 6, 1887; buried "Marlbrook."

CROSS, Michael Hurley, musician; b. Phila., Apr. 13, 1833; studied music. Organist, St. Patrick's Ch., 1848, later at several other chs., at the cathedral, Phila., 18 years, Holy Trinity Episcopal Ch., 17 years; dir. several local socs., also socs. in N.Y.C. and Bklyn. Died Phila., Sept. 26, 1897.

CROSS, Peter F., engraver; b. N.Y.C., circa 1820; m. Harriet; children—Maria, Hannah, William E., Edward. Engraver, N.Y.C., 1846-48; employed at U.S. Mint, Phila., 1855.

CROSSLAND, Edward, congressman; b. Hickman County, Ky., June 30, 1827; studied law. Admitted to bar, 1852, began practice of law, Clinton, Ky.;

sheriff Hickman County, 1851-52; mem. Ky. Ho. of Reps., 1857-58; commd. capt. 1st Ky. Regt., Confederate Army in Civil War, then commd. col. 7th Ky. Regt., served until end of war; judge Ct. of Common Pleas, 1st Jud. Dist. Ky., 1867-70; mem. U.S. Ho. of Reps. (Democrat) from Ky., 42d-43d congresses, 1871-75; judge circuit ct. 1st Jud. Dist. Ky., 1880-81. Died Mayfield, Ky., Sept. 11, 1881; buried Maplewood Cemetery.

CROSSWELL, William, clergyman; b. Hudson, N.Y., Nov. 7, 1804; son of Harry Crosswell; grad. Yale, 1822, Gen. Theol. Sem., 1826; D.D. (hon.), Trinity Coll., 1846. Tchr., pvt. sch., New Haven, Conn., 1822-24; co-editor Albany Argus; ordained to ministry Episcopal Ch., 1828; pastor Ch. of the Advent, Boston, 1828-51; censured for a time because of his ch. views. Author: Poems: Sacred and Secular, published 1859. Died Boston, Nov. 9, 1851.

CROSWELL, Edwin, journalist; b. Catskill, N.Y., May 29, 1797; s. Mackay Croswell. Asst. editor Catskill Recorder, 1811-23; editor Argus, Albany, N.Y., 1823-54; N.Y. State printer, 1824-40, 44-47; a leading partisan Democratic editor. Died Princeton, N.J., June 13, 1871.

CROSWELL, Harry, journalist, clergyman; b. West Hartford, Conn., June 16, 1778; s. Caleb and Hannah (Kellogg) C.; m. Susan Sherman, Aug. 16, 1800. Editor, Catskill (N.Y.) Packet, 1800-01; publisher, editor Balance, Hudson, N.Y., 1801-09; publisher Wasp (Federalist paper), 1802; convicted of libel and fined by Republican judge; moved Balance to Albany, N.Y., 1809, failed financially; ordained deacon Protestant Episcopal Ch., 1814; pastor Christ Ch., Hudson, N.Y., 1814, Trinity Ch., New Haven, Conn., 1815-58. Died Mar. 13, 1858.

CROUCH, Edward, congressman; b. Walnut Hill, nr. Highspire, Lancaster (now Dauphin) County, Pa., Nov. 9, 1764; attended common schs. Served in Revolutionary War; commanded co. in Whiskey Insurrection, 1794; mcht., Walnut Hill; mem. Pa. Ho. of Reps., 1804-06; presdl. elector on Democratic ticket, 1812; asso. judge Dauphin County, 1813; mem. U.S. Ho. of Reps. (Democrat) from Pa., 13th Congress, Oct. 12, 1813-15. Died Walnut Hill, Feb. 2, 1827; buried Paxtang Cemetery.

CROWELL, John, congressman, Indian agt.; b. Halifax County, N.C., Sept. 18, 1780; ed. public schs. Apptd. govt. agt. to Muscogee Indians, Ala., 1815; settled in St. Stephens, Ala., 1817; del. to U.S. Congress, 15th Congress, Jan. 29, 1818-19; mem. U.S. Ho. of Reps. from Ala., 16th Congress, Dec. 14, 1819-21; agt. to Creek Indians, Western Ga. and Eastern Ala., 1821-36. Died Ft. Mitchell, Russell County, Ala., June 25, 1846; buried pvt. cemetery, Ft. Mitchell.

CROWELL, John, congressman, coll. pres.; b. East Haddam, Conn., Sept. 15, 1801; attended Warren (O.) Acad., 1822-25; studied law. Admitted to bar, 1827, began practice of law, Warren; part owner, editor Western Reserve Chronicle, Warren; mem. Ohio Senate, 1840; mem. U.S. Ho. of Reps. (Whig) from Ohio, 30th-31st congresses, 1847-51; moved to Cleve., O., 1852, resumed practice of law; served with Ohio Militia, 20 years, to rank of maj. gen.; editor Western Law Monthly, Cleve.; mem. faculty Homeopathic Med. Coll.; pres. Ohio State and Union Law Coll. of Cleve., 1862-76. Died Cleve., Mar. 8, 1883; buried Lake View Cemetery.

CROWNE, John, dramatist, playwright; b. Shropshire, Eng., 1640; s. William and Agnes (Mackworth) C.; attended Harvard, 1657-60. Came to New Eng., 1657, returned to Eng., 1661; began career with romance Pandion and Amphigenia, 1665; produced Juliana, 1671; won favor of King Charles II with masque Calisto; produced The Country Wit, 1675, The Destruction of Jerusalem (1st success), 1677, comedy City Politiques; at request of king adapted Spanish play into Sir Courtly Nice or It Cannot Be, 1685; other comedies include The English Friar, 1690; The Married Beau, 1694. Died London, Eng., April, 1712.

CROWNE, William; b. Eng., 1617; m. Agnes (Mackworth) Watts, 1639, at least 1 son, John. Created Rouge Dragon in Coll. of Arms, 1638; fought under Oliver Cromwell during Puritan Revolution; county commr. for Shropshire for 4 years; mem. Parliament, 1654; purchased Nova Scotia (in partnership with Col. Thomas Temple), 1656; came to Am., 1657; his proprietary rights ignored by Charles II who ceded N.S. to France, 1667; 1st town register of Mendon, Mass., 1667; moved to R.I., 1674, to Boston, 1679. Died Boston, 1683.

CROWNINSHIELD, Benjamin Williams, banker, U.S. sec. of navy; b. Salem, Mass., Dec. 27, 1772; s. George and Mary (Derby) C.; m. Mary Boardman, Jan. 1, 1804. Pres., Mchts. Bank of Salem; mem. Mass Ho. of Reps., 1811, 21, 33; Mass. Senate, 1812; U.S. sec. of navy, 1814-18; mem. U.S. Ho. of Reps. from Mass., 18th-21st congresses 1823-31. Died Boston, Feb. 3, 1851; buried Mt. Auburn Cemetery, Cambridge, Mass.

CROWNINSHIELD, George, sea capt., mcht.; b. May 27, 1766; s. George and Mary (Derby) C. Sea capt., until 1800; with father's firm George Crowninshield & Sons, 1800-15; built 1st Am. yacht Jefferson; built Cleopatra's Barge (1st sea going vessel of her class). Died Salem, Mass., Nov. 26, 1817.

CROWNINSHIELD, Jacob, mcht., sea capt., congressman; b. Salem, Mass., May 31, 1770; s. George and Mary (Derby) C.; m. Sarah Gardner, June 5, 1796. Brought to N.Y. 1st live elephant ever seen in U.S., 1796; mem. Mass. Senate, 1801; mem. U.S. Ho. of Reps. from Mass., 8th-10th congresses, 1803-08; declined appointment as U.S. sec. of navy under Pres. Jefferson, 1805. Died Washington, D.C., Apr. 15, 1808.

CROZER, John Price, mfg., philanthropist; b. West Dale, Pa., Jan. 13, 1793; s. James and Sarah (Price) C.; m. Sallie Knowles, 1825, 1 son, Samuel A. Acquired large fortune in mfg. cotton goods; built a Baptist ch., Upland, Pa., 1852; built an $845,000 coll. bldg., 1858; endowed professorship at Bucknell U..; pres. Pa. Bapt. Edn. Soc., 1855-66; founder, working mem. U. S. Christian Commn.; Crozer Theol. Sem. built as meml. to him, 1866. Died Upland, Mar. 11, 1866.

CROZET, Claude, mil. engr., educator; b. Villefrauche, France, Jan. 1, 1790; ed. Polytechnic Sch. in Paris, France. Came to U.S., 1816; served as engr. U.S. Army; asst. prof. U.S. Mil. Acad., 1816, prof., head dept., 1817-23; state engr. Va., 1823; mem. original bd. visitors Va. Mil. Inst., pres. until 1845; prin. Richmond Acad., 1858-64; introduced study of descriptive geometry to Am. Author: A Treatise of Descriptive Geometry for the Use of the Cadets of the United States Military Academy (1st Am. textbook on the subject), 1821. Died Jan. 29, 1864.

CROZIER, John Hervey, congressman; b. Knoxville, Tenn., Feb. 10, 1812; grad. U. Tenn. at Knoxville, 1829; studied law. Admitted to Tenn. bar, practiced law in Knoxville; mem. Tenn. Ho. of Reps., 1837-39; presdl. elector on Whig ticket, 1844; mem. U.S. Ho. of Reps. (Whig) from Tenn., 29th-30th congresses, 1845-49; became Democrat, 1856; ret. from law practice, circa 1866, did writing and hist. research. Died Knoxville, Oct. 25, 1889; buried Old Gray Cemetery.

CROZIER, Robert, senator, jurist; b. Cadiz, O., Oct. 13, 1827; studied law, Carrollton, O. Admitted to bar, 1848; pros. atty. Carroll County, 1848-50; moved to Leavenworth, Kan., 1856, practiced law, established Leavenworth Daily Times; mem. Kan. Territorial Council, 1857-58; U.S. atty. Dist. of Kan. (apptd. by Pres. Lincoln), 1861-64; chief justice Kan. Supreme Ct., 1864-67; cashier, mgr. 1st Nat. Bank of Leavenworth; mem. U.S. Senate (Republican, filling vacancy) from Kan., Nov. 24, 1873-Feb. 12, 1874; judge 1st Jud. Dist. Kan., 1876-92; bd. dirs. Kan. Hist. Soc., 1886-89. Died Leavenworth, Oct. 2, 1895; buried Mt. Muncie Cemetery.

CRUDUP, Josiah, clergyman, congressman; b. Wakelon, Wake County, N.C., Jan. 13, 1791; attended Columbian Coll. (now George Washington U.), Washington, D.C.; studied theology. Ordained to ministry Baptist Ch., a pastor most of his life; also engaged in farming; mem. N.C. Senate, 1820, N.C. Ho. of Reps., 1821-23; mem. U.S. Ho. of Reps. (Whig) from N.C., 17th Congress, 1821-23; del. N.C. Constl. Conv., 1835. Died nr. Kittrell, Vance County, N.C., May 20, 1872; buried family burial ground, nr. Kittrell.

CRUGER, Daniel, congressman; b. Sunbury, Pa., Dec. 22, 1780; attended public schs.; studied law. Learned printer's trade; publisher Owego (N.Y.) Democrat; admitted to bar, 1805, started practice of law, Bath, N.Y.; served as maj. in War of 1812; mem. N.Y. State Assembly, 1814-16, 26, speaker, 1816; mem. U.S. Ho. of Reps. (Democrat) from N.Y., 15th Congress, 1817-19; dist. atty. 7th Dist. N.Y., 1815-18, Steuben County, 1818-21; moved to Wheeling, Va. (now W.Va.). Died Wheeling, July 12, 1843; buried Stone Ch. Cemetery.

CRUGER, Henry, mcht., state legislator; b. N.Y.C., Dec. 3, 1739; S. Henry and Elizabeth (Harris) C.; attended King's Coll., Cambridge (Eng.) U.; m. Peach Blair; m. 2d, Elizabeth Blair; m. 3d, Caroline Smith, 1799. Mcht., Bristol, Eng.; mem. Eng. Ho. of Commons, 1774-80, 84-90; advocated reconciliation with Am. colonies; mayor of Bristol, 1781; came to U.S., 1790; took over N.Y.C. br. of business; mem. N.Y. State Senate, 1792. Died Apr. 24, 1827.

CRUGER, John, colonial legislator, mayor N.Y. C., mem. last Colonial Assembly; b. N.Y.C., July 18, 1710; s. John and Maria (Cuyler) C. Alderman, N.Y.C., 1754-55, mayor, 1756-65; mem. Gen. Assembly, 1759-68; mem. N.Y.C. delegation Stam Act Congress, 1765, author Declaration of th Rights and Grievances of the Colonists in Americ (sent to Eng.), 1765; an organizer New York Ci C. of C., 1768, 1st pres., 1769; represented N.Y.C in last Colonial Assembly, 1769-75, speaker b unanimous consent. Died Bristol, N.Y., Dec. 27 1791.

CRUMP, George William, congressman; b. Pow hatan County, Va., Sept. 26, 1786; attended Wash ington Coll. (now Washington and Lee U.), Lex ington, Va.; grad. Princeton, 1805; studied medi cine U. Pa., Phila., 1806-08. Mem. Va. Ho. o Dels., 1817-22, 25-28; mem. U.S. Ho. of Reps (Jackson Democrat, filling vacancy) from Va., 19t Congress, Jan. 21, 1826-27; chief clk. Pensio Bur. (apptd. by Pres. Jackson), 1832-48. Die Powhatan County, Oct. 1, 1848; buried "Log Cas tle," nr. Colonial House, Va.

CRUMP, William Wood, jurist; b. Henrico Coun ty, Va., Nov. 25, 1819; s. Sterling Jamieson an Elizabeth (Wood) C.; grad. Coll. William an Mary, 1838; m. Mary Tabb. Admitted to Va. ba 1840; judge Circuit Ct. for City of Richmond (Va.) 1851; asst. sec. treasury Confederate States Am. pres. bd. visitors Coll. William and Mary; defens lawyer for Jefferson Davis in treason trial, 1867 Died Richmond, Feb. 27, 1897.

CRUTCHFIELD, William, congressman; b. Greene ville, Tenn., Nov. 16, 1824; attended commo schs. Became farmer, Jacksonville, Ala., 1844 moved to Chattanooga, Tenn., 1850; served a hon. capt. Union Army during Chickamauga cam paign in Civil War, with Gen. Thomas during sieg of Chattanooga; served as asst. to Gen. Steedmar other comdrs. until close of war; mem. U.S. Ho of Reps. (Republican) from Tenn., 43d Congress 1873-75. Died Chattanooga, Jan. 24, 1890; burie Old Citizens Cemetery.

CUFFE, Paul, seaman, colonist; b. Cuttyhunk Elizabeth Islands, nr. New Bedford, Mass., Jan 17, 1759; s. Cuffe and Ruth (Moses) Slocum; m Alice Pequit, Feb. 25, 1873. Made large fortun as owner and capt. several mcht. ships manne completely by Negroes; active in passage Mass. Ac of 1783 which gave Negroes legal rights and privi leges; visited Africa, 1811; transported 38 colonist to Sierra Leone (Africa) at own expense, 1815 Died Sept. 9, 1817.

CULBERSON, David Browning, congressman; b Troup County, Ga., Sept. 29, 1830; s. David B. and Lucy (Wilkinson) C.; studied law in office Wil liam P. Chilton, Tuskegee, Ala.; m. Eugenia Kimbal Dec. 2, 1852, at least 1 son, Charles A. Admittec to Ala. bar, 1851; practiced in Dadeville, Ala. 1851-56, Upshur County, Tex., 1856-60, Jefferson Tex., 1865-1900; mem. Tex. Ho. of Reps., 1859-60 64; commd. lt. col., later col. 18th Tex. Inf., Con federate States Am., 1862, resigned, 1863; adjutan and insp. gen. of Tex., 1863-64; mem. Tex. Senate 1873-75; mem. U.S. Ho. of Reps. (Democrat) fron Tex., 44th-54th congresses, 1875-97; mem. commn to codify laws of U.S., 1897-1900. Died Jefferson May 7, 1900; buried Jefferson.

CULBERTSON, Alexander, fur trader; operated Ft. McKenzie, nr. Bear Mountains and Marias River in N.W. U.S. for Am. Fur Co., 1830's; tried unsuc cessfully to discourage native traders during small pox epidemic of 1837, caught and survived the dis ease; explored in Blackfoot region; left valuable jour.

CULBRETH, Thomas, congressman; b. Ken County, Del., Apr. 13, 1786; ed. public schs. an pvt. tutors. Moved to Denton, Md., 1806, becam clk. in store; mem. congressional com., Hillsboro 1810; mem. Md. Ho. of Dels., 1812-13; cashie State Bank, Denton, 1813; mem. U.S. Ho. o Reps. (Democrat) from Md., 15th-16th congresses 1817-21; apptd. chief judge Caroline County Or phans' Ct., 1822; clk. Md. Exec. Council, 1825-38; later moved to "Orrell Farm," nr. Greensboro, Md. Died "Orrell Farm," Apr. 16, 1843; buriec family cemetery on farm.

CULLEN, Elisha Dickerson, congressman; b. Mills boro, Del., Apr. 23, 1799; attended Princeton; studied law. Admitted to bar, 1821, began practice of law, Georgetown, Del.; mem. U.S. Ho. of Reps. (Am. Party) from Del., 34th Congress, 1855-57. Died Georgetown, Feb. 8, 1862; buried Presbyn. Churchyard, Lewes, Del.

CULLIS, Charles, homeopathic physician; b. Boston, Mar. 7, 1833; s. John Cullis; m. Lucretia Ann Cullis, 3 children. Founded 1st of many homes for consumptives, Boston, 1865; sincere believer in cure of disease by faith; operated half dozen homes in Boston as well as faith tng. sch. and several missions; had other missions in Va. W.Va., N.Y., Pa., S.C., Cal., India. Author: History of the Consumptives' Home, 1869; Faith Cures, 1879. Died June 18, 1892.

CULLOM, Alvan, congressman; b. Monticello, Ky., Sept. 4, 1797; studied law. Admitted to bar,

823, began practice of law, Monroe, Tenn.; mem. enn. Ho. of Reps., 1835-36; mem. U.S. Ho. of eps. (Democrat) from Tenn., 28th-29th congresses, 1843-47; judge 4th Jud. Circuit Tenn., 850-52; mem. Washington (D.C.) Peace Conf., 861. Died Livingston, Tenn., July 20, 1877; uried Bethlehem Cemetery, nr. Livingston.

CULLOM, William, congressman; b. nr. Monticello, Wayne County, Ky., June 4, 1810; attended ublic schs.; studied law, Lexington, Ky. Admitted bar, practiced in cts. of Ky. and Tenn.; moved Carthage, Tenn.; mem. Tenn. Ho. of Reps., also enn. Senate; mem. U.S. Ho. of Reps. (Whig) rom Tenn., 32d-33d congresses, 1851-55; clk. .S. Ho. of Reps., 1856-57. Died Clinton, Tenn., ec. 6, 1896; buried Clinton Cemetery.

CULLUM, George Washington, army officer; b. .Y.C., Feb. 25, 1809; s. Arthur and Harriet Sturges) C.; grad. U.S. Mil. Acad., 1833; m. lizabeth Hamilton Halleck, Sept. 23, 1875. ommd., Corps Engrs., U.S. Army, 1833; asst. to hief engr., Washington, D.C., 1834-36; superinending engr. govt. works, notably those at Fts. rumball, Warren, Independence, Winthrop, Sumer, and at Battery Griswold; staff aide-de-camp o Gen. Winfield Scott, comdr.-in-chief U.S. Army; apt., 1838, maj., 1861; brig. gen. U.S. Voluneers, 1861, lt. col. engrs., 1863; engaged in a umber of engring. operations during Civil War, ncluding fortification of Nashville, 1864; supt. .S. Mil. Acad., 1864-66; commd. col., 1867; an rganizer Assn. Grads. U.S. Mil. Acad., 1870; ret., 874; v.p. Am. Geog. Soc. of N.Y., 1877-92; left equests of $250,000 for bldg. at U.S. Mil. cad., $100,000 to Am. Geog. Soc. Author: Biographical Register of the Officers and Graduates of he United States Military Academy. Died N.Y.C., eb. 28, 1892.

CULPEPER, John, colonial leader; b. Eng.; flourshed 1678-80. Leader of insurrection for popular iberty in Albemarle colony, Carolina, 1678; led group which deposed pres. and deputies of proprietaries, onfiscated public funds and set up new govt.; went to Eng. to negotiate a treaty, indicted for igh treason, but acquitted; returned to Carolina; urveyed site of Charles Town (now Charleston), 1680.

CULPEPER, Thomas (2d baron), colonial gov., . Eng., 1635; s. John and Judith C.; m. Margaretta van Hesse, Aug. 3, 1659, 1 dau. Received from King Charles II grant of Colony of Va., gov., 1680-83. Died London, Eng., Jan. 27, 1689.

CULPEPPER, John, congressman; b. nr. Wadesboro, Anson County, N.C., 1761; attended pub. schs. Became minister in Baptist Ch.; mem. U.S. Ho. of Reps. (Federalist) from N.C., 10th, 13th-14th, 16th, 18th, 20th congresses, 1807-09, 13-17, 19-21, 23-25, 27-29. Died Darlington County, S.C., Jan. 1841; buried cemetery, Society Hill, S.C.

CULVER, Erastus Dean, diplomat, congressman; b. Champlain, Washington County, N.Y., Mar. 15, 1803; grad. U. Vt. at Burlington, 1826; studied law. Admitted to bar, 1831, began practice of law, Ft. Ann, N.Y.; moved to Greenwich, N.Y., 1836; mem. N.Y. State Assembly, 1838-40; mem. U.S. Ho. of Reps. (Whig) from N.Y., 29th Congress, 1845-47; moved to Bklyn., 1850; judge City Ct. Bklyn., 1854-61; U.S. minister resident to Venezuela (apptd. by Pres. Lincoln), 1862-66. Died Greenwich, N.Y., Oct. 13, 1889; buried Greenwich Cemetery.

CUMING, Sir Alexander, English agt.; b. Scotland, 1690; s. Sir Alexander and Elizabeth (Swinton) C. Came to Am. 1729; mem. Royal Soc.; under guise of scientific explorer travelled among Creek and Cherokee Indians, persuading them to ally with English rather than French; pursued unsuccessful plans for annexing to Eng. all lands from Appalachians to Mississippi River, from Can. to the Gulf; tried unsuccessfully to secure reforms of colonial currency; returned to Eng. 1730. Died Eng., Aug. 1775.

CUMING, Fortescue, traveller; b. Strabane, Ireland, Feb. 26, 1762; m. Phoebe Harisson Butler, 1784, 7 children. Came to Am., circa 1782; bought land in Ohio, travelled on Ohio and Mississippi rivers, 1807-09. Author: Sketches of a Tour to the Western Country (description of social and polit. conditions on frontier), 1810. Died Vermilionville, La., 1828.

CUMMING, Alfred, territorial gov.; b. Augusta, Ga., Sept. 4, 1802; s. Thomas and Ann (Clay) C. Mayor, Augusta, 1839; served with U.S. Army during Mexican War; supt. Indian affairs on Upper Mo. River; gov. Territory of Utah, 1857-60; known for connection with Mormon War, 1857-58. Died Augusta, Oct. 9, 1873.

CUMMING, Thomas William, congressman; b. Frederick, Md., 1814-15. Apptd. midshipman U.S. Navy, 1832, passed midshipman, 1838; mem. Wilkes exploring expdn., 1838, resigned, 1841; moved to Bklyn., became druggist and drug importer, N.Y.C.; engaged in bus., Bklyn., 1843-53; mem. U.S. Ho. of Reps. (Democrat) from N.Y., 33d Congress, 1853-55. Died Bklyn., Oct. 13, 1855; buried Greenwood Cemetery.

CUMMING, William, Continental congressman; b. Edenton, N.C.; studied law. Admitted to bar, practiced law; mem. N.C. Provincial Congress, 1776; mem. N.C. Ho. of Commons, 1781, 83, 84, 88; mem. Continental Congress, 1784-86; nominated for judge, 1790.

CUMMINGS, Gordon Parker, architect. Practiced as architect, San Francisco (one of 1st architects in city); designed and built Washington Block later known as Montgomery Block), completed 1853, only downtown bldg. undamaged by the 1906 fire; apptd. supervising architect Cal. State Capitol, Sacramento, 1865.

CUMMINGS, Jeremiah Williams, clergyman; b. Washington, D.C., 1814. Ordained priest Roman Catholic Ch., Rome, Italy; apptd. an asst. St. Patrick's Cathedral, N.Y.C.; became pastor St. Stephen's (which he built), 1848; became popular for sermons and musical taste; a friend of Orestes Brownson, brought Brownson from Boston to N.Y., contbd. to his Review; the center of group of clergy and laymen which roused wide hostility with its objections of European grasp on seminary teaching in U.S. and its demands for better colls. and univs.; also suggested more ecumenical approach to those outside Roman Catholic Ch. Died N.Y.C., Jan. 4, 1866.

CUMMINGS, John, tanner; b. Woburn, Mass., Feb. 12, 1785; s. Ebenezer and Jemina (Hartwell) C.; m. Marcia Richardson, May 2, 1811, 3 children including John C. Owned leather tanning business, Woburn, 1804-50; began manufacture of chaise leather, 1830, later manufactured enameled leather; 1st tanner to use splitting machine invented by Samuel Parker. Died June 8, 1867.

CUMMINGS, Joseph, clergyman, coll. pres.; b. Falmouth, Me., Mar. 3, 1817; grad. Wesleyan U., 1840, D.D., 1854, S.T.D. (hon.), 1854; D.D., Harvard, 1861, S.T.D. (hon.), 1861; LL.D., (hon.), Northwestern U., 1866; m. Deborah S. Haskell, Aug. 15, 1842, 1 child, 2 adopted children. Prin. Amenia Sem., N.Y.C., 1843-46; admitted to New Eng. Conf., Methodist Episcopal Ch., 1846; pres. Genesee Coll., Lima, N.Y., 1854-57; pres. Wesleyan U., 1857-75, prof. mental philosophy and polit. economy, 1875-77; resumed preaching, 1877; pres. Northwestern U., 1881-90. Editor: Life of the Late Daniel Stillman Newcomb, 1855; Butler's Analogy of Religion, 1875. Died Evanston, Ill., May 7, 1890.

CUMMINGS, Thomas Seir, painter; b. Bath, Eng., Aug. 26, 1804; s. Charles and Rebecca C.; m. Jane Cook, 1822. A founder N.A.D., 1825, elected to council, treas., 40 years; prof. design Univ. City N.Y.; commd. brig. gen. N.Y. Light Infantry, 1838; an organizer N.Y. Sketching Club, 1844; early engraved works still prized by collectors, including The Bracelet, The Bride, The Exchange of Queens. Died Hackensack, N.J., Sept. 24, 1894.

CUMMINS, Alexander, theatre mgr. Met Noah Miller Ludlow, Nashville, Tenn., 1818, accepted proposal to become joint mgr. of Ludlow Co., was sent ahead to arrange for 1st profl. season (lasting 10 weeks) in Ala., Huntsville, 1818.

CUMMINS, George David, clergyman; b. Smyrna, Del., Dec. 11, 1822; s. George C. and Maria (Durborow) C.; grad. Dickinson Coll., 1841; m. Alexandrine Balch, June 24, 1847. Ordained deacon Protestant Episcopal Ch., 1845, priest, 1847; asst. rector Christ Ch., Balt., 1845-47; rector Christ Ch., Norfolk, Va., 1847-53, St. James's, Richmond, Va., 1853-54, Trinity Ch., Washington, D.C. 1854-58, St. Peter's Ch., Balt., 1858-63, Trinity Ch., Chgo., 1863-66; asst. bishop of Ky., 1866-73; withdrew from Episcopal Ch. because of his opposition to ritualism, founded Reformed Episcopal Ch., 1873. Died Lutherville, Md., June 26, 1876.

CUMMINS, John D., congressman; b. Pa., 1791; grad. Jefferson Coll., Canonsburg, Pa., 1834; studied law. Admitted to bar, started practice of law, New Philadelphia, O.; pros. atty. Tuscarawas County, 1836-41; mem. U.S. Ho. of Reps. (Democrat) from Ohio, 29th-30th congresses, 1845-49. Died while attending circuit ct. session, Milw., Sept. 11, 1849.

CUMMINS, Maria Susanna, author; b. Salem, Mass., Apr. 9, 1827; d. David and Mehitable (Cave) Cummins; never married. Lived and wrote in Boston; contbr. to Atlantic Monthly, other mags. Author: The Lamplighter, 1854; Mabel Vaughan, 1857; El Fureidis, 1860; Haunted Hearts, 1864. Died Dorchester, Mass., Oct. 1, 1866.

CUNNINGHAM, Ann Pamela, assn. leader; b. Rosemont, Laurens County, S.C., Aug. 15, 1816; d. Robert and Louisa (Bird) Cunningham; never married. Founded Mt. Vernon Ladies' Assn. of Union to preserve George Washington's home as nat. shrine, 1853, regent, 1853-75, assn. purchased Mt. Vernon, 1859; lived at Mt. Vernon to supervise estate, 1868-74. Died Rosemont, May 1, 1875; buried First Presbyn. Ch. Churchyard, Columbia, S.C.

CUNNINGHAM, Francis Alanson, congressman; b. Abbeville Dist., S.C., Nov. 9, 1804; studied medicine, law. Moved to Eaton, O., 1826, became sch. tchr.; started practice of medicine, 1829; became clk. of ct. Preble County (O.), 1833; mem. U.S. Ho. of Reps. (Democrat) from Ohio, 29th Congress, 1845-47; admitted to bar, 1847, began practice of law, Eaton; apptd. additional paymaster U.S. Volunteers by Pres. Polk, 1847; commd. paymaster U.S. Army, 1849, served, 1849-63. Died Eaton, Aug. 16, 1864; buried Mt. Hill Cemetery.

CURLEY, James, astronomer; b. Athleague, Roscommon, Ireland, Dec. 26, 1796. Came to U.S., 1817, became bookkeeper in Phila.; taught mathematics, Frederick, Md.; joined Soc. of Jesus, 1827; ordained priest Roman Catholic Ch., 1833; tchr. philosophy and mathematics at Georgetown, also chaplain Visitation Convent, Washington, D.C., nearly 50 years; planner, 1st dir. and historian Georgetown Observatory. Died Georgetown, July 24, 1889.

CURRIER, Moody, banker, gov. N.H.; b. Boscawen, N.H., Apr. 22, 1806; s. Moody Morse and Rhoda (Putney) C.; grad. Dartmouth, 1834, LL.D. (hon.), 1885; LL.D. (hon.), Bates Coll., 1881; m. Lucretia Dustin, Dec. 8, 1836; m. 2d, Mary Kidder, Sept. 5, 1847; m. 3d, Hannah Slade, Nov. 16, 1869. First practiced law at Manchester, N.H.; mem. N.H. Senate, 1856-57, pres., 1857; pres. Amoskeag Nat. Bank, 1864; founder, chief mgr., dir. People's Savs. Bank; pres. Eastern R.R. in N.H., Gas Light Co.; dir. Concord & Portsmouth R.R.; gov. N.H., 1885-87. Died Manchester, Aug. 23, 1898.

CURRIER, Nathaniel, printer, publisher; b. Roxbury, Mass., Mar. 27, 1813; s. Nathaniel and Hannah C.; m. Eliza Farnsworth; m. 2d, Miss Ormsbee; 1 son, Edward W. Founder lithographic firm, 1824, became Currier & Ives, 1850; inaugurated series of popular lithographic prints; issued lithograph showing Ruins of the Merchants' Exchange, 1835; all prints after 1857 bear name Currier and Ives; ret., 1880, firm discontinued, 1907; prints gave picture of Am. life, history, character from 1835-95. Died N.Y.C., Nov. 20, 1888.

CURRY, George Law, territorial gov.; b. Phila., July 2, 1820; s. George Curry; m. Chloe Boone, Mar. 1848. Served 2 terms as pres. Mechanics Apprentices' Library Assn. of Boston, 1838; editor newspaper Ore. Spectator, founder Ore. Free Press (1st weekly pub. in Ore. Territory), 1848; mem. legislature Ore. Provisional Govt., 1848-49; chief clk. Ore. Territorial Council, 1850-51; mem. lower house Ore. Territorial Legislature, 1851-52; sec. of Ore. Territory, 1853; gov. Ore. Territory (last territorial gov.), 1854-59; Curry County (Ore.) named for him. Died Portland, Ore., July 28, 1878.

CURTIN, Andrew Gregg, gov. Pa., diplomat, congressman; b. Bellefonte, Pa., Apr. 23, 1815; s. Roland and Jean (Gregg) C.; grad. Dickinson Coll., 1837; m. Catherine Wilson, May 30, 1844. Admitted to Pa. bar, 1839; sec. Pa., 1854; ex-officio supt. common schs. Pa.; gov. Pa., 1860-66; leader in support of Civil War; father of Pa. Reserve Corps; candidate for U.S. vice presdl. nomination, 1868, lost to Schuyler Colfax; U.S. minister to Russia, 1869-72; mem. U.S. Ho. of Reps. from Pa., 47th-49th congresses, 1881-87. Died Bellefonte, Oct. 7, 1894; buried Union Cemetery, Bellefonte.

CURTIS, Benjamin Robbins, asso. justice U.S. Supreme Ct.; b. Watertown, Mass., Nov. 4, 1809; s. Benjamin and Lois (Robbins) C.; grad. Harvard, 1829, attended Law Sch., 1829-31; m. Eliza Woodward; m. 2d, Anna Curtis, 1846; m. 3d, Maria Allen, 1861. Mem. lower house Mass. Legislature, 1851; asso. justice U.S. Supreme Ct., 1851-57, noted for dissenting opinion to Taney's Dred Scott decision, 1857; defense counsel Pres. Johnson's impeachment, 1868; mem. Hasty Pudding Club, the "Institute." Author: Reports of Cases in the Circuit Courts of the United States, 1854; Decisions of the Supreme Court; Digest of the Decisions of the Supreme Court; Memoirs, 1879. Died Newport, R.I., Sept. 15, 1874.

CURTIS, Carlton Brandaga, congressman; b. Madison County, N.Y., Dec. 17, 1811; studied law. Admitted to bar, Erie, Pa., 1834, began practice of law, Warren, Pa., 1834; mem. Pa. Ho. of Reps., 1836-38; mem. U.S. Ho. of Reps. (Democrat) can), 43d Congress, 1873-75; became a Republi- from Pa., 32d-33d congresses, 1851-55, (Republican, 1855; served from lt. col. to col. 58th Regt. Pa. Volunteer Inf., U.S. Army, 1862-63; moved to Erie, 1868, continued practice of law, also engaged in banking and oil prodn.; an originator and builder Dunkirk & Venango R.R. Died Erie, Mar. 17, 1883; buried Oakland Cemetery, Warren.

CURTIS, Edward, congressman; b. Windsor, Vt., Oct. 25, 1801; grad. Union Coll., Schenectady, N.Y., 1821; studied law. Admitted to bar, 1824, began practice of law, N.Y.C.; mem. common council, 1834; pres. bd. of asst. aldermen; mem. U.S. Ho. of Reps. (Whig) from N.Y., 25th-26th congresses, 1837-41; collector Port of N.Y., 1841-44; resumed practice of law, Washington, D.C. Died N.Y.C., Aug. 2, 1856.

CURTIS, George, banker; b. Worcester, Mass., Feb. 23, 1796; s. David and Susannah (Stone) C.; m. Mary Burrill, Mar. 6, 1821; m. 2d, Julia Bridgham, Apr. 3, 1834; 6 children including James Burrill, George William, Edward, John Green. Mem. R.I. Legislature, speaker of House, 1837-38; pres. Continental Bank of N.Y., 1844-56; helped organize N.Y. Clearing House. Died Jacksonville, Fla., Jan. 9, 1856.

CURTIS, George Ticknor, lawyer; b. Watertown, Mass., Nov. 28, 1812; s. Benjamin and Lois (Robbins) C.; grad. Harvard, 1832; m. Mary Story, Oct. 17, 1844; m. 2d, Louise Nystrom, Jan., 1851; 8 children. Admitted to Mass. bar, 1836; mem. Mass. Ho. Reps., 1840-43; U.S. commr., 1852, enforced the fugitive slave laws by returning to slavery the Negro, Thomas Sims, who had lived in Mass. for several years; lawyer for plaintiff Dred Scott Case, U.S. Supreme Ct. Author: The Law of Copyright, 1847; The Law of Patents, 1849, 4th edit., 1873; A History of the Origin, Formation and Adoption of the Constitution of the United States, 1854-58; Life of Daniel Webster, 1870; Last Years of Daniel Webster, 1878; Life of James Buchanan, 1883. Died N.Y.C., Mar. 28, 1894.

CURTIS, George William, editor, univ. chancellor, reformer; b. Providence, R.I., Feb. 24, 1824; s. George and Mary (Burrill) C.; m. Anna Shaw, Thanksgiving Day, 1856. Mem. Brook Farm Community, 1842-43; traveled abroad, 1846-50; mem. editorial staff N.Y. Tribune, 1850, asso. editor, 1852-57; editor Harper's Weekly, 1863; chmn. N.Y. State, Nat. civil service reform assns.; mem. bd. regents Univ. State N.Y., apptd. chancellor, 1890; pres. Met. Mus. Art. Author: Nile Notes of a Howadji, 1851; Lotus Eating, 1852; Prue and I, 1857; Trumps, 1861. Died Staten Island, N.Y., Aug. 31, 1892.

CURTIS, Moses Ashley, botanist, clergyman; b. Stockbridge, Mass., May 11, 1808; s. Jared and Thankful (Ashley) C.; grad. William Coll., 1827; m. Mary de Rosset, Dec. 3, 1834. Ordained to ministry Episcopal Ch., 1835; missionary, .N.C., 1835-37; tchr. Episcopal Sch., Raleigh, .N.C., 1837-39; pastor in Hillsboro, .N.C., 1841-47, 56-72, Society Hill, S.C., 1847-56; studied vegetation of N.C. during his many missionary travels, specialized in study of fungi. Author: Natural History Survey of North America, Part III, Botany; Containing a Catalogue of the Plants of the State, with Descriptions of History of the Trees, Shrubs, and Woody Vines, 1860. Died Hillsboro, Apr. 10, 1872.

CURTIS, Samuel Ryan, army officer, engr., congressman; b. Champlain, N.Y., Feb. 3, 1805; s. Zarah and Phalley (Yale) C.; grad. U.S. Mil. Acad., 1831; m. Belinda Buckingham, Nov. 3, 1831. Served as col. 3d Ohio Inf. during Mexican War; chief engr. of improvement Des Moines River; city engr. St. Louis, 1850; mayor Keokuk (Ia.), 1856; mem. U.S. Ho. of Reps. from Ia., 35th-38th congresses, 1857-62; commd. brig. gen. U.S. Army, 1861; commanded U.S. Army which defeated Confederates at Pea Ridge (Ark.); commd. maj. gen., in command Dept. of Mo., 1862, Dept. of Kan., 1864, Dept. of N.W., 1865; peace commr. to Indians, 1865; commr. to insp. Union Pacific R.R., 1865-66. Died Council Bluffs, Ia., Dec. 26, 1866; buried Oakland Cemetery, Keokuk, Ia.

CURWEN, Samuel, Loyalist; b. Salem, Mass., Dec. 28, 1715; s. George and Mehitable (Parkman) C.; grad. Harvard, 1735; m. Abigail Russell, May 1750. Capt. of Mass. Militia in expdn. against Louisbourg, 1744; impost officer, Essex, Mass.; Mass. judge of admiralty; Loyalist, went to England, 1775-84; wrote accounts of boredom and trivia of Loyalist life in London; not prosecuted for polit. sympathies after his return to Mass. Author: Journal and Letters, 1864. Died Salem, Apr. 9, 1802.

CUSHING, Caleb, atty. gen. U.S., diplomat; b. Salisbury, Mass., Jan. 17, 1800; s. John and Lydia (Dow) C.; grad. Harvard, 1817; m. Caroline Wilde, Nov. 23, 1824. Admitted to Mass. bar, 1821; mem. U.S. Ho. of Reps. from Mass., 24th-27th congresses, 1835-43; spl. U.S. envoy to China, 1843-45, negotiated Treaty of Wang Huja, July 3, 1844, which opened for trade 5 Chinese ports and limited Am. citizens to jurisdiction of Am. laws and ofcls.; served as col., brig. gen. in Mexican War, 1847; atty. gen. U.S., 1852-57; chmn. commn. to revise and codify statutes of U.S., 1865-67; U.S. diplomat to Bogota, Colombia, 1868; sr. counsel for U.S. before tribunal of arbitration Treaty of Washington, 1871-72, negotiated settlement Ala. claims; U.S. minister to Spain, 1874-77. Author: History of the Town of Newburyport, 1826; The Practical Principles of Political Economy, 1826; Historical and Political Review of the Late Revolution in France, 2 vols., 1833; Reminiscences of Spain, 2 vols., 1833; Growth and Territorial Progress of the United States, 1839; Life of William H. Harrison, 1840; The Treaty of Washington, 1873. Died Newburyport, Mass., Jan. 2, 1879; buried New Burial Ground, Newburyport.

CUSHING, Frank Hamilton, ethnologist; b. North East, Erie County, Pa., July 22, 1857; s. Thomas and Sarah Ann (Harding) C.; attended Cornell U., 1875; m. Emily Magill. Employed by Smithsonian Instn., 1875-79, Bur. Am. Ethnology, 1879-1900; studied ancient and contemporary Indians particularly Zuni Pueblo, lived with Zuni Indians, 5 years. Author: Zuni Breadstuff; Zuni Creation Myths, 1896; Zuni Folk Tales, 1901. Died Apr. 10, 1900.

CUSHING, John Perkins, mcht., yachtsman; b. Boston, Apr. 22, 1787; s. Robert and Ann (Perkins) C.; m. Mary Gardiner. Agt., Perkins & Co., Canton, China; constructed The Sylph, won earliest Am. yacht race on record, 1832. Died Watertown, Mass., Apr. 12, 1862; buried Mt. Auburn Cemetery, Cambridge, Mass.

CUSHING, Luther Stearns, jurist, author; b. Lunenberg, Mass., June 22, 1803; s. Edmund and Mary (Stearns) C.; LL.B., Harvard, 1826; m. Mary Otis Lincoln, May 19, 1840; m. 2d, Elizabeth Dutton Cooper, Oct. 29, 1853; 3 children. Editor, The American Jurist and Law Mag., 1826-32; clk. Mass. Ho. of Reps., 1832-44; judge Boston Ct. Common Pleas, 1844-48; reporter Mass. Supreme Ct., 1848-53; lectr. Roman law Harvard Law Sch. 1848-49, 50-51. Author: An Inquiry into the Present State of the Remedial Law of Massachusetts; with Suggestions for its Reform, 1837; A Manual of Parliamentary Practice, 1844; A Practical Treatise on the Trustee Process, 1853; An Introduction to the Study of Roman Law, 1854; Elements of the Law and Practice of the Legislative Assemblies in the United States, 1856. Died Boston, June 22, 1856.

CUSHING, Thomas, Continental congressman; b. Boston, Mar. 24, 1725; s. Thomas and Mary (Bromfield) C.; grad. Harvard, 1744, LL.D. (hon.), 1785 fellow, 1786-88; M.A. (hon.), Yale, 1750; m. Deborah Fletcher, 1747. A prominent mcht., Boston; mem. Mass. Gen. Ct., 1761-74, speaker, 1766-74; mem. Boston Com. Correspondence, 1773; mem. Mass Com. of Safety, also Provincial Congress of Mass., 1774; mem. 1st, 2d Continental congresses, 1774-76; commissary gen. Mass., 1775; pres. New Haven Price Hartford Conv., 1780; a founder Am. Acad. Arts and Scis., 1780; lt. gov. Mass., 1780-1788. Died Boston, Feb. 28, 1788, buried Granary Burial Ground.

CUSHING, William, justice U.S. Supreme Ct.; b. Scituate, Mass., Mar. 1, 1732; s. John and Mary (Cotton) C.; grad. Harvard, 1751, LL.D. (hon.), 1785; A.M. (hon.), Yale, 1753; m. Hannah Phillips, 1774. Admitted to bar, 1755; judge Probate Ct. for Lincoln County, Mass (now Me.), 1760-61; judge Mass. Superior Ct., 1772, chief justice, 1777-89; 1st Mass. Constl. Conv., 1779; v.p. Mass Conv. which ratified U.S. Constn., 1788; asso. justice U.S. Supreme Ct., 1789-1810; a founder Am. Acad. Arts and Scis., fellow, 1780-1810. Died Scituate, Sept. 13, 1810.

CUSHING, William Barker, naval officer; b. Delafield, Wis., Nov. 4, 1842; s. Milton and Mary (Smith) C.; ed. U.S. Mil. Acad., 1857-61; m. Katherine Forbes, Feb. 19, 1870, 2 children. Master's mate U.S. Navy, captured 1st Civil War prize, a tobacco schooner, 1861; lt. in command gunboat Ellis, 1862; exec. officer ship Commodore Perry; commanded ship Commodore Barney; commanded ships Strokokon and Monticello, 1863; noted for torpedoing Confederate ram Albemarle, 1864; lt. comdr., 1853; commanded ships Lancaster, 1865-67, Maumee, 1868-69; promoted comdr., 1872. Died Washington, D.C., Dec. 17, 1874.

CUSHMAN, Charlotte Saunders, actress; b. Boston, July 23, 1816; d. Elkanah and Mary Eliza (Babbit) C. Studied for operatic career; made debut as Countess Almaviva in Marriage of Figaro, 1835; became actress, appeared as Lady Macbeth, New Orleans, 1835; played various roles, Albany, N.Y. and N.Y.C.; joined Park Co., N.Y.C., 1837, played role of Nancy Sykes in Oliver Twist; stage mgr. Walnut St. Theatre, Phila., 1842-44; made London debut as Bianca in Fazio (with Edwin Forrest), 1845; toured Am., 1849-52 (generally acclaimed as leading Am. actress, also well received in her interpretation of male roles, Romeo, Hamlet, Claude Melnotte); in semi-retirement, Eng., 1852-57; gave various "farewell" performances, 185[illegible]-70, never actually retired; returned to Am., 187[illegible] gave readings, appeared in plays; last N.Y.C. ap[illegible]pearance, 1874, Boston, 1875, Easton, Pa., 187[illegible] (last on any stage). Died Boston, Feb. 17, 187[illegible] buried Mount Auburn Cemetery, Cambridge, Mas[illegible]

CUSHMAN, George Hewitt, artist; b. Windhan[illegible] Conn., June 5, 1814; s. John H. and Pamel[illegible] (Webb) C.; studied drawing under Washington Al[illegible]ston; learned line-engraving from Asaph Willard [illegible] Hartford, Conn.; m. Susan Wetherill, 1849, at lea[illegible] 1 dau., Ida. Moved to Phila., 1843; engaged chief[illegible] with engraving notes for state banks; engrave[illegible] plates for 34 editions of James Fenimore Cooper[illegible] novels, 1859-61, for Frances S. Osgood's Poem[illegible] 1850, for Horatio Alger's Life of Edwin Forres[illegible] 1877, moved to N.Y.C., 1862, primarily engage[illegible] in miniature painting; a self-portrait appeared [illegible] Anne Hollingsworth Wharton's Heirlooms in Minia[illegible]tures, 1898; only public exhbn. of his miniature[illegible] appeared in Retrospective Exhibit at Columbia[illegible] Expn., Chgo., 1893. Died Jersey City Heights, N.J[illegible] Aug. 3, 1876; buried South Laurel Hill Cemetery[illegible] Phila.

CUSHMAN, John Paine, congressman; b. Pom[illegible]fret, Conn., Mar. 8, 1784; attended Plainfiel[illegible] Acad.; grad. Yale, 1807; studied law. Admitted [illegible] bar, 1809, began practice of law, Troy, N.Y[illegible] mem. U.S. Ho. of Reps. from N.Y., 15th Congres[illegible] 1817-19; trustee Union Coll., Schenectady, N.Y[illegible] 1833-48; recorder Troy, 1834-38; judge circui[illegible] ct. of 3d Circuit, 1838-44; engaged in real esta[illegible] bus. Died Troy, Sept. 16, 1848; buried Oakwoo[illegible] Cemetery.

CUSHMAN, Joshua, clergyman, congressman; [illegible] Abner and Mary (Tillson) C.; A.B., Harvard, 1791[illegible] m. Lucy Jones, Sept. 13, 1802. Ordained religiou[illegible] tchr. Congregational Ch., Winslow, Mass. (late[illegible] Me.); mem. Mass. Senate from Kennebec Count[illegible] 1810; mem. Mass. Ho. of Reps. Winslow, 1811-12[illegible] mem. U.S. Ho. of Reps. from Mass. (later Me.)[illegible] 16th-18th congresses, 1819-25; mem. Me. Senate[illegible] 1828. Died Augusta, Me., Jan. 27, 1834.

CUSHMAN, Pauline, Union spy, actress; b. Ne[illegible] Orleans, June 10, 1833; m. Charles Dickinson; m[illegible] 2d, August Fichtner, 1872; m. 3d, Jerry Fryer[illegible] 1879. Appeared in The Seven Sisters, Wood's The[illegible]ater, Louisville, Ky., 1863, during one performanc[illegible] publicly toasted Southern cause, fired from cast[illegible] took oath of allegiance to U.S. Govt., commd[illegible] Union secret agt.; expelled from Nashville (Tenn.[illegible] under guise as ardent Southern sympathizer; he[illegible] mission was to penetrate as far South as possibl[illegible] and collect mil. information; apprehended near Gen[illegible] Bragg's hdqrs. (Tullahoma, Tenn.) with mil. docu[illegible]ments, tried and sentenced to be hanged, left be[illegible]hind as Bragg retreated under Gen. Rosecrans ad[illegible]vance from North, 1863, supplied Rosecran's force[illegible] with valuable information, became too well know[illegible] to continue spying; returned to stage as lectr. afte[illegible] Civil War; Committed suicide San Francisco, Dec[illegible] 2, 1893; buried plot of Grand Army of Republic[illegible]

CUSHMAN, Robert, colonial organizer; b. Canter[illegible]bury, Eng., 1579; m. Mary Singleton, 1617. Ar[illegible]rived in Holland, where he joined the Pilgrims a[illegible] Leyden, 1609; went to Eng. to negotiate paten[illegible] with mchts. for prospective journey to Am.; co[illegible] organizer Mayflower expdn., 1620; remained i[illegible] Eng. to act as agt. for Pilgrims, 1620-25; came t[illegible] Am. with 2d Colonial expdn. on the Fortune, Jul[illegible] 1621; at Plymouth, he delivered the first Am[illegible] sermon published anywhere; returned to Eng. a[illegible] agt. for colonists, 1621. Died Eng., 1625.

CUSHMAN, Samuel, congressman; b. Portsmouth[illegible] N.H., June 8, 1783; attended common schs.[illegible] studied law. Admitted to bar, began practice o[illegible] law, Portsmouth; judge Portsmouth Police Ct.[illegible] county treas., 1823-28; mem. N.H. Ho. of Reps.[illegible] 1833-35; mem. U.S. Ho. of Reps. from N.H. (Dem[illegible]ocrat), 24th-25th congresses, 1835-39; U.S. nav[illegible] officer at Portsmouth, 1845-49. Died Portsmouth[illegible] May 20, 1851; buried Proprietors' Burying Ground[illegible]

CUSHMAN, Susan Webb, actress; b. Boston, Mar. 17, 1822; d. Elkanah and Mary Eliza (Babbitt) Cushman; m. Nelson M. Meriman, Mar. 14, 1836[illegible] m. 2d, Dr. James Sheridan Muspratt, Mar. 1848. Made profl. debut as Laura Costelli in Epes Sargent's play The Genoese, Park Theater, N.Y.C., 1837; acted Grace Harkaway in N.Y.C., Phila., 1841; acclaimed in Satan in Paris; played Desdemona opposite George Vandenhoff's Othello; playe[illegible] Juliet opposite her sister Charlotte Cushman's Romeo, Haymarket Theater, London, 1845, then toure[illegible] England; retired from stage, 1847. Died Liverpool, Eng., May 10, 1859.

CUSTER, George Armstrong, army officer; b. New Rumley, O., Dec. 5, 1839; s. Emmanuel and Maria (Ward) C.; grad. U.S. Mil. Acad., 1861; m. Elizabeth Bacon, Feb. 9, 1864. Commd. 2d lt. 2d U.S. Cav., 1861, 1st lt. U.S. Army, 1862; served in 1st Battle of Bull Run and Peninsular campaign; promoted brig. gen. U.S. Volunteers for conduct at Battle of Aldie, 1863; promoted capt.

U.S. Army, 1864, later brevetted lt. col., then col.; brevetted maj. gen. U.S. Volunteers, 1864; had distinguished Civil War record; brevetted brig. gen., maj. gen. U.S. Army, 1865; promoted maj. gen. U.S. Volunteers, 1865; reverted to rank of capt. U.S. Army, 1865; became lt. col. in command of 7th U.S. Cavalry upon its orgn., 1866, served in various Indian campaigns in Kan., N.D.; sent to take part in Sioux campaign, 1876, in course of fighting his regt. became divided; met (with 5 troops of cavalry) an overwhelmingly large Indian force under Sitting Bull. Killed with all his command in Battle of Little Bighorn, nr. present day Little Bighorn, Mont., June 25, 1876.

CUSTIS, George Washington Parke, playwright; b. Mt. Airy, Md., Apr. 30, 1781; s. John Parke and Eleanor (Calvert) C.; attended St. John's Coll., Princeton; m. Mary Lee Fitzhugh, 1804, 1 dau., Mary. Commd. col. U.S. Army and a.d.c. to Gen. Charles Cotesworth Pinckney, 1799; volunteer for defense Washington (D.C.) during War of 1812; began series "Recollections of Washington" in United States Gazette, 1826, continued in National Intelligencer, published in book form, 1860; his 1st play The Indian Prophecy performed Chestnut Street Theater, Phila., 1827, published, 1828; Pocahontas, or the Settler of Virginia performed Walnut Street Theater, Phila., 1830, published, 1830, The Railroad, 1830; North Point or Baltimore Defended, performed in Balt., 1833; Eighth of January appeared Park Theater, N.Y.C., 1834. Died Arlington House, Fairfax County, Va., Oct. 10, 1857.

CUTBUSH, James, chemist; b. Pa., 1788; s. Edward and Anne (Marriot) C. Authored 15 article series "Application of Chemistry to the Arts and Manufactures," Phila. Aurora, beginning 1808; contbr. article about mercury fulminate to Med. Museum, 1808, article describing method of purifying ether and production of ethylene, 1809, article about value of hop to brewers, 1811; contbr. article "Subjects and Importance of Chemistry" to Freemason's Mag., 1811; founder, 1st pres. Columbian Chemistry Soc., 1811; v.p. Linnaean Soc.; mem. Soc. for Promotion Rational System of Edn.; prof. chemistry, mineralogy and natural philosophy St. John's Coll., Phila.; apptd. asst. apothecary gen. U.S. Army, 1814; chief med. officer U.S. Mil. Acad., 1820, acting prof. chemistry and mineralogy; article on improvement Voltaic electric lamp to Am. Jour. of Science, 1820. Author: A Useful Cabinet, 1808; An Oration on Education, 1812; Philosophy of Experimental Chemistry, 1813; A Synopsis of Chemistry, 1821; A System of Phyrotechny, 1825. Died West Point, N.Y., Dec. 15, 1823; buried West Point.

CUTHBERT, Alfred, senator; b. Savannah, Ga., Dec. 23, 1785; grad. Princeton, 1803; studied law. Admitted to bar, circa 1805, but did not practice; served as capt. of volunteer inf. co., 1809; mem. Ga. Ho. of Reps., 1810-13; mem. U.S. Ho. of Reps. (Democrat) from Ga., 13th-14th congresses, Dec. 13, 1813-Nov. 9, 1816, 17th-19th congresses, 1821-27; mem. Ga. Senate, 1817-19; mem. U.S. Senate from Ga., 1835-43. Died on estate nr. Monticello, Jasper County, Ga., July 9, 1856; buried Summerville Cemetery, Augusta, Ga.

CUTHBERT, John Alfred, congressman, jurist; b. Savannah, Ga., June 3, 1788; grad. Princeton, 1805; studied law. Admitted to bar, 1809, began practice of law, Eastonton, Ga.; mem. Ga. Ho. of Reps., 1811, 13, 17, 22; commanded volunteer co. during War of 1812; mem. Ga. Senate, 1814-mem. U.S. Ho. of Reps. (Democrat) from Ga., 16th Congress, 1819-21; apptd. commr. to treat with Creek and Cherokee Indians by Pres. Monroe, 1822; sec. Ga. Senate, 1830, 33, 34; editor, then propr. Fed. Union, Milledgeville, Ga., 1831-37; moved to Mobile, Ala., 1837; elected judge Mobile County Ct., 1840; apptd. judge circuit ct. Mobile County, 1852. Died "Sans Souci," on Mon Luis Island, nr. Mobile, Sept. 22, 1881; buried pvt. burying ground, Mon Luis Island.

CUTLER, Augustus William, congressman; b. Morristown, N.J., Oct. 22, 1827; attended Yale; studied law. Admitted to bar, 1849, began practice of law, Morristown; prosecutor of pleas Morris County (N.J.), 1856-61; pres. bd. of edn., 1870; mem. N.J. Senate, 1871-74; del. N.J. Constl. Conv., 1873; mem. U.S. Ho. of Reps. (Democrat) from N.J., 44th-45th congresses, 1875-79. Died Morristown, Jan. 1, 1897; buried Evergreen Cemetery.

CUTLER, Carroll, clergyman, coll. pres.; b. Windham, N.H., Jan. 31, 1829; s. Calvin and Rhoda Bartlett (Little) C.; grad. Yale, 1854; attended Union Theol. Sem., N.Y.C., 1856; m. Frances Gallagher, Aug. 10, 1856. Licensed to preach by Congregational West Assn. of New Haven, 1858; traveled abroad, 1859; prof. intellectual philosophy and rhetoric Western Res. Coll., Hudson, O., 1860-89, pres., 1871-86; prof. Biddle U., Charlotte, N.C., Talladega (Ala.) Coll., circa 1889-94. Author: A History of Western Reserve College During Its Firsrt Half Century, 1826-76, 1876; The Beginnings of Ethics, 1889. Died Talladega, Jan. 24, 1894.

CUTLER, Lizzie Petit, author; b. Milton, Va., 1831; d. Peter G. Cutler. Author: Light and Darkness, a Story of Fashionable Life, 1855; Household Mysteries, a Romance of Southern Life, 1856; The Stars of the Crowds, or Men and Women of the Day, 1858. Died Richmond, Va., Jan. 16, 1902.

CUTLER, Manasseh, clergyman, congressman; b. Windham County, Conn., May 13, 1742; s. Hezekiah and Susanna (Clark) C.; grad. Yale, 1765, A.M., 1768, LL.D. (hon.), 1789; m. Mary Balch, Sept. 7, 1766. Admitted to Mass. bar, 1767; licensed to preach, 1770; ordained, Congregational Ch., 1771, pastor, Ipswich Hamlet (now Hamilton), Mass., 1771-1823; served as chaplain in Revolutionary War; an organizer Ohio Co., colonizers Ohio River Valley, 1786; a founder Marietta (O.), 1787; instrumental in drafting Ordinance of 1787 for adminstrn. N.W. Territory; declined position as judge Supreme Ct. of Ohio Territory, 1795; rep. from Ipswich to Mass. Gen. Ct., 1800; mem. U.S. Ho. of Reps. (Federalist) from Mass., 7th-8th congresses, 1801-05; botanist, systematized and catalogued flora of New Eng. by Linnean system; mem. Am. Philos. Soc. (1784), Am. Acad. Arts and Scis. (1791), Phila. Linnaean Soc. (1809), Am. Antiquariran Soc. (1813), New Eng. Linnaean Soc. (1815). Died Hamilton, Mass., July 28, 1823.

CUTLER, Timothy, clergyman; b. Charlestown (now part of Boston), Mass., May 31, 1684; s. Maj. John and Martha (Wiswall) C.; grad. Harvard, 1701; m. Elizabeth Andrew, Feb. 1, 1711. Ordained to ministry Congregational Ch., 1710; became pastor Congregational Ch., Stratford, Conn., 1710; rector Yale, 1718; declared himself independent of validity of his ordination, 1722; travelled to London, ordained to ministry Ch. of Eng.; returned to Am., became rector Christ Ch., Boston. Died Aug. 17, 1765.

CUTLER, William Parker, railroad exec., congressman; b. Marietta, O., July 12, 1812; attended Ohio U. at Athens. Engaged in farming; mem. Ohio Ho. of Reps., 1844-47, speaker, 1847; trustee Marietta Coll., 1845-89; del. Ohio Constl. Conv., 1850; pres. Marietta & Cincinnati R.R., 1850-60; mem. U.S. Ho. of Reps. (Republican) from Ohio, 37th Congress, 1861-63. Died Marietta, Apr. 11, 1889; buried Oak Grove Cemetery.

CUTTER, George Washington, army officer, poet; b. Quebec, Can., 1801; m. Mrs. Frances Ann Drake; married a 2d time. Mem. Ind. Legislature, 1838-39; helped raise a co. of volunteers, 1847; commd. capt. 2d Ky. Regt., 1847; served in Battle of Buena Vista during Mexican War; works include: Buena Vista and Other Poems, 1848; The Song of Stream and Other Poems. 1857; Poems, National and Patriotic, 1857. Died Washington, D.C., Dec. 25, 1865; buried St. John's Masonic Lodge's plot, Congressional Cemetery, Washington.

CUTTING, Francis Brockholst, congressman; b. N.Y.C., Aug. 6, 1804; attended Litchfield (Conn.) Law Sch. Admitted to bar, 1827, began practice of law, N.Y.C.; mem. N.Y. State Assembly, 1836-37; mem. bd. aldermen, 1843; city recorder; mem. U.S. Ho. of Reps. (Democrat) from N.Y., 33d Congress, 1853-55. Died N.Y.C., June 26, 1870; buried Greenwood Cemetery, Bklyn.

CUTTING, Hiram Adolphus, scientist, physician; b. Concord, Vt., Dec. 23, 1832; s. Stephen Church and Eliza Reed (Darling) C.; A.M. (hon.), Norwich (Vt.) U., 1868, Ph.D. (hon.), 1870; M.D. (hon.), Dartmouth, 1870; m. Maranda E. Haskell, Feb. 3, 1856, no children. An extremely precocious child, headed a sch. in Guildhall, Vt., by age 16; mainly self-educated, attended formal sch. for only brief periods; surveyor for a time; partner (with an uncle) in dry goods store, Lunenburg, Vt., 1854-79, sole owner, 1879-92; examining surgeon U.S. War Dept., 1861-65; prof. gen. science Norwich U., various times before and after Civil War; lectr. in med. coll. Dartmouth, 1870; became state geologist Vt., 1870; also practiced medicine during this period, later (1885-92) specialized solely in practice of medicine; became mem. Vt. Bd. of Agr., 1880; chmn. Vt. Fish Commn., for a time; Vt. del. to Internat. Forestry Congress, 1885; credited with devising improved camera lens; did research on capability of various building stones; also interested in agrl. improvements; contbd. many articles to mags. and newspapers. Author works including: Mining in Vermont, 1872; Microscopic Revelations, 1878; Scientific Lectures, 1884. Died Lunenburg, Apr. 18, 1892.

CUTTING, James Ambrose, inventorr; b. Hanover, N.H., 1814; s. Abijah Cutting. Invented a bee hive, patented 1844; patented photographic process "ambrotype," 1850, photolithographic process, 1858; committed to an asylum, Worcester, Mass., 1862. Died Worcester, Aug. 6, 1867.

CUTTS, Charles, senator; b. Portsmouth, N.H., Jan. 31, 1769; grad. Harvard, 1789; studied law. Admitted to bar, 1795; mem. N.H. Ho. of Reps., 1803-10, speaker, 1807, 08, 10; mem. U.S. Senate (Federalist) from N.H., 1810-13, sec., 1814-25. Died nr. Lewinsville, Fairfax County, Va., Jan. 25, 1846; buried pvt. cemetery nr. Lewinsville.

CUTTS, Marsena Edgar, congressman; b. Orwell, Vt., May 22, 1833; attended St. Lawrence Acad., Potsdam, N.Y. Moved to Sheboygan Falls, Wis., 1853; taught sch., 2 years; moved to Oskaloosa, Ia., 1855, admitted to bar, began practice of law, Montezuma, Ia.; pros. atty. Poweshiek County, 1857-58; mem. Ia. Ho. of Reps., 1861, 70-72, Ia. Senate, 1864-66; atty. gen. Ia., 1872-77; mem. U.S. Ho. of Reps. (Republican) from Ia., 47th-48th congresses, 1881-83. Died Oskaloosa, Sept. 1, 1883; buried Forest Cemetery.

CUTTS, Richard, congressman; b. Cutts Island, Saco, Mass. (now Me.), June 28, 1771; grad. Harvard, 1790; studied law. Became engaged in comml. and navigation pursuits; mem. Mass. Ho. of Reps., 1799-1800; mem. U.S. Ho. of Reps. (Democrat) from Mass., 7th-12th congresses, 1801-13; supt. gen. of mil. supplies, 1813-17; 2d comptroller U.S. Treasury, 1817-29. Died Washington, D.C., Apr. 7, 1845; buried St. John's Graveyard, reinterred, Oak Hill Cemetery, 1857.

CUYLER, Theodore, lawyer; b. Poughkeepsie, N.Y., Sept. 14, 1819; s. Cornelis and Eleanor (de Graaff) C.; grad. U. Pa., 1838; studied law under Charles Chauncey; m. Mary Elizabeth de Witt, Dec. 21, 1853. Admitted to Pa. bar, 1841; advocate Christiana treason case, defending persons who had helped fugitive slaves from Md., 1851; mem. Select Council of Phila., 1856-62; solicitor Pa. R.R. Co., 1857-69; del.-at-large from Phila. to Pa. Constl. Conv., 1872. Died Phila., Apr. 5, 1876.

D

DABLON, Claude, missionary; b. Dieppe, France, Feb. 1618, or Jan. 21, 1619. Came as Jesuit missionary Iroquois Mission, New France (now Can.), 1655; co-leader exploratory expdn. up Saquenay River and Lake St. John, 1661; went to N.W. as superior Ottowa Mission, 1669; explored Central Wis., 1670; superior Canadian missions, 1671-80, 86-93; apptd. Father Marquette to accompany Joliet on his voyage which discovered Mississippi River; compiled an account of Marquette's journey. Died Quebec, Can., 1697.

DABNEY, Richard, poet; b. Louisa County, Va., 1787; s. Samuel and Jane (Meriwether) D. Published Poems, Original and Translated, 1812, revised edit., 1815; went to Phila., employed by Mathew Carey, publisher; collaborated with Carey in writing The Olive Branch; or Faults on Both Sides, Federal and Democratic, 1814. Died Louisa County, Nov. 25, 1825.

DABNEY, Robert Lewis, clergyman, educator; b. Louisa County, Va., Mar. 5, 1820; s. Charles and Elizabeth R. (Price) D.; attended Hampden-Sydney Coll., 1836-37, U. Va., 1840-42, Union Theol. Sem., 1844-46; m. Lavinia Morrison, Mar. 28, 1848. Ordained minister Presbyn. Ch., 1846; tchr. Union Theol. Sem., Richmond, Va., also preacher chapel, occasionally tchr. at Hampden-Sydney Coll., 1853-83; became prof. Princeton, also minister Fifth Avenue Presbyn. Ch., N.Y.C., 1860; opposed secession before Civil War, but supported South with religious fervor when war began; served as chaplain Confederate Army, 1862, commd. maj. Thomas J. (Stonewall) Jackson's staff; proposed saving "spiritual" South by mass migrations from conquered "geographical" South to Australia or Brazil; became prof. philosophy U. Tex., 1883, a founder Austin Sch. of Theology; infirm and totally blind, 1890 until death, but continued to lecture until 1897. Author: Life and Campaigns of Lt.-Gen. Thomas J. Jackson, 1866; A Defense of Virginia and the South, 1867; (theologically Calvinist, politically reactionary) Practical Philosophy, 1897; also many other philos. books and essays. Died Victoria, Tex., Jan. 3, 1898.

DABNEY, Thomas Smith Gregory, planter; b. "Bellevue," King and Queen County, Va., Jan. 4, 1798; s. Benjamin and Sarah (Smith) D.; attended Coll. William and Mary; m. Mary Adelaide Tyler, June 6, 1820; m. 2d, Sophia Hill, June 26, 1826, 1 son, Virginius. Mgr. family estate "Elmington," Gloucester County, Va., raised wheat and tobacco, 1820-35; moved to Hinds County, Miss., 1835, engaged in cotton planting; lost his fortune during Civil War. Died Feb. 28, 1885.

DABNEY, Virginius, educator; b. "Elmington," Gloucester County, Va., Feb. 15, 1835; s. Thomas Smith Gregory and Sophia (Hill) D.; attended U. Va., 1853-55, 57-58; m. Ellen Maria Heath; m. 2d, Anna Wilson Noland. Served in Confederate Army during Civil War, discharged as capt.; established Loudoun Sch., Middleburg, Va., 1867; in charge of prep. sch., Princeton, N.J., 1873-74, N.Y. Latin Sch., N.Y.C.; mem. editorial staff N.Y. Comml. Advertiser. Author: The Story of Don Miff, 1886; Gold that did not Glitter, 1889. Died N.Y.C., June 2, 1894.

DABOLL, Nathan, mathematician, educator; b. Groton, Conn., Apr. 24, 1750; s. Nathan and Anna (Lynn) D.; m. Elizabeth Daboll; m. 2d, "Widow Elizabeth Brown." Discovered errors in almanac prepared by Clark Elliott and published by Timothy Green, 1770, employed to revise the calculations; responsible for New England Almanack by Nathan Daboll Philomath (published by Timothy Green), 1773, 74, 75; prof. mathematics and astronomy Plainfield (Conn.) Acad., 1783-88; taught navigation aboard frigate President, 1811. Author: Daboll's Complete Schoolmaster's Assistant, 1799; Daboll's Practical Navigation, published posthumously, 1820. Died Mar. 9, 1818.

DABROWSKI, Joseph, clergyman; b. Russian Poland, Jan. 19, 1842; attended U. Warsaw (Poland), Polish Coll., Rome, Italy. Fought in Polish revolt of 1863; fled to Dresden; ordained priest Roman Catholic Ch., 1869; mem. Congregation of Resurrection, Rome; came to Am., 1869; in charge of Polish congregation, Polonia, Portage County, Wis., 1870; persuaded Felician Sisters of Cracow to come to Am., 1874, aided their settlement in Detroit; chaplain Felician Sisters, 1883; established S. S. Cyril and Methodius Sem., Detroit, 1887; established weekly newspaper Niedziela (published by sem.), 1891. Died Feb. 15, 1903.

da GAMA, Vasco, navigator, explorer; b. Sines, Portugal, circa 1460. Named to command expdn. to complete sea route to India around Southern Africa, 1497; rounded Cape of Good Hope, Nov. 22, 1497; landed at various places on both Eastern and Western African coasts during voyage; took on an Arab pilot to conduct him to India, at Malindi; reached India, May 20, 1498; left to return to Portugal, Aug. 1498; 1st European to have also landed at Mozambique and Zanzibar; returned to Portugal, Sept. 1499; commanded another expdn. to India, 1502-03; created count of Vidiguerira, 1519, viceroy of India, 1524. Died Cochin, Ind., Dec. 24, 1524.

DAGG, John Leadley, clergyman, univ. pres.; b. Middleburg, Va., Feb. 13, 1794; s. Robert and Sarah (Davis) D.; m. Fannie H. Thornton, Dec. 18, 1817; m. 2d, Mrs. Mary (Young) Davis, 1831. Ordained to ministry Baptist Ch., 1817; pastor 5th Bapt. Ch., Phila., 1825-34; in charge of Haddington Instn., nr. Phila.; prin. Ala. Female Athenaeum, Tuscaloosa, 1836-43; prof. theology Mercer U., Penfield, Ga., 1843-55, pres., 1855-56. Author: Manual of Theology, 1857; Elements of Moral Science, 1859 Evidences of Christianity, 1868; An Essay in Defence of Strict Communism. Died Haynesville, Ala., June 11, 1884.

DAGGETT, David, senator, jurist; b. Attleboro, Mass., Dec. 31, 1764; s. Thomas and Sibulah (Stanley) D.; grad. Yale, 1783, LL.D., 1827; m. Wealthy Munson, Sept. 10, 1786; m. 2d, Mary Lines, Mar. 4, 1840. Admitted to Conn. bar, 1786; mem. lower house Conn. Legislature, 1791-97, 1805-09, speaker, 1794-97; mem. Conn. Council, 1797-1803, 1809-13; mem. U.S. Senate from Conn., 1813-19; asso. justice Conn. Superior Ct., 1826-28; Kent prof. law Yale, 1826-48; mayor New Haven (Conn.), 1828-30; chief justice Conn. Supreme Ct. of Errors, 1832-34; upheld right of state legislatures to deprive free colored persons of sch. instrn. except by permission of town selectmen under rule that they were not U.S. citizens (Prudence Crandall case, 1833). Died New Haven, Apr. 12, 1851.

DAGGETT, Naphtali, clergyman, coll. pres.; b. Attleboro, Mass., Sept. 8, 1727; s. Ebenezer and Mary (Blackington) D.; grad. Yale, 1748; m. Sarah Smith, Dec. 19, 1753. Ordained 1st pastor Presbyn. Ch., Smithtown, L.I., N.Y., 1751; prof. divinity Yale, 1756-66, 77-80; pastor Ch. of Christ, Yale, 1766; pres. Yale, 1766-77, resigned after students petitioned for his removal; took part in defense of New Haven (Conn.), 1779, captured by British. Author: The Great Importance of Speaking in the Most Intelligible Manner in Christian Churches, 1768; The Excellency of a Good Name, 1768; The Testimony of Conscience, a Most Solid Foundation of Rejoicing, 1773. Died New Haven, Nov. 25, 1780.

DAHLGREN, John Adolphus Bernard, naval officer; b. Phila., Nov. 13, 1809; s. Bernard Ulric and Martha (Rowan) D.; m. Mary C. Bunker, Jan. 8, 1839; m. 2d, Sarah Madeleine Vinton Goddard, Aug. 2, 1865; 10 children, including Capt. Charles Bunker, Lt. Paul, John Vinton, Ulric, Eric. Apptd. acting midshipman U.S. Navy, 1826, passed midshipman, 1832, lt., 1837; assigned to make observations of solar eclipse, 1836; on leave to undergo treatment for oncoming blindness, 1837-43; patented percussion lock, 1847; chief Bur. of Ordnance, Washington, D.C., 1847-63, 68-69, established ordnance system used by U.S. Navy during Civil War; formulated and equipped Navy Ordnance Yard, Washington; inventor 11 inch Dahlgren gun; introduced boat howitzers to navy, 1850; commd. comdr., 1855, capt., 1862, rear adm., 1863; commanded S. Atlantic blockading squadron, 1868; prof. gunnery U.S. Naval Acad.; mem. A.A.A.S.; comdr. Washington Navy Yard, 1869-70. Author: 32 Pounder Practice for Ranges, 1850; The System of Boat Armament in the United States Navy, 1852; Naval Percussion Locks and Primers, 1853; Shells and Shell Guns, 1856. Died Washington Navy Yard, July 12, 1870.

DAHLGREN, Sarah Madeleine Vinton, author; b. Gallipolis, O., July 13, 1825; d. Samuel Finley and Romaine Madeline (Bureau) Vinton; m. Daniel C. Goddard, June 1840; m. 2d, Rear Adm. John Adolphus Dahlgren; 5 children. Began to write under pseudonyms Corinne and Cornelia, 1859; founder Washington Lit. Soc., 1873; writings include: Idealities, 1859; An Essay on Catholicism, Authority and Order, 1862; Thoughts on Female Suffrage, 1871; Memoir of Ulric Dahlgren, 1872; Etiquette of Social Life in Washington, 1873; South Sea Sketches, 1881; South Mountain Magic, 1882; Memoir of John A. Dahlgren, 1882; A Washington Winter, 1883; The Last Name, 1886; Lights and Shadows of a Life, 1887; Divorced, 1887; Chim: his Washington Winter, 1892; Samuel Finley Vinton, 1895; The Secret Directory, 1896; The Woodley Lane Ghost and Other Stories, 1899; translator: Pius IX and France (Montalembert), 1861; An Essay on Catholicism, Authority and Order from the Spanish of Don Juan Donono Cortes), 1862; The Executive Power in the United States Adolphede de Chambrun), 1874. Died Washington, D.C., May 28, 1898; buried South Mountain, Md.

DAILY, Samuel Gordon, congressman; b. Trimble County, Ky., 1823; attended Hanover (Ind.) Coll.; studied law. Admitted to Indpls. bar, began practice of law, Madison, Ind.; engaged in cooperage bus., Indpls. moved to Neb. Territory, 1857, settled in Peru, Nemaha County; built sawmill on Missouri River; mem. Neb. Territorial Ho. of Reps., 1858; mem. U.S. Congress (Republican) from Neb. Territory, 37th-38th congresses, May 18, 1860-65; dep. collector of customs (apptd. at spl. request of Pres. Lincoln), New Orleans, 1865-66. Died New Orleans, Aug. 15, 1866; buried Mt.Vernon Cemetery, Peru, Neb.

DALE, James Wilkinson, clergyman; b. Odessa, Del., Oct. 16, 1812; grad. U. Pa., 1831, M.D., 1838, D.D. (hon.); studied theology Andover, 1832-33, Princeton Theol. Sem., 1834-35. Agt. for Am. Bd. Commrs. for Fgn. Missions, 1835-38, for Pa. Bible Soc., 1838-45; pastor, Ridley, Delaware County, also Middleton, Dauphin County (both Pa.), 1845-66; pastor Media, Pa., 1866-71, Wayne, Pa., 1871-76. Author: Classic Baptism, 1867; Judaic Baptism, 1869; Christic and Patristic Baptism, 1874. Died Media, Apr. 19, 1881.

DALE, Richard, naval officer; b. Norfolk County, Va., Nov. 6, 1756; s. Winfield and Ann (Sutherland) m. Dorothea Grathorne, Sept. 15, 1791; children —Richard, John M. served with Brit. Navy, 1776-77; joined colonial cause, 1777; served as 1st lt. on Bon Homme Richard under John Paul Jones in battle with Serapis, 1779; commd. lt., 1781; served with Mcht. Marine, 1783-94; commd. capt. U.S. Navy, 1794; commanded squadron in Mediterranean during hostilities with Tripoli, 1801-02. Died Phila., Feb. 26, 1826.

DALE, Samuel, pioneer, soldier; b. Rockbridge County, Va., 1772. Govt. scout on Southern Frontier, 1793-96; became guide for immigrants going to Miss.; took part in Creek War, 1812-14; mem. Gen. Assembly Ala., 1817-29; one of those charged with transporting Choctaw to West of the Mississippi River, 1832; Dale County (Ala.) named after him. Died Lauderdale County, Miss., May 24, 1841.

DALE, Thomas, army officer, colonial gov.; b. England; m. Elizabeth Throckmorton, 1611. Created knight, 1606; apptd. marshal of Va., 1609; acting gov. Colony of Va. 1611, 14-16; placed colonists under marshall law for insubordination, noted for his discipline, his legislative code (known as "Dales Code") precipitated the phrase "five years of slavery," 1611-16; gained disfavor with the colonists but favor from the Linden Co.; returned to Eng. with Thomas Rolfe and his wife, Pocahontas, 1616; comdr. East India Co. Fleet, 1617. Died Masulipatam, India, Aug. 9, 1619.

DALLAS, Alexander James, sec. of treasury; b. Island of Jamaica, B.W.I., June 21, 1759; s. Robert and Sarah (Cormack) D.; m. Arabella Smith. Sept. 4, 1780; 1 son, George Mifflin. Came to U.S. and naturalized, 1783. Admitted to Pa. bar, 1785; apptd. a master in chancery, 1785; counselor Supreme Ct. Pa., 1785; editor Columbian mag., 1787; sec. Commonwealth of Pa., 1791; U.S. dist. atty. Eastern Dist. Pa., 1801-14; sec. of treasury U.S., 1814-16, secured bill establishing 2d Bank of U.S., 1816; acting sec. of war U.S., 1815-16; his govt. finance policies pulled U.S. out of post-war of 1812 depression, restored public credit, advocated nat. banks and protective tariff. Author: Features of Mr. Jay's Treaty, 1795; Laws of the Commonwealth of Pennsylvania, 4 vols., 1793-1801; Reports of Cases Ruled and Adjudged in the Several Courts of the U.S. and Pa., 4 vols., 1790-1807; Treasury Reports: An Exposition of the Causes and Character of the War, 1815; editor 1st Reports of U.S. Supreme Court. Died Trenton, N.J., Jan. 16, 1817.

DALLAS, George Mifflin, vice pres. U.S., diplomat; b. Phila., July 10, 1792; s. Alexander James and Arabella (Smith) D.; grad. Princeton, 1810; m. Sophia Nicklin, May 23, 1813. Admitted to the bar, 1813; sec. to Albert Gallatin on mission to obtain Russian mediation to end War of 1812 with Gt. Britain; chosen by Am. peace commn. to carry back Brit. peace terms from Ghnet to Britain, 1814; dep. atty. gen. Phila. City and County; mayor Phila., 1829-31; U.S. atty. for Eastern dist. Pa., mem. U.S. Senate (Democrat) from Pa., 1831-33; atty. gen. Pa., 1833; minister to Russia, 1837; vice pres. U.S. under James K. Polk, 1844-48; minister to Gt. Britain, 1856-61, negotiated Dallas-Claredon conv. relating to U.S.-Brit. differences in Central Am., 1856. Died Phila., Dec. 31, 1864; buried St. Peter's Churchyard, Phila.

DALLAS, Jacob A., artist; b. Phila., 1825; grad. Ames Coll., circa 1843; studied painting at Pa. Acad. Lived in N.Y.C., circa 1850-57; worked in assn. with several others on a number of large panoramas. Died N.Y.C., Sept. 9, 1857.

DALTON, John Call, physiologist, coll. pres. b. Chelmsford, Mass., Feb. 2, 1825; s. Dr. John Call and Julia (Spalding) D.; grad. Harvard, 1844; M.D., Harvard, 1847; studied physiology under Claude Bernard, Paris, France; never married. Never practiced medicine; became 1st U.S. physician to devote life to exptl. physiology and related scis.; recipient annual prize from A.M.A. for essay on Corpus Luteum, 1851; prof. physiology U. Buffalo (N.Y.), 1851-54, U. Vt., 1854-56; prof. physiology Coll. Physicians and Surgeons, N.Y.C., 1855-83, pres., 1884-89; with L.I. Coll. Hosp., 1859-61; served as surgeon with rank of brig. gen. med. corps. 7th N.Y. Regt., in Civil War, 1861-64; became mem. Nat. Acad. Scis., 1864. Author: Treastise on Human Physiology, 1859; A Treastise on Physiology and Hygiene, 1868; Doctrines of the Circulation, 1884; other med. works. Died N.Y.C., Feb. 12, 1889.

DALTON, Robert, outlaw; b. Cass County, Mo., 1867; s. Louis and Adaline (Younger) D. Moved with family to Coffeyville, Kan., circa 1882; U.S. dep. marshall Indian Territory, 1888; began criminal career by killing a rival in a love affair; organized (with brothers Grattan and Emmet) band of horse-thieves, operated around Baxter Springs, Kan.; went with brothers to Cal., 1890; held up So. Pacific train at Alila, Tulare County, Cal., 1891 (Grattan captured and sentenced, but escaped); robbed train (with Emmet and Charley Bryant), Okla. Territory, 1891 (Bryant killed); robbed train (with Grattan, Emmet, "Bill" Doolin, 2 others), Red Rock, Okla. Territory, 1892; robbed train, Adair, Okla. Territory, 1892. Killed (with Grattan and 2 others) in battle with townsfolk in attempted robbery of 2 banks, Coffeyville, Oct. 5, 1892.

DALTON, Tristram, senator; b. Newbury, Mass., May 28, 1738; grad. Harvard. 1755; studied law. Admitted to bar, did not practice law; became a businesman; del. from Mass. to conv. of coms. of New Eng. Provinces, Providence, R.I., 1776; mem. Mass. Ho. of Reps., 1782-88, speaker, 1784, 85; mem. U.S. Senate from Mass., 1789-91; surveyor Port of Boston, 1814-17. Died Boston, May 30, 1817; buried St. Paul's Episcopal Churchyard, Newburyport, Mass.

DALZELL, Robert M., millwright, inventor; b. Belfast, Ireland, 1793; s. John Dalzell; m. Lucy S., 2 children. Came to Vernon, N.Y., 1801; apprentice to a millwright in N.Y.; worked as a millwright until 1826; moved to Rochester, N.Y., 1826, millwright for flour mill, 1826-51; designed almost all flour mills in Rochester (became known as "Flour City"); perfected and introduced elevator storage system for grain and meal. Died Rochester, Jan. 19, 1873.

DAMON, Howard Franklin, physician; b. Scituate, Mass., 1833; grad. Harvard, 1858, M.D., 1861. Supt., Boston Dispensary, 1862-64; admitting physician Boston City Hosp., 1864-84; mem. Boston Microscopical Soc., Boston Soc. for Med. Improvement. Author: Leucothythaemia: A Boylston Prize Essay, 1864; Neurosis of the Skin, 1868; Structural Lesion of the Skin, 1869; Photographs of Skin Diseases, 1870. Died Boston, Sept. 1, 1884.

DAMRELL, William Shapleigh, congressman; b. Portsmouth, N.H., Nov. 29, 1809; attended public schs. Became owner of large printing firm, Boston; mem. U.S. Ho. of Reps. from Mass., 34th Congress (Am. Party), 1855-57, 35th Congress (Republican), 1857-59. Died Dedham, Mass., May 17, 1860; buried Forest Hills Cemetery.

DAMROSCH, Leopold, conductor, composer; b. Posen, Prussia (now Poznan, Poland), Oct. 22, 1832; M.D., U. Berlin, 1854; Mus. D. (hon.), Columbia, 1880; m. Helena von Heimburg, 1857. Concert master Grand Ducal Opera, Weimar, Germany, 1857; conductor Breslau Philharmonic Orch., 1858-60; organized Breslau Orch. Soc., Choral Soc., and a string quartet, 1862; conductor Soc. for Classical Music; came to U.S. as conductor Arion Soc. of N.Y.C., 1871; made 1st public appearance at Steinway Hall, 1871; founded N.Y. Oratoria Soc., 1873,

N.Y. Symphony Soc., 1878; opened season at Met. Opera House, 1884; composer 3 violin concertos and 7 cantatas. Died N.Y.C., Feb. 15, 1885.

DANA, Amasa, congressman; b. Wilkes-Barre, Pa., Oct. 19, 1792; attended Dana Acad., Wilkes-Barre; studied law, Owego, N.Y. Admitted to bar, 1817, began practice of law; moved to Ithaca, N.Y., 1821; dist. atty. Tompkins County (N.Y.), 1823-37; mem. N.Y. State Assembly, 1828-29; pres., trustee Village of Ithaca, 1835-36, 39; judge Ct. of Common Pleas, Tompkins County, 1837; mem. U.S. Ho. of Reps. (Democrat) from N.Y., 26th, 28th congresses, 1839-41, 43-45; resumed practice of law, 1845, also a banker. Died Ithaca, Dec. 24, 1867; buried Ithaca City Cemetery.

DANA, Charles Anderson, editor; b. Hinsdale, N.H., Aug. 8, 1819; s. Anderson and Ann (Denison) D.; ed. Harvard; A.B. (hon., as of Class of 1843), 1861; m. Eunice Macdaniel, 1846, 4 children. Tchr., mng. trustee Brook Farm, 1841-46; asst. editor Boston Daily Chronotype, 1846-47; city, then mng. editor N.Y. Tribune, 1847-62, covered European revolutions, 1848; editor (with George Ripley) New American Cyclopedia, 16 vols., 1858-63; asst. sec. of war U.S., 1863-64; field observer Union Army, 1863-64; editor Chgo. Republican, 1865; owner, editor N.Y. Sun, 1868-97, fought against Tweed Gang, also Grant's adminstrn.; pioneer modern news editing, noted for new style of journalism, stressing "human interest". Author: The Art of Newspaper Making, 1895; Recollections of Civil War, 1898; Eastern Journeys, 1898. Died West Island, L.I., N.Y., Oct. 17, 1897.

DANA, Francis, Continental congressman, jurist; b. Charlestown, Mass., June 13, 1743; s. Richard and Lydia (Trowbridge) D.; grad. Harvard, 1762, A.M., 1765; m. Elizabeth Ellery, 1773, 2 children, Richard Henry, Martha. Admitted to bar, 1767; mem. Sons of Liberty; declined appointment as del. to Mass. Provincial Congress, traveled to Gt. Britain to determine for himself whether reconciliation between colonies and Britain was possible, decided separation inevitable; mem. Mass. Council, 1776-80; del. to Continental Congress, 1776-78, 84-85, chmn. on army, 1778; unofcl. minister to Russia to secure recognition of U.S. and aid in war with Gt. Britain, 1780-83, at close of war presented his credentials to Russian govt. seeking recognition of U.S. and acceptance as U.S. minister to Russia, 1783, Russia refused; asso. justice Mass. Supreme Ct., 1785-91, chief justice, 1791-1806; elected del. U.S. Constl. Conv., 1787, unable to attend because of illness. Died Cambridge, Mass., Apr. 25, 1811; buried Old Cambridge Cemetery.

DANA, James, clergyman; b. Cambridge, Mass., May 11, 1735; s. Caleb and Phoebe (Chandler) D.; grad. Harvard, 1753; D.D. (hon.), U. Edinburgh Scotland), 1768; m. Catherine Whittelsey, May 8, 1759; m. 2d, Mrs. Abigail (Porter) Belden, July 10, 1796; m. 3d, Mrs. Mary (Miles) Rice, Sept. 14, 1798; 1 son, Samuel Whittelsey. Called to pastorate Congregational Ch., Wallingford, Conn., 1758; involved in "Wallingford Controversy" over his beliefs (belonged to "Old Light" party, his ch. declared separate by "New Light" group); pastor 1st Congregational Ch., New Haven, Conn., 1789-1805 (dismissed). Author: An Examination of the Late Reverend President Edward's Enquiry on Freedom of Will, published anonymously, 1770; The "Examination . . ." Continued, 1773. Died New Haven, Aug. 18, 1812.

DANA, James Dwight, geologist, educator; b. Utica, N.Y., Feb. 12, 1813; s. James and Harriet (Dwight) D.; grad. Yale, 1833; Ph.D. (hon.), U. Munich (Germany), 1872; LL.D. (hon.), Harvard, 1886, U. Edinburgh (Scotland), 1890; m. Henrietta Silliman, June 5, 1844, 4 children. Geologist, mineralogist on capt. Weekes expdn. to South Seas, 1837-40; editor Am. Jour. Science, 1840; Silliman prof. natural history Yale, 1849, prof. geology and mineralogy, 1864-90; pres. A.A.A.S., 1854. Recipient Woolaston medal Geol. Soc. London (Eng.), 1872; Copley medal Royal Soc. London, 1877; $1,000 Walker prize Boston Soc. Natural History, 1892. Author: Manual of Geology, 1862; Textbook of Geology, 1864; Corals and Coral Islands, 1872; Characteristics of Volcanoes, 1890. Died New Haven, Conn., Apr. 14, 1895.

DANA, James Freeman, chemist; b. Amherst, N.H., Sept. 23, 1793; s. Luther and Lucy (Giddings) D.; A.B., Harvard, 1813; M.D., 1817; studied under Friedrich Accum, London, Eng., 1815; m. Matilda Webber, 1818. Changed name from Jonathan to James by legislative act, 1820; organizer Hermetic Soc. at Harvard for informal scientific study; received Boylston prize for paper Tests for Arsenic; selected by Corp. of Harvard to purchase new chem. equipment in London, 1815; received 2d Boylston prize for Composition of Oxymuriatic Acid, 1817; lectr. in chemistry to med. students Dartmouth, 1817-20, prof. chemistry and mineralogy, 1820-26; prof. chemistry Coll. Physicians and Surgeons, N.Y.C., 1826. Author: (with brother Samuel) Outlines of Mineralogy and Geology of Boston and its Vicinity, 1818; Epitome of Chymical Philosophy, 1825. Died N.Y.C., Apr. 14, 1827.

DANA, Judah, senator; b. Pomfret, Conn., Apr. 25, 1772; s. John Winchester and Mrs. (Putnam) D.; grad. Dartmouth, 1795; studied law; at least 1 son, John. Admitted to bar, 1798, began practice of law, Fryeburg, Mass. (now Me.); pros. atty. Oxford County, 1805-11; judge of probate, 1811-22; judge Ct. of Common Pleas, 1811-23; also circuit judge; del. Me. Constl. Conv., 1819; mem. Me. Exec. Council, 1834; mem. U.S. Senate (Democrat, filling vacancy) from Me., Dec. 7, 1836-37. Died Fryeburg, Me., Dec. 27, 1845; buried Village Cemetery.

DANA, Richard, jurist, patriot; b. Cambridge, Mass., June 26, 1700; s. Daniel and Naomi (Croswell) D.; grad. Harvard, 1718; m. Lydia Trowbridge, May 31, 1737, 4 children including Francis. Admitted to Mass. bar; prominent mem. Boston bar; practiced in Marblehead and Charlestown, Mass., also Boston; prominent figure in colonial cause in years preceding Am. Revolution; served with the Adamses, Otis, Quincy, Hancock and Warren in preparing addresses to patriots and petitions to the King and Parliament; mem. Boston Sons of Liberty. Died Boston, May 17, 1772.

DANA, Richard Henry, poet, essayist; b. Cambridge, Mass., Nov. 15, 1787; s. Francis and Elizabeth (Ellery) D.; grad. Harvard, 1808; studied law in Boston, Balt., Newport, R.I.; m. Ruth Charlotte Smith, 1813, 4 children including Richard Henry, Edmund Trowbridge. Admitted to Mass. bar, 1811; mem. Mass. Legislature, 1811; became mem. Anthology Club (made up of men from Cambridge and Boston including John Quincy Adams, William Tudor), 1814; editor, contbr. to N. American Review, 1815; wrote for N.Y. Review, The Biblical Repository, The Literary and Theol. Review, Am. Quarterly Observer at various times; active in Congregational Ch. controversy, 1825-35, sided with Trinitarians (as opposed to Unitarians); lectured on Shakespeare at Boston, N.Y., Phila., other cities, 1839-40. Author: The Idle Man, 1821; The Buccaneer and Other Poems, 1827; Poems and Prose Writings, 1833. Died Boston, Feb. 2, 1879.

DANA, Richard Henry, lawyer, author; b. Cambridge, Mass., Aug. 1, 1815; s. Richard Henry and Ruth (Smith) D.; grad. Harvard, 1837, LL.D. (hon.), 1866; m. Sarah Watson, Aug. 25, 1841, 6 children. Instr. elocution Harvard, 1839-40, lectr. Harvard Law Sch., 1866-68; a founder Free Soil Party, del. to conv., Buffalo, N.Y., 1848; U.S. atty for Mass., dist. 1861-66; counsel for U.S. in treason proceedings against Jefferson Davis, 1867-68; sr. counsel for U.S. before Fisheries Commn. at Halifax, 1877. Author: Two Years Before the Mast (based on his experiences sailing on brig from Boston around Cape Horn to Cal. 1834-36), 1840; Seaman's Friend (standard work), 1841; To Cuba and Back, 1859; editor: Wheaton's Elements of International Law, 1866. Died Rome, Jan. 6, 1882; buried Protestant Cemetery, Rome.

DANA, Samuel, congressman; b. Groton, Mass., June 26, 1767; studied law. Admitted to bar, 1789, began practice of law, Groton; apptd. postmaster Groton, 1801; mem. Mass. Ho. of Reps., 1803, 25-27; atty. Middlesex County, 1807-11; mem. U.S. Ho. of Reps. (Democrat, filling vacancy) from Mass., 13th Congress, Sept. 22, 1814-15; mem. Mass. Senate, 1805-12, 17, pres., 1807, 11-12; chief justice Ct. of Common Pleas, 1811-12. Died Charlestown, Mass., Nov. 20, 1835; buried Groton Cemetery.

DANA, Samuel Luther, chemist; b. Amherst, N.H., July 11, 1795; s. Luther and Lucy (Giddings) D.; grad. Harvard, 1813, M.D., 1818; m. Ann Willard, June 5, 1820; m. 2d, Augusta Willard; 4 children. Served in War of 1812; discovered system of bleaching cotton known as Am. system of bleaching; devised improvements in printing calicoes. Author: Outlines of Mineralogy and Geology of Boston and its Vicinity, 1818; A Muck Manual for Farmers (one of 1st sci. works on agr. written and published in U.S.), 1842. Died Lowell, Mass., Mar. 11, 1868.

DANA, Samuel Whittelsey, senator; b. Wallingford, Conn., Feb. 13, 1760; s. James and Catherine (Whittelsey) D.; grad. Yale, 1775; m. Mary Wyllys Pomeroy, July 13, 1821. Admitted to Conn. bar, 1778; commd. brig. gen. Conn. Militia, 1790; mem. Conn. Gen. Assembly, 1789-96; mem. U.S. Ho. of Reps. from Conn., 5th-11th congresses, 1797-1810; mem. U.S. Senate, 1810-21; mayor Middletown (Conn.), 1822-30; chief judge Middlesex County Ct., 1825. Died Middletown, July 21, 1830; buried Washington Street Cemetery, Middletown.

DANCEL, Christian, inventor; b. Cassel, Germany, Feb. 14, 1847; 2 children. Learned machinist trade in Germany; came to N.Y.C., circa 1865; machinist in various N.Y. shops, 1865-67; devised shoe-sewing machine (bought by Charles Goodyear, Jr. for his shoe-machine factory), became supt. Goodyear's factory; began making machinery for stitching outsoles and sewing shoe-welts, circa 1870; invented machine to sew both welts and turns, 1874 (still used with minor improvements); opened own machine shop and patented some small machines, 1876; called by Goodyear Co. to perfect machine to sew upper and outer sole of shoe, finished it (machine with curved needle sewing a lock-stitch), 1885; patented straight-needle machine, 1891; organized Dancel Machine Co., Bklyn., circa 1895; invented many other shoe-making devices; co-patentee machines for making leather buttonholes, barbed-wire fence, rubbing type. Died Bklyn., Oct. 13, 1898.

DANCKAERTS, Jasper, colonist. A leader Dutch sect of Labadists who settled at head of Chesapeake Bay in 1680's; sketched views of N.Y.C. and Manhattan Island, 1679-80; kept jour. which included his sketches, published in 1800's as Journal of a Voyage to New York; returned to Holland.

DANE, Joseph, congressman; b. Beverly, Essex County, Mass., Oct. 25, 1778; attended Phillips Acad., Andover, Mass.; grad. Harvard, 1799; studied law. Admitted to bar, 1802, began practice of law, Kennebunk, Mass. (now Me.); del. Mass. constl. convs., 1816, 19; declined to become mem. Mass. Exec. Council, 1817; mem. U.S. Ho. of Reps. (Federalist, filling vacancy) from Me., 16th-17th congresses, Nov. 6, 1820-23; mem. Me. Ho. of Reps., 1824-25, 32-33, 39-40, Me. Senate, 1829; declined to serve as exec. councilor Me., 1841. Died Kennebunk, May 1, 1858; buried Hope (Me.) Cemetery.

DANE, Nathan, lawyer, Continental congressman; b. Ipswich, Mass., Dec. 29, 1752; s. Daniel and Abigail (Burnham) D.; ed. Harvard, 1774-78; m. Mrs. Mary Brown, Nov. 1779. Admitted to Mass. bar, 1782; rep. to Mass. Gen. Ct., 1782-85; del. Continental Congress from Mass., 1785-87; co-drafter adminstrn. ordinance N.W. Territory, 1787; judge Mass. Ct. Common Pleas for Essex County, 1793; apptd. commr. to revise laws of Commonwealth of Mass., 1795; presdl. elector, 1812; established Dane Professorship of Law, founder Dane Hall, Harvard; a founder Mass. Temperance Soc. (1st established soc. of its kind). Author: General Abridgement and Digest of American Law, 8 vols., 1825, final vol. published, 1829. Died Beverly, Mass., Feb. 15, 1835.

DANENHOWER, John Wilson, naval officer; b. Chgo., Sept. 30, 1849; s. William W. Danenhower; grad. U. S. Naval Acad., 1870; 2 children. Served in ships Plymouth and Juniata in European Squadron, 1870; served in vessel Portsmouth in survey of North Pacific, 1873-74; rank of master, 1873; spent 2 months in insane asylum, 1878; after release served in ship Vandalia, in Mediterranean; while in Smyrna (Turkey) heard of proposed Arctic expdn. in ship Jeannette, offered services and was accepted; exec. officer in Jeannette from Havre (France) to San Francisco; began trip via Bering Strait to Arctic; 1879; commd. lt., 1879; incapacitated by inflammed left eye, 1879; when Jeannette was crushed in ice (latitude 77°15' north, longitude 155° east), 1881, escaped (with others) over ice to Asia mainland, arrived in U.S., 1882; asst. comdr. of cadets U.S. Naval Acad., Annapolis, Md.; assigned command in Constellation, 1887, grounded vessel going out of harbor, Norfolk, Va.; returned to Annapolis, committed suicide (probably because of this incident). Author: Lieutenant Danenhower's Narrative of the Jeannette, 1882. Died Annapolis, Apr. 20, 1887.

DANFORTH, Charles, inventor, mfr.; b. Norton, Mass., Aug. 30, 1797; s. Thomas and Betsey (Haskins) D.; m. Mary Willett, Oct. 18, 1823, at least 2 children. Foreman cotton-mfg. factory, Matteawan, N.Y.; factory worker Sloatsburg, N.Y., 1825; patented cap-spinner (important spinning frame improvement), 1828; machinist for firm Godwin, Rogers & Clark, Paterson, N.J., took over Roger's place in firm, but continued to work in machine-shop, designed and patented 5 improvements on original cap-spinner; purchased machine-shop branch of firm, 1840, bought firm's cotton mill, 1842 (became Danforth, Cooke & Co., 1854), expanded to build locomotives; incorporated Danforth Locomotive and Machine Co. 1865, pres., 1865-71. Died Paterson, Mar. 22, 1876.

DANFORTH, Joshua Noble, clergyman; b. Pittsfield, Mass., Apr. 1, 1798; grad. Williams Coll., 1818; attended Princeton Theol. Sem.; D.D. (hon.), Del. Coll., 1855. Ordained to ministry, 1825; pastor, New Castle, Del.; pastor, Washington, D.C., 1828-32; became agt. Am. Colonization Soc., 1832; minister Congregational Ch., Lee, Mass., 1834-38; became pastor 2d Presbyn. Ch., Alexandria, Va., 1838. Author: Gleanings and Groupings from a Pastor's Portfolio, 1852. Died Nov. 14, 1861.

DANFORTH, Moseley Isaac, engraver, painter; b. Hartford, Conn., Dec. 11, 1800; s. Edward and Jerusha (Moseley) D.; m. Mrs. Hannah B. Duryee, 1843. Began study of engraving under Asaph Willard of Hartford Graphic Co., 1818; moved to New Haven, Conn., 1821, then to N.Y.C.; a founder

N.A.D., 1826; studied at Royal Acad., London, Eng., 1827-37; formed firm Danforth, Underwood, & Co., N.Y.C., 1850 (merged with Am. Bank Note Co., 1858), v.p. Am. Bank Note Co., 1852-62; engravings include: Don Quixote, Sir Walter Scott, Lord Holland's Daughter, Andrew Jackson, Landing at Jamestown; also painted portraits (only a few of his paintings still in U.S.). Died N.Y.C., Jan. 19, 1862.

DANFORTH, Thomas, colonial gov.; b. Suffolk, Eng., Nov. 1623; s. Nicholas and Elizabeth Danforth; m. Mary Withington, Feb. 1644, 12 children. Came to Am., 1634; treas. Harvard, 1650-68, chosen clk. of overseers, 1654, steward, 1669-82; 1st recorder of deeds Essex County (Mass.), 1652-86; mem. Mass. Gen. Ct. from Cambridge, 1657-59; assistant and mem. Gov.'s Council, 1658-79; commr. (from Mass.) of New Eng. Confederacy, 1662-82; dep. gov. Mass., 1679-88; pres. Province of Me., 1679-88; a leader in revolution against Gov. Andros in 1689; asso. judge Mass. Superior Ct., 1692-99. Died Cambridge, Nov. 5, 1699.

DANIEL, Henry, congressman; b. Louisa County, Va., Mar. 15, 1786; attended public schs.; studied law. Admitted to bar, started practice of law, Mt. Sterling, Montgomery County, Ky.; mem. Ky. Ho. of Reps., 1812, 19, 26; served as capt. 8th Regt., U.S. Inf. in War of 1812, 1813-15; mem. U.S. Ho. of Reps. (Jackson Democrat) from Ky., 20th-22d congresses, 1827-33. Died Mt. Sterling, Oct. 5, 1873; buried Macphelah Cemetery.

DANIEL, John Moncure, journalist, diplomat; b. Stafford County, Va., Oct. 24, 1825; s. John and Elizabeth (Mitchell) D. Editor, Southern Planter; editor Richmond (Va.) Examiner, 1847-53, 61-65, became a leader of So. pub. opinion through its pages, advocating secession and mil. conscription, noted for fierce attacks upon and distrust of Jefferson Davis' adminstrn.; U.S. rep. at Court of Sardinia, 1853-61. Died Richmond, Mar. 29, 1865.

DANIEL, John Reeves Jones, congressman; b. nr. Halifax, N.C., Jan. 13, 1802; grad. U. N.C. at Chapel Hill, 1821; studied law. Admitted to bar, 1823, began practice of law, Halifax; mem. N.C. Ho. of Commons, 1832-34; elected atty. gen. N.C., 1834; mem. U.S. Ho. of Reps. (Democrat) from N.C., 27th-32d congresses, 1841-53; settled nr. Shreveport, La., 1860, became a planter, also continued practice of law Died Shreveport, June 22, 1868.

DANIEL, Peter Vivian, justice U.S. Supreme Ct.; b. Stafford County, Va., Apr. 24, 1784; s. Travers and Frances (Moncure) D.; grad. Princeton, 1805; m. Lucy Nelson Randolph, 1809; m. 2d, Mary Harris, 1853. Admitted to Va. bar, 1808; mem. Va. Legislature, 1809; mem. Va. Privy Council, 1812-35, ex-officio chmn.; lt. gov. Va.; judge U.S. Dist. Ct., Va., 1836-40; asso. justice U.S. Supreme Ct., 1841-60. Died Richmond, Va., May 31, 1860.

DANIELS, Charles, congressman, jurist; b. N.Y.C., Mar. 24, 1825; studied law, Buffalo, N.Y. Admitted to bar, 1847, began practice of law, Buffalo; asso. justice N.Y. Supreme Ct., 1863-91; mem. U.S. Ho. of Reps. (Republican) from N.Y., 53d-54th congresses, 1893-97. Died Buffalo, Dec. 20, 1897; buried Forest Lawn Cemetery.

DANNER, Joel Buchanan, congressman, businessman; b. Liberty, Md., 1804. Hardware dealer and carriage builder, Gettysburg, Pa.; justice of peace; mem. U.S. Ho. of Reps. (Democrat) from Pa., 31st Congress, Dec. 2, 1850-51. Died Gettysburg, July 29, 1885; buried Evergreen Cemetery.

Da PONTE, Lorenzo, poet, librettist; b. Ceneda, nr. Venice, Italy, Mar. 10, 1749; s. Geremia and Rachele (Pinerchele) Conegliano; m. Ann Celestine Ernestine, 1791. Took last name of Bishop of Ceneda who baptized him; tutor seminary, Portogruaro, Italy, 1770, vice rector, 1771, resigned office and went to Venice, 1773; taught at seminary, Treviso, Italy, 1774-76, relieved of duties because of his authorship Accademic Poetica in Venice, 1776-79; banished from Venice for excessive profligacy, went to Austria, 1779; apptd. "Poet to the Italian Theatre," Vienna, Austria; collaborated with Mozart as librettist for Le Nozze di Figaro, 1786, Don Giovanni, 1797, Cosi fan Tutti, 1790; worte scores for Salieri, Righini, Martini, and Storace; left Vienna, 1790; settled in London, Eng., 1793; discharged from Drury Lane Theatre, 1799, with Drury Lane again for a time, 1803; came to U.S., 1805; operated (unsuccessfully) grocery stores in N.Y.C., Elizabethtown, N.J., Sunbury, Pa.; taught Italian to children in pvt. classes, N.Y.C.; prof. Italian literature Columbia Coll., 1825; built Italian opera house, N.Y.C., 1833. Author: Il Ricco d'un Giorno; Il Barbero di Buon Cuore; Il Finto Cieco. Died Aug. 17, 1838.

DARBY, Ezra, congressman; b. Scotch Plains, N.J., June 7, 1768; attended common schs. Engaged in farming; held offices as chosen freeholder, assessor, justice of peace, 1800-04; mem. N.J. Ho. of Assembly, 1802-04; mem. U.S. Ho. of Reps. (Democrat) from N.J., 9th-10th congresses, 1805-08. Died Washington, D..C, Jan. 27, 1808; buried Congressional Cemetery.

DARBY, John, see Garretson, James Edmund.

DARBY, John, educator, coll pres.; b. North Adams, Mass., Sept. 27, 1804; s. Joseph and Farrand Darby; grad. Williams Coll., Williamstown, Mass., 1831; m. Julia P. Sheldon, Aug. 20, 1833, at least 2 children. Taught at Williamstown Acad., also Barhamville Sem., Columbia, S.C.; prof. natural science Wesleyan Female Coll., Macon, Ga., 1842; prof. mathematics Williams Coll.; dir. Sigoruney Inst., Culloden, Ga., 6 years; dir. Masonic Female Coll., Auburn, Ala., 1855-56; prof. naturel science East Auburn Male Coll., Auburn 1856-61; prof. science, later pres. Ky. Wesleyan Coll., Millersburg, 1869-76. Author: A Botany of the Southern States, 1841. Died N.Y., Sept. 1, 1877.

DARBY, John Fletcher, congressman, mayor St. Louis; b. Person County, N.C., Dec. 10, 1803; attended public schs.; studied law. Moved to Mo., 1818, to Frankfort, Ky., 1825; admitted to bar, practiced law, St. Louis, Mo.; mayor St. Louis, 1835-41; mem. Mo. Senate, 1838; mem. U.S. Ho. of Reps. (Whig) from Mo., 32d Congress, 1851-53; engaged in banking, St. Louis, after 1853. Died nr. Pendleton Station, Mo., May 11, 1882; buried Calvary Cemetery, St. Louis.

DARBY, William, geographer; b. Hanover Twp., Pa., Aug. 14, 1775; s. Patrick and Mary (Rice) D.; m. Mrs. Boardman; m. 2d, Elizabeth Tanner, Feb. 1816; at least 2 children. Became cotton-planter, Natchez, Miss., 1781; dep. surveyor for U.S., 1804-09; mem. Andrew Jackson's topog. staff, 1814-15; a surveyor designating boundary line between U.S. and Canada, 1818; lectured and wrote geog. volumes, during next 35 years. Author: A Geographical Description of the State of Louisiana . . . Being an Accompaniment to the Map of Louisiana, 1816; A Tour from the City of New York to Detroit, 1819; (with Theodore Dwight, Jr.) A New Gazetteer of the United States of America, 1833; The Northern Nations of Europe, Russia and Poland, 1841. Died Oct. 9, 1854.

DARE, Virginia; b. Roanoke Island, N.C., Aug. 18, 1587; d. Ananias and Ellinor (or Elyoner) (White) Dare. Born after English colonists under Gov. White (her grandfather) settled in Roanoke Island, 1587; known to have lived 9 days, Aug. 18-Aug. 27, 1587; Gov. White sailed to Eng. for supplies, Aug. 27, 1587, unable to return until 1591, found no remains of settlers (probably massacred by Indians). Died Roanoke Island, N.C., circa 1587.

DARGAN, Edmond Strother, congressman; b. Montgomery County, N.C., Apr. 15, 1805; m. Roxanna Brack. Admitted to Ala. bar, 1829; elected by Gen. Assembly as judge Circuit Ct., Mobile (Ala.) dist., 1841, 42; mayor Mobile, 1844; mem. U.S. Ho. of Reps. (Democrat) from Ala., 29th Congress, 1845-47; elected by Gen. Assembly as judge Ala. Supreme Ct., 1847, chief justice, 1849-52; mem. Confederate Congress of 1862. Died Mobile, Nov. 24, 1879; buried Magnolia Cemetery, Mobile.

DARKE, William, army officer; b. Philadelphia County, Pa., May 6, 1736; s. Joseph Darke; m. Sarah Delayea, 3 sons including Capt. Joseph, 1 dau. Served as cpl. in Rutherford Rangers during French and Indian Wars, 1758-59; capt. Va. Volunteers at beginning of Revolutionary War; captured at Battle of Germantown, 1777; aboard prison ship, N.Y. until 1780; recruited Berkeley and Hampshire (Va.) regts., 1781; served at siege of Yorktown; retired as lt. col.; mem. Va. Conv. to ratify U.S. Constn., 1788; elected mem. Va. Legislature, 1791, served only 3 days; resigned to accept commn., under Gen. Arthur St. Clair to fight Indians; wounded in defeat by Miami Indians, 1791; promoted brig. gen., given 8,000 acres of public lands for his mil. service. Died Jefferson County, Va., Nov. 26, 1801.

DARLEY, Felix Octavius Carr, illustrator; b. Phila., June 23, 1822; s. John and Eleanora (Westray) D.; m. Jane Colburn, 1859. Published 1st sketches in Saturday Museum, 1842; published Scenes in Indian Life, also stone etchings, 1843; commissioned to make illustrations for Library of Am. Humorous Works, 1843; illustrated Margarert (Sylvester Judd); commd. to illustrate Rip Van Winkle, also Legend of Sleepy Hollow (Washington Irving), 1848; elected to N.A.D., 1852; commd. to illustrate all the works of James Fenimore Cooper for James G. Gregory, 1856; regular illustrator for Appleton's, Harper's mags.; executed book Compositions in Outline from Nathaniel Hawthorne's Scarlet Letter, 1879. Died Claymont, Del., Mar. 27, 1888.

DARLEY, Jane Cooper, artist; b. N.Y.C., Jan. 14, 1807; d. Thomas Sully; m. W. H. W. Darley. Exhibited frequently at Pa. Acad., Artists' Fund Soc., 1825-69; exhibited at N.A.D., Boston Athenaeum, Md. Hist. Soc. Died Phila., Mar. 3, 1877.

DARLING, Henry, clergyman, coll. pres.; b. Reading, Pa., Dec. 27, 1823; s. Judge William and Margaretta (Smith) D.; grad. Amherst Coll., 1842, M.A. (hon.), 1852; grad. Auburn Sem., 1845; D.D. (hon.), Union Coll., 1860; LL.D. (hon.), Hamilton Coll., 1881; m. Julia Strong, 1846; m. 2d, Ophelia Wells, 1853. Ordained to ministry Presbyn. Ch., Dec. 30, 1846; pastor Presbyn. Ch., Hudson, N.Y., 1846-62; clk. Gen. Assembly Presbyn. Ch., 1854; pastor Clinton St. Presbyn. Ch., Albany, N.Y., 1864-81; pres. Hamilton Coll., Clinton, N.Y., 1881-91. Author: The Closer Walk, 1862; Conformity to the World, 1873; Doing Nothing but Receiving, 1875; Preaching and Modern Skepticism, 1881. Died Hamilton Coll., Apr. 20, 1891.

DARLING, Mason Cook, congressman, physician; b. Amherst, Mass., May 18, 1801; grad. Berkshire Med. Coll., 1824. Taught sch., N.Y.; practiced medicine, 13 years; moved to Wis., 1837, an original settler of Fond du Lac, Wis.; mem. Wis. Territorial Legislative Assembly, 1840-46; mem. Wis. Territorial Council, 1847-48; mem. U.S. Ho. of Reps. (Democrat) from Wis., 30th Congress, June 9, 1848-49; 1st mayor Fond du Lac, 1852; resumed practice of medicine, also dealt in real estate, Fond du Lac, 1852-64; moved to Chgo., 1864. Died Chgo., Mar. 12, 1866; buried Rienzi Cemetery, Fond du Lac.

DARLING, William Augustus, businessman, congressman; b. Newark, N.J., Dec. 27, 1817; attended public schs. Moved to N.Y.C., entered wholesale grocery bus.; dir. Merc. Library Assn.; served with N.Y. Nat. Guard, 11 years; dep. receiver taxes N.Y. C., 1847-54; pres. 3d Avenue R.R., 1854-65; Republican presdl. elector, 1860; mem. U.S. Ho. of Reps. (Republican) from N.Y., 39th Congress, 1865-67; unsuccessful candidate for mayor N.Y.C., 1866; collector of internal revenue 9th Dist. N.Y., 1869-71, an appraiser, 1871-76; pres. Murray Hill Bank. Died N.Y.C., May 26, 1895; buried Trinity Cemetery.

DARLINGTON, Edward, congressman; b. West Chester, Pa., Sept. 17, 1795; grad. West Chester Acad.; studied law. Taught sch., 1817-20; admitted to bar, 1821, began practice of law, Chester, Pa., 1851; dist. atty. Delaware County (Pa.), Reps. (Whig) from Pa., 23d-24th congresses, 1833-37, (Anti-Mason), 25th Congress, 1837-39; atty. for county commrs., 1846-56; moved to Media, Pa., 1851; dist. atty. Delaware County (Pa.), 1851-54. Died Media, Nov. 21, 1884; buried Chester Rural Cemetery.

DARLINGTON, Isaac, congressman; b. nr. West Chester, Pa., Dec. 13, 1781; attended Friends Sch., Birmingham, Pa.; studied law. Tchr. in country schs.; admitted to bar, 1801, began practice of law, West Chester; mem. Pa. Ho. of Reps., 1807-09; served as lt. and adj. 2d Regt., Pa. Volunteers, 1814-15; mem. U.S. Ho. of Reps. (Federalist) from Pa., 15th Congress, 1817-19; apptd. dep. atty. gen. Chester County (Pa.), 1820; pres. judge jud. dist. of Chester and Delaware counties, 1821-39. Died West Chester, Apr. 27, 1839; buried Friends Burying Ground, Birmingham.

DARLINGTON, William, botanist, congressman; b. Dilworthtown, Chester County, Pa., Apr. 28, 1782; s. Edward and Hannah (Townsend) D.; studied medicine under Dr. John Vaughan, Wilmington, Del.; M.D., U. Pa., 1804; m. Catherine Lacey, June 1808. Surgeon aboard ship to Calcutta, 1806-08; maj. in "Am. Grays" (Pa. Volunteers), during War of 1812; mem. U.S. Ho. of Reps. from Pa., 14th, 16th-17th congresses, 1815-17, 19-23; organized Chester County Cabinet of Natural Scis., 1826; dir., pres. Nat. Bank of Chester County, 1830-63. Author: Florula Cestrica, 1826; Flora Cestrica, 1837; Reliquiae Baldwinianae, 1843; Agricultural Botany, 1847; Memorials of John Bartram and Humphry Marshall, 1849; American Weeds and Useful Plants, 1859. Died West Chester, Pa., Aug. 23, 1863; buried Oakland Cemetery, West Chester.

DARRAGH, Cornelius, congressman; b. Pitts., 1809; grad. Western U. Pa., 1826; studied law. Admitted to bar, 1829, began practice of law, Pitts.; mem. Pa. Senate, 1836-39; U.S. dist. atty. Western Dist. Pa., 1841-44; mem. U.S. Ho. of Reps. (Whig, filled vacancy) 28th-29th congresses, Mar. 26, 1844-47; atty. gen. Pa., 1849-51. Died Pitts., Dec. 22, 1854; buried Allegheny Cemetery.

DARRAH, Ann Sophia Towne, artist; b. Phila., Sept. 30, 1819; m. Robert K. Darrah. Painted landscape and marine scenes, did pastel portraits; exhibited at Boston Athenaeum, Pa. Acad. Died Boston, 1881.

DAUMONT, Simon Francois (sieur de St. Husson), explorer; m. Marguerite Berin, at least 1 child. Went to Can. with Commr. Gaudais-Dupont, 1663, received grant of land and thereafter acted as agt. for the intendant Jean Talon, 1664; sent by Talon as head of expdn. in Upper Great Lakes area to take formal possession for the King of France and to explore for mines nr. Lake Superior, 1670; sent Nicholas Perrot to Green Bay to summon the chief of the tribe there to a ceremony; proceeded to Sault Ste. Marie, 1671, where the pageant of annexation took place, taking the land from the Indians for France; later advanced into Lake Superior region but found no mine. Died 1674.

DAVEE, Thomas, congressman; b. Plymouth, Mass., Dec. 9, 1797; attended common schs. Moved to Me., engaged in business; mem. Me. Ho. of Reps., 1826-27, Me. Senate, 1830-32, 41; high sheriff Somerset County, 1835; postmaster Blanchard (Me.), 1833-37; mem. U.S. Ho. of Reps. (Democrat) from Me., 25th-26th congresses, 1837-41. Died Blanchard, Dec. 9, 1841; buried Village Cemetery, Monson, Me.

DAVEIS, Charles Stewart, lawyer; b. Portland, Me., May 10, 1788; s. Ebenezer and Mehitabel (Griffin) D., grad. Bowdoin Coll., 1807; m. Elizabeth Taylor Gilman, June 1, 1815. Admitted to Me. bar, 1810; held various state and fed. positions involving Me.-Canadian border dispute (culminated in Webster-Ashburton Treaty 1842), 1827-42; spl. agt. U.S. Govt.; mem. Me. Senate from Cumberland County, 1840. Died Portland, Mar. 29, 1865.

DAVEISS, Joseph Hamilton, lawyer; b. Bedford County, Va., Mar. 4, 1774; s. Joseph and Jean (Hamilton) D.; studied law under George Nicholas; m. Ann Marshall, 1803. Admitted to bar, 1795; dist. atty. for Ky., 1800; argued land case Mason vs. Wilson before U.S. Supreme Ct., 1801-02; removed from office (by Jefferson) after making unsuccessful attempt to establish charges of conspiracy against Aaron Burr, 1806; joined forces under Gen. Harrison in campaign against Indians, 1811. Author: A View of the President's Conduct Concerning the Conspiracy of 1806, published 1807; The Sketch of a Bill for an Uniform Militia of the United States, with Reflections on the State of the Nation, Addressed to the Secretary of War, 1810. Died at Battle of Tippecanoe, Nov. 8, 1811.

DAVENPORT, Edward Loomis, actor; b. Boston, Nov. 15, 1815; s. Asher and Demis (Loomis) D.; m. Fanny Vining (Mrs. Charles Gill), 1849, 9 children, including Fanny Lily Gypsy, Blance Maria, Lily Antoinette, May, Marion Caroline, Edgar Longfellow, Henry George Bryant (all successful on stage). Made debut at Lion Theater or Brick Circus, Providence, R.I.; leading Am. actor, 1854-74; chief roles include: Othello, Iago, Shylock, Virginius, Hamlet, Richelieu, Wolsey, Bautus, King Lear; played Giles Overreach in Massinger's A New Way to Pay Old Debts. Died Canton, Pa., Sept. 1, 1877; buried Forest Hills Cemetery, Boston.

DAVENPORT, Fanny Lily Gypsy, actress; b. London, Eng., Apr. 10, 1850; d. Edward Loomis and Fanny Elizabeth (Vining) D.; m. Edward H. Price, July 30, 1879; m. 2d, Melbourne MacDowell, May 19, 1889. Came with family to Am., 1854; played 1st part as the child in play Metamora; made debut (with her parents) as King Charles of Spain in play Faint Heart Never Won Fair Lady, Niblo's Garden, N.Y.C., 1862; started independent career as Carline in play The Black Crook, Louisville, Ky.; played many roles including Shakespearean, N.Y.C.; play Pique written for her by Augustin Daly, 1876; obtained Am. rights to play Fedora, successful in role. Died South Duxbury, Mass., Sept. 26, 1898.

DAVENPORT, Franklin, senator; b. Phila., Sept. 1755; studied law, Bulrington, N.J. Admitted to bar, 1776, began practice of law, Gloucester City, N.J.; clk. Gloucester County Ct., 1776; enlisted as pvt. Capt. James Sterling's Co., N.J. Militia, commd. brigade maj., 1776; served in battles of Trenton and Princeton; apptd. brigade q.m., 1778; asst. q.m. Gloucester County, 1778-79; commd. col. N.J. Militia, 1779, then maj. gen.; prosecutor of pleas, 1777; moved to Woodbury, N.J., 1781; apptd. 1st surrogate Gloucester County, 1785; mem. N.J. Gen. Assembly, 1786-89; presdl. elector, 1792, 1812; served as col. N.J. Militia during Whisky Rebellion, 1794; apptd. brig. gen. Gloucester County Militia, 1796; mem. U.S. Senate from N.J. (filled vacancy), Dec. 5, 1798-99; mem. U.S. Ho. of Reps. from N.J., 6th Congress, 1799-1801; apptd. master in chancery, 1826. Died Woodbury, N.J., July 27, 1832; buried Presbyn. Cemetery, North Woodbury, N.J.

DAVENPORT, George, army officer, trader; b. Lincolnshire, Eng., 1783. Moved to N.Y., 1804; sgt. U.S. Army, circa 1804-05, circa 1814-15; supply agt. for Col. William Morrison; established trading business, Rock Island, Ill., 1816; postmaster, Rock Island, 1825; with Am. Fur Co., 1826; served as col., acting q.m. during Black Hawk War; founder Davenport (Ia.), 1833; accompanied Sauk and Fox Indian chief delegation to Washington, D.C., assisted in negotiating 2d Black Hawk purchase, 1837. Murdered by robbers, July 4, 1845.

DAVENPORT, James, clergyman; b. Stamford, Conn., 1716; s. Rev. John and Elizabeth (Morris) D.; grad. Yale, 1732. Licensed to preach by Congregational Ch., 1735, ordained as minister church in Southold, L.I., N.Y., 1738; became itinerant preacher travelling through N.Y. and N.J.; conducted revivals in settlements between New Haven and Stonington, Conn., 1741, believed in impulses and impressions as guide to conduct; his influence caused members of First Congl. Ch. (New Haven) to break away and form North Ch.; brought to trial in Hartford for disturbing the peace (2 months after Conn. Gen. Assembly passed law against ministers preaching in parish without consent of pastor), 1742, judged mentally disturbed and sent back to Southold; returned to itinerant work again but judged insane by local authorities in Boston and sent home; censured, but not dismissed by Southold Council of Ministers; went to New London (Conn.) to organize church of his converts, 1743, to cure converts of their pride had them burn their fine clothes, ornaments and books of which he did not approve; dismissed by Southold Ch., 1743; became pastor in Hopewell, N.J. Author: Confession and Retractions (confessed his errors), 1744. Died Hopewell, Nov. 10, 1757; buried nr. Pennington, N.J.

DAVENPORT, James, congressman; b. Stamford, Conn., Oct. 12, 1758; s. Abraham Davenport; grad. Yale, 1777. Served in commissary dept. Continental Army during Revolutionary War; judge ct. of common pleas; mem. Conn. Ho. of Reps., 1785-90, Conn. Senate, 1790-97; judge Fairfield County Ct., 1792-96; mem. U.S. Ho. of Reps. (filled vacancy) from Conn., 4th-5th congresses, Dec. 5, 1796-Aug. 3, 1797. Died Stamford, Aug. 3, 1797; buried North Field (now Franklin Street) Cemetery.

DAVENPORT, John, clergyman; b. Coventry, Eng., 1597 (baptized Apr. 9, 1597); s. Henry and Winifred (Barnabit) D.; attended Merton Coll., Oxford (Eng.) U., B.D., Magdalen Coll., Oxford, 1625; m. Elizabeth Wolley, 1 son, John. Chaplain to Hilton family, Durham, Eng., 1615-16; curate Ch. of St. Lawrence Jewry, London, Eng., 1619-24; vicar St. Stephen's Parish, London, 1624 (opposition to his election because of possible Puritan leanings); spiritual adviser of a staunch Puritan, Lady Mary Vere; showed interest in procuring charter for Mass. Co., 1629, contributed 50 pounds and attended several meetings; involved in plot to form inner orgn. within Ch. of Eng. (plan foiled by higher authorities), escaped London and went to Holland, 1633, became involved in controversy in Holland; then he returned to Eng. to prepare for trip to Am., 1637; arrived at Boston in ship Hector; settled at site of New Haven (Conn.) to form own colony, 1638, chosen pastor new church there; harbored 2 refugees from Eng., 1661, but in letter claimed to have known nothing of their whereabouts; a signer of letter to Gen. Ct. of Conn. asking for delay in granting new charter to Conn. because New Haven wished to remain separate, 1662; pastor First Ch., Boston, 1667 (controversy over his leaving ended in scandal and eventual split in ch.). Author: (pamphlets) Instructions to Elders of the English Church, 1634; Catechism Containing the Chief Heads of Christian Religion, 1659; A Discourse about Civil Government in a New Plantation, 1673. Died Boston, Mar. 15, 1670; buried King's Chapel Burying Ground, Boston.

DAVENPORT, John, congressman; b. Stamford, Conn., Jan. 16, 1752; grad. Yale, 1770; studied law. Taught at Yale, 1773-74; admitted to bar, 1773, began practice of law, Stamford; mem. Conn. Ho. of Reps., 1776-96; served with commissary dept. Continental Army during Revolutionary War, commd. maj., 1777; mem. U.S. Ho. of Reps. (Federalist) from Conn., 6th-14th congresses, 1799-1817. Died Stamford, Nov. 28, 1830; buried North Field (now Franklin Street) Cemetery.

DAVENPORT, John, congressman; b. nr. Winchester, Jefferson County, Va., Jan. 9, 1788; attended common schs. Moved to Ohio, 1818, engaged in business; mem. Ohio Ho. of Reps., 1824, 27, 30, Ohio Senate, 1825-26; mem. U.S. Ho. of Reps. from Ohio, 20th Congress, 1827-29, supporter of John Quincy Adams; elected (by legislature) judge Monroe Jud. Circuit, twice. Died Woodsfield, Monroe County, O., July 18, 1855; buried Green Mount Cemetery, Barnesville, O.

DAVENPORT, Thomas, congressman; b. Cumberland County, Va.; studied law. Admitted to bar, began practice of law, Meadville, Va.; mem. U.S. Ho. of Reps. (Federalist) from Va., 19th-23d congresses, 1825-35. Died nr. Meadville, Nov. 18, 1838.

DAVENPORT, Thomas, inventor; b. Williamstown, Vt., July 9, 1802; s. Daniel and Hannah (Rice) D.; m. Emily Goss, Feb. 14, 1827. Built small circular ry. (1st electric ry. on record) ,1835; invented early model of electric train motor, 1836, patented, 1837, unable to improve and market because of financial difficulties; patented 2d model, 1837. Died Salisbury, Vt., July 6, 1851.

DAVENPORT, William Henry Harrison, illusionist; b. Buffalo, N.Y., Feb. 1, 1841; s. Ira and Virtue (Honeysett) D.; m. Adah Isaacs Mencken ("The Bengal Tiger Woman"), 1863. Gained reputation (with his brother) for being spirit caller and having other supernatural abilities; brought to N.Y.C., 1855, soon exposed as frauds; later perfected their technique and became successful, largely because of trick in which both brothers were tied hand and foot at opposite ends of a large box, doors were closed, various sounds occurred and "spirit hands" appeared; toured Europe, 1864-68, Am., 1868-74; started on world tour, 1874; aroused much controversy as to whether the brothers really had supernatural qualities. Died Australia, July 1, 1877.

D'AVEZAC, Auguste Genevieve Valentin, lawyer, diplomat; b. Santo Domingo, May 1780; s. Jean Pierre Valentin Joseph D'Avezac de Castera and Marie Rose Valentin de Maragon; ed. Mil. Coll. of La Fleche, France. Admitted to La. bar; became personal aide to Andrew Jackson, Battle of New Orleans, 1814; judge advocate New Orleans, 1815; sec. of legation The Hague, 1829; charge d'affaires The Netherlands, 1831-39, 45-50; spl. diplomatic agt. of the Two Sicilies, 1833; elected to N.Y. state Legislature, 1843. Died N.Y.C. Feb. 15, 1851.

DAVID, John Baptist Mary, clergyman; b. Couëron, Brittany, France, June 4, 1761; s. Jean and Jeanne (Aubrain) D.; M.A., Coll. of Nantes (France); attended Sulpician Theol. Sem., Issy, France. Ordained Sulpician priest, 1785; prof. theology and philosophy Sulpician Coll., Angers, France, 1785-90; went into hding from terrorists during French Revolution, 1790-92; came to Am., 1792; assigned to missions in Charles County, Md.; 1st Am. priest to institute spiritual retreats for benefit of laity; prof. philosophy Georgetown Coll., 1804-06; prof. St. Mary's Sem., 1806-10; founder, pres. St. Thomas Sem. (chartered as univ. 1823), Bardstown, Ky.; founder, spiritual dir. Sisters of Charity of Nazareth (Ky.); declined nomination as bishop of Phila.; coadjutor-bishop of Bardstown, 1817-32, bishop, 1832-33; rep. to 2d Provincial Council of Balt., 1833. Author: True Piety, 1814; Compilation of Church Music and Hymns, 1815; Catechism of Christian Doctrine, 1825; Spiritual Retreat for Eight Days, 1864. Died Bardstown, July 12, 1841.

DAVIDGE, John Beale, anatomist, surgeon; b. Annapolis, Md., 1768; s. capt. and Honor (Haward) D.; M.D., St. John's Coll., Annapolis, Md., 1793; m. Wilhelmina Stuart, 1793; m. 2d, Mrs. Rebecca Troup Polk. Asso. with many operations, among them shoulder joint amputation, 1792; wrote treatise on yellow fever, 1798; a founder Coll. Medicine of Md. (now U. Md.), 1813, prof. anatomy and surgery, 1813-29, univ. dean. Died Aug. 23, 1829.

DAVIDGE, William Pleater, actor; b. London, Eng., Apr. 17, 1814; m. Elizabeth Clark, Sept. 30, 1842, 3 children including William. Made debut at Nottingham (London) as Adam Winterton in The Iron Chest, 1836; played in Queens, Olympic, Victoria, and Drury Lane theatres; entertained on works of Charles Dickens, 1845, later met Dickens; came to U.S., 1850; made 1st appearance as Sir Peter Teazle at Old Broadway Theatre, N.Y.C.; travelled about country with several cos., 1850-55; played in various theatres, N.Y.C., 1860-68; with Augustin Daly's co., 1869-77; most noted for portrayal of Dick Deadeye in 1st Am. presentation of H.M.S. Pinafore; joined Madison Square Theatre Co., 1885; played some 1100 different roles in his career; an original member Am. Dramatic Fund Assn. Author: (play) The Family Party; (book) The Drama Defended. Died Cheyenne, Wyo., Aug. 17, 1888.

DAVIDS, James, see Dixwell, John.

DAVIDSON, Alexander Caldwell, congressman; b. nr. Charlotte, Mecklenburg County, N.C., Dec. 26, 1826; grad. U. Ala. at Tuscaloosa, 1848, studied law, Mobile, Ala. Became cotton planter, nr. Uniontown, Perry County, Ala.; mem. Ala. Ho. of Reps., 1880-81, Ala. Senate, 1882-85; mem. U.S. Ho. of Reps. (Democrat) from Ala., 49th-50th congresses, 1885-89. Died "Westwood," nr. Uniontown, Nov. 6, 1897; buried Holy Cross Cemetery of Davidson Meml. Ch., Uniontown.

DAVIDSON, John Wynn, army officer; b. Fairfax County, Va., Aug. 18, 1823; s. William Benjamin Davidson; grad. U.S. Mil. Acad. 1845; m. Miss McGunnegle. Served in battles which secured possession of So. Cal. during Mexican War, 1846; commd. capt., 1855; refused commn. in Confederate Army, 1861; commd. brig. gen. U.S. Volunteers, 1862; brevetted lt. col. and col. U.S. Army, 1862; commanded brigade Army of Potomac during Peninsular campaign, 1862; commanded St. Louis dist. Army of S.E. Mo., 1862; commanded

Army of Ark., 1863-64; chief of cavalry div. W. Miss., 1865; assisted in capture of Little Rock, Ark.; brevetted brig. gen., also maj. gen., 1865; served in Insp. Gen.'s Dept. of Mo., 1866; prof. mil. sci. and tactics Kan. Agrl. Coll., 1868-71; commd. col. 2d Cavalry, 1879. Died St. Paul, Minn., June 26, 1881.

DAVIDSON, Lucretia Maria, poet; b. Plattsburg, N.Y., Sept. 27, 1808; d. Oliver and Margaret (Miller) Davidson. Began writing poetry when 4 years old; attended Mrs. Willard's Sch. (Troy N.Y.) through patronage of James Kent; attended Miss Gilbert's Sch., Albany, N.Y., 1825; poems include "Epitaph on a Robin," "What the World Calls Pleasure." Author: Amir Khan and Other Poems, 1829. Died Plattsburg, Aug. 27, 1825.

DAVIDSON, Margaret Miller, poet; b. Plattsburg, N.Y., Mar. 26, 1823; d. Oliver and Margaret (Miller) Davidson. Began to write when 6 years old; wrote and acted in play Tragedy of Alethia when 10 years old, N.Y.C. Died Saratoga, N.Y., Nov. 25, 1838.

DAVIDSON, Robert, clergyman; b. Elkton, Md., 1750; grad. U. Pa., 1771; m. Margaret Montgomery; m. 2d, Jane Harris, Apr. 17, 1810, at least one son, Robert. Ordained by 2d Presbytery of Phila., 1773; taught history, U. Pa., also asst. First Presbyn. Ch., Phila., 1773-84; pastor Presbyn. Ch., Carlisle, Pa., 1784-1812; v.p. Dickinson Coll., Carlisle, 1784-1804, pres., 1804-09; moderator Gen. Assembly of Presbyn. Ch., Carlisle, 1796. Author: Geography Epitomized, 1784; The Christian's A.B.C. . . ., 1809; New Version of the Psalms, 1812. Died Dec. 13, 1812.

DAVIDSON, Robert, clergyman, univ. pres.; b. Carlisle, Pa., Feb. 23, 1808; son of Dr. Robert Davidson; grad. Dickinson Coll., 1828, Princeton Theol. Sem., 1831. Pastor, 2d Presbyn. Ch., Lexington, Ky., 1832-40; pres. Transylvania U., 1940-42; pastor 1st Presbyn. Ch., New Brunswick, N.J., 1843-59, Spring Street Ch., N.Y.C., 1864-68; mem. Bd. Fgn. Missions of Presbyn. Ch., 25 years; dir. Princeton Theol. Sem., 1867-76. Died Phila., Apr. 6, 1876.

DAVIDSON, Thomas Green, congressman; b. Coles Creek, Jefferson County, Miss., Aug. 3, 1805; studied law. Admitted to bar, began practice of law, Greensburg, La.; apptd. register U.S. Land Office; mem. La. Ho. of Reps., 1833-46, 74-78, 80, 83; mem. U.S. Ho. of Reps. (Democrat) from La., 34th-36th congresses, 1855-61; pres. La. Dem. Conv., 1855. Died Springfield, La., Sept. 11, 1883; buried Springfield Cemetery.

DAVIDSON, William, congressman; b. Charleston, S.C., Sept. 12, 1778. Moved (with parents) to Mecklenburg County, N.C; became a planter; mem. N.C. Senate, 1813, 15-19, 25, 27-30; moved to Charlotte, 1820; mem. U.S. Ho. of Reps. (Federalist, filled vacancy) from N.C., 15th-16th congresses, Dec. 2, 1818-21. Died Charlotte, Sept. 16, 1857; buried Old Cemetery.

DAVIDSON, William Lee, army officer; b. Lancaster, Pa., 1746; s. George Davidson; m. Mary Brevard. Commd. maj. 4th N.C. Regt., 1776; joined Washington's Army in N.J., 1776, participated in battles of Brandywine, Germantown, and Monmouth; commd lt. col., 1777; brig. gen. in command Salisbury (N.C.) dist., 1780; detached by Gen. Greene to interrupt passage of Cornwallis across Catawba, 1781. Killed in action at Cowan's Ford, Mecklenburg County, N.C., Feb. 1, 1781.

DAVIE, William Richardson, officer, gov. N.C.; b. Egremont, Cumberlandshire, Eng., June 20, 1756; s. Archibald Davie; grad. with 1st honors Princeton, 1776; m. Sarah Jones, 1782, 6 children. Helped raise cavalry troop, nr. Salisbury, N.C., 1777-78, commd. lt., then capt., maj.; licensed to practice law, 1780; commissary gen. under Gen. Nathanael Greene in Carolina campaign, 1780; apptd. commissary gen. N.C. Bd. of War, 1781; lawyer, riding N.C. circuits, 1782; mem. N.C. Legislature, 1786-98; gov. N.C., 1793-99; a founder U. N.C.; influential in obtaining state laws, in sending reps. to Annapolis and Phila. constl. convs., also in ceding Tenn. to Union and fixing of state boundaries; commanded N.C. troops, 1797; chmn. boundary commns., 1798; brig. gen. in undeclared naval war with France, 1798-99; peace commr. to France, 1799; under presdl. appointment negotiated Tuscarora treaty, 1802; 1st pres. S.C. Agrl. Soc. Died nr. Waxhaw Church, S.C., Nov. 29, 1820.

DAVIES, Charles, educator; b. Washington, Litchfield County, Conn., Jan. 22, 1798; son of Thomas John Davies; grad. U.S. Mil. Acad., 1815; LL.D. (hon.), Geneva (N.Y.) Coll., 1849; m. Mary Ann Mansfield. Brevetted 2d lt. U.S. Army, 1815, assigned to Engr. Corps., 1816, resigned soon after; prof. mathematics, natural and exptl. philosophy U.S. Mil. Acad., 1816-37; toured Europe, 1836-37; prof. mathematics Trinity Coll., 1837-41; paymaster with rank of maj. West Point, 1841-46; prof. mathematics, philosophy U. City N.Y., 1848-49; prof. higher mathematics Columbia, 1857-65, emeritus prof. mathematics, 1865-76. Died Fishkill-on-Hudson, N.Y., Sept. 17, 1876.

DAVIES, Charles Frederick, army officer; b. N.Y., June 27, 1838; son of Judge Henry E. Davies. Employed by Australian Shipping House, 1858-61; became lt. 5th N.Y. Volunteers, 1861; apptd. maj., paymaster U.S. Volunteers, 1861-65; his task was to distribute pay to volunteers at close of Civil War. Died from exposure in field and exhaustion, Fishkill-on-Hudson, N.Y., Dec. 3, 1865.

DAVIES, Edward, congressman; b. Churchtown, Lancaster County, Pa., Nov. 1779; attended rural schs. Engaged in farming and business pursuits; mem. Pa. Ho. of Reps., 1834-35; mem. U.S. Ho. of Reps. (Whig) from Pa., 25th-26th congresses, 1837-41. Died Churchtown, May 18, 1853; buried cemetery, Pottstown, Pa.

DAVIES, Henry Eugene, army officer; b. N.Y.C., July 2, 1836; s. Henry Ebenezer and Rebecca (Tappan) D.; grad. Columbia Law Sch., 1857; m. Julia Rich, Aug. 10, 1858. Admitted to N.Y. bar, 1858; commd. capt., then maj. 5th N.Y. Inf., U.S. Army, 1861, lt. col., 1862, col., 1863; brig. gen. U.S. Volunteers, 1863, maj. gen., 1865, resigned, 1866; pub. adminstr. N.Y.C., 1866-69; asst. dist. atty. So. dist. N.Y., 1870-72. Author: Ten Days on the Plains, 1871; General Sheridan, published posthumously, 1895. Died Middleboro, Mass., Sept. 6, 1894.

DAVIES, Samuel, clergyman, coll. pres.; b. New Castle County, Del., Nov. 3, 1723; s. David and Martha (Thomas) D.; m. Sarah Kirkpatrick, Oct. 23, 1746; m. 2d, Jean Holt, Oct. 4, 1748. Licensed to preach by Presbytery of New Castle (Del.), 1746; ordained evangelist, 1747; went to Eng. to raise funds for proposed Coll. of N.J., 1753; pres. Coll. of N.J. (now Princeton), 1759-61; a founder 1st Presbytery of Hanover (1st in Va.), 1755. Died Princeton, N.J., Feb. 4, 1761.

DAVIS, Alexander Jackson, architect; b. N.Y.C., July 24, 1803; s. Cornelius and Julia (Jackson) D.; m. Margaret Beale, July 14, 1853. With firm Town & Davis, 1829-43; self employed as architect, 1843-80; architect: New York Customs House, 1832; Ind. (1832-35), N.C. (1831), Ill. (1837), Ohio (1839) state capitols; U.S. Patent Office, Washington, D.C., 1832; Va. Mil. Inst., 1852, 59; Assembly Hall, U. N.C., Alumni Hall, Yale; Gilmer House in Balt. (1832) and U. Mich. (1838) are advanced Gothic designs for that period; a founder Llewellyn Park, West Orange, N.J.; exponent of classic and gothic styles; an early experimenter with structural iron. Died West Orange, Jan. 14, 1892.

DAVIS, Alexander Mathews, congressman; b. Old Mt. Airy, Wythe County Va., Jan. 17, 1833; grad. Emory and Henry Coll., Emory, Va.; studied law. Admitted to bar, 1854, began practice of law, Wytheville, Va.; moved to Independence, Va.; served from capt. to lt. col. Co. C., 45th Va. Inf., Confederate Army, during Civil War; captured nr. close of war, held prisoner on Johnson's Island, Lake Erie; mem. Va. Senate, 1869-71; mem. U.S. Ho. of Reps. from Va. 43d Congress, 1873-Mar. 5, 1874 (succeeded by Christopher Y. Thomas who contested election). Died Independence, Sept. 25, 1889; buried Davis family burial ground.

DAVIS, Amos, congressman; b. Mt. Sterling, Ky., Aug. 15, 1794; studied law. Admitted to bar, began practice of law, Mt. Sterling; sheriff Montgomery County (Ky.); mem. Ky. Ho. of Reps., 1819, 25, 27-28; mem. U.S. Ho. of Reps. (Whig) from Ky., 23d Congress, 1833-35. Died while campaigning for reelection, Owingsville, Ky., June 11, 1835; buried City Cemetery, Mt. Sterling.

DAVIS, Charles Henry, naval officer; b. Boston, Jan. 16, 1807; s. Daniel and Lois (Freeman) D.; m. Harriet Mills, 1842, 6 children including Charles Henry, Anna Cabot, Evelyn. Commd. midshipman U.S. Navy, 1824, lt., 1827, comdr., 1854; served as chief of staff, capt. of fleet in expdn. under Dupont which captured Port Royal, S.C., 1861; exec. head Bur. of Detail for selecting, assigning officers during Civil War; assumed command Upper Mississippi Gunboat Flotilla above Ft. Pillow, 1862; commd. chief Bur. of Navigation, 1862; commd. rear adm., 1863; a founder Nat. Acad. Scis., 1863; supt. Naval Observatory, 1864-66, 70-73; commanded Brazilian Squadron, 1867-69, Norfolk (Va.) Navy Yard, 1870-73. Author: The Coast Survey of the United States, 1849; Narrative of the North Pole Expedition of the U.S.S. Polaris, 1876. Died Washington, D.C., Feb. 18, 1877.

DAVIS, Charles Wellington, architect; b. Newburyport, Mass., Mar. 24, 1826. Came to Cal. during Gold Rush; settled in San Francisco, practiced as architect; credited with design of numerous early public and bus. bldgs. in San Francisco, including Jewish Synagogue, Ch. of Rev. Thomas Starr King, Robert Wait Block; moved to Santa Cruz, Cal., circa 1870; established archtl. office, Los Angeles, 1874 Died Apr. 13, 1897.

DAVIS, Daniel Franklin, gov. Me.; b. Freedom Me., Sept. 12, 1843; s. Rev. Moses Franklin and Mary (French) D.; studied law under Lewis Barker Me., 1867-68; m. Laura Goodwin, Jan. 1, 1867, children. Served with Me. Inf., 1863-65; admitted to Me. bar, 1868; became mem. Me. Ho. of Reps. 1874, Me. Senate, 1878; gov. Me., 1879-80; partner (with Charles A. Baily) in law firm, Bangor, Me. 1881-97. Died Jan. 9, 1897.

DAVIS, David, justice U.S. Supreme Ct.; b. Cecil County, Ind., Mar. 9, 1815; s. Dr. David Davis; grad. Kenyon Coll., 1832, Yale Law Sch. 1835; LL.D. (hon.), Beloit (Wis.) Coll., 1863, Ill Wesleyan U., 1865, Williams Coll., 1873, St. John Coll., 1874; m. Sarah Woodruff, Oct. 30, 1838; m 2d, Adeline Burr, 1883; 2 children. Admitted to Ill bar, 1835; elected to Ill. Legislature, 1844; mem Ill. Constl. Conv., 1847; presiding judge 8th Jud Circuit Ill., 1848-68; sent by Ill. Republican Conv as Chgo. del.-at-large to Nat. Conv., where hi leadership was responsible for Abraham Lincoln' nomination, 1860; apptd. by Pres. Lincoln to in vestigate claims in Western Dept. U.S. (of which Fremont had been head), 1861; asso. justice U.S Supreme Ct., 1862-77; nominated for U.S. Pres. by Labor Reform Conv., 1872, but defeated in Liberal Republican Conv.; mem. U.S. Senate from Ill., 1877-83, pres. pro tem, 1881-83. Died Bloomington, Ill., June 26, 1886.

DAVIS, Edmund Jackson, gov. Tex.; b. St. Augustine, Fla., Oct. 2, 1827; m. Ann Britton 1858. Dep. collector of customs on the Rio Grande under the Filmore adminstrn., 1850-52; dist. atty. Rio Grande Valley Dist., 1853-55; judge Dist. Ct of Austin, Tex., 1855-61; commd brig. gen. U.S. Army after Battle of Mansfield, 1861; del. Tex. Constl. Conv., 1866; pres. Tex. Reconstrn. Conv., 1868-69; gov. Tex., 1869-74. Died Austin, Feb. 7, 1883.

DAVIS, Edwin Hamilton, physician, archeologist; b. Hillsboro, O., Jan. 22, 1811; s. Henry and Avis (Slocum) D.; grad. Kenyon Coll., 1833, Cincinnati Med. Coll., 1838; m. Lucy Woodbridge, 1841, 9 children including John Woodbridge. Prof. materia medica and therapeutics N.Y. Med. Coll., 1850-60; surveyed and described (in collaboration with E.G. Squire) 100 of the more important earthworks of the Mound Builders, So. Ohio; compiled findings in the Ancient Monuments of the Mississippi Valley (1st work published by Smithsonian Instn.; continues to be a standard on the subject); noted for his collections of cultural objects of the Mound Builders. Died N.Y.C., May 15, 1888.

DAVIS, Emerson, clergyman; b. Ware, Mass., July 15, 1798; grad. Williams Coll., 1821; D.D. (hon.), Harvard, 1847. Tchr., Westfield (Mass.) Acad., 1821-22, 24-36; tutor Williams Coll., 1822-33, acting pres., 1861-66; pastor 1st Congregational Ch., Westfield, 1836-66. Author: History of Westfield, 1826; The Teacher Taught, 1839; The Half Century, 1852. Died Westfield, June 8, 1866.

DAVIS, Garret, senator; b. Mt. Sterling, Ky., Sept. 10, 1801; s. Jeremiah Davis; m. Miss Trimble, 1825; m. 2d, Mrs. Elliot, 1846. Admitted to Ky. bar, 1823; mem. Ky. Legislature, 1833-35; mem. U.S. Ho. of Reps. from Ky. 26th-29th congresses, 1839-47; mem. Ky. Constl. Conv. of 1849; mem. U.S. Senate from Ky., 1861-72; regent Smithsonian Instn., 1864; dedicated Unionist, opponent of war party and radical reconstructionists. Died Paris, Ky., Sept. 22, 1872.

DAVIS, George, confederate govt. ofcl.; b. Porter's Neck, N.C., Mar. 1, 1820; s. Thomas and Sarah (Eagles) D.; grad. U. N.C., 1838; m. Mary A. Polk, Nov. 17, 1842; m. 2d, Monimia Fairfax, May 9, 1866. Admitted to Wilmington (N.C.) bar, 1840; del. Washington (D.C.) Peace Conf., 1861; mem. Confederate Senate from N.C., 1862-64; atty. gen., Confederate States Am., 1864-65. Author: Address Before the Literary Societies of the University of North Carolina on the Early History of the Cape Fear Section, 1855; A Study in Colonial History, 1879. Died Wilmington, Feb. 23, 1896.

DAVIS, George Thomas, congressman; b. Sandwich, Mass., Jan. 12, 1810; grad. Harvard, 1829; studied law, Cambridge and Greenfield, Mass. Admitted to bar, 1832 began practice of law, Greenfield; established Franklin Mercury, 1833; mem. Mass. Senate, 1839-40; mem. U.S. Ho. of Reps. (Whig) from Mass., 32d Congress, 1851-53; mem. Mass. Ho. of Reps., 1861. Died Portland, Me., June 17, 1877; buried Green River Cemetery, Greenfield.

DAVIS, Henry, clergyman, coll. pres.; b. East Hampton, L.I., N.Y., Sept. 15, 1771; s. John and Mary (Conkling) D.; grad. Yale, 1796; M.A. (hon.), Williams Coll., 1799; D.D. (hon.), Union Coll., 1810; m. Hannah Treadwell, Sept. 22, 1801, 4 children, including Thomas Treadwell Davis. Tutor Williams Coll., 1796-98; tutor Yale, 1798-1803, prof. divinity, 1801; prof. Greek, Union Coll., 1806;

pres. Middlebury Coll., 1809-17, Hamilton Coll., 1817-33; major influence in establishment Auburn Theol. Sem., trustee, 1820-34, pres. bd. trustees, 1820-24. Author: Narrative of the Embarrassments and Decline of Hamilton College, 1833. Died Clinton, N.Y., Mar. 8, 1852.

DAVIS, Henry Gassett, surgeon; b. Trenton, Me., Nov. 4, 1807; s. Isaac and Polly (Rice) D.; M.D., Yale, 1839; m. Ellen W. Deering, 1856; 3 children. Practiced in Worcester, Mass., also Milbury, Mass., 1838-54; went to N.Y.C., 1855; founder traction sch. of orthopedic surgery; his theories concerning the nature and treatment of club foot, congenital dislocation of the hip, chronic diseases of the joints and poliomyelitis form the basis for the modern approach to these problems; unique treatment of abscesses anticipated the Cassel-Dahin therapy; 1st to devise a splint for traction and the protection of the hip joint. Author: Conservative Surgery, as Exhibited in Remedying some of the Mechanical Causes that Operate Injuriously both in Health and Diseases, 1867 (1st significant textbook in history of Am. orthopedic surgery). Died Everett, Mass., Nov. 18, 1896.

DAVIS, Henry Winter, congressman; b. Annapolis, Md., Aug. 16, 1817; s. Rev. Henry Lyon and Jane (Brown) D.; grad. Kenyon Coll., 1837; m. Constance Gardiner, Oct. 30, 1845; m. 2d, Nancy Morris, Jan. 26, 1857. Whig; mem. U.S. Ho. of Reps. (Know-Nothing Party) from Md., 34th-36th, 38th congresses, 1855-61, 63-65, chmn. com. on fgn. relations, 1863; organized and supported Bell and Everett (Union) Party in Md. in opposition to Md. adminstrn. which recognized right of secession, 1860; radical opponent of Lincoln's plan of reconstrn., attempted to substitute his own program known as congressional plan, which received vest pocket veto from Lincoln; virtual ruler (with Thaddeus Stevens) of Ho. of Rps.; leadership of radical Republicans assured by issuance of Wade-Davis Manifesto, 1864; opposed Johnson's plan of reconstrn., succeeded in pushing through his own congressional program, 1865. Died Balt., Dec. 30, 1865.

DAVIS, Jacob Cunningham, congressman; b. nr. Staunton, Va. Sept. 16, 1820; attended Coll. William and Mary; studied law. Moved to Warsaw, Hancock County, Ill., 1838; admitted to bar, began practice of law, Warsaw; clk. Hancock County; apptd. circuit clk., 1841; mem. Ill. Senate, 1842-48, 50-56; mem. U.S. Ho. of Reps. (Democrat, filled vacancy), 34th Congress, Nov. 4, 1856-57; resumed practice of law, Clark County, Mo. Died Alexandria, Mo., Dec. 25, 1883; buried Mitchell Cemetery, nr. Alexandria.

DAVIS, Jefferson, pres. Confederate States Am.; b. Christian (now Todd) County, Ky., June 3, 1808; s. Samuel and Jane (Cook) D.; entered Transylvania U., 1821 (did not graduate); grad. U.S. Mil. Acad., 1828; m. Sarah Taylor (dau. Zachary Taylor), July 1835; m. 2d, Varina Howell, Feb. 26, 1845. Commd. 2d lt. U.S. Army, 1828; served on frontier, 1828-35, resigned commn., 1835; Miss. planter, 1835-45; mem. U.S. Ho. of Reps. from Miss., 29th Congress, 1845-46; resigned to participate in Mexican War, 1846, led advance regt. in attack on Monterey, resigned, 1846; mem. U.S. Senate from Miss., 1847-51; U.S. sec. of war under Pres. Franklin Pierce, 1853-57; mem. U.S. Senate, 1857-61, announced to Senate the secession of Miss. and his senatorial resignation, Jan. 21, 1861; commd. maj. gen. Miss. Militia, 1861; inaugurated pres. Confederate States Am. by Provisional Congress, Feb. 18, 1861; elected by popular vote, inaugurated, Richmond, Va., Feb. 22, 1862; policies promoted opposition and conflict between states' rights advocates and himself; suspected of planning emancipation of slaves; determined to demand independence for Confederacy following Battle of Gettysburg; fled from Richmond, Apr. 3, 1865; captured, Irwinville, Ga., May 10, 1865; imprisoned at Fortress Monroe, Va., 1865-67; indicted for treason, released on bond, May 14, 1867; last years of life spent in retirement and relative poverty at home provided by a bequest. Author: The Rise and Fall of the Confederate Government, 2 vols., 1878-81. Home: "Beauvoir," Biloxi, Miss. Died New Orleans, Dec. 6, 1889; buried Hollywood Cemetery, Richmond.

DAVIS, Jefferson Columbus, army officer; b. Clark County, Ind., Mar. 2, 1828; s. William and Mary (Drummond) D.; m. Mariette Woodson Achon. Mem. 3d Ind. Regt. during Mexican War; brevetted 2d lt. 1st Arty., U.S. Army for gallantry at Battle of Buena Vista, 1848; commd. 1st lt., 1852; stationed Ft. Sumter at time of bombardment, 1861; commd. capt. 1st Arty., 1861; col. 22d Ind. Infantry Volunteers, 1861; brig. gen., 1861; commanded division at Battle of Pea Ridge and siege of Corinth; murdered Gen. William Nelson after quarrel in hotel lobby, Louisville, Tenn., 1862; returned to duty unpunished (because of his mil. service and polit. influence of Gov. Oliver P. Morton); commanded at Murfreesboro, Chickamauga, Sherman's march to sea and Carolinas' campaign; discharged from volunteer service, 1866; col. 23d Inf., U.S. Army, 1866; fought in Modoc War, Oregon, 1873. Died Chgo., Nov. 30, 1879.

DAVIS, John, jurist; b. Plymouth, Mass., Jan. 25, 1761; s. Thomas and Mercy (Hedge) D.; grad. Harvard, 1781, A.M. (hon.), 1801; m. Ellen Watson, 1786. Admitted to Mass. bar, 1786; del. from Plymouth to Mass. Conv. which ratified U.S. Constn. 1788; mem. Mass. Ho. of Reps., 3 times; mem. Mass. Senate from Plymouth County, 1795; comptroller U.S. Treasury, 1795; U.S. atty. for Dist. of Mass., 1796-1801, U.S. judge, 1801-41; fellow Am. Acad. Arts and Scis.; fellow Harvard, 1803, treas., 1810, mem. bd. overseers, 1827. Died Boston, Jan. 14, 1847.

DAVIS, John, theatrical mgr.; b. Santo Domingo, circa 1780. Arrived New Orleans, circa 1811; built and operated 1st Théâtre d'Orléans, 1813-17 (the atre burned down); opened 2d Théâtre d'Orléans, reported to be "grandest" opera house in Am., 1819, eventually added restaurant, gambling house, and dancing hall (where Orleans Quadroon Balls were given), imported Parisian operas, ballets and comedies for presentation at his theatre (Théâtre d'Orléans used as temporary quarters when old State House of New Orleans burned); through his efforts New Orleans became 1st Am. city to present annual opera season. Died circa 1838.

DAVIS, John, senator, gov. Mass.; b. Northboro, Mass., Jan. 13, 1787; s. Isaac and Anna (Brigham) D.; grad. Yale, 1812; m. Eliza Bancroft, Mar. 29, 1822, 1 son, John Chandler Bancroft. Admitted to Mass. bar, 1815; mem. Mass. Ho. of Reps., 1824-34; gov. Mass., 1834-35, 41-43; mem. U.S. Senate from Mass., Dec. 7, 1835-41, 45-53; pres. Am. Antiquarian Soc. Died Worcester, Mass., Apr. 19, 1854.

DAVIS, John, congressman; b. Bucks County, Pa., Aug. 7, 1788; attended common schs. Lived in Md., 1795-1812; settled in what is now Davisville, Pa., 1812, engaged in farming and business pursuits; served from capt. to maj. gen. of militia in War of 1812; mem. U.S. Ho. of Reps. (Democrat) from Pa. 26th Congress, 1839-41; surveyor Port of Phila. (apptd. by Pres. Polk), 1845-49; del. to several Pa. and nat. Dem. convs. Died Davisville, Apr. 1, 1878; buried Davisville Baptist Ch.

DAVIS, John A. G., jurist; b. Middlesex County, Va., 1801; attended Coll. William and Mary. Edited a weekly journal, Charlottesville, Va.; practiced law, Albemarle County, Va.; prof. law U. Va., 1830-40, chmn. faculty, 1839-40. Author: Estates Tail, Executory Devices and Contingent Remainders under the Virginia Statutes Modifying the Common Law; Treatise on Criminal Law. Killed by a student whom he was trying to arrest, Nov. 14, 1840.

DAVIS, John Givan, congressman; b. nr. Flemingsburg, Ky., Oct. 10, 1810; attended country schs., Ind. Engaged in farming; sheriff Parke County (Ind.), 1830-33; clk. county ct., 1833-50; mem. U.S. Ho. of Reps. (Democrat) from Ind., 32d-33d congresses, 1851-55, (Anti-Lecompton Democrat) 35th-36th congresses, 1857-61; engaged in bus. activities and meat packing, Montezuma, Ind.; moved to Terre Haute, Ind., became dry goods mcht. Died Terre Haute, Jan. 18, 1866; buried Highland Lawn Cemetery.

DAVIS, John Lee, naval officer; b. Carlisle, Ind., Sept. 3, 1825; s. John Wesley and Ann (Hoover) D.; m. Frances Robinson, Dec. 12, 1855, 1 dau. Commd. midshipman U.S. Navy, 1841, lt. comdr., 1862; commanded gun boat Wissahickon in sinking of Confederate ship Georgiana, Charleston Harbor, 1863; lt. comdr. in monitor Montauk, engaged in battles at fts. Sumter, Gregg, Moultrie, Battery Bee, 1863; commd. comdr., 1866, capt., 1873, commodore, 1882, rear adm., 1885; commanded flagship of European Squadron, 1877-78; commanded Asiatic Squadron, 1883-86; ret., 1887. Died Washington, D.C., Mar. 12, 1889; buried Rock Creek Cemetery, Washington.

DAVIS, John Wesley, congressman, territorial gov.; b. New Holland, Lancaster County, Pa., Apr. 16, 1799; s. Rev. John Davis; M.D., Balt. Med. Coll., 1821; m. Ann Hoover, 1823, children include John Lee. Moved to Ind., 1823; Sgt. at arms Ind. Senate, 1827; probate judge Sullivan County (Ind.), 1829-31; mem. Ind. Ho. of Reps., 1831-33, 41-43, 51-52, 57; speaker 1831, 41; mem. U.S. Ho. of Reps. from Ind. (Democrat), 24th, 26th, 28th-29th congresses, 1835-37, 39-41, 43-47, speaker, 1845-47; commr. China, 1848-50; gov. Ore. Territory, 1853-55. Died Carlisle, Ind., Aug. 22, 1859.

DAVIS, Joseph Jonathan, congressman; b. nr. Louisburg, Franklin County, N.C., Apr. 13, 1828; attended Louisburg Acad., Wake Forest (N.C.) Coll., Coll. William and Mary; grad. law dept. U. N.C. at Chapel Hill 1850. Admitted to bar, 1850, began practice of law, Oxford, N.C., later in Louisburg; served as capt. Co. G., 47th Regt., Confederate Army, during Civil War; mem. N.C. Ho. of Reps., 1868-70; mem. U.S. Ho. of Reps. (Democrat) from N.C., 44th-46th congresses, 1875-81; apptd. justice N.C. Supreme Ct., 1887. Died Louisburg, Aug. 7, 1892; buried Oaklawn Cemetery.

DAVIS, Joseph Robert, army officer; b. Woodville, Miss., Jan. 12, 1825; s. Isaac and Susan (Garthy) D.; grad. Miami U., Oxford O.; m. Miss Peyton, 1848; m. 2d, Margaret Green, 1879; 3 children including Jefferson. Mem. Miss. Senate, 1860-61; commd. lt. col. 10th Miss. Regt., Confederate Army, 1861; commanded a brigade of Miss. troops Army of No. Va., 1862; commd. brig. gen. Confederate Army, 1862; served in battles of Cold Harbor, Gettysburg and Wilderness. Died Sept. 15, 1896.

DAVIS, Matthew Livingston, journalist; b. Manhattanville, N.Y., Oct. 28, 1773; s. Matthew and Phoebe (Wells) D.; at least 1 son. Editor, Evening Post, 1794; edited (with Philip Freneau) Time Peace and Literary Companion, 1797-98; recommended for naval officer Port of N.Y.C. by Aaron Burr, appointment refused by Pres. Jefferson; present at Burr-Hamilton duel, Weehawken, N.Y., 1804; went to jail rather than give testimony against Burr; mem. Davis & Strong trading firm before War of 1812; grand sachem of Tammany Soc., 1814-15; indicted for swindling, convicted, later aquitted at another trial; inherited Burr's papers and published Memoirs of Aaron Burr, 1836-37; The Private Journal of Aaron Burr During his Residence of Four Years in Europe, 1838; Washington (D.C.) correspondent for London Times and Morning Courier and New York Enquirer. Died Manhattanville, June 21, 1850; buried Trinity Cemetery, Manhattanville.

DAVIS, Paulina Kellogg Wright, editor, suffragist; b. Bloomfield, N.Y., Aug. 7, 1813; d. Capt. Ebenezer and Polly (Saxton) Kellogg; m. Francis Wright, 1833; m. 2d, Thomas Davis, 1849. Lectured to women's groups on anatomy and physiology, 1844; imported 1st known "femme modéle" from Paris to America; established Una, (1st distinctively woman's suffrage paper published in U.S.), 1853-56; visited Europe, 1859; organized meeting of Nat. Women Suffrage Movement, N.Y., 1870; visited Europe, studied art under Carl Marko of Florence, Italy, 1871-74. Author: A History of the National Women's Rights Movement, 1871. Died Providence, R.I., Aug. 24, 1876.

DAVIS, Phineas, inventor; b. Grafton County, N.H., 1800; s. Nathan and Mary Davis; m. Hannah Taylor, Nov. 15, 1826. Watchmaker, York, Pa., 1815-21; partner (with Israel Gardner) in iron foundry and machine-shop, 1821-32; built iron-clad steamboat Codorus, launched from York on Susquehanna River, 1825; won B.& O. R.R. competition with York locomotive, 1831; supt. B.& O. R.R. mech. shops, 1832-35. Crushed to death when train jumped track while on trial run between Balt. and Washington (D.C.), Sept. 27, 1835.

DAVIS, Reuben, congressman, army officer; b. Winchester, Tenn., Jan. 18, 1813; s. Rev. John Davis; m. Mary Halbert. Dist. atty. 6th Miss. Jud. Dist., 1835-39; judge Miss. High Ct. Appeals, 1842; served as col. 2d Miss. Volunteers in Mexican War; mem. Miss Legislature, 1855-57; mem. U.S. Ho. of Reps. (Democrat) from Miss., 35th-36th congresses, 1857-61; maj. gen. Miss. Militia, 1861; mem. Confederate Congress, 1861-64. Author: Recollections of Mississippi and Mississippians, 1889. Died Huntsville, Ala., Oct. 14, 1890.

DAVIS, Richard Bingham, editor; b. N.Y.C., Aug. 21, 1771; attended Columbia, 1785-88. Engaged in wood carver's trade, 1788-96; editor Diary, daily newspaper, N.Y.C., 1796-97; engaged in merc. bus., N.Y., 1797-99; wrote poetry (collected and published 1807). Died of yellow fever, Branswick, N.J., autumn 1799.

DAVIS, Richard David, congressman; b. Stillwater, Saratoga County, N.Y., 1799; grad. Yale, 1818; studied law. Admitted to bar, 1821, began practice of law, Poughkeepsie, N.Y.; mem. U.S. Ho. of Reps. (Democrat) from N.Y., 27th-28th congresses, 1841-45; later became farmer, Waterford, N.Y. Died Waterford, June 17, 1871; buried Waterford Rural Cemetery.

DAVIS, Roger, physician, congressman; b. Charlestown Village, Pa., Oct. 2, 1762; studied medicine U. Pa. Started practice of medicine, Charlestown, Pa., circa 1785; mem. Pa. Ho. of Reps., 1809-11; mem. U.S. Ho. of Reps. (Democrat) from Pa., 12th-13th congresses, 1811-15. Died Charlestown, Nov. 20, 1815; buried Great Valley Presbyn. Churchyard.

DAVIS, Sam, army scout; b. nr. Smyrna, Tenn., 1842. Joined Confederate Army, circa 1861; sent as scout into Union territory by Gen. Bragg to secure mil. information; captured by Union forces while returning, Giles County, Nov. 19, 1863; brought before Maj. Gen. Dodge of U.S. Army to explain how he received the information; sentenced to be hanged; uttered famous last words from scaffold: "If I had a thousand lives I would lose them all before I would betray my friends or the confidence of my informer." Hanged Nov. 27, 1863.

DAVIS Samuel, mcht., congressman; b. Bath, Mass. (now Me.), 1774. Engaged in business activities; became shipowner, 1801; mem. Mass. Ho. of Reps., 1803, 08-12, 15-16; bd. overseers Bowdoin Coll., 1813-18; became pres. Lincoln Bank, Bath, 1813; mem. U.S. Ho. of Reps. (Federalist) from Mass., 1813-15; mcht. in African and West Indian trade. Died Bath, Apr. 20, 1831; buried Maple Grove Cemetery.

DAVIS, Theodore Russell, illustrator; b. Boston, 1840. Exhibited crayon drawing entitled Washington at Am. Inst., 1856; joined staff of Harper's mag., 1861, illustrator and artist-corr., until 1884; wounded twice during Civil War; traveled for Harper's throughout South and mining dists. of Far West; best known for illustrations of Western life; ret., 1884. Died Asbury Park, N.J., Nov. 10, 1894.

DAVIS, Thomas, congressman, mfr.; b. Dublin, Ireland, Dec. 18, 1806; attended pvt. schs. Came to U.S., settled in Providence, R.I., 1817; became jewelry mfr.; mem. R.I. Senate, 1845-53, 77-78; mem. U.S. Ho. of Reps. (Democrat) from R.I., 33d Congress, 1853-55; mem. R.I. Ho. of Reps., 1887-90; mem. sch. com. Providence. Died Providence, July 26, 1895; buried Swan Point Cemetery.

DAVIS, Thomas Terry, congressman; studied law. Admitted to bar, 1789, began practice of law, Mercer County, Ky.; dep. atty. for Commonwealth; 1st pros. atty. of his dist.; mem. Ky. Ho. of Reps., 1795-97; mem. U.S. Ho. of Reps. from Ky., 5th-7th congresses, 1797-1803; apptd. U.S. judge Indiana Territory, 1803; chancellor Ind. Territory, 1806-07. Died Jeffersonville, Clark County, Ind., Nov. 15, 1807.

DAVIS, Thomas Treadwell, congressman; b. Middlebury, Vt., Aug. 22, 1810; attended Clinton (N.Y.) Acad.; grad. Hamilton Coll., Clinton, 1831; studied law. Moved to Syracuse, N.Y., 1831; admitted to bar, 1833, began practice of law, Syracuse; engaged in railroad and coal mining enterprises; mem. U.S. Ho. of Reps. (Unionist) from N.Y., 38th-39th congresses 1863-67. Died Washington, D.C., May 2, 1872; cremated, ashes deposited Oakwood Cemetery.

DAVIS, Timothy, congressman; b. Newark, N.J., Mar. 29, 1794; attended public schs., studied law. Admitted to bar, began practice of law, Ky.; moved to Mo., then to Dubuque, Ia., 1837; mem. U.S. Ho. of Reps. (Whig) from Ia., 35th Congress, 1857-59; engaged in various merc. activities, Dubuque, also Elkader, Ia., Galesville, Wis., Pickwick, Minn. Died Elkader, Ia., Apr. 27, 1872; buried Elkader Cemetery.

DAVIS, Timothy congressman; b. Gloucester, Mass., Apr. 12, 1821; attended public schs. Employed in printing office, 2 years; engaged in business pursuits, Boston; mem. Mass. Ho. of Reps., 1870-71; mem. U.S. Ho. of Reps. from Mass., 34th Congress (as Am. Party candidate), 1855-57, 35th Congress (as Republican), 1857-59; del. Rep. Nat. Conv., Chgo., 1860; apptd. asst. appraiser Boston Customhouse, 1861, prosecuted claims against govt. Died Boston, Oct. 23, 1888; buried Oak Grove Cemetery.

DAVIS, Varina Anne Jefferson, author; b. Richmond, Va., June 27, 1864; d. Jefferson and Varina (Howell) D. Went to Europe with her parents, 1875; attended boarding sch., Karlsruhe, Germany, 1875-81; went to Paris, France, 1882, returned to Am. speaking French and German more fluently than English; accompanied her father on his trips throughout the South, 1882-89, on 1 of these trips nicknamed "Daughter of the Confederacy" by Gov. J. B. Gordon of Ga.; after her father's death, 1889, moved to N.Y.C., continued her writing. Author works including: The Veiled Doctor; a Novel, 1895; A Romance of Summer Seas, 1899. Died Sept. 18, 1898; buried Richmond.

DAVIS, Warren Ransom, congressman; b. Columbia, S.C., May 8, 1793; grad. S.C. Coll. (now U. S.C.), 1810; studied law. Admitted to bar, 1814, began practice of law, Pendleton, S.C.; state solicitor of Western Circuit, 1818-24; mem. U.S. Ho. of Reps. (State Rights Democrat) from S.C., 20th-23d congresses, 1827-35. Died Washington D.C., Jan. 29, 1835; buried Congressional Cemetery.

DAVIS, William Augustine, govt. ofcl.; b. Barren County, Ky., Sept. 21, 1809; s. Hardin and Elizabeth (Wynne) D.; m. Ann Hopkins, June 25, 1843, 8 children. With Richmond (Va.) Post Office, 1831-56, postmaster several terms; postmaster, St. Joseph, Mo., 1855-61; suggested distbn. of mail for West to be made by railroad, 1862; with approval of U.S. Post Office Dept., successfully inaugurated 1st railroad post office on Hannibal & St. Joseph R.R. (1st r.r. to have cars for that purpose); inventor railroad car mail-sorting system. Died St. Joseph, Jan. 15, 1875.

DAVIS, William Morris, congressman; b. Keene Valley, Essex County, N.Y., Aug. 16, 1815. Became sugar refiner, Phila.; mem. U.S. Ho. of Reps. (Republican) from Pa., 37th Congress, 1861-63. Died Keene Valley Aug. 5, 1891; buried Friends Fair Hill Burial Ground, Germantown, Pa.

DAWES, William, revolutionary leader; b. Boston, Apr. 6, 1745; s. William and Lydia (Boone) D.; m. Mehitable May, May 3, 1768; m. 2d, Lydia Gendall, Nov. 18, 1795; 2 children. Rode with Paul Revere from Lexington, Mass. to Concord, Mass., to spread the alarm British troops were attempting raid on countryside, Apr. 18, 1775; started by way of Brighton Bridge and the Cambridge Rd.; slipped through Brit. lines and met Revere at Parson Clark's, Lexington, where John Hancock and Samuel Adams were staying; either Dawes or his accomplice got through and gave the alarm (it is not known which one); joined Continental Army as commissary. Died Feb. 25, 1799.

DAWKINS, Henry, engraver; probably born in Eng.; flourished 1753-80; m. Priscilla Wood, Oct. 2, 1757, 7 children. Came to N.Y.C., 1753; earliest example of his work in Am. is book plate for John Burnet of N.Y., dated 1754; asst. engraver to James Turner, Phila., 1757; self-employed in Phila., 1758; became mem. Grand Lodge of Masons, while residing in Phila., elected jr. warden 1764; arrested on suspicion of counterfeiting Continental and Provincial currency, N.Y.C., 1776, fined $1,500 for counterfeiting, 1780.

DAWSON, Francis Warrington, journalist; b. London, Eng., May 17, 1840; s. Austin and Mary (Perkins) Reeks; attended common schs., London; m. Virginia Fouregeaud, 1867; m. 2d, Sarah Morgan, Jan. 1874; 2 children. Enlisted in Confederate Navy, London, 1861, in Army of No. Va., 1862; promoted capt. following meritorious service in several battles, 1864; employed by Richmond Examiner, 1865; with 2 others purchased Charleston (S.C.) News, 1867, merged with Courier in 1873 to become News and Courier, edited paper, 1867-89; took moderate polit. position, supported Chamberlain (radical gov. of S.C.) against Wade Hampton in 1876; advocated encouragement of immigration from Europe, industrialization and diversification of agriculture. Killed in altercation with Dr. T. B. McDow, Charleston, Mar. 12, 1889; buried Charleston.

DAWSON, George, journalist; b. Falkirk, Scotland, Mar. 14, 1813; married; children—Capt. George S., Burritt S. Came to Am., 1818; learned printer's trade, Niagara, N.Y., 1824; apprentice Anti-Masonic Enquirer, Rochester, N.Y., 1826; foreman of office Evening Journal, Albany, N.Y., 1831-36, asso. editor, 1846-62, sr. editor, owner, 1862-71; editor Daily Democrat, Rochester, 1836-39, circa 1842-46; editor Detroit Daily Advertiser, 1839-circa 1842; postmaster Albany, 1861-67; mem. Washington Park Commn., Albany, 1869-83; an original incorporator Commerce Ins. Co.; dir. 1st Nat. Bank Albany. Author: The Pleasures of Angling, 1876. Died Albany, Feb. 17, 1883.

DAWSON, Henry Barton, editor; b. Gosberton, Eng., June 8, 1821; s. Abraham and Mary (Barton) D.; m. Catherine Martling, May 28, 1845, several children. Came with family to N.Y.C., 1834; worked for publisher and bookseller, Ithaca, N.Y., 1837-39; engaged in various enterprises, N.Y.C., 1839-56; started writing hist. monographs; editor Yonkers Gazette, 1865; editor, owner Historical Mag., 1866-76, became involved in controversy with other historians over some of his hist. work; published edition of The Federalist which led to quarrel with John Jay and James A. Hamilton. Author: Battles of the United States by Sea and Land (criticized generalship of Israel Putnam), 2 vols., 1858; Westchester County, New York, During the American Revolution (paper), 1886. Died Tarrytown, N.Y., May 23, 1889.

DAWSON, John, congressman; b. Va., 1762; s. Rev. Musgrave and Mary (Waugh) D.; grad. Harvard, 1782. Mem. Va. Ho. of Dels. from Spotsylvania County, 1786-87, 87-88, 89; mem. Va. Conv. to ratify U.S. Constn.; mem. Exec. Council Va.; presdl. elector, 1793; mem. U.S. Ho. of Reps. from Va., 5th-14th congresses, 1797-1814, bearer ratified Conv. of 1800 to France, proposed 12th amendment providing for separate election of U.S. Pres. and vice pres.; served as aide to Gen. Andrew Jackson during War of 1812. Died Washington, D.C., Mar. 30, 1814.

DAWSON, John Bennett, congressman; b. nr. Nashville, Tenn., Mar. 17, 1798; attended Centre Coll., Danville, Ky. Became a planter also entered newspaper bus., La.; unsuccessful candidate for gov. La., 1834; mem. La. Ho. of Reps.; served as brig. gen. and maj. gen. militia; judge of parish ct.; apptd. postmaster New Orleans, 1843; mem. U.S. Ho. of Reps. (Democrat) from La., 27th-29th congresses, 1841-45. Died St. Francisville. La., June 26, 1845; buried Grace Episcopal Church.

DAWSON, John Littleton, congressman; b. Uniontown, Fayette County Pa., Feb. 7, 1813; grad. Washington, (Pa.) Coll., 1833; studied law. Admitted to bar, 1835, began practice of law, Brownsville, Pa.; dep. atty. gen. Fayette County, 1838; del. Democratic nat. convs., Balt., 1844, 48, 60, N.Y.C., 1868; U.S. dist. atty. for Western Dist. Pa. 1845-48; mem. U.S. Ho. of Reps. (Democrat) from Pa., 32d-33d, 38th-39th congresses, 1851-55, 63-67, author Homestead Bill of 1854; declined appointment as gov. Kan. Territory. Died "Friendship Hill." Fayette County, Sept. 18, 1870; buried Christ Episcopal Churchyard, Brownsville.

DAWSON, William Crosby, senator; b. Green County, Ga., Jan. 4, 1798; s. George and Ruth (Skidmore) D.; grad. U. Ga., 1816; attended Litchfield (Conn.) Law Sch.; m. Henrietta Wingfield, 1819; m. 2d, Mrs. Eliza Williams, 1854. Admitted to Ga. bar, 1818; clk. Ga. Ho. of Reps., 1819-31; compiled statutes of Ga. into Compilation of the Laws of the State of Georgia, 1828-31; mem. Ga. Ho. of Reps.; mem. U.S. Ho. of Reps. from Ga., 24th-27th congresses, Nov. 7, 1836-Nov. 13, 1841; apptd. judge Ocmulgee County (Ga.) Circuit, 1843; mem. U.S. Senate from Ga., 1849-55; leading mem. Ga. Conv. which adopted Ga. platform on Compromise of 1850. Died Greensborough, Ga., May 5, 1856.

DAWSON, William Johnston, congressman; b. nr. Edenton, N.C. Mem. N.C. Ho. of Commons, 1791; mem. com. to fix permanent place for seat of N.C. Govt., 1791; mem. U.S. Ho. of Reps. from N.C., 3d Congress, 1793-95. Died Bertie County, N.C., 1798.

DAY, Benjamin Henry, printer, journalist; b. West Springfield, Mass., Apr. 10, 1810; s. Henry and Mary (Ely) D.; m. Eveline Shepherd, Sept. 13, 1831, 4 children. Started N.Y. Sun, 1st one-cent daily newspaper, 1833, the Sun surpassed the 17,000 circulation of the London Times, Aug. 28, 1835, sold the Sun in 1838 for $40,000; first to apply steam power to move printing machine in newspaper office, 1835; founder penny paper True Sun, 1840, monthly Brother Jonathan (reprinted British novels), 1842, publisher, 1842-62; ret. from business, 1862. Died N.Y.C., Dec. 21, 1889.

DAY, David Alexander, missionary; b. Dillsburg, Pa., Feb. 17, 1851; illegitimate child; attended Missionary Inst. (now Susquehanna U.), Selinsgrove, Pa., 1869-74; m. Emily V. Winegarden, May 1874; m. 2d, Anna E. Whitfield, Dec. 6, 1896; 3 children. Spent youth in poverty and loneliness; ordained to ministry Lutheran Ch., 1874, sent as missionary to Muhlenberg Mission, Liberia; absent from mission only twice (1883, 93) until his death; his health ruined by African fever, decided to return to U.S. Died on journey home aboard the Lucania, Dec. 17, 1897; buried Selinsgrove.

DAY, Henry, lawyer; b. South Hadley, Mass., Dec. 25, 1820; grad. Yale, 1845; m. Miss Lord, 1848. In charge of acad., Fairfield, Conn., 1845-47; admitted to N.Y. bar, 1848; partner Lord, Day & Lord, law firm, N.Y.C., 1848-93; legal counsel Equitable Life Ins. Co. of U.S., 1859-93; mem. Presbyn. gen. assemblies, 1868, 69; dir. Princeton Theol. Sem., many years; dir. Union Theol. Sem., N.Y.C., 1869-93. Author: The Lawyer Abroad, or Observations on the Social and Political Condition of Various Countries, 1874; From the Pyrenees to the Pillars of Hercules, 1883. Died N.Y.C., Jan 9, 1893.

DAY, Henry Noble, clergyman, coll. pres.; b. New Preston, Conn., Aug. 4, 1808; s. Noble and Elizabeth (Jones) D.; grad. Yale, 1828; studied law with Charles Chauncey, Phila.; m. Jane Louisa Marble, Apr. 27, 1836. Tchr., John Gummere's sem., Burlington, N.J., 1829; tutor, Yale, 1831-34; traveled in Europe, 1835; ordained to ministry Congregational Ch., 1836; became pastor 1st Ch., Waterbury, Conn., 1836; prof. theology Western Res. Coll., Hudson, O., 1840-52; editor Ohio Observer for a time; dir. Cleve. and Pitts. R.R.; pres. Ohio Female Coll., College Hill, nr. Cincinnati, 1858-64; returned to New Haven, Conn., spent remainder of life writing textbooks. Author: Elements of the Art of Rhetoric, 1850; Rhetorical Praxis, 1861; Elements of Logic, 1867; Elements of Psychology, 1876; The Science of Education, 1889. Died New Haven, Jan. 12, 1890.

DAY, Horace H., mfr.; b. Great Barrington, Mass., July 10, 1813; s. William and Mary (Pixley) D.; m. Sarah Wykoff, Apr. 25, 1838; m. 2d, Catherine Alice Day, Sept. 14, 1844. Experimented with processes for mfg. Indian rubber, circa 1828; opened factory for prodn. of rubber fabrics, New Brunswick, N.J., 1839; obtained patents for rubber manufacture (differed from those of Charles Goodyear); became involved with Goodyear in mutual accusations of violation of patent rights (suit brought to U.S. Circuit Ct.; both agreed to stop violating the other's rights 1846); claimed that Goodyear broke agreement soon after, thus repudiated the agreement himself and began making all kinds of bber fabrics, 1848; bought English patent rights to ake car springs in U.S., late 1840's; had injunction led against him by Goodyear in U.S. Circuit Ct., renton, N.J., 1852 (Daniel Webster was Goodear's lawyer, Rufus Choate was Day's lawyer), injunction was granted and Day's business failed; completed power canal at Niagara Falls, 1860; planned supply Buffalo, N.Y., with 6,000 horse-power in rm of compressed air, 1870, but did not have nough capital. Died Manchester, N.H., Aug. 23, 878.

DAY, James Gamble, jurist; b. Jefferson County, hio, June 28, 1832; s. George and Sarah (Gamble) D.; grad. Cincinnati Law Sch., 1857; m. Minerva Manley, Dec. 1, 1857. Commd. 1st lt., 5th Ia. Inf., 1861, promoted to capt.; judge 3d d. Dist. Ia., 1863-70; justice Ia. Supreme Ct., 870-84, chief justice, 1871, 77, 83. Died Des Moines, Ia., May 1, 1898.

DAY, Jeremiah B., coll. pres.; b. New Preston, onn., Aug. 3, 1773; s. Rev. Jeremiah Osborn and bigail (Noble) D.; grad. Yale, 1795; LL.D. (hon.), Williams Coll., Middlebury Coll., 1817; D.D. (hon.), Union Coll., 1818, Harvard, 1831; m. Martha Sherman, Jan. 14, 1805; m. 2d, Olivia Jones, Sept. 24, 811. Licensed to preach, 1800, ordained to ministry Congregational ch., 1817; prof. mathematics nd natural philosophy Yale, 1803-17, pres., 1817-7. Author: Introduction to Algebra, 1814; An nquiry Respecting the Self-Determining Power f Will, 1838; An Examination of President Edward's Inquiry on the Freedom of the Will, 1841. Died New Haven, Conn., Aug. 22, 1867.

DAY, Luther, jurist; b. Granville, N.Y., July , 1813; s. David and Rhoda (Wheelock) D.; ed. Middlebury Coll.; m. Emily Spalding, July 24, 845; m. 2d, Ellen Barnes, Apr. 1854; 1 child. Admitted to Ohio bar, 1840; pros. atty. Portage ounty (O.), 1843-51; judge Ct. Common Pleas for nited counties of Portage, Trumbull and Mahoning (O.), 1851; judge advocate with rank of col. Ohio Milita, 1862; elected to Ohio Senate, 1863; udge Ohio Supreme Ct., 1864-76, acting chief justice, 1869-73; mem. Ohio Supreme Ct. Commn., 877-79, chief justice, one year. Died Ravenna, O., Mar. 8, 1885.

DAY, Rowland, congressman; b. Chester, Mass., Mar. 6, 1779. Moved with parents to N.Y., 1805; ngaged in business; mem. N.Y. State Assembly, 816-17; mem. N.Y. Constl. Conv., 1821; held everal local offices, Sempronius, N.Y.; mem. U.S. Ho. of Reps. (Democrat) from N.Y., 18th, 23d ongresses, 1823-25, 33-35. Died Moravia, N.Y., Dec. 23, 1853; buried Indian Mound Cemetery.

DAY, Stephen, printer; b. Eng., circa 1594; m. Rebecca Bordman, 1618; married 2d wife, 1664; 2 hildren including Matthew. Became locksmith, Cambridge, Eng., 1618; came to New Eng. in ship John, nder contract to Rev. Jesse Glover, 1638 (Glover ad printing press and paper with him, died on the ourney); Glover's widow bought house for Day and is family, set up the press in Cambridge, Mass.; ssued Freeman's Oath of the Mass. Colony (1st material printed in Am.) about 6 months after arrival; given land grant by Mass. Gen. Ct., 1641; eft mgmt. of press to his son, circa 1643; acquired much land, became keeper of grounds of plantation, Lancaster, Pa.; imprisoned by local court for fraud, 643, but soon released by Gen. Ct.; returned to ocksmith trade, Cambridge, Mass., circa 1655. Died Dec. 22, 1668.

DAY, Timothy Crane, congressman; b. Cincinnati, Jan. 8, 1819; attended public schs. Employed as printer and engraver, 1838-40; an editor nd propr. Cincinnati Enquirer, 1849-52; travelled o Europe, 1852; mem. U.S. Ho. of Reps. (Republican) from Ohio, 34th Congress, 1855-57. Died Cincinnati, Apr. 15, 1869; buried Spring Grove Cemetery.

DAYAN, Charles, congressman; b. Amsterdam, N.Y., July 8, 1792; grad. Lowville (N.Y.) Acad. Became a tchr.; served as lt. col. in War of 1812; dmitted to bar, 1817, began practice of law, Lowville; mem. N.Y. Senate, 1827-28, pres. pro em., 1828; acting lt. gov. N.Y., 1828; Democratic presdl. elector, 1828; supreme ct. commr., 1830-38; mem. U.S. Ho. of Reps. (Democrat) from N.Y., 22d Congress, 1831-33; mem. N.Y. State Assembly, 1835-36; master and examiner in chancery, until 1838; dist. atty. Lewis County, 1840-45. Died Lowville, Dec. 25, 1877; buried Lowville Rural Cemetery.

DAYTON, Elias, army officer, Continental congressman; b. Elizabethtown (now Elizabeth), N.J., May 1, 1737; s. Jonathan Dayton; m. Miss Rolfe, 8 children including Jonathan. Commd. lt. N.J. Militia, 1756, capt., 1760; apptd. to enforce measures recommended by Continental Congress, 1774; muster master Essex County (N.J.), 1775; commd. col. 3d Battalion, N.J. Militia, 1776; commd. brig. gen. Continental Army on recommendation of George Washington, 1783; maj. gen. N.J. Militia; mem. Continental Congress from N.J., 1787-88; recorder Elizabeth (N.J.), 1789; mem. N.J. Assembly, 1791-92, 94-96; pres. N.J. Soc. of Cincinnati. Died Elizabethtown, Oct. 22, 1807.

DAYTON, Jonathan, senator; b. Elizabethtown (now Elizabeth), N.J., Oct. 16, 1760; s. Gen. Elias Dayton; grad. Coll. N.J. (now Princeton); 1776, LL.D. (hon.), 1798. Commd. Continental Army, served at Battle of Yorktown; mem. N.J. Assembly, 1786-87, 1814-15, speaker, 1790; del. U.S. Constl. Conv., 1787; mem. Continental Congress from N.J., 1787-89; mem. N.J. Council, 1789, mem. U.S. Ho. of Reps. from N.J., 2d-5th congresses, 1791-99, speaker, 1795-99; mem. U.S. Senate from N.J., 1799-1805; arrested for treason in conjunction with Aaron Burr, never tried. Dayton (O.) named for him. Died Elizabethtown, Oct. 9, 1824; buried St. John's Churchyard, Elizabethtown.

DAYTON, William Lewis, senator, diplomat; b. Baskingridge, N.J., Feb. 17, 1807; s. Joel and Nancy (Lewis) D.; grad. Princeton, 1825; m. Margaret Van Der Veer, May 22, 1833, 7 children. Admitted to N.J. bar, 1830; mem. N.J. Legislative Council, 1837; asso. judge Supreme Ct. of N.J., 1838-42; mem. U.S. Senate from N.J., July 2, 1842-51; Republican candidate for vice pres. U.S., 1856; atty. gen. N.J., 1857-61; U.S. minister to France, 1861-64. Died Paris, France, Dec. 1, 1864.

DEADY, Matthew Paul, jurist; b. Easton, Md., May 12, 1824; s. Daniel and Mary Ann (McSweeney) D.; m. Lucy Henderson, June 24, 1852. Admitted to Ohio bar, 1847; elected to Ore. Territorial Ho. of Reps., 1850; mem. Ore. Territorial Council, 1851-53, presiding officer, 1852-53; appdt. asso. justice Ore. Territorial Supreme Ct., 1853; presiding officer Ore. Constl. Conv., 1857; apptd. U.S. dist. judge for Ore., 1860; codified all gen. laws of State of Ore., 1864, 72; often acted as judge, adv. for jud. coms. both houses Ore. Legislature; drafted Corporation Act of 1862, Portland Charter Act of 1864; founder, mng. dir. Multnomah County (Ore.) Library; pres. bd. regents Ore. State U., 1873-93. Died Portland, Ore., Mar. 24, 1893.

de ALARCON, Hernando, explorer; b. Trujillo, New Spain (now Mexico); flourished 1540. Sailed from New Spain, May 1540, along coast of Cal. peninsula to support Coronado's land expdn., but failed to meet Coronado; explored for about 100 miles on lower Colorado River; charted coast of Lower Cal., proved it was a peninsula, rather than an island; returned to New Spain, 1541.

DEALY, Patrick Francis, clergyman, coll. pres.; b. Galway, Ireland, Apr. 7, 1827. Mem. Soc. of Jesus; apptd. prof. rhetoric St. John's Coll., Fordham, N.Y., 1863; rector St. Francis Xavier Ch., N.Y.C.; selected by Cardinal McCloskey to take charge of 1st pilgrimage from Am. to Rome; founded Xavier Union, 1871; a founder Catholic Union, appt. spiritual dir. by Cardinal McCloskey; rector Fordham Coll., 1880; founded 4 scholarships for St. John's Coll.; pres. St. John's Coll. Died N.Y.C., Dec. 22, 1891.

DEAN, Amos, lawyer, educator; b. Barnard, Vt., Jan. 16, 1803; s. Nathaniel and Rhoda (Hammond) D.; grad. Union Coll., Schenectady, N.Y., 1826; m. Eliza Joanna Davis, Sept. 14, 1842. Admitted to N.Y. bar, 1829; became partner (with Azor Taber) in law firm, 1833; prof. med. jurisprudence Albany (N.Y.), Med. Coll., 1838-58; procured establishment of law dept. U. Albany, 1851; retired from active practice, 1854; chancellor, prof. history U. Ia., Iowa City, 1855-60. Author: Lectures on Phrenology, 1834; Principles of Medical Jurisprudence, a Course of Lectures, 1850. Died Albany, Jan. 26, 1868.

DEAN, Benjamin, congressman; b. Clitheroe, Eng., Aug. 14, 1824; attended Dartmouth; studied law. Came to U.S. with parents, settled in Lowell, Mass.; admitted to bar, 1845, began practice of law, Lowell; moved to Boston, 1852; mem. Mass. Senate, 1862-63, 69; mem. common council, 1865-66, 72-73; mem. U.S. Ho. of Reps. (Democrat) from Mass., 45th Congress, Mar. 28, 1878-79; mem. bd. park commrs., several years, served as chmn. Died South Boston, Mass., Apr. 9, 1897; buried Lowell Cemetery.

DEAN, Charles, mcht., historian; b. Biddeford, Me., Nov. 10, 1813; s. Dr. Ezra Deane; A.M. (hon.), Harvard, 1856; m. Helen Waterston, 1841. Partner dry goods firm Waterston, Pray & Co., 1840-64; became mem. Mass. Hist. Soc., 1849, Am. Antiquarian Soc., 1851, London Soc. of Antiquaries, 1878; del. Archeol. Congress, Antwerp, Netherlands, 1866. Editor: History of Plymouth Plantation (by Gov. Bradford), 1856. Died Nov. 13, 1889.

DEAN, Ezra, congressman; b. Hillsdale, N.Y., Apr. 9, 1795; attended common schs.; studied law. Apptd. ensign 11th Regt., U.S. Inf., 1814; commd. lt. for meritorious service at Ft. Erie, 1814; in command of revenue cutter on Lake Champlain, at close of War of 1812; admitted to bar, Plattsburg, N.Y., 1823; moved to Ohio, 1824, began practice of law, Wooster, O.; postmaster Wooster, 1828-32; pres. judge Ct. of Common Pleas, 1834-41; mem. U.S. Ho. of Reps. (Democrat) from Ohio, 27th 28th congresses, 1841-45; moved to Ironton, O., 1867. Died Ironton, Jan. 25, 1872; buried Woodland Cemetery.

DEAN, Gilbert, congressman; b. Pleasant Valley, Dutchess County, N.Y., Aug. 14, 1819; attended Amenia Sem., N.Y.; grad. Yale, 1841; studied law. Admitted to bar, began practice of law, Poughkeepsie, N.Y., 1844; mem. U.S. Ho. of Reps. (Democrat) from N.Y., 32d-33d congresses, 1851-July 3, 1854; justice N.Y. Supreme Ct., 1854-55; moved to N.Y.C., 1856. Died Poughkeepsie, Oct. 12, 1870; buried Presbyn. Cemetery, Pleasant Valley; reinterred Portland Evergreen Cemetery, Brocton, N.Y.

DEAN, Josiah, congressman; b. Raynham, Mass., Mar. 6, 1748; attended common schs. Employed in rolling-mill and shipbldg. business; selectman, 1781; town clk., 1805; presdl. elector on Jefferson ticket, 1804; mem. Mass. Senate, 1804-07; mem. U.S. Ho. of Reps. (Democrat) from N.Y., 10th Congress, 1807-09; mem. Mass. Ho. of Reps., 1810-11. Died Raynham, Oct. 14, 1818; buried Pleasant Street Cemetery.

DEAN, Julia, actress; b. Pleasant Valley, N.Y., July 22, 1830; d. Edwin and Julia (Drake) Dean; m. Dr. Arthur Hayne, 1855; m. 2d, James G. Cooper, 1867; at least 1 child. Mem. (with parents) Ludlow & Smith Co., Mobile, Ala., 1844-45; 1st success as Lady Ellen in The Lady of the Lake, 1845; played Julia in The Hunchback at Bowery Theatre, N.Y.C., 1846; went to Cal. with husband, 1856; became famous in San Francisco; toured Rocky Mountain states, ending in Salt Lake City, 1865; divorced husband, Salt Lake City, 1865. Died in childbirth, N.Y.C., Mar. 6, 1868.

DEAN, Sidney, clergyman, congressman, editor; b. Glastonbury, Conn., Nov. 16, 1818; s. Amos and Nancy (Kempton) D.; m. Martha A. Hollister, 1839, 1 son, 1 dau.; m. 2d, Annie Eddy, 3 sons. Ordained to ministry Methodist Ch., minister, 1843-53; mem. Conn. Ho. of Reps., 1854-55; mem. U.S. Ho. of Reps. from Conn., 34th-35th congresses, 1855-59; minister, Pawtucket, R.I., 1859-61; pastor Mathewson Street Ch., Providence, R.I., 1863-65; editor and publishing mgr. Providence Evening Press, Providence Morning Star, R.I. Press, Providence, 1865-80; mem. R.I. Senate, 1870-71. Author: A History of Banking and Banks from the Bank of Venice to the Year 1883, published 1884. Died Brookline, Mass., Oct. 29, 1901; buried South Cemetery, Warren, R.I.

De ANDREIS, Andrew James Felix Bartholomew, clergyman; b. Demonte, Italy, Dec. 12, 1778; s. Maurice De Andreis; grad. Alberoni Coll., Italy, 1802. Began novitiate, Mondovi, Italy, 1797; ordained priest Roman Catholic Ch., 1801; prof. Alberoni Coll., 1802-06; transferred to Monte Citorio, Italy, 1806; came to U.S., 1816; tchr. theology St. Thomas's Sem., Bardstown, Ky., 1816-17; became rector of cathedral, St. Louis, 1818; cause of beatification formally introduced by decree of Pope Benedict XV, 1918. Died Oct. 15, 1820.

DEANE, Samuel, clergyman; b. Dedham, Mass., July 10, 1733; s. Samuel and Rachel (Dwight) D.; grad. Harvard, 1760, M.A.; D.D., Brown U., 1790; m. Eunice Pearson, Apr. 3, 1776. Tutor and librarian Harvard, 1760-63; ordained to ministry Congregational Ch., 1764; colleague of Rev. Thomas Smith, Portland, Me., 1764-75; vice pres. and trustee Bowdoin Coll., 1794-1813; pastor, Portland, 1795-1814. Author: The New England Farmer or Georical Dictionary, 1790. Died Portland, Nov. 12, 1814.

DEANE, Silas, continental congressman; b. Groton, Conn., Dec. 24, 1737; s. Silas and Sarah (Barker) D.; grad. Yale, 1758, A.M., 1763; m. Mehitabel Webb, 1763; m. 2d, Elizabeth Saltonstall, 1767; 1 son, Jesse. Admitted to Conn. bar, 1761; a leader Revolutionary movement in Conn.; mem. Conn. Gen. Assembly, 1772; sec. Conn. Com. of Correspondence, 1773, del. to 1st, 2d Continental congresses, 1774-76; secret agt. to France to seek aid and support for Am. Revolution (1st Am. to represent united colonies abroad), 1776; secured 8 ship loads of mil. supplies, commd. several European mil. officers, including Lafayette, De Kalb, Von Steuben, Pulaski; came before Congress to give statement of transactions in Europe, 1780, Congress unsatisfied; went to France to obtain audits of accounts, vouchers; while in Europe lost faith in Am. cause, as shown in letters to Am. urging reconciliation with Eng.; publications of these letters resulted in accusation as traitor, embezzler; vindicated by Congress, 1842; 1st person to use invisible ink in U.S. diplomatic correspondence. Died on shipboard outside of Deal, Eng., Sept. 23, 1789; buried Deal.

de ANZA, Juan Bautista, explorer, colonial gov.; b. Fronteras, Sonora, Mexico, 1735. Capt., Presidio of Tubac, 1760; commd. lt. col., 1774; leader Anza expdn. to Alta, Cal., 1775-76; founder San Francisco, 1776; gov. N.M., 1777-88; established Colorado River Colonies, 1780 (wiped out by Yuma Indians, 1781).

DEARBORN, Benjamin, musician; b. Portsmouth, N.H., 1754; son of Dr. Benjamin Dearborn. Began publishing Freeman's Journal; or N. H. Gazette, 1775; opened sch. to instruct "young misses," 1779; opened Portsmouth Acad., 1791; moved to Boston, 1792; developed new notation system for musical instrn., also new type of printing press for songs; composed music including psalms, hymns. Died Boston, Feb. 22, 1838.

DEARBORN, Henry, army officer, physician, congressman, sec. of war; b. North Hampton, N.H., Feb. 23, 1751; s. Simon and Sarah (Marston) D.; m. Mary Bartlett, 1771; m. 2d, Dorcas Marble, 1780; m. 3d, Mrs. Sarah Bowdoin, 1813; 1 son, Henry Alexander Scammell D. Organizer, capt. company, N.H. Militia, 1772; commd. maj. 3d Hampshire Regt., 1777; commd. brig. gen., then maj. gen. N.H. Militia; dep. q.m. gen. with rank of col. on Gen. Washington's Staff, 1781; apptd. U.S. marshall for Dist. of Me., 1790; mem. U.S. Ho. of Reps. from Mass., 3d-4th congresses, 1793-97; U.S. sec. of war under Pres. Jefferson, 1801-09; collector Port of Boston (apptd. by Pres. Madison), 1809-12; apptd. sr. maj. gen. U.S. Army by Madison, 1812, served in War of 1812; U.S. minister to Portugal, 1822-24; Dearborn (Mich.) named after him. Died Roxbury, Mass., June 6, 1829; buried Forest Hills Cemetery, Boston.

DEARBORN, Henry Alexander Scammell, congressman; author; b. Exeter, N.H., Mar. 3, 1783; s. Gen. Henry and Dorcas (Marble) D.; grad. Coll. William and Mary, 1803. Admitted to Mass. bar, 1805; apptd. to superintend erection new fts. in Portland harbor, 1806; officer Boston Custom House, collector, 1812-29; served as brig. gen. Mass. Militia, 1812; mem. Mass. Legislature from Roxbury, 1829-30; mem. Mass. Gov's Council, 1830; del. Mass. Constl. Conv., 1830; mem. Mass. Senate from Norfolk County, 1830; mem. U.S. Ho. of Reps. from Mass., 22d Congress, 1831-33; adj. gen. Mass., 1835-43; mayor Roxbury, 1847-51. Author: Memoir on the Commerce and Navigation of the Black Sea and the Trade and Maritime Geography of Turkey and Egypt, 1819; Defence of General Henry Dearborn Against the Attack of General William Hull, 1824; Letters on Internal Improvements and Commerce of the West, 1839; A Sketch of the Life of the Apostle Eliot, 1850. Translated from French: Monography of the Genius Camellia (Abbe Lorenzo Berlese), 1838. Died Portland, Me., July 29, 1851; buried Forest Hills Cemetery, Roxbury.

DEARBORN, Nathaniel, engraver; b. Mass., 1786; at least 1 son, Nathaniel S. Became wood engraver, Boston, circa 1811, became one of leading local engravers; partner firm Nathaniel Dearborn & Son, 1836-38; did copperplate printing. Died South Reading, Mass., Nov. 7, 1852.

DEAS, Charles, artist; b. Phila., 1818. Exhibited at N.A.D., 1838, elected asso., 1839; visited brother at Ft. Crawford, Prairie du Chien, Wis., became fascinated with Western life; made hdqrs. at St. Louis, sketched among Indians West of Mississippi River; exhibited paintings of Indian and frontier life at Am. Art-Union, Pa. Acad., Artists' Fund Soc., Boston Athenaeum; returned to N.Y.C., 1847; suffered mental breakdown. Died in an asylum, 1867.

DEAS, Zachariah Cantey, mcht., army officer; s. Col. James Sutherland and Margaret (Chunut) D.; m. Helen Gaines, May 16, 1853. Cotton broker, Mobile, Ala.; served as aide-de-camp to Gen. J.E. Johnston, Confederate Army, commd. col., 1861; recruited (with Maj. Robert B. Armistead) 22d Ala. Inf.; commanded brigade, wounded at Battle of Shiloh, 1862; promoted brig. gen., 1862, served in Battle of Murfreesboro; led brigade at Battle of Chickamauga, 1863, Missionary Ridge, 1863; returned to cotton brokerage, N.Y.C., after war. Died N.Y.C., Mar. 6, 1882.

De AYALA, Juan Manuel, explorer; flourished 1775. Comdr. of ship San Carlos in Spanish expdn. to explore Bay of San Francisco; set sail from San Blas, Spain, Mar. 1775, reached Monterrey, Cal., June 27, proceeded to Bay of San Francisco, July 24; spent months of August, September in exploration of Bay; reported to the Viceroy of bay's significance and its excellent potential, Nov. 9, 1775.

De AYLLON, Lucas Vasquez, explorer; b. Toledo, Spain, circa 1475. Came to Hispaniola (Santo Domingo) with Gov. Nicholas de Ovando, 1502; judge of Supreme Ct. of Hispaniola; had 400 Indians to use to work his land; entered partnership with clk. of Audiencia of Hispaniola, sent a ship under Francisco Gordillo (capt.) and Alonzo Sotil (pilot) to sail North until reaching land, 1520 (reached Am. coast in approximate area of N.C. and took possession, June 30, 1521); went to Spain and reported discovery, took along a native of the country who reported on great riches there; granted right to explore Am. coast in effort to find western route to Indies by Emperor Charles V, who also granted him and his descendants title of adelantado and gov.; sent 2 ships to explore new lands, 1525 (they returned same year with gold, silver and pearls); sailed from La Plata, Hispaniola, with 3 ships carrying from 500 to 600 settlers, landed at what is now either North or South Carolina, 1526; possibly went as far south as Santee River (S.C.), began settlement of San Miguel de Gualdape (colony abandoned after fever outbreak which left only about 150 survivors who returned to Hispaniola). Died San Miguel de Gualdape, Oct. 18, 1526; buried at sea.

De BENEVIDES, Alonzo, clergyman; b. San Miguel Island, Azores; s. Pedro and Antonia (Murato) De B.; probably ed. convent in Mexico City, Mexico, circa 1600-03. Took vows as Franciscan, Mexico City, 1603, made master of novices in monastery of Puebla, Mexico; assumed charge of Franciscan mission among Apache Indians in present N.M., 1621; during following decade built convents in Santa Fe, Picuries, Taos, Acoma, Santa Clara de Capoo; went to Spain, 1629, presented his Memorial to king of Spain describing mission work in N.M., revised by order of Pope Urban VIII, 1634, translated into 4 langs.; returned to N.M., 1633-34; went to Goa, Portuguese India, 1634, became archbishop of Goa. Died Portuguese Goa, 1664.

De BERDT, Dennys, colonial agt.; b. circa 1694; s. John De B.; m. Martha; children include Dennis, Esther. Elected agt. for Mass. Colony in London (Eng.) by Mass. Gen. Ct., 1765, also served as agt. for Colony of Del.; helped secure repeal of Stamp Act. Died Apr. 11, 1770.

DEBERRY, Edmund, congressman; b. Lawrenceville (now Mt. Gilead), N.C., Aug. 14, 1787; attended sch., High Shoals. Engaged in agr., also cotton and flour mill operation; mem. N.C. Senate, 1806-11, 13-14, 20-21, 26-28; justice of peace; mem. U.S. Ho. of Reps. from N.C., 21st, 23d-28th, 31st congresses, 1829-31, 33-45, 49-51. Died Montgomery County, N.C., Dec. 12, 1859; buried family cemetery on plantation nr. Mt. Gilead.

De BOLT, Rezin A., congressman; b. nr. Basil, Fairfield County, O., Jan. 20, 1828; attended common schs.; studied law. Employed as a tanner; admitted to bar, 1856, began practice of law, Lancaster, O.; moved to Trenton, Mo., 1858; commr. of common schs. Grundy County, 1859-61; commd. capt. 23d Regt., Mo. Volunteers, U.S. Army, 1861, captured at Battle of Shiloh, 1862, resigned commn., 1863; judge circuit ct. 11th Jud. Circuit Mo., 1863-75; served as maj. 44th Regt., Mo. Volunteer Inf., 1864-65; mem. U.S. Ho. of Reps. (Democrat) from Mo., 44th Congress, 1875-77. Died Trenton, Oct. 30, 1891; buried Odd Fellows Cemetery.

de BONNEVILLE, Benjamin Louis Eulalie, army officer, explorer; b. Paris, France, Apr. 14, 1796; s. Nicholas and Margaret (Brazier) de B.; grad. U.S. Mil. Acad., 1815; m. Ann Lewis; m. 2d, Susan Neis, 1870. Came to Am., Aug. 1803; aided Lafayette on his tour of U.S., 1825; went on leave of absence from Army to exploit Northwestern country for comml. gain, 1832-35; served as maj., then lt. col. in Mexican War; comdt. Benton Barracks, St. Louis, 1862-65, brig. gen., Civil War, 1865; subject of Washington Irving's Adventures of Captain Bonneville. Died Ft. Smith, Ark., June 12, 1878.

De BOW, James Dunwoody Brownson, editor, govt. ofcl.; b. Charleston, S.C., July 10, 1820; s. Garret De Bow; grad. Coll. Charleston, 1843; m. Caroline Poe, 1854; m. 2d, Martha Johns, 1860; children—James Dunwoody Brownson, Benjamin Franklin, Evilina Johns. Editor, So. Quarterly Review, 1844-45 founder, editor Comml. Review of South and S.W. (later known as DeBow's Review, powerful factor in formation of So. sentiment) 1846-67; a founder La. Hist. Soc.; supt. U.S. Census, 1853. Author: Statistical View of the United States, printed by U.S. Senate, 1854. Died Elizabeth, N.J., Feb. 27, 1867.

De BRAHM, William Girard, geographer; b. 1717; m. 2d, Mary (Drayton) Fenwick, Feb. 18, 1776; at least 1 child. Came to Am., 1751; founded Town of Bethany, Ga., 1751; surveyor of Ga., 1754-64, planned towns of Ebenezer, 1757, Ft. George, 1761; supervised constn. of fortifications at Charleston, S.C., 1755, Savannah, Ga., 1762; drew 1st map of Ga. and S.C., 1757; surveyor gen. for So. Dist., 1764-70; commr. to mark No. boundary line of N.J., 1765; drew map of Atlantic Ocean, 1772. Author: The Atlantic Pilot, 1772; The Levelling Balance and Counter-Balance, 1774; DeBrahm's Zonical Tables for the Twenty-Five Northern and Southern Climates, 1774; Time an Apparition of Eternity, 1791; Apocalyptic Gnomon Points Out Eternity's Divisibility, 1795. Died 1799.

de BREHAN, Marquise, artist. Came to Am., 1788; visited "Mt. Vernon," 1822, painted profile of Washington; lived in N.Y.C., 1789, executed an other profile of Washington, watercolor view o N.Y.C.

De CALLIÉRES BONNEVUE, Louis Hector, colo nial gov.; b. Cherbourg, France, 1646. Became capt French Army, sent to Canada, 1684; apptd. gov Montreal (Can.) at request of Sulpicians there 1684; marched to relieve siege of Quebc (Can.) b British, 1690; became gov. New France (succeede Frontenac), 1699; sent Cadillac to found Detroit negotiated Treaty of Montreal (agreed to by reps of all Indian tribes in colony), 1701. Died Quebec May 26, 1703.

de CARDENAS, Garcia Lopez, explorer; flourishe 1540-42. Capt. in Spanish army in Francisco Coro nado's expdn. to N.M., 1540-42; saved Coronado' life during battle at Zuni Pueblo, 1540; discovere Grand Canyon of Colorado River, 1540; led force which put down Indian revolt at Tiguex, winter 1540-41; returned to Spain, 1542.

de CARONDELET, Francisco Luis Hector (baro de Carondelet), colonial governor; b. Noyelle, Flan ders, Belgium, circa 1748; s. Juan Luis Nicolas an Rosa (Plunkett) de C. Took over govt. and inten dency La. and W. Fla., 1791, after sale of W. Fla to France, continued as gov. La., 1795-97; buil Carondelet Canal giving New Orleans outlet to Gul of Mexico, 1794; reformed police, instituted stree lighting system, New Orleans; pres. Royal Audi encia; gov. gen. Quito, Ecuador, 1799-1807. Die Aug. 10, 1807; buried Vault of St. Peter a Cathedral Ch., Quito.

DECATUR, Emmett Daniel, musician; b. 1815 Spent early life as a minstrel; composed Dixie's Land (now generally known as Dixie), 1859, sol copyright for $500; toured with Al G. Field's Minstrels, 1895. Credited with compositions including Old Dan Tucker, My Old Aunt Sally, Jordan is a Hard Road to Travel, The Bluetail Fly (Jim Crac Corn), Early in the Morn. Died Mt. Vernon, O. 1904.

DECATUR, Stephen, naval officer; b. Newport R.I., 1752; s. Stephen and Priscilla (Hill) D. m. Ann Pine, Dec. 20, 1774, 4 children, Ann James, John, Stephen. Master sloop Peggy, 1774 U.S. privateer during Revolutionary War; comdr. part owner mcht. ships Ariel and Pennsylvania 1782-98; commd. capt. U.S. Navy, 1798; commanded Delaware as sr. officer of squadron operating off No. Cuba during hostilities with French 1798-99; commanded Philadelphia as head Guadeloupe Squadron, 1800-01, discharged, 1801 established gunpowder works, Millsdale, Pa. Died Millsdale, Nov. 14, 1808; buried St. Peter's Churchyard, Phila.

DECATUR, Stephen, naval officer; b. Sinepuxent, Md., Jan. 5, 1779; s. Stephen and Priscilla (Hill) D.; m. Susan Wheeler, Mar. 8, 1806. Apptd. midshipman U.S. Navy, 1798, acting lt., 1799; 1st lt. in ship Essex in Commodore Dale's squadron to Tripoli, 1801-02; in command of ship Enterprise in Tripolitan waters, 1803, noted for daring exploit in recapturing and burning Am. frigate Philadelphia, 1804; capt. in command of gunboat div. in attacks on Tripoli, 1804; served as commander ship United States (defeated Brit. ship Macedonia 1812) and ship President (defeated ship Endymion in War of 1812; served in expdn. to Algeria, 1815, forced a peace on U.S. terms with so-called Barbary Pirates; mem. newly-created naval commn., 1816-20. Killed by naval officer James Barron in duel, nr. Bladensburg, Md., Mar. 22, 1820; buried St. Peters Churchyard, Phila.

DE CÉLERON DE BLAINVILLE, Pierre Joseph, army officer, explorer; b. Montreal, Que., Can., Jan. 9, 1694; s. Jean-Baptiste and Hélène (Picoté de Bellestre) de C. de B.; married 3 times; at least 1 son, Paul Louis. Joined French Army, 1715, promoted lt., 1731; commandant French post Michilimackinac, Can., 1734, 37-40, 41-42; accompanied expdn. against Chickasaw Indians, 1739-40; promoted capt., 1740; in command of posts at Detroit, Niagara and St. Frederic (now Crown Point) until 1748; sent on expdn. to drive English from Ohio River Valley, 1749, during this campaign left lead plates buried along river banks claiming that region for France; commandant of Detroit, 1750-53; promoted maj., 1750; served at Battle of Lake George, 1755. Died Apr. 12, 1759.

de CHAMPLAIN, Samuel (sieur de Champlain), explorer; born in Brouage near Rochefort, France, circa 1567; son of Antoine and Marguerite (Le Roy) C.; m. Helene Bouble, 1610. Comdr. ship St. Julien in Spanish flotilla to New Spain, 1599-1601; visited W.I., Mexico, Cartegena, Isthmus of Panama; mem. French exploring and fur-trading expdn. to Gulf of St. Lawrence; prevented from penetrating interior of N.Am. by Lachine River rapids while ascending St. Lawrnece River; 1601; mem. expdn. to Port Royal, 1605; led 3 exploratory expdns. along New Eng. coast from N.S. to Vineyard Sound, 1605-07; founder Quebec

1st French permanent colony in New World), 608; explored Northern N.Y., discovered Lake hamplain, 1609; 1st to describe, name and map ake Huron, 1615, also traced St. Lawrence River its source; prisoner in Eng. during French-Brit. fficulties, 1629-33; gov. Colony of Quebec, 1633-5. Author: Des Savages (a description of both yage and inhabitants of St. Lawrence Valley), 601; Travels of Sieur de Champlain, 1613; Travels nd Discoveries in New France, 1619; Travels in anada, 1632. Died Quebec, P.Q., Can., Dec. 25, 635.

de CHARLEVOIX, Pierre Francois Xavier, explorer, historian; b. St. Quentin, France, Oct. 29, 682; s. Francois and Antoinette (Forester) de C.; udent College Louis le Grand, 1701-04. Ordained diaconate, 1704; came to Can. as prof. rhetoric suit Coll. at Quebec, 1705; returned to France, 709; came back to Can. to ascertain Arcadian oundaries and find new route to West, 1720; urneyed up the St. Lawrence, through Great akes, down Illinois River to the Mississippi, reaching New Orleans and Biloxi early in 1722; upon turn to France compiled Journal historique (series of letters describing his travels, significant because it is only account written in 1st half of 8th century describing interior America). Author: Historie de la Nouvelle France, 1744. Histoire de Paraguay, 1756. Died La Fieche, France, eb. 1, 1761.

de CHEVERUS, Jean Louis Anne Magdelen Lebre (or Lefebvre), clergyman; b. Mayenne, France, an. 28, 1768; s. John Vincent Lefebre and Anne Lemarchand des Noyers); ed. College Louis-le-Grand, Paris, France. Ordained priest Roman Catholic Ch., Paris, 1790; sailed for Boston, 1796; elped plan Holy Cross Ch., 1800; apptd. 1st bishop f Boston by Pope Pius VII, 1810; returned to rance, 1823; made archbishop of Bordeaux France), 1826; named a counselor of state, 1828, omdr. Order Holy Ghost, 1830; elevated to cardinal, 1836. Died Bordeaux, July 19, 1836.

de CLORIVIÈRE, Joseph-Pierre Picot de Limoëan, artist; b. Broons, Brittany, Nov. 4, 1768. harged with attempted assassination of Napoleon, scaped to Am., 1803; employed as miniaturist, Savannah, Ga., 1803-06, Balt., 1806-12, Charleston, .C., 1812-18; spent last years in Jesuit Monastery f the Visitation, Georgetown, D.C. Died Georgetown, ept. 29, 1826.

de CREVECOEUR, Michel-Guillaume Jean, (pseudonym J. Hector St. John), author; b. Caen, ormandy, France, Jan. 31, 1735; s. Guillaume ean and Marie-Anne (Blouet) de C.; m. Mehetable ippet, 1769; 1 dau., America-Frances. Came to an., served under Montcalm in French and Indian Vars; traveled and explored widely in Am. and an.; became naturalized Am. citizen, 1765; returned to France, 1780; renowned for his Letters om an American Farmer, stating farmers' reactions to issues and circumstances of the day, 782; introduced culture of Am. potato into Normandy, and alfalfa into Am., circa 1782; apptd. rench consul, N.Y.C., 1783; returned to France, 790. Author: La Culture des pommes de terre; oyage dans la haute Pensylvanie et dans l'etat e New York, 3 vols., 1801; Sketches of Eighteenth entury America, published posthumously, 1925. ied Sarcelles, France, Nov. 12, 1813.

DEEMS, Charles Force, clergyman, coll. pres.; . Balt., Dec. 4, 1820; s. George W. and Mary Roberts) D.; grad. Dickinson Coll., 1839; m. Anne Disosway, June 20, 1813. N.C. agt. for Am. Bible Soc., 1840-42; prof. humanistic studies U. N.C, 842-48; prof. natural scis. Randolph-Macon Coll., 849; pres. Greensboro (N.C.) Women's Coll., 850-54; dir. boarding sch., Wilson, N.C., 1859-0; founder, editor The Watchman, N.Y.C., 1865; ounded, preached in non-denominational Ch. of he Strangers, N.Y.C., 1866-92, bldg. donated to is church by Cornelius Vanderbilt, 1870; founder Am. Inst. of Christian Philosophy, 1881. Author: esus, 1872; Scotch Verdict in re Evolution, 1885. Died N.Y.C., Nov. 18, 1893.

DEERE, John, mfr.; b. Rutland, Vt., Feb. 7, 804; s. William Rinold and Sarah (Yates) D.; . Damaris Lamb, Jan. 28, 1827; m. 2d, Lucinda amb, 1867. First mfr. plow steel in U.S., organizer arious mfg. firms; incorporated, became pres. rm Deere & Co., 1868. Died May 17, 1886.

DEERFOOT, (Indian name Ha-ga-sa-do-ni, English name Lewis Bennett), Indian runner; b. Cattaragus Reservation, Erie County, N.Y., 1828. eneca Indian. Gained distinction for ability as ong distance runner; competed in races in N.Y. nd Pa.; appeared in track events in England, 861-63, competed against John White, Edward Aills and W. Lang (English champions); set record or 12 mile run (1 hour, 2 minutes, 2.5 seconds), 863; competed in Indian costume using Deerfoot s his profl. name. Died Cattaragus Reservation, an. 18, 1897.

DEERING, Nathaniel, author; b. Portland, Me., June, 25, 1791; s. James and Almire (Ilsley) D.; grad. Harvard, 1810; m. Anna Margaret Holwell, Oct. 1824, 9 children. Admitted to Me. bar, 1815; practiced in Skowhegan, Me., 1815-36; moved to Portland, 1836; editor Independent Statesman, Portland. Author: Corabasset, or the Last of the Norridgeaochs (play); The Clairvoyant (comedy); Bozzaris (tragedy), 1851. Died Mar. 25, 1881.

DEERING, Nathaniel Cobb, congressman; b. Denmark, Oxford County, Me., Sept. 2, 1827; grad. North Bridgeton Acad. Mem. Me. Ho. of Reps. from Penobscot County, 1855-56; moved to Osage, Ia., 1857; engaged in lumber bus.; built, operated sawmill; clk. U.S. Senate, until 1865; spl. agt. Post Office Dept. for dist. Minn., Ia., Neb., 1865-69; nat. bank examiner State of Ia., 1872-77; mem. U.S. Ho. of Reps. (Republican) from Ia., 45th-47th congresses, 1877-83; engaged in agr.; became pres. large cattle co. in Mont. Died Osage, Dec. 11, 1887; buried Osage Cemetery.

De FONTIANE, Felix Gregory, journalist; b. Boston, 1834; s. Louis Antoine and Miss (Allen) De F.; m. Georgia Moore, 1860. Founder, editor Daily South Carolinian, Columbia, S.C., 1860-65; corr. for N.Y.C. newspapers; sent to N.Y. Herald 1st account bombing of Ft. Sumter to appear in Northern press; mil. corr. with rank of maj. 1st S.C. Regt., Confederate States Army, 1861-65; sec. conv. to consider abuses of carpet bag govt., Columbia, 1867; mng. editor N.Y.C. Telegram, 1867-70; financial editor, later art and drama editor N.Y. Herald, 1870-96. Author: A History of American Abolitionism Together with a History of the Southern Confederacy, 1861; Marginalia, 1864; The Fireside Dickens, 1883; De Fontiane's Long-Hand and Rapid-Writer's Companion, 1886. Died Columbia, Dec. 11, 1896.

De FOREST, David Curtis, mcht., diplomat; b. Huntington, Conn., Jan. 10, 1774; s. Benjamin and Mchitable (Curtis) De F.; m. Julia Wooster, Oct. 6, 1811. Served as lt. U.S. Army, 1799-1800; established 1st Am. comml. house at Buenos Aires, Argentina, 1802; exiled by Spanish viceroy after amassing large fortune, 1809, returned, 1812; obtained commn. from revolutionary govt. to finance privateers (which brought him large profit) during Argentinian Revolution against Spain, 1815; returned to U.S., 1818; Argentinian consul gen. to U.S., 1818-22, attempted unsuccessfully to obtain ofcl. U.S. recognition for Argentina; not recognized as rep. when Argentina won recognition, 1822 (because he was Am. citizen); endowed DeForest scholarship and English prize Yale, 1823. Died Feb. 22, 1825.

De FOREST, Erastus Lyman, mathematician; b. Watertown, Conn., June 27, 1834; s. John and Lucy (Lyman De F.; B.A., Yale, 1854, Ph.B., Sheffield Scientific Sch., 1856, M.A., 1867; never married. Inherited fortune from grandfather; went to Cal. as gold miner, 1849; later travelled in Australia, Orient and Europe; devoted time to study of theory of probability and errors; made important contributions to devel. of formulas for graduation by linear compounding; endowed mathematics chair at Yale, 1888. Died June 6, 1888.

de FRANCA, Manuel Joachim, artist; b. Portugal, 1808. Worked in Phila., circa 1830-42; exhibited at Pa. Acad., Artists' Fund Soc., Apollo Assn., N.A.D.; moved to St. Louis, circa 1847; works include portrait of Henry Clay. Died St. Louis, Aug. 22, 1865.

DEFREES, Joseph Hutton, businessman, congressman; b. Sparta, Tenn., May 13, 1812; attended common schs., Ohio. Apprenticed to blacksmith, 1826-29; learned printing trade; moved to South Bend, Ind., 1831; established Northwestern Pioneer, South Bend; became mcht., Goshen, Ind., 1833, later entered banking; apptd. county agt.; sheriff Elkhart County (Ind.), 1835-40; mem. Ind. Ho. of Reps., 1849, 72, Ind. Senate, 1850-54; mem. U.S. Ho. of Reps. (Republican) from Ind., 39th Congress, 1865-67; engaged in milling, linseed oil manufacture, constrn. of Goshen Hydraulic Works; dir., 1st pres. Cincinnati, Wabash & Mich. R.R. Died Goshen, Dec. 21, 1885; buried Oak Ridge Cemetery.

de GALVEZ, Bernardo, provincial adminstr.; b. Macharaviaya, Spain, July 23, 1746; s. Matias and Josefa Gallardo (Madrid) de G.; m. Felicitas de St. Maxent. Served with Spanish Army against Portugal, in New Spain against Apaches, in Algiers, 1772-76; apptd. gov. and intendant Province of La., 1776; captured Baton Rouge, La. and Natchez, Miss. during war with Gt. Britain, 1779, Mobile, Ala., 1780, Pensacola, Fla., 1781, enabled Spain to obtain both Floridas in the peace settlement, 1783, and to control mouth of the Mississippi River and Gulf of Mexico; commd. maj. gen., 1784; capt. gen. La. and the Floridas; capt. gen. Cuba, 1784; viceroy of New Spain, 1785; aided in obtaining comml. cedula of 1782, shaping policy of Spain in regard to Indian affairs, immigration, boundary dispute with U.S., navigation of Mississippi River. Died Mexico, Nov. 30, 1786.

DEGENER, Edward, congressman; b. Brunswick, Germany, Oct. 20, 1809; ed. Germany and Eng. Mem. legislative body, Anhalt-Dessau, 2 times; mem. 1st German Nat. Assembly, Frankfort on the Main, 1848; came to U.S., 1850, settled in Sisterdale, Kendall County Tex.; engaged in agr.; Union sympathizer, court-matrialed and imprisoned by Confederates; entered wholesale grocery bus., San Antonio, Tex.; mem. Tex. constl. convs., 1866, 68; mem. U.S. Ho. of Reps. (Republican) from Tex., 41st Congress, Mar. 31, 1870-71; mem. San Antonio City Council, 1872-78. Died San Antonio, Sept. 11, 1890; buried City Cemetery.

DE GRAFF, John Isaac, congressman, mayor Schenectady; b. Schenectady, N.Y., Oct. 2, 1783; attended Union Coll., Schenectady, 1811. Became mem. U.S. Ho. of Reps. (Democrat) from N.Y., 20th, 25th congresses, 1827-29, 37-39; mayor Schenectady, 1832-34, 36, 42, 45; declined to serve as U.S. sec. of treasury under Pres. Van Buren; active in constrn. Mohawk & Hudson R.R.; engaged in banking. Died Schenectady, July 26, 1848; buried Vale Cemetery.

de GRAFFENRIED, Christopher (baron de Graffenried), adventurer, colonizer; b. Bern, Switzerland, Nov. 21, 1661; s. Anton (lord Wörb) and Catherine (Jenner) de G.; m. Regina Tscharner, 1683, 13 children including Christopher. Received grant of 5,000 acres from lords proprietors of N.C., 1709, apptd. landgrave; became partner of Michel and the Ritter Co., resulted in transp. to N.C. of 92 Palatine families, 1710; started unsuccessful Colony of New Bern; brought another 156 Swiss to New Bern, 1710; returned to Switzerland, 1713. Died Wörb, Switzerland, 1743.

de GRASSE, Francois Joseph Paul, naval officer; b. Bar, Alpes-Maritimes, France, Sept. 13, 1722. Apptd. rear adm., 1778, sent to W.I., 1779; engaged English Squadron in several encounters, captured Tobago, 1781; brought reinforcements to French and Am. troops at Yorktown, 1781; defeated a Brit. fleet (which prevented them from assisting Gen. Cornwallis in Battle of Yorktown), Sept. 1781; taken prisoner when his squadron was defeated at Battle of Dominica, Apr. 1782; censured in France for his defeat, but exonerated in courtmartial, 1784. Author: Memoire justificatif (defense of his naval campaign in Am. Revolution). Died Paris, France, Jan. 11, 1788.

De HAAS, John Philip, army officer; b. Holland, 1735; s. John Nicholas De Haas; m. Eleanor Bingham. Brought to Am., 1737; commd., ensign Provincial Battalion of Pa. during French and Indian Wars. 1757; took part in expdn. against Ft. Duquesne, 1758; magistrate Lancaster County (Pa.), 1765-79; apptd. col. 1st Pa. Battalion, Continental Army, 1776; participated in Canadian campaign under Gen. Benedict Arnold, 1776; commd. brig. gen., 1777 resigned, 1777; organized local militia for campaign against Indians in Wyoming Valley, 1778, relieved of his command by Arnold. Died Phila., June 3, 1786.

DE HART, John, Continental congressman, mayor Elizabethtown; b. Elizabethtown (now Elizabeth) N.J., 1728; studied law. Admitted to bar, began practice of law; became sgt.-at-law, 1770; a signer Articles of Assn., 1774; mem. Continental Congress from N.J., 1774-75, Feb.-June 1776; mem. com. which prepared draft N.J. Constn. 1776; chief justice N.J. Supreme Ct. 1776-77; mayor Elizabethtown, 1789-95. Died Elizabethtown, June 1, 1795; buried St. John's Churchyard.

de HASS, Mauritz Frederick Hendrick, artist; b. Rotterdam, Netherlands, Dec. 12, 1832; s. Jan and Marie (Petronella) de H.; educated at home; pupil of Louis Meyer, marine artist; m. Catherine A. Millar, 1859, 3 children—Marie Petronella, Willemina F., Mauritz Frederick Hendrick. Quickly acquired wide European reputation in marine painting; came to U.S., 1859; opened and maintained studio for remainer of life, N.Y.C.; asso., later academician Acad. of Design, N.Y.; best-known paintings include Shipwreck in the English Channel, Rapids above Niagara Falls, and Moonlight at Sunset. Died N.Y.C., Nov. 23, 1895.

De HAVEN, Edwin Jesse, naval officer; b. Phila., May 7, 1816; s. William and Maria (MacKeever) De H.; m. Mary Norris Da Costa, May 7, 1844. Apptd. midshipman U.S. Navy, 1829; served in West Indies, 1829-32, with Brazil Squadron, 1832-35, in Pacific Squadron, 1837; passed midshipman, 1835, acting master, 1839; with Wilkes expdn. to Antarctic and Pacific, 1839-42; commd. lt., 1841; served in steamer Mississippi during Mexican War; in command expdn. to Arctic region to search for Sir John Franklin (explorer who had disappeared 1845), 1850-51, failed to find Franklin but discovered and named

Grinnell Land; with Coast Survey, 1853-57; ret., 1862. Died Phila. May 1, 1865; buried Old Christ Ch. Graveyard, Phila.

DeHON, Theodore, clergyman; b. Boston, Dec. 8, 1776; grad. Harvard, 1795; studied theology Trinity Coll. Ordained deacon Protestant Episcopal Ch., Newburyport, Mass., 1797; rector Trinity Ch., Newport, R.I., 1798-1801; toured the South, 1802-03; rector St. Michael's Ch., Charleston, S.C., 1809-12; bishop of S.C., 1812-17; attended Gen. Presbyn. Conv., Phila., 1814, N.Y., 1817. Died of yellow fever, Charleston, Aug. 6, 1817.

DEITZLER, George Washington, abolitionist, mayor; b. Pine Grove, Pa., Nov. 30, 1826; s. Jacob and Maria Deitzler; m. Anna McNeil, Sept. 1864. Aide-de-camp to comdr. free-state forces in Kan., 1855; mem. free-state Territorial Lgeislature, Kan., 1857-58; speaker Kan. Ho. of Reps.; mem. Kan. Senate under Topeka Constn.; became mayor Lawrence (Kan.), 1860; active in organizing 1st Regt., Kan. Volunteer Inf., apptd. col., promoted to brig. gen., 1862, became comdr.-in-chief with rank of maj. gen., 1864; dir. Leavenworth, Lawrence & Ft. Gibson R.R. Co.; treas. U. Kan., 1866. Died Ariz., Apr. 10, 1884.

De JARNETTE, Daniel Coleman, congressman; b. "Spring Grove Manor," nr. Bowling Green, Va., Oct. 18, 1822; attended Bethany (Va., now W. Va.) Coll. Engaged in agr.; mem. Va. Ho. of Reps., 1853-58; mem. U.S. Ho. of Reps. (Democrat) from Va., 36th Congress, 1859-61; mem. 1st, 2d Confederate congresses from Va., 1862-65; an arbitrator to define boundary between Md. and Va., 1871. Died White Sulphur Spirngs, W. Va,. Aug. 20, 1881; buried pvt. burying ground "Spring Grove," Caroline County, Va.

De KAY, George Colman, naval officer; b. N.Y.C., Mar. 5, 1802; s. George and Catherine (Colman) De K.; m. Janet Halleck Drake, 1833, 7 children. Became mcht. capt., 1822; commd. capt. Argentine Navy during dispute with Brazil over possession of what is now Uruguay, 1826; promoted lt. col., 1827; engaged in shipbldg. business, 1828-31; in naval service of Sultan of Turkey, 1831-32; returned to shipbldg. business, 1832; in charge of Macedonian in transport foodstuffs (paid for mostly by himself) to Ireland during famine of 1847. Died Washington, D.C., Jan. 31, 1849.

De KAY, James Ellsworth, naturalist; b. Lisbon, Portugal, Oct. 12, 1792; s. George and Catherine (Colman) De K.; attended Yale, 1810-12; M.D., U. Edinburgh (Scotland), 1819; m. Janet Eckford, July 31, 1821. Librarian, editor transactions Lyceum of Natural History, N.Y.C., 1819-30; dabbled in literary life, asso. with Joseph Rodman Drake, James Fenimore Cooper; visited Turkey, 1831-32; commd. to prepare zool. sect. Natural History Survey of State of N.Y., 1836-44. Author: Sketches of Turkey by an America, 1833; Zoology of New York, 5 vols., 1842-44. Died Oyster Bay, L.I., N.Y., Nov. 21, 1851.

De KOVEN, James, clergyman; b. Middletown, Conn., Sept. 19, 1831; s. Henry Louis and Margaret (Sebor) De K.; grad. Columbia, 1851, Gen. Theol. Sem., N.Y.C., 1854. Ordained deacon Protestant Episcopal Ch., 1854, priest, 1855; asst. rector at Delafield, Wis., prof. ecclesiastical history Nashotah Theol. Sem., in charge of St. John's Hall (prep. sch.), 1855-59; rector Racine (Wis.) Coll., 1859-79; rep. from Racine diocese to Gen. Conv. Protestant Episcopal Ch., 1868-79; defended ritualist beliefs in conflict within Ch. over ceremonial uniformity; failed to become bishop because of what his critics called Romanist tendencies. Author: Tracts by Dr. DeKoven and Others, 1875; Sermons Preached on Various Occasions, 1880. Died Racine, Mar. 19, 1879.

De LACY, Walter Washington, engr.; b. Petersburg, Va., Feb. 22, 1819; s. William and Eliza (Lee) De L.; grad. St. Mary's Catholic Coll., 1838; studied engring. informally under Prof. Manhan, U.S. Mil. Acad., 1838. Constn. engr. I.C., Iron Mountain railroads 1839; asst. prof. French, U.S. Mil. Acad., 1840-46; served in Mexican War and Nez Perce War in Wash., 1855; in charge of constn. of a portion of Mullan Rd. from Ft. Benton to Walla Walla, Wash., 1858-60; prospected for gold in Mont., 1861-64; made 1st map of Mont. on commn. from Mont. Legislature, 1864-65; participated in survey for location line of N.P. R.R.; employed in Mont. Surveyor Gen.'s Office, 1890-92; co-founder Mont. Hist. Soc., Mont. Soc. Engrs. Died Helena, Mont., May 13, 1892.

DELAFIELD, Edward, physician, coll. pres.; b. N.Y.C., May 7, 1794; s. John and Ann (Hallett) D.; A.B., Yale, 1812; M.D., Coll. Physicians and Surgeons, N.Y.C., 1816; m. Elina Elwyn, Oct. 1821; m. 2d, Julia Floyd, Jan. 1840; 5 children. Practiced medicine, specializing in opthalmology, surgery; founder Eye Infirmary, 1818; prof. obstetrics and diseases of women and children Coll. of Physicians and Surgeons, 1825-38, pres., 1858-75; physician N.Y. Hosp., 1834-38; founder, 1st pres. Soc. Relief of Widows and Orphans of Med. Men, 1842; a founder, 1st pres. Am. Opthalmol. Soc., 1864. Died N.Y.C., Feb. 13, 1875.

DELAFIELD, John, mcht.; b. England, Mar. 27, 1749; s. John and Martha (Dell) D.; m. Ann Hallett, 11 children including John. Came to U.S., 1783, brought with him 1st copy of provisional peace treaty between England and U.S. to reach America; became one of richest traders in N.Y.C.; dir. Mut. Assurance Co. of N.Y., 1787; retired from merc. business, 1798; pres. United Ins. Co.; lost most of fortune when vessels he had underwrtiten were destroyed during War of 1812. Died July 3, 1824.

DELAFIELD, John, banker, farmer; b. N.Y.C., Jan. 22, 1786; s. John and Ann (Hallett) D.; grad. Columbia, 1802; m. Mary Roberts; m. 2d, Harriet Wadsworth Tallmadge; at least one child, John. Became owner several mcht. ships, later became banker, London Eng.; held technical prisoner of war because of Am. citizenship during War of 1812; returned to U.S. after bad investments cost him his fortune, 1820; became pres. N.Y.C. bank; pres. N.Y. Banking Co., 1838, lost fortune for a 2d time when Western investments failed; bought large farm in Seneca County, N.Y., made farm a model of advanced agrl. techniques; mem. N.Y. Philharmonic Soc.; raised funds for founding U. City of N.Y.; a founder N.Y. Hist. Soc.; 1st pres. N.Y. State Agrl. Soc. Died Geneva, N.Y., Oct. 22, 1853.

DELAFIELD, Richard, mil. engr., ednl. adminstr.; b. N.Y.C., Sept. 1, 1798; s. John and Ann (Hallett) D.; grad. U.S. Mil. Acad., 1818; m. Helen Summers; m. 2d, Harriet Covington; 6 children. Commd. 2d lt. U.S. Army, 1818, advanced through grades to maj. gen., 1855; supt. U.S. Mil. Acad., West Point, Ga., 1838-45, 56-61; superintending engr. N.Y. Harbor Defenses, 1845-56; mem. Mil. Commn. to Crimea, 1855; commd. brig. gen., chief of engrs. U.S. Army, 1864, in command Corps Engrs., also in charge of Engr. Bur., Washington, D.C., 1864-66; ret., 1866; mem. Commn. for Improvement Boston Harbor; regent Smithsonian Instn. Author: Report on the Art of War in Europe in 1854-6 (published by order of U.S. Congress), 1860. Died Washington, D.C., Nov. 5, 1873.

DELAHAY, Mark William, judge; b. June 24, 1817. Began publ. Territorial Register (free state paper), Leavenworth, Kan., 1855, was denounced as traitor by proslavery party; U.S. dist. judge for Kan., 1863-73. Died Kansas City, Kan., May 8, 1879.

DELAMANO, William, artist. Employed as prin. artist P.T. Barnum's Am. Museum, N.Y.C., during 1850's; produced moving panorama of London Crystal Palace Exhbn., 1851; did panorama of Hudson River shown in N.Y.C., 1858.

DELAMATER, Cornelius Henry, mech. engr.; b. Rhinebeck, N.Y., Aug. 30, 1821; s. William and Eliza (Douglass) D.; m. Ruth O. Caller, 6 children. Built iron boats; built 1st steam fire engines used in U.S.; built engines for Monitor; partner (with Peter Hogg, ret. 1856) in iron works, 1850-56, pres. Delameter Iron Works, 1856-89, constructed 30 gunboats for Spanish govt., 1869; noted for propellors, air compressors, for constrn. 1st successful submarine torpedo boat, 1881; an original mem. Am. Soc. Mech. Engrs. Died N.Y.C., Feb. 7, 1889; buried Woodlawn Cemetery, N.Y.C.

DE LA MATYR, Gilbert, clergyman, congressman; b. Pharsalia, Chenango County, N.Y., July 8, 1825; grad. theol. course of Methodist Episcopal Ch., 1854. Became itinerant elder Meth. Episcopal Ch.; mem. Gen. Conf., 1868, presiding elder, 1 term; helped enlist 8th Regt., N.Y. Heavy Arty., U.S. Army, 1862, served as chaplain, 3 years; pastor in several large cities, including Indpls., Ind.; mem. U.S. Ho. of Reps. (Nat. and Democrat) from Ind. 46th Congress, 1879-81; became pastor, Denver, Colo., 1881; pastor 1st Meth. Episcopal Ch., Akron, O., 1889-92. Died Akron, May 17, 1892; buried Mt. Albion Cemetery, Albion, N.Y.

de la MOTHE, Antoine (sieur de Cadillac), colonial gov.; b. Gascony, France, 1660; s. Jean de la Mothe and Jeanne de Malenfant; m. Marie Therese Guyon, 1687. In command post of Mackinac (most important position in Western country), 1694; capt. colonial troops of the Marine, 1699; obtained grant of Detroit and title of lt. of the King; set out with colonists to found Detroit, 1701; gov. La., 1713-16. Died Castle Sarrazin, France, Oct. 18, 1730.

DE LANCEY, James, jurist, colonial govt. ofcl.; b. N.Y.C., Nov. 27, 1703; s. Stephen and Anne (van Cortlandt) De L.; grad. Corpus Christi Coll., Cambridge (Eng.) U., m. Anne Heathcote, circa 1729, 7 children. Admitted to N.Y. bar, 1725; apptd. to N.Y. Gov's Council, 1729; chief framer Montgomery Charter for City N.Y., 1730; judge N.Y. Supreme Ct., 1731-33, chief justice, 1733-60; lt. gov. N.Y., 1753-55, 57-60; presided at Albany Cor 1754; attended Conf. of Govs., 1755. Died N.Y. July 30, 1760.

De LANCEY, James, mcht., horse-racer; N.Y.C., 1732; s. James and Anne (Heathco De L.; attended Cambridge; m. Margaret All 1771, several children. Became capt. Brit. Arm served in Lake George campaign, 1758, Niag campaign, 1759; inherited father's merc. and r estate interests in N.Y.C., 1760; brought thoroughbred race horses to America, circa 176 owned largest stable running horses in coloni boss of faction which controlled N.Y. Provinc Assembly in last years; went to England, 177 property confiscated by N.Y. State, 1779; v.p. agts. to secure restitution for losses suffered Loyalists, 1783. Died Bath, Eng., 1800.

De LANCEY, James, loyalist; b. Westchest N.Y., 1746; s. Peter and Elizabeth (Colden) De m. Martha Tippetts; 10 children. Leader " Lancey Party" in politics of Colony of N.Y.; r from Westchester in N.Y. Colonial Assemb 1750-68; comdr. De Lancey's Horse (a loya raiding cavalry troop outside N.Y.C.), 1776-8 proscribed by N.Y. Act of Attainder, 1779; f to Nova Scotia, Can., 1782; mem. N.S. Assemb apptd. to N.S. Council, 1799. Died May 2, 1804.

De LANCEY, Oliver, colonial legislator, ar officer; b. N.Y.C., Sept. 16 1718; s. Stephen a Anne (van Cortlandt) De L.; m. Phila Franks, children. Alderman for the Outward, 1754-5 raised N.Y.C. Regt. for expdn. against Cro Point, 1758; mem. N.Y.C. delegation to N.Y. A sembly, 1759-60; mem. N.Y. Provincial Counc 1760-76; receiver gen., 1763; col.-in-chief Mil. Dist., 1773; Loyalist, commd. brig. gen. Br Army (highest ranking American), raised 3 b talions of troops which carried his name, beca symbol of Loyalist during Am. Revolution; we to Eng., 1783. Died Beverley, Eng., Oct. 25, 178

De LANCEY, William Heathcote, clergyman; Mamaroneck, N.Y., Oct. 8, 1797; s. John Pe and Elizabeth (Floyd) De L.; grad. Yale, 181 D.D. (hon.), 1827; studied theology under Bish Hobart, N.Y.C. 1817-22; D.C.L. (hon.), Oxf (Eng.) U., 1852; m. Frances Munro, Nov. 22, 182 8 children including Edward. Ordained pri Protestant Episcopal Ch., 1822; asst. minister a sec. Phila. diocese, 1822-28; sec. Ho. of Bish of Gen. Conv., Protestant Episcopal Ch., 1823, 2 provost U. Pa., 1828-33; 1st bishop Diocese Western N.Y., 1839-65; represented Am. Ch. London during 3d Jubilee of Soc. for Propagati of Gospel, 1852; co-founder DeVeaux Coll., Niaga Falls, N.Y. Died Apr. 5, 1865.

De LANGLADE, Charles Michel, army office b. Mackinac, Can., May 1729; s. Augustin Mor and Domitelle (Ottawa Indian) De L.; m. Cha lotte Bourassa, 1754, several children. Comm cadet French Colonial Army, 1750, ensign, 175 lt., 1760; led Indian allies in battles at La Champlain, Ft. William Henry, Quebec, a Montreal during French and Indian War; beca Brit. subject, 1760; as capt. in Brit. army led I dian auxiliaries against Col. George Rogers Cla during Am. Revolution; granted lands in Cana for services to England Died Green Bay, Wis 1801.

DELANO, Amassa, mcht.; b. Duxbury, Mas Feb. 21, 1763; s. Samuel and Abigail (Drew) I m. Hannah Appleton, no children. Served as p Continental Army, 1776-79; engaged in shippi trade with West Indies, until 1787; comman trading ships in trade with China and other pa of world, 1790-1810. Author: Narrative of Voyag and Travels in the Northern and Southern Hen spheres, Comprising Three Voyages Around t World, 1817. Died Boston, Apr. 21, 1823.

DELANO, Charles, congressman, lawyer; New Braintree, Mass., June 24, 1820; grad. A herst (Mass.) Coll., 1840; studied law. Admitt to bar, 1842, began practice of law, Amhers moved to Northampton, Mass., 1848; treas. Ham shire County, 1849-58; mem. U.S. Ho. of Rep (Republican) from Mass., 36th-37th congress 1859-63; trustee Clarke Sch. for Edn. of Dea 1877-83; spl. counsel for Commonwealth of Mas in matters relating to Hoosac Tunnel and Tr & Greenfield R.R., 1878-83. Died Northampto Jan. 23, 1883; buried Bridge Street Cemeter

DELANO, Columbus, congressman, sec. of i terior; b. Shoreham, Vt., June 5, 1809; s. Jam and Lucinda (Bateman) D.; LL.D. (hon.), Keny Coll.; m. Elizabeth Leavenworth, July 13, 183 children—Elizabeth, John. Licensed to practi law, 1831; pros. atty. Knox County (O.), 183 mem. U.S. Ho. of Reps. from Ohio, 28th, 39th-40 congresses, 1845-47, 65-69; del. Republican Na Conv., 1860-64; U.S. commr. internal revenu 1869-70; U.S. sec. of interior, 1870-75, head Bu Indian Affairs, charged with fraud, supported congressional findings of neglect and incompetenc resigned from office, no ofcl. action taken; pre

Nat. Wool Growers Assn.; trustee Kenyon Coll., builder Delano Hall. Died Mt. Vernon, O., Oct. 23, 1896.

DELANY, Martin Robinson, physician, army officer; b. Charles Town, Va. (now Charleston, W. Va.), May 6, 1812; s. Samuel and Pati D.; entered Harvard, 1849, after having been rejected in N.Y., Pa.; m. Kate A. Richards, Mar. 15, 1843, 11 children. Went to Pa., 1822; with Frederick Douglass issued Northern Star, Rochester, N.Y., 1847; originator, pres. Nat. Emigration Conv., 1854, apptd. to lead expdn. to Niger Valley, Africa, to explore possibilities of returning Negroes to the area; commd. maj. U.S. Army (1st Negro maj.), 1865; judge, Charleston, S.C.; fought vigorously against polit. corruption, but defeated when he stood for election on Independent Republican ticket as lt. gov. S.C., 1874. Author: Condition, Elevation and Destiny of the Colored People of the United States Politically Considered, 1852. Died Xenia, O., Jan. 24, 1885.

DELAPLAINE, Isaac Clason, congressman; b. N.Y.C., Oct. 27, 1817; grad. Columbia, 1834; studied law. Admitted to bar, circa 1840, began practice of law, N.Y.C.; mem. U.S. Ho. of Reps. (Fusionist) from N.Y., 37th Congress, 1861-63. Died N.Y.C., July 17, 1866; buried Greenwood Cemetery, Bklyn.

de la PUENTE, Don Juan Joseph Eligio, provincial ofcl.; b. St. Augustine, Fla., 1724; Creole of Spanish descent; ed. Havana, Cuba. Returned to Fla. at age 15, became clk. of Treasury, rising to chief clk. before 1763; also mcht. affiliated with Brit. exporters in N Y. and Charleston; in charge of emigrant non-mil. population in Spanish evacuation of Fla., 1763, persuaded all to leave, rather than remain under Brit. rule; later apptd. chief auditor of Treasury in Havana; bombarded Spanish court with propaganda for recovery of Fla., was largely responsible for Spain's entry into the Revolutionary War. Died Havana, 1781.

DE LARGE, Robert Carlos, congressman; b. Aiken, S.C., Mar. 15, 1842; grad. high sch. Engaged in farming; del. S.C. Constl. Conv., 1868; mem. S.C. Ho. of Reps., 1868-70; a commr. S.C. sinking fund; state land commr., 1870-71; mem. U.S. Ho. of Reps. (Republican contested election) from S.C., 42d Congress, 1871-Jan. 24, 1873; local magistrate until 1874. Died Charleston, S.C., Feb. 14, 1874; buried Brown Fellowship Graveyard.

De La RICHARDIE, Armand, missionary; b. Perigueux, France, June 7, 1686. Joined Soc. of Jesus, Bordeaux, 1703; sent to Can., 1725; spent 2 years learning Huron Indian lang. in Lorette, then served as missionary to Huron Indians of area around present city of Detroit, 24 years; recalled because of illness to Quebec, Can., 1751. Died Quebec, Oct. 4, 1758.

de la RONDE, Louis Denis, naval officer, Am. prospector; b. Canada, 1675; s. Pierre Denis and Catherine (Le Neuf) de la R.; m. Marie Louise Chartier, July 20, 1709, at least 2 children. Served in French Navy, 1688-1728; explored La. and Mississippi River with his commanding officer, 1700-01; participated in secret mission, Boston, 1711, decorated Cross of Order of St. Louis for his service; commanded post on Madeline Island, Chequamegon Bay, Lake Superior for Canadian army, 1727; discovered copper in Lake Superior area, got permission from France to explore area, 1733, sent back copper samples to Que., 1734; with his sons began settlement, called Ft. La Pointe on Madeline Island, 1739 (destroyed in Indian War of 1740). Died Que., Can., Mar. 1741.

de LAUDONNIÉRE, René Goulaine, colonizer; b. France; flourished 1562-82. Lt. in expdn. of French Huguenots under Jean Ribaut to found colony in Am., 1562, came up St. John's River in Fla., settled at Charlesfort (now Port Royal), S.C.; returned to France with Ribaut, 1562; sent back to colony with 3 ships and 300 colonists, 1564, discovered colony had been abandoned; founded new colony Ft. Caroline (for Charles IX) on St. John's River (colony failed as result of problems over labor, food, gold, and warfare with Indians and Spaniards); escaped Spanish massacre of colony, sailed for Europe on one of Ribaut's ships, 1565; reached France, after having been shipwrecked in Wales, 1566, retired to his estate. Author: L'Histoire notable de la Florida, Paris, 1586. Died France.

DELAVAN, Edward Cornelius, reformer; b. Westchester County, N.Y., 1793; m. Abby Smith; m. 2d, Harriet Schuyler. Formed partnership with brother in wine business, 1814, purchcasing agt. in Europe, 1814-16, partner, N.Y.C., 1816-25; in real estate business, Albany, N.Y., 1825-30; became convinced of evils of alcohol, organized N.Y. State Temperance Soc., 1829; published 2 temperance newspapers American Temperance Intelligencer and Temperance Recorder; chmn. exec. com. Am. Temperance Union, 1836; published temperance jour. Enquirer, 1841. Died Schenectady, N.Y., Jan. 15, 1871.

De la WARR, baron, see West, Thomas.

DE LE MONTANYA, James, congressman; b. N.Y.C., Mar. 20, 1798. Supr., Haverstraw (N Y.), 1832-33; mem. N.Y. State Assembly, 1833; mem. U.S. Ho. of Reps. (Democrat) from N.Y., 26th Congress, 1839-41. Died N.Y.C., Apr. 29, 1849; buried Barnes family burial ground, Stony Point, Rockland County, N.Y.

De LEON, Edwin, diplomat; s. Dr. M. Hendricks and Rebecca (Lopez) De L.; grad. S.C. Coll., 1837. Admitted to S.C. bar, 1840; co-editor Republican, Savannah, Ga., 1842-48; founder (with Ellwood Fisher) Southern Press, Washington, D.C., 1850-54; consul gen. and diplomatic agt. to Egypt and dependencies (apptd. by Pres. Pierce), 1854-60; Confederate diplomatic agt. to Europe, 1862-66; revisited Egypt, 1869, established telephone system in prin. Egyptian cities, 1881. Author: Thirty Years of my Life on Three Continents; Egypt Under Its Khedives (1882); Under the Star and Under the Crescent (1882). Died N.Y.C., Dec. 1, 1891.

DELERY, Francois Charles, physician, author; b. St. Charles Parish, La., Jan. 28, 1815; s. Louis Boisclair and Marie (Babin) D.; studied medicine, Paris, France, 1829-42; m. Odile Delery. Physician, City of New Orleans, 1842-49; pres. New Orleans Bd. Health, 1849-51; founder, contbr. to l'Union Medicale; represented New Orleans at Quarantine Congress, Phila., 1858; lived in Havana (Cuba) during Civil War, wrote articles supporting Confederacy; coroner City of New Orleans, 1865. Author: Essai sur la liberte, 1847; Quelques mots sur le Nativisme, 1854; Precis historique de la fievre jaune de 1858, 1859; Le spectre noir ou la radicalisme aux Etats-Unis, 1868; L'Ecole du peuple, 1877; Quantaine, 1878. Died June 12, 1880.

de LÉRY, Joseph Gaspard Chaussegros, engr.; b. July 20, 1721; s. Gaspard Chaussegros and Marie-Renée (Le Gardeur de Beauvois) de Léry; attended Que. Sem., 1731-34; m. Louise Martel de Brouague, 1753. Asst. engr. French-Canadian Army, 1739; travelled to La. in war with Chickasaw Indians, 1739-42; engr. at Crown Point, 1743, supervised finishing of Ft. St. Frederic; commd. 1st ensign, 1748, lt., 1751; surveyed constrns. at Detroit and in Allegheny River Valley, 1754-55; commd. capt., 1757; fought in French and Indian War, 1757; mem. Que. Legislative Council, 1778; mem. Lower Canada Legislative Council, 1791; kept jours. of his trips from 1748-59 (published in Rapport de L'Archiviste de la Province de Quebec, 1926-29). Died Que., Can., Dec. 11, 1797.

de L'HALLE, Constantin, clergyman; flourished 1696-1706. Joined Recollect Order, ordained priest Roman Catholic Ch.; came to Can., 1696, served parishes at Longueuil, Batiscan; in charge of parish of St. Anne at garrison in colony founded by Sieur de la Cadillac at Detroit, 1701-06; active in caring for Indians of Detroit area. Killed by renegade Ottawa Indians during revolt, Detroit, June 6, 1706; buried St. Anne's Ch., Detroit.

DELLET, James, congressman, lawyer; b. Feb. 18, 1788; grad. U. S.C. at Columbia, 1810; studied law. Admitted to bar, 1813, began practice of law; moved to Claiborne, Ala., 1818; mem. 1st Ala. Ho. of Reps., 1819, 21, 25, speaker, 1819; mem. U.S. Ho. of Reps. (Whig) from Ala., 26th, 28th congresses, 1839-41, 43-45; resumed law practice, also engaged in farming. Died Claiborne, Dec. 21, 1848; buried pvt. cemetery, Claiborne.

DELMONICO, Lorenzo, restaurateur; b. Marengo, Switzerland, Mar. 13, 1813; m. Mme. Miege, 1856. Came to Am., 1832. Opened his 1st restaurant in downtown N.Y.C., located on William St., cooked, served foods in Am. manner, also attracted Parisian chefs, destroyed in fire, 1835, succeeded by restaurants at 76 Broad St., Beaver and Williams streets, Broadway and 26th st.; condr. Delmonico hotel at 21-25 Broadway, 1846-56; prin. restaurant located at Broadway and Chambers streets, 1855-75; he won nat. recognition as tchr. gastronomy, made N.Y.C. known as the center of good living, was largely responsible for growth of the restaurant as an instn. in Am. cities; Delmonico chain grew to largest orgn. of its kind. Founder pub. sch., Marengo, Switzerland. Died Sept. 3, 1881.

De LOM D'ARCE, Louis-Armand (baron de Lahontan), army officer; b. Lahontan, France, June 9, 1666; s. Isaac and Jeanne-Francoise le Fascheaux (de Couttes) de Lom D'Arce. Mem. marine corps, came to French colony in Am., 1683; participated in several expdns. against Iroquois Indians, 1684-87; commanded Ft. St. Joseph on St. Clair River, 1687; travelled into western country, explored upper Mississippi River, 1688-89; returned to France, 1690, promoted capt., decorated Order of Notre Dame; returned to New France, 1691, participated in battle against Brit. naval force off Newfoundland, 1692; royal lt. for Newfoundland, 1692-93; spent remainder of life wandering through courts of Europe. Author: Nouveaux Voyages de Mr. le Baron de Lahontan dans l'Amerique Septentrionale (1 of best contemporary descriptions of life in French colony in Am.), published in Holland, 1703. Died probably in Hanover, circa 1713.

De LONG, George Washington, explorer; b. N.Y.C., Aug. 22, 1844; s. Levi and Catherine (Greames) De L.; grad. U.S. Naval Acad., 1865; m. Emma Watton, Mar. 1, 1871, 1 child. Commd. lt. U.S. Navy, 1869; exec. officer on sch. ship St. Mary's, 1873-78; accompanied Capt. D.L. Braine on Arctic expdn. under authority U.S. Govt., 1873; commanded ship Jeanette, sailing from San Francisco on Arctic research project, 1879, proceeded to Siberian Coast, northward until trapped by ice, Sept. 5, 1879, vessel drifted to N.W. and was crushed 77° 15' N., 155° E., June 12, 1881; with 14 others reached mouth of Lena River (Siberia) where all died from cold and starvation except 2 men sent for relief; bodies discovered by chief engr. George W. Melville, Mar. 23, 1882; jour., The Voyage of the Jeanette, published by widow. Died Siberia, Oct. 30, 1881.

de LOUTHERBOURG, Annibale Christian Henry, artist; b. Paris, France, 1765; s. P.J. de Loutherbourg. Exhibited at Royal Acad., London, Eng., 1793; came to Am., 1794, established himself as miniaturist, Phila.; later engaged as soap-boiler, limner; executed sketch of George Washington's farewell to Congress, circa 1798. Died London, 1813.

de LUNA Y ARELLANO, Tristan, explorer; flourished 1530-61; son of Don Carlos de Luna y Arellano; m. Isabel de Rojas. Left Spain as capt. of Francisco Coronado's expdn. to New Spain, 1530; suppressed Indian outbreak in Oaxaco (now N.M.) for viceroy, Mendoza, 1548; apptd. gov., capt. gen. of Fla., with duties of exploring and fortifying area, 1557; gov. Fla., 1557-61.

De MEZIERES Y CLUGNY, Athanase, army officer, explorer; b. Paris, France, c. 1715; s. Louis Christophe de Mezieres and Marie Antoinette Clugny; m. Marie Petronelle Felicione de St. Denis, Apr. 18, 1746; m. 2d, Dame Pelagie Fazende. Served from ensign to lt. col.; a commr. to determine Tex.-La. boundary at Gulf of Mexico, 1756; as ruler Red River Valley, supervised Indian trade, won tribes of La., Tex., Ark. and Okla. to Spanish allegiance; promoted lt. col. by King of Spain, 1772; created knight Order of St. Louis; apptd. gov. Tex., 1779. Died before taking office, Nov. 2, 1779; buried Cathedral of San Fernando, San Antonio, Tex.

De MILLE, Henry Churchill, playwright; b. Washington, N.C., Sept. 17, 1853; s. William Edward and Margaret (Blount) De M.; A.B., A.M., Columbia, 1875; m. Mathilde Beatrice Samuel, 1876, 3 children including William C., Cecil B. Appeared as actor in A.M. Palmer's company for short time; later instr. Am. Acad. Dramatic Arts; wrote most of plays in collaboration with David Belasco including: The Wife, 1887, Lord Chumley, 1888, The Charity Ball, 1889, Men and Women, 1890. Died Pompton, N.J., Feb. 10, 1893.

DEMING, Benjamin F., congressman; b. Danville, Vt., 1790. Became engaged in merc. activities; clk. Caledonia County (Vt.) Ct., 1817-33; county judge of probate, 1821-33; mem. Vt. Gov.'s Council, 1827-32; mem. U.S. Ho. of Reps. (Whig) from Vt., 23d Congress, 1833-34. Died en route home, at Saratoga Springs, N.Y., July 11, 1834; buried Danville Green Cemetery.

DEMING, Henry Champion, congressman, collector internal revenue; b. Colchester, Conn., May 23, 1815; s. David and Abigail (Champion) D.; grad. Yale, 1836; LL.B., Harvard, 1839, B.L. (hon.), 1869; LL.D. (hon.), Trinity Coll., 1869; m. Sarah Clerc, 1850; m. 2d, Annie Putnam, 1871; 4 children. Mem. Conn. Legislature from Hartford, 1849-50, 59-61, speaker pro tem; mem. Conn. Senate, 1851; mayor Hartford, 1854-59, 60-62; commd. lt. col. 14th Conn. Volunteer Regt.; provisional mayor New Orleans, 1862-63; mem. U.S. Ho. of Reps. from Conn., 38th-39th congresses, 1863-67; del. Loyalist Conv., Phila., 1866; U.S. collector internal revenue, 1869-72. Author: The Life of Ulysses S. Grant, General, United States Army, 1868. Translator: Mysteries of Paris; The Wandering Jew, 1840 (both by Eugene Sue). Died Hartford, Oct. 9, 1872; buried Spring Grove Cemetery, Hartford.

De MIRANDA, Francisco, army officer; b. Caracas, Venezuela, 1750. Became officer Spanish Army; served under Bernardo de Gálvez in Spanish attack on Pensacola (when Spain was ally of rebels in Am. Revolution), 1781; fought under Dumouriez in French Revolutionary Wars; fought unsuccessful revolutionary war in Venezuela against Spanish control, 1806-12, captured and imprisoned for rest of life; called the Precursor. Died 1816.

DEMME, Charles Rudolph, clergyman; b. Muhlhausen, Thuringen, Germany, Apr. 10, 1795; s.

Hermann Gottfried and Frederika (Konig) D.; attended U. Gottingen, U. Halle (both Germany); m. Mariana Schaeffer, Oct. 7, 1828, 11 children. Came to U.S., 1818; ordained to ministry Lutheran Ch., 1818; pastor, Hummelstown, Pa., 1818-21; asst. pastor St. Michael's and Zion's Ch., Phila., 1822-34, pastor, 1834-59, pastor emeritus, 1859-63; mem. Am. Philos. Soc., Am. Tract Soc. Author: Die Werke des Flavius Josephus, 1839. Editor: Liturgie und Kirchenagende, 1842, 2d edit., 1855; Deutsches Gesangbuch, 1849. Died Sept. 1, 1863.

De MOKCSA, Agoston Haraszthy, pioneer; b. Futtak, Hungary, circa 1812; s. Charles Haraszthy; m. Eleanor Dodinsky, 3 children. Mem. Royal Hungarian Body Guard; pvt. sec. to viceroy of Hungary; came to U.S., 1840, went to Wis., founded Széptáj, Haraszthy (later Westfield, now Sauk City); erected sch., store and sawmill attracting various emigrants; returned to Hungary, 1842, sold estate and returned with wife; opened brick yard, Sauk City, 1842; operated 1st ferryboat across Wisconsin River at Sauk City, 1844; in need of better climate to settle his asthma condition, moved to Cal., 1849; sheriff San Diego County (Cal.), 1850; mem. Cal. Legislature, 1852; planted 1st imported vines around San Francisco, 1852; worked at San Francisco Mint, 1857; planted 1st vineyard in Cal., 1858; made commr. to seek out best ways of improving grape-vine culture in Cal., 1861; incorporated his properties into Buena Vista Viticultural Soc., 1863; lost all his property, 1866; moved to Nicaragua, started large sugar plantation. Author: Utazás Ejszak-Amerikabán, 2 vols., Pest, 1844; Grape Culture, Wines, and Wine-Making; with Notes upon Agriculture and Horticulture, 1862. Died by drowning nr. Corinto, Nicaragua, July 6, 1869.

de MOSCOSO de ALVARADO, Luis, explorer; b. Zafra, Spain; s. Alonso and Isabel (de Alvarado) Hernández de Diosdado. Served under Pedro de Alvarado in Guatemala and Quito, 1530-35; embarked from San Lucar with Hernando de Soto, 1538, commanded galleon La Concepción; 2d in command under de Soto in Fla.; assumed command upon death of de Soto, 1542; attempted to reach Mexico from Guachoya (nr. now Arkansas City), 1542; managed to reach Gulf of Mexico after much bitter Indian fighting; reached Veracruz with 311 survivors, 1543. Flourished 1530-43.

De MOTT, John, mcht., congressman; b. Readington, N.J., Oct. 7, 1790; attended common schs., Lodi, N.Y. Served as maj. gen. 38th Brigade, N.Y. Militia; supr. Town of Covert, 1823-24, Lodi, 1826-30; prominent mcht. and grain buyer, Lodi, for more than 40 years; mem. N.Y. State Assembly, 1833; mem. U.S. Ho. of Reps. (Democrat) from N.Y., 29th Congress, 1845-47; engaged in banking. Died Lodi, July 31, 1870; buried Evergreen Cemetery, Ovid, N.Y.

DEMPSTER, John, theologian; b. Florida, N.Y., Jan. 2, 1794; 4 children. Methodist pastor in various N.Y. churches, 1816-36; Meth. missionary to Buenos Aires, 1836-42; pastor in N.Y.C., 1842-45; founder Wesley Theol. Inst. (1st Meth. theol. sem. in U.S.; (now Boston U. Theol. Sch.), 1845, prof. theology, 1847-54; a founder Garrett Bibl. Inst., Chgo., 1854, sr. prof., 1855-63. Died Nov. 28, 1863.

de NANCREDE, Paul Joseph Guerard, army officer, educator, publisher; b. Hericy, France, Mar. 16, 1761; s. Jean Joseph and Louise Francoise (Gautier) Guerard; m. Hannah Dixey, Nov. 11, 1788; 9 children, including Joseph Guerard Nancrede. Served in French Army under Rochambeau during Am. Revolution; returned to U.S., 1785; instr. French lang. and lit. Harvard, 1787-98; bookseller, printer, Boston and Phila. compiled L'Abeille Francoise (1st French sch. text composed especially for use in Am. colls.), 1792; published a French paper Courier de Boston, 1789. Died Paris, France, Dec. 15, 1841.

de NARVAEZ, Panfilo, conquistador; b. Valladolidi, Spain, circa 1478; m. Maria de Valenzuela. Served in Spanish Army in Jamaica at early age; was chief capt. in campaign against Cuba under Valásquez; commd. by Valásquez to seize or kill Cortés, 1520; defeated, held prisoner, until 1521; engaged in expdn. to colonize Florida, 1526-28; organized unsuccessful expdn. in pursuit of alleged riches, Apalaches, Mexico, 1528. Died 1528.

De NECKERE, Leo Raymond, clergyman; b. Wevelghem, Belgium, June 6, 1800; studied at Roulers, then at Lazarist sem., Ghent; came to U.S. in response to call for priests, attended St. Thomas Sem., Ky. and St. Mary of the Barrens, Mo. Joined Lazarist Order, 1820, ordained priest Roman Catholic Ch., 1822; taught at St. Mary's, did missionary work in Mo. and La.; apptd. vicar gen. of New Orleans, 1827, bishop, 1829. Died of plague while caring for plague victims, New Orleans, Sept. 4, 1833.

DENISON, Charles, lawyer, congressman; b. Wyoming Valley, Pa., Jan. 23, 1818; grad. Dickinson Coll., Carlisle, Pa., 1838; studied law. Admitted to bar, 1840, began practice of law, Wilkes-Barre, Pa.; mem. U.S. Ho. of Reps. (Democrat) from Pa., 38th-40th congresses, 1863-67. Died Wilkes-Barre, June 27, 1867; buried Forty Fort Cemetery, Kingston, Pa.

DENISON, George, congressman, lawyer; b. Kingston, Pa., Feb. 22, 1790; attended Wilkes-Barre (Pa.) Acad. Engaged in business; clk. Wilkes-Barre Borough Council, 1811-14, mem., many years, pres., 1823-24; recorder, registrar Luzerne County (Pa.), 1812-15; admitted to bar, 1813, began practice of law, Luzerne County; mem. Pa. Ho. of Reps., 1815-16, 27-31; mem. U.S. Ho. of Reps. (Democrat) from Pa., 16th-17th congresses, 1819-23; dep. atty. gen. Luzerne County, 1824; burgess Wilkes-Barre Borough, 1829-30. Died Wilkes-Barre, Aug. 20, 1831; buried Hollenbeck Cemetery.

de NIZA, Marcos, missionary, explorer; b. Nice, Duchy of Savoy (now France). Franciscan missionary to Santo Domingo, 1531; traveled with Spanish troops in Peru; missionary, Neuva Galicia, New Spain (now Mexico), 1538; vice-commissary-gen. Franciscan Order for New Spain, 1539; traveled into parts of N.M. and Ariz., reported existence of great cities (with result that Coronado was sent to conquer region); guide on Coronado's exploration, 1540. Died Mexico, Mar. 25, 1558.

DENMAN, William, publisher; b. Edinburgh, Scotland, Mar. 17, 1784; of German descent; at least 1 son, William. An asso. of publisher William Andrews, London, Eng.; came to N.Y., 1824; founded (with George Pardow) weekly newspaper The Truth Teller, 1825, asso. with paper for 30 years. Died Bklyn., Sept. 12, 1870.

DENNETT, Jonn Richard, journalist; b. Chatham, N.B., Can., 1837; grad. Woburn (Mass.) High Sch.; grad. Harvard, 1862. Editor, Harvard Mag., while in coll.; wrote class-day poem praised by James Russell Lowell; supt. plantation, Beaufort, S.C., throughout Civil War; later traveled extensively in South, wrote series of articles on So. polit. and social situation, pub. in N.Y. Nation (pub. in 1 vol. as The South as It Is, 1865-66, H.M. Christman, 1965); later became mem. editorial staff of Nation, asst. prof. rhetoric at Harvard. Died 1874.

DENNIE, Joseph, editor, author; b. Boston, Aug. 30, 1768; s. Joseph and Mary (Green) D.; grad. Harvard, 1790; studied law under Benjamin West, Charlestown, N.H. Admitted to N.H. bar, 1794; editor Tablet, Boston, 1795, Farmer's Weekly Museum, Walpole, N.H., 1796-99; sec. to Timothy Pickering (U.S. sec. state), Phila., 1799-1800; weekly Port Folio, 1801-12; wrote series of uncollected essays entitled "Lay Preacher" written between 1795-1808, published in his various mags., mostly in Farmer's Museum. Died Phila., Jan. 7, 1812; buried St. Peter's Ch. Graveyard, Phila.

DENNING, William, cannon-maker; b. 1736. Said to have made 1st successful attempt at manufacturing wrought iron cannons; served as artificer in Continental Army; made 2 small cannons, Middlesex, Pa. (one used in Battle of Brandywine, captured by British and placed in Tower of London, still there); declined offer by British to show them how to make cannons. Died Mifflin Twp., Pa., Dec. 19, 1830.

DENNING, William, congressman; probably born St. John's Newfoundland, Apr. 1740. Moved to N.Y.C. in youth, became a businessman; mem. Com. of One Hundred, 1775; dep. N.Y. Provincial Congress, 1775-77; mem. conv. of state reps., 1776-77; mem. N.Y. State Assembly, 1784-87, N.Y. Senate, 1798-1808; mem. Council of Appointment, 1799; mem. U.S. Ho. of Reps. from N.Y., 11th Congress, 1809-1810. Died N.Y.C., Oct. 30, 1819; buried St. Paul's Churchyard.

DENNIS, George Robertson, senator, physician; b. Whitehaven, Somerset County, Md., Apr. 8, 1822; grad. Resselaer Poly. Inst., Troy, N.Y.; attended U. Va. at Charlottesville; grad. in medicine U. Pa. at Phila., 1843. Practiced medicine, Kingston, Md., many years, later engaged in agr.; mem. Md. Senate, 1854, 71; del. Whig Nat. Conv., Phila., 1856, Democratic Nat. Conv., N.Y.C., 1868; mem. Md. Ho. of Dels., 1867; mem. U.S. Senate (Democrat) from Md., 1873-79. Died Kingston, Aug. 13, 1882; buried St. Andrew's Churchyard, Princess Anne, Md.

DENNIS, John, congressman, lawyer; b. "Beverly," Worcester County, Md., Dec. 17, 1771; attended Washington Acad., Yale; studied law; married, at least 1 son, John. Admitted to bar, 1793, began practice of law, Somerset County; mem. Md. Ho. of Dels., 2 terms; mem. U.S. Ho. of Reps. (Federalist) from Md., 5th-8th congresses, 1797-1805, apptd. a mgr. to conduct impeachment proceedings against William Blount (senator from Tenn.), 1798. Died Phila., Aug. 17, 1806; buried Old Christ Church Graveyard.

DENNIS, John, congressman, lawyer; b. "Beckford," nr. Princess Anne, Md., 1807; s. John Dennis; studied law. Admitted to bar, began practice of law; also engaged in agr.; mem. Md. Ho. of Dels.; mem. U.S. Ho. of Reps. (Whig) from Md., 25th-26th congresses, 1837-41; del. Md. Constl. Conv., 1850. Died "Beckford," Nov. 1, 1859.

DENNIS, Littleton Purnell, congressman, lawyer; b. "Beverly," Worcester County, Md., July 21, 1786; attended Washington Acad.; grad. Yale, 1803; studied law. Admitted to bar, began practice of law; mem. Md. Ho. of Dels., 1815-16, 19-27; presdl. elector, 1800, 12, 16, 24, 28; mem. Md. Exec. Council, 1829; an elector Md. Senate, 1831; mem. U.S. Ho. of Reps. (Whig) from Md., 23d Congress, 1833-34. Died Washington, D.C., Apr. 14, 1834; buried Congressional Cemetery.

DENNISON, Aaron Lufkin, watch mfr.; b. Freeport, Me., Mar. 6, 1812; s. Andrew and Lydia (Lufkin) D.; m. Charlotte W. Foster, Jan. 15, 1840, 5 children. Designed 1st factory made watches in world; conducted firm 1st known as Am. Horologue Co., later as Boston Watch Co., (both Roxbury, Mass.), firm moved to Waltham, Mass., became known as Am. Watch Co., 1859, finally as Am. Waltham Watch Co. (developed into Am.'s largest watch co.), supt. until 1861; organizer Tremont Watch Co., 1864; known as father of Am. watchmaking; interested in application of interchangeable parts prodn. method as means of lowering cost and increasing accuracy of Am. watches. Died Jan. 9, 1895.

DENNISON, William, gov. Ohio; b. Cincinnati, Nov. 23, 1815; s. William and Mary (Carter) D.; grad. Miami U., Oxford, O., 1835; m. dau. William Neil, circa 1840. Admitted to Ohio bar, 1840; practiced law, 1840-48; mem. Ohio Senate (Whig), 1848-50; attended preliminary conv., mem. com. on resolutions Republican Nat. Conv., 1856; acting chmn. Ohio delegation Phila. Conv., 1856; gov. Ohio, 1860-62; chmn. Rep. Nat. Conv., 1864; postmaster gen. U.S. under by Pres. Lincoln, 1864-66. Died Columbus, O., June 15, 1882.

DENNY, Ebenezer, army officer, mayor Pitts.; b. Carlisle, Pa., Mar. 11, 1761; s. William and Agnes (Parker) D.; m. Nancy Wilkins, July 1, 1793, 3 sons—Harmer, William, St. Clair, also 2 daus. Commd. ensign 1st Pa. Regt., 1776, fought nr. Williamsburg, Va.; served with advance units at siege of York, 1776; served under St. Clair in Carolinas, became adjutant to Harmer, aide-de-camp to St. Clair; mem. 1st Pa. Constl. Conv. from Bedford County, 1777; commd. capt., 1794, commanded Le-Boeuf expdn.; treas. Allegheny County (Pa.), 1803, 08; 1st mayor Pitts., 1816; dir. br. of Bank of U.S., Bank of Pitts. Died July 21, 1822.

DENNY, Harmar, congressman, lawyer; b. Pitts., May 13, 1794; grad. Dickinson Coll., Carlisle, Pa., 1813; studied law. Admitted to bar, 1816, began practice of law, Pitts.; mem. Pa. Ho. of Reps., 1824-29; mem. U.S. Ho. of Reps. from Pa. (as Anti-Mason, filled vacancy) 21st Congress, Dec. 15, 1829-31, 24th-25th congresses, 1831-35, (as Whig) 24th Congress, 1835-37; del. Pa. Constl. Conv., 1837; Whig presdl. elector, 1840; commr. under act of incorporation Pa. R.R. Co., 1846; incorporator Ohio & Pa. R.R. Co., 1848; pres. Pitts. & Steubenville R.R. Co., 1851-52; trustee Western U. Pa.; bd. dirs. Western Theol. Sem. Died Pitts., Jan. 29, 1852; buried Allegheny Cemetery.

de NOYAN, Pierre-Jacques Payen, army officer; b. Montreal, Que., Can., Nov. 3, 1695; s. Pierre Payen and Catherine Jeanne (Le Moyne) P. de N.; m. Louise Catherine d'Aillebout, Nov. 17, 1731. Comdt. of Ft. Frontenac (now Kingston, Ont.), 1721; took part in expdn. to Sioux Nation, 1728; believed that England could be kept away from Great Lakes by better regulation of Indian trade, strict control of traders and permanent settlements; commandant of Detroit, 1738-42; in command Ft. Frontenac, 1758, surrendered to Col. John Bradstreet, 1758, exchanged for Col. Peter Schuyler; put on trial in France for mismanagement, 1761, imprisoned until 1762. Died circa 1763.

DENOYELLES, Peter, congressman; b. Haverstraw, N.Y., 1766. Became a brick mfr.; held several local offices; mem. N.Y. State Assembly, 1802-03; mem. U.S. Ho. of Reps. from N.Y., 13th Congress, 1813-15. Died Haverstraw, May 6, 1829; buried Mt. Repose Cemetery.

DENT, Frederick Tracy, army officer; b. St. Louis County, Mo., Dec. 17, 1821; s. Frederick F. and Ellen (Wienshall) D.; grad. U.S. Mil. Acad., 1843. Apptd. brevet 2d lt. 6th Inf., U.S. Army, 1843; served in Indian Territory; served in battles of Veracruz, San Antonio, Contreras, Churubusco, and Molino del Rey during Mexican War; commd. 1st lt., capt., 1848; later served on Pacific R.R.

Survey, Yakima and Spokane expdns., various Indian campaigns in N.W.; commanded regt. in Army of Potomac during Civil War; commd. lt. col., 1864; a.d.c. to Gen. Grant, 1864-65, 66; mil. gov. of Richmond (Va.), 1865; promoted brig. gen. U.S. Volunteers, 1865, col. U.S. Army, 1866; mil. sec. to Pres. Grant, 1868-73; resigned commn., 1883. Died Dec. 24, 1892.

DENT, George, congressman; b. "Windsor Castle" on the Mattawoman. Charles County, Md., 1756. Served as 1st lt. militia of Charles and St. Marys counties under Capt. Thomas H. Marshall, in Revolutionary War, then as 1st lt. 3d Battalion, Flying Camp Regular Troops of Md., 1776; commd. capt. 26th Battalion, Md. Militia, 1778; mem. Md. Ho. of Assembly, 1782-90; speaker pro tem, 1788, speaker, 1789-90; justice Charles County Ct., 1791-92; mem. Md. Senate, 1791-92; pres., 1792; mem. U.S. Ho. of Reps. (Democrat) from Md., 3d-6th congresses, 1793-1801, speaker pro tem, various times, 1797-99; apptd. by Pres. Jefferson U.S. marshall of Dist. Ct. for Potomac Dist., Washington, D.C., 1801; moved to Ga., 1802. Died nr. Augusta, Ga., Dec. 2, 1813; buried on his plantation nr. Augusta.

DENT, William Barton Wade, congressman, businessman; b. Bryantown, Charles County, Md., Sept. 8, 1806; grad. Charlotte Hall Mil. Acad. 1823. Became sch. tchr., Mallorysville, Wilkes County, Ga., 1824; engaged in business, Bullsboro, Ga., 1827; a founder City of Newman (Ga.), 1828; engaged in agr. and milling, Coweta, Carroll, Heard counties; interested in large land holdings in Ala. Ga., Ark., Tenn., Tex.; served as col. Ga. Militia during Creek War; mem. Ga. Ho. of Reps., 1843; judge Inferior Ct. Coweta County, Newnan, 1849; mem. U.S. Ho. of Reps. (Democrat) from Ga., 33d Congress, 1853-55. Died Newnan, Sept. 7, 1855; buried Oak Hill Cemetery.

DENVER, James William, army officer, territorial gov.; b. Winchester, Va., Oct. 23, 1817; s. Frederick and Jane (Campbell) D.; grad. Cincinnati Law Sch., 1844; m. Louisa Rombach, 1856; 1 son, Matthew Rombach. Raised co. for 12th U.S. Volunteer Inf., commd. capt., 1847; mem. Cal. Senate, 1852-53; sec. of state Cal., 1853; mem. U.S. Ho. of Reps. from Cal., 34th Congress, 1855-57; active in promotion transcontinental railroad, 1857; sec. Territory of Kan., 1857-58, gov., 1858; U.S. commr. Indian affairs, 1858-59; commd. brig. gen. U.S. Volunteers, 1861; del. Soldiers Conv., Cleve. 1866; City of Denver (Colo.) named in his honor. Died Washington, D.C., Aug. 9, 1892.

de ONATE, Juan, explorer; b. New Spain (Mexico), circa 1549; s. Cristobal de Onate and Cathalina de Salazar; m. Isabel Tolosa, 2 children. Contracted with Spanish govt. to conquer N.M., 1595, took formal possession, 1598; explorer on expdns. to Kan., 1601, Gulf of Cal., 1605; elected gov. ad interim N.M., refused to serve; tried on charges of misrepresenting value of N.M., mistreatment soldiers and Indians, disobedience to vice-regal orders, 1614, sentenced to perpetual banishment from N.M. Died circa 1624.

de OTERMEN, Antonio, colonial gov. Apptd. Spanish gov. N.M., 1678; gov. N.M. during Pueblo uprising of 1680 which forced the Spaniards to abandon N.M. for 12 years; with his settlers withstood 9-day siege of Pueblo Indians at Santa Fe, were defeated, Aug. 20, 1680; tried unsuccessfully to reconquer N.M. with a force of 146 soldiers, 1681-82. Died 1683.

de PADILLA, Juan, missionary; b. Andalusia, Spain, circa 1500. Came to New Spain as Franciscan missionary, 1528; chaplain expdn. of Nuño de Guzman to Nueva Galicia and Culiacán, 1529-32; in next several years built monasteries at Zapotlan, Túipam and Tulancingo; established 1st mission in Southwestern N.Am. at Quivira (placed variously in Kan. and Tex.), 1542. Killed by Quivira Indians, circa 1544.

de PAUGHER, Adrien, engr.; b. France. Apptd. engr., 1707; chevalier of St. Louis, 1720; apptd. asst. engr. La., 1720; arrived in Biloxi, La., 1720; began to lay out Town of New Orleans, 1721, drew up plan for a town about one sq. mile in area which is now the French Quarter of New Orleans; sent copy of plan to Paris; became chief engr. Colony of La., 1723. Died New Orleans, June 9, 1726.

DePAUW, Washington Charles, mfr., philanthropist; b. Salem, Ind., Jan. 4, 1822; s. John and Elizabeth (Battiste) DeP.; m. Sarah Malott, 1846; m. 2d, Katharine Newland 1855; m. 3d, Frances Leyden, Jan. 8, 1867; 9 children. Clk., Washington County, Ind., 1844-53; established saw and grist mill and bank, Salem; became one of leading bankers in Ind.; built plate-glass plant, New Albany, Ind., 1865; trustee Ind. U.; del. to Gen. Conf., Methodist Episcopal Ch., 1872, 76; del. to Ecumenical Meth. Council, London, Eng., 1881; trustee Ind. Asbury U., Greencastle, Ind., contbd. funds which made it possible for univ. to continue, name changed to DePauw U., 1884. Died May 5, 1887.

de PENALOSA BRICENO, Diego Dionlso, gov. N.M.; b. Lima, Peru, circa 1622; s. Alonso de Peñalosa. Came to New Spain, 1654; apptd. gov. and capt.-gen. of N.M. by viceroy of New Spain, 1661; became embroiled with the church; fined and exiled from New Spain and West Indies, 1668; sold his services to Eng., then France, including plans conquest of New Spain and Mississippi Valley in his bitterness against Spain. Died Paris, France, 1687.

de PERALTA, Pedro, colonial gov.; b. circa 1584; married 1638, 2 children. Went to Mexico City, 1680; apptd. gov. N.M., 1609; founded Sante Fe as capital of province, 1609; had difficulties with church authorities by upholding perogatives of crown; apptd. lt.-comdr. at Port of Acapulco; alcalde of royal warehouse in Mexico City, 1621-22; auditor Royal Treasury, Caracas, Venezuela, 1644-45, treas., 1651-52. Died 1666.

De PEYSTER, Abraham, colonial mcht., jurist; b. New Amsterdam (now N.Y.C.) July 8, 1658; s. Johannes and Cornelia (Lubberts) De P.; m. Catherine, 1684; 13 children, including Abraham. Alderman, New Amsterdam, 1685, mayor, 1691-94; col. N.Y. Militia; mem. N.Y. Gov.'s Council, 1698-1702, 09, 10-22; acting gov. Province of N.Y., 1701, dep. auditor gen., 1701 treas., 1706-21; receiver gen. Port of N.Y., 1708; justice N.Y. Supreme Ct., 1698-1702, chief justice 1701-02. Died N.Y.C., Aug. 10, 1728.

de PORTOLA, Gaspar, colonial gov.; b. Balaguer, Catalonia, Spain, circa 1723. Capt., 1764; became gov. Upper Cal. to take charge of expulsion Jesuits from the territory, 1767, marched 1000 miles from Velicata, Lower Cal. to Monterey, Upper Cal., 1769-70; founder San Diego and Monterey (Cal.), 1769; laid beginnings of mission and presidio of San Carlos Borromeo, Monterey, 1770; gov. City of Puebla, 1776-84. Died Spain, 1784.

de POUILLY, Jacques Nicholas Bussiere, architect; b. Burgundy, France, 1805; studied architecture Ecole des Beaux Arts, Paris, France. Came to U.S., circa 1830, settled in New Orleans; built old St. Louis Hotel (his archtl. masterpiece, no longer standing), 1835-40; believed to have designed Old Citizens Bank (no longer standing), St. Augustine's Ch., present facade and sanctuary of old Cathedral (all New Orleans). Died 1875.

de POURTALES, Louis Francois, naturalist; b. Neuchatel, Switzerland, Mar. 4, 1823; m. Elise Bachmann, 1 child. Accompanied Jean Agassiz on expdns. to study glaciers of Alps, 1840; came to U.S., 1846; with U.S. Coast Survey, 1848-73, in charge of tidal div., 1864-73; keeper Museum of Comparative Zoology, Harvard, 1873-80; collected and studied animal life at great depths; engaged in explorations carried on by Coast Survey steamer Bibb in waters of So. Fla., No. Cuba, Western Bahamas, located Pourtales Plateau off Southeastern Fla.; accompanied Agassiz on voyage in Hassler around Cape Horn to San Francisco, in charge of dredging and other deep sea work, 1871; did his most important work Deep Sea corals, published 1871; collected sea-urchin off So. Fla., named Pourtalesia. Died Beverly Farms, Mass., July 18, 1880.

De QUILLE, Dan, see Wright, William.

DERBIGNY, Pierre Auguste Charles Bourguignon, judge, gov. La.; b. Laon, France, 1767; s. Auguste B. and Louise Angeline (Blondel) d'Herbigny; m. Felicite Odile Schauet de Lassus, 7 children. Sec., Municipality of New Orleans (under French rule); ofcl. interpreter Am. Territorial govt. of New Orleans under Claiborne, 1803; a regent U. of Orleans; clk. La. Ct. Common Pleas; sec. La. Legislative Council; mem. 1st La. Legislature; judge 1st La. Supreme Ct., 1813-20; candidate for gov. La., 1820; sec. of state La., 1820-27; gov. La., 1828-29. Died Gretna, La., Oct. 6, 1829.

DERBY, Elias Hasket, mcht., shipowner; b. b. Salem, Mass., Aug. 16, 1739; s. Capt. Richard and Mary (Hodges) D.; m. Elizabeth Crowninshield, Apr. 23, 1761, 7 children. One of wealthiest mchts. in New Eng. at close of Revolutionary War; sent ship Light Horse from Salem to St. Petersburg, Russia with cargo of sugar (1st ship to display Stars and Stripes to the Baltic), 1784; sent ship Grand Turk to Canton, China (1st New Eng. ship to Orient), 1785 most of fleet built under his personal supervision; his advice led to adoption by govt. of bonded warehouse system; built mansion, Salem, 1797. Died Salem, Sept. 8, 1799.

DERBY, Elias Hasket, mcht.; b. Salem, Mass., Jan. 10, 1766; s. Elias Hasket and Elizabeth (Crowninshield) D.; m. Lucy Brown, 9 children. Made trading voyage to Far East, 1787-90; became largest Am. trading firm on Isle of France (Mauritius); made profitable voyage to Mediterranean, captured several French vessels, 1799; 1st to bring large numbers of Merino sheep to Am.; manufactured broadcloth during War of 1812. Died Londonderry, N.H., Sept. 16, 1826.

DERBY, Elias Hasket, lawyer; b. Salem, Mass., Sept. 24, 1803; s. Elias Hasket and Lucy (Brown) D.; grad. Harvard, 1824; studied law in office of Daniel Webster; m. Eloise Lloyd Strong, Sept. 4, 1834, 7 children. Admitted to N.H. bar, 1827, N.H. Supreme Ct. bar, 1829; specialized in railroad cases; became dir. numerous railroads, influential in seeing completion Hoosac Tunnel; also wrote articles for various newspapers and mags.; performed 2 notable services in field of fgn. affairs by helping prepare Preliminary Report on the Treaty of Reciprocity with Great Britain To Regulate the Trade between the United States and the Provinces of Brit. North America, 1866, also in writing report which aided in drawing up fisheries treaty between U.S. and Gt. Britain, 1867. Died Boston, Mar. 31, 1880.

DERBY, George Horatio, humorist; b. Dedham, Mass., Apr. 3, 1823; s. John Barton and Mary (Townsend) D.; grad. U.S. Mil. Acad., 1846; m. Mary Ann Coons. Very early noted for his wit and practical jokes, especially at Mil. Acad.; apptd. to Engr. Corps shortly after graduation; served in Mexican War; brevetted 1st lt. for gallantry; served in Topographical Bur., 1847-48; mem. various U.S. Army exploring expdns. in Minn. Territory, 1848-49; had duty on Pacific Coast, 1849-56; managed to get some humorous sketches published, 1850, continued writing them thereafter; while temporary editor San Diego Herald, 1853, became famous even in East for his humor; transferred to East by army, 1856; promoted capt., 1860; one of foremost and earliest writers of so-called Western style of humor. Author: (sketches) Phoenixiana; or Sketches and Burlesques, 1856; The Squibob Papers, 1865. Died N.Y.C., May 15, 1861.

DERBY, Richard, ship owner, mcht.; b. Salem, Mass., Sept. 16, 1712; s. Richard and Martha (Hasket) D.; m. Mary Hodges, 1735; m. 2d, Mrs. Sarah (Langley) Hersey, 1771; children—John, Elias Hasket. Went to sea at early age; capt. mcht. sloop Ranger by 1736; bought own vessel, retired to Salem as mcht. owning own fleet by 1756; profited by various European wars of the time by trading with all belligerants; supported revolutionary cause; his ship Quero used to go to Eng. after battles of Lexington and Concord in effort to get support of Brit. public for colonists with dispatches stating Brit. soldiers had fired first, 1775. Died Nov. 9, 1783.

De ROSSET, Moses John, physician; b. Wilmington, N.C., July 4, 1838; s. Dr. Armand John and Eliza Jane (Lord) De R.; attended U. Cologne (Germany), 1856-57; studied medicine under Dr. Gunning Bedford, N.Y.C.; M.D., U. City of N.Y., 1860; m. Adelaide Savage Mears, Oct. 13, 1863, 7 children Resident physician Bellevue Hosp., N.Y.C., 1860-61; commd. asst. surgeon Confederate Army, 1861, promoted surgeon 1863; in charge of Gen. Hosp. Number 4, Richmond, 1863, later became insp. hospitals for Dept. of Henrico; prof. chemistry med. dept. U. Md., Balt. Dental Coll., 1865-73; began to specialize in eye and ear diseases; practiced medicine specializing in eye and ear diseases, Wilmington, Del., 1873-78. N.Y.C., 1878-81; wrote many articles. Translator: Annual Abstract of Therapeutics Materia Medica, Pharmacy and Toxicology for 1867 by A. Bouchardet (French physician). Died May 1, 1881.

De SAINT-MEMIN, Charles Balthazar Julien Fevret, artist, engraver; b. Dijon, France, Mar. 12, 1770; s. Benigne Charles Fevret and Victoire Marie (de Motmans) de S.-M.; grad. Ecole Militaire, Paris, France, 1785. Became ensign in French Guards, 1788; came to U.S., 1793; started engraving work, 1796, 1st Am. work was a panoramic pencil sketch of N.Y., 1796; engraved profile portraits of many distinguished 19th Century Americans; worked as engraver and oil and water color painter in U.S., 1796-1810, 12-14; returned to France, 1814; served as dir. of museum at Dijon, France, 1817-52; painted portrait of Washington said to be the last one done from life; The St.-Memin Collection of Portraits (to which is prefixed a memoir to Madame de St.-Memin) (a collection of his portraits and engravings; new in Corcoran Gallery of Art, Washington, D.C., published 1862. Died Dijon, France, June 23, 1852.

De SAUSSURE, Henry William, jurist; b. Pocotaligo, S.C., Aug. 16, 1763; s. Daniel and Mary (McPherson) De S.; m. Eliza Ford, 1785. Fought in Am. Revolution; admitted to Phila. bar, 1784; mem. S.C. Constl. Conv., 1790; mem. lower house S.C. Gen. Assembly, 1790-94, 96-98, 1800-02, 07-08; dir. U.S. Mint, 1795; intendant (adminstr.) Charleston (S.C.), 1797-98; active in establishment S.C. State U. at Columbia, 1801; chancellor S.C., 1808-37. Died Charleston, Mar. 29, 1839.

de SCHWEINITZ, Edmond Alexander, clergyman; b. Bethlehem, Pa., Mar. 20, 1825; s. Lewis David and Louisa Amelia (Ledoux) van S.; attended theol. sem., Bethlehem, 1843; grad. U. Berlin (Germany) 1844; S.T.D. (hon.), Columbia, 1871; m. Lydia J. de Tschirschky, 1850; m. 2d, Isabel Allison Boggs, 1868; 1 child. Tchr., Nazareth Hall, Pa., 1846-50; pastor Moravian Ch., Lebanon, Pa., 1850; pastor First Ch., Phila.; prof. theology Moravian sem., Phila., 1855; 1st editor of Moravian, (weekly ch. paper) 1856-66; del. from U.S. to Synod in Saxony, Germany, 1857; in charge of church, Lititz, Pa., during Civil War; transferred to Bethlehem, 1864-80; pres. theol. sem. at Bethlehem, 1867-84; elevated to Episcopate, 1870; pres. Gen. Synod, Saxony, 1879; active in work of Moravian missionary society. Author: The Moravian Manual, 1859; Some of the Fathers of the Moravian Church, 1881; The History of the Church Known as the Unitas Fratrum, 1885. Died Bethlehem, Dec. 18, 1887.

DESHA, Joseph, gov. Ky., congressman; b. Monroe County, Pa., Dec. 9, 1768; m. Peggy Bledsoe, 1789. Served in campaign against Indians under Gen. Wayne, Gen. Harrison; mem. Tenn. Ho. of Reps., 1797-1802; mem. Tenn. Senate, 1802-07; mem. U.S. Ho. of Reps. from Ky., 10th-16th congresses, 1807-19; maj. gen. Ky. Volunteers., 1813; commanded a div. in Battle of Thames; gov. Ky., 1824-28. Died Georgetown, Scott County, Ky., Oct. 12, 1842; buried Georgetown Cemetery.

DESHA, Robert, congressman, mcht.; b. nr. Gallatin, Sumner County, Tenn., Jan. 14, 1791; attended public schs. Became a mcht., Gallatin; served as capt., later brevetted maj. 24th Regt., U.S. Inf., in War of 1812, 1812-15; mem. U.S. Ho. of Reps. from Tenn., 20th-21st congresses, 1827-31; mcht., Mobile, Ala., until 1849. Died Mobile, Feb. 6, 1849; buried Magnolia Cemetery.

De SMET, Pierre Jean, missionary; b. Termonde, Belgium, Jan. 31, 1801. Joined Soc. of Jesus, 1821, sent to Jesuit missions in U.S., 1821; ordained priest Roman Catholic Ch., 1827; became instr. Indian Sch., Florissant, Mo. (became St. Louis U.), 1828; started missionary activities among Pottowatomie, Sioux, Blackfoot, Flathead and other Indian tribes in valleys of Missouri, Yellowstone, Platte and Columbia rivers, 1838; often commd. by U.S. Govt. as negotiator with Indians; concluded peace terms with Sitting Bull, 1868. Author: Indian Letters and Sketches; New Indian Sketches. Died St. Louis, May 23, 1873.

De SOTO, Hernando, explorer; b. Barcarrota, Spain, 1500; grad. U. Salamanca (Spain); m. Isabel Davila; at least 1 child (dau., by Inca mistress Curicuillar). Served as capt. Spanish Army, under Gov. Pedrarias Davila in Central Am., 1519-32; served in conquest of Peru, 1532-33; led group which captured Inca chieftain Atahualpa, 1532; received contract from King Charles V of Spain to conquer Fla., 1537; gov. Cuba, 1537-42; landed with army of 100 men in Fla., 1539; wandered through what is now Southern U.S. in search of gold and Indian treasures similar to those found in Mexico and Peru, 1539-42; conquered those Indian tribes he encountered enroute; suffered severe defeat by Mauvilian Indians in Ala., fall 1540; discovered and crossed Mississippi River nr. what is now Memphis, Tenn., 1541; wintered nr. what is now Ft. Smith, Ark., 1541-42; turned back to Fla., Apr. 1542. Died on bank of Mississippi River nr. what is now Arkansas City, Ark., May 21, 1542; buried in Mississippi River.

de ST. DENIS, Louis Juchereau, explorer, colonizer; b. Beauport, Que., Can., Sept. 17, 1676; s. Nicholas and Marie-Thérèse (Giffard) St. Denis (or Denys); m. Mañuela Sánchez Ramón, Feb. 17, 1716. Joined expdn. of Pierre le Moyne to found La., 1698; accompanied Jean Baptiste le Moyne on expdn. to Red River of La., 1700; in charge of post on lower Mississippi River, 1702-05; sent to open route across Tex. and begin Indian trade, 1713; guide for Spanish expdn. sent to found missions in region north of Mexico, 1716; engaged in escapades and smuggling enterprises which created internat. incident when King of France asked his agt. at Madrid to find out secretly what Spain meant to do with this adventurer; commanded Ft. St. Jean, Natchitoches, La., maintained outpost for France for quarter of a century; name also spelled St. Denys. Died Natchitoches, June 11, 1744.

de ST. VRAIN, Ceran De Hault Delassus, fur trader, army officer; b. Spanish Lake, nr. St. Louis, Mo., May 5, 1802; s. Jacques Marcellin Ceran DeHault DeLassus and Marie Felicite Chauvet (Dubreuil) de St. V.; m. Luisa Branch, 3 children. Embarked in fur trade, circa 1823; with Francois Guerin conducted expdn. to the Southwest outfitted by Bernard Pratte & Co. of St. Louis, 1824; received passport at Santa Fe to State of Sonora for pvt. trade, 1826; formed partnership with Charles Bent under name Bent, St. Vrain & Co. (became one of leading fur-trading cos. of West), 1831; became citizen of Mexico; with Cornelio Vigil received land grant from Mexican govt., 1844, comprising 4 million acres in valleys Huerfano, Apishapa, Purgatoire, other tributaries; organizer,, capt. of a volunteer co., 1846-48, lt. col., 1854-55, apptd. col. 1st N.M. Cavalry, 1861. Died Mora, N.M., Oct. 28, 1870.

DESTREHAN, John Noel, mcht., planter, legislator; b. in what became St. Charles Parish, La., 1780. Became a mcht. and planter; mem. com. of 3 Creoles who protested to Congress against provisions of 1st Territorial Govt. (resulted in formation of more liberal govt.); mem. legislative council Territory of Orleans, pres., 1806, 11; del. La. Constl. Conv. (but opposed to admission of Territory to statehood); mem. La. Senate, 1812-18; elected mem. U.S. Senate, 1812, resigned without serving. Died 1824; buried nr. Destrehan, La.

DETMOLD, Christian Edward, civil engr.; b. Hanover, Germany, Feb. 2, 1810; s. Johann Detmold; m. Phoebe Crary. 2 children. Came to U.S., 1826; became surveyor, Charleston, S.C.; completed survey for Charleston & Hamburg R.R. & Canal Co., 1830, won $500 prize for designing best locomotive used by this company; worked for U.S. War Dept., 1833-34, supervised constrn. Ft. Sumter, S.C.; surveyor on various Eastern railroads, 1834-44; iron mfr., Md., 1845-52; constrn. engr. of famous crystal palace, World's Fair "Exhibition of the Industry of All Nations" (opened 1853); lived for time in Europe. Author: The Historical, Political and Diplomatic Writings of Niccolo Machiavelli; Translation from the Italian, 1882. Died N.Y.C., July 2, 1887.

de TOCQUEVILLE, Alexis Henri Maurice Clérel, fgn. minister, author; b. Verneuil, France, July 29, 1805; studied law; married an English woman. Sent to Am. by French Govt. to study penitentiary system, 1831; wrote accounts of his travels which have become classics in study of Am. democracy. Author works including: De la démocratie en Amérique (detailed study of Am. democratic system in its instns. and polit. relations), 1835, published in Eng. as Democracy in America, 1835-40. Died Cannes, France, Apr. 16, 1859.

de TONTY, Henry, explorer; b. Gaeta, Italy, 1650; s. Lorenzo and Isabelle (de Liette or Desliettes) Tonti. Entered French Army, 1668; enlisted under the explorer LaSalle, 1678; arrived in Can., circa 1679; built (with LaSalle) Fort Crevecoeur on Lake Peoria, winter 1679-80, left in command by LaSalle, 1680, left fort after Iroquois raids and desertion of men, 1680, reached Michilemackinac, 1681; built (with LaSalle) Fort St. Louis on the Illinois River; explored Mississippi River, 1682; commd. capt., 1683; made unsuccessful search for LaSalle down Mississippi River, 1686, later returned in search of colonists after La Salle's death, 1689; brought settlers, supplies, missionaries from Can. to Ill., until 1700; joined le Moyne's settlement nr. mouth of Miss. River, 1700; wrote brief memoirs, 1678-83, 78-91; respected by both French and Indians; considered true founder of Ill. Died nr. Mobile, Ala., 1704.

de TOUSARD, Anne Louis, army officer, diplomat; b. Paris, France, Mar. 12, 1749; s. gen. Charles Germain and Antoinette de Poitevin (de la Croix) de T.; grad. Arty. Sch., Strasbourg, France, 1769; m. Maria Francisca Joubert, Jan. 1788; m. 2d, Anna Maria Geddes, 1795. Commd. 2d lt. Royal Arty. Corps, French Army, 1769; arrived in Portsmouth, N.H., 1777; took part in battles of Brandywine and Germantown; brevetted lt. col. by Congress and voted a life pension for gallantry, 1778; decorated chevalier of St. Louis (France), 1779; commd. maj. Provincial Regt. of Toul, France, 1780, lt. col. Regt. du Cap, 1784; went to Santo Domingo, 1784, served with distinction against Negro revolt; accused of counter revolutionary principles, resistance to orders, 1792, arrested, sent to prison in France; released, 1793, returned to U.S.; reinstated in U.S. Army, 1795, commd. maj. 2d Arty., col., 1800; promoted to insp. of arty., 1800; returned to Santo Domingo, then France, 1802; sent to Am. in charge of comml. relations at New Orleans, 1805; moved to Phila. as vice consul; ordered to New Orleans as consul ad interim, 1811-16. Died Paris, May 8, 1817.

de TROBRIAND, Régis Denis de Keredem, army officer, author; b. nr. Tours, France, June 4, 1816; s. Baron Joseph and Rochine (Haghin de Courbeville) de T.; grad. Collège de Tours, 1834; grad. in law, Poitiers, 1837; m. Mary Mason Jones, 1843, 1 dau. Came to U.S., 1841; lived with wife in Venice, Italy, until 1847; a leading figure in N.Y. society and literary circles; editor Revue de Nouveau Monde, 1849-50; contbr. to Le Courrier des États-Unis; became Am. citizen, 1861, also col. "Gardes Lafayette" of N.Y. State Militia; brevetted maj. gen. U.S. Volunteers, 1865; apptd. col. U.S. Army, 1866; made many trips to France; served on frontier wit[h] Army while in Am.; succeeded to title of count o[n] death of his brother, 1874; ret. from Army, 1879 lived in New Orleans. Author: Les Gentilshommes de L'Ouest, 1840; Quatre Ans de Campagnas á L'Arme du Potomoc, 2 vols., 1867-68. Died Bayport, L.I. N.Y., July 15, 1897.

de ULLOA, Antonio, Spanish gov. La.; b. Seville Spain, Jan. 23, 1717; s. Bernardo de Ulloa y Sous[a] and Josefa de la Torre Guiral; m. Francisca Ramire[z] de Lacedo, 9 children including Francisco Javie[r] de Ulloa. Accompanied French scientists on expdn to S.Am., 1735-44; wrote report describing cor[-]rupt conditions in Viceroyalty of Peru, 1749; gov and supt. quicksilver mine, Huancavelica, Peru 1758-64; 1st Spanish gov. of La., 1766-68, force[d] to allow last French gov. to continue administerin[g] province in name of King of Spain due to inade[-]quate Spanish strength; expelled from La. afte[r] Creole uprising, 1768; subsequently rose to hig[h] rank in Spanish Navy. Author: Relacion historic[a] del viage a la America meridinaol, 1748; Noticia Secretas de America, 1749, published 1826. Die[d] July 5, 1795.

de VARGAS ZAPATA y LUJAN PONCE DE LEON, Diego, Spanish gov. N.M.; b. Madrid, Spain circa 1650; s. Alonso and Maria Margarita (de Con[-]tréras) de Vargas Zapata y Lujan; m. Juana. Chie[f] magistrate Real de Minas de Talpugajua in Mexico apptd. colonial gov. and capt. gen. of N.M., 1688 controlled much land in Spain and Mexico throug[h] his wife; reconquered upper Rio Grande Valley fro[m] Pueblo Indians who had defeated Spanish settler[s] in 1680, 1692; engaged in suppressing Indian up[-]risings, 1693-97; reapptd. gov. of N.M. by vicero[y] of New Spain (Mexico), 1696, imprisoned by gov apptd. by Spanish king on charges brought by tow[n] council of Santa Fe; gov. N.M. (reapptd. by king) 1701-03; created marqués de La Nava de Brazi[-]ñas. Died Sandia mountains, N.M., on campaig[n] against Faraon Apaches, Apr. 4, 1704.

DEVENS, Charles, army officer, jurist, atty gen.; b. Charlestown, Mass., Apr. 4, 1820; s. Charle[s] and Mary (Lithcow) D.; grad. Harvard, 1838 LL.D., 1877; Admitted to Mass. bar, 1840; mem. Mass. Senate, 1848-49; U.S. marshal for dist Mass., 1849-53; city solicitor Worcester (Mass.) 1856-58; commd. brig. gen. Mass. Militia; commd. maj. 3d Mass. Battalion, 1861, col. 15th Mass. Regt., 1861; commd. brig. gen. U.S. Volunteers, 1862; brevetted maj. gen., 1865; served in battles of Balls' Bluff, Fredericksburg, Chancellorsville, Cold Harbor during Civil War; apptd. justice Mass. Superior Ct., 1867; judge Mass. Supreme Ct., 1873; U.S. atty. gen., 1877-81; pres. Harvard Alumni Assn., 1886; comdr. Mil. Order, Loyal Legion, Mass.; nat. comdr. Grand Army Republic, 1874; Camp Devens, Ayer, Mass., named for him. Died Boston, Jan. 7, 1891.

DEVEREUX, John C., mayor Utica; b. nr. Enniscorthy, Wexford, Ireland, Aug. 5, 1774. Came to N.Y., 1797; opened store, Utica, N.Y., 1802; became mayor Utica, 1840; founded (with brothe[r] Nicholas) a savings bank, Utica. Died Utica, Dec 11, 1848.

DEVEREUX, John Henry, civil engr., railroad exec.; b. Apr. 5, 1832; son of John Devereux; m Antoinette Kelsey, 1851. Went to Cleve., 1848; di[d] constrn. work, later became apprentice engr. o[n] various railroads; railroad engr. worked on differ[-]ent roads in Ohio; supt. mil. railroads in Ohio, 1862-64; 1st supt., then v.p. Cleve. and Pitts. R.R., 1864-68; v.p., gen. mgr. Lake Shore & Mich. Southern R.R., 1868-73; pres. Big Four R.R., 1873-86 receiver of Atlantic and Gt. Western R.R., 1874-80, pres., 1881; attempted consolidations and engaged in pooling practices; later advocated a[n] interstate commerce commn.; agt. for N.Y. Central R.R., for a time. Died Mar. 17, 1886.

DEVEREUX, Nicholas, bus. exec.; b. nr. Enniscorthy, Ireland, June 7, 1791, Came to N.Y., 1806; founded Irish colony, upstate N.Y.; became wealthy mcht. and banker, Utica, N.Y.; philanthropist, donated to St. Bonaventure's Coll., N. Am. Coll. in Rome, also churches and an orphanage. Died Utica, Dec. 29, 1855.

DEVIN, Thomas Casimer, army officer; b. N.Y.C., Dec. 10, 1822. Joined N.Y. Militia, lt. col. at start of Civil War; apptd. capt. 1st N.Y. Cavalry, 1861; col. 6th N.Y. Calvalry, 1861; served in battles of 2d Bull Run and Antietam; after Battle of Fredericksburg (1862) apptd. brigade comdr., 1863; took part in battles of Chancellorsville and Gettysburg; apptd. brig. gen. U.S. Volunteers, 1865; apptd. lt. col. 8th U.S. Cavalry, 1866; col. 3d U.S. Cavalry, 1877; served mostly on frontier duty, after Civil War, ret., 1878. Died N.Y.C., Apr. 4, 1878.

De VRIES, David Pieterson, mcht. skipper, colonizer; b. La Rochelle, France, 1592. Mcht. skipper to Am., 1631, 32-33, 34-36, 38-44; founded colonies on Staten Island, also nr. what is now Tappan,

Y. (both destroyed in Indian War of 1643). thor: Voyages from Holland to America from 32-1644, published 1655. Died 1655.

DEW, Thomas Roderick, economist, coll. pres.; Md., Dec. 5, 1802; s. Thomas and Lucy E. atewood) D.; A.B,. Coll. William and Mary, 20; m. Natilia Hay, 1845. Prof. polit. law Coll. lliam and Mary, 1827-36, pres., 1836-46, largely sponsible for bringing coll. back to its former eminence; believer in free trade; pro-slavery polit. and econ. theories; became leading pro-very intellectual of South. Author: Lectures the Restrictive System, 1829; Review of the bate in the Virginia Legislature of 1831 and 32, published 1832 (better known in its 2d edit. e Pro-Slavery Argument, 1852); Digest of the ws, Customs Manners, and Institutions of the cient and Modern Nations, published post-mously 1853. Died Paris, France, Aug. 6, 1846.

DEWART, Lewis, congressman, businessman; Sunbury, Pa., Nov. 24, 1780; attended common hs.; at least 1 son, William Lewis. Clk. in s father's store, several years; later became al operator and banker; postmaster Sunbury, 06-16; mem. Pa. Ho. of Reps., 1812-20, 35-40, eaker, 1840; mem. Pa. Senate, 1823-26; an or-nizer, builder Danville & Pottsville R.R., an iginal dir.; mem. U.S. Ho. of Reps. (Jackson emocrat) from Pa., 22d Congress, 1831-33; chief rgess Sunbury, 1837. Died Sunbury, Apr. 26, 352; buried Sunbury Cemetery.

DEWART, William Lewis, congressman, law-er; b. Sunbury, Pa., June 21, 1821; s. Lewis ewart; grad. Dickinson Prep. Sch., Carlisle, Pa.; ad. Princeton, 1839; studied law. Admitted to orthumberland County (Pa.) bar, 1843, began actice of law, Sunbury; chief burgess Sunbury, 345-46; pres. sch. bd.; del. Democratic nat. convs., alt., 1852, 60, Cincinnati, 1856, Chgo., 1884; em. U.S. Ho. of Reps. (Democrat) from Pa., 35th ongress, 1857-59; Dem. presdl. elector, 1860. ied Sunbury, Apr. 19, 1888; buried family ult, Sunbury Cemetery.

DEWEES, William Potts, physician, obste-ician; b. nr. Pottstown, Pa., May 5, 1768; studied edicine under 2 neighboring doctors; M.D., U. a.; m. Martha Rogers; m. 2d, Mary Lorrain, 802. Practiced medicine, Abington, Pa.; moved Phila., 1793; specialized in obstetrics at time hen women were mainly midwives and was onsidered beneath dignity of doctor to do so; s health failed for time, returned to practice, 817; adjunct prof. obstetrics U. Pa., 1825-34, rof., 1834-35; forced to retire by failing health. uthor: (chief work) A Compendious System of idwifery. Died Phila., May 20, 1841.

DEWEY, Chester, clergyman, educator; b. heffield, Mass., Oct. 25, 1784; s. Stephen and lizabeth (Owen) D.; grad. Williams Coll., 1806; . Sarah Dewey, 1810; m. 2d, Olivia Hart Pomeroy, 825; 15 children. Licensed to preach by Berk-hire Conglist. Assn., 1807; tutor Williams Coll., lso preached for a time; prof. mathematics and atural philosophy Williams Coll., 1810-27; an rganizer 1st Anti-Slavery Soc. in Mass., 1823; id work in physics and chemistry in spare time, lso started bot. and geol. college; prin. Berk-hire Gymnasium, Pittsfield, Mass., 1827-36; prin. ymnasium high school (later known as Collegiate nst. of Rochster), 1836-50; prof. chemistry and atural sciences U. Rochester (N.Y.), 1850-61; ectr. various times on chemistry and med. botany erkshire Med. Inst.; lectr. med. sch., Woodstock, t., 1842-49; wrote articles and papers; Deweya umbelliferous plants of Cal.) named after him. uthor: Report on the Herbageous Plants and in he Quadrupeds of Massachusetts, 1840. Died ochester, Dec. 15, 1867.

DEWEY, Daniel, congressman, lawyer; b. Shef-ield, Mass., Jan. 29, 1766; attended Yale; studied aw. Admitted to bar, 1787, began practice of aw, Williamstown, Mass.; treas. Williams Coll., Villiamstown, 1798-1814; mem. Mass. Gov.'s Coun-il, 1809-12; mem. U.S. Ho. of Reps. (Whig) from Mass., 13th Congress, 1813-Feb. 24, 1814; asso. udge Mass. Supreme Ct., 1814-15. Died Williams-own, May 26, 1815; buried West Lawn Cemetery.

DEWEY, Orville, clergyman; b. Berkshire County, Mass., Mar. 28, 1794; s. Silas and Polly (Root) D.; grad. Williams Coll., 1814, Andover Theol. Sem., 1819; D.D. (hon.), Harvard, 1839; m. Louisa Farn-ham, Dec. 26, 1820. Agt. for Am. Edn. Soc. and pastor Congregational Ch., Gloucester, Mass. for a time; changed to Unitarian faith; Unitarian min-ister Federal Street Ch., Boston, 1823-33, First Ch., New Bedford, Mass., 1835-48, Second Congre-gational Ch. of N.Y., 1835-48, New South Ch., Boston, 1857-61; pres. Am. Unitarian Assn., 1845-47; a founder N.Y. Employment Soc. Author: Dis-courses on Various Subjects, 1835; The Old World and the New, 1836; The Works of Orville Dewey, 3 vols., 1844. Died Sheffield, Mass., Mar. 21, 1882.

DEWING, Francis, engraver; b. England; flourished 1716-22; m. Katherin Hart, Dec. 8, 1719. Came to Am., 1716; settled in Boston, es-tablished himself as engraver specializing in copper; arrested on suspicion of counterfeiting (when the 1st Mass. Bay Colony currency was successfully counterfeited to great degree and all engravers were suspected), 1718; subsequently released. Important engravings include: Sea Coast of English America and the French New Settlements, 1716; Casco Bay, 1720; The Town of Boston, 1722. Died after 1745.

De WITT, Alexander, congressman, textile mfr.; b. New Braintree, Mass., Apr. 2, 1798. Became a textile mfr., Oxford, Mass.; mem. Mass. Ho. of Reps., 1830-36, Mass. Senate, 1842, 44, 50-51; mem. Mass. Constl. Conv., 1853; mem. U.S. Ho. of Reps. (Am. Party candidate) from Mass., 33d-34th congresses, 1853-57. Died Oxford, Jan. 13, 1879; buried South Cemetery.

De WITT, Charles, Continental congressman; b. Kingston, N.Y., 1727. Served as col. of militia; mem. colonial assembly, 1768-76; del. to provisi-onal conv., 1775; mem. Provisional Congress which approved Declaration of Independence, 1775-77, mem. constl. com. 1776, com. of safety. 1777; mem. Continental Congress from N.Y., 1784; ed-itor Ulster Sentinel, several years; mem. N.Y. State Assembly, 1781, 85-86; mem. com. to draft N.Y. Constn. Died Kingston, Aug. 27, 1787; buried Dutch Reformed Cemetery, Hurley, N.Y.

De WITT, Charles Gerrit, congressman, lawyer; b. Greenhill, Ulster County, N.Y., Nov. 7, 1789; studied law. Became a lawyer; clk. in Navy Dept.; editor Ulster Sentinel; mem. U.S. Ho. of Reps. (Jackson Democrat) from N.Y., 21st Congress, 1829-31; charge d'affaires to Central Am., 1833-39. Died on board river steamer nr. Newburgh, N.Y., Apr. 12, 1839; buried Dutch Reformed Ceme-tery, Hurley, N.Y.

De WITT, Jacob Hasbrouck, congressman; b. Marbletown, Ulster County, N.Y., Oct. 2, 1784; attended Kingston (N.Y.) Acad. Engaged in ag-riculture; served as adj. in War of 1812; mem. U.S. Ho. of Reps. (Clinton Democrat) from N.Y., 16th Congress, 1819-21; supr. Ulster County, 1827, 40; mem. N.Y. State Assembly, 1839, 47. Died Kingston, Jan. 30, 1867; buried Sharpe Cem-etery on Albany Av.

DeWITT, Simeon, univ. chancellor, state ofcl.; b. Wawarsing, N.Y., Dec. 25, 1756; s. Dr. Andries and Jannetje (Vernooy) DeW.; B.A., Queen's Coll. (now Rutgers), 1776, M.A., 1788; m. Elizabeth Lynott, Oct. 12, 1789; m. 2d, Jane Varick Hard-enberg; m. 3d, Susan Linn, Oct. 29, 1810; 6 chil-dren. Left coll. to join N.Y. Militia; served as asst. geographer Continental Army, 1778-80, chief geographer 1780-81; surveyor gen. State of N.Y., 1784-1834; a commr. to settle N.Y.-Pa. boundary dispute, 1786-87; surveyor of various canal routes for N.Y.; published map of N.Y. State, 1802; regent, then vice-chancellor Univ. State of N.Y., 1798-1829, chancellor, 1829-34; a founder N.Y. Soc. for Promotion of Agr., Arts and Manufactures (later became part of Albany Inst.), v.p. Albany Inst., many years; mem. Am. Philos. Soc. Author: The Elements of Perspective (collection of writings), 1813; contbr. scientific papers to various journals. Died Ithaca, N.Y. Dec. 3, 1834.

De WOLF, James, slave trader, mfr., senator; b. Bristol County, R.I., Mar. 18, 1764; s. Mark A. and Abigail (Porter) De W.; m. Nancy Brad-ford. Most successful of slave traders up to War of 1812; built one of earliest cotton-mills in U.S., Coventry, R.I., 1812; mem. R.I. Legislature from Bristol, 30 years, speaker of house; mem. U.S. Senate from R.I., 1821-25 (resigned). Died N.Y.C., Dec. 21, 1837.

DEXTER, Franklin, jurist, legislator; b. Charles-town, Mass., Nov. 5, 1793; s. Samuel and Catherine (Gordon) D.; grad. Harvard, 1812, LL.D., 1857; m. Catherine Prescott, Sept. 28, 1819. Admitted to practice Ct. Common Pleas, Suffolk County, N.Y., 1815; judge N.Y. State Supreme Jud. Ct., 1818; mem. Mass. Ho. of Reps. from Boston, 1825; mem. Common Council of Boston, 1825; mem. Mass. Senate, 1835; rep. from Boston on Select Com. on Revision of Statutes, 1836; U.S. dist. atty. for Mass., 1841-45, reapptd., 1849. Died Beverly, Mass., Aug. 14, 1857.

DEXTER, Henry, sculptor; b. Nelson, N.Y., Oct. 11, 1806; s. Smith and Clarasa (Dexter) D.; studied painting with Francis Alexander (his wife's uncle); largely self taught as sculptor; m. Calista Kelley, 1828; m. 2d, Mrs. Martha Billilngs, 1859. Apprenticed to blacksmith in Conn., 1822-28, worked as blacksmith, 1828-36; opened portrait studio, Providence, R.I., 1836; moved to Boston, 1836, started sculpting, 1838; did numerous busts including Charles Dickens, Pres. James Buchanan (circa 1859); toured country doing busts of govs. of most of states (most have since been lost); ex-ecuted marble statues (8 still in existence). Died Boston, June 23, 1876.

DEXTER, Henry Martyn, clergyman; b. Plymp-ton, Mass., Aug. 13, 1821; s. Rev. Elijah and Mary (Morton) D.; grad. Yale, 1840, Andover Theol. Sem., 1844; m. Emeline Augusta Palmer, Nov. 19, 1844. Prin., Rochester (Mass.) Acad., 1840-41; ordained to ministry Congregational Ch., 1844; pas-tor ch., Manchester, N.H., 1844-49, Pine Street Congregational Ch., Boston, 1849-67; contbr. to The Congregationalist, mem. editorial staff, 1851-56, editor-in-chief, 1856-90; sometime correspondent N. Y. Independent; drew up resolution protesting Kan.-Neb. Bill, 1854; a founder Congregational Quarter-ly, 1858; part-owner, editor combined publ. Con-gregationalist and Boston Recorder, 1867-90; wrote on ch. and New Eng. history. Author: Congregation-alism, 1865; The Church Policy of the Pilgrims, 1870; As to Roger Williams, 1876; The Congrega-tionalism of the Last 300 Years, 1880; A Hand-book of Congregationalism, 1880. Died New Bed-ford, Mass., Nov. 13, 1890.

DEXTER, Samuel, mcht.; b. Dedham, Mass., Mar. 16, 1726; s. Rev. Samuel and Catherina (Mears) D.; m. Hannah Sigournet, several chil-dren including Samuel. Apprenticed to mcht., Boston, later owner of merc. firm., ret. to Dedham, 1762; mem. Mass. Gen. Ct., 1764-68, 85; mem. Gov.'s Council, 1768-74; mem. 1st Mass. Provin-cial Congress, 1774-75; lived in Woodstock, Conn., 1775-85; left $5,000 to Harvard. Author: Thoughts Upon Several Passages of Scripture, Both in the Old and New Testament, Relative to Jacob and Esau with Incidental Excursions. 1791. Died Mendon, Mass., June 10, 1810; buried Wood-stock.

DEXTER, Samuel, congressman, sec. treasury; b. Boston, May 14, 1761; s. Samuel and Hannah (Sigourney) D.; grad. with highest honors, Har-vard, 1781, LL.D. (hon.), 1813; m. Catherine Gor-don, Mar. 7, 1786, 1 son, Franklin. Admitted to Worcester County bar, 1784; mem. Mass. Ho. of Reps. from. Charlestown, 1788-90; mem. U.S. Ho. of Reps. (Federalist) from Mass., 3d congress, 1793-95; mem. U.S. Senate from Mass., Dec. 2, 1799-June 1800; U.S. sec. of war under Pres. Ad-ams, 1800, sec. of treasury, 1801-02; unsuccessful candidate for gov. Mass., 1814, 15; pres. 1st Mass. soc. to promote temperance, overseer Harvard. Died Athens, N.Y., May 4, 1816.

DEXTER, Timothy, mcht.; b. Malden, Mass., Jan. 22, 1747; s. Nathan and Esther (Brintnall) D.; m. Elizabeth (Lord) Frothingham, children—Sam-uel, Nancy. Worked on farm, 1756-63; apprenticed to leather dresser, Charlestown, Mass., 1763-69; leather dresser, Newburyport, Mass., 1770-91; bought up depreciated certificates of indebtedness of Revolutionary War, became wealthy man upon as-sumption of Hamilton's funding policy, 1791; be-came mcht. with many eccentric traits; sold 42,-000 warming pans as cooking utensils in Cuba, also cornered whalebone market; called himself "Lord" Timothy Dexter, maintained luxurious mansion in Newburyport; engaged a ship carver to make over 40 life-size statutes of likenesses of George Wash-ington, Lord Nelson, Louis XIV and others, which he placed on his front grounds; also had statute made of himself with inscription "I am first in the East"; subsidized an ex-fish peddlar to write odes in his honor; once had a coffin made, kept it in his front room and held mock funeral over him-self, beat his wife when she did not shed any tears; offered to finance various public improvements in Newburyport on condition that all these projects be named for him; had gilded eagle placed on roof of his house; left substantial sums of money to char-ity. Author: (pamphlet) A Pickle for the Knowing Ones (privately printed; had no punctuation, added 2 pages containing word "stop" at end of pamphlet, telling his readers to insert them as they wished), 1802. Died Newburyport, Oct. 23, 1806.

DEXTER, Wirt, lawyer; b. Dexter, Mich., Oct. 25, 1832; s. Samuel William and Millisent (Bond) D.; attended Cazenovia Sem., N.Y., U. Mich.; m. Kate Augusta Dusenberry, June 15, 1858; m. 2d, Josephine Moore, Dec. 18, 1866. Engaged in lumber bus. in Mich., for a time; moved to Chgo., 1853; admitted to bar, became prominent lawyer Chgo.; dir. Chgo., Burlington and Quincey R.R.; a founder Chgo. Relief and Aid Soc., chmn. exec. com. to distribute aid in aftermath of Chgo. Fire, 1871. Died Chgo., May 17, 1890.

DEYMANN, Clementine, clergyman; b. Klein-Stavern, Oldenburg, Germany, June 24, 1844; brought to U.S., 1863; studied in Teutopolis, Ill. Became a Franciscian; ordained priest Roman Catholic Ch. 1872, taught until 1879; pastor German chs., Joliet and Chillicothe; became definitor of province, superior of an orphanage, Watsonville, Cal.; became commissary Pacific province, shortly before death. Author of ascetic treatises. Died Santa Barbara, Cal., Dec. 4, 1896.

DEZENDORF, John Frederick, congressman, businessman; b. Lansingburg, Rensselaer County, N.Y., Aug. 10, 1834. Learned carpenter's trade, also studied architecture, civil engring.; engaged in railroad and other constrn., Toledo, also Cleve., O., 1850-60; engaged in merc. activities, 1860-62; entered shipping bus., Norfolk, Va. 1863; surveyor Norfolk City and County, 1866-69; asst. assessor U.S. Internal Revenue, 1870-72; appraiser of mdse. Norfolk Customhouse, 1872-77; del. Republican Nat. Conv., Cincinnati, 1876; mem. U.S. Ho. of Reps. (Rep.) from Va., 47th Congress, 1881-83; engaged in constrn. bus. Died Norfolk, June 22, 1894; buried Elmwood Cemetery.

DIAS, Bartholomeu de Novaes, navigator; b. Portugal, circa 1450. Probably an ivory trader on African Guinea coast, circa 1478; commd. by King John II of Portugal to extend Portuguese exploration of West African coast, and attempt to find sea route to India, 1486; went farther South along African coast than any previous attempts, as far as Rio de Infante (now known as Great Fish River); proved that sea route to India around Africa was possible; turned back because of discontent of his crew; according to tradition, named tip of South Africa Cabo Tormentoso (Cape of Storms; name later changed to Cabo de Bõa Esperança, meaning Cape of Good Hope, by King John II); reached Lisbon, Dec. 1488; did not receive command of expdn. to India (Vasco da Gama named instead of him), 1497; mem. expdn. to Brazil, 1500. Died in storm at sea on return to Portugal, May 29, 1500.

DIBRELL, George Gibbs, congressman, industrialist; b. White County, Tenn., Apr. 12, 1822; s. Anthony and Mildred (Carter) D.; m. Mary Leftwich, Jan. 13, 1842; children—Wamcen, Joseph. Clk. of Sparta, br. Bank of Tenn., 1840-46; clk. White County Ct., 1846-60; mem. Tenn. Gen. Assembly, 1860-62; commd. lt. col. of a regt. Confederate Army, 1861; in command Nathan B. Forrest's "Old Brigade," 1863; commd. brig. gen., 1864; dir. Southwestern R.R., 1866, became pres., 1869; participated in Tenn. Constl. Conv., 1870; mem. U.S. Ho. of Reps. from Tenn., 44th-48th congresses, 1875-85. Died Sparta, May 6, 1888.

DICK, Elisha Cullen, physician; b. nr. Macus Hook, Pa., Mar. 15, 1762; s. Archibald and Mary (Barnard) D.; grad. U. Pa., 1782; m. Hannah Harman, Oct. 1783, several children. Practiced medicine, Alexandria, Va., 1782-1825; attended George Washington during his final illness (with Dr. James Craik), 1799; helped organize Masonic lodge, Alexandria, served as worshipful master; col. Va. Cavalry in Pa. during Whiskey Rebellion, 1794; mayor Alexandria, 1804. Died Alexandria, Sept. 22, 1825.

DICK, John, congressman, businessman; b. Pitts., June 17, 1794; attended common schs., Pa.; at least 1 son, Samuel Bernard. Commd. maj. 1st Battalion, 1821, col. 1st Regt., 1825, brig. gen. 2d Brigade, 16th Div., Pa. Militia, 1831; engaged in merc. and banking activities; Whig presdl. elector, 1840; founder banking house J. & J. R. Dick, 1850; asso. judge Crawford County, 1850; a promoter Atlantic & Gt. Western R.R.; trustee Allegheny Coll., Meadville, Pa.; pres. Crawford Mut. Ins. Co., also Greendale Cemetery; mem. U.S. Ho. of Reps. from Pa., (as Whig) 33d Congress, 1853-55, (as Republican) 34th-35th congresses, 1855-59. Died Meadville, May 29, 1872; buried Greendale Cemetery.

DICK, Robert Paine, jurist; b. Greensboro, N.C., Oct. 5, 1823; s. John McClintock and Parthenia (Williamson) D.; grad. U. N.C., 1843; m. Mary Adams. Admitted to bar, 1845; del. to Democratic Nat. Conv., Balt., 1852; U.S. dist. atty. for N.C., 1853-61; mem. N.C. Council, 1862; mem. N.C. Senate (peace candidate), 1864; U.S. dist. judge for N.C., 1866-68, 72-98; asso. justice N.C. Supreme Ct., 1868-72. Died Sept. 12, 1898.

DICK, Samuel, Continental congressman; b. Nottingham, Prince Georges County, Md., Nov. 14, 1740; studied medicine, Scotland. Began practice of medicine, Salem, N.Y., 1770; mem. N.J. Provincial Congress, 1776; served as col. 1st Battalion, Salem County (N.J.) Militia, 1776, then as asst. surgeon Continental Army in Canadian campaign; mem. 1st N.J. Gen. Assembly; apptd. collector of customs Western Dist. N.J., 1778; mem. Continental Congress from N.J., 1783-84; del. N.J. Conv. to ratify U.S. Constn., 1787; surrogate Salem County, 1785-1804. Died Salem, Nov. 16, 1812; buried St. John's Episcopal Churchyard.

DICKENS, Charles, author; b. Landport, Portsea, Eng., Feb. 7, 1812; s. John and Elizabeth (Barrow) D.; m. Catherine Hogarth, Apr. 2, 1836, 10 children. Clk. in office of Mr. Mallory, New Square, Lincoln's Inn, Eng., 1827-28; reporter in Doctor's Commons, other courts, 1829-31; reporter to True Sun in Ho. of Commons, 1831-35; had his 1st article (signed "Boz") printed in a periodical, Monthly Mag., 1833; published Pickwick Sketches, Apr. 1836-Nov. 1837, installments of Oliver Twist, Jan. 1837-Mar. 1839; published weekly installments of Master Humphrey's Clock, 1837-40; toured and visited Am., Jan. 4-May 1842, was shocked by level of slavery in Am.; published American Notes, Oct. 1842, Martin Chuzzlewit, 1843 (both sharply critical of Am. character, commercialism and customs); wrote The Christmas Carol, Christmas 1843; editor Daily News, London, Jan.-Feb. 1846; lived in Switzerland, writing Dombey and Son, also Battle of Life, 1846-48; mgr. theatrical co. in Liverpool and Manchester (Eng.), 1847-52; editor Household Works (later called All The Year Round), 1849-70; made 2d trip to Am., Nov. 9, 1867-May 1868, lectured and read his works, received payment of 20,000 pounds. Other works include: Nicholas Nickleby, 1839; The Old Curiosity Shop, 1841; Barnaby Rudge, 1841; David Copperfield (partly autobiog.), 1849-50; Bleak House, 1853; Hard Times, 1854; Little Dorrit, 1857; A Tale of Two Cities, 1859; Great Expectations, 1860-61; Our Mutual Friend, 1864-65; Mystery of Edwin Drood (unfinished), 1870. His books stimulated needed social reform, influenced other writers including James and Brecht. Died Gadshill, nr. Rochester, Eng., June 9, 1870; buried Westminster Abbey.

DICKENS, Samuel, congressman; b. nr. Roxboro, Person County, N.C. Mem. N.C. Ho. of Commons, 1813-15, 18; mem. U.S. Ho. of Reps. from N.C. (filled vacancy), 14th Congress, Dec. 2, 1816-17; moved to Madison County, Tenn., 1820. Died Madison County, 1840.

DICKERSON, Edward Nicoll, lawyer; b. Paterson, N.J., Feb. 11, 1824; s. Philemon and Sidney (Stotesbury) D.; attended Princeton. Admitted to N.J. bar, 1845; practiced in Paterson, 1845-52, N.Y.C., 1852-89, specialist in patent law, represented Samuel Colt, Charles Goodyear and Thomas Edison, many other inventors; interested in mech. engring.; drove 1st locomotive used between Paterson and Jersey City. Died Wave Crest, L.I., N.Y., Dec. 12, 1889.

DICKERSON, Mahlon, senator, gov. N.J., b. Hanover Neck, N.J., Apr. 17, 1770; s. Jonathan and Mary (Coe) D.; grad. Princeton, 1789. Admitted to N.J. bar, 1793, Pa. bar, 1797; elected Phila. Common Council, 1799; state commr. of bankruptcy Pa., 1802; adj. gen. Pa., 1805-08; recorder Phila., 1808-10; mem. N.J. Assembly from Morris County, 1811-13; law reporter N.J. Supreme Ct., 1813-14, justice, 1813-15; gov. N.J., 1815-17; mem. U.S. Senate (Democrat) from N.J., 1817-33; mem. N.J. Council, 1833; U.S. sec. of navy, 1834-38; judge U.S. Dist. Ct. for N.J., 1840; del. N.J. Constl. Conv., 1844; pres. Am. Inst., 1846-48; owner Succasunna Ironworks (N.J.). Died Succasunna, Oct. 5, 1853.

DICKERSON, Philemon, jurist, gov. N.J.; b. Succasunna, N.J., June 26, 1788; s. Jonathan and Mary (Coe) D.; grad. U. Pa., 1808. Admitted to N.J. bar, 1813, admitted counselor at law, 1817; mem. N.J. Assembly, 1821-22; sgt.-at-law N.J., 1834; mem. U.S. Ho. of Reps. from N.J., 23d-24th congresses, 1833-Nov. 3, 1836; gov. N.J., 1836-37; chancellor N.J. Legislature, 1836; apptd. U.S. dist. judge for N.J., 1841-62; instrumental in obtaining Paterson (N.J.) City Charter, 1851. Author: The City of Paterson, Its Past, Present and Future, 1856. Died Paterson, Dec. 10, 1862.

DICKEY, Jesse Column, congressman, farmer; b. New Castle, Pa., Feb. 17, 1808; grad. New London (Pa.) Acad. Became tchr. Hopewell Acad., 1828; engaged in farming; mem. Pa. Ho. of Reps., 1842-45; mem. U.S. Ho. of Reps. (Whig) from Pa., 31st Congress, 1849-51; served as q.m., later paymaster U.S. Army during Civil War. Died New London, Feb. 19, 1890; buried Presbyn. Cemetery.

DICKEY, John, congressman; b. Greensburg, Pa., June 23, 1794; at least 1 son, Oliver James. Postmaster, Old Brighton (Pa.), 1818-21; sheriff, 1824-27; mem. Pa. Senate, 1835, 37; mem. U.S. Ho. of Reps. (Whig) from Pa., 28th, 30th congresses, 1843-45, 47-49; apptd. U.S. marshall for Western Dist. Pa., 1852. Died Beaver Pa., Mar. 14, 1853; buried Old Cemetery.

DICKEY, Oliver James, congressman, lawyer; b. Old Brighton, Pa., Apr. 6, 1823; s. John Dickey; attended Beaver Acad., Dickinson Coll.; studied law. Admitted to bar, Lancaster, Pa., 1844, practice of law; dist. atty. Lancaster County (Pa.), 1856-59; served as lt. col. 10th Regt., Pa. Volunteers, during Civil War; mem. U.S. Ho. of Reps. (Republican, filled vacancy) from Pa., 40th-42d congresses, Dec. 7, 1868-73; del. Pa. Constl. Conv., Harrisburg, 1873; del. several Rep. nat. convs. Died Lancaster Apr. 21, 1876; buried Woodward Hill Cemetery.

DICKEY, Theophilus Lyle, jurist, army officer; b. Paris, Ky., Oct. 2, 1811; s. James Henry and Polly (De Pew) D.; grad. Miami U., Oxford, O., 1831; m. Juliet Evans, Dec. 6, 1831; m. 2d, Mrs. Beulah Hirst, summer 1870. Admitted to Ill. bar, 1835; raised co. for 1st Ill. Inf., at outbreak Mexican War, commd. capt.; judge Ill. Circuit Ct., 1848-52; del. 1st Republican Conv., Bloomingt 1854; raised 4th Ill. Cavalry, 1861, commd. ca fought under Gen. Grant in West, 1861-63; no nated for congressman-at-large Ill., 1866; a atty. gen. U.S., 1868-70; corp. counsel, 18 judge Ill. Supreme Ct., 1875-85. Died Atla City, N.J., July 22, 1885.

DICKINS, John, clergyman; b. London, Eng., A 31, 1747; m. Elizabeth Yancey. Came to Am., ci 1770; converted to Methodism, 1774; evangelist N.C. and Va., 1774-81; admitted to itinerant m istry, 1777; pastor John Street Ch., N.Y.C., 17 89, serving Bertie circuit, N.C., 1785; atten Christmas Conf., Balt. (organized Methodist Epis pal Ch. in Am.), 1784; ordained deacon, 17 elder, 1787; attended Conf. of 1789; may have nanced 1st Methodist Book Concern, 1789, B Steward, 1789-98; publisher Arminian Mag., 17 90, Methodist Mag., 1797-98; pastor St. Georg Ch., Phila., circa 1789-98. Died during Phila. y low fever epidemic, Sept. 27, 1798.

DICKINSON, Anson, artist; b. Milton, Con Apr. 19, 1779; s. Oliver and Anna (Landon) m. Sarah B. Dickinson, 1818, 2 adopted childr Began career as portrait artist, 1800, worked N.Y.C., 1800-04, 11-18, Albany, N.Y., 1805- wandered in New Eng., working in Boston, N Haven and Hartford, Conn., 1818-52; painted min tures and oils; subjects include Gilbert Stuart, R ert Fulton and Sam Houston. Died Milton, M 9, 1852.

DICKINSON, Daniel Stevens, senator; b. Gos en, Conn., Sept. 11, 1800; s. Daniel T. and M (Caulkins) D.; m. Lydia Knapp, 1822. Admitt to bar, 1828; 1st pres. Binghampton (N.Y.), 18 mem. N.Y. State Senate, 1837-41, Democra leader; lt. gov. N.Y., 1842-44; mem. U.S. Sena from N.Y., 1844-51; del. Nat. Democratic Con 1848, 52; U.S. atty. gen. on Union ticket, 186 63; mem. N.W. Boundary Commn., 1863; del. U ion Conv. of 1864; U.S. dist. atty. for So. N.Y 1865. Died N.Y.C., Apr. 12, 1866.

DICKINSON, David W., congressman, lawy b. Franklin, Tenn., June 10, 1808; grad. U. N.C. Chapel Hill; studied law. Admitted to bar, beg practice of law; mem. U.S. Ho. of Reps. fr Tenn. (as Democrat), 23d Congress, 1833-35, (Whig), 28th Congress, 1843-45. Died "Grantlan (father's home) nr. Murfreesboro, Tenn., A 27, 1845; buried family burying ground "Gra land."

DICKINSON, Edward, lawyer, congressman; Amherst, Mass., Jan. 1, 1803; s. Samuel Fowl Dickinson; grad. Yale, 1823; attended law sch Northampton, Mass. Admitted to bar, began pra tice of law, Amherst, 1826; treas. Amherst Coll 1835-73; mem. Mass. Ho. of Reps., 1838-39, 7 Mass. Senate, 1842-43, Mass. Gov.'s Council, 184 47; mem. U.S. Ho. of Reps. (Whig) from Mass 33d Congress, 1853-55. Died Boston, June 1 1874; buried West Cemetery, Amherst.

DICKINSON, Edward Fenwick, congressma lawyer; b. Fremont, O., Jan. 21, 1829; grad. S Xavier Coll., Cincinnati. Admitted to bar, bega practice of law, Fremont; pros. atty. Sandusk County (O.), 1852-54; commd. lt. U.S. Arm during Civil War, promoted capt., served as reg mental q.m. Co. G., 8th Regt., Ohio Volunte Inf.; probate judge Sandusky County, 1866-6 77-79, 85-91; mem. U.S. Ho. of Reps. (Democra from Ohio, 41st Congress, 1869-71; elected may Fremont, 1871, 73, 75. Died Fremont, Aug. 2 1891.

DICKINSON, Emily Elizabeth, poet; b. Am herst, Mass., Dec. 10, 1830; d. Edward and Emi (Norcross) Dickinson; ed. Mt. Holyoke Fema Sem., 1847-48. Began writing poetry, 1861; a re cluse, never leaving her home after 1871; only poems published during lifetime; poetry publishe after death by Mrs. Mabel Loomis Todd, majority it after 1929. Work published as Poems, 189 Poems, 1891; Poems, 1896; The Single Houn 1914; Further Poems, 1929. Died Amherst, Ma 15, 1886.

DICKINSON, John, Continental congressman; b Talbot County, Md., Nov. 8, 1732; s. Samuel an Mary (Cadwalader) D.; LL.D., Coll. of N.J. (no Princeton), 1768; m. Mary Norris, July 19, 177 Admitted to Middle Temple, London, Eng.; admitte to Phila. bar, 1757; mem. Assembly of Lower Coun ties (Del.), 1760, later became speaker; mem Pa. Legislature from Phila., 1762-64, 70-76; print ed pamphlet The Late Regulations Respecting th British Colonies on the Continent of America Co sidered, 1765; del. to Stamp Act Congress fro Pa., 1765; chmn. Com. of Correspondence, 1774 mem. Continental Congress, 1774-76, 79-81 chmn. of a com. of safety and defense, 1775; ad vocated conciliation with Eng.; voted against De laration of Independence; col. 1st Battalion raise in Phila.; pres. Supreme Council Del., 1781; pre Supreme Council Pa., 1782-85; del. U.S. Const nv. from Del., 1787; noted for published series letters urging adoption of Constn., signed Fabi- Author: Letters from a Farmer in Pennsylvania the Inhabitants of the British Colonies (urged n-importation instead of violence), 1768. Died lmington, Del., Feb. 14, 1808.

DICKINSON, John Dean, congressman, lawyer, ker; b. Middletown, Conn., June 28, 1767; d. Yale, 1785. Moved to Lansingburg, N.Y., 90; admitted to bar, 1791, began practice of , Lansingburg; moved to Troy, N.Y.; pres. rmer's Bank of Troy, 1801-41; founder, dir. nsselaer & Saratoga Ins. Co., 1814; mem. N.Y. te Assembly, 1816-17; 1st pres. Troy Lyceum Natural History, 1818; mem. U.S. Ho. of Reps. ederalist) from N.Y., 16th-17th congresses, 19-23 (Whig), 20th-21st congresses, 1827-31; original trustee Rensselaer Poly. Inst., 1824; m. com. which received Lafayette on visits Troy, 1824, 25; Died Troy, Jan. 28, 1841; ied Oakwood Cemetery.

DICKINSON, John Woodbridge, educator; b. Ches- , Mass., Oct. 12, 1825; s. William and Elizabeth orthington) D.; grad. Williams Coll., 1852; m. exene Parsons, 1857, 2 children. Instr., Westfield ass.) State Normal Sch., 1852-57, prin., 1857- ; sec. Mass. Bd. Edn., 1877-93; trustee Williams ll., 1886-90; instr. Emerson Sch. Oratory, Bos- , circa 1895-1901. Author: The Limits of Oral aining, 1890; Brief Descriptive Sketch of the Mas- husetts Public School System, 1893; Principles l Method of Teaching, Derived from a Knowledge the Mind, 1899; Rhetoric and Principles of Writ- n Composition, 1901. Died Newton, Mass., Feb. 1901.

DICKINSON, Jonathan, clergyman, coll. pres.; Hatfield, Mass., Apr. 22, 1688; grad. Yale, 1706; Joanna Melyen, circa 1709; m. 2d, Mary Crane, r. 1747. Ordained, Congregational Ch., Eliza- thtown, N.J., 1709, pastor, 1709-47; persuaded ngregation to join Presbytery of Phila., 1717, derator, 1721, 42; obtained 1st charter Coll. of J. (now Princeton), 1746, 1st pres., 1747. Au- or: Reasonableness of Christianity: Four Serm- s, 1732; The True Scripture of Doctrine Con- rning Some Important Points of Christian Faith, 41. Died Elizabethtown, Oct. 7, 1747.

DICKINSON, Philemon, army officer, Continen- congressman; b. Croisia-dore, Talbot County, l., Apr. 5, 1739; s. Judge Samuel and Mary (Cad- lader) D.; grad. U. Pa., 1759; m. Mary Cad- lader, July 14, 1767; m. 2d, Rebecca Cadwala- r. Commd. col. Hunterdon County (N.J.) Bat- ion, 1775; commd. brig. gen. N.J. Militia, 1775, j. gen., comdr.-in-chief, 1776; defeated a Corn- llis raiding expdn. interrupting Brit. retreat to Y. before Battle of Monmouth, 1777; apptd. mmr. N.J. Loan Office, 1781; mem. Continental ngress from Del., 1782-83; v.p. N.J. Council, 83-84; apptd. a commr. by Continental Congress select site for U.S. Capitol, 1785. Died nr. Tren- , N.J., Feb. 4, 1809.

DICKINSON, Rodolphus, congressman, lawyer; Hatfield, Mass., Dec. 28, 1797; attended Wil- ms Coll., Williamstown, Mass., 1818-21; studied v. Admitted to bar, began practice of law, fin, O.; apptd. pros. atty. Seneca County, 24, Williams County, 1826, Sandusky County, 27; moved to Lower Sandusky, O., 1826; mem. io Bd. of Public Works, 1836-45; mem. U.S. . of Reps. (Democrat) from Ohio, 30th-31st ngresses, 1847-49. Died Washington, D.C., Mar. , 1849; buried Washington, reinterred Oakwood metery, Fremont, O.

DICKSON, David, congressman, physician; b. .; studied medicine. Practiced medicine, Pike unty, Miss.; del. Miss. Constl. Conv. 1817; ved as brig. gen. Miss. Militia, 1818; mem. ss. Senate, 1820-21, sec., 1833; lt. gov. Miss., 21; postmaster Jackson (Miss.), 1822; unsuc- sful candidate for gov. Miss., 1823; del. Miss. nstl. Conv., 1832; sec. of state, 1835; mem. U.S. . of Reps. (Democrat) from Miss., 24th Con- s, 1835-36. Died Hot Springs, Ark., July 31, 36.

DICKSON, David, farmer; b. Hancock County, ., July 6, 1809; s. Thomas Dickson. Owned store, arta, Ga., 1835-46; invested profits in cotton antation, Hancock County (became one of most ccessful in South); raised only foodstuffs for Con- lerate Army, 1862-65, property destroyed by Gen. T. Sherman's army, 1865; owned large plantation Hancock County and another in Tex. after Civil ar; 1st in South to use guano to fertilize cotton, 46. Author: A Treatise on Agriculture, to which Added the Author's Published Letters, by David ckson, 1870. Died Hancock County, Feb. 18, 1885.

DICKSON, John, congressman, lawyer; b. ene, N.H., June 1, 1783; grad. Middlebury t.) Coll., 1808; studied law. Admitted to bar, 12, began practice of law, West Bloomfield, Y.; mem. N.Y. State Assembly, 1829-30; mem. U.S. Ho. of Reps. (Whig) from N.Y., 22d-23d congresses, 1831-35. Died West Bloomfield, Feb. 22, 1852; buried Pioneer Cemetery.

DICKSON, Joseph, planter, congressman; b. Chester County, Pa., Apr. 1745; ed. in Rowan County, N.C. Became cotton and tobacco planter; mem. Rowan County Com. of Safety, 1775; commd. capt. Continental Army, 1775, served under Col. McDowell, 1780, as maj. "Lincoln County Men" at Battle of Kings Mountain; promoted col. for bravery in opposing Lord Cornwallis' invasion of N.C., 1781; commd. brig. gen. before end of Revolutionary War; clk. Lincoln County Ct., 1781; mem. N.C. Senate, 1788-95; a commr. to establish U. N.C. at Chapel Hill; mem. U.S. Ho. of Reps. from N.C., 6th Congress, 1799-1801, helped elect Thomas Jefferson over Aaron Burr; moved to Tenn., 1803, became planter, Davidson (now Rutherford) County; mem. Tenn. Ho. of Reps., 1807-11, speaker, 1809-11. Died Rutherford County, Apr. 14, 1825; buried on his plantation N.E. of Murfreesboro, Tenn.

DICKSON, Robert, fur trade; b. Dumfries, Scotland, 1765; s. John Dickson; m. To-to-Win (sister of a Sioux chief), 1797. Began fur trading career in Canada, 1783; interpreter, storekeeper for British at Indian council at Machilemackinac, 1787; traded among Sioux, 1797-1823; formed firm Robert Dickinson & Co., 1805, merged with Machilemackinac Co., 1807; justice of peace St. Clair County (Ind.), 1803; led Sioux Indians in alliance with British, 1812-15; Brit. agt. for Indians West of Lake Huron with rank of lt. col., 1813-15. Died Drummond Island, Mich., June 20, 1823.

DICKSON, Samuel, physician, congressman; b. Bethlehem (now New Scotland), Albany County, N.Y., Mar. 19, 1807; grad. Union Coll., Schenectady, N.Y., 1825; diploma Censors of Med. Soc. State of N.Y., 1829. Began practice of medicine, New Scotland, 1829; mem. U.S. Ho. of Reps. (Whig) from N.Y., 34th Congress, 1855-57; suffered spinal disease after accident while attending session of U.S. Ho. of Reps. Died New Scotland, May 3, 1858; buried New Scotland Presbyn. Ch. Cemetery.

DICKSON, Samuel Henry, physician; b. Charleston, S.C., Sept. 20, 1798; s. Samuel and Mary (Neilson) D.; B.A., Yale, 1814; M.D., U. Pa., 1819; m. Elizabeth Robertson; m. 2d, Jane Robertson, 1834; m. 3d, Marie DuPre 1845. A founder Med. Coll. S.C., 1833, prof., 1833-47, 50-58; prof. N.Y.U., 1847-50, Jefferson Med. Coll., Phila., 1858-72. Author: Manual of Pathology and Practice, 1839; Elements of Medicine, 1855; Studies in Pathology and Therapeutics, 1867. Died Phila., Mar. 31, 1872.

DICKSON, Thomas, mfr.; b. Leeds, Eng., Mar. 26, 1824; s. James and Elizabeth (Linen) D.; m. Mary Marvine, Aug. 31, 1846, 1 dau., Elizabeth Linen. Came to Am., 1832; went to N.E. Pa., 1834; founder Dickson & Co., Carbondale, Pa., 1856, later Scranton, Pa., pres. reorganized co. Dickson Mfg. Co., 1862; a founder 1st Nat. Bank of Scranton, 1863; dir. Moosic Powder Co., 1865; became pres. Delaware & Hudson Canal Co., 1869; largely responsible for making Scranton an important indsl. center; promoted extension ry. line to Can. Died Morristown, N.J., July 31, 1884.

DICKSON, William, congressman, physician; b. Duplin County, N.C., May 5, 1770; ed. Grove Acad., Kenansville, N.C.; studied medicine. Moved with family to Tenn., 1795; practiced medicine, Nashville, Tenn., many years; mem. Tenn. Ho. of Reps., 1799-1803, served as speaker; mem. U.S. Ho. of Reps. from Tenn., 7th-9th congresses, 1801-07; trustee U. Nashville, 1806-16. Died Nashville, Feb. 1816; buried rural cemetery nr. Nashville.

DIEGO Y MORENO, Francisco Garcia, clergyman; b. Lagos, Jalisco, Mexico, Sept. 17, 1785/86; attended Tridentino Sem., also Apostolic Coll., Guadalupe. Became a Franciscan at age 17; ordained priest Roman Catholic Ch., 1808; taught in Guadalupe; vicar in Zacatecas; rector Apostolic Coll., Zapopan; did missionary work, apptd. prefect of Indian missions in Cal., 1830; settled in Santa Clara, Cal., restored many missions, until Mexican Congress passed decree of secularization, 1834; secured repeal of decree in Mexico, 1836; apptd. 1st bishop of Two Cals., 1840, worked toward restoring the missions (which were almost in ruins); founded sem., Santa Ynez, 1844. Died Santa Barbara, Cal., Apr. 30, 1845.

DIETRICKSON, Johannes Wilhelm Christian, clergyman; b. Fredrickstad, Norway, Apr. 4 (or Aug. 23), 1815; s. Frederick Battington and Karen (Radich) D.; grad. U. Christiania (now Oslo), 1837, postgrad., 1839-43; m. Jörgine Laurense Broch, 1839; m. 2d, Charlotte Mueller, 1845/46. Ordained pastor Lutheran Ch., 1844; came to U.S., 1844; organized and drew up constns. for several Norwegian Am. Luth. chs. in Wis., 1844-45; recruited pastors for work in Wis., Norway, 1845-46; continued work of establishing churches in Am., 1846-50; returned to Norway, 1850. Author: Travels among the Norwegian Emigrants in the "United North American Free States," 1846. Died Porsgrund, Norway, Nov. 14, 1883.

DIETZ, William, congressman, farmer; b. Schoharie, N.Y., June 28, 1778; attended dist. schs. Engaged in farming; town clk., 1804-05; supr. Schoharie, 1812; mem. N.Y. State Assembly, 1814-15, 23; mem. U.S. Ho. of Reps. (Democrat) from N.Y. 19th Congress, 1825-27; mem. N.Y. Senate, 1830-33; Democratic presdl. elector, 1832; served as col. militia. Died Schoharie, Aug. 24, 1848; buried St. Paul's Lutheran Cemetery.

DIGGES, Thomas Atwood, writer; b. Md., circa 1741. Friend of Washington, Jefferson, Franklin, Madison; spent several years in Lisbon during Revolutionary War; generally accepted as author of The Adventures of Alonzo: Containing Some Striking Anecdotes of the Present Prime Minister of Portugal, written by "a native of Maryland some years resident in Lisbon," 1775 (book is imitation of picaresque novel). Died circa 1821.

DILLINGHAM, Paul, Jr., gov. Vt., congressman, lawyer; b. Shutesbury, Mass., Aug. 10, 1799; attended dist. sch. Waterbury, Vt.; studied law; at least 1 son, William Paul. Admitted to bar, 1823, began practice of law, Waterbury; justice of peace, 1826-44; town clk. Waterbury, 1829-44; mem. Vt. Ho. of Reps., 1833-35, 37-40; pros. atty. Washington County, 1835-38; del Vt. constl. convs., 1836, 57, 70; mem. Vt. Senate, 1841-42, 61; mem. U.S. Ho. of Reps. (Democrat) from Vt., 28th-29th congresses, 1843-47; lt. gov. Vt., 1862-65, gov., 1865-66. Died Waterbury, July 26, 1891; buried Village Cemetery.

DILLON, Sidney, railroad builder; b. Northampton, N.Y., May 7, 1812; s. Timothy Dillon; m. Hannah Smith, 1841, 2 daus. Participated in constrn. Rutland & Burlington R.R., Central R.R. of N.J., Phila. & Erie R.R., Morris & Essex R.R., Pa. R.R., New Orleans, Mobile & Chattanooga R.R., Can. So. R.R., also tunnel from Grand Central Sta. to Harlem River, N.Y.C.; constructed U.P. R.R., with which co. he became actively asso. in 1865, dir., 1864-92, pres., 1874-84, 90-92. Elected fellow Am. Soc. Civil Engrs., 1870. Died N.Y.C., June 9, 1892.

DIMAN, Jeremiah Lewis, clergyman, educator; b. Bristol, R.I., May 1, 1831; s. Byron and Abby (Wight) D.; grad. Brown U., 1851, Andover Theol. Sem., 1856; m. Emily Stimson, May 15, 1861. Ordained pastor First Congregational Ch., Fall River, Mass., 1856-60; pastor Harvard Congregational Ch., Brookline, Mass., 1861-64; prof. history and polit. economy Brown U., 1864-81; mem. editorial staff Providence (R.I.) Jour.; reviewed hist. works for The Nation, 1877-81; Lowell lectr., Boston, 1880. Author: The Theistic Argument as Affected by Recent Theories, 1881; Orations and Essays: with Selected Parish Sermons, 1882. Died Feb. 3, 1881.

DIMITRY, Alexander, educator, diplomat; b. New Orleans, Feb. 7, 1805; s. Andrew and Celeste (Pragon) D.; grad. Georgetown Coll., LL.D., 1867. m. Mary Mills, 1835. Clk., Washington (D.C.) Post Office, 1834-42; mem. Union Literary Soc.; established sch., St. Charles Parish (La.), 1842, pres., 1842-47; translator U.S. Dept. State, Washington, 1854-59; U.S. minister to Costa Rica and Nicaragua, 1859-61; asst. postmaster gen. Confederate States Am. during Civil War. Died New Orleans, Jan. 30, 1883.

DIMMICK, Milo Melankthon, congressman, lawyer; b. Milford, Pa., Oct. 30, 1811; studied law. Admitted to bar, 1834, began practice of law, Stroudsburg, Pa.; mem. U.S. Ho. of Reps. (Democrat) from Pa., 31st-32d congresses, 1849-53; unsuccessful candidate for pres. judge 22d Jud. Dist. Pa., 1853; moved to Mauch Chunk, Carbon County, Pa., 1853, continued practice of law, also became a banker. Died Mauch Chunk, Nov. 22, 1872; buried Mauch Chunk Cemetery.

DIMMICK, William Harrison, congressman, lawyer; b. Milford, Pa., Dec. 20, 1815; studied law. Admitted to bar, 1835, began practice of law, Bethany, Pa.; moved to Honesdale, Pa., 1842; pros. atty. Wayne County, 1836-37; mem. Pa. Senate, 1845-47; mem. U.S. Ho. of Reps. (Democrat) from Pa., 35th-36th congresses, 1857-61. Died Honesdale, Aug. 2, 1861; buried Glen Dyberry Cemetery.

DIMOCK, Davis, Jr., congressman, lawyer; b. Exeter, nr. Wilkes-Barre, Pa., Sept. 17, 1801; attended Susquehanna County Acad., Montrose, Pa.; studied law. Admitted to bar, 1833, began practice of law, Montrose; also engaged in editorial work; apptd. county treas., 1834; mem. U.S. Ho. of Reps. (Democrat) from Pa., 27th Congress, 1841-42. Died Montrose, Jan. 13, 1842; buried Montrose Cemetery.

DINGLEY, Nelson, editor, gov. Me., congressman; b. Durham, Me., Feb. 15, 1832; s. Nelson and Jane (Lambert) D.; grad. Dartmouth, 1855; m.

Salome McKenney, June 11, 1857; 1 son, Edward Nelson. Admitted to Me. bar, 1856; editor Lewiston (Me.) Evening Jour., 1856; mem. Me. Legislature (Republican), 1862-65, 68, 73, speaker, 1863-64; gov. Me., 1874-75; mem. U.S. Ho. of Reps. from Me., 47th-55th congresses, 1881-99, mem. ways and means com., 1889, chmn., 1895; declined appointment by McKinley as U.S. treasury; sponsored Dingley Tariff Act of 1897 (highest tariff to that time). Died Washington, D.C., Jan. 13, 1899; buried Oak Hill Cemetery, Auburn, Me.

DINSMOOR, Robert, poet; b. Windham, N.H., Oct. 7, 1757; s. William and Elizabeth (Cochran) D.; m. Mary Park; m. 2d, Mary Anderson; 11 children. Served with N.H. Militia at Battle of Saratoga during Am. Revolution; deacon, clk. Presbyn. Ch., Windham; works collected as Poems of Robert Dinsmoor, the Rustic Bard (compiled and arranged by Leonard Morrison), 1898. Died Mar. 16, 1836.

DINSMOOR, Samuel, gov. N.J., congressman; b. Windham, N.H., July 1, 1766; grad. Dartmouth, 1789; studied law. Admitted to bar, began practice of law, Keene, N.H.; mem. U.S. Ho. of Reps. (War Democrat) from N.H., 12th Congress, 1811-13; councilor N.H., 1821; presdl. elector on Monroe ticket, 1820; judge probate Cheshire County (N.H.), 1823-31; mem. commn. to establish boundary line between N.H. and Mass., 1825; gov. N.H., 1831-33. Died Keene, Mar. 15, 1835; buried Washington Street Cemetery.

DINWIDDIE, Robert, colonial gov. Va.; b. Glasgow, Scotland, 1693; s. Robert and Sarah (Cumming) D.; m. Rebecca Affleck, 2 children. In charge admiralty affairs, Bermuda, 1721; customs collector, Bermuda, 1727-38; made surveyor-gen. customs for So. part America with jurisdiction over Carolinas, Va., Md., Pa., Bahama Islands and Jamaica, Apr. 11, 1738; insp. gen., 1743; lt. gov. Va., July 20, 1751; with approval Bd. of Trade led colonial govs. in opposing French domination of N.Am., thereby greatly affecting course Am. history; attended conf. govs., Annapolis, Apr. 1755; dispatched George Washington and detachment to Ohio region to combat French attack, 1754; supplied provisions for Braddock's campaign; left Va., 1758; noted for his role in French and Indian Wars and promotion of western movement; checkmated French in obtaining interests of Ohio Co. land venture. Died Clifton Bristol, Eng., July 27, 1770.

DISNEY, David Tiernan, congressman, lawyer; b. Balt., Aug. 25, 1803; attended common schs., Ohio; studied law. Admitted to bar, began practice of Reps. (Democrat) from Ohio, 31st-33d con-1825; mem. Ohio Ho. of Reps., 1829, 31-32, speaker, 1832; mem. Ohio Senate, 1833-34, 43-44, pres., 1833; a commr. to adjust boundary line between Ohio and Mich., 1834; chmn. commn. to adjust taxes of Ohio counties, 1840; del. Democratic Nat. Conv., Balt., 1848; mem. U.S. Ho. of Reps. (Democrat) from Ohio, 31st-33d congresses, 1849-55; declined appointment by Pres. Buchanan as U.S. minister to Spain. Died Washington, D.C., Mar. 14, 1857; buried Spring Grove Cemetery, Cincinnati.

DISSTON, Henry, mfr.; b. Tewkesbury, Eng., May 23, 1819; s. Thomas and Ann (Harrod) D.; m. Amanda Mulvina Bickley; m. 2d, Mary Steelman. Came to Am. with father, 1833; became saw maker's apprentice; started successful saw-making business, Phila., 1840; introduced mfg. innovations, including use of steam power and conversion of waste steel; helped free U.S. saw mfrs. from dependence on imported steel. Died Mar. 16, 1878.

DISTURNELL, John, guide book compiler; b. Lansingburg, N.Y., Oct. 6, 1801. Printer, Albany, N.Y.; bookdealer, N.Y.C., 1830-65; librarian Cooper Union, N.Y.C., 1865-70; bookdealer, Phila.; noted for his guide and travel books, including: A Guide to the City of New York, 1836; Emigrant's Guide to New Mexico, California and Oregon, 1849; The United States National Register Containing Authentic Political and Statistical Information, complied yearly, 1851-77; Springs, Waterfalls, Seabathing Resorts, and Mountain Scenery, 1855; New York as It Was and As It Is, 1876. Died N.Y.C., Oct. 1 ,1877.

DITSON, George Leighton, diplomat, author: b. Westford, Mass., Aug. 5, 1812; s. William and Mary (Leighton) D.; attended U. Vt., 1863-64; m. Oralie Bartlett, 1860. Travelled abroad because of health for 2 years; Am. consul at Neuvitas (Cuba) under Presidents Tyler and Polk; tchr. English, Puerto-Principe, Cuba, 1842-43. Author: The Para Papers on France, Egypt and Ethiopia, 1858; The Crescent and French Crusaders, 1859; (novels) Crimora, or Love's Cross, 1852; The Federati of Iataly, 1871. Died N.Y.C., Jan. 29, 1895.

DITSON, Oliver, music publisher; b. Boston, Oct. 20, 1811; s. Joseph and Lucy (Pierce) D.; m. Catherine Delano, circa 1840, 5 children. Founder largest music publishing bus. in N.Am., 1835, became Oliver Ditson & Co., 1857 (firm's income reached $2,000,000 after Civil War); pres. Continental Bank, 1866-68; trustee, organizer Franklin Savs. Bank, also dir. other banks; founder Home for Aged Men in Mass.; a subscriber to New Eng. Conservatory of Music. Died Boston, Dec. 21, 1888 buried Trinity Ch., Boston.

DIVEN, Alexander Samuel, army officer, railroad promoter; b. Tioga County, N.Y., Feb. 10, 1809; s. John and Eleanor (Means) D.; m. Amanda Beers, 1835; m. 2d, Maria Joy, 1876; 8 children. Admitted to N.Y. bar, 1832; an organizer Republican Party in N.Y.; dir. N.Y. & Erie R.R., 1844; chiefly instrumental in orgn. of company which built Binghamton-Corning Line and the Williamsport & Elmira R.R. (pres. latter throughout constrn.), 1849, mem. N.Y Senate from Chemung County, 1858-59; Free Soil candidate for gov. N.Y., 1859; mem. U.S. Ho. of Reps. from N.Y., 37th Congress, 1861-63, mem. judiciary com., 1861-63; commd. lt. col. U.S. Army, col. 1862, asst. adj. gen., 1863, brig. gen., 1864, distinguished service in Va. campaigns, 1862, 63; v.p. N.Y. & Erie R.R., 1865-68; mayor Elmira, N.Y., 1868. Died Elmira, June 11, 1896.

DIX, Dorothea Lynde, reformer; b. Hampden, Me., Apr. 4, 1802; d. Joseph and Mary (Bigelow) Dix; never married. Conducted a girl's sch., Boston, circa 1817-35, put primary emphasis on devel. of moral character, gave up sch. because of poor health; began Sunday sch. class East Cambridge (Mass.) House of Correction, 1841; visits to the jails made her aware of inhuman treatment of insane as criminals; made a thorough investigation of the treatment of the insane in Mass., 1841-43; demanded intelligent and humane treatment of insane by keepers of almshouses and jails, later realized that state-supported asylums with intelligent personnel were necessary; responsible for re-founding or enlarging of state mental hosps. in Mass., R.I., N.J., Pa., and Toronto, Ont., Can., 1841-45; convinced state legislatures to found state hosps. in Ky., Ill., Ind., Tenn., Mo., Miss., La., Ala., S.C., N.C., Md., 1845-52; a 12 million dollar bill for land to be set aside for taxation to support the care of insane vetoed by Pres. Pierce, 1854; travelled in Europe, 1854-57; due to her efforts on this trip hosps. were founded on Isle of Jersey and Rome, and Queen Victoria began a royal commn. to investigate condition of insane in Scotland; apptd. supt. Women Nurses, 1861; continued activities on behalf of insane after Civil War. Died Trenton, N.J., July 17, 1887.

DIX, John Adams, army officer, gov. N.Y.; sec. of treasury; b. Boscowen, N.H., July 24, 1798; s. Col. Timothy and Abigail (Wilkins) D.; m. Catharine Morgan, 1826, 1 son, Morgan. Served in War of 1812; admitted to Washington (D.C.) bar, 1824; travelling aide to Maj. Gen. Jacob Brown; spl. U.S. messenger to Copenhagen, (Denmark), 1826; practiced law, active in politics, Cooperstown, N.Y., 1828; adj. gen. sec. of state N.Y., 1833-39; founder lit. and sci. jour. Northern Light, 1840-43; mem. U.S. Senate (Democrat) from N.Y., 1845-49; unsccessful Free Soil nominee for gov. N.Y., 1848; pres. Chgo. and Rock Island R.R., also Miss. and Mo. R.R., 1854-57; U.S. sec. treasury, served as maj. gen. U.S. Army, comdr. depts. Md. and the East during Civil War; U.S. minister to France, 1866-69; gov. N.Y., 1873-75. Author: A Winter in Madeira; A Summer in Spain and Florence, 1850; Speeches and Occasional Addresses, 2 vols., 1864; Stabat Mater, 1868. Died N.Y.C., Apr. 21,1879.

DIX, John Homer, opthalmologist; b. Boston, Sept. 30, 1811; s. John and Sarah Taffrey (Eddy) D.; grad. Harvard, 1833; M.D., Jefferson Med. Coll., 1836; m. Helen Perhan Curtis, June 9, 1859. Became mem. Mass. Med. Soc., 1837; practiced medicine, specializing in eye and ear diseases, Boston; became interested in opthalmology, one of 1st to import opthalmoscope developed by Helmholtz; built one of 1st apt. houses in U.S., Boston, 1856-57; mem. Am. Opthal. Soc.; Author: Treatise on Strabismus, or Squinting, and the New Mode of Treatment, 1841; also wrote papers on rare diseases of eyes. Died Aug. 25, 1884.

DIXEY, John, sculptor; b. Dublin, Ireland, circa 1760; studied at Royal Acad., London, Eng.; at least 2 sons, George, John V. Exhibited at Royal Acad., 1788; came to Am., 1789; established himself as carver and gilder, N.Y.C., 1801; exhibited at Am., Pa. acads.; made copy of Ceracchi's bust of Alexander Hamilton (owned by N.Y. Hist. Soc.); executed statues of Justice for City Hall, N.Y.C., State House, Albany, N.Y. Died N.Y.C., 1820.

DIXON, Archibald, lawyer, senator; b. nr. Redhouse, Caswell County, N.C., Apr. 2, 1802; s. Wynn Dixon; studied law. Admitted to bar, 1824, began practice of law, Henderson, Ky.; mem. Ky. Ho. of Reps., 1830, 41, Ky. Senate, 1836; lt. gov. Ky., 1843; mem. Ky. Constl. Conv., 1849; mem. U.S. Senate (Whig, filled vacancy) from Ky., Sept. 1, 1852-55; engaged in planting; del. Frankfort Pe Conv., 1863; author bill to repeal Mo. Comprom Died Henderson, Apr. 23, 1876; buried Fernw Cemetery.

DIXON, James, congressman; b. Enfield, Cor Aug. 5, 1814; s. William and Mary (Field) grad. Williams Coll., 1834, A.M., 1837; LL. Trinity Coll., 1862; m. Elizabeth Cogswell, 1, 1840, 4 children. Admitted to bar, 1834; M Conn. Legislature from Enfield, 1837-38- from Hartford, 1854, speaker, 1837; became der Whig Party in Hartford (Conn.), 1839; m U.S. Ho. of Reps. (Whig) from Conn., 29th-3 congresses, 1845-49; pres. Hartford Life Co., 1849-56; mem. Conn. Senate, 1856; m U.S. Senate (Republican) from Conn., 1857- supported Lincoln and Johnson adminstrns., fused to join majority of his party in movement impeach Johnson; declined post of U.S. minis to Russia, 1869. Died Hartford, Mar. 27, 18

DIXON, Joseph, inventor, mfr.; b. Marblehe Mass., Jan. 18, 1799; s. Joseph and Elizal (Reed) D.; m. Hannah Martin, July 28, 18 Inventor machine for cutting files, in his you took up printing, made wood type, became skil in wood-engraving and lithography; later vented matrix for casting metal type; recogni value of mineral graphite, helped open up mark that used this substance (such as pencils and st polish); opened mfg. plant, Salem, Mass., 18 invented photolithographic process and proc for producing colored inks to prevent count feiting, 1832; granted patent for anti-frict bearing metal, 1845; relocated his mfg. pla Jersey City, N.J., 1847; received patents on p cessing graphite crucible, 1850, also received o patents on mfg. improvements; organizer, h Joseph Dixon Crucible Co., 1867-69. Died June 1869.

DIXON, Joseph, congressman; b. Green Cour nr. Farmville, N.C., Apr. 9, 1828; attended pul schs. Engaged in agriculture and business; comr col. N.C. Militia soon after Civil War; judge cou ct., 1864-65; mem. N.C. Ho. of Commons, 18 67; mem. U.S. Ho. of Reps. (Republican, fil vacancy) from N.C., 41st Congress, Dec. 5, 18 71; U.S. commr. of claims, 1871-72; del. fr Greene County to N.C. Constl. Conv., 1875. D nr. Fountain Hill, Pitt County, N.C., Mar. 3, 18 buried Edwards Chapel Cemetery, Lenoir Cour

DIXON, Luther Swift, jurist; b. Underh Vt., June 17, 1825; s. Col. Luther Dix Admitted to Vt. bar, 1850; dist. atty. Colum County, Wis., 1851-55; judge 9th jud. circ Wis., 1858-59; chief justice Wis. Supreme 1859-74; declined Republican nomination U.S. Senate, 1874; practiced law in Wis., 18 79; Denver, Colo., 1879-91. Died Milw., Dec. 1891.

DIXON, Nathan Fellows, senator, lawyer; Plainfield, Conn., Dec. 13, 1774; attended Pla field Acad.; grad. Coll. R.I. (now Brown U 1799; studied law; married, at least 1 son, Nat Fellows. Admitted to bar, 1801, began pract of law, New London County, Conn.; moved Westerly, R.I., 1802, continued practice of also became a banker; pres. Washington Bank Westerly, 1829-42; mem. R.I. Ho. of Reps., 18 30; served as col. R.I. Militia; mem. U.S. Sen (Whig) from R.I., 1839-42. Died Washingt D.C., Jan. 29, 1842; buried River Bend Ceme Westerly.

DIXON, Nathan Fellows, congressman, law b. Westerly, R.I., May 1, 1812; s. Nathan Fell Dixon; attended Plainfield (Conn.) Acad.; g Brown U., 1833; attended Cambridge (Mass New Haven (Conn.) law schs.; married, at least son, Nathan Fellows. Admitted to bar, 18 began practice of law, Westerly; also a bank mem. R.I. Ho. of Reps., 1841-49, 51-54, 58- 71-77; apptd. mem. R.I. Gov.'s Council, 18 Whig presdl. elector, 1844; mem. U.S. Ho. of Re from R.I. (as Whig), 31st Congress, 1849- (as Republican), 38th-41st congresses, 18 71; del. Union Nat. Conv., Phila., 1866. D Westerly, Apr. 11, 1881; buried River Bend Cer tery, Westerly.

DIXON, Nathan Fellows, senator, lawyer; b. We erly, R.I., Aug. 28, 1847; s. Nathan Fellows Dix attended Phillips Acad., Andover, Mass.; grad. Br U., 1869, Albany (N.Y.) Law Sch., 1871. Admit to bar, 1871, began practice of law, Westerly; U atty. for Dist. R.I., 1877-85; mem. U.S. Ho. of Re (Republican, filled vacancy) from R.I., 48th C gress, Feb. 12-Mar. 3, 1885; mem. R.I. Sena 1885-89; mem. U.S. Senate (filled vacancy) fr R.I., Apr. 10, 1889-95; resumed activities as law and banker. Died Westerly, Nov. 8, 1897; bur River Bend Cemetery, Westerly.

DIXWELL, John, polit. refugee; b. Engla circa 1607; s. William and Elizabeth (Brent) m. Mrs. Joanna Ling, Nov. 3, 1673; m. 2d, Ba ıeba Howe, Oct. 23, 1677; 3 children. Upon ɛath of his brother Mark managed his estate in ːent; supported Parliamentary forces during English civil war; M.P. from Dover, 1646; mem. igh ct. of justice which tried Charles I, a signer f death warrant; commd. col. Parliamentary rmy, 1650; mem. Council of State, 1651-52; ov. Dover Castle, 1652; mem. Cromwell Parliament, 1654, 56; mem. Restored Long Parliament, 654; fled to Germany upon restoration of crown, 660; came to New Eng., circa 1664, settled in ew Haven (Conn.) taking name of James avids. Died New Haven, Mar. 29, 1689; buried lew Haven.

DOAK, Samuel, clergyman, coll. pres.; b. Augusta County, Va., Aug. 1749; s. Samuel and Jane (Mitcheall) D.; grad. Coll. of N.J. (now Princeton), 775; m. Esther H. Montgomery; m. 2d, Margaretta I. McEwen; 4 children inclding John W., Samuel V. Tchr., tutor at various acads.; licensed to preach y Presbytery of Hanover; became frontier preacher; ounded Salem Ch., Little Limestone, Tenn., also chs. n Concord, New Providence and Carter's Valley Tenn.); mem. conv. which formed State of Franklin (later part of Tenn.); founded log cabin sch. n his farm, incorporated as Martin Acad., 1783, ecame Washington Coll. (1st seat of higher learnng West of Alleghenies), 1795, pres., 1795-1818; tarted Tusculum Acad., Bethel, Tenn., 1818, later ecame Tusculum Coll. Died Bethel, Dec. 12, 1830.

DOAN, William, congressman, physician; b. Me., ıpr. 4, 1792; studied medicine, New Richmond; rad. Ohio Med. Coll. at Cincinnati, 1827, Began ractice of medicine, Withamsville, O., 1818; mem. hio Ho. of Reps., 1831-32, Ohio Senate, 1833-4; mem. U.S. Ho. of Reps. (Democrat) from hio, 26th-27th congresses, 1839-43. Died Vithamsville, June 22, 1847; buried Union Twp. Mt. Moriah) Cemetery, Tobasco, O.

DOANE, George Washington, clergyman; b. Trenton, N.J. May 27 1799; s. Jonthan and Iary (Higgins) D.; grad. Union Coll., 1818; ttended Gen. Theol. Sem., 1818-21; m. Eliza allahan; children—William Coswell, George H. rdained deacon Protestant Episcopal Ch., 1821, riest, 1823; asst. at Trinity Ch., 1821-25; prof. hetoric and belles-lettres Washington (now Trinty) Coll. Hartford, Conn., 1825-28; rector Trinty Ch., Boston, 1828-32; consecrated bishop of N.J., 1832; a prin. promoter missionary moveient in Episcopal Ch.; founder St. Mary's Hall for girls), Burlington, N.J., 1837, Burlington Coll. (for men), 1846; edited 1st Am. edit. Christian Year (Keble), 1834; leader High Ch. arty in Am.; supporter Tractarian Movement. uthor hymns including Softly now the light of ay, Thou art the way, to Thee alone, Lord, hould we leave Thy hallowed feet, Father of merıes, hear, Thy pardon we implore, Fling out the anner, let it float. Died Burlington, Apr. 27, 1859.

DOANE, Thomas, mech. engr.; b. Orleans, Mass., ept. 20, 1821; s. John and Polly (Eldredge) D.; n. Sophia Dennison Clarke, Nov. 5, 1850; m. 2d, ouisa Amelia Barber; 4 children. Served 3 year aprenticeship with Samuel Felton, civil engr., Charlesown, Mass.; worked for Vt. Central R.R.; resident ngr. Cheshire R.R. in N.H., 1847-49; pvt. engring., urveying practice, Charlestown, 1849-97; apptd. hief engr. in charge of constrn. Hoosac Tunnel, 1863; ntroduced new methods of engring. including new ıses of explosives and compressed-air machinery; chief ngr. Burlington & Missouri River R.R., 1869-73; ompleted constrn. Hoosac Tunnel, 1873-77; mem. Am. Soc. C.E., 1882; pres. Boston Soc. Civil Engrs.; ounder, trustee Doane Coll., Crete, Neb., 1872. Died West Townsend, Vt., Oct. 22, 1897.

DOBBIN, James Cochran, congressman, sec. of ıavy; b. Fayetteville, N.C., Jan. 17, 1814; s. John Moore and Anness (Cochran) D.; grad. U. N.C., 1832; m. Louisa Holmes. Admitted to N.C. bar, 1835; mem. U.S. Ho. of Reps. (Democrat) from N. C. 29th Congress, 1845-47; mem. N.C. Ho. of Commons, 1848-52, speaker, 1850; U.S. sec. of ıavy, 1853-57, noted for enlargement and improvenent of navy, inaugurated new retirement system for officers, merit system for promotion, naval apprentice system, provisions for better treatment and terms for seamen. Died Fayetteville, Aug 4, 1857.

DOBBINS, Samuel Atkinson, congressman, farmer; b. nr. Vincentown, Burlington County, N.J., Apr. 14, 1814; attended pvt. and public schs. Engaged in agriculture; moved to Mt. Holly, N.J., 1838; high sheriff Burlington County, 1854-57; mem. N.J. Ho. of Assembly, 1859-61; del. Republican Nat. Conv., 1864; trustee Pennington (N.J.) Sem., 1866-86, pres. bd., 10 years; mem. U.S. Ho. of Reps. (Rep.) from N.H., 43d-44th congresses, 1873-77. Died Mt. Holly, May 26, 1886; buried Mt. Holly Cemetery.

DOBBS, Arthur, colonial gov. N.C.; b. Castle Dobbs, County Antrim, Ireland, Apr. 2, 1689; s. Richard and Mary (Stewart) D.; m. Justina Davis, 1762. Sheriff, Antrim Ireland 1720; mem. Ho. of Commons, Irish Parliament, 1727; engr.-in-chief, surveyor-gen. Ireland, 1730; co-purchaser 400,000 acres land, N.C., 1745; noted for attempt to discover N.W. passage to Japan, China and India; gov. N.C. (anti-democratic, autocratic policies), 1754-62. Author: Trade and Improvement of Ireland, 1729; An Account of the Countries Adjoining Hudson Bay, 1748. Died Town Creek, N.C., Mar. 28, 1765.

DOCK, Christopher, educator; b. circa 1698. Came to Pa., circa 1712; conducted Mennonite sch., Montgomery County, Pa., circa 1716-26; farmer, circa 1726-38; opened and taught schs. at Skippack and Salford, Pa., taught both at 3 day intervals, 1738-71, used modern teaching methods, composition exercises, constructive writing; his chief principle of disciple was understanding love; wrote articles for Geistliches Magazien in Pa., 1764. Died 1771.

DOCKERY, Alfred, congressman, planter; b. nr. Rockingham, Richmond County, N.C., Dec. 11, 1797; attended public schs.; married, at least 1 son, Oliver Hart. Became a planter; mem. N.C. Ho. of Commons, 1822; mem. N.C. Constl. Conv., 1835; mem. N.C. Senate, 1836-44; mem. U.S. Ho. of Reps. (Whig) from N.C., 29th, 32d congresses, 1845-47, 51-53; unsuccessful Whig candidate for gov. N.C., 1854. Died nr. Rockingham, Dec. 7, 1875; buried family cemetery.

DOD, Albert Baldwin, clergyman, educator; b. Mendham, N.J., Mar. 24, 1805; s. Daniel and Nancy (Squier) D.; grad. Coll. of N.J. (now Princeton), 1822; studied at Princeton Theol. Sem., 1825-26; m. Caroline Bayard, 1830. Tutor at Coll. of N.J., 1827, prof. mathematics, 1831-45; licensed to preach by Presbytery of N.J., 1828; contbr. articles to Biblical Repertory, Princeton Review, after 1835. Author: Beecher's Views in Theology, 1837; Transcendentalism, 1839; Capital Punishment, 1842; Vestiges of Creation, 1845. Died Nov. 19, 1845.

DOD, Daniel, inventor, steam engine builder; b. Va., Sept. 28, 1788; s. Lebbens and Mary (Baldwin) D.; ed. Rutgers; m. Nancy Squier, 1801, 8 children, including Albert Baldwin. Granted U.S. patents on steam engines, including boilers and condensers, for use in steamboats and mills, 1811, manufactured ferryboats, put 1st product into service, 1813; greatest contbn. was machinery for Savannah (first steamboat to cross Atlantic Ocean, 1819). Died in boiler explosion in steamboat test on East River, N.Y.C., May 9, 1823.

DOD, Thaddeus, clergyman, educator; b. Newark, N.J., Mar. 18, 1741; s. Stephen and Deborah (Brown) D.; grad. Coll. of N.J. (now Princeton), 1773; m. Phebe Baldwin, circa 1773. Licensed to preach as Presbyn. minister, 1775, ordained to ministry Presbytery of N.Y., 1777; preached on Western frontier; founded ch., Ten Mile, Pa., 1779, began to teach sch., 1782; received charter to organize Washington Acad., 1789, prin., 1789-90, also organized sch., Canonsburg, Pa. (two schs. later became Jefferson Coll. and Washington Coll., later merged into Washington and Jefferson Coll.). Died Ten Mile, May 20, 1793.

DODD, Edward, congressman, editor; b. Salem, Washington County, N.Y., Aug. 25, 1805; attended public schs. Became a mcht.; moved to Argyle, N.Y., 1835; county clk. Washington County, 1835-44; del. N.Y. Constl. Conv., 1846; mem. U.S. Ho. of Reps. (Whig) from N.Y., 34th-35th congresses, 1855-59; U.S. marshall for No. Dist. N. Y., 1863-69; editor County Post, 30 years; Republican presdl. elector, 1884; trustee Argyle Acad., 51 years; pres. Village of Argyle, 8 years; mem. Rep. State Com., many years. Died Argyle, Mar. 1, 1891; buried Prospect Hill Cemetery.

DODDRIDGE, Joseph, clergyman, physician; b. Bedford, Pa., Oct. 14, 1769; s. John and Mary (Wells) D.; attended Jefferson Acad., Canonsburg, Pa., 1792; studied medicine under Dr. Benjamin Rush, Phila.; m. Jemina Bukey, 1795, 1 dau., Narcissa. Itinerant preacher of Weslyean Methodist Ch. in Pa.; ordained to ministry Episcopal Ch., Phila., circa 1793; practiced medicine and preached in Pa., Va., Ohio. Author: Treatise on the Culture of Bees, 1813; Logan, 1823; Notes on the Settlement and Indian Wars of the Western Parts of Virginia and Pennsylvania, from 1763 to 1783 Inclusive, 1824. Died Nov. 9, 1826.

DODDRIDGE, Philip, congressman; b. Bedford County, Pa., May 17, 1772; s. John and Mary (Wells) D.; m. Julia Musser, Apr. 30, 1800. States atty. Ohio County, W.Va., 1808; mem. Va. Ho. of Dels. from Brooke County, 1815-16, 22-23, 28; del. Va. Constl. Conv., Richmond, 1829; mem. U.S. Ho. of Reps. from Va. 21st, 22d congresses, 1829-32. Died Washington, D.C., Nov. 19, 1832; buried Congressional Cemetery, Washington.

DODDS, Ozro John, congressman, , lawyer; b. Cincinnati, Mar. 22, 1840; attended Miami U., Oxford, O., 4 years, received degree after Civil War; attended Cincinnati Law Sch. Organized Capt. Dodd's Univ. Co. during Civil War, enlisted as capt. Co. B., 20th Oho Volunteer Regt., 1861; served as capt. Co. F, 81st Ohio Volunteer Inf., and acting asst. q.m., 1861-63; promoted lt. col. 1st Ala. Union Cavalry, 1863; admitted to bar, 1866, began practice of law, Cincinnati; mem. Ohio Ho. of Reps., 1870-71; mem. U.S. Ho. of Reps. (Democrat, filled vacancy) from Ohio, 42d Congress, Oct. 8, 1872-73. Died Columbus, O., Apr. 18, 1882; buried Spring Grove Cemetery, Cincinnati.

DODGE, Augustus Ceasar, senator, diplomat; b. Ste. Genevieve, Mo., Jan. 2, 1812; s. Henry and Christina (McDonald) D.; m. Clara Hertich, Mar. 19, 1837. Registrar pub. land office Territory of Ia., Burlington, 1838-41; mem. U.S. Congress from Ia. Territory, 1840-46; mem. U.S. Senate from Ia., 1848-55, supported Compromise of 1850, the Kan.-Neb. Bill, the fugitive-slave law condemning abolitionism; U.S. minister to Spain, 1855-59; mayor Burlington, 1874-75. Died Burlington, Nov. 20, 1883.

DODGE, David Low, mcht.; b. Brooklyn, Conn., June 14, 1774; s. David and Mary Stuart (Earle) D.; m. Sarah Cleveland, June 7, 1798, 1 son, William Earl. Tchr., dist. schs., Conn., 1793-circa 1798; learned dry-goods bus. with aid of wife's family; partner firm Higgenson, Dodge & Co., circa 1807-13; managed cotton mill, Norwich, Conn., for a time; interested in peace movement, became main founder, 1st pres. N.Y. Peace Soc.; presided at organization meeting of Am. Peace Soc., 1818, life mem. bd. dirs.; a founder N.Y. Bible Soc., N.Y. Tract Soc. Author: The Mediator's Kingdom Not of This World, 1809; War Inconsistent with the Religion of Jesus Christ, 1812. Died N.Y.C., Apr. 23, 1852.

DODGE, Ebenezer, clergyman, univ. pres.; b. Salem, Mass., Apr. 21, 1819; s. Ebenezer and Joanna (Appleton) D.; grad. Brown U., 1840, Newton Theol. Instn., 1845; m. Sarah Abbot Putnam, 1846; m. 2d, Eleanor F. Rogers, 1863. Pastor, Baptist Ch., New Hampton, N.H., 1846-49; prof. Bibl. criticism Theol. Instn. of Hamilton (N.Y.), also prof. evidences of revealed religion Madison (now Colgate) U., 1853-61; prof. doctrinal theology Madison U. Sem., 1861-67, pres. univ., 1868-90. Author: The Evidences of Christianity, 1869. Died Jan. 5, 1890.

DODGE, Henry, army officer, senator, territorial gov.; Vincennes, Ind., Oct. 12, 1782; s. Israel and Mary Ann (Hunter) D. m. Christina McDonald, 1800, 1 son, Augustus Caesar. Succeeded his father as sheriff Ste. Genevieve, Missouri Dist., 1805-21; marshall Territory of Mo., 1813; rose to maj. gen. Mo. Militia; apptd. by Pres. Jackson as maj. of bn. of mounted rangers recruited to patrol the frontier of Upper Mississippi Valley; commd. col., 1833; gov. Territory of Wis., 1836-41, 45-48; del. U.S. Congress from Territory of Wis., 27th-29th congresses, 1841-45; mem. U.S. Senate from Wis., 1848-57. Died Burlington Ia., June 19, 1867.

DODGE, Jeremiah, figurehead carver; b. 1781; studied ship carving with Simeon Skillin, circa 1798; at least 1 son, Charles J. Practiced ship carving in partnership with Skillin, 1806-11, with Cornelius N. Sharpe, 1815-28, with his son, 1828-38; known to have carved a Hercules for U.S.S. Ohio, 1820, heads for ships Lexingten and Vincenns, 1825, Andrew Jackson for U.S.S. Constitution, 1835; employed in U.S. Customs House, N.Y.C., 1844-49. Died 1860.

DODGE, John Wood, artist; b. N.Y.C., Nov. 4, 1807. Worked as miniaturist, N.Y.C., 1830-44; exhibited at N.A.D., Apollo Gallery; exhibited series of dioramas including View of New York, The Opening of the Sixth Seal, Interior of St. Peter's Church at Rome, The Departure of the Israelites from Egypt, New Orleans, 1848-49; elected asso. N.A.D. Died Dec. 16, 1893.

DODGE, Mary Abigail, author; b. Hamilton, Mass., Mar. 31, 1833; d. James Brown and Hannah (Stanwood) Dodge; grad. Ipswich Female Sem., 1850. Tchr., Hartford (Conn.) High Sch., 1851-58; contbd. articles to papers under pseudonym Gail Hamilton (name used throughout career); governess, Washington, D.C., 1858-60, also wrote for Nat. Era; an editor, contbr. essays Our Young Folks (mag.), 1865-67; co-editor Wood's Household Mag., 1872-73; opposed women's suffrage. Author: The Battle of the Books, 1870; Woman's Worth and Worthlessness, 1872; Our Common School System, 1880; Biography of James G. Blaine, 1895; X Rays, 1896. Died Aug. 17, 1896.

DODGE, William Earl, mcht., philanthrophist; b. Hartford, Conn., Sept. 4, 1805; s. David Low and Sarah (Cleveland) D.; m. Melissa Phelps, June 24, 1828; at least 1 child, William Earl. Entered wholesale dry goods bus., 1826; an organizer Phelps, Dodge & Co. (firm dealing in copper and other metals), an organizer supporter YMCA in Am.; worked with Evang. Alliance; identified with temperance reforms, Washingtonian movement; leader in fight to make N.Y. a prohibition state; pres. Nat. Temperance Soc., 1865-83; attended Peace Conf., Washington, D.C., 1861; mem. U.S. Ho. of Reps. (Republican) from N.Y., 39th Congress, 1866-67; sought moderate Reconstruction measures after Civil War. Died N.Y.C., Feb. 9, 1883; buried Woodland Cemetery, N.Y.C.

DODS, John Bovee, spiritualist; b. N.Y.C., 1795; married 3 times; 1st wife: Mercy Hodgdon; 5 children including Jennie. Itinerant preacher in Me. for a time, preached mainly on universalism and psychic phenomena; later gave up these theories for spiritualism, did experiments in drugs, hypnotism and electricity. Author: Thirty Short Sermons on Various Important Subjects, Doctrinal and Practical; Six Lectures on the Philosophy of Mesmerism, 1843; Immortality Triumphant, 1852; Spirit Manifestations Examined and Explained, 1854. Died Bklyn., Mar. 21, 1872.

DOE, Charles, jurist; b. Derry, N.H., Apr. 4, 1830; s. Joseph and Mary (Ricker) D.; grad. Dartmouth, 1849; m. Edith Haven, Apr. 11, 1865. Admitted to N.H. bar, Jan. 1852; solicitor for Strafford County (N.H.); asst. clk. N.H. Senate, 1853-54; asso. justice N.H. Supreme Jud. Ct., 1859-74; chief justice newly-formed Supreme Ct. N.H., 1876-96. Died Rollinsford, N.H., Mar. 9, 1896.

DOE, Nicholas Bartlett, congressman, lawyer; b. N.Y.C., June 16, 1786; grad. Phillips Exeter (N.H.) Acad.; studied law. Admitted to bar, began practice of law; settled in Saratoga County, N.Y.; mem. U.S. Ho. of Reps. (Whig, filled vacancy) from N.Y., 26th Congress, Dec. 7, 1840-41; trustee Village of Waterford (N.Y.), 1841. Died Saratoga Springs, N.Y., Dec. 6, 1856; buried Greenridge Cemetery.

DOIG, Andrew Wheeler, congressman, businessman; b. Salem, N.Y., July 24, 1799. Moved to Lowville, N.Y., became a mcht.; town clk. Lowville, 1825; clk. Lewis County, 1825-31; mem. N.Y. State Assembly, 1832; moved to Martinsburg, N. Y., 1833; cashier Lewis County Bank, 1833-34; returned to Lowville; surrogate Lewis County, 1835-40; mem. U.S. Ho. of Reps. (Democrat) from N. Y., 26th-27th congresses, 1839-43; bd. dirs., v.p. Bank of Lowville, 1843-47; moved to Cal., 1849, engaged in mining; returned to Lowville, 1850 clk. customhouse, N.Y.C., 1853-57. Died Bklyn., July 11, 1875; buried Rural Cemetery, Lowville.

DOLCHO, Frederick, physician, clergyman; b. London, Eng., 1770; studied medicine and botany, Balt.; m. Mary E. Threadcraft, 1808. Came to Balt. after death of father; surgeon's mate U.S. Army, 1792, lt., 1794-99; practiced medicine, Charleston, S.C., 1799-1807; established public bot. garden, Charleston; co-editor Federalist paper Chartleston Courier, 1807-11; lay reader Episcopal Ch., St. Paul's Parish, Colleton, S.C., 1811; ordained deacon Episcopal Ch., 1814, priest, 1818; asst. minister St. Michael's Ch., Charlestown, 1819; mem. med. socs. of S.C. and Phila., Acad. Arts, Sciences and Belles-Lettres of Marseilles (France). Author: Ahiman Rezon (handbook for Masons), 1807; An Historical Account of the Protestant Episcopal Church in South Carolina, 1820. Died Charleston, Nov. 24, 1836; buried St. Michael's Ch.

DOLLARD, William, clergyman; b. Ballytarina, Kilkenny, Ireland; attended seminary, Quebec, Can. Ordained priest Roman Catholic Ch., served as missioner Cape Breton and Miramichi; became vicar gen. Charlettetown; became bishop New Brunswick, 1843. Died Aug. 29, 1851.

DOLPH, Joseph Norton, senator; b. Watkins, N.Y., Oct. 19, 1835; s. Chester V. and Eliza (Vanderbilt) D.; m. Augusta Mulkey, Oct. 1864. Admitted to N.Y. bar, 1861; city atty. Portland, Ore., 1864; U.S.dist. atty., 1865; chmn. Ore. Republican Com., 1866; mem. Ore. Senate, 1866-76; v.p. No. Pacific R.R.Co.; mem. U.S. Senate from Ore., 1883-95, chmn. com. on coast defenses, 1886. Died Portland, Mar. 10, 1897, buried Riverview Cemetery, Portland.

DOMENEC, Michael, clergyman; b. Ruez, Tarragona, Spain, 1816; studied in Madrid, Spain, also Lazarist Sem., Paris, France; attended St. Mary's Sem., Mo. Joined Lazarists, Paris, 1832; came to U.S., 1838; ordained priest Roman Catholic Ch., 1839; missionary in Mo., tchr. at sem.; sent (with group of Lazarists) to oversee St. Vincent's Sem., Germantown, Pa., 1845; pastor St. Vincent de Paul Ch., Germantown; bishop of Pitts., 1860-67; 1st bishop Diocese of Allegheny City, 1876-77; ret. to Spain because of ill health, 1877. Died Tarragona, Jan. 5, 1878.

DONAHOE, Patrick, publisher; b. Munnery, Ireland, Mar. 17, 1811; s. Terrence and Jane (Christy) D.; m. Kate Griffin, Nov. 23, 1836; m. 2d, Annie E. Davis, Apr. 17, 1853. Came with father to U.S., 1821; printer for Columbian Sentinel, later for Boston Transcript; worked for The Jesuit, or Catholic Sentinel, 1829-36; founder, co-owner, publisher Boston Pilot, 1836-76, owner and publisher, 1891-1901; published works of various Irish-Am. writers of period; became mcht. and banker, Boston; donated to various charities of Boston; his fortune wiped out during Boston Fire of 1872 and Panic of 1872; started Donahoe's Mag., 1876; recipient Laetare medal Notre Dame U., 1893. Died Boston, Mar. 18, 1901; buried Boston.

DONAHUE, Peter, iron mfr.; b. Glasgow, Scotland, Jan. 11, 1822; m. Mary Jane Maguire, 1852; m. 2d, Annie Downey, 1864; 4 children. Came with parents to U.S., 1833; machinist apprentice, Paterson, N.J., 1837-45; worked on constrn. of ship for Peru, 1845, went with ship as asst. engr. to Peru, lived in Peru, 1845-49; went to gold mines, Cal., 1849, after short time opened (with his 2 brothers) blacksmith and boiler making shop, San Francisco (foundation of 1st iron works in Cal., grew into Union Iron Works), sole owner of iron works, by 1856; contracted to build 2 steamships (1st ever built on West Coast), 1860-63; sold iron works to H.J. Booth & Co., 1865; organized 1st street car line in San Francisco; treas. San Francisco and San Jose R.R.; dir. various other railroads; Town of Donahue (Cal.) named for him. Died San Francisco, Nov. 26, 1885.

DO-NE-HO-GA-WA, see Parker, Ely Samuel.

DONELSON, Andrew Jackson, diplomat; b. Aug. 25, 1799; s. Samuel and Mary (Smith) D.; grad. U.S. Mil. Acad., 1819; m. Emily Donelson (a cousin), 1824; m. 2d, Mrs. Elizabeth Randolph, 1841. Served as aide-de-camp to Gen Andrew Jackson during Seminole War; admitted to Tenn. bar, 1823; sec. to Jackson during presdl. campaign of 1828; invited by Jackson to Washington (D.C.) as pvt. sec. (with his wife as mistress of White House); charge d'affaires Republic of Tex., 1844, successfully concluded negotiations concerning annexation of Tex. to U.S.; U.S. minister to Prussia, 1846-48, to Germany, 1848-49; unsuccessful vice presdl. nominee with Fillmore on ticket of Am. (Know-Nothing) Party, 1856. Author: Reports of Explorations, 1855. Died Memphis, Tenn., June 26, 1871.

DONGAN, Thomas (2d Earl Limerick), colonial gov.; b. Castletown, Ireland, 1634; son of John (1st baronet Limerick); Lt. gov. Tangier, circa 1677-80; gov. N.Y., 1682-88; his governmental policies led to stiffening of defenses against French, establishment of protectorate over Iroquois Indians; superseded by Sir Edmund Andros (when N. Y. was added to the dominion of New Eng.), 1688, returned to Eng., 1691; became 2d earl Limerick, 1698. Died London, Eng. Dec. 14, 1715.

DONIPHAN, Alexander William, lawyer, army officer, b. Maysville, Ky., July 9, 1808; s. Joseph and Anne (Smith) D.; grad. Augusta Coll., 1826; m. Elizabeth Thornton, Dec. 21, 1837, 2 children. Began practice of law in Mo., 1830, became leading Mo. lawyer specialized in criminal cases; mem. Mo. Legislature, 1836, 40, 54; commanded a brigade against Mormons, refused to carry out the later revoked ct. martial sentence of death against Joseph Smith; comdg. officer in N.M. during Mexican War, 1846-48; lead regt. of Missourians from Valverde, N.M. to Chihuahua, Mexico (one of most brilliant long marches ever made), 1846-47; Mo. del. to Washington (D.C.) Peace Conf., 1861; maj. gen. in command Mo. Militia, 1861. Died Richmond, Mo., Aug. 8, 1887.

DONNELL, Richard Spaight, congressman, lawyer; b. New Bern, N.C., Sept. 20, 1820; attended New Bern Acad., Yale; grad. U. N.C. at Chapel Hill, 1839; studied law. Admitted to bar, 1840, began practice of law, New Bern; mem. U.S. Ho. of Reps. (Whig) from N.C., 30th Congress, 1847-49; del. N.C. Secession Conv., 1861, N.C. Constl. Conv., 1865; mem. N.C. Ho. of Commons, 1862, 64, speaker, Died New Bern, June 3, 1867; buried Cedar Grove Cemetery.

DONNELL, Robert, clergyman; b. Guilford County, N.C., Apr. 1784; s. William and Mary (Bell) D.; m. Ann Smith, 1818; m. 2d, Clarissa Lindley, 1832. Took part in many revival meetings, became itinerant preacher, 1801; rode circuit in Cumberland-Ohio rivers area, circa 1805, later went into No. Ala.; ordained by Independent Cumberland Presbytery (organized 1810), 1813; helped bring this independent ch. into prominence, became 1st pres. of its missionary bd., also moderator its gen. assembly; made home in Ala., preached over wide area; a founder Cumberland U., Lebanon, Tenn. Author: Thoughts on Various Theological Subjects, 1852. Died Athens, Ala., May 24, 1855.

DONNER, George, pioneer; b. N.C., 1784; married 3 times; 13 children. Made small fortune as farmer in Ill.; set out with his brother Jacob, their families, several neighbors and employees for Cal., Apr. 1846; joined wagon train under Col. William Henry Russell, Independence, Mo., May 1846; due to mismanagement, dissension, drought and disease, train lost much time and equipment; elected capt. at Ft. Bridger, Utah; influenced by Lansford Hastings (Cal. land promoter) to try a new trail through Great Salt Desert of Utah; lost more time and equipment due to misinformation concerning size of desert, many team animals killed or stolen by Indians; caught by snow at what is now Donner Lake and Alder Creek, on East side of Sierra Nevada mountains, Nov. 1846; party of 17 set out to cross divide for help, Dec. 1846 (7 survived, living off corpses of less fortunate fellows); those who remained behind lived off frozen animals and by cannibalism; 47 survivors (from party of 82 emigrants who reached mountains in Nov. 1846) were brought out by 3 separate relief parties, Feb.-Apr. 1847. Died Donner Lake, Cal., Apr. 1847.

DONNER, Tamsen, pioneer, school tchr.; 3d wife of George Donner (a leader Donner party 1846); 3 daus. Mem. of Donner party, planned book on Donner tragedy, but notes and diary were lost.

DOOLITTLE, Amos, engraver; b. Cheshire, Conn. May 18, 1754; s. Ambrose and Martha (Munson) D.; m. Sally; m. 2d, Phebe Tuttle, Nov. 8, 1797. Apprenticed to silversmith, Cheshire; later turned to engraving, moved to New Haven; mem. Gov.'s Foot Guards during Am. Revolution; engraved 4 copper plates entitled "The Battle of Lexington and Concord," 1775; engraved 2 maps printed in Jedidiah Morse's Geography Made Easy, 1784 other engravings include "Display of United States of America," also 2 "New Displays" on same theme. Died New Haven, Jan. 30, 1832; buried Grove Street Cemetery, New Haven.

DOOLITTLE, James Rood, senator; b. Washington County, N.Y., Jan. 3, 1815; s. Reuben and Sarah (Rood) D.; grad. Hobart Coll., 1834, A.M., 1837, LL.D., 1854; LL.D., Racine (Wis.) Coll., 1887; m. Mary Cutting, 1837, 6 children. Admitted to N.Y. bar, 1837; introduced "Cornerstone" resolution upon which Free Soil Party was founded, 1847; dist. atty. Wyoming County (N. Y.), 1847-50; judge 1st Jud. Circuit of Wis., 1853-56; mem. U.S. Senate from Wis. (Republican) 1857-69, mem. senate com. of 13 to arrange compromise between North and South, 1860; author epigram at time of Lincoln's election "I believe in God Almighty, and under him, I believe in Abraham Lincoln"; supported policies of Pres. Johnson; presided over Union Nat. Conv., Phila., 1866, Democratc Nat. Conv., Balt., 1872; trustee, acting pres., prof. Law Sch., Chgo. U. Author: United States in the Light of Prophecy. Died Edgewood, R.I., July 27, 1897; buried Mound Cemetery, Racine.

DOREMUS, Sarah Platt Haines, social worker; b. N.Y.C., Aug. 3, 1802; d. Elias and Mary (Ogden) Haines; m. Thomas C. Doremus, 1821, 9 children including Robert Ogden. Became interested in religious and reform movements at early age; began activities by getting aid in Am. for Greek revolutionaries; made humanitarian efforts embracing a wide range of interests; influential in improving conditions of prison immates, N.Y.C.; organized a home that gave temporary help to discharged women prisoners; a founder House and Sch. of Industry, 1850, Nursery and Child's Hosp., 1854; a founder Woman's Union Missionary Soc., 1860; expecially successful in enlisting aid of other women in her causes. Died N.Y.C., Jan. 29, 1877.

DORION, Marie; born circa 1791; m. Pierre Dorion, circa 1806; m. 2d, Mr. Venier, circa 1819; m. 3d, Jean Baptiste Toupin; 6 children including Baptiste Dorion, Marguerite Venier. Mem. Ia. Indian tribe; accompanied her husband (an interpreter) to Astoria, 1811; went with husband on hunting trip to Ida. (where he was killed, along with all other males in the party), 1814; managed to escape with her 2 children, survived severe winter, reached safety and related her adventures, Spring 1815; lived for a time at Ft. Okanagon, later at Ft. Walla Walla (both Wash.); became well-known through Washington Irving's Astoria, 1836. Died Willamette Valley, nr. Salem, Ore., Sept. 3, 1850.

DORNIN, Bernard, publisher; b. Ireland, 1761. Came to N.Y., 1803, established bookselling and publishing firm; printed a New Testament, Bklyn., 1805; moved business to Balt., 1809, to Phila., 1817; ret. to Ohio shortly before death. Died 1836.

DORNIN, Thomas Aloysius, naval officer; b. Ireland, May 1, 1800; s. Bernard and Eliza Dornin; ed. St. Mary's Coll., Balt.; m. Mrs. Jane Thorburn Howison, 1837. Entered U.S. Navy, 1815, served in Mediterranean and against W. Indian pirates; promoted lt., 1825; served in Pacific, 1826; served in ship Falmouth in Pacific, 1831-34; in command of receiving ship, Phila., 1834-36; promoted commander, 1841; with Ordnance Dept., Washington, D.C., 1844-51; stationed in Pacific to watch over William Walker's expdn. to Lower Cal., also blocked Brit. and French aggressive naval moves in Hawaii, 1851-55; promoted capt., 1855, commanded Norık Navy Yard, 1855-59; on duty in Mediterranean d in suppression of African slave trade, 1859-61; omoted commodore, 1862; commanded Balt. ıvy Yard, 1862-65. Died Savannah, Ga., Apr. ;, 1874; buried Norfolk, Va.

DORR, Thomas Wilson, polit. reformer; b. Provi-ınce, R.I., Nov. 5, 1805; s. Sullivan and Lydia ıllen) D.; grad. Harvard, 1823; studied law under ıancellor James Kent, N.Y. Admitted to bar, 327; mem. R.I. Legislature, 1834; mem. com. to ite address advocating enlargement of R.I. fran-ıise, 1834; old colonial charter did not have any eans of calling constl. conv., "People's Party" drew new constn. which most of people favored; elected v. under new constn., 1842 (another gov. had been ected under old charter), pleaded case unsuccessful-in Washington (D.C.); other state gov. had de-ıred martial law; voluntarily surrendered, tried for eason and sentenced to hard labor for life, 1844; leased from prison under amnesty act, 1845, civil ghts restored, 1851. Died Dec. 27, 1854.

DORRELL, William, founder religious sect; b. orkshire, Eng., Mar. 15, 1752; m. Molla Chase, 779. Came to Am. with Brit. Army under Gen. ırgoyne, 1775, deserted, 1777; experienced a ligious revelation, began to preach, had a group followers in No. Mass. (known as Dorrellites), 1794; Dorrellites discredited their sect by un-cial behavior; held vegetarianism as his original ɔctrine, experienced numerous subsequent reve-tions; claimed that each generation had a Mes-ah and he was the Messiah of his generation, ıat those who were resurrected from the state of n of the spiritual life were not responsible to civil ıw; claimed that he could not be harmed by a hu-ıan being, beaten by Capt. Ezekiel Foster until he as forced to renounce this doctrine, resulted in end sect; starved himself to death because he thought would live forever if he continued to eat; name so spelled Dorrel, Dorril, Dorriel, Dorral. Died eyden, Mass., Aug. 23, 1846.

DORSCH, Eduard, physician, poet; b. Würzburg, avaria, Germany, Jan. 10, 1822; s. Francis L. and izabeth D.; M.A., U. Munich (Germany), 1845; Sophia Hartung; m. 2d, Augusta (Korte) Uhl, 385. Surgeon to rebels in Bavarian uprising, 1848, so wrote in support of cause; arrived U.S., 1849; ttled in Monroe, Mich., practiced medicine; mem. lich. Bd. Edn., 1872-78; pension examining physi-an for govt. Author: Kurze Hirtenbriefe an das eutsche Volk Diesseits und Jenseits des Ozean, 851; Parabasen, 1875; Aus der Alten und Neuen Velt, 1884. Died Jan. 10, 1887.

DORSEY, Clement, congressman, lawyer; b. nr. aklands, Anne Arundel County, Md., 1778; ttended St. John's Coll., Annapolis, Md.; studied ıw. Admitted to bar, began practice of law; served maj. Md. Militia, 1812-18; mem. U.S. Ho. of eps. from Md., 19th-21st congresses, 1825-31; ıdge 5th circuit ct. Md., until 1848. Died Leon-rdtown, St. Marys County, Md. Aug. 6, 1848; uried pvt. burial ground at "Summerseat," r. Laurel Grove, Md.

DORSEY, James Owen, ethnologist; b. Balt., Oct. 1, 1848; s. Thomas Anderson and Mary Sweetser Hance) D.; attended Protestant Episcopal Theol. em. Ordained deacon Episcopal Ch., 1871; mission-ry to Pawnee Indians, Dakota Territory, 1871-80; orked with Omaha Indians as mem. Bur. Am. thnology; mem. Anthrop. Soc. Washington, A.A.-.S. Author: The Cegiha Language, 1890; contbr. Annual Reports of U.S. Bur. Am. Ethnology. ied Feb. 4, 1895.

DORSEY, John Syng, surgeon; b. Phila., Dec. 23, 783; s. Leonard Dorsey; M.D., U. Pa., 1802; stud-ed medicine, London, Paris, 1803-04; m. Maria alston, Apr. 30, 1807. Staff mem. Pa. Hosp., 807; surgeon, 1810; adjunct prof. U. Pa., 1807, rof. materia medica, 1816. Author: The Elements Surgery, 1813. Died Phila., Nov. 12, 1818.

DORSEY, Sarah Ann Ellis, author; b. Natchez, liss., Feb. 16, 1829; d. Thomas E. and Mary Routh) Ellis; m. Samuel W. Dorsey, 1853. Contbr. N.Y. Churchman; taught reading, writing, reli-ion to her husband's slaves; served as nurse in onfederate hosp.; friend, long time hostess of Jef-erson Davis. Author: Recollections of Henry Wat-ins Allen, 1866; Agnes Graham, 1869; Panola, a ale of Louisiana, 1877. Died July 4, 1879.

DORSHEIMER, William Edward, lawyer, jour-alist, congressman; b. Lyons, N.Y., Feb. 5, 832; s. Philip and Sarah D.; attended Harvard, 849-51, A.M. (hon.), 1859; m. Isabella Patc-en. Admitted to N.Y. bar, 1854; U.S. dist. atty. or No. N.Y., 1867-71; mem. Liberal Republican onv., Cincinnati, 1872; lt. gov. N.Y., 1874-80; racticed law, N.Y.C., 1879-85; mem. U.S. Ho. f Reps. from N.Y., 48th Congress, 1883-85, mem. oint com. to arrange celebration upon completion Vashington Monument; U.S. dist. atty. for So. N. ., 1885; editor N.Y. Star, 1885; a founder Buffalo (N.Y.) Hist. Soc., Buffalo Acad. Fine Arts. Died Savannah, Ga., Mar. 26, 1888.

DOTY, Elihu, missionary; b. Berne, N.Y., Sept. 20, 1809; s. Stephen Holmes and Phebe (Nelson) D.; grad. Rutgers Coll., 1835, attended Rutgers Sem., 1836; m. Clarissa Dolly Ackley, May 13, 1836; m. 2d, Eleanor Augusta Smith, Feb. 17, 1847. Ordained to ministry Dutch Reformed Ch., Berne, 1836; missionary in Java and Singapore, 1836-39; did unsuccessful mission work in Borneo, 1839-44; missionary, Amoy, China, 1844-58. Author: Narrative of a Tour in Borneo; Some Thoughts on the Proper Term for God in the Chinese, 1850; Manual of the Amoy Dialect, 1855. Died Nov. 30, 1864.

DOTY, James Duane, speculator, congressman, territorial gov.; b. Salem, N.Y., Nov. 5, 1799; s. Chilius and Sarah (Martin) D.; m. Sarah Collins, Apr. 14, 1823. Admitted to Mich. bar, 1819; began practice of law in Mich. Territory, 1819; clk. Supreme Ct. Mich. Territory, 1819, also of Territorial Council; sec. to Gen. Lewis Cass on tour of Gt. Lakes Mississippi River, 1820; atty. U.S. Supreme Ct., Washington, D.C., 1821-23; judge Jud. Dist. of No. Mich., 1823-33; commd. by War Dept. to survey mil. roads in Wis., 1823; mem. Mich. Legislative Council from region West of Lake Michigan, 1834-35, introduced bill creating Wis., Ia territories; land speculator, Wis.; mem. U.S. Ho. of Reps. from Wis., 26th, 31st-32d congresses, 1839-41, 49-53; gov. Wis. Territory, 1841-44; supt. Indian affairs, 1861; gov. Utah Territory, 1863-65. Died Salt Lake City, Utah, June 13, 1865; buried Ft. Douglas Cemetery, Salt Lake City.

DOUBLEDAY, Abner, army officer, originator baseball; b. Ballston Spa, N.Y., June 26, 1819; s. Ulysses Freeman and Hester (Donnelly) D.; grad. U.S. Mil. Acad., 1842; m. Mary Hewitt, 1852. Commd. 2d lt. arty., U.S. Army, 1845, 1st lt., 1847; served in battles of Monterey, Buena Vista during Mexican War, 1846-48; capt., 1855; maj. 17th Inf., 1861; aimed 1st shot fired from Ft. Sumter against Confederate attack; brig. gen. U.S. Volunteers, then maj. gen. 1862; commanded brigade in 2d Battle of Bull Run; led div. at battle of Antietam, Fredericksburg; commanded corps during 1st day Battle of Gettysburg, div. on 2d, 3d days; lt. col. U.S. Army, 1863, col., 1867. Author: Reminiscences of Forts Sumter and Moultrie in 1860-61, published 1876; Chancellorsville and Gettysburg, 1882. Declared originator of baseball (Cooperstown, N.Y., 1839) by high commn. of baseball experts in formal report, 1907. Died Mendham, N.J., Jan. 26, 1893; buried Arlington (Va.) Nat. Cemetery.

DOUBLEDAY, Ulysses Freeman, congressman, businessman; b. Otsego County, N.Y., Dec. 15, 1792; learned printing trade. Employed as a printer, Cooperstown, Utica, Albany, N.Y.; served at Sackets Harbor in War of 1812; founded Saratoga Courier, Ballston Spa; publisher Cayuga Patriot, Auburn, N.Y., 1819-39; mem. U.S. Ho. of Reps. (Jackson Democrat), 22d, 24th congresses,, 1831-33, 35-37; engaged in farming, Scipio, N.Y., 1837-46; mcht., N.Y.C., 1846-60. Died Belvidere, Boone County, Ill., Mar. 11, 1866, probably buried North Street Cemetery, Auburn.

DOUGAL, William H., engraver; b. New Haven, Conn., Jan. 30, 1822; married, 1850, at least 3 children. Worked as engraver, Washington, D.C., 1844; commd. to engrave plates for reports of Wilkes expdn.; sketched in Cal., 1849-50; returned to Washington, employed as engraver for govt. publs., banks, publishers; exhibited at Washington Art Assn., 1857. Died Washington, 1895.

DOUGHTY, Thomas, painter; b. Phila., July 19, 1793. Worked in leather, 1809-19; turned to landscape painting, worked in London and Paris; exhibited in Boston Athenaeum, Pa. Acad. Fine Arts, N.A.D.; prospered during 1830's, impoverished thereafter. Died July 22, 1856.

DOUGLAS, Benjamin, banker, mayor; b. Northford, Conn., Apr. 3, 1816; s. Capt. William and Sarah (Kirtland) D.; m. Mary Parker, Apr. 3, 1838, 6 children. Organizer (with brother) firm W. & B. Douglas, foundry, 1832; inventor (with brother) revolving cistern stand pump, 1842; a prin. founder 1st Nat. Bank, Middletown, Conn., pres., many years; pres. Farmers & Mechanics Savs. Bank; trustee Middlesex Banking Co., Asylum Line R.R.; mayor Middletown, 1849-55; mem. Conn. Assembly, 1854; a founder Conn. Republican Party; nominated John B. Fremont, 1856; a presdl. elector who voted for Lincoln, 1860; lt. gov. Conn., 1861-62; pres. Middlesex br. Conn. Bible Soc., Conn. State Temperance Union; trustee Wesleyan U., 1862-85, Conn. State Asylum for the Insane. Died Middletown, June 26, 1894.

DOUGLAS, Beverly Browne, congressman, lawyer; b. Providence Forge, New Kent County, Va., Dec. 21, 1822; attended Rumford Acad., Yale, U. Edinburgh (Scotland); grad. law dept. Coll. William and Mary, 1843. Admitted to bar, 1844, began practice of law, Norfolk, Va., then practiced in King William County, from 1846; del. Va. Constl. Conv., 1850, 51; mem. Va. Senate, 1852-65; Democratic presdl. elector, 1860; commd. 1st lt. Lee's Ranger's, Confederate Army, in Civil War, promoted maj. 5th Va. Cavalry; mem. U.S. Ho. of Reps. from Va. (as Conservative), 44th Congress, 1875-77, (as Democrat), 45th Congress, 1877-78. Died Washington, D.C., Dec. 22, 1878; buried family burying ground at "Zoar," nr. Aylett, Va.

DOUGLAS, Silas Hamilton, chemist; b. Fredonia, N.Y., Oct. 16, 1816; s. Benjamin and Lucy (Townsend) D.; M.D., Coll. Surgeons and Physicians, Balt. Practiced medicine, Dearborn, Mich., for a time; instr. chemistry U. Mich., 1844-45, lectr. in chemistry and geology, 1845-46, prof. chemistry, geology, mineralogy, 1846-51; an organizer dept. of medicine, prof. chemistry and pharmacy, dept. of medicine, 1855-70, prof. chemistry, 1870-75, prof. mineralogy, 1875-77. Author: Tables for Qualitative Chemical Analysis, 1864; co-author: Qualitative Chemical Analysis: A Guide in the Practical Study of Chemistry, 3d edit., 1880. Died Ann Arbor, Mich., Aug. 26, 1890.

DOUGLAS, Stephen Arnold, senator; b. Brandon, Vt., Apr. 23, 1813; s. Dr. Stephen A. and Sarah (Fisk) Douglass; attended Brandon Acad., Canadaigua (N.Y.) Acad.; m. Martha Martin, Apr. 7, 1847; m. 2d, Adele Cutts, circa 1856. Moved to Winchester, Ill., 1833; admitted to Ill. bar, 1834; states atty. for 1st Jud. Dist. Ill., 1834-35; leader in building Democratic Party orgn. in Ill., which became powerful by 1848; mem. Ill. Legislature from Morgan County, 1836-37; U.S. register, land office, Springfield, Ill., 1837-39; sec. of state Ill., 1840; judge Ill. Supreme Ct., 1841-42; mem. U.S. Ho. of Reps. from Ill., 28th-29th congresses, 1843-47; mem. U.S. Senate from Ill., 1847-61, chmn. com. on territories (chiefly concerned with organizing Western territories because of transcontinental railroad problem, slavery became involved as secondary issue); helped frame compromise bills establishing territorial govt. for Utah and N.M., 1850, secured passage of I.C. R.R. Bill, 1850; in debates on Kan.-Neb. Bill (1854) originated term "popular sovereignty" (his idea of easiest and best way to handle slavery question in building a commercially close-knit ocean-to-ocean republic); alienated So. Democrats by condemning Lecompton Constn. in Kan., 1857; engaged in Lincoln-Douglas debates in campaign for reelection to U.S. Senate, 1858, defeated Lincoln in election but lost Southern support with "popular sovereignty" stand; nominated for Pres. U.S. by Northern Democrats at Nat. Conv., Balt., 1860 (following Dem. Party split at conv., Charleston, S.C.), defeated by Lincoln, largely due to Democratic split; called "Little Giant." Died Chgo., June 3, 1861; buried Douglas Monument Park, Chgo.

DOUGLAS, William, army, naval officer; b. Plainfield, Conn., Jan. 16, 1743; s. John and Olive (Spaulding) D.; m. Hannah Manfield, July 5, 1767, children—William, John, Olive, Hannah. Commd. maj. Conn. Militia, 1775, maj. in a volunteer regt., 1776; commd. col. under Gen. Washington, 1776; participated in battles of L.I., Philips Manor, Croton River, White Plains, Harlem Heights; apptd. commodore of vessels on Lake Champlain by Continental Congress; elected to Conn. Assembly, 1777. Died Northford, Conn., May 28, 1777.

DOUGLASS, David Bates, civil engr., army officer, coll. pres.; b. Pompton, N.J., Mar. 21, 1790; s. Nathaniel and Sarah (Bates) D.; grad. Yale, 1813, LL.D. (hon.); m. Ann Eliza Ellicott, Dec. 1815. Commd. 2d lt. engrs., sent to U.S. Mil. Acad., 1813; commd. 1st lt., brevetted capt., 1814; asst. prof. natural philosophy U.S. Mil. Acad., Jan. 1, 1815; prof. natural philosophy Univ. City N.Y., 1832-33; became civil engr., architect; designed N.Y.U. bldg. in Washington Sq.; as engr. N.Y. commrs. selected Croton water shed, determined essential features of system including crossing Harlem River on a high bridge; system supplied N.Y.C. with water, 75 years; pres. Kenyon Coll., 1840-45; prof. mathematics and natural philosophy Hobart Coll.. 1848. Died Geneva, N.Y., Oct. 21, 1849; buried Greenwood Cemetery, N.Y.C.

DOUGLASS, Frederick, diplomat, journalist; b. Tuckahoe, Md., circa Feb. 1817; unknown White father and Harriet Bailey; m. Anna Murray, Sept. 1838; m. 2d, Helen Pitts, 1884. Born a slave to Capt. Aaron Anthony, escaped, 1838; employed as agt. Mass. Anti-Slavery Soc., 1841; became central figure in "One Hundred Conventions" of New Eng. Anti-Slavery Soc.; visited Gt. Britain and Ireland to avoid possible re-enslavement as result of his biography Narrative of the Life of Frederick Douglass, 1845-47; returned to America with money to buy his freedom, established newspaper North Star (for Negro race), 1847; assisted in recruiting 54th and 55th Mass. Colored regts. during Civil War; sec. Santa Domingo Commn., 1871; marshal and recorder of deeds D.C., 1877-86; U.S. minister to Haiti, 1889-91; vigorous supporter of woman suffrage. Died Washington, D.C., Feb. 20, 1895.

DOUGLASS, Robert M. J., artist, lithographer; b. Phila., Feb. 8, 1809 (of Negro parentage); studied under Thomas Sully; m. Sarah. Worked in Phila.; visited Haiti and Eng.; exhibited a portrait at Pa. Acad., 1834. Died Phila., Oct. 26, 1887.

DOUGLASS, William, physician; b. Gifford, Scotland, circa 1691; studied medicine, Paris, Leyden and Edinburgh. Arrived in Boston, 1718; strongly opposed smallpox innoculation, wrote 4 pamphlets on subject. Author: The Practical History of a New Epidemical Eruptive Military Fever. . ., 1736; A Summary, Historical and Political of the First Planting, Progressive Improvements and Present State of the British Settlements in North America, 2 vols., 1749-51. Did Oct. 21, 1752.

DOVE, David James, educator; b. Portsmouth, Eng., circa 1696; s. David and Mary D.; married. Arrived Phila., 1750; tchr. Phila. Acad., 1750; founder acad. for girls, 1751; English master Germantown (Pa.) Union Sch., 1761-63; opened acad. Germantown, 1763-68; later taught in Phila. Author: Labour in Vain; or, an Attempt to Wash a Black-Moor White, 1757; The Quaker Unmask'd;. . ., 1764. Died Phila., Apr. 1769; buried Christ Ch., Phila.

DOW, Henry, judge; b. Ormsby, Norfolkshire, Eng., 1634; s. Henry and Joan D.; m. Hannah Page, June 17, 1659; m. 2d, Mary Hussey; 4 sons. Selectman, Hampton, N.H., 1661, often reelected; dep. marshall N.H., 1680; town clk. Hampton, 1681-1701, town litigator, 1686; ensign Hampton Militia, 1689-92, capt., 1692; justice N.H., Ct.; justice Inferior Ct. of Common Pleas of N.H., 1695-99, sr. judge, 1699; mem. N.H. Legislature from Hampton; treas. N.H. Province; mem. N.H. Gov.'s Council, 1702-07. Died May 6, 1707.

DOW, Lorenzo, inventor, businessman; b. Sumner, Me., July 10, 1825; s. Huse and Zilpha (Drake) D.; grad. Wesleyan U., 1849; studied law, N.Y.C., 1853, Topeka, Kan., 1854-57; m. Elizabeth Penfield, Dec. 25, 1853; m. 2d, Mrs. Sabrina Smith, Oct. 2, 1862, 1 son, 1 dau. Went to Cal., 1850-53; judge Kan. Supreme Ct., 1858; mayor Topeka, 1859; editor Kan. Tribune, Topeka, 1859; patented waterproof cartridge, 1861; experimenter for Remington Arms Co., N.Y., 1861-62, 64-66; went to S.Am., 1866, established steamboat service in Colombia; engaged in mining, Venezuela, 1870-73; returned to U.S., 1873, became mining engr. in Colo., 1873-circa 1883; lived in N.Y.C., circa 1883-99; organized Dow Composing Machine Co. of W.Va., N.Y.C., 1896. Died N.Y.C., Oct. 12, 1899.

DOW, Neal, temperance reformer; b. Portland, Me., Mar. 20, 1804; s. Josiah and Dorcas (Allen) D.; m. Maria Maynard, Jan. 20, 1830, 9 children. Del. from Portland Young Men's Temperance Soc. to Me. Temperance Conv., 1834; organized Me. Temperance Union, 1838; mayor Portland, 1851-58; secured passage of anti-liquor bill ("Maine law") in Me. Legislature, 1851; pres. World's Temperance Conv., N.Y.C., 1853; mem. Me. Legislature, 1858-59; col. 13th Regt., Me. Volunteers, 1861; brig. gen. U.S. Volunteers, 1862; captured, imprisoned, later exchanged for Gen. Fitzhugh Lee, 1864; Prohibition Party candidate for U.S. Pres., 1880; known as "father of the Maine law." Died Portland, Oct. 2, 1897.

DOWDELL, James Ferguson, congressman, lawyer; b. nr. Monticello, Jasper County, Ga., Nov. 26, 1818; grad. Randolph-Macon Coll., Ashland, Va., 1840; studied law. Admitted to bar, 1841, began practice of law, Greenville, Ga.; engaged in agriculture, Chambers County, Ala., 1846; Democratic presdl. elector, 1852; mem. U.S.Ho. of Reps. (States Rights Democrat) from Ala., 33d-35th congresses, 1853-59; served as col. 37th Regt., Ala. Volunteer Inf., under Gen. PRICE, Confederate Army, 1862-65; pres. E. Ala. Coll., Auburn, 1868-70. Died nr. Auburn, Sept. 6, 1871; buried City Cemetery, Auburn.

DOWDNEY, Abraham, congressman, businessman; b. Youghal, Ireland, Oct. 31, 1841; attended pvt. schs. Came to U.S. with his parents, settled in N.Y.C.; engaged in constrn. and contracting bus.; served as capt. 132d Regt., N.Y. Volunteer Inf. in Civil War, 1862-63; chmn. public sch. trustees N.Y.C., 1882-85; mem. U.S. Ho. of Reps. (Democrat) from N.Y., 49th Congress, 1885-86. Died N.Y.C., Dec. 10, 1886; buried Calvary Cemetery, Long Island City, N.Y.

DOWELL, Greensville, physician; b. Albemarle County, Va., Sept. 1, 1822; s. James and Francis (Dawton) D.; attended U. Louisville, 1845-46; M.D., Jefferson Med. Sch., 1847; m. Sarah Zelinda White, June 29, 1849; m. 2d, Mrs. Laura Baker Hutchinson, 1868. Practiced medicine, Como, Miss., Memphis, Tenn., also Tex.; surgeon Cook's Heavy Arty., Confederate Army, later surgeon-in-chief Confederate Hosp. Dept.; prof. anatomy Soulé U. (now Tex. Med. Coll.); in charge of Galveston (Tex.) Hosp.; founded Galveston Med. Jour., 1869. Author: The Radical Cure for Hernia, 1873; Yellow Fever and Malarial Diseases,. . ., 1876. Died June 9, 1881.

DOWNER, Eliphalet, surgeon; b. Norwich (now Franklin), Conn., Apr. 3, 1744, s. Joseph and Mary (Sawyer) D.; m. Mary Gardner, 1766. Practiced medicine, Brookline, Mass., 1766-74; served as surgeon on board Continental privateer Yankee, captured and imprisoned in England; escaped to France, 1777; surgeon on Continental sloop Dolphin, 1777; shipped on Lexington, again captured and escaped; surgeon-gen. Continental Army on Penobscot Expdn., 1779. Died Brookline, Apr. 1806; buried Walnut Street Cemetery, Brookline.

DOWNER, Samuel, mfr.; b. Dorchester, Mass., Mar. 8, 1807; s. Samuel and Catherine (Ayers) D.; m. Nancy Melville, Oct. 13, 1836, 8 children. Joined father's merc. firm Downer & Baldwin, 1828-31; in merc. partnership with Silas P. Merriam, 1831-34; rejoined father and Capt. William R. Austin in manufacture and sale of sperm whale products, 1834; aided in introducing hydrocarbon oils in U.S.; invested in newly discovered petroleum wells. Died Sept. 20, 1881.

DOWNES, John, naval officer; b. Canton, Mass., Dec. 23, 1784; s. Jesse and Naomi (Taunt) D.; m. Maria Gertrude Hoffman, Oct. 30, 1821, at least 1 son John. Purser's steward in U.S. frigate Constitution; apptd. acting midshipman, 1800, midshipman, 1802; served in war against Tripoli pirates; promoted lt., 1807; as 1st lt. joined Essex, 1812; served as prize capt. from Essex, capturing ships which he turned into tiny flotilla; promoted master comdr., 1813, capt., 1817; on tour of duty in Mediterranean Sea, 1815-18; served in Pacific, 1818-28; comdr. in Java in Mediterranean 1828-30; commanded Potomac in Pacific, 1830-34; commandant Boston Navy Yard, 1835-42, 49-52; port capt. of Boston, 1843-45. Died Charleston, Mass., Aug. 11, 1854.

DOWNEY, John, educator; b. Germantown, Pa., circa 1765; s. Capt. John and Sarah Downey; m. Alice Ann Beatty, June 5, 1798. Opened sch., Harrisburg, Pa., 1796; justice of peace Harrisburg, 1807-26; town clk.; mem. Pa. Legislature, 1817-18; author several humorous polit. essays. Died Harrisburg, June 21, 1826.

DOWNING, Andrew Jackson, landscape architect; b. Newburgh, N.Y., Oct. 30, 1815; s. of Samuel Downing; m. Caroline Elizabeth DeWitt, June 7, 1838. Partner with brother in nursery, then became owner, 1838; met Calvert Vaux on trip to Eng. and France, 1850, worked with him on landscaping Capitol, White House, Smithsonian Instn. Author: A Treatise on the Theory and Practice of Landscape Gardening, Adapted to North America, 1841; The Fruits and Fruit Trees of America, 1845; Architecture of Country Houses, Including Designs for Cottages, Farmhouses, and Villas, 1850. Died in steamboat fire, July 28, 1852.

DOWNING, Charles, congressman; b. Va.; studied law. Admitted to bar, began practice of law, St. Augustine, Fla.; mem. legislative council Territory of Fla., 1837; mem. U.S. Congress from Territory of Fla., 25th-26th congresses, 1837-41. Died St. Augustine, 1845.

DOWNING, Charles, pomologist; b. Newburgh, N.Y., July 9, 1802; son of Samuel Downing; m. Mary Wait. Took over father's nursery, 1822, shared bus. with brother Andrew, 1834-39; operated a nursery, 10 years, later devoted efforts to pomology; prepared (with brother Andrew) The Fruits and Fruit Trees of America, published 1845, later issued by him in revised edits. Died Jan. 18, 1885.

DOWNING, Frances Murdaugh, author; b. Portsmouth, Va., circa 1835; dau. of John W. Murdaugh; m. Charles W. Downing, 1851. Lived in Fla., from 1851; published much prose and poetry, frequently under pseudonyms Viola and Frank Dashmore, from 1860's; poems include: Pluto, the Origin of Mint Julep (1876), Flowers of Shakespeare (1882), The Legend of Catawba. Author: (prose works) Nameless, 1865; Florida; Five Little Girls and Two Little Boys, 1878. Died Fla., circa 1894.

DOWNING, George, diplomat; b. Dublin, Ireland, Aug. 1623; s. Emmanuel and Lucy (Winthrop) D.; grad. Harvard, (1st graduating class), 1642. Came with family to Am., 1638; tutor Harvard, 1643; returned to Eng., 1645; served in Parliament, 1654-56, later held other posts including Brit. minister to The Hague, Netherlands; Downing Street (London, Eng.) named after him. Died July 1684.

DOWNING, Maj. Jack, see Smith, Seba.

DOWNS, Solomon Weathersbee, senator, lawyer; b. Montgomery County, Tenn., 1801; grad. Transylvania U., Lexington, Ky., 1823; studied law. Admitted to bar, 1826, began practice of law, Bayou Sara, West Feliciana Parish, La.; practiced law, New Orleans, from 1845; U.S. atty. for Di La., 1845-47; mem. La. Constl. Conv.; mem. U Senate (Democrat) from La., 1847-53; appt by Pres. Pierce collector Port of New Orlea 1853. Died Crab Orchard Springs, Lincoln Coun Ky., Aug. 14, 1854; buried Old City Cemete Monroe, La.

DOWSE, Edward, congressman; b. Charlestow Mass., Oct. 22, 1756. Moved to Dedham, Mas became a shipmaster in East Indian and Chi trade, after Am. Revolution; mem. U.S. Ho. Reps. (Democrat) from Mass., 16th Congre 1819-20. Died Dedham, Sept. 3, 1828; buried O Cemetery.

DOWSE, Thomas, book collector; b. Charlestow Mass., Dec. 28, 1772; s. Eleazer and Mehital (Brentnall) D.; never married. Worked 10 yea for wool-puller and leather-dresser, Roxbury, Mass began collecting library which he donated to Ma Hist. Soc. Died Nov. 4, 1856.

DOX, Peter Myndert, congressman, lawyer; Geneva, N.Y., Sept. 11, 1813; attended Gene Acad.; grad. Hobart Coll., Geneva, 1833; studi law. Admitted to bar, began practice of law, Ge eva; mem. N.Y State Assembly, 1842; jud Ontario County Cts., 1855-56; moved to Madis County, Ala., 1856, engaged in agriculture; me Ala. Constl. Conv., 1865; mem. U.S. Ho. of Rep (Democrat) from Ala., 41st-42d congresses, 186 73. Died Huntsville, Ala., Apr. 2, 1891; buri Maple Hill Cemetery.

DRAKE, Benjamin, editor, author; b. Mays Lic Ky., 1795; s. Isaac D. and Elizabeth (Shotwell) D read law, 1825-26. A founder, editor Cincinna Chronicle, 1826-34; author: Tales and Sketches fro the Queen City, 1838; The Life and Adventure Black Hawk, 1838; The Life of Tecumseh, 184 contbr. to Literary Gazette, Western Monthly Mag So. Literary Messenger. Died Apr. 1, 1841.

DRAKE, Charles Daniel, senator, jurist; b. Ci cinnati, Apr. 11, 1811; s. Dr. Daniel and Harri (Sesson) D.; attended St. Josephs Coll., Bard town, N.Y., 1823-24, U.S. Naval Acad., 1827-3 LL.D. (hon.), Hanover Coll., 1863, U. Woost (Ohio), 1875; m. Margaret Drake. Admitted Cincinnati bar, 1833; originated St. Louis La Library, 1838; mem. Mo. Ho. of Reps., 1859-6 filled vacancy in Mo. Conv., 1863; mem., v.p. M Constl. Conv. which abolished slavery and adopt a constn. called the Drake Constitution, 186 mem. U.S. Senate from Mo. (Republican), 186 70; chief justice U.S. Ct. of Claims, 1870-85. A thor: A Treatise on the Law of Suits by Attachme in the U.S., 1854; Union and Anti-Slavery Speec es Delivered During the Rebellion, 1864; Life Daniel Drake, 1871. Died Washington, D.C. Ap 1, 1892; buried Bellfontaine Cemetery, St. Loui

DRAKE, Daniel, physician; b. Plainfield, N.J Oct. 20, 1785; s. Isaac and Elizabeth (Shotwell) D attended Med. Coll. of U. Pa., 1805-06, M.D 1815; m. Harriet Sisson, 1807. Studied with D William Goforth at Ft. Washington (Cincinnati) 1800-05; practiced medicine, Mays Lick, O., 180 taught materia medica Transylvania U., Lexingto Ky., 1817-18, became dean, 1825-27; found Ohio Med. Coll. (now Med. Coll. of U. Cincinnati) 1819; tchr. Jefferson Med. Coll., 1828; taught various med. schs., Ohio, Pa., in 20 year perio hon. mem. Phila. Acad. Natural Scis., Am. Philo Soc., Wernerian Acad. Natural Scis. of Edinburg contbr. to many med. jours. Author: A Systemat Treatise, Historical, Etiological and Practical, on th Principal Diseases of the Interior Valley of Nor America; As They Appear in the Caucasian, Africa Indian and Eskimoux Varieties of Its Populatio 1850-54. Died Nov. 6, 1852.

DRAKE, Edwin Laurentine, oil driller; b. Green ville, N.Y., Mar. 29, 1819; married, 1845; m. 2d Laura Dow, 1857; 4 children. Night clk. on steam boat between Buffalo and Detroit; engaged in farm ing 1 year; employed as hotel clk., 2 years, d goods clk.; express agt. Boston & Albany R.R Springfield, Mass., 1845-50; conductor N.Y. & Ne Haven R.R., 1850-57; 1st to tap oil at its source Titusville, Pa., 1859; became impoverished, grante $1500 annual stipend by Pa. Legislature, 187 Died Bethlehem, Pa., Nov. 8, 1880; buried Titus ville.

DRAKE, Frances Ann Denny, actress; b. Schenec tady, N.Y., Nov. 6, 1797; m. Alexander Drake circa 1822; children—Col. A. E. Drake, Richard Samuel, Mrs. Harry Chapman; m. 2d, G. W. Cutter Joined group of actors at age 17; toured West; re turned to N.Y.C. via Canada, 1820; starred c N.Y.C. stage, 1820's-30's. Died Sept. 1, 1875.

DRAKE, Sir Francis, privateer, adventurer; b. nr Tavistock, Devonshire, Eng., circa 1540; marrie twice; m. 2d, 1585. Capt. English ship Judith, Sa Juan de Ulloa in Gulf of Mexico, circa 1568; be came privateer by commn. of Queen Elizabeth, 1570 plundered Nombre de Dios on Isthmus of Panama ırned Portobeio, circa 1572; planned to sail into outh Seas through Straits of Magellan, started on s journey, 1577, reached Brazil, then entered traits, 1578; continued up coast of Chile and Peru nd America trying to discover passage to Atlantic; ailed possibly to 48° latitude (Wash. State), reaired his ship (The Golden Hind) at San Francisco ay, 1579; named new country New Albion in name Queen Elizabeth; sailed West to Molucca Islands, he Celebes, Java, 1580, then set sail for home; rrived in Eng., 1580, becoming 1st Englishman to ail around world (2 years, 10 months); created night by Queen Elizabeth; sailed against Spanish ndies, 1585, plundered St. Augustine settlement, 'la.; rescued Roanoke Island (N.C.) colony; vicedm. of fleet that defeated Spanish Armada, 1858; nade unsuccessful expdn. against Spanish West Inies, 1595, became ill. Died off Portobelo, Jan. 8, 1596.

DRAKE, Francis Samuel, hist. writer; b. Northood, N.H., Feb. 22, 1828; s. Gardiner and Louisa Elmes) D. Lt., Boston Light Guards, 1848; served s adjutant to Union Army during Civil War; became ist. writer after Civil War; works include: Dictionry of American Biography Containing Nearly Ten housand Notices, 1872; The Life and Correspondence f Henry Knox; The Town of Roxbury, 1878; Indian listory for Young Folks, 1885. Died Washington, .C., Feb. 22, 1885.

DRAKE, John Burroughs, hotel exec.; b. Lebanon, ., Jan. 17, 1826; s. John and Nancy (Hurry) .; m. Josephine C. Corey, Feb. 24, 1863, 3 sons, daus. Hotel clk. at Peak Street and Burnett Houses, incinnati, 1845-55; part, later full owner Tremont louse, Chgo., 1855-71; bought Michigan Avenue Hoel, 1871, Grand Pacific Hotel, 1873; organizer Jnion Stock Yards; dir. Chgo. & Alton R.R. Died hgo., Nov. 12, 1895.

DRAKE, John Poad, artist, naval architect; b. evon, Eng., circa 1794. Designed several improveients in naval constrn. and ordnance; made paintng of Napoleon on board H.M.S. Bellerophon, 1815; ame to Am.; visited N.S. and Montreal (Can.), ainted portraits; came to N.Y.C., 1821, exhibited is painting of Napoleon: returned to Eng., 1827; vorked as naval designer and draftsman. Died Fowey, ornwall, Eng., Feb. 26, 1883.

DRAKE, John Reuben, congressman; b. Pleasnt Valley, Dutchess County, N.Y.,, Nov. 28, 782. Engaged in business and agriculture; supr. 'own of Owego (N.Y.), 1813; 1st judge Broome ounty, 1815-23; mem. N.Y. State Assembly, 817-19, 34; mem. U.S. Ho. of Reps. from N.Y., 5th Congress, 1817-19; judge Tioga County Ct. f Common Pleas, 1833-38; pres. Owego Village, 841-45. Died Owego, Mar. 21, 1857; buried Everreen Cemetery.

DRAKE, Joseph Rodman, poet; b. N.Y.C., Aug. 7, 1795; s. Jonathan and Hannah (Lawrence) D.; n. Sarah Eckford, Oct. 1816. Toured Europe, circa 1816-19; contbd. series of poems Croaker Papers to Evening Post, N.Y.C., 1819. Author: The Culprit Fay and Other Poems, published 1835. Died Sept. 21, 1820; buried Hunts Point, N.Y.C.

DRAKE, Samuel, actor, theatrical mgr.; b. England, Nov. 15, 1768; m. Miss Fisher, 3 sons, 2 daus. including Alexander, Martha, Julia. Came to U.S., 1810; mem. Boston Theatre Co., 1810-13; acted and managed in Albany, N.Y., 1813-15; acted and managed theatre troup composed largely of immediate family, successfully toured Pa., Ky., Tenn. and Ohio. Died Oldham County, Ky., Oct. 16, 1854.

DRAKE, Samuel Gardner, antiquarian; b. Pittsfield, N.H., Oct. 11, 1798; s. Simeon and Love Muchmore (Tucke) D.; studied law with John Kelly, Pittsfield, read medicine with Dr. Thomas Shannon, Pittsfield, 1820-21; A.M. (hon.), Union Coll., Schenectady, N.Y., 1843; m. Louisa Elmes, Apr. 12, 1825; m. 2d, Sarah Jane Drake; 5 children including Samuel Adams, Francis Samuel. Headmaster sch., London, N.H., 1818; taught at various local schs.; became bookseller; founder New Eng. Hist. General. Soc., sec., 12 years, pres., 1858. Author: Book of the Indians, 1841; The Witchcraft Delusion in New England, 3 vols., 1866. Editor: Mather's Indian War of 1675-6, 1862, Early History of New England, 1864. Died June 14, 1875.

DRAPER, Henry, astronomer; b. Prince Edward County, Va., Mar. 7, 1837; s. John William and Antonia Coetana de Paiva Pereira (Gardner) D.; M.D., U. City N.Y., 1858; m. Mary Anna Palmer, 1867. Mem. staff Bellevue Hosp., N.Y.C., 1858-60; prof. natural science U. City N.Y., 1860-66, prof. physiology, 1866-73, dean of faculty, also prof. analytical chemistry, 1870-82, prof. chemistry, 1882; built observatory at Hastings-on-Hudson, N.Y., 1860; devoted career to study of stellar spectroscopy; directed photographic work in U.S. govt. expdn. to observe transit of Venus, 1874; led expdn. to Wyo. to observe total eclipse of sun, 1878; mem. Nat. Acad. Scis., Am. Philos. Soc. Died N.Y.C., Nov. 20, 1882.

DRAPER, Ira, inventor, mfr.; b. Dedham, Mass., Dec. 24, 1764; s. Abijah and Alice (Eaton) D.; m. Lydia Richards, May 31, 1786; m. 2d, Abigail Richards, Mar. 9, 1812; 16 children including George. Developed several minor improvements for textile looms; chief invention was 1st rotary temple, 1816; organized Draper Co., became world's largest rotary temple mfr. Died Saugus, Mass., Jan. 22, 1848.

DRAPER, John, publisher; b. Oct. 29, 1702; s. Richard and Sally (Kilby) D.; m. Deborah Green, May 24, 1726; m. 2d, Eliza Avery, Oct. 1737; 1 son Richard. Apprentice to father-in-law from whom he inherited Boston News Letter, 1733, publisher, 1733-62; printer to gov. and council of Mass. Died Boston, Nov. 29, 1762.

DRAPER, John William, scientist, historian; b. St. Helen's, Eng., May 5, 1811; s. Rev. John Christopher Draper; attended London U.; M.D., U. Pa., 1836; m. Antonia Coetana de Paiva Pereira Gardner, circa 1830; children—Henry, John Christopher, Daniel, Virginia, Antonia. Came to Am., circa 1832; operated own scientific lab.; prof. chemistry and natural philosophy Hampden-Sydney (Va.) Coll., 1836-38; prof. chemistry Univ. of City N.Y. (now N.Y.U.), 1838; pioneer in photography, took 1st complete portrait of person by sunlight, circa 1839; founder sch. of medicine of Univ. City of N.Y., 1839, prof. chemistry and physiology, 1839-50, pres. med. sch., 1850. Author: A Treatise on the Forces Which Produce the Organization of Plants, 1844; Human Physiology, Statical and Dynamical, 1856; History of the Intellectual Development of Europe, 1863; Thoughts on the Future Civil Policy of America, 1865; History of the American Civil War, 3 vols., 1867-70; History of the Conflict Between Religion and Science, 1874. Died Jan. 4, 1882.

DRAPER, Joseph, congressman, lawyer; b. Draper Valley, Va., Dec. 25, 1794; attended pvt. schs.; studied law. Admitted to bar, 1818, began practice of law, Wytheville, Va.; served as pvt. in War of 1812; mem. Va. Senate, 1828-30; mem. U.S. Ho. of Reps. from Va. (filled vacancies), 21st, 22d congresses, Dec. 6, 1830-31, Dec. 6, 1832-33. Died Wytheville, June 10, 1834; buried Oglesbies Cemetery, Drapers Valley.

DRAPER, Lyman Copeland, antiquarian; b. N.Y., Sept. 4, 1815; s. Luke Draper; attended coll. in Granville, O., 2 years, also Hudson River Sem.; married, 1853; m. 2d, Mrs. Catherine T. Hoyt; Oct. 1889. Held Many unrelated jobs; sec. Wis. Hist. Soc., 1854-86; devoted life to collecting histories of pioneer figures; contbr. to Appleton's Cyclopaedia; King's Mountain and Its Heroes, 1881; editor Wisconsin Historical Collections. Died Aug. 26, 1891.

DRAPER, Margaret Green, journalist; b. circa 1730; m. Richard Draper, May 30, 1750. Published The Mass. Gazette and Weekly News-Letter (became publisher after death of husband, 1774), 1774-76; left Boston with British, 1776. Died London, Eng., 1807.

DRAPER, Richard, journalist; b. Boston, Mar. 1727; s. John and Deborah (Green) D.; m. Margaret Green, May 30, 1750, no children. Silent partner with father in publishing Boston News-Letter, took over printing following father's death, 1762-74, changed name to Boston Weekly News-Letter and New Eng. Chronicle (became Mass. Gazette and Boston News-Letter, 1763); govt. printer, 1762-74. Died Boston, June 5, 1774.

DRAYTON, John, gov. S.C., jurist; b. Charleston, S.C., June 22, 1767; s. William Henry and Dorothy (Golightly) D.; attended Coll. of N.J., (now Princeton), 1779-80; LL.D. (hon.), U. S.C., 1807; m. Hester Tidyman, Oct. 6, 1794, 7 children. Admitted to S.C. bar, 1788; practiced law, S.C., 1788-94; a warden of Charleston, 1789; mem. S.C. Ho. of Reps., 1792-98; lt. gov. S.C., 1798-1800, gov., 1800-04, 08-10; as result of his recommendation to S.C. Gen. Assembly, U. S.C. was established, 1801, pres. bd. dirs., 1801-02; mem. S.C. Senate, 1805-08; judge U.S. Dist. Ct. for S.C., 1812-22. Author: Letters Written during a Tour through the Northern and Eastern States of America, 1794; A View of South Carolina, as Respects her Natural and Civil Concerns, 1802. Editor: Memoirs of the American Revolution from its Commencement to the Year 1776, Inclusive: as Relating to the State of South-Carolina and Occasionally Referring to the States of North-Carolina and Georgia, 2 vols., 1821 (a collection of his father's papers). Died Charleston, Nov. 27, 1822.

DRAYTON, Percival, naval officer; b. S.C., Aug. 25, 1812; s. William and Ann (Gadsden) D. Apptd. midshipman U.S. Navy, 1827, passed midshipman, 1833, lt., 1838, comdr., 1855; apptd. aide to Commodore William Branford Shubrick, 1858; apptd. to command ship Pocahontas in Samuel Francis DuPont's expdn. against Port Royal, S.C., 1861; served as capt. in command of monitor Passaic, 1862; fleet capt. West Gulf Blockading Squadron, 1863; chief Bur. of Navigation, 1865. Died Washington, D.C., Aug. 4, 1865.

DRAYTON, Thomas Fenwick, planter, railroad pres., army officer; b. S.C., 1807; s. William and Ann (Gadsden) D.; grad. U.S. Mil. Acad., 1828; m. Catherine Pope, 8 children. Commd. lt. 6th Inf., U.S. Army, 1828; capt. of a company S.C. Militia, 1842-47; mem. S.C. Bd. Ordnance, 1851-52; mem. upper house S.C. Gen. Assembly, 1853-56; pres. Charleston & Savannah R.R. (constructed and successfully operated under his direction), 1853-61; commd. brig. gen. Provisional Confederate Army, 1861; in command Port Royal, S.C. when attacked by Union ships under DuPont, 1861; commanded brigade in Dist. of Ark., later in charge of sub-dist. in Tex.; pres. S.C. Immigrant Soc., 1878. Died Charlotte, S.C., Feb. 18, 1891.

DRAYTON, William, jurist; b. Ashley River, S.C., Mar. 21, 1732; s. Thomas and Elizabeth (Bull) D.; ed. Middle Temple, London, Eng., 1750-54; m. Mary Motte; m. 2d, Mary Gates, 1780; 10 children, including William Drayton. Went to E. Fla. after 1763; chief justice E. Fla. Province, 1767; judge S.C. Admiralty Ct., 1780; asso. justice S.C. Supreme Ct., 1789; 1st judge U.S. Ct. for S.C., 1789. Died S.C. May 18, 1790.

DRAYTON William, army officer, congressman; b. St. Augustine., Fla., Dec. 30, 1776; s. William and Mary (Motte) D.; ed. English prep. schs.; m. Ann Gadsden; m. 2d, Maria Miles; 9 children including Thomas Fenwick, Percival. Asst. in clk.'s office S.C. Ct. Gen. Sessions; admitted to S.C. bar, 1797; mem. S.C. Ho. of Reps., 1806-08; commd. lt. col. 10th Inf., U.S. Army, 1812, col. 18th Inf., 1812, insp. gen., 1814; recorder, judge City Ct. Charleston, 1819-24; mem. U.S. Ho. of Reps. from S.C. (Union Democrat filling vacancy), 19th-22d congresses, Dec. 15, 1825-Mar. 3, 1833; declined appointments as U.S. sec. war and minister to Eng. under Pres. Jackson; opposed nullification, 1830; moved to Phila., 1833; pres. Bank of U.S., 1840-41. Died Phila., May 24, 1846; buried Laurel Hill Cemetery, Phila.

DRAYTON, William Henry, Continental congressman, jurist; b. "Drayton Hall," nr. Charleston, S.C., Sept. 1742; s. John and Charlotte (Bull) D.; attended Westminster Sch., also Balliol Coll., Oxford (Eng.) U.; m. Dorothy Golightly, Mar. 29, 1764. Admitted to S.C. bar, 1764; became mem. S.C. Assembly, 1765; apptd. privy councilor S.C. by King George III, 1770, suspended for protesting system of filling govt. positions with appointees from Eng.; mem. Gov.'s Council of Province of S.C., 1772-75, pres., 1775, suspended for again protesting appointment system; asst. judge Colony of S.C., 1774-75; pres. S.C. Provincial Congress, 1775; commander of armed ship Prosper, actively engaged Brit. sloops Tamar and Cherokee (beginning revolutionary hostilities in South), summer 1775; chief justice S.C. Supreme Ct., 1776; mem. Continental Congress from S.C., 1778-79. Author: A Memoir of the American Revolution from its Commencement to the Year 1776 as Relating to South Carolina, 1821. Died Phila., Sept. 3, 1779; buried Christ Ch. Cemetery, Phila.

DRESEL, Otto, pianist, composer; b. Geisenheim-on-the Rhine, circa 1826; s. Johann Dietrich and Luise (Ephardt) D. Came to N.Y.C., 1848; taught music, concert pianist; visited Germany; returned, settled in Boston; compositions include: Army Hymn (for solo, chorus and orch.), 1863; Longfellow's In Memoriam (for soprano and orch.). Died Boston, July 26, 1890.

DREW, Daniel, businessman; b. Carmel, N.Y., July 29, 1797; s. Gilbert and Catherine (Muckelworth) D.; m. Roxana Mead, 1832; at least 1 son, William H. Served briefly in War of 1812; a cattle drover, horse trader; cattle buyer, 1828; entered Hudson River steamboat bus., 1834; began Wall St. speculation 1844, invested in railroads, 1850's; joined alliance with Jay Gould and James Fisk against Cornelius Vanderbilt for control of Erie R.R. (became archtype of grasping capitalist or "robber barons" of post Civil War era); lost control of railroad when his former assos. Gould and Fisk combined against him; suffered complete financial ruin as result of Depression of 1873, went into bankruptcy, 1876; large benefactor Drew Theol. Sem., Madison, N.J. and Drew Sem. for Young Ladies, Carmel, N.Y. Died Sept. 18, 1879.

DREW, John, actor; b. Dublin, Ireland, Sept. 3, 1827; m. Louisa Lane, 1850, 3 children, John, Georgiana, Louisa. Shipped on mcht. ship, left sea and began acting in England; came to U.S., played at Richmond Hill Theatre, N.Y.C., 1842; became renowned in Irish roles; played in Phila. in early 1850's; toured Europe in late 1850's; returned to Phila., mgr. Arch Street Theatre, until 1861. Died Phila., May 21, 1862.

DREW, Louisa Lane, actress, theatrical mgr.; b. London, Eng., Jan. 10, 1820; m. Henry B. Hunt;

m. 2d, George Mossop; m. 3d, John Drew, 1850, 3 children, John, Georgiana, Louisa. Made 1st stage appearance at age of 1 year; acted unitl 1861; assumed mgmt. of her husband's Arch Street Theatre, Phila., mgr. (following her husband's death in 1862), 1862-93. Died Larchmont, N.Y., Aug. 31, 1897.

DREXEL, Anthony Joseph, banker, philanthropist; b. Phila., Sept. 13, 1826; s. Francis Martin and Catherine (Hookey) D.; m. Ellen Rozet. Inherited (with brother Francis) firm Drexel & Co., 1847, responsible for expansion and emergence as investment brokerage after Civil War; contbr. to charitable, ch. orgns.; part owner Phila. Pub. Ledger; a founder Childs Drexel Home for Aged Printers, Colorado Springs, Colo.; founder Drexel Inst. Tech., Phila. (opened to students, 1892), contbr. $3,000,000. Died Carlsbad, Germany, June 30, 1893.

DREXEL, Francis Anthony, banker; b. Phila., June 20, 1824; son of Francis Martin Drexel; m. Hannah Langstroth, at least 2 daus., Elizabeth (Mrs. Walter George Smith), Katharine; m. 2d, Emma Bouvier, 1 dau., Louise (Mrs. Edward Morrell). Became asso. with his father's banking firm with offices in Paris, France, also (in assn. with J.P. Morgan), N.Y.C., at age 13, became sr. mem. (upon father's death), 1863; left large bequests to charity in his will; St. Francis Indsl. Sch., Eddington, Pa., also Drexel chair in moral theology at Catholic U., established by daus. out of fortune left to them. Died Phila., Feb. 15, 1885.

DREXEL, Francis Martin, banker, adventurer; b. Dornbirn, Austria, Apr. 7, 1792; s. Franz Joseph and Magdalen (Willhelm) D.; m. Catherine Hookey, 1821, at least 3 children including Joseph William. Studied in Italy; traveled throughout Europe as portrait painter; came to Phila., 1817; portraitist in Phila., 1817-26; made trip to South America, 1826-30; financial broker, 1837-63; founded banking firm Drexel & Co., Phila. Died June 5, 1863.

DREXEL, Joseph William, banker; b. Phila., Jan. 24, 1833; s. Francis Martin and Catherine (Hookey) D.; m. Lucy Wharton, Apr. 18, 1865. Made grand tour of Europe; represented Drexel & Co. (father's banking house) in Germany and Chgo.; returned to Phila., 1863; partner Drexel, Hartes & Co. of Paris, 1867; asso. with Drexel, Morgan & Co., 1871; dir. 11 banks; collector music and painting, donated some of collection to Lenox Library and Met. Museum of N.Y.; pres. Philharmonic Soc. of N.Y.; dir. Met. Museum of N.Y. Died Mar. 25, 1888.

DRIGGS, John Fletcher, congressman, businessman; b. Kinderhook, N.Y., Mar. 8, 1813. Moved to N.Y.C., 1827; apprenticed in sash, door and blind mfg. trade, 1829, journeyman 2 years, master mechanic, 1831-56; supt. N.Y. penitentiary and public instns. on Blackwells Island, 1844; moved to Mich., 1856, engaged in real estate, also salt mfg.; pres. East Saginaw (Mich.) Common Council, 1858; mem. Mich. Ho. of Reps., 1859-60; served as col. during Civil War, organized 29th Mich. Inf., 1864; mem. U.S. Ho. of Reps. (Republican) from Mich., 38th-40th congresses, 1863-69; mem. com. apptd. to accompany Pres. Lincoln's body to Springfield, Ill. Died East Saginaw, Dec. 17, 1877; buried Brady Hill Cemetery, Saginaw, Mich.; reinterred Forest Lawn Cemetery.

DRIPPS, Isaac L., machinist, innovator; b. Belfast, Ireland, Apr. 14, 1810; married, 1830, at least 1 child, William. Apprenticed to steamboat machinery mfr. Thomas Holloway, Phila., 1826-31; with Camden & Amboy R.R., 1831-53; partner Trenton Locomotive & Machine Works, 1853-59; supt. motive power and machinery Pitts., Fort Wayne & Chgo. R.R., 1859-70, completely redesigned, rebuilt mech. dept.; supt. motive power and machinery Pa. R.R., 1870-72, spl. agt., 1872-78. Died Phila., Dec. 28, 1892.

DRISLER, Henry, classical scholar, coll. dean; b. S.I., N.Y., Dec. 27, 1818; grad. Columbia, 1839. Tutor Latin and Greek, Columbia, 1843; became 1st prof. Latin as separate field, 1857, Jay prof. Greek, 1867, interim pres., 1878, 88-90, 1st dean of coll., 1890, ret., 1894; trustee Astor Library, N.Y. Pub. Library; pres. Archaeol. Inst. Am., 1886-89; published a number of textbooks and scholarly classical works. Died Nov. 30, 1897.

DROMGOOLE, George Coke, congressman, lawyer; b. Lawrenceville, Va., May 15, 1797; studied law. Admitted to bar, began practice of law; mem. Va. Ho. of Reps., 1823-26, Va. Senate, 1826-35; del. Va. Constl. Conv., 1829; mem. U.S. Ho. of Reps. (Democrat) from Va., 24th-26th, 28th-30th congresses, 1835-41, 43-47. Died on estate, Brunswick County, Va., Apr. 27, 1847; buried family burying ground S. of Meherrin River.

DRUILLETTES, Gabriel, clergyman; b. France, Sept. 29, 1610. Arrived in New Canada, 1643; Roman Catholic missionary in St. Lawrence River Valley, 1643-48; visited Boston, 1648; came to New Haven (Conn.) to ask New Eng. Confederation to help in warring against Iroquois Indians, 1652, request refused; continued mission work until 1671. Died Que., Can., Apr. 8, 1681.

DRUM, Augustus, congressman; b. Greensburg, Pa., Nov. 26, 1815; attended Greensburg Acad.; grad. Jefferson Coll. (now Washington and Jefferson U.), Canonsburg, Pa.; studied law. Admitted to bar, 1836, began practice of law, Greensburg; held several local offices; mem. Pa. Senate, 1852-53; mem. U.S. Ho. of Reps. (Democrat) from Pa., 33d Congress, 1853-55. Died Greensburg, Sept. 15, 1858; buried St. Clair Cemetery.

DRUMGOOLE, John Christopher, clergyman; b. Granard, Ireland, Aug. 15, 1816; attended St. Francis Xavier Coll., N.Y., 1863, St. John's Coll. at Fordham, 1865, Sem. of Our Lady of Angels, Niagara Falls, N.Y., 1869. Apprenticed to cobbler, N.Y.C.; became ch. sexton, 1844; prepared for priesthood Roman Catholic Ch., 1863-69; returned as priest to ch. where he had been sexton, N.Y.C.; head Cath. Home for Waifs, 1871-88. Died N.Y. C., Mar. 28, 1888.

DRURY, Lacy, clergyman, educator; b. Chesterfield County, Va., Oct. 5, 1758; s. William and Elizabeth (Rice) D.; attended MacRae's Sch., Cumberland County, Va.; B.A., Hampden-Sydney Coll., 1788; m. Anne Smith, Dec. 25, 1789. Tutor, Hampden-Sydney (Va.) Coll., 1784-87, vice pres., 1788-89, acting pres., 1789-97; licensed to preach Presbyn. Ch., 1787, active in religious revival in So. Va., 1787; operated pvt. sch. at his home, nr. Hampton-Sydney, 1797-1815; del. to Gen. Assembly Presbyn. Ch., many times, moderator of Assembly, Phila., 1809. Died Phila., Dec. 6, 1815; buried 3d Presbyn. Ch. cemetery, Phila.

DUANE, James, jurist, mayor, N.Y.C.; b. N.Y.C., Feb. 6, 1733; s. Anthony and Althea (Kettetas) D.; m. Mary Livingston, Oct. 21, 1759, 10 children. Admitted to N.Y. bar, 1754; mem. Com. of Correspondence, 1774; del. Continental Congress, 1774-84; mem. N.Y. Provincial Conv., 1775, 76, 77; helped draft Articles of Confederation; mem. N.Y. Com. of 60 to carry out the Association and of subsequent Com. of 100; as mem. Poughkeepsie Conv. (1788) advocated ratification of U.S. Constn.; 1st mayor N.Y.C., 1784; mem. N.Y. Senate, 1782-85, 89-90; 1st U.S. judge dist. of New York, 1789-94. Died Schenectady, N.Y., Feb. 1, 1797; buried beneath Christ Ch., Duanesburg, N.Y.

DUANE, James Chatham, mil. and civil engr.; b. Schenectady, N.Y., June 30, 1824; s. James and Harriet (Constable) D.; grad. Union Coll., 1844, U.S. Mil. Acad., 1848; m. Harriet Brewerton, 1850, 3 children including Alexander. Participated in Utah expdn. under Albert S. Johnston, 1858; instr. engring. U.S. Mil. Acad., 1858; treas., 1859-61; with McClellan's Army of Potomac during Civil War, made notable contbn. with his orgn. of engr. battalion and equipment; chief engr. Army of Potomac, 1862; brevetted lt. col. and col. U.S. Army for distinguished service; commd. brig. gen., chief of engrs. U.S. Army, 1886-88; ret., 1888; mem. Croton Aqueduct Commn. after 1888. Died N.Y.C., Nov. 8, 1897.

DUANE, William, journalist; b. Lake Champlain, N.Y., May 17, 1760; m. Catharine Corcoran; m. 2d, Margaret Bache, 1800; 5 children. Went to India, 1787, established Indian World, Calcutta, deported because of resistance to East India Co.; returned to London; Parliamentary reporter Gen. Advertiser, came to Phila.; co-editor Phila. Aurora, editor 1798-1822 (made it a powerful Jeffersonian newspaper); was arrested under Sedition Act, charges dropped under influence of Pres. Jefferson; served as lt. col. Rifles, 1808, adjutant gen. during War of 1812; traveled to S.Am., 1822-23; prothonotary Pa. Supreme Ct., 1823-35. Author: A Visit to Colombia in the Years 1822 and 1823, pub. 1826; Military Dictionary, 1810; Handbook for Riflemen, 1813. Died Phila., Nov. 24, 1835.

DUANE, William John, legislator, sec. of treasury; b. Clonmel County, Tipperary, Ireland, May 9, 1780; s. William and Catharine (Corcoran) D.; m. Deborah Bache. Became mem. Pa. Ho. of Reps., 1809 (Republican, later Democrat), chmn. com. roads and inland navigation, com. to consider case of Gideon Olmstead, 1810, com. on banks, 1819; admitted to bar, 1815; pros. atty. for Phila. Mayor's Ct., 1820; mem. Dem. Com. of Correspondence for Phila., 1828, Select Council of Phila., 1829; U.S. sec. of treasury under Pres. Jackson, 1833, removed on Jackson's order for refusing to withdraw govt. deposits from U.S. Bank before meeting of U.S. Congress, 1833. Died Phila., Sept. 27, 1865.

DuBOIS, John, clergyman; b. Paris, France, Aug. 24, 1764; attended Collège Louis-Le-Grand, Sem. St. Magloire. Ordained priest Roman Catholic Ch., 1787; served in ch., St. Sulpice, Paris, 1787-91; came to Norfolk, Va.; built 1st Cath. Ch. in Western Md., 1794; trained aspirants for priesthood, founded sem., Emmitsburg, Md., 1807; joined Soc. of St. Sulpice, 1808; became bishop Diocese of N. Y., 1826; traveled to Europe, 1829; ret. 1839. Died N.Y.C., Dec. 20, 1842; buried St. Patrick's Ch. ((Cathedral), N.Y.C.

DuBOIS, Samuel F., artist; b. Doylestown, P. 1805; s. Rev. Uriah DuB.; studied under Thon Sully. Painted portraits around Doylestown a Phila.; much of his work hung in U.S. Mint, Phil exhibited at Artists' Fund Soc., 1836-37, Pa. Aca 1855-56. Died Doylestown, Oct. 20, 1889.

Du BOIS, William Ewing, numismatist, writer; Doylestown, Pa., Dec. 15, 1810; s. Uriah and M tha (Patterson) Du B.; m. Susanna Eckfeldt, 184 Admitted to Pa. bar; editor's clk. U.S. Mint, 183 35, worked in assay dept., 1833-72, assayer, 187 81. Author: Manual of Gold and Silver Coins of Nations, 1842; On the Natural Dissemination Gold, 1861; a genealogy of Du Bois, 1860. Di Phila., July 14. 1881.

DU BOSE, Dudley McIver, congressman, lawy b. Shelby County, Tenn., Oct. 38, 1834; attend U. Miss. at Oxford; grad. Lebanon (Tenn.) L Sch., 1856. Admitted to bar, 1857, began pract of law, Memphis, Tenn moved to Augusta, G 1860; served as col. 15th Regt., Ga. Volunteer In Confederate Army, during Civil War, promot brig. gen. Western Army; moved to Washingt Ga.; mem. U.S. Ho. of Reps. (Democrat) fr Ga., 42d Congress, 1871-73. Died Washingt Ga., Mar. 2, 1883; buried Rest Haven Cemete

Du BOURG, Louis Guillaume Valentin, clergyma b. Cap Français, St. Domingo, Feb. 13, 176 s. Chevalier Pierre Du Bourg de la Loubère a Marguerite Armand de Vogluzan; grad. Collège Guyenne Sem. of St. Suplice, 1784. Ordained prie Roman Catholic Ch., 1788; rector sch. at Issy; le France for Spain because of French Revolution, th came to Am.; arrived in Balt., 1794; mem. So St. Suplice, Balt., 1795; pres. Georgetown Col 1796-98; took trip to Cuba; head master acad. f West Indian boys at St. Mary's in Md. (became S Mary's Coll. for Am. Boys, 1812); adminstr. apo tolic of New Orleans, 1812-26; trip to Europ 1815-17; built sch. for boys, St. Louis, Mo.; r signed New Orleans post; returned to France a Archdiocese at Besançon. Died Besançon, Franc Dec. 12, 1833.

DUBOURJAL, Savinien Edmé, artist; b. Pari France, Feb. 12, 1795; studied painting, Paris. E hibited at Paris Salon, 1814; work shown at P. Acad., 1824, N.A.D., 1832; visited Am., 1844, se tled in Am., 1845; exhibited at Pa. Acad., N.A.D Boston Athenaeum, Am. Art-Union; friend of An portrait painter G.P.A. Healy, supported by Hea when his health failed in his last years. Died Pari Dec. 8, 1865.

DUBUIS, Claude Mary, clergyman; b. Ich Loire, France, Mar. 10, 1817. Ordained prie Roman Catholic Ch., as mem. Congregation Holy Cross, Lyons, 1844; came to U.S., did missio ary work in Tex.; consecrated bishop of Galvesto Tex., 1862, resigned, 1881, held title until 189 apptd. titular bishop of Acra, 1892. Died Verna son, France, May 22, 1895.

DUBUQUE, Julien, pioneer; b. St. Pierre les Bee quets, Que., Can., Jan. 10, 1762; s. Noel Augusti and Marie (Mailhot) D. Settled in Prairie du Chien Wis., 1785; secured permission from Fox Indian to work lead mines west of Mississippi River, 1788 gov. of La. granted him 7 leagues of land alon west bank of Miss. River; his mining operations im poverished him and enriched St. Louis mcht. Chou teau. Died Dubuque, Ia., Mar. 24, 1810; burie Dubuque.

DUCHÉ, Jacob, clergyman; b. Phila., Jan. 31 1737 (or 1738); s. Col. Jacob and Mary (Spence D.; grad. Coll. of Phila., 1757; attended Cambridg U.; m. Elizabeth Hopkinson, June 19, 1759, a least 1 child, Thomas Spence. Ordained deacon, 1759 ordained to ministry Anglican Ch., in Eng., 1762 taught oratory; became asst. rector Christ and St Peters Chs., Phila., later rector, 1775-77; chaplai Continental Congress, 1775-77; imprisoned whe British took Phila., became strong Loyalist, wen to Eng., 1777; sec., chaplain Orphan Asylum, St George's Fields, Lambeth Parish, Eng.; allowed t return to Am., 1792. Author: The Life and Death o the Righteous, 1760; Pennsylvania, A Poem, 1756 The Duty of Standing Fast in Our Spiritual an Temporal Liberties, 1775; Discourses on Variou Subjects, 1779. Died Phila., Jan. 3, 1798.

DUCHESNE, Rose Philippine, nun; b. Grenoble France, Aug. 29, 1769; d. Pièrre François an Rose Euphrosyne (Périer) Duchesne. Became novic Convent of St. Mary, Grenoble; joined Soc. of Sa cred Heart after French Revolution, sent to Am. 1818; taught at girls sch., St. Charles, Mo., late at sch. for Indian Girls, Florissant, Mo.; tchr., Gran Coteau, La., 1821-25, St. Michael's, La., 1825-29 founded convent, St. Louis, Mo.; established India mission, Kan. Territory. Died St. Charles, Mo., Nov 18, 1852.

DU COUDRAY, Philippe Charles Jean Tronson, my officer; b. Rheims, France, Sept. 8, 1738. n army engr., adj. gen. of arty.; volunteered rvice in Am. Revolution; promised rank of maj. n. by Benjamin Franklin, but named insp. gen. stead (compromise to allay jealousy of colonial aders); placed in charge of fortifications along elaware River. Drowned nr. Phila. after 4 months service, Sept. 11, 1777.

DUCRUE, Francis Bennon, clergyman; b. Mu-ch, Bavaria, June 10, 1721. Joined Soc. of Jesus, 738; missionary in Cal., 1748-67, superior at me Soc. was expelled. Author of an account of s journey through Cal. to Mexico (praised by storian Bancroft) and report on expulsion. Died unich, Mar. 30, 1779.

DUDLEY, Benjamin Winslow, surgeon; b. Spotsyl-nia County, Pa., Apr. 12, 1785; s. Ambrose udley; M.D., U. Pa., 1806; m. Anna Maria Short, 821, 3 children. Studied medicine under Dr. Fred idgely; began practice of medicine, Lexington, y.; traveled, studied in Europe, 4 years; mem. Roy- Coll. Surgeons; returned to Lexington, 1814; prof. natomy and surgery Transylvania U., 1817-50; per-rmed 1st successful cataract operation in West, 836; ret., 1853. Died Lexington, Jan. 20, 1870.

DUDLEY, Charles Edward, senator; b. Stafford-nire, Eng., May 23, 1780; s. Charles and Cath-rine (Cooke) D.; m. Blandina Bleeker, Came to .S., 1794; mem. N.Y. State Senate, 1820-25; ayor Albany (N.Y.), 1821-28; mem. U.S. Senate om N.Y. (sent to take Martin Van Buren's seat), 829-33; mem. so-called Albany Regency (polit. rgn. set up by Van Buren); his widow founded udley Observatory, Albany, in his honor. Died lbany, Jan. 23, 1841.

DUDLEY, Edward Bishop, gov. N.C., congress-an, railroad exec.; b. Onslow County, N.C., Dec. 5, 1769; s. Christopher Dudley; m. Eliza Hay-ood. Mem. N.C. Ho. of Commons, 1811-13; ommd. lt. col. Onslow Volunteer Regt. during War f 1812; mem. N.C. Senate, 1814, 16-17, 34-35; em. U.S. Ho. of Reps. from N.C., 21st Congress, 829-31; gov. N.C. (Whig, 1st N.C. gov. elected hrough popular sovereignty), 1836-40, adminstrn. arked beginning of period of econ. and social evel. in N.C.; secured charter, led in subscribing apital for Wilmington & Raleigh R.R. (his great-st achievement; later became Wilmington & Wel-on R.R., longest in world for several years), pres., 836-37, 41-47. Died Wilmington, N.C., Oct. 30, 855; buried Oakdale Cemetery, Wilmington.

DUDLEY, Henry C., architect. Practiced as archi-ect, N.Y.C.; mem. firm Wills & Dudley, N.Y.C., rm responsible for design of Holy Trinity Ch., 852, 1st Christian Science Ch., 1856-58, Ch. of dvent, 1857-66, all Nashville, Tenn., Christ Epis-opal Ch., New Brunswick, N.J., St. Paul's Episcopal h., Syracuse, N.Y.; charter mem. A.I.A., 1857, ir., 1857-59, 60-65, also fellow. Flourished mid 9th Century.

DUDLEY, Joseph, colonial gov.; b. Roxbury, lass., Sept. 23, 1647; s. Thomas and Catherine Dighton) Hackburn D.; grad. Harvard, 1663; m. ebecca Tyng, 1668, 13 children. Became freeman, 672; mem. Mass. Gen. Ct. from Roxbury, 1673-6; participated in battle with Narragansett Indi-ns during King Phillip's War, 1675; mem. upper ouse Mass. Legislature, 1676-83, 84; commr. nited Colonies of New Eng. until arrival of Sir dmund Andros, 1677-81; pres. Mass. Council, 684; gov. Mass., N.H., also King's Province, 1688-7, 1702-15; mem. Gov. Andros's Council, censor f press, chief justice Colonial Superior Ct., 1687-89; chief Council of N.Y., 1690-92; dep. gov. Isle f Wight; gov. Mass., 1702-15. Died Roxbury, Apr. , 1720.

DUDLEY, Paul, jurist; b. Roxbury, Mass., Sept. , 1675; s. Gov. Joseph and Rebecca (Tyng) D.; rad. Harvard, 1690; studied law, Temple, London, ng.; m. Lucy Wainwright, 1703; children—Thom-s, Joseph. Admitted to Mass. bar, 1700; commd. by ueen Anne atty. gen. Province of Mass. Bay, 1702-18; advocate in Vice Admiralty Ct. Boston; pptd. atty. gen. by Mass. gov. and council; mem. Mass. Legislature, Mass. Exec. Council; judge Mass. uperior Ct. of Judicature, 1718-51; chief justice Mass., 1745-51; known chiefly as founder Dudleian ecture on Religion at Harvard Coll. Died Roxbury, an. 25, 1751.

DUDLEY, Thomas, colonial gov.; b. Northamp-on, Eng., 1576; s. Capt. Roger Dudley; m. Doro-hy Yorke, Apr. 25, 1603; m. 2d, Catherine Digh-on, Apr. 14, 1644; 8 children, including Joseph. Helped form Mass. Bay Colony, dep. gov., 1630-34, 37-40, gov., 1634-35, 40-41, 45-46, 50-51; as-istant in Mass. Ho. of Reps. in interims of above ffices; one of Mass. commrs. to New Eng. Confed-ration, 1643; a founder 1st Ch. at Charlestown, 1630; signer (as gov. Mass.) charter Harvard Coll., 1650, one of 1st overseers. Died Roxbury, Mass., July 31, 1653.

DUELL, Robert Holland, congressman, lawyer; b. Warren, N.Y., Dec. 20, 1824; studied law. Admitted to bar, 1845, began practice of law, Fabius, N.Y.; moved to Cortland, N.Y., 1847; dist. atty. Cortland County, 1850-55; judge Cortland County, 1855-59; assessor internal revenue for 23d Dist. N.Y., 1869-71; mem. U.S. Ho. of Reps. (Republican) from N.Y., 36th-37th, 42d-43d congresses, 1859-63, 71-75; U.S. commr. of pa-tents (apptd. by Pres. Grant), 1875-77. Died Cortland, Feb. 11, 1891; buried Cortland Rural Cemetery.

DUER, John, jurist; b. Albany, N.Y., Oct. 7, 1782; s. William and Catherine (Alexander) D.; m. Anna Bunner. Admitted to N.Y. bar, 1806; del. from Orange County to N.Y. Constl. Conv., 1821; apptd. to commn. to revise N.Y. statutes, 1825; apptd. U.S. dist. atty. for So. N.Y., 1827; judge N.Y.C. Superior Ct., 1849-58; chief justice, 1857-58. Author: Law of Representations in Marine In-surance, 1845; Law and Practice of Marine Insur-ance, 1845-46. Died Staten Island, N.Y., Aug. 8, 1858.

DUER, William, Continental congressman; b. Devonshire, Eng., Mar. 18, 1747; s. John and Fran-ces (Frye) D.; ed. Eton Coll.; m. Catherine Alex-ander, 1779; 2 children—William Alexander, John. Commd. ensign Brit. Army; aide-de-camp to Lord Clive, 1762, accompanied Clive to India, 1764; came to N.Y., 1768; cotton mfr., N.Y. and N.J., prior to Am. Revolution; del. to N.Y. Provincial Congress, 1775; col., dep. adj. gen. N.Y. Militia; del. to N.Y. Constl. Conv., 1776, mem. com. to draft constn.; mem. N.Y. Com. of Public Safety, 1776; del. from N.Y. to Continental Congress, 1777-79, mem. bd. of war; 1st judge common pleas Charlotte (now Washington) County (N.Y.), 1777-86; signer Articles of Confederation; instru-mental in causing failure of Conway Cabal's plan to remove Washington from command; chmn. commn. for conspiracies (established by Congress), 1780; a founder Bank of N.Y., 1784; sec. to Bd. of Treasury under Articles of Confedn., N.Y.C., 1786; mem. N.Y. Assembly, 1786; asst. sec. U.S. 1786; mem. N.Y. Assembly, 1786; asst. sec. U.S. Dept. of Treasury (founded 1789), 1789; became involved in land and other speculations, imprisoned for debt, 1792. Died in prison, N.Y.C., May 7, 1799; buried Jamaica, L.I., N.Y.

DUER, William, congressman, lawyer; b. N.Y.C., May 25, 1805; grad. Columbia, 1824; studied law. Admitted to bar, 1824, began practice of law, N.Y.C.; moved to New Orleans, 1832, to Oswego, N.Y., 1836; mem. N.Y. State Assembly, 1840-41; del. Whig Nat. Conv., 1844; dist. atty. Oswego County, 1845-47; mem. U.S. Ho. of Reps. (Whig) from N.Y., 30th-31st congresses, 1847-51; U.S. consul to Valparaiso, Chile (apptd. by Pres. Fill-more), 1851-53; settled in San Francisco, 1854; clk. San Francisco County, 1858-59; lived in re-tirement, Staten Island, N.Y., 1859-79. Died New Brighton, N.Y., Aug. 25, 1879; buried Silver Mount Cemetery, Thompkinsville, S.I., N.Y.

DUER, William Alexander, jurist, coll. pres.; b. Rhinebeck, N.Y., Sept. 8, 1780; s. William and Catherine (Alexander) D.; m. Hannah Denning, Sept. 11, 1806. Admitted to bar, 1802; mem. N.Y. State Assembly, 1814-20, chmn. com. on colls. and acads.; judge Supreme Ct. N.Y., 1822-29; pres. Columbia, 1829-42. Author: Constitutional Jurisprudence of the United States, 1856. Died N.Y.C., May 30, 1858.

DUFF, Mary Ann Dyke, actress; b. London, Eng., 1794; m. John Duff, 1810; m. 2d, Charles Young; m. 3d, Mr. Beaver; 10 children including Mary Duff. Became actress as a child; gave 1st Am. performance, 1810, became noted tragic actress, N.Y.C., 1810-27; returned to Eng. to play at Drury Lane Thea-tre, London; played in N.Y.C., Balt., Phila., 1828-35; lived in New Orleans, 20 years, acted through-out South; a religious recluse in N.Y.C., during her last years. Died N.Y.C., Sept. 5, 1857.

DUFFIELD, George, clergyman; b. Lancaster Coun-ty, Pa., Oct. 7, 1732; s. George and Margaret Duf-field; grad. Coll. of N.J. (now Princeton), 1752; m. Elizabeth Blair, Mar. 8, 1756; m. 2d, Margaret Armstrong, Mar. 5, 1759; at least 1 son George. Tutor, Coll. of N.J., 1754-56; licensed to preach, 1756; pastor Presbyn. Ch., Carlisle, Pa., 1757-72, 3d Presbyn. Ch., Phila., 1772-90; ordained to min-istry Presbyn. Ch., 1759; capt. local militia; strong patriot, commd. chaplain Pa. Militia, co-chaplain Continental Congress; trustee Coll. of N.J., 1777-90; clk. Pa. Gen. Assembly. Author: A Sermon Preached in the Third Presbyterian Church in the City of Phila-delphia on Thursday, Dec. 11, 1783, published 1784. Died Feb. 2, 1790.

DUFFIELD, George, clergyman; b. Strasburg, Pa., July 4, 1794; s. George and Faithful (Slaymaker) D.; grad. U. Pa., 1811; m. Isabella Graham Bethune. Licensed to preach by Phila. Presbytery, 1815, or-dained to ministry, 1816; pastor Presbyn. Ch., Car-lisle, Pa., 1816-35; pastor 5th Presbyn. Ch., Phila., also Broadway Tabernacle; pastor Protestant Ch., De-troit, 1838-68. Author: The Principles of Presbyterian Discipline, 1835; The Bible Rule of Temperance, 1858. Died Detroit, June 26, 1868.

DUFFIELD, Samuel Augustus Willoughby, clergy-man; b. Bklyn., Sept. 24, 1843; s. Rev. George and Anna Augusta (Willoughby) D.; grad. Yale, 1863; m. Hattie S. Haywood, Oct. 1, 1868. Licensed to preach by Knox Presbytery of Ill., 1866; head of Mosely Mission, Chgo., 1866; ordained to ministry Presbyn. Ch., 1867; preached in Kenderton Presbyn. Ch., Phila., 1867-70; pastor in Jersey City, N.J., 1870, 1st Presbyn. Ch., Ann Arbor, Mich., 1871-74, 8th Presbyn. Ch., Chgo., 1874-76, Central Presbyn. Ch., Auburn, N.Y., 1876-78, 2d Presbyn. Ch., Al-toona, Pa., 1878-81, Westminster Presbyn. Ch., Bloomfield, N.J., 1881-86. Author: Warp and Woof, 1870; English Hymns: Their Authors and History, 1886. Died May 12, 1887.

DUFOUR, John James, grape grower; b. Chatelard, Canton de Vaud, Switzerland, 1763; son of Jean Jacques Dufour. Came to U.S. to establish vine-yards; began his 1st vineyard nr. Lexington Ky., 1798, after failure of vineyard returned to Europe, 1806-16; later established successful vineyard at Vevay, Ind. Author: The American Vine Dresser's Guide, 1826. Died Vevay, Feb. 9, 1827.

DUGANNE, Augustine Joseph Hickey, author; b. Boston, 1823; married. Became newspaper writer; moved to Phila., circa 1845, N.Y.C., 1850; mem. N.Y. Assembly (Know-Nothing Party) from 6th Dist., 1855-56; helped raise 176th N.Y. Volunteers, commd. lt. col., 1862; imprisoned by Confederates, 1863-64. Author: Home Poems, 1844; Parnassus in Pillory, 1851; Art's True Mission in America, 1853; Poetical Works, 1856; Camps and Prisons . . ., 1865. Died N.Y.C., Oct. 20, 1884; buried Cypress Hills Cemetery, N.Y.

DUGDALE, Richard Louis, social reformer; b Paris, 1841; s. Richard John and Anna (Cuddon) D.; attended Cooper Union, N.Y.C. Came to U.S., 1851, traveled and worked in various locations, then settled in N.Y.C.; his home became gathering place for various groups of social reformers; mem. exec. com. Prison Assn. of N.Y., 1868; mem. com. to inspect county jails, 1874, helped publish com. report "The Jukes, A Study in Crime, Pauperism, Disease and Heredity"; 1st sec. Soc. for Polit. Edn., 1880. Died N.Y.C., July 23, 1883.

DUGUÉ, Charles Oscar, journalist, poet; b. New Orleans, May 1, 1821; s. Francois and Jeanne Marie (Pligne) D.; attended Collège St. Louis, Paris, France, also Transylvania Coll., Ky.; m. Elodie Au-gustine de Livaudais. Contbr. to papers L'Abeille, La Lorgnette, Le Propagateur Catholique, New Or-leans; editor L'Orléanais; judge dist. ct. at St. Ber-nard, Jefferson, Plaquemines; asst. supt. schs. New Orleans; pres. Jefferson Coll., St. James Parish, La.; taught sch. during Civil War; made trip to France to publish poem "Homo." Author: Philosophie Mor-ale, 1847; Essais Poétiques, 1847; Mila ou Là Mort de La Salle, 1852. Died Paris, Aug. 29, 1872; buried St. Louis Cemetery Number 2.

DULANY, Daniel, lawyer, mem. gov.'s council Md.; b. Queen's County, Ireland, 1685; s. Thomas Delaney; m. Charity Courts; m. 2d, Rebecca Smith, at least 1 child, Daniel; m. 3d, Henrietta Maria Lloyd. Came to Am., 1703; admitted to Charles County (Md.) bar, 1709; land speculator; mem. Md. Legislative Assembly from Annapolis, 1722-42; atty. gen. of Md.; proprietor's agt., receiver gen., commissary gen., 1733; admiralty judge, 1734; mem. gov.'s council Md. Colony, 1742-53. Died Annapolis, Dec. 5, 1753.

DULANY, Daniel, lawyer; b. Annapolis, Md., June 28, 1722; s. Daniel and Rebecca (Smith) D.; at-tended Eton Coll., Clare Hall of Cambridge (Eng.) U., Middle Temple, London, Eng.; m. Rebecca Task-ier, 1749. Admitted to Md. bar, 1747; mem. lower house Md. Legislature, 1751-54; mem. Md. Council 1757-74; commissary gen. Province of Md., 1759-61, sec., 1761-74; a Loyalist, but urged representa-tion for colonies in Parliament; one of most power-ful colonial lawyers until Revolution when his proper-ty and position suffered due to his politics. Author: Considerations on the Propriety of Imposing Taxes in the British Colonies for the Purpose of Raising a Revenue, by Act of Parliament (pamphlet), 1765. Died Balt., Mar. 17, 1797.

DULUTH, Daniel Greysolon (Sieur Duluth), explorer; b. St. Germain-en-Laye, France, 1636. Came to Can., circa 1670; set out on expdn. with instrns. from Count de Frontenac (gov. Can.) to explore Lake Superior and routes west, 1678; ne-gotiated peace between the Chippewa and Sioux, 1679; made alliance with Sioux, took possession of what is now Minn. for France; led expdns. against Iroquois Indians, 1684, 87; often called upon to settle Indian disputes; commd. capt. French Army, 1690; comdr. Ft. Frontenac, 1690; ret. because of illness, 1695; City of Duluth (Minn.) mamed after him; name also spelled Dulhut. Died Montreal, Que., Can., Feb. 27, 1710.

DUMETZ, Francisco, missionary; b. Majorca, Spain. Became a Franciscan; sent to Mexico City, 1770, to Cal., 1771; missionary at Monterey, other missions, until 1797; founded San Fernando mission, continued work among Indians. Died San Gabriel, Cal., Jan. 14, 1811.

DUMMER, Jeremiah, silversmith, colonial govt. ofcl.; b. Newbury, Mass., Sept. 14, 1645; s. Richard and Frances (Burr) D.; m. Anna Atwater, 1672, at least 2 children, Jeremiah, William. Apprenticed to mint master John Hull, 1659-71, then opened his own silversmithy; served with Boston Arty. Co., 1671-86; constable, 1675; mem. Council of Safety, 1689; selectman of Boston, 1691-92; justice of Peace, 1693-1718; treas. Suffolk County, 1701. Died Boston, May 25, 1718.

DUMMER, Jeremiah, colonial agt.; b. Boston, circa 1679: s. Jeremiah and Anna (Atwater) D.; grad. Harvard, 1699; Ph.D., U. Utrecht (Holland), 1703; never married. Settled in Eng., circa 1705; secret negotiator for Lord Bolingbroke; became wealthy lawyer; influenced Elihu Yale to give money to coll. which became Yale, collected, sent books to sch., 1714; colonial agt. for Conn., 1712-33, for Mass., 1721. Author: A Letter to A Noble Lord, Concerning the Late Expedition to Canada, 1712; Defence of the New England Charters, 1721. Died Plaistow, Eng., May 19, 1739; buried West Ham, Essex, Eng.

DUMONT, Ebenezer, congressman, lawyer; b. Vevay, Ind., Nov. 23, 1814; studied law. Admitted to bar, began practice of law, Vevay; mem. Ind. Ho. of Reps., 1838; Democratic presdl. elector, 1852; served as col. 7th Regt., Ind. Volunteer Inf., during Civil War, promoted brig. gen. U.S. Volunteers, 1861, resigned, 1863; mem. U.S. Ho. of Reps. (Unionist) from Ind., 38th-39th congresses, 1863-67; apptd. gov. Ida. Territory by Pres. Grant, died before taking office. Died Indpls., Ind., Apr. 16, 1871; buried Crown Hill Cemetery.

DUNBAR, Moses, Loyalist; b. Wallingford, Conn., June 14, 1746; s. John and Temperance (Hall) D.; m. Phebe Jerome, 1764, 7 children; m. 2d, Esther Adams. Held Loyalist sympathies, joined English at Long Island, given duty of encouraging enlistment in King's Forces; betrayed and tried, 1777. Hanged (only person ever executed for treason in Conn.) Mar. 19, 1777.

DUNBAR, Robert, businessman; b. Carnbee, Scotland, Dec. 13, 1812; m. Sarah M. Howell, Aug. 26, 1840, at least 1 son, 1 dau. Designed, constructed equipment for shipyard, Niagara, Ont., Can.. 1832-34; held various engring. jobs; partner of C. W. Evans in bldg. grain elevators, 1838-53; established Eagle Iron Works Co., Buffalo, N.Y., 1838, Dunbar & Howell, later R. Dunbar & Son, designed and built grain elevators; patented some of his elevator improvements, in 1880's. Died Buffalo, Sept. 18, 1890.

DUNBAR, William, planter, scientist; b. Elgin, Scotland, 1749; s. Sir Archibald Dunbar; married, 7 children. Came to Fort Pitt (now Pitts.), began trading with Indians, 1771-73; partner John Ross in plantation, West Fla., 1773; founded 2d plantation, nr. Natchez, Miss., 1792; surveyor gen. Dist. of Natchez, 1798; conducted 1st meteorol. observations in Miss. Valley, 1799; mem. Am. Philos. Soc.; apptd. explorer of Hot Springs, Ark. area, 1804, for Red River area, 1805; mem. Territorial Legislature, Miss.; chief justice Ct. of Quarter Sessions; contbr. numerous articles on natural and phys. science to various jours. including Jour. Am. Philos. Soc. Died "The Forest," nr. Natchez, Oct. 1810.

DUNBAR, William, congressman, lawyer; b. Va., 1805. Moved to Alexandria, Va., began practice of law, early 1830's; moved to La., 1852; asso. justice La. Supreme Ct. (apptd. to fill vacancy), 1852-53; mem. U.S. Ho. of Reps. (Democrat) from La., 33d Congress, 1853-55. Died on his sugar plantation, Parish of St. Bernard, Mar. 18, 1861.

DUNCAN, Alexander, physician, congressman; b. Bottle Hill (now Madison) N.J., 1788; studied medicine. Practiced medicine; moved to Cincinnati; mem. Ohio Ho. of Reps., 1828-29, 31-32, Ohio Senate, 1832-34; mem. U.S. Ho. of Reps. (Whig) from Ohio, 25th-26th, 28th congresses, 1837-41, 43-45. Died Madisonville (now part of Cincinnati), Mar. 23, 1853; buried Laurel Cemetery.

DUNCAN, Daniel, congressman, businessman; b. Shippensburg, Cumberland County, Pa., July 22, 1806; attended Jefferson Coll., Canonsburg, Pa., 1825. Moved to Newark, O., 1828; became mcht.; mem. Ohio Ho. of Reps., 1843; mem. U.S. Ho. of Reps. (Whig) from Ohio, 30th Congress, 1847-49. Died Washington, D.C., May 18, 1849; buried Newark Graveyard.

DUNCAN, (William) Garnett, congressman; b. Louisville, Ky., Mar. 2, 1800; grad. Yale, 1821; studied law. Admitted to bar, 1822, began practice of law, Louisville; mem. U.S. Ho. of Reps. (Whig) from Ky., 30th Congress, 1847-49; moved to New Orleans, 1850, continued practice of law; ret., 1860, traveled in Europe, lived for a time in Paris, France, returned to U.S., 1875. Died Louisville, May 25, 1875; buried Cave Hill Cemetery.

DUNCAN, James, congressman; b. Phila., 1756; attended Princeton. Served as 1st prothonotary Adams County; commd. lt. in Col. Hazen's Regt., Revolutionary War, 1776, promoted capt., 1778; elected mem. U.S. Ho. of Reps. from Pa., 17th Congress, resigned before Congress assembled. Died Mercer County, Pa., June 24, 1844.

DUNCAN, James Henry, congressman, lawyer; b. Haverhill, Mass., Dec. 5, 1793; attended Phillips Exeter Acad.; grad. Harvard, 1812; studied law. Admitted to bar, 1815, began practice of law, Haverhill; served to rank of col. in militia; pres. Essex Agrl. Soc.; mem. Mass. Ho. of Reps., 1827, 37, 38, 57, Mass. Senate, 1828-31; del. Whig Nat. Conv., Harrisburg, Pa., 1839; apptd. commr. in bankruptcy, 1841; mem. U.S. Ho. of Reps. (Whig) from Mass., 31st-32d congresses, 1849-53; engaged in real estate bus. Died Haverhill, Feb. 8, 1869; buried Linwood Cemetery.

DUNCAN, Joseph, gov. Ill.; b. Paris, Ky., Feb. 22, 1794; s. Maj. Joseph and Ann Maria (McLaughlin) D.; m. Elizabeth Caldwell Smith, May 13, 1828. Commd. ensign 17th U.S. Infantry, 1812, promoted 2d lt., 1813; moved to Ill., 1818, farmed, expanded his land holdings; served as maj. gen. Ill. Militia, 1821-23, commanded militia troops in Black Hawk War, 1831; mem. Ill. Senate (Democrat) from Jackson County, 1824-26; mem. U.S. Ho. of Reps. from Ill., 20th-23d congresses, 1827-34; gov. Ill., 1834-38. Died Jacksonville, Ill., Jan. 15, 1844; buried Diamond Grove Cemetery, Jacksonville.

DUNCAN, William Addison, congressman; b. Cashtown, Adams County, Pa., Feb. 2, 1836; grad. Franklin and Marshall Coll., Lancaster, 1857; studied law. Admitted to bar, 1859, began practice of law, Gettysburg, Pa.; elected dist. atty., 1862, 68; mem. U.S. Ho. of Reps. (Democrat) from Pa., 48th Congress, 1883-84. Died Gettysburg, Nov. 14, 1884; buried Evergreen Cemetery.

DUNCANSON, Robert S., artist; b. N.Y. State, circa 1817; s. of a Scotch-Canadian father and a Negro mother. Exhibited in Cincinnati, 1842; commd. to paint series of mural landscapes for "Belmont" (home of Nicholas Longworth; now Taft Museum); made 2 visits to Europe, to Italy, 1853, to Britain, 1863-66, possibly a 3d visit, to Scotland, 1870-71; had mental and phys. breakdown. Died Detroit, Dec. 21, 1872.

DUNGLISON, Robley, med. educator; b. Keswick, Eng., Jan. 4, 1798; s. William and Elizabeth D.; attended Royal Coll. of Surgeons, 1818, Soc. of Apothecaries; M.D., U. Erlangen (Germany), 1823; M.D. (hon.), Yale, 1825; m. Harriette Leadham, Oct. 5, 1824, at least one child, Dr. Richard J. Prof. medicine U. Va., 1825-33; prof. U. Md., 1833-36, Jefferson Med. Coll., Phila., 1836-68; v.p. Am. Philos. Soc. Author: Human Physiology, 1832; Elements of Hygiene, 1835; The Practice of Medicine, 1842; A Dictionary of the English Language for the Use of the Blind, 1860. Died Apr. 1, 1869.

DUNHAM, Cyrus Livingston, congressman, lawyer; b. Dryden, Tompkins County, N.Y., Jan. 16, 1817; attended common schs.; studied law. Taught sch. for a time; admitted to bar; began practice of law, Salem, Ind., 1841; pros. atty. Washington County (Ind.), 1845; mem. Ind. Ho. of Reps., 1846-47; Democratic presdl. elector, 1848; mem. U.S. Ho. of Reps. (Democrat) from Ind., 31st-33d congresses, 1849-55; sec. of state (apptd. by Gov. Willard), 1859-60; served as col. 50th Regt., Ind. Volunteer Inf., U.S. Army, during Civil War; resumed practice of law, New Albany, Ind.; mem. Ind. Ho. of Reps., 1864-65; moved to Jeffersonville, Ind., 1871; judge Clark County Criminal Ct., 1871-74. Died Jeffersonville, Nov. 21, 1877; buried Walnut Ridge Cemetery.

DUNHAM, Ransom Williams, congressman, businessman; b. Savoy, Mass., Mar. 21, 1838; attended high sch., Springfield, Mass. Clk. life ins. co., 1855-57; moved to Chgo., 1857, became grain and provision commn. mcht.; pres. Chgo. Bd. of Trade, 1882; mem. U.S. Ho. of Reps. (Republican) from Ill., 48th-50th congresses, 1883-89. Died while on his way to attend Savoy centennial celebration, Springfield, Mass., Aug. 19, 1896; buried Mt. Hope Cemetery, Chgo.

DUNLAP, George Washington, congressman, lawyer; b. Walnut Hills, nr. Lexington, Ky., Feb. 22, 1813; grad. Transylvania U., Lexington, 1834; studied law. Admitted to bar, began practice of law, Lancaster, Ky.; commr. circuit ct., 1843-47; mem. Ky. Ho. of Reps., 1853; mem. U.S. Ho. of Reps. (Unionist) from Ky., 37th Congress, 1861-63, a mgr. apptd. by Ho. of Reps. to conduct i[m]peachment proceedings against West H. Humphre[ys] (U.S. judge for several dists. Tenn.), 1862; mem Border State Conv., 1861; Democratic presd[l.] elector, 1864. Died Lancaster, June 6, 188[6]; buried Lancaster Cemetery.

DUNLAP, James Boliver, artist; b. Indpls., Ma[r.] 7, 1825. Went to Cal., 1850, opened studio, Sa[n] Francisco; executed marble bust of John Sutter r[e]turned to Indpls., circa 1860 made bust of Lincoln 1860; painted portraits and landscapes; drew ca[r]toons for Indpls. Locomotive. Died Indpls., Sep[t.] 4, 1864.

DUNLAP, John, printer; b. Strabane, Irelan[d], 1747; m. Mrs. Elizabeth (Hayss) Ellison, Feb. 4, 1773. Came to Phila., 1757; apprenticed to unc[le] William Dunlap as printer, took over shop, 176[6]; founder weekly The Pa. Packet, 1771, became 1s[t] daily in Am., 1784; founder 1st troop Phila. Ci[ty] Cavalry, 1774, promoted 1st lt., 1781, capt., 179[4]; printed Declaration of Independence; printer t[o] Continental Congress, 1778; published U.S. Constr[itution] (its 1st publication) in Pa. Packet and Daily Ad[vertiser]; mem. Phila. Common Council, 1789-9[2]; maj. in charge of all Pa. Cavalry during suppressi[on] of Whisky Rebellion, 1794. Died Nov. 27, 181[2]; buried Christ Ch., Phila.

DUNLAP, Robert Pinckney, gov. Me.; b. Brun[s]wick, Me., Aug. 17, 1794; s. Capt. John and Ma[ry] (Tappan) D.; grad. Bowdoin Coll., 1815; m. Lyd[ia] Chapman, 1825, 4 children. Admitted to ba[r], 1818; mem. Me. Legislature, 1821-22, Me. Sen[]ate, 1824-28, 31-33; mem. Me. Exec. Council 1829; gov. Me., 1834-38; bd. overseers Bowdoi[n] Coll., 1821-59, pres. bd., 1843-59; mem. U.S. Ho. of Reps. from Me., 28th-29th congresses 1843-47; collector Port of Portland (Me.), 184[8]-49; postmaster Brunswick, 1853-57. Died Bruns[]wick, Oct. 20, 1859.

DUNLAP, William, theatre mgr., painter, au[]thor; b. Perth Amboy, N.J., Feb. 19, 1766; s. Samuel and Margaret (Sargeant) D.; at least [] children, John Alexander, Margaret Ann. Portraitis[t] N.Y.C., 1782; traveled in Europe 3 years, develope[d] interest in theatre; began writing plays; bough[t] part interest in Old American Co., N.Y.C., 179[6]; acting mgr., 1796-98, sole mgr., 1798-1805, wer[e] bankrupt; traveling miniaturist, 1805-06; gen. ass[t.] Park Theatre, 1806-11; established Monthly Re[]corder, 1811; asst. paymaster N.Y. Militia, 1814-16; painter, 1816-39; a founder N.A.D., 182[6]; wrote over 30 plays, best-known include: The Fa[]ther of an Only Child, The Italian Father, Leices[]ter, Andre; outstanding books include: History o[f] the American Theatre, 1832; History of the Ris[e] and Progress of the Arts of the United States 1834; A History of New York, for Schools, 1837. Died N.Y.C., Sept. 28, 1839; buried Perth Amboy.

DUNLAP, William Claiborne, congressman lawyer; b. Knoxville, Tenn., Feb. 25, 1798; at[]tended Ebenezer Acad., Maryville (Tenn.) Coll. 1813-17; studied law. Admitted to bar, bega[n] practice of law, Knoxville, 1819; served in India[n] campaign, 1818-19; moved to Bolivar, Tenn 1828; commd. in U.S. Volunteers, 1830; mem U.S. Ho. of Reps. (Democrat) from Tenn., 23d-24th congresses, 1833-37; judge 11th Circuit Ct of Tenn., 1840-49; mem. Tenn. Senate, 1851, 5[3]-57, Tenn. Ho. of Reps., 1857-59. Died nr. Mem[]phis, Tenn., Nov. 16, 1872; buried Elmwoo[d] Cemetery, Memphis.

DUNLOP, James, state senator; b. Chambers[]burg, Pa., 1795; s. Andrew and Sarah (Chambers) D.; grad. Dickinson Coll., Carlisle, Pa., 1812; m Maria Madeira. Admitted to Franklin County (Pa.) bar, 1817; mem. Pa. Senate from Franklin County 1824-Dec. 1827, Pa. Ho. of Reps. from Frankli[n] County, 1831; rep. dist. of Franklin, Cumberlan[d] and Adams counties in Pa. Conv., 1837; prepare[d] The General Laws of Pennsylvania, 1700-1846 Chronologically Arranged with Notes and Refer[]ences to all the Decisions of the Supreme Court o[f] Pennsylvania, Giving Construction to Such Laws 1847; published Digest of the General Laws of th[e] United States with References and Notes of De[]cisions, 1856. Died Balt., Apr. 9, 1856.

DUNMORE, 4th earl, see Murray, John.

DUNN, Alexander Gordon, artist; b. Glasgow Scotland, Dec. 16, 1815; married. Pattern designer Glasgow, until 1854; came to N.Y.C., 1854, re[]turned to Scotland, 1858, remained until 1867 settled permanently in U.S., 1867; lived in Bklyn. until 1885; moved to Holton, Kan., circa 1885 exhibited at Watercolor Soc. Bklyn., in 1870's Died Holton, Oct. 2, 1887.

DUNN, Charles, jurist; b. Bullitt's Old Lick Bullitt County, Ky., Dec. 28, 1799; s. John an[d] Amy (Burks) D.; m. Mary Schrader, 1821. Ad[]mitted to Ill. bar, 1820; acting commr. Ill. an[d] Mich. Canal, 1829; organizer, capt. of a company ring Black Hawk War; mem. Ill. Ho. of Reps., 35; chief justice Territory of Wisconsin, 1836-; mem. Wis. Constl. Conv., 1847-48, chmn. judiary com.; mem. Wis. Senate, 1853-56. Died r. 7, 1872; buried Mineral Point, Wis.

DUNN, George Grundy, congressman, lawyer; Washington County, Ky., Dec. 20, 1812; tended Ind. U. at Bloomington; studied law. ught sch., Bedford, Ind., 1833; admitted to bar, 35, began practice of law, Bedford; pros. atty. wrence County, Ind., 1842; mem. U.S. Ho. of ps. (Whig) from Ind., 30th Congress, 1847-49, Republican), 34th Congress, 1855-57; mem. Ind. nate, 1850-52. Died Bedford, Sept. 4, 1857; ried Green Hill Cemetery.

DUNN, George Hedford, congressman, lawyer; N.Y.C., Nov. 15, 1794; studied law. Admitted bar, 1822, began practice of law, Lawrencerg, Ind.; mem. Ind. Ho. of Reps., 1828, 32-33; omoter 1st railway in Ind.; mem. U.S. Ho. of ps. (Whig) from Ind., 25th Congress, 1837-39; eas. State of Ind., 1841-44; judge Dearborn ounty (Ind.); pres. Cincinnati & Indpls. R.R. ed Lawrenceburg, Jan. 12, 1854; buried New wn Cemetery.

DUNN, William McKee, congressman, judge adv., my officer; b. Hanover, Indiana Territory, Dec. , 1814; s. Williamson and Miriam (Wilson) D.; ad. State Sem. (later Ind. State U.), 1832; .M., Yale, 1835; m. Elizabeth Lanier. Prin. prep. pt. Hanover Coll., 1832; admitted to Ind. bar, 837; mem. lower house Ind. Legislature, 1837; l. Ind. Costl. Conv., 1850; mem. U.S. Ho. of eps. (Republican), Ind., 36th-37th congresses, 859-63, mem. com. mil. affairs, 1861-63; ensted Ind. Inf., 1861, aide-de-camp to Gen. Mcellan, 1861; commd. brig. gen. U.S. Volunteers, dge adv. of volunteers for Dept. of Mo., 1863-; del. Phila. Loyalists Conv., 1866; judge adv. n. U.S. Army, 1875-81. Died "Maplewood," airfax County, Va., July 24, 1887; buried Oak ll Cemetery, Washington, D.C.

DUNN, Williamson, pioneer, jurist; b. Crow's tation, Ky., Dec. 25, 1781; s. Samuel and Eleaor (Brewster) D.; m. Miriam Wilson, Sept. 1806, children, including William McKee. Pioneer in . Indiana; justice of peace, judge Ct. Common eas of Jefferson County, Indiana Teritory, 1811; ommd. capt. rangers by Pres. Madison during War 1812; asso. judge Circuit Ct. of Jefferson Coun-, 1814-16; became mem. Ind. Ho. of Reps., 816, speaker, 3d, 4th legislatures; commd. reister of land offices for Dist. of Terre Haute Ind.) 1820; helped lay out Town of Crawfordslle (Ind.), 1823; a founder Hanover Coll., 1829; lled vacancy Ind. Senate (Whig), 1837; probate dge Jefferson County, 1846. Died Hanover, Ind., ov. 11, 1854.

DUNSTER, Henry, coll. pres.; b. Lancashire, ng., 1609; s. Henry Dunster; B.A., Magdalene oll., Cambridge (Eng.) U., 1631, M.A., 1634; . Elizabeth Glover, June 22, 1641; m. 2d, Elizaeth Atkinson, 1644. Arrived in Mass., 1640; 1st res. Harvard, 1640-54, thought to be petitioner r act of Mass. Gen. Ct. establishing Harvard Coll., 642, also charter, 1650, forced out of presidency r religious reasons; minister, Scituate, Mass., 654-59. Died Scituate, Feb. 16, 1659.

DUPALAIS, Virginia Poullard, artist; b. Phila., Mar. 20, 1804; m. William Albert Twigg. Accomanied uncle Charles A. LeSueur to New Harmony, nd. (an exptl. utopian community), 1826; amaeur artist, did portraits in pen and pencil, includng that of Maximilian, Prince of Wied (who visted New Harmony, 1842). Died New Harmony, an. 8, 1864.

DuPONCEAU, Pierre Etinne (known in U.S. as uPonceau, Peter Stephen), lawyer, author; b. Isle e Rhe, France, June 3, 1760; hon. LL.D., Harvrd, 1820; m. Anne Perry, May 21, 1788. Apptd. apt. Continental Army, Feb. 18, 1788; became ide-de-camp to newly apptd. Maj. Gen. Von Steuen at Valley Forge, Feb. 1788; Livingston's nder-sec., Oct. 22, 1781-June 4, 1783; admitted s atty. Ct. Common Pleas, Phila., June 24, 1785; tty. Supreme Ct., 1786; translated from Bynkerhoek's original Latin, A Treatise on the Law of War . . . Being the First Book of his Quaestiones uris Publici, with notes, 1810; internationally ecognized for his contbns. to philology, includng work on N.Am. Indian langs.; founded Law cad. Phila., 1821; elected pres. Am. Philos. Soc., 828; mem. Acad. Arts and Scis. Author: A Disertation on the Nature and Extent of the Jurisdicion of the Courts of the United States, 1824; A rief View of the Constitution of the United tates, 1834; English Phonology, 1817; A Disourse on the Early History of Pennsylvania, 1817. ied Phila., Apr. 2, 1844.

Du PONT, Eleuthère Irénée, mfr.; b. Paris, rance, June 24, 1771; s. Pierre Samuel and Nicole Charlotte Marie Louise (Le Dée) Du Pont de Nemours; m. Sophie Madelaine Palmas, Nov. 26, 1791, at least 2 children including Henry. Trained in French state gunpowder works; came with family to Newport, R.I., 1801; founded gunpowder firm E. I. Du Pont de Nemours & Co., Wilmington, Del., 1802; successfully fulfilled various govt. contracts which helped firm to grow and branch out. Died Phila., Oct. 31, 1834.

Du PONT, Henry, mfr.; b. Eleutherian Mills, Wilmington, Del., Aug. 8, 1812; s. Eleuthère Irénée and Sophie Madelaine (Palmas) Du P.; grad. U.S. Mil. Acad., 1833; m. Louisa Bernard, 1837. Served as 2d lt. Del. Militia, 1833-34, maj. gen.; joined father in mfg. gunpowder, became head E. I. Du Pont de Nemours & Co., 1850, expanded co. with Crimean War profits, bought mills in Pa., began using Peruvian nitrate soda instead of saltpetre, set up factory in Cal., 1861, bought out Hazard and Cal. Powder cos., 1876. Died Del., Aug. 8, 1889.

Du PONT, Samuel Francis, naval officer; b. Bergen Point, N.J., Sept. 27, 1803; s. Victor Marie and Gabrielle de la Fire (de Pelleport) Du P.; m. Sophie Madeleine (du Pont), June 27, 1833. Apptd. midshipman U.S. Navy by Pres. Madison, 1815; commd. lt., 1826, comdr., 1843; mem. Sec. Bancroft's bd. organizers naval sch. at Annapolis, Md.; comdr. ship Congress, sailed from Norfolk, 1845; mem. bd. apptd. to consider appropriate study course and prepare regulations for govt. of naval acad., 1849; apptd. mem. bd. to investigate light-house establishment by U.S. sec. of treasury, 1851; naval officer representing govt. at N.Y. World's Fair, 1853; mem. naval efficiency bd., 1855; commd. capt., 1855; comdt. Phila. Navy Yard, 1860-61; sr. mem. commn. of conf. which prepared naval operations plans, 1860; in command of S. Atlantic Blockading Squadron, 1861, led successful expdn. against Port Royal, Va.; commd. rear adm., 1862, led operations along So. coast; directed unsuccessful attack on defenses of Charleston, S.C., 1863; mem. naval bd., 1865; monument erected by Act of Congress at Du Pont Circle, Washington, D.C., 1884. Died Phila., June 23, 1865.

Du PONT, Victor Marie, diplomat; b. Paris, France, Oct. 1, 1767; s. Pierre Samuel and Nicole Charlotte Marie Louise (Le Dée) Du Pont de Nemours; m. Gabrielle Josephine de la Fite de Pelleport, Apr. 9, 1794, at least 1 son, Samuel Francis. Employed by father (head commerce bur. in France); attaché to French legation in U.S., 1787-89, sec., 1791-92, 1st sec., 1795; a.d.c. to Gen. Lafayette, 1789-91; returned to France; acting French consul for Carolinas and Ga., 1796, consul, 1797; apptd. consul gen. in U.S., 1798; arrived in Newport, R.I.; founded V. Du Pont de Nemours Co. (commn. house), 1801, failed, 1805; partner in unsuccessful land speculation scheme, 1806-09; joined brother Irénée's mfg. interest in Del.; mem. Del. Legislature; dir. Bank of U.S. Died Phila., Jan. 30, 1827.

DUPRATZ, Antoine Simon Le Page, historical writer; b. in France, circa 1690. Came to La. as adventurer, 1718; granted duchy in Ark. area; overseer of plantation of Co. of the Indies; returned to La Rochelle, France, 1734. Author: Histoire de la Louisiane . . ., 1758. Died circa 1775.

DuPUY, Eliza Ann, novelist; b. Petersburg, Va., 1814. Governess to Thomas G. Ellis family, Natchez, Miss.; lived entire life in South. Author: Merton, a Tale of the Revolution; The Conspirator, 1850; The Huguenot Exiles, 1856; The Cancelled Will, 1872; All for Love, 1873; The Clandestine Marriage, 1875. Died New Orleans, Jan. 15, 1881.

DUQUESNE De MENNEVILLE, Marquis, colonial gov.; b. France; flourished circa 1740-55. Apptd. gov. New France, 1752; strengthened French forces in Am., built forts along western frontier, repulsed English and colonial advances into French territory; built Ft. Duquesne (became site of Pitts.); aided victory of French over English at Coulon de Villiers, 1754; returned to France, 1755.

DURAN, Narcisco, missionary; b. Castellon de Ampurias, Spain, Dec. 16, 1776. Became a Franciscan, 1792; worked at mission of San Jose, Cal., 1806-44; pres. of missions, 3 times, struggled unsuccessfully to stem the despoliation and seizure of ch. property, was so active in legal moves that Gov. Figueroa tried to have him exiled; protected by govt. at Mexico City; adminstr. Diocese of Cal., for brief time. Died Santa Barbara, Cal., June 1, 1846.

DURAND, Asher Brown, engraver, painter; b. Jefferson Village, N.J., Aug. 21, 1796; s. John and Rachel (Meyer) D.; m. Lucy Baldwin, Apr. 2, 1821; m. 2d, Mary Frank, 1834; at least 1 son, John. Apprenticed to steel-engraver Peter Maverick, 1812-17, partner, 1817-20; his 1st major work was engraving John Trumbull's painting The Signing of Declaration of Independence, 1823; engraved portraits, books, bank notes, until 1830's, then concentrated on painting; toured Europe, 1840-41, painted primarily landscapes; founder (with Thomas Cole) Am. sch. of landscape painting; mem. Lunch Club, Century Club; pres. N.A.D., 1845-61. Died Jefferson Village, Sept. 17, 1886; buried Greenwood Cemetery, Bklyn.

DURAND, Cyrus, engraver, inventor; b. Feb. 27, 1787; s. John and Rachel (Meyer) D.; m. Mrs. Phoebe Woodruff. Inherited his father's silversmithie, Newark, N.J., 1814; served with U.S. Army in War of 1812 for short time; made carding and weaving machines, 1815; patented "grammatical mirror," also machine to ornament columns, 1818; in engraving partnership with brother Asher, 1824-32; govt. engraver, Washington, D.C. Died Irvington, N.J., Sept. 18, 1868.

DURAND, Élie Magloire, pharmacist, botanist; b. Mayenne, France, Jan. 25, 1794; s. André Durand; m. Polymnia Rose Ducatel, Nov. 20, 1820; m. 2d, Marie Antoinette Berauld, Oct. 25, 1825; at least 1 son. Apprenticed to pharmacist; pharmacist in French army, 1813-14; came to U.S., 1816; in pharmacy partnership with Edme Ducatel, Balt., 1817-24; made trip to France, 1824-25; began drugstore, Phila., 1825 (became profl. and social center of Phila.'s physicians and botanists); mem. Phila. Acad. Natural Scis., Am. Philos. Soc.; v.p. Coll. of Pharmacy, 1844; retired, 1851, devoted rest of life to bot. studies; transported his herbarium to Paris, France, 1868, gave it to Jardin des Plantes. Co-translator: Manual of Materia Medica and Pharmacy, 1829. Author: Memoirs of Francois André Michaux and Thomas Nuitall. Died Aug. 14, 1873.

DURANT, Charles Person, aeronaut; b. N.Y.C., Sept. 19, 1805; s. William and Elizabeth (Woodruff) D.; m. Elizabeth Hamilton Freeland, Nov. 14, 1837. First native Am. balloonist, made about 40 ascensions; printer, lithographer. Author: Algae and Corallines of the Bay and Harbor of New York; Exposition, or a New Theory of Animal Magnetism with a Key to the Mysteries, 1837. Died Mar. 2, 1873.

DURANT, Henry, clergyman, coll. pres.; b. Acton, Mass., June 17, 1803; s. Henry and Lucy (Hunt) D.; grad. Yale, 1827; m. Mary Buffett, Dec. 10, 1833. Tutor, Yale, 1829-33; ordained pastor Congl. Ch., Byfield, Mass., 1833; head Dummer Acad., 1849; as result of his petition Coll. of Cal. chartered, 1855, elected 1st pres., 1870, resigned 1872; twice elected mayor of Oakland, Cal. Died Oakland, Jan. 22, 1875.

DURANT, Henry Fowle, lawyer, coll. founder; b. Hanover, N.H., Feb. 20, 1822; s. William and Harriet (Fowle) Smith; grad. Harvard, 1842; read law with father; m. Pauline Adeline Fowle, May 23, 1854, at least 2 children, Henry F., Pauline C. Admitted to Mass. bar, 1843; practiced in Lowell, Mass., 1843-48, Boston, 1848-63; sought solace in religion after death of his son; held revival meetings; trustee Mt. Holyoke, 1867; founded Wellesley Coll., 1870, served in various adminstrv. capacities rest of his life. Died Oct. 3, 1881.

DURANT, Thomas Clark, railroad promoter; b. Lee, Mass., Feb. 6, 1820; s. Thomas and Sybil (Wright) D.; grad. Albany Med. Coll., 1840; m. Heloise Timbrel, 2 children. Joined Henry Farnam in constrn. Mich. So. R.R., 1851, later (with Farnam) contracted for Chgo. & Rock Island and Miss. & Mo. railroads; v.p. U.P. R.R., Oct. 30, 1863-69, became chief figure in its mgmt.; secured charter of Credit Mobiler, became pres., largest stockholder; agreed to build 667 miles U.P. R.R., Aug. 16, 1867, became 1 of 7 trustees, virtual dictator of co., constrn. completed May 10, 1869 when U.P. tracks westward met Central Pacific tracks coming eastward, dropped from U.P. R.R. directorate, May 25, 1869, due to Credit Mobiler scandal. Died North Creek, N.Y., Oct. 5, 1885.

DURANT, Thomas Jefferson, lawyer; b. Phila., Aug. 8, 1817; s. John Waldo and Sarah (Heyliger) D.; m. Mary Harper. Admitted to La. bar; elected to La. Senate, 1846; U.S. dist. atty.; headed movement to organize La. as free state, 1862, pres. Free State Gen. Com., 1863; atty. gen. Mil. Govt. of La., commr. for purpose of carrying out registration of loyal citizens entitled to vote; pleaded Slaughter House Cases before Supreme Ct., won, 1876; retained as counsel for U.S. before Spanish and Am. Claims Commn., 1881. Died Washington, D.C., Feb. 3, 1882.

DURBIN, Elisha John, clergyman; b. Madison County, Ky., Feb. 1, 1800; studied at sem. of St. Thomas, also at Bardstown. Ordained priest Roman Catholic Ch., 1822; given parish which included a third of Ky., 1824, covered region (11,000 miles) on horeseback for next 60 years; later dir. small mission, Princeton, Ky., chaplain of acad., Shelbyville, Ky. Died Shelbyville, 1887.

DURBIN, John Price, clergyman, coll. pres.; b. Paris, Ky., Oct. 10, 1800; s. Hozier and Elizabeth (Nunn) D.; attended Miami U.; grad. Cincinnati Coll., 1825; m. Frances B. Cook, Sept. 6, 1827; m. 2d, Miss Cook. Licensed as preacher Methodist Episcopal Ch., 1818; itinerant preacher in Ind. and Ohio for 7 years; prof. langs. Augusta (Ky.) Coll., 1825-31; chaplain U.S. Senate, 1831; editor Christian Advocate and Jour., 1832-34; pres. Dickinson Coll., 1834-45; pastor in Phila., 1845-50; sec. of missionary soc., 1850-72. Author: Observations in Europe, 1844; Observations in the East, 1845. Died N.Y.C., Oct. 19, 1876; buried Laurel Hill Cemetery, Phila.

DURELL, Daniel Meserve, congressman, lawyer; b. Lee, N.H., July 20, 1769; grad. Dartmouth, 1794; studied law. Admitted to bar, 1797, began practice of law, Dover, N.H.; mem. U.S. Ho. of Reps from N.H., 10th Congress, 1807-09; mem. N.H. Ho. of Reps., 1816; chief justice Dist. Ct. of Common Pleas, 1816-21; U.S. atty. for Dist. N.H., 1830-34. Died Dover, Apr 29, 1841; buried Pine Hill Cemetery.

DURELL, Edward Henry, jurist b. Portsmouth, N.H., July 14, 1810; s. Daniel Meserve and Elizabeth (Wentworth) D.; grad. Harvard, 1831; m. Mary Gebhart, June 8, 1875. Admitted to N.H. bar, 1834; mem. New Orleans Common Council, 1854; drafted city charter for New Orleans which became law, 1856; pres. New Orleans Bur. Finance, 1862; mayor New Orleans (by mil. appointment), 1863; judge Eastern dist. La., 1863, extended jurisdiction over entire state, 1866-74; pres. N.H. Constl. Conv., 1864; del. to Republican Nat. Conv. Balt., 1864. Died Schoharie, N.Y., Mar. 29, 1887.

DURFEE, Job, jurist; b. Tiverton, R.I., Sept. 20, 1790; s. Thomas and Mary (Lowden) D.; grad. Brown U., 1813; m. Judith Borden. Admitted to R.I. bar, 1814; mem. R.I. Gen. Assembly (Republican) from Tiverton, 1816-20; me. U.S. Ho. of Reps. from R.I. 17th-18th ocngresses, 1821-25; mem. R.I. Ho. of Reps., 1826-29, speaker, 1827-29; elected asso. justice R.I. Supreme Ct., 1833, chief justice, 1835-47. Author: Panidea, 1846. Died Tiverton, July 26, 1847; buried Quacket Neck, R.I.

DURFEE, Nathaniel Briggs, congressman; b. Tiverton, R.I., Sept. 29, 1812. Engaged in agriculture, maintained fruit orchard; mem. R.I. Ho. of Reps., 11 years; mem. U.S. Ho. of Reps. from R.I. (Am. Party candidate), 34th Congress, 1855-57, (Republican), 35th Congress, 1857-59; served as county clk. Died Tiverton, Nov. 9, 1872; buried family burial ground nr. Tiverton.

DURFEE, Zoheth Sherman, steel mfr.; b. New Bedford, Mass., Apr. 22, 1831; s. Thomas and Delight (Sherman) D. Trained as blacksmith; obtained patent rights of William Kelly (Bessemer's Am. counterpart), set up Kelly Pneumatic Process Co., Mich., 1863, produced 1st Am. steel by Bessemer blast process, 1864; combined his firm with similar N.Y. co. to form joint-stock co., sec.-treas. of co., 1866-80. Died Providence, R.I., June 8, 1880.

DURIVAGE, Francis Alexander, journalist; b. Boston, 1814; s. Francis and Lucy (Everett) D.; m. Almira Alderworth. Paris corr. for Am. papers; devotée of Delsarte system of theatrical staging; contbd. to many periodicals and papers; wrote some unacted plays; co-editor Ballou's Pictorial. Translator: History of the Revolution of 1848 (Lamartine). Compiler: Popular Cyclopedia of History, 1845; Life Scenes from the World Around Us, 1853. Died Feb. 1, 1881.

DURKEE, Charles, senator, businessman; b. Royalton, Vt., Dec. 10, 1805; attended Burlington (Vt.) Acad. Became a mcht. moved to Wis., 1836; a founder Southport (now Kenosha, Wis.); engaged in agriculture and lumbering; mem. Territorial Legislature, 1836-38, 47-48; mem. U.S. Ho. of Reps. (Free-Soiler) from Wis., 31st-32d congresses, 1849-53; del. World's Peace Conv., Paris; mem. U.S. Senate (Republican) from Wis., 1855-61; apptd. gov. Utah Territory, 1865, resigned due to failing health. Died Omaha, Neb., Jan. 14, 1870; buried Green Ridge Cemetery, Kenosha.

DURKEE, John, b. Windham, Conn., Dec. 11, 1728; s. William and Susannah (Sabin) D.; m. Martha Wood, Jan. 3, 1753. Innkeeper, justice of peace, Norwich, Conn.; mem. Conn. Gen. Assembly; served from 2d lt. to maj. Conn. Militia, French and Indian Wars; apptd. mem. com. to arrange correspondence system between Conn. Sons of Liberty and those of other colonies; chosen mem. com. to recommend Norwich's refraining from importation of some Brit. manufacture; founder Ft. Durkee (Pa.), 1769, renamed it Wilkes-Barre (for John Wilkes and Col. Isaac Barre); served with Continental Army, 1775-81, maj., then lt. col. 3d Conn. Regt., lt. col., then col. 20th Regt., col. 4th, 1st Conn. regts.; served with Sullivan's expdn. against the Six Nations, 1779. Died Norwich, Conn., May 29, 1782.

DURRIE, Daniel Steele, librarian; b. Albany, N.Y., Jan. 2, 1819; s. Horace and Johannah (Steele) D.; m. Ann Holt, Oct. 15, 1844. Apprenticed to his uncle, a bookseller, took over shop, 1844, lost everything in Albany's 1848 fire; moved to Madison, Wis., 1850; became interested in Wis. Hist. Soc. through acquaintance with L. C. Draper; became librarian of soc., 1856-92. Author: A History of Madison, The Capital of Wisconsin, Including the Four Lake Country, 1874; Bibliographia Genealogica Americana; . . ., 1868. Died Madison, Aug. 31, 1892.

DURRIE, George Henry, artist; b. Hartford, Conn., June 6, 1820; received instrn. from Nathaniel Jocelyn, 1839. Painted portraits around New Haven and Bethany (Conn.), later in Conn. and N.J., 1840-42; settled in New Haven; made occasional profl. trips to N.J., N.Y. and Va.; became landscape painter, circa 1850, did landscapes which were engraved and published by Currier & Ives. Died Oct. 15, 1863.

DURYEE, Abram, mcht., army officer; b. N.Y.C., Apr. 29, 1815; s. Jacob and Eliza Duryee; m. Caroline Allen, 1838, 4 children. Became sgt. 142d Regt., N.Y. Militia, 1833, sgt. maj., 1835; sgt. 7th Regt., 1838, commd. capt., 1843, maj., 1845, lt. col., 1845, col., 1849, acting brig. gen., 1861; organized voluntary regt. Duryee's Zouaves, 1861, served at Battles of Big Bethel and Fed. Hill in Civil War; police commr. N.Y.C., 1873, dockmaster, 1884. Died N.Y.C., Sept. 27, 1890.

du SABLE, Jean Baptiste Point, see Point du Sable, Jean Baptiste.

DU SIMITIÉRE, Pierre Eugéne, artist; b. Geneva, Switzerland, circa 1736. Spent 10 years in W.I. as portrait painter; arrived N.Y.C., 1765; moved to Burlington, N.J., then to Phila., 1766; elected mem. Am. Philos. Soc. (because of studies in natural history), curator, 1776-81; America's 1st good portraitist, painted many of leaders of Revolution. Died Phila., Oct. 1784; buried St. Peter's Cemetery, Phila.

DUSTIN, Hannah, pioneer; b. Haverhill, Mass., Dec. 23, 1657; d. Michael and Hannah (Webster) Emerson; m. Thomas Dustin, Dec. 3, 1677, at least 13 children. Carried off by Indians in raid, 1697, killed 10 of her captors, returned safely to Boston bearing 10 scalps; rewarded with 25 pounds by Gen. Ct. Died circa 1732.

DUTTON, Henry, jurist, gov. Conn.; b. Litchfield County, Conn., Feb. 12, 1796; s. Thomas and Tenty (Punderson) D.; grad. Yale, 1818, LL.D., 1822; m. Elizabeth Toy, 1823, 4 children including Henry Melzar. Tutor, Yale, 1821-23, became prof. law, 1847; admitted to Conn. bar, 1823; mem. Conn. Senate, 1849; mem. lower house Conn. Legislature from New Haven, 1850-52; judge New Haven County Ct., 1852; gov. Conn., 1854-55; judge Supreme Ct. Errors and Superior Ct. of Conn., 1861-66. Author: Swift's Digest Revised, 2 vols., 1848-51; co-author Digest of the Connecticut Reports, 1833. Died New Haven, Apr. 12, 1869.

DUVAL, William Pope, lawyer, congressman; b. Richmond, Va., 1784; s. William and Ann (Pope) D.; m. Nancy Hynes, 1804; children—Elizabeth, Harrison, Thomas Howard, John Crittenden, Mary, Laura, Marcia. Admitted to bar, 1803; mem. U.S. Ho. of Reps. (Republican) from Ky., 13th Congress, 1813-15; judge Superior Ct. E. Fla., 1821; 1st civil gov. E. Fla. (effected peaceable transfer of Seminole Indians to S. Fla.), 1822-34, governed ably until 1833, became symbol of Washington rule as desire for statehood increased with population, conflicts arose, removed from office by Pres. Jackson; rep. from Calhoun County in Constl. Conv., St. Joseph, Fla., 1838, chmn. com. on Fla. exec. dept., helped write Fla. Constn., 1838; mem. Fla. Senate from middle dist., 1839-42, pres., 1840; law agt. for Fla., 1841-48; commr. to settle No. boundary Fla., 1845; unsuccessful candidate for U.S. Congress, 1848. Model for 2 lit. characters: Ralph Ringwood in Wolfert's Roost (Washington Irving); James K. Paulding's Nimrod Wilfire. Died Washington, D.C., Mar. 19, 1854; buried Congressional Cemetery, Washington.

DUVALL, Gabriel, asso. justice U.S. Supreme Ct.; b. "Marietta" nr. Buena Vista, Prince George's County, Md., Dec. 6, 1752; s. Benjamin and Susanna (Tyler) D.; m. Mary Bryce, July 24, 1787; m. 2d, Jane Gibbon, May 5, 1795; 1 son, Edmund Bryce. Elected mustermaster and commissary of stores for Md., 1776; served as pvt. Md. Militia in battles of Brandywine, Morristown; admitted to Md. bar, 1778; mem. Md. Gov.'s Council, 1783, 84; mem. Md. Ho. of Dels., 1787-94; mem. U.S. Ho. of Reps. from Md., 3d-4th congresses, Nov. 11, 1794-Mar. 28, 1796; chief justice Md. Gen. Ct., 1796-1802; 1st comptroller U.S. Treasury under Thomas Jefferson, 1802-11; as justice U.S. Supreme Ct., 1812-35; dissented cases The Trustees of Dartmouth College vs. Wo ward, Mima Queen and Child vs. Hepburn (uph use of hearsay evidence in proving freedom of slave's ancestor). Died Prince George's Coun Mar. 6, 1844; buried "Marietta".

DUVERNAY, Ludger, journalist; b. Verché Que., Can., Jan. 22, 1799. Became editor La zette, at Three Rivers, 1817, L'Argus, 1826, fou er (with N. Morin) La Minerve, Montreal, Qu Can., 1827, editor for many years; founded Soc. St. John the Baptist, 1834; chose maple leaf Canada's nat. emblem; extremely active in cause French Can.; forced to flee Can. after rebelli 1837-38; settled in Burlington, Vt., founded Patriote Canadien, 1849; returned to Montreal a union of Can., again edited La Minerve. Died N 28, 1852.

DUYCKINCK, Evert Augustus, editor; b. N.Y. Nov. 23, 1816; s. Evert D. and Harriet June D ckinck; grad. Columbia, 1835; read law with J Anthon; m. Margaret Wolfe Panton, Apr. 1840, sons (all died young). Admitted to N.Y. bar, 18 made trip to Europe, 1838-39; co-editor Arctur A Journal of Books and Opinion, 1840-42; edi Literary World, 1847; owner, publisher (with bro er George) of a jour., 1848-53; editor Cyclopae of Am. Literature, 1855; edited some of Thackera 1st Am. editions; corr. sec. N.Y. Hist. Soc.; trus Columbia Coll., N.Y. Soc. Library; contbr. to N Portrait Gallery of Eminent Americans; Lives a Portraits of the Presidents of the United Stat wrote memorials of John Allen, 1864, Frances Hawks, 1871, Fitz-greene Walleck, 1877. Died A 13, 1878.

DUYCKINCK, George Long, writer; b. N.Y. Oct. 17, 1823; s. Evert and Harriet June Duyckin attended Geneva (now Hobart) Coll., grad. U City of N.Y., 1843. Took trips to Europe, 18 48, 57; an editor (with brother Evert) Liter World, 1848-53, Cyclopaedia of Am. Literatu 1855; mem. exec. com. Gen. Protestant Episco Sunday Sch. Union Ch. Book Soc., 1855-57, tre soc., 1857. Author: biographies of George Herbe 1858, Thomas Ken, 1859, Jeremy Taylor, 18 Hugh Latimore, 1861. Died Mar. 30, 1863.

DUYCKINCK, Gerrit, glazier; b. New Amsterd (now N.Y.C.), circa 1660; s. Evert Duyckinck. A mitted freeman of city, 1698/99; assisted his fat in making and painting of glass for churches a pvt. homes of Dutch towns in New Eng.; credit with painting several portraits in oil. Died N.Y.C circa 1710.

DVORÁK, Antonin, composer; b. Mühlhause Bavaria (now Milevsko, Czechoslovakia), Sept. 1841; grad. Prague (Czechoslovakia) Organ Sc 1862; Mus. Doc., Cambridge U., 1891. Became vi player at Nat. Theatre, Prague; produced his important composition (hymn for male chorus a orch.), circa 1874; received govt. stipend, 18 allowing him to devote himself to compositi gained wide reputation with Stabat Mater, 18 dir. Nat. Conservatory of Music, N.Y.C., 1892-9 composed 9th Symphony (From the New Worl while in U.S. (during summer vacation in Spillvil Ia.); returned to Prague, 1895; proponent of natio alism in music. Other works include: Humoresq (best known single melody), The Spectre's Bri (cantata), St. Ludmilla (oratorio), numerous oper symphonies, concertos, songs, dances. Died Prag May 1, 1904.

DWENGER, Joseph, clergyman; b. Stallotov (now Minster), O., Sept. 7, 1837; s. Gerhard and Maria C. (Wirdt) D.; attended Mt. St. Mary of the West. Ordained priest, Roman Catholic Ch 1859; sec. and missionary Congregation of the Pr cious Blood, 1867-72; bishop of Fort Wayne, In 1872-93; founder orphan asylum for boys, Lafayett Ind., 1875, orphanage for girls, Fort Wayne, 18 Died Fort Wayne, Jan. 22, 1893; buried Fo Wayne Cathedral.

DWIGHT, Benjamin Franklin, architect; b. Bo ton; ed. Boston. Apprenticed to George Snell; draft man with Arthur Gilman, designed several count houses; established archtl. office, 1862; design and built comml. and public bldgs. in Boston, 18 73, including Eastern Express Bldg., Selwyn Theat Burnham Store, several large warehouses; later d signed Globe Theatre, Hotel Berkeley, Hathaw Bldg., several country and city residences; archite Music Hall, Worcester, Mass., Town Hall, Glouce ter, Mass., bldgs. for Mil. Acad., Togus, Me. Di Oct. 1893.

DWIGHT, Benjamin Woodbridge, educator; b. Ne Haven, Conn., Apr. 5, 1816; s. Benjamin Wesl and Sophia Woodbridge (Strong) D.; grad. Hamilt Coll., N.Y., 1835; grad. Yale Divinity Sch., 18 m. Wealthy Jane Dewey, 1846, 3 daus., 1 son; 2d, Charlotte Sophia Parish, 1 dau. Tchr., Hamilt Coll., 1838-41; founder 1st Congregational (n esbyn.) Ch., Joliet, Ill., 1844; ordained by Presbytery of Chgo., 1845; established Dwight's High h. (comml. and classical boys' sch.), Bklyn., 1846-; founder rural art assn., Clinton, N.Y., 1854; tablished boarding sch., Clinton, 1858-63, N.Y.C., 63-68. Died Sept. 18, 1889.

DWIGHT, Edmund, cotton mfr., philanthropist; Springfield, Mass., Nov. 28, 1780; s. Jonathan d Margaret (Ashley) D.; grad. Yale, 1799; m. ary Eliot, Apr. 19, 1809; 1 son, Edmund B. Mem. ass. Gen. Ct. from Springfield, 1810-13, 15; ected 4 cotton mills, by 1831, called 1st Boston Springfield Mfg. Co., later Chicopee Mfg. Co.; omoter of Western R.R. (from Worcester, Mass. Albany, N.Y.), mem. 1st bd. dirs., 1836-39, ected a dir. on behalf of state by Mass. Legisture, 1842, pres., 1843; influenced passing of h. law, 1837, mem. Mass. Bd. Edn. established law; contbr. $10,000, later $5,000 for establishment of normal schs., on condition that state atch amounts; posthumously praised by Mass. Bd. Edn. as key figure in its establishment; privately id part of Horace Mann's salary, 16 years; a under of cotton mfg. in New Eng. Died Boston, pr. 1, 1849.

DWIGHT, Francis, educator; b. Springfield, Mass., ar. 14, 1808; s. James Scutt and Mary (Sanford) .; grad. Harvard, 1827, Harvard Law Sch., 1830; udent law sch. Northampton, Mass.; m. Catherine an Rensselaer Schermerhorn, July 4, 1834, m. 2d, atherine Waters Yates, Apr. 20, 1843. Took 1 year and tour of Europe; engaged in unsuccessful pracce law; moved to Mich. Territory for short period; under Dist. Sch. Jour. of the State of N.Y., 1840 became ofcl. state publ.); supt. sch., Albany, N.Y.; l. dirs. Albany Normal Sch. Died Dec. 15, 1845.

DWIGHT, Henry Williams, congressman, lawyer; Stockbridge, Mass., Feb. 26, 1788; attended illiams Coll., Williamstown, Mass.; studied law. dmitted to bar, 1809, began practice of law, ockbridge; served as aide-de-camp with rank of l. on staff Gen. Whiton, during War of 1812; em. Mass. Ho. of Reps., 1818, 34; mem. U.S. o. of Reps. from Mass., 17th-21st congresses, 321-31; breeder of purebred sheep and cattle. ied N.Y.C., Feb. 21, 1845; buried Stockbridge emetery.

DWIGHT, Jeremiah Wilbur, congressman, businessan; b. Cincinnatus, Cortland County, N.Y., Apr. , 1819; attended Burhan's Sch., Dryden, N.Y.; arried, at least 1 son, John Wilbur. Engaged in siness pursuits, farming, real-estate, mfg. and le of lumber; chmn. bd. suprs. Town of Dryn, 1857-58; mem. N.Y. State Assembly, 1860-; apptd. mem. senatorial dist. war com. by ov. Morgan, 1861; del. Republican nat. convs., 368, 72, 76, 80, 84; dir., mem. exec. com., v.p. . Central R.R. for many years; mem. U.S. Ho. Reps. (Rep.) from N.Y., 45th-47th congresses, 877-83. Died Dryden, Nov. 26, 1885; buried reen Hills Cemetery.

DWIGHT, John Sullivan, music critic, editor; b. oston, May 13, 1813; s. Dr. John and Mary (Cor-y) D.; grad. Harvard, 1832, Harvard Divinity Sch., 336; m. Mary Bullard, Feb. 12, 1851. A founder en. Assn. of Mems. of Pierian Sodality (Harvard usical assn.), 1837; ordained to ministry Unitarian h., pastor ch., Northampton, Mass., 1840; mem. ranscendentalist Club; joined Brook Farm Settleent, 1841, taught music, Latin there; editor mus. our. Harbinger; choir dir. W. H. Channing's Regious Union Associationists, 1847-51; lectr., writer n music; publisher-editor Dwight's Jour. of Music: Paper of Literature and Art, 1851-58, editor, 358-81; trustee Perkins Inst. for the Blind; mem. aturday Club; v.p. Harvard Musical Assn., 1855-73, res., 1873-93. Author: (translator) Select Minor oems Translated from the German of Goethe and chiller, 1839; The History of Handel and Haydn ociety of Boston, Mass., 1883. Died Boston, Sept. , 1893.

DWIGHT, Nathaniel, physician; b. Northampton, Mass., Jan. 31, 1770; s. Maj. Timothy and Mary Edwards) D.; studied medicine with Dr. M. F. ogswell, Hartford, Conn.; m. Rebecca Robbins, June 4, 1798, 8 children. Began practice medicine, artford; served as army surgeon, for short period; racticed medicine Westfield, Mass., New London nd Wethersfield, Conn.; entered ministry, 1812-20; esumed practice medicine Providence, R.I. and Norich, Conn.; strong advocate of improving conditions insane. Author: A Short But Comprehensive Sysem of the Geography of the World: By Way of uestion and Answer, 1795; Sketches of the Lives f the Signers of the Declaration of Independence, 830. Died Oswego, N.Y., June 11, 1831.

DWIGHT, Sereno Edwards, educator, clergyman; b. airfield, Conn., May 18, 1786; s. Timothy and Mary (Woolsey) D.; grad. Yale, 1803; m. Susan dwards Daggett, Aug. 28, 1811. Tchr., Litchfield, onn., 1803-04; amanuensis (sec.) to his father pres. of Yale); tutor at Yale, 1806-10; practiced aw, New Haven, Conn., 1810-16; licensed to preach by West Assn. of Ministers of New Haven, 1816; chaplain U.S. Senate, 1816-17; ordained to ministry; pastor Park Street Ch., Boston, 1817-26; traveled to Europe, 1824-25; founder (with brother Henry) boarding sch. for boys, New Haven, 1828-31; tchr., pres. Hamilton Coll., 1833-35; agt. Pa. Colonization Soc., 1835-38. Author: The Hebrew Wife, 1836; The Works of Pres. Edwards: With Memoir of His Life, 1830; Select Discourses of S. E. Dwight, D.D., 1851. Died Phila., Nov. 30, 1850; buried New Haven.

DWIGHT, Theodore, congressman, journalist; b. Northampton, Mass., Dec. 15, 1764; s. Maj. Timothy and Mary (Edwards) D.; m. Abigail Alsop, Sept. 9, 1792. Admitted to bar, 1787; spoke against slavery before Conn. Soc. for Promotion Freedom, 1794; mem. U.S. Ho. of Reps. (federalist) from Conn., 4th Congress, 1806-07; mem. Conn. Council, 1809-15; sec. Hartford Conv., 1815 (published jour. of this conv. with review of steps to War of 1812, 1833); founder Daily Advertiser, Albany, N.Y., 1815, N.Y. Daily Advertiser, 1817; editor Hartford Couvant, Conn. Mirror; cousin of Aaron Burr. Author: History of the Hartford Convention, 1833; Life and Character of Thomas Jefferson as Exhibited in his Own Writings, 1839. Died N.Y.C., June 12, 1846; buried Greenwood Cemetery, Bklyn.

DWIGHT, Theodore, author, editor; b. Hartford, Conn., Mar. 3, 1796; s. Theodore and Abigail (Alsop) D.; grad. Yale, 1814; m. Eleanor Boyd, Apr. 24, 1827. Took European grand tour, 1818-19, lived abroad until 1833; worked on father's N.Y. Daily Advertiser; author, editor, translator English books into Spanish; worked on various jours.; established Dwight's Am. Mag. and Family Newspaper, 1845-52; with George Walter encouraged some 3000 Free-Soilers to settle in Kan., 1854-58. Author: A Journal of A Tour in Italy in the Year 1821, published 1824; Lessons in Greek, 1833; Open Covenants, or Nunneries and Popish Seminaries Dangerous to the Morals and Degrading to the Character of A Republican Community, 1836; The Roman Republic of 1849, published 1851; Life of Gen. Garibaldi, Translated from His Private Papers with the History of His Splendid Exploits in Rome, Lombardy, Sicily and Naples of the Present Time, 1861. Died N.Y.C., Oct. 16, 1866; buried N.Y.C.

DWIGHT, Theodore William, lawyer, educator; b. Catskill, N.Y., July 18, 1822; s. Benjamin Woolsey and Sophia (Strong) D.; grad. Hamilton Coll., 1840; LL.D. (hon.), Rutgers Coll., 1859, Columbia, 1860, Yale, 1892; attended Yale Law Sch., 1841; m. Mary Bond, Aug. 24, 1847, 3 children. Tutor, Hamilton Coll., 1842-46; admitted to N.Y. bar, 1845; apptd. Maynard prof. of law history, civil polity and polit. economy Hamilton Coll., 1846, head Law Sch., 1855; prof. municipal law Columbia Law Sch., 1858; apptd. to com. to examine N.Y. State Prison Systems, 1866; published Report on the Prisons and Reformatories of the United States and Canada, 1867; del. N.Y. Constl. Conv., 1867; mem. U.S. Judiciary Com., 1867; chmn. legislative com. of Com. of Seventy, 1873; mem. Commn. of Appeals, 1873; v.p. N.Y. State Bd. Pub. Charities; pres. N.Y. State Prison Assn.; N.Y. state commr. to Internat. Prison Congress, Stockholm, Sweden, 1878. Author: Argument in the Court of Appeals in the Rose Will Case, 1863; Cases Extracted from the Report of the Commissioners of Charities in England and the Disposition of Property for Charitable Uses, 1864. Asso. editor Am. Law Register. Died Clinton, N.Y., June 29, 1892.

DWIGHT, Thomas, congressman, lawyer; b. Springfield, Mass., Oct. 29, 1758; grad. Harvard, 1778; studied law. Admitted to bar, began practice of law, Springfield; mem. Mass. Ho. of Reps., 1794-95, Mass. Senate, 1796-1803; mem. U.S. Ho. of Reps. (Federalist) from Mass., 8th Congress, 1803-05; selectman Town of Springfield, 1806-09, 11; mem. Mass. Gov.'s Council, 1808-09. Died Springfield, Jan. 2, 1819; buried Peabody Cemetery.

DWIGHT, Timothy, coll. pres., author; b. Northampton, Mass., May 14, 1752; s. Maj. Timothy and Mary (Edwards) D.; grad. Yale, 1769, M.A., 1772; LL.D. (hon.), Harvard, 1810; m. Mary Woolsey, Mar. 3, 1777. Headmaster, Hopkins Grammar Sch., New Haven, Conn., 1769-71; tutor Yale, 1771-77; licensed to preach, 1777; chaplain Gen. S.H. Parson's Conn. Brigade, Continental Army, 1777-79; mem. Mass. Legislature, 1781-82; ordained to ministry Congregational Ch., 1783; pres. Yale, 1795-1817, prof. theology, founder med. dept.; a projector Andover Theol. Sem.; missionary for Soc. of Conn.; mem. Am. Bd. Commrs. for Fgn. Missions; mem. group called "Hartford Wits." Author: The Conquest of Canaan (1st Am. epic poem), 1785; Greenfield Hill, 1794; Theology, Explained and Defended, 5 vols., 1818-19; Travels in New England and New York, 1821. Died New Haven, Jan. 11, 1817.

DWIGHT, William, army officer, cotton mfr.; b. Springfield, Mass., July 14, 1831; s. William and Elizabeth (White) D.; attended U.S. Mil. Acad., 1849-53; m. Anna Robeson, Jan. 1, 1856. Cotton mfr., Boston and Phila.; commd. capt. 13th Inf., U.S. Army, 1861; commd. lt. col. 70th N.Y. Volunteers, 1861, col., 1861; brevetted brig. gen. for gallantry at Battle of Williamsburg, 1862; helped arrange surrender of Port Hudson, 1863; chief of staff under N.P. Banks on Red River expdn., 1864; commanded 1st div. XIX Corps, Sheridan's Army; mgr., dir. White Water Valley R.R. after Civil War. Died Boston, Apr. 21, 1888.

DWINELL, Justin, congressman, lawyer; b. Shaftsbury, Vt., Oct. 28, 1785; attended Williams Coll., Williamstown, Mass.; grad. Yale, 1808; studied law. Admitted to bar, 1811, began practice of law, Cazenovia, N.Y.; mem. N.Y. State Assembly, 1821-22; mem. U.S. Ho. of Reps. from N.Y., 18th Congress, 1823-25; judge Madison County (N.Y.) Ct. of Common Pleas, 1828-33; dist. atty. Madison County, 1837-45. Died Cazenovia, Sept. 17, 1850; buried Evergreen Cemetery.

DYER, Alexander Brydie, soldier, ordnance expert; b. Richmond, Va., Jan. 10, 1815; s. William Hay and Margaret (Brydie) D.; grad. U.S. Mil. Acad., 1837; m. Elizabeth Allen, Feb. 6, 1840, 6 children. 2d lt., 3d Arty., 1837, in Fla. War, 1837-38; chief ordnance Army in N.M., 1846; capt. Ordnance Corps, Mar. 3, 1853; assigned command Nat. Armory, Springfield, Mass., Aug. 21, 1861; maj. Ordnance Corps, Mar. 3, 1863; chief ordnance U.S. Army (brig. gen.), Sept. 1864; invented cannon projectile; brevetted capt. Mexican War, brevetted maj. gen., Mar. 13, 1865. Died Washington, D.C., May 20, 1874.

DYER, Eliphalet, Continental congressman, jurist; b. Windham, Conn., Sept. 14, 1721; s. Col. Thomas and Lydia (Backus) D.; gra A.B., A.M., Yale, 1740, LL.D. (hon.), 1787; A.M. (hon.), Harvard, 1744; m. Huldah Bowen. Apptd. capt. Conn. Militia, 1745, lt. col. regt., 1755; admitted to Conn. bar, 1746; dist. rep. (to Conn. Gen. Assembly, 1747-62; organizer Susquehanna Co., 1753, purchased lands from Six Nations, 1754, laid out Conn. settlement in Wyoming Valley, West of what was then N.Y. Province, 1774, disputed title with Pa., 1763, argued case before congressional com., 1782, lost title for Conn.; mem. Conn. Gov.'s Council, 1762-84; comptroller Port of New London (Conn.), 1764; Conn. del. to Stamp Act Congress, 1765; asso. judge Conn. Superior Ct., 1766; mem. 1st Continental Congress from Conn., 1774; mem. Conn. Com. of Safety, 1775; Conn. commr. at Hartford Conv., 1780; chief justice Conn. Supreme Ct., 1789-93. Died Windham, May 13, 1807.

DYER, Mary, heretic; b. Eng., circa 1610; m. William Dyer, 7 children. Came to Mass. Bay Colony, 1635; mem. Wilson's Boston Ch., 1635-37; supported Anne Hutchinson during Antinomian controversy, 1636, went to R.I. with her, 1637; lived in Eng., 1650-57, became a Quaker; returned to R.I., 1657, preached Quaker beliefs; expelled from New Haven, 1658; visited Boston, was expelled, 1659; returned to Boston, was condemned, reprieved and expelled; made 3d visit to Boston, was again condemned. Hung for heresy (after refusing offer of life if she would leave Boston), June 1, 1660.

DYLANDER, John, clergyman; b. Sweden, circa 1709; m. Miss Koch. Pastor of Swedish Lutheran congregation, Wicacoa (Southwark), Pa., 1737-41; established relief fund for poor, held services in German, Swedish and English, generally strengthened the ch. Author: Free Grace in Truth. . ., 1741. Died Southwark, Nov. 2, 1741; buried Gloria Dei Ch., Southwark.

DYOTT, Thomas W., glass mfr.; b. London, Eng., 1771. Came to U.S., circa 1795, settled in Phila.; opened drug store, Phila., became largest mfr. and distbr. of patent medicines in U.S., by 1820's; also sold bottles and window glass at store in Phila.; became owner Kensington Glass Works on Delaware River, nr. Phila., 1833, produced 5 grades of glass, employed over 400 workers; decorated many glass bottles with insignias and images of famous people (now collectors' items); established Dyottville, community for workers in which life was strictly regimented, 1833-34; published newspaper Democratic Herald, Dyottville, circa 1834-36; founded Manual Labor Bank for workers in Dyottville with his own resources, went bankrupt when this instn. failed during Panic of 1837; imprisoned for debt, 1837, then returned to drug store business, Phila., eventually recouped fortune. Author: An Exposition of the System of Moral and Mental Labor Established at the Glass Factory at Dyottville, 1833. Died Phila., Jan. 17, 1861.

E

EACHES, Hector, artist; b. Alexandria, Va., 1840; s. Joseph Eaches; studied with Christopher P. Cranch. Opened studio, Louisville, Ky.; returned to Alexandria, 1861, joined Confederate Army; wounded in battle, ret. from active service; became govt. draftsman, Richmond, Va.: had studio,

N.Y.C., circa 1865-73; best known for portraits of Gen. Robert E. Lee. Died N.Y.C., 1873.

EADS, James Buchanan, engr., inventor; b. Lawrenceburg, Ind., May 23, 1820; s. Thomas C. and Ann (Buchanan) E.; LL.D. (hon.), U. Mo., 1877; m. Martha Dillion; m. 2d, Eunice Eads, 1857; 5 children. Inventor diving bell; became partner in steamboat salvaging firm, 1842; called by Pres. Lincoln to Washington, D.C., 1861, recommended means of employing Western rivers for Union war operations, undertook constrn. of fleet of steam-powered armor-plated gunboats which he had proposed, built total of 14 armoured vessels (in record time), featuring his own patented ordnance inventions; constructed Eads Bridge (steel and masonry bridge across Mississippi at St. Louis, best known achievement), incorporated engring. features conquering difficulties considered insuperable by prominent authorities of day, 1867-74; reputation as hydraulic engr. established by river control work completed 1879 at South Pass in Mississippi River, controlled placement of river's sediment so as to keep channel clean; improved harbor facilities at Liverpool (Eng.), Toronto (Ont., Can.), Tampico and Veracruz (Mexico); mem. Am. Soc. C.E., v.p., 1882; fellow A.A.A.S.; mem. Brig. Instn. Civil Engrs., Brit. Assn.; recipient Albert medal from Brit. Soc. for Encouragement of Art, Manufacture and Commerce, 1884. Died Nassau, Bahama Islands, Mar. 16, 1887.

EAGER, Samuel Watkins, congressman, lawyer; b. Neelytown, Orange County, N.Y., Apr. 8, 1789; attended Montgomery (N.Y.) Acad.; grad. Princeton, 1809; studied law. Admitted to bar, 1811, began practice of law, Newburgh, N.Y.; moved to Montgomery, 1826; mem. U.S. Ho. of Reps. (Republican) from N.Y., 21st Congress, Nov. 2, 1830-31; engaged in literary pursuits, Newburgh, from 1836. Died Newburgh, Dec. 23, 1860; buried St. George Cemetery.

EAGLE, The, see Pushmatahaw.

EAGLESON, Thomas R., see Keene, Thomas Wallace.

EAMES, Charles, lawyer, diplomat; b. New Braintree, Mass., Mar. 20, 1812; grad. Harvard, 1831. Held prominent position in Navy Dept. under Sec. Bancroft, 1845; asso. editor Washington (D.C.) Union, 1845; apptd. U.S. commr. to Hawaii by Pres. Polk, 1849; editor Nashville (Tenn.) Union, 1849, Washington Union, 1850; U.S. minister resident to Venezuela, 1854-56; Civil War counsel for Navy Dept. Died Washington, Mar. 16, 1867.

EARL, Augustus, artist; b. Eng., 1793; s. James Earl; attended Royal Acad., London, Eng., circa 1813. Came to U.S., 1818, spent time in N.Y.C. and Phila., visited many parts of country; exhibited at Pa. Acad.; left for S.Am., 1820; became known as "the wandering painter," painted and travelled in S.Am., South Seas, Australasia, East Indies, India; returned to Eng.; many of his sketches used for Burford's panoramas; became draftsman on H.M.S. Beagle on S.Am. expdn. Died circa 1833.

EARL, Ralph Eleaser Whiteside, artist; b. Eng., before 1785; s. Ralph Earl; m. a niece of Mrs. Andrew Jackson, 1818. Brought to Am. as child; worked with father, Conn., 1800; went to Eng., 1809, visited France, 1813, returned to U.S., 1815; itinerant artist in Ga., Ala., Tenn., along Mississippi River; specialized in portraits of Andrew Jackson, after, 1828; mem. Jackson's entourage in Washington, D.C., called (jocularly) "The King's Painter." Died "The Hermitage" (Jackson's home), nr. Nashville, Tenn., Sept. 16, 1838.

EARLE, Elias, congressman, ironmaster; b. Frederick County, Va., June 19, 1762; attended pvt. sch. Moved to Greenville County, S.C., 1787, became one of earliest ironmasters in South; prospected in iron region of Ga.; mem. S.C. Senate, 1800; mem. U.S. Ho. of Reps. (Democrat) from S.C., 9th, 12th-13th, 15th-16th congresses, 1805-07, 11-15, 17-21. Died Centerville, S.C., May 19, 1823; buried Old Earle Cemetery, Greenville, S.C.

EARLE, James, painter; b. Paxton, Mass., May 1, 1761; s. Ralph E. and Phebe (Whittemore) E.; m. Caroline Georgiana Pilkington, circa 1789. Went to Eng., became popular portraitist; exhibited at Royal Acad. of Art; also painted in Charleston, S.C. Died Charleston, Aug. 18, 1796.

EARLE, John Baylis, congressman, planter; b. nr. Landrum, Spartanburg County, S.C., Oct. 23, 1766. Served as drummer boy and soldier during Revolutionary War; engaged in agriculture; mem. U.S. Ho. of Reps. from S.C., 8th Congress, 1803-05; adj., insp. gen. S.C., 16 years; served throughout War of 1812; mem. Nullification Conv., 1832-33. Died Anderson County, S.C., Feb. 3, 1863; buried cemetery on his plantation "Silver Glade," Anderson County.

EARLE, Joseph Haynsworth, senator, lawyer; b. Greenville, S.C., Apr. 30, 1847; orphaned at early age, reared by his aunt; attended pvt. schs., Sumter, S.C.; grad. Furman U., Greenville, 1867; studied law. Enlisted in Confederate Army at outbreak of Civil War, served throughout war; engaged in teaching, 2 years; admitted to bar, 1870, began practice of law, Anderson, S.C.; also engaged in logging bus. and agriculture; mem. S.C. Ho. of Reps., 1878-82, S.C. Senate, 1882-86; del. Democratic Nat. Conv., Cincinnati, 1880, Chgo., 1884; atty. gen. S.C., 1886-90; declined nomination for gov. S.C., 1888; unsuccessful candidate for gov. S.C., 1890; elected circuit judge, 1894; mem. U.S. Senate (Democrat) from S.C., 1897. Died Greenville, S.C., May 20, 1897.

EARLE, Pliny, mfr.; b. Leicester, Mass., Dec. 17, 1762; s. Robert and Sarah (Hunt) E.; m. Patience Buffum, June 6, 1793, at least 5 sons including Thomas, 4 daus. Produced cotton and wool hand cards, Leicester, 1786-1832; produced cards for Almy & Brown, Providence, R.I., 1789; formed partnership Pliny Earle & Bros., expanded to include manufacture machine card clothing, profited greatly until wiped out by Brit. competition after War of 1812; invented leather pricking machine, 1790's; agriculturist after 1820. Died Leicester, Nov. 29, 1832.

EARLE, Pliny, physician, writer; b. Leicester, Mass., Dec. 31, 1809; s. Pliny and Patience (Buffum) E.; M.D., U. Pa., 1837. Supt. Friend's Hosp. for the Insane, Frankford, Pa., 1840-44, Bloomingdale (N.Y.) Asylum, 1844-49; lectr. on mental diseases Coll. Physicians and Surgeons, N.Y.C., 1853-55; supt. State Lunatic Hosp., Northampton, Mass., 1864-85. mem. Phila. Med. Soc. (1837), N.Y. Med. and Surg. Soc. (1845), A.M.A. (a founder, pres. 1845), Am. Medico-Physchol. Assn. (co-founder, pres. 1884), N.Y. Psychol. Assn. (1st pres. 1874), Mass. Med. Soc. (councillor 1876). Author: A Visit to Thirteen Asylums for the Insane in Europe, 1841; Marathon and Other Poems, 1841; The Curability of Insanity, 1887; Institutions for the Insane in Prussia, Germany and Austria, 1853. Died Northampton, May 17, 1892.

EARLE, Ralph, painter; b. Shrewsbury, Mass., May 11, 1751; s. Ralph E. and Phebe (Whittemore) E.; m. Sarah Gates, 1774; m. 2d Anne Whitesides; 4 children including Ralph E.W. Became portraitist, New Haven, 1774; painted early Revolutionary War battle scenes, 1774; became established as painter in London, 1779, painted portraits of mems. of royal family; returned to Am., 1780's, continued painting in Mass., Conn. and N.Y.C. Died Aug. 16, 1801.

EARLE, Samuel, congressman; b. Frederick County, Va., Nov. 28, 1760. Moved to S.C., 1774; served from ensign to capt. (of co. of rangers (Continental Army, during Revolutionary War, 1777-82; mem. S.C. Ho. of Reps., 1784-88; del. S.C. Conv. which ratified U.S. Constn., 1788; del. S.C. Constl. Conv., 1790; mem. U.S. Ho. of Reps. from S.C., 4th Congress, 1795-97. Died Pendleton dist., S.C., Nov. 24, 1833; buried Beaverdam Cemetery, Oconee County, S.C.

EARLE, Thomas, journalist, reformer; b. Leicester, Mass., Apr. 21, 1796; s. Pliny and Patience (Buffum) E.; m. Mary Hussey, July 1820. Attempted various merc. pursuits, for about 10 years; admitted to bar, 1825, practiced law, Phila.; editor Columbian Observer, The Standard, The Mechanic's Free Press and Reform Advocate, The Pennsylvanian; leading proponent of Pa. constl. reformation, 1837; a leading abolitionist. Author: Essay on Penal Law in Pennsylvania, 1827; Treatise on Railroad and Internal Communications, 1830; The Life, Travels and Opinions of Benjamin Lundy, 1847. Died July 14, 1849.

EARLL, Jonas, Jr., b. 1786; attended common schs., Onondaga County, N.Y. Sheriff, Onandaga County, 1815-19; mem. N.Y. State Assembly, 1820-21, N.Y. Senate, 1823-27; mem. U.S. Ho. of Reps. (Democrat) from N.Y., 20th-21st congresses, 1827-31; canal commr., 1832-40, 42-46; postmaster Syracuse (N.Y.), 1840-42. Died Syracuse, Oct. 28, 1846; buried Walnut Grove Cemetery, Onandaga Hill, N.Y.

EARLL, Nehemiah Hezekiah, congressman, lawyer; b. Whitehall, N.Y., Oct. 5, 1787; attended Fairfield Acad., 2 years; studied law. Admitted to bar, 1809, began practice of law, Salina (now part of Syracuse), N.Y.; served as adj. U.S. Army at Oswego during War of 1812; postmaster Onondaga Hill, 1816; justice of peace, 1816-20; master in chancery, 6 years; 1st judge Onondaga County, 1823-31; supt. Onondaga Salt Springs, 1831-36; engaged in milling bus., Jordan; mem. U.S. Ho. of Reps. (Democrat) from N.Y., 26th Congress, 1839-41; ret., blind for many years. Died Mottville, N.Y., Aug. 26, 1872; buried Oakwood Cemetery, Syracuse.

EARLY, John, clergyman; b. Bedford Coun Va., Jan. 1, 1786; s. Joshua and Mary (Leftwi E.; m. Anne Jones; m 2d, Elizabeth Browne Ri 1822. Joined Methodist Ch., 1804, licensed preach, circa 1806; became presiding elder, 18 bishop, 1854-66; pres. colonization soc.; ea advocate of free public schs.; trustee Metho Randolph-Macon Coll., 1830-73; conver thousands in camp meetings; an organizer Met dist Ch. South, 1844. Died Lynchburg, Va., N 5, 1873.

EARLY, Jubal Anderson, lawyer, army offic b. Franklin County, Va., Nov. 3, 1816; s. Joab a Ruth (Hairston) E.; grad. U.S. Mil. Acad., 18 studied law, 1838. Commd. 2d lt. 3d Arty., U Army, 1837, served in Seminole war in F commd. 1st lt., 1838, resigned, 1838; admitted Va. bar, 1840; mem. Va. Ho. of Dels. (Wh youngest mem.), 1841-42; served as maj. 1st Regt., Mexican War, 1847; commanded a d 1862; brig. gen. Army of No. Va., 18 then maj. gen.; served in battles of Chancello ville, Gettysburg and Wilderness campaign; gen., 1864, commanded corps ordered to Shen doah Valley, defeated Lew Wallace at Monoca made unsuccessful attempt to take Washingt D.C., 1864; led raids as far North as Pa., 18 driven back by Sheridan at battles of Winches and Cedar Creek, 1864; his command nearly wi out by Custer at Battle of Waynesboro, 1865; lieved of command by Robert E. Lee, set westward to join Confederate Army in Miss., upon hearing of Confederate surrender, fled Mexico, then to Can.; returned to law practi Lynchburg, Va., 1869; never took oath of alle ance to U.S. after war, although he had origina opposed secession; asso. with P.G.T. Beaureg in La. State Lottery, circa 1870-90. Author: Memoir of the Last Year of the War for I dependence in the Confederate States of Ameri 1866. Died Lynchburg, Mar. 2, 1894.

EARLY, Peter, gov. Ga., congressman; b. Ma son County, Va., June 20, 1773; s. Joel Ear grad. Coll. of N.J. (now Princeton), 1792; Anne Smith, 1793. Mem. U.S. Ho. of Reps., 7t 9th congresses, 1803-07; 1st judge Ocmulgee C cuit, Greensboro, Ga., 1807-13; gov. Ga., 1813- mem. Ga. Senate, 1815-17. Died Greensboro, A 15, 1817.

EASTMAN, Arthur MacArthur, mfr.; b. G manton, N.H., June 8, 1810; s. Ebenezer a Deborah (Greeley) E.; m. Elizabeth H. Moulto 1836, at least 2 children (daus.). Conduct diverse bus. activities, then turned to mfg. m nitions during Crimean War; made huge prof during Civil War, used profits to promote 1st su cessful Anglo-Am. submerged telegraph cab 1874; commd. col. N.H. Militia, 1872; mem. N Constl. Conv., 1876. Died Sept. 3, 1877.

EASTMAN, Ben C., congressman, lawyer; Strong, Me., Oct. 24, 1812; attended public sch studied law. Admitted to bar, 1840, began practi of law, Green Bay, Wis.; moved to Platteville, Wi 1840; sec. legislative council Wis. Territory, 184 46; dist. atty. Grant County; mem. U.S. Ho. Reps. (Democrat) from Wis., 32d-33d congress 1851-55. Died Platteville,, Feb. 2, 1856; bur Forest Hill Cemetery, Madison, Wis.

EASTMAN, Charles Gamage, journalist; b. Fry burg, Me., June 1, 1816; s. Benjamin Clement a Mary Rebecca (Gamage) E.; attended U. Vt.; Susan S. Powers, 1846. Published Lamoille Ri Express (Vt.), 1838, Spirit of the Age, 1840-4 editor Vt. Patroit, Montpelier, 1846-51, so owner, 1851-60; del. Democratic nat. conv 1844, 48, 52, 56,, 60; mem. Vt. Senate (Dem crat) from Washington County, 1852-54; pos master Montpelier, 6 years. Author: Poems, 184 Died Montpelier, Sept. 16, 1860.

EASTMAN, Enoch Worthen, state polit. leade b. Deerfield, N.H., Apr. 15, 1810; s. John and Ma (James) E.; m. Sarah Greenough, Jan. 8, 184 m. 2d, Amanda Hall, 1865. Admitted to N.H. ba 1840; elected lt. gov. Ia., 1863; elected mem. I Senate from Hardin County, 1883; leading figu in Ia. politics, 1844-85. Died Jan. 9, 1885.

EASTMAN, Harvey Gridley, pres. business sch b. Waterville N.Y., Oct. 16, 1832; s. Horace a Mary (Gridley) E.; m. Minerva Clark, 1857. Ope ated bus. coll., Oswego, N.Y., 1855-58, moved sc to St. Louis, 1858, to Poughkeepsie, N.Y., 185 employed cunning advt. which made him, sch. a town prosper; mem. Poughkeepsie Ice Club; offic Poughkeepsie Nat. Bank, Poughkeepsie & Easte R.R.; mayor Poughkeepsie, 1871-74, 77-78; Republi can mem. N.Y. State Assembly, 1872, 74. Di Denver, July 13, 1878.

EASTMAN, Ira Allen, congressman; b. Gilmar ton, N.H., Jan. 1, 1809; grad. Dartmouth Coll 1829; studied law. Admitted to bar, 1832, bega practice of law, Troy, N.H.; returned to Gilmanto

34, continued practice law; clk. N.H. Ho. of ps., 1835, mem., 1836-38, speaker, 1837-38; m. U.S. Ho. of Reps. (Democrat) from N.H., th-27th congresses, 1839-43; judge Ct. of Com-n Pleas, 1844-49; asso. judge N.H. Supreme ., 1849-55; judge Superior Jd. Ct., 1855-59; successful Democratic candidate for gov. N.H., 63, for U.S. senator from N.H., 1866; practiced v, Concord and Manchester, N.H. Died Man-ster, Mar. 21, 1881; buried Valley Cemetery.

EASTMAN, Nehamiah, congressman; b. Gilman-, Belknap County, N.H., June 16, 1782; at-nded acad., Gilmanton; studied law. Admitted bar, 1807; began practice of law, Farmington, H.; mem. N.H. Ho. of Reps., 1813, N.H. Senate, 20-25; mem. U.S. Ho. of Reps. (Democrat) m N.H., 19th Congress, 1825-27. Died Farm-gton, Jan. 11, 1856; buried Farmington Ceme-y.

EASTMAN, Seth, army officer, artist; b. Bruns-ck, Me., Jan. 24, 1808; attended U.S. Mil. Acad., 24-29. Served at Ft. Crawford, Wis., Ft. Snell-g, Minn., 1829-31; served with Topog. Corps, 31-33; asst. tchr. drawing U.S. Mil. Acad., 1833-; served in Fla. War, 1840-41; returned to Ft. elling, 1841-48; went to Tex., 1848-49; worked illustrations for Henry R. Schoolcraft's History d Statistical Information Respecting the . . . In-an Tribes of the United States, 6 vols., 1853-56; rved in Tex., 1855-56, in Office of Q.M. Gen., ashington, D.C., 1857-58; ret., 1863; brevetted ig. gen. U.S. Army, 1866; engaged in painting dian scenes and views of western forts for Capitol, 67-70. Died Washington, Aug. 31, 1875.

EASTMAN, Timothy Corser, meat packer; b. oydon, N.H., May 30, 1821; s. Joseph and Lucy owers) E.; m. Lucy Putnam, 1845, 1 son, 1 dau. ught sch.; became farmer, Wis.; dairy farmer, ttle buyer, Ohio, N.Y.; moved to N.Y.C., 1859; came mgr. all cattle business for N.Y. Central R.; expanded to meat packing, pioneered internat. ipping of refrigerated meat, 1875; mem. N.Y. oduce Exchange. Died Tarrytown, N.Y., Oct. 11, 93.

EASTON, John, colonial gov.; b. Wales circa 17; s. Nicholas Easton; m. Mehitable Grant, n. 4, 1660; m. 2d, Alice Easton; 5 children. Atty. n. United Govts. of Portsmouth and Newport .I.), 1653-54, 56-57, 60-63, 64-70, 72-74; dep. v. R.I., 1674-76, gov., 1690-95. Author: The uses which led to Philip's Indian War. Died Dec. , 1705; buried Newport.

EASTON, Nicholas, colonial gov.; b. Wales, Gt. itain, 1593; m. Christian Bucher, 1638; m. 2d, n Clayton, 1671; 9 children. Came to Boston, 34; rep. to Mass. Gen. Ct., 1635; assistant 1st n. Ct., Newport, R.I., 1640-49; moderator R.I. n. Assembly; pres. R.I. Colony, 1650-51, 54, dep. v. 1666-69, gov., 1672-74. Died Newport, Aug. , 1675.

EASTON, Rufus, congressman; b. Litchfield, nn., May 4, 1774; studied law. Admitted to bar, arted practice of law, Rome, N.Y.; settled in ncennes, Ind. Territory, 1804; moved to St. uis, apptd. judge Dist. of La., 1805; 1st post-aster St. Louis, 1805-15; mem. U.S. Congress emocrat) from Territory of Mo., 1814-16; ty. gen. State of Mo., 1821-26; engaged in actice of law, also real estate bus. Died St. arles, Mo., July 5, 1834; buried Lindenwood ll. Cemetery.

EATON, Amos, scientist; b. Chatham, N.Y., May , 1776; s. Capt. Abel and Azuba (Hurd) E.; ad. Williams Coll., 1797; attended Yale, 1815-; m. Polly Thomas, Oct. 16, 1799, 1 son; m. , Sally Cady, Sept. 16, 1803, 5 sons; m. 3d, n Bradley, Oct. 20, 1816, 3 children; m. 4th, ice Johnson, Aug. 5, 1827, 1 son. Admitted to Y. bar, 1802; became lawyer and land agt., atskill, N.Y., also studied science; lectured on tany and geology throughout Northeast; prof. atural history Med. Sch., Castleton, Vt., 1820-24; of. Rensselaer Sch. (now Poly. Inst.), 1824-42; rote papers in all scientific fields. Author: A Manu-of Botany for the Northern States, 1817. Died ay 10, 1842.

EATON, Charles H., actor; b. Boston, June 10, 13. Began acting career at Warren Street Thea-e, Boston, 1833; appeared as Richard III, N.Y.C., 33; toured U.S., 1833-42; gave last performance s William Tell), Pitts., 1842; known for out-anding interpretations of Shakespearean characters, pecially Shylock, Othello, Macbeth, Hamlet. Died itts., 1842.

EATON, Cyrus, educator; b. Farmingham, Mass., eb. 11, 1784; s. Benjamin and Mary (Stacey) E.; .M. (hon.), Bowdoin Coll., 1848; m. Mary Ler-ond, 1806. Shoemaker, Farmingham, 1800-03; ught sch., Southboro, Mass., 1803-04, Warren Me.) Acad., 1804-75; town clk., 13 years; jus-ice of peace, 32 years; assessor, 9 years; mem. Me. Legislature, 5 years; mem. Me. Constl. Conv., 1826; elected corresponding mem. Mass., Wis. hist. socs., 1851. Author: The Annals of Warren, Maine; A Nar-ration of Events from 1605-1850. Died Warren, Jan. 21, 1875.

EATON, Daniel Cady, botanist; b. Ft. Gratiot, Mich., Sept. 12, 1834; s. Gen. Amos B. and Eliza-beth (Seldon) E.; grad. Yale, 1857; attended Har-vard, 1857-60; m. Caroline Ketcham, Feb. 13, 1866. Served with army commissary, N.Y.C., during Civil War, 1860-64; prof. botany Yale, 1864-95; spe-cialized in study of ferns, did much field work; wrote bot. definitions for Webster's Internat. Dictionary. Author: The Ferns of North America, 2 vols. Died New Haven, Conn., June 29, 1895.

EATON, John Henry, senator, sec. of war; b. Halifax County, N.C., June 18, 1790; s. John and Elizabeth E.; ed. U. N.C.; m. Myra Lewis; m. 2d, Peggy O'Neill. Went to Franklin, Tenn., 1809; served in War of 1812; early supporter and polit. adviser of Andrew Jackson; mem. U.S. Senate from Tenn., 1818-29; U.S. sec. of war in Jackson's cabinet, 1829-31; his 2d wife became the center of a battle in Washington society between Jackson forces and their opponents, which contributed to reshuffling of cabinet and Eaton's resignation, 1829; apptd. gov. Territory of Fla. by Jackson, 1834-36; U.S. minister to Madrid, Spain, 1836-40. An author The Life of Andrew Jackson, Major General in the Service of the U.S., 1817. Died Nov. 17, 1856, Washington, D.C.; buried Oak Hill Cemetery, Washington.

EATON, Joseph Horace, artist; b. Salem, Mass., Oct. 12, 1815; grad. U.S. Mil. Acad., 1835. Served in La., mapped Sabine River; instr. tactics U.S. Mil. Acad., 1839-43; became aide to Gen. Zachary Tay-lor, 1845, served in Mexican War; painted portrait of Taylor; stationed at Ft. Defiance, N.M., 1848-56; made drawings of Zuni and Navajo Indians, studied their langs.; contbd. article to Schoolcraft's History and Statistical Information Respecting the . . . Indian Tribes of the United States, 6 vols., 1853-56; resigned from army to supervise constrn. of Chgo. Customs House, 1856; returned to U.S. Army during Civil War; went to Ore., 1874. Died Portland, Ore., Jan. 20, 1896.

EATON, Joseph Oriel, painter; b. Newark, O., Feb. 8, 1829; s. William and Margaret (Adams) E.; m. Emma Jane Goodman, 1855. Studied art, opened studio in N.Y.C.; portrait painter, specialized in children; asso. Nat. Academician. Died Yonkers, N. Y., Feb. 7, 1875.

EATON, Lewis, congressman; b. N.Y. Sheriff, Schenectady County, 1821-22; lived in Duanes-burg; mem. U.S. Ho. of Reps. (Democrat) from N.Y., 18th Congress, 1823-25; mem. N.Y. State Senate, 1829-32.

EATON, Nathaniel, coll. pres.; b. Eng., 1609; s. Rev. Richard Eaton; attended Trinity Coll., Cam-bridge (Eng.) U., also U. Leyden; Ph.D., M.D., U. Padua, 1647; married twice; m. 2d, Miss Graves; some children. Came to Mass., 1637; pres. Har-vard (1st colonial coll.), 1637-39, his presidency characterized by poor food, poor treatment of stu-dents, embezzlement, tried by Gen. Ct., dismissed with fines; fled to Va., became asst. rector; returned to Eng.; vicar Bishop's Castle, Shropshire, 1661; rector, Bideford, Devonshire, 1668; died in debtor's prison. Died 1674.

EATON, Samuel, clergyman; b. Eng., circa 1596; s. Rev. Richard Eaton; B.A., Magdalene Coll., Cam-bridge (Eng.) U., 1625, M.A., 1628. Came to New Eng., 1637; colleague of John Davenport, New Haven, Conn.; returned to Eng., 1640, continued as clergy-man, wrote several religious tracts. Died Jan. 9, 1665.

EATON, Theophilus, colonizer, colonial gov.; b. Stony Stratford, Eng., circa 1590; s. Rev. Richard Eaton; 1st wife unknown; m. 2d, Ann Lloyd. Dep. gov. East-Land Co.; visited No. countries; apptd. agt. of King Charles I at Ct. of Denmark; a founder, dir. Mass. Bay Co. which sent 1st settlers to Mass. 1628; explored land around New Haven, Conn., 1637; led 1st settlers there, 1638; founder Puritan Ch., New Haven; civil gov. (rule with aid of John Davenport) New Haven Colony (1st gov.), 1639-58; one of commrs. United Co-lonies of New Eng., 1643; apptd. by colony to draw up new code of governing laws, 1655; new code printed in London, Eng., 1656. Died New Haven, June 7, 1658.

EATON, William, diplomat; b. Woodstock, Conn., Feb. 23, 1764; s. Nathan and Sarah (Johnson) E.; grad. Dartmouth, 1790; m. Eliza Sykes, Aug. 22, 1792. Commd. capt. U.S. Army, 1792, served Army of West, later Ga., 1792-95, Phila., 1795-97; U.S. consul in Tunis, 1798-1804; navy agt. to Barbary States, forced to return to U.S. while attempting to guide faction in Tripolitan civil war, 1804; mem. Mass. Legislature, 1 term. Died Brimfield, Mass., June 1, 1811.

EATON, Wyatt, painter; b. Philipsburg, Que., Can., May 6, 1849; s. Jonathan and Mary (Smith) E.; attended N.A.D., N.Y.C., 1857; m. Laura Con-stance Papelard, Sept. 24, 1872; m. 2d, Charlotte Amelia Collins, July 23, 1887. Made trip to Europe, 1872-77, studied in Eng. and France; returned to Am., became successful portraitist. Died Newport, R.I., June 7, 1896.

EBERLE, John, physician; b. Hagerstown, Md., Dec. 10, 1787; grad. U. Pa., 1809. Practiced medi-cine, Lancaster, Pa.; surgeon Lancaster Militia, 1813-14; a founder, editor Am. Med. Recorder, 1818-20; mem. German Acad. Natural Scis.; 1st prof. materia medica Jefferson Med. Coll., Phila., 1825-31; editor; Am. Med. Review, 1824-26; organized med. dept. Miami U., Oxford, O., 1830; a founder Western Med. Gazette, 1832; prof. theory and prac-tice of medicine Transylvania U., Lexington, Ky., 1837-38. Author: Treatise of the Materia Medica and Therapeutics, 1823; Notes of Lectures on the Theory and Practice of Medicine, 1834. Died Feb. 2, 1838.

ECCLESTON, Samuel, clergyman; b. nr. Chester-town, Md., June 27, 1801; studied at St. Mary's Coll., Balt., also in France. Ordained a Sulpician, 1825; became pres. St. Mary's Coll., 1829; became coadjutor bishop of Balt., 1834, archbishop, 1 month later; active in devel. of ednl. opportunities; held 5 provincial councils. Died Washington, D.C., Apr. 22, 1851.

ECHOLS, John, lawyer, army officer, railroad ofcl.; b. Lynchburg, Va., Mar. 20, 1823: s. Joseph and Elizabeth (Lambeth) E.; grad. Washington and Lee U., 1842; post-grad. Va. Mil. Inst., 1843, also Harvard Law Sch.; m. Mary Caperton; m. 2d, Mrs. Mary Cochran Reid. Admitted to Va. bar, 1843; mem. Va. Gen. Assembly; commanded 27th Va. Regt. at 1st Battle of Manassas; commd. brig. gen. Confederate Army, resumed command Dept. of Southwestern Va., 1864; his brigade fought with the Army of No. Va. from Hanover Junction to Cold Harbor; pres. Bank of Staunton (Va.); undertook reorgn. Chesapeake & Ohio & South-western R.R. (now C. & O. Ry.), directed rail-road for 20 years; active mem. bd. visitors Va. Mil. Inst., Washington and Lee U. Died Staunton, May 24, 1896.

ECIJA, Juan de, missionary; b. Fuenteovejuna, Spain, 1510. Went to Mexico, became a Dominican, circa 1531; took name Domingo de la Anunciacion; very successful in teaching Indians; worked zeal-ously during plague of 1545; shipwrecked off Fla., 1559; became blind, 1585. Died 1591.

ECKARD, James Read, educator, clergyman; b. Phila., Nov. 22, 1805; s. Joachim Frederick and Susan (Read) E.; grad. U. Pa., 1823; grad. Prince-ton Theol. Sem., 1833; D.D. (hon.), Lafayette Coll., 1858; m. Margaret E. Bayard, 1833. Practiced law, Phila., 1826-30; missionary to Ceylon, 1833-43; prin. Chatham Acad., Savannah, Ga., 1843-46; pas-tor 2d Presbyn. Ch., Washington, D.C., 1848-58; prof. rhetoric Lafayette Coll., 1858-71. Author: Faith and Justification (in Tamil lang.); The Hin-doo Traveler, 1836; Outline of English Law from Blackstone, 1844. Died Abington, Pa., Mar. 12, 1887.

ECKERT, George Nicholas, congressman, phy-sician; b. Womelsdorf, Berks County, Pa., July 4, 1802; grad. med. dept. U. Pa., Phila., 1824. Began practice of medicine, Reading, Pa.; an organizer Berks County Med. Soc., 1824; moved to Pine Grove, Pa., engaged in coal and iron busi-ess; mem. U.S. Ho. of Reps. (Whig) from Pa., 30th Congress, 1847-49; dir. U.S. Mint, Phila. (apptd. by Pres. Fillmore), 1851-53. Died Phila., June 28, 1865; buried Laurel Hill Cemetery.

ECKFORD, Henry, marine architect, shipbuild-er; b. Irvine, Scotland, Mar. 12, 1775; s. John and Janet (Black) E.; m. Marion Bedell, Apr. 13, 1799, 2 daus. Settled in N.Y.C., 1786; supr. ship-bldg. in Lake Ontario during War of 1812; reduced size of stern frame, altered details of rigging; naval constructor Bklyn. Navy Yard, 1817-20; built steamer Robert Fulton (made 1st successful steam voyage from N.Y.C. to New Orleans and Havana, Cuba, 1822). Died Turkey, Nov. 12, 1832.

ECKSTEIN, Frederick, sculptor; b. Berlin, Ger-many, circa 1775; s. Johann Eckstein; studied at Acad., Berlin. Came to Am., 1794, settled in Phila.; a founder Pa. Acad.; became sch. tchr., after 1817, taught at Harmony, Ind., Pa., Wheeling and Charles-ton, Va. (now W.Va.); settled in Cincinnati, 1823; sculpted heads of Jackson and Lafayette, 1825; founded Cincinnati Acad. Fine Arts; taught sch., Frankfort, Millersburg and Augusta (Ky.), 1830-38, Cincinnati, 1838-40, Louisville, 1840. Died Cincinnati, Feb. 10, 1852.

ECKSTEIN, John, painter, sculptor, engraver; b. Germany (probably Mecklenburg), circa 1750. Settled in Phila., 1794; one of original mems.

Columbian Soc. Artists; asso. Pa. Acad. Fine Arts. Died circa 1817.

EDBROOKE, Willoughby J., architect; b. England, 1843. Came to U.S.; began practice as architect, Chgo., circa 1867, engaged in designing and bldg. in various Midwestern cities; asso. with Franklin P. Burnham in preparing plans for State Capitol, Atlanta, Ga., 1887-91; apptd. supervising architect U.S. Treasury Dept. by Pres. Harrison, 1891, designed several court houses in Ill.; awarded commn. in competition for main bldg. of U. Notre Dame. Died Mar. 29, 1896.

EDDIS, William, colonial ofcl.; b. Eng.; flourished 1769-77; married, 1 son, Eden. Came to Annapolis, Md., 1769; became gov.'s sec., 1769; apptd. loan office commr., 1772; surveyor of customs, Annapolis; forced to return to Eng., 1777.

EDDY, Daniel Clarke, clergyman; b. Salem, Mass., May 21, 1823; s, Daniel and Martha (Honeycomb) E.; attended N.H. Theol. Inst.; m. Elizabeth Stone, Apr. 9, 1846, 4 children. Became Baptist, 1842; pastor 1st Bapt. Ch., Lowell, Mass., 1846-56; mem. Mass. Gen. Ct. (Know-Nothing Party), speaker, 1854-56; pastor Harvard Street Bapt. Ch., Boston, 1856, 1st Bapt. Ch., Bklyn., 1881-96, also held pastorates in Phila., Boston, Fall River, Hyde Park, N.Y. Author: The Young Man's Friend, 1850. Died Martha's Vineyard, July 26, 1896.

EDDY, Isaac, engraver, printer; b. Weathersfield, Vt., Feb. 17, 1777; at least 1 son, Oliver Tarbell. Worked as engraver and printer, Weathersfield, until 1826, engraved plates for 1st Vt. Bible, 1812; operated printing establishment which used Stephen Daye press, 1814-16; moved to Troy, N.Y., 1826, made fortune as mfr. of printer's ink. Died Waterford, N.Y., July 25, 1847.

EDDY, Norman, congressman; b. Scipio, N.Y., Dec. 10, 1810; grad. med. dept. U. Pa. at Phila., 1835; studied law. Practiced medicine, Mishawaka, Ind., until 1847; admitted to bar, 1847, began practice of law, South Bend, Ind.; mem. Ind. Senate, 1850; held various local offices; mem. U.S. Ho. of Reps. (Democrat) from Ind., 33d Congress, 1853-55; apptd. atty. gen. Territory of Minn. by Pres. Pierce, 1855; served as col. 48th Ind. Volunteer Inf. during Civil War; collector internat. revenue, 1865-70; sec. of state Ind., 1870-72. Died Indpls., Ind., Jan. 28, 1872; buried City Cemetery, South Bend.

EDDY, Oliver Tarbell, artist; b. Greenbush, Vt., Nov. 14, 1799; s. Isaac Eddy; m., 1822. Began engraving, circa 1814; in N.Y.C., 1826-29, exhibited at N.A.D., 1827; worked in Elizabeth, N.J., 1831-35, Newark, N.J., 1835-40, Balt., 1842-50, Phila., 1850-68; patented a forerunner of the typewriter; work represented at Newark Museum, Md. Hist. Soc. Died Phila., Oct. 8, 1868.

EDDY, Samuel, congressman, jurist; b. Johnston, nr. Providence, R.I., Mar. 31, 1769; grad. Brown U., 1787; studied law. Admitted to bar, 1790, practiced law, Providence, for short time; clk. R.I. Supreme Ct., 1790-93; sec. of state, 1798-1819; mem. U.S. Ho. of Reps. (Democrat) from R.I., 16th-18th congresses, 1819-25; asso. justice R.I. Supreme Ct., 1826-27, chief justice, 1827-35. Died Providence, Feb. 3, 1839; buried North End Cemetery.

EDDY, Thomas, reformer; b. Phila., Sept. 5, 1758; s. James and Mary (Darragh) E.; m. Hannah Hartshorne, Mar. 20, 1782. Drew up (with Gen. Philip Schuyler) bill for establishment of penitentiary system in N.Y. State, 1796; bd. govs. N.Y. Hosp., 1796-1827; helped De Witt Clinton carry through Erie Canal project; a founder Bloomingdale Asylum for the Insane, free school for poor children, N.Y.C., 1805, House of Refuge, N.Y. Savs. Bank, N.Y. Bible Soc. Author: Account of the State Prison or Penitentiary House in the City of New York, 1801. Died N.Y.C., Sept. 16, 1827.

EDDY, Thomas Mears, clergyman; b. Hamilton County, O., Sept. 7, 1823. Circuit preacher Indiana Methodist Conf., 1842-53; preaching elder Indpls. dist., 1853-56; editor Northwestern Christian Advocate, 1856-68; pastor, Balt., 1868-72; minister Meth. Ch., Washington, D.C., 1872-74; corr. sec. Meth. Missionary Soc., 1872-74. Died N.Y.C., Oct. 7, 1874.

EDDY, Zachary, clergyman; b. Stockbridge, Vt., Dec. 19, 1815; D.D. (hon.), Williams Coll., 1858. Ordained to ministry Cumberland Presbyn. Ch., 1835; missionary in Pa., Ohio, Western N.Y., 1835-38; pastor various congregations, N.Y., Mass., Mich., 1838-87; settled in Augusta, Ga., 1887-91. Author: Immanuel; or, the Life of Christ, 1868; Hymns of the Church, Compiled for the General Synod of the Reformed Church in America, 1869; (with R. D. Hitchcock and L. Ward Mudge) Carminia Sanctorum, 1886. Died Detroit, Nov. 15, 1891.

EDEN, Charles, colonial gov.; b. 1673; m. Mrs. Penelope Golland. Gov. of N.C., 1714-22; instrumental in effecting death of pirate Edward Teach (known as Black Beard); Town of Edenton (N.C.) named for him, 1720. Died N.C., Mar. 17, 1722; buried Berrie County, N.C.

EDEN, Robert, colonial gov.; b. Durham, Eng., Sept. 14, 1741; s. Robert and Mary (Davidson) E.; m. Caroline Calvert (sister Lord Baltimore), 1765, 2 sons. Commd. gov. Md., 1768, served as gov., surveyor gen., chancellor of province during period of preliminary action which lead to Am. Revolution, 1769-76; Continental Congress requested Md. Council of Safety to arrest him, believing him an enemy of colonists; returned to Eng.; created baronet for faithful service to Eng. in colonies, 1776; returned to Annapolis (Md.) to recover his property after Revolutionary War. Died Annapolis, Sept. 2, 1784.

EDES, Benjamin, journalist; b. Charlestown, Mass., Oct. 14, 1732; s. Peter and Esther (Hall) E.; m. Martha Starr, circa 1754, children—Benjamin, Peter. Founder, co-owner, editor and publisher, Boston Gazette and Country Journal, 1755-98, leading New Eng. radical paper advocating cause of liberty, published editorials and propaganda by Samuel and John Adams, John Hancock, other leaders of Revolution; mem. Sons of Liberty; took part in Boston Tea Party. Died Boston, Dec. 11, 1803.

EDGERTON, Alfred Peck, congressman; b. Plattsburgh, N.Y., Jan. 11, 1813; s. Bela and Phebe (Ketchum) E.; m. Charlotte Dixon, Feb. 9, 1841. Mem. Ohio Senate, 1845-47; mem. U.S. Ho. of Reps. from Ohio, 32d-33d congresses, 1851-55; financial agt. Ohio Bd. Fund Commrs., 1853-56; mem. U.S. Civil Service Commn., pres., 1885-89; pres. Ft. Wayne (Ind.) Bd. Edn. Died Hicksville, O., May 14, 1897; buried Lindenwood Cemetery, Ft. Wayne.

EDGERTON, Alonzo Jay, senator; b. Rome, N.Y., June 7, 1827; grad. Wesleyan U., Middletown, Conn., 1850; studied law. Moved to Mantorville, Minn., 1855; admitted to bar, 1855, began practice of law, Mantorville; pros. atty. Dodge County; mem. Minn. Senate, 1858-59, 77-79; commd. capt. 10th Minn. Volunteer Regt. in Civil War, 1862, promoted col., 1864, brevetted brig. gen., 1865; railroad commr., 1871-75; Republican presdl. elector, 1876; moved to Kasson, Minn., 1878; mem. U.S. Senate (Republican) from Minn., Mar.-Oct. 1881 (filled vacancy); apptd. chief justice Territorial Supreme Ct. Dakota; U.S. judge Dist. of S.C.; pres. S.D. Constl. Conv. Died Sioux Falls, S.D., Aug. 9, 1896; buried Evergreen Cemetery, Mantorville.

EDIE, John Rufus, congressman, lawyer; b. Gettysburg, Pa., Jan. 14, 1814; attended Emmitsburg (Md.) Coll., U.S. Mil. Acad.; studied law. Prin. schs., Gettysburg, several years; admitted to bar, 1840, began practice of law, Somerset, Pa.; mem. Pa. Senate, 1845-46; dep. atty. gen., 1847-50; dist. atty., 1850-54; mem. U.S. Ho. of Reps. (Whig) from Pa., 34th-35th congresses, 1855-59; commd. maj. 15th Regt., U.S. Inf., 1861, promoted lt. col., 1863; brevetted col. for services during Atlanta campaign, 1864; served with 15th, 8th regts. U.S. Inf., until 1871. Died Somerset, Pa., Aug. 27, 1888; buried Union Cemetery.

EDMANDS, John Wiley, congressman, mfr.; b. Boston, Mar. 1, 1809; grad. English High Sch., Boston. Asso. with woolen mills, Dedham, Mass.; with Pacific Mills Co., Lawrence, Mass., became treas. 1855; mem. U.S. Ho. of Reps. (Whig) from Mass., 33d Congress, 1853-55; Republican presdl. elector, 1868. Died Newton, Mass., Jan. 31, 1877; buried Mt. Auburn Cemetery, Cambridge, Mass.

EDMOND, William, congressman; b. Woodbury, Conn., Sept. 28, 1755; grad. Yale, 1778; studied law. Served in Continental Army during Revolutionary War, wounded at Battle of Danbury (town burned by British), 1777; admitted to bar, 1780, began practice of law, Newtown, Conn.; mem. Conn. Ho. of Reps., 1791-97, 1801-02, Conn. Senate, 1797-99; mem. U.S. Ho. of Reps. (Federalist, filled vacancy) from Conn., 5th-6th congresses, Nov. 13, 1797-1801; asso. judge Conn. Supreme Ct., 1805-19. Died Newtown, Aug. 1, 1838; buried Newtown Cemetery.

EDMONDS, Francis William, painter; b. Hudson, N.Y., Nov. 22, 1806; s. Samuel and Lydia (Worth) E.; student N.A.D., 1826-63; m. Martha Norman, circa 1831; m. 2d, Dorothea Lord, Nov. 4, 1841; at least 6 children. Cashier, Hudson River Bank, 1830-32, Leather Mfrs. Bank, N.Y.C., 1832-39, Mechanics Bank, N.Y.C., 1839-53; an organizer N.Y. Clearing House, 1853, Bank Note Engraving Co. (later Am. Bank Note Co.), 1853; elected academician N.A.D., 1840, rec. sec., trustee; mem. Sketch Club; incorporator Century Assn.; mem. N.Y. Hist. Soc.; paintings include Scene from Butler's Hudibras, 1827; Sammy, the Tailor, 1836; The Penny Paper, 1839; The Ba[illegible] ful Cousin, 1842; The New Scholar, 1845. D[illegible] Bronxville, N.Y., Feb. 7, 1863.

EDMONDS, John Worth, jurist b. Huds[illegible] N.Y., Mar. 13, 1799; s. Samuel and Lydia (Wor[illegible] E.; grad. Union Coll., Schenectady, N.Y., 18[illegible] Commd. lt. N.Y. State Militia, 1814, later c[illegible] admitted to Columbia County (N.Y.) bar, 18[illegible] recorder Columbia County, 1828-30; elected [illegible] N.Y. Assembly (Democrat), 1830; mem. N[illegible] State Senate, 1831-36; spl. commr. to Indians [illegible] borders of lakes Huron and Superior, 1836-[illegible] apptd. insp. state prisons N.Y., 1843; an organi[illegible] Prison Discipline Soc., Prison Soc., Wome[illegible] Prison Assn. of N.Y.C., 1844; apptd. judge [illegible] N.Y. Circuit, 1845; justice N.Y. State Supre[illegible] Ct., 1847-52; judge N.Y. Ct. Appeals, 1852-[illegible] Author: (with George T. Dexter) Spiritualis[illegible] 1853-55; Reports of Select Cases Decided in [illegible] Courts of State of New York, 1868; editor [illegible] vised Statutes of New York, 1869-72. Died N.Y.[illegible] Apr. 5, 1874.

EDMUNDSON, Henry Alonzo, congressm[illegible] lawyer; b. Blacksburg, Va., June 14, 1814; gr[illegible] Georgetown U., Washington, D.C.; studied l[illegible] Admitted to bar, 1838, began practice of l[illegible] Salem, Va.; mem. U.S. Ho. of Reps. (Democr[illegible] from Va., 31st-36th congresses, 1849-61; ser[illegible] as lt. col. 54th Va. Regt., Confederate Ar[illegible] until 1862; assigned to command of 27th [illegible] Cavalry, 1862; resumed practice of law after C[illegible] War; engaged in agriculture, 1880. Died "Fall[illegible] Waters," Shawsville, Va., Dec. 16, 1890; bur[illegible] Fotheringay Cemetery, Montgomery County, [illegible]

EDOUART, Alexander, artist; b. London, Eng., N[illegible] 5, 1818; s. Auguste Edouart; ed. Edinburgh, Sc[illegible] land; studied art in Italy. Came to Am.; lived [illegible] N.Y.C., 1848-50, exhibited at N.A.D., Am. A[illegible] Union; went to Cal., 1852; best known as photog[illegible] pher, San Francisco; painted some Cal. landscap[illegible] travelled to Europe, 1859; moved to Los Angel[illegible] 1889/90. Died Los Angeles, 1892.

EDOUART, Auguste, silhouettist; b. Dunquerq[illegible] France, 1789; children include Alexander. Served [illegible] French Army, until 1813; went to Eng., 18[illegible] made hair devices, painted landscapes and anim[illegible] portraits, exhibited at Royal Acad., London, En[illegible] 1815-16; began career as silhouettist, 1835; went [illegible] Scotland. 1830, to Ireland, 1833; came to U.S[illegible] 1839; cut silhouettes throughout U.S., including B[illegible] ton, Washington, D.C., 1841, Cambridge, Mas[illegible] New Orleans, 1842, Phila., 1843, New Orlea[illegible] 1844, Charleston, S.C., 1845, 47, N.Y.C., 184[illegible] lost most of his duplicates (said to have been o[illegible] 50,000) in a shipwreck while returning to Fran[illegible] never resumed his profession. Died Guines, nr. Cala[illegible] France, 1861.

EDSALL, Joseph E., congressman, mcht.; [illegible] Rudeville, nr. Hamburg, N.J., 1789; attend[illegible] common schs. Engaged in various business p[illegible] suits, operated distillery, also tannery; cou[illegible] clk.; mem. N.J. Ho. of Assembly; judge Ct. [illegible] Common Pleas; mem. U.S. Ho. of Reps. (Democr[illegible] from N.J., 29th-30th congresses, 1845-49. D[illegible] Hamburg, 1865; buried Baptist Burying Grou[illegible]

EDSON, Tracy R., engraver; b. Otsego Count[illegible] N.Y., 1809. Worked as engraver, N.Y.C., 1834-3[illegible] New Orleans, 1841-42, N.Y.C., 1847-60; mem. fi[illegible] Rawdon, Wright, Hatch & Edson, 1835, 47-5[illegible] merged to form Am. Bank Note Co., 1858, pre[illegible] 1860-63. Died Nov. 30, 1881.

EDWARDS, Bela Bates, clergyman, editor; [illegible] Southampton, Mass., July 4, 1802; s. Elisha a[illegible] Anne (Bates) E.; grad. Amherst Coll., 18[illegible] Andover Theol. Sem., 1830; m. Jerusha Willia[illegible] Billings, Nov. 3, 1831, 3 children. Editor, A[illegible] Quarterly Register, 1827-43; founder Am. Qu[illegible] terly Observer, 1833, merged with Am. Bibl. R[illegible] pository, 1835; prof. Hebrew langs. and lit. An[illegible] over Theol. Sem., 1837, apptd. prof. Bibl. lit[illegible] 1848; ordained to ministry, 1837; editor Bibli[illegible] theca Sacra, 1844-52; trustee Amherst Coll., A[illegible] bott Acad. Author: Biography of Self-Taug[illegible] Men, 1831; Writings of Professor B.B. Edwar[illegible] 2 vols. (edited by Edward A. Park), publish[illegible] posthumously, 1853. Died Athens, Ga., Apr. 2[illegible] 1852.

EDWARDS, Benjamin, congressman; b. Sta[illegible] ford County, Va., Aug. 12, 1753; attended comm[illegible] schs.; married, at least 1 son, Ninian. Engag[illegible] in agriculture and business, Montgomery Coun[illegible] Md.; mem. Md. Ho. of Dels., serveral years; d[illegible] Md. Conv. which ratified U.S. Constn., 1788; me[illegible] U.S. Ho. of Reps. (filled vacancy) from Md., [illegible] Congress, Jan. 2, Mar. 3, 1795; moved to To[illegible] County, Ky. Died Elkton, Ky., Nov. 13, 182[illegible] buried on his estate, Elkton.

EDWARDS, Charles, lawyer; b. Norwich, Eng[illegible] Mar. 17, 1797; attended Cambridge (Eng.) U. A[illegible] mitted to N.Y. bar; standing counel to Brit. co[illegible] sulate gen., N.Y.C. for 25 years; counsel to Bri[illegible] vt. in prize cases, 1862. Author: On Receivers in ancery, 1839; Reports on Chancery Cases Decided the First Circuit of the State of New York by e Honorable William J. M'Coun, 4 vols., 1833-51; e History and Poetry of Finger-Rings, 1855. Died ay 30, 1868.

EDWARDS, Henry Waggaman, senator, gov. Conn.; New Haven, Conn., Oct. 1779; s. Pierpont and ances (Ogden) D.; grad. Coll. of N.J. (now Prince- n), 1797; attended Litchfield (Conn.) Law h.; m. Lydia Miller, at least 1 son, Henry P. acticed law, New Haven; mem. U.S. Ho. of Reps. epublican) from Conn., 16th-17th congresses, 19-23; mem. U.S. Senate from Conn., 1823-27; em. Conn. Senate, 1827-29, Conn. Ho. of Reps., 30; gov. Conn., 1833, 35-38. Died July 22, 1847.

EDWARDS, John, congressman; b. Dutchess unty, nr. Poughkeepsie, N.Y., Aug. 6, 1781; tended common schs. Sheriff, Montgomery Coun- , also keeper Johnstown Jail, 1806-12; moved Ephratah, N.Y.; mem. U.S. Ho. of Reps. Democrat) from N.Y., 25th Congress, 1837-39; came a mcht., also engaged in mfg. Died Johns- wn, N.Y., Dec. 28, 1850; buried Johnstown emetery.

EDWARDS, John, silversmith; b. London, Eng., rca 1671; m. Sybil Newmann; m. 2d, Abigail owle; at least 3 children, Thomas, Samuel, Jo- ph. Tithing-man in Boston, 1701, 08, 11; served as t. Boston Militia, 1704; constable, 1715, city sessor, 1720-27; created large quantities of finely orked silver. Died Apr. 8, 1746.

EDWARDS, John, planter, senator; b. Stafford ounty, Va., 1748; s. Hayden and Penelope (San- rd) E. Mem. Va. Ho. of Dels., 1781-83, 85-86, ; del. Ky. statehood convs., 1785-88, partici- ated in Ky. Constl. Conv., mem. U.S. Senate from y., 1791-95; mem. Ky. Ho. of Reps., 1795, Ky. enate, 1796-1800. Died Bourbon County, Ky., 837; buried at family estate nr. Paris, Ky.

EDWARDS, John, congressman; b. Ivy Mills, a., 1786; studied law. Admitted to bar, 1807, egan practice of law, Chester, Pa.; dep. atty. en. Delaware County (Pa.), 1811; counsel for efense in Wellington's trial for murder of Bonsall, 824; moved to West Chester, 1825, became en- aged in iron mfg.; later became mfr. nails, nr. len Mills, Pa.; mem. U.S. Ho. of Reps. (Whig) om Pa., 26th-27th congresses, 1839-43. Died n estate nr. Glen Mills, June 26, 1843; buried riend's (Hicksite) Cemetery of Middletown Meet- g House, Delaware County.

EDWARDS, John, congressman; b. Louisville, y., Oct. 24, 1805; studied law. Admitted to ar, moved to Ind.; mem. Ind. Ho. of Reps., 845-46; moved to Cal., elected an alcalde, 1849; eturned to Ind., 1852; mem. Ind. Senate, 1853; oved to Chariton, Ia., 1855; mem. Ia. Constl. onv.; mem. Ia. Ho. of Reps., 1856-60, speaker, 858-60; founder newspaper Patriot, 1857; ommd. lt. col. on staff of gov. Ia., during Civil Var, 1861; commd. col. 18th Regt., Ia. Volunteer nf., 1862; promoted brig. gen. U.S. Volunteers, 864; settled in Ft. Smith, Ark., at close of ivil War; U.S. assessor of internal revenue (apptd. y Pres. Johnson), 1866-69; mem. U.S. Ho. of eps. (Liberal Republican) from Ark., 42d Con- ress, 1871-Feb. 9, 1872 (contested election); ettled in Washington, D.C. Died Washington, Apr. 8, 1894; buried Arlington (Va.) Nat. emetery.

EDWARDS, John Cummins, gov. Mo., congress- nan; b. Frankfort, Ky., June 24, 1804; grad. lack's Coll., Ky.; studied law. Admitted to bar, 1825, began practice of law, Murfreesboro, Tenn., ater in Jefferson City, Mo.; sec. of state Mo., 1830-35, 37; dist. judge Cole County (Mo.), 1832-37; mem. Mo. Ho. of Reps. (Democrat) from Mo., 27th Congress, 1841-43; gov. Mo., 1844-48; moved to Stockton, Cal., 1949; mayor Stockton, 1851; engaged in cattle raising, merc. pursuits, eal estate bus. Died Stockton, Oct. 14, 1888; uried Rural Cemetery.

EDWARDS, Jonathan, clergyman, coll. pres.; b. East Windsor, Conn., Oct. 5, 1703; s. Rev. Timothy and Esther (Stoddard) E.; grad. Yale, Sept. 1720; m. Sarah Pierpont, July 1727, 4 chil- dren. Tutor, Yale, 1723-26; ordained to ministry Congregational Ch., 1727; expelled for reaction- ary ideas from Northampton, Mass., 1750; held stern belief in predestination, original sin; played important role in "Great Awakening" in 1730's; revived argument over test for ch. membership centering around Half-Way Convenant of 1662; a great preacher; disciples included Joseph Bellamy, Samuel Hopkins; Pres. Coll. of N.J. (now Prince- ton), 1757-58. Author: A Treatise Concerning Religious Affections, 1746; A Careful and Strict Enquiry into the Modern Prevailing Notions of that Freedom of Will which is Supposed to be Essential to Moral Agency, Vertue and Vice, Re- ward and Punishment, Praise and Blame, (resulted in his appearance as 1st great Am. philosopher), 1754. Died Princeton, N.J., Mar. 22, 1758; buried Princeton.

EDWARDS, Jonathan, clergyman, coll. pres.; b. Northampton, Mass., May 26, 1745; s. Jonathan and Sarah (Pierpont) E.; A.M., Coll. of N.J. (now Princeton), 1765, D.D (hon), 1785; m. Mary Porter, 1770; m. 2d, Mercy Sabin, 1783. Licensed to preach, 1766; pastor, White Haven, Conn., 1769; pres. Union Coll., Schenectady, N.Y., 1799-1801; editor and publisher History of the Works of Redemption (written by his father). Died Schenectady, Aug. 1, 1801.

EDWARDS, Justin, clergyman, reformer, coll. pres.; b. Westhampton, Mass., Apr. 25, 1787; s. Justin and Elizabeth (Clark) E.; grad. (valedictorian) Williams Coll., 1810; D.D. (hon.), Yale, 1827; m. Lydia Bigelow, Sept. 17, 1817, 6 children. Helped found New Eng. Tract Soc., 1814, later a dir. organized Andover (Mass.) South Parish Soc. for Doing Good, 1814; trustee Andover Theol. Sem., 1820-53, pres., 1836-42, pres. bd. trustees, 1850-53; 1st agt. Am. Temperance Soc., Boston, 1827-29, corr. sec., 1829; sec. Am. and Fgn. Sabbath Union, 1842. Author: Well Conditioned Farm; Joy in Heaven over One Sinner That Repenteth; The Way To Be Saved; On the Traffic in Ardent Spirits; Temperance Manual; Sabbath Manual. Died Bath Alum Springs, Va., July 23, 1853; buried Andover.

EDWARDS, Morgan, clergyman; b. Trevethin Parish, Monmouthshire, Eng., Apr. 28, 1722; attended Baptist Coll., Bristol, Eng.; married twice; m. 2d, Mrs. Singleton. Began preaching, 1738; pastor, Cork, Ireland, 1750-59; ordained to ministry Bapt. Ch., 1757; pastor Bapt. Ch., Phila., 1761-71; moved to Newark, Del., lectured and helped plan proposed 12 vol. history of Baptists in Am. Died Jan. 28, 1795.

EDWARDS, Ninian, senator, gov. Ill.; b. Montgomery county, Md., Mar. 17, 1775; s. Benjamin and Markaret (Beall) E.; grad. Dickinson Coll., Carlisle, Pa., 1792; m. Elvira Lane, 1803; children—Ninian Wirt, Albert Gallatin, Benjamin Stevenson, Julia, Margaret. Admitted to Ky. bar, 1798, Tenn. bar, 1799; Ky. circuit judge, 1803; chief justice Ky. Ct. Appeals, 1808; gov. Ill. Territory, 1809-18; mem. U.S. Senate from Ill., 1818-25; U.S. minister to Mexico, 1824; gov. Ill., 1826-30. Author: Life and Times of Ninian Edwards; History of Illionis, 1870; The Edwards Papers, 1884. Died Belleville, Ill., July 20, 1833.

EDWARDS, Ninian Wirt, supt. of schs.; b. Frankfort, Ky., Apr. 15, 1809; s. Ninian and Elvira (Lane) E.; law degree, Transylvania U., 1833; m. Elizabeth P. Todd, Feb. 16, 1832. Atty.-gen., State of Ill., 1834-35; businessman, Springfield, Ill., 1835; mem. Ill. Ho. of Reps. (Whig) from Sangamon County, 1836-40, 48-51; mem. Ill. Senate, 1844-48; mem. Ill. Constl. Conv., 1847; 1st supt. Ill. Pub. Schs., 1854-57; served as capt., commissary of supplies, 1862-65. Author: History of Illinois from 1778 to 1883; Life and Times of Ninian Edwards, 1870. Died Sept. 2, 1889.

EDWARDS, Pierpont, jurist; b. Northampton, Mass., Apr. 8, 1750; s. Jonathan and Sarah (Pierpont) E.; grad. Coll. of N.J. (now Princeton), 1768; m. Frances Ogden, May, 1769; m. 2d, Mary Tucker. Began law practice, New Haven, Conn., 1771; mem. lower house Conn. Legislature, 1777, 84-85, 87-90, speaker, 1787-90; mem. Continental Congress from Conn., 1787-88; mem. Conn. Conv. to ratify U.S. Constn.; leader of Jefferson Republicans in Conn.; judge U.S. Dist. Ct. Conn., 1806-26; attempted to prosecute libel cases against certain newspapers in a grand jury charge, overturned by U.S. Supreme Ct. in case U.S. vs Hudson & Goodwin, 1812; leader of Conn. Constl. Conv. which drew up a new constn. including disestablishment of church and state, 1818. Died Bridgeport, Conn., Apr. 5, 1826; buried Grove St. Cemetery, New Haven.

EDWARDS, Samuel, congressman; b. Delaware County, Pa., Mar. 12, 1785; attended common schs.; studied law. Admitted to bar, 1806, began practice of law, Chester, Pa.; served in War of 1812; mem. Pa. Ho. of Reps., 1814-16; mem. U.S. Ho. of Reps. (Federalist) from Pa., 16th-19th congresses, 1819-27; insp. of customs, 1838-42. Died Chester, Nov. 21, 1850; buried Chester Rural Cemetery.

EDWARDS, Talmadge, glove mfr.; b. Eng., 1747; m. Mary Sherman, 1780, 8 children including John. Came to Am., 1770; fought in Am. Revolution; father glove and mitten industry in Am.; first sold gloves in wholesale lots, Albany, N.Y., 1810; organized manufacture of gloves; improved process of tanning glove leather, originated "oil-tan" method for preparing buckskin. Died Johnstown, N.Y., June 4, 1821.

EDWARDS, Thomas McKey, congressman, businessman; b. Keene, N.H., Dec. 16, 1795; grad. Dartmouth, 1813; studied law. Admitted to bar, 1817, began practice of law, Keene; postmaster Keene, 1818-29; mem. N.H. Ho. of Reps., 1834, 36, 38-39; supervised constrn. of Cheshire R.R., 1st pres.; pres. of a bank, also fire ins. co.; Republican presdl. elector, 1856; mem. U.S. Ho. of Reps. (Rep.) from N.H., 36th-37th congresses, 1859-63. Died Keene, May 1, 1875; buried Woodlawn Cemetery.

EDWARDS, Thomas Owen, congressman, physician; b. Williamsburg, Ind., Mar. 29, 1810; studied medicine U. Md. Moved to Lancaster, O., 1836, practiced medicine; mem. U.S. Ho. of Reps. (Whig) from Ohio, 30th Congress, 1847-49; attended John Quincy Adams when stricken with apoplexy while making speech in Ho. of Reps. (Adams died in his arms); insp. marine hosps.; moved to Cincinnati, entered drug bus.; mem. pres. city council; prof. Ohio Med. Coll., Cincinnati; moved to Madison, Wis., then to Dubuze, Ia.; served as surgeon 3d Regt., Ia. Volunteer Inf., during Civil War; resumed practice of medicine, Lancaster, circa 1870; moved to Wheeling, W.Va., 1875. Died Wheeling, Feb. 5, 1876; buried Mt. Wood Cemetery.

EDWARDS, Weldon Nathaniel, planter, congressman; b. Nothampton County, N.C., Jan. 25, 1788; s. Benjamin Edwards; m. Lucy Norfleet, 1823. Mem. N.C. Ho. of Commons from Warren County, 1814-15; mem. U.S. Ho. of Reps. from N.C., 14th-19th congresses, 1815-27, supported John C. Calhoun; mem. NC.. Senate, 1833-46, 50-54, speaker, 1850-54; del. N.C. Constl. Conv., 1835; leader secession party, organized in N.C., 1861; pres. N.C. conv. to consider secession, 1861. Died Dec. 18, 1873.

EDWARDS, William, tanner; b. Elizabethtown, N.J., Nov. 11, 1770; s. Timothy and Rhoda (Ogden) E.; m. Rebecca Tappan, 1793, 11 children. Built tannery which was for years largest in U.S., 1815; a founder hide and leather industry in U.S.; introduced process used in 11 Am. tanneries by which leather was made in one-fourth the time used in European process; reduced cost of tanning sole leather from 12c to 4c a pound. Died Bklyn., Dec. 29, 1851.

EFNER, Valentine, congressman; b. Blenheim Hill, Schoharie County, N.Y., May 5, 1776. Engaged in agriculture; commd. maj. in War of 1812; mem. N.Y. Ho. of Reps., 1829; mem. U.S. Congress (Democrat) from N.Y., 24th Congress, 1835-37. Died Blenheim Hill, Nov. 20, 1865; buried Blenheim Hill Cemetery.

EGAN, Michael, clergyman; b. Ireland, 1761. Came to U.S., circa 1800; asst. priest Roman Catholic ch., Lancaster; pastor St. Mary's Ch., Phila., 1803-10; 1st bishop of Phila., 1810; preached in English and German. Died Phila., July 22, 1814.

EGBERT, Albert Gallatin, congressman; b. nr. Sandy Lake, Mercer County, Pa., Apr. 13, 1828; attended Austinburg (O.) Acad.; grad. med. dept. Western Res., Cleve., O., 1856, began practice of medicine, Clintonville, Pa.; moved to Cherrytree, Pa., practiced medicine until 1861; ret. from med. practice to become oil producer and farmer; served as volunteer surgeon during Civil War; mem. U.S. Ho. of Reps. (Democrat) from Pa., 44th Congress, 1875-77. Died Franklin, Pa., Mar. 28, 1896; buried Franklin Cemetery.

EGBERT, Joseph, congressman; b. nr. Bull Head, S.I., N.Y., Apr. 10, 1807; attended common schs. Engaged in agriculture; mem. U.S. Ho. of Reps. (Democrat) from N.Y., 27th Congress, 1841-43; supr. Southfield, Richmond County, 1855-56; clk. Richmond County, 1869. Died nr. New Dorp, S.I., July 7, 1888; buried Moravian Cemetery, New Dorp.

EGE, George, congressman; b. nr. Womelsdorf, Berks County, Pa., Mar. 9, 1748; attended common schs. Engaged in land and iron interests; mem. Pa. Ho. of Reps., 1783; an asso. judge Berks County, 1791-1818; mem. U.S. Ho. of Reps. (filled vacancy) from Pa., 4th-5th congresses, Dec. 8, 1796-Oct. 1797; builder, operator Schuylkill County Forge, nr. Port Clinton, Pa., 1804. Died Charming Forge, Berks County, Pa., Dec. 14, 1829; buried Zion's Ch. Cemetery, Womelsdorf.

EGGLESTON, Benjamin, congressman; b. Corinth, N.Y., Jan. 3, 1816. Moved (with parents) to Hocking County, O., 1831; moved to Cleve., O.; employed on canal boat, later became owner of several boats and asso. with various cos.; engaged in merc. pursuits, Cincinnati, 1845; presiding officer Cincinnati City Council; del. Republican Nat. Conv., Chgo., 1860; Rep. presdl. elector, 1860; mem. Ohio Senate, 1862-65,, 80-81; mem. U.S. Ho. of Reps. (Rep.) from Ohio, 39th-40th congresses, 1865-69. Died Cincinnati, Feb. 9, 1888; buried Spring Grove Cemetery.

EGGLESTON, Joseph, congressman; b. Middlesex County, Va., Nov. 24, 1754; grad. Coll. William and Mary, Williamsburg, Va., 1776. Served as capt. and maj. Lee's Lighthorse Cavalry in Continental Army, distinguished himself at Battle of Guilford Court House, capture of Augusta (Ga.), 1781; mem. Va. Ho. of Dels., 1785-88, 91-99; mem. Va. Privy Council, 1787; mem. U.S. Ho. of Reps. (Democrat, filled vacancy) from Va., 5th-6th congresses, Dec. 3, 1798-1801; engaged in agriculture; justice of peace, 1801-11. Died Amelia County, Va., Feb. 13, 1811; buried Old Grubhill Ch. Cemetery, nr. Amelia Court House, Va.

EGLOFFSTEIN, Frederick W. Von, see Von Egloffstein, Frederick W.

EICHBERG, Julius, violinist, composer; b. Dusseldorf, Germany, June 13, 1824; grad. Brussels Conservatory, 1845. Conservatory prof., ch. music leader, Geneva, Switzerland, 1846-56; came to U.S., 1857; mus. leader Boston Mus.; founded Boston Conservatory Music, 1867, dir., 1870-72; founded Eichberg Violin Sch.; composed a nat. hymn To Thee, O Country, light operas The Doctor of Alcantara, 1862, The Rose of Tyrol, 1865, The Two Cadis, 1868, A Night in Rome, 1874. Died Boston, Jan. 18, 1893.

EICHHOLTZ, Jacob, painter; b. Lancaster, Pa., Nov. 2, 1776; s. Leonard and Catharine Eichholtz; m. Catharine Hatz, 4 children; m. 2d, Catharine Trissler, 9 children. Apprenticed to coppersmith; worked as coppersmith, portraitist, later became full-time painter; painted in Boston, Phila., Balt., did 250 portraits, 1810-42. Died Lancaster, May 11, 1842.

EICKEMEYER, Rudolf, inventor, mfr.; b. Altenbamberg, Bavaria, Germany, Oct. 31, 1831; s. Christian and Katherine (Brehm) E.; m. Mary True Tarbell, July 1856 6 children. Came to America, 1850; devised 1st "whip-stitch" for hatbands, 1st successful hat stretching machines; patented 1st hatblocking machine, 1865; designed machine to pounce hats, 1869; developed 1st direct-connected ry. motor for use on N.Y. Elevated R.R.; developed differential gear for mowing and reaping, 1870; secured about 150 patents in U.S. and abroad, including 1st symmetrical drum armature, iron clad dynamo; discovered and was 1st employer of Charles P. Steinmetz; bus. consol. with Gen. Electric Co., 1892; v.p. Yonkers Sch. Bd., trustee 23 years. Died Washington, D.C., Jan. 23, 1895.

EIELSEN, Elling, clergyman; b. Voss, Norway, Sept. 19, 1804; s. Eiel Ingelzigtsen and Anna (Sunve) E.; m. Sigrid Tufte, July 3, 1843. Preached throughout Norway, Sweden and Denmark; came to Am., 1839; missionary among Indians; ordained minister, 1843, organized Evangelical Lutheran Ch. of America, 1846. Died Chgo., Jan. 10, 1883.

EINHORN, David, rabbi, leader Reform Judaism, abolitionist; b. Dispeck, Bavaria, Nov. 10, 1809; s. Maier and Karoline Einhorn; ed. Furth Talmudic Acad., U. Erlangen, U. Wurzburg, U. Munich (all Germany); m. Julie Ochs, 1844. Came to Am. to escape Jewish orthodoxy, 1855; rabbi Har Sinai Synagogue, Balt., 1855-61; strong abolitionist views led to forced flight during Balt. riot, 1861; officiated at Congregation Beth El, N.Y.C., 1874-79; founder mag. Sinai (organ for Reform Judaism), 1856. Published: Das Prinzip des Mosaismus und dessen Verhaeltnis zum Heidenthum und Rabbinischen Judenthum (his theol. system), 1854; Olath Tamid (reform modification of traditional Jewish prayer book which became basis of Union Prayer Book, ofcl. liturgy of Reform Judaism in Am.), 1856. Died N.Y.C., Nov. 2, 1879.

EINSIDEL, D., architect; b. Germany, 1852. Served in Franco-Prussian War, 1870; came to Am., circa 1875; settled in New Orleans, practiced as architect; designed numerous early bldgs. in New Orleans, including Hotel Victor, Wengers Theatre, Olympic Club, YMCA Bldg., Teutonic Bldg., most of Rice Mills in New Orleans. Died Feb. 19, 1896.

EISFELD, Theodor, musician; b. Wolfenbüttel, Germany, Apr. 11, 1816. Kapellmeister, Wiesbaden (Germany) court theater, 1839-43, Converts Viviennes, Paris, France; became hon. mem. Acad. of St. Cecilia, Italy; came to U.S., 1848; lived in N.Y.C., 1848-66; conducted N.Y. Philharmonic Soc., several years; 1st condr. Harmonic Soc., N.Y.C.; established quarter soirées, 1851; ret. to Wiesbaden, 1866. Died Wiesbaden, Sept. 2, 1882.

ELA, Jacob Hart, congressman; b. Rochetser, N.H., July 18, 1820; attended village sch., Rochester. Apprenticed in woolen mfg. bus., circa 1834, later learned printer's trade; engaged in agriculture; mem. N.H. Ho. of Reps., 1857-58; U.S. marshal, 1861-66; mem. U.S. Ho. of Reps. (Republican) from N.H., 40th-41st congresses, 1867-71; 5th auditor of treasury (apptd. by Pres. Grant), 1872-81; auditor of treasury for Post Office Dept., 1881-84. Died Washington, D.C., Aug. 21, 1884; buried North Side Cemetery, Rochester.

ELAM, Joseph Barton, congressman; b. nr. Hope, Hempstead County, Ark., June 12, 1821; studied law. Admitted to bar, 1843, began practice of law, Alexandria, La.; moved to De Soto Parish, 1851; mem., speaker La. Ho. of Reps., 1851-61; del. La. Constl. Conv., 1861, signed ordinance of secession; mem. U.S. Ho. of Reps. (Democrat) from La., 45th-46th congresses, 1877-81. Died Mansfield, De Soto Parish, July 4, 1885; buried Mansfield Cemetery.

ELBERT, Samuel, gov. Ga.; b. Prince William Parish, S.C., 1743; m. Elizabeth Rae, 6 children. Commd. capt., grenadier co. Ga. Militia, 1774; mem. Ga. Council Safety, 1775; commd. lt. col. Continental Army, 1776, col. 1776; brevetted brig. gen., 1783; gov. Ga., 1785-86; sheriff Chatham County; v.p. Ga. Soc. Cincinnati; grand master Ga. Masonic Order. Died Savannah, Ga., Nov. 1, 1788.

ELDER, George, clergyman, coll. pres.; b. Hardin's Creek, Ky., Aug. 11, 1793; studied at Mt. St. Mary's Coll., Md., also St. Mary's Sem., Balt. Ordained priest Roman Catholic Ch., 1819, became an asst. at cathedral, Bardstown, Ky.; founder, pres. of coll., Bardstown, 1830-38; an editor Louisville Catholic Advocate, 1836, wrote satirical columns Letters to Brother Jonathan. Died Sept. 28, 1838.

ELDER, John Adams, artist; b. Fredericksburg, Va., Feb. 3, 1833. Went to N.Y.C., 1850, to Düsseldorf, Germany, 1851; returned to N.Y.C., 1856, to Fredericksburg, 1861; served with Confederate Army during Civil War; worked in Richmond, Va., after Civil War; painted portraits, genre, landscape and battle paintings. Died Fredericksburg, Feb. 24, 1895.

ELDER, William, journalist; b. Somerset, Pa., July 23, 1806; s. William Gore and Magdalen (Armstrong) E.; attended Jefferson Med. Coll., Phila.; m. Sara Maclean, Dec. 24, 1833. Practiced medicine, Juniata County, Pa., 1833; settled in Pitts., 1838; recorder of deeds (Whig) Allegheny County, Pa., 1839; admitted to Pa. bar, 1842; practiced in Pitts., 1842-45; moved to Phila., wrote, lectured; editor Liberty Herald, 1847; contbd. to The Republic, 1848, Nat. Era, other Liberty Party jours.; statistician U.S. Treasury Dept., 1861-66, clk. Comptroller's Office, 1873-85. Author: Periscopics, 1854; Questions of the Day: Economic and Social, 1871. Died Phila., Apr. 5, 1885.

ELDREDGE, Charles Augustus, congressman, lawyer; b. Bridport, Vt., Feb. 17, 1820; attended common schs.; studied law. Admitted to bar, 1846, began practice of law, Canton, N.Y.; moved to Fond du Lac, Wis., 1848; mem. Wis. Senate, 1854-56; mem. U.S. Ho. of Reps. (Democrat) from Wis., 38th-43d congresses, 1863-75. Died Fond du Lac, Oct. 26, 1896; buried Rienzi Cemetery.

ELDREDGE, Nathaniel Buel, congressman; b. Auburn, N.Y., Mar. 28, 1813; attended common schs.; financially unable to accept appointment as cadet to U.S. Mil. Acad., 1829; attended Fairfield Med. Coll. Began practice of medicine, Commerce, Mich.; clk. Mich. Senate, 1845; mem. Mich. Ho. of Reps., 1848; judge of probate, 1852-56; admitted to bar, began practice of law, 1854; held various minor offices; served as capt. Co. G., 7th Regt., Mich. Volunteers, during Civil War, 1861; promoted maj., 1861, lt. col., 1862; sheriff Lenawee County, 1874; mem. U.S. Ho. of Reps. (Democrat) from Mich., 48th-49th congresses, 1883-87. Died Adrian, Mich., Nov. 27, 1893; buried Oakwood Cemetery.

ELDRIDGE, Shalor Winchell, businessman; b. West Springfield, Mass., Aug. 29, 1816; s. Lyman and Phoebe (Winchell) E.; m. Mary Norton, 1839. Railroad contractor, Southampton, Mass., 1838-55; entered hotel business, Kansas City, Mo., 1855; became leader anti-slavery forces in Kan.; his hotel (also several anti-slavery newspapers) destroyed by mob, 1856; mem. delegation of Kan. citizens who obtained appointment of J. W. Geary as territorial gov. Kan. in Washington, D.C.; active in Republican Party, del. Rep. Nat. Conv., Phila., 1856; mem. from Kan. of Hyatt Com. to enlist mems. for Free-State Party, 1856-57, led groups of recruits into Kan.; q.m. gen. Kan., 1858-61; q.m. 2d Kan. Regt. of Volunteers, 1861; served as paymaster U.S. Army, 1863-64; building contractor, Kan., 1865-73; engaged in mining enterprises, Colo., Ark., after 1873. Died Lawrence, Kan., Jan. 16, 1899; buried Lawrence.

ELIOT, Charles, landscape architect; b. Cambridge, Mass., Nov. 1, 1859; s. Charles William and Ellen (Peabody) E.; B.A., Harvard, 1882, postgrad. Bussey Inst., Harvard; m. Mary Pitkin, Nov. 28, 1888. With firm Frederick Law Olmsted, landscape architects, Brookline, Mass., 1883-85; an organizer, adviser Met. Park Commn., Boston, 1892, assisted in attempt to develop park system; an organizer firm Olmsted, Olmsted and Eliot to handle Chgo. World's Fair, 1893; Charles Eliot Professorship of Landscape Architecture, Charles Eliot Travelling Fellowship, Charles Eliot Bo Collection (all at Harvard) in his honor; wr tech. papers collected and edited by Charles Eliot, published under title Charles Eliot, Lan scape Architect, 1902. Died Mar. 25, 1897.

ELIOT, Jared, clergyman, physician; b. Gu ford, Conn., Nov. 7, 1685; s. Joseph and Ma (Wyllys) E.; grad. Yale, 1706; m. Hannah Smi son, 1710, 11 children. Ordained to ministry Co gregational Ch.; pastor Killingworth (now Cli ton) (Conn.) Ch., 1708-63; trustee Yale Cor 1730-63; fellow Royal Soc. of London, 1757-6 one of 1st to develop iron ore beds in Northwes ern Conn.; helped introduce silk culture in colony; his med. practice wide and successfu Author: Essay on Field Husbandry in New En land, 1759. Died Killingworth, Apr. 22, 1763.

ELIOT, John, missionary; b. Widford, Eng., Au 1604; s. Bennett and Lettice (Aggar) E.; gra Jesus Coll., Cambridge (Eng.) U., 1622; m. An Mumford, Oct. 1632, 6 children. Came to Bosto 1631; tchr. in ch., Boston, 1631-32; pastor, Ro bury, Mass., 1632-90; preached to Indians, 1st English, later in their own langs.; translated Ne Testament (1661) and Old Testament (1663) int langs. of various Indian tribes in Mass.; a found Soc. for Propagation of Gospel in New Eng.; founde 1st Indian ch., Natick, Mass., 1660; his entire mis sionary program was destroyed by King Philip's Wa Author: A Primer or Catechism, in the Massachuset Indian Language, 1654; The Christian Commor wealth, 1659; The Indian Primer, 1669. Died Ma 21, 1690.

ELIOT, Samuel, coll. pres., philanthropist; Boston, Dec. 22, 1821; s. William Harvard an Margaret (Bradford) E.: grad. Harvard. 183 LL.D. (hon.), 1880; LL.D. (hon.), Columbia, 186 m. Emily Otis, June 7, 1853. Prof. history Trini Coll., Hartford, Conn., 1856-60, pres., 1860-6 lectr. Harvard, 1870-73, mem. bd. overseer 1866-72; headmaster Girls' High and Normal Sch. 1872-76; apptd. supt. city schs., Boston, 1878; d rected energies to charitable endeavors includir Mass. Gen. Hosp., Perkins Inst. for Blind, Mas Sch. for Feeble Minded, Boston Mus. Fine Art Author: Passages from the History of Libert 1847; The Liberty of Rome, 1849; The Ear Christians, 1853. Died Beverley Farms, Mass. Sept. 14, 1898; buried Mt. Auburn Cemetery, Cam bridge, Mas.

ELIOT, Samuel Atkins, mayor, congressmar b. Boston, Mar. 5, 1798; s. Samuel and Catherin (Atkins) E.; grad. Harvard, 1817, grad. Harvar Sch. Divinity, 1820; m. Mary Lyman, June 1 1826, 5 children including Charles William. Mem Mass. Gen. Ct., several terms; 1st pres. Bosto Acad. Music; introduced to music Boston Pub Schs.; mayor Boston, 1837-39; treas. Harvard 1842-53; mem. U.S. Ho. of Reps., 31st Congress Aug. 22, 1850-Mar. 3, 1851; 1st pres. Boston Prov dent Assn.; organizer 1st paid fire dept., 1st da police in Boston. Author: A Sketch of the Histor of Harvard College and of Its Present State, 1848 Slavery and Its Prospects in the United States A Memoir of Ephraim Peabody. Died Cambridge Mass., Jan. 29, 1862.

ELIOT, Thomas Dawes, congressman; b. Boston ton, Mar. 20, 1808; grad. Columbian Coll. (no George Washington U.), 1825. Admitted to bar 1831, began practice of law, New Bedford Mass.; mem. Mass. Ho. of Reps., 1839; Mass Senate, 1846; mem. U.S. Ho. of Reps. from Mass (as Whig, filled vacancy), 33d Congress, 1854-55 (as Republican), 36th-40th congresses, 1859-69 del. Free-Soil Conv., Worcester, Mass., 1855. Die New Bedford, June 14, 1870; buried Oak Grov Cemetery.

ELIOT, William Greenleaf, clergyman, univ. chancellor; b. New Bedford, Mass., Aug. 5, 1811; s. William Greenleaf and Margaret (Dawes) E.; grad. Columbian Coll., 1829; attended Harvard Divinity Sch., 1834, S.T.D., 1854; m. Abby A. Cranch, 1837, 5 children. Founder Ch. of the Messiah, St. Louis (1st Unitarian Soc. West of Mississippi River), 1834, pastor, 1834-73; pres. St. Louis Sch. Bd., 1848; founder Mission Free Sch., 1856; pres. State Inst. for Blind, 1853; obtained state charter for Eliot Sem. (now Washington U.), St. Louis, 1853, organized corp., 1854, became pres. bd., acting chancellor, 1870, chancellor, 1872-87. Author: A Manual of Prayer, 1851; Discourses on the Doctrines of Christianity, 1852; Lectures to Young Men, 1853; Lectures to Young Women, 1853; The Unity of God, 1854; Early Religious Education, 1855; Discipline of Sorrow, 1855. Died Pass Christian, Miss., Jan. 23, 1887.

ELLERY, Christopher, senator; b. Newport, R.I., Nov. 1, 1768; grad. Yale, 1787; studied law. admitted to bar, began practice of law, Newport; clk. Superior Ct. Newport County, 1794-98; mem. U.S. Senate (Democrat, filled vacancy) from R.I., May 6, 1801-05; apptd. U.S. commr. of loans at Providence by Pres. Jefferson, 1806; collector of customs Newport, 1820-34. Died Midetown, R.I., Dec. 2, 1840; buried Island Cemetery, Newport.

ELLERY, Frank, naval officer; b. Newport, R.I., ly 23, 1794; s. Christopher and Clarissa (Bird) ; m. Elizabeth Martin, Aug. 4, 1835. Became idshipman U.S. Navy, 1812; wounded at 1st sea attle; received sword and reward from Congress, 314; served against Algerian pirates; promoted lt., 320; served under Capt. Jesse D. Elliot, 1825-; lt. in command in Enterprise, short period in 339; resigned, rescinded, reinstated waiting for ders until 1861 (became oldest lt. in service); rmed in poverty, Vt.; in command Naval renezvous, Boston, Phila., later converted ships for ockade; ret. as commodore, 1867. Died Castleton, t., Mar. 24, 1871.

ELLERY, William, Continental congressman, rist; b. Newport, R.I., Dec. 22, 1727; s. William nd Elizabeth (Almy) E.; grad. Harvard, 1747; m. nn Remington, 1750; m. 2d, Abigail Cary, 1767. n original incorporator R.I. Coll., 1764; admitted) R.I. bar, 1770; mem. Continental Congress, 776-80, 81-82, 82-86; signer Declaration of Inependence; apptd. chief justice R.I. Superior Ct., 785; commr. Continental Loan Office for R.I., 786-90; collector customs Newport Dist., 1790-820. Died Newport, Feb. 15, 1820.

ELLET, Charles, civil engr.; b. Penn's Manor, a., Jan. 1, 1810; s. Charles and Mary (Israel) E.; ttended Ecole Polytechnique, Paris, France; m. lvira Daniel, 1837, 1 son, Charles Rivers. Chief ngr. James River and Kanawha Canal, 1836; degned, built wire suspension bridge across Schuyill River nr. Phila., 1842; designed, built susension bridge across Niagara River below the alls, 1847; completed Wheeling (W.Va.) Bridge or B. & O. R.R., 1849; engr. Hempfield R.R., 851-55, Va. Central R.R., 1853-57; served as col. ngrs. U.S. Army 1861-62; converted fleet of Misssippi steamers into rams, sank or disabled sevral Confederate vessels off Memphis, 1862; conidered one of Am.'s great engrs. Author: Physical eography of the Mississippi Valley with Sugestions as to the Improvement of Navigation f the Ohio and Other Rivers, 1853; Coast and larbor Defenses, or the Substitution of Steam attering-rams for Ships of War, 1855. Died Cairo, ll., June 21, 1862.

ELLET, Elizabeth Fries Lummis, author; b. Sodus oint, N.Y., Oct. 1818; d. Dr. William Nixion nd Sarah (Maxwell) Lummis; attended Female em., Aurora, N.Y.; m. Dr. William H. Ellet, 835. Lived in Columbia, S.C., 1835-49; fluent in rench, German, Italian, studied history; settled n N.Y.C., 1850; a writer her entire life. Author: he Characters of Schiller, 1839; Women of the merican Revolution, 1848; Watching Spirits, 1851. ditor: The New Cyclopaedia of Domestic Economy nd Practical Housekeeper, 1872. Died N.Y.C., June , 1877.

ELLETT, Henry Thomas, congressman, lawyer; . Salem, N.J., Mar. 8, 1812; attended Princeon; studied law. admitted to bar, 1833, began ractice of law, Bridgeton, N.J.; moved to Port ibson, Miss, 1837; mem. U.S. Ho. of Reps. (Demorat, filled vacancy) from Miss., 29th Congress, an. 26-Mar. 3, 1847; mem. Miss. Senate, 1853-65; emocratic presdl. elector, 1856; code commr., 857; mem. Miss. Secession Conv., 1861, mem. om. that framed and reported Miss. secession rdinance; declined appointment as postmanter en Confederate States Am., 1861; judge Miss., upreme Ct., 1865-68; moved to Memphis, Tenn., 868; elected chancellor 12th Div. Tenn., 1886. ied while delivering welcome address to Pres. rover Cleveland, Memphis, Oct. 15, 1887; buried lmwood Cemetery.

ELLICOTT, Andrew, surveyor, mathematician; . Bucks County, Pa., Jan. 24, 1754; s. Joseph nd Judith (Bleaker) E.; m.Sarah Brown, 1775; 9 hildren. Founder Ellicott City, (Md.) 1774; erved to maj. during Am. Revolution; pubsher U.S. Almanack, from 1782; completed Mason Dixon Line in West Pa., 1784; mem. Md. Legisature, 1786; mem. Pa. commns. for running Westrn (1785) and No. (1786) state boundaries; sureyed islands in Ohio, Allegheny rivers, 1788; pubished 1st map of "Territory" of Columbia (now).C.), 1793; drew up Ellicott Plan (survey of Vashington, D.C.; redrew L'Enfant's plans of Vashington under direction of Thomas Jefferson; commr. to lay out town of Presqu' Isle (Erie), Pa., 1794; commd. to survey frontier between Fla. nd U.S., 1796; prof. mathematics U.S. Mil. Acad., 1813. Died West Point, N.Y., Aug. 28, 1820

ELLICOTT, Benjamin, congressman; b. nr. Balt., Apr. 17, 1765. Accompanied his brothers to pper Can. on survey to determine western boundary of N.Y. State, 1789; surveyor and draftsman or Holland Land Co., N.Y. and Pa.; judge Geneee County (N.Y.) Ct. of Common Pleas, 1803; an xtensive landowner; mem. U.S. Ho. of Reps. Democrat) from N.Y., 15th Congress, 1817-19; et., moved to Williamsville, N.Y., 1826. Died Williamsville, Dec. 10, 1827; buried graveyard at Williamsville, reinterred Batavia (N.Y.) Cemetery, 1849.

ELLICOTT, Joseph, engr., land agt.; b. Bucks County,. Pa., Nov. 1, 1760; s. Andrew and Judith (Bleaker) E. Began survey of Holland Purchase, 1797; local agt. Holland Land Co., Western N.Y., 1800-20; chose site and laid out plans for City of Buffalo (N.Y.) (similar to plan of Washington, D.C.), originally named New Amsterdam by Holland Land Co., renamed by act of legislature "Town of Buffaloe," 1810. Died Batavia, N.Y., Aug. 19, 1826.

ELLIOT, Charles, clergyman, editor, univ. pres.; b. County Donegal, Ireland, May 16, 1792. Came to U.S., 1814. Supt., Wyandote Indian Mission, Upper Sandusky, O. 1822; presiding elder Ohio dist. Methodist Ch., 1824-25, Pitts. dist., 1833-34, Dayton (O.) dist., 1850-51; prof. langs. Madison Coll., Uniontown, Pa., 1827-31; editor Pitts. Conf. Jour., 1834-48, Western Christian Advocate, 1852-56, 52; pres. Iowa Wesleyan U., 1856-61, 63-66. Author: Treatise on Baptism, 1834; Delineation of Roman Catholicism, 2 vols., 1842; Sinfulness of American Slavery, 2 vols., 1851. Died Mt. Pleasant, Ia., Jan. 8, 1869.

ELLIOT, James, congressman; b. Gloucester Mass., Aug. 18, 1775. s. James and Martha (Day). E.; m. Lucy Dow. Enlisted as 1st non-commd. officer in co. of 2d U.S. Sub-Legion, Springfield, Mass., 1793; admitted to Mass. bar, 1803; mem. U.S. Ho. of Reps. from Mass., 8th-10th congresses, 1803-09; commd. capt. U.S. Army, 1812; edited Freeman's Journal, Phila.; clk. Windham County Ct., 1817-35; mem. Vt. State Ho. of Reps., 1818, 19, 37; register Probate Ct., 1822-34. Author: The Poetical and Miscellaneous Works of James Elliot, 1798. Died Newfane, Vt., Nov. 10, 1839; buried Prospect Hill Cemetery, Battleboro, Vt.

ELLIOT, Jonathan, editor, publisher, author; b. Carlisle, Eng., 1784; married twice; 4 children including Jonathan, Henry. Came to N.Y.C., 1802; fought in war for independence in Granada under Bolivar, 1810, War of 1812; formed partnership to produce 1st Washington (D.C.) daily evening newspaper, 1813, became printer Washington City Gazette (1st published 1814), became publisher and editor, 1815; published Debates, Resolutions and Other Proceedings in Convention on the Adoption of the Federal Constitution, 5 vols., (most complete source of debates, still used today as basic source material), 1827-34; published Diplomatic Code, 1827, 2d edit. 1834. Author: Sketches of the District of Columbia, 1830; Funding System of the U.S., 1845. Died Washington, D.C., Mar. 12, 1846.

ELLIOTT, Benjamin, lawyer; b. Charleston, S.C., Mar. 1787; s. Thomas and Mary (Pinckney) E.; grad. Coll. of N.J. (now Princeton), 1806; studied law with Thomas Parker, Charleston, 1807-10; m. Catherine Savage. Admitted to bar, Charleston, began practice law, 1810; mem. S.C. Legislature from Charleston, circa 1814-18; mem. Charleston City Council, circa 1820; achieved reputation as author polit. pamphlets and legislative compilations. Author: (pamphlet) A Refutation of the Calumnies Circulated Against the Southern and Western States Respecting the Institution of Slavery, 1822; The Militia System of South Carolina, 1835. Died Charleston, Sept. 1836; buried Charleston.

ELLIOTT, Charles Loring, painter; b. Scipio, N.Y., Oct. 12, 1812; s. Daniel and Mehitable (Booth) E.; studied under John Trumbull and John Quidor; m. Mary Elizabeth Shire, 1 child. Painter over 700 portraits of famous people, including Fitz-Greene Halleck, James E. Freeman, Matthew Vassar, James Fenimore Cooper, Gov. Bouck, Gov. Seymour, Gov. Hunt, Erastus Corning; exhibited portrait of Fletcher Harper at Paris Exhbn.; elected to N.A.D., 1846. Died Albany, N.Y., Aug. 25, 1868; buried Greenwood Cemetery, Bklyn.

ELLIOTT, James, congressman, lawyer; b. Gloucester, Mass., Aug. 18, 1775; studied law. Worked on farm, clerked in store, during early years; moved to Guilford, Vt., 1790; served as sgt. in Indian war in Ohio, 1793; published several works of poems and essays, 1798; clk. Vt. Ho. of Reps., 1801-03, 18-19, 37-38; admitted to bar, 1803, began practice of law, Brattleboro, Vt.; mem. U.S. Ho. of Reps. (Federalist) from Vt., 8th-10th congresses, 1803-09; became newspaper publisher, Phila.; served as capt. for short time during War of 1812; clk. Windham County Ct., 1817-35; moved to Newfane, Vt.; register Probate Ct., 1822-34; states atty. Windham County, 1837-39. Died Newfane, Nov. 10, 1839; buried Prospect Hill Cemetery, Brattleboro.

ELLIOTT, James Thomas, congressman; b. Columbus, Ga., Apr. 22, 1823; studied law. Admitted to bar, 1854, began practice of law, Camden, Ark.; became pres. Miss., Ouachita & Red River R.R., 1858; circuit judge 6th Jud. Dist. Ark., 1865-66; founder, editor South Ark. Journal, 1867; mem. U.S. Ho. of Reps. (Republican, filled vacancy) from Ark., 40th Congress, Jan. 13-Mar. 3, 1869; mem. Ark. Senate, 1870; judge 9th Jud. Dist., 1872-74. Died Camden, July 28, 1875; buried Oakland Cemetery.

ELLIOTT, Jesse Duncan, naval officer; b. Hagerstown Md., July 14, 1782; s. Robert and Ann E.; m. Frances Vaughan, Apr. 7, 1812; at least 1 son, Washington Lafayette. Commd. lt. U.S. Navy, 1810; in command naval forces on Lake Erie, 1812; master comdt., 1813; in command ship Niagara, 1813; 2d in command to Commodore Perry at Battle of Lake Erie; mem. Stephen Decatur's squadron against Algiers, 1815; commanded sloop Ontario, 1815-16; commd. capt., 1818; commanded W. Indian Squadron, 1829-32; comdt. Boston Navy Yard, 1833-35; comdr.-in-chief Mediterranean Squadron, 1835-38; commanded Phila. Navy Yard, 1844. Died Phila., Dec. 10, 1845.

ELLIOTT, John, senator; b. St. Johns Parish (now Liberty County), Ga., Oct. 24, 1773; grad. Yale, 1794; studied law. Admitted to bar, began practice of law, Sunbury, Ga., 1797; held several local offices; mem. U.S. Senate from Ga., 1819-25. Died Sunbury, Aug. 9, 1827; buried Old Midway Cemetery, Liberty County.

ELLIOTT, John Milton, congressman; b. Scott County, Va., May 20, 1820; grad. Emory and Henry Coll., Emory, Va., 1841; studied law. Admitted to bar, 1843, began practice of law, Prestonsburg, Ky.; mem. Ky. Ho. of Reps., 1847, 61; mem. U.S. Ho. of Reps. (Democrat) from Ky., 33d-35th congresses, 1853-59; rep. from Ky. 1st, 2d Confederate congresses; circuit judge, 1868-74; judge Ct. of Appeals, 1876-79. Assassinated, Frankfort, Ky., Mar. 26, 1879; buried State Cemetery, Frankfort.

ELLIOTT, Robert Brown, congressman; b. Boston, Aug. 11, 1842; attended High Hollow Acad., London, Eng., 1853; grad. Eton Coll., Eng., 1859; studied law. Admitted to bar, began practice of law, Columbia, S.C.; mem. S.C. Constl. Conv., 1868; mem. S.C. Ho. of Reps., 1868-70, 74-76, speaker; asst. adj. gen. S.C., 1869-71; mem. U.S. Ho. of Reps. (Republican) from S.C., 1871-Nov. 1, 1874; moved to New Orleans, 1881. Died New Orleans, Aug. 9, 1884; buried St. Louis Cemetery Number 2.

ELLIOTT, Stephen, legislator, banker, coll. pres.; b. Beaufort, S.C., Nov. 11, 1771; s. William and Mary (Barnwell) E.; grad. Yale, 1791, L.L.D. (hon.), 1819; LL.D. (hon.), Harvard, 1822, Columbia, 1825; m. Esther Habersham, 1796. Mem. S.C. Ho. of Reps., 1794; mem. S.C. Senate, 1808-12, author 1st free schooling act; 1st pres. Bank of State of S.C., 1812-30; a founder Lit. and Philos. Soc. S.C., pres., 1814-30; pres. Library Soc., 1816; elected pres. S.C. Coll., 1820; a founder Med. Coll. S.C., elected 1st prof. botany and natural history, 1824; co-founder So. Review, 1828. Author: The Botany of South Carolina and Georgia, 2 vols., 1821-24. Died Charleston, S.C., Mar. 28, 1830.

ELLIOTT, Washington Lafayette, army officer; b. Carlisle, Pa., Mar. 31, 1825; s. Jesse Duncan and Frances (Vaughan) E.; ed. Dickinson Coll.; attended U.S. Mil. Acad., 1841-44. Commd. 2d lt. U.S. Army, 1846, 1st lt. 1847, capt., 1854, col., 1861, maj., 1861; commd. brig. gen. U.S. Volunteers, 1862; chief of cavalry, 1862; in command Dept. of N.W., 1862-63; commanded 3d div. III Corps, Army of Potomac, 1863; commd. lt. col., 1866, col., 1878; ret. as maj. gen., 1879; received 5 brevets for distinguished conduct during Civil War; v.p. Cal. Safe Deposit and Trust Co. Died San Francisco, June 29, 1888.

ELLIOTT, William, state legislator; b. Beaufort, S.C., Apr. 27, 1788; s. William and Phoebe (Waight) E.; grad. Harvard, 1809; m. Anne Hutchinson Smith, 1817. Gentleman farmer on father's plantation; mem. S.C. House of Reps. from St. Helena Parish; mem. S.C. Senate, resigned rather than vote for nullification, 1832. Author: Carolina Sports by Land and Water, 1846; The Letters of Agricola, 1852. Died Charleston, S.C., Feb. 3, 1863.

ELLIS, Caleb, congressman; b. Walpole, Mass., Apr. 16, 1767; grad. Harvard, 1793; studied law. Admitted to bar; moved to Newport, N.H., then to Claremont, N.H.; mem. U.S. Ho. of Reps. from N.H.,, 9th Congress, 1805-07; mem. N.H. Ho. of Reps., 1803; mem. N.H. Gov.'s Council, 1809-10; mem. N.H. Senate, 1811; presdl. elector on Clinton-Ingersoll ticket, 1812; judge N.H. Superior Ct., 1813-16. Died Claremont, May 6, 1816; buried Broad Street Cemetery.

ELLIS, Calvin, physician, educator; b. Boston, Aug. 15, 1826; s. Luther and Betsey E.; grad. Harvard, 1846, M.D., 1849. Mem. 1st Harvard Boat Club; asst. in pathology Harvard Med. Sch., prof., 1867-83, dean, 1869; admitting physician, pathologist Mass. Gen. Hosp.; leading exponent of diagnosis by elimination of symptoms of disease; bequeathed $150,000 to Harvard Med. Sch. Mem. Am. Acad. Arts and Scis. 1859. Author: Obstruction of the Lungs, caused by Pressure on the Primary Bronchus; The Tendency of Disease in One Part to Excite it in Another; also 40 or more med. articles, including Boylston prize essay "Tubercle", 1860. Died Boston, Dec. 14, 1883.

ELLIS, Chesselden, congressman, lawyer; b. New Windsor, Vt., 1808; grad. Union Coll., Schenectady, N.Y., 1823; studied law. Admitted to bar, 1829, began practice of law, Waterford, N.Y.; pros. atty. Saratoga County (N.Y.), 1837-43; mem. U.S. Ho. of Reps. (Democrat) from N.Y., 28th Congress, 1843-45; moved to N.Y.C., 1845, continued practice of law. Died N.Y.C., May 10, 1854; buried Albany (N.Y.) Cemetery.

ELLIS, Ezekiel John, congressman, lawyer; b. Covington, La., Oct. 15, 1840; attended Centenary Coll., Jackson, La., 1855-58; grad. law dept. La. State U. at Pineville (now at Baton Rouge), 1861. Commd. 1st lt. Confederate Army, Civil War, promoted capt. 16th Regt., La. Inf., served 2 years; captured at Battle of Missionary Ridge (Tenn.), held prisoner on Johnsons Island, Lake Erie, until end of war; admitted to La. bar, 1866, began practice of law, Convington; mem. La. Senate, 1866-70; mem. U.S. Ho. of Reps. (Democrat) from La., 44th-48th congresses, 1875-85. Died Washington, D.C., Apr. 25, 1889; buried Ellis family cemetery, "Ingleside," nr. Amite, La.

ELLIS, George Edward, clergyman, historian; b. Boston, Aug. 8, 1814; s. David and Sarah (Rogers) E.; grad. Harvard, 1833, grad. Harvard Divinity Sch., 1836, S.T.D. (hon.), 1857, LL.D. (hon.), 1883; m. Elizabeth Eager, Apr. 15, 1840; m. 2d, Lucretia Goddard Gould, Oct. 22, 1859; 1 son. Ordained to ministry Unitarian Ch., 1840; pastor Harvard Unitarian Ch., Charlestown, Mass., 1840-69; co-editor Christian Editor, 1842-45; an editor Christian Examiner, 1849-55; overseer Harvard, 1850-79, sec. bd. overseers, 1853-54, 1st prof. systematic theology Harvard Divinity Sch., 1857-63; v.p. Mass. Hist. Soc., 1877-85, pres., 1885-94; Author: A Half Century of Unitarian Controversy, 1857; The Aims and Purposes of the Founders of Massachusetts, 1869; The Puritan Age and Rule in the Colony of Massachussetts Bay 1629-1685, 1888; also hist. biographies John Mason, 1844, Anne Hutchinson, 1845, William Penn, 1847. Died Boston, Dec. 20, 1894.

ELLIS, Henry, colonial gov.; b. County Monaghan, Ireland, Aug. 29, 1721; s. Francis and Joan (Maxwell) E.; studied law Middle Temple, London, Eng. Led expdn. commd. by Parliament to find N.W. Passage to Pacific, 1746-47; achieved fame as explorer, though failed to discover passage; gov. Colony of Ga., 1757-60, reformed law of land titles, helped establish Anglican Ch., pacified Creek Indians; provided protection against French and Spanish naval attacks along coast during French and Indian War; gov. Nova Scotia, 1761-63; fellow Royal Soc., Eng. Author: Voyage to Hudson's Bay. . ., 1748. Died Naples, Italy, Jan. 21, 1806.

ELLIS, John Willis, gov. N.C.; b. Rowan County, N.C., Nov. 23, 1820; s. Anderson and Judith (Bailey) E.; grad. U. N.C., 1841; m. Mary White, Aug. 25, 1844; m. 2d, Mary Daves, Admitted to N.C. bar, 1842; mem. N.C. Ho. of Commons, 1844-48; judge N.C. Superior Ct., 1848-58; gov. N.C., 1858-61; on behalf of Confederate cause, took formal possession of Ft. Macon, Beaufort, N.C., powder works, Wilmington, N.C., U.S. Arsenal, Fayetteville, N.C.; gov. during secession of N.C. Died Red Sulphur Springs, Va., July 7, 1861; buried Salisbury, N.C.

ELLIS, Powhatan, jurist, senator, diplomat; b. Amherst County, Va., Jan. 17, 1790; s. Maj Josiah and Jane (Shelton) E.; grad. Dickinson Coll., 1810; grad. in law from Coll. William and Mary, 1813; m. Eliza Winn, Feb. 28, 1831, 2 children. Admitted to Va. bar, 1813; moved to Miss., 1816; judge Miss. Supreme Ct., 1818-25; mem. U.S. Senate from Miss., Dec. 3, 1827-32; U.S. judge Miss. dist., 1832-36; U.S. charge d'affaires Mexico City, 1836-39; U.S. minister to Mexico, 1839-42; Ellisville (Miss.) named for him. Died Richmond, Va., Mar. 18, 1863; buried Shockoe Cemetery, Richmond.

ELLIS, William Cox, congressman, lawyer; b. Ft. Muncy, Pa., May 5, 1787; grad. Friends' Sch. nr. Pennsdale, Pa., 1803; studied law. Dep. surveyor gen., 1803-10; cashier Union and Northumberland County Bank, 1810-18; admitted to bar, 1817, began practice of law, Muncy; elected mem. U.S. Ho. of Reps. (Federalist) from Pa., 17th Congress, 1820, resigned before Congress assembled, served in 18th Congress, 1823-25; mem. Pa. Ho. of Reps., 1825-26; became a Republican, 1856. Died Muncy, Dec. 13, 1871; buried Muncy Cemetery.

ELLISON, Andrew, congressman, lawyer; b. West Union, O., 1812; attended public schs.; studied law. Admitted to bar, Adams County, O., 1835, began practice of law, Georgetown, O., 1835; pros. atty. Brown County (O.), 1840-43; mem. Ohio Ho. of Reps., 1846; mem. U.S. Ho. of Reps. (Democrat) from Ohio, 33d Congress, 1853-55. Died circa 1860.

ELLMAKER, Amos,, lawyer; b. "Walnut Bottom" farm, Lancaster County, Pa., Feb. 2, 1787; grad. Princeton; studied law, Lancaster, also Litchfield, Conn. Admitted to bar, began practice of law, Harrisburg, Pa.; dep. atty. gen. Dauhpin County, 1809-15; mem. Pa. Ho. of Reps., 1813-14; elected mem. U.S. Ho. of Reps. from Pa., 14th Congress, did not qualify due to jud. appointment; pres. judge 12th Jud. Dist., 1815-16; atty. gen. Pa., 1816-19, 28-29; declined appointment as sec. of war under Pres. Monroe; moved to Lancaster, Pa., 1821; unsuccessful Anti-Masonic candidate for vice pres. U.S., 1832, for U.S. senator, 1833. Died Lancaster, Nov. 28, 1851; buried St. James' Episcopal Churchyard.

ELLSBERRY, William Wallace, congressman, physician; b. New Hope, O., Dec. 18, 1833; attended pvt. acad., Clermont County; studied medicine with his father; grad. Cincinnati Coll. of Medicine and Surgery, Ohio Med. Coll. Taught sch., 2 years; practiced medicine, Georgetown, O., until 1855, 1887-94; declined appointment as supt. Central Insane Asylum, Columbus, 1878; county auditor; del. Democratic Nat. Conv., Cincinnati, 1880; mem. U.S. Ho. of Reps. (Democrat) from Ohio, 49th Congress, 1885-87. Died Georgetown, Sept. 7, 1894; buried Confidence Cemetery.

ELLSWORTH, Elmer Ephraim, army officer; b. Malta, N.Y., Apr. 11, 1837; s. Ephraim D. and Phoebe (Denton) E. Held various jobs as clk.; became patent-solicitor, Chgo.; became comdr. volunteer mil. co., introduced "Zouave" drill method (which co. popular with public); took U.S. Zouave Cadets on Eastern tour; became maj. Ill. Nat. Guard; became mem. Abraham Lincoln's campaign staff; mem. of Three Years Regt., became 1st well-known Civil War death. Died Washington, D.C., May 24, 1861; buried Mechanicsville, N.Y.

ELLSWORTH, Henry Leavitt, agriculturist, U.S. commr. of patents; b. Windsor, Conn., Nov. 10, 1791; s. Chief Justice Oliver and Abigail (Wolcott) E.; grad. Yale, 1810; m. Nancy Goodrich, 1813, 3 children; m. 2d, Marietta Mariana Bartlett; m. 3d, Catherine Smith. Practiced law, Windsor, Conn., 1813; sec. Hartford County Agrl. Soc., 1818; pres. Aetna Ins. Co., 1819-21; commr. to superintend the settlement of Indian tribes south and west of Ark., 1832; mayor Hartford (Conn.), 1835; 1st U.S. commr. patents, 1835-45; influential in gaining 1st Congl. appropriation for agrl. research, 1839; land commr. U.S., 1845; called father of Dept. of Agri. Died Fair Haven, Conn. Dec. 27, 1858.

ELLSWORTH, Oliver, chief justice U.S. Supreme Ct.; b. Windsor, Conn., Apr. 29, 1745; s. Col. David and Jemima (Leavitt) E.; B.A., Princeton, 1766, LL.D. (hon.), 1797; LL.D. (hon.), Yale, 1790, Dartmouth, 1797; m. Abigail Wolcott, 1772. Admitted to Conn. bar, 1771; mem. Conn. Gen. Assembly from Windsor, 1775; state's atty. Hartford County, Conn., 1777; mem. Conn. Com. of the Pay Table, during Revolutionary War; del. to Continental Congress, 1777-83; mem. Conn. Council of Safety, 1779; mem. Gov.'s Council, 1780-84; judge Superior Ct., 1784-89; del. U.S. Constl. Conv., took part in bringing about Conn. Compromise which provided for equality of representation in Senate, also probably originated term "United States"; mem. U.S. Senate from 1789-96, reported 1st set of Senate rules, framed measure admitting R.I. and N.C. to Union, drew up 1st bill regulating consular service; most important work in Senate—chmn. com. apptd. to bring in bill organizing fed. judiciary (still part of laws of U.S.); 2d chief justice U.S. Supreme Ct., 1796-99; commr. to France, Feb.-Nov. 1799; mem. Conn. Gov.'s Council, 1801-07. Died Windsor, Nov. 26, 1807.

ELLSWORTH, Samuel Stewart, congressman; b. Pownal, Vt., Oct. 13, 1790. Moved to Penn Yan, N.Y., 1819, became a mcht.; supr. Milo, Yates County, 1824-28; judge Yates County, 1824-29; mem. N.Y. State Assembly, 1840; mem. U.S. Ho. of Reps. (Democrat) from N.Y., 29th Congress, 1845-47. Died Penn Yan, June 4, 1863; buried Lake View Cemetery.

ELLSWORTH, William Wolcott, gov. Conn., congressman; b. Windsor, Conn., Nov. 10, 1791; s. Oliver and Abigail (Wolcott) E.; grad. with honors Yale, 1810; LL.D. (hon.), U. N.Y., 1838; m. Emily Webster (dau. Noah Webster), Sept. 14, 1813, 6 children Admitted to Conn. bar, 1813; mem. U.S. Ho. of Reps. from Conn., 21st-23d congresses, 1829-July 8, 1834; gov. Conn., 1838-42; asso. judge Conn. Supreme Ct., 1847-61. Died Hartford, Conn., Jan.18, 1868.

ELLWOOD, Reuben, congressman; b. Mind N.Y., Feb. 21, 1821; attended Cherry Vall (N.Y.) Sem. Became mfr. of agrl. implemen mem. N.Y. State Assembly, 1851; moved to Syc more, Ill., circa 1854, continued in mfg. bus., a engaged in hardware bus.; mem. U.S. Ho. of Rep (Republican) from Ill., 48th-49th congress 1883-85. Died Sycamore, Ill., July 1, 1885; buri Elmwood Cemetery.

ELMENDORF, Lucas Conrad, congressman; Kingston, N.Y., 1758; grad. Princeton, 178 studied law. Admitted to bar, 1785, began pra tice of law; mem. U.S. Ho. of Reps. (Dem crat) from N.Y., 5th-7th congresses, 1797-180 mem. N.Y. State Assembly, 1804-05, N.Y. Sena 1814-17; 1st judge Ulster County Ct. of Comm Pleas, 1815-21; surrogate Ulster County, 1835-4 Died Kingston, Aug. 17, 1843; buried crypt Fir Dutch Ch.

ELMER, Ebenezer, congressman, physicia coll. pres.; b. Cedarville, N.J., Aug. 23, 1752; Daniel and Abigail (Lawrence) E.; m. Hann Seeley, 1784; 1 son, Lucius Quintus Cincinnatu Commd. ensign 3d N.J. Regt., 1776, promoted lt.; served as surgeon's mate, 1777, surgeon N.J. Regt., 1778; a founder Soc. of Cincinna pres. N.J. br.; v.p. state council, 1807-17, 22-3 mem. N.J. Assembly, 1789-91, 93-95, 1817, 1 speaker, 1791, 95, 1817; mem. U.S. Ho. of Rep from N.J. 7th-9th congresses, 1801-07, collecti of customs, Bridgeton, N.J., 1808; v.p. Burlin ton Coll., 1808-17, 22-32; last surviving Revol tionary officer of N.J.; adj. gen. N.J. Militia War of 1812, brig. gen. Cumberland Brigade. Di Bridgeton, Oct. 18, 1843; buried Presbyn. Cemeter Bridgeton.

ELMER, Jonathan, physician, Continental co gressman, senator; b. Fairfield, N.J., Nov. 29, 174 s. Daniel and Abigail (Lawrence) E.; M.D., U. Pa 1769; m. Mary Seeley, 1769. Mem. Am. Philo Soc., 1772; del. Continental Congress, 1776-78, 8 84, mem. bd. treasury; mem. N.J. Legislatur 1780, 84, N.J. Council, 1780, 84; trustee Coll. N.J. (now Princeton), 1782-95; mem. Congress Confedn., 1787-88; surrogate Cumberland Coun (N.J.), 1784-1802; pres. N.J. Med. Soc. 178 mem. U.S. Senate (Federalist) from N.J., 1789-9 Died Burlington, N.J., Sept. 3, 1817.

ELMER, Lucius Quintius Cincinnatus, congres man, jurist; b. Bridgeton, N.J., Feb. 3, 1793; Ebenezer and Hannah (Seeley) E.; attended Pa.; A.M. (hon), Coll. of N.J. (now Princeton 1824, LL.D. (hon.), 1865; m. Catharine Hay, Oc 6, 1818. Licensed as atty., 1815; mem. N.J. As sembly, 1820-23, speaker, 1823; apptd. U.S. dis atty. for N.J., 1824; Trustee Coll. of N.J., 1829-6 1843-45; mem. U.S. Ho. of Reps. from N.J., 28t Congress, atty. gen. N.J., 1850-52; justice N. Supreme Ct., 1852-59, 62-69. Died Bridgeto Mar. 11, 1883.

ELMORE, Franklin Harper, banker, senator; b Laurens dist., S.C., Oct. 15, 1799; s. John Arch and Sarah (Saxon) E.; grad. S.C. Coll., 1819; m Harriet Chesnut, Admitted to S.C. bar, 182 solicitor So. circuit, 1822-37; trustee S.C. Coll mem. U.S. Ho. of Reps. from S.C., 24th-25th con gresses, Dec. 19, 1836-39; pres. Bank of S.C 1839-50; mem. U.S. Senate from S.C., 1850. Di Washington, D.C., May 29, 1850; buried 1 Presbyn. Church Yard, Columbia, S.C.

ELSBERG, Louis, laryngologist; b. Iserlohn Prussia, Apr. 2, 1836; s. Nathan and Adelaide E. M.D., Jefferson Med. Coll., 1857; m. Mary Va Hagen Scoville, 1876. Resident physician Mt Sinai Hosp., N.Y.C.; one of editors North Am Med. Reporter, 1859; mem. faculty med. dept Univ. City N.Y.; held 1st course of lectures o diseases of throat in U.S., 1862; recipient gol medal A.M.A. for publ. Laryngoscopal Surger Illustraated in the Treatment of Morbid Growth within the Larynx, 1865; published Regeneration or the Preservation of the Organic Molecules (hi most important contbn. to med. science), 1874 founder, 1st pres. Am. Laryngological Assn., 187 founder quarterly Archives of Laryngology, 1880 other publs. include: Neuroses of Sensation, 1882 Structure of Hyaline Cartilage, 1881-82; On An gioma of the Larynx, 1884. Died N.Y.C. Feb. 19, 1885.

ELWELL, John Johnson, physician, lawyer; b Warren, O., June 22, 1820; M.D., Cleve. Med Coll., 1846; studied law, 1852-54; m. Nancy Chittenden. Began practice medicine, Cleve., 1846; admitted to Ohio bar, 1854, began practice law specializing in medico-legal area; mem. Ohio Legislature from Ashtabula County, 1853-54; lectr. on med. jurisprudence Ohio U., also Western Res. Coll., 1850's; founder Western Law Monthly, 1857, editor, 1857-61; served with Q.M.'s Corps, U.S. Army, 1861-65, became chief q.m. 10th Corps; practiced law, Cleve., from 1865; contbr. articles to many legal jours.; an editor Bouvier's Law Dictionary. Author. A Medico-Legal Treatise on Malpractice and Medical Evidence, Comprising the Elements of Medical Jurisprudence, 1860. Died Cleve., Mar. 13, 1900; buried Cleve.

ELWYN, Alfred Langdon, philanthropist; b. Portsmouth, N.H., July 9, 1804; s. Thomas and Elizabeth (Langdon) E.; grad. Harvard, 1823; M. D.; U. Pa., 1831; m. Mary Middleton Mease, 1832, 2 children including Mary Middleton. Pres. and philanthropic contbr. to Pa. Agrl. Soc.; Sch. for Feeble-Minded Children, Soc. for Prevention Cruelty to Animals; mem. Pa. Agrl. Soc.; an early lexicographer. Author: (poem) Bonaparte; A Glossary of Supposed Americanisms, 1859. Editor: Papers Relating to Public Events in Masschusetts Preceding the American Revolution. Died Phila., Mar. 15, 1884.

ELY, Alfred, congressman, lawyer; b. Lyme, Conn., Feb. 15, 1815; attended Bacon Acad., Colchester, Conn.; studied law. Admitted to bar, 1841, began practice of law, Rochester, N.Y.; mem. U.S. Ho. of Reps. (Republican) from N.Y., 36th-37th congresses, 1859-63; taken prisoner by Confederate Army while witnessing Battle of Bull Run, imprisoned in Richmond, nearly 6 months. Died Rochester, May 18, 1892; buried Ely vault, Mt. Hope Cemetery.

ELY, John, congressman, physician; b. Saybrook, Conn., Oct. 8, 1774; studied medicine. Practiced medicine, Coxsackie, N.Y.; mem. N.Y. State Assembly, 1806, 12; an organizer N.Y. State and Greene County med. socs., 1807, also Albany Female Acad.; mem. U.S. Ho. of Reps. (Democrat) from N.Y., 26th Congress, 1839-41. Died Coxsackie, Aug. 20, 1849; buried Old Coxsackie Cemetery.

ELY, William, congressman, lawyer; b. Longmeadow, Mass., Aug. 14, 1765; grad. Yale, 1787; studied law. Admitted to bar, 1791, began practice of law, Springfield, Mass.; mem. Mass. Ho. of Reps., 1801-03, 15-16; mem. U.S. Ho. of Reps. (Federalist) from Mass., 9th-13th congresses, 1805-15. Died Springfield, Oct. 9, 1817; buried Springfield.

ELZEY, Arnold, army officer; b. Elmwood, Md., Dec. 18, 1816; s. Arnold Elzey and Anne (Jackson) E.; grad. U.S. Mil. Acad., 1837; m. Ellen Irwin, 1845, 1 son. Served as lt. U.S. Army in Seminole War; fired 1st gun of Mexican War; commd. capt. arty. Confederate Army, 1861; promoted brig gen., 1862; commanded Dept. of Richmond, 1862-64; chief of arty. Army of Tenn. Died Balt., Feb. 21, 1871.

EMBREE, Elihu, abolitionist; b. Pa., Nov. 11, 1782; s. Thomas and Esther Embree. An early iron mfr. in Tenn.; joined Soc. of Friends, freed his slaves, circa 1815; established Manumission Intelligencer (Emancipator), which may have been 1st U.S. journal completely devoted to anti-slavery movement, 1819-20; petitioned Tenn. Legislature to end slavery; recognized as being 1 of earliest anti-slavery advocates. Died Tenn., Dec. 4, 1820.

EMBREE, Elisha, congressman, lawyer; b. Lincoln County, Ky., Sept. 28, 1801; studied law. Moved (with father) to Knox County, Ind., 1811; engaged in agriculture; admitted to bar, 1836, began practice of law, Princeton, Ind.; judge 4th Circuit Ind., 1835-45; mem. U.S. Ho. of Reps. (Whig) from Ind., 30th Congress, 1847-49; resumed legal and agrl. pursuits. Died Princeton, Feb. 28, 1863; buried Warnock Cemetery.

EMBRIE, Jonas Reece, congressman; b. Hillsboro, O., Apr. 25,, 1812; studied law. Admitted to bar, began practice of law, Hillsboro; editor and publisher Hillsboro Gazette, 1839-48, 54-56; an organizer Hillsboro Female Coll.; postmaster Hillsboro, 1839-41; mem. Ohio Senate, 1847-48; 1st probate judge Highland County, 1851-54; mem. U.S. Ho. of Reps. (Republican) from Ohio, 34th Congress, 1855-57; moved to Mound City, Ill., 1857, engaged in merc. pursuits, conducted newspaper, practiced law; police magistrate Mound City, 1858; twp. treas. of schs.; master in chancery Pulaski County (Ill.). Died Mound City, June 5, 1869; buried Beech Grove Cemetery.

EMBURY, Philip, clergyman; b. Ireland, 1728; m. Margaret Switzer, Nov. 27, 1758, at least 1 son, Samuel. Became preacher Methodist Ch., in Limerick, 1749; came to N.Y.C., 1760, worked as carpenter and tchr.; began preaching, 1766; 1 of 1st Methodist preachers in Am.; established Wesley Chapel, N.Y.C., 1768. Died N.Y., 1773; buried Woodland Cemetery, Cambridge, N.Y.

EMERSON, George Barrell, educator; b. Wells, Me., Sept. 12, 1797; s. Samuel and Olive (Barrell) E.; grad. Harvard, 1817, LL.D. (hon.), 1857; m. Olivia Buckminster, June 11, 1823, 3 children m. 2d, Mrs. Mary Rotch Fleming, Nov. 12, 1834. Became mathematics tutor Harvard, 1819; prin. English High Sch., Boston, 1821-23; opened pvt. sch. for young ladies, Boston, 1823; an organizer Boston Mechanics Inst.; a founder Am. Inst. Instrn., 1830; pres. Boston Soc. Natural History, 1837-43; mem. Am. Acad. Arts and Scis. Author: Report on the Trees and Shrubs Growing Naturally in the Forests of Massachusetts, 1846, 2d ed., 1875; Mnual of Agriculture, 1861. Died Newton, Mass., Mar. 4, 1881.

EMERSON, Gouverneur, physician; b. Dover, Del., Aug. 4, 1795; s. Jonathan and Ann (Beel) E.; M.D., U. Pa., 1816; never married. Practiced medicine, Silver Lake, Pa., 1816-18, Phila., 1820; surgeon in ship Superior on China voyage; apptd. attending physician Phila. Dispensary, 1820-22; mem. Phila. Bd. Health, 1823; in charge of hosp. for orphans during cholera epidemic of 1832; mem. conv. which resulted in formation of A.M.A., 1847; mem. Am. Philos. Soc., Union League Club, Phila. Author: (with Dr. Isaac Hays) Code of Medical Ethics; Cotton in the Middle States, 1862. Translator: Organization of Labor (Le Play). Died Phila., July 2, 1874.

EMERSON, Joseph, clergyman; b. Hollis, N.H., Oct. 13, 1777; s. Daniel and Ama (Fletcher) E.; grad. Harvard, 1798; m. Nancy Eaton, Oct. 1803; m. 2d, Eleanor Reed, July 1805; m. 3d, Rebecca Hasseltine, Jan. 16, 1810. Licensed to preach, 1801; tutor Harvard, 1801; pastor Congregational Ch., Beverly, Mass., 1803-16; founded Women's Sem., Byfield, Mass., 1816-21, moved sch. to Saugus, Mass., 1821, Wethersfield, Conn., 1824-33; pastor in Saugus; mem. Am. Inst. Instrn. Author: Prospectus of the Female Seminary at Wethersfield. . ., 1826. Died Wethersfield, May 14, 1833.

EMERSON, Ralph, clergyman, educator; b. Hollis, N.H., Aug. 18, 1787; grad. Yale, 1811, D.D., 1830; grad. Andover Theol. Sem., 1814; m. Eliza Rockwell, Nov. 27, 1817, several children including Joseph, Charlotte. Tutor, Yale, 1814-16; pastor 1st Congregational Ch., Norfolk, Conn., 1816-29; prof. eccles. history Andover Theol. Sem., also pastor South Ch., Andover, 1829-53; pastor Congregational Ch., Newburyport, Mass., 1853-58, Rockford, Ill., 1858-63; also lectr. Chgo. Theol. Sem., 1858-63. Author: Life of Rev. Joseph Emerson, 1834. Translator: Augustinianism and Pelagianism (Wiggins), 1840. Died Rockford, May 20, 1863; buried Rockford.

EMERSON, Ralph Waldo, poet, writer; b. Boston, May 25, 1803; s. William and Ruth (Haskins) E.; grad. Harvard, (class poet), 1821, attended Harvard Sch. Divinity, 1825, 27, LL.D. (hon.), 1866; m. Ellen Tucker, Sept. 30, 1829; m. 2d, Lydia Jackson, Sept. 1855; 4 children, including Waldo, Edward Waldo. Tchr., headmaster sch. for young ladies, 1821-25; licensed as clergyman, 1826; pastor 2d Ch. of Boston, 1829-32; left ministry except for guest preaching; went to Europe, 1832, asso. with Carlyle, Coleridge, Wordsworth; moved to Concord, Mass., 1834; circle of friends included Margaret Fuller, Amos Bronson Alcott, Theodore Parker, Henry David Thoreau, Nathaniel Hawthorne; began his "Journals," 1820; ideas from jours. became lectures, later books; made living as lectr. throughout Am.; author Nature (established his Transcendentalist position with emphasis on nature, idealism), 1836; gave address The American Scholar (called by Oliver Wendell Holmes "our intellectual Declaration of Independence"), 1837, Address before the Divinity College (of Harvard) (contains plea for a modern religion, new ch.), 1838; founder, co-editor The Dial (an early important Am. lit. mag.), 1840-44; an organizer Transcendentalist experiment Brook Farm; advocated reform, abolition of slavery; went to Europe, 1847, 72, asso. with Dickens, Tennyson, Froude, Harriet Martineau, Macaulay, Paine, Turgenev, Ruskin; greatest disciple was Henry David Thoreau, also encouraged Walt Whitman; asso. in later years with Longfellow, Dana, Agassiz, Oliver Wendell Holmes, James Russell Lowell; other works include Essays, 1841, 44; Poems, 1847; English Traits, 1856; May Day and Other Pieces, 1868; Society and Solitude, 1870; Parnassus, 1874; Letters and Social Arms, 1876; Letters from Ralph Waldo Emerson to a Friend (Samuel Gray Ward), published 1899. Died Concord, Apr. 27, 1882; buried Sleepy Hollow Cemetery, Concord.

EMERSON, William, clergyman; b. Concord, Mass., May 6, 1769; s. Rev. William and Phebe (Bliss) E.; grad. Harvard, 1789; m. Ruth Haskins, Oct. 25, 1796, 8 children including Ralph Waldo. Ordained to ministry Unitarian Ch., Harvard, Mass., 1792; pastor 1st Ch. of Boston, 1799; chaplain U.S. Senate; overseer Harvard; mem. Mass. Hist. Soc.; editor Monthly Anthology; founder Anthology Club. Author: An Historical Sketch of the First Church in Boston, 1812. Died Boston, May 12, 1811.

EMERY, Charles Edward, engr.; b. Aurora, N.Y., Mar. 29, 1838; s. Moses Little and Minera (Prentiss) E.; attended Canandaigua Acad., circa 1852-56; Ph.D. (hon.), U. City N.Y., 1876; m. Susan Livingston, 1863. Served as asst. engr. U.S. Navy, 1861-65; engr., Bklyn. Navy Yard, 1865-68, resigned from Navy, 1868, served as cons. engr. to Navy, from 1868; supt. Am. Inst. Fair, N.Y.C., 1869; cons. engr. to Coast Survey, designed over 20 revenue cutters, 1870's; chief engr., mgr. N.Y. Steam Co., N.Y.C., from 1879; cons. engr. to many communities and orgns.; expert on isochronism of timepieces; constructed dynamos and motors which operated by direct current without commutator; recipient Watt medal Instn. Civil Engrs. of Britain, 1889; results of his experiments with steam engines published in Tables and Diagrams Relating to Non-Condensing Engines and Boilers (W. P. Trowbridge), 1872, also in Transactions of Am. Soc. C.E., Vol. III, 1875. Died N.Y.C., June 1, 1898.

EMERY, Stephen Albert, music educator; b. Paris, Me., Oct. 4, 1841; s. Stephen and Jenett (Loring) E.; ed. Colby Coll., 1859-60, U. Lepzeig and U. Dresden (Germany), 1862-63. Prof. harmony and piano New Eng. Conservatory, 1864; prof. composition and theory Boston U.; asst. editor Musical Herald. Author: Elements of Harmony, 1879; Foundation Studies in Pianoforte Playing, 1882. Died Boston, Apr. 15, 1891.

EMMET, John Patten, physician, artist; b. Dublin, Ireland, Apr. 8, 1797; s. Thomas Addis Emmet; attended U.S. Mil. Acad.; studied in Italy; received M.D., N.Y.C. Came with father to Am., 1804; practiced medicine, Charleston, S.C., 1822-24; prof. chemistry U. Va., 1824-circa 1842; executed many sketches, a few oil paintings, marble busts. Died N.Y.C., Aug. 13, 1842.

EMMET, Thomas Addis, Irish patriot, lawyer; b. Cork, Ireland, Apr. 24, 1764; s. Robert and Elizabeth (Mason) E.; grad. Trinity Coll., Dublin, Ireland, 1782; Doctorate of Medicine, U. Edinburgh (Scotland), 1784; m. Jane Patten, Jan. 11, 1791. Admitted to Irish bar, 1790; sec. Soc. United Irishmen, 1795, dir., 1797, imprisoned for activities as mem.; came to U.S., 1804; admitted to N.Y. bar, 1804; became atty. gen. N.Y. State, 1812, a famous early U.S. Supreme Ct. lawyer; his most important case Gibbons vs. Ogden was tried before Chief Justice John Marshall; active in helping Irish immigrants become adjusted to life in Am. Died N.Y.C., Nov. 14, 1827; buried St. Paul's Churchyard, N.Y.C.

EMMETT, Daniel Decatur, minstrel, composer; b. Clinton, O., Oct. 29, 1815; s. Abraham and Sarah (Zerick) E.; m. Catherine Rives; m. 2d, Mary Louise (Brower) Bird, 1879. With Huron Reflector, Norwalk, O., 1828, then with Western Aurora, Mt. Vernon, N.Y., before 1832; fifer U.S. Army, 1832-35; composed song Old Dan Tucker, circa 1830; organized Virginia Minstrels, 1842-43, made 1st appearance at Bowery Amphitheatre, N.Y.C., Feb. 1843; joined Bryant Minstrels, 1857; traveled with own co., 1865-78. Composed songs including Old Dan Tucker (circa 1830); Dixie, 1859; The Road to Richmond; Walk Along, John; Here We Are, or Cross Ober Jordan, (1864). Died nr. Mt. Vernon, June 28, 1904.

EMMONS, Ebenezer, physician, geologist, educator; b. Middlefield, Mass., May 16, 1799; s. Ebenezer and Mary (Mack) E.; grad. Williams Coll., 1818, Rensselaer Inst., 1826; attended Berkshire Med. Sch., 1826-28; m. Maria Cone, 1818. Apptd. lectr. chemistry Williams Coll., 1828; apptd. jr. prof. Rensselaer Inst., 1830; prof. chemistry Albany Med. Sch., 1838, later prof. obstetrics until 1852; apptd. state geologist N.C., 1851. Author: Manual of Mineralogy and Geology (5 papers dealing with investigation of agrl. resources of N.Y. State), 1846-54; Zoology of Mass., 1840; American Geology, 3 vols., 1855. Died Brunswick County, N.C., Oct. 1, 1863.

EMMONS, George Foster, naval officer; b. Clarendon, Vt., Aug. 23, 1811; s. Horatio and Abigail (Foster) E.; m. Frances Thornton, Jan. 10, 1843. With Wilkes surveying expdn., 1838-42; commd. lt. U.S. Navy, 1841, advanced through grades to comdr., 1856, capt., 1863, commodore, 1868; captured Cedar Keys, Fla., 1862; fleet capt. of South Atlantic blockading squadron under Rear Adm. Dahlgren, 1867; duties after Civil War include head Hydrographic Office, Washington, D.C., also comdt. Phila. Navy Yard; promoted rear Adm., 1872, ret., 1873. Author: The Navy of the United States from the Commencement, 1775-1853, with a Brief History of Each Vessel's Service and Fate, 1853. Died Princeton, N.J., July 23, 1884.

EMMONS, Nathanael, clergyman; b. East Haddam, Conn., Apr. 20, 1746; s. Deacon Samuel and Ruth (Cone) E.; grad. Yale, 1767; m. Deliverance French, Apr. 6, 1775; m. 2d, Martha Williams, Nov. 4, 1779; m. 3d, Mrs. Abigail (Moore) Mill, Sept. 28, 1831. Pastor, Congregational Ch., Franklin, Mass., 1773-1827; zealous patriot during Am. Revolution, strong Federalist thereafter. Author: Works of Nathanael Emmons, D.D., 6 vols., published 1842. Died Sept. 23, 1840.

EMORY, John, clergyman; b. Queen Annes County, Md., Apr. 11, 1789; s. Robert and Frances (Thomas) E.; attended Washington Coll., Md.; m.

Caroline Sellers, Oct. 12, 1813; m. 2d, Ann Wright, May 12, 1818; 1 son, Robert. Admitted to Md. bar, 1808; ordained to ministry, 1812; minister Methodist Conf. Phila., 1814; mem. Gen. Conf. Phila. and Balt., 1816-32; bishop Meth. Episcopal Ch., 1832-35; editor Meth. Mag. and Quarterly Review, 1830-32; an organizer Wesleyan U., N.Y.U.; pres. bd. trustees Dickinson Coll. Died Reisterstown, Md., Dec. 16, 1835; buried Eutaw Street Ch., Balt.

EMORY, William Hemsley, army officer; b. Queen Annes County, Md., Sept. 7, 1811; s. Thomas and Anna Maria (Hemsley) E.; grad. U.S. Mil. Acad., 1831; m. Matilda Bache, May 1838. Commd. 1st lt. Topog. Engrs., 1838; prin. asst. on N.E. bondary survey between U.S. and Can., 1844-46; commr. and chief astronomer for running boundary line between Cal. and Mexico, 1848-54; commd. capt. Army of the West, 1851; commd. maj. 2d Cavalry, 1855, lt. col. Army of West, 1857; commanded Indian Territory from Ft. Leavenworth, 1861; commanded a div. under Gen. Banks in La., 1863; commanded 19th Army Corps in Red River Expdn., 1864; distinguished at Fisher's Hill, 1864; commd. maj. gen. U.S. Volunteers, 1865; commanded Dept. of W. Va., 1865-66, Dept. of Washington, Dist. of Republican, 1869-71, Dept. of Gulf, 1871-75; ret. as brig. gen., 1876. Author: Notes of a Military Reconnaissance from Fort Leavenworth in Missouri to San Diego in California, 1848; Report on the U.S. and Mexican Boundary Survey, 1858-59. Died Dec. 1, 1887, Washington, D.C.

EMOTT, James, congressman, jurist; b. Poughkeepsie, N.Y., Mar. 14, 1771; s. William and Celia (Polmantere) E.; A.M. (hon.), Union Coll., 1800; LL.D. (hon.), Columbia, 1833; m. Malissa White, Sept. 20, 1818; m. 2d, Esther Crary, Jan. 27, 1821, 1 son, James. Admitted to N.Y. bar, 1790; mem. N.Y. State Assembly from Albany County, 1804, 14-17, speaker, 1804-14; mem. U.S. Ho. of Reps. from N.Y., 11th-12th congresses, 1809-13; judge N.Y. Ct. of Common Pleas, 1817-27; judge 2d N.Y. Jud. Dist., 1827-31; an incorporator, pres. Dutchess Mut. Ins. Co.; a founder Poughkeepsie Savs. Bank. Died Poughkeepsie, Apr. 7, 1850; buried Poughkeepsie Rural Cemetery.

EMOTT, James, mayor, jurist; b. Poughkeepsie, N.Y., Apr. 23, 1823; s. James and Esther (Crary) E.; grad. Columbia, 1841; m. Mary Helen Crooke, July 16, 1846. Admitted to N.Y. Supreme Ct. bar, 1844; dist. atty. Dutchess County (N.Y.), 1849; pres. Mchts. Bank of Poughkeepsie, 1852-84; 1st mayor Poughkeepsie, 1854-55; judge N.Y. Supreme Ct., 1856-64, presiding judge, 1863; a founder Assn. Bar City N.Y., 1869. Died Poughkeepsie, N.Y., Sept. 11, 1884.

ENDECOTT, John, colonial gov.; b. Chagford, Devon, Eng., circa 1589; s. Thomas and Alice (Westlake) E.; m. Anne Gower; m. 2d, Elizabeth Gibson; at least 2 sons. Sailed in ship Abigail to Mass. Bay, 1628; incorporator of land on Mass. Bay, 1629; leader of earliest settlers at Naumkeag (now Salem), 1628-30; replaced by Gov. Winthrop in great migration of 1630; assistant Colony of Mass., 1630-34, 36-40, 45-48, dep. gov., 1641-43, 50, 54, gov., 1644-49, 51-53, 55-64; overseer Harvard. Died Boston, Mar. 15, 1665.

ENDICOTT, Charles Moses, sea capt.; b. Danvers, Mass., Dec. 6, 1793; s. Moses and Anna (Towne) E.; m. Sarah Rolland Blythe, June 18, 1818, 2 sons. Clk. in merc. houses; super cargo on voyage to Russia, 1812, trip to Far East, 1814; promoted capt.; engaged in pepper trade in East Indies for 15 years; retired from sea, 1835; became bank clk., antiquarian; wrote under name Junius Americanus; contbr. to New Eng. Hist. and Geneal. Register, Boston Gazette. Author: Sailing Directions for the Pepper Ports on the West Coast of Sumatra, 1833; Memoir of John Endicott, 1847. Died Dec. 14, 1863.

ENDICOTT, George, lithographer; b. Canton, Mass., June 14, 1802. Worked as ornamental painter, Balt., circa 1828; formed lithographic firm Endicott & Swett, Balt., 1830, moved to N.Y.C., 1831, carried on firm alone, 1834-45, with brother William as G.&W. Endicott, 1845-48; firm exhibited specimens of lithography at Am. Inst., 1845, 46, 47, twice cited for excellent work. Died Aug. 21, 1848.

ENDICOTT, William, lithographer; b. Canton, Mass., Aug. 20, 1816. Went to N.Y.C., circa 1841; in partnership with brother as G.&W. Endicott, N.Y.C., 1845-48, carried on bus. as William Endicott & Co., 1848-51; awarded diploma for 8 specimens of lithography shown at Annual Fair of Am. Inst., 1848. Died Canton, Oct. 18, 1851.

ENGELMANN, George, botanist, physician; b. Frankfurt-am-Main, Germany, Feb. 2, 1809; s. George and Julia (May) E.; M.D., U. Wurzburg, 1831; m. Dorothea Horstmann, June 11, 1840, 1 son, George J. Came to U.S., 1832; an early user of quinine for treatment of malaria; discoverer adaptation of Pronuba moth for accomplishing pollination of yuccas; discovered immunity of Am. grape to phylloxera; a pioneer meteoroligist; organizer St. Louis Acad. Science, 1856. Works collected in Botanical Works of the Late George Englemann Collected for Henry Shaw, 1887. Died St. Louis, Feb. 4, 1884.

ENGLAND, John, clergyman; b. Cork, Ireland, Sept. 23, 1786; s. Thomas and Honora (Lordan) E.; ed. Coll. of St. Patrick, Caslow, Ireland. Ordained priest Roman Catholic Ch., 1808; consecrated bishop in St. Finnbars Cathedral, Cork, Ireland, 1820; 1st Roman Cath. bishop of S.C., arrived in Charleston, S.C., 1820; preached at St. Peter's Ch., N.Y.C., 1822; opened Philos. and Classical Sem. of Charleston, 1822; induced Sisters of Mercy to establish girls acad. in Charleston, 1829; founder U.S. Catholic Miscellany (1st distinctly Cath. paper), 1822-61; 1st priest to address U.S. Ho. of Reps., 1826; apostolic del. to Haiti, 1833-37; Outstanding lectures: The Pleasures of the Scholar, 1840; American Citizenship, 1841. Died Charleston, Apr. 11, 1842.

ENGLIS, John, shipbuilder; b. Bklyn., Nov. 27, 1808; s. John Englis; m. Mary A. Quackenbush, Feb. 1832, 1 son, John. Founder shipbldg. firm, specializing in steamships, 1837, built total of 89 vessels, including Milwaukee, Red Jacket, Empire City (for service on Gt. Lakes), Hendrick Hudson, Isaac Newton (Hudson River boat 1855), Columbia (steamboat built in 42 days); mem. Gen. Soc. Mechanics and Tradesmen. Died Bklyn., Oct. 25, 1888.

ENGLISH, Elbert, Hartwell, jurist; b. Madison County, Ala., Mar. 16, 1816; s. James and Nancy (McCracken) E.; m. Julia Agnes Fisher, Sept. 30, 1840; m. 2d, Mrs. Susan A. Wheless, July 1872. Admitted to Ala. bar, 1839; mem. Ala. Legislature, 1840-44; reporter Ark. Supreme ct., 1846; chief justice Ark., 1854-64, 74-84 (following adoption of Ark. Constn., 1874) Author: A Digest of the Statutes of Arkansas, 1848. Died Asheville, N.C., Sept. 1, 1884.

ENGLISH, George Bethune, adventurer; b. Cambridge, Mass., Mar. 7, 1787; s. Thomas and Penelope (Bethune) E.; grad. Harvard, 1807, M.A., Harvard Divinity Sch. Rural newspaper editor; mem. New Harmony Community; apptd. lt. U.S. Marines (appointment secured by J. Q. Adams), sent to Mediterranean; resigned commn. at Alexandria, became Muslim officer in Turkish army; served under Ismail Ali (son of Pasha of Egypt) in campaigns to Sudan, 1820-21; returned to U.S.; apptd. U.S. secret agt. to discover Ottoman attitude to possible comml. treaty allowing U.S. ships to trade in Black Sea, conducted these preliminaries, 1823-26, finally failed; was left broke, unemployed and distrusted. Author: The Grounds of Christianity Examined by Comparing the New Testament with the Old, 1813; A Narrative of the Expedition to Dongola and Senaar, 1822. Died Washington, D.C., Sept. 20, 1828.

ENGLISH, James Edward, mfr., senator, gov. Conn.; b. New Haven, Conn., Mar. 13, 1812; s. James and Nancy (Griswold) E.; ed. Common Sch., New Haven; m. Caroline Fowler, Jan. 25, 1837; m. 2d, Anna R. Morris, Oct. 7, 1885; 1 son, Henry F. Established lumber co. English and Welch, New Haven, 1835; mem. New Haven Bd. Selectmen, 1847-61, Common Council, 1848-49; rep. to Conn. Assembly, 1855, 1872; mem. Conn. Senate, 1856, 58; mem. U.S. Ho. of Reps. from Conn., 37th-38th congresses, 1861-65; gov. Conn., 1867-69, 70-71; mem. U.S. Senate from Conn. (filled vacancy), 1875-77. Died New Haven, Mar. 2, 1890; buried Evergreen Cemetery, New Haven.

ENGLISH, William Hayden, congressman; b. Lexington, Ind., Aug. 27, 1822; s. Elisha G. and Mahala (Eastin) E.; attended Hanover Coll., 3 years; m. Emma Mardulia Jackson, 1847, 2 children. Admitted to Ind. bar, 1840; postmaster Lexington, 1841; prin. clk. Ind. Ho. of Reps., 1843; admitted to U.S. Supreme Ct. bar; clk. U.S. Senate, 1850; speaker Ind. Ho. of Reps., 1851-52; mem. U.S. Ho. of Reps. from Ind., 33d-36th congresses, 1853-61; sec. Ind. Constl. Conv., 1851; an organizer Indpls. 1st Nat. Bank (Ind.), 1863, pres., until 1877; Democratic candidate for vice pres. U.S. on ticket with Winfield S. Hancock, 1880; regent Smithsonian Instn.; pres. Ind. Hist. Soc. Died Indpls., Feb. 7, 1896.

ENOCHS,, William Henry, congressman; b. nr. Middleburg, O., Mar. 29, 1842; attended Ohio U. at Athens; grad. Cincinnati Law Sch., 1866. Served as pvt. Co. B, 2d Regt., Ohio Inf., during Civil War, 1861; commd. 1st lt. 5th Regt., W. Va. Inf., 1861, capt., 1862, lt. col., 1863; promoted col. 1st Regt., W. Va. Inf., 1864; brevetted brig. gen. U.S. Volunteers, 1865; admitted to bar, began practice of law, Ironton, O.; mem. Ohio Ho. of Reps., 1870-71; mem. U.S. Ho. of Reps. (Republican) from Ohio, 52d-53d congresses, 1891-93. Died Ironton, July 13, 1893; buried Arlington (Va.) Nat. Cemetery.

ENSLEY, Enoch, planter, mfr., economist; b. Nashville, Tenn., Nov. 8, 1836; s. Enoch and Mary (Rains) E.; ed. Hardeman's Acad., Wilamstown County, Cumberland U.; m. Laura Martin, 1860; m. 2d Mary Leavenworth Beecher, 1889; 4 children who lived to maturity. Pres. Memphis Gas Light Co. (Tenn.), 1872-86; an organizer, also dir. Union and Planters Bank; organizer Tenn. Coal, Iron & Ry. Co.; advocated exemption of personal property from taxation. Author: What Should be Taxed and How it should be Taxed, 1873. Died Nov. 18, 1891.

EPPES, John Wayles, senator, congressman; b. City Point, Va., Apr. 7, 1773; s. Francis and Elizabeth (Wayles) E.; m. Maria Jefferson, Oct. 13, 1797; m. 2d, Martha Jones, Apr. 17, 1804; at least 5 children including Francis. Began study under his uncle Thomas Jefferson, Phila., 1791; admitted to Va. bar, 1794; mem. Va. Ho. of Dels., 1801-03; mem. U.S. Ho. of Reps. from Va., 8th-11th, 13th congresses, 1803-11, 13-15; formed polit. antagonism against John Randolph of Va., with Jefferson's support moved his residence into Randolph's dist.; lost to Randolph for seat in U.S. Ho. of Reps., 1810, 14, won, 1812; mem. U.S. Senate from Va., 1817-19; important aide and polit. supporter of Thomas Jefferson. Died Buckingham County, Va., Sept. 15, 1823; buried Buckingham County, Va.

ERDMAN, Jacob, congressman; b. Coopersburg, Pa., Feb. 22, 1801; attended common schs. Engaged in agriculture; mem Pa. Ho. of Reps., 1834-36; mem. U.S. Ho. of Reps. (Democrat) from Pa., 29th Congress, 1845-47; asso. judge Lehigh County Ct., 1866-67. Died Coopersburg, July 20, 1867; buried Blue Church Cemetery, nr. Coopersburg.

ERICKSON, Reinhart, clergyman; b. Amsterdam, Holland, 1700; attended U. Gröningen (Holland); m. Maria Provoost, 1726; m. 2d, Sarah Luyster. Ordained to ministry Dutch Reformed Ch., 1725; came to Am. as minister to Dutch Congregation, Hackensack, N.J., 1725; pastor Dutch Reformed Ch., Schenectady, N.Y., 1728-36, Middletown, N.J., 1736-63; an organizer, 1st pres. Am. Classis (ruling body which ordains new ministers); advocated establishment coll. for tng. new ministers; a founder Queens Coll. (now Rutgers U.); deprived of his ch., 1764. Died New Brunswick, N.J., 1772

ERICSSON, John, engr., inventor; b. Province of Vermland, Sweden, July 31, 1803; s. Olof ond Brita (Yngstrom) E.; m. Amelia Byam, Oct. 15, 1836. Came to U.S., 1839; built a caloric engine, 1833; developer transmission of power by compressed air, use of centrifugal blowers for boiler forced draft, new types of steam boilers; placed warship engines below water line for protection; constructed railroad steam locomotive, 1829; introduced screw propellers for boats, 1840, designed much of U.S.S. Princeton (1st screw-propelled vessel of war), 1844; designed and built the Monitor (with a friction recoil mechanism for its guns) for U.S. Navy, 1861; designer, builder 13 inch wrought iron gun for U.S. Govt., 1863. Died N.Y.C., Mar. 8, 1889; buried Sweden.

ERICSSON, Leif, explorer; b. Iceland, circa 980; s. Eric Thorvaldsson (Eric the Red). Moved with family to Brattahlid, Greenland at age of 2; made trip to Norway, circa 999; converted to Christianity in Norwegian court; attempted to eliminate usual stop at Iceland on return trip to Greenland, landed on coast of N. Am., which he named Helluland (Land of Flat Stones); landed farther south in flat, wooded area which he named Markland (Forest Land); made 3d landing still farther south in area he named Vinland because of grapes found there (exact location of these areas undetermined); some sagas and reports cite his wish to spread Christianity as reason for making trip to N. Am. mainland; credited with being 1st European discoverer of Am.

ERIC THE RED (Eric Thorvaldsson), explorer; b. Norway; flourished late 10th Century; son of Thorvald; at least 1 son, Leif Ericsson. Nicknamed Eric the Red in youth; accompanied his father into exile, settled (with other families) in Western Iceland; later exiled for outlawry from both Norway and Iceland for 3 year period; decided to spend his exile in exploring area which is now Greenland (known to Icelandic settlers as it could be seen on clear days from extreme N.W. tip of Iceland); sailed 175 miles to Iceland, 982, lived mainly on coast, 982-85, named area Greenland because he thought it better suited to stock raising than Iceland; returned to Iceland to get settlers for Greenland, 986; made 1st settlement, called Brattahild (nr. present town of Julianehaab) on So. coast of Greenland, 986; hero of Icelandic saga Eric the Red.

ERMATINGER, Francis (Frank), pioneer; b. circa 1798; ed. in Eng.; m. Indian woman (dec. 1837); 1 son, Lawrence. Joined Hudson's Bay Co. as clk.,

1818, trans. to Ft. Okanogan on Columbia River in N. Central Wash., 1826; traveled up Columbia River by canoe with Nathaniel Wyeth to take charge of Flathead post, Clark's Fork, Mont., 1833; met and traveled with J.A. Sutter on journey to take charge of Ft. Hall, 1838.

ERRETT, Isaac, clergyman, coll. pres., editor; b. N.Y.C., Jan. 2, 1820; s. Henry and Sophia (Kemmish) E.; LL.D. (hon.), Butler U., 1886; m. Harriet Reeder, Oct. 18, 1841. Ordained minister Disciples of Christ, 1840; corresponding sec. Am. Christian Missionary Soc., 1857-60, pres., 1866; founder, editor Christian Standard, 1866; co-editor Millenial Harbinger; prof. evang. and pastor tng. Hiram coll.; pres Alliance Coll., 1868-69; an organizer Christian Woman's Bd. Missions; a founder Fgn. Christian Missionary Soc., pres. until 1888; delievered chief address at funeral services for Pres. Garfield, 1881. Author: A Brief View of Christan Missions, Ancient and Modern, 1857; First Principles, 1867; Talks to Bereans, 1872; Life and Writings of General Edward Flower, 1885. Died Cincinnati, Dec. 19, 1888.

ERRETT, Russell, congressman; b. N.Y.C., Nov. 10, 1817. Moved to Pitts., 1829; engaged in newspaper work; elected comptroller Pitts., 1860; clk. Pa. Senate, 1860-61, 72-76, mem., 1867; served as additional paymaster U.S. Army, during Civil War, 1861-66; assessor internal revenue, 1869-73; mem. U.S. Ho. of Reps. (Republican) from Pa., 45th-47th congresses, 1877-83; U.S. pension agt. at Pitts. (apptd. by Pres. Arthur), 1883-87. Died Carnegie, Pa., Apr. 7, 1891; buried Chartiers Cemetery.

ERSKINE, John, jurist; b. Strabane, County Tyrone, Ireland, Sept. 13, 1813; m. Rebecca Smith, 1851, 1 dau. (Mrs. Willard P. Ward). Admitted to Fla. bar, 1846; moved to Newman, Ga., then to Atlanta, Ga., 1855; strongly opposed succession; U.S. judge for Dist of Ga., 1866-82. Died Atlanta, Jan. 27, 1895.

ERSKINE, Robert, army officer; b. Dunfermline, Scotland, Sept. 7, 1735; s. Rev. Ralph and Margaret (Simson) E.; attended U. Edinburgh (Scotland), 1748, 52; m. Elizabeth Erskine. Engaged in unsuccessful business venture in London, Eng.; invented centrifical hydraulic engine which led to his election as fellow Royal Soc., 1771; sent to America as rep. Brit. investors in Am. Iron Co., 1771; became supporter of colonists, formed mil. regiment; commd. capt. Bergen County (N.J.) Militia, 1775; geographer, surveyor-gen. Continental Army, 1777-80. Died Oct. 2, 1780.

ERVIN, James, congressman; b. Williamsburg Dist., S.C., Oct. 17, 1778; grad. R.I. Coll. (now Brown U.), 1797; studied law. Admitted to bar, 1800, began practice of law, Peedee, S.C.; mem. S.C. Ho. of Reps., 1800-04, 10-11; solicitor No. Jud. Circuit, 1804-16; trustee S.C. Coll., 1809-17; mem. U.S. Ho. of Reps. (Protectionist) from S.C., 15th-16th congresses, 1817-21; engaged in agriculture; mem S.C. Senate, 1826-29; del. S.C. Conv., 1832. Died Darlington, S..C, July 7, 1841; buried in garden in rear of his home.

ERVING, George William, diplomat; b. Boston, July 15, 1769; s. George and Lucy (Winslow) E.; ed. Oriel Coll., Oxford (Eng.) U. Agt. for claims and appeals of Am. seamen, London, Eng.; charge d'affaires of legation, Madrid, Spain, 1804; spl. U.S. minister to Copenhagen, Denmark, 1811; U.S. minister to Madrid, 1814, largely responsible for Fla. boundary treaty with Spain, 1819; resigned from diplomatic service, 1819; mem. Mass. Hist. Soc., 1822. Died N.Y.C., July 22, 1850.

ESBJORN, Lars Paul, clergyman, educator; b. Delsbo, Sweden, Oct. 16, 1808; s. Esbjorn and Karin (Lindstrom) Paulson; m. Amalia Planting-Gyllenbaga; m. 2d, Helen Magnusson; m. 3d, Gustafa Manusson. Ordained to ministry Swedish Lutheran Ch., 1832; came to U.S., 1849; Scandinavian prof. Ill. State U., 1858; leader of secession of Swedish Lutherans from Synod of No. Ill., organizer independent Augustana Synod, Jefferson Prairie, Wis., 1860; 1st pres. Augustana Sem, Chgo., 1863; founder Swedish Luth. Ch. in U.S. Died July 2, 1870.

ESCALANTE, Silvestre Velez de, clergyman; b. Spain; flourished 1768-92. Franciscan monk, arrived San Francisco, New Spain, 1769; missionary in Sonora and Laguna; head mission Our Lady of Guadalupe, Zuñi; accompanied expdns. to area of Grand Canyon, 1775, 77; left N.M., went to Franciscan Coll., Queretaro, 1792.

ESPEJO, Antonio de, explorer; b. Spain; flourished 1581-83. A Spanish mcht, in Mexico, prospected for precious metals in area Valley of San Bartolomé; led relief expdn. which became trip of prospecting and exploration in American Southwest; extended Spain's knowledge of area further North than Coronado's explorations, 1582-83.

ESPY, James Pollard, educator, meteorologist; b. Westmoreland County, Pa., May 9, 1785; s. Josiah and Elizabeth (Patterson) E.; grad. Transylvania U., Lexington, Ky., 1808; m. Margaret Pollard, 1812. Tchr. mathematics and classics Franklin Inst., Phila., 1817; recipient Magellanic prize Am. Philos. Soc., 1836; apptd. meteorologist U.S. War Dept., 1842; submitted 1st annual weather report, 1843; formulated convectional theory of precipitation (his chief contbn.), laid foundation of weather forecasting; 1st govt. ofcl. to use telegraph to get weather reports from across nation. Author: Philosophy of Storms, 1841. Died Cincinnati, Jan. 24, 1860.

ESTABROOK, Experience, congressman, lawyer; b. Lebanon, N.H., Apr. 30, 1813; attended Dickinson Coll., Carlisle, Pa.; grad. Chambersburg (Pa.) Law Sch. Admitted to bar, Bklyn., 1839; clk. Bklyn. Navy Yard, later began practice of law, Buffalo; moved to Geneva, Wis., 1840; del. 2d Wis. Constl. Conv., 1848; mem. Wis. Ho. of Reps., 1851; atty. gen. Wis., 1852-53; atty. gen. Neb. Territory (apptd. by Pres. Pierce), 1855-59; mem. U.S. Congress from Neb. Territory, 36th Congress, 1859-May 18, 1860 (contested election); apptd. by gov. to codify Neb. state laws, 1866; pros. atty. Douglas County, 1867-68; mem. Neb. Constl. Conv., 1871. Died Omaha, Neb., Mar. 26, 1894; buried Forest Lawn Cemetery.

ESTABROOK, Joseph, coll. pres.; b. Lebanon, N. H., Dec. 7, 1793; s. Hobart and Anna (Hyde) E.; grad. Dartmuth, 1815; m. Nancy Dickinson, 1823. Pres., Amherst (Mass.) Acad., 1817-21; prof. Latin and Greek, Amherst Coll., 1821-24; pres. East Tenn. Coll. became East Tenn. U. 1840; now U. Tenn.), 1834-50. Died Anderson County, Tenn., May 18, 1855.

ESTAING, Charles Hector (Comte d'Estaing), naval officer; b. Château de Ravel, Auvergne, France, Nov. 28, 1729. Served as col. of inf., French Army, later brig. gen., taken prisoner at siege of Madras, 1759; entered service of French East India Co., led naval expdn. which destroyed Brit. holdings in Sumatra; captured by British, released; named lt. adm. French Navy, 1763, vice adm., 1777, in charge of fleet sent to aid Am. colonies; prevented by storm from engaging in a planned battle nr. Newport, R.I., sailed to W.I. and captured Grenada and St. Vincent, damaged Adm. Byron's fleet, 1779; returned to France, 1780, was out of favor with the court, but regained his status, 1783; commandant French Nat. Guard, 1789; promoted adm. French Navy, 1792; favored French Revolution at its beginning, but remained loyal to King, testified in defense of Marie Antoinette at her trial. Author: Les Thermopyles (tragedy), 1755; also book on Am. and poetry. Guillotined, Paris, France, Apr. 28, 1794.

ESTAUGH, Elizabeth Haddon, town founder, religious worker; b. Southwick, Eng., 1680; d. John and Elizabeth (Clark) Haddon; m. John Estaugh, Oct. 1, 1702, 1 adopted son, Ebenezer Hopkins. Came to U.S., settled on 500 acres of her father's land in Western N.J., 1701; her plantation became stopping place for traveling Quakers; village of Haddonfield grew around her house; clk. Women's Meeting, Haddonfield for 50 years. Died Haddonfield, Mar. 30, 1762.

ESTERBROOK, Richard, mfr.; b. Liskeard, Eng., Feb. 21, 1813; s. Richard and Anna (Olver) E.; m. Mary Dale, 1835, 2 children. Came to Phila. to invest his fortune, 1858; founded Esterbrook Pen Co., 1858, pres., 1858-95. Died Camden, N.J., Oct. 11, 1895.

ESTERLY, George, inventor, mfr.; b. Plattekill N.Y., Oct. 17, 1809; s. Peter and Rachel (Griffith) E.; m. Jane Lewis, Mar. 4, 1832; m. 2d, Mrs. Amelia Shaff Hall, Mar. 1855; m. 3d, Caroline Esterly, May 1884; 7 children. One of earliest farm machinery mfrs.; patented horsepushed harvester (1st successful Am. harvester), 1844; invented 1st sulky cultivator, 1854, seeder, 1865, self-rake reaper, 1870. Author: A Consideration of the Currency and Finance Question, 1874; A Plan for Funding the Public Debt, and a Safe Return to Specie Payment, 1875. Died Hot Springs, S.D., June 7, 1893.

ESTEY, Alexander R., architect; probably born Framingham, Mass., 1826; attended acad., Framingham; archtl. trainee in office Richard Bond, Boston. Began archtl. career as draftsman with Gridley Bryant, architect, Boston; later began pvt. practice architecture, Framingham; apptd. to joint com. to report on remodelling Boston State House, 1867 (report not adopted); mem. com. to report on provisions for Congressional Library, Washington, D.C., 1880. Prin. works include: Emanuel Ch. (Gothic style, 1861), Monks Bldg. (1873), Union Congregational Ch. (1877), Baptist Theol. Sch., Boston & Albany Depot (1881) (all Boston); Methodist Ch., Burlington, Vt., 1861; Ch. of Our Savior, Longwood, Brookline, Mass., 1866; Grace Ch., Newton, Mass., 1869; Harvard Ch. (Gothic), Cambridge, Mass., 1877; state normal schs., Framingham, Worcester, Mass.; bldgs. at Colby Coll., Waterville, Me., U. Vt. at Burlington, U. Rochester (N.Y.); also several residences, Framingham. Died July 2, 1881.

ESTEY, Jacob, organ mfr., legislator; b. Hinsdale, N.H. , Sept. 30, 1814; s. Isaac and Patty (Forbes) E.; m. Desdemona Wood, 1837. Pioneer Am. organ mfr.; established Estey Organ Co., mfg. Estey cottage organs, 1860 (largest organ mfg. firm in world by 1890); one of 1st to use easy payment plan to further sale of expensive organs; mem. Vt. Ho. of Reps., 1869, 70, Vt. Senate, 1872; presdl. elector, 1876; organized Estey Piano Co., 1885; a founder Shaw U. (for negro students), Raleigh, N.C. Died Apr. 15, 1890.

ESTIL, Benjamin, congressman, jurist; b. Hansonville, (now Russell County), Va., Mar. 13, 1780; attended Washington Acad. (now Washington and Lee U.), Lexington, Va.; studied law. Admitted to bar, began practice of law, Abingdon, Va.; pros. atty. Washington County; mem. Va. Ho. of Dels., 1814-17; mem. U.S. Ho. of Reps. from Va., 19th Congress, 1825-27; judge 15th Jud. Circuit, 1831-52; ret. to farm, Oldham County, Ky. Died Oldham County, July 14, 1853.

ETHEL, Agnes, actress; b. 1852. Became a star as Gilberte in adaptation by John Augustin Daly of Parisian melodrama Frou-Frou (ran for 103 performances), Fifth Avenue Theater, N.Y.C., 1870; acted in plays Twelfth Night, Much Ado About Nothing, The Hunchback; after a dispute with Daly, joined Albert Marshall Palmer co., Union Square Theater, N.Y.C., 1872; acted for 100 performances in play Agnes (written for her by French dramatist Victorien Sardou), which established Palmer's reputation as a respected theatrical mgr., 1872. Died 1903.

ETTWEIN, John, clergyman; b. Freudenstadt, Würtemberg, June 29, 1721; m. Johanna Maria Kymbel, 1746. Shoemaker; convert to Moravian ch., moved to Marienborn, became missionary; ordained deacon, 1746; came to America, 1754; missionary in Middle states, 1754-63; head Moravian conversions, N.C., 1763-66; asst. to Bishop N. Seidel, Bethlehem, Pa., 1766; arrested as Loyalist; later became Moravian rep. to Continental Congress and Pa. Assembly; chaplain Continental Army hosp., Bethlehem, 1776-77; revived Soc. of United Brethren for Propagating Gospel among Heathen, pres., 1787; bishop Moravian Ch. in N.Am., 1784-1801. Died Bethlehem, Jan. 2, 1802.

EUMENES, see Green, Jacob.

EUSTIS, George, jurist; b. Boston, Oct. 20, 1796; s. Jacob and Elizabeth (Gray) E.; grad. Harvard, 1815; LL.D. (hon.), Tulane U., 1849; m. Clarisse Allain, 1825, 6 children including George, James. Admitted to New Orleans bar, 1822; atty. gen. La., 1830-32; sec. of state La., 1832-34; a founder of a med. coll., chartered 1835; justice La. Supreme Ct., 1838, resigned, 1839, chief justice, 1846-52; mem. La. Constl. Conv., 1845; a founder Tulane U., 1845. Died New Orleans, Dec. 22, 1858.

EUSTIS, George, congressman; b. New Orleans, Sept. 29, 1828; s. George and Clarissa (Allain) E.; attended Jefferson Coll., La.; attended Harvard, 1844-45; m. Louise Corcoran, 3 children. Practiced law; mem. U.S. Ho. of Reps. (American Party) from La., 34th-35th congresses, 1855-59; sec. Confederate legation, Paris, France; arrested with Slidell and Mason in Trent affair; following Civil war became expatriot living in France; aided U.S. minister to France during Franco-Prussian War. Died Cannes, France, Mar. 15, 1872; buried Oak Hill Cemetery, Washington, D.C.

EUSTIS, Henry Lawrence, engr., educator, army officer; b. Boston, Feb. 1, 1819; s. Gen. Abraham and Rebecca (Sprague) E.; grad. Harvard, 1838, A.M., 1850; grad. U.S Mil. Acad., 1842; m. Sarah Eckley, May 2, 1844; m. 2d, Caroline Hall, July 10, 1856; 6 children. Asst. prof. engring. U.S. Mil. Acad., 1847-49; prof. engring. Harvard, 1849-85, organized dept. engring. Harvard's Lawrence Scientific Sch., dean sci. faculty, 1862-63, 71-85; commd. brig. gen. U.S. Volunteers, 1863, served in many important battles; fellow Am. Acad. Arts and Scis. Died Cambridge, Mass., Jan. 11, 1885.

EUSTIS, James Biddle, senator, diplomat; b. New Orleans, Aug. 21, 1834; s. Judge George and Clarisse (Allain) E.; LL.B., Harvard Law Sch., 1854; m. Ellen Buckner, Sept. 3, 1857, 7 children. Admitted to La. bar, 1856; served as judge adv. Confederate Army on Gen. Margruder's staff, 1861, Gen. J. E. Johnston's staff, 1862-65; mem. La. Legislature, 1866; leader La. Democratic Party; mem. La. Senate, 1874; mem. U.S. Senate from La., Jan. 1876-79, 85-91; prof. civil law, lectr. Tulane U., New Orleans, 1879-84; U.S. ambassador to France, 1892; later mem. Tammany Hall, N.Y.C.; practiced law. Died Newport, R.I., Sept. 9, 1899.

EUSTIS, William, gov. Mass., U.S. sec. of war; b. Cambridge, Mass., June 10, 1753; s. Benjamin and Elizabeth (Hill) E.; grad. Harvard, 1772, A.M. (hon.), 1784, LL.D. (hon.), 1823; m. Caroline Langdon, Sept. 24, 1810. Served as surgeon during Am. revolution; surgeon in expdn. to suppress Shay's Rebellion, 1786-87; mem. Mass. Gen. Ct., 1788-94; mem. U.S. Ho. of Reps. from Mass., 7th-8th congresses, 1801-05, 16th-17th congresses, 1820-23; U.S. sec. of war, 1807-13; U.S. minister to Holland, 1814-18; gov. Mass., 1823-25; v.p. Soc. of Cincinnati, 1786-1810, 20. Died Boston, Feb. 6, 1825; buried Granary Burying Ground, Boston.

EVANS, Alexander, congressman, lawyer; b. Elkton, Md., Sept. 13, 1818; attended public schs., also acad., Elkton; studied law. Asst. to a civil engr.; admitted to bar, 1845, begin practice of law, Elkton; mem. U.S. Ho. of Reps. (Whig) from Md., 30th-32d congresses 1847-53; practiced law, Elkton, 1853-88. Died Elkton, Dec. 5, 1888; buried Elkton Presbyn. Cemetery.

EVANS, Anthony Walton Whyte, civil engr.; b. New Brunswick, N.J., Oct. 31, 1817; s. Thomas M. and Eliza (Whyte) E.; grad. Rensselaer Poly. Inst., 1836; m. Anna Zimmerman, at least 1 dau. Worked on Erie Canal; asst. to Allan Campbell in constrn. N.Y. & Harlem R.R., also Copiapo R.R., Chile; built other S.Am. railroads; became cons. engr., N.Y.C., continued designing S.Am. railroads, served as agt. for fgn. railroad cos. Died Nov. 28, 1886.

EVANS, David Ellicott, congressman; b. Ellicotts Upper Mills, Md., Mar. 19, 1788; attended common schs. Moved to Batavia, N.Y., 1803; became clk., then accounting clk. Holland Land Co., resident agt., 1827-37; mem. N.Y. Senate, 1819-22; mem. council of appointment, 1820-21; mem. U.S. Ho. of Reps. (Democrat) from N.Y., 20th Congress, Mar. 4-May 2, 1827; also engaged in banking; del. to conv. to advocate protective tariff, Albany, N.Y., 1827; retired to attend to his extensive land interests, 1837. Died Batavia, May 17, 1850; buried Batavia Cemetery.

EVANS, David Reid, congressman; b. Westminster, Eng., Feb. 20, 1769; came to U.S., 1784; attended Mr. Zion Coll.; studied law. Admitted to bar, 1796, began practice of law, Winnsboro; mem. S.C. Ho. of Reps., 1800-04; solicitor Middle Jud. Circuit, 1804-11; mem. Ho. of Reps. (Democrat) from S.C., 13th Congress, 1813-15; mem. S.C. Senate, 1818-26; 1st pres. Fairfield Bible Soc. Died Winnsboro, S.C., Mar. 8, 1843; buried Winnsboro.

EVANS, Frederick William, reformer; b. Worcestershire, Eng., June 9, 1808; s. George and Sarah (White) E. Came to U.S. (N.Y.), 1820; mem. Owenite community, Massillon, O., 1828-29; an editor and publisher Working Man's Advocate, Daily Sentinel, Young America; converted to Shakerism, mem. Shaker Soc., Mt. Lebanon, N.Y., 1830-93. Author: Tests of Devine Inspiration, 1853; Ann Lee, a Biography, 1858; Shakers . . ., 1866; Shaker Communism, 1871. Died Mt. Lebanon, Mar. 6, 1893.

EVANS, George, congressman; b. Hallowell, Me., Jan. 12, 1797; s. Daniel and Joanna (Hains) E.; grad. Bowdoin Coll., 1815, A.M. (hon.), 1818, LL.D. (hon.), 1847; m. Ann Dearborn, Oct. 1820, 3 children. Admitted to Me. bar, 1818; mem. Me. Legislature (Republican), 1825-29, speaker, 1829; mem. U. S. Ho. of Reps. from Me., 21-26th congresses, 1829-41; mem. U.S. Senate from Me., 1841-45, chmn. com. on finance, atty. gen. Me., 1853-56; pres. Portland & Kennebec R.R. Co.; active mem. Me. Hist. Soc.; an overseer Bowdoin Coll., 1827-45, trustee, 1845-67, Died Portland, Me., Apr. 6, 1867.

EVANS, George Henry, reformer; b. Herefordshire, Eng., Mar. 25, 1805; s. George and Sarah (White) E. Came to U.S., 1820; edited The Man, 1822, Working Man's Advocate, intermittently, 1829-45; leader various attempts to form working men's parties and orgns.; called for land reform as basis of better society. Author: History of the Origin and Progress of the Working Men's Party, 1840. Died Granville, N.J., Feb. 2, 1856.

EVANS, John, Continental congressman. Mem. Del. Assembly, 1774-76; dep. Del. Constl. Conv., 1776; mem. Continental Congress, 1776-77 (did not serve due to ill health); justice Del. Supreme Ct., 1777.

EVANS, John, physician, railroad builder, territorial gov.; b. Waynesville, O., Mar. 9, 1814; s. David and Rachel (Burnet) E.; grad. Lynn Med. Coll., 1838; m. Hannah Canby, 1838; m. 2d, Margaret Patten Gray, Aug. 18, 1853. Began practice medicine, 1838; leader in movement to establish 1st hosp. for insane in Ind., served as 1st supt.; became prof. obstetrics Rush Med. Coll., Chgo., 1848; an editor, propr. Northwestern Med. and Surg. Jour.; promoter Mercy Hosp.; chmn. Chgo. Com. on Schs., 1854; a prin. founder Northwestern U.; dir., part builder Ft. Wayne & Chgo. R.R.; became territorial gov. Colo., 1862; elected to U.S. Senate by those who hoped for Colo. statehood, 1865, never took seat; founder U. Denver (Colo.); leader movement resulting in incorporation Denver Pacific R.R. & Telegraph Co.; promoter S. Park R.R. (across Continental Divide), Denver & New Orleans R.R. (giving Denver access to South); Evanston (Ill.) named after him; Mt. Evans (nr. Denver, 14,260 feet) named in his honor by legislative act, 1895. Died Denver, July 3, 1897.

EVANS, Joshua, Jr., congressman; b. Paoli, Pa., Jan. 20, 1777; attended common schs. Hotel keeper, also farmer; mem. Pa. Ho. of Reps., 1820; 1st postmaster Paoli, 1826-30; pres. Tredyffrin Twp. Sch. Bd., 1836-46; served as brig. gen. Pa. Militia; mem. U.S. Ho. of Reps. (Democrat) from Pa., 21st-22d congresses, 1829-33. Died Paoli, Oct. 2, 1846; buried Great Valley Baptist Ch., New Centerville, Pa.

EVANS, Josiah James, senator, jurist; b. Marlboro Dist., S.C., Nov. 27, 1786; grad. S.C. Coll. at Columbia, 1808; studied law. Admitted to bar, began practice of law, Marlboro Dist., 1811; mem. S.C. Ho. of Reps., 1812-13; moved to Darlington Dist., 1816; state solicitor No. Dist. S.C., 1816-29; judge Circuit Ct., 1829-35; judge S.C. Supreme Ct., 1829-52; mem. U.S. Senate (States Rights Democrat) from S.C., 1853-58. Died Washington, D.C., May 6, 1858; buried pvt. cemetery, Society Hill, Darlington County, S.C.

EVANS, Lemuel Dale, congressman, jurist; b. Tenn., Jan. 8, 1810; studied law. Admitted to bar; moved to Marshall, Tex., 1843, engaged in practice of law; mem. Tex. Conv. that annexed Tex. to U.S., 1845; mem. U.S. Ho. of Reps. (Am. Party candidate), 34th Congress, 1855-57; collector of internal revenue, 1867; mem. Reconstrn. Conv., 1868; chief justice Tex. Supreme Ct., 1870-71; asso. justice, presiding judge, 1872-73; U.S. marshal for Eastern Jud. Dist. Tex., 1875. Died Washington, D.C., July 1, 1877; buried Congressional Cemetery.

EVANS, Nathan, congressman, lawyer; b. Belmont County, O., June 24, 1804; studied law. Clk., Belmont County, 1827-28; taught sch.; admitted to bar, 1831, began practice of law, Hillsboro, O.; moved to Cambridge, O., 1832; mayor Cambridge, 1841, 55-57; pros. atty. Guernsey County, 1842-46; mem. U.S. Ho. of Reps. (Whig) from Ohio, 30th-31st congresses, 1847-51; judge Ct. of Common Pleas, 1859-64. Died Cambridge, Sept. 27, 1879; buried South Cemetery.

EVANS, Oliver, inventor, steam-engine builder; b. New Castle County, Del., 1755; s. Charles Evans; m. Miss Tomlinson, 1780; 2 children. Perfected machine for wool manufacture that could produce 1500 cards a minute; completed series of improvements in flour-mill machinery operated by means of water-power in 1785, then petitioned legislatures Pa. and Md. for exclusive rights to use his "improvements in flour mills and steam carriages" in those states (partially granted in Pa., wholly granted in Md.); in engine building bus., 1803; established Mars Iron Works, 1807; designed and constructed water works in Phila., 1817; 1st steam engine builder in Am., 50 of his engines in use throughout Atlantic coast states by 1819. Author: The Young Mill-Wright and Miller's Guide, 1795; The Abortion of the Young Engineer's Guide. 1805. Died N.Y.C., Apr. 5, 1819.

EVANS, Thomas, congressman; b. Accomac County, Va.; attended Coll. William and Mary; studied law. Admitted to bar; mem. Va. Ho. of Dels., 1780-81, 94-96; mem. U.S. Ho. of Reps. from Va., 5th-6th congresses, 1797-1801; a mgr. apptd. by Ho. of Reps. to conduct impeachment proceedings against Senator William Blount of Tenn., 1798; moved to Wheeling Va. (now W. Va.), 1802; mem. State Ho. of Reps., 1805-06.

EVE, Joseph, inventor, scientist; b. Phila., May 24, 1760; s. Oswald and Anne (Moore) E.; m. Hannah Singletary, 1800, 1 son Joseph Adams. Inventor machine for separating seed from cotton (an early version of cotton gin); manufactured gunpowder and cotton gins, nr. Augusta, Ga., 1810, also experimented with steam; inventor cottonseed huller, 1803, metallic bands for power transmission, 1828, 2 steam engines, 1818, 26. Contbr. several short poems, also long poems "Better to Be" (pub. in book form 1823) and "The Projector" to Augusta newspapers. Died Augusta, Nov. 14, 1835; buried "The Cottage," nr. Augusta.

EVE, Paul Fitzsimons, surgeon; b. Augusta, Ga., June 27, 1806; s. Capt. Oswell and Aphra (Pritchard) E.; B.A., Franklin Coll. (now U. Ga.), 1826; M.D., U. Pa., 1828; m. Sarah Twiggs; m. 2d, Sarah Duncan, 1852; 3 children including 2 sons who became doctors. Practiced medicine in clinics, London, Eng., also Paris, France, 1828-30; participated as physician in Revolution of July 1831, Paris; offered services to Polish Govt., served in hosp., Warsaw; an organizer Med. Coll. Ga., 1832, prof. surgery, 1839-50; prof. surgery U. Louisville; (Ky.), 1850, U. Nashville (Tenn.), 1851-61, 70-77, Nashville Med. Coll., 1877; served in Mexican War; served as surgeon gen. Tenn., then chief surgeon Gen. Joseph E. Johnston's Army, also surgeon Gate City Hosp., Atlanta, Ga., in Civil War; pres. A.M.A., 1857-58; leading surgeon and tchr. of surgery in South; perfected operation for vesical calculus; 1st Am. surgeon to perform hysterectomy; co-editor So. Med. and Surg. Jour.; asst. editor Nashville Jour. of Medicine and Surgery. Author (most noted med. works): A Collection of Remarkable Cases in Surgery, 1857; A Contribution to the History of the Hip-join Operations Performed During the Late Civil War, 1867. Died Nashville, Nov. 3, 1877.

EVELEIGH, Nicholas, Continental congressman; b. Charleston, S.C., circa 1748; educated in Eng. Commd. capt. 2d S.C. Regt., Continental Army, 1775, served in battle with British at Ft. Moultrie, 1776; promoted col., dep. adj. gen. for S.C. and Ga., 1778; served in Ga. campaign at Ft. Tonyn, 1778; engaged in agriculture; mem. S.C. Ho. of Reps., 1781; mem. Continental Congress from S.C., 1781-82; mem. S.C. Legislative Council, 1783; 1st comptroller U.S. Treasury, 1789-91. Died Phila., Apr. 16, 1791; probably buried Phila.

EVERENDON, Walter, gun powder mfr.; b. Eng.; 1 child. Apptd overseer of powder mill (established to provide Colonial forces with ammunition to fight Indians in King Phillip's War), Neponset, Mass., 1675, became sole owner by 1701, gave over mgmt. to son, 1724; 1st producer gunpowder in Am. Died 1725.

EVERETT, Alexander Hill, editor, diplomat; b. Boston, Mar. 19, 1790; s. Rev. Oliver Everett and Lucy (Hill) E.; grad. Harvard, 1806; m. Lucretia Peabody, Sept. 1817. Sec. to John Quincy Adams (minister to Russia), 1809-11; sec. Am. legation The Hague, 1815-16, charge d'affaires, 1818-24; U.S. minister to Spain, 1825-29; held controlling interest in N. American Review, 1830, editor, 1830-35; mem. Mass. Legislature; pres. Jefferson Coll., La.; commr. to China, 1845-47. Author: Europe, or a General Survey of the Political Situation of the Principal Powers with Conjectures on their Future Prospects, 1822; New Ideas on Population, 1822; America, or a General Survey of the Political Situation of the Several Powers of the Western Continent with Conjectures on their Future Prospects, 1827. Died Canton, China, June 29, 1847.

EVERETT, Edward, senator, gov. Mass., coll. pres.; b. Dorchester, Mass., Apr. 11, 1794; s. Rev. Oliver and Lucy (Hill) E.; grad. Harvard, 1811, MA., 1814; Ph. D. (1st awarded to an American) U. Gottingen (Germany); m. Charlotte Brooks, 1822, 6 children. Minister, Brattle Street Unitarian Ch., Cambridge, Mass., 1814-15; prof. Greek literature Harvard, 1815-20, pres., 1846-49, mem. bd. overseers, 1827-46, 49-54, 62-65; editor N. Am. Review, 1819; mem. U.S. Ho. of Reps from Mass., 19th-23d congresses, 1825-35; gov. Mass., 1836-40, created Mass. Bd. of Edn. and normal sch. system, aided in constrn. railroad to Hudson River; U.S. minister to Ct. of St. James, Eng., 1841-45; U.S. sec. of state, 1852-53; mem. U.S. Senate from Mass., 1853-June 1, 1854, worked for compromise of slavery question; lectured for purchase and preservation of Mt. Vernon as nat. monument; unsuccessful candidate for vice pres. U.S. on Constl. Union Party ticket, 1860; made many speeches supporting Union cause, 1860-64; delivered speech preceding Lincoln's Gettysburg Address, Nov. 19, 1863; pres. Union Club of Boston; Republican presdl. elector, 1864. Died Boston, Jan. 15, 1865; buried Mt. Auburn Cemetery, Cambridge, Mass.

EVERETT, Horace, congressman; b. Foxboro, Mass., July 17, 1779; grad. Brown U., 1797; studied law. Admitted to bar, 1801, began practice of law, Windsor, Vt.; pros. atty. Windsor County, 1813-18; mem. Vt. Ho. of Reps., 1819-20, 22, 24, 34; del. Vt. Constl. Conv., 1828; mem. U.S. Ho. of Reps. (Whig) from Vt., 21st-27th congresses, 1829-43. Died Windsor, Jan. 30, 1851; buried Old South Burying Ground.

EVERHART, James Bowen, congressman, lawyer; b. nr. West Chester, Pa., July 26, 1821; s. William Everhart; grad. Princeton, 1842; studied law Harvard, also in Phila.; attended univs. Berlin (Germany) and Edinburgh (Scotland), 2 years. Admitted to bar, 1845; began practice of law, West Chester, circa 1847; served to maj. Co. B, 10th Regt., Pa. Militia, 1862-63; mem. Pa. Senate, 1876-82; mem. U.S. Ho. of Reps. (Republican) from Pa., 48th-49th congresses, 1883-87. Died West Chester, Aug. 23, 1888; buried Oakland Cemetery, nr. West Chester.

EVERHART, William, congressman; b. Chester County, Pa., May 17, 1785; attended common schs.; married, at least 1 son, James Bowen. Became a civil engr.; served as capt. co. of riflemen in War of 1812; the only passenger saved from shipwreck of Albion, off coast of Ireland, 1822; plotted large addition to City of West Chester (Pa.), after 1822; mem. U.S. Ho. of Reps. (Whig) from Pa., 33d Congress, 1853-55; engaged in business. Died West Chester, Oct. 30, 1868; buried Oakland Cemetery.

EVINS, John Hamilton, congressman; b. Spartanburg Dist., S.C., July 18, 1830; grad. S.C. Coll. at Columbia, 1853; studied law. Admitted to bar, 1856, began practice of law, Spartanburg; served from lt. to lt. col. Confederate Army during Civil War; mem. S.C. Ho. of Reps., 1863-64; del. Democratic Nat. Conv., St. Louis, 1876; mem. U.S. Ho. of Reps. (Democrat) from S.C., 45th-48th congresses, 1877-84. Died Spartanburg, Oct. 20, 1884; buried Magnolia Street Cemetery.

EWBANK, Thomas, inventor, govt. ofcl.; b. Durham, Eng., Mar. 11, 1792. Came to N.Y.C., 1819; developed improved methods of tinning lead, patented 1832, improved steam safety valves, patented 1831; U.S. commr. patents, 1849-52; founder, active mem. Am. Ethnol. Soc. Author: Descriptive and Historical Account of Hydraulic and Other Machines Ancient and Modern, 1842 (16th edit. 1870); The World a Workshop or the Physical Relation of Men to the Earth, 1855; Thoughts on Matter and Force, 1858. Died N.Y.C., Sept. 16, 1870.

EWELL, James, physician; b. Dumfries, Va., Feb. 16, 1773; s. Jesse and Charlotte Ewell; m. Margaret Roberston, Dec. 2, 1794. Pioneer of vaccination in Am.; wrote The Planters' and Mariners' Medical Companion, 10 edits., 1807; attended to wounded Brit. soldiers when British occupied his home opposite U.S. Capitol Bldg. during War of 1812; criticized for helping British, published 3d edit. (1816) of earlier work to justify his conduct, also presented valuable record of events during the war. Died Covington, La., Nov. 2, 1832.

EWELL, Richard Stoddert, army officer; b. Georgetown, D.C., Feb. 8, 1817; s. Dr. Thomas and Elizabeth (Stoddert) E.; grad. U.S. Mil. Acad., 1840; m. Leczinska Campbell, 1865. Served in battles of Verz Cruz, Cerro Gordo, Contreras, Churubusco, Molena del Ray, Chapultepec during Mexican War, 1846-48; commd. capt., 1849; participated in Gila and Pinal Apache expdns., 1857-59; commd. col. Confederate Army, brig. gen., 1861, commanded div. in Battle of Blackburn's Ford, promoted maj. gen., 1861; served under Gen. Thomas (Stonewall) Jackson, 1862, in battles of Ft. Royal, Cross Keys, Cedar Mountain, Bull Run; commd. lt. gen., 1863, led 2d Corps at capture of Winchester, battles of Gettysburg, Wilderness, Spotsville Courthouse, 1864; given command defenses of Richmond; considered one of the great Confederate gens. Died Spring Hill, Tenn., Jan. 25, 1872.

EWER, Ferdinand Cartwright, clergyman, author; b. Nantucket, Mass., May 22, 1826; s. Peter Folger and Mary (Cartwright) E.; attended Harvard (did not graduate), A.B. (hon.), 1848, A.M. (hon.), 1868; S.T.D., Columbia, 1867; m. Sophia Mandell Congdon, Dec. 9, 1854, 6 children. A pioneer editor, vigilante, mem. San Francisco Bd. Edn.: mem. Episcopal Ch., 1843; reporter. editor Pacific News, 1849; part owner, editor The Sacramento Transcript; founded The Pioneer (earliest Cal. lit. mag.), 1854; ordained deacon Episcopal Ch., 1857, priest 1858: asst. pastor St. Ann's Ch., N.Y.C., circa 1860, Christ Ch., N.Y.C;. founded parish of St. Ignatius; published Sermons on the Failure of Protestantism and on Catholicity, 1869. Author: Manual of Instruction for Classes Preparing First Communion, 1878: Catholicity in its Relationship to Protestantism and Romantism, 1878; The Operation of the Holy Spirit, 1880; Grammar of Theology, 1880; What Is the Anglican Church, 1883. Died Montreal, Que., Can., Oct. 10, 1883.

EWING, Andrew, congressman; b. Nashville, Tenn., June 17, 1813; grad. U. Nashville, 1832; studied law. Admitted to bar, 1835, began practice of law, Nashville; trustee U. Nashville, 1833-64; mem. U.S. Ho. of Reps. (Democrat) from Tenn., 31st Congress, 1849-51; del. Dem. Nat. Conv., Balt., 1860; served as judge Gen. Braxton Bragg's mil. ct., during Civil War. Died Atlanta, Ga., June 16, 1864; buried Nashville City Cemetery.

EWING, Charles, jurist; b. Bridgeton, N.J., June 8, 1780; s. James and Martha (Boyd) E.; grad. Coll. of N.J. (now Princeton), 1798, A.M. (hon.); LL.D. (hon.), Jefferson Coll., 1830; m. Eleanor Armstrong. Admtited to N.J. bar, 1802; admitted as councillor at law, N.J. 1805; recorder City of Trenton (N.J.), 1812-15; commr. to revise laws of N.J., 1819; trustee Coll. of N.J., 1820-32; chief justice N.J. Supreme Ct., 1824-32. Died Trenton, Aug. 5, 1832.

EWING, Charles, lawyer, army officer; b. Lancaster, O., Mar. 6, 1835; s. Thomas and Maria Ewing; attended Dominican and Gonzaga colls. Began practice of law, St. Louis, 1860; served as capt. 13th Inf., U.S. Army at beginning of Civil War, served in Ark. and Miss. campaigns; wounded 3 times at Vicksburg; promoted lt. col.; joined Gen. Sherman (his brother-in-law) on march through Ga.; promoted brig. gen., cited for gallantry at Vicksburg and Atlanta; returned to practice of law, 1867; became Indian commr., 1873. Died Washington, D.C., June 20, 1883.

EWING, Finis, clergyman; b. Brevard County, Va., July 10, 1773; s. Robert and Mary (Baker) E.; m. Peggy David, 1793. Prosperous frontier farmer, Ky.; licensed by heretic Presbyns. of Westminster Confessions (Ky. Synod refused to recognize license); with 2 others formed Presbytery of Cumberland, 1810, became leader of synod, expanded it, continued revivals, conversions; part-time pastor Lebanon Ch., Christian County, Ky., 1814-20; moved to Central Mo. accompanied by many church people; pastor ch., Lexington, Mo., 1836-41; register of land office. Died July 4, 1841.

EWING, James, army officer, legislator; b. Lancaster County, Pa., Aug. 3, 1736; s. Thomas and Susanna (Howard) E.; m. Patience Wright. Served as lt. Pa. Militia during French and Indian War, 1758; mem. Pa. Gen. Assembly, 1771-75; apptd. brig. gen. Pa. Militia, 1776; v.p. Pa., 1782-84; mem. Pa. Senate, 1795-99; trustee Dickinson Coll., 1783-1806. Died Hellam, Pa., Mar. 1, 1806.

EWING, John, clergyman, univ. provost; b. East Nottingham, Md., July 22, 1732; s. Alexander Ewing; grad. Coll. of N.J. (now Princeton), 1754; D.D. (hon.), U. Edinburgh (Scotland), 1774; m. Hannah Sergeant, circa 1758. Tutor, Princeton, 1756-58; taught philosophy Coll. of Phila., 1758-59: ordained minister Presbyn. Ch., 1758; pastor First Presbyn. Ch., Phila., 1759; provost, prof. natural philosophy. State U. Pa., 1779-1802 (merged with Coll. of Phila. into U. Pa. 1791); served on several boundary commns.; v.p. Am. Philos. Soc. Author papers published as A Plain Elementary and Practical System of Natural Experimental Philosophy, 1809. Died Norristown, Pa., Sept. 8, 1802.

EWING, John, congressman; b. Cork, Ireland, May 19, 1789; came (with parents) to U.S.; attended public schs. Engaged in comml. pursuits, Vincennes, Ind., 1813; founded Wabash Telegraph; asso. justice Knox County Circuit Ct., 1816-20; apptd. lt. col. Ind. Militia, 1825; mem. Ind. Senate, 1825-33, 42-44; mem. U.S. Ho. of Reps. (Whig) from Ind., 23d, 25th congresses, 1833-35, 37-39. Died Vincennes, Apr. 6, 1858; buried City Cemetery.

EWING, John Hoge, congressman; b. nr. Brownsville, Pa., Oct. 5, 1796; grad. Washington (now Washington and Jefferson) Coll., 1814; studied law. Admitted to bar, 1818, began practice of law, Washington, Pa.; engaged in agriculture; trustee Washington Coll., 1834-87, Washington Female Sem., 1846-87; mem. Pa. Ho. of Reps., 1835-36, Pa. Senate, 1838-42; mem. U.S. Ho. of Reps. (Whig) from Pa., 29th Congress, 1845-47; del. Republican Nat. Conv., Chgo., 1860. Died Washington, Pa., June 9, 1887; buried Washington Cemetery.

EWING, Philemon, jurist; b. Lancaster, O., 1820; son of Thomas Ewing; grad. Miami U. Admitted to bar, 1841, went into partnership with his father; active as Whig and Republican; became judge Ct. of Common Pleas, 1862, Ohio Supreme Ct., 1873; a strong opponent of reconstructionist policies. Died Lancaster, Apr. 15, 1896.

EWING, Presley Underwood, congressman; b. Russellville, Ky., Sept. 1, 1822; grad. Centre Coll., Danville, Ky., 1840; grad. law sch. Transylvania U., Lexington, Ky., 1843; studied theology Baptist Sem., Newton, Mass., 1845-46. Traveled in Germany for a time, them returned to Ky., began practice of law, Russellville; mem. Ky. Ho. of Reps., 1848-49; mem. U.S. Ho. of Reps. (Whig) from Ky., 32d-33d congresses, 1851-54. Died Mammoth Cave, Ky., Sept. 27, 1854; buried Maple Grove Cemetery, Russellville.

EWING, Thomas, senator, cabinet officer; b. West Liberty, Va., Dec. 28, 1789; s. George and Rachel (Harris) E.; B.A., Ohio U., 1815; m. Maria Boyle, Jan. 7, 1820, 6 children, including Hugh B., Thomas, Jr.; adopted son, William T. Sherman (later gen. U.S. Army). Admitted to Ohio bar, 1816; pros. atty. Fairfield County (O.); mem. U.S. Senate from Ohio, 1830-36: (filling unexpired term of Thomas Corwin), 1850-51; U.S. sec. of treasury under Harrison (tried to re-charter Bank of U.S.), 1841; resigned in protest an in attempt to force Henry Clay's theories on separation of govt. powers on Tyler; U.S. sec. of interior under Taylor, 1849-50; mem. U.S. Senate del. to Peace Conv., 1861. Died Lancaster, O., Oct. 26, 1871; buried St. Mary's Cemetery, Lancaster.

EWING, Thomas, army officer. congressman; b. Lancaster, O., Aug. 7, 1829; s. Thomas and Maria (Boyle) E.; ed. Brown U., A.M. (hon.); LL.D. (hon.), Georgetown (D.C.) Coll., 1870; m. Ellen Cox, Jan. 8, 1856. Pvt. sec. to Pres. U.S., 1848-50; leader of anti-Lecompton Constn. forces in Kan.; rep. from Kan. to Peace Conv., Washington, D.C., 1861; 1st chief justice Kan. Supreme Ct., 1861-62; commd. col. 11th Kan. Volunteers, 1862, served in battles of Ft. Wayne, Cane Hill and Prairie Grove; promoted brig. gen., 1863, served in battles in Mo., 1864, held Ft. Davidson, Pilot Knob, Mo.; commanded Border dist. 1863-64; St. Louis dist., 1864; brevetted maj. gen., 1865; mem. Ohio Constl. Conv., 1873-74; mem. U.S. Ho. of Reps. from Ohio, 45th-46th congresses, 1877-81; unsuccessful candidate for gov. Ohio, 1879 founder, pres. Ohio Soc. N.Y.; trustee Ohio U., 1878-83; acting v.p. Cincinnati Law Coll., 1881. Died N.Y.C., Jan 21, 1896.

EWING, William Lee Davidson, senator; b. Paris, Ky., Aug. 31, 1795; studied law. Admitted to bar, began practice of law, Shawneetown, Ill.; apptd. by Pres. Monroe receiver of land office, Vandalia, Ill., 1820; served as brig. gen. Ill. Militia; served as col. "Spy Battalion" during Black Hawk War; clk. Ill. Ho. of Reps., 1826-28, 42, mem., speaker, 1830, 38, 40; mem. Ill. Senate, 1832-34, pres. pro tem, 1832; commd. acting lt. gov., 1833; became gov. Ill. for 15 days, 1834; mem. U.S. Senate (Jackson Democrat, filled vacancy), Dec. 30, 1835-37; apptd. auditor public accounts, 1843. Died Vandalia, Mar. 25, 1846; buried Oak Ridge Cemetery, Springfield, Ill.

F

FABENS, Joseph Warren, diplomat; b. Salem, Mass., July 23, 1821; son of Benjamin Fabens; attended Harvard, 1837-38. U.S. consul at Cayenne, S.Am., 1843-circa 1850; U.S. consul at Nicaragua, circa 1850-59; visited Santo Domingo, became prominent advocate of annexing island to U.S. because of its rich natural resources, from 1859; wrote songs including The Last Cigar, Life on the Isthmus, The Camel Hunt. Died N.Y.C., Mar. 13, 1875; buried N.Y.C.

FABER, John Eberhard, pencil mfr.; b. Stein, Bavaria, Germany, Dec. 6, 1822; s. George L. and Albertine Frederika (Kupfer) F.; attended Gymnasium at Nürnberg, U. Erlangen, U. Heidelberg (all Germany); m. Jenny Haag, 1854, 2 children. Came to N.Y.C. after Revolution of 1848; set up pencil factory acting as agt. of his father's firm in Stein; acquired large tracts of cedar forest in Fla., exported wood to pencil factories abroad; due to labor costs his factory dependent on his father's for finished product; eventually acquired machinery that offset labor costs, made his factory independent by 1861; built new factory in Bklyn. (after East Side factory destroyed by fire), 1872; also operated factory for prodn. rubber bands, erasers and pen holders, Newark, N.J.; 1st mfr. to attach rubber tips and metallic point protectors to his pencils. Died Mar. 2, 1879.

FAESCH, John Jacob, ironmaster; b. Basle, Switzerland, 1729; m. Elizabeth Brinckerhoff; m. 2d, Susan Leonard; 4 children. Built furnace, Mt. Hope, N.J.; commd. judge Morris County (N.J.), 1773; mfr. shot for Continental Army during Am. Revolution; del. to N.J. Constl. Conv., 1787; signer N.J. ratification of U.S. Constn. Died May 26, 1799.

FAGAN, James Fleming, army officer; b. Clarke County, Ky., Mar. 1, 1828; s. Steven and Kittie (Stevens) F.; m. Mura Ellisiff Beal, 3 children; m. 2d, Lizzy Rapley, 5 children. Mem. Ark. Legislature (Whig) 1 term; served in Gen. Archibald Yell's regt. during Mebican War, discharged with rank of lt.; receiver Ark. State Bank, 1856-57; raised troops, became col. 1st Ark. Infantry at outbreak of Civil War; after battle of Shiloh promoted brig. gen., 1862; transferred to Trans-Miss. Dept., took part in Battle of Prairie Grove, defense of Ark. and repulse of Frederick Steele's Camden expdn.; promoted maj. gen.; did not surrender until 1865; apptd. U.S. marshall of Western dist. at Ft Smith by Pres. Ulysses S. Grant, 1875; became receiver for Land Office, Little Rock, Ark., 1877. Died Sept. 1, 1893.

FAGES, Pedro, Mexican gov. Cal.; flourished 1767-96; m. Eulalia Callis, 2 chidren. Served as lt. 1st Bn., 2d Regt. Catalonia Volunteers (Mexico), promoted lt. col., later capt., 1771; discovered present location of San Francisco; appt. Mexican gov. of Cal., 1782. Died 1796.

FAGET, Jean Charles, physician, author; b. New Orleans, June 26, 1818; s. Jean Baptiste and Mrs. (Le Mormand) F.; attended Collège Rolin, Paris, France, 1830-37; M.D., Faculté de Paris, 1844; m. Glady Ligeret de Chazet, many children. Practiced medicine, New Orleans, 1845; published articles in La Gazette Médicale, also New Orleans Med. Jour.; published discovery of difference in symptoms between yellow fever and malaria, 1859; apptd. to La.

Bd. Health; mem. San. Commn. apptd. by Gen. Nathaniel Banks, 1864. Author: Memoires et Lettres sur la Fièvre Jaune et la Fièvre Pauludeénne, 1864 (named chevalier Legion of Honor by France for this work, 1864). Died New Orleans, Dec. 7, 1884.

FAIR, James Graham, senator, mining exec.; b. Belfast, Ireland, Dec. 3, 1831; s. James and Miss (Graham) F.; m. Theresa Rooney, 1861 (div. 1883), children—Theresa Alice, James, Virginia, Charles Lewis. Came to Ill., 1843; went to Cal. in gold rush, prospected for quartz rather than gold, 1849; operated mill on Washoe River in Nev.; organized (with S. W. Mackay, others) Bank of Nev.; pursued a thin vein of gold in Consol. Va. Mine, which led to discovery of gold in Comstock lode (most valuable pocket of gold ever found in U.S.); became multi-millionaire from this discovery; mem. U.S. Senate from Nev., 1881-87. Died Dec. 28, 1894.

FAIRBANK, Calvin, abolitionist; b. Allegany (now Wyoming) County, N.Y., Nov. 3, 1816; s. Chester and Betsey (Abbott) F.; m. Mandarra Tileston, June 9, 1864; m. 2d, Adeline Winegar, June 5, 1879. His pious background and encounters with runaway slaves made him militant abolitionist; steered lumber raft down Ohio River taking aboard slave from Va. and freeing him in Ohio, 1837; passenger agt. for Underground Ry.; ordained elder Methodist Ch., 1842; arrested in Lexington (Ky.) for helping family to escape, 1842, held in Frankfort (Ky.) penitentiary, 1845-49; kidnapped at Jeffersonville, Ind., sent back to Frankfort penitentiary, 1851-64; supt., gen. agt. Moore Street Indsl. Inst., Richmond, Va. Died Angelica, N.Y., Oct. 12, 1898.

FAIRBANKS, Erastus, gov. Vt.; b. Brimfield, Mass., Oct. 28, 1792; s. Maj. Joseph and Phebe (Paddock) F.; m. Lois Crossman, May 3, 1815, 8 children. Developer (with bro., Thaddeus) Fairbanks platform scale, patented, 1830; founder (with brothers) E. & T. Fairbanks & Co., 1834 (incorporated as Fairbanks Scale Co. 1874); mem. lower house Vt. Legislature from St. Johnsbury, 1836-39; presdl. elector, 1844, 48; gov. Vt., 1852-53, 60-61 (as war gov. actively supported war effort, pledged his co. to raise emergency funds); made liberal benefactions to town of St. Johnsbury. Died St. Johnsbury, Nov. 20, 1864.

FAIRBANKS, Thaddeus, inventor, scale mfr.; b. Brimfield, Mass., Jan. 17, 1796; s. Joseph and Phebe (Paddock) F.; m. Lucy Barker, Jan. 17, 1820, 2 children including Henry. In partnership with brother Erastus Fairbanks, 1792-1864; established iron foundry E. & T. Fairbanks Co., 1823; patented a plow, 1826, flax and hemp dressing machine, 1830, platform scale, 1831; devised parlor stove, cook stove; invented draft mechanism for furnaces, 1843, hot water heater, 1881, also feed-water heater; established St. Johnsbury (Vt.) Acad., 1842. Recipient knightly cross Order St. Joseph from Emperor Austria, Golden medal from King of Siam, token of comdr. Order of Iftikar from Bey of Tunis. Died St. Johnsbury, Apr. 12, 1886.

FAIRCHILD, Lucius, gov. Wis., diplomat; b. Dec. 27, 1831; s. Jairus and Sally (Clair) F.; ed. Carroll Coll.; LL.D. (hon.), U. Wis., 1864; m. Frances Bull, Apr. 27, 1864, 3 children. Clk., Circuit Ct. of Dane County (Wis.), 1858; joined 1st Wis. Volunteer Regt., 1861; lt. col. in command 2d Wis. Volunteer Regt. at 2d Battle of Bull Run; commd. col., 1862; commd. brig. gen. U.S. Vols.; sec. State of Wis., 1863-64; gov. Wis., 1866-72; U.S. consul to Liverpool, Eng., 1872-78; U.S. consul gen. to Paris, France, 1878-80; state comdr. Grand Army Republic, 1886, became nat. comdr.-in-chief, 1886; a fed. commr. to settle Cherokee Indian affairs in Okla.; comdr.-in-chief Mil. Order Loyal Legion. Died Madison, Wis., May 23, 1896.

FAIRFAX, Donald McNeill, naval officer; b. Va., Mar. 10, 1821; s. George William and Isabella (McNeill) F.; m. Josephine Foote. Apptd. Midshipman from N.C., U.S. Navy, 1837, promoted passed midshipman, 1843, lt., 1851; exec. officer ship San Jacinto, 1861; commanded ships Cayuga, 1862, Nantucket and Montauk, 1863; comdt. of midshipmen U.S. Naval Acad., 1864-65; in charge of ship Susquehanna, 1867; promoted commodore, 1873, comdt. Naval Sta., New London, Conn.; gov. Naval Asylum, New London; 1878; promoted rear adm., 1880. Died Hagerstown, Md., Jan. 10, 1894.

FAIRFAX, Thomas, colonial ofcl.; b. Leeds Castle, County Kent, Eng., Oct. 23, 1693; s. Thomas and Catherine (Culpeper) F.; ed. Oriel Coll., Oxford (Eng.) U., 1710-13. Secured commn. in House Guards Blue, 1719; held post of treas. of the Household under Lord Chamberlain; settled permanently in Am., 1747; commd. justice of the peace in all counties of northern neck of Va.; assumed active duty of county lt. as commandant frontier militia; friend of George Washington, entrusted him with surveying and mapping of his property in the Shenandoah Valley. Died "Greenway Court" nr. Winchester, Va., Dec. 9, 1781; buried under Altarop Frederick Parish Church, "Greenway Court."

FAIRFIELD, John, lawyer, gov. Me.; b. Saco, Me., Jan. 20, 1797; s. Ichabod and Sarah (Nason) F.; m. Anna Thornton, Sept. 25, 1825. Admitted to Me. bar, 1826; reporter Supreme Ct. decisions, 1832-35; mem. U.S. Ho. of Reps. from Me., 24th, 25th congresses, 1835-38, resigned to become gov. Me., 1838-39, re-elected, 1841-43; resigned to become mem. U.S. Senate from Me., 1843. Died Washington, D.C., Dec. 24, 1847.

FAIRFIELD, Sumner Lincoln, poet; b. Warwick, Mass., June 25, 1803; s. Abner and Lucy (Lincoln) F.; attended Brown U., 1818-20; m. Jane Frazee, Sept. 1826. Tchr. in Ga., 1821, S.C., 1822; acted in tragedy Douglas (Home), 1826; headmaster Newton Acad., 1828-29; editor, publisher N.Am. Mag., 1832-38. Author: The Siege of Constantinople, 1822; Poems, 1823; Lays of Melpomene, 1824; Mina, 1825; The Passage of the Sea, 1826; The Cities of the Plain, 1827; The Heir of the World, 1829; Abaddon, 1830; The Last Night of Pompeii, 1832; The Poems and Prose Writings of Sumner Lincoln Fairfield, 1841. Died New Orleans, Mar. 6, 1844.

FAIRMAN, Gideon, engraver; b. Newtown, Conn., June 26, 1774. Apprenticed to blacksmith; worked as engraver, Albany, N.Y.; moved to Phila., 1810, became prominent engraver of banknote vignettes; with firm Murray, Draper, Fairman & Co., Phila., 1814-18; went to Eng. to compete (unsuccessfully) for banknote-engraving contract from Bank of Eng., 1819; returned to Phila., 1822, established firm Fairman, Draper & Co. (later Fairman, Draper, Underwood & Co.); painted portraits; frequent exhibitor at Soc. of Artists, Pa. Acad. Died Phila., Mar. 18, 1827.

FAIRMAN, James, artist; b. Glasgow, Scotland, 1826; attended N.A.D., 1842. Brought to U.S., 1832; exhibited at Am. Inst., 1844; went to Eng., circa 1851; served in Civil War; opened studio, N.Y.C.; went to Europe, 1871, studied in Italy, France, Germany and Eng., 10 years; returned to Am., circa 1880, became prominent critic and lectr.; taught at Olivet Coll. Died N.Y.C., Mar. 12, 1904.

FALCKNER, Daniel, clergyman; b. Langen-Reinsdorf, Saxony, Nov. 25, 1666; son of Daniel Falckner. Licentiate in theology at Erfurt, circa 1690, asso. with leaders of Pietist movement; joined group of Millenarians who planned to go to Pa. and wait for coming of the Lord, 1693; came to Am., settled nr. Germantown, Pa., 1694; returned to Germany to report on group's activities and recruit new members, 1868-69; obtained 22,025 acres of meadowland on Manatawny River, Montgomery County (known as Falckner's Swamp); organized 1st German Lutheran congregation in province, 1700, built log ch. and served as its minister; left Pa., impoverished, 1709; minister to Lutherans of Raritan Valley, N.J., 1709-41. Author: Curieuse Nachricht von Pennsylvania in Norden-America, 1702. Died circa 1741.

FALCKNER, Justus, clergyman; b. Langen-Reinsdorf, Saxony, Nov. 22, 1662; son of Daniel Falckner; attended U. Halle; m. Gerritge Hardick, 1717, 2 daus., 1 son. Came to Pa. to join millenarians, 1700; burgess of Germantown, Pa., 1700; ordained to ministry Lutheran Ch., 1703; minister to Dutch Luth. congregations, N.Y. and Hudson Valley, 1703-23; author hymn Rise, Ye Children of Salvation. Died 1723.

FANEUIL, Peter, mcht.; b. New Rochelle, N.Y., June 20, 1700; s. Benjamin and Anne (Bureau) F.; never married. Engaged in business, Boston, from 1718; became favorite of his wealthy mcht. uncle, inherited uncle's fortune, 1738; gave town hall (later known as Faneuil Hall) as gift to City of Boston. Died Mar. 3, 1743.

FANNIN, James Walker, army officer; b. circa Jan. 1, 1804; son of Dr. Isham Fannin; adopted by his maternal grandfather, J. W. Walker; attended U.S. Mil. Acad. (under name James F. Walker), 1819-21; m. Minerva Fort, 2 daus. Raised on plantation nr. Marion, Ga.; moved to Tex., 1834; active in organizing revolutionary coms. for revolt against Mexico, 1835-36; participated in 1st skirmish of Tex. War for Independence, Oct. 2, 1835; proposed seizure of Mexican port of Matamoras, against wishes of Sam Houston; apptd. to organize and lead expdn. to Mexico, 1836; established control (with force of 420 volunteers) of Goliad on south bank San Antonio River, Feb. 1836; forced to retreat, Mar. 19, 1836, overtaken by Orrea's advance, forced to surrender, Mar. 20. Shot (with over 300 other prisoners) by order of Santa Anna, Mar. 27, 1836.

FANNING, Alexander Campbell Wilder, army officer; b. Boston, 1788; s. Barclay and Caroline Henson (Orne) F.; grad. U.S. Mil. Acad., 1812; m. Miss Fowler. Commd. 1st lt., 3d Arty., U.S. Army, 1812, promoted capt., 1813; severely wounded at capture of York, Upper Canada, Apr. 1813; brevetted maj. for his defense of Ft. Erie, 1814; served with Jackson in Seminole campaign, 1818; occupied Spanish post of St. Mark's with force of 200 men; apptd. by Jackson as mem. of court martial which tried and sentenced Robert Ambrister and Alexander Arbuthnot, provost marshall at execution, Apr. 29, 1819; served at Ft. Gadsen, Detroit, Mackinaw, Columbus, arty. sch. at Fortress Monroe, Va, 1821-24; brevetted lt. col., 1824; commd. maj. 4th Arty., 1832; brevetted col. for service in battle at Withlacoochee, Seminole War, 1835; defended Camp Monroe against surprise Seminole attack, 1837; transferred to Canadian frontier, 1840-41. Died Cincinnati, Aug. 18, 1846.

FANNING, David, Loyalist; b. Amelia County, Va., circa 1755; son of David Fanning; married, Apr. 1782. Became Loyalist, 1775, commenced marauding expdns. against Whigs; commd. col. in militia, 1781; captured the ofcl. of a jud. ct. (or court martial) sitting at Pittsboro, N.C., July 1781; captured Gov. Burke, Hillsboro, N.C., Sept. 1781; 1 of 3 persons who were excluded from pardon by gen. amnesty act at end of Revolutionary War; mem. provincial parliament, New Brunswick, 1791-1801. Died Mar. 14, 1825.

FANNING, Edmund, colonial ofcl., army officer; b. L.I., N.Y., Apr. 24, 1739; s. James and Hannah (Smith) F.; grad. Yale, 1757, LL.D. (hon.), 1803; A.M. (hon.), Harvard, 1764, Kings Coll. (now Columbia), 1772; D.C.L. (hon.), Oxford (Eng.) U., 1774; LL.D. (hon.), Dartmouth, 1803; m. Phoebe Burns, Nov. 30, 1785, 4 children. Admitted to N.C. bar, 1762; col. N.C. Militia; register of deeds N.C.; mem. N.C. Assembly, 1776, 78; apptd. judge Superior Ct. for Salisbury Dist. (N.C.), 1766; pvt. sec. to Gov. Tryon of N.Y., 1771; surrogate N.Y.C., 1771; surveyor gen. Province of N.Y., 1774; raised and commanded corps known as Associated Refugees or King's Am. Regt. of Foot, 1777; property confiscated by N.C., 1779; moved to Nova Scotia; became councillor and lt. gov. N.S., 1783; lt. gov. Prince Edward Island, 1786; commd. col. Brit. Army, 1782, maj. gen., 1873, lt. gen., 1790, gen., 1808. Died London, Eng., Feb. 28, 1818.

FANNING, Edmund, sea capt., explorer; b. Stonington, Conn., July 16, 1769; s. Gilbert and Huldah (Palmer) F.; m. Sarah Sheffield, June 14, 1790, 3 children. Commanded a West Indian brig, 1793, ship Betsey, 1797-98; discovered Fanning Island nr. Cape Horn, also Washington (now called New York Island) and Palmyra Island, 1798 (group known as Fanning's Islands); promoted South Sea trade, as agt. for group N.Y.C. mchts. promoted more than 70 expdns. to South Seas; helped secure authoriziation of ofcl. naval South Seas Exploration Expdn., 1838-42; nicknamed "Pathfinder of the Pacific." Author: Voyages Around the World (memoirs), 1833. Died N.Y.C., Apr. 23, 1841.

FANNING, Nathaniel, privateersman, naval officer; b. Stonington, Conn., May 31, 1755; s. Gilbert and Huldah (Palmer) F.; m. Elizabeth Smith, Nov. 21, 1784, 6 children. Sea-fighting privateersman under Franco-Am. auspices, 1778-83; midshipman, pvt. sec. to John Paul Jones in ship Bonhomme Richard; his action in fight with the Serapis, Sept. 22, 1779, did much to bring about Am. victory; commd. lt. U.S. Navy, 1804. Author: Narrative of the Adventures of an American Naval Officer, 1801. Died Charleston, S.C., Sept. 30, 1805.

FANNING, Tolbert, clergyman, coll. pres., editor; b. Canno County, Tenn., May 10, 1810; s. William and Nancy (Bromley) F.; grad. U. Nashville, 1835; m. Sarah Shreeve; m. 2d, Charlotte Fall, Dec. 25, 1836. On extensive preaching tour for Disciples of Christ, 1833; opened boarding and day sch. for girls, Franklin, Tenn., 1837; promoter Tenn. Agrl. Soc.; editor Agriculturalist and Journal of the State and County Societies, 1840-44; began Christian Revue (later Christian Mag.), 1844; opened 1st sch. in U.S. to combine courses in practical agr. with academic subjects, 1843, success of sch. led to establishment of Franklin Coll., became 1st pres., 1845; started Naturalist, 1850, merged with So. Agriculturist, 1851; belonged to conservative group of Disciples of Christ (opposed organized cooperation). Author: Naturalist and Journal of Natural History, Agriculture, Education and Literature, 1846; Religious Historian, 1872. Died May 3, 1874.

FARAN, James John, congressman, editor; b. Cincinnati, Dec. 29, 1808; s. Charles P. and Phoebe Faran; attended Miami U., 1831; m. Angelina Russell, 1840. Admitted to Ohio bar, 1833; mem. Ohio Ho. of Reps., 1835, 37-39, speaker, 1838; mem. Ohio Senate, 1839, 41-43, speaker, 1841-43; mem. U.S. Ho. of Reps. from Ohio, 29th-30th congresses, 1845-49; editor Cincinnati Enquirer, 1843 a propr., 1844-81; mayor Cincinnati (Democrat), 1854; apptd. postmaster Cincinnati by Pres. Buchanan, 1856. Died Dec. 12, 1892.

FARGO, William George, expressman, mayor; b. Pompey, Onondago County, N.Y., May 20, 1818; s. William C. and Tacy (Strong) F.; m. Anna Williams, Jan. 1840. Rode mail route, 1831; failed as grocery store owner; 1st freight agt. Auburn & Syracuse R.R., Auburn, N.Y.; Buffalo (N.Y.) agt. Pomeroy & Co., 1843; messenger, one of 3 owners Wells & Co., 1844-50; pres. Am. Express Co. (formed by merger Wells & Co. with 2 other firms, 1850), 1850-68, operated in East and Midwest; an organizer Wells, Fargo & Co. for express bus. to Cal., 1852 (merged with Pacific Express Co., 1869); pres. Am. Mchts. Union Express Co. (merged with Am. Express Co. to form Am. Mchts. Union Express Co., 1868), pres., 1868-81 (name of co. changed back to Am. Express Co., 1873); mayor Buffalo (Democrat), 1862-66; unsuccessful candidate for N.Y. Senate, 1871. Died Buffalo, Aug. 3, 1881.

FARIBAULT, Jean Baptist, pioneer; b. Berthier, Que., Can., Oct. 29, 1775; s. Barthelemy and Catherine (Veronneau) F.; m. Pelagie Hanse, 1805, 2 children including Alexander. Apprenticed to N.W. Fur Co., 1796; stationed at a trading post among Sioux Indians, 1800, later at trading post at Little Rapids on Minnesota River; served with Brit. Militia in attack on Prairie du Chien (Wis.), 1814; became naturalized Am. citizen, 1817; trader Columbia Fur Co., 1822; his influence helped maintain peace between Sioux and pioneers for many years; Faribault County (Minn.) named for him (City of Faribault named for his son). Died St. Paul, Minn., Aug. 20, 1860.

FARLEE, Isaac Gray, congressman; b. White House, Hunterdon County, N.J., May 18, 1787; attended public schs. Engaged in business, Flemington, N.J.; mem. N.J. Gen. Assembly, 1819, 21, 28, 30; clk. Hunterdon County, 1830-40; served as brig. gen. N.J. Militia; mem. U.S. Ho. of Reps. from N.J., 28th Congress, 1843-45; mem. N.J. Senate, 1847-49; judge Ct. of Common Pleas, 1852-55. Died Flemington, Jan. 12, 1855; buried Presbyn. Cemetery.

FARLEY, Ephraim Wilder, congressman, lawyer; b. Newcastle, Me., Aug. 29, 1817; grad. Bowdoin Coll., Brunswick, Me., 1836; studied law. Admitted to bar, began practice of law, Newcastle; mem. Me. Ho. of Reps., 1843, 51-53; mem. U.S. Ho. of Reps. (Whig) from Me., 33d Congress, 1853-55; mem. Me. Senate, 1856. Died Newcastle, Apr. 3, 1880; buried in tomb on family estate.

FARLEY, James Thompson, senator, lawyer; b. Albemarle County, Va., Aug. 6, 1829; studied law. Admitted to bar, 1854, began practice of law, Amador County, Cal.; mem. Cal. Assembly, 1855-56, speaker, 1856; mem. Cal. Senate, 1869-76, pres. pro tem, 1871-72; mem. U.S. Senate (Democrat) from Cal., 1879-85. Died Jackson, Cal., Jan. 22, 1886; buried City Cemetery.

FARLIN, Dudley, congressman, businessman; b. Norwich, Conn., Sept. 2, 1777. Engaged in lumber and grain bus., Warren County, N.Y.; supr. Town of Warrensburg (N.Y.), 1818-20, 27-28; sheriff Warren County, 1821-22, 28; mem. N.Y. State Assembly, 1824; Democratic presdl. elector, 1832; mem. U.S. Ho. of Reps. (Democrat) from N.Y., 24th Congress, 1835-37. Died Warrensburg, Sept. 26, 1837; buried Warrensburg Cemetery.

FARMER, Ferdinand (original surname: Steinmeyer), missionary; b. Swabia, Germany, Oct. 13, 1720. Studied under Loyola at Landsberg, Germany, 1743; came to Am., 1752; in charge of a mission, Lancaster, Pa. 1752-58, in charge of German Parish of St. Joseph, Phila.; organized 1st Roman Catholic congregation in N.Y.C. (now St. Peter's) 1775; refused to accept position of chaplain in co. of Loyalist Roman Cath. volunteers the British hoped to form, 1778; an original trustee U. State of Pa., 1779; mem. Am. Philos. Soc.; astronomer, mathematician. Died Phila., Aug. 17, 1786.

FARMER, John, antiquarian, genealogist; b. Cheemsford, Mass., June 12, 1789; s. John and Lydia (Richardson) F.; M.A. (hon.), Dartmouth, 1822. Taught school, 1810; wrote A Family Register of the Descendants of Edward Farmer of Billerica, in the Youngest Branch of his Family, 1813; prepared An Historical Memoir of Billerica, Mass., 1816, Note on the County of Hillsborough, N.H. (paper, published by Mass. Hist. Soc.), 1818; opened apothecary store, 1821; wrote A Genealogical Register of the First Letters of New England (most important work), 1829; corr. sec. N.H. Hist. Soc., 1825-38; apptd. cataloger N.H. collection of state papers, 1836; other works include: Ecclesiastical Register of New Hampshire, 1822; The New Military Guide, 1822; The New Hampshire Annual Register and U.S. Calendar, 1822-38; A Gazetteer of the State of New Hampshire, 1822-38; Memoir of the Penacook Indians, 1824; A Catechism of the History of New Hampshire, 1829, 2d edit., 1830; The Concord Directory, 1830. Died Concord, Mass., Aug. 13, 1838.

FARMER, John, cartographer; b. Halfmoon, N.Y., Feb. 9, 1798; s. John and Catharine (Stoutenburgh) F.; m. Roxana Hamilton, Apr. 5, 1826, 3 children. Tchr., Lancasterian sch., Albany, N.Y.; in charge one of U. Mich. schs., Detroit, 1821; engaged in surveying, map-making, 1825; made map of Mich., accompanied by small gazetteer, 1830; influential in promoting extensive immigration into Mich., 1825-40; produced map of Detroit, 1831, published in Am. State Papers, Public Lands, Vol. VI; sold copyrights to a N.Y. map house; produced new map of Mich., 1844; noted for large map of Mich. and Wis., published 1859. Died Detroit, Mar. 24, 1859.

FARMER, Moses Gerrish, inventor, electrician; b. Boscawen, N.H., Feb. 9, 1820; s. Col. John and Sally (Gerrish) F.; attended Dartmouth, 1840-43; m. Hannah Shapleigh, Dec. 25, 1844, 1 child. Civil engr., Portsmouth, N.H., 1842; asst. in pvt. sch., Portsmouth, 1843; accepted preceptorship Eliot (Me.) Acad., 1843; prin. Belknap Sch. for Girls, Dover, N.H., 1844; devised machine that printed paper shades for lamps; experimented with electric railroad, 1845, constructed miniature electric train of 2 cars; wire examiner of new electric telegraph between Boston and Worcester (Mass), 1847; telegraph operator between Boston and Newburyport (Mass.), 1848; invented electric-striking apparatus for fire alarm service, 1848; supt. 1st electric fire alarm system in Am., installed Boston, 1851; discovered means for duplex and quadruplex telegraph, 1855; became supt. of tobacco-extracting manufactory, Somerville, Mass., 1861; invented an incadescent electric lamp, 1858-59, "self-exciting" dynamo, 1866; electrician U.S. Torpedo Sta., Newport, R.I., 1872-81; cons. electrician for U.S. Electric Light Co. of N.Y.; established public library, Eliot, Me. Died Chgo., May 25, 1893; buried Eliot.

FARNAM, Henry, railroad builder, philanthropist; b. Scipio, N.Y., Nov. 9, 1803; s. Jeffrey Amherst and Mercy (Tracy) F.; m. Ann Whitman, 1839. Surveyor on Erie Canal, 1821-24; asst. engr. in constrn. Farmington Canal, 1825, chief engr., 1827 until canal abandoned, 1846, then engr. and supt. railroad replacing canal; completed Mich. So. R.R. from Hillsdale connecting to East, 1852; built Chgo. & Rock Island R.R., 1852-54, pres. until 1863; designed and built 1st railroad bridge crossing Mississippi River, extended Miss. & Mo. R.R. to Grinnell (Ia.); contbr. to Yale, also civic causes. Died New Haven, Conn., Oct. 4, 1883.

FARNHAM, Eliza Woodson Burnhans, feminist, author; b. Rensselaerville, N.Y., Nov. 17, 1815; d. Cornelius and Mary (Wood) Burhans; m. Thomas Jefferson Farnham, 1836; m. 2d, William Fitzpatrick; 4 children. Apptd. matron female dept. State Prison, Sing Sing, N.Y., 1844-48; with Instn. for Blind, Boston, 1848; organized soc. to assist destitute women in finding homes in West, N.Y.C., 1849; studied medicine; urged women to develop intellectual interests. Author: California, Indoors and Out, 1856; Woman and Her Era (most significant work), 1864; My Early Days, 1859. Editor; Rationale of Crime, and Its Appropriate Treatment, 1846. Died N.Y.C., Dec. 15, 1864.

FARNHAM, Russel, fur trader; b. Mass., 1784; s. John and Susan (Chapin) F.; m. Susan Bosseron, Oct. 27, 1829. Sailed in ship Tonquin in Astoria sea expdn., from N.Y., 1810; selected to bring to J. J. Astor the co. records and net proceeds from sale of Astoria to N.W. Co., 1813; sailed in ship Pedlar, landing at Kamtchatka in Siberia, Apr. 1814, with few provisions made his way across Sibera to St. Petersburg, eventually returned to Balt.; mgr. of upper Mississippi for Am. Fur Co., 1817-19; arrested (with Parling) for violating trade laws, 1817, was acquitted. Died St. Louis, Oct. 23, 1832; buried Catholic Cemetery, St. Louis.

FARNHAM, Thomas Jefferson, lawyer, traveler; b. Vt., 1804; m. Eliza Burhans, 1836, 3 children. Practiced law, Peoria, Ill., before 1839; led a party of travelers to Ore., 1839; wrote petition to U.S. Govt. requesting that Ore. be taken into its protection; sailed to Sandwich Islands, claimed to have liberated from prison Americans and Englishmen implicated in local revolution; contbd. to knowledge of Far West geography; practiced law, San Francisco, 1846-48. Author: Travels In the Great Western Prairies, the Anahuac and Rocky Mountains and in the Oregon Territory (most important book), 1841; Travels in Oregon Territory, 1842; Travels in California and Scenes in the Pacific, 1845; A memoir of the Northwest Boundary Line, 1846. Died San Francisco, Sept. 13, 1848.

FARNSWORTH, Elon John, b. Greek Oak, Mich., July 30, 1837; s. James Patten and Achsah (Hudson) F.; ed. U. Mich., 1855-58. Joined Gen. A. S. Johnston's Utah expdn. against Mormons, 1857-58; joined 8th Ill. Cavalry, 1861, Commd. 1st lt., regimental adjutant; promoted capt., 1861; commended for gallant service, 1863; appt. aide-de-camp by Gen. Pleasanton; acting chief q.m. IV Corps, U.S. Army; commd. brig. gen. U.S. Volunteers, 1863; led charge of right flank of Confederate lines at Battle of Gettysburg, (Pa.), forced several Confederate inf. regts. to withdraw from front lines. Died in Battle of Gettysburg, July 3, 1863; buried Rockton, Ill.

FARQUHAR, John Hanson, congressman; b. Union Bridge, Md., Dec. 20, 1818; attended public schs.; studied law. Moved (with family) to Richmond, Ind., 1833; asst. engr. White River Canal, until 1840; admitted to bar, began practice of law, Brookville, Ind.; sec. Ind. Senate, 1842-43; chief clk. Ind. Ho. of Reps., 1844; Republican presdl. elector, 1860; served as capt. 19th Inf., U.S. Army, during Civil War; mem. U.S. Ho. of Reps. (Rep.) from Ind., 39th Congress, 1865-67; moved to Indpls., 1870, became a banker; apptd. sec. of state by Gov. Baker. Died Indpls., Oct. 1, 1873; buried Crown Hill Cemetery.

FARR, Evarts Worcester, congressman; b. Littleton, N.H., Oct. 10, 1840; attended Dartmouth; studied law. Commd. 1st lt. Co. G, 2d Regt., N.H. Volunteer Inf., during Civil War, promoted capt., 1862; served as maj. 11th Regt., N.H. Volunteer Inf., 1862-65; asst. assessor internal revenue, 1865-69, assessor, 1869-73; admitted to bar, 1867, began practice of law, Littleton; solicitor for Grafton County, 1873-79; mem. N.H. Exec. Council, 1876; mem. U.S. Ho. of Reps. (Republican) from N.H., 46th Congress, 1879-80. Died Littleton, Nov. 30, 1880; buried Glenwood Cemetery.

FARRAGUT, David Glasgow, naval officer, b. Knoxville, Tenn., July 5, 1801; s. George and Elizabeth (Shine) F. (adopted by Commodore David Porter); m. Susan Marchant, Sept. 24, 1823; m. 2d, Virginia Loyall, Dec. 26, 1843, 1 child, Loyall. Commd. midshipman U.S. Navy 1810 (at age 9); served 1st sea duty off U.S. coast, 1811; prize master ship Alexander Barclay during War of 1812; served on board Independence, then Washington, then Franklin in Mediterranean Sea, 1815-20; aide to commodores Bainbridge and Chauncey, also Capt. Gallagher, accompanied Folsom to Tunis; spoke French, Italian, Spanish and Arabic; served as acting lt. brig Spark, 1821; 1st orders were to Greyhound; commanded Ferret (1st naval vessel. command); commd. lt., 1825; exec. officer sloop Natchez, 1833; commanded sloop Erie in Mexican waters to protect Am. citizens and property, 1838; comdr. ship Decatur, 1841; in command of sloop Saratoga, 1847; ordnance duties in Washington and Norfolk, 1850-52, drew up book of ordnance regulations entitled Experiments to Ascertain the Strength and Endurance of Navy Guns; ordered to establish navy yard Mare Island (Cal.), 1854; commd. capt., 1855; went North when Va. seceded; mem. naval bd. N.Y. Navy Yard to select officers for retirement, 1861; apptd. to command West Gulf Blockading Squadron, 1862; went up Mississippi River; contrary to orders ran by Confederate forts before they were reduced, but New Orleans was taken, 1862; given thanks of the nation by resolution of U.S. Congress; after unsuccessful atempt to take Vicksburg, captured Galveston, Corpus Christi and Sabine Pass; promoted rear adm., 1862; suffered several reverses, 1863; captured Port Hudson (an achievement ranking next to New Orleans), 1863, honored by C. of C. of N.Y.C., Union League Club; comdr. flagship Hartford, led attack against Confederate defenses in Mobile Bay, 1864 (most memorable event of his life; uttered "Damn the torpedoes! Go ahead!" here); promoted vice adm., 1864, adm., 1866 (both ranks created for him by Congress); took command European Squadron, 1867, led goodwill tour that ended 1868; honored in Am. Hall of Fame. Died Portsmouth, N.H., Aug. 14, 1870; buried Woodlawn Cemetery, Westchester County, N.Y.

FARRAGUT, George, naval, army officer; b. Ciudadela, Minorca, Sept. 29, 1755; s. Anthony and Juana (Mesquida) Ferragut; m. Elizabeth Shine, 1795, 5 children including David Glasgow, William A.C. With Brit. mcht. marine in Mediterranean Sea, 1765-72; mariner in Am. seas, trading chiefly between Havanna, Cuba and Veracruz, Mexcio, 1773-75; came to Am., 1776, joined colonial cause, became lt. on privateer; commd. 1st. lt. S.C. Navy, 1778; served in defense of Savannah (Ga.), 1779, seige of Charleston (S.C.), 1780; volunteer for Gen. Marion, Battle of Cowpens, 1780; served in N.C. Volunteer Arty. Co. in Battle of Beaufort Bridge; capt. of cavalry troop that he raised; with Am. mcht. marine, 1783-92; sailing master U.S. Navy, 1807; served as sailing master of expdn. dispatched by Gov. William C.C. Claiborne of La. to take possession from Spain of disputed Gulf Coast of Miss. and La. Territory; accompanied personal friend, Andrew Jackson, on Indian campaigns, 1813-14; resigned from U.S. Navy, 1814. Died Point Plaguet, Miss., June 4, 1817.

FARRAR, John, educator; b. Lincoln, Mass., July 1, 1779; s. Deacon Samuel and Mary (Hoar) F.; B.A., Harvard, 1803, M.A., 1806; LL.D. (hon.), Brown U., 1833; m. Lucy Buckminster; m. 2d, Eliza Rotch. Tutor of Greek, Harvard, 1805, Hollis prof. mathematics and natural philosophy, 1807-36; fellow Am. Acad. Arts and Scis., 1808, recording sec., 1811-23, mem. com. on publs., 1828-29, v.p., 1829-31, contbr. articles to its Transactions; author various monographs on meteorology and astronomy; helped make European astron. and math. lit. known in America through translations. Died Cambridge, Mass., May 8, 1853.

FARRAR, Timothy, jurist, b. New Ipswich, N.H., Mar. 17, 1788; s. Timothy and Anna (Bancroft) F.; grad. Dartmouth, 1807; m. Sarah Adams, 1817. Admitted to Rockingham County (N.H.) bar, 1810; practiced law as partner of Daniel Webster, 1813-16, practiced alone, 1816; sec., treas., librarian Dartmouth Coll., 1822-24; judge N.H. Ct. of Common Pleas, 1824-33; engaged in financial bus. Exeter, N.H., 1836; moved to Boston, 1844, practiced law, did literary and hist. work; represented Boston in Mass. Gen. Ct., 1854. Author: Report of the Case of the Trustees of Dartmouth College against William H. Woodward, 1819; Review of the Dred Scott Decision, 1857; Manual of the Constitution of the United States, 1867. Died Mt. Bowdoin, Boston, Oct. 27, 1874.

FARRELLY, John Wilson, congressman, lawyer; b. Meadville, Pa., July 7, 1809; s. Patrick Farrelly; grad. Allegheny Coll., Meadville, 1826; studied law. Admitted to bar, 1828, began practice of law, Meadville; mem. Pa. Senate, 1828, 38-42, Pa. Ho. of Reps., 1837; mem. U.S. Ho. of Reps. (Whig) from Pa., 30th Congress, 1847-49; 6th auditor of treasury (apptd. by Pres. Taylor), 1849-53. Died Dec. 20, 1860; buried Greendale Cemetery.

FARRELLY, Patrick, congressman, lawyer; b. Ireland, 1770; studied law; married, at least 1 son, John Wilson. Came to U.S., 1798, admitted to bar, 1803, began practice of law, Meadville, Pa.; mem. Pa. Ho. of Reps., 1811-12; served as maj. Pa. Militia in War of 1812; mem. U.S. Ho. of Reps. (Democrat) from Pa., 17th-19th congresses, 1821-26. Died Meadville, Jan. 12, 1826; buried Greendale Cemetery.

FARREN, George P., actor; m. Marie Ann Russell, 1832. Popular standby at theaters in New Orleans, St. Louis, Mobile, Ala., 1832-46.

FARREN, Marie Ann Russell, actress; dau. of Richard Russell; m. George P. Farren, 1832. Made debut as the Page in play Purse, Chatham Garden Theater, N.Y.C., 1824; engaged as Young Norval and Little Pickle at Park Theatre, N.Y.C., 1828; popular standby at theaters in New Orleans, St. Louis, Mobile, Ala., 1832-46; appeared at Broadway Theater, Niblo's Theater, Wallack's Theatre, N.Y.C., 1845-46.

FARRINGTON, James, congressman, physician; b. Conway, N.H., Oct. 1, 1791; grad. Fryeburg (Me.) Acad., 1814; studied medicine. Began practice of medicine, Rochester, N.H., 1818; mem. N.H. Ho. of Reps., 1828-31, N.H. Senate, 1836; mem. U.S. Ho. of Reps. (Democrat) from N.H., 25th Congress, 1837-39; apptd. a trustee N.H. Insane Asylum, 1845; an organizer Rochester Bank, pres. until 1859. Died Rochester, Oct. 29, 1859; buried Old Cemetery.

FARROW, Samuel, congressman; b. Va., 1759; studied law. Served and was wounded in Revolutionary War; admitted to bar, 1793, began practice of law, Spartanburg, S.C.; also engaged in agriculture nr. Cross Anchor; lt. gov. S.C., 1810-12; mem. U.S. Ho. of Reps. (War Democrat) from S.C., 13th Congress, 1813-15; mem. S.C. Ho. of Reps., 1816-21. Died Columbia, S.C., Nov. 18, 1824 buried family burial ground on plantation, nr. battlefield of Musgrove Mill, Spartanburg County, S.C.

FARWELL, Nathan Allen, senator, businessman; b. Unity, Me., Feb. 24, 1812; attended common schs. Taught sch., 1832-33; moved to East Thomaston, 1834, engaged in lime mfg., ship bldg.; became master mariner and trader; moved to Rockland, Me.; founder, pres. Rockland Marine Ins. Co.; mem. Me. Senate, 1853-54, 61-62, presiding officer, 1862; mem. Me. Ho. of Reps., 1860, 63, 64; del. Republican Nat. Conv., Balt., 1864; mem. U.S. Senate (Republican, filled vacancy) from Me., Oct. 27, 1864-65; del. So. Loyalists Conv., Phila., 1866. Died Rockland, Dec. 9, 1893; buried Achorn Cemetery.

FASSETT, Cornelia Adele Strong (Mrs. Samuel Montague Fassett), artist; b. Owasco, N.Y., Nov. 9, 1831; d. Capt. Walter and Elizabeth (Gonsales) Strong; m. Samuel Montague Fassett, Apr. 26, 1851. Studied under Castiglione, La Tour, and Matthieu; mem. Washington (D.C.) Art Club; her studio entertainments became notable feature in Washington social life; portraits painted from life include U.S. Presidents Grant, Hayes, Garfield, Vice Pres. Henry Wilson, also prominent people of Chgo. and Washington; outstanding oil painting was The Florida Case before the Electoral Commn., 1877 (now hangs in Capitol Bldg., Washington). Died Washington, D.C., Jan. 4, 1898.

FAULK, Andrew Jackson, territorial gov.; b. Milford, Pa., Nov. 26, 1814; s. John and Margaret (Heiner) B.; m. Charlotte McMath, 1835. Admitted to Pa. bar, 1866; edited, published Armstrong County (Pa.) Democrat, 1837-41; advocate Col. Samuel Black's anti-slavery resolution in Pa. Dem. Conv., Pitts., 1849; held various county offices, 1840-60; shifted to Republican Party; post trader Yankton Indian Reservation on Missouri River, 1861-64; an organizer and supt. Latonia Coal Co. of N.Y., 1864-66; promoter Paxton Oil Co. of Pitts.; gov. Territory of Dakota, also supt. Indian affairs, 1866-68; adv. mem. Sherman's commn. which negotiated Treaty of Ft. Laramie, establishing Indians West of Missouri River; aided in opening Black Hills to white settlers; mayor and alderman Yankton (Dakota Territory); clk. territorial cts. for 2d Jud. Dist.; pres. Dakota Bar Assn. Died Yankton, Sept. 4, 1898.

FAULKNER, Charles James, congressman, diplomat; b. Martinsburg, Va. (now W. Va.), July 6, 1806; s. Maj. James and Sarah (Mackey) F.; grad. Georgetown U., 1822; m. Mary Wagner Boyd, 1833; 8 children including Charles James. Admited to Va. bar, 1829; mem. Va. Ho. of Dels., 1829, 31-34; Va. commr. to adjust boundary dispute with Md., 1832; mem. Va. Senate, 1838-42; prominent advocate Mexican War, 1843; mem. Va. Constl. conv. 1850; mem. U.S. Ho. of Reps. from Va., 32d-35th congresses, 1851-59; U.S. minister to France, 1859-61, returned, arrested, 1861, no charges investigated; entered Confederate Army, 1861, asst. adj. gen., prepared ofcl. battle reports; resumed law practice; pres. Berkley County Agrl. and Mech. Assn., Martinsburg & Potomac R.R.; temporary pres. W. Va. Constl. Conv. 1872. Died Boydville, W. Va., Nov. 1, 1884.

FAUQUIER, Francis, colonial ofcl.; b. Eng., circa 1704; s. Dr. John F. and Elizabeth (Chamberlayne) F.; m. Catharine Dalston. Dir. of South Sea Co., 1751; elected fellow Royal Soc., 1753; lt. gov. Va., 1758-68; warned Pitt of colonial resistance if policy of taxation were continued, 1760; dissolved Va. Legislature for passing Patrick Henry's resolution against Stamp Act, 1765. Died Williamsburg, Va., Mar. 3, 1768.

FAY, Francis Ball, congressman; b. Southboro, Mass., June 12, 1793. Engaged in merc. activities; postmaster Southboro, 1817-32; dep. sheriff Worcester County (Mass.), 1824-30; mem. Mass. Gen. Ct., 1830-31, 34-36, 40, Mass. Senate, 1843-45, 48, 68; mem. U.S. Ho. of Reps. (Whig, filled vacancy) from Mass., 32d Congress, Dec. 13, 1852-53; mayor Chelsea (Mass.), 1857; founder public library, Southboro; settled in Lancaster, Mass., 1858; founder state reform sch., Lancaster. Died South Lancaster, Mass., Oct. 6, 1876; buried Woodlawn Cemetery, Everett, Mass.

FAY, John, congressman; b. Hardwick, Mass., Feb. 10, 1773. Moved to Northampton, N.Y., 1804, became land surveyor; later engaged in agriculture, milling and mfg.; held various local offices; postmaster Northampton, several years; mem. N.Y. State Assembly, 1808-09, 12; mem. U.S. Ho. of Reps. (Democrat) from N.Y., 16th Congress, 1819-21; sheriff Jefferson County, 1828-31; Democratic presdl. elector, 1844. Died Northampton, June 21, 1855; buried Old Presbyn. Ch. Cemetery.

FAY, Jonas, physician; b. Westborough, Mass., Jan. 28, 1737; s. Stephen and Ruth (Child) F.; m. Sarah Fassett, May 1, 1760; m. 2d, Lydia Warner, Nov. 20, 1777; several children, including Maj. Heman A. Agt. of settlers of N.H. grants (now State of Vt.) for complaints to Gov. Tyron at N.Y., 1772; clk. of conv. to take action in the controversy, 1774, sec. various convs. held by the settlers; surgeon to Green Mountain Boys, 1775; mem. com. to inform Continental Congress that settlers of N.H. grants declared themselves a separate state (independent of both N.Y. and N.H.) and to present petition asking Congress for recognition as such, 1777; mem. Windsor Conv. which drafted Vt. Constn., 1777; sec. Vt. Council of Safety; mem. Vt. Gov.'s Council, 1778-1785; apptd. "to transact the necessary business opening a free trade to foreign powers," 1784; judge Supreme Ct. Vt., 1782, judge probate, 1782-87; practiced medicine, Bennington, Vt. Author: (with Ethan Allen) A Concise Refutation of the Claims of New Hampshire and Massachusetts Bay to the Territory of Vermont, 1780. Died Bennington, Mar. 6, 1818.

FAY, Theodore Sedgwick, diplomat, author; b. N.Y.C., Feb. 10, 1807; s. Joseph and Caroline (Broome) F.; m. Laura Gardenier, 1833. Admitted to N.Y. bar, 1828; editor N.Y. Mirror, 1828; sec. Am. legation, London, Eng., 1836, St. Petersburg, Russia, 1837-41, Berlin, Germany, 1841-53; resident minister to Switzerland, 1853. Author: Dreams and Reveries of a Quiet Man, 1832; The Minute-Book, 1833; Norman Leslie, 1835; Views of Christianity, 1836; Sydney Clifton, 1839; Hoboken, a Romance, 1843; History of Switzerland, 1860; Die Sklavenmacht, 1865, The Three Germanys (most substantial work), 1889; also school books. Died Berlin, Nov. 24, 1898.

FAYERWEATHER, Daniel Burton, leather mcht., philanthropist; b. Stepney, Conn., Mar. 12, 1822; s. Lucius and Amelia (Beardsley) F.; m. Lucy Joyce. Learned shoemaking and "tin peddling" (door-to-door selling), took hides in payment, began leather bus.; clk., Hoyt Bros. (became largest leather bus. in U.S.), N.Y.C., 1854, admitted to firm, 1855, became sr. partner; contbd. $50,000 to $300,000 to each of score of Am. colls. Died N.Y.C., Nov. 15, 1890.

FAYSSOUX, Peter, physician, surgeon; b. Charleston, S.C., 1745; stepson of Dr. James Hunter; grad. U. Edinburgh (Scotland), 1769; m. Sarah Wilson, Jan. 29, 1772; m. 2d, Ann Smith, Mar. 1777; at least 13 children. Elected curator 1st mus. of natural history in Am., at Charleston, S.C., 1773; mem. com. to collect signatures for Patriots' Assn., 1775; signer S.C.'s paper money, 1776; sr. physician S.C. Militia; served under Gen. Nathanael Greene in Continental Army; apptd. chief physician and surgeon of hosp. So. Dept., 1781; mem. S.C. Legislature; mem. privy council of Gov. Moultrie; incorporator Santee Canal Co., 1786; charter mem. S.C. Soc. of Cincinnati; an organizer Med. Soc. S.C., 1789, 1st pres., 1790-92. Died Feb. 1, 1795.

FEARING, Paul, congressman; b. Wareham, Mass., Feb. 28, 1762; grad. Harvard, 1785; studied law, Windham, Conn. Admitted to bar, 1787; moved to Northwest Territory, 1788, began practice of law, Ft. Harmer (now part of Marietta, (O.); apptd. U.S. counsel for Washington County, 1788; probate judge, 1797; mem. Territorial Legislature, 1799-1801; mem. U.S. Congress (Federalist) from Territory N.W. of Ohio River, 7th Congress, 1801-03; resumed practice of law, also engaged in fruit and stock raising; apptd. asso. judge Ct. of Common Pleas, 1810, master in chancery, 1814. Died near Marietta, Aug. 21, 1822; buried Harmer Cemetery, Marietta.

FEARN, John Walker, lawyer, diplomat; b. Huntsville, Ala., Jan. 13, 1832; s. Richard Lee and Mary Jane (Walker) F.; grad. Yale, 1851; studied law under Judge John A. Campbell; m. Fanny Hewitt, 1 dau., 1 son. Admitted to Ala. bar, 1853; U.S. minister to Belgium, 1853-56; sec. U.S. legation in Mexico, 1856-69; went to Madrid with 1st commn. sent by Confederate States Am. to secure European support, Feb. 1862; ran Charleston blockade, Oct. 1862, was apptd. to staff of Gen. J. E. Johnston; sec. on mission to St. Petersburg to secure Russian aid for Confederacy, Nov. 1862 (mission was not received); practiced law, New Orleans, 1866-84; U.S. minister resident, consul gen. to Greece, Rumania and Servia, 1885-87; chief of Dept. of Fgn. Affairs at World's Columbian Exposition, Chgo., 1893; a judge Internat. Mixed Tribunal in Egypt. Died Hot Springs, Va., Apr. 7, 1899.

FEATHERSTON, Winfield Scott, congressman; b. Murfreesboro, Tenn., Aug. 8, 1819; s. Charles and Lucy (Pitts) F.; m. Mary Harris, 1848; m. 2d, Elizabeth McEwen, 1858. Served as volunteer in war against Creek Indians; admitted to bar, Houston, Miss.; mem. U.S. Ho. of Reps. (Democrat) from Miss., 30th-31st congresses, 1847-51; commd. col. 17th Miss. Regt., 1861, brig. gen., 1862; important in overthrow of Ames regime in Miss. at close of war; pres. Miss. Taxpayers Conv., 1874-75; introduced impeachment of Gov. Ames; mem. Miss. Legislature, 1876-78, 80-82, chmn. judiciary com.; assisted in revision of Miss. Code, 1880; judge Miss. 2d Jud. Circuit, 1882; mem. judiciary com. Miss. Constl. Conv., 1890. Died Holly Springs, Miss., May 28, 1891.

FEBIGER, Christian, army officer; b. Funen, Denmark, 1746; m. Elizabeth Carson. Toured Am. colonies engaging in lumber, fish and horse trade, 1772; enlisted in Essex and Middlesex regt. Mass. Militia; maj. in Benedict Arnold's brigade Continental Army, taken prisoner, 1775; commd. lt. col. 11th Va. Regt., Jan. 1777; commd. col., 1777; chosen by Washington to command one of 4 light regts. for storming Stony Point, 1779; agt. for obtaining and forwarding stores to So. army under Gen. Nathanael Greene, 1780; aided in suppressing Loyalist insurrection in Hampshire County, Va., 1781; superintending officer Va. Militia, 1781; brevetted brig. gen. by Continental Congress, 1783; treas. of Phila., 1789-96. Died Phila., Sept. 20, 1796.

FECHTER, Charles Albert, actor; b. London, Eng., Oct. 23, 1824; s. Jean Maria and Marie (Regis) F.; m. Mlle. Robert, Nov. 29, 1847; m. 2d, Lizzie Price, 1874 (never divorced 1st wife). Joined amateur acting co. at Salle Molière, Paris, France, 1840; enjoyed greatest success as Armand Duval in La Dame aux Camelias, 1852; became joint mgr. Odéon theatre, 1857; left Paris when govt. prohibited prodn. of plays that were property of Théâtre Française; went to London, made successful debut in title role of Hugo's Ruy Blas, 1860; became prominent figure in Brit. theatre with performances of Hamlet and Iago, 1860-69; began career on Am. stage, 1870; mgr. Globe Theatre, N.Y.C., 1870-72. Died Bucks County, Pa., Aug. 5, 1879; buried Mt. Vernon Cemetery, Phila.

FEE, John Gregg, abolitionist; b. Bracken County, Ky., Sept. 9, 1816; s. John and Elizabeth (Gregg) F.; grad. Augusta Coll.; attended Lane Theol. Sem., 1842-44; m. Mathilda Hamilton, Sept. 26, 1844. Became ardent abolitionist; established anti-slavery chs. in Lewis and Bracken counties; founded Berea Union Ch., Madison County, Ky., 1853, Berea Coll. as abolitionist sch., 1855; banned from Ky. for his abolitionist activities, 1859-63; asso. with John Brown's Raid. Died Jan. 11, 1901.

FEKE, Robert, portrait painter; b. Oyster Bay, L.I., N.Y., 1705; s. Robert and Clemence (Ludlam) F.; m. Elinor Cozzens, Sept. 23, 1742; 5 children. Either learned to paint from John Smibert or influenced by Smibert; painted more than 20 of his finest portraits including those of Bowdoin family, 1748-49; strongly influenced by conventions of pose; pictures appear as life-like reproductions; considered one of best early Am. portrait painters. Died Bermuda or Barbados, 1750.

FELCH, Alpheus, senator, gov. Mich.; b. Limerick, Me., Sept. 28, 1804; s. Capt. Daniel and Sally (Piper) F.; grad. Bowdoin Coll., 1827, LL.D., 1877; m. Lucretia Lawrence, Sept. 14, 1837; 5 children. Admitted to Me. bar 1830; advised by physician to go West; reached Monroe, Mich., 1833; contracted cholera, stayed in Mich.; village atty. of Monroe, 1834; mem. Mich. Legislature, 1835-38; bank commr. Mich., 1838, auditor-gen., 1842; regent U. Mich., 1842-47; justice Mich. Supreme Ct., 1843; gov. Mich., 1846-47; mem. U.S. Senate (Democrat) from Mich., 1846-52; responsible for constrn. of canal at Sault Ste. Marie; appointed pres. commn. to adjust and settle Spanish and Mexican land claims under Treaty of Guadalupe-Hidalgo, 1853-56; opened law office, Ann Arbor, Mich., 1856; Tappan prof. law U. Mich., Ann Arbor, 1879-83, left more than 4,000 books and pamphlets to univ.; wrote articles on Mich. history. Died Ann Arbor, June 13, 1896.

FELDER, John Myers, congressman; b. Orangeburg Dist., S.C., July 7, 1782; grad. Yale, 1804; attended Litchfield (Conn.) Law Sch. Admitted to bar, 1808, began practice of law, Orangeburg; served as maj. militia in War of 1812; elected trustee S.C. Coll., 1812; mem. S.C. Ho. of Reps., 1812-16, 22-24, S.C. Senate, 1816-20, 40-51; mem. U.S. Ho. of Reps. (Democrat) from S.C., 22d-23d congresses, 1831-35; engaged in agriculture and lumber bus. Died Union Point, Ga., Sept 1, 1851; buried family burial ground on plantation "Midway," nr. Orangeburg.

FELIX, Elizabeth Rachel (stage name Rachel), actress; b. Munf, Switzerland, 1820. Debuted at Théâtre Francais, Paris, France, 1838; made Am. debut at Met. Theatre, N.Y.C., 1855; appeared in prodns. in French, in roles of Camille (Les Horaces), Phèdre, Adrienne Lecouvreur (written for her by Scribe and Legouvé), Marie Stuart, Hermione (Andromaque), La Tisbe, Roxana (Bajazet), Pauline (Polyeucte), Jeanne d'Arc, Lesbie, Celimene (Le Misanthrope); performed at Walnut Street Theatre, Phila., also New Boston Theatre, and in Charleston, S.C., 1855; known as 1st actress of the world: 1st fgn.-lang. star to make Am. tour. Died Cannes, France, 1858.

FELL, John, mcht., Continental congressman, jurist; b. N.Y.C., Feb. 5, 1721; m. Susanna Moskhk, 1 child. Sr. partner John Fell & Co., 1859; settled nr. Paramus, Bergen County, N.J.; judge N.J. Ct. of Common Pleas, 1766-74, 76-86; leader in meting of Bergen County citizens signing patriotic resolutions at Hackensack Ct. House, June 25, 1774; chmn. Bergen County com. which supervised local war effort; chmn. Com. of Correspondence; mem. 1st N.J. Provincial Congress, Trenton, 1775; mem. Provincial Council, 1776; captured by Loyalist leaders, 1777, released 1778; mem. Continental Congress, 1778 made prin. contbn. as mem. standing com. on conduct of U.S. comml. affairs, mem. spl. fgn. affairs com., 1779; mem. N.J. Council, 1782-83. Died Dutchess County, N.Y., May 15, 1798.

FELLOWS, John R., congressman, lawyer; b. Troy, N.Y., July 29, 1832; attended country schs.; studied law. Admitted to bar, 1855, began practice of law, Camden, Ark.; presdl. elector on Constl.-Union ticket, 1860; del. Ark. Secession Conv., 1861; served with 1st Ark. Regt., Confederate Army, during Civil War; became adj. and insp. gen., after Battle of Shiloh; assigned to Brig. Gen. W.N.R. Bell's staff, commanded dist. in Gen. Van Dorn's dept.; captured at surrender of Port Hudson, La., 1863, imprisoned, released, 1865; mem. Ark. Senate, 1866-67; moved to N.Y.C., 1868, continued practice of law; del. Democratic Nat. Conv., N.Y.C., 1868; asst. dist. atty., N.Y.C., 1869-72, 85-87, dist. atty., 1888-90, 94-96; mem. U.S. Ho. of Reps. (Democrat) from N.Y., 52d-53d congresses, 1891-Dec. 31, 1893. Died N.Y.C., Dec. 7, 1896; buried Trinity Church Cemetery.

FELT, Joseph Barlow, antiquarian; b. Salem, Mass., Dec. 22, 1789; s. John and Elizabeth (Curtis) R.; grad. Dartmouth, 1813; LL.D., 1856; m. Abigail Shaw, Sept. 18, 1816; m. 2d, Mrs. Catherine (Bartlett) Meacham, Nov. 16, 1862. Published Annals of Salem, 1827, 2d edit. 2 vols., 1845-49; elected to Mass. Hist. Soc., 1830, librarian, 1842-54; classified and arranged ancient papers in Mass. Archives, 1836-39; pres. New Eng. Historic Geneal. Soc., 1850-53. Author: Historical Account of Massachusetts Currency, 1839; Hugh Peters, 1851; Ecclesiastical History of New England (most ambitious work), 2 vols., 1851, 62. Died Salem, Sept. 8, 1869.

FELTON, Cornelius Conway, classical scholar, coll. pres.; b. Newbury, Mass., Nov. 6, 1807; s. Cornelius Conway and Anna (Morse) F.; grad. Harvard, 1827; LL.D., Amherst Coll., 1848, Yale, 1860; m. Mary Whitney, 1838; m. 2d, Mary Carey, 1846. Latin tutor Harvard, 1829, Greek tutor, 1830-32, prof. Greek, 1832-44, became Eliot prof. Greek lit., 1834; editor classical texts and selections from Greek writers for academic use; mem. Cambridge (Mass.) Sch. Com.; mem. Mass. Bd. Edn.; bd. regents Smithsonian Instn., 1856-62; became regent of Harvard, 1849, pres., 1860. Author: Life of William Eaton for Sparks' American Biographies, 1853; prepared revised edit. of Smiths' History of Greece, 1855, Selections from Modern Greek Writers, 1856; Greece, Ancient and Modern, 1867 (most popular work); translator: Menzel's German Literature, 3 vols., 1840; Classical Studies, 1843; Guyots' The Earth and Man, 1849; Selections from Prof. Papkin with Memoir, 1852. Died Chester, Pa., Feb. 2, 1862.

FELTON, Samuel Morse, civil engr., railroad exec.; b. Newbury, Mass., July 17, 1809; s. Cornelius and Anna (Morse) F.; grad. Harvard, 1834; m. Eleanor Stetson, 1836; m. 2d, Maria Lippitt, 1850. Engr. for Loammie Baldwin, Jr., 1836, took over business after Baldwin's death, 1838; built Fresh Pond R.R. to transport ice into Boston, 1841; began constrn. Fichtburg R.R., 1843, supt., 1845; pres. Phila., Wilmington & Balt. R.R., 1851-64 (important in Civil War Union troops movements); officially commended by War Dept. for his role in transporting Gen. Butler's troops to Annapolis and preparing plans for cooperation of all railroads centering in Phila.; commr. Hoosac Tunnel, 1862-65; pres. Pa. Steel Co., 1865; organizer, dir. N.P. R.R. Died Jan. 24, 1889.

FENDALL, Josias, colonial gov.; b. Eng., circa 1620; m. Mary Fendall, 1 child. Gov. Md., 1656-60; went to Eng., 1657, brought back agreement restoring Md. to proprietary rule; made unsuccessful attempt to overthrow proprietary govt., 1659-60; punished with disfranchisement and disqualification for office; ret. to estate in Charles County, Va.; charged with seditious utterances, 1679, could not be found when warrant was issued for his arrest; became influential in No. Va. in movement to overthrow proprietary govt., arrested, 1681, found guilty of attempting to raise a mutiny, was banished and fined. Died circa 1687.

FENN, Stephen Southmyd, congressman; b. Watertown, Conn., Mar. 28, 1820; attended public schs. Moved to Jackson County, Ia., 1841; held several local offices; moved to Cal., 1850, became miner and rancher; admitted to bar, 1862, began practice of law, Washington Territory (became part of Ida. Territory 1863); also engaged in mining; mem. Ida. Territorial Council, 1864-67; dist. atty., 1st Jud. Dist., 1869; mem. Territorial Ho. of Reps., 1872, speaker; engaged in agriculture; mem. U.S. Congress (Democrat, contested election) from Ida. Territory, 44th-45th congresses, June 23, 1876-79. Died Blackfoot, Ida., Apr. 13, 1892; buried Asylum Cemetery.

FENNELL, James, actor; b. London, Eng., Dec. 11, 1766; s. John and Miss (Brady) F.; attended Trinity Coll., Cambridge (Eng.) U.; m. B. H. Porter, May 10, 1792. Made his debut as Othello, 1787; made Am. debut, Phila., 1794; patented process to extract salt from sea water (salt works never became profitable; appeared regularly on N.Y. stage, 1797-1806; played King Lear in his farewell performance, Phila., 1814. Author: An Apology for the Life of James Fennell Written by Himself, 1814. Died June 13, 1816.

FENNER, Arthur, gov. R.I.; b. Providence, R.I., Dec. 10, 1745; s. Arthur and Mary (Olney) F.; m. Amey Comstock. Apptd. to Com. of Inspectors of Continental Congress, 1774; clk. Ct. of Common Pleas, Providence; opposed to adoption of U.S. Constn. as Anti-Federalist; gov. R.I., 1790-1805, convened R.I. Gen. Assembly in spl. session (all officers took oath to support R.I. Constn.), 1790. Died Providence, Oct. 15, 1805.

FENNER, James, gov. R.I.; b. Providence, R.I., Jan. 22, 1771; s. Arthur and Amy (Comstock) F.; grad. Brown U., 1789, LL.D., 1825; m. Sarah Jenckes, Nov. 1792. Mem. R.I. Gen. Assembly; mem. U.S. Senate from R.I., 1804-07; gov. R.I., 1807-11, 24-31, 43-45; elected chief justice of R.I. Supreme Ct., 1818, declined office; pres. R.I. Hist. Soc., 1822-33; opposed to Dorr Rebellion. Died Providence, Apr. 17, 1846.

FENNO, John, editor; b. Boston, Aug. 23, 1751; s. Ephrain and Mary (Chapman) F.; m. Mary Curtiss, May 8, 1777, 1 son, John Ward. Founder, editor Gazette of U.S., Phila., 1790-98. Died Phila., Sept. 14, 1798.

FENTON, Reuben Eaton, senator, gov. N.Y.; b. Carroll, N.Y., July 4, 1819; s. George and Elsie (Owen) F.; m. Jane Frew, 1838; m. 2d, Elizabeth Scudder. Supr. town of Carroll, 1843-51; became mem. N.Y. Assembly, 1849; seceded from Democratic Party on slavery question, led in formation of Republican Party; presiding officer 1st N.Y. State Rep. Conv., 1855; mem. U.S. Ho. of Reps. (Rep.) from N.Y., 33d, 35th-38th congresses, 1853-55, 57-Dec. 20, 1864 (resigned); gov. N.Y., 1864-69, asso. with reforms in registry law and prison system, with numerous ednl. reforms including establishment of Cornell U. and state normal schs.; built up 1 of most powerful polit. machines in history of N.Y.; mem. U.S. Senate from N.Y., 1869-75; pres. 1st Nat. Bank of Jamestown (N.Y.); chmn. U.S. Commn. Internat. Monetary Conf., Paris, France, 1878. Died Jamestown, Aug. 25, 1885; buried Lakeview Cemetery.

FENWICK, Benedict Joseph, clergyman; b. St. Mary's County, Md., Sept. 3, 1782; s. Col. Richard and Dorothy (Plowden) F.; grad. Georgetown Coll., 1796. Novice, Soc. of Jesus, Georgetown Coll., 1806-08; ordained priest Roman Catholic Ch., 1808, in charge St. Peter's Ch., N.Y.C., 1809-17; founder N.Y. Literary Instn.; prepared plans for St. Patrick's Cathedral; pres. Georgetown Coll., 1817-18, 1822-25, minister, 1822; pastor Trinity Ch., 1817-18; vicar-gen. Diocese of Charleston (S.C.), 1818-22; procurator-gen. Soc. of Jesus in U.S., 1822; apptd. bishop of Boston, consecrated in Cathedral of Balt., 1825, contbd. to edn. of young, expanded diocese from 3 to 40 chs.; founder publ. The Jesuit or Cath. Sentinel (name changed to The Pilot), Boston, Sept. 5, 1829; founder Cath. colony of Benedicta, Aroostook County, Me., 1834. Died Boston, Aug. 11, 1846.

FENWICK, Edward Dominic, clergyman; b. St. Marys County, Md., Aug. 19, 1768; s. Ignatius and Sarah (Taney) F.; entered Holy Cross Coll., Bornhem, Belgium, 1784. Joined Dominicans, took vows of a friar preacher, 1790; ordained Priest Roman Catholic Ch., Ghent, 1793; obtained consent to establish an Am. Dominican province; sailed from London, Eng., to Norfolk, Va., 1804; founder, prior convent of St. Rose of Lima (mother-house of Dominican Order in U.S.), Springfield, Ky., also Coll. St. Thomas Aquinas (erected Springfield), 1807; did itinerant missionary work throughout Ky., Ohio, and into the North; built small church outside Cincinnati; consecrated bishop at Cincinnati, 1822; went to Italy to recruit volunteer priests for Ky. and Ohio; provincial Dominican Order in U.S., 1828; founded Catholic Telegraph, 1831. Died Wooster, O., Sept. 26, 1832; buried St. Joseph's Cemetery, Cincinnati.

FENWICK, George, colonist; b. 1603; s. George and Dorothy (Forster) F.; m. Alice Apsley Boteler; m. 2d, Katherine Hesilrige, 1652; children—Elizabeth, Dorothy, also 1 son. Granted land West of Narragansett River (New Eng.) by Council for New Eng., 1632; visited his lands, 1636; soon returned to Eng.; came to New Eng., summer 1639; resided in Saybrook (town at mouth Connecticut River), 1639-44; commr. New Eng. Confedn., 1643-45; magistrate Conn. Colony, 1644, 45, 47, 48; returned to Eng., 1645; mem. Long Parliament, 1645, 54, 56; gov. of Tynemouth, 1648, of Berwick, 1649, of Edinburgh and Leith, 1650. Died Eng., Mar. 26, 1657.

FENWICK, John, colonist; b. Byrnfield, Eng., 1618; s. Sir William Fenwick; studied law Gray's Inn, London, Eng., 1640; m. Elizabeth Covert; m. 2d, Mary Burdette; children—Elizabeth, Anna, Priscilla. Commd. maj. in Cromwell's army; commanded squadron of cavalry present to preserve order at execution of Charles I, 1649; joined Soc. of Friends; mem. group which originated idea of Quaker colony in Am.; obtained Lord Berkeley's share of N.J. in trust for Quaker mcht. Edward Byllynge; established 1st Quaker settlement in N.J. at Salem on Delaware River, 1675; ordered by Gov. Andros to desist from exercising authority at Salem; twice imprisoned by Andros. Died Dec. 1683.

FERDON, John William, congressman; b. Piermont, N.Y., Dec. 13, 1826; grad. Rutgers Coll., 1847; studied law. Admitted to bar, practiced law; mem. N.Y. State Assembly, 1855, N.Y. Sen-

..., 1856-57; del. Republican Nat. Conv., Balt., 1864, Cincinnati, 1876; mem. U.S. Ho. of Reps. (Republican) from N.Y., 46th Congress, 1879-81. Died Monmouth Beach, N.J., Aug. 5, 1884; buried pvt. cemetery on Ferdon estate, Piermont.

FERGUSON, Fenner, congressman; b. Nassau, N.Y., Apr. 25, 1814; attended common schs.; studied law. Admitted to bar, 1840, began practice of law, Albany, N.Y.; moved to Albion, Mich., 1846; master in chancery; dist. atty.; mem. Mich. Ho. of Reps., 1854-59; chief justice Neb. Territory (apptd. by Pres. Pierce), 1854-57; moved to Bellevue, Neb., 1854; organized 1st dist. and supreme cts. of Neb.; assisted 1st Territorial Legislature in drafting 1st code of laws enacted for govt. of Neb. Territory; mem. U.S. Congress from Neb. Territory, 35th Congress, 1857-59.Died Bellevue, Oct. 11, 1859; buried Bellevue Cemetery.

FERN, Fanny, see Parton, Sara Payson Willis.

FERON, Madame, soprano; b. London, Eng., 1797. Made debut at Covent Garden, London, 1811; toured Continent, 1811-26, became pupil of composer Rossini; returned to Eng., 1827, then left for Am.; appeared with Sol Smith's company at theater of the Thespian Soc., Montgomery, Ala., 1829.

FERREL, William, meteorologist; b. Fulton County, Pa., Jan. 29, 1817; s. Benjamin and Miss (Miller) F.; grad. Bethany (W.Va.) Coll., 1844. Taught sch., Liberty, Mo., 1844-46, Todd County, Ky., 1847-54; founded sch., Nashville, Tenn., spring 1854; published Essay on the Winds and the Currents of the Ocean in Nashville Jour. Medicine and Surgery, 1856; worked on Am. Ephemeris and Naut. Almanac, Cambridge, Mass., 1857; mem. Coast and Geodetic Survey, 1867; mem. Signal Service, 1882-86, Author: Meteorological Researches, 1877-82; Recent Advances in Meteorology, 1886; A Popular Treatise on the Winds, 1889. Died Sept. 18, 1891.

FERRIS, Charles Goadsby, congressman; b. "The Homestead," Throgs Neck, Bronx, N.Y., circa 1796; studied law. Admitted to bar, began practice of law, N.Y.C.; mem. bd. aldermen, 1832-33; mem. U.S. Ho. of Reps (Jackson Democrat) from N.Y., 23d Congress, 1841-43; instrumental in securing congressional appropriation for building 1st telegraph line. Died N.Y.C., June 4, 1848.

FERRIS, George Washington Gale, civil engr.; b. Galesburg, Ill., Feb. 14, 1859; s. George W.G. and Martha (Hyde) F.; engring. degree Rensselaer Poly. Inst., 1881; m. Margaret Beatty. Helped locate 78 miles of proposed Balt., Cincinnati & Western R.R. in W. Va., also a narrow-gauge rd., Putnam County, N.Y.; engr., later gen. mgr. Queens City Coal Mining Co. (W. Va.), 1882; organized firm G.W.G. Ferris & Co., 1886, conducted mill and shop-work inspection and testing throughout country, interested in large structural engring. projects; constructed bridges across Ohio River at Wheeling, Cincinnati and Pitts.; designed Ferris wheel for World's Columbian Exposition, Chgo., 1893, considered most spectacular feature of Exposition. Died Pitts., Nov. 22, 1896.

FERRIS, Isaac, clergyman, univ. chancellor; b. N.Y., Oct. 9, 1798; s. John and Sarah (Watkins) F.; grad Columbia, 1816, LL.D., 1853; grad. New Brunswick (N.J.) Theol. Sem., 1820; D.D., Union Coll., 1833; m. Catherine Burchan, Dec. 30, 1820; m. 2d, Sarah J. Crygier; m. 3d, Letitia Storm, Oct. 1, 1850; 12 children. Served in War of 1812; missionary, Mohawk Valley, 1820; minister Dutch Reformed Ch., New Brunswick, N.J., 1821-24, 2d Ch., Albany, N.Y., 1824-36, Market St. Ch., N.Y.C., 1836-53; founded Rutgers Female Sem., com. on distbn., 1848-73; an organizer YMCA, N.Y.C.; 1852; 1st corr. sec. on bd. fgn. missions Reformed Dutch Ch., 1858; elected chancellor U. City N.Y., 1852, sec. financial com. univ. council, prof. moral philosophy, ret. as chancellor emeritus, 1870. Author: Domestic Christian Education, 1835; Ecclesiastical Characteristics of the Reformed Protestant Dutch Church, 1848. Died Roselle, N.J., June 16, 1873.

FERRISS, Orange, congressman; b. Glens Falls, N.Y., Nov. 26, 1814; attended U. Vt. at Burlington; studied law. Admitted to bar, 1840, began practice of law, Glens Falls; justice of peace, 1838-41, 45-48; insp. public schs., 1839-40; corp. clk., 1839-42; judge, surrogate Warren County (N.Y.), 1851-63; mem. U.S. Ho. of Reps. (Republican) from N.Y., 40th-41st congresses, 1867-71; commr. of So. claims (apptd. by Pres. Grant), 1871-77; 2d auditor of treasury, 1880-85. Died Glens Falls, Apr. 11, 1894; buried Glens Falls Cemetery.

FERRY, Elisha Peyre, gov. Wash.; b. Monroe, Mich., Aug. 9, 1825; s. Pierre Ferry; m. Sarah B. Kellogg, Feb. 4, 1849. Admitted to Mich. bar, 1845; 1st mayor Waukegan, Ill.; presdl. elector, 1852, 56; mem. Ill. Constl. Conv., 1862; bank commr. Ill., 1862-64; asst. adj. gen. to Gen. Yates; surveyor gen. Wash. Territory, 1869-72, gov., 1872-80; resumed work as lawyer and banker, 1880; 1st gov. State of Wash. when admitted to Union, 1889; Ferry County (Wash.) named for him. Died Seattle, Wash., Oct. 14, 1895.

FERRY, Orris Sanford, senator; b. Bethel, Conn., Aug. 15, 1823; s. Starr and Esther (Blackman) F.; grad. Yale, 1844; m. Charlotte Bissell, 1847. Editor, Yale Lit. Mag. admitted to Conn. bar, 1846; judge Conn. Probate Ct., 1849-56; states atty. for Fairfield County (Conn.) 1857-59; mem. Conn. Senate, 1855-56, chmn. judiciary com.; mem. U.S. Ho. of Reps. from Conn. 36th Congress, 1859-61, mem. com. Revolutionary claims, also com. of 33; entered U.S .Army, 1861; commd. col. 5th Conn. Volunteers, brig. gen., 1862; changed from radical to moderate polit. course; mem. U.S. Senate from Conn., 1866-75, supported in election of 1873 by Independent Republicans and Democrats. Died Norwalk, Conn., Nov. 21, 1875.

FERRY, Thomas White, senator; b. Mackinac Island, Mich., June 1, 1827; s. William Montague and Amanda (White) F.; never married. Mem. bd. suprs. Grand Haven, Mich., 1848; mem. Mich. Legislature, 1850-52; mem. Mich. Senate, 1857-58; del. Republican Nat. Conv., Chgo., 1860; mem. U.S. Ho. of Reps. from Mich., 39th, 41st congresses, 1865-67, 69-71; mem. U.S. Senate from Mich., 1871-83, submitted plan for recovery after financial crises of 1873, presided over impeachment trial of Sec. of War Belknap, 1876, reclassified rules of Senate (adopted unanimously), pres. pro tem (due to death of U.S. vice pres. Henry Wilson), 1875-77. Died Grand Haven, Oct. 14, 1896; buried Lake Forest Cemetery, Grand Haven.

FESSENDEN, James Deering, lawyer, army officer; b. Portland, Me., Sept. 28, 1833; s. William P.H. and Ellen (Deering) F.; grad. Bowdoin Coll., 1852; m. Frances C. Greeley, Nov. 5, 1856. Admitted to Me. bar, 1856; recruited co. 2d U.S. Sharpshooters, 1861, served as capt.; mem. staff Gen. Hunter, 1862; organized, disciplined 1st regt. of Negro soldiers in nat. service; commd. col., 1862; mustered, disbursed troops, 1863; fought under Gen. Hooker at battles of Lookout Mountain, Missionary Ridge; participated in Sherman's campaign against Atlanta (Ga.), 1864; commd. brig. gen., 1864; led brigade in Grand Review, Washington, D.C., 1865; commd. maj. gen. U.S. Volunteers, 1866; U.S. register of bankruptcy, 1868-78; mem. Me. Legislature, 1872-74. Died Portland, Nov. 18, 1882.

FESSENDEN, Samuel, lawyer; b. Fryeburg, Me., July 16, 1784; s. William and Sarah (Clement) F.; grad. Dartmouth, 1806; studied law under Judge Dana; LL.D., Bowdoin Coll., 1846; m. Deborah Chandler, Dec. 16, 1813, 1 son, William Pitt. Admitted to Me. bar, 1809; practiced in New Gloucester, Me., 1809-22; mem. Mass. Gen. Ct., 1815-16, Mass. Senate, 1818-19, maj. gen. 12th Div., Mass. Militia, 1819-33; moved to Portland, Me., 1822; mem. Me. Legislature, 1825-26; (with Thomas A. Deblois) in law firm, Portland, circa 1822-circa 1852. Died Portland, Mar. 19, 1869.

FESSENDEN, Samuel Clement, congressman, clergyman, lawyer; b. New Gloucester, Me., Mar. 7, 1815; grad. Bowdoin Coll., Brunswick, Me., 1834, Bangor (Me.) Theol. Sem., 1837; studied law. Ordained to ministry Congregational Ch., 1837; pastor 2d Congregational Ch., Thomaston (now Rockland) Me., 1837-56; admitted to bar, began practice of law, 1858; judge Rockland Municipal Ct.; mem. U.S. Ho. of Reps. (Republican) from Me., 37th Congress, 1861-63; examiner U.S. Patent Office, 1865-79; U.S. consul at St. John, New Brunswick, 1879-81. Died Stamford, Conn., Apr. 18, 1882; buried Woodland Cemetery.

FESSENDEN, Thomas Amory Deblois, congressman; b. Portland, Me., Jan. 23, 1826; attended North Yarmouth Acad., Dartmouth; grad. Bowdoin Coll., Brunswick, Me., 1845; studied law. Admitted to bar, 1848, began practice of law, Mechanic Falls, Me.; moved to Auburn, Me., 1850; del. Republican Nat. Conv., Phila., 1856, Chgo., 1868; mem. Me. Ho. of Reps., 1860, 68; pros. atty. Androscoggin County, 1861-62; mem. U.S. Ho. of Reps. (Rep., filled vacancy) from Me., 37th Congress, Dec. 1, 1862-63; Rep. presdl. elector, 1868. Died Auburn, Sept. 28, 1868; buried Riverside Cemetery, Lewiston, Me.

FESSENDEN, Thomas Green, journalist, inventor; b. Walpole, N.H., Apr. 22, 1771; s. Rev. Thomas and Elizabeth (Kendall) F.; grad. (valedictorian) Dartmouth, 1796, A.M., 1799; m. Lydia Tuttle, Sept. 1813. An important Am. satirist of his time; most popular poems include The Country Lovers or Jonathan's Courtship, 1795, The Rutland Ode; sailed for Eng. to secure English patent rights for a hydraulic device which proved fraudulent, 1801; attempted to perfect this device, also a new type of grain mill, 1801-03; returned to U.S., 1804; editor Weekly Inspector (Federalist partisan mag.) under pen name Dr. Caustic, 1806-07; editor Brattleboro (Vt.) Reporter, 1815-16, Bellows Falls (Vt.) Advertiser, 1817-22; established New Eng. Farmer, 1822; patented 2 heating devices, 1827, 30; mem. Mass. Gen. Assembly (Whig) from Boston, 1835-36. Author: Terrible Tractoration (under alias "Christopher Caustic, M.D., LL.D., A.S.S."), 1803; Democracy Unveiled: or Tyranny Stripped of the Garb of Patriotism (an assault on Jefferson and minor Democratic leaders), 1805; Essay on Law of Patents, 1810; American Clerk's companion, 1815; Miniature Bible, 1816; The Ladies' Monitor, 1818. Died Boston, Nov. 11, 1837.

FESSENDEN, William Pitt, lawyer, senator, financier, sec. treasury; b. Boscawen, N.H., Oct. 16, 1806; s. SaSmSuel and Ruth (Greene) F.; grad Bowdoin Coll., 1823, hon. LL.D., 1858; m. Ellen Deering, Apr. 23, 1832. Admitted to Me. bar, 1827; mem. Me. Legislature (elected on Anti-Jackson ticket), 1831, again in 1839, 1845-46, 53-54; accompanied Daniel Webster on tour western states, 1837; mem. U.S. Ho. of Reps. from Me., 27th Congress, 1840-42; an active organizer new Republican Party, active in Whig Party councils; mem. U.S. Senate from Me. (elected by anti-slavery combination in legislature), Feb. 3, 1854-64, 65-69, gave outstanding 1st speech in opposition to Kan.-Neb. Bill, Mar. 3, 1854, mem. finance com., 1857, 61; leader opposition to Buchanan adminstrn., 1857, gave a speech on the evils of irredeemable paper and dangers of inflation, recognized need for drastic taxing program; became U.S. sec. treasury, June 29, 1864; 1 of North's most important leaders during Civil War, majority leader in Senate, chmn. joint com. on reconstrn. (report best statement defending Congl. reconstrn.), 1865; voted "not guilty" in Johnson's impeachment proceedings; mem. governing bds. Bowdoin Coll., 1843-69. Died Portland, Me., Sept. 8, 1869.

FETTERMAN, William Judd, army officer; b. circa 1833; s. Lt. George and Anna Maria C. (Judd) F. Entered U.S. Army at outbreak Civil War, 1861; brevetted for gallant service at battles of Murfreesboro and Jonesboro; promoted capt. 27th Inf., U.S. Army, 1866; stationed at Ft. Phil Kearny, Wyo. Killed (together with force of 80 men) in ambush by Chief Red Cloud nr. Lodge Trail Ridge, Wyo., Dec. 21, 1866.

FEW, Ignatius Alphonso, coll. pres.; b. nr. Augusta, Ga., Apr. 11, 1789; s. Ignatius and Mary (Chandler) F.; m. Selina Carr, circa 1811. Became minister Methodist Ch., 1828; founder, pres. Emory Coll., 1837-39; mem. 1st conf. of Meth. Ch. South, Louisville, Tenn., 1845. Died Athens, Ga., Nov. 28, 1845.

FEW, William, banker, senator; b. balt., June 8, 1748 s. Wliam and Mary (Wheeler) F.; m. Catherine Nicholson, 3 children. Mem. Ga. Gen. Assembly, 1776, 83 mem. Exec. Council of Ga., 1776; surveyor gen. Ga., 1778; served as lt. col. Continental Army, also commr. to Indians during Revolutionary War; mem. Continental Congress from Ga., 1780-82, 85-88; a rep. from Ga. drafting U.S. Constn., signer, 1787; mem. U.S. Senate from Ga., 1789-93; judge 2d U.S. Jud. Circuit of Ga., 1794-97; moved to N.Y.C., 1799; mem. N.Y. Gen. Assembly, 1802-05; insp. N.Y. prisons; alderman N.Y.C.; dir. Manhattan Bank, 1804-14; pres. City Bank of N.Y. Died Fishkill-on-the-Hudson, July 16, 1828.

FFRENCH, Charles Dominic, clergyman; b. Galway, Ireland, 1775. Ordained priest Roman Catholic Ch., Coll. of Corpo Santo, Lisbon, 1799; resided in Ireland, circa 1801-circa 1809; came to Can., 1812; vicar of Que., Can.; missionary among Indians, St. John, N.B., Can., 1813; mem. N.Y. Diocese, 1817; missionary throughout N.J. and N.Y.; said 1st mass in Claremont, N.J.; worked under Bishop Fenwick, Boston, 1826; established Indian mission, Pleasant Point, Me.; pastor in Dover, N.H., 1827; built St. Aloysius's Ch., Dover, St. Dominic's Ch., Portland Me.; went to Rome, 1839; pastor in Greece (N.Y.) upon his return; pastor in Lawrence, Mass., 1846. Died Jan. 5, 1851.

FICKLIN, Orlando Bell, congressman, lawyer; b. Scott County, Ky., Dec. 16, 1808; grad. Transylvania Law Sch., Lexington, Ky., 1830. Admitted to bar, 1830, began practice of law, Mt. Carmel, Ill.; served as q.m. in Black Hawk War, 1832; col. Wabash County Militia, 1833; states atty. for Wabash Circuit, 1835; mem. Ill. Ho. of Reps., 1835, 38, 42, 78; moved to Charleston, Ill., 1837; mem. U.S. Ho. of Reps. (Democrat) from Ill., 28th-30th, 32d congresses, 1843-49, 51-53; Dem. presdl. elector, 1856, 84; del. Dem. Nat. Conv.; Cincinnati, 1856, Charleston, S.C. 1860, Chgo., 1864, del., Ill. Constl. Conv., 1869-70. Died Charleston, Ill., May 5, 1886; buried Mound Cemetery.

FIELD, Benjamin Hazard, exporter, philanthropist; b. Yorktown, N.Y., May 2, 1814; s. Hazard and Mary (Bailey) F.; m. Catherine M. Van Cortlandt de Peyster, 1838. Took charge uncle's fgn.

trade bus., 1838; ret. from comml. activities, 1865; pres. Home for Incurables, N.Y.C., 1866, presented chapel, 1885; a founder N.Y. Free Circulating Library (now N.Y. Pub. Library), 1880, later pres., until 1893; life mem., pres., treas. N.Y. Hist. Soc.; gave support to Am. Geog. Soc., Am. Mus. Natural History, Soc. Prevention Cruelty to Children, N.Y. Eye and Ear Infirmary, Working Women's Protective Union. Died N.Y.C., Mar. 17, 1893.

FIELD, Charles William, army officer; b. Airy Mount, Woodford County, Ky., Apr. 6, 1828; s. Willis and Isabella (Buck) F.; grad. U.S. Mil. Acad., 1849; m. Monimia Mason, 1857, 2 children. Commd. 2d lt. 2d Dragoons, U.S. Army; served in N.M., Tex., Kan., 1849-55; promoted 1st lt., 1855; instr. cavalry tactics U.S. Mil. Acad., 1856; commd. capt., 1861, resigned to enter Confederate Army; commd. capt. Confederate Army, 1861; col. 6th Va. Cavalry, 1861, brig. gen., 1862; commanded brigade at Fredericksburg and Seven Day's battles; served in battles of Cedar Mountain and 2d Bull Run; maj. gen., 1864; present at Appomattox Court House when Lee surrendered; col. engrs. Egyptian Army, 1875, insp. gen. during Abyssinian War; returned to U.S., 1877; doorkeeper U.S. Ho. of Reps., 46th Congress, 1878; U.S. civil engr., 1881-85; supt. Hot Springs (Ark.) Indian Reservation, 1885-89. Died Washington, D.C., Apr. 9, 1892.

FIELD, Cyrus West, mcht., promoter 1st Atlantic cable; b. Stockbridge, Mass., Nov. 30, 1819; s. David Dudley and Submit (Dickinson) F.; A.M. (hon.), Williams Coll., 1859, LL.D., 1875; m. Mary Stone, 1840, 7 children. Asst. to his brother (a paper mfr.), 1837; started paper mfg. bus., Westfield, Mass., 1839; became partner wholesale paper firm E. Root & Co. (firm failed, 1840); built up firm of Cyrus W. Field & Co.; ret. from bus., formed (with a group of prominent New Yorkers) co. to build cable communication between Newfoundland and Ireland; copper wire 1950 miles long and 2 miles deep connected Trinity Bay, Newfoundland and Valentia, Ireland, Aug. 5, 1858, stopped working after 3 weeks of operation; engaged the Great Eastern (world's largest steamer) to lay new cable, successfully laid, 1866; helped establish elevated trains in N.Y.C.; participated with Jay Gould in devel. of Wabash R.R. and control of newspaper Mail and Express, N.Y.C. Died Ardsley, N.Y., July 12, 1892; buried Stockbridge.

FIELD, David Dudley, lawyer; b. Haddam, Conn., Feb. 13, 1805; s. Rev. David Dudley and Submit (Dickinson) F.; attended Williams Coll.; m. Jane Hopkins; m. 2d, Mrs. Mary Carr. Admitted to N.Y. bar, 1828; del. Nat. Dem. Conv., Syracuse, N.Y., 1847, introduced "Cornerstone" resolution; attended Nat. Republican Conv., Chgo., 1860; chmn. N.Y. delegation to Peace Conf., Washington, D.C., 1861; mem. U.S. Ho. of Reps. from N.Y., 44th Congress, 1877; prominent lawyer, 60 years; handled litigation following Civil War, Milligan Case before U.S. Supreme Ct., 1867, Cummings and McCardle cases, 1868, Cruikshank Case, 1875; counsel for Jay Gould, James Fish, later charged with unprofl. conduct, no vote taken; chief counsel for defendant in prosecution of Boss Tweed; counsel for Tilden before Hayes-Tilden Electoral Commn., 1876; counsel for plaintiff in case of N.Y. vs. La. before U.S. Supreme Ct.; his efforts effected addition of Article I, Sect. 7, also Article VI, Sect. 24 to N.Y. State Constn. of 1846, appointing 3 commrs. to "reduce into a written and systematic code the whole body of the law of this state"; apptd. one of 3 commrs. (N.Y. State Codes completed 1865); Cal. adopted all 5 of "Field" Codes; headed movement for codification of laws of nations; visited Europe, attended confs. devoted to internat. affairs, 1866-94; an early fighter for internat. law, published Draft Outline of an International Code, 1872. Died N.Y.C., Apr. 13, 1894.

FIELD, Erastus Salisbury, artist; b. Leverett, Mass., May 19, 1805; studied with S.F.B. Morse, 1824-25; m. Phebe Gilmore, 1831. Painted portraits; best remembered for scenes from classical mythology and Bibl. history, also Historical Monument of the American Republic; lived in Hartford, Conn., Monson and Palmer (Mass.), 1832-42, N.Y.C., 1842-48, Leverett and Palmer, 1849-59; settled in Sunderland, Mass., 1859. Died Sunderland, 1900.

FIELD, Eugene, journalist, author; b. Sept. 23, 1850; s. Roswell and Frances (Reed) F.; attended Williams Coll., 1868-69, Knox Coll., Galesburg, Ill., U. Mo.; m. Julia Comstock, Oct. 16, 1873, 8 children. Connected with press in Mo. and Colo., 1873-83; editorial positions St. Joseph (Mo.) Gazette, St. Louis Jour., Kansas City (Mo.) Times, Denver (Colo.) Tribune; mem. staff Chgo. Morning News (later called Chgo. Record); conducted editorial column Sharps and Flats until 1895; strongly influenced devel. Am. journalism, introduced lit., bibliog. material into a newspaper column, aided many young journalists; one of key people in early Chgo. lit. history. Author: The Tribune Primer, 1882; Culture's Garland, 1887; poems, including humorous poems The Little Peach, Little Boy Blue; lullaby Wynken, Blynken and Nod. Died Chgo., Nov. 4, 1895.

FIELD, Joseph M., actor, playwright, journalist; b. Dublin, Ireland, 1810; s. Matthew Field; m. Eliza Riddle, 1837, 1 dau., Mary Katherine Keemle. Began profl. career as actor Park Theatre, N.Y.C., 1830; toured Southwestern circuit under mgmt. of Sol Smith, 1833; European corr. for New Orleans Picayune, 1840; co-founder St. Louis Reveille, 1845-51; mgr. Mobile (Ala.) Theatre, 1850-52; owner Varieties Theatre, St. Louis, 1852-53. Author: (plays) Victorica, 1838; Family Ties, 1846; The Drama in Pokerville; The Bench and Bar Jurytown, and Other Stories, 1847. Died Mobile, Jan. 28, 1856.

FIELD, Mary Katherine Keemle, author, actress; b. St. Louis, Oct. 1, 1838; d. Joseph M. and Eliza (Riddle) Field. Went to Europe, 1859, travelled among literary sets of Paris, Rome, Florence; returned to Am.; began acting career Booth's Theatre, N.Y., 1874; co-starred with John T. Raymond in The Gilded Age; London corr. N.Y. Herald and N.Y. Tribune; editor Kate Field's Washington, 1891-96. Author: Adelaide Ristori, 1867; Hap-Hazard, 1867; History of Bell's Telephone, 1878; Charles Albert Fechter, 1882. Died Honolulu, Hawaii, May 19, 1896.

FIELD, Maunsell Bradhurst, govt. ofcl.; b. N.Y.C., Mar. 26, 1822; s. Moses and Susan (Osgood) F.; grad. Yale, 1841; m. Julia Stanton, Jan. 7, 1848. Admitted to N.Y. bar, 1848; sec. to U.S. minister to France, 1854; commr. for N.Y. State to Paris Universal Expn. of 1855, pres. U.S. bd. commrs.; dep. asst. treas. of U.S., N.Y.C., 1861, asst. sec. of treasury, Washington, D.C., 1863; collector of internal revenue for 6th dist. N.Y., 1865-69; apptd. judge 2d Judicial Dist. Ct. of N.Y.C. Author: Memories of Many Men and of Some Women, 1874; Adrian, or the Clouds of the Mind (best known works). Died N.Y.C., Jan. 24, 1875.

FIELD, Moses Whelock, congressman; b. Watertown, N.Y. Feb. 10, 1828; grad. acad., Victor, N.Y. Moved to Detroit, 1844; engaged in business and agriculture; alderman Detroit, 1863-65; mem. U.S. Ho. of Reps. (Republican) from Mich., 1873-75; an organizer Independent Greenback Party, called nat. conv., Indpls., Ind., 1876; donated 50 acres of land for Linden Park, Detroit, 1875; regent U. Mich., 1888. Died on his farm "Linden Lawn," nr. Detroit, Mar. 14, 1889; buried Woodmere Cemetery.

FIELD, Richard Stockton, senator, jurist; b. White Hill, N.J., Dec. 31, 1803; s. Robert and Abigail (Stockton) F.; grad. Coll. of N.J. (now Princeton), 1821, LL.D. (hon.), 1859; m. Mary Ritchie, 1831. Admitted to N.J. bar, 1825; mem. N.J. Assembly, 1833; atty. gen. N.J., 1838-41; mem. N.J. Constl. Conv., 1844; prof. constl. law and jurisprudence Coll. of N.J., 1847-55; advocated establishment of N.J. State Normal Sch., 1st pres., 1855-70; mem. U.S. Senate from N.J., Nov. 1862-63 (filled vacancy); judge U.S. Dist. Ct. for N.J., 1863-70; a founder N.J. Hist. Soc., 1845. Author: The Provincial Courts of New Jersey, 1849. Died Princeton, N.J., May 25, 1870.

FIELD, Robert, painter, engraver; b. Gloucestershire, Eng., circa 1769; entered Royal Acad. Sch., London, Eng., 1790. Came to U.S., 1794; engraved portraits of Washington and Hamilton; painted Martha Washington in oil; miniaturist; moved to Halifax, N.S., Can., 1808, to Jamaica, B.W.I., 1816. Died Jamaica, Aug. 9, 1819.

FIELD, Stephen Johnson, asso. justice U.S. Supreme Ct.; b. Haddam, Conn., Nov. 4, 1816; s. David Dudley, and Submit (Dickinson) F.; grad. Williams Coll., 1837; studied law with John Van Buren, N.Y.C., 1838-40; m. Virginia Swearingen, June 2, 1859. Admitted to N.Y.B. bar, 1841; practiced in partnership with brother David, N.Y.C. until 1848; moved to Cal., 1849, practiced in Marysville, Cal.; mem. Cal. Legislature, 1850-51; introduced civil and criminal law codes; justice Cal. Supreme Ct., 1857-63, chief justice, 1859-63, wrote important opinions dealing with land titles and mineral rights; active in supporting Unionism in Cal., 1861; asso. justce U.S. Supreme Ct., 1863-97; held theory of concurrent powers of fed. and state govts.; dissents well known, especially in Slaughterhouse cases, 1873; opposed paper money, powers of ICC and income tax; as judge on Cal. circuit delivered important opinion concerning Chinese immigration in Queue Case, became involved in sensational incident with David Terry concerning Sharon will litigation, 1889. Author: Reminiscences of Early Days in California, 1877. Died Washington, D.C., Apr. 9, 1899.

FIELD, Thomas Warren, author, educator; b. nr. Syracuse, N.Y., 1821; m. Charlotte E. Weir; m. 2d, Helen Tuttle; m. 3d, Emiline Van Siclen; m. 4th, Alice E. Martin, 1876. Prin., Public Sch. Number 18, Bklyn.; mem. Bklyn. Bd. Edn., 1854-75; supt. public instrn., Bklyn., 1873-81. Author: Historic and Antiquarian scenes in Brooklyn and Its Vicinity, 1868; An Essay Towards an Indian Bibliography, 1873. Editor: Alexander Garden's Anecdotes of the American Revolution, 1865. Died Nov. 25, 1881.

FIELDS, James Thomas, publisher, author; b. Portsmouth, N.H., Dec. 31, 1817; LL.D. (hon.), Dartmouth, 1867; m. Eliza Williard, 1850; m. 2d, Annie Adams, 1854. Became jr. partner publishing house Ticknor, Reed & Fields (became Ticknor & Fields 1854), 1838, pres., 1862-70; editor Atlantic Monthly (Ticknor & Fields publ.), 1861-70. Author: Poems, 1849, 2d edit., 1854; A Few Verses for a Few Friends, 1858; Yesterdays with Authors, 1872; Hawthorne, 1876; In and Out of Doors with Charles Dickens, 1876. Underbrush (collection of essays), 1877. Died Boston, Apr. 24, 1881.

FIELDS, William Craig, congressman; b. N.Y.C., Feb. 13, 1804; attended common schs. Became engaged in merc. activities, Laurens, N.Y., 1836; became mfr. cotton and linen goods, 1847; justice of peace, 16 years; clk. Otsego County (N.Y.), 1852-55; supr. Otsego County, 1865-66; mem. U.S. Ho. of Reps. (Republican) from N.Y., 40th Congress, 1867-69. Died Laurens, Oct. 27, 1882; buried Laurens Cemetery.

FILLMORE, John Comfort, musician, theorist; b. nr. Franklin, Conn., Feb. 4, 1843; s. John L. and Mary Ann (Palmer) F.; grad. Oberlin Coll., 1865; studied music under Moritz Hauptmann, Ernst Richter, Benjamin Papperitz, Leipzig, Germany; m. Eliza Hill, at least 2 sons. Instr. instrumental music Oberlin (O.) Coll., 1867-68; prof. music Ripon (Wis.) Coll., 1868-78, Milw. Coll. for Women, 1878, Pomona Coll., Claremont, Cal., 1895-98; founder, dir. Milw. Music Sch., 1884-95. Author: Pianoforte Music: Its History, with Biographical Sketches . . . of Its Greatest Masters, 1883; New Lessons in Harmony, 1887; Lessons in Musical History, 1888. Died Taftville, Conn., Aug. 14, 1898.

FILLMORE, Millard, Pres. U.S.; b. Locke, N.Y., Jan. 7, 1800; s. Nathaniel and Phoebe (Millard) F.; m. Abigail Powers, Feb. 5, 1826; m. 2d, Caroline Carmichael McIntosh, Feb. 10, 1858; children—Mary Abigail, Millard Powers. Admitted to N.Y. bar, 1823; mem. Anti-Masonic Party; mem. N.Y. State Legislature, 1828-32; mem. U.S. Ho. of Reps. from N.Y. State, 23d, 25th-27th congresses, 1833-35, 37-41, chmn. ways and means com., 1840-42; comptroller N.Y. State, 1847; became vice pres. U.S., Feb. 1849, became 13th Pres. U.S. at death of Pres. Taylor, July 9, 1850, allied with moderate Whigs who favored compromises; achieved Compromise of 1850 regulating slavery boundaries; approved treaty opening Japan to Western commerce; lost Whig presdl. nomination, 1852, unsuccessful candidate on Know Nothing ticket, 1856; 1st chancellor U. Buffalo (N.Y.); a founder of Buffalo Hist. Soc.; a founder, 1st pres. Buffalo Gen. Hosp.; declined D.C.L. from Oxford (Eng.) U., on grounds that his literary or sci. attainments were not great enough, 1855. Died Buffalo, Mar. 8, 1874; buried Forest Hill Cemetery, Buffalo.

FILSON, John, explorer, historian; b. Chester County, Pa., c. 1747; s. Davidson Filson. Recorded narrative given by Daniel Boone of his expdn. up the Chillicothe River, 1782; explored Ohio River area to Lexington, Ky.; acquired 12,000 acres land, Fayette County, Ky.; made 1st map of Ky.; wrote an account of Daniel Boone; a backer of the founding of Cincinnati; Filson Club (hist. soc. with hdqrs., Louisville, Ky.) named in his honor. Author: Discovery, Settlement, and Present State of Kentucke (1st history of Kentucky), 1st edit., 1784. Killed by an Indian while surveying Cincinnati area, Little Miami, Ky., Oct. 1788.

FINCH, Isaac, congressman; b. Stillwater, N.Y., Oct. 13, 1783; attended public schs.; studied law. Engaged in agriculture, nr. Jay, Essex County, N.Y.; served as maj. 26th Inf. Regt. during War of 1812; mem. N.Y. State Assembly, 1822-24; mem. U.S. Ho. of Reps. (Democrat) from N.Y., 21st congress, 1829-31. Died Jay, June 23, 1845; buried Central Cemetery.

FINDLAY, James, congressman; b. Franklin County, Pa., Oct. 12, 1770; s. Samuel and Jane (Smith) F.; m. Jane Irwin. Practiced law, Cincinnati; mem. Ohio Territorial Legislative Council, 1798; U.S. receiver public moneys, Cincinnati, 1800; 1st U.S. marshal of Ohio, 1802; mem. Ohio Ho. of Reps., 1803; mayor of Cincinnati, 1805-06, 10-11; col. 2d Ohio Volunteer Inf., 1812; promoted brig. gen. Ohio Militia; mem. U.S. Ho. of Reps. from Ohio, 19th-22d congresses, 1825-33; built Ft. Findlay, 1812, later became town of Findlay, Hancock County, O.; partner Cincinnati Bell, Brass, and Iron Foundry, Liberty Hall and Cincinnati Gazette. Died Cincinnati, Dec. 28, 1835; buried Spring Grove Cemetery, Cincinnati.

FINDLAY, John, congressman; b. Mercersburg, Pa., Mar. 31, 1766. Prothonotary, 1809-21; served as capt. in War of 1812; moved to Chambersburg. Pa.; register and recorder of deeds; clk. of orphans' ct.; clk. ct. of quarter sessions, 1809-18; mem. U.S. Ho. of Reps. (Democrat, filled vacancy) from Pa., 17th-19th congresses, Oct. 9, 1821-27; postmaster Chambersburg, 1829-38. Died Chambersburg, Nov. 5, 1838; buried Falling Spring Presbyn. Ch. Cemetery, Chambersburg.

FINDLAY, William, senator, gov. Pa.; b. Mercersburg, Pa., June 20, 1768; attended publc schs.; studied law. Engaged in agriculture; served as brigade insp. Pa. Militia; admitted to bar, began practice of law, Franklinton, Pa.; mem. Pa. Ho. of Reps., 1797, 1804-07; treas. Pa., 1807-17; gov. Pa., 1817-20; mem. U.S. Senate (Democrat, filled vacancy), Dec. 10, 1821-27; dir. U.S. Mint, 1827-41. Died Harrisburg, Pa., Nov. 12, 1846; buried Harrisburg Cemetery.

FINDLEY, William, congressman; b. No. Ireland, circa 1741. Mem. Pa. Council of Censors, 1783, Pa. Assembly, 1785-86; mem. Pa. Supreme Exec. Council, 1789-90; del. Pa. Constl. Conv., 1790; mem. U.S. Ho. of Reps. from Pa., 2d-5th, 8th-14th congresses, 1791-99, 1803-17; involved in Whiskey Insurrection of 1794; mem. Pa. Senate, 1799-1802. Author: History of the Insurrection in the Four Western Counties of Pennsylvania, 1796. Died nr. Greensburg, Pa., Apr. 4, 1821; buried Unity Meeting House Cemetery, nr. Latrobe, Pa.

FINE, John, congressman, jurist; b. N.Y.C., Aug. 26, 1794; grad. Columbia, 1809; attended Litchfield (Conn.) Law Sch. Admitted to bar, 1815, began practice of law, Ogdensburg, N.Y.; treas. St. Lawrence County (N.Y.), 1821-33; judge St. Lawrence County Ct. of Common Pleas, 1824-39; 43-47; mem. U.S. Ho. of Reps. (Democrat) from N.Y., 26th Congress, 1839-41; unsuccessful candidate for judge N.Y. Supreme Ct., 1847, 49; mem. N.Y. State Senate, 1848. Died Ogdensburg, Jan. 4, 1867; buried Ogdensburg Cemetery.

FINK, Albert, railroad engr., exec.; b. Lauterbach, Germany, Oct. 27, 1827; s. Adres S. and Margaret (Jacob) F.; grad. in engring. and architecture Darmstadt schs., 1848; m. Sarah Hunt, Apr. 14, 1869. Came to U.S., 1849; invented bridge truss that bears his name; became constrn. engr. L. & N. R.R., 1857, chief engr., 1860, gen. supt., 1865; wrote The Fink Report on Cost of Transportation, (regarded as basis of Am. ry. econs.), 1874; exec. dir. So. Ry. & S.S. Assn.; organized Trunk Line Assn., 1877, became commr. Died Sing Sing (now Ossining), N.Y., Apr. 3, 1897.

FINLAY, Hugh, colonial ofcl.; b. Scotland, 1731. Came to Canada, 1760; mcht., Que., also justice of peace; in charge of Canadian sect. Colonial Post Office, 1763; mem. Que. Gov.'s Council, 1765-1801; post office insp., 1772-74; joint dep. postmaster gen., 1774-84; dep. postmaster gen. of Canada, 1784-87; in charge of all postal service in Brit. N. Am., 1787-99; largely responsible for extension service throughout Maritime Provinces; concluded postal agreement with U.S., 1792. Died Que., Dec. 26, 1801.

FINLEY, James, bridge designer; judge Ct. Common Pleas, also justice of peace Fayette County, Pa.; designed cast iron eye-bar chain suspension bridge with suspended level roadway (important feature of modern suspension bridge); his 1st bridge (70 foot span, 12½ feet wide) was built over Jacob's Creek on contract to Fayette and Westmoreland counties, 1801; patented his design, 1808; 40 of his bridges built in Am. in next 7-8 years, most famous being Newburyport Bridge (by John Templeman) over Merrimack River, 1810; 1 bridge fell at Brownsville, Pa., winter 1820.

FINLEY, James Bradley, clergyman; b. N.C., July 1, 1781; s. Robert W. and Rebecca (Bradley) F.; m. Hannah Strane, Mar. 3, 1801. Joined Western Conf., Methodist Ch., 1812; supt. of missionary dists., 21 years; missionary among Indians, 6 years; chaplain, state penitentiary, 3 years; del. to Gen. Conf. of Methodist Ch., 8 times. Author: History of the Wyandott Mission at Upper Sandusky, O., 1840; Memorials of Prison Life, 1850; Life Among the Indians, 1857. Died Sept. 6, 1856.

FINLEY, Robert, clergyman, coll. pres.; b. Princeton, N.J., Feb. 15, 1772; s. James Finley; grad. Coll. of N.J. (now Princeton), 1787; m. Esther Caldwell, May 1798, 1 son, Rev. Robert Smith F. Licensed to preach, 1794; ordained to ministry Presbyn. Ch., 1795; trustee Coll. of N.J., 1807-17; prin. organizer Am. Colonization Soc. (promoted idea of founding African colony for Am. Negro slaves to solve slavery problem), 1816; wrote pamphlet "Thoughts on the Colonization of Free Blacks," 1816; pres. U. Ga., 1817. Died Athens, Ga., Oct. 3, 1817.

FINLEY, Samuel, clergyman, coll. pres.; b. County Armagh, Ireland, 1715; D.D., U. Glasgow (Scotland), 1763; m. Sarah Hall; m. 2d, Anne Clarkso 1761. Licensed to preach, New Brunswick, N.J., 1740; ordained to ministry Presbyn. Ch., 1742; pastor ch., Nottingham, Pa., 1744-61; pres. Coll. of N.J. (now Princeton), 1761-66. Author: Faithful Ministers, the Fathers of the Church, 1752; The Madness of Mankind, 1754; The Power of Gospel Ministers, 1755. Died Phila., July 17, 1766; buried 2d Presbyn. Ch. Cemetery, Phila.

FINN, Henry James William, actor; b. Sydney, N.S., June 17, 1787; s. George and Elizabeth Finn; m. Elizabeth Powell. Went to Eng., circa 1810; acted in minor roles, Haymarket Theatre, London, Eng., 1811-12; appeared at Park Theatre, N.Y.C., 1818; editor Savannah Georgian, 1820; co-mgr. Federal Street Theatre, circa 1825; appeared in plays Removing the Deposits, Casper Hauser; or, the Down Easter, 1835. Died Jan. 13, 1840.

FINNEY, Charles Grandison, clergyman, coll. pres.; b. Warren, Conn., Aug. 29, 1792; s. Sylvester and Rebecca (Rice) F.; attended Hamilton Oneida Acad., Clinton, N.Y., 2 years; studied law privately; m. Lydia Andrews, July 1824; m. 2d, Mrs. Elizabeth Ford Arkinson; m. 3d, Rebecca Allya Rayl. Entered law office of Benjamin Wright, Adous, N.Y., 1818; admitted to N.Y. bar; study of Bible resulted in his conversion; candidate for ministry, St. Lawrence Presbytery, 1823; licensed to preach, 1824; conducted revivals in Middle and Eastern states; pastor Second Free Presbyn. Ch., N.Y., 1832-37; withdrew from Presbyn. Ch., 1836, became Conglist.; established theology dept. Oberlin (O.) Coll., 1835, pres., 1851-66; pastor First Congl. Ch., Oberlin, 1835-72; regular contbr. to Oberlin Evangelist; emphasized individual's ability to repent, also taught that sin and holiness cannot co-exist in a person; strong advocate of temperance. Author: Lectures on Systematic Theology, 1846, 47; Sermons on Gospel Themes, 1876; Sermons on the Way of Salvation, 1891 (both published posthumously). Died Oberlin, Aug. 16, 1875.

FINNEY, Darwin Abel, congressman, lawyer; b. Shrewsbury, Vt., Aug. 11, 1814; grad. mil. acad.. Rutland, Vt.; grad. Allegheny Coll., Meadville, Pa., 1840; studied law. Clk. in law office, Kingsbury, N.Y., 1834-35; admitted to bar, 1842, began practice of law, Meadville; mem. Pa. Senate, 1856-61; mem. U.S. Ho. of Reps. (Republican) from Pa., 40th Congress, 1867-68. Died while traveling in Europe, at Brussels, Belgium, Aug. 25, 1868; buried Greendale Cemetery, Meadville.

FINOTTI, Joseph Maria, clergyman; b. Ferrara, Italy, Sept. 1817; s. Francis M. and Rose (Tassinavi) F. Came to U.S., 1845; joined Soc. of Jesus, ordained priest Roman Catholic Ch., Georgetown, D.C., 1847; left Jesuit Order, 1852; priest Boston Cathedral under Bishop Fitzpatrick, 1852-56; priest under Bishop Macheboeuf, Denver, circa 1876; pastor, Central City, Colo., circa 1876-78. Compiler: Bibliographia Catholica Americana: A List of Works Written by Catholic Authors and Published in the United States: Pt. I, 1784-1820, published 1872. Died Jan. 10, 1879.

FISH, Hamilton, senator, gov. N.Y., sec. of state; b. N.Y., Aug. 3, 1808; s. Nicholas and Elizabeth (Stuyvesant) F.; grad. with highest honors Columbia, 1827; m. Julia Kean, Dec. 15, 1836, 8 children including Stuyvesant. Admitted to N.Y. bar, 1830; mem. U.S. Ho. of Reps. (Whig) from N.Y., 28th Congress, 1843-45; lt. gov. N.Y., 1847, gov., 1848; mem. U.S. Senate from N.Y., 1851-53; mem. Union Defense Com., also U.S. commr. for relief of prisoners during Civil War; U.S. sec state under Grant, 1869-77, a pillar of the adminstrn., settled controversy with Gt. Britain over damages suffered by No. commerce (Ala. claims) through Brit. govt. conduct as neutral during Civil War (treaty of Washington, 1871); trustee Columbia, pres.-gen. Soc. of Cincinnati; pres. Union League Club, N.Y. Hist. Soc. Died Garrison-on-Hudson, N.Y., Sept. 6, 1893.

FISH, Nicholas, army officer; b. N.Y.C., Aug. 28, 1758; s. Jonathan and Elizabeth (Sackett) F.; attended Coll. of N.J.; m. Elizabeth Stuyvesant, Apr. 30, 1803; children including Hamilton. Commd. maj. Gen. Scott's Brigade, 1776; commd. maj. 2d, N.Y. Regt., Continental Army, 1776; 2d in command Yorktown campaign; served in battles of L.I., Bemis Heights and Monmouth, commd. lt. col. at war's end; Federalist leader in early N.Y. politics, close friend of Alexander Hamilton; adj. gen. N.Y. State, 1784; alderman N.Y.C., 1806-17; pres. N.Y. Soc. of Cincinnati; chmn. bd. trustees Columbia. Died N.Y.C., June 20, 1833.

FISH, Preserved, mcht.; b. Portsmouth, R.I., July 3, 1766; s. Preserved Fish; married 3 times. Went to sea as merchantman and whaler, in youth; became capt. of own ship, by 1787; a broker of N.Y. Exchange Bd. (nucleus of N.Y. Stock Exchange), 1817; founder Fish & Grinell (a firm which became 1st in N.Y.C. and shipping circles), 1815; pres. Tradesman's Bank, 1836; Quaker, later Episcopalian. Died N.Y.C., July 23, 1846.

FISHER, Alvan, painter; b. Needham, Mass., Aug 9, 1792; s. Aaron and Lucy (Stedman) F.; studied art under John R. Penniman, 1810-12; m. Lydia Ellis, June 3, 1827, 1 son. Painter in Dedham, Mass., 1814-19; began specializing in portraits, 1819, went to Europe for a time, 1825, then opened studio in Boston. Paintings include: The Escape of Sargeant Champ, Mr. Dustin Saving Children from the Savages, Lost Boy. Died Dedham, Feb. 13, 1863.

FISHER, Charles, congressman; b. nr. Salisbury, Rowan County, N.C., Oct. 20, 1789; ed. by pvt. tutors, Raleigh, N.C.; studied law. Admitted to bar; mem. N.C. Senate, 1818; mem. U.S. Ho. of Reps. (Democrat, filled vacancy) from N.C., 15th-16th, 26th congresses, Feb. 11, 1819-21, 39-41; mem. N.C. Ho. of Commons, 1821-36, speaker, 1831, 32; mem. N.C. Constl. Conv., 1835; declined to be Dem. candidate for gov. N.C., 1846. Died while visiting Hillsboro, Miss., May 7, 1849.

FISHER, Charles, comedy actor; b. 1816. Made Am. debut as Ferment in The School of Reform, Burton's Chambers Street Theater, N.Y.C., 1852; leading comedy actor with John Augustin Daly Co., 1872-91. Died 1891.

FISHER, Clara, actress, singer; b. London, Eng., July 14, 1811; d. Frederick George Fisher; m. James Gaspard Maeder, Dec. 6, 1834, 7 children. Made debut at Drury Lane Theater, London, Dec. 10, 1817, appeared in starring roles Eng. for a decade; made Am. debut at Park Theatre, N.Y.C., 1827, became instant success; appeared in starring roles on extensive Am. tour through West and South; considered one of most accomplished artists on Am. stage after 1837; best parts include: Ophelia, the Fool in King Lear, Viola, Clare in Maid of Milan, Lady Teazle, Lady Gay. Died Metuchen, N.J., Nov. 12, 1898.

FISHER, David, congressman, journalist; b. Somerset County, Pa., Dec. 3, 1794. Moved (with parents) to Point Pleasant, O., 1799; became lay preacher, newspaper contbr.; mem. Ohio Ho. of Reps., 1834; unsuccessful candidate for gov. Ohio, 1844; became editor, propr. newspaper, Wilmington, O., 1846; mem. U.S. Ho. of Reps. (Whig) from Ohio, 30th Congress, 1847-49; city magistrate Cincinnati, 1849-50. Died nr. Mt. Holly, O., May 7, 1886; buried Wesleyan Cemetery, Cincinnati.

FISHER, Ebenezer, clergyman, educator; b. Plantation Number 3 (now Charlotte), Me., Feb. 6, 1815; s. Ebenezer and Sally (Johnson) F.; m. Amy W. Leighton, Sept. 27, 1841. Mem. Me. Legislature, 1840; mem. Me. Universalist Conv., 1840; pastor Universalist Ch., Addison Point, Me., 1841-47, Salem, Mass., 1847-53, South Dedham (Mass.) Universalist Ch., 1853-58; 1st prin. St. Lawrence U. (1st Universalist theol. sch. in U.S.), Canton, N.Y., 1858-79. Died Feb. 21, 1879.

FISHER, George, congressman; b. Franklin, Mass., Mar. 17, 1788; attended Brown U.; studied law. Admitted to bar, Oswego County, N.Y., 1816, began practice of law, Oswego, N.Y.; apptd. insp. of schs., 1818; trustee village of Oswego, 1828, 33; mem. U.S. Ho. of Reps. (contested election) from N.Y., 1829-Feb. 5, 1830; trustee schs., 1830; practiced law, Oswego, until 1833; took family to France, spent 5 years there for edn. of his children; returned to Oswego, engaged in real estate bus.; pres. Northwestern Ins. Co., several years; moved to N.Y.C., circa 1856. Died N.Y.C., Mar. 26, 1861.

FISHER, George Jackson, physician, bibliophile; b. North Castle, N.Y., Nov. 27, 1825; attended U. Buffalo; M.D., U. of N.Y., 1849; M.A. (hon.), Madison U., 1859. Settled in Sing Sing (now Ossining), N.Y., 1851; pres. N.Y. State Med. Soc., 1874; del. Internat. Med. Congress, 1876. Author: Biographical Sketches of the Deceased Physicians of Westchester County, New York, 1861; Old Masters of Anatomy, Surgery and Medicine, 1881-84. Died Feb. 3, 1893.

FISHER, George Purnell, congressman, jurist; b. Milford, Del., Oct. 13, 1817; s. Thomas and Nancy (Owens) F.; attended St. Mary's Coll., Balt., 1834; grad. Dickinson Coll., Carlisle, Pa., 1838; m. Eliza McColley, 1840. Admitted to Del. bar, 1841; clk. Del. Ho. of Reps., 1844; sec. State of Del., 1846-47, atty. gen., 1855-60; mem. U.S. Ho. of Reps. from Del., 37th Congress, 1861-63; judge Supreme Ct. of D.C., 1863-70; U.S. atty., D.C., 1870-75; 1st auditor U.S. Treasury, 1889-93. Died Washington, D.C., Feb. 10, 1899.

FISHER, Horatio Gates, congressman, businessman; b. Huntingdon, Pa., Apr. 21, 1838; grad. Lafayette Coll., Easton, Pa., July 1855. Engaged in mining, shipping and wholesale coal bus.; mem. borough council, 1862-65; auditor Huntingdon County, 1865-68; burgess Borough of Huntingdon, 1874-76; mem. Pa. Senate, 1876-79; mem. U.S Ho. of Reps. (Republican) from Pa., 46th-

47th congresses, 1879-83; apptd. by Gov. Beaver mem. bd. mgrs. Huntingdon Reformatory, 1888. Died Punxsutawney, Pa., May 8, 1890; buried River View Cemetery, Huntingdon.

FISHER, John, congressman, businessman; b. Londonderry, N.H., Mar. 13, 1806; attended common schs. Engaged in merc. pursuits; mgr. iron mfg. establishment, Hamilton, Can., 1836-56; mem. Hamilton City Council, 1848-49, mayor, 1850; moved to Batavia, N.Y., 1856; state commr. for erection of instn. for blind, Batavia, 1866-68; pres. of fire ins. co.; mem. U.S. Ho. of Reps. (Republican) from N.Y., 41st Congress, 1869-71. Died Batavia, Mar. 28, 1882; buried Batavia Cemetery.

FISHER, John Dix, physician; b. Needham, Mass., Mar. 27, 1797; s. Aaron and Lucy (Stedman) F.; grad. Brown U., 1820, Harvard Med. Sch., 1825. One of 1st in America to utilize auscultation (an aid to diagnosis); pioneer in use of etherization in childbirth; acting physician Mass. Gen. Hosp.; mem. Mass. Med. Soc.; introduced in Am. movement for educating the blind, largely responsible for creation Perkins Instn., Mass. Sch. for Blind, 1829, v.p., dir., 1829-50. Author: Description of the Distinct, Confluent, and Inoculated Smallpox, 1829. Died Mar. 3, 1850.

FISHER, Jonathan, artist; b. New Braintree, Mass., Oct. 7, 1768; grad. Harvard, 1792. Pastor, Blue Hill (Me.) Congregational Ch., 1796-1837; wood engraver, portrait and landscape painter; work includes a self-portrait, a copy of Henry Dawkins' view of Nassau Hall, Princeton, N.J., a series of wood engravings showing animals and other creatures of the Bible, at least 20 canvases (now owned by Howard Collection, Blue Hill). Died Blue Hill, Sept. 22, 1847.

FISHER, Joshua Francis, lawyer; b. Phila., Feb. 17, 1807; s. Joshua and Elizabeth Powel (Francis) F.; grad. Harvard, 1825; studied law under Joseph R. Ingersoll; m. Eliza Middleton, Mar. 1837. Mem. Hist. Soc. of Pa., 1828-65; admitted to Pa. bar, 1829; attaché U.S. legation, France, 1829; a founder Pa. Inst. for the Instrn. of the Blind, Phila. Author: Concessions and Compromises, 1860; The Degradation of Our Representative System and Its Reform, 1863; Reform in Our Municipal Elections, 1866. Died Jan. 21, 1873.

FISHER, Samuel Ware, clergyman, coll. pres.; b. Morristown, N.J., Apr. 5, 1814; s. Samuel and Alice (Cogswell) F.; grad. Yale, 1835, Union Theol. Sem., 1839; m. Anna Johnson, Oct. 1839; m. 2d, Jane Jackson, May 1842. Ordained to ministry Presbyn. Ch., 1839; became pastor Presbyn. Ch., West Bloomfield, N.J.; pastor, Albany, N.Y., then Cincinnati, 1843-58; moderator gen. assembly new sch. wing of Presbyn. Ch., 1857; pres. Hamilton Coll., Clinton, N.Y., 1858-66; pastor Westminster Presbyn. Ch., Utica, N.Y., 1867-71; mem. Am. Bd. Commrs. for Fgn. Missions. Author: Three Great Temptations, 1852. Died Cincinnati, Jan. 18, 1874.

FISHER, Sidney George, lawyer, author; b. Phila., Mar. 2, 1809; s. James L. and Anna Eliza (George) F.; grad. Dickinson Coll., 1827; studied law under Joseph Ingersoll, Phila.; m. Elizebeth Ingersoll, 1851; at least 1 child, Sydney. Admitted to Pa. bar, 1828. Author: Winter Studies in the Country, 1856; Kansas and the Constitution, 1856; Rustic Rhymes, 1859; The Law of the Territories, 1859; The Trial of the Constitution, 1862. Died Phila,, July 25, 1871.

FISK, Clinton Bowen, army officer, founder Fisk U.; b. Western N.Y., Dec. 8, 1828; s. Benjamin Bigford and Lydia (Aldrich) F.; m. Jeanette Crippen, 1850. Col., 33d Mo. Volunteers, 1862; commd. brig. gen. U.S. Volunteers, 1862, promoted maj. gen. before mustered out; asst. commr. of bureau of refugees, freedmen and abandoned lands for Ky. and Tenn., Freedmen's Bur., 1865; opened Fisk U. (sch. for Negroes), Nashville, Tenn., 1866; mem. Bd. Indian Commrs., 1874, pres., 1881-90; mem. governing com. of Methodist Book Concern after 1876; Prohibitionist candidate for U.S. Pres., 1888. Died N.Y.C., July 9, 1890.

FISK, James, senator, congressman; b. Greenwich, Mass., Oct. 4, 1763; s. Stephen and Anna (Bradish) F.; m. Priscilla West, Apr. 27, 1786, 6 children. Served with regt. of Mass. Militia in Revolutionary War, 1779-82; mem. Mass. Gen. Assembly, 1785; mem. Mass. Gen. Ct. from Greenwich, 1791-96; ordained to ministry Universalist Ch., circa 1797; moved to Barre, Vt., 1798; admitted to Vt. bar, circa 1799; mem. Vt. Ho. of Reps., 1800-05, 09-10, 15; judge Orange County (Vt.) Ct., 1802-09, 16; chmn. com. to settle Canadian-Vt. boundary, 1804; mem. U.S. Ho. of Reps. (Republican) from Vt., 9th-10th, 12th-13th congresses, 1805-09, 11-15, supported doctrines of Thomas Jefferson and James Madison, Embargo Act and War of 1812 (felt that Can. could be easily conquered); judge Vt. Superior Ct., 1815-16; mem. U.S. Senate from Vt., Nov. 4, 1817-Jan. 8, 1818; moved to Swanton, Vt., 1819; U.S. collector or revenues for dist. of Vt., 1818-26. Died Swanton, Nov. 17, 1844; buried Church Street Cemetery, Swanton.

FISK, James, financier; b. Bennington, Vt., Apr. 1, 1834; s. James and Love (Ryan) F.; m. Lucy Moore, Nov. 1855. Made fortune handling cotton contracts from Union occupied areas in South during Civil War; in assn. with Jau Gould and Daniel Drew took part in "Erie War" (struggle against Cornelius Vanderbilt for control of Erie R.R.), 1866-68; established (with Drew) brokerage firm Fisk & Beldon, 1866; launched campaign to tighten credit and raise price of gold, 1868; netted large profits with raids on U.S. Express Co. and Albany & Susquehana R.R.; regarded as public enemy; attempted to corner gold market, resulting in stock market disaster known as "Black Friday," Sept. 24, 1869; controlled Fall River and Bristol steamboat lines; served as col. 9th regt. N.Y. Militia; called "Jubilee Jim;" fatally shot by Edward Stokes at Grand Central Hotel, in quarrel over Fisk's last mistress, Jan. 6, 1872. Died N.Y.C., Jan. 7, 1872.

FISK, Jonathan, congressman, lawyer; b. Amherst, N.H., Sept. 26, 1778; attended public schs.; studied law. Became a sch. tchr.; moved to Newburgh, N.Y., 1800; admitted to bar, 1802, began practice of law, Newburgh; mem. U.S. Ho. of Reps. (Democrat) from N.Y., 11th, 13th-14th congresses, 1809-11, 13-15 (resigned); U.S. atty. for So. Dist. N.Y. (apptd. by Pres. Madison), 1815-19. Died Newburgh, July 13, 1832; buried Old Town Cemetery.

FISK, Wilbur, clergyman; b. Brattleboro, Vt., Aug. 31, 1792; s. Isaiah and Hannah (Bacon) F.; grad. Brown U., 1815; m. Ruth Peck, June 9, 1823. Mem. New Eng. Conf., Methodist Ch., 1820, ordained elder, 1822; prin. Wesleyan Acad., Wilbraham, Conn., 1825-30; mem. Meth. gen. confs., 1824, 28, 32; 1st pres. Wesleyan U., Middletown, Conn., 1830-39. Author: Travels in Europe, 1838. Died Middletown, Feb. 22, 1839; buried College Cemetery, Conn.

FISKE, Fidelia, missionary; b. Shelburne, Mass., May 1, 1816; d. Rufus and Hannah (Woodward) Fiske; grad. Mt. Holyoke Sem., 1842. Missionary to Nestorians, Oroomiah, Persia, 1843-58. Author: Memorial, Twenty-fifth Anniversary of Mount Holyoke Female Sem., 1862; Recollections of Mary Lyon, 1866. Died July 26, 1864.

FISKE, John, naval officer, mcht.; b. Salem, Mass., Apr. 11, 1744; s. Rev. Samuel and Anna (Gerrish) F.; m. Lydia Phippen, 1766; m. 2d, Martha Lee Hibbert, 1783; m. 3d, Sarah Gerry, 1786; 3 children. Mem. Salem Com. Safety and Correspondence, 1775; capt. brigantine Tyrannicide, 1776; commanded brigantine Massachussetts, harassed enemy shipping off coasts of Western Europe, 1777; mcht., traded with Mediterranian, East and West Indies, purchased several ships after Am. Revolution; mem. Salem Marine Soc., 1791; commd. maj. gen. Mass. Militia, 1792. Died Sept. 28, 1797.

FITCH, Asa, congressman, physician; b. Groton, Conn., Nov. 10, 1765; studied medicine. Served as sgt. Capt. Livingston's Co. during Revolutionary War; practiced medicine, Duanesburg, also Salem, N.Y.; justice of peace, 1799-1810; pres. Washington County Med. Soc., 1806-26; county judge, 1810-21; mem. U.S. Ho. of Reps. (Federalist) from N.Y., 12th Congress, 1811-13. Died Salem, Aug. 24, 1843; buried Evergreen Cemetery.

FITCH, Asa, entomologist; b. Fitch's Point, Salem, N.Y., Feb. 24, 1809; s. Dr. Asa and Abigail (Martin) F.; grad. Vt. Acad. of Medicine, Castleton, 1829; m. Elizabeth McNeil, Nov. 15, 1832. Asst. prof. natural history Rensselaer Poly. Inst., Troy, N.Y., 1830; practiced medicine, Fort Miller, N.Y., 1831-38; moved to Salem, N.Y., 1838; commd. to categorize insects of N.Y. State by N.Y. State Cabinet of Natural History; state entomologist, N. Y., 1854-71. Died Apr. 8, 1879.

FITCH, Graham Newell, senator, physician; b. Le Roy, N.Y., Dec. 5, 1809; attended Middlebury Acad., Geneva (N.Y.) Coll.; grad. Coll. Physicians and Surgeons. Began practice of Medicine, Logansport, Ind., 1834; mem. Ind. Ho. of Reps., 1836, 39; prof. anatomy Rush Med. Coll., Chgo., 1844-48, Indpls. (Ind.) Med. Coll., 1878; Democratic presdl. elector, 1844, 48, 56; mem. U.S. Ho. of Reps. (Democrat) from Ind., 31st-32d congresses, 1849-53; mem. U.S. Senate (filled vacancy; from Ind., Feb. 4, 1857-61; raised 46th Regt., Ind. Volunteer Inf. during Civil War, served as col. 46th Regt., 1861-62, resigned because of battle wounds; commanded brigade at capture of Ft. Thompson (Mo.), Island Number 10, also fts. Pillor and Charles; del. Dem. Nat. Conv., N.Y.C., 1868. Died Logansport, Nov. 29, 1892; buried Mt. Hope Cemetery.

FITCH, John, metal craftsman, inventor, steamboat developer; b. Windsor, Conn., Jan. 21, 1743; s. Joseph and Sarah (Shaler) F.; m. Lucy Roberts, Dec. 29, 1767, 1 child. Established brass shop, East Windsor, Conn., 1764; in charge of Trenton Gun Factory during Revolutionary War; surveyed lands along Ohio Valley and N.W. Territory, 1780-85; organized co. to acquire and exploit lands in N.W. Territory, 1782; invented steamboat successfully launched and operated, 1787; launched 60-foot steam paddle propelled boat used to carry passengers from Phila. to Burlington, N.J., 1788; received French and U.S. patents for steamboat, 1791; lost financial support through inefficient handling of financial affairs, even though he had perfected and constructed 4 steamboats. Died Bardstown, Ky., July 2, 1798.

FITCH, Samuel, lawyer, Loyalist; b. Lebanon, Conn., Jan. 16, 1724; s. Joseph and Anne (Whiting) F.; grad. Yale, 1742; m. Elizabeth Lloyd, Mar. 1753, 4 children including William. Admitted to Conn. bar; began practice law, Lloyd's Neck, L.I., N.Y., 1850; acting advocate gen. Ct. of Admiralty, 1768-76; banished from Boston, his property confiscated by Act of September, 1778; settled in London, Eng., 1776. Died London, Oct. 4, 1799; buried St. Mary's Ch., Battersea, Eng.

FITCH, Thomas, colonial gov.; b. Norwalk, Conn., June 1700; s. Thomas (Jr.) and Sarah F.; grad. Yale, 1721; m. Hannah Hall, Sept. 24, 1724, 8 children. Dep. to Conn. Gen. Assembly from Norwalk, 1726-30, 72, assistant, 1734-35, 40-50; helped to complete revision of laws of Conn., 1749; dep. gov. Conn., 1750-54; chief justice Conn. Superior Cts., 1750-54; gov. Conn., 1754-66; supporter British cause during French and Indian Wars; against Stamp Tax, felt it was his duty to enforce it, thereby lost his polit. following. Author: Reasons Why the British Colonies in America, Should not be Charged with Internal Taxes, by Authority of Parliament, Humbly Offered for Consideration in Behalf of the Colony of Connecticut, 1764. Died Norwalk, July 18, 1774.

FITLER, Edwin Henry, mfr., mayor Phila.; b. Phila., Dec. 2, 1825; s. William and Elizabeth (Wonderly) F.; m. Josephine Baker, 1850. Became partner firm George J. Weaver & Co., 1848, later known as Weaver, Fitler & Co. (Phila. Cordage Works), name changed to Edwin H. Fitler and Co., 1870, introduced labor-saving machinery; pres. Am. Cordage Mfrs. Assn.; an organizer Centennial Exposition, mem. bd. finance, 1875-76; a founder Phila. Art Club; mayor Phila., 1887; pres., dir. Nat. Bank of Northern Liberties. Died Phila., May 31, 1896.

FITTON, James, clergyman; b. Boston, Apr. 10, 1803; s. Abraham and Sarah (Williams) F. Ordained priest Roman Catholic Ch., 1827; 2d resident priest in what is now Diocese of Hartford (Conn.), 1830; opened Mt. St. James Sem., Worcester (later became site of Coll. Holy Cross, 1st Cath. coll. in New Eng.); in charge of Ch. Sts. Peter and Paul, Providence, R.I., 1843; built Our Lady of the Isle Ch., Newport, R.I., 1846, pastor, 1846-55; completed bldg. for Ch. of Most Holy Redeemer, Boston, 1855, pastor, 1855-81. Died Sept. 15, 1881.

FITZ, Henry, telescope maker; b. Newburyport, Mass., Dec. 31, 1808; s. Henry and Susan (Page) F. Began as a locksmith; became interested in optics, circa 1835; exhibited 6 inch refracting telescope at Am. Inst. Fair, 1845; became maker of telescopes in N.Y.C.; constructed two 12 inch telescopes for U. Mich., two 13 inch telescopes for Dudley Obs., Albany, N.Y. Died Nov. 6, 1863.

FITZGERALD, Thomas, senator, lawyer; b. Germantown, N.Y., Apr. 10, 1796; studied law. Served under Gen. Harrison in 5th Regt., N.Y. Militia, during War of 1812, severely wounded; sch. tchr., Marcellus, N.Y.; moved to Boonville, Ind., 1819, taught sch.; admitted to bar, 1821, began practice of law, Boonville; mem. Ind. Ho. of Reps., 1821; apptd. keeper lighthouse at mouth of St. Joseph River, 1832, moved to St. Joseph Mich.; clk. Berrien County, 1834; regent U. Mich., 1837; apptd. bank commr., 1838; mem. Mich. Ho. of Reps., 1839; mem. U.S. Senate (Democrat, filled vacancy) from Mich., June 8, 1848-49 moved to Niles, Mich., 1851, continued practice of law; probate judge Berrien County, 1852-55. Died Niles, Mar. 25, 1855; buried Silverbrook Cemetery.

FITZGERALD, Thomas, editor, playwright; b. N. Y.C., Dec. 22, 1819; m. Sarah Levering Liter, 5 children. Editor, Tallahassean, Tallahassee, Fla.; moved to Phila., 1847, became publisher City Item, 1848; publisher Pa. Volunteer, Fireside Visitor, Bazaar, Phila., 1850; pres. Athletic Base Ball Club, 1860-65; publisher Evening City Item, Phila., 1870. Author: (plays) Light at Last (produced Arch Street Theatre, Phila., 1867); Patrice, or the White Lady of Wicklow; Wolves at Bay; Tangled Threads: Bound to the Rock. Died London, June 25, 1891; buried Phila.

FITZGERALD, William, congressman; b. Port Tobacco, Md., Aug. 6, 1799; studied law. Admitted to bar, Dover, Tenn., 1821; clk. Stewart County (Tenn.) Circuit Ct., 1822-25; mem. Tenn. Legislature, 1825-27; atty. gen. 16th Jud. Circuit Tenn., 1826; mem. U.S. Ho. of Reps. (Jackson Democrat) from Tenn., 22d Congress, 1831-33; moved to Paris, Tenn.; judge 9th Jud. Circuit Tenn., 1845-61. Died Paris, Mar. 1864; buried Fitzgerald Cemetery, nr. Paris.

FITZGIBBON, Catherine (Sister Irene), nun; b. London, Eng., May 12, 1823. Joined Sisters of charity taking name (Mary) Irene, 1850; taught St. Peter's Sch., N.Y.C., 1850-65; 1st dir. foundling home run by Sisters of Charity (became Foundling Hosp.), 1869; founded Seton House (TB hosp.). Died Aug. 14, 1896.

FITZHUGH, George, lawyer; b. Prince William County, Va., Nov. 4, 1806; s. Dr. George and Lucy (Stuart) F.; m. Mary Brockenbrough, 1829, 9 children. Began practice law, Port Royal, Caroline County, Va., circa 1829. Author: Sociology for the South; or, the Failure of Free Society, 1854; Cannibals All! or, Slaves Without Masters, 1857. Died Huntsville, Tex., July 30, 1881.

FITZHUGH, William, lawyer; b. Bedford, Eng., 1651; son of Henry Fitzhugh; m. Sarah Tucker, May 1, 1674. Came to Va., circa 1670; defense counsel for Maj. Robert Beverley, 1682-83; mem. Va. Ho. of Burgesses. Died Stafford County, Va., Oct. 1701.

FITZHUGH, William, Continental congressman; b. Eagles Nest, King George County, Va., Aug. 24, 1741; educated privately. Engaged in agriculture; del. Va. Constl. Conv., 1776; mem. Va. Ho. of Dels., 1776-77, 80-81, 87-88; mem. Continental Congress from Va., 1779-80; mem. Va. Senate, 1781-85. Died Ravensworth, Va., June 6, 1809; buried pvt. cemetery on Ravensworth estate.

FITZPATRICK, Benjamin, senator, gov. Ala.; b. Greene County, Ga., June 30, 1802; s. William and Anne (Phillips) F.; m. Sarah Elmore, 1827; m. Aurelia Blassingame, 1846. Admitted to Montgomery (Ala.) bar, 1823; gov. Ala., 1841-45, revised state banking system; mem. U.S. Senate from Ala. (Democrat, filling vacated seat), 1848-53, elected mem., 1855-61, pres. pro tem, 1857-60, withdrew from U.S. Senate in support of So. cause, 1861; declined nomination for vice pres. U.S. on ticket with Stephen A. Douglas, 1860; pres. Ala. Constl. Conv. assembled in pursuance of Pres. Johnson's plan of reconstrn., 1865. Died Wetumpka, Ala., Nov. 21, 1869; buried Oakwood Cemetery, Montgomery.

FITZPATRICK, John Bernard, clergyman; b. Boston, Nov. 15, 1812; s. Bernard and Eleanor (Finn) F.; entered College de Montreal, 1829; studied for priesthood Grand Seminaire de Saint-Sulpice, Paris; S.T.D., Harvard (1st Cath. bishop to receive degree), 1861. Regent (tutor) College de Montreal, 1833; ordained priest Roman Cath. Ch. 1840; became bishop of Callipolis, coadjutor Boston, 1844; bishop of Boston, 1846-66, organized diocese to meet needs of Irish immigration; European agt. for founding of Provincial Sem., Troy, N.Y.; mem. Thursday Evening Club; mem. Am. Acad. Arts and Scis., 1862. Died Boston, Feb. 13, 1866; buried crypt Cathedral of Holy Cross, Boston.

FITZPATRICK, Thomas, trapper, guide, Indian agt.; b. County Cavan, Ireland, circa 1799; s. Mary Kiernan; m. Margaret Poisal, 1850. Came to U.S., 1815; commanded group penetrating Wyo. wilderness, discovered South Pass; with William Ashley in trapping expdns. in N.W., 1823-30; a founder Rocky Mountain Fur Co., 1830; led 1st Pacific-bound emigrant train, 1841; guide to Fremont's 2d expdn. (to Cal.), 1843-44, Kearny's expdn. to South Pass, 1845; with Lt. J.W. Albert's expdn. along Purgatory and Canadian rivers; guide Kearney's Army of West to Santa Fe, 1846; Indian agt. Upper Platte and the Arkansas, 1846-50; arranged great Indian Council nr. Ft. Laramie, 1851-54, negotiated treaties signed there with plains tribes north of the Arkansas, induced Comanches, Kiowas and Kiowa Apaches to sign peace treaty; called "Broken Hand" and "White Hair" by Indians. Died Feb. 7, 1854; buried Congressional Cemetery, Washington, D.C.

FITZSIMMONS, Thomas (or Fitzsimons), congressman; b. County Tubber, Wicklow, Ireland, 1741; m. Catharine Meade, Nov. 23, 1761. Mem. Continental Congress, 1782, 83; mem. Pa. Ho. of Reps., 1786-87; del. U.S. Constl. Conv., 1787; mem. U.S. Ho. of Reps. from Pa., 1st-3d congresses, 1789-95; pres. Phila. C. of C.; trustee U. Pa.; founder, dir. Bank of N.Am., 1781. Died Phila., Aug. 26, 1811; buried St. Mary's Roman Catholic Churchyard, Phila.

FITZWILLIAM, Fanny, actress. Imitated Fanny Elssler with great success in Foreign Airs and Native Grace at Ludlow and Smith's Poydras Street Am. Theater, New Orleans, 1841; sent by Ludlow and Smith to stimulate failing business at St. Emmanuel Theatre (known as "swamp theater"), Mobile, Ala., 1841, drew capacity crowds (for 1st time in theatre's history) for 2 weeks until her return to New Orleans.

FLACCUS, see Ward, Thomas.

FLAD, Henry, engr., inventor; b. Rennhoff, Germany, July 30, 1824; s. Jacob and Franziska (Brunn) F.; grad. U. Munich (Germany), 1846; m. Helen Reichard, 1848; m. 2d, Caroline Reichard, Sept. 12, 1855 6; 3 children. Served as capt. co. of army engrs. in Bavaria during German Revolution 1848; fled to U.S., 1849; ry. constrn. engr., 1849-60; served from pvt. to col. U.S. Army during Civil War; asst. to James B. Eads in constrn. Eads Bridge over Mississippi River; mem. bd. water commrs. St. Louis 1868-76 (during which time city water-works were completed); mem. Am. Soc. C.E., pres., 1866; founder Engrs. Club of St. Louis, pres. 1868-80; pres. St. Louis Bd. Pub. Improvements, 1877-90; mem. Mississippi River Commn., 1890-98; patented filters, water meters, methods of preserving timber and sprinkling streets, systems rapid transit and cable rys.; devised hydrostatic and hydraulic elevator, deep-sea sounding apparatus, pressure gauges, pile driver. Died Pitts., June 20, 1898.

FLAGET, Benedict Joseph, clergyman; b. Contournat, Auvergne, France, Nov. 7, 1763; attended U. Clermont (France), circa 1780. Ordained Sulpician priest Roman Catholic Ch., 1786; prof. dogma and moral theology Sulpician Sem. of Nantes (France); came to Am., circa 1789; missionary to Vincennes, 1792-95; vice rector, prof. Georgetown Coll., 1795-98; sent to Cuba, 1798-1801; prof. St. Mary's Coll., Balt., 1801-09; 1st bishop of Bardstown, 1810-32. Died Feb. 11, 1850.

FLAGG, Azariah Cutting, editor, state ofcl.; b. Orwell, Vt., Nov. 28, 1790; s. Ebenezer and Elizabeth (Cutting) F.; m. Phoebe Maria Coe, Oct. 20, 1814. Served as lt., q.m. 36th Regt., N.Y. Militia, War of 1812; editor Plattsburg (N.Y.) Republican, 1813-25; mem. N.Y. State Assembly, 1823; sec. of state N.Y., 1826-33; state comptroller N.Y., 1834-39, 42-46; moved to N.Y.C., 1846; prominent leader of Barnburners (radical faction Democratic Party); comptroller N.Y.C., 1852-59. Author: A Few Historical Facts Respecting the Establishment . . . of Banks . . . in the State of New York from 1777 to 1864, published 1868. Died Nov. 24, 1873.

FLAGG, Edmund, journalist, diplomat; b. Wiscasset, Me., Nov. 24, 1815; s. Edmund and Harriet (Payson) F.; grad. Bowdoin Coll., 1835; m. Kate Adeline Gallaher, Feb. 18, 1862. Contbr. to Daily Journal, Louisville, Ky., 1836-61; publisher Literary News Letter, Louisville, 1839; editor Weekly Gazette, Marietta, O., 1842-43; sec. to U.S. minister in Berlin, 1849; U.S. consul to Venice, 1850-52; statistician U.S. Dept. of State, Washington, D.C., 1854-70. Author: The Far West, 1838; Mutual Insurance, 1846; Edmond Dantes, 1849; Venice, the City of the Sea, 1797-1849, published 1853; Report of the Commercial Relations of the United States with All Foreign Nations, 4 vols., 1856-57; De Molai, 1888. Died Nov. 1, 1890.

FLAGG, George Whiting, painter; b. New Haven, Conn., June 26, 1816; s. Henry Collins and Martha (Whiting) F.; studied art, London (Eng.), Paris (France), Rome (Italy), circa 1834; m. Louisa Henriques, Feb. 14, 1849. Became mem. N.A.D., 1842; lived in London, 1861-66; paintings include: A Young Greek, Jacob and Rachel at the Well, Murder of the Princess in the Tower, Laying of the Atlantic Cable, Landing of the Pilgrims, Washington Receiving his Mother's Blessing, Haidee, The Match Girl. Died Jan. 5, 1897.

FLAGG, Josiah, musician; b. Woburn, Mass., May 28, 1737; s. Gershom and Martha F.; m. Elizabeth Hawkes, Apr. 7, 1760. Established a liaison between psalmody and classical music in New Eng.; introduced anthem to English colonies, 1764; founded, drilled mil. band, 1769; served as lt. col. in Elliott's Regt. during Revolutionary War. Died circa 1795.

FLAGG, Josiah Foster, dentist, artist; b. Boston, Jan. 10, 1788; son of Josiah Flagg, Jr.; grad. Boston Med. Coll., 1815; m. Mary Wait, Oct. 18, 1818. Engraved plates for Dr. J. C. Warren's book Anatomical Description of the Arteries of the Human Body; designed extracting forceps adaptable to any size tooth; pioneered use of porcelain for artificial teeth; founder Sch. of Design for Women, Boston. Died Dec. 20, 1853.

FLAGG, Thomas Wilson, naturalist, author; b. Beverly, Mass., Nov. 5, 1805; s. Isaac and Elizabeth (Wilson) F.; ed. Harvard Med. Sch., 1824-25; m. Caroline Eveleth, Jan. 2, 1840. Wrote for Atlantic Monthly; works include: Analysis of Female Beauty, 1834; The Birds and Seasons of New England, 1875. Died Cambridge, Mass., May 6, 1884.

FLAGLER, Thomas Thorn, congressman, business man; b. Pleasant Valley, N.Y., Oct. 12, 1811; attended common schs.; learned printer's trade. Became an owner and publisher Chenango Republican, Oxford, N.Y.; publisher Niagara Courier, Lockport, N.Y., 1836-42; entered hardware bus., 1842; mem. N.Y. State Assembly, 1842-43; 60; treas. Niagara County, 1849-52; mem. U.S. Ho. of Reps. (Whig) from N.Y., 33d-34th congresses, 1853-57; mem. N.Y. Constl. Conv., 1867-68; organizer, pres. Holly Mfg. Co., 1859, also headed 8 other mfg. firms. Died Lockport, Sept. 6, 1897; buried Glenwood Cemetery.

FLANAGAN, James Winright, senator; b. Gordonsville, Va., Sept. 5, 1805; attended common schs., also ed. privately; studied law. Became engaged in merc. pursuits, Cloverport, Ky., circa 1816; justice of peace, 1823-33; admitted to bar, 1825; practiced law, Breckenridge County circuit, 1833-43; moved to Henderson, Tex., 1843, continued practice of law, also engaged in business and agriculture; mem. Tex. Ho. of Reps., 1851-52, Tex. Senate, 1855-56; mem. Tex. constl. convs., 1866, 68; lt. gov. Tex., 1869-70; mem. U.S. Senate (Republican) from Tex., Mar. 30, 1870-75; del. Rep. nat. convs., Phila., 1872, Cincinnati, 1876, Chgo., 1880. Died Longview, Tex., Sept. 28, 1887; buried family burying ground, East Henderson, Tex.

FLANAGIN, Harris, gov. Ark.; b. Roadstown, N.J., Nov. 3, 1817; s. James and Mary Flanagin; m. Martha Nash, July 3, 1851. Mem. Ark. Legislature, 1842; attended Ark. Secession Conv., 1861; served from capt. to col. Company E, 2d Regt., Ark. Mounted Rifles in Civil War; gov. Ark., 1862-65; mem. Ark. Constl. Conv., 1874. Died Arkadelphia, Ark., Oct. 23, 1874.

FLANDERS, Alvan, congressman, territorial gov.; b. Hopkinton, N.H., Aug. 2, 1825; attended public schs.; learned machinist trade, Boston. Moved to Humboldt County, Cal., 1851, engaged in lumber bus., until 1858; moved to San Francisco, 1858; a founder, propr. San Francisco Daily Times; mem. Cal. Ho. of Reps., 1861; officer U.S. br. mint, 1861; commd. by Pres. Lincoln as register U.S. Land Office at Humboldt, 1862, did not serve; moved to Washington Territory, 1863, engaged in merc. pursuits, Wallula; 1st postmaster Wallula, 1865-67; mem. U.S. Congress (Republican) from Washington Territory, 40th Congress, 1867-69; gov. Washington Territory (apptd. by Pres. Grant), 1869-70. Died San Francisco, Mar. 14, 1884; buried Laurel Hill Cemetery.

FLANDERS, Benjamin Franklin, congressman, mayor New Orleans; b. Bristol, N.H., Jan. 26, 1816; attended New Hampton (N.H.) Acad.; grad. Dartmouth, 1842; studied law. Moved to New Orleans, 1843; editor New Orleans Tropic, 1845; alderman New Orleans, 1847, 52; supt. public schs., 1850; an organizer New Orleans, Opelousas & Gt. Western R.R. Co., sec. and treas., 1852-61; city treas. (apptd. by Gen. Butler), July-Dec. 1862; served as capt. Co. C, 5th Regt. La. Volunteer Inf., 1863-; mem. U.S. Ho. of Reps. (Unionist) from La., 37th Congress, Dec. 3, 1862-63; apptd. spl. agt. Treasury Dept. for So. Dist. (La., Tex., Miss., Ala., western Fla.), 1863, reapptd., 1866; unsuccessful candidate for gov. La., 1864; 1st pres. First Nat. Bank of New Orleans, 1864; mil. gov. La., 1867-68; mayor New Orleans, 1870-72; asst. treas. of U.S. at New Orleans, 1873-82. Died "Ben Alva," nr. Youngsville, Lafayette Parish, La., Mar. 13, 1896; buried Metairie Cemetery, New Orleans.

FLASCH, Kilian Casper, clergyman; b. Retzstadt, Bavaria, July 9, or 16, 1831; brought to U.S., 1847; studied at Notre Dame, also St. Francis Sem., Milw. Ordained priest Roman Catholic Ch., La Crosse, Wis., 1859; tchr. at St. Francis, became rector, 1879; consecrated bishop of La Crosse, 1881. Died La Crosse, Aug. 3, 1891.

FLEEGER, George Washington, congressman, lawyer; b. Butler County, Pa., Mar. 13, 1839; attended West Sunbury Acad.; studied law. Entered Union U.S. Army as pvt. Co. C, 11th Regt., Pa. Reserves, 1861, commd. 1st lt., 1862, later brevetted capt., served until 1865; admitted to bar, 1866, began practice of law, Butler, Pa.; mem. Pa. Ho. of Reps., 1871-72; chmn. Pa. Republican Central Com.; del. Rep. state convs., 1882, 90; mem. U.S. Ho. of Reps. (Rep.) from Pa., 49th Congress, 1885-87. Died Butler, June 25, 1894; buried North Cemetery.

FLEET, Thomas, printer; b. Shropshire, Eng., Sept. 8, 1685; m. Elizabeth Vergoose, June 8, 1715; 3 sons, 2 daus. Came to Boston, circa 1712; printer for Mass. Ho. of Reps., 1729-31; printer, owner Weekly Rehearsal, Boston, 1732-35; printer, publisher Boston Evening Post, 1735-58. Printer: The Redeemed Captive (John Williams), 1720; The New England Primer Enlarged, 1737-38; A Brief Narrative of the Case and Tryal of John Peter Zenger, 1738; The Day of Doom (Michael Wigglesworth). Died Boston, July 21, 1758.

FLEISCHMANN, Charles Louis, yeast mfr.; b. nr. Budapest, Hungary, Nov. 3, 1834; s. Abraham Fleischmann; m. Henrietta Robertson, 3 children including Julius, Max. Formed partnership (with James W. Gaff) to make yeast by Hungarian method, presented huge exhibit of product at Phila. Centennial Expn., 1870, bought Gaff's share of bus. after his death, 1879; patented plow, cotton gin, several distilling improvements and devices, 1866-72; dir. about 25 Cincinnati enterprises; pres. Market Nat. Bank, large vinegar co., cooperage co., newspaper; fire commr. Cincinnati, 1890; mem. Ohio Senate, 1879, 95. Died Dec. 10, 1896.

FLEMING, John, printer; flourished 1764-1800; m. Alice Church, Aug. 8, 1770. Came to Boston, 1764; partner (with William Macalpine and John Mein) in printing bus.; publisher Boston Chronicle (1st regular semi-weekly news mag. in New Eng.), 1767-70. Died France.

FLEMING, John, missionary; b. Mifflin County, Pa., Apr. 17, 1807; s. John and Mary (McEwen) F.; grad. Jefferson Coll., Canonsburg, Pa., 1829; m. Margaret Scudder, Nov. 1, 1832; m. 2d, Rebecca Patterson, Apr. 26, 1843, 7 children. Ordained to ministry Presbyn. Ch., 1832; began missionary work among Creek Indians, 1833; 1st to reduce Creek lang. to writing; missionary in LaSalle County (Ill.), 1849-75. Author: Muskokee Teacher (most important work). Died Ayr, Neb., Oct. 27, 1894.

FLEMING, William, army officer, colonial ofcl.; b. Jedburgh, Scotland, Feb. 18, 1729; s. Leonard and Dorothea Fleming; attended U. Edinburgh (Scotland); m. Anne Christian, Apr. 9, 1763. Came to Norfolk, Va., 1755; served as ensign in regt. under Col. George Washington, 1755-63; col. Botetourt Regt. at Battle of Point Pleasant, 1774; county lt. Botetourt County (Va.), 1776; mem. Va. Legislature, 1777-79, Va. Council, 1780; mem. Danville Conv. (for separate statehood for Ky.), 1784; acting gov. Va., June 1-12, 1781. Died Aug. 5, 1795.

FLEMING, William, Continental congressman, jurist; b. Cumberland County, Va., July 6, 1736; grad. Coll. William and Mary, Williamsburg, Va., 1763; studied law. Admitted to bar, began practice of law; mem. Va. Ho. of Burgesses, 1772-75; del. Revolutionary convs., 1775, 76; mem. com. of independence, 1776; mem. Va. Ho. of Dels., 1776-78, mem. Continental Congress from Va., 1779-81; judge Gen. Ct., 1788; mem. 1st Supreme Ct. of Appeals, 1789-24, became pres. of ct., 1809. Died "Summerville," Chesterfield County, Va., Feb. 15, 1824; buried family cemetery on his estate.

FLEMING, William Bennett, congressman, jurist; b. on plantation nr. Flemington, Ga., Oct. 29, 1803; grad. Yale, 1825; studied law. Admitted to bar, began practice of law, Savannah, Ga.; judge Superior Ct. Chatham County (Ga.), 1847-49, 53-68, 79-81; became recorder City of Savannah, 1868; mem. U.S. Ho. of Reps. (Democrat, filled vacancy) from Ga., 45th Congress, Feb. 10,-Mar. 3, 1879; ret. to Walthourville, Ga., circa 1881. Died Walthourville, Aug. 19, 1886; buried Laurel Grove Cemetery, Savannah.

FLEMING, William Maybury, actor; b. Danbury, Conn., Sept. 29, 1817; s. Emily Sophia Chippendale, 1852. Made 1st profl. acting appearance as Shylock, N.Y.C., 1839; toured Kingston, Jamaica, with acting co., 1840-41; acted at Bowery Theatre, 1843; toured New Orleans circuit, 1846-47; mgr. Odeon Theatre, Albany, N.Y., 1847; appeared as Hamlet, Othello and Romeo at St. Charles Theatre, New Orleans, 1848; mgr. Nat. Theatre, Boston, 1853-circa 1861; served as paymaster on Gen. William T. Sherman's staff U.S. Army, circa 1861-66. Died N.Y.C., May 7, 1866; buried Greenwood Cemetery, Bklyn.

FLETCHER, Benjamin, army officer, colonial gov.; b. London, Eng.; s. William and Abigail (Vincent) F.; m. Elizabeth Hodson, at least 3 children including Benjamin. Served from cornet to capt. Brit. Army under Duke of Ormonde, 1663-85; arrived N.Y.C., 1692; gov. N.Y. and Pa., 1692-97; commanded Conn. Militia; brought William Bradford from Phila. prison, set him up as royal printer; liberal benefactor Trinity Ch. (for which he signed charter 1697); deposed and superseded in 1697 (colonists complained of rule), sent to Eng. under arrest, investigated for fraudulent land grants, protection given to piracy. Died Boyle, Ireland, May 28, 1703.

FLETCHER, Calvin, lawyer, banker; b. Ludlow, Vt., Feb. 4, 1798; s. Jesse and Lucy (Keyes) F.; m. Sarah Hill, May 1, 1821; m. 2d, Keziah Backhurst, Nov. 5, 1855. Admitted to Ohio bar, 1820; moved to Indpls., Ind., 1821; state's atty. 5th Judicial Dist. Ind., 1825; mem. Ind. Legislature, 1826-32; mem. com. which organized the 2d Ind. state bank, 1834; pres. br. office State Bank, Indpls., 1843; head Indpls. Banking Co. Died Indpls., May 26, 1866.

FLETCHER, Isaac, congressman; b. Dunstable, Mass., Nov. 22, 1784; grad. Dartmouth, 1808; studied law; grad. U. Vt. at Burlington, 1825 Taught in acad., Chesterfield, N.H.; admitted to bar, 1811, began practice of law, Lyndon, Vt., 1812; mem. Vt. Ho. of Reps., 1819-24, speaker one term; pros. atty. Caledonia County (Vt.), 1820-29; mem. Vt. Constl. Conv., 1822; mem. U.S. Ho. of Reps. (Anti-Masonic Democrat) from Vt., 25th-26th congresses, 1837-41; adj. gen. on staff Gov. Van Ness. Died Lyndon, Oct. 19, 1842; buried Lyndon Town Cemetery.

FLETCHER, James Cooley, missionary; b. Indpls., Apr. 15, 1823; s. Calvin and Sarah (Hill) F.; grad. Brown U., 1846; attended Princeton Theol. Sem.; m. Henrietta Malan, Aug. 28, 1850, at least 2 children; m. 2d, Frederica Jane Smith, Oct. 22, 1872; m. 3d, Mrs. Elizabeth Murton Curreyer, Jan. 2, 1897. Licensed as preacher by Presbytery of New Brunswick, N.J., Apr. 25, 1849; ordained by Presbytery of Muncie, Ind., 1851; went to Brazil, 1851; acting sec. U.S. legation Rio de Janeiro, 1852-53; agt. for Am. Bible Soc. in Brazil, 1855-56; settled in Newburyport, Mass., 1856-62; agt. of Am. Sunday Sch. Union to Brazil, 1862-63, of Am. Tract Soc., 1868-69; U.S. consul Oporto, Portugal, 1869-73; U.S. chargé d'affaires, Lisbon, Portugal, 1870; missionary, Naples, Italy, 1873-90; moved to Los Angeles, 1890; pres. Los Angeles Sch. of Art and Design, 1895-1901. Died Los Angeles, Apr. 23, 1901.

FLETCHER, Richard, jurist; b. Cavendish, Vt., Jan. 8, 1788; s. Asaph and Sarah (Green) F.; A.B., Dartmouth, 1806; LL.D. (hon.), Brown U., 1846, Harvard, 1849. Admitted to N.H. bar, 1811, to Suffolk County (Mass.) bar, 1820; greatest triumph as lawyer was in Charles River Bridge Case before Mass. Supreme Ct.; mem. U.S. Ho. of Reps. from Mass., 25th Congress, 1837-39; judge Mass. Supreme Ct., 1848-53; trustee Brown U., 1832-35, Dartmouth, 1848-57; overseer Harvard, 1854-56; bequeathed over $100,000 to Dartmouth. Died Boston, June 21, 1861.

FLETCHER, Thomas, congressman; b. Westmoreland County, Pa., Oct. 21, 1779. Settled in Montgomery County, Ky.; mem. Ky. Ho. of Reps., 1803, 05-06, 17, 20-21, 23, 25; served as maj. Ky. Volunteers under Gen. Harrison in War of 1812, distinguished himself at Ft. Meigs, 1813; mem. U.S. Ho. of Reps. (filled vacancy) from Ky., 14th Congress, Dec. 2, 1816-17. Died nr. Sharpsburg, Ky.; buried pvt. burial ground nr. Sharpsburg.

FLETCHER, Thomas Clement, gov. Mo.; b. Herculaneum, Mo., Jan. 22, 1827; s. Clement B. and Margaret (Byrd) F.; m. Mary Clara Honey, 1851. Admitted to Mo. bar, 1856; land agt. S.W. Br. of Pacific R.R. (now St. Louis & San Francisco R.R.), St. Louis, 1856; asst. provost-marshal gen., St. Louis, circa 1861; served as col. 31st Mo. Regt., 1862, in battles of Vicksburg and Chattanooga; organized 47th and 50th Mo. regts., 1864; gov. Mo., 1865-69; practiced law, Washington, D.C., circa 1870-99. Died Washington, Mar. 25, 1899.

FLETCHER, William Asa, jurist; b. Plymouth, N. H., June 26, 1788; s. Joshua and Sarah (Brown) F.; studied law, Esperance, N.Y.; married twice; m. 2d, Adeline D. Doyle, 1843. Moved to Mich., circa 1820; practiced law, Detroit, 1821-23; chief justice Wayne County (Mich.) Ct., 1823-25; atty. gen. Mich. Territory, 1825-circa 1830; mem. Mich. Territorial Council, 1830; judge Mich. Jud. Circuit, Ann Arbor, 1833-36; 1st chief justice Mich. State Supreme Ct., 1836-42; prepared The Revised Statutes of the State of Michigan (adopted by Mich. 1837); regent U. Mich., 1842-46. Died Sept. 19, 1852.

FLINT, Austin, physician, educator; b. Petersham, Mass., Oct. 20, 1812; s. Dr. Joseph Henshaw Flint; med. degree, Harvard, 1833; m. Anne Skillings, 1 son, Austin. Prof. med. theory and practice Rush Med. Coll., Chgo., 1844-45; established Buffalo Med. Jour., 1845; a founder Buffalo Med. Coll., 1847, prof. 1847-61; with U. Louisville, 1852-59; prof. New Orleans Med. Coll., 1859-61; prof. pathology and parctical medicine L.I. Coll. Hosp., 1861; a founder, prof. internal medicine Bellevue Hosp. Med. Coll.; pres. N.Y. Acad. Medicine, 1873; del. to Internat. Med. Congress, London, 1881; pres. A.M.A., 1883-84; Author: A Treatise on the Principles and Practice of Medicine, 1866. Died Mar. 13, 1886.

FLINT, Charles Louis, agriculturist; b. Middleton, Mass., Mar. 8, 1824; s. Jeremiah and Polly (Howard) F.; grad. Harvard, 1849, attended Harvard Law Sch.; m. Ellen E. Leland, 1857, 2 sons, 1 dau. Admitted to N.Y. bar, circa 1852; sec. Mass. Bd. of Agr., Boston, 1853-80; commr. from Mass. to Internat. Exbn., Hamburg, Germany, 1863; a founder Mass. Inst. Tech.; a founder Mass. Agrl. Coll., circa 1862, sec. bd. trustees, 1863-65; pres. New Eng. Mortgage Security Co., circa 1885-89. Author: A Practical Treatise on Grasses and Forage Plants, 1857; Manual of Agriculture for the School, the Farm and the Fireside, 1862. Died Hillman, Ga., Feb. 26, 1889; buried Grafton, Mass.

FLINT, Timothy, clergyman, author; b. nr. North Reading, Mass., July 11, 1780; s. William and Martha (Kimball) F.; grad. Harvard, 1800; m. Abigail Hubbard, circa 1801. Preacher, Lunenburg, Mass., 1802-14; agt. for Missionary Soc. of Conn., 1815-16; published Western Monthly Review, Cincinnati, 1827-30. Author: Recollections of the Last Ten Years, Passed in Occasional Residences and Journeyings in the Valley of the Mississippi, 1826; Francis Berrian; or the Mexican Patriot, 2 vols., 1826; The Life and Adventures of Arthur Clenning, 1828; The Biographical Memoir of Daniel Boone, the First Settler of Kentucky, 1833. Died Salem, Mass., Aug. 16, 1840.

FLORENCE, Elias, congressman; b. Fauquier County, Va., Feb. 15, 1797; attended public schs. Engaged in agriculture; moved to Circleville, O.; mem. Ohio Ho. of Reps., 1829-30, 34, 40, Ohio Senate, 1835; mem. U.S. Ho. of Reps. (Whig) from Ohio, 28th Congress, 1843-45; mem. Ohio Constl. Conv., 1850; resumed agrl. pursuits, also engaged in buying and shipping of cattle. Died Pickaway County, O., Nov. 21, 1880.

FLORENCE, Thomas Birch, congressman, editor; b. Phila., Jan. 26, 1812; s. David Florence. Served as col. 5th Regt., Pa. Militia, before Mexican War; mem. bd. mercantile appraisers City and County Phila., 1850; mem. U.S. Ho. of Reps. from Pa., 32d-36th congresses, 1851-61; del. Phila. "Nat. Union Conv.," 1866; founder secret orgn. The Brotherhood of the Union; editor Constl. Union, Washington, D.C., 1863-68; founder and owner Sunday Gazette, Washington, 1868. Died Washington, July 3, 1875; buried Monument Cemetery, Phila.

FLORENCE, William Jermyn, actor, author; b. Albany, N.Y., July 26, 1831; s. Peter and Mary (Flynn) Conlin; m. Malvina Pray, 1853. Expert dialect comedian with talent for impersonation, skill in drawing vivid and convincing characters; starred with his wife, enjoyed unbroken success, 1853-89; wrote and starred in The Irish Boy and the Yankee Girl; most enduring characterization said to have been Bardwell Slote in The Mighty Dollar; other outstanding characterizations include: Bob Brienly in The Ticket-of-Leave Man, Obenseizer in No Thoroughfare; won ribbon of Societe Histoire Dramatique of France. Died Phila., Nov. 19, 1891.

FLORIDABLANCA, conde de (José Moñino y Redondo), Spanish statesman; b. Hellin, Murcia, Spain, Oct. 21, 1728; studied law U. Salamanca. Prosecutor, Council of Castile, for a time; Spanish ambassador to Pope Clement XIV, 1772-76; created knight; prime minister of Spain, 1776-92, aided Am. colonies during Revolution in effort to increase internat. prestige of Spain; hoped to restore Gibralter to Spain (all attacks on it were unsuccessful); regained Fla. and Minorca as Spanish possessions under terms Treaty of Paris, 1783 (ended Am. Revolution); fell out of favor with Queen Maria Louisa, imprisoned, 1792, later banished to his estates. Died Seville, Spain, Dec. 28, 1808.

FLOURNOY, Thomas Stanhope, congressman; b. Prince Edward County, Va., Dec. 15, 1811; attended Hampden-Sydney (Va.) Coll.; studied law. Became a pvt. tchr.; admitted to bar, began practice of law, Halifax, Va., 1834; mem. U.S. Ho. of Reps. (Whig) from Va., 30th Congress, 1847-49; unsuccessful Am. Party candidate for gov. Va., 1855; mem. Va. Secession Conv., Richmond, 1861; raised cavalry co., Confederate Army, served as capt.; promoted col. 6th Va. Cavalry, wounded, 1864; unsuccessful candidate for gov. Va., 1863; settled in Danville, Va., after Civil War, resumed practice of law; del. Democratic Nat. Conv., St. Louis, 1876. Died Halifax County, Va., Mar. 12, 1883; buried family plot on his estate.

FLOWER, George, colonizer; b. Hertford, Eng., 1788; son of Richard Flower; m. Eliza Julia Andrews, at least 2 sons, 1 dau. Visited U.S., 1816; began colonization project in Edwards County, Ill., 1817; made trip to Eng., 1818; planned Village of Albion (Ill.); settled in New Harmony, Ind., 1849. Died Grayville, Ill., Jan. 15, 1862.

FLOWER, Richard, brewery exec.; b. Eng., 1761; son of George Flower; m. Miss Fordham. Owner of brewery, Herford, Eng., 20 years; came to U.S. 1818; settled in Albion, Ill., 1819; founded 1st library in Ill.; returned to Eng., 1824. Author: Observations on Beer and Brewers, in Which the Inequality, Injustice, and Impolicy of the Malt and Beer Tax are Demonstrated, 1802. Died Albion, Sept. 2, 1829.

FLOWER, Rosewell Pettibone, gov. N.Y., congressman; b. Theresa, N.Y., Aug. 7, 1835; s. Nathan Monroe and Mary Ann (Boyle) F.; m. Sarah M. Woodruff, 1859. Asst. postmaster, Watertown, N.Y., 1854-60; mem. N.Y. Stock Exchange, 1873; mem. U.S. Ho. of Reps. from N.Y., 47th, 51st-52d congresses, Nov. 8, 1881-83, 1889-Sept. 16, 1891; gov. N.Y., 1892-95. Died L.I., N.Y., May 12, 1899; buried Brookside Cemetery, Watertown.

FLOY, James, clergyman; b. N.Y.C., Aug. 20, 1806; s. Michael and Margaret (Ferris) F.; attended Columbia; studied horticulture at Royal Gardens, London, Eng.; m. Jane Thacker, 1829; m. 2d, Emma Yates. Taught Sunday Sch.; admitted to N.Y. Methodist Conf. on trial, 1835, ordained deacon, 1837, elder, 1839; became mem. of an anti-slavery conv., prepared anti-slavery tract; charged (with 2 others) of insubordination at Conf. of 1838, was suspended (suspension lifted when he promised to conform); rose to importance in N.Y. East Meth. Conf., became presiding elder of N.Y. dist.; mem. gen. confs., 1848, 56, 60; made motion that resulted in revision of Ch. hymnal in Gen. Conf. of 1848; corr. sec. Am. Tract Soc., 1856-58; editor Nat. Mag., 1856-58. Author works including: Graduated Sunday School, 3 vols., 1861-62. Died N.Y.C., Oct. 14, 1863.

FLOYD, Charles Albert, congressman; b. Smithtown, N.Y., 1791; attended common schs.; studied law. Engaged in agriculture; county clk., 1820-21; admitted to bar, began practice of law; dist. atty., 1830; mem. N.Y. State Assembly, 1836, 38; pres. bd. trustees Huntington, 1837-40; mem. U.S. Ho. of Reps. (Democrat) from N.Y., 27th Congress, 1841-43; judge Suffolk County, 1843-67. Died Commack, L.I., N.Y., Feb. 20, 1873; buried Methodist Church Cemetery.

FLOYD, John, congressman; b. Beaufort, S.C., Oct. 3, 1769; learned carpenter's trade. Moved (with father) to Camden County Ga., 1791, engaged in boat building; served as brig. gen. 1st (Floyd's) Brigade, Ga. Militia, in War of 1812, also served in expdns. against Creek Indians; mem. Ga. Ho. of Reps., 1820-27; mem. U.S. Ho. of Reps. from Ga., 20th Congress, 1827-29. Died nr. Jefferson, Ga., June 24, 1829.

FLOYD, John, surgeon, gov. Va., congressman; b. Floyds Station, Ky., Apr. 24, 1783; s. John and Jane (Buchanan) F.; attended Dickinson Coll., Carlisle, Pa.; M.D., U. Pa., 1806; m. Letita Preston, May, 1804, 9 children. Justice of peace, 1807; surgeon with rank of maj. in War of 1812, became brig. gen. Va. Militia; mem. Va. Ho. of Dels., 1814-15; mem. U.S. Ho. of Reps. from Va., 15th-20th congresses, 1817-29, was 1st to propose occupation and territorial orgn. of Ore. County, 1821; gov. Va., 1830-34; received electoral vote of S.C. for U.S. Pres., 1832. Died Sweetsprings, Va. (now W. Va.), Aug. 1837; buried Sweetsprings.

FLOYD, John Buchanan, gov. Va., sec. of war, army officer; b. Blacksburg, Va., June 1, 1806; s. Gov. John and Letitia (Preston) F.; grad. S.C. Coll., 1829; m. Sally Preston, 1830; 1 adopted dau. Del. to Va. Gen. Assembly from Montgomery County, 1847-49, 55; gov. Va., 1849-52; ex officio chmn. Va. Bd. Pub. Works; presdl. elector Democratic Party, 1852; apptd. sec. of war by Pres. Buchanan, 1857, served until Dec. 29, 1860 (when S.C. seceded); joined Confederate cause, 1860; raised a brigade of volunteers, entered Confederate Army; promoted to maj. gen. by Gen. Assembly of Va., 1863. Died Abingdon, Va., Aug. 26, 1863.

FLOYD, John Gelston, congressman; b. Mastic, L.I., N.Y., Feb. 5, 1806; grad. Hamilton Coll., Clinton, N.Y., 1824; studied law. Admitted to bar, 1825, began practice of law, Utica, N.Y.; clk., pros. atty. Utica (N.Y.), 1829-33; founder Utica Democrat (later Observer-Dispatch), 1836; apptd. judge Suffolk County; mem. N.Y. State Assembly, 1839-43; mem. U.S. Ho. of Reps. (Democrat) from N.Y., 26th-27th congresses, 1839-43; joined Republican Party, 1856. Died Mastic, Oct. 5, 1881; buried family cemetery.

FLOYD, William, congressman; b. Brookhaven, N.Y., Dec. 17, 1734; s. Nicoll and Tabetha (Smith) F.; m. Isabella Jones; m. 2d, Joanna Strong. Served as maj. gen. Suffolk County Regt., N.Y. Militia; mem. Continental Congress from N.Y., 1774-77, 78-83; dep. N.Y. Provincial Conv., 1775; 1st N.Y. del. to sign Declaration of Independence; mem. N.Y. State Senate, 1777-78, 83-88, 1808; mem. N.Y. Council, 1787, 89; mem. U.S. Ho. of Reps. from N.Y., 1st Congress, 1789-91; del. N.Y. Constl. Conv., 1801. Died Westerville, N.Y., Aug. 4, 1821; buried Presbyn. Ch. Cemetery, Westerville.

FLYE, Edwin, congressman, businessman; b. Newcastle, Me., Mar. 4, 1817; attended Lincoln Acad., Newcastle. Engaged in merc. pursuits, also shipbuilding; mem. Me. Ho. of Reps., 1858; pres. 1st Nat. Bank of Damariscotta (Me.), many years; served as paymaster with rank of maj. U.S. Army, during Civil War; del. Republican Nat. Conv., Cincinnati, 1876; mem. U.S. Ho. of Reps. (Rep., filled vacancy) from Me., 44th Congress, Dec. 4, 1876-77. Died while visiting his dau., Ashland, Ky., July 12, 1886; buried Congregational Cemetery, Newcastle.

FLYNN, Thomas, theater manager. Purchased (with Henry Willard) Italian Opera House, N.Y.C., 1836, renamed it National Theatre; managed New Chatham Theatre (which he and Willard financed), N.Y.C., 1839.

FOGG, George Gilman, editor, diplomat; b. Meredith Center, N.H., May 26, 1813; s. David and Hannah (Vickery) F.; grad. Dartmouth, 1839; studied law Harvard; LL.D. (hon.), Bates Coll., 1874. Admitted to N.H. bar, 1842; sec. of state N.H., 1846; mem. N.H. Legislature, 1846; founder, editor-in-chief Independent Democrat, Concord, N.H., 1846-61, 1865-71; active in orgn. Republican Party; N.H. law reporter and state printer, 1855-59; U.S. minister to Switzerland, 1861-65; mem. Geneva Conf. on conditions for sick and wounded in time of war, 1864; del. to Loyalists' Conv., Phila., 1866; mem. U.S. Senate (Republican) from N.H. (serving out unexpired term), 1866-67; trustee Bates Coll., fellow, 1875-81. Died Concord, Oct. 5, 1881.

FOLEY, James Bradford, congressman; b. nr. Dover, Mason County, Ky., Oct. 18, 1807. Worked on flatboat on Mississippi River, 1823; moved to Greensburg, Ind., 1834; engaged in merc. pursuits, 1834-37, later in farming; treas. Decatur County, 1841-43; mem. Ind. Constl. Conv., 1850; apptd. comdr. 4th Brigade, Ind. Militia, 1852; mem. U.S. Ho. of Reps. (Democrat) from Ind., 35th Congress, 1857-59. Died Greensburg, Dec. 5, 1886; buried South Park Cemetery.

FOLEY, Margaret F., artist; b. probably Vt. Began carving and modelling while attending sch., Vergennes, Vt.; worked in silk factory, Lowell, Mass.; contbr. to The Lowell Offering; established herself in Boston as cameo portraitist, Boston, 1848; taught sch., Westford, Mass., 1853-54; returned to Boston; went to Rome, circa 1860; returned to Am. for a visit, 1865; work exhibited at Boston Athenaeum, Pa. Acad., N.A.D., Centennial Expn., Phila., 1876. Died Meran, Austria, Dec. 7, 1877.

FOLEY, Thomas Patrick Roger, clergyman; b. Balt., Mar. 6, 1822; attended St. Mary's Coll., also Sem., Balt. Ordained priest Roman Catholic Ch., Balt., 1846; did missionary and parish work in Balt. and Washington (D.C.) area; apptd. rector Balt. Cathedral; became chancellor of diocese, 1851; sec. 1st Plenary Council of Balt., 1852, notary Plenary Council of 1866; consecrated titular bishop of Pergamum, coadjutor and adminstr. of Diocese of Chgo., 1870; rebuilt many of the instns. of Chgo. Diocese, including cathedral (destroyed in Chgo. fire), greatly expanded facilities of the see. Died Chgo., Feb. 19, 1879.

FOLGER, Charles James, jurist, sec. of treasury; b. Nantucket, Mass., Apr. 16, 1818; s. Thomas F.; grad. Hobart Coll., 1836, M.A., 1840, LL.D., 1870; LL.D., Rutgers U., 1870; m. Susan Worth, June 17, 1844. Admitted to Albany (N.Y.) bar, 1839; judge Ontario County (N.Y.) Ct. Common Pleas, 1844; county judge Ontario County, 1851-55; mem. N.Y. State Senate, 1861-69, pres. pro tem, 4 years, chmn. judiciary com., 1861-69; mem. N.Y. State Constl. Conv. (concerned with material changes in jud. system), 1867; asst. U.S. treas., N.Y.C., 1869-71; asso. judge N.Y. State Ct. Appeals, 1870-71; chief justice N.Y. Supreme Ct., 1880; U.S. sec. of treasury under Pres. Arthur, 1881-84; trustee Cornell U., 1865-73. Died Geneva, N.Y., Sept. 4, 1884.

FOLGER, Peter, town ofcl.; b. Norwich, Norfolk, Eng., 1617; s. John and Mirriba (Gibs) F.; m. Mary Morrils, 1644; 1 dau., Abiah (mother of Benjamin Franklin). Came to Mass., 1635, became tchr., Indian interpreter, town clk. and ct. clk., Nantucket, Mass.; became mem. Baptist Ch., Newport, R.I., 1675. Author: A Looking-Glass for the Times, or The Former Spirit of New England Revived in this Generation, 1676. Died Nantucket, 1690.

FOLGER, Walter, congressman, scientist; b. Nantucket, Mass., June 12, 1765; s. Walter and Elizabeth (Starbuck) F.; m. Anna Ray, Dec. 29, 1785. Exhibited Folger's astronomic clock, 1790; discovered a process of annealing wire; admitted to Mass. bar, 1807; mem. Mass. Gen. Ct. from Nantucket, 1808; mem. Mass. Senate, 1809-14, 22; established cotton and woolen mill, Nantucket, 1812; mem. U.S. Ho. of Reps. (Democrat) from Mass., 15th-16th congresses, 1817-21; judge Nantucket Ct. Common Pleas and Sessions, 1828-34. Author: Description of Nantucket, 1794; Observations of the Solar Eclipse of 1811. Died Nantucket, Sept. 8, 1849; buried Friend's Burying Ground, Nantucket.

FOLINGSBY, George Frederick, artist; b. County Wicklow, Ireland, 1830; married. Went to Can. 1848, later to N.Y.C.; draftsman Harper's mag. pictorial editor Am. edition of Magazine of Art exhibited at N.A.D., 1859; left Am., circa 1852 travelled in Europe, settled in Munich, Germany dir. Nat. Gallery of Victoria, Australia, 1884-91 Died Melbourne, Australia, Jan. 4, 1891.

FOLLEN, Charles F.C., educator; b. Giessen Germany, Sept. 4, 1796; s. Christoph Follenius D.C.L., U. Giessen, 1817; m. Eliza Lee Cabot Sept. 1828. Leader radical youth in Giessen Burschenschaft; lectr. jurisprudence and metaphysic U. Basel; came to U.S., 1824; instr. German Harvard, 1825-30, 1st prof. German lit., 1830-35 instr. ethics Harvard Div. Sch., 1829; mem. New Eng. Anti-Slavery Soc., 1834; drafted anti-slavery Address to People of U.S. (which resulted in his severance from Harvard), 1834; ordained to ministry Unitarian Ch., 1836. Died L.I. Sound, N.Y. Jan. 13, 1840.

FOLLEN, Eliza Lee Cabot, author, abolitionist b. Boston, Aug. 15, 1787; d. Samuel and Sarah (Barrett) Cabot; m. Charles Follen, Sept. 15 1828; 1 child. Editor, Christian Tchr.'s Manual 1828-30, The Child's Friend, 1843-50; active mem Am. Unitarian Assn.; mem. exec. com. Am. Anti-Slavery Soc.; counselor Mass. Soc.; mem. Boston Female Anti-Slavery Soc. Author: A Well-Spent Hour, 1827; The Skeptic, 1835; Poems, 1839; To Mothers in the Free States; Anti-Slavery Hymns and Songs, 1855; Twilight Stories, 1858; Home Dramas, 1859. Died Brookline, Mass., Jan. 26, 1860.

FOLSOM, Charles, librarian, educator, editor; b. Exeter, N.H., Dec. 24, 1794; s. James and Sarah (Gilman) F.; grad. Harvard, 1813; m. Susanna McKean, Oct. 19, 1824. U.S. consul ad interim, Tunis, 1817; tchr. Harvard, 1821-26, librarian Harvard Library, 1823-26; partner University Press, 1824-39; co-editor United States Review and Lit. Gazette, 1826-27, Select Jour. of Fgn. Periodical Literature, 4 vols., 1833-34; conducted sch. for young ladies in Temple Pl., Boston, 1841-45; librarian Boston Athenaeum, 1846-56; active N.Y. conf. of Librarians, 1853. Editor: Cicero's Select Orations with notes, 1811; Additional Selections from Livy with notes, 1829. Died Cambridge, Mass., Nov. 8, 1872.

FOLSOM, George, historian; b. Kennebunk, Me., May 23, 1802; s. Thomas and Edna (Ela) F.; grad. Harvard, 1822; LL.D. (hon.), U. Vt., 1860; m. Margaret Winthrop, 1839, 3 children. Admitted to bar, 1824; practiced law in Mass.; librarian, edited Collections of N.Y. Hist. Soc., 1841; mem. N.Y. Senate, 1844; charge-d'affaires The Netherlands, 1850-53; editor Historical Mag., 1858-59; pres. Am. Ethnol. Soc., 1859-69; mem. Am. Geog. and Statis. Soc., Deaf and Dumb Soc., Union League Club. Author: History of Saco and Biddleford, 1830; Dutch Annals of New York, 1841; Dispatches of Hernando Cortez, 1843; Political Condition of Mexico, 1843; Documents Relating to Early History of Maine, 1858. Died Rome, Italy, Mar. 27, 1869.

FOLSOM, Nathaniel, Continental congressman, army officer; b. Exeter, N.H., Sept. 18, 1726; s. Jonathan and Anna (Foster) F.; m. Dorothy Smith; m. 2d, Mary Sprague. Served in Crown Point expdn. in French and Indian War, 1755; mem. Continental Congress, 1774-75, 77-78, 79-80; signed the Association; mem. N.H. Provincial Congress, 1775; maj. gen. in command of entire N.H. Militia, 1775; served repeatedly in N.H. Legislature; mem. N.H. Com. of Safety; judge Ct. Common Pleas. Died Exeter, May 26, 1790.

FOLWELL, Samuel, miniature painter, engraver; b. circa 1768. Miniature painter and engraver, Phila., 1798-1813; conducted art sch.; few of his engravings have been seen; did silhouette of George Washington. Died Phila., Nov. 26, 1813; buried German Presbyn. burial ground, Phila.

FONDA, John H., frontiersman; b. Watervliet, N.Y., circa 1797; m. Sophia Gallerno, Sept. 4, 1834. Set out for Tex. with a small party, 1819; separated from his group nr. Ft. Towson, Okla., decided to visit Sante Fe, N.M., 1823; returned from S.W. by Oct., 1824, worked as bricklayer and mason, St. Louis; went by steamboat up Mississippi River, 1825, got off at mouth of Illinois River, journeyed to Ft. Dearborn, then went by boat to Juneau's trading house (now Milw., Wis.), then to Green Bay; dispatch-bearer out of Green Bay, 1827-28; enlisted as soldier at Ft. Crawford (Prairie du Chien, Wis.), 1829, discharged because of continued illness, 1831; fought in ship Warrior in Black Hawk War, 1832. Died circa 1868.

FONT, Pedro, missionary. Franciscan missionary in charge Indian mission San Jose de los Pimas, Sonora, Mexico, before 1774 until 1781; apptd. cartographer of Juan Bautista de Anza's expdn. to establish mission and presidio on Bay of San Francisco, 1774-76, determined elevation of Farallon Islands, figured latitude of entrance to San Francisco Bay, made extensive sketches and maps of Bay area, aided in selecting site on which presidio and mission were later built; wrote diary which contains a graphic account of expdn. resulting in selection of site for San Francisco. Died Pitique, Sonora, Mexico, Sept. 6, 1781.

FOOT, Samuel, senator, gov. Conn.; b. Cheshire, Conn., Nov. 8, 1780; s. John and Abigail (Hall) Foote; grad. Yale, 1797; m. Eudovia Hall, 3 children including Andrew Hull. Entered Yale when he was thirteen, 1793; built up a shipping bus., trading chiefly with the West Indies, New Haven, Conn., 1803; mem. Conn. Ho. of Reps., 1817-18, 21-23, 25-26, speaker, 1825-26; mem. U.S. Ho. of Reps. from Conn., 16th, 18th, 23rd congresses, 1819-21, 23-25, 33-34; mem. U.S. Senate from Conn., 1827-33, offered pub. land resolution resulting in the noted Webster-Hayne debate, 1829; gov. Conn., 1834-35. Died Cheshire, Conn., Sept. 15, 1846; buried Hillside Cemetery, Cheshire.

FOOT, Solomon, senator, congressman; b. Cornwall, Vt., Nov. 19, 1802; s. Solomon and Betsey (Crossett) F.; grad. Middlebury Coll., 1826; m. Emily Foy, July 9, 1839; m. 2d, Mary Ann Hodges, Apr. 2, 1844. Principal Castleton Sem., 1826-27, 28-31; tutor U. Vt., 1827-28; admitted to Vt. bar, 1831; mem. Vt. Ho. of Reps., 1833, 36-38, 47, speaker, 1837, 38, 47; mem. Vt. Constl. Conv., 1836; pros. atty. Rutland County (Vt.), 1836-42; mem. U.S. Ho. of Reps. from Vt., 28th-29th congresses, 1843-47; mem. U.S. Senate from Vt., 1851-66; radical Republican in the post Civil War era, pushed through impeachment of Pres. Andrew Johnson, pres. pro tem 36th-37th congresses, chmn. comm. pub. bldgs. and grounds, pushed through the completion of the capital. Died Washington, D.C., Mar. 28, 1866; buried Evergreen Cemetery, Rutland, Vt.

FOOTE, Andrew Hull, naval officer; b. New Haven, Conn., Sept. 12, 1806; s. Senator Samuel A. and Eudocia (Hull) F.; m. Caroline Flagg, June 22, 1828; m. 2d, Caroline Street, Jan. 27, 1842; 3 children. Became acting midshipman U.S. Navy, 1822; 1st lt. in ship Cumberland in Mediterranean, 1843, formed temperance soc. on board, making Cumberland 1st temperance ship in Navy, chiefly responsible for abolishing liquor ration in U.S. Navy (finally accomplishedl 1862); in command ship Perry to help destroy slave ships and trade on African Coast, 1849-51; mem. naval efficiency bd., 1855; captured Canton (China) forts in punishment for attacks on Am. flag, 1856; in charge Bklyn. Navy Yard, Civil War, 1861, then in command naval operations on upper Mississippi; in charge naval side of operations in Grant's capture of Ft. Henry, 1862, then in command of naval force at Ft. Donelson (broke Confederate line of defense in No. Tenn.); commd. rear adm., 1862; chief of bureau of equipment and recruiting, 1863; apptd. to succeed DuPont in command of Charleston Squadron, died enroute to South. Author: Africa and the American Flag, 1854. Died N.Y.C., June 26, 1863; buried New Haven.

FOOTE, Charles Augustus, congressman; b. Newburgh, N.Y., Apr. 15, 1785; grad. Union Coll., Schenectady, N.Y., 1805; studied law. Admitted to bar, 1808, began practice of law, N.Y.C.; later practiced in Delhi, N.Y.; served as col. 6th div. N.Y. State Militia; trustee Delaware Acad.; pres. Village of Delhi; mem. U.S. Ho. of Reps. (Democrat) from N.Y., 18th Congress, 1823-25. Died Delhi, Aug. 1, 1828; buried pvt. burying ground on father's estate "Arbor Hill."

FOOTE, Henry Stuart, senator, gov. Miss.; b. Fauquier County, Va., Feb. 28, 1804; s. Richard Helm and Jane (Stuart) F.; grad. Washington and Lee U., 1819; m. Elizabeth Winters; m. 2d, Mrs. Rachel D. Smiley. Admitted to bar, Richmond, Va., 1823; mem. Miss. Legislature from Hinds County, 1839; mem. U.S. Senate from Miss., 1847-51; gov. Miss., 1851-54; mem. lower house Confederate Congress, 1861-65, became Confederate ofcl. in spite of Unionist sympathies, resigned after Davis refused to accept Pres. Lincoln's peace proposals; after brief imprisonment crossed Union lines, tried unsuccessfully to discuss peace terms with Lincoln and Sec. Seward, then sailed for Europe. Author: The War of Rebellion, 1866; Casket of Reminiscences, 1874; Bench and Bar of the South and Southwest, 1876. Died Nashville, Tenn., May 20, 1880.

FOOTE, William Henry, clergyman; b. Colchester, Conn., Dec. 20, 1794; s. Stephen and Hannah (Waterman) F.; A.B., Yale, 1816; m. Eliza Wilson, Feb. 21, 1822; m. 2d, Arabella Gilliam, Oct. 31, 1839; children—Ann, Eliza, Mary. Tchr., Falmouth, Va., 1816-18; licensed to preach by Winchester (Va.) Presbytery, 1819; itinerant preacher in Va., 1819-22; pastor, Woodstock, Va., 1822-24, Romney congregation (included chs. of Romney, Moorefield and Springfield, Va.), 1824-38; established an acad., Romney; agt. Central Bd. Fgn. Missions, 1838-45; pastor, Romney, 1845-61; prin. Romney Classical Inst., 1845-49; founded Potomac Sem. for girls (under Presbyn. control), Romney, 1850; pastor several chs., So. Va., 1861-63; hosp. chaplain, Farmville and Petersburg, Va., 1864; agt. to raise funds for Hampden-Sydney Coll., 1865, trustee, 1851-69; moderator home missions com. Winchester Presbytery, 1826, clk., 1834-38; moderator Va. Synod, 1839; mem. Va. Presbyn. Gen. Assembly, 1827-28, 33, 37, 44; commr. to Gen. Assembly Presbyn. Ch. of U.S., 1861; trustee Union Theol. Sem., 1838-69, pres. bd., 1864-66. Author: Sketches of North Carolina, Historical and Biographical, 1846; Sketches of Virginia, Historical and Biographical, 1850, 55; The Huguenots, or Reformed French Church, 1870. Died Romney, W.Va., Nov. 22, 1869.

FORBES, Edwin, artist; b. N.Y.C., 1839; s. Joseph C. and Ann Forbes; pupil of A.F. Tait, 1859. Staff artist for Frank Leslie's Illustrated Newspaper, 1861-65; executed Lull in the Fight, 1865; copperplate etchings from his war sketches published as Life Studies in the Great Army; mem. French Etching Club; hon. mem. London Etching Club, 1877. paintings include: A Night March; Returning from Picket Duty; The Rebelle; Early Morning in an Orange County Pasture, 1879; On the Skirmish Line; Stormy March; Roughing; On the Meadows, 1880; Evening in the Sheep Pasture, 1881. Author: 30 Years After, an Artist's Story of the Great War, 1891. Died Bklyn., Mar. 6, 1895.

FORBES, James, Continental congressman; b. nr. Benedict, Md., circa 1731. Apptd. justice of peace Charles County (Md.), 1777; tax commr. Charles County, 1777; mem. Md. Gen. Assembly, 1777; mem. Continental Congress from Md., 1778-80. Died Phila., Mar. 25, 1780; buried Christ Protestant Episcopal Churchyard.

FORBES, John, army officer; b. Dunfermline, Scotland, 1710; s. Col. John Forbes. Joined Scots Greys Regt. of 2d Royal North Brit. Dragoons, 1735, served in War of Austrian Succession; maj., dep. q.m. gen. in Europe, circa 1743, commd. lt. col. Brit. Army, 1745; col. 17th Foot, Eng., 1757; adj. gen. until 1758; brig. gen. Brit. Army in Am. 1757, commanded expdn. against Ft. Duquesne, built forts along the way to preserve eastern communication lines, finally took fort with no resistance from French; raised Brit. flag over Ft. Duquesne (renamed Ft. Pitt), Nov. 25, 1758. Died shortly after successful expdn., Mar. 11, 1759; buried Christ Ch., Phila.

FORBES, John, clergyman; b. Strathdon, Scotland, circa 1740; son of Archibald Forbes; M.A., U. Aberdeen (Scotland), 1763; m. Dorothy Murray, Feb. 2, 1769; children—James Grant, John Murray, Ralph Bennet. Recommended for ordination to the bishop of Ch. of Eng.; licensed as minister Anglican Ch., sent to St. Augustine, East Fla., 1764; only English clergyman in East Fla. during most of Brit. occupation (a ch. built in St. Augustine during his stay); became mem. Fla. Colonial Council, 1771; judge surrogate Vice-Admiralty Ct., also asst. judge Cts. of Common Law, interim chief justice, 1776-77; returned to Eng., 1783. Died Eng., Sept. 17, 1783.

FORBES, John Murray, diplomat; b. St. Augustine, Fla., Aug. 13, 1771; s. Rev. John and Dorothy (Murray) F.; grad. Harvard, 1787; studied law, Newburyport, Mass., 1787. Practiced law, Boston, 1794-96; went to Europe, 1796; signed testimonial to James Monroe (upon Monroe's recall), Paris, 1796; U.S. consul, Hamburg, Germany, also Copenhagen, Denmark, 1801-circa 1819; U.S. agt. for commerce and seamen to Buenos Aires, 1820-23, sec. of legation, 1823-25, chargé d'affaires, 1825-31, obtained change in Buenos Aires policy toward privateering (1821), modification of its maritime police ordinance (1822). Died June 14, 1831.

FORBES, John Murray, railroad exec.; b. Bordeaux, France, Feb. 23, 1813; s. Ralph Bennet and Margaret (Perkins) F.; m. Sarah Hathaway, Feb. 8, 1834, 6 children including William Hathaway. Came to U.S., 1828; head group of financiers which purchased unfinished M.C. R.R. from State of Mich. for $2,000,000, extended it to Lake Michigan and Chgo.; financed, put into operation railroads from Chgo. to Mississippi River and across Iowa; builder Hannibal & St. Joseph R.R. in Mo.; pres. Chgo., Burlington & Quincy R.R., 1878-81; served as Gov. John A. Andrew's most active helper in organizing Mass. for war at outset of Civil War; made unsuccessful attempt to buy Laird rams for Confederacy in Eng., 1863; organizer Loyal Publication Soc.; mem. nat. exec. com. Republican Party. Died Milton, Mass., Oct. 12, 1898.

FORBES, Robert Bennet, sea capt.; b. Jamaica Plain, Mass., Sept. 18, 1804; s. Ralph Bennet and Margaret (Perkins) F.; m. Rose Green Smith, Jan. 20, 1834. Became sailor in his uncles' mcht. bus., took command of 1 of firm's ships, sailed around world, 1824-27; received storeship from his uncles when their co. merged with another to form most powerful Am. mcht. house in China, 1830; almost ruined by Panic of 1837, went to Canton (China) and became involved in Opium War; refused to flee city when the destruction of all opium at Canton was ordered by Chinese commr., 1839, reaped huge fortune until blockade was put into effect, 1840; inventor of Forbes rig for sailing ships; 1 of 1st to advocate screw propeller and iron hulls; owner of 3 steamers, Midas, Edith and Massachusetts, 1844-45; sent ice to Orient, and small iron steamers to China, S.Am. and Cal. on decks of sailing vessels, carried supplies to Irish during Famine of 1847; in charge of shipping co. in China, 1849-51, also served as U.S. and French vice consul; organized a "Coast Guard" during Civil War, supervised constrn. of 9 gunboats, investigated constrn. of Laird rams in Eng. Author: Remarks on China and the China Trade, 1844; Remarks on Ocean Steam Navigation, 1855; The Forbes Rig, 1862; Notes on Ships of the Past, 1888. Died Nov. 23, 1889.

FORBES, William C., theater manager. Managed New Charleston Theater, Charleston, S.C., 1841-47, brought record number of stars and opera companies to Charleston.

FORCE, Peter, mayor Washington, D.C., archivist; b. nr. Passaic Falls, N.J., Nov. 26, 1790; s. William and Sarah (Ferguson) F. Pres., N.Y. Typo. Soc., 1812; served from pvt. to lt., U.S. Army, War of 1812; elected to City Council, Washington, D.C., 1822, later to Bd. Aldermen; mayor Washington (Whig), 1836, 37; established semi-weekly paper Nat. Jour., Washington, 1823, editor, 1823-30; pres. Nat. Inst. for Promotion Science; mem. bd. mgrs. Washington Nat. Monument Soc.; collected and published tracts and other papers, relating principally to origin, settlement and progress of N.Am. colonies (known as Force's Tracts), 1836-46; greatest work: American Archives (considered finest source collection on Am. Revolution and one of best sources of Am. history), 9 vols., 1837-53. Died Washington, Jan. 23, 1868.

FORD, Gordon Lester, lawyer, bibliophile; b. Lebanon, Conn., Dec. 16, 1823; s. Lester and Eliza (Burnham) F.; m. Emily Ellsworth, 1856, 8 children including Paul Leicester, Worthington Chauncey. Admitted to N.Y. County bar, 1850; pres. New London, Willimantic & Palmer R.R., 1852-56; instrumental in founding Bklyn. Union, 1863; U.S. collector internal revenue for 3d collection dist., 1869-72; del. from Bklyn. to Liberal Republican Conv., Cincinnati, 1873; bus. mgr. N.Y. Tribune, 1873-81; a founder Bklyn. Acad. Music, Bklyn. Art Assn.; his library collections (most value able pvt. library in Am. (at the time) given to N.Y. Pub. Library by his sons, 1889. Died Bklyn., Nov. 14, 1891.

FORD, Jacob, army officer, powder maker; b. Feb. 10, 1738; s. Jacob and Hannah (Baldwin) F.; m. Theodosia Johnes, Jan. 27, 1767, 6 children. Owner, Middle Forge, Morristown, N.J., 1764, cast shot and shell for Washington's army; built powder-mill, 1776; commd. col. Morris County (N.J.) Militia, 1775; successfully defended Morristown against Brit. raids. Died Jan. 11, 1777; buried 1st Presbyn. Churchyard, Morristown.

FORD, James, congressman; b. Perth Amboy, N.J., May 4, 1783; attended common schs. Moved to N.Y.C., 1797, then to Lindsley Town (later Lindley), N.Y., 1803; employed as office clk., moved (with employer) to Tioga County, Pa.; purchased land on banks of Cowanesque River, built home there, 1816, named place Lawrence (later Lawrenceville, N.Y.) for Capt. Lawrence of War of 1812; mem. Pa. Ho. of Reps., 1824-25; mem. U.S. Ho. of Reps. (Jackson Democrat) from Pa., 21st-22d congresses, 1829-33; operated sawmill and gristmill, Lawrenceville. Died Lawrenceville, Aug. 18, 1859; buried old Lindsley family cemetery, Lindley.

FORD, James W., artist; b. probably Phila.; m. 2d, Ann Binney. Exhibited at Pa. Acad., 1815, 20; painted portraits of dels to Va. constl. convs., 1829, 50; lived in home of Elliotte DeJarnette, Spotsylvania County, Va., painted over 20 portraits of mems. of family; painted portrait from life of Black Hawk, his son, and The Prophet (now in State Capitol, Richmond, Va.), 1833. Died 1866; buried Mt. Moriah Cemetery, Phila.

FORD, John Baptiste, mfr.; b. Danville, Ky., Nov. 17, 1811; probably son of Jonathan and Margaret (Baptiste) F.; m. Mary Bower, 1831, at least 2 children including Edward. Learned saddle trade, Greenville, Ind., later became owner of saddle shop for a time; opened gen. store, Greenville; set up foundry and rolling mill, prior to Civil War; built and sold river boats (with his 2 sons), also operated steamboat line serving both North and South during Civil War; sold his iron bus. for $150,000, established plate glass factory, New Albany, Ind., 1863-73; almost ruined in Panic of 1873, financed factory by selling a glass tube invention for $30,000; moved to Creighton, Pa., 1884, established Ford Plate Glass Co. (became "the glass city"); majority stockholder (with his sons) in Pitts. Plate Glass Co.; built and equipped several Methodist chs., financially supported Allegheny Coll. (Pa.), built YMCA at Tarentum, Pa.; hon. mem. French Acad. of Scis. Died May 1, 1903.

FORD, John Thompson, theatre exec.; b. Balt., Apr. 16, 1829; s. Elias and Anna (Greanor) F.; m. Edith Andrew, 11 children. In charge of Holliday St. Theatre, Balt., 1854-79; pres. Balt. City Council, 1857-58; built Ford's Theatre, Washington, D.C., mgr. at time of assassination of Pres. Lincoln, imprisoned (with his brother) after shooting, but freed when no evidence could be found of their participation in the crime; built Grand Opera House, Balt., 1781; built 3 theatres, Washington, D.C.; mgr. theatres, Alexandria, Va., Phila., Richmond, Va.; dir. Balt. & Ohio R.R.; v.p. West Balt. Improvement Assn. Died Balt., Mar. 14, 1894.

FORD, Melbourne Haddock, congressman; b. Salem, Mich., June 30, 1849; attended Mich. State Coll. Agr., East Lansing; studied law. Entered U.S. Navy, 1864, apptd. midshipman U.S. Naval Acad., Annapolis, 1867, resigned, 1868; moved to Grand Rapids, Mich., 1873, became ofcl. stenographer several municipal, state and fed. cts.; admitted to bar, 1878; mem. Mich. Ho. of Reps., 1885-86; mem. U.S. Ho. of Reps. (Democrat) from Pa., 50th, 52d congresses, 1887-89, 91; began practice of law, Grand Rapids, 1889; chmn. Mich. Dem. Conv., 1890. Died Grand Rapids, Apr. 20, 1891; buried Oak Hill Cemetery.

FORD, Nicholas, congressman; b. Wicklow, Ireland, June 21, 1833; attended Maynooth Coll., Dublin, Ireland. Came to U.S., 1848, settled in Chgo.; moved to Mo., 1859, later engaged in mining, Colo. and Mont.; became a mcht., Rochester, Mo.; mem. Mo. Ho. of Reps., 1875; mem. U.S. Ho. of Reps. (Liberal Republican) from Mo., 46th-47th congresses, 1879-83; unsuccessful Rep. candidate for gov. Mo., 1884; moved to Virginia City, Nev.; mem. 1st city council. Died Miltonvale, Kan., June 18, 1897; buried Catholic Cemetery, Aurora, Kan.

FORD, Thomas, gov. Ill.; b. Fayette County, Pa., Dec. 5, 1800; s. Robert and Elizabeth (Farquer) F.; m. Frances Hambaugh, June 12, 1828, 5 children. Admitted to bar, 1823; state's atty. for Galena and Quincy (Ill.), 1829-35; judge 6th Circuit, Ill. Dist. Ct., 1835-37, 39-41; judge Chgo. Municipal Ct., 1837; judge Ill. Supreme Ct., 1841-42; gov. Ill., saved state's credit and assured its integrity and future prosperity, 1842-46. Author: History of Illinois from 1818 to 1847, published 1854. Died Peoria, Ill., Nov. 3, 1850.

FORD, William D., congressman, lawyer; b. Herkimer County, N.Y., 1779; attended Fairfield (N.Y.) Sem.; studied law. Admitted to bar, 1809, began practice of law, Fairfield; mem. N.Y. State Assembly, 1816-17; apptd. commr. to perform duties of judge of supreme ct., 1817; moved to Watertown, N.Y., 1817; mem. U.S. Ho. of Reps. (Democrat) from N.Y., 16th Congress, 1819-21; dist. atty. Jefferson County; master in chancery; trustee Village of Watertown, 1827. Died Sackets Harbor, N.Y., Oct. 1, 1833; buried Village Cemetery.

FOREPAUGH, Adam, showman; b. 1831. Learned butcher's trade, owned shop in Cincinnati; supplied horses for circuses, taking shares in Johnny O'Brien Circus as payment, 1862 ,divided show, 1864; made 1st road tour under his own name with clown Dan Rice, trick horse and trained Burmese cattle, 1867; put his circus into 2 tents, one for menagerie, one for performance, 1869; in open conflict with Barnum's Greatest Show on Earth, 1880, reached agreement whereby they divided the routes, 1882. Died Jan. 22, 1890.

FORESTER, Frank, see Herbert, William Henry.

FORESTER, John B., congressman; b. McMinnville, Tenn.; studied law. Admitted to bar, practiced law; mem. U.S. Ho. of Reps. from Tenn., 23d-24th congresses, 1833-37. Died Aug. 31, 1845.

FORESTI, Eleutario Felice, educator, diplomat; b. Conselice, Papal States, Italy, 1793; Dottore in Legge, U. Bologna, 1809. A Carbonari, became Guelph Cavalier; arrested as Carbonari, 1819, taken to Piombi Prison, sentenced to life imprisonment; liberated by decree of Ferdinand on condition of exile to Am., 1835; arrived in N.Y.C., 1836; prof. Italian lang. and lit. Columbia, 1839, N.Y. U., 1842-1856, U. City of N.Y., 1856; ofcl. Am. rep. Giovine Italia (orgn. established by Mazzini); became pres. Central Assn. of N.Y., 1841; del. of Triumvirate in Am., 1850; founder L'Esule Italiano, N.Y.C.; apptd. U.S. consul, 1853, received at Genoa, Italy, 1856. Author: Twenty Years in the Dungeons of Austria, 1856. Died Genoa, Sept. 14, 1858.

FORMAN, David, army officer, jurist; b. Monmouth County, N.J., Nov. 3, 1745; s. Joseph and Elizabeth (Lee) F.; ed. Coll. of N.J.; m. Ann Marsh, Feb. 28, 1767, 11 children. Suppressed Loyalist uprising in Monmouth County, 1776; commd. brig. gen. N.J. Militia, 1777; commanded Jersey Militia at Battle of Germantown, 1777; attached to Maj. Gen. Charles Lee's staff by Gen. Washington's order; judge Monmouth County Ct. of Common Pleas. Died Sept. 12, 1797.

FORMAN, Joshua, lawyer; b. Pleasant Valley, N.Y., Sept. 6, 1777; s. Joseph and Hannah (Ward) F.; grad. Union Coll., 1798; studied law, Poughkeepsie, N.Y., also N.Y.C., 1798-1800; m. Margaret Alexander; m. 2d, Sarah Garrett; at least 1 child (dau.). Practiced law, Onondaga Hollow, N.Y., 1800-19; became mem. N.Y. Legislature, 1807, introduced bill for constrn. of canal between Hudson River and Lake Erie, 1808 (not the original plan, but an important factor in eventual bldg. of Erie Canal); 1st judge Ct. of Common Pleas of Onondaga County, 1813-23; moved to present site of Syracuse, N.Y., 1819, recognized as founder of city; responsible for rapid buildup of Syracuse community; established public instns., gained passage of an act to lower level of Lake Onondaga (thus draining nearby swamp); speculated in land; influential in passage of Safety Fund Act, 1829; purchased large land holdings in N.C., 1829. Died Aug. 4, 1848.

FORMES, Karl Johann, opera singer; b. Mülheim-on-Rhine, Germany, Aug. 7, 1816. Made debut as bass at Cologne as Sarastro in Magic Flute, 1841; played engagements at Mannheim, 1843-48, Royal Italian Opera, London, Eng., 1852-57; made 1st Am. tour, 1857, later divided his time between Europe and Am. Author: Aus meinem Kunst- u. Bühnenleben (memoirs), 1888. Died San Francisco, Dec. 15, 1889.

FORNANCE, Joseph, congressman; b. Lower Merion Twp., Montgomery County, Pa., Oct. 18, 1804; attended Old Acad., Lower Merion; studied law. Admitted to bar, 1832, began practice of law, Norristown, Pa.; pres. council Borough of Norristown; mem. Pa. Ho. of Reps., 1834; mem. U.S. Ho. of Reps. (Democrat) from Pa., 26th-27th congresses, 1839-43. Died Norristown, Nov. 24, 1852; buried Montgomery Cemetery.

FORNEY, Daniel Munroe, congressman; b. nr. Lincolnton, N.C., May 1784; s. Peter Forney; attended U. N.C. at Chapel Hill. Engaged in agriculture; served as maj. in War of 1812; held several local offices; mem. U.S. Ho. of Reps. from N.C., 14th-15th congresses, 1815-18 (resigned); apptd. by Pres. Monroe a commr. to treat with Creek Indians, 1820; mem. N.C. Senate, 1823-26; moved to Lowndes County, Ala., 1834. Died Lowndes County, Oct. 15, 1847; buried family burying ground, Lowndes County.

FORNEY, John Wien, journalist, govt. ofcl.; b. Lancaster, Pa., Sept. 30, 1817; s. Peter and Margaret (Wien) F.; m. Elizabeth Reitzel, 1840. Editor, part owner newspaper Lancaster Intelligencer, 1837 (prosperous enough to merge with Lancaster Jour., 1839); dep. surveyor Port of Phila., 1845; editor, partner Pennsylvanian, Phila., circa 1845; clk. U.S. Ho. of Reps., 1851-56, 60-61; partner Washington (D.C.) Daily Union, 1854, gained lucrative printing contracts of Ho. of Reps.; active in Buchanan's campaign; established Phila. Press., 1857; sec. U.S. Senate, 1861-68; founded Sunday Morning Chronicle, 1861, Daily Morning Chronicle, 1862; actively supported Lincoln administration; founded, edited weekly mag. Progress, Phila., 1878. Author: Letters from Europe, 1869; What I Saw in Texas, 1872; Anecdotes of Public Man, 1873; Forty Years in American Journalism, 1877; The News Nobility, 1882. Died Phila., Dec. 9, 1881.

FORNEY, Peter, congressman; b. nr. Lincolnton, N.C., Apr. 21, 1756; attended public schs.; married, at least 1 son, Daniel Munroe. Served as capt. during Revolutionary War. Engaged in iron mfg.; mem. N.C. Ho. of Commons, 1794-96, N.C. Senate, 1801-02; Democratic presdl. elector, 1804, 08, 16, 24, 28; mem. U.S. Ho. of Reps. (Democrat) from N.C., 13th Congress, 1813-15. Died "Mt. Welcome," Lincoln County, N.C., Feb. 1, 1834; buried pvt. burying ground "Mt. Welcome."

FORNEY, William, congressman, army officer; b. Lincolnton, N.C., Nov. 9, 1823; s. Peter and Sabina Swope (Hoke) F.; grad. U. Ala., 1844; m. Mary Eliza Woodward, Oct. 4, 1854. Commd. 1st lt. 1st Ala. Volunteers at Siege of Vera Cruz, Mexican War; admitted to Ala. bar, 1848; trustee U. Ala., 1851-60; mem. Ala. Ho. of Reps., 1859; entered Confederate Army as capt. 10th Ala. Regt., 1861, promoted to col. after Battle of Gettysburg (where he was crippled for life), promoted to brig. gen. shortly after Appomattox; mem. Ala. Senate, 1865-66; mem. U.S. Ho. of Reps. from Ala., 44th-52d congresses, 1875-93. Died Jacksonville, Ala., Jan. 16, 1894; buried City Cemetery, Jacksonville.

FORREST, Edwin, actor; b. Phila., Mar. 9, 1806; s. William and Rebecca (Lauman) F.; m. Catherine Sinclair, June 23, 1837. Made debut as Douglas in Hone's play Douglas, Walnut Street Theatre, Phila., 1820; performed perhaps the earliest Am. black-face impersonation, 1823; best features of style shaped by study of Edmund Kean; played Othello, Park Theatre, N.Y.C. (1st notable success), 1826; 1st actor to encourage Am. playwriting; recipient medal and banquet honoring him as 1st great Am. actor, N.Y.C., 1834; played Spartacus, Drury Lane, London, Eng., 1845; rival of actor William Macready, blamed Macready's influence when hissed in Macbeth, 1845, in turn hissed Macready's performance of Hamlet (believed to be original cause of Astor Place Riot, 1849, when Forrest's admirers attempted to prevent Macready from appearing in Astor Place Opera House, resulting in 22 deaths); lost popularity as result of riot, further lost public favor through a divorce trial scandal, 1851; willed nearly his entire estate as home for aged players. Died Phila., Dec. 12, 1872.

FORREST, French, naval officer; b. St. Mary's County, Md., Oct. 4, 1796; s. Maj. Joseph and Elizabeth (Dulany) F.; m. Emily Douglas Simms, 1830. Apptd. midshipman U.S. Navy, 1811; served in battles on Lake Erie under Commodore Perry, including battle of Hornet and Peacock during War of 1812 distinguished in operations against Mexican ports in Mexican War; head Washington (D.C.) Navy Yard, 1855-56; commd. capt. Va. Navy in Civil War, 1861, capt. Confederate Navy, 1861, head bur. orders and detail, 1862; commanded James River Squadron, 1863-64. Died Georgetown, D.C., Nov. 22, 1866.

FORREST, Nathan Bedford, army officer; b. Chapel Hill, Tenn., July 13, 1821; s. William and Mariam (Beck) F.; m. Mary Ann Montgomery, 1845. Traded in land, livestock, cotton and slaves; alderman, Memphis, Tenn., after 1849; commd. lt. col. Confederate Army, 1861; led a regt. out of Ft. Donelson, refused to be included in the surrender of that garrison, 1862; commanded a regt. at Battle of Shiloh, 1862; promoted brig. gen., 1862; maj. gen., 1863; commanded a brigade at Battle of Chickamauga, 1863; commanded brigade of Hood's Cavalry in Tenn. Campaign of 1864; considered in some degree responsible for slaughter of Negro soldiers following his capture of Ft. Pillow (Tenn.), Apr. 12, 1864; his fame rests upon his record in independent command on long cavalry raids behind Union lines in Tenn., Ky., Miss. and in such engagements as Okolona, Miss., Brice's Cross Rds.; promoted lt. gen., Feb. 1865; surrendered last Confederate command in arms east of Miss., at Gainesville, Ala., May 9, 1865; briefly involved in early activities of Ku Klux Klan; pres. Selma, Marion and Memphis R.R.; considered 1 of greatest Confederate gens. Died Memphis, Tenn., Oct. 29, 1877.

FORREST, Thomas, congressman; b. Phila., 1747; attended common schs. Commd. capt. Col. Thomas Proctor's Pa. Arty. during Revolutionary War, 1776, promoted maj., 1777, lt. col., 1778, resigned, 1781; mem. U.S. Ho. of Reps. from Pa., 16th, 17th congresses, 1819-21, Oct. 8, 1822-23. Died Germantown (now part of Phila.), Mar. 20, 1825.

FORREST, Uriah, congressman; b. nr. Leonardtown, St. Marys County, Md., 1756. Served as 1st lt., capt., maj. Md. Militia in Revolutionary War; wounded at Battle of Germantown, lost leg at Battle of Brandywine; mem. Continental Congress from Md., 1786-87; mem. U.S. Ho. of Reps. (Federalist) from Md., 3d Congress, 1793-Nov. 8, 1794 (resigned); commd. maj. gen. Md. Militia, 1795; clk. D.C. Circuit Ct., 1800-05. Died "Rosedale," nr. Georgetown, D.C., July 6, 1805; buried Oak Hill Cemetery, Washington, D.C.

FORSYTH, John, senator, gov. Ga., sec. of state; b. Fredericksburg, Va., Oct. 22, 1780; s. Robert and Fanny (Johnson) F.; grad. Princeton, 1799; m. Clara Meigs, several children. Admitted to Ga. bar, 1802; atty. gen. Ga., 1808; mem. U.S. Ho. of Reps. from Ga., 13th-15th congresses, 1813-Nov. 23, 1818, 18th-20th congresses, 1823-29; mem. U.S. Senate from Ga., Nov. 23, 1818-Feb. 17, 1819, Nov. 9, 1829-June 27, 1834; U.S. minister to Spain, 1819-23, secured ratification of treaty of 1819 which ceded Fla. to U.S.; gov. Ga., 1827-29; led opposition at Nullification Conv., Milledgeville, S.C., 1832; U.S. sec. of state under Jackson and Van Buren, 1834-41, opposed annexation of Tex., other chief concerns were rebellion in Canada, French spoilation claims, dispute over Me. boundary. Died Washington, D.C., Oct. 21, 1841; buried Congressional Cemetery, Washington.

FORSYTH, John, clergyman, educator; b. Newburgh, N.Y., Dec. 31, 1810; s. John and Jane (Currie) F.; grad. Rutgers Coll., 1829; studied theology U. Edinburgh (Scotland); m. Ann B. Heyer, 1833. Licensed by Presbytery of Aberdeen (Scotland), 1833; ordained to ministry by N.Y. Presbytery, July 1834; prof. Latin, Coll. of N.J. (now Princeton), 1847-53; prof. Bibl. lit. Newburgh Theol. Sem., 1848; prof. English lit. and rhetoric Rutgers Coll., 1859-62, lectr. history, 1864-72; chaplain, prof. geography, history and ethics U.S. Mil. Acad., 1871-81; contbr. to various church papers especially Christian Intelligencer; pres. Newburg Bd. Edn., 20 years; dir. Nat. Bank of Newburgh; corr. sec. Newburgh Bible Soc.; mem. Soc. for Prevention Cruelty to Animals, Soc. for Improving Condition of Poor. Author: Memoirs of Alexander Proudfit, D.D., the Rev. W. Romaine, Thomas DeWitt D.D., Joseph McCarrell D.D., and the Rev. R. Howard Wallace; History of the Associate Reformed Ch.; Sketches of the Lives of the Early Governors of New York, 1863; Additional Notes to the Epistle of James in Matthew Henry's Commentary. Died Newburgh, Oct. 17. 1886.

FORSYTH, Thomas, Indian agt., fur trader; b. Detroit, Dec. 5, 1771; s. William and Ann (Kinzie) Forsyth; m. Keziah Malotte, 1804, at least 1 child. Entered fur trade, 1790, worked among Ottawa Indians, Saginaw, Mich.; became partner (with Richardson) in fur trading post at Quincy, Ill., after U.S. took possession of Detroit, 1796; became partner (with his half-brother), 1804, worked around Peoria Lake, Ill., until War of 1812, when he moved with his family to St. Louis; U.S. Indian sub-agt., before War of 1812, prevented Potawatomi Indians from entering the war (and they kept him from being killed by British, who put a price on his head); returned to his post at Peoria, 1814-19; sent to negotiate with Indians of Upper Mississippi River, 1819; stationed at Ft. Armstrong (nr. Rock Island, Ill.), was known as Mah-tah-win (The Corn) to the Indians; ret., 1830, lived in St. Louis. Died Oct. 29, 1833.

FORT, George Franklin, gov. N.J.; b. Pemberton, N.J., May 1809; M.D., U. Pa., 1830. Practiced medicine, N.J., soon turned to politics; mem. N.J. Constl. Conv., 1844; mem. N.J. Senate; gov. of N.J., 1850-54; judge N.J. Ct. Errors and Appeals. Author: Early History and Antiquities of Freemasonry. Died Egypt, Ocean County, N.J., Apr. 22, 1872.

FORT, Greenbury Lafayette, congressman, lawyer; b. French Grant, Scioto County, O., Oct. 17, 1825; attended Rock River Sem.; studied law. Admitted to bar, 1847, began practice of law, Lacon, Ill.; sheriff, 1850; clk. Marshall County (Ill.), 1852; county judge, 1857; apptd. 2d lt. 11th Regt., Ill. Volunteer Inf. during Civil War, 1861, promoted 1st lt. with rank of q.m., 1861, capt., 1861, lt. col. and q.m., 1864; brevetted maj., lt. col. U.S. Volunteers, 1865; mem. Ill. Senate, 1866; mem. U.S. Ho. of Reps. (Republican) from Ill., 43d-46th congresses, 1873-81. Died Lacon, Jan. 13, 1883; buried Lacon Cemetery.

FORT, Tomlinson, congressman, physician; b. Warrenton, Ga., July 14, 1787; grad. Phila. Med. Coll. Began practice of medicine, 1810; served as capt. of volunteer co. in War of 1812; mem. Ga. Ho. of Reps., 1818-26; mem. U.S. Ho. of Reps. (Democrat) from Ga., 20th Congress, 1827-29; resumed practice of medicine, Milledgeville, Ga.; pres. State Bank of Ga., 1832-59. Died Milledgeville, May 11, 1859; buried City Cemetery.

FORTEN, James, sail maker; b. Sept. 2, 1766; s. Thomas Forten; married, circa 1790, 8 children. Foreman of working force Robert Bridge's sail making shop, 1787; later became owner of a sail loft; secured 2500 negro volunteers to protect Phila. from Brit. attack, 1814; recipient certificate of appreciation from Humane Soc. Phila., 1821; opposed plans of Am. Colonization Soc. for returning Negroes to Africa; advocated temperance, peace socs., women's rights; refused to do business with owners of slave vessels; one of foremost Negroes of his time. Died Mar. 4, 1842.

FORWARD, Chauncey, congressman; b. Old Granby, Conn., Feb. 4, 1793; studied law. Admitted to bar, Pitts., 1817, began practice of law, Somerset, Pa.; mem. Pa. Ho. of Reps., 1820-22; mem. U.S. Ho. of Reps. (Democrat, filled vacancy) from Pa., 19th-21st congresses, Dec. 4, 1826-31; apptd. prothonotary, recorder Somerset County (Pa.), 1831. Died Somerset, Oct. 10, 1839; buried Aukeny Square Cemetery.

FORWARD, Walter, congressman, sec. of treasury; b. Old Granby, Conn., Jan. 24, 1783; s. Samuel and Susannah (Holcombe) F.; m. Henrietta Barclay, Jan. 31, 1808. Editor, Democratic paper Tree of Liberty for Henry Baldwin, Pitts.; admitted to Pa. bar, 1806; mem. U.S. Ho. of Reps. from Pa., 17th-18 congresses, 1822-25; del. Gen. Conv. of the Nat. Republic, Balt., 1830; an organizer Whig party, 1834; mem. Pa. Constl. Conv., 1837-38; 1st comptroller of currency for Dist. of Pa., 1841; U.S. sec. of treasury under Pres. William Tyler, 1841-43; U.S. charge d'affaires to Denmark, 1849-51; pres. judge Dist. Ct. of Alleghany County (Pa.), 1851; a founder Pitts. Philos. and Philol. Soc.; supporter of temperance. Died Pitts., Nov. 24, 1852; buried Alleghany.

FOSDICK, Nicoll, congressman; b. New London, Conn., Nov. 9, 1785. Moved to Norway, N.Y.; presdl. elector on Monroe ticket, 1816; mem. N.Y. Assembly, 1818-19; mem. U.S. Ho. of Reps. (Whig) from N.Y., 19th Congress, 1825-27; collector of customs, 1849-53; engaged in merc. pursuits. Died New London, May 7, 1868; buried Cedar Grove Cemetery.

FOSDICK, William Whiteman, author; b. Cincinnati, Jan. 28, 1825; s. Thomas R. and Julia (Drake) F.; attended Cincinnati Coll., Transylvania U.; studied law, Louisville, Ky. Practiced law, N.Y.C., 1852-58. Author works including: Malmiztic the Toltec, and the Cavaliers of the Cross, 1851; Ariel and Other Poems, 1855. Died Cincinnati, Mar. 8, 1862.

FOSTER, A. Lawrence, congressman; attended public schs.; studied law, Vernon. Admitted to bar, began practice of law, Morrisville, circa 1827; mem. U.S. Ho. of Reps. (Whig) from N.Y., 27th Congress, 1841-43; settled permanently in Va.

FOSTER, Abiel, clergyman, congressman; b. Andover, Mass., Aug. 8, 1735; s. Asa and Elizabeth (Abbott) F.; grad. Harvard, 1756; m. Hannah Badger, May 15, 1761; m. 2d, Mary Rodgers, Oct. 11, 1769. Ordained to ministry, Cantebury, N.H., 1761; mem. N.H. Provincial Congress, Exeter, 1775; mem. N.H. Ho. of Reps., 1779-83; N.H. del. to Continental Congress, 1783-85; judge N.H. Ct. Common Pleas, 1784-88; mem. U.S. Ho. of Reps. from N.J., 1st, 4th-7th congresses, 1789-91, Dec. 7, 1795-1803; mem. N.H. Senate, 1791-93, pres., 1793; mem. N.H. Constl. Conv., 1791-92. Died Canterbury, N.H., Feb. 6, 1806; buried Center Cemetery, Canterbury.

FOSTER, Abigail Kelley, reformer; b. Pelham, Mass., Jan. 15, 1810; d. Wing and Diana (Daniels) Kelley; m. Stephen Symonds Foster, Dec. 31, 1845. Conducted (with Angelina Grimke) anti-slavery campaign in Mass., 1837; 1st Mass. woman to regularly address mixed audiences; mem. exec. com. Am. Anti-Slavery Soc., 1840; del. to World Anti-Slavery Conv., London, 1840; leader in radical abolitionist group; active in support of prohibition and minor humanitarian interests; considered the leader in women's rights movement after 1850. Died Worcester, Mass., Jan. 14, 1887.

FOSTER, Charles James, editor; b. Bicester, Oxford, Eng., Nov. 24, 1820; s. Samuel and Elizabeth Foster; never married. Reared on horse racing farm, Eng.; went to sea as merchantman, 1838; came to Boston, 1848, settled in Columbus, O.; became friend of Salmon P. Chase, Samuel S. Cox; became asso. editor Ohio Statesman, 1857; contbd. sports articles (signed Privateer) to Porter's Spirit of the Times; an editor Wilkes' Spirit of the Times, 1860; established (with 2 others) N.Y. Sportsman, 1875, asso. with publ. until 1883; had extensive knowledge of horses, prize fighting and game cocks. Author: Lives and Battles of Distinguished Pugilists (series of articles), 1860; Turf (article for Appleton's Am. Cyclopaedia), 1876; The White Horse of Wooton (novel), 1878. Died Astoria, N.Y., Sept. 12, 1883; buried Columbus.

FOSTER, Dwight, senator, congressman; b. Brookfield, Mass., Dec. 7, 1757; grad. Brown U., 1774; studied law. Admitted to bar 1778, began practice of law, Providence, R.I.; justice of peace Worcester County (Mass.), 1781-1823; spl. justice Ct. of Common Pleas, 1792; sheriff Worcester County, 1792; mem. Mass. Ho. of Reps., 1791-92, 1808-09; mem. U.S. Ho. of Reps. (Federalist) from Mass., 3d-6th congresses, 1793-June 6, 1800; del. Mass. Constl. Conv., 1799; mem. U.S. Senate (filled vacancy), June 6, 1800-03; chief justice Ct. of Common Pleas, 1801-11; mem. Mass. Gov.'s Council, also held other state and local offices. Died Brookfield, Apr. 29, 1823; buried Brookfield Cemetery.

FOSTER, Ephraim Hubbard, senator; b. Bardstown, Ky., Sept. 17, 1794; s. Robert Coleman and Ann (Hubbard) F.; grad. Cumberland Coll., 1812; m. Jane Mebane Lytle, 1817. Admitted to Nashville (Tenn.) bar, 1814; mem. Tenn. Ho. of Reps., 1829-31, 35-37, speaker 1835-37; mem. U.S. Senate from Tenn., 1838-39-43-45. Died Nashville, Sept. 6, 1854.

FOSTER, Hannah Webster, author; b. 1759; d. Grant Webster; m. Rev. John Foster, Apr. 1785, 2 children. Published The Coquette; or, The History of Eliza Wharton . . . By a Lady of Massachusetts (story of illicit love affair, became sensation of time in New Eng.), 1797, 3 edits. published by 1837; published The Boarding School; or, Lessons of a Preceptress to her Pupils, 1798. Died Montreal, Que., Can., Apr. 17, 1840.

FOSTER, Henry Allen, senator, congressman; b. Hartford, Conn., May 7, 1800; attended common schs., N.Y.; studied law. Admitted to bar, 1822, began practice of law, Oneida County, N.Y.; surrogate Oneida County, 1827-31, 35-39; supr. Town of Rome (N.Y.), 1829-30, 33-34; mem. N.Y. State Senate, 1831-34, 41-44; mem. U.S. Ho. of Reps. (Democrat) from N.Y., 25th Congress, 1837-39; mem. U.S. Senate (filled vacancy) from N.Y., Nov. 30, 1844-Jan. 27, 1845; del. Democratic Nat. Conv., N.Y., 1848; judge Supreme Ct. for 5th Dist., 1864-72; sr. mem., pres. bd. trustees Hamilton Coll.; v.p. Am. Colonization Soc. Died Rome, May 11, 1889; buried Rome Cemetery.

FOSTER, Henry Donnel, congressman, lawyer; b. Mercer, Pa., Dec. 19, 1808; grad. Coll. of Mead ville; studied law. Admitted to bar, 1829, began practice of law, Greensburg, Pa.; mem. U.S. Ho. of Reps. (Democrat) from Pa., 28th-29th, 42d congresses, 1843-47, 71-73; mem. Pa. Ho. of Reps., 1857-58; unsuccessful candidate for gov. Pa., 1860; moved to Irwin, Pa., 1879. Died Irwin, Oct. 16, 1880; buried St. Clair Cemetery, Greensburg.

FOSTER, John, engraver, printer; b. Dorchester, Mass., 1648; s. Hopestill and Mary (Bates) F.; grad. Harvard, 1667. Became earliest wood-engraver of English Am., 1671; chief among some 10 woodcuts are ¾ length portrait Rev. Richard Mather (considered earliest portrait engraved in colonies), Map of New Eng. (for Hubbard's Narrative of the Troubles with the Indians, 1677), view of Boston and Charlestown from Noodles Island; pioneer printer of Boston, 1675, published 1st med. treatise in Am., also almanacs. Died Sept. 9, 1681; buried Dorchester Burying Ground.

FOSTER, John Gray, army officer; b. Whitefield, N.H., May 27, 1823; s. Perley and Mary (Gray) F.; grad. U.S. Mil. Acad., 1846; m. Mary Moale, Jan. 21, 1851; m. 2d, Nannie Davis, Jan. 9, 1872. Commd. 2d lt. C.E., served in Mexican War; asst. prof. engring. U.S. Mil. Acad., 1855-57; capt. Engrs., July 1, 1860; at Ft. Sumter when bombarded by Confederates, Apr. 1861; brig. gen. Vols., Oct. 23, 1861; col. U.S. Army in command brigade under Gen. Burnside at Roanoke Island, Feb. 1862, at Newbern, Mar., 1862; in command Dept. N.C., July 1, 1862; maj. gen. Vols., July 18, 1862; in command Dept. of South, 1864; brevetted maj. gen. U.S. Army, Mar. 13, 1865; in command Dept. Fla., 1865-67; lt. col. C.E., Mar. 7, 1867; asst. to chief Engrs., 1871-74. Died Nashua, N.H., Sept. 2, 1874.

FOSTER, John Wells, geologist; b. Petersham, Mass., Mar. 4, 1815; s. Festus Foster; grad. Wesleyan U., Middletown, Conn., 1833; studied law, Zanesville, O.; m. Lydia Conerse, Oct. 24, 1838. Practiced law for time, Zanesville; asst. Ohio Geol. Survey, 1837; asso. U.S. geologist, 1847-52; a founder Native Am. Party in Mass., 1852; an organizer Republican Party in Mass., 1855; land commr. I.C. R.R., 1858-63; lectr. geology U. Chgo., 1863-65; pres. A.A.A.S. Author: The Mississippi Valley: Its Physical Geography, Including Sketches of the Topography, Botany, Climate, Geology and Mineral Resources; And of the Progress of Development in Population and Material Wealth, 1869; Prehistoric Races of the United States of America, 1873. Died June 28, 1873.

FOSTER, LaFayette Sabine, editor, senator, judge; b. Norwich, Conn., Nov. 22,, 1806; s. Daniel and Welthea (Ladd) F.: grad. Brown U.. 1828. LL.D. (hon.), 1851; m. Joanna Lanman, Oct. 2, 1837; m. 2d, Martha Lanman, Oct. 4, 1860; 3 children. Admitted to New London (Conn.) bar, 1831; edited Norwich Republican, 1835; mem. Conn. Gen. Assembly from Norwich, 1839, 40, 46-49, 54, 70; mayor Norwich, 1851, 52; mem. U.S. Senate from Conn., 1855-67, became pres. pro. tem at death of Lincoln, presiding officer, Apr. 5, 1865-Mar. 2, 1867; conservative Republican, opposed repeal of Fugitive Slave Act, of Missouri Compromise and of Lecompton Constn. for Kan.; judge Conn. Superior Ct., 1870-76; Conn. commr. to settle N.Y.-Conn. boundary dispute and buy Fisher's Island, 1878-79. Died Norwich, Sept. 19, 1880.,

FOSTER, Nathaniel Greene, congressman; b. nr. Madison, Ga., Aug. 25, 1809; grad. U. Ga. at Athens, 1830; studied law. Admitted to bar, 1831, began practice of law, Madison, Ga.; served as capt. of co. in Seminole War; solicitor gen. Ocmulgee Circuit, 1838-40; mem. Ga. Ho. of Reps., 1840, Ga. Senate, 1841-43, 51-52; mem. U.S. Ho. of Reps. (Am. Party candidate) from Ga., 34th Congress, 1855-57; became a Democrat; pastor Baptist Ch., Madison, 1855-69; judge Ocmulgee Circuit, 1867-68. Died Madison, Oct. 19, 1869; buried Madison Cemetery.

FOSTER, Stephen Clark, congressman; b. Machias, Me., Dec. 24, 1799; attended common schs.; learned blacksmith's trade. Became a shipbuilder; mem. Me. Ho. of. Reps., 1834-37; mem. Me. Senate, 1840, pres.; mem. U.S. Ho. of Reps. (Republican) from Me., 35th-36th congresses,

1857-61; mem. Washington (D.C.) Peace Conv., 1861. Died Pembroke, Me., Oct. 5, 1872; buried Forest Hill Cemetery.

FOSTER, Stephen Collins, song writer; b. Pitts., July 4, 1826; s. William Barclay and Eliza (Tomlinson) F.; attended Allegheny and Athens acads., Jefferson Coll.; m. Jane Denny McDowell, July 1850. Composed The Tioga Waltz for 4 flutes (performed at Athens Acad. commencement); published 1st ballad Open Thy Lattice, Love, 1844; wrote several ballads which became popular, including Louisiana Belle, O Susanna, Uncle Ned and Away Down South (published in Songs of Sable Harmonists), 1848; believed that his popular songs were not respectable, wrote numerous popularly unsuccessful songs which he considered more artistic; allowed Old Folks at Home (better known as Way Down upon the Swanee River) to be published under name of E.P. Christy of Christy's Minstrels, 1851; had financial arrangement with Christy to premier many of his ballads before publication; traveled to New Orleans (perhaps only trip South), 1852; moved to N.Y.C., 1860, drank heavily, sold new songs to music stores for pittance, lived in poverty; wrote Old Black Joe (only success in his final years), 1860; other well known songs include Nelly Was a Lady, 1849, Camptown Races, 1850, Massa's in de Cold, Cold Ground, 1852, My Old Kentucky Home, 1853, Old Dog Tray, 1853, Jeanie with the Light Brown Hair, 1854. Died in Bellevue Hosp. charity ward after fall in his Bowery lodginghouse, N.Y.C., Jan. 13, 1864.

FOSTER, Stephen Symonds, Abolitionist reformer; b. Canterbury, N.H., Nov. 17, 1809; s. Asa and Sarah (Morrill) F.; grad. Dartmouth, 1838; m. Abigail Kelley, Dec. 31, 1845. Famous early New Eng. anti-slavery leader and lectr. ("Slavery is an American and not a Southern institution."); also advocate women's suffrage, temperance worker, supporter rights of labor. Author: The Brotherhood of Thieves, a True Picture of the American Church and Clergy, 1843. Died Worchester, Mass., Sept. 8, 1881.

FOSTER, Theodore, senator; b. Brookfield, Mass., Apr. 29, 1752; s. Jedidiah and Dorothy (Dwight) F.; grad. R.I. Coll. (now Brown U.), 1770; M.A. (hon.), Dartmouth, 1786; m. Lydia Fenner, Oct. 27, 1771; m. 2d, Esther Millard, June 18, 1803; 3 children. Admitted to R.I. bar, 1770; dep. R.I. Gen. Assembly from Providence, 1776-82, from Foster, 1812-16; Town of Foster (R.I.) created in his honor, 1781; trustee Brown U., 1794-1822; mem. U.S. Senate from R.I., May 1790-1803, supported Hamilton's financial policy, Jay Treaty with Gt. Britain. Died Providence, Jan. 13, 1828.

FOSTER, Thomas Flournoy, congressman, lawyer; b. Greensboro, Ga., Nov. 23, 1790; grad. Franklin Coll., 1812; attended Litchfield Law Sch. Admitted to bar, 1816; began practice of law, Greensboro; mem. Ga. Ho. of Reps., 1822-25; mem. U.S. Ho. of Reps. (Democrat) from Ga., 21st-23d, 27th congresses, 1829-35, 41-43; mem. Ga. Conv. to reduce membership of Gen. Assembly, 1833; moved to Columbus, Ga., 1835. Died Columbus, Sept. 14, 1848; buried Linwood Cemetery.

FOSTER, Wilder De Ayr, congressman; b. Orange County, N.Y., Jan. 8, 1819; attended common schs. Moved to Mich., 1837, entered hardware bus., Grand Rapids, 1845; treas., alderman Grand Rapids; mayor Grand Rapids, 1854, 56, 66; mem. Mich. Senate, 1855-56; mem. U.S. Ho. of Reps. (Republican, filled vacancy) from Mich., 42d-43d congresses, Dec. 4, 1871-73. Died Grand Rapids, Sept. 20, 1873; buried Fulton Street Cemetery.

FOUKE, Philip Bond, congressman, lawyer; b. Kaskaskia, Ill., Jan. 23, 1818; attended public schs.; studied law. Became civil engr.; founder, publisher Belleville Advocate, 1841; admitted to bar, 1845, began practice of law, Belleville; pros. atty. Kaskaskia Dist., 1846-50; mem. Ill. Ho. of Reps., 1851; mem. U.S. Ho. of Reps. (Democrat) from Ill., 36th-37th congresses, 1859-63; served as col. 30th Regt., Ill. Volunteer Inf., during Civil War, wounded at Battle of Belmont; practiced law, Washington, D.C. Died Washington, Oct. 3, 1876; buried Congressional Cemetery.

FOULK, George Clayton, naval officer, diplomat; b. Marietta, Pa., Oct. 30, 1856; s. Clayton and Caroline (Rudisill) F.; grad. U.S. Naval Acad., 1876; m. Kane Murase, 1887. Served on 2 cruises, Asiatic duty, U.S. Navy, circa 1876; crossed Siberia into Russia (with 2 other naval officers), reported on area to U.S. govt.; commd. ensign upon return to U.S., assigned to Naval Library, 1877; naval attache to Am. legation, Korea, 1883-85, in charge of legation, 1885-87; declined personal offer to become adviser to Korean king; recalled to Washington, D.C., commd. lt. (j.g.), 1884; with Am. Trading Co., Yokahama, Japan, 1888-90; prof. mathematics Doshisha Coll., Kyoto, Japan, 1890-93. Died Aug. 6, 1893; buried Kyoto.

FOWLE, Daniel, printer; b. Charlestown, Mass., Oct. 1715; s. John and Mary (Barrell) F.; m. Lydia Hall, Apr. 11, 1751, no children. Apprenticed to printer, Boston; partner (with Gamaliel Rogers) in Rogers & Fowle, printing firm, 1740-50; published Boston Weekly Mag., 1743, Am. Mag. and Hist. Chronicle, 1743-46, Independent Advertiser, 1748; in business alone, 1750-54; moved to Portsmouth, N.H., became state printer N.H., 1756-87. Author: (pamphlets) A Total Eclipse of Liberty, 1755; An Appendix to the Total Eclipse of Liberty, 1756. Died June 8, 1787.

FOWLE, William Bentley, educator; b. Boston, Oct. 17, 1795; s. Henry and Elizabeth (Bentley) F.; m. Antoinette Moulton, Sept. 28, 1818; m. 2d, Mary Baxter Adams, Nov. 26, 1860. Apprentice Caleb Bingham's Bookstore; established sch. where he utilized advanced teaching methods; became head of female monitorial sch., 1823; editor, publisher Common Sch. Jour., 1848-52; mem. Mass. Legislature; published over 60 lectures, 500 newspaper essays; wrote more than 50 books. Died Medfield, Mass., Feb. 6, 1865.

FOWLER, John, congressman; b. Va., 1755; attended common schs. Served as capt. in Revolutionary War; mem. conv. held at Danville, Va. (now Ky.), 1787; mem. Va. Ho. of Dels., 1787; mem. Va. Conv. which ratified U.S. Constn.; moved to Lexington, Ky.; mem. U.S. Ho. of Reps. from Ky., 5th-9th congresses, 1797-1807; postmaster Lexington, 1814-22. Died Lexington, Aug. 22, 1840; buried Old Episcopal Cemetery.

FOWLER, Orin, clergyman, congressman; b. Lebanon, Conn., July 29, 1791; s. Capt. Amos and Rebecca (Dewey) F.; grad. Yale, 1814; m. Amaryllis Payson, Oct. 16, 1821. Licensed to preach by Assn. Western Dist. of Fairfield County, 1817; ordained by North Assn. of Hartford County, 1818; pastor Congregational Ch., Plainfield, Conn., 1820-31; mem. Mass. Senate, 1847-48; mem. U.S. Ho. of Reps. from Mass., 31st-32d congresses, 1849-Sept. 3, 1852. Author: Disquisition on the Evils Attending the Use of Tobacco, 1833; Lectures on the Modes and Subjects of Baptist, 1835; A History of Fall River, 1841. Died Washington, D.C., Sept. 3, 1852; buried North Burial Ground, Fall River, Mass.

FOWLER, Orson Squire, phrenologist; b. Cohocton, N.Y., Oct. 11, 1809; s. Horace and Martha (Howe) F.; grad. Amherst Coll., 1834; m. Mrs. Martha Chevalier Brevoort, June 10, 1835; m. 2d, Mrs. Mary Poole Aiken, Oct. 26, 1865; m. 3d, Abbie L. Ayres, Mar. 21, 1882. Partner (with brother Leonard) in firm O. S. & L. N. Fowler, publishers Phrenological Almanac, N.Y.C., 1840-42; editor Am. Phrenological Journal and Miscellany, 1842; partner Fowlers & Wells, 1844-63. Co-author: Phrenology Proved, Illustrated, and Applied, 1837; Love and Parentage, Applied to the Improvement of Offspring, including Important Directions and Suggestions to Lovers and the Married Concerning the Strongest Ties and the Momentous Relations of Life. Died Sharon Station, Conn., Aug. 18, 1887.

FOWLER, Samuel, congressman; b. Newburgh, N.Y., Oct. 30, 1779; attended Montgomery Acad., Pa. Med. Coll. at Phila. Began practice of medicine, Hamburg, N.J., 1800; moved to Franklin, N.J.; mem. N.J. Council, 1827; mem. U.S. Ho. of Reps. (Jackson Democrat) from N.J., 23d-24th congresses, 1833-37; discovered rare mineral Fowlerite (named in his honor), also franklinite (named by him); owner, developer zinc mines, Franklin, N.J.; owner Franklin Furnace Iron Works. Contbr. to many scientific publs. Died Franklin, Feb. 20, 1844; buried North Church Cemetery, nr. Hamburg.

FOWLER, Trevor Thomas, artist. Exhibited portrait at Royal Acad., London, Eng., 1829; exhibited 35 portraits at Royal Hibernian Acad., Dublin, Ireland, 1830-35; came to N.Y.C., circa 1837; exhibited at N.A.D., 1837-38; painted portraits of Harrison and Clay, 1840; went to New Orleans; returned to Europe, circa 1842; exhibited in Dublin, 1843-44; returned to New Orleans, 1844, worked in New Orleans and Cincinnati, until 1853; lived in Germantown (Pa.) and Phila., 1854-69; frequent exhibitor at Pa. Acad.

FOX, Charles Kemble, actor; b. Boston, Aug. 15, 1833; s. George Howe and Emily (Wyatt) F.; m. Kate Denin; m. 2d, Mary Hewins; m. 3d, Mrs. Dulaney. Mem. Howard-Fox Dramatic Co., 1846-50; appeared in Uncle Tom's Cabin at Museum, Troy, N.Y., 1852; last engagement Fox's Broadway Theatre appearing as Pantaloon in Humpty Dumpty at Home, 1874, his miming of part has been called best ever presented before Am. audience. Died N.Y.C., Jan. 17, 1875; buried Mt. Auburn Cemetery, Cambridge, Mass.

FOX, George Washington Lafayette, actor, mgr.; b. Boston, July 3, 1825; s. George Howe and Emily (Wyatt) F.; m. Caroline Gould; m. 2d Mattie Temple. Mem. Howard-Fox Dramatic Co. Providence, R.I., 1846-50; made N.Y. debut in A Pleasant Neighbor at Nat. Theater, 1850, played until 1858; a mgr. Bowery Theater, 1858-59 commd. lt. 8th N.Y. Inf., 1860; played Bottom in revival of A Midsummer Night's Dream, 1867 made pantomime famous in Am. with character "Humpty Dumpty," 1868, made last appearance in Humpty Dumpty in Every Clime at Booth's Theatre, 1875. Died Cambridge, Mass., Oct. 24 1877.

FOX, Gilbert, actor, engraver; b. Eng., 1776 married. Apprenticed to engraver, London, Eng. came to Am., completed apprenticeship under Edward Trenchard, Phila., 1795; taught drawing at girls' seminary; sang with Chestnut Street Theatre Phila., 1798; worked with N.Y. Theatre, 1799-1802 also did engraving; mem. Boston Theatre, 1804-07. Died circa 1807.

FOX, Gustavus Vasa, govt. ofcl.; b. Saugus Mass., June 13, 1821; s. Dr. Jesse and Olivia (Flint) F.; m. Virginia Woodbury, 1856. Apptd midshipman U.S. Navy, 1841, lt., 1852, resigned 1856; in charge of evacuation of Ft. Sumter, transported Anderson and his 70 men to N.Y., 1861 chief clk. Navy Dept., 1861, asst. U.S. sec. of navy, 1861, selected Farragut to command expdn resulting in capture New Orleans and opening of the Mississippi; agt. for U.S. Congress sent to Russia to congratulate Czar Alexander II, 1867; agt Middlesex Co., Lowell, Mass., 1867; ofcl. papers published posthumously as: Confidential Correspondence of Gustavus Vasa Fox, Assistant Secretary of the Navy, 1861-65 (edited by Robert Thompson) 2 vols., 1918-19. Died N.Y.C., Oct 29, 1883.

FOX, Harry, contractor; b. Westfield, Mass., Sept. 29, 1826; s. Hiram Fox; m. Emeline Chamberlain, Nov. 25, 1852, 2 children. Chief operator Northern N.H. R.R., 1846; formed partnership with John P. Chapin, Chgo., 1856; in partnership with bridgebuilder William B. Howard, 1860-75 responsible for numerous topog. improvements in Chgo., including dozen bridges spanning Chicago River, improvement of many Lake Michigan harbors; asso. with firm Fitz-Simons & Connell. Died Salt Lake City, Sept. 4, 1883.

FOX, Margaret, spiritualist medium; b. Bath, Can., Oct. 7, 1833; d. John D. and Margaret Fox. Started seances with her sister in N.Y., summer 1850; toured U.S. with an aunt, Mrs. Leah Fish, in fake act known as "Rochester Rappings," also appeared in London, 1876; became Catholic, exposed her aunt as a fake at Am. Acad. Music in N.Y., Oct. 21, 1888. Died Bklyn., Mar. 8, 1893

FOXALL, Henry, foundry owner; b. Mammouthshire, Eng., May 24, 1758; m. Ann Howard; married a 2d time. Supt. of important iron works, Dublin, Ireland, 1794; lay minister; came to Phila., 1797, formed a partnership (with Robert Morris, Jr.) in Eagle Fire Works; owner Columbian Foundry, Georgetown, D.C., 1800-15; gave ground and funds for Foundry Chapel, Washington, D.C., 1814; mayor Georgetown, 1821-23. Died Mandsworth, Eng., Dec. 11, 1823.

FRALEY, Frederick, mcht., banker; b. Phila., May 28, 1804; s. John Urban and Ann Elizabeth (Laskey) F.; ed. by pvt. tutors; m. Jane Chapman Cresson, 1832. Employed in Thomas Cooper's hardware store, Phila., 1821-26; partner Reeves, Buck & Co., Phila., wholesale hardware firm, 1826-40; mem. Phila. Common Council, 1834-37, Pa. Senate, 1837-40; sec. Am. Fire Ins. Co., 1840-47; pres. Schuykill Navigation Co., 1847-88; treas. Centennial Bd. of Finance, 1873-93; mgr. Western Saving Fund Soc., 1858-78, pres., 1878-1901; a founder Franklin Inst., Phila.; became mem. Am. Philos. Soc., 1842, sec., v.p., pres., various times, 1880-1901; became trustee U. Pa., 1853; a founder Phila. Bd. of Trade, 1833, dir., 1833-38, sec., 1838-66, mem. exec. council 1866-67, v.p., 1867-87, pres. bd. dirs., 1887-1901; an organizer Nat. Bd. of Trade, 1868, pres., 1868-1901. Died Phila., Sept. 23, 1901.

FRANCA, Manuel Joachim de, see de Franca, Manuel Joachim.

FRANCHERE, Gabriel, fur trader; b. Montreal, Can., Nov. 3, 1786; s. Gabriel and Felicite (Martin) F.; m. Charlotte Osborn, 1837. Under auspices of John J. Astor participated in Columbian River Expdn. to develop fur trade beyond Rocky Mountains, 1810; established fur trading co. in N.Y. Author: Relation d'un Voyage a la Cote du Nord Ouest de L'Amerique Septentrionale, dan les annees 1810, 11, 12, 13 et 14 (1st history of Astor expdns., forming basis of Washington Irving's Astoria), 1820. Died St. Paul, Minn., Apr. 12, 1863.

FRANCHOT, Richard, congressman; b. Morris, N.Y., June 2, 1816; attended Hartwick and Cherry Valley acads.; studied civil engring. Polytechnic Inst., Troy, N.Y. Became engaged in agriculture, then in railroad constrn.; pres. Albany & Susquehanna R.R. Co.; mem. U.S. Ho. of Reps. (Republican) from N.Y., 37th Congress, 1861-63; moved to Schenectady, N.Y.; raised 121st Regt., N.Y. Volunteer Inf., during Civil War, commd. col., 1862; brevetted brig. gen. U.S. Volunteers, 1865; asso. with Central Pacific R.R. Co. Died Schenectady, Nov. 23, 1875; buried Vale Cemetery.

FRANCIS, Charles Stephen, bookseller, publisher; b. Boston, Jan. 9, 1805; s. David and Mary (Moore) F.; m. Catharine Rebecca Jewett, Sept. 2, 1830; m. 2d, Averic Parker Allen, Sept. 29, 1849; 5 children including Harriet Moore. Moved to N.Y.C., 1826, opened bookstore in wealthiest residential dist., moved his shop to follow moves of wealthy population; maintained agt. in London, Eng., to fill orders for fgn. publications; published many books including Zenobia (William Ware), 1838, Discourse Occasioned by the Death of William Ellery Channing (H. W. Bellow, 1842; retired from bookselling, 1870. Author: Francis's New Guide to the Cities of New York and Brooklyn, and the Vicinity, 1853. Died Tarrytown, N.Y., Dec. 1, 1887.

FRANCIS, Convers, clergyman, educator; b. West Cambridge, Mass., Nov. 9, 1795; s. Convers and Susannah (Rand) F.; grad. Harvard, 1815, postgrad. in divinity studies, 1815-18; hon. D.D., Cambridge, 1837; m. Abby Allyn, May 15, 1822. Ordained Unitarian minister, June 23, 1819; prof. pulpit eloquence and pastoral care Harvard Divinity Sch., 1842 until death; one of 1st Americans to study German lang. and lit. in religious field; active in Mass. Hist. Soc., helped prepare its "Collections." Author: Errors in Education, 1828; An Historical Sketch of Watertown, in Massachusetts, from the First Settlement of the Town to the Close of its Second Century, 1830; Dudlean Lecture at Cambridge, 1833; Life of Rev. John Eliot, 1836; Rev. John Allyn, D.D., 1836; Judge Davis, 1849; Life of Sebastian Rale, 1848. Died Cambridge, Mass., Apr. 7, 1863.

FRANCIS, James Bicheno, hydraulic engr.; b. Southleigh, Eng., May 18, 1815; s. John and Eliza (Bicheno) F.; m. Sarah Brownell, July 12, 1837, 6 children. Arrived in N.Y.C., 1833; chief engr. group known as "Proprs. of the Locks & Canals on the Merrimack River," 1837-1840; chief engr., gen. mgr. devel. water-power facilities, Lowell, Mass., 1845; began constrn. of Northern Canal, 1846; following trip to Eng., 1849, built machines for timber preservation; devised water supply for fire protection, Lowell, 1850's; designed and constructed hydraulic lifts for guard gates of Pawtucket Canal, 1870; original mem. Boston Soc. Civil Engrs., pres. 1874, 80; pres. Stonybrook R.R., 20 years; dir. Lowell Gas Light Co., 43 years. Author: Lowell Hydraulic Experiments, 1855, 68, 83; Strength of Cast Iron Columns, 1865. Died Boston, Sept. 18, 1892.

FRANCIS, John Brown, senator, gov. R.I.; b. Phila., May 31, 1791; s. John and Abby (Brown) F.; grad. Brown U., 1808; attended Litchfield (Conn.) Law Sch.; m. Anne Brown, June 18, 1822; m. 2d, Elizabeth Harrison, May 22, 1832. Mem. R.I. Ho. of Reps., 1821-29, R.I. Senate, 1831-32, 42-43, 45-56; gov. R.I., 1833-38; mem. U.S. Senate from R.I., 1844-45; life mem. R.I. Soc. for Encouragement Domestic Industry; treas., v.p. R.I. Hist. Soc.; trustee Brown U., 1828-57, chancellor, 1841-54. Died Warwick, R.I., Aug. 9, 1864.

FRANCIS, John F., artist; b. Phila., circa 1808. Exhibited at Artists' Fund Soc., 1840-41; painted in numerous small towns in Pa. and Del., Washington D.C., Nashville, Tenn.; painted in Jeffersonville, Pa., 1866-86; painted portraits and still lifes, also did silhouettes. Died Jeffersonville, Nov. 15, 1886.

FRANCIS, John Morgan, editor, publicist, diplomat; b. Prattsburg, N.Y., Mar. 6, 1823; s. Richard and Mary (Stewart) F.; m. Harriet Tucker, Dec. 8, 1846. Asst. editor Daily Advertiser, Rochester, N.Y., 1846, Northern Budget, Troy, N.Y., 1846-49; in charge of Daily Whig, Troy, 1850; founder (with R.D. Thompson) Daily Times, 1851, editor-in-chief, sr. propr., 1851-97, under his guidance it became one of leading Republican jours. of N.Y. State; del. 1st Republican Conv.; mem. N.Y. State Constl. Conv., 1867-68, 94; U.S. minister to Greece, 1871-74, to Lisbon (Portugal), 1882; envoy extraordinary and minister plenipotentiary to Austria-Hungary, 1884. Died Troy, June 18, 1897.

FRANCIS, John Wakefield, physician; b. N.Y.C., Nov. 17, 1789; s. Melchior Francis; grad. Columbia, 1809, LL.D. (hon.), 1860; M.D., Coll. Phys. and Surg. (1st grad. of coll.), N.Y.C., 1811; LL.D. (hon.), Trinity Coll., Hartford, Conn., 1850; m. Mary Eliza Cutler, Nov. 16, 1829, 1 son, Samuel Ward. Apptd. lectr. in medicine and materia medica Coll. Phys. and Surg.; prof. medicine and materia medica, med. dept. Columbia, prof. forensic medicine, 1817, prof. obstetrics, 1819-26; prof. obstetrics Rutgers Med. Sch., 1826-28; edited (with Hosack) Am. Med. and Philos. Register, 1810-14; founder N.Y. Acad. Medicine, 1846, pres., 1847-48; financially responsible for establishment Woman's Hosp. Author: Use of Mercury, 1811; Introduction to the Practice of Medicine, 1821; Denmans' Practice of Midwifery, 1825. Died N.Y.C., Feb. 8, 1861.

FRANCIS, Joseph, inventor, mfr.; b. Boston, Mar. 12, 1801; s. Thomas and Margaret F.; m. Ellen Creamer. Produced a wooden boat that withstood severest tests; constructed life boats for U.S. vessels Santee and Alabama, 1829; all U.S. Govt. ships equipped with boats of his invention by 1841; contracted with Novelty Iron Works of N.Y. to manufacture the boats; granted patent for corrugated metal boat, 1845; constructed fleet of light-draft corrugated iron steamers for Russian govt., sometime between 1855-63. Recipient medal Franklin Inst., 1854, Gold medal King Ferdinand III. of Sicily, gold snuffbox from Napoleon III, 1856, Congressional medal presented by Pres. Harrison, 1890; named to Royal Order Knighthood St. Stanislaus by Czar of Russia. Died Cooperstown, N.Y., May 10, 1893; buried Mpls.

FRANCIS, Samuel Ward, physician, inventor; b. N.Y.C., Dec. 26, 1835; s. John W. and Maria (Cutler) F.; B.A., Columbia, 1857; M.D., U. City N.Y., 1860; m. Harriet McAllister, June 16, 1859. Patented printing machine which anticipated the typewriter, 1860; invented heating and ventilating device for railroad cars, 1868; developed a sewing machine, 1875; devised signal for telephone and telegraph lines, 1879; active in Sanitary Protection Assn. (founded 1878). Author: Report of Valentine Motts' Surgical Cliniques in the University of New York, 1859-60, pub. N.Y., 1860; Inside and Out, 1862; Biographical Sketches of Distinguished Living New York Surgeons, 1866; Life and Death, 1871. Died Newport, R.I., Mar. 25, 1886.

FRANCIS, Tench, colonial ofcl.; b. Ireland; s. John Francis; m. Elizabeth Turbutt, Dec. 29, 1724. Came to Am. before 1720; atty. for Lord Baltimore, 1720-26; clk. Talbot County (Md.), 1726-34; burgess for Talbot County in Md. Assembly, 1735-38; apptd. atty. gen. Pa., 1741-45; recorder City of Phila., 1750-55. Died Phila., Aug. 16, 1758.

FRANK, Augustus, congressman, businessman; b. Warsaw, N.Y., July 17, 1826; attended common schs. Engaged in merc. pursuits; dir., v.p. Buffalo & N.Y.C. R.R. Co.; del. Republican Nat. Conv., Phila., 1856; mem. U.S. Ho. of Reps. (Rep.) from N.Y., 36th-38th congresses, 1859-65; dir. Wyoming County Nat. Bank, 1865; mem. N.Y. State Constl. Conv., 1867, 68; a mgr. Buffalo State Hospital for the Insane, 1870-82; organizer Bank of Warsaw, 1871, pres., 1871-95; dir. Rochester Trust & Safe Deposit Co., Buffalo, Rochester & Pitts. R.R.; Rep. presdl. elector, 1888; del. at large N.Y. Constl. Conv., 1894. Died N.Y.C., Apr. 29, 1895; buried Warsaw Cemetery.

FRANKENSTEIN, Godfrey N., artist; b. Germany, Sept. 8, 1820. Brought to Cincinnati by parents, 1831; apprenticed to sign painter, 1832; propr. sign painting bus., 1833-39; opened portrait studio, Cincinnati, 1839; 1st pres. Cincinnati Acad. Fine Arts, 1841; specialized in landscape paintings, after 1844; painted panorama of Niagara Falls shown in Phila. and N.Y.C., 1853, Cincinnati, 1854; made sketching trips to White Mountains of N.H. Died Springfield, O., Feb. 24, 1873.

FRANKENSTEIN, John Peter, artist; b. Germany, 1816-17. Came to Cincinnati with parents, 1831; began to paint portraits, 1831; moved to Phila., circa 1839; exhibited portraits at Artists' Fund Soc., Apollo Assn.; returned to Cincinnati, circa 1847, moved to Springfield, O., 1849; had studio, Cincinnati, 1856-75, moved to N.Y.C., 1875; published poem American Art, Its Awful Attitude; spent last years as apparently poverty-stricken recluse, but a considerable sum of money was found in his rooms at his death. Died East New York, N.Y., Apr. 16, 1881.

FRANKLAND, Lady Agnes Surriage, social leader; b. Marblehead, Mass., Apr. 1726; d. Edward and Mary (Pierce) Surriage; m. Sir Crarles Henry Frankland, 1755; m. 2d, John Drew, 1782. Educated by her future husband, became his mistress, 1746, his wife, 1755; leader in Boston Society, 1756-58; accompanied husband to Lisbon, then to Eng. Died Apr. 23, 1783; buried St. Pancras' Ch., Chichester, Eng.

FRANKLIN, Benjamin; b. Boston, Jan. 17, 1706; s. Josiah and Abiah (Folger) F.; self-educated; M.A. (hon.), Yale, 1753, Harvard, 1753, Coll. William and Mary, 1756; LL.D. (hon.), St. Andrews Coll., 1759; D.C.L. (hon.) Oxford (Eng.) U., 1762; took Deborah Read as common law wife, Sept. 1, 1730, later married, 2 children including Francis Folger, Sarah; 2 illegitimate children including William. Contbr. articles to New Eng. Courant (newspaper pub. and printed by his bro. James to whom he was apprenticed), Boston, until 1723; in London, 1724-26; owner Pa. Gazette, 1730-50; established circulation library, Phila., 1731; wrote and published Poor Richard's Almanac (one of 1st Am. lit. prodns. to attain internat. renown, largely because of his common-sense philos. aphorisms), 1732-57; clk. Pa. Assembly, 1736-51, mem. from Phila., 1751-64; dep. postmaster Phila., 1737-53; aided British in French and Indian War; inventor Pa. Fireplace (known as Franklin Stove), Fergusson's Clock, circa 1744, also bifocals; founder Am. Philos. Soc., 1743, Phila. City Hosp., 1751; a founder Acad. for Edn. of Youth, 1751, incorporated, 1753 (later Coll. of Phila., now U. Pa.); performed kite expt. to test theory of identity of lightning and electricity, 1752; joint dep. postmaster gen. Am. colonies, 1753-74; Pa. rep. at Albany (N.Y.) Congress, 1754, submitted "Plan of Union" adopted by Congress but vetoed by colonial legislatures (later important in drafting Articles of Confedn. and U.S. Constn.); polit. agt. Pa. Assembly, sent to Eng. to present case against Penn family for refusing to support defense expenditures, 1757-62, returned to Eng. to obtain recall of Pa. Charter, 1766; questioned before Ho. of Commons during debates on repeal of Stamp Act, 1766; colonial agt. of Ga., 1768, N.J., 1769, Mass., 1770; aided William Pitt in fruitless conciliation efforts, in Eng.; mem. 2d Continental Congress, 1775, sketched plan of union for colonies, organized post office, became 1st postmaster gen.; mem. com. to draft Declaration of Independence, also a signer, 1776; del. of mission to persuade Can. to join Am. cause; commr. to negotiate treaty with France (only American with whom French Prime Minister Vergennes would deal), 1776, signed final commerce and defense alliance treaties, 1778; apptd. minister to France, 1778; apptd. a commr. to negotiate peace with Gt. Britain, 1781, assumed responsibility for preliminary talks, peace treaty signed, 1783; returned to Phila., 1785; pres. Pa. Exec. Council, 1785-87; mem. U.S. Constl. Conv., 1787, largely responsible for representation compromise actually incorporated in Constn.; signed meml. to Congress for abolition of slavery (last public act). Author: Edict by the King of Prussia, Rules by Which a Great Empire May be Reduced to a Small One (both satires), early 1770's; Observations on the Increase of Mankind, of the Peopling of Countries, 1775; Autobiography (never finished); also essays (some of earliest signed Silence Dogood). Died Phila., Apr. 17, 1790; buried Christ Ch. Burial Ground, Phila.

FRANKLIN, Benjamin, clergyman; b. Ohio, Feb. 1, 1812; s. Joseph and Isabella (Devold) F.; m. Mary Personnett, Dec. 15, 1833. Carpenter, 1833-37; operator grist-mill, 1837-40; preacher of Disciples of the West, 1840, became roving evangelist; editor Reformer (also called Western Reformer, Proclamation and Reformer), 1845-56; editor Am. Christian Review, 1856-78. Author: An Oral Debate on the Coming of the Son of Man, Endless Punishment, and Universal Salvation, 1848. Died Oct. 22, 1878; buried Anderson, Ind.

FRANKLIN, James, printer; b. Boston, Mass., Feb. 4, 1697; s. Josiah and Abiah (Folger) F. Started paper New Eng. Courant (an imitation of Addison and Steele's Spectator), Aug. 7, 1721, forbidden to publish it by the court, 1723; taught printing trade to his half-brother, Benjamin Franklin; brought 1st press to R.I.; printed part of an edit. Laws of R.I., 1731; started R.I. Gazette, 1st newspaper pub. in R.I., 1732. Died Newport, R.I., Feb. 1735.

FRANKLIN, Jesse, senator, gov. N.C.; b. Orange County, Va., Mar. 24, 1760; s. Bernard and Mary (Cleveland) F.; m. Meeky Perkins. Served as capt. and adj. N.C. Regt., during Am. Revolution, rose to mem. N.C. Ho. of Commons, 1784, 93, 94, 97, 98; mem. U.S. Ho. of Reps. from N.C., 4th Congress, 1795-97; mem. U.S. Senate from N.C., 1799-1805, 07-13; trustee U. N.C., 1805; mem. N.C. Senate, 1805-06; U.S. commr. to deal with Chickasaws and Cherokees, 1816; gov. N.C., 1820-21. Died Surry County, N.C., Aug. 31, 1823; buried Nat. Park at Guilford Battleground, nr. Greensboro, N.C.

FRANKLIN, John Rankin, congressman, jurist; b. nr. Berlin, Md., May 6, 1820; grad. Jefferson Coll., 1836; studied law. Admitted to bar, 1841, began practice of law, Snow Hill,, Md.; mem. Md. Ho. of Dels., 1840-43, 59, speaker 1 term; pres. Md. Bd. of Public Works, 1851; mem. U.S. Ho. of Reps. (Whig) from Md., 33d Congress, 1853-55; judge 1st Jud. Circuit Md., 1867-78. Died Snow Hill, Jan. 11, 1878; buried Makemie Meml. Presbyn. Churchyard.

FRANKLIN, Meshack, congressman; b. Surry County, N.C., 1772. Mem. N.C. Ho. of Commons, 1800-01, N.C. Senate, 1828-29, 38; mem. U.S. Ho. of Reps. (Democrat) from N.C., 10th-13th congresses, 1807-15. Died Surry County, Dec. 18, 1839.

FRANKLIN, William, colonial gov.; b. Phila., 1731; illegitimate son of Benjamin Franklin and Deborah Read; M.A. (hon.), Oxford, (Eng.) U., 1762; married twice; m. Elizabeth Downes (1st wife), Sept. 4, 1762; 1 illegitimate son, William Temple Franklin. Often accompanied his father to Europe, also helped in father's scientific experiments; served in King George's War, 1748; comptroller Gen. Post Office, clk. Pa. Provincial Assembly, 1754-56; admitted to Middle Temple, London, Eng., later elected to bar; last royal gov. N.J., 1762-76; began controversy with patriot party in N.J., 1765; at outbreak of Revolutionary War, captured and imprisoned as Loyalist; pres. Bd. Asso. Loyalists, N.Y.C., 1778; Loyalist leanings led to break with father; went permanently to Eng., 1782; reconciled with father, 1784. Died Eng., Nov. 16, 1813.

FRASER, Charles, artist; b. Charleston, S.C., Aug. 20, 1782; s. Alexander and Mary (Grimke) F. Admitted to Charleston bar, 1807; trustee Coll. Charleston, 1817-circa 57; chosen by City of Charleston to paint a miniature of Marquis de Lafayette on his visit to the city, 1825; known for his miniatures. Died Charleston, Oct. 5, 1860.

FRAUNCES, Samuel, tavern keeper; b. Brit. West Indies, circa 1722; m. Elizabeth, 7 children. A West Indian French Negro; propr. Masons' Arms on Broadway, N.Y.C., 1759-62; founder, propr. Fraunces Tavern, N.Y.C., 1762-65, 70-95, became favorite rendezvous of Am. revolutionists, scene of Gen. Washington's farewell to his officers, most noted hostelry of colonial N.Y.; voted money by Congress of Confederation and N.Y. State for kindness to Am. prisoners and other services to patriot cause; steward of Pres. Washington's household, N.Y.C. and Phila., 1789-94; dubbed "Black Sam" by Philip Freneau, 1786. Died Oct. 10, 1795.

FRAZEE, John, sculptor; b. Rahway, N.J., July 18, 1790; s. Reuben Frazee; m. Jane Probasco, 1813; m. 2d, Lydia Place; 10 children. Opened marble shop with brother William, N.Y.C., 1818; maker tombstones, ch. memls.; executed portrait of John Wells (1st marble bust carved in this country by native Am.), 1824; a founder N.A.D., 1826; architect, supt. N.Y. Custom House, 1834-41; busts include those of John Jay, Daniel Webster, Andrew Jackson, Nathaniel Bowditch, De Witt Clinton, Marquis de Lafayette. Died Compton Mills, R.I., Feb. 24, 1852.

FRAZER, John Fries, scientist, univ. ofcl.; b. Phila., July 8, 1812; s. Robert and Elizabeth (Fries) F.; grad. U. Pa., 1830, M.A., 1833; LL.D., Harvard, 1857; m. Charlotte Cave, Sept. 1, 1838, 3 children including Persifor. Experimented (with Alexander Dallas Bache) on determination of daily variations of magnetic needle in Am., circa 1828; participated in geol. survey of Pa., 1836; prof. chemistry and natural philosophy U. Pa., 1844-72, vice provost, 1855-68; lectr. Franklin Inst., editor its journal, 1850-66; a founder Nat. Acad. Scis., 1863. Died Phila., Oct. 12, 1872.

FRAZER, Oliver, painter; b. Jessamine County, Ky., Feb. 4, 1808; s. Alexander and Nancy (Oliver) F.; studied painting with Mathew H. Jovett and Thomas Sully; m. Martha Mitchell, 1838. Studied, painted in Europe, 1834-35; studied portraiture in Eng., 1834-38; successful portrait painter, Lexington, Ky.; portraits include Henry Clay, Chief Justice George Robertson. Died Lexington, Feb. 9, 1864.

FRAZER, Persifor, army officer; b. Newton Twp., Pa., Aug. 9, 1736; s. John and Mary (Smith) F.; m. Mary Taylor, Oct. 2, 1766. Took over Sarum Iron Works, 1766; del. to Pa. Provincial Council, 1775; mem. Pa. Com. of Safety; apptd. capt. Pa. Militia, 1776, maj., 1776; lt. col. 5th Pa. Militia, 1776; treas. Chester County (Pa.), 1781; mem. Pa. Gen. Assembly, 1781-82; commd. brig. gen. Pa. Militia, 1782; commr. to Wyoming Valley, 1785; justice Pa. Ct. of Common Pleas, 1786-92; register of wills, Pa., 1786. Died Apr. 24, 1792.

FREDERIC, Harold, journalist; b. Utica, N.Y., Aug. 19, 1856: s. Henry De Motte Frederic. Reporter, Utica Observer, 1876; editor-in-chief Albany (N.Y.) Evening Jour., 1882; London corr. for N.Y. Times, 1884-98; went to Russia to investigate persecution of Jews, 1891. Author: The Lawton Girl, 1890; In the Valley, 1890; The New Exodus: A Study of Israel in Russia, 1892; The Copperhead, 1893; Marsena and Other Stories, 1894; The Damnataion of Theorn Ware, 1896 (his masterpiece); Gloria Mundi, 1898; The Market Place, 1899. Died Henley-on-the-Thames, Eng., Oct. 19, 1898.

FREEDLEY, John, congressman; b. Norristown, Pa., May 22, 1793; attended Norristown Acad.; studied law. Became asst. in his father's brickyard; admitted to bar, 1820, began practice of law, Norristown; asso. with marble and soapstone quarries; mem. U.S. Ho. of Reps. (Whig) from Pa., 30th-31st congresses, 1847-51. Died Norristown, Dec. 8. 1851.

FREEMAN, Bernardus, clergyman; b. Gilhuis, Netherlands, 1660; m. Margareta Van Schaik, Aug. 25, 1705. Tailor in Netherlands during early life; ordained to ministry Reformed Dutch Ch., 1700; became pastor Reformed Ch., Schenectady, N.Y.; apptd. by gov. N.Y. to preach among Indians, worked mainly among Mohawks; involved in eccles. quarrel in L.I., 1702-16; missionary in Queens County, also Monmouth County, N.J.; pastor emeritus, 1741. Author: De Spiegel der Self-Kennes, 1720, De Weegshale de Gerade Gods, 1721 (both printed by William Bradford); Verdeediging van D. Bernardus Freeman (printed by J. Peter Zenger), 1726. Died circa 1742.

FREEMAN, George, artist; b. Spring Hill, Conn., Apr. 21, 1789; probably 1 dau., Anna Mary. Painted miniatures around Hartford, Conn., circa 1810; left for Eng., 1813, had successful career, subjects included Queen Victoria and Prince Albert; returned to Am., circa 1840, worked in N.Y.C. and Phila.; exhibited at N.A.D., Am. Acad., Artists' Fund Soc., Boston Athenaeum. Died Hartford, Mar. 7, 1868.

FREEMAN, James, clergyman; b. Charlestown, Mass., Apr. 22, 1759; s. Constant and Lois (Cobb) F.; grad. Harvard, 1777, D.D. (hon.), 1811; m. Martha Curtis, July 17, 1783, 1 adopted child. Chosen reader by vestry of King's Chapel (1st Episcopal Ch. in New Eng.), Boston, 1782; ordained to ministry Protestant Episcopal Ch., 1787; converted to Unitarianism; his break with Episcopal Ch. and Trinitarianism resulted in establishment of King's Chapel as 1st Unitarian Ch. in Am., minister, 1787-1826; a founder Mass. Hist. Soc., recording sec., 1798-1812; mem. Mass. Constl. Conv., 1820-21; mem. Am. Acad. Arts and Scis. Author: Sermons on Particular Occasions, published 1812. Died Newton, Mass., Nov. 14, 1835.

FREEMAN, James Crawford, congressman, businessman b. Clinton (later Gray), Jones County, Ga., Apr. 1, 1820; attended common schs. Engaged in agriculture; moved to Griffin, Ga. 1865 continued as farmer, also became mcht. and banker; mem. U.S. Ho. of Reps. (Republican) from Ga., 43d Congress, 1873-75; moved to Atlanta, Ga. Died Atlanta, Sept. 3, 1885; buried Oakland Cemetery.

FREEMAN, James Edwards, genre painter, writer; b. Indian Island, New Brunswick, Can., 1808; s. Joshua and Eliza (Morgan) F.; attended N.A.D.; m. Horatia Augusta Latella, 1845. Elected to N.A.D., 1833; left for Italy, 1836; U.S. consul, Ancona, Italy, 1840-49; seldom exhibited in U.S.; largely unknown at time of death; better known pictures include The Beggars, The Savoyard Bay in Italy, An Indian Girl, The Crusader's Return, Flower Girl, Young Italy, Girl and Dog on the Campagna, The Bad Shoe. Author: Gatherings from an Artist's Portfolio, 1877; Gatherings from an Artist's Portfolio in Rome, 1883. Died Rome, Italy, Nov. 21, 1884.

FREEMAN, John D., congressman; b. Cooperstown, N.Y.; attended common schs.; studied law. Admitted to bar, began practice of law, Miss.; dist. atty.; moved to Natchez, Miss.; atty. gen. Miss., 1841-51; author 1st volume reports of decisions of Chancery Ct. of Miss., published 1844; mem. U.S. Ho. of Reps. (Unionist) from Miss., 32d Congress, 1851-53; atty. gen.; mem., chmn. Miss. Democratic Central Com.; moved to Canon City, Colo., 1882, resumed practice of law. Died Canon City, Jan. 17, 1886; buried Jackson, Miss.

FREEMAN, Jonathan, congressman; b. Mansfield, Conn., Mar. 21, 1745; attended public schs. Moved to Hanover, N.H., 1769, engaged in agriculture; town clk., justice of peace; exec. councilor, 1789-97; mem. N.H. Ho. of Reps., 1787-89, N.H. Senate, 1789-94; del. Constl. Conv., 1791; mem. N.H. Council; overseer Dartmouth, 1793-1808, treas., over 40 years; mem. U.S. Ho. of Reps. (Federalist) from N.H., 5th-6th congresses, 1797-1801. Died Hanover, Aug. 20, 1808; buried Hanover Center Cemetery.

FREEMAN, Nathaniel, jurist, physician; b. Dennis, Mass., Mar. 28. 1741: s. Edmund and Martha (Otis) F.; studied medicine under Dr. Cobb, Thompson, Conn.; studied law under James Otis, Sr. (his great-uncle), Sandwich, Mass., 1765; m. Tryphosa Colton, May 5, 1763; m. 2d, Elizabeth Gifford, Apr. 7, 1799; 20 children including Frederick, Nathaniel. Practiced medicine, Sandwich, 1765-1804; also practiced law; favored colonial cause during Am. Revolution; mem. Sandwich Com. of Correspondence; del. from Sandwich to Watertown Provincial Congress, 1775; apptd. lt. col., then col. 1st Barnstable (Mass.) Regt.; negotiated with Penobscot Indians, served in expdn. against British in R.I.; mem. Mass. Legislature, 1778-80; employed by Gen. George Washington on mission to West Point, 1779; resigned as brig. gen. from Mass. Militia, 1793; chief justice Mass. Ct. of Common Pleas; a founder Sandwich Acad. Author: Charge to the Grand Jury. . .at Barnstable, 1802. Died Sandwich, Sept. 20, 1827.

FREEMAN, Nathaniel, Jr., congressman; b. Sandwich, Mass., May 1, 1766; grad. Harvard, 1787; studied law. Admitted to bar, circa 1791, began practice of law, Sandwich and Cape Cod dist.; served as brigade maj. Mass. Militia, 16 years; justice of peace, 1793; mem. U.S. Ho. of Reps. from Mass., 4th-5th congresses, 1795-99. Died Sandwich, Aug. 22, 1800; buried Old Burial Ground.

FREEMAN, Thomas civil engr., explorer; b. Ireland. Came to Am., 1784; sureveyor for new capitol of U. S., 1794-96, surveyed entire No. portion of the dst.; started 1st topographic survey of Washington, D.C., resigned to accept. commn. as U. S. surveyor to chart boundary between U.S. and Spain; explored Red and Arkansas rivers, 1806; surveyed boundary between Tenn. and Ala., 1807; commd. U.S. surveyor pub. lands South of Tenn., 1811; 1st to accurately chart course of lower Red River. Died Huntsville, Ala., Nov. 8, 1821.

FRELINGHUYSEN, Frederick, army officer, senator; b. Somerville, N.J., Apr. 13, 1753; s. Rev. John and Dinah (Van Berg) F.; grad. Princeton (formerly Coll. of N.J.), 1770; m. Gertrude Schenck, children include Theodore; m. 2d,, Ann Yard. Admitted to N.J. bar, 1774; rep. to N.J. Provincial Congres from Somerset County, 1775-76; served as maj. Minute Men; capt. arty. N.J.Militia, then maj., col., aide-de-camp to Gen. Philemon Dickinson; commanded arty. corps at battles of Trenton, Springfield, Eizabethtown; participated in Batle of Monmouth Ct. House, 1778; mem. Continental Congress, 1778-83; mem. N.J. Legislative Council until 1782; mem. N.J. Gen. Assembly, 1784, 1800, 1804; mem. N.J. Conv. which ratified U.S. Constn., 1787; brig. gen. in campaign against Western Indians; 1790; served as maj. gen. N.J. Militia during Whiskey Rebellion, 1794; mem. U.S. Senate from N.J., 1793-96; trustee Princeton, 1802-04. Died Millstone, N.J., Apr. 13, 1804; buried Old Cemetery, Weston, N.J.

FRELINGHUYSEN, Frederick Theodore, senator, sec. of state; b. Millstone, N.J., Aug. 4, 1817; s. Frederick and Jane (Dumont) F.; grad. Rutgers U., 1836; m. Matilde Griswold, Jan. 25, 1842, 6 children. Admitted to N.J. bar, 1839; city atty. Newark, (N.J.), 1849; mem. Newark City Council; rep. from N.J. to Peace Conf., Washington, D.C., 1861; atty. Gen. N.J., 1861-66; mem. U.S. Snate from N.J., 1866-69, 71-77, during latter period was one of so-called "Stalwarts", desired impeachment of Andrew Johnson; declined appointment as U.S. minister to Gt. Britain, 1870 (preferred to have his children educated in Am.); sec. of state U.S., 1881-85; supported Am. comml. interests in Germany and France, closer ties with Latin Am. through reciprocal trade agreements, opened treaty negotiations with Korea; mem. electoral commn. which decided election in favor of Rutherford B. Hayes, 1877. Died Newark, May 20, 1885.

FRELINGHUYSEN, Theodore, senator, coll. pres.; b. Franklin Twp., N.J., Mar. 28, 1787; s. Gen. Frederick and Gertrude (Schenck) F.; grad. Princeton, 1804; m. Charlotte Mercer, 1809; m. 2d, Harriet Pumpelly, Oct. 14, 1857. Admitted to NJ.. bar, 1808; sgt. at law, 1817; atty. gen. N.J., 1817-27; mem. U.S. Senate from N.J., 1829-35, best known for stand against removing Cherokee Indians west of Mississippi River; pres. Am. Bd. Commrs. for Fgn. Missions; mayor Newark (N.J.), 1836-39; chancellor Univ. City of N.Y., 1838-50; pres. Am. Tract Soc., 1842-48; Whig Party candidate for vice pres. U.S., 1844; pres. Am. Bible Soc., 1846-62; v.p. Am. Sunday Sch. Union, 50 years; pres. Rutgers Coll., 1850-62. Died New Brunswick, N.J., Apr. 12, 1862.

FRELINGHUYSEN, Theodorus Jacobus, clergyman; b. Lingen, Germany, 1691; s. Johannes Hendricus Frielinghausen; m. Eva Terhune, 7 children including John. Ordained to ministry Reformed Dutch Ch., 1717; chaplain, Logumer Voorwerk, East Friesland, Netherlands, 1718; subrector, Enkhuizen, West Friesland, Netherlands, 1718; came to N.Y., 1720, missionary in N.J. Valley; involved in quarrel with Dominie Henricus Boel over teachings, 1720-25, defeated Boel with help of Peter Henry Dorsius and Bernardus Freeman; published many sermons; advocated establishment of coll. and theol. sem. Died N.J., circa 1748.

FREMONT, John Charles, army officer, explorer; senator, territorial gov.; b. Savannah, Ga., Jan. 21, 1813; s. Jean Charles and Ann Whiting (Pryor) F.; attended Charleston Coll., 1829-31 (expelled); m. Jessie Benton, Oct. 19, 1841; 1 dau., Elizabeth. Commd. 2d lt. Topog. Corps, U.S. Army explored Des Moines River; helped make surveys in Carolina mountains, also in Ga.; accompanied expdn. of J.N. Nicollet to plateau between Upper Mississippi and Missouri rivers; mapped parts of Ia. Territory, 1841; made 1st important exploration to Wind River, Chain of the Rockies (with Kit Carson as guide), 1842; published Report of the Exploring Expedition of the Rocky Mountains, 1843; explored West to Ore. and South to Santa Fe, N.M., 1843-44 (expdn. left early because his wife informed him that expdn. was to be recalled); made survey of Central Rockies, Gt. Salt Lake Region, also part of Sierra Nevada; participated prominently in conquest of Cal.; helped capture Los Angeles during Mexican War, 1846; apptd. civil gov. Cal., 1847; involved in Stockton-Kearny mil. quarrel, refused to obey orders, arrested for mutiny, court martialled, Wahington, 1847-48, found guilty of mutiny, disobedience, conduct prejudicial to order; penalty remitted by Pres. Polk; resigned from U.S. Army to lead an expdn. subsidized by pvt. interests in Cal. to locate railroad passes from Upper Rio Grande into Cal., largely unsuccessful, 1848-49; mem. U.S. Senate from Cal. (one of 1st 2 senators from Cal.) Sept. 9, 1850-Mar. 4, 1851; led expdn. in search of So. route for Pacific R.R., 1852-54; 1st Republican and Nat. Am. (Know Nothing) Party candidate for U.S. Pes., 1856; in quartz mining bus., Mariposa, Cal.; served as maj. gen. U.S.Army in charge of Dept. of West during Civil War, removed because of his ordering of the "confiscation of rebel property" (including slaves); comdr. Mountain Dept. in Western Va., 1862; Radical Republican nominee for U.S. Pres. (withdrew before elections), 1864; pres., promoter Memphis & El Paso R.R., circa 1865-73; lost fortune in railroad ventures, 1870; territorial gov. Ariz., 1878-83; restored to U.S. Army as maj. gen., 1890; called "Pathfinder". Died N.Y.C., July 13, 1890; buried Piermont on the Hudson, N.Y.

FRENCH, Aaron, mfr., inventor; b. Wadsworth, O., Mar. 23, 1823; s. Philo and Mary (McIntyre) F.; m. Euphrasia Terrill, 1848; m. 2d, Caroline B. Speer. Learned blacksmith trade, 1835; with Ohio Stage Co., Cleve., 2 years, Gayoso House, Memphis, Tenn., 1 year; lived in St. Louis, 1844-45; built wagons for Peter Young, Carlyle, Ill., 1845; became ill, returned to Ohio as semi-invalid, 1845-49; with Cleve. & Pitts. R.R., 1853; supt. blacksmithing Racine & Miss. R.R., Racine, Wis., until 1861; sheriff Racine County, 1861-62; partner (with Calvin Wells) in manufacture of 1st steel springs for railroad cars, Pitts., 1862; invented coiled and elliptic springs (revolutionized railroad industry); owned A. French Spring Co. (merged with Ry. Steel Spring Co.), Pitts.; left some money to Ga. Sch. Tech. Died Mar. 24, 1902.

FRENCH, Augustus C., gov. Ill.; b. N.H., Aug. 2, 1808. Lawyer, settled in Crawford County, Ill.; mem. 10th, 11th Ill. Gen. Assemblies; receiver Palestine Land Office; presdl. elector, 1844; elected gov. Ill. (Democrat), 1846, 48; apptd. bank commr.; prof. law McKendree Coll., Lebanon, Ill.; unsuccessful nominee for state supt. pub. instrn., 1858; del. from St. Clair County to Constl. Conv., 1862. Died Lebanon, Ill., Sept. 4, 1864.

FRENCH, Ezra Bartlett, congressman, govt. ofcl; b. Landaff, N.H., Sept. 23, 1810; studied law, Bath, also Plymouth, N.H. Admitted to bar, 1833, began practice of law, Portland and Woldoboro Me.; moved to Nobleboro (now Damariscotta), Me.; mem. Me. Ho. of Reps., 1838-40, Me. Senate, 1842-45; sec. of state Me., 1845-50; bank commr.; newspaper editor, 1856; an organizer Republican Party, 1856; mem. U.S. Ho. of Reps. (Rep.) from Me., 36th Congress, 1859-61; mem. Washington (D.C.) Peace Conv., 1861; 2d auditor of treasury (apptd. by Pres. Lincoln), 1861-80. Died Washington, D.C., Apr. 24, 1880; buried Hillside Cemetery, Damariscotta.

FRENCH, Jacob, composer; b. Stoughton, Mass., July 15, 1754; s. Jacob and Miriam (Downs) F.; m. Esther Neale, May 26, 1779. Taught singing schs., Providence, 1796-97. Published The New Am. Melody, 1789; The Psalmodist's Companion, 1793; The Harmony of Harmony, 1802. Best known for anthem The Heavenly Vision, tune Dormant. Possibly living in Northampton, Mass. at time of death.

FRENCH, John Robert, congressman, editor; b. Gilmanton, N.H., May 28, 1819; received academic edn., learned printer's trade. Publisher, asso. editor N.H. Statesman, Concord, 5 years; editor Eastern Journal, Biddeford, Me., 2 years; moved to Lake County, O., 1854; editor Telegraph, also Press.; editor Cleve. Morning Leader, 1856; mem. Ohio Ho. of Reps., 1858-59; apptd. to position in Treasury Dept., Washington, D.C., 1861; apptd. by Pres. Lincoln mem. bd. direct-tax commrs. for N.C., 1861; moved to Edenton, N.C., at close of Civil War; del. N.C. Constl. Conv., 1867; mem. U.S. Ho. of Reps. (Republican) from N.C., 40th Congress, July 6, 1868-69; sgt. at arms U.S. Senate, 1869-79; apptd. sec. Ute Commn., 1880; editor Boise City (Ida.) Sun, until 1890. Died Boise City, Oct. 2, 1890; buried Boise City Cemetery.

FRENCH, Lucy Virginia Smith, author; b. Md., Mar. 16, 1825; d. Mease W. and Elizabeth (Parker) Smith; grad. Washington (Pa.) Female Sem.; m. Col. Johns Hopkins French, Jan. 12, 1853, at least 1 dau., Mrs. P.D. Benham. A tchr., moved to Memphis, Tenn.; writer for Louisville (Ky.) Journal under name L'Inconnue; editor paper So. Ladies' Book, New Orleans, 1852; lived at "Forest Home," nr. McMinnville, Tenn., 1853-81; literary editor of newspapers and mags. including So. Homestead (Nashville, Tenn.), Rural Sun, Sunny South, Crusader, Ladies' Home (all Atlanta, Ga.), So. Literary Messenger (Richmond, Va.), 1856-79 Author: (poems) Wind Whispers, 1856; Istalixo, the Lady of Tula, Tragedy of Mexico before Hernando Cortes, 1856; Legends of the South, 1867; (poems) My Roses, 1872; (novel) Darlingtonia, 1879. Died McMinnville, Mar. 31, 1881; buried McMinnville.

FRENCH, Richard, congressman, lawyer; b. nr. Boonesborough, Ky., June 20, 1792; attended pvt. schs.; studied law. Admitted to bar, 1820, began practice of law, Winchester, Ky.; mem. Ky. Ho. of Reps., 1820-26; Democratic presdl. elector, 1828; judge circuit ct., 1829; mem. U.S. Ho. of Reps. (Democrat) from Ky., 24th, 28th, 30th congresses, 1835-37, 43-45, 47-49; unsuccessful Dem. candidate for gov. Ky., 1840. Died Covington, Ky., May 1, 1854; buried family burial ground nr. Mt. Sterling, Ky.

FRENCH, Thomas, colonist; b. Nether Heyford, Northamptonshire, Eng., Oct. 1639; s. Thomas and Sara French; m. Jane Atkins, 9 children. After being converted to Quakerism served several jail terms for his beliefs; signed (with William Penn and others) Concessions and Agreements for West Jersey (liberal charter for settlers of that colony), 1676; came to Burlington County, N.J., 1688; held large land grants in N.J. and Pa. Died Rancocas, Burlington County, 1699.

FRENCH, William Henry, army officer; b. Balt., Jan. 13, 1815; s. William French; grad. U.S. Mil. Acad., 1837. Commd. 1st lt. U.S. Amy, 1838, capt., 1848; served in Seminole and Mexican wars; commd. maj., arty. U.S. Amy, also brig. gen. U.S. volunteers, 1861; served in Army of Potomac; promoted maj. gen. U.S. Volunteers, 1862, served in battles of Fredericksburg, Chancellorsville and Harper's Ferry; commanded 3d Corps, 1863, mustered out of Volunteer Service, 1864, saw no further active duty in Civil War; commd. lt. col. U.S. Army, 1864, col., 1877, ret., 1880. Died Washington, D.C., May 20, 1881.

FRENEAU, Philip Morin, journalist, poet; b. N.Y.C., Jan. 2, 1752; s. Pierre and Agnes (Watson) F.; grad. Coll. of N.J. (now Princeton), 1771; m. Eleanor Forman, 1789. Served as privateer during Revolutionary War, captured and held in prison-brig Aurora (experience later described in poem The British Prison Ship, 1781); an editor, contbr. poetry to Freeman's Jour., Phila., 1781-84; master of brig bound for Jamaica, 1784, lived for several years in West Indies; editor N.Y. Daily Advertiser, 1790; translating clk. U.S. Dept. of State, 1791; editor Nat. Gazette (partisan Jefferson paper), 1791-93; later became editor N.Y. Timepiece; called Poet of Am. Revolution; earned reputation as 1st important Am. lyrical poet with such poems as The Indian Burying Ground, The Wild Honeysuckle and Eutaw Springs; other poems include A Poem on the Rising Glory of America, 1771, Voyage to Boston, 1774, General Gage's Confession, General Gage's Soliloquy, 1775, A Journey from Philadelphia to New York by Robert Slender, 1787, The Village Merchant, 1794. Lost in snow storm and died nr. Freshold, N.J., Dec. 19, 1832.

FRENZENY, Paul, artist; b. France; served with French Army in Mexico, before 1868; toured western U.S. with his partner, Jules Tavernier, making series of illustrations for Harper's Weekly, 1873-74; remained in San Francisco until 1878; illustrator for Harper's. Leslie's Weekly, N.Y.C., circa 1879-89.

FRERET, James, architect; b. New Orleans, Apr. 15, 1839; grad. Jesuit Coll., New Orleans; attended Ecole des Beaux Arts, Paris, France. Returned to U.S. to serve in Confederate Army during Civil War; began archtl. practice, New Orleans, after Civil War; designed La. Sugar Exchange, Produce Exchange, Masonic Temple, St. Patrick's Hall, several instnl. bldgs. for Jesuit order, all New Orleans; asso. with Claude Beroujon on main bldg. of Spring Hill (Ala.) Coll. Died Dec. 11, 1897.

FREY, Joseph Samuel Christian Frederick, clergyman; b. Mainstockheim, Franconia, Germany, Sept. 21, 1771; s. Samuel Levi Frey; m. Hannah Cohen, 1806. Jewish cantor, 1793; baptized Lutheran, 1798; agt. London Soc. for Promoting Christianity Among Jews; came to N.Y., 1816; ordained to ministry Presbyn. Ch., 1818; agt. Am. Soc. for Meliorating the condition of the Jews, 1822-26, 36-39; became Baptist clergyman, 1827; Author: The Converted Jew, 1809; Narrative of My Life, 1809; Hebrew Bible, 1811; Hebrew Grammar, 1813-23; Judah and Israel, 1837; Course of Lectures on the Scripture Types, 1841. Died Pontiac, Mich., June 5, 1850.

FRICK, Henry, congressman, journalist; b. Northumberland, Pa., Mar. 17, 1795; attended public schs. Apprenticed to printer, Phila.; served in War of 1812; moved to Milton, Pa., 1816; founder polit. journal Miltonian, asso. with paper over 20 years; mem. Pa. Ho. of Reps., 1828-31; mem. U.S. Ho. of Reps. (Whig) from Pa., 28th Congress, 1843-44. Died Washington, D.C., Mar. 1, 1844; buried Congressional Cemetery.

FRIDAY, Indian sub-chieftain; b. Kan.- Colo. plains, 1822. Lost by parents as a child, found by Thomas Fitzpatrick (head Rocky Mountain Fur Co.), named for day he was found; sent to sch., St. Louis; parents found out about his rescue and he was returned to tribe; mem. Arapaho delegation to Washington, D.C., 1851; leader of independent band which roamed North Colo.; one of few tribes which refused to attack whites on frontier during Civil War; joined No. Arapahoes under chief Medicine Man, 1869; lived on Shoshone Reservation nr. Wind River in Wyo., 1878; employed by U.S. Govt. as interpreter. Died Shoshone Reservation, May 13, 1881.

FRIEDENWALD, Aaron, physician; b. Balt., Dec. 20, 1836; s. Jonas and Merle (Bar) F.; M.D., U. Md., 1860; postgrad. in opthalmology and gen. medicine in Europe (Berlin, Paris, Prague, Vienna, London), 1860-62; m. Bertha Bamberger, 2 sons including Julius. Returned to Balt., 1862; imprisoned as suspected Confederate, 1 night, 1863; attending surgeon in temporary hosp. caring for both Union and Confederate wounded, during Civil War; started practice medicine, Balt., 1868; became prof. diseases of eye and ear Coll. Physicians and Surgeons, U. Md., 1873; co-founder Md. Opthal. Soc.; pres. Medico-Chirur. Faculty of Md., 1889-90; an organizer Assn. Am. Med. Colls. Died Aug. 26, 1902.

FRIES, Francis, mfr., mayor; b. Wachovia (later Salem, now part of Winston-Salem), N.C., Oct. 17, 1812; s. John Christian and Elizabeth (Nissen) F.; m. Lizetta Volger, 1838. 7 children. Apptd. clk. ct., also master in equity, N.C.; agt. Salem Mfg. Co.; with brother built, operated cotton factory, 1848-80; mem. N.C. Legislature, 1857; mayor Salem; a builder, dir. N.C.R.R., until 1863. Died Aug. 1, 1863.

FRIES, George, congressman, physician; b. Pa., 1799; attended common schs.; studied medicine. Began practice of medicine, Hanoverton, O., 1833; mem. U.S. Ho. of Reps. (Democrat) from Ohio, 29th-30th congresses, 1845-49; moved to Cincinnati, resumed practice of medicine; treas. Hamilton County, 1860-62. Died Cincinnati, Nov. 13, 1866; buried Catholic Cemetery.

FRIES, John, insurgent; b. Montgomery County, Pa., 1750; s. Simon Fries; m. Margaret Brunner, 1770. Cooper's apprentice, itinerant auctioneer in early life; moved to Bucks County, Pa., 1775; capt. of a co. Pa. Militia during Am. Revolution, also Whiskey Insurrection; largely responsible for Pa. opposition to direct fed. property tax levied in anticipation of war with France, 1798, promised to raise regt. of 700 men to oppose collection of tax; tried for treason, twice sentenced to death, pardoned by Pres. John Adams (against advice of his cabinet), 1799. Died Bucks County, Feb. 1818.

FRIETCHIE, Barbara (also spelled Fritchie), legendary Civil War figure; b. circa 1776; resident of Frederick, Md., said to have defied Confederate troops under Stonewall Jackson by flying union flag from her dormer window, Sept. 1862; visited by Col. Jesse Reno a few days before his death, Sept. 1862, declined to give him flag she had flown, but gave him home-made bunting flag which later covered his casket; eulogized in play by Clyde Fitch, 1899, also in poem Barbara Frietchie in J.G. Whittier's In War Time and Other Poems, 1864 (Whittier later stated that a Mrs. Mary A. Quantrell was actually the original heroine).

FRIEZE, Henry Simmons, educator, acting univ. pres.; b. Boston, Sept. 15, 1817; s. Jacob and Betsey (Slade) F.; grad. Brown U., 1841, LL.D. (hon.), 1882; LL.D. (hon.), Chgo. U., 1870, U. Mich., 1885; m. Anna Roffee, 1847. Founded Univ. Grammar Sch., Providence, R.I., 1844; prof. Latin, U. Mich., 1854-89, acting pres., 1869-71, 80-82, introduced diploma system, admitted women, 1870, secured a professorship of msic, led in establishment Sch. of Music. Author: Ancient and Modern Education, 1867; Life and Works of Henry Philip Tappan, 1867; Notes on the Tenth and Twelfth Books on Quintilian, 1867; Giovanni Dupre, the Story of a Florentine Sculptor, 1886. Editor: Virgil's Aeneid (sch. edit.), 1860. Died Ann Arbor, Mich., Dec. 7, 1889.

FRISBIE, Levi, educator; b. Ipswich, Mass., Sept. 15, 1783; s. Levi and Mehitable (Hale) F.; grad. Harvard, 1802; m. Catherine Mellen, Sept. 10, 1815. Able to perform duties as educator, despite eye affliction; tutor Latin, Harvard, 1805-11; prof. Latin, 1811-17, Alford prof. of natural religion, moral philosophy civil polity, 1817-22; mem. Am. Acad. Arts and Scis.; his main precept was prins. of ethics should be derived from Bible; pointed out that great literature can, but rarely does serve morality. Author: Inaugural Address, 1817; Adam Smith's Theory of Moral Sentiments; The Right and Duty of Government To Provide for the Support of Religion by Law. Died Cambridge, Mass., July 9, 1822.

FRITSCHEL, Conrad Sigmund, clergyman; b. Nürnberg, Germany, Dec. 2, 1833; s. Martin Heinrich and Katharina (Kässler) F.; grad. Mission Inst., Neuendettelsan-Bavaria, 1854; D.D., Muhlenberg Coll., Allentown, Pa., 1879; m. Margarethe Prottengeier, Jan. 20, 1856, 11 children including John, Max. Ordained to ministry Lutheran Ch., Hamburg, Germany, 1854; moved to Dubuque, Ia., 1854; became mem. Evang. Luth. Synod of Ia., 1854; missionary Platteville (Wis.) area, 1854-56; pastor, Detroit; prof. Wartburg Sem. of Ia. Synod, 1858-1900, travelled to Germany and Russia to collect money for sem., 1860; del. Gen. Council Evang. Luth. Ch. in N.Am. Died Dubuque, Apr. 26, 1900; buried Mendota, Ill.

FRITSCHEL, Gottfried Leonhard Wilhelm, clergyman; b. Nurnberg, Germany, Dec. 19, 1836; s. Martin Heinrich and Katharina (Kassler) F.; grad. U. Erlangen (Germany), 1856; D.D. (hon.), Muhlenberg Coll., Allentown, Pa., 1879; m. Elise Eleanore Koberle, Aug. 29, 1858, 10 children including Prof. George J. Came to U.S., 1857; ordained to ministry Lutheran Ch., Dubuque, Ia., 1857, became prof. theology Wartburg Sem. of Ia. Synod (sem. moved to Sebald, Ia. to cut expenses, 1857); learned English, Norwegian and Swedish langs.; Author: Passionsbetrachtungen, 1868, 2d edit., 1876; Geschichte der Christlichen Missionen unter den Indianern Nordamerikas in 17 und 18 Jahrhundert, published Nurnberg, 1870; Theophilus, 1889. Died Mendota, Ill., July 13, 1889.

FROBISHER, Sir Martin, navigator; b. Doncaster, Eng., circa 1536. Became acquainted with Sir Humphrey Gilbert; attempted to discover N.W. Passage; made 3 voyages to New World (1576, 77, 78) under patronage of Queen Elizabeth and various nobles; discovered bay that is named for him on 1st voyage; mem. Sir Francis Drake's expdn. to W.I., 1585; served in sea battle against Spanish Armada, 1588; created knight for services against Spain, 1588. Died Plymouth, Eng., Nov. 7, 1594.

FROMENTIN, Eligius, senator; b. France. Ordained priest Roman Catholic Ch.; minister, Etampes, France; fled during Reign of Terror, came to U.S., settled in Pa.; moved to Md., taught sch. and studied law; admitted to bar, began practice of law, New Orleans; clk. Orleans Territory Ho. of Reps., 1807-11; sec. La. Constl. Conv., 1812; sec. La. Senate, 1812-13; mem. U.S. Senate from La., 1813-19; apptd. judge New Orleans Criminal Ct., 1821. Died New Orleans, Oct. 6, 1822.

FRONTENAC, Louis de Buade, colonial gov.; b. Paris, France, 1620; married. Became col. French Army, at age of 23, brig. gen. at age 26, served in Holland, Italy, Germany, Crete; gov. Can., 1672-82, 89-98; during 1st term as gov., built forts to control Iroquois Indians, sent La Salle to explore Mississippi River; came into conflict with many leaders when he tried to exercise more power than permitted by his office; tried to overrule missionaries' objections to liquor trade (especially with Indians); quarreled with Gov. Perrot of Montreal, finally was removed; returned to office after French had suffered disastrous defeats; sent 3 armies into N.Y., N.H. and Me., defeated the British and Iroquois Indians, also English fleet under Adm. Phipps, razed strongholds in Acadia, captured St. John's, Newfoundland; honored by French Govt. for his last successful drive against Mohawk Indians, 1696. Died Quebec, Can., 1698.

FROST, George, Continental congressman; b. Newcastle, N.H., Apr. 26, 1720. Became businessman, Kittery Point, nr. Portsmouth; sea capt., 20 years; returned to Newcastle, 1760, moved to Durham, N.H., 1770; judge Stafford County Ct. of Common Pleas, 1773-91, chief justice several years; mem. Continental Congress from N.H., 1777-79; exec. councilor, 1781-84. Died Durham, June 21, 1796; buried Pine Hill Cemetery, Dover, N.H.

FROST, Joel, congressman; b. Westchester County, N.Y.; attended public schs. Mem. N.Y. State Assembly, 1806-08; surrogate Putnam County, 1812-13, 15-19, 21-22; mem. N.Y. State Constl. Conv., 1821; moved to Schenectady; mem. U.S. Ho. of Reps. from N.Y., 18th Congress, 1823-25.

FROST, Rufus Smith, congressman, businessman; b. Marlboro, N.H., July 18, 1826; attended public schs. Became a mcht.; mayor Chelsea (Mass.), 1867-68; mem. Mass. Senate, 1871-72, Mass. Gov.'s Council, 1873-74; mem. U.S. Ho. of Reps. (Republican, contested election) from Mass., 44th Congress, 1875-July 28, 1876; pres. Nat. Assn. Woolen Mfrs., 1877-84, Boston Bd. of Trade, 1878-80; pres. New Eng. Conservatory of Music; a founder New Eng. Law and Order League, Boston Art Club; del. Rep. Nat. Conv., Mpls., 1892. Died Chgo., Mar. 6, 1894; buried Woodlawn Cemetery, Chelsea.

FROTHINGHAM, James, artist; b. Charlestown, Mass., 1786; at least 1 dau., Sara C. Began career as portrait painter, Boston; moved to N.Y.C., 1826; lived in Bklyn., after 1843; best known for copies of portraits by Gilbert Stuart; exhibited at Pa. Acad., Boston Athenaeum N.A.D., Am. Acad., Apollo Assn.; mem. N.A.D. Died Bklyn., Jan. 6, 1864.

FROTHINGHAM, Nathaniel Langdon, clergyman; b. Boston, July 23, 1793; s. Ebenezer and Joanna (Langdon) F.; grad. Harvard, 1811; m. Ann Gorham Brooks, 1818, 1 son. Instr. rhetoric Harvard, 1812; ordained to ministry Unitarian Ch.; pastor 1st Ch. of Boston, 1815-50, pastor emeritus, 1850; Author: Deism or Christianity, 1845; Sermons in the Order of a Twelve-month, 1852; Metrical Pieces, Translated and Original, 1855; Metrical Pieces, Part Two, 1870; also hymns, including: O God, Whose Presence Glows in All (most famous), We Meditate the Day, O Lord of Life and Truth and Grace. Died Boston, Apr. 4, 1870.

FROTHINGHAM, Octavius Brooks, clergyman; b. Boston, Nov. 26, 1822; s. Nathaniel Langdon and Ann (Brooks) F.; grad. Harvard, 1843, Harvard Divinity Sch., 1846; m. Caroline E. Curtis, Mar. 23, 1847. Ordained to ministry Congregational Ch., 1847; became pastor North Ch., Salem, Mass., 1847; pastor Unitarian Soc., Jersey City, N.J., 1855; organized 3d Congl. Unitarian Soc. (later Independent Liberal Ch.) to further his influence, N.Y.C., 1859; a founder Free Religious Assn., 1867, pres., 1867-78. Author: The Religion of Humanity, 1872; Life of Theodore Parker, 1874; Knowledge and Faith, 1876; A History of Transcendentalism in New England, 1876; Visions of the Future, 1879; Boston Unitarianism, 1890) Recollections and Impressions 1822-90, 1891; also hymn "The Lord of Hosts, Whose Guiding Hand." Died Boston, Nov. 27, 1895.

FROTHINGHAM, Richard, journalist, historian; b. Charlestown, Mass., Jan. 31, 1812; s. Richard and Mary (Thompson) F.; m. Vrylena Blanchard, Dec. 18, 1833, 6 children. Treas., Middlesex Canal Co., 1834-60; propr. Boston Post, mng. editor, 1852-65; del. Nat. Democratic Conv., 1852, 76; mem. Mass. Legislature, 1840, 42, 44, 50-51; del. Mass. Constl. Conv., 1853; mayor Charlestown, 1851-53; mem. Mass. Hist. Soc., treas., 1847-77; layman active in Universalist Ch.; trustee, treas. Tufts Coll., 8 years. Author: The History of Charlestown, Massachusetts, 1845-49; History of the Siege of Boston, 1849; The Command in the Battle of Bunker Hill, 1850; Life and Times of Joseph Warren, 1865; Tribute to Thomas Starr King, 1865; The Rise of the Republic, 1872; The Centennial: Battle of Bunker Hill. Died Charlestown, Jan. 29, 1880.

FRY, Birkett Davenport, lawyer, army officer, cotton mfr.; b. Kanawha County, Va., June 24, 1822; s. Thornton and Eliza (Thompson) F.; attended Va. Mil. Inst., Washington (Pa.) Coll., U.S. Mil. Acad., 2 years; m. Martha Micou, 1853. Admitted to Va. bar, 1846; commd. 1st lt. inf. U.S. Army during Mexican War, 1847; moved to Cal., 1849; commd. brig. gen. during William Walker's expdn. to Nicaragua while attempting to create a state ruled by Walker with gradual introduction of slavery, 1855; had returned to Cal. to recruit more troops when Walker's regime fell, 1857; mgr. cotton mill, Tallasee, Ala., 1859; commd. col. 13th Ala. Inf. Regt., 1861; commd. brig. gen. Army of Va., 1864; pres. Marshall Mfg. Co., 1886-91. Died Jan. 21, 1891.

FRY, Jacob, Jr., congressman, mcht.; b. Trappe, Pa., June 10, 1802; attended public schs. Taught sch,. Trappe; clk. of cts. Montgomery County, 1830-33; mem. U.S. Ho. of Reps. (Democrat) from Pa., 24th-25th congresses, 1835-39; entered merc. business, Trappe; mem. Pa. Ho. of Reps., 1853-54; auditor gen. Pa., 1857-60. Died Trappe, Nov. 28, 1866; buried Lutheran Cemetery.

FRY, James Barnet, army officer, writer; b. Carrollton, Ill., Feb. 22, 1827; s. Jacob and Eily (Turney) F.; grad. U.S.Mil. Acad., 1847. Served in Meixcan War; apptd. asst. adj. gen. U.S. Army, brevetted capt., 1861; chief of staff to U.S.Army under McDowell 1861; commd. lt. col., 1862; chief of staff Gen. Buell's Army of Ohio, 1 year; 1st provost marshall gen. U.S., 1863, organized Bur. of Provost Marshall Gen.; served as brig gen., 1864-66; brevetted maj. gen., 1868, col., brig. gen., 1865; commd. col., 1875; adj. gen. of mil. divs. Pacific, South, Atlantic. Author: Operations of the Army Under Buell from June 10th to October 30th, 1862; Sketch of the Adjutant-General's Department United States Army, from 1775 to 1875, published 1875; The History and Log of Effect of Brevets in the Armies of Great Britain and the United States, 1877; The Buell Commission, 1884; McDowell and Tyler in the Campaign of Bull Run, 1884. Contbr. to Battles and Leaders of the Civil War; also articles to North Am. Review. Died Newport, R.I., July 11, 1894; buried Phila.

FRY, Joseph, Jr., congressman; b. Northampton (now Lehigh) County, Pa., Aug. 4, 1781; attended rural schs. Engaged in business, Fryburg (later Coopersburg), Pa.; mem. Pa. Ho. of Reps., 1816-17, Pa. Senate, 1817-21; served to col. Pa. Militia; mem. U.S. Ho. of Reps. (Democrat) from Pa., 20th-21st congresses, 1827-31; mem. Pa. Constl. Conv., 1837, 38. Died Allentown, Pa., Aug. 15, 1860; buried Union Cemetery.

FRY, Joshua, surveyor, educator; b. Crewkerne, Eng., circa 1700; s. Joseph Fry; ed. Wadham Coll., Oxford (Eng.) U., 1718; m. Mary (Micou) Hill, circa 1720. Came to Va., before 1720; prof. mathematics and natural philosophy Coll. William and Mary, 1731; 1st presiding justice Albemarle Cunty; justice Ct. Chancery; county surveyor; mem. Ho. of Burgesses from Abemarle County until death; county lt., 1745; mapmaker (with Peter Jefferson) Map of the Inhabited Parts of Virginia; surveyor (with P. Jefferson) ran part of Va.-Carolina boundary, 1749; commr. to the Six Nations, 1752, aided in drawing up Treaty of Logstown; col., comdr.-in-chief of a regt. Va. Militia, started for Ohio in expdn. against French, 1754, died enroute, succeeded by George Washington. Died Ft. Cumberland, Md., May 31, 1754.

FRY, Richard, paper mfr.; flourished 1731-41; m. Martha Brook Contracted by Samuel Waldo to come from London, Eng. to Boston, Mass. as paper mfr., 1731; sold stationers' supplies, 1731-34, printed 1,200 copies of Stephen Duck's poems; leased paper mill on Stroudwater River nr. Portland, Mass., 1734, paper-making machinery seized for due rent, 1736, appealed case for 5 years before release from jail in Boston; wrote treatise on currency while in jail, 1739. Died before Aug., 1745.

FRY, William Henry, composer, journalist; b. Phila., Aug. 10, 1815; s. William and Ann (Flesson) F.; attended Mt. St. Mary's Coll., Emmettsburg, Md.; studied under Leopold Meignen. Composed 1st overture at age 14; received gold medal for one of his overtures performed by Phila. Philharmonic Soc., 1835; presented 1st opera Lenora, (1st publically performed grand opera written by native Am., 1845, complete work never published; composer 4 symphonies, The Breaking Heart; A Day in the Country; Santa Claus, or the Christmas Smphony, Childe Harold; became editor Phila. Pub. Ledger, 1844; Paris (France) and London (Eng.) corr. N.Y. Tribune, also Phila. Ledger, 1846-52; editorial writer, music editor N.Y. Tribune, 1852. Died Santa Cruz, West Indies, Dec. 21, 1864.

FRYE, Joseph, army officer; b. Andover, Mass., Mar. 19, 1712; s. Sgt. John and Tabitha (Farmam) F.; m. Mehitable Poor, Mar. 31, 1733. Ensign in Hale's 5th Mass. Regt., 1744-45, served in capture of Louisburg; capt. during King George's War, 1747-49; commd. maj., 1755; commanding officer Ft. Cumberland, Acadia (now Nova Scotia), Can., 1759-60; moved to new settlement, Fryeburg, Mass. Militia, 1775, brig. gen. Continental Army, favored separation of Me. from Mass., del. to conv. which met to consider the measure, 1786. Died July 25, 1794.

FULLER, Andrew S., horticulturist, editor; b. Utica, N.Y., Aug. 3, 1828; m. Jennie Clippens, 1851. Moved to Bklyn., 1857, began culture of small fruits; contbr. articles on horticulture to Life. Illustrated, New York Tribune; editor Woodward's Record of Horticulture, 1866-67; agrl. editor N.Y. Weekly Sun, 1868-94; asso. editor Moore's Rural New Yorker, 1871, became part owner, editor-in-chief, 1876; a founder N.J. Hort. Soc., 1875. Author: Practical Forestry, 1884; The Nut Culturalist, 1896. Died May 4, 1896.

FULLER, George, painter; b. Deerfield, Mass., Jan. 17, 1822; s. Aaron and Fanny (Negus) F.; ed. Deerfield Acad.; studied painting in studio of Henry Kirke Brown, 1841-42; attended N.A.D.; m. Agnes Higginson, 1861. Participated in surveying expdn. to Ill.; elected asso. N.A.D., 1857, exhibited, 1879; exhibited in Boston, 1875-76; works include Winifred Dysart (considered his masterpiece), completed 1881; And She Was a Witch, 1879; The Quadroon, 1880; Maidenhood, 1881; Lutti, 1882; Priscilla Fauntleroy, 1882; The Romany Girl; Aerthusa (last picture), 1884. Died Brookline, Mass., Mar. 21, 1884.

FULLER, Henry Mills, congressman, lawyer; b. Bethany, Pa., Jan. 3, 1820; grad. Princeton, 1839; studied law. Admitted to bar, 1842, began practice of law, Wilkes-Barre, Pa.; mem. Pa. Ho. of Reps., 1848-49; mem. U.S. Ho. of Reps. (Whig) from Pa., 32d, 34th congresses, 1851-53, 55-57. Died Phila., Dec. 26, 1860; buried Hollenback Cemetery, Wilkes-Barre.

FULLER, Hiram (pseudonym: Belle Brittan), journalist; b. Halifax, Mass., Sept. 6, 1814; s. Thomas and Sally (Sturtevant) F.; m. Emilie Delaplaine, Oct. 1844, 1 adopted child, Prin. of a small sch., Providence, R.I., 1836; financed The Rhode Island Book, 1841-43; helped conduct N. Y. Mirror; owner Evening Mirror, N.Y.C.; embroiled with Edgar Allan Poe, reprinted defamatory attack on him by Thomas Dunn (Poe won damage suit of $225); started weekly newspaper Cosmopolitan, London, Eng.; supported So. cause during Civil War. Author: The Groton Letters, 1845; Belle Brittan on a Tour, 1845; Sparks from a Locomotive; or Life and Liberty in Europe, by Belle Brittan, 1859; Grand Transformation Scenes in the United States, 1875. Died Paris, France, Nov. 19, 1880.

FULLER, John Wallace, army officer; b. Cambridge, Eng., July 28, 1827; s. Benjamin Fuller; m. Anna Rathbun, 1851. Came to U.S., 1833; city treas. Utica, N.Y., 1852-54; established publishing, bookselling bus., Toledo, O., 1858; commd. col. 27th Ohio Inf., 1861; commanded Ohio Brigade or Fuller's Brigade at Battle of Iuka, 1862; defeated Gen. Nathan Bedford Forrest's cavalry at Parker's Cross Roads, 1862; captured Decatur, Ala., 1864; participated in Atlanta Campaign, including Gen. Sherman's march to the sea; commd. brig. gen. U. S. Volunteers, 1864; sr. mem. Fuller, Childs & Co., whole-sale boot and shoe mchts., 1865; collector of customs Port of Toledo, 1874-81. Died Toledo, Mar. 12, 1891.

FULLER, Levi Knight, inventor, mfr., gov. Vt.; b. Westmoreland, N.H., Feb. 24, 1841; so. Washington and Lucinda (Constantine) F.; m. Abby Estey, May 8, 1865. Self-taught in practical science, telegraphy, and electricity; mech. engr. J. Estey & Co., 1860, v.p., 1866-68; holder about 50 patents on inventions, most of which were appliances for organs; mem. Vt. Senate, 1880-82; lt. gov. Vt., 1886; gov. Vt. (Republican), 1892-94; trustee Shaw U.; adoption of internat. pitch for mus. instruments due largely to his efforts; mem. A.A.A.S., Soc. Am. Engrs. Died Brattleboro, Vt., Oct. 10, 1896.

FULLER, Philo Case, congressman, businessman; b. nr. Marlboro, Mass., Aug. 14, 1787; attended common schs.; studied law. Admitted to bar, 1813; served in War of 1812; pvt. sec. to Gen. Wadsworth, Geneseo, N.Y.; practiced law, Albany, N.Y.; mem. N.Y. State Assembly, 1829-30, N.Y. Senate, 1831-32; mem. U.S. Ho. of Reps. (Whig) from N.Y., 23d-24th congresses, 1833-Sept. 2, 1836; moved to Adrian, Mich., 1836, engaged in banking; pres. Erie & Kalamazoo R.R. Co.; speaker Mich. Assembly, 1841; unsuccessful Whig candidate for gov. Mich., 1841; returned to Geneseo; apptd. 2d asst. postmaster gen., 1841; comptroller State of N.Y., 1850-51. Died nr. Geneva, N.Y., Aug. 16, 1855; buried Temple Hill Cemetery, Geneseo.

FULLER, Richard, clergyman; b. Beaufort, S.C.; Apr. 22, 1804; s. Thomas and Elizabeth (Middleton) F.; grad. Harvard, 1824, D.D. (hon.), 1853; D.D. (hon.), Columbia, U., Washington, D.C., 1844; m. Charlotte Bull, Aug. 1831. Amitted to S.C. bar, 1825; converted to Baptist religion, entered ministry, 1831; pastor Bapt. ch., Beaufort, S.C., 1832-47; contbd. articles advocating prohibition to Charleston Courier, also tried to justify slavery by scripture; pastor 7th Bapt. Ch., Balt., 1847-71, Eutaw Place Ch., Balt., 1871-76; pres. So. Bapt. Conv., several times. Author: Our Duty to the African Race (address delivered before Am. Colonization Soc., Washington, D.C.) 1851; Sermons; Letters; Argument on Baptist and Close Communion, 1849; Psalmist. Died Balt., Oct. 20, 1876.

FULLER, Sarah Margaret, journalist, social reformer; b. Cambridge, Mass., May 23, 1810; d. Timothy and Margaret (Crane) Fuller; ed. by father; m. Angelo Ossoli; 1 son, Angelino. Educationally precocious; generally considered that enforced edn. impaired her health; in early youth formed lasting associations with Oliver Wendell Holmes, William Henry Channing, James Freeman Clarke, Richard Henry Dana, Amos Bronson Alcott; organized club Boston Conservationalists, including some of most intelligent women in area, 1839-44; main interest lay in potentialities of women in modern society; editor (with Ralph Waldo Emerson and George Ripley) The Dial (Transcendentalist organ), 1840-44; mem. staff N.Y. Tribune, 1844-46, won reputation as Am. critic; assisted in orgn. of hosps. during Roman Revolution (became involved through Assn. with Giuseppe Mazzini). Author: Conversations with Goethe (1st published work), 1839; Summer on the Lakes, 1843; Women in the Nineteenth Century, 1845. Died in shipwreck off Fire Island, N.Y., July 19, 1850.

FULLER, Thomas Charles, jurist; b. Fayetteville, N.C., Feb. 27, 1832; s. Thomas and Catherine (Raboteau) F.; attended U. N.C., 1849-52; studied law under Judge Richmond M. Pearson, 1855; m. Caroline Douglas Whitehead, Nov. 5, 1857. Admitted to N.C. bar, began practice law, Fayetteville, 1856; a Union Whig, opposed secession, but joined 1st N.C. Regt. (upon Abraham Lincoln's call for arms), served in Battle of Bethel (Va.); commd. 1st lt. N.C. battery light inf., Confederate Army; mem. Confederate Congress from N.C., 1863-65; elected to U.S. Ho. of Reps. from N.C., 39th Congress, not seated; moved to Raleigh, N.C., 1873; U.S. justice Ct. of Pvt. Land Claims (to settle titles in area acquired from Mexico), 1891-1901. Died Raleigh, Oct. 20, 1901.

FULLER, Thomas James Duncan, congressman, lawyer; b. Hardwick, Vt., Mar. 17, 1808; attended common schs.; studied law. Admitted to bar, began practice of law, Calais, Me.; mem. U.S. Ho. of Reps. (Democrat) from Me., 31st-34th congresses, 1849-57; 2d auditor of treasury (apptd. by Pres. Buchanan), 1857-61; practiced law before U.S. Supreme Ct. and Ct. of Claims, Washington, D.C. Died while visiting his son, nr. Upperville, Va., Feb. 13, 1876; buried Oak Hill Cemetery, Washington.

FULLER, Timothy, congressman; b. Chilmark, Mass., July 11, 1778; grad. Harvard, 1801; studied law. Tchr., Leicester Acad.; admitted to bar, began practice of law, Boston, 1804; mem. Mass. Senate, 1813-17; mem. U.S. Ho. of Reps. (Democrat) from Mass., 15th-18th congresses, 1817-25; mem. Mass. Ho. of Reps., 1825-28, 31; state councilor, 1828. Died Groton, Mass., Oct. 1, 1835; buried Mt. Auburn Cemetery, Cambridge, Mass.

FULLER, William Kendall, congressman, lawyer; b. Schenectady, N.Y., Nov. 24, 1792; grad. Union Coll., 1810; studied law. Admitted to bar, 1814, began practice of law, Schenectady; adj. gen. N.Y., 1823; dist. atty. Madison County, 1821-29; mem. N.Y. State Assembly, 1829-30; mem. U.S. Ho. of Reps. (Democrat) from N.Y., 23d-24th congresses, 1833-37. Died Schenectady, Nov. 11, 1883; buried Vale Cemetery.

FULLERTON, David, congressman, businessman; b. Cumberland Valley, nr. Greencastle, Pa., Oct. 4, 1772; attended public schs. Served as maj. in War of 1812; became mcht. and banker, Greencastle; mem. U.S. Ho. of Reps. from Pa., 16th Congress, 1819-May 15, 1820 (resigned); mem. Pa. Senate, 1827-39. Died Greencastle, Feb. 1, 1843; buried Cedar Hill Cemetery.

FULTON, Andrew Steele, congressman, jurist; b. nr. Waynesboro, Va., Sept. 29, 1800; attended Hampden-Sydney Coll.; studied law, Staunton, Va. Admitted to bar, 1825, began practice of law, Abingdon, Va., 1826; moved to Wytheville, 1828; mem. Va. Ho. of Dels., 1840, 45; pros. atty. Wythe County (Va.); mem. U.S. Ho. of Reps. (Whig) from Va., 30th Congress, 1847-49; judge 15th Jud. Circuit Pa., 1852-69. Died nr. Austinville, Va., Nov. 22, 1884; buried family cemetery on New River, nr. Austinville.

FULTON, John Hall, congressman, b. Augusta County, Va., grad. Hampden-Sydney Coll., studied law. Admitted to bar, began practice of law, Abingdon, Va., mem. Va. Ho. of Dels., 1823-24, Va. Senate, 1829-31, mem. U.S. Ho. of Reps. (Whig) from Va., 23d Congress, 1833-35. Died Abingdon, Jan. 28, 1836; buried Sinking Spring Cemetery.

FULTON, Robert, civil engr., inventor, artist; b. Little Britain, Pa., Nov. 14, 1765; s. Robert and Mary (Smith) F.; m. Harriet Livingston, Jan. 8, 1808; 4 children. Devised successful manually operated mechanism to propel a boat by paddle wheels, 1779; engaged in a variety of engring. ventures connected with devel. of inland waterways; went to Eng.; worked and lived in Europe, 1786-1806; secured British patent for "double inclined plane" for raising and lowering canal boats; patented machine for sawing marble for which he received medal Soc. for Encouragment of Arts, Commerce and Mfg.; invented dredging machine or power shovel for cutting canal channels; published A Treatise on the Improvement of Canal Navigation, 1796; proposed constrn. of cast iron aqueducts to Bd. Agr. Gt. Britain, 1796, ultimately used; experimented unsuccessfully with self-propelling torpedo; painted what is "L'Incendie de Moscow (thought to be 1st panorama), Paris, France; built diving boat Nautilus, 1800-01, to prove its worth he was to destroy Brit. shipping, but was unsuccessful in sinking ships, later attempted to prove worth to Brit., failed to sink French ships (torpedo failure), 1801-03; entered legal agreement with Robert Livingston (minster to France), to construct steamboat for purpose of navigating Hudson River between Albany (N.Y.) and N.Y.C., 1802; successful in experiments in France, 1803; returned to U.S., 1806; Steamboat Clermont began voyage up Hudson River, Aug. 17, 1807; engaged in establishment, mgmt. steamboat lines, constrn., 1807-15; constructed steam war vessell authorized by U.S. Congress, 1814; dir. company which produced a commercially successful steamboat; ensured introduction, continued operation of steamboats. Died N.Y.C., Feb. 24, 1815; buried Old Trinity Churchyard, N.Y.C.

FULTON, William, architect; b. circa 1802. Credited with design and constrn. of Taylor Blow Bldg., St. Louis, (built 1848), also Robert Campbell residence, James H. Lucas house (built 1849). Died 1868.

FULTON, William Savin, senator; b. Cecil County, Md., June 2, 1795; grad. Balt. Coll., 1813; studied law. Served with volunteer co. during War of 1812; moved to Tenn. after war; admitted to bar, 1817, began practice of law, Gallatin, Tenn.; mil. sec. to Gen. Jackson in Fla. campaign, 1818; moved to Florence, Ala., 1820; elected judge county ct., 1822; apptd. by Pres. Jackson sec. of Ark. Territory, 1829; apptd. gov. Ark., 1835-36; mem. U.S. Senate (Democrat) from Ark., Sept. 18, 1836-44. Died Little Rock, Ark., Aug. 15, 1844; buried Mt. Holly Cemetery.

FURBER, Pierce T., architect. Practiced as architect, St. Louis; rep. of Boston firm Peabody & Stearns, St. Louis, supervised erection of Unitarian Ch. of the Messiah, 1881, Crow Meml. Art Gallery, 1881, St. Louis Club; mem. A.I.A. Died 1893.

FURGUSON, Elizabeth Graeme, poet; b. Phila., Feb. 3, 1737; d. Dr. Thomas and Ann (Diggs) Graeme; m. Henry Hugh Furguson, Apr. 21, 1772. Engaged to William Franklin (son of Benjamin Franklin), 1754-57; translated Télémaque (Fénelon) into English; went to London (Eng.) for health reasons, 1764; after mother's death became mistress of her father's home, Phila., turned home into gathering place for Phila.'s writers; became unknowing tool of English (through her Loyalist husband) by carrying letter to Gen. George Washington which urged his surrender during Revolutionary War. Died Phila., Feb. 23, 1801; buried Christ Ch., Phila.

FURLONG, Thomas J., architect; Practiced as architect, St. Louis, designed several bldgs.; mem. firm Furlong & Brown; designed Central High Sch. (1st public high sch. in St. Louis), 1895; mem. A.I.A. Died Mar. 1897.

FURMAN, James Cement, clergyman, univ. pres.; b. Charleston, S.C., Dec. 5, 1809; s. Richard and Dorothea (Burn) F.; grad. Coll. of Charleston, 1826; attended Furman Theol. Instn.; m. Harriet E. Davis, 1833; m. 2d Mary Davis, 1855. A convert to Baptist Ch., 1828; licensed as Bapt. minister, 1828, ordained, 1832; sr. prof. with duties of pres. Furman Theol. Instn., 1844; pres. Furman U. (Bapt. sch.) 1852-79; del. S.C. Secession Conv.; asso. editor Bapt. Courier; mem. So. Assn. Baptists (pres. 5 terms), S.C. Bapt. Assn. (pres. 7 terms). Died nr. Greenville, S.C., Mar. 3, 1891.

FURMAN, Richard, clergyman, educator; b. Esopus, N.Y., Oct. 9, 1755; s. Wood and Rachel (Brodhead) F.; m Elizabeth Haynesworth, Nov. 1775; m. 2d, Dorothea Burn, May 5, 1789. Ordained pastor Baptist Ch., Esopus, 1774; became outstanding S.C. Bapt. leader; pastor of a Bapt. Ch., Charleston, S.C., 1787; influential mem. S.C. Constl. Conv.; produced plan for incorporation of Charleston Bapt. Assn., 1785; 1st pres. S.C. Bapt. Conv., 1821; leader in plan for Baptists of S.C. and Ga. to unite in founding a collegiate instn. (now known as Furman U.), Greenville, S.C.; pres. Bapt. Triennial Conv. of U.S., 1814, reelected 1817; a founder George Washington U., Washington, D.C. Died Aug. 25, 1825.

FURNESS, William Henry, clergyman; b. Boston, Apr. 20, 1802; s. William and Rebekah (Thwing) F.; grad. Harvard, 1820, grad. Harvard Sch. Divinity, 1823, D.D., 1847; m. Annis Jenks, 1825, 4 children including Horace Howard, William Henry. Ordained to ministry Unitarian Ch., 1825; Minister 1st Unitarian Ch., Phila., 1825-75, became pastor emeritus, 1875; editor Diadem, 1845-48; pioneer in pointing out distinction between Jesus of history and Christ of theology; well-known anti-slavery advocate; one of 1st A. scholars to study and translate German lit. Author: Remarks on the Four Gospels, 1836; A History of Jesus, 1850; Thoughts on the Life and Character of Jesus of Nazareth, 1859; The Veil Partly Lifted, 1864; also hymns, best of which are included in Singers and Songs of the Liberal Faith (A. P. Putnam), 1875. Translator: Character of Jesus Portrayed (Daniel Schenkel), 1866; also German verse, including Song of the Bell (Schiller), 1850. Died Phila., Jan. 30, 1896.

FURST, Moritz, engraver; b. Bosing, nr. Presburg, Hungary, Mar. 1782; studied die-sinking, Vienna, Austria. Came to Am. to be engraver for U.S. Mint (enlisted by Am. consul at Leghorn, Italy, 1807), arrived in Phila., 1808, found no place for him at the Mint; set up bus. as seal engraver, diesinker, steel engraver, Phila.; executed many medals for U.S. Govt., including those honoring heroes of War of 1812, Indian Peace medals from Monroe to Van Buren; moved to N.Y.C., circa 1830; visited Charleston, S.C., 1834; returned to Europe, 1841.

FUSSELL, Bartholomew, physician, reformer; b. Chester County, Pa., Jan. 9, 1794; a. Bartholomew and Rebecca (Bond) F.; M.D., U. Md., 1824; m. Lydia Morris; m. 2d Rebecca Hewes. Stationmaster on the underground R.R.; mem. Phila. conv. which organized Anti-Slavery Soc., 1833; advocate of temperance, free elementary edn., profl. opportunities for women; prin. organizer Female Med. Coll. Pa. (inc. 1850). Died Chester Springs, Pa., Feb. 15, 1871.

FUTHEY, John Smith, jurist; b. Chester County, Pa., Sept. 3, 1820; s. Robert and Margaret (Parkinson) F.; attended Unionville (Pa.) Acad., 1838-40;

m. Elizabeth Miller, Sept. 18, 1845, 3 children. In charge of Moscow Acad., Pa., circa 1840-41; admitted to bar, 1843, began practice law, Chester County; dep. atty. gen. Chester County dist., 1849-53, dist. atty., 1853-54; Republican, active in Pa. politics, from 1850's; presiding judge Chester County Cts., 1879-88. Author: History of Chester County, Pennsylvania, 1881. Died Carlisle, Pa., Nov. 26, 1888; buried Chester County.

FYAN, Robert Washington, congressman, lawyer; b. Bedford Springs, Pa., Mar. 11, 1835; attended common schs.; studied law. Admitted to bar, 1858, began practice of law, Marshfield, Mo.; county atty., 1859; commd. lt. col. Webster County Home Guards, 1861, at start of Civil War; commd. capt., maj., 24th Regt., Mo. Volunteer Inf., then col. 46th Regt., 1861; circuit atty., 1865-66; judge 14th Jud. Circuit Mo., 1866-83; mem. Mo. Constl. Conv., 1875; mem. U.S. Ho. of Reps. (Democrat) from Mo., 48th, 52d-53d congresses, 1883-85, 91-95. Died Marshfield, July 28, 1896; buried Lebanon (Mo.) Cemetery.

G

GABB, William More, paleontologist; b. Phila., Jan. 20, 1839; s. Joseph H. and Christiana Gabb; B.A., Central High Sch., 1857; studied with James Hall, Albany, N.Y., 1857-60; became mem. Acad. Natural Scis., 1860; paleontologist Geol. Survey cal., 1861-67, classified cretaceous, tertiary fossils; recognized as Am.'s leading expert on cretaceous marine paleontology (at age 22); made report on area of Lower Cal., made geol. map which gave true structure on Mexican peninsula, 1867; made topog. and geol. survey of Santo Domingo, 1868-71, Province of Talamanca(for Costa Rica), 1873-76; mem. Nat. Acad. Scis. Author: sects. 1, 4 of 1st vol., and entire 2d vol. of Whitney's Geological Survey of California, 1864; On the Topography and Geological Survey of San Domingo, 1873; On the Indian Tribes and Languages of Costa Rica, 1876; also monographs, papers on gen. paleontol. studies. Died Phila., May 30, 1878.

GADSDEN, Christopher, Continental congressman; b. Charleston, S.C., Feb. 16, 1724; s. Thomas and Elizabeth Gadsden; m. Jane Godfrey, Aug. 28, 1746; m. 2d, Mary Hassell, Dec. 29, 1775; m. 3rd, Anne Wragg, 1776; at least 1 child. Mem. S.C. Assembly, 1757-84; owned 2 stores in Charleston, 2 stores in rural area, also a plantation, by 1761; mem. Stamp Act Congress, 1765; leader S.C. radicals; del. 1st, 2d continental congresses, 1774-75; sr. col. in commad of S.C. Militia, commd. brig. gen. Continental Army, 1776; mem. S.C. constl. convs., 1778, 90; lt. gov. S.C., 1778-80, signed surrender of Charleston to Sir Henry Clinton, 1780, imprisoned by British, exchanged, 1781; mem. S.C. Conv. which ratified U.S. Constn., 1788; S.C. presdl. elector, 1789. Died Charleston, Aug. 28, 1805.

GADSDEN, James, railroad exec., diplomat; b. Charleston, S.C., May 15, 1788; s. Philip and Catherine (Edwards) G.; grad. Yale, 1806; m. Susanna Gibbes Hort. Served as lt. of engrs. U.S. Army during War of 1812; promoted capt., charged with constrn. of defense on Gulf frontier, 1818; insp. gen. So. div. U.S. Army, 1820; commd. col., 1820; adj. gen., 1821; appointed commr. to effect removal of Seminole Indians to reservations in S. Fla., 1823 (accomplished by Treaty of Ft. Moultrie); mem. 1st Fla. Legislative Council, 1824; pres. Louisville, Cincinnati & Charleston R.R., 1840-50, (reincorporated as S.C. R.R. Co. 1842), unsuccessfully urged constrn. of a ry. to Pacific at various So. convs., Augusta, Ga., 1837-38, Charleston, 1839, Memphis, Tenn., 1845; U.S. minister to Mexico, purchased a small strip of territory known as the Gadsden Purchase now part of N.M. and Ariz. through which the major roads to the West traveled, added 45,535 sq. miles to U.S. Died Charleston, Dec. 26, 1858.

GAGE, Frances Dana Barker, author, reformer; b. Marietta, O., Oct. 12, 1808; d. Joseph and Elizabeth (Dana) Barker; m. James L. Gage, Jan. 1, 1829, 8 children. Wrote and lectured in Ohio on temperance, slavery, women's rights; with family moved to St. Louis, Mo., (where she was branded an abolitionist), 1853; engaged in newspaper editing, circa 1854-61; taught freedmen in parts of the South occupied by U.S. Army, 1862; supt. refuge for freedmen, Paris Island, S.S., 1863-64; became unsalaried agt. Western Sanitary Commn; lectured on temperance movement, 1866-67; wrote children's stories under name Aunt Fanny. Author: Elsie Magoon; or the Old Still House in the Hollow, 1867; Gertie's Sacrifice, 1869; Steps Upward, 1870. Died Greenwich, Conn., Nov. 10, 1884.

GAGE, Joshua, congressman; b. Harwich, Mass., Aug. 7, 1763. Moved to Augusta, Mass. (now Me.), 1795; master mariner, engaged in merc. pursuits; mem. Mass. Ho. of Reps., 1805, 07, Mass. Senate, 1813, 15; treas. Kennebec County (Me.), 1810-31; mem. U.S. Ho. of Reps. (Democrat) from Me., 15th Congress, 1817-19; mem. Me. Exec. Council, 1822, 23. Died Augusta, Me., Jan. 24, 1831; buried Augusta.

GAGE, Matilda Joslyn, suffragette; b. Cicero, N.Y., Mar. 24, 1826; d. Dr. Hezekiah and Helen (Leslie) Joslyn; attended Clinton Sem.; m. Henry H. Gage, 1844. Attended Nat. Women's Rights Conv., Syracuse, N.Y., 1852, made 1st public appearance as women's rights advocate; a founder N.Y. State Woman's Suffrage Assn., Nat. Woman's Suffrage Assn., 1869, pres of both for many years; founded Woman's Nat. Liberty League, 1878. pres. 1878-98; edited and published The Nat. Citizen and Ballot Box, Syracuse, 1878-81. Author: Woman, Church and State, 1893; author and editor (with Susan B. Anthony, Clara B. Stanton) History of Woman Suffrage. Died Chgo., Mar. 18, 1898.

GAGE, Thomas, army officer, royal gov.; b. Firle, Sussex, Eng., 1721; s. Thomas (1st viscount Gage) and Benedicta (Hall) G.; m. Margaret Kemble, Dec. 8, 1758, 11 children. Commd. lt. Brit. Army, 1741, lt. col., 1751; came with his regt. to Am., 1754; served under Braddock in expdns. against Ft. Duquesne, 1755, wounded; participated in Ticonderoga expdn., 1758; commd. brig. gen., 1759; served under Amherst against Montreal, 1760; mil. gov. Montreal, 1760; commd. maj. gen., 1761; succeeded Amherst as comdr.-in-chief in N.Am. with hdqrs. in N.Y.C., reapptd., 1775; commd. lt. gen., 1773; commd. vice adm., capt. gen., gov.-in-chief Province of Mass., 1774; attempted to suppress colonial resistance to parliamentary acts, but his efforts (such as an expdn. to Concord, Mass. to seize colonial arms) resulted in open fighting, eventual war; Battles of Lexington, Bunker Hill took place during his rule; established martial law, took offered amnesty to all but Samuel Adams, John Hancock, 1775; sailed from Boston to Eng., 1775; served as col. 17th, later 11th Dragoons; commd. gen. Brit. Army, 1782. Died Eng., Apr. 2, 1787.

GAGLIARDI, Tommaso, sculptor; b. Rome, Italy, 1820. Employed in studio of Thomas Crawford; came to U.S., 1855; sculptor at U.S. Capitol, Washington, D.C., 1855-58; executed bust of Crawford; returned to Italy, circa 1860, active in campaigns of Garibaldi; went to Japan, after 1870, founded sch. of sculpture in Royal Acad., Tokyo; went to India, executed many portrait busts; returned to Italy. Died 1895.

GAILLARD, Edwin Samuel, surgeon, editor; b. Charleston S.C.,Jan 16, 1827; grad. S.C. Coll. (now U.S.C.), 1845; M.D.,Med. Coll. State of S. C., Charleston M.A. (hon.) also LL.D. (hon.), U.N.C., 1873; m. Jane Marshall Thomas, 1856; m. 2nd, Mary Elizabeth Gibson, 1865; 4 children. Practiced medicine, Fla., 1855-57; after trip to Europe settled in Balt., 1861; became asst. surgeon 1st M. Regt., Congederated Army, 1861; mem. examining bd. Army of Va., 1861; lost right arm at Battle of Seven Pines, 1862; apptd. mem. dir. mil. hosps., Va. and N.C.,1862, insp. gen. Confederate hosps., 1863-65; prof. principles and practice medicine and gen. pathology Med. Coll. Va., Richmond, 1865; founded Richmond Med. Journal (changed name to Richmond and Louisville Med. Journal 1868), publisher,1865-79; prof medicine Ky. Sch. Medicine, 1868; an organizer, 1st dean, prof. gen. medicine and pathology Louisville (Ky.) Med. Coll., 1869; established Am. Med. Weekly, Louisville, 1874, editor, 1874-83; moved to N.Y.C. , 1879; published Gaillards's Med. Jour., until 1883. Author numerous papers including Ozone: Its Relation to Health and Disease (received Fiske Fund prize 1861), essay on diphtheria (received Ga. Med. Assn. prize 1866). Died Feb. 1885.

GAILLARD, John, senator; b. St. Stephen's Parish, S.C., Sept. 5, 1765; s. John and Judith (Peyre) G.; m. Mary Lord, Nov. 24, 1792, 2 children. Admitted to Middle Temple, 1782, never practiced law; mem. S.C. Ho. of Reps., 1794; mem S.C. Senate, 1796-1804, pres., 1804; mem. U.S. Senate from S.C., 1805-26, pres. pro tem, 1814-17; opposed bill to re-charter 1st U.S. Bank, also establishment of 2d Bank of U.S.; against fed. aid for internal improvements. Died Washington, D.C., Feb. 26, 1826; buried Congressional Cemetery.

GAILLARDET, Theodore Frederick, journalist, author; b. Auxerre, France, Apr. 7, 1808. Produced own plays in Paris, 1832-36; came to U.S., 1837; contbd. articles on U.S. to French newspapers; travelled through So. U.S.; published Courier des Ettats-Uniis (French lang. newspaper), N.Y.C., 1840-48; returned to France, 1848; polit. corr. for Courier, 1848-82; mayor of Plessis-Bouchard, France, 1882. Author: (plays) La Tour de Nesle, 1832; Georges, ou le criminal par Amour, 1833; Struensee, ou le Medicine de la Reine, 1833; (essays) Memoirs du Chevalier d'Eon, 2 vols., 1836; L'Aristocratie en Amerique, 1883. Died Plessis-Bouchard, Aug. 13, 1882.

GAINE, Hugh, printer; b. Belfast, Ireland, 1727; m. Sarah Robbins, Oct. 24, 1759; m. 2d, Cornelia Wallace, Sept. 5, 1769; 5 children. Came to U.S., 1745; worked in printing office of James Parker, N.Y.C., 1745-52; established own printing bus. and bookstore The Bible and Crown, 1752, changed name to The Bible, 1783; began publishing series of Hutchin's Almanacks, 1752; published newspaper N.Y. Mercury, 1752-83, printed polit. articles called The Watch Tower in paper, 1754-55; public printer Province of N.Y., also ofcl. printer N.Y.C., 1768-83; mem. Soc. of Freemasons, St. Patrick's Soc., N.Y.C.; vestryman Trinity Ch., N.Y.C. Died N.Y.C., Apr. 25, 1807; buried Trinity Ch. Graveyard.

GAINES, Edmund Pendleton, Army officer; b. Culpeper County, Va., May 20, 1777; s. James and Elizabeth (Strother) G.; m. Frances Toulmin; m. 2d, Barbara Blount; m.3d, Myra Clark, 1839. Served as lt. in co. of riflemen, 1795; commd. lt. U.S. Army, 1797; surveyed road from Nashville, Tenn. to Natchez, Miss., 1801-04; made arrest of Aaron Burr; commd. maj., 1812; served as col. in engagement at Chrysler's Field, 1813; adj. gen. in command Fort Erie, 1813. brig. gen. successfully defending Ft. Erie against a superior Brit. force, 1814; recipient gold medal U.S. Congress; commr. to treat with Creek Indians in South, 1817; participated under Jackson in Creek and Seminole wars; in command Eastern Dep. of U.S. Army; led successful campaign against Black Hawk, 1832; for his unofcl. participation in Mexican War, (in which he commanded a large force of volunteers), deprived of his command by U.S. Pres., summoned to Ft. Monroe for trial by ct. martial; successfully defended himself, proceedings were dropped; bitter enemy of Gen. Winfield Scott; at odds with War Dept. through most of his career, especially in regard to methods of frontier defense. Died New Orleans, June 6, 1849.

GAINES, George Strother, Indian agt., mcht., planter; b. Stokes County, N.C., circa 1784; s. James and Elizabeth (Strother) G.; m. Ann, 1812. Asst. factor govt. trading house, Stephens, Miss. Territory, 1805-19; Indian agt. on Spanish border; largely responsible for success of Am. trade with Spain; mem. Ala. Senate, 1825-27; mcht., Mobile, Ala., 1830-56; a promoter Mobile and Ohio R.R.; pres. Mobile br. State Bank; mem. Miss. Legislature, 1861; owned plantation, State line, Miss., retired to plantation, 1856; Gainesville (Ala.) named after him. Author: Reminiscences of Early Times in Miss. Territory, 1872. Died Miss., Jan. 21, 1873.

GAINES, John Pollard, congressman, territorial gov.; b. Augusta County, Va., Sept. 22, 1795; s. Abner and Elizabeth (Mathews) G.; m. Elizabeth Kincaid, June 22, 1819; m. 2d, Margaret B. Wand, circa 1852. Admitted to Ky. bar; served in War of 1812; served as maj. gen. cavalry brigade Ky. Militia, Mexican War; mem. Ky. Legislature; mem. U.S. Ho. of Reps. (Whigs) from Ky., 30th Congress, 1847-49; apptd. gov. Ore. Territory by Pres. Taylor, 1850-55. Died Salem, Ore., Dec. 9, 1857; buried Odd Fellows Cemetery, Salem.

GAITHER, Nathan, congressman, physican; b. nr. Mocksville, N.C., Sept. 15, 1788; attended Bardstown Coll.; grad. Jefferson Med. Coll. Began practice of medicine, Columbia, Ky. served as asst. surgeon in War of 1812, mem. Ky. Ho. of Reps., 1815-18, 55-57; Democratic presdl. elector, 1829; mem. U.S. Ho. of Reps. (Democrat) from Ky., 21st-22d congresses, 1829-33; del. Ky. Constl. Conv., 1849. Died Columbia, Aug. 12, 1862; buried Columbia Cemetery.

GALBERRY, Thomas, clergyman; b. Naas. County Kildare, Ireland, 1833; s. Thomas and Margaret (White) G.; grad. Villanova Coll., 1851 Came to U.S. , 1876; entered Augustinian novitiate, 1852; ordained priest Roman Catholic Ch., 1856; pastor ch., Lansingburg, N.Y , 1860-70, established a cemetery, built a parochial sch., erected St. Augustine's Ch.; apptd. superior of Augustinian missions in U.S., 1866; pres. Villanova Coll., 1872-74; prior-provincial Province of St. Thomas of Villanova, 1874; consecrated bishop of Hartford (Conn.), 1876, began constrn. St. Joseph's Cathedral, founded publ. The Conn. Catholic, built 2 chs., opened a boys' sch., 1876-78; supported temperance movement. Died N.Y.C., Oct. 10, 1878; buried Hartford.

GALBRAITH, John, congressman, lawyer; b. Huntingdon, Pa., Aug. 2, 1794; attended common schs.; studied law. Apprenticed in printer's trade; taught sch.; admitted to bar, 1817, began practice of law, Butler, Pa.; moved to Franklin, Pa., 1822; mem. Pa. Ho. of Reps., 1829-32; mem. U.S. Ho. of Reps. (Democrat) from Pa., 23d-24th, 26th congresses, 1833-37, 39-41; moved to Erie, Pa., 1837; pres. judge 6th Jud. Dist., 1851-60. Died Erie, June 15, 1860; buried Erie Cemetery.

GALE, Benjamin, physician, author; b. Jamaica, L.I.. N.Y., Dec. 14, 1715; s. John and Mary Gale; M.A., Yale, 17; studied medicine and surgery with Dr. Jared Eliot; m. Hannah Eliot, June 6, 1739, 8 children. Began practice of medicine, Killingworth, Conn., circa 1739, became highly espected for abilites as physician; mem. Conn. Gen. Assembly, 1747-67; helped devise the Am. Turtle (a depth bomb); Author: The Present State of the Colony of Connecticut Considered, 1755; Historical Memoirs, Relating to the Practice of Inoculation for the Small-Pox, in the British American Provinces, Particularly in New England, 1765; A Brief Essay, or, An Attempt to Prove, from the Prophetick Writings of the Old and New Testaments, What Period of Prophecy the Church of God is Now Under (his chief theol. work), 1788. Died Killingworth, Conn., May 6, 1790; buried Conn.

GALE, George, congressman; b. Somerset County, Md., June 3, 1756; attended common schs.; married, at least 1 son, Levin. Served during Revolutionary War; mem. Md. Conv. which ratified U.S. Constn., 1788; mem. U.S. Ho. of Reps. from Md., 1st Congress, 1789-91; apptd. supr. of distilled liquors Dist. of Md. by Pres. Washington, 1791. Died "Brookland," Cecil County, Md., Jan. 2, 1815; buried family burying ground on estate.

GALE, George Washington, clergyman, educator; b. Stanford, N.Y., Dec. 3, 1789; s. Josiah and Rachel (Mead) G.; grad. Union Coll., 1814, Princeton Theol. Sem., 1819; m. Harriet Selden, 1820; m. 2d, Esther Williams, 1841; m. 3d, Lucy Merriam, 1844. Ordained by Presbytery of St. Laurence, 1819; princ. founder, head Oneida Inst., Whitesboro, N.Y. (where 1st coll. students payed for instrn. by doing manual labor) 1827-44; a founder Town of Galesburg, (Ill.), 1st pastor local ch.; a founder Knox Coll., 1837, trustee, 1837-61, acting prof. langs., 1837-42, prof. moral philosophy and belles-lettres, 1843-57. Died Galesburg, Sept. 13, 1861.

GALE, Levin, congressman, lawyer; b. Elkton, Md., Apr. 24, 1784; s. George Gale; attended common schs.; studied law. Admitted to bar, began practice of law, Elkton; mem. Md. Senate, 1816; mem. U.S. Ho. of Reps. from Md., 20th Congress, 1827-29. Died Elkton, Dec. 18, 1834.

GALES, Joseph, journalist, reformer, mayor; b. Eckington, Eng., Feb. 4, 1761; s. Thomas Gales; m. Winifred Marshall, May 4, 1784, 3 children including Weston Raleigh, Joseph. Founder Sheffield (Eng.) Register, 1787-94; sold Rights of Man (by Thomas Paine), befriended the author; active supporter England's Constl. Soc.; advocated abolition of slavery, universal manhood suffrage, abolition of imprisonment for debt; fled to Altona, Schleswig-Holstein, Germany 1794; came to Phila., 1795; reporter Am. Daily Advertiser, made 1st verbatim report of proceedings in U.S. Congress; owner, editor Independent Gazeteer, N.C.; founder weekly Raleigh (N.C.) Register, 1799; mayor Raleigh, 19 years; state printer N.C.; compiled 1st 2 vols. Annals of Congress, 1834; sec. Peace Soc., Washington, D.C.; sec., treas. Am. Colonization Soc. until 1839. Died Raleigh, Aug. 24, 1841.

GALES, Joseph, journalist, mayor; b. Eckington, Eng., Apr. 10, 1786; s. Joseph and Winifred (Marshall) G.; attended U. N.C.; m. Sarah Lee, Dec. 14, 1813. Reported Congressional proceedings for Nat. Intelligencer 1807-33, Washington, D.C., 1807-20, became partner of S. Harrison Smith in ownership of paper, 1809, sole owner, 1810-12, partner of William Seaton (his brother-in-law), 1812-60, (only record of Congl. proceedings, began daily publ., 1813; supported War of 1812; his printing equipment destroyed, when British occupied Washington, 1813; mayor of Washington, 1827-30; contbd. funds to Am. Colonization Soc. Author: A Register of Debates in Congress, 29 vols., 1825-37; American State Papers, 38 vols., 1832-61. Died Washington, July 21, 1860.

GALITZEN, Elizabeth, nun; b. St. Petersburg, Russia, Feb. 22, 1797; d. Prince Alexis Andrevitch and Countess Protasof. Became a convert to Roman Catholic Ch., joined Soc. of Sacred Heart, Metz, Lorraine, 1826; was professed, Rome, Italy, 1832; served as sec. gen. to Madeleine Sophie Barat (later canonized); 1834; became asst. gen. and visitor to convents of the order in U.S. Died while nursing victims of yellow fever, La., Dec. 8, 1843.

GALL, (Indian name Pizi), Indian chieftain; b. Moreau River, S.C., circa 1840. War chief Hunkpapa Sioux Indians; mil. lt. to Chief Sitting Bull; prin. war chief in Battle of Little Big Horn, 1876; forced into Can. with Sitting Bull, 1876, returned to U.S., 1880 still belligerent; surrendered after Battle of Poplar River Agy., Mont., 1881; settled as farmer on Standing Rock Reservation, 1881; influenced Indian Offenses, 1889-94; del. to Washington, D.C. on behalf of Sioux Indians, 1889; brought about ratification of Act of Mar. 2, 1889 (last agreement with Siuox regarding div. of their reservation). Died Oak Creek, S.D., Dec. 5, 1894.

GALLAGHER, Hugh Patrick, clergyman; b. Killygordon, Ireland, Mar. 26, 1815; came to Am., 1837; studied Sem. of St. Charles Borromeo, Overbrook, Pa. Ordained priest Roman Catholic Ch., 1840; assigned to Pottsville, Pa.; formed a total abstinence soc.; introduced Sisters of Mercy into Pitts. Diocese, 1843; founder editor Catholic, 1844; a founder St. Francis' Coll. for Boys, 1844; theologian at 1st Plenary Council of Balt.; leader Irish priests and congregations in Western U.S., 1852; helped construct chs. in various mining camps frontier towns; began Ch. of Immaculate Conception, Oakland, Cal.; helped build St. Mary's Cathedral, San Francisco; founder Cath. Standard (1st Cath. newspaper on West Coast), 1853; enlisted group of Presentation nuns to come to Cal. from Ireland; entrusted with savings of miners, laborers, 1855; credited with introduction of parochial sch. system into Diocese of Cal., founder St. Mary's Hosp., San Francisco; founder Magdalen Asylum, 1865. Died St. Mary's Hosp., Mar. 10, 1882.

GALLAGHER, William Davis, journalist; b. Phila., Aug. 21, 1808; s. Bernard and Abigail (Davis) G.; m. Emma Adamson, 1830. Editor newspaper The Backwoodsman, Xenia, O., 1830, Cincinnati (O.) Mirror, 1831, Western Literary Jour. and Monthly Review, Cincinnati, 1836-38, Ohio State Jour., Columbus, O., 1838; asso. editor Gazette, Cincinnati, 1839-50; sec. to Thomas Corwin (U.S. sec. treasury), 1850-52; editor, owner Louisville (Ky.) Daily Courier, 1852-54; editor Western Farmer's Jour., Louisville, 1854-60; del. Republican Nat. Conv., 1860; sec. to Salmon P. Chase (U.S. sec. treasury), 1861; U.S. collector customs for Upper Miss. Valley. Author: The Wreck of the Hornet (poem), 1835; (collected poetry) Erato, 3 vols., 1835-37, Miami Woods, a Golden Wedding and other Poems, 1881. Editor: Selections from the Poetical Literature of the West, 1841. Died June 27, 1894.

GALLATIN, (Abraham Alfonse) Albert, senator, U.S. sec. of treasury; b. Geneva, Switzerland, Jan. 29, 1761; s. Jean and Sophie Albertine (Rolaz) G.; grad. Geneva Acad., 1779; m. Sophie Allegre, 1789; m. 2d, Hannah Nicholson, 1793; at least 2 sons, Albert, Francis. Came to U.S., 1780; tutor French, Harvard, 1781; leader of settlers to Western Pa., 1784; mem. Harrisburg Conf. to revise U.S. Constn., 1788; mem. Pa. Constl. Conv., 1789; mem. Pa. Ho. of Reps. from Fayette County, 1790-93, instrumental in establishing state system of publ. edn., proposed establishment of state paper money and a Bank of Pa.; chiefly responsible for quelling Whiskey Rebellion of 1794 (thus preventing civil war in Pa.); mem. U.S. Ho. of Reps. from Pa., 4th-6th congresses, 1795-1801, Republican minority leader, caused creation of standing com. on finance (now ways and means com.); U.S. sec. treasury under Jefferson and Madison, 1801-14, favored natural growth of industry, opposed excessive govt. taxation, reduced mil. appropriations and public debt, believed that Fed. money should be used to further an expanding internal economy; changed policies when they became unpopular during War of 1812, revived internal taxes visited St. Petersburg (Russia) to attempt to secure Russian mediation to end war with Eng., 1813; peace commr. to Eng. negotiating Treaty of Ghent, 1814, concluded (with Adams and Clay) favorable comml. treaty with British, 1815; U.S. minister to France, 1815-23, to Eng., 1826-27; pres. Nat. (later Gallatin) Bank of N.Y.C.; a founder, 1st pres. council U. City N.Y. (now N.Y.U.), 1831; founder Am. Ethnol. Soc., 1842; pres. N.Y. Hist. Soc., 1843. Author: Considerations on the Currency and Banking System of the United States, 1831; Memorial of the Committee Appointed by the "Free Trade Convention" Held in Philadelphia in . . . 1831, published 1832. Died Astoria, L.I., N.Y., Aug. 12, 1849; buried Trinity Churchyard, N.Y.C.

GALLAUDET, Thomas Hopkins, educator; b. Phila., Dec. 10, 1787; s. Peter Wallace and Jane (Hopkins) G.; grad. Yale, 1805; grad. Andover Theol. Sem., 1814; LL.D. (hon.), Western Res. Coll., 1851; m. Sophia Fowler, Aug. 29, 1821; children—Thomas, Edward Miner. Tutor, Yale, 1808-10; raised money for 1st free Am. sch. for deaf, Hartford, Conn., 1817, prin. until 1830; helped establish pub. normal schs. in Conn.; advocated higher edn. of women; chaplain Insane Hosp., Worcester, Mass., 1838. Author: Child's Book on the Soul; Child's Book on Repentance; Child's Book of Bible Stories; The Youth's Book on Natural History. Contbr. to Am. Annals of the Deaf; Discourses on Various Points of Christian Faith and Practice, 1818. Died Hartford, Sept. 10, 1851.

GALLEGOS, Jose Manuel, congressman; b. in what is now Rio Arriba County, N.M., Oct. 30, 1815; grad. in theology Coll. of Durango, Mexico, 1840. Mem. legislative assembly Dept. of N.M., Republic of Mexico, 1843-46; mem. 1st N.M. Territorial Council, 1851; mem. U.S. Congress (Democrat) from N.M. Territory, 33d-34th, 42d congresses, 1853-July 23, 1856, 71-73; mem. Territorial Ho. of Reps., 1860-62; imprisoned by Tex. Confederate troops, 1862; treas. N.M. Territory, 1865-66. Died Santa Fe, N.M., Apr. 21, 1875; buried Catholic Cemetery.

GALLIER, James, architect; b. Ravensdale, County Louth, Ireland, July 24, 1798; s. Thaddeus and Margaret (Taylor) G.; attended Sch. of Fine Arts, Dublin, Ireland 1818-16; m. Elizabeth Tyler, 1823; m. 2d, Catherine Robinson, July 1850; at least 2 children including James, Jr. Came to U.S., 1832; worked as draftsman, N.Y.C., 1832-33; partner (with Minard Lafever) in archtl. firm, N.Y.C.; 1833-34, (with Charles B. Dakin), New Orleans, 1834-35; won 1st prize in competition for design of Mobile (Ala.) City Hall, 1835 (bldg. never constructed); designed St. Charles Hotel, New Orleans, 1835; owner building firm, speculator in real estate, 1836-50; responsible for revisions and reconstrns. of St. Patrick's Roman Catholic Ch. and U.S. Mint, designed Mcht's Exchange, City Hall, Christ Ch., many large residences (all New Orleans); travelled, Europe and North Africa, 1850-68. Drowned in shipwreck of Evening Star off Cape Hatteras, May 16, 1868.

GALLITZIN, Demetrius Augustine, clergyman, missionary; b. The Hague, Netherlands, Dec. 22, 1770; s. Prince Dmitrie and Countess Amalia (Von Schmettau) G.; ed pvt. tutor. Entered Catholic Ch. taking name of Augustine, 1787; arrived Balt. 1792; ordained priest Roman Catholic Ch., 1795 (1st priest to receive full theol. tng. in Am.); assigned to Allegheny Mountains, 1790, founded mission of Lorretto (Cath. colony on Pa. frontier); naturalized, 1802; sold farms on easy terms to Swiss, German, Irish colonists; erected grist mill, tannery; helped train a militia co. during War of 1812; a series of his letters to Huntington Gazette published as Defence of Catholic Principles, 1816; issued pamphlet Six Letters of Advice to the Gentleman Parsons who Lately Met at Columbia for the Purpose of Declaring War Against the Catholic Church; vicar gen. Western Pa. Died in the Allegheny Mountains, May 6, 1840.

GALLOWAY, Joseph, continental congressman; Loyalist; b. West River, Md., 1731; s. Peter Bines and Elizabeth (Rigbie) G.; LL.D., Princeton; m. Grace Growden, Oct. 18, 1753. Mem. Pa. Assembly, 1756-63, 65-76, speaker, 1766-75; v.p. Am. Philos. Soc., 1769-75; del. to 1st Continental Congress, 1774; famous for Galloway plan for a constl. scheme of Brit. Empire (rejected in favor of independence); joined Brit. Army under Gen. Howe, 1776; Loyalist in Am. Revolution; civil adminstr. of Port of Phila., 1777; went to Eng. as spokesman of Am. Loyalists, 1778. Author: Historical and Political Reflections on the Rise and Progress of the American Rebellion, 1780; Cool Thoughts on the Consequences to Great Britain of American Independence, 1780; The Claim of the American Loyalists Reviewed and Maintained upon Incontrovertible Principles of Law and Justice, 1788. Died Watford, Hertfordshire, Eng., Aug. 29, 1803.

GALLOWAY, Samuel, congressman; b. Gettysburg, Pa., Mar. 20, 1811; s. James and Mrs. (Buchanan) G.; grad. Miami U., Oxford, O., 1833; attended Princeton Theol. Sem., 1835-36; m. Joan Wallin, 1843. Prof. Greek, Miami U., 1837-38; prof. classical langs. Hanover (Ind.) Coll., 1838-40; admitted to Ohio bar, 1842; sec. of state Ohio, 1844-50, reconstructed Ohio public sch. system; mem. U.S. Ho. of Reps. from Ohio, 34th Congress, 1855-57; judge adv. Camp Chase, Columbus, O.; apptd. to investigate conditions in South during Reconstrn. Died Columbus Apr. 5, 1872; buried Greenlawn Cemetery, Columbus.

GALLUP, Albert, congressman; b. East Berne, N.Y., Jan. 30, 1796; studied law. Admitted to bar, began practice of law, Albany, N.Y.; sheriff Albany County, 1831-34; mem. U.S. Ho. of Reps. (Democrat) from N.Y., 25th Congress, 1837-39; apptd. by Pres. Polk collector of customs at Albany. Died Providence, R.I., Nov. 5, 1851; buried Swan Point Cemetery.

GALLUP, Joseph Adams, physician; b. Stonington, Conn., Mar. 30, 1769; s. William and Lucy (Denison) G.; M.D., Dartmouth, 1798; m. Abigail Willard, Sept. 1792. Active in formation of med. socs. including Vt. Med. Soc., 1813, pres., 1818-29; prof. theory and practice of medicine Vt. Acad. Medicine 1821-25, pres. corp., 1822; prof. materia medica med. sch. Burlington, Vt., 1825; founded a clinical sch. of medicine, Woodstock, Vt., 1827; published Domestic Medical and Dietetical Monitor or Journal of Health, 1815. Author: Sketches of Epidemic Diseases in the State of Vermont, 1815; Pathological Reflections on the Supertonic State of Disease, 1822; Outlines of the Institutes of Medicine, 1839. Died Woodstock, Oct. 12, 1849.

GALT, Alexander, sculptor; b. Norfolk, Va., June 26, 1827; studied in Florence, Italy, 1848-54, 56-60. Opened studio, Richmond, Va., 1860; executed busts of several noted Americans before and during Civil War; mem. staff of gov. Va.; made many drawings for Confederate Engrs., circa 1861-63. Died of smallpox, Richmond, Jan. 19, 1863.

GALVEZ, Bernardo de, see de Galvez, Bernardo.

GAMBEL, William, ornithologist; b. N.J., circa 1819. Protege of Thomas Nuttall (for whom he named Nuttall's woodpecker 1843); crossed continent via Santa Fe Trail, 1841, then went with

Workman party over Mormon Trail to Cal.; his writings are most important of early works on birds of Cal.; Gambel's quail named in his honor. Died of typhoid fever on Feather River, Cal., Dec. 1849.

GAMBLE, Hamilton Rowan, gov. Mo., jurist; b. Winchester, Va., Nov. 29, 1798; s. Joseph and Anne (Hamilton) G.; ed. Hampden-Sydney Coll.; m. Caroline Coalter, 1827, 3 children. Admitted to Va. bar, 1816; went to Mo., 1818; sec. of state Mo. Territory; mem. Mo. Legislature, 1846; presiding justice Mo. Supreme Ct., 1851-54, a dissenter in one of Dred Scott's early cases; mem. Mo. Conv. called to consider Mo.'s relation to the Union, leader Conditional Unionists, 1861; provisional gov. Mo. (Republican), favored gradual emancipation, incurred wrath of Radicals, 1861-64. Died St. Louis, Jan. 31, 1864.

GAMBLE, James, congressman, jurist; b. Jersey Shore, Pa., Jan. 28, 1809; attended Jersey Shore Acad.; studied law. Admitted to bar, 1833, began practice of law, Jersey Shore; county treas., 1834-36; mem. Pa. Ho. of Reps., 1841-42; mem. U.S. Ho. of Reps. (Democrat) from Pa., 32d-33d congresses, 1851-55; pres. judge Clearfield County, 1859-60; pres. judge Lycoming County (Pa.) Ct. of Common Pleas, 1868-78. Died Williamsport, Pa., Feb. 22, 1883; buried Wildwood Cemetery.

GAMBLE, John Rankin, congressman, lawyer; b. Alabama, Genesee County, N.Y., Jan. 15, 1848; attended common schs.; grad. Lawrence U., Appleton, Wis., 1872; studied law. Admitted to bar, 1873, began practice of law, Yankton, Dakota Territory (now S.D.); dist. atty. Yankton County, 1876-78; U.S. atty. for Dakota Territory, 1878; mem. Dakota Territorial Ho. of Reps., 1877-79, Territorial Council, 1881-85; elected mem. U.S. Ho. of Reps. (Republican) from S.C., 52d Congress, 1891. Died Aug. 14, 1891; buried Yankton Cemetery.

GAMBLE, Roger Lawson, congressman; b. nr. Louisville, Ga., 1787; studied law. Admitted to bar, circa 1815, began practice of law, Louisville; became cotton planter; served as officer in War of 1812; mem. Ga. Ho. of Reps., 1814-15; mem. U.S. Ho. of Reps. from Ga. (as Democrat), 23d Congress, 1833-35, (as Whig), 27th Congress, 1841-43; judge Ga. Superior Ct., 1845-47. Died Augusta, Ga., Dec. 20, 1847; buried Old Capitol Cemetery, Louisville.

GAMBRILL, Charles D., architect; b. Roxbury, Mass., 1832; attended Harvard; archtl. student in office of George Snell, Boston. Draftsman for George B. Post, N.Y.C.; partner with Henry Hobson Richardson in firm Gambrill & Richardson, N.Y.C., 1867-74; designed and built Brattle Sq. Baptist Ch., Boston, 1870-74; specialized in residences in Queen Anne style. One of 1st fellows A.I.A., sec. 1861-80. Died Sept. 13, 1880.

GAMMON, Elijah Hedding, clergyman, mfr., philanthropist; b. Gilmore Pond Plantation (now Lexington, Me.), Dec. 23, 1819; s. Samuel and Melinda (Quint) G.; m. Sarah Cutler, 1843; m. 2d, Jane Colton, 1856. Admitted to Me. Conf., Meth. Episcopal Ch., 1843; pastor, Wilton, Me., 1843-51, St. Charles, Ill., 1853, Jefferson St. Ch., Chgo., 1854-58; presiding elder St. Charles Dist., Rock River Conf., M.E. Ch., 1855-58; partner Newton and Co., Batavia, Ill., mfrs. farm equipment, 1858-61; partner in mfg. harvesting equipment with J.D. Easter, 1861-68, with William Prindle, 1868-70; partner mfg. firm Gammon and Deering, 1870-79; with William Jones formed Plano Mfg. Co., Chgo., 1880-91; gave funds to Me. Wesleyan Sem. and Garret Bibl. Inst.; founded, endowed Gammon Theol. Sem. for tng. Negro Meth. clergymen, Atlanta, Ga. Died July 3, 1891.

GANIODAIIO, see Skaniadariio.

GANNETT, Barzillai, congressman; b. Bridgewater, Mass., June 17, 1764; grad. Harvard, 1785; studied theology. Selectman, Pittston (Mass., now Me.), 1793-94, 96-98, 1801-02; town clk., 1794; moderator, 1797-1802; selectman and assessor Gardiner (Me.), 1803-08; 1st postmaster Gardiner, 1804-09; moderator, 1804-06, 08-09, 11; mem. Mass. Ho. of Reps., 1805-06; mem. Mass. Senate, 1807-08; mem. U.S. Ho. of Reps. (Democrat) from Mass., 11th-12th congresses, 1809-12 (resigned). Died N.Y.C., 1832.

GANNETT, Ezra Stiles, clergyman; b. Cambridge, Mass., May 4, 1801; s. Rev. Caleb and Ruth (Stiles) G.; grad. with 1st honors, Harvard, 1820, D.D. (hon.), 1843, grad. Harvard Divinity Sch., 1823; m. Anna Linzee Tilden, Oct. 6, 1835, 3 children. Ordained to Unitarian ministry at Federal St. Ch., Boston, 1824 assistant, then pastor; an organizer Am. Unitarian Assn., served as 1st sec., 6 years, pres., 1847-51; editor Scriptural Interpreter, 1831-35; an organizer Benevolent Fraternity of Ch. for the Support of the Ministry-at-Large, 1834, sec., also pres., 1857-62; an overseer Harvard, 1835-58; helped to edit Christian Register; edited Monthly Miscellany of Religion and Letter, 1839-43; co-editor Christian Examiner, 1844-49. Died nr. Boston, Aug. 26, 1871.

GANO, John, clergyman; b. Hopewell, N.J., July 22, 1727; s. Daniel and Sarah (Britton) G.; attended Princeton; m. Sarah Stites, 1755; m. 2d, Mrs. T. Bryant, 1790; children—Stephen, John. Ordained pastor Baptist Ch., Morristown, N.J., 1754; pastor in N.Y. helping in reorgn. Baptist Ch., 1762; a founder R.I. Coll. (now Brown U.); chaplain Continental Army; regent Univ. State N.Y., 1784; trustee King's Coll. (now Columbia), 1787; preached in Ky. and N.C. Died Aug. 10, 1804.

GANO, Stephen, clergyman; b. N.Y.C., Dec. 25, 1762; s. John and Sarah (Stites) G.; A.M. (hon.), R.I. Coll. (now Brown U.), 1800; m. Cornelia Vavasour, Oct. 25, 1782; m. 2d, Polly Tallmadge, 1789; m. 3d, Mary Brown, July 18 1799; m. 4th, Joanna Lattine, Oct. 8, 1801. Surgeon's mate Continental Army, 1779-82; practiced medicine, Tappan, N.Y., 1782-86; ordained to ministry Baptist Ch., 1786; pastor, Hudson, O., 1790-92, 1st Bapt. Ch., Providence, R.I., 1792-1828; mem. Providence Sch. Com., 1794-1824; overseer R.I. Coll. (now Brown U.), 1794-1828; moderator Warren Assn. of Bapt. Ch., 1808-28; del. to Bapt. Triennial Conv., Phila. Died Providence, Aug. 18, 1828.

GANSEVOORT, Leonard, continental congressman, jurist; b. July 1751; s. Harmen and Magdalena (Douw) G.; m. Hester Cuyler. Licensed to practice law, 1772; mem. Albany (N.Y.) Com. of Correspondence, treas. until 1775; mem. 2d, 3rd provincial congresses of N.Y., 1775, 76; mem. Conv. of Reps. of State of N.Y., 1777, pres. pro tem, clk. Albany County, 1777, city recorder, 1780; mem. N.Y. State Assembly, 1778, 87; mem. Continental Congress, 1787-88; N.Y. State Senate, 1791-93, 96-1802; apptd. col. of light cavalry, 1794; judge Albany County, 1794-97; judge Ct. of Probates, 1799-1810. Died Albany, Aug. 26, 1810.

GANSEVOORT, Peter, army officer; b. Albany, N.Y., July 1749; s. Harmen and Magdalena (Douw) G.; m. Catherina Van Schaick, Jan. 12, 1778. Served with Gen. Montgomery in expdn. against Que., Can., 1775; commd. maj. 2nd N.Y. Regt., 1775, lt. col., 1776, col. 3d N.Y. Regt., 1776; comdr. Ft. George, defended Ft. Stanwix against Brit. and Indians under St. Leger for 20 days, 1777; commanded F.T. Schuyler, Rome, N.Y., 1777; in temporary command, Albany, 1777; with Sullivan in expdn. against Indian allies of British, 1779; in command, Saratoga, N.Y.,1780; commd. brig. gen. N.Y. Militia, 1781, maj. gen. 1793; accompanied Gen. Washington in tour of Northern battlefields, 1783; mil. agt. Northern Dept., U.S. Army, 1802; dir. N.Y. State Bank, 1803-12; U.S. commr. Indian affairs; regent Univ. State N.Y., 1808-12; commd. brig. gen. U.S. Army, 1809. Died Albany, July 2, 1812.

GANSON, John, congressman, lawyer; b. Le Roy, N.Y., Jan. 1, 1818; attended Le Roy Acad.; grad. Harvard, 1839; studied law. Admitted to bar, 1846, began practice of law, Canandaigua, N.Y.; moved to Buffalo, N.Y., 1846; mem. N.Y. State Senate, 1862-63; mem. U.S. Ho. of Reps. (Democrat) from N.Y., 38th Congress, 1863-65; railroad dir.; del. Dem. Nat. Conv., Chgo., 1864. Died Buffalo, Sept. 28, 1874; buried Forest Lawn Cemetery.

GARAKONTHIE, Daniel, Indian chief; b. circa 1600. mem., councilor Onondaga Tribe; councilor Iroquois confederacy; visited Montreal, Que., Can., seeking peace with the French, stayed behind as evidence of tribe's good faith; publicly announced himself as protector to the French when Father Simon le Moyne visited Iroquois Indians; called by colonists "Father of the French", rescued over 60 white captives from death and torture; on visit to Que. declared himself a Christian convert, baptized Catholic, 1669-70; opposed sale of liquor in his country. Died Onondaga, N.Y., 1676.

GARCES, Francisco Tomas Hermenegildo, missionary, explorer; b. Aragon, Spain, April 12, 1738; s. Juan and Antonia (Maestro) G.; ed. Coll. of Santa Cruz de Queretaro. Took holy orders, 1754; ordained priest, 1763; missionary to Province of Sonora (Mexico),1768; made 4 expdns. to points along Gila, Colorado rivers, 1768-74; reached present-day Colo., 1780; founded 2 pueblo missions; became convinced of reaching area of No. Cal. because of these expdns.; descended Colorado River to its mouth, 1775; killed when Indians of the region attacked the 2 missions he had founded. Died Mission on Colorado River, July 18, 1781.

GARDEN, Alexander, naturalist, physician; b. Aberdeenshire, Scotland, circa 1730; s. Rev. Alexander Garden; M.D., Marischal Coll., Aberdeen, Scotland, 1753; m. Elizabeth Peronneau, Dec. 24, 1755; 1 son, Maj. Alexander. Came to U.S., 1754; discovered vermifugal properties of pink-root (Spigelia marilandica); discovered Congo snake, mud eel; corresponded with various Am. and European naturalists and was instrumental in sending 1st electric eels to Europe; mem. Royal Soc. Upsula (Sweden), 1763; became fellow Royal Soc. London (Eng.), 1773; sided with King in Am. Revolution banished, property confiscated by Act of Feb. 26 1782; v.p. Royal Soc., Eng.; flower gardenia named after him. Died London, Apr. 15, 1791.

GARDEN, Alexander, army officer, author; b. Charleston, S.C., Dec. 4, 1757; s. Alexander and Elizabeth (Peronneau) G.; M.A., U. Glasgow (Scotland), 1779; m. Mary Anna Gibbes, 1784, 1 adopted child, Alester Gibbes. Commd. lt. Lee's Legion, Continental Army, 1780, a.d.c. to Gen Nathanael Greene, 1781, promoted maj., 1781 mem. S.C. Assembly, 1784; mem. S.C. Soc. of Cincinnati, 1808-29, v.p., 1814-26, pres., 1826-29; best known for accounts of the Revolution published as Anecdotes of the Revolutionary War in America, 1822, Anecdotes of the American Revolution, 2d series, 1828. Died Charleston, Feb. 24, 1829.

GARDENIER, Barent, congressman; b. Kingston, N.Y.; studied law. Admitted to bar, began practice of law; held several local offices; mem. U.S. Ho. of Reps. (Federalist) from N.Y., 10th-11th congresses, 1807-11; practiced law, Ulster and Columbia counties; dist. atty. 1st Dist., 1813-15. Died Kingston, Jan. 10, 1822; buried beneath 1st Reformed Dutch Ch., Kingston.

GARDINER, Sir Christopher, land agt.; flourished 1630-33; married twice. Came to Mass. as secret land agt. for Sir Ferdinando Gorges who claimed holdings and planned to establish colony in Plymouth Grant, 1630; arrested by Mass. authorities for living with a mistress, Mary Grove, and for being Roman Catholic, 1631; while being held, was discovered to be agt. for Gorges, also was found to have 2 wives in Eng.; his mistress was sentenced to be sent to London to join the wives (sentence never carried out); after Mary Grove married Thomas Purchase, a fisherman from Me., Gardiner accompanied them to Brunswick, Me.; appeared as witness for Gorges in attempt to persuade Privy Council to break Mass. Charter, London, 1633.

GARDINER, John, lawyer; b. Boston, Dec. 11, 1737; s. Silvester and Anne (Gibbins) G.; M.A., U. Glasgow (Scotland), 1755; studied law Inner Temple, 1758-61; m. Margaret Harries, 1764, 1 son, John Sylvester John. Admitted to English bar, 1761; practiced law Welsh circuit of Eng., 1761-68; atty. gen. Island of St. Christopher, W.I., 1768-70, practiced law, 1770-83; became naturalized citizen U.S., 1784; practiced law, Boston, 1784-86, Pownalboro, Mass., 1786-93; mem. Mass. Gen. Ct., 1789-93; advocated repeal of laws against theatres, also laws of primo-geniture. Drowned in wreck of Londoner off Cape Ann, Mass., Oct. 15, 1793.

GARDINER, John, Continental congressman; b. South Kingstown, R.I., 1747. Engaged in agriculture, Narragansett, R.I.; served as capt. "Kingston Reds" in Revolutionary Way, 1775-76; Paper Money Party rep. to Gen. Assembly, 1786-87; mem. Continental Congress from R.I., 1789; justice of peace South Kingstown, 1791. Died South Kingstown, Oct. 18, 1808.

GARDINER, John Sylvester, clergyman; b. Haverfordwest, Wales, June 1765; s. John and Margaret (Harris) G.; m. Mary Howard, Sept. 24, 1794, at least 1 child. Ordained deacon Episcopal Ch., N.Y.C., 1789, priest, 1791; asst. rector Trinity Ch., Boston, 1792-1805, rector, 1805-39; taught at large classical sch.; pres. Anthology Club, 1805-10; helped conduct Monthly Anthology and Boston Review; a founder Boston Athenaeum; wrote poem Jacobiniad (satirized French politicians of revolution). Died Harrowgate, Eng., July 29, 1830.

GARDINER, Lion, colonist, mil. engr.; b. 1599; m. Mary Wilemson, children—David, Mary, Elizabeth. Arrived in Boston, 1635; employed by Mass. Bay Colony to design new fort at mouth of Connecticut River (became Ft. Saybrook); leader in defense against Indians, 1636; defended Ft. Saybrook against an attack which culminated in destruction of the Pequot Indian fort, also extermination of most of tribe, 1637; purchased Isle of Wight (now Gardiner's Island), on N.E. coast of L.I., N.Y. Died L.I., 1663.

GARDINER, Robert Hallowell, philanthropist; b. Bristol, Eng., Feb. 10, 1782; s. Robert and Hannah (Gardiner) H.; grad. Harvard, 1801; m. Emma Tudor, June 25, 1805. Inherited large estate on Kennebec River (Me.) at age of 5 from maternal grandmother; moved to Boston, 1792; conceived, initiated founding Gardiner Lyceum, 1821-32 (forerunner of Am. agrl. and tech. schs.), probably 1st instn. of kind to receive pub. money from a state legislature, but financial problems caused closing, 1832; active in missionary, edn. work Protestant Episcopal Ch.; founded a Sunday sch., Gardiner, Me.; mem. Me. Ho. of Reps., 1822; overseer Bowdoin Coll., 1811-41, trustee, 1841-60; pres. Me. Hist. Soc., 1846-55. Died Gardiner, Mar. 22, 1864.

GARDINER, Silvester, physician; b. South Kingston, R.I., June 29, 1708; s. William and Abigail (Remington) G.; m. Anne Gibbins, Dec. 1, 1732; m. 2d, Abigail Eppes, 1772; m. 3d, Catherine Goldthwait, Feb. 18, 1785; 6 children including John. Established apothecary shop in Boston, 1744, later established similar stores in Hartford and Meriden, Conn.; practiced medicine in Boston; proposed the establishment of hosp. for smallpox, 1761; purchased land in Me., 1753, founded Town of Pittston (now Gardiner), Me.; Loyalist during Am. Revolution, lands confiscated, banished, 1778; went to Halifax, N.S., Can., later to Eng.; returned to U.S., 1785, settled in Newport, R.I. Died Newport, Aug. 8, 1786; buried Trinity Ch. Graveyard, Newport.

GARDINER, Sylvester, colonial ofcl.; b. South Kingstown, R.I., circa 1730. Admitted freeman from West Greenwich, R.I., 1757; commd. maj. for Kings County, 1769-70; justice of peace North Kingstown (R.I.), 1774; dep. from North Kingstown, 1775-78, 80-81, 90; apptd. (with others) to take account of powder, arms and ammunition, 1775; mem. com. to remove livestock, 1775; apptd. maj. Kings County Militia, 1780, 6th asst., 1781-83; justice Washington County Ct. of Common Pleas, 1781-88; elected mem. Continental Congress from R.I., 1787, did not take seat; chief justice Ct. of Common Pleas, 1792. Died North Kingstown, 1803.

GARDNER, Caleb, mcht., army officer; b. Newport, R.I., Jan. 24, 1739; s. William and Mary (Carr) G.; m. Sarah Robinson, June 3, 1770; m. 2d, Sarah Fowler, Apr. 17, 1788; m. 3d, Mary Collins, Oct. 20, 1799. Connected with slave trade as mcht. marine; 1st capt. Col. Richmond's Regt., R.I. Militia, 1775; maj., then lt. col. 1st R.I. Regt., 1776; dep. from Newport to R.I. Gen. Assembly, 1777, 79; adviser to French officers in R.I., also Gen. Washington throughout Revolutionary War; mem. R.I. Council of War, 1777-79 noted for piloting French fleet into Newport, 1780; assistant R.I. Gen. Assembly, 1780, 87-90, 92; French vice consul; bank pres.; warden Trinity Ch. Died Newport, Dec. 24, 1806.

GARDNER, Charles Kitchel, army officer, govt. ofcl.; b. Morris County, N.J., June 24, 1787; s. Thomas and Sarah (Kitchel) G.; m. Ann McLean, 1818. Apptd. ensign 6th Regt. Inf., U.S. Army, 1808; promoted capt. 3d Inf., 1812; adj. gen. of Div. of North 1815, 16-18; promoted lt. col., 1815; served in battles of Chippewa and Niagara, siege of Ft. Erie during War of 1812; police justice and dep. commr. gen. N.Y.C., 1818-20; editor Literary and Scientific Repository, and Critical Review, N.Y.C., 1820-22, N.Y. Patriot, N.Y.C., 1822-24; sr. asst. postmaster gen., 1829-36; auditor of treasury for Post Office Dept., 1836-41; sec. bd. commrs. apptd. to adjust claims under treaty with Cherokee Indians 1842-44; postmaster Washington (D.C.), 1845-49; surveyor gen. Ore., 1853-56; clk. U.S. Dept. Treasury, Washington, 1856-67. Author: Compend of the United States System of Infantry Exercise and Manoeuvres, 1819 Regulations for Light Infantry and Riflemen, 1820 A Dictionary of All Officers in the Army of the United States, 1789-1853, published 1853, 2d edit.1860. Died Washington, Nov. 1, 1869.

GARDNER, Francis, congressman; b. Leominster, Mass., Dec. 27, 1771; grad. Harvard 1793; studied law. Admitted to bar, Cheshire County, N.H., 1796, began practice of law, Walpole, N.H.; moved to Keene, N.H., 1806; solicitor Cheshire County, 1807-20; mem. U.S. Ho. of Reps from N.H., 10th Congress, 1807-09. Died Roxbury Mass., June 25, 1835.

GARDNER, Gideon, congressman; b. Nantucket Mass., May 30, 1759. Became successful ship master, later shipowner; also engaged in merc activities; mem. U.S. Ho. of Reps. from Mass. 11th Congress, 1809-11; took petition for tax relief from citizens of Nantucket to Congress, 1813. Died Nantucket, Mar. 22, 1832; buried Friends Burying Ground.

GARDNER, Henry Joseph, gov. Mass.; b. Dorchester, Mass., June 14, 1818; s. Dr. Henry and Clarissa (Holbrook) G.; ed. Bowdoin Coll., A.M. (hon.); LL.D. (hon.), Harvard, 1855; m. Helen Cobb, Nov. 21, 1843, 7 children. Owner dry goods firm Henry J. Gardner & Co.; resident agt. Mass. Life Ins. Co., 1876-92; mem. Boston Common Council, 1850-52, 53, 54, pres., 1852, 53; mem. Mass. Gen. Ct., 1851-52; del. Mass. Constl. Conv., 1853; gov. Mass. (Know Nothing Party), 1854-58. Died Milton, Mass., July 21, 1892.

GARDNER, John Lane, army officer; b. Boston, Aug. 1, 1793; s. Robert Gardner; m. Caroline Goldsborough, 1835. Commd. 3d lt., 4th Inf., U.S. Army, 1813, 2d lt., 1814; served on Northern frontier in War of 1812; transferred to arty., 1814; commd. 1st lt., 1818; q.m. gen., stationed Washington, D.C., 1819-30; promoted capt., 1823; served in Fla. War, also on garrison duty, Fla., 1830-45; commd. maj., 1845; served under Gen. Winfield Scott in campaign from Cerro Gordo to Mexico City during Mexican War; brevetted lt. col. for services at Cerro Gordo, col. for services at Contreras, 1847; in command of dist. of Fla., 1848-50; promoted lt. col., 1852; in command of Ft. Moultrie, Charleston, S.C., 1860, replaced after vowing to defend ft. from confiscation by secessionists, 1860; commd. col., ret., 1861; brevetted brig. gen., 1865. Died Wilmington, Del., Feb. 19, 1869.

GARDNER, Joseph, Continental congressman, physician; b. Chester County, Pa., 1752; studied medicine. Began practice of medicine; raised co. of Volunteers, 1776, commanded 4th Battalion, Chester County Militia; mem. com. of safety, 1776-77; mem. Pa. Assembly, 1776-78, Supreme Exec. Council, 1779; mem. Continental Congress from Pa., 1784-85; resumed practice of medicine, Phila., 1785-92, Elkton, Md., 1792-94. Died Elkton, 1794.

GARFIELD, James Abram, 20th Pres. U.S.; b. Cuyahoga County, O., Nov. 19, 1831; s. Abram and Eliza (Ballou) G.; attended Western Res. Eclectic Inst. (now Hiram Coll.); grad. Williams Coll., 1856; m. Lucretia Rudolph, Nov. 11, 1858, at least 5 children including James Rudolph, Harry Augustus. Admitted to Ohio bar, 1860; tchr., prin. Hiram Coll., 1856-71, pres., 1856-61; mem. Ohio Senate (Republican), 1859; an organizer 42d Ohio Volunteer Inf. Regt., 1861, served as lt. col. and col.; fought at Battle of Middle Creek, 1862; promoted brig. gen. U.S. Volunteers; chief of staff under Rosencrans' Army of Cumberland, 1863; served under Buell in battles of Shiloh and Corinth; organized Div. of Mil. Information; maj. gen. U.S. Volunteers, 1863; mem. U.S. Ho. of Reps. from Ohio, 38th-46th congresses, 1863-Nov. 8, 1880; gained reputation as orator and defender of sound finance; charged with having received gift of stock in Credit Mobilier, 1873, also assailed for not having prevented passage of "Salary Grab Act;" a leader Republican Party, after 1874; mem. Electoral Commn., 1876, active in framing compromise legislation that settled electoral contest between Hayes and Tilden; elected to U.S. Senate, 1880, never took seat; head Ohio delegation to Rep. Nat. Conv., Chgo., 1880, nominated as dark horse candidate, broke deadlock between Blaine and Grant; elected 20th Pres. U.S., Nov. 8, 1880 (defeated Gen. Winfield Scott Hancock), became involved before inauguration in controversy with N.Y. "Stalwarts" led by Roscoe Conkling over claim to control N.Y. patronage appointments (presdl. authority upheld by Senate); shot by Charles J. Guiteau (a disappointed office seeker of "Stalwart" faction), July 2, 1881. Died Elberon, N.J., Sept. 19, 1881; buried Lake View Cemetery, Cleve.

GARFIELDE, Selucius, congressman, lawyer; b. Shoreham, Vt., Dec. 8, 1822; studied law. Moved to Gallipolis, O., later to Paris, Ky.; engaged in newspaper work, Paris; mem. Ky. Constl. Conv., 1849; moved to Cal., 1851; mem. Cal. Ho. of Reps., 1852; elected by legislature to codify Cal. laws, 1853; admitted to bar, 1854, began practice of law, San Francisco; returned to Ky., 1855; del. Democratic Nat. Conv., Cincinnati, 1856; moved to Washington Territory, 1857; receiver public moneys, 1857-60; surveyor gen. Wash. Territory, 1866-69; mem. U.S. Congress (Republican) from Wash. Territory, 41st-42d congresses, 1869-73; apptd. collector of customs for Puget Sound dist., 1873; moved to Seattle, Wash., practiced law; then practiced law, Washington, D.C. Died Washington, Apr. 13, 1881; buried Glenwood Cemetery.

GARIBALDI, Guiseppe, Italian patriot; b. Nice, Italy, July 4, 1807; m. Anite Riveira de Silva; children—Anita, Ricciotti, Menotti. Began fighting for unification of Italy, 1834; fled Italy after defeat by French, 1849; came to N.Y.C., employed as candlemaker, Staten Island; later became trading shipper; returned to Italy to fight again for unification, 1854. Died Island of Caprera, Italy, June 2, 1882.

GARLAND, Augustus Hill, senator, U.S. atty. gen.; b. Tipton County, Tenn., June 11, 1832; s. Rufus and Barbara (Hill) G.; attended St. Mary's Coll., Lebanon, Ky.; grad. St. Joseph's Coll., Bardstown, Ky., 1849; m. Virginia Sanders, 1853. Admitted to Ark. bar, 1850; practiced law, Washington, Ark., 1850-56; partner (with Ebenezer Cummins) in law firm, Little Rock, Ark., 1856-61; admitted to practice before U.S. Supreme Ct., 1860; del. Ark. Secession Conv., 1861; del. Confederate Provisional Congress, 1861; mem. 1st, 2d Confederate congresses from Ark., 1861-64; mem. Confederate Senate, 1864-65; pardoned for Confederate activities by Pres. Andrew Johnson, 1865; readmitted to practice before U.S. Supreme Ct., 1865; elected to U.S. Senate from Ark., 1867, not seated; gov. Ark., 1874-77; mem. U.S. Senate from Ark., 1877-85; U.S. atty. gen. under Pres. Grover Cleveland, 1885-89. Author: Experience in the Supreme Court of the United States, 1898; (with Robert Ralston) A Treatise on the Constitution and Jurisdiction of the United States Courts, 2 vols., 1898. Died Washington, D.C., Jan. 26, 1899; buried Mt. Holly Cemetery, Little Rock.

GARLAND, David Shepherd, congressman, lawyer; b. nr. New Glasgow (now Clifford), Va., Sept. 27, 1769; studied law. Admitted to bar, began practice of law, Va.; mem. Va. Ho. of Dels., 1799-1802, 05-09, 14-15, 19-26, 32-36; mem. Va. Senate, 1809-11; mem. U.S. Ho. of Reps. (Democrat, filled vacancy) from Va., 11th Congress, Jan. 17, 1810-11. Died Clifford, Oct. 7, 1841; buried Meredith and Garland families' graveyard, Clifford.

GARLAND, James, congressman, lawyer; b. Ivy Depot, Albemarle County, Va., June 6, 1791; studied law. Admitted to bar, began practice of law, Lovingston, Va.; served in War of 1812; mem. Va. Ho. of Dels., 1829-31; mem. U.S. Ho. of Reps. (Democrat) from Va., 24th-26th congresses, 1835-41; moved to Lynchburg, Va., 1841; judge corp. ct., 1841-82; commonwealth atty. for Lynchburg, 1849-72. Died Lynchburg, Aug. 8, 1885; buried Spring Hill Cemetery.

GARLAND, Landon Cabell, univ. chancellor; b. Nelson County, Va., Mar. 21, 1810; s. Spotswood and Lucinda (Rose) G.; grad. Hampden-Sydney Coll., 1829; m. Louisa Garland, Dec. 1835. Prof. natural science Washington Coll. (now Washington and Lee U.), 1829-32; prof. natural philosophy Randolph-Macon Coll., 1832-36, pres., 1836-46; became prof. U. Ala., 1847, pres., 1855-65; prof. physics and astronomy U. Miss., 1866; wrote a series of articles for Christian Advocate, Nashville, Tenn; resulted in plan for sectionwide Methodist univ. to be established, Nashville, 1868; 1st chancellor Vanderbilt U., Nashville, 1875-93, Author: Trigonometry, Plane and Spherical, 1841. Died Nashville, Feb. 12, 1895.

GARLAND, Rice, congressman, lawyer; b. Lynchburg, Va., circa 1795; studied law. Admitted to bar, began practice of law; moved to Opelousas, La., 1820; mem. U.S. Ho. of Reps. (Whig, filled vacancy) from La., 23d-26th congresses, Apr. 28, 1834-July 21, 1840 (resigned); judge La. Supreme Ct., 1840-46; practiced law, Brownsville, Tex., 1846-61. Died Brownsville, 1861; buried Brownsville.

GARLICK, Theodatus, surgeon, sculptor; b. Mar. 30, 1805; s. Daniel and Sabra (Kirby) G.; grad. U. Md. Med. Sch., 1834; m.3d, Mary Chittenden, 1845. Practiced surgery, Youngstown, O., 1834-52, had reputation as plastic surgeon; inventor new splints, surg. instruments; made models of surg. and pathol. anatomy; sculpted bas-reliefs of Andrew Jackson, Henry Clay, full length miniature of Chief Justice John Marshall; constructed camera which took daguerreotypes (photographing a person not in direct sunlight for 1st time), 1840; did experiments in artificial trout-breeding (1st of kind in Am.). Died Dec. 9, 1884.

GARNET, Henry Highland, educator, clergyman; b. New Market, Md., Dec. 23, 1815; s. George and Henny Garnet; attended Oneida Inst., Whitestown, N.Y.; m. Julia Williams, 1841. Escaped from slavery, 1824; went to sch. with other escaped slaves at Canaan, N.H. (sch. broken up by a mob, 1835); became preacher and abolition agitator for Am. Anti-Slavery Soc.; licensed to preach, 1842; delivered address before nat. conv. of free people of color at Buffalo urging slaves to rise and slay their masters, 1843; opposed in that conv. by Frederick Douglass; urged establishment of a press to promote emancipation; pastor of Liberty Street Presbyn. Ch., Troy, N.Y., 1843-48; sent as missionary to Jamaica, B.W.I., by U.P. Ch. of Scotland, 1852; went on lecture tour through Eng. as pres. of African Civilization Soc., 1861; chaplain of 20th, 26th, and 31st colored regts. during Civil War; went to Washington, D.C. as pastor of 15th St. Presbyn. Ch. where he did much for relief of distressed during the Civil War, 1864; pres. Avery Coll., 1869-70; apptd. minister to Liberia, 1881. Died Monrovia, Liberia, Feb. 13, 1882.

GARNETT, Alexander Yelverton Peyton, physician; b. Essex County, Va., Sept. 19, 1819; s. Muscoe and Maria (Battaile) G.; M.D., U. Pa., 1841; m. Mary Wise, June 13, 1848. Commd. Asst. surgeon Med. Corps, U.S. Navy, 1841; prof. clin. medicine Nat. Med. Coll., Washington, D.C., 1850-61, 67-70; served as med. officer Confederate Army in charge of 2 mil. hosps., Richmond, Va., also Pres. Davis' personal physician; considered a leading gen. practitioner; mem. bds. dirs. of charitable instns. and hosps. in Washington; pres. A.M.A., 1885-88. Autho: Observations on the Sanitary Advantages of Tide-Water Virginia, 1877. Died Rehoboth Beach, Del., July 11, 1888.

GARNETT, James Mercur, congressman, agriculturist, educator; b. Essex County, Va., June 8, 1770; s. Muscoe and Grace Fenton (Mercur) G.; m. Mary Mercer, Sept. 21, 1793. Mem. Va. Ho. of Reps., 1799, 1800, 25-26; mem. U.S. Ho. of Reps. from Va., 7th-8th congresses, 1805-09; mem. grand jury that indicted Aaron Burr, 1807; pres. Fredericksburg Agrl. Soc., 1817-37; mem. Anti-Tariff Conv., Balt., 1821; attended Anti-Tariff Conv., Phila., 1831; a founder Va. Agrl. Soc.; 1st pres. U.S. Agrl. Soc.; mem. Va. Constl. Conv., 1829-30; prepared constl. charts of legislative, exec. and judiciary depts. in all states of union including Fed. govt.; opened sch. for young ladies in early 1820's; advocate of improved methods of edn. Author: Seven Lectures on Female Education (advocated wider edn for women). 1824; An Address on the Subject of Literary Associations to Promote Education, 1854. Died Rappahannock, Va., Apr. 23, 1843; buried family burial ground, Loretto, Va.

GARNETT, Muscoe Russel Hunter, congressman; b. Essex County, Va., July 25, 1821; s. James Mercur and Maria (Hunter) G., Jr.; m. Mary Stevens. Admitted to Va. bar, 1842; del. Va. Constl. Conv., 1850, 61; del. Nat. Democratic Conv., Balt., Cincinnati, 1856; mem. Va. Ho. of Dels., 1853-56; bd. visitors U. Va., 1855-59; mem. U.S. Ho. of Reps. from Va., 34th-36th congresses, Dec. 1, 1856-61; strong advocate of secession; chosen to fill vacancy at Va. Secession Conv., 1861; mem. 1st Confederate Congress, 1862-64. Author: The Union Past and Future: How It Works and How To Save It (pamphlet), 1850. Died Feb. 14, 1864.

GARNETT, Robert Selden, congressman, lawyer; b. "Mt. Pleasant," nr. Loretto, Va., Apr. 26, 1789; attended Coll. of N.J. (now Princeton); studied law. Admitted to bar, began practice of law, Lloyds, Va.; mem. Va. Ho. of Dels., 1816-17; mem. U.S. Ho. of Reps. (Democrat) from Va., 15th-19th congresses, 1817-27. Died on his estate "Champlain," nr. Lloyds, Aug. 15, 1840; buried family burying ground on estate.

GARNETT, Robert Selden, army officer; b. Essex County, Va., Dec. 16, 1819; s. Robert Selden and Olympia Charlotte (DeGouges) G.; grad. U.S. Mil. Acad, 1841; m. Mary Neilson, 1857. Asst. instr. tactics U.S. Mil. Acad., 1843-44; aide-de-camp to Gen. Wood, 1845; brevetted capt. in Battle of Monterey during Mexican War, 1846-48; aide-de-camp to Zachary Taylor, 1846-49; commd. 1st lt. with brevets of capt., maj., 1850; capt. inf., 1848-50; comdt. of cadets, instr. inf. tactics U.S. Mil. Acad., 1852-54; commd. maj., 1855; commanded Puget Sound, also Yakima expdns. in N..W, 1856; commd. brig. gen. in command Confederate Army in N.W. Va., 1861; served in Battle of Carricks Ford, Va., covered the retreat of his force from Laurel Hill across Cheat River in face of McClellan's Army. Killed in Battle of Carricks Ford (1st gen. to fall in Civil War), July 13, 1861.

GARNSEY, Daniel Greene, congressman, lawyer; b. Canaan, N.Y., June 17, 1779; attended pvt. schs.; studied law, Norwich, N.Y. Became mem. N.Y. Militia, 1805; brigade insp., Saratoga County, N.Y., 1810-11; admitted to bar, 1811, began practice of law, Rensselaer and Saratoga counties; served (with rank of maj.), as aide-de-camp to maj. gen. in War of 1812; moved to Pomfret, 1816; a promoter devel. of Village of Dunkirk; commr. to perform spl. jud. duties at chambers of Supreme Ct.; surrogate Chautauqua County (N.Y.), 1813-31; brigade insp. Chautauqua County, 1817; dist. atty. Chautauqua County, 1818-26; mem. U.S. Ho. of Reps. (Jackson Democrat) from N.Y., 19th-20th congresses, 1825-29; moved to vicinity of Battle Creek, Mich., 1831; apptd. postmaster, govt. supt. public works, nr. Detroit and Ypsilanti, Mich.; served with Gen. Scott in Black Hawk War, 1836; moved to Rock Island, Ill.; receiver of public moneys at land office, Dixon, Ill. (apptd. by Pres. Harrison), 1841-43; pres. of Harrison celebration, Galena, Ill., 1840. Died (while on way to attend celebration of completion of Erie R.R.), Gowanda, N.Y., May 11, 1851; buried Pine Hill Cemetery.

GARRARD, James, gov. Ky., clergyman; b. Stafford County, Va., Jan. 14, 1749; s. William Garrard; m. Elizabeth Mountjoy, Dec. 20, 1769, 12 children including James. Commd. col. Stafford County Regt., Va. Militia, 1781; mem. Va. Ho. of Dels., 1779; helped organize Cooper's Run Ch., nr. Mt. Lebanon, Ky., 1787; mem. Va. Ho. of Dels. from Fayette County, 1785; rep. Fayette and Bourbon counties in convs. for establishment of Ky. statehood, 1784-90; mem. 1st Ky. Constl. Conv.; gov. Ky., 1796-1804, used great influence in adoption Ky. Resolutions of 1798; dropped from Baptist Ch. and Nat. Bapt. Assn. for possessing and spreading Unitarian views, 1803. Died Bourbon County, Ky. Jan. 19, 1822.

GARRARD, Kenner, army officer; b. Ky., circa Sept. 1828; s. Zeptha Dudley and Sarah (Ludlow) G.; grad. U.S. Mil. Acad., 1851. Served frontier duty before Civil War; served as col. 146th N.Y. Volunteers in Rappahannock (Va.) and Pa. campaigns, 1861; brevetted lt. col. U.S. Army; commd. brig. gen. U.S. Volunteers, 1863; transferred to Army of Cumberland as comdr. cavalry comm. in Tenn., Ga.; in charge of Cavalry Bur., Washington, D.C.; brevetted col. for leading expdn. to Covington, Ga., 1864; commanded 2d div. XVI U.S. Army Corps, 1864-65; brevetted maj. gen., also brig. gen. U.S. Volunteers for gallantry; brevetted maj. gen. U.S. Army 1865; comdg. officer Dist. of Mobile until 1865; asst. insp. gen. Dept. of Mo. until 1866; mem. Hist. and Philos. Soc. of Ohio. Died Cincinnati, May 15, 1879; buried Spring Grove Cemetery, Cincinnati.

GARREAU, Armand, author; b. Cognac, France, Sept. 13, 1817; s. Louis and Marie (Dumontet) G.; m. Marie Anais Boraud, Nov. 1838, 6 children. Came to U.S., circa 1840; conducted sch., New Orleans; contbd. articles to French newspaper La Revue de la Semaine, New Orleans; returned to France, 1848; editor-publisher newspaper Ne Narrateur impartial, Barbezieux, France, 1850-54; published mag. Légendes et Chroniques de l'Angoumois, de la Saintonge et des provinces limitrophes, 1854-57; returned to New Orleans, 1858, resumed teaching. Author: (novels) Louisiana, 1849; Ogine, 1852; Leudaste, 1854. Died New Orleans, Mar. 28, 1865.

GARRETSON, James Edmund, (pseudonym John Darby), oral surgeon; b. Wilmington, Del., Oct. 4, 1828; s. Jacob M. and Mary (Powell) G.; grad. Phila. Coll. Dental Surgery, 1856; M.D., U. Pa., 1859; m. Beulah Craft, Nov. 10, 1859, 2 daus. With Phila. Dental Coll., 1874-95, prof. anatomy and surgery, 1878, dean of faculty, 1880; prof. clin. surgery Medico-Chirurg. Coll. of Phila.; pres. Med. and Chirurg. Soc. Phila., 1883; originator of oral surgery as a splty. of dentistry; 1st surgeon to employ dental engine as modified for surg. operations, 1882. Author: A Treatise on the Diseases and Surgery of the Mouth, Jaws and Associated Parts, 1869; A System of Oral Surgery, 1873, 81, 84, 90, 95; Man and His World, 1889. Died Lansdowne, Pa., Oct. 26, 1895.

GARRETT, John Work, railroad exec., banker; b. Balt., July 31, 1820; s. Robert and Elizabeth (Stouffer) G.; attended Lafayette Coll. (Pa.), 2 years; m. Rachel Harrison. Became pres. B.& O. R.R., 1858 (after stockholders' challenge to mgmt., which he led); managed road successfully, improved earnings, freed bd. of dirs. from polit. control; instrumental in preventing Md. Confederates from taking Washington (D.C.) during Civil War; continued railroad service throughout war, although line twice crossed Confederate territory; obtained direct routes to Chgo. and Pitts., after war, also acquired independent line to N.Y.C.; arranged for N. German Lloyd line to unload ships at Balt., re-establishing city as major seaport; built B.& O. R.R. into integrated co. by having line build its own cars and operate its own express and telegraph cos.; solved problem of rate wars by formation of pools; attempted to manipulate state legislature (because of charges of discrimination), 1870's. Died Deer Park, Garrett County, Md., Sept. 26, 1884.

GARRETT, Robert, businessman; b. Lisburn, County Down, Ireland, May 2, 1783; son of John Garrett; m. Elizabeth Stouffer, May 19, 1817, at least 2 children including John Work. Came to U.S., 1790; clk. for produce and commn. bus., Balt., 1800-04; partner Wallace & Garrett, western trading firm, Balt., 1804-12; established and headed Robert Garrett and Sons, wholesale grocery and commn. bus., Balt., 1820-57; an original investor in B.& O. R.R., 1827; established trade connections with Latin Am. and Europe; Am. rep. for several European firms; dir. Balt. Water Co., Gas Co., Shot Tower Co., Savs. Bank Balt.; founder, dir. Western Bank of Balt., 1836-57, Eutaw Says. Bank, 1847-57; owner Eutaw House, Wheatfield Inn (hotels), Balt. Died Balt., Feb. 4, 1857.

GARRETT, Thomas, abolitionist; b. Upper Darby, Pa., Aug. 21, 1789; s. Thomas and Sarah (Price) G.; m. Mary Sharpless; m. 2d, Rachel Mendenhall. Joined Pa. Abolition Soc., 1818; his home in Wilmington, Del. was a refuge for slaves and an Underground R.R. Station which caused Md. to offer reward of $10,000 for his arrest; arrested 1848, convicted, fined; helped about 2000 slaves to escape; Wilmington Negroes celebrating 15th Amendment drew him through streets in open carriage with a picture of him called Our Moses. Died Wilmington, Jan. 25, 1871; buried Wilmington.

GARRETTSON, Freeborn, clergyman; b. Md., Aug. 15, 1752; s. John and Sarah (Hanson) G.; m. Catharine Livingston, June 30, 1793. Inherited father's plantation in Md., 1773; became Methodist, freed his slaves, 1775; itinerant preacher, Md., Va., Pa., N.Y., 1776-84; attended conf. which organized Methodist Ch. of U.S., Balt., 1784; ordained to ministry Methodist Ch., 1784; missionary in Nova Scotia, 1785-87; travelling preacher, primarily in N.Y., 1787-1827; a founder Missionary and Bible Soc. Author: The Experience and Travels of Mr. Freeborn Garretson, 1791; A Dialogue Between Do-Justice and Professing Christian, 1820. Died Sept. 26, 1827.

GARRISON, Cornelius Kingsland, financier, mayor San Francisco; b. Ft. Montgomery, N.Y., Mar. 1, 1809; s. Oliver and Catherine (Kingsland) G.; m. Mary Re Tallack, Aug. 1, 1831, a son, William Re Tallack; m. 2d, Letitia Randall, Oct. 10, 1878. Gen. mgr. Canadian bus. for Upper Can. Co. until 1833; went to St. Louis, 1833; designed, built, ran steam boats; organized regular freight service to New Orleans and other ports; established comml. and banking house in Panama, 1849; managed Pacific agy. at San Francisco of Nicaragua S.S. Co., 1853; elected mayor San Francisco, 1853, effected permanent civic reforms, suppressed pub. gambling halls, closed theaters on Sundays; supported Pony Express transcontinental mail service; returned to N.Y.C., 1859, started banking firm Garrison & Fretz; initiated steamship service between N.Y.C. and Brazil, promoted extensive trading operations with other S. Am. countries; pres. Mo. Pacific R.R., 1876. Died N.Y.C., May 1, 1885.

GARRISON, Daniel, congressman; b. nr. Salem, N.J., Apr. 3, 1782. Engaged in agriculture; mem. N.J. Gen. Assembly, 1806-08; surrogate Salem County, 1809-23; mem. U.S. Ho. of Reps. (Democrat) from N.J., 18th-19th congresses, 1823-27; insp. of revenue, collector of customs Port of Bridgeton (N.J.) (apptd. by Pres. Jackson), 1834-38. Died Salem, Feb. 13, 1851; buried St. John's Episcopal Cemetery.

GARRISON, George Tankard, congressman, lawyer; b. Accomack County, Va., Jan. 14, 1835; grad. Dickinson Coll,. Carlisle, Pa., 1853, law dept. U. Va. at Charlottersville, 1857. Admitted to bar, began practice of law, Accomac; served as pvt. Confederate Army during Civil War; mem. Va. Ho. of Dels., 1861-63, Va. Senate, 1863-65; also engaged in agriculture; judge 8th Va. Circuit, 1870, later judge 17th Circuit; mem. U.S. Ho. of Reps. (Democrat) from Va., 47th-48th congresses, 1881-83, Mar. 20, 1884-85; judge Accomack County Ct. Died Accomac, Nov. 14, 1889; buried Edge Hill Cemetery.

GARRISON, William Lloyd, abolitionist, reformer; b. Newburyport, Mass., Dec. 10, 1805; s. Abijah and Frances (Lloyd G., m. Helen Benson Sept. 4, 1834, 7 children. Editor, Free Press, Newburyport, 1826; co-editor Nat. Philanthropist Boston,, 1828; condr. Journal of the Times, Bennington, Vt.; co-editor weekly Genius of Universal Emancipation, Balt., 1829; founded The Liberator, 1831 (paper so embittered South that Ga. even offered $5,000 reward for arrest and conviction); a founder, corresponding sec. New Eng. Anti-Slavery Soc.; one of 1st abolitionists to demand complete and immediate emancipation; a founder Am. Anti-Slavery Soc., 1833, fgn. sec., 1833, pres. pro tem, 1840, pres., 1843-65; attended meeting Friends of Universal Reform, 1840; leader anti-slavery group Old Ogs; became disunionist, 1841; conducted lecture tour beyond Alleghanies against defenders of Union, 1847; prevented abolition socs. from openly condemning Lincoln's administrn.; responsible for reconciling 2 factions of Abolitionists; worked for women's suffrage and fair treatment of Indians, after Civil War. Author: Thoughts on African Colonization, 1832; Sonnets and Other Poems, 1843. Died N.Y.C., May 24, 1879; buried Boston.

GARRISON, William Re Tallack, financier; b. Goderich, Can., June 18, 1834; s. Cornelius Kingsland and Mary (Re Tallack) G.; m. Mary Estill, 1865. Moved to St. Louis, circa 1834 assumed charge of his father's banking and maritime interests on Pacific Coast, 1859-64; managed all family enterprises N.Y.C., from 1864; pres. Garrison line to Brazil; pres. M.P. R.R., circa 1878-79; pres. Wabash R.R.; accomplished permanent unification of elevated railroads, opened way for extension and successful operation, N.Y.C.; pres. Manhattan Co., dir. until 1882. Died Elberson, N.J., July 1, 1882.

GARROW, Nathaniel, congressman; b. Barnstable, Mass., Apr. 25, 1780; attended public schs. Became a seaman; moved to Auburn, N.Y., 1796; apptd. justice of peace, 1809; sheriff Cayuga County (N.Y.), 1815-19, 21-25; mem. U.S. Ho. of Reps. (Democrat) from N.Y., 20th Congress, 1827-29; Dem. presdl. elector, 1832; U.S. marshal No. Dist. N.Y., 1837-41. Died Auburn, Mar. 3, 1841; buried family burying ground on his estate; reinterred Ft. Hill Cemetery, Auburn.

GARRY, Spokane, Indian chief; b. Spokane fishery (now Spokane County), Wash., 1811; s. Illim-Spokanee. Named for Nicholas Garry, dep. gov. Hudson Bay Co.; received limited edn. in mission sch. in Can.; returned to his tribe, opened a sch., 1832; became chief of upper and middle bands Spokane Indians, kept peace between his people and white men; signed treaty relinquishing land claims of his tribes, 1887. Died in poverty with treaty still unratified, Jan. 13, 1892; buried Greenwood Cemetery, Spokane, Wash.

GARTRELL, Lucius Jeremiah, congressman, army officer; b. Wilkes County, Ga., Jan.7, 1821; s. Joseph and Miss (Boswell) G., Jr.; attended U. Ga, Randolph-Macon Coll.; m. Louisiana O. Gideon, 1841; m. 2d, Antoinette T. Burke, 1855; m. 3d, Maud Condon, circa 1888; 11 children. Admitted to Ga. bar, 1842; elected to Ga. Gen. Assembly, 1847-51, radical pro-Southern, pro-slavery leader, 1849; mem. U.S. Ho. of Reps. from Ga., 35th-36th congresses, 1857-59, strongly advocated secession; organized 7th Ga. Regt., Confederate Army, 1861; elected col.; mem. Confederate Congress, 1861; commd. brig. gen., 1864; noted criminal lawyer; leading mem. Ga. Constl. Conv., 1877; regent Smithsonian Instn. Died Atlanta, Ga., Apr. 7, 1891.

GARVIN, William Swan, congressman, journalist; b. Mercer, Pa., July 25, 1806. Editor, Western Press, Mercer, 50 years; postmaster Mercer, 1837-41, 67-69; mem. U.S. Ho. of Reps. (Democrat) from Pa., 29th Congress, 1845-47; flour insp., Pitts. Died Mercer, Feb. 20, 1883; buried Citizens' Cemetery.

GARY, Martin Witherspoon, army officer; b. Cokesbury, S.C., Mar. 25, 1831; s. Thomas Reader and Mary Anne (Porter) G.; attended S.C. Coll.; grad. Harvard, 1854. Admitted to S.C. bar, 1855; mem. S.C. Legislature, 1860; leader S.C. secession movement; commd. capt. Watson Guards, 1861; commd. lt. col. of inf. Confederate Army, col. of regt.; brig. gen., 1864, in charge troops conducting Jefferson Davis to Cokesbury where last Confederate cabinet meeting was held at Gary's mother's home; a foremost defender of 'straightout policy,' white supremacy, no compromise with negroes; opposed payment of reconstrn. debts; mem. S.C. Senate, 1876-80. Died Apr. 9, 1881.

GASKILL, Harvey Freeman, inventor, engr.; b. Royalton, N.Y., Jan. 19, 1845; s. Benjamin F. and Olive G.; grad. Comml. Coll., 1866; m. Mary Moore, Dec. 25, 1873. Designed revolving hay-rake, 1858; mem. clock mfg. firm Penfield, Martin & Gaskill; draftsman Holly Mfg. Co., 1873; engr., supt., 1877, dir., v.p., 1885; invented Gaskill pumping engine (1st crank and fly-wheel high duty pumping engine built as standard for waterworks service),1882; mem. Am. Soc. M.E. Died Apr. 1, 1889.

GASS, Patrick, explorer; b. Falling Springs, Pa., June 12, 1771; probably s. Henry Gass; m. Maria Hamilton, 1831, 7 children. Joined Lewis and Clark expdn. as pvt., 1803, promoted sgt., 1804; kept journal of trip, published 1807; served under Andrew Jackson against Creek Indians in War of 1812, fought in Battle of Lundy's Lane, 1814; joined Campbellites in later life. Died Apr. 30, 1870.

GASTON, William, congressman, jurist; b. New Bern, N.C., Sept. 19, 1778; s. Alexander and Margaret (Sharpe) G.; grad. Coll. of N.J. (now Pirnceton), 1796; m. Susan Hay; m. 2d, Hannah McClure; m. 3d, Eliza Worthington; 5 children including Alexander. Admitted to N.C. bar, 1798; mem. N.C. Ho. of Commons, 1807-09, 24, 27-29, 31, N.C. Senate, 1800, 12, 18, 19, helped write act which established N.C. Supreme Ct., 1818; mem. U.S. Ho. of Reps. from N.C., 13th-14th congresses, 1813-17; chief justice N.C. Supreme Ct., 1833-44; mem. N.C. Constl. Conv., 1835; trustee U. N.C., 1802-44. Died Raleigh, N.C., Jan. 23, 1844; buried Cedar Grove Cemetery, New Bern.

GASTON, William, gov. Mass.; b. Killingly, Conn., Oct. 3, 1820; s. Alexander and Kesia (Arnold) G.; grad. with honors Brown U., 1840, LL.D., 1875; LL.D., Harvard, 1875; m. Louisa Beeches, May 27, 1852. Opened law office, Roxbury, Mass., 1844; mem. Mass. Legislature, 1853-54, 56; city solicitor Roxbury, 1856-60, mayor, 1861-62; mem. Mass. Senate, 1868; mayor Boston, 1871-72; gov. Mass. (Democrat) 1874-75; a founder law firm Jewell, Gaston and Field, 1865-99; leading Mass. trial lawyer; pres. Boston Bar Assn.; head Mass. Bar Assn. Died Boston, Jan. 19, 1894; buried Forest Hills Cemetery.

GATES, Horatio, army officer; b. Maldon, Essex, Eng., circa 1728; s. Robert and Dorothy (Parker) G.; m. Elizabeth Phillips, Oct. 20, 1754, 1 son, Robert; m. 2d, Mary Vallance, July 31, 1786. Lt. in Nova Scotia, 1749-50; commd. capt. in N.Y. Independent Co. of Foot, 1754; served as capt. with Braddock's army at Ft. Duquesne, 1755; with Gen. Nicholas Herkimer during defense of Ft. Herkimer against French and Indians, 1758; with Gen. Monckton in expdn. that took Martinique; commd. maj. 45th Regt., 1762; lt. col. in Va. Militia; commd. adj. gen. Continental Army with rank of brig. gen. 1775; promoted maj. gen., 1776; in supreme command of No. army, late summer 1777; in charge of Continental forces during Saratoga campaign which brought about defeat of Burgoyne's army (key in gaining French alliance); implicated in congressional conspiracy known as Conway Cabal (he was to replace George Washington as comdr.-in-chief); recipient medal from Congress, 1777; pres. Bd. of War, 1777; again commanded No. dept., Apr. 1778; took command of troops in Eastern dept., Oct. 1778; directed by Congress to command army in So. dept., 1780; largely responsible for defeat at Camden, Aug. 1780; relieved of command, Dec. 1780; rejoined army, 1782; pres. State Soc. of Cincinnati, 1783; mem. N.Y. Legislature, 1800-06, Whig. Died N.Y.C., Apr. 10, 1806.

GATES, Seth Merrill, congressman; b. Winfield, N.Y., Oct. 10, 1800; attended Middleburg Acad., Wyoming, N.Y.; studied law. Became insp. of common schs., also dep. sheriff Le Roy (N.Y.), circa 1825; admitted to bar, 1827, began practice of law, Le Roy; supr. Le Roy, 1830; mem. N.Y. State Assembly, 1832; owner, editor Le Roy Gazette, 1838; mem. U.S. Ho. of Reps. (Anti-Slavery Whig) from N.Y., 26th-27th congresses, 1839-43; moved to Warsaw, N.Y., 1843, continued practice of law, also engaged in lumber, ha-rdware and dry-goods businesses; unsuccessful Free-Soil candidate for lt. gov. N.Y., 1848; sec. Wyoming County Ins. Co., 1851-65; postmaster Warsaw, 1861-70; v.p. Genesee County Pioneer Assn., 1872. Died Warsaw, Aug. 24, 1877; buried Warsaw Cemetery.

GATES, Sir Thomas, colonial gov; b. Colyford, Devonshire, Eng., circa 1560; children--Anthony, Thomas, Margaret, Elizabeth. Sailed to Am. with Sir Francis Drake, 1585, helped carry back survivors of Roanoke Colony; created knight after battle which captured Cadiz for Eng., 1596; 1st named of grantees in charter of Apr. 10, 1606 to Va. and Plymouth Co.; lt. gen. and investor (2,000) pounds in Va. Co.; left for Va., his ship Sea Adventure separated from main body and believed lost, ship reached Bermuda where colonists lived for 10 months, arrived in Va., 1610 (incident inspired Shakespeare's The Tempest); took over govt. of Va. from Percy, May-June 1610; went to Eng. to attract settlers from Eng. and Holland and gain support for Co. and colony, 1610, returned, 1611; gov. Va., 1611-14, organized econ. activities, stalilized polit. instns. of colony; went back to Eng., 1614, active in Va. Co. affairs. Died Holland, 1621.

GATLIN, Alfred Moore, congressman; b. Edenton, N.C., Apr. 20, 1790; grad. U. N.C. at Chapel Hill, 1808; studied law. Admitted to bar, 1823, began practice of law, Camden, N.C.; mem. U.S. Ho. of Reps. from N.C., 18th Congress, 1823-25; moved to Territory of Fla.

GAUSE, Lucien Coatsworth, congressman, lawyer; b. nr. Wilmington, N.C., Dec. 25, 1836; grad. U. Va. at Charlottesville; studied law; grad. Cumberland U., Lebanon, Tenn. Admitted to bar, began practice of law, Jacksonport, Ark., 1859; served from lt. to col. Confederate Army, during Civil War; mem. Ark. Ho. of Reps., 1866; commr. to represent state govt. at Washington; mem. U.S. Ho. of Reps. (Democrat) from Ark. 44th-45th congresses, 1875-79. Died Jacksonport, Nov 5, 1880; buuried pvt. burying ground nr. Jacksonport.

GAVIT, John E., engraver; b. N.Y.C., Oct., 29, 1817; Learned engraver's trade, Albany, N.Y.; established engraving, printing and lithographic bus., Albany, circa 1840; became banknote engraver; a founder Am. Bank Note Co., 1858, sec., several years, pres., 1866-74; moved to N.Y.C., 1859, established engraving firm Gavit & Co. Died Stockbridge, Mass., Aug. 25, 1874.

GAY, Ebenezer, clergyman; b. Dedham, Mass., Aug. 15, 1696; s. Nathaniel and Lydia (Lusher) G.; grad. Harvard, 1712, D.D. (hon.), 1795; m. Jerusha Bradford, Nov. 3, 1719, 11 children. Ordained and installed as minister Congregational Ch., Hingham, Mass, 1718; theologically an Arminian, opposed rigid articles of faith, anticipated Unitarian movement in his liberal attitudes; published sermons including The Old Man's Calendar 1781, The Massachusetts Election Sermon, 1745. Dudleian Lecture at Harvard on Natural and Revealed Religion, 1759. Died Hingham, Mar. 18, 1787.

GAY, Edward James, congressman, businessman; b. Liberty, Va., Feb. 3, 1816; attended Augusta Coll., Ky., 1833-34. Engaged in business, St. Louis, 1838-60; engaged in mfg. and agriculture, La.; 1st pres. La. Sugar Exchange, New Orleans; mem. U.S. Ho. of Reps. (Democrat) from La., 49th-51st congresses, 1885-89. Died on his plantation, Iberville Parish, La., May 30, 1889; buried Bellefontaine Cemetery, St. Louis.

GAY, Sydney Howard, journalist; b. Hingham, Mass., May 22, 1814; s. Ebenezer and Mary (Otis) G.; B.A., Harvard, 1833; m. Elizabeth Neall, 1845. Joined group of Abolitionists led by William L. Garrison, Boston, 1842; speaker for Am. Anti-Slavery Soc., Boston, 1842; editor Am. Anti-Slavery Standard, N.Y.C., 1843-57; agt. for underground ry., 1843-57; mem. editorial staff N.Y. Tribune, 1857-62, mng. editor, 1862-65; mng. editor Chgo. Tribune, 1867-71; mem. editorial staff N.Y. Evening Post, 1872-74. Died June 25, 1888.

GAYARRE, Charles Etienne Arthur, state ofcl., historian; b. New Orleans, Jan. 9, 1805; s. Don Carlos and Marie (de Bore) G.; grad. Coll. of Orleans, 1825; m. Mrs. Annie Sullivan Buchanan, circa 1843. Published an influential pamphlet opposing criminal code prepared by Edward Livingston, 1826; admitted to Phila. bar, 1829; published Essai historique sur la Louisiane, 1830; elected to La. Legislature, 1830; apptd. asst. atty. gen. La., 1831; presiding judge city cts. of New Orleans, 1832; elected to U.S. Senate, 1835, resigned because of ill health; went to France; stayed until 1843, while there started Histoire de la Luisiane, published 1846-47; mem. La. Legislature, 1844-46; sec. of state La., 1846-53, established 1st state library, defeated for reelection (perhaps by use of fraudulent opposition voting), 1853; because of this experience wrote School for politics (a satirical novel); participated in formation of Know-Nothing Party in La.; supported Confederacy during Civil War, but realizing its hopeless position he advocated freeing and arming of slaves; pres. La. Hist. Soc., 1860-88; reporter of decisions La. Supreme Ct., 1873-76. Author: Romance of the History of Louisiana, 1848; Louisiana, Its Colonial History and Romance, 1851; Philip II of Spain, 1866; History of Louisiana—The American Domination, 1866; Ferdinand de Lemos, Truth and Fiction, 1872. Died New Orleans, Feb. 11, 1895.

GAYLE, John, gov. Ala., congressman; b. Sumter Dist., S.C., Sept. 11, 1792; s. Matthew and Mary (Reese) G.; grad. S.C. Coll., 1815; m. Sarah Haynesworth, Nov. 14, 1819, 6 children including Amelia; m. 2d, Clarissa Peck, Nov. 1, 1839, 4 children. Admitted to S.C. bar, 1813; practiced in Mobile, Ala.; mem. 1st council Ala. Territory, 1818; solicitor Monroe County, Ala., 1819; mem. Ala. Ho. of Reps., 1822-23, 29, speaker; circuit judge, justice Ala. Supreme Ct., 1823; gov. Ala., 1831-35, rejected doctrine of nullification until 1833; mem. U.S. Ho. of Reps. from Ala., 30th Congress, 1847-49; U.S. dist. judge for Ala., 1849-59. Died Mobile, July 28, 1859; buried Magnolia Cemetery, Mobile.

GAYLER, Charles, playwright; b. N.Y.C., Apr.1, 1820; s. C.J. Gayler; m. Grace Christian, 1846. Editor Cincinnati Evening Dispatch; became actor, appeared in Hamlet, Othello and Richelieu, in Ohio; wrote reviews for Tribune and Herald, 1862; credited with authorship over 400 plays (tragedies, comedies, melodramas, operettas), over 100 of which were produced on Am. and English stage; produced 1st play The Buckeye Gold Hunters, Cincinnati, 1849; other noted plays include: Bull Run (1st Civil War play), Taking Chances (1851), The Love of a Prince, The Son of Night, The Magic Marriage, A Mistress of Arts. Died Bklyn., May 28, 1892; buried Greenwood Cemetery, Bkly.

GAYLORD, Charles Seely, artist; b. Gaylordsville, Conn., Dec. 30, 1811; attended Yale. Painted in Gaylordsville most of life; resided in Catskill, N.Y., 1838-41; exhibited at N.A.D., Am. Art-Union; 2 extant works privately owned. Died of injuries received when he was gored by a cow while painting a farm scene, Oct. 26, 1862.

GAYLORD, James Madison, congressman; b. Zanesville, O., May 29, 1811; attended Ohio U. at Athens; studied law. Admitted to bar, began practice of law; apptd. clk. Ct. of Common Pleas, 1834; mem. U.S. Ho. of Reps. from Ohio, 32d Congress, 1851-53; probate judge, 1853; apptd. dep. U.S. marshal, 1860; justice of peace, 1865-74. Died McConnelsville, O., June 14, 1874; buried McConnelsville Cemetery.

GAYLORD, Willis, agrl. editor; b. Bristol, Conn., 1792; s. Lemon and Rhoda (Plumb) G.; Began writing for Genesee Farmer, circa 1833; asst. editor, 1837, later sr. editor; editor of the combined Genesee Farmer and Cultivator; published a series of articles in Cultivator "Dictionary of Terms used in Agriculture", 1840-43 (had only reached letter U at his death); wrote "Treatise of Insects Injurious to Crops, Fruit Orchards, Vegetable Gardens, and Domestic Animals" (won N.Y. State Agrl. Soc. prize 1843, published in Soc.'s Transactions). Author: (with Luther Tuckes American Husbandry; Being a Series of Essays on Agriculture, 1840. Died Camillus, N.Y., Mar. 27, 1844.

GAYOSO de LEMOS, Manuel, colonial ofcl.; b. 1752; m. Teresa y Pereira, circa 1788; m. 2d, Margaret Watts, 1797. Lt. col. of inf. Lisbon Regt., 1783; commd. gov. Dist. of Natchez, 1787; arrived in La., 1789; commd. col., 1789; contbd. to Northward extension of Spanish frontier by building forts at Walnut Hills, 1790-92, Chickasaw Bluffs, 1795; duties included inducing Am, frontiersmen to settle on Sanish soil and trying to promote separation of West from U.S. (conspirator with Gen. James Wilkinson); persuaded Southern Indians to form confederacy and enter into defensive alliance with

Spain vs. U.S., 1793; commd. brig. gen., 1795; took possession of Govt. of La., 1797, excluded Americans from settlement in La., while encouraging their commerce. Died July 18, 1799.

GAZLEY, James William, congressman; b. N.Y.C., July 23, 1784; attended common schs.; studied law, Poughkeepsie, N.Y. Admitted to bar, 1809, began practice of law; moved to Cincinnati, 1813; mem. U.S. Ho. of Reps. (Jackson Free-Statesman) from Ohio, 18th Congress, 1823-25; editor weekly paper Western Tiller, 1826-27; engaged in literary work. Died Cincinnati, June 8, 1874; buried Spring Grove Cemetery.

GEAR, Joseph, artist; b. Eng., 1768; at least 1 son, John William. Served as chorister St Paul's Cathedral, London, Eng.; exhibited marine views at Royal Acad., London, 1815-21; came to Am., 1824; prominent in musical acitvities, N.Y.C., 1826-31; moved to Boston, circa 1831, active as artist and musician; exhibited at Boston Athenaeum, 1829-37. Died Boston, 1853.

GEARY, John White, gov. Pa., territorial gov. Kan.; b. Mt. Pleasant, Pa., Dec. 30, 1819; s. Richard and Margaret (White) G.; attended Jefferson Coll.; m. Margaret Logan, 1843; m. 2d, Mary Church Henderson, 1858. Admitted to Pa. bar; asst. supt. and engr. of Allegheny Portage R.R.; lt. in militia, 1835; elected first alcalde of San Francisco, 1843; served as lt. col. in Mexican War, 1846, col., 1848; apptd. 1st postmaster of San Francisco and mail agt. for Pacific Coast, 1848; also performed duties of chief civil officer of city; 1st mayor of San Francisco, 1850; active in making Cal. free state; returned to Pa., 1852; chmn. Democratic Territorial Com.; gov. of Kan. Territory, 1856; substituted U.S. troops for pro-slavery militia, organized a new territorial militia, arrested irregular bands of free-state sympathizers; resigned due to trouble with legislature and some pro-slavery ofcls., 1857; set up recruiting office in Pa., 1861; became col. 28th Pa. Volunteers, 1861, promoted brig. gen., 1862; served in Battle of Cedar Mountain, 1862, commanded div. at Chancellorsville, Gettysburg, Lookout Mountain, and in Sherman's March to the Sea; mil. gov. of Savannah after capture; brevetted maj. gen., 1865; gov. of Pa., 1867-73, tried to reduce state debt by tight monetary policies; advocated gen. railroad law, state control of ins., gas cos., safeguards for public health. Died Pa., Feb. 8, 1873.

GEBHARD, John, congressman, lawyer; b. Claverack, N.Y., Feb. 22, 1782; attended public schs.; studied law. Admitted to bar, began practice of law; surrogate Schoharie County (N.Y.), 1811-13, 15-22; mem. U.S. Ho. of Reps. from N.Y., 17th Congress, 1821-23. Died Schoharie, N.Y., Jan. 3, 1854; buried St. Paul's Lutheran Cemetery.

GEDDES, George Washington, congressman; b. Mt. Vernon, Knox County, O., July 16, 1824; attended common schs.; studied law. Admitted to bar, 1845, began practice of law; judge Ct. of Common Pleas, 6th Jud. Dist., 1856-73; unsuccessful Democratic candidate for judge Ohio Supreme Ct., 1872; mem. U.S. Ho. of Reps. (Democrat) from Ohio, 46th-49th congresses, 1879-87. Died Mansfield, O., Nov. 9, 1892; buried Mansfield Cemetery.

GEDDES, James, congressman, civil engr.; b Carlisle, Pa., July 22, 1763; m. Lucy Jerome, 1799, 1 child. Began production of salt, Liverpool, N.Y., 1794; admitted to N.Y. bar, 1800; justice of peace, Onondaga County, N.Y., 1800-04; mem. N.Y. State Assembly, 1804-22, asso. justice Onondaga County Ct., 1809; judge Ct. Common Pleas, Onondaga County, 1809; mem. U.S. Ho. of Reps. (Federalist) from N.Y., 13th Congress, 1813-15; mem. N.Y. Assembly 1822; one of prin. engrs. engaged by N.Y. Canal Commn. to construct Erie and Champlain canals, 1816-22; surveyed canal from Ohio River to Lake Erie for State of Ohio, 1822; chief engr. Chesapeake and Ohio Canal, 1827. Died Geddes, N.Y., Aug.19, 1838; buried Oakwood Cemetery, Syracuse, N.Y.

GEDDES, James Loraine, army officer, educator; b. Edinburgh, Scotland, Mar. 19, 1827; s. Capt. Alexander and Elizabeth (Careless) G.: m. Margaret Moore, Oct. 14, 1856; m. 2d, Elizabeth Evans, Apr. 14, 1876. Served as col. Canadian Cavalry, 1854-57; moved to Benton County, Ia., 1857; commd. lt. col. Co. D, 8th Ia. Inf., 1861; promoted col., 1862; commd. brig. gen. U.S. Volunteers, 1865; commanded Ia. regt., served in battles of Shiloh, Vicksburg, Jackson; in charge of a brigade, 1863; provost marshal Memphis (Tenn.); supt. Ia. Instn. for Edn. of Blind, 1867-69; became steward Ia. land-grant coll. at Ames, 1870, prof. mil. tactics, v.p., dep. treas. coll., treas., 1884, initiated mil. instrn. in a land-grant coll., became coll. land agt., 1886. Author war songs including The Soldier's Battle-Prayer, The Stars and Stripes. Died Ames, Feb. 21, 1887.

GEER, George Jarvis, clergyman; b. Waterbury, Conn., Feb. 24, 1821; grad. Trinity Coll., Hartford, Conn., 1842, Gen. Theol. Sem., 1845; S.T.D. (hon.), Columbia; D.D. (hon.), Union Coll. Rector, Christ Ch., Ballston Spa, N.Y., 1846-52; asso. rector Ch. of Holy Apostles, N.Y.C., 1852-57; rector St. Timothy's Ch., N.Y.C., 1857-85; revised, edited Tune Book of Protestant Episcopal Ch., 1858. Author: The Conversion of St. Paul, 1871. Died N.Y.C., Mar. 16, 1885.

GELSTON, David, Continental congressman; b. Bridgehampton, N.Y., July 4, 1744. Signer, Articles of Assn., 1775; del. 2d-4th provincial congresses N.Y., 1775-77; mem. N.Y. State Constl. Conv., 1777; mem. N.Y. State Assembly, 1777-85, speaker, 1784-85; apptd. a commr. on specie, 1780; mem. Continental Congress, 1789; mem. council of appointment, 1792-93; mem. N.Y. Senate, 1791-94, 98, 1802; canal commr., 1792; surrogate N.Y. County, 1787-1801; collector Port of N.Y., 1801-20; engaged in business, N.Y.C. Died N.Y.C., Aug. 21, 1828; buried 1st Presbyn. Church Cemetery.

GEMUNDER, August Martin Ludwig, violin maker; b. Ingelfingen, Wurtemberg, Germany, Mar. 22, 1814; s. Johann Georg Heinrich Gemunder. Specialized in copying violins of old Italian masters before 1840's succeeded in producing an entirely original violin, after 1844, used by internationally known artists; came to U.S., 1846; opened shop (with his brother George), N.Y.C, 1852; pioneer quality violin building in U.S.; made reprodns. of 18th century violins of greatest Italian violin makers; submitted a model so skillfully made that experts believed it to be a genuine Guarnerius, at Vienna Exposition, 1873; won medals all over world, circa 1860-80. Author: Fine Violins, 1884. Died N.Y.C., Sept. 7, 1895.

GENET, Edmond Charles (Citizen Genet), diplomat; b. Versailles, France, Jan. 8, 1763; s. Edmé Jacques and Marie Ann Louise (Cardon) G.; studied at Giessen, Germany, 1780; m. Cornelia Clinton, Nov. 6, 1794; m. 2d, Martha Osgood, July 31, 1814. Mem. bur. of interpretations of fgn. affairs at Versailles, 1781-87; went to Eng. as acting sec. of legation to secure information useful for treaty of commerce between Gt. Britain and France, 1783; sec. to Comte de Ségur, minister to Ct. of Catherine II, 1787; expelled from Russia, June 1792; went on temporary mission to Geneva, summer 1792; 1st French minister plenipotentiary to U.S., 1793-94; unsuccessfully tried to get U.S. aid for France in war with Eng., and to take Fla. and La. from Spain; commd. privateers to prey on Brit. commerce and to intrigue against Spanish territory (Jeffersonians wished to support his work, but Washington was strongly against war with Britain); disregarded Washington's request to stop these activities (feeling that Jeffersonians would support him); his recall requested by Washington, 1794; replaced as minister, 1794, but remained in U.S. and settled in N.Y. State. Died Rensselaer County, N.Y., July 15, 1834.

GENGEMBRE, Charles Antoine Colomb, artist, engr.; b. Paris, France, 1790; children—Sophie Gengembre) Anderson, Philip Hubert. Practiced as architect, France, until 1848; came to Am., 1849, settled in Cincinnati, later in Manchester and Allegheny City (Pa.); painted landscapes; designed several bldgs., including Allegheny City Hall; changed name to Hubert, before 1863. Died Allegheny City, 1863.

GENIN, John Nicholas, mcht.; b. N.Y.C., Oct. 19, 1819. Became prominent mcht. by use of novel advt. methods, N.Y.C.; gained nat. recognition by paying $250 for 1st choice of seats to Jenny Lind's 1st Am. concert, 1850; as publicity stunt had pavement on Broadway (N.Y.C.) cleaned at his own expense; one of 1st retail mchts. to make wide use of publicity to increase sales. Author: (booklet) An Illustrated History of the Hat from the Earliest Ages to the Present Time, 1845. Died Apr. 30, 1878.

GENIN, Sylvester, artist; b. St. Clairsville, O., Jan. 22, 1822. Painted portraits, hist. subjects; travelled to La. for reasons of health, 1848, to Jamaica, 1849; his father published Selections from the Works of the Late Sylvester Genin, Esq., in Poetry, Prose and Historical Design, with a Biographical Sketch, 1855. Died of consumption, Kingston, Jamaica, Apr. 4, 1850.

GENT, Mrs. Sophia, S. Daniell, artist; b. Eng., circa 1818. Exhibited at London (Eng.) galleries, 1826-31; came to Am.; exhibited at Md. Hist. Soc., 1848; lived in Balt., 1849-50; moved to Phila., circa 1853; exhibited Pussy, Are You Awake at Pa. Acad., 1868.

GENTH, Frederick Augustus (original name Friedrich August Ludwig Karl Wilhelm Genth), chemist; b. Wachtersbach, Hesse-Cassel, Germany, May 17, 1820; s. George Fredrich and Karoline (Freyin von Swartzenau) G.; attended U. Heidelberg, U. Giessen (both Germany); PH.D., U. Marburg (Germany), 1845; m. Karolina Jager, 1847, 3 children; m. 2d, Minna Fischer, 1852, 9 children. Became asst. to Robert Wilhelm Bunsen in Europe; came to U.S., 1848; opened analytical chem. lab. in Phila., 1848; prof. chemistry U. Pa., 1872-88, re-opened pvt. lab., 1888; chemist to Pa. Bd. Agr., 1877-84; expert in mineral chemistry, discovered 23 new mineral species, genthite (nickelgymnite) named in his honor; best example of work is paper "Corundum, its Alterations and Associated Minerals," 1873; did study ammonia-cobalt bases, 1847-56; wrote most important paper; mem. Nat. Acad. Scis., 1872, A.A. A.S., 1875. Died Feb. 2, 1893.

GENTRY, Meredith Poindexter, congressman; b. Rockingham County, N.C., Sept. 15, 1809; studied law. Admitted to bar, began practice of law, Franklin, Tenn.; mem. Tenn. Ho. of Reps., 1835-39; mem. U.S. Ho. of Reps. (Whig) from Tenn., 26th-27th, 29th-32d congresses, 1839-43, 45-53; unsuccessful candidate for gov. Tenn., 1855; retired to plantation in Tenn.; mem. 1st, 2d Confederate congresses, 1862-63. Died Nashville, Tenn., Nov. 2, 1866; buried Mt. Olivet Cemetery.

GEORGE I (George Louis of Hanover), King of Eng.; b. Hanover, Germany, Mar. 28, 1660; s. Ernest Augustus and Sophia of Hanover; m. Sophia Dorothea, 1682, children—George Augustus (became George II), Sophia Dorothea. Crowned King of Eng., Oct. 20, 1714, ruled until 1727; unable to speak English, involved in affairs of Germany and his mistressess; left his rule, including Am. colonial policies, to his ministers; responsible for English entrance into War of Spanish Succession (called Queen Anne's War in Am.), 1701-14. Died at or nr. Osnabrück, Prussia, night of June 10-11, 1727.

GEORGE II (George Augustus), King of Eng. b. Herrenhausen, Germany, Nov. 10, 1683; son of George I and Sophia Dorothea; m. Wilhelmina Caroline of Anspach, 1705; children—Frederick Louis, George William, William Augustus, Anne, Amelia Sophia Eleondra, Elizabeth Caroline, Mary, Louisa. Ruled as king of Eng., 1727-60; his reign was marked by rule of his ministers (Robert Walpole helped keep Eng. out of war); entered war with Spain as result of Spanish depredations of English commerce in Am., 1739; involved Eng. in War of Austrian Succession, 1739-48 (called King George's War in Am.), in 7 Years' War, 1756-63 (called French and Indian War in Am); during his reign the period of "Salutary Neglect" began, a period of econ. prosperity for the Am. colonies, when they were left to their own governmental devices (a cause of Am. Revolution, as colonies did not want to relinquish their perogatives when Eng. tried to assert her supremacy later). Died London, Eng., Oct. 25, 1760.

GEORGE III (George William Frederick), King of Eng.; b. London, Eng., June 4, 1738; s. Frederick Louis (Prince of Wales) and Princess Augusta of Saxe-Gotha; m. Charlotte Sophia, Princess of Mecklenburg-Strelitz, Sept. 8, 1761; children—George A., Frederick, William H., Ernest A., Edward A., Augustus F., Adulphus F., Octavius, Alfred, Charlotte A., Augusta S., Elizabeth, Mary, Sophia, Amelia. King of Eng., 1760-1820; determined to be true ruler of country; enforced own policy in ending Seven Years War (French and Indian War in Am.) at Peace of Paris, 1763 (Gt. Britain gained Can. in treaty); supported and led English govt. in its colonial policies which brought on Am. Revolution; his polit. opposition in Eng. referred to him as tyrant, and his policies as subversive to liberty of Englishmen (especially in Wilkes case); completely opposed to any liberalization of Am. colonial govt.; by actions of his prime ministers, and by his own disregard of Am. petitions and appeals, proved himself to be (according to the Am. Declaration of Independence) "A Prince, whose character is thus marked by every act which may define a Tyrant. . . unfit to be the ruler of a free people"; gave up his efforts at personal govt. after loss of Am. colonies, 1783; suffered successively longer periods of insanity, 1780-1810; became permanently insane, 1810, and Prince of Wales was made regent for last 10 years, 1810-20. Died Windsor Castle, Eng., Jan. 29, 1820.

GEORGE, Henry, economist, reformer; b. Phila., Sept. 2, 1839; s. Richard Samuel Henry and Catherine (Vallance) G.; m. Annie Fox, Dec. 3, 1861. Compositor on Home Jour., c. 1860; a founder and publisher Evening Jour.; returned to San Francisco as printer on newly established Times, 1866, became reporter editorial writer, then mng. editor; 1st of his articles appeared in Overland Monthly, Oct. 1868; revisited East as agt. for San Francisco Herald, late 1868; established independent news service; returned to Cal., became editor Oakland Transcript, 1869; became partner and editor Daily Evening Post, 1871; state insp. of gas meters, 1876; advanced theory of the single tax on unearned increment of land values in book Progress and Poverty, 1879; became leader of reform element in Am. and traveled throughout country; founded single tax party; probably most important polit. reformer of early

1880's; pub. The Irish Land Question (became very popular, had heavy influence on Fabian Socialists), 1881; correspondent for Irish World in N.Y., 1881-82; lectured in Gt. Britain under auspices of Land Reform Union, 1883-84, for Scottish Land Restoration League, 1884; ran for mayor of N.Y.C. on social reform platform, lost to Tammany leader Abrams Hewitt (but ran ahead of Theodore Roosevelt) 1886; ran for mayor again, 1897; published weekly Standard, 1887-92; lectured in Gt. Britain, 1888, 89, Australia, 1890; The Science of Political Economy, 1897. Author: Our Land and Land Policy (contained essentials of econ. philosophy which he later expanded), 1871; Progress and Poverty, 1879; Social Problems (originally series of articles in Frank Leslie's Newspaper), 1883; Protection or Free Trade, 1886; An Open Letter to the Pope, 1891; A Perplexed Philosopher, 1892. Died N.Y.C., Oct. 29, 1897; buried Bklyn.

GEORGE, James Zachariah, senator, jurist; b. Monroe County, Ga., Oct. 20, 1826; s. Joseph Warren and Mary (Chamblis) G.; m. Elizabeth Young, c. 1848. Admitted to Miss. bar, circa 1848; elected reporter of Miss. Supreme Ct., 1854, 60; mem. Miss. Secession Conv., 1861; served from capt. to brig. gen. of Miss. state troops, during Civil War; published 10 vols. of Miss. Reports; prepared Digest of the Reports, 1872; became partner (with Wiley P. Harris) in law firm, Jackson, Miss., 1872; led in restoration of native white supremacy in Miss.; chief justice Miss. Supreme Ct., 1879-81; mem. U.S. Senate from Miss., Mar. 4, 1881-97; led in defense of Miss. and South from fed. interference; only Democrat to play important part in framing Sherman Anti-Trust Law of 1890; mem. Miss. Constl. Conv., 1890. Author: The Political History of Slavery in the United States, published 1915. Died Jackson, Miss., Aug. 14, 1897.

GERARD, James Watson, lawyer, reformer; b. N.Y.C., 1794; s. William and Christina (Glass) G.; grad. Columbia, 1811; m. Elizabeth Sumner, Oct.3, 1820, 4 children. Admitted to N.Y. bar, 1816; an organizer debating soc. The Forum; joined Soc. for Prevention of Pauperism; incorporated Soc. for Reformation of Juvenile Delinquents 1824, mem. bd. mgrs; induced great reforms in police system; school trustee; insp. 5th sch. dist. N.Y.C., raised standards of public edn; leader N.Y. State bar. Died N.Y.C., Feb. 7, 1874.

GERHARD, William Wood, physician; b. Phila., July 23, 1809; s. William and Sarah (Wood) G.; A.B., Dickinson Coll., Carlisle, Pa., 1826; M.D., U. Pa., 1830; m. Miss Dobbyn, 1850, 3 children. Wrote thesis on endermic application of medicaments, 1830; went to Paris to study Asiatic cholera epidemic of 1831-32; published paper on pathology of smallpox, 1833, pneumonia in children 1834; wrote On Cerebral Affections of Children (study of tuberculosis meningitis), 1834; published his most important paper, On the Typhus Fever, which Occurred at Philadelphia in 1836. . .showing the Distinction between this Form of Disease and. .Typhoid Fever with Alteration of the Follicles of the Small Intestine (clearly distinguished typhus from typhoid fever for 1st time;, 1837; published paper on epidemic meningitis, 1963; resident physician Pa. Gen. Hosp., Phila., 1834-68; prof. physiology U. Pa., 1838-72. Author: Lectures on the Diagnosis, Pathology, and Treatment of the Diseases of the Chest, 1842; Diagnosis of Thoracic Diseases, 1835. Editor: Grave's System of Clinical Medicines. Died Phila., Apr. 28, 1872.

GERMAIN, George (Lord Sackville), govt. ofcl., army officer; b. Jan. 26, 1716; s. Lionel and Elizabeth (Colyear) Sackville; B.A., Trinity Coll., U. Dublin (Ireland), 1733, M.A., 1734; m. Diana Sambroke, Sept. 1755, 5 children. Apptd. clerk of Council of Dublin, 1737; mem. English Ho. of Commons, 1741-61; served with Brit. Army, became col., 1746, maj. gen. 1755, lt. gen., 1757; comdr.-in-chief Lower Army of Rhine, 1758, relieved of command and court martialled for disobeying orders, 1760; regained rank by 1765, also became mem. Privy Council, Lord North's cabinet; lord commr. of trade and plantations, 1775-79, in this capacity supervised Am. colonies, supported and ineptly implemented colonial legislation, thereby furthering discontent which led to Am. Revolution. Died Stoneland Lodge, Sussex, Eng., Aug. 26, 1785.

GERMAN, Obadiah, senator; b. Amenia, N.Y., Apr. 22, 1766; attended dist. schs.; studied law. Admitted to bar, 1792, began practice of law, Norwich, N.Y.; mem. N.Y. State Assembly, 1798, 1804-05, 07-09, 19, speaker, 1819; mem. U.S. Senate (Democrat) from N.Y., 1809-15; judge Chenango County, 1815-19; apptd. commr. public works, 1817; became a Whig. Died Norwich, N.Y., Sept. 24, 1842; buried Riverside Cemetery, North Norwich, N.Y.

GERRY, Elbridge, vice pres. U.S.; b. Marblehead, Mass., June 17, 1744; s. Thomas and Elizabeth (Greenleaf) G.; grad. Harvard, 1762; m. Ann Thompson, Jan. 12, 1786, 3 sons, 4 daus. Mem. Mass. Gen. Assembly, 1772-75; rep. to Mass. Gen. Ct., 1772-73; mem. Com. of Correspondence, 1773; mem. 1st and 2d Mass. provincial congresses, 1774-75; mem. 1st and 2d coms. of safety; active in raising troops and supplies for Continental Army; mem. Continental Congress from Mass., 1776-85; pres. Treasury Bd., 1776-89; a signer Declaration of Independence, 1776, Articles of Confederation; del. to New Haven price-fixing conv. to eliminate profiteering, 1778; engaged successfully in trade and profiteering, 1780-83; mem. Mass. Ho. of Reps., 1786; del. U.S. Constl. Conv., Phila., 1787; mem. U.S. Ho. of Reps. (Anti-Federalist) from Mass., 1st-2d congresses, 1789-93; went to France with Marshall and Pinckney on diplomatic mission, 1797; gov. Mass., 1810-12; vice pres. U.S. under Madison, 1812-14; presented bill to change electoral dists. of Mass. so as to elect more Republican state senators than actual Rep. voting strength (originated term Gerrymander). Author: Observations on the New Constitution and On the Federal and State Conventions by a Columbian Patriot (anti-Const.), 1788. Died Washington, D.C., Nov. 23, 1814; buried Congressional Cemetery, Washington.

GERRY, Elbridge, congressman, lawyer; b. Waterford, Me., Dec. 6, 1813; attended Bridgton Acad.; studied law. Admitted to bar, 1839, began practice of law, Waterford; clk. Me. Ho. of Reps,. 1840; apptd. U.S. commr. in bankruptcy, 1841; mem. Me. Ho. of Reps., 1846; mem. U.S. Ho. of Reps. (Democrat) from Me., 31st Congress, 1849-51; resumed practice of law, Portland, Me. Died Portland, Apr. 10, 1886; buried Evergreen Cemetery.

GERRY, James, congressman, physician; b. nr. Rising Sun, Md., Aug. 14, 1796; grad. West Nottingham Acad.; studied medicine U. Md. at Balt. Began practice of medicine, Shrewsbury, Pa., 1824; mem. U.S. Ho. of Reps. (Democrat) from Pa., 26th-27th congresses, 1839-43; retired from practice of medicine, 1870. Died Shrewsbury, July 19, 1873; buried Lutheran Cemetery.

GERSTLE, Lewis, businessman; b. Ichenhausen, Bavaria (now Germany), Dec. 17, 1824; m. Hannah Greenebaum, 1858, 7 children. Came to U.S., 1847; became partner in wholesale grocery bus. Louis Sloss & Co. (later became mining stock brokers and dealers in wool and leather), 1850; established Alaska Comml. Co,. 1867, pres, 1867-1902; obtained monopoly on seal fishing in Alaskan waters from U.S. Govt., 1870; built trading posts, schs. and chs. in Alaska; established steamship line between San Francisco and Alaska; original investor in Union Iron Works, Pioneer Woolen Mills (both San Francisco), San Joaquin Valley R.R.; dir. Nev. Nat. Bank, Union Trust Co., Cal.-Hawaiian Sugar Co.; treas. U. Cal., 1902; bd. dirs. Hebrew Asylum and Home Soc., San Francisco. Died Nov. 19, 1902.

GERVAIS, John Lewis, Continental congressman; b. probably in France; son of Huguenot parents; ed. Hanover, Germany. Came to U.S., arrived Charleston, S.C., 1764; became mcht., planter and landowner; del. provincial conv., also Provincial Congress, 1775-76; mem. Council of Safety, 1775-76, 81; apptd. by Congress dep. postmaster gen. for S.C., 1778; served in organizing troops and defense of Charleston (1780) in Revolutionary War; mem. S.C. Senate, 1781-82, served as pres.; mem. Continental Congress from S.C., 1782-83; mem. com. to which were referred letters from U.S. reps. abroad, 1783; commr. public accounts for S.C., 1794-95. Died Charleston, Aug. 18, 1798; buried St. Philip's Churchyard.

GETTY, George Washington, army officer; b. Georgetown, D.C., Oct. 2, 1819; s. Robert and Margaret (Wilmot) G.; grad. U.S. Mil. Acad., 1840; m. Elizabeth Stevenson, 1848. Commd. 2d lt., 4th Arty., U.S. Army, 1840, 1st lt., 1845; served at battles of Contreras, Churubusco, Molino del Rey, Chapultepec during Mexican War; brevetted capt., 1847; served in wars against Seminole Indians, 1849-50, 56-57; promoted capt., 1853, lt. col., 1861; served in Peninsular campaign, battles of South Mountain, Antietam, Fredericksburg, also Wilderness and Shenandoah campaigns; apptd. brig. gen. U.S. Volunteers, 1862; commd. maj. U.S. rmy, 1863, col., 1866; commanded post and arty. sch., Ft. Monroe, 1871-77; led troops in suppressing riots along B. & O. R.R., 1877; ret., 1883. Died Forest Glen, Md., Oct. 1, 1901.

GETZ, James Lawrence, congressman, journalist; b. Reading, Pa., Sept. 14, 1821; studied law. A founder newspaper Reading Gazette, 1840, became sole owner, later purchased Jefferson Democrat, merged 2 papers into Reading Gazette and Democrat, owner until 1868; admitted to bar, 1846, never practiced law; mem. Pa. Ho. of Reps., 1856-57, speaker, 1857; mem. U.S. Ho. of Reps. (Democrat) from Pa., 40th-42d congresses, 1867-73; city comptroller Reading, 1888-91. Died Reading, Dec. 25, 1891; buried Charles Evans Cemetery.

GEYER, Henry Sheffie, senator; b. Frederick, Md., Dec. 9, 1790; s. John and Elizabeth (Sheffie) G.; m. Clarissa B. Starr, Jan. 1, 1818; m. 2d, Joanna Easton, Apr. 26, 1831; m. 3d, Jane Stoddard, Feb. 12, 1850. Began practice law, 1811; served as 1st lt. in War of 1812, became regt. paymaster 38th Regt., Md. Inf., 1813; moved to St. Louis, 1813; mem. Mo. Territorial Legislature, 1818; played principal part in Mo. "Solemn Public Act," prominent part in struggle for statehood; mem. Mo. Ho. of Reps., 1820-24, 34-35, speaker, 1820-22, 24, effected maj. revision of Mo. statute law in legislative sessions 1825, 35; mem. U.S. Senate (Whig) from Mo., 1851-57; leading atty. for defendant slave-owner in Dred Scott case. Died St. Louis, Mar. 5, 1859.

GHOLSON, James Herbert, congressman, lawyer; b. Gholsonville, Va., 1798; grad. Princeton, 1820; studied law. Admitted to bar, began practice of law, Percivals, Va.; mem. Va. Ho. of Dels., 1824-28, 30-33; mem. U.S. Ho. of Reps. (Democrat) from Va., 23d Congress, 1833-35; judge Brunswick Circuit Ct., many years. Died Brunswick County, Va., July 2, 1848.

GHOLSON, Samuel Jameson, congressman, jurist; b. Madison County, Ky., May 19, 1808; m. Miss Ragsdale, 1838. Admitted to Miss. bar, 1829; mem. Miss. Ho. of Reps., 1835, 36, 39; mem. U.S. Ho. of Reps. from Miss., 24th-25th congresses, 1836-38; judge U.S. Dist. Ct. for Miss., 1839-61; pres. Miss. Democratic Conv., 1860; mem. Miss. Constl. Conv. which passed Ordinance of Secession, 1861; capt. of Monroe Volunteers, promoted col., brig. gen. Miss. Militia, 1861, maj. gen., 1863; brig. gen. Confederate Army, 1864, commanded brigade of cavalry; mem. Miss. Ho. of Reps., 1865, speaker, 1866; mem. Miss. Legislature, 1878. Died Aberdeen, Miss., Oct. 16, 1883; buried Odd Fellows Cemetery, Aberdeen.

GHOLSON, Thomas, Jr., congressman, lawyer; b. Brunswick, Va.; studied law. Admitted to bar, began practice of law, Brunswick County (Va.); mem. Va. Ho. of Dels., 1806-09; mem. U.S. Ho. of Reps. (Democrat, filled vacancy) from Va., 10th 14th congresses, Nov. 7, 1808-16. Died Brunswick County, July 4, 1816.

GHOLSON, Thomas Saunders, lawyer; b. Gholsonville, Va., Dec. 9, 1808; s. William and Mary (Saunders) G.; grad. U. Va., 1827; m. Cary Ann Gholson (cousin), May 14, 1829; Practiced law, Brunswick County, Va., 1827-40; partner (with brother James) in law firm, Petersburg, Va., 1840-48; visitor of Coll. of William and Mary, 1844; pres. Bank of Petersburg; founder public library, Petersburg; judge 5th Jud. Circuit of Va., 1859-63; mem. 2d Confederate States Congress from Va., 1863-65; went to Eng., 1865; owner cotton and tobacco commn. house, Liverpool, Eng., 1865-68. Died Savannah, Ga., Dec. 12, 1868; buried Blandford Ch. Graveyard, Petersburg.

GHOLSON, William Yates, jurist; b. Southampton County, Va., Dec. 25, 1807; s. Thomas and Ann (Yates) G.; grad. Coll. of N.J. (now Princeton), 1825; m. Ann Taylor, Dec. 25, 1827, m. 2d, Elvira Wright, May 21, 1839. Admitted to Miss. bar, 1834; a founder U. Miss., 1844; practiced law, Cincinnati, 1844-54; judge Cincinnati Superior Ct., 1854-59; asso. justice Ohio Supreme Ct., 1859-63; resumed practice of law, 1863-70. Died Cincinnati, Sept. 21, 1870.

GIBAULT, Pierre, missionary; b. Montreal, Can., Apr. 1737; s. Pierre and Marie (Saint-Jean) G.; ed. Seminary of Quebec. Became Roman Catholic missionary in Illinois country in response to call for helpers by Father Sebastian Meurin, 1768; vicar gen. Illinois country, 1796; through his influence new church erected in Vincennes (Ind.); successful in gaining allegiance of French at Vincennes and friendship of Indian tribes of region; assisted in securing volunteers among French for expdns. recapturing Vincennes from British; friend of George Rogers Clark; received thanks of Va. Assembly; settled at New Madrid, Spanish Territory, parish priest until 1804. Died 1804.

GIBBES, Robert Wilson, physician, scientist, mayor; b. Charleston, S.C., July 8, 1809; s. William Hassell and Mary (Wilson) G.; grad. S.C. Coll., Charleston, 1827; M.D., S.C. Med. Coll., 1830; m. Carolina Guignard, Dec. 20, 1827, 12 children. Asst. prof. chemistry, geology and mineralogy S.C. Coll., 1827-35; wrote article "On Typhoid Pneumonia, as it Occurs in the Neighborhood of Columbia, S.C.," (revolutionized treatment of the disease), 1842; took over, edited The South Carolinian (Democratic paper), 1852-58; edited Weekly Banner, 1852-60; mayor Charleston, 2 terms; surgeon gen. S.C. during Civil War; owned Saluda factory mfg. cotton shirting. Author: Monograph on Fossil Squalidae; Memoir on Monosaures and the Three Allied New Genera, 1849; Documentary History of the American Revolution, 3 vols., 1853-57. Died Columbia, S.C., Oct. 15, 1866.

GIBBON, John, army officer; b. Holmesburg, Pa., Apr. 20, 1827; s. John Heysham and Catharine (Lardner) G.; grad. U.S. Mil. Acad., 1847; m. Frances Moale, Oct. 16, 1855. Served in Seminole War in Fla., 1849, commd. 1st lt., 1850; prepared The Artillerists' Manual, 1859, adopted by War Dept., 1859, published 1860; promoted capt., 1859; commanded a brigade at battles of Antietam, 1862, Gettysburg, 1863; commd. brig. gen. U.S. Volunteers, 1862, maj. gen., 1864; assigned to command of Iron Brigade; commanded a draft depot., 1864; div. comdr., 1864; served in battles of Wilderness, Spatsville and Cold Harbor, 1864; commanded XXIV Corps in last operations in No. Va., 1865; a commr. designated to arrange details of surrender of South; commd. col. U.S. Army, 1866; Indian fighter; commanded column of inf.; participated in Yellowstone expdn. against Sitting Bull, 1876; promoted brig. gen., 1885; commanded Dept. of Columbia; maintained peace during threatened anti-Chinese outbreak in Seattle, 1885-86; chief of Loyal Legion, 1896. Author: Personal Recollections of the Civil War, 1885. Died Balt., Feb. 6, 1896; buried Arlington (Va.) Nat. Cemetery.

GIBBONS, Abigail Hopper, abolitionist, reformer; b. Phila., Dec. 7, 1801; d. Isaac Tatem and Sarah (Tatum) Hopper; ed. at home and in Quaker day schs.; m. James Sloan Gibbons, Feb. 14, 1833, 6 children. Set up Phila. Sch. for Elementary Edn. of Children of Soc. of Friends, 1821-30; went to N.Y., 1830; became head of Friends Sch.; devoted abolitionist, made her home a refuge for escaping slaves; resigned membership in Quaker Soc. after being disowned because of her anti-slavery views; worked to improve conditions of poor, blind, crippled children in city poor-house in N.Y.C.; nurse and helper in camps and hosps. in Civil War, 1861-65; during draft riots of 1863 her home greatly destroyed by rioters; helped start Labor and Aid Soc. (to assist returning soldiers in finding employment and new opportunity); a founder Protestant Asylum for Infants; pres. N.Y. Com. for Prevention of State Regulation of Vice; pres. Women's Prison Assn; through her efforts provision made for arrested women to be searched by persons of their own sex. Died N.Y.C., Jan. 16, 1893.

GIBBONS, Henry, physician, editor; b. Wilmington, Del., Sept. 20, 1808; s. William and Rebecca (Donaldson) G.; grad. med. sch. U. Pa., 1829; m. Martha Poole, May 1833, 4 children. Practiced medicine, Wilmington, 1829-41, Phila., 1841-50; active mem. Phila. Acad. Natural Science, Coll. Physicians; practiced medicine, Cal., 1850-84; pres. Cal. Med. Soc., 1857-71; a founder Med. Soc. County of San Francisco, pres., 1856-66; del. Internat. Med. Congress, Phila., 1876; prof. materia medica Med. Coll. of Pacific, 1861-68, prof. med. practice, 1868-84; vis. physician St. Mary's, San Francisco County hosps., 18 years; 1st pres. Soc. for Prevention Cruelty to Animals; editor Med. Press. (later merged with Pacific Med. and Surg. Jour.), 1864-84. Died Wilmington, Nov. 4, 1884.

GIBBONS, James Sloan, abolitionist; b. Wilmington, Del., July 1, 1810; s. William and Rebecca (Donaldson) G.; m. Abigail Hopper, 1833, 6 children. An organizer Ocean City and Broadway Bank, N.Y.C.; prominent in work of Am. Anti-Slavery Soc.; chief supporter of newspaper Nat. Anti-Slavery Standard, N.Y.C.; disowned by N.Y. Meeting of Friends because of his abolitionist activities, 1842. Author: The Banks of N.Y., Their Dealers, The Clearing House and The Panic of 1857, 1859; The Public Debt of the U.S., 1867. Composer war song: We Are Coming Father Abraham. Three Hundred Thousand Strong, 1862. Died Oct. 17, 1892.

GIBBONS, Thomas, lawyer, steamboat operator; b. Savannah, Ga., Dec. 15, 1757; s. Joseph and Hannah (Martin) G. Loyalist during Am. Revolution; responsible for one of 1st disputed elections to Congress; mayor of Savannah, Ga., 1791-92, 94-95, 99-01; operated steamboats from Elizabethtown Point up Raritan River, to New Brunswick where they connected with Aaron Ogden's steamers, 1817-18; broke with Ogden, 1818; ran his own ferries from Elizabethtown to N.Y. (thus infringing upon Ogden's monopoly grant); sued by Ogden in case that eventually came to U.S. Supreme Ct. (Gibbons vs. Ogden, 1824); Gibbons won verdict; (case resulted in abolishment of state chartered monopolies and establishment of fed. jurisdiction over inter-state commerce. Died N.Y.C., May 16, 1826.

GIBBONS, William, Continental congressman; b. Bear Bluff, S.C., Apr. 8, 1726. Admitted to Ga. bar; mme. Sons of Liberty, 1774; leader in opposition to Crown; mem. party which broke into King's powder magazine, Savannah, Ga., 1775; mem. Ga. Provincial Congress, 1775; mem. Ga. Com. of Safety, 1775; mem. exec. council created by Ga. Provincial Congress, 1777-81; mem. Ga. Ho. of Reps., 1783, 85-89, 91-93, speaker, 1786, 87; del to Continental Congress, 1784-86; asso. justice Chatham County (Ga.) Ct.; pres. Ga. Constl. Conv., 1789; leading rice planter in region. Died Savannah, Sept. 27, 1800.

GIBBONS, William, physician, editor; b. Phila., Aug. 10, 1781; s. James and Eleanor (Peters) G.; M.D., U. Pa., 1805; m. Rebecca Donaldson, May 14, 1806, 14 children including James Sloan, Henry, William Peters. Practiced medicine, 1806-45; devout Quaker; 1st pres. Del. State Temperance Soc. Del. Acad. Natural Scis.; became editor, publisher of religious paper, Berean, 1824. Author: (pamphlets) Truth Advocated in Letters Addressed to the Presbyterians, 1822, Exposition of Modern Scepticism, 1829. Died Wilmington, Del., July 25, 1845.

GIBBS, George, mineralogist; b. Newport, R.I., Jan. 7, 1776; s. George and Mary (Channing) G.; M.A., R.I. Coll. (now Brown U.), 1800; attended Yale, 1808; m. Laura Wolcott, children include George, Oliver Wolcott, Alfred. Amassed collection of minerals by 1805 (largest and most valuable yet seen in U.S.), offered to deposit collection at Yale, 1810, sold collection to Yale, 1825; initiated suggestion for founding Journal of Science; v.p. N.Y. Lyceum of Natural History, 1822. Died Astoria, L.I., N.Y., Aug. 5, 1833.

GIBBS, George, enthnologist, geologist; b. Astoria, L.I., N.Y., July 17, 1815; grad. Harvard, 1838; m. Mary Gibbs, 1871. Collector, Port of Astoria, 1850-53; geologist U.S. Govt. commn. laying N.W. boundary; mem. N.W. boundary survey, 1857; important mem. Loyal Nat. League and Loyal Publication Soc., at outbreak of Civil War; contbd. to study of Indian langs., specialized in N.W. Indian langs. and customs. Author: Memoirs of the Administrations of Washington and John Adams (of great importance for history of Federalist Party), 1846; Instructions for Research Relative to the Ethnology and Philology of America. Died New Haven, Conn., Apr. 9, 1873.

GIBBS, James Ethan Allen, inventor; b. Rockbridge County, Va., Aug. 1, 1829; s. Richard and Isabella (Poague) G.; m. Catherine Givens, 1883; m. 2d, Margaret Craig, 1893; at least 3 children. Asso. with father's machine carding bus., Rockbridge County, until 1846; made unsuccessful attempt to establish wool-carding bus. utilizing machine of own design, Mill Point, Pocahontas County, W. Va., 1846; engaged in agr., 1846-50; built a sewing machine (from pictures of sewing machines appearing in advertisements), patented 2 improvements (a forerunner of automatic tensions system and a material feeding device), 1856; patented several chain and lock stitch machines, 1857; invented twisted loop rotary hook machine, 1857; formed partnership with James Willcox, introduced Willcox and Gibbs sewing machine, 1858; patented a lock and clutch driven bicycle; mfr. gunpowder for Confederate Army during Civil War; ret. from bus., 1890; traveled around U.S. and to Europe; gave name to Town of Raphine (from Greek: to sew), Rockbridge County. Died Raphine, Nov. 25, 1902.

GIBBS, Josiah Willard, educator, philologist, b. Salem, Mass., Apr. 30, 1790; s. Henry and Mercy (Prescott) G.; grad. Yale, 1809; m. Mary Van Cleve, Sept. 30, 1830, 5 children. Tutor at Yale, 1811; licensed to preach, New Haven, Conn., 1815; studied Hebrew, other oriental langs. under Moses Stuart, 1815, helped prepare Hebrew Grammar (Stuart's most important work), 1821; published Hebrew and English Lexicon of the Old Testament including the Biblical Chaldee (translation of German work by Wilhelm Gesenius, the standard work on subject until 1836;, 1824; prof. sacred lit., coll. librarian Yale Divinity Sch., 1826; leading Am. scholar of time in study of comparative philology; one of 1st mems. Am. Oriental Soc., contbr. articles to its journal. Died New Haven, Mar. 25, 1861.

GIBBS, William Hasell, lawyer, b. Charleston, S.C., Mar. 16, 1754; s. William and Elizabeth (Hasell) G.; read law under John Rutledge; attended Inner Temple, London, Eng., 1774; m. Elizabeth Allston, Aug. 29, 1772, m. Mary Philip Wilson, Jan. 21, 1808; at least 10 children including Robert W. Signed petition protesting Intolerable Acts to Ho. of Commons, during stay in Eng., 1774; refused passport to Am. when Am. Revolution began, but managed to get to S.C.; commd. capt. lt. Ancient Arty. Co., Charleston, S.C., served in defense of Charleston and Savannah; arrested by Cornwallis, 1780, held prisoner in St. Augustine, Fla; admitted to S.C. bar, circa 1782; master in equity S.C., 1783-25, impeached by S.C. Legislature on charges resulting from a sale of slaves, 1811, acquitted by large majority on all charges; engaged in pvt. practice of law, 1825-34. Died Charleston, Feb. 13, 1824; buried St. Philip's Churchyard, Charleston.

GIBSON, George, army officer; b. Lancaster, Pa., Oct. 1747; s. George and Elizabeth (deVinez) G.; m. Anne West, 1772; 1 son, John Banister. Organized, commanded company of frontiersmen for service in West, 1775; negotiated purchase of powder from Spanish at New Orleans for use of Va. and Continental troops, 1776; served as col., 1777-78; in charge of Am. prison camp, York, Pa., 1779; joined Maj. Gen. Arthur St. Clair's expdn. as lt. col. in command 2d Regt., 1791; fatally wounded in battle against Miami Indians on Wabash River. Died Fort Jefferson, O., Dec. 14, 1791.

GIBSON, James King, congressman; b. Abingdon, Va., Feb. 18, 1812; attended common schs. Became a mcht., Abingdon, 1834; dep. sheriff Washington County, 1834-35; postmaster Abingdon, 1837-49; mem. U.S. Ho. of Reps. (Democrat) from Va., 41st Congress, Jan. 28, 1870-71; engaged in agriculture and banking. Died Abingdon, Mar. 30, 1879; buried Sinking Spring Cemetery.

GIBSON, John, army officer, territorial ofcl.; b. Lancaster, Pa., May 23, 1740; s. George and Elizabeth (de Viner) G.; m. Ann; possibly married an Indian wife, Took part in Forbes Expdn. which won Ft. Duquesne from the French, 1758; at Ft. Duquesne as Indian trader, 1758-63; captured by Indians during Pontiac's uprising, 1763; took part in Lord Dunmores' War, 1774; aided in negotiations resulting in Treaty of Pitts., 1775; Western agt. for Va., 1775; mem. Western Pa. Com. of Correspondence; active in securing peace with Indians; served as lt. col. Continental Army, 1776, col., 1777-81; judge ct. common pleas and maj. gen. of militia, Allegheny County, Pa., 1781; mem. Pa. Constl. Conv., 1790; helped negotiate purchase for Pa. of Erie Triangle from Iroquois Confederacy, 1789; organizer Ind. Territorial Govt., 1800-16; sec. Ind. Territory, acting gov. during War of 1812; fluent speaker of various Indian dialects. Died Braddock's Field, Pa., Apr. 16, 1822.

GIBSON, John Bannister, jurist; b. Westover Mills, Pa., Nov. 8, 1780; s. George and Anne (West) G.; attended Dickinson Coll., Carlisle, Pa., 1880; m. Sarah Work, Oct. 8, 1812, 8 children. Admitted to Cumberland County (Pa.) bar, 1803; mem. Pa. Legislature (Democrat), 1810-12; apptd. president judge 11th Jud. Dist. Pa. Ct. of Common Pleas, 1813; asso. justice Pa. Supreme Ct., 1816-27, 51-53, chief justice, 1827-51, a decisive influence in devel. of Pa. law; most known for opinion in De Chastellux vs. Fairchild which laid down limits of legislative power in regard to state cts.; other important opinions include: Commonwealth vs. Green & Others, and Donoghue vs. The County, also outstanding property law cases Lyle et al vs. Richards, Hillyard vs. Miller, and Hileman et al vs. Bouslaugh; profound student of Shakespeare; also known as excellent piano tuner and dentist, devised a peculiar plate for his own teeth after profl. assistance had failed. Died Phila., May 3, 1853; buried Carlisle.

GIBSON, Randall Lee, senator; b. Woodford County, Ky., Sept. 10, 1832; s. Tobias and Louisiana (Hart) G.; grad. Yale, 1853, law dept. U. La. (now Tulane U.), 1855; m. Mary Montgomery, Jan. 25, 1868, 3 sons. Served as capt. 1st Regt., La. Arty., Confederate Army, 1861; col. 13th Regt., La. Inf., 1861, brig. gen., 1864; mem. U.S. Ho. of Reps. from La., 44th-47th congresses, 1875-83, influential in securing adoption of J.B. Eads plan for constructing jetties at mouth of Mississippi River, 1878, urged creation of Mississippi River Commn., 1879; mem. U.S. Senate from La., 1883-Dec. 15, 1892; 1st pres. bd. adminstrs. Tulane U., 1884-92; mem. bd. adminstrs. Howard Meml. Library, New Orleans, bd. regents Smithsonian Instn.; trustee Peabody Edn. Fund. Died Hot Springs, Ark., Dec. 15, 1892; buried Lexington (Ky.) Cemetery.

GIBSON, Walter Murray, adventurer; b. at sea on Atlantic Ocean, 1823; m. Miss Lewis, 3 children. Came to U.S., 1823, lived with Indians for a time; commission mcht., N.Y., 1844; went to Cal., 1849; imprisoned by Dutch at Batavia (following visit of his mcht. vessel to Sumatra) during native East Indian uprising against Dutch, 1852, escaped, 1853, later sued for damages but did not collect; became Mormon, inspired scheme for selling Salt Lake Territory to U.S. and moving Mormon colony to Hawaiian Islands; sent to Hawaii to execute plan, 1861, expelled from ch., 1864; publisher the Nuhou (advocated "Hawaii for the Hawaiians"); became premier of Hawaii, 1882, attempted to create protectorates over other South Pacific islands and aroused enmity of some European powers (primarily Germany), dismissed when fgn. element split into opposing camps, 1887; returned to U.S. Author: The Prisoner of Weltevreden, 1855. Died Jan. 21, 1888.

GIBSON, William, surgeon, educator; b. Balt., Mar. 14, 1788; s. John Gibson; ed. St. John's Coll., Annapolis; M.D., U. Edinburgh (Scotland), 1809; studied with Sir Charles Bell in Eng.; m. Sarah Hollingsworth, 8 children including Charles Bell. Prof. surgery U. Md., 1811-19; tied common iliac artery for aneurism (1st time done in Am.), 1812; prof. surgery U. Pa., 1819-55; did much to advance knowledge and practice surgery; performed Caesarean section twice on same patient who lived

50 years after 1st operation (most striking surg. success). Author: The Institutes and Practice of Surgery (prin. publ.), 1824. Died Savannah, Ga., Mar. 2, 1868.

GIBSON, William Hamilton, artist, naturalist; b. Sandy Hook, Conn., Oct. 5, 1850; s. Edmund Trowbridge Hastings and Elizabeth (Sanford) G.; attended Bklyn. Poly. Inst.; m. Emma Blanchard, Oct. 29, 1873. Contbr. bot. sketches to Am. Agriculturist, Art Jour., Appleton's Am. Cyclopaedia; published drawings as Providence and Vicinity and The Connecticut Shore of the Sound in W.C. Bryant's Picturesque America, 2 vols., 1872-74; author and illustrator of a long and varied succession of nature articles appearing in Harper's, Scribner's and Century mags. (popularized nature study); annual contbr. exhbns. of Am. Water Color Soc., became member, 1885; illustrated The Heart of the White Mountains, 1882, Nature's Serial Story, 1885; author and illustrator Traps and Trap Making, 1875, The Complete American Trapper, 1876, Pastoral Days, Complete American Trapper, 1882, Hyways and Byways, 1883, Happy Hunting Grounds, 1886, The Master of the Gunnery, 1887, Strolls by Starlight and Sunshine, 1891, Sharp Eyes, 1892. Died Washington, Conn., July 16, 1896.

GIDDINGS, Joshua Reed, congressman, abolitionist; b. Bradford County, Pa., Oct. 6, 1795; s. Joshua and Elizabeth (Pease) G.; m. Laura Waters, Sept. 24, 1819. Served in War of 1812; admitted to Ohio bar, 1821; mem. Ohio Ho. of Reps., 1826-28; mem. U.S. Ho. of Reps. from Ohio, 26th-36th congresses, 1839-59; worked for greater freedom of debate on slavery issues in Congress, fought against anti-slavery "gag-rule" in force in Ho., 1836-44; to circumvent this rule, introduced resolutions on Creole Case (involving 135 slaves on brig Creole who had revolted and taken ship to Nassau, for which U.S. was trying to gain compensation from British who had liberated slaves); argued in his resolutions that the slaves were now beyond state laws and had returned to their natural state of liberty; censored by Ho. of Reps. by vote of 125 to 69, forced to resign, 1842, but re-elected in same year; opposed annexation of Tex., Mexican War; broke with Whigs, 1848, joined Free-Soil Party; became a Republican, 1854, took active part in Republican Conv., 1860; consul gen. to Can., 1861-64. Author: The Exiles of Florida, 1858; The History of the Rebellion, 1864. Died Montreal, Can., May 27, 1864; buried Oakdale Cemetery, Jefferson, O.

GIDDINGS, Napoleon Bonaparte, congressman; b. nr. Boonsborough, Ky., Jan. 2, 1816; attended common schs., Mo.; studied law. Served as sgt. maj. of regt. in Tex. War of Independence; apptd. chief clk. auditor's office Republic of Texas, served as acting auditor until 1838; returned to Fayette, Mo., admitted to bar, 1841, began practice of law, Fayette; served as capt. Co. A, 2d Regt., Mo. Mounted Volunteers during Mexican War, 1846-47; editor Union Flag (1st paper published in Franklin County, Mo.), after Mexican War; mined gold in Cal.; then practiced law, Savannah, Mo., later in Nebraska City, Neb.; mem. U.S. Congress (Democrat) from Neb. Territory, 33d Congress, Jan. 5-Mar. 3, 1855; served as lt. col. 51st Regt., Mo. Volunteer Inf., during Civil War, 1865. Died Savannah, Mo., Aug. 3, 1897; buried City Cemetery.

GIDEON, Peter Miller, pomologist; b. Woodstock, O., Feb. 9, 1820; s. George and Elizabeth (Miller) G.; m. Wealthy Hull, Jan. 2, 1849. Moved to land claim "Gideon's Bay," Lake Minnetonka Minn., 1858; engaged in developing varieties of fruit to withstand Northern climates for 41 years; developed "Wealthy" apple from seeds of Siberian crabtree; head of Minn. state exptl. fruit farm, 1878; originated new varieties of crab apples. Author: Growing Hardy Fruits, 1885; Our Seedling and Russian Apples, 1887. Died Oct. 27, 1899.

GIESLER-ANNEKE, Mathilde Franzisha, educator, author; b. Westphalia, Germany, Apr. 3, 1817; d. Karl and Elizabeth (Hulswitt) Giesler; m. Gerichstrat Alfred von Tabouillot, 1836, 1 dau.; m. 2d, Fritz Anneke, June 3, 1847, 6 children. Started 2 papers Neue Kolnische Zeitung and Frauenzeiting (quickly suppressed by German govt.); became orderly in revolutionary force to which her husband belonged in Baden and Palatinate; served in Battle of Ubstadt, 1849; came to Milw., 1849; edited Frauenzeitung, Newark, N.J., 1852-58; newspaper correspondent, Switzerland, 1860-65; founded and conducted Milw. Tochter Institut, 1865-84. Author: Des Christen Freudiger Aufblick zum Himmlischen Vater: Gebete und Betrachtungen, 1839; Heimathgruss, 1840; Damenalmanach fur das Jahr, 1842, published 1842; Das Weib in Konflict mit den Sozialen Verhaltnissen, 1846; Das Geisterhaus in New York, 1863. Died Nov. 25, 1884.

GIFFORD, Sanford Robinson, landscape painter; b. Greenfield, N.Y., July 10, 1823; s. Elihu and Eliza (Starbuck) G.; attended Brown U., 1842-44; pupil of John Rubens Smith, N.Y.C.; m. 1877. elected asso. N.A.D., 1851, academician, 1854; painted landscapes Tivoli and Palermo (products of European tour, 1868-70); other works include Villa Malta, Lago Maggiore, Lake George, Venice, 1870, Fire Island Beach. Died N.Y.C., Aug. 29, 1880.

GIGNOUX, Régis Francois, artist; b. Lyon, France, 1816; studied under Paul Delaroche. Came to Am., circa 1841, opened studio, Bklyn.; frequent exhibitor at galleries in N.Y.C., Boston, Phila.; mem. N.A.D.; 1st Pres. Bklyn. Acad.; returned to France, 1870. Died Paris, France, Aug. 6, 1882.

GILBERT, Abijah, senator; b. Gilbertsville, Otsego County, N.Y., June 18, 1806; attended Gilbertsville Acad.; grad. Hamilton Coll., Clinton, N.Y., 1822. Engaged in business, N.Y.C., 1822-50; moved to St. Augustine, Fla., 1865: mem. U.S. Senate (Republican) from Fla., 1869-75. Died Gilbertsville, Nov. 23, 1881; buried Brookside Cemetery.

GILBERT, Edward, congressman, journalist; b. Cherry Valley, N.Y., circa 1819; attended public schs. Became compositor Albany Argus, 1839, later asso. editor; served as 1st lt. Co. H., Col. J.D. Stevenson's N.Y. Volunteer Regt. during Mexican War; in command of detachment, also dep. collector Port of San Francisco, 1847-48; founder, editor Alta California, 1849; mem. Cal. Constl. Conv., 1849; mem. U.S. Ho. of Reps. (Democrat) from Cal., 31st Congress, Sept. 11, 1850-51. Killed in duel with Gen. James W. Denver, nr. Sacramento, Cal., Aug. 2, 1852; buried Lone Mountain (now Laurel Hill) Cemetery, San Francisco.

GILBERT, Eliphalet Wheeler, clergyman, coll. pres.; b. New Lebanon, N.Y., Dec. 19, 1793; s. Elisha and Ellen G.; grad. Union Coll., 1813; post-grad. Princeton Theol. Sem., 1814-16 (did not grad.); m. Lydia Munro, Oct. 21, 1819; m. 2d, Mary Singer. Licensed to preach, 1817; ordained by Presbytery of New Castle (Del.), 1818; pastor of new congregation Hanover St. Ch., Wilmington, Del., 1829-34, 35-40; apptd. trustee Newark (Del.) Coll. (now U. Del.), chosen permanent pres. bd., 1833, pres. coll., 1834-35, again pres. (on condition that sch. dispose of lottery which previously had been used to support it, 1840-47; co-editor Presbyn. Quarterly. Died Phila., July 31, 1853.

GILBERT, Ezekiel, congressman, lawyer; b. Middletown, Conn., Mar. 24, 1756; grad. Yale, 1778; studied law. Admitted to bar, began practice of law, Hudson, N.Y.; mem. N.Y. State Assembly, 1789-90, 1800-01; mem. U.S. Ho. of Reps. from N.Y., 3d-4th congresses, 1793-97; clk. Columbia County, 1813-15. Died Hudson, July 17, 1841.

GILBERT, Sir Humphrey, explorer; b. Compton, Eng., circa 1539; ed. Oxford (Eng.) U. Served with Brit. Army in France, 1563, Ireland, 1566-68, Netherlands, 1572; M.P. for Plymouth, 1571; unsuccessfully petitioned Queen Elizabeth for permission to attempt discovery of N.E. and N.W. passages, 1566; received royal charter for discovery and colonization, 1578; made unsuccessful 1st voyage, 1579; explored Newfoundland coast, took possession in Queen's name, 1583; established colony in Harbor of St. John's (1st successful English colony in N.Am). Author: Discourse (argued fact that a N.W. passage actually existed), 1576. Lost at sea on return voyage to Eng., Sept. 9, 1583.

GILBERT, John Gibbs, actor; b. Boston, Feb. 27, 1810; s. John Neal and Elizabeth (Atkins) G.; m. Maria Campbell, 1836; m. 2d, Sarah H. Gavett, 1867. Made acting debut as Jaffies in Venice Preserved, Tremont Theatre, Boston, 1828; played in New Orleans and Mississippi River towns, 1829-34; actor Tremont Theatre (associated with Booth family, Edwin Forrest, Thomas Hamblin, J.W. Wallack, Tyrone Power, Charlotte Cushman, Ellen Tree, others), Boston, also periodically mgr., 1834-47, played at Princess Theatre, London, Eng., 1847; actor Wallack's Co., N.Y.C., 1862-88, Joseph Jefferson's Co., 1888-89; played wide range of characters, notably Sir Peter Teazle, Sir Anthony Absolute, Old Dornton, Job Thornberry. Died Boston, June 17, 1889.

GILBERT, Linda, philanthropist; b. Rochester, N.Y., May 13, 1847; d. Horace Gilbert; ed. Acad. of Our Lady of Mercy. Established 1st county jail library in Chgo.; worked for prisons, N.Y.C., 1873; established and incorporated Gilbert Library, also Prisoners Aid Soc., N.Y., 1876; firm believer in idea that it is society's duty to provide for rehab. of prisoners. Author: Sketch of the Life and Work of Linda Gilbert, 1876. Died Mt. Vernon, N.Y., Oct. 24, 1895.

GILBERT, Marie Dolores Eliza Rosanna, see Montez, Lola.

GILBERT, Rufus Henry, physician, inventor; b. Guilford, N.Y., Jan. 26, 1832; s. William Dwight Gilbert; attended Coll. Phys. and Surg., N.Y.C.; m. Miss Maynard; m. 2d, Miss Price; 2 children. Began practice medicine, Corning, N.Y., circa 1853; went to Europe, circa 1857, became convinced that public health problems could best be solved by building rapid transp. facilities to permit urban residents to live outside cities in cleaner atmosphere; surgeon to Duryée Zouaves, 1861, later served as med. dir. XIV Corps, U.S. Army; to implement his ideas on rapid transp., became asst. supt. Central R.R. of N.J.; obtained patents for pneumatic tube system, 1870; instrumental in incorporation of Gilbert Elevated R.R. Co., 1872 (opened for travel, 1878), forced out of mgmt. of co., circa 1878. Died N.Y.C., July 10, 1885.

GILBERT, Sylvester, congressman, lawyer; b. Hebron, Conn., Oct. 20, 1755; grad. Dartmouth, 1775; studied law. Admitted to bar, 1777, began practice of law, Hebron; mem. Conn. Ho. of Reps., 1780-1812. 26; states atty. Tolland County 1786-1807; chief judge county ct., judge probate ct., 1807-18; prin. of a law sch., 1810-18; mem. Conn. Senate, 1815-16; mem. U.S. Ho. of Reps. from Conn., 15th Congress, Nov. 16, 1818-19; judge county ct., 1820-25. Died Hebron, Jan. 2, 1846; buried Old Cemetery.

GILBERT, William Augustus, congressman; b. Gilead, Conn., Jan. 25, 1815; attended public schs.; studied law. Admitted to bar, 1843, began practice of law, Adams, N.Y.; mem. N.Y. State Assembly, 1851-52; mem. U.S. Ho. of Reps. (Whig) from N.Y., 34th Congress, 1855-Feb. 27, 1857; pres. Village of Adams, 1859-60; engaged in banking. Died Adams, May 25, 1875; buried Rural Cemetery.

GILBERT, William Lewis, businessman; b. Litchfield, Conn., Dec. 30, 1806; s. James and Abigail (Kinney) G.; m. Clarinda Hine, 1835; m. 2d, Anna Westcott, 1876. Clock-maker, Bristol and Farmington, Conn., 12 years; moved to Winsted, Conn.; became owner (with Lucius Clarke and Ezra Baldwin) Riley Whiting Clock Factory (became William L. Gilbert Clock Co. 1871); founded banking house Gilbert and Gay; pres. Hurlbut Nat. Bank; promoter, treas., pres. Conn. Western R.R.; mem. Conn. Legislature, 1848, 68; left money for founding of William L. Gilbert Home for Friendless Children and Gilbert Sch. (both Winsted). Died Oshawa, Ont., Can., June 29, 1890.

GILCHRIST, Robert, state ofcl., lawyer; b. Jersey City, N.J., Aug. 21, 1825; s. Robert and Frances (Vacher) G.; m. Fredericka Beardsley. Admitted to N.J. bar, 1847, later to U.S. Supreme Ct. bar; mem. N.J. Assembly, 1859; commd. capt. N.J. Volunteers, 1861; atty gen. N.J., 1869-75; authority on constl. law; one of most important opinions proclaimed right of Negroes to vote in N.J., circa 1870; a commr. to revise N.J. Constn., 1873; drew up N.J. riparian-rights act. Died Jersey City, July 6, 1888.

GILDER, William Henry, journalist, explorer; b. Phila., Aug. 16, 1836; s. Rev. William Henry and Jane (Nutt) G. Served as pvt. 5th N.Y. Inf., 1861; commd. 2d lt. Co. H, 40th N.Y. Inf., 1862, promoted lt., capt., asst. adj. gen.; transferred to Co. D, 40th N.Y. Inf., 1863; wounded at Battle of Gettysburg, discharged; re-enlisted, 1864, wounded at Hatcher's Run, 1864; correspondent for N.Y. Herald; accompanied Lt. Frederick Schwatka on expdn. to discover bodies and records of Sir John Franklin's expdn. in No. Can., 1878-80; explored (with Lt. Robert M. Berry) for missing ship Jeannette in Bering Strait, 1881-82; correspondent in China when French took Cochin; editor Sunday Standard, Newark, N.J., Sunday Times, Trenton, N.J.; mem. staff N.Y. Journal, N.Y.C.; Author: Schwatka's Search, 1881; Ice Pack and Tundra, 1883. Died Feb. 5, 1900.

GILES, Chauncey, clergyman, coll. pres.; b. Charlemont, Mass., May 11, 1813; s. John and Almira (Avery) G.; B.A. (hon.), M.A. (hon.), Williams Coll., 1876; m. Eunice Lakey, Sept. 8, 1841, at least 1 child. Influenced by writings of Emanuel Swedenborg, 1844, became main interest of his life; moved to Cincinnati, 1853, became pastor Ch. of New Jerusalem until 1864 (had no theol. training); pastor Ch. of New Jerusalem, N.Y.C., 1864-78, Phila., 1878-93; consecrated ordaining minister of Ch. of New Jerusalem, 1863; editor New Jerusalem Messenger (now New Church Messenger), 1871-78, part of Gen. Conv. of New Jerusalem; published weekly periodical Helper, Phila.; pres. Urbana U., Cincinnati, several years; pres. Gen. Conv. of New Jerusalem, 1875-93. Author: Lectures on the Nature of Spirit, and of Man as a Spiritual Being, 1867; Heavenly Blessedness, 1872; Perfect Prayer, 1883; The Sanctity of Marriage, 1896. Died Nov. 6, 1893.

GILES, William Branch, senator, gov. Va.; b. nr. Amelia Court House, Va., Aug. 12, 1762; grad. Princeton, 1781; studied law. Admitted to bar, began practice of law, Petersburg, Va., 1784; mem. U.S. Ho. of Reps. (Anti-Federalist, filled vacancy) from Va., 1st-5th congresses, Dec. 7, 1790-Oct. 2, 1798 (resigned); Democratic presdl. elector,

1800; mem. Va. Ho. of Dels., 1798-1800, 16-17, 26-27; mem. U.S. Ho. of Reps. (Democrat) from Va., 7th Congress, 1801-03; mem. U.S. Senate from Va., Aug. 11, 1804-1815; gov. Va., 1827-30; mem. Va. Constl. Conv., 1829-30. Died "Wigwam," nr. Amelia Court House, Dec. 4, 1830; buried pvt. cemetery "Wigwam."

GILES, William Fell, congressman, jurist; b. Harford County, Md., Apr. 8, 1807; attended Bel Air Acad.; studied law. Admitted to bar, 1829, began practice of law, Balt.; mem. Md. Ho. of Dels., 1838-40; mem. U.S. Ho. of Reps. (Democrat) from Md., 29th Congress, 1845-47; U.S. dist. judge for Dist. of Md., 1853-79; officer Am. Colonization Soc., more than 30 years; a commr. State of Md. for removing free Negroes to Liberia, more than 20 years. Died Balt., Mar. 21, 1879; buried Greenmount Cemetery.

GILL, John, journalist; b. Charlestown, Mass., May 17, 1732; s. John and Elizabeth (Abbot) G.; m. Ann Kneeland, Jan. 1756, several children. Began publication (with Benjamin Edes) Boston Gazette and Country Jour., 1755, became prominent radical organ (Boston Tea Party group met in its office before setting out), ofcl. printers Mass. for several years, partnership dissolved, 1775; arrested because of liberal and radical content of paper, 1775, liberated, 1775; published Continental Jour. and Weekly Advertiser, 1776-1785, disposed of paper as protest against state stamp act; reapptd. ofcl. printer Mass., 1785. Died Aug. 25, 1785.

GILLAM, Bernhard, political cartoonist; b. Banbury, Eng., Apr. 28, 1856; s. John Sewell and Lucy (Clarke) G.; m. Bartelle Arkell, 1889. Came (with family) to N.Y., 1866; copyist in lawyer's office, N.Y.; began study engraving, sold 1st drawings in 1876; began career as polit. cartoonist by drawing caricatures for Leslie's Weekly and New York Graphic; engaged by Puck, 1881, did cartoons of James G. Blaine in campaign of 1884; part owner (with W.J. Arkell) mag. Judge, 1886-96; in campaigns of 1888 and 1892 stressed importance of Republican Party's protectionist policies as opposed to Democrats' free trade, cartoons included "Easter Eggs—Both Addled," 1888, "Mud-Slingers," 1888, "Benjamin Where Am I At." 1892. Died Canajoharie, N.Y., Jan. 19, 1896.

GILLEM, Alvan Cullem, army officer; b. Jackson County, Tenn., July 20, 1830; s. Samuel J. Gillem; grad. U.S. Mil. Acad., 1851; m. Margaret Jones. Served in Seminole War, also on garrison duty and duty on Tex. frontier; commd. capt. U.S. Army, 1861; col. 10th Tenn. Volunteers, chief q.m. Army of Ohio during Tenn. campaign; provost marshal Nashville (Tenn.); adj. gen. Tenn. (apptd. by Gen. Andrew Johnson), 1863-65; commanded troops guarding Nashville & Northwestern R.R., 1863-64; commd. brig. gen. U.S. Volunteers, 1863, brevetted lt. col., col., brig. gen., promoted maj. gen. for gallantry at capture of Salisbury, 1865; prominent in reorgn. of Tenn. civil govt., v.p. of reorgn. conv., Jan. 1865; mem. Tenn. Legislature, 1865; commanded Dist. of East Tenn., 1865-66; commd. col. U.S. Army, 1866; commanded 4th Mil. Dist. (Miss. and Ark.), 1868-69; transferred to Tex., took part in Modoc campaign, 1873. Died Nashville, Dec. 2, 1875.

GILLESPIE, George, clergyman; b. Glasgow, Scotland, 1683; attended U. Glasgow. Licensed to preach by Presbyn. Ch., in Eng., 1712; came to New Eng., 1712; rector ch., White Clay Creek, Del., 1713-41; temporarily retired from ministry, 1741-44; worked in New Eng. Presbyn. Synod, 1744-60. Author: Treatise Against Deists and Free Thinkers, 1735; Letters to Presbytery of New York, 1740; Sermon Against Divisions in Christ's Church, 1740. Died Jan. 2, 1760.

GILLESPIE, James, congressman; b. Kenansville, N.C. Mem. N.C. Const. Conv., 1776; mem. N.C. Ho. of Commons, 1779-83, N.C. Senate, 1784-86; mem. U.S. Ho. of Reps., 3d-5th, 8th congresses, 1793-99, 1803-05. Died Washington, D.C., Jan. 11, 1805; buried Congressional Cemetery.

GILLESPIE, Neal Henry, educator; b. Pa., Jan. 19, 1831; grad. Notre Dame U., 1849. Joined Congregation of Holy Cross, 1853; ordained priest Roman Catholic Ch., Rome, Italy, 1856; v.p. Notre Dame U., 1856-59; pres. Coll. of St. Mary of the Lake, Chgo., until 1863; stationed at Le Mans, France, until 1866; later editor of Ave Maria, until 1874. Died Notre Dame, Ind., Nov. 12, 1874.

GILLESPIE, William Mitchell, civil engr., educator; b. N.Y., 1816; s. James and Ann (Waldron) G.; grad. Columbia, 1834, LL.D. (hon.) 1859; studied at Ecole des Ponts et Chaussees, France; m. Harriet Emily Bates, Apr. 7, 1864, at least 1 son, T. Waldron. First prof. civil engring. Union Coll., Schenectady, N.Y., 1845-68, stressed importance of humanities to engring.; after trip to France lost voice and lectured by whispering to an asst., 1867. Author: Rome: As Seen by a New-Yorker in 1843-44, published 1845; A Manual of the Principles and Practice of Road-Making, 1847; The Philosophy of Mathematics, 1851; A Treatise of Land-Surveying, 1855. Died N.Y., Jan. 1, 1868.

GILLET, Ransom Hooker, congressman; b. New Lebanon, N.Y., Jan. 27, 1800; s. Capt. John and Lucy Gillet; studied law under Silas Wright, 1821; m. Eleanor C. Barhydt, 1825. Admitted to N.Y. bar, circa 1822; partner (with Silas Wright) in law firm, circa 1823; served as maj., insp. local brigade N.Y. Militia, 1827-37; postmaster Ogdensburg (N.Y.), 1830-33; mem. 1st Nat. Democratic Conv., 1832; mem. U.S. Ho. of Reps. (Dem.) from N.Y., 23d-24th congresses, 1833-37; U.S. Indian commr. for N.Y., 1837-39; mem. Dem. nominating conv., 1840, helped draw up resolutions used as platform for every Dem. conv. until 1864; U.S. register of treasury, 1845-47, U.S. solicitor of treasury, 1847-49; asst. U.S. atty. gen., 1855-58; solicitor to U.S. Ct. of Claims, 1858-60. Author: Democracy in the United States, 1868; The Federal Government, 1871; The Life and Times of Silas Wright, 2 vols., 1874. Died Washington, D.C., Oct. 24, 1876; buried Glenwood Cemetery, Washington.

GILLETT, Ezra Hall, clergyman, editor; b. Colchester, Conn., July 15, 1823; s. Ely Hall and Mary (Williams) G.; grad. Yale, 1841; attended Union Theol. Sem., until 1845; D.D. (hon.), Hamilton Coll., 1864; m. Maria Huntington Ripley, Oct. 15, 1851; m. 2d, Mary Kendall, June 19, 1854; 3 children. Ordained to ministry Presbyn. Ch., 1845; asst. librarian Union Theol. Sem., 1844-45; later began McAlpin Collection of British History and Theology; most important work The Life and Times of John Huss led to appointment as ofcl. historian of Presbyn. Ch., 1863; prof. polit. sci., ethics and history U. City of N.Y., 1868, prof. polit. sci., 1870-75. Author: History of the Presbyterian Church in the United States, 1864; Life Lessons, 1864; England Two Hundred Years Ago, 1866; What Then?, 1866; Ancient Cities and Empires: Their Prophetic Doom Read in the Light of History and Modern Research, 1874; The Moral Life, 1874. Died N.Y.C., Sept. 2, 1875.

GILLETTE, Francis, senator; b. Bloomfield, Conn., Dec. 14, 1807; s. Ashbel and Achsah (Francis) Gillet; grad. Yale, 1829; m .Eliza Hooker, 1834, 6 children. Mem. Conn. Ho. of Reps., 1832-40; chmn. bd. trustees Conn. State Normal Sch., 1849-65; mem. U.S. Senate from Conn., May 24, 1854-55; abolitionist, prominent in founding of Republican Party in Conn., 1856; silent partner Hartford Evening Press; incorporator Am. Temperance Life Ins. Co.; mem. Phi Beta Kappa. Died Hartford, Conn., Sept. 30, 1879.

GILLIS, James Lisle, congressman; b. Hebron N.Y., Oct. 2, 1792; attended public schs. Became a tanner; served in War of 1812; moved to Ridgway, Pa., 1822; asso. judge Jefferson County; mem. Pa. Ho. of Reps., 1840, 51; a judge Jefferson County, 1842; mem. Pa. Senate, 1845; mail agt. in San Francisco; mem. U.S. Ho. of Reps. (Democrat) from Pa., 35th Congress, 1857-59; apptd. agt. Pawnee Indians. Died Mt. Pleasant, Ia., July 8, 1881; buried Forest Home Cemetery.

GILLISS, James Melville, naval officer, astronomer; b. Georgetown, D.C., Sept. 6, 1811; s. George and Mary (Melville) G.; attended U. Va., 1833; m. Rebecca Roberts, Dec. 1837. Entered U.S. Navy, 1826; commd. midshipman, 1833; studied in Paris for 6 months, 1835, ordered back to Washington (D.C.), assigned to Depot of Charts and Instruments; in charge of depot, 1837; commd. to make astron. observations in Washington necessary for evaluation of longitude observation of Lt. Charles Wilkes' expdn., 1838; pointed out inadequacy of existing building and equipment for astron. research to Bd. Naval Commrs., 1841 (led to act of Congress providing for establishment U.S. Naval Observatory at Washington); visited Europe in interests of observatory, circa 1842-1843, authorized by Congress to go to Santiago (Chile) to observe Venus and Mars, 1849-52; became supt. U.S. Naval Observatory, 1861; mem. Nat. Acad. Sci. Died Feb. 9, 1865.

GILLMORE, Quincy Adams, army officer; b. Black River, O., Feb. 28, 1825; s. Quartus and Elizabeth (Reid) G.; grad. U.S. Mil. Acad., 1849; m. Mary O'Maher, 1849; m. 2d, Mrs. Briggs; 4 children. Commd. 2d lt. engrs. U.S. Army, 1849, 1st lt., 1856, capt., 1861; chief engr. Port Royal expdn.; brevetted lt. col. for services during capture of Ft. Pulaski, 1862; commd. brig. gen. U.S. Volunteers, 1862, maj. gen., 1863; brevetted col. U.S. Army for gallantry, 1863; commanded 10th Army Corps, then Dept. of South; wounded during defense of Washington (D.C.), 1864; pres. bd. to test wrought iron cannon; brevetted brig. gen. and maj. gen. U.S. Army for bravery; pres. Mississippi River Commn. Author various engring. works including: Practical Treatise on Limes, Hydraulic Elements and Mortars, 1863; Report on Experiments with the Seely and Bethell Processes for the Preservation of Timber, 1879. Died Bklyn., Apr. 7, 1888; buried U.S. Mil. Acad., West Point, N.Y.

GILLON, Alexander, naval officer, congressman; b. Rotterdam, Holland, Aug. 13, 1741; s. Mary Gillon; m. Mary Cripps, July 6, 1766; m. 2d, Ann Purcell, Feb. 10, 1789; 1 son, 2 daus. Commanded Brit. mcht. vessels with hdqrs. at Charleston, S.C., 1764-65; engaged in trading enterprises, 1766-76; mem. S.C. Provincial Congresses, 1775-77, strongly favored Am. independence; apptd. commodore in state navy of S.C., 1778, sent to France as financial agt. to borrow money and purchase ships; obtained from Chevalier Luxembourg frigate which he named South Carolina, 1780, took command of ship, captured prizes in North Sea, 1781, commanded expdn. which took Bahamas, 1782, his ship captured by British, 1782, lost money in the enterprise (claims for payment made by Chevalier Luxembourg continued in courts for many years); del. to Congress of Confederation, 1784; mem. S.C. Assembly, 1786-88; mem. U.S. Ho. of Reps. from S.C., 3d Congress, 1793-94. Died at estate Gillon's Retreat, Oct. 6, 1794.

GILMAN, Arthur Delevan, architect; b. Hingham, Eng., Nov. 5, 1821; s. Arthur and Elizabeth (Marquand) G.; attended Trinity Coll., Hartford, Conn., 1837-40; m. Frances Juliet, Apr. 7, 1859. Became interested in architecture after leaving college, wrote articles on subject and lectured at Lowell Inst., Boston, 1844-45; studied architecture in Europe, late 1840's, returned to Boston as profl. architect, circa 1852; moved to N.Y.C., 1868; critical of Greek revival structures, based his designs on Georgian and Italian Renaissance styles; designed Boston City hall, 1862-65; commd. to build N.Y. State Capitol at Albany, 1867; designed Equitable Life Assurance Soc. Bldg., N.Y.C., circa 1869, St. John's Episcopal Ch., S.I., N.Y., 1869. Died N.Y.C., July 11, 1882; buried N.Y.C.

GILMAN, Caroline Howard, writer; b. Boston, Oct. 8, 1794; d. Samuel and Anna (Lillie) Howard; attended common schs., Mass.; m. Samuel Gilman, Dec. 1819, 1 dau., Caroline (Gilman) Jervey, Published first poem in Cambridge, Mass., 1810; published poem Jairus's Daughter in North American Review, 1817; lived in Charleston S.C., 1819-70; Cambridge, 1870-circa 1880, Washington, D.C., circa 1880-84; editor Southern Rosebud (children's paper), 1832-39; edited Revolutionary War memoirs of Eliza Wilkinson; other works include: Recollections of a Housekeeper (1st book, collection domestic anecdotes), 1834; Oracles from the Poets, 1844; Oracles for youth, 1852; Poems by Mother and Daughter, 1872. Died Washington, Sept. 15, 1888.

GILMAN, John Taylor, gov. N.H.; b. Exeter, N.H., Dec. 19, 1753; s. Nicholas and Ann (Taylor) G.; attended common schools, Exeter; m. Deborah Folsom, Jan. 13, 1776; m. 2d, Mary Folsom, July 5, 1792; m. 3d, Mrs. Charlotte Hamilton, Dec. 29, 1814. In father's merc. and shipbuilding trade, circa 1767-75; clk. under his father (treas. of N.H.), 1775-83; mem. N.H. Legislature, 1779-81; mem. Continental Congress from N.H., 1782-83; treas. N.H., 1783-88, 91-94; mem. fed. bd. commrs. for settlement Confederation's accounts with various states, 1788-90; elected Federalist gov. N.H., 1794-1805, 13-16, during 1st tenure aroused Republican faction in N.H. by opposing creation of any banks other than 1 chartered bank in Portsmouth (of which he was pres.), during 2d term supported war effort (War of 1812) in state; trustee Dartmouth, 1794-1819, in Dartmouth controversy (1816-19) opposed removal of pres. Wheelock and remained neutral between contending groups. Died Portsmouth, N.H., Aug. 31, 1828.

GILMAN, Nicholas, senator, congressman; b. Exeter, N.H., Aug. 3, 1755; s. Nicholas and Ann (Taylor) G.; attended common schools, Exeter. Commd. capt. N.H. Militia 1775, served with adj. gen. until 1782; returned to Exeter, 1783, active politically; commanded local militia during currency troubles, 1786; del. to Congress of Confederation, 1786-88; del. to U.S. Constl. Conv., Phila.,, 1787; mem. U.S. Ho. of Reps. (Federalist) from N.H., 1st-4th congresses, 1789-97; mem. N.H. Senate, 1804-05; changed allegiance to Republican Party; mem. U.S. Senate (Rep.) from N.H., 1805-14. Died Phila., May 2, 1814; buried Exeter.

GILMAN, Samuel, clergyman, writer; b. Gloucester, Mass., Feb. 16, 1791; s. Frederick and Abigail (Hillier) G.; attended acad., Atkinson, N.H., 1803-07; grad. Harvard, 1811; m. Caroline Howard, Dec. 1819, at least 1 dau. Taught school, Boston, 1812-17; tutor Harvard, 1817-19; ordained to ministry Unitarian Ch., 1819; minister 2d Independent (Unitarian) Ch., Charleston, S.C., 1819-58; devoted much time to writing prose and poetry; contributed to N. Am. Review; prominent literary figure in Charleston. Author: Monody on the Victims of the Late Conflagration in Richmond, Va., 1812; Memoirs of the New England Village Choir, 1829; many of his publications collected in Contributions to Literature, 1856. Died Kingston, Mass., Feb. 9, 1858; buried Charleston.

GILMER, Francis Walker, lawyer, author; b. Pen Park, Albemarle County, Va., Oct. 9, 1790; s. George and Lucy (Walker) G.; attended school at Georgetown, D.C., 1808-09; grad. Coll. William and Mary, 1810; studied law with William Wirt, Richmond, Va., 1811-14. Admitted to Richmond bar, 1815; practiced in Winchester, Va., 1815-17, Richmond, 1817-24; went to Britain, induced 5 scholars to come to new U. Va., 1824, apptd. prof. law, 1825, died before assuming duties. Author: Sketches of American Orators, 1816; Reports of Cases Decided in the Court of Appeals of Virginia, 1821; Sketches, Essays, and Translations (collected miscellaneous writings), 1828. Died Feb. 25, 1826; buried Pen Park.

GILMER, George Rockingham, gov. Ga., congressman; b. Lexington, Ga., Apr. 11, 1790; s. Thomas Meriwether and Elizabeth (Lewis) G.; attended acad., Abbeville, S.C., 1804-08, pvt. law school, Lexington, 1808-circa 1811; m. Eliza Grattan, 1822. Began practice of law, Lexington, circa 1811; commanded Ga. Militia in expdn. against Creek Indians, 1813; elected to Ga. Legislature, 1818, 24; mem. U.S. Ho. of Reps. from Ga., 17th Congress, 1821-23, 20th Congress, 1826, 23d Congress, 1833-35; an adherent Troup faction in Ga. politics and advocate slavery and states' rights; gov. Ga., 1828-31, 37-39; bequeathed Gilmer Fund to U. Ga. for teacher tng. Author: Sketches of Some of the First Settlers of Upper Georgia (recollections of early years), 1885. Died Lexington Nov. 16, 1859; buried Presbyn. Cemetery, Lexington.

GILMER, John Adams, congressmna; b. Guilford County, N.C., Nov. 4, 1805; s. Robert and Anne (Forbes) G.; attended acad., Greensboro, N.C., 1824-26; studied law with A.D. Murphy, Greensboro, 1828-32; m. Juliana Paisley, Jan. 3, 1832. Taught school, S.C., 1822-24, 26-29; admitted to bar; began law practice in Greensboro, 1832; active local politics as Whig; as N.C. senator urged moderation on slave issue, 1846-56; mem. U.S. Ho. of Reps. (Know-Nothing Party rep.) from N.C., 35th-36th congresses, 1857-61, opposed Le-Compton constn. in Kan., one of strongest Southern Unionists, 1860-61; considered for appointment to Lincoln's cabinet, 1861; became loyal supporter of Confederacy; mem. 2d Confederate Congress, 1864-65; del. Nat. Union Conv., Phila., 1866. Died Greensboro, May 14, 1868; buried Presbyn. Ch. Cemetery, Greensboro.

GILMER, Thomas, gov. Va., congressman; b. Gilmerton, Albemarle County, Va., Apr. 6, 1802; s. George and Elizabeth (Hudson) G.; educated privately by tutors; m. Anne Baker, 1826. Admitted to bar, opened law office, Charlottesville, Va., circa 1825; supporter of Andrew Jackson, 1828; elected to Va. Legislature, 1828-39 (except 1834, 37), speaker Ho. of Dels. during last 2 terms; broke with Jackson over nullification crisis, 1833, became Whig; elected gov. Va., 1840, resigned over dispute with Legislature concerning some extradition porceedings with N.Y., 1841; mem. U.S. Ho. of Reps. (Whig) from Va., 27th-28th congresses, 1841-45, powerful advocate of economy in govt., supported Pres. Tyler in opposition to Clay Whigs, urged annexation of Tex. in famed "Texas Letter"; apptd. sec. of navy by Pres. Tyler, 1844, Killed by explosion on board ship Princeton, nr. Washington, D.C., Feb. 28, 1844; buried Mt. Air Cemetery, Albemarle County, Va.

GILMOR, Harry, army officer; b. Balt., Jan. 24, 1838; s. Robert and Ellen (Ward) G.; tutored at home; m. Mentoria Strong; Engaged in farming in Wis. and Neb., later with father in Md., circa 1848-61, joined Confederate Army under Ashby in Va., 1861; commd. capt. 21st Va. Cavalry, 1862; served in Shenandoah Valley throughout war, captured and exchanged, 1862; commd. maj. 2d Md. Cavalry, 1863; cut B. & O. R.R. during raid nr. Harper's Ferry, 1864, acquitted by Confederate court martial for robberies which occurred at that time; burned Chambersburg, Pa., 1864; leader of many raids, highly successful at guerilla style warfare; captured again, 1865; in business in Balt., 1865-74; police commr. of Balt., 1874-79. Died Balt., Mar. 4, 1883; buried Balt.

GILMORE, Alfred, congressman, lawyer; b. Butler, Pa., June 9, 1812; s. John Gilmore; grad. Washington (Pa.) Coll., 1833; studied law. Admitted to bar, 1836, began practice of law, Butler; mem. U.S. Ho. of Reps. (Democrat) from Pa., 31st-32d congresses, 1849-53; practiced law, Phila., then moved to Lenox, Mass., 1866. Died while visiting N.Y.C., June 29, 1890; buried Lenox Cemetery.

GILMORE, John, congressman; b. Somerset County, Pa., Feb. 18, 1780; s. Alfred Gilmore; attended common sch.; studied law. Admitted to bar, 1801, began practice of law, Washington, Pa.; moved to Butler, Pa., 1803; apptd. dep. dist. atty. Butler County (Pa.), 1803; mem. Pa. Ho. of Reps., 1816-21, speaker, 1821; mem. U.S. Ho. of Reps. (Jackson Democrat) from Pa., 21st-22d congresses, 1829-33; elected treas. Pa. by Pa. Legislature, 1841. Died Butler, May 11, 1845; buried North Cemetery.

GILMORE, Joseph Albree, gov. N.H.; b. Weston, Vt., June 10, 1811; s. Asa and Lucy (Dodge) G.; attended common schools, Weston; m. Ann Whipple, July 10, 1832. In business in Boston, circa 1830; established wholesale grocery firm, Concord, N.H., 1842, became constrn. agt. Concord & Claremont R.R., 1848, supt., 1856-66; mem. N.H. Senate (Republican), 1858-59; gov. N.H., 1863-64, provided effective leadership in areas of finance and mil. organization in which Legislature had performed inadequately. Died Apr. 17, 1867.

GILMORE, Patrick Sarsfield, musician; b. Dublin, Ireland, Dec. 25, 1829; 1 dau. Moved to Salem, Mass., circa 1848, became mil. band master; toured U.S. with own band in 1850's; bandmaster 24th Mass. Regt., U.S. Volunteers, 1861; headed all army band units in Dept. of La., 1863; originated "monster concerts" utilizing thousands in choruses and hundreds in band, performed in this manner at Nat. Peace Jubilee, Boston, 1869, also Chgo. (Peace) Jubilee, 1873; served as bandmaster 22d Regt. N.Y. Nat. Guard, 1870's, toured with group in Canada, 1878, also Europe; composed much band music, many songs. Died Sept. 24, 1892.

GILMOUR, Richard, clergyman; b. Glasgow, Scotland, Sept. 28, 1824; s. John and Marian (Callender) G.; ed. common schools, Cumbola, Pa.; grad. St. Mary's Coll., Emmitsburg, Md., 1848. Ordained priest Roman Catholic Ch., 1852; served missions in Portsmouth, O., 1852-57; rector St. Patrick's Ch., Cincinnati, 1857-68; prof. theology Mt. St. Mary's of West, Cincinnati, 1868; rector St. Joseph's Ch., Dayton, O., 1869-72; designated bishop, 1872, in charge of Diocese of Cleve., 1872-91; leader in securing religious freedom for Catholics in prisons and obtaining exemption church properties from local taxes; established 40 parochial schools in diocese; founder St. Ignatius Coll., Cleve.; hostile to militant Irish nationalist groups in diocese; served at 3d Plenary Council, Balt., 1884, defended principles of independence of Am. hierarchy. Died St. Augustine, Fla., Apr. 13, 1891; buried Cleve.

GILPIN, Edward Woodward, jurist; b. Wilmington, Del., July 13, 1803; s. William and Ann (Dunwoody) G.; read law with Senator John Wales, Wilmington, 1822; m. Eleanor LaMotte, Mar. 15, 1842. Employed as clerk in Wilmington retail business, 1820-21; apprenticed to a tanner, Phila., 1821; admitted to Wilmington bar, 1827; became prominent lawyer in Wilmington during 1830's; atty. gen. of Del., 1840-50; a Whig; apptd. chief justice Del. Supreme Ct., 1857-76; strong supporter of Union during Civil War. Died Dover, Del., Apr. 29, 1876; buried Wilmington.

GILPIN, Henry Dilworth, U.S. atty. gen.; b. Lancaster, Eng., Apr. 14, 1801; s. Joshua and Mary (Dilworth) G.; attended pvt. sch. (Dr. Hamilton's), nr. London, Eng., 1811-15; grad. U. Pa., 1819; read law with Joseph Ingersoll, Phila. 1819-22; m. Eliza Johnson, Sept. 3, 1834. Admitted to Phila. bar, 1822, practiced in Phila.; sec. Chesapeake & Ohio Canal Co.; editor Atlantic Souvenir (annual gift book), 1825; became frequent contbr. to Am. Quarterly Review and Democratic Review, 1820's; became identified with Jacksonian Democrats in Pa., circa 1829; U.S. atty. for Eastern Dist. of Pa., 1831-37; dir. Bank of U.S. (apptd. by Pres. Jackson), 1833, defended Jackson's anti-U.S. Bank policies; solicitor of U.S. Treasury (apptd. by Pres. Van Buren), 1837-40; U.S. atty. gen. in Van Buren's cabinet, 1840-41; retired from polit. life, 1841, devoted himself to classical and literary pursuits, 1840's-50's; pres. Pa. Acad. Fine Arts; v.p. Pa. Hist. Soc.; trustee U. Pa. Editor: The Papers of James Madison, 1840; Opinions of the Attorneys-General of the United States, 1841. Died Phila., Jan. 29, 1860; buried Phila.

GILPIN, William, territorial gov. Colo.; b. Brandywine, Pa., Oct. 4, 1813; s. Joshua and Mary (Dilworth) G.; grad. U. Pa., 1833; attended U.S. Mil. Acad., 1834-35; m. Mrs. Julia Dickerson, Feb. 12, 1874. Served as 2d lt. U.S. Army, in Seminole War 1836, resigned as 1st lt., 1838; editor Mo. Argus, (newspaper which he made organ of Democratic Party), St. Louis, 1838; accompanied Fremont's expdn. to Pacific coast, 1843; served as maj. in volunteer Mo. regt., Mexican War, 1846-47, then engaged in Indian wars in Rockies, mustered out as lt. col. of Mo. Volunteers, 1848; lectured often on theme of establishing Denver as capital of new civilization in West in 1850's; apptd. territorial gov. of Colo., 1861, held territory for U.S. during early stages of Civil War, raised 1st Regt. of Colo. Volunteers, autumn, 1861, served until 1862 (recalled after dispute); owned interest in land devel. in N.M., 1870's; continued propagandizing on behalf econ. and polit. devel. of West in 1870's-80's. Author: The Central Gold Region, 1860; The Cosmopolitan Railway (urged uniting Asia and U.S. via railroad across Bering Straits), 1890. Died Denver, Jan. 20, 1894; buried Denver.

GIMBREDE, Thomas, artist; b. France, 1781; children include Joseph Napoleon. Came to Am., 1802; worked as miniaturist, took up engraving, circa 1810; worked in N.Y.C., 1802-18; drawing master U.S. Mil. Acad., West Point, N.Y., 1819-32. Died West Point, Oct. 25, 1832.

GINTER, Lewis, tobacco mfr.; b. N.Y.C., Apr. 4, 1824; s. John and Elizabeth Ginter. Founded retail merchandise firm, Richmond, Va., 1842; partner (with John F. Alvey) in import dry-goods firm, Richmond, circa 1851-61; served as q.m. under Gen. J.R. Anderson of Confederate Army of Northern Va., 1861-65; his activity in battle gave him title of "fighting commissary"; asso. with a brokerage business, N.Y.C., 1865-69; returned to Richmond, 1869, established tobacco firm Allen & Ginter (mfg., selling smoking and chewing tobacco) 1872; introduced manufacture of cigarettes, 1875 (1st manufacturer to use Va. tobacco successfully produced); "Richmond Gem" and other brands of cigarettes, which led to expansion of firm and its absorption into Am. Tobacco Co. in 1890; realized large fortune in this transaction, devoted wealth to civic improvements and projects in Richmond. Died Richmond, Oct. 2, 1897; buried Hollywood Cemetery, Richmond.

GIRARD, Charles Frederic, zoologist; b. Mulhausen, Upper Alsace, France, Mar. 9, 1822; ed. Sch. at Neuchatel (Switzerland), circa 1843-47; M.D., Georgetown (D.C.) Coll., 1856. Came to U.S. with Louis Agassiz, 1847, lived in Cambridge (Mass.) until 1850, published papers on flatworms and fish; moved to Washington (D.C.), 1850, served as asst. to Spencer Baird at Smithsonian Instn. until 1860, in this capacity helped plan U.S. Nat. Museum, 1857; published many reports on fish and reptiles, especially dealing with collections made by exploring and survey parties in Far West during 1850's; went to France, 1860; became Confederate sympathizer, 1861, travelled through Va. and Carolinas as Confederate agt. for drug and surg. supplies, 1863; practiced medicine, Paris, France, 1865-85; published "Herpetology" of Wilkes expdn., 1858; published essay on fish in reports of the railroad explorations to the Pacific (Vol. X), 1859; published paper on typhoid fever during Franco-Prussian War, 1872, paper on fishes, also bibliography of his works, 1888, paper on N.Am. flatworms, 1891. Died Neuilly-sur-Seine, France, Jan. 29, 1895.

GIRARD, Stephen, financier, philanthropist; b. Bordeaux, France, May 20, 1750; s. Pierre and Odette (Lafargue) G.; m. Mary Lum, 1777, no children. Made 1st voyage as capt. of French mcht. ship to Port-au-Prince, 1774; employed as capt. by shipping firm, N.Y.C., 1775; settled in Phila., engaged in merc. business, 1776; owned mcht. fleet based at Phila. following Revolutionary War; served as supr. of improvised hosp. for 2 months during yellow fever epidemic of 1793; a supporter Bank of U.S., (purchased bldg. and opened Bank of Stephen Girard when Bank of U.S. expired, 1811), established credit in U.S. and abroad, played a key role in helping govt. through financial crisis during War of 1812; instrumental in founding 2d Bank of U.S., 1816, served as govt. dir. of bank, 1816-17; bequeathed large sums to City of Phila. and State of Pa. for public improvements; contbd. approximately $6,000,000 to Phila. for education orphan boys, (resulted in Girard Coll., opened 1848). Died Phila., Dec. 26, 1831; buried Phila.

GIRARDEAU, John Lafayette, clergyman; b. James Island, S.C., Nov. 14, 1825; s. John Bohum and Claudia (Freer) G.; attended sch. of German Friendly Soc., Charleston, S.C., 1835-39; grad. Coll. of Charleston, 1843, Columbia (S.C.) Theol. Sem., 1848; m. Penelope Hamlin, 1849. Licensed to preach, 1848, preacher in rural congregations, S.C., 1848-53; pastor of a negro ch., Charleston, 1853-60; served as chaplain Confederate Army, 1861-65; pastor Zion Presbyn. Ch., Charleston, 1866-75; prof. theology Columbia Sem., 1875-95; advocated church (rather than state) edn., opposed Darwinist ideas. Author: The Will in its Theological Relations, 1891. Died June 23, 1898.

GIRSCH, Frederick, engraver; b. Budingen, Hesse, Germany, Nov. 14, 1825; attended Royal Acad. of Darmstadt, circa 1845-48. Came to U.S., 1849, became engraver for New-Yorker Criminal Zeitung, N.Y.C.; became well-known bank note engraver, during Civil War; work includes head of Liberty on many small bills, proposed Legion of Honor (which Pres. Lincoln had planned to give to Civil War vets.; widely-known engravings included Grand Ma's Toast, The Gypsy Girl; large engraving Niagara now in collection of N.Y. Hist. Soc. Died Dec. 18, 1895.

GIRTY, Simon, renegade; b. Pa., 1741; s. Simon and Mary (Newton) G.; m. Catharine Malott, 1784. Captive of Indians, 1756-59; interpreter, Ft. Pitt, Pa., 1759-74; served as scout in Lord Dunmore's War, 1774-75; employed as interpreter by Continental Congress, 1776, deserted and became interpreter for British, Detroit, 1778, led many Indian attacks on Am. settlers; notorious for cruel tortures he and his Indian friends inflicted on their Am. victims; received pension from British, settled on farm nr. Amherstburg, Ont., Can., 1781; continued to incite Indians to attack Am. settlers; led Indians in defeat of Gen. Arthur St. Clair, 1791, and at Battle of Fallen Timbers, 1794. Died Amherstburg, Feb. 18, 1818.

GIST, Christopher, explorer; b. Md., circa 1706; s. Richard and Zipporah (Murray) G.; learned surveying from father; m. Sarah Howard, 5 children. Started from Cumberland, Md. to explore territory nr. Ohio River for Ohio Co., 1750; passed through what is now Pitts., explored as far as mouth of Scioto River; explored country S. of Ohio River, 1752; 1st Am. to explore So. Ohio and Northeastern Ky. from Monongahela to Great Kanawha rivers; started with George Washington on journey to Ft. Duquesne, 1753, twice saved Washington's life during travels; with Washington at surrender of Ft. Necessity (nr. present Uniontown, Pa.), 1754; served as guide to Gen. Braddock during campaign of 1755; Indian agt. in what is now Eastern Tenn., 1756-58. Died probably in Ga., 1759.

GIST, Joseph, congressman, lawyer; b. Union Dist., S.C., Jan. 12, 1775; grad. Charleston (S.C.) Coll.; studied law. Admitted to bar, 1799, began practice of law, Pinckneyville, S.C., 1800; mem. S.C. Ho. of Reps., 1801-19; bd. trustees S.C. Coll. at Columbia, 1809-21; mem. U.S. Ho. of Reps. (Democrat) from S.C., 17th-19th congresses, 1821-27. Died Pinckneyville, Mar. 8, 1836. buried family burial ground.

GIST, Mordecai, army officer; b. Reisterstown, Md., Mar. 6, 1743; s. Thomas and Susannah (Cockey) G.; attended common schs.; m. Cecil Carnan; m. 2d, Mary Sterrett, Jan. 23, 1778; m. 3d, Mrs. Mary Cattell, 1783; 2 sons, Independent, States. Engaged in merc. pursuits, Balt., circa 1770; served as capt. Balt. volunteer unit, 1774; commd. maj., then col. 1st Md. Battalion (under Gen. Smallwood), 1776; served in Battle of Germantown, 1777; commd. brig. gen., 1779, commended for role in Battle of Camden (1779) by Congress, 1780; served in recruiting and supply depts., 1780-81. Died Aug. 2, 1792.

GIST, William Henry, gov. S.C.; b. Charleston, S.C., Aug. 22, 1807; s. Francis Fincher Gist; attended S.C. Coll., 1823-27; m. Louisa Bowen, 1828; m. 2d, Mary Price. Managed family plantations, Union dist., S.C., from circa 1829; mem. lower house S.C. Legislature, 1840-44, S.C. Senate, 1844-56; gov. S.C., 1858-60; played prominent role in S.C.'s secession from U.S., 1860, tried to secure cooperation of other So. govs. in secession movement; signed S.C. secession ordinance, Dec. 10, 1860 (3 days after leaving office as gov.); mem. S.C. Exec. Council (which supervised defenses of state), 1860-61. Died Union dist.. Sept. 30, 1874; buried Union dist.

GLADDING, Timothy, artist; b. probably Bristol, R.I., circa 1775; children include Timothy Allen, Freeman. Established house painting and decorating bus. with his brother, Albany, N.Y., 1810; painted portraits. Died Albany, May 2, 1846.

GLADWIN, Henry, army officer; b. Derbyshire, Eng., Nov. 19, 1729; s. Henry and Mary (Dakeyne) G.; m. Frances Berridge, Mar. 30, 1762. Commd. lt. 48th Regt., Brit. Inf., 1753; served with Gen. Braddock's expdn. to Ft. Duquesne, 1755; commd. capt. 80th Regt., Brit. Inf., 1757, maj., 1759; served in relief of Ft. Niagara, 1760; in command at Detroit, 1761-64, supervised successful defense of fort during Pontiac's War, 1763; commd. lt. col., 1763; dep. adj. gen. in Am., 1764-80, but returned to Eng., 1764, never returned to Am. colonies; promoted col., 1777, maj. gen., 1782. Died Chesterfield, Eng., June 22, 1791; buried Wingerworth Churchyard, nr. Chesterfield.

GLASCOCK, Thomas, congressman, lawyer; b. Augusta, Ga., Oct. 21, 1790; attended public schs.; studied law. Admitted to bar, began practice of law, Augusta; del. Constl. Conv., 1798; served as capt. Volunteers in War of 1812, as brig. gen. in Seminole War, 1817; mem. Ga. Ho. of Reps., 1821, 23, 31, 34, 39, speaker, 1833, 34; mem. U.S. Ho. of Reps. (Union Democrat, filled vacancy) from Ga., 24th-25th congresses, Oct. 5, 1835-39; moved to Decatur, Ga. Died Decatur, May 19, 1841; buried City Cemetery, Augusta.

GLASGOW, Hugh, congressman; b. Nottingham, Chester County, Pa., Sept. 8, 1769; attended public schs.; studied law. Engaged in agriculture; admitted to bar, practiced law; judge York County (Pa.), 1800-13; mem. U.S. Ho. of Reps. from Pa., 13th-14th congresses, 1813-17. Died Peach Bottom, Pa., Jan. 31, 1818; buried Slate Ridge Burying Ground.

GLASS, Hugh, trapper, adventurer. A captive of pirate Lafitte, off New Orleans, circa 1818; after release from Lafitte, captured by Indians in Tex., circa 1820; mem. Ashley's 2d Mo. expdn., 1823; with Andrew Henry's expdn. to mouth of Yellowstone River, later in 1823 (an alleged bout with grizzly bear on this trip celebrated in song and myth); later conducted trapping enterprises in N.M. and other parts of West, served in battles with Indians. Supposedly killed by Blackfeet Indians on Upper Yellowstone River, 1833.

GLASS, James William, Jr., artist; b. Cadiz, Spain, circa 1825 (parents Am. citizens); Became engr. U.S. Coast Survey and Fortification Service; became painter, 1844; went to Europe, 1847/48; painted equestrian portrait of Duke of Wellington; returned to U.S., 1855; hon. mem. N.A.D.; painted hist. subjects and portraits. Committed suicide, Dec. 22, 1855.

GLEN, Henry, congressman; b. Schenectady, N.Y., July 13, 1739. Clk., Schenectady County, 1767-1809; served as dep. q.m. gen. in Revolutionary War; mem. 1st-3d provincial congresses, 1774-76; mem. N.Y. State Assembly, 1786-87, 1810; mem. U.S. Ho. of Reps. from N.Y., 3d-6th congresses, 1793-1801. Died Schenectady, Jan. 6, 1814.

GLESSING, Thomas B., artist; b. London, Eng., 1817. Came to Am., circa 1846; painted scenery for Arch Street Theatre, Phila., 1846; painted panorama of voyage to Cal. from sketches by W. B. Meyers, 1849; moved to Cincinnati; settled in Indpls., 1861; prin. scenic artist Met. Theater, Indpls., 1861-73; painted several pictures for local celebrations; became scenic painter Boston Museum, 1873. Died Boston, 1882.

GLONINGER, John, congressman, jurist; b. Lancaster County, Pa., Sept. 19, 1758; attended common schs. Served as subaltern officer Associaters during Revolutionary War, later commanded militia battalion; apptd. by supreme exec. council a lt. upon orgn. of Dauphin County, 1785; mem. Pa. Ho. of Reps., 1790, Pa. Senate, 1790-92; apptd. justice of peace Dauphin County, 1790; commd. asso. judge, 1791; commd. asso. judge Lebanon County, 1813; mem. U.S. Ho. of Reps. (Democrat) from Pa., 13th Congress, Mar. 4-Aug. 2, 1813 (resigned); again apptd. asso judge Lebanon County. Died Lebanon, Pa., Jan. 22, 1836; buried 1st Reformed Churchyard.

GLOSSBRENNER, Adam John, congressman; b. Hagerstown, Md., Aug. 31, 1810; learned printing trade. Publisher, Western Telegraph, Hamilton, O., 1827-28; moved to York, Pa., 1829; founded York County Farmer, 1831; partner York Gazette, 1835-60; clk. U.S. Ho. of Reps., 28th-29th congresses, 1843-47; clk. U.S. Dept. of State, Washington, D.C., 1848-49; sgt. at arms U.S. Ho. of Reps., 1860-61; founded Phila. Age, 1862; mem. U.S. Ho. of Reps. (Democrat) from Pa., 39th-40th congresses, 1865-69; became banker, York, 1872; with Pa. R.R. Co., Phila., until 1889. Died Mar. 1, 1889; buried Prospect Hill Cemetery, York.

GLOVER, John Montgomery, congressman; b. Harrodsburg, Ky., Sept. 4, 1822; attended Marion and Masonic Colls., Philadelphia, Mo.; studied law. Admitted to bar, began practice of law, St. Louis; practiced law, Cal., 1850-55; served as col. 3d Regt., Mo. Volunteer Cavalry, during Civil War, 1861-64; collector internal revenue 3d Dist. Mo., 1866-67; mem. U.S. Ho. of Reps. (Democrat) from Mo., 43d-45th congresses, 1873-79; engaged in agriculture. Died nr. Newark, Mo., Nov. 15, 1891; buried on his farm nr. Newark; reinterred Woodland Cemetery, Quincy, Ill.

GLOVER, Townend, entomologist; b. Rio de Janeiro, Brazil, Feb. 20, 1813 (parents English citizens); s. Henry and Mary (Townend) G.; ed. in Eng.; m. Sarah T. Byrnes, Sept. 1840, 1 adopted dau.; studied art in Germany under Mattenheimer (insp. Munich Art Gallery), 1834-35; came to New Rochelle, N.Y., 1836; took his collection of modelled fruits to Washington, D.C., 1853-54, resulted in appointment by Bur. Agr., U.S. Patent Office until 1878; had plans for work illustrating insects of U.S., never completed; ret. to Balt. due to ill health, 1878. Died Balt., Sept. 7, 1883.

GLOVER, William Howard, musician; b. London, Eng., June 6, 1819; studied violin under Wagstaff. Mem. English Opera orchestra; made artistic tours of Italy, Germany, France; founded sch. for music and drama, London; also sang in opera; came to U.S., 1868, settled in N.Y.C.; critic Morning Post, N.Y.C. Composer: Ruy Blas (grand opera), 1861; operettas The Coquette, 1845, Aminta, 1855, Once too Often, 1862, Palomita; cantata Tam O'Shanter, 1855; orchestral overture Manfred; other pieces and songs. Died N.Y.C., Oct. 28, 1875.

GLYNN, James, naval officer; b. Phila., June 28, 1801; s. James Anthony Glynn; m. Anne Stoddard. Entered gunboat service at New Orleans, 1810; served as acting midshipman in ships General Pike and Superior, Lake Ontario, 1815; apptd. midshipman, 1815; promoted lt., 1825, comdr., 1841; commanded sloop Preble on Cal. coast, 1848; transferred to East India Squadron, 1848, took part in rescue of several Am. seamen held captive by Japanese; credited by Commodore Geisinger with 1st successful negotiation with Japan; returned to U.S., expressed view that relations could be opened with Japanese govt., 1851, published article stating this view, 1851; put on reserve list, 1855, restored and given back pay, 1858; served in ship Macedonian against Confederate raider, 1862; ret. as capt. Died New Haven, Conn., May 13, 1871.

GOBRECHT, Christian, engraver; b. Hanover, Pa., Dec. 23, 1785; s. Rev. John C. Gobrecht; m. Mary (Hamilton) Hewes, May 31, 1818. Apprenticed in Manheim, Pa., them became engraver of ornamental works for clocks, Balt.; moved to Phila., circa 1811; became employed by Murray, Draper, Fairman and Co., banknote engravers, Phila., 1816; furnished model dies for U.S .Mint, Phila., 1826; engraver for U.S. Mint, 1830-44; engraved brass dies for Morocco covers of Boston Token, also eagle cover of Phila. Token, 1831-36; engraved medals including Charles Willson Peale Medal, Franklin Inst. Medal. Died Phila., July 23, 1844; buried Monument Cemetery, Phila.

GODBE, William Samuel, mine operator, editor; b. London, Eng., June 26, 1833; s. Samuel and Sarah (La Riviere) G.; m. Mary Hamilton, Nov. 10, 1856, at least 1 son. Became convert to Ch. of Jesus Christ of Latter Day Saints, moved to Salt Lake City, Utah, 1851, set up merchandise bus.; began publishing Utah Mag. (in which he supported growing mining industry), 1868; accused of heretical views, 1869, disfellowed as a result; terminated Utah Mag., 1869, started Salt Lake Tribune (became voice of growing liberal party); went to London, Eng., 1871, organized Chgo. Silver Mining Co. there, returned to open and operate mines, Dry Canyon, Utah; founder Bullionville Smelting Co., 1879, Piuche Consol. & Smelting Co., 1885; forced to halt all operations by depression of 1893. Died Brighton, Utah, Aug. 1, 1902.

GODDARD, Calvin, congressman, lawyer; b. Shrewsbury, Mass., July 17, 1786; attended Plainfield (Conn.) Acad.; grad. Dartmouth, 1786; studied law. Admitted to bar, 1790, began practice of law, Plainfield; mem. Conn. Ho. of Reps., 1795-1801, speaker, 1807; mem. U.S. Ho. of Reps. (Federalist, filled vacancy) from Conn., 7th-9th congresses, May 14, 1801-05 (resigned); resumed practice of law, Norwich, Conn., 1807; mem. Exec. Council, 1808-15; presdl. elector on Peace Party ticket, 1812; del. Hartford Conv., 1814; judge Superior Ct., 1815, 18; mayor Norwich, 1814-34. Died Norwich, May 2, 1842; buried City Cemetery.

GODDARD, Calvin Luther, inventor; b. Covington, N.Y., Jan. 22, 1822; s. Levi and Fanny (Watson) G.; grad. Yale, 1845; m. Gertrude Griggs Quimby, Dec. 19, 1846, 4 children. Tchr. in classical sch., N.Y.C., 1846; clk. in burring-machine mfg. firm, 1846-54; worked on machine that efficiently removed dust, burs, other extraneous matter from wool, 1854-66, patented machine, 1866, organized firm to manufacture burring machines, N.Y.C., moved business to Worcester, Mass., 1875-95; received Gold medal for invention at World's Fair, London, Eng., 1862, Paris, France, 1867. Died Mar. 29, 1895.

GODDARD, John, cabinetmaker; b. Dartmouth, Mass., Jan. 9, 1724; s. Daniel and Mary (Tripp) G.; m. Hannah Townsend, Aug. 7, 1745, at least 2 sons, Stephen, Thomas. Apprenticed to cabinetmaker Job Townsend, Newport, R.I.; became freeman R.I. Colony, 1745; recognized as leading cabinetmaker of Newport, by 1760, with customers including Moses Brown of Providence and Gov. Stephen Hopkins; identified with block front style in woodwork; records of his work lost during Am. Revolution; partner in firm Goddard & Engs, opened sales warehouse, Providence, R.I., 1782. Died Newport, July 1785.

GODDARD, Paul Beck, physician, photographic pioneer; b. Balt., Jan. 26, 1811; grad. Washington (now Trinity) Coll., Hartford, Conn., 1828; M.D., U. Pa., 1832. Practiced medicine, Phila.; asst. to Dr. Robert Hare (prof. chemistry U. Pa.), circa 1833, later prof. anatomy med. dept.; began experimenting with photography after Louis Daguerre's discovery that pictures could be produced with sun and sensitized plate as agt.; later discovered that process could be accelerated by using vapor of bromide on silvered plate, presented his discoveries before Am. Philos. Soc., 1839, elected mem., 1840; his discovery ignored by some Brit. writers and credit erroneously given to John Frederick Goddard (London optician). Author: Plates of the Cerebro-Spinal Nerves with References, 1837; Plates of the Arteries, with References, 1839. Died Phila., July 3, 1866; buried Laurel Hill Cemetery, Phila.

GODDARD, William, printer, journalist; b. New London, Conn., 1740; s. Dr. Giles and Sarah (Updike) G.; m. Abigail Angell, May 25, 1785. Apprenticed to printer John Holt, New Haven, Conn., 1755, then moved to James Parker's plant, N.Y.C.; journeyman, N.Y.C., 1761; opened printing office, Providence, R.I., 1762; established Providence Gazette, also Country Journal, 1762 (suspended Journal due to lack of support, 1765); partner with John Carter (an asso. of Benjamin Franklin), 1767-68; published Constl. Courant, Woodridge, N.Y., 1765; left his mother in charge of Providence Gazette, 1766, went to Phil. to open printery in partnership with Joseph Galloway and Thomas Wharton; published (at 1st with partners, then alone) Pa. Chronicle and Universal Adviser, 1767-74; founded Md. Journal and Balt. Adviser, Balt., 1773; established independent postal system (later taken over by Continental Congress), Balt.; ret. to Johnston, R.I., 1793. Died Dec. 23, 1817.

GODEFROY, Maximilian, architect, engr. Came to U.S. from France, 1805; taught architecture at "au College de Baltimore" (probably St. Mary's Sem.); designer Chapel of St. Mary's Sem. (1st ch. of Gothic revival in Am.), 1807; exhibited some of his projects in Phila., 1811, 13; bid for contract of Washington Monument by submitting triumphal arch design of restrained classical design, 1813; employed in designing fortification for Balt. which withstood attack Brit. attack, 1814; designed Court House and formal terraces of Capitol grounds, Richmond, Va., 1815; collaborated with B.H. Latrobe in designing U.S. Bank, Phila., 1818; went to London, Eng., 1819, exhibited water colors and archtl. views of Am. subjects, 1820-24. Flourished 1806-24.

GODEY, Louis Antoine, publisher; b. N.Y.C., June 6, 1804; s. Louis and Margaret G.; m. Maria Duke, Aug. 31, 1833, at least 5 children. Clk. for Charles Alexander on Daily Chronicle, Phila., 1820-30; published (with Alexander) Ladies' Book (later known as Godey's Ladies' Book), Phila., 1830, later propr., until 1877, devoted to women authors and women's fashions, later published contbns. from leading men authors; an organizer Saturday News and Literary Gazette, 1836; published Ladies' Mag., Boston, 1837. Died Phila., Nov. 29, 1878.

GODFREY, Benjamin, financier; b. Chatham, Mass., Dec. 4, 1794; m. 2d, Miss Pettit. Ran away to sea, 1803, spent 9 years in Ireland; served with U.S. Navy during War of 1812; later capt. of merchantman sailing from Chatham to Spain and West Indies; became mcht., Matamoros, Mexico, moved back to U.S. when he was robbed of his fortune; mcht., New Orleans; moved to Alton, Ill., 1832, in partnership with Winthrop S. Gillman in storage and commn. business, 1833; got control State Bank of Ill., 1835, within few years embezzled close to $800,000, lost all of it in Panic of 1837, resigned his position, 1837; founder Monticello Female Sem., Godfrey, Ill.; projector, pres. Alton and Sangamon R.R. (chartered, 1847, completed, 1852); presented by citizens of Alton with silver pitcher with representations of 1st train of the railroad and of original bldg. of sem. on it. Died Godfrey, Apr. 13, 1862.

GODFREY, Thomas, inventor, mathematician; b. Bristol Twp., Pa., 1704; s. Joseph Godfrey; married, at least 1 child, Thomas. Apprenticed to glazier; invented guadrant for ascertaining latitude which he claimed to be more reliable than what was then in use, 1730; gave guadrant to Joshua Fisher to test in Delaware Bay; James Hadley (v.p. Royal Soc., London, Eng.), claimed to have invented the quadrant; Godfrey's cause pleaded unsuccessfully by Gov. Logan of Pa. Died Dec. 1749; buried Laurel Hill Cemetery, Phila.

GODFREY, Thomas, writer; b. Phila., Dec. 4, 1736; s. Thomas Godfrey; probably attended Coll. of Phila. (now U. Pa.). Commd. ensign Pa. Militia, 1758; participated in campaign against Ft. Duquesne; became factor, Wilmington, N.C.; published lyric and love poems in William Smith's American Mag.; wrote play Prince of Parthia (1st drama written by native Am. to be produced on profl. stage), produced by David Douglass's Am. Co. at Southwark Theatre, Phila., 1767; wrote The Court of Fancy (poem), 1762. Died Wilmington, Aug. 3, 1763.

GODMAN, John Davidson, naturalist, anatomist; b. Annapolis, Md., Dec. 20, 1794; s. Capt. Samuel and Anna (Henderson) G.; studied medicine; M.D., U. Md., 1818; m. Angelica Kauffman Peale, Oct. 6, 1821. Practiced medicine, New Holland, Pa.; moved to village nr. Balt.; gave series of lectures on anatomy and physiology, Phila.; became prof. surgery Med. Coll. of Ohio, Cincinnati; editor 1st issue of Quarterly Reports of Med., Surg. and Natural Science (1st med. jour. published West of Allegheny Mountains), 1822. Mem. editorial bd. Phila. Jour. of Med. and Phys. Scis. (became Am. Jour. Med. Scis., 1827), 1825-27; prof. anatomy Rutgers Med.Coll., N.Y.C., 1826-27; suffered attack of tuberculosis; ret. to Germantown, Pa., devoted remainder of his life to naturalist studies and writing. Author: American Natural History, 3 vols., 1826-28; Rambles of a Naturalist, 1833. Died Apr. 17, 1830.

GODSHALK, William, congressman; b. East Nottingham, Pa., Oct. 25, 1817; attended Union Acad., Doylestown, Pa. Learned miller's trade, entered milling bus., Doylestown Twp., 1847; served with Co. K, 153d Regt., Pa. Volunteer Inf., U.S. Army, during Civil War, 1862-63; elected asso. judge Bucks County (Pa.), 1871, served 5 years; mem. U.S. Ho. of Reps. (Republican) from Pa., 46th-47th congresses, 1879-83. Died New Britain, Pa., Feb. 6, 1891; buried Presbyn. Ch. Cemetery, Doylestown.

GOEBEL, William, gov. Ky.; b. Carbondale, Pa., Jan. 4, 1856; s. William and Augusta (Guenaclay) G.; studied law with Gov. John W. Stephenson of Ky.; grad. Cincinnati Law Sch., 1877; attended Kenyon Coll., Gambier, O. Began practice of law in Ky. as partner of John G. Carlisle, later entered Stephenson's firm; mem. Ky. Senate (Democrat) from Kenyon County, 1887-99; killed John Sandford, 1895, pleaded self-defense and was acquitted; nominated for gov. Ky., 1899, defeated in election, charged fraud and contested election before Ky. Legislature which declared him legal gov.; shot by an assassin, Jan. 30, 1900. Died Feb. 3, 1900.

GOETSCHIUS, John Henry, clergyman; b. Bernick, Switzerland, Mar. 8, 1718; s. Maurice and Esther (Werndi) G.; studied theology with Rev. John Philip Dorsius, Neshaminy, Pa.; m. Rachel Zabiowisky, Aug. 26, 1750. Missionary, German Reformed Ch. in Pa., 1735, began preaching to German Reform settlers in Phila., 1735; refused ordination by Presbytery of Phila., later ordained after studying theology, 1841; served as minister in Dutch chs. on L.I., N.Y., until 1748; submitted to reexamination and reordination when his ordination was contested, 1748; colleague pastor Hackensack and Schraalinburgh, N.J., 1748-74; an original trustee Queens Coll. (now Rutgers U.), Died Nov. 14, 1774.

GOETZ, George Washington, metallurgist; b. Milw., Feb. 17, 1856; s. August W. and Augusta (Stottyr) G.; attended U. Wis., Sch. Mines, Berlin, Germany; m. Elsie Luedecke, 1886, 3 children. Telegraph operator Milw. Iron Co., 1870; began metall. studies with Otis Steel Co., 1881, in charge of open hearth steel dept.; became foremost iron and steel metallurgist in Am.; established metall. lab., Milw., 1890, cons. metallurgist Ill. Steel Co., Westinghouse Co., others. Died Jan. 15, 1897.

GOFF, Emmet Stull, horticulturist; b. Elmira, N.Y., Sept. 3, 1852; s. Gustavus A. and Mary (Stull) G.; m. S. Antoinette Carr, Oct. 2, 1880. Fruit grower and farmer, nr. Elmira, 13 years; horticulturist N.Y. Exptl. Sta., Geneva, 1882-89, experimented on culture of many economically important plants; 1st prof. horticulture U. Wis., 1889-1902; did his most notable research in field of differentiation of flower buds of fruit plants. Author: Principles of Plant Culture, 1897; Lessons in Commercial Fruit Growing, 1902. Died June 6, 1902.

GOFFE, William, army officer; b. Sussex, Eng.; s. Stephen Goffe; M.A. (hon.), Oxford (Eng.)U., 1649; m. Frances Whalley; children—Anne, Elizabeth, Frances. Col. in Puritan Army during Puritan Revolution; mem. High Ct. Justice apptd. by Parliament to try Charles I; signed death warrant of the king, 1649; mem. from Yarmouth, Eng. of Oliver Cromwell's parliament of 1654; maj.-gen. for Sussex, Hampshire and Berkshire (Eng.); served in Parliament from Hampshire, 1656; mem. Cromwell's House of Lords; fled to New Eng. after Restoration, 1660, lived as fugitive in Boston, and Hadley, Mass., also New Haven, Milford and Hartford (Conn.); aided in def. of Hadley in battle with Indians during King Philip's War. Died Hartford, Conn., circa 1679.

GOFORTH, William, physician; b. N.Y.C., 1766; s. Judge William and Catharine (Meeks) G.; studied medicine under Drs. Joseph Young and Charles McKnight, N.Y.C.; m. Miss Wood, circa 1790. Went to Ky., 1788, to Cincinnati, 1800; probably 1st to vaccinate West of Alleghanies; made 1st vaccinations in N.W. Territory, 1801; commd. surgeon-gen. 1st Div., Ohio Militia, 1804; at Big Bone Lick (Ky.) dug up collection of prehistoric fossils of interest to natural science, 1803; signed 1st med. diploma given in N.W. Ty. (given Daniel Drake), 1805; considered leading physician of Cincinnati, 1800-07; went to New Orleans as parish judge, 1807; mem. La. Constl. Conv.; served as surgeon in a volunteer regt. during Brit. attack on New Orleans. Died Cincinnati, May 12, 1817.

GOGGIN, William Leftwich, congressman, lawyer; b. nr. Bunker Hill, Va., May 31, 1807; grad. Tucker's Law Sch., Winchester, Va. Admitted to bar, 1828, began practice of law, Liberty (now Bedford), Va.; also engaged in agriculture; mem. Va. Ho. of Dels., 1836-37; mem. U.S. Ho. of Reps. (Whig) from Va., 26th-27th, (filled vacancy) 28th, 30th congresses, 1839-43, Apr. 25, 1844-45, 47-49; unsuccessful Whig candidate for gov. Va., 1859; del. Va. Constl. Conv., 1861; served as capt. Home Guards, Confederate Army, during Civil War. Died on his estate nr. Liberty, Jan. 3, 1870; buried Goggin Cemetery on family estate nr. Bunker Hill.

GOING, Jonathan, clergyman, coll. pres.; b. Reading, Vt., Mar. 7, 1786; s. Capt. Jonathan and Sarah (Kendall) G.; grad. Brown U., 1809; A.M. (hon.), U. Vt., 1812; D.D., Waterville (Vt.) Coll., 1832) m. Lucy Thorndike, Aug. 1811. Converted to Baptist faith, 1805; ordained to ministry Bapt. Ch., 1811; a founder Worcester Acad., Newtown Theol. Instn.; trustee Brown U., 1825-44; an original trustee Amherst Coll.; his activities led to orgn. Mass. Bapt. Conv.; an organizer Am. Bapt. Home Mission Soc., corr. sec., 1832-37; editor weekly Baptist and Home Missionary Record; pres. Denison U., Granville, O., 1837-44. Died Granville, Nov. 9, 1844.

GOLD, Thomas Ruggles, congressman, lawyer; b. Cornwall, Conn., Nov. 4, 1764; grad. Yale, 1786; studied law. Admitted to bar, began practice of law, Goshen, Conn.; moved to Whitesboro, N.Y., 1792; asst. atty. gen. N.Y., 1797-1801; mem. N.Y. State Senate, 1796-1802; mem. N.Y. State Assembly, 1808; mem. U.S. Ho. of Reps. (Federalist) from N.Y., 11th-12th, 14th congresses, 1809-13, 15-17; resumed practice of law, Whitesboro. Died Whitesboro, Oct. 24, 1827; buried Grand View Cemetery.

GOLDSBOROUGH, Charles, gov. Md., congressman; b. Hunting Creek, nr. Cambridge, Md., July 15, 1765; s. Charles and Anna (Tilghman) Goldsborough; B.A., U.Pa., 1784, M.A., 1787; m. Elizabeth, Sept. 22, 1793, 2 children; m. 2d, Sarah, 1804, 15 children. Admitted to Md. bar, 1790; mem. Md. Senate, 1791-95, 99, 1801; mem. U.S. Ho. of Reps. from Md., 9th-15th congresses, 1805-17; gov. Md., 1818-19. Died Cambridge, Dec. 13, 1834; buried Christ Protestant Episcopal Ch. Cemetery, Cambridge.

GOLDSBOROUGH, Louis Malesherbes, naval officer; b. Washington, D.C., Feb. 18, 1805; s. Charles Washington and Catharine (Roberts) G.; m. Elizabeth Wirt, Nov. 11, 1833, 3 children. Commd. midshipman U.S. Navy, 1812, lt., 1825, comdr., 1841, capt., 1855, rear adm., 1862; originator plan for depot of charts and instruments Washington, in charge, 1830; commanded mounted volunteers in Seminole War, 1833; served in Mexican War; sr. naval mem. commn. which explored Cal. and Ore., 1849-50; supt. Naval Acad., 1853-57; commanded Brazil Squadron, 1859-61, Atlantic Blockading Squadron, 1861, N. Atlantic Blockading Squadron, 1861; cooperated with Gen. Burnside in capture of Roanoke Island, 1862; adminstrv. duties, Washington until 1865; in charge of European Squadron, 1865. Died Washington, Feb. 20, 1877.

GOLDSBOROUGH, Robert, Continental congressman; b. Cambridge, Md., Dec. 3, 1733; s. Charles and Elizabeth (Ennalls) G.; grad. Phila. Coll. (now U. Pa.), 1760; m. Sarah Yerbury, Mar. 27, 1755. Admitted to Middle Temple, London, Eng.; admitted to English bar, 1757; mem. Md. Ho. of Dels., 1764; atty. gen. Md., 1766-68; mem. Continental Congress, 1774-75, 76; del. Md. Conv., 1775; mem. Md. Council of Safety, 1775; elected mem. Md. Constl. Conv., 1776; mem. 1st Md. Senate; del. to Md. Conv. which ratified U.S. Constn., apparently did not attend, 1788. Died Cambridge, Dec. 22, 1788.

GOLDSBOROUGH, Robert Henry, senator; b. "Myrtle Grove", nr. Easton, Md., Jan. 4, 1779; grad. St. John's Coll., Annapolis, 1795. Engaged in agriculture; mem. Md. Ho. of Dels., 1804, 25; commanded troop of horsemen in Md. Militia during War of 1812; mem. U.S. Senate (Federalist, filled vacancy) from Md., May 21, 1813-19, Jan. 13, 1835-36; a founder Easton Gazette, 1817; Nat.-Republican presdl. elector, 1832; mem. bd. public works Eastern Shore Md., 1836. Died "Myrtle Grove," Oct. 5, 1836; buried "Ashby," Talbot County, Md.

GOLDSMITH, Deborah, artist; b. North Brookfield, N.Y., 1808; m. George Addison Throop, Dec. 1833. Itinerant portrait and miniature painter in oils and watercolors; travelled in N.Y. State, painted to support her family; gave up profl. painting after her marriage. Died Hamilton, N.Y., Mar. 16, 1836.

GOLDSMITH, Jonathan, architect; b. New Haven, Conn., 1783. Employed as carpenter; moved to Ohio, 1811, built houses in Willoughby, Mentor and Cleve.; settled in Painesville, O., practiced as architect; designed Doctor Mathews residence, Painesville, 1831, credited with design of St. James Episcopal Ch., Painesville, old Gauega Bank (later Painesville Bank). Died 1847.

GOLDSMITH, Middleton, surgeon; b. Port Tobacco, Md., Aug. 5, 1818; s. Dr. Alban and Talia Ferro (Middleton) Smith; attended Hanover (Ind.) Coll.; grad. Coll. Physicians and Surgeons, N.Y.C., 1840; m. Frances Swift, June 1843, 2 daus. Introduced (with his father) the practice of lithority (method of crushing bladder stones) in Am. A founder 1st Alumni Assn. Coll. Physicians and Surgeons, N.Y. Path. Soc., 1844; prof. surgery Castleton (Vt.) Med. Coll., 1844-45; pres. Vt. Med. Soc., 1851; prof. surgery Ky. Sch. Medicine, Louisville, 1856; brigade surgeon Army of Cumberland; med. dir. U.S. Army under Gen. Buell at Battle of Shiloh; insp. hosps. under Gen. Grant at Battle Corinth; surgeon gen. Ky. and Dept. of Ohio mil. hosps.; in charge of Gen. Army Hosp., Jeffersonville, Ind.; wrote pamphlet A Report on Hospital Gangrene, Erysipelas, and Pyaemin as Observed in the Departments of the Ohio and the Cumberland: With Cases Appended, 1863; pioneer in antiseptic surgery; established Rutland (Vt.) Free Dispensary; spl. commr. to investigate state insane asylum, Vt., which resulted in its improvement and reform; drew up game laws of Vt. Died Nov. 26, 1887.

GOLDTHWAITE, George, senator, jurist; b. Boston, Dec. 10, 1809; s. Thomas and Anne (Wilson); student U.S. Mil. Acad.; m. Oliva Price, Nov. 30, 1835, 6 children. Admitted to Ala. bar, 1827; circuit judge, 1843-52, 66; elected to Ala. Supreme Ct., 1852-56, chief justice, 1856; represented Ala. in Nashville (Tenn.) Conv.; adj. gen. State of Ala., 1861-64; did not sympathize with slavery, but followed Ala. into secession; mem. U.S. Senate from Ala., 1870-77. Died Montgomery, Ala., Mar. 16, 1879.

GOLDTHWAITE, Henry Barnes, jurist; b. Concord, N.H., Apr. 10, 1802; s. Thomas and Anne (Wilson) G.; m. Eliza Witherspoon, Apr. 10, 1839; 4 children. Admitted to Ala. bar; edited a newspaper in conjunction with law practice; circuit solicitor, 1825; mem. Ala. Legislature, 1829; judge Ala. Supreme Ct., 1836-47; Democrat. Died Oct. 19, 1847.

GOLLADAY, Edward Isaac, congressman, lawyer; b. Lebanon, Tenn., Sept. 9, 1830; grad. literary dept. Cumberland U., Lebanon, 1848, law dept., 1849. Admitted to bar, 1849, began practice of law, Lebanon; mem. Tenn. Ho. of Reps., 1857-58; Constl.-Union presdl. elector, 1860; served as col. Confederate Army, throughout Civil War; mem. U.S. Ho. of Reps. (Democrat) from Tenn., 42d Congress, 1871-73. Died while visiting dau., Columbia, S.C., July 11, 1897; buried Cedar Grove Cemetery, Lebanon.

GOLLADAY, Jacob Shall, congressman; b. Lebanon, Tenn., Jan. 19, 1819; attended public schs. Moved to Nashville, Tenn., 1838, to Ky., 1845; mem. Ky. Ho. of Reps., 1851-53; mem. Ky. Senate, 1853-55; mem. U.S. Ho. of Reps. (Democrat, filled vacancy) from Ky., 40th-41st congresses, Dec. 5, 1867-Feb. 28, 1870 (resigned). Died nr. Russellville, Ky., May 20, 1887; buried Maple Grove Cemetery, Russellville.

GONS, James Walker, clergyman, educator; b. Albemarle County, Va., Dec. 29, 1812; s. Rev. John and Jane (Walker) G.; attended U. Va.; m. Jane Ashley Grigsby, Sept. 29, 1835; licensed to preach by Baptist Ch., 1832; began preaching views of Alexander Campbell, lead to div. in his congregation, formed ch., Charlottesville, Va., 1836; minister Disciples of Christ, made preaching tours, established chs.; participated in publication of Christian Publisher (1st periodical published by Disciples of Christ), 1836-40, sole editor and publisher, 1843-45, changed name to Christian Intelligencer; established sch. for girls, Gordonsville, Va., 1851, moved to Albemarle County, 1856, renamed Piedmont Female Acad., conducted sch., until 1867; took charge of So. Ky. Female Inst., Hopkinsville, 1867-69. Died Piedmont, Va., Nov. 26, 1870.

GOOCH, Daniel Wheelwright, congressman, lawyer; b. Wells, York County, Me., Jan. 8, 1820; grad. Dartmouth, 1843; studied law. Admitted to bar, began practice of law, Boston, 1846; mem. Mass. Ho. of Reps., 1852; mem. Mass. Constl. Conv., 1853; mem. U.S. Ho. of Reps. (Republican, filled vacancy) from Mass., 35th-39th, 43d congresses, Jan. 31, 1858-Sept. 1, 1865 (resigned), 73-75; Navy agt. Port of Boston, 1856-66; pension agt., Boston, 1876-86; resumed practice of law, also engaged in writing. Died Melrose, Mass., Nov. 11, 1891; buried Wyoming Cemetery.

GOOCH, Sir William, colonial gov.; b. Yarmouth, Eng., Oct. 21, 1681; s. Thomas and Frances (Lone) G.; m. Rebecca Staunton. Lt. gov. (served as acting gov.) 1727-40, 41-49; defended colonists before Bd. Trade urging repeal Parliamentary Act requiring that tobacco not be stripped from stalk before shipping (resulting in unnecessary but taxable bulk), also urged repeal tax on imported liquors and slaves; in command Va. battalions in British attack on Carthagena, New Granada (on coast of S.Am.), 1741; urged Va. Assembly to pass legislation for promotion religion and morality; negotiated Treaty of Lancaster with the Six Nations to insure protection of colonists on Va.'s N.W. frontier, 1744; created baronet, 1746; commd. maj. gen. Brit. Army, 1747. Died London, Eng., Dec. 17, 1751; buried Yarmouth.

GOOD, Adolphus Clemens, Missionary, naturalist; b. West Mahoning, Pa., Dec. 19, 1856; s. Abram and Hannah (Irwin) G.; grad. Washington and Jefferson Coll., 1879, Western Theol. Sem., 1882; m. Lydia Walker, June 21, 1883. Ordained to ministry Presbyn Ch., 1882; active in missionary work, Baraka, French Congo, Africa, 1882-85, Kangwe, French Congo, 1885-92; worked in Bulu country in German Territory, 1892-94 (penetrated further inland than any other white man up to that time); prepared a Bulu primer; translated Gospels into Bulu; added more to knowledge of insect forms of Africa than any other single collector. Died Efulen, German Territory, North of French Congo, Dec. 13, 1894.

GOOD, Jeremiah Haak, clergyman; b. Rehrersburg, Pa., Nov. 22, 1822; s. Philip Augustus and Elizabeth (Haak) G.; grad. Marshall Coll., Chambersburg, Pa., 1842; m. Susan Root, Dec. 23, 1846. Licensed to preach by the Mercersburg Classis of German Reformed Ch., 1846; edited ch. paper Western Missionary, Columbus, O., 1848-53; prof. math. Heidelberg Coll., Tiffin, O., 1850-69, prof. dog-matics and practical theology, also pres. sem., 1869-87, prof. emeritus, 1887; pres. Ohio Synod, 19 years; founder, pastor 2d Reformed Ch., Tiffin. Died Tiffin, Jan. 25, 1888; buried Green Lawn Cemetery, Tiffin.

GOODALE, Stephen Lincoln, agriculturist; b. South Berwick, Me., Aug. 14, 1815; s. Enoch and Lucy (Lincoln) G.; m. Prudence Nourse, Sept. 23, 1838. Moved with family to Saco, Me., 1816; bought a place in Saco, began cultivating and studying trees and shrubs, 1841; 1st sec. Me. Bd. Agr., 1856-73; founder, trustee State Coll. of Agr. and Mech. Arts (later U. Me.); pres. Saco & Biddeford Savs. Instn.; pres., mgr., chemist Cumberland Bone Co. Author: The Principles of Breeding: or, Glimpses at the Physiological Laws Involved in the Reproduction and Improvement of Domestic Animals, 1861. Died Saco, Nov. 5, 1897.

GOODALL, Albert Gallatin, engraver; b. Montgomery, Ala., Oct. 31, 1826. Served as midshipman Tex. Navy during Mexican-Texan war; went to Havana, Cuba, 1844, learned copperplate engraving; established himself as banknote engraver, Phila., 1848; asso. with a co. which merged to form Am. Bank Note Co., 1858, pres., 1874-87; visited several European and S.Am. countries to obtain fgn. contracts for firm. Died N.Y.C., Feb. 19, 1887.

GOODALL, Harvey L., publisher; b. Lunenburg, Vt., May 28, 1836; m. Ellen F. Sullivan, 1883. Travelled to Europe; returned to U.S., worked in cotton mill in New Eng.; ofcl. reporter Pa. Senate, 2 sessions; journalist, Harrisburg, Pa., Lancaster, Pa., Phila., N.Y.C.; served with 2d Ill. Cavalry during Civil War, 1861-64; publisher Cairo (Ill.) Daily Times, 1865-68; established weekly Sun, Chgo., 1869, publisher, 1869-1900; established weekly Drover Jour. (1st live-stock paper), 1873, became daily, 1877, publisher, 1873-1900. Died Mar. 28, 1900.

GOODE, George Brown, naturalist, govt. ofcl.; b. New Albany, Ind., Feb. 13, 1851; s. Francis Collier and Sarah (Crane) G.; grad. Wesleyan U., Middletown, Conn., 1870; m. Sarah Lamson Ford Judd, 4 children. Moved to N.Y., 1857; in charge Orange Judd Mus. Natural History, 1871-77; mem. staff Smithsonian Instn., 1873, asst. sec., 1887; employed in Atlantic Coast explorations of Fish Commn.; U.S. commr. fish, 1887-88; supervised Smithsonian exhibits at Phila. Centennial - Expn., 1876; U.S. commr. at fisheries exhbns., Berlin, Germany, 1880, London, Eng., 1883; conducted survey Am. fisheries for 10th census, 1880. Author: Catalogue of the Fishes of the Bermudas, 1876; Oceanic Ichthyology (added 156 new species of fish from Atlantic), 1895; An Account of the Smithsonian Institution, 1895, and The Smithsonian Institution 1846-96, 1897 (best known hist. treatises); Virginia Cousins (his own family record), 1887; The Game Fishes of North America; American Fishes, 1888; The Beginnings of American Science; The Origin of the Scientific and Educational Institutions of the United States, 1890; The Museums of the Future, 1891. Died Washington, D.C., Sept. 6, 1896.

GOODE, Patrick Gaines, congressman, clergyman; b. Cornwall parish, Charlotte County, Va., May 10, 1798; attended Xenia (O.) Acad.; studied law. Admitted to bar, 1821, practiced law Madison, Ind., then Shelby County, O.; mem. Ohio Ho. of Reps., 1833-35; mem. U.S. Ho. of Reps. (Whig) from Ohio, 25th-27th congresses, 1837-43; served as a local preacher nearly all his life, preached in Washington, D.C., during congl. career; became clergyman Central Ohio Conf., Methodist Episcopal Ch.; judge Ct. of Common Pleas, 1844-51. Died Sidney, O., Oct. 17, 1862; buried Graceland Cemetery.

GOODE, Samuel, congressman; b. "Whitby," Chesterfield County, Va., Mar. 21, 1756; studied law. Admitted to bar, practiced law; served as lt. Chesterfield Troop of Horse, later as col. militia during Revolutionary War; mem. Va. Ho. of Dels., 1778-85; mem. U.S. Ho. of Reps. from Va., 6th Congress, 1799-1801. Died Invermay, Va., Nov. 14, 1822; buried on estate nr. Invermay.

GOODE, William Osborne, congressman, lawyer; b. Inglewood, Va., Sept. 16, 1798; grad. Coll. William and Mary, 1819; studied law. Admitted to bar, 1821, began practice of law, Boydton, Va.; mem. Va. Ho. of Dels., 1822, 24-32, 39-40, 45-46, 52, speaker 3 terms; mem. Va. constl. convs., 1829-30, 50; mem. U.S. Ho. of Reps. (Democrat) from Va., 27th, 33d-36th congresses, 1841-43, 53-59. Died Boydton, July 3, 1859; buried on his estate "Wheatland," nr. Boydton.

GOODELL, William, missionary; b. Templeton, Mass., Feb. 14, 1792; s. William and Phebe (Newton) G.; grad. Dartmouth, 1817; grad. Andover Theol. Sem., 1820; D.D., Hamilton Coll., 1854; m. Abigail Davis, Nov. 19, 1822, at least 8 children including Henry Hill, William. Ordained to ministry, 1822; missionary in Near East, 1823-51, 53-65; helped establish mission, Beirut, Lebanon, 1823; superintended mission press, Malta, 1828-31; established mission, Constantinople, Turkey, 1831; helped lay foundation of Am. Bd. Commrs. for Fgn. Missions' work in Turkey; translated Bible into Armeno-Turkish, later revised it. Author: The Old and the New, 1853. Died Phila., Feb. 18, 1867.

GOODELL, William, reformer; b. Coventry, N.Y., Oct. 25, 1792; s. Frederic and Rhoda (Guernsey) G.; m. Clarissa Cady, July 4, 1823, at least 2 children. Active in promoting Merc. Library Assn., N.Y.C., dir., 1827; edited reform weekly Investigator and Gen. Intelligencer, Providence, R.I., 1827; published Female Advocate and Youth's Temperance Lecturer, N.Y.C., 1830-36; helped organize Am. Anti-Slavery Soc., 1833, began publishing the Emancipator; edited Friend of Man, 1836-42, Anti-Slavery Lecturer; founded Christian Investigator; helped organize Liberty Party, 1840; induced to set up Honeoye (N.Y.) church, 1843, his "ideal church", founded Liberty League, 1847; settled in N.Y. to edit American Jubilee, 1854; an organizer Nat. Prohibition Party, 1869. Author: Views upon American Constitutional Law, in its Bearing upon American Slavery, 1844. Died Janesville, Wis., Feb. 14, 1878.

GOODENOW, John Milton, congressman, judge; b. Westmoreland, N.H., 1782; m. Mrs. Sarah (Wright) Campbell, 1813; married a 2d time. Admitted to Ohio bar, 1813; apptd. collector of direct taxes and internal duties Ohio 6th Collection Dist.; responsible to some extent for the fact that today Ohio has no common-law crimes; mem. Ohio Ho. of Reps., 1823; mem. U.S. Ho. of Reps. from Ohio, 21st Congress, 1829-30; justice Ohio Supreme Ct., 1830; presiding judge Ct. Common Pleas, Cincinnati. Died New Orleans, July 20, 1835; buried Spring Grove Cemetery, Cincinnati.

GOODENOW, Robert, congressman, lawyer; b. Henniker, N.H., Apr. 19, 1800; studied medicine, law. Admitted to bar, 1822, began practice of law, Wilton, Me.; county atty., 1828-34, 69-70; moved to Farmington, Me., 1832; mem. U.S. Ho. of Reps. (Whig) from Me., 32d Congress, 1851-53; apptd. state bank commr., 1857; treas. Franklin County, 1866-68; treas. Franklin County Savings Bank, 1868-74. Died Farmington, May 15, 1874; buried Riverside Cemetery.

GOODENOW, Rufus King, congressman; b. Henniker, N.H., Apr. 24, 1790. Engaged in agriculture; also a seaman, made several trips to European ports; served as capt. 33d Regt., U.S. Inf. in War of 1812; moved to Paris, Me., 1821; clk. Oxford County Cts., 1821-37; mem. Me. Ho. of Reps., 1837-38; del. Whig Nat. Conv., Harrisburg, Pa., 1839; Whig presdl. elector, 1840; admitted to bar, practiced in courts of Me.; mem. U.S. Ho. of Reps. (Whig) from Me., 31st Congress, 1849-51. Died Paris, Mar. 24, 1863; buried Riverside Cemetery, South Paris, Me.

GOODHUE, Benjamin, senator, congressman; b. Salem, Mass., Sept. 20, 1748; s. Benjamin and Martha (Hardy) G.; grad. Harvard, 1766; m. Frances Richie, Jan. 6, 1778; m. 2d, Anna Willard, Nov. 25, 1804. Mem. Mass. Constl. Conv., 1779-

0; mem. Mass. Ho. of Reps., 1780-82; represented Salem in Mass. Gen. Ct., 1780-82; mem. ass. Senate, 1786-88; mem. U.S. Ho. of Reps. rom Mass., 1st-4th congresses, 1789-June 1796; taunch Federalist, supported Jay Treaty; mem. .S. Senate from Mass., June 11, 1796-Nov. 8. 800. Died Salem, July 28, 1814; buried Broad treet Cemetery, Salem.

GOODHUE, James Madison, lawyer, editor; b. Hebron, N.H., Mar. 31, 1810; s. Stephen and Betsey Page) G.; grad. Amherst Coll., 1833; m. Henrietta Knuland, Dec. 22, 1843. Settled in Lancaster, Wis., racticed law; bought Wis. Herald, 1845, editor, 845-49; began publishing Minn. Pioneer, St. Paul, 849; staunch conservative, condemned any kind of peculation; accompanied Indian commrs. to signing f 1st treaties with Sioux Indians at Traverse des ioux, 1851; Goodhue County (Minn.) named for im by Minn. Legislature, 1853. Author: Struck a ead (novel) Died Aug. 27, 1852.

GOODIN, John Randolph, congressman; b. Tiffin, O., Dec. 14, 1836; attended Geneva Coll.; tudied law. Admitted to bar, 1857, began practice f law, Kenton, O.; moved to Humboldt, Kan., 859; mem. Kan. Ho. of Reps., 1866; judge 7th ud. Dist. of Kan., 1868-76; mem. U.S. Ho. of Reps. Democrat) from Kan., 44th Congress, 1875-77; ditor The Inter State, Humboldt. Died Kansas ity, Kan., Dec. 18, 1885; buried Oak Grove Cemetery.

GOODLOE, Daniel Reaves, abolitionist, editor; b. Louisburg, N.C., May 28, 1814; s. Dr. Kemp Strother and Mary (Reaves) G.; studied law under Robert B. Gilliam. Apprenticed to printer, Oxford, N.C.; erved in Creek and Seminole wars in Ala. and Fla.; editor Whig Standard, Washington, D.C., 1844-52; editor Georgetown Advocate, Christian Statesman; became asst. editor Nat. Era (anti-slavery paper), 1852, later became editor; Washington correspondent N.Y. Times, 1861-62; apptd. chmn. commn. to carry out compensation of provision of act emancipating slaves in D.C., 1862; apptd. U.S. marshall for N.C., 1865; favored drastic punishment of South, opposed carpet-baggers, bitterly opposed ratification of "carpet-bag constn." in N.C., 1868. Died Warrenton, N.C., Jan. 18, 1902; buried Warrenton.

GOODLOE, William Cassius, diplomat, legislator; b. Madison County, Ky., June 27, 1841; s. David Short and Sally Ann (Smith) G.; ed. Transylvania U.; m. Mary E. Mann, June 8, 1865, 6 children. Acting sec. of legation, St. Petersburg, Russia, 1861; served as capt. U.S. Army in Civil War; an organizer Republican Party in Ky., 1867; published Kentucky Statesman (advocating principles of Republican Party), 1867; speaker Ky. Ho. of Reps., 1871; mem. Ky. Senate, 1873; U.S. minister to Belgium, 1878-80; apptd. U.S. collector internal revenue, 1889. Died in fight with polit. enemy Armistead Swope, Lexington, Ky., Nov. 10, 1889.

GOODMAN, Charles, engraver, lawyer; b. Phila., 1796; s. John and Mary (Roach) G.; m. Margaret Thatcher, Dec. 14, 1824; Became accomplished stipple-engraver; formed partnership with Robert Piggot, circa 1815, did portraits of Peyton Randolph, Samuel Adams, folio print of Pres. James Monroe (published 1817); admitted to Pa. bar, 1819, practiced in Phila.; noted for portrait of Benjamin Franklin published in Analectic, 1818, portrait of John Wesley as described by Henry Fielding. Died Phila., Feb. 11, 1835.

GOODNOW, Isaac Tichenor, educator; b. Whitingham, Vt., Jan. 17, 1814; s. William and Sybil (Arms) G.; grad. Wesleyan Acad., 1838; m. Ellen Denison, Aug. 28, 1838. Became prof. natural scis. Wesleyan Acad., Mass., 1838, Providence (R.I.) Conf. Sem., 1848-59; active in New Eng. Emigrant Aid Co., raised company of 200 emigrants who left Boston, 1855, and founded Town of Manhattan (Kan.); mem. Free-State Conv., Kan., 1855; mem. conv. which drew up Leavenworth (Kan.) Constn., 1858; a founder, regent ex officio Bluemont Central Coll. (later Kan. State Agrl. Coll., now Kan. State U.); mem. 1st Kan. Legislature, 1861-62; supt. public instrn. state of Kan., 1862, 64; land commr. M.-K.-T. R.R., 1873-80. Died Manhattan, Mar. 20, 1894.

GOODRICH, Benjamin Franklin, rubber mfr.; b. Ripley, N.Y., Nov. 4, 1841; s. Anson and Susan (Dinsmore) G.; grad. Cleve. Med. Coll., Feb. 1861; m. Mary Marvin, Nov. 4, 1869; 3 children. State certificate of asst. surgeon, 1861; contract surgeon with Army of Potomac, 1862; asst. surgeon 9th N.Y. Cavalry, 1863-64; obtained control (with partner J.P. Morris) of Hudson River Rubber Co., Hastings-on-the-Hudson, N.Y., 1867, became pres.; formed new firm Goodrich, Tew & Co., Akron, O., 1870; incorporated, became pres. B.F. Goodrich Co., 1880; became leading rubber mfr. Died Manitou Springs, Colo., Aug. 3, 1888.

GOODRICH, Charles Augustus, clergyman, state senator, author; b. Ridgefield, Conn., Aug. 19, 1790; s. Samuel and Elizabeth (Ely) G.; grad. Yale, 1812; m. Sarah Upson, June 24, 1818; 7 children. Ordained to ministry Congregational Ch., 1816; became pastor 1st Conglist Ch., Worcester, Mass., 1816; dismissed by his request after being vindicated in a doctrinal-polit. conflict, 1820; mem. Conn. Senate, 1838; most popular works: History of the United States of America, 1822; A Child's History of the United States, 1846; other works include: Cabinet of Curiosities: Natural, Artificial and Historical, 2 vols., 1822; Outlines of Modern Geography on a New Plan, 1827; Pictorial and Descriptive View of All Religions, 1829; Lives of the Signers of the Declaration of Independence, 1829; The Universal Traveller, 1837. Died Hartford, Conn., June 4, 1862.

GOODRICH, Chauncey, senator, congressman; b. Durham, Conn., Oct. 20, 1759; s. Rev. Elizur and Catharine (Chauncey) G.; grad. Yale, 1776; m. Abigail Smith; m. 2d, Mary Ann Wolcott, Oct. 13, 1789. Taught at Yale, 1778-81; admitted to Conn. bar, 1781; mem. Conn. Ho. of Reps., 1793-94; mem. U.S. Ho. of Reps. (Federalist) from Conn., 4th-7th congresses, 1795-1801; mem. Conn. Exec. Council, 1802-07; mem. U.S. Senate from Conn., Oct. 25, 1807-May 1813; mayor Hartford (Conn.), 1813-15; lt. gov. Conn., 1813-15; del. to Hartford Conv., 1814. Died Hartford, Aug. 18, 1815; buried Old North Cemetery, Hartford.

GOODRICH, Chauncey, printer, horticulturist; b. Hinsdale, Mass., Sept. 10, 1798; s. Elyah Hubbard and Mabel (Nicholson) G.; m. Arabella Marsh, 1828, 2 children. Printed Statutes of Vt., also 1st Am. edition of Aids to Reflection (Coleridge), 1829; active in improvement of fruit growing in Vt. and No. N.Y.; a leading organizer and supporter of Champlain Hort. Soc. Author: The Northern Fruit Culturist, or the Farmer's Guide to the Orchard and Fruit Garden, 1849. Died Sept. 11, 1858.

GOODRICH, Chauncey Allen, clergyman, educator, lexicographer; b. New Haven, Conn., Oct. 23, 1790; s. Elizur and Anne (Allen) G.; A. M., Yale, 1810; D.D. (hon.), Brown U., 1835; m. Julia Webster, Oct. 1, 1816. Tutor, Yale, 1812-14; prepared textbook Elements of Greek Grammar, 1814; licensed to preach by New Haevn Assn. of Ministers, 1814; ordained to ministry installed at Congregational Ch., Middleton, Conn., 1816; prof. rhetoric Yale, 1817-39, helped establish theol. dept., 1822, proposed establishment of professorship for tng. students in preaching and pastoral work, 1838, prof. pastoral theology, until 1860; purchased Christian Spectator, 1828, edtied it as Quarterly Christian Spectator, 1828-36; prepared Lessons in Greek Parsing, 1829, Lessons in Latin Parsing, 1832; made thorough revision of Webster's American Dictionary of the English Language, 1847; most important work: Select British Eloquences, 1852. Died New Haven, Feb. 25, 1860.

GOODRICH, Elizur, clergyman; b. Wethersfield, Conn., Oct. 26, 1734; s. David and Hepzibah (Boardman) G.; grad. Yale, 1752; m. Catharine Chauncey, Feb. 1, 1759, 7 children including Chauncey, Elizur, Chauncey Allen. Ordained to ministry Congregational Ch., 1756; pastor Congregational Ch., Durham, Conn., 1756-97; elected to Corp. of Yale Coll., 1776; mem. convs. of dels. from Synod of N.Y. and Phila., also Assn. of Conn., 1766-75; urged participation in Am. Revolution as religious duty. Died Nov. 22, 1797.

GOODRICH, Elizus, congressman, mayor; b. Durham, Conn., Mar. 24, 1761; s. Elizus and Catharine (Chauncey) G.; grad. Yale, 1779; m. Anne Allen, 1785. Tutor, Yale, 1781-83; practiced law, New Haven, Conn., 1783; mem. New Haven City Council, 1789-95; mem. Conn. Legislature, 1795-1802; mem. U.S. Ho. of Reps. from Conn., 6th Congress, 1799-1801; apptd. collector Port of New Haven, 1801; probate judge, New Haven, 1802-18; chief judge county court, 1805-18; mayor New Haven, 1803-22; prof. law Yale, 1801-10, ex officio mem. Yale corp., 1809-18, sec., 1818-46. Died New Haven, Nov. 1, 1849; buried Grave St. Cemetery, New Haven.

GOODRICH, Frank Boott, journalist, author; b. Boston, Dec. 14, 1826; s. Samuel Griswold and Mary (Boott) G.; grad. Harvard, 1845; m. Ella Schmidt, 1859. Author: "Dick Tinto" letters to N.Y. Times describing Louis Napoleon's coup d'etat, 1852; published Tricolored Sketches in Paris, 1855, Man upon the Sea; or a History of Maritime Adventure, Exploration and Discovery, 1858 (final revision 1873); author plays (with Frank L. Warden) Fascination, Romance after Marriage, or the Maiden Wife (3-act comedy), (with Dion Boucicault) The Poor of New York; translated 4 novels of Balzac, 1860-63; other writings include: The Court of Napoleon, 1857; Women of Beauty and Heroism, 1859; The Tribute Book, 1865. Died Morristown, N.J., Mar. 15, 1894.

GOODRICH, John Zacheus, congressman; b. Sheffield, Mass., Sept. 27, 1804; attended Lenox (Mass.) Acad.; studied law. Admitted to bar, practiced law; also became a mfr.; Whig presdl. elector, 1840; mem. Mass. Senate, 1848-49; mem. U.S. Ho. of Reps. (Whig) from Mass., 32-33d congresses, 1851-55; Republican presdl. elector, 1860; mem. Washington (D.C.) Peace Conv., 1861; lt. gov. Mass. (Republican), 1861; collector of customs, Boston, 1861-65. Died Stockbridge, Mass., Apr. 19, 1885; buried Stockbridge Cemetery.

GOODRICH, Levi, architect; b. N.Y.C., 1822; received archtl. tng. in father's office. Began practice as architect, N.Y.C.; went to Cal. during Gold Rush, settled in San Francisco; designed numerous early bldgs. in San Francisco and in Cal.; moved to San Jose, Cal., continued practice, charter mem. San Francisco chpt. A.I.A., 1880. Died 1887.

GOODRICH, Milo, congressman, lawyer; b. East Homer, N.Y., Jan. 3, 1814; attended Cortland Acad., Homer, N.Y., also Oberlin (O.) Coll.; studied law. Taught sch., N.Y., Pa. and Ohio; admitted to bar, Worcester, Mass., 1840, practiced in Beloit, Wis., 2 years; settled in Dryden, N.Y., 1844; postmaster Dryden, 1849-53; mem. N.Y. Constl. Conv., 1867-68; mem. U.S. Ho. of Reps. (Republican) from N.Y., 42d Congress, 1871-73; moved to Auburn, N.Y., 1875, continued practice of law. Died Auburn, Apr. 15, 1881; buried Green Hills Cemetery, Dryden.

GOODRICH, Samuel Griswold, (pseudonym Peter Parley), author, publisher; b. Ridgefield, Conn., Aug. 19, 1793; s. Rev. Samuel and Elizabeth (Ely) G.; M.A. (hon.), Williams Coll., 1836; M.A. (hon.), Yale, 1848; m. Adeline Bradley, 1818; m. 2d, Mary Boott, 1826. Served in War of 1812; entered publishing bus., 1816; publisher, editor The Token (frequently included works of Nathaniel Hawthorne including 1st publ. Twice Told Tales), Boston, 1826-42; author The Tales of Peter Parley About America, 1827, 100 other books under pen name Peter Parley; founder Parley's Mag. for children, 1833; mem. Mass. Senate (Federalist), 1837-39; established, edited Robert Merry's Museum, 1841-50; U.S. consul in Paris, France, 1851-53; other writings include: Peter Parley's Tales, 36 vols.; Parley's Historical Compends, 36 vols., Parley's Miscellanies, 70 vols.; The Outcast and Other Poems, 1836; Poems, 1851; Recollections of a Lifetime, 1856. Died N.Y.C., May 9, 1860.

GOODRICH, William Marcellus, organ maker; b. Templeton, Mass., July 21, 1777; s. Ebenezer and Beulah (Childs) Goodridge (later changed his name to Goodrich); m. Hannah Geald, on February 1822. Employed in shop of Benjamin Crekor, Milton, Mass., 1798; established himself in organ-bldg. bus., Boston, 1799; constructed duplicate of J. M. Maelyel's panharmonicon, sent to Europe for exhbn. after Maelyel's was lost at sea, 1809; moved factory to East Cambridge, Mass., 1809, asso. with Thomas Appleton (a cabinetmaker); directed bldg. of organ for Catholic Cathedral, Franklin Street, Boston; built some organs which are still in use. Died Sept. 15, 1833.

GOODRIDGE, Sarah, artist; b. Templeton, Mass., Feb. 5, 1788; d. Ebenezer and Beulah (Childs) Goodridge; studied with Gilbert Stuart, 1820-24. Accompanied brother William to Milton, Mass., later to Boston, kept house for him, took drawing lessons; taught at Templeton Sch.; began painting portraits for her friends; work noted for its simplicity and directness; best portraits include those of Gilbert Stuart, Daniel Webster, Gen. Henry Lee, Isaiah Thomas. Died Boston, Dec. 28, 1853.

GOODWIN, Daniel Raynes, clergyman, coll. pres.; b. North Berwick, Me., Apr. 12, 1811; s. Samuel and Anna (Gerrish) G.; grad. Bowdoin Coll., 1832; postgrad. Andover Theol. Sem.; m. Mary Merrick, Jan. 2, 1838. Prof. modern langs. Bowdoin Coll., Brunswick, Me., 1835-53, librarian, circa 1838-53; confirmed in Episcopal Ch. during 1840's, ordained deacon, 1847, priest, 1848, helped organize church, Brunswick; elected pres. Trinity Coll., Hartford, Conn., 1853, prof. modern langs., later prof. moral and intellectual philosophy; provost U. Pa., 1860, ret., 1868; dean Phila. Divinity Sch., 1868-83, prof. systematic divinity, 1865-90; most influential leader Evang. party of Episcopal Ch. of his time. Died Phila., Mar. 15, 1890.

GOODWIN, Elijah, clergyman; b. Champaign County, O., Jan. 16, 1807; s. Aaron and Mary (Chapman) G.; m. Jane Davis, Aug. 5, 1828; m. 2d, Marcia Bassett, June 19, 1864. Licensed to preach by Ind. Christian Conf., 1825; apptd. by Ind. and Wabash confs. to travel among their chs., 1827, established many chs. in Southwestern Ind.; became a Campbellite, circa 1835; co-publisher, editor Christian Record, 1847-59, owner, editor, 1851-54; pastor St. Paul Ch., Newark, N.J., 1854-1859-66; a founder Ind. Christian Home Missionary Soc., 1849; mem. bd. commrs. which organized Northwestern Christian U. (now Butler U.) Indpls., agt. 1855-59, mem. bd. dirs., 1854-79, treas., circa 1860-70, twice pres. Died Cleve., O., Sept. 4, 1879.

GOODWIN, Hannibal Williston, clergyman, inventor; b. Taughannock, N.Y., Apr. 30, 1822; s. George and Cynthia Williston (Gregory) G.; grad. Union Coll., Schenectady, N.Y., 1848; grad. Gen. Theol. Sem. of Episcopal Ch., N.Y.C., 1851; attended Yale Law Sch.; m. Rebecca Goodwin, 2 children. Apptd. rector Christ Ch., Bordentown, N.J., 1851-54; pastor St. Paul Ch., Newark, N.J., 1854-59; moved to San Francisco to regain health, 1860-67; rector House of Prayer, Newark, 1867-87; studied photography to find substitute for glass negatives; applied for patent for "Photographic Pellicle," 1887, however Henry M. Reichenback of Eastman Dry Plate Co. also applied and received patent for "manufacture of flexible photographic films," 1889, patent contested 12 years, obtained patent just before his death. Died Dec. 31, 1900

GOODWIN, Henry Charles, congressman, lawyer; b. De Ruyter, N.Y., June 25, 1824; studied law. Admitted to bar, 1846, began practice of law, Hamilton, N.Y.; dist. atty. Madison County (N.Y.), 1847-50; mem. U.S. Ho. of Reps. (Republican, filled vacancy), 33d, 35th congresses, Nov. 7, 1854-55, 57-59. Died Hamilton, Nov. 12, 1860; buried Madison Street Cemetery.

GOODWIN, Ichabod, financier, gov. N.H.; b. North Berwick, Me., Oct. 8, 1794; s. Samuel and Anna (Gerrish) G.; m. Sarah Parker Rice, Sept. 3, 1827, 7 children. Mcht. in fgn. trade, Portsmouth, N.H., circa 1832; 1st pres. Eastern R.R., 25 years, also dir.; mem. 1st bd. dirs. Portland, Saco & Portsmouth R.R. Co., pres. 1847-71; del.-at-large several Whig. nat. convs.; mem. N.H. Legislature, 1838-56; mem. N.H. Constl. Conv., 1859; gov. N.H., 1859, 60-61, announced that N.H. would stand by Union and Constn., borrowed $680,000, gathered men and supplies to meet 1st call for troops; pres., dir. Piscataqua Exchange Bank (now First Nat. Bank), Portsmouth Savs. Bank; pres. several Portsmouth enterprises. Died Portsmouth, July 4, 1882.

GOODWIN, John Noble, territorial gov., congressman; b. South Berwick, Me., Oct. 18, 1824; s. John and Mary (Noble) G.; grad. Dartmouth, 1844; m. Susan Robinson, Nov. 1857. Admitted to Me. bar, 1848; mem. Senate 1854; mem. U.S. Ho. of Reps. from Me., 37th, 39th congresses, 1861-63, 65-67; chief justice Ariz. Territory, 1863-65, gov., 1863-65, responsible for orgn. of Ariz. state govt. Died Paraiso Springs, Cal., Apr. 29, 1887; buried Forest Grove Cemetery, Augusta, Me.

GOODWYN, Peterson, congressman, lawyer; b. "Sweden," nr. Petersburg, Va., 1745; studied law. Admitted to bar, 1776, began practice of law, Petersburg; also a planter; served from capt. to maj. during Revolutionary War; equipped his own company; promoted col. for gallantry at Battle of Smithfield; mem. Va. Ho. of Dels., 1789-1802; mem. U.S. Ho. of Reps. (Democrat) from Va., 8th-15th congresses, 1803-18. Died "Sweden," Feb. 21, 1818; buried family burying ground on his estate.

GOODYEAR, Charles, inventor; b. New Haven, Conn., Dec. 29, 1800; s. Amasa and Cynthia (Bateman) G.; m. Clarissa Beecher, Aug. 24, 1824; m. 2d, Fanny Wardell, 1854; 7 children. Began expts., 1834; obtained 1st patent for acid and metal coating to destroy the adhesive properties of rubber, 1837; discovered (with N.M. Hayward, whom he employed to expt. with effects of sulphur on rubber) what became vulcanization process, patented 1844; went to Europe to extend his patent, 1851; recipient Grand Medal of Honor and cross of Legion of Honor (France), 1855; obtained fgn. patents in all countries but Eng.; sold mfg. licenses and thus was largely responsible for establishment of rubber industry in Europe. Died N.Y.C., July 1, 1860.

GOODYEAR, Charles, congressman; b. Cobleskill, Schoharie County, N.Y., Apr. 26, 1804; attended Hartwick Acad., Otsego County; grad. Union Coll., Schenectady, N.Y., 1824; studied law. Admitted to bar, 1826, began practice of law, Schoharie, N.Y.; 1st judge Schoharie County, 1838-47; mem. N.Y. State Assembly, 1840; mem. U.S. Ho of Reps. (Democrat) from N.Y., 29th, 39th congresses, 1845-47, 65-67; founder, pres. Schoharie County Bank, 1852; del. Union Nat. Conv. of Conservatives Phila., 1866, Democratic Nat. Conv. N.Y.C., 1868; ret., 1869, moved to Charlottesville, Va.; judge Albemarle County Ct. Died Charlottesville Apr. 9, 1876; buried Maplewood Cemetery.

GOODYEAR, Charles, industrialist; b. Germantown, Pa., Jan. 1, 1833; s. Charles and Clarissa (Beecher) G.; m. Mary Colt, July 14, 1858, 7 children survived him. Assisted in his father's business, continued alone after father's death, 1860; became pres. Am. Shoe-tip Co., 1861; organized Goodyear Shoe Machinery Co., 1864; organized co. in Eng., 1870; reorganized N.Y. firm as Goodyear Boot & Shoe Machinery Co., 1871, (consolidated with Gordon McKay into a welt-shoe bus., 1880-88). Died May 22, 1896.

GOOKIN, Daniel, colonial ofcl.; b. Kent, Eng., 1612; s. Daniel and Mary (Byrd) G.; married 3 times; m. 2d, Mary Dalling, 1639; m. 3d, Hannah Tyng, 1685; children including Nathaniel, Daniel. Mem. Va. House of Burgesses, 1641-42; captain in charge of train bands, circa 1641-42, 49-circa 1687; ardent Puritan, a signer of Nansemond Petition asking ch. elders in Mass. to send clergy to Va.; settled in Roxbury, Mass., 1644; a founder of free grammar sch., Roxbury; dep. to Mass. Gen. Ct., 1649-52, spl. magistrate, 1652; supt. of all Indians acknowledging govt. of Mass., 1656, 61; went to Eng., collector customs and Dep. Treas. at war, Dunkirk, Eng., 1658; supporter Indian Rights which made him unpopular with many colonists, 1661; sgt.-maj. Middlesex Regt., 1680; maj. gen. all forces in Mass. colony, 1681. Author: Historical Collections of the Indians of Massachusetts, written 1674, published 1792. Died Cambridge, Mass., Mar. 30, 1687.

GORDON, Adoniram Judson, clergyman; b. New Hampton, Belknap County, N.H., Apr. 19, 1836; s. John Calvin and Sally (Robinson) G.; grad. Brown U., 1860, Newton Theol. Sem., 1863; m. Maria Hale, 1863, 8 children. Pastor, Baptist Ch., Jamaica Plain, Mass., 1863-69, Clarendon Street Bapt. Ch., 1869-95. Author: In Christ, 1872; Congregational Worship, 1872; Grace and Glory, 1880; The Twofold Life, 1884; Ministry of the Spirit, 1894; How Christ Came to Church, 1895. Died Boston, Feb. 2, 1895.

GORDON, Andrew, missionary; b. Putnam, N.Y., Sept. 17, 1828; s. Rev. Alexander and Margaret (Martin) G.; grad. Franklin Coll., New Athens, O., 1850; attended Theol. Sem., Canonsburg, Pa.; m. Rebecca Campbell Smith, May 18, 1852, 1 dau. Licensed to preach by Albany Presbyter, 1853; ordained to ministry Presbyn. Ch.; missionary to India, 1854-85, arrived in Calcutta, 1855, traveled to Sialkot in Pujab, established mission; organized 8 chs., theol. and lit. instns. returned to Am., 1885. Author: Our Indian Mission, 1886. Died Phila., Aug. 13, 1887; buried West Laurel Hill Cemetery, Phila.

GORDON, Archibald D., playwright; b. Ceylon, October 11, 1835; son of Rev. Alexander Gordon. Arrived in N.Y., 1865; employed by a publishing house, later became contbr. to several newspapers, N.Y. and Chgo. Author: (plays) Trixie; The Ugly Duckling; Is Marriage a Failure; The Girl from Mexico. Died Port Richmond, S.I., N.Y., Jan. 9, 1895.

GORDON, George Henry, army officer; b. Charlestown, Mass., July 19, 1823; s. Robert and Elizabeth (Carlisle) G.; grad. U.S. Mil. Acad., 1846, Harvard Law Sch., 1856; m. Mary Scott, June 1864. Served in Mexican War, brevetted 1st lt., 1847; served in Washington, D.C., then frontier duty in Kan., 1850-54; admitted to bar, 1857; raised 2d Mass. Inf., 1861; commd. col., 1861, served in Shenandoah Valley operations; commd. brig. gen., 1862, participated in battles of Winchester, Cedar Mountain and Antietam; in command of Eastern dist., 1865; brevetted maj. gen. U.S. Volunteers, 1865; a founder Mil. Hist. Soc. of Mass. Author: Brook Farm to Cedar Mountain . . . 1861-2, published 1863; History of the Campaign of the Army of Virginia . . . from Cedar Mountain to Alexandria, 1862, 1879; A War Diary of Events in the War of the Great Rebellion, 1882. Died Framingham, Mass., Aug. 30, 1886.

GORDON, George Phineas, inventor; b. Salem, N.H., Apr. 21, 1810; s. Phinias and Mary (White) G.; m. Sarah Cornish, 1846; m. 2d, Lenore May, 1856; 1 child. Apprenticed to printer, N.Y.C.; opened small job-printing office, N.Y.C.; began experimenting on improved press for card printing, 1835; obtained 1st patent for "Yankee" job press, 1851; introduced "Firefly" job press, 1854, turned out 10,000 cards per hour; built more than 100 kinds of presses; established factory in Rahway, N.J., with offices in N.Y.C., 1872. Died Norfolk, Va., Jan. 21, 1878.

GORDON, James, congressman; b. County Antrim, Ireland, Oct. 31, 1739; attended local schs. Came to U.S., 1758, settled in Schenectady, N..Y; an Indian trader; served as lt. col. Albany County (N.Y.) Militia Regt. during Revolutionary War, captured and imprisoned in Can.; mem. N.Y. State Assembly, 1777-80, 86, 90; moved to Ballston Spa, N.Y.; mem. U.S. Ho. of Reps. (Federalist) from N..Y, 2d-3d congresses, 1791-95; trustee Union Coll., Schenectady, 1795-1809; mem. N.Y Senate, 1797-1804. Died Ballston Spa, Jan. 17, 1810; buried Briggs Cemetery.

GORDON, Samuel, congressman, lawyer; b. Wattle's Ferry, Delaware County, N.Y., Apr. 28, 1802; attended public schs.; studied law, Delhi, N.Y. Admitted to bar, 1829, began practice of law, Delhi; postmaster Delhi, 1831-41; mem. N.Y. State Assembly, 1834; dist. atty. Delaware County, 1841-44; supr. Town of Delhi, several terms; mem. U.S. Ho. of Reps. (Democrat) fro N.Y., 27th, 29th congresses, 1841-43, 45-57; apptd provost marshal 19th Dist. N.Y., during Civil Wa 1863-65. Died Delhi, Oct. 28, 1873; buried Wood land Cemetery.

GORDON, William, clergyman, historian; b. Hert fordshire, Eng., 1728; ed. for ministry, London Eng.; m. Elizabeth Fields. Minister, Independan Ch., Ipswich, Eng., 1752-64; pastor Old Gravel Lan Ch., Southwick, Eng., 1764-70; came to Am., 1770 began preaching to Mass. Hist. Soc.; ordained pasto 3d Congregational Ch., Roxbury, Mass., 1772; pub lished Plan of a Society for Making Provision fo Widows (advocated old age pensions), 1772; apptd chaplain Mass. Provincial Congress, 1775; delivere 1st independence anniversary sermon before Mass Gen. Ct., 1777, sermon widely published; collecte materials, letters, interviewed generals and states men in order to write an objective history of Am Revolution, 1776-86, forced to revise manuscript be cause both English and Americans thought it wa too objective, 1786, published work as The Histor of the Rise, Progress and Establishment of the Unit ed States of America, 4 vols., 1788; pastor in Hunt ingdonhire, Eng., 1789-1802; returned to Ipswich, 1802. Died Ipswich, Oct. 19, 1807.

GORDON, William, congressman; b. nr. Boston, Apr. 12, 1763; grad. Harvard, 1779; studied law. Admitted to bar, 1787, began practice of law, Amherst, N.H.; apptd. register of probate, 1793 mem. N.H. Senate, 1794-95; solicitor Hillsboroug County, 1794-1801; mem. U.S. Ho. of Reps. from N.H., 5th-6th congresses, 1797-June 12, 1800 (resigned), a mgr. apptd. by Ho. of Reps. to conduct impeachment proceedings against Senator William Blount from Tenn.; atty. gen. N.H., 1800-02. Died Boston, May 8, 1802; buried Amherst Cemetery.

GORDON, William Fitzhugh, congressman; b. Germanna, Va., Jan. 13, 1787; s. James and Elizabeth (Gordon) G.; m. Mary Rootes, Dec. 12, 1809; m. 2d, Elizabeth Lindsay, Jan. 21, 1813. Admitted to Va. bar, circa 1808; atty. Commonwealth of Va., 1812; served as brig. gen., maj. gen. Va. Militia in War of 1812; mem. Va. Ho. of Dels., 1818-29; mem. Va. Constl. Conv., 1829-30, framer successful compromise measure fixing representation in the 2 houses on the mixed basis of population and taxation; mem. U.S. Ho. of Reps. (Democrat) from Va., 21st-23d congresses, Jan. 25, 1830-35, introduced bill providing for establishment of independent treasury, (1st step in separation of bank and state) 1834; leading figure in So. Conv., Nashvillee, Tenn., 1850. Died Albemarle County, Va., Aug. 28, 1858; buried Springfield, nr. Gordonsville, Va.

GORDON, William Robert, clergyman; b. N.Y.C., Mar. 19, 1811; s. Robert and Elizabeth (Postley) G.; grad. U. N.Y., 1834, New Brunswick Theol. Sem., 1837. Ordained to ministry Dutch Reformed Ch., 1837; pastor Dutch Reformed Ch., North Hempstead, N.Y., 1838-43; pastor, Flushing, N.Y., 1843-49, Houston Street Ch., N.Y.C., 1849-58; pastor, Schraalenburgh, N.J., 1858-80. Author: A Rebuke to High Churchism, 1844; Peter Never in Rome, 1847; The Reformed Church in America: Its History, Documents and Government, 1869. Died Manhasset, N.Y., Mar. 30, 1897

GORDON, William Washington, lawyer, railroad ofcl.; b. Screven County, Ga., Jan. 17, 1796; s. Ambrose and Elizabeth (Meade) G.; grad. U.S. Mil. Acad., 1815; m. Sarah Anderson Stites, 1826. 1 son. Practiced law, Savannah, Ga., 1818; helped acquire charter from Ga. Legislature authorizing constrn. Cenrtal R.R. of Ga., 1833, obtained amendment to original railroad charter authorizing banking privileges, became 1st pres., 1835, caused constrn. costs under his admintsrn. to be lower by half than nat. average of the time. Died Savannah, Mar. 20, 1842.

GORE, Christopher, senator, gov. Mass.; b. Boston, Sept. 21, 1758; grad. Harvard, 1776; studied law. Admitted to bar, began practice of law, Boston; mem. Mass. Ho. of Reps., 1788, 89, 1808; U.S. atty. for Dist. of Mass., 1789-96; commr. to Eng., 1796-1803; charge d'Affaires, London, Eng., 1803-04; mem. Mass. Senate, 1806-07; gov. Mass., 1809; mem. U.S. Senate (filled vacancy) from Mass., May 5, 1813-May 30, 1816 (resigned); Federalist presdl. elector, 1816; overseer Harvard, 1810-15, fellow, 1812-20. Died Waltham, Mass., Mar. 1, 1827; buried Granary Burying Ground, Boston.

GORGAS, Josiah, army officer, educator; b. Dauphin County, Pa., July 1, 1818; s. Joseph and Sophia (Atkinson) G.; grad. U.S. Mil. Acad., 1841; went abroad to study ordnance and arsenals of European armies, 1845; m. Amelia Gayle, Dec. 1853; children—William C., Jesse, Mary, Amelia, Maria, Richard H. Served as lt. Ordnance, Mexican War, 1847-48, commd. capt., 1855; commd. maj., chief of ordnance Confederate Army, 1861; established armories for making arms, Richmond, Va. and Faytteville, N.C.; set up arsenals throughout South; sponsible for founding a cannon foundry and cenal lab. at Macon, Ga.; brought about steady improvements in products of foundries and armories espite difficulties of Confederate system; brig. gen., Nov. 1864; became mgr. Brierfield Iron Works Ala. after war; became headmaster jr. dept. U. South, Sewanee, Tenn., 1869, prof. engring., 870, vice chancellor, 1872; pres. U. Ala., 1878-79, brarian of univ., 1879-82. Died Tuscaloosa, Ala., lay 15, 1883.

GORGES, Sir Ferdinando, landowner; b. Ashton hillips, Somerset, Eng., circa 1565; children—Robert, John. Apptd. gov. of Plymouth (Eng.), 1604; an rganizer Plymouth Co. (had trading and settlement ights in area 34th-45th North latitude, known as orth Va.), 1606; sent out expdn. which founded t. George on Kennebec River in what is now Me., 607 (settlement later abandoned); sent out 2 more nsuccessful expdns., 1615; founded (with assos.) new corp., Plymouth, 1620 (this was foundation all future New Eng. land grants); becam lord ropr. Province of Me., 1639; known as Father of olonization in New Eng.; his heirs were involved in any law suits because of tangled legal character grant. Died Eng., 1647.

GORHAM, Benjamin, congressman, lawyer; b. harlestown, Mass., Feb. 13, 1775; s. Nathaniel orham; grad. Harvard, 1795; studied law. Aditted to bar, began practice of law, Boston; em. Mass. Ho. of Reps., 1814-18, 41, Mass. enate, 1819-21, 23; mem. U.S. Ho. of Reps. (filled cancies) from Mass., 16th-17th, 20th-21st, 23d ngresses, Nov. 6, 1820-23, July 23, 1827-31, 33-5. Died Boston, Sept. 27, 1855; buried old burial ound Phipps Street Cemetery, Charlestown.

GORHAM, Jabez, silversmith, mcht.; b. Provience, R.I., Feb. 18, 1792; s. Jabez and Catherine Tyler) G.; m. Amey Thurber, Dec. 4, 1816; m. d, Lydia Dexter, Apr. 16, 1822. Apprenticed to ehemiah Dodge, 1807; mem. jewelry firm, 1813-8; in jewelry firm with Stanton Beebe, 1818-31; gan making spoons, forks and thimbles, 1831 1st silversmiths to use machinery), bought silverare part of bus., 1842, formed new firm (origin Gorham Mfg. Co.); mem. R.I. Gen. Assembly om Providence; mem. Providence Common Coun-l, 1842-44; capt. of a co. R.I. Militia. Died rovidence, Mar. 24, 1869.

GORHAM, John, physician, chemist; b. Boston, eb. 24, 1783; s. Stephen and Molly (White) G.; A., Harvard, 1801, M.B., 1804, M.D., 1811; udied exptl. chemistry under Friedrich Accum, ondon, Eng.; m. Mary Warren, June 2, 1808. Adnct prof. chemistry and materia medica Harvard, 809-15, Ewing prof. chemistry and mineralogy, 815-27; librarian Mass. Med. Soc., 1814-18; felw Am. Acad. Arts and Scis.; ret., 1827. Author: he Elements of Chemical Science (1st systematic hemistry textbook written by an Am. and published this country), 2 vols., 1819-20; contbr. articles on edicine and chemistry to profl. jours., including ew Eng. Jour. of Medicine, New Eng. Jour. of ledicine and Surgery. Died Mar. 27, 1829.

GORHAM, Nathaniel, businessman, Continental ongressman; b. Charlestown, Mass., May 1738; Nathaniel and Mary (Soley) G.; m. Rebecca all, 1763, 9 children. Mem. Mass. Legisature, 1771-75; del. to Mass. Provincial Congress, 774-75; mem. Mass. Bd. of War, 1778-81; del. lass. Constl. Conv., 1779-80; mem. Mass. Senate, 780; mem. Mass. Ho. of Reps., 1781-87, speaker, 781, 82, 85; mem. Continental Congress, 1782-3, 85-87, pres., 1786; an incorporator Charles iver Bridge, 1785; apptd. judge Ct. of Common leas, Middlesex, Mass., 1785; del. to U.S. Constl. onv., 1787; mem. Mass. Conv. which ratified U.S. onstn., 1788; engaged in land speculation, obained (with Oliver Phelps) title to 6,000,000 cres of land; strain of meeting his financial oblitations to Mass. led to breakdown of health. Died harlestown, June 11, 1796.

GORMAN, Willis Arnold, army officer, territorial ov.; b. Flemingsburg, Ky., Jan. 12, 1816; s. David and Elizabeth G.; LL.B. (hon.), U. Ind. Law ch., 1845; m. Martha Stone, Jan. 1836; m. 2d, mily Lewington, Apr. 27, 1865. Admitted to Ind. ar, 1835; clk. Ind. Senate, 1837-38, enrolling ec., 1839-40; mem. Ind. Ho. of Reps., 1841-44; ommd. maj. 3d Ind. Regt. under Gen. Lane, 846; col. 4th Ind. Regt. in Mexican War, 1847; ivil and mil. gov. Puebla (Mexico), 1848; mem. S. Ho. of Reps. (Democrat) from Ind., 31st-2d congresses 1849-51; gov. Minn. Territory, 852-57; supt. Indian affairs, negotiated several eaties; responsible for Minn.'s system of taxing andgrants; del. Minn. Constl. Conv.; mem. Minn. egislature, 1859; commd. col. 1st Minn. Voluneers 1861, brig. gen., 1861; served in 1st Battle f Bull Run, 1861; commanded a brigade at battles f Savage's Station, South Mountain, Edwards Fery, Antietam, 1862; atty. City of St. Paul Minn.), 1869-76. Died St. Paul, May 20, 1876.

GORRIE, John, physician, mayor, inventor; b. Charleston, S.C., Oct. 3, 1803; grad. Coll. Physicians and Surgeons, N.Y.C., 1833; m. Caroline (Myrick) Beeman, May 1838. Postmaster, Apalachicola, Fla., 1834-38, mem. city council, 1835-36, treas., 1835-36, mayor, 1837; received patent on mech. refrigeration, 1851 (discovery was result of plan to cool hospital rooms). Died Apalachicola, June 16, 1855.

GORRINGE, Henry Honeychurch, naval officer; b. Barbados, W.I., Aug. 11, 1841. Entered U.S. Navy, 1862, served under Porter on Upper Mississippi River, 1862-65, commd. lt. comdr., 1869; with Hydrographic Office, Washington, D.C., prepared several volumes of sailing directions for South Atlantic, 1871-74; in charge of bringing Egyptian Obelisk Cleopatra's Needle from Alexandria to N.Y.C., 1880; resigned commn., 1883; organized, became mgr. Am. Shipbldg. Co. Author: Egyptian Obelisks; contbr. letters to N.Y. Nation. Died N.Y.C., July 6, 1885; buried Sparkill, N.Y.

GORTON, Samuel, religious leader; b. Gorton, Eng., 1593; m. Mary Maplet, at least 9 children including Samuel. Came to Am. in attempt to find tolerant climate for heterodox religious beliefs, 1637; repeatedly persecuted in colonies; fined, imprisoned, banished from Boston, 1637; banished from Plymouth, 1637; publicly whipped, banished from Portsmouth (now R.I.), 1639; later settled at Pawtuxet, Mass., but forced to leave; bought land from Narragansett Indians, 1643, founded Shawomet (later Warwick), Mass.; arrested, imprisoned for blasphemy by Mass. Council, 1643-44; went to Eng., 1644-48, secured letter of safe conduct in Mass. from Earl of Warwick, guaranteeing him religious liberty; his followers (sect known as Gortonites) existed for over a century after his death; believed in divinity of Christ, denounced doctrine of Trinity, also denounced paid ministry and absolute moral law; mem. Mass. Assembly from Warwick, 1649, 51-52, 55-57, 59-60, 62-66; mem. Warwick Town Council, 1677. Author: Simplicities' Defence against Seven-Headed Policy, 1646; An Incorruptible Key Composed of the CX Psalme, 1647; Saltmarsh Returned from the Dead, 1655; An Antidote against the Common Plague of the World, 1657. Died Warwick, Mass., 1677.

GOSNOLD, Bartholomew, navigator, colonizer; b. Suffolk, Eng.; flourished 1572-1607; s. Anthony and Dorothy (Bacon) G.; ed. Jesus Coll., Cambridge Eng. U.; m. Catherine Barrington, 1596, 6 children. Commanded ship Concord sailing from Falmouth on expdn. to start colony in Va., Mar. 1602; explored Northeastern Am., landed at Me. and Mass., gave names to Cape Cod and Martha's Vineyard, 1602; erected fort on Elizabeth's Isle; traded with Indians and returned to Eng., July 1602; made 2d trip to Am. to colonize Va., 1606-07, sailed from Thames River as vice adm. of fleet in command of ship God Speed carrying 52 pioneers bound for projected settlement, Dec. 1606; landed Cape Henry, Va., Apr. 1607; mem. local council for colony, in charge of searching country for minerals; signed 1st report drawn up for information of home authorities; protested choice of site of Jamestown, overruled. Died of malaria, Jamestown, Va.

GOSS, Nathaniel Stickney, ornithologist; b. Lancaster, N.H., June 6, 1826. State ornithologist Kansas; gave Goss Ornithol. Collection (one of largest and most complete in U.S.) to Kan. State Hist. Soc., 1881; first postmaster at Neosho Falls, Kan.; pres. So. branch U.P. R.R., Emporia, Kan. Author: A History of the Birds of Kansas. Died Neosho Falls, Mar. 10, 1891.

GOSTELOWE, Jonathan, cabinetmaker; b. Passyank, Pa. (now part of Phila.), 1744; s. George and Lydia G.; m. Mary Duffield, June 16, 1768; m. 2d, Elizabeth Towers, Apr. 19, 1789. Made cabinets in mahogany and walnut; made clock cases for Edward Duffield; served as maj. arty. Continental Army, 1776, later chief commissary mil. stores in Phila.; capt. of a co. 3d Bn., Pa. Militia, 1783-84, lt. arty., 1787; elected chmn. Gentleman Cabinet and Chair Makers, Phila., 1788; presented carved font to Christ Ch., Phila., 1789. Died Phila., Feb. 3. 1795: buried Christ Ch. Graveyard.

GOTT, Daniel, congressman, lawyer; b. Hebron, nr. New London, Conn., July 10, 1794; attended public schs.; studied law. Began teaching sch. at age 16; moved to Pompey, N.Y., 1817; admitted to bar, 1819, began practice of law, Pompey; mem. U.S. Ho. of Reps. (Whig) from N.Y., 30th-31st congresses, 1847-51; moved to Syracuse, N.Y., 1853, resumed practice of law. Died Syracuse, July 6, 1864; buried Pompey Hill Cemetery, Pompey.

GOTTSCHALK, Louis Moreau, pianist, composer; b. New Orleans, May 8, 1829; s. Edward and Aimée Marie (de Brusle) G. Made piano debut at Salle Pleyel, Paris, France, Apr. 1845; played concert series with Hector Berlioz at Italian Opera, 1846-47; successfully toured Savoy, Switzerland and French Provinces, 1850; played for Queen of Spain, Nov. 1851 who conferred on him Order of Isabella the Catholic (1851); named chevalier Royal Order of Charles III, 1856; performed 80 concerts in N.Y., 1855-56; organizer large festival in Rio de Janeiro, Brazil, 1869; best known compositions include Last Hope, Tremolo, Gran Tarantella, The Dying Poets, Etude, Banjo, Bamboula, Cuban Dances, Negro songs; also wrote 2 operas (never performed) and 2 symphonies; considered one of greatest pianists of his period and best Am. performer. Author: Notes of a Pianist (edited by his sister, Clara Gottschalk). Died Tijuca, Brazil, Dec. 18, 1869; buried Rio de Janeiro; reinterred Greenwood Cemetery, N.Y.C.

GOUDY, William Charles, lawyer; b. Ind., May 15, 1824; s. Robert and Jane (Ansley) G.; grad. Ill. Coll., 1845; m. Helen M. Judd, 1849. Admitted to Ill. bar, 1847; state atty. 10th Jud. Dist. Ill., 1852-55; mem. Ill. Senate from Fulton and McDonough counties, 1856-61; del. Nat. Democratic Conv., 1868; prominent Midwest lawyer, expert on real estate law; gen. counsel Chgo. & Northwestern Ry., 1893; counsel for defense in Wabash, St. Louis & Pacific Ry. Co. vs. Ill. case. Died Apr. 27,

GOUGE, William M., editor, govt. ofcl.; b. Phila. Nov. 10, 1796. Propr. and editor (with Stevenson Smith) Phila. Gazette, 1823; opposed banks and paper money because of resultant currency inflation and unfavorable trade balance; apptd. clk. U.S. Treasury Dept., 1834; editor Jour. of Banking, 1841; apptd. examiner of books of all U.S. Treasury branches except San Francisco, 1854; an accountant state banks of Ark., 1857-58. Author: A Short History of Money and Banking in the United States, (gave detailed description of orgn. of state banks and abuses associated with their mgmt.), 1833; Died Trenton, N.J., July 14, 1863. 1893.

GOUGH, John Bartholomew, temperance lectr.; b. Sandgate, Eng., Aug. 22, 1817; s. John and Jane Gough; m. Lucretia Fowler, Dec. 18, 1839; m. 2d, Mary Whitcomb, Nov. 23, 1843; at least 1 child. Came to U.S., 1829; set up bookbinding shop, Newburyport, Mass., 1839; signed total-abstinence pledge after 3 years as alcoholic, 1842; became one of foremost platform orators in Am.; lectr. on temperance reform, 1843-86; made trips to Eng. to speak for London Temperance League, 1853-57-60, 78; personally induced 215,179 people to take the pledge. Author: Orations Delivered on Various Occasions by John B. Gough, 1859. Died Frankford, Pa., Feb. 18, 1886.

GOULD, Augustus Addison, physician, conchologist; b. New Ipswich, N.H., Apr. 23, 1805; s. Nathaniel Duren and Sally (Prichard) G.; grad. Harvard, 1825, M.D., 1830; m. Harriet Sheafe, Nov. 25, 1833. Became one of leading physicians in Mass.; influential in devel. of conchology in Am.; wrote Report on the Invertebrata of Mass., 1841, Mollusca and Shells, 1852 (his most important contbns. to Am. science); editor The Terrestrial-Air-Breathing Mollusks of the United States and the Adjacent Territories of North America; introduced such subjects as principles of classification, geog. distbn. of genera and species, geol. relationships, and anatomical structures; mem. Boston Soc. Natural History, pres., several years; an original mem. Nat. Acad. Arts and Scis. Author: Invertebrate Animals of Mass., 1841; Mollusca and Shells of the United States Exploring Expedition under Capt. Wilkes, 1852; A System of Natural History Containing Scientific and Popular Descriptions of Various Animals, 1833; (with Louis Agassiz) Principles of Zoology, 1848. Died Boston, Sept. 15, 1886.

GOULD, Benjamin Apthorp, astronomer; b. Boston, Sept. 27, 1824; s. Benjamin Apthorp and Lucretia (Goddard) G.; grad. Horvard, 1884, LL.D. (hon.), 1885; Ph.D., U. Gottingen (Germany), 1848; LL.D. (hon.), Columbia, 1887; m. Mary Quincy, 1861, 5 children. Established and conducted Astronomical Journal, 1849-51, re-established, 1886; in charge of longitude dept. U.S. Coast Survey, 1852-67; organized and directed Dudley Observatory, Albany, N.Y., 1855-59; gauged (by aid of submarine cable) difference in longitude between Am. and Europe, 1860; prepared "standard catalogue," applying for 1st time systematic corrections to various star catalogues, 1862; built pvt. observatory, nr. Cambridge, Mass., 1862; dir. Nat. Observatory, Cordoba, Argentina, 1870-circa 1884, did greatest work in observation of stars of So. hemisphere; 1st astronomer to use telegraph in geodetic work, made 15 determinations before method introduced in Europe. Fellow U. Chile, Royal Soc., London, Acad. of Sci., Paris, Imperial Acad., St. Petersburg, Bureau des Langitudes, Paris, Astronomical Gesellschaft, Berlin; v.p. Am. Acad. Arts and Scis., recipient Watson medal; charter mem. Nat. Acad. Scis.; pres. Colonial Soc. of Mass., 1892; hon. prof. U. Argentine Republic; created knight Order Pour le merite by Emperor of Germany. Author: Investigation of the Orbit of the Comet U., 1847; Reports on the Discovery of the Planet Neptune, 1850; Uranometria Argentina, 1879; Resultados Del Observatorio Nacional

Argentino en Cordoba (most important work, contains zone catalogues giving positions of 73,160 stars and gen. catalogue of 32,448 stars in So. hemisphere), 1879-96. Died Cambridge, Nov. 26, 1896.

GOULD, Edward Shuman, author; b. Litchfield, Conn., May 11, 1805; s. Judge James and Sally McCurdy (Tracy) G.; 2 children. Moved to N.Y.C. after graduation from secondary sch.; delivered series of lectures titled Am. Criticism on Am. Literature, denouncing Am. authors and praising Brit. writers (later published as Lectures Delivered Before the Mercantile Library Association); published The Sleep-Rider, or the Old Boy in the Omnibus (short novel), 1843; published Good English; or, Popular Errors in Language (an attempt to correct current stylistic and philological errors), 1867. Died N.Y.C., Feb. 21, 1885; buried Litchfield.

GOULD, Hannah Flagg, poet; b. Lancaster, Mass., Sept. 3, 1789; d. Benjamin and Griselda Apthorp (Flagg) Gould. Moved to Newburyport, Mass., 1808; began writing and contributing poetry to mags. and annuals, 1820's; a popular poet for 20 years, wrote nature poems for children (her best work), religious and patriotic verse. Works include: Poems (verses collected by friends and presented to her as her 1st published vol., 1832, republished 1833, 35, 36, 41); The Golden Vase: A Gift For the Young, 1844; Gathered Leaves, 1846; New Poems, 1850. Died Newburyport, Sept. 5, 1865; buried New Hill Cemetery, Newburyport.

GOULD, Herman Day, congressman; b. Sharon, Conn., Jan. 16, 1799. Engaged in business; pres. Delhi Nat. Bank (N.Y.), 1839-49; mem. U.S. Ho. of Reps. (Whig) from N.Y., 31st Congress, 1849-51. Died Delhi, Jan. 26, 1852; buried Woodland Cemetery.

GOULD, James, jurist, educator; b. Branford, Conn., Dec. 5, 1770; s. William and Mary (Foote) G.; grad. Yale, 1791; attended Tapping Reeve's Law Sch., Litchfield, Conn., 1795; m. Sally McCurdy Tracy, Oct. 21, 1798, 9 children. Sch. tchr., Wethersfield, Conn., later, Balt., 1791-93; tutor Yale, 1793-95; asso. in conducting Tapping Reeve's Law Sch., 1798-1820, took charge of sch., 1820; judge Conn. Superior Ct. and Ct. of Errors, 1816-19 (retired because of Conn. Constn. of 1818); forced to close law sch. due to ill health, 1833. Author: Principles of Pleading in Civil Actions, 1832. Died May 11, 1838.

GOULD, Jay (christened Jason), financier; b. Roxbury, N.Y., May 27, 1836; s. John Burr and Mary (Moore) G.; m. Helen Miller, 6 children including George Jay. Helped prepare maps of upper N.Y. State, 1854-57, saved $5,000; established (with Zadock Pratt) large tannery, No. Pa., 1857; mem. brokerage firm Smith, Gould and Martin, N.Y.C., 1860; speculated in small eastern railroads, became pres. Washington & Rutland R.R., mgr. Renssalaer & Saratoga R.R.; became mem. bd. dirs., then pres. Erie R.R., 1867, (with James Fisk and Daniel Drew) defeated Cornelius Vanderbilt for control by throwing 50,000 Erie shares on market, 1868, forced to flee Jersey City, went to Albany and bribed N.Y. Legislature to achieve legalization of the Erie stock issue and prevent union of Erie and N.Y. Central railroads; in complete control of Erie R.R. (with Fisk) after peace developed between Vanderbilt and Gould interests and Drew retired; added William Marcy ("Boss") Tweed and Peter B. Sweeney to partnership, then looted Erie R.R. by watering stock, and attempted to corner gold market, resulting in Panic of 1869 (Black Friday, Sept. 24); ejected from control of Erie R.R. (Fisk died and Tweed Ring destroyed); expanded activities to West, became dir. U.P. R.R., 1874, also bought control Kan. Pacific R.R.; bought control Denver Pacific, Central Pacific and Mo. Pacific railroads, 1879, forced U.P. R.R. (by threatening to compete by forming new transcontinental railroad with Kan. Pacific R.R.) to consolidate with Kan. Pacific R.R. at par; owned half of all railroad mileage in S.W., by 1890; owner N.Y. World, 1879-83; part owner N.Y. Elevated R.R., became practically full owner, 1886; bought control of Western Union Telegraph Co., made it one of world's greatest telegraph systems. Died N.Y.C., Dec. 2, 1892.

GOULD, Nathaniel Duren, musician; b. Bedford, Mass., Nov. 26, 1781; s. Reuben and Mary (Gould) Duren; m. Sally Prichard, Nov. 15, 1801, at least 2 children including Augustas Addison, Charles. Taught dist. sch., 1797; gave music lessons; conductor Middlesex Musical Soc., 1805; mem. N.H. Legislature from New Ipswich, 1809-12, 14-16; became deacon, 1812; founder Hubbard Soc., New Ipswich, N.H., 1815; trustee New Ipswich Acad., 1817-24; moved to Boston, 1820, taught music; joined Handel and Hadyn Soc., 1820. Author: Social Harmony of A Compilation of Airs, Duetts and Trion, 1823; Musical Prosody, 1830; Church Music in America, 1853. Died Boston, May 28, 1864.

GOULD, Thomas Ridgeway, sculptor; b. Boston, Nov. 5, 1818; s. John Ridgeway and Ann (Ridgeway) G.; m. Rebecca Sprogell; children—Marshall S., Alfred. Represented a Boston merc. firm. established in New Orleans by brother John M. Gould; exhibited heads of Christ and Satan in Boston Athenaeum, 1863 (received 1st serious recognition as sculptor); opened studio, Florence, Itayl, 1868; most noted work was The West Wind; Shakespearian subjects include The Ghost in Hamlet; commd. by Grand Army of Republic to execute statue of John A. Andrew, 1875; other works include: busts of Ralph Waldo Emerson, Michelangelo, Edwin Booth, Imogene, Childhood; heroic statue Timon of Athens, Ascending Spirit, Ariel, Undine, Puritan. Author: The Tragedian, 1868. Died Florence, Nov. 26, 1881.

GOULDING, Francis Robert, clergyman; b. Midway, Ga., Sept. 28, 1810; s. Thomas and Ann (Holbrook) G.; grad. U. Ga., 1829; grad. Theol. Sem., Columbia, S.C., 1832; m. Mary Wallace Howard, 1833; m. 2d, Matilda Rees, 1855. Preached in Sumter County, S.C., Greenboro and Washington, Ga.; became agt. Am. Bible Soc.; preached in Eatonton and Bath, Ga., 1843-51; moved to Kingston, Ga., 1853, set up sch. for boys and began research on instincts of birds and beasts; served unofficially as chaplain in Confederate Army during Civil War; taught sch. for girls after Civil War, Macon, Ga. Author: Robert and Harold (later entitled The Young Marooners on the Florida Coast), 1852 (went through 10 editions); Marooners' Island, 1869. Died Roswell, Ga., Aug. 21, 1881.

GOUPIL, St. Rene, missionary, lay brother of Soc. of Jesus; b. Anjou, France circa 1607. Missionary in Can., 1640-42; captured and tortured by Iroquois, Aug. 1642. Killed with tomahawk, Ossernenon, N.Y., Sept. 29, 1642. Beatified by Roman Catholic Ch. as martyr for the Christian Faith, June 21, 1925; canonized by Pope Pius XI, June 29, 1930.

GOURDIN, Theodore, congressman; b. nr. Kingstree, Williamsburg County, S.C., Mar. 20, 1764; ed. Charleston, S.C., also in Europe. Became a planter; mem. U.S. Ho. of Reps. (Democrat) from S.C., 13th Congress, 1813-15. Died Reinville, S.C., Jan. 17, 1826; buried Episcopal Cemetery, St. Stephen, S.C.

GOVAN, Andrew Robison, congressman; b. Orange Parish, S.C., Jan. 13, 1794; grad. S.C. Coll. at Columbia, 1813; mem. S.C. Ho. of Reps., 1820-22; mem. U.S. Ho. of Reps. (filled vacancy) from S.C., 17th-19th congresses, Dec. 4, 1822-27; a planter, Miss., 1828-41. Died Marshall County, Miss., June 27, 1841; buried family cemetery on estate "Snowdown," Marshall County.

GOWANS, William, bibliophile; b. Lanark County, Scotland, Mar. 29, 1803; m. Susan Bradley. Emigrated to Phila., 1821; moved to N.Y., 1828, engaged in various occupations; played minor part with Edwin Forrest at Old Bowery Theatre, N.Y.C., 1830; set up bookstall on Chatham St., N.Y.C.; issued 28 catalogues of his books, 1842-70; 250,000 volumes sold by executors of his will. Author: Gowans Bibliothica Americana, 5 vols., 1845-69. Died N.Y.C., Nov. 27, 1870.

GOWEN, Franklin Benjamin, lawyer, railroad exec.; b. Mt. Airy, Phila., Pa., Feb. 9, 1836; s. James and Mary (Miller) G.; LL.D., Washington and Lee U., 1879; Held various posiitons in mining operations of coal-fields Pa. in youth; admitted to Pa. bar, 1860; became dist. atty. Schuylkill County, Pa., 1862; counsel Phila. & Reading R.R., 1864, pres., 1870-85; mem. Pa. Constl. Conv., 1872; counsel for Commonwealth of Pa. in prosecution of the Molly Maguires, procured conviction and execution of a number of the leaders, broke up orgn. Committed suicide for no apparent reason, Washington, D.C., Dec. 14, 1889.

GRABAU, Johannes Andreas August, clergyman; b. Ovenstedt, Prussia, Mar. 18, 1804; s. Johann Andreas and Anna (Jericho) G.; grad. U. Halle (Germany), 1830; m. Christine Sophie Burggraf, July 15, 1834, 3 children. Taught sch., Magdeburg, Sachsa, Germany, circa 1830-34; elected pastor St. Andreas, Erfurt, 1834; ordained to ministry Lutheran Ch., 1834; opposed Union liturgy and carried on services in pvt. homes while he was not in prison, 1836-38, finally allowed to emigrate with group of about 1000 parishioners; settled in Buffalo, N.Y., 1839; pastor Derifaltigkets-Kirche, 1839-79; opened sch. later known as Martin Luther Sem., 1840, trained candidates for ministry; met at Milw. with Heinrich von Rohr (his 1st pupil) and 3 other clergymen, 1845, organized Synod of Luth. Ch. Emigrated from Prussia (became known as Buffalo Synod); visited Germany with von Rohr to confer with William Lohe on matters of doctrine, 1853-54; Buffalo Synod split into 3 factions over subject of ordination, 1866, largest splinter joined Mo. Synod; started new paper Die Wachende Kirche to defend his synod's views. Died June 2 1879.

GRACE, Thomas Langdon, clergyman; b Charleston, S.C., Nov. 16, 1814; studied at Cincinnati Sem., also St. Rose's Priory, Ky., late at the Minerva, Rome, Italy. Became a Domin ican, Ky., 1830; ordained priest Roman Catholi Ch., Rome, 1839; returned to parish and mission ary work in Ky. and Tenn., 1844; bishop of St Paul, Minn., 1859-84; encouraged immigration extension of Catholic ednl. facilities and chari table works; apptd. titular bishop of Menith, 1884 titular archbishop of Siunia, 1889. Died St. Paul Feb. 22, 1897.

GRACIE, Archibald, army officer; b. N.Y.C. Dec. 1, 1832; s. Archibald and Elizabeth (Beth une) G.; studied in Heidelberg, Germany; grad U.S. Mil. Acad., 1854; m. Josephine Mayo, Nov 19, 1856. Took part in Snake River expdn., 1855 moved to Mobile, Ala., 1856; capt. Washingtor Light Inf. Co., Mobile; commd. maj. 11th Ala Regt., 1861; raised 43d Ala. Regt., 1862, electe col., led expdn. across Cumberland Mountains t attack and capture Ft. Cliff (Tenn.) commd brig. gen. Confederate Army, 1862; served in en gagements at Chickamauga and Beans Station posthumously commd. maj. gen. Died Petersburg Ky., Dec. 2, 1864; buried N.Y.C.

GRADY, Henry Woodfin, orator, journalist; b Athens, Ga., May 24, 1850; s. William S. and Anr Elizabeth (Gartrell) G.; grad. State U. Ga., 1868; postgrad. in law, U. Va., 1868-69; m. Julia King 1871. Known for his efforts on behalf of So. readjustment after Civil War; joined Methodist Ch., 1865; went to Rome, Ga., as editor of Courier, 1871; editor-publisher Daily-Comml., 1871; founded (with 2 others) Atlanta (Ga.) Herald, 1872; spl. reporter in Atlanta for N.Y. Herald, 1876-77; bought ¼ interest in Atlanta Constitution, 1879, through his journalism (1879-89) helped restore Southern confidence and economy; coined phrase "The New South" in address before New Eng. Club of N.Y.C., Dec. 1886, Best known orations include: The South and her Problems (Dallas, Tex., 1887), The Race Problem in the South (Boston, 1889), Against Centralization (1889), The Position of the South on the Race Problem (1889). Died Atlanta, Dec. 23, 1889.

GRAESSL, Lawrence, clergyman; b. Ruemannsfelden, Germany, Aug. 18, 1753; s. Lorenz Graessl. Ordained priest Roman Catholic ch., engaged in parochial duties and as tutor in Munich, Germany; urged to come to Phila. by Father Ferdinand Farmer; arrived in Phila., 1787, apptd. asst. St. Mary's Ch., Phila., curate, 1788; missionary throughout Pa., Del. and N.J.; represented Phila. at 1st Provincial Synod, Balt., 1791; recommended by Bishop Carroll to succeed him, appointment did not come through until after his death. Died during yellow fever plague, Phila., circa Oct. 12, 1793; buried St. Joseph's Ch., Phila.

GRAFF, Frederic, civil engr.; b. Phila., May 23, 1817; s. Frederick and Judith (Swyer) G.; m. Elizabeth Mathieu. Asst. engr. Phila. Water Dept., 1842-47, chief engr., 1847-56, 66-62, reorganized dept. by combining dist. works with prin. city works, planned and directed constrn. of 3 reservoirs and 1 dam, modernized Phila. water sysetm; park commr. City of Phila., 1851, established Fairmount Park System; experimented with pumping machinery, suggested water-supply systems for many of larger cities in East; pres. Am. Soc. Civil Engrs., 1885, dir. several years; pres. Engrs. Club of Phila., 1880, pres. Franklin Inst. Died Phila., Mar. 30, 1890.

GRAFF, Frederick, engr.; b. Phila., Aug. 27, 1774; s. Jacob Graff; m. Judith Sawyer, 1 son Frederic. Draftsman, Phila. Water Works (1st steam-powered water works in U.S.) 1797, apptd. supt., 1805; selected (with John Davis) Mt. Morris (now Fairmount), Pa. as site for new reservoir, 1810; designed mains (over 113 miles of which were laid by 1842), connections, stipcocks, and fire plugs for water system of Phila. (1st efficient hydraulic water system in nation), chief engr. for Phila. Water Dept. until 1847; mem. Franklin Inst., 1826. Died Apr. 13, 1847.

GRAFFENRIED, Christopher, see de Graffenried, Christopher.

GRAHAM, Charles Kinnaird, naval and army officer, civil engr.; b. N.Y.C., June 3, 1824; m. Mary Graham. Commd. midshipman U.S. Navy, 1841; served with Gulf Squadron during Mexican War, 1846-48; one of surveyors employed in laying out Central Park, N.Y.C.; became constrn. engr. Bklyn. Navy Yard, 1857; commd. maj. Army of Potomac, U.S. Army, 1862, later lt. col.; apptd. col. 74th Inf.; promoted brig. gen. for services with Army of Potomac, 1863; commanded brigade of III Corps at battles of Chancellorsville and Gettysburg, captured and exchanged, 1863; comdr. gunboat flotilla under Gen. B.F. Butler on James River, took part in attack on Ft. Fisher; chief engr. dock epot, N.Y.C., 1873-75; surveyor Port of N.Y., 878-83, naval officer, 1883-85. Died Lakewood, J., Apr. 15, 1889.

GRAHAM, David, lawyer; b. London, Eng., Feb. , 1808; s. David Graham; studied law under his ather, N.Y.C. Came with family to N.Y.C. when e was youth; admitted to N.Y. bar, 1829; practiced law in partnership with his father; mem. com. hat drafted new charter of N.Y.C., 1832; elected lderman N.Y.C., 1834; apptd. by N.Y. State egislature to commn. on practice and pleadings, 848, drafted much of resultant code of civil proedure; ret. from practice, 1851; went to Europe ue to ill health. Author: A Treatise on the Practice f the Supreme Court of the State of New York, 832; A Treatise on the Law of New Trials in Cases ivil and Criminal, 1834. Died Nice, France, May 7, 1852.

GRAHAM, George Rex, editor, publisher; b. hila., Jan. 18, 1812; m. Elizabeth Fry, 1839. dmitted to Pa. bar, Mar. 27, 1839; asst. editor at. Evening Post, 1839; bought Casket mag. from amuel C. Atkinson, 1839; bought Gentleman's lag., 1840; issued Graham's Mag., 1841; bought hila. North Am., merged it with U.S. Gazette; ent bankrupt, 1853. Died Orange, N.J., July 13, 894; buried Laurel Hill Cemetery, Phila.

GRAHAM, Isabella Marshall, philanthropist; b. anark, Scotland, July 29, 1742; d. John and Janet Hamilton) Marshall; m. Dr. John Graham, 1765, children. Came to Am., 1789; established sch. or young women, N.Y.C., 1789; directress Soc. or Relief Poor Widows with Small Children (earliest rgn. of kind in Am.), 1797; presided over meeting or orgn. of Orphan Asylum Soc., 1806; pres. bd. irs. Magdalen Soc., 1811; active in organ. Soc. for romotion Industry Among Poor, 1814. Died N.Y.C., July 27, 1814.

GRAHAM, James, provincial ofcl.; b. Scotland; . John and Isabella (Auchinlick) G.; m. 2d, Elizaeth Windebank, 1684; 2 sons, 4 daus. Came to N.Y.C., 1678; apptd. alderman N.Y.C. by Gov. dmund Andros, 1680; 1st appointee to office of ecorder N.Y.C., 1683; atty. gen. Province of N.Y.; lk. 1st N.Y. Ct. of Chancery, 1684; speaker 1st en. Assembly of N.Y., 1691-99: mem. N.Y. ov.'s Council. Died Morrisania, N.Y., Jan. 1701.

GRAHAM, James, congressman, lawyer; b. Lincoln County, N.C., Jan. 7, 1793; grad. U. N.C. at hapel Hill, 1814; studied law. Admitted to bar, 1818, began practice of law, Rutherford County; mem. N.C. Ho. of Reps., 1822-24, 28-29; mem. U.S. Ho. of Reps. from N.C., 24th-27th congresses, (as Whig) 29th Congress, 1835-43, 45-47; engaged n agriculture, nr. Rutherfordton, N.C. Died Rutherfordton, Sept. 25, 1851.

GRAHAM, James Duncan, army officer; b. Prince William County, Va., Apr. 4, 1799; s. Dr. William and Mary (Campbell) G.; grad. U.S. Mil. Acad., 1817; m. Charlotte Meade, July 6, 1828; m. 2d, Frances Wickham; 1 son, William M. First asst. on Maj. Stephen H. Long's expdn. to Rocky Mountains, 1819-21; served topog. duty, 1819-38; commd. maj. Topog. Engr. Corps, 1838; astronomer in surveying party that fixed boundary between U.S. and Republic of Tex., 1839; astronomer, head scientific corps in joint demarcation of Me.-Canadian boundary, 1840-43; brevetted lt. col., circa 1847; directed resurvey of Mason-Dixon line, 1848-50; astronomer and head scientific corps that surveyed part of Mexican border, 1850-51; served on Gt. Lakes, 1854-64; promoted lt. col., 1861, col., 1863; supt. engr. of sea-walls in Boston Harbor, 1864-65; Mt. Graham (Ariz.) named after him. Died Dec. 28, 1865.

GRAHAM, James Harper, congressman; b. Bovina, N.Y., Sept. 18, 1812; attended public schs. Supr. Town of Delhi (N.Y.); chmn. bd. suprs. Delaware County (N.Y.); engaged in agriculture; mem. U.S. Ho. of Reps. (Republican) from N.Y., 36th Congress, 1859-61; Rep. presdl. elector, 1868; mem. N.Y. State Assembly, 1871, N.Y. Senate, 1872-73. Died Delhi, June 23, 1881; buried Woodland Cemetery.

GRAHAM, John, colonial ofcl.; b. Scotland, 1718; m. Frances Crooke, 1755, 4 sons. Came to Ga., 1753; mcht., Savannnah, Ga., 1753-65; mem. Ga. Gov.'s Council, 1763-76; planter, 1765-76; opposed sending dels. to Continental Congress, 1775; lt. gov. Colony of Ga., 1776; fled to Eng., 1776, returned, 1779; apptd. supt. Indian affairs for Miss. region with hdqrs. in Charleston, S.C., 1782; moved to Fla. when British evacuated Charleston, 1782; returned to Eng., 1782, became mcht., London, Eng. Died Naples, Italy, Nov. 1795.

GRAHAM, John, diplomat, govt. ofcl.; b. Dumfries, Va., 1774; s. Richard and Jane (Brent) G.; grad. Columbia Coll., 1790; m. Susan Hill. Went to Ky., 1790; mem. Ky. Legislature, 1800; attached to Am. embassy, Madrid, Spain, 1st as sec. of legation, later charge d'affaires, 1801-03; apptd. sec. Territory of Orleans, 1804, investigated activities of Aaron Burr regarding his scheme to seize Western lands; chief clk. U.S. Dept. of State, 1807-17; U.S. sec. of state ad interim, 1817; named minister plenipotentiary to Portugal, 1819. Died Washington, D.C., Aug. 6, 1820.

GRAHAM, John Andrew, lawyer, author; b. Southbury, Conn., June 10, 1764; s. Andrew and Martha (Curtiss) G.; studied law under Edward Himnan, Southbury, 1781-85; m. Rachel Freeman; m. 2d, Margaret Lorimer. Admitted to Conn. bar, 1785, Vt. Supreme Ct. bar, 1790, N.Y. bar, 1805; practiced in Rutland, Vt.; del. from Rutland to Episcopal Conv. of Vt., 1794; moved to Washington, D.C., 1803, later to N.Y.C. Author: A Descriptive Sketch of the Present State of Vermont, 1797; Speeches Delivered at the City-Hall of the City of New York, in the Courts of Oyer and Terminer, Common Pleas and General Sessions of the Place, 1812. Died Aug. 29, 1841.

GRAHAM, John Hugh, congressman; b. Belfast, Ireland, Apr. 1, 1835; brought to U.S., 1836; attended public schs., Bklyn. Recruited Co. A, 5th Regt., Heavy Arty., N.Y. Volunteers, during Civil War, served as capt., 3 years; commd. maj., brevetted lt. col. for services at Harpers Ferry and in Shenandoah Valley (Va.); engaged in hardware bus., Bklyn., after Civil War; mem. U.S. Ho. of Reps. (Democrat) from N.Y., 53d Congress, 1893-95. Died Bklyn., July 11, 1895; buried Greenwood Cemetery.

GRAHAM, Joseph, army officer; b. Chester County, Pa., Oct. 13, 1759; s. James and Mary (McConnell) G.; ed. Queen's Museum, Charlotte, S.C.; m. Isabella Davidson, 1787. Joined Continental Army as enlisted man, 1778, became capt. of a company of mounted inf.; in command reserve during defense of Charlotte, 1780; organizer company of dragoon, maj., 1781; del. to N.C. Conv. that ratified U.S. Constn., 1788; del. to N.C. Conv. that ratified Bill of Rights, 1789; mem. N.C. Senate, 1788-94, N.C. Council of State, 1814-15; an original trustee U. N.C.; started writing series letters and articles for Archibald D. Murphy, 1820, which provide valuable record of Revolutionary times in N.C. Died Lincoln County, N.C., Nov. 12, 1836.

GRAHAM, Sylvester, reformer, author; b. West Suffield, Conn., July 5, 1794; s. John and Ruth G.; m. Miss Earl, 1826. Worked as farm hand, clk. and tchr. during early life; prepared himself for ministry during long illness; preached in Berkshire Valley and Morris County, N.J., 1831; delivered addresses on human physiology, diet and regiment, Phila., N.Y.C., 1830-31, began cross country lecture tour; lectr. on cholera, 1832-33, chastity, 1834; his influence and popularity declined by 1840; Graham flour named for him. Author: The Young Man's Guide to Chastity, 1834; Lectures on the Science of Human Life, 2 vols., 1839. Died Northampton, Mass., Sept. 11, 1851.

GRAHAM, William, congressman; b. at sea, Mar. 16, 1782; settled (with parents) in Harrodsburg, Ky.; attended public schs. Moved to Vallonia, Ind., 1811; engaged in agriculture; mem. Ind. Territorial Ho. of Reps., 1812; del. Ind. Constl. Conv., 1816; mem. Ind. Ho. of Reps., 1816-21, served as speaker; mem. Ind. Senate, 1821-33; mem. U.S. Ho. of Reps. (Whig) from Ind., 25th Congress, 1837-39. Died nr. Vallonia, Aug. 17, 1858; buried White Church Cemetery, Vallonia.

GRAHAM, William Alexander, gov. N.C.; b. Lincoln County, N.C., Sept. 5, 1804; s. Joseph and Isabella (Davidson) G.; grad. with high honors U. N.C., 1824; m. Susannah Sarah Washington, June 8, 1836, 10 children. Admitted to bar, 1826; mem. N.C. Ho. of Commons, 1833-40, twice speaker; mem. U.S. Senate from N.C., Nov. 24, 1840-43; gov. N.C., 1845-49; U.S. sec. of navy, 1850-52; unsuccessful candidate for vice pres. U.S. (on Whig ticket with Gen. Winfield Scott), 1852; mem. N.C. Legislature, 1854, anti-secessionist, but stayed with Confederacy; mem. Confederate Senate, 1864; an original trustee Peabody Fund. Died Saratoga Springs, N.Y., Aug. 11, 1875.

GRANGER, Amos Phelps, congressman, businessman; b. Suffield, Conn., June 3, 1789; attended public schs. Moved to Manlius, N.Y., 1811; pres. Town of Manlius, several years; served as capt. at Sackets Harbor and on Canadian border, during War of 1812; moved to Syracuse, N.Y., 1820, engaged in various business enterprises; trustee City of Syracuse, 1825-30; delivered welcoming address when Gen. Lafayette visited Syracuse, 1825; del. Whig Nat. Conv., Balt., 1852; mem. U.S. Ho. of Reps. (Whig) from N.Y., 34th-35th congresses, 1855-59. Died Syracuse, Aug. 20, 1866; buried Oakwood Cemetery.

GRANGER, Bradley Francis, congressman, lawyer; b. Lowville, N.Y., Mar. 12, 1825; attended public schs.; studied law. Admitted to bar, 1847, began practice of law, Tecumseh, Mich.; moved to Ann Arbor, Mich.; mem. U.S. Ho. of Reps. (Democrat) from N.Y., 37th Congress, 1861-63. Died Ann Arbor, Nov. 4, 1882; buried Forest Hill Cemetery.

GRANGER, Francis, congressman; b. Suffield, Conn., Dec. 1, 1792; s. Gideon and Mindwell (Pease) G.; grad. Yale, 1811; m. Cornelia Ruston Van Rensselaer, 1817. Admitted to N.Y. bar, 1816; mem. N.Y. Assembly, 1826-28, 30-32; del. Anti-Masonic Nat. Conv., Phila., 1830; mem. N.Y. Ho. of Reps. from N.Y., 24th, 26th-27th, 28th congresses, 1835-37, 39-41, Nov. 27, 1841-43; Whig candidate for vice pres. U.S., lost election by 33-16 vote in U.S. Senate, 1836; postmaster gen. U.S., Mar.-Sept. 1841; mem. Washington (D.C.) Peace Conv., 1861. Died Canandaigua, N.Y., Aug. 31, 1868; buried Woodlawn Cemetery, Canandaigua.

GRANGER, Gideon, postmaster gen. U.S.; b. Suffield, Conn., July 19, 1767; s. Gideon and Tryphosa (Kent) G.; grad. Yale, 1787; m. Mindwell Pease, June 14, 1790, 3 children. Mem. Conn. Legislature, 1792-1801; prin. founder Conn. Common Law Sch. of 1795; postmaster-gen. U.S., 1801-14; mem. N.Y. State Senate, 1820-21; ardent supporter of DeWitt Clinton and Erie Canal project. Author: Political Essays. Died Canandaigua, N.Y., Dec. 31, 1822.

GRANGER, Gordon, Union soldier; b. Joy, N.Y., Nov. 6, 1822; s. Gaius and Catherine (Taylor) G.; grad. U.S. Mil. Acad., 1845; m. Maria Letcher, 1869. Soldier in Mexican War; 1st lt., 1852; stationed mostly on frontier before Civil War; capt., 1861, col., 1861; served under Gen Nathaniel Lyon in Battle Wilson's Creek, Aug. 1861; commanded cav. brigade in Miss., 1862, brig. gen., Mar. 26, 1862; maj. gen. Vols., commanding div. in Tenn., Sept. 17, 1862; in command Army of Ky., spring 1863; most famous for aid to Gen. Thomas at Battle Chickamauga; comdr. army aiding Adm. Farragut in capture Ft. Morgan (Ala.), Aug. 1864; col. inf. Regular Army, July 28, 1866; commanded Dist. N.M. Died Santa Fe, N.M., Jan. 10, 1876.

GRANGER, Miles Tobey, congressman, jurist; b. New Marlboro, Mass., Aug. 12, 1817; grad. Wesleyan U., Middletown, Conn., 1842; studied law. Moved to La., 1843; admitted to bar, Wilkinson County, Miss., also Litchfield County, Conn., 1845; practiced law, Canaan, Conn., 1847-67; mem. Conn. Ho. of Reps., 1857, Conn. Senate, 1866-67; judge probate ct., 1849-67; judge Conn. Superior Ct., 1867-76, Conn. Supreme Ct., 1876-87; mem. U.S. Ho. of Reps. (Democrat) from Conn., 50th Congress, 1887-89; state referee, 1893-95. Died North Canaan, Conn., Oct. 21, 1895; buried Lower Cemetery.

GRANT, Abraham Phineas, congressman, lawyer; b. New Lebanon, N.Y., Apr. 5, 1804; grad. Hamilton Coll., Clinton, N.Y.; studied law. Admitted to bar, 1828, began practice of law, Oswego, N.Y.; dist. atty. Oswego County, 1835; mem. U.S. Ho. of Reps. (Democrat) from N.Y., 25th Congress, 1837-39. Died Oswego, Dec. 11, 1871; buried Riverside Cemetery.

GRANT, Asahel, physician, missionary; b. Marshall, N.Y., Aug. 17, 1807; s. William and Rachel (Wedge) G.; studied medicine under Dr. Seth Hastings, Clinton, N.Y.; m. Electa Spafford Loomis, Aug. 23, 1827; m. 2d, Judith Lathrop; 2 children. Practiced medicine, Utica, N.Y., later volunteered for work among Nestorians under auspices of Am. Bd. Commrs. for Fgn. Missions; sailed for dist. of Oroomiah in Western Persia, 1835; established 2 missions at Oroomiah and Ashitha; his work came to end when Turks made war on Nestorians, massacred thousands, 1843; fled to Mosul, Persia, ministered to refugees, until 1844. Author: The Nestorians: or the Lost Tribes: Containing Evidence of their Identity; Account of their Manners, Customs and Ceremonies; Together with Sketches of Travel in Ancient Assyria, Armenia, Media, and Mesopotamia; and Illustrations of Scripture Prophecy, 1841. Died Mosul, Apr. 24, 1844.

GRANT, John Thomas, railroad builder; b. Greene County, Ga., Dec. 13, 1813; s. Daniel and Lucy (Crutchfield) G.; grad. U. Ga., 1833; m. Martha Cobb, 1834, at least 1 son, William. Acquired huge tract of land, Walton County, Ga., 1844, owned largest plantation in Ga. (2000 acres and 100 slaves); executed large railroad bldg. contracts in Ga., Ala., Tenn., Miss., Tex.; mem. Ga. Senate, 1856; served with rank of col. on staff Gen. Howell Cobb during Civil War; moved to Atlanta (Ga.) after Civil War, owned large tracts of real estate, furthered railroad constrn. Died Atlanta, Jan. 18, 1887.

GRANT, Ulysses Simpson, 18th Pres. U.S.; b. Point Pleasant, O., Apr. 27, 1822; s. Jesse Root and Hannah (Simpson) G.; grad. U.S. Mil. Acad., 1843; m. Julia T. Dent, Aug. 22, 1848, 4 children including Frederick Dent, Jesse. Commd. lt. 4th Inf., U.S. Army, 1843; served under Gen. Zachary

Taylor in Mexico, 1845-47; joined Gen. Winfield Scott's army 1847, active in all battles from Buena Vista to Mexico City; promoted 1st lt., brevetted capt., 1848; stationed in Miss., 1848-52; transferred to Ft. Vancouver, Ore., 1852; promoted capt., Humboldt Bay, Cal., 1853; resigned commn., 1854; unsuccessful as farmer, real estate salesman, clk. in brother's leather bus., 1854-61; commd. col. 21st Ill. Volunteers, 1861, promoted brig. gen., 1861, hdqrs. at Cairo, Ill.; 1st action was indecisive battle, Belmount, Mo., 1861; captured Ft. Henry and Ft. Donelson in Tenn. (1st major Union victory), 1862; promoted maj. gen. U.S. Volunteers; led U.S. Army Battle of Shiloh, 1862, saved from defeat by reinforcements headed by Gen. D.C. Buell; captured Vicksburg (Miss.) by siege, 1863 (gave U.S. Army complete control of Mississippi River, divided Confederacy); given supreme command U.S. Army in West, 1863; defeated Confederate Army under Gen. Braxton Bragg at Battle of Chattanooga (Tenn.), 1863; promoted comdr. in chief U.S. Army with rank lt. gen., 1864; directed Army of the Potomac in Wilderness Campaign; adopted policy of attrition, although suffering great losses at battles of Spotsylvania and Cold Harbor finally defeated Gen. Robert E. Lee by sheer force of numbers; accepted Lee's surrender at Appomattox Courthouse, Va., Apr. 9, 1865; promoted full gen. (1st since George Washington to hold rank), 1866; apptd. U.S. sec. of war by Pres. Andrew Johnson (to replace E.M. Stanton), 1867, served for 5 months, turned office back to Stanton when U.S. Senate refused to approve Stanton's removal; elected Pres. U.S. (Republican), 1868, reelected, 1872, his adminstrn. characterized by corruption, scandal, gave polit. appointments to friends and relatives without regard for ability or merit; signed bill providing for specie-payment legal tender notes issued during Civil War, 1869, other bills included inflation bill of 1874 which favored indsl., comml. interests; attempted to annex Dominican Republic, 1869; backed punitive Reconstrn. measures; apparently unaware of illegal conduct of some subordinates; when his pvt. sec Orville Babcock and Sec. of War William E. Belknap were implicated in graft scandals (1875) allowed them to resign before they could be impeached; made world tour, 1877-79; candidate for Rep. nomination for Pres., 1880, defeated by James Garfield; involved in fraudulent unsuccessful banking bus., N.Y.C., 1884; began writing his memoirs, 1884, published posthumously as Personal Memoirs, 1885. Died of cancer of the throat, Mt. McGregor, N.Y., July 23, 1885; buried Grant's Tomb, Riverside Dr., N.Y.C.

GRANTLAND, Seaton, congressman; b. New Kent County, Va., June 8, 1782; studied law. Admitted to bar, began practice of law, Milledgeville, Ga.; mem. U.S. Ho. of Reps. (Unionist) from Ga., 24th-25th congresses, 1835-39; Whig presdl. elector, 1840. Died "Woodville," nr. Milledgeville, Oct. 18, 1864; buried Milledgeville Cemetery.

GRASSE, Francois Joseph Paul de, see de Grasse, Francois Joseph Paul.

GRATIOT, Charles, fur trader; b. Lausanne, Switzerland, 1752; s. David and Marie (Bernard) G.; m. Victoire Chouteau, June 25, 1781; at least 1 son Charles. Came to Montreal, Que., Can., 1769, learned fur trading; joined firm David McCrae and Co., 1777; opened store, Chokia, Ill., 1777; moved to St. Louis, 1781; fur trader, operated distillery, tannery and salt works; transfer of Upper La. made at his house, 1804; 1st presiding justice Ct. of Quarter Sessions of St. Louis; elected trustee when St. Louis was incoporated as town, 1809; close asso. of George Rogers Clark. Died Apr. 20, 1817.

GRATZ, Bernard, mcht.; b. Langensdorf, Upper Silesia, 1738; s. Soloman Gratz; m. Richea Myers, Dec. 10, 1760, 2 children including Rachel. Came to Phila., 1754; employed by David Franks, fur trader, 1754-58; formed partnership with Benjamin M. Clava, 1758, conducted business by himself, 1759; partner firm B. & M. Gratz (with his brother Michael); signed non-importation resolutions, protest by mchts. of Phila. against Stamp Act, 1765; 1st recorded pres. Mickveh Israel Congregation; laid cornerstone 1st synagogue in Phila., 1782; throughout his life fought for rights of Jews in Pa. Died Balt., Apr. 20, 1801.

GRATZ, Michael, mcht.; b. Langensdorf, Upper Silesia,, 1740; s. Soloman Gratz; m. Miriam Simon, June 20, 1769, 12 children including Rebecca. Emigrated to London, Eng., apprentice in counting-house of his cousin Soloman Henry, entered firm, 1756; came to Phila., 1758, employed by David Franks; later entered partnership (with his brother Bernard), firm B. & M. Gratz firm secured great tracts of land in Va., Western Pa., Ohio, Ind., Ill. (through influence of Michael's father-in-law); also operated steamboat line from Pitts.; moved to Va. during Am. Revolution, continued bus. until 1798. Died Sept. 8, 1811; buried Old Cemetery on Spruce St., Phila.

GRATZ, Rebecca, philanthropist; b. Phila., Mar 4, 1781; d. Michael and Miriam (Simon) Gratz. Elected sec. Female Assn. for Relief of Women and Children in Reduced Circumstances, 1801, served many years; founder Hebrew Sunday Sch Soc. (1st instn. of its kind in U.S.), 1838, pres., 1838-64; a founder Jewish Foster Home, Phila., 1850; she is probably the original of character Rebecca in Ivanhoe (Sir Walter Scott). Died Aug. 29, 1869.

GRAUPNER, Johann Christian Gottlieb, musician; b. Verden, Prussia, Oct. 6, 1767; s. Johann Georg and Anna Maria (Schoenhagen) G.; m. Catherine Comeford Hillier, Apr. 6, 1796. Went to London, Eng., 1788; 1st oboist with London Orch. under direction of Franz Joseph Haydn, 1791-92; went to Charleston, S.C., 1795, to Boston, 1796; organizer, 1st (and only) pres. Philharmonic Soc. in Boston (1st symphony orch. in Am.), 1810; an organizer Handel and Haydn Soc. (gave 1st oratorio performance in U.S.) 1815. Author: Rudiments of the Art of Playing on the Pianoforte, 1825. Died Apr. 16, 1836.

GRAVELY, Joseph Jackson, congressman; b. nr. Leatherwood, Va., Sept. 25, 1828; attended public schs.; studied law. Engaged in agriculture, also taught schs.; admitted to bar, practiced law; mem. State Ho. of Reps., 1853-54; moved to Mo., 1854; del. Mo. Constl. Conv., 1860; mem. Mo. Senate, 1862, 64; served as col. 8th Regt., Mo. Volunteer Cavalry, U.S. Army, during Civil War; mem. U.S. Ho. of Reps. (Republican) from Mo., 40th Congress, 1867-69; lt. gov. Mo., 1871-72 Died Stockton, Mo., Apr. 28, 1872; buried Lindley Prairie Cemetery, nr. Bear Creek, Mo.

GRAVES, James Robinson, clergyman, publisher; b. Chester, Vt., Apr. 10, 1820; s. Zuinglius Calvin and Lois (Schnell) G.; m. Florence Spencer, 1845; m. 2d, dau. of Dr. George Snider; m. 3d, dau. of Lou Snider. Prin., Kingsville Acad., O., circa 1838-39; in charge of Clear Creek Acad., Jassamine County, Ky., also studied for ministry, 1840-44; ordained to ministry Baptist Ch., 1844; became head of classical and math. acad., Nashville, Tenn., 1844; became editor Tenn. Baptist (weekly), 1846; established So. Publishing House, 1848 (suspended during Civil War); established So. Bapt. Publ. Soc., after Civil War; participated in many doctrinal debates, most important against Rev. Jacob Dietzhe (Methodist). Author: Great Iron Wheel or Republican Backwards and Christianity Reversed, 1855; The Work of Christ in the Convenant of Redemption; Developed in Seven Dispensations, 1883. Died June 26, 1893.

GRAVES, William Jordan, congressman; b. New Castle, Ky.,, 1805; studied law. Admitted to bar, practiced law; mem. Ky. Ho. of Reps., 1834, 43; mem. U.S. Ho. of Reps. (Whig) from Ky., 24th-26th congresses, 1835-41; killed Jonathan Cilley in duel on Marlboro Rd., Md., 1838; Whig presdl. elector, 1844. Died Louisville, Ky., Sept. 27, 1848; buried pvt. burial grounds, Henry County, Ky.

GRAVES, Zuinglius Calvin, coll. pres.; b. Chester, Vt., Apr. 15, 1816; s. Zuinglius C. and Lois (Schnell) G.; m. Adelia C. Spencer, July 1841, at least 1 son, James. Licensed to preach; pastor Ludlow Baptist Ch., Chester; taught in dist. sch., 4 years; conducted acad., Ashtabula, O.; moved to Winchester, Tenn., 1850; 1st pres. Mary Sharpe Coll. (for women), admitted at least 300 women per year by 1861, coll. closed for last 2 years of Civil War, reopened shortly after war, pres. until 1891; pres. Soule Coll., Murfreesboro, Tenn., 1891-93; tried to reopen Mary Sharpe Coll., 1893-96, forced to close due to financial difficulties. Died May 18, 1902.

GRAVIER, Charles (comte de Vergennes), diplomat; b. France, 1717. French minister to Treves, 1750; French ambassador to Constantinople, 1755; minister to Sweden, 1771-74; encouraged anti-English revolt which established Gustavus III as absolute monarch, 1772; French fgn. minister, 1774-87, signed Franco-Am. Alliance that brought France into war against Eng., Feb. 1778; a negotiator Peace of Teschen, 1779; chief French rep. negotiating Treaty of Paris, 1783; signed trade agreement with Eng., which in effect established free trade, 1786. Died 1787.

GRAVIER, Jacques, missionary; b. Moulins, France, May 17, 1651; performed his novitiate, Paris, France, 1670-72. Designated for missionary work in Canada, 1685, worked at mission of Sillery, Can., 1686; stationed at St. Ignace on Straits of Mackinac, 1687-88; sent to aid Father Allouez in Ill., became vicar gen. of Ill. missions after Father Allouez's death (1689), with hdqrs. among Kaskaskia and Peoria tribes on Illinios River; baptized over 200 Indians during 9 months of 1693; served 3 years at Superior of Western missions, then returned to Ill. mission, 1700; accompanied Indians who intended to set up new colony at Biloxi; upon return to mission at Lake Peoria, found Indians hostile to him; author of an Illinois Indian lang. grammar (now in Harvard library). Died as result of severe wound suffered when he was attacked by Indians of his mission, Apr. 23, 1708.

GRAY, Asa, botanist; b. Paris, N.Y., Nov. 8, 1810; s. Moses and Roxana (Howard) G.; M.D. Fairfield Med. Sch., Jan. 25, 1831; hon. degree from Oxford and Cambridge (Eng.), Aberdeen (Scotland) univs.; A.M. (hon.), Harvard, 1844; LL.D., Hamilton Coll., 1860; m. Jane Lathrop Loring, May 4, 1848. Mem. U.S. exploring expdn under command of Capt. Charles Wilkes, 1834-37; prof. botany U. Mich., 1837; Fisher prof natural history at Harvard, 1842-73, 79, organized dept. botany; recognized authority in area of plant geography; wrote famous study of Japanese botany and its relationship to that of N.Am.; described N. American plants in hundreds of publs. a founder Nat. Acad. Arts and Scis.; pres. A.A.A.S., 1863-73; regent Smithsonian Inst., 1874-88; mem. Hall of Fame, Author: North American Gramineae and Cyperaceae, 1835; Elements of Botany, 1836; First Lessons in Botany and Vegetable Physiology, 1857, revised edit., 68; How Plants Grow, 1858; Field, Forest and Garden Botany 1868, 70; How Plants Behave, 1872; Elements of Botany, 1887; Botanical Textbook, 1842, Natural Science and Religion, 1880. Died Cambridge Mass., Jan. 30, 1888; buried Mt. Auburn Cemetery, Cambridge.

GRAY, David, journalist; b. Edinburgh, Scotland Nov. 8, 1836; m. Martha Terry Gutherie, 1869. Came with family to Am., 1848; reporter Courier, Boston 1860-68, wrote articles while touring Eng., Germany, Sweden, Russia, Switzerland, 1865-68, editor 1868-82, editorially supported Samuel J. Tilden in campaign of 1876; visited Europe, 1882-84; sec. Niagara Park Commn., 1884-88. Died Binghamton N.Y., Mar. 18, 1888.

GRAY, Edwin, congressman; b. Southampton County, Va., July 18, 1743; ed. Coll. William and Mary. Mem. Va. Ho. of Burgesses, 1769-75; mem Va. convs., 1774, 75, 56; mem. Va. Ho. of Dels. 1776, 79, 87-88, 91; mem. U.S. Ho. of Reps. from Va., 6th-12th congresses, 1799-1813. Died Nansemond County, Va.

GRAY, Francis Calley, state legislator, philanthropist; b. Salem, Mass., Sept. 19, 1790; s. William and Elizabeth (Chipman) G.; grad. Harvard 1809. Sec. to U.S. legation at St. Petersburg Russia, also pvt. sec. to John Quincy Adams, 1809 admitted to Mass. bar, 1814; mem. Mass. Senate 1825, 26, 28, 29, 31, 43; elected fellow of Harvard, 1826; pres. Boston Athenaeum; bequeathed to Harvard 3,000 rare engravings, $50,000 for a mus of comparative zoology, $25,000 of Harvard library; Gray's Hall, Harvard, named in his honor. Author: Mass. Body of Liberties, 1841; Prison Discipline, 1847. Died Boston, Dec. 29, 1856.

GRAY, George Zabriskie, clergyman; b. N.Y.C. July 14, 1838; s. John A. C. and Susan M (Zabriskie) G.; grad. U. N.Y., 1858; grad. theol sch., Phila., 1862; m. Kate Forrest, 1862. Ordained priest Episcopal Ch., 1863; rector St. Paul's Ch., Kinderhook, N.Y., 1863-65, Trinity Ch., Bergen Point, N.J., 1865-76; dean Episcopal Theol. Sch. Cambridge, Mass., 1876-82; warden Racine (Wis.) Coll., 1882-89. Author: The Spiritual Doctrine of Recognition in the World to Come, 1875; Husband and Wife; or The Theory of Marriage and its Consequences, 1885. Died Sharon Springs, N.Y., Aug. 4, 1889.

GRAY, Henry Peteers, painter; b. N.Y.C., June 23, 1819; s. George W. Gray; m. Miss Clark, 1843. Exhibited at N.A.D., 1839, mem. council, 1842, v.p., 1861, pres., 1869; studied, toured in Europe, 1840-42; paintings include: The Flower of Fiesole, Venus and Paris, Pride of the Village (exhibited at Paris Expn., 1867), The Origin of Our Flag, Cupid Begging His Arrows, Proserpine and Bacchus, Teaching A Child to Pray, Wages of War, Hagar and the Angel, Cleopatra, St. Christopher, Charity, Genevieve, Portia and Bassanio, The Model from Cadore, The Immortality of the Soul, Twilight Musings, Greek Lovers, Normandy Girl, Apple of Discord. Died N.Y.C., Nov. 12. 1877.

GRAY, Hiram, congressman, jurist; b. Salem, N.Y., July 10, 1801; attended Salem Acad.; grad. Union Coll., 1821; studied law. Admitted to bar, 1823, practiced law, Elmira, N.Y., 1825-28; mem. U.S. Ho. of Reps. (Democrat) from N.Y., 25th Congress, 1837-39; apptd. circuit judge and vice chancellor 6th Jud. Dist. N.Y., 1846; justice N.Y. Supreme Ct., 1847-60; commr. of appeals, 1870-75. Died Elmira, May 6, 1890; buried Woodlawn Cemetery.

GRAY, Isaac Pusey, gov. Ind., diplomat; b Chester County, Pa., Oct. 18, 1828; s. John and Hannah (Worthington) G.; m. Eliza Jaqua, 1850. Admitted to Ind. bar before the Civil War; served as officer in Civil War, 1862-63; col. in "minute men" emergency in Ind., 1863; mem. Ind. Senate, 1868-72; largely responsible for Ind. ratification of 15th Amendment to U.S. Constn. (Ind. was ast state to vote on it and her ratification was ieeded); lt. gov. Ind., 1876-80; filled out term is gov. Ind., Nov. 1880-Jan. 1881; gov. Ind., 1885-39; appted. U.S. minister to Mexico, 1893. Died Mexico City, Mexico, Feb. 14, 1895.

GRAY, John Cowper, congressman; b. Southampton County, Va., 1783. Mem. Va. Ho. of Dels., 1804-06, 21-23; mem. U.S. Ho. of Reps. (filled vacancy) from Va., 16th Congress, Aug. 28, 1820-21. Died May 18, 1823.

GRAY, John Purdue, physician, alienist; b. Center County, Pa., Aug. 6, 1825; s. Peter B. and Elizabeth (Purdue) G.; A.M., Dickinson Coll., 1846; M.D., U. Pa., 1849; LL.D., Hamilton Coll., 1874; m. Mary B. Wetmore, Sept. 6, 1854. Resident physician Blockley Hosp., Phila., 1849; 1st asst., acting med. supt. N.Y. State Lunatic Asylum, Utica, 1853; med. supt. Mich. State Lunatic Asylum, 1853; full editor Am. Jour. of Insanity, 1854; prof. psychol. medicine and med. jurisprudence Bellevue Hosp. Med. Coll., 1874-82, Albany Med. Coll., 1876-82; pres. Assn. Med. Supts. of Am. Instn. for the Insane; revolutionized asylum construction, introduced steam heat and ventilation; abolished as far as possible mechanical restraint and solitary feeding for patients. Died Utica, Nov. 29, 1886.

GRAY, Joseph W., journalist; b. Bridport, Vt., Aug. 5, 1813; s. Urel and Betsey (Case) G.; m. Catherine Foster. 2 sons, 1 dau. Tchr., Cleve. 1836-40; started law practice, 1840; bought newspaper Plain Dealer, Cleve., 1840, owner, editor, 1840-62; pioneered illustrated journalism, especially use of cartoons; postmaster Cleve., 1853-58. Died May 26, 1862.

GRAY, Robert, navigator, fur-trader; b. Teverton, R.I., May 10, 1755; s. Edward Gray; m. Martha Atkins, Feb. 3, 1794, 4 sons, 1 dau. Took part in Revolutionary War on the sea; made a voyage around the world in command of sloop Washington, transferred and completed voyage in Columbia, 1787-90; made 2d trip around world in the Columbia (1st vessel to enter Columbia River), 1790-93; discovered Gray's Harbor (named for him) and Columbia River (named after his own vessel), 1792; his discovery gave U.S. a basis for later Ore. claims. Died Charleston, S.C., 1806.

GRAY, William, mcht., state ofcl.; b. Lynn, Mass., July 8, 1750; s. Abraham and Lydia (Calley) G.; m. Elizabeth Chipman, Mar. 29, 1782, 10 children. Served in Revolutionary War; one of 1st N.E. mchts. to enter trade with Russia, India, China, became one of leading mchts., Salem, Mass., annually employed about 300 seamen; del. to Mass. Conv. which ratified U.S. Constn., 1788; mem. Mass. Senate, 1807-09; supported embargo policies of Jefferson and Madison (unlike other Salem mchts.); lt. gov. Mass., 1810-12; pres. Boston br. Bank of U.S., 1811-16. Died Boston, Nov. 3, 1825.

GRAY, William H., missionary; studied medicine briefly, 1835; m. Mary Dix, Feb. 23, 1838. Protestant missionary, went west in party with Marcus Whitman and Henry Spalding, 1838, but returned east in same year, unsuccessfully seeking mission of his own; worked on Spalding's mission in Ida., then Whitman's mission, Waiilatpu, Ore, removed in mission's reorgn., 1842. Author: History of Oregon, 1870.

GRAYDON, Alexander, author; b. Bristol, Pa., Apr. 10, 1752; s. Alexander and Rachel (Marks) G.; m. Miss Wood, 1778; m. 2d, Theodosia Pettit Dec. 16, 1799. Forced to study law by his father, more interested in poetry, metaphysics and women; joined volunteers in Phila. at outbreak of Am. Revolution, shocked by punishment of Loyalists; commd. capt., 1776, saw action under Gen. Philip Schuyler at Lake George, 1776, covered George Washington's retreat from L.I. to N.Y.; taken prisoner at Battle of Harlem Heights, paroled and returned to Phila., 1777; moved to Harrisburg, Pa., 1785; mem. Pa. Conv. to ratify U.S. Constn., 1789; contributed many articles to John Fenno's Gazette. Author: Memoirs of a Life, Chiefly Passed in Pennsylvania within the Last Sixty Years; with Occasional Remarks upon the General Occurrences, Character, and Spirit of the Eventful Period (one of most valuable hist. sources of period), 1811. Died May 2, 1818.

GRAYDON, William, lawyer; b. Bristol, Bucks County, Pa., Sept. 4, 1759; son of Col. Alexander Graydon. Admitted to Pa. bar, 1786; practiced law, Harrisburg, Pa., 1786-1840; became 1st notary public of Harrisburg, 1791. Author: Digest of the Laws of the United States, 1803; Justice and Constable's Assistant, 1820; Forms of Conveyancing, and of Practice in the Various Courts and Public Offices. Died Harrisburg, Oct. 13, 1840.

GRAYSON, William, army officer, Continental congressman, senator; b. Prince William County, Va., 1736; s. Benjamin and Susanah (Monroe) G.; attended Coll. of Phila. (now U. Pa.); m. Eleanor Smallwood. Commd. lt. col., a.d.c. to George Washington, 1776; promoted col., in command of a Va. Regt., 1777; took part in battles of L.I., White Plains, and Brandywine; testified at trial of Maj. Gen. Charles Lee regarding confusion prior to Battle of Monmouth; ret. from Army, 1779; commr. Bd. of War, 1780-81; mem. Va. Ho. of Dels., 1784-85, 88; mem. Continental Congress, 1785-87; mem. U.S. Senate from Va., 1789; strong supporter of So. interests; influential in procuring passage Ordinance of 1787. Died Dumfries, Va., Mar. 12, 1790.

GRAYSON, William John, congressman; b. Beaufort, S.C., Nov. 2, 1788; s. William Grayson; grad. S.C. Coll. at Columbia, 1809; studied law. Admitted to bar, 1822, began practice of law, Beaufort; mem. S.C. Ho. of Reps., 1822-26; mem. S.C. Senate, 1826-31; elected commr. in equity for Beaufort Dist., 1831; mem. U.S. Ho. of Reps. (Whig) from S.C., 23d-24th congresses, 1833-37; collector of customs at Charleston, S.C., 1841-53; retired to his plantation; frequent contbr. to So. Quarterly Rev. Died Newberry, S.C., Oct. 4, 1863; buried Magnolia Cemetery, Charleston.

GREATHOUSE, Clarence Ridgeby, lawyer, diplomat; b. Ky., circa 1845; s. Dr. Ridgeby Greathouse. Practiced law, San Francisco, 1870; gen. mgr. San Francisco Examiner, 1883-86; apptd. U.S. consul gen. at Kanagawa (now Yokohama), Japan, 1886-90; engaged as legal adviser to Korean Govt., 1890, v.p. home office in charge of matters pertaining to legal affairs, 1891-98; most notable work was in connection with trial of those Koreans implicated in murder of queen of Korea by Japanese and Korean conspirators, 1895, due to his influence trials were free from many faults which were then characteristic of Korean courts; confidential adviser to king of Korea, circa 1898-99. Died Seoul, Korea, Oct. 21, 1899.

GREATON, John, army officer; b. Roxbury, Mass., Mar. 10, 1741; s. John and Catherine (Lenton) G.; m. Sara Humphreys, 1760, several children including Ann, Richard. A trader; joined Sons of Liberty, 1774; commd. lt. Mass. Militia, 1774, col., 1775, served in 24th Mass. Regt., 36th Mass. Regt., 3d Mass. Regt., Continental Army; commd. col. 24th Inf., Continental Army, 1776, brig. gen., 1783; took part in expdn. to Can. Died Roxbury, Dec. 16, 1783.

GREATON, Joseph, clergyman; b. London, Eng., Feb. 12, 1679. Ordained Jesuit priest, 1719; emigrated secretly to Md. where he lived in Jesuit-owned manor in Anne Arundel County, 1720, celebrated mass in pvt. chapels and homes; moved to Phila., 1729, purchased through John Dixon a lot on Walnut St. on which he built St. Joseph's Ch., 1st Catholic pastor in Pa.; parish grew to such numbers that he was given an assistant (Henry Neale, S.J.); Cath. congregation suspected of French sympathies during King George's War but Quakers protected Cath. chapel from Presbyn. mob, 1750. Died Bohemia, Md., Aug. 19, 1753.

GREATOREX, Eliza Pratt, artist; b. Manor Hamilton, Ireland, Dec. 25, 1820; m. Henry W. Greatorex, 1849; 2 daus., Kathleen Honora, Elizabeth Eleanor. Came to N.Y.C., 1840; became profl. artist, 1858; best known for views of N.Y.C.; elected asso. N.A.D., 1869; travelled in Europe, died Paris, France, Feb. 9, 1897.

GREBLE, John T., army officer; b. Phila., Jan. 19, 1834; s. Edwin and Susan Greble; grad. U.S. Mil. Acad., 1854; m. Sarah B. French, Aug. 4, 1858, 2 children. Commd. 2d lt. arty. U.S. Army, 1854, stationed Newport Barracks, Fla., 1854-56, explored lakes of area, served against Seminole Indians; asst. prof. ethics and English, U.S. Mil. Acad., 1856-60; promoted 1st lt., 1859; joined regt. at Fortress Monroe, Va., 1860; transferred to construct batteries and instruct volunteers in arty., Newport News, Va., 1861; ordered by Gen. Benjamin F. Butler to lead attack against Big Bethel, Va., 1861. Killed while covering retreat of his men from Big Bethel, June 9, 1861.

GREELEY, Horace, editor; b. Amherst, N.H., Feb. 3, 1811; s. Zaccheus and Mary (Woodburn) G.; m. Mary Young Cheney, July 5, 1836, 7 children including Gabriella, Ida. Journeyman printer, N.Y.C., 1831-33; became partner with Francis Story in job-printing bus., 1833, later in partnership with Jonas Winchester; founder The New Yorker, 1834, publisher, 1834-41; contbr. to Daily Whig; editor The Jeffersonian, 1838, Log Cabin, 1840 (both Whig campaign papers); editor and publisher weekly N.Y. Tribune (merger Log Cabin and New Yorker 1841), 1841-72; credited with establishing 1st inexpensive daily which concentrated on intelligent reporting rather than sensationalism; supported cooperative shops, labor unions, protective tariffs, abolition; advocated Charles Fourier's plans for establishing small socialist agrl. communities, invested in communities at Red Bank, N.J., Greeley, Colo.; urged free land for settlers; popularized phrase "Go West, young man, go west!"; opposed Mexican War; mem. U.S. Ho. of Reps. (Whig, filled vacancy) from N.Y., 30th Congress, Dec. 4, 1848-49; 1st pres. N.Y. Printers Union, 1850; toured Europe, 1851; opposed Kan.-Neb. Act, Fugitive Slave Law; provided arms for Free-Soilers in Kan.; commr. Paris Expdn., 1855; joined Republican Party, 1856; attacked Dred Scott decision, also Know-Nothingism, 1857; supported Lincoln at Rep. Nat. Conv., 1860; strong supporter of Union during Civil War, felt that secession was act of small minority which had gained power in South; favored gen. amnesty after war, signed bail bond to release Jefferson Davis from prison; del. N.Y. State Constl. Conv., 1867; Liberal Rep. candidate for Pres. U.S. (endorsed by Democrats), 1872, soundly defeated by U.S. Grant; his wife's death (Oct. 30, 1872), plus election defeat, combined to drive him insane. Author: Hints Toward Reforms, 1850; History of the Struggle for Slavery Extension or Restriction in the United States, 1850; Glances at Europe, 1851; Recollections of a Busy Life (autobiography), 1868; An Overland Journey from New York to San Francisco in Summer of 1859, pub. 1860; What I Know of Farming, 1871. Died Pleasantville, N.Y., Nov. 29, 1872.

GREELY, Edward, mcht., author; b. Sandwich, Kent, Eng., Dec. 1, 1835. Mem. Brit. naval expdn. to Japan, 1855-56; commd. capt., served in China, then as attaché Brit. legation in Japan, 1860-68; came to Am., 1868, became mcht., N.Y.C. Author: (plays) Vendome, Mirah, The Third Estate; Blue Jackets (1871); The Golden Lotus (1883). Died N.Y.C., Oct. 1, 1888.

GREEN, Alexander Little Page, clergyman; b. Sevier County, Tenn., June 26, 1806; s. George and Judith (Sillmon) G.; m. Mary Ann Elliston, Oct. 19, 1831. Admitted to Tenn. Conf. of Methodist Ch. on trial, 1824, ordained elder, 1827; moved to Nashville, Tenn., 1829; del. quadrennial Gen. Conf. of Meths., 1832-44; spent most of his time in Ala. during Civil War; mem. coms. to amend Discipline, to supervise ecclestiastical books and periodicals at Gen. Conf., Meth. Ch., 1866; proposed and partly carried through series of reforms in church adminstrn.; chiefly interested in publication house he had brought to Nashville in latter part of his life. Died July 15, 1874.

GREEN, Asa, physician, author; b. Ashby, Mass., Feb. 11, 1789; s. Oliver and Dorothy (Hildreth) G.; grad. Williams Coll., 1813; M.D., Brown U., 1822, Berkshire Med. Instn., 1827. Practiced medicine, Lunenberg, Townsend, North Adams, Mass.; publisher Berkshire American, Pittsfield, Mass., Socialist, North Adams, 1828; went to N.Y. C. to begin career as author (apparently after these newspapers failed), wrote novels which were chiefly autobiographical, considered representative of early Am. prose fiction. Author: The Life and Adventures of Dr. Dodimus Duckworth, A.N.Q., 1833; A Yankee among the Nullifiers, 1833; A Glance at New York, 1837. Died circa 1837.

GREEN, Ashbel, clergyman, univ. pres.; b. Hanover, N.J., July 6, 1762; s. Jacob and Elizabeth (Pierson) G.; grad. Coll. of N.J. (now Princeton), 1782; LL.D. (hon.), U. N.C., 1812; m. Elizabeth Stockton, 1785; m. 2d, Christiana Anderson, 1809; m. 3d, Mary McCulloh, 1815; 1 son, Jacob. Participated in Revolutionary War; prof. mathematics and natural philosophy Coll. of N.J., 1785-87, pres., 1812-22 (1st coll. pres. to introduce study of Bible into the curriculum), trustee, 1790-1848, founder Princeton Theol. Sem., pres. bd. dirs., 1812-48, licensed to preach, 1786; asst. pastor 2d Presbyn. Ch., Phila., 1787-93, pastor, 1793-1812; mem. Gen. Assembly Presbyn. Ch., 1790-1839; chaplain U.S. Congress, 1792-1800; editor Christian Advocate, 1822-34. Author: Sermons on the Assembly Catechism, 1818; Presbyterian Missions, 1820; Discourse Delivered in the College of New Jersey, 1822. Died Phila., May 19, 1848.

GREEN, Bartholomew, printer, journalist; b. Cambridge, Mass., Oct. 12, 1666; s. Samuel and Sarah (Clark) G.; m. Mary Green, 1690; m. 2d, Jane Toppen, June 16, 1710; 11 children. Assisted his half-brother Samuel in managing Samuel Sewall's Press, Boston, 1682-84; operated another press, 1684-90; worked with his father in Cambridge, 1690-92; returned to Boston, 1692, chief printer of Mass. Colony for 40 years; printed Boston News-Letter, 1704-07, 11-32; refused to become involved in quarrels of colonists with England, 1723-27; deacon South Ch., Boston, 1719. Died Dec. 28, 1732.

GREEN, Beriah, reformer; b. Preston, Conn., Mar. 24, 1795; s. Beriah and Elizabeth (Smith) G.; grad. (valedictorian) Middlebury Coll., 1819; m. Marcia Deming, Jan. 21, 1821; m. 2d, Daraxa Foote, Aug. 30, 1826; 9 children. Ordained minister Congregational Ch., 1823; prof. sacred lit., theol. dept. Western Res. Coll., 1830; pres. Am. Anti-Slavery Soc., 1833; pres. Oneida Inst., Whitestown, N.Y., 1833. Author: History of the Quakers; Sermons and Discourses with a Few Essays and Addresses. Died Whitestown, May 4, 1874.

GREEN, Byram, congressman; b. East Windsor, Mass., Apr. 15, 1786; grad. Williams Coll., Williamstown, Mass., 1808; studied law. Prof., coll. at Beaufort, S.C., 1810; admitted to bar, practiced law; judge Wayne County Circuit Ct., 1814; served in Battle of Sodus Point during War of 1812; mem. N.Y. State Assembly, 1816-22, N.Y. Senate, 1823-24; mem. U.S. Ho. of Reps. from N.Y., 28th Congress, 1843-45. Died Sodus, N.Y., Oct. 18, 1865; buried Rural Cemetery.

GREEN, Duff, businessman; b. Woodford County, Ky., Aug. 15, 1791; s. William and Lucy (Marshall) G.; m. Lucretia Edwards, Nov. 26, 1813; 11 children including Benjamin Edwards. Served from pvt. to capt. in War of 1812; engaged in land speculation and merc. ventures in Mo. after war; established 1st stage-coach line West of Mississippi River; admitted to Mo. bar; brig. gen. 1st Mo. brigade; mem. Mo. Constl. Conv.; mem. Mo. Legislature from Howard County, 1823; became owner St. Louis Enquirer, 1823, editorially supported Jackson in nat. election of 1824; became owner-editor U.S. Telegraph, Washington, D.C., 1825; mem. of Jackson's kitchen cabinet, 1828-32; printer to Congress, 1827-33; broke with Jackson, backed Clay for presidency, 1832, Harrison, 1836; founded Balt. Pilot, 1840; unofcl. rep. of U.S. in Eng. and France, 1840-44; established the Republic, N.Y., 1844; apptd. consul at Galveston, Tex. by Tyler; unsuccessfully attempted to maneuver U.S. Govt. into acquiring area of Tex., N.M. and Cal., circa 1844; founded the Reformer, 1857; built portion of East Tenn. & Ga. R.R.; organized Sabine & Rio Grande R.R., Selma, Rome & Dalton R.R., others; organized numerous business firms including Union Potomac Co., Va., 1836, The Union Co., Md., 1839, Am. Land Co., Md., 1840, Jonesboro Iron Works (Tenn.), 1861, The Planters Ins. Trust & Loan Co., Ga., 1861; The Md. Indsl. Agy., 1867, Miss. Am. Indsl. Agy., 1867; operated iron mfg. plants for Confederacy during Civil War, acted as adviser on fiscal and fgn. policy to Confederate leaders; founded Dalton, Va.; aided in indsl. recovery of South after Civil War. Author: Facts and Suggestions on the Subjects of Currency and Direct Trade, 1861; The Treasury Notes of the Confederate Government, 1861; Facts and Suggestions, Biographical, Historical, Financial and Political, 1866; How To Pay off the National Debt, Regulate the Value of Money and Maintain Stability in the Values of Property and Labor, 1872. Died Dalton, June 10, 1875.

GREEN, Frances Harriet Whipple, reformer, author; b. Smithfield, R.I., Sept. 1805; m. Charles C. Green, July 1, 1842 (div. 1847); m. 2d, William C. McDougall, 1861. Had gained some notice with her poetic contbns. to R.I. papers, 1830; editor Original (book of local sketches), 1830; devoted herself to various causes, including temperance, labor, abolition, 1830-78; editor, publisher Wampanoag and Operatives Jour., Fall River, R.I., 1842-43; became interested in spiritualism, 1847, contributed to S.B. Brittan's paper Univercoelum and Spiritual Philosopher, N.Y.C.; moved to Cal., 1860. Author: Nanuntenoo, or Legend of the Narragansetts, 1848; Shalmak in Pursuit of Freedom; or the Branded Hand, 1858; Beyond the Veil, 1878. Died June 10, 1878.

GREEN, Francis, Loyalist, philanthropist; b. Boston, Aug. 21, 1742; s. Benjamin and Margaret (Pierce) G.; grad. Harvard, 1760; m. Susannah Green, Oct. 18, 1769, 3 children; m. 2d, Harriet Matthews, 1785, 6 children. Ensign in French and Indian War, 1754; present at battles of Louisburg, 1758, Martinique and capture of Havana, 1762; capt. 3d Co. of Loyal Asso. Volunteers, 1775; apptd. magistrate, Halifax, N.S., Can., 1776; went to N.Y., 1777; banished to Eng. because of Loyalist sympathies, 1778-84; sheriff of Halifax County (N.S.), 1784-87; went to Mass., 1797; 1st joint treas. of Mass.; published many articles and translations concerning tng. of deaf-mutes (1st Am. writer in this field, became interested in subject because one of his children was a deaf mute); helped to establish a sch. for deaf-mutes, London, Eng. Author: The Art of Imparting Speech, 1783. Died Medford, Mass., Apr. 21, 1809.

GREEN, Frederick William, congressman; b. Fredericktown (now Frederick), Md., Feb. 18, 1816; settled in Tiffin, O., 1833; studied law. Admitted to bar, began practice of law, Tiffin, O.; auditor Seneca County, 6 years; mem. U.S. Ho. of Reps. (Democrat) from Ohio, 32d-33d congresses, 1851-55; clk. U.S. Dist. Ct. for No. Dist. Ohio, Cleve., 1855-66; Ohio commr. to Phila. Centennial Exposition; editor Cleve. Plain Dealer, 1866-74; state oil insp., 1878-79. Died Cleve., June 18, 1879; buried Woodland Cemetery.

GREEN, Henry Woodhull, jurist; b. Maidenhead (now Lawrenceville), N.J., Sept. 20, 1804; s. Caleb Smith and Elizabeth (Van Cleve) G.; grad. Coll. of N.J. (now Princeton), 1820; studied law with Charles Ewing, Trenton, N.J.; m. Emily Augusta Ewing, Mar. 22, 1831; m. 2d, Susan Mary Ewing, Jan. 2, 1840. Admitted to N.J. bar as atty., 1825, as counselor, 1859; practiced in Trenton; elected recorder of Trenton, 1832; recorder Ct. of Chancery, Trenton, 1837-44; mem. N.J. Assembly from Mercer, 1842; del. Nat. Whig Conv., Balt., 1844; del. to N.J. Constl. Conv., 1844, opposed popular election of judges; chief justice N.J. Supreme Ct., 1846-60; chancellor, judge N.J. Prerogative Ct., 1860-66; declined appointment by Pres. Lincoln as justice U.S. Supreme Ct. because of failing health, 1864. Died Dec. 19, 1876.

GREEN, Horace, laryngologist; b. Chittenden, Vt., Dec. 24, 1802; s. Zeeb and Sarah (Cowee) G.; M.D., Castleton Med. Coll., 1825; m. Mary Butler, Oct. 20, 1829; m. 2d, Harriet Douglas, Oct. 27, 1841; 11 children. First Am. physician to specialize in diseases of the throat; wrote Treatise on Diseases of the Air Passages: Comprising an Inquiry into the History, Pathology Causes and Treatment of those Affectations of the Throat Called Bronchitis, Chronic Laryngetis, Clergyman's Sore Throat (advocated application of local medication in the larynx, created a controversy; this was before invention of laryngscope); prof. medicine and pres. Castleton Med. Coll., 1840-43; a founder N.Y. Med. Coll., 1850, prof. medicine, 1850-60; founded Am. Med. Monthly, 1854; contbr. numerous articles to med. jours. Died Ossining, N.Y., Nov. 29, 1866.

GREEN, Innis, congressman, jurist; b. Hanover Twp., Pa., Feb. 26, 1776; studied law. Admitted to bar, practiced law. apptd. an asso. judge Dauphin County (Pa.), 1818-27, also in 1830's; mem. U.S. Ho. of Reps. (Democrat) from Pa., 20th-21st congresses, 1827-31. Died Dauphin, Pa., Aug. 4, 1839; buried Dauphin Cemetery.

GREEN, Isaiah Lewis, congressman; b. Barnstable, Mass., Dec. 28, 1761; grad. Harvard, 1781; studied law. Admitted to bar, practiced law; mem. U.S. Ho. of Reps. from Mass., 9th-10th, 12th congresses, 1805-09, 11-13; collector of customs Dist. of Barnstable (apptd. by Pres. Madison), 1814-37. Died Cambridge, Mass., Dec. 5, 1841; buried Old Cambridge Cemetery.

GREEN, Jacob (pseudonym Eumenes), clergyman; b. Malden, Mass., Feb. 2, 1722; s. Jacob and Dorothy (Lynde) G.; grad. Harvard, 1744, hon. A.M., 1749; m. Anna Strong, June 1747; m. 2d, Elizabeth Pierson, Oct. 1757; 10 children including Ashbel. Licensed to preach, 1745; pastor Presbyn. Ch., Hanover, N.J., 1746; an original trustee Coll. of N.J. (now Princeton), 1748-64, acting v.p., in charge of sch., 1758-59; mem. N.J. Provincial Congress, 1776; Author: Sermons, 1768; A Pamphlet on the Jewish Church, 1768; Sermons, 1769; wrote widely circulated tract "Observations on the Reconciliation of Great Britain and the Colonies in which are Exhibited Arguments for and against that Measure, by a Friend of American Liberty"; wrote many articles on the currency under pen-name Eumenes. Died Morristown, N.J., May 24, 1790.

GREEN, Jacob, educator; b. Phila., July 26, 1790; s. Ashbel and Elizabeth (Stockton) G.; grad. U. Pa., 1807; M.D. (hon.), Yale, 1827. Prof. chemistry and exptl. philosophy Coll. of N.J. (now Princeton), 1818-22; prof. chemistry Jefferson Med. Coll., Phila., 1825-41; published theoretical books on science, textbooks and other scientific works; known for scholarly but popular presentation of science. Author: Electro-Magnetism, 1827; Monography of the Trilobetes in America, 1832; Diseases of the Skin, 1841. Died Phila., Feb. 1, 1841.

GREEN, James Stephen, senator; congressman; b. Rectortown, Va., Feb. 28, 1817; s. James S. and Francis G.; m. Elizabeth Reese; m. 2d, Mary Evans, Nov. 28, 1847. Admitted to Mo. bar, 1840; del. to Mo. Constl. Conv., 1845; mem. U.S. Ho. of Reps. from Mo., 30th-31st congresses, 1847-51; counsel for Mo. in boundary controversy with Ia., 1848; U.S. charge d'affaires to Columbia, 1853-54, apptd. minister resident but did not present his credentials, 1854; mem. U.S. Senate from Mo., Jan. 12, 1857-61, presented majority report on congressional com. favoring admission of Kan. Territory under Lecompton Constn., 1858. Died St. Louis, Jan. 19, 1870; buried Old Cemetery, Canton, Mo.

GREEN, John Cleve, mcht., philanthropist; b. Maidenhead (now Lawrenceville), N.J., Apr. 4, 1800; s. Caleb Smith and Elizabeth (Van Cleve) G.; m. Sarah Griswold, 3 children. Entered employ N.L. & G. Griswold & Co., N.Y. mchts., 1823, spent great deal of time at sea; head Russell & Co. (most powerful Am. house in China trade), 1834; financial backer Mich. Central R.R.; dir. N.Y. Bank Commerce; a founder Home for Ruptured and Crippled; gov. N.Y. Hosp.; gave half-million dollars to Princeton, financed constrn. 3 bldgs., endowed 3 chairs in science; trustee Princeton Theol. Sem. 25 years, endowed chair in ch. history. Died N.Y.C., Apr. 29, 1875; buried Ewing Cemetery, Trenton, N.J.

GREEN, Jonas, printer, journalist; b. New Lon don, Conn., circa 1712; s. Deacon Timothy Greer m. Anne Catherine Hoof, Apr. 25, 1738, 14 chil dren. Learned printing, New London; moved t Boston, worked as printer for firm Kneeland Green; moved to Phila., circa 1735, worked a printer for both Benjamin Franklin and Andre Bradford; moved to Annapolis, Md., 1738, becam public printer; established Md. Gazette, Annapolis 1745, opposed Stamp Act, paper suspended 1777; revived during Revolutionary War by 2 of hi sons, 1779; supposed to be one of best printers i colonies, Green's known for neatness and correct ness; alderman and postmaster Annapolis; vestry man St. Anne's Ch.; printed Thomas Bacon's Law of Maryland (considered his best work), 1765 Died Annapolis, Apr. 11, 1767.

GREEN, Joseph, mcht., author; b. probably Bos ton, 1706; grad. Harvard, 1726; m. Elizabet Green. After graduation started mcht. business also for a time distiller in Boston; became Loyalist did not sign Non-Importation Agreement of 1769 joined group of mchts. who protested to Gov. Thoma Hutchinson about mcht. patriots, 1744; forced t take refuge in London, Eng., 1775; known in hi day as occasional poet and wit; published man poems in literary mags. in Boston and London. Au thor: The Grand Arcanum Detected, 1755; Th Dying Speech of Old Tenor, 1750. Died London Dec. 11, 1780.

GREEN, Lewis Warner, clergyman, coll. pres.; b Boyle County, Ky., Jan. 28, 1806; s. Willis an Sarah (Reed) G.; grad. Centre Coll., Danville, Ky. 1824; attended Yale, Princeton Theol. Sem.; m Eliza J. Montgomery, Feb. 1827; m. 2d, Mary Fry Apr. 1834. Prof. belles-lettres and polit. econ Centre Coll., 1832, v.p., 1838, pres., 1858-63 licensed to preach by Transylvania Presbytery 1833, ordained, 1838; apptd. prof. Oriental an Bibl. lit. in Theol. Sem. of Hanover (Ind.) Coll. 1838; colleague-pastor of Danville (Ky.) Presbyn Ch., 1838; prof. Oriental lit. and Bibl. criticism Western Theol. Sem., Allegheny, Pa., 1840; pres Hampden-Sydney Coll., 1848-56, Transylvania U. 1856-57. Died Danville, May 26, 1863.

GREEN, Nathan, privateer; b. Salem, Mass. circa 1787; probably son of Capt. John and Patt (Sampson) G.; m. Thankful Goodale, July 15 1813. Given command of privateer Grand Turk 1814 (only fully recorded period of his life), too 8 prizes in 1st voyage, burned 4 other vessels an stopped 23 neutral ships around Bay of Biscay 1814; captured 2 Brit. ships (1 contained 1 nail kegs containing some $17,500 in gold) in 2 voyage in Brazilian waters; narrowly escaped cap ture by Brit. frigate disguised as mcht. ship; pro ceeds of last voyage totaled some $73,000 (Green' share $4,000); one of 2 most successful privateer in War of 1812. Drowned N.Y.C., 1825.

GREEN, Norvin, physician, legislator, telegrap exec.; b. New Albany, Ind., Apr. 17, 1818; s. Jo seph and Susan (Ball) G.; grad. Med. Coll., U Louisville, 1840; m. Martha English, Apr. 1, 1840 Practiced medicine, 1841-53; mem. Ky. Ho. c Reps., 1850,51-53; commr. Custom House, Louis ville, Ky., 1853-57; pres. South Western Telegrap Co.; 1st to conceive idea of nat. consolidation c telegraph cos., formed N.Am. Telegraph Co (formed basis of Western Union); v.p. Wester Union, 1866-78, pres., 1878-93; mem. Ky. Ho. c Reps. from Louisville, 1867; pres. Louisville, Cin cinnati & Lexington Ry., 1870-73. Author: Th Government and the Telegraph. Died Louisville Feb. 12, 1893.

GREEN, Robert Stockton, congressman; b Princeton, N.J., Mar. 25, 1831; grad. Coll. c N.J. (now Princeton), 1850; studied law. Ad mitted to bar, 1853, began practice of law, Eliza beth, N.J.; prosecutor borough cts., 1857; cit atty. Elizabeth, 1857-68; del. Dem. nat. convs. 1860, 80, 88; surrogate Union County, 1862-67 mem. city council, 1863-73; presiding judg Union County Ct. of Common Pleas, 1868-73 mem. commn. to suggest amendments to N.J Constn., 1873; admitted to bar, N.Y., 1874; mem U.S. Ho. of Reps. (Democrat) from N.J., 49t Congress, 1885-Jan. 17, 1887 (resigned); go N.J., 1887-89; vice chancellor N.J., 1890-95 judge Ct. of Errors and Appeals, 1894-95. Die Elizabeth, May 7, 1895; buried Greenwood Ceme tery, Bklyn.

GREEN, Samuel, printer; b. Eng., 1615; s Bartholomew and Elizabeth Green; m. Jane Ban bridge, Nov. 16, 1657; m. 2d, Sarah Clark, Ma 6, 1663; about 19 children. Came with parents t Cambridge, Mass., 1633; after retirement of Steph en Day became mgr. of press which Pres. Dunst of Harvard had acquired (only printing office colonies until 1665); managed printing work f Soc. for Propagation of Gospel in New Eng., 1654 90 (when soc.'s press was placed under Harva control); clk. of writs Middlesex County (Mass.) from 1652; town clk. Boston, 1694-97; most fa ous printing accomplishments: Sir Thomas Eliot

Indian Bible, completed 1663; The Book of the General Lawes and Libertyes Concerning the Inhabitants of Massachusetts, 1681. Died Jan. 12, 1702.

GREEN, Seth, fish culturist; b. Monroe County, N.Y., Mar. 19, 1817; s. Adonijah Green; m. Helen M. Cook, Feb. 14, 1848. Established fish stall in city market, Rochester, N.Y.; began experimenting on artificial hatching of salmon and trout, 1837, resulted in location of trout ponds nr. Caledonia, N.Y., 1864; apptd. to N.Y. State Fish Commn., 1868, later became supt. of fisheries; established hatchery adjacent to his own which had been acquired by the state, 1875; noted for expts. with hatching shad, sturgeon and white fish; contbr. many articles on fish culture to sportsman's periodicals. Author: Trout Culture, 1870. Died Aug. 20, 1888.

GREEN, Thomas, printer, editor; b. New London, Conn., Aug. 25, 1735; s. Samuel and Abigail (Clark) G.; m. Desire Sanford, Sept. 1761; m. 2d, Abigail Green; m. 3d, Abigail Miles, 1782; 2 children. Employed by James Parker and Co., printers Conn. Gazette, New Haven, 1757; printed Conn. Courant, Hartford (now Hartford Courant), 1764-67; returned to New Haven, 1767; printed Conn. Jour. and New Haven Post Bay, 1767-1809; ret., 1809; conservative as editor; paper had slight Federalist bent after Am. Revolution. Died May 1812.

GREEN, William, lawyer; b. Fredericksburg, Va., Nov. 10, 1806; s. William and Mary (Brown) G.; studied law with his father; m. Columbia Slaughter, Apr. 6, 1837. Admitted to Va. bar, 1827, practiced in Culpeper County, Va.; contbr. articles to Culpeper Gazette and So. Lit. Messenger; moved to Richmond, Va. to practice before Ct. of Appeals, most known for Shelley case (Moon vs. Stone, 19 Grattan, 130), his arguments printed by court order in Reports; served in Confederate Dept. Justice during Civil War; apptd. prof. law Richmond Coll., 1870-71, resigned; practiced law; wrote articles on profl. topics in preparation for projected works on legal and hist. subjects, including "Stare Decises" in American Law Review (his most famous article), 1880. Died July 29, 1880.

GREEN, William Mercer, clergyman; b. Wilmington, N.C., May 2, 1798; s. William and Mary (Bradley) G.; grad. U. N.C., 1818, LL.D. (hon.), 1880; D.D. (hon.), U. Pa., 1845; m. Sarah Williams, Dec. 22, 1818, 5 children; m. 2d, Charlotte Isabella Fleming, Dec. 16, 1835, 8 children. Ordained deacon, Christ Ch., Raleigh, N.C., 1820; rector St. John's Ch., Williamsborough, N. C., 1821-25; founder St. Matthew's Ch., Hillsborough, N.C., 1825, rector, 1825-37; chaplain, prof. belles-lettres and rhetoric U. N.C., 1837-49; Protestant Episcopal bishop Miss. Diocese, 1850-83; a founder U. of South, Sewanee, Tenn., 1857, became chancellor, 1867. Author: Memoir of the Rt. Rev. Bishop Ravenscroft of North Carolina, 1830; The Influence of Christianity Upon the Welfare of Nations, 1831. Died Sewanee, Feb. 13, 1887.

GREEN, Willis, congressman; b. Shenandoah Valley, Va.; attended public schs. Clk. of ct. Lincoln County, 1783; mem. Ky. Constl. Conv., 1792; surveyor for locating land warrants; mem. Ky. Ho. of Reps., 1836-37; mem. U.S. Ho. of Reps. (Whig) from Ky., 26th-28th congresses, 1839-45.

GREENBERRY, Nicholas, colonial ofcl.; b. Eng., 1627; m. Ann; children—Charles, Catherine. Came to Md., 1674, established plantation on Severn River; a justice Anne Arundel County, Md., 1686-89; mem. Md. Gov.'s Council, 1692-97; pres. of council, also chancellor Md., 1693-94; acting gov. Md., 1693; judge Md. High Ct. of Chancery, 1695-97; a commr. to lay out City of Annapolis (Md.). Died Dec. 17, 1697.

GREENE, Albert Collins, senator; b. East Greenwich, R.I., Apr. 15, 1791; grad. Kent Acad., East Greenwich; studied law. Admitted to bar, 1812, began practice of law, East Greenwich; mem. R.I. Ho. of Reps., 1815-25, 57, speaker, 1821-25; served as brig. gen. 4th Brigade R.I. Militia, 1816-21, maj. gen., 1821-23; atty. gen. R.I., 1825-43; mem. R.I. Senate, 1843-44, 51-52; mem. U.S. Senate (Whig) from R.I., 1845-51. Died Providence, Jan. 8, 1863; buried Grace Ch. Cemetery.

GREENE, Albert Gorton, lawyer, poet; b. Providence, R.I., Feb. 10, 1802; s. John H. and Elizabeth (Beverly) G.; grad. Brown U., 1820; studied law under John Whipple; m. Mary Ann Clifford, 1824. Admitted to R.I. bar, 1823; clk. Providence City Council, 1832-67; clk. Providence Municipal Ct., 1832-57, justice, 1858-67; also occasional poet and editor; contbr. 5 poems to The Rhode Island Book (edited by Anne C. Lynch), 1841; most famous poem was Ode on the Death of Rev. Dr. William E. Channing; pres. R.I. Hist. Soc., 1854-68; had notable collection of original engravings and library which contained 18,000 volumes and 2,000 pamphlets (now embodied in Harris Collection of Am. Poetry at Brown U.). Died Cleve., Jan. 3, 1868.

GREENE, Christopher, army officer; b. Warwick, R.I., May 12, 1737; s. Philip and Elizabeth (Wickes) G.; m. Ann Lippitt, Jan. 6, 1757, several children. Asso. with relatives in operation of extensive mfg. works built on South br. Pawtuxet River; freeman Colony of R.I., 1759; mem. R.I. Legislature from Warwick, 1771-72; chosen lt. in Kentish Guards established by R.I. Legislature, 1774; apptd. maj. in regt. of King's and Kent County Militia under Col. James Mitchell Varnum, 1775; commd. lt. col. in command of 1st bn. R.I. Militia in Benedict Arnold's expdn. to Can., captured and imprisoned in Que. until 1777, promoted col. 1st R.I. Inf., 1777, placed in command of Ft. Mercer on Delaware River, 1777; voted sword by Continental Congress for gallant defense of fort against Col. (Count) Donop's troops; transferred to R.I., 1778, took part in Battle of R.I. commanding regiment Negro troops recruited from slaves; transferred to Westchester County, N.Y., 1781, with hdqrs. on Croton River. Killed in Westchester County, May 14, 1781.

GREENE, George Sears, army officer, engr.; b. Apponaug, R.I., May 6, 1801; s. Caleb and Sarah (Robinson) G.; grad. U.S. Mil. Acad., 1823; m. Elizabeth Vinton, July 14, 1828; m. 2d, Martha Barrett Dana, Feb. 21, 1837; 3 children. Taught mathematics U.S. Mil. Acad., 1823-27; served in various arty. posts throughout New Eng., 1827-36; promoted 1st lt., 1829; became engr. after leaving army; engr. in charge of Croton water-works extension and Croton Reservoir, Central Park, N.Y., at outbreak of Civil War; apptd. col. 60th N.Y. Volunteers, 1862, served at Washington, D.C., 1862, apptd. brig. gen. volunteers serving in Shenandoah Valley; fought in battles of Antietam, Chancellorsville and Gettysburg (where he commanded defense of Culp's Hill); transferred to Tenn., 1863, wounded at Battle of Wauhatchie, 1863; resigned commn., 1866, resumed engring. work, N.Y.C., did notable work in other Eastern cities; planned sewerage system for Washington, extension of water system in Detroit, Troy and Yonker, N.Y.; a founder Am. Soc. C.E., pres., 1875-77; returned to U.S. Army as lt. by spl. act of Congress, placed on retired list, 1894. Died Morristown, N.J., Jan. 28, 1899; buried Warwick, R.I.

GREENE, George Washington, educator, historian; b. East Greenwich, R.I., Apr. 8, 1811; s. Nathanael and Anna Maria (Clarke) G.; ed. Brown U.; m. Catharine Porter, Feb. 9, 1852. Went to Europe because of poor health, 1827; became interested in lit. through friendship with Henry Wadsworth Longfellow; U.S. consul at Rome, Italy, 1837-45; instr. modern langs. Brown U.; mem. R.I. Legislature, 1865; lectr. Am. history Cornell U. (1st chair Am. history in U.S.), 1871. Author: Historical Studies, 1850; Historical View of the American Revolution, 1851; History and Geography of the Middle Ages, 1851; Biographical Studies, 1860; Life of Nathanael Green (a not-too-well received attack on George Bancroft's version), 1st vol., 1867, 2d, 3d vols., 1871; The German Element in the War of American Independence, 1876; Short History of Rhode Island, 1877. Died East Greenwich, Feb. 2, 1883.

GREENE, George Woodward, congressman; b. Mt. Hope, N.Y., July 4, 1831; grad. U. Pa. at Phila.; studied law. Taught sch.; admitted to bar, 1860, began practice of law, Goshen, N.Y.; sch. commr. Orange County (N.Y.); judge Orange County Cts., 1861-64; mem. U.S. Ho. of Reps. (Democrat, contested election) from N.Y., 41st Congress, 1869-Feb. 17, 1870; mem. N.Y. State Assembly, 1885-88. Died N.Y.C., July 21, 1895; buried "The Plains" Cemetery, Otisville, N.Y.

GREENE, John Holden, architect; b. 1777; trained for carpenter's trade. Became self-trained architect, Providence, R.I., designed some public bldgs., several residences. Prin. works include: St. Joseph's Episcopal Ch. (Gothic style, 1810), Congregational (now Unitarian) Ch., Sullivan-Dorr house (1809), St. John's Ch. (1810), Gov. Elisha Dyer house (1818), William Watson house (1819), Friends' Sch. (1819), Candace Allen house (1819), Roger Williams Bank Bldg. (built 1830, no longer standing), Granite Block on Market St. (circa 1820, razed 1939), John Larcher house (1823, now home of Handicraft Club), 1st Universalist Ch. (1825, no longer standing), Rufus Greene house (razed), Truman Beckwith house, Benoni Cooke house (1826), Dexter Asylum (1830), Franklin Hotel, Woodward house (all Providence); perhaps designed hotel on Market St., Bristol, R.I. Died 1850.

GREENE, Nathanael, army officer; b. Warwick, R.I., Aug. 7, 1742; s. Nathanael and Mary (Mott) G.; m. Catharine Littlefield, July 20, 1774; children—George Washington, Martha Washington, Cornelia Lott, Nathanael Ray, Louisa Catherine. Dep. to R.I. Gen. Assembly, 1770-72, 75; organized militia co. known as Kentish Guards, 1774; commd. brig. gen. Continental Army, 1775; present at siege of Boston, later commanded army of occupation in Boston, Mar. 1776; then commanded Continental troops in N.J.; promoted maj. gen. Continental Army, took part in fighting around N.Y., Aug. 1776; led left wing of Am. force in Battle of Trenton; served at Valley Forge, 1777-78; promoted q.m. gen., Mar. 1778; led right flank at Battle of Monmouth, June 1778; in supreme command of Continental Army during Washington's absence, Sept. 1780; pres of bd. which condemned Maj. John André to be hanged, 1780; in command of post at West Point, Oct. 1780; in command of Army of South, 1780; noted for his strategy in the Carolinas, which ultimately forced Cornwallis, to Yorktown; lived on plantation outside Savannah, Ga., after war. Died Savannah, June 19, 1786; buried Christ Episcopal Ch., Savannah.

GREENE, Nathaniel, editor, postmaster, translator; b. Boscawen, N.H., May 20, 1797; s. Nathaniel and Ruth (Fowler) G.; m. Susan Batchelder, winter 1817-18. Apprentice in office of N.H. Patriot, 1809; editor Concord Gazette, 1812; founder, editor Essex Patriot (Mass.), 1817-21; a founder of Am. Statesman (foremost Democratic paper in Mass.), Boston, 1821; postmaster Boston, 1829-41, 44-49; contbd. more than 200 poems to Boston jours. under name of Boscawen. Translator: Tales from the German (K.F. Van der Velde), 2 vols., 1837; History of Italy (G. Sforzosis), 1836; Tales from the German, Italian and French, 1843; Improvisations and Translations, 1852. Died Boston, Nov. 29, 1877.

GREENE, Ray, senator, lawyer; b. Warwick, R.I., Feb. 2, 1765; grad. Yale, 1784; studied law. Admitted to bar, began practice of law, Providence, R.I.; atty. gen. R.I., 1794-97; mem. U.S. Senate (filled vacancy) from R.I., Nov. 13, 1797-1801 (resigned). Died Warwick, Jan. 11, 1829; buried family burying ground on his estate, Warwick.

GREENE, Samuel Dana, naval officer; b. Cumberland, Md., Feb. 11, 1840; s. Gen. George Sears and Martha (Dana) G.; grad. U.S. Naval Acad., 1859; m. Mary Willis, Oct. 9, 1863; m. 2d, Mary Babbitt, Nov. 8, 1876; 3 children. Entered U.S. Navy, 1855, commd. lt., 1861; only exec. officer in iron-clad Monitor during 1st battle with Merrimac, 1862, criticized for allowing Merrimac to escape, although his orders had been to keep Monitor on defensive, rather than to follow Merrimac; served in Monitor until its sinking, 1862, commended for his bravery; exec. officer ship Florida, 1863-64; promoted lt. comdr., 1865; instr. mathematics, head dept. astronomy, navigation and surveying, asst. in charge bldgs. and grounds, sr. aide to supt. U.S. Naval Acad., 1866-84; served with Pacific Squadron, 1868-71; commd. comdr., 1872; comdr. ships Juniata, 1875, Monongahela, 1876-77, Dispatch, 1882-84; exec. officer Portsmouth (N.H.) Navy Yard. Committed suicide, Portsmouth, Dec. 11, 1884.

GREENE, Samuel Stillman, educator; b. Belchertown, Mass., May 3, 1810; s. Ebenezer and Sybil (Hitchcock) G.; grad. Brown U., 1837; m. Edna Amelia Bartlett, Aug. 29, 1839; m. 2d, Mary Adeline Bailey, Aug. 10, 1854. Taught at Worcester (Mass.) Acad., 1837-40, public schs., Boston, 1842-49; apptd. supt. public schs., Springfield, Mass., 1840-42; agt. Mass. Bd. Edn. (1st office of its kind in U.S.), 1849-51; supt. schs., Providence, R.I., 1851; prof. didactics Brown U., 1851, prof. mathematics and civil engring., 1855, prof. natural philosophy and astronomy, 1864-75, prof. mathematics and astronomy, 1875; opened pvt. normal sch., Providence, 1852, later taken over by state, now R.I. Coll. Edn.; pres. Nat. Tchrs. Assn., 1856-60, Am. Inst. Instrn., 1864-65, 69-70. Author: Greene's Analysis: A Treatise on the Structure of the English Language, 1848; The Elements of English Grammar, 1853; An Introduction to the Study of English Grammar, 1868. Died Jan. 24, 1883.

GREENE, Thomas Marston, congressman; b. James City County, Va., Feb. 26, 1758. Engaged in planting, Miss. Territory; mem. 1st Miss. Territorial Gen. Assembly; mem. U.S. Congress (filled vacancy) from Miss. Territory, Dec. 6, 1802-03. Died Feb. 7, 1813.

GREENE, William, colonial gov.; b. Warwick, R.I., Mar. 16, 1696; s. Samuel and Mary (Gorton) G.; m. Joan Tattersall; m. 2d, Catharine Greene, Dec. 30, 1719; 12 children including John, Benjamin, Samuel, William, Margaret, Catherine, Christopher. Practical surveyor, 1728, 36, 41, helped fix line between Conn. and R.I., 1728, 36; dep. gov. Colony of R.I., 1740-43; gov. 1743-45, 46-47, 48-55, 57-58, terms marked by struggles over paper currency and boundary disputes in which he favored R.I. and Newport trade mchts. Died Warwick, Feb. 1758.

GREENE, William, gov. R.I.; b. Warwick, R.I., Aug. 16, 1731; s. Gov. William and Catharine Greene; m. Catharine Ray, 1758, 4 children including Ray. Mem. R.I. Ho. of Deps. from Warwick, 1773, 74, 76, 77, speaker, 1777; a signer Declaration of Independence, 1776; 1st asso. justice Superior Ct .R.I., 1776, chief justice, 1777; a commr. from R.I. to conv. of Northern states to regulate prices commodities, New Haven, Conn., 1777; gov. R.I., 1778-86. Died Warwick, Nov. 29, 1809.

GREENHALGE, Frederick Thomas, gov. Mass.; b. Clitheroe, Eng., July 19, 1842; s. William and Jane (Slater) G.; attended Harvard, 1859-62, awarded degree, 1870; m. Isabel Nesmith, 1872, 4 children. Admitted to Mass. bar, 1865; mem. Common Council of Lowell (Mass.), 1868-69, mayor, 1880-81; del. Republican Nat. Conv., Chgo., 1884; mem. Mass. Legislature, 1885; solicitor of Lowell, 1888; mem. U.S. Ho. of Reps. from Mass., 51st Congress, 1889-91; gov. Mass., 1894-96, dispersed mob over 5,000 unemployed through effective speech, 1894; trustee Rogers Hall Sch., Westford Acad., Lowell Gen. Hosp.; pres., trustee Lowell Savs. Bank. Died Lowell, Mar. 5, 1896; buried Lowell Cemetery.

GREENHOW, Robert, physician, linguist, historian; b. Richmond, Va., 1800; s. Robert and Mary Ann (Wills) G.; grad. Coll. William and Mary, 1816; studied medicine under John W. Francis, N.Y.C.; M.D., Coll. Physicians and Surgeons, N.Y.C., 1821; m. Rose O'Neil, 4 children. Went to Europe, 1821-25; practiced medicine, N.Y.C., 1825-28; lectr. chemistry to a N.Y. literary and scientific soc.; translator Dept. of State, Washington, 1828-50; moved to Cal., 1850; with law office U.S. Land Commn. in Cal., 1852-54; used original sources such as jours. of explorers in Spanish, English, French, in addition to literary and hist. works, did all translating himself. Author: The History and Present Condition of Tripoli, 1835; The History of Oregon and California, 1844, English edit., 1844 (written at request of Senator Lewis F. Linn, head Congressional com. on Am. claims to Ore. Territory, 1839). Died San Francisco, Mar. 27, 1854.

GREENLEAF, Benjamin, educator; b. Haverhill, Mass., Sept. 25, 1786; s. Caleb and Susanna (Emerson) G.; grad. Dartmouth, 1813; m. Lucretia Kimball, Nov. 20, 1821, 9 children. Taught sch., 1805-10; prin. grammar sch., Haverhill, 1813; preceptor Bradford (Mass.) Acad., 1814-36; mem. Mass. Legislature, 1837-39, advocated normal schs., chmn. com. which recommended geol. and natural history surveys of state which were later made; founded, became head Bradford Tchrs. Sem., 1839-48; spent last years in making calculations for almanacs and in gen. activities on behalf of edn. Died Oct. 29, 1864.

GREENLEAF, Edmund, silk dyer, army officer; b. Ipswich, Suffolk, Eng., circa 1574; s. John and Margaret Greenleaf; m. Sarah Dale; m. 2d, Sarah Hill; at least 9 children. Became silk dyer, Eng.; came to Am., 1635, established silk dyeing business, Boston; admitted as freeman to Newbury, Mass., 1639, opened house of entertainment; commanded mil. co. which fought Indians, 1637-39; ensign mil. co. at Newbury, 1639-42; became lt. comdr. Mass. provincial forces under Capt. William Gerrish, 1642, capt., 1644-47; returned to silk-dyeing, Boston, 1650-71. Died 1671.

GREENLEAF, Jonathan, clergyman; b. New Gloucester, Me., Sept. 4, 1785; s. Capt. Moses and Lydia (Parsons) G.; studied theology under Rev. Francis Brown, North Yarmouth; D.D. (hon.), Bowdoin Coll., Princeton. Licensed to preach by Cumberland Assn., Congregational Ch., at Saco, Me., 1814; pastor 1st Congregational Ch., Wells, Me., 1814-28, Mariner's Ch., Boston, 1828-33; corresponding sec. Am. Seamen's Friend Soc., 1833-41; editor Sailor's Mag., 1833-42; founder Presbyn. Ch., Franklin Av., Bklyn., 1843, pastor, 1843-65. Author: Sketches of the Ecclesiastical History of Maine, 1821; History of the Churches of New York, 1846; Genealogy of the Greenleaf Family, 1854. Died Bklyn., Apr. 24, 1865.

GREENLEAF, Moses, army officer; b. Newburyport, Mass., May 19, 1755; s. Jonathan and Mary (Presbury) G.; m. Lydia Parsons, Sept. 1776. Asso. with his father in ship-bldg. bus., Mass., 1781-90; served as pvt. Mass. Militia, 1775, 2d lt., 1775-76, lt., 1776, took part in siege of Boston; commd. capt., 1779; served with 11th Mass. Regt. under Col. Benjamin Tupper, 1777-81; retired from Continental Army, 1790; farmer, New Gloucester, Me., until 1812. Died New Gloucester, Dec. 18, 1812.

GREENLEAF, Moses, cartographer; b. Newburyport, Mass., Oct. 17, 1777; s. Moses and Lydia (Parsons) G.; m. Persis Poor, Feb. 11, 1805. Kept gen. store, New Gloucester, Bangor, Me., 1799-1806; entered into real estate partnership with William Dood of Boston; helped settle what is now Williamsburg (Me.); spent rest of his life in furthering settlement interior of Me.; surveyed roads, located stone and mineral deposits, secured charter for Picataquis Canal and R.R. Co., 1833, provided valuable information to miners, purchasers and legislators through his publications and maps. Author: Map of the District of Maine from the Latest and Best Authorities, 1815. Died Mar. 20, 1834.

GREENLEAF, Simon, lawyer, educator; b. Newburyport, Mass., Dec. 5, 1783; s. Moses and Lydia (Parsons) G.; A.M. (hon.), Bowdoin Coll., 1817; LL.D. (hon.), Harvard, 1834, Amherst, 1845, U. Ala., 1852; m. Hannah Kingman, Sept. 18, 1806. Admitted to Cumberland County (Me.) bar, 1806, became a leader in Portland bar, 1818; mem. Me. Legislature, 1820; reporter Me. Supreme Jud. Ct., 1820-32; Royall prof. law Harvard, 1833, prof. emeritus, 1848; foremost expert on common law of his time. Author: A Brief Inquiry into the Origin and Principles of Free Masonry; Reports of Cases Argued and Determined by the Supreme Judicial Court of the State of Maine, 9 vols., 1820-32; A Treatise on the Law of Evidence, 1st vol., 1842, 2d vol., 1846, 3d vol., 1853; Cruise's Digest of the Law of Real Property, Revised and Abridged for the Use of American Students, 7 vols. in 5, 1849-50. Died Oct. 6, 1853.

GREENLEAF, Thomas, printer, journalist; b. Newburyport, Mass., 1755; s. Joseph and Abigail (Payne) G.; m. Ritsana (or Anna) Quakenbos, Oct. 31, 1791, 4 children. Learned printing in shop of Isiah Thomas, Boston; moved to N.Y.C., 1785, became mgr. Eliazer Oswald's New York Jour. or the Weekly Register, became owner, 1787, became daily newspaper under title New-York Jour. and Daily Patriotic Register, 1787-88, became weekly, 1788, published semi-weekly under title New-York Jour. and Patriotic Register, 1790, name changed to Greenleaf's New-York Jour., 1793; established Argus and Greenleaf's New Daily Advertiser, N.Y.C., mgr. 1795-98; supported Aaron Burr's party against Federalists, often printed attacks against George Washington. Died N.Y.C., Sept. 14, 1798.

GREENOUGH, Henry, architect, painter, author; b. Newburyport, Mass., Oct. 5, 1807; attended Harvard, 1823-26; studied painting under Prof. Bezzioli, Royal Acad. of Fine Arts, Florence, Italy, 1829-32; m. Frances Boott, Mar. 18, 1837, 2 children. Tchr., Mr. Greene's sch., Jamaica Plain, Mass., 1826-29; through Washington Allston received commn. to design Orthodox Ch., Cambridge, Mass., 1829; returned to Boston, 1833, worked at various jobs attempting to redeem his father's finances; lived in Italy, 1845-50, spent much time with artists of times, especially the Brownings; designed Cambridgeport Athanaeum, 1850; supervised decoration (working with Italian fresco painters) of Crystal Palace, N.Y.C., 1852; designed houses in Boston and Cambridge; Author: (novels) Ernest Carroll, 1859, Apelles, 1860; wrote many articles on art for leading periodicals. Died Oct. 31, 1883.

GREENOUGH, Horatio, sculptor; b. Boston, Sept. 6, 1805; s. David and Betsey (Bender) G.; grad. Harvard, 1825; studied art, Rome, Italy, 1825-26; m. Louisa Gore, 1837. Designed Bunker Hill Monument, 1825 (while still student at Harvard); maintained studio, Florence, Italy, 1828-31, 33-51, Paris, France, 1831-33, returned to U.S., 1851. Prin. works include: Chanting Cherubs (marble group commd. by James Fenimore Cooper, 1831; The Child and The Angel (marble group), circa 1831; seated figure of George Washington (originally intended for U.S. Capitol, now in Smithsonian Instn.), 1843; The Rescue (1st colossal group in marble by an American, placed on buttress of Capitol portico), 1837-51; The Guardian Angel, The Angel Abdiel, Lucifer. Busts include: John Quincy Adams (now in N.Y. Hist. Soc.), 1826; Chief Justice Marshall, circa 1827; Lafayette, 1831; Henry Clay, Josiah Quincy, Josiah Mason, James Fenimore Cooper, Thomas Cole, Samuel Appleton, John Jacob Astor. Author: Aesthetics in Washington, 1851; Travels, Observations, and experiences of a Yankee Stonecutter, 1852. Died Somerville, Mass., Dec. 12, 1852.

GREENUP, Christopher, gov. Ky., congressman; b. Loudoun County, Va., circa 1750; m. Mary Pope. Served as capt. in Revolutionary War; admitted to Va. bar, 1783; mem. Va. Legislature, 1785; helped secure statehood for Ky.; clk. Militia Conv., Danville, Ky., 1784; mem. convs. at Danville to consider separation from Va., 1785, 88; mem. Ky. Soc. for Promoting Useful Knowledge, 1787; an organizer Ky. Mfg. Soc., 1789; mem. U.S. Ho. of Reps. from Ky., 2d-4th congresses, 1792-97; clk. Ky. Senate, 1799-1802; gov. Ky., 1804-08; dir. Bank of Ky., 1807; an original trustee Transylvania U.; mem. Danville Polit. Club; justice of peace Franklin County (Ky.), 1812. Died Blue Lick Springs, Ky., Apr. 27, 1818; buried State Cemetery, Frankfort, Ky.

GREENWALD, Emanuel, clergyman; b. Frederick, Md., Jan. 13, 1811; s. Christian and Mary Magdalena (Smith) G.; studied theology under Rev. David Frederick Schaeffer, Frederick, 1827-31; m. Lavina Williams, Dec. 17, 1834. Licensed to preach in Lutheran Ch., 1831; settled in New Philadelphia, O., remained until 1851; established 14 preaching stations throughout area; ordained to ministry Luth. Ch., Lancaster, O., 1836; established, edited Lutheran Standard, Lancaster, 1842-44, 1851-54, became involved in religious controversy with Benjamin Kurtz, held conservative views; pres. English Dist. Synod of Ohio, 1848-50; moved to Columbus (O.) to organize English Luth. congregation in conjunction with Capital U., 1851; pastor Christ Ch., Easton, Pa., 1854-67 (this parish disagreed with his conservative views); pastor Holy Trinity Ch., Lancaster until 1885. Author: The Lutheran Reformation, 1867; Discourses on Romanticism and the Reformation, 1880. Died Lancaster, Dec. 21, 1885.

GREENWOOD, Alfred Burton, congressman; b. Franklin County, Ga., July 11, 1811; grad. U. Ga. at Athens; studied law. Admitted to bar, 1832, began practice of law, Bentonville, Ark.; mem. Ark. Ho. of Reps., 1842-45; state pros. atty., 1845-51; circuit judge Ark., 1851-53; mem. U.S. Ho. of Reps. (Democrat) from Ark., 33d-35th congresses, 1853-59; commr. Indian affairs, 1859-61; mem. Confederate Ho. of Reps., 1862-65. Died Bentonville, Oct. 4, 1889; buried Odd Fellows Cemetery.

GREENWOOD, Ethan Allen, artist; b. Hubbardstown, Mass., May 25, 1779; attended Dartmouth, studied law; studied painting with Edward Savage, N.Y.C., 1806. Taught sch.; opened studio, Boston, 1812, painted many portraits; took charge of Savage's Museum, Boston, 1818; returned to Hubbardstown, 1827, entered politics. Died Hubbardstown, May 3 or 6, 1856.

GREENWOOD, Isaac, mathematician; b. Boston, May 11, 1702; s. Samuel and Elizabeth (Bronsdon) G.; grad. Harvard, 1721; m. Sarah Clarke, July 31, 1729, 5 children. Influenced by lectures on exptl. philosophy by John T. Pesaguliers while in London (Eng.); prof. mathematics Harvard, 1728-38. Author: Experimental Course on Mechanical Philosophy, 1726; Arithmetic, Vulgar and Decimal: with the Application Thereof to a Variety of Cases in Trade and Commerce (1st textbook of its kind by an American), 1729. Died Charlestown, Mass., Oct. 12, 1745.

GREENWOOD, John, dentist; b. Boston, May 17, 1760; s. Isaac and Mary (I'ans) G.; m. Elizabeth Weaver, Mar. 22, 1788. Apprenticed to a cabinetmaker; served as rifleman and scout during Revolutionary War; became dentist, N.Y.C., 1785; credited with originating foot-power drill, also springs which held plates of false teeth in position, and use of porcelain in manufacture of false teeth; George Washington was one of his patients, (found Greenwood to be most satisfactory of his numerous dentists). Died N.Y.C., Nov. 16, 1819.

GREENWOOD, Miles, ironmaster; b. Jersey City, N.J., Mar. 19, 1807; s. Miles Greenwood; m. Miss Mills, 1832; m. 2d, Phoebe Hopson, 1836. moved with family to Ind., 1825; in charge of a foundry under exptl. colony led by Robert Owen, New Harmony, Ind., 1828; established (with Joseph Webb) Eagle Iron Works, Cincinnati (became largest iron-mfg. concern in old West), 1832; mem. Cincinnati City Council, 1840; built 1st steam fire engine in U.S. for use by Cincinnati Volunteer Fire Dept.; an organizer 1st paid fire dept. in Cincinnati, 1853; manufactured 1st steam engine in U.S., put in use, 1852; his factories were burned 3 times by So. sympathizers during Civil War; dir. Cincinnati So. Ry., pres. bd., 1869. Died Cincinnati, Nov. 5, 1885.

GREGG, Alexander, clergyman; b. Society Hill, Darlington Dist., S.C., Oct. 8, 1819; grad. S.C. Coll., 1838, D.D. (hon.), 1859; studied law. Admitted to S.C. bar, 1840, practiced law briefly; ordained priest Protestant Episcopal Ch., 1847; rector St. David's Parish, Cheraw, S.C., 1846-59; in charge of Presbyn. mission, So. Tex., 1874-93. Author: History of old Cheraw; A Brief Sketch of the Church in Texas (published in Ch. Ency. 1884). Died Galveston, Tex., July 11, 1893.

GREGG, Andrew, senator; b. Carlisle, Pa., June 10, 1755; s. Andrew and Jane (Scott) G.; m. Martha Potter, Jan. 29, 1787. Tutor, U. Phila., 1779-83; mem. U.S. Ho. of Reps. (Republican) from Pa., 2d-9th congresses, 1791-1807; mem. U.S. Senate (Constitutionalist) from Pa., 1807-1813, pres. pro tem, 1809-10; pres. Centre Bank, Bellefonte, Pa., 1814-20; sec. Commonwealth of Pa., 1820-23. Died Bellefonte, May 20, 1835; buried Union Cemetery, Bellefonte.

GREGG, James Madison, congressman, lawyer; b. Patrick County, Va., June 26, 1806; attended public schs.; studied law. Admitted to bar, 1830, began practice of law, Danville, Ind.; surveyor Hendricks County, 1834-37; clk. circuit ct., 1837-45; mem. U.S. Ho. of Reps. (Democrat) from Ind., 35th Congress, 1857-59; mem. Ind. Ho. of

Reps., 1862. Died Danville, June 16, 1869; buried South Cemetery.

GREGG, John, army officer; b. Lawrence County, Ala., Sept. 28, 1828; s. Nathan and Sarah (Pearsall) G.; grad. La Grange Coll., 1847; m. Mary Garth, 1856. Moved to Tex., 1852; dist. judge Freestone County (Tex.), 1856; mem. irregularly assembled secessionist conv. which voted Tex. out of Union; Tex. rep. Confederate Provisional Congress, Montgomery Ala., 1861; commd. col. 7th Tex. Inf., 1861; captured at Ft. Donelsen, 1862, later exchanged; commd. brig. gen. Confederate Army, 1862; commanded brigade of Tenn. and Tex. troops; participated in battles of Vicksburg, Chickamauga, also Campaign of 1864. Killed in battle before Richmond (Va.), Oct. 7, 1864.

GREGG, Josiah, adventurer, author; b. Overton County, Tenn., July 19, 1806; s. Harmon and Susannah (Schmelzer) G.; Family moved from Ill. to Mo., 1812-25; because of ill health made many journeys to S.W., beginning in 1831, kept notes of these trips; took his complete manuscript to N.Y.C. with letter of introduction from John Bigelow, winter 1843-44; made several trips to Mexico on horseback, 1846-48; set out for Cal. via Sante Fe, 1849; died in upper Cal. while commanding expdn. of 7 men exploring Trinity mountains. Author: Commerce of the Prairies, 1814, 45, 50, 57. Died Cal., Feb. 25, 1850.

GREGG, Maxcy, army officer; b. Columbia S.C., 1814; s. James and Cornelia (Maxcy) G ; grad. Coll. of S.C., 1830. Admitted to S.C. bar, 1839; commd. maj. 12th Inf., U.S. Volunteers, 1847, mem. central com. framing S.C. ordinance of secession, adopted 1860; commd. col. Confederate Army, 1861, brig. gen., commanded brigade of reserves at battle of Beavers Dam Creek, 1862, also 2d battle Manassas, 1862, battles of Mechanicsville, Cold Harbor, Frazers Farm, Malvern Hill, Cedar Mountain; held center reserve of Gen. Jackson's line at Battle of Fredricksburg, 1862. Engaged in astron.; ornithol. and bot. studies; an early advocate of So. Rigrhts; leading mem. Conv. So. Rights Assns., Charleston; advocated reopening of African slave trade as means of separation from North. Died in Battle of Fredericksburg (Va.), Dec. 14, 1862; buried Columbia.

GREGG, William, cotton mfr.; b. Carmichaels, W. Va., Feb. 2, 1800; s. William and Elizabeth (Webb) G.; m. Marina Jones, 1829. Made fortune in jewelry bus., Columbia, S.C., reorganized and expanded cotton factory nr. Edgefield, S.C., 1829-43; wrote Essays on Donestic Industry, advocating devel. of new econ. basis for the South which would include concentration on cotton mfr. (textiles) rather than prodn. supported by internal improvements and protective tariffs, 1845; pres. Graniteville Mfg. Co. (1st cotton mill in South), 1846; mem. S.C. Ho. of Reps., 1856, 57; organized 1st factory community in South planned for workers welfare; prin. organizer S.C. Inst. for encouragement of mech. arts. Died Kalmia, S.C., Sept. 13, 1877.

GREGORY, Dudley Sanford, congressman; b. Redding, Conn., Feb. 5, 1800; attended public schs., N.Y. Mem. honor guard to receive Gen. Lafayette on his visit to U.S., 1824; moved to N.Y.C., 1824, to Jersey City, N.J., 1834; freeholder Hudson County, 3 terms; elected 1st mayor Jersey City, 1838, served 3 terms; dir. 16 railroads; mem. U.S. Ho. of Reps. (Whig) from N.J., 30th Congress, 1847-49; engaged in banking. Died Jersey City, Dec. 8, 1874; buried Greenwood Cemetery.

GREGORY, John Milton, clergyman, coll. pres.; b. Sand Lake, N.Y., July 6 1822; s. Joseph G. and Rachel (Bullock) G.; grad. Union Coll., 1846; LL.D. (hon.), Madison U., 1866; m. Julia Gregory, 1848, 5 children; m. 2d, Louisa C. Allen 1879, 1 dau. Ordained to ministry Baptist Ch., 1847; founder, editor Mich. Jour. of Edn.; supt. pub. instrn. State of Mich., 1859-64; pres. Kalamazoo Coll., 1864-67; sec. Mich. Bd. Edn.; 1st regent (pres.) Ill. Indsl. U. (now U. Ill.), 1867-80; U.S. Commr. to Vienna Expn., 1873; judge ednl. dept. Centennial Expn., 1876; Ill. commr. to Paris Expn. of 1878; pres. Ill. Bd. Health, 1881. gen. supt. ednl. work Am. Bapt. Home Mission Soc.; mem. 1st U.S. civil Service Commn., 1883-85 (resigned). Author: A New Political Economy, 1882; The Seven Laws of Teaching, 1884. Died Washingotn D.C., Oct. 19, 1898; buried Champaign, Ill.

GREGORY, Samuel, physician, educator; born Guilford, Vt., Apr. 19, 1813; A.B., Yale, 1840, Masters degree, 1845, M.D. (hon.), 1853. Opened Boston Female Med. Sch. (earliest sch. of its kind in U.S.), 1848, reorganized with class of 12 students as New Eng. Female Med. Coll., 1856; sec., 1st instr. med. edn. of women 1848-72; later prof. chemistry; continuing sec. Female Med. Edn. Soc. (organized 1848). Died Boston, Mar. 23, 1872.

GREIG, John, congressman, banker; b. Moffat, Dumfriesshire, Scotland, Aug. 6, 1779; attended Edinburgh High Sch.; came to U.S., 1797; studied law. Admitted to bar, 1804, began practice of law, Canandaigua, N.Y.; pres. Ontario Bank, 1820-56; regent U. State N.Y., 1825-58, vice chancellor 1845-58; a founder Ontario Female Sem.; mem. U.S. Ho. of Reps. (Whig, filled vacancy) from N.Y., May 21,-Sept. 25, 1841 (resigned); pres. Ontario Agrl. Soc. Died Canandaigua, Apr. 9, 1858; buried West Avenue Cemetery.

GRELLET, Stephen, clergyman; b. Limoges, France, Nov. 2, 1773; s. Gabriel Marc Antoine and Susanne (de Senamaud) de Grellet; attended Coll. of Oratorians, Lyons, France; m. Rebecca Collins, July 11, 1804, 1 child. Joined royal forces in Germany at outbreak of French Revolution; mem. King's Horse Guards, 1792; captured, escaped to Amsterdam, Holland, eventually went to S. Am., 1793; moved to Newtown, L.I., N.Y., 1795, became disciple of Voltaire; converted to Soc. of Friends after reading William Penn; moved to Phila., 1795; officially recorded as minister of Christ by Monthly Meeting of North Dist., 1798; moved to N.Y.C. because of yellow fever plague in Phila., 1799; itinerant preacher in U.S., 1799-1807; traveled to France, 1807-08; made 3d European tour with William Allen of London, Eng., 1818-20; ret. to Burlington, N.J., 1823; made another trip to Europe, 1831-34. Author: Scripture Lessons for Schools, 1820. Died Burlington, Nov. 16, 1855.

GRENNELL, George, Jr., congressman; b. Greenfield, Mass., Dec. 25, 1786; attended Deerfield Acad.; grad. Dartmouth, 1808. Admitted to bar, 1811; pros. atty. Franklin County, 1820-28; mem. Mass. Senate, 1825-27; mem. U.S. Ho. of Reps., 21st-25th congresses, 1829-39; Whig presdl. elector, 1840; trustee Amherst Coll., 1838-59; judge of probate, 1849-53; clk. Franklin County Cts., 1853-56; 1st pres. Troy & Greenfield R.R. Died Greenfield, Nov. 19, 1877; buried Green River Cemetery.

GRESHAM, Walter Quintin, army officer, cabinet officer; b. Lanesville, Ind., Mar. 17, 1832; s. William and Sarah (Davis) G.; attended Ind. U.; m. Matilda McGrain, Feb. 11, 1858. Admitted to Ind. bar, 1854; mem. Ind. Legislature, 1860; served as div. comdr. in Gen. Blair's Corps, U.S. Army, before Atlanta, 1861; commd. brig. gen., 1863, brevetted maj. gen., 1865; U.S. dist. judge for Ind., 1869-82; U.S. postmaster gen., 1882-84; suggested as Republican candidate for presidency, did not receive nomination, 1884, 88; U.S. sec. of treasury, 1884; apptd. circuit judge 7th U.S. Jud. Dist., 1884; broke with Rep. Party over McKinley tariff; offered nomination as Populist Party candidate for Pres. U.S., 1892; supported Cleveland in 1892 election; sec. of state under Pres. Cleveland, 1893-95; advised against Hawaiian annexation treaty, settled Nicaraguan-Brit. dispute and Allianca affair between U.S. and Spain. Died Washington, D.C., May 28, 1895; buried Arlington (Va.) Nat. Cemetery.

GREVILLE, Mr., actor. Left school at Princeton to join company of David Douglass, 1767, appeared with company in Phila., N.Y.C.; 1st native American to become profl. actor.

GREW, Theophilus, mathematician; M.A. (hon.), Coll. and Acad. of Phila., 1757; m. Elizabeth Cossins, 1735; m.2d, Frances Bowen, 1739; m. 3d, Rebecca Richards, 1747. Published widely circulated almanacs in N.Y.C., Phila., Annapolis, Md., Williamsburg, Va., 1732-57; headmaster Kent County (Md.) Pub. Sch., 1740-42; conducted pvt. sch. for study of mathematics, Phila., 1742-50; cons. for Pa. in survey to determine boundary between Pa. and Md., 1750; apptd. 1st prof. mathematics Coll. and Acad. od Phila., 1750. Died Phila., 1759.

GREY, Benjamin Edwards, congressman; b. "Shiloh," nr. Bardstown, Ky.; studied law. Admitted to bar, began practice of law, Hopkinsville, Ky.; mem. Ky. Ho. of Reps., 1838-39; mem. Ky. Senate, 1847-51; presiding officer Ky. Senate, acting lt. gov., 1850; mem. U.S. Ho. of Reps. (Whig) from Ky., 32d-33d congresses, 1851-55. Died Selma, Ala.

GRIDER, Henry, congressman; b. Garrard County, Ky., July 16, 1796; studied law. Admitted to bar, began practice of law, Bowling Green, Ky.; served in War of 1812; mem. Ky. Ho. of Reps., 1827-31, Ky. Senate, 1833-37; mem. U.S. Ho. of Reps. (Whig) from Ky., 28th-29th,, 37th-39th congresses, 1843-47, 61-66. Died Bowling Green, Sept. 7, 1866; buried Old College Street Cemetery.

GRIDLEY, Charles Vernon, naval officer; b. Logansport, Ind., Nov. 24, 1844; s. Franklin and Ann (Sholes) G.; grad. U.S. Naval Acad., 1863; m. Harriet Frances Vincent, May 1, 1872, 3 children including Ruth. Took part in Battle of Mobile Bay, 1864; commd. lt., assigned to South Pacific Squadron 1867; assigned to ship Michigan on Gt. Lakes, 1870-73, to South Atlantic stas., 1873-74; instr. U.S. Naval Acad., 1875-79; promoted comdr., 1882; navigation officer Boston Navy Yard, 1882-84; commanded vessels Jamestown and Portsmouth, 1884-86, cruiser Marion, 1892-94; commd. capt., 1897, commanded receiving ship Richmond; commanded Olympia, flagship of Commodore (later Adm.) Dewey in Asiatic Squadron, 1897, received Dewey's order "You may fire when ready, Gridley," in Battle of Manila Bay, 1898; a destroyer named in his honor, 1918. Died Kobe, Japan, June 5, 1898; buried Lakeside Cemetery, Erie, Pa.

GRIDLEY, Jeremiah, atty. gen. Mass.; b. Boston, Mar. 10 1702; s. Richard and Rebecca Gridley; grad. Harvard, 1725. m. Abigail Lewis, 3 daus. A founder Marine Soc., 1742; became Free Mason, 1748, grand master for all N. Am., 1749-67; mem. Mass. Gen. Ct., 1755-57; atty. gen. Province of Mass., 1757-67, defended legality of writs of assistance (requiring colonists to contribute to support of Brit. Army) against James Otis, before Superior Ct. of Judication, 1761. Died Brookline, Mass., Sept. 10, 1767.

GRIDLEY, Richard, army officer, mil. engr.; b. Boston, Jan. 3, 1711; s. Richard Gridley; m. Hannah Deming, Feb. 25, 1730, 9 children. Served as engr. during Siege of Louisbourg, 1745; drew plans for battery and other fortifications Boston Harbor, 1746; built Ft. Western (Augusta, Me.) and Ft. Halifax, 1752; commd. col. Brit. Army, served under Winslow in expdn. to Crown Point, 1756, under Amherst, 1758, under Wolfe in expdn. to Quebec, 1759; commanded Mass. arty., 1759; commd. chief engr., comdr. arty. Continental Army at Cambridge, Mass., 1775; commd maj. gen., 1775, planned defensive works of Bunker Hill on the night before battle, 1775; commd. col., 1775; engr. gen. Eastern Dept., 1777-80. Died Stoughton, Mass., June 21, 1796.

GRIER, Robert Cooper, asso. justice U.S. Su-Ct.; b. Cumberland County, Pa., Mar. 5, 1794; s. Isaac and Elizabeth (Coopes) G.; grad. Dickinson Coll., 1812; m. Isabella Rose, 1829. Instr., Dickinson Coll., 1813; prin. Acad. of Northumberland, 1815; admitted to bar, Bloomsburg, Pa., 1817; pres. judge Allegheny County Dist. Ct., 1833-46; asso. justice U.S. Supreme Ct., 1846-70, concurred in Dred Scott case, wrote letter to incoming Pres. James Buchanan on probable outcome; upheld power of Pres. to establish by proclamation a blockade of Confederate coast in Prize cases involving Rebel claims for destroyed ships. Died Phila., Sept. 25, 1870.

GRIEVE, Miller, journalist, diplomat; b. Edinburgh, Scotland, Jan. 11, 1801; s. John and Marion (Miller) G.; m. Sarah Caroline Grantland, 1833, 2 children. Came to Savannah, Ga., 1817, moved to Oglethorpe County, Ga., 1820; practiced law in Lexington, Ga.; pvt. sec. to Gov. George Rockingham Gilmer, moved to Milledgeville, Ga., 1829-30; mgr., publisher So. Recorder, Milledgeville, 1833-53, became organ for Whig party in Ga., influence of paper is said to have affected reelection of Gilmer in 1837, and to have been determining factor in Ga. voting for William Henry Harrison, 1840, for Zachary Taylor, 1848; mem. Ga. Legislature, 1841-45, chmn. bank com.; commd. U.S. charge d'affaires in Denmark, 1852. Died Milledgeville, circa 1878.

GRIFFIN, Charles, army officer; b. Granville, O., Dec. 18, 1825; s. Appolus Griffin; grad. U.S. Mil. Acad., 1847; m. Sallie Carroll, Dec. 10, 1861. Served in Mexican War; commd. 1st lt. U.S. Army, 1849; served against Navajo Indians in N. M., 1849-54; instr. in tactics U.S. Mil. Acad., 1860; organizer Battery D, 5th Arty., 1860; promoted capt., 1861; brig. gen., 1862; commanded West Point battery in 1st Battle of Bull Run served at Battle of Malvern Hill commanded div. at battles of Antietam and Fredericksburg in Hooker's Campaign, served in Peninsular Campaign under Gen. John Pope (relieved of command after 2d Battle of Bull Run pending investigation because of remarks about Pope but restored to command), 1862; comdr. 5th Army Corps, 1865, directed by Grant to receive arms and colors of Army of North Va. after surrender at Appomattox Court House; commd. maj. gen., 1865, col., 1866, in charge Mil. Dist. of Tex., stationed at Galveston 1866-67. Died of yellow fever (after refusing to leave his duty station when epidemic broke out), Sept. 15, 1867.

GRIFFIN, Cyrus, Continental congressman; b. Farnham Parish, Va., July 16, 1748; s. LeRoy and Mary Ann (Bertrand) G.; student law Edinburgh (Scotland) U.; m. Lady Christina Stuart, 1770. Admitted to Middle Temple, London, Eng.; Began law practice in Va. 1774; addressed Plan of Reconciliation between Great Britain and her Colonies to Earl of Dartmouth 1775; mem. Va. Legislature from Lancaster County 1777-78 mem. Continental Congress 1778-81, 87-88, pres.; 1788-89; judge Ct. Appeals in Cases of Capture (which helped familiarize public with idea of some sort of superior fed. judiciary), 1780-87; a commr. to attend treaty between Creek Indians and State of Ga., 1789; U.S. judge for Dist. of Va. (apptd. by Pres. Washington), 1789-1810, presided at Aaron Burr's trial. Died Yorktown, Pa., Dec. 14, 1810.

GRIFFIN, Edward Dorr, clergyman, coll. pres.; b. East Haddam, Conn., Jan. 6, 1770; s. George and Eve (Dorr) G.: grad. Yale, 1790; D.D., Union Coll., 1808; m. Frances Huntington, May 17, 1796; 2 children. Studied theology under Jonathan Edwards (the younger), who instilled a revival sense; ordained to ministry Congregational Ch., 1794; prof. pulpit eloquence Adnover Theol. Sem., 1809-11, a founder Am. Bible Soc.; active in United Fgn. Mission Soc.; pres. Williams Coll., 1821-36, largely responsible for saving it from financial disaster,Author: Lectures in Park Street Church, 1813. Died Newark, N.J., Nov. 8, 1837.

GRIFFIN, Isaac, congressman; b. Kent County, Del., Feb. 27, 1756; attended public schs. Engaged in agriculture, Fayette County, Pa.; commd. capt. during Revolutionary War; apptd. justice of peace, 1794; mem. Pa. Ho. of Reps., 4 terms, from 1807; mem. U.S. Ho. of Reps. (Democrat, filled vacancy) from Pa., 13th-14th congresses, Feb. 16, 1813-17. Died on his estate, Nicholson Twp., Pa., Oct. 12, 1827; buried Nicholson Twp.

GRIFFIN, John King, congressman; b. nr. Clinton, S.C., Aug. 13, 1789. Became a planter; mem. S.C. Ho. of Reps., 1816-18, S.C. Senate, 1820-24, 28; mem. U.S. Ho. of Reps. (State Rights Whig) from S.C., 22d-26th congresses, 1831-41. Died nr. Clinton, S.C., Aug. 1, 1841; buried Little River Church Cemetery.

GRIFFIN, Samuel, congressman; b. Richmond County, Va.; studied law. Admitted to bar, practiced law; served as col. in Revolutionary War, wounded at Harlem Heights, 1776; mem. state bd. of war; mem. Va. Ho. of Dels., 1786-88; mem. U.S. Ho. of Reps. from Va., 1st-3d congresses, 1789-95. Died Nov. 3, 1810.

GRIFFIN, Thomas, congressman, jurist; b. Yorktown, Va., 1773; studied law. Admitted to bar, practiced law; also engaged in farming; mem. Va. Ho. of Dels., 1793-1800, 19-23, 27-30; justice Ct. of Oyer and Terminer, 1796-1810, chmn. ct., 1814-20; mem. U.S. Ho. of Reps. from Va., 8th Congress, 1803-05; chief justice Ct. of Quarter Sessions, 1805-10; justice York County Ct., 1810-12; served as maj. Inf., in War of 1812; Died "The Mansion," nr. Yorktown, Oct. 7, 1837.

GRIFFING, Josephine Sophie White, social reformer; b. Hebron, Conn., Dec. 18, 1814; d. Joseph and Sophie (Waldo) White; m. Charles S.S. Griffing, 1836, 1 child. Moved to Ohio where she and her husband worked with various anti-slavery socs., 1842, their home station of Underground R.R.; became advocate for women's sufferage, 1848; she became worker in Loyal League and in sanitary commn. units when Civil War broke out, 1861; went to Washington (D.C.) to urge Fed. aid for freed Negro slaves, 1863, urged modern edn. and colonization on deserted plantations for them; became agt. Nat. Freedman's Relief Assn. of D.C., 1863; asst. commr. Freedman's Bur., 1865; organized, became pres. Universal Franchise Assn. of D.C., 1867; corr. sec. Nat. Women's Suffrage Assn. Died Feb. 18, 1872.

GRIFFITH, Benjamin, clergyman, historian; b. County Cardigan, South Wales, Eng., Oct. 16, 1668; m. Sarah Miles, Dec. 7, 1720. Came to Del. 1710; joined Welsh Tract Baptist Ch.; moved to Montgomery County, Pa., 1720, became pastor of church; ordained, 1725; commd. by Phila. Assn. to collect accounts of Bapt. churchs in colonies, 1746, presented his findings to Assn. in folio form (now in possession Am. Bapt. Hist. Soc.), regarded as one of important source books on early Bapt. history. Author: A Short Treatise of Church-Discipline, 1743. Died circa Oct. 5, 1768.

GRIFFITH, Robert Eglesfield, physician; b. Phila., Feb. 13, 1798; grad. med. dept. U. Pa., 1820. Practiced medicine, Phila., 1820-36; physician to Phila. Bd. Health, 1834-36; prof. materia medica U. Md., 1836-38; prof. medicine U. Va., 1838-49; v.p. Phila. Acad. Natural Science, 1849-50. Author: Medical Botany, 1847; Universal Formulary, 1848. Died Phila., June 26, 1850.

GRIFFITH, Samuel, congressman, lawyer; b. Merthyr Tydfil, South Wales, Gt. Britain, Feb. 14, 1816; grad. Allegheny Coll., Meadville, Pa.; studied law. Admitted to bar, 1846, began practice of law, Mercer, Pa.; del. Democratic Nat. Conv., Balt.; mem. U.S. Ho. of Reps. (Democrat) from Pa., 42d Congress, 1871-73. Died Mercer, Oct. 1, 1893; buried Mercer Cemetery.

GRIFFITH, William, lawyer, author; b. Boundbrook, N.J., 1766; s. Dr. John Griffith; studied law under Elisha Boudinot, Newark, N.J.; married, at least 1 dau., Susan. Admitted to N.J. bar as atty., 1788, counselor, 1791; practiced in Burlington, N.J.; became N.J.'s leading lawyer on land titles; best known for legal writings; one of midnight judicial appointments of John Adams, 1801, his court abolished by act of Congress, returned to law practice; mem. N.J. Assembly, 1823-24; mayor Burlington, 1824-26. Author: A Treatise on the Jurisdiction and Proceedings of Justices of the Peace in Civil Suits, 1796; The Scriveners Guide, 1797; New Jersey State Gazette (series of essays on what he considered defective structure and unsound principles of N.J. Constn.), 1798-99; Historical Notes of the American Colonies and Revolution from 1754 to 1775, 1836, 43. Died June 7, 1826.

GRIFFITHS, John Willis, naval architect; b. N.Y.C., Oct. 6, 1809; s. John Griffiths. Wrote series of articles on naval architecture in portsmouth Advocate, 1836; delivered 1st formal lecture on naval architecture, N.Y.C.; editor American Ship, 1878-82; one of 1st to specialize in designing; designed Rainbow (1st "extreme clipper ship"); designed Sea Witch; developed improved form of rivet; invented machine for bending timber into crooked forms used in shipbldg.; designed New Era (1st ship with mechanically bent timber), 1870. Author: Treatise on Marine and Naval Architecture, 1850; Ship Builder's Manual, 1853; Progressive Ship-Builder, 1875. Died Bklyn., Mar. 30, 1882.

GRIGEBY, Hugh Blair, lawyer, journalist, historian; b. Norfolk, Va., Nov. 22, 1806; s. Rev. Benjamin and Elizabeth (McPherson) G.; attended Yale; m. Mary Venerable Carrington, Nov. 19, 1840. Admitted to Va. bar but started journalistic career because of his increasing deafness; owner, editor Norfolk American Beacon for 6 years; mem. Va. Ho. of Dels. from Norfolk, 1828-29, 29-30; del. Va. Constl. Conv., 1829-30; bd. visitors Coll. William and Mary, elected chancellor, 1871; mem., contbr. to Va. Hist. Soc., pres., 1870; most of his life spent studying history of U.S. and Va. Author: The Virginia Convention of 1776, 1855; Discourse on the Life and Character of the Honorable Littleton Waller Tazewell, 1860; The Founders of Washington College, 1890. Died Charlotte County, Va., Apr. 28, 1881.

GRIM, David, tavern keeper, artist; b. Zweiburcken, Bavaria, Germany, Aug. 25, 1737; s. Philip Grim; m. 2d, Mary Barwick, Dec. 24, 1781; 3 children including Elizabeth, Catherine, Philip. Came to N.Y.C, 1739; cruised about West Indies aboard King of Prussia, 1757; innkeeper at "Sign of the Three Tuns." Chapel St., N.Y.C. (popular place among German patriots), 1767-89; joined German Soc. of City N.Y., 1784, as pres., 1784-1802 (succeeded Baron von Steuben); mcht., 1789; most remembered for pen-and-ink sketches he made during last years of his life of N.Y.C. as he remembered it as a boy, among them Plan and Elevation of the City Hall, A Plan of the City and Environs of New York as They Were in the Years 1742-43, 1744. Died Mar. 26, 1826.

GRIMES, James Stanley, natural philosopher, author; b. Boston, May 10, 1807; probably son of Andrew (or Joseph) and Polly (or Sally) (Robbins) Grimes. Practiced law, Boston and N.Y.C.; prof. med. jurisprudence Castleton Med. Coll., also Willard Inst.; one of 1st Am. evolutionists; became interested in phrenology, 1832; in mesmerism; published Phreno-Geology (which he claimed to be 1st essay on theistic evolution), 1851; took part in series of 8 debates with Leo Miller, Boston, 1860; moved to Evanston, Ill. Author: A New System of Phrenology, 1839; Etherology, 1845; The Mysteries of Human Explained, 1857; Phreno-Physiology, 1893. Died Evanston, Sept. 27, 1903.

GRIMES, James Wilson, senator, gov. Ia.; b. Deering, N.H., Oct. 20, 1816; s. John and Elizabeth (Wilson) G.; A.B., Dartmouth (as of class of 1836), 1845; m. Elizabeth Nealley, Nov. 9, 1846. Moved to Ia., 1836; elected to legislative assembly Ia. Territory, 1838, 43, 68, became chmn. judiciary com.; leader in promoting railroads for Ia.; charter mem. So. Ia. Hort. Soc.; gov. Ia. (Whig), 1854-58; his administrn. established state univ. at Iowa City; a founder of Rep. Party in Ia.; mem. U.S. Senate (Republican) from Ia., 1859-69; carried into Senate chamber (because of paralytic stroke) during voting at impeachment trial of Andrew Johnson, voted not guilty (which resulted in Johnson's acquittal); his polit. reputation and leadership suffered as result of this action; instrumental in keeping Naval Acad. at Annapolis. Died Burlington, Ia., Feb. 7, 1872.

GRIMKÉ, Angelina Emily, reformer; b. Charleston, S.C., Feb. 20, 1805; d. Judge John Faucheraud and Mary (Smith) G.; m. Theodore Dwight Weld, May 14, 1838; 1 son, Charles Stuart. Moved North following her sister, Sarah Moore; published letter in William Lloyd Garrison's Liberator which encouraged him in his abolitionist views, 1835; wrote Appeal to the Christian Women of the South, 1836; threatened with imprisonment if she returned to Charleston; wrote Letters to Catherine E. Becker in reply to her Essay on Slavery and Abolitionism Addressed to A. E. Grimke, 1838; interested in women's rights; wrote Appeal to the Women of the Nominally Free States, 1837; aided husband and sister in conducting a sch., Bellville, N.J. Died Hyde Park, Mass., Oct. 26, 1879.

GRIMKÉ, Frederick, jurist; b. Charleston, S.C., Sept. 1, 1791; s. John Faucheraud Grimké; grad. Yale, 1810. Practiced law, Charleston, S.C., 1810-18, Columbus, O., 1818-63; judge Ohio Supreme Ct., 1836-41. Author: Ancient and Modern Literature, 1848; The Nature and Tendency of Free Institutions, 1848. Died Chillicothe, O., Mar. 8, 1863.

GRIMKÉ, John Faucheraud, army officer, jurist; b. Charleston, S.C., Dec. 16, 1752; s. John Paul and Mary (Faucheraud) G.; A.B., Trinity Coll., 1774; m. Mary Smith, Oct. 12, 1784, 14 children including Thomas Smith, Sarah Moore, Angelina Emily. Commd. capt. S.C. Arty., Continental Army, 1776, promoted lt. col.; dep. adj; gen. for S.C. and Ga., 1776-80. imprisoned at surrender of Charleston (S.C.), 1780, parolled, 1781; mem. S.C. Ho. of Reps., 1781-86; sr. asso. of S.C. Superior Court 1799-1819; mem. S.C. Conv. which ratified U.S. Constn., 1788; presdl. elector, 1789. Died Long Branch, N.J., Aug.9, 1819.

GRIMKÉ, Sarah Moore, reformer; b. Charleston, S.C., Nov. 26 1792; d. John Faucheraud and Mary (Smith) Grimke. After death of her father, she and her sister Angelina freed slaves they had inherited; moved to Phila. to escape slavery and "the shrieks of the tortured victims,"1821; joined Soc. of Friends; joined Am. Anti-slavery Soc., began speaking career; became champion of women,s rights. Author: Epistle to the Clergy of the Southern States, 1836; Letters of the Equality of the Sexes and the Condition of Woman, 1838. Died Hyde Park, Mass., Dec. 23, 1873.

GRIMKÉ, Thomas Smith, reformer; b. Charleston, S.C., Sept. 26, 1786; s. John Faucheraud and Mary (Smith) G.; grad. Yale, 1807; m. Sarah Daniel Dragton, Jan. 25, 1810, 6 sons. Partner (with Robert Y. Hayne) in law firm, S.C. mem. S.C. Senate, 1826-30; a pacifist, argued for maintenance of the Union; mem. Am. Peace Soc.; active in temperance movement; advocated manual training in public schs.; favored higher edn. for women. Author: Address on the Truth, Dignity, Power and Beauty of the Principles of Peace, 1832. Died Columbus, O., Oct. 11, 1834; buried Columbus.

GRINNELL, Henry, mcht., philanthropist; b. New Bedford, Mass., Feb. 13, 1799; s. Cornelius and Sylvia (Howland) G.; ed. New Bedford Acad.; m. Sarah Minton, 1822; 1 son, Henry Walton. Partner, Grinnell, Minton & Co. (became one of strongest merc. houses in N.Y.C.), 1825-50 U.S. Mgr. for Liverpool & London Ins. Co. for a number of years; bore entire expense of outfitting vessels Advance and Rescue for Franklyn Polar Expdn.; outfitted expdn. sent in search of Sir John Franklyn under command of Lt. E.J. DeNaven, 1850 (DeNaven discovered land at latitude 80° N. which became known as Grinnell Land, but did not find Franklyn), helped send 2nd expdn. under ship Advance (attained highest latitude ever achieved by sailing vessel); a founder Am. Geog. and Statis. Soc., pres., 1862-63. Died N.Y.C., June 30, 1874.

GRINNELL, Joseph, mcht., mfr.; b. New Bedford Mass., Nov. 17, 1788; s. Cornelius and Sylvia (Howland) G.; m. Sarah Russell, May 14, 1812; m. 2nd Rebecca (Chase) Kinsman, Sept. 19, 1865; 1 adopted dau., Cornelia. Apptd. dep. collector Portsmouth (R.I.) 1809; established firm Fish & Grinnell, 1815; pres. 1st Nat. Band, New Bedford; 1832-73; became asso. with Boston & Providence R.R.,1841, dir. and pres. 5 years; mem. R.I. Gov.'s Council, 1838, 39, 40; mem. U.S. Ho. of Reps. from Mass., 28th-31st congresses, Dec. 3, 1843-51; pres. 1st unit Wamsutta Mills 1847. Died New Bedford, Mass., Feb. 7, 1885.

GRINNELL, Josiah Bushnell, congressman, clergyman; b. New Haven, Vt., Dec. 22, 1821; s. Myron and Catherine (Hastings) G.; grad. Auburn Theol. Sem., 1847; m. Julia Ann Chapin, Feb. 5, 1852. Pastor, Congregational Ch., Union Village, N..Y, 1847-50; started First Congl. Ch., Washington, D.C., 1851; a founder Grinnell (Ia.), 1854; dir. Rock Island R.R.; mem. Ia. Senate, 1856-60; admitted to Ia. bar, 1858; mem. U.S. Ho. of Reps. (Republican) from Ia., 38th-39th congresses, 1863-67; introduced Devon cattle and Norman and Clydesdale horses into Ia.; pres. Am. Agrl. Soc., 1885; pres. Central R.R. of Ia.; a founder Grinnell Coll., trustee 1854-84; pres. Ia. Hort. Soc.; said to have been the man to whom Horace Greeley said "Go West,, young man, go West." Died Marshaltown, Ia., Mar. 31, 1891; buried Hazelwood Cemetery, Marshaltown.

GRINNELL, Moses Hicks, mcht., congressman; b. New Bedford, Mass., Mar. 3, 1803; s. Cornelious and Sylvia (Howland) G.; m. Susan Russell, 1826; m. 2d, Julia Irving, 1836. Entered firm Fish, Grinnell & Co. (important Am. importing houses), 1824; established firm which became Grinnell, Minturn & Co.; mem. U.S. Ho. of Reps. from N.Y., 26th Congress, 1839-41; pres. N.Y.C. C.of C., 1843-48; pres. Instn. for Savs. of Mchts. Clks.; mem. original Central Park Commn., N. Y.C.; trustee Univ. City N.Y., 1851; contbr. to outfitting 2d Franklin Expdn. under Kane, 1853-55; presdl. elector supporting Fremont and Dayton, 1856; commr. charties and corrections N.Y. C., 1860-65; mem. Union Defense Com.; collector Port of N.Y., 1869-70, naval officer of customs, 1870-71. Died N.Y.C., Nov. 24, 1877; buried Sleepy Hollow Burying Ground, Tarrytown, N.Y.

GRISCOM, John, educator, chemist; b. Hancock's Bridge, N.J., Sept. 17,1774; s. William and Rachel (Denn) G.; m. Abigail Hoskins, 1800; m. 2d, Rachel Denn, Dec. 13, 1843; children--Abigail, John. First Am. educator to teach chemistry and give lectures on subject to classes, 1803; prof. chemistry and natural history Queens Coll. (now Rutgers U.), 1812-28; organized N.Y. High. Sch. for Boys 1825; instituted Lancasterian system of monitorial instrn.; prin. Friends' Sch., Providence, R.I.; prof. chemistry Columbia; made known med. properties of cod-liver oil and value iodine in treatment of goiter; a founder N.Y. Soc. for Prevention Pauperism, Soc. for Reformation Juvenile Delinquents; prin. founder House of Refuge (1st reformatory in U.S.). Author: Year in Europe, 2 vols., 1823; Discourse on Character and Education, 1823; Monitorial Instruction, 1825. Died Burlington, N.J., Feb. 26, 1852.

GRISWOLD, Alexander Viets, clergyman; b. Simsbury, Conn., Apr. 22, 1766; s. Elisha and Eunice (Viets) G.; D.D. (hon.), Brown U., 1810, Princeton, 1811, Harvard, 1812; m. Elizabeth Mitchelson, 1785; m. 2d, Mrs. Amelia Smith, 1827; 14 children. Ordained deacon Episcopalian Ch., 1795, priest, Plymouth, Conn., 1795; rector St. Michael's Ch., Bristol, R.I., 1804; 1st and only bishop of Eastern Diocese, 1810-30; reorganized and revitalized Episcopal Ch. in New Eng. Author: Discourses on the Most Important Doctrine and Duties of the Christian Religion, 1830; The Reformation and the Apostolic Religion, 1830; Remarks on Social Prayer Meetings, 1858. Died Boston, Feb. 15, 1843.

GRISWOLD, Gaylord, congressman, lawyer; b. Windsor, Conn., Dec. 18, 1767; grad. Yale, 1787; studied law. Admitted to bar, 1790, began practice of law, Windsor; moved to Herkimer, N.Y., 1792 (becoming 1st lawyer in Herkimer County); mem. N.Y. State Assembly, 1796-98; mem. U.S. Ho. of Reps. (Federalist) from N.Y., 8th Congress, 1803-05. Died Herkimer, Mar. 1, 1809; buried Oak Hill Cemetery.

GRISWOLD, John Augustus, congressman; b. Nassau, N.Y., Nov. 11, 1822; s. Chester and Abbey (Moulton) G.; m. Elizabeth Hart, Sept. 14, 1843. Head Bessemer Steel Works and Rensselaer Iron Works; mayor Troy (N.Y.), 1855; mem. U.S. Ho. of Reps. from N.Y., 38th-40th congresses, 1863-69; during Civil War raised 3 regts. of inf. Griswold Light Cavalry, Black-horse Cavalry; aided John Ericsson in building Monitor; constructed many iron-clad monitors during Civil War; pres. Troy & Lansingbargh R.R. Co., Troy & Cohoes R.R. Co., New Orleans, Mobile & Tex. R.R. Co.; dir., stockholder Port Henry Iron Ore Co., Fall Creek Bituminous Coal Co.; elected regent U. State N.Y., 1869. Died Troy, Oct. 31, 1872; buried Oakwood Cemetery, Troy.

GRISWOLD, Matthew, gov. Conn., jurist; b. Lyme, Conn., Mar. 25, 1714; s. John and Hannah (Lee) G. ; LL.D., Yale, 1779; m. Ursula Wolcott, Nov. 10, 1743; 7 children including Matthew, Robert. Admitted to bar, 1743; rep. Lyme to Conn. Gen. Assembly, 1751-59; mem. Conn. Gov.'s Council, 1759-66; judge Conn. Superior Ct., 1766-69; chief justice, 1769-84; dep. gov. Conn., 1769-84; gov., 1784-86; presided over Conn. Conv. which ratified U.S. Constn., 1788. Died Lyme, Apr. 28, 1799.

GRISWOLD, Roger, gov. Conn.; b. Lymme, Conn., May 21, 1762; s. Matthew and Ursula (Wolcott) G.; grad. Yale, 1780, LL.D. (hon.), 1812; LL.D. (hon.), Harvard, 1811; m. Fanny Rogers, Oct. 27, 1788. Admitted to Conn. bar, 1783; mem. U.S. Ho. of Reps. from Conn., 4th-8th congresses, 1795-1805, engaged in brawl on floor of House with Matthew Lyon; judge Supreme Ct. of Conn., 1807; lt. gov. Conn., 1809-11; gov., 1811;1812. Died Norwich, Conn., Oct. 25, 1812; buried Griswold Cemetery, Lyme, Conn.

GRISWOLD, Rufus Wilmot, editor, critic, author; b. Benson, Vt., Feb. 15, 1815; s. Rufus and Deborah (Wass) G.; m. Caroline Searles, Mar. 1837; m. 2d, Charlotte Myers, Aug. 10, 1845; m. 3d, Harriet Stanley McCrillis, 1853; 3, children. Licensed to preach by Baptist Ch., 1837, never held regular pastorate; edited Vergennes Vermonter, 1838-39; advocated abolition of slavery and laws against imprisonment for debt and capital punishment; worked for Horace Greeley, N.Y. C., 1838-40; established library in N.Y.C. Prison; wrote for Daily Standard and Gazette in Phila., 1840-41; asst. editor Graham's Mag. 1842-43 (succeeded his friend Edgar Allan Poe); began to write literary criticism, surrounded himself with minor writers who sought his favors; Griswold wrote frank obituary at death of Poe (1849) published in N.Y. Daily Tribune, included writer's good and bad traits, made him unpopular in many literary circles; named literary executor by Poe; edited Internat; Monthly Mag., 1850-52, P.T. Barnum's Illustrated News, 1852-53. Author: The Poets and Poetry of America, 1842; The Songs of Beranger in English, 1844; The Poetical Works of W.M. Praed, 1844,52; The Poets and Poetry of England in the Nineteenth Century, 1844; The Prose Works of John Milton, 2 vols., 1845,47; The Prose Writers of America, 1847; The Female Poets of America, 1848; The Republican Court, or American Society in the Days of Washington, 1855. Died N.Y. C., Aug. 27, 1857; buried Greenwood Cemetery, Bklyn.

GRISWOLD, Stanley, clergyman, editor, senator; b. Torrington, Conn., Nov. 14, 1763; s. Shubael and Abigail (Stanley) G.; grad. Yale, 1786; m. Elizabeth Flagg, Aug. 5, 1789. Ordained to ministry Congregational Ch., 1790; colleague pastor, New Milford, Conn., 1790-1802; expelled by Litchfield South Ministerial Assn. for liberal polit. views, 1797 (favored new state constn. and ch. disestablishment); editor Polit. Observatory, Walpole, N.H., 1804; sec. Michigan Territory, 1805-08; mem. U.S. Senate from Ohio, June 2, 1809-Jan. 12, 1810; apptd. judge in Ill. Territory, 1810. Died Shawneetown, Ill. Territory, Aug. 21, 1815.

GRISWOLD, Victor Moreau, artist; b. Worthington, O., Apr. 14, 1819; studied law. Began painting portraits, circa 1840; exhibited at Am. Art-Union, N.A.D., 1849-58; became profl. photographer, Tiffin, O., 1851, Lancaster, O., 1853; invented ferrotype plate, 1856, manufactured plate, Lancaster, 1856-61, Peekskill, N.Y., 1861-72. Died Peekskill, June 18, 1872.

GRISWOLD, William McCrillis, bibliographer; b. Oct. 9, 1853; s. Rufus W. and Harriet Stanley (McCrillis) G.; grad. Harvard, 1875; m. Anne Deering Merrill, Sept. 14, 1882, 4 children. Spent several years in Europe, contbd. articles to Am. jours., after 1875; clk. patent office Library of Congress, 1882-88; engaged in prodn. of periodical indexes published at his own expense under pseudonym Q.P. Index (bibliographies marked by eccentricities in abbreviations and spelling), works include: A General Index to the Nation, Vols. I-III, 1880; A Directory of Writers for the Literary Press in the United States, 1884; The Novels of 1897, published 1897; Passages from the Correspondence and Other Papers of Rufus W. Griswold, 1898. Died Seal Harbor, Me., Aug. 3, 1899; buried Bangor, Me.

GROESBECK, William Slocum, congressman; b. Schenectady, N.Y., July 24, 1815; s. John H. and Mary (Slocum) G.; grad. Miami U., Oxford, O., 1834; m. Elizabeth Burnet, Nov. 12, 1837, 5 children. Admitted to Ohio bar, 1836; mem. Ohio Constl. Conv., 1851; commr. to codify laws of Ohio, 1852; mem. U.S. Ho. of Reps. from Ohio, 35th Congress, 1857-59; mem. Washington (D.C.) Peace Conv., 1861; mem. Ohio Senate, 1864; del. Nat. Union Conv., 1866; served as defense counsel to Pres. Andrew Johnson in his impeachment trials, 1868; presdl. candidate of a small group of liberal Republicans, 1872, received one electoral vote for vice pres. U.S.; del. Internat. Monetary Conf., Paris, France, 1878. Died Cincinnati, July 7, 1897; buried Spring Grove Cemetery, Cincinnati.

GRONLUND, Lawrence, author, lectr.; b. Denmark, July 13, 1846; M.A., U. Copenhagen (Denmark), 1865. Came to Milw., 1867, taught German in public schs.; admitted to Chgo. bar, 1869; became interested in Socialist movement; elected mem. exec. com. Socialist Labor Party, 1888; started movement for orgn. of secret soc. to be known as Am. Socialist Fraternity, 1891. Author: The Coming Revolution: Its Principles, 1878; The Cooperative Commonwealth (1st comprehensive works in English on socialism), 1884; Ca Ira! or Danton in the French Revolution, 1887; New Economy; A Peaceable Solution of the Social Problem, 1898; Socializing a State, 1898. Died N.Y.C., Oct. 15, 1899.

GROOMBRIDGE, William, artist; b. Tunbridge, Kent, Eng., 1748; m. Catherine. Landscape and portrait painter, Kent and London, Eng., 1773-90; arrived in Phila., circa 1794; painted in Phila., 1794-1804; moved to Balt., 1804; exhibited at Soc. of Artists, Phila., posthumously at Md. Hist. Soc. Died Balt., May 24, 1811.

GROOME, James Black, senator, gov. Md.; b. Elkton, Cecil County, Md., Apr. 4, 1838; attended Tennant Sch., Hartsville, Pa.; studied law. Admitted to Md. bar, 1838, began practice of law in Elkton; mem. Md. Constl. Conv., 1867; mem. Md. Ho. of Dels., 1871-72, 73-74; Democratic presdl. elector, 1872; gov. Md., 1874-76; resumed law practice, 1876; mem. U.S. Senate (Democrat) from Md., 1879-85; collector customs Port of Balt., 1889-93. Died Balt., Oct. 5, 1893; buried Elkton Presbyn. Cemetery.

GROS, John Daniel, clergyman, educator, philosopher; b. Webenheim, Bavarian Palatinate, Germany, 1738; s. Lorenz Gross: student U. Marburg, 1759, U. Heidelberg, 1761; S.T.D. (hon.), Columbia: Came to Am., 1764; founded ch., Allentown, Pa.; pastor German Reformed Ch., N.Y.C.; mem. Coetus which successfully freed itself from control of Dutch Synods; prof. German and geography Columbia, 1784-89, prof. moral philosophy, 1789-95; trustee, 1787-92; regent U. State N.Y., 1784-87. Author: Natural Principles of Rectitude, 1795. Died Canajoharie, N.Y., May 25, 1812.

GROSE, William, state legislator, army officer; b. Montgomery County, O., Dec. 16, 1812; s. William and Mary (Hubbel), G.; m. Rebecca Needham, Dec. 1836; m. 2d, Mrs. Martha Black, 1884. Admitted to Ind. bar, 1843, began practice of law, Newcastle, Ind., 1846; Democratic presdl. elector, 1852; mem. Ind. Legislature (Republican), 1857-59; commanded 36th Ind. Volunteer Inf. in Gen. Don Carlos Buell's army, 1861, took part in battles of Shiloh, Corinth, Chickamauga, Chattanooga, Missionary Ridge; commd. brig. gen. U.S. Volunteers, 1864, later transferred to Gen. George Henry Thomas' army; pres. of court-martial in Nashville, Tenn., June-Dec. 1865; commd. maj. gen. U.S. Volunteers, 1865; collector internal revenue 5th Dist. (apptd. by Andrew Johnson), 1866-74; mem. commn. that supervised building of 3 state hosps. for insane, 1884-86; mem. Ind. Senate, 1888. Author: The Story of the Marches, Battles, and Incidents of the 36th Regiment, Indiana Volunteer Infantry, 1891. Died Newcastle, July 30, 1900.

GROSEILLIERS, sieur de (Medart Chouart), explorer; b. Charly-Saint-Cyr, France; flourished 1625-84; s. Medard and Marie (Poirier) C.; m. Helene Martin, Sept. 3, 1647; m. 2d, Marguerite Radisson, Aug. 24, 1653. Went to Can., 1637 (or 1641), spent several years in mission to Hurons on Manitoulin Island; went to Three Rivers to open up fur trade, circa 1647; went on trapping expdn. with Pierre Esprit Radisson, 1658-60 (their furs confiscated since they did not have a license); went (with Radisson) to Boston where they met Col. George Cartwright (royal commr. of Charles II) and proposed voyage to Hudson Bay in Brit. interest; obtained audience with King Charles II, 1666, resulted in promise of ship with which to make trading venture to Hudson Bay; sailed with Groseilliers aboard ship Nonsuch and Radisson aboard ship Eaglet, 1668 (Eaglet never reached Hudson Bay); reached South Bay (now James Bay), built stockade called Ft. Charles; collected numerous furs and both Groseillers and Radisson honored by Charles II; this expdn. stimulated formation Hudson Bay Co., 1670; they made other expdns. for both England and France; Groseilliers settled in Can.

GROSS, Ezra Carter, congressman; b. Hartford, Vt., July 11, 1878; grad. U. Vt., 1806; studied law. Admitted to the bar, 1810; practiced law, Elizabethtown, N.Y., later in Keeseville, N.Y.; admitted as master in chancery, 1812; served in War of 1812; officer N.Y. Militia, 1814-21; surrogate Essex County (N.Y.), 1815-19; supr. Elizabethtown, 1818, 23-24; mem. U.S. Ho. of Reps. (Democrat) from N.Y., 16th Congress, 1819-21; resumed law practice, 1821; mem. N.Y. State Asembly, 1828-29. Died Albany, N.Y., Apr. 9, 1829; buried Evergreen Cemetery, Keeseville.

GROSS, Samuel, congressman; b. Upper Providence, Montgomery County, Pa., 1774; attended pub. schs. Farmer; mem. Pa. Ho. of Reps., 1803-07, Pa. Senate, 1811-15; mem. U.S. Ho. of Reps. (Democrat) from Pa., 16th-17th congresses, 1819-23; ret. from pub. life. Died Trappe, Pa., Mar. 19, 1844; buried Augustus Lutheran Cemetery, Trappe.

GROSS, Samuel David, surgeon, educator; b. Easton, Pa., July 8, 1805; s. Philip and Johanna (Brown) G.; grad. Jefferson Med. Coll., 1828; D. C.L., Oxford (Eng.) U. ; LL.D., Cambridge (Eng.) U., U. Edinburgh (Scotland), U. Pa.; m. Louisa Weissell, 1828. Apptd. demonstrator anatomy Med. Coll., Ohio, 1833; prof. pathological anatomy Cincinnati Med. Coll., 1835; prof. surgery U. Louisville, 1840; Jefferson Med. Coll., 1856; a founder A.M.A.; founder Phila. Path. Soc., Phila. Acad. Surgery, Am.

Surg. Soc.; established Acad. Surgery prize for original articles; presided over Internat. Congress Surgeons, 1876; v.p. German Surg. Soc.; inventor numerous instruments; translator from French and German med. texts. Author: Elements of Pathological Anatomy (1st work on subject in English lang.), 1839; A Practical Treatise on Foreign Bodies in the Air Passages, 1854; A System of Surgery, Pathological, Diagnostic, Theraputive and Operative, 1859. Died Phila., May 6, 1884.

GROSS, Samuel Weissell, surgeon; b. Cincinnati, Feb. 4, 1837; s. Samuel David and Louisa (Weissell) G.; grad. Jeffersoon Med. Coll., 1857; m. Grace Linzee Revere, Dec. 28, 1876. Served as surgeon U.S. Army during Civil War; commd. lt. col. Med. Corps, 1865; surgeon Phila. Hosp; surgeon hosp. of Jefferson Med. Coll.; founded, developed present-day radical operation for cancer; prof. principles of surgery and clin. surgery Jefferson Med. Coll., 1882; one of 1st physicians in Phila. to use antiseptic surgery. Author : Practical Treatise on Tumors of the Mammary Gland, 1880; Practical Treatise on Impotence, Sterility and Allied Disorders of the Male Sexual Organs, 1881. Died Phila., Apr. 16, 1889.

GROSSMAN, Georg Martin, clergyman, coll. pres.; b. Grossbieberau, Germany, Oct. 18, 1823; s. Ludwig and Maria (Rotenhauser) G.; studied theology under Friedrich Bauer, Nürnberg Germany, U. Erlangen (Germany); m. Nannie Steppes. Immigrated to U.S. to conduct sch. for tchrs., Saginaw, Mich., 1852; involved in controversy with Mo. Synod, went to Ia., 1853; settled in Dubuque, Ia., an organizer German Lutheran Synod of Ia., 1854, pres., 1854-93, synod grew with influx of German immigrants; pres. theol. sem., until 1874; pres. Wartburg Normal Coll., Waverly, Ia., 1878-94. Died Waverly, Aug. 24, 1897.

GROSVENOR, Thomas Peabody, congressman; b. Pomfret, Conn., Dec. 20, 1778; grad. Yale, 1800; studied law. Admitted to the bar, 1803; began law practice, Hudson, N.Y.; mem. N.Y. State Assembly, 1810-12; dist. atty. Essex County (N.Y.), 1810-11; mem. U.S. Ho. of Reps. (Federalist), 12th Congress (filled vacancy), 13th-14th congresses, Jan. 29, 1813-17; practiced law, Balt. Died Waterloo, nr. Balt., Apr. 24, 1817; buried Hudson.

GROSVENOR, William Mason, journalist, author; s. Rev. Mason and Esther D. (Scarborough) G.; attended Yale, 1861-53; m. Ellen M. Stone, 1867; m. 2d, Ellen Sage, 1870. Editor, New Haven (Conn.) Palladium, 1859-61; enlisted in 13th Regt. Conn. Volunteers, 1861, promoted capt., 1862; commd. col. 2d Regt., La. Native Guards, 1863; editor Jour.-Courier, New Haven, 1864-66; editor St. Louis Democrat, 1866-70, 72-75, helped Carl Schurz in his election to U.S. Senate, 1872, provided evidence leading to conviction of more than 100 leaders St. Louis Whiskey Ring, 1873-74; econ. editor N.Y. Times, 1875-1900; frequently gave aid to U.S. Govt. in connection with tariff acts and other financial measures; controlled Electro Matrix Printing Co. during Panic of 1893. Author: Does Protection Protect, 1871; American Securities, 1885. Died July 20, 1900.

GROTE, Augustus Radcliffe, entomologist, author; b. Aigburth, Eng., Feb. 7, 1841; ed. in Europe, after 1857; married, 1880; m. 2d, Minna Ruyter. Came to Am., 1846, settled in Staten Island, N.Y.; published Noctuidae in Proc. Acad. Natural Sci. and of the Entomol. Soc., Phila., 1862; gave series of lectures on cotton caterpillar in South; moved to Buffalo, N.Y., 1873, became curator Buffalo Soc. Natural Scis.; became publisher N.Am. Entomologist, 1879; v.p., sectional chmn. A.A.A.S., 1878; returned to Europe, 1884, spent rest of life in Bremen and Hildesheim, Germany; hon. asst. Romer Museum, 1894-1903. Author: Genesis I-II: An Essay on the Bible Narrative of Creation, 1880; The New Infidelity, 1881; contbr. numerous articles to various publs., 1862-1903. Died Sept. 12, 1903.

GROUARD, Frank, scout; b. Paumotu Archipelago, Sept. 20, 1850; son of Benjamin Grouard. Came to U.S. with parents, 1852; captive of Sioux Indians, 1869-75, thoroughly learned their lang.; escaped, Camp Robinson, Neb., 1875; scout for Gen. George Crook in Sioux War, 1876-77; participated in battles of Powder River, Rosebud, 1876; attached to Pine Ridge Agy. during Messiah craze among Sioux, 1890-91. Died St. Joseph, Mo., Aug. 15, 1905.

GROUT, Jonathan, congressman; b. Lunenburg, Mass. (now Vt.), July 23, 1737; studied law. Served in expdn. against Can., 1757-60; admitted to the bar, began practice of law, Petersham, Mass.; served in Revolutionary War; mem. Mass. Ho. of Reps., 1781, 84, 87, Mass. Senate, 1788; mem. Mass. Constl. Conv., 1788; mem. U.S. Ho. of Reps. (Democrat) from Mass., 1st Congress, 1789-91. Died Dover, N.H., Sept. 8, 1807; buried Pine Hill Cemetery, Dover.

GROVE, Asa Porter, congressman; b. nr. Phelps, Ontario County, N.Y., Feb. 18, 1819; attended common schs., N.Y., Centre Coll., Danville, Ky.; studied law. Moved to Ky., 1837, taught sch., Woodford and Franklin counties; admitted to the bar, 1843, began practice of law, Owenton, Ky.; mem. Ky. Senate, 1857-65; mem. Ky. Democratic Conv., 1863; mem. U.S. Ho. of Reps. (Democrat) from Ky., 40th Congress, 1867-69; resumed practice of law; moved to Georgetown, Ky., 1881, practiced law, 1881-87. Died Georgetown, July 20, 1887; buried Georgetown Cemetery.

GROVE, William Barry, congressman; b. Fayetteville, N.C., Jan. 15, 1764; studied law. Admitted to the bar, practiced law; mem. N.C. Ho. of Commons, 1786, 88, 89; del. N.C. Conv. to ratify U.S. Const., 1788, voted against postponement, del. Conv. which ratified Constn., 1789; trustee U. N.C.; pres. Fayetteville br. Bank of U.S.; mem. U.S. Ho. of Reps. (Federalist) from N.C., 2d-7th congresses, 1791-1803, unsuccessful candidate for re-election, 1802. Died Fayetteville, Mar. 30, 1818; buried Grove Creek Cemetery, Fayetteville.

GROVER, Cuvier, army officer; b. Bethel, Me., July 29, 1828; s. John and Fanny (Lary) G.; grad. U.S. Mil. Acad., 1850; m. Susan Flint, Aug. 1, 1865; m. 2d, Ella Miller, Jan. 28, 1875. Engr. on exploring expdn. to Far N.W., 1853, made report on expdn. (removed many objections to feasibility of a No. Pacific railroad), 1854; commd. 1st lt. 10th Inf., U.S. Army, 1855, capt., 1858; served in expdn. against Mormons in Utah, circa 1856, apptd. provost marshall Utah Territory, circa 1857; promoted brig. gen., 1862, in command of 1st Brigade, 2d Div., 3d Corps, Army of Potomac, served in Battle of Williamsburg; brevetted lt. col., then col.; commanded 4th Div., 19th Corps; served in 2d Battle of Bull Run; took possession of Baton Rouge, La.; commanded div. 19th Corps, Dept. of Gulf, 1862-64; served in 1st Battle of Winchester, 1864; brevetted maj. gen., 1864; fought in battles of Fisher's Hill and Cedar Creek; comdr. Dist. of Savannah: 1865; commd. brig. gen., 1865, then maj. gen.; returned to frontier duty; promoted col. 1st Cavalry, U.S. Army, 1875. Died Atlantic City, N.J., June 6, 1885.

GROVER, Martin, congressman; b. Hartwick, N.Y., Oct. 20, 1811; attended common schs.; studied law. Admitted to N.Y. bar, began law practice, Angelica; mem. U.S. Ho. of Reps. (Native Am. Democrat) from N.Y., 29th Congress, 1845-47; elected justice N.Y. Supreme Ct., 1857, 59; judge N.Y. Ct. Appeals, 1867-69, asso. judge, 1870-75. Died Angelica, Aug. 23, 1875; buried Angelica Cemetery.

GRUBE, Bernhard Adam, missionary; b. Thuringen, nr. Erfurt, Germany, June 24, 1715; married twice, 1754, 78. Entered Moravian ministry, 1740, taught in sem. at Lindheim; came to Am., 1748, taught at Bethlehem, Pa.; volunteered for missionary work among Indians; moved to Mineolagomeka, Monroe County, Pa., 1752-63, missionary Shamokin, Pa., 1752-53, Gnadenhutten, Pa., 1753-55, Pachgatgoch Conn., 1758-60, Wechquetauc, Pa., 1760-63; forced to flee to Phila. at outbreak of Pontiac's War, 1763; pastor at Lititz, Pa., 1765-85; spent his last years ministering to congregations at Nazareth (Pa.) and Bethlehem. Died Mar. 20, 1808.

GRUND, Francis Joseph, journalist; b. Klosterneuburg nr. Vienna, Austria, 1798; attended U. Vienna. Prof. mathematics mil. sch., Rio de Janeiro, Brazil, 1825; came to U.S., 1827; chmn. Conv. of German Citizens of U.S., Pitts., 1837; U.S. consul, Antwerp, Belgium, 1854-60; editor Whig newspapers Standard, Grund's Pennsylvanischer Deutscher, Phila.; opposed Van Buren, 1840; consul at Bremen, Germany, 1841-42; founder newspaper Age, Phila., 1842; contbr. to Phila. Public Ledger, polit. corr., 1842; credited as father of sensational style of journalism; began attacks on Franklin Pierce in the Public Ledger, 1853; consul at Le Havre, France, 1860 known for oratorial abilities. Author: Martin Van Buren als Staatsmann und Kunftiger President der der Vereinigton Staten von Nordamerika, 1835; The Americans in the Moral, Social and Political Relations, 1837; Thoughts and Reflections on the Present Position of Europe, and its Probable Consequence to the United States, 1860. Died Phila., Sept. 29, 1863.

GRUNDY, Felix, senator, congressman, U.S. atty. gen.; b. Berkley County, Va., Sept. 11, 1777; s. George Grundy; m. Ann P. Rodgers. Admitted to Ky. bar, 1797; mem. Ky. Ho. of Reps., 1799-1806; asso. justice Ky. Supreme Ct. Errors and Appeals, 1806-07; moved to Nashville, Tenn., 1807; mem. U.S. Ho. of Reps. from Tenn., 12th-13th congresses, 1811-15; mem. Tenn. Ho. of Reps., 1819-25; supporter relief laws, fostered state-owned loan office, extending credit of govt. to debtors; mem. U.S. Senate from Tenn., Oct. 19, 1829-July 4, 1838, 39-Dec. 19, 1840; U.S. atty. gen. under Pres. Van Buren, 1838. Died Nashville, Dec. 19, 1840; buried Mt. Olivet Cemetery, Nashville.

GRUNEWALD, Gustavus, artist; b. Gnadau, Germany, Dec. 10, 1805. Came to Am., 1831, settled in Bethlehem, Pa.; taught drawing and painting Young Ladies' Sem., Bethlehem, 1836-66; exhibited frequently at Artists' Fund Soc., Pa. Acad., Md. Hist. Soc., N.A.D., Apollo Assn., Am. Art-Union; returned to Germany, 1868. Died Gnadenburg, Germany, Aug. 1, 1878.

GUERIN, Anne-Therese (Mother Theodore), educator; b. Etables, France, Oct. 2, 1798; d. Laurent and Isabeth (Le Fevre) Guerin. Entered community Sisters of Providence, Ruille-sur-Loire, France, 1823, apptd. superior convent at Rennes, served until 1833; taught sch., Soulaines, France, 1833-40, at same time took courses in medicine and pharmacy; came to U.S. as superior with 6 sisters on appeal from Bishop Celestine de la Hailandiere of Vincennes (Ind.), 1840, arrived at St. Mary-of-the-Woods, Ind., 1840,, established 1st acad. for women in Ind., sch. chartered and granted power to confer academic honors and degrees, 1846, sch. successful primarily due to her academic ability and spiritual integrity. Died May 14, 1856.

GUERNSEY, Henry Newell, physician; b. Rochester, Vt., Feb. 10, 1817; s. Joseph and Phoebe (Jefferson) G.; M.D., U. N.Y., 1844; M.D. (hon.), Homoeopathic Med. Coll. Pa., 1862; m. Statira Colburn, Apr. 27, 1845, 3 children. Practiced medicine, Frankford, Pa., 1844-57, Phila., 1857-84; specialized in diseases of women and children; prof. materia medica, dean Hahnemann Med. Coll., Phila., 1871-74; went to Europe for health reasons, 1879, 82. Author: Obstetrics and Diseases of Women and Children. Died June 27, 1885.

GUESS, George, see Sequoyah.

GUGLER, Henry, engraver; b. Germany, 1816; children include Henry. Came to Am., 1833; engraver with banknote engraving firm, N.Y.C., several years; one of 1st vignette engravers Nat. Note Bur., Washington, D.C., during Civil War; noted for life size steel engraving of Lincoln; founded lithographic firm H. Gugler & Son (now Gugler Lithographing Co.), Milw., 1878. Died Milw., 1880.

GUIGNAS, Michel (Louis Ignace Guignas), missionary; b. Condom, France, Jan. 22, 1681. Joined Soc. of Jesus, 1703, sent to do missionary work in New France, 1716; with mission at Mackinac, Can., 1717-27; set up mission at St. Michel Archange among Sioux Indians near what is now Frontenac, Minn., 1727, forced to evacuate mission because of French invasion of Fox country; captured, spent 5 months in prison, escaped to Ill. country, 1729; with Godefroy de Lingtot rebuilt Sioux mission at Ft. Trumpealeau in Wis., 1731-36, moved mission to Ft. Pepin, Wis., 1736; went to Mackinac when fort was attacked by Sioux, 1737; lived in Que., Can., 1740-52, regional prefect of Jesuit order until 1749. Died Feb. 6, 1752.

GUILD, LaFayette, physician, army officer; b. Tuscaloosa, Ala., Nov. 23, 1825; s. James and Mary (Williams) G.; M.D., Jefferson Med. Coll., Phila., 1848; m. Martha Aylette Fitts, 1851, 2 adopted Indian sons. Entered med. service U.S. Army as asst. surgeon, 1849; served in South and S.W.; assigned to 2d Dragoons, 1857-61; accompanied regt. in actions against Indians of No. Cal.; entered Confederate Army as surgeon, 1861, commd. maj.; insp. hosps., 1861-62; med. dir. Army of No. Va., 1862-65; pvt. practice medicine, Mobile, Ala., 1865-66; quarantine officer Port of Mobile, 1866-69; moved to San Francisco, 1869; vis. surgeon San Francisco City and County Hosp., 1869-70. Died Marysville, Cal., July 4, 1870; buried Tuscaloosa.

GUILD, Reuben Aldridge, librarian; b. West Dedham, Mass., May 4, 1822; s. Reuben and Olive (Morse) G.; grad. Brown U., 1847; LL.D. (hon.) Shurtleff Coll., 1874; m. Jane Clifford Hunt, Dec. 17, 1849, 6 children. Librarian, Brown U., 1848-93, sec. alumni assn., 15 years; a founder Am. Library Assn., 1876; Author: Librarian's Manual, 1858; Life of James Manning, 1864; History of Brown University, 1864-67; An Introduction to the Writings of Roger Williams, 1866; Life and Letters of Chaplain Smith, 1885. Died Providence, R.I., May 13, 1899.

GUILFORD, Nathan, supt. schs., editor; b. Spencer, Mass., July 19, 1786; s. Dr. Jonas and Lydia (Hobbs) G.; grad. Yale, 1812; m. Eliza Farnsworth, Aug. 29, 1819. Admitted to Ohio bar, 1816; editor Solomon Thrifty's Almanac, 1818-25; mem. Ohio Senate, 1824; owner, editor Cincinnati Daily Atlas, 1843-47; supt. Cincinnati Pub. Schs., 1850-52; elected city magistrate Cincinnati, 1854. Author: The Western Spelling Book, 1831; The Juvenile Arithmetic, 1836. Died Cincinnati, Dec. 18, 1854.

GUINEY, Patrick Robert, lawyer, army officer; b. Parkstown, Ireland, Jan. 15, 1835; brought to Portland, Me., at age 6; attended Holy Cross Coll.; m. Janet Doyle. Admitted to bar, 1856; moved to Boston; served from pvt. to brig. gen. 9th Mass. Regt. during Civil War, served in 30 engagements, was decorated; partially blinded at Battle of Wilderness; asst. dist. atty.; founder Catholic Union; mem. various civic orgns., Boston. Died Boston, Mar. 21, 1877.

GUIRAUD, Ernest, musician; b. New Orleans, June 23, 1837; s. Jean-Baptiste Guiraud; studied music, Paris (France) Conservatory later in Rome, Italy 1860-63. Wrote opera Le roi David, 1852; won Grand Prix de Rome for cantata Bajazet et le joueur de flute, 1859; played at Concerts Populaires; composed orchestral suite which established him as composer, 1872; apptd. prof. harmonics and accompaniment Paris Conservatory, 1876, prof. composition (pupils included Debussy), 1880; became mem. French Acad., 1891; other compositions include (operas) Sylvie, 1846, En prison, 1869, Le Kobold, 1870, Mme. Turlupin, 1872, Gretna Green, 1873, Piccolino, 1876, La galante aventure, 1882, Brunhilde (completed by Saint-Saëns), produced posthumously, 1895; a solemn mass, an overture, a Traité d' Instrumentation; recitatives to Bizet's Carmen. Died Paris, May 6, 1892.

GUITEAU, Charles Julius, assassin, lawyer; b. circa 1840. Republican supporter for election of James Garfield; went to Washington, D.C. to secure a fed. office (presumedly that of U.S. consul to Marseilles, France), 1880, did not secure position; became further incensed at Garfield's support of civil service reform and his stand against stalwart wing of Republican Party (which Guiteau favored); shot Garfield in waiting room of Balt. & Potomac R.R., Washington, July 2, 1881; his trial long and sensational, found guilty almost a year after the shooting. Hanged, Washington, June 30, 1882.

GULICK, Luther Halsey, missionary; b. Honolulu, Hawaii, June 10, 1828; s. Rev. Peter Johnson and Fanny (Hinckley) G.; grad. med. coll. City of N.Y., 1850; m. Louisa Lewis, Oct. 29, 1851, 7 children including Luther Halsey. Ordained to ministry Congregational Ch., 1850; sent by Am. Bd. Commrs. for Fgn. Missions as missionary to Caroline Islands, 1851; sec. Hawaiian Evang. Assn., 1863-70; inspected, organized mission posts, Spain, Italy, Turkey, Bohemia, 1870-75; agt. Am. Bible Soc. in China, Japan, 1875-85; editor Chines Recorder and Missionary Jour., 1885-89; founder Med. Missionary Jour. Author: A Sermon on the Foolishness of Preaching, 1853; Notes on the Grammar of the Ponape Dialect, 1858. Died Springfield, Mass., Apr. 8, 1891.

GULLAGER, Christian, artist; b. Copenhagen, Denmark, Mar. 1, 1759; attended Royal Acad., Copenhagen; married, May 9, 1786. Came to Am., circa 1782; lived in Newburyport, Mass., moved to Boston, 1786-97; theatrical painter, N.Y.C., 1797; settled in Phila., 1798; left family in Phila. to seek work, 1806; best known work is portrait of George Washington, painted 1789; Died Phila., Nov. 12, 1826.

GUMMERE, John, educator, mathematician; b. Willow Grove, Pa., 1784; s. Samuel and Rachel (James) G.; m. Elizabeth Bugby, 1808, at least 1 son Samuel James. For most part self-educated; taught mathematics, Horsham, Pa., 1803-05; taught in Rancocas, N.J., 1806-11; opened, operated boarding sch., Burlington, N.J., 1814-33; elected to Am. Philos. Soc., 1814, began contbg. articles to their Transactions; taught mathematics Haverford (Mass.) Sch., 1833-44, supt., several years; reestablished (with son Samuel James) sch., Burlington, 1843-45; recognized as one of ablest mathematicians in U.S. at that time. Author: A Treatise on Surveying, 1814; Elementary Treatise on Astronomy, 1822. Died May 31, 1845.

GUMMERE, Samuel James, coll. pres.; b. Rancocas, N.J., Apr. 28, 1811; s. John and Elizabeth (Buzby) G.; m. Abigail Griscom, Jan. 1835; m. 2d, Elizabeth Hooten Barton, Jan. 9, 1845, 1 son, Francis Barton. Head classics dept. Friends Sch., Providence, R.I., until 1834; tchr. Haverford (Pa.) Sch. (became Haverford Coll.), 1834-43; tchr. in father's sch., Burlington, N.J., 1843-62; travelled in Europe, 1854; prof. mathematics, physics, astronomy Haverford Coll., 1862-64, pres., 1864-74; mem. Am. Philos. Soc. Died Oct. 23, 1874.

GUNN, Frederick William, educator; b. Washington, Conn., Oct. 4, 1816; s. John and Mary (Ford) G.; grad. Yale, 1837; m. Abigail I. Binsmade, Apr. 16, 1848. Taught sch., New Preston, Conn., 1838-39; opened, taught acad., Washington, 1840-45, held abolitionist views which made him unpopular, forced to leave; opened, taught sch., Towanda, Pa., 1847-49; returned to Washington, 1849, taught sch.; operated family sch. later called The Gunnery, Washington, 1850-81. Died Aug. 16, 1881.

GUNN, James, senator; b. Va., Mar. 13, 1753; attended common schs.; studied law. Admitted to the bar; began law practice, Savannah, Ga.; served in Revolutionary War, capt. dragoons defending Savannah, 1782; col. 1st Regt., Chatham County Militia; promoted brig. gen. Ga. Militia; elected to Continental Congress, 1787, did not serve; mem. U.S. Senate from Ga., 1789-1801. Died Louisville, Ga. July 30, 1801; buried Old Capitol Cemetery, Louisville.

GUNNISON, John Williams, army officer, engr.; b. Goshen, N.H., Nov. 11, 1812; s. Samuel and Elizabeth (Williams) G.; grad. U.S. Mil. Acad., 1837; m. Martha A. Delony, Apr. 15, 1841, 3 children. Served with 2d Artillery as 2d lt. in Seminole War, 1837-38; aided transfer of Cherokees to Indian Territory, 1838; participated in surveys in Ga. and lake region of Northwest, 1840-49; spent winter in Salt Lake City, made study of Mormon religion; commd. capt., 1853, assigned to survey Huerfano River, Cochetopa Pass and Grand and Green valleys to Santa Clara in S.W. Utah, expdn. attacked by band of Pahvant Indians. Author: The Mormons, 1852. Killed in Indian attack, Utah, Oct. 26, 1853.

GURLEY, Henry Hosford, congressman; b. Lebanon, Conn., May 20, 1788; attended Williams Coll., 1805-08; studied law. Admitted to the bar, began practice in Baton Rouge, La.; mem. U.S. Ho. of Reps. (Whig) from La., 18th-21st congresses, 1823-31; judge dist. ct., Baton Rouge, 1831-33. Died Baton Rouge, Mar. 16, 1833.

GURLEY, John Addison, congressman; b. East Hartford, Conn., Dec. 9, 1813; attended dist. schs.; studied theology. Learned hatter's trade; pastor Universalist Ch., Methuen, Mass., 1835-38; moved to Cincinnati, 1838; pastor, Cincinnati, 1838-50; owner, editor Star and Sentinel (later Star in the West), 1838-54; mem. U.S. Ho. of Reps. (Republican) from Ohio, 36th-37th congresses, 1859-63, unsuccessful candidate for re-election, 1862; served as col. and a.d.c. on staff of Gen. John Fremont during Civil War; apptd. gov. Ariz. by Pres. Lincoln, died before taking office. Died Green Twp. nr. Cincinnati, Aug. 19, 1863; buried Spring Grove Cemetery, Cincinnati.

GURLEY, Ralph Randolph, assn. adminstr., editor; b. Lebanon, Conn., May 26, 1797; s. Rev. John and Mary (Porter) G.; grad. Yale, 1818; m. Eliza McLellan, 13 children. Ordained to ministry Presbyn. Ch.; successively agt., sec., v.p., life (adminstrv.) dir. Am. Colonization Soc., 1822-72; edited African Repository 25 years; chaplain U.S. Ho. of Reps.; went to Liberia to report on colony's condition for U.S. Govt., 1824, drew up Plan for the Civil Government of Liberia (adopted as Liberian Constn.), made other trips to Liberia, 1849, 67; worked among poverty stricken Negroes in Washington, D.C. Died Washington, July 30, 1872.

GURNEY, Ephraim Whitman, educator; b. Boston, Feb. 18, 1829; s. Nathan and Sarah (Whitman) G.; grad. Harvard, 1852; m. Ellen Sturgis Hooper, Oct. 3, 1868. Tutor Greek and Latin, Harvard, 1857, asst. prof., 1863, asst. prof. philosophy, 1867, prof. history, 1869-86, McLean prof. ancient and modern history, 1896, 1st dean faculty, 1870-76, fellow corp., 1884; editor (with James Russell Lowell) N Am. Review, 1868-70; fellow Am. Acad. Arts and Scis., 1860. Died Beverly, Mass., Sept. 12, 1886.

GUROWSKI, Adam, reformer; b. Kalisz, Poland, Sept. 10, 1805; s. Ladislas Gurowski; attended U. Berlin (Germany); grad. U. Heidelberg (Germany), 1823; m. Theresa de Ibijewska, 1827, 2 children. Participated in revolutionary movement in Poland, 1825-31, sentenced to death, fled to Paris, France, 1831; prof. polit. economy U. Bern (Switzerland), 1848-49; came to U.S., 1849; lectr. history of Roman law Harvard, 1849-51; contbd. articles to Boston Mus., N.Y. Tribune, New Am. Ency.; supported Russian cause during Crimean War; wrote pamphlets and books denouncing slavery, favored war as means of freeing slaves, favored establishment of Negro troops; apptd. to position in U.S. State Dept. to translate fgn. newspapers and advise sec. of state on internat. affairs, 1861, discharged for publishing criticisms of high govt. ofcls., 1862. Author: The Turkish Question, 1854; Russia as It is, 1854; A Year of the War, 1855; America and Europe, 1857; Slavery in History, 1860; Diary, Vol. I, 1862, Vol. II, 1864, Vol. III, 1866; and Europe, 1857. Died Washington D.C., May 4, 1866; buried Congressional Cemetery, Washington.

GUSTINE, Amos, congressman; b. 1789; Mem. bd. mgrs. Mifflin Bridge Co., Mifflin County, Pa., 1828; sheriff Juniata County (Pa.), 1831-34; awarded contract for 1st courthouse erected at Mifflintown, Pa., 1832; mem. 1st town council, mcht., Mifflintown, 1833; elected treas. Juniata County, 1837; mem. U.S. Ho. of Reps. (Democrat) from Pa., 27th Congress, May 4, 1841-43; farmer, miller. Died Jericho Mills, Juniata County, Mar. 3, 1844; buried Presbyn. cemetery, Mifflintown.

GUTHRIE, Alfred, engr.; b. Sherburne, N.Y., Apr. 1, 1805; s. Dr. Samuel and Sybil (Sexton) G.; studied medicine and chemistry under his father; m. Nancy Piper, Oct. 2, 1823; m. 2d, Phoebe Guthrie, Mar. 31, 1857. Moved West due to financial distress, 1845; engr., designed and constructed hydraulic works on Ill. and Mich. Canal in order to carry Chgo. sewerage to Mississippi River; aided devel. of fed. system of steamship inspection, inspected over 200 vessels and determined their defects, succeeded in having bill introduced into Congress providing for regulation, 1851, placed at head of enforcement bureau when bill passed, 1852, number of steamboat accidents steadily decreased under his leadership. Died Chgo., Aug. 17, 1882.

GUTHRIE, James, railroad promoter, senator, univ. pres.; b. Bardstown, Ky., Dec. 5, 1792; s. Adam and Hannah (Polk) G.; m. Eliza C. Prather, May 13, 1821, 3 daus. Admitted to bar; apptd. commonwealth's atty.; mem. lower house Ky. Legislature, 1827-31; mem. Ky. Senate, 1831-41, twice speaker pro. tem; outstanding ry. promoter in Ky.; organized pub. sch. system, Louisville, Ky.; founder U. Louisville, pres., 1846-66; pres. Ky. Constl. Conv., 1851; U.S. sec. treasury, 1853-57; pres. L. & N. R.R.; mem. U.S. Senate from Ky., 1867-Feb. 1868. Died Louisville, Mar. 13, 1869.

GUTHRIE, Samuel, chemist; b. Brimfield, Mass., 1782; s. Samuel and Sarah Guthrie; attended Coll. Physicians and Surgeons, N.Y.C., 1810-11, U. Pa., 1815; m. Sybil Sexton, 1804, 4 children including Alfred, Edwin. Moved from Sherburne (N.Y.) to Sacketts Harbor, N.Y., 1817, practiced medicine, set up exptl. chem. lab.; said to have invented an effective priming powder called "percussion pill" and punch lock for exploding it which together made the flintlock musket obsolete; devised process for rapid conversion of potato starch into molasses, 1830; made "chloric ether" by distilling chloride of lime with alcohol in copper (proved to be chloroform). Author: The Complete Writings of Samuel Guthrie (collection of letters and comments), 1832. Died Sacketts Harbor, Oct. 19, 1848.

GUY, Francis, artist; b. Lorton, nr. Keswick, Eng., circa 1760. Silk dyer, London, Eng.; came to Am., 1795; established silk dyeing plant, Bklyn.; moved to Phila., later to Balt.; landscape painter, Balt., circa 1798-1817; commd. to paint view of new Balt. Cathedral, 1812; painted several marine battle scenes during War of 1812; returned to Bklyn., 1817. Died Bklyn., Aug. 12, 1820.

GUYON, James, Jr., congressman; b. Richmond, N.Y., Dec. 24, 1778; s. James Guyon. Apptd. capt. 2d Squadron, 1st Cavalry Div., N.Y. Militia, 1807; mem. N.Y. State Assembly, 1812-14; promoted maj., 1814, col. 1st Regt. of Horse Arty., 1819; mem. U.S. Ho. of Reps. (Federalist) from N.Y., 16th Congress, Jan. 14, 1820-21; engaged in farming. Died Richmond, Mar. 9, 1846; buried St. Andrew's Cemetery, Richmond.

GUYOT, Arnold Henry, geographer, educator; b. Boudevilliers, Switzerland, Sept. 28, 1807; s. David Pierre and Constance (Favarger) G.; grad. Coll. of Neuchatel, 1825; Ph.D., U. Berlin, 1835; LL.D. (hon.), Union Coll., 1873; m. Sarah Doremus Haines, July 2, 1867. Prof. history and phys. geography Acad. of Neuchatel, 1839-48; 1st to formulate laws of structure and movement of glaciers; came to U.S., 1848; published The Earth and Man; lectured under Mass. Bd. Edn. 6 years; published geography textbooks, 1866-75, made 1st definite attempt at scientific presentation of geography in Am. schs.; prof. phys. geography and geology Princeton, 1854-84; founded museum at Princeton; selected and equipped weather observation stations in N.Y. and Mass. Died Princeton, N.J., Feb. 8, 1884.

GWIN, William McKendree, senator; b. Sumner County, Tenn., Oct. 9, 1805; s. James and Mary G.; M.D., Transylvania U., 1828; m. Caroline Sampson; m. 2d, Mary Bell; 6 children. U.S. marshal for Dist. of Miss., 1833; mem. U.S. Ho. of Reps. from Miss., 27th Congress, 1841-43; mem. U.S. Senate from Cal., Sept. 1850-61; given credit for establishing Cal. mint and initiating plans to survey Pacific Coast. Died N.Y.C., Sept. 3, 1885; buried Mountain View Cemetery, Oakland, Cal.

GWINNETT, Button, Continental congressman; b. Down Halherley, Eng., circa 1735; s. Samuel and Anne (Emes) G.; m. Ann Bourne, Apr. 19, 1757. Planter, St. Catherine Island off coast of Ga., 1765, justice of peace, 1767-68; mem. Ga. Colonial Assembly, 1769; del. Continental Congress, 1776; signer Declaration of Independence; mem. Ga. Assembly, 1776-77, speaker, 1776; played important part in drafting 1st Ga. Constn.; pres. State of Ga., and comdr. in chief Ga. Militia, 1777; activities investigated after unsuccessful Ga. Militia expdn. against British in Fla., cleared of charges of negligence but died as result of wounds suffered in duel with Lachlan McIntosh (his chief polit. opponent). Died nr. Savannah, Ga., May 16, 1777.

H

HABERSHAM, Alexander Wylly, naval officer, mcht.; b. N.Y.C., Mar. 24, 1826; s. Richard W. and Sarah (Elliott) H.; grad. U.S. Naval Acad., 1848; m. Jessie Steele, several children. Assigned to Pacific Squadron, U.S. Navy, 1848-50; served with Coast Survey, 1851-52; served in ship J. P. Kennedy in expdn. to North Pacific and China Seas as acting lt., 1853; assigned to John Hancock at Hong Kong, 1854; assigned to Phila. Navy Yard, 1855-57; assigned to ship Powhatan of East India Squadron, 1857-60, resigned to engaged in business in Japan; one of 1st Am. importers of Japanese tea; returned to U.S., 1861, arrested as Southern sympathizer; became part owner firm Habersham & Barrett, importers and dealers in teas and East Indian goods, Balt., 1865; engaged in coffee and canned goods brokerage business, 1870-71-83. Author: My Last Cruise, or Where We Went and What We Saw, circa 1856. Died Annapolis, Md., Mar. 26, 1883.

HABERSHAM, James, mcht., planter, colonial gov.; b. Beverley, Eng., Jan. 1713; s. James Hebersham; m. Mary Bolton, Dec. 26, 1740, 10 children. Came to Savannah, Ga., 1738; organized firm Harris & Habersham, 1744; raised 1st cotton in colony, advocated intro. of slavery; apptd. councillor and sec. Province of Ga., 1754; pres. upper house Ga. Gen. Assembly, 1767-71; acting gov. Ga., 1771-73; Loyalist; dissolved assembly which refused his choice of speaker; established Bethesda Orphanage. Died New Brunswick, N.J., Aug. 28, 1775; buried Savannah.

HABERSHAM, John, Continental congressman; b. "Beverly" nr. Savannah, Ga., Dec. 23, 1754; s. James Habersham; attended Coll. of N.J. (now Princeton). Engaged as mcht.; served as 1st lt., brigade maj. 1st Ga. Regt., Continental Army during Revolutionary War, taken prisoner twice; mem. Continental Congress from Ga., 1785-86; apptd. Indian agt. by Gen. Washington; commr. to Beaufort Conv. to adjust Ga.-S.C. boundary; mem. 1st bd. trustees U. Ga.; 1st sec. Ga. br. Soc. of Cincinnati; collector customs Port of Savannah, 1789-99. Died nr. Savannah, Dec. 17, 1799; buried Colonial Park Cemetery, Savannah.

HABERSHAM, Joseph, patriot, postmaster gen.; b. Savannah, Ga., July 28, 1751; s. James and Mary (Bolton) H.; ed. Coll. of N.J. (now Princeton); m. Isabella Rae, May 1776, 10 children. An organizer firm Joseph Clay & Co., 1773; mem. Ga. Council of Safety, 1775, raised body of volunteers which captured Sir James Wright (Ga. gov.) and held him under guard in his own home for a month; mem. Ga. Provincial Congress, Savannah, July 4, 1775; commd. col. 1st Ga. Battalion, Continental Army; mem. Continental Congress, 1785-86; speaker Ga. Gen. Assembly, 1785-90; mem. Ga. Conv. which ratified U.S. Constn., 1788; mayor Savannah, 1792; postmaster-gen. U.S. under Presidents Washington, Adams and Jefferson, 1795-1801; pres. branch of Bank of U.S., 1802-15. Died Savannah, Nov. 17, 1815.

HABERSHAM, Richard Wylly, congressman; b. Savannah, Ga., Dec. 1786; s. Joseph Habersham; grad. Princeton, 1810; studied law. Admitted to Ga. bar, began practice in Savannah; U.S. dist. atty., until 1825; atty. gen. Ga.; mem. U.S. Ho. of Reps. from Ga. (States Rights Democrat), 26th-27th congresses, 1839-42. Died Clarksville, Ga., Dec. 2, 1842; buried Old Cemetery, Clarksville.

HACK, George, mcht., physician; b. Cologne, Germany, circa 1623; M.D., Cologne U.; m. Anna Verlett, 4 children including George Nicholas, Peter. Came to New Amsterdam, gradually left practice of medicine; partner (with Augustine Herrman) in Va. tobacco trade, circa 1648-51 (prospering co. ruined by English Navigation Act, stating that only English ships could carry trade to and from colonies 1651); went to Va., 1651, practiced medicine and grew tobacco; became naturalized citizen of Va., 1658. Died circa 1665.

HACKETT, James Henry, actor; b. N.Y.C., Mar. 15, 1800; s. Thomas C. Hackett; attended Columbia 1815; m. Catharine Lee Sugg, 1819; m. 2d, Clara Cynthia Morgan, Mar. 27, 1864; children--John K., James Keteltas. Made 1st stage appearance in Love in a Village, playing Justice Woodcock to his wife's Rosseta, Park Theatre, N.Y.C., 1826; played Falstaff in Henry IV, Park Theatre, 1828; made stage version of Rip Van Winkle, 1830; played Melodious Migrate in The Moderns, or a Trip to the Springs, 1831; played Col. Nimrod Wildfire in The Lion of the West, or a Trip to Washington; mgr. Astor Place Opera House, 1849, The National, N.Y.C., Howard Athenaeum, Boston; founded 1st Am.-born theatrical family; played in London, Eng.; helped develop Am. character comedy into popular art; maintained extensive correspondence on Shakespeare with John Quincy Adams. Died Jamaica, L.I., N.Y., Dec. 28, 1871.

HACKETT, Thomas C., congressman; b. Ga.; attended common schs. Solicitor gen. Cherokee circuit, 1841-43; mem. Ga. Senate, 1845; mem. U.S. Ho. of Reps. (Democrat) from Ga., 1849-51. Died Marietta, Ga., Oct. 8, 1851.

HACKLEY, Aaron, Jr., congressman; b. Wallingford, Conn., May 6, 1783; s. Aaron Hackley; grad. Williams Coll., 1805. Moved to Herkimer, N.Y.; elected clk. Herkimer County, 1812, 15; judge adv. during War of 1812; mem. N.Y. State Assembly, 1814, 15, 18, 37; mem. U.S. Ho. of Reps. from N.Y., 16th Congress, 1819-21; dist. atty. Herkimer County, 1828-33; justice St. Lawrence County (N.Y.) Ct., 1823-24; master in chancery; recorder Utica (N.Y.). Died N.Y.C., Dec. 28, 1868; buried Trinity Ch. Cemetery, N.Y.C.

HADDOCK, Charles Brickett, educator; b. Salisbury, N.H., June 20, 1796; s. William and Abigail Eastman (Webster) H.; grad. Dartmouth, 1816, Andover (Mass.), Theol. Sem., 1818; m. Susan Saunders Lang, Aug. 19, 1819; m. 2d, Caroline Young, July 21, 1841; at least 1 son Charles. First prof. rhetoric and oratory Dartmouth, 1819-38, prof. intellectual philosophy and polit. economy, 1838-50; mem. N.H. Ho. of Reps., 1845-48; 1st commr. N.H. Common Schs., 1846-47; chargé d'affaires to Portugal (apptd. by Pres. Millard Fillmore), 1850-54; retired to West Lebanon, N.H., 1854; contbr. articles on academic and polit. subjects, to New Eng. periodicals. Author: Addresses and Miscellaneous Writings (his collected speeches and articles), 1846; Report of the Commissioner of Common Schools (survey N.H. sch. system), 1847. Died Lebanon, N.H., Jan. 15, 1861.

HADFIELD, George, architect; b. Leghorn, Eng., circa 1764; s. Charles and Isabella Hadfield; ed. (traveling studentship) schs. Royal Acad. Art. Supt. constrn. U.S. Capitol, Washington, D.C., 1795-98 (dismissed due to controversy over design and actual superintendence of capitol work); furnished adopted design for Treasury and Exec. Offices, 1798 (both burned by British in 1814); patented 1st machine for brick-making in U.S., 1800; councilman Washington, 1803; designed Washington Arsenal, 1803. Commodore Porter's house, 1816-19, City Hall. 1820, Assembly Rooms, 1822, Br. Bank U.S., 1824. "Arlington" (later home of Robert E. Lee; now preserved in Arlington Nat. Cemetery). Died Washington, Feb. 5, 1826.

HADLEY, James, philologist, educator; b. Fairfield, N.Y., Mar. 30, 1821; s. James and Maria (Hamilton) H.; grad. Yale, 1842, attended Divinity Sch., 1843-44; m. Anne Loring Twining, Aug. 31, 1851, at least 1 son, Arthur Twining. Tutor, Yale, 1845-48, asst. prof. Greek, 1848-51, prof., 1851-72; published frequently in Am. Jour. of Science, The Nation; worked for Am. Commn. for Revision of Bible. Author: Greek Grammar for Schools and Colleges, 1860; Essays Philological and Critical Selected Papers of James Hadley, (edited by William Dwight Whitney), 1873. Died Nov. 14, 1872.

HAGEN, Hermann August; educator; b. Konigsberg, Germany, May 30, 1817; s. Carl Heinrich and Anna (Linck) H.; grad. Gymnasium, Konigsberg, 1836; degree in medicine U. Konigsberg, 1830, Ph.D. (hon.), 1863; D.S. (hon.), Harvard, 1887; m. Johanna Maria Gerhards, 1851. Came to U.S., 1867; developed entomol. dept. Museum Comparative Zoology, Harvard; apptd. prof. entomology Harvard, (1st prof. entomology at any U.S. coll.) 1870; mem. Am. Acad. Arts and Scis., Am. Philos. Soc., Am. Entomol. Soc. Author: (at request Smithsonian Instn.) Synopsis of North American Neuroptera, 1861; Bibliotheca Entomologica, 1862-63; contbr. over 400 articles to profl. publs. Died Cambridge, Mass., Nov. 9, 1893.

HAGER, Albert Davis, geologist; b. Chester, Vt., Nov. 1, 1817. Asst. geologist of Vt. under Edward Hitchcock, 1857-61; curator Vt. Cabinet of Natural History, 1862-70; geologist Mo., 1870-72; librarian Hist. Soc., Chgo., 1877-88. Contbr. to Report on the Geology of Vermont, 2 vols., 1861, Annual Report of Vermont Fish Commission, 1866-69. Died Chgo., July 29, 1888.

HAGER, John Sharpenstein, senator, jurist; b. Morris County, N.J., Mar. 12, 1818; s. Lawrence and Mary (Sharpenstein) H.; grad. Coll. of N.J. (now Princeton), 1836; m. Elizabeth (Lucas) Hicks, 1872. Admitted to N.J. bar, 1840; moved to Cal., 1840; mem. Cal. Senate, 1853-55, 65-69; dist. judge San Francisco, 1855-61; regent U. Cal., 1869; mem. U.S. Senate (anti-monopoly Democrat) from Cal., 1873-75; collector Port of San Francisco, 1885. Died San Francisco, Mar. 19, 1890; buried Bellefontaine Cemetery, St. Louis.

HAGNER, Peter, accountant, auditor; b. Phila., Oct. 1, 1772; s. John V. and Margaretta (Hanckin) H.; attended U. State of Pa. (now U. Pa.); m. Sarah Nichols, Dec. 8, 1799; m. 2d, Frances Randall, 1805. Apprenticed to Peter Borger, mcht., Phila., 1788-90; clk. firm Phillips, Crammon & Co., mchts., Phila., 1790-93; given clerkship in Office of U.S. Accountant of War through his acquaintance with James Madison, 1793; apptd. U.S. accountant of war, 1809; appdt. 3d auditor U.S. Treasury, 1817-49. Died July 16, 1850.

HAGOOD, Johnson, army officer, gov. S.C.; b. Barnwell County, S.C., Feb. 21, 1829; s. James O. and Indina (Allen) H.; grad. The Citadel, Charleston, S.C., 1847; m. Eloise Butler, Nov. 21, 1856. Admitted to S.C. bar, 1850; master in equitp Barnwell County, 1851-61; dep. adj. gen. S.C. Militia, circa 1850; served as col. 1st Regt. of S.C. under Gen. Beauregard in capture of Ft. Sumter, 1861; commd. brig. gen. Confederate Army, 1862, serving in defense of coast and siege of Morris Island; comdr. 1st brigade Gen. R.F. Hokes div. Anderson's Corps, Army of No. Va., 1864, served in battles of Walthall Junction, Swift Creek, Drewry's Bluff, Cold Harbor, the Burmuda Hundred; served under Beauregard in defense of Petersburg, 1864; 1st pres. S.C. Agrl. and Mech. Soc., 1869; v.p. S.C. Democratic Conv., 1876; comptroller-gen. S.C., 1876-80; gov. S.C., 1880-82; chmn. S.C. Bd. of Agr., twice; chmn. bd. visitors The Citadel, 14 years. Died Barnwell, S.C., Jan. 4, 1898.

HAGUE, William, clergyman; b. Pelham, Westchester County, N.Y., Jan. 4, 1808; grad. Hamilton Coll., 1826, Newton Theol. Sem., 1829; D.D. (hon.), Brown U., 1849, Harvard, 1863. Pastor, 2d Baptist Ch., Utica, N.Y., 1829-31, 1st Bapt. Ch., Boston, 1831-37, 1st Bapt. Ch., Providence, R.I., 1837-40, Federal Street Ch., Boston, 1840-48; pastor, Jamaica Plain, Mass., 1848-50, Newark, N.J., 1850-53, Pearl Street Bapt. Ch., Albany, N.Y., 1853-58, Madison Avenue Bapt. Ch., N.Y.C., 1858-62; pastor in Boston, 1862-69, 1st Bapt. Ch., Orange, N.J., 1870-74, Wallaston Heights, nr. Boston, 1876-87. Author: Historical Discourse on the Two Hundredth Anniversary of the First Baptist Church, Providence, R.I., 1839; The Authority and Perpetuity of the Christian Sabbath, 1863; Self-Witnessing Character of the New Testament Christianity, 1871; Life Notes; or Fifty Years Outlook, 1888. Died Boston, Aug. 1, 1887.

HAHN, John, congressman; b. New Hanover Twp., Montgomery County, Pa., Oct. 30, 1776; attended common schs.; studied medicine. Practiced medicine; mem. U.S. Ho. of Reps. (Democrat) from Pa., 14th Congress, 1815-17; resumed med. practice, also engaged in farming. Died New Hanover Twp., Feb. 26, 1823; buried Falkner Swamp Graveyard, New Hanover Twp.

HAHN, Michael Georg Decker, gov. La., congressman; b. Klingenmünster, Bavaria, Germany, Nov. 24, 1830; s. Margaretta (Decker) H.; LL.B., U. La. Law Sch. (now Tulane U.), 1851. Pres., New Orleans Sch. Bd., 1852; mem. U.S. Ho. of Reps. (Anti-Secessionist) from La., 37th Congress, 1861-63; purchased, edited True Delta, 1864, advocated emancipation, supported Lincoln and Grant; gov. La., 1864-65; elected to U.S. Senate from La., 1865, never served; founder, editor New Orleans Republican, 1867-71; founder Village of Hahnville (La.), 1871; issued St. Charles Herald, 1872-86; mem. La. Ho. of Reps., 1872-76; judge U.S. 26th Jud. Dist., 1879-85. Died Washington, D.C., Mar. 15, 1886; buried Metairie Cemetery, New Orleans.

HAIDT, John Valentine, artist; b. Danzig, Germany, Oct. 4, 1700; attended Berlin (Germany) Acad. Joined Moravian Ch., London, Eng., circa 1725; came to Am., 1754, settled at Moravian community, Bethlehem, Pa.; painted portraits of many Moravians, also numerous religious pictures to decorate Moravian chs. around Bethlehem. Died Bethlehem, Jan. 18, 1780.

HAIGHT, Charles, congressman; b. Colts Neck, N.J., Jan. 4, 1838; grad. Princeton, 1857; studied law. Admitted to N.J. bar, 1861, began practice in Freehold; mem. N.J. Assembly, 1860-62, speaker, 1861-62; commd. brig. gen. N.J. Militia, 1861; in command of Camp Vredenburgh, 1862-65; organized, equipped 14th, 28th, 29th N.J. regts.; mem. U.S. Ho. of Reps. (Democrat) from N.J., 40th-41st congresses, 1867-71; resumed law practice; chmn. N.J. delegation; Dem. Nat. Conv., Balt., 1872; apptd. prosecutor of pleas; pres. atty. Monmouth County (N.J.), 1873-91. Died Freehold, Aug. 1, 1891; buried Maplewood Cemetery, Freehold.

HAIGHT, Edward, banker, congressman; b. N.Y. C., Mar. 26, 1817; attended common schs. Engaged in wholesale dry-goods bus., banking; moved to Westchester, N.Y., 1850; dir. Nat. Bank of N.Y.; organized Bank of Commonwealth of N.Y.C., 1856, pres., 1856-70; mem. U.S. Ho. of Reps. (Democrat) from N.Y., 37th Congress, 1861-63, unsuccessful Republican-Union Party candidate for re-election, 1862; dir. several banks and ins. cos. Died Westchester, Sept. 15, 1885; buried Trinity Ch. Cemetery, N.Y.C.

HAIGHT, Henry Huntly, gov. Cal.; b. Rochester, N.Y., May 20, 1825; s. Fletcher M. and Elizabeth Stewart (MacLachlan) H.; grad. Yale, 1844; m. Anna Bissell, Jan. 1855. Moved to St. Louis, 1846; admitted to St. Louis bar, 1846; went to Cal., 1850; chmn. Cal. Republican Com., 1859; gov. Cal., 1867-71, opposed Chinese immigration, Negro suffrage, approved proposals for 8-hour day; bd. regents U. Cal. Died San Francisco, Sept. 2, 1878.

HAILE, William, congressman; b. 1797. Moved to Woodville, Miss.; mem. Miss. Ho. of Reps., 1826-27, 30; mem. U.S. Ho. of Reps. from Miss., 19th-20th congresses, July 10, 1826-Sept. 12, 1828; del. Miss. Constl. Conv., 1832. Died nr. Woodville, Mar. ?, 1837.

HAINES, Charles Glidden, lawyer, author; b. Canterbury, N.H., Jan. 24, 1792; s. Samuel and Hannah (Johnson) H.; grad. Middlebury (Vt.) Coll., 1816; studied law under U.S. Senator Seymour, Middlebury, under Pierre Van Wyck, N.Y.C. Admitted to N.Y. bar, 1821, U.S. Supreme Ct. bar, 1824; pvt. sec. to Gov. DeWitt Clinton; wrote on current topics (especially canal question); publisher U.S. Law Jour. and Civilian Mag., 1822-23 (one of earliest law jours. in country); supported Clinton when he was removed as state canal commr. and campaigned for Clinton's reelection as gov., 1824; apptd. adjutant gen. N.Y. State by Gov. Clinton, 1825, died before assuming his office. Author: Considerations on the Great Western Canal from the Hudson to Lake Erie (pamphlet defending Clinton's position), 1818. Died July 3, 1825.

HAINES, Daniel, gov. N.J., jurist; b. N.Y.C., Jan. 6, 1801; s. Elias and Mary (Ogden) H.; A.B., Coll of N.J. (now Princeton), 1820; m. Ann Maria Austin, June 28, 1827; m. 2d, Mary Townsend, July 6, 1865. Admitted to bar, 1823; mem. N.J. Council, 1837, upper house N.J. Legislature, 1839-40; gov. N.J., 1843-44, 47-51; asso. justice N.J. Supreme Ct., 1852-66; mem. N.J. Boundary Commn., 1870-76; trustee Coll. of N.J., 1845-77; founder state normal sch., 1843; v.p. Nat. Prison Assn. of U.S., 1872. Died Hamburg, N.J., Jan. 26, 1877.

HAJI ALI, dey of Algiers. Succeeded to deyship of Algiers, 1809; maintained friendly relations with U.S., 1809-12; demanded and received from U.S. sum of $27,000, 1812; captured brig Edwin and imprisoned crew, 1812, released 2 crew mems. on payment of $4,000. Murdered by palace guard, 1815.

HAKLUYT, Richard, geographer, clergyman; b. circa 1552; attended Oxford (Eng.) U., 1570. Lectr. on geography Oxford; ordained to ministry Anglican Ch., 1578; chaplain to Sir Edward Stafford, English ambassador to France, 1583; in Paris, France, 1583-88; prebendary Bristol Cathedral, circa 1584; rector, Wetheringsett, Suffolk, Eng., circa 1589; chaplain of Savoy, archdeacon Westminster Abby, circa 1600. Author: Divers Voyages Touching the Discovery of America, 1578; A Particular Discourse Concerning Western Discoveries, 1584; The Principall Navigations, Voiages, and Discoveries of the English Nation . . . within the Compass of these 1500 Yeares, 1589. Died London, Eng., Nov. 23, 1616.

HALDEMAN, Richard Jacobs, congressman; b. Harrisburg, Pa., May 19, 1831; grad. Yale, 1851; attended Heidelberg and Berlin (Germany) univs. U.S. Attaché of legation at Paris, France, 1853, later at St. Petersburg, Russia, and Vienna, Austria; owner, editor Daily and Weekly Patriot, Harrisburg, until 1860; del. Democratic Nat. Conv., Balt. and Charleston, 1860; mem. U.S. Ho. of Reps. (Dem.) from Pa., 41st-42d congresses, 1869-73. Died Harrisburg, Oct. 1, 1886; buried Harrisburg Cemetery.

HALDEMAN, Samuel Steman, scientist, philologist; b. Locust Grove, Pa., Aug. 12, 1812; s. Henry and Frarce (Steman) H.; attended Dickinson Coll., Carlisle, Pa.; m. Mary A. Hough, 1835. Operated sawmill, Locust Grove, 1831-36, at same time studied natural history; asst. to Darwin Rodgers (geologist of Pa.), 1836-42; prof. natural history U. Pa., 1851-55, 1st prof. comparative philology, 1868-80; prof. chemistry Pa. Agrl. Coll., 1853-58; prof. natural scis. Del. Coll., 1853-58; made study of Am. Indian dialects, became expert in field. Author: Monograph on the Freshwater Mollusca of the United States, 1842; Elements of Latin Pronunciation, 1851; Outlines of Etymology, 1877; Word Building, 1881. Died Chickies, Pa., Sept. 10, 1880.

HALE, Artemas, congressman; b. Winchendon, Mass. Oct. 20, 1783. Sch. tchr., Hingham, Mass., 1804-14; mfr. cotton gins, Bridgewater, Mass.; mem. Mass. Ho. of Reps., 1824, 25, 27, 28, 38-42, Mass. Senate, 1833, 34; del. Mass. Constl. Conv., 1853; mem. U.S. Ho. of Reps. (Whig) from Mass., 29th-30th congresses, 1845-49; engaged in farming; presdl. elector Republican Party, 1864. Died Bridgewater, Aug. 3, 1882; buried Mt. Prospect Cemetery, Bridgewater.

HALE, Benjamin, educator, coll. pres.; b. Newburyport, Mass., Nov. 23, 1797; s. Thomas and Alice (Little) H.; grad. Bowdoin Coll., 1818; A.M., M.D. (hon.), Dartmouth, 1827; S.T.B., Columbia, 1836; m. Mary King, Apr. 9, 1823, 2 children. Licensed to preach, 1822; prin. Gardiner (Me.) Lyceum, 1822-27; prof. chemistry and mineralogy Dartmouth, 1827-35; ordained deacon Protestant Episcopal Ch., 1828, priest, 1831; pres. Geneva Coll. (later became Hobart Coll.), 1836-58, trustee, 1836-60. Author: Introduction to the Mechanical Principles of Carpentry, 1827; Scriptural Illustrations of Liturgy, 1835; Sermons, 1836-58, published 1883. Died Newburyport, July 15, 1863.

HALE, Charles, journalist, diplomat; b. June 7, 1831; s. Nathan and Sarah (Everett) H.; grad. Harvard, 1850. Jr. editor Boston Daily Advertiser, his father's paper, 1850; founder, contbr. to Today: A Boston Literary Journal, 1853-54; contbr. articles exposing how Roman Catholic schs. were being inspected by Know-Nothing politicians of state legislature to Daily Advertiser; mem. Mass. Ho. of Reps., 1855-61, 74-78, speaker, 1859; traveled to Egypt due to illness, visited W. S. Thayer the consul gen., 1861; apptd. consul gen. to Egypt on Thayer's death, 1864-70; active in devel. of internat. tribunals to replace old consular courts; mem. Mass. Senate, 1871; asst. sec. state under Hamilton Fish, 1872-74; admitted to Mass. bar, 1874. Died Mar. 1, 1882.

HALE, David, journalist; b. Lisbon, Conn., Apr. 25, 1791; s. Rev. David and Lydia (Austin) H.; m. Laura Hale (cousin), Jan. 18, 1815; m. 2d, Lucy S. Turner, Apr. 22, 1825; at least 1 son, David A. Clk. commn. house, Boston, 1809-12; taught dist. sch., Coventry, Conn., 1812-15; with importing and jobbing dry goods firm, 1815-17; bus. mgr. New York Jour. of Commerce (owned by Arthur Tappan), 1827, co-editor with Gerard Hallock, 1831-49, contb. editorials and articles; active mem. Broadway Tabernacle (completed 1836; 1st strong Congregational Ch. in N.Y.C.), purchased church property sold, 1840, used bldg. for large public meetings as well as religious services. Died Jan. 20, 1849.

HALE, David C., architect; b. Boston; grad. in architecture, Mass. Inst. Tech. Began as draftsman in office of Henry Hudson Richardson, later with firm Shepley, Rutan & Coolidge, 1886, in charge of constrn. of numerous bldgs., including Cincinnati Chamber of Commerce, became head drafting dept., Boston, in charge of plans for Amos Office Bldg., Boston Chamber of Commerce, others. Died Nov. 10, 1896.

HALE, Edwin Moses, physician, educator; b. Newport, N.H., Feb. 2, 1829; s. Dr. Syene and Betsy (Dow) H.; attended Western Coll. Homeopathic Medicine, Cleve., 1850-52; m. Abba Ann George, 1855. Practiced medicine, Jonesville, Mich., 1852-64; asst. editor North Am. Jour. of Homeopathy, 1860-69; prof. materia medica Hahnemann Med. Coll., Chgo., 1864-70, prof. med. botany, 1870, spl. lectr. on heart, 1871, tchr. therapeutics and new remedies, 1872-77, resigned; asst. editor Am. Homeopathic Observer, 1867-74; prof. materia medica Chgo. Homeopathic Coll., 1877-90. Author: New Remedies: Their Pathogenetic Effects and Therapeutical Applications in Homeopathic Practice, 1864; Lectures on the Heart, 1871; The Practice of Medicine, 1894. Died Jan. 15, 1899.

HALE, Enoch, physician, author; b. Westhampton, Mass., Jan. 19, 1790; s. Rev. Enoch and Octavia (Throop) H.; M.D., Harvard, 1813; m. Almira Hooker, 1813; m. 2d, Sarah Hooker, 1822; m. 3d, Jane Murdock, 1829. Practiced medicine Gardiner, Me., 1813-18, Boston, 1818; taught medicine, Boston, 1818; apptd. dist. physician Boston Dispensary, 1819; won Boylston prize for med. dissertations, 1819, 21; a founder Boston Soc. for Med. Improvement, 1828; recording sec. Mass. Med. Soc., 1832-35. Author: History and Description of an Epidemic Fever, Commonly Called Spotted Fever (observations on meningitis), 1819; Observations on the Typhoid Fever of New England, 1839. Died Nov. 12, 1848.

HALE, Horatio Emmons, ethnologist; b. Newport, N.H., May 3, 1817; s. David and Sarah Josepha (Buell) H.; grad. Harvard, 1837; m. Margaret Pugh, 1854. Before entering coll. wrote Remarks on the Language of the St. John's or Wlastukweek Indians, with a Penobscot Vocabulary; mem. Wilkes Exploring Expdn., 1838-42; admitted to Ill. bar, 1855; specialized in Am. Indian and Polynesian studies and the migrations of these peoples; practiced law, Clinton, Can.; v.p. A.A.A.S., 1886; pres. Am. Folklore Soc. Author: Ethnology and Philology, 1846; (paper) The Tutelo Tribe and Language, 1883; The Iroquois Book of Rites, 1883; An International Idiom, 1890; The Fall of Hochlega, 1893. Died Dec. 28, 1896.

HALE, James Tracy, congressman; b. Towanda, Pa., Oct. 14, 1810; attended pub. schs.; studied law. Admitted to Pa. bar, 1832, began practice, Bellefonte; apptd. pres. judge 20th Jud. Dist., 1851; mem. U.S. Ho. of Reps. (Republican) from Pa., 36th-38th congresses, 1859-65. Died Bellefonte, Apr. 6, 1865; buried City Cemetery, Bellefonte.

HALE, John Parker, senator; b. Rochester, N.H., Mar. 31, 1806; s. John Parker and Lydia (O'Brien) H.; grad. Bowdoin Coll., 1827; m. Lucy Lambert, 1 dau., Lucy Lambert. Admitted to N.H. bar, 1830; mem. N.H. Ho. of Reps., 1832-34; U.S. dist. atty., 1834-41; mem. U.S. Ho. of Reps. from N.H., 28th Congress, 1843-45; mem. U.S. Senate from N.H., 1847-53, 55-65, secured abolition of flogging in navy urged abolition of grog ration; outspoken opponent of slavery; U.S. presdl. nominee on Free Soiler's ticket, 1852; U.S. minister to Spain, 1865-69. Died Dover, N.H., Nov. 19, 1873; buried Pine Hill Cemetery, Dover.

HALE, Nathan, patriot; b. Coventry, Conn., June 6, 1755; s. Richard and Elizabeth (Strong) H.; grad. Yale, 1773. Taught sch., East Haddam, Conn., 1773-74, New London, Conn., 1774-75; commd. lt. Continental Army, 1775, distinguished in siege of Boston; commd. capt., 1776; capt. of a co. of Conn. rangers known as Congress' Own in Battle of L.I., with Gen. Washington in his retreat across the East River from Bklyn.; served as capt. Knowlton's Rangers, 1776; offered his services when Washington called for volunteers to gather intelligence concerning the condition and intentions of British; went from Harlem Heights to L.I. disguised as sch tchr., captured as spy on his return, Sept. 21, 1776, execution ordered by Gen. Howe; supposed to have said before being hanged: "I only regret that I have but one life to lose for my country." Hanged by British, Sept. 22, 1776.

HALE, Nathan, journalist; b. Westhampton, Mass., Aug. 16, 1784; s. Rev. Enoch and Octavia (Throop) H.; grad. Williams Coll., 1804; A.M., Dartmouth, 1810; m. Sarah Preston Everett, 1816; children—Lucretia Peabody, Charles, Edward Everett, Nathan, Susan. Tchr. mathematics Phillips Exeter (N.H.) Acad., 1804-10; admitted to Suffolk (Mass.) bar, 1810; editor Boston Weekly Messenger, 1814; owner, editor 1st Boston daily newspaper Boston Daily Advertiser, 1814-54; mem. Mass. Ho. of Reps., 1820-22, Mass. Senate, 1829-30; 1st pres. Boston & Worcester R.R., 1831-49; a founder North Am. Review, 1815, Christian Examiner, 1824; editor Monthly Chronicle, 1840-46. Author: Journal of Debates and Proceedings in the Convention of Delegates Chosen to Revise the Constitution of Massachusetts, 1821. Died Feb. 8, 1863.

HALE, Robert Safford, congressman; b. Chelsea, Vt., Sept. 24, 1822; s. Harry and Lucinda (Eddy) H.; grad. U. Vt., 1842; m. Lorina Sibley Stone, at least 1 son, Harry. Admitted to N.Y. bar, 1847; county judge, surrogate Essex County (N.Y.), 1856-65; counsel for Sec. of War Stanton in impeachment trial of Pres. Johnson, 1868; mem. bd. regents U. State N.Y., 1859-81; mem. U.S. Ho. of Reps. from N.Y., 39th, 43d congresses, Dec. 3, 1866-67, 73-75; spl. counsel U.S. Treasury Dept., 1868; agt., counsel for U.S. before Am.-Brit. Mixed Claims Commn., 1871-73; 1st pres. Elizabethtown (N.Y.), 1875; commr. N.Y. Topog. Survey, 1876. Died Elizabethtown, Dec. 14, 1881; buried Riverside Cemetery, Elizabethtown.

HALE, Salma, congressman; b. Alstead, Cheshire County, N.H., Mar. 7, 1787; s. David Hale; children include George Silsbee. Became a printer; editor Walpole Polit. Observatory, 1805; apptd. clk. Cheshire County Ct. Common Pleas, moved to Keene, N.H., 1813; mem. U.S. Ho. of Reps. (Democrat) from N.H., 15th Congress, 1817-19; clk. N.H. Supreme Ct., 1817-34; mem. N.H. Ho. of Reps., 1823, 28, 44, N.H. Senate, 1824-25, 45-46; admitted to N.H. bar, 1834; sec. commn. apptd. under Treaty of Ghent for determining N.W. boundary of U.S. Author: The Administration of John Q. Adams and the Opposition by Algernon Sidney, 1826; A New Grammar of the English Language, rev. edit., 1831; others. Died Somerville, Mass., Nov. 19, 1866; buried Woodland Cemetery, Keene.

HALE, Sarah Josepha Buell, editor, author; b. Newport, N.H., Oct. 24, 1788; d. Gordon and Martha (Whittlesey) Buell; m. David Hale, Oct. 1813, 5 children including Horatio Emmons. Wrote occasional articles for newspapers; began writing career after husband's death, 1822; editor Ladies Mag., Boston, 1828-37, she became literary editor when editor, Lewis Godey bought the mag. and started Godey's Lady's Book, 1837, editor, Phila., 1841-77; writings include: The Genius of Oblivion, 1823; Northwood, A Tale of New England, 1827; Poems for Our Children, 1830; Woman's Record, or Sketches of Distinguished Women, 3d edit., 1876. Died Phila., Apr. 30, 1879.

HALE, William, congressman; b. Portsmouth, N.H., Aug. 6, 1765; attended pub. schs. Mcht., shipowner; mem. N.H. Senate, 1796-1800; mem.

N.H. Gov.'s Council, 1803-05; mem. U.S. Ho. of Reps. (Federalist), 11th, 13th-14th congresses, 1809-11, 13-17. Died Dover, N.H., Nov. 8, 1848; buried Pine Hill Cemetery, Dover.

HALE, William, gov. Wyo. Territory; b. London, Henry County, Ia., Nov. 18, 1837. Admitted to Ia. bar, 1859; Republican presdl. elector for Ia., 1868; gov. Wyo. Territory, 1882-85. Died Cheyenne, Wyo., Jan. 13, 1885.

HALEY, Elisha, congressman; b. Groton, Conn., Jan. 21, 1776; attended common schs. Engaged in farming, later in civil engring.; mem. Conn. Ho. of Reps., 1820, 24, 26, 29, 33, 34; Conn.Senate, 1830; served as capt. Conn. Militia; mem. U.S. Ho. of Reps. (Democrat) from Conn., 24th-25th congresses, 1835-39. Died Groton, Jan. 22, 1860; buried Crary Cemetery, Groton.

HALL, Abraham Oakey, mayor, author; b. Albany, N.Y., July 26, 1826; s. Morgan James and Elsie (Oakey) H.; B.A., U. City of N.Y., 1844, M.A., 1847; attended Harvard Law Sch., 1 year; studied law under Charles W. Sanford, N.Y.C., Thomas and John Slidell, New Orleans; m. Katharine Louise Barnes; m. 2d, Mrs. John J. Clifton, 1896; 6 children. Admitted to New Orleans bar, 1849, N.Y. bar, 1851, also English bar; asst. dist. atty. N.Y. County, 1851, dist. atty., 1855-58, 62-68; became mem. Tammany Hall, 1864; mayor N.Y.C., 1868-72, covered up for Tweed Ring while in office; accused of being part of Tweed Ring, 1871, claimed innocence, but was indicted, brought to trial, 1872, gained acquittal; dir. Manhattan Club, 1868-71; pres. Lotus Club, 1870-73; city editor N.Y. World, 1879-82; London rep. N.Y. Herald, 1882-87; London rep. N.Y. Morning Jour., 1890-91. Author: (works include) The Manhattaner in New Orleans or Phases of Crescent City Life, 1851; Sketches of Travel, 1859; Ballads of Hans York, 1880. Died N.Y.C., Oct. 7, 1898.

HALL, Arethusa, educator, author; b. Norwich (now Huntington), Mass., Oct. 13, 1802; d. Aaron and Sarah (Richardson) Hall. Tchr. sch., Greenland, N.H., 1826; head instr. female dept. Haverhill (N.H.) Acad., circa 1827-31; injured in fall from carriage, 1831; taught for brief periods, New Eng., 1831-49; mem. faculty Bklyn. Female Acad., 1849-51; a founder, asst. prin. Bklyn. Heights Sem., 1851-circa 1860. Author: Thoughts of Blaise Pascal, 1846; A Manual of Morals, 1849; The Literary Reader, 1850; her autobiography, 1875-76. Died Northampton, Mass., May 24, 1891.

HALL, Augustus, congressman, jurist; b. Batavia, N.Y., Apr. 29, 1814; attended Middleburg (N.Y.) Acad.; studied law. Admitted to the bar, 1836; began law practice, Mt. Vernon, Ohio; asst. U.S. marshal, 1839; pros. atty. Union County (Ohio), 1840-42; moved to Keosauqua, Ia., 1844; Democratic presdl. elector, 1852; mem. U.S. Ho. of Reps. (Dem.) from Ia., 34th Congress, 1855-57; chief justice Neb. Territory (apptd. by Buchanan), 1858-61. Died Bellevue, Neb., Feb. 1, 1861; buried Prospect Hill Cemetery, Bellevue.

HALL, Baynard Rush, clergyman, educator; b. Phila., Jan. 28, 1798; s. Dr. John and Elizabeth (Baynard) H.; grad. Union Coll., 1820; grad. Princeston Theol. Sem., 1823; m. Miss Young, 1821. First prin. Ind. State Sem., Bloomington, Ind., 1824-28, prof. ancient langs., 1828-31; ordained to ministry Presbyn. Ch., Ind., 1825; Preacher Bloomington, Presbyn. Ch., 1826-30; an organizer Synod of Ind., 1826; opened and taught in an acad., Bedford, Pa., 1831-38; prin. Park Inst., also pastor Dutch Ref. Ch., Bklyn., 1852-62. Author: (works include) Latin Grammar, 1828; The New Purchase; or, Seven and A Half Years in the Far West, 1st edit., 1843; Something for Everybody, 1846. Died Bklyn., Jan. 23, 1863.

HALL, Benton Jay, congressman, govt. ofcl.; b. Mt. Vernon, O., Jan. 13, 1835; attended Knox Coll., Galesburg, Ill.; grad. Miami U., Oxford, O., 1855; studied law. Moved to Ia., 1840; admitted to Ia. bar, 1857, practiced law; mem. Ia. Ho. of Reps., 1872-73, Ia. Senate, 1882-86; mem. U.S. Ho. of Reps. (Democrat) from Ia., 49th Congress, 1885-87; U.S. commr. of patents (apptd. by Cleveland), 1887-89; resumed law practice. Died Burlington, Ia., Jan. 5, 1894; buried Aspen Grove Cemetery, Burlington.

HALL, Bolling, congressman; b. Dinwoddie County, Va., Dec. 25, 1767. Served in Revolutionary War; moved to Hancock County, Ga., 1792; mem. Ga. Ho. of Reps., 1800-02, 04-06; mem. U.S. Ho. of Reps. (War Democrat), 12th-14th congresses, 1811-17; became engaged in planting, nr. Montgomery, Ala., 1808; chmn. reception com. to welcome Gen. Lafayette, 1824. Died "Ellerslie," Autauga (now Elmore) County, Ala., Feb. 25, 1836; buried "Ellerslie."

HALL, Chapin, mfr., congressman; b. Busti, Chautauqua County, N.Y., July 12, 1816; attended Jamestown (N.Y.) Acad.; moved to Pine Grove (now Russell), Pa., circa 1841, engaged as mcht., also in lumber bus.; moved to Warren, Pa., 1851, engaged in banking; mem. U.S. Ho. of Reps. (Republican) from Pa., 36th Congress, 1859-61; mfr. lumber products, Louisville, Ky., Fond du Lac, Wis., Newark, N.J.; mfr. worsted goods, Jamestown. Died Jamestown, Sept. 12, 1879; buried Lake View Cemetery, Jamestown.

HALL, Charles Francis, explorer; b. Rochester, N.H., 1821. As a restless youth held various jobs; became interested in fate of Arctic explorer Sir John Franklin and his party, left New London, Conn. in search of relics and survivors of expdn., May 1860; landed alone at Frobisher Bay in Arctic region, July 1860; lived with and gained help of Eskimos until his return to New London, Sept. 1862, having found relics of Frobisher's expdn. of 1577-78 but none of Franklin expdn.; made similar journey, 1864-69, during which he found relics of Franklin expdn. as well as traces of possible survivors; on June 29, 1871, with backing of U.S. Congress, he undertook last voyage to North in command of ship Polaris, penetrated to 82° 11' N and 61° W, the farthest point attained up to that time by vessel; Hall died on trip, but crew members survived extremely severe winter to return to U.S.; trip proved to have important geographic results. Author: Arctic Researches and Life Among the Esquimaux, 2 vols., 1865. Died Thank God Harbor, Greenland, Nov. 8, 1871.

HALL, Charles Henry, clergyman, author; b. Augusta, Ga., Nov. 7, 1820; s. Charles and Margaret (Reid) H.; grad. Yale, 1842; studied Bibl. literature, Andover, Mass., Hartford, Conn., also Gen. Theol. Sem., N.Y.C.; m. Annie Maria Cumming, Mar. 2, 1848; m. 2d, Lizzie Ames, Sept. 10, 1857. Ordained deacon Episcopal Ch., 1844; pastor St. John's Ch., Huntington, L.I., N.Y., 1845; ordained presbyter, Fair Haven, Conn., 1845; rector Ch. of Holy Innocents, West Point, N.Y., 1847-48; chaplain U.S. Mil. Acad., West Point; pastor St. John's Ch., John's Island, S.C., 1848-56; rector Ch. of the Epiphany, Washington, D.C., 1856-69; rector Holy Trinity Ch., Bklyn., 1869-95. Author: (works include) Notes, Practical and Expository, on the Gospels, 2 vols., 1857; The Valley of the Shadow, 1878; The Church of the Household, 1877. Died Bklyn., Sept. 12, 1895.

HALL, David. printer; b. Edinburgh, Scotland, 1714; m. Mary Lacock, Jan. 7, 1748. Learned printing trade, London, Eng.; came to Phila. as journeyman in office of Benjamin Franklin, 1743, became partner under name Franklin & Hall, 1748, sole owner, 1766, then took in partner. Died Phila., Dec. 24, 1772; buried Christ Ch. Graveyard, Phila.

HALL, Dominick Augustin, jurist; b. probably S.C., circa 1765. Judge, 5th U.S. Circuit Ct., 1801-03, Dist. Ct., Territory of Orleans, 1804-13; U.S. dist. judge La. Dist., 1813-20; while New Orleans still under martial law because of War of 1812 he granted writ of habeas corpus for release of Louis Louillier who had been arrested by Gen. Andrew Jackson for inciting discontent among troops, 1815, Gen. Jackson refused to recognize authority of court, rearrested Louillier and committed him to trial (Hall had been sent out of city by Jackson); came back and fined Jackson $1,000 for contempt of court and disregarding writ of habeas corpus; Jackson paid fine, peace with Britain had meanwhile been made ofcl., Jackson withdrew martial law. Died New Orleans, Dec. 19, 1820.

HALL, Fitzedward, philologist; b. Troy, N.Y., Mar. 21, 1825; s. Daniel and Anjinette (Fitch) H.; grad. Rensselaer Poly. Inst., 1842; A.M., Harvard, 1846, LL.D. (hon.), 1895; D.C.L., Oxford (Eng.) U., 1862; m. Amy Schuldham, 1854. Became interested in the study of langs. while in India; instr. local govt. coll., Benares, India, 1850-53, prof. Anglo-Sanskrit, 1853-55; insp. pub. instrn. for Ajmere-Merwara, India, 1855; insp. pub. instrn. Central Provinces of India, 1856-57; prof. Sanskrit, Hindustani and Indian jurisprudence King's Coll., London, Eng., 1862-64; examiner in Hindustani, Hirdi and Sanskrit for Civil Service Commrs., 1864-80. Author: Recent Exemplifications of False Philology, 1872; editor: The Vishnu Purana, 1864-77; Benares Ancient and Medieval, 1868. Died Feb. 1, 1901.

HALL, George, congressman; b. Chesire, Conn., May 12, 1770; studied law. Admitted to N.Y. bar, practiced in Onondaga County; moved to Town of Onondaga, 1802, practiced law; postmaster Onondaga Hollow, 1802; surrogate Onondaga County, 1800-12, supr., 1811-12; justice of peace, 1818-22; mem. N.Y. State Assembly, 1816-17; mem. U.S. Ho. of Reps. (Democrat) from N.Y., 16th Congress, 1819-21, unsuccessful candidate for re-election, 1820; resumed law practice. Died Onondaga Valley, N.Y., Mar. 20, 1840; buried Onondaga Valley Cemetery.

HALL, Henry Bryan, engraver, portrait painter; b. London, Eng., Mar. 11, 1808; tutored in art and engraving by Benjamin Smith, Sir Thomas Lawrenc Henry Meyer in London; m. Stepney Holloway, se eral children including Alice, Henry Jr., Alfred Br an, Charles B. Apprentice to hist. engraver of t Crown, H. T. Ryall, London, 4 years; became portra painter, portrait of Napoleon III one of best work came to Am., 1850, did engraving for vario publishers; began engraving and portrait publishi bus.; some of best engravings include those of Geor Washington. Died Morrisania, N.Y., Apr. 25, 188

HALL, Hiland, gov. Vt., congressman; b. Ber nington, Vt., July 20, 1795; s. Nathaniel and Ab gail (Hubbard) H.; LL.D. (hon.), U. Vt., 185 m. Dolly Tuttle Davis, Oct. 27, 1818, 8 childre including Charles. Admitted to Bennington Coun (Vt.) bar, 1819; state's atty. for Benningt County, 1829-31; mem. U.S. Ho. of Reps. fro Vt., 23d-27th congresses, 1833-43; commr. Vt. Sta Bank, 1843-46; judge Supreme Ct. Vt., 1846-5 2d comptroller of treasury, 1850-51; U.S. land com mr. for Cal., 1851-54; gov. Vt., 1858-60; pres. V Hist. Soc., 1859-65. Author: History of Vermo from Its Discovery to Its Admission to the Unic in 1791. Died Springfield, Mass., Dec. 18, 188 buried Bennington (Vt.) Center Cemetery.

HALL, Isaac Hollister, Orientalist; b. Norwalk Conn., Dec. 12, 1837; s. Edwin and Fanny (Hollis ter) H.; grad. Hamilton Coll., 1859; grad. La Dept., Columbia, 1865; Litt.D., Tercentenary (Dublin U.; m. Fannie M. Dederick, Sept. 5, 187 Became 1st to translate entire Cypriote inscriptio instr. Syrian Protestant Coll. (now Am. U. of Be rut), Beirut, Lebanon, 1875-77; discovered Syria manuscript of New Testament of about 800 A.D 1876, contained 4 Gospels in Philoxenian versio Book of Acts, several Epistles; mem. editorial sta Sunday Sch. Times, 1877-84; mem. staff Met. Mu Art, N.Y.C., curator dept. sculpture, 1886. Mem Am. Philol. Assn. (pres.), Am. Oriental Soc. (v.p. dir.), Soc. Bibl. Lit. and Exigesis (mem. council) Author: Williams Manuscript: The Syrian Antile gomena Epistles, 1886; The American Greek Tes tament: A Critical Bibliography of the Greek Ne Testament as Published in America, 1883. Die Mount Vernon, N.Y., July 2, 1896.

HALL, James, clergyman; b. Carlisle, Pa., Au 22, 1744; s. James and Prudence (Roddy) H grad. with distinction Princeton, 1774. Licensed t preach by Presbytery of Orange, 1775; comdr. chaplain of self-organized company of cavalry o expdn. into S.C. during Revolution; an organizer Gen. Assembly of Presbyn. Ch., modertor, 1803 moderator Synod of the Carolinas, 1812; an organ izer Am. Bible Soc., N.C. Bible Soc. (1st pres.) established 1st Protestant mission of lower Missis sippi valley at Natchez, 1800 (1st in series of mis sionary efforts in lower valley Mississippi); earl patron U. N.C.; one of chief promoters Princeto Theol. Sem. Author: Narrative of a Most Extraordi nary Work of Religion in North Carolina; Report o a Missionary Tour through the Mississippi and th Southwestern County. Died Bethany, N.C., July 25 1826; buried Bethany.

HALL, James, author, jurist, banker; b. Phila. Aug. 19, 1793; s. John and Sarah (Ewing) H. m. Mary Harrison Posey, 1823; m. 2d, Mary Lou isa (Anderson) Alexander, Sept. 3, 1839. Commd 3d lt. in 2d Arty. Regt. under Winfield Scott 1813; served under Gen. Brown in Army Buffalo 1814, in battles Chippewa, Lundy's Lane, Niagar and Ft. Erie; admitted to bar, 1818; pros. atty for area extending from Ohio to Mississippi rivers circuit judge, 1825; treas. Ill., 1828; leader i state agrl. soc.; 1st pres. state antiquarian soc. held offices in state Bible Soc.; pres. state Lyce um; trustee Ill. Coll.; editor Ill. Intelligences 1829-32; established Ill. Monthly Magazine, 1830 pres. Comml. Bank Cincinnati, 1853. Author: Let ters from the West, 1829; Legends of the West, 1832; The Soldiers Bride, 1832; The Harpes' Head, 1833; Tales of the Border, 1835; Sketches of the West, 1835; Life of Gen. William Henry Harrison, 1830; Statistics of the West, 1836 (new edit. 1839), History and Biography of the Indians o North America, 3 vols., 1838-44; The Wilderness and the Warpath, 1845; Romance of Western History, 1847. Died Cincinnati, July 5, 1868.

HALL, James, geologist; b. Hingham, Mass., Sept. 12, 1811; s. James and Susanna (Dourdain) H.; grad. Rensselaer Poly. Inst. (then Rensselaer Sch.), 1832; A.M. (hon.), Union Coll., 1842; M.D. (hon.), U. Md., 1846; LL.D. (hon.), Hamilton Coll., 1863, McGill U., 1884, Harvard, 1886; m. Sarah Aiken, 1838, 4 children. Asst. prof. chemistry Rensselaer Poly. Inst., 1832-36, prof. geology, 1836; began explorations, Western N.Y., 1838; state geologist Ia., 1855-58, Wis., 1857-60; dir. N.Y. State Museum, 1866-98; recipient Wollaston medal of Geol. Soc. of London, 1858, Walker prize of Boston Soc. Natural History, 1884, Hayden medal from Acad. Natural Scis. of Phila., 1890; 1st pres. Geol. Soc. Am.; v.p. Internat. Congress of Geologists, Paris, 1878, at Bologna, 1881, at Berlin, 1885; charter mem. Nat. Acad. Scis. Author: The Paleontology of New York, Part

IV Comprising the Survey of the Fourth Geological District, 1843, (classic of early geol. lit.); New York State Natural History Survey: Paleontology, 8 vols., 1847-94. Died Albany, N.Y.; Aug. 7, 1898.

HALL, John, Continental congressman; b. nr. Annapolis, Md., Nov. 27, 1729; studied law. Admitted to Md. bar, began practice in Annapolis; declined office of judge of admiralty; mem. Md. Council of Safety; del. Md. Conf., 1775; mem. Continental Congress from Md., 1775, 77, 80, 83, 84; continued practice of law; Died "The Vineyard" (now known as "Iglehart") nr. Annapolis, Mar. 8, 1797; buried family burial ground, "The Vineyard."

HALL, John, clergyman; b. County Armagh, Ireland, July 31, 1829; s. William and Rachel (McGowan) H.; B.A., Belfast (Ireland) Coll., 1846, grad. theology sch., 1849; m. Mrs. Emily (Bolton) Irwin, 1852, 4 children including T. C. (son.). Missionary, Connaught, Ireland, 1849-52; pastor First Ch. of Armagh, 1852-58; asst. Mary's Abbey, Dublin, Ireland, 1858-67, founded, edited monthly paper Evangelical Witness; a commr. of edn. of Ireland, 1860; sent to U.S. on visit by Irish Ch., 1867, became minister Fifth Av. Presbyn. Ch., N.Y.C., 1867-98; chancellor U. City of N.Y., 1881-91. Died Bangor, Ireland, Sept. 17, 1898.

HALL, John Elihu, lawyer, writer; b. Phila., Dec. 27, 1783; s. John and Sarah (Ewing) H.; attended Princeton; studied law, Phila.; m. Fanny M. Chew. Admitted to Pa. bar, 1805, U.S. Supreme Ct. bar; co-defender of Alexander C. Hansen, Jr. of Balt. who was attacked by anti-British mob for publishing Fed. Republican, 1812; prof. ancient and modern langs. U. Md., 1813; mem. Am. Philos. Soc., 1814; editor Port Folio, Phila., 1816-27. Author: American Law Journal, 6 vols., 1808-17; To The People of the United States (pamphlet); The Philadelphia Souvenir: A Collection of Fugitive Pieces from the Philadelphia Press, 1826. Died Phila., June 12, 1829.

HALL, John H., engraver, lithographer; b. Cooperstown, N.Y. Apprentice, Albany, N.Y., 1825; received instrn. in wood engraving from Dr. Alexander Anderson, N.Y.C.; with Carter, Andrews & Co. Lancaster, Mass., 1830; a founder Boston Bewick Co., 1834; best known work was for Nuttall's Manual of Ornithology; sr. partner firms Hall, Packard & Cushman, 1839, Hall & Cushman, 1839 (both Albany); went to Cal. during Gold Rush, 1849. Died Cal.

HALL, Joseph, congressman; b. Methuen, Mass., June 26, 1793; attended Andover (Mass.) Acad. Moved to Camden, Me., 1809, engaged as mcht.; served as ensign in Col. Forte's Regt., Mass. Militia during War of 1812, later apptd. col.; became dep. sheriff, 1821, sheriff, 1827; postmaster of Camden, 1830-33, 37-38; U.S. Ho. of Reps. (Democrat), 23-24th congresses, 1833-37; measurer Boston Customshouse, 1838-46, clk., 1857-59; naval agt., Boston, 1846-49; unsuccessful candidate for mayor Boston, 1849; farmer, 1850-57. Died Boston, Dec. 31, 1859; buried Mountain Cemetery, Camden, Me.

HALL, Lawrence Washington, congressman; b. Lake County, O., 1819; grad. Hudson Coll., 1839; studied law. Admitted to Ohio bar, 1843, began practice in Bucyrus, 1844; pros. atty. Crawford County (O.), 1845-51; judge Ct. Common Pleas, 1852-57; mem. U.S. Ho. of Reps. (Democrat) from Ohio, 1857-59, unsuccessful candidate for re-election, 1858; resumed law practice; imprisoned for alleged disloyalty to Union, 1862. Died Bucyrus, Jan. 18, 1863; buried Oakwood Cemetery, Bucyrus.

HALL, Louisa Jane Park, poet; b. Newburyport, Mass., Feb. 7, 1802; dau. of Dr. John Park; m. Rev. Edward B. Hall, 1840, at least 1 child. Published her 1st writings in Literary Gazette, 1823. Author: Miriam (1830); Joanna of Naples; Life of Elizabeth Carter (1838); Dramatic Fragment. Died Cambridge, Mass., Sept. 8, 1892.

HALL, Lyman, statesman, signer Declaration of Independence, gov. Ga.; b. Wallingford, Conn., Apr. 12, 1724; s. John and Mary (Street) H.; grad. Yale, 1747; m. Abigail Burr, May 20, 1752; m. 2d, Mary Osborn, 1 son. Ordained to ministry, 1749, dismissed from his pulpit, 1751, then reinstated, filled various vacant pulpits for 2 years, then abandoned ministry and studied medicine; moved to Ga. as part of a S.C. colony, about 1756; mem. Provincial Congress Ga., 1775; took part in colonizing Midway Dist. Ga.; del. to Continental Congress from Ga., Mar. 1775; signed Declaration of Independence; gov. Ga., 1783; one of early advocates of setting aside public land for purposes higher edn. Died Burke County, Ga., Oct. 19, 1790.

HALL, Nathan Kelsey, U.S. postmaster gen., jurist; b. Marcellus, N.Y., Mar. 28, 1810; s. Ira and Katherine (Rose) H.; studied law under Millard Fillmore, Aurora, N.Y., 1828; m. Emily Paine, Nov. 16, 1832, 5 children. Admitted to N.Y. bar, 1832; partner (with Fillmore) in law firm, Buffalo, N.Y., 1832; clk. bd. suprs. Erie County (N.Y.), 1832-38; city atty. Buffalo, 1833-34, alderman, 1837; master in chancery Buffalo, 1839-41; judge Erie County Ct. of Common Pleas, 1841; mem. U.S. Ho. of Reps. from N.Y., 30th Congress, 1847-49; postmaster gen. U.S., 1850-52; U.S. judge No. Dist. N.Y., 1852-74. Died Buffalo, Mar. 2, 1874; buried Forest Lawn Cemetery, Buffalo.

HALL, Obed, congressman; b. Raynham, Mass., Dec. 23, 1757; Moved to Madbury, N.H., later to Upper Bartlett, N.H.; engaged in farming, later became innkeeper; surveyor of hwys., 1790; mem. bd. selectmen Bartlett (N.H.), 1791, 98, 1800, 02, 10, 14-19, 23; mem. N.H. Ho. of Reps., 1801-02; judge N.H. Ct. Common Pleas; mem. U.S. Ho. of Reps. (Democrat) from N.H., 12th Congress, 1811-13; mem. N.H. Senate, 1819. Died Bartlett, Apr. 1, 1828; buried Garland Ridge Cemetery, nr. Bartlett; reinterred Evergreen Cemetery, Portland, Me.

HALL, Robert Bernard, clergyman, congressman; b. Boston, Jan. 28, 1812; entered Boston Latin Sch., 1822; studied theology, New Haven, 1833-34; LL.D., Ia. Central Coll., 1858. Ordained to ministry Congregational Ch., later to Episcopal Ch.; an original mem. Garrison's New Eng. Anti-Slavery Soc., 1832; a founder Am. Anti-Slavery Soc., 1833; moved to Plymouth, Mass.; mem. Mass. Senate, 1855; mem. U.S. Ho. of Reps. from Mass. as Am. (Know-Nothing) Party rep., 34th Congress, 1855-57, was Republican, 35th Congress, 1857-59; del. Union Conv., Phila., 1866. Died Plymouth, Apr. 15, 1868; buried Oak Grove Cemetery, Plymouth.

HALL, Samuel, printer; b. Medford, Mass., Nov. 2, 1740; s. Jonathan and Anna (Fowle) H. With Newport Mercury, 1762-68; founded 1st printing house in Salem (Mass.), 1768, published Essex Gazette (a major agt. of colonial cause); founded New Eng. Chronicle, 1776, Salem Gazette, 1781, Mass. Gazette, 1785, Courier of Boston, 1789; known for publishing children's books; ret., 1805. Died Boston, Oct. 30, 1807.

HALL, Samuel, shipbuilder; b. Marshfield, Mass., Apr. 23, 1800; s. Luke and Anna (Tuels) H.; m. Christina Kent; m. 2d, Huldah B. Sherman; 2 sons including Samuel, Jr., 6 daus. Established shipbldg. yard, East Boston, Mass., 1839; launched 110 clipper ships from yard including Surprise (1st clipper built in Mass.), Game Cock, Race Horse (all 1850), RB Forbes, 1851; John Gilpin, Flying Children, Hoogby, Polynesia (all 1852), Amphitrite, Mystery, Wizard, Oriental (all 1853); set style for New Eng. fishing schooners with Express, Telegraph; instrumental in having water piped to East Boston, 1851; pres. East Boston Ferry Co., Dry Dock Co., Maverick Nat. Bank (all Boston). Died Princeton, Ind., Nov. 13, 1870.

HALL, Samuel Read, educator, clergyman; b. Croydon, N.H., Oct. 27, 1795; s. Samuel Read and Elizabeth (Hall) H.; m. Mary Dascomb, June 17, 1823; m. 2d, Mary Holt, June 6, 1837; 10 children. Tchr. in Rumford, Me., 1814, credited with 1st use of blackboards in U.S.; prin. of an acad., Fitchburg, Mass., circa 1822; licensed as Congregational minister, 1822; established tchrs. tng. sch. (1st normal sch. in U.S.), Concord, Vt., 1823; a founder Am. Inst. of Instrn., Boston, 1830 (oldest ednl. assn. in Am.); prin. Phillips Acad., Andover, Mass., 1830-37, Holmes Plymouth Acad. (N.H.), 1837-40, Craftsbury (Vt.) Acad., 1840-46; pastor ch., Craftsbury, 1840-58, Browington, Vt., 1858-67, Granby, Vt., 1872-75. Author: (works include) Lectures on School-Keeping, 1829; Lectures to Female Teachers on School-Keeping, 1832. Died June 24, 1877.

HALL, Sarah Ewing, essayist; b. Phila., Oct. 30, 1761; d. Rev. John and Hannah (Sergeant) Ewing; m. John Hall, 1782, at least 4 children, Harrison, John Elihu, James, Thomas Mifflin. Contbr. to Port Folio, Phila., 1801-27; works include Waverly, 1815; conversations on the Bible, 1818; essays published by son Harrison as Selections from the Writings of Mrs. Sarah Hall, Author of Conversations on the Bible, 1833. Died Phila., Apr. 8, 1830; buried Third Presbyn. Churchyard, Phila.

HALL, Sherman, missionary; b. Weathersfield, Vt., Apr. 30, 1800; s. Aaron and Sarah (Brigham) H.; grad. Dartmouth, 1828; grad. Andover Theol. Sem., 1831; m. Betsey Parker, 1831. Ordained to ministry Congregational Ch., Woburn, Mass., 1831; sent to Lake Superior region by Am. Bd. Commrs. for Fgn. Missions, 1831, founded mission on Madeline Island in Lake Superior (1st mission among the Chippewa Indians since the Jesuits); opened at least 2 schs. on island for which he received large grants from U.S. govt.; translated textbooks, hymns, parts of the Bible into Chippewa, 1833-56; supt. manual labor sch. for Chippewas at junction of Crow Wing and Mississippi rivers, 1852-54; pastor Congregational Ch., Sauk Rapids, Minn., 1854-79. Died Sauk Rapids, Sept. 1, 1879.

HALL, Thomas H., congressman; b. Prince George County, Va., June 1773; studied medicine. Practiced medicine, Tarboro, N.C.; mem. U.S. Ho. of Reps. (Democrat) from N.C., 15th-18th, 20th-24th congresses, 1817-25, 27-35; resumed practice of medicine, engaged in farming; mem. N.C. Senate, 1836. Died Tarboro, June 30, 1853; buried Macnail-Hall Cemetery, nr. Tarboro.

HALL, Thomas Seavey, mfr. automatic railroad and highway signal devices; b. Upper Bartlett, N.H., Apr. 1, 1827; s. Elias and Hannah (Seavey) H.; m. Sarah C. Phillips, 1 son. A prominent woolen mfr. in New Eng.; a victim of a railroad accident, 1866, led to interest in signal devices to avoid such accidents; patented electric automatic signals, 1867; organized Hall Drawbridge & Signal Co., Stamford, Conn., 1867; 1st signal installed, Stamford, 1868; devised electric enclosed disc or "banjo" signal, 1869; 1st automatic block signalling system installed, 1871; patented highway-crossing signal, 1879. Died Meriden, Conn., Dec. 1, 1880.

HALL, Willard, congressman, jurist; b. Westford, Mass., Dec. 24, 1780; attended Westford Acad.; grad. Harvard, 1799; studied law. Admitted to Del. bar, 1803, began practice in Dover; sec. of state Del., 1811-14, 21; mem. U.S. Ho. of Reps. (Democrat) from Del., 15th-16th congresses, 1817-21, unsuccessful candidate for re-election, 1820; mem. Del. Senate, 1822; U.S. dist. judge for Del., 1823-71; compiler Revised Code of Del., 1829; del. Del. Constl. Conv., 1821; pres. Wilmington (Del.) Sch. Bd., 1852-70. Died Wilmington, May 10, 1875; buried Wilmington and Brandywine Cemetery.

HALL, Willard Preble, gov. Mo.; b. Harper's Ferry, Va. (now W.Va.), May 9, 1820; s. John and Statica (Preble) H.; grad. Yale, 1839; m. Ann Eliza Richardson, Oct. 28, 1847; m. 2d, Ollie C. Oliver, June 22, 1864; 7 children. Admitted to Mo. bar, 1841; apptd. circuit atty. in Mo., 1843; Democratic presdl. elector, 1884; served as lt. in 1st Mo. Cavalry during Mexican War; with Col. Alexander Doniphan drew up code of laws for governing N.M. Territory; mem. U.S. Ho. of Reps. (Dem.) from Mo., 30th-32d congresses, 1847-53; mem. Mo. Constl. Conv. which made decision to remain in Union, 1861; provisional lt. gov. of Mo., 1861-64; brig. gen. Mo. Militia, 1861-63; gov. Mo., 1864-65. Died St. Joseph, Mo., Nov. 3, 1882; buried Mt. Moriah Cemetery, St. Joseph.

HALL, William, congressman, gov. Tenn.; b. Surry County, N.C., Feb. 11, 1775; attended country schs. Moved to New River, N.C., 1779, Sumner County, Tenn., 1785; engaged in farming; mem. Tenn. Ho. of Reps., 1797-1805; served as brig. gen. during War of 1812; served under Andrew Jackson in Creek War; mem. Tenn. Senate, 1821-29, speaker, 1827-29; gov. Tenn., 1829; maj. gen. Tenn. Militia; mem. U.S. Ho. of Reps. (Democrat) from Tenn., 22d Congress, 1831-33. Died "Locust Land" nr. Castalian Springs, Sumner County, Oct. 7, 1856; buried family cemetery, "Locust Land."

HALL, William Augustus, congressman; b. Portland, Me., Oct. 15, 1815; attended Yale; children include Uriel Sebree. Moved to Randolph County, Mo., 1840; admitted to Mo. bar, 1841, began practice in Huntsville; moved to Fayette, Mo., continued practice of law; Democratic presdl. elector, 1844; judge circuit ct., 1847-61; served as capt. during Mexican War; del. Mo. Constl. Conv., 1861; mem. U.S. Ho. of Reps. (Dem.) from Mo., 37th-38th congresses, Jan. 20, 1862-65; del. Nat. Dem. Conv., Chgo., 1864; resumed law practice, engaged in farming. Died nr. Darkville, Randolph County, Mo., Dec. 15, 1888; buried family cemetery.

HALL, William Whitty, physician, author; b. Paris, Ky., Oct. 15, 1810; s. Stephen and Mary (Wooley) H.; grad. Centre Coll., Danville, Ky., 1830; M.D., Transylvania U., Lexington, Ky., 1836; m. Hannah Matlock; m. 2d, Magdalen Matilda Robertson. Ordained to ministry Presbyn. Ch., 1836, did missionary work, Tex., 1837; abandoned preaching, practiced medicine in New Orleans and Cincinnati, until 1851, practiced in N.Y.C., from 1851; published periodical Hall's Jour. of Health, N.Y.C., 1854-76. Author: Consumption a Curable Disease, Illustrated in the Treatment of 150 Cases, 1845; Bronchitis and Kindred Diseases, 1852; Sleep, 1861; How to Live Long, 1875. Died N.Y.C., May 10, 1876.

HALLAM, Lewis, actor, theatrical mgr.; b. in Eng., circa 1740; son of Lewis Hallam; married twice; m. 2d, Miss Tuke, circa 1793; 3 children including Mirvan. Came to Am. with parents in acting co., circa 1752; made 1st stage appearance in Merchant of Venice, Williamsburg, Va., 1752, fled from stage when he forgot his one line; travelled with co., N.Y.C., Phila., 1752-54, Jamaica, 1754-58; leading man when co. returned to Am., 1758; returned to Eng., 1775, appeared in Covent Garden, London; returned to Am. as sole owner of the co., from end of Revolutionary War to 1797, again became actor in co., 1797. Died Phila., Nov. 1, 1808.

HALLAM, Robert Alexander, clergyman; b. New London, Conn., Sept. 30, 1807; grad. Yale, 1827, Gen. Theol. Sem., N.Y., 1832; S.T.D. (hon.), Oxford, 1853. Rector St. Andrew's Ch., Meriden, Conn., 1832-34, St. James Ch., New London, 1835-77; mem. standing com. Conn. Diocese, 1846-72; del. gen. convs., 1850-68. Author: A Course of Lectures Delivered in the Chapel of St. Andrew's Church, New London, 1869; Sketches of Travel in Europe, 1869. Died New London, Jan. 14, 1877.

HALLECK, Fitz-Greene, poet; b. Guilford, Conn., July 8, 1790; s. Israel and Mary (Eliot) H. Went to N.Y., 1811; wrote (with Joseph Rodman Drake) Croaker Papers in N.Y. Evening Post, 1819; wrote best known poem, beginning "Green be the turf above thee," as tribute at Drake's death, 1820; wrote Fanny, 1819 (expanded 1821); wrote poems Alnwick Castle (published with other poems 1827) and Burns during European tour, 1822; clk in counting house of John Jacob Astor, 1832-49; v.p. Author's Club, 1837; wrote poems Connecticut, 1852, Young America, 1865; also wrote "The world is bright before thee;" poetical works and letters edited and published by James Grant Wilson, 1869. Died Guilford, Nov. 19, 1867.

HALLECK, Henry Wager, army officer, businessman; b. Westernville, N.Y., Jan. 16, 1815; s. Joseph and Catherine (Wager) H.; A.B., Union Coll., 1837, A.M. (hon.), 1843, LL.D., 1862; grad. U.S. Mil. Acad., 1839; m. Elizabeth Hamilton, Apr. 10, 1855; 1 son, Henry Wager. Asst. prof. chemistry and engring. U.S. Mil. Acad., 1839-40; asst. to bd. of engrs., Washington, D.C., 1841-42; commd. 1st lt. U.S. Army, 1846; served as chief of staff under Col. Burton on expdn. into Lower Cal. in Mexican War; brevetted capt., 1847; author of constn. for state of Cal., 1849; lt. gov. Mazatlan (Cal.); commd. capt., 1853; head of law firm Halleck, Peachy and Billings, 1854; dir.-gen. New Almaden quicksilver mine; pres. Pacific & Atlantic R.R.; maj. gen. Cal. Militia; commd. maj. gen. U.S. Army, 1861, commanded Dept. of the Missouri, 1861, Dept. of the Mississippi, 1862; commanded seizure of Corinth, 1862; assumed command as gen.-in-chief U.S. Army, hdqrs. Washington, D.C., 1862, superseded by Gen. Grant, 1864; mil. adviser to Pres. Lincoln, 1862; chief of staff to Grant, 1864-65; commanded Div. of the James, 1865, mil. div. of Pacific, 1865-69, div. of South, 1869, 72; mem. Phi Beta Kappa. Author: The Science of War, 1845 Elements of Military Art and Science, 1846; A Collection of Mining Laws of Spain and Mexico, 1859; International Law, 1861. Died Louisville, Ky., Jan. 9, 1872; buried Greenwood Cemetery, Louisville.

HALLET, Étienne Sulpice, architect; b. Paris, France, Mar. 17, 1755; m. Mary Gormain, 3 children. Came to Am., 1786, as part of an attempt by Quesnay de Beaurepaire to found an Academie des Sciences et Beaux-Arts, Richmond, Va.; won 2d place in competition sponsored by Thomas Jefferson for design of new U.S. Capitol Bldg., 1791 (William Thorton of Phila. won competition; Thorton's designs later were criticized); commd. to revise Thorton's plans and supervise bldg., 1793, dismissed in controversy over the designs, 1794. Died New Rochelle, N.Y., Feb. 1825.

HALLETT, Benjamin, mcht., reformer; b. Barnstable, Mass., Jan. 18, 1760; s. Jonathan and Mercy (Bacon) H.; m. Abigail Lovell, 13 children including Benjamin Franklin. Served on Am. frigate Deane during Revolutionary War; established packet line of mail steamers between Boston and Albany, N.Y., 1788; built Ten Sisters (his best sloop) in Catskill, N.Y., 1808; founder Bethel Movement for social and religious reform among seamen. Died Dec. 31, 1849.

HALLETT, Benjamin Franklin, lawyer, editor; b. Osterville, Mass., Dec. 2, 1797; s. Benjamin and Abigail (Lovell) H.; grad. Brown U., 1816; studied law in Providence, R.I.; m. Laura Larned, June 25, 1822. Admitted to R.I. bar, 1819, practiced intermittently; editor Providence Jour., 1821-28 (credited with bringing about R.I. Supreme Ct. reform); editor Providence Daily Advertiser, 1829-31; editor Boston Daily Advocate (anti-Masonic paper), 1838; dist. atty., Boston, 1852. Author: (pamphlets) The Rights of the Marshpee Indians, 1834; The Right of the People to Establish Forms of Government, 1848. Died Boston, Sept. 30, 1862.

HALLIDIE, Andrew Smith, engr., inventor; b. London, Eng., Mar. 16, 1836; s. Andrew and Julia (Johnstone) Smith; m. Martha Elizabeth Woods, Nov. 1863, 1 child. Adopted godfather's name Hallidie (legalized by Cal. Legislature); came to Cal. in search of gold, 1853; constructed flume across Middle Fork of American River, 1855; built various flumes and suspension bridges along Pacific coastal area, 1855-circa 67; became mfr. wire rope, circa 1857, constructed 1st wire rope factory on West Coast, 1858; invented rigid suspension bridge, 1867, perfected means of transporting freight over canyons and difficult areas by use of endless wire rope (Hallidie ropeway); devised method to pull streetcars up a steep slope by means of underground endless moving cable, 1871, made 1st installation in San Francisco, 1873; regent U. Cal., 1868-1900, chmn. finance com., 1874-1900, also acting pres.; pres. Mechanics Inst. of San Francisco; v.p. James Lick Sch. Mech. Arts; a founder San Francisco Public Library and Art Soc.; mem. exec. com. World's Columbian Expn., 1892-93. Died San Francisco, Apr. 24, 1900.

HALLOCK, Gerard, journalist; b. Plainfield, Mass., Mar. 18, 1800; s. Rev. Moses and Margaret (Allen) H.; grad. Williams Coll., 1819; m. Eliza Allen, June 2, 1825. Opened a pvt. sch., Salem, Mass., 1821, taught Hebrew and German; publisher weekly paper Boston Telegraph, 1824-25; editor weekly Telegraph and Recorder, Boston, 1825-26; co-owner, editor New York Observer, 1826-28; editor N.Y. Jour. of Commerce, 1828-30, co-owner, 1830-61; his paper a mem. of Assn. Morning Papers which shared ann. expense of maintaining boats to secure newspapers from incoming fgn. ships; obtained his own boat (due to rivalry), expelled from assn.; secured 6 more boats (at cost of $25,000 per year), 1831; his paper became mem. of Asso. Press, 1848; pres. Gen. News Assn. of City of N.Y., 1856; opposed Union aggression during Civil War (U.S. postmaster gen. excluded his paper from mails because of position). Died New Haven, Conn., Jan. 4, 1866.

HALLOCK, John, Jr., congressman; b. Oxford, Orange County, N.Y., July 1783. Mem. N.Y. Assembly, 1816-21; mem. N.Y. Constl. Conv., 1821; mem. U.S. Ho. of Reps. (Democrat) from N.Y., 19th-20th congresses, 1825-29. Died Ridgebury, N.Y., Dec. 6, 1840; buried family cemetery, nr. Ridgebury.

HALLOCK, William Allen, orgn. exec.; b. Plainsfield, Mass., June 2, 1794; s. Rev. Moses and Margaret (Allen) H.; grad. Williams Coll., 1819; attended Andover Theol. Sem., 1819-22; m. Fanny Leffingwell Lathrop, Sept. 1, 1829; m. 2d, Mrs. Mary Lathrop. Mem. New Eng. Tract Soc., 1822-25; 1st corr. sec. New Am. Tract Soc., 1825-70, sec. emeritus, 1870-80; editor Am. Messenger, 1830-70. Author: Memoir of Harlan Page, 1835; Brief Sketch of the Hallock Ancestry in the United States, 1866. Died Oct. 2, 1880.

HALLOWAY, Ransom, congressman; b. Beekman, N.Y., circa 1793. Engaged in farming; brigade paymaster N.Y. Militia, 1818; mem. U.S. Ho. of Reps. (Whig) from N.Y., 31st Congress, 1849-51. Died Mount Pleasant, N.Y., Apr. 6, 1851.

HALLOWELL, Benjamin, coll. pres., educator; b. Cheltenham Twp., Pa., Aug. 17, 1799; s. Anthony and Jane (Shoemaker) H.; studied natural science and mathematics under John Gummere, Burlington, N.J., 1817; m. Margaret E. Farquhar, Oct. 13, 1824. Apprentice to carpenter, 1814, fall from ladder prevented his entering this profession; taught sch., Westfield, N.J., Fair Hill, Md., Westtown, Pa., 1818-24; opened sch., Alexandria, Va., 1824-58, offered excellent math. tng. (Robert E. Lee received his early edn. there); a founder Lyceum of Alexandria; prof. chemistry med. dept. Columbian Coll. (now George Washington U.), Washington, D.C.; 1st pres. Md. Agrl. Coll., 1859; minister Soc. of Friends, 1859; 1st pres. Alexandria Water Co.; made religious tour of West, 1863. Author: Young Friend's Manual, 1867; Astronomy, 1869; Memoir of Margaret Brown, 1872. Died Sandy Spring, Neb., Sept. 7, 1877.

HALPINE, Charles Graham, journalist, humorist; b. Oldcastle, Ireland, Nov. 20, 1829; s. Nicholas John and Anne (Grehan) H.; ed. Trinity Coll. Came to U.S., 1851; pvt. sec. to P.T. Barnum; co-editor Carpet Bag, 1852; French translator N.Y. Herald; Nicaraguan corr., asso. editor N.Y. Times; prin. editor Leader (helped lead reform movement against Fernando Wood), 1857; editor N.Y. Citizen, 1864; brevetted lt. col. 47th Regt., N.Y. Volunteers, 1864, helped prepare 1st order for enlistment of Negro regt.; col., brig. gen., 1865; wrote lyric "Tear down the flaunting lie! Half mast the starry flag" (often attributed to Horace Greeley). Author: Miles O'Reilly, His Book, 1864; Baked Meats of the Funeral, 1866. Died N.Y.C., Aug. 3, 1868.

HALSEY, George Armstrong, congressman; b. Springfield, N.J., Dec. 7, 1827; attended Springfield Acad. Engaged in leather mfg., Newark, N.J., later in wholesale clothing bus.; mem. N.J. Assembly, 1861-62; U.S. assessor of internal revenue, 1862-66; mem. U.S. Ho. of Reps. (Republican) from N.J., 40th, 42d congresses, 1867-69, 71-73; resumed leather mfg. bus.; pres. of an ins. co.; active N.J. Hist. Soc., Newark Library Assn. Died Newark, Apr. 1, 1894; buried Mt. Pleasant Cemetery, Newark.

HALSEY, Jehiel Howell, congressman; b. Southampton, L.I., N.Y., Oct. 7, 1788; s. Silas Halsey; attended common schs. Moved to Lodi, N.Y., 1793, engaged in farming; clk. Seneca County (N.Y.) 1819-21; mem. U.S. Ho. of Reps. (Jacksonian Democrat), 21st Congress, 1829-31; mem. N.Y. Senate, 1832-35; surrogate Seneca County, 1837-43; supr. Town of Lodi, 1845-46. Died Lodi, Dec. 5, 1867; buried West Lodi Cemetery.

HALSEY, John, pirate; b. Boston, Mar. 1, 1670; s. James and Dinah H. In his youth went to sea, later comdr. small trading fleet; master in sloop Adventure trading between Boston and Va., 1693; secured privateering commn. to prey on French shipping in Newfoundland area, 1703; brought 3 French ships valued at 1,000 pounds into Barbados, 1703, refused to pay 1/10 tax on them; capt. Boston privateer vessel Charles, 1704; commd. by gov. of R.I. to prey on French and Spanish vessels during War of Spanish Succession; abandoning privateering and took up piracy; involved in battles with Moorish ships in African area; captured some 50,000 pounds from English fleet. Died Madagascar, 1716.

HALSEY, Leroy Jones, clergyman; b. Goochland County, Va., Jan. 28, 1812; s. John and Lucy (Teller) H.; grad. U. Nashville (Tenn.), 1834, Princeton Theol. Sem., 1839; D.D. (hon.), Hanover Coll., 1851; LL.D. (hon.), Southwestern U. of Tenn., 1880; m. Caroline Augusta Anderson, at least 1 child. Ordained to ministry Presbyn. Ch.; pastor ch., Dallas County, Ky., 1840-43, Jackson, Mo., 1843-48, Louisville, Ky., 1848-59; prof. pastoral theology, ch. govt. and homiletics at Presbyn. theol. sem., Chgo., 1859-80; asso. editor Interior, 1880-85. Author: Literary Attractions of the Bible, 1858; The Beauty of Immanuel, 1861; Life Pictures from the Bible, 1861. Died Chgo., June 18, 1896.

HALSEY, Nicoll, congressman; b. Southampton, L.I., N.Y., Mar. 8, 1782; s. Silas Halsey. Moved to Lodi, N.Y., 1793, Trumansburg, N.Y., 1808; engaged in farming, milling; supr. Town of Ulysses (N.Y.), 1812, 14, 15, 18, 21, 26; mem. N.Y. Assembly, 1816, 24; sheriff Tompkins County (N.Y.), 1819-21; mem. U.S. Ho. of Reps. (Democrat) from N.Y., 23d Congress, 1833-35; apptd. judge Tompkins County Ct., 1834. Died Marshall, Mich., Mar. 3, 1865; buried Grove Cemetery, Trumansburg.

HALSEY, Silas, congressman; b. Southampton, L.I., N.Y., Oct. 6, 1743 (old style); attended pub. schs.; studied medicine, Elizabethtown (now Elizabeth), N.J. Practiced medicine, Southampton, 1764-76; undersheriff of Suffolk County, 1784-87, sheriff, 1787-92; moved to Lodi, N.Y., 1793, practiced medicine, operated a grist mill; supr. Town of Ovid (N.Y.), 1794-1804; mem. N.Y. Assembly from Onondaga County, 1797-98, from Cayuga County, 1800-01, 03-04; mem. N.Y. Constl. Conv., 1801; clk. Seneca County (N.Y.), 1804-13, 15; mem. U.S. Ho. of Reps. (Democrat), from N.Y., 9th Congress, 1805-07; mem. N.Y. Senate, 1808-09. Died Lodi, Nov. 19, 1832; buried Old Halsey Cemetery, South Lodi, N.Y.

HALSEY, Thomas Lloyd, diplomat; b. Providence, R.I., circa 1776; s. Thomas Lloyd and Sarah (Bowen) H.; grad. Coll. of R.I. (now Brown U.), 1793; at least 3 children including Maria Louisa Andrea del Valle. After college entered into comml. business; U.S. consul to Buenos Aires, 1814-18, supplied United Provinces of Rio de la Plata with arms from U.S., most of these being used by José de San Martín in his revolutionary activities, became involved in privateering enterprise against Spain, recalled by Sec. State John Q. Adams, 1818; trustee Brown U., 1809-39. Died Feb. 2, 1855.

HALSTEAD, William, congressman; b. Elizabeth, N.J., June 4, 1794; s. grad. Princeton, 1812; studied law. Admitted to N.J. bar, 1816, began practice in Trenton; reporter N.J. Supreme Ct., 1821-32; pros. atty. Hunterdon County (N.J.), 1827-29, 33-37; mem. U.S. Ho. of Reps. (Whig) from N.J., 25th, 27th congresses, 1837-39, 41-43; U.S. dist. atty. for N.J., 1849-53; organized 1st Regt. of N.J. Volunteer Cavalry for Civil War, col. until 1862. Died Trenton, Mar. 4, 1878; buried Riverview Cemetery, Trenton.

HAMBLETON, Samuel, congressman; b. "Waterloo," Talbot County, Md., Jan. 8, 1812; attended Easton (Md.) Acad.; studied law. Admitted to Md. bar, began practice in Easton; mem. Md. Ho. of Dels., 1834-35; states atty. for Talbot County, 1836-44; Democratic presdl. elector, 1844; pres. Chesapeake & Ohio Canal, 1853-54; mem.U.S.Ho. of Reps. (Democrat) from Md., 41st-42d congresses, 1869-73; Died Easton, Dec. 9, 1886; buried Spring Hill Cemetery, Easton.

HAMBLIN, Joseph Eldridge, army officer; b. Yarmouth, Mass., Jan. 13, 1828; s. Benjamin and Hannah (Sears) H.; m. Isabella Gray, Oct. 15, 1868. Served with various militia cos. before Civil War; served from lt. to maj., 65th N.Y. Volunteers (1st U.S. Chasseurs) under Gen. B.F. Butler at siege of Yorktown (Va.) and battles of Williamsburg, Fair Oaks, Glendale, Malvern Hill (Va.); commd. lt. col., assigned to 1st Brigade, 1862, col., 1863; commanded regt. at Gettysburg; served in Chancellorsville campaign, 1863; distinguished at Hazel Run, 1864; brig. gen., 1864; served with Grant's army from the Wilderness to Petersburg, with Sheridan's army in Shenandoah Valley; commanded 2d Brigade in Appomattox campaign; commd. maj. gen., 1865; adj. gen., chief of staff. N.Y. Nat. Guard, 1867-70. Died N.Y.C., July 3, 1870.

HAMBLIN, Thomas Sowerby, actor, theatrical mgr.; b. England, May 14, 1800; m. Elizabeth Blanchard; m. 2d, Mrs. Eliza Mary Ann (Trewar) Shaw, 1849; several children. Mem. Sadler's Wells Theatre, London, Eng., 1815; appeared at Drury Lane, London, 1818; leading actor at Bath Theatre, 1820-23; came to U.S. after engagements at Brighton and Dublin theatres; made Am. debut as Hamlet in Park Theatre, N.Y.C., 1825; played leading roles in various Am. cities, 1825-30; mgr. Bowery Theatre, N.Y.C., 1830-53, bldg. burned to ground, shortly after he bought it; 1836; visited and acted in Europe until 1839; opened new Bowery Theatre, 1839, burned, 1845, again became mgr., 1848; leased and refitted Park Theatre which he opened, 1848, totally destroyed by fire, 1848. Died N.Y.C., Jan. 8, 1853.

HAMER, Thomas Lyon, congressman; b. Northumberland County, Pa., July 1800; studied law under Thomas Morris; m. Lydia Higgins; m. 2d, Catherine Johnston, 1845. Admitted to Ohio bar, 1821; mem. Ohio Ho. of Reps., 1825, 28-30, speaker, 1829-30; mem. U.S. Ho. of Reps. from Ohio, 23d-25th congresses, 1833-39, elected to 30th Congress, 1845, died before taking office; presided over Ohio Democratic Conv., 1840; commd. brig gen. 1st Ohio Volunteers in Mexican War; posthumously awarded sword for gallantry at Monterey, Mexico (presented by Congress to his nearest male relative). Died Monterey, Dec. 2, 1846; buried Georgetown (O.) Cemetery.

HAMET KARAMANLI, pasha of Tripoli; b. Tripoli; s. Ali Karamanli. Forced from throne by younger brother Yusuf, circa 1795; offered aid by Americans in attempt to regain his throne in return for granting a favorable treaty to U.S., 1801; persuaded by Am. consul William Eaton at Tunis to refuse post of gov. of Derna (Tunisia) offered by Yusuf, 1801, accepted post, 1802; fled from Derna to Egypt and started raising troops for rebellion against Yusuf, 1803; participated in Battle of Derna under command of William Eaton; outcome of battle unsuccessful, but U.S. had meanwhile concluded peace with Yusuf, 1805; treaty arrangements enabled him to recover his family (imprisoned by Yusuf), 1806, also received some financial aid from U.S. Govt.; spent rest of life in exile.

HAMILL, Patrick, congressman; b. Allegany County, Md., Apr. 29, 1817; attended common schs., Westernport, Md. Engaged in real estate bus., mcht.; collector of taxes, 1841-42; mem. Md. Ho. of Dels., 1843-44; judge Orphans' Ct. of Allegany County, 1854-69; elected chief judge, 1867; mem. U.S. Ho. of Reps. (Democrat) from N.Y., 41st Congress, 1869-71; Died Oakland, Md., Jan. 15, 1895; buried Odd Fellows Cemetery, Oakland.

HAMILTON, Alexander, physician, historian; b. Edinburgh, Scotland, 1712; s. Dr. William Hamilton; studied medicine under Dr. John Knox, Edinburgh; m. Margaret Dulany, 1747. Came to America, 1738; practiced medicine, Annapolis, Md.; supported inoculation in pamphlet A Defence of Dr. Thomson's Discourse, 1752; author hist. works, including Itinerarium, History of the Tuesday Club (2 surviving works; both deal with his contemporary scene;) vestryman St. Anne's Anglican Ch., Annapolis, 1749-52. Died Annapolis, May 11, 1756.

HAMILTON, Alexander, 1st U.S. sec. of treasury; b. Nevis, B.W.I., Jan. 11, 1757; s. James and Rachel (Faucette) H.; attended King's Coll. (Columbia), 1773-76; m. Elizabeth Schuyler, 1780, 8 children including James Alexander, Philip, John C. Worked as clk. for a time; came to Am., 1772; wrote pamphlets and newspaper articles defending colonists' position against British, circa 1773-76; apptd. capt. of arty. Continental Army, 1776; sec., aide-de-camp to Gen. George Washington, 1777-81, served in battles of L.I., Yorktown; admitted to N.Y. bar, 1781; became noted lawyer in N.Y.; del. from N.Y. to Continental Congress, 1782-83, 87-88; developer and exponent of theory of stronger central govt.; mem. Annapolis Conv., 1786; mem. N.Y. Legislature, 1787; largely responsible for sending N.Y. delegation (including himself and 2 anti-constn. Clinton Democrats, Robert Yates and John Lansing) to U.S. Constl. Conv., Phila., 1787; played only a minor role in drafting U.S. Constn.; signed U.S. Constn. for State of N.Y., 1787; wrote (with John Jay, James Madison) series of articles The Federalist Papers, favoring adoption of U.S. Constn., 1787-88; attended N.Y. Conv. to ratify U.S. Constn., was highly influential in securing ratification; U.S. sec. of treasury (apptd. by Washington), 1789-95; identified with Federalist Party, became probably its main spokesman; conducted (as sec. of treasury) financial program based on paying U.S. domestic debt, founding Bank of U.S., assuming state debts, raising excise taxes and imposing protective tariffs; presented plan to Congress in series of reports (final one the famous report on manufactures), 1790, defended his plan largely through the implied powers argument of U.S. Constn.; met strong opposition, but all measures were adopted except the imposition of protective tariffs (assumption of state debts came about only because Jefferson agreed to swing votes for it in return for Hamilton's support on locating nat. capital in South); adoption of excise taxes was main cause of Whiskey Rebellion in Pa., 1794; clashed with Jefferson both personally and in policy matters (basic theory of govt., fgn. policy); his conflict with Jefferson led to development of 2-party system in Am.; resigned cabinet post, 1795, continued to attempt to advise Washington, wrote part of Washington's Farewell Address, 1796; apptd. insp. gen. U.S. Army in anticipation of war with France, 1798 (John Adams managed to avert war, which caused break in Federalist Party ranks); put his influence on Jefferson's side during tie for presidency that developed between Jefferson and Aaron Burr, swung many Federalist votes in U.S. Ho. of Reps. to Jefferson (start of enmity between Burr and Hamilton); practiced law, N.Y.C., 1795-1804; a founder N.Y. Evening Post (1801), Bank of N.Y.; influential in preventing the election of Burr as gov. N.Y., 1804; challenged to duel by Burr, mortally wounded at Weehawken Heights, N.J. Died N.Y.C., day after duel, July 12, 1804; buried Trinity Churchyard, N.Y.C.

HAMILTON, Andrew, colonial ofcl.; b. Scotland; married 3 times, 2d wife Anne Rudyard; son, John. Mem. N.J. Gov.'s Council, 1686; dep. gov. N.J., 1687; gov. East and West N.J., 1692-97, 99-1701, upheld Jersey proprietory policies against anti-proprietory factions; dep. postmaster gen. Am. colonies, 1692, established successful postal system; dep. gov. Pa. under William Penn, 1701. Died Perth Amboy, N.J., Apr. 26, 1703.

HAMILTON, Andrew, colonial legislator, jurist; b. Scotland, circa 1676; m. Anne Brown, Mar. 6, 1706, a son, James. Dep. to Md. Assembly from Kent County; went to Eng., 1712-13, admitted to Gray's Inn; moved to Pa., 1717; atty. gen. Pa., 1717; recorder Phila., 1727; prothonotary Pa. Supreme Ct., 1727; mem. Pa. Assembly, 1727, speaker after 1729, except 1733; defended John Peter Zenger (charged for seditious libel in his newspaper), 1735, argued that truth is a defense in libel cases, upheld by jury (thus helping to establish freedom of press in Am.); judge Vice Admiralty Ct. for Pa., 1737; amateur architect, designed Independence Hall. Died Phila., Aug. 4, 1741; buried "Bush Hill," reinterred Christ Church, Phila.

HAMILTON, Andrew Holman, congressman; b. Ft. Wayne, Ind., June 7, 1834; grad. Wabash Coll., 1854; studied law, Harvard. Admitted to Ind. bar, 1859, began practice in Ft. Wayne; mem. U.S. Ho. of Reps. (Democrat), 44th-45th congresses, 1875-79. Died Ft. Wayne, May 9, 1895; buried Lindenwood Cemetery, Ft. Wayne.

HAMILTON, Andrew Jackson, congressman, army officer; b. Madison County, Ala., Jan. 28, 1815; s. James and Abagail (Bayless) H.; m. Mary Jane Bowen, 1843. Admitted to Ala. bar, 1841; atty. gen. Tex., 1849; mem. Tex. Legislature, 1851-53; mem. U.S. Ho. of Reps. from Tex., 36th Congress, 1859-61; elected to Tex. Legislature, 1861, refused to take seat under Confederate States Am.; served as grig. gen. Tex. Volunteers, U.S. Army during Civil War, 1862; apptd. mil. gov. Tex., 1862; provisional gov. Tex., 1865-66; justice Tex. Supreme Ct., 1866. Died Austin, Tex., Apr. 11, 1875; buried Oakwood Cemetery, Austin.

HAMILTON, Charles Memorial, congressman; b. Pine Creek Twp., Clinton County, Pa., Nov. 1, 1840; grad. Columbia (Pa.) Law Sch. Enlisted as pvt. U.S. Army during Civil War, 1861; captured at Battle of Fredericksburg, imprisoned in Libby Prison, Richmond, Va., until 1863; exchanged, 1863; commd. ensign, transferred to Vets. Res. Corps; promoted 1t lt., later capt.; judge advocate of gen. ct. martial, gen. pass officer for Army of Potomac; mem. staff of mil. gov. Washington (D.C.), transferred to Marianna, Fla., 1865; admitted to Fla. bar, 1867, began practice in Marianna; mem. U.S. Ho. of Reps. (Republican) from Fla., 40th-41st congresses, July 1, 1868-71; apptd. sr. maj. gen. Fla. Militia, 1871; postmaster of Jacksonville (Fla.), 1871-72; collector of customs Key West (Fla.), 1873. Died Pine Creek Twp., Oct. 22, 1875; buried Jersey Shore Cemetery, Pa.

HAMILTON, Charles Smith, army officer; b. Oneida County, N.Y., Nov. 16, 1822; s. Zane A. and Sylvia (Putnam) H.; grad. U.S. Mil. Acad., 1843; m. Sophia Shepard, Feb. 1849. Served in Mexican War, brevetted capt. for gallantry; served in Indian Wars, resigned commn., 1853, settled in Fond Du Lac, Wis.; commd. col., recruited and organized 3d Wis. Volunteers, 1861; commd. brig. gen., served under Gen. Banks during Shenandoah campaign, 1861; commd. maj. gen. on recommendation of Gen. Grant, 1862, transferred to Army of W.Va., primarily responsible for success of Battle of Corinth; command of XVI Army Corps and dist. of Tenn., in command of left wing of Grant's Army, 1863; resigned his commn. in 1863 because he thought his mil. talents were not duly recognized U.S. marshal at Milw., 1869; pres. Hamilton Paper Co., 1878; mem. bd. regents U. Wis., 1866-75, pres. bd. 1869-75. Died Milw., Apr. 17, 1891.

HAMILTON, Cornelius Springer, congressman; b. Gratiot, O., Jan. 2, 1821; attended Granville (O.) Coll. Moved to Union County, O., 1821, engaged in farming; admitted to Ohio bar, 1845, began practice in Marysville; land appraiser and assessor, 1845; del. Ohio Constl. Conv., 1850-51; editor, propr. Marysville Tribune, 1850-53; mem. Ohio Senate, 1856-57; assessor 8th Congressional Dist. of Ohio (apptd. by Pres. Lincoln), 1862-66; mem. U.S. Ho. of Reps. (Republican) from Ohio, 40th Congress, Mar. 4-Dec. 22, 1867. Killed by an insane son, Marysville, Dec. 22, 1867; buried Oakdale Cemetery, Marysville.

HAMILTON, F. F., architect; b. Me., 1853; ed. in Boston. Went to Cal., circa 1870; did archtl. work in Los Angeles, until 1877; became partner (with George W. Percy) in archtl. firm Percy & Hamilton, San Francisco, 1877. Prin. works of firm include: old Acad. of Science, Children's Playhouse and grounds in Golden Gate Park, 1st Unitarian Ch. (all San Francisco); Alameda (Cal.) City Hall; Museum, Library and Assembly Hall at Stanford U., Palo Alto; Lick Observatory, Mt. Hamilton. Died Dec. 1, 1899.

HAMILTON, Frank Hastings, surgeon; b Wilmington, Vt., Sept. 10, 1813; s. Calvin and Lucinda H.; grad. Union Coll., 1830; M.D., U. Pa., 1835; m. Mary (van Arsdale) McMurran, Oct. 15, 1834; m. 2d, Mary Gertrude Hart, Sept. 1, 1840. Licensed to practice medicine, N.Y., 1833; prof. surgery Fairfield Sch., 1839, Geneva Med. Sch., 1840-44; helped found med. dept. U. Buffalo, 1846, 1st prof. surgery until 1858; prof. surgery L.I. Coll. Hosp.; prof. clin. and mil. surgery Bellevue Hosp. Med. Coll., 1861, became full prof. surgery and surg. pathology, 1868; med. insp. U.S. Army; cons. physician to Pres. Garfield, in attendance until Garfield died after assassination. Author: A Practical Treatise on Fractures and Dislocations, 1860; Treatise on Military Surgery and Hygiene, 1862; Surgical Memoirs of the War of the Rebellion, 2 vols., 1870-71; The Principles and Practice of Surgery, 1872. Died N.Y.C., Aug. 11, 1886.

HAMILTON, Gail, see Dodge, Mary Abigail.

HAMILTON, Henry, army officer; b. England. Served in Canada and West Indies during French and Indian Wars; apptd. lt. gov. of Detroit, 1775; served in West during Am. Revolution; became notorious for inciting Indians to attack Am. frontier settlements; accused of paying Indians for Am. scalps which were brought to him; captured (with his command) by George Rogers Clark, Vincennes (now Ind.), 1779, exchanged; held various imperial adminstrv. posts until death. Died 1796.

HAMILTON, James, lawyer, mayor Phila., colonial govt. ofcl.; b. Accomac County, Va., circa 1710; s. Andrew and Ann (Brown) Preeson H. Prothonotary of Pa. Supreme Ct., 1733; mem. Pa. Assembly, 1734-39; mayor Phila., 1745; 1st subscriber The Phila. Contributionship for the Ins. of Houses from Loss by Fire (1st ins. co. in Am.); pres. bd. trustees Coll. of Phila.; mem. Pa. Provincial Council, 1734 and 1745-47; lt. gov. Pa., 1748-54, 59-63, acting gov. 1771, 73; pres. Pa. Council, 1771, 73; during his service as lt. gov. was constantly at odds with assembly over such matters as defense and Indians; did not favor patriot cause during Revolutionary War, but was not avowed Loyalist; arrested, 1777, released, 1778. Died N.Y.C., Aug. 14, 1783.

HAMILTON, James, artist; b. Entrien, nr. Belfast, Ireland, Oct. 1, 1819. Came with parents to Phila., 1834; established himself as landscape artist and drawing tchr., Phila., circa 1840; exhibited at Artists' Fund Soc., 1840, later at other galleries in Phila., N.Y.C., Boston, Balt., Washington, D.C.; in London, 1854-55; commd. to illustrate Arctic Explorations (Kane), and Memoirs (John C. Frémont). Died while on trip around world, San Francisco, Mar. 10, 1878.

HAMILTON, James, Jr., gov. S.C., congressman; b. Charleston, S.C., May 8, 1786; s. Maj. James and Elizabeth (Lynch) H.; studied law; m. Elizabeth Heyward, Nov. 15, 1813. Admitted to S.C. bar, 1810, began practice in Charleston; served as maj. during War of 1812; mayor of Charleston; mem. S.C. Ho. of Reps., 1820-23; mem. U.S. Ho. of Reps. from S.C., 17th-20th congresses, Dec. 13, 1822-29;

leader Jacksonian forces against Pres. John Q. Adams; gov. S.C., 1830-32, militant exponent doctrine nullification in opposition to Pres. Jackson, chiefly responsible for passage of nullification ordinance, 1832; led armed force designed to support state's rights against Fed. encroachment after leaving office; organizer, pres. Bank of Charleston; dir. S.C. & Louisville, Cincinnati & Charleston r.r.'s; mem. S.C. Senate, 1836; commr. loans for Republic of Tex., 1838; diplomatic agt. from Tex. to France, Gt. Britain, Belgium, and Netherlands, 1839. Drowned in Gulf of Mexico, Nov. 15, 1857.

HAMILTON, James Alexander, lawyer; b. N.Y.C., Apr. 14, 1788; s. Alexander and Elizabeth (Schuyler) H.; grad. Columbia Coll., 1805; m. Mary Morris 1810. Admitted to N.Y. bar 1809; served as brig. maj. and insp. N.Y. Militia, War of 1812; U.S. sec. of state Mar. 4-27, 1829; mem. Jackson's so-called Appointing Council, 1829; U. S. dist. atty. for So. Dist. N.Y.; became a Whig, 1840; strong supporter of his father's fiscal policies; believed slavery was protected by Constn. at outset of Civil War but swung over to emancipation viewpoint; mem. Tammany Hall, asso. with Charles King; publisher (with Johnston Ver Planck) N.Y. American. Author: State Sovereignty: Rebellion against the U.S. by the People of a State in Its Political Suicide 1862; The Public Debt and the Public Credit of the U.S., 1864; Martin Van Buren's Calumnies Repudiated: Hamilton's Conduct as Secretary of the Treasury Vindicated, 1870. Died N.Y. C., Sept. 24, 1878.

HAMILTON, John, colonial gov.; b. Eng. Mem. N.J. Gov.'s Council under Robert Hunter, William Burnet, John Montgomerie and William Crosby, 1713-35; asso. justice N.J. Provincial Supreme Ct., 1735-36; gov. N.J., 1736-38, 46, granted 1st charter to Coll. of N.J. (now Princeton), gave aid to Canadian expdn. in French and Indian War. Died Perth Amboy, N.J., 1746.

HAMILTON, John, congressman; b. York (now Adams) County, Pa., Nov. 25, 1754. Commd. lt. col. Pa. Militia, 1786, brig. gen., 1800; maj. gen. 14th Div. of Militia of Washington and Greene Counties, 1807; high sheriff of Washington County (Pa.), 1793-96; mem. Pa. Senate, 1796-1805; mem. 1st bd. trustees Jefferson (now Washington and Jefferson) Coll., 1802-31; asso. judge Washington County, 1802-05, 20-37. presdl. elector, 1804, 20; mem. U.S. Ho. of Reps. (Democrat) from Pa., 9th Congress, 1805-07. Died nr. Ginger Hill, Washington County, Aug. 22, 1837; buried Mingo Cemetery, nr. Monongahela, Pa.

HAMILTON, Morgan Calvin, senator; b. nr. Huntsville, Ala., Feb. 25, 1809; attended pub. schs. Mcht., Elyton, Ala.; moved to Tex., 1837; clk. War Dept., Republic of Tex., 1839-45, sec. of war and marine ad interim, 1844-45; apptd. comptroller of treasury State of Tex., 1867; del. Tex. Constl. Conv., 1868; mem. U.S. Senate (Republican) from Tex., Mar. 30, 1870-77. Died San Diego, Cal., Nov. 21, 1893; buried Oakwood Cemetery, Austin, Tex.

HAMILTON, Paul, gov. S.C., sec. of navy; b. St. Paul's Parish S.C. Oct. 16 1762; s. Archibald and Rebecca (Branford) H.; m. Mary Wilkinson, Oct. 10, 1782. Fought in Revolutionary War; justice of peace, St. Paul's Parish, 1786; mem. lower house S.C. Legislature, 1787-89, S.C. Senate, 1794, 98-99; comptroller S.C., 1800-04; gov. S. C. 1804-06, although a slave-owner, urged S.C. Legislature to prohibit African slave trade; U.S. sec. of navy, 1809-13, hampered throughout adminstrn. by lack of funds, but helped secure act for constrn. of naval hosps., 1811, endeavored to enforce govt. embargo policy at beginning War of 1812. Died Beaufort, S.C., June 30, 1816.

HAMILTON, Peter, state senator; b. Harrisburg, Pa., Nov. 7, 1817; s. William Thomas and Charlotte (Cartledge) H.; grad. Princeton, 1835; m. Anna Martha Beers, Dec. 27, 1842; m. 2d, Caroline (Cunningham) Goodman, May 23, 1863. Taught at Barton Acad., Mobile, Ala., 1835-38; admitted to Ala. bar, 1838; practiced with his brother, Ala.; mem. Ala. Legislature, 1847-circa 1860; counsel for Mobile & Ohio R.R., 1860-76, helped restore railroad after war had brought severe losses; mem. Ala. Senate, 1872-76, mem. finance com., author act for funding state debt; assisted in preparation of state code, 1886. Died Mobile, Nov. 22, 1888.

HAMILTON, Peter Myers, lawyer, author; b. Herkimer, N.Y., Aug. 4, 1812. Began practice law, Bklyn., circa 1835; wrote poetry and fiction, from 1840; his poem on Science read before Hobart Coll., 1841; contbr. short stories to Dollar Newspaper, Phila., 1840's. Author: (novels) The First of the Knickerbockers: A Tale of 1673, published 1848; The Young Patroon, 1849; The Prisoner of the Border: A Tale of 1838, published 1857. Died Bklyn., Oct. 30, 1878; buried Bklyn.

HAMILTON, Robert, congressman; b. Hamburg, N.J., Dec. 9, 1809; studied law. Admitted to N.J. bar, 1835, began practice in Newton; prosecutor of pleas Sussex County (N.J.), 1848-58, 68-69; del. Dem. Nat. Conv., Charleston (S.C.) and Balt., 1860; mem. N.J. Assembly, 1863-64, speaker; pres. Mcht's. Nat. Bank, 1865-78; mem. U.S. Ho. of Reps. (Democrat) from N.J., 43d-44th congresses, 1873-77; dir. Morris & Essex R.R. Co. Died Newton, Mar. 14, 1878; buried Newton Cemetery.

HAMILTON, William Thomas, senator, gov. Md.; b. Hagerstown, Md., Sept. 8, 1820; s. Henry and Anna (Hess) H.; attended Jefferson Coll., Canonsburg, Pa.; m. Clara Jenness, 1859, 6 children. Admitted to Md. bar, 1845; Democratic mem. Md. Ho. of Dels., 1846-47; mem. U.S. Ho. of Reps. from Md., 31st-33d congresses, 1849-55; mem. U.S. Senate (Dem.) from Md., 1869-75, voted against 15th Amendment, opposed "salary grab" act which would greatly increase salaries govt. ofcls.; opposed secession although he upheld right to secede; gov. Md., 1879-83. Died Hagerstown, Oct. 26, 1888; buried Rose Hill Cemetery, Hagerstown.

HAMLIN, Edward Stowe, congressman; b. Hillsdale, N.Y., July 6, 1808; studied law. Admitted to the bar, 1831, began practice in Elyria, O.; pros. atty. Lorain County (O.), 1833-35; mem. U.S. Ho. of Reps. (Whig) from Ohio, 28th Congress, Oct. 8, 1844-45; engaged in newspaper bus.; published True Democrat (now Cleve. Plain Dealer), 1846; mem. Free Soil Conv., Buffalo, 1848; pres. bd. pub. works, 1849-52; declined appointment as atty. gen. Ohio, 1855; atty. Cincinnati, Indpls. & Lafayette R.R. many years; moved to Williamsburg, Va. to supervise his extensive land holdings at Newport News, Va., 1844. Died Washington, D.C., Nov. 23, 1894; buried Cedar Grove Cemetery, Williamsburg.

HAMLIN, Emmons, inventor, mfr.; b. Rome, N.Y., Nov. 16, 1821; s. Henry and Laura (Munson) H.; m. Elvira J. Patrick, Feb. 12, 1843. With George A. Prince & Co., melodeon mfrs., Buffalo, N.Y., circa 1840-52; discovered means of perfecting melodeon by clearing up thin nasal tones, 1850; went to Boston, became partner Mason & Hamlin Organ Co., 1854-85, new co. made its 1st Organ-Harmonium, 1855, this instrument (with improvements) became popular as Am. Cabinet Organ, 1861; Mason and Hamlin Organs won 1st prize at Paris Expdn., 1876; took up art of violin-making in later years. Died Boston, Apr. 8, 1885.

HAMLIN, Hannibal, vice pres. U.S.; b. Paris Hill, Me., Aug. 27, 1809; s. Cyrus and Anna (Livermore) H.; m. Sarah J. Emery, Dec. 10, 1833; m. 2d, Ellen V. Emery, Sept. 25, 1856; 1 son Charles. Admitted to Me. bar, 1833; mem. Me. Ho. of Reps., 1836-40, 47, speaker, 1837, 39-40; mem. U.S. Ho. of Reps. from Me., 28th-29th congresses, 1843-47; mem. U.S. Senate from Me., as Democrat, 1848-57, as Republican, 57-61, 69-81; gov. Me., 1857; outspoken opponent of slavery; vice pres. U.S. under Pres. Lincoln, 1861-65; strong proponent of emancipation as presiding officer of Senate, became asso. with Radicals of Congress; collector Port of Boston, 1865; opposed Chinese exclusive law and "salary grab" act; U.S. minister to Spain, 1881-82. Died Bangor, Me., July 4, 1891; buried Mt. Hope Cemetery, Bangor.

HAMLIN, William, engraver; b. Providence, R.I., Oct. 15, 1772; s. Capt. Samuel and Thankful (Ely) H.; m. Eliza Bowen, Apr. 2, 1810. Began bus. career in making and repairing of naut. instruments, Providence; became interested in engraving, made at least 3 plates of George Washington; engraved The Burning of the Frigate Philadelphia in Tripoli Harbor, February 1804 (his best work). Died Providence, Nov. 22, 1869.

HAMLINE, Leonidas Lent, clergyman, philanthropist; b. Burlington, Conn., May 10, 1797; s. Mark and Roxanna (Moses) Hamlin (added "e" to family name for no known reason); m. Eliza Price, Mar. 6, 1824; m. 2d, Mrs. Melinda Truesdell, 1836. Pushed toward ministry by his father, suffered mental breakdown, 1825, after recovery felt law better suited him; admitted to Ohio bar, 1827 (according to his claim, records place his admittance in 1825); became converted to Methodism on trip to N.Y.; licensed to preach in Ohio as Meth., 1829, ordained deacon, 1834, elder, 1836; jr. pastor Wesley Chapel, Cincinnati, 1834-36; asst. editor Western Christian Advocate, Cincinnati, 1836; del. Gen. Conf. of Methodsts, 1840, recommended his supervising writing of female periodical; supr., editor Ladies' Repository, 1840-44; elected bishop by Conf., 1844, resigned 1852, this raised question of whether bishop was merely ecclesiastical officer or distinct order chosen for life (former positon accepted); spent his later years in Mt. Pleasant (Ia.) engaging in philanthropy with inheritance left by his 1st wife; contributed $25,000 toward founding of Hamline U., St. Paul, Minn., $25,000 to Mt. Vernon Inst., Ia. Writings published as Works of Rev. Leonidas L. Hamline, D.D. (edited by F. G. Hibbard), Vol. I, 1869, Vol. II, 1871. Died Mar. 23, 1865.

HAMMETT, Henry Pinckney, mfr., industrialist; b. Greenville County, S.C., Dec. 31, 1822; s. Jesse and Nancy (Davis) H.; m. Deborah Jane Bates. Clk. Matthews & Co., cotton firm, Augusta, Ga., 1840; bookkeeper Batesville Cotton Mill. (S.C.), married owner's daughter, became part owner, in charge of cotton purchasing and sale; became tax assessor Greenville County; when firm sold out, 1863; mem. S.C., Legislature, 1865-69; pres. Greenville & Columbia R.R., 1866-70; pres. Piedmont Mfg. Co., 1873-91, began bldg. cotton factory on Saluda River (S.C.), 1875, built 2d mill, 1878, 3d, 1890, most of products were sheeting exported mainly to China. Died May 8, 1891.

HAMMETT, Samuel Adams, author; b. Jewett City, Conn., Feb. 4, 1816; s. Augustus and Mary (Wright) H. Wandered about Tex. for about 12 years, served in Tex. Militia, worked as clk. in Montgomery County Dist. Ct.; became flour mcht., N.Y.C., 1848; wrote for Spirit of the Times, Knickerbocker Mag., Literary World, U.S. and Democratic Review, Am. Whig Review. Author: (under pseudonym Philip Paxton) A Stray Yankee in Texas, 1853; (under name "by the author of A Stray Yankee in Texas") The Wonderful Adventures of Captain Priest, 1855, Piney Woods Tavern, or Sam Slick in Texas, 1858. Died Bklyn., Dec. 24, 1865.

HAMMETT, William H., congressman; b. Va.; studied theology. Chaplain, U. Va., 1832-34, also of Va. Ho. of Dels.; moved to Princeton, Miss.; mem. U.S. Ho. of Reps. (Democrat) from Miss., 28th Congress, 1843-45.

HAMMON, Jupiter, poet; b. circa 1720. African slave owned by Henry Lloyd, Lloyd's Neck, L.I., N. Y.; inherited by Joseph Lloyd, Henry's son, 1763; inherited by John Lloyd, Jr. (Joseph's grandson), during Revolutionary War; author: An Evening Thought on Salvation by Christ, with Penetential Cries; Composed by Jupiter Hammon, a Negro Belonging to Mr. Lloyd, of Queen's Village, on Long Island, the 25th of December, 1760, N.Y., 1761; An Essay on the Ten Virgins, 1779; A Winter Piece, Hartford, 1782; An Address to the Negroes of the State of New York, 1787. Died circa 1800.

HAMMOND, Charles, state senator, journalist; b. Balt., Sept. 19, 1779; s. George and Elizabeth (Wells) H.; studied law under Philip Doddridge, 1800; m. Sarah Tillinghast, 1803; m. 2d, Miss Morehead. Admitted to Va. bar, 1801, fed. ct. bars, 1803; wrote some strong Federalist articles for Scioto Gazette, Chillicothe, O., circa 1802; moved to Belmont County, O., 1810; became leader Ohio Federalist party; mem. Ohio Senate, 1813-15; published Ohio Federalist, 1813-17; mem. Ohio Ho. of Reps., 1817-19, 20-21; revised Ohio laws; 1st reporter Ohio Supreme Ct., 1823-40, prepared 1st 9 vols. of Ohio Reports; editorial writer Cincinnati Gazette, 1823-25, editor, 1825-40; attacked slavery and Andrew Jackson; lost case to Henry Clay but gave excellent review of John Marshall's decision in McCulloch vs. Md., 1819; became known as lawyer for case Osborn vs. Bank of U.S. (9 Wheaton, 938), 1824. Died Apr. 3, 1840.

HAMMOND, Edward, congressman; b. "Font Hill" nr. Ellicott City, Md., Mar. 17, 1812; grad. Yale, 1830; studied law, New Haven (Conn.) and Balt. Admitted to Md. bar., 1833; began practice in Annapolis; mem. Md. Ho. of Dels. from Anne Arundel County, 1839, 41, 42, from Howard County, 1861, 67; mem. Md. Senate, 1848; mem. U.S. Ho. of Reps. (Democrat) from Md., 31st-32d congresses, 1849-53; assos. judge 5th jud. dist., 1867-82. Died "Font Hill," Oct. 19, 1882; buried St. John's Cemetery, nr. Ellicott City.

HAMMOND, Edwin, sheep breeder; b. Middlebury, Vt., May 20, 1801; s. Elnathan and Deborah (Carr) H.; m. Alpha Olmstead, Dec. 29, 1828, 3 children. Foremost contbr. to improvement of breed Merion sheep (one of most profitable branches of animal husbandry in Northern New Eng. at the time); founder Vt. State Agrl. Soc., 1851, pres., several years; aided and advised in formation New Eng. Agrl. Soc.; mem. exec. com. Nat. Woolgrowers Assn., asso. with Nat. Mfrs.' Assn. in framing schedule on wool and woolens in connection with tariff of 1867; mem. Vt. Legislature, 1858, 59; del. Republican Nat. Conv., 1864; trustee Middlebury Coll. Died Dec. 31, 1870.

HAMMOND, George Henry, meat packer; b. Fitchburg, Mass., May 5, 1838; s. John and Sarah (Huston) H.; m. Ellen Barry, 1857, 11 children. Worked at various jobs in East before arriving in Detroit, 1854, worked for mattress and furniture co. until 1856; began mfg. chairs, 1856, opened meat market when this concern burned down, adding slaughter house later, became very prosperous; began using refrigerator cars to transport his meat (1st packer to see usefulness of these cars), 1868-69, had 800 cars in operation by 1885; established other slaughter houses at Omaha (Neb.) and Hammond (Ind.; named for him). Died Detroit, Dec. 29, 1886.

HAMMOND, Jabez Delano, congressman; b. New Bedford, Mass., Aug. 2, 1778; s. Jabez and Priscilla (Delano) H.; A.M. (hon.), Union Coll., 1826; LL.D. (hon.), Hamilton Coll., 1845; m. Miranda Stoddard, 1810; m. 2d, Laura Williams, 1834; 3 children including Wells Stoddard. Admitted to N.Y. bar, 1805; trustee Village of Cherry Valley (N.Y.), 1812; mem. U.S. Ho. of Reps. (Democrat) from N.Y., 14th Congress, 1815-17; mem. N.Y. Senate, 1817-21; commr. to settle claims of N.Y. against fed. govt., 1825, 26; judge Otsego County, N.Y., 1839-47; supt. of schs., Otsego County; regent N.Y.U., 1845; mem. N.Y. Council of Appointment, 1812-15. Author: The History of Political Parties in the State of New York, 1842; The Political History of New York to December 1840, 1843; Life and Opinions of Julius Melbourne, 1847; Life of Silas Wright, 1848; Evidence, Independent of Written Revelation, of the Immortality of the Soul, 1851. Died Cherry Valley, Aug. 18, 1885; buried Cherry Valley Cemetery.

HAMMOND, James Henry, senator, gov. S.C., congressman; b. Stoney Battery, Newbury Dist., S.C. Nov. 15, 1807; s. Elisha and Catherine (Spann) H.; grad. S.C. Coll., 1825; m. Catherine FitzSimmons, June 23, 1831. Admitted to S.C. bar, 1828; founded the Southern Times, 1830, supporter of nullification and advocate of states rights; gov. S.C., 1842-44, in favor of secession; founded S.C. Agrl. Soc.; mem. U.S. Ho. of Reps. from S.C., 34th Congress, 1835-37; mem. U.S. Senate (Democrat) from S.C., 1857-60, gave speech known as the cotton king speech, referred to slaves and wage earners as "the very mudsills of society," a charge answered by Lincoln directly in an address. Died Beech Island, S.C., Nov. 13, 1864.

HAMMOND, John, congressman; b. Crown Point, N.Y., Aug. 17, 1827; grad. Rensselaer Poly. Inst. Cal. pioneer, 1849; served as pvt. during Civil War, promoted capt. cavalry, later brig. gen.; iron mfr., 25 years; pres. Crown Point Iron Co.; mem. U.S. Ho. of Reps. (Republican) from N.Y., 46th-47th congresses, 1879-83; ret. from bus. Died Crown Point, May 28, 1889; buried Forest Dale Cemetery, Crown Point.

HAMMOND, Nathaniel Job, congressman, jurist; b. Elbert County, Ga., Dec. 26, 1833; s. Amos W. Hammond; grad. U. Ga., 1852, LL.D. (hon.), 1896; m. Laura Lewis, 1858, 1 son. Admitted to Ga. bar, circa 1853; solicitor gen. Atlanta (Ga.) circuit during Civil War; reported Supreme Ct. Ga., 1865; atty. gen. Ga., 1872; mem. Atlanta Bd. Edn., 25 years; trustee U. Ga.; pres. bd. trustees Atlanta Coll. Physcians and Surgeons; mem. U.S. Ho. of Reps. from Ga., 46th-49th congresses, 1879-87; asso. justice Ga. Supreme Ct., 1887-89. Died Atlanta, Apr. 20, 1899; buried Oakland Cemetery, Atlanta.

HAMMOND, Robert Hanna, congressman, army officer; b. Milton, Pa., Apr. 28, 1791; attended acads., Milton. Engaged in merc. business; brig. gen. Pa. Militia; enlisted as lt. U.S. Army, 1817, resigned; register, recorder Northumberland County (Pa.); postmaster Milton, 1833-37; mem. U.S. Ho. of Reps. (Van Buren Democrat) from Pa., 25th-26th congresses, 1837-41; commd. paymaster U.S. Army during Mexican War, wounded and ordered home on sick leave; sailed on steamship Orleans for New Orleans, 1847. Died on the high seas, June 2, 1847; buried Milton Cemetery.

HAMMOND, Samuel, army officer, congressman; b. Richmond County, Va., Sept. 21, 1757; s. Charles and Elizabeth (Steele) H.; m. Rebecca (Elbert) Rae, 1783; m. 2d, Eliza A. O'Keefe, May 25, 1807. Served as volunteer during Lord Dunmore's War, 1774; commd. capt. Va. Volunteers, 1775; commd. capt. Continental Army, 1779, maj. LeRoy Hammond's Regt., 1780; participated in battles of Kings Mountain, Cowpens, Eutaw, others in S.C. and Ga.; commd. lt. col. at end of Revolutionary War; mem. Ga. Legislature from Chatham County; fought against Creek Indians, 1793; surveyor gen. Chatham County; mem. U.S. Ho. of Reps. from Ga., 8th Congress, 1803-05; col., mil. and civil comdt. No. part of Dist. of La., 1804-06; judge Ct. Common Pleas, Dist. of La., 1811; pres. Territorial Council of Mo., 1813; surveyor gen. S.C., 1827; sec. State of La., 1831-35. Died Hamburg, S.C., Sept. 11, 1842.

HAMMOND, William Gardiner, legal educator; b. Newport, R.I., May 3, 1829; s. William Gardiner and Sarah (Bull) H.; grad. Amherst Coll., 1849; studied law under Samuel E. Johnson, Bklyn.; attended U. Heidelberg (Germany) for 1 year; m. Lydia Bradford Torrey, May 26, 1852; m. 2d, Juliet Martha Roberts, May 3, 1865. Admitted to N.Y. bar, 1851; practiced in Bklyn., 1851-56; spent 3 years in Europe for recovery of health and for study; began practice of law in Ia., 1860; founder, editor Western Jurist, Des Moines, Ia., 1867-70; partly responsible for Ia. Law Code of 1873; opened pvt. law sch. which became part of U. Ia., chancellor, 1869, head law dept., 1869-81; dean Washington U. Law Sch., St. Louis, 1881-94; chmn. com. on legal edn. Am. Bar Assn., 1889-94; most eminent authority in U.S. on history of common law in his time; published editions of Institutes of Justinian (Thomas Collett Sandar), 1876, Legal and Political Hermeneutics (Francis Lieber), 1880, Blackstone's Commentaries, 1890. Died Apr. 12, 1894.

HAMMONS, David, congressman; b. Cornish, Me., May 12, 1808; attended common schs.; studied law. Admitted to Me. bar, 1836, began practice in Lovell; mem. Me. Senate, 1840-41; mem. U.S. Ho. of Reps. (Democrat) from Me., 30th Congress, 1847-49; resumed law practice. Died Bethel, Me., Nov. 7, 1888; buried Woodland Cemetery, Bethel.

HAMMONS, Joseph, physician, congressman; b. Cornish, Me., Mar. 3, 1787; studied medicine, Ossipee, N.H. Began practice of medicine, Farmington, N.H., 1817; mem. N.H. Med. Soc.; mem. U.S. Ho. of Reps. (Jacksonian Democrat) from N.H., 21st-22d congresses, 1829-33; postmaster Dover (N. H.), 1833-36. Died Farmington, Mar. 29, 1836; buried old family cemetery.

HAMPTON, James Giles, congressman; b. Bridgeton, N.J., June 13, 1814; grad. Princeton, 1835; studied law. Admitted to N.J. bar, 1839, began practice, Bridgeton; collector Port of Bridgeton, 1841-44; mem. U.S. Ho. of Reps. (Whig) from N.J., 29th-30th congresses, 1845-49; resumed law practice; solicitor bd. chosen freeholders of Cumberland County (N.J.), 1852. Died Bridgeton, Sept. 22, 1861; buried Broad St. Presbyn. Cemetery, Bridgeton.

HAMPTON, Moses, congressman; b. Beaver, Pa., Oct. 28, 1803; grad. Washington Coll. (now Washington and Jefferson U.), 1827; studied law, Uniontown, Pa. Admitted to Pa. bar, 1829, began practice in Somerset; moved to Pitts., 1838, practiced law; mem. U.S. Ho. of Reps. (Whig) from Pa., 30th-31st congresses, 1847-51; pres. judge Allegheny County Dist. Ct., 1853-73. Died "Hampton Place" nr. Wilkinsburg, Pa., June 27, 1878; buried Allegheny Cemetery, Pitts.

HAMPTON, Wade, congressman, army officer, planter; b. Halifax County, Va., 1752; s. Anthony and Anne (Preston) H.; m. Mrs. Martha Epps Howell, 1783; m. 2d, Harriet Flud, 1786; m. 3d, Mary Cantey, 1801; 2 children including Wade. Commd. lt. col. Continental Army, 1781, served with distinction under Gen. Thomas Sumter in Revolutionary War; mem. Va. Legislature, 1782-92; justice of peace Richmond County; mem. conv. which ratified U.S. Constn., 1788; sheriff Camden Dist.; mem. U.S. Ho. of Reps. (Republican) from Va., 4th Congress, 1795-97, 8th Congress, 1803-05; presdl. elector, 1801; commd. col. U.S. Army, 1808, brig. gen., 1809; in charge of fortification of Norfolk, Va., 1812-13; commd. maj. gen., 1813, in command of army on Lake Champlain in Mil. Dist. 9, repulsed in attack on Sir George Prevost at Chateaugay, and in expdn. against Montreal, 1813; owner cotton plantation, Richland County, S.C., also sugar plantations, Ark. and Miss.; reputed to have been wealthiest planter in Am. at time of death. Died Columbia, S.C., Feb. 4, 1835; buried Trinity Churchyard, Columbia.

HAMTRAMCK, John Francis, army officer; b. Ft. Wayne, Ind., Apr. 19, 1798; s. Col. John Francis and Rebecca (Mackenzie) H.; grad. U.S. Mil. Acad., 1819; m. Miss Williamson; m. 2d, Ellen Selby; m. 3d, Sarah Selby; several children including Selby Mackenzie. Left under guardianship of William Henry Harrison at death of his father, 1803; served as sgt. 1st inf. under Zachary Taylor in War of 1812; commd. 2d lt. of arty., 1819, stationed at Ft. McHenry, Balt., resigned 1822; U.S. Indian agt. (apptd. by Pres. John Q. Adams) to Osage Indians, 1826-31; planter, nr. Shepherdstown, Va. (now W. Va.), 1831-46; apptd. col. 1st Va. Volunteer Regt., 1846; joined Zachary Taylor in Mexico; mil. gov. of Saltillo (Mexico); mustered out 1848; mayor Shepherdstown, 1850-54; justice Jefferson County (Va.) Ct., 1854-58. Died Apr. 21, 1858.

HAMUDA PASHA, bey of Tunis. Succeeded as bey of Tunis, 1782; preyed on European and Am. shipping; seized Am. schooner Eliza, demanded $10,-000 ransom, 1796; unsuccessfully approached by Am. commr. Richard O'Brien, 1796; Joel Barlow (Am. commr. to Algiers) succeeded in persuading Algiers to go to war against Tunis for a financial settlement, but war was inconclusive, 1797; ratified treaty with Am. for $107,000, 1798; ratified revised treaty (more favorable to U.S.), 1800; continued depredations on U.S. shipping; threatened war when U.S. seized some Tunisian ships, 1804; troubled during his rule with famine and civil discontent; forced because of a strong showing by U.S. Navy to abrogate all demands on America; took advantage of War of 1812 to act in concert with British as regards Am. shipping. Died 1814.

HANBACK, Lewis, congressman; b. Winchester, Ill., Mar. 27, 1839; attended Cherry Grove Sem., Knox County, Ill., 3 years. Sch. tchr., Morgan County, Ill., 1860-61; enlisted as pvt. U.S. Army during Civil War, promoted to capt., 1861; brigade insp., 1862-64; admitted to Kan. bar, 1865, practiced law; elected justice of peace, 1867; probate judge Shawnee County (Kan.), 1868-72; asst. chief clk. Kan. Ho. of Reps.; asst. sec. Kan. Senate, 1877; asst. U.S. dist. atty. for Kan., 1877-79; receiver public moneys, Salina, Kan.; mem. U.S. Ho. of Reps. (Republican) from Kan., 48th-49th Congresses, 1883-87. Died Kansas City, Kan., Sept. 7, 1897; buried Topeka (Kan.) Cemetery.

HANBY, Benjamin Russel, songwriter; b. Rushville, O., July 22, 1833; s. William and Ann (Miller) H.; grad. Otterbein U., Westerville, O., 1858; m. Mary Kate Winter, June 1858. Prin. acad. Sevenmile, O., 1859-60; pastor United Brethren Ch., Lewisburg, O., 1861-63; employed by John Church Music Co., Cincinnati, 1864; worked for Root & Cady Music House, Chgo., 1865-67; wrote while in coll. "Darling Nelly Gray" (his 1st song) wrote "Little Tillie's Grave," 1861, "Now den, now den." Author (with George F. Root) Our Song Birds, (contained 60 of his tunes), 2 vols., 1866-67. Died Chgo., Mar. 16, 1867.

HANCHETT, Luther, congressman; b. Middlebury, Portage County, O., Oct. 25, 1825; attended common schs.; studied law. Admitted to Ohio bar, 1846, began practice in Fremont; moved to Portage County (Wis.), 1849, engaged in lumber and mining bus.; county atty., 4 years; mem. Wis. Senate, 1856-60; mem. U.S. Ho. of Reps. (Republican) from Wis., 37th Congress, 1861-62. Died Plover, Wis., Nov. 24, 1862; buried Plover Cemetery.

HANCOCK, George, congressman; b. Chesterfield County, Va., June 13, 1754. Served as col. inf. Va. Regt., Continental Army, during Revolutionary War; mem. staff of Count Pulaski at siege of Savannah, taken prisoner, paroled; admitted to Va. bar, 1774, began practice in Chesterfield County; apptd. ensign, Chesterfield County, 1776, later promoted capt.; apptd. col. Botetourt County (Va.) Militia, 1785; commonwealths atty. Botetourt County, 1787-89, dep. states atty., 1789-93; mem. U.S. Ho. of Reps. (Democrat) from Va., 3d-4th congresses, 1793-97. Died "Fotheringay," Elliston Valley, Montgomery County, Va., July 18, 1820; buried in tomb at "Fotheringay."

HANCOCK, John, mcht., gov. Mass., signer Declaration of Independence; b. Quincy, Mass., Jan. 12, 1736; s. Rev. John and Mary (Hawke) H.; grad. Harvard, 1754; m. Dorothy Quincy, Aug. 28, 1775. Partner, Thomas Hancock & Co., 1763; mem. Mass. Gen. Assembly, 1766; involved in opposition to Brit. colonial policy in the celebrated Liberty affair (his ship and its cargo of Madeira wine seized for failure to pay duty; faced with bankruptcy if penalties resulting from suits against him were to be enforced), 1768; mem. Mass. Gen. Ct., 1769; head of town com. Boston, 1770; treas. Harvard, 1773; pres. Provincial Congress, 1774-75; exempted from Gen. Thomas Gage's amnesty proclamation, 1775; escaped arrest by Brit. troops sent to Concord to arrest him and Samuel Adams, (warned by either William Dawes or Samuel Prescott), Apr. 1775; pres. Continental Congress, 1775-77; 1st signer of Declaration of Independence, 1776; pres. Mass. Constl. Conv., 1780; gov. Mass., 1780-85, 1787-93; presided at Mass. Conv. to ratify U.S. Constn., 1788. Died Oct. 8, 1793; buried Old Granary Burying Ground, Boston.

HANCOCK, John congressman; b. Jackson County, Ala., Oct. 24, 1824; s. John Allen and Sarah (Ryan) H.; attended East Tenn. U.; m. Susan E. Richardson, 1855. Admitted to Ala. bar, 1846; dist. judge, Austin, Tex., 1851-55; mem. Tex. Legislature, 1860-61; refused to take oath of allegiance to Confederate States Am.; mem. U.S. Ho. of Reps. from Tex., 42d-44th, 48th congresses, 1871-77, 83-85. Died Austin, Tex., July 19, 1893; buried Oakwood Cemetery, Austin.

HANCOCK, Thomas, mcht.; b. Cambridge Farms (later Lexington), Mass., July 13, 1703; s. Rev. John and Elizabeth (Clark) H.; m. Lydia Henchman, Nov. 5, 1730. Apprentice to bookseller and bookbinder, 1716-23; started bookstore in Mass., 1723; engaged in partnership supplying Newfoundland fishing fleet with various supplies, also owned fleet of freighters; became one of wealthiest Boston mchts. of his era; engaged in partnership to supply Brit. forces in Novia Scotia, 1746-58; supplied Col. Edward Cornwallis, 1749, enabled him to found Halifax; with his partner acted as agt. for Province of N.S., 1755; increased his wealth by smuggling. Died Mass., Aug. 1, 1764.

HANCOCK, Winfield Scott, soldier, presdl. candidate; b. Montgomery Square, Pa., Feb. 14, 1824; s. Benjamin Franklin and Elizabeth (Hoxworth) H.; grad. U.S. Mil. Acad., 1844; m. Almira Russell, Jan. 24, 1850; 2 children. Served as 2d lt.

U.S. Army during Mexican War, 1846, distinguished at battles of Contreras and Churubusco, brevetted 1st lt., 1847; regimental q.m. and adj. on Upper Missouri, 1848-55; served as q.m. with rank capt. under Gen. Harvey during Seminole War, 1855; accompanied Gen. Harvey expdn. to Utah; commd. brig. gen., organized and trained newly assembled Army of Potomac, 1861; served under McClellan in Peninsular Campaign at battles of Antietam and Fredricksburg, 1862, commanded a corps at Battle of Gettysburg, 1863, and at Spottsylvania Ct. House, where he took 4000 prisoners, 1864; commd. maj. gen., 1862; in command of II Army Corps, 1863; commd. brig. gen. U.S. Army, 1864, maj. gen., 1866; command of Central Mil. Dept., 1867 commanded Dept. of La. and Tex., 1867; commanded Dept. of Dakota, 1870-72, Div. of the Atlantic, 1872-86, and Dept. of East; unsuccessful Democratic candidate for U.S. Pres., 1880. Died Governors Island, N.Y., Feb. 9, 1886; buried Norristown, Pa.

HAND, Augustus Cincinnatus, congressman; b. Shoreham, Vt., Sept. 4, 1803; attended Litchfield (Conn.) Law Sch. Admitted to N.Y. bar, 1828, began practice at Crown Point; moved to Elizabethtown, N.Y., 1831; surrogate Essex County (N.Y.), 1831-39; mem. U.S. Ho. of Reps. (Democrat) from N.Y., 26th Congress, 1839-41; mem. N.Y. Senate, 1844-47; asso. justice N.Y. Supreme Ct., 1847-55; del. Dem. Nat. Conv., N.Y.C., 1868. Died Elizabethtown, Mar. 8, 1878; buried Riverside Cemetery, Elizabethtown.

HAND, Daniel, mcht., philanthropist; b. East Guilford (now Madison), Conn., July 16, 1801; s. Daniel Hand; m. Elizabeth Ward. Took over his uncle's mcht. business, Augusta, Ga., extended business to br. in Charleston, S.C., branch outgrew home office; arrested and sent to Libby Prison, Richmond, Va. during Civil War, released on parole; established Daniel Hand Edn. Fund for Colored People by leaving over $1 million to Am. Missionary Assn. of N.Y., 1888 (at this time largest gift ever given to benevolent soc.). Died Dec. 17, 1891.

HAND, Edward, physician, army officer; b. Kings' County, Ireland, Dec. 31, 1744; s. John Hand; ed. Trinity Coll.; m. Catharine Ewing, Mar. 13, 1775. Served as surgeon's mate Brit. Navy, came to Phila., 1767; lt. col. of brigade under Gen. William Thompson Continental Army, 1775, took part in seige of Boston, battles of L.I., Trenton, Princeton; Lancaster County Associators, col. riflemen, 1776; commd. brig. gen., 1777; brevetted maj. gen. Pa. Militia, 1783; mem. Continental Congress from Pa., 1784-85; mem. Pa. Assembly, 1785-86; presdl. elector, 1789; mem. Pa. Constl. Conv., 1789-90; maj. gen. provisional U.S. Army, 1798; U.S. insp. revenue, 1791-1801. Died "Rockford," Lancaster, Pa., Sept. 3, 1802.

HANDY, Alexander Hamilton, jurist; b. Princess Anne, Somerset County, Md., Dec. 25, 1809; s. Col. George and Betsy (Wilson) H.; m. Susan Wilson Stuart, 1835. Admitted to Md. bar, 1834; moved to Canton, Miss., practiced law; asso. justice Miss. Ct. Errors and Appeals, 1853-64, chief justice, 1864-67; apptd. by gov. after Miss. secession to go to Md. to invoke people there to secede, 1860; taught U. Md. Law Sch., 1870-71. Died Canton, Sept. 12, 1883.

HANNA, John, congressman; b. nr. Indpls., Ind., Sept. 3, 1827; grad. Ind. Asbury (now De Pauw) U., Greencastle, Ind., 1850; studied law. Admitted to Ind. bar, began practice in Greencastle; mayor Greencastle, 1851-54; moved to Kan.; mem. Kan. Territorial Legislature, 1857-58; returned to Ind.; Republican presdl. elector, 1860; U.S. dist. atty., 1861-69; mem. U.S. Ho. of Reps. (Rep.) from Ind, 45th Congress, 1877-79. Died Plainfield, Ind., Oct. 24, 1882; buried Forest Hill Cemetery, Greencastle.

HANNA, John Andre, congressman; b. Flemington, N.J., 1762; grad. Coll. of N.J. (now Princeton), 1782; studied law. Admitted to Lancaster County (Pa.) bar, 1783, began practice in Lancaster, Pa.; moved to Harrisburg, Pa., admitted to Dauphin County (Pa.) bar, 1785; del. Pa. Conv. to ratify U.S. Constn., 1787; sec. Anti-Federal Conf., 1788; mem. Pa. Ho. of Reps., 1791; elected lt. col. 3d Battalion of Dauphin County, 1792; apptd. brig. gen. Dauphin County Brigade, 1793, in command during Whiskey Rebellion, 1793; apptd. maj. gen. 6th Div. of Dauphin and Berks counties, 1800; mem. U.S. Ho. of Reps. (Anti-Federalist) from Pa., 5th-9th congresses, 1797-1805. Died Harrisburg, July 23, 1805; buried Mt. Kalmia Cemetery, Harrisburg.

HANNA, Robert, senator; b. nr. Fountainius, Laurens Dist., S.C., Apr. 6, 1786. Settled in Brookville, Ind., 1802; sheriff of Ct. Common Pleas, 1811-20; mem. Ind. Constl. Conv., 1816; brig. gen. Ind. Militia; register land office, 1820-30; moved to Indpls., 1825; mem. U.S. Senate (Whig) from Ind., Aug. 19, 1831-Jan. 3, 1832; mem. Ind. Ho. of Reps., 1832-33, 36-39; contractor for nat. roads, 1835; mem. Ind. Senate, 1842-46. Killed by a train while walking on the track, Indpls., Nov. 16, 1858; buried Crown Hill Cemetery, Indpls.

HANNEGAN, Edward Allen, senator, congressman; b. Hamilton County, O., June 25, 1807; attended pub. schs., Bourbon County, Ky.; studied law; m. Margaret Chambers Duncan. Admitted to Ky. bar, 1827; moved to Terre Haute, Ind., began practice of law, 1827; moved to Crawfordsville, Ind., 1830, to Covington, Ind., 1830, practiced law; mem. Ind. Ho. of Reps., 1832-33, 41-42; mem. U.S. Ho. of Reps. (Democrat) from Ind., 23d-24th congresses, 1833-37; register land office, Laporte, Ind., 1839; mem. U.S. Senate from Ind., 1843-49; U.S. minister to Prussia, 1849-50; resumed law practice, Covington; moved to St. Louis, 1857, practiced law. Died St. Louis, Feb. 25, 1859; buried Woodlawn Cemetery, Terre Haute.

HANSON, Alexander Contee, jurist; b. Annapolis, Md., Oct. 22, 1749; s. John and Jane (Contee) H.; grad. Coll. of Phila.; m. Rebeca Howard, June 4, 1778, 2 children, including Alexander C. Admitted to Md. bar, 1772; asso. judge Gen. Court of Md., 1778-81; his decision to have hanged, drawn and quartered Tories accused of treason resulted in passage of Md. law providing for imprisonment instead, 1782; Md. presdl. elector, 1789; favored adoption of U.S. Constn.; chancellor of Md., 1789-1806; wrote legal tracts and pamphlets. Died Annapolis, Jan. 16, 1806.

HANSON, Alexander Contee, senator; b. Annapolis, Md., Feb. 27, 1786; s. Alexander Contee Hanson; grad. St. John's Coll., 1802; m. Priscilla Dorsey, June 24, 1805. Editor-in-chief, founder Federal Republican, 1808; his anti-war policy led to violence by Republicans against him and other Federalists, resulted in destruction of his newspaper plant, 1812; mem. U.S. Ho. of Reps. from Md., 13th-14th congresses, 1813-16; mem. U.S. Senate from Md., 1817-19. Died "Belmont," Elkridge, Md., Apr. 23, 1819; buried family burial ground.

HANSON, John, Continental congressman; b. Mulberry Grove, Charles County, Md., Apr. 13, 1721; s. Samuel and Elizabeth (Story) H.; m. Jane Contee, 9 children, including Alexander Contee. An early advocate of colonial independence; mem. Md. Assembly, 1757-73; mem. Md. Conv., 1775; active in raising troops and providing arms and ammunition for Revolutionary Army; established gun-lock factory, Frederick, Md.; del. to Continental Congress, 1779; Md. refused to ratify articles of Confederation until Va. and other states had relinquished their claims to unsettle Western lands, for which Hanson (with colleague Daniel Carroll) labored successfully; pres. Congress of Confederation (sometimes called 1st pres. of U.S.), 1781-82. Died Oxon Hill, Prince Georges County, Md., Nov. 22, 1783.

HANSON, Roger Weightman, army officer; b. Winchester, Ky., Aug. 27, 1827; s. Samuel and Matilda (Calloway) H. Served as 1st lt. U.S. Army in Mexican War, 1846-48; mem. Ky. Legislature, 1853-55; col. Ky. State Guards, regt. formed nucleus of 2d, 3d, 4th and 5th Ky. Regts.; held Confederate right wing at Ft. Donelson repulsing 2 attacks, 1862; commanded 2d Ky. Inf., then 1st Brigade (2d, 4th, 6th, 9th, Ky. inf. regts.), 1862; brig. gen., 1862; under Gen. J.H. Morgan in expdn. against Hartsville, 1862, captured and destroyed Union force of 2,000 men with loss of only 68 Confederate soldiers. Died Battle of Stone's River, Jan. 4, 1863; buried Nashville, Tenn., reinterred, Lexington, Ky.

HAPPER, Andrew Patton, missionary; b. Washington County, Pa., Oct. 20, 1818; s. Baptist and Ann (Arrell) H.; grad. Jefferson Coll., Phila., 1835; attended Western Theol. Sem., Pa., 1840-43; M.D., U. Pa., 1844; m. Elizabeth S. Ball, Nov. 11, 1847; m. 2d, Miss A. L. Elliott, Oct. 6, 1869; m. 3d, Hannah J. Shaw, Mar. 18, 1875; at least 4 children. Ordained to ministry Presbyn. Ch., 1844; arrived in China as missionary, 1844, set up hdqrs. in a suburb of Canton, 1847-84; baptized his 1st convert, 1854; conducted sch., in charge of 1st Presbyn. Ch. of Canton; editor Chinese Recorder, 1880-84; returned to U.S., 1884, raised over $100,000 for establishment of Christian coll. in China (Canton Christian Coll., later Lingan U.), 1888; returned to Canton, took care of coll., 1888-91; spent his later years in Wooster, O. Died Wooster, Oct. 27, 1894.

HARADEN, Jonathan, naval officer, privateer; b. Gloucester, Mass., Nov. 11, 1744; s. Joseph and Joanna (Emerson) H.; m. Hannah Deadman, June 8, 1767; m. 2d, Mrs. Eunice (Diman) Mason, Mar. 11, 1782; m. 3d, Mrs. Mary Scallon, Oct. 12, 1797. Lt. in sloop (later brigantine) Tyrannicide of Mass. Navy 1776, comdr., 1777; together with another ship he sailed around Brit. Isles and France searching for prizes; cruised in W.I., 1777; comdr. privateering ship General Pickering, 1778, engaged and captured 3 ships at one time, encountered larger ship Brit. privateer Achilles, 1780, forced Achilles to run off; captured with General Pickering at St. Eustatius, W.I., 1781; commanded privateer Julius Caesar after obtaining freedom, 1782. Died Salem, Mass., Nov. 23, 1803.

HARALSON, Hugh Anderson, congressman; b. nr. Penfield, Ga., Nov. 13, 1805; grad. Franklin Coll. (now U. Ga.), 1825; studied law. Admitted to Ga. bar, 1825, began practice in Monroe; moved to Lagrange, Ga., 1828, practiced law; engaged in farming; mem. Ga. Ho. of Reps., 1831-32; Ga. Senate, 1837-38; served as maj. gen. Ga. Militia, 1838-40; mem. U.S. Ho. of Reps. (Democrat) from Ga., 28th-31st congresses, 1843-51; resumed practice of law. Died Lagrange, Sept. 25, 1854; buried Hill View Cemetery, Lagrange.

HARBAUGH, Henry, clergyman, author; b. Washington Twp., Pa., Oct. 28, 1817; s. George and Anna (Snyder) H.; attended Marshall Coll., sem., Mercersburg, Washington Twp., 1840-43; m. Louisa Goodrich, Dec. 14, 1843; m. 2d, Maria Louisa Linn, Nov. 14, 1848; 7 children. Left home, 1836, went to Ohio, became carpenter, singing tchr., public speaker; licensed to preach by German Reformed Ch., Va., 1843; pastor, Lewisburg, Pa., 1843-50, 1st Ch., Lancaster, Pa. 1850-60 St. John's Ch., Lebanon, Pa., 1860-63; editor Guardian (monthly mag.), 1850-66; prof. theology Mercersburg Theol. Sem., 1863. Author: The Sainted Dead, 1848; The Heavenly Home, 1853; The True Glory of Woman, 1858. Died Mercersburg, Dec. 28, 1867.

HARBY, Isaac, journalist, playwright; b. Charleston, S.C., Nov. 9, 1788; s. Solomon and Rebecca (Moses) H.; studied law under Langdon Cheves, 1805; m. Rachel Mordecai. Started acad., Charleston, 1809; co-owner, editor So. Patriot and Comml. Advertiser, 1814-22; worked for City Gazette and Comml. Daily Advertiser, Charleston, 1822; a founder Reformed Soc. of Israelites of Charleston. Author: Alexander Severus (play), 1805; The Gordian Knot, or Causes and Effects (tragedy), 1810; Alberti, 1819. Died N.Y.C., Dec. 14, 1828.

HARD, Gideon, congressman; b. Arlington, Vt., Apr. 29, 1797; grad. Union Coll., Schenectady, N.Y., 1822; studied law. Taught sch.; admitted to the bar, 1825; began practice of law, Newport (now Albion), N.Y., 1826; mem. U.S. Ho. of Reps. (Whig) from N.Y., 23d-24th congresses, 1833-37; commr. schs. Barre Twp., Orleans County, N.Y., 1841-48; mem. N.Y. Senate, 1841-48; canal appraiser, 1849-50; county judge and surrogate Orleans County, 1856-60. Died Albion, Apr. 27, 1887; buried Mt. Albion Cemetery.

HARDEE, William Joseph, army officer; b. Camden County, Ga., Oct. 12, 1815; s. John and Sarah (Ellis) H.; grad. U.S. Mil. Acad., 1838; m. Mary Lewis, Jan. 1863, 1 child. Commd. 1st lt. 2d Dragoons, 1839, capt., 1844, accompanied Gen. Taylor across Rio Grande, commd. lt. col., 1848; published Rifle and Light Infantry Tactics (known as Hardee's Tactics, adopted as textbook by Army), 1855; sr. maj. 2d Cav., 1855; lt. col., comdt. of cadets U.S. Mil. Acad., 1856; commd. brig. gen. Confederate Army, 1861, maj. gen., 1861; commanded corps at Battle of Shiloh, 1862; commanded left wing Confederate Army at Battle of Perryville, 1862; organized original Ark. Brigade (known as Hardee's Brigade); commd. lt. gen., 1862; commanded mil. depts. of S.C., Ga. and Fla., 1864; commanded army defending Savannah (Ga.) against Gen. Sherman, 1864. Died Wytheville, Va., Nov. 6, 1873; buried Selma, Ala.

HARDEMAN, Thomas, Jr., congressman; b. Eatonton, Ga., Jan. 12, 1825; grad. Emory Coll., 1845; studied law. Admitted to Ga. bar, 1847; engaged in warehouse and commn. bus.; mem. Ga. Ho. of Reps., 1853, 55, 57; mem. U.S. Ho. of Reps. (Democrat) from Ga., 36th, 48th congresses, 1859-Jan. 23, 1861, 83-85; capt. Floyd Rifles; maj. 2d Ga. Battalion during Civil War, later col. 45th Ga. Inf., Confederate Army; mem. Ga. Ho. of Reps., 1863 64, 74, speaker; del. Nat. Dem. Conv., Balt., 1872; pres. Ga. Dem. Conv., also chmn. Ga. Dem. Exec. Com., 4 years. Died Macon, Ga., Mar. 6, 1891; buried Oak Hill Cemetery, Macon.

HARDENBERGH, Jacob Rutsen, clergyman, coll. pres.; b. Rosendale, N.Y., 1736; s. Col. Johannes and Maria (DuBois) H.; student theology under John Frelinghuysen; D.D., Coll. N.J. (now Princeton), 1771, A.M. (hon.), 1777; S.T.D., Columbia, 1789; m. Mrs. Dinah Van Bergh Frelinghuysen, 1756, several children, including John, Jacob Rutsen. Ordained to ministry Dutch Reformed Ch., 1758 (among 1st of faith to be ordained in Am.); leader Coetus, group which sought independence from parent ch. in Holland and the establishment of Dutch Ref. theol. sch. in Am., authorized to petition governing Classis in Amsterdam for independent Am., classis, 1763, was refused; obtained royal charter for founding Queen's Coll. (now Rutgers U.), 1766, apptd. to 1st bd. trustees 1771, 1st pres., 1786-90; reward offered by Eng. for his capture during Revolutionary War because of his ardent support of patriot cause; del. Provincial Congress of N.J. which ratified Declaration of Independence and framed N.J. Constn.; mem. N.J. Gen. Assembly. Died New Brunswick, N.J., Nov. 2, 1790.

HARDENBURGH, Augustus Albert, congressman; b. New Brunswick, N.J., May 18, 1830; attended Rutgers Coll., 1844. Employed in a banking house, N.Y.C; clk. Hudson County Nat. Bank, 1852, pres., 1878; mem. N.Y. Assembly, 1853-54; mem. bd. edn. Jersey City, N.J., 1855-56, mem. common council, 1857-63, pres., 1860; mem. city council Bergen (N.J.); elected state dir. railroads of N.J., 1868; del. Nat. Democratic Conv., Balt., 1872; elected pres. No. R.R. of N.J., 1874; mem. U.S. Ho. of Reps. (Dem.) from N.J., 44th-45th, 47th congresses, 1875-79, 81-83; mem. Jersey City Bd. of Finance and Taxation, 1883-89; trustee state reform sch., 1884; Dem. presdl. elector, 1884. Died Jersey City, Oct. 5, 1889; buried Mt. Pleasant Cemetery, Newark, N.J.

HARDEY, Mother Mary Aloysia, educator; b. Piscataway, Md., Dec. 8, 1809; d. Frederick and Sarah (Spalding) Hardey. Entered convent of Soc. of Sacred Heart of Jesus, Grand Coteau, La., 1821, received highest honors, 1824, order to habit, 1825; asst. superior St. Michael's (La.), 1835, superior, 1836; trans. to N.Y., 1841; founder and superior 1st convent of her order in East, which became popular ednl. instn., center of far-spread influence; provincial of houses of Eastern states and Can., 1844; visited convents of N.Am., 1871, also visited Spain, Belgium, Eng. and Ireland. Died Paris, France, June 17, 1886; buried Kenwood, Albany, N.Y.

HARDIE, James Allen, army officer; b. N.Y.C., May 5, 1823; s. Allen Wardwell and Caroline (Cox) H.; grad. U.S. Mil. Acad., 1843; m. Margaret Hunter, 1851, 5 children. Asst. prof. geography, history and ethics U.S. Mil. Acad., 1844-46; served as maj. N.Y. Volunteers, 1846-48; became Roman Catholic; helped raise money to build 1st cathedral ch. in San Francisco during Mexican War; commd. 1st lt. 3d Arty., U.S. Army, 1848; adj. gen. Dept. of Oregon; lt. col. on staff Gen. McClellan during Peninsular and Md. campaigns, 1861, on staff Gen. Ambrose Burnside in battles around Fredericksburg (in controversy between Burnside and William Franklin over responsibility for disaster on the Rappahannock, 1862, both contestants agreed to use his accurate field dispatches as true record of events); asst. adj. gen. Army of Potomac; commd brig. gen. Volunteers, 1862; carried secret personal message making George Meade comdr. in place of Joseph Hooker just before Gettysburg, 1863; asst. sec. to U.S. Sec. of Army Edwin M. Stanton; judge advocate gen. Army of Potomac, 1863; promoted maj. U.S. Army, 1863, maj., 1865; maj. chief of Insp. Gen.'s Office, 1865. Died Washington, D.C., Dec. 14, 1876.

HARDIN, Benjamin, congressman; b. Westmoreland County, Pa., Feb. 29, 1784; s. Benjamin and Sarah H.; m. Elizabeth Barbour, Mar. 31, 1807. Admitted to Ky. bar, 1806; mem. Ky. Ho. of Reps., 1810, 11, 24, 25; mem. Ky. Senate, 1828-32; mem. U.S. Ho. of Reps. from Ky., 14th, 16-17th, 23d-24th congresses, 1815-17, 19-23, 33-37; sec. of state Ky., 1844-47; del. Ky. Constl. Conv., 1849-50. Died Bardstown, Ky., Sept. 24, 1852; buried nr. Springfield, Ky.

HARDIN, Charles Henry, gov. Mo.; b. Trimble County, Ky., July 15,, 1820; s. Charles and Hannah (Jewell) H.; grad. Miami U., 1841; LL.D., William Jewell Coll., 1890; m. Mary Barr Jenkins, Oct. 6, 1844. Admitted to Mo. bar, 1843; circuit atty. 2d Jud. Dist. Mo., 1842-52; became mem. lower house Mo. Gen. Assembly, 1852; mem. com. to prepare revised statutes Mo., 1855-56; organizer American Party in Mo.; leader Bell-Everett forces, 1860; mem. Mo. Senate (Conservative-Unionist), 1860-62, (Democrat), 72-74; gov. Mo. (1st Dem. gov. since Civil War), 1874-77; founder Hardin Coll. for Women, Mexico, Mo., 1873. Died Mexico, Mo., July 29, 1892.

HARDIN, John, army officer, Indian fighter; b. Fauquier County, Va., Oct. 1, 1753; s. Martin Hardin; m. Jane Davies, before 1786, at least 1 son, Martin D. Ensign in Dunmore's Indian campaign, 1774; served with Daniel Morgan's Riflemen at Saratoga during Revolutionary War; lt. col. Ky. Militia in Wabash expdns. led by George Rogers Clark, 1786, then served with every U.S. expdn. into Ky. Indian territory except that of Gen. Arthur St. Clair; fought Indians in Western Pa., 1786-92; col. in charge of Nelson County (Ky.) Militia; 1788, 89; commd. brig. gen. Ky. Militia; Hardin County (O.), (formed 1792) named in his honor, also Hardin County (Ky.); killed by Indians while on peace mission to Miami tribes Died Hardin County, O., Apr. 1792.

HARDIN, John J., congressman, army officer; b. Frankfort, Ky., Jan. 6, 1810; s. Martin and Elizabeth (Logan) H.; grad. Transylvania U., Lexington, Ky.; m. Sarah Smith, Jan .13, 1831, 4 children including Martin D. Maj. gen. Ill. Militia during Blackhawk War, 1832; mem. Ill. Gen. Assembly from Morgan County, 1836-42; mem. U.S. Ho. of Reps. from Ill., 28th Congress, 1843-45; comdr.-in-chief Ill. Militia, 1845, conducted campaign against Mormons, inducing them to leave Ill. peacefully; col. 1st Regt., Ill. Volunteers during Mexican War, 1846-47, joined army of occupation under Gen. Zachary Taylor. Killed in Battle of Buena Vista, Feb. 23, 1847; buried East City Cemetery, Jacksonville, Ill.

HARDIN, John Wesley, outlaw; b. Bonham, Tex., 1853; studied law in prison. Gambler and outlaw, evaded capture until 1877; sentenced to 25 year imprisonment for killing sheriff, 1877, pardoned, 1894; practiced law, El Paso, Tex., 1894-95. Shot down, died 1895.

HARDIN, Martin D., army officer; senator; b. in Southwestern Pa., June 21, 1780; s. John and Jane (Davies) H.; ed. Transylvania Sem.; m. Elizabeth Logan, 1 son, Col. John J. Hardin. Family moved to Ky., 1786; mem. Ky. Ho. of Reps., 1805, 19-20, speaker, 1819-20; published Reports of Cases Argued and Adjudged in the Court of Appeals, Kentucky, 1810; sec. of state Ky., 1812; served as maj. in a Ky. regt. during War of 1812; mem. U.S. Senate from Ky. (Democrat), 1816-17; known as a nationalist, favored liberal interpretation of U.S. Constn. Died Frankfort, Ky., Oct. 18, 1823.

HARDING, Aaron, congressman; b. nr. Campbellsville, Ky., Feb. 20, 1805; attended rural schs.; studied law. Admitted to Ky. bar, 1833, began practice, Greensburg; elected pros. atty. Green County, 1833; mem. Ky. Ho. of Reps., 1840; mem. U.S. Ho. of Reps. (Union Democrat) from Ky., 37th-39th congresses, 1861-67; del. Union Nat. Conv., Phila., 1866; resumed practice of law, Danville, Ky. Died Georgetown, Ky., Dec. 24, 1875; buried Georgetown Cemetery.

HARDING, Abner Clark, congressman, army officer, financier; b. East Hampton, Conn., Feb. 10, 1807; s. Nathan and Philena Sears (Clark) H.; m. Mrs. Rebecca L. (Laybricks) Byers, Jan. 30, 1829; m. 2d Susan A. Ickes, June 30, 1835; 2 children. Admitted to Pa. bar, 1828; county sch. commr., 1847-49; mem. Ill. Ho. of Reps., 1848-50; organizer 2d Nat. Bank Monmouth (Ill.); engaged in constrn. of Peoria & Oquawka R.R.; mem. 1st bd. trustees Monmouth (Ill.) Coll., 1853, later endowed a professorship; commd. brig. gen. U.S. Volunteers, 1863; mem. U.S. Ho. of Reps. from Ill., 39th-40th congresses, 1865-69. Died Monmouth, July 19, 1874; buried Monmouth Cemetery.

HARDING, Chester, artist; b. Conway, Mass., Sept. 1, 1792; s. Abiel and Olive (Smith) H.; m. Caroline Woodruff, 4 children including Margaret E. White. A drummer in War of 1812; made drums for army when dismissed from army; engaged in cabinet-making, Caledonia, N.Y.; opened sign painter's shop, Caledonia; became interested in portrait painting, moved to Paris, Ky., set up shop; painted portrait of Daniel Boone; went East, became very popular as portrait painter; at one time painted 80 portraits in 6 months; went to England with family, 1823-26, painted important people including Robert Owen; painted such people as John Marshall, John C. Calhoun, Daniel Webster, 1826-66. Died Boston, Apr. 1, 1866.

HARDING, Jesper, publisher; b. Phila., Nov. 5, 1799; s. George and Mary (Hudd) H.; m. Maria Wilson, at least 2 sons, William White, George. Apprenticed to publisher of U.S. Gazette, Phila.; opened publishing bus., 1815, added book binding to bus., by 1820; absorbed several jours. of Phila. into his bus. including Pa. Inquirer and Democratic Press; became largest publisher of Bibles in U.S.; erected paper mill, Phila., 1835, moved it to Trenton, N.J., operator, 1840-59; U.S. internal revenue collector for 1st Dist. of Pa., 1862-65. Died Phila., Aug. 21, 1865.

HARDING, Robert, clergyman; b. Nottinghamshire, Eng., Oct. 6, 1701. Ordained Jesuit priest, 1722; came to Am., 1732; worked as missionary in Pa. until 1749; pastor St. Joseph's Ch., Phila., 1749-59; became friendly with Protestants in area who later contbd. to bldg. of St. Mary's Ch., Phila., 1763; mem. Am. Philos. Assn., 1768. Died Phila., Sept. 1, 1772.

HARDING, Seth, naval officer; b. Eastham, Mass., Apr. 17, 1734; s. Theodore and Sarah (Hamilton) H.; m. Abigail Doane, Apr. 27, 1753; m. 2d, Ruth Reed, Nov. 24, 1760. In his youth served on mcht. vessels to West Indies, also during French and Indian War; assumed command brig Defence at start of Revolutionary War; consummated most brilliant Am. naval feat up to that time by forcing 2 Brit. armed transports in Mass. Bay to surrender, 1776; commanded Continental frigate Confederacy, 1778; became comdr. Diana, engaged in commerce raiding and convoy service between Am. and W.I. until captured, 1781; was exchanged in 1782, became 2d in command ship Alliance under John Barry; in mcht. service after war; ret. on capt.'s half-pay, 1807. Died Schoharie, N.Y., Nov. 20, 1814.

HARDING, William White, publisher; b. Phila., Nov. 1, 1830; s. Jesper and Maria (Wilson) H.; m. Catharine Hart, 6 children. Clk. bookstore of George S. Appleton, Phila., 1846-49; made partner in his father's publishing business, 1856; Sole propr. Pa. Inquirer and father's huge Bible-publishing bus., 1859, changed paper's name to The Phila. Inquirer; served as col. on staff of Gov. James Pollack during Civil War; maintained circulation to armies during war; his paper became a sch. for journalists; established paper mill, Manayunk Pa., 1864; 1st attempted to make paper out of wood (by permission of the inventor), received medal for this at Phila. Centennial Expn., 1876; ret. from active mgmt. of Inquirer, 1889. Died Phila., May 15, 1889.

HARDY, Josiah, colonial gov.; flourished circa 1715-63. Gov. of N.J., 1761-63, dismissed for violating his appointment orders, 1763; Brit. consul at Cadiz, Spain.

HARDY, Samuel, Continental congressman; b. Isle of Wight County, Va., 1758; s. Richard Hardy; grad. Coll. William and Mary, 1778. Admitted to Va. bar, 1781; elected to Va. Ho. of Dels., 1781; lt. gov. Va., 1782; del. Continental Congress, 1783-85; effective in keeping central govt. operating despite weaknesses of Articles of Confederation; mem. Phi Beta Kappa. Died N.Y.C., Oct. 17, 1785; buried St. Paul's Ch., N.Y.C.

HARE, Darius Dodge, congressman; b. nr. Adrian, O., Jan. 9, 1843; attended law dept. U. Mich. Entered U.S. Army as pvt., 1864, served during remainder of Civil War; assigned to spl. duty at hdqrs. of Maj. Gen. Canby after Civil War, later with Maj. Gen. Sheridan at New Orleans; discharged from army, 1866; admitted to the bar, 1867; began practice of law in Carey, O.; moved to Upper Sandusky, O., 1868; mayor Upper Sandusky, 1872-72; mem. U.S. Ho. of Reps. (Democrat) from Ohio, 52d-53d congresses, 1891-95. Died Upper Sandusky, Feb. 10, 1897; buried Oak Hill Cemetery, Upper Sandusky.

HARE, George Emlen, clergyman, educator; b. Phila., Sept. 4, 1808; s. Charles Willing and Ann (Emlen) H.; attended Dickinson Coll.; grad. Union Coll., Schenectady, N.Y., 1826; attended Gen. Theol. Sem., N.Y.C.; m. Elizabeth C. Hobart, June 4, 1830, at least 1 son Bishop William Hobart. Ordained deacon Episcopal Ch., Phila., 1829; ordained priest; pastor Trinity Ch., Princeton, N.J., 1834-43; asst. prof. Latin and Greek, U. Pa., 1844-45; headmaster acad., Phila., 1846-57; dean, faculty Episcopal tng. sch., Phila., 1857, sch. expanded, became Divinity Sch. of Protestant Episcopal Ch., prof. emeritus, 1889. Author: Christians and Their Offspring, a Holy People (sermon), 1840; Visions and Narratives of the Old Testament, 1889. Died Feb. 15, 1892.

HARE, Robert, chemist, educator; b. Phila., Jan. 17, 1781; s. Robert and Margaret (Willing) H.; studied chemistry under James Woodhouse; A.M., M.D. (both hon.), Yale, 1806; M.D. (hon.), Harvard, 1816; m. Harriett Clark, Sept. 11, 1811; 1 son, John Clark. Discovered oxy-hydrogen blow-pipe (source of highest degree of heat then known, which enabled him to fuse the most refractory substances and led to founding of platinum industry), 1801; prof. chemistry U. Pa.; inventor calorimeter, 1816; received 1st Rumford medal from Am. Acad. Arts and Scis., prof. chemistry Coll. William and Mary, 1818; prof. chemistry, med. dept. U. Pa., 1818-47; for discovery of mercury cathode in electrolysis of aqueous solutions of metallic salts, 1839; developed means of using tar for lighting; hon. mem. Smithsonian Instn.; inventor deflagrator, 1820; author chem. process for denarcotizing laudanum. Author: Brief View of the Policy and Resource of the United States, 1810; Chemical Aparatus and Manipulations, 1836; Compendium of the Course of Chemical Instruction in the Medical Department of the University of Pennsylvania, 1840. Died Phila., May 15, 1858.

HARING, John, Continental congressman; b. Tappan, N.Y., Sept. 28, 1739; attended sch., N.Y.C.; studied law. Admitted to the bar; practiced law in N.Y.C. and Rockland County (N.Y.); mem. Continental Congress, 1774, 75, 85-88; judge Orange County (N.Y.), 1774, 75, 78-88; mem. N.Y. Provincial congresses, 1775-77, pres. pro tem, 2d and 3d congresses; mem. N.Y. State Senate, 1781-82; mem. N.Y. State Bd. Regents, 1784; mem. N.Y. Conv. to consider U.S. Constn., 1788, voted to reject Constn.; mem. N.Y. Assembly, 1806. Died Blauveltville, N.Y., Apr. 1, 1809; buried Tappan Ch. Cemetery.

HARKEY, Simeon Walcher, clergyman; b. Iredell County, N.C., Dec. 3, 1811; grad. Lutheran Sem.,

1834; D.D. (hon.), Wittenburg Coll., 1852. Pastor, Woodsborough and Frederick, Md., 1834-50; prof. theology Ill. State U., 1850-67; in charge of English Mission, St. Louis, 1867-69. Author: Sermon on National Thanksgiving; True Greatness; Prisons for Women; Mission of the Lutheran Church. Died Knoxville, Ill., Mar. 1, 1889.

HARLAN, Aaron, congressman; b. Warren County, O., Sept. 8, 1802; attended pub. schs.; studied law. Admitted to Ohio bar, began practice in Xenia, 1825; mem. Ohio Ho. of Reps., 1832-33, Ohio Senate, 1838, 39, 49; moved to a farm nr. Yellow Springs, O., 1841, continued law practice; presdl. elector, 1844; del. Ohio Constl. Conv., 1850; mem. bd. trustees Antioch Coll., 1852; mem. U.S. Ho. of Reps. (Whig) from Ohio, 33d-35th congresses, 1853-59; served as lt. col. 94th Regt., Ohio Minutemen during Civil War, 1862; moved to San Francisco, 1864. Died San Francisco, Jan. 8, 1868; buried Laurel Hill Cemetery, San Francisco.

HARLAN, James, congressman; b. Mercer County, Ky., June 22, 1800; s. James and Sarah (Caldwell) H.; m. Eliza Davenport, Dec. 23, 1822, 9 children including James, John Marshall. Admitted to Ky. bar, 1823; pros. atty. Commonwealth of Ky., 1829-35; mem. U.S. Ho. of Reps. from Ky., 24th-25th congresses, 1835-39; sec. of state Ky., 1840-44; mem. lower house Ky. Legislature, 1845; atty. gen. Ky., 1851-63. Author: The Code of Practice in Civil and Criminal Cases, 1854. Died Frankfort, Franklin County, Ky., Feb. 18, 1863.

HARLAN, James, senator, univ. pres., jurist; b. Clark County, Ill., Aug. 26, 1820; s. Silas and Mary (Conley) H.; grad. Indiana Asbury U. (now De Pauw U.), 1845; m. Ann Eliza Peck, 1845. Prin., Ia. City Coll.; admitted to Ia. bar, 1848; pres. Ia. Wesleyan U., 1853-55, 69-70; mem. U.S. Senate from Ia., (Freesoiler) 1855-65, (Republican), 1867-73, U.S. sec. of interior, 1865-66, accused of corruption while in office, exonerated; presiding judge Ct. Commrs. of Ala. Claims, 1882-85. Died Mt. Pleasant, Ia., Oct. 5, 1889; buried Forest Home Cemetery, Mt. Pleasant, Ia.

HARLAN, Josiah, army officer, adventurer; b. Newlin Twp., Pa., June 12, 1799; s. Joshua and Sarah (Hinchman) H.; m. Elizabeth Baker, May 1, 1849, 1 child. Journeyed to Far East, 1823; asst. surgeon East India Co.; med. officer Col. George Pollock's Bengal Arty. in 1st Burmese war; left army, 1826, became friend of Shah Shooja-ool-Moolk (ex-king of Kabul), apptd. secret agt. to start revolution in Afghanistan, 1828 (unsuccessful); became friend of Maharajah Ranjit Singh (sovereign of Punjab), apptd. gov. of Goozerath; unable to dethrone Shah Shooja successfully, and returned to U.S. after Brit. intervention, 1841; raised Pa. regiment known as Harlan's Light Cavalry during Civil War, 1861; commd. col. and served in Army of Potomac until 1862. Died San Francisco, Oct. 1871.

HARLAN, Richard, naturalist, physician; b. Phila., Sept. 19, 1796; s. Joshua and Sarah (Hinchman) H.; grad. U. Pa., 1818; m. Margaret (Simons)Howell, Jan. 30, 1833. Prof. anatomy, surgeon Phila. Museum, 1821; mem. commn. to Canada and N.Y. to study epidemic of Asiatic cholera, 1822; corr. sec. Geol. Soc. of Pa., 1832-36; v.p. La. Med. Soc., 1843; Author: Anatomical Investigations, 1824; Fauna Americana, 1825; contbr. article "Critical Notices of Various Organic Remains Hitherto Discovered in North America" in Transactions, 1834. Died New Orleans, Sept. 30, 1843.

HARLAND, Thomas, watch and clock maker, silversmith; b. England, 1735; m. Hannah Leffingwell, 1779. Supposed to have come to Am. aboard a tea ship; opened shop as watch and clock maker and silversmith, Norwich, Conn.; superintended constrn. of fire engine, Norwich, 1788; became master craftsman by 1790; his shop produced some 200 watches and 40 clocks per year. Died Norwich, Mar. 31, 1807.

HARMANSON, John Henry, congressman; b. Norfolk, Va., Jan. 15, 1803; grad. Jefferson Coll., Washington, Miss. Moved to Avoyelles Parish, La., engaged in farming; admitted to the bar, practiced law; mem. La. Senate, 1844; mem. U.S. Ho. of Reps. (Democrat) from La., 29th-31st congresses, 1845-50. Died New Orleans, Oct. 24, 1850; buried Moreau Plantation Cemetery, Pointe Coupee Parish, La.

HARMAR, Josiah, army officer; b. Phila., Nov 10, 1753; m. Sarah Jenkins, Oct. 19, 1784. Served as maj. 3d Pa. Regt., 1776, lt. col. 6th Pa. Regt., 1777; served in Continental Army under Washington, 1778-80, Greene's div. in South, 1781-82; commd. col., 1783; Indian agt. for N.W. Territory, took part in Treaty of Ft. McIntosh, 1785; commd. brig. gen., 1787; commanded expdn. against Miami Indians, not entirely successful, 1790 (court of inquiry held, did not find against him); adj. gen. Pa., 1793-99. Died Phila., Aug. 20, 1813.

HARMON, Daniel Williams, fur trader; b. Bennington, Vt., Feb. 19, 1778; s. Daniel and Lucrecia (Dewey) H.; m. Elizabeth Harman, Oct. 10, 1805 (not legal marriage date). Clk., regional supt. for North-West Co., Man., Sask. and Alta., Can., 1800-10, worked in Brit. Columbia, 1810-19, eventually became partner. Author: Journal of Voyages and Travels in the Interior of North America, 1820. Died Montreal, Que., Can., Mar. 26, 1845.

HARNDEN, William Frederick, pioneer expressman; b. Reading, Mass., Aug. 23, 1812; s. Ameriah and Sally (Richardson) H.; m. Sarah Wright Fuller, Dec. 1835. Conductor, ticket agt. for Boston & Worcester R.R., 1834-39; established messenger service between N.Y.C. and Boston, 1839, established many European offices, 1840-41; induced about 100,000 workers to come to U.S. to furnish labor power for devel. of West, 1841. Died Jan. 14, 1845.

HARNETT, Cornelius, patriot, Continental congressman; b. Chowan County, N.C., Apr. 20, 1723; s. Cornelius and Mary (Holt) H.; m. Mary Harnett. Mem. N.C. Gen. Assembly from Wilmington, 1754-75; chmn. Cape Fear (N.C.) Sons of Liberty, 1765-66, a leader of opposition to Stamp Act; known as "Sam Adams of N.C.;" pres. N.C. Provincial Congress, 1776; mem. com. which drafted 1st N.C. state constn., author clause forbidding established ch. and guaranteeing religious freedom, 1776; mem. Continental Congress, 1777-80; a signer Articles of Confederation. Died while a British prisoner on parole, Wilmington, Apr. 28, 1781.

HARNEY, John Milton, poet; b. Sussex County, Del., Mar. 9, 1789; son of Thomas Harney; studied medicine; m. dau. of Judge John Rowan, 1814. Toured Europe, 1816-25; served in naval service of Buenos Aires. Author: Crystalina: A Fairy Tale; The Fever Dream; Echo and the Lover. Died Bardstown, Ky., Jan. 15, 1825.

HARNEY, William Selby, army officer; b. Haysboro, Tenn., Aug. 22, 1800; s. Thomas and Margaret (Hudson) H.; m. Mary Mullanphy, 1833; m. 2d, Mrs. St. Cyr; 3 children. Served as 2d lt. 10th U.S. Inf., 1818; participated in Seminole War; commd. lt. col., 1836; brevetted col., 1840; served as col. during Mexican War, 1846; brevetted brig. gen. for bravery, ranking cavalry officer, 1847; defeated Sioux Indians at Sand Hill on the Platte River, 1855; brig. gen. in command Dept. of Ore., 1858; as consequence of his mil. seizure of Island of San Juan (claimed by Brit. as part of Brit. Columbia), dispute with Gt. Britain led to his recall from Ore., 1860; commanded Dept. of West, 1861; ret. as maj. gen., 1863. Died Orlando, Fla., May 9, 1889.

HARPER, Alexander, congressman; b. nr. Belfast, Ireland, Feb. 5, 1786; studied law. Came to U.S., settled in Zanesville, O.; admitted to Ohio bar, 1813, began practice in Zanesville; mem. Ohio Ho. of Reps. 1820-21; pres. judge Ct. Common Pleas, 1822-36; mem. U.S. Ho. of Reps. (Whig) from Ohio, 25th, 28th-29th, 32d congresses, 1837-39, 43-47, 51-53; resumed law practice. Died Zanesville Dec. 1, 1860; buried Greenwood Cemetery, Zanesville.

HARPER, Fletcher, printer, publisher; b. Newtown, L.I., N.Y., Jan. 31, 1806; s. Joseph and Elizabeth (Kolyer) H.; m. Jane Freelove Lyon, 1825, 2 children. Joined firm later known as Harper & Bros., 1825; created Harper's Weekly, 1857, Harper's Bazaar, 1867; mgr. Harper's New Monthly Mag. (founded by brother James). Died N.Y.C., May 29, 1877; buried Greenwood Cemetery, Bklyn.

HARPER, Francis Jacob, congressman; b. Frankford, Pa., Mar. 5, 1800. Mem. Pa. Ho. of Reps., 1832; Pa. Senate, 1834-35; elected to U.S. Ho. of Reps. (Democrat) from Pa., 24th Congress, died before assembling of Congress. Died Frankford, Mar. 18, 1837; buried Frankford Cemetery, reinterred Congressional Cemetery, Washington, D.C., Dec. 1848.

HARPER, James, congressman; b. Castlederg, County Tyrone, Ireland, Mar. 28, 1780; attended pub. schs. Came to U.S., settled in Phila.; engaged in brick mfg., wholesale grocery bus., 1820-30; mem. U.S. Ho. of Reps. from Pa. as Clay Democrat, 23d Congress, 1835-37, as Whig, 24th Congress, 1837-39; mem. bd. guardians of the poor, bd. prison insps. Died Phila., Mar. 31, 1873; buried Laurel Hill Cemetery, Phila.

HARPER, James, publisher, mayor N.Y.C.; b. Newtown, L.I., N.Y., Apr. 13, 1795; s. Joseph and Elizabeth (Kolyer) H.; m. Maria Arcularius; m. 2d, Julia Thorne; 4 children. Apprenticed to a printer, 1811; established (with brother John) J & J Harper, 1817, admitted brothers Joseph Wesley and Fletcher as partners, changed firm name to Harper and Bros., 1833; 1st large printing job was 2,000-copy edition of Seneca's Morals; published Locke's Essay Concerning the Human Understanding, 1818; 1st to use steam-run presses; 1st to introduce electrotyping on large scale; originated idea of Harper's New Monthly Mag.; mayor N.Y.C., 1844. Died N.Y.C., Mar. 27, 1869.

HARPER, James Clarence, congressman; b. Cumberland County, Pa., Dec. 6, 1819; attended common schs., Ohio. Moved to Darke County, O., 1831, to Lenoir, N.C., 1840; land surveyor, civil engr., draftsman; laid out Town of Lenoir, 1841; engaged in merc. bus., later in mfg. cotton and woolen goods; served as col. N.C. Militia; mem. N.C. Ho. of Commons, 1865-66; mem. U.S. Ho. of Reps. (Conservative) from N.C., 42d Congress, 1871-73. Died nr. Patterson, N.C., Jan. 8, 1890; buried Cemetery at Harpers Chapel, Patterson.

HARPER, John Adams, congressman; b. Derryfield, N.H., Nov. 2, 1779; attended Phillips Exeter (N.H.) Acad., 1794; studied law. Admitted to N.H. bar, circa 1802, began practice in Sanbornton; 1st postmaster of Sanborton; moved to Meredith Bridge (now Laconia), N.H., 1806; clk. N.H. Senate, 1805-08; mem. N.H. Ho. of Reps., 1809-10; served with N.H. Militia, 1809-12; mem. U.S. Ho. of Reps. (War Democrat) from N.H., 12th Congress, 1811-13. Died Meredith Bridge, June 18, 1816; buried Union Cemetery, Meredith Bridge.

HARPER, Joseph Morrill, congressman; b. Limerick, Me., June 21, 1787; attended Fryeburg, Acad.; studied medicine. Practiced medicine, Sanbornton, N.H., 1810, Canterbury, N.H., 1811; served as asst. surgeon 4th Inf., U.S. Army, War of 1812; mem. N. H. Ho. of Reps., 1826-27; justice of peace, Canterbury, 1826-65; mem. N.H. Senate, 1829-30, pres., 1830; ex offico gov. N.H., 1831; mem. U.S. Ho. of Reps. (Democrat) from N.H., 22d-23d congresses, 1831-34; justice of the peace and quorum, 1835-65; pres. Mechanics' Bank of Concord, 1847-56. Died Canterbury, Jan. 15, 1865; buried Village Cemeter, Canterbury.

HARPER, Robert Goodloe, senator; b. Fredericksburg, Va., Jan. 1765; s. Jesse and Diana (Goodloe) H.; grad. Princeton, 1785, LL.D., 1820; m. Catherine Carroll, May 1801. Admitted to S.C. bar, 1786; mem. U.S. Ho. of Reps. from S.C., 3d-6th congresses, Feb. 9, 1795-1801, elected as Republican, became a leader in Federalist Party, chmn. ways and means com., 1799-1801; organizer Balt. Exchange Co.; maj. gen. Md. Militia, 1814; mem. U.S. Senate from Md., 1816-22; unsuccessful candidate (Federalist) for vice pres. U.S., 1816; an original mem. Am. Colonization Soc. Died Balt., Jan. 14, 1825; buried Greenmount Cemetery, Balt. Died Apr. 15, 1825.

HARPER, William, senator, jurist; b. Antigua, Brit. West Indies, Jan. 17, 1790; s. John Harper; grad. S.C. Coll. (now U. S.C.), 1808; m. Catherine Coalter, July 4, 1816. Admitted to S.C. bar, 1813; chancellor Mo. Territory, 1819-21, State of Mo., 1821-23; reporter S.C. Supreme Ct., 1823-25; mem. U.S. Senate from S.C., Mar. 28-Dec. 7, 1826; speaker S.C. Ho. of Reps., 1828; chancellor S.C., 1828-30, 35-47; judge S.C. Ct. of Appeals, 1830-35; del. S.C. Nullification Conv., wrote nulificataion ordinance, 1832. Author: Memoir on Slavery (pro-slavery argument), 1837. Died Columbia, S.C., Oct. 10, 1847.

HARPUR, Robert, educator, colonial ofcl.; b. Ballybay, Ireland, Jan. 25, 1731; s. Andrew and Elizabeth (Creighton) H.; ed. U. Glasgow; m. Elizabeth Crygier, Sept. 29, 1773; m. 2d, Myra Lackey, Apr. 1789; 5 children. Came to Am., 1761; prof. mathematics and natural philosophy King's Coll. (now Columbia), N.Y.C., 1761-67, 1st librarian, 1762-67; mem. 3d, 4th Provincial congresses, 1776-77; sec. of regents U. State N.Y., 1784, mem. and clk. bd. trustees, 1787-95; mem. N.Y. Council of Safety; mem. N.Y. Assembly, 1777-84; dep. sec. of state N.Y., 1795; sec. N.Y. Land Bd.; interested in possibilities of Am. frontier; founder Village of Harpursville (N.Y.), 1795.

HARRAH, Charles Jefferson, promoter, b. Phila. Jan. 1, 1817; s. John Hurrah; m. Anna Margaret Riehl, Apr. 14, 1839. Began working in shipyards in Phila., 1836; established shipyard in Brazil, 1843-52; returned to Brazil 1858, to construct mountainous portion Dom Pedro II R.R., completed constrn. in 6 years, but was financially ruined; entered merc. bus. to recoup losses; cooperated in organizing Bot. Garden R.R. Co., constructed and operated 1st street railroad in Brazil), 1868; pres. 1st telegraph co. in Brazil; aided in formation Brazilian Navigation Co., engaged in confidential mission for the Emperor; established 1st pub. sch. in Rio de Janeiro, 1870; returned to Phila., 1873; pres. Peoples' Passenger Ry. Phila., Midvale Steel Works; mem. hosp. and charity bds. Died Phila., Feb. 18, 1890.

HARRELL, John, clergyman; b. Perquimans County, N.C., Oct. 21, 1806; m. Eliza Williams, 1832. Licensed to preach, 1823; admitted to Tenn. Conf., 1829; preacher in Ark. Dist. of Mo. Conf., 1831; organized 1st preaching circuit among Cherokees; preached in Indian Mission Conf., 1850-76; chaplain Confederate Army during Civil War; supt., pres.

Indian Mission Conf. Died Dec. 8, 1876; buried Old Asbury Mission, Eufala, Okla.

HARRIMAN, Walter, army officer, gov. N.H.; b. Warner, N.H., Apr. 8, 1817; s. Benjamin Evans and Hannah (Flanders) H.; m. Apphia K. Hoyt, Sept. 1841; m. 2d, Almira Andrews, Oct. 1844; 3 children. Ordained to ministry Universalist Ch., minister, 10 years; mem. N.H. Ho. of Reps., 1849-51, 53-54, 58-59; mem. commn. for classification of Indian lands in Kan., 1856; mem. N.H. Senate, 1859-61; editor, part owner Union Democrat (renamed Weekly Union) in N.H., 1861; commd. col. 11th N.H. Volunteers, 1862-65; served at 1st Battle of Fredricksburg, 1862; commanded a brigade at Battle of Petersburg; brevetted brig. gen. U.S. Volunteers, 1865; sec. of state N.H., 1865; gov. N.H. (Republican), 1867-68; U.S. naval officer for Port of Boston, 1869-77; mem. N.H. Legislature, 1881. Author: History of Warner, N.H., 1879. Died Concord, N.H., July 25, 1884.

HARRINGTON, Henry William, congressman; b. nr. Cooperstown, N.Y., Sept. 12, 1825; entered Temple Hill Acad., Livingston County, N.Y., 1845; studied law, Geneseo, N.Y. Admitted to N.Y. bar, 1848, began practice in Nunda; moved to Madison, Ind., 1856, practiced law; moved to St. Louis, 1872, returned to Ind., 1874, settled in Indpls.; del. Nat. Dem. Conv., 1860, 68, 72; mem. U.S. Ho. of Reps. (democrat) from Ind., 38th Congress, 1963-65; collector of internal revenue for 3d Dist. of Ind., 1866-67. Died Indpls., Mar. 20, 1882; buried Evergreen Cemetery, Alpena, Mich.

HARRINGTON, Samuel Maxwell, jurist, railroad pres.; b. Dover, Del., Feb. 5, 1803; grad. with 1st honors, Washington Coll., (Md.), 1823; LL.D. (hon.), Del. Coll., 1845; m. Mary Lofland, 1836. Admitted to Dover bar, 1826; sec. of state Md., 1828-30; chief justice Del. Supreme Ct., 1830; asso. justice Del. Superior Ct., 1832-35, also ct. reporter, compiled 5 vols. of reports and prepared code whereby state legislature revised statute law of Del., chief justice, 1855-57; pres. Eastern Shore R.R., 1952; developer Del. R.R.; chancellor Del., 1857-65. Died Phila., Nov. 28, 1865.

HARRIS, Benjamin, journalist, publisher; b. Eng.; flourished 1673-1716. Publisher and journalist London, Eng., until 1686; an Anabaptist, joined with Shaftesbury, the Whigs and Titus Oates in exposing Popish Plot, 1679; with failure Monmouth's Rebellion and acession James II, came to Boston, 1686, became 1st Am. journalist; publisher Boston Almanach, 1687; published Publick Occurrences Both Forreign and Domestick (1st newspaper printed in America, contained mostly Am. news, 1st issue suppressed), 1690; published famous New Eng. Primer, also opened coffee house, 1690; ofcl. printer to gov. Mass., 1692; returned to London, 1695, published Intelligence Domestick and Foreign, 1695, London Post, 1699-1706.

HARRIS, Benjamin Gwinn, congressman; b. nr. Leonardtown, Md., Dec. 13, 1805; attended Yale, Cambridge (Mass.) Law Sch. Admitted to the bar, 1840; mem. Md. Ho. of Dels., 1833, 36; mem. U.S. Ho. of Reps. (Democrat) from Md., 38th-39th congresses, 1863-67; tried by a mil. ct., Washington, D.C., for harboring 2 paroled Confederate soldiers, sentenced to 3 years imprisonment, disqualified from holding any govtl. office, sentence later remitted by Pres. Andrew Johnson. Died "Ellenborough" nr. Leonardtown, Apr. 4, 1895; buried family burying ground, "Ellenborough."

HARRIS, Caleb Fiske, mcht., bibliophile; b. Warwick, R.I., Mar. 9, 1818; s. Dr. Stephen and Eliza (Greene) H.; attended Brown U.; m. Emily Stevenson Davis, Jan. 17, 1866. Engaged in commission business, N.Y.C., circa 1836-56; collected over 4,000 books, many rare, bequeathed collection to Brown U. Died by drowning in Moosehead Lake, Me., Oct. 2. 1881.

HARRIS, Chapin Aaron, dentist; b. Pompey N.Y., May 6, 1806; s. John and Elizabeth (Brundage) H. A.M., M.D.; m. Lucinda Heath Hawley, Jan. 11, 1826, 9 children. Licensed as dentist by Med. and Chirurg. Faculty of Md., Balt., 1833; editor Am. Journal Dental Science (1st dental periodical), 1839; organizer Balt. Coll. of Dental Surgery (world's 1st dental coll.), 1839, 1st dean, 1st prof. operative dentistry and dental prosthesis, 1840-44, pres., 1844-60; an organizer Am. Soc. of Dental Surgeons (1st nat. dental assn.), 1840, 1st corr. sec., pres. 1844; an organizer Am. Dental Conv., 1855, pres., 1856-57. Author: The Dental Art, a Practical Treatise on Dental Surgery, 1839; translator: A Treatise on Second Dentition (C.F. Delabarre), 1845; Complete Elements of the Science and Art of the Dentist (A.M. Desiraback), 1847; editor: Natural History and Diseases of the Human Teeth (Joseph Fox). Died Balt., Sept. 29, 1860; buried Mt. Olivet Cemetery, Balt.

HARRIS, Charles Murray, congressman; b. Munfordsville, Ky., Apr. 10, 1821; attended common schs.; studied law. Admitted to Ky. bar; moved to Ill., settled in Oquawka, practiced law; mem. U.S. Ho. of Reps. (Democrat) from Ill., 38th Congress, 1863-65, unsuccessful candidate for re-election, 1864. Died Chgo., Sept. 20, 1896; buried Oquawka.

HARRIS, Daniel Lester, engr.; b. Providence, R. I., Feb. 6, 1818; s. Allen and Hart (Lester) H.; grad. Wesleyan U., 1838; m. Harriet Corson, May 25, 1843, 11 children. Engr. for Erie R.R., also Troy-Schenectady R.R., 1839-43; mem. engring. firm Boody, Stone & Harris, Springfield, Mass., 1845-79; an owner Howe Truss patent, designed many railroad bridges for firm; pres. Conn. River R.R. 1856-79; mem. Mass. Legislature, 1857, 73; mayor Springfield, 1860; dir. U.P. R.R., from 1869; sec. Eastern R.R. Assn., 1866-78. Died Springfield, July 11, 1879; buried Springfield.

HARRIS, Elisha, physician, public health ofcl.; b. Westminister, Vt., Mar 5, 1824; s. James and Eunice (Foster) H.; grad. Columbia Coll. Phys. and Surg., N.Y.C., 1849; m. Eliza Andrews, 1849. Supt., quarantine hosp., Staten Island, N.Y., 1855; mem. Nat. Quarantine and Sanitary Assn., largely responsible for code of marine hygiene adopted 1860; an organizer, mem. U.S. Sanitary Commn., 1861; designer railroad hosp. car; originator system of nat. records of death and burial of soldiers; sec. Council of Hygiene, also Citizens' Assn. N.Y.; registrar of records N.Y.C. Bd. of Health, later sanitary supt.; organizer 1st free public vaccination service, 1869; an organizer, 1st sec. Am. Public Health Assn., pres., 1877; registrar of vital statistics N.Y. State, 1873-76; original commr., sec. N.Y. State Bd. Health, 1880. Died Albany, N.Y., Jan. 31, 1884.

HARRIS, George Washington, humorist; b. Allegheny City, Pa., Mar. 20, 1814; m. Mary Nance, Sept. 3, 1835; m. 2d, Mrs. Jane Pride, Oct. 1869; 6 children. Capt. of steamboat Knoxville, out of Knowville, Tenn., 1835; contbr. articles to Argus (Whig paper), Knoxville, 1839; in jewelry business, Knoxville, from 1843; contbr. Tenn. local humor pieces to N.Y.C. Spirit of the Times, 1843-57; known for stories involving mountaineer character Sut Lovingood (appeared in many newspapers in Tenn.); postmaster Knoxville, 1857-58; supt. Wills Valley R.R., 1866-69. Author: The Sut Lovinggood Yarns, 1867. Died Knoxville, Dec. 11, 1869; buried Knoxville.

HARRIS, Ira, senator, jurist; b. Charleston, N.Y., May 31, 1802; s. Frederic Waterman and Lucy (Hamilton) H.; grad. Union Coll., 1824; m. Louisa Tubbs, before 1845; m. 2d, Mrs. Pauline Penny Rathbone; 6 children. Admitted to N.Y. bar, 1827; a founder Albany (N.Y.) Med. Coll., 1838; mem. N.Y. Assembly, 1844-47; mem. N.Y. Senate, 1847; judge N.Y. Supreme Ct., 1847-59; trustee, chancellor U. Rochester, 1850-75; mem. faculty Albany Law Sch., 1851-75; mem. U.S. Senate (Republican) from N.Y., 1861-67; trustee Vassar Coll., Union Coll. Died Albany, Dec. 2, 1875.

HARRIS, Isham Green, senator, gov. Tenn.; b. Tullahoma, Tenn., Feb. 10, 1818; s. Isham Green and Lucy (Davidson) H.; m. Martha Travis, 1843, 8 children. Admitted to Tenn. bar, 1841; mem. Tenn. Senate, 1847-48; mem. U.S. Ho. of Reps. from Tenn., 31st-32d congresses, 1849-53; gov. Tenn., 1857-63, strongly advocated secession and alignment with Confederacy; served as aide-de-camp to generals Albert Sidney Johnston, G.T. Beauregard, Braxton Bragg, Joseph E. Johnston, Joseph B. Hood, participated in all Civil War battles in Tenn. and N. Ga., 1862-65; mem. U.S. Senate from Tenn., 1877-97, pres. pro tem, 1893-95. Died Washington, D.C., July 8, 1897; buried Elmwood Cemetery, Memphis, Tenn.

HARRIS, John, trader; b. Harris Ferry, Pa., 1726; s. John and Esther (Say) H.; m. Elizabeth McClure. Propr. of Indian trading post, from 1748; leader in protecting frontier settlements in Pa. from Indian attack; built stockade at post at Paxtang on Susquehanna, during French and Indian War (1756-63); maintained close relations with Indian tribes of Six Nations; established Town of Harrisburg (named for him), 1785 (became seat of Dauphin County, Pa.). Died Harrisburg, July 29, 1791; buried Harrisburg.

HARRIS, John, congressman; b. Harris Ferry (now Harrisburg), Pa., Sept. 26, 1760; moved to Aurelias, N.Y., 1789; operated 1st ferry across Cayuga Lake; Indian interpreter; opened 1st store and tavern in Cayuga County (N.Y.), 1789; apptd. col. N.Y. State Militia, 1806; mem. U.S. Ho. of Reps. from N.Y., 10th Congress, 1807-09; commanded 158th N.Y. Regt. during War of 1812. Died Bridgeport, N.Y., Nov. 1824; buried local cemetery.

HARRIS, John Woods, lawyer; b. Nelson County, Va., 1810; grad. U. Va., 1837; m. Annie Fisher, 1852. Went to Tex., 1837; mem. 1st Congress Republic of Tex., 1839, chmn. judiciary com., 1841 (made successful proposal to abolish Mexican laws, replacing with common law on jurisprudence of Republic, but retaining Spanish "community property" system, an innovation in Anglo-Saxon countries, later adopted by some other states); 1st atty. gen. State of Tex., 1846; mem. com. to revise Tex. laws, 1854; mem. 14th Tex. Legislature (which passed bill calling for Tex. Constl. Conv. 1875), 1874-75. Died Galveston, Tex., Apr. 1, 1887.

HARRIS, Joseph, journalist; b. Shrewsbury, Eng., June 29, 1828; s. Henry and Anne (Webb) H.; studied with Sir Joseph Gilbert at Rothansted farm in Eng. Came to U.S., 1849, settled in N.Y.C.; became regular contbr. to agrl. journals; asso. editor mag. Country Gentleman, N.Y.C., 1855; propr. Genesee Farmer (agrl. mag.), circa 1857-66; contbr. Am. Agriculturist, 1866-92; operated seed bus., Coldwater, N.Y., 1879-92. Author: Harris on the Pig, 1870; Talks on Manure, 1878; Gardening for Young and Old, 1883. Died "Moreton Farm," nr. Rochester, N.Y., Nov. 18, 1892; buried Rochester.

HARRIS, Mark, congressman; b. Ipswich, Mass., Jan. 27, 1779; attended common schs. Moved to Portland, Mass. (now Me.), 1800; engaged as mcht.; mem. Mass. Senate, 1816; mem. U.S. Ho. of Reps. from Me., 17th Congress, Dec. 2, 1822-23; mem. Me. Ho. of Reps., 1830; treas. Cumberland County (Me.), 1824-32, 34-40; treas. State of Me., 1828, 32-34; moved to N.Y.C., 1842, engaged as mcht. Died N.Y.C., Mar. 2, 1843; buried (probably) Old Eastern Cemetery, Portland.

HARRIS, Moses (Black), pioneer scout; traveled with William Sublette in N.W., 1827; adj. to Thomas Fitzpatrick of Am. Fur Co. on ann. pack train, 1836; led party to Ore., 1844; renowned scout and mountain man, specialist in winter and solitary travel.

HARRIS, Robert, congressman; b. Harris Ferry (now Harrisburg), Pa., Sept. 5, 1768; attended pub. schs. Assisted in building bridge over Susquehanna River, orgn. Harrisburg Bank, constrn. Middletown Turnpike Rd.; surveyor to lay out road from Chambersburg (Pa.) to Pitts., also for improving Susquehanna River; apptd. commr. to choose location of Pa. capitol bldg., Harrisburg; paymaster U.S. Army during War of 1812; mem. U.S. Ho. of Reps., 18th-19th congresses, 1823-27; prothonotary Dauphin County. Died Harrisburg, Sept. 3, 1851; buried Harrisburg Cemetery.

HARRIS, Sampson Willis, congressman; b. Elbert County, Ga., Feb. 23, 1809; grad. U. Ga., 1828; studied law. Admitted to Ga. bar, 1830, began practice in Athens; mem. Ga. Ho. of Reps., 1834-35; moved to Wetumpka, Ala., 1838; elected solicitor 8th circuit, 1841; mem. Ala. Senate, 1844-45; mem. U.S. Ho. of Reps. (Democrat) from Ga., 30th-34th congresses, 1847-57. Died Washington, D.C., Apr. 1, 1857; buried Oconee Cemetery, Athens.

HARRIS, Samuel, clergyman, coll. pres.; b. East Machias, Me., June 14, 1814; s. Josiah and Lucy (Talbot) H.; grad. Bowdoin Coll., 1833, LL.D., 1871; attended Andover Theol. Sem., 1835-38; D.D. (hon.) Williams Coll., 1855; A.M. (hon.), Yale, 1872; m. Deborah Robbins Dickinson, Apr. 30, 1839; m. 2d, Mrs. Mary Sherman Skinner Fitch, Oct. 11, 1877. Prin. Limerick (Me.) Acad., 1833-34; ordained to ministry Congl. Ch., 1841; pastor Congl. Ch., Conway, Mass., 1841-51; pastor South Congl. Ch., Pittsfield, Mass., 1851-55; prof. systematic theology Bangor Theol. Sem., 1851-55; pres., prof. mental and moral philosophy Bowdoin Coll., 1867-71; Dwight prof. systematic theology Yale Divinity Sch., 1871-95. Author: Zaccheus: The Scriptural Plans of Beneficience, 1844; Kingdom of Christ on Earth, 1874; The Philosophical Basis of Theism, 1883; The Self-Revelation of God, 1886; God the Creator and Lord of All, 1896. Died Litchfield, Conn., June 25, 1899.

HARRIS, Samuel Smith, clergyman; b. Autauga County, Ala., Sept. 14, 1841; grad. U. Ala., 1859, LL.D. (hon.), 1879; D.D. (hon.) Coll. William and Mary, 1874. Admitted to Ala. bar, 1860; ordained to ministry Presbyn. Ch., 1869; pastor, Montgomery, Ala., Columbus, O., New Orleans, Chgo., 1870-88; del. Gen. Conv., 1874, 77; founder, editor Living Church, 1878-89; bishop Diocese of Mich., 1879-88. Died Detroit, Aug. 21, 1888.

HARRIS, Thaddeus Mason, clergyman; b. Charlestown, Mass., July 7, 1768; s. William and Rebekah (Mason) H.; grad. Harvard, 1787, A.M., 1790, S.T.D. (hon.), 1813; m. Mary Dix, Jan. 28, 1795, 1 son, Thaddeus William. Licensed to preach, 1789; librarian Harvard, 1791-93, later overseer; ordained minister Unitarian Ch., 1793; pastor 1st Ch., Dorchester, Mass., 1793-1839; disliked denominational titles, believed doctrine of Trinity to be contradictory, believed in atonement and supernatural grace; edited Mass. Mag., 1795, 96; librarian Mass. Hist. Soc., 1837-42; supt. pub. schs., Dorchester; satirized by Leonard Withington (writing under name John Oldbury) as Dr. Snivelwell in The Puritan. Author: Discourses in Favor of Free Masonry, 1803; Journal of a Tour of the Territory Northwest of the Alleghany Mountains (based on Western tour 1802), 1805; A Natural History of the Bible, 1821; Memoirs of James Ogelthorpe, 1841. Died Dorchester, Apr. 3, 1842.

HARRIS, Thaddeus William, entomologist, librarian; b. Dorchester, Mass., Nov. 12, 1795; s. Thaddeus Mason and Mary (Dix) H.; grad. Harvard, 1815; med. degree, 1820; m. Catherine Holbrook, 1824. Librarian, Harvard, 1831-56; instr. in nat. history, 1837-42; mem. com. apptd. to make bot. and geol. survey of Mass., 1837. Author: A Treatise, Some of the Insects of New England Which are Injurious to Vegetation, 1842. Died Jan. 16, 1856.

HARRIS, Thomas K., congressman; studied law, Admitted to Tenn. bar; practiced law in Sparta and McMinnville (Tenn.); trustee Priestly Acad., Sparta; mem. Tenn. Senate, 1809-11; mem. U.S. Ho. of Reps. (Democrat) from Tenn., 13th Congress, 1813-15. Died from wounds received in an encounter with Col. John W. Simpson at Shells Ford of Collins River, between Sparta and McMinnville, Mar. 18, 1816.

HARRIS, Thomas Langrell, congressman; b. Norwich, Conn., Oct. 29, 1816; grad. Washington (now Trinity) Coll., Hartford, Conn., 1841; studied law. Admitted to the bar, 1842; began practice of law, Petersburg, Menard County, Ill.; sch. commr. Menard County, 1845; raised and commanded a co. during Mexican War, joined 4th Regt., Ill. Volunteer Inf., later elected maj. of the regt.; elected mem. Ill. Senate (in absentia), 1846; presented with sword by State of Ill. for gallantry at Battle of Cerro Gordo; mem. U.S. Ho. of Reps. (Democrat), from Ill. 31st, 34th-35th congresses, 1849-51, 55-58. Died Springfield, Ill., Nov. 24, 1858; buried Rose Hill Cemetery, Petersburg, Ill.

HARRIS, Townsend, mcht., diplomat; b. Sandy Hill, N.Y., Oct. 3, 1804; s. Jonathan Harris. Elected to N.Y.C. Bd. of Edn., 1846, pres., 2 years; a founder N.Y. Free Coll. (now Coll. City N.Y.); acquired ship, engaged in S. Pacific trade, 1847; Am. consul at Ning-Po, China, 1854; 1st U.S. consul gen. in Japan (apptd. under provisions of Treaty of 1854 effected by Commodore Perry), 1855, became minister resident and consul gen., 1859; en route to Japan, negotiated comml. treaty with Siam; one of few westerners who had influence in an Eastern govt.; resigned, 1861. Died N.Y.C., Feb. 25, 1878.

HARRIS, Wiley Pope, congressman; b. Pike County, Miss., Nov. 9, 1818; s. Early and Mary Vivian (Harrison) H.; m. Frances Mayes, 1851. Elected circuit judge 2d Dist. Miss., 1847; del. Miss. Constl. Conv., 1851; mem. U.S. Ho. of Reps. from Miss., 33d Congress, 1853-55; mem. Miss. Constl. Conv. which adopted secession, 1861; del. Provisional Congress of Confederate States Am., 1861; mem. Miss. Constl. Conv., 1890. Died Jackson, Miss., Dec. 3, 1891; buried Greenwood Cemetery, Jackson.

HARRIS, William, clergyman, coll. pres.; b. Springfield, Mass., Apr. 29, 1765; s. Daniel and Sarah (Pynchon) H.; grad. Harvard, 1786, A.M. (hon.), 1789, S.T.D. (hon.); S.T.D. (hon.), Columbia, 1811; m. Martha Clark, Nov. 3, 1791. Ordained deacon, priest Protestant Episcopal Ch., 1791; prin. acad., Marblehead, Mass.; rector St. Mark's in the Bowery, N.Y.C., 1802; pres. Columbia, 1811-29, initiated planning, opening Columbia Grammar Sch. Died N.Y.C., Oct. 18, 1829.

HARRIS, William Alexander, congressman; diplomat; b. nr. Warrenton, Va., Aug. 24, 1805; studied law. Admitted to Va. bar, began practice in Luray; mem. Va. Ho. of Dels., 1830-31; Democratic presdl. elector, 1840; mem. U.S. Ho. of Reps. (Democrat) from Va., 27th Congress, 1841-43; editor Spectator and Constitution, Washington, D.C.; chargé d'affaires to Argentine Republic, 1846-51; editor Washington Union, also printer to U.S. Senate, 1857-59. Died Pike County, Mo., Mar. 28, 1864; buried Riverview Cemetery, Louisiana, Mo.

HARRIS, William Littleton, jurist; b. Elbert County, Ga., July 6, 1807; s. Jeptha and Sarah (Hunt) H.; grad. U. Ga., 1825; m. Frances Semmes, May 13, 1830. Admitted to bar, Ga., 1826, began practice of law, Washington, Ga.; practiced in Columbus, Miss., 1837-53; judge Miss. Circuit Ct., 1853-57; judge Miss. High Ct. of Appeals, 1857-58, 65; commr. to Ga. from Miss., Dec. 1860; continued as circuit judge in Miss. under Confederate Govt.; strong supporter of Confederacy; resigned as judge, 1867, practiced law, Memphis, Tenn., until 1868. Died Memphis, Nov. 26, 1868.

HARRIS, William Logan, clergyman; b. Mansfield, O., Nov. 14, 1817; s. James and Mary (Logan) H.; ed. Norwalk (O.) Sem.; m. Anna Atwell, Aug. 9, 1840. Converted to Methodism, 1834; ordained deacon Meth. Episcopal Ch., 1839, elder, 1841; tutor Ohio Wesleyan U., 1845-46, prin. academic dept., 1851, prof. chemistry and natural sci., 1852; prin. Baldwin Inst., Berea, O., 1848; mem., sec. annual Gen. confs., 1856-72, opposed membership for slave-holders; asst. corr. sec. Missionary Soc., 1860-72; became bishop Meth. Episcopal Ch., 1872. Author: Powers of the General Conference . . . The Relation of the Episcopacy to the General Conference, 1854. Died Bklyn., Sept. 2, 1887.

HARRISON, Albert Galliton, congressman; b. Mount Sterling, Ky., June 26, 1800; grad. Transylvania U., Lexington, Ky., 1820; studied law. Admitted to Ky. bar, began practice in Mount Sterling; moved to Fulton, Mo., 1827, practiced law; mem. bd. visitors U.S. Mil. Acad., 1828; mem. commn. to adjust land titles arising from Spanish grants, 1820-35; mem. U.S. Ho. of Reps. (Van Buren Democrat) from Mo., 24th-25th congresses, 1835-39. Died Fulton, Sept. 7, 1839; buried Congressional Cemetery, Washington, D.C.

HARRISON, Benjamin, gov. Va., Continental congressman; b. "Berkeley," Charles City County, Va., circa 1726; s. Benjamin and Anne (Carter) H.; ed. Coll. William and Mary; m. Elizabeth Bassett, circa 1745; children—Benjamin, William Henry. Mem. Va. Ho. of Burgesses, 1749-75, frequently speaker, mem. com. that drew up Va.'s protest to Stamp Act although he opposed Patrick Henry's resolutions, 1764; mem. Va. Revolutionary Conv., 1775; mem. Continental Congress from Va., 1774-78, mem. bd. war and ordnance, also marine com.; mem. Va. Ho. of Dels., 1776-82, 87-91, speaker, 1778-82, 85, 86; signer Declaration of Independence, 1776, Articles of Confedn., 1777; mem. Va. Conv. to ratify U.S. Constn., 1788; gov. Va., 1782-84. Died Charles City, Va., Apr. 24, 1791.

HARRISON, Carter Bassett, congressman; b. Charles City County, Va.; s. Benjamin Harrison; attended Coll. William and Mary. Mem. Va. Ho. of Dels., 1784-86, 1805-08; mem. U.S. Ho. of Reps. from Va., 3d-5th congresses, 1793-99. Died at the Maycock plantation, Prince George County, Va., Apr. 18, 1808.

HARRISON, Carter Henry, congressman, mayor Chgo.; b. Lexington, Ky., Feb. 15, 1825; s. Carter Henry and Caroline (Russell) H.; grad. Yale, 1845; LL.B., Transylvani U., 1855; m. Sophorisba Preston, 1855; m. 2d, Marguerite Stearns, 1882; 1 son, Carter Henry (5 times mayor Chgo.). County commr. Cook County (Ill.), 1871-74; mem. U.S. Ho. of Reps. from Ill., 44th-45th congresses, 1875-79; mayor Chgo., 1879-87, 93; unsuccessful candidate for gov. Ill., 1884; owner Chgo. Times. Author: A Race with the Sun, 1890. Assassinated by a disappointed officer-seeker, Oct. 28, 1893.

HARRISON, Christopher, artist; b. Cambridge, Md., 1775; ed. St. John's Coll. Confidential clk. to mcht., Balt.; moved to Jefferson County, Ind., circa 1808, to Salem, Ind., 1815; engaged in farming, storekeeping, painting; elected 1st lt. gov. Ind., 1816; a commr. to lay out and survey site of Indpls.; returned to Md., circa 1830. Died Md., 1863.

HARRISON, Gessner, educator; b. Harrisonburg, Va., June 26, 1807; s. Peachy and Mary (Stuart) H.; M.D., U. Va., 1828; m. Eliza Tucker, Dec. 1830, 6 sons, 3 daus. Prof. of Greek, U. Va., 1828-59, established several publs. (adopted as classical texts in other colls.), employed study of comparative grammar as means of learning Greek; owned and conducted pvt. boarding sch. for boys, Nelson County, Va., 1859-62. Author: The Geography of Ancient Italy and Southern Greece (pamphlet), 1834; Exposition of Some of the Laws of the Latin Grammar, 1852; Treatise on the Greek Prepositions, 1858. Died Nelson County, Apr. 7, 1862; buried Nelson County.

HARRISON, Horace Harrison, congressman; b. Lebanon, Tenn., Aug. 7, 1829; attended Carroll Acad. Moved to McMinnville, Tenn., 1841; clk. county ct., master chancery ct., register of deeds; clk. Tenn. Senate, 1851-52; admitted to Tenn. bar, 1857, began practice at McMinnville; moved to Nashville, 1859, practiced law; U.S. dist. atty., 1863-66, 72-73; chancellor Nashville div. Tenn. Ct. Chancery, 1866; judge Tenn. Supreme Ct., 1867-68; Republican presdl. elector, 1868-84; mem. U.S. Ho. of Reps. (Rep.) from Tenn., 43d Congress, 1873-75, unsuccessful candidate for re-election; del. Rep. Nat. Conv., Chgo., 1880; mem. Tenn. Legislature, 1880-81. Died Nashville, Dec. 20, 1885; buried Mt. Olivet Cemetery, Nashville.

HARRISON, James, mfr.; b. Bourbon County, Ky., Oct. 10, 1803; s. John and Betsy (McLanahan) H.; m. Maria Prewitt, 1832, 4 children. Moved to Fayette, Mo., entered grain bus., 1822; conducted many trading expdns. to Chihuahua, Mexico, maintained trading posts for Indians in Ark., 1834-40; a promoter Am. Iron Mountain Co., St. Louis (became one of leading iron ore producers in nation), 1843; established Chouteau, Harrison & Valle (firm which constructed largest rolling mill in West), 1850; a founder Iron Mountain R.R. Co., circa 1852; Confederate supporter during Civil War. Died St. Louis, Aug. 3, 1870; buried St. Louis.

HARRISON, John, mfg. chemist; b. Phila., Dec. 17, 1773; s. Thomas and Sarah (Richards) H.; studied chemistry under J.B. Priestly; m. Lydia Leib, Nov. 27, 1802; 8 children, including George Leib, Thomas, Michael. Served as capt. Phila. Militia, 1792; 1st mfg. chemist in U.S., 1801; pioneer in manufacture of sulfuric acid, 1806; 1st to attempt prodn. of nitric acid; recorder City and County of Phila., 1821-24; mem. 1st bd. mgrs. Franklin Inst.; established firm Harrison & Sons, chem. mfrs., 1831. Died Phila., July 19, 1833.

HARRISON, John Scott, congressman; b. Vincennes, Ind., Oct. 4, 1804; s. Pres. William Henry and Anna (Symmes) H.; studied medicine; children include Pres. Benjamin Harrison. Engaged in farming; mem. U.S. Ho. of Reps. (Whig) from Ind., 33d-34th congresses, 1853-57, unsuccessful candidate for re-election. Died "Point Farm" nr. North Bend, Ind., May 25, 1878; buried Harrison Tomb, North Bend.

HARRISON, Joseph, mech. engr.; b. Phila., Sept. 20, 1810; s. Joseph and Mary (Crawford) H.; m. Sarah Poulterer, Dec. 15, 1836, 7 children. Apprenticed to steam-engine builders, 1825; foreman Garrett, Eastwick & Co., mfrs. locomotives, 1835; designed locomotive "Samuel D. Ingham", became partner 1837; designed 1st practical 8-wheel engine with 4 driving and 4 truck wheels; patented method for equalizing weight on driving wheels, 1839; among first to successfully burn anthracite coal in locomotives; built Gowan and Marx locomotive which attracted attention of Russia, 1841; went to Russia to build 162 locomotives, 2500 freightcars, 1843; decorated by Czar Nicholas I; returned to Phila., 1852; patented Harrison Steam Boiler, 1859; mem. Am. Philos. Soc., 1864; recipient Gold and Silver Rumford medals Am. Acad. Arts and Scis., 1871. Author: An Essay on the Steam Boiler, 1867; (essay) The Iron Worker and King Solomon, 1869; (book) The Locomotive Engine and Philadelphia's Share in Its Early Improvements, 1872. Died Phila., May 27, 1874.

HARRISON, Mark Robert, artist; b. Hovringham, Yorkshire, Eng., 1819; studied art, Toronto, Ont., Can., Rochester, N.Y., N.Y.C.; attended Royal Acad., London, Eng., also studied at Brit. Museum. Came to Am. with family, circa 1822; lived in Hamilton, Ont., and Oshkosh, Wis.; settled in Fond du Lac, Wis., 1852, lived as recluse; painted hist. and religious subjects, some portraits and Indian scenes; exhibited at N.A.D., 1871-72. Died Fond du Lac, 1894.

HARRISON, Peter, architect; b. York, Eng., June 14, 1716; s. Thomas Jr. and Elizabeth (Denison) H.; m. Elizabeth Pelham, June 6, 1746, 4 children. Came to Newport, R.I., 1740; designed Redwood Library, Newport, the Brick Market (1761), Christ Church (1761), Cambridge (1761) The Synagogue (1762-63); collector of customs New Haven (Conn.), 1768-75. Died Apr. 30, 1775.

HARRISON, Samuel Smith, congressman; b. Va., 1780; studied law. Admitted to the bar, practiced law; moved to Kittanning, Pa.; mem. U.S. Ho. of Reps. (Democrat) from Pa., 23d-24th congresses, 1833-37. Died Kittanning, Apr. 1853; buried Old Kittanning Cemetery.

HARRISON, William, Jr., Continental congressman; b. Md.; s. William Harrison. Mem. Continental Congress from Md., 1785-87; engaged in shipbldg., St. Michaels, Md., 1810; served as 1st lt. Ind. Light Dragoons, 9th Cavalry Regt., Md. Militia, 1812, later capt., comdr. troop; justice ct. at St. Michaels, 1813.

HARRISON, William Henry, 9th Pres. U.S.; b. "Berkeley," Charles City County, Va., Feb. 9, 1773; s. Benjamin and Elizabeth (Bassett) H.; attended Hampden-Sydney Coll., 1787-90; studied medicine under Dr. Benjamin Rush, Phila., 1790-91; m. Anna Symmes, 1795, 6 sons including John Scott (father of Benjamin Harrison, 23d Pres. U.S.), Col. William Henry, 4 daus. Apptd. ensign 1st Inf., U.S. Army, 1791; served on frontier duty old N.W. Territory; promoted capt., 1797; in command at Ft. Washington (now Cincinnati), 1797-98; resigned commn., 1798; sec. N.W. Territory, 1798-99, del. to U.S. Congress, 1799-1800; gov. and Indian commr. for Territory of Ind., 1800-13; defeated Indian confederation under Tecumseh and Elskwatawa (the Prophet) at Battle of Tippecanoe, Nov. 6-7, 1811; brevetted maj. gen. U.S. Volunteers and brig. gen. U.S. Army, 1812, comdg. gen. Army of N.W.; commd. maj. gen., 1813; victor in Battle of Thames (assured Am. control of N.W.), 1813, brought about pacification of most of Indians at death of Tecumseh; resigned commn., 1814; mem. U.S. Ho. of Reps. from Ohio, 14th-15th congresses, Oct. 8,

1816-19; mem. Ohio Senate, 1819-21; mem. U.S. Senate from Ohio, 1825-28; U.S. minister to Colombia, S. Am., 1828-29; unsuccessful Whig candidate for U.S. Pres., 1836; elected 9th Pres. U.S. after extensive popular campaign (included slogan "Tippecanoe and Tyler too"), 1840, served from Mar. 4-Apr. 4, 1841 (1st pres. to die in office). Died of pneumonia, Washington, D.C., Apr. 4, 1841; buried Harrison Tomb, opposite Congress Green Cemetery, North Bend, O.

HARRISON, William Pope, clergyman, editor; b. Savannah, Ga., Sept. 3, 1830; attended Emory Coll., Ga., circa 1849; m. Mary Hodges, 1850. Admitted to Ga. Conf. Methodist Ch., 1850, to Ala. Conf., 1852; pastor in Ala., until 1860; prin. Auburn Female Coll., Ala., 1860-62; pastor St. Luke's Ch., Columbus, Ga., 1863-65, 1st Methodist Ch., Atlanta, Ga., 1865-77; editor New Monthly Mag. (Methodist publ.), 1870-77; chaplain U.S. Ho. of Reps., 1877; pastor Mt. Vernon Place Ch., Washington, D.C., 1877-82; book editor So. Methodist Ch., Nashville, Tenn., 1882-94; editor Quarterly Review, Nashville, 1886-94. Author: The Living Christ, 1883; The High Churchman Disarmed, 1886; Methodist Union, 1892. Died Columbus, Ga., Feb. 7, 1895; buried Columbus.

HARROD, James, frontiersman; b. Bedford County, Pa., 1742; m. Anne, 1 dau. Served with Gen. Forbes' forces in Pa. during French and Indian War, 1756-63; explored on Ohio River to present site of Louisville, Ky., 1773; founded 1st settlement in Ky. (later became Harrodsburg), 1774; opposed activities of Transylvania Co. in Ky.; leader in resistance to Indian attacks, organized expdns., 1777; participated in Bowman expdn. against Chillicothe 1779; mem. George R. Clarke's expdn. to Shawnee Territory, 1782; mem. Va. Legislature, 1779; lived in Harrodsburg, from 1770's. Probably murdered on exploring expdn., Ky., July 1793.

HART, Abraham, publisher; b. Phila., Dec. 15, 1810; s. Abraham and Sarah (Stork) H.; m. Rebecca Isaacks, Nov. 23, 1831. Partner, E.L. Carey & A. Hart, book publishing bus., 1829-45, partner (with Henry Carey Baird), 1845-49, sole owner, 1849-54; published annual anthology The Gift; pres. Centennial Button-hole Machine Co.; v.p. Am. Button-hole Machine Co.; pres. Jewish Congregation Mickveh Israel, Phila. Died Long Branch, N.J., July 23, 1885.

HART, Edmund Hall, horticulturist; b. Poughkeepsie, N.Y., Dec. 26, 1839; s. Benjamin Hall and Elizabeth (Nichols) H.; m. Isabella Howland, Dec. 1, 1870, 3 children. Settled in Fla., 1867; imported and bred bananas; imported seeds and developed ornamental palm trees; introduced Valencia orange to Fla.; mem. Fla. Fruit Growers' Assn.; charter mem. Am. Pomological Soc.; chmn. Fla. State Fruit Com. Died Apr. 22, 1898.

HART, Elizur Kirke, congressman; b. Albion, N.Y., Apr. 8, 1841; attended Albion Acad. Engaged in banking; mem. N.Y. Assembly, 1872; dir. Niagara Falls Internat. Bridge Co.; mem. U.S. Ho. of Reps. (Democrat) from N.Y., 45th Congress, 1877-79; founder, pres. Rochester (N.Y.), Post-Express, 1882; pres. Orleans County Nat. Bank, 1890-93. Died Albion, Feb. 18, 1893; buried Mt. Albion Cemetery.

HART, Emanuel Bernard, congressman; b. N.Y.C., Oct. 27, 1809; student pub. schs. Engaged in merc. bus.; served as col. N.Y. Militia; mem. bd. aldermen N.Y.C., 1845; mem. U.S. Ho. of Reps. (Democrat) from N.Y., 1851-53; surveyor Port of N.Y. (apptd. by Pres. Buchanan), 1857-61; mem. bd. assessors N.Y.C.; admitted to N.Y. bar, 1868, practiced law; Democratic presdl. elector, 1868; pres. Mt. Sinai Hosp., 1870-76; commr. of immigration, 1870-73; excise commr., 1879; treas. Soc. for Relief of Poor Hebrews. Died N.Y.C., Aug. 29, 1897; buried Cypress Hills Cemetery, Bklyn.

HART, Joel Tanner, sculptor; b. Winchester, Ky., Feb. 10, 1801; s. Josiah and Judith (Tanner) H. Began career as sculptor with Shobal V. Clevinger, Lexington, Ky., 1831; produced busts of Casius M. Clay, Andrew Jackson, John J. Crittenden, Robert Wickliffe, 1830's-40's; modeled life-size statue of Henry Clay, 1846; lived in Florence, Italy, from 1850, executed many portrait busts including 1 of Millard Fillmore, several of Henry Clay; his busts of Clay and Crittenden now in Corcoran Gallery, Washington, D.C.; most famous original work: "Woman Triumphant." Died Florence, Mar. 2, 1877; buried Frankfort.

HART, John, Continental congressman; b. Stonington, Conn., 1711; s. Edward and Martha H.; m. Deborah Scudder, 1740; Justice of peace Hunterdon County, N.J., 1755; mem. 20th N.J. Assembly, 1761, 21st Assembly, 1771; opposed Stamp Act of 1765; mem. 1st Provincial Congress of N.J., 1774; judge N.J. Ct. Common Pleas, 1775-76; del. Continental Congress, 1776, v.p., 1776; mem. Com. of Correspondence; signer Declaration of Independence, 1776; mem. 1st Assembly under new N.J. Constn., chosen speaker, 1776. Died Hopewell, N.J., May 11, 1779.

HART, John Seely, educator; b. Stockbridge, Mass., Jan. 28, 1810; s. Isaac and Abigail (Stone) H.; grad. Coll. of N.J. (now Princeton), 1830, Princeton Theol. Sem., 1834; m. Amelia Morford, Apr. 21, 1836. Prof. classics Coll. of N.J., 1834-36; owner Edgehill Sch., N.J., 1836-37; prin. Central High Sch., Phila., 1837-44; editor Pa. Common Sch. Journal, 1844; an editor Sartain's Union Mag. of Literature and the Arts, 1849; editor Sunday Sch. Times, 1859-71; prin. N.J. State Normal Sch., 1862-72; prof. English, Coll. of N.J., 1872-74. Author: Elementary Grammar of the English Language, 1845; Essay on the Life and Writings of Edmund Spencer, 1847; In the School Room, 1868. Died Princeton, Mar. 26, 1877.

HART, Roswell, congressman; b. Rochester, N.Y., Aug. 4, 1824; grad. Yale, 1843; studied law. Admitted to N.Y. bar, 1847; engaged in various bus. activities; mem. U.S. Ho. of Reps. (Republican) from N.Y., 39th Congress, 1865-67; supt. Ry. Mail Service for states of N.Y. and Pa., 1869-76. Died Rochester, Apr. 20, 1883; buried Mt. Hope Cemetery, Rochester.

HART, William, painter; b. Paisley, Scotland, Mar. 31, 1823; s. James and Marion (Robertson) H.; m. Janet Wallace. Came to Am., 1831; began as carriage painter, later painted portraits and landscapes; asso. N.A.D., 1855, full mem., 1858; 1st pres. Bklyn. Acad. Design, 1865; an organizer Am. Soc. Water-Colorists, pres., 3 years; encouraged other artists; paintings include: Autumn in the Woods of Maine, 1867; Scene on the Peabody River, 1868; Twilight on the Brook, 1869; A Brook Study, 1870; Easter Sky at Sunset, 1871; The Golden Hour, 1872; Morning in the Clouds, 1874; Cattle Scenes, 1876; The Ford, 1878; Scene of Napanock Creek, 1884; A Modern Cinderella, 1885; After a Shower, 1886. Died Mt. Vernon, N.Y., June 17, 1894; buried Greenwood Cemetery, Bklyn.

HARTER, Michael Daniel, congressman; b. Canton, O., Apr. 6, 1846; attended pub. schs. Engaged as mcht., banker; treas., mgr. Aultman & Taylor Co., Mansfield, O.; mem. U.S. Ho. of Reps. (Democrat) from Ohio, 52d-53d congresses, 1891-95. Died Fostoria, O., Feb. 22, 1896; buried Mansfield Cemetery.

HARTLEY, Thomas, congressman; b. Colebrookdale Twp., Pa., Sept. 7, 1748; s. George Hartley; m. Catherine Holtzinger. Admitted to Pa. bar, 1769, U.S. Supreme Ct. bar (1st Pa. lawyer admitted), 1791; dep. Pa. provincial confs., Phila., 1774-75; elected lt. col. 6th Battalion, Pa. Regt., Continental Army, 1776, commanded Pa. brigade, 1777; mem. Pa. Council of Censors, 1783-84; mem. U.S. Ho. of Reps. from Pa. 1st-6th congresses, 1789-Dec. 21, 1800; Federalist. Died York, Pa., Dec. 21, 1800; buried St. John's Churchyard, York.

HARTRANFT, John Frederick, army officer, gov. Pa.; b. Fagleysville, Pa., Dec. 16, 1830; s. Samuel Engle and Lydia (Bucher) H.; grad. Union Coll., 1853; m. Sallie D. Sebring, Jan. 26, 1854, 3 children. Admitted to Pa. bar, 1860; commd. col. 51st Regt., Pa. Inf., U.S. Army, 1861; commd. brig. gen. U.S. Volunteers, 1864, served in 2d Battle of Bull Run, battle of Chantilly, South Mountain and Fredericksburg; led famous charge which captured stone bridge at Antietam, (one of most brilliant achievements of war); a comdr. Army of West, 1863, engaged in battles of Campbell's Station, Vicksburg, Knoxville, brevetted maj. gen. U.S. Volunteers, 1865; auditor gen. Pa. (Republican), 1865,68; gov. Pa. (Rep.), 1872-74; comdr. Pa. Nat. Guard, 1879-89; postmaster Phila., 1879; collector Port of Phila. 1881-85. Died Norristown, Pa., Oct. 17, 1889.

HARTRIDGE, Julian, congressman; b. Savannah, Ga., Sept. 9, 1829; grad. Brown U., 1848, Harvard Law Sch., 1850. Admitted to Ga. bar, 1851, began practice in Savannah; solicitor gen. Eastern Jud. Circuit of Ga., 1854-58; mem. Ga. Ho. of Reps., 1858-59; del. Dem. Nat. Conv., 1860, 72, 76; served as lt. Chatham (Ga.) Arty, during Civil War, 1 year; mem. 1st and 2d Confederate congresses, 1862-65; Dem. presdl. elector at large, 1872; mem. U.S. Ho. of Reps. (Dem.) from Ga., 44th-45th congresses, 1875-79. Died Washington, D.C., Jan. 8, 1879; buried Laurel Grove Cemetery, Savannah.

HARTSHORNE, Henry, physician; b. Phila., Mar. 16, 1823; s. Dr. Joseph and Anna (Bonsall) H.; grad. Haverford Coll., 1839; M.D., U. Pa., 1845, LL.D. (hon), 1884; m. Mary Brown, Jan. 8, 1849. Resident physician Pa. Hosp., Phila., 1846-48; prof. insts. of medicine Phila. Coll. Medicine, 1853-54; lectr. natural history Franklin Inst., Phila., 1857-58; prof. theory and practice medicine Gettysburg (Pa.) Coll., 1859-61; prof. hygiene U. Pa., Phila., 1865; prof diseases of children, then prof. physiology and hygiene Woman's Med. Coll., Phila., 1867-76; instr., lectr. Phila. Central High Sch., Pa. Coll. Dental Surgery, Girard Coll., circa 1869-76; advocate of edn. of women, particularly right of women to study medicine; engaged in religious and missionary work in Japan, 1893-97; active in Am. Philos. Soc., Acad. Natural Scis.; a founder Am. Public Health Assn; Died Tokyo, Japan, Feb. 10, 1897; buried Tokyo.

HARTSUFF, George Lucas, army officer; b. Tyre, N.Y., May 28, 1830; grad. U.S. Mil. Acad., 1852; m. Sarah Maine, Dec.11, 1858. Participated in Seminole War, severely wounded; asst. instr. tactics U.S. Mil. Acad., 1856-59; asst. adj. gen. during Civil War; commd. capt., 1861; served at Ft. Pickens, Fla., 1861; served under Rosecrans in W. Va., 1861-62; in command Abercrombie's brigade at battles of Cedar Mountain and Antietam; commd. brig. gen. U.S. Volunteers, 1862, promoted maj. gen., 1862; commanded XXIII Army Corps in Ky., Tenn., 1863; brevetted brig. gen., also maj. gen., 1864; ret. as maj. gen. U.S. Army. Died N.Y.C., May 16, 1874.

HARTT, Charles Frederick, geologist; b. Fredericton, N.B., Can., Aug. 23, 1840; s. Jarvis William Hartt; grad. Arcadia Coll., N.S., Can., 1860. Studied at Mus. of Comparative Anatomy on invitation of Louis Agassiz, Cambridge, Mass., 1861-64; geologist on Thayer expdn. to Brazil, 1865-66; prof. geology Vassar Coll., 1866-67; prof. geology and phys. geography Columbia, 1868-75; chief Geol. Commn. of Brazil, 1875-78. Author: Geography of Brazil, 1870; Notes on the Modern Tupi of the Ana, 1872; Crustacea Collected on the Coast of Brazil, 1866-73. Died Rio de Janeiro, Brazil, Mar. 18, 1878.

HARTWIG, Johann Christoph, clergyman; b. Thuringen, Germany, Jan. 6, 1714. Ordained to ministry Lutheran Ch., London, 1745; came to Am., 1746; pastor Lutheran ch., Rhinebeck, N.Y., 1746-48; maintained close relations with Livingstons and Van Rensselaers of N.Y.; confidante of Henry Melchior Muhlenberg; known for extreme asceticism and Pietism; held many brief pastorates, including Waldeboro (Me.), Winchester (Va.), Reading (Pa.), N.Y.C., Federick (Md.), also spent much of life as wandering preacher; provided in will for founding of Indian sch. (resulted in establishment of Hartwicke Coll., Otsego County, N.Y.). Died Clermont, N.Y., July 17, 1796.

HARVARD, John, clergyman; b. Southwark, Eng., Nov. 1607; s. Robert and Katherine (Rogers) H.; grad. Emmanuel Coll., Cambridge (Eng.) U., 1632; m. Anne Sadier, 1636. Came to Am., 1637, settled in Charlestown, Mass.; became landowner, freeman of colony, colleague minister of Charlestown (Puritan) Ch.; mem. com. which compiled Body of Liberties for Charlestown; willed 400 volumes plus approximately 700 pounds for erection of coll. (named Harvard Coll. in his honor by Mass. Gen. Ct., 1639). Died Charlestown, Sept. 14, 1638; buried Cambridge, Mass.

HARVEY, George, artist; b. Tottenham, Eng., circa 1800. Came to U.S., circa 1820, spent several years in the West; established himself as artist; settled in Bklyn., later moved to Boston; painted many miniatures; elected asso. N.A.D., 1828; visited Eng., circa 1833; built home nr. Hastings-on-the-Hudson (N.Y.); helped to design "Sunnyside" (home of Washington Irving); began series of atmospheric views of Am. scenery in watercolor to be engraved and published (project failed for lack of subscribers); made home in Eng., after 1840, made painting trips to N.Am. and Bermuda. Died Eng., 1878.

HARVEY, Haywood Augustus, inventor, mfr.; b. Jamestown, N.Y., Jan. 17, 1824; s. Thomas William and Melinda (Hayward) H.; m. Matilda Winant, Dec. 29, 1849, 1 child; m. Emily Halsey, June 21, 1865, 1 child. Patented corrugated blind staple; invented hay-cutter; joined Harvey Iron & Steel Co., Mott Haven, N.Y., 1852; patented ry. chair, 1859, peripheral grip bolt, 1874; original inventor of cold-forged screw; organized Harvey Steel Co., 1886; developed Harvey process of treating armour plate (to harden surface of steel for combat ships, adopted by U.S. and several European navies), became world famous. Recipient Silver medal Am. Inst. Fair, 1847. Died Aug. 28, 1893.

HARVEY, James Madison, senator, gov. Kan.; b. nr. Salt Sulphur Springs, Va. (now W.Va.), Sept. 21, 1833; attended common schs. Civil engr.; engaged in farming; served as capt. 4th and 10th regts. Kan. Volunteer Inf., U.S. Army, during Civil War, 1861-64; mem. Kan. Ho. of Reps., 1865-66, Kan. Senate, 1867-68; gov. Kan., 1868-72; mem. U.S. Senate (Republican) from Kan., Feb. 2, 1874-77; govt. surveyor in N.M., Utah, Nev. and Okla. Died nr. Junction City, Kan., Apr. 15, 1894; buried Highland Cemetery, Junction City.

HARVEY, Sir John, colonial gov. Va.; b. Dorsetshire, Eng.; m. Elizabeth Piersey. Attempted to establish English colony in Guiana, 1616; invested in Va. Co., 1620-22; apptd. a commr. to investigate conditions in Va. prior to dissolution of Va. Co. by the Crown; secured commn. from court of Va. Co. to transport people and goods to Va.; created knight, 1628; gov., capt.- gen. Va., 1630-35, 37-39; attempted to secure royal monopoly on tobacco; developed grain prodn., fostered increase in trade; unpopular with people and Council because of use of proclamations and taxation policies; deposed and arrested by Va. Ho. of Burgesses, 1635, sent to Eng. for trial; re-apptd. by King Charles; recalled due to opposition, 1639; property confiscated by creditors; returned to Eng., 1641. Died 1646.

HARVEY, Jonathan, congressman; b. Sutton, N. H., Feb. 25, 1780; attended common schs. Engaged in farming; mem. N.H. Ho. of Reps., 1811-16, 31-34, 38-40; mem. N.H. Senate, 1816-23, pres., 1817-23; mem. N.H. Exec. Council, 1823-25; mem. U.S. Ho. of Reps. from N.H., 19th-21st congresses, 1825-31. Died North Sutton, N.H., Aug. 23, 1859; buried North Sutton Cemetery.

HARVEY, Louis Powell, gov. Wis.; b. East Haddam, Conn., July 22, 1820; s. David and Almira (Powell) H.; attended Western Res. U., 1837-39; m. Cordelia Perrine, 1847. Went to Wis., 1841; mem. conv. framing Wis. Constn., 1847; mem. Wis. Senate, 1853-57, pres. pro tem, 1855-57; sec. of state Wis., 1860-61; gov. Wis., 1862; drowned in accident while visiting Wis. soldiers wounded at Battle of Shiloh. Died Savannah, Tenn., Apr. 19, 1862; buried Forest Hill Cemetery, Madison, Wis.

HARVEY, Matthew, gov. N.H., congressman; b. Sutton, N.H., June 21, 1781; grad. Dartmouth, 1806; studied law. Admitted to N.H. bar, began practice in Hopkinton, 1809; mem. N.H. Ho. of Reps., 1814-20, speaker, 3 terms; mem. U.S. Ho. of Reps. (Democrat) from N.H., 17th-28th congresses, 1821-25; mem. N.H. Senate, 1825-27, pres.; mem. N.H. Exec. Council, 1828-29; gov. N.H., 1830; U.S. dist. judge for N.H. (apptd. by Pres. Jackson), 1831-66. Died Concord, N.H., Apr. 7, 1866; buried Old North Cemetery, Concord.

HARVIE, John, Continental congressman, mayor; b. Albemarle County, Va., 1742; s. John and Martha (Gaines) H.; m. Margaret Jones. Engaged in practice law; commd. col. Va. Militia, 1776; del. to Va. convs. 1775, 76, mem. com. to prepare declaration of rights and form of govt.; apptd. commr. for Indian affairs, 1776; mem. Continental Congress, 1777-79, a signer Articles of Confederation, mem. various coms. for provisioning army; purchasing agt. for Va.; register Va. Land Office, 1780; mayor Richmond, Va., 1785-86. Died Richmond, Feb. 6, 1807.

HARWOOD, Andrew Allen, naval officer; b. Settle, Pa., 1802; son of John Edmund Harwood. Apptd. midshipman U.S. Navy, 1818, served in suppression of slave trade and piracy in W.I., 1818-23; commd. lt., 1827, capt., 1855; insp. of ordnance, 1858-61; promoted commodore, 1862, rear-adm. on ret. list, 1869. Died Marion, Mass., Aug. 28, 1884.

HARWOOD, John, see Miner, Charles.

HARWOOD, John E., comedian; b. London, Eng., 1771. Brought to Phila. by Thomas Wignell, 1793; established reputation as outstanding comedian of polished, refined comedy at Chestnut Street Theatre, Phila., 1793-1803; secured by William Dunlap for Park Theater, N.Y.C., 1803; recognized as best portrayer of Falstaff then seen in U.S. Died 1809.

HASBROUCK, Abraham Bruyn, congressman, coll. pres.; b. Kingston, N.Y., Nov. 29, 1791; s. Jonathan and Catharine (Wynkoop) H.; grad. Yale, 1810, A.M., 1819; LL.D. (hon.), Columbia, 1840; m. Julia Ludlum, Sept. 12, 1819, Admitted to N.Y. bar, 1813; mem. U.S. Ho. of Reps. from N.Y., 19th Congress, 1825-27; pres. Ulster County Bank, (N.Y.), 1831; pres. Rutgers Coll., 1840-50; 1st pres. Ulster Hist. Soc., 1859. Died Kingston, Feb. 23, 1879; buried Pine St. Cemetery, Kingston.

HASBROUCK, Abraham Joseph, congressman; b. "Guilford," N.Y., Oct. 16, 1773. Engaged in merc. bus., Kingston, N.Y.; an incorporator Del. & Hudson Canal; apptd. 1st lt. cavalry N.Y. Militia; organizer, dir. Middle Dist. Bank of Kingston; mem. N.Y. Assembly, 1811; mem. U.S. Ho. of Reps. (Clintonian Democrat) from N.Y., 13th Congress, 1813-15; mem. N.Y. Senate, 1822; became Whig. Died Kingston, Jan. 12, 1845; buried Albany Avenue Cemetery, Kingston.

HASBROUCK, Josiah, congressman; b. New Paltz, N.Y., Mar. 5, 1755. Operated a gen. merchandising bus.; 2d lt. 3d Regt., Ulster County (N.Y.) Militia, 1780; supr. New Paltz, 1784-86, 93, 94, 99-1805; mem. N.Y. Assembly, 1796, 97, 1802, 06; mem. U.S. Ho. of Reps. from N.Y., 8th, 15th congresses, Apr. 28, 1803-05, 17-19. Died nr. Plattekill, N.Y., Mar. 19, 1821; buried family burial ground, re-interred New Paltz Rural Cemetery.

HASCALL, Augustus Porter, congressman; b. Hinsdale, Mass., June 24, 1800; attended pub. and pvt. schs.; studied law. Admitted to N.Y. bar, began practice in Le Roy; justice of peace, supr., judge ct. common pleas; Whig presdl. elector, 1848; mem. U. S. Ho. of Reps. (Whig) from N.Y., 32d Congress, 1851-53; resumed law practice; trustee Village of Le Roy, 1858. Died Le Roy, June 27, 1872; buried Myrtle St. Cemetery, Le Roy.

HASENCLEVER, Peter, iron mfr.; b. Remscheid, Prussia, Nov. 24, 1716; s. Luther and Clara (Moll) H.; studied Liege, Belgium, 1732; m. Katharine Wilds, 1745, 1 dau., Katharine. Came to Am., 1764, settled in Morris County, N.J.; established iron works, Morris County, also Orange County, N. Y.; raised flax and hemp, engaged in mining and prodn. of potash; built bridges, dams and factories on 50,000 acres of land; became involved in financial difficulties (due to fraudulent partners), 1768; left Am., 1773. Died Silesia, Prussia, June 13, 1793.

HASKELL, Dudley Chase, congressman; b. Springfield, Vt., Mar. 23, 1842; s. Franklin and Almira (Chase) H.; m. Harriet Kelsey, 2 children. Mem. lower house Kan. Legislature (Republican), 1871-77, speaker, 1876; mem. U.S. Ho. of Reps. from Kan., 45th-48th congresses, 1877-83. Died Washington, D.C., Dec. 16, 1883; buried Oak Hill Cemetery, Lawrence, Kan.

HASKELL, William T., congressman; b. Murfreesboro, Tenn., July 21, 1818; attended U. Nashville (Tenn.). fought in Seminole War, 1836; admitted to Tenn. bar, 1838, began practice in Jackson; mem. Tenn. Ho. of Reps., 1840-41; served in Mexican War; apptd. col. 1st Brigade, 2d Regt., Tenn. Volunteers, 1846; mem. U.S. Ho. of Reps. (Whig) from Tenn., 30th Congress, 1847-49. Died in an asylum, Hopkinsville, Ky., Mar. 12, 1859; buried Riverside Cemetery, Jackson.

HASKET, Elias, gov. Bahamas; b. Salem, Mass., Apr. 25, 1670; s. Stephen and Elizabeth (Hill) H.; m. Elizabeth Rich. Comdr. ship New London, made frequent sea voyages, 1696; gov. New Providence (largest of Bahama Islands), 1700, adminstrn. included a colonist' revolt against his tyranny and illicit trading with both pirates and French, imprisoned, deported to N.Y.; given command of a ship on petition to Crown for his losses. Lost at sea, Mar. 1739.

HASKIN, John Bussing, congressman; b. Fordham (now part of N.Y.C.), N.Y., Aug. 27, 1821; attended pub. schs.; studied law. Admitted to N.Y. bar, 1843; began law practice in N.Y.C., 1845; civil justice of N.Y.C., 1847-49; supr. of Fordham, 1850-53; corp. atty., 1853-56; mem. U.S. Ho. of Reps. (Democrat) from N.Y., 35th-36th congresses, 1857-61; supr. Town of West Farms (N.Y.), 1863; del. serveral Dem. convs. Died Friends Lake, N.Y. Sept. 18, 1895; buried Woodlawn Cemetery, N.Y.C.

HASSARD, John Greene, journalist; b. N.Y.C., Sept. 4, 1836; s. Thomas and Augusta (Greene) H.; grad. Fordham Coll., 1855; m. Isabella Hargous, 1872. Reporter, N.Y. Tribune, circa 1856-62, mng. editor, editorial writer, music critic, various times from 1866; editorial asst. on New Am. Cyclopaedia, circa 1857-64; editor Catholic World, 1865; co-editor Chgo. Republican, 1866; N.Y. correspondent for London Daily News, 1870's. Author: Reflections and Meditations Selected from the Writings of Fenelon, 1865; Life of the Most Reverend John Hughes, 1866; A History of the United States, 1878. Died Apr. 18, 1888.

HASSAUREK, Friedrich, journalist, diplomat; b. Vienna, Austria, Oct. 8, 1831; s. Franz and Johanna (Abele) H.; married 3 times, 3d wife Eunice Marshall. Came to Am., 1849; became asst. editor Ohio Staatszeitung, 1849; editor Hochwaechter, 1850-55; mem. Cincinnati City Council, 1852; admitted to Ohio bar, 1855; an organizer Republican Party in Cincinnati; strong anti-slavery advocate; apptd. U.S. minister to Ecuador, 1861-66; editor, part-owner Tagliches Cincinnatier Volksblatt, from 1865. Author: Hierarchie und Aristokratie, 1855; Four Years Among Spanish Americans, 1867; The Secret of the Andes, 1879; (collection of poems) Welke Blatter und Bluthen, 1877. Died Paris, France, Oct. 3, 1885.

HASSELQUIST, Tuve Nilsson, clergyman, coll. pres.; b. Hasslarod, Sweden, Mar. 2, 1816; s. Nils and Lissa (Svensdotter) H.; grad. Lund U., Sweden, 1839; m. Eva Cervin, May 24, 1852. Ordained to ministry Lutheran Ch., in Sweden, 1839; came to U.S., 1852, became pastor Swedish Lutheran congregation, Galesburg, Ill.; pres. Augustana Synod of Lutheran Ch., 1860-70; pres. Augustana Coll. and Theol. Sem., 1863-91; an opponent of particularism in Lutheran Ch., upheld need for 1 synod and 1 coll. for area (No. Ill.); advocated connection of synod with Gen. Council, 1870. Died Galesburg, Feb. 4, 1891.

HASSLER, Fredinand Rudolph, geodesist, mathematician; b. Aarau, Switzerland, Oct. 7, 1770; s. Jakob Hassler; m. Marianne Gaillard, 1798, 9 children. Acting prof. mathematics U.S. Mil. Acad., 1807-09; prof. natural philosophy and mathematics Union Coll., 1809-11; 1st supt. U.S. Coast Survey, 1816-18, 32-43; U.S. supt. weights and measures, 1830-32. Died Phila., Nov. 20, 1843.

HASTINGS, George, congressman; b. Clinton, N. Y., Mar. 13, 1807; grad. Hamilton Coll., Clinton, 1826; studied law. Admitted to N.Y. bar, 1830, began practice in Mount Morris; dist. atty., 1839-48; mem. U.S. Ho. of Reps. (Democrat) from N. Y., 33d Congress, 1853-55; judge Livingston County (N.Y.) Ct., 1855-66. Died Mount Morris, Aug. 29, 1866; buried City Cemetery, Mount Morris.

HASTINGS, John, congressman; b. Ireland, 1778; studied law, Lisbon, O. Came to Am.; admitted to the bar; practiced law in Miss., engaged in various bus. activities; engaged in farming, Hanover Twp., O.; mem. U.S. Ho. of Reps. (Jacksonian Democrat) from Ohio, 26th-27th congresses, 1839-43. Died nr. Hanoverton, O., Dec. 8, 1854; buried Grove Hill Cemetery, Hanoverton.

HASTINGS, Lansford W., pioneer; displayed Elijah White as capt. of White's emigrant party shortly after it left Independence, Mo. for Ore., 1842 (1st emigrant party to reach Ore.); had ambitions to govern new republic in Cal., tried to lure Ore.-bound settlers there; wrote much used but unreliable handbook The Emigrants Guide to Oregon and California, which refers to dubious route labeled Hastings' Cut-Off, 1845 (some attribute 1846 Donner tragedy to this); officer in Fremont's batallion, 1846.

HASTINGS, Serramus Clinton, congressman, jurist; b. Watertown, N.Y., Nov. 14, 1813; s. Robert Collins and Patience (Brayton) H.; grad. Hamilton Coll.; m. Azalea Brodt, 1845; m. Lillian Knust, 1885; 7 children. Prin., Norwich Acad., 1834; editor Indiana Signal, 1836; admitted to Ind. bar, 1836; mem. Ia. Territorial Council, 1838-46; mem. U.S. Ho. of Reps. from Ia., 29th Congress, Dec. 28, 1846-47; chief justice Ia. Supreme Ct., 1848-49; 1st chief justice Cal. Supreme Ct., 1850-52; atty. gen. Cal., 1852-59; provided endowment of $100,000 for establishment of Hastings Coll. of Law, San Francisco, 1878. Died San Francisco, Feb. 18, 1893; buried St. Helena (Cal.) Cemetery.

HASTINGS, Seth, congressman; b. Cambridge, Mass., Apr. 8, 1762; grad. Harvard, 1782; studied law; children include William Soden. Admitted to Mass. bar, 1786, began practice in Mendon; treas. Town of Mendon, 1794-95; elected one of 1st sch. commrs., 1796; mem. U.S. Ho. of Reps. (Federalist) from Mass., 7th-9th congresses, Aug. 24, 1801-07; mem. Mass. Senate, 1810, 14; chief justice Worcester County (Mass.) Ct. Sessions, 1819-28. Died Mendon, Nov. 19, 1831; buried Old Cemetery, Mendon.

HASTINGS, Thomas, composer; b. Washington, Conn., Oct. 15, 1784; s. Seth and Eunice (Parmele) H.; m. Mary Seymour, Sept. 15, 1822. Taught music, Clinton, N.Y., 1806; gathered hymns and sacred songs for publication, circa 1806-16; moved to Troy, N.Y., 1817, taught music, directed choirs; moved to Utica, N.Y., 1823-32, taught and edited religious publ. Western Recorder; lived in N.Y.C., 1832-72; directed several choirs including Bleecker Street Presbyn. Ch.; taught music, published works on ch. music, compiled hymnals. Author: Musica Sacra, 1816; Dissertation on Musical Taste, 1822; The Musical Miscellany, 1836; The Psalmodist, 1844; Devotional Hymns and Religious Poems, 1850; History of Forty Choirs, 1854. Died N.Y.C., May 15, 1872; buried N.Y.C.

HASTINGS, William Soden, congressman; b. Mendon, Mass., June 3, 1798; grad. Harvard, 1817; studied law. Admitted to Mass. bar, 1820, began practice in Mendon; mem. Mass. Ho. of Reps., 1828, Mass. Senate, 1829-33; mem. U.S. Ho. of Reps. (Democrat) from Mass., 25th-27th congresses, 1837-42. Died Red Sulphur Springs, Va. (now W. Va.), June 17, 1842; buried Old Cemetery, Mendon.

HASWELL, Anthony, publisher; b. Portsmouth, Eng., Apr. 6, 1756; s. William and Elizabeth Haswell; m. Lydia Baldwin, Apr. 23, 1778; m. 2d, Betsey Rice, Sept. 30, 1799; 17 children. Came to Am. 1769; wrote crude songs for Mass. Sons of Liberty; served in Revolutionary War, 1776-77; moved to Hartford, Conn., 1781; became postmaster-gen. Vt., 1784; publisher various papers, mags., books and pamphlets including newspaper Mass. Spy, 1777, New England Almanac for 1781, (with Elisha Babcock), Mass. Gazette or Springfield and Northhampton Weekly Advertiser (weekly paper), 1782, paper. Vt. Gazette or Freemen's Depository, 1783, Monthly Miscellany, or Vt. Mag., 1794; an early victim of Sedition Act, tried in 1800, sentenced to 2 months in prison and $200 fine. Author: Memoirs of Capt. Matthew Phelps, 1802. Died Bennington, Vt., May 22, 1816.

HATCH, Edward, army officer; b. Bangor, Me., Dec. 23, 1832; s. Nathaniel and Mary (Scott) H.;

attended Norwich (Vt.) U., 2 years; m. Evelyn Barrington. Served as capt. troop 2d Iowa Cavalry, U.S. Army, 1861, commd. col., 1862, commanded 2d Ia. Cavalry in Grant's western campaign; served in battles of Corinth, Franklin, Nashville, also Grant's Miss. campaign; in command of cavalry div. Army of Tenn.; commd. brig. gen. 1864, in command of cavalry div. participating in actions at Florence, Lawrenceburg, Campbellville, Spring Hill, Franklin; brevetted maj. gen. U.S. Volunteers, 1864; commd. col. 9th U.S. Cavalry, 1866, brevetted brig. gen. and maj. gen. U.S. Army, 1867; commanded Dept. of Ariz. and N.M., 1866-67. Died Ft. Robinson, Neb., Apr. 11, 1889.

HATCH, Israel Thompson, congressman; b. Johnstown, N.Y., June 30, 1808; grad. Union Coll., Schenectady, N.Y., 1829; studied law. Admitted to N.Y. bar, 1828; asst. sec. of state N.Y., 1829-31; practiced law, Buffalo, N.Y., 1831-40; mem. N.Y. Assembly, 1833, 34, 51; surrogate Erie County (N.Y.), 1833-36; pres. Comml. Bank of Buffalo, 1840-42; grain mcht.; mem. U.S. Ho. of Reps. (Democrat) from N.Y., 35th Congress, 1857-59; postmaster of Buffalo (apptd. by Pres. Buchanan), 1859-61; resumed law practice, engaged in banking; mem. N.Y. Constl. Conv., 1867-68; commr. to negotiate a reciprocity treaty between U.S. and Can., 1869-70; built Marine and Empire elevators, Buffalo. Died Buffalo, Sept. 24, 1875; buried Forest Lawn Cemetery, Buffalo.

HATCH, Rufus, financier; b. Wells, Me., June 24, 1832; s. Rufus and Huldah (Littlefield) H.; m. Charlotte Hatch, 1853; m. 2d, Mary Gray; 7 children. Moved to Ill., 1851; mem. original Chgo. Bd. Trade; after unsuccessful attempt to get control Northwestern R.R. after Civil War, managed Northwestern R.R. pool for Henry Keep for several years; attacked Vanderbilt interests in "Rufus Hatch's Circulars," exposing stock-watering plans of N.Y.C Central R.R.; organized Open Bd. Brokers, 1869-70 (due to competition merged with Stock Exchange, 1870), declined presidency Stock Exchange important N.Y. broker during Wall St. campaigns of the Erie and N.Y. Central railroads and failure of Jay Cooke; pres. Pacific Mail S.S. Co., 1874; suffered gt. losses in No. Pacific crash of 1883. Died N.Y.C., Feb. 23, 1893.

HATCH, Stephen D., architect; b. 1839. Practiced as architect, N.Y.C.; designed numerous bus. and comml. structures in N.Y.C., including Norwell, Coring, and Roosevelt bldgs., old Murray Hill Hotel. Died Plainfield, N.J., Aug. 1, 1894.

HATCH, William Henry, congressman; b. Georgetown, Ky., Sept. 11, 1833; s. Rev. William and Mary (Adams) H.; m. Jennie Smith; m. 2d, Thetis Hawkins, 1861. Admitted to Ky. bar, 1854; circuit atty. 16th Jud. Dist. Mo., 1858-62; served as lt. col. Confederate Army during Civil War; mem. U.S. Ho. of Reps. from Mo., 46th-53d congresses, 1879-95, proposed and sponsored act to create Bur. of Animal Industry, 1884, 1st oleomargarine act, 1886; author Hatch Act calling for fed. aid to encourage study of scientific agr. (passed 1887), meat inspection act, 1890. Died Hannibal, Mo., Dec. 23, 1896; buried Riverside Cemetery, Hannibal.

HATCHER, Robert Anthony, congressman; b. Buckingham County, Va., Feb. 24, 1819; attended pvt. schs., Lynchburg, Va.; studied law. Admitted to Ky. bar; began practice of law, New Madrid, Mo., 1847; circuit atty.; mem. Mo. Ho. of Reps., 1850-51; served to maj. Confederate Army during Civil War; mem. Confederate Congress, 1864-65; mem. U.S. Ho. of Reps. (Democrat) from Mo., 43d-45th congresses, 1873-79. Died Charleston, Mo., Dec. 4, 1886; buried Odd Fellows Cemetery, Charleston.

HATFIELD, Edwin Francis, clergyman; b. Elizabeth, N.J., Jan. 9, 1807; s. Oliver and Jane (Mann) H.; grad. Middlebury Coll., 1829; D.D. (hon.), Marietta Coll., 1850; m. Mary Taylor, Apr. 27, 1837, 5 children. Ordained to ministry Presbyn. Ch., 1832; pastor 7th Presbyn. Ch., N.Y.C., 1835-56; dir. Union Theol. Sem., 1846-64, financial agt., 1864-65, recorder bd. dirs.; clk. Gen. Assembly of New School Presbyn. Ch., 1846-83, moderator, 1883. Author: Universalism as It Is, 1841; Memoir of Reverend Elihu W. Baldwin, 1843; Church Hymn Book, 1872,74; The Early Annals of the Union Theological Seminary, 1876. Died Summit, N.J., Sept. 22, 1883.

HATFIELD, Oliver Perry, architect; b. Elizabeth, N.J., 1819. Began archtl. practice in partnership with brother R. G. Hatfield, N.Y.C., 1851; became treas. A.I.A., 1879, also pres. N.Y. chpt. Died Aug. 1, 1894.

HATFIELD, R. G., architect; b. Elizabeth, N.J., 1815. Employed in bldg. trade; practiced as architect, N.Y.C., joined in partnership by his brother Oliver Perry Hatfield, 1851; works in firm include: bldgs. for Dept. of Charities and Correction on Randall's Island, Inst. for Deaf and Dumb, Seamen's Savs. Bank, Wall St., Security Ins. Co., all N.Y.C., Westchester County Ct. House, White Plains, N.Y.; charter mem. 1st treas. A.I.A., 1857-79, also pres. N.Y. chpt. Died Feb. 18, 1879.

HATHAWAY, Samuel Gilbert, congressman; b. Freetown, Mass., July 18, 1780; student pub. schs. Moved to Chenango County, N.Y., 1803, Cincinnatus, N.Y., 1805, engaged in farming; justice of peace, 1810-58; mem. N.Y. Assembly, 1814, 18; moved to Solon, N.Y., 1819; mem. N.Y. Senate, 1822; served as maj. gen. N.Y. Militia, 1823-58; mem. U.S. Ho. of Reps. (Democrat) from N.Y., 23d Congress, 1833-35; Dem. presdl. elector, 1852; del. Dem. Nat. Conv., Charleston, S.C., 1860. Died Solon, May 2, 1867; buried family cemetery nr. Solon.

HATHORN, Henry Harrison, congressman; b. Greenfield, N.Y., Nov. 28, 1813; grad. from pub. schs., Greenfield. Discovered Hathorn Mineral Spring; mcht., Saratoga Springs, N.Y., 1839-49; sheriff of Saratoga County (N.Y.), 1853-56, 62-65; supr. of Saratoga Springs, 1858, 60, 66, 67; mem. U.S. Ho. of Reps. (Republican) from N.Y., 43d-44th congresses, 1873-77. Died Saratoga Springs, Feb. 20, 1887; buried Greenridge Cemetery, Saratoga Springs.

HATHORN, John, congressman; b. Wilmington, Del., Jan. 9, 1749. Surveyor, sch. tchr.; capt. N.Y. Colonial Militia; apptd. col. 4th Orange County (N.Y.) Regt., 1776, served throughout Revolutionary War; commd. brig. Gen. Orange County Militia, 1786, maj. gen. N.Y. State Militia, 1793; mem .N.Y. Assembly, 1778, 80, 82-85, 95, 1805, speaker, 1783-84; mem. N.Y. Senate, 1786-90, 99-1803; mem. council of appointment, 1787, 89; elected to Continental Congress, Dec. 1788, no further sessions held; mem. U.S. Ho. of Reps. (Federalist) from N.Y., 1st, 4th congresses, 1789-91, 95-97. Died Warwick, N.Y., Feb. 19, 1825; buried cemetery on family estate, reinterred Warwick Cemetery.

HATHORNE, George, architect; b. Springfield, Mass. Practiced as architect, Springfield, circa 1860-70; best known bldgs. include City Library, Inst. of Savs., Springfield, Walker Hall at Amherst Coll. (built 1871); moved to N.Y.C., practiced as architect; an early mem. A.I.A. Died 1889.

HATHORNE, William, colonial ofcl.; b. Binfield, Eng., circa 1607; s. William and Sara Hathorne; m. Anne. Came to Am., 1630; mem. bd. selectmen Dorchester (Mass.), 1634; dep. Mass. Gen. Ct., 1635-37; speaker, 1644-50; served to ranks capt. and maj. Mass. Militia; mem. Mass. Bd. of Assts., 1662-69; 1 of 5 principal citizens of Mass. ordered to Eng. by Charles II, 1666. Died 1681.

HATTON, Frank, journalist, postmaster gen.; b. Cambridge, O., Apr. 28, 1846; s. Richard and Sarah (Green) H.; m. Lizzie Snyder, 1867, 1 child. Served in Civil War; family moved to Ia., 1866; owner Burlington (Ia.) Daily Hawk-Eye, 1874; local postmaster, 1879; apptd. asst. postmaster gen. U.S., 1881, postmaster gen., 1884-95, extended carrier service, created spl. delivery system; wrote for Nat. Republican, Washington, D.C.; editor Mail, Chgo., 1885-88; a founder N.Y. Press, circa 1888; owner, editor Washington (D.C.) Post, 1889-94. Died Washington, D.C., Apr. 30, 1894.

HATTON, Robert Hopkins, congressman; b. Steubenville, O., Nov. 2, 1826; grad. Cumberland U., Lebanon, Tenn., 1847, attended law sch., 1848-49. Tutor, Cumberland U., 1847-48, trustee, 1854-62; prin. Woodland Acad., Sumner County, Tenn., 1849-50; admitted to Tenn. bar, 1850, began practice in Lebanon; mem. Tenn. Ho. of Reps., 1855-57; unsuccessful candidate for gov. Tenn., 1857; mem. U.S Ho. of Reps. (Am. Party rep.) from Tenn., 36th Congress, 1859-61; commd. col. 7th Regt., Tenn. Volunteer Inf., 1861, brig. gen. Confederate Army, 1862; assigned to command 5th Brigade, 1st Corps, Army of Va. Killed in Battle of Seven Pines, nr. Richmond, Va., May 31, 1862; buried Cedar Grove Cemetery, Lebanon.

HAUGHEY, Thomas, congressman; b. Glasgow, Scotland, 1826; diploma New Orleans Med. Coll. Came to U.S., settled in N.Y.C.; moved to Jefferson County, Ala., 1841; tchr., St. Clair County, Ala.; practiced medicine, Elyton, Ala.; served as surgeon 3d Regt., Tenn. Volunteer Inf., U.S. Army, 1862-65; resumed practice of medicine, Decatur, Ala.; del. Ala. Constl. Conv., 1867; mem. U.S. Ho. of Reps. (Republican) from Ala., 40th Congress, July 21, 1868-69, candidate for renomination. Assassinated while making a polit. speech, Courtland, Ala., Aug., 1869; buried Green Cemetery, nr. Pinson, Ala.

HAUN, Henry Peter, senator; b. nr. Newtown, Ky., Jan. 18, 1815; attended Transylvania U., Lexington, Ky.; studied law. Admitted to Ky. bar, 1839, began practice in Lexington; pros. atty. Scott County (Ky.), 1845; moved to Clinton County, Ia., settled in Hauntown, 1845; practiced law, formed partnership with his brother in distillery, sawmill and store; moved to Marysville, Cal., 1849, practiced law, engaged in farming; county judge Yuba County (Cal.), 1851-54; mem. U.S. Senate (Democrat) from Cal., Nov. 3, 1859-60. Died Marysville, June 6, 1860; buried Marysville Cemetery.

HAVELL, Robert, engraver, painter; b. Reading, Berkshire, Eng., Nov. 25, 1793; s. Robert and Lydia (Phillips) H.; m. Amelia Jane Eddington, 4 children. Learned engraving trade in publishing firm Colnaghi & Co., Eng., 1825-27; engraver in partnership with his father, 1827-28, contracted to engrave plates for Audubon's Birds of America, did Audubon engravings, 1828-38; came to U.S., 1838, settled in Tarrytown, N.Y.; painted and sketched in N.Y. area around Hudson River, 1857-78. Died Tarrytown, Nov. 11, 1878; buried Sleepy Hollow, N.Y.

HAVEMEYER, William Frederick, sugar refiner, mayor N.Y.C., Feb. 12, 1804; s. William Havemeyer; grad. Columbia Coll., 1823; m. Sarah Craig, 1828; several children. Successful sugar refiner, 1828-42; mayor N.Y.C., (Democrat) 1845-46, 1849-50; pres. Bank of N.Am. and N.Y. Savs. Bank from 1850's to 1861; mayor N.Y.C., 1873-74, on reform platform after "Tweed Diary" disclosures, term was stormy, warned about his conduct by N.Y. Gov. John A. Dix, but no corruption charges brought against him or proved. Died N.Y.C., Nov. 30, 1874.

HAVEN, Emily Bradley Neal, editor, author; b. N.Y., Sept. 13, 1827; d. George and Sarah (Brown) Bradley; m. Joseph C. Neal, Dec. 1846; m. 2d, Samuel L. Haven, Jan. 1, 1853; 5 children. Contbr. poems and sketches (under pen name Alice G. Lee) to Neal's Saturday Gazette and Lady's Literary Museum, Phila., before 1846; asst. editor (under name Clara Cushman) Neal's Paper, 1846-47; owner, editor (with Charles J. Peterson) Neal's Saturday Gazette and Lady's Literary Museum, 1846-53. Author: Helen Morton's Trial, 1849; The Gossips of Rivertown, 1850; Contentment Better than Wealth, 1853; Out of Debt, Out of Danger, 1855; The Good Report, published 1867. Died Mamaroneck, N.Y., Aug. 23, 1863; buried Rye, N.Y.

HAVEN, Erastus Otis, educator, clergyman; b. Boston, Nov. 1, 1820; s. Jotham and Betsy (Spear) H.; grad. with honors Wesleyan U., 1842; m. Mary Frances Coles, 5 children. Joined N.Y. Methodist Conf., 1848; taught Aminia (N.Y.) Sem., 1843-46, princ. 1846-48; prof. Latin, U. Mich., 1853, prof. history and English literature, 1854-56, prof. rhetoric, English literature, also pres. coll., 1863-69, conceived plan of annual state legislative appropriations to support univ.; editor Meth. Weekly, Zion's Herald, Boston, 1856-63; not anabolitionist, nevertheless advocated excluding slave owners from ch. membership; mem. Mass. Bd. Edn.; a founder Mass. Agrl. Coll.; mem. Mass. Senate, 1862-64; Mass. rep. on bd. overseers Harvard; pres. Northwesrern U., 1869-72; corr. sec. Bd. of Edn. of Meth. Episcopal Ch., 1872; chancellor Syracuse U., 1874-78; bishop Diocese of San Francisco, 1880-81. Author: The Young Man Advised, 1856; The Pillars of Truth, 1865; Textbook Rhetoric, 1869. Died Salem, Ore., Aug. 2, 1881.

HAVEN, Gilbert, clergyman; b. Malden, Mass., Sept. 19, 1821; s. Gilbert and Hannah (Burrill) H.; grad. Wesleyan U., 1846; m. Mary Ingraham, 1851, 2 children. Taught Greek and German in Amenia Sem., N.Y., 1846-51, prin., 1848-51; became minister New Eng. Conf. of Methodist Episcopal Ch., 1851; held several pastorates in Mass., 1851-61; chaplain 8th Mass. Div., 1861-62; editor Zion's Herald, 1867-72, advocated civil rights and absolute civil equality; mem. M.E. Gen. Conf., 1868; bishop of Atlanta (Ga.), 1872-80. Author: The Pilgram's Wallet, 1866; National Sermons. 1869; Father Taylor, the Sailor Preacher, 1872; A Winter in Mexico, 1875. Died Malden, Jan. 3, 1880.

HAVEN, Henry Philemon, whaling mcht.; b. Norwich, Conn., Feb. 11, 1815; s. Philemon and Fanny (Manwaring) H.; m. Elizabeth Douglas, Feb. 23, 1840. Partner, Haven & Smith, whaling and sealing co., 1838; formed co. of Eastern and Western shipowners which obtained monopoly of seal fisheries at St. Paul's and St. George's islands, Alaska, 1870; reorganizer, pres. New London & No. R.R. Co.; prominent in 3 Conn. banks; major New London (Conn.), 1852; mem. Conn. Assembly, 1852; unsuccessful Republican candidate for gov. Conn., 1873; tchr. Sunday Sch. at age 15; supt. Sunday sch. 2d Congregational Ch., New London, 1858; one of 1st and prin. contbrs. to Internat. Sunday Sch. Lessons. Died New London, Apr. 30, 1876.

HAVEN, Joseph, clergyman, educator; b. Dennis, Mass., Jan. 4, 1816; s. Rev. Joseph and Elizabeth (Sparrow) H.; grad. Amherst Coll., 1835, Andover Theol. Sem., 1839; m. Mary Emerson, Sept. 23, 1840, 10 children. Tchr. in instn. for deaf mutes, N.Y.C., 1835-37; pastor Congregational Ch., Andover, Mass., 1839-46, Harvard Congregational Ch., Brookline, Mass., 1846-50; prof. mental and moral philosophy Amherst Coll., 1850-57; prof. systematic theology Chgo. Theol. Sem., 1858-70; prof. mental and moral philosophy U. Chgo., 1873-74. Author: Mental Philosophy, 1857; Mental Science as a Branch of Education, 1857; Moral Philosophy, 1859; Studies in Philosophy and Theology, 1869. Died May 23, 1874.

HAVEN, Nathaniel Appleton, congressman; b. Portsmouth, N.H., July 19, 1762; grad. in medicine Harvard, 1779. Practiced medicine, Portsmouth, also engaged as mcht.; served as ship's surgeon in Revolutionary War; mem. U.S. Ho. of Reps. (Federalist) from N.H., 11th Congress, 1809-11. Died Portsmouth, Mar. 13, 1831; buried Proprietor's Burying Ground, Portsmouth.

HAVEN, Solomon George, congressman; b. Chenango County, N.Y., Nov. 27, 1810; studied medicine, law. Admitted to N.Y. bar, 1835, began practice in Buffalo; commr. of deeds; dist. atty. Erie County (N.Y.), 1844-46; mayor Buffalo, 1846-47; mem. U.S. Ho. of Reps. (Whig) from N.Y., 32d-34th congresses, 1851-57. Died Buffalo, Dec. 24, 1861; buried Forest Lawn Cemetery, Buffalo.

HAVENS, Jonathan Nicoll, congressman; b. Shelter Island, N.Y., June 18, 1757; grad. Yale, 1777. Mem. N.Y. State Assembly, 1786-95; town clk., 1783-87; mem. N.Y. Conv. which ratified U.S. Constn., 1788; chmn. com. for establishing pub. schs. in N.Y., 1795; justice of peace Suffolk County (N.Y.), 1795; mem. U.S. Ho. of Reps. (Democrat) from N.Y., 4th-6th congresses, 1795-99. Died Shelter Island, Oct. 25, 1799; buried South burial ground of Presbyn. Ch., Shelter Island.

HAVERLY, Christopher, theatrical mgr.; b. Boiling Springs, Pa., June 30, 1837; s. Christopher and Eliza (Steel) H.; m. Sarah Duval; m. 2d, Eliza Duval (sisters). Owned and operated variety theater, Toledo, O., 1864-66; opened his 1st minstrel show, Adrian, Mich., 1864; mgr. Cal Wagner's Minstrels, 1870-75; part owner New Orleans Minstrels, 1876, Callender's Colored Minstrels, 1878; became owner Adelphi Theatre, Chgo., 1876, also owned theaters in Phila., N.Y., San Francisco; organized Haverly's Mastodon Minstrels, 1878, toured Europe with troup, 1880-81; lost fortune in unsuccessful tour, London, Eng., 1884; spent last years of life mining in West. Died Salt Lake City, Utah, Sept. 28, 1901.

HAVILAND, John, architect; b. Gundenham Manor, Somerset, Eng., Dec. 15, 1792; s. James and Ann (Cobley) H.; studied architecture with James Elmes, London, Eng.; m. Miss Von Sonntag, Sept. 1816. Came to U.S., 1816; conducted (with Hugh Bridport) archtl. drawing school, Phila.; most notable work was creation archtl. radiating plan of modern prison design (as in Pitts. Penitentiary); began career in prison architecture with design and constrn., Eastern State Penitentiary, Cherry Hill, Pa., 1821; also designed Western Penitentiary, Pitts., state penitentiaries of N.J., Mo., R.I.; jails of Allegheny, Dauphin, Lancaster, Berks counties, also Halls of Justice and City Prison in N.Y.; a founder Am. Instn. of Architects, 1836; other works include: 1st Presbyn. Ch., St. Andrews Episcopal Ch., Pa. Inst. for Deaf and Dumb (all Phila.), U.S. Naval Asylum, Norfolk, Va., State Insane Asylum, Harrisburg, Pa., U.S. Mint, Phila., County Hall, Newark, N.J. Author: (with Bridport) The Builders Assistant for the Use of Carpenters and Others, 1818-19. Died Phila., Mar. 28, 1852.

HAWES, Albert Gallatin, congressman; b. nr. Bowling Green, Va., Apr. 1, 1804; attended Transylvania U., Lexington, Ky. Moved to Ky. ,1810; settled nr. Hawesville, Ky., engaged in farming; mem. U.S. Ho. of Reps. (Jacksonian Democrat) from Ky., 22d-24th congresses, 1831-37; farmer, nr. Yelvington, Ky. Died nr. Yelvington, Mar. 14, 1849; buried Hawes family burial ground, nr. Yelvington.

HAWES, Aylett, congressman; b. Culpeper County, Va., Apr. 21, 1768; studied medicine U. Edinburgh (Scotland). Practiced medicine, Va.; engaged as planter; mem. Va. Ho. of Dels., 1802-06; mem. U.S. Ho. of Reps. (Democrat) from Va., 12th-14th congresses, 1811-17; resumed practice of medicine, planting; extensive landowner. Died Rappahannock County, Va., Aug. 31, 1833; buried on a farm nr. Sperryville, Va.

HAWES, Joel, clergyman; b. Medway, Mass., Dec. 22, 1789; grad. Brown U., 1813; attended Andover Theol. Sem.; at least 1 child. Pastor, 1st Congregational Ch., Hartford, Conn., 1818-69. Author: Memoir of Norman Smith, 1839; Religions of the East, with Impressions of Foreign Travel, 1845; An Offering to Home Missionaries, 1865; Sermons, Experimental and Practical, 1866. Died Gilead, Conn., June 5, 1867.

HAWES, Richard, congressman, Confederate gov. Ky.; b. nr. Bowling Green, Va., Feb. 6, 1797; attended Transylvania U., Lexington, Ky.; studied law. Moved to Ky., 1810, settled nr. Lexington; admitted to Ky. bar, 1824, began practice in Winchester; served in Black Hawk War; mem. Ky. Ho. of Reps., 1828, 29, 34; mem. U.S. Ho. of Reps. (Whig) from Ky., 25th-26th congresses, 1837-41; moved to Paris, Ky., 1843, practiced law; Confederate provisional gov. Ky., 1862-65; county judge, master commr. of circuit and common pleas cts., 1866-77. Died Paris, May 25, 1877; buried Paris Cemetery.

HAWES, William Post, lawyer; b. N.Y.C., Feb. 4, 1803; s. Peter and Nancy (Post) H.; grad. Columbia, 1821. Admitted to N.Y. bar, 1824; practiced law, also did writing, N.Y.C., 1824-42; contbd. articles to N.Y. Mirror, Am. Monthly Mag., Spirit of the Times and Turf Register. Died N.Y.C., 1842.

HAWK, Robert Moffett Allison, congressman; b. nr. Rushville, Ind., Apr. 23, 1839; attended Eureka (Ill.) Coll.; studied law. Commd. 1st lt. U.S. Army during Civil War, 1862, promoted capt., 1863, brevetted maj., 1865; moved to Mount Carroll, Ill., 1865, engaged in farming; clk. Carroll County (Ill.) Ct., 1865-79; mem. U.S. Ho. of Reps. (Republican) from Ill., 46th-47th congresses, 1879-82. Died Washington, D.C., June 29, 1882; buried Oak Hill Cemetery, Mount Carroll.

HAWKES, James, congressman; b. Petersham, Mass., Dec. 13, 1776; attended common schs. Taught sch., Richfield, N.Y., later in Burlington, N.Y.; sheriff of Otsego County (N.Y.), 1815-19; mem. N.Y. Assembly, 1820; mem. U.S. Ho. of Reps. from N.Y., 17th Congress, 1821-23. Died Rochester, N.Y., Oct. 2, 1865; buried Mt. Hope Cemetery, Rochester.

HAWKINS, Benjamin, senator; b. Granville (now Warren) County, N.C., Aug. 15, 1754; s. Philemon and Delia (Martin) H.; attended Princeton, 1773-76. French interpreter for George Washington, 1776-78; mem. N.C. Ho. of Commons, 1778-79, 84; chosen by N.C. Legislature to procure arms and munitions to defend N.C., 1780; mem. Continental Congress, 1781-84, 86-87; apptd. by Congress to negotiate treaties with Creek and Cherokee Indians, 1785; del. N.C. Conv. to ratify U.S. Constn., 1789; mem. U.S. Senate from N.C., 1789-95; Indian agt. for all tribes south of Ohio River, 1796-1816. Died Crawford County, Ga., June 6, 1816; buried on plantation nr. Roberta, Ga.

HAWKINS, Benjamin Waterhouse, sculptor, naturalist; b. London, Eng., Feb. 8, 1807; studied at Coll. of St. Aloysius; studied art under William Behnes. Made models of living animals at Knowsley Park, seat of Earl of Derby, 1842-47; came to U.S., 1868; commd. to make models of extinct animals, Central Park Museum, N.Y.C.; mem. Royal Geog. Soc., from 1854. Author: Popular Comparative Anatomy, 1840; Elements of Form, 1842; The Science of Drawing Simplified, 1843. Died 1889.

HAWKINS, Dexter Arnold, lawyer, educator; b. Canton. Me., June 24, 1825; s. Rev. Henry and Abigail (Fuller) H.; grad. Bowdoin Coll., 1848; attended L'Ecole des Droit, Paris, France; m. Sophia Meeks, Apr. 12, 1859. Apptd. lectr. on public instrn. before teachers' institutes by Me. Bd. Edn., 1848; began practice law, N.Y.C., 1854; active in establishing U.S. Dept. Edn., 1867; advocated system of free independently controlled public schools; drew up "Act to Secure to Children the Benefits of Elementary Education," passed into law by N.Y. State, 1874; instrumental in overthrowing Tammany ring and in correcting polit. irregularities in N.Y.C. Died N.Y.C., July 24, 1886.

HAWKINS, George Sydney, congressman, jurist; b. Kingston, N.Y., 1808; grad. Columbia; studied law. Admitted to N.Y. bar, practiced law; moved to Pensacola, Fla.; served as capt. during Seminole War, 1837; mem. Legislative Council of Territory of Fla.; apptd. dist. atty., 1841; apptd. U.S. dist. atty. for Apalachicola dist., 1842; asso. justice Fla. State Supreme Ct., 1846-60; judge circuit ct., 1851; mem. Fla. Ho. of Reps., Fla. Senate; collector of customs Port of Apalachicola; mem. U.S. Ho. of Reps. (Democrat) from Fla., 35th-36th congresses, 1857-Jan. 21, 1861; judge dist. ct. under Confederacy, 1862-65; commd. by Fla. Legislature to prepare a digest of state laws, 1877. Died Marianna, Fla., Mar. 15, 1878; buried St. Luke's Episcopal Cemetery, Marianna.

HAWKINS, Isaac Roberts, congressman, army officer; b. nr. Columbia, Tenn., May 16, 1818; attended common schs.; studied law. Admitted to Tenn. bar, 1843, began practice in Huntingdon; served as lt. during Mexican War; resumed law practice; del. from Tenn. to Washington (D.C.) Peace Conf., 1861; elected to conv. for consideration of fed. relations; judge circuit ct., 1862; commd. lt. col. 7th Regt., Tenn. Volunteer Cavalry, U.S. Army, 1862, captured at Union City, Tenn., 1864, imprisoned, one of officers who were placed under fire at Charleston (S.C.); exchanged, 1864, in command of cavalry force in Western Ky. until end of Civil War; declined appointment as chancellor of Tenn., 1865; del. Republican Nat. Conv., Chgo., 1868; mem. U.S. Ho. of Reps. (Rep.) from Tenn., 39th-41st congresses, July 24, 1866-71. Died Huntingdon, Aug. 12, 1880; buried Hawkins family burial ground, nr. Huntingdon.

HAWKINS, Joseph, congressman; b. N.Y., Nov. 14, 1781; studied law. Admitted to N.Y. bar, began practice in Henderson, also engaged in farming; mem. U.S. Ho. of Reps. (Adams Democrat) from N.Y., 21st Congress, 1829-31. Died Henderson, Apr. 20, 1832; buried Clark Cemetery, Henderson.

HAWKINS, Joseph H., congressman; b. Lexington, Ky.; studied law. Admitted to Ky. bar, practiced law; mem. Ky. Ho. of Reps., 1810-13, speaker, 2 years; mem. U.S. Ho. of Reps. (Federalist) from Ky., 13th Congress, Mar. 29, 1814-15; resumed practice of law, engaged in merc. bus. Died New Orleans, La., 1823.

HAWKINS, Micajah Thomas, congressman; b. nr. Warrenton, N.C., May 20, 1790; attended U. N.C. Engaged in farming; mem. N.C. Ho. of Commons, 1819-20; mem. N.C. Senate, 1823-27, 46; served to maj. gen. N.C. Militia; mem. U.S. Ho. of Reps. (Democrat) from N.C., 22d-26th congresses, Dec. 15, 1831-41; mem. N.C. Council, 1854-55. Died nr. Warrenton, Dec. 22, 1858; buried family burying ground, nr. Warrenton.

HAWKS, Francis Lister, clergyman; b. New Bern, N.C., June 10, 1798; s. Francis and Julia (Stephens) H.; grad. with 1st honors U. N.C., 1815; attended Tapping Reeve's Law Sch., Litchfield, Conn.; m. Emily Kirby, 1823: m. 2d, Olivia Trowbridge; 8 children. Reporter, N.C. Supreme Ct., 1820-26; mem. N.C. Ho. of Commons from New Bern, 1821; ordained deacon, then priest Protestant Episcopal Ch., 1827; prof. divinity sch. Washington (now Trinity) Coll., Hartford, Conn., 1830; rector St. Stephen's Ch., later St. Thomas' Ch., N.Y.C., 1831-43; asst. sec. Gen. Conv., 1832; sec. N.Y. Diocesan Conv., 1834; prof. eccles. history Gen. Theol. Sem., 1833-35; founder ch. sch. St. Thomas Hall, Flushing, L.I., N.Y., 1839; an original trustee U. Miss.; rector Christ Ch., New Orleans, 1844; 1st pres. U. La., 1844-49; a founder Ch. Journal, N.Y., 1853; founder parish of our Savior and Iglesia de Santiaga, N.Y.C., 1865; leader reorgn. of N.Y. Hist. Soc.; a founder Am. Ethnol. Soc., v.p., 1855-59; a founder Am. Geog. and Statis. Soc., pres. for several years. Author: sects. "Va." (1836) and "Md." (1839) in Ecclesiastical History of the United States; Journals of the General Convention of the Protestant Eipscopal Church in the United States, 1861; (with W.S. Perry) Documentary History of the Protestant Episcopal Church in the United States of America, 2 vols., 1863-64. Died Sept. 27, 1866.

HAWKS, John, architect; b. Dragley, Lincolnshire, Eng., 1731; m. Mary Fisher, 1770, 1 child. Came to N.C., 1764; commd. by English Ct. to construct mansion for colonial gov. N.C., constructed mansion, 1767-70; commr. of finance for Gov. Tryon of Colony of N.C., 1770-73; clk. upper house N.C. Gen. Assembly, 1773-84; justice of peace for Craven County, N.C., 1773-84; 1st auditor N.C., 1784-90. Died New Bern, N.C., Feb. 16, 1790.

HAWLEY, Gideon, missionary; b. Stratfield, Conn., Nov. 5, 1727; s. Gideon and Hannah (Bennett) H.; grad. Yale, 1749; m. Lucy Fessenden, June 14, 1759; m. 2d Mrs. Elizabeth Burchard, Oct. 7, 1778; 5 children. Licensed to preach by Fairfield East Assn., Congressional Ch., 1750; missionary to Indians at Stockbridge, Mass., 1752; established mission among the Six Nations on the Susquehanna River, 1754-56, acted as interpreter; went on temporary mission to Indians, Marshpee, Mass., 1758, Indians petitioned to have him made permanent minister, requested granted by Commrs. of Soc. for Propagating Gospels. Died Marshpee, Oct. 3, 1807.

HAWLEY, Gideon. ednl. adminstr.; b. Huntington, Conn., Sept. 26, 1785; s. Gideon and Sarah (Curtiss) H.; B.A., Union Coll., 1809; m. Margarita Lansing, Oct. 19, 1814, 2 children. Admitted to Albany (N.Y.) bar, 1812; dir. Mohawk & Hudson R.R.; treas. Utica & Schenectady R.R.; pioneer in railroad devel. in N.Y.; 1st supt. of public instrn. for N.Y. State, 1812-21; laid foundations for public elementary schools N.Y. State, circa 1821, sec. bd. regents State U. N.Y., mem bd., 1842-70; 1814-41; dominant figure N.Y. State end., a founder 1st normal sch. in N.Y. (now Coll. of Edn. of State U. N.Y.), 1844; bd. regents Smithsonian Instn., 1846-61. Author: Essays on Truth and Knowledge, 1856. Died Albany, July 17, 1870.

HAWLEY, John Baldwin, congressman; b. Hawleyville, Conn., Feb. 9, 1831; attended Jacksonville (Ill.) Coll.; studied law. Admitted to Ill. bar, 1854, began practice in Rock Island; state's atty., 1856-60; served as capt. Co. H., 45th Regt., Ill.

Volunteer Inf. during Civil War, ret. because of injuries, 1862; apptd. postmaster of Rock Island, 1865, removed from office by Pres. Johnson, 1866; mem. U.S. Ho. of Reps. (Republican) from Ill., 41st-43d congresses, 1869-75; asst. sec. of treasury U.S., 1877-80; resumed law practice, Chgo., 1880; gen. atty. for Western brs. Northwestern R.R. Co., Omaha, Neb. Died Hot Springs, S.D., May 24, 1895; buried Prospect Hill Cemetery, Omaha.

HAWLEY, Joseph, patriot; b. Northampton, Mass., Oct. 8, 1723; s. Joseph Hawley; grad. Yale, 1742; m. Mercy Lyman, Nov. 30, 1752. Admitted to Mass. bar, 1749; largely influential in Jonathan Edwards' dismissal from the church; mem. bd. selectmen Northhampton, 1747-88, often chmn.; commd. maj. 2d Hampshire County Regt., Mass. Militia, 1754; mem. Mass. Gen. Ct., 1751, 54, 55 56; settled boundary dispute between Mass. and N.Y., 1773; leading proponent of Revolution in Connecticut Valley, 1774-76; favored disestablishment of church; refused to take seat in Mass. Senate because of religious oath qualification, 1780; active in maintaining law and order during Western Mass. riots, 1782. Died Hampshire County, Mass., Mar. 10, 1788.

HAWS, John Henry Hobart, congressman; b. N.Y.C., 1809; grad. Columbia, 1827; studied law. Admitted to N.Y. bar, began practice of law; mem. U.S. Ho. of Reps. (Whig) from N.Y., 37th Congress, 1851-53. Died N.Y.C., Jan. 27, 1858; buried St. Stephen's Cemetery, reinterred Greenwood Cemetery, Bklyn.

HAWTHORNE, Nathaniel, author; b. Salem, Mass., July 4, 1804; s. Nathaniel and Elizabeth (Manning) H.; grad. Bowdoin Coll., 1825; m. Sophia Peabody, July 9, 1842; children—Una, Julian, Rose. Lived and wrote in Salem, 1825-36, turned to short story writing after failure of Fanshawe (his 1st novel, pub. anonymously), 1828; his early stories include Ethan Brand, The Gentle Boy, The Maypole of Merry Mount, The Birthmark (many stories of this period collected and published as Twice Told Tales, 1837); editor Am. Mag. of Useful and Entertaining Knowledge, Boston, 1836; compiled Peter Parley's Universal History, 1837; weigher and gager Boston Custom House, 1839-41; invested in Brook Farm (founded by Transcendentalists), West Roxbury, Mass., lived there briefly, 1841, 42; moved to Concord, Mass., 1842, wrote short stories including Young Goodman Brown, Rappaccini's Daughter (collected and published as Mosses from An Old Manse, 1846); surveyor Port of Salem, 1845-49; U.S. consul in Liverpool, Eng. (apptd. by Pres. Franklin Pierce, a coll. classmate), 1853-58. Author: (novels) Scarlet Letter, 1850, The House of Seven Gables, 1851, Blithedale Romance (idea attributed to Brook Farm stay), 1852, The Marble Faun (based on European experiences), 1860; (children's books) A Wonder Book, 1852, Tanglewood Tales, 1853; (short stories) The Minister's Black Veil, The Snow Image, The Great Stone Face. Died Plymouth, N.H., May 18 or 19, 1864; buried Sleepy Hollow Cemetery, Concord.

HAY, Andrew Kessler, congressman, businessman; b. nr. Lowell, Mass., Jan. 19, 1809; Employed in mfg. window glass; engaged in mfg. glass, Winslow, N.J., also active in real estate and agr.; mem. U.S. Ho. of Reps. (Whig) from N.J., 31st Congress, 1849-51; Republican presdl. elector, 1872; pres. Camden & Atlantic R.R. Co., 1872-76. Died Winslow, Feb. 7, 1881; buried Colestown Cemetery, nr. Haddonfield, N.J.

HAY, Charles Augustus, clergyman; b. York, Pa., Feb. 11, 1821; s. John and Eliza (Ebert) H.; grad. Pa. Coll. (now Gettysburg Coll.), 1839, Gettsburg Theol. Sem.. 1841; postgrad. U. Berlin, U. Halle, 1841-43; m. Sarah Barnitz, May 5, 1845, 8 children. Licensed to preach, 1843; prof. Bibl. lit. and German, Gettysburg Theol. Sem., 1844-48, pres. bd. dirs., 1861-63, prof. Hebrew and Old Testament theology and German, 1865-93; minister Zion Ch., Harrisburg, Pa., 1849-65; Unionist; joined Synod of East Pa, 1857, pres., 1860,74; pres. Gen. Synod, 1881; trustee Pa. Coll., 40 years; noted as histo.ian of Luth. Ch. in Am.; curator Luth. Hist. Soc., many years; Died Gettysburg, Pa., June 26, 1893; buried Harrisburg, Pa.

HAY, George, jurist; b. Williamsburg, Va., Dec. 15, 1765; s. Anthony and Elizabeth (Davenport) H.; m. 2d, Elizabeth Monroe; 3 children, including Charles, Hortense. Mem. Va. Ho. of Dels.; U.S. dist. atty. for Va. dist., 1801; conducted prosecution of Aaron Burr for treason; apptd. judge U.S. Ct. for Eastern dist. Va., 1825. Author: Treatise on Expatriation, 1814; Treatise Against the Usury Laws; The Life of John Thompson; also 2 pamphlets on liberty of the press, 1799, 1803. Died Richmond, Va., Sept. 21, 1830.

HAYDEN, Amos Sutton, clergyman; b. Youngstown, O., Sept. 17, 1813; s. Samuel and Sophia Hayden; m. Sarah M. Ely, May 31, 1837. Converted to Disciples of Christ by Walter Scott; became independent evangelist for Disciples of Christ, 1832; pastor of ch., Collamer, Cuyahogan County, O., 1840-57, 59-80; a founder Western Reserve Eclectic Inst., Hiram, O., 1850, pres., 1850-57; prin. McNeely Normal Sch., Hopedale, O., 1858-59. Author: The Christian Hymn and Tune Book, 1870; The Early History of the Disciples in the Western Reserve, 1875. Died Sept. 10, 1880.

HAYDEN, Ferdinand Vandiveer, geologist; b. Westfield, Mass., Sept. 7, 1829; s. Asa and Melinda (Hawley) H.; A.B., Oberlin Coll., 1850; M.D., Albany Med. Coll., 1853; LL.D., U. Rochester, 1876, U. Pa., 1887; m. Emma Woodruff, Nov. 9, 1871. Went to Badlands of S.D. on collecting trip, 1853; 1st contbn. to geology was a vertical geol. sect. showing order of superposition of the strata; geologist on staff Lt. G. K. Warren of Topog. Engrs. in the surveying expdn. of Yellowstone and Missouri rivers and Badlands of S.D., 1856-57; with F. B. Meek in explorations in Kan. Territory, 1858; explored Yellowstone and Missouri rivers with Capt. W. F. Raynolds, 1859-62; served as surgeon U.S. Army, 1861-65, promoted to lt. col., 1864; prof. geology U. Pa., 1865-72; entered upon a survey of Neb. Territory in 1867 which laid foundation for U.S. Geol. Survey as it exists today; his work resulted in the setting aside of land for Yellowstone Nat. Park. Mem. Acad. Natural Scis. of Phila., Nat. Acad. Scis., Geol. Socs. of London and Edinburgh, Geologosche Reichsanstalt of Vienna, Société Impériale of Moscow. Died Phila., Dec. 22, 1887.

HAYDEN, Horace H., dentist, geologist, coll. pres.; b. Windsor, Conn., Oct. 13, 1769; s. Thomas and Abigail (Parsons) H.; received D.D.S. as mem. Am. Soc. Dental Surgeons, 1840; M.D. (hon.), Med. Sch., U. Md., 1840; m. Marie Robinson, Feb. 23, 1805, 6 children including Handel. Licensed as dentist by Med. and Chirurgical Faculty of Md., 1810; asst. surgeon, sgt. Md. Militia, 1814; 1st sec. Balt. Phys. Assn., 1818; pres. Md. Acad. Scis. and Lit. 1826; prin. founder Balt. Coll. Dental Surgery (world's 1st dental coll.), 1840, 1st pres., 1st prof. principles of dental science, prof. dental physiology and pathology until 1844; influenced orgn. of Am. Soc. Dental Surgeons, N.Y.C., 1840; discovered nr. Balt. a form of chalazite (named Haydenite after him. Author: Geological Essays; or An Inquiry into Some of the Geological Phenomena to be Found in the Various Parts of America and Elswhere, 1820. Died Balt., Jan. 26, 1844.

HAYDEN, Joseph, inventor, mfr.; b. Foxborough, Mass., July 31, 1802; s. Daniel and Abigail (Shepard) H.; m. Ruhamah Guilford, 1819, 1 son, Hiram Washington. Started in mech. work with his father in Mass.; moved to Waterbury, Conn., entered brass industry; invented machine to manufacture cloth-covered buttons, 1828; patented invention of wire-eyed buttons, also machines for making them, 1830. Died Feb. 17, 1877.

HAYDEN, Moses, congressman; b. nr. Westfield, Mass., 1786; grad. Williams Coll., 1804; studied law. Admitted to N.Y. bar, began practice in York; 1st judge Ct. Common Pleas of Livingston County (N.Y.), 1821-23; mem. U.S. Ho. of Reps. from N.Y., 18th-19th congresses, 1823-27; mem. N.Y. Senate, 1829-30. Died Albany, N.Y., Feb. 13, 1830; buried Mt. Pleasant Cemetery, York.

HAYDEN, William, pioneer evangelist Disciples of Christ; b. Rosstrevor Twp., Pa., June 30, 1799; s. Samuel and Sophia Hayden; m. Mary McCollum, Dec. 20, 1818. Converted to and joined Bapt. Ch.; adopted views of the Disciples, circa 1821; licensed to preach, May 1828, ordained, 1828; evangelistic worker, chiefly in Western Res.; established Western Res. Eclectic Inst. (Hiram Coll.). Died Chargin Falls, O., Apr. 7, 1863.

HAYES, Augustus Allen, chemist; b. Windsor, Vt., Feb. 28, 1806; s. Thomas Allen and Sophia (West) H.; attended med. sch. Dartmouth, M.D. (hon.), 1846; m. Henrietta Bridge Dana, July 13, 1836. Published account of he isolation of alkaloidal compound which he called sanguinaria; 1825; investigated certain chromium compounds, 1826-28; became dir. of large plant mfg. colors and other chemicals, Roxbury, Mass.; consulting chemist for several large dyeing, bleaching, gas-making and smelting establishments in New Eng.; state assayer Mass.; devised methods for shortening the time needed in smelting iron and refining copper; work led to fundamental inprovements in constrn. of furnaces and arrangement of steam boilers; conducted investigation of water supply, Charlestown, Mass., 1859-60; devised and used simple elec. method of detecting the limits of slight impurities in drinking water; 1st to suggest application of oxides of iron in refining of pig iron mem. Am. Acad. Arts and Scis., contbr. scientific papers to its Proceedings, also to Am. Jour. of Science. Died Brookline, Mass., June 21, 1882.

HAYES, Isaac Israel, physician, explorer; b. Chester County, Pa., Mar. 5, 1832; s. Benjamin and Ann (Borton) H.; M.D., U. Pa., 1853. Surgeon, 2d Arctic expdn. of Elisha Kent Kane, 1853; explored unknown coast of Ellismere Land northwest of Cape Sabine; organized new expdn. to determine extent of Arctic Ocean (financed largely by Am. Geog. Soc. and Henry Grinnell), sailed from Boston, 1860, expdn. helped open way to North Pole; in charge Satterlee Hosp., West Philadelphia, during Civil War; promoted maj., then col. U.S. Army; made 3d voyage to Arctic, 1869; attended Iceland millennial as correspondent for N.Y. Herald, 1874; mem. N.Y. Assembly (Republican); a promoter Hudson River Tunnel. Author: The Open Polar Sea, 1876; The Land of Desolation (sketch of Greenland), published London, 1871, N.Y.C., 1872. Died N.Y.C., Dec. 17, 1881.

HAYES, John Lord, lawyer, editor; b. South Berwick, Me., Apr. 13, 1812; s. William Allen and Susan (Lord) H.; grad. Dartmouth, 1831; attended Harvard Law Sch., 1833-34; m. Caroline S. Ladd, May 29, 1839. Admitted to N.H. bar, 1835; clk. U.S. Circuit Ct. for N.H., 1840-43; became mem. Boston Soc. of Natural History, 1845; rep. Iron Masters of New Eng., 1850-51; practiced law, Washington, D.C., 1851-61; chief clk. U.S. Patent Office, 1861-65; sec. Nat. Assn. of Wool Mfrs., 1865-69, editor of its Bulletin, 1869-87; headed U.S. Tariff Commn., 1882-83; wrote and studied in field of tariffs, 1883-87. Died Cambridge, Mass., Apr. 18, 1887.

HAYES, Lucy Webb, 1st lady; b. 1831; dau. of Dr. James Webb; attended Wesleyan Female Coll., Cincinnati; m. Rutherford Birchard Hayes, Dec. 30, 1852; children—Birchard A., Webb C., Rutherford P., Joseph T., George C., Frances, Scott R., Manning F. An advocate of temperance, did not allow alcoholic beverages in White House, even on ofcl. state occasions. Died Fremont, O., June 25, 1889.

HAYES, Rutherford Birchard, 19th Pres. U.S.; b. Delaware, O., Oct. 4, 1822; s. Rutherford and Sophia (Birchard) H.; grad. Kenyon Coll., Gambier, O., 1842, LL.D. (hon.), 1868; grad. Harvard Law Sch., 1845; LL.D. (hon.), Harvard, 1877, Yale, 1880, Johns Hopkins, 1881; m. Lucy Webb, Dec. 30, 1852; children—Birchard Austin, Webb Cook, Rutherford Platt, Joseph T., George C., Frances, Scott R., Manning F. Admitted to Ohio bar, 1845; mem. Literary Club of Cincinnati; city solicitor Cincinnati, 1858; commd. maj. 23d Regt., Ohio Volunteers, 1861; in command of Gen. George Crook's 1st Inf. Brigade, 1863-64; promoted brig. gen., 1864; brevetted maj. gen. U.S. Volunteers, 1865; mem. U.S. Ho. of Reps. from Ohio, 39th-40th congresses, 1865-June 20, 1867 (resigned), sided with radical Republicans in U.S. Congress; gov. Ohio (Rep.), 1868-72, 75-77, obtained reforms in treatment of insane, helped create Ohio Geol. Survey; Republican candidate for Pres. U.S. (against Democrat Samuel J. Tilden), 1876, elected (after disputed Electoral Commn. results) by spl. electoral commn. created by Congress; Pres. U.S., 1877-81, withdrew last fed. troops from South, attempted to reform Civil Service, opposed free and unlimited coinage of silver as legal tender; pres. Nat. Prison Assn., 1883-93; trustee Peabody Edn. Fund, Slater Fund. Died Fremont, O., Jan. 17, 1893; buried Spiegel Grove Park, Fremont.

HAYGOOD, Atticus Green, bishop, educator; b. Watkinsville, Ga., Nov. 19, 1839; s. Green B. and Martha (Askew) H.; grad. Emory Coll., 1859; m. Mary Yarbrough, 1859. Admitted to trial into Ga. Conf. of Methodist Episcopal Ch. South, 1859; served as chaplain in Confederate Army; Sunday Sch. sec. Ga. Conf. Meth. Episcopal Ch.s., 1870; pres. Emory Coll., 1875-84; edited Wesleyan Christian Advocate, 1878-82; elected bishop but declined to serve (1st in his church to reject this honor), 1882; became agt. of John F. Slater Fund, established for edn. of Negroes, 1883; bishop, Los Angeles, 1890-93; advocated fed. aid for Negro edn., opposed leasing of convicts as common laborers. Author: Our Children, 1877, Our Brother in Black, 1881, Sermons and Speeches, 1883; Pleas for Progress, 1889. Died Oxford, Ga., Jan. 19, 1896.

HAYGOOD, Laura Askew, missionary; b. Watkinsville, Ga., Oct. 14, 1845; d. Green B. and Martha Ann (Askew) H. Tchr., Palmer Inst., Oxford, Ga., 1862-66; opened and conducted sch. for girls, Atlanta, Ga., 1866-72; instr. Girl's High Sch., Atlanta, 1872-77, prin., 1877-84; missionary for Woman's Bd. of Missions of Methodist Episcopal Ch. South, in China, 1884-1900; established McTyeire Home and Sch., Shanghai, China, 1889; traveled and lectured in U.S., 1894-96, returned to China, 1896; Laura Haygood Home and Sch., Soochow, China, established as a meml. to her. Died Shanghai, Apr. 29, 1900.

HAYMOND, Thomas Sherwood, congressman; b. nr. Fairmont, Va. (now W.Va.), Jan. 15, 1794; attended Coll. William and Mary; studied law. Served as pvt. during War of 1812; admitted to Va. bar, 1815, began practice in Morgantown, Va. (now W. Va.); mem. U.S. Ho. of Reps. (Whig) from Va., 31st Congress, Nov. 8, 1849-51; served as brig. gen.

Va. Militia; commd. col. Confederate Army, 1861, served throughout Civil War. Died Richmond, Va., Apr. 5, 1869; buried Palatine Cemetery, nr. Fairmont.

HAYMOND, William Summerville, physician, congressman, coll. dean; b. nr. Clarksburg, Va. (now W.Va.), Feb. 20, 1823; grad. Bellevue Hosp. Med. Coll., N.Y.C. Began practice of medicine, Monticello, Ind., 1852; served as surgeon U.S. Army during Civil War, 1862-63; unsuccessful candidate for state senator, 1866; pres. Indpls., Delphi & Chgo. R.R. Co., 1872-74; mem. U.S. Ho. of Reps. (candidate of both Democrats and Liberals) from Ind., 44th Congress, 1875-77; organizer Central Med. Coll., Indpls., 1877, dean, 1877-85; published a history of Ind. 1879. Died Indpls., Dec. 24, 1885; buried Crown Hill Cemetery, Indpls.

HAYNE, Arthur Peronneau, senator, army officer; b. Charleston, S.C., Mar. 12, 1790. Engaged in bus.; served as 1st lt. at Sackets Harbor, during War of 1812, maj. of cavalry on St. Lawrence River, insp. gen., 1814; brevetted lt. col. for gallantry at Battle of New Orleans; admitted to the bar, practiced law; served as comdr. Tenn. Volunteers during Fla. War; ret., 1820; mem. S.C. Ho. of Reps.; Democratic presdl. elector, 1828; U.S. naval agt. in Mediterranean for 5 years; declined Belgian mission; mem. U.S. Senate from S.C., May 11-Dec. 2, 1858. Died Charleston, Jan. 7, 1867; buried St. Michael's Churchyard, Charleston.

HAYNE, Isaac, planter, army officer; b. Colleton Dist., S.C., Sept. 23, 1745; s. Isaac and Sarah (Williamson) H.; m. Elizabeth Hutson, July 18, 1765, 2 children. Planter and breeder of fine horses in S.C., before Am. Revolution; served as capt. Colleton Militia, during Revolutionary War; swore allegiance to Crown after fall of City of Charlston (S.C.), with assurance that mil. service would not be required of him, later ordered to join Brit. Army; considering this a release from his oath of allegiance, joined S.C. Militia, captured Gen. Andrew Williamson. Captured by Col. Nisbet Balfour, July 1781, hung at Charleston, Aug. 4, 1781.

HAYNE, Paul Hamilton, poet; b. Charleston, S.C., Jan. 1, 1830; s. Lt. Paul Hamilton (USN) and Emily (McElhenny) H.; grad. Charleston Coll., 1850; LL.D. (hon.), Washington and Lee Coll., 1882; m. Mary Michel, 1852; 1 son, William Hamilton. Mem. editorial staffs So. Literary Gazette and Washington Spectator; helped make Charleston literary center of the South; a founder, an editor Russell's Mag., 1857-60; poet in Charleston during Civil War; lost property as result of war. Author: (1st poem) On the Ashley River; Poems, 1855, Sonnets and Other Poems, 1857, Avolia, A Legend, 1860, Legends and Lyrics (considered his best), 1872, The Mountain of the Lovers and Other Poems, 1875; Lives of Robert Young Hayne and Hugh Swinton Legare, 1878. Editor: Henry Timrod: Poems with a Memoir, 1872. Died Augusta, Ga., July 6, 1886.

HAYNE, Robert Young, senator, gov. S.C.; b. St. Paul's Parish, S.C., Nov. 10, 1791; s. William and Elizabeth (Peronneau) H.; m. Frances Pinckney; m. 2d, Rebecca Alston. Admitted to S.C. bar, 1812; mem. S.C. legislature, 1814-18, speaker of house, 1818; atty. gen. S.C., 1819-20; mem. U.S. Senate from S.C., 1823-32, an exponent of strict constl. constrn., noted for debate with Daniel Webster over tariff and states' rights (touched off by Foot Resolution on restraint of sale of public lands, Dec. 29, 1829) which developed into 2-week bout of oratory covering wide range of subjects; gov. S.C., 1832-34, supported Calhoun during nullification crisis but moderated views when Clay called for compromise; mayor Charleston (S.C.), 1835-36; pres. Louisville, Cincinnati & Charleston R.R. Co., 1836-39. Died Asheville, N.C., Sept. 24, 1839.

HAYNES, Charles Eaton, physician, congressman; b. Brunswick, Va., Apr. 15, 1784; grad. in medicine, U. Pa., Practiced medicine; mem. U.S. Ho. of Reps. from Ga., as Democrat, 19th-21st congresses, 1825-31, as Unionist, 24th-25th congresses, 1835-39. Died Aug. 29, 1841; buried Sparta, Ga.

HAYNES, John, colonial gov.; b. Essex, Eng., 1594; s. John and Mary (Mitchell) H.; m. Mary Thornton; m. 2d, Mabel Harlakenden; 8 children including John, Roger, Joseph, Ruth, Mabel. Came to Am., 1633; assistant Mass. Bay Colony, 1634, gov., 1635-36, pronounced sentence of banishment upon Roger Williams, considered John Winthrop's adminstrn. of justice too lenient; commd. col. Mass. Regt., 1636; moved to Conn., 1637; 1st gov. Colony of Conn., 1639, chosen gov. Conn. every alternate year until death under rules of Fundamemtal Orders adopted 1638-39; worked to establish union of New Eng. colonies, 1637-43, mem. New Eng. Confederation 1643; rep. from Conn. to meetings of commrs. of united colonies, 1646, 50. Died Hartford, Conn., Jan. 1653/4.

HAYS, Alexander, army officer; b. Franklin, Pa., July 8, 1819; s. Samuel and Agnes (Broadfoot) H.; grad. U.S. Mil. Acad., 1844; m. Annie Adams McFadden, Feb. 19, 1846. Served with U.S. Army on frontier in La. after 1844; brevetted 1st lt. for services at battles of Palo Alto and Resaca-de-la-Palma in Mexican War; resigned commn., 1848; prospected for gold in Cal., 1849-51; engaged in constrn. bus. in Pa., 1851-61; returned to U.S. Army with rank of capt. 16th Inf., 1861; promoted to col. 63d Pa. Regt. in defense of Washington (D.C.), 1861; served in Army of Potomac, 1862-64; brevetted maj. for services at battles of Fair Oaks, Peach Orchard and Glendale (Va.); brevetted lt. col. after Battle of Malvern Hill, 1862; wounded at Battle of Manassas; given command of div., 1863; brevetted col. for conduct in Battle of Gettysburg. Killed on 2d day of Battle of Wilderness, May 5, 1864.

HAYS, Charles, congressman; b. "Hays Mount" nr. Boligee, Ala., Feb. 2, 1834; attended U. Ga., U. Va. Cotton planter; del. Democratic Nat. Conv., Balt., 1860; served as maj. Confederate Army; mem. Ala. Constl. Conv., 1867; mem. Ala. Senate, 1868; mem. U.S. Ho. of Reps. (Republican) from Ala., 41st-44th congresses, 1869-77. Died "Myrtle Hall," Greene County, Ala., June 24, 1879; buried family cemetery, "Hays Mount."

HAYS, Edward Retilla, congressman; b. nr. Fostoria, Ohio, May 26, 1847; attended Heidelberg Coll., Tiffin, O. Served as pvt. 1st Regt., Ohio Heavy Arty., 1862-65; admitted to the bar, 1869; began law practice, Knoxville, Ia.; mem. U.S. Ho. of Reps. (Republican) from Ia., 51st Congress, Nov. 4, 1890-91; resumed law practiced. Died Knoxville, Feb. 28, 1896; buried Graceland Cemetery, Knoxville.

HAYS, Harry Thompson, lawyer, army officer; b. Wilson County, Tenn., Apr. 14, 1820; s. Harmon and Elizabeth (Cage) H.; grad. St. Mary's Coll., Balt.; m. Elizabeth Cage, circa 1859. Served in Mexican War; formed successful legal practice with W.C. Harmon, New Orleans, 1848; del. to Whig Nat. Nominating Conv., 1852, Scott ticket presdl. elector, 1852; commd. col. 7th La. Regt., Army No. Va., 1861, brig. gen., 1862, maj. gen., 1865; sheriff Orleans Parish, 1866. Died New Orleans, Aug. 21, 1876; buried Washington St. Cemetery, New Orleans.

HAYS, Isaac, ophthalmologist, med. editor; b. Phila., July 5, 1796; s. Samuel and Richea (Gratz) H.; B.A., U. Pa., 1816, M.D., 1820; m. Sarah Minis, 1834, 4 children including Isaac Minis. One of first to study colorblindness and astigmatism; invented spl. knife for cataract operations; mem. staff Infirmary for Diseases of the Eye and Ear, Phila., 1822-27; surgeon Wills' Ophthalmic Hosp., Phila., 1834-54; fellow Coll. of Physicians, Phila., 1835-79; editor-in-chief Am. Jour. Med. Scis., 1827-79; established Med. News, 1843; published Monthly Abstract of Med. Science, 1874-79; a founder Franklin Inst., A.M.A.; mem. Acad. Natural Scis. of Phila., pres., 1865-69. Died Phila., Apr. 13, 1879.

HAYS, John Coffee, army officer; b. Wilson County, Tenn., Jan. 28, 1817; s. Harmon and Elizabeth (Cage) H.; m. Susan Calvert, 1857, 6 children. Went to Tex., 1836; served in Texan Army against Indians and Mexicans, 1836-40; capt. Tex. Rangers, serving in the region between Rio Grande and Nueces rivers, 1840-47; col. Tex. Volunteer Ca., Mexican War; moved to Cal., 1849; sheriff San Francisco County, 1850-53; apptd. surveyor-gen. Cal., 1853; engaged in real estate, banking, indsl. affairs. Died Apr. 28, 1885.

HAYS, Samuel, congressman; b. County Donegal, Ireland, Sept. 10, 1783. Came to U.S., 1792; treas. Venango County (Pa.), 1808, sheriff, 1808, 20, 29, 33; mem. Pa. Ho. of Reps., 1813, 16, 23, 25, Pa. Senate, 1822, 39; trustee Allegheny Coll., Meadville, Pa., 1837-61; served as brig. gen. in command 1st Brigade, 7th Div., Pa. Militia, 1841-43; mem. U.S. Ho. of Reps. (Democrat) from Pa., 28th Congress, 1843-45; mfr. of iron, nr. Franklin, Pa.; apptd. U.S. marshal for Western dist. Pa., 1847; asso. judge dist. ct., 1856. Died Franklin, July 1, 1868; buried Old Town Cemetery, Franklin, Reinterred, New Franklin Cemetery.

HAYS, Samuel Lewis, congressman; b. nr. Clarksburg, Va. (now W.Va.), Oct. 20, 1794; Engaged in farming, Stewarts Creek Va. (now Glenville, W.Va.); mem. Va. Assembly; mem. U.S.,Ho. of Reps. (Democrat) from Va., 27th Congress, 1841-43; Dem. presdl. elector, 1844, 52, 56; del. Va. Constl. Conv., 1850; receiver of pub. moneys, Sauk Rapids, Minn. (apptd. by Pres. Buchanan), 1857-60. Died Sauk Rapids, Mar. 17, 1871; buried original Old Benton County (Minn.) Cemetery.

HAYS, William Jacob, painter; b. N.Y.C., Aug. 8, 1830; s. Aaron Burr and Sarah Pool (Foreman) H.; m. Helen Dummer, 1865. Exhibited 1st picture Dogs in a Field at Nat. Acad. Design, 1850; asso. N.A.D., 1852-57; made study of fauna and landscape of Colo., Wyo. and Rocky Mountains, 1860 (The Wounded Buffalo most important picture of the group); considered one of ablest painters in the country. Prin. works include: Head of Bull Dog, 1852, The Stampede, A Herd on the Move, Setter and Game, Prairie-dog Village. Died N.Y.C., Mar. 13, 1875.

HAYWARD, George, surgeon; b. Boston, Mar. 9, 1791; s. Lemuel Hayward; grad. Harvard, 1809; M.D., U. Pa., 1812. Physician to the almshouse, Boston; fellow Am. Acad. Arts and Scis., 1818; asst. surgeon Mass. Gen. Hosp., 1826; founder (with John Collins Warren and Enoch Hale) med. sch., Boston, 1830-38; sc. Mass. Med. Soc., 1832-35; lectr. Harvard Med. Sch., 1834, prof. principles of surgery, clin. surgery, 1835-49; surgeon-in-chief Mass. Gen. Hosp., 1838; performed 1st maj. operation (amputation) using ether 1846; pres. Mass. Med. Soc., 1825-55; fellow Harvard, 1852-63. Translator: Anatomie Generale (Bechat), 1822. Author: (1st Am. text of physiology) Outlines of Human Physiology, 1834. Died Boston, Oct. 7, 1863.

HAYWARD, Nathaniel Manley, inventor, mfr.; b. Easton, Mass., Jan. 19, 1808; s. Jerahmeel Hayward; m. Louisa Buke, 7 children. Discovered that sulphur is agt. which prevents rubber from softening when warm; successfully produced rubber which would not become soft and sticky in summertime, 1835; result of discovery, employed as gen. supt. Eagle India Rubber Corp., Woburn, Mass., 1835, became co-owner, 1836, sole owner, 1838, sold factory to Charles Goodyear, 1838; brought about superficial vulcanization; granted patent on volcanization, 1839; discovered method of giving rubber shoes a luster; mgr. Hayward Rubber Co., Colchester, Conn., 1847-54, pres. co., 1855-65, obtained large govt. contracts during Civil War. Died Colchester, July 18, 1865.

HAYWARD, William, Jr., congressman; b. "Shipshead" nr. Easton, Md., 1787; attended Easton Acad.; grad. Princeton, 1808; studied law. Admitted to Md. bar, 1809, began practice in Easton; mem. Md. Ho. of Dels., 1818-20; del. Md. Democratic Conv., 1818; mem. U.S. Ho. of Reps. (Dem.) from Md., 18th Congress, 1823-25; practiced law, Easton, 1825-36. Died Easton, Oct. 19, 1836; buried "Shipshead."

HAYWOOD, John, jurist, historian; b. Halifax, County, N.C., Mar. 16, 1762; s. Egbert and Sarah (Ware) H.; m. Martha Edwards, 1785. Solicitor gen. N.C., 1790, 1790-91, atty. gen., 1791-93; judge Superior Ct. N.C., 1793-1800, compiled decisions (earliest series of law reports in N.C.); moved to Tenn. to practice law, 1807; judge Supreme Ct. Tenn., 1818-26; founder, 1st pres. Tenn. Antiquarian Soc.; interviewed many settlers and wrote 1st history books about Tenn. Author: The Christian Advocate, 1819; The Natural and Aboriginal History of Tenn., 1823; The Civil and Political History of Tenn., 1823. Died Nashville, Tenn., Dec. 22, 1826.

HAYWOOD, William Henry, Jr., senator; b. Raleigh, N.C., Oct. 23, 1801; grad. U. N.C., 1819; studied law. Admitted to N.C. bar, 1822, began practice in Raleigh; mem. N.C. Ho. of Commons, 1831, 34-36, speaker, 1836; declined appointment as chargé d'affaires Belgium; mem. U.S. Senate (Democrat) from N.C., 1843-July 25, 1846; resumed law practice, Raleigh. Died Raleigh, Oct. 7, 1852; buried Old City Cemetery, Raleigh.

HAZARD, Augustus George, businessman; b. South Kingstown, R.I., Apr. 28, 1802; s. Thomas S. and Silence (Knowles) H.; m. Salome Goodwin Merrill, 1822, 8 children. Engaged in oil and paint bus., Savannah, Ga., 1822-27; co-owner of N.Y. to Savannah shipping line, N.Y.C., circa 1828; partner Loomises, Hazard & Co., 1837-43 (became Hazard Powder Co., 1843-68); Hazardville (Conn.) named for him. Died Enfield, Conn., May 7, 1868.

HAZARD, Ebenezer, govt. ofcl.; b. Phila., Jan. 15, 1744; s. Samuel and Catherine (Clarkson) H.; grad. Coll. of N.J. (now Princeton), 1762, A.M., 1765; m. Abigail Arthur, Sept. 11, 1783; 1 son, Samuel. Partner, publishing firm Noel & Hazard, N.Y.C., 1769-75; authorized by N.Y. Cm. of Safety to reorganize local postal service, 1775; commd. 1st postmaster N.Y.C. by Continental Congress, 1775; apptd. surveyor-gen. U.S. Post Office,1 776-82, postmaster-gen., 1782-89; 1st sec. Ins. Co. of N.Am.; mgr. Schuylkill Bridge Co., also Del. & Schuylkill Canal Co.; trustee Presbyn. Gn. Assembly; curator Am. Philos. Soc.; corresponding mem. Mass. Hist. Soc.; mem. N.Y. Hist. Soc.; pioneer collector and publisher of original hist. records, responsible for publ. Belknap's History of New Hampshire, 1784. Editor: Historical Collections, 2 vols., 1792-94. Died Phila., June 13, 1817.

HAZARD, Jonathan J. ((called Beau Jonathan), Continental congressman; b. Newport, R.I., 1744; s. Jonathan and Abigail (Mac Coun)) H.; m. Patience Hazard; m. 2d, Hannah Brown; m. 3d, Marian Gage. Mem. R. I. Ho. of Reps., 1776, 78, 90-1805; paymaster R.I. Battalion, Continental Army,

'77; joined George Washington's Army, 1777; em. R.I. Council of War, 1778; mem. Continental ongress from R.I., 1787-89; del. R.I. Conv. at outh Kingstown, 1790; opposed ratification U.S. nstn. Died on an estate in the friends' settlement Verona, N.Y., after 1824.

HAZARD, Rowland Gibson, mfr.; b. South Kingsn R.I., Oct. 9, 1801; s. Rowland and Mary Peace) H.; m. Caroline Newbold, Sept. 25, 1828. sso. with his brother Isaac Peace in woolen indusy, Peacedale, R.I., 1819-48; mem. R.I. Ho. of eps., 1851, 54, 89, R.I. Senate, 1866; del. Reiblican nat. convs., 1856, 60, 68; retired from isiness, 1866, devoted himself to writing and studyg; trustee Brown U., 1869-75. Author Language: Connexion with the Present Condition and Future Prospects of Man, 1836; Our Resources, 1864; reedom of Mind in Willing; or Every Being that 'ills a Creative First Cause, 1864; Two Letters on ausation and Freedom in Willing, Addressed to ohn Stuart Mill, 1869. Died June 24, 1888.

HAZARD, Samuel, editor; b. Phila., May 26, 784; s. Ebenezer and Abigail (Arthur) H.; m. bigail Clark Hetfield, Mar. 18, 1819. Mcht. in hila., in early years; conducted cotton brokerage isiness, Huntsville, Ala. Territory, 1818-27; found- Register of Pa. (weekly periodical), Phila., 1828-6; editor U.S. Comml. and Statis. Register, 1839-2; editor (commd. by gov. Pa.) Pennsylvania Arcives: Selected and Arranged from Original Docuents in the Office of the Secretary of the Commonealth, 1852-56; edited The Annals of Pennsylvania, om the Discovery of the Delaware, 1609-1682, ublished 1850. Died Germantown, Pa., May 22, 870.

HAZARD, Thomas, abolitionist; b. Narragansett, .I., Sept. 15, 1720; s. Robert and Sarah (Borden) .; attended Yale; m. Elizabeth Robinson, 1742. ne of 1st mems. Soc. of Friends to take stand gainst slavery, mem. com. of Yearly Meeting which ent to R.I. Gen. Assembly with bill affirming ersonal freedom, 1774 (resulted in abolishment f slavery in R.I. 1784); mem. com. of Yearly Meetig which brought to Gen. Assembly a petition for bolition of slavery, 1783; a founder Providence Soc. r Abolishing Slave Trade; an incorporator R.I. Coll. now Brown U.) a founder Friends' Sch., Providence, .I. Died Aug. 26, 1798.

HAZARD, Thomas Robinson, agriculturalist, soial reformer; b. South Kingston, R.I., Jan. 3, 1797; . Rowland and Mary (Peace) H.; m. Frances Minurn, Oct. 12, 1838. Began raising sheep, Narraganett, R.I., before 1821, also manufactured textiles, 821-40; worked for cause known as Modern Spiritalism, 1854-60; v.p. Am. Colonization Soc.; pronoted relief work in U.S., 1846-47; wrote against lavery, war, exclusion of women from suffrage. Died Mar. 26, 1886.

HAZELIUS, Ernest Lewis, clergyman; b. Neusaly, ilesian Prussia, Sept. 6, 1777; s. Eric and Chrisiana (Brahty) H.; D.D. (hon.), Union and Columbia colls., 1824; m. Hulda Cummings, 1810. Licensed o preach Moravian Ch., 1800, sent to Nazareth, Pa.; taught Latin, Greek, theology Moravian Sch., Nazareth, 1800-09; ordained to ministry Lutheran Ch., 1809; pastor New Germantown, German Valley nd Spruce Run in Hunterdon and Morris counties (N.J.), 1809-15; prof. theology Hartwick Sem., Otego County, N.Y., 1815-30; prof. Gettysburg Theol. Sem., 1830-33; prof. theology Classical and Theol. Inst. of Synod of S.C., Lexington, 1834-53. Died Feb. 20, 1853.

HAZELTINE, Abner, congressman; b. Wardsboro, Vt., June 10, 1793; grad. Williams Coll., 1815; studied law, Jamestown, N.Y. Admitted to N.Y. bar, 1819, began practice in Chautauqua County; 1st located county lawyer, Warren, Pa.; resumed law practice, Jamestown, 1823; editorial writer Jamestown Jour., 1826-29; mem. N.Y. Assembly, 1829-30; mem. U.S. Ho. of Reps. (Whig) from N.Y., 23d-24th congresses, 1833-37; pros. atty. Chautauqua County, 1847-50, judge, 1859-63, apptd. spl. county judge, 1873, did not qualify; U.S. commr. for No. dist. N.Y., until 1879. Died Jamestown, Dec. 20, 1879; buried Lakeview Cemetery, Jamestown.

HAZELTON, John Wright, congressman; b. Mullica Hill, N.J., Dec. 10, 1814; attended common schs. Engaged in farming; del. Republican Nat. Conv., Phila., 1856, Chgo., 1868; Rep. presidential elector, 1868; mem. U.S. Ho. of Reps. (Rep.) from N.J., 42d-43d congresses, 1871-75; resumed farming. Died nr. Mullica Hill, Dec. 20, 1878; buried Friends Cemetery, Mullica Hill.

HAZELWOOD, John, naval officer; b. Eng., circa 1726; m. Mary Edgar, Aug. 10, 1753; m. 2d, Esther Fleeson. Came to Pa.; in command various mcht. ships; apptd. to Pa. Com. of Safety in constrn. of warships, floating batteries, fire rafts, 1775; supt. fleet of rafts, 1776; commodore Pa. Navy, 1777, full command, 1777, successfully defended fleet against Brit. in Port of Phila.; commr. purchases Continental Army, Phila., 1780; receiver provisions Pa. Militia, 1780; port warden Phila., 1785; owner or part owner vessels engaged in fgn. trade; a founder St. George Soc., Phila. Died Phila., Mar. 1, 1800.

HAZEN, Moses, army officer; b. Haverhill, Mass., June 1, 1733; s. Moses and Abigail (White) H.; m. Charlotte de la Saussaye, Dec. 1770. Served in French and Indian Wars, other colonial wars, as lt. in expdns. against Crown Point, N.Y., 1756, against Louisbourg, French stronghold on Cape Breton Island, N.S., Can., 1758; with Gen. James Wolfe's expdn. against Quebec, Can., 1759; settled in Que.; British seized his property at outbreak of Revolutionary War because he was suspected of loyalty to colonies, 1776; joined colonial side; formed 2d Canadian Regt. known as Hazen's Own, col., 1776; took part in battles of Brandywine and Germantown with Continental Army under Washington; began constrn. of mil. road to Canadian border, 1779; commd. brig. gen., 1781. Died Troy, N.Y., Feb. 3, 1803.

HAZEN, William Babcock, army officer; b. West Hartford, Vt., Sept. 27, 1830; s. Stillman and Sophrona (Fenno) H.; grad. U.S. Mil. Acad., 1855; m. Mildred McLean, 1 child. Commd. capt. inf. U.S. Army, 1861; col. 41st Ohio Volunteers, 1862, maj. gen., 1865; commanded 15th Corps, Army of Tenn., 1865, comdr. division in Sherman's march to the sea, opened up communications between army and fleet; served at battles of Shiloh, Corinth, Perryville, Stone River, Chickamauga, Chattanooga; commd. col. U.S. Army, 1868, responsible for forcing Custer not to attack friendly Kiowa Indian camp, 1868; mil. observer with German armies in War of 1870; wrote articles in N.Y. papers pointing out corruption in adminstrn. of post-trader system of West and false claims of railroad promoters regarding real value of their land; 1872; chief signal officer U.S. War Dept., 1880; organized scientific expdn. under Lt. Greely sent to Lady, Franklin's Bay, 1881; reprimanded for criticizing what he felt to be negligent inaction in War Dept. in sending relief expdns. to Ft. Greely, 1885. Died Washington, D.C., Jan. 16, 1887.

HEADE, Martin Johnson, artist; b. Lumberville, Pa., Aug. 11, 1819; studied with Thomas Hicks; studied in Italy, France and Eng., circa 1837-40; began exhibiting in major galleries after returning to Am.; worked as portrait and landscape painter in East and Mid-West; visited Brazil, 1863-64, made painting trips to Nicaragua, Colombia, Puerto Rico and Jamaica, later to B.C., Can., Cal. and Fla.; settled at St. Augustine, Fla., 1885; naturalist and poet; best known for paintings of tropical birds and flowers. Died St. Augustine, Sept. 4, 1904.

HEADLEY, Joel Tyler, author; b. Walton, Delaware County, N.Y., Dec. 30, 1813; s. Isaac and Irene (Benedict) H.; grad. Union Coll., 1839; attended Auburn Theol. Sem.; m. Anna Allston Russel, May 1850. Poor health prevented continuation of ministerial career; went to Italy, 1842; asso. editor N.Y. Tribune, 1846; mem. N.Y. Assembly, 1854; sec. of state N.Y.,1855-58; Author: Italy and the Italians, 1844, Letters from Italy, 1845; Napolean and his Marshals, 1846, Washington and his Generals, 1847, (two most important works); Life of Cromwell, 1848; Sacred Scenes and Characters, 1849; Life of Havelock, 1859; Champlains of the Revolution, 1861; The Great Rebellion, 2 vols., 1864; Grant and Sherman, their Campaigns and Generals, 1865; Farragut and our Naval Commanders, 1867; Sacred Heroes and Martyrs, 1865; dubbed by Edgar Allen Poe"the autocrat of all the quacks". Died Newburgh, N.Y., Jan. 16, 1897.

HEALY, George Peter Alexander, painter; b. Boston, July 15, 1813; s. William and Mary (Hicks) H.; m. Louisa Phipps; 9 children. Opened studio, exhibited paintings, at age of 18; went to Paris, France, 1834; admitted to studio of Baron Gros, 1834; painted portraits of King Louis-Philippe, Marshal Souet; received medal at Universal Exposition for painting Franklin Urging the Claims of the American Colonies before Louis XVI 1855; returned to U.S., 1855; mem. N.A.D.; returned to Europe, 1865; invited to contribute a portrait of himself to collection of self-portraits at Uffizi Gallery, Florence, Italy (1st Am. to receive this honor); executed portraits of Daniel Webster, Longfellow, series of Presidents of U.S.; executed Webster Replying to Hayne (his best known hist. work; contains 150 portraits); exhibited Paris Salon of 1878, also at N.A.D.; other works include portraits of Gen. McClellan, Adm. Porter, Liszt, Bismarck, Abraham Lincoln, Joseph Hume, Sir Arthur and Lady Faulkner, The Duke of Sussex, Lady Agnes Buller, Lord and Lady Waldegrave, Audubon, Prescott, Gen. Cass, Andrew Jackson, Henry Clay, John Quincy Adams, Gen. Grant, Gen. Sherman. Died Chgo., June 24,1894.

HEALY, Joseph, congressman; b. Newton, Mass. Aug. 21, 1776. Hotel keeper, engaged in farming; mem. N.H. Senate, 1824; mem. U.S. Ho. of Reps. (Democrat) from N.H., 19th-20th congresses, 1825-29; mem. N.H. Exec. Council, 1829-32. Died Washington, N.H., Oct. 10, 1861; buried Old Cemetery, Washington.

HEAP, Samuel Davies, diplomat, naval officer; b. Carlisle, Pa., Oct. 8, 1781; s. Judge John and Margaret (Kerr) H.; m. Margaret Porter, 1810, 5 children. Commd. surgeon's mate U.S. Navy, 1804, promoted surgeon, 1808; stationed at New Orleans, Norfolk, Boston, Phila., 1808-17; in charge of hosp. of Am. Mediterranean fleet, 1817-23; chargé d'affaires, Tunis, 1823-24, Am. consul to Tunis, 1824-53. Died Oct. 2, 1853; buried Protestant Cemetery, Tunis.

HEARD, Augustine, sea captain, mcht.; b. Ipswich, Mass., Mar. 10, 1785; s. John and Sally (Staniford) H. Sailed as master on brig Caravan acting as both capt. and supercargo, 1812; became a leading capt. in East-India Trade; sailed for Canton, China, 1830, became partner firm Samuel Russell & Co.; established Augustine Heard & Co., 1840; returned to China to assume charge of co., 1841; returned to Am., 1844; incorporator Ipswich Mfg. Co. 1828, sole owner, 1852; founded and endowed Ipswich Pub. Library. Died Ipswich, Sept. 14, 1868.

HEARD, Franklin Fiske, lawyer; b. East Sudbury (now Wayland), Mass., Jan. 17, 1825; s. Jonathan Fiske and Harriet (Stratton) H.; grad. Harvard, 1848; m. Harriet Hildreth, Apr. 24, 1855; m. 2d, Martha B. Stone, Apr. 5, 1868. Admitted to Mass. bar, 1850, practiced law, Saxonville, Mass., 1850-84; began writing legal works, 1853. Author: A Treatise on the Law of Libel and Slander, 1860; Criminal Abortion, 1868; The Principles of Criminal Pleading, 1870; Precedents of Equity Pleading, 1884. Editor: Practical Treatise upon the Authority and Duty of Justices of the Peace in Criminal Prosecutions (Davis). Died Boston, Sept. 29, 1889.

HEARST, George, senator, prospector, mine owner; b. Franklin County, Mo., Sept. 3, 1820; s. William G. and Elizabeth (Collins) H.; ed. Franklin Mining Sch. (Mo.); m. Phoebe Apperson, June 15, 1862; 1 son, William Randolph. Acquired great fortune through rich mineral finds in western Nev.; holdings included Ophir Mine (Nev.), Ontario Mine (Utah), Homestake Mine (S.D.), Anaconda (Mnt.) Mine; mem. Cal. Assembly, 1865-66; acquired San Francisco Daily Examiner (later called Examiner), 1880, turned mgmt. over to son, 1867; mem. U.S. Senate from Cal., 1886-90. Died Washington, D.C., Feb. 28, 1891.

HEATH, James Ewell, state ofcl.; b. Northumberland County, Va., July 8, 1792; s. John and Sarah (Ewell) H.; m. Fannie Weems; m. 2nd, Elizabeth Macon, 1820. Mem. Va. Legislature, 1814; mem. Va. Privy Council, 1816; auditor State of Va., 1819-49; commr. of pensions Va., 1850-53; one of 1st officers Va. Hist and Philos. Soc.; editorial adviser So. Literary Messenger (sometimes inaccurately described as 1st editor); Author: Edgehill, or the Family of the Fitzroyals; published anonymously, 1828; (3 act comedy). Whigs and Democrats or the Love of No Politics (satire of rural election practices; it is thought he was removed from auditorship by Democrats as result of this writing), published anonymously, 1839. Died June 28, 1862.

HEATH, James P., congressman; b. Del., Dec. 21, 1777. Served as lt. engrs. U.S. Army, 1799-1802; register in chancery, Annapolis, Md.; served as a.d.c. to Gen. Winder throughout War of 1812; mem. U.S. Ho. of Reps. (Democrat) from Md., 23d Congress, 1833-35. Died Georgetown, D.C., June 12, 1854; buried Oak Hill Cemetery, Washington, D.C.

HEATH, John, congressman; b. Wicomico Parish, Northumerland County, Va., May 8, 1758; attended Coll. William and Mary. An organizer Phi Beta Kappa (1st Greek letter soc. established in an Am. coll.), 1776, elected pres.; served in Revolutionary War; admitted to Va. bar, practiced in Northumberland County; commonwealth's atty., 1781-84, 87-93; mem. Va. Privy Council, several years; mem. Va. Ho. of Dels., 1782; mem. U.S. Ho. of Reps. (Republican) from Va., 3d-4th congresses, 1793-97. Died Richmond, Va., Oct. 13, 1810.

HEATH, William, army officer; b. Roxbury, Mass., Mar. 2, 1737; s. Samuel and Elizabeth (Payson) H.; m. Sarah Lockwood, Apr. 19, 1759. Mem. Mass. Gen. Ct., 1761; joined Ancient and Honorable Arty. Co. of Boston, 1765; mem. Mass. Provincial Congress, 1774-75; commd. brig. gen., organized forces at Cambridge before Battle of Bunker Hill, 1774; served as brig. gen. Continental Army under Washington, 1775-76; comnd. maj. gen., 1776; in charge of unsuccessful attack on Ft. Independence (N.Y.), 1777; severely reprimanded by Washington, received no more field commands from then until close of war, restricted mainly to staff duty; in command Eastern Mil. Dist., 1777-78, Dist. of Lower Hudson, 1779; mem. Mass. Conv. which ratified U.S. Constn., 1788; mem. Mass. Senate, 1791-92; judge Probate Ct., Norfolk, Mass. 1792; elected lt. gov. Mass. but declined to serve. Died Roxbury, Mass., Jan. 24, 1814.

HEATHCOTE, Caleb, mcht., jurist, mayor N.Y. C.; b. Chesterfield, Eng., Mar. 6, 1666; s. Gilbert and Anne (Dickens) H.; m. Martha Smith, Sept. 7 1699; children-Anne, Martha. Came to N.Y., 1692; mem. N.Y. Gov.'s Council, 1692-98, 1702-21; col. N.Y. Militia, 1692; presiding judge Ct. of Sessions, Westchester County, N.Y.; judge Perrogative Ct., Westchester County; 1st judge Ct. Common Pleas for Westchester County, 1693; commr. to conduct offices of collector and receiver gen., 1695, 1702-03; patented Great Nine Partners tract in Dutchess County, N.Y., engaged in other land speculation; received manor of Scarsdale, N.Y., (last such land grant made by Brit. Govt.); 1701; mayor N.Y.C., 1711-13; surveyor gen. customs for all Brit. colonies north to Delaware River; judge vice admiralty of N.Y.. Conn. and the Jerseys, 1715; led in founding Trinity Parish, also bldg. the edifice; established day sch., Sunday sch., Rye, N.Y. Died N.Y.C., Mar. 1, 1721.

HEATON, David, congressman; b. Hamilton, Ohio, Mar. 10, 1823; studied law. Adimitted to Oho bar; mem. Ohio Senate, 1855; moved to St. Anthony Falls, Minn., 1857; mem. Minn. Senate, 1858-63; apptd. spl. agt. Treasury Dept. and U.S. Depository, New Bern, N.C., 1863; declined appointment as 3d auditor of the Treasury, 1864; mem. N.C Constl. Conv., 1867; mem. U.S. Ho. of Reps. (Republican) from N.C., 40th-41st congresses, July 15, 1868-70. Died Washington, D.C., June 25, 1870; buried Nat. Cemetery, New Bern.

HEBARD, William, congressman; b. Windham, Conn., Nov. 29, 1800; attended Orange County Grammar Sch., Randolph, Vt.; studied law. Admitted to Vt. bar, 1827, began practice in East Randolph; pros. atty. Orange County, 1832-36; mem. Vt. Ho. of Rep., 1835, 40-42, 58, 59, 64, 65, 72, Vt. Senate, 1836, 38; judge of probate Randolph dist., 1838, 40-41; elected asso. judge Vt. Supreme Ct., 1842, 44; mem. U.S. Ho. of Reps. (Whig) from Vt., 31st-32d Congresses, 1849-53; del. Vt. Constl. Conv., 1857; del. Republican Nat. Conv., Chgo., 1860. Died Chelsea, Vt., Oct. 20, 1875; buried Old Cemetery, Randolph Center, Vt.

HEBERT, Paul Octave, army officer, gov. La.; b. Iberville Parish, La., Dec. 12, 1818; s. Paul Gaston and Mary (Hamilton) H.; grad. Jefferson Coll., 1836, U.S. Mil. Acad., 1840; m. Cora Vaughn, Aug. 2, 1842; m. 2nd Penelope Lynch Andrews, Aug. 3, 1861. Asst. prof. engring. U.S. Mil. Acad., 1840-42; chief engr. of La., 1845; lt. col. 14th Inf., U.S. Army, participated in all important battles of Mexican War; brevetted col., 1848; mem. La. Constl. Conv., 1852; gov. La., 1852; commd. brig. gen. Confederate Army, 1861; commanded Dept. of Tex., in charge of defenses of Galveston; commanded sub-dist. of North La.; engr. State of La., 1873; commr. and civil engr. of Mississippi levees. Died New Orleans, Aug. 29, 1880; buried Bayou Goula, La.

HECK, Barbara Ruckle, religious leader; b. County Limerick, Ireland, 1734; d. Sebastian Ruckle; m. Paul Heck, before 1760. Came to N.Y., 1760; responsible for beginning of Wesleyan movement in Am., 1766, resulted in erection 1st Wesleyan chapel in Am., 1768; helped found a Wesleyan Soc., Washington County, N.Y., 1770; Loyalist; forced to move to Can.; called mother of Methodism in Am. Died Augusta, Can., Aug. 17, 1804.

HECKER, Friedrich Karl Franz, army officer; b. Eichtersheim, Baden, Germany, Sept. 28, 1811; attended U. Heidelberg (Germany); LL.D., U. Munich (Germany); m. Josephine Eisenhardt, 5 children. Practiced law, Mannheim, Germany, 1835-42; mem. 2d Chamber of Baden, 1842-47; expelled from Prussia because he opposed German incorporation of Schleswig-Holstein area, 1845; agitated Germans in Lake Dist. to fight for German Republic which he had proclaimed, defeated by Gen. Von Gagern, 1848, fled to Sweden; came to U.S., 1849, successful farmer in St. Clair County, Ill., 1849-61; enlisted as pvt. under Gen. Sigel, 1861, became col. 24th Ill. Volunteers; led 82d Ill. Volunteers for greater part of war; served in battles of Chattanooga, Missionary Ridge and Chancellorsville; returned to farm, St. Clair County, 1866; active in Liberal Republican Movement of 1872; visited Germany, 1873; lived on farm, St. Clair County, 1872-81. Died Summerfield, St. Clair County, Mar. 24, 1881.

HECKER, Isaac Thomas, clergyman; b. N.Y.C., Dec. 18, 1819; s. John and Caroline (Freund) H. Baptized as Roman Catholic, 1844, confirmed in Redemptorist Order, 1845; novitiate at St. Trond, Belgium, 1845; ordained priest Roman Cath. Ch., London, Eng., 1849; returned to U.S. as Redemptorist missionary to German immigrants, 1851; founder Missionary Priests of St. Paul the Apostle, 1858, superior of order, 1858-88; founder Catholic World, 1865; organized Cath. Publicaton Soc., 1866; began publ. Young Catholic, 1870. Author: Questions of the Soul, 1852; Aspirations of Nature, 1857. Died N.Y.C., Dec. 22, 1888.

HECKEWELDER, John Gottlieb Ernestus, missionary; b. Bedford, Eng., Mar. 12, 1743; s. Rev. David Heckewelder; m. Sarah Ohneberg, 1780. Came to U.S.,1754; occasionally dispatched as a messenger to Indian settlement, Wyalusing, Pa., and to Indian towns on West br. of Susquehanna River, 1763-77, learned various Indian customs and langs.; began regular mission service with Moravian Christian Indians, guided them from the Susquehanna to Schoenbrunn and Gnadenhuetten on the Muskingum River, (O.), 1771; captured by British, 1781, accused of being an Am. spy, released to continue missionary work; mem. com. to arrange peace treaty at Vincennes, Ind., 1792; administered to Indian "estate" on Muskingum, 1801-10. Writings include: Account of the History, Manners and Customs of the Indian Nations Who Once Inhabited Pennsylvania and the Neighboring States. Died Bethlehem, Pa., Jan. 31, 1823.

HEDBROOKE, Andrew, see Sill, Edward Rowland.

HEDGE, Frederic Henry, clergyman, educator; b. Cambridge, Mass., Dec. 12, 1805; s. Levi and Mary (Kneeland) H.; grad. Harvard, 1825, attended Sch. Divinity, 1825-29; m. Lucy Pierce, 1830. Memorized Virgil's Eclogues before age of 7; studied in Germany under George Bancroft, 1818-22; ordained to ministry Unitarian Ch., 1829; minister several Unitarian chs.; established (with Ralph Waldo Emerson and George Ripley) Transcendental Club, 1836; minister Westminster Congl. Soc., Providence, R.I., 1850-56; editor Christian Examiner, 1857-61; prof. eccles. history Harvard Sch. Divinity, 1857-76, prof. German lit. Harvard Coll., 1872-84, specially apptd. instr. eccles. history, 1877-78; leader Unitarian movement, pres. Am. Unitarian Assn., 1859-62; influential in Am. German studies. Author: Prose Writers of Germany, 1848; Ways of the Spirit and Other Essays, 1877; Conservation and Reform, 1843; Hymns for the Church of Christ; Recent Inquiries into Theology; Reason in Religion, 1865; Hours with German Classics, 1886; Personality and Theism, 1887. Translator; Ein Feste Burg (Martin Luther), 1877. Died Cambridge, Aug. 21, 1890.

HEDGE, Levi, educator; b. Warwick, Mass., Apr. 19, 1766; s. Rev. Lemuel and Sarah (White) H.; grad. Harvard, 1792; A.M. (hon.), Brown U., 1808; LL.D. (hon.), Yale, 1823; m. Mary Kneeland, Jan. 15, 1801, at least 1 child. Tutor in philosophy Harvard, 1795-1800, prof. logic and metaphysics, 1810-27, Alford prof. natural religion, moral philosophy and civil polity, 1827-32. Author: Elements of Logick or a Summary o the General Principles and Different Modes of Reasoning, 1816. Editor: Treatise on the Philosophy of the Human Mind (Thomas Brown), 1827. Died Jan. 3, 1844.

HEENAN, John Carmel, pugilist; b. West Troy, N.Y., May 2, 1835; s. Timothy and Mary (Morrissey) H.; m. Adah Isaacs Menken, Apr. 3, 1859; m. 2d, Sarah Stevens, 1862. Went to Cal. to prospect for gold, 1852, fought bouts with all comers; returned to N.Y., 1857, fought John Morrissey in Long Point, Can. for $2,500 (defeated); fought holder of English belt, Tom Sayers, 1860 (defeated); fought (with Joe Cushing as mgr.) several exhibition matches with Sayers in England. Died Oct. 25, 1873.

HEERMANN, Adolphus L., physician, ornithologist; b. S.C., circa 1827; M.D., U. Md., 1846. Joined Phila. Acad. Natural Scis., 1845; made trip to Cal., 1849-52, collected many specimens of birds, nests and eggs; apptd. acting asst. surgeon U.S. Army on railroad survey of So. Cal., 1853; used word oology for his collection of birds' nests and eggs(possibly 1st usage of term in Am. Ornithology); Heermann's gull named in his honor, 1852. Died nr. San Antonio, 1865.

HEERMANS, Augustyn, surveyor, artist; b. Prague, Bohemia, circa 1605. Served in Thirty Years' War; came to Am., 1633; settled at New Amsterdam as agt. for a Dutch comml. house; became prominent member of colony; known as talented amateur artist, sketched a view of New Amsterdam which was sent to Holland, 1660; employed by authorities of Md. to survey and map Colony of Md., received in payment a grant of land in Md., moved to Md., 1662. Died Md., 1686.

HEILMAN, William, congressman; b. Albig, Duchy of Hesse-Darmstadt, Germany, Oct. 11, 1824. Came to U.S., 1843, settled in Ind.; became pres. of a cotton mill; founder machine shop for mfg. drills, 1847; mem. Evansville (Ind.) City Council, 1852-65; mem. Ind. Ho. of Reps., 1870-76; del. Republican Nat. Conv., Cincinnati, 1876; mem. Ind. Senate, 1876-79; mem. U.S. Ho. of Reps. (Rep.) from Ind., 46th-47th congresses, 1879-83. Died Evansville, Sep 22, 1890; buried Oak Hill Cemetery, Evansville.

HEILPRIN, Michael, editor; b. Poland, 1823; Phineas Mendel and Hannah (Lipschitz) H.; Henrietta Silver, 1843, 5 children. Emigrated Hungary, 1842, took part in Hungarian Revol tion, 1842-48; came to U.S., 1856; editor for Ar Cyclopaedia, 1858-88; wrote numerous articles history and biography especially for the Natio worked for establishment of farms for refugee Je from Russia, 1881-88. Author: The Historical Poet of the Ancient Jews, 2 vols., 1879-80. Died M 10, 1888.

HEINE, Peter Bernard William, artist; b. Dre den, Germany, Jan. 30, 1827. Came to U.S., 184 partner of Julius H. Kummer, N.Y.C.; artist wi Perry expdn. to Japan, 1852-54; lived in N.Y.C until 1859, returned to Europe, 1859. Died n Dresden, Oct. 5, 1885.

HEINRICH, Antony Philip, musician; b. Schör büchel, Bohemia, Mar. 11, 1781; m. twice. Came Am., 1805; 1st white composer to attempt use Am. Indian mus. themes in modern mus. compos tions; dir. music Southwark Theatre, Phila., 181 published The Dawning Music in Kentucky, or, Th Pleasure of Harmony in the Solitudes of Nature, Oper Prima, 1820; violinist Drury Lane Theatre, Eng 1831; presided at meeting for founding N.Y. Phi harmonic Soc., 1842; known as Father Heinrich grand festivals of his music held at Broadway Tabe nacle, N.Y.C., 1842, Tremont Temple, Boston, 184 wrote book Memoranda; conducted concerts, als played violin, piano, Bardstown, Ky., Louisville Ky.; presented 1st Am. performance of Beethoven' First Symphony in Ky. Led an erratic career an died in poverty, N.Y.C., May 3, 1861.

HEINTZELMAN, Samuel Peter, soldier; b. Ma heim, Pa., Sept. 30, 1805; s. Peter and An (Grubb) H.; grad. U.S. Mil. Acad., 1826; m. Mar garet Stewart, Dec. 5, 1844. Commd. capt. U.S Army, 1838; served in battles of Pasolos Ovejas Huamantla and Atexco in Mexican War, 1846-48 brevetted maj., 1847; promoted to maj. 1st Inf in Cal., 1855; founder Ft. Yuma (Ariz.); comm col. 17th Inf., 1861, brig. gen. U.S. Volunteers 1861; commanded 3rd Div., U.S. Army under Ge Irvin McDowell at 1st Battle of Bull Run; com manded III Corps. right wing of army under Ge John Pope, 2d Battle of Bull Run, 1862; too part in Peninsula campaign, battles of Malver Hill and Seven Days; promoted maj. gen. U.S. Vol unteers, 1862, participated in battles of Williams burg, Seven Pines and Fair Oaks; assigned t defenses of Washington, D.C., 1862-63; sent to com mand No. (Central) States Dept., 1864; comman 17th Inf. in Tex., 1865-69; promoted gen., ret 1869. Died Washington, D.C., May 1, 1880.

HEINZEN, Karl Peter, journalist; b. Greven brioich, Rhenish Prussia, Feb. 22, 1809; s. Josep and Marie (Schmitz) H.; m. Henriette Schiller 1840, 1 son Karl Frederick. Wrote 2 importan satires Die Ehre, 1842, Die Geheime Konduiten liste, 1842; came to U.S.,1848; edited (with Iva Tyssowske), Die Deutsche Schmellpost (later Ne Yorker Deutsche Zeitung; a failure); the Janu (a failure); edited Herold des Westens, Louis ville, Ky.; founded, edited Pionier, 1854-78 abolitionist and revolutionary, opposed all strongl centralized govts.; essays collected in Teutsche Radikalismus in Amerika: Ausgewahlte Vortrage 4 vols., 1867-79. Died Boston, Nov. 12, 1880.

HEISS, Michael, clergyman, educator; b. Pfah ldorf, Bavaria, Apr. 12, 1818; s. Joseph and Gert rude (Frei) H.; entered Gymnasium of Newburg on the Danube, 1831; attended U. Munich, 1835-39 Diocesan Sem. of Eichstatt, 1839-40. Ordaine priest Roman Catholic Ch., 1840; came to U.S., 1842; a founder, 1st rector St. Francis Sem., Milw., 1856-68; 1st bishop of LaCrosse (Wis.), 1868-80; 2d archbishop of Milw., 1880-90; called to Rome to advise pope on Am. ch. affairs, 1883; planned, directed 1st Provincial Council of Milw., 1886, also helped secure repeal of the Bennett Law (a pub. sch. act); one of 5 bishops who helped establish Cath. U. Am., Washington, D.C. Author: De Matrimonio, 1861; The Four Gospels, 1863. Died LaCrosse, Mar. 26, 1890.

HELBRON, Peter, missionary; b. Hilbringen, Rhenish Province, Germany, 1739; s. Joannes Matthias and Maria Magdalene (Gottlieb) H. Ordained priest Capuchin Order, Roman Catholic Ch.; came to Am., 1787; missionary in area of Goshenhoppen, Berks County, Pa., 1789-91; pastor Ch. of Holy Trinity, Phila., 1791-96; curate St. Joseph's Ch., Phila., 1796-99; missionary in Central Pa., 1799-1804, built chs., established congregations in area of Pitts.; pastor, Greensburg, Pa., 1804-16. Died Carlisle, Pa., Apr. 24, 1816.

HELFENSTEIN, Ernest, see Smith, Elizabeth Oakes Prince.

HELFFENSTEIN, John Albert Conrad, clergyman; b. Mosbach, Palatinate, Germany, Feb. 16, 1748;

Peter and Anna Margaretha (Dietz) H.; attended , Heidelberg (Germany), 1764-67; m. Catharine ircher, Feb. 11, 1773, 4 children. Vicar to his ther, Mosbach, 1767-71; ordained to ministry for etus of Pa., German Reform Ch., 1771; came to S., 1772; pastor German Reform Ch., Germanwn, Pa., 1772-75, 79-90, Reform Ch., Lancaster, ., 1775-79. Died May 17, 1790.

HELM, John Charles, diplomat; b. Hornellsville, Y., June 21, 1817; s. Francis T. and Sallie (Mcinney) H.; studied law in office of John W. Tibtts, Newport, Ky.; m. Louise A. Whistler, 1854, children. Admitted to Ky. bar, 1842; served with th Ky. Regt. under Col. John Tibbatts during exican War, 1846-48; practiced law, Newport, 48-51; mem. Ky. Legislature, 1851-52; U.S. mml. agt. on Island of St. Thomas, 1853-58; U.S. nsul gen., Havana, Cuba, 1858-61; spl. agt. for nfederate States Am. to West Indies, residing in avana, 1861-66; lived in Toronto, Can., 1866-68. ed Toronto, Feb. 1868.

HELM, John Larue, gov. Ky.; b. Elizabethtown, ., July 4, 1802; s. George and Rebecca (Larue) ; m. Lucinda Hardin, 1830, 12 children incling Ben Hardin. Admitted to Ky. bar, 1823; unty atty., 1824; mem. Ky. Ho. of Reps., 1826- , 30, 32-37, 39, 42-43; speaker, several times; der in state politics until cira 1837; mem. Ky. nate, 1844-48; 65-67; largely responsible for reval all restrictive and punitive laws against exnfederates; lt. gov. Ky. (Whig), 1848-51; pres. uisville & Nashville R.R., 1854-60; gov. Ky., Sept. 8, 1867. Died Elizabethtown, Sept. 8, 1867.

HELMICK, William, congressman; b. nr. Canton, , Sept. 6, 1817; student pub. schs.; studied law. lmitted to Ohio bar, 1845, began practice in New iladelphia; pros. atty. Tuscarawas County (O.), 51; mem. U.S. Ho. of Reps. (Republican) from io, 36th Congress, 1859-61; chief clk. Pension fice (apptd. by Pres. Lincoln), 1861-65; apptd. stice of peace by Pres. Hayes, 1877. Died Washgton, D.C., Mar. 31, 1888; buried Congressional metery, Washington.

HELMPRAECHT, Joseph, clergyman; b. Niederinkling, Bavaria, Jan. 14, 1820; attended U. Mun-. Novice, Congregation of Most Holy Redeemer, tötting, 1843; came to Balt., 1843; ordained iest Roman Catholic Ch., Balt., 1844; superior . Mary's Ch. and Redemptorist House, Buffalo, Y., 1848-54; rector Ch. of Holy Redeemer, Y.C., 1854-60; went to Rome, 1865; provincial n. Redemptorists, 1865-77. Died N.Y.C., Dec. , 1884.

HELMS, William, congressman; b. Sussex County, J. Served from 2d lt. to capt. during Revolutionary ar; brevetted maj., 1783; mem. N.J. Assembly, '91-92; mem. U.S. Ho. of Reps. (democrat) from .J., 7th-11th congresses, 1801-11. Died Hamilton ounty, O., 1813.

HELMSLEY, William, Continental congressman; b. over Fields Farm nr. Queenstown, Md., 1737; Enged in planting; provincial treas. of Eastern Shore Md.), 1773; surveyor Talbot County (Md.); col.)th Battalion, Queen Annes County Militia, 1777; stice of peace Queen Annes County, 1777; mem. d. Senate, 1779-81, 86, 90, 1800; Mem. Connental Congress from Md., 1782-84. Died Queen nnes County, June 5, 1812; buried Clover Fields arm Cemetery.

HELMUTH, Justus Henry Christian, clergyman; Helmstedt, Germany, May 16, 1745; s. Johann hristoph and Justina (Helmuth) H.; attended U. alle (Germany); m. Maria Barbara Keppele, 5 ildren. Came to Am., 1769; pastor Lutheran Ch., ancaster, Pa., 1769-79; co-pastor St. Michael's d Zion's Ch., Phila., 1779-1820; founder Evangesches Magazin (1st Lutheran ch. paper in U.S.), 312. Author: Empfindungen des Herzens in einigen edern, 1781; Denkmal der Liebe und Achtung, elches, Seiner Hockwurden dem Herrn D. Heinrich elchoir Muhlenberg. . .ist Gesetzet Worden, 1788; tliche Kirchenlieder, 1809. Died Feb. 5, 1825.

HEMENWAY, Mary Porter Tileston, philanthrost; b. N.Y., Dec. 20, 1820; d. Thomas and ary (Porter) Tileston; m. Augustus Hemenway, ne 25, 1840. Devoted her wealth to numerous ilanthropic projects; helped establish schs. on uthern coast after Civil War; founded sch. for eaching sewing, Boston, 1865, indsl.-vocational sch., oston, 1883; opened kitchen in a public sch. (1st U.S.), Boston, 1885; founder Boston Normal Sch. Cooking, 1887; promoted Hemenway Southwestrn Archaeological Expdn. (headed by Frank H. ushman), 1886; organized conf. for introduction of ymnastics into public sch. curriculum, 1889. Died ar. 6, 1894.

HEMPEL, Charles Julius, homeopathic physian, translator; b. Solingen, Germany, Sept. 5, 811; ed. College de France, Paris; M.D., U. ity N.Y., 1845; m. Mary Coggeshall Calder, 1855. ssisted Jules Michelet in writing Histoire de France; came to U.S., 1835; became leading homeopathic physician; prof. materia medica Hahnemann Med. Coll., Phila., 1856-61; mem. Swedenborgian Ch. Author: A New and Comprehensive System of Materia Medica and Theraputics, 1859; Grammar of the German Language, 2 vols., 1842; Schiller's Complete Works, 2 vols., 1870; translator outstanding German and French books on homeoathy; Died Grand Rapids, Mich., Sept. 24, 1879.

HEMPHILL, John, senator; b. Blackstock, S.C., Dec. 18, 1803; s. Rev. John and Jane (Lind) H.; grad. Jefferson Coll., 1825. Admitted to practice S.C. Ct. Common Pleas, 1829, S.C. Ct. of Chancery, 1831; went to Tex., 1838; dist. judge in Tex., 1840-42; chief justice Republic of Tex. Supreme ct., 1840-45; adj. gen. to Gen. Somerville in expdn. to Rio Grande; mem. Tex. Constl. Conv. of 1845; 1st chief justice State of Tex., 1845-58; mem. U.S. Senate from Tex. (Democrat), 1861; rep. from Tex. to Confederate Congress, 1861-62; gave form and content to community property system, also homestead exemption law in Tex.; helped effect a blending of law and equity in Tex. courts. Died Richmond, Va., Jan. 4, 1862.

HEMPHILL, Joseph, congressman; b. Thornbury Twp., Pa., Jan. 7, 1770; s. Joseph and Ann (Wills) H.; B.A., U. Pa., 1791; m. Margaret Coleman, Sept. 11, 1806. Admitted to Pa. bar, 1793, practiced law, West Chester, Pa.; mem. Pa. Ho. of Reps., 1797-1800, 05, 31-32; active in securing Compromise Act of 1799 to settle Wyoming land controversy between Conn. and Pa.; mem. U.S. Ho. of Reps. (Federalist) from Pa., 7th Congress, 1801-03, 16th-19th, 21st congresses, 1819-26, 29-31, chmn. com. on slave trade, attacked Mo's discrimination of free Negores and mulattoes as unconstl., 1820, advocated internal improvements and relief for war veterans; moved to Phila., 1804; 1st pres. judge Dist. Ct. of City and County of Phila., 1811, 17-19; engaged in porcelain mfg. after polit. career. Died Phila., May 29, 1842; buried Laurel Hill Cemetery, Phila.

HEMPSTEAD, Edward, territorial ofcl.; b. New London, Conn., June 3, 1780; studied law. Admitted to the bar, 1801, began practice in R.I.; moved to St. Louis (then part of Dist. of La.), 1805; atty. gen. Territory of Upper La., 1809-11; served in several expdns. against Indians North of Mississippi River; mem. 3d Mo. Territorial Gen. Assembly, 1812, speaker; del. to U.S. Congress from Territory of Mo., 1812-14. Died as a result of being thrown from a horse, St. Louis, Aug. 10, 1817; buried Hempstead Farm (now part of Bellefontaine Cemetery), St. Louis.

HENCHMAN, Daniel, publisher, mcht.; b. Boston, Jan. 21, 1689; s. Hezekiah and Abigail Henchman; m. Elizabeth Gerrish, Jan. 14, 1713, 1 dau., Lydia Henchman Hancock. Served as lt. col. Boston regt. Mass. Militia; justice of peace, Boston; publisher, bookseller, Boston, 1710-61, said to have published 1st Am. edit. of Bible, 1749; imported manufactured goods from Eng.; established 1st paper mill in New Eng., Milton, Mass., 1728-40; contbd. large gifts to Harvard. Died Boston, Feb. 15, 1761.

HENDEL, John William, clergyman; b. Durkheim, Germany, Nov. 20, 1740; s. Johann Jacob and Anna Sybilla (Otten) H.; student U. Heidelberg (Germany). 1759-62; m. Elizabeth IeRay, 1766; 1 son, William. Sent to Pa. by Synods of Holland, 1764; pastor, Lancaster, Pa., 1765-69, 82-94, Tulpehocken, Pa., 1769-82; Phila., 1794-98; pres. Coetus, 1768,79,89,91; v.p. Franklin Coll., 1787-94; leader movement that resulted in separation from Dutch Synods and orgn. of Synod of U.S., 1793. Died Phila., Sept. 19, 1798; buried Franklin Sq., Phila.

HENDERSON, Archibald, congressman; b. Granville County, N.C., Aug. 7, 1768; s. Richard and Elizabeth (Keeling) H.: grad. Springer Coll. (N. C.); studied law under Judge John Williams; m. Sarah Alexander, 1801. Admitted to N.C. bar, circa 1790; practiced in Salisbury N.C.; clk., master in equity county ct. N.C., 1795-98; mem. U.S. Ho. of Reps. (Federalist) from N.C., 6th-7th congresses, 1799-1803, favored Judiciary Act of 1801 and continuation of Sedition Law; mem. N.C. Ho. of Commons, 1807-09, 14, 19-20; pres. Salisbury br. State Bank of N.C.; v.p. Raleigh chpt. Am. Colonization Soc., 1819; considered by John Marshall as one of ablest lawyers of that area. Died Salisbury, Oct. 21, 1822; buried City Cemetery, Salisbury.

HENDERSON, Bennett H., congressman; b. Bedford, Va., Sept. 5, 1784. Moved to Tenn.; mem. U.S. Ho. of Reps. from Tenn., 14th Congress, 1815-17. Died Summitville, Tenn.

HENDERSON, David English, artist; b. Jefferson County, Va. (now W.Va.), 1832. Worked in Georgetown (Va.) and N.Y.C.; worked in Bklyn. after Civil War; executed pen and wash drawings of scenes in W.Va. and Tenn. for General Atlas (Mathew Carey), published 1841 (now owned by Princeton U. Library). Died Jefferson County, 1887.

HENDERSON, James Henry Dickey, congressman; b. nr. Salem, Ky., July 23, 1810; attended pub. schs. Learned printing; ordained to ministry; pastor, Washington County, Pa., 1843-51; published a literary mag., Mo.; settled in Yamhill County, Ore., 1852, homesteaded; engaged in farming, Eugene, Ore., specialized in fruit raising; supt. pub. schs. Lane County (Ore.), 1859; mem. U.S. Ho. of Reps. (Republican), from Ore., 39th Congress, 1865-67; preached, lectured, wrote for periodicals. Died Eugene, Dec. 13, 1885; buried Odd Fellows Cemetery, Eugene.

HENDERSON, James Pinckney, senator, gov. Tex.; b. Lincoln County, N.C., Mar. 31, 1808; s. Lawson and Elizabeth (Carruth) H.; attended U. N.C., did not graduate; m. Frances Cox, Oct. 1839. Admitted to N.C. bar, 1829; col. N.C. Militia; commd. brig. gen., 1836; appointed atty. gen. Republic of Tex., 1836, sec. of state, 1836-37; diplomatic agt. to Eng. and France with power to secure recognition of Tex. independence and to effect treaties of commerce, amity and navigation, 1837-1840, in Eng. negotiated informal comml. trading arrangement between Eng. and Tex., in France made similar treaty, 1838, signed, 1839; special envoy to U.S. to assist with Tex. annexation, 1844; del. to Tex. Constl. Conv. 1845; 1st gov. of Tex. (Democrat), 1845-47; took command of 4 regts. furnished by Tex., commd. brig. gen. U.S. Volunteers during Mexican War, 1846; mem. U.S. Senate (Dem.) from Tex., 1857-58. Died Washington, D.C., June 4, 1858.

HENDERSON, John, senator; b. Bridgeton, N.J., Feb. 28, 1795; m. 2d, Louisa Fourniquet, 1830. Moved to Miss. in youth; mem. Miss. Senate from Wilkinson County, 1835, 36, constl. criticism of Miss. Ho. of Reps. resulted in adjournment both houses, Jan. 31, 1835; mem. U.S. Senate (Whig), from Miss., 1839-45; helped Lopez prepare for invasion of Cuba, thus violating Neutrality Law 1818, arrested and acquitted, 1851; name carved on meml. to Am. citizens who took part in long struggle for independence erected by Cuba in Havana; also interested in annexation of Texas. Died Pass Christian, La., Sept. 16,1857.

HENDERSON, Joseph, physician, congressman; b. Shippensburg, Pa., Aug. 2, 1791; grad. Jefferson Med. Coll., Phila., 1813. Commd. 1st lt. 22d Regt., Pa. Volunteers during War of 1812, promoted capt.; brevetted maj., given command of a regt., 1814; participated in battles of Chippewa and Lundy's Lane, siege of Ft. Erie; practiced medicine, Browns Mills, Pa.; mem. U.S. Ho. of Reps. from Pa., 23d-24th congresses, 1833-37; practiced medicine, Lewistown, Pa., 1850-63. Died Lewistown, Dec. 25, 1863; buried St. Mark's Cemetery, Lewistown.

HENDERSON, Leonard, jurist; b. Granville County, N.C., Oct. 6, 1772; s. Richard and Elizabeth (Keeling) H.; studied law in office of Judge John Williams, Hillsboro, N.C.; m. Frances Starr, 4 children. Admitted to N.C. bar, 1794; clk. of dist. ct., Hillsboro, 1794-1800; pvt. practice of law, Hillsboro, 1800-08; judge N.C. Superior Ct., 1808-16; judge N.C. Supreme Ct., 1818-29, chief justice, 1829-33. Died Aug. 13, 1833.

HENDERSON, Peter, horticulturist; b. Pathhead, Scotland, June 9, 1882; s. James and Agnes (Gilchrist) H.; m. Emily Gibbs, 1851; m. 2d, Jean H. Reid, 1871. Apprenticed to George Stirling, head gardener at gardens of Melville Castle, Dalkeith, Scotland, 1837-43; came to N.Y., 1843; gardener for George Thorburn at Astoria, L.I., 1843-44, for Charles F. Spang, Pitts., 1844-47; partner (with his brother James) in market-gardening bus., Jersey City, N.J., 1847-50; sold greenhouse plants, N.Y.C., 1853-64; owner seed store in N.Y., 1864-71; established Peter Henderson & Co. (seed and garden supply house), 1871-90; contbr. articles to Mag. of Horticulture, Rural New Yorker, Country Gentleman. Author: Gardening for Profit, 1866; Gardening for Pleasure, 1875; Henderson's Hand Book of Plants, 1881. Died Jersey City, Jan. 17, 1890.

HENDERSON, Richard, colonizer; b. Hanover County, Va., Apr. 20, 1735; s. Samuel and Elizabeth (Williams) H.; m. Elizabeth Keeling, Dec. 28, 1763, several children including Archibald, Leonard. Family moved to N.C., 1742; admitted to N.C. bar; asso. justice N.C. Superior Ct., 1768; became acquainted with Daniel Boone; organizer Richard Henderson & Co., 1764; organizer Louisa Co. (Transylvania Co.) with intention of establishing proprietary colony in the West, 1774, bought land from Cherokee Indians between Ky. and Cumberland rivers; Revolutionary War made it impossible for him to secure recognition of his colony from Eng., also he was opposed by Va. and N.C.; a N.C. commr. working with Va. commrs. to survey boundary between Va. and N.C., 1779-80; promoted, carried out colonization of what is now W. Tenn., established settlement at Nashville, 1779-80; elected to N.C. Legislature, 1781; mem. N.C. Council of State, 1782. Died Hillsborough, N.C., Jan. 30, 1785.

HENDERSON, Samuel, congressman; b. Eng., Nov. 27, 1764; attended sch., Eng. Came to U.S., 1782, settled in Montgomery, Pa.; owner, operator Henderson Marble Quarries, Montgomery County (Pa.); mem. U.S. Ho. of Reps. (Republican) from Pa., 13th Congress, Oct. 11, 1814-15. Died on estate at Upper Merion, Pa., Nov. 17, 1841; buried family burying ground, Montgomery County.

HENDERSON, Thomas, physician, army officer, congressman; b. Freehold, N.J., Aug. 15, 1743; s. John and Ann (Stevens) H.; grad. Coll. of N.J. (now Princeton), 1761; m. Mary Hendricks, Sept. 23, 1767; m. 2d, Rachel Burrowes, Jan. 2, 1778; 7 children. Mem. N.J. Com. of Safety, 1774; mem. Freehold Com. of Observation and Inspection, 1774; lt. local militia in N.J., 1775; maj. Minutemen, 1776; commd. maj. Continental Army, 1776; surrogate Monmouth County (N.J.), 1776; lt. col. Forman's Additional Continental Regt., 1777; mem. N.J. Provincial Council, 1777, N.J. Assembly, 1780-84; became mem. local com. of retaliation, 1780; mem. N.J. Gen. Assembly, 1780-84; judge of common pleas, 1783, 99, master of chancery, 1790; mem. N.J. Council, 1793-94; 1812-13, v.p., 1794; acting gov. N.J., 1794; mem. U.S. Ho. of Reps. (Federalist) from N.J., 4th Congress, 1795-97; mem. N.J. Med. Soc., 1766; trustee, elder Tennent Ch. N.J. Died Freehold, Dec. 15, 1824; buried Old Tennent Cemetery, Freehold.

HENDRICK (Tiyanoga), Indian chief; b. circa 1680. Mohican by birth, adopted by Mohawks. Elected Mohawk sachem as young man; visited Eng., presented to Queen Anne, 1710; ofcl. spokesman for Mohawks, in close contact with those responsible for English policy along N.Y. frontier; consulted by Jonathan Edwards about project for educating Mohawks, 1751; often rep. of Mohawks at councils between Six Nations and English leaders; joined Am. forces in French and Indian War on request of Gen. Johnson, 1754; made greatest speech at Albany Congress, 1754, upbraided English for leaving only their Indian allies standing between them and the French and for generally neglecting frontier defenses (speech published in Eng. in Gentleman's Mag., 1755); considered the outstanding N. Am. Indian of his time, often referred to as King Hendrick. Died Battle of Lake George (N.Y.), Sept. 8, 1755.

HENDRICKS, Thomas Andrews, vice pres. U.S.: b. nr. Zanesville, O., Sept. 7, 1819; s. John and Jane (Thomson) H.; grad. Hanover (Ind.) Coll., 1841; attended law sch., Chambersburg, Pa., 1843; m. Eliza Morgan, Sept. 26, 1845, 1 child. Admitted to Ind. bar, 1843; mem. Ind. Ho. of Reps., 1848, Ind. Senate, 1849; mem. U.S. Ho. of Reps. from Ind., 32d-33th congresses, 1851-55; commr. Gen. Land Office, 1855-59; mem. U.S. Senate from Ind., 1863-69; gov. Ind., 1872; unsuccessful vice presdl. nominee Democratic Party on Tilden ticket, 1876, disputed election being decided by electoral commn.; U.S. vice pres. under Grover Cleveland, 1885. Died Indpls., Nov. 25, 1885; buried Crown Hill Cemetery, Indpls.

HENDRICKS, William, senator, gov. Ind., congressman; b. Ligonier, Pa., Nov. 12, 1782; s. Abraham and Ann (Jamison) H.; grad. Washington and Jefferson Coll., 1810; LL.D. (hon.), Washington Coll., Pa., 1833; m. Ann Paul, May 19, 1816. Admitted to Ohio bar, 1812; publisher Western Eagle, 1813; sec. Ind. Gen. Assembly, 1814-15; mem. U.S. Ho. of Reps. from Ind., 14th-17th congresses, Dec. 11, 1816-July 25, 1822; gov. Ind., 1822-25; mem. U.S. Senate from Ind., 1825-27. Died Madison, Ind., May 16, 1850; buried Fairmont Cemetery, Madison.

HENING, William Waller, lawyer; b. Va., 1767; m. Agatha Banks. Practiced law, Fredericksburg, Va., at early age; practiced law, Albemarle County, Va., 1791-1828; mem. Va. Legislature, 1804-05; clk. of Chancery Ct. for Dist. of Richmond (Va.), 1807-28. Author: The New Virginia Justice, 1795; The American Pleader and Lawyer's Guide, 1811; Maxims of Law and Equity, 1811; The Statutes at Large; Being a Collection of All the Laws of Virginia (accomplished under enactment of Va. Legislature; represents compilation of all Va. laws, 1619-1792), published 1809-23. Died Apr. 1, 1828.

HENKEL, Paul, clergyman; b. Rowan County, N. C., Dec. 15, 1754; s. Jacob and Mary Barbara (Teter) H.; m. Elizabeth Negeley, Nov. 20, 1776, 9 children. Learned coppers trade as youth; preached 1st sermon, 1781; licensed to preach by Ministerium of Pa. at York, Pa., 1783, ordained, 1792; preached in Va., N.C., Tenn., Ky. and Ohio, 1790-1825; a founder N.C. Synod, 1803, Joint Synod of Ohio, 1818, Tenn. Synod, 1820. Died New Market, Va., Nov. 27, 1825; buried Emmanuel Cemetery, New Market.

HENKLE, Eli Jones, congressman; b. Westminster, Md., Nov. 24, 1828; grad. U. Md., 1850. Taught sch., Anne Arundel County, Md.; practiced medicine, Brooklyn, Md.; prof. anatomy, physiology and Hygiene Md. Agrl. Coll., also trustee; mem. Md. Ho. of Dels., 1863, 72-75, Md. Constl. Conv., 1864, Md. Senate, 1867, 68, 70; del. Democratic Nat. Conv., Balt., 1872; mem. U.S. Ho. of Reps. (Dem.) from Md., 44th-46th congresses, 1875-81, unsuccessful candidate for re-election, 1880; supt. vaccination, Balt., 1883. Died Balt., Nov. 1, 1893; buried Druid Ridge Cemetery, Balt.

HENLEY, Robert, naval officer; b. Williamsburg, Va., Jan. 5, 1783; s. Leonard and Elizabeth (Dandridge) H.; attended Coll. William and Mary, before 1799; married, no children. Obtained midshipman's warrant in U.S. Navy, 1799; served in ship Constellation in war with France, circa 1800; studied navigation and naval science, Williamsburg, Va., 1806-07; commd. lt. U.S. Navy, 1807; commanded brig Eagle at Battle of Lake Champlain in War of 1812; captured pirate schooner Moscow off Santo Domingo, 1821; promoted capt., 1825; stationed at Naval Sta., Charleston, S.C., 1825-28. Died Sullivan's Island, Charleston, Oct. 6, 1828.

HENLEY, Thomas Jefferson, congressman; b. Richmond, Ind., Apr. 2, 1810; attended Ind. U., Bloomington; studied law. Admitted to Ind. bar, 1828, began practice in Richmond; engaged in banking; mem. Ind. Ho. of Reps., 1832-43, speaker, 1840; mem. U.S. Ho. of Reps. (Democrat) from Ind., 28th-30th congresses, 1843-49; moved to Cal., 1849, engaged in banking, Sacramento; mem. 1st Cal. Ho. of Reps., 1851-53; supt. Indian affairs of Cal., 1855-58; postmaster of San Francisco, 1860-64. Died San Francisco, Jan. 2, 1865; buried Santa Rosa (Cal.) Cemetery.

HENN, Bernhart, congressman; b. Cherry Valley, N.Y., 1817; attended common schs.; studied law. Admitted to Ia. bar; apptd. register U.S. Land Office, 1845; mem. U.S. Ho. of Reps. (Democrat) from Ia., 32d-33d congresses, 1851-55; engaged in banking, real estate dealings. Died Fairfield, Ia., Aug. 30, 1865; buried Evergreen Cemetery, Fairfield.

HENNEPIN, Louis, clergyman, explorer; b. Ath, Belgium, Apr. 7, 1640; s. Gaspard and Robertine (Leleup) H. Baptized as Johannes, changed name on becoming a Recollect friar; missionary in Canada, 1675-78; became chaplain to La Salle's forces in Can., 1678, accompanied La Salle on expdn. to central Ill., 1679; mem. Michel Aco's expdn. on upper Mississippi, 1680, captured by Sioux Indians, later rescued by Duluth; returned to France, 1682,, expelled (for unknown reasons) from France, 1690; appealed unsuccessfully to both Eng. and France to be sent back to Can.; no record of him after 1701. Author: Description de la Louisiane, 1683; Nouveau Voyage, 1696; Nouvelle Decouverte, 1697. Died circa 1701.

HENNI, John Martin, clergyman; b. Masanenga, Switzerland, June 15, 1805; s. Johann Georg and Maria (Henni) H.; ed. Lyceum and Gymnasium, Lucerne, Switzerland. Arrived in N.Y.C., May 28, 1828; ordained priest Roman Catholic Ch., Sem., Bardstown, Ky., 1829; apptd. vicar gen. Cincinnati, pastor of Germans in Cincinnati, 1834-44; founder, editor Wahrheitsfreund (1st German Cath. newspaper in U.S.), Cincinnati, 1837-43; 1st bishop of Milw., 1844-75, established St. Francis Sem.; introduced Capuchins and Jesuits into diocese; became archbishop, 1875. Died Milw., Sept. 7, 1881.

HENNINGSEN, Charles Frederick, army officer, author; b. Brussels, Belgium, Feb. 21, 1815; m. Williamina (Belt) Connelly. Entered service of Carlists in Spain, 1834; knighted, made capt. Lancers in Spain, 1835-36; came to U.S. with Louis Kossuth, (leader of Hungarian freedom movement), after fighting with Hungarians against Austrians, 1851; joined expdn. to Nicaragua as brig. gen. in charge of arty. under William Walker, 1856; col. 59th Regular Va. Inf., Confederate Army, 1861-62; an accomplished linguist. Author: Revelations of Russia (gave Americans 1st idea of Russia through a book), 1844; The White Slave, 1845; Eastern Europe and the Emperor Nicholas, 3 vols., 1846; Sixty Years Hence, 1847; Analogies and Contrasts, 2 vols., 1848; The Past and Future of Hungary, 1852. Died Washington, D.C., June 14, 1877; buried Congressional Cemetery, Washington.

HENRY, Albert P., sculptor; b. Versailles, Ky., Jan. 8, 1836. Clk. iron works; taught himself modelling, cast early pieces in iron for doorstops; captured by Confederate Army during Civil War, spent time in prison carving in bone; apptd. U.S. consul at Ancona (Italy) after Civil War; best known works include busts of Henry Clay (now in U.S. Capitol), Abraham Lincoln. Died Paris, Ky., Nov. 6, 1872.

HENRY, Alexander, fur trader; b. New Brunswick, N.J., Aug. 1739; m. widow of John Kittson, 4 children including William and Alexander. Mc trading between Albany, N.Y. and Michilimack ac (now Mackinac, Mich.), 1760-63; captured Indians during Pontiac Conspiracy, 1763, saved French comdt. at Michilimackinac; fur trader Lake Superior area, 1764-76, discovered copper region; went as far west as Saskatchewan in trading expdns.; lived in Montreal, Can., af 1776; capt. militia, Montreal; an original me Beaver Club (orgn. of men who had been fur tra ers in Old N.W.), 1786. Author: Travels and A ventures of Alexander Henry, 1809. Died Mc treal, Apr. 4, 1824.

HENRY, Andrew, fur trapper; b. York County, P circa 1775; s. George and Margaret (Young) m. Marie Villars, Dec. 16, 1805; m. 2d, Mary Fle ing, 1819. Organizer (with Manuel Lisa) St. Lo Mo. Fur Co., 1809-11, set up 1st trapping Co. W of Rockies; served as maj. of local regt. under Col. W. H. Ashley; joined Ashley in establish trapping areas in Rocky Mountains, 1822, constru ed forts as protection against Blackfoot India Died June 10, 1833.

HENRY, Caleb Sprague, clergyman; b. Rutla Mass., Aug. 2, 1804; grad. Dartmouth, 1825; Cornelia M. Heard, Mar. 1838. Ordained to m istry Congregational Ch., 1829; pastor Congre tional chs., Greenfield, Mass., 1829-31, West Ha ford, Conn., 1833-35; ordained priest, 1836; pr moral philosophy Bristol Coll., Pa., 1835-38, City N.Y., 1838-52; rector St. Clement's Ch., N. C., 1847-50; best known for his work as an edi and author. Author: Dr. Oldham at Greystones a His Talk There, 1860, also other works. Edit Elements of Psychology (Victor Cousin), 1834; G eral History of Civilization in Europe (W. Hazlit translation of Guizot's work), 1842. Died Mar. 1884.

HENRY, Heth, army officer; b. Chesterfield Cou ty, Va., Dec. 16, 1825; attended Georgetown Co 1837; grad. U.S. Mil. Acad., 1847; m. Harriet S den, 3 children. Brevetted 2d lt., 1847, served Mexican War; promoted 1st lt., 1853, capt., 185 served against Sioux Indians; joined Confeder Army, 1861, organized Floyd's command for W.V. Fall 1861; commd. brig. gen. in command of m dist. around Lewisburg, Va., 1862; post and d comdr. in Bragg's Army during expdns. into K transferred to Army of No. Va., 1863; commd. m gen. 1863; his most conspicuous action was at B tle of Gettysburg (which he precipitated by eng ing U.S. Army early); civil engr. for U.S. Gov 1880-84; spl. agt. Office of Indian Affairs, 18 98. Died Washington, D.C., Sept. 27, 1899.

HENRY, James, Continental congressman; b. comac County, Va., 1731; studied law U. Edinbu (Scotland). Admitted to the bar, practiced la mem. Va. Ho. of Burgesses, 1772-74, Va. Ho. Dels., 1776, 77, 79; mem. Continental Congress fr Va., 1780-81; judge Va. Ct. Admiralty, 1782- Va. Gen. Ct., 1788-1800. Died "Fleet Bay," Nor umberland County, Va., Dec. 9, 1804.

HENRY, John, actor, theatrical mgr.; b. Du lin, Ireland, circa 1746; ed. Trinity Coll., Du lin; m. Maria Storer. Made debut at Drury La London, 1762, Am. debut at Southwark Theat Phila., Oct. 6, 1767; adapted "The School Soldiers; Or, The Deserter" for Old Am. Co., 178 partnership with Lewis Hollman produced monop Am. theatre from N.Y. to Annapolis (despite co flicting natures of the partners), 1785-91; 1 most accomplished men on early Am. stage. Di at sea, Oct. 1794.

HENRY, John, senator, gov. Md.; b. Dorches County, Md., Nov. 1750; s. Col. John and Dorot (Rider) H.; grad. Coll. of N.J. (now Princeton 1769; m. Margaret Campbell, Mar. 6, 1787; children. Admitted to Middle Temple, London, En del. Continental Congress from Md., 1778-81, 8 87, strong advocate of provisioning and strengthe ing army and authority of George Washington; me U.S. Senate from Md., 1789-97; gov. Md., 179 98. Died Dorchester County, Dec. 16, 1798.

HENRY, John, adventurer; b. Ireland, circa 177 flourished 1807-20; m. a French émigrée, 2 childre Served as arty. officer U.S. Army, 1800-02; lived estate in Vt., 1802-07; student-at-law, Montre Can., 1807; defended fur-barons of N.W. Co. Can., 1807-08; commd. by Sir James Craig (go gen. of Can.) to determine Am. public opini toward possible war with Eng., 1809-10; with h of Count de Crillon, sold letters of corresponden between himself and Can. to Pres. James Madis for $50,000, 1811; a paid informer sent to Ita to discover evidence against Queen Caroline of Eng 1820.

HENRY, John, congressman; b. nr. Stanford, K Nov. 1, 1800; attended pub. schs. Served as p Capt. Arnett's Co., Ill. Volunteers, during Bla Hawk War; mem. Ill. Ho. of Reps., 1832-40; p icipated in constrn. of 1st ry. in Ill., 1838; mem. Ill. Senate, 1840-47; mem. U.S. Ho. of Reps. (Whig) from Ill., 29th Congress, Feb. 5-Mar. 3, 1847; supt. Ill. State Insane Asylum, Jacksonville, 1850-55; served with Q.M. Dept., U.S. Army, Jackson, Tenn., 1862-63. Died St. Louis, Apr. 28, 1882; buried Bellefontaine Cemetery, St. Louis.

HENRY, John Flournoy, physician, congressman; b. Henrys Mill, Ky., Jan. 17, 1793; attended Georgetown (Ky.) Acad., Jefferson Med. Coll., Phila.; grad. Coll. Physicians and Surgeons, N.Y.C., 1817. Served as surgeon's mate Ky. Militia, 1813; engaged in farming; practiced medicine; mem. U.S. Ho. of Reps. from Ill., 19th Congress, Dec. 11, 1826-27, unsuccessful candidate for re-election; prof. Med. Coll. of Ohio, 1831; practiced medicine, Bloomington, Ill., 1834-45, Burlington, Ia., 1845-73. Died Burlington, Nov. 12, 1873; buried Aspen Grove Cemetery, Burlington.

HENRY, Joseph, scientist; b. Albany, N.Y., Dec. 17, 1797; s. William and Ann (Alexander) H.; received numerous hon. degrees including A.M., Union Coll., 1829; LL.D., S.C. Coll. (now U. S.C.), 1838, U. State N.Y., 1850, Harvard, 1851; m. Harriet Alexander, May 1830, 6 children. Conducted research in self-induction; 1st to detect the induced current, 1832; invented an electromagnetic motor; prof. natural philosophy Coll. of N.J (now Princeton), 1832-46; did research which anticipated some of the modern developments in science of electricity, 1838-42; invented low and high resistance galvonometers; 1st sec. and dir. Smithsonian Instn., 1846-78, (instn. as known today largely a result of his work); initiated system of basing weather forecasts on weather reports received by telegraph, 1850; became mem. Light House Bd., 1852, pres., 1871-78; became mem. Am. Philos. Soc., 1835; an organizer A.A.A.S., pres. 1849; a founder Philos. Soc. of Washington, 1871, pres. 1871-78; charter mem. Nat. Acad. Scis., v.p., 1866, pres., 1868-78; scientific unit of self-induction named "Henry" in his honor. Died Washington, D.C., May 13, 1878.

HENRY, Morris Henry, physician; b. London, Eng., July 26, 1835; s. Henry A. Henry; M.D., U. Vt., 1860; m. Elizabeth Hastings, 1872; m. 2d, Mrs. Harrison Everett Maynard, 1880; survived by 1 child. Came to N.Y.C., 1852; surgeon Northern Dispensary, 1864; surgeon N.Y. Dispensary, 1869; surgeon-in-chief N.Y. State Emigrant Hosp., 1873-80; chief police surgeon of N.Y.C., 1872-84, organized ambulance service; founder, editor Am. Jour. Syphilography and Dermatology, 1870-75; published Am. edit. Skin Diseases: Their Description, Pathology, Diagnosis, and Treatment (W.T. Fox), 1871; invented numerous instruments including forceps, scissors for many purposes; decorated by sovereigns of Greece and Turkey. Died May 19, 1895.

HENRY, Patrick, gov. Va., Continental congressman; b. Hanover County, Va., May 29, 1736; s. John and Sarah (Winston) H.; m. Sarah Shelton, 1754; m. 2d, Dorothea Dandridge, 1776. Licensed to practice law, 1760; elected to Va. Ho. of Burgesses, 1765; claimed legislative independence for Va. in response to Stamp Act, 1765; gave one of his most famous speeches against Stamp Act, contained phrase "If this be treason, make the most of it;" organized (with Thomas Jefferson and Richard Henry Lee) Com. of Correspondence, 1773; mem. 1st Continental Congress from Va., 1774-75, offered resolution providing that "this Colony be immediately put into a position of defense" (contained famous phrase, "give me liberty or give me death"); took seat in 2d Continental Congress, May 18, 1775, participated in legislation by which Continental Army was organized; resigned commn. as col. Va. Militia, 1776; elected mem. 3d Va. Revolutionary Conv., 1776, took decisive part in drafting new Va. constn., took part in urging passage of resolutions authorizing Congress to declare independence and to appeal to France for aid; gov. Va., 1776-79, 84-86, sent George Rogers Clark to Illinois Country to expel British from N.W. Territory, 1778; del. to Va. Conv. to ratify U.S. Constn., 1788, opposed ratification, largely responsible for addition of Bill of Rights; elected to Va. Ho. of Dels. (Federalist), 1799, died before taking office. Died Va., June 6, 1799; buried Red Hill Plantation, Staunton River, Va.

HENRY, Robert, clergyman, educator; b. Charleston, S.C., Dec. 6, 1792; s. Peter and Anne (Schwiers) H.; M.A., U. Edinburgh (Scotland), 1814; m. Elizabeth Connors, 1818, 6 children. Ordained to ministry Ch. of Scotland, 1817; ordained deacon Episcopal Ch., 1841, priest, 1842; prof. logic and moral philosophy S.C. Coll. (now U. S.C.), 1818-34, pres. pro tem, 1834-35, prof. metaphysics, logic and belles-lettres, 1839, chmn. faculty, 1841, pres., coll., 1842-45, pro. Greek lit., 1845-56. Died Columbia, S.C., Feb. 6, 1856; buried Columbia.

HENRY, Robert Pryor, congressman; b. Henrys Mills, Ky., Nov. 24, 1788; grad. Transylvania Coll., Lexington, Ky.; studied law. Admitted to Ky. bar, 1809, began practice in Georgetown; pros. atty., 1819; served in War of 1812; mem. U.S. Ho. of Reps. (Clay Democrat) from Ky., 18th-19th congresses, 1823-26. Died Hopkinsville, Ky., Aug. 25, 1826; buried Pioneer Cemetery, Hopkinsville.

HENRY, Thomas, congressman; b. County Down, Ireland, 1779. Came to Am., settled in Beaver, Pa., 1798; apptd. justice of peace, 1808; elected county commr., 1810; capt. of a co. which went from Beaver to help in defense of No. frontier against a threatened British invasion, 1814; mem. Pa. Ho. of Reps., 1815; prothonotary and clk. of cts., 1816-21; county sheriff, 1821; propr., editor Western Argus, 1821-31; county treas., 1828-29; mem. U.S. Ho. of Reps. (Whig) from Pa., 25th-27th congresses, 1837-43. Died Beaver, July 20, 1849; buried Old Beaver Cemetery.

HENRY, William, gunsmith, Continental congressman, inventor; b. West Caln Twp., Pa., May 19, 1729; s. John and Elizabeth (DeVinne) H.; m. Ann Wood, Jan. 1755, 7 children including William, Joseph. Went to Lancaster, Pa., 1744, apprenticed to gunsmith; formed partnership with Joseph Simon for making of firearms, prin. armorers of colonial troops during French and Indian Wars, 1750; went on business trip to Eng., 1761, learned from James Watt about his steam engine; aided Robert Fulton and Benjamin West in their youth; pioneer steam propulsion in Am.; built stern-wheel steamboat (1st in U.S.) 1762-63; joined Am. Philos. Soc., 1768; credited with invention of a screw auger; perfected steam-heating system; justice of peace, Pa., 1758; asst. burgess of Lancaster, 1765-75; del. to Pa. Assembly, 1776; mem. Pa. Council of Safety, 1777; treas. Lancaster County, 1777-86; elected by Assembly as del. Continental Congress, 1784; asst. commissary gen. and disbursing officer U.S. Govt. for dist. of Lancaster, 1775-81. Died Lancaster, Dec. 15, 1786.

HENRY, William, congressman; b. Charlestown, N.H., Mar. 22, 1788; attended common schs. Engaged in bus., Chester, Vt., in mfg., Vt., N.Y., and Jaffery, N.H., in banking, Bellows Falls, Vt.; mem. Vt. Ho. of Reps., 1834-35, Vt. Senate, 1836; dir. Rutland & Burlington R.R. Co.; del. Whig Nat. Conv., Harrisburg, Pa., 1839; Whig presdl. elector, 1840; mem. U.S. Ho. of Reps. (Whig) from Vt., 30th-31st congresses, 1847-51; Republican presdl. elector, 1860. Died Bellows Falls, Apr. 16, 1861; buried South St. Cemetery, Chester.

HENSCHEL, Lillian June Bailey, concert soprano; b. Columbus, O., Jan. 18, 1860; studied with Mme. Rudersdorff, later with Mme. Viardot-Garcia; m. George Henschel, Mar. 9, 1881. Made successful debut, Boston, 1876; made English debut at Philharmonic concert, 1879; asso. with husband in recital and concert, until 1901. Died Kensington, London, Eng., Nov. 4, 1901.

HENSHAW, David, state polit. leader, sec. of navy; b. Leicester, Mass., Apr. 2, 1791; s. David and Mary (Sargent) H. With assos. established Boston Statesman, 1821; established an ins. co., 1824; incorporator Western R.R.; dir. Boston and Worcester R.R.; collector Port of Boston, 1827; recognized as Democratic boss of Mass.; mem. Mass. Legislature, 1839; U.S. sec. of navy, 1843-1884. Author: Remarks Upon the Rights and Powers of Corporations, 1837; Letters on Internal Improvements and Commerce of the West, 1839. Died Leicester, Nov. 11, 1852.

HENSLEY, Samuel J., guide; horseman with Chiles' party, 1843; leader various pioneer parties to Cal.; pioneered route known as Salt-Lake Cut-off, 1848; officer Fremont's battalion, 1847.

HENSON, Josiah, escaped slave; b. Charles County, Md., June 15, 1789; m. slave girl, 1811, 12 children; m. 2d, circa 1870. Became supt. of slaves on his master's farm in Md., assigned to conduct master's slaves to Ky., 1825; urged to escape while passing through Ohio, but kept promise to his master; admitted as preacher to Methodist Episcopal Ch., 1828; made unsuccessful attempt to purchase his freedom, was sent to New Orleans to be sold; escaped to Can., 1830; worked for cultural and indsl. betterment of his race; made 3 trips to Eng.; awarded bronze medal for black walnut boards exhibited at World's Fair, on 2d trip to Eng., 1851; told his story to Harriet Beecher Stowe, reputed to be original of Uncle Tom of Uncle Tom's Cabin. Author: The Life of Josiah Henson, Formerly a Slave, Now an Inhabitant of Canada, as Narrated by Himself, 1849. Died Dresden, Ont., Can., May 5, 1883.

HENTZ, Caroline Lee Whiting, author; b. Lancaster, Mass., June 1, 1800; d. John and Orpah Whiting; m. Nicholas Marcellus Hentz, Sept. 30, 1824, 4 children. Assisted husband in sch. work; wrote play De Lara or the Moorish Bride, 1843; story Aunt Patty's Scrap Bag, 1846; series of popular novels The Mob Cap, 1848; Linda, or the Young Pilot of the Belle Creole, 1850; Rena or the Snow Bird, 1851; Marcus Warland or the Long Moss Spring, 1852; Wild Jack, 1852; Helen and Arthur, 1853; Love After Marriage, 1854; The Lost Daughter, 1855. Died Marianna, Fla., Feb. 11, 1856; buried Marianna.

HENTZ, Nicholas Marcellus, artist; b. France, July 25, 1797. Came to Am., circa 1816, settled in Wilkes-Barre, Pa.; taught sch., Phila. and Boston; taught at Round Hill Sch., Northampton, Mass.; exhibited miniature of a Creole lady at Pa. Acad., 1819; prof. modern langs. U. N.C., 1824-30; head several So. acads. and female sems., 1830-49; pioneer in Am. entomology, authority on spiders. Died Mariana, Fla., 1856.

HERBERT, John Carlyle, congressman; b. Alexandria, Va., Aug. 16, 1775; grad. St. John's Coll., Annapolis, Md., 1794; studied law. Admitted to Va. bar, began practice in Richmond, circa 1795; mem. Va. Ho. of Dels., 1798-99; settled in Prince Georges County, Md., 1805; mem. Md. Ho. of Dels., 1808-13, speaker, 1812-13; served as capt. Bladensburg Troop of Horse, during War of 1812; mem. U.S. Ho. of Reps. (Federalist) from Md., 14th-15th congresses, 1815-19; resumed practice of law; presdl. elector at large from Md., 1824, 32. Died Buchanan, Va., Sept. 1, 1846; buried Greenmount Cemetery, Balt.

HERBERT, Louis, army officer, engr.; b. La., Mar. 13, 1820; s. Valéry and Clarisse (Bush) H.; grad. Jefferson Coll., 1840, U.S. Mil. Acad., 1845; m. Malvina Lambremont, 1848, 3 children. Asst. engr. in constrn. of Ft. Livingston, La., 1845-47; served as maj. La. Militia, 1847-50, col., 1858-61; mem. La. Senate, 1853-55; chief engr. La., 1855-59; served as col. 3d La. Inf., Confederate Army, from 1861, commd. brig. gen., 1862; editor Iberville South, Plaquemine, La., 1866-circa 1870; taught sch., Iberville and St. Martin Parish, La., 1870-1901. Died Jan. 7, 1901.

HERBERT, Philemon Thomas, congressman; b. Pine Apple, Ala., Nov. 1, 1825; attended U. Ala.; Moved to Mariposa City, Cal., circa 1850; mem. Cal. Assembly, 1853-54; mem. U.S. Ho. of Reps. (Democrat) from Cal., 34th Congress, 1855-57; moved to El Paso, Tex., circa 1859, practiced law; served as lt. col. 7th Tex. Cavalry, Confederate Army, during Civil War; fatally wounded at Battle of Mansfield, 1864. Died Kingston, La., July 23, 1864; buried Evergreen Cemetery, Kingston.

HERBERT, William Henry, author; b. London, Eng., Apr. 7, 1807; s. Rev. William and Hon. Letitia Emily Dorothea (Allen) H.; grad. Caius Coll., 1830; m. Sarah Barker, 1839; m. 2d, Adela R. Budlong, 1858. Came to U.S., 1831; published (with A. D. Patterson) Am. Monthly Mag., 1833-35; wrote series of articles under pseudonym Frank Forester for Am. Turf Register, 1839. Author: The Brothers, A Tale of the Fronde (1st novel), 1835; The Knights of England, France and Scotland, 1852; The Captains of the Roman Republic, 1854; (novels under pseudonym Frank Forester) The Warwick Woodlands, or Things as They were Ten Years Ago, 1845, My Shooting Box, 1846, The Deer Stalkers, 1849; Frank Forester's Horse and Horsemanship of the United States and British Provinces of North America, 1857. Shot himself after desertion by 2d wife, N.Y.C., May 17, 1858; buried Mt. Pleasant Cemetery, Newark, N.J.

HERDIC, Peter, lumberman, inventor; b. Ft. Plains, N.J., Dec. 14, 1824; m. Amand Taylor, Dec. 25, 1849; m. 2d, Encie E. Maynard, Jan. 12, 1860; at least 2 children. Worked for lumberman, Pipe Creek, N.Y., 1844-46; operated shingle mill, Williamsport, Pa. (town which he had built by purchasing land surrounding his original lumber mill and developing it), 1846-78; obtained patent for improved vehicle running gear, 1880, later patented fare-collecing box to be used on coach or cab; organizer, operator Herdic Coach Co., Phila., 1880's. Died Williamsport, Mar. 2, 1888; buried Williamsport.

HEREFORD, Frank, senator, congressman; b. nr. Warrenton, Va., July 4, 1825; grad. McKendree Coll., Lebanon, Ill., 1845; studied law. Admitted to the bar, practiced law; moved to Cal., 1849; dist. atty. Sacramento County (Cal.), 1855-57; moved to W.Va.; mem. U.S. Ho. of Reps. (Democrat) from W.Va., 42d-44th congresses, 1871-Jan. 31, 1877; mem. U.S. Senate from W.Va., Jan. 31, 1877-81; resumed law practice; Dem. presdl. elector, 1888. Died Union, W.Va., Dec. 21, 1891; buried Green Hill Cemetery, Union.

HERING, Constantine, homeopathic physician; b. Oschatz, Saxony, Jan. 1, 1800; s. Christian Karl and Christiane (Kreutzberg) H.; attended Surg. Acad. of Dresden, U. Leipzig; diploma in medicine, surgery, obstetrics U. Würzburg, 1826; m. Charlotte Kemper, 1829; m. 2d, Marianne Hussmann; m. 3d,

Theresa Buckheim, 1845; children—Carl, Rudolph. Tchr. mathematics Blochmann Inst., 1826; delegated to go to S.Am. to make researches in zoology in Surinam, 1827; practiced medicine in Paramaribo; came to U.S., 1833; an organizer N.Am. Acad. of Homeopathic Healing Art (1st sch. of homeopathic therapeutics in world), Allentown, Pa., 1835, pres. and prin. instr., 1836-42; presided at 1st meeting of Am. Inst. of Homeopathy, 1844; founded (with Jacob Jeanes and Walter Williamson), Homeopathic Med. Coll. of Pa., 1848, prof. insts. of homeopathy, practice of medicine, 1864-67; formed Hahnemann Med. Coll. of Phila., 1867 (joined with Homeopathic Med. Coll., 1869), dean, 1867-71, prof. insts. and materia medica, 1867-69, 70-71, prof. insts. and practice, 1869-70, prof. emeritus, 1876-80; an editor N.Am. Homoeopathic Jour., 1851-53, Homoeopathic News, 1854-56, Am. Homoeopathic Materia Medica, 1867-71. Author: The Homoeopathist or Domestic Physician, 1835; Analytical Therapeutics, 1875, Guiding Symptoms, 10 vols., 1878-91. Died Phila., July 23, 1880.

HERIOT, George, govt. ofcl., artist; b. Island of Jersey, 1766. Settled in Can., before 1800; clk. Ordnance Depot, Que., Can., later dep. postmaster gen. and postmaster gen. of Brit. N.Am.; painted many watercolor views in Can. and Northeastern U.S.; kept sketchbooks which are now at N.Y. Hist. Soc. Author: Travels through the Canadas, 1807. Died 1844.

HERKIMER, John, congressman; b. Tryon (now Herkimer) County, N.Y., 1773; attended pub. schs. Mem. N.Y. Ho. of Reps., 1800, 04, 06; mem. N.Y. Constl. Conv., 1801; served as maj. during War of 1812, commanded a battalion of N.Y. Volunteers in defense of Sackets Harbor, 1813; judge circuit ct.; mem. U.S. Ho. of Reps. (Democrat) from N.Y., 15th, 18th congresses, 1817-19, 23-25. Died Danube, N.Y., June 8, 1848; buried General Herkimer Cemetery, Danube.

HERKIMER, Nicholas, army officer; b. in what is now Herkimer, N.Y., 1728; s. Johan Jost and Katharine Herkimer; m. Lany Tygert; m. 2d, Myra Tygert. Served as lt. N.Y. Militia during French and Indian Wars; comdr. Ft. Herkimer, 1758; chmn. Com. of Safety of Tyron County (Mohawk Valley), N.Y.; brig. gen. N.Y. Militia in charge of defense against Indian and Tory attacks (because of large Loyalist following in Mohawk Valley), 1776; in charge of relief expdn. to Ft. Stanwix which was besieged by British, ambushed by Tories and Indians at Oriskany, forced to retreat; although it appeared to be a Brit. victory, its adverse effect on larger Brit. strategy of Gen. Burgoyne was influential to overall Am. cause. Died nr. Little Falls (N.Y.) of wounds received in Battle of Oriskany, Aug. 16, 1777.

HERMAN, Lebrecht Frederick, clergyman; b. Güsten, Germany, Oct. 2, 1761; s. Johann Friedrich Gottlieb and Dorothea (Wartman) Herrmann; attended U. Halle, 1781-84; m. Maria Johanna Feidt, 1787, at least 6 children. Ordained to ministry German Reformed Ch. for Coetus of Phila., 1786; pastor at Easton, Plainfield, Dryland, Greenwich (all Pa.), 1786-90; pastor, Falkner Swamp, Pottstown, Pa., 1848, organized "Swamp Coll." which gave instrn. in classical langs., exigesis and dogmatics; organized (with friends) Synod of Free German Reformed Congregations of Pa., 1822-37, returned synod to main body of German Reformed Ch., 1837. Died Jan. 30, 1848.

HERNANDEZ, Joseph Marion, territorial del.; b. St. Augustine, Fla., Aug. 4, 1793. Transferred his allegiance from Spain to U.S.; del. to U.S. Congress from Territory of Fla., Sept. 30, 1822-23; mem., presiding officer Fla. Territorial Ho. of Reps.; apptd. brig. gen. volunteers in Seminole War; served with U.S. Army, 1835-38; commanded expdn. which captured Indian chief Oceola, 1837; apptd. brig. gen. Mounted Volunteers, 1837; unsuccessful Whig Candidate for U.S. Senate, 1845; moved to Cuba, engaged as planter in Dist. of Coliseo, nr. Matanzas. Died "Audaz," Dist. of Coliseo, Matanzas Province, June 8, 1857; buried Junco family vault, San Carlos Cemetery, Matanzas.

HERNDON, Thomas Hord, congressman; b. Erie, Ala., July 1, 1828; grad. U. Ala., 1847; attended Harvard Law Sch., 1848. Admitted to Ala. bar, 1849, began practice in Eutaw; editor Eutaw Democrat, 1850; moved to Mobile, Ala., 1853, practiced law; mem. Ala. Ho. of Reps., 1857-58; trustee U. Ala., 1858-59; mem. Ala. Secession Conv., 1861; served as maj., lt. col., then col. 36th Regt., Ala. Inf., Confederate Army, during Civil War, twice wounded in battle; volunteered to command troops at evacuation of Spanish Fort after Civil War, credited with saving hundreds of lives; resumed law practice, Mobile. Unsuccessful candidate for gov. Ala., 1872; mem. Ala. Constl. Conv., 1875; mem. Ala. Ho. of Reps., 1876-77; mem. U.S. Ho. of Reps. (Democrat) from Ala., 46th-48th congresses, 1879-83. Died Mobile, Mar. 28, 1883; buried Magnolia Cemetery, Mobile.

HERNDON, William Henry, lawyer, biographer; b. Greensburg, Ky., Dec. 25, 1818; s. Archer G. and Rebecca (Day) Johnson H.; attended Ill. Coll.; m. Mary Maxey, Mar. 26, 1840; m. 2d, Anna Miles, July 31, 1861; 8 children. An anti-slavery advocate, purported to have influenced Abraham Lincoln in his anti-slavery views; jr. law partner of Lincoln, Springfield, Ill., 1844; mayor of Springfield 1 term, also state bank examiner; chiefly known as biographer of Lincoln; sold his researches (due to financial necessity) to persons engaged in preparing Lamon Life of Abraham Lincoln, 1870; later published (with Jesse W. Weik) Herndon's Lincoln: The True Story of a Great Life, 3 vols., 1889; book criticized for his statements regarding birth of Lincoln's mother and other details; his biography also responsible for exaggeration of Anne Rutledge influence on Lincoln's life; gave Lincoln more human quality than earlier biographers had done. Died Mar. 18, 1891.

HERNDON, William Lewis, naval officer; b. Fredericksburg, Va., Oct. 25, 1813; s. Dabney and Elizabeth (Hull) H.; m. Frances Elizabeth Hansbrough, Mar. 9, 1836, 1 child. Became midshipman U.S. Navy, 1828; commd. lt., 1841; commanded ship Iris in Mexican War, 1847-48; stationed at Naval Observatory, Washington, D.C., 1848-51; head of Amazon River exploration trip, 1851-53; promoted comdr., 1855; commanded Pacific Mail steamer Central America, 1855-57; a naval destroyer named for him, 1919. Author: Exploration of the Valley of the Amazon, 2 vols., 1853-54. Died Sept. 25, 1857.

HERNE, Katherine Corcoran (Mrs. James A. Herne), actress; m. James A. Herne, Apr. 1878; children—Julie, Chrystal, Dorothy. Appeared as Chrystal in Hearts of Oak, Baldwin Theatre, San Francisco, Chgo., other cities, 1879-86; appeared in Margaret Fleming, N.Y.C., 1891, as Helen in Shore Acres, McVicker's Theatre, Chgo., 1892; dominant influence in life of her actor-playwright husband; succeeded in rewriting from memory her husband's play Margaret Fleming when fire destroyed only existing copy in Herne home on L.I., N.Y.

HEROD, William, congressman; b. Bourbon County, Ky., Mar. 31, 1801; studied law. Admitted to Ky. bar, later to Ind. bar, 1825; began law practice, Columbus, Ind.; mem. Ind. Ho. of Reps., 1829-30, 44, Ind. Senate, 1834, 45-46; pros. atty. Bartholomew County (Ind.), 1833-37; mem. U.S. Ho. of Reps. (Whig) from Ind., 24th-25th congresses, Jan. 25, 1837-39; resumed law practice, Columbus; clk. Bartholomew County Circuit Ct., 1853; became a Republican. Died Columbus, Oct. 20, 1871; buried City Cemetery, Columbus.

HERON, Matilda Agnes, actress; b. County Londonderry, Ireland, Dec. 1, 1830; d. John and Mary (Loughlin) Heron; m. Henry Byrne, June 10, 1854; m. 2d, Robert Stoepel, circa 1858; 1 dau., Helene Stoepel. Made debut at Walnut St. Theatre, Phila., 1851; contrived debut in San Francisco, 1853; translated La Dame aux Camelias (Dumas) into English while in Paris, played Camille (one of her greatest roles), N.Y.C., 1855; leading lady of Bowery Theatre, N.Y.C.; appeared in a translation of Legouve's Medea (another great role) Drury Lane Theatre, London, Eng., 1858; trained aspirants for theatre, including her dau.; unsuccessful in plays she had written, reduced to poverty; benefit for her relief (in which Edwin Booth participated), given in N.Y.C., Jan. 17, 1872. Died N.Y.C., Mar. 7, 1877.

HERON, William, Revolutionary spy; b. Cork, Ireland, 1742; ed. Trinity Coll., Dublin, Irleand; m. Mary; 8 children. Little known of him before Am. Revolution; mem. Conn. Assembly, 1778, 82; engaged as Hiram the Spy in secret correspondence with Maj. Oliver De Lancey (head of Brit. secret service), 1780-82; revealed important facts about Am. forces, also did some spying on British for Am.; captured as rebel with his boat by band of Loyalists, 1781; mem. Conn. Assembly several terms, 1784-96; spying done more out of self-interest than patriotism; not suspected of treasonable activity until after death. Died Conn., Jan. 8, 1819.

HERR, John, clergyman; b. West Lampetes, Pa., Sept. 18, 1781; s. Francis and Fanny (Barr) H.; m. Betsey Groff, Apr. 7, 1807. Founded Reformed Mennonite Church, Strasburg, Pa., 1812; believed Mennonites had become too secular and were not true followers of Menno Simons; elected pastor and bishop, 1812. Author: The True and Blessed Way, 1816; The Illustrating Mirror, 1834. Died Humberstone, Ont. Can., May 3, 1850.

HERRICK, Anson, congressman; b. Lewiston, Mass. (now Me.), Jan. 21, 1812; s. Ebenezer Herrick; attended pub. schs. Established Citizen (newspaper), Wicasset, Me., 1833, N.Y. Atlas, N.Y.C., 1838; mem. bd. aldermen N.Y.C., 1854-56; naval storekeeper Port of N.Y., 1857-61; mem. U.S. Ho. of Reps. (Democrat) from N.Y., 38th Congress, 1863-65; del. Union Nat. Conv., Phila., 1866. Died N.Y.C., Feb. 6, 1868; buried Greenwoo Cemetery, Bklyn.

HERRICK, Ebenezer, congressman; b. Lewistor Mass. (now Me.), Oct. 21, 1785; attended commo schs.; studied law. Admitted to Mass. bar, bega practice in Bowdoinham, Mass. (now Me.); engage in merc. bus., 1814-18; mem. Mass. Ho. of Reps 1819; mem. 1st Me. Constl. Conv., 1820; sec. M Senate, 1821, 28-29; mem. U.S. Ho. of Reps. fro Me., 17th-19th congresses, 1821-27. Died Lewis ton, May 7, 1839; buried Old Herrick Buryin Ground, Lewiston.

HERRICK, Edward Claudius, scientist, librarian b. New Haven, Conn., Feb. 24, 1811; s. Claudiu and Hannah (Pierpont) H.; A.M. (hon.), Yale 1838. Clk. in bookstore at age 16; advanced theor of periodic occurance of large number of meteors 1837; contbr. to Am. Jour. of Sci., 1837-62; pub lished A Brief Preliminary Account of the Hessia Fly and Its Parasites, 1841; 1st to find and de scribe parasites of eggs of spring canker-worm moth one of best early econ. entomologists; librarian Yale 1843-58. Died New Haven, June 11, 1862.

HERRICK, Joshua, congressman; b. Beverly, Mass. Mar. 18, 1793; attended common schs. Moved t Me. dist. of Mass., 1811, engaged in lumber bus. served in War of 1812; moved to Brunswick, Me. connected with 1st cotton factory in Me.; dep. sher iff Cumberland County (Me.), many years; dep. col lector, insp. customs, Kennebunkport, Me., 1829-41, 47-49, town clk., 1832-42, selectman, assessor overseer of the poor 1839-42; county commr. Yor County (Me.) 1842-43; mem. U.S. Ho. of Reps (Democrat) from Me., 28th Congress, 1843-45; reg ister of probate York County, 1849-55. Died Al fred, Me., Aug. 30, 1874; buried Village Cemetery, Kennebunkport.

HERRICK, Richard Platt, congressman; b. Greenbush, (now Rensselaer), N.Y., Mar. 23, 1791; mem N.Y. Assembly, 1839; mem. U.S. Ho. of Reps. (Whig) from N.Y., 29th Congress, 1845-46. Die Washington, D.C., June 20, 1846; buried Greenbus Cemetery.

HERRICK, Samuel, congressman; b. Amenia, N.Y., Apr. 14, 1779; studied law, Carlisle, Pa.; Admitte to the bar, 1805; began law practice, St. Clairsville, O.; apptd. pros. atty. Guernsey County (O.), als U.S. dist. atty., 1810; apptd. pros. atty. Licking County (O.); commd. brig. gen. Ohio Militia, 1814; mem. U.S. Ho. of Reps. (Democrat) from Ohio, 15th-16th congresses, 1817-20; presdl. elector, 1828; U.S. dist. atty. for Ohio, 1829-30. Died Zanesville, O., June 4, 1852; buried City (now Greenwood) Cemetery, Zanesville.

HERRING, James, painter; b. London, Eng., Jan. 12, 1794; s. James Herring; married, 1812, 1 son, Frederick W. Came to U.S., 1804; started bus. as distiller, Bowery, N.Y.C.; began painting when his business was disrupted by War of 1812, became portrait painter employed throughout Northern N. J.; established sutdio, N.Y.C., 1822, Enterprise Library, 1830; published (with J.B. Longacre) The National Portrait Gallery, 4 vols., 1834-39; painted portrait of Noah Webster; projected Apollo Gallery, 410 Broadway, N.Y.C., proposed Catalogue of First Fall Exhibition of Works of Modern Artists at The Apollo Gallery, 1838, led to orgn. Apollo Assn. for Promotion Fine Arts in U.S., served as corr. sec.; Mason (grand sec. N.Y. State 1829). Died Paris, France, Oct. 8, 1867; buried Bklyn.

HERRING, Silas Clark, safe mfr.; b. Salisbury, Vt., Sept. 7, 1803; s. Otis and Mary (Olds) H.; m. Mary Draper, 1831; m. 2d, Caroline Tarbell, May 9, 1843; at least 1 child, Francis. Apptd. paymaster and col. 5th regt. N.Y. Arty.; began building Salamander safes (1st fire-proof safes in U.S.), constructed of metal with plaster of paris lining (mfg. rights for lining purchased from patentee Enos Wilder, who received 1 cent per pound royalty), 1840; added improvements to makes safes burglarproof; eventual fire and burglar-proof Herring Champion safe awarded 1st Prize at World's Fair, N.Y.C., also at Exposition Universelle, Paris, 1862. Died Plainfield, N.J., June 23, 1881.

HERRMAN, Augustine, cartographer, mcht.; b. Prague, Bohemia, circa 1605; s. Augustine Ephraim and Beatrix (Redel) H.; m. Jannetje Veslett (or Vasleth), Dec. 10, 1651; m. 2d, Catherine Ward; 5 children including Ephraim. Claimed to have been founder Dutch West India Co.'s Va. tobacco trade, 1629; came to Am., 1644; became agt. for Peter Gabry & Sons, merc. firm, Amsterdam, 1644; conducted beaver trade, New Amsterdam, also grew indigo and exported tobacco; apptd. one of Gov. Stuyvesant's "Nine Men" (adv. council) in New Netherland, 1647; became citizen Md., 1663; made map of Va. and Md. (his outstanding achievement), 1673, received manor in Cecil County, Md. in compensation for map. Died Bohemia Manor, Md., 1686.

HERRMANN, Alexander, magician; b. Germany, Feb. 10, 1844; s. Samuel and Anna (Meyer) H.;

n. Adelaide Scarsey. Asst. in his brother's magician show, 1859-62; came to U.S., 1860; established own magician show, 1862-67, in partnership with his brother, 1867-69; traveled in many parts of world giving magical performances, 1869-96; called Chevalier Alexander Herrmann, also Herrmann the Great. Author: Herrmann's Handbook of Parlor Magic, 1898; Herrmann's Conjuring for Amateurs, 1901; Herrmann's Book of Magic, 1902. Died Dec. 17, 1896.

HERSEY, Samuel Freeman, congressman; b. Sumner, Me., Apr. 12, 1812; attended common schs., Sumner and Buckfield, Me.; grad. Hebron (Me.) Acad., 1831. Taught sch., 1828-31; engaged in merchandising bus., Lincoln, Me., 1833, Milford, Me., 1837, in lumber bus., Stillwater, Me., 1842, Bangor, Me., 1850, extended bus. to Minn., Wis., and Ia., continued in bus. until 1863; mem. Me. Ho. of Reps., 1842, 57, 65; mem. Me. Exec. Council, 1852-54; del. Republican Nat. Conv., Chgo., 1860; mem. Me. Senate, 1868-69; mem. Rep. Nat. Com., 1864-68; unsuccessful candidate for Gov. Me., 1870; mem. U.S. Ho. of Reps. (Rep.) from Me., 43d-44th congresses, 1873-75. Died Bangor, Feb. 3, 1875; buried Mt. Hope Cemetery, Bangor.

HERTER, Christian, interior designer; b. Stuttgart, Germany, Jan. 8, 1840; s. Christian and Christiana (Schaeffer) H.; ed. Stuttgart Polytechnic, also Ecole des Beaux Arts, Paris, France; m. Mary Miles, 1864, 1 son, Christian Archibald. Came to U.S., 1860; became designer Tiffany's, N.Y.C.; worked for half-brother, Gustave Herter, bought out firm, 1870; worked on interiors of houses of Gov. Latham, San Francisco, Pierpont Morgan, William H. Vanderbilt, N.Y.C.; 1st to use Chinese porcelains, Persian pottery and embroideries, Japanese art objects, employ Oriental motifs in U.S.; revolutionized textile design. Died N.Y.C., Nov. 2, 1883.

HERVÁS Y PANDURO, Lorenzo, missionary, philologist; b. Horjaco, Spain, May 1, 1735. Joined Soc. of Jesus, Madrid, Spain; studied at Alcalá de Henares, taught at Murcia; a missioner in Am., for a number of years; went to Italy when soc. was suppressed in Spanish world, 1767; in Spain, 1799-1803, then returned to Rome; made prefect of Quirinal Library by Pope Pius VII. Author: (chief work) Idea dell' universo (explored origins and ethnol. relationship of nations from study of langs.), 21 vols., 1778-87; also wrote on paleography, Am. colonies and ednl. work for deaf mutes. Died Rome, Aug. 24, 1809.

HESSELIUS, Gustavus, painter, organ builder; b. Folkarna, Dalarne, Sweden, 1682; m. Lydia, 4 children including John. Came to Phila., 1711; 1st known portrait painter in Am.; commd. by vestry to paint large and elaborate altar piece The Last Supper for St. Barnabas Ch., Prince Georges County, Md. (1st publicly commd. altar piece in country); active as portrait painter, Phila., 1735-50, painted portraits of himself and wife (now in collection of Pa. Hist. Soc.), Thomas Bardley, atty. gen. Md.; 1st Am. organ builder; built organ for Moravian Brethren Ch., Bethlehem, Pa., 1746. Died Phila., May 25, 1755.

HESSELIUS, John, portrait painter; probably b. Prince George's County, Md., 1728; s. Gustavus Hesselius; m. Mary Woodward, Jan. 30, 1763, 1 son, 3 daus. Probably most prolific painter of pre-Revolutionary period; did greater part of family portraits in Md., Va. and Phila., including portrait of Samuel Chew and wife; style is credited to influence of John Wollaston; vestryman, warden St. Anne's Ch., Annapolis. Died nr. Annapolis, Md., Apr. 9, 1778; buried "Bellefield," Annapolis.

HETH, Henry, army officer; b. Chesterfield County, Va., Dec. 16, 1825; attended Georgetown Coll., 1837; grad. U.S. Mil. Acad., 1847; m. Harriet Selden, 3 children. Brevetted 2d lt., 1847, served in Mexican War; promoted 1st lt., 1853, capt., 1855, served against Sioux Indians; joined Confederate Army, 1861, organized Floyd's command for W.Va., Fall 1861; commd. brig. gen. in command of mil. dist. around Lewisburg, Va., 1862; post and div. comdr. in Bragg's Army during expdns. into Ky.; transferred to Army of No. Va., 1863; commd. maj. gen. 1863; his most conspicuous action was at Battle of Gettysburg (which he precipitated by engaging U.S. Army early); civil engr. for U.S. Govt., 1880-84; spl. agt. Office of Indian Affairs, 1884-98. Died Washington, D.C., Sept. 27, 1899.

HEWAT, Alexander, clergyman, historian; b. Scotland, 1745; grad. U. Edinburgh, D.D. (hon.), 1780; m. Eliza Barksdale. Came to Am., 1763; pastor 1st Presbyn. Ch., Charleston, S.C., 1763-75; returned to Eng. because of Loyalist sympathies, 1775; witness before Royal Commn. on losses and services of Am. Loyalists, 1785. Author: An Historical Account of the Rise and Progress of the Colonies of South Carolina and Georgia (1st history of S.C.), 2 vols., 1799; Sermons, 2 vols., 1803-05. Died London, Eng., 1829.

HEWES, Joseph, Continental congressman; b. Kingston, N.J., Jan. 23, 1730; s. Aaron and Providence (Worth) H. Founder, merc. and shipping bus., Edenton, N.C., 1763; borough rep. N.C. Colonial Assembly, 1766-75; mem. Com. of Correspondence, 1773; del. to all 5 N.C. provincial congresses; a signer Declaration of Independence; mem. Continental Congress, 1774-77, 79, mem. secret com., com. on claims, com. to prepare plan of confederation, chmn. com. of marine (directed U.S. naval affairs 1776-77; apptd. John Paul Jones a naval officer and provided him with ship); aided Washington in planning mil. operations, 1776; borough mem. N.C. Ho. of Commons, 1778. Died during session of Continental Congress, Phila., Nov. 10, 1779; buried Phila.

HEWES, Robert, mfr.; b. Boston, 1751; son of Mr. and Ann (Frye) Hewes. Made unsuccessful attempt to start glass factory, Temple, N.H., 1780; organized Essex Glass Works, Boston, 1787 (name changed to Boston Crown Glass Co. 1809); granted patent on manufacture of glass in Mass., 1787-1802; retired, 1824; part owner of a glue factory, a soapworks, a slaughter-house; taught fencing to Boston elite. Author: Rules and Regulations for Sword Exercise of Cavalry, 1802; On the Formation and Movements of Cavalry, 1804. Died Boston, July 1830; buried burying ground on Boston Common.

HEWIT, Augustine Francis (christened Nathaniel Augustus), clergyman; b. Fairfield, Conn., Nov. 27, 1820; s. Rev. Nathaniel and Rebecca (Hillhouse) H.; grad. Amherst Coll., 1839; attended Theol. Inst. of Conn., East Windsor, 1840-42; studied theology under Dr. Patrick N. Lynch, 1846-47. Licensed to preach in Congregational Ch., 1842, ordained deacon, 1843; mem. Episcopal Ch. until 1846; converted to Roman Catholicism, 1846; ordained priest Roman Cath. Ch., 1847, took name Augustine Francis; vice prin. Charleston (S.C.) Collegiate Inst., 1847-48; became mem. Congregation of Most Holy Redeemer, Balt., 1849, took vows, 1850, missionary until 1858, released from vows, 1858; a founder Missionary Soc. of St. Paul the Apostle, N.Y., wrote its constn.; editor Cath. World, N.Y., 1869-74; superior new order, 1869-74, pledged order to support of Cath. U. of Am., Washington, D.C., secured establishment of St. Thomas Aquinas Coll. at Cath. U. Am., 1889. Author: The Life of Reverend Francis A. Baker, 1865; Problems of the Age, with Studies in St. Augustine on Kindred Subjects, 1868. Died N.Y.C., July 3, 1897.

HEWITT, Goldsmith Whitehouse, congressman; b. nr. Elyton, Ala., Feb. 14, 1834; grad. law dept. Cumberland U., 1866. Enlisted as pvt. Confederate Army, 1861; promoted capt. Co. G, 28th Regt., Ala. Inf., 1862; participated in several battles, wounded at Battle of Chickamauga; admitted to Ala. bar, 1866, began practice in Birmingham; mem. Ala. Ho. of Reps., 1870-71, 86-88, Ala. Senate, 1872-74; mem. U.S. Ho. of Reps. (Democrat) from Ala., 44th-45th congresses, 1875-79; resumed law practice. Died Birmingham, May 27, 1895; buried Oak Hill Cemetery, Birmingham.

HEWITT, James, violinist, composer; b. Dartmoor, Eng., June 4, 1770; s. John Hewitt; m. Miss Lamb, 1790; m. 2d, Eliza King, Dec. 1795. Leader of court orch. King George III; came to U.S. (N.Y.C.), 1792, gave 1st concert at Corre's Hotel, Jan. 25, 1793; established self as violinist and concert mgr.; orch. leader of Old Am. Co.; bought N.Y. br. of Carr's Mus. Repository to facilitate carrying on business of publishing music, 1797; took charge of music at Federal Street Theatre, 1812. Composer Grand Sinfonie Characteristic of the Peace of the French Republic, 1802; Tammany or the Indian Chief (became symbol of anti-federalist feeling, libretto written by Anne J. Halton, poetess of Tammany Soc., N.Y.C.), 1794; also wrote incidental music for plays and dramas. Died Boston, Aug. 1827.

HEWITT, John Hill, journalist, poet; b. N.Y.C., July 11, 1801; s. James and Eliza (King) H.; attended U.S. Mil. acad.; m. Estella Mangin, 7 children; m. 2d, Alethia Smith, 4 children. Established newspaper 1st known as Republican, then Mountaineer, Greenville, S.C.; asso. with Rufus Dawes in editing Balt. Minerva and Emerald, 1829, (became Minerva and Saturday Post 1830), sole editor, after 1830; Balt. Saturday Visitor, 1832; editor, part owner daily Balt. Clipper; edited Evening Mirror, Savannah, Ga. Author: Song of the Winds (won poetry competition over Edgar Allen Poe), 1833; (oratorio) Jeptha's Daughter; Miscellaneous Poems, 1838; also numerous popular ballads. Died Balt., Oct. 7, 1890.

HEWITT, William Keesey, artist; b. Phila., 1817. Worked in N.Y.C.; made sketch of burning of steamboat Lexington (on which Nathaniel Currier based his 1st popular lithograph), 1840; lived in Phila., after 1843; exhibited frequently at Pa. Acad. Died Phila., 1893.

HEYER, John Christian Frederick, missionary; b. Helmstedt, Germany, July 10, 1793; s. Johann Gottlieb and Frederike (Wagener) H.; studied theology under Dr. Justus H. C. Helmuth and Dr. Frederick D. Schaeffer, 1809-14; attended Göttingen (Germany) U., 1815-16; studied medicine and Sanskrit, Balt., 1840-41; m. Mary (Webb) Gash, 1819, 6 children. Came to Phila., circa 1807; taught Zion Ch. Sch., Southwark, Phila., 1813-15; licensed as Lutheran preacher by Pa. Ministerium, 1817; itinerant preacher in Pa., 1817-18; preacher Cumberland parish, Md., 1818-24; ordained to ministry Luth. Ch., Lancaster, Pa., 1820; pastor at Somerset, Pa., 1824-27, 32-37, Carlisle, Pa., 1827-28; sec. West Pa. Synod, 1828-31, pres., 1831; agt. Sunday Sch. Union of Evang. Luth. Ch. in U.S., 1830-32; missionary German Fgn. Missionary Soc. in India, 1842-72, took furlough periods, 1846-47, 57-69; founded 1st fgn. mission of his ch., Guntur, India, 1842; spent his 2d furlough as missionary in Minn., 1857-69; chaplain Luth. Theol. Sem., Phila., 1872-73. Died Phila., Nov. 7, 1873; buried Friedensburg, Pa.

HEYWARD, Thomas, army officer, jurist; b. St. Helena's Parish, S.C., July 28, 1746; s. Daniel and Mary (Miles) H.; m. Elizabeth Mathewes, Apr. 20, 1773; m. 2d, Susanna Savage, May 4, 1786. Admitted to S.C. bar, 1771; elected to S.C. Ho. of Commons, 1772; del. S.C. Provincial Conv., Charleston, 1774; mem. 1st, 2d S.C. provincial congresses, Charleston, 1775; mem. S.C. Council of Safety; served on Com. of 11 to prepare Constn. for S.C., 1776; mem. 2d Continental Congress, 1776-78; signer Declaration of Independence, 1776; circuit judge, 1778-79, 84-89; capt. arty. battalion S.C. Militia in Charleston, 1780, served in Battle of Port Royal Island, 1779, defense of Charleston, 1780; mem. S.C. legislature from Charleston, 1782-84; a founder, 1st pres. Agrl. Soc. of S.C., 1785. Died St. Luke's Parish, S.C., Mar. 6, 1809; buried St. Luke's Parish.

HEYWOOD, Ezra Hervey, reform publisher; b. Princeton, Mass., Sept. 29, 1829; s. Ezra and Dorcas (Roper) Hoar; grad. Brown U., 1856; m. Angela Fiducia Tilton, June 6, 1865, 4 children—Hermes, Angelo, Vesta, Psyche Ceres. Took name Heywood by Mass. legislation, 1848; after meeting with William Lloyd Garrison in Framingham (Mass.) became mem. Mass. Anti-Slavery Soc.; opposed to Civil War; set up Coop. Pub. Co. with his wife and children, Princeton, Mass., 1871; published monthly reform jour. The Word, 1872-93; organized (with wife) Union Reform League, Princeton, also New Eng. Free Love League (1873); arrested for violating Fed. law of 1873 which forbade mailing of obscene matter, 1877, convicted in U.S. Ct., 1878, sentenced to 2 years imprisonment in Dedham (Mass.) jail, and $100 fine; pardoned (after pleas from some 6,000 of his followers) by Pres. Rutherford B. Hayes after serving only 6 months; arrested again for mailing obscene literature, 1882 (acquitted), arrested 3d time under Mass. obscenity law, 1883 (acquitted); convicted for obscene articles in The Word, 1890, served 2 year prison term. Author: (pamphlets) Uncivil Liberty; Social Ethics . . . Free Rum . . . Assures Temperance; The Labor Movement; Hard Cash; Free Trade; The Great Strike . . . of 1877. Died Boston, May 22, 1893; buried Princeton.

HEYWOOD, Levi, mfr., inventor; b. Gardner, Mass., Dec. 10, 1800; s. Benjamin and Mary (Whitney) H.; m. Martha Wright, Dec. 29, 1825; 5 children. Became mfr. wooden chairs, Gardner, 1826; formed partnership (with brother and friend) to start sawmill, Charlestown, Mass., 1831; invented method for sawing veneers from mahogany and other woods; partner Heywood Bros. & Co., chair mfg. firm, 1835-41, became sole owner, 1841; invented many furniture mfg. devices including rattan-processing machine, wood-bending machine; partner (with W. B. Washburn) in chair and wooden ware mfg. firm, Erving, Mass.; a major stockholder Am. Rattan Co., 1876; erected foundry to make various iron posts used in chair mfg., 1876; del. Mass. Const. Conv., 1853; mem. lower house Mass. Legislature, 1871. Died Gardner, July 21, 1882.

HIACOOMES, clergyman; b. Great Harbor (now Edgartown), Martha's Vineyard, Mass., circa 1610; 1 son. Mem. Pokanauket tribe (subdiv. Narragansetts); believed to be 1st Indian in New Eng. to be converted to Christianity, converted by younger Thomas Mayhew (to whom he acted as an interpreter); called The Christian Indian; the immunity of Hiacoomes and his family during great sickness of 1645 impressed other Indians and marked the beginning of his preaching to natives who wanted to be converted; made 199 converts and started 2 Indian congregations, by 1651; founded (with Mayhew) an Indian ch., 1659; ordained to ministry Puritan (now Congregationalist) Ch. by John Eliot and John Cotton, 1670. Died 1690.

HIBBARD, Freeborn Garrettson, clergyman, author; b. New Rochelle, N.Y., Feb. 22, 1811; s. Rev. Billy and Sybil (Russ) H.; m. Mary Whipple; m. 2d, Maria Hyde, 1846; 1 child. Admitted to N.Y. Conf., Methodist Episcopal Ch., 1830, ordained deacon, 1832, elder, 1834; transferred to Genesee Conf. (called Central N.Y. Conf. 1872-82), 1837-95; a mem. of six N.Y. gen. confs., 1844, five from 1856-

72; editor No. Christian Advocate, N.Y., 1856-60. Author: A Treatise on Infant Baptism, 1843; The Religion of Childhood, 1864; History of the Late East Genesee Conference, 1887. Died Jan. 27, 1895.

HIBBINS, Ann, alleged witch; m. Mr. Moore; m. 2d, William Hibbins; at least 2 children. Admitted to Boston Ch., July 28, 1639, censured by ch. because of temper; accused of being a witch, 1655, found guilty in jury trial, verdict found unacceptable by local magistrates, case taken to Mass. Gen. Ct.; found guilty, sentenced to be hanged (even though examinations indicated her innocence). Hanged June 19, 1656.

HIBSHMAN, Jacob, congressman; b. nr. Ephrata, Pa., Jan. 31, 1772; attended pvt. sch., Harrisburg, Pa. Engaged in farming; asso. judge Lancaster County (Pa.), 1810-19; mem. U.S. Ho. of Reps. (Republican) from Pa., 16th Congress, 1819-21; dep. surveyor Lancaster County, 20 years; justice of of peace, chmn. bd. canal suprs. Served as maj. gen. Pa. Militia, 12 years; organizer No. Mut. Ins. Co., 1844, 1st pres. Died nr. Ephrata, May 19, 1852; buried Hibshman Cemetery, nr. Ephrata.

HICKMAN, John, congressman; b. West Bradford Twp., Pa., Sept. 11, 1810; studied medicine and law. Admitted to Pa. bar, 1833, began practice in West Chester; del. Nat. Democratic Conv., Balt., 1844; mem. U.S. Ho. of Reps. from Pa., as Democrat, 34th-36th congresses, 1855-61, as Republican, 1861-63; a mgr. apptd. by U.S. Ho. of Reps. to conduct impeachment proceedings against West H. Humphreys (U.S. judge for Tenn.); resumed practice of law; mem. Pa. Ho. of Reps., 1869. Died West Chester, Mar. 23, 1875; buried Oaklands Cemetery, nr. West Chester.

HICKOK, James Butler (known as Wild Bill Hickok), army officer, scout, U.S. marshall; b. Troy Grove, Ill., May 27, 1837; s. William and Polly (Butler) H.; m. Mrs. Agnes Lake, Mar. 1876. Went to Kan., 1855, took part in border wars of area; constable Monticello Twp. (Kan.), 1856, fought McCanles gang at Rock Creek Station, Neb., killing McCanles and 2 of gang, 1861; stage driver on Santa Fe Trail, later on Oregon Trail; served as scout and spy for U.S. Army during Civil War; dep. U.S. Marshal Ft. Riley (Kan.), 1866; U.S. marshal Hays City (Kan.), 1869; marshall Abilene (Kan.), 1871; toured East with Buffalo Bill, 1872-73; went to Deadwood, Dakota Territory, 1874; known as good shot, frontier legends (pro and con) grew up around him. Shot by Jack McCall, Deadwood, Aug. 2, 1876; buried Mt. Moriah Cemetery, Deadwood.

HICKOK, Laurens Perseus, clergyman, coll. pres.; b. Bethel, Conn., Dec. 29, 1798; s. Ebenezer and Polly (Benedict) H.; grad. Union Coll., 1820; m. Elizabeth Taylor, Oct. 9, 1822. Ordained to ministry Presbyn. Ch., 1823; prof. Christian theology Western Res. Coll., 1836-44, Auburn Theol. Sem., 1844-52; v.p. Union Coll., Schenectady, N.Y., 1852-66, prof. mental and moral philosophy, 1852-68, pres., 1866-68; moderator Presbyn. Gen. Assembly, 1856. Author: Rational Psychology, 1849; System of Moral Science, 1853; Rational Cosmology, 1858; Creator and Creation, 1872; Rational Logic, 1875. Died Amherst, Mass., May 6, 1888.

HICKS, Edward, artist; b. Attleboro (now Langhorne), Pa., Apr. 4, 1780. Engaged in coach, sign and ornamental painting, Newtown, Pa.; painted hist. and religious scenes, including The Peaceable Kingdon (best known); prominent Quaker preacher, participated in separation led by his cousin Elias Hicks. Died Newtown, Aug. 23, 1849.

HICKS, Elias, clergyman; b. Hempstead Twp., L.I., N.Y., Mar. 19, 1748; s. John and Martha (Smith) H.; m. Jemima Seaman, 1771, 11 children. Carpenter's apprentice, N.Y.C., 1765; became Quaker minister, circa 1775, preached in almost every state and Can., opponent of slavery; recognized as a champion of liberal views, 1815-30, inclined toward extreme Quietism, emphasized an inward aspect of religion (an aspect which led to separation in Quaker Ch. 1827-28), his branch became known as "Hicksite" as opposed to "orthodox" br. Author: Observations on Slavery, 1811; Elias Hick's Journal of His Life and Labors, 1828; The Letters of Elias Hicks, 1834. Died Jericho, N.Y., Feb. 27, 1830.

HICKS, Thomas, painter; b. Bucks County, Pa., Oct. 18, 1823; s. Joseph and Jane (Bond) H.; attended Pa. Acad., N.A.D.; studied under Thomas Couture, Paris, France. Returned to Am., 1849; elected to N.A.D., 1851; portraits include those of Abraham Lincoln, Henry Wadsworth Longfellow, William Cullen Bryant, Edwin Booth (as Iago), General Meade, Stephen Foster. Died Thornwood, Trenton Falls, N.Y., Oct. 8, 1890.

HICKS, Thomas Holliday, senator, gov. Md.; b. Dorchester County, Md., Sept. 2, 1798; s. Henry and Mary (Sewell) H.: m. Ann Thompson; m. 2d, Leah Raleigh; m. 3d, Mrs. Jane Wilcox. Mem. Md. Ho. of Dels., 1830, 36-37, 48-58; registrar wills Dorchester County, Md., 1837-51; mem. Md. Constl. Conv., 1850-51; gov. Md., 1857-62, anti-secessionist, exercised authority in suppressing riot caused by Mass. troops passing through Balt., 1861; mem. U.S. Senate (Republican) from Md., 1862-65. Died Washington, D.C., Feb. 13, 1865; buried Cambridge, Md.

HIESTAND, John Andrew, congressman; b. East Donegal Twp., Pa., Oct. 2, 1824; attended Pa. Coll., Gettysburg; studied law. Admitted to Pa. bar, 1849, began practice in Lancaster; mem. Pa. Ho. of Reps. (Whig), 1852-53, 56; purchased interest in Lancaster Examiner (printing firm), 1858; mem. Pa. Senate, 1860; Republican presdl. elector, 1864, chosen to carry the electorial vote of Pa. to Washington, D.C.; unsuccessful candidate for congressman, 1868; naval officer Port of Phila. (apptd. by Pres. Grant), 1871-79; mem. U.S. Ho. of Reps. (Rep.) from Pa., 49th-50th congresses, 1885-89. Died Lancaster, Dec. 13, 1890; buried Marietta (Pa.) Cemetery.

HIESTER, Daniel, congressman; b. Upper Salford Twp., Pa., June 25, 1747; s. Daniel and Catharine (Schuler) H.; m. Rosanna Hager, 1770. Mgr. of father's farm and tannery, also father-in-law's estate, 1774; mem. Pa. Assembly, 1778-81; commd. col. and brig. gen. Pa. Militia, 1782, served in Revolutionary War; mem. Supreme Council Pa., 1784-86; commr. Conn. land claims, 1787; mem. U.S. Ho. of Reps. from Pa., 1st-4th congresses, 1789-1796, from Md., 7th, 8th congresses, 1801-04. Died Washington, D.C., Mar. 7, 1804; buried Zion Reformed Graveyard, Hagerstown, Md.

HIESTER, Daniel, congressman; b. Chester County, Pa., 1774; s. John Hiester. Prothonotary and clk. of cts. Chester County, 1800-09; mem. U.S. Ho. of Reps. from Pa., 11th Congress, 1809-11; a founder Bank of Chester County, 1st cashier, 1814-17; burgess of West Chester (Pa.), 1815-17; apptd. register of wills and recorder of deeds, 1821. Died Hagerstown, Md., 1834.

HIESTER, Isaac Ellmaker, congressman; b. New Holland, Pa., May 29, 1824; s. William Hiester; grad. Yale, 1842; studied law. Admitted to Pa. bar, 1845, began practice in Lancaster; dist. atty. Lancaster County (Pa.), 1848-51; mem. U.S. Ho. of Reps. (Whig) from Pa., 33d Congress, 1853-55, unsuccessful candidate for re-election, 1854-56; resumed practice of law; del. Democratic Nat. Conv., N.Y.C., 1868. Died Lancaster, Feb. 6, 1871; buried Lancaster Cemetery.

HIESTER, John, congressman; b. Goshenhoppen, Pa., Apr. 9, 1745; attended common schs. Engaged in lumbering bus., Berne Twp., Pa.; served as capt. Pa. Militia during Revolutionary War; mem. U.S. Ho. of Reps. from Pa., 10th Congress, 1807-09. Died Goshenhoppen, Oct. 15, 1821; buried Union Ch. Cemetery, Parker Ford, Pa.

HIESTER, Joseph, gov. Pa; b. Berks County, Pa.; Nov. 18, 1752; s. John and Mary (Epler) H.; m. Elizabeth Whitman, 1771. Del. to Provincial Conf., Phila., 1776; served as col. Continental Army, commanded co. in Col. Henry Haller's Battalion in Battle of L.I., 1776; promoted lt. col., 1777; mem. Pa. Assembly, 1780-90, Pa. Senate, 1790-94; presdl. elector, 1792, 96; mem. U.S. Ho. of Reps. from Pa., 5th-8th congresses, 1797-1805, 14th-16th congresses, 1815-Dec. 1820; gov. Pa., 1820-25. Died June 10, 1832; buried Charles Evans Cemetery, Reading, Pa.

HIESTER, William, congressman; b. Berne Twp., nr. Reading, Pa., Oct. 10, 1790; attended common schs. Served as lt. during War of 1812; engaged in farming, merc. bus., Lancaster County, Pa.; justice of peace, 1823-28; mem. U.S. Ho. of Reps. (Whig) from Pa., 22d-24th congresses, 1831-37; del. Pa. Constl. Conv., 1837; mem. Pa. Senate, 1840-42, speaker, 1842. Died New Holland, Pa., Oct. 13, 1853; buried Lancaster Cemetery.

HIGBY, William, congressman; b. Willsboro, N.Y., Aug. 18, 1813; grad. U. Vt., 1840; studied law. Admitted to the bar, 1847; began practice in Elizabethtown, N.Y.; moved to Cal., 1850; practiced law, Calaveras County, Cal.; dist. atty., 1853-59; mem. Cal. Senate, 1862-63; mem. U.S. Ho. of Reps. (Republican) from Cal., 38th-40th congresses, 1863-69; editor Calaveras Chronicale; collector of internal revenue, 1877-81. Died Santa Rosa, Cal., Nov. 27, 1887; buried Mountain View Cemetery, Oakland, Cal.

HIGGINSON, Francis, clergyman; b. Claybrooke, Eng., circa 1586; s. Rev. John and Elizabeth H.; B.A., Jesus Coll., Cambridge (Eng.) U., 1610, M. A., 1613; m. Anna Herbert, Jan. 8, 1616, 8 children including John. Ordained deacon Anglican Ch., Cawood Castle, Eng., 1614, priest, 1614; lectr. at St. Nicholas, Leicester, Eng., 1617; met Thomas Hooker and other Puritans, followed their faith without officially breaking from Anglican faith; accepted offer of Mass. Bay Co. to go to New Eng., left on ship Talbot, 1629; drew up confession of faith and a covenant for colony in Salem (Mass.) which became separatist from Anglican Ch. Author: (jour. of trip to New Eng.) New-England's Plantation, or, A Short and True Description of the Commodities an Discommodities of that Country, 1630. Died Salem Aug. 6, 1630.

HIGGINSON, John, clergyman; b. Claybrooke Eng., Aug. 6, 1616; s. Rev. Francis and Anna (Her bert) H.; m. Sarah Whitefield, circa 1642; m. 2d Mary Blakeman; 7 children including Nathaniel Came to Mass. with father, 1629; sec. Cambridg (Mass.) Synod of 1637; chaplain fort, Saybrook Mass., 1637-41; tchr., Hartford, 1639; ordained t ministry Congregationalist Ch., 1660; pastor, Salem Mass., 1660-1708, Author: Survey of the Sum o Church Discipline, 1648; The Application of Redemp tion by the Effectual Work of the Word an spirit of Christ, for the Bringing Home of Lost Sin ners to God; The Poor Doubting Christian Draw to Christ. Died Salem, Dec. 9, 1708.

HIGGINSON, Nathaniel, colonial gov.; b. Guil ford, Conn., Oct. 11, 1652; s. Rev. John and Sara (Whitfield) H.; grad. Harvard, 1670, master's de gree, 1672; m. Elizabeth Richardson, May 1692, children including Richard. Went to Eng. to see employment, 1674; tutor for children of Lord Thom as Wharton, circa 1674-81; as writer for East Indi Co. sailed for Ft. St. George, Madras, India 1684, asst. custom and warehouse agt. of Ft. St George, 1684-85, factor, 1685-86, mem. gov.' council, 1686-89, also held concurrent positions a judge admiralty and municipal courts, mayor, min master, chief accountant, bookkeeper, paymaster, jus tice of the peace, commr. of customs, in charge o mayor's ct. (all Ft. St. George), 1685-89; lef Ft. St. George, 1689, returned as gov., 1692-98 apptd. lt. gen. of India, 1694, disputes over lan and occupation led to minor war with Asad Khan 1697-98; mem. Thomas Pitt's Council, Ft. St. George, 1698; returned to Eng., 1700; with 1 others petitioned Queen Anne for removal of Gov. Joseph Dudley of Mass., 1706; mem. Soc. for Propagation of the Gospel in New Eng. Died Pancreas Parish, Eng., Oct. 31, 1708; buried Bow Ch., Cheapside, Eng.

HIGGINSON, Stephen, mcht.; b. Salem, Mass., Nov. 28, 1743; s. Stephen and Elizabeth (Cabot) H.; m. Susan Cleveland, 1764; m. 2d, Elizabeth Perkins, 1789; m. 3d, Sarah Perkins, 1792. Became privateer in Am. Revolution, 1776; mem. Mass. Legislature, 1782; mem. Continental Congress, 1782-83; lt. col. Mass. Militia, served in suppression of Shays' Rebellion, 1786; navy agt. at Boston, 1797-1801; a leading Mass. Federalist. Author: Examination of Jay's Treaty by Cato, 1795. Died Boston, Nov. 22, 1828.

HILDRETH, Richard, author, editor; b. June 28, 1807; s. Rev. Hosea and Sarah (McLeod) H.; grad. Harvard, 1826; m. Caroline Neagus, June 7, 1844. Admitted to Mass. bar, 1830, practiced law in Boston and Newburyport, 1830-32; co-editor paper Boston Daily Atlas, 1832-34, part owner, 1834, wrote editorials for paper, 1836-38; in Brit. Guiana, 1840-43; writer N.Y. Tribune, 1855-61; U.S. consul at Trieste, 1861-64. Author: The People's Presidential Candidate, 1839; The Contrast: or William Henry Harrison versus Martin Van Buren, 1840; Despotism in America, 1840; A Letter to Andrews Norton on Miracles as the Foundation of Religious Faith, 1840; Local Guide to British Guiana, 1843; The White Slave, 1852; History of the United States, 6 vols. 1852; Theory of Politics, 1853; Japan As It Was and Is, 1855. Died Florence, Italy, July 11, 1865; buried Protestant Graveyard, Florence.

HILDRETH, Samuel Prescott, physician, historian; b. Methuen, Mass., Sept. 30, 1783; s. Dr. Samuel and Abigail (Bodwell) H.; studied medicine with father, then with Dr. Thomas Kittredge, Andover, Mass.; M.D., Med. Soc. of Mass., 1805; m. Rhoda Cook, Aug. 19, 1807, 6 children. Practiced medicine, Hampstead, N.H., 1805; moved to Marietta, O., 1806, practiced medicine, 1806-61; recorded discoveries of curative effect of malaria on epilepsy and value of charcoal and yeast in malignant fevers; mem. Ohio Legislature, 1810-11, secured passage of law providing for med. socs. and regulating practice of medicine; wrote med. papers on epidemics, especially great epidemic of 1822-23; as naturalist contbd. articles to Am. Jour. Science, 1826-33, wrote one of earliest papers of presence of petroleum in salt springs; pres. 3d Med. Conv. of Ohio; hist. writings include: "A Brief History of the Floods of the Ohio River from the Year 1772 to the Year 1832" (in Jour. of Hist. and Philos. Soc. Ohio, Vol. I), 1838; Genealogical and Biographical Sketches of the Hildreth Family, 1840; Pioneer History, 1848; Biographical and Historical Memoirs of the Early Pioneer Settlers of Ohio, 1852; reports of meteorol. observations published in Smithsonian. Contributions to Knowledge, Vol. XVI, 1870. Died Marietta, July 24, 1863.

HILGARD, Ferdinand Heinrich Gustav, see Villard, Henry.

HILGARD, Julius Erasmus, geodesist; b. Zweibrucken, Bavaria, Jan 7, 1825; s. Theodor Erasmus and Margaretha (Paule) H.; m. Katherine Clements, Aug. 1848, 4 children. Chief bur. U.S. Coast Survey under Alexander Bache, 1856; made 1st reliable determination of differences of longitude between Washington, Greenwich and Paris, 1872; U.S. del. to Internat. Bur. Weights and Measures 1872; dir. Office Weights and Measures; charter mem. Nat. Acad. Scis., pres., 1875; mem. A.A.A.S.; supt. U.S. Coast Survey, 1881-85. Died Washington, D.C., May 8, 1891.

HILL, Ambrose Powell, army officer; b. Culpeper, Va., Nov. 9, 1825; s. Maj. Thomas and Fannie (Baptist) H.; grad. U.S. Mil. Acad., 1847; m. Kitty Morgan, May 1859, 4 children including Lucy. Served in Mexican War, 1846-48, in Seminole War in Fla., 1849-50; commd. 1st lt., 1851; commd. col. 13th Va. Inf., Confederate Army, 1861, brig. gen., 1862; maj. gen., 1862, served in 3 engagements in Battle of Seven Days, 1862; served with Stonewall Jackson at battles of Cedar Mountain, 2d Bull Run, 1862; directed Confederate attack at Battle of Chancellorsville after Jackson was wounded, until he himself was wounded; promoted lt. gen., 1863; directed Confederate action of 1st day at Battle of Gettysburg, July 1, 1861; served in Batle of Wilderness, also in actions from North Anna and Cold Harbor; killed during last Union attack on Petersburg (Va.), 1865; served in all great battles of Civil War in Va., considered one of ablest Confederate gens., famed for ability to move troops rapidly. Killed in Battle of Petersburg, Apr. 2, 1865; buried Richmond, Va.

HILL, Benjamin Harvey, senator; b. Jasper County, Ga., Sept. 14, 1823; s. John and Sarah (Parham) H.; grad. U. Ga., 1843; m. Caroline Holt, Nov. 27, 1845, 6 children. Admitted to Ga. bar, 1845; mem. Ga. Assembly, 1851; mem. Confederate States Senate from Ga. (Jefferson Davis' champion and spokesman), 1861-65; delivered "Davis Hall Speech" against Reconstrn. Acts of 1867, 1867; mem. U.S. Ho. of Reps. from Ga., 44th-45th congresses, May 5, 1875-77, resigned, 1877; mem. U.S. Senate from Ga., 1877-82. Died Atlanta, Ga., Aug. 16, 1882; buried Oakland Cemetery, Atlanta.

HILL, Daniel Harvey, army officer, coll. pres.; b. York Dist., S.C., July 12, 1821; s. Solomon and Nancy (Cabeen) H.; grad. U.S. Mil. Acad., 1842; m. Isabella Morrison, Nov. 2, 1852. served as 2d lt. U.S. Army in every important battle in Mexican War, 1846-48; prof. mathematics Washington Coll., 1849-54, Davidson (N.C.) Coll., 1854-59; pres. N.C. Mil. Inst., 1859-61; commd. brig. gen. Confederate Army, 1861, maj. gen., 1862, held the pass in Blue Ridge nr. Boonesboro until Stonewall Jackson had captured Harper's Ferry and Lee had crossed Potomac River during Md. Campaign, 1862; promoted lt. gen., 1863, in command of corps under Gen. Braxton Bragg at Battle of Chickamauga; publisher mag. The Land We Love, 1866-77; pres. U. Ark., 1877-84; directed Ga. Mil. Coll., 1885-89. Author: A Consideration of the Sermon on the Mount, 1858; The Crucifixion of Christ, 1860; The Elements of Algebra. Died Charlotte, N.C., Sept. 24, 1889; buried Davidson Coll.

HILL, Frederic Stanhope, actor; b. Boston, 1805; m. Mary Welland Blake, June 7, 1828, 1 son, Frederic Stanhope. Inherited small fortune from his father, 1827, began publishing Boston Lyceum, literary journal; owner Galaxy, weekly mag., 1830-31; made 1st stage appearance as Hotspur, Richmond Hill Theatre, N.Y., 1832, played Romeo, also Orlando (in As You Like It), later in season; appeared as Romeo, Tremont Theatre, Boston, 1832; actor, stage mgr. Warren Theatre (became Nat. Theatre 1836), Boston, 1832-38; played at Arch Street Theatre, Phila., 1834; ret. from stage, returning only for brief appearances, after 1838; made last appearance as Cassio, Howard Athenaeum, Boston, 1851. Author: The Harvest Festival with Other Poems, 1826. Died Apr. 7, 1851.

HILL, George Handel, actor; b. Boston, Oct. 8, 1809; s. Ureli K. and Nancy (Hull) H.; m. Cordelia Thompson, 1828. Made debut as interpreter in a musical, Bklyn., 1826; joined strolling co. as low comedian, circa 1830; minor actor Arch Street Theatre, Phila., 1832; appeared at Park Theatre, N.Y.C., 1832; became know nas "Yankee" Hill for his part in Yankee plays; toured Gt. Britain, 1836-37, played at Drury Lane Theatre, London, other theatres; appeared in Paris, France, 1838; leased Franklin Theatre, N.Y.C., 1840, named it Hill's Theatre; opened Hill's N.Y. Museum (formerly Peale's Museum), 1842; made last performance at Saratoga Springs, N.Y. Died Saratoga, Sept. 27, 1849.

HILL, Hugh Lawson White, congressman; b. nr. McMinnville, Tenn., Mar. 1, 1810; attended Carroll Male Acad., McMinnville; grad. Cumberland Coll., Nashville, Tenn. Taught Sch.; engaged in farming, fruit growing; mem. Tenn. Ho. of Reps., 1837-38, 41; mem. U.S. Ho. of Reps. (Democrat) from Tenn., 30th Congress, 1847-49; mem. Tenn. Constl. Conv., 1870. Died Hills Creek, Tenn., Jan. 18, 1892; buried Hill Graveyard, nr. McMinnville.

HILL, Isaac, senator, gov. N.H.; b. Cambridge, Mass., Apr. 6, 1789; s. Isaac and Hannah (Russell) H.; m. Susanna Ayer, Feb. 2, 1814, 1 son, John McClary. Took charge of Am. Patriot, 1809, changed name to N.H. Patriot (an organ. of N.H. Democratic Party, soon controlled large portion of state's public opinion); mem. N.H. Senate, 1820-23, 27-28; 2d comptroller Nat. Treasury under Jackson, 1829-30, also mem. "Kitchen Cabinet;" mem. U.S. Senate from N.H., 1831-36; published Farmers' Monthly Visitor, 1835-51; gov. N.H., 1836-39; in Boston sub-treasury, 1840-41. Died Washington, D.C., Mar. 22, 1851.

HILL, James, army officer, shipbuilder, legislator; b. Kittery, Me., Dec. 20, 1734; s. Benjamin and Mary (Neal) H.; m. Sarah Coffin; m. 2d, Sarah Hoyt; m. 3d, Martha Wiggin; 17 children. Participated in expdn. against French at Crown Point (N.Y.), 1755; shipwright on warship Achilles to Jamaica and Eng.; served as capt. under Gen. John Sullivan; Continental Army; in Revolution, 1775; signer of "Association Test", 1776; lt. col., 1777; served as brig. gen. N.H. Militia, 1788-93; fought with Gates against Burgoyne; mem. N.H. Provincial Congress, 1775; mem. 1st session N.H. Legislature under new N.H. Constn., 1784. Died Aug. 22, 1811.

HILL, John, engraver; b. Eng., 1770; m. Ann Musgrove, 1 son, John William. Came to Am., 1816, settled in Phila.; moved to N.Y.C., 1819; his earliest Am. works include magazine plates in black and white; later did a series of larger plates colored by hand entitled Picturesque Views of American Scenery (using paintings by Joshua Shaw), published in Landscape Album, 1820; engraved set of plates called Hudson River Portfolio, later aquatinted in water colors; ret. to farm, nr. West Nyack, N.Y., 1836. Died West Nyack, 1850.

HILL, John, congressman; b. nr. Germanton, N. C., Apr. 9, 1797; grad. U. N.C., 1816. Planter; clk. Stokes County (N.C.) Ct., 30 years; mem. N.C. Ho. of Commons, 1819-23; N.C. Senate, 1823-25, 30-31; mem. U.S. Ho. of Reps. (Democrat) from N.C., 26th Congress, 1839-41; reading clk. N.C. Senate, 1850; del. N.C. Constl. Conv., 1861. Died Raleigh, N.C., Apr. 24, 1861; buried Old Hill Burying Ground, nr. Germanton.

HILL, John, congressman; b. New Canton, Va., July 18, 1800; grad. Washington Acad. (now Washington and Lee U.), Lexington, Va., 1818; studied law. Admitted to the bar, 1821, practiced law; mem. U.S. Ho. of Reps. (Whig) from Va., 26th Congress, 1839-41; resumed law practice; mem. Va. Constl. Conv., 1850-51; commonwealth atty., several years; county judge Buckingham County (Va.), 1870-79. Died Buckingham Ct. House, Va., Apr. 19, 1880; buried Presbyn. Cemetery.

HILL, John, congressman; b. Catskill, N.Y., June 10, 1821; attended pvt. schs. Bank clk., bookkeeper, engaged in merc. bus.; postmaster Boonton (N. J.), 1849-53; mem. twp. com., 1852-56, 63-67; justice of peace, 1856-61; mem. N.J. Assembly, 1861-62, 66, speaker, 1866; raised troops during Civil War; mem. U.S. Ho. of Reps. (Republican) from N.H., 40th-42d, 47th congresses, 1867-73, 81-83; del. Rep. Nat. Conv., Chgo., 1868; mem. N.J. Senate, 1875-77. Died Boonton, July 24, 1884; buried Boonton Cemetery.

HILL, John Henry, clergyman, educator; b. N.Y.C., Sept. 11, 1791; grad. Columbia, 1807; attended Protestant Episcopal Sem., Alexandria, Va., 1827-30; m. Frances Mulligan, 1821. Businessman, 1807-27; ordained priest Protestant Episcopal Ch., Norfolk, Va., 1830; went to Greece as missionary; opened schs. for girls and boys in Athens (1st schs. in Athens after expulsion of Turks), 1831; devoted himself (with his wife) to educating girls, conducted best sch. for girls in Greek-speaking world; chaplain Brit. legation in Greece, 30 years; received letter of thanks from King George I of Greece on 50th anniversary of his schs., 1881; continued work, although blind, 1877-82; monument erected over his grave by City of Athens; sch. remained as Hill Meml. Sch. Died Athens, July 1, 1882.

HILL, John William, artist; b. London, Eng., Jan. 13, 1812; s. John Hill; at least 1 son, John Henry. Came to Am. with family, 1819; lived in Phila., N.Y.C. and West Nyack, N.Y.; topog. artist N.Y. State Geol. Survey; topog. artist with firm Smith Bros., N.Y.C., drew many views of Am. cities for lithographs; in his later years painted primarily landscapes; considered leading spirit of "naturalism" of "Pre-Raphaelitism" in Am.; work included in An Artist's Memorial, written by his son and illustrated with etchings done from his landscapes. Died nr. West Nyack, Sept. 24, 1879.

HILL, Joshua, senator; b. Abbeville Dist., S.C., Jan. 10, 1812; m. Emily Read, 4 sons, 4 daus. Mem. U.S. Ho. of Reps. from Ga., 35th-36th congresses, 1857-61, opposed Civil War, resigned office Jan. 23, 1861, rather than take part in seccession; mem. U.S. Senate from Ga., 1871-73; mem. Ga. Constl. Conv., 1877. Died Madison, Ga., Mar. 6, 1891; buried Madison Cemetery.

HILL, Mark Langdon, congressman; b. Biddeford, Mass. (now Me.), June 30, 1772; s. Jeremiah and Mary (Langdon) Storer H.; attended pub. schs.; m. Mary McCobb, Feb. 14, 1797 (dec. 1817), 10 children including John Langdon, Mark Langdon; m. 2d, Abigail Sewall, 1821. Mcht., shipbuilder, Phippsburg, Mass. (now Me.); overseer, trustee Bowdoin Coll., 1796-1842; mem. Mass. Ho. of Reps., 1797-1808, 10, 13, 14, Mass. Senate, 1804, 15-17; judge Ct. Common Pleas, 1810; mem. U.S. Ho. of Reps. from Mass., 16th Congress, 1819-21, from Me., 17th Congress, 1821-23; postmaster of Phippsburg, 1819-24; apptd. collector of customs, Bath, Me., 1824. Died Phippsburg, Nov. 26, 1842; buried Congregational Churchyard, Phippsburg Center, Me.

HILL, Nathaniel Peter, metallurgist, senator; b. Montgomery, N.Y., Feb. 18, 1832; s. Nathaniel P. and Matilda (Crawford) H.; grad. Brown U., 1856; m. Alice Hale, July 1860, 2 daus., 1 son. prof. chemistry Brown U., 1860-64; mem. commn. of Mass. and R.I. mfrs. to investigate mineral deposits in Colo., 1864; studied metallurgy in Europe, 1865-66, 66-67; organized Boston & Colo. Smelting Co. (introduced smelting process increasing gold ore yield), 1867; mayor Blackhawk (Colo.), 1871; mem. Colo. Territorial Council, 1872-73; developed refining process for separating precious metals from copper, 1873; mem. U.S. Senate from Colo., 1879-85; propr. Denver (Colo.) Republican, 1886; mem. Internat. Monetary. Commn. (studying question of internat. metal currency), 1891; del. Bimetallic Conf., 1893. Died Denver, May 22, 1900; buried Fairmount Cemetery, Denver.

HILL, Richard, colonial legislator, mayor Phila., jurist; b. Md., 1673; s. Richard Hill; m. Hannah Lloyd, 1700. Moved to Phila., 1700; mem. Pa. Provincial Council, 1703, Pa. Gov's Council, 1704-29, Pa. Assembly, 1705-06, 10-21; mayor Phila., 1710, 15, 16, 17; asso. justice Pa. Provincial Supreme Ct., 1711-29; Pa. del. in Md.-Pa. boundary dispute, 1713. justice Pa. Ct. of Common Pleas,; 1715-24 del. Five Nations Council, Albany, N.Y., 1722; permanent mem. Pa. Supreme Council's Commn. on Proprietary Lands; mem. Soc. of Friends; friend of William Penn. Died Phila., Sept. 4, 1729; buried Phila.

HILL, Robert Andrews, jurist; b. Iredell County, N.C., Mar. 25, 1811; s. David and Rhoda (Andrews) H.; m. Mary Andrews, 1833. Moved with family to Tenn., 1816; constable Williamson County (Tenn.), 1834-36, justice of peace, 1836-44; began practice law, 1844; atty. gen. Tenn. Circuit Ct., 1847-55; went to Miss. 1855; judge Tishimingo County (Miss.) Ct. of Probate, 1858-65; chancellor of his dist., 1865-66; mem. Miss. Constl. Conv., 1865; judge U.S. Dist. Ct., Miss., 1866-91, upheld as constl. various U.S. laws giving civil and polit. rights to Negroes; trustee U. Miss. Died Oxford, Miss., July 2, 1900.

HILL, Thomas, clergyman, coll. pres.; b. New Brunswick, N.J., Jan. 7, 1818; s. Thomas and Henrietta (Barker) H.; A.B., Harvard, 1843, A.M., 1846, S.T.D. (hon.), 1860; S.T.D., Harvard Divinity Sch., 1845; LL.D. (hon.), Yale, 1863; m. Ann Bellows, 1845; m. 2d, Lucy Shepard, 1866; 7 children. Ordained to ministry Unitarian Ch., 1845; minister, Waltham, Mass., 14 years; pres. Antioch Coll., Yellow Springs, O., 1859-62; pres. Harvard (introduced system of elective courses), 1862-68, overseer, 1871-73; mem. Mass. Legislature from Waltham, 1871; fellow Am. Acad. Arts and Scis.; accompanied Louis Agassiz on expdn. to S.Am. Author: Christmas Poems on Slavery, 1843; Arithmetic, 1845; Geometry and Faith, 1849; Curvature, 1850; First Lessons in Geometry, 1855; Liberal Education, 1855; Jesus, the Interpreter of Nature, 1859; The Natural Sources of Theology. Died Waltham, Nov. 21, 1891.

HILL, Ureli Corelli, violinist, conductor; b. Conn., circa 1802; s. Ureli K. and Nancy (Hull) H. Played 1st violin N.Y. Sacred Music Soc., 1828; conducted 1st complete performance of Messiah (1st full length oratorial performance in U.S.), N.Y.C., 1831; founder Philharmonic Soc. of N.Y., pres. 1st 6 years, later v.p., mem. bd. dirs.; tchr. Conservatory of Music, Newark, N.J.; frequent conductor N.Y. Philharmonic Orch.; founder 1st String Quartet, N.Y.C. Died Paterson, N.J., Sept. 2, 1875.

HILL, Whitmel, Continental congressman; b. Bertie County, N.C., Feb. 12, 1743; grad. U. Pa., 1760; connected with early Revolutionary activities; served to col. during Revolutionary War; engaged in farming; del. Assembly of Freemen, Hillsboro, N.C., 1775; mem. N.C. Congress, 1776; del. N.C.

Constl. Conv., 1776; mem. N.C. Ho. of Commons, 1777; mem. Continental Congress from N.C., 1778-81; mem. N.C. Senate, 1778-80, 84-85. Died Hills Ferry, nr. Hamilton, N.C., Sept. 26, 1797; buried family cemetery on his estate, reinterred Trinity Cemetery, nr. Scotland Neck, N.C., 1887.

HILL, William, ironmaster, army officer; b. North Ireland, 1741; m. Jane McCall, 6 children. Came to Am., circa 1761, settled in Pa.; moved to S.C., 1762, acquired extensive land grants nr. Bowers's Mill Creek, before Am. Revolution; began iron works (with Isaac Hayne), Allison's Creek, S.C., 1776; supplied most of cannonballs used at seige of Charleston (S.C), 1780; works burned by British, 1780; commd. lt. col. S.C. Militia, distinguished in several battles; mem. S.C. Legislature after Am. Revolution; justice Camden Dist., S.C., 1783, York County (S.C.) Ct., 1785-99; rebuilt iron furnace, 1787, built another, 1788, paid his employees in iron. Died Dec. 1, 1816; buried Bethel Presbyn. Churchyard, York, S.C.

HILL, William Henry, congressman; b. Brunswick, N.C., May 1, 1767; attended pub. schs., studied law, Boston. Engaged in farming; admitted to the bar, practiced law; apptd. U.S. dist. atty. for N.C., 1790; mem. N.C. Senate, 1794; mem. U.S. Ho. of Reps. (Federalist) from N.C., 6th-7th congresses, 1799-1803; apptd. judge U.S. Dist. Ct. for N.C. by John Adams, appointment withdrawn by Thomas Jefferson. Died "Hilton" nr. Wilmington, N.C., 1809; buried family burial ground, "Hilton."

HILLARD, George Stillman, lawyer, state legislator; b. Machias, Me., Sept. 22, 1808; s. John and Sarah (Stillman) H.; grad. Harvard, 1828, A.M., 1831, LL.B., 1832; LL.D. (hon.), Trinity Coll., 1857; m. Susan Howe, 1835, 1 child. Admitted to Mass. bar, 1833; editor the Jurist; mem. Mass. Ho. of Reps., 1835; pres. Boston Common Council, 1846-47; mem. Mass. Senate, 1850; del. to Mass. Constl. Conv., 1853; city solicitor Boston, 1854-55; U.S. atty. for Mass. dist., 1866-71; bd. overseers Harvard, 1871-75. Author: Memorial of Daniel Webster, 1853; Six Months in Italy, 1863; Political Duties of the Educated Classes. Editor: The Poetical Works of Edmund Spenser, 5 vols., 1835; translator: Guizot's Essay on the Character and Influence of George Washington, 1840. Died Longwood, Mass., nr. Boston, Jan. 21, 1879.

HILLEGAS, Michael, mcht., treas. U.S.; b. Phila., Apr. 22, 1729; s. Michael and Margaret Hillegas; m. Henrietta Boude, May 10, 1753, 10 children. Mem. Provincial Assembly Pa., 1765-75; treas. Province of Pa., 1776; treas. Continental Congress, 1776; contbd. large part of his fortune to support of Am. Revolution; treas. U.S., 1777-89; one of 1st subscribers to Bank of N.Am.; formed Lehigh Coal Mining Co.; alderman Phila., 1793-1804; mem. Am. Philos. Soc., 1768. Died Phila., Sept. 29, 1804.

HILLEN, Solomon, Jr., congressman, mayor; b. Hillen Road, nr. Balt., July 10, 1810; s. Solomon Hillen; grad. Georgetown Coll.; studied law. Admitted to Md. bar, began practice in Balt.; mem. Md. Ho. of Reps., 1834-38; mem. U.S. Ho. of Reps. (Democrat) from Md., 26th Congress, 1839-41; mayor of Balt., 1842-45. Died N.Y.C., June 26, 1873; buried Greenmount Cemetery, Balt.

HILLHOUSE, James, senator; b. Montville, Conn., Oct. 21, 1754; s. William and Sarah (Griswold) H.; grad. Yale, 1773, LL.D. (hon.), 1823; m. Sarah Lloyd, Jan. 1, 1774; m. 2d, Rebecca Woolsey, Oct. 10, 1782; 5 children including James Abraham. Admitted to Conn. bar, 1773; lt. co. New Haven (Conn.) Volunteers, 1776; capt. Gov.'s Foot Guards when New Haven attacked by British under Tryon, 1779; mem. Conn. Ho. of Reps., 1778-85; mem. U.S. Ho. of Reps. from Conn., 2d-4th congresses, 1791-96; mem. U.S. Senate from Conn., Dec. 6, 1796-June 10, 1810, pres. pro tem, 1801-10; commr. Conn. sch. funds, 1810-25; treas. Yale Coll., 1782-1832. Died New Haven, Dec. 29, 1832; buried Grove St. Cemetery, New Haven.

HILLHOUSE, James Abraham, poet; b. New Haven, Conn., Sept. 26, 1789; s. James and Rebecca (Woolsey) H.; A.B. with high honors, Yale, 1808, M.A., 1811; m. Cornelia Lawrence, 1822. Author: The Education of a Poet, 1811, The Judgment, 1812, Percy's Masque, 1820, Hadad, 1825, Some Considerations which should Influence an Epic or a Tragic Writer in the Choice of an Era, 1826, Relations of Literature to a Republican Government, 1836, Demetria (written 1813, published 1839); almost all his writings appeared in Dramas, Discourses and Other Pieces, 1839. Died New Haven, Jan. 4, 1841.

HILLHOUSE, William, Continental congressman, jurist; b. Montville, Conn., Aug. 25, 1728; studied law; children include James. Admitted to the bar, practiced law; mem. Conn. Ho. of Reps., 1756-60, 63-85; served as maj. 2d Regt., Conn. Cavalry, during Revolutionary War; mem. Continental Congress from Conn., 1783-86; judge Ct. Common Pleas, 1784-1806; mem. Conn. Senate, 1785-1808; judge of probate for New London (Conn.) dist., 1786-1807. Died Montville, Jan. 12, 1816; buried Raymond Hill Cemetery, Montville.

HILLIARD, Francis, lawyer; b. Cambridge, Mass., Nov. 1, 1806; s. William and Sarah (Lovering) H.; mem. class of 1823, Harvard (received degree, 1842), attended Harvard Law Sch., 1826; m. Catherine Dexter Haven. Admitted to bar, Mass., 1830; practiced law, Boston, later, Roxbury, Mass.; 1st judge Roxbury Police Ct., 1855-78; wrote various legal treatises; one of 1st writers to supply texts of Am. decisions. Author: Elements of Law, 1835; The Law of Mortgages, 1853; Law of Torts (started new trends in legal thought), 1859, The Law of Remedies for Torts, 1867; American Law: A Comprehensive Summary of the Law in its Various Departments, 2 vols., 1877-78. Died Worcester, Mass., Oct. 9, 1878.

HILLIARD, Henry Washington, congressman, diplomat; b. Fayetteville, N.C., Aug. 4, 1808; grad. S.C. Coll., 1826; m. Miss Bedell; m. 2d, Mrs (Glascock) Mays. Admitted to Ga. bar, 1829; 1st prof. English lit. U. Ala., 1831-34; mem. Ala. Legislature, 1836-38; charge d'affaires to Belgium, 1842-44; mem. U.S. Ho. of Reps. from Ga., 29th-31st congresses, 1845-51; U.S. commr. to Tenn., 1861; U.S. minister to Brazil, 1877-81. Author: De Vane: A Story of Plebeians and Patricians, 1865; Politics and Pen Pictures at Home and Abroad, 1892; translated Roman Nights (Alesandro Verri), 1850. Died Dec. 17, 1892; buried Oakwood Cemetery, Montgomery, Ala.

HILLIS, David, pioneer, state ofcl.; b. Washington County, Pa., Nov. 1788; s. William and Jane (Carruthers) H.; m. Ealia Werden, 1812; m. 2d, Margaret Burk; 5 children. Moved to Ind. Territory, 1808, became one of largest landowners in the area; commd. lt. col. 6th Regt., Ind. Militia, War of 1812, lt., 1813-14; asso. judge Ind. Circuit Ct., 1816-18; mem. Ind. Gen. Assembly, 1823-32, Ind. Senate, 1832-35; lt. gov. Ind., 1837-40; mem. Ind. Ho. of Reps., 1842-44. Died Jefferson County, Ind., July 8, 1845.

HILLYER, Junius, congressman; b. Wilkes County, Ga., Apr. 23, 1807; s. Shaler and Rebecca (Freeman) H.; A.B., U. Ga., 1828; m. Jane Watkins, Oct. 1831. Admitted to Ga. bar, 1828; solicitor gen. Western Jud. Circuit of Ga., 1834; judge Ga. Superior Ct., 1841-45; mem. U.S. Ho. of Reps. from Ga., 32d-33d congresses, 1851-55; solicitor U.S. Treasury, 1857-61; trustee U. Ga., Mercer U. Died Decatur, Ga., June 21, 1886; buried Oakland Cemetery, Atlanta, Ga.

HIMES, Charles Francis, educator; b. Lancaster, Pa., June 2, 1838; s. William D. and Magdalen (Lanius) H.; A.B., Dickinson Coll., 1855; post-grad. U. Giessen (Germany), 1863-64; m. Mary E. Murray, 1868, 2 daus. Prof. mathematics Troy (N.Y.) U., 1860-63; prof. natural sci. Dickinson Coll., Carlisle, Pa., 1865-96, a pioneer in elective lab. courses, 1865, prof. physics, 1885-88, acting pres., 1888-89; mem. U.S. Govt. Expdn. to observe total eclipse of sun, Ottumwa, Ia., 1869; organized 1st summer sch. of photography, Mountain Lake Park, Md., 1884. Author: Some of the Methods and Results of Observation of the Total Eclipse of the Sun, August 7th, 1869, published 1869; (with Spencer Fullerton Baird of Smithsonian Instn.) Annual Record of Science and Industry for 1871-78, pub. 1872-79. Died Johns Hopkins Hosp., Balt., Dec. 6, 1918.

HIMES, Joshua Vaughan, reformer, leader religious sect; b. North Kingstown, R.I., May 19, 1805; s. Stukeley and Elizabeth (Vaughan) H.; m. Mary Thompson Handy, 1826; m. 2d, Hannah Harley, 1879. Apprenticed to cabinet maker in his youth; became exhorter of Christian church, then a minister; pastor 1st Christian (Episcopal) Ch., Boston, 1830-37; pastor, builder 2d Christian (Episcopal) Ch., Boston, 1837-42; became active in abolitionist movement; an organizer Non-Resistance Soc. of Boston; became asst. to William Miller who preached 2d coming of Christ in 1843, chiefly responsible for making Miller well known through publicity; began publishing Signs of the Times (Boston weekly), 1840; founded The Midnight Cry, N.Y.C., 1842, movement spread world wide; sold newspapers and moved West in 1850's; published Advent Christian Times in Mich.; returned to Episcopal Ch., 1878; head various Episcopal missions until his death. Died Elk Point, S.D., July 27, 1895.

HINDMAN, Thomas Carmichael, army officer, congressman; b. Knoxville, Tenn., Jan. 28, 1828; s. Thomas and Sallie (Holt) H.; m. Mary Biscoe, Nov. 11, 1856; 1 son, Biscoe. Served as lt. U.S. Army in Mexican War, 1846-48; admitted to Miss. bar, 1851; mem. Miss. Legislature, 1854; moved to Ark.; mem. U.S. Ho. of Reps. from Ark., 36th Congress, 1859-61, reelected, 1860, but declined seat to join Confederate Army; commd. maj. gen., enforced Jefferson Davis' western policy; served at Battle of Praire Grove, 1862, in fighting around Chattanooga and against Gen. Sherman; moved to Mexico, 1865, returned to Ark., 1867. Assassinated for opposition to Reconstrn., Helena, Ark., Sept 27, 1868; buried Maple Hill Cemetery, Helena.

HINDMAN, William, senator; b. Dorcheste County, Md., Apr. 1, 1743; s. Jacob and Mar (Trippe) H.; grad. U. Pa., 1761; studied Inns c Ct., London, Eng., 1765. Admitted to Md. bar 1765; mem. Md. Senate, 1777-84; mem. Con tinental Congress from Md., 1784-88; mem. Gov Md.'s Exec. Council, 1789-92; mem. U.S. Ho. o Reps. from Md., 2d-5th congresses, 1793-99; mem Md. Ho. of Dels., 1799-1800; mem. U.S. Senat from Md., Dec. 12, 1800-1801. Died Balt., Jan 19, 1822; buried St. Paul's Burial Ground, Balt

HINDS, James, congressman; b. Hebron, N.Y., Dec. 5, 1833; attended State Normal Sch., Albany, N.Y., law sch., St. Louis; grad. Cincinnati Law Coll., 1856. Admitted to Minn. bar, began practice in St. Peter; dist. atty., 3 years; U.S. dist. atty. for Minn.; joined expdn. under Gov. Sibley against Indians on Western frontier, 1862; Democrat, but supported Lincoln; moved to Little Rock, Ark., 1865, practiced law; del. from Pulaski County to Ark. Constl. Conv., 1867; commr. to codify Ark. laws; mem. U.S. Ho. of Reps. (Republican) from Ark., 40th Congress, June 22-Oct. 22, 1868. Assassinated nr. Indian Bay, Ark., Oct. 22, 1868; buried East Norwich, N.Y.

HINDS, Thomas, congressman; b. Berkeley County, Va., Jan. 9, 1780. Moved to Greenville, Miss., served as maj. cavalry during War of 1812, distinguished at Battle of New Orleans, brevetted brig. gen. for gallantry; unsuccessful candidate for gov. Miss., 1820; mem. U.S. Ho. of Reps. (Democrat) from Miss., 20th-21st congresses, Oct. 21, 1828-31. Died Greenville, Aug. 23, 1840.

HINES, Richard, congressman; b. Tarboro, N.C.; studied law. Admitted to N.C. bar, 1816; practiced law, Raleigh, N.C.; mem. N.C. Ho. of Commons, 1824; mem. U.S. Ho. of Reps. (Democrat) from N.C., 19th Congress, 1825-27, unsuccessful candidate for re-election, 1826; resumed law practice, Raleigh. Died Raleigh, Nov. 20, 1851; buried Old City Cemetery, Raleigh.

HINMAN, Elisha, naval officer; b. Stonington, Conn., Mar. 9, 1734; s. Capt. Andrew and Mary (Noble) H.; m. Abigail Solbear, Mar. 1, 1777. Commd. lt. Continental Navy, served as capt. sloop Cabot also frigate Alfred, 1777; captured, imprisoned, 1778; became privateer in command ships Deane, later Marquis de Lafayette; became mcht. after Revolutionary War. Died Stonington, Aug. 29, 1805.

HINMAN, Joel, jurist; b. Southbury, Conn., Jan. 27, 1802; s. Joel and Sarah (Curtis) H.; m. Alathea Scovill, Oct. 9, 1825. Judge of probate for Waterbury (Conn.) Dist., 1830-40; mem. Conn. Senate, 1836; judge Conn. Superior Ct., 1842-51; judge Conn. Supreme Ct., 1851-60, chief justice, 1860-70. Died Cheshire, Eng., Feb. 21, 1870.

HIRST, Henry Beck, poet, lawyer; b. Phila., Aug. 23, 1817; s. Thomas Hirst; studied law privately and with half-brother William; married. Admitted to bar, 1843; wrote poetry for various magazines; a friend of Edgar Allan Poe, friendship terminated due to Hirst's claim to have authored The Raven; his mind had become disarranged by 1869, later deteriorated into insanity. Author: The Coming of the Mammoth (1st collection of poems), 1845; Endymion (best poem), 1848; The Penance of Roland, 1849. Died Blockley Almshouse, Phila., Mar. 30, 1874.

HISE, Elijah, congressman, jurist; b. Allegheny County, Pa., July 4, 1802; s. Frederick Hise; LL.B., Transylvania U., 1823; m. Elvira L.D. Stewart, 1832. Developed large law practice, Logan County, Ky., 1823-48; mem. Ky. Ho. of Reps., 1829; charge d'affaires to Guatemala, 1848-49; judge Ky. Ct. of Appeals, 1851-54, rendered noted dissenting opinion in Slack vs. Maysville and Lexington R.R. Co.; mem. U.S. Ho. of Reps. from Ky., 39th-40th congresses, Dec. 3, 1866-1867. Committed suicide, Russellville, Ky., May 8, 1867; buried Maple Grove Cemetery, Russellville.

HITCHCOCK, Alfred, physician; b. Westminster, Vt., Oct. 17, 1813; son of David Hitchcock; grad. med. dept. Dartmouth, 1838, Jefferson Med. Coll., 1845. Practiced medicine, Ashby, Mass., 1844-47; mem. Mass. Legislature, 1847, 55, Exec. Council, 1862-64; apptd. spl. agt. to superintend care of wounded in Mass. during Civil War, 1863-64, designed a stretcher, wheel chair and splints; retired from practice medicine, 1865, pursued literary interests, 1865-74. Author: Christianity and Medical Science, 1867. Died Fitchburg, Mass., Mar. 30, 1874.

HITCHCOCK, Edward, geologist, coll. pres.; b. Deerfield, Mass., May 24, 1793; s. Justin and Mercy (Hoyt) H.; grad. Yale Theol. Sem., 1820; m. Orra White, 1821, 6 children including Charles Henry, Edward. Prin, Deerfield Acad., 1815-19; pastor Congregational Ch., Conway, Mass., 1821-25; prof. chemistry and natural history Amherst

(Mass.) Coll., 1825-45, pres., 1845-54, prof. theology and geology, 1854-64; made 1st complete geol. survey of Mass., 1830; state geologist Vt., 1857-61. Author: Geology of Connecticut Valley, 1823; Elementary Geology, 1840; Fossil Footsteps, 1848; Religion of Geology, 1851; Illustrations of Surface Geology, 1857. Died Amherst, Feb. 27, 1864.

HITCHCOCK, Enos, clergyman; b. Springfield, Mass., Mar. 7, 1744; s. Peletiah and Sarah (Parsons) H.; grad. Harvard, 1767; m. Achsah (Upham) Jordan, Jan. 13, 1771, 1 dau., 1 adopted dau. Ordained to ministry Congregational Ch., 1771; served as chaplain during Revolutionary War, also preached in Beverly (Mass.) and Providence (R.I.) when not on duty; pastor Benevolent Congl. Ch., Providence, 1783-1803. Author: Discourse on Education, 1785 (sermon which advocated free pub. schs.). Died Feb. 26, 1803.

HITCHCOCK, Ethan Allen, soldier, author; b. Vergennes, Vt., May 18, 1798; s. Samuel and Lucy (Allen) H.; grad. U.S. Mil. Acad., July 17, 1817; m. Martha Nicholls, 1868. Commd. Capt. U.S. Army, 1824; asst. instr. U.S. Mil. Acad, 1824-27, comdt. cadets, 1829-33; acting insp. gen. in Gen. Gaine's campaign, 1836; commd. lt. col., 1842; served in Mexican War; insp. gen. U.S. Army; col. in command Mil. Div. of Pacific, 1851-54; mil. adviser to Pres. Lincoln, 1861-65; commissary gen. of prisoners of war, 1865; called the "pen of the army" works include: Remarks on Alchemy and Alchemists, 1857; Swedenborg, a Hermetic Pilosopher, 1858; Christ, the Spirit, 1860; Red Book of Appin and Other Fairy Tales, 1863; Notes on the Vita Nuova of Dante; edited The Sonnets of Shakespeare, 1865. Died Sparta, Ga., Aug. 5, 1870.

HITCHCOCK, Peter, congressman, jurist; b. Cheshire, Conn., Oct. 19, 1781; s. Valentine and Sarah (Hotchkiss) H.; grad. Yale, 1801; LL.D. (hon.), Marrietta Coll., 1845, Western Res. U., 1849; m. Nabby Cook, Dec. 12, 1805. Admitted to Ohio bar, 1804; mem. Ohio Ho. of Reps., 1810, Ohio Senate, 1812-15, 33-34; served as lt. col. 4th Regt., Ohio Militia, 1814; mem. U.S. Ho. of Reps. from Ohio, 15th Congress, 1817-19; judge Ohio Supreme Ct., 1819-32, 45-52; del. Ohio Constl. Conv., 1850. Died Painesville, O., Mar. 4, 1854; buried Welton Cemetery, Burton, O.

HITCHCOCK, Phineas Warrener, senator; b. New Lebanon, N.Y., Nov. 30, 1831; s. Gad and Nancy (Prime) H.; B.A., Williams Coll., 1855; m. Annie Monell, 1857. Established 1st Republican paper in Omaha (Neb.); del. to 2d Rep. Nat. Conv.; U.S. marshal for Nebraska Territory; del. to U.S. Congress from Nebraska Territory, 1864-67; surveyor gen. for Dist. Nebraska and Iowa, 1867; mem. U.S. Senate from Neb., 1871-77. Died Omaha, July 10, 1881.

HITCHCOCK, Roswell Dwight, clergyman, educator; b. East Machias, Me., Aug. 15, 1817; s. Roswell and Betsey (Longfellow) H.; grad. Amherst Coll., 1836; attended Andover Theol. Sem., 3 years, U. Halle, U. Berlin; D.D. (hon.), Bowdoin, 1855, U. Edinburgh (Scotland), 1855; LL.D. (hon.) Williams Coll., 1873, Harvard, 1886; m. Elizabeth Anthony Brayton, Jan. 2, 1845, 3 children. Tutor, Amherst Coll., 1839, became life trustee, 1869; ordained to ministery Congressional Ch., 1845; pastor 1st Congressional Ch., Exeter, N.H., 1845-52; prof. natural and revealed religion Bowdoin Coll., 1852; prof. ch. history Union Theol. Sem., N.Y.C., 1855-87, pres. faculty, 1880-87; editor Am. Theol. Review, 1863-70. pres. Palestine Exploration Soc., 1871. Author: Life of Edward Robinson, 1863; Analysis of the Holy Bible, 1869; Socialism, 1879; Eternal Atonement, 1888. Died Somerset, Mass., June 16, 1887.

HITE, Jost, colonizer; b. Strasbourg, France; m. Anna Marie Du Bois; m. 2d, Maria Magdalena Nuschwanger, 1741. Emigrated to Holland; sailed to Am. on his own ship with Dutch and German immigrants, 1710; settled in N.Y.C.; moved to Pa., 1716; purchased contracts from Va. for settlement of 40,000 acres in Western Va., 1731, later that year purchased contract to settle additional 100,-000 acres (with Robert McKay); started taking families to Va., 1732, placed required number and became owner of 94,000 acres; Lord Fairfax proved however that land patents fell in Northern Neck area where Hite was not supposed to go, Fairfax promised to issue other patents but gave many of them to other persons and encroached on Hite's grants, resulting litigation became one of most famous land controversies with courts finally deciding in favor of Hite's heirs. Died 1760.

HOADLEY, David, architect; b. Waterbury, Conn., Apr. 29, 1774; s. Lemuel and Urania (Mallory) H.; m. Jane Hull, circa 1798; m. 2d, Rachel Beecher, 1805. Began his career as carpenter; entirely selftaught in archtl. tng.; credited with designing Congregational and Episcopal chs. in Waterbury; designed and built mansion for Col. William Leavenworth, 1800 (remained standing until 1905), built North Ch., New Haven, Conn., 1814-15; designed and built many mansions and churches in Conn.; built Tontine Hotel, New Haven, 1824-27. Died Waterbury, July 1839.

HOADLEY, John Chipman, civil engr., mfr.; b. Martinsburg, N.Y., Dec. 10, 1818; s. Maj. Lester and Sarah (Chipman) H.; m. Charlotte Kimball, Aug. 24, 1847; m. 2d, Catherine Melville, Sept. 15, 1853. Moved to Utica, N.Y., 1824; held various surveying and engring. jobs in youth; helped form McKay and Hoadley, firm mfg. mill machinery, steam engines and water wheels, 1848; also engaged in constrn. railroad locomotives; developed 1st single valve automatic steam engine; in charge constrn. with McKay Sewing Machine Assn., 1868; organizer Clinton Wire Cloth Co.; pres. Archibald Wheel Co.; mem. Mass. Legislature, 1858; founder Am. Soc. M.E.; original trustee Mass. Inst. Tech. Author various papers for sci. and engring. socs., best known being The Portable Steam Engine, 1863; Steam Engine Practice in the United States, 1884. Died Oct. 21, 1886.

HOAG, Joseph, clergyman; b. Oblong, N.Y., Apr. 22, 1762; s. Elijah and Phebe H.; m. Huldah Case, 1782. Confirmed as minister in Soc. of Friends; moved to Charlotte, Vt., circa 1785; became well-known as itinerant Quaker preacher; experienced vision which foretold of dividing spirit which would divide Protestant churches, Soc. of Friends and eventually the U.S. resulting in abolition of slavery, 1803; opposed liberal preaching of Elias Hicks. Died Nov. 21, 1846.

HOAG, Truman Harrison, congressman; b. Manlius, N.Y., Apr. 9, 1816; attended pub. schs. Moved to Syracuse, N.Y., 1832, employed as retail clk., also in canal collector's office; moved to Oswego, N.Y., 1839, worked for a commn. mchts. co., became agt. for same firm, Toledo, O., 1849; engaged in transp. and merc. bus., mfr. illuminating gas and coke; unsuccessful candidate for mayor Toledo, 1867; mem. U.S. Ho. of Reps. (Democrat) from Ohio, 41st Congress, 1869-70. Died Washington, D.C., Feb. 5, 1870; buried Forest Cemetery, Toledo.

HOAGLAND, Moses, congressman; b. nr. Balt., June 19, 1812; attended pub. schs.; studied law. Admitted to the bar, 1842; began practice of law, Millersburg, O.; served in Mexican War, promoted maj. for bravery in action; mem. U.S. Ho. of Reps. (Democrat) from Ohio, 31st Congress, 1849-51; resumed law practice; declined appointment as asso. justice Territory of Washington, 1853. Died Millersburg, Apr. 16, 1865; buried Oak Hill Cemetery, Millersburg.

HOAR, Ebenezer Rockwood, atty. gen., congressman; b. Concord, Mass., Feb. 21, 1816; s. Samuel and Sarah (Sherman) H.; B.A., Harvard, 1835, LL.B, 1839, LL.D. (hon.), 1868; LL.D. (hon.), Williams, 1861; m. Caroline Brooks, Nov. 20, 1840, 7 children including Sherman. Mem. Mass. Senate, 1840; judge Mass. Ct. of Common Pleas, 1849-55; asso. justice Supreme Jud. Ct. of Mass., 1859-69; atty. gen. U.S. under Pres. Grant, 1869-70; mem. joint high commn. to consider Ala. Case, establishing tribunal of arbitration which awarded U.S. $15,500,000 gold in damages, 1871; mem. U.S. Ho. of Reps. from Mass., 43d Congress, 1873-75. Died Concord, Jan. 31, 1895; buried Sleepy Hollow Cemetery, Concord.

HOAR, Leonard, coll. pres.; b. Gloucester, Eng., 1630; s. Charles and Joanna (Hinksman) Hoare; A.B., Harvard, 1650, M.A., 1653; M.A., U. Cambridge (Eng.), 1654, M.D. (hon.), 1671; m. Bridget Lisle. Rector, Wanstead, Essex, Eng.; pres. Harvard, 1672-75, published 1st catalogue of graduates. Author: Index Biblicus, 1669. Died Boston, Nov. 28, 1675.

HOAR, Samuel, congressman; b. Lincoln, Mass., May 18, 1778; s. Samuel and Susanna (Pierce) H.; B.A., Harvard, 1802, LL.D., 1838; m. Sarah Sherman, Oct. 13, 1812, 6 children including E. Rockwood, George F. Admitted to Mass. bar, 1805; del. to Mass. Constl. Conv., 1820; mem. Mass. Senate, 1826, 32,33; mem. U.S. Ho. of Reps. from Mass., 24th Congress, 1835-37; del. from Mass. Senate to S.C. to test constitutionality of state's barring free Negroes from S.C., expelled by S.C. Legislature, 1844; mem. Mass. Ho. of Reps., 1850; chmn. conv. which formed Mass. Republican Party, 1855. Died Concord, Mass., Nov. 2, 1856; buried Sleepy Hollow Cemetery, Concord.

HOARD, Charles Brooks, congressman; b. Springfield, Vt., June 5, 1805; attended pub. schs. Postmaster, Antwerp, N.Y.; mem. N.Y. Assembly, 1837; clk. Jefferson County (N.Y.), 1844-46; mem. U.S. Ho. of Reps. (Republican) from N.Y., 35th-36th congresses, 1857-61; engaged in mfg. portable engines, converted factory to manufacture arms for U.S. Govt. during Civil War. Died Ceredo, W.Va., Nov. 20, 1886; buried Spring Hill Cemetery, Huntington, W.Va.

HOBAN, James, architect; b. Callan, Ireland, 1762; s. Edward and Martha (Bayne) H.; m. Susannah Sewell, Jan. 1799, 10 children including James. Designer S.C. State Capitol at Columbia, completed 1791; designer, supr. constrn. of future White House, 1792, rebuilt (after destruction by British 1814), 1815-29; a supt. at Washington, D.C., designed, erected State and War Offices, begun 1818; mem. Washington City Council, 1802-31. Died Washington, Dec. 8, 1831.

HOBART, Aaron, congressman; b. Abington, Mass., June 26, 1787; grad. Brown U., 1805; studied law. Admitted to Mass. bar, 1809, began practice in Abington; mem. Mass. Ho. of Reps., 1814, Mass. Senate, 1819; mem. U.S. Ho. of Reps. (Democrat) from Mass., 16th-19th congresses, Nov. 24, 1820-27; mem. Mass. Exec. Council, 1827-31; judge of probate, 1843-58. Died East Bridgewater, Mass., Sept. 19, 1858; buried Central Cemetery, East Bridgewater.

HOBART, John Henry, clergyman; b. Phila., Sept. 14, 1775; s. Enoch and Hannah (Pratt) H.; attended U. Pa., 1788-90; grad. Princeton, 1793, A.M., 1796; D.D. (hon.), Union Coll., 1816; m. Mary Chandler, May 6, 1800. Ordained deacon Protestant Episcopal Ch., 1798, priest, 1801; sec. N.Y. Diocesan Conv., 1801; dep. Gen. convs. Episcopal Ch., 1801,04, 08, sec. of deps., 1804; trustee Columbia; founder Protestant Episcopal Theol. Soc. (became Gen. Theol. Sem.), N.Y.C., 1806, prof. pastoral theology, 1821-30; Bible and Common Prayer-Book Soc. of N.Y., 1809; asst. bishop Diocese of N.Y., 1811-16, bishop 1816-30; rector Trinity Ch., N.Y.C., 1816-30; founder N.Y. Sunday Sch. Soc., 1817, Protestaant Episcopal Press, 1817, Geneva (N.Y.) Coll. (now Hobart Coll.), 1825. Author: Festivals and Fasts, 1804; Companion for the Altar, 1804; The Christian Manual, 1805; Apology for Apostolic Oders, 1807. Died Auburn, N.Y., Sept. 12, 1830; buried Trinity Ch., N.Y.C.

HOBART, John Sloss, senator, jurist; b. Fairfield, Conn., May 6, 1738; s. Rev. Noah and Ellen (Sloss) H.; grad. Yale, 1757, LL.D. (hon.), 1793; m. Mary Grinnell, 1764. Mem. N.Y. Stamp Act Congress, 1765; mem. Sons of Liberty, 1765, Com. of Correspondence, 1774; dep. to N.Y. Provincial Conv. 1775; mem. N.Y. Provincial Congress, 1775-77; justice N.Y. Supreme Ct., 1777-98; del. to Poughkeepsie Conv. that ratified U.S. Constn., 1788; mem. U.S. Senate from N.Y., Jan. 11-May 5, 1798; U.S. dist. judge for N.Y., 1798-1805. Died N.Y.C., Feb. 4, 1805.

HOBBIE, Selah Reeve, congressman; b. Newburgh, N.Y., Mar. 10, 1797; studied law. Admitted to N.Y. bar, began practice in Delhi; dist. atty. Delaware County (N.Y.), 1823-27; mem. N.Y. Ho. of Reps., 1827-29; served as brigade maj., insp. N.Y. Militia; mem. U.S. Ho. of Reps. (Jacksonian Democrat) from N.Y., 20th Congress, 1827-29; asst. postmaster gen. U.S., 1829-51, 1st asst. postmaster gen., 1853-54. Died Washington, D.C., Mar. 23, 1854.

HOBBS, Alfred Charles, mfr.; b. Boston, Oct. 7, 1812; 2 children. Apprenticed to glass-cutting works Boston & Sandwich Glass Co., 1834-36; invented and patented new cutglass doorknob with new attachment to door socket; partner Jones and Hobbs, lockmakers; became salesman of safes for Edwards & Holman Co., later Day & Newell Co., became expert lock picker to demonstrate uselessness of his competing locks; partner firm Hobbs, Ashley Co., 1851-60; recipient Telford medal from Inst. Civil Engrs. for his paper On the Principles and Construction of Locks, 1854; engr., supt. for Elias Howe Jr. Sewing Machine Co., 1860-66; supt. Union Metallic Cartridge Co., Bridgeport, Conn., 1866-90. Died Bridgeport, Nov. 5, 1891.

HODGE, Archibald Alexander, educator; b. Princeton, N.J., July 18, 1823; s. Charles and Sarah (Bache) H.; A.B., Princeton, 1841, A.M.,1844, attended Princeton Theol. Sem., 1847, D.D., 1862; LL.D., Coll. of Wooster, 1876; m. Elizabeth Holliday, 1847; m. 2d, Mrs. Margaret McLean Woods, 1862. Tutor, Princeton, 1844-46; missionary in India, 1847; prof. theology Western Sem., Pa., 1864, theology Princeton Theol. Sem., 1878-86. Author: Outlines of Theology, 1860; The Atonement, 1868; A Commentary on Confession of Faith, 1869; The Life of Charles Hodge, 1880; Manual of Forms, 1883; Popular Lectures on Theological Themes, 1887. Died Princeton, N.J., Nov. 11, 1886.

HODGE, Charles, clergyman, educator; b. Phila., Dec. 27, 1797; s. Dr. Hugh and Mary (Blanchard) H.; grad. Coll. N.J. (now Princeton), 1815; grad. Princeton Theol. Sem., 1819; m. Sarah Bache, 1822, 8 children; m. 2d, Mrs. Mary (Hunter) Stockton, 1852. Instr., Princeton Theol. Sem., 1820, prof. Oriental and Bibl. lit., 1822-40, prof. theology, 1840-78; conservative leader Presbyn. Ch. Author: A Commentary on the Epistle to the Romans, 1835; The Constitutional History of the Presbyterian Church in the United States of America, 2 vols., 1839-40; Systematic Theology, 3 vols., 1872-73. Died June 19, 1878.

HODGE, Hugh Lenox, obstetrician; b. June 27, 1796; s. Dr. Hugh and Mary (Blanchard) H.; grad. Coll. of N.J. (now Princeton), 1814; grad. U. Pa. Med. Sch., 1818; m. Margaret E. Apsinwall, Nov. 12, 1828. In charge of lying-in dept. Pa. Hosp., 1832; prof. obstetrics U. Pa., 1835-63 (resigned because of failing vision); fellow Coll. Physicians of Phila.; mem. Am. Philos. Soc. Author: On Diseases Peculiar to Women, 1860; The Principles and Practice of Obstetrics, 1864. Died Feb. 26, 1873.

HODGEN, John Thompson, surgeon, educator; b. Hodgenville, Ky., Jan. 29, 1826; s. Jacob and Frances (Brown) H.; grad. McDowell's Coll. Medicine (now med. dept. U. Mo.), St. Louis, 1848; m. Elizabeth Mudd, Mar. 28, 1854. Asst. resident physician, then resident physician St. Louis City Hosp., until 1849; prof. anatomy Mo. Med. Coll., 1854-64, prof. physiology, 1858-64; surgeon gen. Mo. during Civil War; prof. physiology and anatomy St. Louis Med. Coll., 1864, dean, 1865; pres. A.M.A., 1881; pres. Mo. Med. Soc. Died St. Louis, Apr. 28, 1882.

HODGES, Charles Drury, congressman, jurist; b. Queen Anne, Md., Feb. 4, 1810; grad. Trinity Coll., Hartford, Conn., 1829; studied law, Annapolis, Md. Admitted to Md. bar, 1831, began practice in Annapolis; moved to Carrollton, Ill., 1833, practiced law; engaged in merc. bus.; mem. Ill. Ho. of Rep., 1851-53; judge Greene County (Ill.), 1854-59; sec., treas. St. Louis, Jacksonville, & Chgo. R.R., 1858; mem. U.S. Ho. of Reps. (Democrat) from Ill., 35th Congress, Jan. 4-Mar. 3, 1859; resumed law practice, Carrollton; circuit judge, 1867-73; mem. Ill. Senate, 1873-77. Died Carrollton, Apr. 1, 1884; buried City Cemetery, Carrollton.

HODGES, George Tisdale, congressman; b. Clarendon, Vt., July 4, 1789; attended common schs. Engaged in bus., Rutland, Vt.; mem. Vt. Ho. of Reps., 1827-29, 39-40; mem. Vt. Senate, 1845-47, pres. pro tem, 1846-47; presdl. elector, 1848; pres. Bank of Rutland, 25 years; mem. U.S. Ho. of Reps. (Republican) from Vt., 34th Congress, Dec. 1, 1856-57. Died Rutland, Aug. 9, 1860; buried Evergreen Cemetery, Rutland.

HODGES, James Leonard, congressman; b. Taunton, Mass., Apr. 24, 1790; attended common schs.; studied law. Admitted to the bar, practiced law; bank cashier; postmaster of Taunton; mem. Mass. Constl. Conv., 1820; mem. Mass. Senate, 1823-24; mem. U.S. Ho. of Reps. from Mass., 1823-24; mem. U.S. Ho. of Reps. from Mass., 20th-22d congresses, 1827-33. Died Taunton, Mar. 8, 1846; buried Plain Burying Ground, Taunton.

HODGKINSON, John, actor; b. England, circa 1767; s. Mr. Meadowcroft and Miss (Hodgkinson); m. Miss Brett, circa 1792, 2 children—Fanny, Rosina. Made Am. debut, Phila., 1792; opened in N.Y.C., 1793, widely acclaimed; mgr. of a Boston theatre, 1798; returned to N.Y.C. because of financial difficulties, 1799; got into difficulties because of his desire for best parts and greater control of acting co. Died Sept. 12, 1805.

HODGSON, William Brown, orientalist; b. Georgetown, D.C., Sept. 1, 1801; s. Joseph and Rebecca (Hersey) H.; A.M. (hon.), Princeton, 1824, LL.D. (hon.), 1858; m. Margaret Telfair, July 11, 1842. First dragoman to U.S. consulate, Algiers, 1826-29; with State Dept., Washington, D.C., 1829-32; dragoman to U.S. legation, Constantinople (now Istanbul), 1832-34; served in Washington, 1837; consul gen. Tunis, 1841-42; made comparison of N. African geog. names as reported by early Greeks and Romans with modern Berber words; translated parts of Bible into Kabyle (Berber dialect); believed that doctrine of race was involved with that of language, and that those peoples speaking Aryan langs. were superior in all ways to peoples of other langs.; a founder Am. Oriental Soc.; mem. Am. Philos. Soc. Author: Grammatical Sketch and Specimens of the Berber Language (paper presented before Am. Philos. Soc., Phila.), 1829; Notes on Northern Africa, the Sahara and Soudan, 1844. Died N.Y.C., June 26, 1871.

HOE, Richard March, inventor, mfr.; b. N.Y.C., Sept. 12, 1812; s. Robert and Rachel (Smith) H.; m. Lucy Gilbert; m. 2d, Mary Gay Corbin; 5 children. Patented new method of grinding circular saws; designed and put into prodn. single large cylinder press (1st flat bed and cylinder press ever used in U.S.); introduced rotary press which remained world leader for 25 years, 1847; introduced stop cylinder press, 1853; built web press, 1871; his printing inventions (by increasing speed and volume) made possible modern day journalism and immense circulation of daily newspapers. Died Florence, Italy, June 7, 1886.

HOE, Robert, mfr.; b. Hoes, Eng., Oct. 29, 1784; s. Thomas and Elizabeth H.; m. Rachel Smith, 3 children including Richard M. Came to N.Y., 1803; with Smith, Hoe & Co., carpentry firm specializing in printer's presses, 1805-23; began mfg. power press, circa 1830; improved upon Napier's cylinder press which soon replaced all English presses. Died Jan. 4, 1833.

HOECKEN, Christian, missionary; b. Tilburg, North Brabant, Feb. 28, 1808. Joined Soc. of Jesus, 1832; arrived in Mo., 1832; worked in Kickapoo mission, nr. Leavenworth, Kan., 1836-39; worked with Potawatomi Indians, 1841-51. Author: Peoria and Potawatomi Prayerbook, 1846. Died June 19, 1851; buried cemetery of St. Stanislaus Novitiate, Florissant, Mo.

HOEN, August, lithographer, cartographer; b. Nassau, Germany, Dec. 28, 1817; s. Martin and Eliza (Schmidt) H.; m. Caroline (Muth) Weber, Feb. 1849, at least 1 son, Albert B. Came with his family to U.S., 1835; worked for E. Weber & Co. (lithography firm operated by his cousin), Balt., circa 1837, name changed to A. Hoen & Co. upon Weber's death, 1849, printed 1st color show cards in U.S., 1830; printed lithographed maps illustrating Fremont's expdn. in 1840's; patented method of reproduction known as Lithpkaustic, 1860; developed method of map symbolism making it possible to differentiate subdivisions of geol. periods. Died Sept. 20, 1886.

HOFFMAN, Charles Fenno, editor, poet; b. N.Y.C., Feb. 7, 1806; s. Josiah Ogden and Maria (Fenno) H.; A.M. (hn.), Columbia, 1837. Admitted to N.Y. bar, 1827; co-editor N.Y. American, 1830-34; established Knickerbocker Magazine, 1833; editor Am. Monthly mag., 1835-37, N.Y. Mirror, 1837; asso. with Horace Greeley of New Yorker mag., 1840; editor Literary World, 1847; became insane, confined in Harrisburg (Pa.) Insane Asylum, 1849-84. Author: Greyslaer: a Romance of the Mohawk (novel), 1839; also collections of poems: The Vigil of Faith and Other Poems, 1842; The Echo, or Borrowed Notes for Home Circulation, 1844; Lays of the Hudson and Other Poems, 1846. Died Harrisburg, June 7, 1884.

HOFFMAN, David, lawyer, educator; b. Balt., Dec. 24, 1784; s. Peter and Dorthea (Lloyd) H.; ed. St. John's Coll.; hon. degrees U. Md., U. Gottingen (Germany), Oxford (Eng.) U.; m. Mary McKean, Jan. 8, 1816, 3 children. Admitted to Md. bar; prof. law U. Md., 1816-36. Author: A Course on Legal Study, 1817; Legal Outlines, 1836; Miscellaneous Thoughts on Men, Manners and Things by Anthony Grumbler of Grumbleton Hall, Esq., 1837; Viator, or a Peep Into My Notebook, 1841; Legal Hints, 1846. Died N.Y.C., Nov. 11, 1854.

HOFFMAN, David Murray, jurist; b. N.Y.C., Sept. 29, 1791; s. Martin and Beulah (Murray) H.; grad. Columbia, 1809; m. Frances Burrall, Dec. 16, 1817; m. 2d, Mary Murray Ogden, Apr. 18, 1837; 9 children including Wickham. Admitted to N.Y. bar, 1811; vice-chancellor N.Y., 1839-43; judge Superior Ct., N.Y.C., 1853-61. Author: The Office and Duties of Masters in Chancery and Practice in the Master's Office, 1824; A Treatise upon the Practice of the Court of Chancery, 3 vols., 1834-40; Ecclesiastical Law in the State of New York, 1868. Died Flushing, N.Y., May 7, 1878.

HOFFMAN, Henry William, congressman; b. Cumberland, Md., Nov. 10, 1825; grad. Jefferson Coll., 1846; studied law. Admitted to the bar, 1848; mem. U.S. Ho. of Reps. (American Party rep.) from Md., 34th Congress, 1855-57; treas. Chesapeake & Ohio Canal Co., 1858-60; sgt. at arms U.S. Ho. of Reps., 1860-61; collector of customs Port of Balt. (apptd. by Lincoln), 1861-66; resumed practice of law, Cumberland; asso. judge 6th Md. Circuit Ct., 1883-95. Died Cumberland, July 28, 1895; buried Rose Hill Cemetery, Cumberland.

HOFFMAN, John Thompson, gov. N.Y., mayor N.Y.C.; b. Ossining, N.Y., Jan. 10, 1828; s. Adrian and Jane (Thompson) H.; grad. Union Coll., 1846, LL.D. (hon.), 1869; LL.D. (hon.), Coll. of N.J. (now Princeton), 1870; m. Ella Starkweather, 1854. Admitted to N.Y. bar, 1849; joined Tammany Soc., 1859; recorder of N.Y.C., 1860-66, mayor, 1865, re-elected 1867, 68; gov. N.Y., 1869-72. Died Wiesbaden, Germany, Mar. 24, 1888.

HOFFMAN, Josiah Ogden, lawyer; b. Newark, N.J., Apr. 14, 1766; s. Nicholas and Sarah (Ogden) H.; m. Mary Colden, Feb. 16, 1789; m. 2d, Maria Fenno, Aug. 7, 1802; 7 children including Ogden, Matilda, Charles. Mem. N.Y. Ho. of Reps. (Federalist), 1791-95, 97; atty. gen. N.Y., 1798-1801; recorder N.Y.C., 1808-15; asso. judge N.Y. Superior Ct., 1828-37; lawyer with large and successful practice, argued case of The Nereide before U.S. Supreme Ct., 1815. Died Jan. 24, 1837.

HOFFMAN, Michael, congressman; b. Half Moon, N.Y., Oct. 11, 1787; studied medicine and law. Admitted to N.Y. bar, began practice in Herkimer; dist. atty., 1823-25; mem. U.S. Ho. of Reps. (Democrat) from N.Y., 19th-22d congresses, 1825-33; judge Herkimer County (N.Y.), 1830-33; canal commr. N.Y., 1833-35; register land office, Saginaw, Mich., 1836; mem. N.Y. State Assembly, 1841-42, 44; del. N.Y. Constl. Conv., 1846; naval officer of N.Y.C., 1845-48. Died Bklyn., Sept. 27, 1848.

HOFFMAN, Ogden, congressman, lawyer; b. N Y.C., May 3, 1793; s. Josiah Ogden and Ma (Colden) H.; grad. Columbia, 1812; m. Emily Bu rall, June 27, 1819; m. 2d, Virginia E. Southard 2 children including Ogden. Warranted midshipma U.S. Navy, 1814, resigned, 1816; admitted to N.Y bar, 1818; dist. atty. Orange County (N.Y.), 1823 mem. N.Y. Ho. of Reps., 1825, 28; dist. atty. Cit and County N.Y., 1829-35; mem. U.S. Ho. of Reps (Whig) from N.Y., 25th-26th congresses, 1837-41 opposed Sub-Treasury Bill; a leading criminal law yer of N.Y.; judge-advocate in Navy-Yard trial c Spencer mutiny plot, 1842; U.S. dist. atty. for So Dist. N.Y., 1844-45; atty. gen. N.Y., 1853-55 Died N.Y.C., May 1, 1856; buried St. Mark' Church, N.Y.C.

HOFFMAN, Wickham, army officer, diplomat, b N.Y.C., Apr. 2, 1821; s. David Murray and France (Burrall) H.; grad. Harvard, 1841; m. Elizabet Baylies, May 14, 1844. Admitted to N.Y. bar, prac ticed law until Civil War; a.d.c. to Gov. Edwin Mor gan, also insp. of N.Y. troops at Fortress Monroe 1861; commd. asst. adj. gen. U.S. Volunteers, 1862 assigned to staff of Brig. Gen. Thomas Williams i expdn. at Baton Rouge, La.; ordered to Gen. W. T Sherman's staff as asst. adj. gen., 1862-63; wit Maj. Gen. W. B. Franklin in Red River Campaign 1863; on Maj. Gen. Quincy Gillmore's staff in Va. asst. adj. gen. of E. Va. and N.C. dist.; ordered t New Orleans as adj. gen. and chief of staff to Maj Gen. Edward Canby, 1865; commd. col. U.S. Volunteers for meritorious service in war, 1865; asst. sec. U.S. legation in Paris, France, 1866, 1st sec. of legation, 1867-74; sec. legation, London, Eng., 1874-77, St. Petersburg, Russia, 1877-83; U.S. minister to Denmark, 1883-85. Author: Camp, Court, and Siege, 1877; Leisure Hours in Russia, 1883. Died Atlantic City, N.J., May 21, 1900.

HOFFY, Alfred M., lithographer; b. Eng., circa 1790. Came to U.S., circa 1835; drew on stone a view of N.Y.C. fire of Dec. 16, 1835; worked in N.Y.C., until 1838, produced illustrations for U.S. Mil. Mag., Phila., 1839-41; editor Orchardist's Companion, Phila., 1841-43; published North American Pomologist, with 36 color plates, 1860; exhibited at Artists' Fund Soc., Pa. Acad.

HOGAN, John, congressman, businessman; b. Mallow, County Cork, Ireland, Jan. 2, 1805; s. Thomas and Mary (Field) H.; m. Mary Mitchell West, 1830; m. 2d, Harriet Garnier, May 18, 1847; 9 children. Came to U.S., 1817; Methodist preacher, 1826-92; engaged in gen. mdse. bus., Edwardsville and Alton, Ill., 1830-35; pres. Ill. Bd. Pub. Works, 1834-37; became pres. Alton br. State Bank of Ill., 1835; moved to St Louis, 1845; v.p. Mo. State Mut. Fire & Marine Ins. Co., 1853; organized Dollar Savs. Instn., St. Louis, 1854; wrote Thoughts About the City of St. Louis, 1854, circulated in Germany and Ireland, resulted in increased immigration to St. Louis; postmaster St. Louis, 1857-61: mem. U.S. Ho. of Reps. from Mo., 39th Congress, 1865-67. Author: The Resources of Missouri, 1858; Sketches of Early Western Pioneers, 1859; History of Western Methodism, 1860. Died St. Louis, Feb. 5, 1892; buried Bellefontaine Cemetery, St. Louis.

HOGAN, William, congressman; b. London, Eng., July 17, 1792; grad. Columbia, 1811. Came to U.S., 1803; served with War of 1812, participated in Battle of Plattsburg; admitted to the bar, did not practice; interested in undeveloped lands in Franklin County (N.Y.); mem. N.Y. Assembly, 1822-23; county judge Franklin County, 1829-37; mem. U.S. Ho. of Reps. (Jacksonian Democrat) from N.Y., 22d Congress, 1831-33; apptd. examiner of claims, 1855; translator Dept. of State, Washington, D.C., until 1869. Died Washington, Nov. 25, 1874; buried Trinity Ch. Cemetery, N.Y.C.

HOGE, John, congressman; b. nr. Hogestown, Pa., Sept. 10, 1760; served in Revolutionary War as ensign 9th Pa. Regt.; founder (with brother William) Town of Washington (Pa.), 1782; del. Pa. Constl. Conv., 1790; mem. Pa. Senate, 1790-95; mem. U.S. Ho. of Reps. (Democrat) from Pa., 8th Congress, Nov. 2, 1804-05. Died Meadow Lands, nr. Washington, Pa., Aug. 4, 1824; buried City Cemetery, Washington.

HOGE, John Blair, congressman; b. Richmond, Va., Feb. 2, 1825; studied law. Admitted to Va. bar, 1845, began practice in Martinsburg, Va. (now W.Va.); became pres. Bank of Berkeley (Va., now W.Va.), 1853; mem. Va. Ho. of Dels., 1855-59; del. Democratic Nat. Convs., Charleston, S.C., and Balt., 1860; served with Confederate Army during Civil War; engaged in journalism; resumed law practice, Martinsburg, 1870; del. W.Va. Constl. Conv., 1872; mem. Dem. Nat. Com., 1872-76; judge 3d judicial circuit, 1872-80; mem. U.S. Ho. of Reps. (Dem.) from W.Va., 47th Congress, 1881-83; U.S. dist. atty. for D.C., 1885-89. Died Martinsburg, Mar. 1, 1896; buried Norborne Cemetery, Martinsburg.

HOGE, Joseph Pendleton, congressman; b. Steubenville, O., Dec. 15, 1810; grad. Jefferson Coll.; studied law. Admitted to the bar, 1836; moved to Ill., began practice of law, Galena, 1836; mem. U.S. Ho. of Reps. (Democrat) from Ill., 28th-29th congresses, 1843-47; resumed law practice, Galena; moved to Cal., 1853, practiced law; unsuccessful candidate for U.S. Senate, 1869; pres. Cal. Constl. Conv., 1878; pres. bd. freeholders, 1880; judge Cal. Superior Ct., 1889-91. Died San Francisco, Aug. 14, 1891; buried Laurel Hill Cemetery, San Francisco.

HOGE, Moses, clergyman, coll. pres.; b. Cedargrove, Va., Feb. 15, 1752; s. James and Nancy (Griffiths) H.; received theol. instrn. from Rev. James Waddel ("the blind preacher" immortalized by William Wirt); S.T.D. (hon.), Coll. of N.J. (now Princeton); m. Elizabeth Poage, Aug. 23, 1783; m. 2d, Mrs. Susan Watkins Hunt, Oct. 25, 1803; 2 sons, James, Samuel Davies. Fought in Revolutionary War; ordained to ministry Presbyn. Ch., 1782; trustee Washington Coll., 1791-1807; pres. Hampden-Sydney Coll., 1807-20. Author: Strictures on a Phamphlet by the Rev. Jeremiah Walker, entitled Fourfold Foundations of Calvinism Examined and Shaken, 1793; Christian Panoply: An Answer of Paine's Age of Reason, 1799. Died Phila., July 5, 1820.

HOGE, Moses Drury, clergyman; b. Hampden-Sydney, Va., Sept. 17, 1819; s. Samuel Davies and Elizabeth Rice (Lacy) H.; grad. Hampden-Sydney Coll., 1839; m. Susan Wood, Mar. 20, 1844. First pastor Second Presbyn. Ch., Richmond, Va., 1845-99; volunteer chaplain to Confederate soldiers, Richmond, 1861; ran blockade to get supply of Bibles from England, 1862; del. to Evang. Alliance, N.Y., 1873; co-editor Central Presbyn. of Richmond. Died Jan. 6, 1899.

HOGE, William, congressman; b. nr. Hogestown, Pa., 1762. Founder (with brother John) Town of Washington (Pa.), 1782; mem. Pa. Ho. of Reps., 1796-97; mem. U.S. Ho. of Reps. (Federalist) from Pa., 7th-8th, 10th congresses, 1801-Oct. 15, 1804, 07-09. Died nr. Washington, Pa., Sept. 25, 1814; buried Old Graveyard, Washington.

HOGE, William James, clergyman; b. Athens, O., Aug. 14, 1824; s. Samuel and Elizabeth (Lacy) H.; grad. Ohio U. at Athens, 1841; m. Mary Ballard, 1847; m. 2d, Virginia Randolph; 6 children. Prof. mathematics Ohio U., circa 1843-51; ordained to ministry Presbyn. Ch., 1851; moved to Richmond, Va., assisted his brother in ch. and ednl. work; pastor Westminster Presbyn. Ch., Balt., 1852-56; prof. Biblical literature Union Theol. Sem., Hampden-Sydney, Va., 1856-59; asso. pastor Brick Presbyn. Ch., N.Y.C., 1859-61; pastor, Charlottesville, Petersburg, Va., 1861-64, also worked in mil. hosps. and camps. Died Chesterfield, Va., July 5, 1864.

HOGEBOOM, James Lawrence, congressman; b. Ghent, N.Y., Aug. 25, 1766; Mcht.; mem. N.Y. Ho. of Reps., 1804-05, 08; judge Rensselaer County (N.Y.), 1805-08; mem. N.Y. Constl. Conv., 1821; mem. U.S. Ho. of Reps. (Whig) from N.Y., 18th Congress,. 1823-25; engaged in merc. bus. Died Castleton, N.Y., Dec. 23, 1839; buried Castleton Cemetery.

HOGG, George, mfr., mcht.; b. Cramlington, Eng., June 22, 1784; s. John and Mary (Crisp) H.; m. Mary Ann Breading, Mar. 7, 1811, 6 children. Founder wholesale drygoods bus. Breading & Hogg, Pitts. also wholesale grocery Dalzell, Taylor & Co. with brs. all along East coast (1st to develop chain store system in Am.); a founder, mgr. Monongahela Navigation Improvement Co.; founder Brownsville Glass Factory, 1828. Died Pitts., Dec. 5, 1849.

HOGG, Samuel, congressman; b. Halifax, N.C., Apr. 18, 1783; attended pub. schs., Caswell County, N.C.; studied medicine, Gallatin, Tenn., circa 1804. Taught sch.; served as surgeon 1st Regt., Tenn. Volunteer Inf., 1812-13; hosp. surgeon on staff of Maj. Gen. Andrew Jackson in expdn. against Creek Indians, 1814, on staff of Maj. Gen. William Carroll, 1814-15; mem. Tenn. Ho. of Reps.; mem. U.S. House of Representatives (Democrat) from the State of Tennessee, Fifteenth Congress, 1817-19; practiced medicine, Lebanon, Tenn., until 1828, Nashville, Tenn., 1828-36, Natchez, Miss., 1836-38; pres. Tenn. Med. Soc., 1840. Died Rutherford County, Tenn., May 28, 1842; buried Nashville City Cemetery.

HOGUN, James, army officer; b. Ireland; m. Ruth Norfleet, 1 child. Came to N.C., 1751; rep. from Halifax County to N.C. Provincial congresses, 1775, 76; elected 1st maj. Halifax Militia by N.C. Provincial Congress, 1776; assigned to command N.C. Brigade, Continental Army under Washington, fought at battles of Brandywine, Germantown; assigned by Washington to command Phila., 1779; in charge of brigade in defense of Charleston, S.C., 1780; captured by British, offered pardon, but elected to stay with men of his brigade. Died as result of strain of imprisonment, Haddrell's Point, S.C., Jan. 4, 1781.

HOISINGTON, Henry Richard, clergyman; b. Vergennes, Vt., Aug. 23, 1801; s. Job and Sarah H.; grad. Williams Coll., 1828, Auburn Theol. Sem., 1831; m. Nancy Lyman, Sept. 21, 1831. Ordained to ministry Congregational Ch., 1831; missionary in India and Ceylon, 1833-41; prin. Batticotta Sem., Ceylon, 1836-41, 44-49; returned to Am. because of poor health, 1841-44; lectr. Hinduism, Williams Coll., 1854-56. Author: Origins and Developments of the Existing System of Religious Belief in India, 1852; Treatises on Hindu Philosophy, (translation of religious texts), 1854. Died Centerbrook, Conn., May 16, 1858.

HOLBROOK, Edward Dexter, congressman; b. Elyria, O., May 6, 1836; attended Oberlin (O.) Coll.; studied law. Admitted to Ohio bar, 1859, began practice in Elyria; moved to Cal., 1859, practiced law, Weaverville; moved to Placerville, Ida., 1863, practiced law; mem. U.S. Ho. of Reps. (Democrat) from Ida., 39th-40th congresses, 1865-69; fatally shot by Charles H. Douglas, June 17, 1870. Died Idaho City, Ida., June 18, 1870; buried Masonic Burial Ground, Idaho City.

HOLBROOK, John Edwards, physician, zoologist; b. Beaufort, S.C., Dec. 30, 1794; s. Silas and Mary (Edwards) H.; grad. Brown U., 1815; M.D., U. Pa., 1818; m. Harriott Pinckney Rutledge, May 1827. A founder Med. Coll. of S.C., 1824, prof. anatomy, 1824-54; med. officer Confederate Army, head S.C. Examining Bd. of Surgeons, 1861-65; specialized in study of Am. reptiles and fishes; considered most important Am. zoologist of his time. Author: American Herpetology: or a Description of Reptiles Inhabiting the United States, 1842; Ichthyology of South Carolina, 1855, 2d edition., 1860. Died Norfolk, Mass., Sept. 8, 1871.

HOLBROOK, Josiah, ednl. reformer; b. Derby, Conn., 1788; s. Col. Daniel and Anne (Hitchcock) H.; grad. Yale, 1810; m. Lucy Swift, May 1815, at least 2 children, including Alfred. Opened pvt. sch., Derby, 1810, Indsl. Sch., 1819, Agrl. Sem., 1824-25; an originator lyceum idea of adult edn.; organizer Millbury (Mass.) Lyceum no. 1 (1st group of its type in Am.) br. Am. Lyceum Assn., 1826; editor Family Lyceum, 1832; corr. sec. Sch. Agts. Soc., 1831-37; sec. control bur. Am. Lyceum Assn., 1842-49. Died nr. Lynchburg, Va., June 17, 1854.

HOLBROOK, Silas Pinckney, author; b. Beaufort, S.C., June 1, 1796; s. Silas and Mary (Edwards) H.; grad. Brown U., 1815; m. Esther Gourdine. Admitted to Mass. bar, began practice law, Medfield, Mass.; devoted career to literary pursuits, from circa 1818; contbd. short stories and essays to publs. including New Eng. Galaxy, Boston Courier; contbd. to European portion of Peter Parley's Pictorial Geography; wrote travel sketches, Letters from a Mariner, Travels of a Tin Pedlar under pseudonym Jonathan Farbink; editor Tribune, Boston, 1820's. Author: Sketches by a Traveler, 1834. Died Pineville, S.C., May 26, 1835; buried Pineville.

HOLCOMB, Amasa, telescope maker; b. Southwick, Mass., June 18, 1787; s. Elijah and Lucy (Holcomb) H.; m. Gillett Kendall, 1808; m. 2d, Maria Holcomb, circa 1861. Began mfg. telescopes, circa 1825, his telescopes described as being same quality as more expensive European makes; recommended by com. on science and arts of Franklin Inst. (Phila.) for award and medal from John Scott Legacy Fund, 1835; mem. Mass. Ho. of Reps. from Southwick, 1832-33; justice of peace for Hampden County (Mass.), 1834-75. Died Southwick, Feb. 27, 1875.

HOLCOMBE, George, congressman; b. West Amwell (now Lambertsville), N.J., Mar. 1786; grad. Princeton, 1805; attended med. dept. U. Pa.; studied medicine, Trenton, N.J. Practiced medicine, Allentown, N.J., 1808-15; mem. N.J. Gen. Assembly, 1815-16; mem. U.S. Ho. of Reps. (Democrat) from N.J., 17th-20th congresses, 1821-28. Died Allentown, Jan. 14, 1828; buried Congressional Cemetery, Washington, D.C.

HOLCOMBE, Henry, clergyman; b. Prince Edward County, Va., Sept. 22, 1762; s. Grimes and Elizabeth (Buzbee) H.; D.D. and A.M. (hon.), Brown U., 1800; D.D. (hon.), S.C. Coll.; m. Frances Tanner, 1786. Served in Revolutionary War; ordained to ministry Baptist Ch., 1785; mem. S.C. Conv. which ratified U.S. Constn., 1788; founder Beaufort Coll., 1795-99, Savannah Female Asylum (orphanage), 1801; founder, editor Analytical Repository; helped found Bapt. Acad., Mt. Enon, Burke County, Ga., 1804, Ga. Bapt. Missionary Soc., 1806; an originator of penitentiary system which abolished death sentence for ordinary crimes; baptized 1st white person ever immersed in Savannah, Ga. Died Phila., May 22, 1824.

HOLCOMBE, James Philemon, Confederate agt., educator; b. Powhatan County, Va., Sept. 20, 1820; s. Dr. William James and Ann Eliza (Clopton) H.; ed. Yale, U. Va.; m. Anne Selden Watts, Nov. 4, 1841, 6 children. Adjunct prof. law U. Va., 1851, full prof. law and belleslettres, 1854; mem. Va. Secession Conv., 1861; a signer agreement between Va. and Confederacy, 1861; mem. Confederate Congress, 1862-64; mem. Confederate Comm. to Can., 1863-65. Author: Leading Cases on Commercial Law; Digest on the Decisions of the Supreme Court; Merchants' Book of Letters; Literature and Letters. Died Capon Springs, W. Va., Aug. 22, 1873.

HOLCOMBE, William Henry, physician; b. Lynchburg, Va, May 29, 1825; s. William James and Ann (Clopton) H.; attended Washington Coll. (now Washington and Lee U.); grad. med. dept. U. Pa., 1847; m. Rebecca Palmer, 1852. Practiced medicine, Cincinnati, 1850-52, Natchez, Miss., 1852-55, 62-93, Waterproof, La., 1855-62; staff mem. Miss. State Hosp., Natchez, 1853-55; chmn. Yellow Fever Commn. of Am. Inst. of Homeopathy, 1879; pres. Am. Inst. Homeopathy, 1874. Author: The Scientific Basis of Homeopathy, 1852; On the Nature and Limitations of the Homeopathic Law, 1858; Poems, 1860; The Alternative: A Separate Nationality, or the Africanization of the South, 1860; What Is Homeopathy?, 1864; Our Children in Heaven, 1868; The Sexes Here and Hereafter, 1869; Song Novels, 1873; Helps to Spiritual Growth, 1886. Died New Orleans, Nov. 28, 1893.

HOLDEN, Oliver, carpenter, musician; b. Shirley, Mass., Sept. 18, 1765; s. Nehemiah and Elizabeth Holden; m. Nancy Rand, May 12, 1791, 6 children. Settled at Charlestown, Mass., 1787, became carpenter and real estate investor; an incorporator Andover Turnpike, 1805; Freemason, King Solomon's Lodge, 1795-1805; mem. Mass. Ho. of Reps., 1818, 25, 26, 28-33; wrote hymn "Coronation," 1793; pastor Puritan church, Charlestown. Author: The American Harmony, 1792; Union Harmony, 2 vols., 1793; The Worcester Collection, 1797; Modern Collection of Sacred Music, 1800; Vocal Companion, 1807. Died Sept. 4, 1844.

HOLDEN, William Woods, editor, gov. N.C.; b. Orange County, N.C., Nov. 24, 1818; m. Ann Augusta Young, 1841; m. 2d, Louisa Virginia Harrison. Writer for Whig paper Raleigh (N.C.) Star, 1837-43; changed polit. party to become editor Democratic organ N.C. Standard, 1843; unsuccessful candidate for gov. N.C., 1858, 64; advocated seccession policy, 1860; a leader in peace movement, 1863; provisional gov. N.C., May 1865, defeated for re-election; apptd. minister to San Salvador, 1866, refused confirmation by U.S. Senate; gov. N.C., 1868-71, impeached for corruption and convicted, 1871; editor Daily Morning Chronicle, Washington, D.C., 1872; postmaster Raleigh, 1873-81. Died Raleigh, Mar. 1, 1892.

HOLDER, Joseph Basset, physician, naturalist; b. Lynn, Mass., Oct. 26, 1824; s. Aaron Lummus and Rachael (Bassett) H.; m. Emily Augusta Cove, at least 1 child, Charles Frederick. City physician, Lynn; surgeon-in-chief to U.S. Engrs. on Fla. reef, 1859; studied reef formation, plant and animal life; health officer, surgeon mil. prison Ft. Jefferson, Fla., 1861-65; curator zoology sect. Am. Mus. Natural History, N.Y.C., 1881. Author: The Florida Reef; (with H.G. Wook) Our Living World. Died N.Y.C., Feb. 27, 1888.

HOLLADAY, Alexander Richmond, congressman; b. Prospect Hill, Va., Sept. 18, 1811; attended U. Va.; studied law. Admitted to Va. bar, practiced in Spotsylvania, Orange and Louisa counties; mem. Va. Ho. of Dels., 1845-47; mem. U.S. Ho. of Reps. (Democrat) from Va., 31st-32d congresses, 1849-53; practiced law, Richmond, Va.; pres. Va. Bd. Pub. Works, 1857-61. Died Richmond, Jan. 29, 1877; buried family burial ground called Prospect Hill, Spotsylvania County.

HOLLADAY, Ben, financier; b. Carlisle County, Ky., Oct. 1819; s. William Holladay; m. Notley Ann Calvert; m. 2d, Esther Campbell; 9 children. Bought Central Overland Cal. & Pikes Peak Express Co.; organized Cal., Ore. & Mexican S.S Co., 1863; formed No. Pacific Transp. Co., 1867; chief owner Ore. Central R.R. Co., 1868. Died Portland, Ore., July 8, 1887.

HOLLAND, Cornelius, congressman; b. Sutton, Mass., July 9, 1783; attended common schs.; studied medicine. Began practice of medicine, Livermore, Me., 1814; engaged in farming; del. Me. Constl. Conv., 1819; mem. Me. Ho. of Reps., 1821-22; Me. Senate, 1822, 25, 26; justice of peace, 1826-55; mem. U.S. Ho. of Reps. (Democrat) from Me., 21st-22d congresses, Dec. 6, 1830-33; resumed practice of medicine, farming. Died Canton Point, Me., June 2, 1870; buried Hillside Cemetery, Canton Point.

HOLLAND, Edwin Clifford, author; b. Charleston, S.C., 1794; s. John and Jane Holland. Editor, Charleston Times; wrote for Southern papers under name Orlando. Author: Odes, Naval Songs, and Other Occasional Poems, 1813; a dramatization of Lord Byron's Corsair, 1818; Omnium Botherum, 1821;

Refutation of the Calumnies Circulated Against the Southern and Western States Respecting the Institution and Existence of Slavery among Them, 1822. Died Sept. 11, 1824.

HOLLAND, George, comedian; b. London, Eng., Dec. 6, 1791; m. 2d, Catherine De Lucy; 4 children, Edmund Milton, Joseph Jefferson, George, Kate. Came to U.S., 1827; made 1st U.S. appearance in A Day After the Fair at Bowery Theatre, N.Y.C., 1827; traveled as comedian, 1827-43; treas. St. Charles Theatre, New Orleans, 1834-42; in N.Y.C., 1842-55; toured with Wallack's company, 1855-67. Died N.Y.C., Dec. 20, 1870.

HOLLAND, James, congressman; b. Anson County, N.C., 1754. Served as maj. N.C. Militia, also in Continental Army, 1775-83; sheriff of Tryon County (N.C.), 1777-78; justice of peace Rutherford County (N.C.), 1782-85; mem. N.C. Senate, 1783, 97, N.C. Ho. of Commons, 1786, 89; del. 2d N.C. Constl. Conv. which adopted U.S. Constn., 1789; mem. 1st bd. trustees U. N.C., 1789-95; admitted to N.C. bar, 1793, began practice in Rutherfordton; mem. U.S. Ho. of Reps. (Anti-Federalist) from N.C., 4th, 7th-11th congresses, 1795-97, 1801-11; engaged in farming, nr. Columbia, Tenn.; justice of peace, 1812-18. Died on his estate, Maury County, Tenn., May 19, 1823; buried Holland Family (now Watson) Cemetery, nr. Columbia.

HOLLAND, John Joseph, artist; b. Eng., circa 1776. Came to Am., 1796; scene painter Phila. Theatre, 1796-1807; moved to N.Y.C., 1807; designed New Theatre, N.Y.C., prin. scene painter, until 1813, returned as co-mgr., 1814; scene painter Theatrical Commonwealth, N.Y.C., 1813-14; scene painter Park Theatre, until 1820; painted several watercolor views of N.Y.C. which are extant. Died N.Y.C., Dec. 15, 1820.

HOLLAND, Josiah Gilbert, editor, author; b. Belchertown, Mass., July 24, 1819; s. Harrison and Anna (Gilbert) H.; grad. Berkshire Med. Coll., 1844; m. Elizabeth Chapin, Oct. 7, 1845, 3 children. Became editor Springfield (Mass) Republican, 1850; a founder Scribner's Mag., 1870; editor Scribner's Monthly (became Century Mag),. 1870-81. Author: Bitter Sweet (poem), 1858; Miss Gilbert's Career, 1860; Lessons in Life, 1861; Letters to the Joneses, 1863; Plain Talk on Familiar Subjects, 1865; Life of Abraham Lincoln, 1865; Kathrina, 1867; Arthur Bonnicastle, Seven Oaks, Nicholas Minturn (all novels). Died N.Y.C., Oct. 12, 1881.

HOLLEMAN, Joel, congressman; b. nr. Smithfield, Isle of Wight County, Va., Oct. 1, 1799; grad. Chapel Hill Coll., Wake Forest, N.C.; studied law. Admitted to Va. bar, began practice at Burwell Bay; mem. Va. Ho. of Dels., 1832-36, 41-44, served as speaker; mem. Va. Senate, 1836-39; mem. U.S. Ho. of Reps. (Democrat) from Va., 26th Congress, 1839-40; resumed law practice. Died Smithfield, Aug. 5, 1844; buried Ivy Hill Cemetery, Smithfield.

HOLLENBACK, George Matson, industrialist; b. Wilkes-Barre, Pa., Aug. 11, 1791; s. Matthias Hollenback; m. Emily Lindsley, Sept. 23, 1816, no children. Operated (with his father) Matthias Hollenback & Son (one of largest merc. firms in Pa.), operated firm under his own name, after 1818; county treas., 1820-22; mem. Pa. Gen. Assembly, 1824-25; pres. Wyoming Bank, circa 1836-66; canal commr. of Pa., 1842, contbd. financial support to extension and bldg. of Pa. canal system. Died Nov. 7, 1866; buried G. M. Hollenback Cemetery.

HOLLENBACK, Matthias, mcht., jurist; b. Lancaster (now Lebanon) County, Pa., Feb. 17, 1752; s. John and Eleanor (Jones) H.; married, 3 daus., 1 son, George Matson. Went to Wyoming Valley, Pa., 1769; commd. ensign 24th Regt. Conn. Militia, 1775; apptd. ensign Capt. Durkee's Co. of Wyoming Minute Men, 1776; served in battles of Millstone, Brandywine and Germantown; established trading posts, acquired land, became one of largest landowners in Susquehanna Valley; commdg. justice of peace and of Ct. of Common Pleas, 1787; asso. judge Pa. Supreme Ct., 1791-1829. Died Feb. 18, 1829.

HOLLEY Alexander Lyman mech engr. b Lakeville, Conn., July 20, 1832; s. Alexander H. and Jane (Lyman) H.; grad. Brown U., 1853; m. Mary Slade, 2 children. With N.J. Locomotive works, Jersey City, 1855. published Holley's Railroad Advocate, N.J., 1855-57; mem. staff N.Y. Times, 1858-75; tech. editor Am. Ry. Review; chiefly responsible for introducing Bessemer process in U.S.; designer and builder Bessemer plant, Harrisburg, Pa., 1867; became leading engr. and designer of steel plants in U.S., including Edgar Thomeson Works, Pitts; patentee 5 mech. improvements on Bessemer process; mem. Am. Soc. C.E., U.S. Bd. for Testing Structural Materials; pres. Am. Inst. Mining Engrs., 1876; a founder Am. Inst. Mech. Engrs.; trustee Rensselaer Poly. Inst.; mem. Instn. Civil Engrs. (Eng.), 1877. Author: American and European Railway Practice, 1860. Died Bklyn., Jan. 29, 1882.

HOLLEY, John Milton, congressman; b. Salisbury, Conn., Nov. 10, 1802; grad. Yale, 1822; studied law. Admitted to N.Y. bar, began practice at Black Rock, 1825; moved to Lyons, N.Y., 1826, practiced law; mem. N.Y. Assembly, 1842-45; mem. U.S. Ho. of Reps. (Whig) from N.Y., 30th Congress, 1847-48. Died Jacksonville, Fla., Mar. 8, 1848; buried Rural Cemetery, Lyons.

HOLLEY, Horace, clergyman, univ. pres.; b. Salisbury, Conn., Feb. 13, 1781; s. Luther and Sarah (Dakin) H.; grad. Yale, 1803; m. Mary Austin, Jan. 1805, 2 children. Ordained to ministry Unitarian Ch., 1805; pastor Greenfield Hill Unitarian Ch., Fairfield, Conn., 1806-09, South End Ch., Boston, 1809-18; mem. bd. overseers Harvard; pres. Transylvania U., Lexington, Ky., 1818-27. Died at sea, July 31, 1827; buried at sea.

HOLLEY, Myron, editor, abolitionist; b. Salisbury, Conn., Apr. 29, 1779; s. Luther and Sarah (Dakin) H.; grad. Williams Coll., 1799; m. Sally House, 1804, 6 daus. Became bookseller, Canandaigua, N.Y., 1804; mem. N.Y. Gen. Assembly from Canandaigua, 1816; mem. commn. for Erie Canal, 1816-24, served as treas.; del. from N.Y. to Nat. Anti-Masonic Conv., Phila., 1830; wrote Address to the People of the United States (argued that Masonic socs. were inimical to free govt.); editor Lyons Countryman, 1831-34, Free Elector, Hartford, Conn., 1834; del. to Anti-Slavery Conv., Cleve., O., 1839; a founder Liberty Party (gave polit. action to agitation of abolitionists; nominated James G. Birney for U.S. Pres.), 1840; editor Freeman, Rochester, N.Y., 1839-41. Died Rochester, Mar. 4, 1841; buried Mt. Hope Cemetery, Rochester.

HOLLIDAY, Cyrus Kurtz, railroad exec.; b. nr. Carlisle, Pa., Apr. 3, 1826; s. David and Mary (Kennedy) H.; grad. Allegheny Coll., Meadville, Pa., 1852; m. Mary Jones, June 11, 1854, 2 children. Founder, Topeka (Kan.), 1854; pres. Topeka Town Co., 1854-59; successful in persuading Constl. Conv. of 1859 to declare Topeka state capital, 1859; mem. Kan. Territorial Council, 1859; drafted, largely responsible for bill which chartered Atchison and Topeka R.R. Co. (now A.T.& S.F. Ry.), 1859, dir., 1859-1900; at various times mem. Kan. Legislature; pres. Mchts.' Nat. Bank, also Excelsior Gas & Coke Co., Topeka. Died Mar. 29, 1900.

HOLLINS, George Nichols, naval officer; b. Balt., Sept. 20, 1799; s. John and Janet (Smith) H.; m. twice, the Steritt sisters; 2 children. Apptd. midshipman U.S. Navy, 1814; served under Capt. Stephen Decatur during War of 1812 and in Tripolitan War; promoted lt., 1825, comdr., 1845, capt., 1855, resigned, 1861; commd. capt. Confederate States Navy, 1861; captured steamer St. Nicholas and converted it into gunboat, capturing several Union trading vessels; promoted commodore, 1861; commanded Confederate Naval Station, New Orleans, 1861-62; commanded Confederate forces on Upper Mississippi River, 1862; served in battles of Columbus, New Madrid, Island Number 10, Ft. Pillow, and Memphis. Died Balt., Jan. 18, 1878.

HOLLISTER, Gideon Hiram, state legislator, diplomat; b. Washington, Conn., Dec. 14, 1817; s. Gideon and Harriet (Jackson) H.; grad. Yale, 1840; studied law with Judge Origen S. Symour, Litchfield, Conn.; m. Mary S. Brisbane, June 1847. Admitted to Conn. bar, 1842; Clk., Litchfield County Ct., 1843-52 (except for 1 year); elected to Conn. Senate, 1856; apptd. U.S. minister to Haiti by Pres. Johnson, 1868-69; mem. Conn. Legislature, 1880-81. Author: Mount Hope, 1851; Thomas a Becket, 1866; Kinley Hollow, 1882. Died Litchfield, Conn., Mar. 24, 1881.

HOLLOWAY, David Pierson, journalist, congressman; b. Waynesville, O., Dec. 7, 1809; attended common schs., Cincinnati. With Cincinnati Gazette, 4 years; moved to Richmond, Ind., 1823; purchased Richmond Palladium, 1832, editor, propr., 1832-83; mem. Ind. Ho. of Reps., 1843-44, Ind. Senate, 1844-50; apptd. examiner land offices, 1849; mem. U.S. Ho. of Reps. (Peoples Party rep.) from Ind., 34th Congress, 1855-57; U.S. commr. of patents, 1861-65; patent atty. Washington, D.C., until 1883. Died Washington, Sept. 9, 1883; buried Maple Grove Cemetery, Richmond, reinterred Earlham Cemetery.

HOLLOWAY, John, colonial ofcl.; b. Eng., 1666; m. Elizabeth Catesby, 1720. Came to Am.; apptd. judge vice-admiralty Va. Cts. by Gov. Spotswood; 1st mayor Williamsburg (Va.), 1722; mem. Va. Ho. of Burgesses, 1710-14, 23-34, speaker, 1720-34; treas. Colony of Va., 1723-24, tenure marked by scandal, left office 1,850 pounds in arrears. Died Dec. 14, 1734.

HOLLOWAY, Joseph Flavius, mech. engr.; b. Uniontown, O., Jan. 18, 1825; s. Joseph T. Holloway. Worked for Cuyahoga Steam Furnace Co., 1846; designed machinery for screw-propelled boat Niagara, 1847; designed equipment for iron steamers, 1851; supt., later pres. Cuyahoga Steam Furnace Works, 1857-87; v.p. H. R. Worthington firm of hydraulic engrs., 1887-94. Died Sept. 1, 1896.

HOLLY, Henry Hudson, architect. Practiced as architect in partnership with Horatio F. Jelliff, N.Y.C., after 1887; known to have designed Va. Mil. Inst., Lexington, St. Luke's Meml. Hall at U. of South, Sewanee, Tenn., and a palatial residence in Colo. Author: Country Seats, 1863; Church Architecture, 1871. Died Sept. 1892.

HOLMAN, Jesse Lynch, jurist, legislator; b. Danville, Ky., Oct. 24, 1784; s. Henry and Jane Holman; m. Elizabeth Masterson, circa 1807. Wrote and published Errors of Education (under auspices Henry Clay), 2 vols., 1804; pros. atty. Dearborn County (Ind.), 1811; elected to Ind. Territorial Legislature, 1814, became speaker; circuit judge Indian Territory, 1814-16; U.S. dist. judge for Ind., 1834-42; a founder Ind. U.; founder Franklin Coll. Died Aurora, Ind., Mar. 28, 1842.

HOLMAN, William Steele, congressman; b. Aurora, Ind., Sept. 6, 1822; s. Jesse Lynch and Elizabeth (Masterson) H.; attended Franklin (Ind.) Coll. 1840-42; m. Abigail Knopp, circa 1842. Probate judge Dearborn County (Ind.), 1843-46, pros. atty., 1847-49; del. Ind. Constl. Conv., 1850; mem. Ind. Legislature, 1851-52; judge Ind. Ct. of Common Pleas, 1852-56; mem. U.S. Ho. of Reps. from Ind., 36th-38th, 40th-45th, 47th-53d, 55th congresses, 1859-65, 67-77, 81-95, 97. Died Washington, D.C., Apr. 22, 1897; buried Veraestau Cemetery, Aurora.

HOLME, Thomas, surveyor, mapmaker, colonial legislator; b. Waterford, Ireland, 1624; 5 children. Came to Am., 1682; on arrival in Province of Pa., apptd. by William Penn as one of his councillors, sitting with lord propr. in his 1st ct., 1682, and 1st council, Phila., 1683; surveyor gen. Pa., 1682, laid out city of Phila.; mem. 1st assembly Phila.; mem. Pa. Provincial Council, 1683-86, acting pres., acting gov., 1685, 86; noted for maps Province of Pennsylvania, 1687, Portraiture of the City of Philadelphia (1st map of city), 1683. Died Phila., Apr. 1695.

HOLMES, Abiel, clergyman, historian; b. Woodstock, Conn., Dec. 24, 1763; s. David and Temperance (Bishop) H.; grad. Yale, 1783; m. Mary Stiles, 1790; m. 2d, Sarah Wendell, Mar. 26, 1801; 5 children including Oliver Wendell. Ordained to ministry Congregational Ch., 1785; mem. faculty Yale, 1786-87; minister First Ch., Cambridge, Mass., 1792-1829; mem. Mass. Hist. Soc., 1798-1837, corr. sec., 1813-33; pastor Shepard Congl. Soc. of Cambridge, 1829-31. Author: The Life of Ezra Stiles, D.D., LL.D., 1798; The Annals of America, from the Discovery by Columbus in the Year 1492 to the Year 1826, published 1829. Died Cambridge, June 4, 1837.

HOLMES, Charles Horace, congressman; b. Albion, N.Y., Oct. 24, 1827; grad. Albany Law Sch. Admitted to N.Y. bar, 1855, began practice, Albion; mem. U.S. Ho. of Reps. (Republican) from N.Y., 41st Congress, Dec. 6, 1870; resumed law practice, Albion. Died Albion, Oct. 2, 1874; buried Mt. Albion Cemetery.

HOLMES, David, senator, gov. Miss.; b. York County, Pa., Mar. 10, 1769; s. Joseph and Rebecca (Hunter) H. Admitted to Va. bar, 1791; commonwealth's atty. Rockingham County (Va.), 1793-97; mem. U.S. Ho. of Reps. from Va., 5th-10th congresses, 1797-1809; gov. Territory of Miss., 1809-17; del. Miss. Constl. Conv., 1817; gov. Miss., 1817-20, Jan.-July, 1826; mem. U.S. Senate from Miss., Aug. 30, 1820-Sept. 25, 1825. Died nr. Winchester, Va., Aug. 20, 1832; buried Mt. Hebron Cemetery, Winchester.

HOLMES, Edward, music critic, author; b. nr. London, Eng., 1797; studied with V. Novello. Became a piano tchr.; visited Germany, 1827, published A Ramble among the Musicians of Germany, 1828; became music critic The Atlas; wrote The Life of Mozart, 1845; contbd. articles to musical Times, other jours.; came to Am., 1849, engaged as editor and music critic; other works include: Life of Purcell; Analytical and Thematic Index of Mozart's Piano-works. Died U.S., Aug. 28, 1859.

HOLMES, Elias Bellows, congressman; b. Fletcher, Vt., May 22, 1807; attended St. Albans (Vt.) Acad.; studied law, Pittsford, N.Y. Admitted to N.Y. bar, 1830; began practice in Brockport; engaged in farming, transp. bus.; ran canal packets between Rochester and Buffalo (N.Y.), 1840-55; a promoter, dir. Rochester & Niagara Falls R.R.; mem. U.S. Ho. of Reps. (Whig) from N.Y., 29th-30th congresses, 1845-49; resumed farming. Died Brockport, July 31, 1866; buried City Cemetery, Brockport.

HOLMES, Ezekiel, agriculturalist; b. Kingston, Mass., Aug. 24, 1801; s. Nathaniel and Asenath (Chandler) H.; grad. Brown U., 1821; M.D., Bowdoin Coll., 1824; m. Sarah E. Benson, Aug. 14, 1825, 2 children. Practiced medicine in Me.; discovered great tourmaline desposit on Mt. Mica, Me., 1823; instr. in agr. Gardiner Lyceum, 1825-29, prin., 1829-32; lectr. chemistry, mineralogy, botany and geology Colby Coll., 1833-37; founder and editor Kennebec Farmer and Jour. of the Useful Arts (1st newspaper in Me. devoted to sci. study of agr.), 1833-65; a founder Me. Bd. Agr., 1852, sec., 1852-55; a founder Me. Agrl. Soc., 1855, sec., 1855-65; mem. Me. Legislature, 1835-39, 50, Me. Senate, 1840-41; a founder U. Me., 1865. Author: Report of an Exploration and Survey of the Territory on the Aroostook River during the Spring and Autumn of 1838. Died Feb. 9, 1865.

HOLMES, Gabriel, gov. N.C., congressman; b. nr. Clinton, N.C, 1769; attended Harvard; studied law, Raleigh, N.C. Admitted to N.C. bar, 1790, began practice in Clinton; mem. N.C. Ho. of Commons, 1794-95, N.C. Senate, 1797-1802, 12-13; gov. N.C., 1821-24; mem. U.S. Ho. of Reps. from N.C., 19th-21st congresses, 1825-29. Died nr. Clinton, Sept. 26, 1829; buried family burial plot.

HOLMES, George Frederick, educator, coll. pres.; b. Staebrock, Brit. Guiana, Aug. 2, 1820; s. Joseph Henry and Mary Anne (Pemberton) H.; D.C.L., U. Durham (Eng.), 1891; m. Eliza Floyd, circa 1844. Admitted to S.C. bar, 1842; writer for So. Literary Messenger, 1843; prof. ancient langs. U. Richmond, 1845; prof. history, and polit. economy Coll. William and Mary, 1847; chosen 1st pres. U. Miss., 1848; with U. Va., 1857-97, became prof. history and lit., 1857, prof. hist. science, including polit. economy, 1882, prof. polit. economy and science of society, 1889. Died Charlotteville, Va., Nov. 4, 1897; buried Sweet Springs, Va.

HOLMES, Isaac Edward, congressman; b. Charleston, S.C., Apr. 6, 1796; s. John Bee and Elizabeth (Edwards) H.; grad. Yale, 1815; m. Mary Fisher Holmes, 1818. Admitted to S.C. bar, 1818; a founder S.C. Assn. (orgn. for countering abolitionist influences from North), 1823; mem. S.C. Ho. of Reps., 1826-33; mem. U.S. Ho. of Reps. from S.C., 26th-31st congresses, 1839-51, chmn. com. on naval affairs, 1846-47; delivered meml. address for John Quincy Adams, 1848; practiced law, San Francisco, 1851-54, 57-61; returned to S.C., 1861; commr. from S.C. to confer with U.S. Govt. concerning provisional govt., 1865. Died Charleston, Feb. 24, 1867; buried Circular Churchyard, Charleston.

HOLMES, Israel, brass mfr.; b. Waterbury, Conn., Dec. 19, 1800; s. Israel and Sarah (Judd) H.; m. Ardelia Hayden, 6 children. Became partner (with Horace Hotchkiss) in mfg. hats, Augusta, Ga., circa 1818; became one of 7 partners firm Holmes & Hotchkiss, mfrs. of sheet brass and wire (1st venture of its kind in U.S.), 1830; went to Eng., 1831, returned with 1st wire drawing and tube-making machinery seen in U.S.; founder Wolcottville Brass Co. (1st U.S. firm to employ battery process in mfg. brass kettles), 1833; pres. Waterbury Brass Co., 1845-53; organizer Holmes, Booth & Haydens (1st U.S. co. to both roll and manufacture brass on large scale), 1853-69; leader in constrn. Naugatuck R.R.; mem. Conn. Legislature from Torrington, 1839, from Waterbury, 1870. Died July 15, 1874.

HOLMES, John, senator; b. Kingston, Mass., Mar. 14, 1773; s. Melatiah and Elizabeth (Bradford) H.; attended R.I. Coll. (now Brown U.), 1796; m. Sally Brooks, Sept. 22, 1800; m. 2d, Caroline F. Swan, July 31, 1837. Admitted to Mass. bar, 1799; mem. Mass. Gen. Ct. (Federalist), 1802, 03; mem. Mass. Senate (Democrat), 1813, 14; commr. under Treaty of Ghent (to divide islands of Passamaquoddy Bay between U.S. and Gt. Britain), 1814-15; mem. U.S. Ho. of Reps. from Mass., 15th-16th congresses, 1817-Mar. 15, 1820; del. to Brunswick Conv. for separation of Me. from Mass., 1816; mem. U.S. Senate from Me., June 13, 1820-27, Jan. 15, 1829-33; mem. Me. Ho. of Reps., 1835-38; U.S. dist. atty. for Me., 1841-43. Author: The Statesman, 1840. Died Portland, Me., July 7, 1843; buried Eastern Cemetery, Portland.

HOLMES, Oliver Wendell, physician, poet, educator; b. Cambridge, Mass., Aug. 29, 1809; s. Rev. Abiel and Sarah (Wendell) H.; grad. Harvard, 1829, M.D., 1836; LL.D. (hon.), Cambridge (Eng.) U, 1887, Oxford (Eng.) U., 1887; m. Amelia Lee Jackson, June 15, 1840, 3 children including Chief Justice Oliver Wendell. Wrote poem Old Ironsides which caused preservation of U.S.S. Constitution, 1830; winner Boylston prize for med. essay, 1836; prof. anatomy Dartmouth, 1838-40; Parkman prof. anatomy and physiology Harvard Med. Sch., 1847-82, dean, 1847-53, prof. emeritus, 1882-94; established Atlantic Monthly, 1857, contbd. essays noted for humor and common sense later published as The Autocrat of the Breakfast-table, 1858, The Professor at the Breakfast-table, 1860, The Poet at the Breakfast-table, 1872, Pages from an Old Volume of Life, 1883, Over the Teacups, 1891; mem. Saturday Club (also included James Russell Lowell, Louis Agassiz, William Wadsworth Longfellow, Ralph Waldo Emerson, others); poems The Chambered Nautilus, The Deacon's Masterpiece or, The Wonderful One-Hoss Shay included in Poems, 1836; other works include Songs in Many Keys, 1862; Songs of Many Seasons, 1875; The Iron Gate and Other Poems, 1880; Before the Curfew and Other Poems, 1887. Author: novels including Elsie Venner, 1861; The Guardian Angel, 1867; A Mortal Antipathy, 1885 (novels were anti-Calvinist, dealt with med. problems, were ahead of their time in understanding of psychology). Died Boston, Oct. 7, 1894.

HOLMES, Sidney Tracy, congressman; b. Schaghticoke, N.Y., Aug. 14, 1815; grad. Morrisville (N.Y.) Acad. Taught sch.; civil engr. on Chenango and Black River canals, 5 years; admitted to N.Y. bar, 1841, began practice in Morrisville; loan commr. Madison County (N.Y.), 1848-51, judge and surrogate, 1851-64; mem. U.S. Ho. of Reps. (Republican) from N.Y., 39th Congress, 1865-67; resumed law practice, Morrisville, later in Utica, N.Y., until 1872, Bay City Mich., 1872-90. Died Bay City, Jan. 16, 1890; buried Cedar St. Cemetery, Morrisville.

HOLMES, Theophilus Hunter, army officer; b. Sampson County, N.C., Nov. 13, 1804; s. Gov. Gabriel H. and Mary (Hunter) H.; grad. U.S. Mil. Acad., 1829; m. Laura Wetmore, 1841. Served as 2d lt. U.S. Army on frontier duty in La., Ark. and Indian lands, 1830-36; served in Mexican War; in command of recruiting Governor's Island, N.Y., 1859-61; commd. brig. gen. Confederate Army, in command of brigade at Aquia Creek, Va., June 5, 1861; in command brigade at 1st Battle of Bull Run; fought in N. Va. campaign; maj. gen. in command div. under Magruder's command in Battle of Seven Days before Richmond; served as lt. gen. at Battle of Vicksburg, 1862. Died nr. Fayetteville, N.C., June 21, 1880.

HOLMES, Uriel, congressman; b. East Haddam, Conn., Aug. 26, 1764; grad. Yale, 1784; studied law. Admitted to Conn. bar, 1798, began practice in Litchfield; mem. Conn. Ho. of Reps., 1803-05; pros. atty. Litchfield County (Conn.), 1807-14; judge Litchfield County Ct., 1814-17; mem. U.S. Ho. of Reps. (Federalist) from N.Y., 15th Congress, 1817-18. Died Canton, Conn., May 18, 1827; buried East Cemetery, Litchfield.

HOLSEY, Hopkins, congressman; b. nr. Lynchburg, Va., Aug. 25, 1779; attended U. Va.; grad. Litchfield (Conn.) Law Sch. Admitted to the bar; began law practice, Hamilton, Ga.; mem. Ga. Ho. of Reps. from Hancock County, several years; mem. U.S. Ho. of Reps. (Union Democrat) from Ga., 24th-25th congresses, Oct. 5, 1835-39; publisher So. Banner, Athens, Ga.; unsuccessful candidate for U.S. Congress, 1852; resumed practice of law, Butler, Ga. Died "Brightwater," nr. Butler, Mar. 31, 1859; buried "Brightwater."

HOLST, Edvard, composer; b. Copenhagen, Denmark, 1843. Came to U.S., circa 1874, settled in N.Y.C.; engaged as actor, stage-dancer, dancing master, playwright; composer numerous songs, pianoforte pieces, pieces for mil. band, including Marine Band March, Battle of Manila; composed comic opera Our Flats, produced in N.Y.C., 1897; compositions total over 2,000 works. Died N.Y.C., Jan. 1899.

HOLT, Edwin Michael, mfr.; b. Orange County, N.C., Jan. 14, 1807; s. Michael and Rachel (Rainey) H.; m. Emily Farish, Sept. 30, 1828, 10 children. Founder cotton mfg. firm Holt & Carrigan (became one of largest cotton mills in South), 1837; dir. N.C. R.R.; established Comml. Nat. Bank of Charlotte; one of wealthiest men in N.C. Died May 15, 1884.

HOLT, Hines, congressman; b. nr. Milledgeville, Ga., Apr. 27, 1805; grad. Franklin Coll. (now U. Ga.), 1824; studied law. Admitted to Ga. bar, began practice in Columbus; mem. U.S. Ho. of Reps. (Whig) from Ga., 26th Congress, Feb. 1-Mar. 3, 1841; resumed law practice; mem. Ga. Senate, 1859; mem. 1st Confederate Ho. of Reps., 1862-64; del. Ga. Constl. Conv., 1865. Died Milledgeville, Nov. 4, 1865; buried Linwood Cemetery, Columbus.

HOLT, John, publisher; b. Williamsburg, Va., 1721; m. Elizabeth Hunter, 1749. Began Conn. Gazette (1st paper printed in Conn.), 1755; jr. partner James Parker & Co., published New York Gazette and Weekly Post-Boy, 1760, published journal intermittently and under several names, 1763-83; published Virginia Gazette or Norfolk Intelligencer, 1775. Died N.Y.C., Jan. 30, 1784; buried St. Paul's Churchyard, N.Y.C.

HOLT, Joseph, judge adv. gen.; b. Breckenridge County, Ky., Jan. 6, 1807; s. John and Eleanor (Stephens) H.; ed. St. Joseph's Coll., Centre Coll.; m. Mary Harrison; 2d, Margaret Wickliffe. Commonwealth's atty. for 4th Louisville (Ky.) dist., 1833-35; U.S. commr. patents, 1857-59; U.S. postmaster gen., 1859-61; apptd. U.S. sec. of war, 1861; judge adv. gen. U.S. Army, 1862-75, prosecuted Clement Vallandigham, John Wilkes Booth and compatriots for assassination of Pres. Lincoln. Died Washington, D.C., Aug. 1, 1894.

HOLT, Orrin, congressman; b. Willington, Conn., Mar. 13, 1792. Engaged in farming; mem. Conn. Ho. of Reps., 1830-32, Conn. Senate, 1835-36; mem. U.S. Ho. of Reps. (Democrat) from Conn., 24th-25th congresses, Dec. 5, 1836-39; active Conn. mil. orgns., served as insp. gen. Died East Willington, June 20, 1855; buried Old Cemetery, Willington Hill, Conn.

HOLTEN, Samuel, physician, congressman, jurist; b. Salem Village (now Danvers), Mass., June 9, 1738; s. Samuel and Hannah (Gardner) H.; m. Mary Warner, Mar. 30, 1758. Began practice of medicine, Gloucester, Mass., circa 1756; practiced in Danvers, 1758; mem. Mass. Gen. Ct., 1768-76; mem. Mass. provincial congresses, 1774, 75; abandoned Med., profession, 1775 mem. Mass. Com. of Safety, 1776, mem.; Continental Congress from Mass., 1778-80, 82-83, 84-85, 86-87 Mass. mem.; Senate, 1787; an incorporator Mass. Med. Soc., 1781; signer Articles of Confederation; mem. U.S. Ho. Reps. from Mass., 3d Congress, 1793-95; judge Essex County (Mass.) Probate Ct., 1796-1815. Died Danvers, Jan. 2, 1816; buried Holten Cemetery, Danvers.

HOLYOKE, Edward Augustus, physician; b. Marblehead, Mass., Aug. 1, 1728; s. Rev. Edward and Margaret (Appleton) H.; grad. Harvard, 1746, M. D. (hon.), 1783, LL.D. (hon.), 1815; m. Judith Pickman, June 1755; m. 2d, Mary Viall, Nov. 22, 1758; 12 children. Practiced medicine, Salem, Mass., 1749-1821; in charge of smallpox hosp. in Salem during epidemic, 1777; a pioneer in smallpox vaccination in U.S.; taught medicine privately; a founder Mass. Med. Soc., pres., 1782-84, 86-87; a founder Am. Acad. Arts and Scis., pres., 1814-20; a founder Essex Hist. Soc., pres., 1821-29. Died Salem, Mar. 31, 1829.

HOLYOKE, Samuel, educator, composer; b. Boxford, Mass., Oct. 15, 1762; s. Rev. Elizur and Hannah (Peabody) H.; grad. Harvard, 1789. Organizer, Groton (now Lawrence) Acad., Groton, Mass., 1793; composed Arnheim (his 1st tune), 1777, Harmonica Americana, 1791; compiler Christian Harmonist (collection of tunes), 1804, Columbian Repository (largest collection of tunes published up to that time), 1809. Author: The Istrumental Assistant, 2 vols., 1800-07. Died East Concord, N.H., Feb. 21, 1820.

HOMES, Henry Augustus, missionary, librarian; b. Boston, Mar. 10, 1812; s. Henry and Dorcas (Freeman) H.; grad. Amherst Coll., 1830; attended Andover Theol. Sem., 1831-32, Yale, 1832-34; m. Anna Whiting Heath, Apr. 15, 1841. Ordained by Église Reformée, Paris, France, 1835; did missionary work in Turkey, 1836-54; interpreter, chargé d' affaires Am. legation, Constantinople, 1851-53; asst. librarian N.Y. State Library, 1854-62, chief librarian, 1862-87; author pamphlets and papers "Observations on the Design and Import of Metals," "The Palatine Emigration to England in 1709," "The Correct Arms of the State of New York," 1880. Died Nov. 3, 1887.

HONE, Philip, businessman, mayor N.Y.C.; b. N.Y.C., Oct. 25, 1780; m. Catharine Duncomb, Oct. 1, 1801, 6 children. Became partner in his brother John's action business, N.Y.C., 1789, ret. with fortune of over half-million dollars, 1821; mayor N.Y.C., 1825; local leader Whig Party; trustee Columbia, Merc. Library; supported Delaware & Hudson Canal; maintained diary which is one of best extant records of contemporary life, 1828-51. Died May 5, 1851.

HONEYWELL, Miss M.A., silhouettist; b. probably Lempster, N.H., circa 1787. Born with no hands and only 3 toes on one foot; learned to make paper cut-outs and silhouettes, embroider and write with her mouth and toes; had career as prodigy, 1806-circa 1848, in Salem, Mass., Charleston, S.C., and Louisville, Ky.

HOOD, John Bell, army officer; b. Bath County, Ga., June 1, 1831; s. Dr. John and Theodocia (French) H.; grad. U.S. Mil. Acad., 1853; m. Anna Marie Hennen, 1868, 10 children. Cavalry instr. U.S. Mil. Acad., 1859-60; commd. 1st lt. in charge of cavalry under Gen. John B. Magruder, Confederate Army, 1861; brig. gen. in command of Tex. Brigade, led at battles of Gaine's Mill, 2d Bull Run and Antietam, 1862; wounded at Battle of Gettysburg, 1863; directed corps and 3 divs. Army of Tenn. at Battle of Chickamauga; commd. lt. gen. in command of corps under Joseph E. Johnston, 1864; tried to stop Sherman, but lost in battles at Atlanta, Franklin and Nashville; gave up his command, Jan. 1865, surrendered, May 1865; became commn. mcht., New Orleans, after Civil War. Died New Orleans, Aug. 30, 1879; buried New Orleans.

HOOD, Washington, topog. engr.; b. Phila., Feb. 2, 1808; s. John McClellan and Eliza Forebaugh) H.; grad. U.S. Mil. Acad., 1827. Commd. 2d lt. 4th Inf., U.S. Army, 1827, on topog. duty, 1831-36, commd 1st lt., 1835, capt. Topog. Engrs., 1837; drew (with Robert E. Lee) boundary line between Ohio and Mich., 1835; drew map of Ore. which was used as part of basis for U.S. claims to that territory. Died Bedford Springs, Pa., July 17, 1840.

HOOK, Enos, congressman; b. Waynesburg, Pa., Dec. 3, 1804: studied law. Admitted to Pa. bar, 1826, began practice in Waynesburg; mem. Pa. Ho. of Reps., 1837-38; mem. U.S. Ho. of Reps. (Democrat) from Pa., 26th-27th congresses, 1839-Apr. 18, 1841. Died Waynesburg, July 15, 1841; buried Green Mount Cemetery, Waynesburg.

HOOKER, Joseph (nickname Fighting Joe), army officer; b. Hadley, Mass., Nov. 13, 1814; s. Joseph and Mary (Seymour) H.; grad. U.S. Mil. Acad., 1837; m. Olivia Groesbeck, 1865. Served with U.S. Army in campaigns under Taylor and Scott in Mexican War, 1846-48; served in Florida War, 1836-43; supt. mil. roads in Ore., 1858-59; commd. col. Cal. Militia, 1859-61; commd. brig. gen. U.S. Volunteers, aided in defense of Washington (D.C.), 1861; leader div. in Peninsular Campaign, 1862; in command 1st Corps in Md. Campaign, 1862, wounded at Battle of Antietam, promoted brig. gen. U.S. Army, fought at Battle of Fredricksburg; comdr. Army of Potomac, 1863, failed to take initiative at Battle of Chancellorsville, resulting in Union retreat, 1863; brevetted maj. gen. U.S. Army at Battle of Lookout Mountain, Nov. 24, 1863; comdr. 11th and 12th Corps under Gen. Thomas and Gen. Sherman, battles of Mill Creek Expdn., Pasaca, Cassville, New Hope Church, Pine Mountain and siege of Atlanta; in command No. Dept., Cincinnati, 1864, Dept. of East, N.Y.C., 1865, Dept. of the Lakes, Detroit, 1866. Died Garden City, N.Y., Oct. 31, 1879; buried Laurel Grove Cemetery, Cincinnati.

HOOKER, Philip, builder, architect, surveyor, city ofcl.; b. Rutland, Mass., Oct. 28, 1766; s. Samuel and Rachel (Hinds) H: M. Sarah Monk, 1814. Apptd. to Common Council of Albany (N.Y.), 1818-21, city supt., 1821-27, city surveyor, 1819-32; designed (and in some cases, built) 6 churches, N.Y. State Capitol, City Hall, 2 municipal markets, 2 acads., theater in Albany, also 2d Union Coll. Bldg., steeple and front of Hamilton Coll. Chapel, 1797-1830. Died Albany, Jan. 31, 1836.

HOOKER, Thomas, clergyman, colonist; b. Marfield, Eng., circa 1586; s. Thomas Hooker; attended Queen's Coll., Cambridge (Eng.) U., A.B., Emmanuel Coll., 1608, A.M., 1611; m. Susanna, at least 3 children. Ordained to ministry Congregational Ch.; rector, Eshor, Surrey, Eng., circa 1620; preacher St. Mary's, Chelmsford, Eng., circa 1626; scheduled to appear before High Commn. (spiritual ct.), 1630, fled to Holland, soon returned to Eng.; came to Boston, 1633, became pastor at Newtown (now Cambridge), Mass., 1633; moved to and founded Conn. (with majority of congregation), 1636; his democratic ideas form the basis of "Fundamental Orders" (constn. of Conn.), adopted 1639. Author: A Survey of the Summe of Churchdiscipline (preface contains statement of principles of Congregationalism in Am.), 1648. Died Hartford, Conn., July 19, 1647.

HOOKER, William, engraver, flourished 1804-46. An artist who made maps for Pinkerton's Modern Geography, 1804; executed copperplate engraving of Wolfe Tavern for the proprs., 1807; assisted in prodn. of Blunt's Stranger's Guide to City of New York, 1817; published New Pocket Plan of the City of New York, 1824; did chart of Atlantic Ocean, 1831.

HOOKER, Worthington, physician, author; b. Springfield, Mass., Mar. 3, 1806; s. John and Sarah (Dwight) H.; grad. Yale, 1825; M.D., Harvard, 1829; m. Mary Ingersoll, Sept. 30, 1830; m. 2d, Henrietta Edwards, Jan. 31, 1855. Prof. theory and practice of medicine Med. Instn. of Yale Coll., 1852-67; a dir. Conn. Hosp. Soc.; v.p. A.M.A., 1864 Author: Physician and Patient, 1849; Homoeopathy, 1852; Human Physiology for Colleges and Schools, 1854; Rational Therapeutics, 1857. Died New Haven, Conn., Nov. 6, 1867.

HOOKS, Charles, congressman; b. Bertie County, N.C., Feb. 20, 1768. Engaged in planting, N.C.; mem. N.C. Ho. of Commons, 1801-05, N.C. Senate, 1810-11; mem. U.S. Ho. of Reps. (Democrat) from N.C., 14th, 16th-18th congresses, Dec. 2, 1816-17, 19-25; engaged in planting, nr. Montgomery, Ala. Died nr. Montgomery, Oct. 18, 1843; buried Molton family cemetery, nr. Montgomery.

HOOPER, Johnson Jones, author; b. Wilmington, N.C., June 9, 1815; s. Archibald and Charlotte (De Berniere) H.; m. Miss Brantley. Solicitor, 9th Ala. Jud. Circuit, 1849-53; editor The Mail, Montgomery, Ala., 1853-61; known as a humorist. Author: Some Adventures of Captain Simon Suggs, Late of the Tallapoosa Volunteers, 1846; The Widow Rugby's Husband, A Night at the Ugly Man's and Other Tales of Alabama, 1851; Dog and Gun, A Few Loose Chapters on Shooting, 1858. Died June 7, 1862.

HOOPER, Lucy Hamilton, journalist; b. Phila., Jan. 20, 1835; dau. of Battalle Muse Jones; m. Robert M. Hooper, 1854, 2 children. Asso. editor of Our Daily Fare, 1864; an editor Lippincott's Mag., 1868; lived in Paris, France (where her husband was Am. consul-gen.), 1874-93; contbd. to Lippincott's Mag., Appleton's Journal, Phila. Evening Telegraph. Author: Poems: with Translations from the German of Geibel and Others, 1864; Poems, 1871; Under the Tricolor; or the American Colony in Paris, 1880; The Tsar's Window, 1881. Died Paris, Aug. 31, 1893; buried Pére-Lachaise Cemetery, Paris.

HOOPER, Samuel, mcht., congressman; b. Marblehead, Mass., Feb. 3, 1808; s. John and Eunice (Hooper) H.; m. Anne Sturges, 1832. Became jr. partner in father-in-law's shipping firm, 1832; joined importing firm William Appleton & Co. (became Samuel Hooper & Co., 1862), 1843; dir. Mchts.' Bank of Boston, Eastern R.R. Co.; mem. Mass. Ho. of Reps., 1851-54, Mass. Senate, 1858; mem. U.S. Ho. of Reps. from Mass., 37th-43d congresses, Dec. 2, 1861-Feb. 14, 1875. Author: Currency or Money, 1855; An Examination of the Theory and the Effect of Laws Regulating the Amount of Specie in Banks, 1860. Died Washington, D.C., Feb. 14, 1875; buried Oak Hill Cemetery, Washington.

HOOPER, William, Continental congressman; b. Boston, June 17, 1742; s. Rev. William and Marie (Dennie) H.; grad. Harvard, 1760; m. Anne Clark, 1767; children— William, Thomas, Elizabeth. Admitted to Mass. bar, 1764; dep. atty. gen. N.C.; mem. N.C. Gen. Assembly, 1773; del. to Continental Congress, 1774-77; speaker Hillsboro and Halifax (N.C.) convs., 1776; signer Declaration of Independence, Aug. 2, 1776; borough mem. N.C. Ho. of Commons, 1777-82, 84; one of U.S. commrs. who decided territorial rights controversy between N.Y. and N.J., 1786. Died Hillsboro, N.C., Oct. 14, 1790; buried Guilford Battle Ground, N.C.

HOOPER, William Henry, territorial ofcl., businessman; b. Cambridge, Md., Dec. 25, 1813; attended common schs. Engaged in merc. bus.; moved to Galena, Ill., 1835, engaged in trade on Mississippi River; moved to Salt Lake City, Utah, 1850; sec. Utah Territory, 1857-58; del. U.S. Congress from Utah Territory, 1859-61; engaged in merc. bus., mining, Salt Lake City; supt. Zion's Co-op. Merc. Instn., 1873-77, pres., 1877-82; pres. Deseret Nat. Bank, Salt Lake City, 1872-82. Died Salt Lake City, Dec. 30, 1882; buried Salt Lake City Cemetery.

HOPE, James, artist; b. Drygrange, Roxboroughshire, Scotland, Nov. 29, 1818/19; attended Castleton (Vt.) Sem. Brought to Can.; apprenticed to wagonmaker, Fairhaven, Vt.; began portrait painting, West Rutland, Vt., 1843; painted portraits, Montreal, Que., Can., 1844-46; taught at Castleton Sem.; began painting landscapes; served in Civil War; made numerous studies which he later developed into a series of large battle paintings, exhibited throughout country after Civil War; lived in Watkins Glen, N.Y., after 1872, painted landscapes. Died Watkins Glen, 1892.

HOPE, James Barron, poet; b. Norfolk, Va., Mar. 23, 1829; s. Wilton and Jane (Barron) H.; grad. Coll. William and Mary, 1847; m. Anne Beverly Whiting, 1857. Sec. to Commodore Samuel Barron (his uncle), 1848-51; practiced law; commonwealth atty. Va., 1856; served to maj. Confederate Army during Civil War; journalist with Norfolk Day Book and Norfolk Virginian, after Civil War; editor Norfolk Landmark, 1873-87; supt. Norfolk Pub. Schs., 1885. Author: Leoni di Monta and Other Poems, 1857; A Collection of Poems, 1859; Little Stories for Little People, 1874; Under the Empire, 1878; Arms and the Man (in celebration of Cornwallis' surrender at Yorktown), 1882. Died Norfolk, Sept. 15, 1887.

HOPKINS, Arthur Francis, jurist; b. Pittsylvania County, Va., Oct. 18, 1794; s. James and Frances (Carter) H.; ed. U. N.C.; m. Pamela Thorpe Mosley, 1815; m. 2d, Juliet Opie, 1854. Admitted to Va. bar, 1814; mem. 1st Ala. Constl. Conv., 1819; mem. Ala. Senate, 1822-24; chief justice Ala. Supreme Ct., 1834; temporary chmn. Whig Nat. Conv., 1844; pres. Mobile & Ohio R.R., 1855. Died Mobile, Ala., Nov. 10, 1865.

HOPKINS, Benjamin Franklin, congressman; b. Hebron, N.Y., Apr. 22, 1829; attended common schs. Telegraph operator; moved to Madison, Wis., 1849; pvt. sec. to gov. Wis., 1856-57; mem. Wis. Senate, 1862-63, Wis. Assembly, 1866; mem. U.S. Ho. of Reps. (Republican) from Wis., 40th-41st congresses, 1867-70. Died Madison, Jan. 1, 1870; buried Forest Hill Cemetery, Madison.

HOPKINS, Edward, colonial gov.; b. Shrewsbury, Eng., 1600; s. Edmund and Katherine (Lello) H.; m. Ann Yale. Mem. Davenport's Puritan colony, 1637; asst. gov. Conn., 1639-42, 55-56, gov., 1644, 46, 50, 52, 54, dep. gov., 1643, 45, 47, 49, 51, 53; commr. to New Eng. Confederation, 1644; mem. English Parliament, 1656 (while serving as asst. gov. Conn.). Died London, Eng., Mar. 1657.

HOPKINS, Edward Augustus, diplomat, transp. promoter; b. Pitts., Nov. 29, 1822; s. Rt. Rev. John Henry Hopkins and Melusina (Muller) H.; m. Jeanne Arnaud de la Coste, Mar. 24, 1858; m. 2d, Marie Antoinette de Renthel, Marquise de Sainte Croix Molay, Apr. 27, 1888. Apptd. spl. U.S. agt. to report on recognition of Paraguay, 1845; commd. U.S. consul to Paraguay, 1853; established steam navigation on Parana River, built steam ry. between Buenos Aires and San Fernando, Argentina; sent by Argentina as consul gen. to N.Y., 1864; sec. Argentine delegation to Intercontinental R.R. Commn., 1890-91. Died Washington, D.C., June 10, 1891.

HOPKINS, Edward Jerome, musician; b. Burlington, Vt., Apr. 4, 1836; attended U. Vt., N.Y. Med. Coll. Organist for various churches, N.Y.C., until 1869; founder The Am. Music Assn. for performing native works, 1856; founded and supported N.Y. Orpheon Free Schs., 1865-87; founder, editor N.Y. Philharmonic Jour., 1868-85; originated Lecture-Concerts, made many concert-tours in U.S., Eng.; composed over 700 works; published 2 collections of ch. music, also Orpheon Class-book. Died Athenia, N.J., Nov. 4, 1898.

HOPKINS, Esek, 1st comdr.-in-chief Continental Navy; b. Scituate, R.I., Apr. 26, 1718; s. William and Ruth (Wilkinson) H.; m. Desire Burroughs, Nov. 28, 1741, 10 children. Privateer during French and Indian Wars; brig. gen. in charge all mil. forces of R.I., 1775; became comdr.-in-chief Continental Navy, 1775, met difficulties in equipping and manning the few Am. ships available, censured by Congress for failure, 1776, suspended from command, 1777, dismissed 1778; dep. to R.I. Gen. Assembly, 1779-86; collector imposts, 1783; trustee Brown U., 1782-1802. Died North Providence, R.I., Feb. 26, 1802.

HOPKINS, George Washington, congressman; b. nr. Goochland Court House, Va., Feb. 22, 1804; attended common schs.; studied law. Admitted to Va. bar, 1834, began practice in Lebanon; mem. Va. Ho. of Dels., 1833-35, 50-51, 59-61; mem. U.S. Ho. of Reps. (Democrat) from Va., 24th-29th, 35th congresses, 1835-47, 57-59; chargé d'affaires to Portugal, 1847-49; mem. Va. Constl. Conv., 1850-51; judge circuit ct. Died Richmond, Va., Mar. 1, 1861; buried Sinking Springs Cemetery, Abingdon, Va.

HOPKINS, James Campbell, judge; b. Rutland County, Vt., Apr. 27, 1819; s. Ervin Hopkins; m. Mary Allen, 1845; m. 2d, Cordelia Bradley. Admitted to N.Y. bar, 1845; postmaster Granville (N.Y.), 5 years; mem. N.Y. Senate, 1853; U.S. judge of U.S. Court for Western dist. Wis., 1870-77; prof. U. Wis. Law Sch., 1877. Died Sept. 3, 1877.

HOPKINS, John Burroughs, naval officer; b. Providence, R.I., Aug. 25, 1742; s. Esek and Desire (Burroughs) H.; m. Sarah Harris, Oct. 2, 1768. Took part in burning of Brit. ship Gaspee, 1772; apptd. capt. ship Cabot, 1775; took command ship Warren, 1777; captured Brit. ships Jason and Hibernia, 1779, dismissed from command because of irregularities in his conduct on this cruise; commanded privateers, 1780-81. Died Dec. 5, 1796.

HOPKINS, John Henry, clergyman; b. Dublin, Ireland, Jan. 30, 1792; s. Thomas and Elizabeth (Fitzakerly) H.; D.C.L., Oxford (Eng.) U., 1867; m. Melusina Muller, May 8, 1816, 13 children. Admitted to Pa. bar, 1818; rector Trinity Episcopal Ch., Pitts., 1823; asst. minister Trinity Ch., Boston, 1831; helped open divinity sch., Cambridge, Mass.; elected 1st Protestant Episcopal bishop Vt., 1832; presiding bishop Protestant Episcopal Ch. (helped in reunion of Southern Branch), 1865-68. Author: Christianity Vindicated, 1833; The Primitive Creed, 1834; The Primitive Church, 1835; The Church of Rome in her Primitive Purity, 1837; The History of the Confessional, 1850; The End of Controversy Controverted, 1854; The American Citizen, 1857; A Scriptural, Historical and Ecclasiastical View of Slavery, 1864; The Law of Ritualism, 1866. Died Rock Point, Vt., Jan. 9, 1868.

HOPKINS, John Henry, Jr., lithographer, clergyman; b. Pitts., Oct. 28, 1820; s. John Henry Hopkins; grad. U. Vt., 1839; attended Gen. Theol. Sem., N.Y.C. Assisted his father in publishing series of Vermont Drawing Books; taught sch., Savannah, Ga., 2 years; editor Church Jour., 1853-68; rector Episcopal Ch., Plattsburgh, N.Y., 1872-76, Williamsport, Pa., 1876-87. Author: Champion of the Cross,

Being the Life of John Henry Hopkins (biography of his father). Died Troy, N.Y., Aug. 14, 1891.

HOPKINS, Johns, businessman, philanthropist; b. Anne Arundel County, Md., May 19, 1795; s. Samuel and Hannah (Janney) H.; organizer wholesale grocery and commission mcht. bus., 1819, later organized (with brothers Philip, Mahlon and Gerard) firm Hopkins Bros., expanded into banking, warehousing and railroads; became dir. B. & O. R.R., 1847, chmn. finance com., 1855, became 3d largest stockholder; pres. Mchts. Bank; made will, 1870, left $7,000,000 equally divided between Johns Hopkins U. and Johns Hopkins Hosp. (to fulfill his desire to found a great hosp. and a univ. with med. sch. and tng. course for nurses in connection with hosp.; Johns Hopkins U. became 1st U.S. univ. founded upon European ideas under influence of George Peabody). Died Balt., Dec. 24, 1873.

HOPKINS, Juliet Ann Opie, nurse; b. Jefferson County, Va., May 7, 1818; d. Hierome and Margaret (Muse) Opie; m. Comdr. Alexander Gordon, 1837; m. 2d, Judge Arthur F. Hopkins, 1854. Established hosps., Richmond, Va., 1861; matron Ala. hosps.; wounded while rescuing casualties at Battle of Seven Pines; her portrait appears on 25 cent pieces and 50 dollar bills issued by Ala. during Civil War. Died Washington, D.C., Mar. 9, 1890; buried Arlington (Va.) Nat. Cemetery.

HOPKINS, Lemuel, physician, satirist; b. Waterbury, Conn., June 19, 1750; s. Stephen and Dorothy (Talmadge) H.; M.A. (hon.), Yale, 1784. Projector, asso. editor The Anarchiad; hon. mem. Mass. Med. Soc.; a founder Conn. Med. Soc.; one of group called "Hartford wits." Author: Hypocrite's Hope; The Echo; The Political Greenhouse; The Guillotine. Died Hartford, Conn., Apr. 14, 1801.

HOPKINS, Mark, clergyman, coll. pres.; b. Stockbridge, Mass., Feb. 4, 1802; s. Archibald and Mary (Curtis) H.; A.B., Williams Coll., 1824; M.D., Berkshire Med. Coll., 1829; m. Mary Hubbell, Dec. 25, 1832, 10 children. Prof. moral philosophy and rhetoric Williams Coll., 1830-37, pres., 1836-72; Licensed to preach by Am. Bd. Commrs. for Fgn. Missions, 1833, pres., 1857-87; ordained Congregational Ch., 1836; Pres. Garfield said, "The ideal college is a log, with the student at one end and Mark Hopkins at the other." Author: Lectures on the Evidences of Christianity, 1846; Lectures on Moral Sciences, 1862; The Law of Love and Love as Law, 1869; An Outline Study of Man, 1873; Strength and Beauty, 1874; The Scriptural Idea of Man, 1883. Died Williamstown, Mass., June 17, 1887.

HOPKINS, Samuel, theologian, author; b. Waterbury, Conn., Sept. 17, 1721; s. Timothy and Mary (Judd) H.; grad. Yale, 1741; m. Joanna Ingersoe, Jan. 13, 1748, 8 children. Ordained pastor, Great Barrington, Mass., 1743; minister 1st Conglist. Ch., Newport, R.I., 1770-1803; close friend of Jonathan Edward's and the two influenced each other in their theol. views; one of 1st Conglist. ministers to speak out against slavery. Author: Sin, through Divine Interposition and Advantage to the Universe, 1759; An Inquiry whether the Promises of the Gospel are made to the Exercises and Doings of Persons in the Unregenerate State, 1765; The True State and Character of the Unregenerate, 1769; An Inquiry into the Nature of True Holiness, 1773; System of Doctrines contained in Divine Revelation, 1793; A Life of Pres. Jonathan Edwards, 1796; Susannah Anthony, 1798; Mrs. Osborn, 1798; A Dialogue on the Nature and Extent of True Christian Submission, 1805. Died Newport, R.I., Dec. 20, 1803.

HOPKINS, Samuel, congressman, army officer; b. Albemarle County, Va., Apr. 9, 1753; s. Dr. Samuel and Isabella (Taylor) H.; m. Elizabeth Branch Bugg, Jan. 18, 1783. Fought under George Washington at battles of Trenton, Princeton, Monmouth, Brandywine and Germantown during Am. Revolution; served as lt. col. 10th Va. Regt. at seige of Charleston; original mem. Soc. of Cincinnati; moved to Ky., 1796; chief justice 1st Ct. Criminal Common Law and Chancery Jurisdiction in Ky., 1799-1801; mem. Ky. Ho. of Reps., 1800, 01, 03-06, Ky. Senate, 1809-13; commd. maj. gen. U.S. Army, 1812; comdr.-in-chief Western frontier; led 2000 volunteers against Kickappo Indian villages on Illinois River, 1812; mem. U.S. Ho. of Reps. from Ky., 13th Congress, 1813-15. Died Henderson, Ky., Sept. 16, 1819; buried family burial plot "Spring Garden" nr. Henderson.

HOPKINS, Samuel, clergyman; b. Northampton, Mass., Apr. 11, 1807; s. John and Lydia (Thomson) H.; grad. Dartmouth, 1827, Andover Theol. Sem., 1831; m. Caroline Dwight, May 29, 1832. Ordained to ministry Congregational Ch., 1831; served as pastor Congregational chs., Montpelier, Vt., Saco, Me., Standish, Mass. Author: Lessons at the Cross, 1854; The Youth of the Old Dominion, 1856; The Puritans; or the Court, Church, and Parliament of England during the Reigns of Edward VI and Elizabeth, 3 vols., 1859-61. Died Northampton, Feb. 10, 1887; buried Northampton.

HOPKINS, Samuel Miles, congressman; b. Salem, Conn., May 9, 1772; grad. Yale, 1791; studied law. Admitted to N.Y. bar, began practice in Le Roy, 1793; moved to N.Y.C., 1794, practiced law; mem. U.S. Ho. of Reps. from N.Y., 13th Congress, 1813-15; mem. N.Y. Assembly, 1820-21, N.Y. Senate, 1822; reporter N.Y. Ct. Chancery, 1823-26; mem. commn. to superintend constrn. of Sing Sing Prison, 1825-30; judge N. Y. Circuit Ct., 1832-36. Died Geneva, N.Y., Mar. 9, 1837; buried Washington St. Cemetery, Geneva.

HOPKINS, Stephen, colonial gov., Continental congressman; b. Providence, R.I., Mar. 7, 1707; s. William and Ruth (Wilkinson) H.; m. Sarah Scott, 1726; m. 2d, Anne Smith, 1755; 7 children. Laid out Town of Providence, 1731, town clk., 1732, pres. town council, 1735; mem. R.I. Gen. Assembly, 1732-33, 35-38, 41-42, 44-52, 69-74, 77, speaker, 1742-43; asst. justice R.I. Superior Ct., 1747-49, chief justice, 1751-55; gov. R.I., 1755-57, 58-62, 63-65, 67-68; mem. Gen. Colonial Congress, Albany, N.Y., 1754, 55, 57; a founder Providence Gazette and Country Jour., 1762 1st chancellor R.I. Coll. (now Brown U.), 1764; del. to Continental Congress, 1774-76, 78; signer Declaration of Independence, Aug. 2, 1776; del. to convs. of New Eng. states, 1776, 80; mem. Philos. Soc. of Newport (R.I.). Author: The Rights of Colonies Examined, 1765; The Grievances of the American Colonies Candidly Explained, 1765. Died Providence, Apr. 13, 1785.

HOPKINS, Stephen Tyng, congressman; b. N. Y.C., Mar. 25, 1849; attended Anthon Grammar Sch., N.Y.C. Iron mcht., broker; mem. N.Y. Assembly, 1885-86; asso. with coal and iron syndicates in W.Va. and Tenn.; mem. U.S. Ho. of Reps. (Republican) from N.Y., 50th Congress, 1887-89; watchman N.Y.C. Customhouse, 1890. Found dead by a train crew along the railroad tracks nr. Pleasantville, N.J., Mar. 3, 1892; buried Greenwood Cemetery, Bklyn.

HOPKINSON, Francis, Continental congressman; b. Phila., Oct. 2, 1737; s. Thomas and Mary (Johnson) H.; A.B., Coll. of Phila. (1st diploma granted by coll.), 1757, A.M., 1760; received hon. degree from Coll. of N..J (now Princeton), 1763; m. Ann Borden, Sept. 1, 1768, 1 son, Joseph. Began study of harpsichord, 1754, gave 1st public performance, 1757, later set poems and psalms to music; became 1st native Am. composer of secular songs, 1759; admitted to Pa. bar, 1775, N.J. bar, 1775; practiced law in Phila. and Bordentown, N.J.; apptd. collector of customs Port of Salem (N.J.), 1763, New Castle, Del., 1772; mem. N.J. Gov.'s Council, 1774, N.J. Provincial Congress, 1774-76; mem. Continental Congress, 1776, signer Declaration of Independence; mem. Continental Navy Bd., 1776-78; treas. Continental Loan Office, 1778-81; apptd. judge of admiralty for Pa., 1779, 80, 87; mem. Pa. Conv. which ratified U.S. Constn., 1787; judge U.S. Dist. Ct. for Eastern Pa., 1789-91; sec. conv. which organized Protestant Episcopal Ch., 1789; mem. com. which designed seal of Am. Philos. Soc., 1770; a designer Great Seal of N.J., 1776; designed Am. Flag, 1777; prepared seal for U. State Pa., 1782. Author: A Prophecy (essay which predicted that Am. would declare independence); Letter to Lord Howe, 1777, A Letter Written by a Foreigner, 1777, An Answer to Gen. Burgoyne's Proclamation, 1777, Letter to Joseph Galloway, 1778 (all pamphlets); The Battle of the Kegs (his most effective and popular verse), 1778; contbr. poetry and essays to Am. Mag., 1757-58, Pa. Mag., 1775-76; composer Seven Songs (1st book of music published by an Am. composer), 1788. Died Phila., May 9, 1791; buried Christ Ch. Burial Ground, Phila.

HOPKINSON, Joseph, congressman, jurist; b. Phila., Nov. 12, 1770; s. Francis and Mary (Johnson) H.; grad. U. Pa., 1786; m. Emily Mifflin. Sec. bd. trustees U. Pa., 1790-91, mem., 1806-19, 22-42; admitted to Pa. bar, 1791; wrote "Hail Columbia" at request of Gilbert Fox to tune of "The President's March," 1798; defense counsel for Justice Samuel Chase in his impeachment trial, 1804; mem. U.S. Ho. of Reps. from Pa., 14th-15th congresses, 1814-19; moved to N.J., 1819, mem. N.J. Assembly; returned to Pa.; judge U.S. Dist. Ct. for Eastern Pa., 1828-42; chmn. Pa. Constl. Conv., 1837; Died Phila., Jan. 15, 1842; buried Borden-Hopkinson Burial Ground, Bordentown, N.J.

HOPPER, Isaac Tatem, reformer; b. Deptford, N.J., Dec. 3, 1771; s. Levi and Rachel (Tatem) H.; m. Sarah Tatum, Sept. 18, 1795; m. 2d, Hannah Athmore, Feb. 1824; 10 children. Became mem. Soc. of Friends, 1793, disowned by ch. for anti-slavery activities, 1841; owner tailor shop, Phila.; agt. for Underground Ry., Phila.; mem. Pa. Abolition Soc.; moved to N.Y.C., 1829, opened bookshop there; continued to aid runaway slaves by arranging passage by sea from N.Y.C. to Boston; asso. editor Nat. Anti-Slavery Standard, 1841-45; became agt. for Prison Assn. of N.Y., 1845; active in defending persons who could not afford legal counseling, in prison reform and edn. of prisoners, and in aiding ex-convicts in readjustment to society. Died N.Y.C., May 7, 1852.

HOPPIN, Augustus, illustrator; b. Providence, R.I., July 13, 1828; s. Thomas Coles and Harriet (Jones) H.; grad. Brown U., 1848; attended Harvard Law Sch., 1848-50. Admitted to R.I. bar, 1850; abandoned law to become an illustrator; drawings appeared in many mags.; illustrated numerous books including Potiphar Papers (G. W. Curtis), 1853, Autocrat of the Breakfast Table (Oliver W. Holmes), 1858; other publs. include Hay Fever, 1873, A Fashionable Sufferer, 1883, Two Compton Boys, 1885. Author: (anonymous romance) Married for Fun, 1885. Died Flushing, L.I., N.Y., Apr. 1, 1896.

HOPPIN, William Warner, gov. R.I.; b. Providence, R.I., Sept. 1, 1807; s. Benjamin and Esther (Phillips) H.; grad. Yale, 1828, LL.D., 1830; m. Frances Street, June 26, 1832; children—Frederick, William Warner, Jr. Admitted to R.I. bar, 1830; mem. R.I. Senate, 1853-66; gov. R.I., 1854-57; del. to Nat. Peace Conf., Washington, D.C., 1861; registrar in bankruptcy, 1867-72; mem. R.I. Ho. of Reps., 1874-75; mem. Providence Sch. Bd. Died Providence, Apr. 19, 1890.

HORN, Charles Edward, musician; b. London, Eng., June 21, 1786; s. Karl Friedrich Horn. Made debut as opera singer, 1809; came to Am., 1833, produced several operas at Park Theatre, N.Y.C.; became voice tchr. after his voice failed, later an importer and publisher of music; produced oratorio The Remission of Sin (later renamed Satan); returned to Eng., 1843; apptd. music dir. Princess' Theatre; returned to Am., 1847, condr. Handel and Haydn Soc., Boston, 1848-49; works include: oratorio Daniel's Prediction, 1848; cantata Christmas Bells; 26 English operettas; canzonets, glees, songs. Died Boston, Oct. 21, 1849.

HORN, George Henry, physician, entomologist; b. Phila., Apr. 7, 1840; s. Philip Henry and Frances Isabella (Brock) H.; M.D., U. Pa., 1861. Served as mil. surgeon U.S. Army, Civil War, regtl. surgeon Cal. Volunteers, 1864; mem. Entomol. Soc. of Phila., 1860, pres., 1866; vice dir. Acad. of Natural Scis., 1876-83, dir. entomol. sect., 1883-97; prof. entomology U. Pa., 1889; prin. contbr. to study and classification of Coleoptera, responsible for naming and describing more than 1,550 species; pres. Am. Entomol. Soc., 1883-97; hon. mem. Entomol. Soc. France. Author papers: "Description of New North American Coleoptera in the Cabinet of the Entomological Society of Philadelphia," 1860; The Classification of the Coleoptera of North America, 1883. Died Beesley's Point, N.J., Nov. 24, 1897.

HORN, Henry, congressman; b. Phila., 1786; studied law. Admitted to Pa. bar, practiced law in Phila.; mem. U.S. Ho. of Reps. (Jacksonian Democrat) from Pa., 22d Congress, 1831-33; resumed law practice, Phila.; collector of customs, Phila., 1845-46. Died Flourtown, Pa., Jan. 12, 1862; buried Woodlands Cemetery, Phila.

HORNBECK, John Westbrook, congressman; b. Montague, N.J., Jan. 24, 1804; grad. Union Coll., Schenectady, N.Y., 1827; studied law. Admitted to Northampton County (Pa.) bar, 1829; began practice of law, Allentown, Pa., 1830; dep. atty. gen. Pa. for Lehigh County, 1836-39; mem. U.S. Ho. of Reps. (Whig) from Pa., 30th Congress, 1847-48. Died Allentown, Jan. 16, 1848; buried Allentown Cemetery.

HORNBLOWER, Joseph Coerten, jurist; b. Belleville, N.H., May 6, 1777; s. Josiah and Elizabeth (Kingsland) H.; A.M. (hon.), Princeton, 1823, LL.D. (hon.), 1841; m. Mary Burnet, Apr. 9, 1803; m. 2d, Mary Ann Kinney, Mar. 9, 1840; 8 children. Admitted to N.J. bar, 1803; elected to N.J. Legislature, 1829; chief justice N.J., 1834-46; 1st pres. N.J. Hist. Soc., 1845-64; prof. law Princeton, 1847-55; pres. N.J. Electoral Coll., 1860. Died Newark, N.J., June 11, 1864.

HORNBLOWER, Josiah, engr., jurist; b. Straffordshire, Eng., Feb. 23, 1729; s. Joseph and Rebecca H.; m. Elizabeth Kingsland, 1755, 12 children. Built 1st steam engine constructed in Am., Belleville, N.J., 1753; served in defense of N.J. during French and Indian War, 1755; commd. capt., 1756; commr. for tax appeals, Newark, N.J., 1778; mem. N.J. Legislature, 1779-80, speaker, 1780; mem. N.J. Council, 1781-84, Congress of Confederation, 1785; judge Essex County (N.J.) Ct. Common Pleas, 1790-1809. Died Newark, Jan. 21, 1809.

HORNER, William Edmonds, anatomist; b. Warrenton, Va., June 3, 1793; s. William and Mary (Edmonds) H.; grad. U. Pa., 1814; m. Elizabeth Welsh, Oct. 26, 1820, 10 children. Adj. prof. anatomy U. Pa., 1819, later prof., dean med. dept.,

1822-52; described for 1st time tensor tarsi, spl. muscle connected with lachrymal apparatus, 1824; a founder St. Joseph's Hosp. Author: The American Dissector, 1819; A Treatise on Pathological Anatomy for the Use of Dissectors, 1823; Treatise on Special and General Anatomy, 2 vols., 1826; Treatise on Pathological Anatomy (1st path. text pub. in America), 1829. Died Phila., Mar. 13, 1853.

HORR, Roswell Gilbert, congressman; b. Waitsfield, Vt., Nov. 26, 1830; grad. Antioch Coll., 1857; studied law. Clk., Ct. Common Pleas of Lorain County (O.), 1857-62; admitted to Ohio bar, 1862, began practice in Elyria; engaged in mining, S.E. Mo., 1866-72; mem. U.S. Ho. of Reps. (Republican) from Mich., 46th-48th congresses, 1879-85; del. Rep. Nat. Conv., Chgo., 1884; asso. editor N.Y. Tribune, 1890-96. Died Plainfield, N.J., Dec. 19, 1896; buried Greenwood Cemetery, Wellington, O.

HORROCKS, James, clergyman, coll. pres.; b. Eng., circa 1734; s. James Horrocks; B.A., Trinity Coll., Cambridge (Eng.) U., 1775, M.A., 1778. Licensed to preach by Ch. of Eng., 1761; sent to Va. by Bishop of London as master grammar sch. connected with Coll. William and Mary, 1762-64; pres. Coll. William and Mary, 1764-71; rector of Bruton Parish, commissary of Bishop of London, and mem. Council of Va. by 1771. Died Oporta, Portugal, Mar. 10, 1772.

HORSEY, Outerbridge, senator; b. nr. Laurel, Del., Mar. 5, 1777; studied law. Admitted to Del. bar, 1807, began practice in Wilmington; mem. Del. Ho. of Reps., 1800-02; atty. gen. Del., 1806-10; mem. U.S. Ho. of Reps. (Federalist) from Del., Jan. 10, 1810-21. Died "Needwood" nr. Petersville, Md., June 9, 1842; buried St. John's Cemetery, Frederick, Md.

HORSFIELD, Thomas, naturalist, physician; b. Bethlehem, Pa., May 12, 1773; s. Timothy and Juliana Sarah (Parsons) H.; M.D., U. Pa., 1798. Surgeon, Dutch Colonial Army, Java, 1801; joined Brit. East India Co., 1811; went to London with collections of Java flora, 1819; curator East India Co. Museum, 1820-59. Author: An Experimental Dissertation on Rhus Vernix, Rhus Radicans and Rhus Glabrum (pioneer contbn. to study of poison ivy and sumac in exptl. pharmacology), 1798; Plantae Javanicae Rariores, 5 vols., 1838-52. Died July 24, 1859.

HORSFORD, Eben Norton, chemist; b. Moscow, N.Y., July 27, 1818; s. Jerediah and Charity (Norton) H.; grad. Rensselaer Poly. Inst., 1838; A.M., Harvard, 1847; studied analytical chemistry with Liebig, Giessen, Germany, 1844-46; m. Mary L'Hommedieu Gardiner, 1847, 4 daus.; m. 2d, Phoebe Dayton Gardiner, 1857, 1 dau. Prof. mathematics and natural scis. Albany (N.Y.) Female Acad., 1840-44; taught chemistry, research Lawrence Scientific Sch. (now part of Harvard), Cambridge, Mass., 1847-63; pres. bd. visitors Wellesley Coll.; early mem. Am. Chem. Soc. Author: The Theory and Art of Breadmaking, 1861; contbr. many articles to scientific jours. Died Cambridge, Jan. 1, 1893.

HORSFORD, Jerediah, congressman; b. Charlotte, Vt., Mar. 8, 1791; attended common schs. Engaged in farming; served in War of 1812; missionary to Seneca Indians, Moscow (now Leicester) N.Y., 1815; mem. N.Y. Assembly, 1831; mem. U.S. Ho. of Reps. (Whig) from N.Y., 32d Congress, 1851-53; served as col. light inf. N.Y. Militia, resumed farming, Livonia, N.Y. Died Livonia, Jan. 14, 1875; buried Moscow Cemetery.

HORSMANDEN, Daniel, jurist; b. Purleigh, Eng., June 4, 1694; s. Rev. Daniel and Mrs. Susannah (Bowyer) H.; m. Mary Reade, 1745; m. 2d, Anne Jevon. Admitted to Middle Temple, London, Eng., 1721, Inner Temple, 1724; admitted to N.Y. bar, 1732; atty. N.Y. Supreme Ct., 1732; vestryman Trinity Parish, 1734-72; judge N.Y. Supreme Ct., 1736-47, 53-63; judge N.Y. Ct.; Admiralty recorder N.Y.C., 1736; reapptd. to N.Y. Supreme Ct., 1753-63; last chief justice Province of N.Y., 1763-78; mem. commn. to inquire into burning of Eng. ship Gospel, circa 1772. Author: A Journal of the Proceedings in the Detection of the Conspiracy Formed by Some White People, in Connection with Negro and Other Slaves, 1744. Died Flatbush, N.Y., Sept. 23, 1778; buried Trinity Churchyard, N.Y.C.

HORSTMANN, William H., inventor, mfr.; b. Cassel, Germany. Came to Am., 1815; became silk goods mfr., Phila.; invented and patented various machines and improvements for silk goods manufacture; introduced Jacquard loom into Am.; founder firm William H. Horstmann & Sons (oldest silk mfg. firm in U.S.). Died Phila., 1852.

HORTON, Samuel Dana, economist; b. Pomeroy, O., Jan. 16, 1844; s. Valentine B. and Clara Alsop (Pomeroy) H.; grad. Harvard. 1864. A. M., Harvard Law Sch., 1867, LL.B., 1868; attended U. Berlin (Germany), 1870; m. Blanche Lydiard, Aug. 28, 1877, 1 child Lydiard. Won Bowdoin prize for resident grads. at Harvard, 1866; admitted to Ohio bar, 1871; practiced in Cincinnati and Pomeroy, 1871-85; advocate of bimetalism (use of silver and gold as currency at ratio of 16 to 1); sec. Am. delegation to Internat. Monetary Conv., Paris, 1878, del. to 2d Paris Monetary Conf., 1881. Author: Silver and Gold in Their Relation to the Problem of Resumption, 1876; The Silver Pound and England's Monetary Policy Since the Restoration, 1887. Died Washington, D.C., Feb. 23, 1895.

HORTON, Thomas Raymond, congressman; b. Fultonville, N.Y., Apr., 1822; attended pub. schs.; studied law. Admitted to the bar, practiced law; mem. bd. trustees of Fultonville, 1848; clk. bd. suprs. Montgomery County (N.Y.), 6 years; justice of peace, 8 years; editor, publisher Amsterdam (N.Y.) Recorder, 1841-57; mem. U.S. Ho. of Reps. (Republican) from N.Y., 34th Congress, 1855-57; del. Republican Nat. Conv., Chgo., 1860; served as adj. 115th Regt., N.Y. Volunteer Inf., 1862-64; editor, publisher Montgomery County Republican. Died Fultonville, July 26, 1894; buried Village Cemetery, Fultonville.

HORTON, Valentine Baxter, bituminous coal operator, towboat builder; b. Windsor, Vt., Jan. 29, 1802; s. Zenas and Nancy (Seaver) H.; grad. Norwich (Vt.) Acad., 1825; m. Clara Pomeroy, 1833, 6 children including Clara Pomeroy, Frances Dabney, Samuel Dana. Admitted to Conn. bar; designed "Condor" towboat to tow barges back up Ohio River in early shipping of coal from Ohio mines; mem. Ohio Constl. Conv., 1850; organizer Pomeroy Salt Co. (O.), 1851; reorganizer, pres. Ohio River Salt Co.; mem. U.S. Ho. of Reps. from Ohio, 34th-35th, 37th congresses, 1855-59, 61-63; trustee Ohio U., Athens. Died Pomeroy, Jan. 14, 1888.

HOSACK, Alexander Eddy, surgeon; b. N. Y.C., Apr. 6, 1805; s. Dr. David and Mary (Eddy) H.; M.D., U. Pa., 1824; studied under Dupuytren, France; m. Celine B. Hosack. Introduced Syme's operation for exsection of elbow to Am.; known for his improvements in cleft palate operation by 1833; a pioneer urological surgeon; 1st N.Y. surgeon to use ether as anesthetic; author paper on removal tumors in female uretha in New York Jour. Medicine and Surgery, 1839. Died Mar. 2, 1871.

HOSACK, David, physician; b. N.Y.C., Aug. 31, 1769; s. Alexander and Jane (Arden) H.; attended Columbia, 1786; grad. Princeton, 1789; m. Catharine Warner, 1792; m. 2d, Mary Eddy, 1797; m. 3d, Magdalena Coster; 10 children including Alexander Eddy. Began med. practice, Alexandria, Va., 1791; prof. botany Columbia, 1795-1811, prof. materia medica, 1795-1811, prof. materia medica Coll. Phys. and Surg., 1807-08, prof. theory and practice of physic, 1811; attending surgeon at Burr-Hamilton duel, 1804; 1st American to litigate femoral artery for aneurysm, 1808; an incorporator Am. Acad. Fine Arts, 1808; a founder Rutgers Med. Coll., pres. until 1830; a founder Bellevue Hosp., N.Y.C., 1820; a founder N.Y. Hist. Soc., pres., 1820-28; established Am. Med. and Philos. Register, editor, 1810-14. Author: A Tribute to the Memory of the Late Caspar Wistar, M.D., 1818; A System of Practical Nosology, 1819; Memoir of DeWitt Clinton, 1829. Died N.Y.C., Dec. 22, 1835.

HOSHOUR, Samuel Klinefelter, clergyman, univ. pres.; b. Heidelburg Twp., Pa., Dec. 9, 1803; attended York (Pa.) Acad., 1822-24; m. Lucinda Savage, Feb. 7, 1826. Prin., New Market Acad., Va., 1827; ordained to ministry Lutheran Ch., 1827; pastor Smithsburg (Md.) parish, 1828-31; shared views of Disciples of Christ, expelled from Luth. Synod, circa 1835; settled in Wayne County, Ind., 1835; prin. Wayne County Sem., 1836; opened, conducted Cambridge Sem., Cambridge City, Ind., 1839-46; pres. North Western Christian U. (now Butler U.), 1858-61, prof. langs., 1861-75; supt. public instruction State of Ind., 1862. Author: Letters to Esq. Pedant in the East by Lorenzo Altisonant an Emigrant to the West, 1844. Died Nov. 29, 1883.

HOSKINS, George Gilbert, congressman; b. Bennington, N.Y., Dec. 24, 1824. Engaged in merc. bus.; town clk., justice of peace, Bennington, postmaster, 1849-53, 61-66; mem. N.Y. Assembly, 1860, 65-66, speaker, 1865; commr. pub. accounts Attica (N.Y.), 1868-70; collector internal revenue 29th Dist. of N.Y., 1871-73; mem. U.S. Ho. of Reps. (Republican) from N.Y., 43d-44th congresses, 1873-77; lt. gov. N.Y., 1880-83; del. Rep. Nat. Conv., Chgo., 1880. Died Attica, June 12, 1893; buried Forest Hill Cemetery, Attica.

HOSMER, Hezekiah Lord, congressman; b. June 7, 1765; studied law. Admitted to practice in mayor's ct. of Hudson, N.Y., 1785; recorder of Hudson, 1793-94, 1810-11, 13-14; mem. U.S. Ho. of Reps. from N.Y., 5th Congress, 1797-99; one of mgrs. apptd. by Ho. of Reps. to conduct impeachment proceedings against William Blount (senator from Tenn.). Died Hudson, June 9, 1814.

HOSMER, Hezekiah Lord, jurist; b. Hudson, N.Y., Dec. 10, 1814; s. Hezekiah Lord and Susan (Throop) H.; m. Sarah Seward (Dec. 1839); m. 2d, Jane Thompson (Dec. 1848); m. 3d, Mary Stower (Dec. 1858). Admitted to Ohio bar, 1835; editor, part propr. Toledo (O.) Blade, 1844; sec. com. on territories U.S. Ho. of Reps., 1861-64; chief justice Mont. Territorial Supreme Ct., 1864; postmaster Virginia City (Mont.), 1869-72. Author: Early History of the Maumee Valley, 1858; Adela, the Octoroon, 1860; A Trip to the States; Bacon and Shakespeare in the Sonnets, 1887. Died San Francisco, Oct. 31, 1893.

HOSMER, Titus, jurist; b. Middletown, Conn., 1737; s. Stephen and Deliverance (Graves) H.; A.B., Yale, 1757; m. Lydia Lord, Nov. 1761, 7 children including Stephen Titus. Held several town offices, including justice of peace, Middletown, 1758-72; admitted to Conn. bar, 1760, began law practice, Middleton; mem. Conn. Gen. Assembly, 1773-78, an assistant,1778-80; speaker Conn. Ho. of Reps., 1777; mem. Conn. Com. of Safety; mem. Continental Congress, 1778; a signer Articles of Confederation, 1778; elected to U.S. Maritime Ct. Appeals created by act of U.S. Congress, 1780. Died Middletown, Aug. 4, 1780.

HOSMER, William Howe Cuyler, poet; b. Avon, N.Y., May 25, 1814; s. George and Elizabeth (Berry) H.; grad. Hobart Coll., 1837; m. Stella Avery, Oct. 16, 1838; 2 sons, William, Charles. Clk., N.Y. Customs House, 1854-58; rejected as volunteer U.S. Army because of poor health. Author: The Pioneers of Western New York, 1838; The Months, 1847; The Poetical Works of William H.C. Hosmer, 2 vols., 1854. Died Avon, May 23, 1877.

HOSTETTER, Jacob, congressman; b. nr. York, Pa., May 9, 1754; attended common schs. Pioneer in mfg. tall 8-day clock; mem. Pa. Gen. Assembly, 1797-1802; mem. U.S. Ho. of Reps. (Democrat) from Pa., 15th-16th congresses, Nov. 16, 1818-21. Died Columbiana, O., June 29, 1831.

HOTCHKISS, Benjamin Berkeley, inventor, mfr.; b. Watertown, Conn., Oct. 1, 1826; s. Asahel A. and Althea (Guernsey) H.; m. Maria Bissell, May 27, 1850. Inventor (with his brother) new form of cannon projectile, demonstrated at Washington (D.C.) Navy Yard, 1855; made gift of some projectiles to liberal govt. of Mexico, 1859; furnished several hundred projectiles to Japanese, 1860, succeeded in getting small order from U.S., 1860; founder factory, N.Y.C., when Civil War produced demand for projectiles; patentee practical machine gun, 1872; inventor magazine rifle, 1875, exhibited in Phila., sold patent rights to Winchester Repeating Arms Co., New Haven, Conn. (rifle used by U.S. Army, then by U.S. Navy); organizer Hotchkiss & Co., with hdqrs. in U.S., factories in Eng., Germany, Austria, Russia and Italy, 1882; other patents include an explosive shell and packing for projectiles. Died Paris, France, Feb. 14, 1885; buried Sharon, Conn.

HOTCHKISS, Giles Waldo, congressman; b. Windsor, N.Y., Oct. 25, 1815; attended Windsor Acad., Oxford Acad.; studied law. Admitted to N.Y. bar, 1837, began practice in Binghamton; a founder Republican Party; del. Rep. Nat. Conv., Chgo., 1860; mem. U.S. Ho. of Reps. (Rep.) from N.Y., 38th-39th, 41st congresses, 1863-67, 69-71; resumed law practice, Binghamton. Died Binghamton, July 5, 1878; buried Spring Forest Cemetery, Binghamton.

HOTCHKISS, Julius, congressman; b. Waterbury, Conn., July 11, 1810; attended common schs. Engaged in mfg.; mayor of Waterbury, 1852; mem. Conn. Ho. of Reps., 1851, 58; mem. U.S. Ho. of Reps. (Republican) from Conn., 40th Congress, 1867-69; lt. gov. of Conn., 1870. Died Middletown, Conn., Dec. 23, 1878; buried Pine Grove Cemetery, Middletown.

HOUCK, Jacob, Jr., congressman; b. Schoharie, N.Y., Jan. 14, 1801; s. Jacob Houck; grad. Union Coll., Schenectady, N.Y., 1822; studied law. Admitted to N.Y. bar, practiced in Schoharie; dist. atty. Schoharie County (N.Y.), 1831-36; mem. U.S. Ho. of Reps. (Democrat) from N.Y., 27th Congress, 1841-43; resumed law practice. Died Schoharie, Oct. 2, 1857; buried Lutheran Cemetery, Schoharie.

HOUGH, David, congressman; b. Norwich, Conn., Mar. 13, 1753; attended common schs. Ship carpenter; moved to Lebanon, N.H., 1778; mem. N.H. Ho. of Reps., 1788-89, 94; justice of peace; Col. N.H. Militia; del. N.H. Constl. Conv., 1783; commr. of valuation, 1798; mem. U.S. Ho. of Reps. from N.H., 8th-9th congresses, 1803-07; engaged in farming. Died Lebanon, Apr. 18, 1831; buried cemetery nr. Lebanon.

HOUGH, Franklin Benjamin, physician, forester; b. Martinsburg, N.Y., July 22, 1822; s. Dr. Horatio G. and Martha (Pitcher) H.; grad. Union Coll., 1843; M.D., Western Res. Med. Coll., 1848; m. Maria S. Eggleston, July 9, 1845; m. 2d, Mariah E. Kilham, May 16, 1849; 9 children. Became prin. Gustavus Acad. in Ohio, 1845; chosen to direct N.Y. State Census, 1854; insp. U.S. Sanitary Commn., early in Civil War; served as regimental surgeon 97th N.Y. Volunteers, 1862-63; supt. N.Y. State Census, 1865, D.C. Census, 1867; edited N.Y. Conv. Manual, 2 vols., 1867; elected supt. U.S. Census, 1870; apptd. forestry agt. U.S. Dept. Agr. (1st fed. ofcl. in forestry) with responsibilty to investigate consumption of timber and preservation of forests, 1876, received new commn. with larger appropriation from U.S. Congress, 1881. Author: A Catalogue of Plants in Lewis and Franklin Counties, N.Y., 1847; History of St. Lawrence and Franklin Counties, N.Y., 1847; Papers Relating to Cromwell County, N.Y., 1856; Proceedings of the Commission of Indian Affairs, 1861; Military and Hospital Camps, 1862; History of Duryea's Campaign, 1864; Washingtoniana, 1865; The Siege of Charleston, 1867; American Biographical Notes, 1875; Report on Forestry, 1878-80. Died Lowville, N.Y., June 11, 1885.

HOUGH, William Jervis, congressman; b. Cazenovia, N.Y., Mar. 20, 1795; studied law. Practiced law Syracuse, N.Y.; mem. N.Y. Assembly, 1835-36; served as gen. N.Y. Militia; mem. U.S. Ho. of Reps. (Democrat) from N.Y., 29th Congress, 1845-47; resumed practice of law, Syracuse. Died Syracuse, Oct. 4, 1869; buried Oakwood Cemetery, Syracuse.

HOUGHTON, Douglass, geologist, mayor Detroit; b. Troy, N.Y., Sept. 21, 1809; s. Jacob and Maria (Douglas) H.; grad. Rensselaer Poly. Inst., Troy, 1829; m. Harriet Stevens, 1833, 2 daus. Asst. prof. chemistry and natural history Rennselaer Poly. Inst., 1829; Lectured on biology, geology and chemistry, Detroit, 1830; licensed as med. practicioner, 1831; apptd. surgeon and botanist H.R. Schoolcraft's expdn. to find sources of Mississippi River, 1831; practicing physician and surgeon, Detroit, 1832-37; prof. geology and mineralogy U. Mich. 1838-45; mayor Detroit, 1842-43; mem. Literary and Hist. Soc. of Que., Boston Soc. Natural History. Drowned in Lake Superior, Oct. 13, 1845.

HOUGHTON, George Heindric, clergyman; b. Deerfield, Mass., Feb.1, 1820; s. Edward C. and Fanny (Smith) H.; grad. U. City N.Y., 1842; m. Caroline Anthon. Ordained deacon Episcopal Ch., 1845, priest, 1846; founder, pastor Ch. of Transfiguration became known as Little Ch. Around the Corner. N.Y.C., 1849-97; prof. Hebrew, Gen. Theol. Sem., 1850-97. Died N.Y.C., Nov. 17, 1897.

HOUGHTON, Henry Oscar, publisher; b. Sutton, Vt., Apr. 30, 1832; s. Capt. William and Marilla (Clay) H.; grad. U. Vt., 1846; m. Nanna W. Manning, Sept. 12, 1854, 1 son, Henry, 3 daus. Printers apprentice Burlington Free Press, 1836; established printing firm which became known as Riverside Press, circa 1850; founder (with M.M. Hurd) firm Hurd & Houghton, 1864, later merged to form Houghton, Osgood & Co., changed name to Houghton Mifflin Co., 1880; mayor Cambridge (Mass), 1872. Died North Andover, Mass., Aug. 25, 1895.

HOUK, George Washington, congressman; b. nr. Mt. Holly Springs, Cumberland County, Pa., Sept. 25, 1825; attended E.E. Barney Acad., Dayton, O.; studied law. Admitted to Ohio bar, 1847, began practice in Dayton, mem. Ohio Ho. of Reps., 1852-53; del. Democratic Nat. Conv., 1860, 76; Dem. presdl. elector, 1884; mem. U.S. Ho. of Reps. (Dem.) from Ohio, 52d-53d congresses, 1891-94. Died Washington, D.C., Feb. 9, 1894; buried Woodland Cemetery, Dayton.

HOUK, Leonidas Campbell, congressman, jurist; b. Boyds Creek, Tenn., June 8, 1836; a son, John Chiles. Admitted to Tenn. bar, 1859; enlisted as pvt. U.S. Army, 1861; promoted lt. 1st Regt., Tenn. Volunteer Inf., col. 3d Regt., 1862-63; mem. Tenn. Constl. Conv., 1865; judge 17th Jud. Circuit of Tenn., 1866-70; mem. Tenn. Legislature, 1873-75; mem. U.S. Ho. of Reps. from Tenn., 46th-52d congresses, 1879-91. Died Knoxville, Tenn., May 25, 1896; buried Old Gray Cemetery, Knoxville.

HOUSE, Royal Earl, inventor; b. Rockland, Vt., Sept. 9, 1814; s. James N. and Hepsibah (Newton) H.; m. Theresa Thomas, 1846, no children. Patented machine to saw barrel staves, 1839; worked on electric telegraph of teletype model, 1840-44; exhibited his printing telegraph at Am. Inst. Fair, N.Y., 1844, patented it, 1846; telegraph lines equipped with printing telegraph constructed from N.Y. to Boston, Washington, Cleve. and Cincinnati, 1847-55; spanned Hudson River with his telegraph lines, established permanent telegraphic communication between N.Y. and Phila., 1849. Died Feb. 24, 1895.

HOUSE, Samuel Reynolds, physician, missionary; b. Waterford, N.Y., Oct. 16, 1817; s. John and Abby (Platt) H.; grad. Union Coll., Schenectady, N.Y., 1837; M.D., Coll. of Physicians and Surgeons, N.Y., 1845; m. Harriet Petit, Nov. 27, 1855. Conducted floating dispensary on the Menam in Siam, 1847-51; in charge of boy's sch. established by Presbyn. Mission in Bangkok, 1852-76; ordained to ministry Presbyn. Ch., 1856; discovered 2 varieties of shells: Cyclostoria Housei, Spiraculum Housei. Author: Notes on Obstetric Practices in Siam, 1879. Died Waterford, Aug. 13, 1899.

HOUSEMAN, Julius, congressman; b. Zechendorf, Bavaria, Germany, Dec. 8, 1832; attended common schs., Zenkendorf, comml. sch., Munich, Bavaria. Came to U.S., 1848, settled in Battle Creek, Mich.; engaged in lumber and merc. bus., Grand Rapids, Mich., 40 years; alderman Grand Rapids; 1861-70; mem. Mich. Ho. of Reps., 1871-72; mayor of Grand Rapids, 1873-75; unsuccessful candidate for lt. gov. Mich., 1876; mem. U.S. Ho. of Reps. (Democrat) from Mich., 48th Congress, 1883-85. Died Grand Rapids, Feb. 8, 1891; buried Oak Hill Cemetery, Grand Rapids.

HOUSTON, George Smith, senator, gov. Ala.; b. Williamson County, Tenn., Jan. 17, 1808; s. David and Hannah (Regan) H.; m. Mary Beatty, 1835; m. 2d, Ellen Irvine, 1861; 10 children. Admitted to Ala. bar, 1831; mem. Ala. Legislature, 1832; states atty. for Florence Jud. Dist., 1836; mem. U.S. Ho. of Reps. from Ala., 27th-30th, 32d-36th congresses, 1841-49, 1851-61, senator-elect for term ending 1867, not permitted to take seat; del. Union Nat. Conv., Phila., 1866; gov. Ala., 1874-78; mem. U.S. Senate from Ala., 1879. Died Athens, Ala., Dec. 31, 1879; buried Athens City Cemetery.

HOUSTON, Henry Howard, railroad exec.; b. Wrightsville, Pa., Oct. 3, 1820; s. Samuel N. and Susan (Strickler) H.; m. Sallie Bonnell, 1856, 6 children. Clk., David Leech & Co., Phila., 1847-50; managed freight line Pa. R.R. Co. between Phila., and Pitts., 1850-52; gen. freight agt. Pa. R.R. Co., 1852-67, mem. bd. dirs., 1881-95; promoter of Union and Empire lines; made fortune from investments in Pa. oil fields, western gold mines; built Protestant Episcopal Ch. of St. Martin's-in-the-Fields, nr. Phila., 1886-95; trustee Washington and Lee U., U. Pa. Died Phila., June 21, 1895.

HOUSTON, John Wallace, congressman; b. Concord, Del., May 4, 1814; grad. Yale, 1834; studied law, Dover, Del. Admitted to Del. Bar, 1837; began practice of law, Georgetown, Del., 1839; sec. of state Del., 1841-44; mem. U.S. Ho. of Reps. (Whig) from Del., 29th-31st congresses, 1845-51; asso. judge Del. Superior Ct., 1855-93; mem. Washington (D.C.) Peace Conf., 1861. Died Georgetown, Apr. 26, 1896; buried Presbyn. Cemetery, Lewes, Del.

HOUSTON, Samuel, pres. Republic of Tex.; b. Timber Ridge Church, nr. Lexington, Va., Mar. 2, 1793; s. Maj. Samuel and Elizabeth (Paxon) H.; ed. Maryville (Tenn.) Acad. (now Maryville Coll.); m. Eliza Allen, Jan. 22, 1829; m. 2d, Margaret Lea, 1840; 8 children. Adopted by Chief Jolly of Cherokee Indians, circa 1806; enlisted as pvt. 39th Inf. Regt., U.S. Army, 1813, promoted ensign, 1813; served as sgt. 7th Inf. Regt. under Gen. Andrew Jackson during Creek War; promoted lt., 1814; admitted to Tenn. bar, 1818; dist. atty. Nashville (Tenn.), 1819; adj. gen. Tenn., 1820; commd. maj. gen. Tenn. Militia, 1821; mem. U.S. Ho. of Reps. from Tenn., 18th-19th congresses, 1823-27; gov. Tenn., 1827-29; moved to Cherokee Indian territory, 1829, to Tex., 1833; mem. San Felipe de Austin Conv. to establish separate statehood for Tex., 1833; mem. Tex. Constl. Conv., 1835; became comdr.-in-chief Tex. Army, 1836, routed Mexican forces and captured Santa Anna at Battle of San Jacinto, Apr. 21, 1836; 1st pres. Republic of Tex., 1836-38, 3d pres., 1841-44; mem. Tex. Congress, 1838-40; mem. U.S. Senate from Tex., Feb.21, 1846-57; gov. Tex., 1859-61, deposed because he refused to take oath of allegiance to Confederate States of Am., Mar. 18, 1861; Houston (Tex.) named for him. Died Huntsville, Tex., July 26, 1863; buried Oakwood Cemetery, Huntsville.

HOUSTON, William Churchill, Continental congressman; b. S.C., circa 1746; s. Archibald and Margaret Houston; A.B., Coll. of N.J. (now Princeton), 1768; m. Jane Smith, 4 children. Prof. mathematics and natural philosophy Coll. of N.J., 1771-83; capt. Somerset County Foot Militia, 1776-77; mem. Continental Congress from N.J., 1775-76, 79-82, 84-85, dep. sec., 1775, 76; mem. N.J. Assembly, 1776, mem. com. to settle public accounts, clk. pro tem; mem. N.J. Council of Safety 1778; admitted to N.J. bar, 1781; clk. N.J. Supreme Ct., 1781-88; receiver Continental taxes in N.J., 1782-85; del. to Annapolis (Md.) Conv., also U.S. Constl. Conv., Phila. did not sign U.S. Constn. Died Frankford, Pa., Aug. 12, 1788.

HOUSTOUN, John, gov. Ga., Continental congressman; b. nr. Waynesboro, Ga., Aug. 31, 1744; s. Sir Patrick Houstoun; m. Miss Bryan. An organizer 1st Ga. Provincial Congress, 1775; del to Continental Congress, 1775-76; gov. Ga., 1778-84; chief justice Ga., 1786; commr. to settle boundary dispute between Ga. and S.C., 1787; justice Chatham County, Ga., 1787; mayor Savannah (Ga.), 1789-90; judge Superior Ct., Eastern Circuit Ga., 1792. Died White Buff, nr. Savannah, July 20, 1796.

HOUSTOUN, William, Continental congressman; b. Savannah, Ga., 1755; attended higher schs., Eng., studied law. Admitted to Inner Temple, London, Eng., 1776; participated in revolutionary activities; mem. Continental Congress from Ga., 1784-87; an agt. from Ga. to settle boundary dispute with S.C., 1785; del. U.S. Constl. Conv., Phila., 1787, declined to sign Constn; an original trustee U. Ga. Died Savannah, Ga., Mar. 17, 1813; buried St. Paul's Chapel, N.Y.C.

HOVENDEN, Thomas, artist; b. Dunmanway, Ireland, Dec. 23, 1840; s. Robert and Ellen (Bryan) H.; attended Cork Sch. of Design, Sch. of N.A.D., N.Y.; attended École des Beaux-Arts, 1874; m. Helen Corson, 1881, 1 dau., Martha. Artist specializing in hist. and genre paintings in academic tradition of his tng. École de Beaux-Arts; elected to Nat. Acad. of Art, 1882. Paintings include: The Last Moments of John Brown, Jerusalem the Golden, Elaine. Died Plymouth Metting, Pa., Aug. 14, 1895.

HOVEY, Alvin Peterson, gov. Ind., jurist, army officer; b. nr. Mt. Vernon, Ind., Sept. 6, 1821; s. Abiel and Frances (Peterson) H.; m. Mary Ann James Nov. 24, 1844; m. 2d, Rosa Smith, 1863; 5 children. Admitted to Ind. bar, 1842; 1st lt. company of volunteers, during Mexican War; mem. Ind. Constl. Conv. 1850; circuit judge, 1851-54; mem. Ind. Supreme Ct., 1854-56; pres. Democratic State Conv., 1855; U.S. dist. atty. for Ind., 1856-58; served as col. 1st regt. Ind. Legion and col. 24th Ind. Inf. in Civil War, promoted Brig. gen., 1862, fought at Battle of Shiloh, brevetted maj. gen. U.S. Volunteers, 1864, in command Dist. of Ind., 1864-65; U.S. minister to Peru, 1865-70; mem. U.S. Ho. of Reps. from Ind., 50th Congress, 1887-89; gov. Ind., 1888-91. Died Indpls., Nov. 23, 1891.

HOVEY, Charles Edward, educator, army officer; b. Thetford, Vt., Apr. 26, 1827; s. Alfred and Abigail (Howard) H.; grad. Dartmouth, 1852; m. Harriette Spofford, Oct. 9, 1854, 3 children including Richard. Prin. free high sch., Framingham, Mass., 1852-54; 1st prin. boys' high sch., Peoria, Ill., 1854-56; supt. Peoria pub. schs., 1856-57; elected pres. Ill. State Tchrs. Assn., 1856; mem. 1st Ill. Bd. Edn., 1857; editor Illinois Teacher, 1856-58; founder Ill. State Normal U., 1857, apptd. prin., served as col. of regiment largely composed of students and tchrs. of the univ. in Civil War; commd. col. 33d Ill. Volunteer Inf., 1861, brig. gen., 1862; brevetted maj. gen. for gallant battle conduct, Sept. 5, 1862 particularly at Ark. Post, 1863; commd. maj. gen. U.S. Volunteers, 1865; practiced law, Washington D.C., until 1897. Died Washington, Nov. 17, 1897.

HOVEY, Charles Mason, horticulturist; b. Cambridge, Mass., Oct. 26, 1810; s. Phineas and Sarah (Stone) H.; m. Anna Chaponil, Dec. 25, 1835. Established nursery, Cambridge, 1832; developed Hovey strawberry (1st variety of fruit to be developed by planned breeding in N. Am.), 1834; founder, editor, Mag. of Horticulture, Botany, and All Useful Disconeries and Improvements in Rural Affairs, 1835-68; mem. Am. Pomol. Soc.; pres. Mass. Hort. Soc., 1863-66. Author: Fruits of America, 3 vols., 1847-56. Died Sept. 2, 1887.

HOWARD, Benjamin, territorial gov., congressman; b. Va., 1760; s. John Howard. Mem. Ky. Legislature, 1801-02; mem. U.S. Ho. of Reps. from Ky., 10th - 11th congresses, 1807 - Apr. 1810; resigned to become gov. Dist. of La.(later Territory of Mo.), 1810; commd. brig. gen. 8th Mil. Dept., U.S. Army, 1813; Howard County (Mo.) named for him, 1816. Died St. Louis, Sept. 18, 1814; buried Bellefontaine Cemetery, St. Louis.

HOWARD, Benjamin Chew, army officer, congressman; b. "Belvedere" nr. Balt., Nov. 5, 1791; s. Col. John Eager and Peggy (Chew) H.; B.A., Coll. of N.J. (now Princeton) 1809, M.A., 1812; m. Jane Grant Gilmore, 1818. Served as capt. Mech. Volunteers of Balt. during War of 1812; participated in Battle of North Point, 1814; admitted to Md. bar, circa 1816; elected mem. Balt. City Council, 1820; mem. Md. Ho. of Dels., 1824; mem. 1829-33, 35-39, chmn. fgn. relations com.; mem. U.S. Ho. of Reps., 21st-22d, 24th-25th congresses, Md. Senate, 1840-41; reporter U.S. Supreme Ct., 1843-61, wrote 24 vols. of Supreme Court Reports; unsuccessful candidate for gov. Md., 1861; del. Washington (D.C.) Peace Conf. from Md., 1861. Died Balt., Mar. 6, 1872; buried Green Mount Cemetery, Balt.

HOWARD, Blanche Willis, author; b. Bangor, Me., July 21, 1847; d. Daniel Mosley and Eliza Anne (Hudson) Howard; m. Dr. Julius von Teuffel, 1890. Published One Summer, her 1st novel, 1875; European correspondent for Boston Transcript, 1875; lived in Germany, 1877-98; taught sch. for visiting Am. girls, Germany; writings include: Aunt Serana, 1881; Aulnay Tower, 1885; No Heros, 1893; The Garden of Eden, published posthumously, 1900, translated various work from German to English. Died Munich, Germany, Oct. 7, 1898.

HOWARD, George C., theater mgr., actor; 1 dau., Cordelia. Produced play and appeared as St. Clair in Uncle Tom's Cabin at Troy (N.Y.) Museum (theater under his mgmt), 1852, play ran 100 nights; toured as St. Clair at Albany, Nat. Theatre, N.Y.C. (200 performances), through West, South, later in England, 1852-54.

HOWARD, Henry, architect; b. 1818; worked in New Orleans; designed Belle Grove, Grecian-style villa of John Andrews, White Castle, La., 1857 (masterpiece of Deep South Mansions, later destroyed). Died 1884.

HOWARD, Jacob Merritt, senator; b. Shaftsbury, Vt., July 10, 1805; s. Otis and Polly (Millington) H.; grad. Williams Coll., 1830; m. Catherine Shaw, Oct. 8, 1835, at least 2 daus., 3 sons. Admitted to Mich. bar, 1833; city atty. Detroit, 1834; mem. Mich. Ho. of Reps., 1838; mem. U.S. Ho. of Reps. from Mich., 27th Congress, 1841-43, drafted 1st clause of 13th amendment; formed 1st Republican Party conv. platform, 1854; atty. gen. Mich., 1854; mem. U.S. Senate from Mich., Jan. 17, 1862-71; mem. reconstrn. commn. to investigate conditions in Va., N.C. and S.C., 1865-66; Translator: Historical and Secret Memoirs of the Empress Josephine (from French work by A. Le Normand), 1848. Died Detroit, Apr. 2, 1871; buried Elmwood Cemetery, Detroit.

HOWARD, John Eager, army officer, senator, gov. Md.; b. Baltimore County, Md., June 4, 1752; s. Cornelius and Ruth (Eager) H.; m. Peggy Chew May 18, 1787; 1 son, Benjamin Chew. Commd. capt. in Col. Carvil Hall's "Flying Camp," 1776, served at Battle of White Plains, Oct. 28, 1776; commd. maj. 4th Md. Regt., 1777; lt. col. 5th Md. Regt. at Battle of Camden, Mar. 11, 1778 led charge at critical moment in Battle of Cowpens, Jan. 17, 1781, received gold medal and thanks of Continental Congress; del. to Continental Congress, 1787-88; gov. Md., 1788-91; mem. U.S. Senate from Md., 1796-1803; commd. brig. gen. U.S. Army, 1803; Federalist candidate for vice pres. U. S., 1816. Died Belvedere, Md., Oct. 12, 1827.

HOWARD, Tilghman Ashurst, congressman; b. nr. Pickensville, S.C., Nov. 14, 1797; attended pub. schs.; studied law. Admitted to Tenn. bar, 1818, began practice in Knoxville; mem. Tenn. Senate, 1824; Democratic presdl. elector, 1828; practiced law; Bloomington, Ind., 1830-33, Rockville, Ind., 1833; U.S. dist. atty. for Ind., 1830-37; unsuccessful candidate for U.S. Senate, 1839; mem. U. S. Ho. of Reps. (Democrat) from Ind., 26th Congress, 1839-Aug. 1, 1840; unsuccessful candidate for gov. Ind., 1840; apptd. chargé d'affaires to Republic of Tex., 1844. Died Washington, Tex., Aug. 16, 1844; buried Rockville Cemetery.

HOWARD, Volney Erskine, congressman, jurist; b. Norridgewock, Somerset County, Me., Oct. 22, 1809; attended Waterville (now Colby) Coll.; m. Catherine Elizabeth Gooch, Mar. 6, 1837. Admitted to Miss. bar, 1832; mem. Miss. Ho. of Reps., 1836; reporter Miss. High Ct. Errors and Appeals; co-editor The Mississippian, 1836; wrote (with Anderson Hutchinson) The Statutes of the State of Mississippi, 1840; published Howard's Reports (1834-43); moved to San Antonia, Tex., 1844; del. Tex. Constl. Conv., 1845; mem. U.S. Ho. of Reps. from Tex., 31st-32d congresses, 1849-53; legal agt. U.S. Land Comm., Cal., 1853-54; apptd. maj. gen. Cal. Militia to put down vigilante activities, San Francisco, 1856; dist. atty., Los Angeles, 1861-70; mem. Cal. Constl. Conv., 1878-79; judge Los Angeles Superior Ct., 1880-84. Died Santa Monica, Cal., May 14, 1889; buried Ft. Hill Cemetery, Los Angeles.

HOWARD, William, congressman; born in Jefferson County, Va., Dec. 31, 1817; attended common schs.; studied law. Admitted to the bar, practice law; moved to Batavia, O.; pros. atty., 1845-49; served as 2d lt. Co. C, 2d Regt., Ohio Volunteer Inf., during Mexican War, 1847-48; mem. Ohio Senate, 1850-52; mem. U.S. Ho. of Reps. (Democrat) from Ohio, 36th Congress, 1859-61; served as maj. 59th Regt., Ohio Volunteer Inf., during Civil War, 1861-63; resumed law practice. Died Batavia, June 1, 1891; buried Union Cemetery, Batavia.

HOWARD, William Alanson, territorial gov., congressman; b. Hinesburg, Chittenden County, Vt., Apr. 8, 1813; s. Dan and Esther (Spencer) H.; grad. Middlebury (Vt.) Coll., 1839; m. Ellen Jane Birchard, Mar. 1, 1841, 2 sons including James Birchard, 2 daus. Admitted to Mich. bar, 1842; chmn. Mich. Whig Central Com., 1852; mem. U.S. Ho. of Reps. from Mich., 34th-35th, 36th congresses, 1855-59, May 15, 1860-61; postmaster of Detroit, 1861-66; declined appointment as U.S. minister to China, 1869; land commr. Grand Rapids & Ind. Ry., 1869-71, N.P. Ry., 1872-78; unsuccessful candidate for U.S. Senate, 1871; territorial gov. Dakota, 1878-80. Died Washington, D.C., Apr. 10, 1880; buried Elmwood Cemetery, Detroit.

HOWE, Albert Richards, congressman; b. Brookfield, Mass., Jan. 1, 1840. Enlisted as pvt. U.S. Army during Civil War, 1861, advanced through grades to maj., mustered out, 1865; engaged in cotton planting, Como, Miss.; mem. Miss. Constl. Conv., 1868; del. Republican Nat. Conv., Chgo, 1868; treas. Panola County (Miss.), 1869; mem. Miss. Ho. of Reps. 1870-72; mem. U.S. Ho. of Reps. (Rep.) from Miss., 43d Congress, 1873-75; engaged as broker, Chgo., 1875-84. Died Chgo., June 1, 1884; buried Brookfield (Mass.) Cemetery.

HOWE, Albion Parris, army officer; b. Standish, Me., Mar. 25, 1818; s. Dr. Ebenezer and Catherine (Spring) H.; grad. U.S. Mil. Acad., 1841; m. Elizabeth Mehaffey, 1859. Asst. prof. mathematics U.S. Mil. Acad., 1843-46; served with 4th Arty. Regt., U.S. Army, in Mexican War; brevetted capt. for service in battles of Contreras and Churubusco, 1847; sent with his battery to help restore peace at Harper's Ferry after John Brown's Raid, 1859; served in Civil War campaigns and battles including W.Va. and Peninsular campaigns, battles of Manassas, S. Mountain, Antietam, Fredericksburg, Gettysburg; commanded arty. depot, Washington, D.C., 1864-66; a guard of honor after Lincoln's assassination; mem. Arty. Bd., U.S. Army, 1866; mem. Bur. of Refugees, Freedmen and Abandoned Lands; retired, 1882. Died Cambridge, Mass., Jan. 25, 1897; buried Mt. Auburn Cemetery, Cambridge.

HOWE, Andrew Jackson, surgeon; b. Paxton, Mass., Apr. 14, 1825; s. Samuel H. and Elizabeth H. (Moore) H.; grad. Harvard, 1853, Worcester Med. Inst., 1855; m. Georgianna Lakin, Feb. 2, 1858. Became prof. anatomy Eclectic Med. Inst., Cincinnati, 1859, prof. surgery, 1861-92; mem. A.A.A.S., Cincinnati Soc. of Natural History. Author: A Practical and Systematic Treatise on Fractures and Dislocations, 1870; Manual of Eye Surgery, 1874; Art and Science of Surgery, 1876. Died Jan. 16, 1892; buried Paxton.

HOWE, Elias, inventor sewing machine; b. Spencer, Mass., July 9, 1819; s. Elias and Polly (Bemis) H.; m. Elizabeth J. Ames, Mar. 3, 1841; married a 2d time. Invented sewing machine that equated speed of 5 of swiftest hand sewers, making 250 stitches per minute, 1844-45, granted patent, 1846; made and marketed a number of sewing machines, N.Y.C.; royalties reached $4,000 a week; organized Howe Machine C., Bridgeport, Conn., 1865; won Gold medal for Howe Machine at Paris Exhbn., 1867. Died Bklyn., Oct. 3, 1867.

HOWE, Frederick Webster, machine tool mfr.; b. Danvers, Mass., Aug. 28, 1822; s. Frederick and Betsey (Dale) H.; m. Anna Clafton, 1 dau. Asst. machine tool designer Robbins, Kendall & Lawrence, 1847, plant supt., 1848-54; designed profiling machine (became widely used in gun shops), 1848; built plain milling machine (forerunner of Lincoln type miller), 1849; designed 1st comml. universal milling machine, 1850; operated own armory, Newark, N.J., 1856-58, Middletown, Conn., 1858-60; supt. armory Providence Tool Co. (R.I.), 1861-65; sewing machine mfr., Bridgeport, Conn., 1865-68; pres. Brown & Sharpe Mfg. Co., 1868-76; aided in devel. Wilcox and Gibbs sewing machine; built (with Charles Goodyear, Jr.) Shoe-making machinery. Died Apr. 25, 1891.

HOWE, George, clergyman; b. Dedham, Mass., Nov. 6, 1802; s. William and Mary (Gould) H.; grad. Middlebury Coll., 1822, Andover Theol. Sem., 1825; m. Mary Bushnell, Aug. 25, 1831; m. 2d, Mrs. Sarah (Walthour) McConnell, Dec. 19, 1836. Ordained to ministry Presbyn. Ch., 1827; Phillips prof. sacred theology Dartmouth, 1827-30; prof. Biblical literature Columbia Theol. Sem., S.C., 1831-83. Author: A Discourse on Theological Education, 1844; History of the Presbyterian Church in South Carolina, 1870-83. Died Apr. 15, 1883.

HOWE, George Augustus, army officer; b. circa 1724; s. Emanud and Maria (von Kielmansegge) H. Mem. Brit. Parliament from Nottingham borough, 1747-58; became ensign Grendadier Guards, 1745, promoted lt. col., 1749; col. 3d Battalion of Royal Americans, 1757; col., then brig. gen. 55th Battalion, Upper N.Y., 1757; 2d in command of Abercromby's Ticonderoga expdn., 1758. Killed in skirmish with French nr. Lake George, July 6, 1758; buried St. Peter's Ch., Albany, N.Y.

HOWE, Henry, historian; b. New Haven, Conn., Oct. 11, 1816; s. Hezekiah and Sarah (Townsend) H.; m. Frances A. Tuttle, Sept. 1847, at least 1 son, Frank Henry. Lived in Cincinnati, 1847-77, died bankrupt because of cost of 2d edit. of Historical Collections of Ohio (3 vols., 1st edit. 1847), 1890. Author: Eminent Americans, 1839; Historical Collections of the State of New York, 1841; Historical Collections of the State of New Jersey, 1844; Historical Collections of Virginia, 1845. Died Oct. 14, 1893.

HOWE, John H., jurist; b. Monroe County, N.Y. Admitted to Ohio bar; moved to Ill., 1854, became judge 6th Jud. Dist. of Ill.; joined Republican Party, 1860; served as brig. gen. during Civil War; 1st chief justice Wyoming Territory, 1869-71, upheld law which gave women right to vote and hold office; mem. commn. to settle boundary dispute between U.S. and Mexico. Died Laredo, Tex., Apr. 3, 1873; buried Kewanee, Ill.

HOWE, John Ireland, inventor, mfr.; b. Ridgefield, Conn., July 20, 1793; s. William and Polly (Ireland) H.; grad. Coll. Physicians and Surgeons, N.Y.C., 1815; m. Cornelia Ann Ireland (cousin), May 20, 1820. Practiced medicine, N. Y.C., 1815-29; resident physician N.Y. Alms House; gave up practice, 1829, started experimenting in mfr. of rubber; set up rubber mfg. plant, North Salem, N.Y., 1829-30; attempted to find mech. way of making straight pins, 1830-31, designed successful pin-making machine, 1832; obtained fgn. patents for machine in England, France, Scotland, Ireland, 1832-33; manufactured pins, North Salem, 1835-38, Darby, Conn., 1838-68; lived in retirement, Birmingham, Conn., 1868-76. Died Birmingham, Sept. 10, 1876.

HOWE, John W., congressman; b. Me., 1801; studied law. Admitted to the bar; moved to Franklin, Pa., 1829, began practice of law; justice of peace; mem. U.S. Ho. of Reps. (Free Soil Whig) from Pa., 31st-32d congresses, 1849-53. Died Rochester, N.Y., Dec. 1, 1873; buried Greendale Cemetery, Meadville, Pa.

HOWE, Jonas Holland, artist; b. Petersham, Mass., 1821. Went to Boston, 1844, studied with his aunt Caroline Negus; set up portrait studio with his cousin George Fuller, Boston; moved to Minn., before 1860, became prominent as farmer and agrl. publicist; resumed painting in later years, painted landscapes (4 of which are owned by Hennepin County Hist. Soc.). Died 1898.

HOWE, Mark-Anthony De Wolfe, clergyman; b. Bristol, R.I., Apr. 5, 1808; s. John and Louisa (Smith) H.; attended Middlebury (Vt.) Coll., 1824-26; grad. Brown U., 1828; studied law in father's office. Taught at Boston Sch., 1829-30; tutor Brown U., 1831-32; ordained to ministry Episcopal Ch.; minister Episcopal Ch., South Boston, Mass., 1833-34; rector St. James Ch., Roxbury, Mass., 1834-46; editor Christian Witness, 1836-46; rector St. Luke's Ch., Phila., 1846-71; consecrated 1st bishop Diocese of Central Pa., 1871-75. Died July 31, 1895.

HOWE, Robert, army officer; b. Bladen County, N.C., 1732; s. Job and Sarah (Yeamans) H.; m. Sarah Grange. Justice of peace Bladen, 1756, Brunswick County, N.C., 1764; mem. N.C. Assembly, 1764-75; in command of Ft. Johnston, 1766-67, 69-73; commd. col. Arty.; mem. N.C. Colonial Asembly, 1772-73; del. to Colonial Congress, New Bern, N.C., 1774; mem. N.C. Com. of Correspondence; commd. col. 2d N.C. Regt., 1775, with Gen. Woodford at Norfolk, Va. drove Lord Dunmore out of that part Va.; commd. brig. gen. Continental Army, 1776; in command of So. Dept.; commd. maj. gen., 1777; commanded Savannah, 1778, later West Point, N.Y.; elected to N.C. Ho. of Commons, 1786, died before taking seat. Died Brunswick County, Dec. 14, 1786.

HOWE, Samuel, jurist; b. Belchertown, Mass., June 20, 1785; s. Dr. Estes and Susanna (Dwight) H.; grad. Williams Coll., 1804; m. Susan Tracy, Sept. 1807; m. 2d, Sarah Robbins, Oct. 1813; 7 children. Admitted to Berkshire (Mass.) bar, 1807; mem. Mass. Legislature from Worthington, 1812-13; apptd. asso. justice of newly established Mass. Ct. of Common Pleas, 1821; elected mem. Am. Acad. Arts and Scis., 1823; opened law sch. with partners Elijah Hunt Mills and John Hooker Ashmun, 1823; trustee Amherst (chosen by legislature to fill vacancy), 1826. Died Jan. 20, 1828.

HOWE, Samuel Gridley, philhellenist, reformer; b. Boston, Nov. 10, 1801; s. Joseph Neals and Patty (Gridley) H.; grad. Brown U., 1821; M.D., Harvard, 1824; m. Julia Ward, Apr. 27, 1843. Fought for Greece in War of Independence from Turkey, 1824-30; started sch. for blind, Boston, 1832; campaigned for establishment of schs. for blind, deaf and mentally retarded, 1832-66; co-editor anti-slavery paper The Commonwealth, 1844-45; worked for Free-Soilers in Kan.; chmn. Mass. Bd. State Charities, 1865-74; raised funds for people of Crete who were fighting war for independence from Turkey, 1866-67; apptd. by Pres. U.S. Grant to report on advisability of annexing Island of Santo Domingo, 1871. Died Jan. 9, 1876.

HOWE, Thomas Marshall, businessman, congressman; b. Williamstown, Vt., Apr. 20, 1808; grad. Warren (O.) Acad. Clk. wholesale drygoods establishment, Pitts., 1829; began his own bus., 1833; cashier, pres. Exchange Nat. Bank of Pitts., 1839-59; engaged in copper mining, copper and steel mfg.; mem. U.S. Ho. of Reps. (Whig) from Pa., 32d-33d congresses, 1851-55; del. Republican Nat. Conv., Chgo., 1860; Rep. presdl. elector, 1860; asst. adj. gen. on staff of gov. Pa.; chmn. Allegheny County (Pa.) com. for recruiting Union soldiers during Civil War; an organizer, 1st pres. Pitts. C. of C. Died Pitts., July 20, 1877; buried Allegheny Cemetery, Pitts.

HOWE, Thomas Y., Jr., congressman; b. Auburn, N.Y., 1801. Insp., Auburn Prison, 1834-38; surrogate Cayoga County (N.Y.), 1836-40; mem. U.S. Ho. of Reps. (Democrat) from N. Y., 32d Congress, 1851-53; mayor of Auburn, 1853-54. Died Auburn, July 15, 1860; buried Ft. Hill Cemetery, Auburn.

HOWE, Timothy Otis, senator, U.S. postmaster gen.; b. Livermore, Me., Feb. 24, 1816; s. Dr. Timothy and Betsy (Howard) H.; ed. Me. Wesleyan Sem.; m. Linda Ann Haynes, Dec. 21, 1841, 2 children. Admitted to bar, 1839; judge 4th Wis. Circuit, also justice Wis. Supreme Ct., 1850-53; mem. U.S. Senate from Wis., 1861-77, advocated emancipation, Negro suffrage, voted for impeachment of Pres. Johnson; apptd. commr. to Internat. Monetary Conf. in Paris by Pres. Garfield, 1881; postmaster gen. U.S., 1882-83. Died Kenosha, Wis., Mar. 25, 1883.

HOWE, William, army officer; s. Emanuel Scrope and Mary (Sophia) H.; m. Frances Conolly, June 4, 1765, no children. Cornet in Duke of Cumberland's Light Dragoons, 1746, promoted lt., 1747; capt. Lord Bury's Regt., 1750; maj. 60th Foot, Brit. Army, 1756; took part in capture of Louisbourg in French and Indian War, 1758; served under Gen. James Wolfe in capture of Quebec, 1759; apptd. col. 46th Foot in Ireland, 1764; mem. Parliament for Nottingham, 1768-80; commd. maj. gen., 1772; came to Am. with Gen. Gage, 1775; created knight of Bath, commd. lt. gen., 1775; succeeded Gage in command in Am., 1775; defeated Washington at L.I., N.Y., captured N.Y.C., 1776; resigned his command, 1778; charges on his conduct in Am. brought before Ho. of Commons but without result either way, 1779. Died Plymouth, Eng., July 12, 1814.

HOWE, William, inventor; b. Spencer, Mass., May 12, 1803; s. Elijah and Fanny (Bemis) H.; m. Azubah Towne Stone, Mar. 12, 1828. Commd. to construct bridge at Warren, Mass., 1838, devised 2 features which he later patented, designed bridge as a truss with wooden diagonals and vertical iron ties in single or double systems; spent last years building bridges in Mass. Died Springfield, Mass., Sept. 19, 1852.

HOWELL, David, educator, Continental congressman, jurist; b. Morristown, N.J., Jan. 1, 1747; s. Aaron and Sarah H.; grad. Coll. of N.J. (now Princeton), 1766; A.M., R.I. Coll. (now Brown U.) 1769, LL.D., 1793; A.M., Phila. Coll., 1769, Yale, 1772; m. Mary Brown, Sept. 30, 1770, 5 children, including Jeremiah. Tutor, Brown U., 1766-69, mem. bd. fellows, 1773-1824, sec. of corp., 1780-1806, prof. jurisprudence, 1790-1824, pres. ad interim, 1791-92; admitted to R.I. bar, 1768; del. Continental Congress from R.I., 1782-85; asso. justice Supreme Ct. of R.I., 1786-87; atty. gen. R.I., 1789; a boundary commr. in connection with Jay Treaty, 1794; U.S. judge for R.I., 1812-24. Died Providence, R.I., July 30, 1824.

HOWELL, Edward, congressman; b. Newburgh, N.Y., Oct. 16, 1792; attended pub. schs., studied law. Taught sch., Unadilla, N.Y.; postmaster of Bath (N.Y.), 1817-21; clk. Steuben County (N.Y.), 1818-21; admitted to N.Y. bar, 1823, began practice in Bath; dist. atty. Steuben County, 1829-34, 36-40; mem. N.Y. Assembly, 1832; mem. U.S. Ho. of Reps. (Democrat) from N.Y., 23d Congress, 1833-35; resumed law practice. Died Bath, Jan. 30, 1871; buried Grove Cemetery, Bath.

HOWELL, Elias, congressman; b. N.J., 1792; attended pub. schs.; children include James Bruen. Moved to Newark, O., 1819; mem. Ohio Senate, 1830-32; mem. U.S. Ho. of Reps. (Whig) from Ohio, 24th Congress, 1835-37. Died nr. Newark, May 1844.

HOWELL, James Bruen, senator, journalist; b. Morristown, N.J., July 4, 1816; s. Elias and Eliza H.; attended Miami U., Oxford, O., 1837; LL.D. (hon.), Ia. Coll., 1871; m. Isabella Richards, Nov. 1, 1842; m. 2d, Mary Ann Bowen, Oct. 23, 1850. Admitted to Ohio bar, 1839; owner Des Moines Valley Whig (Ia.), 1845; established daily Whig, Keokuk, Ia., 1854, renamed Gate City, 1855; del. to 1st Republican Nat. Conv., 1856; mem. U.S. Senate from Ia. (filled vacancy), Jan. 18, 1870-71; apptd. to Ct. of Southern Claims, 1871-80. Died Keokuk, June 17, 1880.

HOWELL, Jeremiah Brown, senator; b. Providence, R.I., Aug. 28, 1771; s. David Howell; grad. Brown U., 1789; studied law. Admitted to R.I. bar, 1793, began practice in Providence; served as brig. gen. R.I. Militia; mem. U.S. Senate (Federalist) from R.I., 1811-17. Died Providence, Feb. 5, 1822; buried North Burial Ground, Providence.

HOWELL, Nathaniel Woodhull, congressman; b. Blooming Grove, N.Y., Jan. 1, 1770; grad. Coll. of N.J. (now Princeton), 1788; studied law. Taught sch., Montgomery County, N.Y., 1789-92; admitted to N.Y. bar; practiced law in N.Y.C., in Tioga County (N.Y.), 1794-96, in Canandaigua, N.Y., 1796-1851; atty. gen. for Western N.Y., 1799-1802; mem. N.Y. Assembly, 1804; mem. U.S. Ho. of Reps. from N.Y., 13th Congress, 1813-15; mem. commn. to appraise Western Inland Lock Navigation Co., 1817; 1st judge Ontario County (N.Y.), 1819-32. Died Canandaigua, Oct. 15, 1851; buried West Avenue Cemetery, Canandaigua.

HOWELL, Richard, army officer, gov. N.J.; b. Newark, Del., Oct. 25, 1754; s. Ebenezer and Sarah (Bond) H.; m. Keziah Burr, Nov. 1799, 9 children. Mem. Greenwich (N.J.) tea party on ship Greyhound, 1774; commd. capt. N.J. Militia, serving at battles of Ticonderoga and Quebec, 1775; wounded in Battle of Brandywine, 1777; served as maj. of a brigade; licensed atty., 1779; succeeded William C. Houston as clk. N.J. Supreme Ct., 1788; gov. N.J., 1793-1801, commanded right wing of troop sent to put down Whiskey Rebellion in Pa.; mem. Soc. of Cincinnati. Died Burlington, N. J., Apr. 28, 1802.

HOWELL, Robert Boyté Crawford, clergyman; b. Wayne County, N.C., Mar. 10, 1801; s. Ralph and Jane (Crawford) H.; attended Columbian Coll. (now George Washington U.), 1824-26; m. Mary Ann Morton Toy, Apr. 23, 1829. Pastor Cumberland Street Bapt. Ch., Norfolk, Va., 1827-34, First Bapt. Ch., Nashville, Tenn., 1834-50, 57-67, Second Bapt. Ch., Nashville, 1850-57. Author: The Terms of Sacramental Communion, 1841; The Deaconship, 1846; The Way of Salvation, 1849. Died Apr. 5, 1868.

HOWEY, Benjamin Franklin, congressman; b. Pleasant Meadows, nr. Swedesboro, N.J., Mar. 17, 1828; attended acads., Swedesboro and Bridgeton, N.J. Engaged as flour and grain commn. mcht., Phila., 1847, later in quarrying and mfg. slate; served as capt. Co. G, 31st Regt., N.J. Volunteers during Civil War, 1862-63; sheriff of Warren County (N.J.), 1878-81; mem. U.S. Ho. of Reps. (Republican) from N.J., 48th Congress, 1883-85. Died Columbia, N.J., Feb. 6, 1895; buried Trinity Ch. Cemetery, Swedesboro.

HOWLAND, Benjamin, senator; b. Tiverton, R.I., July 27, 1755; attended common schs. Engaged in farming; collector of taxes, 1801; town auditor, 1802, town moderator, 1805; mem. R.I. Ho. of Reps., 1810; served as gen. R.I. Militia during War of 1812; mem. U.S. Senate (Democrat) from R.I., Oct. 29, 1804-09. Died Tiverton, May 1, 1821; buried family lot on his estate.

HOWLAND, Gardiner Greene, merchant; b. Norwich, Conn., Sept. 4, 1767; s. Joseph and Lydia (Bell) H.; m. Louisa Edgar, Dec. 16, 1812; m. 2d, Louisa Meredith, 1829. Family moved to N.Y.C., 1800; formed mcht. bus. with brother Samuel Shaw Howland, 1816; built frigate Liberator for revolutionary Greeks, 1825; mcht. bus. extended all over world, specializing in Latin Am.; a dir. Hudson River R.R., 1847. Died Nov. 9, 1851.

HOWLEY, Richard, colonial gov., Continental congressman; b. Liberty County, Ga., 1740. Mem. Ga. Legislature, 1779; gov. Ga. (elected by legislature), 1780; mem. Continental Congress, 1780-81; chief justice Ga., 1782. Co-author: (pamphlet) Observations upon the Effects of Certain Late Political Suggestions by the Delegates of Georgia, 1781. Died Savannah, Ga., Dec. 1784.

HOYME, Gjermund, clergyman; b. Valdres, Norway, Oct. 8, 1847; s. Gjermund Guldbrandsen and Sigrid Christophersen (Ridste) H.; attended Marshall (Wis.) Theol. Sem.; attended U. Wis., 1861-72, also Augsburg Sem., Duluth, Miss.; m. Mrs. Ida Othelia Larsen Olsen. Came with parents to U.S., 1851; ordained to ministry Lutheran Ch., 1873; pastor, Menominie, Wis., 1874-76; pastor of largest Norwegian Lutheran Ch. in U.S., at Eau Claire, Wis., 1876-1902; pres. United Norwegian Luth. Ch. of Am., 1890-1902. Co-compiler book of sacred songs Harpen (The Harp). Author: (sermons)) G. Hoyme Prest og Formand, I Hvilestunder (In Moments of Peace), issued 1904. Died Eau Claire, June 9, 1902.

HOYT, Henry Martyn, gov. Pa.; b. Kingston, Pa., June 8, 1830; s. Ziba and Nancy (Hurlbut) H.; A.B., Williams Coll., 1849, A.M., 1865; LL.D. (hon.), U. Pa., 1881, Lafayette Coll., 1881; m. Mary Loveland, Sept. 25, 1855, 1 son, Henry Martin. Admitted to Pa. bar, 1853; served with U.S. Army, from lt. col. to brig. gen. Army of Potomac, 1861-63, in battles of Bottom's Bridge, Seven Pines, Fair Oaks, Morris Island, Ft. Wayner; apptd. temporary judge Luzerne County (Pa.), 1867; became collector internal revenue for Luzerne and Susquehanna counties (Pa.), 1869; chmn. Pa. Republican Com., 1875; gov. Pa., 1878-82; v.p. Nat. Prison Assn.; mem. Pa. Bd. Public Charities; served as gen. sec. and mgr. Am. Protective Tariff League during presdl. campaign of 1888. Died Wilkes-Barre, Pa., Dec. 1, 1892.

HOYT, Ralph, poet; b. N.Y.C., Apr. 18, 1806. Engaged in teaching, N.Y.C., from circa 1826, also contbd. articles to local newspapers; ordained to ministry Protestant Episcopal Ch., 1842, rector Ch. of Good Shephard, N.Y.C., until circa 1856; contbd. numerous poems to newspapers and mags., from 1840's; collection of poems privately printed, 1875-76. Author: Echoes of Memory and Emotion, 1859; Sketches of Life and Landscape, 1873; The True Life, 1875. Died N.Y.C., Oct. 11, 1878; buried N.Y.C.

HUBARD, Edmund Wilcox, congressman; b. nr. Farmville, Va., Feb. 20, 1806; attended U. Va. Engaged in farming; justice of peace; mem. U.S. Ho. of Reps. (Democrat) from Va., 27th-29th congresses, 1841-47; served as regtl. col. Va. Militia, 1864; appraiser to regulate value of dollar for Confederate Govt. Died nr. Farmville, Dec. 9, 1878; buried family cemetery.

HUBARD, William James, artist; b. Whitchurch, Shropshire, Eng., Aug. 20, 1807. Child prodigy as silhouettist in Eng.; brought to Am. by his mgr., 1824, spent 3 years in N.Y.C. and Boston; left his mgr., turned to oil painting under encouragement from Gilbert Stuart; settled in Gloucester County (Va.) after 1832; moved to Richmond, Va., 1841; became interested in sculpture, established a foundry for casting bronzes, Richmond; manufactured ammunition for Confederate Army during Civil War; fatally injured in an explosion at his factory. Died Feb. 15, 1862.

HUBBARD, Asahel Wheeler, congressman; b. Haddam, Conn., Jan. 19, 1819; attended sch., Middletown, Conn.; studied law; children include Elbert Hamilton. Employed as book agt., sch. tchr., Rushville, Ind.; admitted to Ind. bar, 1841, began practice, Rushville; mem. Ind. Ho. of Reps., 1847-48; engaged in real estate bus., Sioux City, Ia., 1857; judge 4th Jud. Dist., 1859-62; mem. U.S. Ho. of Reps. (Republican) from Ia., 38th-40th congresses, 1863-69; an organizer 1st Nat. Bank of Sioux City, 1871, pres., 1871-79; interested in railroad bldg. in Ia., mining property, Leadville, Colo. Died Sioux City, Sept. 22, 1879; buried Floyd Cemetery, Sioux City.

HUBBARD, Chester Dorman, congressman; b. Hamden, Conn., Nov. 25, 1814; grad. Wesleyan U., Middletown, Conn., 1840. Engaged in banking, mfg. iron and lumber; mem. Va. Ho. of Dels., 1852-53; del. Va. Conv., Richmond, 1861, opposed secession; del. W.Va. Conv., Wheeling, 1861; del. Republican Nat. Conv., Balt., 1864, Chgo., 1880; mem. U.S. Ho. of Reps. (Rep.) from W.Va., 39th-40th congresses, 1865-69. Died Wheeling, Aug. 23, 1891; buried Greenwood Cemetery, Wheeling.

HUBBARD, David, congressman, Confederate govt. ofcl.; b. Old Liberty (now Bedford City), Va., circa 1792; s. Thomas and Margaret H.; m. Eliza Campbell; m. 2d, Rebecca Stoddert; 6 children. Served as maj. Q.M. Corps in War of 1812; admitted to Ala. bar, circa 1820; solicitor Florence (Ala.), 1823-26; mem. Ala. Senate, 1827, 28; trustee U. Ala., 1828-35; mem. Ala. Ho. of Reps., 1831, 42, 43, 45, 53; mem. U.S. Ho. of Reps. from Ala., 26th Congress, 1839, 31st Congress, 1849-51; mem. Confederate Ho. of Reps., 1861-63; 1st Confederate commr. Indian affairs, 1863-65; constructed one of 1st railroads in U.S. from Tuscumbia to Decatur (Ala.). Died Pointe Coupeé Parish, La., Jan. 20, 1874; buried Trinity Episcopal Churchyard, Rosedale, La.

HUBBARD, Demas, Jr., congressman; b. Winfield, N.Y., Jan. 17, 1806; s. Demas Hubbard; attended pub. schs.; studied law. Admitted to N. Y. bar; began practice in Smyrna, N.Y., 1835; mem. N.Y. Assembly, 1838-40; supr. of Smyrna, 1859-64; chmn. bd. suprs. Chenango County (N. Y.); mem. U.S. Ho. of Reps. (Republican) from N.Y., 39th Congress, 1865-67; resumed practice of law. Died Smyrna, Sept. 2, 1873; buried Smyrna East Cemetery.

HUBBARD, Gardiner Greene, telephone pioneer; b. Boston, Aug. 25, 1822; s. Samuel and Mary Anne (Greene) H.; grad. Dartmouth, 1841; m. Gertrude McCurdy, Oct. 21, 1846, children include Mabel G. (wife of Alexander Graham Bell). Introduced gas lighting into Cambridge (Mass.), 1857, also secured fresh water supply for city and built one of earliest U.S. street-car lines between Cambridge and Boston; leader movement which incorporated Clarke Instn. for Deaf Mutes, Northampton, Mass., 1867, pres., 1867-77; mem. Mass. Bd. of Edn., 12 years; became interested in elec. work invention of telephone, 1875; became exec. of 1st telephone orgns. (became Bell Telephone Co.), directed early bus. devel., his system of renting (rather than selling) phones led to present federated structure of Bell System; mem. commn. to investigate transp. of the mails and make recommendations for improvement to Congress, 1876; trustee Columbian (now George Washington) U., 12 years; founder (with Alexander Graham Bell) Science (organ of A. A. A. S.), 1883; asso. with Bell in founding Am. Assn. to Promote Teaching of Speech to the Deaf, 1890, v.p., 1890-97; interested in Alaskan explorations, Hubbard Glacier named for him, 1890; became regent Smithsonian Instn., 1895; pres., joint commn. of scientific socs. of Washington (D.C.) which later organized Washington Acad. of Scis., 1895-97; founder Nat. Geog. Soc., 1888, 1st pres., 1888-97; Hubbard Hall (home of Nat. Geog. Soc.), Washington, named for him. Died Washington, Dec. 11, 1897.

HUBBARD, Gurdon Saltonstall, fur trader, meat packer; b. Windsor, Vt., Aug. 22, 1802; s. Elizur and Abigail (Sage) H.; m. Elenora Berry, 1831; m. 2d, Mary Ann Hubbard, 1843; 1 child. Went to Montreal, Can., in youth; apprentice to Am. Fur Co., 1818-23, ran trading station on Iroquois River in Ill., for a time, later became supt. all trading posts in Ill. region, then partner in co., 1827; bought out Ill. interests of Am. Fur Co., 1828, became sole owner of his own fur co.; early recognized advantages of meat packing trade, became one of 1st to open meat packing hdqrs. in Chgo., 1834; organized Eagle Line Transp. Co.; mem. Ill. Legislature, 1823-33; largely responsible for passage of bill (1836) setting up 1st canal in Chgo. (which connected it with western trade routes); his meat packing plant (known as Hubbard's Folly) housed 1st bank in Chgo., also 1st Chgo. ins. co.; lost much of his property during Great Chgo. Fire of 1871. Died Chgo., Sept. 14, 1886.

HUBBARD, Harry, congressman; b. Concord, Vt., June 1, 1816; grad. Dartmouth, 1835; studied law. Admitted to N.H. bar, 1838, began law practice, Bath; asst. clk., then clk. N.H. Ho. of Reps. 1840-42; mem. N.H. Ho. of Reps., 1843-45, speaker, 1844-45; mem. N.H. Senate, 1845, 47-48, pres. 1847-48; del. Dem. Nat. Conv., 1848, 56; mem. U.S. Ho. of Reps. (Dem.) from N.H., 31st-33d congresses, 1849-55; resumed practice of law, Bath; declined appointment as judge N.H. Supreme Ct. Died in a sanatorium, Somerville, Mass., July 28, 1872; buried Village Cemetery, Bath.

HUBBARD, Henry, senator, gov. N.H.; b. Charlestown, N.H., May 3, 1784; grad. Dartmouth, 1803; studied law, Portsmouth, N.H. Admitted to N.H. bar, circa 1806, began practice in Charlestown; moderator of Charlestown, 1810, re-elected for 16 terms; 1st selectman, 1819-20, 28; mem. N.H. Ho. of Reps., 1812-13, 18, 20, 23-27, speaker, 3 years; state solicitor for Cheshire County (N.H.), 1823-28; probate judge Sullivan County (N.H.), 1827-29; mem. U.S. Ho. of Reps. (Democrat) from N.H., 21st-23d congresses, 1829-35, speaker pro tem, May 16, 1834; mem. U.S. Senate (Dem.) from N.H., 1835-41; gov. N. H., 1841-43; U.S. subtreas. at Boston, 1846-49. Died Charlestown, June 5, 1857; buried Forest Hill Cemetery, Charlestown.

HUBBARD, Henry Griswold, inventor, mfr.; b. Middletown, Conn., Oct. 8, 1814; s. Elijah and Lydia (Mather) H.; attended Wesleyan U., Middletown, Conn.; m. Charlotte Rosella Macdonough, June 19, 1844. Clk., J.&.S. Baldwin's store, Middletown, 1831-33; owner, operator dry goods store, Middletown, 1833-37; perfected 1st successful elastic web woven on power looms, 1841; purchased control of Russell Mfg. Co., 1850, began mfg. elastic and non-elastic webbing; mem. Conn. Senate, 1866-67; dir. Middletown Bank; trustee Middletown Savs. Bank. Died July 29, 1891.

HUBBARD, Henry Guernsey, entomologist; b. Detroit, May 6, 1850; s. Bela and Sarah (Baughman) H.; grad. Harvard, 1873; m. Kate Laiser, 1887, 4 children, Started museum for study of entomology, Detroit, 1874; took several expdns. with E.A. Schwartz to Lake Superior Region in search for Coleoptera, 1877-78; naturalist Geol. Survey of Ky., 1879-80; agt. U.S. Entomol. Commn. of Dept. Agr., 1880-84; engaged in research of insects attacking orange trees for U.S. Dept. Agr., 1894-99. Died Jan. 18, 1899.

HUBBARD, John, educator; b. Townsend, Mass.; s. John and Mary (Bell) H.; grad. Dartmouth, 1785. Tchr., 1st preceptor New Ipswich (N.H.) Acad., 1787-95; town clk. New Ipswich, 1795-98; judge probate Cheshire County (N.H.), 1798-99; postmaster Walpole (N.H.), 1799-1802; presented comic opera, Lionel and Clarissa, Walpole; preceptor Deerfield (Mass.) Acad., 1802-05; prof. mathematics and natural philosophy Dartmouth, 1805-10. Author: Rudiments of Geography, 1803; The American Reader, 1805. Died 1810.

HUBBARD, John, physician, gov. Me.; b. Mar. 22, 1794; s. Dr. John and Olive (Wilson) H.; grad. Dartmouth, 1816; M.D., U. Pa., 1822; LL.D. Colby U., 1851; m. Sarah Barrett, July 12, 1825, 6 children including Thomas Hamlin. Tchr. Hallowell Me., Acad., 1817-18; tchr., Dinwiddie County Va., 1818-20; mem. Me. Senate, 1842-43; gov. Me., 1849-53, signed "Maine Law" (prohibition law), 1851; spl. agt. U.S. Treasury to examine customhouses in Eastern states, 1857-59; commr. under Reciprocity Treaty with Gt. Britain (concluded 1854), 1859-61. Died Hallowell, Me., Feb. 6, 1869.

HUBBARD, John Henry, congressman; b. Salisbury, Conn., Mar. 24, 1804; attended pub. schs.; studied law. Admitted to Conn. bar, 1828, began practice in Lakeville; mem. Conn. Senate, 1847-49; pros. atty., 1849-52; moved to Litchfield, Conn., 1855, practiced law; mem. U.S. Ho. of Reps. (Republican) from Conn., 38th-39th congresses, 1863-67; resumed law practice. Died Litchfield, July 30, 1872; buried East Cemetery, Litchfield.

HUBBARD, Jonathan Hatch, congressman; b Tolland, Conn., May 7, 1768; studied law. Admitted to the bar, 1790; began practice of law, Windsor, Vt.; mem. U.S. Ho. of Reps. (Federalist) from Vt., 11th Congress, 1809-11; judge Vt. Supreme Ct., 1813-15; resumed law practice. Died Windsor, Sept. 20, 1849; buried Old South Cemetery, Windsor.

HUBBARD, Joseph Stillman, astronomer; b. New Haven, Conn., Sept. 7, 1823; s. Ezra Stiles and Eliza (Church) H.; grad. Yale, 1843. Asst. to Sears C. Walker at High Sch. Observatory, Phila., 1844-45; prof. mathematics U.S. Naval Acad., stationed at U.S. Naval Observatory, 1845-63; especially interested in question of parallax of Alpha Lyrae; contbr. numerous articles to Astron. Jour.; calculated orbit of comet of 1843. Died Aug. 16, 1863.

HUBBARD, Levi, congressman; b. Worcester, Mass., Dec. 19, 1762; attended common schs. Engaged in farming, Paris, Mass. (now Me.); active state mil. orgns.; mem. Mass. Ho. of Reps., 1804, 05, 12; Mass. Senate, 1806-11, 16; mem. U.S. Ho. of Reps. (Democrat) from Mass., 13th Congress, 1813-15; mem. Me. Exec. Council, 1829. Died Paris, Feb. 18, 1836; buried in a tomb on his farm.

HUBBARD, Richard Bennett, senator, gov. Tex.; b. Walton County, Ga., Nov. 1, 1832; s. Richard Bennett and Serena (Carter) H.; grad. Mercer Coll., 1851; LL.B., Harvard, circa 1853; m. Eliza Hudson; m. 2d, Janie Roberts. U.S. dist. atty. western dist. of Tex., 1858-60; del. Democratic Nat. Conv., Charleston, S.C., 1860, supported John C. Breckinridge against Stephen A. Douglas; organizer, served to rank of col. 22d Tex. Inf., Confederate Army, 1860-65; del. Dem. Nat. Conv., 1872; gov. Tex., 1873-76; mem. U.S. Senate (Dem.) from Tex., 1876-82; temporary chmn. Dem. Nat. Conv., Chgo., 1884; E.E. and M.P. to Japan, 1884-88. Author: The United States in the Far East, 1899. Died July 12, 1901.

HUBBARD, Richard Dudley, gov. Conn., congressman; b. Berlin, Conn., Sept. 7, 1818; grad. Yale, 1839; studied law. Admitted to Conn. bar, 1842, began practice in Hartford; mem. Conn. Ho. of Reps., 1842, 55, 58; pros. atty. Hartford County (Conn.), 1846-68; mem. U.S. Ho. of Reps. (Democrat) from Conn., 40th Congress, 1867-69; gov. Conn., 1878-79; practiced law, Hartford, 1877-84. Died Hartford, Feb. 28, 1884; buried Cedar Hill Cemetery, Hartford.

HUBBARD, Samuel Dickinson, congressman, cabinet officer; b. Middletown, Conn., Aug. 10, 1799; grad. Yale, 1819; studied law. Admitted to Conn. bar; practiced law, Middletown, 1823-37; engaged in mfg.; mem. U.S. Ho. of Reps. (Whig) from Conn., 29th-30th congresses, 1845-49; U.S. postmaster gen. under Pres. Fillmore, 1852-53. Died Middletown, Oct. 8, 1855; buried Indian Hill Cemetery, Middletown.

HUBBARD, Thomas Hill, congressman; b. New Haven, Conn., Dec. 5, 1781; grad. Yale, 1799; studied law. Admitted to N.Y. bar, 1804, began practice in Hamilton; surrogate of Madison County (N.Y.), 1806-16; presdl. elector, 1812; dist. atty. 6th dist., 1816-18; dist. atty. Madison County, 1818-21; mem. U.S. Ho. of Reps. (Democrat) from N.Y., 15th, 17th congresses, 1817-19, 21-23; 1st clk. Oneida County (N.Y.) Ct. of Chancery, 1823; clk. N.Y. Supreme Ct., 1825-35; a founder Hamilton Coll., Clinton, N. Y., Hamilton (N.Y.) Acad.; trustee Utica (N. Y.) Acad.; Dem. presdl. elector, 1844, 52. Died Utica, May 21, 1857; buried Forest Hill Cemetery, Utica.

HUBBARD, William, clergyman; b. Eng., circa 1621; s. William Hubbard; grad. Harvard, 1642; m. Margaret Rogers, 1646; m. 2d, Mary Pearce, circa 1700; 3 children. Came to Am., 1635; made a freeman in Mass., 1653; joined Thomas Cobbet in Congregational ministry, Ipswich, Mass., 1656, ordained to ministry Congregational Ch., 1658; an elder who protested Mass. Gen. Ct.'s censuring of apostasy in the ch., 1671; opposed taxes of Andros Govt. in Mass., 1687; opposed witch-hunting in Mass. Author: Narrative of the Troubles with the Indians in New England, 1677; The Present State of New England, 1697. Died Sept. 14, 1704.

HUBBELL, Edwin Nelson, congressman; b. Coxsackie, N.Y., Aug. 13, 1815; Supr., Greene County (N.Y.) several years; mem. U.S. Ho. of Reps. (Democrat) from N.Y., 39th Congress, 1865-67; clk. lumber co., East Saginaw, Mich., 1883-87; asst. city treas., 1887-90, dep. city treas., 1894-96.

HUBBELL, James Randolph, congressman; b. Lincoln Twp., O., July 13, 1824; attended common schs.; studied law. Taught sch., Woodbury, O.; admitted to Ohio bar, 1845, began practice in London; moved to Delaware, O., practiced law; mem. Ohio Ho. of Reps., 1849, 58-59, 62-63, speaker, 1863; Republican presdl. elector, 1856; mem. U.S. Ho. of Reps. (Rep.) from Ohio, 39th Congress, 1865-67; apptd. minister to Portugal by Pres. Johnson, appointment not confirmed; mem. Ohio Senate, 1869; unsuccessful candidate for U.S. Ho. of Reps., 1870. Died Bellville, O., Nov. 26, 1896; buried Oak Grove Cemetery, Delaware.

HUBBELL, William Spring, congressman; b. Painted Post, N.Y., Jan. 17, 1801; attended pub. schs. Postmaster of Bath (N.Y.), 1829, town clk., 1831; engaged in banking; mem. N.Y. Ho. of Reps., 1841; mem. U.S. Ho. of Reps. (Democrat) from N.Y., 28th Congress, 1843-45; del. Dem. Nat. Conv., Charleston, S.C., 1860. Died Bath, Nov. 16, 1873; buried Grove Cemetery, Bath.

HUBBS, Rebecca, clergyman; b. Burlington County, N.J., Dec. 3, 1772; d. Paul and Rebecca (Hewlings) Crispin; m. Paul Hubbs, circa 1800. Converted to Quaker religion, began to speak at meetings, 1803; accredited as Quaker minister, 1807; sent on preachng journey through Pa., Va., Ohio, Ind., 1813-15; went to see Pres. James Madison to admonish him about the war, 1814; became famous as a preacher in East and Midwest. Died Sept. 29, 1852.

HUBLEY, Edward Burd, congressman; b. Reading, Pa., 1702; attended pub. schs.; studied law. Admitted to Pa. bar, 1820, began practice in Reading; mem. U.S. Ho. of Reps. (Jacksonian Democrat) from Pa., 24th-25th congresses, 1835-39; canal commr. of Pa., 1839-42; commr. to settle claims under an 1835 treaty with Cherokee Indians, 1842. Died Phila., Feb. 23, 1856; buried Charles Evans Cemetery, Reading.

HUDD, Thomas Richard, congressman; b. Buffalo, N.Y., Oct. 2, 1835; attended Lawrence U., Appleton, Wis.; studied law. Admitted to Wis. bar, 1856, began practice in Appleton; dist. atty. Outagamie County (Wis.), 1856-57; mem. Wis. Senate, 1862-63, 76-79, 82-83, 85; moved to Green Bay, Wis., 1868, practiced law; mem. Wis. Assembly, 1868, 75; city atty. of Green Bay, 1873-74; del. Democratic Nat. Conv., Cincinnati 1880; mem. U.S. Ho. of Reps. (Dem.) from Wis., 49th-50th congresses, Mar. 8, 1886-89. Died Green Bay, June 22, 1896; buried Woodlawn Cemetery, Green Bay.

HUDDE, Andries, surveyor; b. Kampen, Netherlands, 1608; s. Hendricks and Aeltje (Schinckels) H.; m. Geertruy Bornstra, Jan. 1639. Held office as commissary of stores in New Netherland, 1629-32; obtained deed (with Wolphert Gerritsen Van Couwenhoven) to 3,600 acres of land on Long Island, N.Y., 1636; arrived in L.I., 1638, took up residence in New Amsterdam (now N.Y.C.); surveyor of New Amsterdam, 1642-44; commissary of Ft. Nassau, 1644-52; sec. and surveyor on Delaware River, 1655-57; robbed of possessions by Indians, 1660; clk. and reader at

Ft. Altona, New Amsterdam, 1660-61. Died Nov. 4, 1663.

HUDSON, Charles, clergyman, congressman; b. Marlboro, Middlesex County, Mass., Nov. 14, 1795; s. Stephen and Louisa (Williams) H.; m. Ann Rider, July 21, 1825; m. 2d, Martha Rider, May 14, 1830. Ordained to ministry Universalist Ch., 1819; pastor 1st Universalist Parish, Westminster, Mass., 1824-42; seceded from Universalist Ch., founded Mass. Soc. Universal Restorationists; mem. Mass. Ho. of Reps., 1828;33, Mass. Senate, 1833-39, Mass. Bd. Edn., 1837-45, Mass. Exec. council, 1838-41; mem. U.S. Ho. of Reps. from Mass.; 27th-30th congresses May 3, 1841-49; naval officer Port of Boston, 1849-53; editor Boston Daily Atlas; U.S. assessor of internal revenue, Boston, 1864-68. Author: A Reply to Mr. Balfour's Essays, 1829; A History of the Town of Westminster, 1832; Doubts Concerning the Battle of Bunker Hill, 1857; also congressional reports "Protective Policy," "Capital Punishment." Died Lexington, Mass., May 4, 1881; buried Munroe Cemetery, Lexington.

HUDSON, Edward, dentist, Irish patriot; b. County Wexford, Ireland, Oct. 1772; s. Capt. Henry Edward and Jane (de Tracey) H.; studied dentistry under Dr. Hudson at Trinity Coll., Dublin, Ireland; m. Maria Bridget Bryne, Apr. 1804; m. 2d, Maria Elizabeth Becker; m. 3d, Marie Mackie; 8 children. Became involved with Thomas More and Robert Emmet (leaders of Irish Revolution) while at Trinity Coll.; imprisoned by British in Ft. George, Scotland, 1798-1802; exiled to Holland at conclusion of Treaty of Amiens, 1802; came to Am., settled in Phila., 1803; practiced dentistry, Phila., 1810-33; one of 1st to perform operation removing dental pulp and filling root of tooth with gold foil. Died Jan. 3, 1833.

HUDSON, Erasmus Darwin, surgeon; b. Torringford, Conn., Dec. 5, 1805; grad. Berkshire Med. Coll. Mem. Conn. Med. Soc.; gen. agt. Am. Anti-Slavery Soc., 1837-49; moved to N.Y.C., 1850, practiced orthopedic surgery specializing in artificial limbs. Author: Medical and Surgical History of the War of the Rebellion, 1872. Died Riverside, Conn., Dec. 31, 1880.

HUDSON, Frederic, journalist; b. Quincy, Mass., Apr. 25, 1819; s. Barzillai and Rebecca (Eaton) H.; m. Eliza Woodward, 1844, 1 son Woodward. Became reporter N.Y.C. Herald, 1837, mng. editor, circa 1840-66, Herald rep. to N.Y. Asso. Press, 1848-61, set up communication lines between N.Y. C. and New Orleans using telegraph, horse express and railroad during Civil War. Author: Journalism in the United States from 1690-1872 (1st comprehensive book on Am. journalism), 1873. Died Concord, Mass., Oct. 21, 1875.

HUDSON, Henry, explorer; flourished 1607-11; m. Katherine Hudson; children—Oliver, John, Richard. Arranged for voyage for English Muscovy Co. to find N.E. passage to China, Japan and East Indies, London, Eng., 1607; reached Spitzbergen in Arctic Ocean in his ship Hopewell, but forced to return to Eng., 1607, made 2d voyage in Hopewell, 1608; made agreement with Dutch East India Co. to find N.E. passage, 1609, sailed from Amsterdam in Half Moon, was forced to give up hope of finding N.E. passage, turned South towards America in defiance of terms of his orders, entered Delaware Bay, sailed out of Delaware Bay, North to sight of N.Y., and up river (Hudson River) named after him, reaching what is now Albany, N.Y., 1609 (Dutch claim to this area was result of this voyage); made 4th and final expdn. (financed by some English adventurers) in ship Discovery, 1610, sailed through strait between Greenland and Labrador (Hudson Strait), discovered Hudson's Bay, 1610; iced in for winter after several weeks of exploration; his crew mutinied, 1611, set Hudson, his son John and 7 others adrift without any provisions, never seen again.

HUDSON, Henry Norman, clergyman, scholar; b. Cornwall, Vt., Jan. 28, 1814; grad. Middlebury (Vt.) Coll., 1840; m. Emily Sarah Bright, Dec. 18, 1852. Apprenticed to coach maker, 1832-35; tchr., various schs., Ky. and Vt., 1840-44; moved to Boston, began lecturing on Shakespeare; ordained to ministry Protestant Episcopal Ch., 1849; editor The Churchman, 1852-55; rector Episcopal Ch., Litchfield, Conn., 1858-60; chaplain 1st N.Y. Volunteer Engrs., 1862-65, also war correspondent for N.Y. Evening Post; held under detention for his criticism of Gen. Butler, 1864; specialized in Shakespearian studies, from 1865. Author: Lectures on Shakespeare, 1848; Shakespeare, His Life, Art and Characters, 1872; Sermons, 1874; English in Schools: A Series of Essays, 1881; (pamphlet) General Butler's Campaign on the Hudson, 1883; Studies in Wordsworth, 1884. Editor: all of Shakespeare's plays, 11 vols., 1851-56; Harvard Edit. of Shakespeare's Plays, 20 vols., 1880-81. Died Cambridge, Mass., Jan. 16, 1886.

HUDSON, William Smith, mech. engr.; b. Derby, Eng., Mar. 13, 1810; s. Daniel Smith and Anne (Roper) H.; learned trade of machinist; m. Ann Elizabeth Cairns, Oct. 6, 1836; 1 child. Worked in locomotive shop, New Castle, Eng., 1830-35; came to Am., 1835; locomotive engr. Troy & Saratoga R.R., 1835-36; engr. Rochester & Auburn R.R., 1838-49; master mechanic Attica & Buffalo R.R., 1849-51; supt. locomotive works Rogers Locomotive & Machine Works, 1851-81; designed, patented unique feed water-heater, 1860; patented application of cast-iron thimbles to the ends of boiler tubes, 1861; invented an improved valve gear, safety-valves, levers, an equalizing lever, 1868-70. Died July 20, 1881.

HUDSPETH, Benoni, scout, guide; leader (with J.J. Myers) pioneer party from Jackson County, Mo. to Cal., 1849; discovered Emigrants' (also called Hudspeth's or Myers') Cut-off en route, July 1849.

HUFTY, Jacob, congressman; b. N.J. Engaged as blacksmith; served as pvt. N.J. Militia; freeholder Salem Twp. (N.J.), 1792, 1800-04, dir. bd. chosen freeholders, 1801; overseer of poor, collector Salem Twp., 1793; county justice Salem County (N.J.), 1797, county judge, 1798, sheriff, 1801-04, county justice and judge, 1804, county collector, 1805-08, judge orphans ct., 1805-08, surrogate, 1898; mem. N.J. Council, 1804, 06-07; mem. U.S. Ho. of Reps. (Democrat) from N.J., 11th-13th congresses, 1809-14. Died Salem, N.J., May 20, 1814; buried St. John's Episcopal Cemetery, Salem.

HUGER, Benjamin, congressman; b. at or nr. Charleston, S.C., 1768. Engaged in rice planting on Waccamaw River; mem. S.C. Ho. of Reps., 1798-99; mem. U.S. Ho. of Reps. from S.C., 6th-8th, 14th congresses, 1799-1805, 15-17; mem. S.C. Senate, 1818-23, pres., 1819-22. Died on estate nr. Georgetown, S.C., July 7, 1823; buried All Saints' Churchyard, Georgetown.

HUGER, Benjamin, army officer; b. Carleston, S.C., Nov. 22, 1805; s. Francis Kinlock and Harriott (Pickney) H.; grad. U.S. Mil. Acad., 1825; m. Elizabeth Pickney, Feb. 17, 1831, 5 children. Commd. 2d lt. arty., U.S. Army, 1825, capt. of ordnance, 1832, commanded arsenals at Fortress Monroe, Pikesville, Md. and Charleston, S.C., armory at Harpers Ferry; mem. ordinace bd. Dept. of War, 1839-46, sent abroad to study European mil. methods, 1840; chief of ordnance U.S. Army under Gen. Scott, in charge of seige of trains at Vera Cruz during Mexican War, 1846; brevetted maj., lt. col., col.; commd. col. arty. Confederate Army, 1861; commd. brig. gen. Provisional Army of Confederate States, 1861, commanded troops from S.C. at Norfolk, later all troops and defenses around Norfolk, 1861; relieved of command after Battle of Malvern Hill (under charge of failing to cut off McClellan's retreat after Cnfederate victory), 1862; became an insp. arty. and ordnance, 1862. Died Charleston, Dec. 7, 1877.

HUGER, Daniel, congressman; b. "Limerick," St. John's Parish, Berkeley County, S.C., Feb. 20, 1742; attended sch., Charleston, also in Eng.; children include Daniel Elliott. Justice of peace, 1775; mem. S.C. Ho. of Reps., 1778-79; mem. S.C. Gov.'s Council, 1780; del. Continental Congress from S.C., 1786-88; mem. U.S. Ho. of Reps. from S.C., 1st-2d congresses, 1789-93; engaged in mng. his estates. Died Charleston, S.C., July 6, 1799; buried Western churchyard of St. Philip's Ch., Charleston.

HUGER, Daniel Eliott, senator, jurist; b. S.C., June 28, 1779; s. Daniel and Sabina (Elliott) H.; A.B., Coll. of N.J. (now Princeton), 1798, A.M., 1801; m. Isabella Middleton, Nov. 6, 1800, 10 children. Admitted to S.C. bar, 1799; mem. S.C. Legislature, 1804-19, 38-42 (protested against states rights doctrine); commd. brig. gen. S.C. Militia, 1814; circuit judge S.C. Ct. Appeals, 1819-30; became reconciled with Calhoun, adopted moderate states rights position; mem. U.S. Senate from S.C. (States Rights Democrat, replacing John C. Calhoun), 1843-45. Died Sullivans Island, S.C., Aug. 21, 1854.

HUGER, Francis Kinloch, physician, army officer; b. Charleston, S.C., Sept. 17, 1773; s. Benjamin and Mary (Kinloch) H.; studied in London under surgeon John Hunter; M.D., U. Pa., 1797; m. Harriet Lucas Pinckney, Jan. 14, 1802. Served on med. staff Brit. Army, Flanders, 1794-95; unsuccessfully attempted (with Dr. Justus Eric Bollman) to liberate Lafayette imprisoned at Olmütz, Vienna, circa 1796; returned to Am., 1796; served as capt. U.S. Army, 1798-1801, lt. col. arty. during War of 1812; moved to Pendleton, S.C., 1826; lived in Charleston, S.C., circa 1854-55. Died Charleston, Feb. 14, 1855.

HUGER, Isaac, army officer; b. S.C., Mar. 8, 1742; s. Daniel and Mary (LeJan) H.; m. Elizabeth Chalmers, Mar. 23, 1762, 8 children. Mem. S.C. Provincial Congress, 1755, 1778; served as lt. S.C. Militia during Cherokee War, 1760, lt. col. 1st Regt., 1775; col. 5th Regt., Continental Army, 1776; brig. gen. So. Army, 1779, fought at battles of Stone Ferry, Charleston, Guilford Court House (in command Virginians), Hobkirk's Hill; defeated by Tarleton and Webster at Battle of Monk's Corner, 1780; mem. S.C. Gen. Assembly, 1782; v.p. S.C. br. Soc. of Cincinnati, 1783. Died Charleston, S.C. Oct. 17, 1797.

HUGER, John, revolutionary patriot; b. Limerick Plantation, S.C., June 5, 1744; s. Daniel and Mary (Cordes) H.; m. Charlotte Motte, Mar. 15, 1767; m. 2d, Anne Broun, Jan. 11, 1785; 8 children including Alfred. Served as ensign in Cherokee War, 1760; mem. Commons House of Provincial Congress of S.C., 1775; mem. S.C. Council of Safety; became 1st sec. of state under new S.C. Constn., 1776; intendent City of Charleston (S.C.), 1792-1804. Died Charleston, Jan. 22, 1804.

HUGHES, Charles, congressman; b. New Orleans, Feb. 27, 1822; studied law. Admitted to the bar, 1846; began law practice, Sandy Hill (now Hudson Falls), N.Y.; mem. U.S. Ho. of Reps. (Democrat) from N.Y., 33d Congress, 1853-55; clk. ct. appeals, 1860-62; provost marshall 16th Dist. of N.Y., 1862; mem. staff of gov. N.Y., also judge adv. gen. N.Y. Militia, 1875-79; mem. N.Y. Senate, 1878-79; resumed law practice, Sandy Hill. Died Sandy Hill, Aug. 10, 1887; buried Union Cemetery, nr. Sandy Hill.

HUGHES, Christopher, diplomat; b. Balt., 1786; s. Christopher and Margaret (Sanderson) H.; A.B., Coll. of N.J. (now Princeton), 1805, A.M., 1808; m. Laura Smith. Sec. to Am. Peace Commn. at Ghent, 1814; mem. Md. Ho. of Dels., 1815-16; sent on spl. duty to Cartagena, New Granada, 1816; sec. of legation, Stockholm, Sweden, 1816-25, charge d'affaires during most of this period; apptd. charge d'affaires at Ct. of Netherlands by Pres. John Quincy Adams, 1825; charge d'affaires, Stockholm, 1830-42, Netherlands, 1842-45. Died Balt., Sept. 18, 1849.

HUGHES, David Edward, inventor; b. London, Eng., May 16, 1831; son of David Hughes; m. Anna Chadbourne. Came with parents to U.S., 1838; taught music and natural philosophy; became interested in telegraphic experimentation; settled in Bowling Green, Ky., 1853; supported his researches by giving music lessons; worked on improved methods of telegraphic printing, sold his still-uncompleted printing device to Comml. Printing Telegraph Co. for $100,000, 1855, patented invention, 1856; starting working for Am. Telegraph Co., 1856; went to Eng. in unsuccessful attempt to introduce his methods there, 1857-60; had his system adopted by France, 1861, also by all other major European countries, by 1869; lived in London, 1877-1900; considered to be inventor of microphone, 1878; did work in aerial telegraphy, never published results; fellow, v.p., recipient Gold medal Royal Soc.; recipient Albert medal Soc. of Arts. Died London, Jan. 22, 1900; buried London.

HUGHES, George Wurtz, congressman, engr., railroad exec.; b. Elmira, N.Y., Sept. 30, 1806; s. John and Anna (Konkle) H.; attended U.S. Mil. Acad.; m. Ann Sarah Maxey. Became civil engr. for U.S. Govt.; commd. capt. Topog. Engrs., U.S. Army, 1838; served in Mexican War, promoted maj., later col.; mil. gov. Jalapa Province for a time; railroad surveyor employed by W. H. Aspinwall and J.C. Stevens to run line across Panama, 1848-49; resigned commn., 1850; pres. Balt. & Susquehanna R.R., 1854-57, continued as pres. after merger into No. Central R.R., q.m. gen. of Md., 1857-59; mem. U.S. Ho. of Reps. (Democrat) from Md., 36th Congress, 1858-61; engaged as planter and cons. engr. Died West River, Md., Dec. 3, 1870; buried West River.

HUGHES, Henry, stage legislator, writer; b. Miss.; grad. Oakland Coll., Miss., 1847. Practiced in Port Gibson, Miss.; mem. Miss. Senate, 1857; enlisted as pvt. in Confederate Army at start of Civil War; became capt., later col. 12th Miss. Regt., 1861; Author: Treatise on Sociology (defense of Southern slavery), 1854; paper "A Report on the African Apprentice System" (attempted to prove that slavery had improved in South), 1859. Died of illness contracted during Civil War, Port Gibson, Oct. 3, 1862.

HUGHES, James, congressman, jurist; b. Hamstead, Md., Nov. 24, 1823. Admitted to Ind. bar, 1842; served as lt. in Mexican War; judge 6th Jud. Circuit of Ind., 1852-56; prof. law Ind. U., 1853-56; mem. U.S. Ho. of Reps. from Ind., 35th Congress, 1857-59; judge U.S. Ct. of Claims,

1860-64; mem. Ind. Legislature, 1866-67; mem. Ind. Senate, 1868. Died Badensburg, Md., Oct. 21, 1873; buried Rose Hill Cemetery, Bloomington, Ind.

HUGHES, James Madison, congressman; b. Bourbon County, Ky., Apr. 7, 1809; studied law. Admitted to the bar; practiced law, engaged in merc. bus., Liberty, Mo.; mem. Mo. Ho. of Reps., 1839; mem. U.S. Ho. of Reps. (Democrat) from Mo., 28th Congress, 1843-45; engaged in banking bus., St. Louis, 1855. Died Jefferson City, Mo., Feb. 26, 1861; buried Bellefontaine Cemetery, St. Louis.

HUGHES, John Joseph, clergyman; b. Annaloghan, Ireland, June 24, 1797; s. Patrick and Margaret (McKenna) H. Came to Am., 1817 ordained priest Roman Catholic Ch., Phila., 1826; temporarily assigned to St. Augustine's Ch., Phila.; pastor old St. Mary's Ch., Phila.; accepted famous challenge of Rev. John R. Breckenridge to justify Roman Cath. Ch., 1830, continued public controversy until 1835; coadjutor bishop N.Y. with right of succession, 1837; consecrated titular bishop of Basileopolis, 1838, became formal head 1842; founder St. John's Coll., 1841; co-founder Provincial Sem., Troy, N.Y.; an organizer Catholic parochial sch. system in N.Y.; leader in establishment of N. Am. Coll. in Rome; archbishop of N.Y. (newly created archdiocese), 1850, received pollium from Pius IX in Rome 1851; laid cornerstones of St. Patrick's Cathedral, 1858, and of new Cath. U. in Ireland, 1862. Died Jan. 3, 1864.

HUGHES, Price, colonizer; b. Kaullygan, Wales. Conceived plan of Welsh colony in S.C. (with brother Valentine); came to Am., circa 1712, received land grants in Craven County (S.C.); became Indian agt.; formulated plan to have British supplant French in Mississippi Valley; engaged in trade in La., obtained alliances with Chickasaw and Choctaw Indians; captured by French at Manchac, Miss., while visiting various Brit. trading posts during winter of 1714-15, later released. Killed by Tohome Indians nr. Alabama River during gen. Indian uprising against all white settlers, 1715.

HUGHES, Robert Ball, sculptor; b. London, Eng., Jan. 19, 1806; studied under Edward Hodges Baily and Royal Acad. Won gold medal for bas-relief Pandora Brought by Mercury to Epimetheus, 1823; came to U.S., circa 1828; completed marble statute of Bishop John H. Hobart, 1831, later did marble statute of Alexander Hamilton; cast statue of Nathaniel Bowditch (1st bronze statute in Am., 1847; sculpted Little Nell, 1858; also did busts of John Marshall and John Trumball; did wax portraits including William Henry Harrison and Robert Charles Winthrop. Died Boston, Mar. 5, 1868.

HUGHES, Thomas Hurst, congressman; b. Cold Spring, N.J., Jan. 10, 1769; attended pub. schs. Engaged in merc. bus., Cape May City, N.J.; built Congress Hall (a hotel), 1816, conducted it during summer seasons; sheriff of Cape May County, 1801-04; mem. N.J. Gen. Assembly, 1805-07, 09, 12-13; mem. N.J. Council, 1819-23, 24-25; mem. U.S. Ho. of Reps. (Whig) from N.J., 21st-22d congresses, 1829-33; resumed hotel bus. Died Cold Spring, Nov. 10, 1839; buried Cold Spring Cemetery.

HUGHSTON, Jonas Abbott, congressman; b. Sidney, N.Y., 1808; studied law. Admitted to N.Y. bar, 1839, began practice in Delhi; dist. atty. Delaware County (N.Y.), 1842-45; mem. U.S. Ho. of Reps. (Whig) from N.Y., 34th Congress, 1855-57; marshal of consular ct. at Shanghai, China (apptd. by Pres. Lincoln), 1862. Died Shanghai, Nov. 10, 1862; buried Poo-ting Cemetery, Shanghai.

HUGUNIN, Daniel, Jr., congressman; b. Montgomery County, N.Y., Feb. 6, 1790; s. Daniel Hugunin. Served in War of 1812; mem. U.S. Ho. of Reps. (contested election) from N.Y., 19th Congress, Dec. 15, 1825-27; U.S. marshal for Territory of Wis., 1841-50. Died Kenosha, Wis., June 21, 1850; buried Green Ridge Cemetery, Kenosha.

HUIDEKOPER, Frederic, clergyman; b. Meadville, Pa., Apr. 7, 1817; s. Harm Jan and Rebecca (Colhoon) H.; grad. Harvard; attended Geneva, Leipzig and Berlin univs.; m. Harriet Nancy Huidekoper, Nov. 10, 1853, 4 children. Returned to U.S. after 2 years abroad, 1841; ordained evangelist Unitarian Ch., Meadville, 1843; a founder Meadville Theol. Sch., 1844, prof., 1844-77. Author: The Belief of the First Three Centuries Concerning Christ's Mission to the Underworld, 1854; Judaism at Rome, 1876; The Indirect Testimony of History to the Genuineness of the Gospels, 1879. Died Meadville, May 16, 1892.

HUIDEKOPER, Harm Jan, land speculator; b. Hodgeveen, Holland, Apr. 3, 1776; s. Anne Jans and Gesiena Frederica (Wolthers)) H.; m. Rebecca Colhoon, Sept. 1, 1806; children—Anna, Frederic. Arrived in N.Y.C., 1796; joined Dutch settlement at Oldenbarneveld, Pa., 1797; bookkeeper land office of Holland Land Co., Phila., 1802, became local agt., Meadville, Pa., 1805; sec. Pa. Population Soc.; became pvt. agt. for new owners following sale of Holland Land Co. (1810) and Pa. Population Soc. (1813); established home sch. for his children at his manor house with public Unitarian worship on Sabbath, 1825; published monthly The Unitarian Essayist, 1831-32; chief founder Meadville Theol. Sch., 1844. Died May 22, 1854.

HULBERT, John Whitefield, congressman; b. Alford, Mass., June 1, 1770; grad. Harvard, 1795; studied law. Admitted to Mass. bar, began practice in Alford, 1797; dir. Berkshire Bank, Pittsfield, Mass.; mem. U.S. Ho. of Reps. (Federalist) from Mass., 13th-14th congresses, Sept. 26, 1814-17; moved to Auburn, N.Y., 1817; mem. N.Y. Ho. of Reps., 1825; resumed law practice. Died Auburn, Oct. 19, 1831; buried North St. Cemetery, Auburn.

HULBURD, Calvin Tilden, congressman; b. Stockholm, N.Y., June 5, 1809; grad. Middlebury Coll.; attended Yale Law Sch. Admitted to N.Y. bar, 1833; mem. N.Y. Assembly, 1842-44, 62; mem. U.S. Ho. of Reps. (Republican) from N.Y., 38th-40th congresses, 1863-69; supt. constrn. of N.Y. Post Office. Died Brasher Falls, N.Y., Oct. 25, 1897; buried Fairview Cemetery, Brasher Falls.

HULL, Isaac, naval officer; b. Huntington, Conn., Mar. 9, 1773; s. Lt. Joseph and Sarah (Bennet) H.; m. Anna Hart, Jan. 2, 1813, no children. Commanded 1st ship before age of 21, 1793; commd. lt. U.S. Navy, 1798; served on frigate Constitution during naval war with France; commanded ships Enterprise and Argus during war with Tripoli; promoted comdr., 1804; assisted Gen. William Eaton in attacking and seizing Derna in Libya, 1805; commd. capt., 1806; in command of Constitution, 1810, noted for defeating and compelling surrender of Brit. frigate Guerrier during War of 1812 (1st important naval action of war); commanded Boston Navy Yard, Portsmouth Navy Yard, 1812-15; apptd. naval commr., resigned to return to Boston Navy Yard; commanded Pacific Station; commd. commodore; comdt. Washington (D.C.) Navy Yard, 1829-35; chmn. Bd. of Revision, 1838; in command Mediterranean Station, 1839-41. Died Phila., Feb. 13, 1843; buried Laurel Hill Cemetery, Phila.

HULL, John, colonial ofcl., mcht., silversmith; b. Leicestershire, Eng., Dec. 18, 1624; s. Robert and Elizabeth (Storer) H.; attended sch. of Philemon Pormort; m. Judith Quincy, 1647, at least 2 children including Hannah (wife of Judge Samuel Sowall). Came to Am., 1635; elected cpl. Mass. Militia; became head mint Mass. Bay Colony, 1652, designed coins known as Boston or Bay shillings; ensign South Mil. Co., 1654; selectman Boston, 1657, town treas., 1658; mem. Boston Arty. Co., 1660, later ensign, lt. and capt.; dep. to Mass. Gen. Ct., 1669-73; mem. war com. King Philip's War, also treas. for war; 1675; treas. Mass. Bay Colony, 1675-80, asst. to gov., 1680; one of earliest silversmiths in Am. (in partnership with Robert Sanderson), some of his works now in leading Am. museums; leading mcht. and banker in Am. colonies; kept diaries published in Collections and Transactions, Am. Antiquarian Soc., Vol. III, 1857. Died Boston, Sept. 28, 1683.

HULL, William, territorial gov., army officer; b. Derby, Conn., June 24, 1753; s. Joseph and Eliza (Clark) H.; grad. Yale, 1772, A.M. (hon.), 1779; A.M., (hon.) Harvard, 1787; m. Sarah Fuller, 1781, 1 adopted son, Isaac (naval hero). Admitted to Conn. bar, 1775; joined Continental Army as capt. Derby Militia, 1775, advanced through grades to maj., lt. col.; served in battles of White Plains, Trenton, Princeton, Saratoga, Monmouth and Stony Point; helped suppress Shay's Rebellion, 1787; judge Mass. Ct. Common Pleas, circa 1790; mem. Mass. Senate, 1790-1805; an organizer Soc. of Cincinnati; gov. Mich. Territory (apptd. by Pres. Jefferson), 1805-12; brig. gen. U.S. Army in command of defense of Mich. and attack on upper Can., 1812; surrendered to Gen. Isaac Brock after futile attack upon British in upper Can., at Detroit without even giving battle 1812; court martialed, found guilty of cowardice and neglect of duty, sentenced to death; vindicated, 1824. Died Newton, Mass., Nov. 29, 1825.

HULLIHEN, Simon P., surgeon; b. Point Twp., Fla., Dec. 10, 1810; s. Thomas and Rebecca (Freeze) H.; M.D., Washington Coll., Balt.; m. E. Fundenburg, 1834. Practiced surgery and dentistry, Canton, O., 1832; moved to Wheeling, Va. (now W.Va.), 1834; chiefly interested in surgery of face and mouth and plastic surgery; developer numerous dental instruments; contbr. articles "Harelip and its Treatment" (1844), "Cleft Palate and its Treatment" (1845) to Am. Jour. of Dental Science. Died Mar. 27, 1857.

HUMBERT, Jean Joseph Amable, army officer, adventurer; b. Rouvray, France, Nov. 25, 1775. Entered French Army, 1792; gen. of brigade, 1794; aided in suppressing Vendée Revolt; fought for Irish, 1798; served in Santo Domingo; came to U.S., 1814; took part in Battle of New Orleans on U.S. side; fought in Mexico on various filibuster expdns. Died New Orleans, Jan. 2, 1823; buried St. Louis Cemetery, New Orleans.

HUME, William, canning co. exec.; b. Waterville, Me., Nov. 19, 1830; s. William and Harriett (Hunter) H.; m. Emma Lord, 1876. Went to Cal., 1852, returned to Me. to bring his 2 brothers and a friend back to West Coast; formed canning firm Hapgood, Hume & Co., Yoco County, Wash., 1864; built 1st canning co. on Columbia River in order to obtain better grade of fish, 1865; owned more than half of all canning factories in Northwest, by 1865. Died June 25, 1902.

HUMES, Thomas William, coll. pres.; b. Knoxville, Tenn., Apr. 22, 1815; s. Thomas and Margaret (Russell) H.; grad. East Tenn. Coll., 1830, M.A., 1833; attended Princeton Theol. Sem.; m. Cornelia Williams, Dec. 4, 1834; m. 2d, Anna B. Williams, Apr. 12, 1849. Mcht., 1834-39; editor Knoxville Register and Watch Tower; ordained deacon Protestant Episcopal Ch., 1845; rector St. John's Episcopal Ch., Knoxville, 1846; chmn. exec. com. East Tenn. Relief Assn. during and immediately after Civil War; pres. East Tenn. Coll., 1865-83. Author: The Loyal Mountaineers of Tennessee, 1881. Died Jan. 16, 1892.

HUMPHREY, Charles, congressman; b. Little Britain, N.Y., Feb. 14, 1792; attended Newburgh (N.Y.) Acad.; studied law. Entered U.S. Army at beginning of War of 1812, served as capt. 41st Regt., U.S. Inf.; admitted to N.Y. bar, 1816; moved to Ithaca, N.Y., 1818, practiced law; mem. U.S. Ho. of Reps. (Democrat) from N.Y., 19th Congress, 1825-27; pres. Village of Ithaca, 1828-29; surrogate of Tompkins County (N.Y.), 1831-34; mem. N.Y. Assembly, 1834-35, 42, speaker, 1835-36; clk. N.Y. Supreme Ct., 1843-47. Died Albany, N.Y., Apr. 17, 1850; buried City Cemetery, Ithaca.

HUMPHREY, Heman, clergyman, coll. pres.; b. West Simsbury, Conn., Mar. 26, 1779; s. Solomon and Hannah (Brown) H.; grad. Yale, 1805; m. Sophia Porter, Apr. 20, 1808. Taught in local Conn. schs.; licensed to preach by Litchfield North Assn. (Congregational), 1806; ordained to ministry Congregational Ch., Fairfield, Conn., 1807; refused to accept half-way covenant; began temperance agitation, 1810; pastor, Pittsfield, Mass., 1817-23; pres. Charitable Collegiate Instn. (now Amherst Coll.), 1823-45. Author: Domestic Education, 1840; Letters to a Son in the Ministry, 1842; Life and Labors of Reverend T. H. Ballaudt, 1857. Died Apr. 3, 1861.

HUMPHREY, Herman Leon, congressman; b. Candor, N.Y., Mar. 14, 1830; attended Cortland Acad. Clk., Ithaca, N.Y.; admitted to N.Y. bar, 1854; moved to Hudson, Wis., 1855, began practice of law; dist. atty. St. Croix County (Wis.); county judge, 1860-62; mem. Wis. Senate, 1862-63; mayor of Hudson, 1 year; judge 8th Jud. Circuit of Wis., 1866-76; mem. U.S. Ho. of Reps. (Republican) from Wis., 45th-47th congresses, 1877-83; mem. Wis. Assembly, 1887. Died Hudson, June 10, 1902; buried Willow River Cemetery, Hudson.

HUMPHREY, James, congressman; b. Fairfield, Conn., Oct. 9, 1811; grad. Amherst (Mass.) Coll., 1831; studied law. Admitted to the bar, practiced law; moved to Bklyn.; mem. U.S. Ho. of Reps. (Republican) from N.Y., 36th, 39th congresses, 1859-61, 65-66. Died Bklyn., June 16, 1866; buried Greenwood Cemetery, Bklyn.

HUMPHREY, Reuben, congressman; b. West Simsbury, Conn., Sept. 2, 1757. Served from pvt. to capt. during Revolutionary War; keeper Newgate State Prison, Simsbury, Conn., 5 years; moved to N.Y., 1801, settled nr. Marcellus; 1st county judge Onondaga County, 1804-07; mem. U.S. Ho. of Reps. from N.Y., 10th Congress, 1807-09; mem. N.Y. Senate, 1811-15; engaged in farming. Died nr. Marcellus, Aug. 10, 1832; buried Old City Cemetery, Marcellus.

HUMPHREYS, Andrew Atkinson, engr., soldier, scientist; b. Phila., Nov. 2, 1810; s. Samuel and Letitia (Atkinson) H.; grad. U.S. Mil. Acad., 1831; L.L.D. (hon.), Harvard; m. Rebecca Hollingsworth, 1839, 4 children. Commd. lt. arty., U.S. Army, 1831, served as civil engr. in Corps Topog. Engrs.; planned Delaware River fortifications and harbor works, 1837-38; commd. lt. Corps Topog. Engrs., 1838; assigned to duty in Coast Survey, 1844; commd. capt., 1848, maj. on

McClellan's staff, 1861; commd. maj. gen., chief of staff Army of Potomac, 1863-64; commd. brig. gen. U.S. Volunteers, chief Topog. Engrs., fought at battles of Fredericksburg and Chancellorsville, commanded Union div. at Battle of Gettysburg and corps in operations around Gettysburg, 1864-65; command II Army Corps, 1864; chief C.E. with rank brig. gen., 1866-79, brevetted col. Battle of Fredericksburg, brig. gen. Battle of Gettysburg, maj. gen. Battle of Sailor's Creek. Mem. Am. Philos. Soc., Am. Acad. Arts and Scis.; incorporator Nat. Acad. Scis. Died Washington, D.C., Dec. 27, 1883.

HUMPHREYS, Benjamin Grubb, army officer, gov. Miss.; b. Clairborne County, Miss., Aug. 24-26, 1808; s. George Wilson and Sarah (Smith) H.; ed. U.S. Mil. Acad.; m. Mary McLaughlin, 1832; m. 2d, Mildred Hickman, Dec. 1839; 14 children. Mem. Miss. Legislature from Claiborne County, 1838-40, Miss. Senate, 1840-44; commd. capt. 21st Miss. Regt., Confederate Army, 1861; col., led regt. through major battles of Army N. Va.; achieved distinction at Gettysburg and Fredericksburg; brig. gen. commanding 21st, 13th, 17th, 18th Miss. regts. McLaw's Div., Longstreet's Corps, Army No. Va., 1863; gov. Miss, 1865-68 (famous Black Code passed during this period, effecting his removal and downfall of local govt.). Died Ita Bena, Miss., Dec. 20, 1882; buried Port Gibson, Miss.

HUMPHREYS, Charles, Continental congressman; b. Haverford, Pa., Sept. 19, 1714. Engaged in milling; mem. Pa. Provincial Congress, 1764-74; mem. Continental Congress from Pa., 1774-76, voted against Declaration of Independence; Quaker. Died Haverford, Mar. 11, 1786; buried Old Haverford Meeting House Cemetery.

HUMPHREYS, David, army officer, diplomat, writer; b. Derby, Conn., July 10, 1752; s. Rev. Daniel and Sar ah((Riggs) H.; A.B., Yale, 1771, M.A., 1774; m. Ann Frances Bulkeley, 1797. Served as brigade maj., 1777; lt. col., aide-de-camp to Gen. Washington, 1780; apptd. sec. Commn. for Negotiating Treaties of Commerce with Fgn. Powers, 1784; mem. Conn. Assembly, 1786; comdt. new regt. for operations against Indians, 1786; comdr. fed. troops that surpressed Shays' Rebellion, 1787; publisher (with Barlow, Hopkins and Trumbull) The Anarchiad (satirical essay), 1786-87; spl. agt. to obtain information for Am. govt. at London, Lisbon and Madrid; sole commr. for Algerine affairs, 1793; E.E. and M.P. to Spain, 1796; capt.-gen. Vet. Volunteers, War of 1812; mem. group known as "Hartford (or Conn.) Wits;" poetic works include: A Poem Addressed to the Armies of the United States of America, 1780; The Happiness of America, 1786; The Widow of Malabar: A Tragedy; wrote comedy The Yankey in England, 1815. Died New Haven, Conn., Feb. 21, 1818.

HUMPHREYS, James, printer; b. Phila., Jan. 15, 1748; s. James and Susanna (Assheton) H.; attended Coll. of Phila., 1763-64; studied medicine; m. Mary Yorke. Apprenticed to printer William Bradford; began printing house, 1770; published Wetten-Hall's Greek Grammar (1st Greek text published in colonies), 1773; founded newspaper The Pennsylvania Ledger; . . ., 1775-76, 77-78; moved to Loyalist colony, Shelburne, N.S., Can.; established N.S. Packet, mcht., 1780-97; returned to Phila. as printer. Died Phila., Feb. 2, 1810; buried Christ Ch. Burial Ground, Phila.

HUMPHREYS, John J., architect; b. 1860. Practiced as architect in assn. with Frank E. Kidder, Denver, Colo., designed Christ Methodist Ch., Jewish Synagogue, both Denver, Mines and Transp. Bldg. at Trans-Miss. Expn., Omaha, Neb., 1898; maintained independent office after 1891. Died 1896.

HUMPHREYS, Joshua, ship builder; b. Haverford Pa., June 17, 1751; s. Joshua and Sara (Williams) H.; m. Mary Davids, 11 children. Apprentice to ship carpenter, Phila.; later became owner shipyard; built many ships for Continental Navy; his suggestion led to Am.'s decision to build super-frigates of Constitution class; apptd. naval constructor to new U.S. Govt., 1794-1801; built govt. docks and wharfs, 1806. Died Jan. 12, 1838.

HUMPHREYS, Parry Wayne, congressman; b. Lexington, Ky.; studied law. Admitted to the bar, 1801; began practice of law, Nashville, Tenn.; judge Superior Ct. of Tenn., 1807-09; judge Tenn. Jud. Circuit, 1809-13, 18-36; mem. U.S. Ho. of Reps. (Democrat), from Tenn., 13th Congress, 1813-15; unsuccessful Whig candidate for U.S. Senate, 1817; moved to Hernando, Miss., engaged in banking. Died Hernando, Mar. 1, 1839; buried Methodist Cemetery, Hernando.

HUMPHREYS, West Hughes, jurist; b. Montgomery County, Tenn., Aug. 26, 1806; s. Perry Wayne and Mary (West) H.; m. Amanda M. Pillow, Jan. 1839. Admitted to Tenn. bar, 1828; moved to Fayette County; del. Tenn. Constl. Conv., 1834; mem. lower house Tenn. Gen. Assembly, 1835-38; atty. gen. Tenn., 1839-51, also reporter Tenn. Supreme Ct.; U.S. dist. judge of Tenn., 1853-62; supported secession of Tenn.; judge Dist. of Tenn. under Confederate States Am., 1862; impeached by U.S. Congress for being Confederate judge, prevented from holding any fed. office, found not guilty on charge that as judge he had decreed confiscation of property of Andrew Johnson and John Catron. Author: Suggestions on the Subject of Bank Charters, 1859; author and editor Reports of Cases . . . in the Supreme Court of Tennessee, 1839-51, 11 vols., 1841-51. Died nr. Nashville, Tenn., Oct. 16, 1882.

HUNGERFORD, John Newton, congressman; b. Vernon, N.Y., Dec. 31, 1825; grad. Hamilton Coll., Clinton, N.Y., 1846. Settled in Corning, N.Y., 1848, engaged in banking; del. Republican Nat. Conv., Phila., 1872; mem. U.S. Ho. of Reps. (Republican) from N.Y., 45th Congress, 1877-79. Died Corning, Apr. 2, 1883; buried Glenwood Cemetery, Watkins Glen, N.Y.

HUNGERFORD, John Pratt, congressman; b. Leeds, Va., Jan. 2, 1761; studied law. Admitted to the bar, practiced law; served in Revolutionary War; mem. Va. Ho. of Dels., 1797-1801, 23-30, Va. Senate, 1801-09; mem. U.S. Ho. of Reps. from Va., 13th-14th congresses, 1813-17; served as brig. gen. Va. Militia during War of 1812. Died "Twiford," Westmoreland County, Va., Dec. 21, 1833; buried Hungerford Cemetery, Leedstown, Va.

HUNGERFORD, Orville, congressman; b. Farmington, Conn., Oct. 29, 1790; attended pub. schs. Retail clk., Burrville, N.Y., later engaged in merc. bus., Watertown, N.Y.; cashier Jefferson County Nat. Bank, Watertown, 1820-33, pres., 1834-45, also dir., until 1851; Democratic presdl. elector, 1836; mem. U.S. Ho. of Reps. (Democrat) from N.Y., 28th-29th congresses, 1843-47; unsuccessful Dem. candidate for comptroller State of N.Y., 1847; pres. Watertown & Rome R.R. Co., 1847-51. Died Watertown, Apr. 6, 1851; buried Brookside Cemetery, Watertown.

HUNNEWELL, Horatio Hollis, banker; b. Watertown, Mass., July 27, 1810; s. Dr. Walter and Susanna (Cooke) H.; m. Isabelle Pratt Welles, Dec. 24, 1835, probably 2 sons. Worked for Welles & Co., banking house, Paris, France, 1825-37; returned to Mass., 1837; pres. 3 railroads, dir. of many including I.C. R.R. and Mich. Central R.R.; a founder, dir. Webster Bank of Boston; v.p. Provident Instn. for Savs., 1861-1902; established H. H. Hunnewell & Sons., Boston, 1860; interested in horticulture, supported Mass. Hort. Soc., Arnold Arboretum, botany depts. of Harvard and Wellesley Coll. Died Mar. 20, 1902.

HUNNEWELL, James, sea trader; b. Charlestown, Mass., Feb. 10, 1794; s. William and Sarah (Frothingham) H.; m. Susannah Lamson, Sept. 23, 1819. Served in ship that traded along Cal. coast, 1816, ship sold in Honolulu to some Hawaiian chiefs who payed for it in sandalwood, spent several months of extensive travel in Hawaii to collect payment, became acquainted with language and customs of natives; sailed in Thaddeus with 1st Am. missionaries to go to Hawaii, 1819, Thaddeus also sold for sandalwood, remained again to collect payment; sailed around Cape Horn in Missionary Packet, reached Honolulu, 1826; established comml. house later known as C. Brewer & Co.; exported goods from Charlestown to Hawaii and Cal., 1830-66; a founder Oahu Coll., Hawaii. Died May 2, 1869.

HUNT, Alfred Ephraim, metallurgist; b. East Douglas, Mass., Mar. 31, 1855; s. Leander and Mary (Hanchett) H.; grad. Mass. Inst. Tech., 1876; m. Maria McQuesten, Oct. 29, 1878, 1 son. Worked for Bay State Steel Co., 1876, helped build 2d open hearth furnace in U.S., South Boston; reported on iron fields of Northern Mich. and Wis., 1876, important in devel. of these regions; supt. steel dept. Nashua Iron & Steel Co. (N.H.), 1877-81; metall. chemist, supr. Park Bros. & Co., Pitts., 1881-83; established chem. and metall. lab. with George Clapp, 1883; organized Pitts. Reduction Co., company bought control patents for Hall process of reduction of aluminum; commanded Battery B of Pa. in Spanish-Am. War, contracted malaria in P.R. Died Phila., Apr. 26, 1899.

HUNT, Freeman, publisher; b. Quincy, Mass., Mar. 21, 1804; s. Nathan and Mary (Turner) H.; m. Lucia Blake, May 6, 1829; m. 2d, Laura Phinney, Jan. 2, 1831; m. 3d, Elizabeth Parmenter, Oct. 1853; at least 1 son. Established publishing firm Putnam & Hunt, 1828-30; published Ladies Mag. and American Anecdotes, 1830; edited Am. Mag. of Useful and Entertaining Knowledge, published by Boston Bewick Co. (coop. firm of authors, artists, printers and booksellers); established Freeman Hunt & Co., published Letters about the Hudson River and Its Vicinity, 1836, Mchts.' Mag. and Comml. Review, 1839-58 (known as Hunt's Mchts.' Mag. 1850-60). Author: Lives of American Merchants, 2 vols., 1858. Died Mar. 2, 1858.

HUNT, Harriot Kezia, physician, reformer; b. Boston, Nov. 9, 1805; d. Joab and Kezia (Wentworth) Hunt. Practiced medicine (with her sister Sarah) under influence of a Dr. and Mrs. Mott, 1835 (advertised themselves as physicians); formed Ladies' Physiol. Soc., 1843; refused admittance to Harvard Med. Sch., 1847, 50; leader anti-slavery and womans suffrage movements. Author: Glances and Glimpses (autobiography), 1856. Died Jan. 2, 1875.

HUNT, Henry Jackson, army officer; b. Detroit, Sept. 14, 1819; s. Lt. Fanuel Wellington and Julia (Herrick) H.; grad. U.S. Mil. Acad., 1839; m. Emily de Russy; 1 dau., Mary Craig. Commd. 2d lt. 2d Arty., U.S. Army, 1839, served in Mexican War; commd. capt., 1852; revised light mil. tactics, 1856; commd. maj. 5th Arty. and chief of arty. of Washington (D.C.) defenses; commd. col. in charge tng. arty. res. Army of Potomac, 1861; commd. brig. gen. U.S. Volunteers for his participation as arty. expert in Peninsular Campaign; helped break Pickett's charge by concentration of arty. fire at Battle of Gettysburg; in charge of siege of Petersburg; commd. col. 5th Arty., 1869; in command of Dept. of South, 1880-83; gov. Soldier's Home, Washington, D.C., 1885. Died Washington, Feb. 11, 1889.

HUNT, Hiram Paine, congressman; b. Pittstown, N.Y., May 23, 1796; grad. Union Coll., Schenectady, N.Y., 1816; attended Litchfield (Conn.) Law Sch.; Admitted to N.Y. bar, 1819, began practice in Pittstown; town clk. Pittstown, 1822; moved to Lansingburgh, N.Y., 1825, Troy, N.Y., 1831, practiced law; mem. U.S. Ho. of Reps. (Whig) from N.Y., 24th, 26th-27th congresses, 1835-37, 39-43; resumed law practice, Troy, later moved to N.Y.C. and practiced. Died N.Y.C., Aug. 14, 1865.

HUNT, Isaac, writer, clergyman; b. Bridgetown, Barbados, W.I., circa 1742; s. Isaac Hunt; grad. Phila. Acad. (now U. Pa.), 1763, M.A., 1771; m. Mary Shewell, June 17, 1767, 1 son. Published "A Letter from a Gentleman in Transilvania" under pseudonym Isaac Bickerstaff, 1764; published series of satires including "The Substance of the Exercise Had this Morning in Scurrility Hall," 1765; admitted to Pa. bar, circa 1768; opposed colonial independence, escaped to England, 1775; ordained to ministry Anglican Ch. Author: The Political Family, 1775; Rights of Englishmen: An Antidote to the Poison now Vending by. . . Thomas Paine, 1779. Died 1809.

HUNT, James Bennett, congressman; b. Demerara, Brit. Guiana, S.Am., Aug. 13, 1799; studied law, N.Y.C. Admitted to N.Y. bar, 1824, began practice in N.Y.C.; moved to Pontiac, Mich., 1836; judge probate ct., 1836; apptd. commr. of internal improvement by Gov. Mason of Mich., 1837, in charge of Mich. Central R.R. from Detroit to Ann Arbor, also constrn. of part of Clinton & Kalamazoo Canal from Mt. Clemens to Rochester; pros. atty. Oakland County (Mich.), 1841-43; mem. U.S. Ho. of Reps. (Democrat) from Mich., 28th-29th congresses, 1843-46; register land office, Sault Ste. Marie, Mich., 1848-49; circuit ct. commr. of Oakland County; moved to Washington, D.C. Died Washington, Aug. 15, 1857; buried Oak Hill Cemetery, Pontiac.

HUNT, Jonathan, congressman; b. Vernon, Vt., Aug. 12, 1787; grad. Dartmouth, 1807; studied law. Admitted to Vt. bar, began practice in Brattleboro; 1st pres. Old Brattleboro Bank, 1821; mem. Vt. Ho. of Reps., 1811, 16, 17, 24; mem. U.S. Ho. of Reps. (National Republican) from Vt., 20th-22d congresses, 1827-32. Died Washington, D.C., May 15, 1832; buried Brattleboro.

HUNT, Nathan, clergyman; b. Guilford County, N.C., Oct. 26, 1758; s. William and Sarah (Mills) H.; m. Martha Ruckman, 1778, 6 children; m. 2d, Prudence Thornburgh, 1792, 2 children. Ordained Quaker minister, 1793; preached in England, Ireland and Scotland, 1820-21; a founder New Garden Boarding Sch. (later Guilford Coll., N.C.). Died Aug. 8, 1853.

HUNT, Richard Morris, architect, b. Brattleboro, Vt., Oct. 31, 1827; s. Jonathon and Jane (Leawitt) H.; grad. Boston Latin Sch., 1843; LL.D. (hon.) Harvard, 1892; m. Catharine Howland, Apr. 2, 1861, 5 children. Travelled in Europe, Egypt, Asia Minor, 1846-54, studied art; mem.

Beaux Arts (Paris, France), 1846; insp. constrn. additions to Louvre and Tuileries, Paris, 1854; draftsman under Thomas Walter for Washington Capitol; designed Tribune Bldg. (containing 1st office elevators), 1873; designed many town houses, including William Vanderbilt's (most prominent), N.Y.C., begun 1878, Elbridge Gerry's, 1891, John Jacob Astor's 1893, designed country-house "Biltmore," Asheville, N.C. (considered his best country-house); designed Adminstrn. Bldg. World's Fair, 1893, main portion of Met. Mus. Art (N.Y.C.), base of Statue of Liberty, Lenox Library, Scroll and Key Club at Yale U., Nat. Observatory (Washington); a founder A.I.A., 1st sec., 1857-60, pres., 1888-91; mem. fine arts juries in architecture sects. Paris Expn., 1867, Centennial Expn., Phila., 1876, World's Columbian Expn., 1891; recipient Queen's Gold medal Royal Inst. Brit. Architects, 1893, Monument erected to him on Fifth Av., N.Y.C. Died Newport, R.I., July 31, 1895.

HUNT, Robert, clergyman; b. circa 1568; m. Elizabeth Edwards, 1597, 2 children, Thomas, Elizabeth. Vicar of Riculver, 1594-1602, Heathfield, 1602; chaplain expdn. under Capt. John Smith which founded Jamestown (Va.), 1606-08. Died 1608.

HUNT, Samuel, congressman; b. Charlestown, N.H., July 8, 1765; studied law. Admitted to N.H. bar 1790, began practice in Alstead; moved to Keene, N.H., 1790, practiced law, 1790-95; moved to Charlestown, N.H., engaged in farming; mem. N.H. Ho. of Reps., 1802-03; mem. U.S. Ho. of Reps. from N.H., 7th-8th congresses, Dec. 6, 1802-05; founded a colony in Ohio. Died Gallipolis, O., July 7, 1807; buried Mound Cemetery, Marietta, O.

HUNT, Theodore Gaillard, congressman; b. Charleston, S.C., Oct. 23, 1805; grad. law dept. of Columbia; Admitted to S.C. bar, began practice in Charleston; moved to New Orleans, circa 1830; dist. atty. for New Orleans; mem. La. Ho. of Reps., 1837-52; mem. U.S. Ho. of Reps. (Whig) from La., 33d Congress, 1853-55; judge 1st La. Dist., 1859; col. 5th La. Regt., Confederate Army, 1861-62; apptd. adj. gen. of La. with rank of brig. gen. Died New Orleans, Nov. 15, 1893; buried Metairie Cemetery, New Orleans.

HUNT, Thomas Sterry, chemist, geologist; b. Norwich, Conn., Sept. 5, 1826; s. Peleg and Jane (Sterry) H.; attended Yale; m. 1877. Chemist, mineralogist Geol. Survey of Can., 1847-72; taught chemistry Laval U., Que., Can., McGill U., Montreal, Can. 1862-68; prof. geology Mass. Inst. Tech., 1872-78. Author: Chemical and Geological Essays, 1875, 78; A New Basis for Chemistry: A Chemical Philosophy, 1887; Systematic Mineralogy, 1891. Died Feb. 12, 1892.

HUNT, Ward, justice U.S. Supreme Ct.; b. Utica, N.Y., June 14, 1810; s. Montgomery and Elizabeth (Stringham) H.; grad. with honors Union Coll., 1828, LL.D. (hon.) 1870; LL.D. (hon.) Rutgers Coll., 1870; m. Mary Savage, 1837; m. 2d, Maria Taylor, 1853; 2 children. Admitted to N.Y. bar, 1831; mem. N.Y. Assembly (Jacksonian Democrat) from Oneida County, 1838; mayor Utica, 1844; an organizer N.Y. Republican Party, 1856; elected to N.Y. Ct. of Appeals, 1865, chief judge, 1868, remained as commr. of appeals (after constl. amendment, 1869, subsequent jud. reorgn.), 1869-73; asso. justice U.S. Supreme Ct. (nominated by Pres. Grant), 1873-86. Died Washington, D.C., Mar. 24, 1886.

HUNT, Washington, gov. N.Y., congressman; b. Windham, Greene County, N.Y., Aug. 5, 1811; s. Sanford and Fanny (Rose) H.; m. Mary Walbridge, 1834. Admitted to N.Y. bar, 1834; 1st judge Niagara County (N.Y.) Ct. of Common Pleas, 1836-41; mem. U.S. Ho. of Reps. from N.Y., 28th-30th congresses, 1843-49; comptroller state of N.Y., 1849-50, gov., 1850-52; declined Democratic nomination for vice pres. U.S., 1860. Died N.Y.C., Feb. 2, 1867; buried Glenwood Cemetery, Lockport, N. Y.

HUNT, William Gibbes, editor; b. Boston, Feb. 21, 1791; s. Samuel and Elizabeth (Gibbes) H; grad. Harvard, 1810; LL.B., Transylvania U., 1822; m. Fanny Wrigglesworth, Sept. 28, 1820. moved to Lexington, Ky., 1815; editor Western Monitor, 1815 (became Western Monitor and Lexington Advertiser, 1819); editor Western Review and Miscellaneous Mag., 1820-22; editor, owner Nashville Banner, 1825-33, supported Jackson and Freemasonry. Author: Ichthyologia Ohiensis, 1820. Died Aug. 13, 1833.

HUNT, William Henry, sec. of navy, diplomat; b. Charleston, S.C., June 12, 1823; s. Thomas and Louisa (Gaillard) H.; ed. Yale; m. Frances Ann Andrews, Nov. 16, 1848; m. 2d, Elizabeth Ridgely, Oct. 14, 1852; m. 3d, Sarah Harrison, 1864; m. 4th, Mrs. Louise Hopkins, June 1, 1871; 7 children. Admitted to La. bar, 1844; prof. civil law U. La. Law Sch. (Now Tulane U.), 1866; apptd. atty. gen. La., 1876, asso. judge U.S. Ct. Claims, 1878; U.S. sec. of navy under Pres. James Garfield, 1881-82; U.S. minister to Russia, 1882-84. Died St. Petersburg, Russia, Feb. 17, 1884; buried Oak Hill Cemetery, Washington, D.C.

HUNT, William Morris, artist; b. Brattleboro, Vt., Mar. 31, 1824; s. Jonathan and Jane (Leavitt) H.; attended Harvard; studied art under Thomas Couture, Paris, France; m. Louisa Perkins, 1855. Came under artistic influence of Millet at Barbizon, circa 1847; established himself in Boston, 1855, expounded ideas of Barbizon sch. so well that Boston became 1st Am. market for their works (Millet, Rousseau, Diaz, et al); works include Peasant Girl at Barbizon, Girl at a Fountain, The Bathers, portrait of Chief Justice Shaw. Died by drowning, Isles of Shoals, Sept. 8, 1879.

HUNT, Wilson Price, trader; b. Hopewell, N. J., circa 1782; s. John P. and Margaret (Guild) H.; m. Anne (Lucas) Hunt, Apr. 20, 1836. Ran gen. store, St. Louis, 1804-09; became partner in Pacific Fur Co., 1810, organized expdn. to Montreal, Can., trapped in Montreal area, 1811-12, sold furs to Russian-Am. Co.; chartered Albatross and traded in Sandwich Islands area, 1812-14; ran business in St. Louis, 1814-19; purchased, operated gristmill, St. Louis, 1819-24; postmaster of St. Louis, 1822-40. Died Apr. 1842.

HUNTER, Andrew, clergyman; b. York County, N.Y., 1751; s. David and Martha Hunter; grad. Coll. of N.J. (now Princeton), 1772; m. Nancy Riddle, Oct. 2, 1775; m. 2d, Mary Stockton. Licensed to preach by Presbytern of Phila., 1774; made missionary visit to Va.; took part in burning cargo of tea in Greenwich, N.J., 1774; commd. by Provincial Congress of N.J. as chaplain of Col. Philip Van Cortland's batallion, 1776; in charge of Presbyn. chs. in Woodbury and Blackwood, N.J., 1786-97; del. Gen. Assembly of Presbyn. Ch., 1789, 94; trustee Coll. of N.J., 1788, 91, prof. mathematics and astronomy, 1804-08; in charge of acad. Bordentown, N.J., 1808-10; schoolmaster U.S. Naval Service, Washington, D.C., 1812-23. Died Feb. 24. 1823.

HUNTER, David, army officer; b. Washington, D.C., July 21, 1802; s. Rev. Andrew and Mary (Stockton) H.; grad. U.S. Mil. Acad., 1822; m. Maria Kinzie, circa 1829. Commd. 2d lt. 5th Inf., U.S. Army, 1822; capt. 1st Dragoons, 1833; maj., paymaster U.S. Army, 1842; col. calvary, 1861; commd. brig. gen. U.S. Volunteers, in command 2d div. U.S. Army under Gen. McDowell, 1861, served at 1st Battle of Bull Run; comdr. Western Dept., (succeeding Fremont), 1861; assumed command of South, 1862, issued order emancipating all slaves in Union custody in his dept., 1862, sanctioned liberation of all slaves in area, 1862; in command operations in Shenandoah Valley, 1864, won Battle of Piedmont, took Lynchburg (Va.); retreated before Early's troops, enabling Confederate comd. to threaten Washington (D.C.) by way of Shenandoah Valley; served court martial duty, 1865 until end of Civil War; pres. mil. commn. which tried Lincoln's assassins; pres. spl. claims commn. Cavalry Promotion Bd.; brevetted brig. gen. and maj. gen. meritorious conduct during war; ret. as col., 1866. Died Washington, Feb. 2, 1886.

HUNTER, John, senator, congressman; b. S. C., 1732. Engaged in farming, nr. Newberry, S. C.; mem. S.C. Ho. of Reps., 1786-92; Federalist presdl. elector, 1792; mem. U.S. Ho. of Reps. (Federalist) from S.C., 3d Congress, 1793-95; mem. U.S. Senate from S.C., Dec. 8, 1796-Nov. 26, 1798; resumed farming. Died 1802; buried family plot in Presbyn. Ch. Cemetery, Little River, S.C.

HUNTER, Morton Craig, congressman; b. Versailles, Ind., Feb. 5, 1825; grad. law dept. Ind. U., 1849, Admitted to Ind. bar, practice law; mem. Ind. Ho. of Reps., 1858; Republican presdl. elector, 1860; enlisted in U.S. Army during Civil War, 1862; commanded 1st Brigade, 3d Div., 14th Army Corps; with Sherman's march to the sea; brevetted brig. gen. U.S. Volunteers; discharged, 1865; mem. U.S. Ho. of Reps. (Republican) from Ind., 40th, 43d-45th congresses, 1867-69, 73-79; operated a limestone quarry in Ind. Died Bloomington, Oct. 25, 1896; buried Rose Hill Cemetery, Bloomington.

HUNTER, Narsworthy, congressman; b. Va. Served as capt. in a dist. militia, formed 1793; insp. mil. posts on East side of Mississippi River; del. U.S. Congress from Miss. Territory, 1801-02. Died Washington, D.C., Mar. 11, 1802; buried Congressional Cemetery, Washington.

HUNTER, Richard, actor. Petitioned gov. Province of N.Y. for license to stage plays in N.Y.C., between 1699-1702 (petition granted); stated in his petition that he had encountered "great charge and expense in providing persons and necessary's" for presentation of his plays; 1st profl. actor to perform in America.

HUNTER, Robert, royal gov.; b. Hunterston, Scotland; s. James and Margaret (Spalding) H.; m. Elizabeth Orby. Fought at Blenheim, 1704; served as lt. col. Brit. Army until 1707; apptd. lt. gov. Va., 1708, captured on way to Am., exchanged by French for Bishop of Quebec; capt. gen. and gov.-in-chief N.Y. and N.J., 1709-19, arrived to begin his adminstrn., N.Y.C., 1710, one of colonial America's most successful govs., played prominent part in orgn. colonial def. against French in N.Am.; gov. Jamaica, B.W.I., 1727-34. Author: (with Lewis Morris) Androborus (satire, 1st play published and written in Am.). Died Jamaica, Mar. 1734.

HUNTER, Robert Mercer Taliaferro, senator, Confederate ofcl.; b. Essex County, Va., Apr. 21, 1809; s. James and Maria (Garnett) H.; grad. U. Va., 1828; m. Mary Evelina Dandridge, Oct. 4, 1836, 8 children including Martha T. Admitted to Va. bar, 1830; mem. Va. Ho. of Dels. 1833, Va. Senate, 1835-37; mem. U.S. Ho. of Reps. 47, speaker, 1839-41; mem. U.S. Senate from Va., 1847-61; del. from Va. to Confederate Provisional Congress, Richmond, Va., 1861; sec. of state Confederate States Am., 1861-62; mem. Confederate Senate from Va., 1862-65; peace commr. to meeting with Pres. Lincoln, Hampton Roads, Va., 1865; treas. State of Va., 1877. Died "Foothill" nr. Lloyds, Va., July 18, 1887; buried "Elmwood" nr. Loretto, Va.

HUNTER, William, congressman; b. Sharon, Conn., Jan. 3, 1754; attended common schs. Served as sgt. and lt. under Gen. Montgomery during Revolutionary War; mem. Vt. Ho. of Reps., 1795, 1807-08; register of probate, 1798-1801; judge of probate for Dist. of Windsor (Vt.), 1801-16; Democratic presdl. elector, 1804; asst. judge county ct., 1805-16; mem. Vt. Council of Censors, 1806, 20; mem. Vt. Exec. Council, 1810-13, 15; mem. U.S. Ho. of Reps. (Republican) from Vt., 15th Congress, 1817-19. Died Windsor, Nov. 30, 1827; buried Sheddsville Cemetery, West Windsor, Vt.

HUNTER, William, senator, diplomat; b. Newport, R.I., Nov. 26, 1774; s. Dr. William and Deborah (Malbone) H.; grad. with honor R.I. Coll. (now Brown U.), 1791, LL.D., 1819; m. Mary Robinson, July 15, 1804, 8 children. Admitted to bar, 1795; mem. R.I. Gen. Assembly, 1799; 1812, 23-25, speaker house, 1811-12, 23-25; mem. U.S. Senate from R.I., 1813-21; apptd. charge d'affaires to Brazil by Pres. Jackson, 1834, minister plenipotentiary until 1845; trustee R.I. Coll., 1800-38. Died Newport, Dec. 3, 1849.

HUNTER, William Forrest, congressman; b. Alexandria, Va., Dec. 10, 1808; attended common schs.; studied law. Admitted to the bar; began practice of law, Woodsfield, O.; mem. U.S. Ho. of Reps. (Whig) from Ohio, 1849-53. Died Woodsfield, Mar. 30, 1874; buried Woodsfield Cemetery.

HUNTER, William H., congressman; b. Frankfort, Ky.; studied law. Admitted to the bar; began practice of law, Tiffin, O.; moved to Norwalk, O., circa 1825, practiced law; apptd. collector of customs at Sandusky, O., 1835; mem. U.S. Ho. of Reps. (Democrat) from Ohio, 1837-39. Died mysteriously nr. Sandusky, 1842; buried Old Burial Ground, Sandusky.

HUNTINGTON, Abel, congressman; b. Norwich, Conn., Feb. 21, 1777. Practiced medicine, East Hampton, L.I., N.Y.; presdl. elector, 1820; supr. of East Hampton, 1829-32, 44; mem. U.S. Ho. of Reps. (Democrat) from N.Y., 23d-24th congresses, 1833-37; mem. N.Y. Constl. Conv., 1846; collector of customs, Sag Harbor, N.Y., 1845-49. Died East Hampton, May 18, 1858; buried South End Cemetery, East Hampton.

HUNTINGTON, Benjamin, congressman; b. Norwich, Conn., Apr. 19, 1736; grad. Yale, 1761. Apptd. surveyor of lands Windham County (Conn.), 1764; admitted to Conn. bar, 1765, began practice in Norwich; mem. Conn. Ho. of Reps., 1771-80, clk., 1776-77, speaker, 1778-79; del. Conn. Provincial Congress, 1778; mem. Continental Congress from Conn., 1780-87, 87-88; mem. Conn. Senate, 1781-90, 91-93; mayor of Norwich, 1784-96; mem. U.S. Ho. of Reps. from Conn., 1st Congress, 1789-91; judge Conn. Superior Ct., 1793-98. Died Rome, N.Y., Oct. 16, 1800; buried Norwichtown Cemetery, Norwich.

HUNTINGTON, Ebenezer, congressman; b. Norwich, Conn., Dec. 26, 1754; grad. Yale, 1775. Served to lt. col. Continental Army, during Revolutionary War; commd. brig. gen. U.S. Army,

1798; discharged, 1800; mem. U.S. Ho. of Reps. (Whig) from Conn., 11th, 15th congresses, Oct. 11, 1810-11, 17-19. Died Norwich, June 17, 1834; buried Norwichtown Cemetery.

HUNTINGTON, Elisha, physician, state ofcl.; b. Topsfield, Mass., Apr. 9, 1796; s. Rev. Asahel and Alethea (Lord) H..; grad. Dartmouth, 1815; M.D., Yale: 1823; m. Hannah Hinckley, May 31, 1825, children—Mrs. J. P. Cooke, William Reed. Taught in Marietta, O., 1815-19, Marblehead, Mass., 1819-20; elected to 1st Lowell (Mass.) Sch. Bd., 1826; selectman Lowell, 1833-34; mem. council when Lowell became a city, 1836, pres., 1838, mayor, 1839-47; elected lt. gov. Mass. (whig), 1853; pres. Middlesex North Dist. Med. Soc., 1848-49, Mass. Med. Soc., 1855-57; chosen overseer Harvard Coll., 1860, Author: Address on the Life Character, and Writings of Elisha Bartlett, 1856. Died Lowell, Dec. 13, 1865.

HUNTINGTON, Jabez, army officer, jurist; b. Norwich; Conn., Aug. 7, 1719; s. Joshua and Hannah (Perkins) H.; grad. Yale, 1741; m. Elizabeth Backus, Jan. 20, 1742; m. 2d, Hannah Williams, 1746, children- Jedediah, Andrew, Joshua, Ebenezer. Justice of peace, New London, Conn.; mem. Conn. Assembly from Norwich, clk., 1757; speaker Conn. Ho. of Reps., 1760; commd. capt. troop of horse 3d Regt., Conn. Militia, 1754, lt. 1st company 5th Regt., 1760, capt., 1764; made assistant by Conn. Assembly, 1764; lt. col. 3rd regt. Conn. Militia, 1765; apptd. probate judge for Norwich Dist., 1773; moderator of large meeting assembled "to take into consideration the melancholy situation of our civil constitutional liberties, rights and privileges," Norwich, June 6, 1774; mem. Conn. Council of Safety, 1775-1779; apptd. one of 2 maj. gens. from Conn., 1776, maj. gen. entire Conn. Militia, 1777. Died Oct. 5, 1786.

HUNTINGTON, Jabez Williams, senator, congressman; b. Norwich, Conn., Nov. 8, 1788; grad. Yale, 1806; studied law. Taught at Litchfield (Conn.) South Farms Acad., 1 year; admitted to Conn. bar, began practice in Litchfield; mem. Conn. Ho. of Reps., 1829; mem. U.S. Ho. of Reps. from Conn., 21st-23d congresses, 1829-Aug. 16, 1834; apptd. judge Conn. Supreme Ct. Errors, 1834; mem. U.S. Senate (Whig) from Conn., May 4, 1840-47. Died Norwich, Nov. 1, 1847; buried Norwichtown Cemetery.

HUNTINGTON, Jedediah, army officer; b. Norwich, Conn., Aug. 4, 1743; s. Gen. Jabez and Elizabeth (Bachus) H.; grad. Harvard, 1763; m. Faith Trumbull; m. 2d, Ann Moore; 2 sons, Joshua, Daniel. Commd. ensign 1st Norwich Co. by Conn. Assembly, 1769, lt., 1771, capt., 1774; col. 20th Regt., Conn. Militia, 1774, col. 8th Regt., 1775, 17th Inf. Regt., Continental Army, 1776, fought at Battle of L.I.; col. 1st Conn. Regt., 1777; commd. brig. gen. Continental Army, 1777, brevetted maj. gen. at close of Revolutionary War; sheriff New London (Conn.); del. to Conn. Constl. Conv.; treas. Conn.; apptd. collector customs Port of New London by Pres. Washington, 1789. Died New London, Sept. 25, 1818.

HUNTINGTON, Samuel, gov. Conn., pres. Continental Congress; b. Windham, Conn., July 3, 1731; s. Nathaniel and Mehetable (Thurston) H.; LL.D., Dartmouth, 1785, Yale, 1787; m. Martha Devotion, 1761. Admitted to Conn. bar, 1758; mem. Conn. Gen. Assembly from Norwich, 1765; apptd. king's atty. for Conn., 1765; justice of peace, New London, Conn., 1765-75; judge Superior Ct. of Conn., 1773-83; apptd. mem. com. for defense of Conn. by Gen. Assembly, 1775; mem. Continental Congress from Conn., 1775-84, pres., 1779-81; signer Declaration of Independence; mem. com. to meet reps. from Mass., N.H., R.I. and N.Y. to consult on state of currency Springfield, Mass. 1777; chief justice Superior Ct. Conn., 1784; lt. gov. Conn., 1785-86, gov., 1786-96. Died Norwich, Jan. 5, 1796.

HUNTINGTON, Samuel, gov. Ohio; b. Coventry, Conn., Oct. 4, 1765; s. Joseph and Hannah (Devotion) H.; A.B., Yale, 1785, A.M., 1788; attended Dartmouth, 3 years; m. Hannah Huntington, Dec. 20, 1791. Admitted to Conn. bar, 1793; elected to 1st Ohio Senate, 1802, chosen speaker; apptd. judge Ohio Supreme Ct., 1803; gov. Ohio, 1808-10; mem. Ohio Ho. of Reps., 1811-12; dist. paymaster U.S. Army, War of 1812. Died Painesville, O., June 8, 1817.

HUNTSMAN, Adam, congressman; b. Va. Moved to Jackson, Tenn.; mem. U.S. Ho. of Reps. (Jacksonian Democrat) from Tenn., 24th Congress, 1835-37, unsuccessful candidate for re-election, 1836.

HURD, Frank Hunt, congressman; b. Mount Vernon, O., Dec. 25, 1840; grad. Kenyon Coll., Gambier, O., 1858; studied law. Admitted to Ohio bar, 1861, practiced law; pros. atty. Knox County (O.), 1863; mem. Ohio Senate, 1866; apptd. to codify criminal laws of Ohio, 1868; moved to Toledo, O., 1869; city solicitor of Toledo, 1871-73; mem. U.S. Ho. of Reps. (Democrat) from Ohio, 44th, 46th, 48th congresses, 1875-77, 79-81; resumed practice of law, Toledo. Died Toledo, July 10, 1896; buried Mound View Cemetery, Mount Vernon.

HURD, John Codman, legal writer, lawyer; b. Boston, Nov. 11, 1816; s. John R. and Catharine (Codman) H.; grad. Yale, 1836. Admitted to N.Y. bar, 1839; became noted legal author. Author: Law of Freedom and Bondage in the United States (traced history of chattel slavery as foundation for his analysis of contemporary Am. legal situation), 1858; The Theory of Our National Existence, 1881; The Union-State: A Letter to Our States-rights Friend, 1890. Died June 25, 1892.

HURD, Nathaniel, silversmith, engraver; b. Boston, Feb. 13, 1730; s. Jacob and Elizabeth (Mason) H. Trained by father to engrave on silver and gold; experimented with engraving on copper confined mainly to bookplates; engraved cartoon of two counterfeiters who were objects of public interest, 1762; his portrait painted by John Singleton Copely (now in Cleve. Mus. Art). Died Dec. 17, 1777.

HURLBERT, William Henry, journalist, author; b. Charleston, S.C., July 3, 1827; s. Martin Luther and Margaret (Morford) Hurlbert; grad. Harvard, 1847, Harvard Divinity Sch., 1849; m. Katharine Tracy, Aug. 9, 1884. Wrote for Putnam's Mag., drama critic for Albion, 1855-57; worked for N.Y. Times, 1857; arrested in South for anti-slavery views, 1861, confined in Richmond, escaped in summer 1862; stumped for McClellan in presdl. campaign, 1864; part-owner N.Y. Comml. Advertiser, 1864-67; spl. corr. for N.Y. World with spl. commn. to Santo Domingo, 1871, editor-in-chief, 1876-83. Author: (play) Americans in Paris: or A Game of Dominoes, 1858; McClellan and the Conduct of the War, 1864; Ireland under Coercion, 2 vols., 1888; England under Coercion, 1893. Died Cadenabbia, Italy, Sept. 4, 1895.

HURLBUT, Stephen Augustus, congressman, army officer, diplomat; b. Charleston, S.C., Nov. 29, 1815; s. Martin Luther and Lydia (Bunch) H.; m. Sophronia R. Stevens, May 13, 1847. Admitted to S.C. bar, 1837; adj. S.C. Regt. during Seminole War, 1835-43; moved to Ill., 1845; mem. Ill. Constl. Conv. from Boone and McHenry counties, 1847; mem. Ill. Gen. Assembly, 1858-61; commd. brig. gen. U.S. Army, 1861, comdr. 4th Div. at Battle of Shiloh; promoted maj. gen., 1862; stationed Memphis, Tenn., 1862-63; in charge of XVI Army Corps, 1863, defense of Memphis during Vicksburg campaign, 1863; served with Gen. Sherman at Mobile (Ala.), 1864; commanded Dept. of Gulf, 1864; discharged from U.S. Army, 1865; 1st comdr.-in-chief Grand Army of Republic, 1866-68; U.S. minister to Colombia, S.Am., 1869-72; mem. U.S. Ho. of Reps. from Ill., 43d-44th congresses, 1873-77; U.S. minister to Peru, 1881-82. Died Lima, Peru, Mar. 27, 1882; buried Belvidere (Ill.) Cemetery.

HUSBANDS, Hermon, insurrectionist; b. Cecil County, Md., Oct. 3, 1724; s. William and Mary Husbands; married 3 times; m. 2d, Mary Pugh, July 3, 1762; m. 3d, Amy (Emmy) Allen, 1766. Became mem. Soc. of Friends; connected with Regulators (people from back-country of N.C. who were protesting ofcl. corruption and extortion); arrested for inciting riot, 1768, released from jail, acquitted, because he had public support; mem. N.C. Colonial Assembly, 1769-70, expelled from Assembly for writing "false, seditious, and libelous" letter to press, 1770, freed when grand jury failed to indict him, 1771; forced to flee N.C. because of his assn. with Regulators who had been defeated by govt. forces at Battle of Alamance, 1771; settled in Pa.; a leader in Whiskey Rebellion, served on Com. of Safety, 1794, captured, tried and condemned to death, later pardoned. Died 1795.

HUSSEY, Curtis Grubb, mfr.; b. nr. York, Pa., Aug. 11, 1802; s. Christopher and Lydia (Grubb) H.; m. Rebecca Updegraff. Licensed to practice medicine, 1825; built profitable practice in Morgan County, Ind.; bought and managed many stores, Morgan County; mem. Ind. Ho. of Reps., 1829; went to Pitts., 1840; organizer Pitts. & Boston Mining Co., 1842, opened 1st Lake Superior copper Mine (Cliff mine); organizer C. G. Hussey & Co. (became known as Pitts. Copper & Brass Rolling Mills), 1849, one of early large suppliers of Am. copper; bought (with T. M. Howe) steel plant of Blair & Co., 1859, began mfg. steel by "direct process"; established Sch. of Design for Women, Pitts.; founder, pres. Allegheny Observatory; trustee Western U. Pa. (now U. Pitts.), 1864-93. Died Apr. 25, 1893.

HUSSEY, Obed, inventor; b. Me., 1792; m. Eunice Starbuck, 1 dau. Began work on a grain cutting machine, Cincinnati, 1830, obtained patent for reaper, 1833; gave successful demonstration of reaper before Hamilton County (O.) Agrl. Soc., 1833; introduced reaper into Ill., N.Y., Md. and Pa., 1834-38; exhibited reaper along with McCormick reaper at London (Eng.) Exhbn., 1851; forced to sell his bus. because of competition with McCormick reaper, 1858. Died Aug. 4, 1860.

HUSSMAN, George, viticulturist; b. Meyenburg, Prussia, Nov. 4, 1827; s. J. H. and Louise (Wesselhoeft) H.; m. Louise Kielmann, 1854, at least 3 children. Came with family to Phila., 1837; attempted mining in Cal., 1850-52; returned to Mo., planted vineyards and orchards on what became known as model fruit farm of Mo.; served as q.m. 4th Infantry, Mo. Volunteers, 1862-63; pres. Bluffton Wine Co. (Mo.), 1869-72; mem. Mo. Bd. Agr.; mem. bd. curators U. Mo., 1869-72, prof. pomology and forestry, 1878-81; moved to Cal., 1881; U.S. statis. agt. for Cal., 1885-1900; mem. 1st Viticultural Congress, Washington, D.C. Author: American Grape Growing and Wine Making, 1880; Grape Culture and Wine Making in California, 1888. Died Napa, Cal., Nov. 5, 1902.

HUSTON, Charles, physician, mfr.; b. Phila., July 23, 1822; s. Dr. Robert and Hannah (West) H.; grad. U. Pa., 1840; M.D., Jefferson Med. Coll., 1842; m. Isabella Lukens, Apr. 1848. Practiced medicine, Phila.; forced to give up practice due to ill health, 1848; partner Lukens Iron & Steel Mills, 1849; studied properties of iron and steel using phys. and chem. tests; chmn. com. of boiler-plate mfrs. to develop standards for testing boiler-plate used in steamboats, 1877. Died Coatsville, Pa., Jan. 5, 1897.

HUTCHINS, John, congressman; b. Vienna, O., July 25, 1812; attended Western Res. Coll.; studied law. Admitted to Ohio bar, 1837, began practice in Warren; clk. Ct. of Common Pleas for Trumbull County, (O.), 1838-43; mem. Ohio Ho. of Reps., 1849-50; mayor of Warren, 2 years, mem. bd. edn., 6 years; mem. U.S. Ho. of Reps. (Republican) from Ohio, 36th-37th congresses, 1959-63; resumed practice of law, Warren; moved to Cleve., 1868, practiced law. Died Cleve., Nov. 20, 1891; buried Lakeview Cemetery, Cleve.

HUTCHINS, Thomas, mil. engr., geographer; b. Monmouth County, N.J., 1730. Served as officer Pa. Colonial Militia, 1757-59; engr. mil. installations at Ft. Pitt and Pensacola (Fla.); elected mem. Am. Philos. Soc., 1772; refused rank of maj. in a Brit. regt. during Revolutionary War; charged with treason by Brit. Govt., 1779, released from prison, 1780; went to France, recommended to Congress by Benjamin Franklin; apptd. geographer So. Army under Gen. Greene, May 1781, title changed to geographer to the U.S., July 1781; apptd. to determine boundary between Va. and Pa., 1783; geographer of U.S. in charge of surveying Western lands ceded by the states to Congress, 1785-89. Died Apr. 28, 1789.

HUTCHINS, Waldo, congressman; b. Brooklyn, Conn., Sept. 30, 1822; grad. Amherst (Mass.) Coll., 1842; studied law. Admitted to N.Y. bar, 1845, began practice in N.Y.C.; mem. N.Y. Assembly, 1852; declined nomination for judge N. Y. Supreme Ct.; del. N.Y. Constl. Conv., 1867; park commr. N.Y.C., 1857-69, 87-91; mem. U. S. Ho. of Reps. (Democrat) from N.Y., 46th-48th congresses, Nov. 4, 1879-85; resumed law practice. Died N.Y.C., Feb. 8, 1891; buried Woodlawn Cemetery, N.Y.C.

HUTCHINS, Wells Andrews, congressman; b. Hartford, Ohio, Oct. 8, 1818; attended pub. schs.; studied law. Admitted to Ohio bar, 1841, began practice in Warren; moved to Portsmouth, O., 1842; mem. Ohio Ho. of Reps., 1852-54; city solicitor of Portsmouth, 1857-61; U.S. provost marshal for Ohio, 1862; mem. U.S. Ho. of Reps. (Democrat) from Ohio, 38th Congress, 1864-65, unsuccessful candidate for re-election, 1864, 80. Died Portsmouth, Jan. 25, 1895; buried Greenlawn Cemetery, Portsmouth.

HUTCHINSON, Adoniram Judson Joseph, singer; b. Milford, N.H., Mar. 14, 1817; s. Jesse and Mary (Leavitt) H.; m. Jerusha Hutchinson, 2 daus. Moved to Lynn, Mass., 1841, opened grocery store; later formed quartet with 2 bros. and sister, went on singing tours in N.Y. and New Eng., made European tour, 1845; sang in Union Army camps during Civil War; composed most of music used by quartet; compositions include Bridge of Sighs, Away down East; a founder Hutchinson, Minn., 1855; Lake Judson (Minn.) named for him. Committed suicide, Lynn, Jan. 10, 1859.

HUTCHINSON, Anne, colonist; b. Alford, Lincolnshire, Eng., 1591; d. Francis and Bridget (Dryden) Marbury; m. William Hutchinson, Aug. 9, 1612, 14 children including Edward, Faith, Susanna. Arrived in Mass., 1634; advocated religion based on intuition of God's grace and love rather than on obedience to laws; tried for her views, sentenced to banishment from Mass. Bay Colony, 1637; went with her family to Aquidneck Island, R.I., 1638; moved to L.I., 1642. Massacred by Indians, L.I., 1643.

HUTCHINSON, Benjamin Peters, meat packer; b. Middleton, Mass., July 24, 1829; s. Ira and Hannah (Wilson) H.; m. Sarah Ingalls, 1853; 1 son, Charles L. Worked in Plankinton's meat-packing plant, Milw., 1856-58; moved to Chgo., began packing meats privately, 1858; entered firm Burt, Hutchinson & Snow (1st firm to move into Union Stock Yards), Chgo., during Civil War; organized Corn Exchange Bank, Chgo., 1870; became one of most powerful traders on Chgo. Bd. Trade. Died Mar. 16, 1899.

HUTCHINSON, James, physician, educator; b. Wakefield Twp., Pa., Jan. 29, 1752; s. Randall and Catherine (Rickey) H.; studied medicine under Dr. John Fothergill, London, Eng.; m. Lydia Biddle; m. 2d Sidney Evans Howell. Returned to Am., 1778; joined Army as surgeon, later became surgeon gen. of Pa., 1778-84; mem. Phila. Com. of Safety, 1788; trustee U. Pa., 1779-81, prof. chemistry, 1791-93; an incorporator Coll. of Physicians, Phila.; mem. Am. Philos. Soc. Died Sept. 5, 1793.

HUTCHINSON, Thomas, colonial gov.; b. Boston, Sept. 9, 1711; s. Thomas and Sarah (Foster) H.; grad. Harvard, 1727, M.A., 1730; D.C.L., Oxford (Eng.) U.; m. Margaret Sanford, May 16, 1734; children—Thomas, Elisha, William, Sarah, Margaret. Mcht., Boston; chosen selectman of Boston, 1737; mem. Mass. Ho. of Reps., 1737-38, 40-49, speaker, 1746-48; mem. Gov.'s Council of Mass., 1749-66; judge of probate, justice of common pleas Suffolk County (Mass.), 1752; acting gov. Mass. Bay Colony, 1769-71, gov., 1771-74; polit. rival of Samuel Adams. Author: A Letter on the Present State of the Bills of Credit, 1736; History of the Colony of Massachusetts Bay, 3 vols., 1764-1828; Strictures upon the Declaration of the Congress at Philadelphia, 1776. Died Brompton, Eng., June 3, 1780; buried Croydon, Eng.

HUTSON, Richard, jurist, Continental congressman; b. Prince Williams Parish, S.C., July 9, 1748; s. Rev. William and Mary (Ehardon) H.; A.B. Coll. of N.J. (now Princeton), 1765, A.M., 1768. Mem. S.C. Assembly, 1776, S.C. Legislative Council, 1776; del. to Continental Congress, 1778-79; signer Articles of Confederation; mem. lower house S.C. Assembly, 1779, S.C. Assembly meeting at Jacksonborough, 1782; lt. gov. S.C., 1782; 1st intendant City of Charleston (S.C.), 1783; elected one of 1st chancellors S.C. Equity Ct., 1784, sr. judge, 1791-93; mem. S.C. Conv. which ratified U.S. Constn., 1787; mem. S.C. Ho. of Reps., 1789. Died Charleston, Apr. 12, 1795; buried Independent Congregational Ch. Cemetery, Charleston.

HUTTON, John Edward, physician, congressman; b. Polk County, Tenn., Mar. 28, 1828; grad. Pope's Med. Coll., St. Louis; studied law. Taught sch.; began practice of medicine, Warrenton, Mo., 1860; commd. col. 59th Regt., Mo. Volunteer Inf., U.S. Army, during Civil War; admitted to Mo. bar, 1864, began practice of law Warrenton; moved to Mexico, Mo., 1865, practiced law, 1865-73; became owner, publisher Intelligencer (a Democratic newspaper), 1873; mem. U.S. Ho .of Reps. (Dem.) from Mo., 49th-50th congresses, 1885-89; resumed practice of medicine and law. Died Mexico, Mo., Dec. 28, 1893; buried Elmwood Cemetery, Mexico.

HUYLER, John, businessman, congressman; b. N.Y.C., Apr. 9, 1808; attended common schs., Tenafly, N.J. Apprenticed as mason, later engaged in contracting and bldg., N.Y.C., until 1846; moved to N.J., engaged in farming, Pollifly; settled in Hackensack, N.J., circa 1855, engaged in merc. and lumber bus.; pres. bd. freeholders Bergen County (N.J.); mem. N.J. Assembly, 1849-51, speaker, 1851; judge ct. appeals, 1854-57; mem. U.S. Ho. of Reps. (Democrat) from N.J., 35th Congress, 1857-59; resumed lumbr bus. Assassinated in Hackensack, Jan. 9, 1870; buried New York Cemetery, Hackensack.

HYDE, Edward, colonial gov.; b. England, 1650; m. Catherine. Apptd. dep. gov. N.C. by Lord Proprietors 1709, acting gov., 1710-11; approved as gov. N.C. by Privy Council, 1711, gov., 1711-12; contracted yellow fever fighting Tuscarora Indians. Died of yellow fever, N.C., Sept. 8, 1712.

HYDE, Edward (viscount Cornbury) colonial gov..; b. 1661; s. Henry Hyde (earl Clarendon); m. Katherine O'Brian, 1688. Mem. English Ho. of Commons, 1685-1702; apptd. gov. N.Y. and N.J. due to influence of his cousin Queen Anne, 1702, his adminstrn. marked by graft, embezzlement and incompetence; detested by colonists, for habits of vanity, drunkenness, stinginess, and appearing publicly dressed in imitation of his royal cousin, persecuted Presbyns. and Quakers, recalled 1708, held by sheriff of N.Y. for debts until he succeeded his father as earl Clarendon; became mem. Privy Council, 1711. Died Apr. 12, 1723.

HYDE, Henry Baldwin, businessman; b. Catskill, N.Y., Feb. 15, 1834; s. Henry Hazen and Lucy Baldwin (Beach) H.; m. Annie Fitch, 1864, 1 child. Went to N.Y.C., 1852, became clk., Mut. Life Ins. Co.; started Equitable Life Assurance Soc., 1859, due to his youth, signed presidency over to William C. Alexander; in spite various govt. investigations his co. prospered (before his death co. reported assets over $250,000,000, surplus over $60,000,000, and insurance over $1,-000,000); owned majority of co.'s shares by 1899, but was unable to pass them on to his son. Died May 2, 1899.

HYDE, Joseph, architect. Practiced as architect, Charleston, S.C.; designed several pub. bldgs., Charleston, including St. Philip's Protestant Episcopal Ch. (erected 1835-38), 1st Grand Lodge Hall (built 1837, later destroyed by fire), old Market Hall (a Confederate Museum, 1840-1938). Flourished early 19th Century.

HYDE DE NEUVILLE, Anne-Marguerite-Henriette (baroness Hyde de Neuville), artist; b. circa 1779; m. Baron Hyde de Neuville, 1794. Accompanied husband into exile in Am., 1807; lived in N.Y.C. and New Brunswick, N.J., 1807-14; made many pencil and watercolor sketches of Am. scenes and faces; returned to France, 1814; lived in Washington (D.C.) when her husband was minister to U.S., 1816-22, made further sketches of Am. life; collections of her work owned by N.Y. Hist. Soc., N.Y. Pub. Library. Died France, 1849.

HYMAN, John Adams, congressman; b. nr. Warrenton, N.C., July 23, 1840; s. of Negro slave parents. Sold and sent to Ala.; returned to N.C., 1865, engaged in farming; del. N.C. Equal Rights Conv., 1865, N.C. Constl. Conv., 1868; mem. N.C. Senate, 1868-74; mem. U.S. Ho. of Reps. (Republican) from N.C., 44th Congress, 1875-77; spl. dep. collector of internal revenue 4th Dist. of N.C., 1877-78. Died Washington, D.C., Sept. 14, 1891; buried Harmony Cemetery, Washington.

HYNEMAN, John M., congressman; b. Reading, Pa., circa Apr. 25, 1711; ed. common schs. Mem. Pa. Ho. of Reps., 1809; clk. orphans ct., 1810-16; mem. U.S. Ho. of Reps. (Democrat) from Pa., 12th-13th congresses, 1811-Aug. 2, 1813; commd. brig. gen. Pa. Militia; surveyor Berks County (Pa.), 1816. Died Reading, Apr. 16, 1816; buried Trinity Lutheran Cemetery, Reading.

HYRNE, Edmund Massingberd, army officer; b. Jan. 14, 1748; son of Col. Henry Hyrne. Served as capt. 1st S.C. Continental Regt., 1775-79, promoted maj., 1779; dep. adj.-gen. Southern Dept., 1778-83; received Congressional notice for bravery, 1780; aide-de-camp to Gen. Nathanael Green, 1781-82; mem. Jacksonborough (S.C.) Legislature, 1782. Died on his plantation "Ormsby," St. Bartholomew's Parish, S.C., Dec. 1783.

I

IARDELLA, Francisco, sculptor; b. Carrara, Italy, 1793. Came to U.S. to work on U.S. Capitol, Washington, D.C., 1816; succeeded to position in charge of sculpture work on Capitol, 1824. Died Washington, Jan. 23. 1831.

IDE, William B., pioneer; b. Mass., circa 1794; m., several children including Sarah. Farmed in Vt., Ky., Ohio, Ill.; went to Cal. with Grigsby-Ide party, 1845; elected del. by Am. settlers of Sacramento Valley to Mexican-Am. negotiations at Sonoma (estate of Gen. M.G. Vallejo), 1846; assumed leadership of Bear Flag Revolt from Sonoma, June 15, 1846, prepared proclamation urging loyalty to new republic; shouldered out by Fremont, June 25, 1846.

IHRIE, Peter, Jr., congressman; b. Easton, Pa., Feb. 3, 1796; grad. Dickinson Coll., 1815; studied law. Admitted to Pa. bar, 1818, began practice in Easton; charter mem. bd. trustees Lafayette Coll., 1826; mem. Pa. Ho. of Reps., 1826-27; brig. gen. Pa. Militia, 1845; mem. U.S. Ho. of Reps. (Jacksonian Democrat) from Pa., 21st-22d congresses, 1829-33; dir. Easton Bank. Died Easton, Mar. 29, 1871; buried Easton Cemetery.

ILSLEY, Daniel, congressman; b. Falmouth, Mass. (now Me.), May 30, 1740. Engaged in distillery and shipping bus.; mem. Com. of Correspondence and Safety; Served as maj. and mustering officer, Falmouth, during Revolutionary War; del. Mass. Conv. which ratified U.S. Constn., 1788; mem. Mass. Ho. of Reps., 1873-74; mem. U.S. Ho. of Reps. (Democrat) from Mass., 10th Congress, 1807-09. Died Portland, Me., May 10, 1813; buried Eastern Cemetery, Portland.

IMBERT, Antoine, painter, lithographer; b. Calais, France; married. Served in Napoleonic wars, imprisoned, 4 years; arrived N.Y.C., circa 1824; his 1st known painting of Am. subject was "Landing of General Lafayette at Castle Garden, New York, 16th August, 1824; established what was probably 1st Am. lithographic firm. Died N.Y.C., circa 1835.

IMBODEN, John Daniel, army officer; b. Augusta County, Va., Feb. 16, 1823; s. George William and Isabella (Wunderlich) I.; attended Washington Coll., 1841-42; m. Eliza McCue; m. 2d, Mary Wilson McPhail; m. 3d, Edna Porter; m. 4th, Anna Lockett; m. 5th, Mrs. Florence Crockett; at least 5 children. Taught sch., also practiced law, Staunton, Va.; mem. Va. Legislature, 2 terms; organized and commanded Staunton Arty. which aided in Confederate capture of Harper's Ferry; promoted col. Confederate Army, brig. gen., 1863; served under gens. Jackson and Lee; involved in railroad promotion for most of life after Civil War. Died Damascus, Va., Aug. 15, 1895; buried Hollywood Cemetery, Richmond, Va.

IMLAY, Gilbert, adventurer; b. Monmouth County, N.J., circa 1754; lived with Mary Wollstonecraft, 1 dau., Fanny. Served as 1st lt. of Continental Army during Am. Revolution, 1777-78, later capt.; bought land, moved to Ky.; became dep. surveyor; speculated on land., financial difficulties caused him to leave country; became important in French polit. councils which advised taking La. in early 1790's. Author: A Topographical Description of the Western Territory of North America, 1792; The Emigrants, 1793; Observations du Cap. Implay. Died Island of Jersey, Nov. 20, 1828; buried St. Brelade's.

IMLAY, James Henderson, congressman; b. Imlaystown, Monmouth County, N.J., Nov. 26, 1764; grad. Coll. of N.J. (now Princeton), 1786; studied law. Tutor, Coll. of N.J.; admitted to N.J. bar, 1791, practiced law; maj. Monmouth County Militia, during Revolutionary War; mem. N.J. Assembly, 1793-96, speaker, 1796; mem. U.S. Ho. of Reps. from N.J., 5th-6th congresses, 1797-1801; a mgr. apptd. to conduct impeachment proceedings against William Blount (senator from Tenn.), 1798; postmaster of Allentown (N.J.), 1804-05; resumed practice of law, Allentown. Died Allentown, Mar. 6, 1823; buried Presbyn. Ch. Cemetery, Allentown.

INGALLS, Jeremiah, composer, choir leader; b. Andover, Mass., 1764; s. Abijah Ingalls; m. Mary Bigelow, 1791. Tavern-keeper in Newbury, Vt., 1800-10, also worked as cooper and farmer; led Congl. Ch. choir, Newbury, which won wide recognition; taught singing schs., Rochester, Hancock and neighboring towns in Vt. hill country, from 1810. Published The Christian Harmony, 1805; known for fuguing tunes including New Jerusalem, Northfield, The Young Convert. Died 1838.

INGALLS, Marilla Baker, missionary; b. Greenfield Centre, N.Y., Nov. 25, 1828; d. Sealk and Sarah (Tremain) Baker; m. Rev. Lovell Ingalls, Dec. 23, 1850. Converted to Baptist Ch. in youth; accompanied and worked with her husband as missionary under auspices of Am. Bapt. Missionary Union in Burma, 1851-56; in U.S., 1856-58; went back to Burma, 1858; established mission at Thongze, in remote sect. of Burma, ran mission for more than 40 years. Died Thongze, Dec. 17, 1902; buried Thongze.

INGE, Samuel Williams, congressman; b. Warren County, N.C., Feb. 22, 1815; attended pub. schs.; studied law. Moved to Greene County, Ala. Admitted to Ala. bar, began practice in Livingston; mem. Ala. Ho. of Reps., 1844-45; mem. U.S. Ho. of Reps. (Democrat) from Ala., 30th-31st congresses, 1847-51; participated in a duel with Edward Stanly (a rep. from N.C.); apptd. U.S. atty. for. No. Dist. of Cal., 1853. Died San Francisco, June 10, 1868; buried Mount Calvary Cemetery, San Francisco.

INGE, William Marshall, congressman; b. Granville County, N.C., 1802; attended schs., N.C. and Tenn.; studied law. Admitted to Tenn. bar, practiced law; mem. U.S. Ho. of Reps. (Democrat) from Tenn., 23d Congress, 1833-35; moved to Livingston, Ala., 1836, practiced law; mem. Ala. Ho. of Reps., 1840, 44, 45; Died Livingston, 1846; buried Livingston Cemetery.

INGERSOLL, Charles Jared, writer, congressman; b. Phila., Oct. 3, 1782; s. Jared and Elizabeth (Pettit) I.; attended Princeton, 1796-99; m. Mary Wilcocks, Oct. 18, 1804. Staged his play Edwy and Elgiva, Phila., 1801; wrote View of the Rights and Wrongs, Power and Policy, of the United States of America, 1808; wrote Anchiquin, the Jesuit's

Letters, 1810; mem. U.S. Ho. of Reps. from Pa., 13th, 27th-30th congresses, 1813-15, 41-49; U.S. dist. atty. for Pa., 1815-29; mem. Pa. Improvement Conv., 1825; mem. Pa. Ho. of Reps., 1830; wrote Julian: A Tragedy, 1831; mem. Pa. Constl. Conv., 1837; apptd. sec. of legation to Prussia, 1837; wrote Historical Sketch of the Second War Between the United States and Great Britian, 1845-49; apptd. minister to France, appointment not confirmed by Senate, 1847; apptd. U.S. judged for Dist. of Conn., 1853. Died Phila., 1862; buried Woodlands Cemetery, Phila.

INGERSOLL, Ebon Clark, congressman; b. Dresden, N.Y., Dec. 12, 1831; studied law. Admitted to Ill. bar, 1854, began practice in Peoria; mem. Ill. Ho. of Reps., 1856; mem. U.S. Ho. of Reps. (Republican) from Ill., 38th-41st congresses, May 20, 1864-71; practiced law, Washington, D.C. Died Washington, May 31, 1879; buried Oak Hill Cemetery, Washington.

INGERSOLL, Edward, legal writer; b. Phila., Apr. 2, 1817; s. Charles Jared and Mary (Wilcocks) I.; grad. U. Pa., 1835; m. Anne C. Warren, June 5, 1850, 7 children. Admitted to Phila. bar, 1838; engaged only in small practice, concentrated on legal writing. Author: The History and Law of the Writ of Habeas Corpus, with an Essay on the Law of Grand Juries, 1849; editor: The History of the Pleas of the Crown (Matthew Kent), 1847. Died Feb. 19, 1893.

INGERSOLL, Jared, jurist; b. New Haven, Conn., Oct. 27, 1749; s. Jared and Hannah (Whiting) I.; grad. Yale, 1766; m. Elizabeth Pettit, Dec. 6, 1781; children—Charles Jared, Joseph Reed. Admitted to Phila. bar, 1773, Middle Temple, London, Eng., 1773, U.S. Supreme Ct. bar, 1791; mem. Continental Congress, 1780; del. Fed. Conv. of 1787; mem. Phila. Common Council, 1789; atty. gen. Pa., 1790-99, 1811-17; pleaded case Chisholm vs. Ga. before U.S. Supreme Ct., 1792, Hylton vs. United States (1st case to involve constitutionality of an act of Congress), 1796; city solicitor Phila., 1798-1801; U.S. dist. atty. for Pa., 1800-01; nominated for vice pres U.S. by Pa. Federalists, 1811; presiding judge of Dist. Ct. for City and County of Phila., 1821-22. Died Phila., Oct. 31, 1822.

INGERSOLL, Joseph Reed, congressman; b. Phila., June 14, 1786; s. Jared Ingersoll; grad. Princeton, 1804; studied law. Admitted to Pa. bar, began practice in Phila.; mem. U.S. Ho. of Reps. (Whig) from Pa., 24th, 27th-30th congresses, 1835-37, Oct. 12, 1841-49; U.S. minister to Gt. Britain (apptd. by Pres. Fillmore), 1852-53. Died Phila., Feb. 20, 1868; buried St. Peter's Protestant Episcopal Churchyard, Phila.

INGERSOLL, Ralph Isaacs, congressman, diplomat, mayor; b. New Haven, Conn., Feb. 8, 1789; grad. Yale, 1808; studied law; children include Colin Macrae. Admitted to Conn. bar, 1810, began practice in New Haven; mem. Conn. Ho. of Reps., 1820-25, speaker, 1824-25; mem. U.S. Ho. of Reps. (Democrat) from Conn., 19th-22d congresses, 1825-33; states atty. for New Haven County (Conn.), 1833; declined appointment to fill vacancy as U.S. senator, 1835; U.S. minister to Russia, 1846-48; mayor New Haven, 1851. Died New Haven, Aug. 26, 1872; buried Grove St. Cemetery, New Haven.

INGERSOLL, Simon, inventor; b. Stanwich, Conn., Mar. 3, 1818; s. Alexander S. and Caroline (Carll) I.; m. Sarah B. Smith, 1839; m. 2d, Frances Hoyt; 5 children. Farmer, L.I., N.Y., 1839-58; patented rotating shaft for steam engine, 1858; built steam propelled wagon; patented friction clutch, gate latch, spring scale in 1860's; engaged in farming, 1870; patented rock drill, 1871; organized Ingersoll Rock Drill Co.; patented 16 improvements of drill machinery and 4 patents for life line thrower, 1873-83. Died July 24, 1894.

INGHAM, Charles Cromwell, painter; b. Dublin, Ireland, 1796; studied painting Royal Dublin Soc., 1809; student of William Cuming. Accompanied family to N.Y.C., 1816; specialized in portraits of women and children; mem. N.A.D., 1826, later prof.; founder Sketch Club, 1847. Died N.Y.C., Dec. 10, 1863.

INGHAM, Samuel, congressman; b. Hebron, Conn., Sept. 5, 1793; attended com. schs. Vt.; studied law. Admitted to the bar, 1815, began practice in Canaan, Vt.; moved to Jewett City, Conn., later to Essex (then part of Saybrook), Conn., 1819, practiced law; states atty. for Middlesex County (Conn.), 1827-35, 43-44; mem. Conn. Ho. of Reps., 1828, 34, 51-52, speaker, 1851-52; judge of probate, 1829-33; judge Middlesex County Ct., 1849-53; mem. U.S. Ho. of Reps. (Democrat) from Conn., 24th-25th congresses, 1835-39; mem. Conn. Senate, 1843-50; unsuccessful Dem. candidate for U.S. Senate, 1854; U.S. commr. of customs, 1857-61. Died Essex, Nov. 10, 1881; buried River View Cemetery, Essex.

INGHAM, Samuel Delucenna, congressman, sec. of treasury; b. Great Spring, Pa., Sept. 16, 1779; s. Dr. Jonathan and Ann (Welding) I.; m. Rebecca Dodd, 1800, 5 children; m. 2d, Deborah Hall, 1822, 3 children. Mem. Pa. Ho. of Reps. from Bucks County, 1806-08; justice of the peace, 1808; mem. U.S. Ho. of Reps. from Pa., 13th-15th, 18th-20th congresses, 1813-18, 23-29; prothonotary Bucks County Ct. of Pleas, 1818; sec. Commonwealth of Pa., 1819; U.S. sec. of treasury under Andrew Jackson, 1829-31; helped develop inland canal navigation, railroad transp., anthracite coal mining in Pa. Died Trenton, N.J., June 5, 1860; buried Salebury Churchyard, Bucks County.

INGLE, Richard, pirate; b. England, 1609. Came to Md. as tobacco agt., circa 1632; traded in his own ship Reformation; ship seized, imprisoned on charges of piracy and high treason in Md. in 1640's, returned to England after escape, secured letters of marque, came back to Md. where he attacked shipping and plundered shore, 1644-45; escaped punishment, probably died in poverty. Died 1653.

INGLIS, Charles, clergyman; b. Ireland, 1734; m. Mary Vining, Feb. 1764; m. 2d, Margaret Crooke, May 31, 1773; 2 daus., 2 sons. Came to Am., 1755; ordained Anglican deacon, 1758; attached to Dover (Del.) mission, 1759-65, transferred to N.Y.C.; supported Royalist cause; left Am., 1783; bishop of N.S. (Can.), 1787-1816; mem. N.S. Council, 1809. Died Halifax, N.S., Feb. 24, 1816.

INGRAHAM, Duncan Nathaniel, naval officer; b. Charleston, S.C., Dec. 6, 1802; s. Nathaniel and Louisa (Hall) I.; m. Harriot Horry Laurens, 1827, 3 sons, 5 daus. Apptd. midshipman U.S. Navy at age 9 years, 1812; served in ships Congress and Madison during War of 1812; promoted lt., 1825, comdr., 1838; served in Mexican War; participated in Koszta affair (his most celebrated act), 1853; chief Bur. Ordnance, 1856-60; entered Confederate Navy, 1861; chief ordnance, Richmond, Va.; commanded Confederate naval forces on S.C. coast; commanded 2 iron clads, 1863; on shore duty, 1863-65. Died Charleston, Oct. 16, 1891.

INGRAHAM, Edward Duffield, lawyer; b. Phila., Feb. 12, 1793; s. Francis and Elizabeth (Duffield) I.; read law under Alexander J. Dallas, 1811-13; m. Mary Wilson; m. 2d, Caroline Barney. Admitted to Phila. bar, 1813; del. Phila. Free Trade Conv., 1831; sec. Congressional com. investigation U.S. Bank, 1834, dir., 1834-36; commr. Fugitive Slave Act, 1850. Author: A Sketch of the Insolvent Laws of Pennsylvania, 1822; A Sketch of the Events which Preceded the Capture of Washington by the British, 1849; numerous legal books. Died Nov. 5, 1854.

INGRAHAM, Joseph, sea capt.; b. Boston, Mar. 1762; s. Duncan and Susannah (Blake) I.; m. Jane Salter, Oct. 11, 1785, 3 sons. One of earliest sea capts. engaging in Am. Northwest-China trade; became capt. ship Columbia on voyage to Cape Verde Islands; discovered 6 islands in Pacific on trip to N.W., 1791; lt. brig Pickering, U.S. Navy, 1799-1800, brig sailed, never heard from again. Lost at sea, 1800.

INGRAHAM, Joseph Holt, clergyman; b. Portland, Me., Jan. 25, 1809; s. James and Elizabeth (Thurston) I.; m. Mary Brooks, circa 1849, 4 children including Prentiss. Ordained priest Protestant Episcopal Ch., Jackson, Miss., 1852; missionary, Aberdeen, Miss., 1852-54; rector St. John's Ch., Mobile, Ala., 1855-58, Christ Ch., Holly Springs, Miss., 1859-60. Author: Lafitte, 2 vols., 1836; Rafael; or, The Twice Condemned, 1845; The Pillar of Fire, 1859; The Sunny South, 1860. Died Holly Springs, Dec. 18, 1860; buried Hill Crest Cemetery, Holly Springs.

INMAN, George, army officer; b. Boston, Dec. 3, 1775; s. Ralph and Susanna (Speakman) I.; grad. Harvard, 1772; m. Mary Badger, Apr. 23, 1778, 4 daus. Served with British at Bunker Hill, 1775; took part in capture of Am. intelligence officers at Battle of L.I. (perhaps decisive in Am. defeat), 1776; commd. ensign 17th Inf., 1776, served in battles of Princeton, Brandywine, Germantown, Monmouth; exiled in Eng., 1780-88. Died circa Feb., 1789.

INMAN, Henry, artist; b. Utica, N.Y., Oct. 28, 1801; s. William and Sarah Inman; apprenticed to John W. Jarvis; m. Jane O'Brien, 1832, 5 children including Henry, Mary. Opened portrait studio, N.Y.C., 1823; a founder N.A.D., v. p., 1826-30, 38-44; painted portraits of Wordsworth, Macaulay, Dr. Chalmers, others, in Eng., 1844-45. Works include: The Young Fisherman, Rip Van Winkle's Awakening, View of Rydal Water, also portraits of many famous Americans including John Marshall, Martin Van Buren, Nathaniel Hawthorne. Died Jan. 17, 1846.

INMAN, John, editor; b. Utica, N.Y., 1805; s. William and Sarah Inman; m. Miss Fisher, 1833. Practiced law, N.Y.C., 1829-33; mem. editorial staff N.Y. Mirror, 1828-31, 35-36; asst. editor Comml. Advertiser, 1837-44, editor-in-chief, 1844-50; editor Columbian Lady's and Gentleman's Mag., 1844-48. Author: The Little Old Man of Coblentz, 1828; The Sudden and Sharp Doom, 1842. Died Mar. 30, 1850.

INMAN, John Hamilton, mcht., financier; b. Landridge, Tenn., Oct. 6, 1844; s. Shadrach and Jane (Hamilton) I.; m. Margaret McKinney Coffin, 1870. Served in Confederate Army, 1862-75; organized Inman, Swann & Co., N.Y.C., 1870; a founder N.Y. Cotton Exchange; organizer, dir. Tenn. Coal, Iron & R.R. Co.; ofcl. of several Southern railroads; mem. N.Y. Rapid Transit Commn. Died New Canaan, Conn., Nov. 5, 1896.

INNES, Harry, judge; b. Caroline County, Va., Jan. 15, 1753; s. Richard and Catherine (Richards) I.; m. Elizabeth Calloway; m. 2d, Mrs. Ann Shields. Admitted to Va. bar, 1772; elected by Va. legislature to determine claims to unpatented lands in dist. around Abingdon, Ky., 1779; escheator Bedford County (Ky.), 1779; apptd. supt. over tax commrs. of 6 counties by Benjamin Harrison (gov. Va.), 1782; elected by Va. Legislature as atty. gen. for Western dist. of Va., 1784; U.S. dist. judge for Ky., 1789-1816; trustee Transylvania U. Died Frankfort, Ky., Sept. 20, 1816.

INNES, James, lawyer; b. Caroline County, Va., 1754; s. Robert and Catherine (Richards) I.; attended Coll. William and Mary; m. Elizabeth Cooke, 1 dau., Ann. Commd. lt. col., 15th Va. Regt.; aide to Washington; navy commr., 1778; chmn. bd. war for Va., 1779; mem. Va. Assembly from James County and Williamsburg, 1780-82; elected judge adv. Continental Army by Congress, 1782; atty. gen. Va., 1786; orator, selected to deliver final speech for adoption of U.S. Constn. in Va. Constl. Conv., 1788. Died Phila., Aug 2, 1798; buried Christ Ch. Burial Ground, Phila.

INNESS, George, painter; b. nr. Newburgh, N.Y., May 1, 1825; s. John William and Clarissa (Baldwin) I.; studied painting with Regis Gignoux, N.Y.C.; m. Delia Miller, 1848; m. 2d, Elizabeth Hart, 1850; 5 children including George, Helen. With Sherman & Smith, map engraving firm, 1841-42; established own studio, N.Y.C., 1845; exhibited his 1st picture, Afternoon, 1846; studied and painted in Rome, Italy, 1847-48; again lived in Italy, 1851-52, 71-75, Medfield, Mass., 1859-64, Montclair, N.J., 1878-94; became most prosperous landscape artist of his time; sale of his paintings a year after his death totaled $108,670; his works represented in collections of most major U.S. art museums. Died while traveling in Europe, Bridge of Allan, Scotland, Aug. 3, 1894; buried N.Y.C.

INNOKENTII, see Popov-Veniaminov, Ioann.

INSKIP, John Swanel, clergyman; b. Huntington, Eng., Aug. 10, 1816; s. Edward and Martha (Swanel) I.; m. Martha J. Foster, Nov. 1, 1835. Licensed to preach by Methodist Ch., 1835, ordained deacon, 1838, elder, 1840; ministered in Phila. Conf., 1835-45, Ohio Conf., 1845-52; involved in "promiscuous sitting" controversy (favored seating men and women together); transferred to N.Y. Conf., 1852; chaplain 14th Regt., N.Y. State Militia, 1860-61; pres. newly-formed Nat. Camp Meeting Assn. for Promotion of Holiness, 1867; editor Christian Standard, 1876-84. Author: Methodism Explained and Defended, 1851. Died Ocean Grove, N.J., Mar. 7, 1884.

IOASAF, see Bolotov, Ivan Il'ich.

IOOR, William, playwright; b. Dorchester, S. C., circa 1780; s. John Ioor. Wrote comedy Independence, or, Which Do You Like Best, the Peer, or the Farmer, 1st performed at Charleston (S.C.) Theatre, 1805; wrote The Battle of Eutaw Springs, and Evacuation of Charleston, 1807. Died circa 1830.

IREDELL, James, justice U.S. Supreme Ct.; b. Lewes, Eng., Oct. 5, 1751; s. Francis and Margaret (McCulloh) I.; m. Hannah Johnston, July 18, 1773. Comptroller of customs, Edenton, N.C., 1768; collector of customs Port of N.C., 1774-76; judge Superior Ct. of N.C., 1777; atty. gen. N.C., 1779; mem. N.C. Council of State, 1787; wrote Answer to Mr. Mason's Objections to the New Constn. in support of U.S. Constn., also was floor leader N.C. Conv., maj. force in adoption of Constn. in N.C.; asso. justice U.S. Supreme Ct, 1790-99; wrote dissenting opinion in case of Chisholm vs. Ga.; decision in case of Calder vs. Bull. Died Edenton, Oct. 20, 1799.

IREDELL, James, senator, gov. N.C.; b. Edenton, N.C., Nov. 2, 1788; grad. Princeton, 1806; studied law. Admitted to N.C. bar, 1809, began practice in Edenton; served as capt. of a volunteer co. during War of 1812; mem. N.C. Ho. of

Commons, 1813, 16-28, speaker, 1817-28; judge N.C. Superior Ct., 1819; gov. N.C., 1828; mem. U.S. Senate (Democrat) from N.C., 1828-31; moved to Raleigh, N.C., practiced law; reporter N.C. Supreme Ct., 1840-52; commr. to revise N.C. laws, 1836-37. Died Edenton, Apr. 13, 1853; buried Johnston Burial Ground on Hayes plantation, Edenton.

IRELAND, John, army officer, gov. Tex.; b. Millerstown, Ky., Jan. 1, 1827; s. Patrick and Rachel (Newton) I.; m. Matilda Wicks, 1854; m. 2d, Anna Penn, 1857. Dep., Hart County, Ky., 1847-50; admitted to Ky. bar, 1852; 1st mayor Sequin, Tex., 1858; del. to conv. which abrogated articles of annexation between Tex. and U.S., 1861; argued for secession; commd. lt. col. Confederate Army, served in campaigns in Trans-Miss. Dept., 1862; mem. Tex. Ho. of Reps., 1872; mem. Tex. Senate, 1873-75; asso. justice Tex. Supreme Ct., 1875-76; gov. Tex. (Democrat), 1882-86. Died Sequin, Mar. 15, 1896.

IRELAND, Joseph Norton, stage historian; b. N.Y.C., Apr. 24, 1817; s. Joseph and Sophia (Jones) I.; m. Mary Titus, June 10, 1845. Retired from business, 1855; resided at Bridgeport, Conn., 1857-98. Author: Some Account of the Ireland Family, Originally of Long Island, New York, 1644-1880, 1880; Mrs. Puff, 1882; compiler: Records of the New York Stage, from 1750-1860, 2 vols., 1866-67. Died Bridgeport, Dec. 29, 1898; buried Bridgeport.

IRENE, Sister, see Fitzgibbon, Catherine.

IRVIN, Alexander, congressman; b. Penns Valley, Pa., Jan. 18, 1800; attended pub. schs. Moved to Curwensville, Pa., 1820, Clearfield, Pa., 1826, engaged in merc. and lumber bus.; treas. Clearfield County, 1828-30; mem. Pa. Senate, 1837-38; prothonotary Pa. Ct. Common Pleas, 1842; clk. of cts.; recorder of deeds and register of wills of Clearfield County, 1842-44; mem. U.S. Ho. of Reps. (Whig) from Pa., 30th Congress, 1847-49; U.S. marshal for Western Dist. of Pa., 1850; del. Republican Nat. Conv., Cincinnati, 1872. Died Clearfield, Mar. 20, 1874; buried Reed addition to Old Graveyard, Clearfield.

IRVIN, James, congressman; b. Linden Hall, Pa., Feb. 18, 1800; attended common schs. Engaged in merc. bus., milling, mining, mfg., Oak Hill, Milesburg and Bellefonte, Pa.; mem. U.S. Ho. of Reps. (Whig) from Pa., 27th-28th congresses, 1841-45; unsuccessful Whig candidate for gov. Pa., 1857; U.S. naval storekeeper, Phila., 1857. Died Hecla, Pa., Nov. 28, 1862; buried Union Cemetery, Bellefonte.

IRVIN, William W., congressman, jurist; b. nr. Charlottesville, Va., circa 1778; studied law. Admitted to Va. bar, 1800, began practice in Albemarle County; moved to Lancaster, O., circa 1801, practiced law; apptd. asso. judge Ct. Common Pleas for Fairfield County (O.), 1803, impeached, 1804; mem. Ohio Ho. of Reps., 1806-07, 25-27, speaker, 1825-26; justice Ohio Supreme Ct., 1810-15; mem. U.S. Ho. of Reps. (Democrat) from Ohio, 21st-22d congresses, 1829-33; engaged in farming, nr. Lancaster. Died nr. Lancaster, Mar. 28, 1842.

IRVINE, James, army officer; b. Phila., Aug. 4, 1735; s. George and Mary (Rush) I. Commd. ensign 1st Bn., Pa. Provincial Regt., 1760, capt., 1763; del. Provincial Conf., Phila., 1775; commd. lt. col., 1775; commd. rank of col. on charge of 9th Pa. Regt., 1776; served in Can. campaign, 1776; commd. brig. gen. Pa. Militia, 1777, given command of 2d Brigade; commanded right flank of Am. line at Battle of Germantown; mem. Supreme Exec. Council of Pa. (Constitutionalist), 1782-85, v.p. council, 1784-85; mem. Pa. Assembly, 1785-86; maj. gen. Pa. Militia, 1782-93; mem. Pa. Senate, 1795-99. Died Phila., Apr. 28, 1819.

IRVINE, William, army officer, congressman; b. Enniskillen, Ulster Province, Ireland, Nov. 3, 1741; ed. Trinity Coll., Dublin, Ireland; m. Anne Calender, children include Calender, Col. William N., Capt. Armstrong. Served as surgeon on Brit. ship of war during Seven Years War; came to Am., 1763; mem. Pa. Provincial Conv., Phila., 1774; commd. col. 6th (later 7th) Pa. Regt., 1776; participated in Battle of Three Rivers, 1776; commd. brig. gen. Continental Army, 1779; participated in Lord Stirling's expdn. against Staten Island, also unsuccessful attack at Bull's Ferry with Gen. Wayne, 1780; del. from Pa. to Continental Congress, 1786-88; del. Pa. Constl. Conv., 1790; mem. U.S. Ho. of Reps. from Pa., 3d Congress, Dec. 2, 1793-95; pres. Pa. br. Soc. of Cincinnati, 1801-04. Died Phila., July 29, 1804.

IRVINE, William, congressman; b. Whitneys Point, N.Y., Feb. 14, 1820; attended common schs.; studied law. Admitted to N.Y. bar, 1849, began practice in Corning; mem. U.S. Ho. of Reps. (Republican) from N.Y., 36th Congress, 1859-61; an organizer, lt. col. 10th Regt., N.Y. Volunteer Cavalry, 1861; wounded at Battle of Beverly Ford (Va.), taken prisoner, imprisoned in Libby Prison; honorably discharged, 1864; brevetted col. and brig. gen. U.S. Volunteers, 1865; adj. gen. on staff of Gov. Fenton of N.Y., 1865-66; moved to Cal., practiced law. Died San Francisco, Nov. 12, 1882; buried Elmira (N.Y.) Cemetery.

IRVING, John Beaufain, artist; b. Charleston, S.C., Nov. 26, 1825; s. Dr. John Beaufain and Emma (Cruger) I.; pupil of Leutze, 1851. Became asso. N.A.D., 1869, academician, 1872; most of his paintings were of genre or hist. type; works include: Wine Tasters, 1869; The End of the Game, 1876; The Connoisseurs, 1877. Died Apr. 20, 1877.

IRVING, Peter, author; b. N.Y.C., Oct. 30, 1772; s. William and Sarah (Sanders) I.; grad. Columbia, 1794. Owner, editor Morning Chronicle, 1802-04, Corrector, N.Y.C., 1804; member group which produced satire Salmagundi: Or, the Whim-Whams of Lancelot Langstaff Esq. and Others, 1807; a travelling companion of his brother Washington Irving. Author: Giovanni Sbogarro: A Venetian Tale. Died June 27, 1838.

IRVING, Pierre Munro, lawyer, writer; b. 1803; s. William and Julia (Paulding) I.; grad. Columbia, 1821. Collected materials which were basis for Washington Irving's Astoria, 1836; financial and literary mgr. for Washington Irving, 1846-59, literary executor, 1859. Author: The Life and Letters of Washington Irving, 1862-64. Editor: Washington Irving's Spanish Papers and Other Miscellanies, 1866. Died 1876.

IRVING, Roland Duer, geologist; b. N.Y.C., Apr. 29, 1847; s. Pierre Paris and Anna Henrietta (Duer) I.; attended Columbia, 1863-64; grad. Columbia Sch. Mines, 1869; m. Abby Louise McCulloch, 1872, 1 dau., 2 sons including John Duer. Supt. smelting works, Grenville, N.J., 1879; prof. geology and mineralogy U. Wis., 1870; asst. geologist during geol. survey of 1873-76; sponsored by U.S. Geol. Survey to investigate geology of Lake Superior region, 1880-88. Author: Copper-Bearing Rocks of Lake Superior, 1833. Died May 27, 1888.

IRVING, Washington, author; b. N.Y.C., Apr. 3, 1783; s. Deacon William and Sarah (Sanders) I. Entered law office of Henry Masterson, 1798; admitted to N.Y. bar; wrote for Morning Chronicle, also for The Chronicle (his anonymous Burrite sheet) ; offered 1st installment of "The Letters of Jonathan Oldstyle, Gent." in Morning Chronicle, Nov. 15, 1802; leader in group which published Salmagunde (series of whimsical essays in which name Gotham was 1st applied to N.Y.C.); wrote a History of New York (1st great comic lit. work written by an American), published 1809; The Sketch Book (included "Rip Van Winkle") published in N.Y.C. in groups of 4 or 5 essays, 1819-20, complete English edit. compiled, London, 1820; attached to U.S. Embassy, Madrid, Spain, 1826-29; discussed a proposed translation into English of recently published Coleccion de los Viages y Descubrimentos (Columbus) with Everett, 1826, published The History of the Life and Voyages of Columbus, 1828, won him election to Real Academia de la Historia; A Chronicle of the Conquest of Granada (1829) and The Alhambra (1832) identify him as an important 19th century interpreter of Spanish legend and culture; sec. of legation, London, 1829; U.S. minister to Spain, 1843-46; other works include: Bracebridge Hall, 1822; The Stout Gentleman; Dolph Heyliger; Tales of a Traveller, 1824; The Crayon Miscellany, 1835; The Tour; Astoria, 1836; The Adventures of Captain Bonneville, U.S.A., 1837; Oliver Goldsmith, 1849; Wolfert's Roost, 1855; Life of Washington, 5 vols., 1855-59; short stories Rip Van Winkle, The Legend of Sleepy Hollow. Died Tarrytown, N.Y., Nov. 28, 1859.

IRVING, William, congressman; b. N.Y.C., Aug. 15, 1766; s. William and Sarah (Sanders) I.; m. Julia Paulding, Nov. 7, 1793, children include Pierre Munroe. Fur trader among Indians along Mohawk River, Johnstown, Caughnawaga, N.Y.; went to N.Y.C., 1793; contbr. to Washington Irving's Salmagundi; or The Whim-Whams and Opinions of Launcelot Langstaff, Esq. and Others, 1808; mem. U.S. Ho. of Reps. from N.Y., 13th-15th congresses, Jan. 22, 1814-19. Died Nov. 9, 1821.

IRWIN, Jared, congressman; b. Ga., Jan. 19, 1768. Apptd. commr. for valuation of lands and dwellings and enumeration of slaves for 2d Div. of Ga., 1798; engaged in merc. bus., Milton, Pa.; postmaster of Milton, 1802-03; sheriff of Northumberland County (Pa.), 1808-12; mem. Pa. Ho. of Reps., 1811; served as col. 5th Rifle Regt., War of 1812; mem. U.S. Ho. of Reps. (Democrat) from Pa., 13th-14th congresses, 1813-17; moved to S.Am.

IRWIN, Solden, appeared (with wife) as 1st profl. players at Salt Lake Theatre, Salt Lake City, 1863, had successful season, Soldens taught amateur company there some of acting fundamentals.

IRWIN, Thomas, congressman, jurist; b. Phila., Feb. 22, 1785; attended Franklin Coll., Lancaster, Pa.; studied law. Became editor Phila. Repository, 1804; admitted to Pa. bar, 1808, began practice in Uniontown; Indian agt., Natchitoches, La., also practiced law, 2 years; resumed practice of law, Uniontown, 1811; mem. Pa. Ho. of Reps., 1824-28; mem. U.S. Ho. of Reps. (Democrat) from Pa., 21st Congress, 1829-31; U.S. judge for Western Pa. 1831-59. Died Pitts., May 14, 1870; buried Allegheny Cemetery, Pitts.

IRWIN, William Wallace, congressman, mayor; b. Pitts., 1803; attended Allegheny Coll., Meadville, Pa.; studied law. Admitted to Pa. bar, 1828, began practice in Pitts.; mayor of Pitts., 1840; mem. U.S. Ho. of Reps. (Whig) from Pa., 27th Congress, 1841-43; U.S. Chargé d'affaires to Denmark, 1843 47. Died Pitts., Sept. 15, 1856; buried Allegheny Cemetery, Pitts.

ISAACS, Henry G. architect; b. Phila., 1840; ed. in N.Y.C.; received archtl. tng. in office of Richard Upjohn. Practiced as architect in partnership with George L. Barnett, St. Louis; designed numerous bldgs. in St. Louis, including Merc. Library (built 1885), Bank of Commerce, Episcopal Ch. of Holy Communion, Pilgrim Congregational Ch., Southern Hotel, also numerous residences for some of leading citizens of St. Louis; became mem. A.I.A., 1884. Did Sept. 8, 1895.

ISAACS, Samuel Myer, clergyman, journalist; b. Leeuwarden, Netherlands, Jan. 4, 1804; s. Myer Samuel Isaacs; m. Jane Symmons, at least 3 children, Judge Myer S., Isaac S., Abram S. Moved to London (Eng.) with family, 1814; in charge of Neveh Zedek orphan asylum, Eng.; went to N.Y.C. as rabbi B'nai Jeshurum Synagogue, 1839-47; spiritual leader Congregation Shaaray Tefila, 1847-78; founder, editor Jewish Messenger, 1857. Died N.Y.C., May 19, 1878.

ISACKS' Jacob C., congressman; b. Montgomery County, Pa. Moved to Winchester, Tenn.; mem. U.S. Ho. of Reps. from Tenn., 18th-22d congresses, 1823-33, unsuccessful candidate for reelection, 1832. Died Winchester.

IVERSON, Alfred, senator, jurist; probably born Liberty County, Ga., Dec. 3, 1798; s. Robert and Rebecca (Jones) I.; grad. Princeton, 1820; m. Caroline Goode Holt; m. 2d, Julia Forsyth; 4 children including Brig. Gen. Alfred. Mem. lower house Ga. Gen. Assembly, 1827-29; judge Chattahoochee circuit Ga. Superior Ct., 1835-37, 50-54; mem. Ga. Senate from Muscogee County, 1843; mem. U.S. Ho. of Reps. from Ga., 30th Congress, 1847-49; mem. U.S. Senate from Ga., Dec. 3, 1855-Jan. 28, 1861; publicly advocated secession, July 14, 1859. Died Macon, Ga., Mar. 4, 1873; buried Linwood Cemetery, Columbus, Ga.

IVES, Chauncey Bradley, sculptor; b. Hamden, Conn., Dec. 14, 1810; m. Maria Louisa Davis, 1860, 7 children. Woodcarver's apprentice under R. E. Northrop, New Haven, Conn.; moved to Boston to begin career as sculptor; lived in Florence, Italy, 1844-51, in Rome, Italy, 1851-94; produced busts of Prof. Benjamin Silliman and Ithiel Towne; opened studio to exhibit his works including Pandora, Cupid with his Net and Rebecca, N.Y.C., 1855; came to U.S. to marry, 1860; executed sculptures of Jonathan Trumbull and Roger Sherman (placed in Statuary Hall of Capitol, Washington, D.C.), 1872; exhibited portrait busts of Gen. Winfield Scott and William H. Seward at Phila. Centennial, 1876. Died Rome, Aug. 2, 1894.

IVES, Eli, physician; b. New Haven, Conn., Feb. 7, 1778; s. Levi and Lydia (Augur) I.; grad. Yale, 1799; m. Maria Beers, Sept. 1805, 3 sons, 2 daus. Rector, Hopkins Grammar Sch., New Haven, 1799-1800; fellow Conn. Med. Soc., 1806, sec., 1810, 11, 12; prof. materia medica and botany Yale Med. Coll., 1813-29; contbr. to 1st Pharmacopoeia of the United States of America, 1820; pres. A.M.A., 1860. Died Oct. 8, 1861.

IVES, James Merritt, lithographer; b. N.Y.C., Mar. 5, 1824; m. Caroline Clark, 1852. Bookkeeper firm of Nathaniel Currier, lithographers, circa 1852, became partner, firm name changed to Currier & Ives, 1857, handled managerial aspect of business; served as capt. Company F, 23d Bklyn. Regiment during Civil War. Died Rye, N.Y., Jan. 3, 1895.

IVES, Joseph Christmas, army officer; b. N.Y.C., 1828; grad. U.S. Mil. Acad., 1852. Asst. to lt. A. W. Whipple, U.S. Topog. Engrs., to survey Pacific R.R. route, 1853-54; promoted 1st lt. U.S. Army,

1857; in charge of expdn. to explore Colorado River, 1857-58; engr., architect Washington Nat. Monument, 1859-60; commr. to survey border between Cal. and U.S. territories, 1860-61; declined appointment as capt. U.S. Army, 1861; commd. capt. engrs. Confederate Army; chief engr. Southeastern States, 1861; fortified defenses of Savannah and Charleston, 1861-62; commd. col. Confederate Army, 1862; a.d.c. to Jefferson Davis, 1863-65; adviser to Gen. Beauregard in defense of Charleston, 1864. Author: Memoir to Accompany a Military Map of the Peninsula of Florida, South of Tampa Bay, 1856; Military Maps of the Seat of War in Italy, 1859. Died N.Y.C., Nov. 12, 1868.

IVES, Levi Silliman, clergyman; b. Meriden, Conn., Sept. 16, 1797; s. Levi and Fanny (Silliman) I.; attended Hamilton Coll., 1816; studied theology under Bishop J. H. Hobart; m. Rebecca Hobart, 1822. Ordained deacon Protestant Episcopal Ch., 1822, priest, Trinity Ch., Phila., 1823; asst. St. James' Ch., Batavia, N.Y.; rector Trinity Ch. (Southwark), Phila.; asst. minister Trinity Ch., N.Y.C; rector St. James' Ch., Lancaster, Pa.; bishop of N.C., 1831; founded Brotherhood of Holy Cross, Valle Crucis, N.C., dissolved after investigation by conv. of Episcopalian Ch., 1848; resigned as bishop and entered Roman Catholic Ch., 1852; prof. English, St. John's Coll., Fordham, N.Y., also St. Joseph's Sem.; founder, 1st pres. Cath. Male Protectory. Author: New Manual of Devotions, Humility a Ministerial Qualification, 1840; The Apostle's Doctrine and Fellowship, 1844; The Obedience of Faith, 1849; Trials of a Mind in its Progress to Catholicism; a Letter to his Old Friends, 1853. Died Oct. 13, 1867.

IVES, Willard, congressman; b. Watertown, N.Y., July 7, 1806; attended Belleville (N.Y.) Acad., Lowvile (N.Y.) Acad. Engaged in farming, banking; mem. N.Y. Ho. of Reps., 1829-30; del. Methodist World Conv., London, Eng., 1846; mem. U.S. Ho. of Reps. (Democrat) from N.Y., 32d Congress, 1851-53; pres. Ives Sem., Antwerp, N.Y.; an organizer Syracuse U., trustee, 1870-86. Died Watertown, Apr. 19, 1896; buried Brookside Cemetery, Watertown.

IVY, Hardy, pioneer; erected hewn-log cabin and contracted to pay "in produce as he could spare it" for 200 acres in Canebrake (present-day Atlanta), 1833; only inhabitant of area when A.H. Brisbane surveyed what is now downtown Atlanta, 1837; farmed nr. what is now corner Ivy and Auburn; considered 1st Atlanta settler, and believed to be buried beneath parking lot just west of Ivy St.

IZARD, George, army officer, territorial gov.; b. Richmond, Eng., Oct. 21, 1776; s. Ralph and Alice (DeLancey) I.; m. Elizabeth Farley, June 6, 1803, 3 children. Took part in actions along N.Y.-Canadian border during War of 1812; commd. 2d lt. U.S. Army, 1812, sent to N.Y. as brig. gen. by Sec. John Armstrong, 1812; promoted maj. gen., 1814, became sr. officer in command N.Y. on Canadian border; apptd. gov. Ark. Territory by Pres. Monroe, 1825-28; mem. Am. Philos. Soc.; Izard County (Ark.) named for him. Died Little Rock, Ark., Nov. 22, 1828.

IZARD, Ralph, diplomat, senator; b. Charleston, S.C., Jan. 23, 1742; s. Henry and Margaret (Johnson) I.; grad. Christ Coll., Cambridge (Eng.) U., 1762; m. Alice DeLancey, May 1, 1767, 14 children. Selected by Continental Congress as commr. to Tuscany, 1777; del. from S.C. to Continental Congress, 1782-83; mem. S.C. Legislature; mem. U.S. Senate from S.C., 1789-95, pres. pro tem., 1794-95; founder, trustee Coll. of Charleston. Died Southbay, nr. Charleston, May 30, 1804, buried Ch. St. James, Goose Creek, S.C.

J

JACK, William, congressman; b. Greensburg, Pa., July 29, 1788; studied law. Admitted to Pa. bar, practiced law; moved to Brookville, Pa., 1831, engaged in merc. bus.; div. insp. militia for Westmoreland and Fayette counties (Pa.), 1830-35; sheriff of Brookville, 1833; contractor and builder in Miss., assisted in constrn. of a canal; judge Jefferson County (Pa.) Ct., circa 1840; mem. U.S. Ho. of Reps. (Democrat) from Pa., 27th Congress, 1841-43; engaged in farming. Died Greensburg, Feb. 28, 1852; buried Old Cemetery of St. Clair Cemetery Assn., Greensburg.

JACKSON, Abraham Reeves, gynecologist; b. Phila., June 17, 1827; s. Washington and Deborah (Lee) J.; M.D., Pa. Med. Coll., 1848; m. Harriet Hollinshead, 1850; m. 2d, Julia Newell, 1871. Asst. med. dir. Army of Va., U.S. Army, 1862-64; toured Europe with Mark Twain, 1867, became "Doctor" in Twain's Innocents Abroad; moved to Chgo., 1870; founder, chief surgeon Woman's Hosp. of Ill., 1871; lectr. gynecology Rush Med. Coll., Chgo., 1872-77; co-founder,, 1st pres. Chgo. Coll. Physicians and Surgeons, 1882; pres. Chgo. Gynecol. Soc., 1883; toured world for health reasons, 1889; pres. Am. Gynecol. Soc., 1891. Died Chgo., Nov. 12, 1892.

JACKSON, Andrew, 7th Pres. U.S.; b. Waxhaw, S.C., Mar. 15, 1767; s. Andrew and Elizabeth (Hutchinson) J.; read law, Salisbury, N.C.; m. Rachel (Donelson) Robards, 1791 (again in Dec. 1794); 1 adopted son, Andrew, Jr. Served in Battle of Hanging Rock during Am. Revolution, was captured by British and imprisoned at Camden, S.C.; admitted to N.C. bar, 1787; moved to Nashville, Tenn., 1788; apptd. pros. atty. for S.W. Territory under Gov. William Blount, 1791; judge advocate Davidson County (Tenn.) Militia Regt., 1791; del. Tenn. Constl. Conv., 1796; mem. U.S. Ho. of Reps. from Tenn., 4th Congress, Dec. 5, 1796-97; mem. U.S. Senate from Tenn., Mar. 4, 1797-Apr. 1798, 1823-Oct. 14, 1825; judge Tenn. Supreme Ct., 1798-1804; elected maj. gen. Tenn. Militia, 1802; defeated Creek Indians at Horseshoe Bend, Ala., Mar. 1814; apptd. maj. gen. U.S. Army, May 1814; defeated British at Battle of New Orleans, Jan. 8, 1815 (after signing of peace treaty at Ghent); became major hero of War of 1812 because of totality of this victory; sent to punish Seminole Indians who were raiding on Fla. border, 1818, misinterpreted his orders, crossed border into Fla., captured Pensacola (which belonged to Spain) and hung 2 Brit. subjects (gunrunners) who were inciting the Seminoles (incident placed U.S. in danger of war with Spain and Gt. Britain); his actions were defended by John Q. Adams who placed the blame on Spain (only mem. of Pres. Monroe's cabinet to take Jackson's side); was not chastized, but instead apptd. 1st gov. of Fla. Territory (ceded from Spain 1820), Mar. 10, 1821, resigned July 18, 1821; Democratic candidate for Pres. U.S., ran against Henry Clay, John Q. Adams, William Crawford, 1824 (no candidate received majority in Electoral Coll., election went to U.S. Ho. of Reps.); lost election in Ho. of Reps. when Clay threw his support to Adams; defeated Adams in election of 1828 to become 7th Pres. U.S., Mar. 4, 1829-Mar. 3, 1837; considered to be father of "spoils system"; his cabinet became split as result of Peggy O'Neill (wife of Sec. of War John Eaton) incident, basically brought about by polit. differences between Sec. of State Van Buren and Vice Pres. Calhoun; surprised supporters of John C. Calhoun by strength of his support of Union during nullification crisis, 1832; at this time made famous statement: "Our Federal Union! it must and shall be preserved"; became further alienated from Calhoun upon William Crawford's publication of Calhoun's attempt to censure Jackson for his conduct in Seminole campaign of 1818, chose Van Buren to succeed Calhoun as vice pres.; vetoed bill calling for constrn. of road from Maysville to Lexington (Ky.) on grounds it was a matter of local concern, 1830 (polit. rebuff to Clay); vetoed bill for rechartering Bank of U.S. (passed in Congress with Clay's aid), 1832, Bank question thus became leading issue in election of 1832; initiated Dem. Party nat. nominating conv. (replacing previous caucus system), 1832; favored the conv. (ostensibly introduced to better reflect will of the people) as means of getting Van Buren nominated for vice presidency; defeated Clay in presdl. election of 1832 (won by greater margin than in 1828); initiated Force Bill of 1833 in retaliation to S.C.'s decision to prohibit collection of duties within the state, threatened to use force to execute the law if necessary (crisis was eased by Compromise Tariff of 1833; supported states-rights position of Ga. in removal of Cherokee Indians; removed funds from Bank of U.S. and placed them in "pet" state banks; removed Sec. of Treasury McLane for refusing to make this transfer of funds, replaced McLane with James Duane (who also refused); replaced Duane with R. B. Taney, who made the transfer; rewarded Taney for his loyalty by appointing him to U.S. Supreme Ct., 1836; raised power of exec. br. of govt. to new high through use of patronage and veto, and refusal to implement Supreme Ct. decisions; supported Van Buren for Pres. U.S., 1836, 40, James K. Polk, 1844; advocated annexation of Tex. Died "Hermitage," nr. Nashville, June 8, 1845; buried "Hermitage."

JACKSON, Charles, lawyer; b. Newburyport, Mass., May 31, 1775; s. Jonathan and Hannah (Tracy) J.; grad. Harvard, 1793; studied law under Theophilus Parsons; m. Amelia Lee, Nov. 20, 1799, 1 child; m. 2d, Frances Cabot, Dec. 31, 1809, 5 children. Practiced law, Newburyport, 1776-1803, Boston, 1803-13; judge Mass. Supreme Jud. Ct., 1813-23; overseer Harvard, 1816-25. Author: A Treatise on the Pleadings and Practice in Real Actions, With Precedents of Pleadings, 1828. Died Dec. 13, 1855.

JACKSON, Charles Thomas, geologist; b. Plymouth, Mass., June 21, 1805; s. Charles and Lucy (Cotton) J.; M.D., Harvard, 1829; studied at Sorbonne and École des Mines, Paris, France, 1829; m. Susan Bridge, Feb. 27, 1834, 5 children. Became interested in mineralogy after visiting and collecting mineral specimens in Nova Scotia, circa 1828; travelled through Europe studying geology, mineralogy and meeting leading med. men, 1829-32; practiced medicine, Boston, 1832-36; mem. survey team in Me., Mass., 1837-39; became state geologist of Me., 1837; surveyor of R.I., 1839-40; state geologist, N.H., 1840, surveyor of N.H., 1841-44. Involved in controversy with Samuel F. B. Morse over invention of telegraph, claimed to have made 1st working model, 1840; also claimed to have 1st developed surg. anesthesia, 1846; a U.S. geologist in survey of Lake Superior region, 1847-48; contbr. articles to Am. Jour. of Science, 1828-29. Author: A Manual of Etherization, Containing Directions for the Employment of Ether, Chloroform and other Anaesthetic Agents, 1861. Died Aug. 28, 1880.

JACKSON, Claiborne Fox, gov. Mo.; b. Fleming County, Ky., Apr. 4, 1806; s. Dempsey and Mary (Pickett) J.; married (successively) 3 Sappington sisters,. Retired from merc. bus., 1837; mem. Mo. Gen. Assembly, 1836, 42-48, speaker Mo. Ho. of Reps., 1844, 46; mem. Mo. Senate (Democrat), 1848-49; gov. Mo., 1860; a secessionist; when Mo. Legislature failed to pass an act enabling him to gain possession of U.S. Arsenal at St. Louis, he determined to use his power as gov. to accomplish it; helped found banking system of Mo. Died Little Rock, Ark., Dec. 6, 1862.

JACKSON, David, physician, Continental congressman; b. Oxford, Pa., circa 1747; s. Samuel Jackson; B.M., Coll. of Phila. (now U. Pa.), 1768; m. Jane (Mather) Jackson, 1768; m. 2d, Susanna Kemper; 9 children including David, Samuel. Practiced medicine, Phila.; mgr. of the lottery (apptd. by Continental Congress), 1776-77; surgeon, q.m. gen., Pa. Militia, 1779; mem. med. staff Phila. Gen. Hosp., 1779-80; del. Continental Congress from Phila., 1785; trustee U. State of Pa., 1789, U. Pa., 1791-1801; mem. Am. Philos. Soc., 1792; an organizer 1st Democratic Soc. in Am., 1793; alderman Phila., 1801. Died Phila., Sept. 17, 1801.

JACKSON, David E., fur trapper; established firm (with William Sublette and Jedediah S. Smith) to transport people across Rocky Mountains, 1823; bought out (with partners) William H. Ashley's fur trading bus., took charge of trapping operations, extended bus. through Rockies to Cal. and Columbia River; Jackson Hole and Jackson, Wyo., named for him.

JACKSON, David Sherwood, congressman; b. N.Y.C., 1813; attended pub. schs. Alderman, N.Y.C., 1843-46, 56-57; engaged in merc. bus.; mem. U.S. Ho. of Reps. (Democrat) from N.Y., 30th Congress, 1847-Apr. 19, 1848 (seat declared vacant as result of contested election). Died N.Y.C., Jan. 20, 1872; buried Marble Cemetery, N.Y.C.

JACKSON, Ebenezer, Jr., congressman; b. Savannah, Ga., Jan. 31, 1796; s. Ebenezer Jackson; grad. St. Mary's Coll., nr. Balt., 1814 attended Litchfield (Conn.) Law Sch. Admitted to the bar; began practice of law, Phila., 1821; moved to Middletown, Conn., 1826; mem. Conn. Ho. of Reps., 1829-32, 49; mem. U.S. Ho. of Reps. (Whig) from Pa., 23d Congress, Dec. 1, 1834-35. Died Middletown, Aug. 17, 1874; buried Indian Hill Cemetery, Middletown.

JACKSON, Edward Brake, congressman; b. Clarksburg, Va. (now W.Va.), Jan. 25, 1793; s. George Jackson; attended Randolph Acad. Clarksburg; studied medicine. Began practice of medicine, Clarksburg; served as surgeon's mate during War of 1812; mem. Va. Ho. of Dels., 1815-18; clk. U.S. Dist. Ct., 1819; mem. U.S. Ho. of Reps. (Democrat) from Va., 16th-17th congresses, Oct. 23, 1820-23. Died Bedford Springs, nr. Bedford, Pa., Sept. 8, 1826; buried nr. Bedford.

JACKSON, Francis, reformer; b. Newton, Mass., Mar. 7, 1789; son of Maj. Timothy Jackson. Prominent citizen of Boston; active city govt. Boston; pres. Anti-Slavery Soc. Author: History of Newton, 1854. Died Boston, Nov. 14, 1861.

JACKSON, George, congressman; b. Cecil County, Md., Jan. 9, 1757; studied law; children include John George, Edward Brake. Served to col. during Am. Revolution; admitted to Va. bar, 1787, began practice in Clarksburg, Va. (now W.Va.); justice of peace, 1784; mem. Va. Ho. of Dels., 1785-91, 94; mem. Va. Conv. which ratified U.S. Constn., 1788; mem. U.S. Ho. of Reps., from Va., 4th, 6th-7th congresses, 1799-1803; moved to Zanesville, O., circa 1806, engaged in farming; mem. Ohio Ho. of Reps., 1809-12, Ohio Senate, 1817-19. Died Zanesville, May 17, 1831; buried Falls Twp., nr. Zanesville.

JACKSON, George K., organist, author; b. Oxford, Eng., 1758; instructed in music by Dr. James Nares, Eng.; D. Mus., St. Andrew's Coll., Eng., 1791; m. Miss Rogers; 11 children. Came to Norfolk, Va., 1796; music dir. St. George's Chapel, N.Y.C., 1804; organist Brattle St. Ch., Boston, 1812; organist King's Chapel, Trinity Ch. and St. Paul's Ch., Boston, after War of 1812. Author: First Principles; or A Treatise on Practical Thorough Bass, 1795; David's Psalms, 1804; A Choice Collection of Chants, 1816; The Choral Companion, 1817. Died Boston, Nov. 18, 1822.

JACKSON, Hall, surgeon; b. Hampton, N.H., Nov. 11, 1739; s. Dr. Clement and Sarah (Leavitt) J.; studied medicine under father in Portsmouth, N.H., also in London hosps.; m. Mrs. Molly (Dalling) Wentworth, Dec. 1, 1765, 2 children. One of earliest Am. physicians to perform cataract-couching operation of eye; administered innoculations during smallpox epidemic, Boston, 1764; an organizer smallpox hosp. on Henzell's Island, nr. Portsmouth after return from Boston; cared for wounded of Battle of Bunker Hill, 1775; recruited a Mass. arty. co., 1775; surgeon in Pierce Long's regt. at capture Ft. Ticonderoga; received vote of thanks and commn. as chief surgeon in N.H. troops of Continental Army from N.H. Provisional Congress, 1775; hon. mem. Mass. Med. Soc.; charter mem. N.H. Med. Soc. Died Sept. 28, 1797.

JACKSON, Helen Maria Fiske Hunt, author; b. Amherst, Mass., Oct. 15, 1830; d. Nathan Welby and Deborah (Vinal) Fiske; attended Abbott Bros. Sch., N.Y.C.; m. Edward Bissell Hunt, Oct. 28, 1852; m. 2d, William Sharpless Jackson, Oct. 22, 1875; 2 children, Murray, Warren Horsford. Wrote 1st poem for Nation mag., 1865; wrote 1st prose for N.Y. Independent, 1866; apptd. U.S. spl. commr. to investigate needs on Cal. Mission Indians, 1882; writings include: Verses, 1870; Bits of Travel, 1872; Hetty's Strange History, 1877; The Story of Boon (poem), 1847; Ramona (novel), 1884; Between Whiles, 1887. Died Colorado Springs, Colo., Aug. 12, 1885; buried nr. summit of Cheyenne Mountain, Colo., reinterred Evergreen Cemetery, Colorado Springs.

JACKSON, Henry Rootes, jurist, diplomat; b. Athens, Ga., June 24, 1820; s. Henry and Martha (Rootes) J.; grad. Yale, 1839; A.M. (hon.), U. Ga., 1848, LL.D. (hon.), 1893; m. Cornelia Davenport; m. 2d, Florence King; 4 children. Admitted to Ga. bar, 1840; U.S. dist. atty. for Ga., 1842; served as col. of a Ga. regt.; editor Georgian, Savannah, 1848-49; judge Superior Ct. of Eastern Circuit, 1849-53; U.S. charge d'affaires Austria, 1853-54, minister resident, 1854-58; mem. Ga. Secession Conv., 1861; judge Confederate cts. of Ga.; commd. maj. gen. of a div. Ga. Militia, 1861; commd. brig. gen. Confederate Army, 1864; U.S. minister to Mexico, 1885, resigned, 1886; pres. Ga. Hist. Soc.; trustee Peabody Edn. Fund. Author: Talulah and Other Poems, 1850. Died Savannah, Ga., May 23, 1898.

JACKSON, Howell Edmunds, senator, justice U.S. Supreme Ct.; b. Paris, Tenn., Apr. 8, 1832; s. Dr. Alexander and Mary (Hurt) J.; grad. W. Tenn. Coll., 1849; attended U. Va., 1851-52; grad. Cumberland U., Lebanon, Tenn., 1856; m. Sophia Malloy, 1859; m. 2d, Mary Harding, Apr. 1847. Judge Ct. Arbitration for W. Tenn., 1875-79; mem. Tenn. Legislature, 1880; mem. U.S. Senate from Tenn. (Democrat), 1881-86; judge U.S. Circuit Ct. for 6th circuit, 1886-93; 1st presiding judge on a circuit ct. appeals, 1891; asso. justice U.S. Supreme Ct., 1893-95. Died Nashville, Tenn., Aug. 8, 1895; buried Mt. Olivet Cemetery, Nashville.

JACKSON, Jabez Young, congressman; b. Savanah, Ga., July 1790; s. Sen. James Jackson. Mem. U.S. Ho. of Reps. (Union Democrat) from Ga., 24th-25th congresses, Oct. 5, 1835-39. Died Clarksville, Ga.

JACKSON, James, senator, gov. Ga.; b. Moreton-Hampstead, Eng., Sept. 21, 1757; s. James and Mary (Webber) J.; m. Mary Young, 5 children. Came to Am., 1772; mem. 1st Ga. Constl. Conv., 1777; commd. lt. col. Continental Army, 1782; commd. col. Chatham County (Ga.) Militia, 1784, brig. gen. 1786; declined governorship of Ga., 1788; mem. U.S. Ho. of Reps. from Ga., 1st Congress, 1789-91; mem. U.S. Senate from Ga., 1793-95; 1801- Mar. 19, 1806; gov. Ga., 1798-1801. Died Washington, D.C., Mar. 19, 1806; buried Congressional Cemetery, Washington.

JACKSON, James, physician, author; b. Newburyport, Mass., Oct. 3, 1777; s. Johnathan and Hannah (Tracy) J.; A.B., Harvard, 1796, A.M., 1799, M.B., 1802, M..D, 1809; studied anatomy, London, Eng., 1799; m. Elizabeth Cabot, Oct. 3, 1801; m. 2d, Sarah Cabot; 9 children, including James. Learned to vaccinate in Eng., became 1st in Am. to apply scientific investigation to vaccination; apptd. physician to Boston Dispensary, 1802; Hersey prof. of theory and practice of physics Harvard Med. Sch., 1813. Author: On the Theory and Practice of Physics, 1825; Letters to a Young Physician, 1855; Another Letter to a Young Physician, 1861. Died Aug. 27, 1867.

JACKSON, James, congressman, jurist; b. Jefferson County, Ga., Oct. 18, 1819; s. William H. and Mildred (Cobb) J.; grad. U. Ga., 1837; m. Ada Mitchell, 1853; m. 2d, Mrs. Mary Schoolfield, 1870. Admitted to Ga. bar, 1839; mem. Ga. Ho. of Reps., 1845-47; judge Ga. Superior Ct., 1846-59; mem. U.S. Ho. of Reps. from Ga., 35th- 36th congresses, 1857-Jan. 23, 1861; served as judge adv. Confederate Army on staff of Gen. Thomas (Stonewall) Jackson, 1861-65; justice Ga. Supreme Ct., 1875-87, chief justice, 1879-87. Died Alanta, Ga., Jan. 13, 1887; buried Rose Hill Cemetery, Macon, Ga.

JACKSON, James Caleb, abolitionist, physician; b. Manlius, N.Y., Mar. 28, 1811; s. James and Mary Ann (Elderkin) J.; m. Lucretia Brewster, Sept. 10, 1830. Agt. for Mass. Anti-Slavery Soc., 1838; sec. Am. Anti-Slavery Soc., 1840; asst. editor Nat. Anti-Slavery Standard paper, 1840-41; co-founder Madison County Abolitionist, Cazenovia, N.Y., 1841-42; editor Liberty Press, Utica, N.Y., 1842-44; owner, editor Albany (N.Y.) Patriot, 1844-46; a sponsor Liberty League in N.Y. (a 4th party outgrowth of Liberty Party); co-founder Glen Haven Water Cure (hygienic inst.), Skaneateles Lake, N.Y. circa 1848-50; opened Our Home and Hygienic Inst., Dansville, N.Y., 1858-79. Author: How to Treat the Sick Without Medicine, 1868. Died Dansville, July 11, 1895.

JACKSON, James Streshly, congressman; b. Fayette County, Ky., Sept. 27, 1823; attended Centre Coll., Danville, Ky.; grad. Jefferson Coll., Pa., 1844; grad. law dept. Translyvania U., Lexington, Ky., 1845. Admitted to the bar; began practice in Greenupsburg, Ky., 1845; enlisted as pvt. 1st Ky. Cavalry during Mexican War, commd. 3d lt., 1846, resigned, 1846; moved to Hopkinsville, Ky., 1859; mem. U.S. Ho. of Reps. (Unionist) from Ky., 37th Congress, Mar. 4-Dec. 13, 1861; commd. col. 3d Regt., Ky. Volunteer Cavalry, U.S. Army, Dec. 13, 1861; commd. brig. gen. U.S. Volunteers, 1862. Killed in Battle of Perryville, Oct. 8, 1862; buried Riverside Cemetery, Hopkinsville.

JACKSON, John Adams, sculptor; b. Bath, Me., Nov. 5, 1825; s. Thomas and Susan (Smith) J.; studied drawing under D.C. Johnston, Boston; studied anatomy, Paris, France. Made bust of Daniel Webster from a portrait, 1851; made portrait busts of Miss Adelaide Phillips and Thomas Buchanan Read, Florence, Italy, 1853; made bust of John Young Mason, Paris, 1854; had studio, N.Y.C., 1858-60; returned and settled in Florence under grant by Kane Monument Assn. of N.Y.C., 1860; visited N.Y. C., 1867, designed group of busts for So. gatehouse of reservoir in Central Park. Best works include: Reading Girl, 1869; Musidora, 1873; Hylas, 1875. Died Pracchia, Italy, circa Aug. 30, 1879.

JACKSON, John Davies, physician, author; b. Danville, Ky., Dec. 12, 1834; s. John and Margaret (Spears) J.; A.B., Centre Coll., Danville, 1854; student medicine U. La., 1855; M.D., U. Pa., 1857. Surgeon, Confederate Army; established pvt. med. sch., Danville, after Civil War; brought recognition to Ephraim McDowell's work in abdominal surgery. Author: "Anniversary Address before the Boyle County (Ky.) Medical Society," 1869; "Biographical Sketch of Dr. Ephraim McDowell, of Danville, Ky." (published in Richmond and Louisville Med. Jour.), 1873; An Operation Manual, 1874. Died Dec. 8, 1875.

JACKSON, John George, congressman; b. Buckhannon, Va. (now W. Va.), Sept. 22, 1777; s. George and Elizabeth (Von Brake) J.; m. Mary Payne, 1801; m. 2d, Mary Meigs, Sept. 13, 1810. Surveyor of pub. lands West of Ohio, 1793; mem. Va. Ho. of Reps. from Va., 8th-11th, 13th-14th congresses, 1803-Sept. 28, 1810, 13-17; mem. Va. Ho. of Reps., 1811-12; commd. brig. gen. Va. Militia, 1812; U.S. dist. judge for Western dist. Va., 1819-25. Died Clarksburg, Va. (now W. Va.), Mar. 28, 1825; buried Old Jackson Cemetery, Clarksburg.

JACKSON, Jonathan, Continental congressman; b. Boston, June 4, 1743; grad. Harvard, 1761. Engaged in merc. bus., Newburyport, Mass.; mem. Mass Provincial Congress, 1775; mem. Mass. Ho. of Reps., 1777; mem. Continental Congress from Mass., 1782; mem. Mass. Senate, 1789; U.S. marshal for Dist. of Mass., 1789-91; treas. Commonwealth of Mass., 1802-06; insp. and supr. of internal revenue; pres. Mass. State Bank; pres. corp. Harvard. Died Boston, Mar. 5, 1810; buried Granary Burying Ground, Boston.

JACKSON, Joseph Webber, congressman; b. Cedar Hill, nr. Savannah, Ga., Dec. 6, 1796; attended common schs.; studied law. Admitted to the bar, practiced law; mem. municipal council, mayor Savannah; mem. Ga. Ho. of Reps., Ga. Senate; mem. U.S. Ho. of Reps. (Democrat) from Ga., 31st-32d congresses, Mar. 4, 1850-53; served as capt. Savannah Volunteer Guards, also col. 1st Regt., Ga. Militia; judge Ga. Superior Ct. Died Savannah, Sept. 29, 1854.

JACKSON, Mercy Ruggles Bisbe, homeopathic physician; b. Hardwick, Mass., Sept. 17, 1802; d. Constant and Sarah (Green) Ruggles; grad. New Eng. Female Med. Coll., 1860; m. Rev. John Bisbe, June 1823; m. 2d, Capt. Daniel Jackson, 1835; 11 children including Dr. Samuel H. Opened sch. for young ladies after death of 1st husband, Port-physician; b. Hardwick, Mass., Sept. 17, 1802; d. Constant and Sarah (Green) Ruggles; grad. New land, Me., 1832-35; became interested in study of homeopathy, 1848; mem. Am. Inst. Homeopathy, 1871-77; adjunct prof. diseases of children Boston U. Sch. Medicine, 1873-77. Died Dec. 13, 1877.

JACKSON, Mortimer Melville, jurist, diplomat; b. Rensselaerville, N.Y., Mar. 5, 1809; s Jeremiah and Martha (Keyes) J.; m. Catherine Garr, June 1838. Admitted to N.Y.C. bar; head delegation to Young Men's N.Y. State Whig Conv., 1834; dir., later v.p. Mercantile Library, N.Y.C.; atty. gen. Territory of Wis., 1842-45; mem. a com. to prepare plan for improvement in common sch. edn., 1846; 1st circuit judge 5th Judicial Circuit of Wis., 1848-53; apptd. consul at Halifax (N.S., Can.) by Pres. Lincoln, 1861; he made report on fisheries and fishery laws of Canada at request of sec. of state, 1870; apptd. consul gen. at Halifax, 1880. Died Madison, Wis., Oct. 13, 1889.

JACKSON, Patrick Tracy, cotton mfr.; b. Newburyport, Mass., Aug. 14, 1780; s. Jonathan and Hannah (Tracy) J.; m. Lydia Cabot, Nov. 1, 1810, 9 children. An organizer Boston Mfg. Co., built mill on Charles River Waltham, Mass., 1813, in charge of Waltham Mills (1st time all operations in cotton mfg. brought under one roof); founder Lowell, Mass.; founder Merrimac Mfg. Co., Appleton Co., Moston & Lowell R.R. Died Beverly, Mass., Sept. 12, 1847.

JACKSON, Rachel Donelson, first lady; b. N.C.; d. Col. John Donelson; m. Lewis Robards, after 1780; m. 2d, Andrew Jackson (7th Pres. U.S.), Aug. 1791, also 1794. Unhappy in her 1st marriage; went to live with her mother, Nashville, Tenn., 1790, met Andrew Jackson; married Jackson under the impression that Lewis Robards had obtained a divorce, 1791, but Robards did not obtain full divorce until 1793; remarried Jackson, 1794; marriage became significant in Jackson's career because it was used as a weapon by his polit. enemies to impugn his character; died after election of 1828, never entered White House. Died "Hermitage," nr. Nashville, Dec. 22, 1828; buried "Hermitage."

JACKSON, Richard, Jr., congressman; b. Providence, R.I., July 3, 1764; s. Richard Jackson; attended sch., Providence and Pomfret, Conn. Engaged in merc. and cotton mfg. bus.; pres. Washington Ins. Co., Providence, 1800-38; mem. U.S. Ho. of Reps. (Federalist) from R.I., 10th-13th congresses, Nov. 1, 1808-15; trustee Brown U., 1809-38. Died Providence, Apr. 18, 1838.

JACKSON, Samuel, physician; b. Pa., Mar. 22, 1787; s. David and Susanna (Kemper) J.; grad. U. Pa., 1808; married, circa 1832. Mem. 1st Phila. Troop of Cavalry, 1812-15, took part in operations along the Chesapeake; returned to med. practice, 1815; pres. Phila. Dept. Health during yellow fever epidemic; a founder, trustee Phila. Coll. Pharmacy, 1821, prof. materia medica and pharmacy, 1821-27; tchr. physiology, asst. to Nathaniel Chapman at U. Pa., 1827-35, prof. physiology, 1835-63; taught in Phila. Hosp., 1842-45; Author: The Principles of Medicine, Founded on the Structure and Function of the Animal Organism, 1832; contbr. numerous articles to Phila. Jour. of Med. and Phys. Sciences, Am. Jour. Med. Sciences. Died Apr. 5, 1872.

JACKSON, Samuel P., musician; b. Manchester, Eng., Feb. 5, 1818; s. James Jackson; Came to Am., 1825, learned organbldg. trade; played organ St. Clement's Ch., 1830-42, St. Bartholomew's Ch., 1842-61, later at Christ Ch., Ch. of Ascension, Anthon Meml. Ch.; tchr. organ and harmony; music proof reader for G. Schirmer, N.Y.C., many years; composed a variety of sacred music; published Gems for the Organ, 4 books of Organ-Voluntaries. Died Bklyn., July 27, 1885.

JACKSON, Thomas Birdsall, congressman; b. Jerusalem, L.I., N.Y., Mar. 24, 1797; attended pub. schs.; studied law. Engaged in farming; admitted to N.Y. bar, practiced in Jerusalem, Hempstead, and Newtown (now Elmhurst Station), Flushing, L. I., N.Y.; elected county judge, 1832; mem. N.Y. Assembly, 1833-35; moved to Newtown, 1835; justice of peace; mem. U.S. Ho. of Reps. (Democrat) from N.Y., 25th-26th congresses, 1837-41; resumed farming. Died Newtown, Apr. 23, 1881; buried Flushing Cemetery.

JACKSON, Thomas Jonathan (nickname Stonewall), army officer; b. Clarksburg, Va. (now W.Va.), Jan. 21, 1824; s. Jonathan and Julia (Beckwith) J.; grad. U.S. Mil. Acad., 1846; m. Eleanor Junkin, 1853; m. 2d, Mary Anne Morrison, July 16, 1857. Entered U.S. Army; served at battles of Vera Cruz, Cerro Gordo and Chapultepec during Mexican War, 1846-48; brevetted maj., 1847; served at Ft. Columbus and Ft. Hamilton (N.Y.), 1849-51; resigned commn., 1851; prof. artillery tactics and natural philosophy Va. Mil. Inst., 1851-61; commd. brig. gen. Confederate Army, 1861; received nickname Stonewall at 1st Battle of Bull Run; commd. maj. gen., 1861; in command of Shenandoah Valley dist. Dept. of No. Va.; withdrew from Winchester, Va., 1862, beginning Shenandoah Valley campaign which prevented 2 Northern armies from joining attack on Richmond (Va.); made a series of brilliant marches and battles, 1862, including Kernstown, Staunton, Front Royal, Winchester, Cross Keys, Port Republic; fought under Robert E. Lee in Seven Days Campaign, 1862 (including Battle of Gaines Mill); captured Manassas Junction, Aug. 27, defeated (with Lee) Union Army at 2d Battle of Bull Run, Aug. 30, captured Harper's Ferry, Sept. 15, Antietam, Sept. 17, Fredericksburg, Dec. 13 (all 1862), commd. lt. gen., 1862; accidentally shot by his own men after routing Union right wing at Battle of Chancellorsville, May 2, 1863; considered best and most famous Confederate gen. after Lee. Died Fredericksburg, Va., May 10, 1863; buried Lexington, Va.

JACKSON, William, army officer, sec. to Pres. U.S.; b. Cumberland, Eng., May 9, 1759; m. Elizabeth Willing, Nov. 11, 1795. Served as lt. in expdn. against St. Augustine (Fla.), 1778; maj., aide to Gen. Benjamin Lincoln; U.S. asst. sec. of war, 1782-84; sec. U.S. Constl. Conv. Phila., 1787; admitted to Pa. bar, 1788; sec. to Pres. George Washington, 1789-91; U.S. surveyor of customs, Phila., 1796-1801; sec. Soc. of Cincinnati, 1800-28; founder, editor Polit. and Comm. Register, Phila., 1801-17. Died Phila., Dec. 18, 1828; buried Christ Church Cemetery, Phila.

JACKSON, William, railway promoter, congressman; b. Newton, Mass., Sept. 2, 1783; s. Timothy and Sarah (Winchester) J.; m. Hannah Woodward, Dec. 1, 1806; m. 2d, Mary Bennett, 1816; 16 children. Mem. Mass. Gen. Ct. from Boston, 1819, 29-31; active supporter railroad projects in Mass., including constrn. of Western, Boston & Worcester, Boston & Albany, New Bedford & Taunton railroads; mem. U.S. Ho. of Reps. from Mass., 23d-24th congresses, 1833-37; an organizer Liberty Party, 1840; unsuccessful candidate for lt. gov. Mass., 1842, 43, 44; pres. Newton Savs. Bank, 1831-35, Am. Missionary Soc., 1846-54, Newton Nat. Bank, 1848-55; founder, deacon Eliot Ch. of Newton. Died Newton, Feb. 26, 1855; buried Old Burial Ground, Newton.

JACKSON, William Terry, congressman; b. Chester, N.Y., Dec. 29, 1794; attended common schs. Taught sch., Goshen, N.Y., 1813-15; employed as surveyor; engaged in merc. bus., Chester and Oswego, N.Y., also Bermerville, N.J.; moved to Havana, N.Y., 1825, engaged in merc. bus.; justice of peace, 1836-38; judge Ct. Common Pleas and Gen. Sessions of Chemung County (N.Y.), 1839-46; justice of peace for Town of Catherine, N.Y.; mem. U.S. Ho. of Reps. (Whig) from N.Y., 31st Congress, 1849-51. Died Montour Falls, N.Y., Sept. 15, 1882; buried Montour Falls Cemetery.

JACOBS, Ferris, Jr., congressman; b. Delhi, N.Y., Mar. 20, 1836; s. Ferris Jacobs. Grad. Williams Coll., 1856; studied law. Admitted to N.Y. bar, 1859, began practice in Delhi; served in U.S. Army during Civil War; commd. capt. 3d N.Y. Cavalry, 1861, maj., 1863, lt. col., 1864, mustered out, 1864; commd. lt. col. 26th N.Y. Cavalry, 1865; brevetted brig. gen. U.S. Volunteers, 1865, mustered out, 1865; resumed law practice Delhi; elected dist. atty., 1865, 66; del. Republican Nat. Conv., Chgo., 1880; mem. U.S. Ho. of Reps. (Rep.) from N.Y., 47th Congress, 1881-83. Died White Plains, N.Y., Aug. 30, 1886; buried Woodland Cemetery, Delhi.

JACOBS, Israel, congressman; b. nr. Perkiomen Creek, Pa., June 9, 1726; attended pub. schs. Engaged in farming, merc. bus.; mem. Pa. Colonial Assembly, 1770-74; one of 1st to advocate union of colonies; apptd. to distribute aid to families of poor soldiers during Am. Revolution; mem. U.S. Ho. of Reps. from Pa., 2d Congress, 1791-93. Died Providence Twp., Pa., circa Dec. 10, 1796; buried (probably) in graveyard of Friends Meeting House, Providence Twp.

JACOBS, Michael, clergyman, educator; b. Waynesboro, Pa., Jan. 18, 1808; s. Henry and Anna Maria (Miller) J.; grad. Jefferson Coll., Canonsburg, Pa., 1828; m. Julianna M. Eyster, May 3, 1833. Moved to Gettysburg, Pa. to help brother David at Gettysburg Gymnasium, 1829, sch. became Pa. Coll. (now Gettysburg Coll.), 1832, prof. mathematics and natural science, 1832-66; licensed by West Pa. Synod, Lutheran Ch., 1832, pres. synod, 3 terms, treas., 3 terms; devised process of preserving fruit by canning. Author: Notes on the Rebel Invasion of Maryland and Pennsylvania and the Battle of Gettysburg, 1864. Died July 22, 1871.

JACOBSON, John Christian, clergyman, educator; b. Burkhall, Denmark, Apr. 8, 1795; studied theology at Niesky, Denmark; m. Lisetta Schnall, 1826. Came to Nazareth, Pa., taught at Nazareth Hall, 1816-20, later returned as prin.; prof. theology Moravian Theol. Sem., Bethlehem, Pa., 1820-26; pastor, Bethania, N.C., 1826-34; prin. Salem Female Acad., Winston-Salem, N.C., 1834-44; del. Moravian Gen. Synod, Herrnhut, Saxony, 1848; presiding officer Provincial Elders Conf., Bethlehem, 1849-67; made extensive teaching and preaching tour of Western missions, 1852; ordained bishop Moravian Ch., 1854; gave lectures on New Testament at Moravian Coll.; ret., 1867. Died Nov. 24, 1870.

JACOBY, Ludwig Sigmund, missionary; b. Altstrelitz, Germany, Oct. 21, 1813; s. Samuel and Henrietta (Hirsch) J.; m. Amalie T. Nuelson, Sept. 1840, 8 children. Came to Cincinnati, 1838, became English tutor; converted to Lutheranism by Rev. William Nast, 1839; sent to open mission at St. Louis, 1841, set up preaching stas., Dubuque, Ia., Galena, Ill.; presiding elder St. Louis German Dist., 1844, Quincy German Dist., 1845; went to Bremen, Germany, to establish congregation, 1849, pastor, editor publs., founder and dir. of a hosp. and sem., presiding elder Oldenburg Dist., 1849-71; returned to U.S., 1871, became pastor Soulardgemeinde, St. Louis. Author: Handbuck des Methodismus, 1853; Letzte Stonden, Oder Die Kraft der Religion Jesu Christ im Tode, 1870. Died June 20, 1874.

JAMES, Amaziah Bailey, congressman, jurist; b. Stephentown, N.Y., July 1, 1812. Printer's apprentice, Batavia, N.Y.; moved to Ogdensburg, N.Y., 1831, established Northern Light (weekly newspaper); part owner Times and Advertiser (Whig paper); capt. Ogdensburg Arty., 1836; promoted maj. gen. N.Y. Militia; admitted to N.Y. bar, 1838, began practice in Ogdensburg; justice N.Y. Supreme Ct., 1853-76; mem. Washington (D.C.) Peace Conf., 1861; mem. U.S. Ho. of Reps. (Republican) from N.Y., 45th-46th congresses, 1877-81, stricken with paralysis while serving his 2d term, partially recovered. Died Ogdensburg, July 6, 1883; buried City Cemetery, Ogdensburg.

JAMES, Charles Tillinghast, engr., senator, inventor; b. West Greenwich, R.I., Sept. 15, 1805; s. Silas and Phebe (Tillinghast) J.; A.M., Brown Coll., 1838; 4 children. Commd. maj. gen. R.I. Militia; supt. Slater Cotton Mills, Providence, R. I.; built early steampowered cotton mills; built Atlantic DeLaine Mill, Olneyville, R.I., 1849; mem. U.S. Senate (Democrat) from R.I., 1851-57, chmn. com. on patents, 34th Congress; perfected rifle-cannon, projectile. Died Sag Harbor, N. Y., Oct. 17, 1862; buried Swan Point Cemetery, Providence.

JAMES, Edward Christopher, lawyer; b. Ogdensburg, N.Y., May 1, 1841; s. Amaziah B. and Lucia Williams (Ripley) J. Apptd. adjutant 50th N.Y. Volunteers at outbreak of Civil War, promoted col., 1863, ret. due to injuries received in W.Va.; admitted to N.Y. bar, 1863, began practice of law, Ogdensburg; partner of Stillman Foote, 1864-74, of A.R. Herriman, 1881-82; went to N.Y.C., 1882; mem. firm James, Schnell & Elkus, N.Y.C., 1896-1901; took active part cases Laidlaw vs. Sage (158 N.Y., 74), People vs. McLaughlin (150 N.Y., 365), Dittmar vs. Gould (60 A.D., 94). Died Mar. 24, 1901.

JAMES, Edwin, explorer, naturalist, physician, geologist; b. Weybridge, Vt., Aug. 27, 1797; s. Daniel and Mary (Emmes) J.; grad. Middlebury Coll., 1816; m. Clarissa Rogers, Apr. 5, 1827, 1 child. Became botonist, 1820; geologist and surgeon of expdn. commanded by Maj. Stephen H. Long to explore country between Mississippi River and Rocky Mountains; with two companions reached Pike's Peak (1st white men to accomplish the feat), July 14, 1820; asst. surgeon in U.S. Army, 1823-29; resigned, 1833; asso. editor Temperance Herald and Journal, 1836; agt. for Potawatamie Indians at Old Council Bluffs (Ia.), 1837-38. Author: Expedition to the Rocky Mountains, 1819-20, published 1823; The Narrative of John Tanner, 1830; translated New Testament in Ojibway (Indian) Language, 1833. Died Burlington, Ia., Oct. 28, 1861.

JAMES, Francis, congressman; b. Thornbury Twp., Pa., Apr. 4, 1799; attended Gauses' Acad.; studied law. Admitted to Chester County (Pa.) bar, 1825, began practice in West Chester, Pa.; mem. Pa. Senate, 1834-36; mem. U.S. Ho. of Reps. (Whig) from Pa., 26th Congress, 1839-41; chief burgess, 1850. Died West Chester, Jan. 4, 1886; buried Oakland Cemetery, West Chester.

JAMES, Henry, philosopher; b. Albany, N.Y., June 3, 1811; s. William and Catherine (Barber) J.; grad. Union Coll., Albany, N.Y., 1830; attended Princeton Theol. Sem., 1835-37; m. Mary Robertson Walsh, July 28, 1840; children—William, Henry. Went to Europe, 1837-38; editor Robert Sandeman's Letters on Theron and Aspasio, 1838; returned to Europe 1843 after much study converted to ideas of Emanuel Swedenborg; publisher The Harbinger (publ. of Brook Farm Movement, 1845); lived in Europe, 1845-47; contbr. articles on Fourierist Movement to N.Y. Tribune, 1847; went to Europe to further edn. of his sons, 1855-58, 59-60; settled in Newport, R.I., 1860, resumed relations with New Eng. friends including Ralph Waldo Emerson; moved to Cambridge, Mass., 1864; became friend of Thomas Carlyle in Europe, conferred with him on his Recollections of Carlyle. Author: (works mainly concerned with his religious doctrines) Christianity the Logic of Creation, 1857; Substance and Shadow; Or Morality and Religion in Their Relation to Life, 1863; Society the Redeemed Form of Man, and the Earnest of God's Omnipotence in Human Nature, 1879. Died Cambridge, Dec. 18, 1882.

JAMES, Jesse Woodson, desperado; b. nr. Kearney, Mo., Sept. 5, 1847; s. Robert and Zerelda (Cole) J.; m. Zerelda Mimms, Apr. 24, 1874, 2 children. Became Confederate guerrilla (with his brother Alexander Franklin) under William Clarke Quantrill, during Civil War; leader band of outlaws (included brother Frank and Coleman Younger), specialized in bank and train robberies, 1866-81 (most of outlaws arrested when William Wallace elected pros. atty. Jackson County, Mo., 1880); lived in St. Joseph, Mo. under name Thomas Howard, joined Baptist Ch., 1868, professed belief in Christian religion throughout life. Shot in back of head by Robert Ford, (mem. of his band), died St. Joseph, Apr. 3, 1882.

JAMES, Thomas, legislator, trader, author; b. in Md., 1782; s. Joseph Austin and Elizabeth (Hosten) J. Mem. 1st St. Louis Fur Co. expdn. up Mississippi River, 1809; mem. 1st organized exploration Blackfoot region; in river trade, transport between St. Louis, Mo. and Pitts., 1812-14; opened br. of McKight & Brady of St. Louis at Harrisonville, Ill, 1815; accompanied Robert McKnight on expdn. to Santa Fe by way of Mississippi River, 1821-24; opened mill called James' Mill, Monroe City, Ill., 1825; apptd. gen. Ill. Militia, 1825; mem. Ill. Legislature, 1825-28; postmaster of James' Mills (Ill.), 1827-47; comdr. Spy Battalion during Black Hawk War, 1832. Author: Three Years Among the Indians, 1846. Died Dec. 1847.

JAMES, Thomas Chalkley, physician, educator; b. Phila., Aug. 31, 1766; s. Abel and Rebecca (Chalkley) J.; grad. U. State of Pa., 1787, M.D., 1811; studied under Dr. John Hunter, also at Story Street Lying In Hosp. under Drs. Osborne and John Clark, London, Eng.; m. Hannah Morris, 1802. Ship's surgeon on voyage to Cape of Good Hope, 1788-90; returned to Phila., 1793; gave series of lectures on obstetrics, 1802, given at U. Pa., 1810; physician Pa. Hosp., 1807-32, became obstetrician, 1810; frequent lectr., read papers before Phila. Coll. Surgeons; editor Eclectic Repertory, 11 years; published verses, essays anonymously; one of 1st men to deliver children. Died July 5, 1835.

JAMES, Thomas Potts, botanist; b. Radnor, Pa., Sept. 1, 1803; s. Dr. Isaac and Henrietta (Potts) J.; m. Isabella Batchelder, 1851. In wholesale drug bus. with brother in Phila. from 1831 for 35 years; prof., examiner Phila. Coll. Pharmacy, many years; moved to Cambridge, Mass., devoted rest of life to study of mosses, 1866; conferred with W.Ph. Schimper, Europe, 1878, compared Am. and Old World species mosses; became recognized as foremost Am. specialist on mosses, began collaboration with Charles Leo Lesquereux on Manual of North American Mosses, died before its completion in 1884; contbr. to sci. mags including Proceedings Acad. of Natural Sciences of Phila.; mem. Am. Philos. Soc., A.A.A.S.; a founder Am. Pomol. Soc. Died Feb. 22, 1882.

JAMESON, Horatio Gates, physician, educator; b. York, Pa., 1778; s. Dr. David and Elizabeth (Davis) J.; studied medicine under father; M.D., U. Md., 1813; m. Catherine Shevell, Aug. 3, 1797; m. 2d, Hannah (Fearson) Ely, 1852; 7 children. Practiced medicine, Somerset County, Pa., 1795-1810; moved to Balt., 1810; physician to fed. troops, 1812; surgeon Balt. City Jail, 1814-35; cons. physician Balt. Bd. Health, 1821-35; founder Washington Med. Coll., Balt., 1827, obtained univ. charter, built hosp. by 1835, forced to close schs. because of financial difficulties, 1851; prof. surgery Med. Co.. of Ohio, Cincinnati, 1835-36; used animal ligature (his most famous contbn. to surgery). Author: Treatise on Epidemic Cholera, 1855; published accounts of his unusual operations in leading med. jours. including Am. Med. Recorder. Died N.Y. C., Aug. 26, 1855; buried Balt.

JAMESON, John, congressman; b. nr. Mount Sterling, Ky., Mar. 6, 1802; attended common schs.; studied law. Moved to Callaway County, Mo., 1825; admitted to Mo. bar, 1826, began practice in Fulton; mem. Mo. Ho. of Reps., 1830-36, speaker, 1834, 36; mem. U.S. Ho. of Reps. (Democrat) from Mo., 26th, 28th, 30th congresses, Dec. 12, 1839-41, 43-45, 47-49; ordained to ministry Christian Ch.; engaged in farming; served as capt. during Black Hawk War. Died Fulton, Jan. 24, 1857; buried Jameson family cemetery nr. Fulton.

JAMESON, John Alexander, lawyer; b. Irasburgh, Vt., Jan. 25, 1824; s. Thomas and Martha J.; grad. U. Vt., 1846, M.A., 1849; attended Harvard Law Sch., 1852; studied law under Gov. Underwood, Burlington, Vt.; m. Eliza Denison, Oct. 11, 1855,

3 children. Taught, Stanstead, Can., 1846-49; tutor U. Vt., 1849-50; moved to Chgo., 1853, partner with H.N. Hibbard, firm moved to Freeport, Ill., 1853; reestablished law firm, Chgo., 1856-65; judge Chgo. Superior Ct., 1865-83, most famous case was Samuel Chase et al vs. Charles E. Cheney (58 Ill., 509), reversed by Ill. Supreme Ct.; prof. equity and constl. law U. Chgo., 1867-68; resumed law practice, 1883; elected pres. Hyde Park (Ill.) Bd. Trustees, 1888; asst. editor Am. Law Register; collected material which now constitutes John Alexander Jameson Library in Am. History, U. Pa. Author: The Constitutional Convention; It's History, Powers, and Modes of Preceeding, 1867. Died Hyde Park, June 16, 1890.

JAMISON, David, jurist; b. Scotland, 1660; m. Mary Hardenbrook, May 7, 1692; m. 2d, Johanna Meech, Jan. 16, 1703. Came to Am., 1685; dep. sec., clk. N.Y. Council; chief justice J.J., 1711-23; recorder N.Y.C., 1712; acting atty. gen. N.Y., 1712, became atty. gen., 1715; vestryman and warden Trinity Ch., N.Y.C. Died N.Y.C., July 26, 1739.

JANES, Henry Fisk, congressman; b. Brimfield, Mass., Oct. 10, 1792; studied law, Montpelier, Vt. Served in War of 1812, participated in Battle of Plattsburg; admitted to Vt. bar, began practice in Waterbury, 1817; postmaster, 1820-30; mem. Vt. Legislative Council, 1830-34; mem. U.S. Ho. of Reps. (Whig and Anti-Mason) from Vt., 23d-24th congresses, Dec. 2, 1834-37; treas. State of Vt., 1838-41; mem. Vt. Council of Censors, 1848; town rep., 1854, 61-62; mem. Vt. Ho. of Reps., 1855. Died Waterbury, June 6, 1879; buried Village Cemetery, Waterbury.

JANES, Lewis George, author, educator; b. Providence, R.I., Feb. 19, 1844; s. Alphanso R. and Sophia (Taft) J.; m. Gertrude Pool, June 2, 1869; m. 2d, Helen Hall Rawson, June 17, 1882; 4 children. Went to N.Y.C., 1866, engaged in scientific and religious study, also taught Sunday Sch. at 2d Unitarian Ch., Bklyn.; pres. Bklyn. Ethical Assn., 1885-96, delivered many lectures on Spencerian philosophy; lectr. sociology and civics Sch. of Polit. Sci. of Bklyn. Inst. Arts and Scis., 1893-96; instr. history Adelphi Coll., Bklyn., 1894-95; moved to Cambridge, Mass., 1896, devoted rest of life to philos. and intellectual socs., especially Free Religious Assn. (founded by Ralph Waldo Emerson), pres., 1899. Author: A Study of Primitive Christianity, 1866; Samuell Gorton: A Forgotten Founder of Our Liberties, First Settler of Warwick, Rhode Island, 1896. Died Sept. 4, 1901.

JANNEY, Samuel McPherson, author, clergyman; b. Loudoun County, Va., Jan. 11, 1801; s. Abijah and Jane (McPherson) J.; m. Elizabeth Janney, Mar. 9, 1826. Partner cotton factory, Occoquan, Va., 1830-39; opened sch. for girls, Loudoun County, 1839-44; Quaker minister to Hicksite division, Va., advocated emancipation and promoted free public schs.; supported Union during Civil War but ministered to both armies; supt. Indian affairs in Northern Superintendency, 1869-71. Author: The Last of the Lenape, and Other Poems, 1839; The Life of William Penn, 1852; History of the Religious Society of Friends, From It's Rise to the Year 1828, 1860-67. Died Apr. 30, 1880.

JANSEN, Reinier, printer; b. Alkmaar, Holland; at least 1 child. Came to Pa., 1698; only printer in Pa., 1698-1706; operated 1st Quaker press in Am., issued his 1st book God's Protecting Providence, 1699; lace-maker, mcht. Died Phila., Mar. 6, 1706.

JANSSENS, Francis, clergyman; b. Tilburg, North Brabant, Holland, Oct. 17, 1843; s. Cornelius and Josephine (Dawes) J.; attended Am. Coll. of U. Louvain (Belgium). Became subdeacon Roman Catholic Ch., 1866, ordained priest, 1867; arrived in Richmond, Va., 1868; consecrated bishop of Natchez, 1881, responsible for conversion of Choctaw Indians in northern part Miss.; made archbishop of New Orleans, 1888; supreme spiritual dir. Knights of Columbus. Died on board steamer Creole while on way to N.Y.C., June 10, 1897; buried St. Louis Cathedral, New Orleans.

JAQUESS, James Frazier, clergyman, coll. pres., army officer; b. Evansville, Ind., Nov. 18, 1819; s. Jonathan Garrettson and Mary (Smith) J.; A.B., Ind. Asbury (now De Pauw) U., 1845; m. Mary Sciple; m. 2d, Sarah E. Steel, circa 1847. Admitted to Ind. bar, 1846, gave up law; ordained to ministry Methodist Ch., 1847; pres. Ill Female Coll., Jacksonville, 1848-54, Quincy (Ill.) Coll., 1854-60; commd. chaplain 6th Ill. Cavalry during Civil War; recruited and commanded 73d Ill. Volunteers ("preacher's regiment"); believed that he could help bring war to peaceful conclusion, 1863, allowed to go into Confederate territory, failed in his attempt; held peace conf. with Jefferson Davis, 1864, received from him statement that South was fighting for freedom or annihilation; employed by Freedmen's Bur. in South after Civil War. Died St. Paul, Minn., June 17, 1898.

JARDINE, David, architect; b. Scotland, July 2, 1840; trained under his father (a builder-architect). Came to Am., circa 1860; asso. with Edward Thompson, architect, N.Y.C., circa 1860-61; later formed archtl. firm (with his bros.) Jardine & Jardine, N.Y.C.; designs credited to firm include: original Fifth Av. Theatre, Synagogue at 63d St. and Lexington Av., Alpine Bldg., Wilbraham Apt. House, Apprentice Library, remodelling of old Robinson Hall, also several Presbyn. chs. (all N.Y. C.). Died Larchmont, N.Y., June 4, 1892.

JARNAGIN, Spencer, senator; b. Grainger County, Tenn., 1792; grad. Greenville Coll., 1813; studied law. Admitted to Tenn. bar, 1817, began practice in Knoxville; mem. Tenn. Senate, 1833-35; trustee East Tenn. Coll., 1836-51; moved to Athens, Tenn., 1837, practiced law; Whig presdl. elector, 1840; mem. U.S. Senate (Whig) from Tenn., Oct. 17, 1843-47; unsuccessful candidate for judge Tenn. Supreme Ct., moved to Memphis, Tenn., practiced law. Died Memphis, June 25, 1853; buried Elmwood Cemetery, Memphis.

JARRATT, Devereaux, clergyman; b. New Kent County, Va., Jan. 17, 1733; s. Robert and Sarah (Bradley) J.; studied under Alexander Martin, circa 1761; m. Martha Claiborne. Tutor in house of John Cannon; sailed for England, 1762; ordained as priest by Bishop of Chester in Presbyn. Ch., 1863; returned to Va., 1863, became rector Bath Parish, Dinwiddie County; carried on reform work in other Va. counties and N.C.; assisted Methodist preacher Robert Williams, 1773; took keen interest and regularly attended Meth. confs. although closely associated with Episcopal (Presbyn.) Ch. Author: A Brief Narrative of the Revival of Religion in Virginia in a Letter to a Friend (sent to John Wesley), 1773; Thoughts on Some Capital Subjects in Divinity in a Series of Letters to a Friend, 1791; An Argument between an Anabaptist and a Methodist on the Subject and Mode of Baptism, reprinted 1814. Died Jan. 29, 1801.

JARVES, James Jackson, editor; b. Boston, Aug. 20, 1818; s. Deming and Anna (Stutson) J.; m. Elizabeth Swain, Oct. 2, 1838; m. 2d, Isabel Hayden, Apr. 30, 1862; 6 children including James Jackson, Jr., Annabel. Founder, editor, weekly newspaper The Polynesian, Honolulu, Hawaii (1st newspaper published in Hawaiian Islands), 1840; dir. Govt. Press (ofcl. organ Hawaiian Govt.), 1844; commd. to negotiate comml. treaties with U.S., Gt. Britain, France, 1848; U.S. vice consul, Florence, Italy, 1880; decorated Order of Kamehameha I by King of Hawaii, chevalier Order of Crown of Italy; hon. mem. Academia delle Belle Arti of Florence; corr. mem. Am. Oriental Soc.; patron Met. Mus. Art, N.Y.C. Author: History of the Hawaiian Islands or the Sandwich Islands, 1843; Parisian Sights and French Principles Seen through American Spectacles, 1855; Art Hints: Architecture, Sculpture and Painting, 1855; Italian Sights and Papal Principles Seen through American Spectacles, 1855; Art Studies: The Old Masters of Italy, 1861; The Art Idea: Sculpture, Painting and Architecture in America, 1866; Died Tarasp in the Engadine, Switzerland, June 28, 1888; buried English Cemetery, Rome, Italy.

JARVIS, Charles H., pianist, educator; b. Phila., Dec. 20, 1837; s. Charles Jarvis; studied piano under his father and Leopold Meignen; m. Lucretia Hall, July 17, 1861; m. 2d, Josephine E. Roebling, 1879. Gave his 1st concert at Musical Fund Hall, Phila., 1844; began teaching music, 1854; played often with Phila. Symphony Orch., N.Y. Philharmonic Soc., Theodore Thomas Orch.; gave series of chamber music and hist. piano recitals (latter with Dr. Hugh A. Clarke), 1862-92; his musical library presented to Drexel Inst. Died Feb. 25, 1895.

JARVIS, Deming, inventor, mfr.; b. probably Boston, circa 1790 (baptized Dec. 9, 1790); s. John and Hannah (Seabury) J.; m. Anna Smith Stutson, 1815, 2 sons, John, James. Bought (with Amos Binney and Daniel Hasting) Boston Crown Glass Co., Cambridge, Mass., 1817, granted charter to manufacture flint and crown glass; constructed exptl. furnace in which he compounded litharge or red lead which enabled co. to compete with English glass cos.; broke with former assos. and organized Boston and Sandwich Glass Co., Sandwich, Mass., 1826, produced apothecary and chem. supplies in addition to glass products, tableware, chandeliers, mantle lamps; reproduced certain shades of English glass by using barytes earth in his mixture; compiled directions for bldg. kilns, 1828; withdrew from former firm and organized Cape Cod Glass Co., Sandwich, 1858. Author: Reminiscences of Glass Making, (pamphlet) 1854. Died Boston, Apr. 15, 1869.

JARVIS, Edward, physician, statistician; b. Concord, Mass., Jan. 9, 1803; s. Francis and Milicent (Hosmer) J.; grad. Harvard, 1826; studied physiology and anatomy under Dr. Josiah Bartlett; attended Mass. Med. Sch. (now Harvard Med. Sch.); M.D., U. Vt., 1830; m. Almira Hunt, Jan. 9, 1834, 2 children. Taught sch., Concord, 1827; practiced medicine, Northfield, Mass., 1830, Louisville, Ky., 1837-43; became interested in vital statistics due to Lemuel Shattuck's influence; contbr. articles to Louisville Med. Jour.; returned to Dorchester, Mass., opened house for treatment of insane, 1843; consulted by Gen. James A. Garfield (head of Ho. of Reps. com. on census), 1869; mem. commn. that studied condition of insane and idiots in Mass., 1854. Author: (pamphlets) Practical Physiology, 1847, Primary Physiology, 1848; wrote 175 articles, speeches and pamphlets. Died Dorchester, Oct. 31, 1884; buried Concord.

JARVIS, John Wesley, painter; b. South Shields, Eng., 1781; s. John and Ann Jarvis; m. 1808. Left with his uncle John Wesley (founder Methodist religion) when his parents came to Am., 1781, brought to Phila., 1786; apprenticed to Edward Savage, engraver, 1800, firm moved with Jarvis to N.Y.C.; began engraving on his own after apprenticeship; set up studio (with Joseph Wood) to paint miniatures, N.Y.C., 1805; set up studio on Broadway into which he took Thomas Sully, 1807; made yearly winter trips to South due to large demand for his portraits; foremost portrait painter of his time in N.Y.C.; heaving drinking in his later years caused him to lose most of his clientele; most famous for full-length portraits of mil. heroes of War of 1812 made for N.Y.C. City Hall. Died Jan. 14, 1839.

JARVIS, Leonard, congressman; b. Boston, Oct. 19, 1781; grad. Harvard, 1800. Moved to Surrey, Me.; sheriff of Hancock County (Me.), 1821-29; collector of customs for Penobscot Dist., 1829-31; mem. U.S. Ho. of Reps. (Democrat) from Me., 21st-24th congresses, 1829-37; naval agt. for Port of Boston, 1838-41. Died Surry, Oct. 18, 1854; buried Hillside Cemetery, Surry.

JARVIS, William, diplomat, mcht.; b. Boston, Feb. 2, 1770; s. Dr. Charles and Mary (Clapham) J.; m. Mary Pepperrell Sparhawk, 1808; m. 2d, Ann Bailey Bartlett, 1817; 12 children. Opened merc. firm on Long Wharf, Boston, 1791, prospered until 1795; comdr., part owner of a brig, 1797; chargé d'affaires to Portugal (apptd. by Pres. Jefferson) 1802-11; secured purchase of 3,000 Merino sheep with license to export them to U.S. when Napoleon conquered Spain, 1808 (these sheep previously guarded by Spanish govt. against exportation); carried on commn. house, Lisbon; del. Harrisburg Conv., 1827. Died Oct. 21, 1859.

JARVIS, William Chapman, physician, laryngologist; b. Fortress Monroe, Va., May 13, 1855; s. Nathan Sturges Jarvis; M.D., U. Md., 1875; attended Johns Hopkins. Practiced medicine, N.Y.C., 1877; worked as asst. in Prof. Frank H. Bosworth's Nose and Throat Service, Bellevue Hosp., N.Y.C. published account of his "Snare" or cold wire eraseur which revolutionized treatment of intranasal tumors, 1881; offered lectureship in laryngology U. City of N.Y. (now N.Y.U.), prof., 1886-93, prof. emeritus, 1893; famous for innovations in diagnosis and treatment of nasal and laryngeal diseases such as use of local anesthetic; contbr. 31 papers to periodical literature on his spl. subjects, 1880-92. Died West Point, N.Y., July 30, 1895.

JASPER, William, patriot, army officer; b. probably Georgetown, S.C., circa 1750. Enlisted as sgt. in co. recruited by Francis Marion, 1775, company assigned to Ft. Johnson, S.C., 1775-76, assigned to Ft. Sullivan (now Ft. Moultrie), 1776, awarded sword by Gov. John Rutland for bravery during bombardment by Brit. fleet; employed as scout, made 3 trips into Brit. lines in Ga.; used in Black Swamp after capture of Savannah by Brit.; accompanied Benjamin Lincoln's assault upon Savannah, 1799. Killed trying to plant colors of 2d S.C. Inf. upon Spring Hill Redoubt, Oct. 9, 1779.

JAVIS, Abraham, clergyman; b. Conn., May 5, 1740; s. Samuel and Naomi (Brush); grad. Yale, 1761; m. Ann Farmer, May 25, 1766; m. 2d, Lucy Lewis, July 4, 1806. Sailed for England, 1763, ordained priest Episcopal Ch. by Charles Lyttelton (bishop of Carlisle), 1864; chmn. Conv. of Episcopal Clergyman, New Haven,, Conn., 1776, decided to suspend all public worship to avoid reading prayer for king; sec. secret meeting to organize Episcopal Ch. in Conn., Woodbridge, 1783, also decided to send Samuel Seabury to England to be consecrated bishop of Conn.; elected to succeed Seabury, 1797, consecrated bishop of Conn. at Trinity Ch., New Haven, 1797. Died May 3, 1813.

JAY, Sir James, physician; b. N.Y.C., Oct. 27, 1732; s. Peter and Mary (Van Cortlandt) J.; M.D., U. Edinburgh (Scotland), 1753. Began practice of medicine, N.Y.C.; went to Eng. to raise money for King's Coll. (now Columbia), 1762; created knight by King George III; sent mil. information to colonies from Eng. in early part of Am. Revolution; returned to Am., 1778; mem. N.Y. Senate, 1778-82; underwent an apparent change of loyalties, tried unsuccessfully to reunite Eng. and Am., 1782; went to Eng., 1782, practiced medicine in Eng. for a number of years; later returned to Am.; trustee Coll. Physicians and Surgeons, Springfield, N.J., 1807-11. Author: A Letter to Governors of the College of New York, 1771; Reflections and Observations on the Gout, 1772. Died Springfield, Oct. 1815.

JAY, John, chief justice U.S.: b. N.Y.C., Dec. 12, 1745; s. Peter and Mary (Van Cortlandt) J.; grad. Kings Coll. (now Columbia), 1764; m. Sarah Livingston, Apr. 28, 1774, 7 children, including Peter Augustus, William. Admitted to N.Y.C. bar, 1768; sec. royal commn. to settle boundary between N.Y. and N.J., 1773; del. to Continental Congress, 1774-79, pres., 1778-79; N. Y. Provincial Congress (helped draft a state constn.), 1776; chief justice of N.Y., 1776-78; commd. col. N.Y. Militia; minister plenipotentiary to Spain, 1779; called to Paris by Benjamin Franklin as joint commr. for negotiating peace with Gt. Britain, 1782; U.S. sec. fgn. affairs, 1784-89, tried to settle boundary disputes with commerce with Morocco and Prussia; wrote (with Eng. and France, also negotiated treaties of commerce with Morocco and Prussia wrote (with James Madison and Alexander Hamilton) Federalist Papers (written as argument in favor of adoption of U.S. Constn. by N.Y. State), 1787-88; 1st chief justice U.S., 1789-95, wrote Chisholm vs. Ga. decision which resulted in 11th Amendment to U.S. Constn.; formulated Jay Treaty with Gt. Britian, 1794, settling outstanding disputed matters such as debts, navigation of the Mississippi River, boundaries; gov. N.Y., 1795-1801; pres. Westchester Bible Soc., 1818, Am. Bible Soc., 1821. Died Bedford, N.Y., May 17, 1829.

JAY, John, lawyer, diplomat; b. N.Y.C., June 23, 1817; s. Judge William and Hannah (McVickar) J.; grad. Columbia, 1836; m. Eleanor Field, June 23, 1837. Admitted to N.Y. bar, 1839; mgr. N.Y. Young Men's Anti-Slavery Soc., 1834; sec. Irish Relief Com. during potato famine, 1847; U.S. minister to Austria, 1869-75; chmn. commn. to investigate N.Y. Custom House for Treasury Dept., 1877; v.p. Civil Service Reform Assn. State N.Y.; mem. State Civil Service Commn., 1884-87; a framer of state's 1st civil service law; pres. Am. Hist. Soc., 1890; a founder Union League Club, pres., 1866, 77; 1st pres. Huguenot Soc. of Am.; a founder Am. Geog. and Statis. Soc., 1852; active mem. N.Y. Hist. Soc., Met. Mus. Art, Nat. Acad. Design. Author: The Peace Negotiations of 1782 and 1783, published by N.Y. Hist. Soc., 1884; also papers "America Free, or America Slave," 1856; "The Church and the Rebellion," 1863; "On the Passage of the Constitutional Amendment," 1864; "Abolishing Slavery," 1864; "The American Foreign Service," 1877. Died N.Y.C., May 5, 1894.

JAY, Peter Augustus, jurist; b. Elizabethtown, N.J., Jan. 24, 1776; s. John and Sarah (Livingston) J.; grad. Columbia Coll., 1794, LL.D. (hon.), 1835; LL.D. (hon.), Harvard, 1831; m. Mary Clarkson, July 29, 1807, 8 children. Pvt. sec. to father John Jay in Eng., 1794; admitted to N.Y. bar, 1797; a visitor in Paris, France, 1802, brought La. Purchase Treaty and Napoleon's order to evacuate territory back to America; trustee Columbia, 1812-17, 23-43, chmn. bd., 1832; mem. N.Y. Assembly (Fed. Republican), 1816; recorder N.Y., 1819-21; mem. Kent Club; criminal ct. judge N.Y.C., 1820; mem. conv. framing N.Y.'s revolutionary constn., 1821; pres. N.Y. Hosp., 1827-33; a commr. fixing boundary line between N.Y. and N.J., 1833; pres. N.Y. Hist. Soc., 1840-43. Died N.Y.C., Feb. 20, 1843.

JAY, William, jurist, reformer; b. N.Y.C., June 16, 1789; s. John and Sarah Van Brugh (Livingston) J.; grad. Yale, 1807; studied law under John B. Henry, Albany, N.Y.; m. Hannah Augusta McVickar, Sept. 4, 1812; several children including John. A founder Am. Bible Soc., 1816; judge Ct. of Westchester County (N.Y.), 1818-43; strong anti-slavery advocate; a founder N.Y.C. Anti-Slavery Soc., 1833; opposed gradual emancipation and colonization of freed slaves in Africa; a dir. Am. Tract Soc.; pres. Am. Peace Soc.; mgr. father's estate, in Bedford, N.Y. Author: An Inquiry into the Character and Tendency of the American Colonization, and American Anti-Slavery Societies, 1835; Miscellaneous Writings on Slavery, 1853; War and Peace: The Evils of the First and A Plan for Preserving the Last, 1842; The Life of John Jay: with Selections from His Correspondence and Miscellaneous Papers, 2 vols., 1833. Died Oct. 14, 1858.

JAY, William, architect; b. Somersetshire, Eng., 1794; apprenticed to architect and surveyor, London, Eng. Came to Am., circa 1818, settled in Savannah, Ga.; sometimes credited with introducing Greek Revival movement to the South. Prin. works in Savannah include: Richardson-Owens residence (1816-19), Scarborough house (1818-19) Wayne Gordon house (all still standing); Habershorn house (razed 1916); Savannah br. U.S. Bank (razed 1924); Telfair Acad. Arts and Scis. (built circa 1820).

JEFFERS, William Nicholson, naval officer; b. Gloucester County, N.J., Oct. 16, 1824; s. John Ellis and Ruth (Westcott) J.; grad. U.S. Naval Acad., 1846; m. Lucy Smith, Sept. 17, 1850, 2 children. Apptd. midshipman U.S. Navy, 1840; served in ship Vixen during Mexican War; instr. U.S. Naval Acad., 1848-49; served in Gulf of Mexico in ship Honduras on survey for interoceanic ry., 1852-53, 57; commanded Water Witch in Brazil Squadron surveying Parana and LaPlata rivers, 1853-56; promoted lt., 1855; hydrographer in survey for canal route across Chiriqui Isthmus, Honduras, 1859-60; commanded ship Philadelphia in Potomac River, 1861; served in ship Roanoke in Atlantic blockade; commanded gunboat Underwriter in N.C. sounds, 1862; commanded ironclad Monitor, 1862; promoted lt. comdr., 1862; insp. of ordnance Washington (D.C.) Navy Yard, 1863-65, chief of ordnance, 1873-81; promoted capt., 1870, commodore, 1878; introduced system of bronze and steel boat howitzers, 1875; converted smooth-bore guns used on ships to breech-loaded rifles for all calibers up to 12-inch. Author: Nautical Rules and Stowage, 1849; A Concise Treatise on the Theory and Practise of Naval Gunnery, 1850; Nautical Surveying, 1871; Care and Preservation of Ammunition, 1874; editor Ordnance Instructions for the U.S. Navy, 4th edit., 1866, 5th edit., 1880. Died Washington, D.C., July 23, 1883; buried Naval Cemetery, Annapolis, Md.

JEFFERSON, Cornelia Burke (Cornelia Frances Thomas), actress; b. France; m. 1st Thomas Burke, 1 son Charles; m. 2d, Joseph Jefferson II, 1826, 1 son Joseph III. Appeared with Commonwealth or Anthony Street Co., New Olympic Theater, N.Y.C., 1812-14; appeared with family and partner-uncle Alexander MacKenzie for season, Chgo. Theater, 1837; made theatrical tour of West, Galena (Ill.), Dubuque (Ia.), Springfield (Ill.), Memphis (Tenn.), Mobile (Ala.), New Orleans, also Miss. and Tex., 1837-46.

JEFFERSON, Joseph, actor; b. Plymouth, Eng., 1774; s. Thomas and May J.; m. Euphemia Fortune, 8 children. Came to Am., 1795; stock actor Federal Street Theatre, Boston, 1795, John Street Theatre, N.Y.C., 1796-1803; comedian Chestnut Street Theatre Co., Phila., 1803-28. Died Harrisburg, Pa., Aug. 4, 1832.

JEFFERSON, Martha Wayles; b. Charles City County, Oct. 19, 1748; d. John Wayles; m. Bathurst Skelton; m. 2d, Thomas Jefferson (3d Pres. U.S.), 1772. Inherited large property from her father; inherited husband's estate, 1767; known as one of most beautiful women in Va.; in ill-health much of time because of strain of helping to run plantation; Jefferson often turned down important positions to be near her; died before Jefferson became Pres. Died Sept. 6, 1782.

JEFFERSON, Thomas, 3d Pres. U.S.; b. "Old Shadwell," Goochland (now Albemarle County), Va., Apr. 13, 1743; s. Peter and Jane (Randolph) J.; attended Coll. William and Mary, 1760-62; studied law under George Wythe; m. Martha Wayles Skelton, Jan. 1, 1772; 6 children (only Martha and Marie attained maturity). County lt. Albemarle County, 1770, county surveyor, 1773; admitted to bar, 1776; mem. Va. Ho. of Burgesses, 1769-75; mem. com. which created Va. Com. of Correspondence; introduced (with others) resolution for a fast day in Va. in sympathy with Boston Port Bill (resolution resulted in dissolution of Ho. of Burgesses); wrote A Summary View of the Rights of British America, 1774 (not adopted by Va. Ho.); mem. Continental Congress, 1775-76; mem. com. of 5 to draw up Declaration of Independence, personally wrote declaration (with minor changes by John Adams and Benjamin Franklin and by Congress as finally adopted), signed declaration, 1776; mem. Va. Ho. of Dels., 1776-79; gov. Va., 1779-81, struck blow at vested privilege by initiating abolition of primogeniture (achieved in 1785) and entail; originated bill to establish freedom of religion and opinion (passed in 1786); urged public sch. and library system; a resolution calling for inquiry into his mil. conduct as gov. was found groundless by Ho. of Dels. and resolutions of thanks were adopted; went into semi-retirement and finished his scientific work Notes on the State of Virginia (privately printed 1785); again mem. Continental Congress, 1783-84, drafted com. report urging adoption of dollar as unit of money system based on decimal notation, 1784; drafted resolution known as Ordinance of 1784, providing for temporary govt. of western territory; named as commr. to help carry out his formula for negotiating treaties of commerce based on universal reciprocity; succeeded Benjamin Franklin as minister to France, 1785-89; 1st U.S. sec. of state under new constn., 1790-93, chief architect of policy of neutrality; became leader of Anti-Federalist forces (Republicans); resigned, retired to Monticello, 1793; vice pres. U.S., 1796-1801; wrote Ky. Resolutions in answer to Alien and Sedition Acts which grew out of Am.-French trouble of the time, 1798; Pres. U.S., 1801-09; his 1st administrn. marked by La. Purchase, 1803; sent Lewis and Clark to explore new territory; his 2d adminstrn. beset with troubles stemming from English-French wars on the Continent; maintained Am. neutrality largely through econ. measures such as Non-Importation Act, 1806, Embargo Act, 1807; forced by econ. distress to partially ease embargo through Non-Intercourse Act, 1809; retired to Monticello for remainder of his life, 1809; an architect of renown, partly planned City of Washington (D.C.), designed and built Monticello; a prin. founder U. Va., mem. 1st bd. visitors, a rector (1819-26), also conceived univ.'s distinctive architecture and ednl. perspective, personally compiled several thousand titles in all academic fields as basis for its library; pres. Am. Philos. Soc., 1797-1815; maintained scientific interests which led him into studies and writings on paleontology, ethnology, geography and botany; writings include: Manual of Parliamentary Practice, 1801, thereafter used in U.S. Senate. Regarded as 1st great shaper of Am. democracy based on individual liberties, people's capabilities and checks on fed. power. Died Monticello, Albemarle County, July 4, 1826; buried Monticello.

JEFFERY, Rosa Griffith Vertner Johnson, poet, novelist; b. Natchez, Miss., 1828; d. John Y. and Miss (Abercrombie) Griffith; m. Claude M. Johnson, 1845, 6 children; m. 2d, Alexander Jeffery, 1863, no children. Contbr. under name of Rosa to Louisville (Ky.) Jour., 1850; lived in Rochester, N.Y., 1861-65; author: Poems, 1857; Woodburn, 1864; Daisy Dare and Baby Power, 1871; The Crimson Hand, 1881. Died Lexington, Ky., Oct. 6, 1894.

JEFFORDS, Elza, congressman; b. Ironton, O., May 23, 1826; attended common schs., Portsmouth, O.; studied law. Admitted to Ohio bar, 1847, began practice in Portsmouth; served as clk. Q. M. Dept., Army of Tenn. during Civil War; judge Miss. High Ct. Errors and Appeals, 1868-69; del. Republican Nat. Conv., Phila., 1872; mem. U.S. Ho. of Reps. (Rep.) from Miss., 48th Congress, 1883-85. Died Vicksburg, Miss., Mar. 19, 1885; buried Cedar Hill Cemetery, nr. Vicksburg.

JEFFRIES, John, physician, balloonist; b. Boston, Feb. 5, 1745; s. David and Sarah (Jaffrey) J.; grad. Harvard, 1763; M.D., Marischal Coll., U. Aberdeen (Scotland), 1769; m. Sarah Rhoads, 1770; m. 2d, Hannah Hunt, Sept. 8, 1787; 14 children. Asst. surgeon on Brit. naval vessel, 1771-74; surgeon maj. with Brit. troops, 1775-79; surgeon gen. of forces in N.S.; surgeon gen. Am. forces at Charleston, S.C., 1780; 1st to attempt to gather scientific data of free air; made 2 ascents, one over London, 1784, other over English Channel for scientific purposes, Jan. 7, 1785, balloon voyage successful, flew from Dover to Forest of Guines, Ardes, France, 1st crossing of English Channel by air; made baron of Cinque Ports; gave 1st public lecture on anatomy in New Eng., 1789. Author: Narrative of Two Aerial Voyages, 1786. Died Boston, Sept. 16, 1819.

JELLIFF, Horatio F., architect; b. Poughkeepsie, N.Y., 1844. Apprenticed to Henry Hudson Holly, served as chief draftsman, became partner, 1887; practiced independently, designed and built numerous houses in N.Y. State; credited with design of home of Thomas Edison, also a lab. built on estate. Died Oct. 7, 1892.

JEMISON, Mary (Indian name Dehgewanus), colonist; b. on the Atlantic Ocean while parents came from Belfast to Phila., 1743; d. Thomas and Jane Erwin Jemison; m. Sheninjee, circa 1761, 2 children; m. 2d, Hiokatoo, circa 1766, 6 children. Captured by Shawnee Indians at junction of Sharps Run and Conewago Creek, Pa., 1758; adopted by 2 Seneca tribeswomen; married Delaware warrior Sheninjee; went to Little Beard's Town (now Geneseo, N.Y.), turned down chance to return to her people, 1763; became naturalized citizen, 1817; known as "the White Woman of the Genesee." Died Sept. 19. 1833; buried Letchworth Park, N.Y.

JENCKES, Joseph, colonist; b. Eng., 1623; son of Joseph Jenks; m. Esther Ballard, 6 daus., 4 sons. Came to Lynn, Mass. to work in father's iron works, circa 1650; established sawmill and forge, Pawtucket Falls, R.I., 1671, a small community grew up around his bus. location (became Pawtucket, R.I.); dep. to R.I. Gen. Assembly, 1679. Died Jan. 4, 1717.

JENCKES, Joseph, colonial gov.; b. Pawtucket, R.I.,1656; s. Joseph and Esther (Ballard) J.; m. Martha Brown; m. 2d, Alice (Smith) Dexter, 1727; 9 children. Dep. to R.I. Gen. Assembly, 1691, 98, 1700-08, speaker, 1698-99, 1707-08; maj. of mainland R.I. Militia, 1707-11; asst. on R.I. Gov.'s Council, 1708-12; dep. gov. R.I., 1715-27, gov. 1727-32. Died Providence, R.I., June 15, 1740.

JENCKES, Thomas Allen, congressman, b. Cumberland, R.I., Nov.2,1818; s. Thomas B. and Abigail W. (Allen) J.; grad. Brown U.. 1838,

LL.D. (hon.), 1873; m. Mary Fuller, 1842, 7 children. Admitted to R.I. bar, 1840; sec. R.I. "Landholder's Conv.," 1841, R.I. Constl. Conv., 1842, R.I., Gov's Council, 1842; mem. U.S. Ho. of Reps. from R.I., 38th-41st congresses, 1863-71; initiated competitive examinations for admission to U.S. Mil. Acad., West Point, N.Y.; a pros. atty. in Credit Mobilier investigation. Died Cumberland, Nov. 4, 1875; buried Swan Point Cemetery, Providence, R.I.

JENIFER, Daniel (of St. Thomas), colonial statesman; b. Charles County, Md., 1723; s. Dr. Daniel Jenifer. Justice of the peace Charles County; commr. to settle boundary dispute between Pa. and Del., 1760; mem. Provincial Ct. of Md., 1766; mem. Md. Gov.'s Council, 1773-76; pres. Md. Council of Safety, 1775; pres. Md. Senate, 1777-80; mem. Continental Congress from Md., 1778-82; Md. del. to U.S. Constl. Conv., Phila., 1787; signer U.S. Constn.; unsuccessful candidate for gov. Md., 1782, 85; Died Annapolis, Md., Nov. 16, 1790.

JENIFER, Daniel, congressman; b. Charles County, Md., Apr. 15, 1791; studied law. Mem. Md. Ho. of Dels.; mem. U.S. Ho. of Reps. (National-Republican) from Md., 22d, 24th-26th congresses, 1831-33, 35-41; U.S. minister to Austria, 1841-45; register of wills for Charles County, 1846-51. Died Mulberry Grove, nr. Port Tobacco, Md., Dec. 18, 1855; buried on "Charleston" (a farm), Charles County.

JENKINS, Albert Gallatin, congressman, army officer; b. Cabell County, Va., Nov. 10, 1830; s. Capt. William and Janetta (McNutt) J.; grad. Jefferson Coll., 1848, Harvard Law Sch., 1850; m. Virginia Bowlin, 1858. Admitted to Va. bar 1850; del. Democratic Nat. Conv., Cincinnati, 1856; mem. U.S. Ho. of Reps. from Va., 35th-36th congresses, 1857-61; del. Confederate Provisional Congress, 1861; commd. brig. gen. Confederate States Army, 1862; led brigade on 500 mile raid into Ohio, 1862; led advance guard into Pa., 1863; wounded at battles of Gettysburg, 1863, Cloyd's Mountain, 1864. Killed in Battle of Wilderness, May 9, 1864; buried at home, Green Valley, W.Va.

JENKINS, Charles Jones, gov. Ga., jurist; b. Beaufort Dist., S.C., Jan. 6, 1805; s. Charles Jones Jenkins; grad. Union Coll., 1824, LL.D. (hon.), 1874; m. Miss Jones; m. 2d, Miss Barnes. Admitted to Ga. bar, 1826; mem. Ga. Legislature from Richmond County, 1830-31, 36-42, 43-50, speaker 4 terms; atty. gen. Ga., 1831; wrote, supported Ga. platform during Ga. Constl. Conv., 1850; judge Ga. Supreme Ct., 1860-65; gov. Ga. (Democrat), 1865-68; pres. Ga. Constl. Conv., 1877. Died nr. Augusta, Ga., June 14, 1883.

JENKINS, John, pioneer, surveyor; b. East Greenwich, Conn., Feb. 15, 1728; s. Lydia (Alden); m. Lydia Gardner, Feb. 1751, children include John. Explored Wyoming Valley, 1753, leading spirit and chief commissioner; attended Albany congress of the colonies of 1754; obtained deed to disputed lands on Susquehanna River from chief of Six Nations including Wyoming and country Westward of the Alleghanies; began settlement of Kingston, 1769; held all lands from township line to Kingston and Exeter; helped construct Ft. Jenkins; mem. Conn. Assembly from Westmoreland County, 1774, 75, 77; pres. judge of 1st County Ct. of Wyoming (Pa.); participated in Pennamite war in Wyoming until driven out by Pennamites, 1784. Died Pa., Nov. 1785.

JENKINS, John Stilwell, lawyer, editor, author; b. Albany, N.Y., Feb. 15, 1818; s. Ira and Rebecca van Heusen) J.; attended Hamilton Coll., 2 years; m. Miss Fellows, 1843, 4 children. Admitted to N.Y. bar, 1837; established, edited Cayuga Tocsin; wrote novelette Alice Howard, 1846, The New Clerk's Assistant (a volume of practical legal forms which had numerous printings, sold 30,000 copies), 1846; wrote, The History of the War Between the United States and Mexico, from the Commencement of Hostilities to the Ratification of the Treaty of Peace (1st account of the struggle between the two republics), 1848; Died Syracuse, N.Y., Sept. 20, 1852.

JENKINS, Lemuel, congressman; b. Bloomingburg, N.Y., Oct. 20, 1789; studied law. Admitted to Sullivan County (N.Y.) bar, 1815, practiced in Bloomingburg, N.Y.: master in chancery; 1st dist. atty. Sullivan County, 1818-18; mem. U.S. Ho. of Reps. (Democrat) from N.Y., 18th Congress, 1823-25; moved to Albany, N.Y., resumed law practice. Died Albany, Aug. 18, 1862; buried Albany Rural Cemetery.

JENKINS, Micah, army officer; b. Edisto Island, S.C., Dec. 1, 1835; s. Capt. John and Elizabeth (Clark) J.; grad. S.C. Mil. Acad., 1854; m. Caroline Jamison, 1856, 4 children, including Maj. Micah, Maj. Gen. John M. A founder King's Mountain Mil. Sch., Yorkville, S.C., 1855; an organizer, col. 5th S.C. Regt.; commanded a brigade in 7 days battle around Richmond, Va.; commanded a brigade at Battle of Seven Pines; brig. gen. at 2d Battle Bull Run, 1862; commanded Hood's div. at Battle of Chickamauga; accompanied Gen. Longstreet to Tenn. Killed at Battle of Wilderness, Mar. 6, 1864.

JENKINS, Nathaniel, inventor, mfr.; b. Boston, June 7, 1812; s. Nathaniel and Mary (Wheeler) J.; m. Mary W Tucker, Oct. 4, 1835, 4 children including Charles, Alfred B. Founder Rice, Jenkins & Co., coppersmith bus. (name changed to Jenkins & Co. 1853), Boston, 1837; later became silversmith and clock maker, Boston; began work on inventing and producing water faucets with renewable rubber packings, 1864; patentee rubber compound that would with-stand both hot water and steam, 1866; inventor Jenkins (steam) valve, circa 1868. Died May 20, 1872.

JENKINS, Robert, congressman; b. Windsor Forges, Pa., July 10, 1769; attended common and pvt. schs. Ironmaster, Caenarvon Twp., Pa.; mem. Pa. Ho. of Reps., 1804-05; mem. U.S. Ho. of Reps. from Pa., 10th-11th congresses, 1807-11; participated in suppressing Whisky Insurrection. Died Windsor Forges, Apr. 18, 1848; buried Caernarvon Presbyn. Churchyard, Churchtown, Lancaster County, Pa.

JENKINS, Thornton Alexander, naval officer, govt. ofcl.; b. Orange County, Va., Dec. 11, 1811; s. William Jenkins; m. Annie Powers, 1835; m. 2d, Elizabeth Tornton, 1849; 5 children. Apptd. midshipman U.S. Navy, 1828, lt., 1839; sec. 1st temporary lighthouse bd., 1850-52, framed law of 1852 for adminstrn. lighthouse service, sec. permament bd., 1852-58, 61-62; served in Mexican War, also on West Indies duty; capt. in command ship Oneida, 1862, sr. officer, 1862; Farragut's flag capt. on the Mississippi River commanding ship Hartford, 1863, commanded div. blockading entrance to Mobile Bay, 1863-64; chief Bur. Navigation, 1865-69; commd. rear adm., 1870, commanded Asiatic Squadron, 1872-73, rct., 1873. Died Washington, D.C., Aug. 9, 1893.

JENKINS, Timothy, congressman; b. Barre, Mass., Jan. 29, 1799; studied law. Admitted to N.Y. bar, 1825; began practice in Oneida Castle; moved to Vernon, N.Y., 1832; atty. for Oneida Indians in dealings with State of N.Y., 1838-45; dist. atty. for Oneida County, 1840-45; mem. U.S. Ho. of Reps. (Democrat) from N.C., 29th-30th congresses, 1845-49; del. Republican Nat. Conv., Phila., 1856. Died Martinsburg, N.Y., Dec. 24, 1859; buried City Cemetery, Oneida Castle.

JENKS, John Whipple Potter, zoologist; b. West Boylston, Mass., May 1, 1819; s. Nicholas and Betsey (Potter) J.; grad. Brown U., 1838; m. Sarah Tucker, Oct. 30, 1842. Operated sch., Americus, Ga., 1838-40; pastor Baptist Ch., Washington, Ga., 1840-42; headmaster Peirce Acad., Mass., 1842-71; founder natural history museum Brown U., Providence, R.I., 1871, curator, also prof. zoology, from 1872. Author: Fourteen Weeks in Zoology, 1876. Died Providence, 1895; buried Providence.

JENKS, Joseph, inventor; probably born Colnbrook, Eng., 1602; m. Elizabeth, 5 children including Joseph Jenckes. Came to Lynn, Mass. to work in 1st Am. iron works (established by Robert Bridges), 1642; had unusual inventive ability, worked on new and original products to improve the iron works; chosen to cut dies for 1st coins when new mint was erected at Boston; constructed 1st fire engine in Am., 1654; produced new type of scythe (improvement on an old Brit. model), 1655. Died Sangus, Mass., Mar. 1683.

JENKS, Michael Hutchinson, congressman; b. Bridgetown Mills, Pa., May 21, 1795. Engaged in farming; commr. Bucks County (Pa.), 1830-33, treas., 1833-35; moved to Newtown, Pa., 1837; asso. judge Ct. Common Pleas of Bucks County, 1838-43; mem. U.S. Ho. of Reps. (Whig) from Pa., 28th Congress, 1843-45; real estate and gen. bus. agt., 1845-65; chief burgess of Newtown, 1848-53. Died Newtown, Oct. 16, 1867; buried Newtown Friends Meeting Cemetery.

JENKS, William, clergyman; b. Newton, Mass., Nov. 25, 1778; s. Capt. Samuel and Mary (Haynes) J.; grad. Harvard, 1797; m. Betsey Russell, Oct. 22, 1797, 16 children. Pvt. tutor, tchr., student, also officiated at Christ Ch., Cambridge, Mass., 1797-1805; ordained to ministry Congregational Ch., 1805; pastor 1st Ch., Bath, Me., 1805-18; army chaplain during War of 1812; prof. Oriental langs. and English lit. Bowdoin Coll., 1812-16; opened pvt. sch. and chapel Central Wharf, Boston, 1818 (became City Missionary Soc. and Shawmut Ch.); a founder Salem and Green Street chs., pastor Green Street Ch., 1826-45; elected to Mass. Hist. Soc., 1821, librarian, 1823-32; 1st v.p. Am. Oriental Soc., 1842; sr. v.p. Am. Antiquarian Soc., 1853-66. Author: Memoir of the Northern Kingdom, 1808; Comprehensive Commentary on the Holy Bible, 6 vols., 1835-38. Died Nov. 13, 1866.

JENNESS, Benning Wentworth, senator; b. Deer field, N.H., July 14, 1806; attended Bradford Acad. Mass. Engaged in merc. bus., Strafford, N.H., 1826-56; mem. N.H. Ho. of Reps.; judge of probate fo Strafford County, 1841-45; mem. U.S. Senate from N.H., Dec. 1, 1845-June 13, 1846; mem. N.H Constl. Conv., 1850; del. Democratic Nat. Conv. Balt., 1852; withdrew as nominee for gov. N.H., 1861; moved to Ohio, engaged in lumbering, banking. Died Cleve., Nov. 16, 1879; buried family cemetery, Strafford.

JENNINGS, David, congressman; b. Readingtor Twp., N.J., 1787; attended pub. schs.; studied law. Moved to St. Clarisville, O., 1812; admitted to Ohio bar, 1813, began practice in St. Clairsville; pros. atty. Belmont County (O.), 1815-25; mem. Ohio Senate, 1819-24; mem. U.S. Ho. of Reps. from Ohio, 19th Congress, 1825-May 25, 1826 (resigned). Died Balt., 1834.

JENNINGS, John, army officer, jurist; probably born Phila.; circa 1738; probably son of Solomon Jennings. Sheriff, Northampton County (Pa.), various times 1761-78; became prominent in Pennamite War by ejecting Conn. settlers from Wyoming Valley; became pvt. 3d Regt., Continental Army, 1783; elected q.m. 1st Co., 2d Battalion, Northampton County Militia, 1784; moved to Phila., became sec. (or clk.) Mut. Assurance Co.; clk. to commrs. of bankrupts, Phila., 1791; dep.U.S. marshall for dist. of Pa., 1794; alderman Phila., 1796; asso. justice Mayor's Ct., Phila., 1796-1802. Died Jan. 14, 1802.

JENNINGS, Jonathan, gov. Ind., congressman; b. Hunterdon County, N.J., 1784; s. Jacob and Mary (Kennedy) J.; m. Ann Hay, Oct. 19, 1811; m. 2d, Clarissa Barber, 1827. Admitted to Ind. bar, 1807; del. U.S. Congress from Ind. Territory, 1809-16; pres. Ind. Constl. Conv., 1816; 1st gov. Ind., 1816-22; mem. U.S. Ho. of Reps. from Ind., 17th-21st congresses, Dec. 2, 1822-31. Died Charlestown, Ind., July 26, 1834; buried Charlestown Cemetery.

JENNINGS, Louis John, journalist; b. London, Eng., May 12, 1836; never married. Mem. staff London Times, travelled between London, India and N.Y.C., 1860-67; editor N.Y. Times, 1867-76, attacked Tweed Ring, largely responsible for bringing an end to it; returned to Eng., 1876; M.P. from Stockport, 1885-86, 92. Died London, Feb. 9, 1893.

JEROME, Chauncey, clock maker; b. Canaan, Conn., June 10, 1793; s. Lyman and Sallie (Noble) J.; m. Salome Smith, Feb. 1815, 3 children. House carpenter, Plymouth, Conn., 1808-12, also made hands for grandfather clocks; served with militia co. at New London and New Haven (Conn.) during War of 1812; worked with Eli Terry (clock maker), Plymouth, 1816; set up small clock making shop, Plymouth, 1817-22; moved to Bristol, Conn., 1822-24, made clock cases; formed clock co. (with brother Noble and Elijah Darrow), 1824, designed bronze looking-glass clock which made his business extremely profitable; established plant, Richmond, Va., 1835, Hamburg, S.C., 1836; moved main plant to New Haven, 1845; merged with another co. to form Jerome Mfg. Co., 1850 (co. failed by 1855); spent rest of life unsuccessfully trying to recoup his losses. Author: History of the American Clock Business for the Past Sixty Years and a Life of Chauncey Jerome Written by Himself, 1860. Died Apr. 20, 1868.

JERVIS, John Bloomfield, engr.; b. Huntington, N.Y., Dec. 14, 1795; s. Timothy and Phoebe (Bloomfield) J.; LL.D. (hon.), Hamilton Coll., Clinton, N.Y., 1878; m. Cynthia Brayton, 1834; m. 2d, Elizabeth Coates. Axeman and rodman on survey for Erie Canal under Benjamin Wright, in charge of constrn. 17 miles of canal, 1819, became supt. in charge of flow of traffic on 50 miles of completed canal, 1823; prin. asst. to Wright on Del. and Hudson Canal, 1825, became chief engr., 1827; became chief engr. Mohawk and Boston R.R., 1830; designed swivel truck which enabled locomotives to travel 60-80 miles per hour, 1832; chief engr. Schenectady & Saratoga R.R.; became chief engr. Chenango Canal, N.Y., 1833; chief engr. eastern half Erie Canal, 1836; became chief engr. Croton Aqueduct, N.Y., 1836, directed completion of dam, Ossining and Harlem River bridges; engr. in charge of new source of water supply for City of Boston, 1846-48; chief engr. for various railroads and canals, 1866 until retirement. Author: Description of the Croton Aqueduct, 1842; Railroad Property: A Treatise on the Construction and Management of Railroads, 1861; The Question of Labour and Capital, 1877. Died Rome, N.Y., Jan. 12, 1885.

JESUP, Thomas Sidney, army officer; b. Berkeley County, Va. (now W. Va.), Dec. 16, 1788; s. James Edward and Ann (O'Neill) J.; m. Ann Croghan. Commd. 2d lt. 7th Inf., U.S. Army, 1808, 1st lt., 1809; served as brigade maj. and adj. gen. during War of 1812; commd. capt. and maj. of inf., 1813;

brevetted lt. col. for bravery at Battle of Chippewa, 1814; brevetted col. for services at Battle of Niagara, 1814; full lt. col., 1817; adj. gen. U.S. Army with rank of col., 1818; q.m. gen. with rank of brig. gen., 1818; maj. gen., 1828; brig. gen. in command army in Fla., 1836; resumed duties as q.m. gen. 1838-60. Died Washington D.C., June 10, 1860; buried Arlington (Va.) Nat. Cemetery.

JETER, Jeremiah Bell, clergyman; b. Bedford County, Va.; s. Pleasant and Jane Eke (Hatcher) J.; m. Margaret P. Waddy, Oct. 5, 1826; m. 2d, Sarah Ann Gaskins, Dec. 1828; m. 3d, Charlotte E. Wharton, June 1849; m. 4th, Mrs. Mary C. Dabbs, May 5, 1863. Began to preach, 1821; ordained to ministry Baptist Ch., 1824, did evangelistic preaching; pastor 1st Bapt. Ch., Richmond, Va., 1836-49; attended Bapt. Triennial Conv., Phila., 1844; leader of orgn. of So. Bapt. Conv., 1845; pastor 2d Bapt. Ch., St. Louis, 1849-52, Grace Street Ch., Richmond, 1852-70; propr., editor Religious Herald, 1865-80. Author: Campbellism Examined, 1855. Died Feb. 18, 1880.

JEWELL, Harvey, lawyer; b. Winchester, N.H., May 26, 1820; s. Pliny and Emily (Alexander) J.; grad. Dartmouth, 1844; m. Susan Bradley, Dec. 26, 1849, 3 children. Admitted to Suffolk County (Mass.) bar, 1847; justice of peace, Boston, after 1850; mem. Boston Municipal Council, 1851, 52; mem. Mass. Ho. of Reps., 1861-62, 66-71, mem. many important coms., chmn. judiciary com., speaker, 1868-71; apptd. by Pres. Grant to Ct. of Commrs. of Ala. Claims, 1875-76. Died Boston, Dec. 8, 1881.

JEWELL, Marshall, mfr., gov. Conn., postmaster gen.; b. Winchester, N.H., Oct. 20, 1825; s. Pliny and Emily (Alexander) J.; m. Esther Dickinson, Oct. 6, 1852, 2 children. In charge constrn. Louisville and New Orleans Telegraph Line; supt. telegraph line between Boston and N.Y.C., 1849; part owner Hartford (Conn.) Evening Post; pres. Jewell Pin Co., S. New Eng. Telephone Co.; gov. Conn., 1869-70, 71-72; U.S. minister to St. Petersburg, Russia, 1873; U.S. postmaster gen., 1874; initiated fast mail service between N.Y.C. and Chgo.; chmn. Republican Nat. Com., 1880-83; partner Charles Root & Co., Detroit. Died Hartford, Feb. 10, 1883.

JEWETT, Charles Coffin, librarian; b. Lebanon, Me., Aug. 12, 1816; s. Rev. Paul and Eleanor Masury (Punchard) J.; attended Dartmouth; grad. Brown U., 1835, Andover Theol. Sem., 1840; m. Rebecca Green Haskins, Apr. 5, 1848. Librarian, prof. modern langs. Brown U., 1841-43, visited libraries and collected books for Brown U. in Europe, 1843-45, again taught at Brown, 1845-48; asst. sec., librarian under Joseph Henry at Smithsonian Instn., 1848-54, introduced new and original methods of card cataloguing, dismissed from position when he insisted that instn. should be a reference library; purchaser of books for Boston Public Library, 1854-58, supt., 1858-68. Author: Notices to Public Libraries in the United States, 1851; A Plan for Stereotyping Catalogues by Separate Titles, 1851; On the Construction of Catalogues of Libraries. . .with Rules and Examples, 1852. Died Braintree, Mass., Jan. 9, 1868.

JEWETT, David, naval officer; b. New London, Conn., June 17, 1772; s. David Hibbard and Patience (Bulkley) J.; m. Mrs. Eliza Lawrence McTiers, 1827. Served as comdr. U.S. Navy, 1799-1801; in service of United Provinces of the Rio de la Plata (Argentina), commanded the Invincible, 1815; sailed for Port Soledad in command the Heroina; landed and took possession in the name of United Provinces, 1820; commd. capt. Brazilian Navy, 1822, promoted to div. chief, 1823. Died July 26, 1842.

JEWETT, Frederick Stiles, artist; b. Simsbury, Conn., Feb. 26, 1819. Went on whaling voyage, 1835; editor New Eng. Weekly Review, Hartford, Conn.; journalist, West Indies, circa 1841-53; returned to Hartford, worked as ins. agt.; began marine and landscape painting; exhibited at Wadsworth Athenaeum, Yale Art Gallery, 1858, N.A.D., 1859-63; Western rep. Conn. Ins. Co., Cleve., 1864. Died Cleve., Dec. 26, 1864; buried Simsbury.

JEWETT, Freeborn Garrettson, congressman; b. Sharon, Conn., Aug. 4, 1791; studied law. Moved to Skaneateles, N.Y., 1815; justice of peace, 1817; admitted to N.Y. bar, 1818, began practice in Skaneateles; surrogate of Onondaga County (N.Y.), 1824-31; mem. N.Y. Assembly, 1826; Democratic presdl. elector, 1828; mem. U.S. Ho. of Reps. (Jacksonian Dem.), from N.Y., 22d Congress, 1831-33; insp. Auburn Prison, 1838-39; dist. atty. for Onondaga County, 1839; apptd. asso. justice N.Y. Supreme Ct., 1845; judge N.Y. Ct. of Appeals, 1847-53, chief justice, 1847-50. Died Skaneateles, Jan. 27, 1858; buried Lake View Cemetery, Skaneateles.

JEWETT, Hugh Judge, railroad exec., congressman; b. "Lansdowne," Harford County, Md., July 1, 1817; s. John and Susannah (Judge) J.; attended Hiram (O.) Coll.; m. Sarah Ellis; m. 2d, Mrs. Sarah (Guthrie) Kelly; 7 children. Admitted to Md. bar, 1838; pres. Muskingum County br. Ohio State Bank, 1852; mem. Ohio Senate, 1853; U.S. atty. for So. dist. Ohio, 1854; mem. Ohio Ho. of Reps., 1855, 68, 69; pres. Central Ohio R.R. Co., 1857, Little Miami, Columbus & Xenia railroads, 1869, Cincinnati & Muskingum Valley R.R.; mem. U.S. Ho. of Reps. from Ohio, 43d Congress, 1873-June 23, 1874; pres. Erie Ry. Co., 1874-84. Died Augusta, Ga., Mar. 6, 1898; buried Woodlawn Cemetery, Zanesville, O.

JEWETT, John Punchard, publisher; b. Lebanon, Me., Aug. 16, 1814; s. Rev. Paul and Eleanor M. (Punchard) J.; m. Harriette Cobb, 1837; m. 2d, Helen Crane, June 20, 1861. Employed in a bindery and bookstore, Salem, Mass.; opened bookstore-publishing house, Boston, 1847; published Harriet Beecher Stowe's Uncle Tom's Cabin, 1852, followed by Mrs. Stowe's Key to Uncle Tom's Cabin; opened branch, Cleve., O., by 1855, published tracts on temperance, abolition and religion including Maria S. Cummins' Lamplighter and Margaret Fuller's Women In the Nineteenth Century; his business declined after Panic of 1857; tried 1 business after another, finally set up a bookstore in N.Y.C., 1866. Died Orange, N.J., May 14, 1884.

JEWETT, Joshua Husband, congressman; b. Deer Creek, Md., Sept. 30, 1815; attended common schs.; studied law. Admitted to Ky. bar, 1836, began practice in Elizabethtown; pros. atty. Hardin County (Ky.); mem. U.S. Ho. of Reps. (Democrat) from Ky., 34th-35th congresses, 1855-59; resumed law practice. Died Elizabethtown, July 14, 1861; buried City Cemetery, Elizabethtown.

JEWETT, Luther, congressman; b. Canterbury, Conn., Dec. 24, 1772; grad. Dartmouth, 1795; studied medicine and theology. Practiced medicine, Putney, Vt.; mem. Vt. Ho. of Reps.; mem. U.S. Ho. of Reps. (Federalist) from Vt., 14th Congress, 1815-17; moved to St. Johnsbury, Vt.; ordained to ministry; pastor, Newbury, Vt., 1821-28; published Farmer's Herald, St. Johnsbury, 1828-32, Free Mason's Friend, 1830-32. Died St. Johnsbury, Mar. 8, 1860; buried Mt. Pleasant Cemetery, St. Johnsbury.

JEWETT, Milo Parker, educator; b. St. Johnsbury, Vt., Apr. 27, 1808; s. Calvin and Sally (Parker) J.; grad. Dartmouth, 1828; studied law under Josiah Quincy, Rumney, Vt.; grad. Andover Theol. Sem., 1833; m. Jane Augusta Russell, Sept. 17, 1833. Prof., Marietta (O.) Collegiate Inst. (now Marietta Coll.), 1833-38; mem. com. of three to urge Ohio Legislature to establish common sch. system; established Judson Female Inst., Marion, Ala., 1838-55; purchased Cotton Hill Sem., Poughkeepsie, N.Y., from Matthew Vassar, 1856, received charter for Vassar Coll., 1861, became 1st pres.; studied univ. orgn. in Europe, 1862; moved to Milw., 1867, became commr. of public schs., chmn. Milw. Bd. of Health, trustee Milw. Female Coll. (now Milw.-Downer Coll.); Jewett Hall at Vassar Coll. named for him. Died June 9, 1882.

JEWETT, William, painter; b. East Haddam, Conn., Jan. 14, 1792; s. Nathan and Mary (Griffen) H.; studied painting under Samuel L. Waldo. Employed to grind paints for a coach painter, New London; became asst. to S.L. Waldo, N.Y.C., painted landscapes of Hudson River, soon became Waldo's partner (both often worked on same painting); their portraits of John Pinter (founder N.Y. Hist. Soc.), Edward Kellogg, Rev. Gardiner Spring, Gen. Matthew Clarkson, now in collection of Met. Mus. of Art, N.Y.C. Died Jersey City, N.J., Mar. 24, 1874.

JEWETT, William Cornell; b. N.Y.C., Feb. 19, 1823; s. Joseph and Matilda (Cornell) J.; m. Almira Guion, 1848; m. 2d, Charlotte Berna, 1867. Attended Peace Conf. of 1861; m. 2d, Charlotte Berna, 1867. Attended Peace Conf. of 1861; made several trips to Europe during Civil War to seek fgn. intervention to secure peace between North and South; together with George N. Saunders (Confederate agitator) conferred with Horace Greeley and John Hay at Niagara Falls, N.Y., summer 1864 (meeting eventually resulted in alienation of some of Abraham Lincoln's conservative supporters); considered peace to be impossible by Sept., 1864; wrote many articles and pamphlets advocating peace between North and South. Died Geneva, Switzerland, Oct. 27, 1893.

JEWETT, William Samuel Lyon, artist; b. N.Y.C., 1834; s. William and Mary (Lyon) J.; m. Mary Sikes Bliss, 3 daus. Correspondent for Leslie's Illustrated Newspaper, gained notoriety during trial of John Brown when he was expelled from Charleston (Va., now W.Va.), suspected of being a correspondent for N.Y. Tribune; contbr. engravings and sketches to Harper's Weekly, 1859-76; drew at least 20 portraits for Harper's History of the Great Rebellion; painted a few oil portraits. Died of a pistol wound, Bergen, N.J., July 23, 1876.

JEWETT, William Smith, artist; b. South Dover, N.Y., Aug. 6, 1812; married, 1870, 1 son, William Dunbar. Portrait painter, N.Y.C., 1833-49; exhibited at N.A.D., elected asso., 1845; exhibited at Am. Art-Union; had studio at N.Y.U., 1845-49; accompanied Hope Co. to San Francisco, 1849; became 1st profl. portrait painter in Cal.; maintained portrait studios in San Francisco, 1850-69, Sacramento, 1850-55, also painted landscapes and subject paintings; returned to N.Y.C., 1869, ret.; made visit to Cal., then went to Europe; returned to U.S., circa 1873. Died Springfield, Mass., Dec. 3, 1873.

JOCELYN, Nathaniel, engraver, painter; b. New Haven, Conn., Jan. 31, 1796; s. Simeon and Lucina (Smith) J.; m. Sarah Atwater Plant. Became partner Hartford Graphic & Bank Note Engraving Co. (after 3 year apprenticeship), 1817; began painting portraits, Savannah, Ga., also New Haven, 1821; traveled with Samuel F. B. Morse in Eng., Italy and France, 1829; set up studio in New Haven after return to U.S., divided his time between his business and his art; head of art dept. Am. Bank Note Co., until 1865; exhibited at Nat. Acad.; won gold palette for best portrait in Conn., 1844; hon. mem. Nat. Acad. of Design; mem. Conn. Acad. of Arts; most famous painting: portrait of Cinquè, leader of Amistad Africans (now owned by New Haven Colony Hist. Soc.). Died Jan. 31, 1881.

JOCELYN, Simeon Smith, engraver; b. New Haven, Conn., Nov. 21, 1799; s. Simeon Jocelin. Partner firm N. & S. Jocelyn, New Haven, 1818-43; engraved several portraits painted by his brother Nathan; asso. with banknote engraving firms Draper, Toppan & Co., 1840-44, Toppan, Carpenter & Co., after 1844, Toppan, Carpenter, Casilear & Co., circa 1850-53; became sec. Am. Missionary Soc., 1853. Died Tarrytown, N.Y., Aug. 17, 1879.

JOGUES, Isaac, missionary; b. Orleans, France, Jan. 10, 1607; Jesuit novice in Rouen and Paris, France. Joined Soc. of Jesus; ordained priest Roman Catholic Ch., 1636; arrived in Can. for mission work, 1636; missionary among Huron Indians on shores of Lake Huron, Can., 1636-41; worked among Sioux Indians living beyond Lake Superior, 1641-42; captured by Hohawk-Iroquois tribe who mutilated and tortured him, 1642-43, rescued by Dutch at Ft. Orange; resided at Jesuit coll. at Rennes, France, 1644-46; returned to Can., 1646, undertook mission to Mohawks. Beatified by Pope XI, 1925, canonized, 1930. Killed by Hohawk Indians, Ossernenon, N.Y., Oct. 18, 1646.

JOHNS, John, clergyman, coll. pres.; b. New Castle Del., July 10, 1796; s. Chief Justice Kensey and Ann (Van Dyke) J.; grad. Coll. of N.J. (now Princeton), 1815; S.T.D., Columbia, 1834, U. Sate N.Y., 1834; LL.D., Coll. William and Mary, 1855; m. Juliana Johnson, 1820; m. 2d, Jane Schaaf; m. 3d, Mrs. Southgate. Ordained to ministry Protestant Episcopal Ct. 1819; minister All Saints Parish, Frederick, Md., 1819-28, Christ Ch., Balt., 1828-42; became asst. bishop of Va., 1842; pres., prof. moral and intellectual philosophy Coll. William and Mary, 1849-54; became bishop of Va., 1862. Died Apr. 4, 1876.

JOHNS, Kensey, jurist; b. West River, Md., June 14, 1759; s. Kensey and Susannah (Galloway) J.; m. Ann Van Dyke, children- Kensey, John. Del. from New Castle County to Del. Constl. Conv. of 1792; apptd. to Del. vacancy in U.S. Senate, 1794, never seated; asso. judge Del. Supreme Ct., chief justice, 1799; chancellor of Del., 1830; pres. Del. Court of Errors and Appeals. Died New Castle, Del., Dec. 20, 1848.

JOHNS, Kensey, Jr., congressman, jurist; b. New Castle, Del., Dec. 10, 1791; s. Chief Justice Kensey and Ann (Van Dyke) J.; grad. Coll. of N.J. (now Princeton), 1810; LL.D. (hon.), Jefferson Coll., Pa., 1846; m. Maria McCallmont, 1813. Admitted to bar, 1813; mem. U.S. Ho. of Reps. from Del., 20th-21st congresses, Oct. 2, 1827-31; chancellor of Del., 1832-57. Died Sussex, Del., Mar. 28, 1857; buried Presbyn. Cemetery, Sussex.

JOHNSON, Alexander Bryan, businessman; b. Gosport, Eng., May 29, 1786; son of Bryan Johnson; m. Abigail Louisa Adams, 1814; m. 2d, Lydia Masters; m. 3d, Mary Livingston. Came to N.Y. with family, 1801; worked in father's store, Utica, N.Y., 1801-07; operated glass factory, studied finance, 1807-12; banker, Utica, 1812-16; organizer, operator Utica Ins. Co., 1816-19; pres. Utica br. Ont. Bank of Canandaigua, 1819-55. Author: The Philosophy of Human Knowledge; or a Treatise of Language, 1828; Religion in its Relation to the Present Life, 1841; A Guide to a Right Understanding of our American Union, 1857; The Unon as It Was and the Constitution as It Is, 1862; The Advanced Value of Gold, 1862. Died Sept. 9, 1867.

JOHNSON, Alexander Smith, jurist; b. Utica, N.Y., July 30, 1817; s. Alexander B. and Abigail (Adams) J.; grad. Yale, 1835; LL.D. (hon.), Hamilton Coll,. 1859; m. Catherine Crysler, Nov. 1852, 4 children. Admitted to the bar, 1838; judge N.Y. Ct. of Appeals, 1851-59, 73-74, chief judge, 1858-59; practiced law, Utica, 1859-73; mem. N.Y. State Commn. on Appeals, 1873; U.S. circuit judge 2d Jud. Circuit, 1875; regent Univ. State N.Y. Died Nassau, Bahama Islands, Jan. 26, 1878.

JOHNSON, Andrew, 17th Pres. U.S.; b. Raleigh, N.C., Dec. 29, 1808; s. Jacob and Mary (McDonough) J.; m. Eliza McCardle, May 17, 1827; children—Martha, Charles, Mary, Robert, Andrew. Moved to Greeneville, Tenn., 1826, employed as a tailor; alderman Greeneville, 1828-30, mayor, 1830-34; mem. Tenn. Senate, 1835-37, 39-41; mem. U.S. Ho. of Reps. from Tenn., 28th-32d congresses, 1843-53, supported 1st homestead bill which granted land to settlers gratis or at nominal price, 1858 (vetoed by Pres. Buchanan), reintroduced bill and continued support until passage of Homestead Act of 1862; gov. Tenn., 1853-57; mem. U.S. Senate from Tenn., Oct. 8, 1857-Mar. 4, 1862; voted for Jefferson Davis' resolution to permit citizens to take slaves into new territories, 1860; apptd. mil. gov. Tenn. with rank of brig. gen. U.S. Volunteers, 1862; organized provisional govt. for Tenn., held Nashville against Confederate Army; vice pres. U.S., Mar. 4-Apr. 15, 1865; after Lincoln's assassination became Pres. U.S., Apr. 15, 1865-Mar. 3, 1869; issued 2 proclamations continuing Lincoln's reconstrn. policy, May 29, 1865; vetoed Freedmen's Bur. extension act, also Civil Rights act, 1866; vetoed Tenure of Office act, 1867 (act passed over his veto); suspended Edwin M. Stanton as U.S. sec. of war, 1867 (Senate refused the suspension, 1868); impeachment proceedings started against him by Thaddeus Stevens and John A. Bingham, Feb. 1868; acquitted in subsequent impeachment trial (conducted under 11 articles of impeachment, Mar. 5-May 11, 1868) by 35 to 19 vote in U.S. Senate; vetoed reconstrn. legislation passed by Congress during completion of presdl. term; during his adminstrn. French were forced from Mexico and Alaska was purchased from Russia; unsuccessful candidate for U.S. Senate, 1869, for U.S. Ho. of Reps., 1872; mem. U.S. Senate from Tenn., 1875. Died nr. Elizabethon, Cartar County, Tenn., July 31, 1875; buried Andrew Johnson Nat. Cemetery, Greeneville.

JOHNSON, Benjamin Pierce, agriculturist; b. Canaan, N.Y., Nov. 30, 1793; son of William Johnson; grad. Union Coll., Schenectady, N.Y., 1813; studied law under Elisha Williams; m. Anne McKinstry, Dec. 11, 1820; m. 2d, Mary Adams, Mar. 1, 1839; at least 1 son, 1 dau. Practiced law, Rome, N.Y., 1817; mem. N.Y. State Gen. Assembly, 1827-29; v.p. N.Y. State Agrl. Soc., 1841, corr. sec., 1844, 47, pres., 1845; co-editor Central N.Y. Farmer, 1842-44; toured Europe and studied agrl. methods in Eng. and Wales, 1846; moved to Albany, N.Y., circa 1848; commr. from N.Y. to London (Eng.) Exhbn., 1851; mem. Nat. Agrl. Soc. of France, 1851; U.S. commr. to Internat. Exhbn., London, 1862. Author: Report of Benjamin P. Johnson, Agent of the State of New York, Appointed to Attend the Exhibition of the Industry of All Nations, 1852. Died Albany, Apr. 12, 1869; buried Rome.

JOHNSON, Bushrod Rust, army officer; b. Belmont County, O., Oct. 7, 1817; grad. U.S. Mil. Acad., 1840; 1 child. Served as 2d lt. 3d Inf., U.S. Army, commd. 1st lt., 1844; served in Mexican War, 1847; commissary duty, Vera Cruz Mexico, 1847; resigned commn., 1847; instr. philosophy chemistry, Western Mil. Inst., Georgetown, Ky., 1847, instr. natural philosophy, mathematics, engring., supt., 1851-55; commd. lt. col. Ky. Militia, 1849-51; col., 1851-54; col. Tenn. Militia, 1854-61; supt. Mil. Coll., U. Nashville, 1855; commd. col. of engrs. Confederate Army, 1861, brig. gen., 1862; commanded a div. in Battle of Shiloh, in Bragg's invasion of Ky. at Perryville, 1862, Stone's River, 1863, Battle of Chickamauga in siege of Knoxville, 1863; promoted maj. gen., 1863; commanded a S.C. div., surrendered with Lee at Apomattox; chancellor U. Nashville, 1870. Died Brighton, Ill., Sept. 12, 1880; buried Miles Cemetery, Brighton.

JOHNSON, Cave, congressman, cabinet officer; b. Springfield, Tenn., Jan. 11, 1793; s. Thomas and Mary (Noel) J.; m. Elizabeth (Dortch) Brunson, Feb. 20, 1838. Admitted to Tenn. bar, 1814; pros. atty. Montgomery County (Tenn.), 1817; mem. U.S. Ho. of Reps. from Tenn., 21st-24th, 26th-28th congresses, 1829-37, 39-45; postmaster gen. U.S. under Polk, 1845-49, introduced use of stamps; pres. State Bank of Tenn., 1854-60; U.S. commr. to settle dispute between U.S. and Paraguay Navigation Co., 1860. Died Clarksville, Tenn., Nov. 23, 1866.

JOHNSON, Chapman, legislator; b. Louisa County, Va., Mar. 12, 1779; s. Thomas and Jane (Chapman) J.; attended Coll. William and Mary; m. Mary Nicholson, 1816. Admitted to Richmond (Va.) bar, 1802; mem. Va. Senate from Augusta dist., 1810-36; served as capt. of a company of cavalry, aide to Gen. Breckinridge in War of 1812; recodified criminal laws of Va.; mem. Va. Constl. Conv., 1828-30; mem. bd. visitors U. Va., 1819-45, rector, 1836-44. Died Richmond, July 12, 1849.

JOHNSON, Charles, congressman; b. Chowan County, N.C. Engaged in planting; mem. N.C. Senate, 1781-84, 88-90, 92; mem. U.S. Ho. of Reps. from N.C., 7th Congress, 1801-02. Died Bandon, nr. Edenton, N.C., July 23, 1802; buried Edenton Cemetery.

JOHNSON, Edward, colonial legislator; b. Canterbury, Eng., Sept. 1598; s. William and Susan (Porredge) J.; m. Susan Mannter, circa 1618, 7 children. Moved to Boston, 1630; licensed to trade with Indians; became freeman, 1631; returned to Eng., circa 1632; settled with entire family, Charlestown, Mass., 1636; co-founder of Woburn, Mass., 1640; dep. to Mass. Gen. Ct., 1634-46, 49-72. Author: The Wonder-Working Providence of Sion's Saviour in New England, 1653. Died Apr. 23, 1672.

JOHNSON, Edward, army officer, farmer; b. Salisbury, Va., Apr. 16, 1816; s. Dr. Edward Johnson; ed. U.S. Mil. Acad., 1838. Commd. 1st lt. U. S. Army, 1839; brevetted capt., 1847, maj., 1848; participated in siege of Veracruz during Mexican War, 1847, skirmish of Amazoque, 1847, Battle of Churubusco, 1847; storming of Chapultepec, 1847, Molina del Rey, Sept. 18, 1847, also at assault and capture of city of Mexico; commd. capt. 6th Inf., U.S. Army, 1851; col. 12th Ga. Volunteers, Confederate Army, 1861, served as brig. gen. at Battle of McDowell (Va.), commanded div. in battles of Winchester, Martinsburg Pike, 1861; maj. gen., 1863; participated in battles of Carlisle, (Pa.), Gettysburg, 1863; led div. at Battle of Payne's Farm, 1863; participated in battles of Wilderness and Spotsylvania, 1864, taken prisoner; fought under Hood at Nashville, Tenn., again captured, 1864; returned to farming, Chesterfield County, Va. Died Ford's Hotel, Richmond, Va., Mar. 2, 1873; buried Hollywood Cemetery, Richmond.

JOHNSON, Edwin Ferry, civil engr.; b. Essex, Vt., May 23, 1803; s. John and Rachel (Ferry) J.; ed. Am. Literary, Scientific and Mil. Acad., Middletown, Conn. (now Norwich U.); m. Charlotte Shaler, Sept. 7, 1830, 8 children. Instr. mathematics and asst. prof. natural history Am. Lit., Sci. and Mil. Acad., 1825-26, prof. mathematics and civil engring., 1826-29; in charge of land surveys for Erie Canal, 1829, Champlain Canal, 1830-31, Morris Canal, 1831; asst. engr. in charge of surveys for Catskill & Canajoharie R.R., 1831; chief engr. or prin. asst. in location of 14 railroads, including N.Y. & Erie, N.Y. & Boston, Chgo, St. Paul & Fond du Lac, also 4 canals; pres. Stevens Assn. (railroad and steamship lines), Hoboken, N.J.; mem. Conn. Senate, 1856; mayor Middletown, 1856-57; chief engr. N.P. Ry., 1867, consulting engr., 1871; inventor, canal lock improvement, screw power press, 6-wheeled locomotive truck, 8-wheeled locomotive. Author: Report...upon the Defenses of Maine, 1862; Report of a General Plan of Operations to the Secretary of War, 1863 (both at request of U.S. War Dept.); Review of the Project for a Great Western Railway, 1831; The Railroad to the Pacific, Northern Route, Its General Character, Relative Merits, Etc., 1854. Died N.Y.C. Apr. 12, 1872.

JOHNSON, Elijah, Liberian pioneer; b. N.J., circa 1780; 1 son, Hilary R.W. Served in War of 1812; became mem. pioneer co. of emigrants who left N.Y. to establish Am. Negro settlement in Africa, 1820, took charge of group (with Daniel Coker), explored coast, finally chose present site of Liberian capitol for settlement; commissary of stores, leader colonial troops; mem. conf. which made Declaration of Independence, 1847. Died Mar. 23, 1849.

JOHNSON, Elizabeth, comedienne; b. England; m. John Johnson. Appeared with Old Am. Co., Boston, 1795-96; made 1st N.Y.C. appearance at John Street Theatre, 1796, appeared at last performance of John Street Theatre in The Comet and Tom Thumb, 1798; appeared as Rosalind in As You Like It at opening of Park Theatre, N.Y.C., 1798, appeared as comedienne with Park Theatre company, 1802-06; returned to Eng. for 10 years in 1806; returned to Am., 1817-18, appeared for the season at Park Theatre.

JOHNSON, Ellen, actress. Made debut at Park Theatre, N.Y.C., 1817; appeared in premiere of Payne's opera Clari, 1823, sang for 1st time Home, Sweet Home.

JOHNSON, Ellen Cheney, educator, prison reformer; b. Athol, Mass., Dec. 20, 1829; d. Nathan and Rhoda (Holbrook) Cheney; m. Jesse Cram Johnson, 1849. Mem. finance coms. New Eng. br. of U.S. San. Commn.; active supporter Temporary Asylum for Discharged Female Prisoners, Dedham, Mass., 1864; urged establishment separate prisons for women; mem. Mass. Prison Commn., 1879-84; supt. Reformatory Prison for Women, Sherborn, Mass., 1884-99. Died while attending Women's Internat. Congress; London, Eng., June 28, 1899.

JOHNSON, Francis, congressman; b. Caroline County, Va., June 19, 1776; studied law. Admitted to the bar, practiced law; moved to Woodford County, Ky., 1796, Bowling Green, Ky., 1807; mem. Ky. Ho. of Reps., 1812-13, 15; mem. U.S. Ho. of Reps. (Democrat) from Ky., 16th-19th congresses Nov. 13, 1820-27; moved to Louisville, Ky., 1829 practiced law; commonwealth atty. for 5th Dist of Ky.; unsuccessful Republican candidate for gov Ky. Died Louisville, May 16, 1842; buried old family burial ground (later a municipal playground), Louisville.

JOHNSON, Frederick Avery, congressman; b. Fort Edward, N.Y., Jan. 2, 1833; grad. Glen Falls (N.Y.) Acad. Engaged in banking, wool bus., N.Y. C., later in banking, Glens Falls; pres. Village of Glens Falls; mem. U.S. Ho. of Reps. from N.Y. 48th-49th congresses, 1883-87. Died Glens Falls July 17, 1893; buried Bay St. Cemetery, Glens Falls.

JOHNSON, Guy, supt. Indian affairs, loyalist b. Ireland, 1740; m. Mary Johnson. Served throughout French and Indian War; sec. to Sir William Johnson; served as lt. in a N.Y. independent company; commanded company of rangers under Gen. Amherst, 1759-60; col., adj. gen. N.Y. Militia, dep. for Six Nations and Neighbouring Indians, 1762, served occasionally as sec. to supt.; mem. N.Y. Assembly, 1773-75; supt. Northern Dept. of Indians, 1774-82; at beginning of Am. Revolution tried to organize Indians against colonialists, 1775, lead Indian riots, 1778-82; commanded Ft. Niagara, 1780-82; returned to Eng., 1783. Died London, Eng., Mar. 5, 1788.

JOHNSON, Harvey Hull, congressman; b. West Rutland, Vt., Sept. 7, 1808; attended Middlebury Acad.; studied law. Admitted to the bar, 1833; began practice of law, Akron, O.; postmaster of Akron 1837; moved to Ashland, O., circa 1848; mem. U.S. Ho. of Reps. (Democrat) from Ohio, 23d Congress, 1853-55; moved to Winona, Minn., 1855, practiced law; pres. Winona & St. Peter R.R.; moved to Owatonna, Minn., 1865, practiced law; mayor and city justice of Owatonna, 1867-70. Died Owatonna, Feb. 4, 1896; buried Forest Hill Cemetery, Owatonna.

JOHNSON, Henry, senator, gov. La.; b. Va., Sept. 14, 1783; studied law. Admitted to Va. bar; moved to Territory of Orleans, 1809; clk. 2d Superior Ct. of Orleans Territory; dist. judge of Parish Ct., 1811; del. 1st La. Constl. Conv., 1812; practiced law, Donaldsonville, La.; mem. U.S. Senate from La., Jan. 12, 1818-May 27, 1824, Feb. 12, 1844-49; gov. La., 1824-28; mem. U.S. Ho. of Reps. (Whig) from La., 23d-25th congresses, Sept. 25, 1834-39, moved to New River, La., after 1850, practiced law. Died Parish of Pointe Coupee, La., Sept. 4, 1864; buried on his plantation.

JOHNSON, Herschel Vespasian, senator, gov Ga., Confederate senator; b. Burke County, Ga., Sept. 18, 1812; s. Moses and Nancy (Palmer) J. A.B., U. Ga., 1834; m. Ann (Polk) Walker, Dec. 19, 1833. Admitted to Va. bar, 1835; mem. U.S. Senate from Ga., 1848-49; judge Ocmulgee Circuit, Ga., 1849-53; gov. Ga., 1853-57; candidate for vice pres. U.S. on ticket with Stephen A. Douglas, 1860, defeated; opposed secession in Ga. Secession Conv., 1861; elected to Confederate Senate, 1862; pres. Ga. Constl. Conv., 1865; elected to U.S. Senate from Ga., 1866, denied seat by Republicans, judge middle circuit, Ga. Superior Ct., 1873-80. Died Jefferson County, Ga., Aug. 16, 1880; buried Louisville (Ky.) Cemetery.

JOHNSON, James, army officer, congressman; b. Orange County, Va., Jan. 1, 1774; s. Robert and Jemima (Sugget) J.; at least 3 children. Served as lt. col. Ky. Volunteers under command of his brother (Col. Richard M. Johnson) during War of 1812, served at Battle of Thames, 1813, led right wing of U.S. forces against combined forces of British and Indian allies led by Tecumseh; outmaneuvered British at Thames, largely responsible for U.S. success; contractor for supplying U.S. troops on Mississippi and Missouri rivers, 1819-20; mem. U.S. Ho of Reps. (Democrat) from Ky., 19th Congress, 1825-26. Died Great Crossings, Ky., Aug. 13, 1826.

JOHNSON, James, congressman; b. Va.; grad. Coll William and Mary, circa 1795; studied law. Admitted to Va. bar, practiced in Williamsburg; del Va. Constl. Conv., 1788; mem. Va. Ho. of Dels. 1797-1804, 06-07, 08-13; moved to Isle of Wight County, 1807, practiced law; mem. U.S. Ho. of Reps. (Democrat) from Va., 13th-16th congresses 1813-Feb. 1, 1820; collector of customs, Norfolk Va., 1820-25. Died Norfolk, Dec. 7, 1825.

JOHNSON, James, congressman; b. Robeson County, N.C., Feb. 12, 1811; grad. U. Ga., 1832; studied law. Taught sch.; admitted to Ga. bar, 1835; bega ractice of law, Columbus, Ga., 1836; pros. atty. Muscogee County (Ga.); mem. U.S. Ho. of Reps. (Unionist) from Ga., 32d Congress, 1851-53; provisional gov. Ga., 1865; unsuccessful candidate for U.S. Senate, 1866; collector of customs, Savannah, Ga., 1866-69; Republican presdl. elector, 1868; judge Ga. Superior Ct., 1869-75; resumed practice of law, 1875. Died on his plantation, Chattahoochee County, Ga., Nov. 20, 1891; buried Linwood Cemetery, Columbus.

JOHNSON, James Augustus, congressman; b. Spartanburg, S.C., May 16, 1829; grad. Jefferson Med. Coll., Phila.; studied law. Admitted to Cal. bar, 1859; began practice of law in Downieville; mem. Cal. Gen. Assembly, 1859-60; mem. U.S. Ho. of Reps. (Democrat) from Cal., 40th-41st congresses, 1867-71; lt. gov. Cal., 1875-80; moved to San Francisco; registrar of voters, 1883-84; practiced law, San Francisco until 1896. Died San Francisco, May 11, 1897; buried Masonic Cemetery, San Francisco.

JOHNSON, James Hutchins, congressman; b. Bath, N.H., June 3, 1802; attended pub. schs. Owner, operator lumber mill; dep. sheriff Grafton County (N.H.), 1824-25; paymaster 32d Regt., N.H. Militia, 1826, later adj. and col.; mem. N.H. Senate, 1838, N.H. Council, 1842-46; mem. U.S. Ho. of Reps. from N.H., 29th-30th congresses, 1845-49. Died Bath, Sept. 2, 1887; buried Village Cemetery, Bath.

JOHNSON, James Leeper, congressman; b. nr. Smithland, Ky., Oct. 30, 1818; attended pvt. schs.; studied law. Admitted to Ky. bar, 1841, began practice in Owensboro; mem. Ky. Ho. of Reps., 1844; Whig presdl. elector, 1848; mem. U.S. Ho. of Reps. (Whig) from Ky., 31st Congress, 1849-51; resumed law practice, Owensboro, also engaged in farming; judge Daviess County (Ky.) Circuit Ct., 1867. Died Owensboro, Feb. 12, 1877; buried Elmwood Cemetery, Owensboro.

JOHNSON, Jeromus, congressman; b. Wallabout, N.Y., Nov. 2, 1775; attended pub. schs. Engaged in merc. bus., N.Y.C.; mem. N.Y. Assembly, 1822; mem. U.S. Ho. of Reps. (Democrat) from N.Y, 19th-20th congresses, 1825-29; appraiser of mdse. for Port of N.Y., 1830-40. Died Goshen, N.Y., Sept. 7, 1846; buried pvt. cemetery on his estate, Goshen

JOHNSON, Sir John, Loyalist, supt. Indian affairs, b. Johnstown, N.Y., Nov. 5, 1742; s. Sir William and Catharine (Weisenberg) J.; m. Mary Watts, June 30, 1773, 1 son, Sir Adam Gordon. Capt. company N.C. Militia, 1760, col. regt. of horse; created knight in Eng., 1765, baronet, 1774; commd. maj. gen. N.Y. Militia, 1774; commd. lt. col. during Revolutionary War, served at Battle of Oriskany, 1777; supt. gen. of Six Nations of Indians in Province of Que., 1782, renewed, 1791; made home in Can., 1783, was given tract of land to compensate for N.Y. Seizure of Am. lands, became mem. Que. Provincial Council; commd. col. Brit. Army. Died Montreal, Que., Can., Jan. 4, 1830.

JOHNSON, John, congressman; b. nr. Dungannon, County Tyrone, Ireland, 1805. Came to U.S., 1818; settled in Coshocton, O., 1819; engaged in merc. bus., banking; mem. Ohio Senate, 1843-44; del. Ohio Constl. Conv., 1849-50; mem. U.S. Ho. of Reps. (Independent) from Ohio, 32d Congress, 1851-53; engaged in banking and farming, Coshocton. Died Coshocton, Feb. 5, 1867; buried Oakbridge Cemetery, Coshocton.

JOHNSON, John Telemachus, congressman; b. Great Crossings, Scott County, Ky., Oct. 5, 1788; attended Transylvania U., Lexington, Ky.; studied law. Admitted to Ky. bar, 1809, began practice in Georgetown; served as aide to Gen. William Henry Harrison during War of 1812; mem. Ky. Ho. of Reps., 5 terms; mem. U.S. Ho. of Reps. (Jacksonian Democrat) from Ky., 17th-18th congresses, 1821-25; judge ct. appeals, 1826; minister Christian Ch.; became editor Christian Messenger, 1832, Gospel Advocate, 1835, Christian, 1837; a founder Bacon Coll., Georgetown, 1836. Died Lexington, Mo., Dec. 17, 1856; buried Lexington (Ky.) Cemetery.

JOHNSON, Joseph, physician; b. Mt. Pleasant, S. C., June 15, 1776; s. William and Sarah (Nightingale) J.; grad. Coll. of Charleston, 1793; M.D., U. Pa. Med. Coll., 1797; m. Catherine Bonneau, Oct. 1802, 15 children. Began practice of medicine, Charleston, S.C., 1797; mem. S.C. Med. Soc., 1798-1862, pres., 1807; pres. Bank of U.S., Charleston, 1818-25. Author: An Experimental Inquiry into the Properties of Carbonic Acid Gas,,or Fixed Air, 1797; An Address to the Literary and Philosophical Society of South Carolina, 1822; Traditions and Reminiscences Chiefly of the American Revolution in the South, 1851. Died Pineville, S.C., Oct. 6, 1862.

JOHNSON, Joseph, gov. Va., congressman; b. Orang County, N.Y., Dec. 19, 1785. Engaged in farming, Bridgeport, Va. (now W.Va.); served as capt. of a co. Va. Riflemen, during War of 1812; mem. Va. Ho. of Dels., 1815-16, 18-22, 47-48; mem. U.S. Ho. of Reps. (Democrat) from Va., 18th-19th, 22d, 24th-26th, 29th congresses, 1823-27, Jan. 21-Mar. 3, 1833, 35-41, 45-47; del. Dem. Nat. Conv., Balt., 1844; del. Va. Constl. Conv., 1850-51; gov. Va., 1852-56; presdl. elector, 1860. Died Bridgeport, Feb. 27, 1877; buried Brick Church Cemetery, Bridgeport.

JOHNSON, Levi, ship-builder, contractor; b. Herkimer County, N.Y., Apr. 25, 1786; m. Margaret Montier, 1811. Moved to Cleve., 1809; built 1st frame house in Cleve., 1813; traded with U.S. Army during War of 1812, Detroit; built his 1st ship, 1814; built steam boat Enterprise, 1824; building contractor, Cleve., 1830-58. Died Dec. 19, 1871.

JOHNSON, Marmaduke, printer; b. Eng.; m. Ruth Cane, Apr. 28, 1670, 2 children. Contracted by Soc. for Propagation of Gospel in New Eng. to come to Boston for 3 years to print Indian translation of Bible, 1660; returned to Eng., 1664; came back to Boston, opened printshop, 1665, moved shop to Cambridge, Mass., 1665, returned to Boston, 1674. Died Dec. 25, 1674.

JOHNSON, Nathaniel, colonial gov.; b. Kebblesworth, Eng., circa 1645; s. William and Margaret (Sherwood) J.; a son, Robert. Mem. Parliament for Newcastle-on-Tyne, 1680; knighted, 1680; gov. Leeward Islands, 1686; gov. Province of S.C., 1702-08, passed act establishing Ch. of Eng. in colony of S.C.; pioneer silk culture in S.C. Died nr. Charleston, S.C., 1713.

JOHNSON, Noadiah, congressman; b. Conn., 1795; studied law. Admitted to N.Y. bar, began practice in Delhi; dist. atty. Delaware County (N.Y.), 1825-33; a publisher Delaware Gazette; mem. U.S. Ho. of Reps. (Democrat) from N.Y., 23d Congress, 1833-35; mem. N.Y. Senate, 1837-39. Died Albany, N.Y. Apr. 4, 1839; buried cemetery at Delhi.

JOHNSON, Oliver, journalist, reformer; b. Peacham, Vt., Dec. 27, 1809; s. Ziba and Sally (Lincoln) J.; m. Mary Ann White, Sept. 8, 1832; m. 2d, Jane Abbott, Aug. 27, 1875; 1 child. Editor, Christian Soldier, Boston (a newspaper opposed to Universalism), 1831; a founder New Eng. Anti-Slavery Soc., 1832, travelling agt., 1836; edited The Liberator in the absence of William Lloyd Garrison, 1833, 37, 38, 40; Boston correspondent for N.Y. Tribune, 1842-44, asst. to Horace Greeley, 1844-48; editor Anti-Slavery Bugle, Salem, Mass., 1849-53, Nat. Anti-Slavery Standard, N.Y.C., 1853-65; asso. editor The Independent, N.Y.C., 1865-70; editor N.Y. Weekly Tribune, 1870-73; campaigned for Horace Greeley in his unsuccessful presdl. race, 1872; asso. editor N.Y. Evening Post, 1881-89. Died Bklyn., Dec. 8, 1889; buried Kennet Square, Pa.

JOHNSON, Perley Brown, congressman; b. Marietta, O., Sept. 8, 1798; attended pub. schs.; studied medicine. Began practice of medicine, Marietta, 1822; moved to McConnelsville, O., 1823, practiced medicine; clk. ct. common pleas, 1825; mem. Ohio Ho. of Reps., 1833-35; Whig presdl. elector, 1840, mem. U.S. Ho. of Reps. (Whig) from Ohio, 28th Congress, 1843-45; practiced medicine, McConnelsville, 1845-47. Died McConnelsville, Feb. 9, 1870; buried McConnelsville Cemetery.

JOHNSON, Philip, congressman; b. Polkville, N.J., Jan. 17, 1818; attended Lafayette Coll., Easton, Pa., 1842-44, Union Law Sch., Easton. Plantation tutor, Miss., 1844-46; admitted to Pa. bar, 1848, began practice in Easton; clk. county ct., 1848-53; me. Pa. Ho. of Reps., 1853-54; revenue commr. 3d Jud. Dist., 1859-60; mem. U.S. Ho. of Reps. (Republican) from Pa., 37th-39th congresses, 1861-67. Died Washington, D.C., Jan. 29, 1867; buried Easton Cemetery.

JOHNSON, Reverdy, senator, U.S. atty. gen.; b. Annapolis, Md., May 21, 1796; s. John and Deborah (Ghieselen) J.; grad. St. John's Coll., Annapolis, 1811; m. Mary Mackall Bowie, Nov. 16, 1819. Admitted to Md. bar, 1815; dep. atty. gen. Md., 1816-17; mem. Md. Senate, 1821-29, 60-61; mem. U.S. Senate from Md., 1845-49, 63-July 10, 1868; atty. gen. U.S. under Pres. Taylor, 1849-50; mem. Pace Conf., Washington, D.C., 1861; U.S. minister to Eng., 1868-69. Died Annapolis, Feb. 10, 1876; buried Greenmount Cemetery, Balt.

JOHNSON, Richard Mentor, vice pres. U.S.; b. Beargrass, Ky., Oct. 17, 1781; s. Robert and Jemima (Suggett) J.; never married; 2 children by Julia Chinn (slave). Admitted to Ky. bar, 1802; mem. Ky. Ho. of Reps., 1804-07, 1850 drafted law forbidding imprisonment of debtors, 1819; mem. U.S. Ho. of Reps. (Democrat) from Ky., 10th-15th, 21st-24th congresses, 1807-19, 29-37, chmn. com. on mil. affairs; served as col. Ky. Volunteers, 1812-13; commanded U.S. forces in Battle of Thames, 1813, killed Indian chief Tecumseh during the battle; mem. U.S. Senate from Ky., 1819-29; vice pres. U.S. under Martin Van Buren, 1837-41, failed to get majority of electoral votes, only vice pres. ever elected by Senate, unsuccessful candidate for reelection 1840; founder, trustee Georgetown (Ky.) Coll. Died Frankfort, Ky., Nov. 19, 1850; buried State Cemetery, Frankfort.

JOHNSON, Richard W., army officer; b. Smithland, Ky., Feb.7, 1827; s. Dr. James L. and Jane (Leeper) J.; grad. U.S. Mil. Acad., 1849; m. Rachel Steele, 1855; m. 2d, Julia McFarland, 1894; 4 children. Commd. lt. col. 3d Ky. Cavalry, 1861; commd. brig. gen. U.S. Volunteers, 1861; assigned to Gen. Buell's army in engagements at Shiloh, Tenn., siege of Corinth, Miss.; commanded a div. of Army of Ohio in Tenn. campaign; commanded 12th div. Army of Cumberland in battles of Stones River, Chickamauga, Missionary Ridge, New Hope Ch., Ga. brevetted lt. col. for service at Battle of Chickamauga, 1863, col. for Battle of Chattanooga, 1863, maj. gen. U.S. U.S. Volunteers; commanded a div. of cavalry in Battle of Nashville, 1864 subsequently brevetted brig. gen. 1865; commd. maj. gen. U.S. gen. U.S. Army; ret. with rank of maj. gen., 1867; prof. mil. sci. U. Mo., later at U. Minn. Author: A Memoir of Gen. George H. Thomas, 1881; Manual for Colt's Breech-Loading Carbine, 1886. Died St. Paul, Apr. 21, 1897.

JOHNSON, Robert, colonial gov.; b. circa 1676; s. Sir Nathaniel Johnson; m. Margaret; 5 children including Margaret. Freeman of Newcastle-upon-Tyne, 1702/3; proprietary gov. S.C., 1717-19; 1st gov. S.C. under crown, 1731-35; helped in founding colony of Ga., 1732. Died Charleston, S.C., May 3, 1735.

JOHNSON, Robert Ward, senator; b. Scott County, Ky., July 22, 1814; s. Benjamin and Matilda (Williams) J.; grad. St. Joseph's Coll., Bardstown, Ky., 1833, Yale Law Sch., 1835; m. Sarah Smith, 1835; m. 2d, Laura Smith, after 1862; 3 children. Admitted to Ark. bar, 1835; pros. atty. Little Rock (Ark.), also ex offico atty. gen. Ark., 1840-42; mem. U.S. Ho. of Reps. from Ark., 30th-32d congresses, 1847-53; mem. U.S. Senate from Ark., July 6, 1853-61; del. to Provisional Govt. of Confederate States, 1862; mem. Confederate Senate until end of Civil War. Died Little Rock, July 26, 1879; buried Mt. Holly Cemetery, Little Rock.

JOHNSON, Samuel, clergyman, coll. pres.; b. Guilford, Conn., Oct. 14, 1696; s. Samuel and Mary (Sage) J.; grad. Collegiate Sch. (now Yale), 1714; M.A. (hon.), Oxford (Eng.) U., 1723, D.D. (hon.), 1743; M.A. (hon.,) Cambridge (Eng.) U., 1723; m. Charity (Floyd) Nicoll, Sept. 26, 1725; m. 2d, Mrs. Sarah (Hull) Beach, June 18, 1761; 3 children, including William Samuel. Ordained pastor Congl. Ch., West Haven, Conn., 1720; missionary for Soc. Propagation of the Gospel, Stratford, Conn.; ordained priest Protestant Episcopal Ch., 1723; 1st pres. King's Coll. (now Columbia), 1754-63. Author: Ethics, Elementa, or the First Principles of Moral Philosophy, 1746, reprinted with new sect. Elementa Philosophica, 1752. Died Jan. 6, 1772.

JOHNSON, Samuel, clergyman; b. Salem, Mass., Oct. 10, 1822; s. Dr. Samuel and Anna (Dodge) J.; grad. Harvard, 1842, Harvard Divinity Sch., 1846. Began preaching at Unitarian ch., Dorchester, Mass., 1846; in charge of Oxford Street Chapel, Lynn, Mass., 1853-70; visited Europe, 1860-61. Author: Oriental Religions and Their Relations to Universal Religion, India, 1872, China, 1877, Persia, 1885. Died Feb. 19, 1882.

JOHNSON, Waldo Porter, senator; b. Bridgeport, Va., Sept. 16, 1817; grad. Rector Coll., Pruntytown, Va., 1839; studied law. Admitted to Va. bar; began practice in Harrison County, Va., 1841; moved to Osceola, Mo., 1842, practiced law; served with 1st Regt., Mo. Mounted Volunteers, during Mexican War; mem. Mo. Ho. of Reps., 1847; circuit atty., 1848; judge 7th Jud. Circuit, 1851-52; mem. Washington (D.C.) Peace Conf., 1861; mem. U.S. Senate (Democrat) from Mo., Mar. 17, 1861-Jan. 10, 1862 (expelled); served to lt. col. 4th Mo. Inf., Confederate Army, during Civil War; wounded twice in Battle of Pea Ridge, 1862; engaged in recruiting troops for Gen. Price's army; filled vacancy as mem. Confederate States Senate; resumed practice of law, Osceola, 1866; pres. Mo. Constl. Conv., 1875. Died Osceola, Aug. 14, 1885; buried Forest Hill Cemetery, Kansas City, Mo.

JOHNSON, Sir William, army officer, supt. Indian affairs; b. Smithtown, County Meath, Ireland, 1715; s. Christopher and Ann (Warren) J.; m. Catharine Weisenberg, circa 1739; m. 3d, Molly Brant; children—John, Mary, Nancy. Connected with fur trading, Oswego, N.Y., 1743; erected flour mills nr. Amsterdam (N.Y.), 1744; one of his majesty's justices of the peace for Albany County (N.Y.), 1745; commissary of N.Y.for Indian affairs, 1746; responsible for supply of English garrison, Oswego, 1746; attended Albany Council, 1746; col. of Six Nations involved in transferring conduct of Indian affairs to Gov. Clinton, 1746; commanded 14 cos. of N.Y. Militia, for defense of frontiers, 1748, col. Albany Regt., 1748; mem. Council of N.Y., 1750-74; mem. Albany Congress, 1754; commanded expdn. sent against Crown Point; supt. Indian affairs, responsible for mgmt. and direction of affairs of Six Nations and their allies; maj. N.Y. Militia; created baronet, 1755; col. Six Nations, their confederates and affairs, 1756; commanded force which captured Niagara, 1759; mem. Am. Philos. Soc., 1769; trustee Queen's Coll. (now Rutgers U.), 1770; aided in opening up Mohawk Valley to settlement; helped to drive French power from N. Am.; commd. maj. gen., 1772. Died Johnstown, N.Y., July 11, 1774.

JOHNSON, William, court reporter; b. Middletown, Conn., Dec. 17, 1769; s. Asahel and Eunice (Wetmore) J.; grad. Yale, 1788; m. Maria Templeton; June 17, 1809, 4 children. Practiced law, N.Y. C., circa 1788; reporter Ct. of Errors, N.Y. State Supreme Ct., 1806-23, N.Y., Ct. of Chancery, 1814-23. Author: Report of Cases Argued and Determined in the Supreme Court of Judicature and in the Court for Trial of Impeachments and Correction of Errors, February 1806-February 1823, 20 vols.; Cases Argued and Determined in the Court for the Trial and Impeachments and the Correction of Errors, 1799-1803, 3 vols., 1806-12. Died June 25, 1848.

JOHNSON, William, asso. justice U.S. Supreme Ct.; b. Charleston, S.C., Dec. 27, 1771; s. William and Sarah (Nightingale) J.; grad. Princeton, 1790; studied law under Charles Cotesworth Pinckney; m. Sarah Bennett, Mar. 20, 1794. Admitted to S.C. bar, 1793; mem. S.C. Ho. of Reps., 1794-98, speaker, 1798; judge S.C. Ct. Common Pleas, 1798-1804; asso. justice U.S. Supreme Ct., 1803-34; believed in Federalist interpretation of Constn., but dissented from Chief Justice John Marshall's liberal decisions in cases of ex parte Bollman and Swarthwout, 1807, Fletcher vs. Peck, 1810, Dartmouth Coll. vs. Woodward, 1819; mem. Am. Philos. Soc. Author: Sketches of the Life and Correspondence of Nathanael Greene, 1822; Eulogy of Thomas Jefferson, 1826. Died Blyn., Aug. 4, 1834.

JOHNSON, William Bullein, clergyman, educator; b. Beaufort County, S.C., June 13, 1782; s. Joseph and Mary (Bullein) J.; A.M. (hon.), Brown U., 1814; m. Henrietta Kelsall Hornby, 1803. Licensed to preach by Beaufort (S.C.) Baptist Ch., 1805; pastor Euhaw (S.C.) Bapt. Ch., 1806-09, 1st Bapt. Ch., Savannah, Ga., 1811-15, Greenville, S.C., 1822-30, Edgefield (S.C.) Village Ch., 1830-52; founded 1st Bapt. Ch., Columbia, S.C., 1811; prin. Greenville Female Acad., 1822-30; founder Furman Acad. and Theol. Instn. (now Furman U.), Edgefield, 1825, trustee, 1825-52; prin. Edgefield Female Acad.; founder Johnson Female Sem. (later Johnson Female U.), Anderson, S.C., 1848, chancellor, pres. of bd., 1852-circa 1858; a founder Am. Bapt. Missionary Soc., 1814, pres., 1841; an organizer S.C. Bapt. State Conv., 1821, v.p., 1821-25, pres., 1825-52; served several terms as moderator Saluda and Edgefield Bapt. Assns.; an organizer So. Bapt. Conv., 1845, pres., 1845-52; organized Greenville Bapt. Assn., 1860. Died Greenville, Oct. 2, 1862.

JOHNSON, William Cost, congressman; b. nr. Jefferson, Md., Jan. 14, 1806; studied law. Admitted to Md. bar, 1831, began practice in Jefferson; mem. Md. Ho. of Reps., 1831-32; mem. U.S. Ho. of Reps. (Whig) from Md., 23d, 25th-27th congresses, 1833-35, 37-43; del. Md. Constl. Conv., 1835; practiced law, Washington, D.C., 1843-60. Died Washington, Apr. 14, 1860; buried Reformed Church Cemetery, Jefferson.

JOHNSON, William Ransom, legislator, horseman; b. Warren County, N.C., 1782; s. Marmaduke and Elizabeth (Ransom) J.; m. Mary Evans, 1803. Mem. N.C. Ho. of Reps. from Warren County, 1807-08, 10-14; established stables at Oakland, began career on Va. turf; mem. Va. Ho. of Dels. from Petersburg, 1818-20, from Chesterfield, County, 1821-22, reelected resigned; mem. Va. Senate, 1823-26; mem. Va. Ho. of Reps., 1828-30, 33-37; raced Sir Archy, also Pacolet, between 1808-13, won $30,000; leader, mgr. (by common consent) for the South in South-North Races, Washington, D.C., 1823, also in nearly all 30 contests until 1834 (of which the South won 17 races); leading turfman in Am. for a generation; known as The Napoleon of the Turf. Died Mobile, Ala., Feb. 10, 1849; buried Plantation Oakland, Va.

JOHNSON, William Samuel, senator, jurist, coll. pres.; b. Stratford, Conn., Oct. 7, 1727; s. Samuel and Charity (Floyd) Nicoll J: A.B., Yale, 1744, LL.D. (hon.), 1778; A.M., Harvard, 1747; D.C.L., Oxford (Eng.), U., 1766; m. Anne Beach, Nov. 5, 1749; m. 2d, Mary (Brewster) Beach, Dec. 11, 1800. Served as ensign in a Stratford co. Conn. Militia, 1753, advanced to higher grades, mem. Conn. Ho. of Reps. from Stratford, 1761, 65; Conn. del. Stamp Act Congress, 1765; assistant or mem. upper house Conn. Legislature, 1766-74; colonial agt., London, Eng., 1766; mem. Conn. Gov.'s Council, 1766-67, 71; hon. judge Conn. Superior Ct., 1771; refused appointment as del. Continental Congress, 1774; signer Declaration of Independence; mem. Continental Congress, 1784-87; chmn. "the Grand Committee" apptd. to frame U.S. Constn.; proposed measure to form separate body of Senate; 1st pres. Columbia Coll., 1787-1800; a counsellor in trial of the Susquehanna case, 1784-87; mem. U.S. Senate from Conn., 1789-91; active in shaping Judiciary Act of 1789. Died Stratford, Nov. 14, 1819.

JOHNSTON, Albert Sidney, army officer; b. Washington, Ky., Feb. 2, 1803; s. Dr. John and Abigail (Harris) J.; grad. U.S. Mil Acad., 1826; m. Henrietta Preston, Jan. 20, 1829; m. 2d, Eliza Griffin, Oct. 3, 1843; 5 children. Brevetted 2d lt. 2d Inf., U.S. Army, served at Sackett's Harbor, N.Y., 1826; commd. 2d lt., 6th Inf. at Jefferson Barracks, Mo., 1827; adjutant in Black Hawk War; resigned commn., 1834; adj. gen. Army of Tex., 1836, sr. brig. gen., 1837; sec. of war Republic of Tex., 1838-40; col. 1st Tex. Rifle Volunteers and insp. gen. at Monterrey (Mexico) during Mexican war; paymaster U.S. Army for Tex., comdr. Dept. of Tex., 1856-58; led expdn. against Mormons, 1857; comdr. Dept. of Utah, 1858-60; commd. brig. gen. U.S. Army, 1858; comdr. Dept. of Pacific, 1860; joined Confederate Army as gen. in charge of operations in West; loss of Ft. Donelson forced him to retreat, 1862; concentrating his army around Corinth (Miss.) attacked Grant at Pittsburg landing (known in North as Shiloh), Apr. 6, 1862 (a So. victory); Killed in Battle of Shiloh, Apr. 6, 1862; buried Austin, Tex.

JOHNSTON, Alexander, historian, educator; b. Bklyn., Apr. 29, 1849; son of Samuel G. Johnston; grad. Rutgers Coll., 1870; m. Mary Louise Carter, Aug. 29, 1878. Admitted to N.J. bar, 1875; taught at Rutgers Coll. Grammar Sch., 1876-79; founder, prin. Latin Sch., Norwalk, Conn., 1879-83; prof. jurisprudence and polit. economy Coll. of N.J. (now Princeton), 1883-89. Author: History of American Politics, 1879; The Genesis of a New England State (Conn.), 1883; A History of the United States for Schools, 1885; Connecticut, 1887; The United States: Its History and Constitution, 1889; American Political History (collection of articles edited by James A. Woodburn) 1905. Died Princeton, N.J., July 20, 1889.

JOHNSTON, Augustus, colonial ofcl., Loyalist; b. Perth Amboy, N.J., circa 1730; 4 children. Moved to Newport, R.I., circa 1750; helped in preparation bills for R.I. Gen. Assembly, 1754, 56; served as 1st lt. in a regt. against Crown Point; atty. gen. Colony of R.I., 1757-66; stamp distbr., 1765, colonists forced him to sign paper stating he would discontinue distbn., mob attacked his house; refused to give oath of Allegiance to colony, 1776, became Loyalist, property confiscated. Died circa 1790.

JOHNSTON, Charles, congressman; b. Salisbury, Conn., Feb. 14, 1793; attended common schs.; studied law. Admitted to N.Y. bar, practiced law; mem. U.S. Ho. of Reps. (Whig) from N.Y., 26th Congress, 1839-41; practiced law, Poughkeepsie, N. Y., 1841-45. Died Poughkeepsie, Sept. 1, 1845; buried burying ground of Christ Episcopal Ch., reinterred Rural Cemetery, Poughkeepsie, 1861.

JOHNSTON, Charles Clement, congressman; b. Longwood, nr. Farmville, Va., Apr. 30, 1795; studied law. Admitted to Va. bar, 1818, began practice in Abingdon; mem. U.S. Ho. of Reps. (States Rights Democrat) from Va., 22d Congress, 1831-32. Drowned nr. docks in Alexandria, Va., June 17, 1832; buried Congressional Cemetery, Washington, D.C.

JOHNSTON, David Claypoole, lithographer, actor; b. Phila., Mar. 1799; s. William P. and Charlotte (Rowson) J.; m. Sarah Murphy, 1830, 8 children including Thomas Murphy. Apprenticed to Francis Kearny, engraver, Phila., 1815; made debut as Henry in play Speed the Plow, Phila., 1821; actor in Phila. and Boston, 1821-26; later devoted efforts to painting, illustrating books, making drawings for comic prints; exhibited paintings at Boston Atheneum, also N.A.D., N.Y.C.; illustrated Fanny Kemble's Journal, 1835, Joseph C. Neal's Charcoal Sketches, 1838, also others. Author: Scraps (collection of comic engravings), 1830; The House That Jeff Built (satire of Jefferson Davis), 1863. Died Dorchester, Mass., Nov. 8, 1865.

JOHNSTON, Gabriel, royal gov.; b. Scotland, 1699; ed. Univ. of St. Andrews, Scotland; m. Penelope (Golland) Pheney; m. 2d, Frances. 1 dau., Penelope. Editor, The Craftsman, 1730; royal gov. N.C., 1734-54; Johnston County, N.C. named aft him; at his death the colony was near rebelli against him over his rent collection system. Di Chowan County, N.C., July 17, 1752.

JOHNSTON, Henrietta, artist. First woman a tist in America; painted pastel portraits of aristro racy of colonial S.C.; portraits include Col. Willia Rhett, 1711, Col. John Moore, 1725, Col. Daniel Mrs. Robert Brewton, Mrs. Nathaniel Broughto Frances Moore Bayard. Died Charleston, S.C., Ma 1729; buried St. Philip's Churchyard, Charleston.

JOHNSTON, John, agriculturist; b. New Gall way, Scotland, Apr. 11, 1791; m. 1818, several ch dren. Came to U.S., 1821; bought farm nr. Genev N.Y., 1821; 1st in U.S. to drain farm land by bur ing tiles; one of 1st to use lime and plaster ar surface application of manure to increase crop yiel his farm became model of advanced agrl. technique Died Geneva, Nov. 24, 1880.

JOHNSTON, John Taylor, railroad exec., b. N.Y C., Apr. 8, 1820; s. John and Margaret (Taylor J.; grad. N.Y.U., 1839; attended Yale Law Sh 1839-41; m. Frances Colles, 1850, 5 childrer admitted to N.Y. bar 1843; pres. Central R.R. N.J., 1848; acquired Lehigh & Susquehanna R.R art collector; 1st pres. Met. Mus. Art, N.Y.C 1870-89; pres. council N.Y.U., 1872-86, endow professorship of Latin langs. Died N.Y.C., Ma 24, 1893.

JOHNSTON, John Warfield, senator; b. Panice lo, nr. Abingdon, Va., Sept. 9, 1818; attended S.C Coll., law dept. of U. Va. Admitted to Va. ba 1839, began practice in Tazewell; commonwealt atty. for Tazewell County (Va.), 1844-46; mem Va. Senate, 1846-48; judge Va. Circuit Ct., 1866 70; mem. U.S. Senate (Conservative) from Va. Jan. 26, 1870-83; resumed law practice. Died Rich mond, Va., Feb. 27, 1889; buried St. Mary's Ceme tery, Wytheville, Va.

JOHNSTON, Joseph Eggleston, army officer, cor gressman; b. "Cherry Grove", Prince Edward County Va., Feb. 3, 1807; s. Peter and Mary (Wood) J. grad. U.S. Mil. Acad., 1829; m. Lydia McLane July 10, 1845. Commd. 2d lt. 4th Arty., U.S. Army 1829, 1st lt., 1836, resigned, 1837; commd. 1st lt Topog. Engrs., 1838, capt., 1846; served in Mexica War, 1846-48, in battles of Vera Cruz, Contreras Churbusco, Molino del Rey, Mexico City; wounde twice at Battle of Cerro Gordo, 3 times in Battl of Chapultepec; promoted lt. col. 1st Cavalry, U.S Army, 1855, brig. gen. and q.m., 1860, resigned t serve with Confederate Army, 1861; apptd. maj. gen Va. Militia, then brig. gen. Confederate Army 1861; served at 1st Battle of Bull Run, 1861 4th ranking gen. of Confederate Army, 1861-75 wounded at Battle of Fair Oaks; in command c Southwest forces, 1863; engaged in futile effort t reinforce Vicksburg, 1863; in command of Army c Tenn., 1863; defeated Gen. William T. Sherma at Battle of Kenesaw Mountain, June 1864; re lieved of command because he retreated before Sher man's advance to Atlanta, Ga., July 1864; reinstate (after his successor, Gen. Hood, had lost most o Army of Tenn. trying to stop Sherman) by Gen. Le to command Army of Tenn. and all forces in Fla. S.C. and Ga. to drive back Sherman, 1865; sur rendered to Sherman, 1865; railroad pres., Ark. 1866-69; moved to Richmond, 1877; mem. U.S. Ho of Reps. from Va., 46th Congress, 1879-81; U.S commr. of railroads, 1887-91. Author: Narrative o Military Operations, 1874. Died Washington, D.C. Mar. 21, 1891; buried Greenmount Cemetery, Balt

JOHNSTON, Josiah Stoddard, senator; b. Salis bury, Conn., Nov. 24, 1784; s. John and Mary (Stoddard) J.; grad. Transylvania U., 1805; studie law under William T. Barry; m. Eliza Sibley, 1814 Admitted to La. bar; mem. La. Territorial Legis lature, 1805-12; maj. La. Territorial Militia, 1809 me. La. Ho. of Reps., 1812; dist. judge La., 1812 21; commd. col. La. Militia, 1814; mem. U.S. Ho of Reps. from La., 17th Congress, 1821-23; mem U.S. Senate from La., Jan. 24, 1824-33. Killed b explosion while passenger aboard steamship Liones traveling on Red River nr. Alexandria, La., May 19 1833; buried Rapides Cemetery, Pineville, La

JOHNSTON, Peter, army officer, jurist; b Osborne's Landing, Va., Jan. 6, 1763; s. Peter an Martha (Butler) Rogers Johnson; m. Mary Wood June 23, 1788; m. 2d, Ann Bernard, Dec. 13, 1828 10 children including Joseph Eggleston. Commd. lt cavalry Continental Army under command Lt. Col Henry Lee, 1781; adj., capt. light corps, later brig gen. militia; mem. Legislature, 1792; speaker Va Ho. of Dels., 1805-06, 06-07; rep. from Va. o commn. to settle Tenn. boundary question, 1802 judge Va. Gen. Ct., 1811. Died Dec. 8, 1831.

JOHNSTON, Richard Malcolm, author, educator b. Oak Grove, nr. Powelton, Ga., Mar. 8, 1822 s. Malcolm and Catherine (Davenport) J.; grad Mercer U., Penfield (now Macon), Ga., 1841; m Mary Frances Mansfield, 1844, several children. Ad mitted to Ga. bar, 1842; partner with Eli Baxter parta, Ga., 1842-44, with Linton Stephens, 1851-7; taught sch., 1844-51; prof. rhetoric and belles-ettres U. Ga., 1857-61; conducted sch. for boys, Rockby, Ga., 1862-67, later established Pen Lucy Sch., Balt.; clk. U.S. Bur. Edn., Washington, D.C., 1896-98; lectr. Catholic Summer Sch., Plattsburg, N.Y., 1895-98; wrote stories set primarily in pre-war Ga. (idealized Southern life). Author: The English Classics, 1860; Dukesboro Tales, 1871; (with William H. Browne) English Literature, 1872; Life of Alexander H. Stephens, 1878; Old Mark Langston, 1884; Two Gray Tourists, 1885; Ogeechee Cross-Firings, 1889; Widow Guthrie, 1890; The Primes and Their Neighbors, 1891; Mr. Billy Downs and His Likes, 1892; Mr. Fortner's Marital Claims, 1892; Little Ike Templin, 1894; Old Times in Middle Georgia, 1897; Autobiography of Colonel William Malcolm Johnston, 1900. Died Balt., Sept. 23, 1898.

JOHNSTON, Samuel, Continental congressman, senator; b. Dundee, Scotland, Dec. 15, 1733; s. Samuel and Helen (Scrymoure) J.; m. Frances Cathcart. Came to Am., 1736; provincial treas. Northern div. of N.C.; mem. N.C. Assembly, 1760; mem. Com. of Correspondence, 1773; del. 1st-4th N.C. provincial congresses, 1774, pres. 3d-4th congresses; dep. naval officer Port of Edenton (N.C.); moderator Revolutionary Conv., 1775; colonial treas. N.C., 1775; mem. at large N.C. Provincial Council Safety; dist. paymaster of troops; mem. commn. to codify laws then in force; mem. N.C. Senate, 1779, 83, 84; mem. Continental Congress from N.C., 1780-82, declined to serve as pres.; mem. comm. to settle boundary dispute between Mass. and N.Y., 1785; gov. N.C., 1787-89; pres. N.C. Conv. which refused to ratify U.S. Constn., 1788, N.C. Conv. which adopted Constn., 1789; mem. U.S. Senate (Federalist from N.C.; 1st trustee U. N.C., served for 12 years; judge Superior Ct. N.C., 1800-03. Died nr. Edenton, Aug. 18, 1816; buried Johnston Burial Ground, nr. Edenton.

JOHNSTON, Thomas, engraver, painter; b. 1708; m. Rachel Thwing, 1730; m. 2d, Bathsheba Thwing, Aug. 17, 1747; many children including Thomas, John. Worked as engraver, painter, portraitist (scenic and heraldic), topographer and organ builder, Boston; built organ for Old North Ch., Boston, 1759; his maps include the Canada River, The Kennebec and Sagadahoc Rivers; engravings include Prospect of Yale College, Battle of Lake George. Died Boston, May 8, 1767; buried King's Chapel, Boston.

JOHNSTON, Thomas Murphy, artist; b. Boston, 1834; s. David Claypoole Johnston. Commd. to execute crayon portrait of Abraham Lincoln, Springfield, Ill., 1860; practiced lithography; painted landscapes and religious subjects; went to France to study, 1868. Died Paris, France, Feb. 28, 1869.

JOHNSTON, William, congressman; b. Ireland, 1819; attended pub. schs.; studied law. Came to U.S., settled in Ohio; admitted to Ohio bar; practiced law, Mansfield, O., 1859-63; mem. U.S. Ho. of Reps. (Democrat) from Ohio, 38th Congress, 1863-65. Died Mansfield, May 1, 1866; buried Mansfield Cemetery.

JOHNSTON, Zachariah, legislator; b. nr. Staunton, Va., 1742; s. William Johnston; m. Ann Robertson. Commd. capt. Va. Militia, 1776; served in campaigns against Indians in West and in defeat of Cornwallis, 1781; mem. Va. Ho. of Dels. from Augusta County, 1778-92, from Rockbridge County, 1792-circa 1798; leader in securing passage of Va.'s act for establishing religious freedom, 1786; mem. Va. Conv. to ratify U.S. Constn., 1788; worked on scheme to connect rivers of Western Va. with Potomac navigation plan proposed by George Washington. Died Jan. 1800.

JOHNSTONE, Job, jurist; b. Fairfield Dist., S. C., June 7, 1793; s. John and Mary (Caldwell) J.; grad. S.C. Coll., 1810; m. Eliza Johnstone, Nov. 14, 1816; m. 2d, Aelia DeWalt, Aug. 7, 1844; 10 children. Admitted to bar, 1818; mem. S.C. Nullification Conv., 1832; clk. S.C. Senate, 1826; chancellor S.C., 1830-47; pres. Equity Ct. of Appeals, 1847-59; asso. justice Ct. of Appeals S.C., 1859-62. Died Newberry, S.C., Apr. 8, 1862.

JOLIET, Louis, explorer; b. Beaupre, Que., Can., Sept. 21, 1645; s. Johan and Marie (d'Abancour) J.; m. Clair Brissat, Oct. 7, 1675. Went to Europe, studied hydrography in France, 1667; sent to take supplies to Jean Pere and to trade with Indians, 1669, then searched for copper in Lake Superior; his party 1st to pass down Great Lakes by way of Detroit River into Lake Erie, 1669; sent with St. Tusson's party, present at ceremony, to annex western country to crown of France, held at Greenbay, 1670; expert cartographer; chosen to lead expdn. set up by Gov. Frontenac to explore Mississippi River (with Father Marquette as chaplain of the expdn.), left May 17, 1673, went by Fox and Wisconsin rivers to Mississippi River, June 17, 1673; went down Mississippi River, to Arkansas River, then being sure it flowed to sea, returned to Illinois and Des Plaines rivers, thereby passing future site of Chgo.; lost maps and journals when his canoe overturned near Montreal; given Anticosti Island as reward for accomplishing expdn.; became trader in Hudson Bay area; explored coast of Labrador, 1694; made royal pilot for St. Lawrence, 1694; granted seniority of Joliet, south of Que., 1697; royal prof. hydrographer for Can., 1697; (name also spelled Jolliet). Died Can., May 1700; buried Mignan Island, Can.

JONES, Abner, religious leader; b. Royalston, Mass., Apr. 28, 1772; s. Asa and Dorcas (Wade) J.; m. Damaris Pryor, 1796; m. 2d, Nancy F. Clark, Aug. 1, 1839. Baptized in Baptist Ch., 1793; founded ch. based on belief that Bible was only source of religion and that denominational ties were unnecessary, at Lyndon, Vt., 1801; ordained pastor by (as Christian brother without denomination) Free Will Bapt. Council; travelled throughout New Eng. as evangelist; founded chs., Hanover, N.H., 1802, Piermont, Vt., 1803, Portsmouth, N.H., 1805; presiding officer U.S. Christian Conf., Milan, N.Y., 1832; (movement of primitive Christianity developed later as Disciples of Christ). Author: Memoirs of the Life and Experience, Travels and Preaching of Abner Jones, 1807. Died Exeter, N.H., May 29, 1841.

JONES, Alexander, journalist, physician; b. N.C., 1802; M.D., U. Pa. Med. Sch., 1822. Practiced medicine, N.Y.C.; contbd. to newspapers, also corr. for English papers at N.Y.C.; wrote under name "Sandy Hook"; wrote 1st news story to be sent by wire from N.Y.C., 1846; organized N.Y. Asso. Press (1st cooperative newspaper wire service in U.S.), served as 1st gen. agt.; comml. reporter N.Y. Herald 1851-63; mem. St. David's Soc., N.Y.C. Author: Cuba in 1851, published 1851; Historical Sketch of the Electric Telegraph, 1852; The Cymry of '76; or Welshmen and Their Descendants of the American Revolution, 1855. Died N.Y.C., Aug. 22, 1863.

JONES, Allen, Continental congressman; b. Halifax County, N.C., Dec. 24, 1739; s. Robert (Robin) and Sarah (Cobb) J.; attended Eton Coll., Eng.; m. Mary Haynes, Jan. 21, 1762; m. 2d, Rebecca Edwards, Sept. 3, 1768. Clk. of Superior Court for Halifax dist.; mem. N.C. Ho. of Commons from Northampton County, 1873-75; assisted in suppression of "Regulators", 1771; mem. Com. of Safety for Halifax dist., 1775; represented Northampton in 5 N.C. provincial congresses, 1774-76, mem. coms. to provide mil. defense, to establish temporary forms of civil govt., to impower N.C. dels. in Congress to concur with those of other colonies in declaring independence, 1776, and to frame state constn. of 1776; commd. brig. gen. N.C. Militia for Halifax dist. 1776; mem. N.C. Senate, 1777-79, speaker, 1778, 79; mem. Continental Congress, 1779-80, mem. council extraordinary charged with conduct of war, 1781; mem. N.C. Council of State, 1782; mem. N.C. Senate from Northampton County, 1783, 84, 87. Died Northampton County, Nov. 14, 1807.

JONES, Anson, pres. Republic of Tex.; b. Great Barrington, Mass., Jan. 20, 1798; s. Solomon and Sarah (Strong) J.; M.D., Jefferson Med. Coll., 1827; m. Mrs. Mary McCrory, May 17, 1839. Practiced medicine, Phila., 1827-32, New Orleans Brazoria, Tex., 1833; Physician Tex. Army under Sam Houston, 1836; chmn. mass meeting which drew up resolutions in favor of Declaration of Independence of Tex., Dec. 1835; judge adv. gen. in war for Tex. independence, 1836-37; rep. in 2d Tex. Congress, 1837; Tex. minister to Washington (D.C.), 1837-39; elected to Tex. Senate; v.p. ex officio Republic of Tex., 1840, sec. of state, 1841-44, last pres., 1844-47; unsuccessful candidate for U. S. Senate, 1857; Committed suicide at Capital Hotel, Houston, Tex., Jan. 9, 1858.

JONES, Benjamin, congressman; b. Winchester, Va., Apr. 13, 1787; Learned cabinetmaker's trade; moved to Wooster, O., 1812, engaged in merc. bus.; justice of peace, 1815; commr. Wayne County (O.), 1818; mem. Ohio Ho. of Reps., 1821-22; Democratic presdl. elector, 1824; mem. Ohio Senate, 1829-32; mem. U.S. Ho. of Reps. (Dem.) from Ohio, 23d-24th congresses, 1833-37. Died Wooster, Apr. 24, 1861; buried Oak Hill Cemetery, Wooster.

JONES, Calvin, physician; b. Great Barrington, Mass., Apr. 2, 1775; s. Ebeneezer and Susannah (Blackmer) J.; m. Temperance Williams, 1819. Licensed to practice medicine in Mass., 1792; practiced medicine, Great Barrington, 1792-95, Smithfield, N.C., 1795, Raleigh, N.C., 1803-32; a founder N.C. Med. Soc., 1799; mem. lower house N.C. Legislature, 1799, 1802, 07; co-owner newspaper Star, Raleigh, 1808-15; adjutant gen. N.C. Militia, 1808, maj. gen. N.C. Militia during War of 1812, organized coastal defenses of state; one of 1st physicians in state to urge use of inoculation against smallpox; active Freemason; retired, 1832, moved to estate nr. Bolivar, Tenn. Died at estate Pontine, nr. Bolivar, Sept. 20, 1846.

JONES, Catesby Ap Roger, navy officer; b. Fairfield, Va., Apr. 15, 1821; s. Roger and Mary Ann Mason (Page) J.; m. Gertrude Tartt, Mar. 23, 1865, 6 children. Apptd. midshipman U.S. Navy, 1836, served on ships including frigate Columbia and schooner Shark, passed midshipman, 1842; asst. in surveying Tampa Bay, 1843; served in Pacific Squadron during Mexican War, seeing no active service; lt., 1849; assisted John A. Dahlgren in perfecting Dahlgren gun while on ordnance duty, Washington, D.C., 1853; resigned U.S. commn., became capt. Va. Navy, 1861; lt. Confederate Navy, 1861; exec. officer on ironclad Virginia (known in North as Merrimac), acting comdr. during famous fight with Monitor, 1862; became comdr. ship Chattachooche, 1862; commanded naval gun foundry and ordnance works, Selma, Ala., 1863; comdr. Confederate Navy, 1863; became businessman after Civil War. Shot by J.A. Harral during a quarrel, Selma, June 20, 1877.

JONES, Charles Colcock, historian; b. Savannah, Ga., Oct. 28, 1831; s. Charles Colcock and Mary (Jones) J.; grad. Coll. of N.J. (now Princeton); grad. Harvard Law Sch., 1855; m. Ruth Whitehead, 1858; m. 2d, Eva B. Eve, 1863. Admitted to bar, Savannah, 1855; practiced in Savannah; served as col. arty. Confederate Army, 1861-65; practiced in N.Y. C., 1865-77, did research in hist. subjects; moved to Augusta, Ga., 1877-93, lectured and wrote hist. works. Author: Antiquities of the Southern Indians, Particularly of the Georgia Tribes, 1873; The Dead Towns of Georgia, 1878; History of Georgia, 1883; Memorial History of Augusta, Georgia, 1890; History of Savannah, Georgia, 1890. Died Augusta, July 19, 1893; buried Augusta.

JONES, Daniel Terryll, congressman; b. Hebron, Conn., Aug. 17, 1800; grad. med. dept. Yale, 1826. Began practice of medicine, Amboy, N.Y.; moved to Baldwinsville, N.Y., 1841; mem. U.S. Ho. of Reps. (Democrat) from N.Y., 32d-33d congresses, 1851-55; chmn. N.Y. State Republican Conv., 1858; resumed practice of medicine. Died Baldwinsville, Mar. 29, 1861; buried Riverside Cemetery, Baldwinsville.

JONES, David, clergyman; b. New Castle County, Del., May 12, 1736; s. Morgan and Eleanor (Evans) J.; attended Hopewell Acad., N.J., circa 1757-58; m. Anne Stillwell, Feb. 22, 1762. Licensed to preach by Baptist Ch. in N.J., 1761; ordained to ministry Bapt. Ch., 1766; pastor ch., Freehold, N.J., 1766-75, Great Valley Bapt. Ch., Chester County, Pa., 1775-86, 92-1820, Southhampton Bapt. Ch., Bucks County, Pa., 1786-92; an outspoken colonial patriot, served as chaplain Anthony Wayne's div. of Pa. troops, 1776-83; also chaplain to Pa. troops during War of 1812. Author: A Journal of Two Visits Made to . . . Indians on the Ohio River, 1774; The Doctrine of Laying on the Hands Examined and Vindicated, 1786. Died Chester County, Feb. 5, 1820; buried Great Valley Ch. Cemetery.

JONES, David Rumph, army officer; b. Orangeburg Dist., S.C., Apr. 5, 1825; s. Donald Bruce and Mary (Rumph) J.; grad. U.S. Mil. Acad., 1846; m. Rebecca Taylor. Served as 2d lt. 2d Inf., U.S. Army during Mexican War; brevetted 1st lt. for bravery at battles of Contreras, Churubusco, 1852; served in Adj. Gen.'s Dept. on Pacific Coast, also St. Louis; commd. maj. Confederate Army, chief of staff to Gen Beauregard besieging Ft. Sumter, 1861; assigned to command 3d brigade in Army of Potomac; brig. gen. comdg. brigade in Battle of Bull Run, 1861; commd. maj. gen., 1862; participated in Battle of Fair Oaks, 1862; fought under Longstreet at 2d Battle of Bull Run, Battle of Antietam. Died Richmond, Va., Jan. 15, 1863.

JONES, Francis, congressman; studied law. Admitted to Tenn. bar, began practice in Winchester; solictor gen. 3d Tenn. Dist., 1815; mem. U.S. Ho. of Reps. from Tenn., 15th-17th congresses, 1817-23; resumed practice of law, Winchester. Died Winchester.

JONES, Gabriel, lawyer; b. Williamsburg, Va., May 17, 1724; s. John and Elizabeth (Jones); m. Margaret Morton, 1749, 4 children. Served law apprenticeship, London, Eng.; returned to Am. circa 1745; settled in Va., became king's atty. for Frederick and Augusta counties until 1775; friend and mentor of George Washington in 1750's and 1760's; aided Washington in election to Va. Ho. of Burgesses, 1758; had Loyalist sympathies, 1774-76; became adherent Am. cause during Revolution; prosecutor Rockingham County, Va., 1775-circa 1780; commr. Va. Assembly to Ft. Pitt on diplomatic mission, 1777; mem. Va. House of Burgesses, 1783; mem. Va. Conf. to ratify U.S. Constn., 1788; ardent Federalist, favored Constn. Author: (polit. pamphlet) A Refutation of the Charges . . ., 1804. Died Frederick County, Va., Oct. 6, 1806.

JONES, George, senator, mayor; b. Savannah, Ga., Feb. 25, 1766; s. Noble Wymberley Jones; studied medicine. Practiced medicine; participated in Am. Revolution, imprisoned on an English ship, 1780-81; mem. Ga. Ho. of Reps., Ga. Senate; served as capt. of a co. of Savannah reserves during War of 1812; mem. bd. aldermen Savannah, 1793-94, 1802-03, 14-15; mayor of Savannah, 1812-14; judge Eastern Jud. Circuit of Ga., 1804-07; mem. U.S. Senate from Ga., Aug. 27-Nov. 7, 1807. Died Savannah, Nov. 13, 1838; buried Bonaventure Cemetery, Savannah.

JONES, George, naval chaplain; b. York, Pa., July 30, 1800; s. Robert and Elizabeth (Dunnman) J.; grad. Yale, 1823; m. Mary Silliman, 1837. Taught sch., Washington, D.C., 1823-25; sec. to comdr. of ship Brandywine, U.S. Navy, 1825-28; tutor Yale, 1828-30; rector Episcopal ch., Middletown, Conn., 1830-31; ordained to ministry Episcopalian Ch., 1830; served as chaplain U.S. Navy in ship United States, later in Delaware, 1832-36; chaplain Norfolk (Va.) Navy Yard, 1836-40; chaplain several vessels including Columbus and Constitution, 1840-45; prof. English, U.S. Naval Acad., Annapolis, Md., 1845-50, chaplain, 1857-61; accompanied Commodore Matthew C. Perry on expdn. to Japan, aided in writing ofcl. report of journey, 1851-56; retired from Navy, 1862; served in mil. hosps. as chaplain and nurse during Civil War, Washington, D.C., also Annapolis. Author: Narrative of an American Squadron to the China Seas and Japan, 1856; Life Scenes from the Old Testament, 1868. Died Phila., Jan. 22, 1870; buried Phila.

JONES, George, newspaper publisher; b. Poultney, Vt., Aug. 16, 1811; s. John and Barbara (Davis) J.; m. Sarah Gilbert, 1836. Owned retail business, N.Y.C., 1832-41; in business office of newspaper Tribune, N.Y.C., 1841-51; co-owner (with Henry J. Raymond) N.Y. Times, 1851-60, bus. mgr., 1856-69, also directed editorial policy after Raymond's death (1869); pressed Times' expose of Tweed ring in N.Y.C. until Tweed's downfall, 1871; supported Republicans politically. Died N.Y.C., Aug. 12, 1891; buried N.Y.C.

JONES, George Wallace, senator, diplomat; b. Vincennes, Ind., Apr. 12, 1804; s. John Rice and Mary (Barger) J.; grad. Transylvania U., Lexington, Ky., 1825; m. Josephine Gregoire, Jan. 7, 1829. Clk., U.S. cts., Mo., 1826; del. from Mich. Territory (representing Wis. area) to U.S. Congress, 1835-36, from Wis. Territory, 1837-39; surveyor pub. lands for Wis. and Ia. territories, 1840-41, 46-48; mem. U.S. Senate from Ia., Dec. 7, 1848-59; U.S. minister resident to New Granada, 1859-61; arrested (by order of Sec. Seward) and charged with disloyalty because of correspondence with college friend Jefferson Davis, 1861, released by order of Pres. Lincoln, Sept. 1861. Died Dubuque, Ia., July 22, 1896; buried Mt. Olivet Cemetery, Dubuque.

JONES, George Washington, congressman; b. King and Queen County, Va., Mar. 15, 1806; ed. common schs. Apprenticed to saddler's trade; justice of peace, 1832-35; mem. Tenn. Ho. of Reps., 1835-39, Va. Senate, 1838-41; clk. Lincoln County (Tenn.) Ct., 1840-43; mem. U.S. Ho. of Reps. (Democrat) from Tenn., 28th-35th congresses, 1843-59; del. Washington (D.C.) Peace Conv., 1861, did not attend; mem. Confederate Ho. of Reps., from Tenn., 1862-64; del. Tenn. Constl. Conv. 1870; trustee Tenn. Hosp. for Insane, 1871-84. Died Fayetteville, Tenn., Nov. 14, 1884; buried Rose Hill Cemetery, Fayetteville.

JONES, Hugh, clergyman, mathematician, historian; b. England, circa 1670; probably attended Oxford (Eng.) U. Came to Va., circa 1716; apptd. prof. mathematics Coll. William and Mary, also chaplain Va. Ho. of Burgesses, minister of Jamestown, lectr. Bruton Ch., 1717-21; returned to Eng., 1721; returned to Va., did parochial work at St. Stephen's Parish, King and Queen County; minister William and Mary Parish, Charles County, Md., 1726-31; rector St. Stephen's Parish, Cecil County, Md., 1731-60; against popery and Jesuitism, avid Hanoverian. Author: The Present State in Virginia, 1724; A Short English Grammar, 1724. Died Sept. 8, 1760.

JONES, Isaac Dashiell, congressman; b. "Wetcpquin," Somerset County, Md., Nov. 1, 1806; grad. Washington Acad., Somerset County, Md. Asst. tutor Washington Acad.; admitted to Md. bar, began practice in Princess Anne, Md.; mem. Md. Ho. of Dels., 1832, 35, 40, 66; mem. U. S. Ho. of Reps. (Whig) from Md., 27th Congress, 1841-43; del. Md. constl. convs., 1864- 67; atty. gen. Md., 1867; judge Balt. Ct. Arbitration, 1877; mem. Md. Hist. Soc., Md. Bible Soc., bd. dirs. Md. State Sch. for Deaf, Frederick, 1867-93, Md. Sch. for Colored Blind and Deaf, Balt., 1872-93. Died Balt., July 5, 1893; buried Greenmount Cemetery, Balt.

JONES, Jacob, naval officer; b. Smyrna, Del., Mar. 1768; s. Jacob Jones; m. 1st, Miss Sykes; m. 3d, Ruth Lusby, 1821; 6 children, including Richard. Clk., Del. Supreme C.; commd. midshipman U.S. Navy, served on frigate United States, 1799; promoted lt., 1801; 2d lt. on ship Philadelphia grounded and captured off Tripoli, 1803; comdr. Wasp, 1810; awarded gold medal by U.S. Congress; captured Frolic (a Brit. sloop of war, under Capt. Whingates), 1812; commd. capt., given command of ship Macedonian in Stephen Decatur's squadron operating in Mediterranean Sea, 1813, comdr. Mediterranean Squadron, 1821-23; navy commr. Pacific Squadron, 1826-29; in charge of Phila. Naval asylum, until 1850. Died Phila., Aug. 3, 1850.

JONES, James, congressman; b. Md.; attended acad., Augusta, Ga.; studied law. Admitted to Ga. bar, practiced in Savannah; 1st lt. East Co., Chatham County Regt., Ga. Militia, 1790; mem. Ga. Ho. of Reps., 1796-98; del. Ga. Constl. Conv., 1798; mem. U.S. Ho. of Reps. (Republican) from Ga., 6th Congress, 1799-1801. Died Washington, D. C., Jan. 11, 1801; buried Congressional Cemetery, Washington.

JONES, James, congressman; b. Nottoway Parish, Amelia (now Nottoway) County, Va., Dec. 11, 1772; grad. Hampden-Sydney Coll., 1791; attended Jefferson Med. Coll.; M.D., U. Edinburgh (Scotland), 1796. Practiced medicine, engaged in farming, Amelia County; mem. Va. Ho. of Dels., 1804-09, 18, 27-29; mem. Va. Privy Council, 1809-11; served in War of 1812; dir. gen. hosp. and med. stores and rations, 1813; mem. Va. Ho. of Dels., 1818; presdl. elector, 1824, 28, 32, 36, 40; mem. U.S. Ho. of Reps. (Democrat) from Va., 16th-17th congresses, 1819-23. Died "Mountain Hall" nr. Nottoway, Apr. 25, 1848; buried family burying ground "Mountain Hall."

JONES, James Chamberlayne, senator, philanthropist; b. Davidson County, Tenn., Arp. 20, 1809; s. Peter and Catherine (Chappell) J.; m. Sarah Munford, Aug. 1829. Mem. Tenn. Gen. Assembly, 1839; presdl. dist. elector from Wilson County, Tenn. on Harrison ticket, 1840; campaigned against James Polk (known as Polk-Jones Contest), 1841, 43; gov. Tenn., 1841-45; del. to Nat. Whig Conv., 1848; Whig presdl. elector, 1848; prin. achievements include: starting of present state capitol, sch. for blind at Nashville, sch. for deaf mutes at Knoxville; pres. Memphis & Charleston R.R., 1850; mem U.S. Senate from Tenn. (Whig), 1851-57. Died Memphis, Tenn., Oct. 29, 1859; buried Elmwood Cemetery, Memphis.

JONES, James Taylor, congressman; b. Richmond, Va., July 20, 1832; grad. Princeton, 1852; grad. Law Sch., U. Va., 1855. Admitted to the bar, 1856; began practice of law, Demopolis, Ala.; enlisted as pvt. 4th Ala. Regt., Confederate Army, during Civil War, elected capt. Co. D., 1862; judge advocate Confederate War Dept., 1864-65; del. Ala. Constl. Conv., 1865; mem. Ala. Senate, 1872-73; mem. U.S. Ho. of Reps. (Democrat) from Ala., 45th, 48th-50th congresses, 1877-79, Dec. 3, 1883-89; judge 1st Jud. Circuit of Ala., 1890-95. Died Demopolis, Feb. 15, 1895; buried Lyon Cemetery, Demopolis.

JONES, Jehu Glancy, congressman, diplomat; b. Berks County, Pa., Oct. 7, 1811; s. Jehu and Sarah (Glancy) J.; attended Kenyon Coll., Gambier, O.; m. Anna Rodman, June 23, 1832, 9 children. Ordained deacon Episcopal Ch., 1834, priest, 1835; admitted to Easton (Pa.) bar, 1842, Berks County bar, 1845; dist. atty. Berks County, 1847-49; del., v.p. Nat. Democratic Conv., Balt., 1848, Cincinnati, 1856; del. Pa. Dem. Conv., 1848, 49, 55, pres. 1855; mem. U.S. Ho. of Reps. from Pa., 33d-35th congresses, 1851-53, Feb. 4, 1854-Oct. 30, 1858, chmn. ways and means com., 1857-58; del. Dem. Nat. Conv., 1856; U.S. minister to Austria, 1858-61. Died Reading, Pa., Mar. 24, 1878; buried Charles Evans Cemetery, Reading.

JONES, Joel, coll. pres., mayor Phila.; b. Coventry, Conn., Oct. 25, 1795; s. Amasa and Elizabeth (Huntington) J.; grad. Yale, 1817; attended Litchfield (Conn.) Law Sch.; m. Eliza Sparhawk, June 14, 1831, 6 children, including Samuel Huntington, Rev. John Sparhawk. Admitted to bar, Luzerne County, Pa.; founder Lafayette College, Easton, Pa.; a commr. to revise Civil Code of Pa., 1830, wrote Reports of a Commission to Revise the Civil Code of Pennsylvania; asso. judge Dist. Ct. of Phila., 1835, presiding judge, 1845-47; 1st pres. Girard Coll., Phila., 1847-49; mayor Phila., 1849. Author: A Manual of Pennsylvania Land Law. Died Phila., Feb. 3, 1860.

JONES, John, physician; b. Jamaica, L.I., N.Y., 1729; s. Dr. Evan and Mary (Stephenson) J.; grad. U. Rheims, 1751. Prof. surgery and obstetrics King's Coll. (now Columbia), 1767-76; founder (with Dr. S. Bard), attending physician N.Y. Hosp., 1771; credited as an organizer Med. Dept. of Continental Army; attending physician Pa. Hosp., 1780; pres. Humane Soc.; attended Pres. Washington in Phila., 1790; 1st v.p. Coll. Physicians of Phila., 1787; Author: Plain, Concise, Practical Remarks on the Treatment of Wounds and Fractures, Designed for the Use of Young Military Surgones of America (1st surg. text book in Am. colonies), 1775; translated Disease Incident to Armies (VanSwieten). Died Phila. June 23, 1791.

JONES, John B., army officer; b. Fairfield, S.C. Dec. 22, 1834; s. Henry and Nancy (Robertson) J. grad. Mt. Zion Coll., Winnsboro, S.C., circa 1855 m. Mrs. A.J. Anderson, Feb. 25, 1879. Rancher Navarro, Tex., circa 1856-61; adjutant Tex. 15t Inf., Confederate Army, 1861-63; capt. Tex. Inf brigade, 1863-65; elected mem. Tex. Legislature 1868, denied seat by reconstrn. regime; maj. Fron tier Battalion of Tex. Rangers, 1874-79, suppresse Indian violence Western borders of state, pursue outlaws in interior regions; pacified mob in El Pas (Tex.) during "Salt War," 1877; adjutant gen of Tex., 1879-81. Died Austin, Tex., July 19, 1881 buried Austin.

JONES, John Beauchamp, editor, author; b. Balt., Mar. 6, 1810; m. Frances Custis, 1840. Editor, Balt. Sunday Visiter, circa 1839-42; editor Madisonian newspaper (mouthpiece of Tyler adminstrn.), Washington, D.C., 1842; engaged in writing novels and poetry, 1840's, 50's; editor Southern Monitor newspaper, Phila., 1857-61, represented So. polit. viewpoint; clk. War Dept., Confederate States Am., Richmond, 1861-65; published, 1866. Author: (novels) Wild Western Scenes, 1841, The Western Merchant, 1849, The Monarchist, 1852, The War Path, 1858; Rebel War Clerk's Diary (provides useful hist. information about econ. and social aspects of life in Confederate capitol), 2 vols., 1866. Died Burlington, N.J., Feb. 4, 1866; buried Burlington.

JONES, John Paul, naval officer; b. Kirkcudbrightshire, Scotland, July 6, 1747; s. John and Jean (Macduff) Paul. First mate on slave ship Two Friends, 1766; commanded mcht. ship John, on two voyages to West Indies, 1769-70; added Jones to his name, 1773; master ship Betsey of London, 1773; commd. lt., 1775; sr. 1st lt., 1st Continental Navy, 1775, 1st ranking officer in list chosen from colonies south of Pa.; hoisted flag of Colonial Am. on board the Alfred, 1775 (displayed for 1st time); commanded ship Providence, later chosen capt.; commanded sloop Ranger, 1777; made successful offensive cruise in waters around Brit. Isles, captured Drake (1st Brit. warship to surrender to a Continental vessel); commanded French ship Duras, forty guns, renamed Bonhomme Richard, 1779, defeated Brit. ship Serapis, Sept. 23, 1779; received Cross of Instn. of Mil. Merit which entitled him to be called "Chevalier," 1781; unanimously elected to command the America, 1781; presented with Gold medal by U.S. Congress, 1787; served as rear adm. with Russian Navy on Black Sea, 1788-90; decorated Order of St. Ann; resided in Paris, France, 1790-92; remembered for attributed saying (when asked if he was surrendering): "Sir, I have not yet begun to fight." Died Paris, France, July 18, 1792; remains brought to U.S., 1905; buried U. S. Naval Acad., Annapolis, Md.

JONES, John Taylor, missionary; b. New Ipswich, N.H., July 16, 1802; s. Elisha and Persia (Taylor) J.; attended Boston U.; grad. Amherst Coll., 1825; attended Andover Theol. Sem., Newton Theol. Sem.; m. Eliza Coltman Grew, July 14, 1830; m. 2d, Judith Leavitt, 1840; m. 3d, Sarah Sleeper, 1847. Ordained to ministry Baptist Ch., 1830; missionary in Moolmein, Burma, 1831; went to Siam, 1833, 1st English missionary to master Siamese lang., 1833; his major task was to translate religious terminology into Siamese terms. Author: Catechism on Geography and Astronomy, 1834; Brief grammatical Notices of the Siamese Language, 1842; The New Testament Translated from the Greek into Siamese, 1844. Died Bangkok, Siam, Sept. 13, 1851.

JONES, John William, physician, congressman; b. Rockville, Md., Apr. 14, 1806; attended Carlisle (Ky.) Sem.; attended U. Pa., 1830-31; grad. Jefferson Med. Coll., 1836. Began practice of medicine, Washington, Tenn., 1826; apptd. regtl. surgeon 96th Regt., Tenn. Militia, 1827; moved to Monroe, later to Campbellton, Ga., 1829, practiced medicine; regtl. surgeon 73d Regt., Ga. Militia, 1830; moved to Culloden, Ga., 1833; mem. Ga. Ho. of Reps., 1837; moved to Griffin, Ga., 1841, practiced medicine; pres. Griffin Med. Soc.; mem. U.S. Ho. of Reps. (Whig) from Ga., 30th Congress, 1847-49; declined appointment by Pres. Taylor as consul at Havana, Cuba; resumed practice of medicine, Oak Bowery, Ala.; trustee Oak Bowery Female Coll., 1850; moved to Auburn, Ala., 1851; a founder Auburn Masonic Female Coll. (now Auburn Coll.); prof. Atlanta Med. Coll. (now Emory U.), 1856-62, 65-70; moved to Atlanta, Ga., 1856; served as surgeon Confederate Army, during Civil War. Died Decatur, Ga., Apr. 27, 1871; buried Oakland Cemetery, Atlanta.

JONES, John Winston, congressman; b. Amelia County, Va., Nov. 22, 1791; s. Alexander and Mary Ann (Winston) J.; grad. law dept. Coll. Wiliam and Mary, 1803; m. Harriet Boisseau. Admitted to Va., bar, 1813; pros. atty. 5th Va. ud. Circuit, 1818-35; mem. Va. Constl. Conv., 829-30; mem. U.S. Ho. of Reps. from Va., 24th-8th congresses, 1835-45, speaker, 1843-45, began recedent which gave speaker pro tem the right to hoose coms. in which he had a personal interest; em. Va. Legislature from Chesterfield County, 846-47. Died Chesterfield, Va., Jan. 29, 1848; uried family cemetery at "Bellwood" nr. Petersurg, Va.

JONES, Joseph, Continental congressman; b. King George County, Va., 1727; s. James and Hester J.; n. Mary Taliaferro, before 1758. Admitted to Inner Temple, 1749, Middle Temple, 1751; called to English bar, 1751; dep. atty. for King of Eng., 1754; hmn. com. King George County, 1774; mem. Va. Ho. of Burgesses, 1772; mem. 2d Va. Com. Safety, 775, also all Va. revolutionary convs.; mem. Va. Ho. of Dels. 1776, 77, 80, 81, 83-85; mem. com. which framed Va. Declaration of Rights and Va. Constn., 1776; mem. Continental Congress from Va., 1777-78, 80-83; judge Va. Gen. Ct., 1778-83, 89-1805; mem. Va. Conv. which ratified U.S. Constn., 1788; served as maj. gen. Va. Militia. Died Fredericksburg, Va., Oct. 28, 1805.

JONES, Joseph, physician; b. Liberty County, Ga., Sept. 6, 1833; s. Charles Colcock and Mary (Jones) J.; grad. Coll. of N.J. (now Princeton), 1853; M.D., U. Pa., 1856; m. Caroline Davis, 1858; m. 2d, Susan Polk, 1870. Taught medicine, Savannah and Augusta, Ga., 1858-61; surgeon Confederate Army, 1861-65; practiced medicine, New Orleans, 1865-72; prof. medicine U. La., 1872-96; active in public sanitation investigation and promotion in New Orleans; pres. La. Bd. Health, 1880-84; instrumental n securing legal recognition of municipal right to quarantine power; mem. La. Med. Soc., So. Hist. Soc. Author: (articles) Contributions to the Natural History of Specific Yellow Fever, 1874, Contributions to Teratology, 1888; wrote part of Vol. II of Surgical Memoirs of the War of the Rebellion, 1871. Died New Orleans, Feb. 17, 1896; buried New Orleans.

JONES, Joseph Seawell, historian; b. Warren County, N.C., 1808; attended U. N.C., 1823-24; grad. Harvard Law Sch., 1833. Began practice law, N.C., 1833; devoted much of career to writing hist. works. Author: A Defense of the Revolutionary History of North Carolina from the Aspersions of Mr. Jefferson (justification of adminstrns. of govs. Tryon and Martin against Thomas Jefferson's charges), 1834; Memorials of North Carolina, 1838; My Log Cabin in the Prairie, 1855. Died Miss., 1855; buried Miss.

JONES, Joseph Stevens, actor; b. Boston, Sept. 28, 1809; s. Abraham and Mary (Stevens) J.; M.D., Harvard, 1843. Made debut as actor, Providence, R.I., 1827; began career in Boston, 1828, acted and wrote plays, 1828-38; mgr. Tremont Theater, Boston, 1839-41; following graduation from med. sch. continued to write plays for Boston theaters; practiced medicine, 1843-77. Author: (plays) The Silver Spoon or Our Own Folks (best-known drama, produced at Boston Museum 1852), Moll Pitcher, The People's Lawyer, Paul Revere and the Sons of Liberty, 1875, The Carpenter of Rouen; (novel) The Life of Jefferson S. Batkins . . ., 1871. Died Boston, Dec. 29, 1877; buried Boston.

JONES, Morgan, congressman; b. London, Eng., Feb. 26, 1830; attended pub. schs., N.Y.C. Came to U.S., 1833; engaged in plumbing bus., 1850; mem. bd. councilmen of N.Y.C., 1859-63, pres., 1860, 61, 63; mem .bd. aldermen N.Y.C., 1864-65, pres., 1865; mem. U.S. Ho. of Reps. (Democrat) from N.Y., 39th Congress, 1865-67; resumed bus. interests, N.Y.C., ret., 1887. Died N.Y.C., July 13, 1894; buried Greenwood Cemetery, Bklyn.

JONES, Nathaniel, congressman; b. Warwick, N. Y., Feb. 17, 1788; Taught sch.; mem. N.Y. Assembly, 1827-28; engaged in banking, 1834; mem. U.S. Ho. of Reps. (Democrat) from N.Y., 25th-26th congresses, 1837-41; moved to Newburgh, N.Y., 1841; surveyor gen. State of N.Y., 1842-44, canal commr., 1844-47; supt. schs., clk. bd. edn. of Newburgh, 1851; mem. N.Y. Senate, 1852-53. Died Newburgh, July 20, 1866.

JONES, Noble Wymberley, physician, Continental congressman; b. nr. London, Eng., circa 1724; s. Noble Jones; m. Sarah Davis, 6 children including George J. Practiced medicine, Savannah, Ga., 1748-56; served from cadet to 1st lt. Oglethorpe's Regt.; mem. Ga. Commons Ho. of Assembly, 1755-74, speaker, 1768-69; mem. Continental Congress, 1775-76, 81-83; mem. Ga. Council of Safety, various other provincial congresses; mem., speaker Ga. Assembly, 1782; pres. Ga. Constl. Conv., 1795; pres. Ga. Med. Soc. Died Savannah, Jan. 9, 1805; buried Bonaventure Cemetery, Savannah.

JONES, Owen, congressman; b. nr. Ardmore, Pa., Dec. 29, 1819; grad. U. Pa.; studied law, Phila. Admitted to the bar, Montgomery County, Pa., 1842, began practice in Ardmore; mem. U.S. Ho. of Reps. (Democrat) from Pa., 35th Congress, 1857-59; raised a troop of cavalry during Civil War, served from capt. to col., 1861-63; resumed law practice. Died nr. Ardmore, Dec. 25, 1878; buried Laurel Hill Cemetery, Phila.

JONES, Phineas, congressman; b. Spencer, Mass., Apr. 18, 1819; attended common schs. Moved to Elizabethtown (now Elizabeth), N.J., 1855; mem. Elizabethtown City Council, 1856-60; moved to Newark, N.J., 1860, engaged in mfg. and merc. bus.; v.p. N.J. Agrl. Soc.; mem. N.J. Ho. of Assembly, 1873-74; mem. U.S. Ho. of Reps. (Republican) from N. J., 47th Congress, 1881-83; Died Newark, Apr. 19, 1884; buried Evergreen Cemetery, Elizabeth.

JONES, Roland, congressman; b. Salisbury, N.C., Nov. 18, 1813; grad. Cambridge (Mass.) Law Sch., 1838. Admitted to Miss. bar, began practice in Brandon; editor Brandon Republican, 1838-40; moved to Shreveport, La., 1840, practiced law; mem. La. Ho. of Reps., 1844-48; dist. judge Caddo Parish (La.), 1851-52, 60-68; mem. U.S. Ho. of Reps. (Democrat) from La., 33d Congress, 1853-55. Died Shreveport, Feb. 5, 1869; buried Oakland Cemetery, Shreveport.

JONES, Samuel, lawyer; b. Fort Hill, L.I., N. Y., July 26, 1734; s. William and Phoebe (Jackson) J.; m. Eleanor Turk, 1765; m. 2d, Cornelia Haring (also Herring), 1768; 2 children. Mem. N.Y. Com. of 100; apptd. to collect and reduce to proper form for legislative enactment all such statutes of Gt. Britain as were continued in force under N.Y. Constn. of 1777; mem. N.Y. Assembly from Queens County, 1786-90; del. N.Y. Conv. which ratified U.S. Constn., 1788; recorder N.Y.C., 1789-96; mem. N.Y. State Senate, 1791-97; apptd. to draft law for establishing and regulating office of comptroller; comptroller N.Y., 1797-1800. Died West Neck, L.I., Nov. 25, 1819.

JONES, Samuel, jurist; b. N.Y.C., May 26, 1770; s. Samuel and Cornelia (Haring) J.; grad. Yale, 1790; ad eundem degree Columbia, 1793; m. Catharine Schuyler, Jan. 27, 1816, 5 children, including Samuel. Admitted to N.Y. bar, 1791; one of 1st appointees Spl. Justices' Ct., N.Y.C., 1797; asst. alderman N.Y.C., 1809-17; mem. N.Y. State Assembly from N.Y.C., 1812-14; recorder N.Y.C., 1823; chancellor N.Y. State, 1826; 1st chief justice Superior Ct. of N.Y.C., 1828; justice N.Y. State Supreme Ct. under Constn. of 1846; ex officio mem. N.Y. Ct. of Appeals, 1847-49. Died Cold Spring, L.I., N.Y., Aug. 9, 1853.

JONES, Seaborn, congressman; b. Augusta, Ga., Feb. 1, 1788; attended Princeton; studied law. Admitted to Ga. bar, 1808, began practice in Milledgeville; apptd. solicitor gen. Ocmulgee Circuit, 1817, solicitor gen. Ga., 1823; a commr. to investigate trouble among Creek Indians; moved to Columbus, Ga., 1827; mem. U.S. Ho. of Reps. (Democrat) from Ga., 23d, 29th congresses, 1833-35, 45-47. Died Columbus, Mar. 18, 1864; buried Linwood Cemetery, Columbus.

JONES, Sybil, clergywoman; b. Brunswick, Me., Feb. 28, 1808; d. Ephraim and Susannah (Dudley) Jones; m. Eli Jones, June 26, 1833; 5 children including Richard Mott. Taught pub. schs., Providence, R.I., 1825-33; recognized by Friend's chs. as gospel minister, 1833; preached in Nova Scotia, also New Brunswick, Can., 1840-42, New Eng., 1842, Ohio, Ind., Balt., N.C., 1845; made missionary trip to Liberia, 1851; preached in Eng., also several countries on the continent, 1852-54; worked in Union hosps. during Civil War; visited Syria, also Palestine, 1867-68, attempted to explain Quaker concept of equality of the sexes to Moslem women. Died Augusta, Me., Dec. 4, 1873.

JONES, Thomas, jurist; b. Ft. Neck, South Oyster Bay, L.I., N.Y., Apr. 30, 1731; s. David and Anna (Willet) J.; grad. Yale, 1750; m. Anne de Lancey, Dec. 9, 1762; 1 adopted dau., Anne de Lancey. Admitted to N.Y. bar, 1755; clk. Ct. Common Pleas of Queens County, N.Y., 1757; atty., then mem. bd. govs. King's Coll. (now Columbia); recorder N.Y.C., 1769-73; justice N.Y. Supreme Ct., 1773-76; imprisoned for Loyalist sympathies during Am. Revolution; went to England, 1881. Author: History of New York During Revolutionary War. Died Hoddesdon, Hertfordshire, Eng., July 25, 1792.

JONES, Thomas Ap Catesby, naval officer; b. Westmoreland County, Va., Apr. 24, 1790; s. Maj. Catesby and Lettice (Turberville) J.; m. Mary Carter, July 1, 1823, 4 children. Entered U.S. Navy as midshipman under Isaac Hutland and Stephan Decatur, 1805; commd. lt., 1812, master commandant, 1820, capt., 1829; helped suppress slave trade in Gulf of Mexico, 1808-12; comdr. South Seas Surveying and Exploring Expdn., 1836; comdr. Pacific Squadron, 1842, and prematurely seized Monterey, Cal., thinking war had been declared between U.S. and Mexico; commanded Pacific Squadron for 3d time, 1844. Died Sharon, Fairfax County, Va., May 30, 1858.

JONES, Thomas Dow, artist; b. Oneida County, N.Y., Dec. 11, 1811. Stonemason, Cincinnati, circa 1830-40; began to do portrait busts, circa 1842; best known works include busts of Lincoln, 1861, Salmon P. Chase (for Supreme Ct. room of U.S. Capitol), 1876; asso. N.A.D. Died Columbus, O., Feb. 27, 1881.

JONES, Thomas Laurens, congressman; b. White Oak, Rutherford County, N.C., Jan. 22, 1819; grad. Princeton; grad. law dept. of Harvard. Admitted to S.C. bar, 1846; began practice of law, N.Y.C., 1847; moved to Newport, Ky., 1849, practiced law; mem. Ky. Ho. of Reps. from Campbell County, 1853-55; mem. U.S. Ho. of Reps. (Democrat) from Ky., 40th-41st, 44th congresses, 1867-71, 75-77. Died Newport, June 20, 1887; buried Evergreen Cemetery, Newport.

JONES, Thomas P., editor; b. Herefordshire, Eng., 1774. Came to U.S., circa 1800; editor, owner Am. Mechanics' Mag., N.Y.C., 1825, merged his publication with The Franklin Jour., 1826, became Jour. of Franklin Inst., 1827, editor until 1848, during his editorship Jour. contained list of all patents filed with govt. office; prof. natural philosophy Franklin Inst., Phila., 1825; examiner U.S. Patent Office, 1837-38. Editor: Young Mill-Wright and Miller's Guide, 8th edit., 1834. Died Washington, D.C., Mar. 11, 1848; buried Washington.

JONES, Walter, physician, congressman; b. Williamsburg, Va., Dec. 18, 1745; grad. Coll. William and Mary, 1760; M.D., U. Edinburgh (Scotland), 1770; Practiced medicine, Northumberland County, Va.; physician gen. Middle Mil. Dept., 1777; mem. Va. Ho. of Dels., 1785-87, 1802-03; del. Va. Constl. Conv., 1788; mem. U.S. Ho. of Reps. (Democrat) from Va., 5th, 8th-11th congresses, 1797-99, 03-11. Died Westmoreland County, Va., Dec. 31, 1815; buried family burial ground at "Hayfield" nr. Callo, Va.

JONES, Walter, lawyer; b. Northumberland County, Va., Oct. 7, 1776; s. Dr. Walter and Alice (Flood) J.; m. Anne Lucinda Lee, May 1808, 14 children. Admitted to Va. bar, 1796; apptd. U.S. atty. for Dist. of Potomac, 1802, for D.C., 1804 (apptd. by Pres. Jefferson); participated in several noted cases of period; represented Md. in McCullough v. Md., 1819, represented Ogden in Ogden v. Saunders, 1827; other cases include Girard Will case, Myra Clark Gaines case, Randolph Will case; commd. brig. gen. D.C. Militia, 1821, later maj. gen.; a founder Washington Nat. Monument Soc. Died Washington, D.C., Oct. 14, 1861.

JONES, William, army officer, gov. R.I.; b. Newport, R.I., Oct. 8, 1753; s. William and Elizabeth (Pearce) J.; m. Anne Dunn, Feb. 28, 1787, 1 dau., Harriet. Received commn. as lt. from R.I. Gen. Assembly, 1776, capt., 1776; served as capt. of marines on brig Providence, 1778; justice of the peace, Providence, R.I.; rep. R.I. Gen. Assembly, 1807-11; presented a petition against the Embargo Act, 1808; speaker R.I. Gen. Assembly, 1809, 10; gov. R.I., 1811-17; mem. Soc. of Cincinnati; pres. Peace Soc., also R.I. Bible Soc., Am. Bible Soc.; trustee Brown U. Died Providence, Apr. 9, 1822.

JONES, William, sec. of navy, congressman; b. Phila., 1760. Served with Continental Army in Revolutionary War; participated in battles of Trenton, 1776, Princeton, 1777; served as 3d lt. in ship St. James; commd. 1st lt U.S. Navy, 1781; mem. U.S. Ho. of Reps. from Pa., 7th Congress, 1801-03; U.S. sec. of navy under Pres. Madison, 1813-14; pres. Bank of U.S., 1816-19; collector of customs Phila., 1827-29. Died Bethlehem, Pa., Sept. 16, 1831; buried St. Peter's Churchyard, Phila.

JONES, William Palmer, physician; b. Adair County, Ky., Oct. 17, 1819; s. William and Mary (Powell) J.; M.D., Med. Coll. of Ohio, Cincinnati, 1840; m. Jane Currey, 1851. Practiced medicine, Edmonton, Ky., 1840, Bowling Green, Ky., 1841-49, Nashville, Tenn., from 1849; editor periodical Parlor Visitor, Nashville, 1852-circa 1856; co-editor So. Jour. of Med. and Phys. Scis., 1853-56; editor Tenn. Sch. Jour.; a founder Shelby Med. Coll., 1858; supported Union during Civil War; supt. Acad. Hosp. of U.S. Army, Nashville during Civil War; head Tenn. Hosp. for Insane, 1862-69; mem. Tenn. Senate, 1873, worked on behalf of public schools and instns. for insane; pres. faculty Nashville Med. Coll., 1876-97. Died Nashville, Sept. 25, 1897; buried Nashville.

JONES, William Patterson, educator; b. Phila., Apr. 23, 1831; s. William and Ursula (Linderman) J.; grad. Allegheny Coll., Meadville, Pa., 1853. Strong advocate of coll. edn. for women during 1850's; operated Northwestern Female Coll., Evanston, Ill., 1856-62; U.S. consul successively at Macao, Amoy, Canton, 1862-68; wrote many articles on edn. for Chgo. newspapers 1870's; pres. Neb.

State Normal Sch., Fullerton, 1884-86. Author: (poem) The Myth of the Stone Idol, 1876; (with Henry Gannett and R.P. Porter) The West: from the Census of 1880, published 1882. Died Fullerton, Aug. 3, 1886; buried Fullerton.

JONES, William Richard, engr., steel co. exec.; b. Hazleton, Pa., Feb. 23, 1839; m. Harriet Lloyd Apr. 14, 1861, 4 children. Journeyman machinist, 1853; with Cambria Iron Co., Johnston, Pa., 1859; served with Co. A, 133d Pa. Volunteers, 1862-63, served in battles of Fredericksburg and Chancellorsville; served as capt. Co. F., 194th Pa. Regt. of Emergency Men (which he raised), 1864-65; gen. supt. Edgar Thomson Steel Co., Braddock, Pa., 1875-89; cons. engr. Carnegie, Phipps & Co., 1888-89; inventor and patentee numerous devices connected with prodn. steel, most important was Jones mixer (mixed molten iron from blast furnaces for converter), 1889; 1st American to be invited to see Krupp steel works at Essen. Died Pitts., Sept. 28, 1889.

JONES, William Theopilus, congressman; b. Corydon, Ind., Feb. 20, 1842; studied law. Admitted to Ind. bar, 1865, began practice in Corydon; served as maj. 17th Regt., Ind. Volunteer Inf., during Civil War; Republican presdl. elector, 1868; apptd. asso. justice Supreme Ct. of Territory of Wyo., 1869; del. U.S. Congress from Territory of Wyo., 1871-73; resumed practice of law, Corydon. Died Corydon, Oct. 9, 1882; buried Cedar Hill Cemetery, Corydon.

JONES, Willie, Continental congressman, legislator; b. Northampton County, N.C., circa 1741; s. Robert (Robin) and Sarah (Cobb) ap J.; attended Eton (Eng.), several years; m. Mary Montfort, June 27, 1776. Aide to Gov. Tryon of N.C. in Alamance campaign against Regulators; chmn. Halifax Com. of Safety; mem. 5 N.C. provincial congresses from Halifax County, elected supt. Indian affairs for So. colonies during 4th congress, 1774, mem. com. to draft N.C. constn. during 5th congress, influential in determining its form and character, credited with its authorship; mem. N.C. Ho. of Commons from Borough of Halifax, 1777, from Halifax County, 1779-80; mem. Continental Congress, 1780-81; mem. N.C. Council of State, 1781, 87; elected to N.C. Senate, 1782, 84, 88; del. to N.C. Conv. of 1788, to ratify U.S. Constn. (opposed); mem. 1st bd. trustees U. N.C.; mem. of commn. which located capitol of N.C., provided for bldg. of statehouse. Died Raleigh, N.C., June 18, 1801.

JORDAN, Isaac M., congressman; b. Mifflinsburg, Pa., May 5, 1835; attended Northwood (O.) Inst., 2 years; grad. Miami U., Oxford, O., 1857; studied law. Admitted to Ohio bar, 1858, began practice in Dayton; moved to Cincinnati, 1859, practiced law; mem. U.S. Ho. of Reps. (Democrat) from Ohio, 48th Congress, 1883-85. Died from injuries received in an elevator accident, Cincinnati, Dec. 3, 1890; buried Spring Grove Cemetery, Cincinnati.

JORDAN, Thomas, army officer, editor; b. Luray, Va., Sept. 30, 1819; s. Gabriel and Elizabeth (Sibert) J.; grad. U.S. Mil. Acad., 1840; m. Miss Kearney, 2 children. Commd. lt. 3d Inf., U.S. Army, served in Fla. War; 1st lt., 1846; served as capt., q.m. in Mexican War, 1847; served as staff q.m. in 2d Seminole uprising, 1848-50; served on Pacific Coast, and against Indians in Wash., 1850-60; introduced steam navigation on Columbia River above Ft. Dalles, Ore., and initiated successful irrigation project, 1856-60; commd. lt. col. Va. Militia, Confederate Army, 1861; served as adj.-gen., 1st Battle of Bull Run, 1861; promoted brig. gen., 1862; contbr. article attacking Jefferson Davis to Harper's Magazine, aroused widespread interest; editor Memphis (Tenn.) Appeal, 1866; chief of staff, later comdr. Cuban insurgents, 1869; founder, editor Financial and Mining Record of N.Y. Author: The South, Its Products, Its Commerce, and Resources, 1861; The Campaigns of Lieutenant-General N.B. Forrest, 1868. Died N.Y.C., Nov. 27, 1895.

JORGENSEN, Joseph, congressman; b. Phila., Feb. 11, 1844; grad. med. dept. U. Pa. Cadet surgeon U.S. Army, 1864-65, acting asst. surgeon, 1865, 67-70; mem. Va. Ho. of Dels. from Prince Edward County, 1871-73; moved to Petersburg, Va.; postmaster of Petersburg, 1874-77; mem. U.S. Ho. of Reps. (Republican) from Va., 45th-47th congresses, 1877-83; del. Rep. Nat. Conv., Chgo., 1880; register land office, Walla Walla, Wash. (apptd. by Pres. Arthur), 1883-86. Died Portland, Ore., Jan. 21, 1888; buried Mountain View Cemetery, Walla Walla.

JOSSELYN, John, author; b. Essex, Eng.; flourished 1638-75; s. Sir Thomas and Theodora (Cooke Bere) J. Visited New Eng., summer 1638-39, 63-71. Author: New England's Rarities Discovered (1st systematical account of bot. specimens of New Eng.) 1672; An Account of Two Voyages to New England, 1679.

JOUBERT de la MURAILLE, James Hector Marie Nicholas, clergyman; b. St. Jean d'Angely, France, Sept. 6, 1777; attended St. Mary's Sem., Balt. With French tax dept. on Island of Santo Domingo, 1800-04; escaped from native rebellion to Balt., 1804; ordained priest Soc. of St. Sulpice, Roman Catholic Ch., 1810; tchr., disciplinarian, v.p. St. Mary's Coll., Balt.; while working with French West Indian Negroes thought of founding religious soc. of Negro women for edn. Negro children, 1827; founded Oblate Sisters of Providence (confirmed by Ch. as religious soc., 1831). Died Nov. 5, 1843.

JOUETT, John, state legislator; b. Albemarle County, Va., Dec. 7, 1754; s. Capt. John and Mourning (Harris) J.; m. Sallie Robards, Aug. 20, 1784, 1 son, Matthew Harris. Signer oath of allegiance to Va. Commonwealth, 1779; capt. Va. Militia; remembered for daring ride over 40 miles to save Gov. Jefferson and Va. Legislature from capture; mem. Va. Assembly from Lincoln County, 1786-87, Mercer County, 1787-88, 90; a leading mem. Danville Conv., influential in organizing Ky. as separate state; mem. Ky. Legislature from Mercer County, 1 term, from Woodford County, 3 terms. Died Mar. 1, 1822.

JOUETT, Matthew Harris, artist; b. Mercer County, Ky., Apr. 22, 1787; s. John and Sallie (Robards) J.; grad. Transylvania U., 1808; studied law under Judge George M. Bibb; studied art with Gilbert Stuart, 1816; m. Margaret Allen, 1812, 8 children. Enlisted in 3d Mounted Regt., Ky. Volunteers, 1812; paymaster, 1st lt. 28th U.S. Inf., 1813, promoted capt., 1814, resigned, 1815; established himself as portrait painter, Lexington, Ky., 1815; did portraits of Lafayette, Henry Clay, John Grimes. Died Aug. 10, 1827.

JOUTEL, Henri, explorer; b. Rouen, France, circa 1645. Sailed with LaSalle on his expdn. to found settlement at mouth of Mississippi River, 1684, expdn. unknowingly passed up mouth and landed on coast of Tex., began colony at Lavaca Bay; allowed to escape when LaSalle was murdered while leading expdn. to find Missisipi, 1687; his party reached Ft. St. Louis, 1687, then reached Que., sailed from there to Rouen, 1688. Author: A Journal of the Last Voyage Perform'd by Monsr. de la Sale to the Gulph of Mexico To Find out the Mouth of the Mississippi River, 1714. Died circa 1723.

JOUVENAL, Jacques, artist; b. Pinache, Germany, Mar. 18, 1829; studied art, Stuttgart, Germany, circa 1845. Came to U.S., 1853, lived in N.Y.C., 1853-55, Washington, D.C., 1855-1905; worked on finishing capitals of columns of U.S. Capitol, Washington; began portrait sculpting, work includes a bust of Aaron Burr (now in U.S. Capitol). Died Washington, Mar. 8, 1905.

JOY, James Frederick, lawyer, railroad exec.; b. Durham, N.H., Dec. 2, 1810; s. James and Sarah (Pickering) J.; grad. Dartmouth, 1833, Harvard Law Sch., 1836; m. Martha Reed, Aug. 12, 1841; m. 2d, Mary Bourne, Dec. 12, 1860; 7 children. Admitted to Mass. bar, 1836; counsel gen. Mich. Central R.R., 1852, Ill. Central R.R., 1853; pres. Chg. & Aurora Br. R.R., 1853, Central Mil. Tract R.R., 1856 (merged with Chgo. & Aurora Br. R.R., forming Chgo., Burlington & Quincy R.R.); purchased Burlington & Mo. River R.R., extended to Council Bluffs on the Missouri River, by 1869; acquired Hannibal & St. Joseph R.R. (gaining control of So. Ia., No. Mo.); mem. Mich. Legislature, 1861-62, floor leader Ho. of Reps.; pres. Mich. Central R.R., 1867; combined lines for Kansas City, St. Joseph & Council Bluffs R.R., pres., 1870-74; pres. Detroit Post and Tribune, 1881-84, Wabash, St. Louis & Pacific R.R., 1884-87. Died Detroit, Sept. 24, 1896.

JOY, Thomas, architect; b. Eng., circa 1610; m. Joan Gallop, 1637, 10 children. Came to Boston, no later than 1636; agitated for extension of suffrage to non-Puritans, 1646, arrested and forced to leave Boston; operated saw mill, Hingham, Mass., 1646-56; designed bldg. to house public bodies, 1657 (destroyed by fire, 1711). Died Oct. 21, 1678.

JÚAREZ, Benito, pres. Mexico; b. Mexico, 1806. Gov. of Oaxaca (Mexico) for a time; imprisoned for opposition to Santa Anna, 1853; drew up Plan of Ayutta (blueprint of liberal revolution); successfully waged "War of Reform" which defeated Conservatives, 1858-61; led Mexican resistance to French attempt to establish Maximilian as emperor of Mexico, 1864-67; his partisans executed Maximilian, June 19, 1863; pres. of Mexico, 1867-71, 71-72. Died 1872.

JUDAH, Samuel, lawyer; b. N.Y.C., July 10, 1798; s. Dr. Samuel Bernard and Catherine (Hart) J.; grad. Rutgers Coll., 1816; m. Harriet Brandon, 1825, 6 children. Admitted to N.J. bar, 1816; mem. Ind. Ho. of Reps., 1827-29, 37-41, presided over Whig legislative caucus, 1839, speaker, 1840; mem. com. which wrote address of Jackson Conv., 1824; served as counsel for Vincennes U. in case Vincennes U. vs. State of Ind. before U.S. Supreme Ct. 1842. Died Apr. 24, 1869.

JUDAH, Samuel Benjamin Helbert, author, lawyer; b. N.Y.C., circa 1799; s. Benjamin S. and Elizabeth Judah. Admitted to N.Y. bar, 1825. Author: The Mountain Torrent (play), 1820; A Tale of Lexington (play), 1823; Odofriede, the Outcast, 1822; Gotham and the Gothamites, 1823 (for which convicted of libel, sent to prison for 5 weeks); The Maid of Midian, 1833. Died N.Y.C., July 21, 1876.

JUDAH, Theodore Dehone, engr., railroad builder; b. Bridgeport, Conn., Mar. 4, 1826; s. Henry R. Judah; attended Rensselaer Poly. Inst., Troy, N.Y. m. Anna Pierce, May 10, 1847. Built bridge, Vergennes, Vt., 1847-54; planned and built Niagara Gorge R.R.; in charge of constrn. for Buffalo & N.Y. R.R.; chief engr. Sacramento Valley R.R., 1854-56; published widely circulated pamphlet advocating constrn. of transcontinental railroad; 1857 agt. Pacific R.R. Conv., Washington, D.C., 1859-60; organized Central Pacific R.R. Co., 1861, sold his share in co. because of friction with partners 1863. Died N.Y.C., Nov. 2, 1863.

JUDD, Gerrit Parmele, Hawaiian statesman; b. Paris, N.Y., Apr. 23, 1803; s. Dr. Elnathan and Betsey (Hastings) J., Jr.; grad. med. sch. at Fairfield, Herkimer County, N.Y., 1825; m. Laura Fish, 1827, 9 children. Physician to Sandwich Islands, 1827; went to Honolulu as mem. Mission of Am. Bd. of Commrs. for Fgn. Missions, 1828; took service under King of Hawaii, mem. treasury bd.; accompanied Commdr. Wilkes in exploring expdn. through islands, 1840; recorder and translator to King of Hawaii, 1842, sec. of state for fgn. affairs, 1843, minister of foreign affairs, 1843-45, minister of interior, 1845-46, minister of finance, 1846-53 (during all this time prime minister in fact if not in name); represented King in committee which drew up liberal constn. of 1852; an original mem. of board of Hawaiian Evang. Assn., 1863. Died Honolulu, July 12, 1873.

JUDD, Norman Buel, congressman, diplomat; b. Rome, N.Y., Jan. 10, 1815; s. Norman and Catherine (Van der Heyden) J.; m. Adeline Rossiter, 1844. Admitted to N.Y. bar, 1836; moved to Chgo., 1836; drafted Chgo.'s 1st municipal charter, 1836; 1st city atty. Chgo., 1837-38; mem. Ill. Senate, 1844-60; nominated Abraham Lincoln for Pres. U.S., 1860; U.S. minister to Prussia (now Germany), 1861-65; mem. U.S. Ho. of Reps. from Ill., 40th-41st congresses, 1867-71; collector of customs, Chgo., 1872-76. Died Chgo., Nov. 11, 1878; buried Graceland Cemetery, Chgo.

JUDD, Orange, agrl. editor, publisher; b. nr. Niagara Falls, N.Y., July 26, 1822; s. Ozias and Rheuama (Wright) J.; grad. Wesleyan U., Middletown, Conn., 1847; attended Yale, 1850-53; m. Sarah L. Ford, Oct. 10, 1847; m. 2d, Harriet Stewart, May 1, 1855; at least 2 sons. Co-editor, later owner, publisher and editor Am. Agriculturist, N.Y.C., 1853-83; agrl. editor N.Y. Times, 1855-63; owner Health and Home, 1870-73; donated Orange Judd Hall of Natural Science to Wesleyan U., 1871, provided means for establishment State Agrl. Expt. Stas.; editor Prairie Farmer, Chgo., 1884-88; owner-editor Orange Judd Farmer, Chgo., 1888-92. Died Dec. 27, 1892.

JUDD, Sylvester, clergyman, author; b. Westhampton, Mass., July 23, 1813; s. Sylvester and Apphia (Hall) J.; grad. Yale, 1836, Harvard Divinity Sch., 1840; m. Jane Elizabeth Williams, Aug. 31, 1841. Ordained to ministry Unitarian Ch., 1840; became pastor East Parish, Augusta, Me., 1840; chaplain Me. Legislature until 1842. Author: Margaret, 1845; Richard Edney and the Governor's Family, 1850; Philo, an Evangeliad, 1850. Died Jan. 26, 1853.

JUDGE, William Quan, theosophist; b. Dublin, Ireland, Apr. 13, 1851; s. Frederick H. and Alice (Quan) J.; studied law under George P. Andrews, N.Y.C.; m. Ella Smith, 1874. Admitted to N.Y. bar, 1872; partner firm Olcott, Gozalez & Judge; mem. Theosophical Soc., 1875, reorganized N.Y. br. into Aryan Theosophical Soc., 1883; editor The Path, 1886-96; relinquished law practice to devote full time to theosophy, 1893. Author: The Yoga Aphorisms of Pantanjali; An Interpretation, 1889; Echoes of the Orient, 1890; The Ocean of Theosophy, 1893; Notes on the Bhagavad-Gita, pub. posthumously, 1918. Died Mar. 21, 1896.

JUDSON, Adoniram, missionary; b. Malden, Mass., Aug. 9, 1788; s. Adoniram and Abigail (Brown) J.; grad. Brown U., 1807; attended Andover Theol. Sem.; m. Ann Hasseltine, Feb. 5, 1812, 1 child; m. 2d, Sarah Hall Boardman, Apr. 10, 1834, 8 children including Adoniram Brown, Edward; m. 3d, Emily Chubbuck, June 2, 1846, 1 child. Ordained to ministry Congregational Ch., Salem, Mass., 1812; converted to Baptist Ch., 1812; missionary to Calcutta, India, 1812-45; translated Bible into Burmese, 1834; missionary to Maulmain, Burma, 1846.

uthor: Dictionary, English and Burmese, 1849. ied aboard ship while taking sea voyage for health easons, Apr. 12, 1850; buried at sea.

JUDSON, Andrew Thompsen, congressman; b. astford, Conn., Nov. 29, 1784; studied law. Ad- itted to Conn. bar, 1806; moved to Montpelier, t., began practice of law; settled in Canterbury, onn., 1809; states atty. for Windham County Conn.), 1819-33; mem. Conn. Ho. of Reps., 1822- 5; mem. U.S. Ho. of Reps. (Democrat) from onn., 24th Congress, 1835-July 4, 1836; U.S. idge for Dist. of Conn., 1836-53. Died Canter- ury, Mar. 17, 1853; buried Hyde Cemetery, Canter- ury.

JUDSON, Ann Hasseltine, missionary, author; b. radford, Mass., Dec. 22, 1789; d. John and Rebec- a (Burton or Barton) Hasseltine; m. Adoniram udson, Feb. 5, 1812, 1 child. Born Nancy, changed ame to Ann; taught sch. in towns nr. Bradford, lass.; accompanied her husband to Burma (1st oman dedicated to convert heathen to leave Amer- ca); her health suffered and son died in infancy ue to hardships she had to endure; returned to Am., 822-23; rejoined her husband, imprisoned with oth- foreigners at Ava and Oung-pen-la; started new ission at Amherst, Burma after release from pris- n. Author: Account of the American Baptist Mis- ion to the Burman Empire, 1823. Died Oct. 24, 826.

JUDSON, Edward Zane Carroll (Ned Buntline), uthor, adventurer; b. Stamford, N.Y., Mar. 20, 823; s. Levi Carroll Judson; m. Seberina, 1845; m. d, Annie Bennett, circa 1848, 1 child; m. 3d, Ma- ie Gardiner, 1857; m. 4th, Anna Fuller, 1871, 2 hildren. Cabin boy at sea; apprentice in Navy, ommd. midshipman for heroism, 1838, resigned rom Navy, 1842; published story The Captain's ig under pseudonym Ned Buntline; published Ned untline's Mag., Cincinnati, 1844; co-editor West- rn Lit. Jour. and Monthly Mag., 1844-45; re- eived bounty of $600 for capturing 2 murderers, Eddyville, Ky., 1845; published Ned Buntline's Own, Nashville, Tenn.; killed Robert Porterfield, 1846, while waiting for indictment in court house was hot at by Porterfield's brother, escaped through window but was caught and jailed, hanged at night y mob but was cut down and lived (grand jury lid not indict him); went to N.Y., again started Ned Buntline's Mag.; led mob against Astor Place Theatre which ended in riot, 1849; indicted for ausing election riot, St. Louis, 1852; an organizer Know-Nothing Party; enlisted 1st N.Y. Mounted Rifles, 1862; sgt. Company K, 1st N.Y. Mounted Rifles, dishonorably discharged, 1864; became ac- quainted with William Frederick Cody, Ft. Mc- Pherson, Neb., 1869, gave him name "Buffalo Bill" and made him the hero of series of dime novels; wrote and produced successful play Scouts of the Prairies, Niblo's Garden, N.Y., 1873; moved to Stamford, 1871; originator of dime novel. Author of some 400 stories including The Mysteries and Mis- eries of New York, 1848; The Boys of New York; The Gals of New York; War Eagle, or Ossiniwa the Indian Brave; Ned Buntline's Life Yarn, 1848; Navi- gator Ned; Cruisings Afloat and Ashore from the Log of Ned Buntline; Stella Delorme, or the Comanche's Dream, 1860. Died Stamford, July 16, 1886.

JUDSON, Egbert Putnam, inventor, explosives mfr.; b. Syracuse, N.Y., Aug. 9, 1812; s. William and Charlotte (Putnam) J. Founder 1st assay works in San Francisco, 1852; an organizer San Francisco Chem. Works (later Judson & Sheppard), 1867; dir. Giant Powder Co.; founder Judson Power der Co., Kenvil, N.J.; patentee Giant Powder, No. 2, 1873, "gentle" blasting powder, 1876; founder Judson Fuse Works, Judson Iron Works, Judson Can- dle Works, Butterworth & Judson Chem. Works; pres. Judson Mfg. Co., Cal. Paper Co. Died San Francisco, Jan. 9, 1893.

JUDSON, Emily Chubbuck, missionary, author; b. Eaton, N.Y., Aug. 22, 1817; d. Charles and Lavinia (Richards) Chubbuck; attended Utica (N.Y.) Fe- male Sem., 1840; m. Rev. Adoniram Judson, June 2, 1846, 1 dau., 1 son. Taught sch., Morrisville, Smithville, Hamilton (all N.Y.), 1832-40; convert to Baptist Ch., 1834; tchr. English, Utica Female Sem.; missionary to Burma, 1846-47, to Rangoon, 1847; returned to Boston, 1851; lived in Hamilton, 1852-54. Author: Charles Linn, or How To Observe the Golden Rule, 1841; Trippings in Author-Land, 1846; An Olio of Domestic Verses, 1852; My Two Sisters, 1854. Died Hamilton, June 1, 1854.

JUDSON, Sarah Hall Boardman, missionary; b. Alstead, N.H., Nov. 4, 1803; d. Ralph and Abiah Hall; m. George Dana Boardman, July 4, 1825 (dec. 1831); m. 2d, Adoniram Judson, Apr. 10, 1834; 11 children (6 reached maturity including George Dana, Adroniram Brown, Edward). Accompanied 1st hus- band to Burma, 1825, their 1st years in Burma proved to be very hard physically; expert in Bur- mese lang.; set sail for Am. for health, 1845. Trans- lator: (into Burmese) The Pilgrim's Progress. Died on island of St. Helena while returning to U.S., Sept. 1, 1845.

JUENGLING, Frederick, wood-engraver; b. Leipzig, Saxony, Oct. 18, 1846. Came to N.Y.C., 1866; pub- lished woodcuts (in which he attempted to reproduce, rather than interpret, work of the artist) in Scrib- ner's Monthly, 1877; became mem. Art Students' League, 1879, later pres.; recipient honorable men- tions for woodcuts in Paris salons, 1881, 83; en- gravings include: The Longshoreman's Noon, Edison in his Workshop, Poe's Raven. Died N.Y.C., Dec. 31, 1889.

JULIA, Sister, see McGroarty, Susan.

JULIAN, George Washington, congressman, aboli- tionist; b. Wayne County, Ind., May 5, 1817; s. Isaac and Rebecca (Hoover) J.; m. Anne Finch (de- ceased 1860); m. 2d, Laura Giddings, Dec. 31, 1863. Admitted to Ind. bar, 1840; Whig mem. Ind. Ho. of Reps., 1845-46; mem. U.S. Ho. of Reps. (Free- Soiler) from Ind., 31st, 37th-41st congresses, 1849- 51, 61-71; because of abolitionist convictions op- posed compromise measures of 1850; unsuccessful Free-Soil candidate for vice pres. U.S., 1852; chmn. com. on public lands which passed Homestead Act; a Radical, opposed Pres. Johnson; mem. com. to prepare articles of impeachment against Johnson, 1867; proposed a constl. amendment extending suf- frage to women, 1868; surveyor gen. of N.M. (apptd. by Pres. Cleveland), 1885-89, exposed many land grant frauds. Author: Speeches on Political Ques- tions, 1872; The Gospel of Reform (speech support- ing Tilden for presidency, 2 million copies distri- buted), 1876; Political Recollections, 1840-72, pub- lished 1884. Died July 7, 1899.

JUMEL, Stephen, wine mcht.; b. circa 1754; m. Eliza Brown (also known as Betsey Bowen), Apr. 7, 1804. Came from Haiti to N.Y.C., 1795; partner (with Jacques Desobry) in wine bus., ac- cumulated considerable fortune; his widow (who was main cause of his losing his fortune before he died) became famous as wife of Aaron Burr. Died May 22, 1832.

JUNEAU, Solomon Laurent, mayor Milw.; b. L'Assomption, Can., Aug. 9, 1793; s. Francois and Therese Galerneau (LaTulipe) J.; m. Josette Vieau. Began operations at tract of land (now Milw.), 1818; agt. American Fur Co.; formed partnership with Morgan L. Martin to plot a town on Milwaukee River (now Milw.), 1833, accomplished, 1835; be- came 1st postmaster and 1st pres. of town; donated square for a courthouse and land for a lighthouse; later gave lots for Catholic cathedral and Protes- tant Milw. Female Coll.; built 1st store, 1st inn in town; became 1st mayor when city was incorpo- rated in 1846; lived on plot of ground in Dodge County where he founded village of Theresa, 1852; del. to Nat. Democratic Conv., 1856. Died Menom- inee Indian Reservation, Nov. 14, 1856; buried Milw.

JUNGMAN, John George, missionary; b. Hocken- heim, Baden, Apr. 19, 1720; s. Johann Jungman; m. Anna Bechtel Bütner, Aug. 24, 1745. Came to Phila., 1732; took 1st Holy Communion at Moravian Community, Bethlehem, Pa., 1743; Moravian mission- ary at Guadenhüten on the Mahoning, 1746-54, at Christiansbrum, Schonbrum on the Muskingum, De- troit, other locations, 1754-85; captured by English and sent to Detroit, 1781; retired from active missionary activities, 1785. Died July 17, 1808.

JUNKIN, George, clergyman, coll. pres.; b. Cum- berland County, Pa., Nov. 1, 1790; s. Joseph and Eleanor (Cochran) J.; grad. Jefferson Coll., 1813; m. Julia Miller, June 1, 1819; children—Eleanor, Margaret. Licensed to preach, 1816; ordained to ministry Presbyn. Ch., 1818; pastor, Milton, Pa., 1819-30; instigated establishment Milton Acad.; commr. Gen. Synod of Asso. Reformed Ch., 1826; prominent in councils and controversies of Presbyn. Ch.; prin. Manual Labor Acad. of Pa., German- town; 1st pres. Lafayette Coll., Easton, Pa., 1832- 41, 44-48; pres. Miami U., Oxford, O., 1841-44, Washington Coll., Lexington, Va., 1848-61. Died Easton, May 20, 1868.

K

KALB, Johann, army officer; b. Huttendorf, Ba- varia, June 29, 1721; s. Johan Leonhard and Margarethe Seitz (Putz) K.; m. Anna Van Robais, Apr. 10, 1764. Known as "Baron de Kalb"; served as lt. in Count Loewendal's Regt., French Inf. un- der name "Jean de Kalb", capt., adj. officer of detail, 1747; commd. maj. during Seven Years' War, 1756; secret agt. of French Govt. in Am., 1768; returned to Am. to enter patriot cause, 1776; maj. gen. Continental Army, served with Washington at Valley Forge; joined Gen. Gates nr. Camden, S.C., 1780, their combined forces attacked British un- der Cornwallis and Rawdon, Aug. 1780. Died from wound received in battle at Camden, Aug. 19, 1780.

KALBFLEISCH, Martin, congressman, mayor Bk- lyn.; b. Flushing, Holland, Feb. 8, 1804; attended pub. schs.; studied chemistry. Came to U.S., set- tled in N.Y.C., 1826; engaged in mfg. and selling paints, N.Y.C.; health warden, N.Y.C., 1832, sch. trustee, 1836; established chem. factory, Green- point, N.Y., 1844; supr. of Bushwick (N.Y.), 1852- 54; mayor of Bklyn., 1862-64, 67-71; mem. U.S. Ho. of Reps. (Democrat) from N.Y., 38th Con- gress, 1863-65. Died Bklyn., Feb. 12, 1883; buried Greenwood Cemetery, Bklyn.

KALISCH, Isidor, clergyman; b. Posen, Prussia, Nov. 15, 1816; s. Burnham and Sarah (Tobias) K.; attended univs. of Berlin, Breslau, Prague; m. Charlotte Bankman, 1843 (dec. 1856); m. 2d, Adelaide Baer, 1864. Forced to leave Prussia due to radical views, 1848, came to N.Y.C., 1849; rabbi in Cleve., Cincinnati, Milw., Indpls., Detroit, Leaven- worth (Kan.), Newark, Nashville (Tenn.), 1850- 75; a moulder of reform Judaism in U.S.; opened Conf. of Reform Rabbis, Cleve., 1855. Author: A Guide for Rational Enquiries into the Biblical Writ- ings, Being an Examination of the Doctrinal Dif- ference Between Judaism and Primitive Christianity Based Upon A Critical Exposition of the Book of Matthew, 1857. Died Newark, N.J., May 11, 1886.

KAMAIAKAN, Indian chief; b. at what is now Lewiston, Ida., circa 1800; s. Jayayaheha and Kaenoxnith. Chief, Yakima Indians; helped obtain establishment of mission in Yakima Valley, 1847; influenced other tribes not to war with whites; failed in efforts to prevent cessions of land in Treaty of 1855, aroused most of Northwest tribes to fight, defeated, 1858 (his defeat brought out- break to end). Died circa 1880.

KAMEHAMEHA I, Hawaiian king; born on Kohala, circa 1737. Chief of 1 of 4 Hawaiian king- doms, 1781; became 1st King of Hawaiian Islands, recognized as ruler of all territories except Kauai and Niikau (ceded to Kingdom of Hawaii 1810), by 1795; maintained law and order throughout king- dom during reign; successfully resisted Russian en- croachments, 1815-16; permitted trade with fgn. nations. Died Kailua, Hawaii, May 5, 1819; buried Hawaii.

KAMEHAMEHA III, Hawaiian king; b. Mar. 7, 1814. Ascended Hawaiian throne, 1824, ruled in own right, after 1832; issued Declaration of Rights and Edict of Toleration, 1839; during his reign Am. missionaries reduced Hawaiian lang. to writing, be- gan publication of books and newspapers; promul- gated 1st laws in Hawaiian lang., by 1840; promul- gated 1st constn. for Hawaii providing for rep. legislature and supreme ct., 1840; issued 1st legal code, 1842; obtained U.S. recognition of Hawaiian independence, 1842, French and Brit. recognition, 1843; decreed land reform, 1845, new penal code, 1850, new constn., 1852. Died Honolulu, Hawaii, Dec. 15, 1854; buried Honolulu.

KANE, Elias Kent, senator; b. N.Y.C., June 7, 1794; grad. Yale, 1813; studied law. Admitted to the bar; began practice of law, Nashville, Tenn.; moved to Kaskaskia, Ill., 1814; apptd. judge Terri- tory of Ill.; del. 1st Ill. Constl. Conv., 1818; 1st sec. of state Ill., 1820-24; mem. Ill. Ho. of Reps., 1824; mem. U.S. Senate (Democrat) from Ill., 1825-35. Died Washington, D.C., Dec. 12, 1835; buried old Kane farm, nr. Fort Gage, Ill.

KANE, Elisha Kent, naval officer, surgeon, ex- plorer; b. Phila., Feb. 3, 1820; s. John Kintzing and Jane (Leiper) K.; attended U. Va., 1838-39; grad. Med. Dept., U. Pa., 1842. Asst. surgeon U.S. Navy in ship Brandywine, 1843; served as surgeon in China, 1844, African coast, 1846, Mexico, 1848, in Mediterranean, 1849; attached to U.S. Coast Survey, served as surgeon in Advance; sailed for Arctic in Grinnell Expdn. sent by U.S. Govt. in search of English expdn. under Sir. Franklin (which had been lost since 1845), 1850-51; sailed for No. seas in command 2d Grinnell Expdn. (with rank of passed asst. surgeon), 1853-55; abandoned ship, hiked to Upernauik, May 1855, arrived, Aug. 6, 1855, returned home, Oct. 1855; brig. entered unknown waters now called Kane Basin. Author: The U.S. Grinnell Expedition in Search of Sir John Franklin, 1853; Arctic Explorations: The Second Grinnell Expedition in Search of Sir John Franklin in the Years 1853, 1854, 1855, published 1856. Died Havana, Cuba, Feb. 16, 1857.

KANE, John Kintzing, jurist; b. Albany, N.Y., May 16, 1795; s. Elisha and Alida (Van Rens- selaer) K.; grad. Yale, 1814; m. Jane Leiper, Apr. 20, 1819; 7 children including Elisha Kent, Thom- as Leiper. Admitted to Pa. bar, 1817; mem. Am. Philos. Soc., 1825, sec., 1828-48, v.p., 1849-57, pres., 1857-58; city solicitor Phila., 1829-30; apptd. commr. to settle claims with France under Conv. of July 4, 1831; atty. gen. Pa., 1845; judge U.S. Dist. Ct. for Eastern dist. Pa., 1846-58;

mem. 1st bd. trustees Girard Coll.; v.p. Instn. for Instrn. Blind, Phila.; vice provost Law Acad., Phila.; pres. bd. trustees 2d Presbyn. Ch. of Phila.; trustee Gen. Assembly of Presbyn. Ch.; dir. Del. & Chesapeake Canal, Girard Bank. Died Phila., Feb. 21, 1858.

KANE, Nicholas Thomas, congressman; b. County Waterford, Ireland, Sept. 12, 1846; attended common schs. Came to U.S., settled nr. Albany, N.Y.; served with U.S. Army during Civil War; engaged in merc. bus.; mem. Albany County (N.Y.) Bd. Suprs., 1883-85; mem. U.S. Ho. of Reps. (Democrat) from N.Y., 50th Congress, 1887. Died Albany, Sept. 14, 1887; buried St. Agnes Cemetery, Colonie, N.Y.

KANE, Thomas Leiper, army officer; b. Phila., Jan. 27, 1822; s. John Kintzing and Jane (Leiper) K.; m. Elizabeth Ward, Apr. 21, 1853. Admitted to the Pa. bar, 1846; clk. U.S. Dist. Ct. for Eastern dist. Pa.; U.S. commr. Eastern dist. Pa.; chmn. Pa. Central com. Free Soil Party, 1848; became friend of Brigham Young, helped end Mormon War, 1857-58; organizer regt. of woodsmen and hunters known as Bucktails, col. regt., 1861, then. lt. col.; commd. brig. gen. U.S. Volunteers, 1862; comdr. 2d brigade 2d div. XII Army Corps, at Battle of Chancellorsville; brevetted maj. gen., 1865; 1st pres. Pa. Bd. State Charities; mem. Am. Philos. Soc. Died Phila., Dec. 26, 1883.

KAPP, Friedrich, lawyer; b. Hamm, Westphalia, Apr. 13, 1824; s. Dr. Friedrich Kapp; attended U. Heidelberg, U. Berlin (Germany); m. Louise Engels. Admitted to practice law at Hamm, 1845; became disillusioned with revolutionary movement, left Germany, 1849; arrived N.Y.C., 1850, became mem. law firm Fitz, Kapp & Froebel; editor New-Yorker Abendzeitung, 1850; Am. corr. for Kolnische Zeitung, 1861-65; had great influence on German-Am. population, especially in getting them to support Union in Civil War; mem. N.Y. Bd. of Immigration, 1867-70; returned to Germany, 1870; Nat. Liberal mem. German Reichstag, 1871-78, 81-84; mem. Prussian Landtag, 1874-77. Author: Leben des Americanischen Generals Johann Kalb, 1862; Aus und über Amerika, 1876. Died Berlin, Germany, Oct. 27, 1884.

KAUFMAN, David Spangler, congressman; b. Boiling Springs, Pa., Dec. 18, 1813; grad. Princeton, 1833; studied law. Admitted to Miss. bar; began practice of law, Natchitoches, La.; moved to Nacogdoches, Tex., 1837; Indian fighter; mem. Tex. Ho. of Reps., 1838-43, Tex. Senate, 1843-45; chargé d'affaires of Tex. to U.S., 1845; moved to Lowes Ferry, Tex.; mem. U.S. Ho. of Reps. (Democrat) from Tex., 29th-31st congresses, Mar. 30, 1846-51. Died Washington, D.C., Jan. 31, 1851; buried Congressional Cemetery, Washington.

KAUTZ, August Valentine, army officer; b. Ispringen, Baden, Germany, Jan. 5, 1828; s. George and Doratha (Lalwing) K.; grad. U.S. Mil. Acad., 1852; m. Charlotte Tod, Sept. 1865; m. 2d, Fannie Markbreit, 1872; 3 children. Enlisted in 1st Ohio Inf., Mexican War, 1846; assigned to 4th Inf. at Vancouver Barracks, Wash., 1852; commd. 1st lt., 1855; commissioned capt. 6th Cavalry, U.S. Army in Civil War, 1861, participated in Peninsular War, 1862; promoted to col., 1862; chief of cavalry XXIII Army Corps; commd. brig. gen. U.S. Volunteers, 1864; chief of cavalry Dept. of Va.; brevetted maj. U.S. Army, 1863, lt. col. and col., 1864, brig. gen. and maj. gen., 1864; brevetted maj. gen. U.S. Volunteers; comdr. 1st Div. XXV Corps (Negro), 1865, entered Richmond; lt. col. 34th Inf., 1866; col., 1874, placed Mescalero Apaches back on their reservation; promoted brig. gen., 1891; commanded Dept. of Columbia, 1891-92. Author: The Company Clerk, 1863; Customs of Service for Non-Commissioned Officers and Soldiers, 1864; Customs of Service for Officers, 1866. Died Sept. 4, 1895.

KAVANAGH, Edward, gov. Me., diplomat; b. Damariscotta Mills, Me., Apr. 27, 1795; s. James and Sarah (Jackson) K.; grad. St. Mary's Coll., Balt., 1813. Admitted to the bar; mem. Me. Legislature, 1826; sec. Me. Senate, 1830; mem. U.S. Ho. of Reps. from Me., 22d-23d congresses, 1831-35; U.S. charge d'affaires to Portugal, 1835-41; chmn. joint select com. on Me. boundary, commr. sent to negotiate settlement of Northeastern boundary between U.S. and Brit. provinces with Daniel Webster and Lord Ashburton, 1842; mem. Me. Senate, 1842-43; gov. Me., 1843-44. Died Newcastle, Me., Jan. 20, 1844; buried St. Patrick's Catholic Cemetery, Damariscotta Mills.

KEAGY, John Miller, educator; b. Lancaster County, Pa., Aug. 31, 1792; s. Abraham and Barbara (Boehm) K.; m. Helen Hulings, 3 children. Tchr., Asbury Coll., Balt., 1818, Classical Acad., Harrisburg, Pa., 1826, Penn Charter Sch., Phila., 1830-35; trustee Dickinson Coll., 1833-35; a leader in movement to secure profl. tng. for tchrs.; founder, contbr. Monthly Jour. of Edn., 1835 (became the Schoolmaster and Advocate of Edn., 1836). Author: An Essay on English Education, 1824; Pestalozzian Primer, 1827. Died Jan. 13, 1837.

KEAN, Charles, tragedian; b. London, Eng., 1811; s. Edmund and Mary (Chambers) K.; m. Ellen Tree, 1842. Made debut as Young Norval at Drury Lane Theatre, London, 1827; made Am. debut as Richard III at Park Theatre, N.Y.C., 1830, appeared (with wife) in Richard III, other tragedies, 1845-46; appeared as guest star (with wife) at Boston Theatre, 1846, toured St. Louis, New Orleans, other Southwestern cities, 1850; gave farewell performances (with wife) in Shakespearian and classical tragedies at Broadway Theatre, N.Y.C., 1865. Died 1868.

KEAN, Edmund, tragedian; b. London, Eng., 1787; m. Mary Chambers, children—Howard, Charles. Made debut as Shylock at Drury Lane Theatre, London, 1814; made guest appearances in Richard III, Hamlet, Othello, The Merchant of Venice, Julius Caesar, at Anthony Street Theatre, N.Y.C., 1820; toured Phila., Boston, other Am. cities, 1821; appeared as Richard III, also Othello at Park Theatre, N.Y.C., 1825, as Richard III at Charleston (S.C.) Theatre, 1826; because of personal notoriety his dramatic appearances caused riots in N.Y.C. and Boston theaters; considered one of theater's finest tragedians. Died 1833.

KEAN, John, Continental congressman; b. Charleston, S.C., 1756. Engaged in merc. bus.; taken prisoner at capture of Charleston by Gen. Cliinton, 1780; mem. commn. to audit accounts of Continental Army (apptd. by Gen. Washington); mem. Continental Congress from S.C., 1785-87; cashier Bank of U.S. (apptd. by Pres. Washington), Phila., until 1795. Died Phila., May 4, 1795; buried St. John's Churchyard, Phila.

KEAN, Thomas, theatrical mgr., actor, author. With Walter Murray gave earliest recorded performance of standard play Cato in warehouse owned by William Plumstead, Phila., 1749; gave 1st recorded season of standard plays presented on a schedule (plays included Richard III, The Spanish Friar, The Orphan, The Beaux' Stratagem, The History of George Barnwell, Love for Love, also other popular London comedies and dramas), in small auditorium of Hon. Rip Van Dam, Esq., Nassau Street, N.Y.C., 1750-51; left (with Murray and Charles Somerset Woodham) for Williamsburg, Va., 1751, constructed theater and gave season of plays.

KEARNEY, Drye, Continental congressman; b. Kent County, Del.; studied law. Admitted to New Castle County (Del.) bar, 1784; began practice of law, Dover, Del.; mem. Continental Congress from Del., 1787-88. Died Dover, circa Nov. 1, 1791.

KEARNY, Francis, engraver; b. Perth Amboy, N.J., July 23, 1785; s. Michael and Elizabeth (Lawrence) K.; attended Columbia Acad. of Painting; apprenticed to engraver Peter R. Maverick, 1803. Opened engraving studio, N.Y.C., 1806, in Phila., 1810-37. Engraver: The Last Supper (based on Leonardo DaVinci), 1833; Our Savior Healing the Sick; some plates for John Pinkerton's General Collection of the Best and Most Interesting Voyages and Travels, 1810-12. Died Perth Amboy, Sept. 1, 1837; buried St. Peter's Ch., Perth Amboy.

KEARNY, Lawrence, naval officer; b. Perth Amboy, N.J., Nov. 30, 1789; s. Michael and Elizabeth (Lawrence) K.; m. Josephine Hall, Jan. 2, 1834, 2 children. Apptd. midshipman U.S. Navy, 1807, commd. lt., 1813; commanded schooners Caroline, Ferret, Nonsuch during War of 1812; promoted master commandant, 1825; in service against Mediterranean pirates, 1825; promoted capt., 1832; commanded East India Squadron, 1840-43; obtained promise from China that U.S. would be allowed same trading privileges with China as England and Japan; pres. bd. examiners of midshipmen, 1846; commandant Norfolk Navy Yard, 1847; gen. supt. ocean mail steamships at N.Y.C., 1852; retired, 1861; promoted commodore, ret., 1867; mayor of Perth Amboy, 1848-49. Died Perth Amboy, Nov. 29, 1868.

KEARNY, Philip, army officer; b. N.Y.C., June 1, 1814; s. Philip and Susan (Watts) K.; grad. Columbia, 1833; m. Diana Bullett, June 24, 1841; m. 2d, Agnes Maxwell, 1858; 4 children. Commd. 2d lt. 1st U.S. Dragoons, 1837; sent to France to study tactics in cavalry sch. at Saumur, 1839; served with Chausseure Afrique in Algiers, 1840; a.d.c. to Gen. Alexander Macomb (comdr.-in-chief U.S. Army), later Gen. Winfield Scott, 1840-46; lead advance to City of Mexico in Mexican War, 1846; resigned from U.S. Army, 1851; returned to France as mem. staff Gen. Morris, French Army, 1859; command of cavalry of guard under Napoleon II in Italian Wars; decorated cross Legion d'Honneur by French Emperor; commd. brig. gen. 1st N.J. brigade U.S. Volunteers in Gen. Franklin's div. Army of Potomac during Civil War; promoted maj. gen., 1862, in command of 1st div. 3d Corps. Died Chantilly, Va., Sept. 1, 1862; buried Nat. Cemetery, Arlington, Va.

KEARNY, Stephen Watts, army officer; b. Newark, N.J., Aug. 30, 1794; s. Philip and Susannah (Watts) K.; attended Columbia, 1811; m. Mary Radford, Sept. 5, 1830. Served as 1st lt. 13th Inf., U.S. Army during War of 1812; commd. capt., 1813; brevetted maj., 1823; participated Gen. Atkinson's expdn. to mouth of the Yellowstone River, 1825; assumed command of Ft. Crawford, Prairie du Chien, Wis., 1828; maj., 1829; lt. col. dragoons, 1833; commanded 3d Mil. Dept., 1842; leader expdn. to South Pass, 1845; began bldg. 1st Ft. Kearny, Nebraska City, Neb., 1846; commanded Army of West during Mexican War, 1846; commd. brig. gen., 1846; conquered N.M., 1846, mil. gov., 1846; helped draw up code of laws for N.M., 1846; defeated by Mexicans at San Pascual, Cal., 1846; brevetted maj. gen., 1847; leading role in conquest of Cal.; civil gov. Vera Cruz, 1847. Author: Carbine Manual, 1837. Died St. Louis Oct. 31, 1848.

KEARSLEY, John, physician, architect; b. Durham County, Eng., June 4, 1684; s. Rev. John Kearsley; m. Anne Magdalene; m. 2d, Margaret Brand, Nov. 24, 1748; 1 child. Came to Am., 1711; became a leading physician in Pa.; mem. Pa. House of Assembly several terms; wrote essays on yellow fever, smallpox, malaria, pneumonia; architect, builder Christ Ch., Phila., 1727; mem. com. of 3 to plan a state house for Pa., 1729; founded, endowed Christ Ch. Hosp. Died Jan. 11, 1772.

KEATING, John Marie, physician; b. Phila., Apr. 30, 1852; s. William Valentine and Susan (La Roche) K.; grad. med. dept. U. Pa., 1873; m. Edith McCall, 4 children. Vis. physician Phila. Hosp., 1873-80; prof. medicine Women's Med. Coll. of Phila.; gynecologist to St. Joseph's and St. Agnes hosps., asst. physician to Children's Hosp., in charge of children's depts. Howard Hosp. and St. Joseph's Female Orphan Asylum (all Phila.); med. dir. Pa. Mut. Life Ins. Co., 1881-91; visited Far East with Pres. Grant's party, 1879; founder, editor Internat. Clinics, 1891-93; editor Archives of Pediatrics; fellow Coll. Physicians Phila., 1887-93; mem. Am., Brit. gynecol. socs., Assn. Life Ins. Med. Dirs.; pres. Am. Pediatric Soc. Author: With Grant in the East, 1879; Mother's Guide in the Management and Feeding of Infants, 1881; Maternity, Infancy, and Childhood, 1887; Diseases of the Heart and Circulation in Infancy and Adolescence, 1888; Cyclopedia of Diseases of Children, 5 vols., 1889-99; How to Examine for Life Insurance, 1890; A New Pronouncing Dictionary of Medicine, 1892; Mother and Child, 1893. Died Colorado Springs, Colo., Nov. 17, 1893.

KEATING, William Hypolitus, mineral. chemist; b. Wilmington, Del., Aug. 11, 1799; s. John and Eulalia (Deschapelles) K.; grad. U. Pa., 1816, A.M., circa 1820; m. Elizabeth Bollman. Prof. minerology and chemistry U. Pa., 1822-27; largely responsible for discovery of new minerals including red zinc ore, franklinite, dysulsite, zinc carbonate; geologist and historiographer of Maj. Stephen H. Lang's 2d expdn. of 1823; editor Conversations on Chemistry, etc., published 1824; founded Franklin Inst. of Pa., 1824; one of 1st mgrs., elected prof. chemistry; mem. Am. Philos. Soc., 1822, sec.; admitted to Phila. bar, 1834; mem. Pa. Ho. of Reps., 1834; a founder Phila. & Reading R.R. Died London, Eng., May 17, 1840.

KEELER, Ralph Olmstead, journalist; b. No. Ohio, Aug. 29, 1840; s. Ralph and Amelia (Brown) K.; attended St. Vincent Coll., 1854-56, Kenyon Coll., 1858-61, Karl Rupert U. (Germany). As young boy joined minstrel company, became leading attraction as child star; Eastern corr. for Alta California, 1868; apptd. spl. corr. in Cuba for N.Y. Tribune, 1873. Author: Vagabond Adventures (his best work), 1870. Died at sea nr. Cuba, Dec. 17, 1873.

KEELEY, Patrick C., architect; b. Kilkenny, Ireland, 1816. Asso. with his father's archtl. firm, Ireland, until 1841; eame to U.S., 1841, settled in Bklyn.; became noted as designer of Roman Catholic chs., credited with design of over 500 Cath. chs. and cathedrals, N.Y., New Eng. and Can. Prin. works include: Jesuit Ch. of St. Francis Xavier (N.Y.C.); Cathedral of Saints Peter and Paul, Providence, R.I., 1893; Cathedral of Immaculate Conception, Portland, Me., 1866-69; Cathedral of Holy Cross (circa 1867), Ch. of Immaculate Conception (both Boston). Died 1896.

KEELY, John Ernst Worrell, imposter; b. Phila., Sept. 3, 1827; m. Anna M. Keely. Claimed to have made "discovery" of new physical power source, 1873 organized Keely Motor Co., circa 1874, issued stock over entire nation; challenged by stockholders, 1881, rescued from bankruptcy by Mrs. Clara Bloomfield-Moore (who financed co.); his "invention" revealed as hoax in investigation, 1895, and Mrs. Bloomfield-Moore withdrew her support; his "power source" was revealed to public as only a fraud after his death. Died Phila., Nov. 18, 1898.

KEEN, Morris Longstreth, inventor; b. Phila., May 24, 1820; s. Joseph Swift and Ann (Longstreth) K. Organized (with his brother) mfg. firm specializing in flat-irons; secured 1st paper-making patent on a boiler for making paper pulp from poplar wood, 1859; a founder Am. Wood Paper Co., Manyunk, Pa.; established the Experiment Mills, Stroudsburg, Pa. Died Highland Grove nr. Stroudsburg, Nov. 2, 1883.

KEENE, Laura, (stage name; original name unknown) actress; b. Eng., 1826; m. John Taylor; m. 2d, John Lutz; 2 children. Played role of Pauline in Lady of Lyons, 1851; came to N.Y. as leading lady in James W. Wallack's new theatre, 1852; became star Met. Theatre, San Francisco, 1854; mgr. Union, Am. theatres, San Francisco; opened Laura Keene's Varieties, N.Y.C., 1855; mgr., leading lady Laura Keene's Theatre, 1856-63; most successful roles were in Our American Cousin, also The Seven Sisters; during presentation of Our American Cousin at Ford's Theatre, Washington, D.C., the assassination of Pres. Lincoln took place, Apr. 14, 1865; Miss Keene was 1st to reach his box and give assistance to dying Pres. Died Montclair, N.J., Nov. 4, 1873.

KEENE, Thomas Wallace (real name: Thomas R. Eagleson), actor; b. N.Y.C., Oct. 26, 1840; s. Mr. Eagleson; m. Margaret Creighton, at least 2 children. With Cal. Theatre Stock Co., San Francisco, 1857-60; played Henry VI (his 1st important part), Albany, N.Y., 1862; leading man with Kate Fisher, 1865; with Nat. Theatre and Theatre Comique, Cincinnati, 1866-67; at George Wood's Museum, N.Y.C., 1868-69; embarked on tour of country in repertory which included Richard III, Hamlet, Louis XI, circa 1880, tour repeated annually; played Sam with Lucille Western in The Child Stealer, Broadway Theatre, N.Y.C.; appeared with John E. Owens in Salon Shingle. Died Tompkinsville, N.Y., June 1, 1898.

KEEP, Henry, financier; b. Adams, N.Y., June 22, 1818; s. Herman Chandler and Dorothy (Kent) K.; m. Emma Woodruff, 1 child. Invested in depreciated currency during financial crisis of 1837, return to normalcy quadrupled his holdings; opened exchange banking office, Watertown, N.Y.; established several other country banks; began operating in Wall Street, 1850; dealt in stock of Mich. So. & No. Ind. R.R. Co., treas., 1861-63; pres. N.Y. Central R.R., 1866; pres. C. & N.-W. Ry. (of which he had financial control); controlled No. Ind. R.R.; pres., prin. owner Cleve. & Toledo R.R.; left estate of over $4,000,000. Died N.Y.C., July 30, 1869.

KEESE, Richard, congressman; b. Peru (now Ausable) Twp., Clinton County, N.Y., Nov. 23, 1794; attended Keeseville Acad. Engaged in farming; mem. U.S. Ho. of Reps. (Democrat) from N.Y., 20th Congress, 1827-29; engaged in auctioneering; judge Clinton County Ct. Common Pleas, 1835-36. Died Keeseville, Ausable Twp., Feb. 7, 1883; buried Evergreen Cemetery, Keeseville.

KEIM, George May, congressman; b. Reading, Pa., Mar. 23, 1805; attended Princeton; studied law. Admitted to Pa. bar, 1826, began practice in Reading; served as maj. gen. Pa. Militia; del. Pa. Constl. Conv., 1837-38; mem. U.S. Ho. of Reps. (Democrat) from Pa., 25th-27th congresses, Mar. 17, 1838-43; U.S. marshal for Eastern Pa., 1843-50; mayor of Reading, 1852; Dem. presdl. elector, 1860. Died Reading, June 10, 1861; buried Charles Evans Cemetery, Reading.

KEIM, William High, congressman; b. nr. Reading, Pa., June 13, 1813; attended Mt. Airy Mil. Sch. Served to maj. gen. Pa. Militia; mayor of Reading, 1848; mem. U.S. Ho. of Reps. (Democrat) from Pa., 35th Congress, Dec. 7, 1858-59; surveyor gen. of Pa., 1860-62; commd. maj. gen. Pa. Volunteers, U.S. Army, 1861; commd. brig. gen. U.S. Volunteers, 1861. Died Harrisburg, Pa., May 18, 1862; buried Charles Evans Cemetery, Reading.

KEITH, George, clergyman, educator, missionary; b. Peterhead, Scotland, circa 1638; M.A., Aberdeen U., 1658; m. Elizabeth Johnston. Became Quaker, 1664; made missionary expdn. through Holland and Germany, 1677; surveyor gen. N.J., 1685; settled in Phila., 1689; headmaster William Penn Charter Sch., Phila.; mild advocate transmigration of souls; attempted to correct slackness in adminstrn. Quaker discipline; controversy with Pa. Quaker leaders resulted in formation of separatist party "Christian Quakers" or "Keithians", 1690; disowned by London yearly meeting of Quakers, 1695; issued pamphlets against prominent Friends, London, Eng., 1695; entered Anglican Ch., ordained by Bishop of London, 1700; returned to Am. as agt. Soc. for Propagation of the Gospel in Fgn. Parts, 1702; helped expand, establish Episcopal Ch. in N.J. Author: Immediate Revelation Not Ceased, 1668; The Universall Free Grace of The Gospel Asserted, 1671. Died Eng., Mar. 27, 1716.

KEITH, Lawrence Massillon, congressman, army officer; b. Orangeburg Dist., S.C., Oct. 4, 1824; s. George and Mary (Wannamaker) K.; grad. S.C. Coll. (now U. S.C.), 1843; m. Susanna Sparks, 2 children. Admitted to S.C. bar, 1845; mem. U.S. Ho. of Reps. from S.C., 33d-36th congresses, 1853-July 16, 1856, re-elected to fill vacancy caused by his own resignation, Aug. 6, 1856-Dec. 1860; mem. Provisional Congress of Confederacy, Montgomery, Ala., later Richmond, Va., 1861; organized, commd. col. 20th Regt., S.C. Volunteers, later brig. gen.; mortally wounded at Battle of Cold Harbor (Va.), June 1, 1864. Died Cold Harbor, June 2, 1864; buried family cemetery nr. St. Mathews, S.C.

KEITH, Sir William, colonial gov.; b. Peterhead, Eng., 1680; s. Sir William and Jean (Smith) K.; m. Ann Newbury; 5 children. Surveyor gen. customs for So. colonies, 1714-15; gov. Pa. and Del., 1717-26, sided with Assembly; drafted "Report on the Progress of the French Nation," 1719; elected to Pa. Assembly, 1726; assisted in negotiations of treaty of 1730 with a delegation of Cherokee Indians. Author: Discourse (concerning colonial settlement, trade, industry), 1728. Died London, Eng., Nov. 18, 1749.

KELLER, Mathias, composer; b. Ulm, Würtemberg, Germany, Mar. 20, 1813; at least 1 child. First violinist Royal Chapel, Vienna, Austria, 1829-34; bandmaster 3d Royal Brigade, Vienna, 1834-41; came to Am., 1846; established Keller's Patent Steam Violin Manufactory, Phila., 1857. Author: A Collection of Poems, 1874; hymn Speed our Republic, O Father on High, circa 1860, also over 100 songs including The Girls of Dear New England. Died Boston, Oct. 12, 1875; buried Boston.

KELLEY, Alfred, transp. pioneer; b. Middlefield, Conn., Nov. 7, 1789; s. Daniel and Jemima (Stow) K.; m. Mary Willes, Aug. 25, 1817, 11 children. Admitted to Cleve. bar, 1810, Cleve.'s 1st lawyer; pros. atty. Cuyahoga County, 1810-22; pres., village of Cleve., 1814-16; pres. Comml. Bank of Lake Erie, 1816; an incorporator Cleve. Pier Co., 1816; mem. Ohio Legislature, 1814-57; canal commr. State of Ohio, 1822-25, acting canal commr., 1825-34, played major part in promotion of state canal system; commr. Canal Fund, reestablishing Ohio's credit, 1841-43; backed and wrote legislation which reformed state banking system (Act of 1845) and gen. property tax system (Act of 1846); railroad builder after Mexican War; pres. Columbus & Xenia R.R., Cleve., Columbus & Cincinnati R.R.; pres. Cleve., Painesville & Ashtabula R.R., 1851-54. Died Columbus, O., Dec. 2, 1859.

KELLEY, Hall Jackson, propagandist, colonist; b. Northwood, N.H., Feb. 24, 1790; s. Dr. Benjamin and Mary (Gile) K.; A.B., Middlebury (Vt.) Coll., 1813; m. Mary Baldwin, May 4, 1815; m. 2d, Mary Perry, Apr. 17, 1822; 4 children. Projected a settlement West of Rocky Mountains, 1817; helped to establish the Sunday Sch., Boston; secured act of incorporation from Mass. Legislature to encourage settlement of Ore. Territory, 1829; organized Am. Soc. for Encouraging the Settlement of Ore., 1829; organized several Ore. settlers' parties, 1831; visited Ore., 1834; best writing on Ore. question was Memoir, published in 1839; exerted an influence on the popular and governmental thought in favor of Am. occupation of Ore. Author: Geographical Memoir of Oregon (with 1st map of territory ever compiled), 1830; A History of the Settlement of Oregon and of the Interior of Upper California and of Persecutions and Afflictions of Forty Years' Continuance Endorsed by the Author, 1868. Died Palmer, Mass., Jan. 20, 1874.

KELLEY, Harrison, congressman; b. Montgomery Twp., Wood County, O., May 12, 1835; attended common schs. Moved to Coffey County, Kan., 1858; served to capt. 5th Regt., Kan. Volunteer Cavalry, during Civil War; commd. brig. gen. Kan. Militia, 1865; mem. Kan. Ho. of Reps., 1868-70; dir. Kan. State Penitentiary, 1868-73; receiver U.S. Land Office, Topeka, Kan., 1877-78; mem. Kan. Senate, 1880-84; dep. collector internal revenue; chmn. Kan. Livestock San. Commn.; treas. Kan. Bd. Charities, 1889; mem. U.S. Ho. of Reps. (Republican) from Kan., Dec. 2, 1889-91. Died Burlington, Kan., July 24, 1897; buried Bowman Cemetery, Ottumwa, nr. Burlington.

KELLEY, William Darrah, congressman; b. Phila., Apr. 12, 1814; s. David and Hannah (Darrah) K.; m. Isabella Tennant; m. 2d, Caroline Bartram Bonsall; 4 children. Jeweler's apprentice, Phila., 1827-34; admitted to Pa. bar, 1841; dep. pros. atty. for Phila., 1845-46; judge Phila. Ct. of Common Pleas, 1846-56; an organizer Republican Party in Pa.; del. Rep. Nat. Conv., Chgo., 1860; mem. U.S. Ho. of Reps. (Rep.) from Pa., 37th-51st congresses, 1861-90; member of the ways and means committee, for twenty years and chairman from 1881-83; noted for being an extreme advocate of protectionism for Am. industry. Author: Speeches, Addresses, and Letters on Industrial and Financial Questions, 1872; Lincoln and Stanton, 1885; The Old South and the New, 1888. Died Washington, D.C., Jan. 9, 1890; buried Laurel Hill Cemetery, Phila.

KELLOGG, Albert, physician, botanist; b. New Hartford, Conn., Dec. 6, 1813; s. Isaac and Aurilla (Barney) K.; M.D., Transylvania U. First botanist resident in Cal.; surgeon, botanist U.S. Govt.'s 1st expdn. to Bering Sea; a founder Cal. Acad. Scis., 1853, contbr. to its Proceedings, 1855. Author: Forest Trees of California, 1882. Died Alameda, Cal., Mar. 31, 1887.

KELLOGG, Charles, congressman; b. Sheffield, Mass., Oct. 3, 1773; attended common schs.; studied law. Moved to Cayuga County, N.Y., 1798, founded Kelloggsville; engaged in merc. bus.; operated grist mill, New Hope, N.Y.; admitted to the bar, practiced law; county judge; mem. N.Y. Assembly, 1808-10, 20-22; justice of peace for Semphronius Twp.; postmaster of Kelloggsville, 1814-25; mem. U.S. Ho. of Reps. from N.Y., 19th Congress, 1825-27; engaged in farming; moved to Ann Arbor, Mich., 1839. Died Ann Arbor, May 11, 1842; buried Fairview Cemetery, Ann Arbor.

KELLOGG, Edward, mcht.; b. Norwalk, Conn., Oct. 18, 1790; s. James and Lydia (Nash) K.; m. Esther Fenn Warner, 1817, 1 dau., Mary Kellogg Putnam. Established Edward Kellogg & Co., wholesale dry goods firm, N.Y.C., 1820; invested in real estate, Bklyn.; ret., 1843. Author: Currency, the Evil and the Remedy (written in outraged reaction to Panic of 1837; attacked pvt. usury, high interest, advocated instead govt. notes loaned at low interest), 1843, published in later edits. under title A New Monetary System (served as found. of Greenbackism). Died Bklyn., Apr. 29, 1858.

KELLOGG, Elijah, clergyman, author; b. Portland, Me., May 20, 1813; s. Elijah and Eunice (McLellan) K.; grad. Bowdoin Coll., 1840, Andover Theol. Sem., 1844; m. Hannah Pearson Pomeroy, June 3, 1855, 2 children. Ordained to ministry Congregational Ch.; pastor Congregational Ch., Harpswell, Me., 1844-55, 85-1901, Mariners' Ch., Boston, 1855-67; also chaplain Sailors' Home, Boston, 1855-67. Author: (stories for young boys) Good Old Times, 1867; Lion Ben, 1869; The Young Ship-Builders of Elm Island, 1870; The Sophomores of Radcliffe, 1872; The Mission of Black Rifle, 1876; A Strong Arm and a Mother's Blessing, 1881. Died Mar. 17, 1901.

KELLOGG, Elijah Chapman, lithographer; b. Tolland, Conn., June 13, 1811; studied with Jarvis G. Kellogg. Lithographer with D. W. Kellogg & Co., Hartford, Conn.; partner with brother as firm E. B. & E. C. Kellogg, 1842-48; partner firm Kelloggs & Comstock, 1848-50, Kellogg & Bulkley, 1867; noted as fish breeder, made trip to Europe as agt. to stock ponds for Samuel Colt. Died Hartford, Dec. 14, 1881.

KELLOGG, Francis William, congressman; b. Worthington, Mass., May 30, 1810; attended common schs. Moved to Columbus, O., 1833, Grand Rapids, Mich., 1855; engaged in lumber bus., Kelloggville, Kent County, Mich.; mem. Mich. Ho. of Reps., 1857-58; mem. U.S. Ho. of Reps. (Republican) from Mich., 37th-38th congresses, 1859-65; organizer several regts. during Civil War, served as regtl. col.; collector of internal revenue So. Dist. of Ala., 1866-68; mem. U.S. Ho. of Reps. (Rep.) from Ala., 40th Congress, July 22, 1868-69. Died Alliance, O., Jan. 13, 1879; buried Fulton St. Cemetery, Grand Rapids.

KELLOGG, Orlando, congressman; b. Elizabethtown, N.Y., June 18, 1809; studied law. Admitted to N.Y. bar, 1838, began practice in Elizabethtown; surrogate Essex County (N.Y.), 1840-44; mem. U.S. Ho. of Reps. from N.Y., as Whig, 30th Congress, 1847-49, as Republican, 38th-39th congresses, 1863-Aug. 24, 1865; del. Republican Nat. Conv., Chgo., 1860. Died Elizabethtown, Aug. 24, 1865; buried Riverside Cemetery, Elizabethtown.

KELLOGG, Samuel Henry, clergyman; b. Quogue, L.I., N.Y., Sept. 6, 1839; s. Samuel and Mary (Henry) K.; grad. Princeton, 1861, Princeton Theol. Sem., 1864; m. Antoinette Whiting Hartwell, May 3, 1864; m. 2d, Sarah Constance Macrum, May 20, 1879; 8 children. Ordained missionary by Hudson (N.Y.) Presbytery, 1864; missionary, Fategarh, India, 1865-71; tchr. Theol. Sch. of India Synod, Presbyn. Ch., Allahabad, India, 1873-76; pastor 3d Presbyn. Ch., Pitts., 1877-86; prof. systematic theology Alleghany (Pa.) Theol. Sem., 1877-85; pastor St. James Presbyn. Ch., Toronto, Can., 1886-92; attended Internat. Congress of Orientalists, Stockholm, Sweden, 1889; mem. com. to revise Hindi Old Testament, Landour, India, 1893-99.

Author: The Jews, or, Prediction and Fulfillment, 1883; From Death to Resurrection, 1885; The Light of Asia and the Light of the World, 1885; The Book of Leviticus, 1891; The Genesis and Growth of Religion, 1892; Grammar of the Hindi Language, 1893; A Handbook of Comparative Religion, 1899. Died Landour, May 3, 1899.

KELLOGG, William, congressman; b. Kellogsville, O., July 8, 1814; attended pub. schs.; studied law. Admitted to the bar; began law practice, Canton, Ill.; mem. Ill. Ho. of Reps., 1849-50; judge Ill. Circuit Ct., 1850-55; mem. U.S. Ho. of Reps. (Republican) from Ill., 35th-37th congresses, 1857-63; moved to Peoria, Ill., 1864; declined appointment by Pres. Lincoln as minister resident to Guatemala, 1864; chief justice Neb. Territory (apptd. by Pres. Johnson), 1865-67; collector of internal revenue for Peoria Dist., 1867-69; moved to Miss., 1869; unsuccessful candidate for U.S. Ho. of Reps.; returned to Ill. Died Peoria, Dec. 20, 1872; buried Springdale Cemetery, Peoria.

KELLY, Eugene, banker; b. County Tyrone, Ireland, Nov. 25, 1808; s. Thomas Boye O'Kelly; m. Sarah Donnelly, 1830's; m. 2d, Margaret Hughes, 1857. Came to N.Y., circa 1835; a founder Murphy Grant & Co., chief dry-goods firm on West coast, San Francisco; founded Eugene Kelly & Co. (br. of banking house Donohoe, Ralston & Co.), N.Y.C., 1856; became a multi-millionaire; founded So. Bank of Ga., Savannah; dir. Bank of N.Y., Emigrant Savs. Bank, Nat. Park Bank, Equitable Life Assurance Soc.; chmn. electoral com. N.Y., 1884; mem. N.Y. Bd. of Edn., 13 years; trustee, patron Met. Mus. of Art; treas. Irish Parliamentary Fund; pres. Nat. Fedn. of Am.; trustee Seton Hall Coll.; a founder Catholic U. of Am., Washington, D.C., treas., financial consultant, 1887-94; named chamberlain of Cape and Sword by Pope. Died Dec. 19, 1894.

KELLY, James, congressman; b. York County, Pa., July 17, 1760; grad. U. Pa., 1782; studied law, Tutor, U. Pa., 1782-83; admitted to Pa. bar; practiced law, Phila., 1785-1819; mem. Pa. Ho. of Reps., 1793, 94, 97-98; mem. U.S. Ho. of Reps. from Pa., 9th-10th congresses, 1805-09. Died York, Feb. 4, 1819.

KELLY, John, congressman; b. Apr. 21, 1821; s. Hugh and Sarah (Donnelly) K.; m. Miss McIlhargy; m. 2d, Teresa Mullen, 1870; 5 children. Became mem. Tammany Soc., 1853; alderman N.Y. C., 1853; mem. U.S. Ho. of Reps. from N.Y., 34th-35th congresses, 1855-Dec. 25, 1858; sheriff N.Y. City and County, 1859-62, 65-67; unsuccessful candidate for mayor N.Y.C., 1868; instrumental in ousting Tweed ring from Tammany Hall, 1871, grand sachem, 1874-82; comptroller N.Y.C., 1876-79. Died N.Y.C., June 1, 1886; buried Old St. Patrick's Cathedral, N.Y.C.

KELLY, Michael J., baseball player; b. Troy, N.Y., Dec. 31, 1857; s. Michael and Catherine K. Known as King Kelly; played profl. baseball for Olympics, Paterson, N.J., Buckeyes, Columbus, O.; played right field, catcher for Cincinnati team in Nat. League, 1879; right fielder, catcher Chgo. White Stockings, 1880-87, led league in hitting, 1886; sold to Boston team for $10,000 (an unheard of price at that time), 1887-90; played with Boston Players League Club, 1890-92 loaned to N.Y. team of Nat. League, 1893; hero of Song Slide, Kelly, Slide. Author: Play Ball!: Stories of the Diamond Field, 1888. Died Boston, Nov. 8, 1894.

KELLY, William, senator; b. Tenn., 1770; studied law. Admitted to Ala. bar, began practice in Huntsville; mem. U.S. Senate from Ala., Dec. 12, 1822-25; moved to New Orleans. Died New Orleans, 1832.

KELLY, William, inventor; b. Pitts., Aug. 21, 1811; s. John and Elizabeth (Fitzsimons) K.; m. Mildred A. Gracy, circa 1847. Jr. mem. firm McShane & Kelly, 1846; developer Suwanee Iron Works & Union Forge, mfg. sugar kettles; granted U.S. patent for original invention Bessemer process (a process of air-boiling of steel which made possible inexpensive soft steel), 1857; built 1st successful fitted converter at Cambria Iron Works, 1859; founder axe mfg. firm, Louisville, Ky., 1861; honored by Am. Soc. for Steel Treating with bronze tablet at site of Wyandotte Iron Works, 1925. Died Louisville, Feb. 11, 1888.

KELPIUS, Johann, mystic; b. Schassburg, Transylvania, Germany, 1673; s. Georg Kelp; M.A., U. Altdorf, Bavaria, 1689. Came to Am. as leader of German group waiting for the Millenium, 1694, established community at Germantown, Pa. Author: A Diary of the Voyage to America; Inquisitio an Ethicus Ethnicus Aptus sit Christianae Juventutis Hodegus, 1690. Died Roxborough, Phila., 1708.

KELSEY, William Henry, congressman; b. Smyrna, N.Y., Oct. 2, 1812; attended common schs.; studied law. Admitted to N.Y. bar, 1843, began practice in Geneseo; surrogate Livingston County (N.Y.), 1840-44, dist. atty., 1850-53; mem. U.S. Ho. of Reps. from N.Y., as Whig, 34th-35th congresses, 1855-59, as Republican, 40th-41st congresses, 1867-71. Died Geneseo, Apr. 20, 1879; buried Temple Hill Cemetery, Geneseo.

KELSO, John Russell, congressman; b. nr. Columbus, O., Mar. 23, 1831; grad. Pleasant Ridge Coll., Mo., 1859. Served as capt. of a co. Mo. Militia during Civil War; brevetted maj., lt. col., and col.; mem. U.S. Ho. of Reps. (Independent Radical) from Mo., 39th Congress, 1865-67; prin. Kelso Acad., Springfield, Mo., 1867-69; moved to Modesto, Cal., 1872, to Longmont, Colo., 1885; author, lectr. Died Longmont, Jan. 26, 1891; buried on his estate nr. Longmont, later cremated and ashes scattered.

KELTON, John Cunningham, army officer; b. Delaware County, Pa., June 24, 1828; s. Robert and Margaretta (Cunningham) K.; grad. U.S. Mil. Acad., 1851; m. Josephine Campbell, Apr. 30, 1870; 7 children. Commd. 1st lt. U.S. Army, 1855; commanded a brigade of Pope's div., 1861; served as asst. adj. gen. under Gen. Lyon, 1861; col. 9th Mo. Volunteers, 1861; asst. adj. gen. Dept. of Mo., 1862; aide-de-camp to Gen. Halleck (comdr. Mil. Div. of Janus), 1862-65; brevetted lt. col., col., brig. gen., 1865; chief of appointment bur. Adj. Gen.'s Office, Washington, D.C., 1865-70; commd. lt. col., 1866; prin. asst. to adj. gen., 1885-89; adj. gen. U.S. Army, 1889-92; gov. U.S. Soldier's Home, Washington, D.C., 1892; invented many improvements for service rifle, revolver. Author: Manual of the Bayonet, 1861; Information for Riflemen, 1884. Died U.S. Soldier's Home, July 15, 1893; buried U.S. Soldiers Home.

KEMBLE, Frances Anne (Fanny), actress, reader, author; b. London, Eng., Nov. 27, 1809; d. Charles and Maria (DeCamp) K.; m. Pierce Butler, June 1834 (divorced 1849), 2 children. Made debut in Covent Garden playing role of Juliet in Romeo and Juliet, 1829; made Am. debut with Park Theatre Co., N.Y.C., 1832; was success in U.S. as Julia in The Hunchback (a play written for her by Sheridan Knowles); ret., 1834; published Journal of A Residence in America, 2 vols., 1835; gave public readings from Shakespeare in U.S., Gt. Britain, during 1850's, 60's; responsible for fame of Lenox 1st as summer lit. colony, then as resort of fashion; other works include Frances the First (drama), 1832; Journal of a Residence on a Georgia Plantation (an anti-slavery record of her life in the South in 1838-39 published to influence Brit. opinion during Civil War; her best known work), 1863; Records of a Girlhood, 1878; Records of Later Life, 1882. Died London, Jan. 15, 1893.

KEMBLE, Gouverneur, congressman, mfr.; b. N.Y.C., Jan. 25, 1786; s. Peter and Gertrude (Gouverneur) K.; grad. Columbia, 1803; never married. U.S. consul to Cadiz (Spain) under Pres. Monroe; owner factory known as West Point Foundry Assn., produced 1st fairly perfect cannon ever cast in U.S., received spl. patronage of U.S. govt.; sent to Mediterranean as naval agt. during war with Tripoli; mem. U.S. Ho. of Reps. (Democrat) from N.Y., 25th-26th congresses, 1837-41; del. to Dem. Nat. Conv., 1844, 60; del. to N.Y. State Constl. Conv., 1846. Died Cold Spring, N.Y., Sept. 16, 1875; buried Cold Spring Cemetery.

KEMP, James, clergyman; b. Keith Hall, Scotland, May 20, 1764; s. Donald and Isabel K.; grad. Marischal Coll., Aberdeen, Scotland, 1786; D.D. (hon.), Columbia; m. Elizabeth Noel, 1790, 3 children. Came to Am., 1787; ordained deacon, Phila., 1789, to ministry Protestant Episcopal Ch., 1789; rector Great Choptank Parish, Pa., 1790-1813; asso. rector St. Paul's Parish, Balt., 1813-14; elected asst. bishop to Right Rev. Thomas J. Claggett, with jurisdiction over Eastern Shore dist., Md., 1814; became bishop, succeeded to Episcopate of Md., 1816; his work resulted in revival of Md. Diocese. Died New Castle, Del., Oct. 28, 1827.

KEMP, John, educator; b. Auchlossan, Scotland, Apr. 10, 1763; M.A., Marischal Coll., Aberdeen, Scotland, 1783; LL.D., King's Coll., Aberdeen, 1787; 1 child. Came to Am., 1782; prof. mathematics and natural philosophy Columbia, 1786-99, prof. geography, 1795; said to have influenced views of De Witt Clinton on subject of internal improvement and nat. policy; fgn. fellowship Royal Soc. Edinburgh, 1792; became a Federalist, 1799. Died N.Y.C., Nov. 15, 1812.

KEMP, Robert H., businessman, mus. condr.; b. Wellfleet, Mass., June 6, 1820; s. Nathan and Hannah (Wharf) K.; married. With firm Mansfield & Kemp, shoe dealers, Boston, 1840-circa 1850, in bus. alone, after 1861; owner farm, Reading Mass.; founder, condr. Reading Old Folks' Musical Soc., 1854-70, made several concert tours of U.S., toured Eng., 1861. Author: Father Kemp and His Ol Folks: A History of the Old Folks' Concerts, Com prising an Autobiography of the Author. Die Charlestown, Mass., May 15, 1897.

KEMPER, Jackson, clergyman; b. Pleasant Valley N.Y., Dec. 24, 1789; s. Daniel and Elizabeth (Mari us) K.; grad. Columbia (valedictorian), 1809, D.D (hon.), 1829; D.D. (hon.), Oxford (Eng.) U 1868; LL.D. (hon.) Cambridge (Eng.) U., 1868 m. Jerusha Lyman, 1816; m. 2d, Ann Relf, 1821 3 children. Ordained deacon Protestant Episcopa Ch., 1811, priest, 1814; elected 1st missiona bishop Protestant Episcopal Ch. with jurisdictio over N.W., 1835, also apptd. bishop of Wis., 1854 founded Kemper Coll., Nashotah House, Racin Coll. (all for tng. missionaries); established dioceses, opened numerous schs. and acads., es tablished Episcopal Ch. in N.W.; attended Counc of Bishops of Protestant Episcopal Ch., Eng. 1868. Died Delafield, Wis., May 24, 1870.

KEMPER, James Lawson, gov. Va.; b. Madiso County, Va., June 11, 1823; s. William and Mari (Allison) K.; B.A., Washington Coll., 1842; m Cremora Cave, July 4, 1853, 5 children. Commd capt. U.S. Volunteers, 1847; mem. Va. Ho. Dels. 1853-63, speaker, 1861-62; commd. col. 7th Regt Va. Volunteers, Confederate Army, 1861, brig gen., 1862, maj. gen. in command Conscript Bur. 1864; supported Horace Greeley for Pres. U.S. 1872; gov. Va., 1874-77, urged full recognition o civil rights for Negroes; chmn. bd. visitors Va. Mil Inst. Died Gordonsville, Va., Apr. 7, 1895.

KEMPER, Reuben; b. Loudoun or Faquier County Va. Attempted to establish colony (with his brothers Nathan and Samuel, also John Smith), nr. Bato Rouge, La., 1800, later expelled from his land by Spanish; attempted (with small party of followers) to capture Baton Rouge, 1804, failed, retreated to Miss.; continued to harass Spanish from Miss.; kidnapped, taken across border to Spanish Territory and arrested, 1805; freed almost immediately by Americans on Mississippi River; tried to seize Mobile (now Ala.) and Pensacola (now Fla.) from Spain, 1810. Died Natchez, Miss., Jan. 28, 1827.

KEMPSHALL, Thomas, congressman; b. Eng., circa 1796; attended common schs. Came to U.S., settled in Pittsford, N.Y., 1806; moved to Rochester, N.Y., 1813; employed as carpenter; engaged in merc. bus., milling; alderman, Rochester, 1834, 44, mayor, 1837; mem. U.S. Ho. of Reps. (Whig) from N.Y., 26th Congress, 1839-41. Died Rochester Jan. 14, 1865; buried Mt. Hope Cemetery, Rochester.

KENAN, Thomas, congressman; b. Kenansville, N. C., Feb. 26, 1771; ed. privately. Mem. N.C. Ho. of Commons, 1799-1803, N.C. Senate, 1804; mem. U.S. Ho. of Reps. (Democrat) from N.C., 9th-11th congresses, 1805-11; moved to Selma, Ala., 1833, engaged in planting; mem. Ala. Ho. of Reps., several years. Died nr. Selma, Oct. 22, 1843; buried Valley Creek Cemetery, nr. Selma.

KENDALL, Amos, journalist, postmaster gen.; b. Dunstable, Mass., Aug. 16, 1789; s. Zebedee and Molly (Dakin) K.; grad. Dartmouth, 1811; m. Mary Woolfolk, Oct. 1818; m. 2d, Jane Kyle, Jan. 5, 1826. Admitted to Ky. bar, 1814; editor, in charge of Argus of Western Am., Frankfort, Ky., 1816; largely responsible for Jackson's victory in Ky.; 4th auditor Treasury Dept., 1829-34; mem. Jackson's Kitchen Cabinet, speech writer and adviser to Jackson, 1828-36; postmaster gen. U.S., 1835-39; editor Extra Globe, Washington, D.C., circa 1839; established biweekly Kendall's Expositor, 1841, weekly Union Democrat, 1842; an agt. for collection of claims against U.S. Govt., 1843; bus. agt. for Samuel F.B. Morse, organized several telegraph cos., participated in operation; financially responsible for erection of original, also of present Calvary Baptist Ch., Washington, D.C.; helped found Columbia Instn. for Deaf and Dumb (now Gallaudet Coll.), 1st pres. bd. trustees. Author: Autobiography of Amos Kendall, 1872. Died Washington, Nov. 12, 1869.

KENDALL, George Wilkins, journalist; b. Mount Vernon, N.H., Aug. 22, 1809; s. Thaddeus and Abigail (Wilkins) K.; m. Mlle. Adeline de Valcourt. Founder (with Francis Lumsden) the Picayune, New Orleans, 1837, gained nat. fame as humorist; joined Santa Fe expdn., 1841; on return wrote Narrative of the Texan Santa Fe Expedition, 2 vols., 1844; Picayune became famous for its coverage of Mexican War, 1846-48, during which Kendall reported as mem. staff Gen. Taylor; originated art of war correspondence; Kendall County (Tex.) named for him. Died Oak Spring, Tex., Oct. 21, 1867.

KENDALL, John Wilkerson, congressman; b. Morgan County, Ky., June 26, 1834; attended Owingsville Acad.; studied law; children include Joseph Morgan. Admitted to Ky. bar, 1854, began practice in West Liberty; pros. atty. Morgan County, 1854-58; served as 1st lt. and adj. 10th Ky. Cavalry, Confederate Army, during Civil War; mem. Ky. Ho. of Reps., 1867-71; commonwealth atty. 13th Ky. Jud. Dist., 1872-78; mem. U.S. Ho. of Reps. (Democrat) from Ky., 52d Congress, 1891-92. Died Washington, D.C., Mar. 7, 1892; buried Barber Cemetery, West Liberty.

KENDALL, Jonas, congressman; b. Leominster, Mass., Oct. 27, 1757; children include Joseph Gowing. Engaged in paper mfg., Leominster, 1796; mem. Mass. Ho. of Reps., 1800-01, 03-07, 21, Mass. Senate, 1808-11, Mass. Sch. Bd., 1803, 11, 14, Mass. Exec. Council, 1822; Federalist presdl. elector, 1816; mem. U.S. Ho. of Reps. (Federalist) from Mass., 16th Congress, 1819-21. Died Leominster, Oct. 22, 1844; buried Evergreen Cemetery, Leominster.

KENDALL, Joseph Gowing, congressman; b. Leominster, Mass., Oct. 27, 1788; s. Jonas Kendall; grad. Harvard, 1810; studied law. Taught at Harvard, 1812-17; admitted to Mass. bar, 1818, practiced law in Leominster; mem. Mass. Senate, 1824-28; mem. U.S. Ho. of Reps. from Mass., 21st-22d congresses, 1829-33; clk. of cts. Worcester County (Mass.), 1833-47. Died Worcester, Mass., Oct. 2, 1847; buried Evergreen Cemetery, Leominster.

KENDRICK, Asahel Clark, classicist, educator; b. Poultney, Vt., Dec. 7, 1809; s. Rev. Clark and Esther (Thompson) K.; grad. Hamilton Coll., 1831; D.D. (hon.), Union Coll., 1848; LL.D. (hon.), U. Lewisburg, 1872; m. Ann Hopkins, 1838; m. 2d, Helen Morris Hooker, 1857. Prof. ancient history and modern langs. Colgate U., 1831; prof. Greek lang. and lit. U. Rochester (N.Y.), 1850-95, acting pres., 1863, 77-78, acting prof. Bibl. lit. and New Testament exegesis Rochester Theol. Sem., 1865-69, 75-77; mem. Com. on New Testament Revision, 1872; pres. Am. Philological Assn., 1872-73. Author: An Introduction to the Greek Language, 1841; Greek Ollendorf, 1851; Echoes, 1855; Biblical Commentary on the New Testament, 6 vols., 1856-58; contbr. to Baptist Quarterly, other jours. Died Rochester, Oct. 21, 1895.

KENDRICK, John, navigator, trader; b. Cape Cod, Mass., 1740; s. Solomon and Elizabeth (Atkins) Kenwrick; m. Huldah Pease, Dec. 1767. Commanded privateers during Revolutionary War; pioneer in maritime fur trade; commanded expdn. of the ships Columbia and Washington, left for N.W. Am. 1787; sailed for China, 1789; sailed for N.W. coast, 1791, visited Japan; sailed again from China, 1793, traded on N.W. coast, 1793-94; took part in inter-island war in Hawaiian Islands, 1794; one of 1st Am. seamen in Orient trade. Died Honolulu (Hawaii) Harbor, Dec. 12, 1794.

KENNA, John Edward, senator; b. St. Albans, Kanawha County, Va. (now W.Va.), Apr. 10, 1848; s. Edward and Margery (Lewis) K.; attended St. Vincent's Coll., Wheeling, W.Va., 1865-68; m. Rosa Quigg, Sept. 1870; m. 2d, Anna Benninghaus, Nov. 1876. Admitted to W.Va. bar, 1870; pros. atty. Kanawha County, 1872-77; mem. U.S. Ho. of Reps. from W.Va., 45th-47th congresses, 1877-83; mem. U.S. Senate from W.Va., 1883-93. Died Washington, D.C., Jan. 11, 1893; buried Mt. Olivet Cemetery, Charleston, W.Va.

KENNEDY, Andrew, congressman; b. Dayton, O., July 24, 1810; attended common schs.; studied law. Blacksmith's apprentice; admitted to Ind. bar, 1833, began practice in Connersville; moved to Muncytown (now Muncie), Ind., 1834, practiced law; mem. Ind. Ho. of Reps., 1835, Ind. Senate, 1838; mem. U.S. Ho. of Reps. (Democrat) from Ind., 27th-29th congresses, 1841-47; Dem. caucus nominee for U.S. Senate, 1847. Died of smallpox, Indpls., Dec. 31, 1847; buried Greenlawn Cemetery, Indpls., reinterred Beach Grove Cemetery, Muncie.

KENNEDY, Anthony, senator; b. Balt., Dec. 21, 1810; attended Jefferson Acad., Charleston, Va. (now W.Va.); studied law. Engaged in farming, Charlestown; mem. Va. Ho. of Dels., 1839-43; magistrate Jefferson County (Va.) Ct., 10 years; declined appointment by Pres. Fillmore as consul to Havana, Cuba, 1850; returned to Balt., 1851; mem. Md. Ho. of Dels., 1856; mem. U.S. Senate (Unionist) from Md., 1857-63; del. Md. Constl. Conv., 1867. Died Annapolis, Md., July 4, 1892; buried Greenmount Cemetery, Balt.

KENNEDY, Archibald, colonial ofcl., publicist; b. Craigoch, Scotland, 1685; s. Alexander Kennedy; married twice; m. 2d, Mary (Walter) Schuyler, Dec. 1736; 1 son, Capt. Archibald (Royal Navy). Arrived in N.Y.C., 1710; collector of customs and receiver-gen. Province of N.Y., 1722; mem. N.Y. Gov.'s Council, 1727-61; bought Bedlow's Island in 1746, sold it, 1758. Author pamphlets: Observations on the Importance of the Northern Colonies under the Proper Regulations, 1750; Serious Considerations on the Present State of Affairs in the Northern Colonies, 1754. Died N.Y.C., June 14, 1763.

KENNEDY, John Doby, diplomat; b. Camden, S.C., Jan. 5, 1840; s. Anthony M. and Sarah (Doby) K.; studied S.C. Coll., 1855-57; m. Elizabeth Cunningham, 1857; m. 2d, Harriet Boykin, 1882. Admitted to S.C. bar, 1861; became capt. Company E., 2d S.C. Regt. in Civil War, col., 2d Regt., 1862, brig. gen., 1864; elected to U.S. Ho. of Reps., 1865, denied seat when he refused to take oath; mem. Dem. Nat. Conv., St. Louis, 1876; mem. La. Democratic Exec. Com., 1876, chmn., 1878; mem. lower house S.C. Legislature, 1878-79; lt. gov. S.C., 1880-82; U.S. consul gen., Shanghai, China, 1885-89. Died Camden, Apr. 14, 1896.

KENNEDY, John Pendleton, U.S. sec. navy, author; b. Balt., Oct. 25, 1795; s. John and Nancy (Pendleton) K.; grad. Balt. Coll. (now U. Md.), 1812; m. Mary Tennant, 1824; m. 2d, Elizabeth Gray, 1829. Admitted to Balt. bar, 1816; provost U. Md.; pres. bd. trustees Peabody Inst., Balt.; mem. Md. Ho. of Dels., 1821-23, 46; mem. U.S. Ho. of Reps. from Md., 25th, 27th-29th congresses, Apr. 25, 1838-39, 1841-45; Whig presdl. elector, 1840; chosen to Md. Ho. of Dels., speaker, 1846; sec. navy under Pres. Fillmore, 1852-53; organized Commodore Matthew C. Perry's expdn. to Japan, 1852. Author: Swallow Barn (under pseudonym Mark Littleton), 1832; Horse Shoe Robinson, a Tale of the Tory Ascendency, 1835; Rob of the Bowl: A Legend of St. Iniques, 1838; Memoirs of the Life of William Wirt, 1842. Died Newport, R.I., Aug. 18, 1870; buried Greenmount Cemetery, Balt.

KENNEDY, Joseph Camp Griffith, statistician, govt. ofcl.; b. Meadville, Pa., Apr. 1, 1813; s. Thomas Ruston and Judith (Ellicott) K.; student Allegheny Coll., 1829, LL.D. (hon.), 1862; m. Catharine Morrison, Oct. 21, 1834, 4 children. Owner, editor Crawford (Pa.) Messenger; sec. bd. engaged in preparations of plan for taking 7th census, 1849; apptd. superintending clk. U.S. census, 1850; sec. U.S. Commn. to World's Fair, London, Eng., 1851; commr. Internat. Exhbn., London, some years later; authorized in interests of census work to go abroad to examine statis. systems in Europe; chiefly responsible for orgn. 1st Internat. Statis. Congress, Brussels, Belgium, 1853, mem. 2d, 4th congresses, 1855, 60; superintending clk. 8th census, 1860-65. Died Washington, D.C., July 13, 1887.

KENNEDY, William, congressman; b. nr. Washington, N.C., July 31, 1768; grad. U. Pa., 1782; studied law. Admitted to N.C. bar; mem. U.S. Ho. of Reps. (Federalist) from N.C., 8th, 11th, 12th-13th congresses, 1803-05, 09-11, Jan. 30, 1813-15. Died Washington, Oct. 11, 1834; buried Kennedy Cemetery, nr. Washington.

KENNER, Duncan Farrar, planter, Confederate legislator; b. New Orleans, Feb. 11, 1813; s. William and Mary (Minor) K.; grad. Miami U., Oxford, O., 1831; m. Anne Guillelmine Nanine Bringier, June 1, 1839. Sugar planter, horse breeder, La.; elected to La. Ho. of Reps., 1836; mem. La. Constl. Conv., 1844, pres., 1852; del. from La. to Confederate Provisional Congress, Montgomery, Ala., 1861; La. rep. to Confederate Ho. of Reps., 1861-65, chmn. ways and means com.; secretly sent to Europe as minister plenipotentiary to obtain aid for the Confederacy (failed), 1865; an organizer, pres. La. Sugar Planters' Assn., 1877, Sugar Expt. Sta., 1885; mem. La. Senate, 1866-67; mem. U.S. Tariff Commn., 1882; pres. La. Jockey Club. Died New Orleans, July 3, 1887.

KENNETT, Luther Martin, congressman; b. Falmouth, Ky., Mar. 15, 1807; attended pvt. schs. Dep. county clk. Pendleton County (Ky.), 1822-23, Campbell County (Ky.), 1824; moved to St. Louis, 1825, engaged in merc. bus.; engaged in lead mining, shot mfg., Jefferson and St. Francis counties, Mo.; alderman, St. Louis, 1843-46; v.p. Pacific R.R. Co.; mayor St. Louis, 1850-53; pres. St. Louis & Iron Mountain R.R., 1853; mem. U.S. Ho. of Reps. (Am. Party rep.) from Mo., 34th Congress, 1855-57; went to Europe, 1867. Died Paris, France, Apr. 12, 1873; buried Bellefontaine Cemetery, St. Louis.

KENNICOTT, Robert, naturalist, explorer; b. New Orleans, Nov. 13, 1835; s. Dr. John Albert and Mary (Ransom) K. Naturalist, made comprehensive natural history survey of So. Ill., 1855; a founder Chgo. Acad. Scis., 1856, became curator and trustee, circa 1863, later dir.; organized natural history mus. for Northwestern U., 1857; assembled and labeled collection from Cal. at Smithsonian Instn., Washington, D.C., 1858-59; explorer, made 1st expdn. to Canadian Arctic (now Manitoba, Can.), gathered collections of fauna, 1859; apptd. by Western Union Telegraph Co. to lead expdn. to Alaska to survey for overland telegraph line to Asia, 1865. Died Ft. Nulato, Alaska, May 13, 1866.

KENNON, William, Sr., congressman; b. Uniontown, Pa., May 14, 1793; attended Franklin Coll., New Athens, O.; studied law. Admitted to Ohio bar, 1824, began practice in St. Clairsville; mem. U.S. Ho. of Reps. (Democrat) from Ohio, 21st-22d, 24th congresses, 1829-33, 35-37; pres. judge ct. common pleas, 1840-47; del. 2d Ohio Constl. Conv., 1850; judge Ohio Supreme Ct., 1854-56; resumed law practice, St. Clairsville; became Republican. Died St. Clairsville, Nov. 2, 1881; buried Methodist Cemetery, St. Clairsville.

KENNON, William, Jr., congressman; b. Carrickfergus, Ireland, June 12, 1802; grad. Franklin Coll., New Athens, O., 1826; studied law. Came to U.S., 1816; admitted to Ohio bar, began practice in St. Clairsville; pros. atty. Belmont County (O.), 1837-41; mem. U.S. Ho. of Reps. (Democrat) from Ohio, 30th Congress, 1847-49; judge Ct. of Common Pleas for 15th Jud. Dist., 1865-67. Died St. Clairsville, Oct. 19, 1867; buried Union Cemetery, St. Clairsville.

KENRICK, Francis Patrick, clergyman; b. Dublin, Ireland, Dec. 3, 1796; s. Thomas and Jean (Eustace) K.; entered Coll. Propoganda, Rome, Italy, 1814. Ordained to Roman Catholic Ch., Rome, 1821; came to Am., 1821; assigned to missions in Ky. under Bishop Flaget; prof. theology St. Thomas Sem., Bardstown, Ky.; mem. 1st Provincial Council of Balt., 1829; titular bishop of Arath, consecrated at Bardstown; held diocesan synod, 1832; a founder Catholic Herald, 1833; his advocation of moderation during nationalist riots of 1844 in Phila. paved way for better ch.-community relations; apptd. archbishop of Balt., 1851; apostolic del., presided over 1st Plenary Council, 1852; introduced 40 Hours' Devotionists into U.S., 1858. Author: Theologia Dogmaticae, 4 vols., 1839-40; Theologia Moralis, 3 vols., 1841-43; The New Testament, 1862. Died Balt., July 8, 1863.

KENRICK, Peter Richard, clergyman; b. Dubline, Ireland, Aug. 17, 1806; s. Thomas and Jean (Eustace) K.; ed. St. Patrick's Coll., Maynooth. Ordained priest Roman Catholic Ch., 1832; came to Am., 1833; pres. of sem., Phila., also vicar gen. Diocese of Phila.; editor Cath. Herald; consecrated coadjutor in St. Louis with title Bishop of Drasa, 1841; became bishop of St. Louis, 1843, archbishop, 1847; held one synod, one provincial council; prominent participant Ecumenical Council, Vatican; archbishop of Marcianopolis, 1891. Author: The New Month of Mary, 1840; The Validity of Anglican Ordinances, 1841; The Holy House of Loretto, 1842. Died Mar. 4, 1896.

KENRICK, William, nurseryman; b. Newton, Mass., Dec. 24, 1789; s. John and Mehitable (Meriam) K.; m. Harriot (Russell) Jackson, May 13, 1824. A pioneer in founding present-day fruit industry; established a nursery, 1832, inherited father's nursery, 1833; an original mem. Mass. Hort. Soc., mem. council, 1829-41, recipient spl. award, 1835; contbr. public park to Town of Newton. Author: The New American Orchardist, 1833. Died Newton, Feb. 14, 1872.

KENSETT, John Frederick, painter; b. Cheshire, Conn., Mar. 22, 1816; s. Thomas and Elizabeth (Daggett) K.; studied art in Europe, 1840-47. Engraver, Am. Bank Note Co., N.Y.C., 1838-40; landscape painter and engraver of "Hudson River School," often sketched and painted while wandering over the countryside; became mem. N.A.D., 1849, mem. Nat. Art Commn. to supervise decoration of Capitol Bldg., Washington, D.C., 1859; 38 of his works represented in collection of Met. Mus. of Art, N.Y.C.; principal works include: "View of Windsor Castle" (quickly became famous), 1850; "View on the Arno" and "Shrine" (exhibited N.A.D.) 1848; "Mount Washington from North Conway," 1849; "Sketch of Mount Washington," 1851; "Franconia Mountains," 1853; "High Bank on Genesee River," 1857; "Sunset on the Coast," 1858; Autumn Afternoon on Lake George," 1864; "Glimpse of the White Mountains," 1867. Died N.Y.C., Dec. 14, 1872.

KENT, Edward, jurist, gov. Me.; b. Concord, N.H., Jan. 8, 1802; s. William Austin and Charlotte (Mellen) K.; grad. Harvard, 1821; LL.D. (hon.), Colby Coll., 1855; m. Sarah Johnston, July 26, 1827; m. 2d, Abby Rockwood, 1855; 1 child. Admitted to practice in Supreme Jud. Ct. of Penobscot County (Me.), 1827; mem. lower house Me. Legislature, 1828-29; mayor Bangor (Me.), 1836-38; gov. Me. (Whig), 1840-41; apptd. by Me. Legislature as mem. commn. in support of Me.'s claims to N.E. boundary, 1842; U.S. consul to Rio de Janeiro, 1848-53; justice Me. Supreme Jud. Ct., 1859-73. Died Bangor, May 19, 1877.

KENT, James, jurist, legal commentator; b. Fredericksburg, N.Y., July 31, 1763; s. Moses and Hannah (Rogers) K.; B.A., Yale, 1781; m. Elizabeth Bailey, 1785. Admitted to N.Y. Supreme Ct. bar, 1785; mem. N.Y. State Assembly, 1790, 92, 96; prof. law Columbia, 1793-98, 1823-26; master N.Y. Ct. Chancery, 1796-98; recorder N.Y.C., Mar. 1797; justice N.Y. Supreme Ct., 1798, introduced custom of submitting opinions of important cases in writing; mem. council of revision charged with examining bills from the legislature and vetoing them at their discretion, 1798-1821; helped edit revised statutes of State of N.Y., 1802; chief justice N.Y. Supreme Ct., 1804-14; chancellor N.Y., 1814-23; developed, preserved a line of decisions in law and equity which are fundamental in Am.

jurisprudence; pres. N.Y. Hist. Soc., 1828; prepared Course of Reading for Merc. Library Assn. of N.Y.; a founder Phi Beta Kappa chpt. at Yale. Author: Commentaries On American Law, 4 vols., published 1826-30. Died N.Y.C., Dec. 12, 1847.

KENT, Joseph, senator, gov. Md.; b. Calvert County, Md., Jan. 14, 1779; s. Daniel Kent; m. Eleanor Lee Wallace; m. 2d, Alice Lee Contee. Licensed as physician, 1799; mem. U.S. Ho. of Reps. from Md., 12th-13th, 16th-19th congresses, 1811-15, 1819-Jan. 6, 1826; gov. Md., 1826-29; mem. U.S. Senate from Md., 1833-37. Died "Rosemount" nr. Bladensburg, Md., Nov. 24, 1837; buried "Rosemount."

KENT, Moss, congressman; b. Rensselaer County, N.Y., Apr. 3, 1766; studied law. Admitted to N.Y. bar, practiced law; apptd. 1st judge of Jefferson County (N.Y.), 1795, again apptd., 1810; moved to Cooperstown, N.Y.; mem. N.Y. Senate, 1799-1803; N.Y. Assembly, 1807, 10; mem. U.S. Ho. of Reps. (Federalist) from N.Y., 13th-14th congresses, 1813-17; resumed law practice. Died Plattsburg, N.Y., May 30, 1838; buried Riverside Cemetery, Plattsburg.

KENTON, Simon, Indian fighter; b. Culpeper (now Fauquier) County, Va., Apr. 3, 1755; s. Mark and Mary (Miller) K.; m. Martha Dowden, Feb. 15, 1787; m. 2d, Elizabeth Jarboe, Mar. 27, 1798. Served as scout in Lord Dunmore's War, 1774; apptd. scout by Daniel Boone, leading participant in local encounters with Indians around Ky., Ill.; helped to quell Indian riots in Ill. region during Revolutionary War, 1777; capt. of a volunteer co., helped drive British and Indians out of Ky. region, 1779; served as maj. in Wayne's expdn., 1794; brig. gen. Ohio Militia, 1805; a town in Ohio, also a county in Ky. named after him; fought in Can. during War of 1812. Died Bellefontaine, O., Apr. 29, 1836; buried Urbana, O.

KENYON, William Scheuneman, congressman; b. Catskill, N.Y., Dec. 13, 1820; grad. Rutgers Coll., 1842; studied law, Kingston, N.Y. Admitted to N.Y. bar, 1846, began practice in Kingston; an incorporator Ulster County Savs. Bank (N.Y.), trustee, 44 years; mem. U.S. Ho. of Reps. (Republican) from N.Y., 36th Congress, 1859-61; del. Rep. Nat. Conv., Phila., 1872, Cincinnati, 1876; judge Ulster County, 1883-89; chmn. Ulster County Rep. Com. Died Kingston, Feb. 10, 1896; buried Wiltwyck Rural Cemetery, Kingston.

KEOKUK (Watchful Fox), Indian chief; b. nr. present site of Rock River, Ill., 1780; s. Lalotte. Born into Fox clan; became important in tribal councils; took over as chief Sac (also Sauk)-Foxes when Blackhawk joined British fighting against Americans, 1812; received support of U.S. in return for his aid; kept his people from joining Blackhawk during Blackhawk War, his faction received a reservation on lower Iowa River, 1832; took Blackhawk on tour of East, 1833, 37; spokesman for tribe against Sioux Indians, Washington, D.C., 1837; leader tribe when Sacs and Foxes were removed to Kan., 1845; Keokuk (Ia.) named after him. Died Sauk Agency, Franklin County, Kan., June 1848.

KEPPLER, Joseph, cartoonist; b. Vienna, Austria, Feb. 1, 1838; s. John and Josepha (Pellwein) K.; enrolled Akademie der Bildenden Kunste, Vienna, 1856; m. Pauline Pfau, July 1870. Came to St. Louis, 1867; cover artist for Frank Leslie's Illustrated Newspaper, 1870-76; founder (with Adolph Schwarzmann) Puck Humoristisches WocherBatt, 1876, English edit. inaugurated, 1877. Died N.Y.C., Feb. 19, 1894.

KERFOOT, John Barrett, clergyman, coll. pres.; b. Dublin, Ireland, Mar. 1, 1816; s. Richard and Christiana (Barrett) K.; grad. St. Paul's Coll., 1834; D.D., Columbia, 1850, Trinity Coll., 1865; LL.D., Cambridge (Eng.) U., 1867; m. Eliza M. Anderson, 1842. Came to U.S., 1819; ordained deacon Protestant Episcopal Ch., 1837, priest, 1840; pres. Coll. of St. James, Washington County, Md., 1842-64; pres. Trinity Coll., Hartford, Conn., 1864-66; dep. to Gen. Conv. Episcopal Ch., 1865; consecrated 1st bishop Pitts. Diocese, 1866; attended 1st, 2d Lambeth confs., 1867, 78; attended Old Catholic confs., Freiburg and Bonn, Germany. Died Meyersdale, Pa., July 10, 1881.

KERLIN, Isaac Newton, physician; b. Burlington, N.J., May 27, 1834; s. Joseph and Sarah (Ware) K.; M.D., U. Pa., 1856; m. Harriet C. Dix, 1865, 4 children. Pioneer in care and treatment of mentally deficient children and adults; asst. supt. Pa. Tng. Sch. for Feeble-minded Children at Elwyn, nr. Media, Pa., 1856-62, supt., 1864-93; served with U.S. San. Cmmn. in Army of Potomac, 1863; a founder Nat. Assn. Supts. of Instn. for Feebleminded 1876, sec., 1876-93; framed draft of bill to provide instns. in Western part of Pa.; did important pioneer work in field of psycho-pathology. Author: The Manual of Elwyn, 1891. Died Oct. 25, 1893; buried Elwyn.

KERN, Edward Meyer, artist; b. Phila., Oct. 26, 1823. Exhibited at Artists' Fund Soc., 1841; topographer with Frémont's 3d expdn. to S.W., 1845-47; served under Frémont in Cal. during Mexican War; accompanied Frémont's 4th expdn. to Colorado Rockies, 1848-49; topographer with Simpson's expdn. into Navajo country, 1849; ofcl. artist to Ringgold exploring and surveying expdn. in North Pacific; joined U.S. Navy expdn. to survey route from Cal. to China, 1858-60; served under Frémont during Civil War, 1861, discharged, 1861. Died Phila., Nov. 25, 1863.

KERN, Richard Hovenden, artist; b. Phila., Apr. 11, 1821. Exhibited at Artists' Fund Soc., 1840; executed landscape and figure studies in pencil and watercolor; taught drawing, Phila., circa 1845; topog. draftsman with Frémont's 4th expdn. to S.W., 1848-49, with Simpson's expdn. into Navajo country, 1849; accompanied Sitgreaves' expdn. down Zuni and Colorado rivers, Gunnison's exploration of a Pacific R.R. route, 1853. Killed by Indians nr. Sevier Lake, Utah, Oct. 26, 1853.

KERNAN, Francis, senator; b. Wayne, Steuben County (now Tyrone, Schuyler County) N.Y., Jan. 14, 1816; s. William and Rose (Stubbs) K.; grad. Georgetown Coll., Washington, D.C., 1836; m. Hannah Devereaux, May 23, 1843, 6 sons, 2 daus. Admitted to N.Y. bar, 1840; reporter N.Y. Ct. of Appeals, 1854-57; mem. N.Y. State Assembly, 1860; mem. U.S. Ho. of Reps. from N.Y., 38th Congress, 1863-65; mem. N.Y. Constl. Conv., 1867; instrumental in ousting Tweed ring, 1871; mem. U.S. Senate from N.Y., 1875-81; sch. commr. Utica, (N.Y.), 20 years; bd. regents U. N.Y., 1870-92. Died Utica, Sept. 7, 1892; buried St. Agnes Cemetery, Utica.

KERR, John, congressman; b. nr. Yanceyville, N. C., Aug. 4, 1782; attended common schs.; studied theology; children include John. Licensed to preach as Baptist minister, 1802; settled in Halifax County, Va., 1805; mem. U.S. Ho. of Reps. (Democrat) from Va., 13th, 14th congresses, 1813-15, Oct. 30, 1815-17; pastor Bapt. chs., Arbor and Mary Creek, Va.; moved to Richmond, Va., 1825; pastor 1st Bapt. Ch., Richmond, 1825-32; settled on farm nr. Danville, Va., 1836. Died nr. Danville, Sept. 29, 1842; buried Bapt. Cemetery, Yanceyville.

KERR, John, Jr., congressman; b. nr. Danville, Va., Feb. 10, 1811; s. John Kerr; studied law. Admitted to N.C. bar, began practice in Yanceyville; trustee Wake Forest Coll., 1844-56, U. N.C., 1846-68; mem. U.S. Ho. of Reps. (Whig) from N.C., 33d Congress, 1853-55; mem. N.C. Ho. of Reps., 1858, 60; judge N.C. Supreme Ct. during Civil War; judge N.C. Superior Ct., 1874-79. Died Reidsville, N.C., Sept. 5, 1879; buried City Cemetery, Yanceyville.

KERR, John Bozman, congressman; b. Easton, Md., Mar. 5, 1809; s. John Leeds Kerr; grad. Harvard, 1830; studied law. Admitted to Md. bar, began practice in Easton, 1833; mem. Md. Ho. of Dels., 1836-38; dep. atty. gen. for Talbot County (Md.), 1845-48; mem. U. S. Ho. of Reps. (Whig) from Md., 31st Congress, 1848-51; chargé d'affaires to Nicaragua, 1851-53; resumed practice of law, Balt. and St. Michaels, Md., 1854; solicitor Ct. of Claims, Washington, D.C., 1864-68; solicitor Office of 6th Auditor of Treasury Dept., 1869-78. Died Washington, Jan. 27, 1878; buried "Bellville" nr. Oxford Neck, Talbot County.

KERR, John Glasgow, physician; b. Adams County, O., Nov. 30, 1824; s. Joseph and Jane (Loughridge) K.; attended Denison U., 1840-42; M.D, Jefferson Med. Coll., Phila., 1847; m. Abby L. Kingsbury, Sept. 20, 1853; m. 2d, Isabella Jane Moseley, July 4, 1858; m. 3d, Martha Noyes, June 9, 1886. Practiced medicine, Brown and Adams counties, O.; med. missionary for Bd. Fgn. Missions of Presbyn. Ch., Canton, China, 1854-55; supt. hosp. of Med. Missionary Soc., Canton, 1855-98; a founder, 1st pres. Med. Missionary Assn. of China, 1886; founder 1st hosp. for insane in China, Canton, 1897, supt., 1897-1901. Died Aug. 10, 1901.

KERR, John Leeds, senator, congressman; b. Greenbury Point, nr. Annapolis, Md., Jan. 15, 1780; grad. St. John's Coll., Annapolis, 1799; studied law; children include John Bozman. Admitted to Md. bar, 1801, began practice in Easton; dep. state's atty. for Talbot County (Md.), 1806-10; mem. Md. Electoral Coll., 1816; agt. for State of Md. to prosecute claims against U.S. Govt. for War of 1812, 1817; mem. U.S. Ho. of Reps. (Whig) from Md., 18th-20th, 22d congresses, 1825-29, 31-33; Whig presdl. elector, 1840; mem. U.S. Senate from Md., Jan. 5, 1841-43. Died Easton, Feb. 21, 1844; buried "Bellville" nr. Oxford Neck, Talbot County.

KERR, Joseph, senator; b. Kerrtown (now Chambersburg), Pa., 1765. Moved to Ohio, 1792; justice of peace, Manchester, O., 1797; apptd. judge 1st Quarter Session Ct. of Adams County, N.W. Territory, 1797; surveyor and land agt. during opening of Western territory; clk. bd. commrs. Adams County; moved to Chillicothe, O., 1801, farmed a tract of land which he later lost to a prior claimant; dep. surveyor Va. mil. lands in Ohio; industrialist, engaged in shipping produce on Mississippi River; mem. Ohio Senate from Ross County, 1804, 10, Ohio Ho. of Reps., 1808, 16, 18, 19; a commr. to survey road from Cumberland, Md. to Ohio River, 1806; adj. gen. Ohio, 1809-10; apptd. brig. gen. Ohio Volunteers during War of 1812; operated hotel, slaughter house, salting bus., cooperage, boat bldg. works, gen. mdse. bus.; supplied provisions to Army of N.W. during War of 1812; mem. U.S. Senate (Democrat) from Ohio, Dec. 10, 1814-15; propr. of an inn, Chillicothe; went into bankruptcy; moved to Tenn.; engaged in farming, nr. Memphis, until 1828; moved to La., purchased a homestead and plantation. Died nr. Providence, La., Aug. 22, 1837; buried on his homestead (now covered by Mississippi River).

KERR, Michael Crawford, congressman; b. Titusville, Pa., Mar. 15, 1827; grad. law dept. U. Louisville (Ky.), 1851. Admitted to Ky. bar, began practice in New Albany, Ind., 1852; city atty., New Albany, 1854; pros. atty. Floyd County (Ind.), 1855; reporter Ind. Supreme Ct., 1852-65; mem. U.S. Ho. of Reps. (Democrat) from Ind., 39th-42d, 44th congresses, 1865-73, 75-76, speaker, 1875-76. Died Rockbridge, Va., Aug. 19, 1876; buried Fairview Cemetery, New Albany.

KERR, Washington Caruthers, geologist, educator; b. Guilford County, N.C., May 24, 1827; s. William M. and Euphence (Doak) K.; grad. U. N.C., 1850, Ph.D., 1879, LL.D., 1885; attended Lawrence Sci. Sch., Harvard; m. Emma Hall, 1853. Prof., Marshall U., Tex., 1851-52; with Nautical Almanac office, Cambridge, Mass., 1852; prof. chemistry and geology Davidson College, N.C., 1856-65; chemist, supt. Mecklenburg Salt Co., nr. Charleston, S.C., 1862; state geologist N.C.,1864-82; lectr. geology U. N.C., 1869-84; made map of N.C., published 1882; chief So. div. U.S. Geol. Survey, 1882-83; one of 1st to call prominently to attention phenomena soil creep. Author: Report of the Geological Survey of North Carolina, vol. 1, 1875, vol. 2, 1881; Minerals and Mineral Localities of North Carolina, 1881; Ores of North Carolina, 1888. Died Asheville, N.C., Aug. 9, 1885.

KERSHAW, John, congressman; b. Camden, S.C., Sept. 12, 1765; attended Oxford (Eng.) U.; studied law. Admitted to S.C. bar, began practice in Camden; engaged in planting, wheat milling; tobacco insp., 1789; mem. S.C. Constl. Conv., 1790; judge Kershaw County Ct., 1791; escort of Pres. Washington on his visit to Camden, 1791; mem. S.C. Ho. of Reps., 1792, 1800; mayor of Camden, 1798, 1801, 11, 22; served as capt. 1st S.C. Light Dragoons; mem. U.S. Ho. of Reps. (Democrat) from S.C., 13th Congress, 1813-15. Died Camden, Aug. 4, 1829; buried family burial ground.

KERSHAW, Joseph Brevard, army officer, jurist; b. Camden, S.C., Jan. 5, 1822; s. Col. John and Harrietta (Du Bose) K.; m. Lucretia Douglas, 1844, 5 children. Admitted to S.C. bar, 1843; commd. lt. Palmetto Regt., 1843, served in Mexican War; mem. S.C. Legislature, 1852-56; mem. S.C. Secession Conv., 1860; commd. col. 2d S.C. Volunteers, Confederate Army, 1861, brig. gen., 1862, maj. gen., 1864; participated in battles of Bull Run, Chickamauga, prominent in operations in Va. and Md., including battles of Fair Oaks, Savage Station, Malvern Hill, 2d Bull Run, South Mountain, Antietam, distinguished at Battle of Fredericksburg, 1862; pres. S.C. Senate, 1865; judge 5th Circuit Ct. S.C., 1877-93. Died Camden, Apr. 13, 1894.

KETCHUM, Winthrop Welles, congressman; b. Wilkes-Barre, Pa., June 29, 1820; studied law. Instr., Wyoming Sem., Kingston, Pa., 1844-47; Girard Coll., Pa., 1848-49; admitted to Pa. bar, 1850; practiced law; prothonotary of Luzerne County (Pa.), 1855-57; mem. Pa. Ho. of Reps., 1858, Pa. Senate, 1859-61; del. Republican Nat. Conv., 1860, 64; solicitor U.S. Ct. of Claims, 1864-66; Rep. presdl. elector, 1868; mem. U.S. Ho. of Reps. (Rep.) from Pa., 44th Congress, 1875-July 19, 1876; judge U.S. Dist. Ct. for Western Pa., 1876-79. Died Pitts., Dec. 6, 1879; buried Hollenback Cemetery, Wilkes-Barre.

KETTELL, Samuel, editor; b. Newburyport, Mass., Aug. 5, 1800; s. Jonathan and Mary (Noyes) K. Edited Specimens of American Poetry (1st comprehensive anthology of Am. verse), 1829; contbr. satirical and humorous articles to Boston Courier, 1835-48, editor, 1848; mem. Mass. Gen. Ct., 1851-52; translated, published Personal Narrative of the First Voyage of Columbus, 1827, Records of the Spanish Inquisition, 1828. Died Malden, Mass., Dec. 3, 1855.

KEY, Francis Scott, lawyer; b. Carroll County, Md., Aug. 1, 1779; s. John Ross and Ann (Charlton) K.; grad. St. John's Coll., Annapolis, Md., 1796; m.

Mary Lloyd, Jan. 19, 1802, 11 children. Admitted to Md. bar, 1801, began practice of law, Fredericktown, Md.; went on mission to obtain release of prisoner from British, 1814, wrote poem The Star Spangled Banner while witnessing bombardment of Ft. McHenry from deck of ship Surprise, Sept. 13-14, 1814 (poem published in Balt. American, Sept. 21, 1814, rapidly gained popularity throughout nation); practiced law, Washington, D.C., from 1830; U.S. dist. atty. for D.C., 1833-41; negotiated settlement between state and fed. govts. over Creek Indian lands, 1833; monument erected in his honor in Golden Gate Park, San Francisco. Died Balt., Jan. 11, 1843; buried Mt. Olivet Cemetery, Frederick, Md.

KEY, Philip, congressman; b. (probably) nr. Leonardtown, St. Marys County, Md., 1750; ed. in Eng.; studied law. Engaged in farming, Md.; admitted to the bar, practiced law; mem. Md. Ho. of Dels., 1773, 79-90, 95-96, speaker, 1795-96; mem. St. Marys County Com. of Correspondence, 1774; mem. U.S. Ho. of Reps. from Md., 2d Congress, 1791-93; declined a cabinet appointment offered by Pres. Monroe; declined office of gov. Md. Died St. Marys County, Jan. 4, 1820; buried (probably) in churchyard at Chaptico, Md.

KEY, Philip Barton, congressman; b. Charlestown, Cecil County, Md., Apr. 12, 1757; s. Francis and Anne Arnold (Ross) K.; m. Ann Plater, July 4, 1790, 2 sons, 6 daus. Served as capt. Chalmer's Regt. Md. Loyalists, Brit. Army, 1778; went to Eng., 1783; admitted to Middle Temple, Inns of Ct., London, Eng., 1784; returned to Md., 1785; admitted to Md. bar, 1785; mem. Md. Ho. of Dels., 1794-99; chief justice 4th U.S. Circuit Ct., 1800-02; counsel for Justice Samuel Chase in trial before U.S. Senate, 1805; mem. U.S. Ho. of Reps. from Md., 10th-12th congresses, 1807-15. Died Georgetown, D.C., July 28, 1815; buried Oak Hill Cemetery, Washington, D.C.

KEYES, Elias, congressman; b. Ashford, Conn., Apr. 14, 1758; attended common schs.; studied law. Moved to Stockbridge, Vt., 1785; mem. Vt. Ho. of Reps., 1793-96, 98-1802, 18, 20, 23-25; mem. Vt. Gov.'s Council, 1803-13, 15-17; mem. Vt. Constl. Conv., 1814, asst. judge Windsor County (Vt.) Ct., 1803-14, judge, 1815-18; mem. U.S. Ho. of Reps. (Republican) from Vt., 17th Congress, 1821-23. Died Stockbridge, July 9, 1844; buried Maplewood Cemetery, Stockbridge.

KEYES, Erasmus Darwin, army officer, businessman; b. Brimfield, Mass., May 29, 1810; s. Justus and Elizabeth (Corey) K.; grad. U.S. Mil. Acad., 1832; m. Caroline Clarke, Nov. 8, 1837; m. 2d, Mary (Laughborough) Bissell, Nov. 22, 1862; 10 children including Edward Lawrence. Commd. 2d lt., 3d Arty., U.S. Army, 1833, capt., 1841; a.d.c. to Gen. Winfield Scott, 1837-38, 38-41; instr. field arty. and cavalry U.S. Mil. Acad., 1844-48; served primarily on West Coast, 1851-60; commd. maj. 1st Arty., 1858; mil. sec. to Gen. Scott with rank of lt. col., 1860-61; commd. col. 11th Inf., 1861; commd. brig. gen. U.S. Volunteers, 1861, maj. gen., 1862, brig. gen. U.S. Army, 1862; pres. Maxwell Gold Mining Co., 1867-69; v.p. Cal. Vine-Culture Soc. for Napa County; v.p. Humboldt and Savs. and Loan Socs., 1868-70. Author: Fifth Years' Observations of Men and Events, 1884. Died Nice, France, Oct. 14, 1895; buried West Point, N.Y.

KEYT, Alonzo Thrasher, physician, physiologist; b. Higginsport, O., Jan. 10, 1827; s. Nathan and Mary (Thrasher) K.; M.D., Med. Coll. Ohio, 1848; m. Susannah Hamlin, 1848, 7 children. Inventor multigraph sphygmometer cardiograph; important contbr. to knowledge of circulation, perfected clin. methods of diagnosis of diseased conditions of circulation; papers published under title Sphygmography and Cardiography, Physiological and Clinical, 1887. Died Nov. 9, 1885.

KICKING BIRD (Indian name Tené-Angpóte), Indian chief. A Crow Indian, captured and adopted by Kiowa Indians; had peaceful nature, made successful raids in Tex. after he was accused by his tribe of cowardice, became dominant in tribe; after Civil War he accepted fate of White domination and accepted reservation life in present State of Okla.; responsible for establishment of 1st Kiowa sch., 1872; kept his tribe from war when Tex. refused release of 2 of his chiefs, 1873; kept most of tribe from futile war and from coming under leadership of Lone Wolf, when war with Whites seemed inevitable because of broken treaties and aggression. Died May 3, 1875.

KIDD, William, pirate; b. Greenock, Scotland, 1645; m. Sarah Oort, 1691, 2 children. Known as Captain Kidd; ship owner, sea capt., N.Y.C., by 1690; rewarded by British for services against French privateers, 1691; commd. by N.Y. Gov. Richard Coote (Earl of Bellomont) as privateer to defend English ships against pirates in Red Sea and Indian Ocean; became a pirate in 1697; returned to New York City (New York) to clear himself of piracy charges, 1698; imprisoned, sent to London, Eng., tried for piracy and murder. Hanged in London, May 23, 1701.

KIDDER, Daniel Parish, clergyman, educator; b. South Pembroke, N.Y., Oct. 18, 1815; s. Selvey and Mehetabel (Parish) K.; grad. Wesleyan U., Conn., 1836, D.D. (hon.); D.D. (hon.), McKendree Coll., 1851; m. Cynthia Russell, 1836; m. 2d, Harriette Smith, 1842. Converted to Methodist Ch., 1834; apptd. to new Methodist mission in Brazil, 1837-40; joined Genesee Conf., 1839; sec. Sunday Sch. Union, editor literature of its Sunday schs., 1844-56; pioneer in Sunday Sch. normal convs. and inst. work; edited Sunday School Advocate; taught practical theology Garrett Bibl. Inst., Evanston, Ill., 1856-71, Drew Theol. Sem., Madison, N.J., 1871-81; sec. Bd. Edn. of Methodist Ch., 1880-87; del. to Meth. Gen. confs., 1852,68. Author: Sketches of Residence and Travel in Brazil, 1845; Mormonism and the Mormons, 1846; Demonstration of the Necessity of Abolishing a Constrained Clerical Celibacy; Brazil and the Brazilians, 1857; Treatise on Homiletics, 1864; The Christian Pastorate, 1871; Helps to Prayer, 1884. Died Evanston, July 29, 1891.

KIDDER, David, congressman; b. Dresden, Mass. (now Me.), Dec. 8, 1787; studied law. Admitted to Me. bar, began practice in Bloomfield; moved to Skowhegan, Me., 1817, Norridgewock, Me., 1821; pros atty. Somerset County (Me.), 1811-23; mem. U.S. Ho. of Reps. (Whig) from Me., 18th-19th congresses, 1823-27; resumed practice of law, Skowhegan, 1827; mem. Me. Ho. of Reps., 1829. Died Skowhegan, Nov. 1, 1860; buried Bloomfield Cemetery.

KIDDER, Frederic, mcht., author; b. New Ipswich, N.H., Apr. 16, 1804; s. Isaiah and Hepsey (Jones) K.; m. Harriet Maria Hagar, Jan. 12, 1841. Trader in Southern goods, Boston, 1836-68; mem. New Eng. Historic Geneal. Soc.; contbd. articles to soc.'s Register, also other New Eng. mags. Author: The History of New Ipswich, 1852; Military Operations in Eastern Maine and Nova Scotia During the Revolution, 1867; History of the Boston Massacre, 1870. Died Dec. 19, 1885.

KIDDER, Jefferson Parish, congressman; b. Braintree, Vt., June 4, 1815; grad. Norwich Mil. Acad., Northfield, Vt.; studied law, Montpelier, Vt. Engaged in farming, teaching; admitted to Vt. bar, 1839, practiced in Braintree and West Randolph; mem. Vt. Constl. Conv., 1843; state's atty., 1843-47; mem. Vt. Senate, 1847-48; lt. gov. Vt., 1853-54; del. Democratic Nat. Conv., Cincinnati, 1856; moved to St. Paul, Minn., 1857; joined Republican Party, 1860; mem. Minn. Ho. of Reps., 1863-64; moved to Vermillion, Dakota Territory (now S.D.), 1865; asso. justice Supreme Ct. of Dakota Territory, 1865-75, 79-83; del. U.S. Congress from Dakota Territory, 1875-79. Died St. Paul, Oct. 2, 1883; buried Oakland Cemetery, St. Paul.

KIDDLE, Henry, educator; b. Bath, Eng., Jan. 15, 1824; studied law under Samuel J. Tilden. Came to N.Y.C., 1833; prin., 1st ward sch., N.Y.C., 1843; admitted to N.Y. bar, 1848; asst. supt. public schs., N.Y.C., 1856-70; prin. Saturday Normal Sch. (now Normal Coll.), supt. public schs., 1870-79; spent last years of life in literary pursuits. Author: Cyclopedia of Education, 1876. Died N.Y.C., Sept. 25, 1891.

KIDWELL, Zedekiah, congressman; b. Fairfax, Va., Jan. 4, 1814; grad. Jefferson Med. Coll., 1839; studied law. Moved to Clarksburg, Va. (now W.Va.), 1834, retail clk., sch. tchr.; practiced medicine, Fairfax County, Va., 1839-49; moved to Fairmont, Va. (now W.Va.); mem. Va. Ho. of Dels., 1842-45, 49-50, 52; admitted to Va. bar, 1849; del. Va. Constl. Conv., 1849; Democratic presdl. elector, 1852; mem. U.S. Ho. of Reps. (Democrat) from Va., 33d-34th congresses, 1853-57; mem. W.Va. Bd. Pub. Works, 1857-60. Died Fairmont, Apr. 27, 1872; buried Fairmont Cemetery.

KIEFT, Willem, colonial gov.; b. Amsterdam, Holland, Sept. 1597; s. Gerrit Willemszoon and Machteld (Huydecoper) K. Came to New Amsterdam, N.Y., 1638, gov. New Netherland, 1638-45; his adminstrn. noted for massacre of Raritan Indians, and resulting war; instigated murder of 80 Indians, 1643; replaced, 1645; left Am., 1647; caused great financial loss to his superiors in Holland, hardships to his subjects. Died Welsh Coast, Sept. 27, 1647.

KIER, Samuel M., industrialist; b. Livermore, Pa., 1813; s. Thomas Kier; m. Nancy Eicher; 4 children. Partner firm Hewitt & Kier, operator ry. express; organizer Kier, Royer & Co., owners, operators canal boats, 1838; established Independent Line (dealing in section boats which were boats combined with ry. car, could be placed on rails), 1846-54; pioneer in manufacture of firebrick; sold Kier's Rock Oil, 1846; 1st in Am. to produce refined oil (later known as kerosene). Died Pitts., Oct. 6, 1874.

KILBOURNE, James, congressman; b. New Britain, Conn., Oct. 19, 1770; s. Josiah and Anna (Neal) K.; m. Lucy Fitch, Nov. 19, 1789; m. 2d, Cynthia Goodale, 1808. Ordained to ministry Episcopal Ch., 1800; formed colonization co., Scioto Co., 1801; established community of Worthington, O., 1803; rector Episcopal Ch. (1st in Ohio), Worthington, 1803-04; capt. frontier militia, 1804; U.S. surveyor public lands, 1805; founded Western Intelligencer (1st newspaper in central Ohio), 1811; settled Ohio public lands and great Va. reservation boundary line dispute, 1812; mem. U.S. Ho. of Reps. from Ohio, 13th-14th congresses, 1813-17, introduced 1st Homestead Bill, 1814; mem. Ohio Gen. Assembly, 1823, 24, 38-39. Died Worthington, Apr. 9, 1850; buried St. John's Episcopal Ch. Burying Ground, Worthington.

KILBY, Christopher, mcht.; b. Boston, May 25, 1705; s. John and Rebecca (Simpkins) K.; m. Sarah Clark, Aug. 18, 1726; m. 2d, Martha Neaves; children—Sarah, Catharine. A trader, Boston, 1726-33, 35-39; made business trip to West Indies, 1733-35; mem. Mass. Gen. Ct., 1735-39, sent to London, Eng. as advocate, 1739; remained in London as agt. for Mass. and Boston, representing their interests at Privy Council; agt. English Bd. of Ordnance, 1739-48; banker, also London adviser to Colony of Halifax, 1749-53; agt. victualler Brit. Army in colonies, 1756-63. Died Dorking, Surrey, Eng., Oct. 1771.

KILGORE, Constantine Buckley, congressman; b. Newnan, Ga., Feb. 20, 1835; studied law. Served from pvt. to adj. gen. during Civil War; wounded at Battle of Chickamauga; captured and imprisoned in Ft. Delaware, 1864; admitted to Tex. bar, practiced in Rusk County; elected justice of peace, 1869; mem. Tex. Constl. Conv., 1875; Democratic presdl. elector, 1880; mem. Tex. Senate, 1884-86, pres., 1855; mem. U.S. Ho. of Reps. (Democrat) from Tex., 50th-53d congresses, 1887-95; U.S. judge for So. Dist. of Indian Territory (apptd. by Pres. Cleveland), 1895-97. Died Ardmore, Indian Territory (now Okla.), Sept. 23, 1897; buried White Rose Cemetery, Wills Point, Tex.

KILGORE, Daniel, congressman; b. Kings Creek, Va. (now W.Va.), Apr. 3, 1804. Moved to Cadiz, O.; mem. Ohio Senate, 1828-32; mem. U.S. Ho. of Reps. (Democrat) from Ohio, 23d-25th congresses, Dec. 1, 1834-July 4, 1838. Died N.Y.C., Dec. 12, 1851.

KILGORE, David, congressman; b. Harrison County, Ky., Apr. 3, 1804; attended common schs., Franklin County, Ind.; studied law. Admitted to Ind. bar, 1830, began practice in Yorktown; mem. Ind. Ho. of Reps., 1833-36, 38-39, 55, speaker, 1855; pres. judge Yorktown Circuit, 1838-46; del. Ind. Constl. Conv., 1850; mem. U.S. Ho. of Reps. (Republican) from Ind., 35th-36th congresses, 1857-61; del. Union Nat. Conv., Phila., 1866. Died nr. Yorktown, Jan. 22, 1879; buried Mt. Pleasant Cemetery nr. Yorktown.

KILLE, Joseph, congressman; b. nr. Bridgeport, N.J., Apr. 12, 1790. Moved to Salem, N.J.; sheriff of Salem County, 1822-29, clk., 1829-39; mem. N.J. Assembly, 1856; mem. U.S. Ho. of Reps. (Democrat) from N.Y., 26th Congress, 1839-41. Died Salem, Mar. 1, 1865; buried St. John's Episcopal Cemetery, Salem.

KILLINGER, John Weinland, congressman; b. Annville, Pa., Sept. 18, 1824; grad. Franklin and Marshall Coll., Lancaster, Pa., 1843; studied law, Lancaster. Admitted to Pa. bar, 1846, practiced in Lebanon County, 1846-86; pros. atty. Lebanon County, 1848-49; mem. Pa. Ho. of Reps., 1850-51, Pa. Senate, 1854-57; del. Republican Nat. Conv., Phila., 1856; mem. U.S. Ho. of Reps. (Rep.) from Pa., 36th-37th, 42d-43d, 45th-46th congresses, 1859-63, 71-75, 77-81; solicitor Phila. & Reading R.R. Co. Died Lebanon, Pa., June 30, 1896; buried Mt. Lebanon Cemetery.

KILPATRICK, Hugh Judson, army officer, diplomat; b. Deckertown, N.J., Jan. 14, 1836; grad. U.S. Mil. Acad., 1861; m. Alice Nailer, May 6, 1861. Commd. 2d lt. 1st Arty., U.S. Army, 1861; capt. 5th N.Y. Volunteers, 1861; lt. col. 2d N.Y. Calvary, 1861; commd. brig. gen. U.S. Volunteers, 1863, served in battles of Aldie and Gettysburg; brevetted maj. and col. U.S. Army, then brig. gen. and maj. gen., 1865; one of noted Union cavalry leaders in Civil War; U.S. minister to Chile, 1865-81; dir. U.P. R.R.; del. to Republican Nat. Conv., 1880. Died Valparaiso, Chile, Dec. 2, 1881.

KILTY, William, jurist; b. London, Eng., 1757; s. John and Ellen (Ahearn) K.; ed. Coll. St. Omer, France; m. Elizabeth Middleton. Came to U.S., circa 1774; surgeons mate 4th Md. Regt., Apr. 1778, surgeon, 1780; compiler (authorized by act of legislature) Laws of Maryland, 1799-1800; chief justice Circuit Ct. of D.C., 1801-06; chancellor Md., 1806-21; a founder Soc. of Cincinnati. Died Annapolis, Md., Oct. 10, 1821.

KIMBALL, Gilman, surgeon; b. New Chester, N.H., Dec. 8, 1804; s. Ebenezer and Polly (Aiken) K.; M.D., Dartmouth, 1827; studied surgery in Paris with Guillaume Dupuytren, 1829; m. Mary Dewar; m. 2d, Isabella Defries; 1 child. Surgeon, Lowell (Mass.) Corp. Hosp.; pioneer operations in gynecology; 1st surgeon to remove tumor of uterus by abdominal incision; performed 1st successful removal of ovarian tumor; prof. surgery Vt. Med. Coll., 1844; prof. surgery Berkshire Med. Coll., Pittsfield, Mass., 1845; served as brigade surgeon during Civil War; v.p. Mass. Med. Soc., 1878; pres. Am. Gynecol. Soc., 1882-83. Died July 27, 1892.

KIMBALL, Heber Chase, Mormon pioneer, state ofcl.; b. Sheldon, Vt., June 14, 1801; s. Solomon Farnham and Anna (Spaulding) K.; m. Vilate Murray, Nov. 7, 1822; 45 wives; 65 children. Became a Mormon, ordained to ministry, 1832; ordained one of 12 apostles standing next to Joseph Smith in rank and authority, 1835; named head of 1st Mormon mission to Eng., spring 1837, made trips to Eng., 1837-38, 39-41; one of 1st pioneers to penetrate Gt. Salt Lake Valley; became a chief counselor (with Willard Richards) to Brigham Young, 1847 (Young, Richards and Kimball comprised "1st presidency" representing exec. head of church); elected chief justice and lt. gov. when State of Deseret was organized, later mem. legislature; mem. Council of Utah, until 1858, pres., 1855-58; lt. gov. Utah, until death. Died Salt Lake City, Utah, June 22, 1868.

KIMBALL, Jacob, Jr., musician; b. Topsfield, Mass., Feb. 22, 1761; grad. Harvard, 1780; studied law. Drummer, Mass. Militia, 1775; admitted to the bar; taught music in various New Eng. towns; composed hymns, psalm-tunes; compiled collections The Rural Harmony, published 1793, The Essex Harmony, published 1800. Died almshouse, Topsfield, Feb. 6, 1826.

KIMBALL, Nathan, army officer; b. Fredericksburg, Ind., Nov. 22, 1823; s. Nathaniel and Nancy (Furgeson) Kimball; attended DePauw U., 1839-41; m. Martha Ann McPheeters, Sept. 23, 1845. Raised a company and served as capt. 2d Ind. Regt. in Mexican War, 1846; commd. capt. Ind. Militia, 1861; helped raise 14th Ind. Regt., became col.; commd. brig. gen. U.S. Volunteers, 1862; in command V Army Corps at battles of Kernstown, Antietam, Fredericksburg; had commanding division at siege of Vicksburg, 1863, Battle of Franklin, 1864; mustered out of service, 1865; fought at Atlanta, Franklin and Nashville in charge IV Army Corps; brevetted maj. gen., 1865; helped organize Grand Army of Republic in Ind., became comdr.; elected treas., State of Ind., 1866, 68; mem. Ind. Legislature, 1872; surveyor gen. Utah, 1873. Died Ogden, Utah, Jan. 21, 1898.

KIMBALL, Richard Burleigh, author, lawyer; b. Plainfield, N.H., Oct. 11, 1816; s. Richard and Mary (Marsh) K.; grad. Dartmouth, 1834, LL.D. (hon.), 1873; m. Julia Tomlinson, Apr. 17, 1844, 5 children. Admitted to Waterford (N.Y.) bar, 1836; practiced in N.Y.C., 1836-54; founder Kimball (Tex.), early 1850's; built part of Galveston, Houston & Henderson R.R. (1st railroad in Tex.), pres., 1854-60; best known novel: St. Leger; or the Threads of Life (appeared in Knickerbocker Mag. to which he often contbd.), 1849-50; other works include: Cuba and the Cubans, 1850; Romance of Student Life Abroad, 1857. Died N.Y.C., Dec. 28, 1892.

KIMMEL, William, congressman; b. Balt., Aug. 15, 1812; attended St. Mary's Coll., Balt. Coll.; studied law. Admitted to Md. bar, began practice in Balt.; dir. for State of Md. of B.& O. R.R. Co.; dir. Union R.R. Co.; mem. Md. Democratic Com., 1862-66; del. Dem. Nat. Conv., Chgo., 1864; mem. Md. Senate, 1866-71; dir. Canton Co., Balt., 1869-73; mem. U.S. Ho. of Reps. (Dem.) from Md., 45th-46th congresses, 1877-81. Died Balt., Dec. 28, 1886; buried Loudon Park Cemetery, Balt.

KINCAID, John, congressman; b. nr. Danville, Ky., Feb. 15, 1791; attended pub. schs.; studied law. Admitted to Ky. bar, began practice in Stanford; commonwealth atty.; mem. Ky. Ho. of Reps., 1819, 1836-37; mem. U.S. Ho. of Reps. (Democrat) from Ky., 21st Congress, 1829-31; circuit judge, 1836-37; Dem. presdl. elector, 1844; resumed law practice, also engaged in farming; moved to Gallatin, Tenn., 1870. Died Gallatin, Feb. 7, 1873; buried Bellview Cemetery, Danville.

KING, Adam, congressman; b. York, Pa., 1790; studied medicine U. Pa. Began practice of medicine, York; editor and publisher York Gazette, 1818-35; clk. of cts. of York County, 1818-26; mem. U.S. Ho. of Reps. (Democrat) from Pa., 20th-22d congresses, 1827-33; resumed practice of medicine. Died York, May 6, 1835; buried Prospect Hill Cemetery, York.

KING, Andrew, congressman; b. Greenbrier County, Va. (now W.Va.), Mar. 20, 1812; attended common schs.; studied law. Admitted to the bar; began practice of law, St. Charles, Mo.; mem. Mo. Senate, 1846, Mo. Ho. of Dels., 1858; judge cir-cuit ct. for 19th Mo. Jud. Dist., 1859-64; mem. U.S. Ho. of Reps. (Democrat) from Mo., 42d Congress, 1871-73; resumed law practice. Died Jefferson City, Mo., Nov. 18, 1895; buried Oak Grove Cemetery, St. Charles.

KING, Austin Augustus, gov. Mo.; b. Sullivan County, Tenn., Sept. 21, 1802; s. Walter and Mrs. (Sevier) K. Admitted to Tenn. bar, 1822; mem. Mo. Legislature from Boone County, 1834-37; judge Circuit Ct. of N.W. Mo., 1837-48; gov. Mo., 1848-52; mem. U.S. Ho. of Reps. from Mo., 38th Congress, 1863-65. Died St. Louis, Apr. 22, 1870; buried Richmond (Va.) Cemetery.

KING, Charles, mcht., editor, coll. pres.; b. N.Y.C., Mar. 16, 1789; s. Rufus and Mary (Alsop) K.; ed. Harrow, Eng.; m. Eliza Gracie, Mar. 16, 1810; m. 2d, Henrietta Low, Oct. 20, 1826; at least 1 son, Gen. Rufus. Partner merc. house, 1810; capt. regt. N.Y. Militia during War of 1812; mem. N.Y. Gen. Assembly, 1813-14; propr. N.Y. American, 1823, (American merged with Courier and Enquirer), 1845, asso. editor, 1845; dir. Bank of N.Y.; officer N.Y.C. C. of C.; pres. Columbia, 1849-64; during his adminstrn. coll. grew to a univ. with orgn. of Law Sch., 1858, Coll. Physicans and Surgeons, 1859. Died Frascati, Italy, Sept. 27, 1867.

KING, Charles Bird, artist; b. Newport, R.I., 1785; studied under Benjamin West, London, Eng., 1805-12. Returned to Am., spent several years in Phila. and Balt.; settled in Washington; noted for portraits of Indians; hon. mem. N.A.D. Died Washington, Mar. 18, 1862.

KING, Charles William, mcht.; b. 1809; s. Samuel and Harriet (Vernon) K.; attended Brown U., 1823-25; m. Charlotte Mathews, 3 children. Mcht., went to China, 1826, became partner Olyphant & Co., China; contbr. to Chinese Repository, 1832-40; tried to open Japan to trade with America, 1837, failed. Died at sea while returning to U.S., Sept. 27, 1845.

KING, Cyrus, congressman; b. Scarboro, Mass. (now Me.), Sept. 6, 1772; attended Phillips Acad., Andover, Mass.; grad. Columbia, 1794; studied law. Pvt. sec. to Rufus King (his half brother; U.S. minister to Eng.), 1796; admitted to the bar, 1797, began practice in Saco, Mass. (now Me.); served as maj. gen. 6th Div., Mass. Militia; a founder Thornton Acad., Saco.; mem. U.S. Ho. of Reps. (Federalist) from Mass., 13th-14th congresses, 1813-17. Died Saco, Apr. 25, 1817; buried Laurel Hill Cemetery, Saco.

KING, Dan, physician, pamphleteer; b. Mansfield, Conn., Jan. 27, 1791; s. John and Jane (Knight) K.; grad. Yale Med. Sch., 1814; M.D. (hon.), Berkshire Med. Inst., 1852; m. Cynthia Pride, 1816, 11 children. Licensed to practice medicine, 1815; practiced medicine in Charlestown, R.I. until 1841, Woonsocket, R.I., 1841-48, Taunton, Mass., 1848-59; rep. from Charlestown in R.I. Gen. Assembly, circa 1832-34; a Unionist and abolitionist. Author: The Life and Times of Thomas Wilson Door (his most important literary work), 1859; The Draft, or Conscription Reviewed by the People, 1863; contbr. to Boston Med. and Surg. Jour. Died Nov. 13, 1864.

KING, Daniel Putnam, congressman; b. Danvers, Mass., Jan. 8, 1801; grad. Harvard, 1823; studied law. Engaged in farming; mem. Mass. Ho. of Reps., 1836-37, 43-44, speaker, 1844; mem. Mass. Senate, 1838-41, pres. 1840; mem. U.S. Ho. of Reps. (Whig) from Mass., 28th-31st congresses, 1843-50. Died South Danvers, Mass., July 25, 1850; buried King Cemetery, Peabody, Mass.

KING, Edward Smith, journalist, author; b. Middlefield, Mass., Sept. 8, 1848; s. Edward and Lorinda (Smith) K. Mem. staff Springfield Republican as reporter, sub-editor, editorial writer, 1866-70; published The Great South (book form of articles originally published in Scribner's), 1875; correspondent for Boston Morning Journal in Europe, 1875; published Echoes from the Orient volume of verse, 1880; formed Stanley Club, Paris, France; sec. Societe de Gens de Lettres, Paris; returned to Am., 1888; editorial writer N.Y. Morning Journal and Collier's Once A Week; published his best novel Joseph Zalmonah, 1893; other works include: My Paris, 1868; Kentucky's Love, 1872. Died Bridgeport, Conn., Mar. 27, 1896; buried Bridgeport.

KING, George Gordon, congressman; b. Newport, R.I., June 9, 1807; attended Phillips Acad., Andover, Mass.; grad. Brown U., 1825; attended Litchfield (Conn.) Law Sch.; Admitted to R.I. bar, 1827, practiced law, Providence and Newport; mem. speaker R.I. Ho. of Reps., 1845-46; Whig presdl. elector, 1848; mem. U.S. Ho. of Reps. (Whig) from R.I., 31st-32d congresses, 1849-53. Died Newport, July 17, 1870; buried Island Cemetery, Newport.

KING, Henry, congressman; b. Palmer, Mass., July 6, 1790; studied law, New London, Conn. and Wilkes-Barre, Pa. Admitted to the bar, 1815; began practice of law, Allentown, Pa.; mem. Pa. Senate, 1826-28, 30-32; mem. U.S. Ho. of Reps. (Democrat) from Pa., 22d-23d congresses, 1831-35. Died Allentown, July 13, 1861; buried Union Cemetery, Allentown.

KING, Horatio, lawyer, postmaster gen.; b. Paris, Me., June 21, 1811; s. Samuel and Sarah (Hall) K.; m. Anne Collins, May 25, 1835; m. 2d, Isabella Osborne, Feb. 8, 1875; 7 children. Part owner Jeffersonian, 1830, sole owner, 1831, editor, 1832-38; supt. Fgn. Mail Service, 1850; apptd. 1st asst. postmaster gen. by Pres. Pierce, Mar. 28, 1854, served under Pierce and Buchanan, 1854-61; acting postmaster gen., Jan. 1861; postmaster gen., Feb. 1-Mar. 8, 1861; mem. bd. commrs. to carry out Emancipation Proclamation in D.C., 1862; practiced law, Washington, D.C.; sec. Washington Monument Soc.; leader Saturday Evening Lit. Club. Author: Sketches of Travel, 1878. Died Washington, May 20, 1897.

KING, James Gore, congressman, businessman; b. N.Y.C., May 8, 1791; s. Rufus and Mary (Alsop) K.; grad. Harvard, 1810; attended Litchfield (Conn.) Law Sch.; m. Sarah Rogers Gracie, Feb. 4, 1813, 7 children. Served as asst. adj. gen. N.Y. Militia during War of 1812; established commn. house James G. King & Co., N.Y.C., 1815; sr. partner King & Gracie, Liverpool, Eng., 1818-24; partner in banking house Prime Wood & Sands, N.Y., circa 1825; pres. N.Y. & Erie R.R., 1835-39; persuaded Bank of Eng. to loan 1,000,000 pounds to be distributed in N.Y. banks during financial panic (in which specie payments were suspended), 1837; pres. N.Y. C. of C., 1845-48; mem. U.S. Ho. of Reps. from N.J., 31st Congress, 1849-51. Died "Highwood," Weehawken, N.J., Oct. 3, 1853; buried Grace Ch., Jamaica, N.Y.

KING, John, congressman; b. Canaan, N.Y., 1775; attended common schs. Supr., Town of Canaan, 1806-08; sheriff of Columbia County (N.Y.), 1811-13, 15-19; supr. Town of New Lebanon (N.Y.), 1819-23, 26, 29; mem. N.Y. Assembly, 1824; mem. U.S. Ho. of Reps. (Democrat) from N.Y., 22d Congress, 1831-33. Died New Lebanon, Sept. 1, 1836; buried Cemetery of Evergreens, New Lebanon.

KING, John, eclectic physician; b. N.Y.C., Jan. 1, 1813; s. Harman and Marguerite (La Porte) K.; grad. Reformed Med. Coll. of City N.Y., 1838; m. Charlotte M. Armington, 1833; m. 2d, Phebe Rodman, 1853. Sec. 1st nat. conv. Reform Med. Practitioners, 1848; became prof. materia medica and therapeutics, Memphis, Tenn., 1849; prof. obstetrics Eclectic Med. Inst., Cincinnati, 1851; pres. Nat. Eclectic Med. Assn., 1878; 1st pres. Ohio Eclectic Med. Assn.; leader reform in Am. med. therapeutics; a founder eclectic sch. medicine; introduced to gen. use oleo-resin of iris (1st of resin class of drugs); introduced podophyllin, hydrastis, sanguinaria; most notable work was The American Dispensatory, 1852; an early abolitionist. Died North Bend, O., June 19, 1893.

KING, John Alsop, gov. N.Y.; b. N.Y.C., Jan. 3, 1788; s. Rufus and Mary (Alsop) K.; m. Mary Ray, Jan. 3, 1810, 7 children including Dr. Charles Ray. Admitted to N.Y. bar, circa 1812; served as lt. cavalry U.S. Army during War of 1812; mem. N.Y. State Assembly, 1819-21, 32, 38, 40, N.Y. State Senate, 1823-25; sec. of legation, London, Eng., 1825, charge d'affaires, 1826; mem. U.S. Ho. of Reps. from N.Y., 31st Congress, 1849-51; del. 1st Republican Nat. Conv., Phila., 1856; gov. N.Y., 1857-58; mem. Peace Conv., Washington, D.C., 1861; founder, pres. N.Y. Agrl. Soc. Died N.Y.C., July 7, 1867; buried Grace Ch. Cemetery, Jamaica, N.Y.

KING, John Crookshanks, sculptor; b. Kilwinning, Ayrshire, Scotland, Oct. 11, 1806. Came to Am., 1829, worked as machinist, New Orleans, Louisville (Ky.), Cincinnati, until 1833; took up sculpture; moved to Boston, circa 1840; executed marble portrait busts and cameos. Died Boston, Apr. 22, 1882.

KING, John Pendleton, railroad exec., senator; b. Glasgow, Ky., Apr. 3, 1799; s. Francis and Mary (Patrick) K.; entered Acad. of Richmond County, Augusta, Ga., 1817; married, 1842, 4 children. Admitted to Ga. bar, 1819; del. Ga. Constl. Conv., 1830, 33; judge Ga. Superior Ct., 1831; mem. U.S. Senate from Ga. (Democrat), 1833-37; pres. Ga. R.R. & Banking Co., 1841-78; chief promoter, pres. Atlantic & West Point R.R.; responsible for Augusta Canal, on the Savannah River. Died Summerville, Ga., Mar. 19, 1888; buried St. Paul's Churchyard, Augusta.

KING, Jonas, missionary, diplomat; b. Hawley, Mass., July 29, 1792; s. Jonas and Abigail (Leonard) K.; grad. Williams Coll., 1816, Andover Theol. Sem., 1819; studied Arabic in Paris, France, 1 year; m. Annetta Aspasia Mengous, 1829. Ordained as evangelist by S.C. Congl. Assn., 1819; served in Palestine mission Am. Bd. Commrs. for Fgn. Missions, 1822-25; sent to Athens, Greece by Am. Bd. Fgn. Missions, 1830; planned (with his pupil

Mr. Kalopothakes) a Greek Protestant Ch. which later became a permanent orgn.; unofcl. agt. between the U.S. and the Greek Govt.; U.S. consular agt. at Athens, 1851-57. Author: Farewell Letter (outlined his reasons for not joining Roman Catholic Ch., translated into several langs.), 1825. Died Athens, May 22, 1869.

KING, Preston, senator; b. Ogdensburg, N.Y., Oct. 14, 1806; illegitimate s. John King and Margaret Galloway; grad. Union Coll., Schenectady, N.Y., 1827; studied law under Silas Wright. Admitted to N.Y. bar; established St. Lawrence Republican, 1830; postmaster Ogdensburg, 1831-34; mem. N.Y. State Assembly, 1835-38; participated in Canadian Revolution against Eng., 1837-38; mem. U.S. Ho. of Reps. from N.Y., 28th-29th, 31st-32d congresses, 1843-47, 49-53; mem. U.S. Senate from N.Y., 1857-63; collector of customs Port of N.Y.C., 1865. Committed suicide by drowning, Hudson River, N.Y.C., Nov. 12, 1865; buried City Cemetery, Ogdensburg.

KING, Putnam, congressman; b. New Marlboro, Mass., Jan. 12, 1784; studied law. Admitted to the bar; moved to Greenville, N.Y., 1802, began practice of law; town clk., Greenville, 1815; mem. N.Y. Assembly, 1827; mem. U.S. Ho. of Reps. (Democrat) from N.Y., 21st Congress, 1829-31; county judge Greene County (N.Y.), 1838-47. Died Freehold, N.Y., Nov. 29, 1875; buried Snyder Cemetery, Freehold.

KING, Richard, steamboat capt., rancher; b. Orange County, N.Y., July 10, 1825; m. Henrietta Chamberlain, Dec. 10, 1854. Went to Tex., 1847; in 1848 bought small steamboat and engaged in trade on Rio Grande River; partner, organizer Kenedy & Co., builders, operators steamboats on Rio Grande, 1850-72; purchased 75,000 acres southwest of Corpus Christi, Tex., 1852, established King Ranch (1st ranch in that region), owned more than half-million acres, by 1855; built San Diego, Corpus Christi and Rio Grande R.R. (from Corpus Christi to Laredo, Tex.), 1876-80; Town of Kingsville (Tex.) built on former part of the ranch land, named for him. Died Kingsville, Apr. 14, 1885.

KING, Rufus, Continental congressman, senator; b. Scarboro, Me., Mar. 24, 1755; s. Capt. Richard and Isabella (Bragdon) K.; grad. Harvard, 1777; m. Mary Alsop, Mar. 30, 1786, children—John Alsop, Charles, James Gare. Aide to Gen. Sullivan in expn. to R.I. in Revolutionary War; mem. Mass. Ho. of Reps., 1782; del. Mass. Gen. Ct. from Newburyport, 1783, 84, 85; mem. Continental Congress from Mass., 1784-87; mem. U.S. Constl. Conv., Phila., 1787; mem. Mass. Conv. to ratify U.S. Constn., mem. N.Y. Assembly, 1789-90; mem. U.S. Senate from N.Y., 1789-96, 1813-25; dir. Bank of U.S., 1791; minister to Gt. Britain, 1796-03, 1825-26; unsuccessful Federalist candidate for vice pres. U.S., 1804; author Navigation Act 1818; mem. N.Y. Constl. Conv., 1821; opposed admission of Mo. as a slave state, voted against Mo. Compromise, 1820; proposed buying freedom of slaves with proceeds of sales of pub. lands. Died Jamaica, L.I., N.Y., Apr. 29, 1827; buried Gracie Ch., Jamaica.

KING, Rufus, army officer, editor, diplomat; b. N.Y.C., Jan. 26, 1814; s. Charles and Eliza (Gracie) K.; grad. U.S. Mil. Acad., 1833; m. Ellen Eliot, 1836; m. 2d, Susan Eliot, 1843; 3 children including Gen. Charles. Commd. lt. of engrs. U.S. Army, 1833, resigned commn., 1836; asst. engr. Erie R.R., 1836; editor Albany (N.Y.) Daily Advertiser, 1839-41, Albany Evening Jour., 1841-45; adj. gen. N.Y. State, 1839-43; part owner Milw. Sentinel and Gazette, 1845-47, editor, 1845-61; mem. 2d Wis. Constl. Constn., 1846, adopted, 1848; mem. bd. regents U. Wis., 1848-54; mem. bd. visitors U.S. Mil. Acad., 1849; supt. schs. Milw., 1859-60; commd. brig. gen. U.S. Army, 1861; organized Iron Brigade which fought at Gainesville; U.S. minister to Rome, Italy, 1861, 63-68; resigned from active service, 1868; dep. collector of customs N.Y.C., 1869. Died N.Y.C., Oct. 13, 1876.

KING, Rufus H., congressman; b. Rensselaerville, N.Y., Jan. 20, 1820; grad. Wesleyan U., Lima, N.Y.; studied law. Admitted to N.Y. bar, 1843, began practice in Catskill; mem. U.S. Ho. of Reps. (Whig) from N.Y., 34th Congress, 1855-57; pres. Catskill Nat. Bank, 1865-67, dir. after consolidation with Tanners' Nat. Bank; Republican presdl. elector, 1860; del. Rep. nat. convs., Chgo., 1868, 80. Died Catskill, Sept. 13, 1890; buried Village Cemetery, Catskill.

KING, Samuel, mfr., painter; b. Newport, R.I., Jan. 24, 1748; s. Benjamin and Mary (Haggar) K.; m. Amey Vernon, Aug. 26, 1770; m. 2d, Sarah Ward, Nov. 1795; at least 2 children, Samuel K., Jr., William Vernon. Mfr. nautical instruments, Boston; painted portraits as avocation; taught painting to Edward Malbone, Gilbert Stuart, Anne Hall, Charles B. King; portrait subjects include: Benjamin Mumford, Mrs. Richard Derby, Ezra Stiles. Died Dec. 30, 1819; buried Newport, R.I.

KING, Samuel Ward, physician, gov. R.I.; b. Johnston, R.I., May 23, 1786; s. William Borden and Welthian (Walton) K.; med. diploma Brown U., 1807; m. Catherine Angell, May 20, 1813. Surgeon in Chesapeake, attended Lawrence when he died from wounds received in fight between Chesapeake and Shannon, 1813; town clk. Johnston, 1820-43; 1st asst. to gov. R.I., 1839, acting gov. 1839-40, gov. R.I., 1840-43; put down Dorr's Rebellion, 1842. Died Providence, R.I., Jan. 21, 1851.

KING, Thomas Butler, congressman; b. Palmer, Mass., Aug. 27, 1800; s. Daniel and Hannah (Lord) K.; m. Anna Matilda, Dec. 2, 1824; 6 sons including Henry Lord Page, 4 daus. Admitted to Pa. bar, 1822, Ga. bar, 1823; mem. Ga. Senate, 1832, 34, 35, 37, 59; mem. U.S. Ho. of Reps. from Ga., 26th-27th, 29th-31st congresses, 1839-43, 45-50; pres. Brunswick R.R. & Canal Co., 1840; personal adviser to Pres. Taylor on Cal. statehood, went to Cal. to investigate prospects, 1849; collector of customs Port of San Francisco, 1851-52; unsuccessful candidate for U.S. Senate from Cal., 1851; returned to Ga., 1852; commr. to explain Ga.'s trade interests to Eng., France and Belgium during Civil War, 1861-62. Died Waresboro, Ga., May 10, 1864; buried Christ's Churchyard, St. Simons Island, Ga.

KING, Thomas Starr, clergyman, lectr.; b. N.Y.C., Dec. 17, 1824; s. Rev. Thomas Farrington and Susan (Starr) K.; A.M. (hon.), Harvard, 1850; m. Julia Wiggin, Dec. 17, 1848. Prin., West Grammar Sch., Medford, Mass., 1842; ordained to ministry, circa 1846; 1st pastor Universalist Ch., Charlestown, Mass., 1846-48; pastor Hollis St. Ch., Boston, 1848-59; in charge of Unitarian parish in San Francisco, 1860-64; mem. U.S. San. Commn. in Cal.; best known lectures include: Goethe, Substance and Show, The Lost Arts, Socrates, Sight and Insight, The Laws of Disorder, Webster and the Constitution, Lexington and the New Struggle, Washington and the Union. Author: The White Hills, their Legends, Landscapes, and Poetry, 1860; contbr. letters to Boston Transcript. Died San Francisco, Mar. 4, 1864.

KING, William, ship owner, gov. Me.; b. Scarboro, Me., Feb. 9, 1768; s. Richard and Mary (Black) K.; m. Ann Frazier, 1802, 2 children. One of largest ship owners in U.S.; made fortune in lumber and ship bldg.; overseer Bowdoin Coll., 1797-1821, trustee, 1821-49; organizer, pres. 1st bank in Bath, Mass. (now Me.); rep. Mass. Gen. Ct. from Topsham, 1795, 99; mem. Mass. Legislature from Bath, 1804-06; mem. Mass. Senate from Lincoln County, 1807-11, 1818-19; leader in movement for separation of Me. from Mass.; pres. Me. Constl. Conv., 1819; 1st gov. Me. (Whig), 1820-21; U.S. commr. for adjustment of Spanish claims in Fla., 1821; put into effect the treaty in Spain, 1821-24; trustee Colby Coll., 1821-48; commr. pub. bldgs. Me., 1828; collector customs, Bath, 1830-34. Died Bath, June 17, 1852.

KING, William Rufus Devane, vice pres. U.S., senator; b. Sampson County, N.C., Apr. 7, 1786; s. William and Margaret (Devane) K.; grad. U. N.C., 1803. Admitted to N.C. bar, 1806; mem. N.C. Ho. of Commons, 1807-09; city solicitor Wilmington (N.C.), 1810; mem. U.S. Ho. of Reps. from N.C., 12th-14th congresses, 1811-Nov. 4, 1816; sec. legation Naples, Italy, then St. Petersburg, Russia, 1816-18; mem. U.S. Senate from N.C., Dec. 14, 1819-Apr. 15, 1844, July 1, 1848-Dec. 20, 1852; U.S. minister to France, 1844-46; vice pres. U.S., Mar.-Apr. 1853, took oath of office in Havana, Cuba, through privilege granted by spl. act of Congress. Died "Kings Bend" nr. Cahawba, Dallas County, Ala., Apr. 18, 1853; buried City Cemetery, Selma, Ala.

KING OF WILLIAM, James, editor; b. Georgetown, D.C., Jan. 28, 1822; son of William King; m. Charlotte M. Libbey, 1843, 6 children. With Kendell's Expositor, then with Daily Globe, later Corcoran and Riggs, banking firm (all Washington, D.C.), 1840-48; went to Cal., 1848; worked gold mine, Hangtown (Placeville), Cal., for short time; owner bank, San Francisco, 1849-53; cashier Adams & Co., express and banking firm, 1854-55; founder, editor Daily Evening Bulletin, San Francisco, 1855-56; mem. 1st Vigilante Com., 1851; used his paper to expose corrupt firms, public ofcls. and criminals; shot to death by James P. Casey, politician and publisher of San Francisco Sunday Times, after having assailed Casey's character in his newspaper (Casey lynched on day of King's funeral). Died San Francisco, May 20, 1856; buried Lone Mountain Cemetery, San Francisco.

KINGSBURY, John, educator; b. South Coventry, May 26, 1801; s. John and Dorothy (Leavens) K.; grad. Brown U., 1826, LL.D. (hon.), 1856; m. Mary M. Burgess, Aug. 19, 1834, 9 children. A founder Am. Inst. of Instrn., 1830, pres., 1855-57; conducted pvt. high sch. for girls, Providence, 1828-58; pres. R.I. Inst. of Instrn., 1845-56; commr. public instrn. R.I., 1857-58; mem. Am. Bd. Commrs. for Fgn. Missions; distbr. of Bibles to poor of R.I.; officer of R.I. Alpha chpt. Phi Beta Kappa, 17 years; trustee, fellow, sec. corp. Brown U.; pres. Washington Ins. Co., Providence; sec. and pres. Providence Franklin Soc. Died Providence, Dec. 21, 1874.

KINGSBURY, William Wallace, congressman; b. Towanda, Pa., June 4, 1828; attended acads., Towanda and Athens, Pa. Retail clk., surveyor; moved to Endion, Minn. Territory, 1852; mem. Minn. Territorial Ho. of Reps., 1857; del. Minn. Constl. Conv., 1857; del. U.S. Congress from Minn. Territory, 1857-58; returned to Towanda, 1865, engaged in real estate and ins. bus.; commn. mcht., Balt., 3 years; moved to Tarpon Springs, Fla., 1887, engaged in real estate and merc. bus. Died Tarpon Springs, Apr. 17, 1892; buried Cydia Cemetery, Tarpon Springs.

KINGSFORD, Thomas, inventor, mfr.; b. Wickham, Kent County, Eng., Sept. 29, 1799; s. George and Mary (Love) K.; m. Ann Thomson, 1818; m. 2d, Elizabeth Austen, 1839; 1 son, Thomson. Came to U.S., 1831; supt. starch factory William Colgate & Co., Harsimus, N.J., 1833-46, developed method of producing starch from corn (rather than wheat), 1842; manufactured starch in own plant, Bergen, N.J., 1846-48; founder, owner Oswego (N.Y.) Starch Factory, 1848-69; produced cornstarch suitable for food purposes, 1850. Died Oswego, Nov. 28, 1869.

KINGSLEY, Calvin, clergyman; b. Annsville, Oneida County, N.Y., Sept. 8, 1812; s. Oran Kingsley, Jr.; grad. Allegheny Coll., 1841; m. Delia Scudder, 1841. Admitted on trial to Erie Conf., Methodist Episcopal Ch., 1841, ordained deacon, 1843, elder, 1845; prof. mathematics and civil engrng. Allegheny Coll., 1843-56; editor Western Christian Advocate, 1856; elected bishop, Gen. Conf., Meth. Episcopal Ch., 1864, presided at confs. on Pacific Coast, 1865-66; Author: The Resurrection of the Dead: A Vindication of the Literal Resurrection of the Human Body. Died on trip to Holy Land, Beirut, Syria, Apr. 6, 1870.

KINGSLEY, James Luce, educator; b. Scotland, Conn., Aug. 28, 1778; s. Jonathan and Zillah (Cary) K.; B.A., Yale, 1799; LL.D. (hon.), Middlebury (Vt.) Coll., 1831; m. Lydia Coit, Sept. 23, 1811, 4 children. Librarian, Yale, 1805-24, prof. Hebrew, Greek and Latin langs., also eccles. history, 1805-31, tchr. Greek until 1831, Hebrew until 1835, devoted to study of Latin, 1835-51, prof. emeritus, 1851. Author: Eulogy on Professor Fisher, 1822; Review of Stuart's Select Classics (in Am. Monthly Review), Apr. 1833; History of Yale College, 1835; De Oratore (Cicero), 1838; Historical Discourse Delivered on the Two Hundreth Anniversary of the Settlement of New Haven. Died New Haven, Conn., Aug. 31, 1852.

KINLOCH, Cleland, planter; b. Charleston, S.C., 1760; s. Francis and Anne (Cleland) K.; m. Harriott Simmons, Apr. 15, 1786. Inherited rice plantation from his father, S.C., 1784; mem. S.C. Conv. which ratified U.S. Constn., 1788; mem. S.C. Ho. of Reps., 1791-93; pioneered use of tide movement system of flooding ricefields; built 1 of 1st tidal rice-pounding mills in U.S. Died "Acton," S.C., Sept. 12, 1823; buried Statesburg, S.C.

KINLOCH, Francis, Continental congressman, army officer; b. Charleston, S.C., Mar. 7, 1755; grad. Eton Coll., Eng., 1774; studied law Lincoln's Inn, London, Eng. Admitted to the bar, London; traveled and studied in Paris, France and Geneva, Switzerland, 1774-77; served as volunteer, lt. and capt. during Revolutionary War, 1778-81; participated in Battle of Beaufort, defense of Charleston; mem. staffs of gens. Moultrie and Huger, and Gov. Rutledge; wounded in attack on Savannah, 1779; mem. S.C. Ho. of Reps., 1779, 86-88; mem. Continental Congress from S.C., 1780-81; rice planter, "Kensington," Georgetown Dist., S.C.; del. S.C. Conv. which ratified U.S. Constn., 1788; warden City of Charleston, also justice of peace and quorum, 1789; mem. S.C. Legislative Council, 1789, S.C. Constl. Conv., 1790; traveled in Europe, 1790, 1802-06. Died Charleston, Feb. 8, 1826; buried St. Michael's Ch. Cemetery, Charleston.

KINLOCH, Robert Alexander, surgeon; b. Charleston, S.C., Feb. 20, 1826; s. Dr. George and Charlotte (Granby) K.; grad. Charleston Coll., 1845; M.D., U. Pa., 1848; m. Elizabeth Caldwell, 1856, 8 children. Served as surgeon in Confederate Army, 1861-65; insp. of hosps. for S.C., Ga., Fla.; prof. materia medica Med. Coll. of State of S.C., 1866, prof. principles and practice of surgery, 1869, prof. clin. surgery, dean faculty, 1888-91; contbr. to Charleston Med. Jour., editor for a while; mem. Med. Soc. of S.C., Am. Surg. Assn.; asso. fellow Phila. Coll. of Physicians. Died Charleston, Dec. 23, 1891.

KINNARD, George L., congressman; b. Pa., 1803; studied law, Indpls. Admitted to Ind. bar, practiced in Marion County; assessor for Marion County, 1826-27; mem. Ind. Ho. of Reps., 1827-30; county surveyor, 1831-35; state auditor, several years; mem. U.S. Ho. of Reps. (Democrat) from Ind., 23d-24th congresses, 1833-36. Died from injuries received in an explosion on steamer Flora on Ohio River, Nov.

26, 1836; buried (probably) Presbyn. Burying Ground (now Washington Park), Cincinnati.

KINNERSLEY, Ebenezer, educator, elec. experimenter; b. Gloucester, Eng., Nov. 30, 1711; s. William Kinnersley; M.A. (hon.), Coll. of Phila., 1757; m. Sarah Duffield, 1739, 2 children. Came to Am., 1714; ordained to ministry Baptist Ch., 1743; asso. with Benjamin Franklin, Edward Duffield, Philip Synge, Thomas Hopkins in experiments with elec. fire; rediscovered Dr. DuFaye's 2 contrary electricities of glass and sulphur (led to verification of truth of positive-negative theory); delivered 1st recorded exptl. lectures on electricity in Fanneuil Hall, Boston, 1751; elected chief master Coll. of Phila., 1753, prof. English and oratory, 1755-73; demonstrated heat could be produced by electricity, invented elec. air thermometer, 1755; mem. Am. Philos. Soc. Died Phila., July 4, 1778.

KINNEY, Elizabeth Clementine Dodge Stedman, poet, essayist; b. N.Y.C., Dec. 18, 1810; d. David Low and Sarah (Cleveland) Dodge; m. Col. Edmund Burke Stedman, Mar., 1830; m. 2d, William Burnet Kinney, Nov. 1841; 1 son, Edmund Clarence Stedman. Published some of her best essays and critical articles in Newark (N.J.) Daily Advertiser (2d husband was founder and editor of newspaper), 1841-51; lived in Turin, Sardinia, where her husband was chargé d'affaires, 1850-53; lived in Florence, Italy, 1853-63; asso. with Robert Browning, Alfred Tennyson, Kiram Powers and others. Author: Felicita (a hist. romance), 1855; Collected Poems, 1867; Bianca Capello (her 2d verse romance), 1873. Died Summit, N.J., Nov. 19, 1889.

KINNEY, O.S., architect; children include a son, A. J. Known to have designed several public bldgs. in So. Ill. and No. Ind., also numerous ct. houses in Western Reserve area of Ohio, prior to 1865; opened archtl. office, Chgo., 1865; unfinished work of his office completed by his son A. J. Kinney and Dankmar Aldar. Died circa 1869.

KINNEY, William Burnet, journalist, diplomat; b. Speedwell, N.J., Sept. 4, 1799; s. Abraham and Hannah (Burnet) K.; attended U.S. Mil. Acad.; m. Mary Chandler; m. 2d, Elizabeth Clementine Dodge Stedman, Nov. 1841; 4 children including William Burnet, Jr. Editor, N.J. Eagle, weekly, Newark N.J., 1820-25; literary adviser Harper & Bros., publishers, N.Y.C., 1825-35; a founder, later librarian Merc. Library, N.Y.C.; editor Newark Daily Advertiser, 1835-50, became chief stockholder; U.S. chargé de affairs to Sardinia, 1850-53; remained in Europe until 1865. Died N.Y.C., Oct. 21, 1880; buried churchyard 1st Presbyn. Ch., Newark.

KINO, Eusebio Francisco, missionary, explorer; b. Segno, Italy, c. 1645. Entered Jesuit order, Freiburg, Germany, 1665; assigned to fgn. mission being organized in Spain, 1678; arrived Mexico City, 1681; joined Atondo expdn. to lower Cal. as head Jesuit mission, 1682; hdqrs. at Mission Dolores, 1687-1711; explored in So. Ariz. and vicinity; founded missions in San Miguel, Magdalena, Altar, Sonoita, Santa Cruz, San Pedro river valleys; discovered, wrote 1st description of Casa Grande ruins; instrumental in return of Jesuits to Cal. peninsula, 1697; his maps of S.W. territory, jours. are among earliest records of the area. Author: (treatise) Exposicion Astronomica de el Cometa, 1681. Died Magdalena, Mexico, Mar. 15, 1711.

KINSELLA, Thomas, congressman, editor; b. County Wexford, Ireland, Dec. 31, 1832; m. twice; 4 daus. by 1st wife; m. 2d, Emiline Van Siclen. Came to N.Y., 1849; learned printer's trade Cambridge (N.Y.) Post, 1851-54; typesetter, law reporter, contbr. articles Bklyn. Daily Eagle, 1858-61, editor, 1861-84; postmaster Bklyn., 1866; commr. Bklyn. Bd. Edn., 1868, initiated reforms including open bidding for supplies, equal salary for women in sch. system; mem. U.S. Ho. of Reps. from N.Y., 42d Congress, 1871-73. Died Bklyn., Feb. 11, 1884; buried Holy Cross Cemetery, Bklyn.

KINSEY, Charles, congressman; b. Balt., 1773; attended common schs. Engaged in paper mfg., Balt., later in Paterson and New Prospect (now Waldwick), N.J.; mem. N.J. Gen. Assembly, 1812-13, 19, 26, N.J. Council, 1814; mem. U. S. Ho. of Reps., from N.J., 15th, 16th congresses, 1817-19, Feb. 2, 1820-21; mem. 1st bd. fire wardens Town of Paterson, 1821; judge Bergen County Ct. Common Pleas, Bergen County Orphan's Ct., 1830-45. Died New Prospect, June 25, 1849; buried Union Cemetery, nr. New Prospect.

KINSEY, James, Continental congressman, jurist; b. Phila., Mar. 22, 1731; attended common schs.; studied law. Admitted to N.J. bar, 1753, practiced in cts. of Pa. and N.J.; mem. N.J. Gen. Assembly, 1772-75; mem. Com. of Correspondence for Burlington County (N.J.), 1774-75; mem. Continental Congress from N.J., 1774-75; chief justice N.J. Supreme Ct., 1789-1803. Died Burlington, N.J., Jan. 4, 1803; buried St. Mary's Churchyard, Burlington.

KINSEY, John, jurist; b. Burlington, N.J., 1693; s. John and Sarah (Stevens) K.; 2 children. Admitted to N.J. bar; elected to N.J. Assembly as speaker, 1730; elected to Pa. Assembly, 1731-50 (except 1 year), speaker, 1739-50; atty. gen. Pa., 1738-41; chief justice Supreme Ct. of Pa., 1743-50; Quaker. Author: The Acts of the General Assembly of the Province of New Jersey (1st compilation of N.J. laws), 1732. Died Burlington, May 11, 1750.

KINSLEY, Martin, congressman; b. Bridgewater, Mass., June 2, 1754; grad. Harvard, 1778; studied medicine. Purveyor of supplies for Continental Army during Revolutionary War; mem. Mass. Ho. of Reps., 1787-88, 90-92, 95-96; treas. of Hardwick (Mass.), 1787-92; moved to Hampden, Mass., 1797; mem. Mass. Gen. Ct. from Hampden, 1801-04, 06; mem. Mass. Exec. Council, 1810-11; judge ct. common pleas, 1811; judge probate ct.; mem. Mass. Senate, 1814; mem. U.S. Ho. of Reps. from Mass., 16th Congress, 1819-21. Died Roxbury, Mass., June 20, 1835.

KINTPUASH, see Captain Jack.

KINZIE, John, trader; b. Que., Can., Dec. 1763; s. John and Anne (Haliburton) McKinzie (changed name after father died); m. Eleanor Little McKillip, 4 children. Learned silversmith trade from Indian called Silver Man; began trading with Indians on Maumee River, Ft. Wayne, O., 1781; moved to St. Joseph River, 1796; moved to mouth of Chicago River, set up trading post, 1804; saved (with his family) by friendly Indians, 1812 in massacre of Ft. Dearborn; moved to Detroit, jailed by British for having Am. sympathies; returned to Chgo., 1816, aided commrs. in making Indian treaty, 1821; commd. justice of peace, 1825. Died Chgo., Jan. 6, 1828.

KIP, William Ingraham, clergyman; b. N.Y.C., Oct. 3, 1811; s. Leonard and Maria (Ingraham) K.; grad. Yale, 1831, LL.D. (hon.), 1872; grad. Gen. Theol. Sem., N.Y.C., 1835; S.T.D., Columbia, 1847; m. Maria Lawrence, July 1, 1835. Ordained priest 1835; rector St. Peter's Ch., Morristown, N.J., deacon Protestant Episcopal Ch., July 1, 1835 1835-36, St. Paul's Ch., Albany, N.Y., 1838; elected missionary bishop of Cal. by Gen. Conv. of 1853; bishop in sole charge Cal. Diocese (1st bishop Protestant Episcopal Ch. in Cal.), 1857-74; rector Grace Ch., San Francisco, 1862; rector 1st Cathedral of Episcopal Ch. in Am.; examiner U.S. Naval Acad. (apptd. by Pres. Hayes), 1880. Author: The History, Object, and Proper Observance of the Holy Season of Lent, 1843. Died San Francisco, Apr. 7, 1893.

KIRBY, Ephraim, lawyer; b. Litchfield County, Conn., Feb. 23, 1757; s. Abraham and Eunice (Starkweather) K.; studied law under Reynold Marvin, Litchfield, Conn.; M.A. (hon.), Yale, 1787; m. Ruth Marvin, Mar. 17, 1784, 8 children including Frances. Served as pvt. Continental Army, 1776-79; served at battles of Brandywine, Monmouth, Germantown; ensign R.I. Militia, 1782-83; practiced law, Litchfield; a founder Grand Lodge of Conn., also Grand Chpt. of Royal Arch Masons in U.S.; original mem. Conn. Soc. of Cincinnati; del. to nat. meeting Soc. of Cincinnati, 1796; mem. Conn. Ho. of Reps., 1791-1803; U.S. commr. on Spanish Boundary, 1803-04. Died Ft. Stoddart, Mississippi Territory (now Miss.), Oct. 20, 1804.

KIRBY, J. Hudson, actor; b. on board ship nr. Sandy Hook, N.Y., Apr. 3, 1819; m. Mrs. J. Hudson Kirby. First appeared at Walnut Street Playhouse, Phila., 1837; spent most of his 10 year career at Bowery, Nat. and Chatham theatres, N.Y.C., acted in leading roles with Jame W. Wallack and Thomas S. Hamblin; appeared with Edwin Forrest at Chatham Theatre, 1842; went to England, 1845, appeared at Surry and other London threatres. Died London, 1848.

KIRBY-SMITH, Edmund (see Smith, Edmund Kirby).

KIRK, Edward Norris, clergyman; b. N.Y.C., Aug. 14, 1802; s. George and Mary (Norris) K.; ed. Coll. of N.J. (now Princeton), 1820; attended Princeton Theol. Sem., 1822-26. D.D. (hon.), Amherst Coll. Converted to Presbyterianism, 1822; licensed to preach, 1826; agt. Am. Bd. Commrs. for Fgn. Missions, 1826-28; ordained to ministry Presbyn. Ch., 1828; pastor 4th Presbyn. Ch., Albany, N.Y., 1829; founder Troy and Albany Theol. Sch., 1833; sec. Fgn. Evang. Soc., 1839; preached at revivals in prin. cities of East; an organizer Evang. Alliance, London, Eng., 1846; established an Am. chapel, Paris, France, 1857; pres. Am. Missionary Assn., 1865; in charge of Mt. Vernon Congl. Ch., Boston, 1842-71; Sermons Delivered in England And America, 1840; Lectures on Revivals, 1874; Memorial of the Rev. John Chester D.D.; Lectures on Christ's Parables; Sermons; Canon of the Holy Scriptures. Died Boston, Mar. 27, 1874.

KIRKBRIDE, Thomas Story, physician; b. Morrisville, Pa., July 31, 1809; s. John and Elizabeth (Story) K.; M.D., U. P., 1832; m. Ann Jenks, 1839; m. 2d, Eliza Butler, 1866. Resident physician Friends' Asylum for Insane, Phila., 1832, Pa. Hosp., 1833-35; physician-in-chief, supt. Pa. Hosp. for Insane, 1840-83; published set of rules for care of insane stressing importance of recognizing personal dignity; devised plan for constrn. and design of mental hosps.; an organizer Assn. Med. Supts. of Am. Instns. for Insane, 1844, sec., 8 years, pres., 8 years; trustee 1st state hosp. in Pa., also Pa., Instn. for Blind. Died Phila., Dec. 16, 1883.

KIRKLAND, Caroline Matilda Stansbury, author; b. N.Y.C., Jan. 12, 1801; d. Samuel and Elizabeth (Alexander) Stansbury; m. William Kirkland, 1827/28; 1 son, Joseph. Wrote 1st book A New Home--Who'll Follow, 1839; author Forest Life, 1842, Western Clearings, 1845; early works about Western life were popular, later works unimportant; went to Europe, wrote Holidays Abroad, 1848; editor Union Mag., 1847-48, asso. editor, 1849-51; wrote The Helping Hand (pamphlet urging better treatment for female ex-convicts), 1853; other works include Evening Book; or, Fireside Talks on Morals and Manners. Died N.Y.C., Apr. 6, 1864.

KIRKLAND, John Thornton, coll. pres.; b. Herkimer, N.Y., Aug. 17, 1770; s. Rev. Samuel and Jerusha (Bingham) K.; grad. Harvard, 1789, post-grad. study of works of liberal divines; D.D., Coll. of N.J. (now Princeton), S.T.D. (hon.), 1802; A.M. (hon.), Dartmouth, 1792; A.M. (hon.), Brown, 1794, LL.D. (hon.), 1810; m. Elizabeth Cabot, Sept. 1, 1827. Ordained to ministry Unitarian Ch. 1794; a founder Monthly Anthology, also Boston, Athenaeum, 1803; pres. Harvard, 1810-28, coll. became a university under his adminstrn., introduced lecture method, 1st elective courses. Author: Eulogy on Washington, 1799; Biography of Fisher Ames, 1809; Discourse on the Death of Hon. George Cabot, 1823. Died Boston, Apr. 26, 1840.

KIRKLAND, Joseph, congressman; b. in what is now Lisbon, Conn., Jan. 18, 1770; grad. Yale, 1790; studied law. Admitted to the bar, 1794; began law practice, New Hartford, N.Y.; mem. N.Y. Assembly, 1804-05, 18, 20, 21, 25; moved to Utica, N.Y., 1813; dist. atty. 5th Dist. of N.Y., 1813-16; mem. U.S. Ho. of Reps. from N.Y., 17th Congress, 1821-23; mayor of Utica, 1832-36. Died Utica, Jan. 26, 1844; buried Forest Hill Cemetery, Utica.

KIRKLAND, Joseph, army officer, author; b. Geneva, N.Y., Jan. 7, 1830; s. William and Caroline M. (Stansbury) K.; m. Theodosia Burr Wilkinson, 1863, 4 children. Served from pvt. to maj. U.S. Army in Civil War, 1861-63; with U.S. Revenue Service, 1875-80; admitted to Ill. bar, 1880; spl. correspondent, reviewer, literary editor Chgo. Tribune, 1890; influenced literary devel. of Hamlin Garland. Author: Zury: The Meanest Man in Spring County, 1885; The Captain of Company K, 1891; The McVeys; The Story of Chicago. Died Chgo., Apr. 29, 1894.

KIRKLAND, Samuel, missionary; b. Norwich, Conn., Dec. 1, 1741; s. Rev. Daniel and Mary (Perkins) K.; A.B. in absentia, Coll. of N.J. (now Princeton), 1765; m. Jerusha Bingham, Sept. 19, 1769, 1 son, John Thorton. Lived with Seneca Indians, 1764-66; ordained minister Congregational Ch., Lebanon, Conn., 1766; began 40 year career working with Oneida Indians, establishing ch., teaching habits of industry, 1766; placed himself under charge of Boston Commrs. of Honorable Soc. in Scotland for Propagating Christian Knowledge, 1770; instrumental in preventing Lord Dunmore's War from becoming gen. Indian uprising, 1774-75; obtained gen. declaration of neutrality from the Six Nations, 1775; rebuilt the ch., 1784; granted 4,000 acres by Indians and N.Y. State in recognition of his services, 1788; brought together council of the Six Nations, persuaded council to send large delegation of chiefs to Phila. to negotiate with U.S. Govt., resulting in continued friendly relations between the Six Nations and U.S., 1792-93; founded Hamilton Coll. (orginally Hamilton Oneida Acad. for Indians), 1793. Died Clinton, N.Y., Feb. 28, 1808; buried Hamilton Coll. Cemetery.

KIRKPATRICK, Andrew, jurist; b. Minebrook, N.J., Feb. 17, 1756; s. David and Mary (McEowen) K.; grad. Coll. of N.J. (now Princeton), 1775; m. Jane Bayard, Nov. 1, 1792, 7 children. Admitted to N.J. bar, 1785; mem. lower house of N.J. Legislature, 1797; asso. justice N.J. Supreme Ct., 1798, chief justice, 1804-24; original trustee Princeton Theol. Sem., chmn. bd. trustees, 1822-31; trustee Coll. of N.J., 1807-31. Died New Brunswick, N.J., Jan. 6, 1831.

KIRKPATRICK, William, congressman; b. Amwell, nr. Zion, N.J. Nov. 7, 1769; grad. Princeton, 1788; studied medicine, U. Pa. Began practice of medicine, Whitestown, N.Y., 1795; moved to Salina, N.Y., 1806, practiced medicine; supt. Onondaga Salt Springs; mem. U.S. Ho. of Reps. (Democrat) from N.Y., 10th Congress, 1807-09. Died Salina, Sept. 2, 1832; buried Oakwood Cemetery, Syracuse, N.Y.

KIRKWOOD, Daniel, astronomer, educator; b. Harford County, Md., Sept. 27, 1814; s. John and Agnes (Hope) K.; A.M. (hon.), Washington Coll., 1849; m. Sarah McNair, 1845. Prin., Lancaster (Pa.) High Sch., 1843-49, Pottsville Acad., 1849-51; prof. mathematics Del. Coll., 1851-56, pres., 1854-56; prof. mathematics Ind. U., 1856-65, 1867-86; prof. mathematics and astronomy Jefferson Coll., Canonsburg, Pa.; apptd. lectr. Leland Stanford Jr. U., 1891; mem. Am. Philos. Soc., 1852; published his formula for rotation periods of planets in Proceedings of A.A.A.S., 1849, article on comets and meteors in Danville Quarterly Review, 1861. Author: Meteoric Astronomy, 1867; Comets and Meteors, 1873. Died Riverside, Cal., June 11, 1895.

KIRKWOOD, Samuel Jordan, senator, gov. Ia.; b. Harford County, Md., Dec. 20, 1813; m. Jane Clark, 1843. Admitted to Ohio bar, 1843; pros. atty. Richmond County (O.), 1845-49; mem. Ohio Constl. Conv., 1850, 51; moved to Ia., 1855; mem. Ia. Senate, 1856-59; gov. Ia., 1860-64, 76-77; declined appointment as U.S. minister to Denmark, 1863; mem. U.S. Senate from Ia., Jan. 13, 1866-67, 77-81; pres. Ia. & Southwestern R.R. Co.; U.S. sec. of interior under Pres. Garfield, 1881-82. Died Iowa City, Ia., Sept. 1, 1894; buried Oakland Cemetery, Iowa City.

KIRTLAND, Dorrance, congressman; b. Coxsackie, N.Y., July 28, 1770; grad. Yale, 1789; studied law. Admitted to N.Y. bar, began practice in Coxsackie; surrogate of Greene County (N.Y.), 1808-38; mem. U.S. Ho. of Reps. from N.Y., 15th Congress, 1817-19; judge Greene County Ct. of Common Pleas, 1828-38. Died Coxsackie, May 23, 1840; buried Old Coxsackie Cemetery.

KIRTLAND, Jared Potter, physician, naturalist; b. Wallingford, Conn., Nov. 10, 1793; s. Turhand and Mary (Potter) K.; attended Md. Instn., Yale, 1813-14, M.D., 1815; attended Med. Dept., U. Pa., 1814; m. Caroline Atwater, May 22, 1815; m. 2d, Hannah Tousey, 1825. Probate judge, Wallingford, 1818; mem. Ohio Legislature, 1828-34; reformed penitentiary system, substituted indsl. work for inmates in place of previous idleness; trustee Western Res. Coll., 1833-35; prof. theory and practice of medicine Med. Coll. Ohio, Cincinnati, 1837; mem. Boston Soc. Natural History, 1838; pres. Ohio Med. Conv., 1839, 49; a founder Cleve. Med. Coll., 1843, prof. theory and practice of medicine, 1843-64, prof. emeritus, 1864-77; organized Cleve. Acad. Natural Sci. (reorganized as Kirtland Soc. Natural Scis. 1869), 1845, pres. until 1875; mem. A.A.A.S., 1848; editor Ohio Family Visitor, 1851-58; mem. Nat. Acad. Scis., Am. Philos. Soc. Died Rockport, O., Dec. 10, 1877.

KITCHELL, Aaron, senator, congressman; b. Hanover, N.J., July 10, 1744; attended common schs. Became blacksmith; mem. N.J. Gen. Assembly, 1781-82, 84, 86-90, 93-94, 97, 1801-04, 09; mem. U.S. Ho. of Reps. (Democrat) from N.J., 2d, 3d-4th, 6th congresses, 1791-93, Jan. 29, 1795-97, 99-1801. mem. U.S. Senate from N.J., 1805-Mar. 12, 1809; Dem. presdl. elector, 1816. Died Hanover, June 26, 1820; buried Presbyn. Churchyard, Hanover.

KITCHEN, Bethuel, congressman; b. Ganotown, Va. (now W.Va.), Mar. 21, 1812; attended common schs. Engaged in farming, stock raising; mem. Va. Ho. of Dels., 1861-62; mem. W.Va. Senate, 1864-65, 78-79; mem. U.S. Ho. of Reps. (Republican) from W.Va., 40th Congress, 1867-69; pres. Agrl. and Mech. Assn. of Berkeley, Jefferson, and Morgan Counties, 1869-75; master W.Va. Grange, 1873-79; pres. Berkeley County (W.Va.) Ct., 1880-95. Died Shanghai, W.Va., Dec. 15, 1895; buried Presbyn. Churchyard, Shanghai.

KITTERA, John Wilkes, congressman; b. nr. Blue Ball, Pa., Nov. 1752; grad. Coll. of N.J. (now Princeton), 1776; studied law; children include Thomas. Admitted to Pa. bar, 1782, began practice in Lancaster; mem. U.S. Ho. of Reps. (Federalist) from Pa., 2d-6th congresses, 1791-1801; U.S. atty. for Eastern Pa. (apptd. by Pres. Jefferson), 1801. Died Lancaster, June 6, 1801; buried Presbyn. Cemetery, Lancaster.

KITTERA, Thomas, congressman; b. Lancaster, Pa., Mar. 21, 1789; s. John Wilkes Kittera; grad. U. Pa., 1805; studied law. Admitted to Pa. bar, 1808; began practice in Phila.; dep. atty. gen. of Pa., 1817-18, of Phila., 1824-26; pres. Phila. Select Council, 1824-26; mem. U.S. Ho. of Reps. (Federalist) from Pa., 19th Congress, Oct. 10, 1826-27. Died Phila., June 16, 1839; buried St. Paul's Protestant Episcopal Cemetery, Phila.

KITTREDGE, George Washington, congressman; b. Epping, N.H., Jan. 31, 1805; studied medicine Harvard. Began practice of medicine, Newmarket, N.H., 1835; mem. N.H. Ho. of Reps., 1835, 47, 48, 52, speaker, 1852; dir. Boston & Me. R.R. Co., 1836-56; pres. Newmarket Savs. Bank, 40 years; mem. U.S. Ho. of Reps. (Anti-Neb. Democrat) from N.H., 33d Congress, 1853-55. Died Newmarket, Mar. 6, 1881; buried Forest Hills Cemetery, nr. Boston.

KITTSON, Norman Wolfred, fur and transp. exec., mayor; b. Chambly, Lower Canada, Mar. 5, 1814; s. George and Nancy (Tucker) K. Became apprentice Am. Fur Co., 1830, spl. partner at St. Peter's, Minn., asigned to valleys of Upper Minnesota and Red River of the North, 1843; founder trading post at Pembina nr. internat. boundary, engaged in fur competition with Hudson's Bay Co.; mem. Legislative Council, Minn. Territory, 1852-55; Democratic mayor St. Paul (Minn.) 1858; dir. overland and river traffic in Minn. area; founder (with Jerome T. Hill) Red River Transp. Co., 1871; secured control and reorganized (with others) St. Paul, Mpls. & Manitoba Ry., 1878. Died Minn., May 10, 1888.

KLINE, George, editor, publisher; b. Germany, circa 1757; m. Rebecca Weiss, 11 children. Came to Am. at early age, worked as printer, Phila.; moved to Carlisle, Pa., 1785, started Federalist weekly The Carlisle Gazette and the Western Repository of Knowledge, published until 1817, then absorbed by Carlisle Spirit of the Times, approached news from frontiersmen's point of view; published Isaac Watt's Scripture History, 1797, John Brown's Westminster Assembly of Divines. Died Carlisle, Nov. 12, 1800.

KLINGENSMITH, John, Jr., congressman; b. Westmoreland County, Pa., 1785. Elected sheriff of Westmoreland County, 1828; mem. U.S. Ho. of Reps. (Democrat) from Pa., 24th-25th congresses, 1835-39; sec. Land Office of Pa., 1838-42.

KLIPPART, John Hancock, agriculturalist; b. Canton, O., July 26, 1823; s. Henry and Eve (Henning) K.; m. Emeline Rahn, 1847, at least 1 child. Corresponding sec. Ohio State Bd. Agr., 1856-78; mem. Am. Bd. Commrs. of London Internat. Exhbn., 1861-62; sent by Ohio Bd. Agr. to observe agrl. methods in Europe, 1865; asst. geologist Ohio Geol. Survey, 1869; del. from Ohio to Nat. Agrl. Conv., Washington, D.C., 1872; state fish commr. Ohio, 1873; edited reports of Ohio Bd. Agr., 1857-77, also contbd. articles including An Essay on the Origin, Growth, Diseases, Varieties, etc., of the Wheat Plant (1857), An Essay on Practical Drainage (1860), An Essay on the Varieties of Sheep and Sheep Culture in Ohio (1862), Report on an Agricultural Tour in Europe (1865), Address on Agricultural Education (1865), An Essay on Dairy Husbandry (1870). Author: (books) The Wheat Plant, 1860; Principles and Practice of Land Drainage, 1861. Died Oct. 24, 1878.

KLIPSTEIN, Louis Frederick, philologist; b. Winchester, Va., Jan. 2, 1813; s. Peter and Frances (Kimmelmyer) K.; grad. Hampden-Sydney Coll., 1832; attended Union Theol. Sem., 1832-35; Ph. D. in absentia), U. Giessen (Germany); m. Allston Jerman, circa 1845. Licensed to preach by Winchester Presbytery, 1835; became adherent of New School movement in Presbyn. Ch.; founder periodical The Polyglot, Charleston, S.C., 1844; 1st American to publish works on Anglo-Saxon language. Author: A Grammar of the Anglo-Saxon Language (regularized spelling and inflectional endings). Died Fla., Aug. 20, 1878.

KLOTZ, Robert, congressman; b. Northampton (now Carbon) County, Pa., Oct. 27, 1819; attended county schs. First register and recorder Carbon County, 1843; served from pvt. to lt. and adj. 2d Pa. Volunteers during Mexican War, 1846-47; mem. Pa. Ho. of Reps., 1848-49; moved to Pawnee, Kan., 1855; mem. Topeka (Kan.) Constl. Conv., 1855; 1st sec. of state under Topeka Constn.; served as brig. gen. under Gov. Robinson of Kan.; moved to Mauch Chunk, Pa., 1857; treas. Carbon County, 1859; served as col. 19th Pa. Emergency Militia, U.S. Army during Civil War; trustee Lehigh U., Bethlehem, Pa., 1874-82; mem. U.S. Ho. of Reps. (Democrat) from Pa., 46th-47th congresses, 1879-83; agt., dir. Laflin-Rand Powder Co., N.Y.C. Died Mauch Chunk, May 1, 1895; buried City Cemetery, Mauch Chunk.

KNABE, Valentine Wilhelm Ludwig, piano mfr.; b. Kreuzberg, Prussia, Germany, June 3, 1803; s. Martin Friedrich and Ernestine Traugott (Kohler) K.; m. Christiana Ritz, Aug. 18, 1833, 2 children. Came to Am., 1833; entered into a partnership with Henry Gaehle as mfr. pianos, 1840, continued bus. alone, 1854; virtually controlled piano bus. in the South by 1861. Died Phila., May 21, 1864.

KNAPP, Anthony Lausett, congressman; b. Middletown, N.Y., June 14, 1828; studied law. Moved to Ill., 1839, settled in Jerseyville; admitted to Ill. bar, began practice in Jerseyville; mem. Ill. Senate, 1859-61; mem. U.S. Ho. of Reps. (Democrat) from Ill., 37th-38th congresses, Dec. 12, 1861-65; moved to Chgo., 1865, Springfield, Ill., 1867, practiced law. Died Springfield, May 24, 1881; buried Springfield Cemetery, reinterred Oak Ridge Cemetery, Springfield.

KNAPP, Charles, congressman; b. Colchester, N. Y., Oct. 8, 1797; attended common schs.; children include Charles Junius. Engaged in farming; taught sch., Delaware County, N.Y.; engaged in merc. bus., 1825; mem. N.Y. Assembly, 1841; organizer bank, Deposit, N.Y., 1854, pres.; mem. U.S. Ho. of Reps. (Republican) from N.Y., 41st Congress, 1869-71. Died Deposit, May 14, 1880; buried Laurel Bank Cemetery, Deposit.

KNAPP, Chauncey Langdon, congressman; b. Berlin, Vt., Feb. 26, 1809. Newspaperman, Montpelier, Vt.; co-propr., editor State Jour.; sec. of state Vt., 1836-49; moved to Lowell, Mass.; editor Lowell News, other papers; sec. Mass. Senate, 1851; mem. U.S. Ho. of Reps. from Mass., as Am. Party rep., 34th Congress, 1855-57, as Republican, 35th Congress, 1857-59; editor Lowell Daily Citizen, 1859-82. Died Lowell, May 31, 1898; buried Lowell Cemetery.

KNAPP, George, journalist; b. Montgomery, N.Y., Sept. 25, 1814; s. Edward and Frances (Flood) K.; m. Eleanor McCartan, Dec. 22, 1840, 12 children. With newspaper Mo. Republican, 1836-83, part propr. book and job printing dept., 1836, then editor (made it one of leading newspapers in U.S.), 1837-83; an organizer of volunteer militia St. Louis Legion, served as capt. and lt. col., Mexican War; organizer, capt. company called Mo. Republican Guards, 1862; largely responsible for building 1st bridge over Mississippi in St. Louis. Died in S.S. Pennland while returning to U.S. from European trip, Sept. 18, 1883.

KNAPP, Samuel Lorenzo, journalist; b. Newburyport, Mass., Jan. 19, 1783; s. Isaac and Susanna (Newman) K.; grad. Dartmouth, 1804; LL.D. (hon.), from a coll., Paris, France; m. Mary Ann Davis, July 18, 1814, 2 children. Rep. to Mass. Gen. Ct., 1812-16; editor Gazette, Boston, 1824-26; published Boston Monthly Mag., 1825-26; started newspaper Nat. Republican; editor Nat. Journal, Washington, D.C.; Author: Lectures on American Literature (1st critical evaluation of Am. literature), 1829. The Bachelor and Other Tales; Advice in the Pursuit of Literature; Travels of Ali Bey in Boston; The Genius of Free Masonry. Died Hopkinson, Mass., July 8, 1838.

KNEASS, Samuel Honeyman, civil engr.; b. Phila., Nov. 5, 1806; s. William and Mary (Honeyman) K.; studied architecture under William Strickland, Phila., 1821-25; m. Anna Arndt Lombaerdt, Mar. 14, 1837. Prin. asst. engr. in constrn. Susquehanna div. Pa. State Canal, 1825-28, of Del. div., 1828--29; chief engr. Mine Hill & Schuylkill Haven R.R., 1829-31, Phila. & Trenton R.R., 1832; with various railroad and canal cos., 1832-36; engr. Phila. & Wilmington R.R., 1836-40; U.S. consul at Carthagena, New Grenada (now Colombia), 1845-46; city surveyor Phila., 1849-53; chief engr. North Western R.R. of Pa., 1854-58. Died Phila., Feb. 15, 1858.

KNEASS, Strickland, civil engr., railroad exec.; b. Phila., July 29, 1821; s. William and Mary (Honeyman) K.; grad. Rensselaer Poly. Inst., Troy, N.Y., 1839; m. Margaretta Sybilla Bryan, Aug. 17, 1853. Draftsman, bur. engring. U.S. Navy, 1840-42; surveyed map of northeastern U.S.-Canadian boundary, 1842; asst. to chief engr. in constrn. Pa. R.R., 1847, prin. 1st asst. engr., 1848-53, asst. to pres., 1872-78; asso. engr. N. Pa. R.R., 1853-55; chief engr., surveyor City of Phila., 1855-65, designed new drainage system for city; pres. Eastern R.R. Assn., 1878; pres. Pa. & Del. R.R. Co., Trenton R.R. Co., Columbia & Port Deposit & Western R.R. Co., 1880-84; dir. Pitts., Cincinnati & St. Louis R.R., 1880-84. Died Jan. 14, 1884.

KNEASS, William, engraver; b. Lancaster, Pa., Sept. 25, 1780; s. Christopher and Anna (Feltman) K.; m. Mary Turner Honeyman, June 23, 1804; m. 2d, Jane Kramer; 6 children including William Honeyman, Strickland. Became engraver, Phila., 1804; partner (with James H. Young) Kneass, Young & Co., engravers, Phila., 1817-20; engraver and die-sinker to U.S. Mint, Phila., 1814-40; a founder Franklin Inst., 1824; mem. Beef Steak Club of Phila. Engravings include: A View of Quebec, 1813; plates for Analectic Mag., Rees's Cyclopedia; U.S. gold coinage for 1834, 38; U.S. silver coinage for 1836-38. Died Aug. 27, 1840.

KNEELAND, Abner, clergyman; b. Gardner, Mass., Apr. 7, 1774; s. Timothy and Moriah (Stone) K.; m. Waitstill Ormsbee, Apr. 9, 1797; m. 2d, Lucinda Mason, circa 1807; m. 3d, Mrs: Eliza Osborn, Aug. 11, 1813; m. 4th, Mrs. Dolly Rice, 1834; 12 children. Became a Universalist, 1803; licensed to preach, 1804; mem. N.H. Legislature from Langdon, 1810-11; editor Christian Messenger, 1819-21, Phila. Universal Mag. and Christian Messenger, 1821-23, Gazetteer, 1824, Olive Branch, N.Y.C., 1827; left Universalist Ch., 1829; founder First Soc. of Free Enquirers, Boston; tried for religious blasphemy in Boston, 4 times, 1834-35, served 60 days in jail, 1838; founder Salubria (Ia.), 1839. Died Salubria, Aug. 27, 1844.

KNEELAND, Samuel, printer, publisher; b. Boston, Feb. 10, 1698; s. John and Mary (Green) K.; apprenticed to printer Bartholomew Green, Boston; m. Mary Alden, 1721, 9 children. Established printing shop, Boston, 1718; printed, published Boston Gazette, 1720-27, 36-41, New Eng. Weekly Journal, 1727-41; merged papers into Boston Gazette, or Weekly Advertiser, 1741-55; ofcl. printer for Mass. Provincial Govt.; printed Christian History (1st religious periodical in Am.), 1743. Died Boston, Dec. 14, 1769.

KNEELAND, Samuel, physician, naturalist; b. Boston, Aug. 1, 1821; s. Samuel and Nancy (Johnson) K.; A.B., Harvard, 1840, A.M., M.D., 1843; m. Eliza Curtis, 1849. Recipient Boylston prize for M.D. thesis on contagiousness of puerperal fever (published in Am. Jour. of Med. Scis., Jan. 1846); helped found Boylston Med. Sch., 1847; physician to Boston Dispensary, 1845-47; demonstrator of anatomy Harvard Med. Sch., 1851-53; served as surgeon U.S. Army, 1862-66; in charge Univ. Hosp., New Orleans, also gen. hosps. of Mobile, Ala.; brevetted lt. col. U.S. Volunteers; mem. corp. Mass. Inst. Tech., prof. zoology and physiology, 1869-78, sec. of corp. and faculty, 1865-78; an editor The Annual of Scientific Discovery, 1866-69; sec. Am. Acad. Arts and Scis. Author: Hydrotherapy, 1844; Science and Mechanism, 1854. Translator: Andry's Diseases of the Heart, 1847. Died Hamburg, Germany, Sept. 27, 1888.

KNICKERBOCKER, Harmen Jansen, colonist; b. Friesland, Netherlands, circa 1650; 7 children. Settled nr. Albany, N.Y., circa 1674; bought a quarter of the land in Dutchess County (N.Y.), 1704; name used by Washington Irving when he wrote Knickerbocker's History of New York under pseudonym of Deidrich Knickerbocker, 1809; name came to symbolize Dutch settlers of N.Y. State. Died circa 1720.

KNICKERBOCKER, Herman, congressman; b. Albany, N.Y., July 27, 1779; s. Johannes and Elizabeth (Winne) K.; m. Ariantie Lansing, Oct. 10, 1801; m. 2d, Rachel Wendell, Dec. 6, 1814; m. 3d, Mary Buel, July 20, 1826; 14 children. Served as capt. of a new troop of cavalry 1801; admitted to N.Y. bar, 1803; sr. partner law firm Knickerbocker & Piersen; supr. of Troy (N.Y.), 1805-06, 13, 18-23, 25-29; mem. U.S. H. of Reps. (Federalist) from N.Y., 11th Congress, 1809-11; commd. maj. 3d Regt. of Cavalry, N.Y. Militia, 1810, col., 1818; mem. N.Y. State Assembly, 1816; 1st judge Rensselaer County (N.Y.) Ct. of Common Pleas, 1828. Died Williamsburg, N.Y., Jan. 30, 1855; buried Knickerbocker family cemetery, Rensselaer County.

KNIGHT, Edward Collings, business exec., inventor; b. Collingswood, N.J., Dec. 8, 1813; s. Jonathan and Rebecca (Collings) K.; m. Anna Magill, July 20, 1841, 5 children. Founder firm E.C. Knight & Co. (sugar wholesalers, developed into famous monopoly); devised, built sleeper car, 1859, sold to Pullman, 1868; Republican presdl. elector, 1860; helped establish Southwark Sugar Refinery, 1861; pres. Am. Steamship Line; pres. Del. & Bound Brook R.R., 1874-92, N. Pa. R.R., 1887. Died Cape May, N.J., July 21, 1892.

KNIGHT, Edward Henry, mech. expert, lawyer; b. London, Eng., June 1, 1824; s. George and Sarah (Harris) K.; m. Maria Richards, May 29, 1848, 5 children. Came to U.S., 1845; admitted to Ohio bar; with U.S. Patent Office, founded, edited The Official Gazette of the United States Patent Office, 1872-76; granted 7 patents including 3 on steam governors; commr. Universal Exposition, Paris, France, 1878; decorated chevalier Legion d'Honneur (France); Author: A Library of Poetry and Song, 1870; Knight's American Mechanical Dictionary, 3 vols., 1874, 76. Died Bellefontaine, O., Jan. 22, 1883.

KNIGHT, Henry Cogswell, clergyman, poet; b. Newburyport, Mass., Jan. 29, 1789; s. Joseph and Elizabeth (Cogswell) K.; attended Harvard, 1808-11; A.B., A.M., Brown U., 1812; never married. Travelled in South, 1814-21; ordained deacon Protestant Episcopal Ch., 1827; rector Prince George's and St. Bartholomew's parishes, Montgomery County, Md., 1829-30; later lived in Boston. Author: (poetry) The Cypriad, 1809, The Broken Harp, 1815, Poems, 2 vols., 1821; (other works) Letters from the South and West, by Arthur Singleton, Esq. (pseudonym), 1824, Lectures and Sermons, 2 vols., 1831. Died Rowley, Mass., Jan. 10, 1835.

KNIGHT, Jonathan, congressman, civil engr; b. Bucks County, Pa., Nov. 22, 1787; s. Abel and Ann S. Knight; m. Ann Heston, 1809, 10 children. Apptd. by Pa. to make map of Washington County, 1816, elected county commr., 1816; mem. Pa. Ho. of Reps., 1822-28; apptd. U.S. Govt. commr. to extend Nat. Road from Wheeling through Ohio and Ind. to Ill., 1825; apptd. chief engr. B. & O. R.R., 1829-42; cons. engr., 1842; sec. 1st agrl. soc. organized in Washington County; mem. U.S. Ho. of Reps. (Whig) from Pa., 34th Congress, 1855-57. Died East Bethlehem, Pa., Nov. 22, 1858; buried West Land Cemetery, Washington County.

KNIGHT, Jonathan, physician; b. Norwalk, Conn., Sept. 4, 1789; s. Dr. Jonathan and Ann (Fitch) K.; grad. Yale, 1808, M.A., 1811, M.D. (hon.), 1818; m. Elizabeth Lockwood, Oct. 1813. Licensed to practice medicine by Conn. Med. Soc., 1811; asst. prof. anatomy and physiology Yale, 1813, prof. surgery, 1838, founder Med. Sch.; sec. Conn. Med. Soc., 1817; pres. meetings of Nat. Med. Conv. which formed A.M.A., 1846, 47; pres. A.M.A., 1853; 1st surgeon to cure aneurisms by compression. 1848. Died New Haven, Conn., Aug. 25, 1864.

KNIGHT, Nehemiah, congressman; b. "Knightsville," Cranston (now part of Providence), R.I., Mar. 23, 1746; attended common schs.; children include Nehemiah Rice. Engaged in farming; town clk., 1773-1800; mem. Gen. Assembly of R.I. and Providence Plantations, 1783-87; sheriff Providence County (R.I.), 1787; mem. U.S. Ho. of Reps. (Anti-Federalist) from R.I., 8th-10th congresses, 1803-08. Died Cranston, June 13, 1808; buried "Knightsville."

KNIGHT, Nehemiah Rice, senator, gov. R.I.; b. Cranston, R.I., Dec. 31, 1780; s. Nehemiah Knight; attended common schs. Mem. R.I. Ho. of Reps., 1802; clk. ct. common pleas, 1805-11, circuit ct., 1812-17; collector of customs, Providence, R.I., 1812-17; gov. R.I. (Anti-Federalist), 1817-21; pres. Roger Williams Bank, 1817-54; mem. U.S. Senate (as Anti-Federalist, later as Democrat) from R.I., Jan. 9, 1821-41; del. R.I. Constl. Conv., 1843. Died Providence, Apr. 18, 1854; buried Grace Church Cemetery, Providence.

KNIGHT, Sarah Kemble, educator; b. Boston, Apr. 19, 1666; d. Thomas and Elizabeth (Trerice) Kemble; m. Capt. Richard Knight, 1680, 1 dau., Elizabeth, Conducted writing school in Boston; acted as legal adviser and recorder of public documents; travelled alone to N.Y.C., 1704, recorded her experiences and impressions of that trip in her diary The Journals of Madam Knight and Rev. Mr. Buckingham, published 1825; moved to Conn., 1714; owned several farms, kept a shop, speculated in Indian lands. Died Sept. 25, 1727; buried New London, Conn.

KNOWLES, Lucius James, inventor, mfr.; b. Hardwich, Mass., July 2, 1819; s. Simeon, Jr. and Lucetta (Newton) K.; A.M. (hon.), Williams Coll., 1865; m. Eliza Adams; m. 2d, Helen Strong. Perfected Knowles Safety Steam-boiler feed regulator, 1840, began mfg., 1859; began daguerreotype bus., Worcester, Mass., 1841; inventor machine for spooling thread, 1843; engaged in mfg., New Wooster, Mass., 1843-45; partner (with Harrison H. Sibley) to operate Old Draper Mill, mfg. cotton warp, Spencer, Mass., 1846; extended activities to include woolen mill, 1853-59; patented improvements in looms, 1856; erected bldg. near cotton factory to manufacture boiler-feeder water regulator, 1862; mem. Mass. Ho. of Reps. from Warren, New Braintree and West Brookfield, 1862, 65; made steam pumps, exptl. looms, 1863; propr. Knowles Steam Pump Co., L.J. Kowles & Bro. Loom Works (consol. as Crompton & Knowles Loom Works, 1897); mem. Mass. Senate from 3d Worcester dist., 1869; trustee Worcester Free Inst. Tech., 1871. Died Washington D.C., Feb. 25, 1884.

KNOWLTON, Charles, physician; b. Templeton, Mass., May 10, 1800; s. Stephen and Comfort (White) K.; M.D., Dartmouth Med. Coll., 1824; m. Tabitha Stewart, Apr. 17, 1821. Wrote Elements of Modern Materialism (one of 1st Am. books philos. materialism), 1829; pioneer advocate of birth control; wrote Fruits of Philosophy; or, The Private Companion of Young Married People (1st edition anonymous 1832, 2d edit. signed 1833), imprisoned and prosecuted for its contents which are earliest Am. printed matter on birth control; prosecution made book bestseller with 9 Am. editions before 1839; book was popular in Eng. (1st edit. 1834), became subject of famous legal case involving sexual edn. Died Winchendon, Mass., Feb. 20, 1850.

KNOWLTON, Ebenezer, congressman; b. Pittsfield, N.H., Dec. 6, 1815; attended common schs.; studied theology. Moved to South Montville, Me., 1825; entered ministry; mem. Me. Ho. of Reps., 1844-50, speaker, 1846; mem. U.S. Ho. of Reps. (Republican) from Me., 34th Congress, 1855-57. Died South Montville, Sept. 10, 1874; buried City Cemetery, South Montville.

KNOWLTON, Thomas, army officer; b. West Boxford, Mass., Nov. 1740; s. William and Martha (Pinder) K.; m. Anna Keyes, Apr. 5, 1759. Served in Brit. Army during Seven Years War; farmer, Ashford, Mass., 1762-75; elected capt. of an Ashford Company, 1775, served in Battle of Bunker Hill; commd. maj. 20th Inf., Continental Army, 1776; promoted to lt. col. Durkees' Regt. by Continental Congress, 1776, served in Battle of L.I. Killed in Battle of Harlem Heights (N.Y.), Sept. 16, 1776.

KNOX, Henry, army officer, sec. of war; b. Boston, July 25, 1750; s. William and Mary (Campbell) K.; m. Lucy Flucker, June 16, 1774, 12 children. Started London Book Store, 1771; 2d in command Boston Grenadier Corps, 1772; commd. col. in charge arty. Continental Army, 1775; brought arty. equipment from Ft. Ticonderoga, forcing Brit. out of Boston; in charge of arty., N.Y.C., also L.I., 1776; field comdr., Trenton, N.J., 1776; commd. brig. gen., 1776; started govt. arsenal, Springfield, Mass., 1777; led at battles of Brandywine and Germantown, 1777, Monmouth, 1778; prin. founder mil. acad. which became U.S. Mil. Acad., 1779; on ct. martial duty, one of tribunal to try and condemn to death Maj. Andre for treason, 1780; commanded, placed arty. for Siege of Yorktown, 1781; commd. maj. gen., 1781; in command West Point, 1782-85; conceived, organized Soc. of Cincinnati, 1783, 1st sec., v.p., 1805; elected 1st sec. of war U.S. by Continental Congress, 1785, served, 1785-94; founder (with Thomas Jefferson) U.S. Navy; settled in Me., 1796, became brickmaker, cattle-raiser, shipbuilder, lumber-cutter; close friend, adviser George Washington. Died Thomaston, Me., Oct. 25, 1806; buried Thomaston.

KNOX, James, congressman; b. Canajoharie, N.Y., July 4, 1807; attended Hamilton Coll., Clinton, N.Y.; grad. Yale, 1830; studied law. Admitted to N.Y. bar, 1833, began practice in Utica; moved to Knoxville, Ill., 1836, practiced law, also engaged in farming; del. Ill. Constl. Conv., 1847; mem. U.S. Ho. of Reps. (Whig) from Ill., 33d-34th congresses, 1853-57. Died Knoxville, Oct. 8, 1876; buried City Cemetery, Knoxville.

KNOX, John Jay, financier, U.S. comptroller of currency; b. Augusta, N.Y., Mar. 19, 1828; s. John J. and Sarah Ann (Curtiss) K.; grad. Hamilton Coll., 1849; m. Caroline Todd, Feb. 7, 1871, 6 children. An organizer Burnet Bank, Syracuse, N.Y., 1852, Susquehanna Valley Bank, Binghampton, N.Y., 1856; urged establishment of nat. banking system with safe, standard currency; clk. U.S. Treasury Dept., 1862-65, in charge mint and coinage correspondence, dep. comptroller, of currency, 1867-72, comptroller, 1872-84; pres. Nat. Bank of Republic, N.Y.C., 1884-92. Author: United States Notes, A History of the Various Issues of Paper Money by the Government of the United States, 1884. Died N.Y.C., Feb. 9, 1892.

KNOX, Samuel, clergyman, educator; b. Armagh County, Ireland, 1756; s. Samuel Knox; M.A., U. Glasgow (Scotland), 1792; m. Grace Gilmour; m. 2d, Zeraiah McClerry; 4 children. Came to Am., circa 1795; licensed to preach by Presbytery of Belfast, Irleand; 1st prin. Frederick Acad., 1797-03; head of a pvt. acad. which merged into Balt. Coll., 1808, prin., until 1820; prin. Frederick Acad., 1823-27. Author: Essay on the Best System of Liberal Education, adapted to the Genius of the Government of the U.S., 1799; (sermons) Some Prefatory Strictures on the Lately Avowed Religious Principles of Joseph Priestley, 1798, A Vindication of the Religion of Mr. Jefferson and a Statement of his Services in the Cause of Religious Liberty, 1800. Died Aug. 31, 1832.

KNOX, Thomas Wallace, author, inventor; b. Pembroke, N.H., June 26, 1835; s. Nehemiah Critchett and Jane (Wallace) K. Established, became prin. acad., Kingston, N.H., 1857; spl. reporter, then city editor Denver Daily News, 1860; lt. col. on staff Cal. Nat. Guard in Civil War; war corr. N.Y. Herald; granted patent for transmitting plans of battle field by telegraph; explored many unfrequented parts of Orient, secured materials for large number of travel volumes, 1877; decorated Order of White Elephant by Siam. Author: Overland through Asia, 1870; The Boy Travelers in the Far East, 1881; Pocket Guide Around the World 1882; Life of Henry Ward Beecher, 1887, others. Died N.Y.C., Jan. 6, 1896.

KOCH, Henry G., architect; b. Germany, 1840; brought to U.S. in childhood; at least 1 son. Began career as architect, Milw., circa 1865, later organized firm Henry G. Koch & Son. Prin. works include: old City Hall (1895), Hotel Phister (1st fire-proof public bldg. in Milw.), Science Hall at U. Wis., Madison (circa 1888), Catholic Ch. of Il Gesu, Marquette, Wis.; also designed at least 20 court houses, 12 sch. bldgs.

KOCHERTHAL, Josua von, see Von Kocherthal, Josua.

KOERNER, Gustave, lawyer; b. Germany, 1809; univ. legal edn. Came to U.S., 1833, settled in Belleville Ill.; elected mem. Ill. Gen Assembly (Democrat), 1842; apptd. judge Ill. Supreme Ct., 1845; elected lt. gov., 1852; became Republican, del. Rep. Nat. Conv., Chgo., 1860, Cin., 1872; served as col. staffs Gen. Fremont, Gen. Halleck; U.S. minister to Spain, 1862-65; Rep. presdl. elector, 1868; elected mem. Ill. Legislature, 1870;

apptd. to 1st Bd. R.R. and Warehouse Commrs., 1871, served as pres. Pres. 1st bd. trustees Soldiers' Orphans' Home, 1867. Author: Collection of the Important General Laws of Illinois (in German), 1838; From Spain, 1866; The German Element in the U.S., 1880. Died Belleville, Apr. 9, 1896.

KOHLMANN, Anthony, clergyman, coll. pres., missionary; b. Kaiserberg, Alsace, France, July 13, 1771; theol. studies U. Fribourg (Switzerland). Ordained priest Roman Catholic Ch., 1796; entered Soc. of Jesus, 1803; among 1st to arrive in Am. as missionary, 1806; adminstr. Diocese of N.Y., also in charge of St. Peter's Ch., 1808-14; pres. Georgetown Coll., 1818-20; prof. theology Gregoriana (Jesuit univ.), Rome, Italy, 1824. Author: Unitarianism Philosophically and Theologically Examined. Died Rome, Apr. 10, 1836.

KOHUT, Alexander, rabbi, lexicographer; b. Feligyhaza, Hungary, Apr. 22, 1842; s. Jacob and Cecelia (Hoffman) K.; Rabbi, Jewish Theol. Sem. in Breslau (Germany), 1867; Ph.D. honoris causa, U. Leipzig, 1870; married Julia Weissbrunn (deceased 1886), at least 10 children including George A.; m. 2d, Rebekah Bettelheim, Feb. 14, 1887. Rabbi Congregation Ahawath Chesed, N.Y.C., 1885; an organizer, prof. Talmud Jewish Theol. Sem. Am. examiner in rabbinics Columbia Coll., 1891; Kohut Found. established in his memory. Modernized the Aruch Hashalem (Talmudic dictionary originally compiled by Nathan ben Jeciel, Rome, 11th century), 1878-92. Died N.Y.C., May 25, 1894.

KOLB, Dielman, clergyman; b. Germany, Nov. 21, 1691; s. Dielman and Mrs. (Schumacher) K.; m. Elizabeth Schnebli, 1714, 1 dau., Elizabeth Kolb Zeigler. Preacher, Mennonite Ch., Mannheim, Germany; came to Am., 1717; became weaver, farmer, preacher, Montgomery County, Pa.; worked with Com. on Fgn. Needs (Amsterdam, Holland) to encourage and finance immigration to Am.; became naturalized citizen Pa., 1731. Died Dec. 28, 1756.

KOLLOCK, Shepard, publisher, jurist; b. Lewes, Del., Sept. 1750; s. Shepard and Mary (Goddard) K.; m. Susan Arnett, June 5, 1777, 8 children Served as 1st lt. 2d Arty. Regt., Continental Amy, 1777; published N.J. Journal, 1779, U.S. Almanac, 1779-83, N.Y. Gazeteer, 1783-86; published Polit. Intelligencer, 1783, changed name, published as N.J. Journal, 1786-1818; published 1st N.Y.C. directory; published Christian's, Scholar's and Farmer's Mag., 1789-91; judge Ct. of Common Pleas Essex County (N.J.), 1804-39; postmaster Elizabeth (N.J.), 1820-29. Author: Poems on the Capture of General Burgoyne, 1782. Died Phila., July 28, 1839.

KONINGS, Anthony, clergyman; b. Helmond, Holland, 1821; studied at diocesan sem. Entered Redemptorists, 1842, ordained priest Roman Catholic Ch., 1848; became tchr. and master of novices; then apptd. rector of Amsterdam, later of Wittem house of studies, 1860; apptd. provincial of Holland, 1865; sent to U.S. to teach theology and canon law in Redemptorist house of studies, Ilchester, Md., 1870. Died Ilchester, July 30, 1884.

KORNER, Gustav Philipp, diplomat, jurist; b. Frankfurt-am-Main, Germany, Nov. 20, 1809; s. Bernhard and Marie (Kampfe) K.; studied U. Jena; received doctorates from univs. of Munich and Heidelberg; studied law Transylvania U., Lexington, Ky., circa 1836; m. Sophie Engelmann, June 17, 1836. Arrived in N.Y.C. 1833, settled in St. Clair County, Ill.; justice Ill. Supreme Ct., 1845-50; lt. gov. Ill., 1852-56; apptd. U.S. minister to Spain, 1862; became mem. Liberal Republican Party, 1872. Author: Aus Spanien (book on Spain), 1867; Das Deutsche Element in Den Vereinigten Staaten von Nord-Amerika (a history), 1880. Died Apr. 9, 1896.

KOSCIUSZKO, Tadeusz Andrzej Bonawentura, (Americanized as Thaddeus Kosciuszko), army officer, Polish patriot; b. Palatinate of Breescin Grand Duchy of Lithuania, Feb. 12, 1746; grad. with rank of capt., Royal Sch., Warsaw, Poland, 1769. Capt., Polish Army, 1769; came to Am., 1775; commd. col. of engrs. Continental Army, 1776; advised Horatio Gates to fortify Bemis Heights which resulted in victory of Saratoga; in charge bldg. fortifications U.S. Mil. Acad., 1778-80; charge of transp. during Greene's campaign in South, 1781, adjutant to George Washington, 1779; apptd. brig. gen. by Continental Congress, 1783; a founder Soc. of Cincinnati; maj. gen. Polish Army, 1789; vowed to fight for Polish freedom from Russia until his death; head Polish Army against Russians, 1792; led rebellion of 1794; imprisoned, 1794-96; continued efforts for a free Poland until death. Died Switzerland, Oct. 15, 1817; buried Cracow, Poland.

KOSSUTH, Lajos (Louis), Hungarian patriot; b. Monok, Hungary, Sept. 19, 1802. Engaged in revolutions in Hungary, 1848; came to U.S. to arouse public opinion toward freedom for Hungary in 1850's; verbally attacked by other Hungarians in U.S. because he claimed to be only Hungarian nat. hero of revolution; left U.S., lived for a time in Eng.; tried unsuccessfully to stir up revolution in Hungary, 1859, 66. Died Turin, Italy, Mar. 20, 1894; buried Budapest, Hungary.

KRAUS, John, educator; b. Nassau, Germany, Feb. 2, 1815; s. Jacob and Margaretha (Herbst) K.; m. Maria Boelte, 1873. Came to U.S., 1851; established schs., lectured on ednl. theories of Pestalozzi; a pioneer in concentrating on principles of kindergarten; lectr. U.S. Bur. Edn., 1867-73; mem. Nat. Edn. Assn., mem. com. to promote application of Froebel's principles to Am. grammar schs., 1872; founded, conducted sem. for kindergarten tchrs., N Y.C., 1873-96. Author: The Kindergarten Guide, 1877. Died N.Y.C., Mar. 4, 1826.

KRAUTBAUER, Franz Xaver, clergyman; b. Bruck, Bavaria, Jan. 12, 1824; studied at Ratisbon Sem., also Munich. Ordained priest Roman Catholic Ch., 1850; came to U.S., did parish work in Buffalo; became spiritual dir. Am. Sisters of Notre Dame, 1859; consecrated bishop of Green Bay, Wis., 1875. Died Green Bay, Dec. 17, 1885.

KRAUTH, Charles Philip, clergyman, coll. pres.; b. New Goshenhoppen, Pa., May 7, 1797; s. Charles James and Katherine (Doll) K.; D.D., U. Pa., 1832; m. Catherine Heiskell, Dec. 7, 1820; m. 2d, Harriet Brown, 1834; 4 children, including Charles Porterfield. Licensed by Ministerium of Pa., Lutheran Ch., 1819; pastor, Martinsburg, Va., Shepherdstown, Va., 1819-27, St. Matthews Ch., Phila., 1827-33; 1st pres. Gettysburg (Pa.) Coll., 1834-50; a founder Gettysburg Theol. Sem., 1825, prof., 1850-67; founder Synod of Md. and Pa., 1820; editor Evangelical Review, 1850-61; pres. Gen. Synod, Luth. Ch., 1848. Died Gettysburg, May 30, 1867.

KRAUTH, Charles Porterfield, clergyman; b. Martinsburg, Va. (now W.Va.), Mar. 17, 1823; s. Charles Philip and Catharine (Heiskell) K.; grad. Pa. (now Gettysburg) Coll., 1839, Gettysburg Theol. Sem., 1841; m. Susan Reynolds, 1844; m. 2d, Virginia Baker, 1855. Licensed and ordained to ministry Lutheran Ch., 1842; pastor, Canton and Balt. (both Md.), Shepherdstown and Martinsburg (both now W.Va.), Winchester (Va.), 1848-55, later pastor Pitts. and Phila.; leader conservative br. Luth. Ch., advocated close ties to traditional European ch.; editor-in-chief Lutheran and Missionary, 1861-67; 1st prof. systematic divinity Mt. Airy Theol. Sem., Phila., 1864-83; trustee U. Pa., 1866-68, prof. moral and intellectual philosophy, 1868-83, vice provost, 1873-83; editor-in-chief Luth. Ch. Review, 1882-83; mem. Am. Revision Com. of Old Testament, 1871-83. Author: The Conservative Reformation and Its Theology, 1871. Died Phila., Jan. 2, 1883.

KREBS, Jacob, congressman; b. Orwigsburg, Pa., Mar. 13, 1782; attended pub. schs. Engaged in farming; mem. U.S. Ho. of Reps. (Democrat) from Pa., 19th Congress, Dec. 4, 1826-27; resumed farming. Died Orwigsburg, Sept. 26, 1847; buried Lutheran Cemetery, Orwigsburg.

KREMER, George, congressman; b. Middletown, Pa., Nov. 21, 1775; studied law. Admitted to Pa. bar, began practice in Lewisburg; mem. Pa. Ho. of Reps., 1812-13; mem. U.S. Ho. of Reps. from Pa., 18th-20th congresses, 1823-29. Died Middleburg, Pa., Sept. 11, 1854; buried on family estate nr. Middleburg.

KREZ, Konrad, lawyer, poet; b. Landau, Rhenish Bavaria, Apr. 27, 1828; s. Jean Baptiste and Luise (Naas) K.; attended U. Heidelberg (Germany), 1848; m. Addie Stemmler, 1852, 7 children. Came to U.S., 1851; began practice law, Sheboygan, Wis., 1854; commd. col. 27th Wis. Inf., U.S. Volunteers, 1863, brevetted brig. gen., 1865; collector Port of Milw., 1885-89; mem. Wis. Assembly; city atty. Milw., 1892. Author: (poetry) Dornen und Rosen von den Vogesen, 1848; Gesangbuch, 1850; Aus Wisconsin, 1875. Died Milw., Mar. 9, 1897.

KRIMMEL, John Lewis, painter; b. Ebingen, Württemburg, Germany, 1789. Came to U.S., 1810; became portraitist, Phila.; mem. Columbian Soc. Artists; pres. Assn. Am. Artists, 1821. Paintings include: Pepper-Pot (1811); Country Wedding; Procession of Victuallers; The Burning of Masonic Hall; Fourth of July Celebration at the State House (1819); Centre Square, Phila., in 1812; Election Day. Died Germantown, Pa., July 15, 1821.

KROEGER, Adolph Ernst, journalist; b. Schwabstedt, Schleswig, Germany, Dec. 28, 1837; s. Jacob Kroeger; m. Eliza Curren, 1861, 4 children including Ernest Richard, Alice Bertha. Came to U.S., 1848; correspondent for N.Y. Times in St. Louis, 1858-61; served as lt. U.S. Army, under Gen. John C. Fremont, 1861-62; returned to St. Louis as free-lance journalist; treas. City of St. Louis, 1865-67; convicted erroneously of forgery, 1870, pardoned, 1872; noted for translations of German philosophers, most of which appeared in Jour. of Speculative Philosophy. Translator (works of Johann Gottlieb Fichte) New Exposition of the Science of Knowledge, 1868; The Science of Rights, 1869; The Science of Ethics as Based on the Science of Knowledge, 1897. Died St. Louis, Mar. 8, 1882.

KROL, Bastiaen Jansen, colonial ofcl.; b. Harlingen, Friesland, Holland, 1595; son of Annetjen Egberts; m. Annetjen Stoffels, Feb. 18, 1616; m. 2d, Engeltie Baerents; 3 children. Lay clergyman Dutch Reformed Ch., sent to New Netherland (now N.Y.), 1624; commissary at Ft. Orange (now N.Y.), 1626-31; became mem. consistory of Dutch Reformed Ch., 1628; land agt. for Kiliaen Van Rensselaer, 1630; comdr. Ft. Orange, 1631-32, 38-42. Died Amsterdam, Holland, 1674.

KRUESI, John, inventor; b. Speicher, Switzerland, May 15, 1843; m. Emily Zwinger, 1871, 8 children. Came to U.S., 1870; became mechanic and engr. to Thomas Edison, 1871; built many of inventions designed by Edison; foreman machine shop, Menlo Park, N.J., 1877; built 1st Edison phonograph, 1877; helped perfect incandescent lamp; designed machinery for manufacture of electric lighting equipment; supt. Edison Machine Works, N.Y.C., 1881-86; patented waterproof and insulated method for laying underground cables, 1882; gen. mgr., chief mech. engr. Edison Machine Works, Schenectady, N.Y., 1886-95, chief engr., 1895-99. Died Schenectady, Feb. 22, 1899.

KUHN, Adam, physician, botanist; b. Germantown, Pa., Nov. 17, 1741; s. Adam Simon and Anna (Schrack) K.; M.D., U. Edinburgh, 1767; m. Elizabeth Hartman, 1780, 2 children. Prof. materia medica and botany Coll. of Phila. (now U. Pa.), 1768-89; physician Pa. Hosp., 1775-98; cons. physician Phila. Dispensary, 1786; a founder Coll. Physicians of Phila., 1787, pres., 1808; prof. theory and practice medicine U. of State Pa., 1789, prof. practice of physics, 1792-97; mem. Am. Philos. Soc.; 1st prof. botany in Am. colonies; Kuhnia eupatorioides named after him. Died Phila., July 5, 1817.

KUHNS, Joseph Henry, congressman; b. nr. Greensburg, Pa., Sept. 1800; grad. Washington (later Washington and Jefferson) Coll., 1820; studied law. Admitted to Pa. bar, 1823, began practice in Greensburg; mem. U.S. Ho. of Reps. (Whig) from Pa., 32d Congress, 1851-53; practiced law, Greensburg, until 1877. Died Greensburg, Nov. 16, 1883; buried St. Clair Cemetery, Greensburg.

KUMLER, Henry, clergyman; b. Lancaster County, Pa., Jan. 3, 1775; s. Jacob and Elizabeth (Young) K.; m. Susanna Wingert, Sept. 5, 1797, 12 children including Henry, Jr. Became farmer, Franklin County, Pa., 1810; ordained to ministry United Brethren in Christ, 1814; circuit preacher in Pa., 1814-15, Va., 1816-19, Ohio, 1819-25; apptd. presiding elder, 1817; farmer, Butler County, O., after 1819; bishop United Brethren Ch., 1825-45. Died Jan. 8, 1854.

KUNKEL, Jacob Michael, congressman; b. Frederick, Md., July 13, 1822; grad. U. Va., 1843; studied law. Admitted to Md. bar; began practice of law, Frederick, 1846; mem. Md. Senate, 1850-56; mem. U.S. Ho. of Reps. (Democrat) from Md., 35th-36th congresses, 1857-61; del. Loyalist Conv., Phila., 1866. Died Frederick, Apr. 7, 1870.

KUNKEL, John Christian, congressman; b. Harrisburg, Pa., Sept. 18, 1816; grad. Jefferson Coll. (later Washington and Jefferson Coll.), 1839; attended Carlisle Law Sch. Admitted to Dauphin County (Pa.) bar, 1842, began practice in Harrisburg; mem. Pa. Ho. of Reps., 1844-45, 50; mem. Pa. Senate, 1851-53, speaker, 1852-53; mem. U.S. Ho. of Reps. (Whig) from Pa., 34th-35th congresses, 1855-59. Died Harrisburg, Oct. 14, 1870; buried Harrisburg Cemetery.

KUNZE, John Christopher, clergyman, educator; b. Artern, Saxony, Aug. 5, 1744; grad. U. Leipzig (Germany), circa 1767; m. Margaretta Henrietta Mühlenberg, July 23, 1771, 5 children. Taught sch., Germany, 1767-70; called to Phila. as coadjutator to Henry Melchior Mühlenberg, 1770; ordained to ministery Lutheran Ch., 1770; became 2d leading Lutheran in U.S. at the time; primarily interested in teaching English to all Luth. ministers (because he foresaw that English would become the lang. of the ch.); started pre-theol. sch., Phila., 1773, closed at beginning of Am. Revolution; made unsuccessful attempt to establish German Inst. at U. Pa., 1779; chief pastor of Phila., 1779-84; pastor Christ Ch., N.Y.C., 1784-1807; prof. Oriental langs. Columbia, 1784-87, 92-99, prof. theology, 1797-1807. Author: Rudiments of the Shorter Catechism of Luther, 1785; A Hymn and Prayer Book for the Use of Such Lutheran Churches as Use the English Language, 1795. Died July 24, 1807.

KURTZ, Benjamin, clergyman; b. Harrisburg, Pa., Feb. 28, 1795; s. Benjamin and Elizabeth (Gardner) K.; studied theology under John George Lockman,

Lebanon, Pa., 1813-15; m. Ann Barnett; m. 2d, Mary Catharine Baker; m. 3d, Mary Calhoun; 10 children. Asst., Harrisburg Acad., 1810-13; licensed to preach in Lutheran Ch. by Ministerium of Pa., 1815; pastor, Hagerstown, Md., 1815-31; a leading exponent of Am. Lutheranism; a founder Synod of Md. and Va., 1820, Gen. Synod, 1820, Gettysburg (Pa.) Theol. Sem., 1825; went to Europe to obtain financial support for Gettysburg Theol. Sem., 1826; pastor, Chambersburg, Pa., 1831-33; editor Luth. Observer, Balt., 1833-58; advocated union of German and Luth. Reformed Chs.; del. 1st meeting Evang. Alliance, 1846; broke away from Md. Synod, formed Melanchthon Synod, 1857, wrote its Declaration of Faith; founder Missionary Inst., Selinsgrove, Pa., turned out ministers which were insufficiently educated. Author: Why Are You a Lutheran?, 1843. Died Balt., Dec. 29, 1865.

KURTZ, William Henry, congressman; b. York, Pa., Jan. 31, 1804; attended York County Acad.; studied law. Admitted to Pa. bar, 1828, began practice in York; pros. atty. York County; mem. U.S. Ho. of Reps. (Democrat) from Pa., 32d-33d congresses, 1851-55. Died York, June 24, 1868; buried Prospect Hill Cemetery, York.

KUSKOV, Ivan Aleksandrovich, fur trader, colonizer; b. Totma, Russia, 1765; m. Ekaterina Prokhorovna. Met A.A. Baronov in Siberia; became asst. to Baronov in direction of Golikov and Shelekhov fur-trading co. in Alaska, 1791-1822; organized building of new Russian communities in Alaska, promoted ship constrn.; comdr.-in-chief of fortress Novo-Arkhangel'sk (now Sitka), directed all structural work of community, 1806; noted for building of Russian settlement Ft. Ross, approximately 50 miles from San Francisco, 1812, mgr. of ft., 1812-21, built shipyard there; returned to Totma, 1822. Died Totma, Oct. 1823.

KUYKENDALL, Andrew Jackson, congressman; b. Gallatin County, Ill., Mar. 3, 1815; studied law. Admitted to Ill. bar, 1840, began practice in Vienna; mem. Ill. Ho. of Reps., 1842-62; served as maj. 31st Regt., Ill. Volunteers, Union Army, during Civil War; mem. U.S. Ho. of Reps. (Republican) from Ill., 39th Congress, 1865-67; county and probate judge Johnson County (Ill.), 1873-81; mem. Ill. Senate, 1872-82. Died Vienna, May 11, 1891; buried Fraternal Cemetery, Vienna.

KYNETT, Alpha Jefferson, clergyman, reformer; b. Adams County, Pa., Aug. 12, 1829; s. John and Polly (Peterson) K.; m. Althea Pauline Gilruth, 1854. Moved to Ia., 1842; joined Ia. Conf., Methodist Episcopal Ch., 1851, ordained deacon, 1853, elder, 1855; presiding elder Davenport dist., 1860; mem. Gov.'s staff during Civil War, aided in raising and equipping troops; del. Meth. Gen. Conf., 1864-68, leading force in establishment of Ch. Extension Soc., 1864, sec., 1867-99; secured erection of hundreds of chs. in West, 1899; editor Christianity in Earnest (bi-monthly), 1889-99; a founder Anti-Saloon League; organizer Interdenominational Christian Temperance Alliance of Ohio, 1893; an organizer Anti-Saloon League of Am., 1895; influential in formation of Bd. of Temperance, Prohibition and Public Morals of Episcopal Ch. Died Feb. 23, 1899; buried West Laurel Hill Cemetery, Phila.

L

La BARGE, Joseph, navigator, fur trader; b. St. Louis, Oct. 1, 1815; s. Joseph Marie and Eulalie (Hortiz) La B.; attended St. Mary's Coll. (Mo.), 1827-30; m. Pelagie Guerette, Aug. 17, 1842. Clk. in Am. Fur. Co. boat, Yellowstone, traveling on Missouri River, 1831-34, gained 1st experience as navigator when cholera epidemic incapacitated most of crew, 1833; entered fur trade in competition with Am. Fur. Co., 1841, was forced to sell out; pilot of Omega for Am. Fur. Co., 1843-55, master at several times; piloted Audubon expdn. to upper Mo., 1843; organized firm La Barge, Harkness & Co., 1861, encountered severe losses, sold out, 1862; pilot for U.S. Govt., 1880-85; held municipal office, St. Louis, 1890-94; compiled list of all steamboat wrecks on Missouri River from its opening until 1897 for Missouri River Commn., 1896-97; 1 of most famous of Missouri River boatmen. Died St. Louis, Apr. 3, 1899; buried Calvary Cemetery, St. Louis.

La BORDE, Maximilian, physician, educator; b. Edgefield, S.C., June 5, 1804; s. Pierre and Sarah (Crane) La B.; attended Edgefield Acad.; grad. S.C. Coll., 1821, Med. Coll. of S.C., 1825; m. Sophia Carroll, Sept. 28, 1826; m. 2d, Elizabeth Carroll, Dec. 27, 1843. Practiced medicine, Edgefield, 1826-42; editor, owner Edgefield Advertiser, 1836-39; mem. lower house S.C. Legislature, 1837-38; sec. of state S.C., 1839; prof. literature, later philosophy S.C. Coll. (now U. S.C.), Columbia, 1842-61, saved coll. from destruction during Sherman's invasion, prof. English, 1866-73, trustee, 1837-73; organized relief agys. and hosps. for S.C. soldiers during Civil War. Author: Introduction to Physiology, 1855; History of South Carolina College, 1859. Died Columbia, Nov. 6, 1873; buried Columbia.

LA BRANCHE, Alcée Louis, congressman; b. nr. New Orleans, 1806; attended Université de Sorreze, France. Engaged in planting; mem. La. Ho. of Reps., 1831-33, speaker, 1833; chargé d'affaires to Tex., 1837-45; mem. U.S. Ho. of Reps. (Democrat) from La., 28th Congress, 1843-45; naval officer Port of New Orleans, 1847. Died Hot Springs, Va., Aug. 17, 1861; buried Red Church Cemetery, St. Charles Parish, La., reinterred Metairie Cemetery, New Orleans.

LACEY, John, army officer, public ofcl.; b. Buckingham, Pa., Feb. 4, 1755; s. John and Jane (Chapman) L.; m. Anastasia Reynolds, Jan. 18, 1781, 4 children. Commd. capt. of a volunteer co., 1776; organized co., Bucks County, Pa.; served with 4th Pa. Regt. in Canadian campaign of 1776; commd. lt. col. Bucks County Militia, 1777, brig. gen., 1778; sub.-lt., also commr. of confiscated estates for Bucks County; mem. Pa. Assembly from Bucks County, 1778; mem. Provincial Council of Pa., 1779-81; mem. Pa. Supreme Exec. Council, 1779-82, on leave as comdr. of a militia brigade, 1780-81; apptd. justice of the peace, 1801; mem. N.J. Assembly. Died New Mills, N.J., Feb. 17, 1814.

LACLEDE, Pierre Ligueste (real name Pierre Laclede Ligueste), fur trader; b. Bedous, France, 1724; 3 children. Emigrated to New Orleans, 1755, became asso. with trading establishment Maxent, Laclede & Co., became agt. territory which is now Ill., 1763; went to Western bank of Mississippi River after Eastern region came under Brit. rule, founded Village of St. Louis, 1764 (named in honor of Louis IX), laid out and became sole ruler of community. Died nr. mouth of Arkansas River, June 20, 1778.

LACOCK, Abner, senator; b. Alexandria, Va., July 9, 1770; s. William and Lovey L.; m. Hannah Eddy, 3 sons, 4 daus. Justice of peace Beaver, Pa., 1796; mem. Pa. Legislature, 1801-03, 04-08, 32-35; asso. justice Beaver County Ct., 1803; brig. gen. Pa. Militia, 1807; mem. Pa. Senate, 1808-10; mem. U.S. Ho. of Reps. from Pa., 12th-13th congresses, 1811-13, resigned 2d term; mem. U.S. Senate from Pa., 1813-19; supervised constrn. of Western div. canal connecting Delaware and Ohio rivers, 1825; commr. to survey constrn. of Pa. and Ohio "cross-cut canal." Died Freedom, Pa., Apr. 12, 1837; buried Lacock Cemetery, Rochester, Pa.

LADD, Catherine, educator; b. Richmond, Va., Oct. 28, 1808; d. James and Ann (Collins) Stratton; attended Richmond Public Schs.; m. George W. Ladd, Sept. 1828, 1 son, Albert W. Prin., Vineville Acad., Macon, Ga., circa 1836-39, Winnsboro (S.C.) Female Inst., 1840-62; active supporter of Confederacy; pres. Ladies' Relief Assn. of Fairfield, during Civil War; lost her home and possessions during invasion of S.C., 1865; conducted boarding and day sch. for girls, Winnsboro, 1870-80; lived on plantation "Buena Vista" nr. Winnsboro, after 1880. Contbr. poems, essays, stories to Charleston News & Courier, from 1840's; contbd. 2 poems to 2d vol. So. Literary Messenger, many poems (under pseudonyms Arcturus, Alida) to Winnsboro newspaper. Died "Buena Vista," Jan. 30, 1899; buried Presbyn. Cemetery, Salem, S.C.

LADD, George Washington, congressman; b. Augusta, Me., Sept. 28, 1818; attended Kents Hill Sem. Engaged in drug bus., Bangor, Me., later engaged in lumber, commn. and wholesale grocery bus.; del. numerous nat. convs.; mem. U.S. Ho. of Reps. (Democratic and Greenback rep.) from Me., 46th-47th congresses, 1879-83. Died Bangor, Jan. 30, 1892; buried Mt. Hope Cemetery, Bangor.

LADD, Joseph Brown, physician, poet; b. Newport, R.I., July 7, 1764; s. William and Sarah (Gardner) L.; studied medicine, Newport, circa 1780-83. Began writing ballads and satire at age 14; licensed to practice medicine, Newport, 1783; moved to Charleston, S.C., practiced medicine, gained reputation as man of letters; wrote polit. and sci. essays, also poems (many on patriotic themes, most in heroic couplets); delivered address on Am. Revolution before assembly Soc. of Cincinnati of S.C., July 4, 1785. Author: The Poems of Arouet, 1786. Died Charleston, Nov. 2, 1786; buried Charleston.

LADD, William, pacifist leader; b. Exeter, N.H., May 10, 1778; s. Eliphalet and Abigail (Hill) L.; grad. Harvard, 1798; m. Sophia Ann Stidolph, 1799. Operated farm, Minot, Me., from 1812; interested in peace movement, from 1819; organized local peace socs., tried to secure public support through writings and public meetings, 1820's-30's; founded Am. Peace Soc., Boston, 1828, became editor of soc.'s ofcl. publication; pioneered propaganda methods of petitions and delegations to legislative bodies; ordained to ministry Congregational Ch., 1837, used this status to communicate with religious assemblies and seminaries; secured adoption by Am. Peace Soc. of principle of condemnation of all war whether offensive or defensive, 1837; evolved plan for world peace based on congress of all nations and an internat. court. Author A Brief Illustration of the Principles of War and Peace, 1831; On the Duty of Females to Promote the Cause of Peace, 1836; An Essay on a Congress of Nations, 1840. Died Apr. 9, 1841.

LADD, William Sargent, businessman; b. Holland, Vt., Oct. 10, 1826; s. Nathaniel and Abigail (Mead) L.; m. Caroline Elliot, 1854. Tchr. and farmer, N.H., until 1851; went to Portland, Ore., 1851, established retail bus.; founded Ladd & Tilton Bank, Portland, 1859, for next 30 years provided financial support for many new enterprises including Ore. Steam & Navigation Co. (1862), Ore. Central R.R. Co. (1866), Ore. & Ida. Telegraph Co. (1868), Ore. R.R. & Navigation Co. (1879); made contbns. to many schs. and chs. including Presbyn. Theol. Sem. of San Francisco, Portland Library Assn. Died Portland, Jan. 6, 1893; buried Portland.

LA DOW, George Augustus, congressman; b. nr. Syracuse, N.Y., Mar. 18, 1826; attended common schs., McHenry County, Ill.; studied law. Admitted to the bar, 1850; began practice of law, Waupaca, Wis.; dist. atty. Waupaca County (Wis.), 1860-62; moved in Minn., 1862, settled in Wilton; mem. Minn. Ho. of Reps., 1868-69; moved to Pendleton, Ore., 1869, practiced law; mem. Ore. Ho. of Reps., 1872-74; mem. U.S. Ho. of Reps. (Democrat) from Ore., 44th Congress, 1875. Died Pendleton, May 1, 1875; buried Pioneer Park Cemetery, Pendleton.

LAFAYETTE, Marquis de (Marie Joseph Paul Yves Roche Gilbert du Motier), army officer; b. Auvergne, France, Sept. 6, 1757; s. Gilbert (Marquis de Lafayette) and Marie Louise Julie de la Riviere; attended Collège du Plessis, Paris, France, 1768-72; m. Marie Andrienne Francoise de Noailles, Apr. 11, 1774, at least 1 son, George Washington. Served with 2d Co., King's Musketeers, French Army, 1771-73, transferred to regt. commanded by Louis, Vicomte de Noailles, became 2d lt., 1773, promoted capt., 1774; entered Continental Army (volunteered to do so at own expense) during Revolutionary War, 1777, commd. maj. gen. by vote of Continental Congress, July 1777, placed in command of div. of Va. light troops by vote of Congress, Dec. 1777; spent furlough in France, advancing Am. cause, 1778-80; served in Va., took part in Battle of Yorktown, 1781; became mem. Soc. of Cincinnati; an intimate asso. of George Washington; returned to France, Dec. 1781; visited U.S., 1784, 1824-25; became mem. French Assembly of Notables, 1787, French Nat. Assembly, 1789; an organizer Nat. Guard of France; designer of French tri-color flag; a founder Club of the Feuillants (conservative liberals who wished to establish constl. monarchy), 1790; commanded French Army in War with Austria, 1791; declared a traitor by Nat. Assembly, 1792, fled to Flanders, captured and imprisoned by Austrians; returned to France after 7-year exile, 1799; mem. Chamber of Deputies, 1815, 18-24; commander French Nat. Guard in July Revolution, 1830; voted $24,424 for his part in Am. Revolution by U.S. Congress, 1794, given 11,520 acres of land in La., 1803; named hon. citizen of U.S. Died May 20, 1834; buried Picpus Cemetery (grave covered with earth from Bunker Hill), Paris.

LAFEVER, Minard, architect; b. Morristown, N.J., Aug. 10, 1798; s. Isaac and Anna (Stark) L.; married twice, 1st wife; Pamelia Laraway; 6 children. Became architect, N.Y.C., 1828, in partnership with James Gallier, 1833-34, with James Bell, 1835, with Benjamin F. Smith, 1848-50; prin. works include: 1st Reformed Ch., 1834, 1st Bapt. Ch., 1841 (both N.Y.C.); Pierrepont Bapt. Ch., 1843-44, 1st Unitarian Ch. (consecrated as Ch. of the Saviour 1844), Holy Trinity Ch., 1844-47, Bklyn. Sav. Bank, 1847, Packer Collegiate Inst., completed 1856 (all Bklyn.). Author: The Young Builder's General Instructor, 1829; The Beauties of Modern Architecture, 1835; The Architectural Instructor, 1856. Died Williamsburg, L.I., N.Y., Sept. 26, 1854; buried Cypress Hills Cemetery, Williamsburg.

LAFFITE, Jean, pirate; b. probably Bayone, France, circa 1779. Probably went to sea as youth; joint owner (with brother Pierre) blacksmith shop, New Orleans, by 1809, probably used shop as depot for smuggled goods and slaves; became leader of smuggling band operating in violation of U.S. revenue laws, from small islands in Barataria Bay, circa 1810; pardoned by Pres. Madison as reward for service in Battle of New Orleans, 1815; resumed privateering from hdqrs. in Galveston, 1817; apptd. gov. Galveston under republic founded by James Long; forced to abandon his Galveston operation by Am. naval raid under Lt. Kearney, 1821, burned the town and left; some activity on Spanish Main. Disappeared circa 1825.

La FLESCHE, Susette (Bright Eyes), reformer; b. Omaha (Neb.) Reservation, 1854; d. Joseph La Flesche (Iron Eye); m. Mr. Tibbles, 1881. Taught govt. day sch., Omaha Reservation; wrote (with her father) accounts of Ponca Indians (removed forcibly from their reservations by U.S. Govt.) and their sufferings on new reservation; made speaking tour of East (with her brother Francis and Standing Bear, chief of Poncas) in attempt to awaken public opinion to Indian rights; toured Scotland (with her husband), appealing for Indians, after 1881; spent later years at Lincoln, Neb. Author: Ploughed Under, the Story of An Indian Chief, 1881. Died on reservation nr. Bancroft, Neb., May 26, 1903.

LAFLIN, Addison Henry, congressman; b. Lee, Mass., Oct. 24, 1823; grad. Williams Coll., 1843; Moved to Herkimer County, N.Y., 1849; mem. N.Y. Senate, 1858-59; mem. U.S. Ho. of Reps. (Republican) from N.Y., 39th-41st congresses, 1865-71; del. N.Y. Republican Conv., 1867; naval officer Port of N.Y., 1871-77. Died Pittsfield, Mass., Sept. 24, 1878; buried Oakwood Cemetery, Syracuse, N.Y.

LAFON, Thomy, businessman, philanthropist; b. New Orleans, Dec. 28, 1810; born of free Negro parentage; s. Pierre and Modest (Foucher) Laralde. Taught sch., New Orleans, circa 1830-50; operated store, New Orleans, from 1850; accumulated considerable wealth by loaning money, investing in real estate, from late 1850's; patron of arts in New Orleans; contbd. money to many needy persons and charitable enterprises; made bequests to Charity Hosp., Lafon Old Folks Home, Soc. of Holy Family, Shakespeare Almshouse, also several ednl. instns. including Straight U. (all New Orleans). Died New Orleans, Dec. 22, 1893; buried St. Louis Cemetery, New Orleans.

LAHM, Samuel, congressman; b. Leitersburg, Md., Apr. 22, 1812; attended Washington Coll., Pa.; studied law. Admitted to Ohio bar, 1836, began practice in Canton; master of chancery, 1837-41; pros. atty. Stark County (O.), 1841-45; mem. Ohio Senate, 1842; del. Democratic Nat. Conv., Balt., 1844; served as brig. gen. Ohio Militia; mem. U.S. Ho. of Reps. (Dem.) from Ohio, 30th Congress, 1847-49; engaged in farming, sheep raising. Died Canton, June 16, 1876; buried West Lawn Cemetery, Canton.

LAHONTAN, baron de, see De Lom D'Arce, Louis-Armand.

LAIRD, James, congressman; b. Fowlerville, N.Y., June 20, 1849; attended Adrian Coll.; grad. law dept. U. Mich., 1871. Served with 16th Regt., Mich. Volunteer Inf., during Civil War, 1862-65; admitted to the bar; began practice of law, Hastings, Neb., 1872; mem. Neb. Constl. Conv., 1875; Republican presdl. elector, 1880; mem. U.S. Ho. of Reps. (Rep.) from Neb., 48th-51st congresses, 1883-89. Died Hastings, Aug. 17, 1889; buried Parkview Cemetery, Hastings.

LAKANAL, Joseph, educator; b. Serres, France, July 14, 1762. Prof. rehetoric U. Bourges (France); prof. philosophy U. Moulins (France); mem. French Nat. Conv., 1792-95; mem. French Council of 500, 1795; came to Am., 1814, given land in Ala. by Congress; became cotton planter, Ala.; pres. U. La., 1817-25; returned to France, 1838, re-elected to French Acad. Scis. Died Paris, France, Feb. 14, 1845.

LAKE, William Augustus, congressman; b. nr. Cambridge, Md., Jan. 6, 1808; grad. Jefferson Coll., Pa., 1827; studied law. Mem. Md. Ho. of Dels., 1831; moved to Vicksburg, Miss.; admitted to Miss. bar, 1834, began practice in Vicksburg; mem. Miss. Senate, 1848; mem. U.S. Ho. of Reps. (Whig) from Miss., 34th Congress, 1855-57; mem. Miss. Ho. of Reps., 1859-61; resumed law practice; candidate for Confederate Congress, 1861. Killed in a duel with Col. Chambers (his opponent for election to Confederate Congress), Hopefield, Ark., Oct. 15, 1861; buried City Cemetery, Vicksburg.

LALOR, Alice, see Mother Teresa.

LAMAR, Gazaway Bugg, steamship co. exec., banker; b. Richmond County, Ga., Oct. 2, 1798; s. Basil and Rebecca (Kelley) L.; m. Jane Creswell, Oct. 18, 1821; m. 2d, Harriet de Cazenove, circa 1842; 11 children. Active various trading enterprises, Savannah and Augusta, Ga., from 1820's; built ship John Randolph (1st steamship in Am. waters), 1834; a founder Am. Steamboat Co. of Augusta, 1835, operated service on Savannah River; pres. Bank of Republic, N.Y.C., 1845-61; agt. in N.Y.C. for State of Ga. in comml. affairs during secession crisis, 1860-61; pres. Bank of Commerce, Savannah, 1861-65; pres. Bank Conv. of Confederate States, Atlanta, 1861; organized blockade running operations for Confederacy; benefactor of Negro hosps., Augusta, Savannah, also Young Men's Library Assn., Augusta. Died N.Y.C., Oct. 5, 1874; buried Alexandria, Va.

LAMAR, Henry Graybill, congressman; b. Clinton, Ga., July 10, 1798; studied law. Admitted to Ga. bar, began practice in Macon; judge Ga. Superior Ct.; mem. Ga. Ho. of Reps.; mem. U.S. Ho. of Reps. (Democrat) from Ga., 21st-22d congresses, Dec. 7, 1829-33; unsuccessful candidate for gov. Ga., 1857; asso. justice Ga. Supreme Ct. Died Macon, Sept. 10, 1861; buried Rose Hill Cemetery, Macon.

LAMAR, John Basil, congressman; b. Milledgeville, Ga., Nov. 5, 1812; attended Franklin Coll. (now U. Ga.), 1827. Engaged in planting nr. Macon, Ga., 1830; mem. Ga. Ho. of Reps., 1837-38; mem. U.S. Ho. of Reps. (Democrat) from Ga., 28th Congress, Mar. 4-July 29, 1843 (resigned); resumed planting; trustee U. Ga., 1855-58; del. Ga. Secession Conv., 1861; served as aide on staff of Gen. Howell Cobb, Confederate Army, during Civil War; fatally wounded in battle at Cramptons Gap, Md., Sept. 14, 1862. Died Cramptons Gap, Sept. 15, 1862; buried Rose Hill Cemetery, Macon.

LAMAR, Lucius Quintus Cincinnatus, asso. justice U.S. Supreme Ct., senator; b. Eatonton, Putnam County, Ga., Sept. 17, 1825; s. Lucius Q. C. and Sarah (Bird) L.; grad. Emory Coll., Oxford, Ga., 1845; m. Virginia Longstreet, July 15, 1847, 1 son, 3 daus.; m. 2d, Henrietta Dean, Jan. 5, 1887, no children. Admitted to Ga. bar, 1847; prof. mathematics U. Miss., Oxford, 1849; moved to Ga., 1852; mem. Ga. Ho. of Reps., 1853; returned to Miss., 1855; mem. U.S. Ho. of Reps. from Miss., 35th-36th, 43d-44th congresses, 1857-Dec. 1860, 1873-77; member Mississippi Secession Conv., 1861; col. 18th Miss. Regt. during Civil War; Confederate commr. to Russia, 1862-64; judge advocate III Corps, Army of No. Va., 1864-65; mem. Miss. Constl. convs., 1865, 68, 75, 77, 81; prof. econs. and social science U. Miss., 1866, prof. law, 1867; mem. U.S. Senate from Miss., 1877-Mar. 6, 1885; U.S. sec. of interior under Pres. Cleveland, 1885-88; asso. justice U.S. Supreme Ct., 1888-93. Died Vineville, Ga., Jan. 23, 1893; buried St. Peter's Cemetery, Oxford, Miss.

LAMAR, Mirabeau Buonaparte, pres. Republic of Tex., army officer; b. Louisville, Ga., Aug. 16, 1798; s. John and Rebecca (Lamar) L.; m. Tabeta Jordan, Jan. 1, 1826; m. 2d, Henrietta Maffett, 1851. Pvt. sec. to Gov. George M. Troup of Ga., 1823; editor Columbus (Ga.) Enquirer, 1826; went to Tex., 1836; served as comdr. Tex. Cavalry at Battle of San Jacinto; atty. gen., then sec. of war in Pres. Burnet's provisional cabinet, 1836; v.p. Republic of Tex., 1836, pres., 1838-41; a founder City of Austin (Tex.), 1840; fought in Mexican War, participated in Battle of Monterey, 1846; U.S. minister to Argentina, 1855-56; became strong advocate of Southern rights; Lamar State Coll., Tex., named for him. Died Richmond, Tex., Dec. 19, 1859.

LAMB, Alfred William, congressman; b. Stamford, N.Y., Mar. 18, 1824; studied law, Mo. Admitted to Mo. bar, began practice in Hannibal; mem. U.S. Ho. of Reps. (Democrat) from Mo., 33d Congress, 1853-55; resumed law practice. Died Hannibal, Apr. 29, 1888; buried Riverside Cemetery, Hannibal.

LAMB, John, revolutionary patriot, army officer; b. N.Y.C., Jan. 1, 1735; s. Anthony Lamb; m. Catherine Jandine, Nov. 13, 1755. Joined Sons of Liberty, 1765; commd. capt. arty. co., July 1775; maj. in command No. Dept., Continental Army; taken prisoner by British, exchanged, apptd. col. 2d Continental Arty, 1777; commanded arty. at U. S. Mil. Acad., 1779-80; participated in siege and battle of Yorktown, 1781; brevetted brig. gen., 1783; apptd. collector of customs Port of N.Y., 1784; mem. N.Y. Legislature; an original mem. Soc. of Cincinnati. Died May 31, 1800.

LAMB, Martha Joanna Reade Nash, editor, author; b. Plainfield, Mass., Aug. 13, 1829; d. Arvin and Lucinda (Vinton) Nash; m. Charles A. Lamb, Sept. 8, 1852. Active in charity work, Chgo., 1852-66; moved to N.Y.C., 1866, wrote several children's books; editor Mag. of Am. History (only publ. of its time exclusively concerned with Am. history), N.Y.C., 1883-93, also contbr. numerous articles. Author: History of the City of New York: Its Origin, Rise, and Progress, 2 vols., 1877-81; (articles) Wall Street in History, 1883, Unpublished Washington Portraits, 1888. Died N.Y.C., Jan. 2, 1893; buried Plainfield, Mass.

LAMBDIN, James Reid, painter; b. Pitts., May 10, 1807; s. James and Prudence Lambdin; studied painting with Thomas Sully, Phila., 1823-26; m. Mary Cochran, 6 children. Operated museum and gallery, Pitts., 1826-32; painted in Louisville, Ky., 1832-37, travelled widely in South; known for portraits and miniatures; lived in Phila., from 1837; officer Artists' Fund Soc., Phila., 1838-67; dir. Pa. Acad. Fine Arts, 1845-64; apptd. U.S. art commr. by Pres. Buchanan, 1858; prof. fine arts U. Pa., 1861-66. Portraits include: John Marshall, J. Q. Adams, Andrew Jackson, James K. Polk, Abraham Lincoln. Died Phila., Jan. 31, 1889; buried Phila.

LAMBERT, Charles, stonecutter; b. Kirk Deighton, Yorkshire, Eng., Aug. 30, 1816. Joined Mormon Ch., 1843; came to U.S., 1844, settled in Nauvoo, Ill.; carved sun-face capitals of Nauvoo Temple of Latter-day Saints; settled in Utah, 1849. Died Salt Lake City, May 2, 1892.

LAMBERT, John, senator, congressman; b. Lambertville, N.J., Feb. 24, 1746. Engaged in farming; mem. N.J. Gen. Assembly, 1780-85, 88; mem. N.J. Council, 1790-1804, v.p., 1801-04; acting gov. N.Y., 1802-03; mem. U.S. Ho. of Reps. (Democrat) from N.J., 9th-10th congresses, 1805-09; mem. U.S. Senate from N.J., 1809-15; plantation owner. Died nr. Lambertville, Feb. 4, 1823; buried Barber's Burying Ground, Delaware Twp., Hunterdon County, N.J.

LAMBUTH, James William, missionary; b. Greene County, Ala., Mar. 2, 1830; s. John Russell; grad. U. Miss., 1851; m. Mary McClellan, 1 son, Walter R. Preacher in Miss., 1851-54; became mem. Miss. Conf., So. Methodist Ch., 1854, apptd. missionary to China; preached in Chinese lang., Shanghai and area, 1855-61; came back to Miss. because of Civil War, 1861-64; returned to mission work in China, 1864-76; established (with son, Dr. Walter Lambuth) So. Meth. mission in Japan, 1876; active in Kobe, Osaka and Inland Sea area (Japan) until 1892. Died Kobe, Apr. 28, 1892.

LAMON, Ward Hill, lawyer; b. Frederick County, Va., Jan. 6, 1828; s. George and Elizabeth (Ward) L.; studied law, Louisville, Ky., 1847-circa 1849; m. Angelina Turner; m. 2d, Sally Logan; 1 dau. Admitted to bar, began practice of law, Danville, Ill., circa 1850; law partner of Abraham Lincoln, Danville, 1852-53; active in Republican Party in Ill., from 1856; bodyguard to Lincoln on trip from Ill. to Washington, Feb. 1861; sent by Lincoln on mission to Charleston, S.C., Mar. 1861; U.S. marshall of D.C., 1861-65; aroused controversy by opposing abolitionists; partner (with Jeremiah S. Black) in law firm, 1865-79; practiced law, Denver, 1879-86; published The Life of Abraham Lincoln from his Birth to His Inauguration as President (Chauncy Black), 1872. Died Martinsburg, W.Va., May 7, 1893.

LaMOUNTAIN, John, balloonist; b. Wayne County, N.Y., 1830. Began experimenting with balloons, 1850's; made balloon ascension (with O. A. Gager) from Bennington, Vt., circa 1858; planned (with Gager and John Wise) balloon for trans-Atlantic use, 1859; travelled in balloon Atlantic (with Gager and Wise) from St. Louis to Henderson County, N. Y. (1,000 miles, longest air trip on record to that date), July 1, 1859; performed aerial reconnaissance missions for Gen. McClellan in balloon, passed behind Confederate lines, Aug. 1861; later supervised several ascensions for mil. reconnaissance purposes. Died Feb. 14, 1870.

LAMPORT, William Henry, congressman; b. Brunswick, N.Y., May 27, 1811; attended pub. schs., Gorham, N.Y. Engaged in farming; supr. of Gorham, 1848-49; sheriff Ontario County (N.Y.), 1850-53; mem. N.Y. Assembly, 1854; moved to Canandaigua, N.Y., 1864; pres. Village of Canandaigua, 1866-67; mem. U.S. Ho. of Reps. (Republican) from N.Y., 42d-43d congresses, 1871-75. Died Canandaigua, July 21, 1891; buried West Avenue Cemetery, Canandaigua.

LAMPSON, Sir Curtis Miranda, mcht.; b. Sept. 21, 1806; s. William and Rachel (Powell) L.; m. Jane Sibley, Nov. 30, 1827, 1 son, 1 dau. Clk. in store, New Haven, Vt., circa 1820-25; engaged in merc., later exporting bus., N.Y.C., circa 1825-30; established C. M. Lampson Co., importing firm, London, Eng., 1830; became Brit. subject, 1849; a promoter and investor Atlantic Telegraph Co. (laid 1st trans-Atlantic cable, 1866), dir., from 1858; created baronet for telegraph enterprise, 1866; trustee George Peabody Fund for London Poor. Died London, Mar. 12, 1885; buried London.

LAMY, John Baptist, clergyman; b. Lempdes, France, Oct. 11, 1814; s. Jean and Marie Lamy; attended Sem. of Montferrand, France. Ordained priest Roman Catholic Ch., 1838; came to Am., 1839, became missionary, Wooster and Danville, O., later in Covington, Ky.; named vicar apostolic of N.M., bishop of Agathon, 1850; became bishop of Santa Fe, 1853 (diocese included N.M., Ariz., parts of Colo., Utah, Nev., expanded to include whole of Colo., 1860); induced Sisters of Loretto to found settlement in Santa Fe, 1852, Christian Brothers, 1867; built many schs. and chs. in diocese; archbishop of Santa Fe, 1875-85; novel Death Comes for the Archbishop (Willa Cather, 1927) based on his life. Died Santa Fe, Feb. 13, 1888; buried Santa Fe.

LANCASTER, Columbia, congressman; b. New Milford, Conn., Aug. 26, 1803; attended common schs., Canfield, O.; studied law, Detroit. Admitted to Mich. bar, 1830, began practice in Centerville; pros. atty. Mich. Territory; mem. Mich. Territorial Legislature, 1837; settled in Willamette Valley, Ore., 1847;

asso. justice Ore. Provisional Supreme Ct.; settled nr. mouth of Lewis River, Ore. (now Wash.); mem. Ore. Territorial Council, 1850-52; del. U.S. Congress (Democrat) from Territory of Wash. (after separation of territories of Wash. and Ore.), 1854-55; regent U. Wash., 1862; asso. with Puget Sound & Columbia River R.R., 1862. Died Vancouver, Wash., Sept. 15, 1893; buried City Cemetery, Vancouver.

LANDAIS, Pierre, naval officer; b. St. Malo, Brittany, France, 1731. Served as officer French Navy; mem. French exploratory voyage around the world with Louis Bougainville, 1766-69; commd. capt. Continental Navy, 1777; commanded mcht. ship Flamand, delivered supplies from France to Portsmouth, N.H.; commanded frigate Alliance, 1778; became naturalized citizen of Mass., 1778; assigned to fleet of John Paul Jones, 1779; ct. martialed, convicted of insubordination during battle with Brit. ship Serapis, 1781, expelled from U.S. Navy; commd. rear adm. French Navy, 1792; returned to N.Y., 1797. Died N.Y.C., Sept. 17, 1820.

LANDER, Frederick West, explorer, army officer; b. Salem, Mass., Dec. 17, 1821; s. Edward and Eliza (West) L.; m. Jean Davenport, Oct. 1860. Civil engr. during survey of No. Pacific R.R. route, 1853; headed party of exploration to report on feasibility of railroad from Puget Sound to Mississippi River, 1854; supt., chief engr. overland wagon road, 1855; led or participated in 5 transcontinental surveys; served as aide on Gen. McClellan's staff; commd. brig. gen. U.S. Volunteers, 1861; commanded a brigade in Gen. C. P. Stone's div. on Upper Potomac, 1861; wrote patriotic poems during Civil War. Died Va., Mar. 2, 1862.

LANDERS, George Marcellus, congressman; b. Lenox, Mass., Feb. 22, 1813; attended pub. schs., Lenox. Moved to New Britain, Conn., 1830, engaged in hardware mfg.; mem. Conn. Ho. of Reps., 1841, 67, 74, Conn. Senate, 1853, 69, 73; bank commr. State of Conn., 1874; mem. U.S. Ho. of Reps. (Democrat) from Conn., 44th-45th congresses, 1875-79. Died New Britain, Mar. 27, 1895; buried Fairview Cemetery, New Britain.

LANDRETH, David, agriculturist; b. Phila., Sept. 15, 1802; s. David and Sarah (Arnell) L.; ed. common schs., Phila.; m. Elizabeth Rodney, 1825; m. 2d, Martha Burnet, 1842. Became propr. of his father's nursery and seed bus., Phila., 1828; a founder Pa. Horticultural Soc., v.p., 1829-36; became publisher Illustrated Floral Mag., 1832; constructed nursery and arboretum, Bristol, Pa., 1847; a founder Farmers' Club of Pa., 1847; active in agrl. experimentation, cattle breeding, 1850's, 60's; pres. Phila. Soc. for Promotion of Agr., 1856; experimented with steam plowing, digging and chopping, 1870's; published Am. edit. Dictionary of Modern Gardening (George W. Johnson), 1847. Died Bristol, Feb. 22, 1880; buried Bristol.

LANDRUM, John Morgan, congressman; b. Edgefield Dist., S.C., July 3, 1815; grad. S.C. Coll. (now U. S.C.), 1842; studied law. Taught sch.; admitted to the bar, 1844; began practice of law, Shreveport, La.; mayor of Shreveport, 1848-49; mem. U.S. Ho. of Reps. (Democrat) from La., 36th Congress, 1859-61. Died Shreveport, Oct. 18, 1861; buried Oakland Cemetery, Shreveport.

LANDRY, Joseph Aristide, congressman; b. nr. Donaldsonville, La., July 10, 1817; attended sch., Cape Girardeau, Mo. Mem. La. Ho. of Reps., 1840; mem. U.S. Ho. of Reps. (Whig) from La., 32d Congress, 1851-53; pres. policy jury of Ascension Parish (La.), 1861; served as 1st sgt. Chasseurs de la'Ascension, later with Co. B., Cannoneers of Donaldsonville (disbanded before called into Confederate service). Died nr. Donaldsonville, Mar. 9, 1881; buried Donaldsonville Catholic Cemetery.

LANDY, James, congressman; b. Phila., Oct. 13, 1813; attended pub. schs.; studied law. Engaged in merc. bus.; mem. Phila. Bd. Sch. Commrs., 1845; mem. U.S. Ho. of Reps. (Democrat) from Pa., 35th Congress, 1857-59; chief commr. of hwys., 1862. Died Phila., July 25, 1875; buried Monument Cemetery, Phila.

LANE, Amos, congressman; b. nr. Aurora, N.Y., Mar. 1, 1778; attended pub. schs.; studied law; children include James Henry. Admitted to the bar; began practice of law, Lawrenceburg, Ind., 1808; moved to Burlington, Ky., 1814, practiced law; mem. Ky. Ho. of Reps., 1816-17, 39, speaker, 1839; mem. U.S. Ho. of Reps. (Democrat) from Ky., 23d-24th congresses, 1833-37. Died Lawrenceburg, Sept. 2, 1849; buried Lawrenceburg Cemetery, reinterred Greendale Cemetery, Lawrenceburg.

LANE, George Martin, educator; b. Boston, Dec. 24, 1823; s. Martin and Lucretia (Swan) L.; grad. Harvard, 1846; Ph.D., U. Gottingen, 1851; m. Frances E. Gardiner, 1857; m. 2d, Mrs. Fanny Clark, 1878. Instr. Latin, Harvard, 1846-47, prof. Latin, 1851-69, Pope prof. Latin, 1869-94; known for his teaching abilities. Author: Latin Pronunciation, 1871; Latin Grammar for Schools and Colleges, 1898; contbr. articles to Nation, Bibliotheca Sacra, N.Am. Review, Harvard Studies in Classical Philology. An editor Harper's Latin Dictionary, 1879. Died Cambridge, Mass., June 30, 1897.

LANE, Henry Smith, senator; b. Sharpesburg, Bath County, Ky., Feb. 24, 1811; s. James H. Lane; m. Pamela Jameson; m. 2d, Janna Elston, Feb. 11, 1845. Admitted to Ky. bar, 1832; moved to Ind., 1834; mem. Ind. Senate, 1837, Ind. Ho. of Reps., 1838, 39; mem. U.S. Ho. of Reps. from Ind., 26th-27th congresses, Aug. 3, 1840-43; maj. 1st Ind. Regt. and col. Ind. Volunteers during Mexican War; chmn. 1st Republican Nat. Conv., Phila., 1856; gov. Ind., 1861; mem. U.S. Senate from Ind., 1861-67; Indian commr., 1869-71; commr. for improvement of Mississippi River, 1872. Died Crawfordsville, Ind., June 18, 1881; buried Oak Hill Cemetery, Crawfordsville.

LANE, James Henry, senator; b. Lawrenceburg, Ind., June 22, 1814; s. Amos Hawes and Mary (Foote) L.; m. Mary Baldridge, 1841. Admitted to bar; mem. city council; col. 3d Ind. Regt. in Mexican War, also volunteer comdr.; commanded 5th Ind. Inf. led it to Mexico City; lt. gov. Ind., 1849-53; mem. U.S. Ho. of Reps. (Democrat) from Ind., 33d Congress, 1853-55; became leader Free State Party in Kan., 1855; chmn. Exec. Com. of Kan. Territory, 1855; elected pres. Topeka (Kan.) Const. Conv., 1855; led an army in attacks on proslavery strongholds in Kan., 1856; pres. Leavenworth (Kan.) Constl. Conv., 1857; maj. gen. Kan. Militia, circa 1857; apptd. brig. gen. Kan. Volunteers by Pres. Lincoln, 1861; mem. U.S. Senate from Kan., Apr. 4, 1861-July 11, 1866; delegate to Union League, 1864; represented Kan. on Nat. Com. and as chmn. Nat. Union Com. for West which urged Western radicals to support Pres. Lincoln for reelection. Died nr. Leavenworth, July 11, 1866; buried City Cemetery, Lawrence, Kan.

LANE, John, clergyman; b. Fairfax County, Va., Apr. 8, 1789; s. William and Nancy Lane; attended Franklin Coll., Ga., 1813; m. Sarah Vick, 1819. Admitted on trial as preacher S.C. Annual Conf., 1814; mem. 1st Miss. Annual Conf. of Methodist Ch., 1815; executor of estate of Newet Vick (his father-in-law), 1821, instrumental in founding Vicksburg (Miss.); active in comml. affairs, Vicksburg, 1820's; leader in Meth. Ch. in Miss., 1832-55; pres. Missionary Soc. of Miss. Conf.; presiding elder Meth. Ch. in Miss., 1832-48; a founder, trustee Centenary Coll., 1839; del. Gen. Conf. Meth. Episcopal Ch., advocated formation of Meth. Episcopal Ch. South, 1844. Died Vicksburg, Oct. 10, 1855.

LANE, Joseph, senator, territorial gov.; b. Buncombe County, N.C., Dec. 14, 1801; s. John and Elizabeth (Street) L.; m. Polly Pierce, 1820. Moved to Ind., 1821; mem. Ind. Ho. of Reps., 1822, 23, 31-33, 38, 39, Ind. Senate, 1844-46; col. 2d Ind. Volunteer Regt., 1846; brig. gen., 1846; brevetted maj. gen. for gallantry at Battle of Humantla (Mexico), 1847; gov. Ore. Territory, 1849-50, 53; del. from Ore. Territory to U.S. Ho. of Reps., 32d-35th congresses, 1851-Feb. 14, 1859; mem. U.S. Senate from Ore., Feb. 14, 1859-61; unsuccessful candidate for vice pres. U.S., 1860. Died Roseburg, Ore., Apr. 19, 1881; buried Masonic Cemetery, Roseburg.

LANE, La Fayette, congressman; b. nr. Evansville, Ind., Nov. 12, 1842; s. Joseph Lane; attended pub. schs., Washington, D.C., and Stamford, Conn.; studied law. Admitted to the bar; began practice of law, Roseburg, Ore.; mem. Ore. Ho. of Reps., 1864; code commr., 1874; mem. U.S. Ho. of Reps. (Democrat) from Ore., 44th Congress, Oct. 25, 1875-77. Died Roseburg, Nov. 23, 1896; buried Catholic Cemetery, Roseburg.

LANE, Ralph, colonist; b. Northamptonshire, Eng., 1530; s. Sir Ralph and Maud (Parr) L. Apptd. sheriff of County Kerry (Ireland), 1583; commanded unsuccessful colony on Roanoke Island, Va., winter 1585-86; account of Va. published by Hakluyt in The Principal Navigations . . . of the English Nation, 1859; served as muster master of camp at West Tilbury in Essex, 1588; muster master gen. of army sent to Spain under Drake, 1589; muster master gen., clk. of check of garrisons in Ireland, 1592; knighted by lord deputy, 1593. Died Dublin, Ireland, Oct. 1603.

LANE, Tidence, clergyman; b. Balt., Aug. 31, 1724; s. Richard and Sarah Lane; m. Esther Bibbin, May 9, 1743, 7 sons, 2 daus. Settled with family in Yadkin River area, N.C., 1740's; converted through preaching of Shubael Stearns to Separate Baptist faith, 1754; moved to what is now Washington County, Tenn., 1776, founded Buffalo Ridge Bapt. Ch. (1st permanent ch. in Tenn.); moved to what is now Hamblin County, Tenn., circa 1780; founded Bent Creek Bapt. Ch., Hamblin County, 1785, pastor, 1785-1806; moderator 1st Bapt. Assn. in Tenn., 1785. Died Hamblin County, Jan. 30, 1806.

LANE, Walter Paye, army officer; b. County Cork, Ireland, Feb. 18, 1817; s. William and Olive Lane. Came with family to U.S., 1821, went to Tex., 1835; fought under Sam Houston in Texas War for Independence, 1836; fought against Indians in Tex., privateer in Gulf of Mexico; served a capt. under Gen. Zachary Taylor in No. Mexico, under Gen. Winfield Scott at Battle of Veracruz, Mexican War, 1846; mined for gold in Cal., Nev. Ariz., Peru; served as lt. col. 3d Tex. Cavalry in battles around Bentonville (Ark.) during Civil War; participated also in Atchafalaya Raid, conflicts at Fort Defiance, Donaldsonville LaFourche, Berbeaux, under Gen. Richard Taylor in No. La., 1864; rose to brig. gen. Confederate Army. Died Marshall, Tex., Jan. 28, 1892.

LANE, William Carr, physician, mayor St. Louis; b. Fayette County, Pa., Dec. 1, 1789; s. Presley Carr and Sarah (Stephenson) L.; attended Jefferson Coll., Chambersburg, Pa.; grad. Dickinson Coll., Carlisle, Pa.; postgrad. Med. Dept., U. Pa.; m. Mary Ewing, Feb. 26, 1818; 2 children. Served as surgeon's mate at Ft. Harrison during Creek War, 1813; post surgeon, 1816; resigned from army, 1819; became q.m. gen. of Mo., 1822; 1st mayor St. Louis, 1823-29, 38-40; mem. Mo. Legislature (Democrat), 1826; served as suregon with rank brig. gen. in Black Hawk War, 1832; a founder Mo. Med. Coll., 1840, also prof. obstetrics; apptd. gov. N.M. Territory by Pres. Fillmore, 1852; returned to practice medicine, St. Louis, 1853. Author: Water for the City (advocated municipal waterworks for St. Louis), 1860. Died St. Louis, Jan. 6, 1863; buried Bellefontaine Cemetery, St. Louis.

LANGDON, Chauncey, congressman; b. Farmington, Conn., Nov. 8, 1763; grad. Yale, 1787; studied law, Litchfield, Conn. Admitted to the bar, 1787; began practice of law, Castleton, Vt.; moved to "The Grants," 1788; settled in Windsor, Vt., later returned to Castleton; register of probate, 1792-97; judge of probate, 1798-99; mem. Vt. Council, 1808, 23-30; mem. Vt. Ho. of Reps., 1813-14, 17, 18-20, 22; trustee Middlebury (Vt.) Coll., 1811-30; mem. U.S. Ho. of Reps. (Federalist) from Vt., 14th Congress, 1815-17. Died Castleton, July 23, 1830; buried Congregational Cemetery, Castleton.

LANGDON, John, mcht., senator, gov. N.H.; b. Portsmouth, N.H., June 26, 1741; s. John and Mary (Hall) L.; m. Elizabeth Sherburne, Feb. 2, 1777. Aided in seizure and removal of munitions from Portsmouth fort, 1774; mem. N.H. Legislature, 1775-81, 84, 86-87, 1801-05, speaker, 1775, 77-81, 86-87, 1803-05; mem. Continental Congress, 1775, 83-84; apptd. agt. for Continental prizes in N.H., 1776; pres. N.H., 1785; attended U.S. Constl. Conv., Phila., 1787; U.S. Senate from N.H., 1789-1801, pres. pro tem, 1st Congress; gov. N.H., 1805-09, 10-11; declined Democratic nomination as candidate for v.p. of U.S., 1812. Died Portsmouth, Sept. 18, 1819; buried North Cemetery, Portsmouth.

LANGDON, Samuel, clergyman, coll. pres.; b. Boston, Jan. 12, 1723; s. Samuel and Esther (Osgood) L.; A.M., Harvard, 1740; S.T.D. (hon.), U. Aberdeen (Scotland), 1762; m. Elizabeth Brown, 1748, at least 5 children. Went to Louisbourg as capt. N.H. Regt., 1745; became asst. to Rev. Jabez Fitch, North Ch., Portsmouth, N.H., ordained to ministry Congregational Ch., 1747, pastor North Ch., 1747-74; helped prepare map of N.H., 1761; pres. Harvard, 1774-80; became pastor Congl. Ch., Hampton Falls, N.H., 1781; mem. N.H. Conv. to ratify U.S. Constn., 1788; an original mem. Am. Acad. Arts and Scis. Died Hampton Falls, N.H., Nov. 29, 1797.

LANGDON, William Chauncy, clergyman; b. Burlington, Vt., Aug. 19, 1831; s. Kohn Jay and Harriet (Woodward) L.; grad. Transylvania Coll., Ky., 1850; m. Hannah Courtney, 1858. Prof. astronomy Shelby Coll., Ky., 1850-51; asst. examiner U.S. Patent Office, Washington, D.C., 1851-55, chief examiner patents, 1855-56; a founder YMCA of Washington, 1852, active in nat. and internat. efforts to co-ordinate YMCA activities, 1850's; ordained deacon Protestant Episcopal Ch., 1858; in charge of Episcopal Ch. for Americans in Rome, 1859-62; rector St. John's Ch., Havre de Grace, Md., 1862-65; in charge of Episcopal Ch., Florence, Italy, 1865-73; active in Old Catholic religious movement in Europe, from 1859; interested in reunion of Protestant and Roman Catholic chs.; attended Old Catholic congresses, 1872, 73, 74, 75; rector Christ Ch., Cambridge, Mass., 1876-78, St. James Ch., Bedford, Pa., 1883-90; founder St. Martin's Mission, Providence, R.I., 1890. Died Providence, Oct. 29, 1895; buried Providence.

LANGE, Louis, editor, publisher; b. Province of Hesse, Germany, Sept. 19, 1829; s. Andrew and Anna (Still) L.; m. Margarethe Schmidt, 1851, 6 children. Came to Am., 1846; worked for Michigan Staats-Zeitung, Detroit, 1855-57; became financial mgr. to Moritz Niedner (founder Daily Mo. State Jour.), 1861, paper suppressed because of Confederate sympathies (Lange had nothing to do with editorial policy); bought mag. Die Abendschule, 1863, made it one of leading German lang. periodicals; founder Die Rundschau (to express his Republican polit. views). Died St. Louis, Sept. 25, 1893.

LANGSTON, John Mercer, congressman, univ. ofcl.; b. Louisa, Va., Dec. 14, 1829; illigetimate son of Ralph Quarles and Lucy Langston (Negro slave belonging to Ralph Quarles); grad. collegiate dept. Oberlin Coll., 1849, grad. theol. dept., 1853; studied law under Philemon Bliss; m. Caroline M. Wall, Oct. 1854. Emancipated by his father, 1834; admitted to Ohio bar, 1854; clk. Brownhelm Twp., O. (1st Negro elected to public office in U.S.), 1855; helped raise 1st Colored regts., 54th Mass., 55th Mass. and 5th Ohio regts. during Civil War; mem. Council of Oberlin, 1865-67; mem. Oberlin Bd. Edn., 1867-68; insp. gen. Bur. Freedmen, Refugees, and Abandoned Lands, 1868; dean Howard U. Law Dept., 1869-76, v.p., acting pres., 1872; mem. D.C. Bd. Health, 1871; minister resident and consul gen. to Haiti, chargé d'affaires to Santo Domingo, 1877-85; pres. Va. Normal and Collegiate Inst., Petersburg, 1885; mem. U.S. Ho. of Reps. from Va., 51st Congress, Sept. 23, 1890-91. Author: From the Virginia Plantation to the National Capital (autobiography), 1894. Died Washington, D.C., Nov. 15, 1897; buried Woodlawn Cemetery, Washington.

LANGSTROTH, Lorenzo Lorraine, educator, apiarist; b. Phila., Dec. 25, 1810; s. John G. and Rebekah (Dunn) L.; grad. Yale, 1831; m. Anne Tucker, Aug. 22, 1836, 3 children. Prin., Abbot Acad., Andover, Mass., 1838-39; prin. High Sch. for Young Ladies, Greenfield, Mass., 1838-44; prin. school for young ladies at Phila., 1848-52; invented movable-frame beehive. Author: Langstroth on the Hive and the Honeybee, 1853. Died Oxford, O., Oct. 6, 1895.

LANGWORTHY, Edward, Continental congressman; b. Savannah, Ga., 1738; orphan. Organized Ga. Council of Safety, sec., 1775; mem. Continental Congress from Ga., 1777-79; signed Articles of Confederation; moved to Md., 1785; with William Goddard issued Md. Jour. and Balt. Advertiser, 1785-86; tchr. classics Balt. Acad., 1787-91; began 1st attempted history of Ga., 1791; clk. of customs Balt., 1795-1802. Author: Memoirs of the Life of the late Charles Lee, 1792. Died Balt., Nov. 2, 1802.

LANGWORTHY, James Lyon, pioneer; b. Windsor, Vt., Jan. 20, 1800; s. Stephen and Betsy (Massey) L.; m. Agnes Miln, Mar. 17, 1840. Helped open mines, Hardscrabble, Wis., circa 1824; headed a com. which helped to draw up a miner's agreement (1st civil regulation in history of Ia.), 1830; leader in development of Dubuque (Ia.); constructed mil. road from Dubuque to the Iowa City (new territorial capital), in early 1840's Died Mar. 14, 1865.

LANIER, James Franklin Doughty, financier; b. Washington, N.C., Nov. 22, 1800; s. Alexander Chalmers and Drusilla (Doughty) L.; completed law course, Transylvania U., 1823; m. Elizabeth Gardiner, 1819; m. 2d, Mary McClure, 1848; 9 children. Asst. clk. Ky. Ho. of Reps., 1824, chief clk., 1827; 1st pres. Madison br. Ind. State Bank, mem. gen. bd. control; fed. govt. pension agt. in Northwest; helped revive Madison and Indpls. R.R.; a founder Winslow, Lanier & Co., 1849; participated in mng. affairs of Pitts., Ft. Wayne & Chgo. R.R., restored its prosperity; repeatedly saved financial situation of State of Ind., especially during Civil War crisis. Died N.Y.C., Aug. 27, 1881; buried Greenwood Cemetery, Bklyn.

LANIER, Sidney, poet, musician; b. Macon, Ga., Feb. 3, 1842; s. Robert Sampson and Mary Jane (Anderson) L.; grad Oglethorpe U., 1860; m. Mary Day, Dec. 21, 1867, 4 sons including Henry Wysham. Joined Macon Volunteers, Confederate Army, 1861; captured and imprisoned, 1864, returned to Ga. in poor health (already suffering tuberculosis), 1865; variously employed as hotel clk., tchr., lawyer, 1865-73; became flute player Peabody Symphony Orch., Balt., 1873; lectr. English literature Johns Hopkins, 1879-81, wrote many of his prose works for his courses there; began poetic career with publication of 2 poems (Corn, The Sumphony), 1875; best known for his ballads and lyric poetry including The Marshes of Glynn, Psalm of the West, Song of the Chattahoochee. Author: Tiger Lilies (novel based on Civil War experiences), 1867; Poems, 1877; St. Augustine in April, 1878; The Boys' Library of Legend and Chivalry (adaptations of romances and legends for children), 1879-82; The Science of English Verse (work on prosody), 1883; The English Novel (criticism), 1883; Poems, 1884; Music and Poetry, 1898; Shakespeare and his Forerunners (lectures), 1902; Poem Outlines, 1908. Died Lynn, N.C., Sept. 7, 1881.

LANIGAN, George Thomas, journalist; b. St. Charles, Can., Dec. 10, 1845. Covered Fenian disturbances for N.Y. Herald, 1866; co-editor Free Lance, satirical publ., Montreal, Can.; spl. writer Chgo. Times; reporter St. Louis Daily Globe, 1870; staff writer Chgo. Tribune, also western correspondent N.Y. World; mem. editorial staff N.Y. World, N.Y.C., 1874-82; editor Post-Express, Rochester, N.Y., 1883-84; mem. editorial staff Phila. Record, 1884-86. Author: Fables of G. Washington Aesop, Taken "Anywhere, Anywhere Out of the World," 1878; National Ballads of Canada, 1878. Died Phila., Feb. 5, 1886.

LANMAN, Charles, author, explorer, artist; b. Monroe, Mich., June 14, 1819; s. Charles James and Marie (Guie) L.; studied art under Asher B. Durand; m. Adeline Dodge, 1849. Editor Monroe Gazette, 1845; elected asso. Nat. Acad. Design, 1846; asso. editor Cincinnati Chronicle, 1846; mem. editorial staff Express, N.Y.C., 1847; librarian U.S. War Dept., Washington, D.C., 1849; pvt. sec. to Daniel Webster, 1850; head returns office U.S. Interior Dept., 1855-57, 65; published Dictionary of the United States Congress, 1859; librarian U.S. Ho. of Reps., 1861; Am. sec. of Japanese legation, 1871-82; asst. assessor D.C., 1885; librarian Washington City Library, 1888. Author: Essays for Summer Hours (1842); Evenings in My Library; Riverside Essays; Letters from a Motley Crew; Curious Characters and Pleasant Places; My Ships of Thought; A Summer in the Wilderness (1847); A Tour to the River Saguenay (1848); Letters from the Alleghany Mountains (1849); A Winter in the South; From the River Potomac to Mount Desert; Private Life of Daniel Webster (1852); Adventures in the Wilds of America (accountants of explorations in Mississippi Valley, Gt. Lakes and Appalachian regions, 1854); Life of William Woodbridge (1867); Japaniana; In the Evening Twilight. Paintings include Brookside and Homestead; Home in the Woods (1881); Frontier Home (1884). Died Georgetown, D.C., Mar. 4, 1895.

LANMAN, James, senator; b. Norwich, Conn., June 14, 1767; grad. Yale, 1788; studied law. Admitted to Conn. bar, 1791, began practice in Norwich; state's atty. for New London County (Conn.), 1814-19; mem. Conn. Ho. of Reps., 1817, 33; del. Cónn. Constl. Conv., 1818; mem. Conn. Senate, 1819, 32; mem. U.S. Senate (Democrat), from Conn., 1819-25; judge Conn. superior and supreme cts., 1826-29; mayor Norwich, 1831-34. Died Norwich, Aug. 7, 1841; buried City Cemetery, Norwich.

LANMAN, Joseph, naval officer; b. Norwich, Conn., July 11, 1811; s. Peter and Abigail (Trumbull) L.; m. Ann Williams, Sept. 20, 1842; 4 children. Commd. midshipman, U.S. Navy, 1825, lt., 1835, served in Pacific Squadron, 1847-48, commd. comdr., 1855, commodore, 1862; comdr. Washington Navy Yard, 1855-56. In command steam frigate Minnesota, 1864; joined N. Atlantic Blockading Squadron; commd. rear adm., 1867; head Portsmouth Navy Yard, 1867-69; in command of South Atlantic Squadron, 1869-71. Died Norwich, Mar. 13, 1874.

LANSING, Frederick, congressman; b. Manheim, N.Y., Feb. 16, 1838; attended Little Falls Acad., N.Y.; studied law. Admitted to N.Y. bar, 1859; practiced law, Watertown, N.Y.; served with 8th N.Y. Cavalry during Civil War, acting adj., 1863; wounded in Battle of Bristoe Station, Va., 1863, discharged on account of wounds, 1864; mem. N.Y. Senate, 1881-85; mem. U.S. Ho. of Reps. (Republican) from N.Y., 51st Congress, 1889-91. Died Watertown, Jan. 31, 1894; buried Brookside Cemetery, Watertown.

LANSING, Gerit Yates, congressman; b. Albany, N.Y., Aug. 4, 1783; grad. Union Coll., 1800; studied law. Admitted to N.Y. bar, 1804, began practice in Albany; clk. N.Y. Assembly, 1807; judge ct. of probates, 1816-23; regent U. State of N.Y., 1829-62, apptd. chancellor of bd. regents, 1842; mem. U.S. Ho. of Reps. (Jacksonian Democrat) from N.Y., 22d-24th congresses, 1831-37; pres. Albany Savs. Bank, 1854-62, Albany Ins. Co., 1859-62. Died Albany, Jan. 3, 1862; buried Albany Rural Cemetery.

LANSING, Gulian, missionary; b. Lishaskill, N.Y., Feb. 1, 1825; s. John and Eliza L.; grad. Union Coll., 1847; studied theology Asso. Reformed Church, Newburgh, New York; m. Maria Oliver, 1850; m. 2d, Sarah Dales, 1866. Ordained for missionary service Asso. Reformed Ch., 1850; influential in developing Egyptian missions of United Presbyn. Mission; caused establishment of several new missionary stations in Nile Valley; taught in mission's theol. sch.; secured legal standing for Protestantism as a religion in Cairo. Author: Egypt's Princes, 1864. Died Cairo, Egypt, Sept. 12, 1892.

LANSING, John, Continental congressman, jurist; b. Albany, N.Y., Jan. 30, 1754; s. Gerrit Jacob and Jannetje (Waters) L.; studied law under Robert Yates, Albany, James Duane, N.Y.C. Admitted to N.Y. bar, 1775; sec. to Gen. Schuyler, 1776, 77, 89; mem. N.Y. State Assembly, 1780-86; mem. Continental Congress from N.Y., 1784, 85; N.Y. del. to U.S. Constl. Conv., 1787; del. to N.Y. Conv. to ratify Fed. Constn., 1788; mem. commn. to fix N.Y.-Vt. boundary, 1790; justice N.Y. Supreme Ct., 1790-98, chief justice, 1798-1801; chancellor of N.Y., 1801-14; declined unanimous nomination for N.Y. governorship, 1804; regent U. State of N.Y., 1817-29; presdl. elector, 1824. Mysteriously disappeared in N.Y.C., Dec. 12, 1829.

LANSING, William Esselstyne, congressman; b. Perryville, N.Y., Dec. 29, 1821; grad. Cazenovia (N.Y.) Sem., 1841; studied law, Utica, N.Y. Admitted to N.Y. bar, 1845, began practice in Chittenango; dist. atty. Madison County (N.Y.), 1850-53; pres. Village of Chittenango, 1853-55; county clk., 1855-58; mem. U.S. Ho. of Reps. (Republican) from N.Y., 37th, 42-43d congresses, 1871-75; resumed practice of law, Syracuse, N.Y. Died Syracuse, July 29, 1883; buried Oakwood Cemetery, Chittenango.

LAPHAM, Elbridge Gerry, senator, congressman; b. Farmington, N.Y., Oct. 18, 1814; attended Canandaigua (N.Y.) Acad.; studied civil engring. and law. Admitted to N.Y. bar, 1844; practiced law, Canandaigua; mem. N.Y. Constl. Conv., 1867; mem. U.S. Ho. of Reps. (Republican) from N.Y., 44th-47th congresses, 1875-July 29, 1881, a mgr. apptd. to conduct impeachment proceedings against William W. Belknap (former sec. of war), 1876; mem. U.S. Senate from N.Y., Aug. 2, 1881-85; resumed law practice, Canandaigua. Died "Glen Gerry" on Canandaigua Lake, N.Y., Jan. 8, 1890; buried Woodlawn Cemetery, Canandaigua.

LAPHAM, Increase Allen, scientist, state ofcl.; b. Palmyra, N.Y., Mar. 7, 1811; s. Seneca and Rachel (Allen) L.; m. Ann Alcott, 1838, 5 children. Asst. engr. on Ohio Canal, 1829-33; sec. Ohio Bd. Canal Commrs., 1833; published Wisconsin: Its Geography and Topography, History, Geology and Mineralogy (1st good maps of Wis. and Milw. vicinity), 1844; published The Antiquities of Wisconsin, 1855; sch. commr. Milw., aided in establishing Milw.-Downer Coll. (normal sch. for girls), pres. bd. trustees, many years; charter mem. Wis. Acad. of Scis., Arts and Letters; influential in obtaining passage of law which established U.S. Weather Bur., 1869; state geologist Wis., 1873-75; v.p., pres. Wis. Hist. Soc. Died Oconomowoc, Wis., Sept. 14, 1875.

LAPHAM, William Berry, physician, journalist; b. Greenwood, Me., Aug. 21, 1828; s. John and Louvisa (Berry) L.; attended Waterville (now Colby) Coll., 1851, A.M. (hon.), 1871; M.D., N.Y. Med. Coll., 1856; m. Cynthia A. Perham, Nov. 27, 1866, 1 son, 2 daus. Began practice medicine, Bryant's Pond, Me.; became 1st lt. 23d Me. Volunteers, circa 1861, 1st lt., 1st Me. Mounted Arty., 1863, brevetted maj., 1865; mem. Me. Legislature, 1867; examining surgeon Me. Pension Bd.; trustee Me. Insane Hosp., 1867-74; editor Me. Farmer, 1872-81, Me. Genealogist, 1875-78; mem. Me. Hist. Soc., New Eng. Historic Geneal. Soc.; compiled genealogies of Lapham, Ricker, Chase, Chapman, Webster, Hill, Knox families. Author: My Recollections of the War of the Rebellion, 1892. Died Togus, Me., Feb. 22, 1894.

LAPORTE, John, congressman; b. Asylum, Pa., Nov. 4, 1798; attended common schs. County auditor Bradford County (Pa.), 1827-28; mem. Pa. Ho. of Reps., 1828-32, speaker, 1831-32; mem. U.S. Ho. of Reps. from Pa., 23d-24th congresses, 1833-37; asso. judge Bradford County, 1837-45; surveyor gen. State of Pa., 1845-51; engaged in banking, Towanda, Pa., 1850-62. Died Phila., Aug. 22, 1862; buried family cemetery, Asylum.

LARAMIE, Jacques, pioneer, fur trapper. Allegedly 1st white man to explore upper Laramie River; became important figure in legends of West, his name associated with districts he never saw; known accomplishments are few, what is known may be fiction; Laramie Mountains, Laramie (Wyo.), Ft. Laramie, Laramie Plains, Laramie Peak, Laramie River named after him. Died in what is now Wyo., 1821.

LARCOM, Lucy, educator, writer; b. Beverly, Mass., Mar. 5, 1824; d. Benjamin and Lois (Barrett) Larcom. Works 1st appeared in Lowell (Mass.) Offering circa 1840; contbr. to Operative's Mag.; studied and taught at Monticello Sem. nr. Alton, Ill., 1849-52; tchr. Wheaton Sem., Norton, Mass., 1854-62; published Call to Kansas (1st poetic success), 1855; an editor Our Young Folks, 1865-73; helped John Greenleaf Whittier prepare Child Life, 1871, collaborated with him on Songs of 3 Centuries, 1883, contbr. to Independent, Congregationalist mags.; other writings include: A New England Girlhood, 1889; Hannah Binding Shoes, Crayon (poems); Wildroses from Cape Ann (volume of poetry); Home in Beverly Farms Mass. Died Boston, Apr. 17, 1893; buried Beverly.

LARD, Moses E., clergyman, editor; b. Bedford County, Tenn., Oct. 29, 1818; grad. Bethany Coll., circa 1848; m. Mary, 9 children. Engaged in evangelistic work among Disciples of Christ chs., Mo., before Civil War; went to Can., 1862; later became pastor Main Street Ch., Lexington, Ky.; founder Lard's Quarterly, publisher until 1869; editor Apostolic Times, 1869-80. Author: Review of Rev. J. B. Jeter's Book Entitled "Campbellism Examined," 1857. Died Lexington, June 17, 1880; buried Mt. Mora Cemetery, St. Joseph, Mo.

LARDNER, James Lawrence, naval officer; b. Phila., Nov. 20, 1802; s. John and Margaret (Saltar) L.; m. Margaret Wilmer, Feb. 2, 1832; m. 2d, Ellen Wilmer, June 23, 1853; 7 children. Apptd. midshipman U.S. Navy, 1820, lt., 1828; navigating officer on the Vincennes, 1828-31; lt. in command of receiving ship at Phila., 1844-48; commd. comdr., 1851; fleet capt. West India Squadron, 1855; commd. capt., 1861; comdr. Susquehanna of N. Atlantic Squadron aiding in capture of Port Royal and blockading of S.C. and Ga. coasts; in command East Gulf Blockading Squadron, 1862; commodore in command East Coast Squadron, 1862; comdr. West India Squadron, 1863; commd. rear adm., 1866; gov. Naval Asylum, Phila., 1869-72. Died Phila., Apr. 12, 1881; buried Frankford, Pa.

La RICHARDIE, Armand de, see De La Richardie, Armand.

LARKIN, John, educator, clergyman; b. Newcastle-upon-Tyne, Eng., Feb. 2, 1801; grad. Upshaw Coll., nr. Durham, Eng. Joined Sulpician Order in Paris, France, ordained, 1827; taught mathematics and allied subjects Sulpician Coll., Montreal, Que., Can., 1827-39; enlisted as Jesuit, St. Mary's Coll., Ky., 1840; established St. Ignatius' Instn., Louisville, Ky., 1841; taught at St. John's Coll., Fordham, N.Y., 1846; pres., 1851-54; founded Coll. of St. Francis Xavier, N.Y.C., 1847, 1st pres., 1847-49, missionary, 1856-58; declined appointment as bishop of Toronto, 1850; commd. agt. of father-gen. to visit Jesuit houses in Ireland, 1854. Died Fordham, Dec. 11, 1858.

LARKIN, Thomas Oliver, businessman; b. Charlestown, Mass., Sept. 16, 1802; s. Capt. Thomas Oliver and Ann (Rogers) L.; m. Rachel (Hobson) Holmes, June 10, 1833. Went to Monterey, Cal., 1832, engaged in trading and land speculation; U.S. consul to Cal., 1844-48; U.S. confidential agt., 1846-48; naval storekeeper, 1847-48, navy agt., 1847-49; mem. Cal. State Constl. Conv., 1849; engaged in business until 1858. Died Oct. 27, 1858.

LARNED, Joseph Gay Eaton, inventor; b. Thompson, Conn., Apr. 29, 1819; s. George and Anna (Spalding) L.; grad. Yale, 1839; m. Helen Lee, May 9, 1859. Tchr. classics Chatham Acad., Savannah, Ga., 1839; pvt. tchr., Charleston, S.C., 1840; took charge of academy in Waterloo, N.Y., 1841; tutor Yale, 1842; wrote articles for New Englander, Conn., 1845-46; studied law at home, admitted to Conn. bar, 1847; moved to N.Y.C., 1854; in partnership with Wellington Lee to manufacture steam fire engines at Novelty Iron Works, N.Y., 1855-63; invented steam fire engine and demonstrated it in N.Y.C. and other cities; became asst. insp. of ironclads for Navy Dept. in charge of work at Green Point, Bklyn., 1863; returned to law practice, N.Y.C., after Civil War. Author: A Quarter-Century Record of the Class of 1839, Yale College, 1865. Died N.Y.C., June 3, 1870.

LARNED, Simon, congressman; b. Thompson, Conn., Aug. 3, 1753; attended common schs. Sheriff of Berkshire County; served as capt. Col. Shepherd's regt. during Revolutionary War; engaged in merc. bus., Pittsfield, Mass., 1784; mem. Mass. Gen. Ct., 1791; county treas., 1792-1812; served as col. 9th Inf., U.S. Army during War of 1812, participated in Battle of Plattsburg; mem. U.S. Ho. of Reps. from Mass., 8th Congress, Nov. 5, 1804-05; pres. Berkshire Bank. Died Pittsfield, Nov. 16, 1817; buried Pittsfield Cemetery.

La ROCHE, René, physician, author; b. Phila., Sept. 23, 1795; s. René and Marie Jeanne (de la Condemine) La R.; M.D., U. Pa., 1820; m. Mary Jane Ellis, 1824. Capt. volunteers in Col. James Biddle's regt. in War of 1812; after graduation taught medicine in summer sch. of U. Pa.; edited N.Am. Med. and Surg. Journal, Phila., 1826-31; active Coll. of Physicians; pres. Path. Soc. of Phila. Author: Yellow Fever, Considered in Its Historical, Pathological, Etiological and Therapeutical Relations, 2 vols., 1855. Died Phila., Dec. 9, 1872.

LARPENTEUR, Charles, fur trader; b. nr. Fontainebleau, France, May 8, 1807; m. 3d, Rebecca White Bingham, Apr. 1, 1855; several children. His family settled nr. Balt. after Napoleonic Wars; moved to West, 1828; worked for several years in St. Louis; clk. with Sublette and Robert Campbell for Rocky Mountain Fur. Co., 1833; accompanied Campbell to Am. Fur Co.'s post Ft. Union at mouth of Yellowstone River; developed farm in what is now Harrison County, Ia., 1851; moved from one trading post to another in Indian country, 1851-71; retired, wrote autobiography from a journal which he had kept since 1834. Died Ia., Nov. 15, 1872.

LARRABEE, Charles Hathaway, congressman; b. Rome, N.Y., Nov. 9, 1820; s. Charles and Elizabeth (Hathaway) L.; m. Minerva Norton, May 13, 1846. Admitted to bar, 1841; elected atty. of Chgo., 1844; became miller, Horicon, Wis., 1847; mem. 2d Constl. Conv. of Wis. Territory from Dodge County, 1847; circuit judge, 1848-58; became ex offico mem. Wis. Supreme Ct.; mem. U.S. Ho. of Reps. (Democrat) from Wis., 36th Congress, 1859-61; commd. maj. 5th Wis. Inf., 1861, col. 24th Wis. Inf., 1862; moved to Cal., 1863, later moved to Seattle, Wash., mem. conv. to frame Wash. Territory Constn.; finally settled in San Bernardino, Cal. Died Los Angeles, Jan. 20, 1883.

LARRABEE, William Clark, clergyman, educator; b. Cape Elizabeth, Me., Dec. 23, 1802; grad. Bowden U., Brunswick, Me., 1828; m. Harriet Dunn, September 28, 1828, 4 children. Licensed to preach by Methodist Ch., 1821; prin. Alfred Acad., Me., 1828-30; apptd. tutor of prep. sch. (later became Wesleyan U.), Middletown, Conn., 1830; prin. Oneida Conf. Sem., Cazenovia, N.Y., circa 1831-32; admitted to Oneida Conf., Meth. Episcopal Ch., 1832; assisted in 1st geol. survey of N.Y., 1837-38; del. Gen. Conf., Meth. Episcopal Ch., Balt., 1840; prof. mathematics and natural sci. Indiana Asbury U. (now De Pauw U.), Greencastle, 1841-50, pres., 1849-50; editor Ladies Repository, Cincinnati, 1852; 1st supt. pub. instrn. State of Ind., 1852-54, 56-59. Author: Lectures on the Scientific Evidences of Natural and Revealed Religion, 1850; Wesley and his Coadjutors, 2 vols., 1851; Asbury and his Coadjutors, 2 vols., 1853; Rosabower, 1854. Died Ind., May 5, 1859.

LA SALLE, sieur de (Robert Cavelier), explorer; b. Rouen, France, Nov. 22, 1643; s. Jean and Catherine (Geest) Cavelier; trained as Jesuit, left order, 1655; Came to Can., 1666, established seignory at Lachine; left Montreal with expdn. to Lake Ontario region, 1669, claimed to have discovered Ohio River; returned to France, 1673, 78, obtained from Louis XIV a patent of nobility, monopoly of Indian trade and extensive tract of land around Ft. Frontenac; commandant Ft. Frontenac; set out to establish the French on the Mississippi, 1678; built Ft. Crevecoeur (now Peoria, Ill.), 1680; explored Mississippi River, 1682, took possession of river valley (which he named Louisiana) for King of France; rebuilt Ft. St. Louis at Starved Rock, Ill., 1682-83; returned to France, 1683, was named viceroy of N.Am. with command from Ill. to Spanish borders; 1st French explorer to trace Mississippi River to its mouth; organized colonizing expdn., 1684, sailed to N.Am., landed by mistake in Tex. Murdered in mutiny by his men while trying to reach mouth of Mississippi, on Brazos River, Tex., Mar. 19, 1687.

LA SÉRE, Emile, congressman; b. Santo Domingo, 1802. Moved to New Orleans, circa 1805; clk. merc. bus., Jackson, La., later in Mexico; elected sheriff New Orleans Parish, 1840; mem. U.S. Ho. of Reps. (Democrat) from La., 29th-31st congresses, Jan. 29, 1846-51; served as maj. 10th La. Regt., Confederate Army during Civil War, later chief q.m. Trans-Miss. Dept.; chmn. La. Dem. Central Com., 15 years; pres. Tehuantepec R.R. Co., Mexico. Died New Orleans, Aug. 14, 1882; buried Metairie Cemetery, New Orleans.

LASH, Israel George, congressman; b. Bethania, N.C., Aug. 18, 1810; attended acad., Bethania. Engaged in merc. bus., cigar mfg.; banker, Salem (now Winston-Salem), N.C.; del. N.C. Conv. which resolved to reenter Union, 1868; mem. U.S. Ho. of Reps. (Republican) from N.C., 40th-41st congresses, July 20, 1868-71. Died Salem, Apr. 1, 1878; buried Moravian Cemetery, Bethania.

LASSEN, Peter, pioneer; b. Copenhagen, Denmark, Aug. 7, 1800. Blacksmith by trade; came to U.S., arriving in Boston, 1829, moved to Katesville, Mo.; traveled (with 12 companions) overland to Ore., 1839; went by sea to Ft. Ross, Cal., 1840; operated saw mill nr. Santa Cruz, until 1842; began ranching nr. J. Sutter's property, working for Sutter and taking stock as payment; received land grant in No. Sacramento Valley, 1844, established ranch which became popular endpoint for many Forty-niners; led a party by haphazard route to Cal., 1848; established Benton City; a mountain, nat. park and forest, county, various other sites named for him.

LATHAM, Louis Charles, congressman; b. Plymouth, N.C., Sept. 11, 1840; grad. U. N.C., 1859; attended Harvard Law Sch. Served as capt., later maj. 1st N.C. Regt., Confederate Army, during Civil War; admitted to N.C. bar, 1868; began practice in Plymouth; mem. N.C. Ho. of Commons, 1864, N.C. Senate, 1870; mem. U.S. Ho. of Reps. (Democrat) from N.C., 47th, 50th congresses, 1881-83, 87-89; resumed law practice, Greenville, N.C. Died Johns Hopkins Hosp., Balt., Oct. 16, 1895; buried City Cemetery, Greenville.

LATHAM, Milton Slocum, senator; b. Columbus, O., May 23, 1827; s. Bela and Juliana (Sterritt) L.; grad. Jefferson Coll., O., 1845; m. Sophie Birsall, 1853; m. 2d, Mary McMullin, 1870; 1 child. Admitted to Cal. bar, 1848; clk. Recorder's Ct., San Francisco, 1850; dist. atty. Sacramento County (Cal.), 1851; mem. U.S. Ho. of Reps. (Democrat) from Cal., 33d Congress, 1853-55; collector Port of San Francisco, 1855-57; gov. Cal., Jan. 9-14, 1860; mem. U.S. Senate from Cal., 1860-63; mgr. San Francisco office London & San Francisco Bank, 1865-72; pres. N.Y. Mining and Stock Exchange, N.Y.C., 1880-82. Died Mar. 4, 1882; buried Lone Mountain Cemetery, San Francisco.

LATHROP, George Parsons, author, editor; b. Honolulu, Hawaii, Aug. 25, 1851; s. Dr. George Alfred and Frances (Smith) L.; attended Columbia Law Sch., N.Y.C., 1870; m. Rose Hawthorne, Sept. 11, 1871. Asso. editor Atlantic Monthly, 1875-77; editor Boston Sunday Courier, 1877-79; founder Am. Copyright League, N.Y.C., 1883, sec., until 1885; proposed internat. copyright law converted (with wife) to Roman Catholic faith, 1891; founded Cath. Summer Sch. of Am., New London, Conn., 1892; founder Apostolate of the Press. Author: (poems) Rose and Roof-tree, 1875; (opera) Scarlet Letter (adapted from novel by Nathaniel Hawthorne), 1896; (with wife), A Story of Courage (history of Order of Sisters of the Visitation), 1894; contbr. travel essays "Spanish Vistas" to Harper's Monthly; editor A Masque of Poets, 1878. Died N.Y.C., Apr. 19, 1898.

LATHROP, John, lawyer; b. Boston, Jan. 13, 1772; s. Rev. John and Mary (Wheatley) L.; grad. Harvard, 1789, A.M., 1792; read law under Christopher Gore; m. Ann Pierce, 1792; m. 2d, Jane Thompson, circa 1801; m. 3d, Grace Eleanor Harrison, circa 1808. Admitted to Mass. bar, practiced law, Boston, also Dedham, Mass.; clk. of cts. Norfolk County (Mass.), 1798; became friends with Robert T. Paine and Charles Prentiss in Boston; left for India to gain a fortune, 1799; opened sch., Calcutta, India, also wrote for papers Hircarrah and Post; unsuccessfully proposed plan for educating Indian youths in their own country (rather than in Eng.); returned to U.S., 1809, opened sch., Boston, edited almanacs, made speeches. Author of works including The Speech of Caunonicus, published Calcutta, 1802, Boston, 1803; contbr. poem, series of papers "The Moral Censor" to mag. Polyanthos, Boston, 1812-14. Died Georgetown, D.C., Jan. 30, 1820.

LATHROP, John Hiram, coll. pres.; b. Sherburne, Chenango County, N.Y., Jan. 22, 1799; s. John and Prudence (Hatch) L.; grad. Yale, 1819; m. Frances Lathrop, 1833, 7 children including Fannie (Lathrop) Smith, Jessie (Lathrop) Ripley, Gardiner. Admitted to Conn. bar, 1826; prin. Gardiner (Me.) Lyceum, 1828; prof. mathematics and natural philosophy Hamilton Coll., 1829, became Maynard prof. law, civil polity and polit. economy, 1835; 1st pres. U. Mo., 1841-49, prof. English lit., 1860, chmn. faculty, prof. moral, mental and polit. philosophy, 1863-65, pres., 1865-66; chancellor U. Wis., 1849-59; pres. Ind. U., 1859-60. Died Madison, Wis., Aug. 2, 1866.

LATHROP, Samuel, congressman; b. West Springfield, Mass., May 1, 1772; grad. Yale, 1792; studied law. Admitted to Mass. bar, began practice in West Springfield; clk. and treas. West Springfield, 1796-98, town moderator, 8 years; mem. U.S. Ho. of Reps. (Republican) from Mass., 16th-19th congresses, 1819-27; engaged in farming; mem. Mass. Senate, 1829-30, served as pres. Died West Springfield, July 11, 1846; buried Park St. Cemetery, West Springfield.

LATIL, Alexandre, poet; b. New Orleans, Oct. 6, 1816; attended College d'Orleans; married. Found to have leprosy, circa 1831; when disease worsened, sent to live in log cabin on Bayou St. John, La. (wife remained with him until death); contbd. poetry to Creole mags. and newspapers; wrote collection of 24 poems, Les Ephemeres, 1841; could not write thereafter because of extreme suffering and blindness. Died Mar. 1851.

LATIMER, Henry, senator, congressman; b. Newport, Del., Apr. 24, 1752; grad. U. Pa., 1773, Edinburgh (Scotland) Med. Coll., 1775. Practiced medicine, Wilmington, Del.; served as surgeon during Revolutionary War; mem. Del. Ho. of Reps., 1787-88, 90, speaker, 1790; mem. U.S. Ho. of Reps., 3d Congress, Feb. 14, 1894-Feb. 7, 1895; mem. U.S. Senate from Del., Feb. 7, 1795-Feb. 28, 1801. Died Phila., Dec. 19, 1819; buried Presbyn. Cemetery, Wilmington.

La TOUR, Le Blonde de, engr., army officer; b. France. A draftsman in Portugal, 1702, engr., 1703; served in Spanish Army, 1704-08, taken prisoner, 1705, exchanged, 1706; served in various battles in War of Spanish Succession (1701-04), decorated Cross of Royal and Mil. Order of St. Louis, 1715; reserve capt. Piedmont Regt., then cpl. His Majesty's

Engrs.; apptd. engr.-in-chief Province of La., arrived in La. to superintend constrn. of public buildings, 1720; supervised building of capital of La. Province, New Biloxi (now Biloxi), 1721; claimed to have drawn up plans for building of New Orleans (claims false); left New Biloxi to supervise building of new capital in New Orleans, 1722; lt. gen. Province of La. Died New Orleans, Oct. 14, 1723.

LATROBE, Benjamin Henry, engr., architect; b. Fulneck, Eng., May 1, 1764; s. Benjamin and Anna Margaret (Antes) L.; studied architecture under Samuel Pepys Cockerell (pioneer in Greek revival), Eng., 1788-89; m. Lydia Sellon, 1790, 4 children including Henry, Lydia; m. 2d, Mary Hazlehurst, May 2, 1800, children—John, Benjamin Henry. Executed his 1st independent archtl. work "Hammerwood Lodge," East Grinstead, Sussex, Eng., circa 1787; later became surveyor of police force of London (Eng.); came to Am., 1796; cons. on improvement of navigation on James River, 1796; designed prison on principle of solitary confinement, Richmond, Va., 1797; completed exterior of Va. State Capitol (designed by Jefferson); designed Bank of Pa., Phila., 1798; designed and engineered project for pumping Phila.'s water supply from Schuylkill River by using pumps operated by steam engines, 1799; undertook improvement of navigation on Susquehanna River; designed several houses in Phila. including "Sedgby" for William Cramond, the Burd House at Chestnut and 9th Streets; apptd. surveyor of public bldgs. by Pres. Jefferson, 1803; commd. to design South Wing of Capitol Bldg. which would contain U.S. Ho. of Reps.; commd. by Bishop John Carroll to design cathedral for Diocese of Balt., 1804, executed in Gothic revival style; did much work on Washington and N.Y.C. naval yards, 1804; designed 1st bldg. at Dickinson Coll., Carlisle, Pa., 1804, bldg. for Pa. Acad. Fine Arts, Phila., 1805; apptd. engr. Chesapeake and Del. Canal, 1804; became partner of Robert Fulton, Robert R. Livingston and Nicholas J. Roosevelt to build steamboat to navigate Ohio River, 1812 (project collapsed after Fulton's death, 1815); worked on reconstrn. of Capitol Bldg. and White House, Washington, D.C. (after destruction by British), 1815-17; adviser to Thomas Jefferson on design of Pavillions V and III for U. Va., 1817; after death of son Henry, completed building of water works, New Orleans, 1817. Author: View of the Practicability and Means of Supplying the City of Philadelphia with Wholesome Water, 1799. Died of yellow fever, New Orleans, Sept. 3, 1820.

LATROBE, Benjamin Henry, civil engr.; b. Phila., Dec. 19, 1806; s. Benjamin Henry and Mary (Hazlehurst) L.; m. Maria Eleanor Hazlehurst, Mar. 12, 1833, 5 children including Charles Hazlehurst. Mem. engr. corps B. & O. R.R., 1831-35, in charge of survey locating line from Balt. to Washington, 1832, built Thomas Viaduct (outstanding piece of railroad architecture); became chief engr. Balt. & Port Deposit R.R., 1835, directed survey of line from Point of Rocks to Harpers Ferry (Md.), 1836, built road through mountains from Harpers Ferry to Cumberland; apptd. chief engr. B. & O. R.R., 1842, completed survey of line from Wheeling, Va. (now W.Va.) to the Ohio, 1848, built Northwestern Va. R.R., 1851-52; chief engr. Pitts. and Connellsville R.R., 1871. Died Balt., Oct. 19, 1878.

LATROBE, Charles Hazelhurst, engr.; b. Balt., Dec 25, 1834; s. Benjamin Henry and Maria Eleanor (Hazelhurst) L.; attended St. Mary's Coll., Balt.; m. Letitia Breckinridge (Gamble) Holliday, 1861; m. 2d, Rosa Wirt Robinson, 1869; m. 3d, Louise McKim, 1881; 3 children. Worked for B.& O. R.R.; went to Fla. as chief engr. in charge of constrn. Pensacola & Ga. R.R.; commd. lt. of engrs. Confederate Army, 1861; asso. (with father and Charles Shaler Smith) in Balt. Bridge Co., 1866-77; engr. Jones Falls Commn., Balt., 1875-89, designed and constructed several iron bridges, laid out terraced gardens along Mt. Royal Avenue; commd. by Peruvian govt. to construct bridge (highest bridge in world at that time) at Verrugas on Callao-Oroya-Huancayo R.R. Died Balt., Sept. 19, 1902; buried Greenmount Cemetery, Balt.

LATROBE, John Hazlehurst Boneval, lawyer, inventor; b. Phila., May 4, 1803; s. Benjamin Henry and Mary (Hazlehurst) L.; attended U.S. Mil. Acad., 1816-20; m. Margaret Stuart, Nov. 29, 1828; m. 2d, Charlotte Clairborne, Dec. 6, 1832; 8 children. Admitted to Md. bar, 1824; submitted winning design for West Point Kosciuszko Monument, 1825; founder Md. Inst. for Promotion of Mechanic Arts, chartered 1825; helped draft charter for B. & O. R.R., 1827, counsel, 1828-91; inventor Latrobe Stove; mem. bd. visitors U.S. Mil. Acad., 1849, became pres.; pres. Am. Colonization Soc., 1853-90; regent U. Md.; founder Md. Hist. Soc., pres., 1871-91; U.S. rep. (by invitation of King of Belgians) to Internat. Assn. for Exploration and Colonization of Central Africa, 1876, pres. Am. br.; a founder Republic of Liberia. Author addresses: "Justices' Practice," 1828; "Hints for 6 Months in Europe," 1869; "Odds and Ends," 1876; "The Capitol and Washington at the Beginning of the Maryland Historial Society," 1881. Died Balt., Sept. 11, 1891.

LATTA, Alexander Bonner, inventor, mfr.; b. Chillicothe, O., June 11, 1821; s. John and Rebecca (Bonner) L.; m. Elizabeth Ann Pawson, 1847, 2 children. Worked in cotton factory in Ohio, 1831; foreman Harkness Machine Shop, Cincinnati, circa 1841; directed constrn. of locomotive for Little Miami R.R. (1st locomotive built West of Allegheny Mountains), 1845; designed and built locomotive having extra steam cylinders for Boston & Me. R.R.; patented several improvements on locomotives, steam engines and boilers; completed his 1st steam fire engine, (could be pulled by men or horses), 1852, patented self-propelled steam fire engine, 1855; formed partnership with his brother, built 30 engines by 1860; recipient gold medal for fire engine improvements at Ohio Mechanics Inst. Fair, 1854; retired, 1862. Died Ludlow, Ky., Apr. 28, 1865.

LATTIMORE, William, physician, territorial del. U.S. Congress; b. nr. Norfolk, Va., Feb. 9, 1774; s. Charles Lattimore; m. Cecilia Lea; m. 2d, Sabrina Lattimore. Moved to Miss., 1801; apptd. to Miss. Territorial Council by Jefferson, 1802; del. to U.S. Congress from Miss. Territory, 1803-07, 1813-17, responsible for compromise which helped effect division comprising present states of Ala. and Miss.; mem. Miss. Constl. Conv., 1817. Died Amite County, Miss., Apr. 3, 1843.

LAURANCE, John, senator, army officer, jurist; b. Falmouth, Eng., 1750; m. Elizabeth Macdougall, 1774-75; m. 2d, Elizabeth Lawrence, June 30, 1791. Came to N.Y.C., 1767; admitted to N.Y. bar, 1772; served as 2d lt. N.Y. Regt., Continental Army, 1775-76; a.d.c. to Gen. Washington, 1776; judge adv. gen. on staff comdr.-in-chief Continental Army presiding at trial of Maj. John Andre, 1777-82; elected vestryman Trinity Ch., also trustee Columbia, 1784; del. Congress of Confedn., 1785-87; mem. N.Y. State Senate, 1788-90; mem. U.S. Ho. of Reps. from N.Y., 1st-2d congresses, 1789-93; judge U.S. Dist. Ct., 1794-96; dir. Bank of U.S., 1794; mem. U.S. Senate from N.Y., Nov. 8, 1796-Aug. 1800. Died N.Y.C., Nov. 11, 1810; buried 1st Presbyn. Churchyard, Fifth Av., N.Y.C.

LAURENS, Henry, Continental congressman, diplomat; b. Charleston, S.C., Mar. 6, 1724; s. Jean Samuel and Esther (Grasset) L.; m. Eleanor Ball, July 6, 1750, 12 children including Henry, Martha, Eleanor, John. Owner largest export bus. in Charleston; owner plantations in S.C., Ga., Carolinas; mem. S.C. Provincial Commons Ho., 1757-76; served as lt. col. S.C. Militia, 1761; elected to 1st, 2d S.C. provincial congresses, 1774, 75, pres., 1775; pres. Charleston Council of Safety, 1774, drafted form of association signed by those who favored independence, pres., 2d Council of Safety; pres. S.C. Exec. Gen. Com., 1775, vice pres., helped draft temporary constn. for S.C., 1776; mem. Continental Congress, 1777-79, pres., 1777-78; U.S. minister to Holland, 1779; captured by British en route to Holland, 1780, exchanged, 1781; apptd. peace commr., 1782; signed preliminaries of treaty with Eng., 1782; acted as unofcl. minister to Britain, 1782-83; mem. U.S. Constl. Conv., 1787. Died Charleston, Dec. 8, 1792; buried on estate "Mepkin," S.C.

LAURENS, John, army officer, diplomat; b. Charleston, S.C., Oct. 28, 1754; s. Henry and Eleanor (Ball) L.; m. Martha Manning, Sept. 16, 1776. Admitted to Middle Temple, London, 1772; joined Washington's staff as volunteer aide, 1777, served in every battle Washington was in, including battles of Brandywine (1779), Monmouth, Germantown, Savannah, Charleston; commd. lt. col. by Continental Congress; mem. S.C. Assembly, 1779; commd. envoy extraordinary by Congress to France to obtain aid for colonies, 1780; helped organize plan for siege of Yorktown, received Lord Cornwallis' sword at Yorktown, 1781; mem. Jacksonborough Legislature, 1782. Died Aug. 27, 1782.

LAURIE, James, civil engr.; b. Bells Quarry, Scotland, May 9, 1811; Apprentice to math. engring. instrument maker, Bells Quarry, until 1832; worked in civil engr.'s office, became asso. with James P. Kirkwood, came to U.S. with him, 1833; asso. engr. Norwich & Worcester R.R. of Mass., chief engr., supt. constrn., 1835; after completion of railroad became adviser to canal and railroad cos.; a founder Boston Soc. Civil Engrs., 1848; moved to N.Y.C., 1852, invited all engrs. in vicinity to form a civil engrs. soc.; organized Am. Soc. C.E., 1852, 1st pres., 1852-67, at 1st meeting called for elevated railway tracks in his paper "The Relief of Broadway"; examiner railroad bridges for N.Y. State, 1855-56; chief engr. N.S. R.R., 1858-60; worked for Mass. inspecting Troy & Greenfield R.R.; consultant on Hoosac Tunnel for several years, concurrently chief engr. New Haven, Hartford & Springfield R.R., designed and built bridge across Connecticut River at Warehouse Point. Died Hartford, Conn., Mar. 16, 1875.

LAVALLÉE, Calixa, musician; b. Verchéres, Que., Can., Dec. 28, 1842; attended Paris (France) Conservatory. Concert pianist; made debut, 1852; solo pianist of Mme. Gerster's 1st tour in U.S., 1881; gave many concerts and recitals of works by Am. composers in leading Am. cities; pres. Music Tchrs. Nat. Assn., 1886-87; instr. Petersilea Acad., Boston. Composer: O Canada (Canadian nat. song). Died Boston, Jan. 21, 1891.

LAVEILLE, Joseph, architect. Practiced architecture in Pa., before 1820; became partner (with George Morton) in archtl. firm, St. Louis, 1821; designed (with Morton) works in St. Louis including 1st Court House (built circa 1825, razed 1865), Episcopal Ch. (1st built West of Mississippi River), 1st Jefferson Barracks (1828), Ch. of St. Louis of France (Roman Catholic cathedral, completed 1834, now a noted landmark); street commr. St. Louis, 1823-26; alderman from South Ward, St. Louis, until 1842. Died 1842.

LA VERENDRYE, Pierre Gaultier de Varennes (sieur de la Verendrye), explorer; b. Three Rivers, Can., Nov. 17, 1685; s. Rene and Marie (Boucher) Gaultier; m. Marie-Anne Dandonneau de Sable, Oct. 29, 1712, children—Jean Baptiste, Pierre, Francois, Louis Joseph. Sent to France as lt. in Regiment de Bretagne, 1707; commd. ensign local forces, 1712; went to Quebec to obtain permission from gov. to search overland for Western Sea, 1729, received permission to explore at own expense; reached Rainey Lake, built Ft. St. Pierre, 1731, built Ft. St. Charles on Lake of the Woods, 1732, Ft. Maurepas on Lake Winnipeg, 1734, Ft. La Reine on Assiniboin River, Ft. Rouge on site of Winnipeg, Man., 1738; promoted capt., 1746; decorated Cross of St. Louis for services, 1749; discovered Manitoba, The Dakotas, Western plains of Minn., N.W. territories of Can., probably part of Mont.; 1st white man (with his sons) to see Red River of North Assiniboin, probably the Saskatchewan, and great stretches of Upper Missouri River. Died Dec. 6, 1749.

LAVIALLE, Peter Joseph, clergyman; b. Lavialle, Auvergne, France, July 15, 1820; came to U.S. to join Bishop Chabrat (a relative), Louisville, Ky., 1841; studied at St. Thomas' Sem., Bardstown, Ky. Ordained priest Roman Catholic Ch., Bardstown, 1844; served at cathedral; taught at St. Thomas' Sem., 1849; apptd. pres. St. Mary's Coll., 1856; consecrated bishop of Louisville, 1865; attended 2d Plenary Council, Balt., 1866. Died Nazareth, Ky., May 11, 1867.

LAW, Andrew, composer, author; b. Milford, Conn., Mar. 1749; s. Jahleel and Ann (Baldwin Hollingsworth) Law; grad. R.I. Coll., 1775; studied theology with Rev. Levi Hart, Preston, Conn. Successfully petitioned Conn. Assembly for exclusive right to imprint and sell his tune collections, 1781; ordained to ministry Congregational Ch., Hartford, Conn., 1787; preached in Phila., Balt.; became writer tunes and hymns; taught singing, Salem, Mass., 1795-97; patented new way to print music with 4 different note shapes. Author: A Select Number of Plain Tunes Adopted to Congregational Worship, 1767; Select Harmony, 1780; The Musical Primer, 1780; Harmonic Companion, 1807; Essays on Music, Phila., 1814. Died Cheshire, Conn., July 13, 1821.

LAW, George, businessman; b. Jackson (now Shushan), N.Y., Oct. 25, 1806; son of John Law; m. Miss Anderson, 1834, 1 child. Worked on constrn. for Dismal Swamp, Morris, Harlem canals, also Del. & Hudson Canal; took 1st contracting job to build small lock and aqueduct on Del. & Hudson Canal, 1827; became large contractor, 1830-37; secured contract for work nr. Tarrytown on Croton Water Works, 1837; awarded contract for High Bridge crossing Harlem River, 1839; pres. Dry Dock Bank, 1842; later purchased and extended Harlem and Mohawk railroads; founded (with 2 others) U.S. Mail S.S. Co., 1847, received contract for mail service connecting N.Y., Havana and New Orleans; agreed on dividing business with Pacific Mail S.S. Co., 1851; a millionaire by 1856 (having sold his steamships and shifted to horse car business); pres. 8th Av. R.R., N.Y.C., 1854-81; promoter, pres. 9th Av. R.R., 1859; acquired Bklyn. and S.I. ferry lines. Died N.Y.C., Nov. 18, 1881.

LAW, John, congressman, jurist; b. New London, Conn., Oct. 28, 1796; s. Lyman and Elizabeth (Learned) L.; grad. Yale, 1814; m. Sarah Ewing, Nov. 24, 1822, 13 children. Admitted to Conn. bar, 1817; pros. atty. 1st Jud. Circuit of Ind., 1818-20, 25-28; mem. Ind. Ho. of Reps., 1824-25; judge 7th Ind. Circuit, 1830-31, 44-50; receiver pub. money, Vincennes, Ind., 1838-42; judge U.S. Ct. Land Claims, Vincennes (apptd. by Pres. Pierce), 1855-57; mem. U.S. Ho. of Reps. (Democrat) from Ind., 37th-38th congresses, 1861-65; pres. Ind. Hist. Soc., 1859-73. Author: Colonial History of Vincennes, under the French, British, and American Governments, 1858. Died Evansville, Ind., Oct. 7, 1873; buried Greenlawn Cemetery, Vincennes.

LAW, Jonathan, gov. Conn. jurist; b. Milford, Conn., Aug. 6, 1674; s. Jonathan and Sarah (Clark) L.; ed. Harvard, 1695, A.M., 1729; m. Ann Eliot, 1698; m. 2d, Abigail Arnold, 1704/5; m. 3d, Abigail Andrew, 1706; m. 4th, Mrs. Sarah Burr, 1726; m. 5th, Eunice (Hall) Andrew, 1730; 7 children. Dep. to Conn. Assembly from Milford, intermittently, 1706-17, sometimes clk. or speaker lower house; one of 1st men admitted to Conn. bar, 1708; apptd. justice of peace and of quorum for New Haven County, 1709; elected asst. to gov. Conn., 1717; dep. gov. Conn., 1724-41; judge New Haven County Ct.; asst., then chief judge Conn. Superior Cts., 1725-41; gov. Conn., 1941-50. Died Milford, Nov. 6, 1750.

LAW, Lyman, congressman; b. New London, Conn., Aug. 19, 1770; s. Richard Law; grad. Yale, 1791; studied law; children include John. Admitted to Conn. bar, 1793, began practice in New London; mem. Conn. Ho. of Reps., 1801-02, 06, 09-10, 19, 26, speaker, 1806, 09-10; mem. U.S. Ho. of Reps. (Federalist) from Conn., 12th-14th congresses, 1811-17. Died New London, Feb. 3, 1842; buried "Second Burial Ground", reinterred Cedar Grove Cemetery, New London, 1851.

LAW, Richard, Continental congressman, jurist; b. Milford, Conn., Mar. 7, 1733; s. Jonathan and Eunice (Hall) L.; grad. Yale, 1751, LL.D. (hon.), 1802; read law with Jared Ingersoll; m. Ann Prentise, Sept. 21, 1760, 1 son Lyman. Admitted to Conn. bar, 1753; moved to New London, Conn., 1757, practiced law; justice of peace, New London, 1765; mem. Conn. Gen. Ct., 1765; chief judge New London County Ct., 1773-84; mem. Conn. Gov.'s Council, 1776-86; mem. Conn. Council of Safety, 1776; mem. Continental Congress from Conn., 1777, 81-82; mayor New London, 1784-1806; judge Conn. Supreme Ct., 1784, 89, chief justice, 1786; mem. Conn. Conv. to ratify U.S. Constrn., 1788; mem. 1st electoral coll., 1789; U.S. dist. judge for Conn. (apptd. by George Washington), 1789-1806. Author: (with Roger Sherman) Acts and Laws of the State of Connecticut, in America (codification of Conn. laws), 1784. Died New London, Jan. 26, 1806; buried Cedar Grove Cemetery, New London.

LAW, Sallie Chapman Gordon, Confederate patriot; b. Wilkes County, N.C., Aug. 27, 1805; d. Chapman and Charity (King) Gordon; m. Dr. John S. Law, June 28, 1825, 7 children. Organized So. Mothers Hosp., Memphis, Tenn., 1861, under her leadership hosp. expanded from 12 beds to instn. caring for hundreds of wounded after Battle of Shiloh; carried quinine, morphine, opium (bought by treasury of So. Mother's Assn.) into Confederacy on her person, distributed in La Grange (Ga.) hosps.; hosp. named for her La Grange; only pres. So. Mothers Assn.; wrote pamphlet Reminiscences of the War of the Sixties Between the North and South, 1892; called "Mother of the Confederacy." Died June 28, 1894.

LAWLER, Frank, congressman; b. Rochester, N.Y., June 25, 1842; attended pub. schs. Moved to Chgo., 1854; news. agt., brakeman for a railroad, several years; learned shipbldg. trade; an organizer trade and labor unions; pres. Ship Carpenters and Caulker's Assn.; letter carrier Chgo. Post Office, 1869-77; mem. Chgo. City Council, 1876-85; liquor mcht., 1878; mem. U.S. Ho. of Reps. (Democrat) from Ill., 49th-51st congresses, 1885-91; alderman Chgo., 1896. Died Chgo., Jan. 17, 1896; buried Calvary Cemetery, Chgo.

LAWLER, Joab, congressman; b. Union County, N.C.,,June 12, 1796; attended pub. schs., Miss. Territory; studied theology. Licensed to preach; moved to Mardisville, Ala., 1820; minister, Mardisville; mem. Ala. Ho. of Reps., 1826-31, Ala. Senate, 1831-32; receiver of pub. moneys for Coosa Land Dist., 1832-35; treas. U. Ala., Tuscaloosa, 1833-36; mem. U.S. Ho. of Reps. (Whig) from Ala., 24th-25th congresses, 1835-38. Died Washington, D.C., May 8, 1838; buried Congressional Cemetery, Washington.

LAWRENCE, Abbott, mfr., congressman, diplomat, philanthropist; b. Groton, Mass., Dec. 16, 1792; s. Deacon Samuel and Susanna (Parker) L.; m. Katherine Bigelow, June 28, 1819, 7 children. Partner with brother in importing bus. A. & A. Lawrence of Boston, 1814-55; one of 7 businessmen sent to Harrisburg Conv., 1827; became cotton mfr., owner mills, 1830; mem. U.S. Ho. of Reps. from Mass., 24th, 26th congresses, 1835-37, 39-41, mem. ways and means com.; advocated extension of Boston and Worcester Rd. over Berkshires to Albany, 1835; boundary commr. of Mass., 1842; Mass. del.-at-large Whig Conv., 1844; a founder textile city of Lawrence (Mass.), 1845; helped promote constrn. of municipal water works, Boston, 1845; donated $50,000 for establishment of a sch. of science at Harvard (named Lawrence Scientific Sch.) left an additional $50,000 endowment in his will; U.S. minister to Gt. Britain, 1849-52. Died Boston, Aug. 18, 1855; buried Mt. Auburn Cemetery, Cambridge, Mass.

LAWRENCE, Amos, mcht., philanthropist; b. Groton, Mass., Apr. 22, 1786; s. Samuel and Susanna (Parker) L.; m. Sarah Richards, June 6, 1811; m. 2d, Nancy Means Ellis, 1821; 4 children including Amos Adams, William Richards. Mcht.'s apprentice, Dunstable, Mass., 1799-1807; became mcht., Boston, 1807, changed co. name to A. & A. Lawrence, 1814, ret. because of ill health, 1831; engaged in various philanthropies, gave away about $500,000, 1842-52, including gifts to Groton (Mass.) Acad. (also endowed in his will), and Williams Coll., Williamstown, Mass.; prin. contbr. to erection of Bunker Hill Monument. Wrote advice with his benefactions, collected by his sons and published as Extracts from the Diary and Correspondence of the Late Amos Lawrence, 1855. Died Boston, Dec. 31, 1852.

LAWRENCE, Amos Adams, textile mcht., philanthropist; b. Groton, Mass., July 31, 1814; s. Amos and Sarah (Richards) L.; grad. Harvard, 1835; m. Sarah Appleton, Mar. 31, 1842, 7 children. Partner Mason & Lawrence, sales firm for textile mills, 1843-83; became owner Ipswich Textile Mills, 1860; pres. Am. Assn. Knit Goods Mfrs., also Nat. Assn. Cotton Mfrs. and Planters; trustee Mass. Gen. Hosp.; founder Lawrence U., Appleton, Wis.; founder coll., Lawrence, Kan. (later became U. Kan.); treas. Harvard, several years; treas. Episcopal Theol. Sch., Cambridge, Mass., many years; treas. New Eng. Emigrant Aid Co. Died Boston, Aug. 22, 1886.

LAWRENCE, Cornelius Van Wyck, congressman, mayor N.Y.C.; b. Flushing, N.Y., Feb. 28, 1791; attended common schs. Moved to N.Y.C., 1812, engaged in merc. bus.; mem. U.S. Ho. of Reps. (Jacksonian Democrat) from N.Y., 23d Congress, 1833-May 14, 1834 (resigned); mayor of N.Y.C., 1834-37; Dem. presdl. elector, 1836; dir. several banks and trust cos.; collector of customs Port of N.Y., 1845-49. Died Flushing, Feb. 20, 1861; buried family burying ground, Bayside, L.I., N.Y.

LAWRENCE, Effingham, congressman; b. Bayside, L.I., N.Y., Mar. 2, 1820; attended schs., Bayside and Flushing, N.Y. Moved to La., circa 1843, engaged in planting and refining sugar; mem. La. Ho. of Reps.; mem. U.S. Ho. of Reps. (Democrat, contested election) from La., 43d Congress, Mar. 3, 1875; resumed farming. Died "Magnolia," Plaquemines Parish, La., Dec. 9, 1878; buried Greenwood Cemetery, New Orleans.

LAWRENCE, George Newbold, ornithologist, wholesale druggist; b. N.Y.C., Oct. 20, 1806; s. John Burling and Hannah (Newbold) L; m. Mary Ann Newbold, 1834. Became interested in study of birds, circa 1820, collected some 8,000 stuffed birds over the years (collection later became property of Am. Mus. of Natural History); entered father's wholesale drug firm, N.Y.C., 1822, later became partner, then head of firm, 1835; devoted later years to complete study of ornithology; became interested in neotropical birds, circa 1858, became expert on birds of W.I. and Central Am.; a founder, hon. mem. Am. Ornithologists' Union; hon. mem. Zool. Soc. of London, Brit. Ornithologists' Union, others; a founder Coll. of Pharmacy of City of N.Y. Author: (with Spencer F. Baird, John Cassin) report of N.Am. birds published in vol. IX of Reports of Explorations to Ascertain the . . . Route for a Railroad from the Mississippi River to the Pacific Ocean, 1858. Died N.Y.C., Jan. 17, 1895.

LAWRENCE, James, naval officer; b. Burlington, N.J., Oct. 1, 1781; s. John and Martha (Tallman) L.; m. Jula Montaudevret, 1808, 2 children. Apptd. midshipman U.S. Navy 1798, acting lt. on ship Adams, 1800; promoted to sailing master, 1801; served in Tripoli War, 1801-05, 1st lt., comdr. ship Enterprise and Gunboat Number 6; 1801-02; comdt. ship Hornet, captured Brit. ship Peacock, 1813; promoted capt., 1813; in command Navy Yard, N. Y.C., 1813; comdr. Chesapeake during War of 1812, fatally wounded in engagement against Brit. frigate Shannon; known for his dying words "Don't give up the ship!" Died June 4, 1813; buried Trinity Churchyard, N.Y.C.

LAWRENCE, John Watson, congressman; b. Flushing, N.Y., Aug. 1800; attended local schs. Engaged as merc. clk.; pres. Village of Flushing, 1835-45, trustee, 1860-75; mem. N.Y. Assembly, 1840-41; mem. U.S. Ho. of Reps. (Democrat) from N.Y., 29th Congress, 1845-47; declined nomination for lt. gov. N.Y.; resumed banking. Died Flushing, Dec. 20, 1888; buried Flushing Cemetery.

LAWRENCE, Joseph, congressman; b. nr. Hunterstown, Pa., 1786; attended common schs.; children include George Van Eman. Engaged in farming; mem. Pa. Ho. of Reps., 1818-24, 34-36, speaker, 1820-22; mem. U.S. Ho. of Reps. from Pa., 19th-20th, 27th congresses, 1825-29, 41-42; treas. State of Pa., 1837. Died Washington, D.C., Apr. 17, 1842; buried Congressional Cemetery, Washington.

LAWRENCE, Richard Smith, inventor, mfr.; b. Chester, Va., Nov. 22, 1817; s. Richard and Susan (Smith) L.; m. Mary Ann Finney, May 22, 1842, 1 child. With N. Kendall & Co., gun-makers, Windsor, Vt., 1838, in charge of mfg. process, 1838-42; opened gunshop (with Kendall), Windsor, 1843; obtained U.S. contract for 10,000 rifles (with aid of S. E. Robbins), 1844, formed new co. Robbins, Kendall & Lawrence, Windsor, sold out to his partners, 1847; devised barrel-drilling and rifling machines, invented split pulley; introduced practice of lubricating bullets with tallow (led to eventual prodn. of repeating rifle), 1850; contracted to supply all machinery for Enfield Armory (Eng.) and for Brit. Enfield rifles, 1851; contracted to make Sharps carbines and rifles, 1852, went bankrupt before completion of contract because of unsuccessful attempt to make railroads cars in 1850; supt. Sharps Rifle Co., 1856-72; mem. water bd., bd. aldermen, fire bd. of Hartford, Conn. Died Hartford, Mar. 10, 1892.

LAWRENCE, Samuel, congressman; b. Newtown (now part of N.Y.C.), N.Y., May 23, 1773; attended common schs.; studied law. Admitted to N.Y. bar, 1794, began practice in N.Y.C.; clk. to atty. gen. State of N.Y.; judge Marine Ct. (later City Ct.); mem. N.Y. Assembly, 1808, 17-18, 20-21; county clk. N.Y. County, 1811-12; Democratic presdl. elector, sec. Electoral Coll., 1816; mem. U.S. Ho. of Reps. from N.Y., 18th Congress, 1823-25. Died Cayuta Lake, nr. Cayutaville, N.Y., Oct. 20, 1837; buried family cemetery, Cayuta Lake.

LAWRENCE, Sidney, congressman; b. Weybridge, Vt., Dec. 31, 1801; attended common schs., Moira, N.Y.; studied law. Admitted to N.Y. bar, began practice in Moria; justice of peace, 50 years; supr. and assessor of Town of Moira; surrogate of Franklin County (N.Y.), 1837-43; mem. N.Y. Senate, 1843-44, N.Y. Assembly, 1846; mem. U.S. Ho. of Reps. (Democrat) from N.Y., 30th Congress, 1847-49; engaged in real estate bus., banking. Died Moira, May 9, 1892; buried Moira Cemetery.

LAWRENCE, William, businessman; b. Groton, Mass., Sept. 7, 1783; s. Samuel and Susanna (Parker) L.; m. Susan Ruggles Bordman, May 20, 1813, 9 children. Joined his brother in Boston, 1809; set up own business as commn. mcht., Boston, 1810, took his brother Samuel into partnership, 1822; instrumental in formation of Middlesex Mfg. Co. (1st incorporated co. for manufacture of woolen goods), 1825; established Suffolk Bank System, putting New Eng. currency on sound basis (chartered 1818), mem. bd. dirs., 1818-48; helped financially in various improvements in Boston; benefactor of Groton Acad. (name changed to Lawrence Acad. in honor of him and his brother Amos). Died Oct. 14, 1848.

LAWRENCE, William, congressman; b. Washington (now Old Washington), O., Sept. 2, 1814; grad. Jefferson Coll., Canonsburg, Pa., 1835. Engaged in farming; mem. Ohio Ho. of Reps., 1843; Democratic presdl. elector, 1848; del. Ohio Constl. Conv., 1851; mem. Ohio Senate, 1856-57, 67, 85-86; mem. U.S. Ho. of Reps. (Dem.) from Ohio, 35th Congress, 1857-59; engaged in merc. bus., Old Washington; pres. bd. dirs. Ohio Penitentiary; Died Old Washington, Sept. 8, 1895; buried Washington Cemetery.

LAWRENCE, William Beach, lawyer; b. N.Y.C., Oct. 23, 1800; s. Isaac and Cornelia (Beach) L.; grad. Columbia, 1818; studied Litchfield (Conn.) Law Sch., 1821-23; 1st recipient D.C.L. (hon.), U. State N.Y.; LL.D. (hon.), Brown U.; m. Esther Gracie, May 19, 1821. Admitted to N.Y. bar, circa 1820; apptd. sec. of legation, London, Eng., 1826, charge d'affaires, 1827; v.p. N.Y. Hist. Sc., 1836-45; lt. gov. R.I., 1851, acting gov., 1852; mem. commn. to compile code of internat. law; mem. R.I. constl. Conv., 1853; lectr. internat. law Columbian U., Washington, D.C., 1872-73; an original mem. Inst. of Law of Nations. Author: Law of Charitable Uses, 1845; Visitation and Search, 1858; Commentaire sur les elements du droit international, 9 vols., 1868-80. Editor: Wheaton's Elements of International Law. Died N.Y.C., Mar. 26, 1881.

LAWRENCE, William Thomas, congressman; b. N. Y.C., May 7, 1788; attended common schs. Engaged in merc. bus.; served with 4th Regt., N.Y. Arty. during War of 1812; moved to Cayuga County, N.Y., 1823, engaged in farming; justice of peace, 1838; mem. U.S. Ho. of Reps. from N.Y., 30th Congress, 1847-49. Died nr. Cayutaville, N.Y., Oct. 25, 1859; buried family cemetery, N.Y.C.

LAWSON, Alexander, engraver; b. Ravenstruthers, Scotland, Dec. 19, 1773; m. Elizabeth Scaife, June 6, 1805; 3 children including Oscar A., Mary Lockhart. Went to Liverpool to work for his brother, 1788; moved to Manchester, Eng., 1789, experimented in engraving; came to U.S., 1794; worked for Thackara and Vallance, Phila., 1794-96; set up own engraving business, 1796; did series of 4 plates illustrating Thomson's Four Seasons, 1797; engraved plates for supplemental volumes of Thomas Dobson's Encyclopaedia, 1803; partner with J. J. Barralet for short time, engraved plates for The Powers of Genius, by Rev. John Blair Linn, 2d edit., 1802; friend of naturalist Alexander Wilson, agreed to do plates for less than $1 a day for Wilson's American Ornithology, 9 vols., 1808-14; engraved various portraits; made plates for American Ornithology; or, he Natural History of Birds Inhabiting the United tates Not Given by Wilson, by Charles Lucien Bonaarte, 4 vols., 1825-33; his work presented in exhbn. f 100 notable Am. engravers at N.Y. Public Lirary, 1928. Died Phila., Aug. 22, 1846.

LAWSON, James, editor, ins. exec.; b. Glasgow, cotland, Nov. 9, 1799; s. James Lawson; attended J. Glasgow, 1812; m. Mary Eliza Donaldson. Came o N.Y.C., 1815, worked as accountant in office of is uncle Alexander Thomson; partner firm Alexaner Thomson and Co., 1822-26; contbr. articles to N.Y. Literary Gazette and Am. Athenaeum; edited vith John B. Skilman and James G. Brooks Morning ourier, N.Y.C., 1827-29; edited (with Amos Buter) Merc. Adviser, N.Y.C., 1829-33; engaged in narine ins. business, 1833-80. Author: Poems: leanings from Spare Hours of a Business Life, 857. Died Mar. 24, 1880.

LAWSON, John, explorer; m. Hanna Smith, 1 lau., Isabelle. Arrived in Charleston, S.C., 1700, mmediately set out (with 6 Englishmen, 4 Indians) o explore Eastern Carolina area; secured incorporaion of Town of Bath (S.C.), 1705; organized (with Christopher de Graffenried in London, Eng.) immigration of 600 Germans and Swiss to Carolina, 1709, ounded New Bern, N.C.; siezed (with De Graffenide, who was later released) when new settlement vas attacked by Tuscarora Indians. Killed by Tuscaoras, 1711.

LAWSON, John Daniel, congressman; b. Montgomery, N.Y., Feb. 18, 1816; attended pub. schs. Moved to N.Y.C., employed as clk. dry goods store; engaged in merc. bus., importing dry goods, 1843; del. Republican state, county and dist. convs., 30 years; del. all Rep. nat. convs., 1868-92; mem. U.S. Ho. of Reps. (Rep.) from N.Y., 43d Congress, 1873-75. Died N.Y.C., Jan. 24, 1896; buried Greenwood Cemetery, Bklyn.

LAWSON, Leonidas Merion, physician; b. Nicholas County, Ky., Sept. 10, 1812; s. Rev. Jeremiah and Hannah (Chancellor) L.; M.D., Transylvania Coll., Ky., 1838; studied in London, Eng., Paris, France, 1844-45; m. Louise Cailey; m. 2d, Eliza Robinson; 7 children including Louise. Practiced medicine, Mason County, Ky., until 1841; moved to Cincinnati, 1841; founder, publisher Western Lancet, 1842-55; editor Journal of Health, 1844; taught at Transylvania Coll., 1845-47; prof. materia medica, pathology Med. Coll. of Ohio, Cincinnati, 1847-53, prof. principles and practice medicine, 1853, prof. theory and practice medicine, 1860-64; gave 2 courses at Ky. Sch. of Medicine, Louisville, 1854-56. Author: Phthisis Pulmonalis (study of tuberculosis), 1861. Died Jan. 21, 1864.

LAWSON, Thomas, army officer; b. Va., 1781. Apptd. from Va. as surgeon's mate U.S. Navy, 1809; apptd. garrison surgeon's mate U.S. Army, 1811, promoted surgeon 6th Inf., 1813, remained in position throughout War of 1812; apptd. surgeon gen. U.S. Army, 1836, twice had line commands, once commanded a regt.; served as q.m. and adj.; brevetted brig. gen., 1848. Author: Report on Sickness and Mortality, U.S. Army 1819-1839, published 1840; Meteorological Register 1826-30, published 1848; Appendix for 1822-1825, published 1840. Died Norfolk, Va., May 15, 1861.

LAWTON, Alexander Robert, army officer, diplomat; b. St. Peter's Parish, Beaufort Dist., S.C., Nov. 4, 1818; s. Alexander James and Martha (Mosse) L.; grad. U.S. Mil. Acad., 1839, Harvard Law Sch., 1842; m. Sarah Alexander, Nov. 5, 1845; 4 children. Commd. 2d lt. 1st Arty., 1839, resigned, 1841; pres. Augusta & Savannah R.R., 1849-54; mem. Ga. Ho. of Reps., 1855-56, Ga. Senate, 1860; col. 1st Volunteer Regt. of Ga., commd. brig. gen., 1861; fought in Seven Days, 2d Manassas, Sharpsburg engagements; took charge Ewell's div., commanded its advance into Md.; became q.m. gen. Confederacy, 1863; served in lower house Ga. Legislature, 1870-75; chmn. Ga. Electoral Coll., 1876; mem., pres. pro tem Ga. Constl. Conv. of 1877; unsuccessful candidate for U.S. Senate, 1880, elected pres. Am. Bar, 1882; minister to Austria, 1887-89. Died Clifton Springs, N.Y., July 2, 1896.

LAWYER, Thomas, congressman; b. Schoharie, N.Y., Oct. 14, 1785; studied law. Admitted to N.Y. bar, practiced in Schoharie County; mem. N.Y. Ho. of Reps., 1816, 46; served as brig. gen. N.Y. Militia; mem. U.S. Ho. of Reps. from N.Y., 15th Congress, 1817-19; dist. atty. Schoharie County, 1822-31; presdl. elector, 1824. Died Lawyersville, N.Y., May 21, 1868.

LAY, Alfred Morrison, congressman; b. Lewis County, Mo., May 20, 1842; grad. Bethany Coll., Va. (now W.Va.), 1856; studied law. Admitted to Mo. bar, 1857, began practice in Jefferson City; U.S. dist. atty. for Western Mo. (apptd. by Pres. Buchanan), until 1861; served from pvt. to maj. Mo. State Guard; served as capt. of ordnance Confederate Army; captured, imprisoned at Alton, Ill., exchanged at Aikens Landing, Va.; capt. 10th Mo. Cavalry; regtl. q.m., asst. brigade q.m. until end of Civil War; resumed law practice, Jefferson City; mem. Mo. Constl. Conv., 1875; mem. U.S. Ho. of Reps. (Democrat) from Mo., 46th Congress, 1879. Died Washington, D.C., Dec. 8, 1879; buried Woodlawn Cemetery, Jefferson City.

LAY, Benjamin, reformer; b. Colchester, Eng., 1677; m. Sarah Lay. Moved to Barbados, 1718, forced to leave because of his sympathy for slaves; settled in Phila., conducted anti-slavery campaign, also advocated vegetarianism, temperance, prison reform. Author: All Slave-Keepers that Keep the Innocent in Bondage, Apostates Pretending to Lay Claim to the Pure and Holy Christian Religion, 1737. Died Phila., Feb. 3, 1759; buried Friends' Burial Ground, Abington, Pa.

LAY, George Washington, congressman; b. Catskill, N.Y., July 26, 1798; grad. Hamilton Coll., Clinton, N.Y., 1817; studied law. Admitted to N.Y. bar, began practice in Batavia, 1820; treas. Genesee County (N.Y.), 1825-31; mem. U.S. Ho. of Reps. (Whig) from N.Y., 23d-24th congresses, 1833-37; mem. N.Y. Assembly, 1840; chargé d'affaires to Sweden, 1842-45. Died Batavia, Oct. 21, 1860; buried Batavia Cemetery.

LAY, Henry Champlin, clergyman; b. Richmond, Va., Dec. 6, 1823; s. John Olmstead and Lucy (May) L.; grad. U. Va., 1842, theol. sem., Alexandria, Va., 1846; m. Elizabeth Atkinson, May 13, 1847. Ordained to ministry Episcopal Ch., 1848; rector Ch. of the Nativity, Huntsville, Ala., 1848-59; missionary bishop of Southwest in Protestant Episcopal Ch., 1859; became bishop of Ark. when Southern wing of Ch. split from Northern, 1860; resumed work as missionary bishop, worked for church unity, at end of Civil War; became bishop of Easton, Eastern Shore area of Md., 1869. Author: Studies in the Church, 1872; The Church in the Nation, 1885. Died Church Home, Balt., Sept. 17, 1885; buried Easton, Md.

LAY, John Louis, inventor; b. Buffalo, N.Y., Jan. 14, 1832; s. John and Frances (Atkins) L. Commd. 2d asst. engr. U.S. Navy, 1861, 1st asst. engr., 1863; perfected torpedo, patented, 1865; worked as naval engr. for Peruvian Govt., 1865-67; invented self-propelled torpedo (could be directed from a ship), sold many to Russia and Turkey; lived in Europe, 1870-98. Died bankrupt in Bellevue Hosp., N.Y.C., Apr. 17, 1899.

LAZARUS, Emma, poet; b. N.Y.C., July 22, 1849; d. Moses and Esther (Nathan) Lazarus. Began her writing on problem of Jewish immigrants as result of persecution of Jews during period 1879-83; her poem about Statue of Liberty chosen to be placed on its base. Author: Poems and Translations Admetus and Other Poems, 1871 (published privately 1866); Alide (novel), 1874; The Spagnoletto (play), 1876; Songs of a Semite, 1882. Died Nov. 19, 1887.

LAZEAR, Jesse, congressman; b. Rich Hill Twp., Greene County, Pa., Dec. 12, 1804. Taught sch.; engaged in merc. bus., recorder Greene County, 1829-32; cashier Farmers & Drovers Bank, Waynesburg, Pa., 1835-67; mem. U.S. Ho. of Reps. (Democrat) from Pa., 37th-38th congresses, 1861-65; del. Union Nat. Conv., Phila., 1866; pres. Balt. & Powhatan R.R. Co., 1871-74. Died "Windsor Mill Farm," Baltimore County, Md., Sept. 2, 1877; buried Green Mount Cemetery, Waynesburg.

LAZEAR, Jesse William, physician; b. Balt., May 2, 1866; s. William and Charlotte (Pettigrew) L.; A.B., Johns Hopkins, 1889; M.D., Columbia, 1892; postgrad. Pasteur Inst., Paris, France; m. Mabel Houston, 1896, 2 children. Physician, Johns Hopkins Hosp., Balt., 1895; asst. surgeon in U.S. Army at Columbia Barracks, Quemados, Cuba, 1900; mem. Yellow Fever Commn. with Maj. Walter Reed, while in charge of mosquitos was bitten. Died helping to show that mosquitos were carriers of yellow fever, Quemados, Sept. 25, 1900.

LEA, Isaac, malacologist, naturalist; b. Wilmington, Del., Mar. 4, 1792; s. James and Elizabeth (Gibson) L.; LL.D. (hon.), Harvard, 1852; m. Frances Carey, 1821; children--Mathew Carey, Henry Charles, 1 dau. Became mem. Acad. Natural Sciences of Phila., 1815, pres., 1858-63; partner in father-in-law's publishing firm, 1821-51; concentrated on studies of fresh-water mollusks, became recognized authority in field, described more than 1800 species mollusks, recent and fossil; A.A.A.S., 1860: v.p. Am. Philos. Soc. Died Phila., Dec. 8, 1886.

LEA, Luke, congressman; b. Surry County, N.C., Jan. 21, 1783; attended common schs., Hawkins County, Tenn. Clk., Tenn. Ho. of Reps., 1804-06; comdr. regt. under Gen. Andrew Jackson during Creek and Seminole wars, 1818; held local offices, Campbells Station, Tenn.; mem. U.S. Ho. of Reps. (Union Democrat) from Tenn., 23d-24th congresses, 1833-37; sec. of state Tenn., 1837-39; declined appointment by Pres. Taylor as commr. Indian affairs, 1850; Indian agt. (apptd. by Pres. Fillmore), Ft. Leavenworth, Kan., 1850-51. Died nr. Ft. Leavenworth, June 17, 1851; buried Westport Cemetery, Kansas City, Mo.

LEA, Mathew Carey, chemist; b. Phila., Aug. 18, 1823; s. Isaac and Frances (Carey) L.; studied chemistry under James C. Booth; m. Elizabeth Jaudon, July 14, 1852; m. 2d, Eva Lovering. Pioneered use of photography in study of chemistry in U.S.; mem. Franklin Inst., Nat. Acad. Scis. Author: A Manual of Photography, 1868. Died Phila., Mar. 15, 1897.

LEA, Pryor, congressman; b. Knox County, Tenn., Aug. 31, 1794; grad. Greeneville Coll.; studied law. Admitted to Tenn. bar, 1817, began practice in Knoxville; served in Creek War, 1813; U.S. atty. for Tenn., 1824; mem. U.S. Ho. of Reps. (Jacksonian Democrat) from Tenn., 20th-21st congresses, 1827-31; moved to Jackson, Miss., 1836, to Goliad, Tex., 1846; engaged in railroad bldg.; mem. Tex. State People's Conv. which passed secession ordinance, 1861. Died Goliad, Sept. 14, 1879; buried Oak Hill Cemetery, Goliad.

LEACH, Daniel Dyer, clergyman, educator; b. Bridgewater, Mass., June 12, 1806; s. Apollos and Chloe (Dyer) L.; grad. Brown U., 1830; attended Andover Theol. Sem.; m. Mary Lawton, 1834, 3 children. Ordained to ministry Episcopal Ch., 1833; prin. Classical High Sch., Roxbury, Mass., 1838-42; conducted own pvt. school, 1842-48; agt. Mass. Bd. Edn., 1848-55; supt. schs., Providence, R.I., 1855-85; mem. R.I. Bd. Edn., 1870-89; trustee Brown U., 1877-91. Author elementary textbooks. Died Providence, May 16, 1891.

LEACH, James Madison, congressman; b. "Lansdowne," Randolph County, N.C., Jan. 17, 1815; grad. U.S. Mil. Acad., 1838; studied law. Admitted to N.C. bar, 1842, began practice in Lexington; mem. N.C. Ho. of Commons, 1848-58; presdl. elector on Am. Party ticket, 1856; mem. U.S. Ho. of Reps. from N.C., as Whig, 36th Congress, 1859-61, as Conservative, 42d-43d congresses, 1871-75; served as capt. and lt. col. Confederate Army, during Civil War; mem. Confederate States Congress, 1864-65; mem. N.C. Senate, 1865-66, 79. Died Lexington, June 1, 1891; buried Hopewell Cemetery, nr. Trinity, N.C.

LEACH, Shepherd, mfr.; b. Easton, Mass., Apr. 30, 1778; s. Abisha and Patience (Woods) L.; m. Phoebe Torrey, 1804. Bought father's iron factory, Easton, 1802, made iron castings for machinery, became largest iron mfr. in area; wealthiest man in Easton (owned cotton mills, grist mill, saw mill) by 1832; served as maj. gen. Mass. Militia. Died Sept. 19, 1832.

LEADBETTER, Daniel Parkhurst, congressman; b. Pittsfield, Mass., Sept. 10, 1797; attended common schs., Pittsfield; studied law, Steubenville, O. Admitted to Ohio bar, 1821, began practice in Steubenville; commd. capt. 2d Co., 3d Regt., 6th Div., Ohio Militia, 1821, q.m. 4th Div., 1831; moved to Millersburg, O., 1828, practiced law; county recorder, 1831-36; mem. U.S. Ho. of Reps. (Jacksonian Democrat) from Ohio, 25th-26th congresses, 1837-41; resumed law practice, also engaged in farming; mem. Ohio Constl. Conv., 1851; served as capt. during Civil War, 1862. Died Millersburg, Feb. 26, 1870; buried Oak Hill Cemetery, Millersburg.

LEAKE, Shelton Farrar, congressman; b. nr. Hillsboro, Va., Nov. 30, 1812; studied law. Taught sch.; admitted to Va. bar, 1835, began practice in Charlottesville; mem. Va. Ho. of Dels., 1842-43; mem. U.S. Ho. of Reps. (Democrat) from Va., 29th, 36th congresses, 1845-47, 59-61; Dem. presdl. elector, 1848; elected lt. gov. Va., 1851. Died Charlottesville, Mar. 4, 1884; buried Maplewood Cemetery, Charlottesville.

LEAKE, Walter, senator, gov. Miss.; b. Albemarle County, Va., May 25, 1762; studied law. Served in Revolutionary War; admitted to the bar, practiced law; apptd. U.S. judge for Miss. Territory by Pres. Jefferson, 1807; mem. U.S. Senate from Miss., Dec. 10, 1817-May 15, 1820; apptd. U.S. marshal for Miss. Dist., 1820; gov. Miss., 1821-25. Died Mount Salus, Miss., Nov. 17, 1825.

LEAMING, Jacob Spicer, farmer; b. nr. Madisonville, O., Apr. 2, 1815; s. Christopher and Margaret Leaming; m. Lydia Middlesworth, Mar. 1, 1839, 9 children. Through selective process developed Leaming corn (an earlier maturing, more productive strand), raised productivity to over 100 bushels per acre; corn won prizes at Paris Expn., 1878; went into seed business to handle demand. Died May 12, 1885.

LEAMING, Jeremiah, clergyman; b. Durham, Conn., 1717; s. Jeremiah and Abigail (Turner) L.; grad. Yale, 1745; M.A. (hon.), King's Coll., 1765, S.T.D. (hon.), 1789; m. Ann Leaming; m. 2d, Elizabeth Peck. Ordained to ministry Episcopal Ch., 1748; minister Trinity Ch., Newport, R.I., 1748-58, St. Paul's Ch., Norwalk, Conn., 1758-77; fled Norwalk because he was Loyalist, 1777; minister, Stratford, Conn., 1784-90. Died Sept. 15, 1804.

LEAMING, Thomas, army officer; b. Cape May County, N.J., Sept. 1, 1748; s. Thomas and Elizabeth (Leaming) L.; read law under John Dickinson; m. Rebecca Fisher, Aug. 19, 1779, at least 2 sons, Thomas Fisher, Jeromiah Fisher. Admitted to Phila. bar; organized militia in Cape May County, 1776; mem. N.J. Provincial Assembly, 1776; fought at Princeton, Trenton, Germantown and Brandywine; founded firm Bunner, Murray & Co., 1777; his company Thomas Leaming & Co. sponsored privateers, captured over 50 ships; returned to law practice, Phila. Died Phila., Oct. 29, 1797; buried Christ Ch. Burial Grounds, Phila.

LEAR, Tobias, diplomat; b. Portsmouth, N.H., Sept. 19, 1762; s. Capt. Tobias and Mary (Stilson) L.; grad. Harvard, 1783; m. Mary Long, Apr. 18, 1790; m. 2d, Frances Bassett, Aug. 22, 1795; m. 3d, Frances Henley. Pvt. sec. to George Washington, 1785-92; elected pres. Potomac Canal Co., 1795; apptd. by Washington as his mil. sec. with rank of col., 1798; apptd. by Jefferson as consul at Santo Domingo, 1802; consul gen. at Algiers, 1804-11, negotiated treaty with Tripoli which ended exactment of tribute from Am. mcht. vessels; accountant War Dept., 1811-16. Died Washington, D.C., Oct. 11, 1816.

LEARNED, Amasa, congressman; b. Killingly, Conn., Nov. 15, 1750; grad. Yale, 1772; studied theology and law. Taught at Union Sch., New London, Conn.; licensed to preach by Windham Assn., 1773; mem. Conn. Ho. of Reps., 1779, 85-91; mem. Conn. Conv. which ratified U.S. Constn., 1788; mem. Conn. Upper House of Assistants, 1791; mem. U.S. Ho. of Reps. from Conn., 2d-3d congresses, 1791-95; del. Conn. Constl. Conv., 1818; land speculator. Died New London, May 4, 1825; buried Cedar Grove Cemetery, New London.

LEARNED, Ebenezer, army officer; b. Oxford, Mass., Apr. 18, 1728; s. Col. Ebenezer and Deborah (Haynes) L.; m. Jerusha Baker, Oct. 5, 1749; m. 2d, Eliphal Putnam, May 23, 1800. Served as capt. of Rangers to relieve Ft. Henry in French and Indian War, capt. in company in Col. Ruggles' Regt.; del. to Mass. Provincial Congress, Concord, 1774, Cambridge, 1775; served with Mass. Militia at Battle of Bunker Hill; commd. col. 3d Inf., Continental Army, 1776, brig. gen., 1777; in command brigade at Saratoga; mem. Mass. Constl. Conv. from Oxford, 1779; mem. Mass. Legislature, 1783; chmn. Mass. Constl. Conv., 1789. Died Oxford, Apr. 1, 1801.

LEARY, Cornelius Lawrence Ludlow, congressman; b. Balt., Oct. 22, 1813; grad. St. Mary's Coll., Balt. 1833; studied law. Mem. Md. Ho. of Dels., 1838-39; admitted to Md. bar, 1840, began practice in Balt.; presdl. elector on Am. Party ticket, 1856; mem. U.S. Ho. of Reps. (Unionist) from Md., 37th Congress, 1861-63; resumed practice of law, Balt. Died Balt., Mar. 21, 1893; buried Lorraine Cemetery, Balt.

LEAVENWORTH, Elias Warner, congressman; b. Canaan, N.Y., Dec. 20, 1803; grad. Yale, 1824; attended Litchfield (Conn.) Law Sch., 1825-27. Admitted to N.Y. bar, 1827; practiced law in Syracuse, N.Y., 1827-50; served to brig. gen. N.Y. Militia; pres. Village of Syracuse, 1839-41, 46-47; mayor Town of Syracuse, 1849-50, 59-60; mem. N.Y. Assembly, 1850, 57; sec. of state N.Y., 1854-55; pres. N.Y. State Republican Conv., 1860; U.S. commr. under conv. with New Granada, Washington, D.C., 1861-62; apptd. pres. bd. commrs. to locate N.Y. State Asylum for Blind, 1865; trustee N.Y. State Asylum for Insane, 1865; constl. commr., 1872; mem. N.Y. and N.J. Boundary Line Commn., 1875; mem. U.S. Ho. of Reps. (Rep.) from N.Y., 44th Congress, 1875-77. Died Syracuse, Nov. 25, 1887; buried Oakwood Cemetery, Syracuse.

LEAVENWORTH, Henry, army officer; b. New Haven, Conn., Dec. 10, 1783; s. Jesse and Catharine (Conkling) L.; m. Elizabeth Morrison; m. 2d, Electra Knapp, 1810; m. 3d, Harriet Lovejoy, circa 1813. Admitted to N.Y. bar, 1804; commd. capt. 25th Inf., U.S. Army, 1812, maj. 9th Inf., 1813; brevetted col. for services at Battle of Chippewa, 1814, lt. col. for services at Battle of Niagara, 1814; mem. N.Y. Legislature, 1815; commd. lt. col. 5th Inf., 1818, trans. to 6th Inf., made comdt. at Ft. Atkinson (Calhoun), 1821; brevetted brig. gen., 1824; commd. col. 3d Inf., 1824; built post Ft. Leavenworth (now Leavenworth, Kan.), 1827; post comdr. Jefferson Barracks, 1829; comdr. South Western Frontier, 1834. Died Camp Smith, Kan., July 21, 1834; buried Ft. Leavenworth.

LEAVITT, Dudley, publisher, author; b. Exeter, N.H., May 23, 1772; s. Joshua and Elizabeth (James) L.; m. Judith Glidden, Apr. 7, 1795. Issued 1st almanac, 1797; wrote text books; editor N.H. Register, 1811-17; sold over 60,000 copies of Leavitt's Farmer's Almanack by 1846. Died Meredith, N.H., Sept. 15, 1851.

LEAVITT, Humphrey Howe, congressman, jurist; b. Suffield, Conn., June 18, 1796; s. John and Miss (Fitch) L.; m. Maria McDowell, Dec. 1821. Admitted to bar, 1816; prosecutor Jefferson County (O.), 1823-29; mem. Ohio Ho. of Reps., 1825-26, Ohio Senate, 1827-28; clk. ct. Common Pleas and Supreme Cts. of Jefferson County; mem. U.S. Ho. of Reps. (Democrat) from Ohio, 22nd-23d congresses, 1831-34; U.S. dist. judge for Ohio, 1834-71; mem. World's Conv. on Prison Reform, London, Eng., 1872. Died Springfield, O., Mar. 15, 1873; buried Spring Grove Cemetery, Cincinnati.

LEAVITT, John McDowell, coll. pres.; b. Steubenville, O., 1824; grad. Jefferson Coll., 1841; attended theol. sem., Gambier, O.; D.D. (hon.), Ohio U., 1872; LL.D. (hon.), St. John's Coll., 1889. Admitted to Ohio bar; ordained priest Protestant Episcopal Ch., 1848; prof. Kenyon Coll., Ohio U.; pres. Lehigh U., Bethlehem, Pa.; pres. St. John's Coll., Annapolis, Md., 1880-84. Author: Old World Tragedies from New World Life; Hymns to Our King.

LEAVITT, Joshua, clergyman, editor; b. Heath, Mass., Sept. 8, 1794; s. Roger Smith and Chloe (Maxwell) L.; grad. Yale, 1814, Yale Div. Sch., 1825; m. Sarah Williams, 1820. Admitted to Mass. bar, 1819; ordained to ministry Congregational Ch., Stratford, Conn., 1825; sec. Seamen's Friend Soc., N.Y.C., 1828, also editor Sailor's Mag.; lectr. Am. Temperance Soc.; editor Evangelist, 1831-37; mem. exec. com. Nat. Anti-Slavery Soc., 1833; editor Emancipator (reform mag.), 1839-48; asst. editor Independent, 1848-73. Died Jan. 16, 1873.

Le BRUN, Napoleon Eugene Henry Charles, architect; b. Phila., Jan. 2, 1821; s. Charles and Adelaide Le Brun; studied architecture under Thomas A. Walter; m. Adele Louise Lajus, Dec. 20, 1845, 5 children. Practiced in Phila., 1841-61; mem. A.I.A.; designed Tabernacle Presbyn. Ch., Acad. of Music, Girard Bldg., interior of Cathedral of Sts. Peter and Paul (all Phila.); practiced in N.Y.C., 1861-1901; designed Ch. of Epiphany, Ch. of St. John Baptist, Home Life Ins. Bldg., Met. Life Ins. Bldg. (all N.Y.C.). Died July 9, 1901.

LECHFORD, Thomas, lawyer; flourished 1629-42. attended Clemet's Inn., London, Eng.; m. Elizabeth Lechford. Came to Boston, 1637; debarred for trying to influence a jury, 1639; returned to Eng., 1641. Author: Plain Dealing: or, Newes from New-England (anti-New Eng.), 1642.

Le CLEAR, Thomas, painter; b. Owego, N.Y., Mar. 11, 1818; s. Louis Le Clear; m. Miss Wells, 1844; m. 2d, Miss King, 1869. Traveled country painting portraits, 1832-60; settled in N.Y.C., 1860-82; mem. N.A.D., 1863; painted portraits of Presidents Fillmore and Grant, also of Joseph Henry, George Bancroft, Edwin Booth, William Cullen Bryant. Died Rutherford Park, N.J., Nov. 26, 1882.

LECOMPTE, Joseph, congressman; b. nr. Georgetown, Ky., Dec. 15, 1797; attended common schs. Engaged in farming, Lecomptes Bottom, Ky.; served with Ky. Riflemen during War of 1812, participated in Battle of New Orleans; mem. Ky. Ho. of Reps., 1819, 22, 38-39, 44; served as maj. Ky. Militia; mem. U.S. Ho. of Reps. (Democrat) from Ky., 19th-22d congresses, 1825-33; mem. Ky. Constl. Conv., 1850. Died Henry County, Ky., Apr. 24, 1851; buried pvt. family cemetery, Lecomptes Bottom.

LeCONTE, John, physicist, coll. pres.; b. Liberty County, Ga., Dec. 4, 1818; s. Louis and Ann (Quarterman) LeC.; grad. Franklin Coll. (now U. Ga.), 1838; M.D., Coll. Physicians and Surgeons, N.Y.C., 1841; m. Eleanor Graham, June 20, 1841. Prof. physics and chemistry Franklin Coll., 1846-55; prof. physics U. So. Cal., 1856-69; became prof. physics U. Cal., 1869, also pres., 1869, 75-81. Author: (papers) Experiments Illustrating the Seat of Volition in the Alligator, 1845; On the Influence of Musical Sounds on the Flame of a Jet of Coal-gas, 1858; On Sound Shadows in Water, 1882; Physical Studies of Lake Tahoe, 1883, 84. Died probably Berkeley, Cal., Apr. 29, 1891.

LeCONTE, John Lawrence, entomologist; b. N.Y.C., May 13, 1825; s. John and Mary Anne (Lawrence) LeC.; grad. Mt. St. Mary's Coll., 1842; M.D., Coll. Physicians and Surgeons, N.Y.C., 1846; m. Helen Grier, Jan. 10, 1861. Investigated and published papers on entomology and zoogeography, 1846-61; surgeon of volunteers, M.C., U.S. Army, 1861-65, later lt. col., med. insp.; studied mineralogy, geology and entomology, 1865-83; chief clk. U.S. Mint, Phila., 1878-83; an incorporator Nat. Acad. Scis.; pres. A.A.A.S., 1874. Contbr. papers Coleoptera of Europe and North America to Annals of Lyceum of Natural History of N.Y., 1848, The Rhynchophora of America North of Mexico to Proceedings of Am. Philos. Soc., 1876, Classification of the Coleoptera of North America to Smithsonian Miscellaneous Collections, 1883. Died Phila., Nov. 15, 1883; buried Phila.

LEDERER, John, explorer; b. Germany. Came to Va., 1668; condr. expdns. for exploring and discovering passage through mountains; reached top of Blue Ridge Mountains on 1st journey, 1669; traveled from falls of James River West and S.W. through part of N.C. on 2d journey, 1670; traveled from falls of Rappahannock Westward to the mountains, reached the "top of the Apalataen Mountains." on 3d journey, 1670. Author: The Discoveries of John Lederer in Three Several Marches from Virginia to the West of Carolina and Other Parts of the Continent (Mar. 1669- Sept. 1670), written in Latin, translated by Sir William Talbot, published in London, Eng., 1672. Died circa 1670.

LEDYARD, John, explorer; b. Groton, Conn., 1751; s. John and Abigail (Hempstead) L.; divinity student Dartmouth, 1772. Served as cpl. in Marines, accompanied Capt. Cook on his 3d expdn. through No. Pacific, 1776-80, arrested as spy at Irkutsk, Russia, 1788, while attempting to reach West Coast of Am. by crossing Bering Straits and going through Alaska; died during exploratory voyage to Central Africa, undertaken under patronage of African Assn. Author: A Journal of Captain Cook's Last Voyage to the Pacific Ocean, 1783. Died Cairo, Egypt, Jan. 10, 1789.

LEDYARD, William, army officer; b. Groton, Conn., Dec. 6, 1738; s. John and Deborah (Youngs) L.; m. Ann Williams, Jan. 1761, 9 children. Mem. Com. of Correspondence; commd. capt. arty. Continental Army, 1776; fought against Benedict Arnold's Brit. troops at Fort Griswold, Conn., 1781, surrendered after battle in which British suffered heavy losses, after surrender British massacred the Revolutionaries. Killed by British, Sept. 6, 1781.

LEE, Alfred, clergyman; b. Cambridge, Mass., Sept. 9, 1807; s. Benjamin and Elizabeth (Leighton) L.; grad. Harvard, 1827, Gen. Theol. Sem., N.Y.C., 1837; m. Julia White, 1832, 8 children. Ordained priest Episcopal Ch., 1838; pastor in Poquetanuck, Conn., Rockdale, Pa., 1838-41; rector St. Andrew's Ch., Wilmington, Del., 1841-47; became Episcopal bishop of Del., built Episcopal Ch. in Del. from 4 parishes to over 40; rendered episcopal services in Haiti, 1863; made episcopal visit to mission in Mexico (subsequently became fgn. br. P.E. Ch.), 1875; presiding bishop Episcopal Ch., 1884-87. Author: A Life Hid in Christ with God, 1856; Life of the Apostle John in a Series of Practical Discourses, 1857; Eventful Nights in Bible History, 1886. Died Wilmington, Apr. 12, 1887.

LEE, Ann, religious leader; b. Manchester, Eng., Feb. 29, 1736; dau. of John Lee (or Lees); m. Abraham Standerin, Jan. 5, 1762, 4 children. Joined Shaker soc. in Eng., 1758, recognized by sect as its leader in Eng. from 1770; came to Am., 1774; settled in village of Watervliet, nr. Albany, N.Y., 1776, founded Shaker community; called Mother Ann by her followers, who believed her to be 2d appearance of Christ; her group (known as The Millenial Ch.) persecuted because of pacifist doctrines; arrested (with other ch. leaders) for treason for refusal to take oath of allegiance, 1780; conducted religious tour of New Eng. preaching 2d coming of Christ and need for frugality and integrity, 1781. Died Watervliet, Sept. 8, 1784; buried Watervliet.

LEE, Arthur, Continental congressman, diplomatic agt.; b. "Stratford," Westmoreland County, Va., Dec. 20, 1740; s. Thomas and Hannah (Ludwell) L.; M.D., U. Edinburgh (Scotland), 1764; studied law, Lincoln's Inn and Middle Temple, London, Eng., 1766-70; never married. Elected fellow Royal Soc., 1766; wrote Moniter's Letters, also An Appeal to the English Nation, 1769, Junus Americasis (written and published in Eng. in support of Am. colonies), 1770; an agt. (in assn. with Benjamin Franklin) for Mass. in Eng. and France; admitted to London bar, 1775; confidential correspondent for Continental Congress, London, 1775; apptd. (with Benjamin Franklin and Silas Deane) to negotiate a treaty with France, 1776; commr. to Spain, 1777; mem. Va. Ho. of Dels., 1781-83, 85-86; mem. Continental Congress, 1781-84; negotiated Indian treaties of Ft. Stanwix, 1784, Ft. McIntosh, 1785; mem. bd. treasury (apptd. by Continental Congress), 1785-89. Died Urbana, Va., Dec. 12, 1792; buried "Lansdowne," nr. Urbana.

LEE, Charles, army officer; b. Dernhall, Cheshire, Eng., 1731; s. John and Isabella (Bunbury) L. Ensign in father's regt., 1747; lt. 44th Regt., 1751; with Gen. Bradstock's expdn. to Ft. Duquesne, 1755; served under Amherst in capture of Montreal, 1760; maj. 103d Regt., 1761, lt. col., 1762; served under Burgoyne in Portugal in resistance to Spanish invasion, 1762; accompanied Polish embassy to Turkey, 1764; gen. and adjutant Polish Army, 1769; returned and settled in Am., 1773; author "Strictures on a Friendly Address to All Reasonable Americans in Reply to Dr. Myles Cooper" (an incitement to colonial rebellion), 1774; commd. 2d. maj. gen. Continental Army, 1775, in command So. Dept., 1776, played prin. part in victory of Charleston; fought rear guard action in Washington's retreat from N.Y.C.; ambitious to become comdr.-in-chief, became severe critic of Washington, notably in letter to Gen. Gates; captured by British, 1776, while prisoner submitted secret plan to Gen. Howe for defeating Americans; released in prisoner exchange, 1778, put in command of planned attack on Monmouth, retreated instead of attacking and was halted by arrival of Washington, Greene, Steuben and forces; courtmartialed, found guilty of disobedience, misbehavior before enemy and disrespect to comdr.-in-chief, resulting in suspension from command; continued his abuse of Washington, was dismissed from army, 1780. Died Phila., Oct. 2, 1782; buried Christ Ch. Graveyard, Phila.

LEE, Charles, atty. gen.; b. Fauquier County, Va., July 1758; s. Henry and Lucy (Grymes) L.; A.B., Coll. of N.J. (now Princeton), 1775; m. Ann Lee, Feb. 11, 1789; m. 2d, Margaret (Scott) Peyton; 9 children. Served as naval officer of South Potomac, 1777-89; collector Port of Alexandria (Va.), 1789-93; admitted to Pa. bar, 1794; mem. Va. Gen. Assembly from Fairfax County, 1793-95; U.S. atty. gen., 1795-1801; judge of new circuit cts. (created by Judiciary Act of 1801), a leading lawyer before Supreme Ct., successfully pleaded Marbury vs. Madison, defended Aaron Burr in treason trial in Richmond, also before John Marshall; mem. defense staff in impeachment of Judge Chase. Died Fauquier County, June 24, 1815.

LEE, Charles Alfred, physician; b. Salisbury, Conn., Mar. 3, 1801; s. Samuel and Elizabeth (Brown) L.; grad. Williams Coll., 1822; M.D., Berkshire Med. Inst., 1826; m. Hester Mildeberger, 1828, 4 children. Practiced medicine, N.Y.C., 1827; a founder Northern Dispensary, N.Y.C., operator, 1827-32; mem. staff Greenwich Cholera Hosp., 1832-circa 1849; attending physician N.Y. Orphan Asylum, 1832-49; a founder N.Y. Jour. Medicine and Collateral Scis., 1843, editor, 1846-53; prof. pathology Geneva Med. Coll., 1844-47; lectr. medicine Starling Med. Coll., O., 1847; prof. medicine U. Buffalo (N.Y.), 1848-60; lived, practiced medicine, Peekskill, N.Y., from 1850; made study European hosps. for U.S. Govt., 1862-63; sanitation adviser to U.S. Army, 1864-65. Author: (papers) Catalogue of Medicinal Plants in N.Y., 1848, Remarks on Wines and Alcohol, 1871. Editor: Conspectus of Pharmacopeoias . . . (A. T. Thomson), 1843; Principles of Forensic Medicine (W. A. Guy), 1845. Died Peekskill, Feb. 14, 1872.

LEE, Eliza Buckminster, author; b. Portsmouth, N.H., circa 1788; d. Joseph and Sarah (Stevens) Buckminster; m. Thomas Lee, 1827. Established her reputation as literary figure with her translation of autobiography of Jean Paul Richter (published 1842); became well known for biog. and hist. works, especially for translations of German authors, 1840's-50's. Author: Sketches of a New England Village, 1838; Life of Jean Paul Richter, 1842; Naomi, or Boston Two Hundred Years Ago, 1848; Parthenia, or the Last Days of Paganism, 1858. Died Brookline, Mass., June 22, 1864.

LEE, Francis D., architect; b. Charleston, S.C., 1826; grad. City Coll., Charleston, circa 1846; studied architecture in office of Edward C. Jones, Charleston. Became mem. archtl. firm Jones & Lee, Charleston, 1852; designed (with Jones) buildings including St. Luke's Ch. (1859), St. James Methodist Ch., remodeling of old Unitarian Ch., Planters & Mechanics Bank (all Charleston), also Ch. of Holy Cross, Statesburg, N.C.; served to maj., as mil. engr. Gen. Beauregard's staff, Confederate Army, during Civil War; worked on planning and bldg. fortifications in Charleston harbor and improving torpedo defense system; accepted invitation from Napoleon III to visit Paris, France to explain his engring. plans and inventions, after war, later traveled throughout Europe; organized archtl. firm Lee & Annan, St. Louis, 1867; designed (with Annan) works including Mchts. Exchange (1875), Roe, Gay, C. of C. bldgs., 3d Nat. Bank, Bedford Block, Post Grad. Med. Coll., Grand Av. Presbyn. Ch. (all St. Louis). Died 1885.

LEE, Francis Lightfoot, Continental congressman; b. "Stratford," Westmoreland, Va., Oct. 14, 1734; s. Thomas and Hannah (Ludwell) L.; m. Rebecca Tayloe, spring 1769. Mem. Va. Ho. of Burgesses from Loudoun County, 1758-68, from Richmond County, 1769-76; signer Westmoreland Assn. against Stamp Act, 1766; mem. com. forming Va. Com. of Correspondence, 1773; signed call for Va. Conv., 1774, mem. conv., 1775; del. to Continental Congress, 1775-79; a signer Declaration of Independence, 1776; a framer Articles of Confederation, 1777; mem. Va. Senate, 1779-82. Died "Menokin," Richmond County, Va., Jan. 11, 1797.

LEE, Hannah Sawyer, author; b. Newburyport, Mass., 1780; d. Micajah Sawyer; m. George Gardner Lee, Jan. 20, 1807, 3 daus. Began literary career, 1832 (16 years following death of her husband); established reputation for brief works of fiction as well as ednl. tracts and books during 1830's-50's; her works dealing with family finances were widely read. Author: Three Experiments in Living, published in Eng., 1837; Historical Sketches of Old Painters, 1838; The Life and Times of Martin Luther, 1839; The Huguenots in France and America, 1843; Sketches and Stories from Life: for the Young, 1850; Familiar Sketches of Sculpture and Sculptors, 1854. Died Boston, Dec. 27, 1865; buried Boston.

LEE, Henry (Light-Horse Harry), gov. Va.; b. Dumfries, Va., Jan. 29, 1756; s. Henry and Lucy (Grymes) L.; grad. Coll. of N.J. (now Princeton), 1773; m. Matilda Lee, 1782; m. 2d, Anne Hill Carter, June 18, 1793; 7 children including Robert E., Henry. Served as capt. Theodorick Bland's regt. Va. Cavalry, 1776; maj. in charge of Lee's Legion (cavalry corps) which surprised Brit. garrison at Paulus Hook, awarded Gold medal Continental Congress, 1779; maj. Continental Army, 1778, lt. col., 1780, served at Battle of Guilford, beseiged Augusta, Ga., 1781; mem. Va. Ho. of Dels., 1785, 89-91; mem. Congress of Confederation from Va., 1785-88; mem. Va. Conv. that ratified U.S. Constn., 1788; gov. Va., 1792-95; commanded forces sent to suppress Whiskey Insurrection, Pa., 1794; mem. U.S. Ho. of Reps. from Va., 7th Congress, 1799-1801; pronounced George Washington's funeral oration, 1799; imprisoned for debt, 1808-08; injured by mob while in jail for attempting to aid a friend in defending the press of newspaper Fed. Republican, Balt., 1812; spent several years in West Indies recovering health. Author: Memoirs of the War in the Southern Department of the United States, 2 vols., 1812. Died Cumberland Island, Ga., Mar. 25, 1818; buried Cumberland Island, reinterred Lee Chapel, Washington and Lee U., 1913.

LEE, Henry, mcht.; b. Beverly, Mass., Feb. 4, 1782; s. Joseph and Elizabeth (Cabot) L.; attended Phillips Andover Acad.; m. Mary Jackson, June 16, 1809, 6 children. Partner (with his brother Joseph) in trading enterprise, Boston, circa 1800-11; lived in Calcutta, India, 1811-14; in trading ventures with East and West Indies, S.Am., Europe (out of Boston), from 1815; active as spokesman and writer in free trade cause, from 1820; took prominent part in Free Trade Conv., Phila., 1831, prepared appendix of statistics to pamphlet of Gallatin; received electoral votes of S.C. for vice pres. U.S., 1832; ret. from business, 1840. Author: (booklet) Report of a Committee . . . Opposed to a Further Increase of Duties on Importations, 1827; An Exposition of Evidence (printed in Memorial of the Committee Appointed by the Free Trade Convention), 1832. Died Boston, Feb. 6, 1867; buried Boston.

LEE, Henry, author; b. "Stratford," Westmoreland County, Va., May 28, 1787; s. Henry and Matilda Lee; grad. Coll. William and Mary, 1808; m. Anne McCarty, Mar. 1817. Mem. Va. Ho. of Dels. from Westmoreland County, 1810-13; served as maj. 36th Inf., U.S. Army, War of 1812; employee Post Office Dept., also polit. writer for John Calhoun, 1824-26; credited with literary form of Jackson's presdl. inaugural address; apptd. consul-gen. to Algiers, but rejected by unanimous vote of U.S. Senate, 1839; spent later life abroad, mainly in Paris, France. Author: The Campaign of 1781 in the Carolinas, 1824; The Life of Napoleon Bonaparte down to the Peace of Tolentino and the Close of his First Campaign in Italy, 1837. Died Paris, Jan. 30, 1837.

LEE, Jason, missionary; b. Stanstead, Vt. (now Que., Can.), June 28, 1803; s. Daniel and Sarah (Whittaker) L.; attended Wilbraham Acad., Mass., 1829. Minister to Wesleyan Methodists, Stanstead, other Vt. communities, 1830-32; ordained elder New Eng. Conf., Methodist Episcopal Ch., 1832; apptd. to head mission at Ft. Vancouver, 1833 (plan abandoned 1834); established small community on Willamette River, nr. what is now Salem, Ore.; went to Washington, D.C., to petition for territorial status for Ore., 1838; established Methodist missions in Clatsop and Dalles Indian territories, Ore. region; after decline of Indian missions became ardent promoter of settlement in Ore. country; relieved of missionary office, 1844, returned to Mass. Died Stanstead, Mar. 12, 1845; buried Salem, Ore.

LEE, Jesse, clergyman; b. Prince George County, Va., Mar. 12, 1758; s. Nathaniel and Elizabeth Lee. Methodist circuit preacher in Va., Md., N.C., 1783-89; ordained elder Meth. Ch., 1790; pioneer in founding Meth. Ch. in New Eng.; opposed hierarchical authority in Meth. Council and Episcopate; asst. to Bishop Asbury, 1797-1800; presiding elder So. dist. of Meth. Ch. in Va., 1801-15; chaplain U.S. Ho. of Reps., 1809-13, U.S. Senate, 1814; wrote 1st history of Meth. denomination published in U.S., 1808-09; presiding elder, Annapolis, Md., 1816. Author: A Short History of the Methodists in the U.S.A., 1810. Died Hillsborough, Md., Sept. 12, 1816; buried Mt. Olivet Cemetery, Balt.

LEE, John, congressman; b. "Needwood" nr. Frederick, Md., Jan. 30, 1788; s. Thomas Sim Lee; ed. Harvard; studied law. Managed "Needwood"; mem. U.S. Ho. of Reps. (Dem.) from Md., 18th Congress, 1823-25, chmn. com. to escort Marquis de Lafayette from Frederick City to Washington, D.C., 1825; mem. Md. Ho. of Dels., Md. Senate; a proponent Chesapeake & Ohio Canal, Balt. & Ohio R.R. Died N.Y.C., May 17, 1871; buried "Bonnie Brae" (now New Cathedral Cemetery), Balt.

LEE, John Doyle, religious leader; b. Kaskaskia, Ill., Sept. 6, 1812; s. Ralph Lee; m. Agathe Woolsey, July 24, 1833; also 17 polygamous wives; 64 children. Moved to Mo., 1837, became convert Ch. of Jesus Christ of Latter Day Saints; accompanied Mormons in move to Nauvoo, Ill.; Mormon missionary, 1839, 41; active in supporting Joseph Smith's campaign for presidency, 1844; went to Salt Lake City with migration of Mormons, 1847; an organizer band of Mormons and Indians which ambushed group of settlers (falsely alleged to have plundered Mormon settlements), Mountain Meadows, Utah, 1857; tried for murder of settlers, 1875 and 1876, sentenced to death (although several others were equally guilty of perpetrating the massacre). Author: Mormonism Unveiled, 1877. Executed Mountain Meadows, Mar. 23, 1877.

LEE, Joshua, congressman; b. Hudson, N.Y., 1783; studied medicine. Commd. surgeon Col. Avery Smith's Inf. Regt., 1811, served in War of 1812; participated in Battle of Queenstown; supr. Town of Benton (N.Y.), 1815; mem. N.Y. Assembly, 1817, 33; mem. U.S. Ho. of Reps. (Democrat) from N.Y., 24th Congress, 1835-37; unsuccessful candidate for U.S. Senate, 1839. Died Penn Yan, N.Y., Dec. 29, 1842; buried Lake View Cemetery, Penn Yan.

LEE, Luther, clergyman, abolitionist; b. Schoharie, N.Y., Nov. 30, 1800; s. Samuel and Hannah (Williams) L.; m. Mary Miller, July 31, 1835. Admitted on trial as circuit preacher in Methodist Conf., Genesee, N.Y., 1827; preached in frontier N.Y. until 1836; became abolitionist, 1837, organized numerous anti-slavery socs.; Western N.Y. agt. Am. Anti-Slavery Soc., 1838-40; a founder Liberty Party in N.Y., 1840; a founder Wesleyan Meth. Connection of Am. (anti-slavery sect), 1843, pres. Gen. Conf. of this sect, 1844; editor True Wesleyan (ofcl. organ of new group), 1845-circa 1865; held several pastorates in N.Y., Ohio, Mich., 1844-66; prof. Adrian (Mich.) Coll. (founded by Wesleyan Connection) from circa 1860; rejoined Meth. Episcopal Ch., 1867; pastor in Flint, Mich. until 1877. Author: Slavery Examined in the Light of the Bible, 1855; Natural Theology, 1866; Autobiography of the Rev. Luther Lee, 1882. Died Flint, Mar. 23, 1877; buried Flint.

LEE, Moses Lindley, congressman; b. Minisink, N.Y., May 29, 1805; grad. Union Coll., 1827, Coll. Physicians and Surgeons of Western N.Y., 1830. Practiced medicine, Fulton, N.Y.; postmaster Fulton, 1840-44; mem. N.Y. Ho. of Reps., 1847-48; N.Y. Senate, 1855; mem. U.S. Ho. of Reps. (Republican) from N.Y., 36th Congress, 1859-61; resumed practice of medicine, Fulton. Died Petersburg, Va., May 19, 1876; buried Mt. Adnah Cemetery, Fulton.

LEE, Richard, colonial ofcl.; b. Shropshire, Eng., circa 1590; m. Ann, 8 children. Came to Am., 1641, to Northumberland County, Va., 1651; raised tobacco for trade with Eng.; clk. Va. Council; atty. gen. Colony of Va.; mem: Va. Ho. of Burgesses; high sheriff York County, mem. King's Council, sec. of state (all Va.); made treaty (with William Berkely) with Cromwell's forces which ratified in Eng. provided for reorgn. of colony as an independent dominion. Died Northumberland County, Va., 1664.

LEE, Richard Bland, congressman; b. Prince William County, Va., Jan. 20, 1761; s. Henry and Lucy (Grymes) L.; m. Elizabeth Collins, June 19, 1794. Rep. from Loudoun County Va. Ho. of Dels., 1784-88, 96; mem. U.S. Ho. of Reps. (Federalist) from Va., 1st-3d congresses, 1789-95; commr. claims for property destroyed during War of 1812, 1816; judge Orphan's Ct., Washington, D.C., 1819-27; famous for his part in aiding Alexander Hamilton's plan for the assumption of state debts by the fed. govt. in return for setting up the new nation's capital in Washington. Died Mar. 12, 1827.

LEE, Richard Henry, senator; b. "Stratford," Westmoreland County, Va., Jan. 20, 1732; s. Thomas and Hannah (Ludwell) L.; m. Ann Aylett, Dec. 3, 1757; m. 2d, Mrs. Anne Pinckard, 1769; 6 children. Justice of peace Westmoreland County, 1757; mem. Va. Ho. of Burgesses, 1758-75, opposed Stamp Act; mem. com. to draw up address to King, 1764; head of assn. to prevent sale of stamped paper, 1765; helped secure separation of offices of speaker of house and treas., 1765-66; formed Westmoreland Assn. to boycott Brit. goods, 1766; suggested inter-colonial corresponding societies, 1768 (1st used by Mass. and Va., 1773); engaged in tobacco shipping bus., 1768-73; del. to Continental Congress from Va., 1775-79, instructed to propose a gen. colonial independence (resulting in Declaration of Independence); a signer Declaration of Independence, 1776; mem. Va. Ho. of Dels., 1777, 80, 85; del. Congress of Confedn., 1784-87, pres., 1784; del. Va. Conv. to ratify U.S. Constn.; mem. U.S. Senate from Va., 1789-Oct. 8, 1792. Died Chantilly, Va., June 19, 1794; buried family burial ground, "Mt. Pleasant," Va.

LEE, Robert Edward, comdr.-in-chief Confederate Army; b. "Stratford," Westmoreland County, Va., Jan. 19, 1807; s. Henry (Light Horse Harry) and Ann (Carter) L.; grad. U.S. Mil. Acad., 1829; m.

Mary Ann Curtis, June 30, 1831, 7 children including George Washington Custis, William H. Fitzhugh. Brevetted 2d lt. Corps Engrs., U.S. Army; asst. engr. Ft. Monroe, Va., 1831-34; asst. in chief engr.'s office, Washington, D.C., 1834-37; aided in running Ohio-Mich. boundary line, 1835; promoted 1st lt., 1836; supt. engr. for St. Louis harbor, upper Mississippi and Mo. rivers, 1837-41; promoted capt., 1838; stationed Ft. Hamilton, N.Y., 1841-46; asst. engr. U.S. Army, San Antonio, Tex., 1846; served in Mexican War, 1846-48, brevetted col. U.S. Army for gallantry, 1848; in charge of constrn. Ft. Carroll, Baltimore harbor, 1848-52; supt. U.S. Mil. Acad., 1852-55; promoted lt. col. 2d U.S. Cavalry, 1855; commanded detachment which suppressed John Brown's raid at Harper's Ferry, 1859; commanded Dept. of Tex., 1860-Feb. 1861; promoted col. 1st Cavalry, Mar. 1861; declined field command of U.S. Army (privately offered by Francis P. Blair, head of Ho. Com. on Mil. Def.); resigned from U.S. Army, Apr. 20, 1861 (resignation accepted Apr. 25, 1861); accepted command of Va. forces, Apr. 23, 1861; apptd. mil. adviser (with rank of gen.) to Pres. Jefferson Davis, Confederate States Am.; organized defenses of South Atlantic seaboard, Nov. 1861-Mar. 1862; placed in command of Army of No. Va., June 1, 1862; defeated McClellan in Seven Days' Battle, June 25-July 1, 1862; defeated Pope at Battle of 2d Manassas, Aug. 30, 1862; started campaign into Md., was checked at Battle of Antietam (Md.), Sept. 1862; defeated Burnside at Battle of Fredericksburg (Va.), Dec. 1862; defeated Hooker at Battle of Chancellorsville (Va.), May 1863; lost Battle of Gettysburg, July 1-4, 1863; promoted comdr.-in-chief of all Confederate Armies, Feb. 6, 1865; conducted (with inferior forces) defensive operations against Gen. Grant, including battles of Spotsylvania and Cold Harbor, siege of Richmond, May 1864-Apr. 1865; surrendered to Gen. Grant at Appomattox Court House, Va., Apr. 9, 1865; pres. Washington Coll., Lexington, Va., 1866-70 (name later changed to Washington and Lee U. in his honor); spent his last years advocating acceptance of defeat and rebuilding of South; his estate "Arlington" is now site of Arlington Nat. Cemetery. Died Lexington, Oct. 12, 1870; buried Washington and Lee University.

LEE, Samuel Phillips, naval officer; b. Fairfax County, Va., Feb. 13, 1812; s. Francis Lightfoot and Jane (Fitzgerald) L.; m. Elizabeth Blair, Apr. 27, 1843, 1 child, Francis Preston. Apptd. midshipman U.S. Navy, 1825, on coast survey duty, 1842-55, in command coast survey brig. Washington during Mexican War; commanded ship Dolphin, 1851, ship Oneida in Farragut's expdn. against New Orleans, 1862; acting rear adm. in command N. Atlantic blocking squadron off Va. and N.C., 1862; comdr. Mississippi Squadron, 1864; head Signal Service, 1870; promoted rear adm., 1870, commanded N. Atlantic Squadron, 1870-72. Died Silver Spring, Md., June 5, 1897; buried Arlington (Va.) Nat. Cemetery.

LEE, Silas, congressman; b. Concord, Mass., July 3, 1760; grad. Harvard, 1784; studied law. Admitted to the bar; mem. Mass. Ho. of Reps., 1793, 97, 98; mem. U.S. Ho. of Reps. (Federalist) from Mass., 6th-7th congresses, 1799-Aug. 20, 1801; U.S. atty. for Me. dist. (apptd. by Pres. Jefferson), 1802-14; justice of peace and of quorum, 1803; probate judge, 1805-14; chief judge Ct. Common Pleas, 1810. Died Wiscasset, Me., Mar. 1, 1814; buried Evergreen Cemetery, Wiscasset.

LEE, Thomas, jurist; b. Charleston, S.C., Dec. 1, 1769; s. William and Anne (Theus) L.; m. Kezia Miles, Feb. 9, 1792, 5 children including Thomas. Admitted to bar, 1790; asso. judge or judge S.C. cts. of common pleas and sessions, 1791; solictor for So. Circuit of S.C. 1791; cashier lower house S.C. Legislature, 1798, 1800, clk., 1802; comptroller gen. S.C., 1804; presdl. elector, 1816; pres. Bank of S.C., 1817; U.S. dist. judge for S.C., 1823; deacon Unitarian Ch., Charleston. Died Charleston, Oct. 24, 1839; buried Unitarian Churchyard.

LEE, Thomas, congressman; b. Phila., Nov. 28, 1780; attended common schs., Chester Valley, Pa. Moved to Leesburg, N.J., circa 1798, to Port Elizabeth, N.J., 1805; mcht., shipbuilder, landowner; judge ct. common pleas, 1813-15; mem. N.J. Gen. Assembly, 1814-15; postmaster of Port Elizabeth, 1818-33, 46-49; mem. U.S. Ho. of Reps. (Democrat) from N.J., 23d-24th congresses, 1833-37; founder Port Elizabeth Library and Acad. Died Port Elizabeth, Nov. 2, 1856; buried Methodist Episcopal Churchyard, Port Elizabeth.

LEE, Thomas Sim, gov. Md.; b. Prince George's County, Md., Oct. 29, 1745; s. Thomas and Christiana (Sim) L.; m. Mary Diggs, Oct. 27, 1771, 10 children. Mem. Md. Provincial Council, 1777; maj. battalion from Prince George's County; gov. Md., 1779-82, 92-94, supported all efforts to defeat British in Revolutionary War years; del. to Continental Congress, 1783-84; mem. Md. Conv. which ratified U.S. Constn., 1788; presdl. elector, 1792. Died on estate, Frederick County, Md., Nov. 9, 1819; buried Roman Catholic Cemetery nr. Upper Marlboro, Md.

LEE, William, diplomat; b. "Stratford," Westmoreland County, Va., Aug. 31, 1739; s. Thomas and Hannah (Ludwell) L.; m. Hannah Ludwell Mar. 7, 1769. Sheriff of London (Eng.) (only American ever to hold office), 1773, alderman, 1775; apptd. by secret com. of Congress as comml. agt. at Nantes, France, 1777, became involved in Lee-Deane controversy; negotiator treaty of commerce between Netherlands and Am., which (though never ratified) was ostensible cause of war between Eng. and Netherlands; commr. to Berlin and Vienna, 1777, failed in attempts to get Germany and Austria to recognize America. Died nr. Williamsburg, Va., June 27, 1795.

LEE, William Henry Fitzhugh, army officer, congressman; b. Arlington. Va., May 31, 1837; s. Gen. Robert Edward and Mary Ann (Custis) L.; grad. Harvard, 1857; m. Charlotte Wickham, 1859; m. 2d, Mary Bolling, 1867. Served as 2d lt. 6th Inf., U.S. Army, 1857-59; commd. capt., then maj. of cavalry Confederate States Army, 1861; chief of cavalry in W. Va. Campaign, 1861; lt. col., then col. 9th Va. Cavalry, 1861-62, under command of Gen. J. B. Stuart; participated in 2d Battle of Manassas, Battle of Turner's Pass, raid on Chambersburg (Pa.), 1862; commd. brig. gen., commanded brigade at Battle of Chancellorsville, 1862, also in Fredericksburg, Gettysburg campaigns; promoted maj. gen. cavalry, 1864; pres. Va. Agrl. Soc.; mem. Va. Senate, 1875-79; mem. U.S. Ho. of Reps. from Va., 50th-52d congresses, 1887-91. Died Alexandria, Va., Oct. 15, 1891; buried Lee Mausoleum, Lexington, Va.

LEE, William Little, jurist; b. Sandy Hill, N.Y., Feb. 8, 1821; s. Stephen and Mary (Little) L.; grad. Norwich U., 1842; postgrad. Harvard Law Sch.; m. Catherine E. Newton, 1849. Judge for Island of Oahu, Hawaii; chief justice Hawaii, 1847, mem. privy council, 1847; drafted penal code (basis of Hawaiian criminal laws today), 1850; mem. Hawaii Ho. of Reps., 1851, speaker; chief justice of what is now Supreme Ct. of Hawaii, 1852; minister to U.S., 1855; negotiated reciprocity treaty with U.S. sec. of state. Died Honolulu, Hawaii, May 28, 1857.

LEEDOM, John Peter, congressman; b. Adams County, O., Dec. 20, 1847; grad. Smith's Merc. Coll., Portsmouth, O., 1863. Tchr. pub. schs., Portsmouth; engaged in farming; elected clk. Adams County Ct. of Common Pleas, 1874, re-elected, 1877; mem. Ohio Democratic Central Committee, 1879; mem. U.S. Ho. of Reps. (Dem.) from Ohio, 47th Congress, 1881-83; sgt. at arms U.S. Ho. of Reps., 1884-90. Died Toledo, O., Mar. 18, 1895; buried Odd Fellows Cemetery, Manchester, O.

LEEDS, Daniel, surveyor; b. Kent, Eng., 1652; son of Thomas Leeds; m. Ann Stacy, Feb. 1681; m. 2d, Dorothy Young, 1682; m. 3d, Jane Revell, circa 1702; 2 sons, Titan, Felix. Moved to Burlington, N.J., 1677; surveyor gen. of West Jersey Province, 1682-circa 1700, made 1st map of Burlington, 1696; mem. N.J. Provincial Assembly, 1682; published Almanac, Phila., 1687, issued 2d edit. which involved him in controversy with Quakers of Phila., 1688; mem. N.J. Gov.'s Council, 1702-08. Author numerous pamphlets including The Temple of Wisdom for the Little World, 1688, News of a Trumpet Sounding in the Wilderness, 1697, The Great Mistery of Fox-Craft Discovered, 1705. Died Burlington, Sept. 28, 1720; buried Burlington.

LEEDS, John, mathematician, astronomer; b. Bay Hundred, Talbot County, Md., May 18, 1705; s. Edward and Ruth (Ball) L.; m. Rachel Harrison, Feb. 14, 1726, 3 children. Commr. justice of peace Talbot County, 1734; clk. Talbot County Ct., 1738-77; regular mem. commn. from Md. to mark off long-disputed Md.-Pa. boundary line, 1762; observed transit of Venus, obtained results published in Royal Soc. London's Philos. Transactions . . . for the Year 1769 (pub. 1770); treas. Eastern Shore dist., Md., 1766; justice Provincial Ct., 1766; naval officer Port of Pocomoke, 1766; surveyor gen. Md., 1766-circa 1775, after 1783-90. Died Wade's Point, Md., Mar. 1790.

LEESER, Isaac, clergyman, coll. pres.; b. Westphalia, Prussia, Dec. 12, 1806; son of Uri Leeser; attended Gymnasium of Munster (Germany), circa 1822-23. Came to U.S., 1824, settled in Richmond, Va.; rabbi Mikveh Israel Congregation, Richmond, 1819-50, Beth El Emeth Congregation, Richmond, 1857-67; operated sch. in home for Jewish children; founder, editor The Occident and Am. Jewish Advocate, 1843-68; conservative in doctrinal issues; travelled widely in U.S., helped found many Jewish synagogues; a founder Maimonides Coll., Richmond, pres., 1867-68. Author: The Jews and the Mosaic Law, 1833; Hebrew Spelling Book, 1838; Catechism for Young Children, 1839; numerous other textbooks for Jewish students. Died Richmond, Feb. 1, 1868.

LEET, Isaac, congressman; b. nr. Washington, Pa 1801; grad. Washington (now Washington and Je ferson) Coll., 1822; studied law. Admitted to P bar, 1826, began practice in Washington; trea Washington County, 1826-30, dep. atty. gen., 183 34; mem. Pa. Senate, 1834-38; mem. U.S. Ho. Reps. (Democrat) from Pa., 26th Congress, 183 41. Died Washington, Pa., June 10, 1844; buri old Cooke pvt. graveyard nr. Washington.

LEETE, William, colonial gov.; b. Huntingto shire, Eng., circa 1613; s. John and Anna (Shute L.; m. Anna Payne, 1638; m. 2d, Sarah Ruthe ford; m. 3d, Mary Street. Came to Am., 163 founder Guilford, Conn., mem. bd. trustees ac ing as temporary govt., town sec. or clk., 1639-6 magistrate, 1651-83; rep. New Haven (Conn.) C lony in New Eng. Confederation, 1655-64; go New Haven, 1661-65; magistrate's asst., 1662-6 dep. gov. Conn. Colony, 1669-76; rep. from Con in New Eng. Confederation, 1673, 78, pres. b commrs.; gov. Conn., 1676-82. Died Hartford, Ap 16, 1683; buried 1st Ch., Hartford.

LEFEVER, Joseph, congressman; b. Strasbu Twp., nr. Paradise, Pa., Apr. 3, 1760; attende common schs. Engaged in farming; mem. U.S. H of Reps. (Democrat) from Pa., 12th Congress, 181 13; resumed farming. Died Paradise Twp., Pa., Oc 17, 1826; buried Carpenter's Graveyard, Paradis Twp.

LEFEVER, Peter Paul, clergyman; b. Roulers, Be gium; s. Charles and Albertine-Angeline (Muylle L.; studied with Lazarists, Paris, France, circ 1824-27; attended diocesan sem., St. Louis, 182 30. Came to America, 1828, settled in St. Louis ordained priest Roman Catholic Ch., 1831; missio ary Ralls County, Mo., to frontier settlements i Southern Ia. and Western Ill. plus Eastern Mo. 1832-40; consecrated bishop coadjutor of Detroit 1841, head Diocese of Detroit, 1841-69, increase parishes from 18 to over 170; founded (with bisho of Louisville) Am. Coll. at Louvain to obtain priests introduced Sisters of Notre Dame and Sisters of Char ity; founded orphanage, hosp. and insane asylum initiated missions to convert Indians in Diocese Died Detroit, Mar. 4, 1869; buried Cathedral o St. Peter and St. Paul, Detroit.

LEFFEL, James, inventor, mfr.; b. Botetour County, Va., Apr. 19, 1806; m. Mary Croft, Jul 4, 1830, 2 children. Designed, built and operate water power saw mill outside of Springfield, O on Mad River; patented waterwheels, 1845; es tablished and operated by waterpower 1st cotto mill and machine shop in Springfield, 1845; pa tented lever jack, 1850, two types of cookin stoves, 1852, double turbine wheel, 1862; organ ized James Leffel & Co., 1864. Died Springfield June 11, 1866.

LEFFERTS, John, congressman; b. Bklyn., Dec 17, 1785; attended pub. schs. Mem. U.S. Ho. o Reps. (Democrat) from N.Y., 13th Congress, 1813 15; del. N.Y. Constl. Conv., 1821; mem. N.Y. Senate, 1820-25. Died Bklyn., Sept. 18, 1829; buried Greenwood Cemetery, Bklyn.

LEFFERTS, Marshall, engr.; b. Bklyn., Jan. 15, 1821; s. Leffert and Amelia (Cozine) L.; m. Mary Allen, June 4, 1845, 5 sons, 2 daus. Surveyor, engr., Bklyn., circa 1840-49; pres. N.Y. & New Eng. and N.Y. State Telegraph cos., 1849-50; owner iron factory, 1850-60; chief elec. engr. Am. Tel. & Tel. Co., 1860-61, 61-66, devised instruments for detection of elec. flaws; col. N.Y. 7th Regt. of Volunteers, 1861; head news agy. Western Union Co., 1866-71 pres. Gold & Stock Telegraph Co., N.Y., 1871-76; cons. engr. Atlantic Cable Co., 1871-76. Died nr. Phila., July 3, 1876; buried N.Y.C.

LEFFLER, Isaac, lawyer, legislator; b. Washington County, Pa., Nov. 25, 1788; s. Jacob and Jane (Smith) L.; m. Rebecca Forman, Nov. 1814; m. 2d, Lethenia Mitchell, 1832. Admitted to the bar; mem. Va. Legislature, 1817-19, 23-27, 32-33 mem. Va. Bd. Pub. Works, 1827; mem. U.S. Ho. of Reps. from Va., 20th Congress, 1827-29; admitted to practice of law in Territorial Cts. of Mich., 1835; elected to Wis. Territorial Legislature, 1836, reelected, chosen speaker; presided at conv. at Burington (Ia.), 1837, helped organize Ia. country into separate teerritory; mem. Ia. Territorial Ho. of Reps., 1841; U.S. marshall for Ia. dist., until 1845; receiver of public moneys for the Chariton Land Dist. of Ia., 1852. Died Chariton, Ia., Mar. 8, 1866; buried Aspen Grove Cemetery, Burlington.

LEFFLER, Shepherd, legislator; b. Washington County, Pa., Apr. 24, 1811; s. Jacob and Jane (Smith) L.; grad. Jefferson Coll., 1833; m. Elizabeth Parrott, 1840. Went to Ia. Territory, 1835; mem. Ia. Territorial Ho. of Reps., 1839, Ia. Territorial Council, 1841, served in either house or council until 1846; del. from Des Moines County to 1st Ia. Constl. Conv., 1844; mem. of conv. in which constn. was framed with present Ia. boundaries, 1846; mem. U.S. Ho. of Reps. (Democrat) from Ia., 29th-31st congresses, 1846-51. Died Sept. 7, 1879; buried Aspen Grove Cemetery, Burlington, Ia.

LEFLORE, Greenwood, Indian chieftain, state senator; b. Jackson, Miss., June 3, 1800; s. Louis and Rebecca (Cravat) LaFleur (parents French-Canadian and Indian); m. Rosa Donly; m. 2d, Elizabeth Cody (or Coody) (niece of Chief Ross of Cherokees); m. 3d, Priscilla James Donly; 3 children. Became chief of Choctaw Indians, circa 1820; chose to remain in Miss. by treaty of Dancing Rabbit Creek, Sept. 15, 1830, became citizen (majority of tribe were removed to Okla.); mem. Miss Senate, 1841-44; built Town of Leflore (Miss.) for his cotton business; Greenwood (Miss.) named after him. Died Aug. 31, 1865.

LEFTWICH, Jabez, congressman; b. nr. Liberty (now Bedford), Va., Sept. 22, 1765; attended rural schs. Mem. Va. Ho. of Dels., 1801-09; insp. gen. with rank of col. on staff of Gen. Joel Leftwich (his brother) during War of 1812; mem. U.S. Ho. of Reps. from Va., 17th-18th congresses, 1821-25; moved to Madison County, Ala., 1825, engaged in merc. bus., farming; mem. Ala. Ho. of Reps. Died nr. Huntsville, Ala., June 22, 1855; buried Maple Hill Cemetery, Huntsville.

LEFTWICH, John William, congressman; b. Liberty (now Bedford), Va., Sept. 7, 1826; grad. Phila. Med. Coll., 1850. Engaged in merc. bus., Memphis, Tenn.; mem. U.S. Ho. of Reps. (Democrat) from Tenn., 39th Congress, July 24, 1866-67; del. Dem. Nat. Conv., N.Y.C., 1868; mayor Memphis, 1869-70; contested election to 41st U.S. Congress, died en route to Washington (D.C.) to prosecute case. Died Lynchburg, Va., Mar. 6, 1870; buried Elmwood Cemetery, Memphis.

LEGARE, Hugh Swinton, congressman, atty. gen., diplomat; b. Charleston, S.C., Jan. 2, 1797; s. Solomon and Mary (Swinton) L.; grad. S.C. Coll., 1814. Mem. lower house S.C. Legislature from Charleston, 1820-22, 24-30; editor, contbr. Southern Review, 1828-32; atty. gen. S.C., 1830; U.S. charge d'affaires in Belgium, 1832-36; mem. U.S. Ho. of Reps. from S.C., 25th Congress, 1837-39; U.S. atty. gen. under Pres. Tyler, 1841-43; became U.S. sec. of state, May 9, 1843 ad interim after resignation of Daniel Webster). Died Boston, June 20, 1843; buried Magnolia Cemetery, Charleston.

LEGARÉ, James Mathewes, writer, painter; b. Charleston, S.C., Nov. 26, 1823; studied painting St. Mary's Coll., Balt. Exhibited several landscapes, Charleston, 1843, 56; drawing master in pvt. home, Augusta, Ga., 1847; published volume of poems Orta-Undis and Other Poems, 1848; settled in Aiken, S.C., circa 1847. Died Aiken, May 30, 1859.

LEGGETT, Mortimer Dormer, supt. schs., army officer, electric co. exec.; b. Ithaca, N.Y., Apr. 19, 1821; s. Isaac and Mary (Strong) L.; studied Willoughby Med. Coll.; m. Marilla Wells, July 9, 1844; m. 2d, Weltha Post, 1879; 1 child. Admitted to bar, 1844; founder 1st free grade sch. system west of Alleghany Mountains, Akron, O., 1846, supt. schs., 1846-49; supt. schs., Warren, O., 1849-55; prof. law and pleading Ohio Law Coll., 1856; supt. schs., Zanesville, O., 1857; commd. col. 18th Ohio Volunteers; served as brig. gen. in command brigade in fight along the Mississippi River, 1862; brevetted maj. gen., 1863; fought at battles of Corinth, Shiloh, Vicksburg, Atlanta; marched with Sherman through South; commd. maj. gen. U.S. Volunteers, resigned 1866; U.S. patent commr., 1871-74; 1st pres. Brush Electric Co. (later absorbed into Gen. Electric Co.), 1884. Died Jan. 6, 1896.

LEGGETT, William, journalist; b. N.Y.C., Apr. 30, 1801; s. Abraham and Catherine (Wylie) L.; attended Georgetown Coll., 1818-19; m. Almira Waring, 1828. Lived in Ill., 1819-22; midshipman U.S. Navy, 1822-26; contbr. to jours., newspapers, N.Y.C., 1826-28; founder Critic, weekly jour., N.Y.C., 1828; partner, asso. editor (under William Cullen Bryant) Evening Post, newspaper, N.Y.C., 1829-34, editor, 1834-35, adhered to Locofoco group Democratic Party, supported Jackson adminstrn., opposed recharter of Bank U.S. and slavery; editor Plaindealer, newspaper, N.Y.C., 1836-37; editor daily Examiner, 1837-38, advocated free trade, trade unions; apptd. agt. to Guatemala by Pres. Van Buren, 1839, died before assuming duties. Author: A Collection of the Writings of William Leggett, published 1840. Died N.Y.C., May 29, 1839; buried N.Y.C.

LEHMAN, William Eckart, congressman; b. Phila., Aug. 21, 1821; grad. U. Pa., 1841; studied law. Admitted to Pa. bar, 1844, began practice in Phila.; apptd. post office examiner for N.Y. and Pa. by Pres. Polk; mem. U.S. Ho. of Reps. (Democrat) from Pa., 37th Congress, 1861-63; U.S. provost marshal for 1st Pa. dist. with rank of capt., 1863-65. Died Atlantic City, N.J., July 19, 1895; buried St. Peter's Episcopal Ch. Cemetery, Phila.

LEIB, Michael, surgeon, senator; b. Phila., Jan. 8, 1760; s. Johann George and Margaretha (Liebheit) L.; m. Susan Kennedy, 1808, 2 children. Served as surgeon Phila. Militia, 1780-81; physician Phila. Dispensary, 1786-93, Phila. Almshouse an Hosp., 1788-90, Bush Hill Hosp., 1793, Lazaretto Hosp., 1800; corporator Coll. Physicians of Phila.; mem. Pa. Prison Soc.; mem. Pa. Assembly, 1795-98, 1817-18; mem. U.S. Ho. of Reps. (Republican) from Pa., 6th-8th congresses, 1799-1805; Democratic presdl. elector, 1808; served as brig. gen. Pa. Militia, 1807-11; mem. U.S. Senate from Pa., 1809-14; postmaster Phila., 1814-15; mem. Pa. Senate, 1818-21; prothonatary U.S. Dist. Ct. for City and County of Phila. Died Phila., Dec. 22, 1822; buried St. John's Lutheran Churchyard, Phila.

LEIB, Owen D., congressman; b. Pa.; studied medicine. Began practice of medicine, Catawissa, Pa.; mem. U.S. Ho. of Reps. (Democrat) from Pa., 29th Congress, 1845-47. Died Catawissa, June 17, 1848.

LEIDY, Joseph, naturalist; b. Phila., Sept. 9, 1823; s. Philip and Catherine (Mellick) L.; M.D., U. Pa., 1844; m. Anna Harden, Aug. 1864. Lectr., Franklin Med. Coll., Phila., 1846-53; prof. anatomy U. Pa., 1853-91; surgeon Satterlee Army Hosp., Phila., 1861-65; prof. natural history Swarthmore Coll., 1870-85; pioneer investigator in fields of vertebrate paleontology and parasitology; pres. Acad. Natural Scis. Phila., 1881-91; recipient Lyell medal Geol. Soc. London. Author: (articles including) On the Fossil Horse of America, pub. in Proceedings of Acad. Natural Scis. Phila., 1847; The Ancient Fauna of Nebraska, pub. in Smithsonian Contributions to Knowledge, Vol. VI, 1854; Fresh Water Rhizopods of North America, pub. as Monograph XII of Hayden Survey, 1879. Died Phila., Apr. 29, 1891; buried Phila.

LEIDY, Paul, congressman; b. Hemlock Twp., Pa., Nov. 13, 1813; attended common schs.; studied law. Apprenticed as tailor; taught sch., Danville, Pa., several years; admitted to Pa. bar, 1837, began practice in Danville; dist. atty. Montour County (Pa.), 1852-57; mem. U.S. Ho. of Reps. (Democrat) from Pa., 35th Congress, Dec. 7, 1857-59. Died Danville, Sept. 11, 1877; buried Odd Fellows Cemetery, Danville.

LEIGH, Benjamin Watkins, senator; b. Chesterfield County, Va., June 18, 1781; s. Rev. William and Elizabeth (Watkins) L.; grad. Coll. William and Mary, 1802; m. Mary Watkins; m. 2d, Susan Colston; m. 3d, Julia Wickham; numerous children. Admitted to Va. bar, 1802; mem. Va. Ho. of Dels., 1811-13; supervised preparation of state legal code, 1819; represented Va. in boundary dispute with Ky., 1822; mem. Va. Constl. Conv. 1829-30, represented interests of slave-holding planters of Eastern Va.; reporter Va. Supreme Ct. Appeals, 1829-41; commr. from Va. to persuade S.C. to withdraw nullification, 1833; mem. U.S. Senate from Va., 1834-36, refused to comply with Va. Legislature's instrns. to vote for expunging censure of Jackson, 1836. Died Feb. 2, 1849; buried Shockoe Cemetery, Richmond, Va.

LEIGHTON, William, glass mfr.; b. Edinburgh, Scotland, circa 1810; son of Thomas Leighton; m. Mary Needham, Mar. 8, 1829, 1 son, William. With New Eng. Glass Co., Cambridge, Mass., 1826-62, became expert in chemistry of glass mfg.; developed method of producing ruby glass, 1848-49; partner, supt. Hobbs, Brockunier & Co., glass mfg. firm, Wheeling, W.Va., 1863-68; devised numerous improvements in glass making processes, including low cost process for mfg. lime-flint glass (1864). Died Wheeling, 1868.

LEIPER, George Gray, congressman; b. Phila., Feb. 3, 1786; grad. U. Pa., 1803. Moved to "Lapidea," Delaware County, Pa., 1810, engaged in logging; operated bark mills, stone quarries; served as 1st lt. Delaware County Fencibles, 1814; mem. Pa. Ho. of Reps., 1822-23; mem. U.S. Ho. of Reps. (Democrat) from Pa., 21st Congress, 1829-31; asso. judge Delaware County Cts., 1843-51. Died "Lapidea," Nov. 18, 1868; buried Ridley Presbyn. Ch. Cemetery, Ridley Twp., Pa.

LEIPER, Thomas, mcht.; b. Lanark, Scotland, Dec. 15, 1745; s. Thomas and Helen (Hamilton) L.; m. Elizabeth Gray, Nov. 3, 1778. Came to Am., 1763, settled in Md., then in Phila. from 1765; established tobacco and snuff factory, Delaware County, Pa., circa 1770; leader in opposition to British, 1773-74; mem. 1st troop Phila. City Cavalry; participated in battles of Trenton, Princeton, Brandywine, and Germantown; began operation stone quarry nr. factory, 1780; a prominent anti-Federalist in Pa. in 1790's; pres. Phila. Common Council, 1801-05, 08-10, 12-14; dir. Bank of U.S., 1825; a founder Franklin Inst., Phila., 1823. Died Delaware County, July 6, 1825.

LEISLER, Jacob, b. Frankfort, Germany, Mar. 1640; s. Rev. Jacob Victorius and Susanna (Adelheid) Leyssler; m. Elsie Tymens, Apr. 11, 1663. Came to Am. as soldier in service Dutch West India Co., 1660; bought land as refuge for persecuted Huguenots, New Rochelle, N.Y.; judge N.Y. Ct. Admiralty, 1683; served as capt. N.Y. Militia; headed movement parallel with English Revolution of 1689 which disposed Jacobite lt. gov. Francis Nicholson of N.Y., 1689; assumed authority of royal gov. N.Y., 1689; opposed by wealthy traders, large landowners and upper classes, but backed by middle class and artisans; assumed functions of royal lt. gov. without formal authority, underwent military attack in Ft. William, laid down his power on arrival of Henry Slaughter as gov. N.Y., 1691; tried for treason, 1691. Executed N.Y.C., May 16, 1691.

LEITER, Benjamin Franklin, congressman; b. Leitersburg, Md., Oct. 13, 1813; studied law. Sch. tchr., Md., 1830-34, Ohio, 1834-42; admitted to Ohio bar, 1842, began practice in Canton; justice of peace; mayor Canton, 10 years; mem. Ohio Ho. of Reps., 1848-49, speaker, 1849; mem. U.S. Ho. of Reps. (Republican) from Ohio, 34th-35th congresses, 1855-59. Died Canton, June 17, 1866; buried West Lawn Cemetery, Canton.

Le JAU, Francis, clergyman; b. Angers, France, 1665; M.A., Trinity Coll., Dublin, Ireland, 1693, B.D., 1696; m. Jeanette Huguenin, 1690; m. 2d, Elizabeth Harrison, 1706; 2 children. Ordained priest Ch. of Eng., 1696; canon St. Paul's Cathedral, London, Eng., 1696-1700; Anglican missionary in West Indies, 1700-06; came to Am., 1706, settled in Goose Creek, S.C.; pastor Anglican Ch., Goose Creek, 1706-17, active in educating slaves and Indians, worked for humane treatment of slaves; rector St. Phillips's Ch., Charleston, S.C., also commissary of Bishop of London, 1717. Died Charleston, Sept. 15, 1717; buried Charleston.

LELAND, John, clergyman; b. Grafton, Mass., May 14, 1754; s. James and Lucy (Warren) L.; m. Sarah Divine, Sept. 30, 1776, 9 children. Licensed as preacher in Baptist Ch., Mass., 1774; Bapt. preacher in Orange County, Va., 1777-91; leader in movement to disestablish Episcopal Ch. in Va.; advocate abolition of slavery; lived in Cheshire, Mass., 1791-1841, active in preaching and Bapt. missionary work; worked for disestablishment of Congregational ch. in Mass.; Republican mem. Mass. Legislature, 1811. Author: Short Essays on Government, 1820. Died Cheshire, Jan. 14, 1841; buried Cheshire.

LEMKE, Peter Henry, missionary; b. Rhena, Mecklenburg, July 27, 1796; studied U. Rostock (Germany), 1815. Ordained priest Roman Catholic Ch., 1826; came to U.S., 1834, served Holy Trinity Ch., Phila.; in charge of mission, Ebensburg, Pa., 1834-37; engaged in farming, Pa., 1837-40; founded settlement, built ch., Carrolltown, Pa., 1840; served chs., Reading, Pa., also Phila., circa 1846-51; mem. Benedictine Brotherhood, 1851-55; missionary nr. Atchison, Kan., 1855-58; travelled in Germany on behalf of Am. missions, 1859-60; in charge of St. Michael's Parish, Elizabeth, N.J., 1861-71; founded Benedictine Acad., Elizabeth; built and served St. Henry's Ch., Elizabeth, 1871-76. Died Carrolltown, Nov. 29, 1882.

LeMOYNE, Francis Julius, physician, abolitionist; b. Washington, Pa., Sept. 4, 1798; s. John Julius and Nancy (McCulley) LeM.; grad. Washington Coll., 1815; attended Jefferson Med. Coll., circa 1818-20; m. Madeleine Bureau, 1823, 3 sons, 5 daus. Practiced medicine, Washington, Pa., 1823-53; became leader in Abolitionist Movement, 1830's; Liberty Party candidate for vice pres. U.S., 1840; Abolitionist candidate for gov. Pa., 1841, 44, 47; an organizer Underground Railroad in Pa.; pioneer advocate of cremation, 1876-79; endowed LeMoyne Normal Inst. for Negroes, Memphis, Tenn.; founded professorships at Washington and Jefferson Coll., 1872, 79, trustee, from 1830. Died Washington, Pa., Oct. 14, 1879.

Le MOYNE, Jacques de Morgues, artist. Earliest artist known to have visited continental U.S.; accompanied Laudonnière's expdn. to Fla., Ga. and Carolinas, 1564; one of survivors of Huguenot settlement on St. Johns River, Fla. (destroyed by Spanish, 1565); painted watercolor views of Am. scenes and natural curiosities, engraved and published with his narrative of expdn.; settled in London, painted several watercolors of English plants and animals. Died Eng., 1588.

Le MOYNE, Jean Baptiste (sieur de Bienville), Colonial gov.; b. Montreal, Can., Feb. 23, 1680; s. Charles and Catherine (Tierry) Le Moyne. Served with French Navy, 1692-97; explored Red River, 1700; French gov. La., 1701-12, 18-26, 33-43; built Ft. Lewis, 1702; founder Mobile (Ala.), 1710; commanded La., 1717; founder New Orleans, 1718; awarded cross of Order of St. Louis. Died France, Mar. 7, 1767.

LE MOYNE, Pierre (sieur d' Iberville), army officer; b. Canada, July 1661; son of Charles (Sieur de Longueuil) and Catherine Tierry (Primot) Le M.; m. Marie Thérèse Pollet de la Comte Pocatière, Oct. 8, 1693, 2 children. Served in French Navy; mem. Chevalier de Troyes' expdn. against English at James Bay, 1686; led piratical raids against Hudson Bay Co. outposts for over 10 years, until Peace of Ryswick; led expdn. which founded La., 1698. Died July 9, 1706.

LENEY, William Satchwell, engraver; b. London, Eng.; s. Alexander and Susanna Leney; m. Sarah White, 9 children. Engraver, London, 1790-1805; came to Am., 1805, settled in N.Y.C.; produced plates for book and mag. illustrations; did portrait plates of numerous public figures including Patrick Henry (painted by Sully), John Adams (Copley), Capt. Lawrence (Stuart); partner (with William Rollinson) in portrait engraving firm, N.Y. C., 1812-20; moved to Longue Point, nr. Montreal, Can., 1820, became banknote engraver for Bank of Montreal. Died Longue Point.

L'ENFANT, Pierre Charles, army engr., city planner; b. Paris, France, Aug. 2, 1754; s. Pierre and Marie (Leullier) L'E. Brevetted lt. French Colonial Forces, commd. 1st lt. engrs., 1776; came to Am. with Lafayette, 1777, joined Continental Army, commd. capt. engrs., 1778; maj. by spl. resolution of Congress, 1783; surveyor and planner new fed. city of Washington, D.C., forced to resign because his plans were so expensive, 1792 (govt. began remodeling city along his original lines, 1901); employed to lay out "Capital scene of manufactures" for Soc. for Useful Manufactures, 1792; temporary engr. at Ft. Mifflin on Mud Island in Delaware River, 1794; engr. at Ft. Washington on Potomac River, 1812; mem. Soc. of Cincinnati. Died Prince George's County, Va., June 14, 1825; buried Arlington (Va.) Nat. Cemetery.

LENNOX, Charlotte Ramsay, author; b. N.Y., 1720; dau. of James Ramsay; m. Alexander Lennox, Oct. 6, 1747, 1 son, 1 dau. Sent to Eng. for her edn., 1735, remained there rest of her life; published her 1st book, 1747; became friend of Samuel Johnson and Henry Fielding; wrote romances, plays, translated several plays from French; editor Lady's Museum (women's mag.), 1760-61. Author: Poems on Several Occasions, 1747; Shakespeare Illustrated, 1753; (novels) The Life of Harriot Stuart, 1750, The Female Quixote, 1752, The History of Henrietta, 1758; (plays) Old City Manners, 1775; The Sister, 1769. Died London, Eng., Jan. 4, 1804; buried London.

LENOX, James, bibliophile, philanthropist; b. N. Y.C., Aug. 19, 1800; s. Robert and Rachel (Carmer) L.; grad. Columbia. Admitted to bar, N.Y.C., 1822, never practiced law; became partner in father's real estate firm; assembled 1 of best collections of Bibles in nation, including 1st Gutenberg Bible in U.S.; established Lenox Library to house collection of books and art objects, N.Y.C., 1870; donated land for Presbyn. Hosp. and Presbyn. Home for Aged Women; benefactor of Princeton; contbd. over $12,-000,000 to charities during his lifetime. Author: Shakespeare's Plays in Folio, 1861; The Early Editions of King James' Bible in Folio, 1861. Died N. Y.C., Feb. 17, 1880; buried N.Y.C.

LENT, James, congressman; b. Newton, L.I. (now part of Borough of Queens), N.Y., 1782. Engaged in merc. bus., N.Y.C.; judge Queens County, 1823-29; mem. U.S. Ho. of Reps. (Jacksonian Democrat) from N.Y., 21st-22d congresses, 1829-33. Died Washington, D.C., Feb. 22, 1833; buried Congressional Cemetery, Washington, reinterred Presbyn. Cemetery, Newtown.

LENTHALL, John, naval architect; b. D.C., Sept. 16, 1807; s. John Lenthall; studied shipbldg. under father and Samuel Humphreys. Chief naval constructor U.S. Navy, 1849-53; chief of bur. constrn., 1853-71; responsible for design of class of wooden, steam frigates represented by Merrimac, also designed or aided in design of ships Wabash, Niagara, Roanoke, Colorado, Minnesota. Died Washington, D.C., Apr. 11, 1882; buried Rock Creek Parish Cemetery, Washington.

LEONARD, Daniel, Loyalist, jurist; b. Norton, Mass., May 18, 1740; s. Ephraim and Judith (Perkins) L.; grad. Harvard, 1760; m. Anna White, 1767; m. 2d, Sarah Hammock, 1770; 3 daus., 1 son, Charles. Admitted to Mass. bar, circa 1767; King's atty. for Bristol County, Mass., 1769-70; mem. Mass. Gen. Ct., 1770-74, a leading spokesman for royal cause; mandamus councilor of Mass., 1774; entered Brit. lines, 1775, served as a customs commr.; published 17 articles defending royal policy (signed Massachusettensis) in Mass. Gazette, 1774-75 (John Adams directed Novanglus Papers to these articles); left Boston with Brit. forces, 1777, went to Eng.; admitted to English bar; chief justice of Bermuda, 1782-1806. Died London, Eng., June 27, 1829; buried London.

LEONARD, George, congressman, jurist; b. Norton, Mass., July 4, 1729; grad. Harvard, 1748; studied law. Register of probate, 1749-83; admitted to the bar; began practice of law, Norton, 1750; mem. Mass. Provincial Assembly, 1764-66, Mass. Exec. Council, 1770-75; judge probate ct., 1784-90; judge Mass. Ct. of Common Pleas, 1785-89, chief justice, 1798-1804; mem. U.S. Ho. of Reps., 1st, 4th congresses, 1789-91, 95-97; mem. Mass. Senate, 1792-93, Mass. Ho. of Reps., 1801-02. Died Raynham, Mass., July 26, 1819; buried local cemetery, Norton.

LEONARD, George, Loyalist; b. Plymouth, Mass., Nov. 23, 1742; s. Nathaniel and Priscilla (Rogers) L.; m. Sarah Thacher, Oct. 14, 1765. Served as lt. Asso. Loyalists aiding British during blockade of Boston, 1774-75; went with Boston Loyalists to Halifax, N.S., 1776; agt. for Assoc. (Loyalist) Refugees in R.I., 1779; a dir. Asso. Loyalists, 1780-82, engaged in preying on colonials' commerce, Long Island, also Staten Island, 1780-82; land agt., Halifax, 1782-84; supt. trade and fisheries, N.S., 1786-90; mem. N.S. Gov.'s Council, 1790-1826. Died Halifax, Apr. 1, 1826; buried Sussex Vale, N.S.

LEONARD, John Edwards, congressman; b. Fairville, Pa., Sept. 22, 1845; grad. Phillips Exeter (N.H.) Acad., 1863, Harvard, 1867; studied law, Germany. Admitted to La. bar, 1870, began practice in Monroe; dist. atty. 13th La. Jud. Dist., 1871-72; elected asso. justice La. Supreme Ct., 1876; mem. U.S. Ho. of Reps. (Republican) from La., 45th Congress, 1877-78. Died Havana, Cuba, Mar. 15, 1878; buried Friends' (Hicksite) Cemetery of Middletown Meeting House, Middletown Twp., Pa.

LEONARD, Levi Washburn, clergyman; b. Bridgewater, Mass., June 1, 1790; s. Jacob and Mary (Swift) L.; grad. Harvard, 1815, Harvard Divinity Sch., 1818; m. Elizabeth Morison Smith, 1830; m. 2d, Elizabeth Dow Smith, 1851. Tchr., Bridgewater Acad., 1818-20; ordained to ministry Unitarian Ch., 1820; pastor, 1st Unitarian Ch., Dublin, N.H., 1820-55, preacher, 1855-64; active civic affairs, Dublin, founder of local lyceum and library, leader in mgmt. local schs.; editor Exeter (N.H.) News-Letter, 1854-62. Author: (textbooks) The Literary and Scientific Classbook, 1826, Sequel to Easy Lessons, 1830, The North American Spelling Book, 1835; The History of Dublin, New Hampshire, 1855. Died Exeter, Dec. 12, 1864; buried Dublin.

LEONARD, Stephen Banks, congressman; b. N.Y. C., Apr. 15, 1793; attended pub. schs. Learned printer's trade, Owego, N.Y.; newspaperman, Albany, N.Y.; publisher, editor Owego Gazette, 1814-35; trustee Village of Owego; commr. of excise; trustee Owego Acad., many years; established 1st stage route from Owego to Bath, N.Y., 1816; postmaster of Owego, 1816-20; mem. U.S. Ho. of Reps. (Democrat) from N.Y., 24th, 26th congresses, 1835-37, 39-41; engaged in merc. bus., farming; supr. of Owego, 1854-56; dep. U.S. marshal, 1857-61. Died Owego, May 8, 1876; buried Presbyn. Ch. Burying Ground, Owego.

LEONARD, Zenas, trapper; b. Clearfield, Pa., Mar. 19, 1809; s. Abraham and Elizabeth (Armstrong) L.; m. Isabelle Harrelson, 2 children. Trapper in Far West, 1832-35; mem. Walker's Cal. expdn. (1st Americans to explore Yosemite Valley), 1833; Indian trader, Sibley, Mo., 1836. Author: Narrative of the Adventures of Zenas Leonard, 1839. Died Sibley, July 14, 1857.

LERAY, Francis Xavier, clergyman; b. Château Giron, Brittany, France, Apr. 20, 1825; studied at Rennes, France; came to Balt., 1843, attended St. Mary's Sem., also Spring Hill Coll., Ala. Went to Natchez, Miss. with Bishop Chanche; ordained priest Roman Catholic Ch., Natchez, 1852, engaged in missionary work throughout Miss.; became pastor, Vicksburg; served as chaplain Confederate Army during Civil War; consecrated bishop of Natchitoches, at Rennes, 1877; apptd. titular bishop of Janopolis, coadjutor and apostolic adminstr. New Orleans, 1879, became bishop, 1883, instrumental in abolishing bd. of trustees of cathedral and in reducing large debt inherited from previous bishop. Died while visiting France, at Château Giron, Sept. 23, 1887.

Le ROUX, Bartholomew, silversmith; b. Amsterdam, Holland, circa 1665; s. Pierre and Jane Le Roux; m. Gertrude Van Rollegom, Dec. 14, 1688, 11 children including Charles. Came to Am. before 1687, had learned silversmith's trade from father; mem. militia, took part in rebellion in N.Y.C., 1689; signed protest petition sent to King William III, 1690; constable N.Y.C., 1691; collector Port of N.Y.C., 1699; assessor N.Y.C., 1707, alderman, 1702-04, 08-13; did very ornate silver work, examples now owned by Met. Mus., N.Y.C., also Yale. Died N.Y.C., July 1713.

Le ROUX, Charles, silversmith; b. Dec. 1689; s. Bartholomew and Gertrude (Van Rollegom) Le R.; m. Catherine Beekman, 1715. Learned trade from father; ofcl. silversmith of N.Y.C., 1720-43; engraved printing plates for early paper money of N.Y. State; alderman, N.Y.C., 1734; mem. N.Y.C. Common Council, 1734-39; mayor N.Y.C. Militia, 1738; mem. grand jury during Negro Scare of 1741-42. Died Mar. 22, 1745.

LESCHI, Indian chief; b. nr. Nisqually River; flourished 1855-58. A Nisqualli Indian chief, joined uprising of 1855, commanded Indians West of the Cascades in Wash. Territory; attacked Seattle, Wash., 1856; although granted amnesty at end of war, arrested and tried by Wash. Territorial Govt. Hung for murder, Olympia, Wash., Feb. 19, 1858.

LESLIE, Charles Robert, painter; b. London, Eng., Oct. 19, 1794; s. Robert and Lydia (Baker) L.; attended U. Pa.; studied under Benjamin West and Washington Allston at Royal Acad. of Art, London, Eng., 1811; m. Harriet Stone, 1825. Apprenticed to booksellers Bradford & Inskeep, Phila., 1808-11; tchr. drawing U.S. Mil. Acad., 1833; spent most of his life in London; mem., prof. painting Royal Acad.; took most of his paintings from literary sources; paintings include: Touchstone, Olivia, illustrations for an edit. of Don Quixote. Author: Memoirs of the Life of John Constable, 1843; A Handbook for Young Painters, 1855; Autobiographical Recollections, 1860. Died London, May 5, 1859.

LESLIE, Eliza, author; b. Phila., Nov. 15, 1787; dau. of Robert and Lydia (Barker) L. Became wealthy through sales of her cookbooks; also wrote children's stories, contbd. stories to popular women's mags. Author: Seventy-Five Receipts for Pastry, Cakes, and Sweetmeats, 1837; The Domestic Cookery Book (38 edits. published before her death), 1837; The Young Revolutionists (short stories), 1845; The Lady's Receipt Book, 1846; Amelia, or a Young Lady's Vicissitudes (novel), 1848. Died Gloucester, N.J., Jan. 1, 1858.

LESLIE, Frank (real name Henry Leslie), publisher; b. Ipswich, Eng., Mar. 24, 1821; s. Joseph and Mary (Carter) L.; m. Miriam Florence Folline, July 13, 1874, 3 children. Engraver, Illustrated London News, 1842-48; came to N.Y.C., 1848; engraver for Gleason's Pictoral, 1852; supt. engraving dept. Illustrated News, N.Y.C., 1853; founded Frank Leslie's Ladies Gazette of Paris, London, and N.Y. Fashions, 1854, Frank Leslie's N.Y. Journal, 1855, Frank Leslie's Illustrated Newspaper (became influential during Civil War), 1855, Frank Leslie's New Family Mag., 1857, also more than a dozen lesser mags.; introduced new speed in engraving by using as many as 48 engravers for 1 large picture (each man doing a small block of the print); U.S. commr. Paris Worlds Fair, 1867; went bankrupt in depression of 1877. Died Jan. 10, 1880.

LESQUEREUX, Leo, paleobotanist; b. Fleurier, Switzerland, Nov. 18, 1806; s. V. Aimé and Marie Anne Lesquereux; m. Sophia von Reichenberg. Became specialist on peat bogs; dir. peat bogs for Swiss Govt., 1844-48; came to Boston, 1848, worked with Louis Agassiz; expert on coal formation, surveyed Ky., Ill., Ind. and Miss. for coal deposits; mem. Nat. Acad. Sci. Author: Description of the Coal Flora of the Carboniferous Formation in Pennsylvania and Throughout the United States, 2 vols., 1880-84. Died Columbus, O., Oct. 25, 1889.

LESTER, Charles Edward, author; b. Griswold, Conn., July 15, 1815; s. Moses and Sarah (Woodbridge) L.; studied law under Robert J. Walker, Natchez, Miss.; attended Auburn Theol. Sem., 1835-36; m. Ellen Brown, Aug. 8, 1837; 1 dau., Ellen Salisbury. Ordained to ministry Presbyn. Ch., 1836; minister in No. N.Y., for a time, then left ministry; became interested in anti-slavery movement; del. World Anti-Slavery Conv., Eng., 1840; U.S. consul, Genoa, 1842-47; devoted himself to writing, lived chiefly in N.Y.C., after 1847; worked in hosps. in Washington, D.C., during Civil War. Author: Chains and Freedom, 1839; Artists of America, 1846; Our First Hundred Years, 1874-75; America's Advancement, 1876; also 23 other books and translations from Italian writers. Died Detroit, Jan. 29, 1890.

LESUEUR, Charles Alexandre, artist, naturalist; b. Le Havre, France, Jan. 1, 1778; s. Jean-Baptiste Denis and Charlotte Geneviéve (Thieullent) L.; attended Royal Mil. Sch., Beaumont-En-Auge, France, 1787-96. Mem. French scientific expdn. which explored coasts of Australia, 1800-04, took many zool. specimens back to France, including 2,500 new species; in West Indies, 1815-16; came to Am., 1816; made tour (with Am. geologist William Maclure) of much of interior Am., 1816-17, painted and collected specimens on trip; engraver and tchr. of drawing, Phila., 1817-26; curator Acad. Natural Scis. of Phila., 1817-25; tchr. drawing, New Harmony, Ind. (community founded by Robert Owen), 1826-37, also continued scientific work; lived in Paris, France, 1837-45; wrote 29 monographs on Am. fishes; engraved plates for scientific publs. Author: (with others) Voyage de Découvertes aux Terres Australes, 2 vols., 1807-16. Died Dec. 12, 1846.

LE SUEUR, Pierre, explorer, trader; b. Artois, France, circa 1657; s. Victor and Anne (Honneur) le Sueur; m. Marguerite Messier, Mar. 29, 1690. Emigrated to Canada, circa 1679, became interested in fur trade; negotiated with Sioux to keep peace between them and Chippewa, 1693; built forts on Madeline Island, at end of Borulé-St. Croix portage, Prairie Island, Mississippi River, 1695, on West shore of Lake Pepin opposite Chippewa River, Ft. l'Huillier on br. of St. Pierre River; responsible for alliance of Sioux and Chippewa Indians with French Canada. Died at sea, circa 1705.

LETCHER, John, gov. Va.; b. Lexington, Va., Mar. 29, 1813; s. William and Elizabeth (Davidson) L.; grad. Washington Coll. (now Washington and Lee U.), 1833; m. Mary Holt, 9 children. Admitted to Lexington bar, 1839; editor paper Valley star, Lexington, 1839-40, 44-50; active Democratic 1839-40, 44-50; active Democratic presdl. campaigns, 1840, 44, 48; presdl. elector, 1848; mem. Va. Constl. Conv., 1850-51; mem. U.S. Ho. of Reps. (Dem.) from Va., 32d-35th congresses, 1851-59, mem. ways and means com.; gov. Va., 1859-64; mem. Va. Ho. of Dels., 1875-77. Died Lexington, Jan. 26, 1884; buried Presbyn. Cemetery, Lexington.

LETCHER, Robert Perkins, gov. Ky.; b. Goochland County, Va., Feb. 10, 1788; s. Stephen Giles and Betsey (Perkins) L.; m. Mary Epps; m. 2d, Charlotte Robertson; no children. Served as judge advocate in regt. Ky. Mounted Volunteer Militia, 1812; mem. lower house, Ky. Legislature from Garrard County, 1813-15, 17; mem. U.S. Ho. of Reps. from Ky., 18th-23d congresses, 1823-35, mem. com. on fgn. affairs, speaker, 1831; mem. Ky. Ho. of Reps., 1836, 37, 38, speaker, 1837; gov. Ky., 1840-44; presdl. elector, 1836; E.E. and M.P. to Mexico, 1849-52. Died Frankfort, Ky., Jan. 24, 1861; buried State Cemetery, Frankfort.

LETTERMAN, Jonathan, army officer, surgeon; b. Canonsburg, Washington County, Pa., Dec. 11, 1824; s. Jonathan Letterman; grad. Jefferson Coll., 1845; M.D., Jefferson Med. Coll., 1849; m. Mary Lee, Oct. 1863. Asst. surgeon U.S. Army, serving on Western and Southwestern frontiers, 1849-61; assigned to Army of Potomac, 1861; surgeon, maj., 1862, apptd. med. dir. Army of Potomac; organizer system of field med. service featuring mobile hosps. and ambulance service which became standard for entire U.S. Army. Died Mar. 15, 1872.

LEUTZE, Emanuel, painter; b. Gmünd, Wurtemberg, May 24, 1816; married. Received early tng. and support from Edward L. Carey, Phila.; painted hist. scenes and portraits in Europe, 1841-59; returned to U.S., 1859. Best known work: Washington Crossing the Delaware. Died Washington, D.C., July 18, 1868.

LEVADOUX, Michael, clergyman; b. Clermont-Ferrand, Auvergne, France, Apr. 1, 1746. Joined the Sulpicians, 1769; dir. of seminary, Limoges, 1774-91; sent (with group of Sulpicians) to found St. Mary's Sem., Balt., 1791, served as treas., 1 year; then sent as vicar gen. to Bishop Carroll on missionary work in Middle West; began pastoral work, Detroit, 1796; recalled to Balt., 1801, to France, 1803; apptd. superior of sem. in Auvergne, 1803, of Le Puy-en-Velay, France, 1814. Died Le Puy-en-Velay, Jan. 13, 1815.

LEVERETT, John, colonial gov.; b. Eng., July 1616; s. Thomas and Anne (Fisher) L.; m. Hannah Hudson, before 1640; m. 2d, Sarah Sedgwick, 1647, 18 children. Came to Am., 1633; commd. capt. Boston Arty.; mem. Mass. Gen. Ct., 1651-53, 63-65, speaker house, 1664; selectman Boston, 1651; commr. sent to Me. to proclaim settlements there subject to jurisdiction of Mass., 1652; commr. sent to confer with Stuyvesant over difficulties with Dutch in N.Y., 1653; colonial agt. in Eng., 1655-62; maj. gen., commanded all Mass. Militia, 1663-73; custody of colony charter confided to him, 1664; mem. Mass. Council, 1665-70; dep. gov. Mass., 1671-73, gov., 1673-79. Died Boston, Mar. 16, 1679.

LEVERETT, John, coll. pres.; b. Boston, Aug. 25, 1662; s. Hudson and Sarah (Peyton) L.; A.B., Harvard, 1680, A.M., 1683, S.T.D. (hon.), 1692; m. Mrs. Margaret Berry, 1697; m. 2d, Mrs. Sara (Crisp) Harris; 9 children. Fellow and tutor Harvard, 1685-1700; Rep. Mass. Gen. Ct. from Cambridge, 1696-97; justice of peace, 1699; speaker Mass. Ho. of Dels., 1700; judge Superior Ct. and judge probate for Middlesex County, 1702; mem. Mass. Provincial Council, 1706; pres. Harvard, 1707-24; colonial commr. to Port Royal, N.S., 1707; fellow Royal Soc. London (Eng.). Died May 3, 1724.

LEVIN, Lewis Charles, congressman; b. Charleston, S.C., Nov. 10, 1808; attended S.C. Coll. (now U. S.C.); m. Anne Hays; m. 2d, Julia Gist. Settled in Phila.; admitted to Pa. bar, 1838; editor Temperance Advocate; a founder Nativist Party, Phila., 1843; editor Phila. Daily Sun; mem. U.S. Ho. of Reps. (Am. Party), 29th-31st congresses, 1845-51; practiced law in Phila. until insanity resulted in death. Died Phila., Mar. 14, 1860.

LEVINS, Thomas C., clergyman; b. Drogheda, Ireland, Mar. 14, 1789; s. Patrick and Margaret Levins; attended Jesuit colls., Clongowes, Dublin, Ireland and Stonyhurst, Lancashire, Eng. Tchr. natural philosophy and mathematics Georgetown (D.C.) Coll., 1822-25; resigned from Soc. of Jesus to become asst. at St. Peter's Ch., also pastor old St. Patrick's, N.Y.C.; co-editor N.Y. Weekly Register and Catholic Diary, 1833-36; suspended from clergy, 1834; founded publ. Green Banner; contbr. Catholic Register; engr. for N.Y. Croton Aqueduct; reinstated as priest, 1841. Died N.Y.C., May 5, 1843.

LEVY, David, see Yulee, David Levy.

LEVY, Uriah Phillips, naval officer; b. Phila., Apr. 22, 1792; s. Michael and Rachel (Phillips) L.; m. Virginia. Cabin boy, circa 1802-04; apprenticed to mcht.-shipowner John Coulter, Phila., 1806-10; part-owner, master of schooner George Washington, 1811; lt. aboard Argus; captured by British while commanding prize vessel, imprisoned in Eng., 1813-14; court-martialed 6 times and dismissed from U.S. Navy twice during 10 year period following War of 1812; promoted capt., 1844; flag officer Mediterranean Fleet; owned Jefferson's "Monticello" for a time. Died N.Y.C., Mar. 22, 1862.

LEVY, William Mallory, congressman; b. Isle of Wight, Va., Oct. 31, 1827; grad. Coll. William and Mary, 1844; studied law. Served as 2d lt. Va. Volunteers during Mexican War; admitted to Va. bar, 1851, began practice in Norfolk; moved to Natchitoches, La., 1852, practiced law; mem. La. Ho. of Reps., 1859-61; Democratic presdl. elector, 1860; served with Confederate Army during Civil War, commd. capt. Co. A, 2d La. Inf., 1861, later served as maj. Adj. Gen.'s Dept.; mem. U.S. Ho. of Reps. (Dem.) from La., 44th Congress, 1875-77; mem. La. Constl. Conv., 1879; asso. justice La. Supreme Ct., 1879-82. Died Saratoga, N.Y., Aug. 14, 1882; buried American Cemetery, Natchitoches.

LEWIS, Abner, congressman; b. Panama, N.Y.; attended pub. schs. Mem. N.Y. Assembly, 1838-39; mem. U.S. Ho. of Reps. (Whig) from N.Y., 29th Congress, 1845-47; county judge, 1847-52.

LEWIS, Andrew, army officer; b. Donegal, Ireland, 1720; s. John and Margaret (Lynn) L.; m. Elizabeth Givens, 6 children. Served as maj. in Ohio campaigns commanded by Washington, 1754-55; led Sandy Creek expdn., 1756; county lt. of Augusta County, Va.; justice of peace; rep. Botetourt County Legislature; aided in Indian Treaty of Ft. Stanwix; defeated Indians at Battle of Point Pleasant in Lord Dunmore's War, 1774; mem. Revolutionary Colonial Convs. of Va. 1775; commd. brig. gen. Continental Army in command Am. forces stationed at Williamsburg, Va., 1776; defeated British under Lord Dunmore at Gwynn's Island, 1776; resigned from Continental Army, 1777; mem. Va. Exec. Council, 1776-81. Died Bedford County, Va., Sept. 26, 1781.

LEWIS, Barbour, congressman; b. Alburg, Vt., Jan. 5, 1818; grad. Ill. Coll., 1846; grad. law dept. Harvard. Taught sch., Mobile, Ala.; admitted to the bar, practiced law; del. Republican Nat. Conv., Chgo., 1860; served as capt. Co. G, 1st Mo. Volunteers, Union Army, during Civil War; judge Civil Commn. Ct., Memphis, Tenn., 1863-64; pres. bd. commrs. Shelby County (Tenn.), 1867-69; mem. U.S. Ho. of Reps. (Rep.) from Tenn., 43d Congress, 1873-75; resumed practice of law, Memphis; moved to St. Louis, 1878; with U.S. Land Office, Salt Lake City, Utah, 1878-79; moved to Whitman County, Wash. Territory, engaged in farming, stock raising. Died Colfax, Wash., July 15, 1893; buried Colfax Cemetery.

LEWIS, Burwell Boykin, congressman, coll. pres.; b. Montgomery, Ala., July 7, 1838; grad. U. Ala., 1857; studied law, Selma, Ala. Admitted to Ala. bar, 1859, began practice in Montevallo; served to capt. 2d Ala. Cavalry, Confederate Army, during Civil War; Democratic presdl. elector, 1868; mem. Ala. Ho. of Reps., 1870-72; moved to Tuscaloosa, Ala., 1872, engaged in iron and coal bus.; mem. U.S. Ho. of Reps. (Democrat) from Ala., 44th, 46th congresses, 1875-77, 79-Oct. 1, 1800; pres., prof. constl. and internat. law U. Ala., 1880-85. Died Tuscaloosa, Oct. 11, 1885; buried Evergreen Cemetery, Tuscaloosa.

LEWIS, Charles Levin, editor, congressman; b. Charleston, S.C., Nov. 10, 1808; attended S.C. Coll.; m. Anna Hays; m. 2d, Julia Gist. Admitted to Phila. bar, 1838; editor Phila. Sun; a founder Native-Am. Party in Pa., 1843, mem. Pa. State Conv., also Nat. Conf.; mem. U.S. Ho. of Reps. (Native-Am. party) from Pa., 29th-31st congresses, 1845-51. Died Mar. 14, 1860.

LEWIS, Charles Swearinger, congressman; b. Clarksburg, Va. (now W.Va.), Feb. 26, 1821; attended Ohio U.; grad. Augusta (Ky.) Coll., 1844; studied law. Admitted to Va. bar, 1846, began practice in Clarksburg; mem. Va. Ho. of Dels., 1848-52; mem. U.S. Ho. of Reps. (Democrat) from Va., 33d Congress, Dec. 4, 1854-55; resumed law practice, Clarksburg; del. Va. Constl. Conv., 1861; mem. W.Va. Ho. of Reps., 1871; supt. free schs., adj. gen. State of W.Va., 1871-73; judge 2d Jud. Circuit, 1873-78. Died Clarksburg, Jan. 22, 1878; buried Odd Fellows Cemetery, Clarksburg.

LEWIS, Clarke, congressman; b. Huntsville, Ala., Nov. 8, 1840; attended Somerville Inst. Taught sch.; served with Confederate Army during Civil War, 1861-65; resumed teaching, 1866; retail clk., 1866-67; engaged in merc. bus., farming, 1867-79; mem. Miss. Ho. of Reps., 1878; mem. U.S. Ho. of Reps. (Democrat) from Miss., 51st-52d congresses, 1889-93; resumed farming. Died nr. Macon, Miss., Mar. 13, 1896; buried Odd Fellows Cemetery, Macon.

LEWIS, Diocesian, reformer; b. Auburn, N.Y., Mar. 3, 1823; s. John C. and Delecta (Barbour) L.; attended Harvard Med. Sch., 1845-46; M.D. (hon.), Homoeopathic Hosp. Coll., Cleve.; m. Helen Cecilia Clarke, 1847. Established sch., Lower Sandusky (now Fremont), O.; practiced medicine, Buffalo, N.Y.; published monthly Homoeopathist; began gymnastic classes for women; traveled widely preaching temperance; organized gymnastic classes, Boston, 1860; conducted sanitarium and girls' sch., Lexington, Mass. Author: New Gymnastics, 1862. Died N.Y.C., May 21, 1886.

LEWIS, Dixon Hall, senator; b. Dinwiddie County, Va., Aug. 10, 1802; s. Francis and Mary Dixon (Hall) L; grad. S.C. Coll., 1820; m. Susan Elmore, Mar. 11, 1823, 7 children. Admitted to Ala. bar, 1823; mem. Ala. Legislature, 1826-28; mem. U.S. Ho. of Reps. (Democrat) from Ala., 21st-28th congresses, 1829-44, chmn. ways and means com.; mem. U.S. Senate from Ala., 1844-48, states' rights advocate, opposed high protective tariff and internal improvements by fed. govt., chmn. com. on finance. Died N.Y.C., Oct. 25, 1848; buried Greenwood Cemetery, L.I., N.Y.

LEWIS, Ellis, jurist; b. Lewisberry, Pa., May 16, 1798; s. Maj. Eli and Pamela (Webster) L.; m. Josephine Wallis, Nov. 21, 1822. Admitted to Pa. bar, 1822; dep. atty. gen. Lycoming and Tioga counties (Pa.), 1824; del. to Pa. Democratic Conv., 1832; atty. gen. Pa., 1833; president judge 8th Jud. Dist.; president judge 2d Jud. Dist., 1843; judge Pa. Supreme Ct., 1851-54, chief justice, 1854-57. Died Phila., Mar. 19, 1871.

LEWIS, Enoch, educator; b. Rador, Pa., Jan. 29, 1776; s. Evan and Jane (Meredith) L.; m. Alice Jackson, May 9, 1799; m. 2d, Lydia Jackson, May 1815. Became sch. tchr. at age 15, continued teaching for 35 years; opened own sch., 1808; founded African Observer, 1827, Friend's Review, 1847-56. Author: A Vindication of the Society of Friends, 1841; also numerous mathematics text books. Died July 14, 1856.

LEWIS, Estelle Anna Blanche Robinson, author; b. Balt., Apr. 1824; dau. of John N. Robinson; m. Sylvanus D. Lewis, 1841 (div. 1858). Contbr. to Democratic Review, Spirit of the 19th Century, Am. Review, Literary World, Godey's Lady's Book; lived in Europe, after 1858. Author: Records of the Heart, 1844; Child of the Sea and Other Poems, 1848; Sappho; A Tragedy, in Five Acts, 1875. Died London, Eng., Nov. 24, 1880; buried in U.S.

LEWIS, Fielding, planter, colonial ofcl.; b. Gloucester County, Va., July 7, 1725; s. John and Frances (Fielding) L.; m. Catherine Washington, Oct. 18, 1746, 3 children; m. 2d, Betty Washington, May 7, 1750, 11 children. Wealthy planter in Va.; long-time friend, brother-in-law of George Washington; asso. with George Washington's Dismal Swamp Co.; mem. Va. Ho. of Burgesses from Spotsylvania, 10 years; mem. Com. of Correspondence, Spotsylvania County Com.; chief commr. of govt. arms factory (to which he gave part of his wealth), Fredericksburg, Va., 1775-81. Died circa Jan. 1782.

LEWIS, Francis, Continental congressman; b. Llandaff, Wales, Mar. 21, 1713; s. Rev. Francis and Amy (Pettingal) L.; m. Elizabeth Annesley, June 15, 1745; children—Francis Lewis, Morgan. Came to Am. 1738; aide to Gen. Mercer in French and Indian War, 1757, captured at Ft. Oswego; mem. Stamp Act Congress, 1765; mem. Sons of Liberty; del. to N.Y. Provincial Conv., 1774; mem. Com. of Fifty-one and Sixty; mem. Continental Congress, 1775-79; instrumental in drawing up new govt. for N.Y., 1776; mem. Bd. of Admiralty, 1779-81, mem. marine, secret and comml. coms. Died N.Y.C., Dec. 30, 1802.

LEWIS, Henry, artist; b. Scarborough, Kent, Eng., 1819. Came to U.S., 1836, became mechanic, carpenter, St. Louis; conceived idea of moving panorama of Mississippi River, traveled up and down river making sketches, 1846-48; toured U.S. with his panorama, then toured Eng., Germany; U.S. consul to Düsseldorf, Germany, 1851. Author: Das Illustrirte Mississipithal, 1854-58. Died Düsseldorf, 1904.

LEWIS, James, actor; b. Troy, N.Y., Oct. 5, 1837; s. William Hoadly and Arabella (Benson) Demming; m. Medora Frances Herbert, May 8, 1871. Made 1st stage appearance at age 17; acted in many dramas and farces throughout U.S.; traveled internationally with Daly's Co. of N.Y.C., 1880's. Died West Hampton, L.I., N.Y., Sept. 10, 1896.

LEWIS, James Otto, engraver, artist; b. Phila., Feb. 3, 1799. Began career as engraver, Phila., circa 1815; went West with Gov. Lewis Cass of Mich.; employed to paint portraits of Indians for U.S. Govt., 1823-34; worked as engraver, St. Louis, circa 1820-21; settled in Detroit, painted portraits, engraved, did copperplate printing, until 1833; present at several Indian treaties in Wis. and Ind., painted portraits of many Indians participating in treaties (lithographed and published as The Aboriginal Port-Folio, 1835). Died N.Y.C., 1858.

LEWIS, John Francis, senator; b. Lynnwood, Rockingham County, Va., Mar. 1, 1818; s. Gen. Samuel and Nancy (Lewis) L.; m. Serena Sheffey, 1842, 7 children. Opposed secession in Va. Conv., 1861 (supported Union in Civil War); lt. gov. Va., 1869-70, 81-83; mem. U.S. Senate from Va., Jan. 26, 1870-75, chmn. com. on D.C.; U.S. marshal for Western Va., 1872-82. Died Lynnwood, Sept. 2, 1895; buried family burying ground, Lynnwood.

LEWIS, Joseph, Jr., congressman; b. Va., 1772; s. Joseph Lewis. Mem. Va. Ho. of Dels., 1799-1803, 17-18; mem. U.S. Ho. of Reps. (Federalist) from Va., 8th-14th congresses, 1803-17. Died Clifton, Va., Mar. 30, 1834.

LEWIS, Lawrence, lawyer; b. Phila., June 20, 1856; s. Robert and Anna (Shippen) L.; grad. U. Pa., 1876; m. Dora Kelly, 1883. Admitted to Phila. bar, 1879, began practice of law, Phila.; sec. Law Acad. of Phila., 1879-circa 1881; defense counsel in case of Forepaugh vs. Del., Lackawanna & Western R.R. Co., secured recognition of principle of limited liability of partners in businesses; drafted new law of escheats for State of Pa. (simplified legal processes involving land titles); editor Weekly Notes of Cases, 1879-90. Author: A History of the Bank of North America, 1882; (articles) The Constitution, Jurisdiction, and Practice of the Courts of Pennsylvania in the 17th Century, pub. Pa. Mag. of History & Biography, Vol. V, number 2; Memoir of Edward Shippen, pub. Pa. Mag., 1883; A Brief Statement of the Origin, Nature and History of the French Spoliation Claims. Annotator: The American and English Railroad Cases, Vols. X-XX 1883-85. Died West Chester, Pa., Sept. 2, 1890; buried Phila.

LEWIS, Meriwether, explorer, gov. La.; b. Albemarle County, nr. Charlottesville, Va., Aug. 18, 1774; s. Capt. William and Lucy (Meriwether) L. Served with Va. Militia during Whiskey Rebellion; commd. ensign 2d Legion, U.S. Army, 1795, lt., paymaster for regt., 1799; pvt. sec. to Thomas Jefferson, 1801, conveyed annual Presdl. message to Senate, 1801; sent by Jefferson to study astronomy and map-making in Phila. and Lancaster, Pa., 1803; started (with William Clark as companion officer) on famous Lewis and Clark expdn. to explore La. Territory and find land route to Pacific Ocean; obtained guides Sacajawea and her French Canadian husband, Apr. 1805; came to end of navigation on Mo. River by Aug, 1805; went down Columbia River to Pacific Ocean, established Ft. Clatsop for winter hdqrs.; arrived in St. Louis, 1806; gained much new knowledge of La. and Far West, named such rivers as Madison, Jefferson, Gallatin. Maria during expdn.; gov. La., 1806; Lewis County (Tenn.) named for him (monument erected there by Tenn. Govt, 1848); Lewis and Clark County (Mont.) named for him. Died Tenn. (according to 2 accounts either suicide or murder), Oct. 11, 1809.

LEWIS, Morgan, gov. N.Y.; b. N.Y.C., Oct. 16, 1754; s. Francis and Elizabeth (Annesley) L.; grad. Coll. of N.J. (now Princeton), 1773; m. Gertrude Livingston, May 11, 1779. Commd. maj. 2d Regt., N.Y. Militia, 1776, later capt. of a co., commd. maj.; commd. col., dep. q.m. gen., 1776 until end of Revolutionary War, chief of staff at battles of Ticonderoga and Saratoga; admitted to N.Y.C. bar; mem. N.Y. Assembly, 1789-90, 92; atty. gen. N.Y., 1791-92; justice Supreme Ct. N.Y., 1792-1801, chief justice, 1801; gov. N.Y., 1804-07; mem. N.Y. Senate, mem. Council of Appointment; commd. brig. gen., q.m. gen. U.S. Army, 1812; maj. gen. serving on Niagara frontier, 1813; grand master Freemasons of U.S., 1821; pres. N.Y. Hist. Soc., 1832-36; pres. gen. Soc. of Cincinnati, 1839-44; a founder N.Y. U. Died N.Y.C., Apr. 7, 1844.

LEWIS, Samuel, educator; b. Falmouth, Mass., Mar. 17, 1799; s. Samuel and Abigail (Talman) L.; m. Charlotte Goforth, 1823. Admitted to Ohio bar, 1822; 1st supt. common schs. State of Ohio, 1837; a founder Coll. of Tchrs.; founder free pub. sch. system in Ohio; active in anti-slavery movement. Died Cincinnati, July 28, 1854.

LEWIS, Thomas, congressman; b. Augusta County, Va.; attended common schs. Mem. U.S. Ho. of Reps. from Va., 8th Congress, 1803-Mar. 5, 1804, lost seat to Andrew Moore who successfully contested the election.

LEWIS, William, lawyer; b. Edgemont, Pa., Jan. 22, 1752; s. Josiah and Martha (Allen) L.; studied law under Nicholas Waln; m. Rosanna Lort; m. 2d, Frances Durdin; 3 children. Admitted to Pa. bar, 1773, admitted again after new state constn., 1776; mem. Pa. Legislature, 1787, 89; mem. Pa. Constl. Conv.; U.S. atty. Dist. of Pa., 1789; judge U.S. Dist. Ct. for Eastern dist. Pa., 1791-92; successful trial lawyer, defended John Fries, leader of Northampton Insurgents, 1799, counsel for petitioners against election of Albert Gallatin to U.S. Senate, 1794. Died Phila., Aug. 16, 1819.

LEWIS, William Berkeley, planter, govt. ofcl.; b. Loudoun County, Va., 1784; son of John Lewis; m. Margaret Terrell Lewis. Began operating plantation, nr. Nashville, Tenn., circa 1806; served as q.m. for Andrew Jackson during Natchez campaign, 1812, Creek campaign, 1813; became personal friend of Jackson, promoted Jackson's presdl. candidacy during 1820's; 2d auditor U.S. Treasury during Jackson adminstrn., 1829-37, also mem. Jackson's "Kitchen Cabinet"; active supporter of Van Buren's presdl. candidacy, 1830's; retired to plantation, 1845; Unionist during Civil War. Died "Fairfield," nr. Nashville, Nov. 12, 1866; buried Mt. Olivet Cemetery, Nashville.

LEWIS, William David, businessman; b. Christiana, Del., Sept. 22, 1792; attended Clermont (Del.) Sem., circa 1808; m. Sarah Claypoole, June 28, 1825. Apprentice, Samuel Archer & Co., Phila., 1809; partner (with brother) in mcht. enterprise, St. Petersburg, Russia, 1813-24; in merc. bus., Phila., 1825-55; cashier Girard Bank, Phila., 1832-42; instrumental in providing financing for New Castle & Frenchtown R.R., Phila., Germantown & Norristown R.R., Phila., Wilmington & Balt. R.R., 1830's; collector of customs Port of Phila., 1849-53; pres. Pa. Acad. Fine Arts. Died nr. Florence, N.J., Apr. 1, 1881; buried Florence.

LEWIS, William J., congressman; b. Augusta County, Va., July 4, 1766; attended common schs. Mem. Va. Ho. of Dels.; mem. U.S. Ho. of Reps. (Democrat) from Va., 15th Congress, 1817-19. Died "Mount Athos" nr. Lynchburg, Va., Nov. 1, 1828; buried in a vault blasted out of a solid rock at "Mount Athos."

LEWIS, Winslow, mfr., legislator; b. Wellfleet, Mass., May 11, 1770; s. Winslow and Mary (Knowles) L.; m. Elizabeth Greenough, Nov. 7, 1793; m. 2d Martha S. Hurlburt, Nov. 22 1843; at least 1 child, Dr. Winslow. Capt. of mcht. vessels, made several long voyages as comdr. before retiring to business in Boston; mem. 1st Common Council of Boston, 1822, alderman, 1829, 30, 35, 36; mem. lower house Mass. Legislature, 1828-33; pres. Boston Marine Soc., 1818-20; patented a "lantern, reflecting and magnifying" for illuminating lighthouses, 1810, installed in Boston Light for trial, 1811; contracted with Albert Gallatin (sec. treasury) to put his lamps and reflectors in all U.S. lighthouses; patented a binnacle light, 1808, lamps, 1818. Died May 19, 1850.

LEYPOLDT, Frederick, publisher, bibliographer; b. Stuttgart, Germany, Nov. 17, 1835; s. Michael and Christiane (Deible) L.; m. Augusta Garrigue, Sept. 27, 1867. Came to Am., 1854; employed in Christern's Bookstore, N.Y.C.; established bookstore and reading room specializing in fgn. books and periodicals, Phila., 1859; entered publishing bus. with edition of The Ice-Maiden (Hans Christian Andersen), 1863; partner (with Henry Holt) in pub. firm, N.Y.C., 1865-84, edited firm's Literary Bulletin (became Publishers' Weekly 1873), 1868-84; founder Library Journal, 1876, publisher, 1876-84; published annual catalogues of Am. books, 1869-72; founded Uniform Trade List Annual, 1873; a founder Am. Library Assn., 1876; published Index Medicus, 1879-84. Author: A Reading Diary of Modern Fiction, 1881; compiler (with Lynds Jones) The Books of All Time, 1882. Died N.Y.C., Mar. 31, 1884; buried N.Y.C.

LEX, Charles E., lawyer; b. Phila., 1812; grad. U. Pa.; studied law under Joseph R. Ingersoll. Admitted to Pa. bar, 1834, practiced law in Phila., specializing in banking law, became solicitor for many of prin. banks of Phila.; mem. bd. trustees U. Pa.; sec. standing com. Episcopal Diocese of Pa. Died Phila., May 16, 1872.

L'HALLE, Constantin de, see de L'Halle, Constantin.

L'HOMMEDIEU, Ezra, state senator, agriculturist; b. Southold, L.I., N.Y., Aug. 30, 1734; s. Benjamin and Martha (Borune) L'H.; grad. Yale, 1754; m. Charity Floyd, 1765; m. 2d, Mary Havens, 1803. Admitted to bar; mem. N.Y. Provincial Congresses, 1774-77, a framer Constn. of 1777; mem. N.Y. Assembly, 1777-83; del. from N.Y. to Continental Congresses, 1779-83, 87-88; mem. N.Y. State Senate, 1784-1809, Council of Appointment, 1784, 99; clk. Suffolk County, 1784-1809; noted as principal author of U. State N.Y. as reconstituted in 1787, regent, 1784-1811; mem. Interpretative Constl. Conv., 1801; wrote numerous papers on agr. for Transactions of N.Y. Soc. for Promotion Agr. Arts and Manufactures, v.p., many years. Died Southold, Sept. 27, 1811.

LICK, James, businessman, philanthropist; b. Fredericksburg, Pa., Aug. 21, 1796; s. John and Sarah (Long) L. Apprentice piano maker, Balt. 1817-20; engaged in piano and organ mfg. in Buenos Aires, Argentina, also Lima, Peru, 1820-37; engaged in piano mfg. and real estate operations N.Y.C., 1837-47; moved to Cal., 1847, settled in San Francisco; became owner real estate in San Francisco, Santa Clara Valley, Cal., on shores Lake Tahoe, Nev. in 1850's-60's; willed bequests to Soc. Cal. Pioneers, Cal. Acad. Scientists; made $700,000 bequest to build telescope larger than any previously made (completed at Lick Obs., Mt. Hamilton, Santa Clara County, Cal. in 1888). Died San Francisco, Oct. 1, 1876; buried Lick Obs.

LIEBER, Francis, polit. scientist; b. Berlin, Germany, Mar. 18, 1800; s. Friedrich Wilhelm Lieber, Ph.D., U. Jena, 1820; m. Matilda Oppenheimer, Sept. 21, 1829. Adherent of F. L. Jahn in Prussia, 1811-20; participated in expdn. of German volunteers in Greek Revolution, 1822; arrested twice by German Govt. for subversive activities, went to Eng., 1826; came to U.S., 1827, settled in Boston, operated gymnasium until 1834; founder Ency. Americana, 1828, publisher 1829-33; prof. polit. economy S.C. Coll. (now U. S.C.), 1835-56, Columbia, N.Y.C., 1857-65, Columbia Coll. Law Sch. until 1872; adviser to U.S. Govt. during Civil War, wrote A Code for the Government of Armies (adopted by U.S. Army, 1863, became accepted authority in Europe on mil. law); presiding mem. Mexican Claims Commn., 1870. Author: Manual of Political Ethics, 1838-39; A Popular Essay on Subjects of Penal Law, 1828; Legal and Political Hermeneutics, 1839; Essays on Property and Labor, 1841; On Civil Liberty and Self Government, 1853. Died N.Y.C., Oct. 2, 1872.

LIENAU, Detlef, architect; b. Utersen, Germany, Feb. 17, 1818; s. Jacob and Lucia (Heidorn) L.; attended Royal Archtl. Sch., Munich, Germany, 1841-42; m. Catharine Van Giesen Booraem, May 11, 1853; m. 2d, Harriet Jane Wreaks, Nov. 8, 1866; children—August, Detlef Booraem, Cornelia, Eleanor, J. Henry. Came to U.S., 1848; entered partnership with architect Henry Marcotte, N.Y.C., 1848; designed many elaborate residences, N.Y.C.; designed sugar refineries for Matthiesen & Weichus, Jersey City, N.J., 1862, N.J. Sugar Refining Co., 1867, Suydam Hall (1871) and Sage Library (1873) for Theol. Sem., New Brunswick, N.J.; other works include many office bldgs., N.Y.C., some stores, a few model tenement houses. Died N.Y.C., Aug. 29, 1887.

LIGON, Thomas Watkins, gov. Md.; b. nr. Farmville, Prince Edward County, Va., May 10, 1810; s. Thomas D. and Martha (Watkins) L.; attended Hampden-Sydney Coll., 1830, U. Va., 1831, Yale Law Sch., m. Sallie Dorsey, 1840; m. 2d, Mary Dorsey. Admitted to Va. bar, 1833; practiced in Balt., 1835-53; mem. Md. Ho. of Dels., 1843; mem. U.S. Ho. of Reps. (Democrat) from Md., 29th-30th congresses, 1845-49; gov. Md., 1853-58, sought to maintain order with state militia during riots ensuing from Know-Nothing movement; pres. Patapsco Female Inst. Died "Chatham" nr. Ellicott City, Md., Jan. 12, 1881; buried St. John's Cemetery, Ellicott City.

LILIENTHAL, Max, clergyman; b. Munich, Bavaria, Germany, Oct. 16, 1815; s. Loew and Dina (Lichtenstein) L.; grad. U. Munich, 1837; m. Babette Netre, 1845. Supt. schs., Riga, Russia, 1840-45; came to U.S., 1845, settled in N.Y.C.; rabbi at 3 congregations, N.Y.C.; rabbi Bene Israel Congregation, Cincinnati, 1855-82; mem. Cincinnati Bd. Edn.; active in supporting separation ch. and state in U.S., also in fostering friendship between Christians and Jews; an editor Am. Israelite and Sabbath Sch. Visitor in 1860's; instrumental in founding Union of Am. Hebrew Congregations, 1873, Hebrew Union Coll., Cincinnati, 1875, Rabbinical Literary Assn., 1879. Author: Synopsis of the History of the Israelites from the Time of Alexander the Macedonian. . .," 1857. Died Cincinnati, Apr. 5, 1882; buried Cincinnati.

LILLY, Samuel, congressman, jurist; b. Geneva, N.Y., Oct. 28, 1815; grad. med. dept. U. Pa., 1837. Began practice of medicine, Lambertville, N.J.; 1st mayor of Lambertville, 1848-52; mem. U.S. Ho. of Reps. (Democrat) from N.J., 33d Congress, 1853-55; dir. bd. freeholders Hunterdon County (N.J.), 8 years; brig. gen. N.J. Militia; U.S. consul gen. to British India, 1861-62; judge Hunterdon County Ct. of Common Pleas, 1868-73; mem. bd. mgrs. N.J. Insane Asylum, 1871; judge N.J. Ct. Errors and Appeals, 1873-80; mem. N.J. Bd. Pardons, 1873-80. Died Lambertville, Apr. 3, 1880; buried Mt. Hope Cemetery, Lambertville.

LILLY, William, congressman; b. Penn Yan, N.Y., June 3, 1821; moved to Carbon County, Pa., 1838;

elected col. of a militia regt. of Lehigh Valley (Pa.), later brig. gen.; mem. Pa. Ho. of Reps., 1850-51; Democrat; joined Republican Party, 1862; del. to 6 Rep. nat. convs.; del. at large to revise Pa. Constn., 1872-73; engaged in coal mining; mem. U.S. Ho. of Reps. (Rep.) from Pa., 53d Congress, Mar. 4-Dec. 1, 1893; mem. Soc. Am. Mining Engrs.; life mem. Acad. Natural Scis. of Phila. Died Mauch Chunk, Pa., Dec. 1, 1893; buried City Cemetery, Mauch Chunk.

LIMERICK, 2d earl, see Dongan, Thomas.

LINCECUM, Gideon, physician, naturalist; b. Hancock County, Ga., Apr. 22, 1793; s. Hezekiah and Sally (Hickman) L.; studied medicine privately, Ga., 1815-17; m. Sarah Bryan, Oct. 25, 1814. Commr. apptd. by Miss. Legislature to organize County of Monroe, 1821-22; Indian trader in Miss., 1823-circa 1827; practiced medicine, Cotton Gin Port, Columbus, Miss., 1830-48; owned plantation, Long Point, Tex., 1848-74, studied insects and made lengthy investigation of life of mound-building ants; corresponded with many fgn. naturalists including Charles Darwin; sent specimens to Smithsonian Instn., Acad. Natural Scis., Phila., Jardin des Plantes, Paris, France; papers on insects published in Jour. of Proc. of Linnaean Soc., Vol. 6, London, 1852, and in Proc. of Acad. Nat. Scis. of Phila., 2d series, Vol. X, 1866. Died Long Point, Nov. 28, 1874; buried Long Point.

LINCOLN, Abraham, 16th Pres. U.S.; b. nr. Hodgenville, Hardin County (now part of Larue County), Ky., Feb. 12, 1809; s. Thomas and Nancy (Hanks) L.; LL.D., Knox Coll. 1860, Columbia, 1861, Princeton, 1864; m. Mary Ann Todd, Nov. 4, 1842; children—Robert Todd, Edward Baker, William Wallace, Thomas (Tad). As a youth lived usual pioneer life with family in Ky., moved to Ind. with family, 1816; took flat boat trip down Mississippi River to New Orleans, 1828; moved to Macon County, Ill. with family, 1830; moved alone to New Salem, Ill., 1831, resided there, 1831-1837, storekeeper in partnership with William F. Berry, dep. county surveyor, postmaster, odd jobber, studied law in spare time; served as capt. and pvt. in Black Hawk War, 1832; mem. Ill. Legislature (Whig), 1834-42; licensed as atty., 1836; admitted to bar, 1837; moved to Springfield, Ill., 1837, practiced law with John T. Stuart, later with Stephen T. Logan, then with William H. Herndon (author of a biography of Lincoln); mem. U.S. Ho. of Reps. (Whig) from Ill., 30th Congress, 1847-49, opposed Mexican War; resumed law practice, Springfield; re-entered polit. life by opposing Kan.-Neb. Bill (1854) and other policies of Stephen A. Douglas; unsuccessful Whig candidate for U.S. Senate; joined newly formed Republican Party, 1856, received 110 votes for the vice presdl. nomination at Rep. Nat. Conv., 1856; unsuccessful Rep. nominee for U.S. Senate in opposition to S. A. Douglas, 1858, gave acceptance speech in which he said, "a house divided against itself cannot stand" (campaign highlighted by Lincoln-Douglas Debates); Rep. candidate for U.S. Pres., 1860, won election, inaugurated, Mar. 4, 1861; conservative regarding abolition, but definitely opposed to extension of slavery into territories; Confederate States Am. formed in opposition to his election, 1861; called for volunteers to preserve Union when Ft. Sumter was fired upon, Apr. 1861 (beginning of Civil War); restored to conscription, suspension of writ of Habeas Corpus; unsuccessfully recommended to Congress plan for gradual, compensated emancipation, signed act freeing slaves in D.C. Apr. 1862; slavery in territories prohibited by act of Congress, June 1862; issued Emancipation Proclamation, Sept. 1862 (effective Jan. 1, 1863); delivered Gettysburg Address, Nov. 1863; won re-election over Dem. nominee George B. McClellan, 1864, running on Nat. Union ticket; gave inaugural address with memorable phrase "with malice toward none, with charity for all," 1865; began reconstrn. policy when he pardoned certain Confederate ofcls. who would swear allegiance to Union and formed loyal So. state govts.; gen. plan of re-union and reconstrn. one of forgiveness but abolition of slavery prime requisite (Congress favored harsher plan); major Confederate forces under R. E. Lee surrendered Apr. 9, 1865 (signalling coming end of Civil War). Author: Autobiography, 1859, revised and enlarged, 1860; Political Debates between Abraham Lincoln and Stephen A. Douglas . . . , 1860 (with S. A. Douglas); Collected Works of Abraham Lincoln, 9 vols., 1953-55. Shot by John Wilkes Booth at Ford's Theatre, Washington, D.C., Apr. 14, 1865; died Washington, Apr. 15, 1865; buried Oak Ridge Cemetery, Springfield, Ill.

LINCOLN, Benjamin, army officer, sec. of war; b. Hingham, Mass., Jan. 24, 1733; s. Benjamin and Elizabeth (Thaxter) L.; M.A. (hon.), Harvard; m. Mary Cushing, Jan. 15, 1756, 11 children. Town clk. Hingham, 1757, justice of peace, 1762; mem. Mass. Legislature, 1772-73; mem. Mass. Provincial Congress, 1774-75, sec., mem. com. on supplies, 1774-75, pres., 1775; adj. 3d regt. (Suffolk County), Mass. Militia, 1755, commd. maj., 1763, lt. col. 1772; brig. gen., 1776; 3d maj. gen. in command Mass. Militia nr. Boston, 1776; commanded militia regts. to reinforce Continental Army, N.Y.C., 1776; maj. gen. Continental Army in command militia in Vt., 1777; in command So. Dept., Continental Army, 1778, captured with his forces at Charleston by Clinton, 1779; U.S. sec. of war, 1781, resigned after Treaty of Peace; Mass. commr. to deal with Penobscot Indians on land purchases, 1784, 86; led Mass. Militia to suppress Shay's Rebellion; lt. gov. Mass., 1788; collector Port of Boston, 1789; apptd. to negotiate with Creek Indians on borders of So. states, 1789, with Indians North of the Ohio, 1793; mem. Am. Acad. Arts and Scis., Mass. Hist. Soc.; wrote essays on Indian tribes. Died Boston, May 9, 1810.

LINCOLN, Enoch, gov. Me.; b. Worcester, Mass., Dec. 28, 1788; s. Levi and Martha (Waldo) L.; attended Harvard, 1806- circa 1808; A.M. (hon.), Bowdoin coll., 1821. Admitted to Mass. bar, 1811; asst. U.S. dist. atty., Paris, Me., 1815-18; mem. U.S. Ho. of Reps. from Mass., 15th-16th congresses, Nov. 16, 1818-21, from Me., 17th-19th congresses, 1821-26; gov. Me., 1826-29; wrote poetry; studied langs. of Me. Indians. Died Augusta, Me., Oct. 8, 1829.

LINCOLN, James Sullivan, artist; b. Taunton, Mass., May 13, 1811. Apprenticed to engraver, Providence, R.I.; painted portraits, Providence, after 1837; 1st pres. Providence Art Club. Died Providence, Jan. 18, 1888.

LINCOLN, John Larkin, educator; b. Boston, Feb. 23, 1817; s. Ensign and Sophia (Larkin) L.; grad. Brown U., 1836; attended Newton (Mass.) Theol. Inst., 1837-39, univs. of Halle and Berlin (Germany), 1841-43; m. Laura Pearce, 1846. Tutor Latin and Greek, Brown U., 1939-41, prof. Latin lang. and literature, 1844-circa 1890; operated sch. for young women, Providence, R.I., 1859-67; one of 1st mems. Am. Philol. Soc.; known for success in teaching Latin, commentaries on Latin authors; contbr. articles to jours. including N.Am. Rev., Christian Rev., Baptist Quar., Bibliotheca Sacra. Author: Titus Livius: Selections. . ., 1847; The Works of Horace, 1851; Selections from the Poems of Ovid, 1882. Died Providence, Oct. 17, 1891.

LINCOLN, Levi, gov. Mass.; b. Hingham, Mass., May 15, 1749; s. Enoch and Rachel (Fearing) L.; grad. Harvard, 1772; m. Martha Waldo, Nov. 23, 1781, 9 children, including Enoch, Levi. Admitted to Worcester (Mass.) bar; began practice of law. Worcester, 1772; judge probate, Worcester County; 1771-81; mem. 1st Mass. Constl. Conv., 1779-81; mem. Mass. Gen. Ct., 1769; mem. Mass. Senate, 1796-97; mem. U.S. Ho. of Reps. from Mass., 6th Congress, 1800-01; U.S. atty. gen. under Thomas Jefferson, 1801-04; mem. Mass. Gov.'s Council, 1806, 10-12; lt. gov. Mass., 1807-09, gov., 1808-09. Died Worcester, Apr. 14, 1820; buried Rural Cemetery, Worcester.

LINCOLN, Levi, gov. Mass.; b. Worcester, Mass., Oct. 25, 1782; s. Levi and Martha (Waldo) L.; grad. Harvard, 1802; m. Penelope Sever, Sept. 6, 1807, 8 children. Admitted to Worcester bar, 1805, began practice law, Worcester; mem. Mass. Senate, 1812-13; mem. Mass. Ho. of Reps., 1814-22, speaker, 1820-22; mem. Mass. State Constl. Conv., 1820-21; presdl. elector, 1823, 48, 64; lt. gov. Mass., 1823; asso. justice Mass. Supreme Ct., 1824; pres. Worcester County Agrl. Soc., 1824-52; gov. Mass., 1825-34, headed Mass. Bd. of Internal Improvements, 1828, also railroad system instituted in Boston and Lowell (1st railroad constructed 1829), founded Mass. normal schs., 1828, state lunatic asylum, 1829; presided over 1st Mass. Temperance Conv., Worcester, 1833; mem. U.S. Ho. of Reps., 23d-27th congresses, Feb. 17, 1834-Mar. 16, 1841; collector Port of Boston, 1841-43; mem. Mass. Senate, 1844-45, pres., 1845; mem. com. to revise Mass. Militia laws, 1847; mayor Worcester, 1848; founder Am. Antiquarian Soc.; mem. governing bd. Leicester Acad.; bd. overseers Harvard; mem. Mass. Hist. Soc.; pres. Worcester County Bible Soc. Died Worcester, May 29, 1868.

LINCOLN, Mary Todd, first lady; b. Lexington, Ky., Dec. 13, 1818; d. Robert S. and Eliza (Parker) Todd; m. Abraham Lincoln (16th Pres. U.S.), Nov. 4, 1842; children—Robert Todd, Edward Baker, William Wallace, Thomas (Tad). Moved to Springfield, Ill., 1839; wrote newspaper skits for which Lincoln assumed blame, giving rise to Lincoln-Shield newspaper duel; lived in Springfield, 1842-61, in White House, 1861-65; credited with difficult temperament, extravagance (traits which Lincoln described jokingly); object of some nat. malice evolving from her gay social engagements and receptions during Civil War; attended play Our American Cousin at Ford's Theatre during which Lincoln was assassinated, 1865; travelled in Europe before returning to Springfield; granted Congressional pension, 1870; adjudged insane (resulting from depression over deaths of sons William and Thomas and her husband), 1875, spent several months in a pvt. sanitarium, Batavia, Ill., 1875; declared sane, 1875. Died Springfield, July 16, 1882.

LINCOLN, Rufus Pratt, physician; b. Belchertown, Mass., Apr. 27, 1840; s. Rufus S. and Lydia (Baggs) L.; A.B., Amherst Coll., 1862; M.D., Harvard, 1868; m. Caroline C. Tyler, 1869; 1 son, Rufus Tyler. Served to col. Mass. Volunteers, 1862-65; engaged in pvt. practice medicine, specializing in laryngology and intranasal surgery; developed technique for almost painless removal of semi-malignant retronasal growths; a founder N.Y. Laryngol. Soc.; pres. Am. Laryngol. Assn. Died N.Y.C., Nov. 27, 1900.

LINCOLN, William Slosson, congressman; b. Berkshire (now Newark Valley), N.Y., Aug. 13, 1813; attended common schs.; studied law. Admitted to N.Y. bar; engaged in merc. bus., later in leather mfg.; postmaster of Newark Valley, 1838-41, 44-66, supr., 1841, 44, 65-66, justice of peace, 1852-53; mem. U.S. Ho. of Reps. (Republican) from N.Y., 40th Congress, 1867-69; practiced law, Washington, D.C. Died Washington, Apr. 21, 1893; buried Oak Hill Cemetery, Washington.

LIND, Jenny, singer; b. Stockholm, Sweden, Oct. 6, 1821; m. O. Goldschmidt. Appeared on Swedish stage at age of 9; sang various opera roles, Stockholm, 1838-41, various European cities, 1844-45; contracted with P. T. Barnum for Am. concert tour, 1849, was very well received in U.S.; later went on her own tour of U.S.; went into semi-retirement after Am. tours, taught music in London; struck by paralytic stroke shortly before death. Died Malvern, Eng., Nov. 2, 1887.

LINDE, Christian (full name Christian Lemvigh Paul Lövenörn de Linde-Friedenreich), physician; b. nr. Copenhagen, Denmark, Feb. 19, 1817; grad. Royal U. of Copenhagen, 1837; m. Sarah Dickinson, 1843; m. 2d, Sarah Davis, 1852; m. 3d, Hulda Henning Volner, 1858; 3 children including Fred. Came to U.S., 1842; practiced medicine, Oshkosh, Wis. (1st surgeon in that part of Wis.); treated Indians, became very popular with them; 1st to use animal tendons for surg. suture material; v.p. Winnebago County Med. Soc.; pres. Wis. Med. Soc. Died Oshkosh, Nov. 24, 1887.

LINDERMAN, Henry Richard, govt. ofcl.; b. Lehman Twp., Pa., Dec. 26, 1825; s. Dr. John Jordan and Rachel (Brodhead) L. Chief clk. Phila. Mint, 1853-64, dir., 1867-69; assistant in drafting Coinage Act of 1873, 1869-70; examined Western mints, 1872; 1st dir. U.S. Bur. of Mint (when coin act passed), 1873-79. Died Washington, D.C., Jan. 27, 1879.

LINDHEIMER, Ferdinand Jacob, botanist; b. Frankfurt-am-Main, Germany, May 21, 1801; s. Johan H. Lindheimer; attended U. Weisbaden, U. Bonn (Germany); m. Elenore Reinarz, 1846. Came to U.S., 1834; served in Tex. Army in war for independence; travelled throughout Tex. collecting bot. specimens, 1841-52; participated in exptl. communistic colony, Bettina, Tex., 1847; editor Neu Braunfelser (Tex.) Zeitung, 1852-70; his bot. work described in Plantae Lindheimerianae published in Boston Jour. of Natural History, Vol. V, 1845, Vol. VI, 1850. Died New Braunfels, Comal County, Dec. 2, 1879.

LINDLEY, Daniel, clergyman, missionary; b. Washington County, Pa., Aug. 24, 1801; s. Jacob and Hannah (Dickey) L.; grad. Ohio U., 1824; attended Sem., Hampden-Sydney, Va.; m. Lucy Allen, Nov. 20, 1834, children—Mary, Martha, Sarah, Newton, Charlotte, Daniel, John, Lucy, James, Charles, Clara. Ordained minister in Concord Presbytery, Synod of N.C., 1832; pastor, Rock River, N.C.; mem. 1st missionary band to South Africa (sent by Am. Bd. Commrs. for Fgn. Missions), 1834; settled in what is now Marico dist. of Trasvaal to work among Matebele tribe; went to Natal when Boers from Cape Colony attacked the Matebele; minister to Trek-Boren tribe (parish included Natal, Orange Free State and Transvaal), 1841-47; worked among Zulus, Inanda, Natal, 1847-59; came to U.S., 1859-62, returned to Inanda, 1862-73; founded Zulu girls' sem., Inanda; ret., 1873. Died Sept. 3, 1880.

LINDLEY, Jacob, educator; b. Washington County, Pa., June 13, 1774; s. Demas Lindley; grad. Coll. of N.J. (now Princeton), 1800; m. Hannah Dickey, 1800, several children including Lutellus. Licensed to preach by Washington County Presbytery, 1800; pastor at Waterford, O., 1803-09, Athens, O., 1809-28, Walnut Hills, O., 1828-29; apptd. trustee proposed Ohio U., 1805, mem. com. to establish acad. at Athens, 1806, preceptor and 1st instr. in prep. dept. (only dept. then in existence) Ohio U., 1808-22, apptd. prof. mental and moral philosophy and belles-lettres (when coll. faculty organized 1822), 1822-24, prof. mathematics, 1824-26, resigned from bd. trustees, 1838. Died Connellsville, Pa., Jan. 29, 1857.

LINDLEY, James Johnson, congressman; b. Mansfield, O., Jan. 1, 1822; attended Woodville Coll., O.; studied law, St. Louis. Admitted to Mo. bar, 1846, began practice in Monticello; elected circuit atty.,

1848, 52; mem. U.S. Ho. of Reps. (Whig) from Mo., 33d-34th congresses, 1853-57; moved to Davenport, Ia., 1858, practiced law; commd. to investigate condition of Ia. troops during Civil War; practiced law, Chgo., until 1868; judge circuit ct. of 8th Mo. Jud. Dist., 1871-83, moved to Kansas City, Mo. Died Nevada, Mo., Apr. 18, 1891; buried Elmwood Cemetery, Kansas City.

LINDSEY, Stephen Decatur, congressman; b. Norridgewock, Me., Mar. 3, 1828; attended Broomfield Acad.; studied law. Admitted to Me. bar, began practice in Norridgewock, 1853; clk. Somerset County (Me.) jud. cts., 1857-60; mem. Me. Ho. of Reps., 1856; mem. Me. Senate, 1868-70, pres. 1869; del. Republican Nat. Conv., 1860, 68; mem. Me. Exec. Council, 1874; mem. U.S. Ho. of Reps. (Rep.) from Me., 45th-47th congresses, 1877-83. Died Norridgewock, Apr. 26, 1884; buried River View Cemetery, Norridgewock.

LINDSLEY, John Berrien, physician, clergyman, educator; b. Princeton, N.J., Oct. 24, 1822; s. rev. Philip and Margaret (Lawrence) L.; A.B., U. Nashville, 1839; M.D., U. Pa., 1843; D.D. (hon.) Princeton, 1856; m. Sarah McGavock, Nov. 9, 1857, 6 children. Ordained by Presbytery of Nashville (Tenn.), 1846; faculty med. dept. U. Nashville (1st school of kind South of Ohio River), 1850, induced trustees by buy Peabody Normal Coll., dean, 6 years, prof. chemistry and pharmacy, until 1873, chancellor, 1855, dean med. sch., 4 years; mem. Nashville Bd. Edn., 1856-60; in charge of Confederate hosps. in Nashville during Civil War; organized Montgomery Bell Acad. as prep. sch., 1867; an organizer Tenn. Coll. Pharmacy, 1873, later prof. materia medica; health officer, Nashville, 1876-80; contbr. to Theol. Medium; published Military Annals of Tennessee Confederate. Died Nashville, Dec. 7, 1897.

LINDSLEY, Philip, clergyman, coll. pres.; b. nr. Morristown, N.J., Dec. 21, 1786; s. Isaac and Phoebe (Condict) L.; grad. Coll. of N.J. (now Princeton), 1804; m. Margaret Elizabeth Lawrence, Oct. 1813; m. 2d, Mrs. Mary Ann (Sillman) Ayers, Apr. 19, 1849; several children including John Berrien. Tutor, Coll. of N.J., 1807-10, sr. tutor, 1812-13, prof. langs., 1813-17, v.p. 1817-23, acting pres., 1822-23; licensed to preach by Presbytery of New Brunswick, N.J., 1810; pastor in Newton, N.Y., 1810-12; ordained pastor, 1817; pres. U. Nashville (Tenn.), 1825-50; prof. New Albany (Ind.) Theol. Sem., 1850-53; moderator Presbyn. Gen. Assembly, 1834. Died Nashville, May 25, 1855.

LINDSLEY, William Dell, congressman; b. New Haven, Dec. 25, 1812; attended common schs. Moved to Buffalo, N.Y., 1832; moved to Erie County, O., settled nr. Sandusky; engaged in farming; served as capt. Ohio Militia, 1840-43, commd. brig. gen., 1843; mem. U.S. Ho. of Reps. (Democrat) from Ohio, 33d Congress, 1853-55. Died Perkins Twp., Erie County, Mar. 11, 1890; buried Oakland Cemetery, Sandusky.

LINGARD, James W., actor, theatrical mgr. Opened (in partnership with George L. Fox) New Bowery Theater, N.Y.C., 1859, presented Shakespearean plays, also various sensational works including Fast Women of a Modern Time.

LINING, John, physician; b. Scotland, 1708; m. Sarah Hill, 1739, no children. Came to Am., 1730; practiced medicine, Charlestown (now Charleston), S.C.; made extensive studies of epidemic diseases; sent to Europe 1st scientific account of yellow fever in Am., 1748; studied effects of climate on metabolism; kept 1st published weather records in Am. Died Sept. 21, 1760.

LINN, Archibald Ladley, congressman; b. N.Y.C., Oct. 15, 1802; grad. Union Coll., Schenectady, N.Y., 1820; studied law. Admitted to N.Y. bar, began practice in Schenectady; judge Schenectady County, 1840-45; mem. U.S. Ho. of Reps. (Whig) from N.Y., 27th Congress, 1841-43; mem. N.Y. Assembly, 1844. Died Schenectady, Oct. 10, 1857.

LINN, James, congressman; b. Bedminster Twp., N.J., 1749; grad. Coll. of N.J. (now Princeton), 1869; studied law. Admitted to the bar, 1772; began practice of law, Trenton, N.J.; judge Somerset County (N.J.) Ct. of Common Pleas; mem. N.J. Provincial Congress, 1776; served as capt. Somerset County Militia during Revolutionary War, 1776, 1st maj., 1776-81; mem. N.J. Council, 1777, 93-97, N.J. Gen. Assembly, 1790-91; mem. U.S. Ho. of Reps. (Democrat) from N.J., 6th Congress, 1799-1801; supr. of revenue (apptd. by Pres. Jefferson), 1801-09; sec. of state N.J., 1809-20. Died Trenton, Jan. 5, 1821; buried Lamington Presbyn. Ch. Cemetery, Somerset County.

LINN, John, congressman; b. nr. Johnsonburg, N.J., Dec. 3, 1763; attended common schs., Sussex County, N.J. Served as pvt. and sgt. during Revolutionary War; mem. N.J. Gen. Assembly, 1801-04; judge ct. common pleas, 1805-21; sheriff Sussex County, 1812; mem. U.S. Ho. of Reps. from N.J., 15th-16th congresses, 1817-21. Died Washington, D.C., Jan. 5, 1821; buried North Hardyston Cemetery, nr. Franklin Furnace, N.J.

LINN, John Blair, poet; b. Shippensburg, Pa., Mar. 14, 1777; s. William and Rebecca (Blair) L.; grad. Columbia Coll., 1795; studied law under Alexander Hamilton; m. Hester Bailey, 1799, 3 children. Licensed to preach by classis of Albany (N.Y.), 1798; pastor 1st Presbyn. Ch. of Phila., 1798-1804. Author: (play) Bourville Castle, or the Gallic Orphan, 1797; (poetry) Miscellaneous Works, Prose and Poetical, by a Young Gentleman of New York, 1795, The Poetical Wanderer, 1796, The Death of George Washington: A Poem in Imitation of the Manner of Ossian, 1800, The Powers of Genius, 1801; A Discourse Occasioned by the Death of the Reverend John Ewing, 1802. Died Phila., Aug. 30, 1804.

LINN, Lewis Fields, physician, senator; b. Louisville, Ky., Nov. 5, 1796; s. Asahel and Nancy Ann (Hunter) L.; m. Elisabeth Relfe, 1818. Began practice medicine, Sainte Genevieve, Mo., 1816; authority on Asiatic cholera; mem. Mo. Senate, circa 1828; apptd. commr. to settle French land claims in Mo. 1833; mem. U.S. Senate from Mo., 1833-43, chmn. com. on the territories, wrote Oregon Bill providing for occupation, govt. and defense of Ore. Territory. Died Sainte Genevieve, Oct. 3, 1843; buried Protestant Cemetery, Sainte Genevieve.

LINTNER, Joseph Albert, entomologist; b. Schoharie, N.Y., Feb. 8, 1822; s. George Ames and Maria (Wagner) L.; Ph.D. (hon.), U. State of N.Y.; m. Frances C. Hutchinson, 1856. In business, N.Y.C., 1837-48, Schoharie, 1848-60; mfr. woolens, Utica, N.Y., 1860-68; began collecting insects, 1853; asst. in zoology N.Y. State Mus., 1868-74, head entomol. dept., 1874-80; N.Y. State entomologist, 1880-98; entomol. editor Country Gentleman for 25 years; pres. Assn. Econ. Entomologists, 1892. Author: (pamphlet) Entomological Contributions, 4 issues, 1872-79. Died Rome, Italy, May 5, 1898.

LINTON, William James, wood engraver, author; b. London, Eng., Dec. 7, 1812; A.M. (hon.), Yale, 1891; married 3 times; m. 3d, Eliza Lynn, 1858, at least 1 dau., Margaret Linton Mather. Apprenticed to George Wilmot Bonner, wood engraver; partner John O. Smith, wood engraver, London, 1842-66; edited polit. reform mags. Odd Fellow, 1841-42, Leader, 1850, English Republic, 1851-55, No. Tribune, 1854; edited literary jour. Illuminated Mag., 1845; came to U.S., 1866; taught wood engraving Cooper Union, N.Y.C., 1868-70; mem. N.A.D., 1882-97; founder, owner Appledore Press, New Haven, Conn., 1878-97, published limited edits. Author: Life of Paine, 1839; To the Future, 1848; The Plaint of Freedom, 1852; Claribel and Other Poems, 1865; Some Practical Hints on Wood-graving for the Instruction of Reviewers and the Public, 1879; The History of Wood-Engraving in America, 1882; The Golden Apples of Hesperus, 1882; Wood-Engraving: A Manual of Instruction, 1884; Masters of Wood-Engraving, 1889; Poems and Translations, 1889. Illustrator: Snow-Bound (John Greenleaf Whittier), 1868; Building of the Ship (Henry W. Longfellow), 1870; Thanatopsis (William Cullen Bryant), 1878. Died New Haven, Dec. 29, 1897.

LIPPARD, George, author; b. Chester County, Pa., Apr. 10, 1822; s. Daniel B. and Jemina (Ford) L.; m. Rose Newman, May 14, 1847. Reporter, columnist Spirit of the Times, Phila., 1841-42; wrote short stories for The Citizen Soldier, Phila. weekly, 1843-44; lectr. on Am. Revolution in Phila.; published The Quaker City, Phila. weekly., 1849; established his own religion and philosophy in reaction to what he considered hypocrisy of Christianity; organized Brotherhood of the Union, communist orgn. based on brotherhood of man, 1850; short stories include: Philippe de Agramont, 1842, Herbert Tracy, 1842, The Battle Day of Germantown, 1843. Author: (novels) The Quaker City, 1845; The Nazarene, 1846; Blanche of Brandywine, 1846; Legends of Mexico, 1847; Washington and His Generals, 1847; Paul Ardenheim, 1848; Bel of Prairie Eden, 1848; Adonai, The Pilgrim of Eternity, 1851; The Man with the Mask, 1852; The Empire City, 1853; Eleanor; or, Slave-Catching in Philadelphia, 1854. Died Phila., Feb. 9, 1854; buried Odd Fellows Cemetery, Phila.

LIPPINCOTT, James Starr, horticulturist, meteorologist; b. Phila., Apr. 12, 1819; s. John and Sarah (Starr) L.; attended Haverford (Pa.) Coll., 1834-35; m. Susan Haworth Ecroyd, 1857; m. 2d, Anne E. Shepphard, 1861; no children. Farmer at Cole's Landing, later at Haddonfield, N.J.; del. World's Peace Congress, Frankfort, Germany, 1850; invented vapor index for measuring humidity of air; meteorol. observer for Smithsonian Instn. at Cole's Landing, 1864-66, Haddonfield, 1869-70. Author: Universal Pronouncing Dictionary of Biography and Mythology, 1870. Contbr. articles to Reports of Commrs. of Agr., including: Climatology of American Grape Vines, 1862, Geography of Plants, 1863, Market Products of West New Jersey, 1865, Observations on Atmospheric Humidity, 1865, The Fruit Regions of the Northern United States and Their Climates, 1866. Died Greenwich, Cumberland County, N.J., Mar. 17, 1885.

LIPPINCOTT, Joshua Ballinger, publisher; b. Johnstown, N.J., Mar. 18, 1813; s. Jacob and Sarah (Ballinger) L.; m. Josephine Craige, Oct. 16, 1845, 4 children. Founder, J.B. Lippincott & Co., 1836; purchased Grigg, Elliott & Co., 1849, reorganized firm into Lippincott, Grambo & Co., 1850 (again became J.B. Lippincott & Co. with Grambo's retirement 1855), acknowledged leader publishing bus. in Phila.; dir. Farmers' and Mechanics' Bank of Phila., 1854; bd. mgrs. Phila. Savs. Fund Soc., 1861; dir. Pa. Co. for Ins. on Lives and Granting Annuities, 1862; published Lippincott's Pronouncing Gazetteer, 1855, Critical Dictionary of English Literature and British and American Authors, (Samuel Austin Alliborne), 1870-71, Lippincott's Mag., 1868; pres. Soc. Prevention of Cruelty to Animals; a founder, donor to dept. vet. medicine U. Pa.; incorporator J. B. Lippincott Publishing Co., 1885. Died Phila., Jan. 5, 1886.

LIPPITT, Henry, mfr., gov. R.I.; b. Providence, R.I., Oct. 9, 1818; s. Warrenan Eliza (Seamans) L.; grad. acad., Kingston, R.I.; m. Mary Ann Balch, Dec. 16, 1845, 11 children. Organizer, Providence Bd. of Trade, presiding officer, 3 years; asso. with Edward Walcott in firm Walcott & Lippett, bale cotton dealers, 1838-40; organizer, lt. col. Providence Marine Corps of Arty., 1840-42; with Armory Chapin & Co., 1848, Quinebaug Mfg. Co., 1849; commr. for enrolling and drafting men under call for soldiers, 1862-69; organizer, pres. Silver Spring Bleaching & Dyeing Co.; pres. R.I. Nat. Bank, R.I. Instn. for Savs., Wheaton Hotel Co.; pres. Providence Opera House Assn.; treas. Social Mfg. Co.; gov. R.I., 1875-76. Died Providence, June 5, 1891.

LIPSCOMB, Abner Smith, jurist; b. Abbe-ville dist., S.C., Feb. 10, 1789; s. Joel and Elizabeth (Chiles) L.; m. Elizabeth Gaines, Apr. 13, 1813; m. 2d Mary (Hunt) Bullock, May 10, 1843. Admitted to S.C. bar, 1811; mem. Ala. Territorial Legislature, 1818; circuit judge Ala., 1819; chief justice Supreme Ct. Ala., 1823-35; mem. Ala. Legislature, (Democrat) 1838, chmn. judiciary com.; sec. of state Texas, 1839; mem. Tex. Constl. Conv. 1845; justice Tex. Supreme Ct., 1845-56; county in N.W. Tex. named for him. Died Austin, Tex., Dec. 8, 1856.

LIPSCOMB, Andrew Adgate, clergyman, coll. pres.; b. Georgetown, D.C., Sept. 16, 1816; s. Rev. William Corrie and Phoebe (Adgate) L.; D.D. (hon.), U. Ala., 1851; D.D. (hon.), Emory Coll., 1853; m. Henrietta Richardson, 1839; m. 2d, Susan Dowdell; 1 child. Ordained to ministry Methodist Episcopal Ch., 1834, called to Montgomery, Ala., 1842; founder Met. Inst. for Young Ladies, Montgomery; pres. Female Coll., Tuskegee, Ala., 1855-60; chancellor U. Ga., 1860-74; prof. art, philosophy and criticism Vanderbilt U., Nashville, Tenn.; Shakespeare scholar and lectr. Author: Our Country; The Social Spirit of Christianity; Christian Heoism; Lessons in the Life of Saint Peter; Studies in The Forty Days. Died Athens, Ga., Nov. 23, 1890.

LISA, Manuel, fur trader; b. New Orleans, Sept. 8, 1772; s. Christopher and Maria (Rodriguez) de Lisa; m. Mary Charles; m. 2d, Mitain (Omaha Indian), 1814; m. 3d, Mrs. Mary (Hempstead) Keeney, 1819; 5 children including Raymond. Became fur trader, St. Louis, circa 1790; held patent from Spanish govt. granting him monopoly of trade with Osage Indians; established Ft. Raymond (later Ft. Manuel) at mouth of Big Horn River, 1807 (1st ft. on upper Missouri River); a founder Mo. Fur Co., 1808; established Ft. Lisa at mouth of Big Knife River, 1809; U.S. sub-agt. for Indian tribes on Missouri River about mouth of Kansas River, 1814-20. Died St. Louis, Aug. 12, 1820; buried Bellefontaine Cemetery, St. Louis.

LISLE, Marcus Claiborne, congressman; b. nr. Winchester, Ky., Sept. 23, 1862; attended U. Ky.; grad. law dept. Columbia. Admitted to Ky. bar, began practice in Winchester, 1887; county judge Clark County (Ky.), 1890; mem. U.S. Ho. of Reps. (Democrat) from Ky., 53d Congress, 1893-94. Died Winchester, July 7, 1894; buried Winchester Cemetery.

LIST, Georg Friedrich, German, American economist; b. Reutlingen, Wurttemberg, Germany, Aug. 6, 1789; s. Johannes and Mrs. (Schafer) L.; ed. U. Tubingen; m. Catherine (Seybold) Neidhard, circa 1818; 4 children. Entered public service of Wurttemberg, 1806; rose to ministerial undersec.; prof. administrn. and politics U. Tubingen, 1817; lost post, 1819, because of polit., econ. ideas; elected to Diet of Wurttemberg from Reutlingen, 1819; charged with sedition because of his advocacy of reforms, exiled; came to Am., 1825, naturalized; toured Atlantic states with Lafayette; became editor of Readinger Adler, Reading, Pa.; loomed as a leading advocate of protective tariff and "Am. System" with his writings, address to Pa. legislature, 1828, and dispute with Gov. W. B. Giles of Va.; developed anthracite deposits near Tamaqua, Pa.; organized Little Schuylkill Navigation, R. R. & Coal Co. (progenitor of modern Reading System), 1828, opened 1831; exec. agt. Dept. of State, went to Europe, planned to introduce Pa. anthracite coal there; U.S. consul, Baden, Germany, 1831-34, Leipzig, 1834-37, Stuttgart, 1843-45; founder Zollvereinsblatt, polit. economy jour., 1843; visited England in vain attempt to prepare comml. alliance between that nation and Germany, 1846; retired heartbroken to Augsburg. An architect of econ. nationalism. Author: Outlines of American Political Economy, 1827; National System of Political Economy, 1841. Died, a suicide, in the Tyrol, Nov. 30, 1846.

LITCHFIELD, Electus Backus, railroad exec.; b. Delphi Falls, N.Y., Feb. 15, 1813; s. Elisha and Percy (Tiffany) L.; m. Hannah Maria Breed, 1836, 5 children. Wholesale grocer, N.Y.C., 1844-54; treas., later pres. Toledo & Cleve. R.R.; built Fifth Av. and Atlantic Av. street rys., Coney Island Plank Rd., Bklyn.; owned Bklyn., Bath, and West End R.R.; with brothers in firm of E. B. Litchfield and Co. acted as agt., banker and broker for various Am. railroads; owner St. Paul and Pacific R.R., 1862-70, 73-79. Died May 12, 1889.

LITCHFIELD, Elisha, congressman; b. Canterbury, Conn., July 12, 1785; attended common schs. Learned carpenter's trade; moved to Onondaga County, N.Y., settled in Delphi, N.Y., 1812; served as maj. during War of 1812; justice of peace and supr. Onondaga County; postmaster of Delphi, 1817-21; engaged in merc. bus.; mem. N.Y. Assembly, 1819, 31-33, 44, 48, speaker, 1848; mem. U.S. Ho. of Reps. (Democrat) from N.Y., 17th-18th congresses, 1821-25; moved to Cazenovia, N.Y., 1838. Died Cazenovia, Aug. 4, 1859; buried City Cemetery, Delphi Falls, N.Y.

LITTEL, Emlyn T., architect; b. Phila., 1840; grad. U. Pa. Practiced as architect, N.Y.C.; specialized in ecclesiastical design; noteworthy examples of his work include Ch. of Incarnation, Rectory of Zion Ch., House of St. John the Baptist, all N.Y.C., Ch. and Sch. of St. James, Phila.; sec. A.I.A., 1862-63, elected pres. N.Y. chpt., circa 1890. Died Apr. 2, 1891.

LITTELL, Eliakim, editor, publisher; b. Burlington, N.J., Jan. 2, 1797; s. Stephen and Susan (Gardner) L.; m. Mary Frazee Smith, Feb. 12, 1828, 6 children including Robert Smith. Spread European thought in Am. by reprinting articles from fgn. mags.; editor Phila. Register and Nat. Recorder, 1819, name changed to Nat. Recorder, 1819-21, to Saturday Mag., 1821-22, to Museum Fgn. Literature and Science, 1822-43, merged with Am. Eclectic under name Eclectic Museum of Fgn. Literature, Science and Art, 1843; founded, published, edited Littell's Living Age, Boston, 1844-70; published Jour. Fgn. Med. Science and Literature, 1824, The Religious Mag. and Spirit of Fgn. Theol. Jours., 1828, The Panorama of Life and Literature, 1855-70. Died Brookline, Mass., May 17, 1870.

LITTELL, Squier, physician; b. Burlington, N.J., Dec. 9, 1803; s. Stephen and Susan (Gardner) L.; M.D., U. Pa., 1824; m. Mary Graff Emlin, 1834, 2 children. Practiced medicine, Phila.; specialist in opthalmic surgery; surgeon Wills Hosp. for lame, halt and blind, 1834-64; mem. Coll. Physicians of Phila., 1836-86; editor Monthly Jour. of Fgn. Medicine, 1828-29, Banner of the Cross, 1839-41. Author: A Manual of Diseases of the Eye, 1837. Died Bay Head, N.J., July 4, 1886.

LITTELL, William, lawyer, author; b. N.J., 1768; LL.D. (hon.), Transylvania U., 1810; m. Martha McCracken, Jan. 22, 1816; m. 2d, Eliza Hickman, Dec. 9, 1823; 2 children including William. Practiced law, Frankfurt, Ky.; wrote satirical essays; compiled statutes under commn. of State of Ky. Author: Epistles of William, Surnamed Littell, to the People of the Realm of Kentucky, 1806; A Narrative of the Settlement of Kentucky, 1806; Political Transactions in and Concerning Kentucky, 1806; Principles of Law and Equity, 1808; Statute Law of Kentucky, 5 vols., 1809-19; Festoons of Fancy, Consisting of Compositions Amatory, Sentimental, and Humorous in Verse and Prose, 1814. Died Sept. 26, 1824.

LITTLE, Charles Coffin, publisher; b. Kennebunk, Me., July 25, 1799; s. David and Sarah (Chase) L.; m. Sarah Anne Hilliard, Jan. 1, 1829; m. 2d, Abby Wheaton, Jan. 18, 1854; 5 children. Clk., Carter, Hilliard and Co., booksellers, Boston, 1821-27, partner in reorganized firm Hilliard, Gray, & Co., 1827-37; sr. partner (with James Brown; gen. mgr. Little and Brown, 1837-47, renamed Little, Brown, & Co., 1847-69; selectman of Cambridge, Mass., 1836, 41; mem. Mass. Legislature, 1836-37. Died Aug. 9, 1869.

LITTLE CROW V, Indian chief; b. 1803; s. Little Crow IV; 22 children. Signer Treaty of Mendota (in which Mdewakanton Sioux ceded their lands in Southeastern Minn. and agreed to move to upper Minnesota River area), 1851; leader Sioux uprising, 1861, lead unsuccessful attack on Ft. Ridgely, Aug. 20-22, 1861, commanded force defeated by Gen. Henry Sibley at Wood Lake, Minn., Sept. 23, 1861. Died July 3, 1863.

LITTLE, Edward Preble, congressman; b. Marshfield, Mass., Nov. 7, 1791; s. Capt. George Little; attended pub. schs. Commd. midshipman U.S. Navy (at age 9, by suggestion of Pres. Adams), 1800, accompanied his father on frigate Boston; engaged in farming; mem. Mass. Ho. of Reps., 1829-34, 35-38; mem. U.S. Ho. of Reps. (Democrat) from Mass., 32d Congress, Dec. 13, 1852-53; collector of customs Port of Plymouth (Mass.), 1853-57. Died Lynn, Mass., Feb. 6, 1875; buried Congregational Ch. Cemetery, Marshfield Hills, Mass.

LITTLE, George, naval officer; b. Marshfield, Mass., Apr. 15, 1754; s. Lemuel and Penelope (Eames) L.; m. Rachel Rogers, June 24, 1779, at least 1 son, Edward Preble. Commd. 2d lt. Mass. Navy, 1778, promoted 1st lt., 1779; served as 1st officer in Hazard, 1779; promoted capt. in charge of Winthrop, 1782; discharged, 1783; apptd. capt. U.S. Navy, 1799; in command of Boston, 1799-1800, captured several prizes including Danish ship Flying Fish, French ships Deux Anges and Berceau; discharged, 1801. Died Weymouth, Mass., July 22, 1809.

LITTLE, Peter, congressman; b. Petersburg, Pa., Dec. 11, 1775; attended common schs. Watchmaker; engaged in farming, Freedom, Md.; mem. Ho. of Dels., 1806-07; mem. U.S. Ho. of Reps. (Democrat) from Md., 12th, 14th-20th congresses, 1811-13, Sept. 2, 1816-29; served as col. 38th Md. Inf., during War of 1812, 1813-15; judge Baltimore County Orphan's Ct. Died Freedom, Feb. 5, 1830; buried Freedom Methodist Episcopal Cemetery, nr. Eldersburg, Md.

LITTLE TURTLE (Indian name Michi Kini Kwa), Miami chief; b. Eel River, Ft. Wayne, Ind., circa 1752. Led slaughter U.S. troops under Gen. Arthur St. Clair in Ky., 1791; commanded Indian forces, 1792; defeated with loss great numbers by Gen. Wayne, 1794; signed Treaty Greenville, 1795, and many subsequent treaties with U.S. Died Ft. Wayne, July 14, 1812.

LITTLEFIELD, Nathaniel Swett, congressman; b. Wells, Me., Sep. 20, 1804; attended common schs.; studied law. Admitted to Me. bar, 1827, began practice in Bridgton; postmaster of Bridgton, 1827-41; sec. Me. Senate, 1831-32, mem., 1837-39, pres., 1838; mem. U.S. Ho. of Reps. (Democrat) from Me., 27th, 31st congresses, 1841-43, 49-51; mem. Me. Ho. of Reps., 1854; del. Union Conv., Phila., 1866. Died Bridgton, Aug. 15, 1882; buried High St. Cemetery, Bridgton.

LITTLEJOHN, De Witt Clinton, congressman; b. Bridgewater, N.Y., Feb. 7, 1818. Engaged in merc. bus., flour mfg., Oswego, N.Y.; mayor Oswego, 1848-50; mem. N.Y. Assembly, 1853-55, 57, 59-61, 66-67, 70-71, 84; served as col. 110th N.Y. Volunteer Inf., during Civil War; mem. U.S. Ho. of Reps. (Republican) from N.Y., 38th Congress, 1863-65; brevetted brig. gen. U.S. Volunteers, 1865. Died Oswego, Oct. 27, 1892; buried Riverside Cemetery, Oswego.

LITTLEPAGE, Lewis, diplomat; b. Hanover County, Va., Dec. 19, 1762; s. James and Elizabeth (Lewis) L.; attended Coll. William and Mary, 1778-79; never married. Protégé of John Jay (then U.S. minister to Spain), 1780-81; served with Spanish Army, 1781-83; chamberlain to King Stanislaus of Poland, Polish ambassador to Russia, 1786-98; secret Italian envoy to French Court, early 1780's; later engaged in various secret intrigues involving several European countries; returned to U.S., 1801. Died Fredericksburg, Va., July 19, 1802.

LIVERMORE, Abiel Abbot, clergyman; b. Wilton, N.H., Oct. 30, 1811; s. Jonathan and Abigail (Abbot) L.; grad. Harvard, 1835; attended Cambridge (Mass.) Divinity Sch., 1833-36; m. Elizabeth Abbot, May 17, 1838; m. 2d, Mary (Keating) Moore, June 18, 1883; no children. Ordained pastor Congregational Ch., Keene, N.H., 1836-50; pastor Unitarian ch., Cincinnati, 1850-56, Yonkers, N.Y., 1859-63; trustee Cheshire Acad., Keene; founder, corr. sec. Western Unitarian Conf., 1852; editor Christian Inquirer, N.Y.C., 1856-63; pres. Theol. Sch., Meadville, Pa. (now Meadville Theol. Sem., Chgo.), 1863-90. Author: The War with Mexico Reviewed, 1850; Discourses, 1854; Lectures to Young Men on Their Moral Dangers and Duties, 1864. Died Wilton, Nov. 28, 1892.

LIVERMORE, Arthur, congressman, jurist; b. Londonderry (now Derry), N.H., July 29, 1766; s. Samuel and Jane (Browne) L.; studied law under older brother Edward St. Loe Livermore, Concord, N.H.; m. Louisa Bliss, Mar. 27, 1810, 8 children including Arthur. Admitted to N.H. bar, 1791; practiced in Concord, 1791-93, Chester, N.H. after 1793; mem. N.H. Ho. of Reps., 1794-95; solicitor Rockingham County, N.H., 1796-98; judge Superior Ct. of N.H., 1798-1809, chief justice, 1809-13; asso. justice N.H. Supreme Ct., 1813-16; mem. U.S. Ho. of Reps. from N.H., 15th-16th, 18th congresses, 1817-21, 23-25; mem. N.H. Senate, 1820; judge probate Grafton County, N.H., 1822-23; chief justice N.H. Ct. Common Pleas, 1825-32. Died Campton, N.H., July 1, 1853; buried Holderness, N.H.

LIVERMORE, Edward St. Loe, congressman; b. Portsmouth, N.H., Apr. 15, 1762; s. Samuel and Jane (Browne) L.; m. Mehitable Harris, Aug. 7, 1784; m. 2d, Sarah Stackpole, May 2, 1799; 12 children including Samuel, Harriet. Mem. conv. to revise N.H. Constn., 1791; solicitor Rockingham County (N.H.), 1791-93; U.S. dist. atty. for N.H., 1794-97; judge N.H. Supreme Ct., 1797; naval officer Port of Portsmouth, 1798-1802; mem. U.S. Ho. of Reps. (Federalist) from N.H., 10th-11th congresses, 1807-11. Died Tewksbury, Mass., Sept. 15, 1832; buried Old Granary Burying Ground, Boston.

LIVERMORE, George, antiquarian; b. Cambridge, Mass., July 10, 1809; s. Nathaniel and Elizabeth (Gleason) L.; M.A. (hon.), Harvard, 1850; m. Elizabeth Cunningham Odiorne, 3 children. In shoe and leather businesses, Cambridge, 1834-38, then became wool mcht.; authority on hist. bibliography, particularly Bibl. materials; mem. Am. Antiquarian Soc., Mass. Hist. Soc., 1849-65; mem. Am. Acad. Arts and Scis., 1855-65, treas., 1865. Author: The Origin, History, and Character of the New-England Primer, 1849; An Historical Research Respecting the Opinions of the Founders of the Republic, on Negroes as Slaves, as Citizens, and as Soldiers, 1862. Died Aug. 30, 1865.

LIVERMORE, Samuel, Continental congressman, senator; b. Waltham, Mass., May 25, 1732; s. Samuel and Hannah (Brown) L.; grad. Princeton, 1752; m. Jane Brown, 5 children including Edward St. Lowe, Arthur, George Williamson. Admitted to N.H. bar, 1756; mem. N.H. Gen. Ct., 1768-70; King's atty. and judge adv. N.H. Admiralty Ct., 1769-74; an original grantee and chief propr. of Holderness (N. H.); atty.-gen. N.H., 1776; mem. Continental Congress from N.H., 1780-82; chief justice N.H. Supreme Ct., 1782-90; mem. Congress of the Confederation, 1785; mem. N.H. Conv. to ratify U.S. Constn., 1788; mem. U.S. Ho. of Reps. from N.H., 1st-2d congresses, 1789-93; pres. N.H. Constnl. Conv., 1791; mem. U.S. Senate from N.H., 1793-1801, pres. pro tem, 1797, 99. Died Holderness, May 18, 1803; buried Trinity Ch. Cemetery, Holderness.

LIVERMORE, Samuel, lawyer; b. Concord, N.H., Aug. 26, 1786; s. Edward St. Loe and Mehitable (Harris) L.; grad. Harvard, 1804. Admitted to Mass. bar, 1804; practiced in Boston, later New Orleans. Author: A Treatise on the Law Relative to Principals, Agents, Factors, Auctioneers, and Brokers, 1811 (1st Am. work on subject); Dissertations on the Questions which Arise from the Contrariety of the Positive Laws of Different States and Nations, 1828 (1st Am. work on conflict of laws). Died Florence, Ala., July 11, 1833.

LIVINGSTON, Edward, senator, sec. of state, diplomat; b. "Clermont," Columbia County, N.Y., May 26, 1764; s. Robert R. and Margaret (Beekman) L.; grad. Coll. of N.J. (now Princeton), 1791; m. Mary McEvers, Apr. 10, 1788; m. 2d, Madame Louise Moreau de Lassy nee D'Avezac, June 3, 1805; 4 children including Cora, Julia. Admitted to N.Y. bar, 1795; mem. U.S. Ho. of Reps. (Democrat) from N.Y., 4th-6th congresses, Dec. 7, 1795-1801, 18th-2t0h congresses, 1823-29; U.S. atty. for N.Y. Dist., 1801-03; mayor N.Y.C., 1801-03; moved to New Orleans, 1804; aide-de-camp, mil. sec., interpreter, confidential adviser to Andrew Jackson at Battle of New Orleans, 1814; engaged Jean Lafitte to fight with Americans; negotiated with British for exchange of prisoners; mem. La. Ho. of Reps., 1820-22; commd. to revise penal code of La., 1821, presented "Report of the Plan of the Penal Code" to La. Assembly, 1821, finished revision, 1825; mem. Academie des Sciences Morales et Politiques (France); presented "System of Penal Laws for the United States of America" to U.S. Senate, 1828 (no action taken); inherited large fortune from his sister (Mrs. Montgomery), 1828; mem. U.S. Senate from La., 1829-31; U.S. sec. of state, 1831-33, drafted proclamation to the nulifiers of S.C., 1832; U.S. minister to France, 1833-35, attempted to secure payment of U.S. claims against France in Napoleonic Wars (promised in treaty of July 4, 1831). Died Rhinebeck, N.Y., May 23, 1836; buried family vault "Clermont," reinterred, Rhinebeck.

LIVINSTON, Henry Brockholst, asso. justice U.S. Supreme Ct.; b. N.Y.C., Nov. 25, 1757; s. William and Susanna (French) L.; grad. Princeton, 1774;

studied law with Peter Yates, Albany, N.Y., 1782-83; LL.D. (hon.), Harvard, 1810; m. Catherine Keteltas; m. 2d, Ann Ludlow; m. 3d, Catherine (Seaman) Kortright. Commd. capt. Continental Army, 1776, promoted to maj., 1776, lt. col., 1777, serving as aide in siege of Ticonderoga and Battle of Saratoga; left service, 1777; pvt. sec. to John Jay (U.S. minister to Spain), 1779-82; admitted to N.Y. bar, 1783; judge N.Y. State Supreme Ct., 1802-07; asso. justice U.S. Supreme Ct., 1806-23. Mem. N.Y. Soc. Library (trustee), N.Y. Hist. Soc. (v.p. 1805). Died Washington, D.C., Mar. 18, 1823.

LIVINGSTON, Henry Walter, congressman; b. Linlithgo, N.Y., 1768; s. Walter Livingston; grad. Yale, 1786; studied law. Admitted to N.Y. bar, began practice in N.Y.C.; pvt. sec. to Gouverneur Morris (Am. E.E. and M.P. to Paris, France), 1792-94; judge Columbia County (N.Y.), Ct. of Common Pleas; mem. N.Y. Assembly, 1802- 10; mem. U.S. Ho. of Reps., 8th-9th congresses, 1803-07. Died Livingston Manor, Linlithgo, Dec. 22, 1810.

LIVINGSTON, James, state legislator, army officer; b. Montreal, Que., Can., Mar. 27, 1747; s. John and Catryna (Ten Broeck) L.; m. Elizabeth Simpson, 1771; 9 children including Elizabeth, Margaret. Raised and commanded regt. Canadian refugees, Continental Army, 1775; commd. col. by Continental Congress, 1776; mem. 1st bd. regents U. State N.Y., 1784-87; mem. N.Y. Assembly from Montgomery County, 1786-87, 89-91. Died Saratoga County, N.Y., Nov. 29, 1832.

LIVINGSTON, John Henry, clergyman, coll. pres.; b. nr. Poughkeepsie, N.Y., May 30, 1746; s. Henry and Susanna (Conklin) L.; grad. Yale, 1762, U. Utrecht, 1770; m. Sarah Livingstone, Nov. 26, 1775, 1 child. Licensed to preach by Classis of Amsterdam, 1769, ordained, 1770; pastor Dutch Reformed Ch., N.Y.C., 1770-1810; prof. theology Gen. Synod of Dutch Ref. Ch., 1784-1825, thus establishing 1st theol. sem. in U.S.; largely responsible for resolving conflict over sovereignty between Am. and Dutch factions in Ref. Ch.; pres. Queen's Coll. (now Rutgers U.), 1810-25. Author: Oratio Inauguralis de Veritate Religionis Christianae, 1785; The Glory of the Redeemer, 1799; A Funeral Service, or Meditations Adopted to Funeral Addresses, 1812; A Dissertation on the Marriage of a Man with His Sister-in-Law, 1816. Died New Brunswick, N.J., Jan. 20, 1825.

LIVINGSTON, John William, naval officer; b. N.Y.C., May 22, 1804; s. William and Eliza (Livingston) Turk (changed name from Turk to Livingston, 1843); commd. midshipman U.S. Navy, 1823, lt., 1832; served in Mexican War; promoted comdr., 1855; in command ship St. Louis on African coast, 1856-58, steamer Penguin during Civil War; comdt. Norfolk (Va.) Navy Yard, 1862, naval station, Mound City, Ill., 1864; commd. capt., 1861, commodore, 1862, rear adm., 1868. Died N.Y.C., Sept. 10, 1885.

LIVINGSTON, Peter Van Brugh, mcht.; b. Albany, N.Y., Oct. 1710; s. Philip and Catharine (Van Brugh) L.; grad. Yale, 1731; m. Mary Alexander, Nov. 14, 1739; m. 2d, Elizabeth Ricketts, 1767. Became a mcht., N.Y.C., 1731; supplied mil. expdns., financed privateering ventures during French and Indian War; trustee Coll. of N.J. (now Princeton), 1748-61; signed nonimportation agreement prompted by Sugar Act, 1764; mem. N.Y. Com. of 51 organized to choose dels. to 1st Continental Congress, 1774; mem. Com. of 60 and Com. of 100 (which acted successively as provisional govt. of N.Y.), 1775; presiding officer N.Y. Provincial Congress, 1775. Died Elizabethtown, N.J., Dec. 28, 1792.

LIVINGSTON, Philip, Continental congressman; b. Albany, N.Y., Jan. 15, 1716; s. Philip and Catharine (Van Brugh) L.; A.B., Yale, 1737; m. Christina Ten Broeck, Apr. 14, 1740. Established professorship of divinity Yale, 1746; an organizer N.Y. Soc. Library, 1754; alderman E. ward N.Y.C., 1754-63; pres. St. Andrews Soc., N.Y.C., 1756-57; mem. N.Y. Assembly, 1758; mem. N.Y. Ho. of Reps., 1763-69, speaker, 1768; del. Stamp Act Congress, 1765; an organizer N.Y.C. of C., 1768; mem. 1st bd. govs. N.Y. Hosp., 1771; mem. Com. of 51 which named N.Y. dels. to 1st Continental Congress, 1774; mem. Continental Congress, 1774-78; mem. Com. of 60 to enforce terms of Congress, 1775; mem. Com. of 100 to cary on provincial affairs until meeting of 1st Provincial Coongress, 1775; mem. Bd. of Treasury of Continental Congress, 1776; signed Declaration of Independence, 1776; mem. N.Y. State Senate, 1777; a framer N.Y. Constn.; a founder King's Coll. (now Columbia). Died N.Y.C., June 12, 1778; buried Prospect Hill Cemetery, York, Pa.

LIVINGSTON, Robert, sec. Indian affairs; b. Ancrum, Roxburghshire Scotland, Dec. 13, 1654; s. John and Janet (Fleming) L.; m. Alida Van Rensselaer, July 9, 1679; children—Philip, Robert. Town clk. Albany (N.Y.), sec. N.Y. Bd. Commrs. for Indian Affairs, 1675; sec. Indian affairs for N.Y. Province, 1695-1728; mem. N.Y. Provincial Assembly from Albany dist., 1709-11, 16-25, speaker, 1718-25; granted patent by Royal Propr. which made his landholdings into manor and lordship of Livingston. Died Oct. 1, 1728.

LIVINGSTON, Robert Le Roy, congressman; b. Claverack, N.Y.; grad. Coll. of N.J. (now Princeton), 1784. Commd. 1st lt. 12th Inf., U.S. Army, 1799, discharged, 1800; mem. U.S. Ho. of Reps. (Federalist) from N.Y., 11th-12th congresses, 1809-May 6, 1812; served as lt. col. 23d Inf. during War of 1812, 1812-13.

LIVINGSTON, Robert R., jurist; b. N.Y.C., Aug. 1718; s. Robert and Margaret (Howarden) L.; m. Margaret Beekman, Dec. 19, 1742, 9 children including Robert R., Edward. Mem. N.Y. Assembly from Dutchess County, 1758-68; judge N.Y. Admiralty Ct., 1759-63; judge N.Y. Supreme Ct., 1763-68; chmn. N.Y. Com. of Correspondence, 1765; del. Stamp Act Congress, drafted address of congress to King George III, 1765. Died Dec. 9, 1775.

LIVINGSTON, Robert R., Continental congressman, diplomat; b. N.Y.C., Nov. 27, 1746; s. Judge Robert R. and Margaret (Beckman) L.; grad. Kings Coll. (now Columbia), 1765; LL.D. (hon.), U. State of N.Y., 1792; m. Mary Stevens, Sept. 9, 1770, 2 children. Admitted to bar, 1770; recorder N.Y.C., 1773-75; mem. N.Y. Provincial Conv., 1775; del. to Continental Congress, 1775-79, 79-81, 84-85, mem. com. apptd. to draft Declaration of Independence, mem. coms. on financial affairs, supplies, legal orgn., fgn. affairs, mil. problems; del. N.Y. State Constl. Conv., 1777; established N.Y. Ct. of Appeals, drafted commns. for its judges, prepared their instrns., mem. commn. to govern N.Y. after Brit. evacuation; chancellor of N.Y., 1777-1801; U.S. sec. for fgn. affairs, 1781-83; administered oath of office to Gen. Washington as 1st Pres. U.S., 1789; pres. Soc. for Promotion Useful Arts, 1791-1813; U.S. minister to France, 1801, secured U.S.-French treaty resulting in La. Purchase, 1803; mem. 1st N.Y. Canal Commn., 1811; founder, 1st pres. Am. Acad. Fine Arts; trustee N.Y. Soc. Library; friend, patron and partner of Robert Fulton, granted monopoly (with Fulton) on steam navigation by N.Y. State. Died Clermont, N.Y., Feb. 26, 1813; buried estate "Clermont" nr. Clermont.

LIVINGSTON, Walter, Continental congressman; b. Nov. 27, 1740; s. Philip Livingston; children include Henry Walter. Del., N.Y. Provincial Conv., 1775; mem. 1st N.Y. Provincial Congress, 1775; judge Albany County (N.Y.), 1774-75; commissary of stores and provisions for Dept. of N.Y., 1775-76; dep. commissary gen. No. Dept., Continental Army, 1775-76; mem. N.Y. Assembly, 1777-79, speaker, 1778; mem. N.Y. and Mass. Boundary Commn., 1784; mem. bd. regents U. State N.Y., 1784-87; mem. Continental Congress from N.Y., 1784-85; apptd. commr. U.S. Treasury, 1785. Died N.Y.C., May 14, 1797.

LIVINGSTON, William, gov. N.J.; b. Albany, N.Y., Nov. 1723; s. Philip an Catharine (Van Brugh) L.; grad. Yale, 1741, LL.D. (hon.), 1778; m. Susanna French, 1745, 13 children including Henry Brockholst, Susanna, Sarah (Mrs. John Jay). Admitted to N.J. bar, 1748; a counsel for defendants in great chancery suit between proprs. of East Jersey and settlers, 1752; published weekly paper The Independent Reflector, 1752; mem. Essex County Com. of Correspondence, 1774; mem. Continental Congress from N.J., 1774, 75; served as brig. gen. in command N.Y. Militia, 1776; 1st gov. N.J., 1776-90; emm. U.S. Constl. Conv., 1787. Author: (poem) Philosophic Solitude, 1747; A Solioquy, 1770. Editor: A Digest of Laws of New York, 1691-1762, published 1752, 2d edit., 1762. Died Elizabethtown, N.J., July 25, 1790.

LLOYD, David, jurist; b. Manafon, Montgomeryshire, Wales, 1656; m. Sarah Lloyd; m. 2d, Grace Browden, 1697. Atty. gen. Pa., 1686; clk. Philadelphia County Ct.; clk. Pa. Provincial Ct., dep. master of rolls; rep. from Chester County in Pa. Assembly, 1693-95, speaker, 1694; mem. Pa. Provincial Council from Chester County, 1695-96, 98-1700; apptd. dep. judge and advocate to admiralty; mem. Pa. Assembly from Philadelphia County, 1703-10, speaker, 1704-05, 06-09, from Chester County, 1711, 12-14, 15-18, 23-24, 25-29, speaker, 1714-15, 23-24, 25-29, leader Democratic or Antiproprietary party, 1700-29; recorder Phila. City Ct., 1702-08; chief justice Province of Pa., 1717-31. Author: A Vindication of the Legislative Powers, 1725. Died Chester, Pa., Mar. 26, 1731.

LLOYD, Edward, state senator; b. Nov. 15, 1744; s. Edward and Ann (Rousby) L.; m. Elizabeth Tayloe, Nov. 19, 1767. Mem. Md. Ho. of Burgesses from Talbot County, 1771; mem. Com. of Correspondence for Talbot County, 1774; mem. lower house Md. Legislature under new state constn., 1777-80; mem. Exec. Council, 1777-80; mem. Md. Senate from Eastern Shore, 1781-96; Md. del. in Congress of Confedn., 1783-84; del. from Talbot County in Md. Conv. which ratified U.S. Constn. Died July 8, 1796.

LLOYD, Edward, senator, gov. Md.; b. "Wye House," Talbot County, Md., July 22, 1779; s. Edward and Elizabeth (Tayloe) L.; m. Sally Scott Murray, Nov. 30, 1797. Mem. Md. Ho. of Dels., 1800-05; mem. U.S. Ho. of Reps. from Md., 9th-10th congresses, Dec. 3, 1806-09; gov. Md., 1809-11; mem. U.S. Senate from Md., 1819-26, sometimes presiding officer. Died Annapolis, Md., June 2, 1834; buried Wye family burying grounds, Talbot County.

LLOYD, James, physician; b. Oyster Bay, L.I., N.Y., Mar. 24, 1728; s. Henry and Rebecca (Nelson) L.; studied medicine under Dr. William Clark, Boston, 1745-50, obstetrics and surgery under William Smellie and William Cheselden, London, Eng., 1750-52; m. Sarah Corwin, at least 1 child, James. Began practice surgery, Boston, 1752; 1st physician to practise midwifery in Am.; early advocate of vaccination for smallpox; only noted physician to remain in Boston during Am. Revolution. Died Boston, Mar. 14, 1810.

LLOYD, James, senator; b. "Farley" nr. Chestertown, Md., 1745; studied law. Admitted to the bar, practiced law; commd. 2d lt. Kent County (Md.) Militia, 1776, served in Revolutionary War; served as gen. during War of 1812; mem. U.S. Senate (Democrat) from Md., Dec. 11, 1797-Dec. 1, 1800; practiced law. Died "Ratclift Manor" nr. Easton, Md., 1820; buried "Clover," Queen Annes County, Md.

LLOYD, James, senator; b. Boston, Dec. 1769; attended Boston Latin Sch.; grad. Harvard, 1787. Engaged as mcht.; mem. Mass. Ho. of Reps., 1800-01, Mass. Senate, 1804; mem. U.S. Senate (Federalist) from Mass., June 9, 1808-May 1, 1813, June 5, 1822-May 23, 1826; moved to Phila., 1826. Died N.Y.C., Apr. 5, 1831; buried Kings' Chapel Burying Ground, Boston.

LLOYD, Thomas, physician, colonial ofcl.; b. Dolobran, Wales, Eng., Apr. 6, 1640; s. Charles and Elizabeth (Stanley) L.; grad. Jesus Coll., Oxford, Eng., 1662; studied medicine; m. Mary Jones, Nov. 9, 1665; m. 2d, Patience (Gardiner) Story; numerous children. In semi-internment due to his Quaker beliefs, 1665-72; practiced medicine; came to Am., 1683; master rolls of Phila., 1683; mem. Pa. Provincial Council, 1684, pres., 1684-88; keeper of the Great Seal of the Province, 1684; pres. Pa. Council, 1689-91; dep. gov. Pa., 1691-93. Died Phila., Aug. 31, 1694.

LOAN, Benjamin Franklin, congressman; b. Hardinsburg, Ky., Oct. 4, 1819; studied law, Ky. Moved to St. Joseph, Mo., 1838; admitted to Mo. bar, 1840, began practice in St. Joseph; served with U.S. Army during Civil War, brig. gen. Mo. Militia, 1861-63; declined appointment as judge Mo. Supreme Ct., 1863; mem. U.S. Ho. of Reps. from Mo., as Emancipationist, 38th-39th congresses, 1863-67, as Radical, 40th Congress, 1867-69; apptd. a visitor U.S. Mil. Acad. by Pres. Grant, 1869; declined appointments as mem. diplomatic missions to Venezuela and Brazil, gov. N.M., territorial judge; resumed law practice, St. Joseph; del. Republican Nat. Conv., Cincinnati, 1876. Died St. Joseph, Mar. 30, 1881; buried Mt. Mora Cemetery, St. Joseph.

LOCHMAN, John George, clergyman; b. Phila., Dec. 2, 1773; s. Nicolaus and Anna Maria (Schneider) L.; grad. U. Pa., 1789; m. Mary Grotz, Sept. 7, 1795; m. 2d, Susan Hoffman, June 3, 1799; 15 children including Augustus Hoffman. Licensed to preach by Lutheran Ministerium of Pa., 1794; ordained minister Luth. Ch., 1800; pastor Lebanon, Pa., 1794-1815, Harrisburg, Pa., 1815-26; pres. Ministerium of Pa., 1818; a founder Gen. Synod Luth. Ch. in Am., 1821, pres., 1821-26. Author: Haupt-Inhalt der Christlichen Lehre, 1808; The History, Doctrine, and Discipline of the Evangelical Lutheran Church, 1818; Principles of the Christian Religion, 1822; Hinterlassene Predigten, 1828. Died Harrisburg, July 10, 1826.

LOCKE, David Ross, journalist; b. nr. Binghamton, N.Y., Sept. 20, 1833; s. Nathaniel Reed and Hester (Ross) L.; m. Martha Bodine, 3 children. Publisher, Plymouth (O.) Advertiser, 1852; later worked for various newspapers in Ohio; editor Jeffersonian, Findlay, O., 1861-65; editor, part-owner Toledo (O.) Blade, 1865-88; mng. editor Evening Mail, N.Y.C., 1871; began writing polit. satire under name Petroleum V. Nasby, 1861, used Nasby as caricature of Copperhead Democrats to criticize slavery, Democrats, the South and intemperance. Died Toledo, Feb. 15, 1888.

LOCKE, Francis, senator; b. Rowan County, N.C., Oct. 31, 1776; attended U. N.C.; studied law. Admitted to N.C. bar, practiced law; judge N.C. Superior Ct., 1803-14; Democratic Presdl. elector, 1808; elected mem. U.S. Senate from N.C., 1814, resigned without qualifying, Dec. 5, 1815. Died Rowan

County, Jan. 8, 1823; buried Thyatira Churchyard, nr. Salisbury, N.C.

LOCKE, John, philosopher; b. Wrington, Somerset, Eng., Aug. 29, 1632; s. John and Agnes (Keene) L.; B.A., Christ Coll., Oxford (Eng.) U., 1656, M.A., 1658, M.B., 1675. Lectr. of Greek, Christ Coll., 1660; sec. to a propr. of Carolina, Athony Ashley (Earl of Shaftesbury), 1667-73; wrote original draft of the Constitution of Carolina, which permitted wide religious toleration in colony, 1669; became the secretary of the Council of Trade (dealt with Am. colonial problems, was most influential governing body for colonies), after Shaftesbury became Lord Chancellor, 1673-75; fled to Holland after Shaftesbury's polit. downfall, 1683-89; returned with supporters of William of Orange; apptd. commr. of appeals, 1689; worked with Isaac Newton in re-minting of English currency, 1696; mem. Council of Trade, 1696-1704. Author: Essay on Human Understanding, 1690 (imagined men in nominalistic view, denied existence of innate ideas, rather emphasized causality; originated term "tabula rosa"); Two Treatises on Government, 1690 (stated basic natural rights theory and contract theory of govt.; 2d treatise is simply summed up in 1st paragraph of Declaration of Independence; emphasized property more than happiness as basis of govt.; written to justify Glorious Revolution in Eng., 1689, became basic support for polit. theories behind Am. Revolution in 1776). Died Oates, High Laver, Essex, Eng., Oct. 28, 1704; buried Episcopal Churchyard, High Laver.

LOCKE, John, congressman; b. Hopkinton, Mass., Feb. 14, 1764; attended Andover Acad. and Dartmouth Coll.; grad. Harvard, 1792; studied law. Taught sch.; admitted to Mass. bar, began practice in Ashby, 1796; mem. Mass. Ho. of Reps., 1804-05, 13, 23; del. Mass. Constl. Conv., 1820; mem. U.S. Ho. of Reps. from Mass., 18th-20th congresses, 1823-29; mem. Mass. Senate, 1830, Mass. Exec. Council, 1831; moved to Lowell, Mass., 1837, Boston, 1849. Died Boston, Mar. 29, 1855; buried Lowell Cemetery.

LOCKE, John, inventor, educator; b. Lempster, N.H., Feb. 19, 1792; s. Samuel Barron and Hannah (Russell) L.; M.D., Yale, 1819; m. Mary Morris, Oct. 25, 1825, several children. Asst. surgeon U.S. Navy, 1818; curator botany Harvard, 1819-21; founded, conducted Cincinnati Female Acad., 1822-35; prof. chemistry and pharmacy Med. Coll. of Ohio, Cincinnati, 1835-53; studied geology and paleontology of Ohio, Ill., Ia. and Wis., 1835-40, later studied terrestrial magnetism and electricity; invented a surveyors' compass, level, orrery, electromagnetic chronograph (built for U.S. Coast Survey). Author: Outlines of Botany, 1819. Died Cincinnati, July 10, 1856.

LOCKE, Matthew, congressman; b. North of Ireland, 1730; s. John and Elizabeth Locke; m. Mary Brandon, 1749; m. 2d, Mrs. Elizabeth Gostelowe. Settled nr. present city of Salisbury, N.C., circa 1752; justice of peace, vestryman; mem. N.C. Ho. of Commons, 1770-71, 73-75, 77-81, 83-84, 89-92; agt., mem. Rowan Com. of Safety, 1774-76; del. from N.C. to 3d-5th Provincial congresses, 1775-76; paymaster, brig. gen., auditor Salisbury dist., circa 1776-81; mem. N.C. Senate, 1781-82, 84; trustee Salisbury Acad., 1784; mem. U.S. Ho. of Reps. from N.C., 3d-5th congresses, 1793-99. Died Salisbury, Sept. 7, 1801; buried Thyatira Churchyard, Salisbury.

LOCKE, Richard Adams, journalist; b. East Brent, Somersetshire, Eng., Sept. 22, 1800; s. Richard and Anne (Adams) L.; grad. Cambridge (Eng.) U.; m. Esther Bowering, 1826, at least 1 child, Adelaide. Published 2 unsuccessful mags., The Republican, The Cornucopia, London, Eng.; came to U.S., 1832; reporter Courier and Enquirer, N.Y.C., 1832-35; reporter N.Y. Sun, 1835-36, greatly increased paper's circulation by writing Moon Hoax (in which he quoted fictitious scientists as having described the moon as being populated with weird men and freakish animals); publisher (with Joseph Price) New Era, 1836; later editorial writer Bklyn. Daily Eagle. Died N.Y.C., Feb. 16, 1871.

LOCKHART, James, congressman; b. Auburn, N.Y., Feb. 13, 1806; attended pub. schs., Auburn. Moved to Ithaca, N.Y., circa 1826, operated woolen mill; moved to Ind., 1832; admitted to Ind. bar, 1832, began practice in Evansville, 1834; city clk. Evansville, 1836-37; pros. atty. Vanderburg County, (Ind.), 1841-45; judge 4th Jud. Dist., 1846-51; del. Ind. Constl. Conv., 1850; mem. U.S. Ho. of Reps. (Democrat) from Ind., 32d, 35th congresses, 1851-53, 57; apptd. supt. constrn. of marine hosp., Evansville, 1853. Died Evansville, Sept. 7, 1857; buried Oak Hill Cemetery, Evansville.

LOCKWOOD, James Booth, army officer, explorer; b. Annapolis, Md., Oct. 9, 1852; s. Henry Hayes and Anna (Booth) L.; ed. St. John's Coll. Commd. 2d lt. 23d U.S. Inf., 1873; volunteer for duty with Lady Franklin Bay Arctic Expdn., 1881, made scientific observations, crossed Kennedy Channel to Greenland, proved that North Greenland was mountainous glacier-covered region; set out on exploratoy trip, 1882, reached Cape Bryant at latitude 83° 24' 30" and longitude 40 46' 30" (most northerly point reached by any man up to that time), named island Lockwood Island; 2d in command on U.S. expdn., 1882, took over duties as naturalist of expdn., 1883. Died Cape Sabine, Arctic, Apr. 9, 1884, buried Burial Grounds, U.S. Naval Acad.

LOCKWOOD, Ralph Ingersoll, lawyer, author; b. Greenwich, Conn., July 8, 1798; s. Stephen and Sarah (Ingersoll L. Practiced law, N.Y.C.; mem. N.Y. Law Library (later N.Y. Law Inst.), 1838-58; expert in chancery law. Author: Essay on a National Bankrupt Law, 1825; Analytical and Practical Synopsis of All the Cases Argued and Reversed, in Law and Equity, in the Court for the Correction of Errors, of New York, 1799 to 1847, published 1848; (novels) Rosine Laval, 1833, The Insurgents, 2 vols., 1835. Died N.Y.C., Apr. 12, 1858.

LOCKWOOD, Samuel Drake, jurist; b. Poundridge, Aug. 2, 1789; s. Joseph and Mary (Drake) L.; m. Mary Nash, Oct. 3, 1826. Sergeant-maj., regt. N.Y. Militia, 1808, paymaster, 1811; justice of peace, 1812; licensed to practice law, N.Y.; master of chancery, 1812; trustee Presbyn. Ch., 1812; helped Organize N.Y.'s 1st Bible society; atty. gen. Ill., 1821, sec. of state, 1822; asso. justice Ill. Supreme Ct., 1825-48; legislative trustee land dept. I.C. R.R., 1851-74. Died Batavia, Ill., Apr. 23, 1874.

LOEWENTHAL, Isidor, missionary; b. Posen, Prussia (now Poznan, Poland), circa 1827; B.A., Lafayette Coll., Wilmington, Del., 1848, M.A.; grad. Princeton Theol. Sem., 1851; never married. Came to U.S., 1846; taught Hebrew, German and Latin, Lafayette Coll., 1847-48; taught langs., collegiate sch., Mt. Holly, Pa., 1848-50; tutor Princeton, 1854-55; ordained minister by Presbytery of N.Y., 1855; missionary to India, 1855-64; translated New Testament into Pashtu. Died Apr. 27, 1864.

LOFLAND, James Rush, congressman; b. Milford, Del., Nov. 2, 1823; grad. Del. Coll. (now U. Del.), 1845; studied law. Admitted to Del. bar, 1848, began practice in Milford; sec. Del. Senate, 1849; mem. Del. Constl. Conv., 1853; sec. of state Del., 1855-59; paymaster U.S. Army, 1863-67; del. Republican Nat. Conv., Phila., 1872; mem. U.S. Ho. of Reps. (Republican) from Del., 43d Congress, 1873-75. Died Milford, Feb. 10, 1894; buried Odd Fellows Cemetery, Milford.

LOGAN, Benjamin, army officer, legislator; b. Augusta County, Va., 1743; s. David and Jane Logan; m. Ann Montgomery, 1773/4, 8 children including William. Served as sgt. in Gen. Henry Bouquet's expdn. against Shawnee Indians, 1764; commd. lt. of a co. Va. Militia, 1774; county lt. Lincoln County (Va.), 1781; mem. Va. Gen. Assembly from Lincoln County, 1781-82, 85-87; mem. Ky. Constl. Constn., 1792; mem. Bd. of War in the West, also brig. gen. Ky. Militia, 1790; mem. Ky. Ho. of Reps. from Lincoln County, 1793-94, from Shelby County, 1795. Died Dec. 11, 1802; buried Shelbyville, Ky.

LOGAN, Cornelius Ambrose, diplomat; b. Deerfield, Mass., Aug. 24, 1832; s. Cornelius Ambrosius and Eliza (Akeley) L.; m. Zoe Shaw, 1854, at least 1 child, Celia Logan Waterous. Med. supt. St. John's Hosp., Cincinnati, 1856-57, later practiced medicine, Leavenworth, Kan.; surgeon, 1st Regt., Kan. Militia, 1861-65; botanist Kan. Geol. Corps; 1st pres. Kan. Med. Soc., 1866-67; founder Leavenworth Med. Herald, 1867, editor, 1867-71; U.S. envoy extraordinary and minister plenipotentiary to Chile, 1873-79, 82-85; U.S. minister resident to Central Am. states, 1879-82; mem. Ind. Order Odd Fellows, established order in Chile. Author: Physics of the Infectious Diseases, 1878. Died Los Angeles, Jan. 30, 1899.

LOGAN, Cornelius Ambrosius, actor, dramatist; b. Balt., May 4, 1806; studied for priesthood St. Mary's Coll., circa 1822; m. Eliza Akeley, 1 son Cornelius Ambrose, 3 daus., Eliza, Celia, Olive. Engaged in newspaper work, N.Y.C., 1823-24; appeared in Bertram at Tivoli Garden Theater, Phila., 1825, at Bowery Theater, N.Y.C., 1826; mgr. Pitts. theater, 1827-28; toured Western cities with own acting co., 1830's-40's; lived in Cincinnati in 1830's, ran theater; famed for portrayal of Sir Peter Teazle in School for Scandal; made 1st appearance in own play Chloroform or New York a Hundred Years Hence, N.Y.C., 1849. Author: (plays) Yankee Land; The Wag of Maine; The Vermont Wool Dealer. Died Marietta, O., Feb. 22, 1853.

LOGAN, George, senator; b. Germantown, Pa., Sept. 9, 1753; s. William and Hannah (Emlen) L.; grad. U. Edinburgh, 1779; m. Deborah Norris, Sept. 6, 1781, 3 children. Mem. Pa. Assembly, 1785-88; mem. Am. Philos. Soc., 1793; a founder Phila. Soc. for Promotion Agr.; went on successful unofcl. mission to France, secured removal of French embargo on Am. shipping, 1798 (resulted in passage of Logan Act of 1799 making it unlawful for any citizen to intervene in any dispute with a fgn. govt.); mem. U.S. Senate from Pa., 1801-07; went to Eng. as pvt. citizen in unsuccessful attempt to prevent war, 1810. Died Stanton, Pa., Apr. 9, 1821; buried Logan Graveyard, Phila.

LOGAN, Henry, congressman; b. nr. Dillsburg, Pa., Apr. 14, 1784; attended common schs. Engaged in farming; served as capt. Pa. Militia during War of 1812, commd. lt. col., 1814; mem. Pa. Ho. of Reps., 1818-19, Pa. Senate, 1828-31; mem. U.S. Ho. of Reps. (Democrat) from Pa., 24th-25th congresses, 1835-39; mem. bd. commrs. York County (Pa.), 1840, served as county auditor. Died nr. Dillsburg, Dec. 26, 1866; buried Presbyn. Ch. Cemetery, Dillsburg.

LOGAN, James, mayor Phila.; b. Lurgan, County Armaugh, Ireland, Oct. 20, 1674; s. Patrick and Isabel (Hume) L.; m. Sarah Read, Dec. 9, 1714, 5 children. Came to Am., 1699; sec. to William Penn, 1699; sec. Province of Pa.; clk. Pa. Provincial Council, 1701-17, voting mem., 1702, pres. and sr. mem., chief exec. Province of Pa., 1736-38, commr. property and receiver-gen.; alderman Phila., 1717; mayor, 1722; justice Phila. County, 1726; judge Ct. Common Pleas, 1727; chief justice Pa. Supreme Ct., 1731-39; contbr. pvt. library of over 3,000 books to Phila. (forming basis of Phila. Public Library). Died Stenton, Pa., Oct. 31, 1751.

LOGAN, James (Indian name Tahgahjute), Indian leader; b. Sunbury, Pa., circa 1725; son of Shikellamy. Leader Mingo Indians on Ohio and Scioto rivers in 1760's; friendly to white settlers of area, close to Brit. govt. ofcls.; following massacre of his family by white settlers at Yellow Creek (1774) led attacks on white settlements, helped precipitate Lord Dunmore's War; refused to adhere to peace treaty at Chillicothe (O.) in 1774 following Indian defeat at Point Pleasant; ally of British during Am. Revolution, massacred white pioneers in Ohio Valley. Killed by relative in family quarrel, nr. Detroit, 1780.

LOGAN, John Alexander, senator, army officer; b. Jackson County, Ill., Feb. 9, 1826; s. Dr. John and Elizabeth (Jenkins) L.; grad. U. Louisville, grad. law dept., 1851; m. Mary Simmerson Cunningham, Nov. 27, 1855, 2 children. Served as lt. 1st Ill. Inf. in Mexican War, 1846-48; admitted ot Ill. bar, 1852; mem. Ill. Ho. of Reps., 1852, 53, 56, 57; pros. atty. 3d Jud. Dist. Ill., 1853-57; mem. U.S. Ho. of Reps. from Ill., 36th-37th congresses, 1859-Apr. 2, 1862, 41st-42d congresses, 1867-71, apptd. a mgr. to conduct impeachment proceedings against Pres. Andrew Johnson, 1868; commd. col. 21st Ill. Inf., U.S. Army, 1861; commd. brig. gen. Ill. Volunteers, 1862, maj. gen., 1862-65; an organizer Soc. of Army of Tenn., circa 1865, Grand Army of Republic, circa 1865 (3 times pres.); declined appointment as minister to Mexico, 1865; conceived idea of Meml. Day (inaugurated May 30, 1868); mem. U.S. Senate from Ill., 1871-77, 79-86. Author: The Great Conspiracy: Its Origin and History, 1886; The Volunteer Soldier of America, With Memoir of the Author and Military Reminiscences from General Logan's Private Journal, 1887. Died Washington, D.C., Dec. 26, 1886; buried Rock Creek Cemetery, Washington.

LOGAN, John Henry, physician; b. Abbeville, S.C., Nov. 5, 1822; s. John and Susan (Wilson) L.; grad. S.C. Coll., 1844, Charleston Med. Coll., circa 1849; m. Eliza Calhoun. Editor Banner, newspaper, Abbeville, circa 1845; practiced medicine, Greenwood, S.C., 1850's; served as surgeon Confederate Army during Civil War; became prin. Synodical Inst., Talladega, Ala., 1865; prof. chemistry Atlanta (Ga.) Med. Coll., from circa 1870; editor Atlanta Med. Journal. Author: Students' Manual of Chemico-Physics. Died Atlanta, Mar. 23, 1885.

LOGAN, Stephen Trigg, jurist; b. Franklin County, Ky., Feb. 24, 1800; s. David and Mary (Trigg) L.; m. America T. Bush, June 25, 1823, 8 children. Admitted to Ky. bar, circa 1819; dep. in circuit clk.'s office, Barren County, Ky.; commonwealth's atty. for Glasgow (Ky.) Circuit, 1823-32; judge 1st Jud. Circuit Ill., 1835-37; formed law partnership with Lincoln, 1841-44; mem. Ill. Legislature, 1842-48, 54-56; mem. Ill. Constl. Conv., 1846, 47; Ill. del.-at-large to Nat. Republican Conv., Chgo., 1860; rep. Ill. at Washington (D.C.) Peace Conv., 1861. Died Springfield, Ill., July 17, 1880.

LOGAN, Thomas Moldrup, physician; b. Charleston, S.C., July 31, 1808; s. George and Margaret (Polk) L.; grad. Med. Coll. of S.C., 1828; m. Susan Richardson; m. 2d, Mary Greely, 1864. Practiced medicine, Charleston, 1828-43, New Orleans, 1843-50, Sacramento, Cal., 1850-76; taught medicine Med. Coll. of S.C., Charleston; mem. staff Charity Hosp., New Orleans; active in fostering measures for public health protection; instrumental in founding Cal. Bd. Health, 1870, sec. until 1876; made studies of epidemiology and sch. hygiene; pres.

Cal. Med. Soc. (1870), Agassiz Inst. of Sacramento, A.M.A. (1872). Author: (articles) History of Medicine in California, 1858; Report on the Medical Topography and Epidemics of California published in Transactions of A.M.A., Vol. XII, 1859. Died Sacramento, Feb. 13, 1876; buried Sacramento.

LOGAN, William, senator; b. in the fort at Harrodsburg, Ky., Dec. 8, 1776; studied law, Shelby County, Ky. Admitted to Ky. bar, practiced law; del. Ky. Constl. Conv., 1799; commr. Ky. River Co., 1820; mem. Ky. Ho. of Reps., 1803-06, 09, speaker, 2 terms; judge ct. appeals, 1808-12; presdl. elector, 1801, 12, 16; mem. U.S. Senate (Democrat) from Ky., 1819-May 29, 1820; unsuccessful candidate for gov. Ky., 1820. Died Shelby County, Aug. 8, 1822; buried Logan family burial ground nr. Shelbyville, Ky.

LOGUEN, Jermain Wesley, clergyman; b. Davidson County, Tenn., circa 1813; s. David Loguen; attended Oneida Inst., Whitesboro, N.Y., 1837-38; m. Caroline Storum, Nov. 1840. Escaped from slavery in Tenn., circa 1834; went to Can., later N.Y.; ran schs. for Negro children in Utica and Syracuse, N.Y., 1838-43; active in underground railroad in N.Y.; pastor African Meth. Episcopal Zion chs., Ithaca, Syracuse, Troy (all N.Y.), 1843-50; helped fugitive slaves (in assn. with abolition leaders including Gerrit Smith and John Brown, Jr., Syracuse, 1850-60; involved in Jerry Rescue case, 1851; bishop A.M.E. Zion Ch., 1868-70, served in Alleghany-Ky. dist.; served in Genesee, Phila. and Balt. confs., 1870-72. Died Saratoga Springs, N.Y., Sept. 30, 1872.

LOMAX, John Tayloe, jurist, educator; b. Port Tobago, Carolina County, Va., Jan. 19, 1781, s. Thomas and Ann (Taylor) L.; grad. St. John's Coll., Annapolis, Md., 1797; LL.D. (hon.), Harvard, 1847; m. Charlotte Thornton, 1805. Practiced law, Fredericksburg, Va., 1800; militia officer for lower counties of Northern Neck in War of 1812; 1st prof. law U. Va., 1826-30, chmn. faculty, 1827-28; asso. judge Va. Circuit Superior Ct. of Law and Chancery, 1830; conducted pvt. law sch., Fredericksburg, influenced legal edn. in Va.; asso. justice Circuit Ct. of Gen. Ct. of Va., 1851-57. Author: Digest of the Real Laws Respecting Real Property Generally Adopted and in Use in the United States, 1839, 56. Died Fredericksburg, Oct. 10, 1862.

LONG, Alexander, congressman; b. Greenville, Pa., Dec. 24, 1816; studied law. Admitted to the bar; began practice of law, Cincinnati; mem. Ohio Ho. of Reps., 1848-49; mem. U.S. Ho. of Reps. (Democrat) from Ohio, 38th Congress, 1863-65; del. Dem. nat. convs., 1864, 68, 72, 76. Died Cincinnati, Nov. 28, 1886; buried Spring Grove Cemetery, Cincinnati.

LONG, Armistead Lindsay, army officer; b. Campbell County, Va., Sept. 3, 1825; s. Col. Armistead and Calista (Cralle) L.; grad. U.S. Mil. Acad., 1850; m. Mary Heron Sumner, 1860. Brevetted 2d lt. U.S. Army, 1850, commd. 1st lt., 1854, stationed chiefly in Indian Territory, Kan. and Neb., until 1860; a.d.c. to Gen. Sumner, 1861; resigned commn., 1861; Robert E. Lee's mil. sec. with rank of col. until 1863; commd. brig. gen. arty., chief engr. of a Va. canal company 1863. Author: Memoirs of Robert E. Lee, His Military and Personal History, 1886. Died Charlottesville, Va., Apr. 29, 1891.

LONG, Crawford Williamson, anesthesist, surgeon; b. Danielsville, Ga., Nov. 1, 1815; s. James and Elizabeth (Ware) L.; grad. Franklin Coll. (now U. Ga.), 1835; M.D., U. Pa., 1839; m. Caroline Swain, Aug. 11, 1842. Moved to N.Y., 1839, practiced as surgeon; moved to Ga., 1841, practiced surgery; accidently discovered that sulphuric ether could be used as anesthetic in early 1840's; performed operation on neck of James Venable for removal of cystic tumor, 1842, performed 5 other operations using this procedure before 1846; published results of these expts. in So. Med, and Surg. Jour., 1849; practiced medicine and surgery, Athens, Ga., 1850-58; one of earliest users of ether in U.S. Died Athens, June 16, 1878; buried Athens.

LONG, Edward Henry Carroll, congressman; b. Princess Anne, Md., Sept. 28, 1808; grad. Yale, 1828; studied law. Admitted to Md. bar, 1830, began practice in Princess Anne; engaged in farming; mem. Md. Ho. of Dels., 1833-35, 39, 44, 61, Md. Senate, 1860; mem. U.S. Ho. of Reps. (Whig) from Md., 29th Congress, 1845-47; unsuccessful candidate for U.S. Senate, 1860. Died Princess Anne, Oct. 16, 1865; buried family burying ground at "Catalpa" nr. Princess Anne.

LONG, James, mil. officer; b. N.C., circa 1793; m. Jane Wilkinson, 1815. Moved with family to Rutherford, Tenn.; served as physician in War of 1812, 1812-15; attempted unsuccessfully to practice medicine in Tenn., 1815-17; became mcht., Natchez, Miss., 1817; selected by Natchez townsmen to lead expdn. intended to open Tex. to Am. settlement, 1819, gathered 300 men in this cause and marched to Nacogdoches, Tex., established republic, apptd. himself pres. of supreme council and comdr.-in-chief; declared Tex. independence, 1819; negotiated with Jean Laffite to become gov. of new territory, 1819, driven out of Tex. by Spanish militia; went to New Orleans, gained support of John Austin and Ben Milam; gave presidency of republic to E. W. Ripley; entered alliance with Jose Trespalacios (Am. revolutionist), 1820; attacked La Bahia, Mexico, 1820, defeated by Perez, captured and sent to Mexico City. Shot in Mexico City, Apr. 8, 1822.

LONG, John, congressman; b. Loudoun County, Va., Feb. 26, 1785; attended pvt. and pub. schs., N.C. Engaged in farming, Randolph County, N.C.; mem. N.C. Ho. of Reps., 1811-12, N.C. Senate, 1814-15; mem. U.S. Ho. of Reps. (Whig) from N.C., 17th-20th congresses, 1821-29. Died Longs Mill (now Liberty), N.C., Aug. 11, 1857; buried Richland Graveyard, Longs Mill.

LONG, Pierse, Continental congressman; b. Portsmouth, N.H., 1739. Engaged in shipping bus.; del. N.H. Provincial Congress, 1775; served as col. 1st N.H. Regt. during Revolutionary War; participated in battles at Ticonderoga and on Lake George and Lake Champlain; present at surrender of Gen. Burgoyne at Saratoga; brevetted brig. gen.; mem. Continental Congress from N.H., 1784-86; del. N.H. Conv. which ratified U.S. Constn., 1788; apptd. customs collector for Port of Portsmouth by Pres. Washington, 1789, did not take office due to ill health. Died Portsmouth, Apr. 13, 1789; buried Proprietors' Burying Ground.

LONG, Robert Carey, architect; b. 1770. Practiced as architect, Balt.; one of earliest important architects in Md.; designed numerous public bldgs. in Balt., including Rembrandt Peale (now Municipal) Museum, 1814, Sch. of Medicine at U. Md., Union Bank Bldg., St. Paul's Episcopal Ch., 1814 (destroyed by fire, 1854). Died 1833.

LONG, Stephen Harriman, army officer; b. Hopkinton, N.H., Dec. 30, 1784; s. Moses and Lucy (Harriman) L.; grad. Dartmouth, 1809; m. Martha Hodgkins, Mar. 3, 1819, 5 children. Commd. 2d lt. engrs. U.S. Army, 1814; asst. prof. mathematics U.S. Mil. Acad., 2 years; served as topog. engr., brevetted maj.; sent by War Dept. to examine portages of Fox and Wisconsin rivers and explore upper Mississippi River, 1817; explorer on expdn. to Rocky Mountains, 1819-23, reached Rockies, 1820, named peak after himself; examined sources of St. Peter's (Minn.) River and No. boundary U.S. to Gt. Lakes, 1823; cons. engr. B. & O. R.R., 1827, selected route for railroad later pres. bd. engrs.; chief engr. Atlantic & Gt. Western R.R., 1837-40; patentee bracing and counterbracing wooden bridges, 1836; commd. maj., 1838; commd. col., chief Corps of Engrs., 1861; ret., 1863. Author: Railroad Manual, 1829. Died Alton, Ill., Sept. 4, 1864.

LONGACRE, James Barton, engraver; b. Delaware County, Pa., Aug. 11, 1794; s. Peter Longacre. Apprenticed to engraver George Murray, Phila., 1815-19; established engraving bus., 1819; engraved portraits of George Washington, Thomas Jefferson and John Hancock on fascimile of Declaration of Independence (largest engraving of time), 1820; commd. to engrave many of portraits for Biography of the Signers of the Declaration of Independence (John Sanderson), 1820; engraved portraits on actors for Lopez and Wemyss edit. of Acting American Theatre, 1826; worked on engravings for 4 vols. of National Portrait Gallery of Distinguished Americans, 1834-39; chief engraver U.S. Mint, 1844-69, designed and engraved 1st double eagle coin, 1849; helped remodel coinage of Republic of Chile. Died Phila., Jan. 1, 1869.

LONGFELLOW, Henry Wadsworth, poet; b. Portland, Me., Feb. 27, 1807; s. Stephen and Zilpah (Wadsworth) L.; grad. Bowdoin Coll., 1825; LL.D. (hon.), Cambridge (Eng.) U., D.C.L. (hon.), Oxford (Eng.) U., 1868-69; m. Mary Potter, Sept. 14, 1831; m. 2d, Frances Appleton, July 13, 1843; 6 children. Published a poem in Gazette of Me., Portland, 1820; classmate of Nathaniel Hawthorne and Franklin Pierce, (Pres. U.S. 1852-56) at Bowdoin Coll.; studied abroad in preparation for teaching at Bowdoin Coll., 1826-29, prof. modern langs., 1829-35, librarian, 1829-35; Smith prof. modern langs. and belles-lettres Harvard, 1835-54; a popular poet in both Am. and Europe, a friend of many of the leading people of his day including Hawthorne, Lowell, Holmes, Agassiz, Trollope, Tennyson, Liszt, Froude; his home now a museum, Cambridge, Mass.; his was 1st Am. bust placed in Poets' Corner of Westminster Abbey. Most popular poems include: The Village Blacksmith, The Wreck of the Hesperus, Excelsior, Paul Revere's Ride, Stars of the Summer Night, A Psalm of Life. Author: (volumes of poems) Hyperion, 1839; Voices of the Night, 1839; Ballads and Other Poems, 1841; Poems on Slavery, 1842; Evangeline, 1847; The Song of Hiawatha, 1855; The Courtship of Miles Standish and Other Poems, 1858; Tales of a Wayside Inn, 1863; The Hanging of the Crane, 1874. Translator: The Divine Comedy of Dante Alighieri, 3 vols., 1865-67. Died Cambridge, Mar. 24, 1882; buried Mt. Auburn Cemetery, Cambridge.

LONGFELLOW, Samuel, clergyman; b. Portland, Me., June 18, 1819; s. Stephen and Zilpah (Wadsworth) L.; grad. Harvard, 1839, attended Divinity Sch., 1842-44. Taught sch., Elkridge, Md., 1838-40; became interested in Transcendentalism; ordained to ministry Unitarian Ch., 1848; pastor Unitarian Ch., Fall River, Mass., 1848-51, 2d Unitarian Ch., Bklyn., 1853-60, Unitarian Ch., Germantown, Pa., 1878-82; tutor to young student touring Europe, 1851-52; introduced many new religious approaches in Bklyn.; toured Europe, studied, 1860-62; preached at Cambridge, Mass., 1867-68; traveled abroad, wrote essays for Radical (edited by Sidney H. Morse), 1868-78. Author: A Book of Hymns, for Public and Private Devotion, 1846; Thalatta: A Book for the Seaside, 1853; Vespers, 1859; (with Samuel Johnson) Hymns of the Spirit, 1864; Life of Henry Wadsworth Longfellow, 1886; Final Memorials of Henry Wadsworth Longfellow, 1887. Died Oct. 3, 1892.

LONGFELLOW, Stephen, congressman; b. Gorham, Me., June 23, 1775; s. Stephen and Patience (Young) L.; grad. Harvard, 1798; LL.D. (hon.), Bowdoin Coll., 1828; m. Zilpah Wadsworth, Jan. 1, 1804, 8 children including Samuel, Henry Wadsworth. Admitted to Me. bar, 1801; bd. overseers Bowdoin Coll., 1811-17, trustee, 1817-36; del. Hartford Conv., 1814; rep. Mass. Gen. Ct., 1814-16; mem. U.S. Ho. of Reps. from Me., 18th Congress, 1823-25; mem. Me. Legislature from Portland, 1826; pres. Me. Hist. Soc., 1834; compiled 16 vols. of reports of cases in Mass. cts., 12 vols. Me. reports. Died Portland, Me., Aug. 2, 1849; buried Western Cemetery, Portland.

LONGNECKER, Henry Clay, congressman; b. Allen Twp., Pa., Apr. 17, 1820; grad. Norwich Mil. Acad., Vt., Lafayette Coll., Easton, Pa.; studied law. Admitted to Pa. bar, practiced in Easton; served as 1st lt., capt. and adj. during Mexican War; wounded at Battle of Chapultepec, 1847; dist. atty. Lehigh County (Pa.), 1848-50; mem. U.S. Ho. of Reps. (Republican) from Pa., 36th Congress, 1859-61; an organizer Pa. troops during Civil War; served as col. 9th Regt., Pa. Volunteers, U.S. Army; resumed law practice, Allentown, Pa.; asso. judge Lehigh County, 1867. Died Allentown, Sept. 16, 1871; buried Fairview Cemetery, Allentown.

LONGSTREET, Augustus Baldwin, clergyman, coll. pres.; b. Augusta, Ga., Sept. 22, 1790; s. William and Hannah (Randolph) L.; grad. Yale, 1813; attended Litchfield (Conn.) Law Sch.; m. Frances Parke, 1816. Admitted to bar, Richmond County, Ga., 1815; mem. Ga. Legislature, 1821; circuit judge Superior Ct. of Ga., 1822-25; published humorous sketches called Ga. Scenes (1st of a literary genre in Am.), in newspapers, 1827-30, in book form, 1835; founder newspaper The Sentinel, Augusta, 1834-36; ordained to ministry Methodist Ch., 1838; pres. Emory Coll., 1839-48; mem. Meth. Gen. Assembly in N.Y., 1844; pres. Centenary Coll., Jackson, La., 1849, U. Miss., 1849-56, U. S.C., 1857. Author: Letters from Georgia to Massachusetts; Letters to Clergymen of Northern Methodist Church; Master William Mitten, 1864. Died Oxford, Miss., Sept. 9, 1870.

LONGSTREET, William, inventor; b. Allentown, N.J., Oct. 6, 1759; s. Stoffel and Abigail (Wooley) L.; m. Hannah Randolph, 1783, at least 6 children. Interested in mech. instruments at early age; moved to Augusta, Ga., 1783, began to work seriously on steam engines; given patent on steam engine he had constructed by Ga. Legislature, 1788; invented and patented "breast-roller" of cotton gins, before 1801, also designed portable saw mill; built small steam boat which ran on Savannah River, Ga., 1806. Died Augusta, Sept. 11, 1814.

LONGSTRETH, Edward, draftsman; b. Hatboro, Pa., June 22, 1839. Machinist, Baldwin Locomotive Works, Phila., 1857-68, supt., 1868-70, made several drawings of Baldwin engines; partner locomotive firm M. Baird & Co., Phila., 1870-74, Burnham, Parry, Williams & Co., Phila., 1874-86. Died Phila., Feb. 24, 1905.

LONGWORTH, Nicholas, horticulturist; b. Newark, N.J., Jan. 16, 1782; s. Thomas and Apphia (Vanderpoel) L.; studied law in Judge Jacob Burnet's office, Cincinnati; m. Susan Connor, 1807, 4 children. Clk. brother's store, S.C.; moved to Cincinnati, 1803; practiced law; defended horse thief in his 1st case for which he received 2 copper stills, traded these for 33 acres which were later valued at $2,000,000; entered real estate bus., became millionaire; became interested in horticulture, 1828, producted marketable wine from grapes he had raised; also interested in cultivating strawberries, discovered that stamintate and pistillate plants had to be interplanted if crop was to be successful; waged "strawberry war" with those who doubted his findings. 1842, wrote numerous articles on subject. Author: A Letter from N. Longworth . . . On the Cultivation of the Grape and Manufacture of the Wine, Also, On the Character and Habits of the Strawberry Plant, 1846. Died Feb. 10, 1863.

LONGYEAR, John Wesley, congressman; b. Shandaken, N.Y., Oct. 22, 1820; attended Lima (N.Y.) Acad.; studied law. taught sch.; admitted to Ingham County (Mich.) bar, 1846; began practice of law, Lansing, Mich., 1847; mem. U.S. Ho. of Reps. (Republican) from Mich., 38th-39th congresses, 1863-67; del. Loyalist Conv., Phila., 1866, Mich. Constl. Conv., 1867; judge U.S. Dist. Ct. for Eastern Mich. (apptd. by Pres. Grant), 1870-71. Died Detroit, Mar. 11, 1875; buried Mt. Hope Cemetery, Lansing.

LOOMIS, Andrew Williams, congressman; b. Lebanon, Conn., June 27, 1797; grad. in Law, Union Coll., Schenectady, N.Y., 1819. Admitted to N.Y. bar; moved to Canton, O., practiced law; moved to New Lisbon (now Lisbon), O.; del. Ohio National-Republican Conv., 1827-28; mem. U.S. Ho. of Reps. (Whig) from Ohio, 25th Congress, Mar. 4-Oct. 20, 1837; Whig presdl. elector, 1848; mem. Washington (D.C.) Peace Conv., 1861; moved to Cleve., circa 1873. Died Cumberland, Md., Aug. 24, 1873; buried Allegheny Cemetery, Pitts.

LOOMIS, Arphaxed, congressman; b. Winchester, Conn., Apr. 9, 1798; s. Thaddeus and Lois (Griswold) L.; m. Ann Todd, Oct. 5, 1831. Admitted to N.Y. bar, 1822; surrogate Herkimer County (N. Y.), 1828-36; commr. to investigate the govt. and discipline of state prisons; 1st judge Herkimer County, 1835-40; mem. U.S. Ho. of Reps. (Democrat) from N.Y., 25th Congress, 1837-39; mem. N.Y. State Assembly, 1841-42; 53-54; mem. N.Y. Constl. Conv., 1846; mem. comm. to revise, abridge, and simplify proceeding in civil actions, 1857; del. N.Y. nominating convs., 1861, 63. Died Little Falls, N.Y., Sept. 15, 1885.

LOOMIS, Mahlon, dentist, experimenter in electricity; b. Oppenheim, N.Y., July 21, 1826; s. Prof. Nathan and Waitie (Jenks) L.; studied dentistry, Cleve., 1848; m. Achsah Ashley, May 28, 1856, no children. Practiced dentistry, Earlville, N.Y., Cambridgeport, Mass., Phila., 1848-60; began to expt. in electricity, 1860, an early expt. was to force growth of plants by buried metal plates attached to batteries; carried on 2-way "wireless" communication over distance of 18 miles, 1868; founded Loomis Aerial Telegraph Co. (inc. by Act of Congress, 1870), did not receive financial backing necessary to carry on his expts. Died Terre Alta, W.Va., Oct. 13, 1886.

LOOP, Augustus Henry, artist; b. Hillsdale, N.Y., Sept. 9, 1831; s. George H. and Angelica M. (Downing) L.; studied art under Henry Peters Gray, N.Y. C., 1850, under Thomas Couture, Paris, France, 1859-61; m. Jennette Shepherd Harrison, 1865, 3 children. Mem. N.A.D., 1860, regular contbr., 1860-95; most famous works include Undine, 1863, Aphrodite, 1876, Italian Minstrel, 1868, Love's Crown, 1898; portraits include Bishop Gregory T. Bedell, Hon. William G. Choate, Anson Phelps Stokes. Died Lake George, N.Y., Oct. 20, 1895.

LOPEZ, Aaron, mcht.; b. Portugal, 1731; m. Abigail Lopez, before 1752; m. 2d, Sarah Rinera, after 1762; 17 children. Went under name Edward in Portugal to escape persecution for practice of Judaism (which he renewed upon arrival in Am.); arrived in Newport, R.I., 1752; began trading and selling in Newport and Providence, R.I.; engaged in whale oil industry, 1756; opened up trade with London, Bristol (Eng.) and in W.I. after 1765, most prosperous during 1773-74; moved from Newport to Leicester, Mass., during Am. Revolution; bus. destroyed by 1776; lived in Leicester, 1776-82. Died Providence, May 28, 1782.

LORAS, Jean Mathias Pierre, clergyman; b. Lyons, France, Aug. 30, 1792; s. Jean Mathias and Étiennette (Michalet) L.; attended Sem. L'Argentiére, Hautes-Alpes, France, 1807-17. Pres., Petit Seminaire of Meximieux, France, 1817-24; superior Sem. L'Argentiére, 1824-27; pastor Archdiocese of Lyons, 1827-29; left France for U.S. to work in Mobile, Ala., 1829; pastor Cathedral of Mobile, 1828-36, also superior Spring Hill Coll., vicar gen. Diocese of Mobile at same time; consecrated bishop Diocese of Dubuque, Wis. Territory (now Ia.), 1837; bishop of Dubuque, 1837-58; abstained from alcoholic beverages, however urged his congregation to vote for Ia. Liquor Law, 1855; bishopric grew rapidly under his guidance during this time. Died Feb. 19, 1858.

LORD, Asa Dearborn, ednl. adminstr.; b. Madrid, N.Y., June 17, 1816; s. Asa and Lucretia (Dearborn) L.; attended Western Res. Coll., 1839; m. Elizabeth W. Russell, July 21, 1842. Head, Western Res. Tchrs. Sem., Kirtland, O., 1839-47; publisher Ohio Sch. Jour., 1846-49; supt. schs., Columbus, O., 1847-54; an organizer Ohio Tchrs. Assn., 1847; editor The Ohio Jour. of Edn., 1852-55; head Ohio Instn. for Edn. of Blind, 1856-58; licensed to preach by Presbytery of Franklin, O., 1863; head N.Y. State Sch. for Blind, 1868-75. Died Bavaria, N.Y., Mar. 7, 1875.

LORD, Daniel, lawyer; b. Stonington, Conn., Sept. 23, 1795; s. Daniel and Phebe (Crary) L.; grad. Yale, 1814; m. Susan Lockwood de Forest, May 16, 1818. Admitted to Conn. bar, 1817; entered law office George Griffin, Litchfield, Conn.; atty. in case of Aymar and Aymar vs. Astor, led to bus. connection with John Jacob Astor, provided him with reputation in bus. law field; important cases include A. N. Lawrence and Others vs. The Trustees of the Leake and Watts Orphan House, Bascom vs. Lane. Author: The Legal Effect of the Secession Troubles on the Commercial Relations of the Country, 1861. Died Mar. 4, 1868.

LORD, David Nevins, mcht., theologian; b. Franklin, Conn., Mar. 4, 1792; s. Nathan and Mary (Nevins) L.; grad. Yale, 1817; studied theology, 1817-23; m. Eliza J. Lyon, 1824, no children. Lost his voice, 1823, left study of theology, entered dry goods import business, prospered in N.Y.C. until fire of 1835; never gave up interest in theology; published 1st number of quarterly review Theol. and Lit. Jour., 1848. Author: The Characteristics and Laws of Figurative Language, 1854; The Coming and Reign of Christ, 1858; Visions of Paradise, 1867. Died July 14, 1880.

LORD, Eleazar, clergyman, ry. exec.; b. Franklin, Conn., Sept. 9, 1788; s. Nathan and Mary (Nevins) L.; attended Andover Theol. Sem., 1810-12, Coll. of N.J. (now Pinceton), 1813; m. Elizabeth Pierson, July 12, 1824; m. 2d Ruth Thompson, Dec. 31, 1835; 7 children. Licensed to preach in Congregational Ch. by Haverhill Assn., 1812; founder, 1st pres. Manhattan Fire Ins. Co., 1821-34; founder N.Y. and Erie R.R. Co., 1833, pres., 1839-41, 44-45; founder N.Y. Sunday Sh. Union Soc., 1815, sec., 1818-26, pres., 1826-36; 1st sec. Am. Home Missionary Soc.; founder, council mem. U. City of N.Y., 1831-34; a founder Auburn Theol. Sem., 1820. Author: Principles of Currency and Banking, 1829; The Epoch of the Creation, 1851; The Messiah in Moses and the Prophets, 1852; Symbolic Prophecy, 1854; An Historical Review of the New York & Erie Railroad, 1855; National Currency, 1862. Died Piermont, N.Y., June 3, 1871.

LORD, Frederick William, congressman; b. Lyme, Conn., Dec. 11, 1800; grad. Yale, 1821; grad. in Medicine, 1828; studied medicine, Balt. Prof. mathematics, Washington Coll., Chestertown, Md., 2 years; began practice of medicine, Sag Harbor, N.Y.; del. Whig Nat. Conv., 1840; moved to Greenport, L.I., N.Y., 1846, engaged in farming, cultivating fruit and ornamental trees; mem. U.S. Ho. of Reps. (Whig) from N.Y., 30th Congress, 1847-49; elected del. Republican Nat. Conv., Chgo., 1860, became ill on steamer Massachusetts enroute to conv. Died N.Y.C., May 24, 1860; buried East Hampton (N.Y.) Cemetery.

LORD, Henry William, congressman, diplomat; b. Northampton, Mass., Mar. 8, 1821; studied law. Moved to Detroit, 1839, to Pontiac, Mich., 1843; engaged in farming, merc. bus.; U.S. consul to Manchester, Eng. (apptd. by Pres. Lincoln), 1861-67; mem. Mich. Bd. Corrections and Charities, 1871-82; Republican presdl. elector, 1876; mem. U.S. Ho. of Reps. (Rep.) from Mich., 47th Congress, 1881-83; register U.S. Land Office, Creelsburg, N.D., 1883-84, Devils Lake, N.D., 1884-88. Killed in a railroad accident nr. Butte, Mont., Jan. 25, 1891; buried Elmwood Cemetery, Detroit.

LORD, John, historian, lectr.; b. Portsmouth, N.H., Dec. 27, 1810; grad. Dartmouth, 1833, Andover Theol. Sem., 1837; m. Mary Porter, May 1846; m. 2d, Louisa Tucker, 1864; 2 children. Lectr., preacher for Am. Peace Soc., 1837-38; preacher Congl. Ch., New Marlboro, Mass., 2d Presbyn. Ch., Utica, N.Y., 1838-40; toured New Eng. lecturing in history, 1840-43; hist. researcher and lectr., Eng. and Scotland, 1843-46; lectured extensively in New Eng., 1846-52; lectured and studied in Europe, 1852-54, returned to Am., resided permanently in Stamford, Conn., continued to lecture and write on history, 1854-94. Author: A Modern History from the Time of Luther to the Fall of Napoleon, 1849; The Old Roman World, 1867; Beacon Lights of History (collection of his lectures), 8 vols., 1884-96. Died Stamford, Dec. 15, 1894.

LORD, Nathan, clergyman, coll. pres.; b. South Berwick, Me., Nov. 28, 1792; s. John and Mehitabel (Perkins) L.; grad. Bowdoin, 1809, D.D. (hon.), 1828; grad. Andover Theol. Sem., 1815; L.L. D. (hon.), Dartmouth, 1864; m. Elizabeth Leland, July 24, 1816. Ordained Pastor Congl. Ch., Amherst, N.H., 1816, pastor, 1816-28; trustee Dartmouth Coll., 1821-28, pres., 1828-63, left office because of his pro-slavery views, published as A True Picture of Abolition, 1863. Author: Letter to Rev. Daniel Dana D.D. on Parks' "Theology of New England," 1852. Died Sept. 9, 1870.

LORD, Otis Phillips, jurist, state legislator; b. Ipswich, Mass., July 11, 1812; s. Nathaniel and Eunice (Kimball) L.; grad. Amherst Coll., 1832, LL.D. (hon.), 1869; LL.B., Harvard, 1836; m. Elizabeth Farley, Oct. 9, 1843. Admitted to Essex County (Mass.) bar; mem. lower house Mass. Legislature, 1847-48; mem. Mass. Senate, 1849; mem. Mass. Ho. of Reps., 1853-54, speaker, 1854; judge Mass. Superior Ct., 1859; asso. judge Supreme Ct. Commonwealth of Mass., 1875-82. Died Salem, Mass., Mar. 13, 1884.

LORD, Scott, congressman; b. Nelson, N.Y., Dec. 11, 1820; attended acads., Morrisville and Geneseo, N.Y.; studied law. Admitted to N.Y. bar, 1842, began practice in Mount Morris; moved to Geneseo, 1847; judge Livingston County (N.Y.), 1847-56; moved to Utica, N.Y., 1872, practiced law; mem. U.S. Ho. of Reps. (Democrat) from N.Y., 44th congress, 1875-77, a mgr. to conduct impeachment proceedings against William W. Belknap (sec. of war), 1876; moved to N.Y.C., 1877, practiced law. Died Morris Plains, N.J., Sept. 10, 1885; buried Temple Hill Cemetery, Geneseo.

LORILLARD, Pierre, mcht., horse breeder; b. N. Y.C., Oct. 13, 1833; s. Peter and Catherine (Griswold) L.; m. Emily Taylor, 1858, 3 children. A well-known sportsman in his youth; influential in making Newport (R.I.) yachting capital of time; founded Rancocas, breeding farm for trotting and race horses, Jobstown, N.J., 1873; his horses noted for winning many famous internat. races; set up game and fish preserve, Orange County, N.Y.; after death of father, bought out his brothers' interests in family tobacco business, greatly expanded firm. Died N.Y.C., July 7, 1901.

LORIMIER, Pierre Louis, trader, interpreter; b. Lachine, Can., Mar. 1748; m. Charlotte Pemanpieh Bougainville; m. 2d, Marie Berthiaume; at least 3 children. Accompanied father to Miami River, O., 1769, established post known as Lorimier's (became rendevous for British during Revolutionary War); traded with Indians and became interpreter; took part in raids on Am. forces (captured Daniel Boone in 1 raid); his post destroyed by George Rogers Clark's expdn. into Ind. and Ill., 1782; driven to St. Mary's (Mo.) by his creditors, 1787, apptd. agt. of Indian affairs, capt. commandant of Spanish militia in that dist., 1808; apptd. judge Mo. Territory Ct. of Common Pleas by U.S. govt. after La. Purchase; received many land concessions from Spanish, built these into dists. which were later inhabited by Americans. Died June 26, 1812.

LORING, Edward Greely, ophthalmologist; b. Boston, Sept. 28, 1837; s. Judge Edward Greely V. and Harriet (Boott) L.; attended Harvard, 1857-58, M.D., 1864; studied medicine, Florence and Pisa, Italy, 1858-61; m. Chevalita Jarves, Jan. 3, 1866; m. 2d, Helen Swift; no children. Intern in ophthalmology Boston City Hosp., Mass. Charitable Eye and Ear Hosp., 1865-66; practiced medicine, Balt., 1866-67; in partnership with Dr. Cornelius Rea Agnew, 1867-73; practiced in N.Y.C., 1873-88; surgeon Bklyn. Eye and Ear Hosp., Manhattan Eye and Ear Hosp., N.Y. Eye and Ear Family; greatest achievement was improvement of opthalmoscope (instrument for looking into eye). Author: A Text Book on Ophthalmoscopy, 1st vol., 1886, 2d vol., 1891. Died N.Y.C., Apr. 23. 1888.

LORING, Ellis Gray, lawyer, abolitionist; b. Boston, Apr. 14, 1803; s. James Tyng and Relief (Faxon) L.; attended Harvard, 1823; studied law; m. Louisa Gilman, Oct. 29, 1827. Admitted to Mass. bar, 1827; an organizer New Eng. Anti-Slavery Soc., 1831, contbd. much financial support (newspaper Liberator could not have been continued without his help); favored "gradual abolition" approach to problem; successfully presented legal arguments in case of Commonwealth vs. Thomas Aves, involving Negro slave Ned who was brought into Mass., established principle that slave brought to Mass. could not be taken out of that state against his will; practiced law until 1858. Author: An Address to the Abolitionists of Massachusetts on the Subject of Political Action, 1838. Died May 24, 1858.

LORING, Frederick Wadsworth, author, journalist; b. Boston, Dec. 12, 1848; s. David and Mary Hall (Stodder) L.; grad. Harvard, 1870; never married. Wrote play Wild Rose while at Harvard, produced by George Selwyn, Boston; asst. editor Boston Saturday Evening Gazette, 1870-71; also asso. with Boston Daily Advertiser and Every Saturday; contbr. to Atlantic Monthly, N.Y. Independent and N.Y. World; best known poem is "In the Churchyard at Fredericksburg"; accompanied Wheller Expdn. as reporter for Appleton's Jour., 1871. Author: The Boston Dip and Other Verses, 1871. Killed in

Apache stagecoach raid while returning from Wheller Expdn., Nov. 5, 1871.

LORING, George Bailey, physician, congressman; b. North Andover, Mass., Nov. 8, 1817; s. Bailey and Sally (Osgood) L.; grad. Harvard, 1838, M. D., 1842; m. Mary Pickman, Nov. 6, 1851; m. 2d, Anna (Smith) Hildreth, June 1, 1880. Commr. to revise U.S. marine hosp. system; postmaster Salem Mass., 1853-57; mem. Mass. delegation to Nat. Democratic Conv., 1856; mem. Mass. Ho. of Reps., 1866-67; chmn. Mass. Republican Com., 1869-76; del. to Republican Nat. conv., 1868, 72, 76; pres. Mass. Senate, 1873-76; mem. U.S. Ho. of Reps. from Mass. (Republican), 45th-46th congresses, 1877-81; U.S. commr. agriculture, 1881; rep. of Essex Agrl. Soc. on Mass. Bd. Agr., 1888-90; founder New Eng. grl. Sc., 1864, pres. until 1889; U.S. minister to Portugal, 1889-90. Author: Classical Culture, 1866; Eulogy on Louis Agassiz, 1873; The Cobden Club and the American Farmer, 1880. Died Salem, Spt. 14, 1891.

LORING, Joshua, naval officer; b. Boston, Aug. 3, 1716; s. Joshua and Hannah (Jackson) L.; m. Mary Curtis, 1740, at least 1 son Joshua. Apprenticed to tanner James Mears, Roxbury, Mass.; commanded brigantine Privateer which was captured by French during war between French and English, 1744, released from prison, 1744; commd. capt. Brit. Navy, 1757; commanded naval operations on Lakes George, Ontario and Champlain, 1759; severely wounded, 1760; participated in capture of Quebec and conquest of Canada under General Amherst; settled in Roxbury at conclusion of war, appointed mem. Gen. Gage's council, under great pressure from Americans to resign from this council, denounced by Mass. Provincial Council as being enemy of independence, 1775; banished from Mass. by action of Gen. Ct., 1778, property confiscated, left for Eng. Died Highgate, Eng., Oct. 1781.

LORING, Joshua, Loyalist; b. Hingham, Mass., Nov. 1, 1744; s. Joshua and Mary (Curtis) L.; m. Elizabeth Lloyd, Oct. 19, 1769, at least 2 children, Sir John Wentworth, Henry Lloyd. Served with Brit. Colonial Army, commd. ensign, 1761, lt., 1765, ret., 1768; received 20,000-acre grant in N.H. for mil. services; permanent high sheriff Mass., 1769-76; a signer of protest against Mass. Com. of Safety; signed document approving course of action taken by Mass. Gov. Thomas Hutchinson, 1774; signed similar document to Gen. Thomas Gage (who replaced Hutchinson), 1775; apptd. by Gage as sole vender-master and auctioneer of Mass., 1775; forced to flee Boston with Brit. Army, 1776, went to Halifax; commissary of prisoners in Brit. Army, 1777, reported to have been exceptionally cruel to prisoners, sent letter to Gen. George Washington denying cruelty charges; banished from Mass., spent rest of life in Eng. Died Edgefield, Eng., Aug. 1789.

LORING, William Wing, army officer; b. Wilmington, N.C., Dec. 4, 1818; s. Ruben and Hannah (Kenan) L.; ed. Georgetown Coll. Commd. 2d lt., 2d Fla. Volunteers, U.S. Army, 1837; mem. Fla. bar; mem. Fla. Legislature, 3 years; capt. Mounted Rifles, 1846, maj., 1847, brevetted lt. col., 1847; commd. col. U.S. Volunteers, 1847, lt. col., 1848; commanded mil. dept. Ore., 1849-51; col. U.S. Army, 1856, commanded Dept. Mexico, 1860-61; resigned from U.S. Army, 1861, commd. brig. gen. Confederate Army, 1861, maj. gen., 1862; surrendered to Gen. Sherman, 1865; joined mil. service of Khedive of Egypt, 1st insp. gen. with rank brig. gen., in command defenses of Alexandria and all Eyptian coast, 1870, gen. of div.; decorated Egyptian orders Osman and Medjidie. Died N.Y.C., Dec. 30, 1886.

LOSKIEL, George Henry, clergyman; b. Angermuende, Courland, Russia, Nov. 7, 1740; s. John Christian Loskiel; studied theology U. Halle (Germany); m. Maria Magdalena Barlach, June 27, 1771. Joined Moravian Ch., 1759; supt. Livonian Mission, agt. for Moravian Ch. in Russia, 1782-1802; involved in adminstrn. and financial matters of Moravian missions, 1791-1801; ordained bishop, 1802, came to U.S. to take control of Am. missions; successful in securing complete separation of Am. from European branch of Moravian Ch., 1802-11. Author: Geschichte der Mission der Evangelischen Brueder unter den Indianern in Nordamerika, 1789 (translated as History of the Mission of the United Brethren among the Indians in North America, published London, Eng., 1794); Etwas Für' Herz, circa 1791. Died Bethlehem, Pa., Feb. 23, 1814.

LOSSING, Benson John, editor; b. Beekman, N.Y., Feb. 12, 1813; s. John and Miriam (Dorland) L.; studied wood engraving with J. A. Adams; LL.D. (hon.), U. Mich., 1873; m. Alice Barritt, June 18, 1833; m. 2d, Helen Sweet, Nov. 18, 1856. Watchmaker's apprentice, Poughkeepsie, N.Y., 1826-33, partner, 1833-35; joint editor, propr. Poughkeepsie Telegraph, 1835; co-editor literary journal Poughkeepsie Casket, 1836; became wood engraver, N.Y.C., 1838; editor, illustrator Family Mag., N.Y.C., 1839-41; editor Am. Hist. Record and Repertory of Notes and Queries (mag.), probably in N.Y.C., 1872-74. Author: Outline History of the Fine Arts, 1840; Pictorial Field Book of the Revolution, 2 vols., 1850-52; The Life and Times of Philip Schuyler, 2 vols., 1860-73; A Memorial of Alexander Anderson, M.D., the Frst Engraver of Wood in America, 1872; The Empire State, 1887. Died Dover Plains, N.Y., June 3, 1891.

LOTHROP, Daniel, publisher; b. Rochester, N.H., Aug. 11, 1831; s. Daniel and Sophia (Horne) L.; m. Ellen Morrill, July 25, 1860; m. 2d, Harriet Mulford Stone, Oct. 4, 1881; 1 child. Managed his brother's drug store, Rochester, 1844-48; opened drug stores, Laconia, also Newmarket, N.H., 1848; became owner book store, Dover, N.H., 1850; established bank and drug store, St. Peter, Minn. Territory, 1856; established publishing firm D. Lathrop & Co., Boston, 1868, specialized in Sunday Sch. material, juvenile books; founder various periodicals including Wide Awake, 1875; founded Am. Inst. of Civics, Boston, 1880. Died Boston, Mar. 18, 1892.

LOTHROP, George Van Ness, diplomat; b. Easton, Mass., Aug. 8, 1817; s. Howard and Sally Williams) L.; grad. Brown U., 1838, LL.D. (hon.), 1863; m. Almira Strong, May 13, 1847, 7 children. Admitted to Mich. bar, 1843; mgr. Detroit Young Men's Soc., 1844; atty. gen. Mich., 1848-51; recorder Detroit, 1853; gen. counsel Mich. Central R.R. Co., 1854-80; del. Nat. Democratic Conv., Charlestown, S.C., 1860; mem. Mich. Constl. Conv., 1867; pres. Detroit Bar Assn., 1879-96; U.S. minister to Russia, 1885-88. Died Detroit, July 12, 1897.

LOTHROPP, John, clergyman; b. Etton, Yorkshire, Eng., 1584; son of Thomas and Mary Lothropp; B.A., Queens Coll., Oxford (Eng.) U., 1606, M.A., 1609; m. 1st wife, before 1614; m. 2d, Ann, circa 1634; 14 children. Ordained to ministry Anglican Ch., preached in various parishes, Kent, Eng.; became pastor of group of non-conformists in London, Eng., 1625, arrested with group, 1632, imprisoned by Ct. of High Commn., 1632-34; offered to be pastor of ch. in Plymouth Colony; fled to colonies, arriving in ship Griffin in Boston, Sept. 1634; chosen 1st pastor of Puritan Ch., Scituate, Plymouth Colony, ordained to Puritan ministry, Jan. 1635; became freeman Colony of New Plymouth, June 1637; wrote letters of complaint to New Plymouth Colony Ct. of Assts. about scarcity of land in Scituate; after receiving unfavorable grants, moved to Barnstable, Mass., Oct. 1639; pastor, Barnstable, 1639-53. Died Barnstable, Nov. 8, 1653.

LOUDON, Samuel, mcht., publisher; b. circa 1727; m. Sarah Oakes, Jan. 24, 1756; m. 2d, Lydia Griswold; 8 children including Samuel. Mcht. in N.Y.C., 1753, fitted ships, invested in land, sold books; published N.Y. Packet and the Am. Advertiser (newspaper), 1776; supported colonial cause but was against independence; published Deceiver Unmasked; or Loyalty and Interest United (pamphlet against independence), his printing shop looted and most of pamphlets destroyed; fled N.Y.C. when captured by British; published N.Y. Packet from Fishkill, N.Y.; became state printer, published N.Y. State Constn. of 1777, also N.Y. paper money; printed Laws of the State of New York, 1786, also Am. Mag.; changed name of Packet to Diary or Loudon's Register, 1792. Died nr. Middletown Point, N.J., Feb. 24, 1813.

LOUDOUN, 4th earl, see Campbell, John.

LOUGHLIN, John, clergyman; b. Drumboneff, Down, Ireland, Dec. 20, 1817; came to U.S. (Albany, N.Y.), circa 1823; attended Chambly Coll., Montreal, Can., also Mt. St. Mary's, Md. Ordained priest Roman Catholic Ch., 1840, served in Utica, N.Y., also N.Y.C.; vicar gen. under Bishop Hughes, 1849-53; became 1st bishop of Bklyn. (including all of L.I.), 1853; during his episcopate some 125 chs., 93 schs., 2 colls., a sem., and many charitable instns. were built; founded St. John's Coll., Bklyn., 1869; attended 2d, 3d plenary councils of Balt., 1866, 84; attended Vatican Council, 1869-70. Died Bklyn., Dec. 29, 1891.

LOUGHRIDGE, Robert McGill, missionary; b. Laurensville, S.C., Dec. 24, 1809; s. James and Deborah (McGill) L.; grad. Miami (O.) U., 1837; attended Princeton Theol. Sem., 1838; m. Olivia Hills, Dec. 6, 1842; m. 2d, Mary Avery, Dec. 4, 1846; m. 3d, Harriet Johnson, Oct. 15, 1853. Licensed to preach by Presbyn. Ch., 1841, ordained to ministry, 1842; missionary to Creek Indians in Okla., 1842-61; established schs., churches, translated parts of Bible and hymnal into Muskogee (Creek lang.), 1881-88; minister in many Tex. chs., 1861-80; minister Presbyn. Ch., Tulsa, Okla., 1888, Waco, Tex., 1892. Author: English and Muskogee Dictionary, 1890. Died July 8, 1900.

LOUGHRIDGE, William, congressman; b. Youngstown, O., July 11, 1827; attended common schs.; studied law. Admitted to Ohio bar, 1849, began practice in Mansfield; moved to Ia., 1852, settled in Oskaloosa; mem. Ia. Senate, 1857-60; judge 6th Ia. Jud. Circuit, 1861-67; mem. U.S. Ho. of Reps. (Republican) from Ia., 40th-41st, 43d congresses, 1867-71, 73-75. Died nr. Reading, Pa., Sept. 26, 1889; buried Forest Cemetery, Oskaloosa.

LOUTHERBOURG, Annibale Christian Henry de, see de Loutherbourg.

LOVE, Emanuel King, clergyman; b. nr. Marion, Ala., July 27, 1850; s. Cumby J. and Maria Love; attended Lincoln U., Marion, 1871; grad. Augusta (Ga.) Inst., 1877; D.D. (hon.), Selma (Ala.) U., 1888; m. Josephine Leeks, Oct. 30, 1879. Ordained to ministry Baptist Ch., 1875; missionary in Ga., 1877-79; minister First African Bapt. Ch., Thomasville, Ga., 1879-84; supr. Sunday Sch. missions for Negroes in Ga., 1881-85; pastor First African Bapt. Ch., Savannah, Ga., 1885-1900; organizer, pres. Bapt. Fgn. Mission Conv., 1889-91, 93; editor, founder The Baptist Truth (mag. of Ga. Negro Bapt. Conv.); aided Negro edn. Author: History of the First African Baptist Church, 1788-1888. Died Apr. 24, 1900.

LOVE, James, congressman; b. Nelson County, Ky., May 12, 1795; attended common schs., Bardstown, Ky.; studied law. Served as volunteer during War of 1812; admitted to Ky. bar, began practice in Barboursville; mem. Ky. Ho. of Reps., 1819-31; mem. U.S. Ho. of Reps. from Ky., 23d Congress, 1833-35; moved to Galveston, Tex., 1837; mem. Tex. Constl. Conv., 1836; 1st judge Galveston Dist.; clk. U.S. Ct., until 1861; served with Terry Rangers during Civil War; elected 1st judge Galveston and Harris County Criminal Ct. after Civil War, removed by Mil. comdr. Died Galveston, June 12, 1874; buried Trinity Ch. Cemetery, Galveston.

LOVE, John, congressman; studied law. Admitted to Va. bar, 1801, began practice in Alexandria; mem. Va. Ho. of Dels., 1805-07; mem. U.S. Ho. of Reps. (Democrat) from Va., 10th-11th congresses, 1807-11; mem. Va. Senate, 1816-20; resumed law practice. Died Alexandria, Aug. 17, 1822.

LOVE, Peter Early, congressman; b. nr. Dublin, Ga., July 7, 1818; grad. Franklin Coll. (now U. Ga.), 1829, Phila. Coll. Medicine, 1838; studied law. Practiced medicine; admitted to Ga. bar, 1839, began practice in Thomasville; solicitor gen. So. dist. of Ga., 1843; mem. Ga. Senate, 1849; elected judge Ga. Superior Ct. for So. circuit, 1853; mem. U.S. Ho. of Reps. (Democrat) from Ga., 36th Congress, 1859-Jan. 23, 1861; resumed law practice, Thomasville; mem. Ga. Ho. of Reps., 1861. Died Thomasville, Nov. 8, 1866; buried Old Cemetery, Thomasville.

LOVE, Thomas Cutting, congressman; b. Cambridge, N.Y., Nov. 30, 1789; attended common schs.; studied law. Served as volunteer during War of 1812; wounded and captured at Battle of Ft. Erie, 1814, imprisoned in Quebec until end of war; admitted to the bar, practiced law; moved to Batavia, N.Y., later to Buffalo, N.Y.; judge Erie County (N.Y.), 1828-29, dist. atty., 1829-35, surrogate, 1841-45; mem. U.S. Ho. of Reps. (Whig) from N.Y., 24th Congress, 1835-37. Died Buffalo, Sept. 17, 1853; buried Forest Lawn Cemetery, Buffalo.

LOVE, William Carter, congressman; b. nr. Norfolk, Va., 1784; attended U. N.C., 1802-04; studied law. Admitted to N.C. bar, began practice in Salisbury, 1806; mem. U.S. Ho. of Reps. (Democrat) from N.C., 14th Congress, 1815-17; resumed law practice. Died Salisbury, 1835; buried pvt. cemetery, Salisbury.

LOVEJOY, Asa Lawrence, lawyer; b. Groton, Mass., Mar. 14, 1808; s. Dr. Samuel and Betsey (Lawrence) L.; m. Elizabeth McGary, 1845. Admitted to Mass. bar, 1840; rode with Dr. Marcus Whitman back from Waiilatpu to Bent's Fort, then back to Oregon with Whitman's emigrant train, 1842-43; atty. gen. Oregon Territory, 1844; mayor Oregon City, 1845; adjutant gen.; supreme judge Oregon Territory, 1848; speaker of house, 1st Oregon Territorial Legislature; mem. Council, 1851-52; postal agt., 1853; del. to lower house Oregon Territorial Legislature, 1854, 56; mem. Conv. of 1857, active in shaping Ore. Constn.; mem. Oregon City Woolen Mfg. Co., 1863; dir. Ore. Telegraph Co.; dir. East-Side Ore. Central Ry. Co. (1st railroad through Willamette Valley); a founder Portland (Ore.). Died Portland, Sept. 10, 1882.

LOVEJOY, Elijah Parish, printer; b. Albion, Me., Nov. 9, 1802; s. Rev. Daniel and Elizabeth (Pattee) L.; grad. Waterville (Me.) Coll. (now Colby Coll.), 1826; attended Princeton Theol. Sem., 1832; m. Celia French, Mar. 4, 1835. Licensed to preach in Presbyn. Ch., 1833; editor Presbyn. newspaper St. Louis Observer, 1833-36, advocated temperance and abolition of slavery; became editor Alton (Ill.) Observer,, 1836, advocated immediate emancipation of slaves; his press destroyed 3 times by anti-abolitionists; supported by Ohio Anti-Slavery Soc. which provided new presses; founder Ill. br. Am. Anti-Slavery Soc., 1837; his press destroyed 4th time, 1837; received new press from Ohio, placed it under guard in a warehouse; killed while trying to get to warehouse (which mob had set on fire in attempt to destroy his new press); became symbol for abolitionist movement in U.S. Died Alton, Nov. 7, 1837.

LOVEJOY, Owen, abolitionist, congressman; b. Albion, Me., Jan. 6, 1811; s. Rev. Daniel and Elizabeth (Pattee) L.; ed. Bowdoin Coll., 1830-33; m. Eunice (Storrs) Dunham, Jan. 1843, 7 children. Moved to Ill., 1836; ordained to ministry Congregational Ch., 1839; pastor, Princeton, Ill., 1839-56; del. Nat. Abolitionist Conv., Buffalo, N.Y., 1847; mem. Ill. Ho. of Reps., 1854; leading abolitionist in Ill.; mem. U.S. Ho. of Reps. (Republican) from Ill., 35th-39th congresses, 1857-64; supported Lincoln; author of bill which abolished slavery in all territories of U.S. Died Bklyn., Mar. 25, 1864; buried Oakland Cemetery, Princeton.

LOVELACE, Francis, colonial gov.; b. Hurley, Berkshire, Eng., circa 1621; s. Sir William and Anne (Barne) L. Served as col. for Charles I in Civil Wars; gov. Carmarthen Castle; dep. gov. L.I., N.Y., 1665; gov. N.Y., 1667; commd. lt. col. Brit. Army, 1667; gov. N.Y. and N.J., 1668-73; organizer postal route between N.Y.C. and Boston; purchased Staten Island from Indians; returned to Eng. when N.Y.C. was captured by Dutch, 1673. Died Oxford, Eng., 1675.

LOVELAND, William Austin Hamilton, mcht., railroad exec.; b. Chatham, Mass., May 30, 1826; s. Leonard and Elizabeth (Eldridge) L.; attended McKendree Coll., Shurtleff Coll. (both Ill.); m. Philena Shaw, May 13, 1852; m. 2d, Maranda Montgomery, Aug. 25, 1856; at least 1 child. Served as wagonmaster in Mexican War, 1847; went to Cal. in gold rush, 1849; joined Pike's Peak gold rush, 1859, opened store at Golden (Colo.) to supply miners; invested in mines and real estate; owner Denver Rocky Mountain News, 1878-86; mem. Colo. Territorial Council, 1862-70; pres. Colo. Constl. Conv., 1865; through his influence, Golden was capital of Colo., 1862-67; promoter Colo. Central and Pacific R.R. (bought by U.P. R.R.); Loveland (Colo.) named after him. Died Lakeside, Colo., Dec. 17, 1894.

LOVELL, James, Continental congressman; b. Boston, Oct. 31, 1737; s. John and Abigail Lovell; grad. Harvard, 1756; m. Mary Middleton, Nov. 24, 1760, at least 2 children including James. Tchr., Boston Latin Sch., also master North Grammar Sch., 1757-75; chosen 1st orator to commemorate Boston Massacre (which had made him staunch opponent of Brit. measures), 1770; arrested by British for spying after Battle of Bunker Hill, 1775, imprisoned, Halifax, N.S., 1776, exchanged and returned to Boston, 1776; del. from Mass. to Continental Congress, 1776-82, mem. com. on fgn. affairs, 1777; possibly involved in Conway Cabal (plot to remove George Washington as comdr.-in-chief Continental Army), 1777; receiver of continental taxes, Boston, 1784-88; collector of customs Mass., 1788-89; naval officer for Boston, also Charleston (S.C.), 1789-1814. Died Windham, Me., July 14, 1814.

LOVELL, John, educator; b. Boston, Apr. 1, 1710; s. John and Priscilla (Gardiner) L.; grad. Harvard, 1728; m. Abigail Green, circa 1735, 1 son, James. Usher, Boston Latin Sch., 1729-34, master or prin., 1734-75, in this position taught most of boys who became leaders in Boston for next 50 years, especially during Am. Revolution; wrote articles for Weekly Rehearsal, Boston, 1731-35; Loyalist, fled Boston, 1776. Died Halifax, N.S., 1778.

LOVELL, John Epy, educator; b. Colne, Lancashire, Eng., Apr. 23, 1795; s. John and Elizabeth (Epy) L.; m. Harriet Fletcher, 1835; m. 2d, Minerva Camp, Mar. 29, 1845; 3 children. Tutor to family of Duke of Bedford, 1811-13, met Joseph Lancaster (originator Lancasterian method of teaching which uses older pupils to teach younger ones); prin. Lancasterian sch., Burr Rose, Eng., before 1815; came to U.S., 1815; organizer, prin. Lancasterian sch., New Haven, Conn., 1822-27, 30-57; taught elocution Mt. Pleasant Classical Inst., Amherst, Mass., 1827-30; pvt. tutor, 1857-82; lived with his sister, Milw., 1890-92. Author: Introductory Arithmetic, 1827; Rhetorical Dialogues, 1839; Lovell's Progressive Reader, 5 vols., 1855-59. Died Milw., May 3, 1892.

LOVELL, Joseph, physician, army officer; b. Boston, Dec. 22, 1788; s. James and Deborah (Gorham) L.; A.B., Harvard, 1807, M.D., 1811; m. Margaret Mansfield, 11 children including Mansfield. Surgeon, 4th Infantry, U.S. Army, 1812-14; dir. U. S. Army Hosp., Williamsville, N.Y., 1814-17; chief med. officer No. dept. U.S. Army, 1817; surgeon gen. U.S. Army, 1818-36, head new Army med. dept. Died Oct. 17, 1836.

LOVELL, Mansfield, army officer, civil engr.; b. Washington, D.C., Oct. 20, 1822; s. Dr. Joseph and Margaret (Mansfield) L.; grad. U.S. Mil. Acad., 1842; m. Emily Plympton, 1849. Commd. 2d lt., 4th Arty., U.S. Army, 1842, 1st lt., 1846, served in Taylor's campaign, 1846-47, aide-de-camp to Gen. John A. Quitman; brevetted capt. for gallantry at Battle of Chapultepec, 1847; resigned commn., 1854; dep. street commr. N.Y.C., 1858, later supt. street improvements; commd. maj. gen. Confederate Army, 1861, in command New Orleans, fought at Battle of Vicksburg, 2d-in-command in Battle of Corinth. Died N.Y.C., June 1, 1884.

LOVERING, Joseph, educator; b. Charlestown, Mass., Dec. 25, 1813; s. Robert and Elizabeth (Simonds) L.; A.B., Harvard, 1833, LL.D. (hon.), 1879, attended Harvard Divinity Sch., 1835-36; m. Sarah Hawes, 1844, 4 children. Lectr. natural philosophy Harvard, 1837, Hollis prof. mathematics and natural philosophy, Harvard, 1838-88; mem. A.A. A.S., sec., 1854-73, pres., 1873; became mem. Am. Acad. Arts and Scis., 1839, pres., 1880-87. Died Cambridge, Mass., Jan. 18, 1892.

LOVETT, John, congressman; b. in what is now Lisbon, Conn., Feb. 20, 1761; grad. Yale, 1782. Moved to Albany, N.Y., later to Fort Miller, N.Y., gen. agt. and land steward; moved to Lansingburg, N.Y.; mem. N.Y. Assembly, 1800-01; clk. Albany Common Council, until War of 1812; mil. sec. to Gen. Stephen Van Rensselaer on N.W. frontier; wounded at Battle of Queenstown, 1812; clk. Albany County, 1813-15; mem. U.S. Ho. of Reps. (Federalist) from N.Y., 13th-14th congresses, 1813-17; founder Perrysburg (O.). Died Fort Meigs, O., Aug. 12, 1818.

LOVEWELL, John, Indian fighter; b. Dunstable, Mass., Oct. 14, 1691; s. John and Anna (Hassell) L.; m. Hannah Lovewell, 2 children. Farmer at Dunstable, lost wife and children in Indian raid, 1724; petitioned Mass. Legislature for commn. to kill Indians, 1724; organized group of 80 men who surprised and killed 10 sleeping Indians, 1725; built fort at Lake Ossipee, Me.; became subject of New Eng. folk literature and songs. Killed in Indian ambush, Me., May 8, 1725.

LOW, Abiel Abbot, mcht.; b. Salem, Mass., Feb. 7, 1811; s. Seth and Mary (Porter) L.; m. Ellen Dow, Mar. 16, 1841; m. 2d, Ann (Bedell) Low, Feb. 25, 1851; at least 1 child, Seth. Clk. merc. house Russell & Co., Canton, China, 1833, became partner firm, 1837; built up own bus. in China trade A.A. Low & Bros., expanded into large fleet of mcht. ships; helped finance 1st Atlantic cable; asso. with bldg. C. & O. R.R. through W. Va. to the Ohio River; a founder Newport News (Va.), also Huntington (W.Va.); pres. N.Y.C. C. of C., 1863-66; commr. charities Kings County (N.Y.), investigated influence of growth of urban population and unsanitary conditions on the increase of pauperism; pres. bd. trustees Packer Collegiate Inst. Died Bklyn., Jan. 7, 1893.

LOW, Frederick Ferdinand, gov. Cal., banker; b. Frankfort, Me., June 30, 1828; m. Mollie Creed, 1850. Apprentice to East India firm, Russell, Sturgis & Co., Boston, 1843; participated in Cal. gold rush of 1849; accomplished merger of almost all inland steamship lines on San Francisco Bay and Sacramento River, 1854; mem. U.S. Ho. of Reps. from Cal., 37th Congress, June 3, 1862-63; U.S. Collector Port of San Francisco, 1863; gov. Cal. (1st to serve 4 year term), 1863-67; a founder U. Cal.; U.S. minister to China, 1870-74; joint mgr. Anglo-Cal. Bank, San Francisco, 1874-91. Died San Francisco, July 21, 1894; buried Laurel Hill Cemetery, San Francisco.

LOW, Isaac, Continental congressman; b. Raritan Landing, N.J., Apr. 13, 1735; s. Cornelius, Jr. and Johanna (Gouverneur) L.; m. Margarita Cuyler, July 17, 1760, 1 son, Isaac. Del. from N.Y. to Stamp Act Congress, 1765; head of com. of inspection to enforce non-importation agreement, 1768; chmn. Com. of 51, also a drafter of proposals for gen. congress to deal with non-importation; mem. 1st Continental Congress from N.Y., 1774-75; mem. Provincial Congress from N.Y., 1775; a founder N.Y. C. of C., 1775, pres., 1775-83; accused of treason and arrested, 1776, property confiscated by Am. authorities because of treason, 1779; moved to Eng., 1783. Died Cowes, Isle of Wight, Eng., July 25, 1791.

LOW, Nicholas, mcht.; b. nr. New Brunswick, N.J., Mar. 30, 1739; s. Cornelius and Johanna (Gouverneur) L., Jr.; m. Alice Fleming, 3 children. Clk. to mcht. Hayman Levy, N.Y.C.; founded mcht. firm Low & Wallace, N.Y.C., during Am. Revolution; dir. Bank of N.Y., 1785; mem. N.Y. State Assembly, 1787; mem. N.Y. State Conv. to ratify U.S. Constn., 1788; had large land holdings in upper N.Y. and N.Y.C.; helped develop Town of Ballston (N.Y.) by building hotel and cotton factory there; Lowville (N.Y.) named after him. Died N.Y.C., Nov. 15, 1826.

LOWE, Charles, clergyman; b. Portsmouth, N.H., Nov. 18, 1828; s. John and Sarah (Simes) L.; grad. Harvard, 1847, Divinity Sch., 1851; attended U. Halle (Germany), 1854-55; m. Martha Perry, Sept. 16, 1857. Pastor, North Ch., Salem, Mass., 1855-57, Unitarian Ch., Somerville, Mass., 1859-65; chmn. Army com. Am. Unitarian Assn., 1864, exec. sec., 1865-71, tried to organize nat. union for his church; editor Unitarian Review and Religious Mag., 1873-74. Died Boston, June 20, 1874.

LOWE, David Perley, congressman; b. nr. Utica, N.Y., Aug. 22, 1823; grad. Cincinnati Law Coll., 1851. Admitted to Ohio bar, began practice in Cincinnati; moved to Mound City, Kan., 1861, practiced law; mem. Kan. Senate, 1863-64; judge 6th Kan. Jud. Dist., 1867-71, 79-82; moved to Fort Scott, Kan., 1870; mem. U.S. Ho. of Reps. (Republican) from Kan., 42d-43d congresses, 1871-75; apptd. chief justice Utah Territory, 1875. Died Fort Scott, Apr. 10, 1882; buried Evergreen Cemetery, Fort Scott.

LOWE, Ralph Phillips, gov. Ia., jurist; b. Warren County, O., Nov. 27, 1805; s. Jacob Derrick and Martha (Per-Lee) L.; grad. Miami U., Oxford, O., 1829; m. Phoebe Carleton, 1837. Admitted to Ala. bar, 1832; served on Ia. Constl. Conv., 1844; dist. atty. Ia., judge 1st dist. of Ia., 1852-57; 1st gov. of Ia. (under constn. of 1857), 1858-60; justice Ia. Supreme Ct., 1860-68, chief justice, 1866-68. Died Washington, D.C., Dec. 22, 1883.

LOWELL, Edward Jackson, historian; b. Boston, Oct. 18, 1845; s. Francis and Mary (Gardner) L.; grad. Harvard, 1867; m. Mary Goodrich, Jan. 1868; m. 2d, Elizabeth Jones, June 1877; 3 children including Guy. Admitted to Mass. bar, 1872; practiced with Brooks Adams, 1872-74, retired to study history, 1874; mem. Mass. Hist. Soc., Am. Acad. Arts and Scis. Author: The Hessians and the Other German Auxiliaries of Great Britain in the Revolutionary War, 1884; The Eve of the French Revolution, 1892. Died Cotuit, Mass., May 11, 1894.

LOWELL, Francis Cabot, mfr.; b. Newburyport, Mass., Apr. 7, 1775; s. Judge John and Susanna (Cabot) L.; grad. Harvard, 1793; m. Hannah Jackson, Oct. 31, 1798, 4 children including John. Mcht. with William Cabot, Boston, 1793-1810; went to Eng. for health, 1810, studied textile mills; formed Boston Mfg. Co. which bought land at Waltham, Mass., designed from memory or invented machines for cotton factory (1st factory in world to unite all processes of cloth under one roof); lobbied for tariff of 1816 which protected his cloth mill; Lowell (Mass.) named after him. Died Boston, Aug. 10, 1817.

LOWELL, James Russell, author, educator, diplomat; b. "Elmwood," Cambridge, Mass., Feb. 22, 1819; s. Rev. Charles and Harriet (Spence) L.; B.A., Harvard, 1838, grad. Law Sch., 1840; D.C.L. (hon.), Oxford (Eng.) U., 1872; LL.D. (hon.) Cambridge (Eng.) U., 1874; m. Maria White, Dec. 26, 1844 (dec. Oct. 1853), children—Blanche, Mabel, Rose, Walter; m. 2d, Frances Dunlop, Sept. 1857; Editor, The Pioneer (literary and critical mag.), 1843; corresponding editor The Nat. Anti-Slavery Standard, 1848; editorial writer Pa. Freeman; Smith prof. French and Spanish langs. and lits. Harvard, 1855-86, prof. emeritus, 1886-91; editor Atlantic Monthly, 1857-61, N.Am. Review, 1864-72; del. Nat. Republican Conv., 1876; mem. Electoral Coll., 1876; U.S. minister to Spain, 1877-80; U.S. minister to Ct. of St. James, 1880-85. Author: A Year's Life, 1841; Poems, 1844; Conversations on Some of the Old Poets, 1845; Poems by James Russell Lowell, Second Series, 1848; A Fable for Critics, 1848; The Biglow Papers, 1st vol., 1848; The Vision of Sir Launfal, 1848; Under the Willows (poems), 1869; The Cathedral, 1870; Fireside Travels, 1870; Among My Books, 1870; My Study Windows, 1871; Among My Books, Second Series, 1876; Three Memorial Poems, 1877; Heartsease and Rue, 1888; Last Poems of James Russell Lowell, published posthumously, 1895. Died "Elmwood," Aug. 12, 1891.

LOWELL, John, Continental congressman, jurist; b. Newburyport, Mass., June 17, 1743; s. Rev. John and Sarah (Champney) L.; grad. Harvard, 1760, LL.D. (hon.), 1792; m. Sarah Higginson, Jan. 3, 1767; m. 2d, Susanna Cabot, May 31, 1774; m. 3d, Rebecca (Russell) Tyng; 9 children including John, Francis Cabot, Charles. Admitted to Mass. bar; del. to Essex County Conv., 1776; rep. from Newburyport in Mass. Provincial Assembly, 1771, 72, 74, 76; rep. from Boston to Mass. Gen. Ct., 1778; del. to Mass. Constl. Conv., 1779-80; mem. Continental Congress, 1781-83; judge to hear appeals in admiralty cases, 1782; mem. corp. Harvard, 1784-1802, elected to bd., 1784; mem. commn. apptd. to settle boundary dispute between Mass. and N.Y., 1784; U.S. judge for dist. Mass., 1789; chief judge 1st Circuit, 1801; pres. Mass. Agrl. Soc.; founder Am. Acad. Arts and Scis. Died Roxbury, May 6, 1802.

LOWELL, John, lawyer; b. Newburyport, Mass., Oct. 6, 1769; s. Judge John and Sarah (Higginson) L.; grad. Harvard, 1786; m. Rebecca Amory, June 8, 1793; 1 son, John Amory. Admitted to Mass. bar,

1789; mem. Mass. Legislature from Boston, 1798-1800; mem. corp. Harvard, 1810-22, overseer, 1823-27; founder Mass. Gen. Hosp.; mem. Boston Athenaeum, Mass. Hist. Soc., Am. Antiquarian Soc., Mass. Agrl. Soc. Author: Mr. Madison's War, 1812. Died Mar. 12, 1840.

LOWELL, John, mcht., philanthropist; b. Boston, May 11, 1799; s. Francis Cabot and Hannah (Jackson) L.; entered Harvard, 1813; m. Georgina Amory, Apr. 6, 1825, 2 children. Mem. Boston City Council, Mass. Legislature; went to India as mcht. dealing with East Indies, 1816; provided funds to found Lowell Inst. in his will, 1832. Died Bombay, India, Mar. 4, 1836.

LOWELL, John, judge; b. Boston, Oct. 18, 1824; s. John A. and Susan (Lowell) L.; grad. Harvard, 1843, Law Sch., 1845; m. Lucy Emerson, 1853, 7 children including James, John. Admitted to Mass. bar, 1846; practiced law with partner William Sohier, 1846-57; founded own firm, Boston, 1857; editor Monthly Law Reporter, 1856-60; U.S. dist. judge for Mass., 1865-78; U.S. circuit judge for 1st Circuit, 1878-84; overseer Harvard; chmn. commn. to revise Mass. tax laws, 1896. Author: A Treatise on the Law of Bankruptcy, 2 vols., published posthumously 1899. Died May 14, 1897.

LOWELL, Joshua Adams, congressman; b. Thomaston, Me., Mar. 20, 1801; attended common schs.; studied law. Taught sch.; admitted to Me. bar, began practice in East Machias, 1826; mem. Me. Ho. of Reps., 1832-33, 35, 37; mem. U.S. Ho. of Reps. (Democrat) from Me., 26th-27th congresses, 1839-43; resumed law practice; Dem. presdl. elector, 1844. Died East Machias, Mar. 13, 1874; buried Village Cemetery, East Machias.

LOWELL, Robert Traill Spence, clergyman, educator; b. Boston, Oct. 8, 1816; s. Rev. Charles and Harriet (Spence) L.; grad. Harvard, 1833, attended Med. Sch., 1833-36; m. Mary Ann Duane, Oct. 28, 1845, 7 children. Ordained priest Protestant Episcopal Ch., 1843; missionary in Newfoundland, 1843-47, Newark, N.J., 1848-59; rector Christ Ch., Duanesburg, N.Y., 1859-68; prof. belles lettres Racine (Wis.) Coll., 1868; headmaster St. Mark's Sch., Southboro, Mass., 1869-73; prof. Latin lang. and literature Union Coll., 1873-79. Author: The New Priest in Conception Bay, 1858; A Story or Two from an Old Dutch Town, 1878; Poems, 1864. Died Sept. 12, 1891.

LOWER, Christian, congressman; b. Tulpehocken Twp., Berks County, Pa., Jan. 7, 1740; attended sch. Engaged as blacksmith, later propr. iron foundry; col. asso. battalions, 1775, sub-lt., 1780; commr. Berks County, 1777-79; mem. Pa. Ho. of Reps., 1783-85, 93-94, 96, Pa. Senate, 1797-1804; mem. U.S. Ho. of Reps. (Democrat) from Pa., 19th Congress, 1805-06. Died Tulpehocken Twp., Dec. 19, 1806; buried Tulpehocken Ch. Burial Ground.

LOWNDES, Rawlins, colonial ofcl.; b. St. Kitts, B.W.I., Jan. 1721; s. Charles and Ruth (Rawlins) L.; m. Amarinthia Elliott, Aug. 15, 1748; m. 2d, Mary Cartwright, Dec. 23, 1751; m. 3d, Sarah Jones, Jan. 1773; 12 children including William. Provost marshall S.C., 1740-52; mem. S.C. Legislature from St. Paul's Parish, 1749, from St. Bartholomew's Parish, 1751-66, 72-75, speaker lower house, 1763-65, 72-75; asso. judge S.C. Ct. Common Pleas, 1766-73; mem. S.C. Provincial congresses of 1775, S.C. Council of Safety; mem. S.C. Legislative Council (formed after S.C.'s declaration of independence from Eng.), 1776; pres. S.C., 1778-79; mem. S.C. Senate from Charleston, 1882-87; opposed adoption of U.S. Constn., 1787. Died Charleston, Aug. 24, 1800.

LOWNDES, Thomas, congressman; b. Charleston, S.C., Jan. 22, 1766; studied law. Admitted to S.C. bar, 1789, began practice in Charleston; mem. S.C. Ho. of Reps., 1796-1800; mem. U.S. Ho. of Reps. (Federalist) from S.C., 7th-8th congresses, 1801-05. Died Charleston, July 8, 1843; buried St. Paul's Churchyard, Charleston.

LOWNDES, William (Jones), congressman; b. Horseshoe Plantation, Colleton County, S.C., Feb. 11, 1782; s. Rawlins and Sarah (Jones) L.; m. Elizabeth Pinckney, Sept. 16, 1802. Admitted to S.C. bar, 1804; mem. S.C. Ho. of Reps., 1806-10; capt. S.C. Militia, 1807; mem. U.S. Ho. of Reps. from S.C., 12th-17th congresses, 1811-May 8, 1822, mem. com. for commerce and manufactures, com. for mil. affairs, chmn. ways and means com., 1815-18, author sinking fund act which payed off nat. debt in 14 years, 1816, chmn. com. on fgn. affairs, 1819, also chmn. spl. com. on coinage (submitted report on relative value of coins of different nations in relation to Am. coinage), speaker of Ho., 1820, chmn. com. of 3 to report on acceptance Mo. Constn. Died at sea, Oct. 27, 1822, buried at sea.

LOWREY, Mark Perrin, clergyman, army officer, educator; b. McNairy County, Tenn., Dec. 30, 1828; s. Adam and Margaret (Doss) L.; m. Sarah Holmes, 1849. Ordained to ministry by Farmington Baptist Ch., 1853; col. 4th Regt. of sixty-day volunteers, 1861; organized, became col. 32d Miss. Regt.; commd. brig. gen., 1863; founded Blue Mountain Female Instn., 1873, pres., prof. history and moral science, 1873-85; mem. bd. trustees U. Miss., 1872; pres. Miss. Bapt. Conv., 1868-77. Died Middleton, Tenn., Feb. 27, 1885.

LOWRIE, Walter, senator; b. Edinburgh, Scotland, Dec. 10, 1784; s. John and Catherine (Cameron) L.; m. Amelia McPherrin, Jan. 14, 1808; m. 2d, Mary K. Childs, 1834; 8 children. Came to Huntington County, Pa., circa 1792; served as clk., mem. bd. commrs., justice of peace, Butler County, Pa.; mem. Pa. Ho. of Reps., 1811-12, Pa. Senate, 1812-19; mem. U.S. Senate from Pa., 1819-25, sec,. 1825-36; corresponding sec. Western Fgn. Missionary Soc. (became Bd. Fgn. Missions of Presbyn. Ch. 1837) 1836-68; Died N.Y.C., Dec. 14, 1868; buried 1st Presbyn. Ch., N.Y.C.

LOYALL, George, congressman; b. Norfolk, Va., May 29, 1789; grad. Coll. William and Mary, 1808; studied law. Visited Eng., 1815; mem. Va. Ho. of Dels., 1818-27; del. Va. Constl. Conv., 1829; mem. U.S. Ho. of Reps. from Va., 21st, 23d-24th congresses, Mar. 9, 1830-31, 33-37; naval agt., Norfolk, 1837-61 (except for 2 years). Died Norfolk, Feb. 24, 1858; buried Elmwood Cemetery, Norfolk.

LOZIER, Clemence Sophia Harned, physician; b. Plainfield, N.J., Dec. 11, 1813; d. David and Hannah (Walker)) Harned; grad. Syracuse Med. Coll., 1853; m. Abraham Lozier, 1830, 1 son Abraham. Moved to N.Y.C., lectured on hygiene and physiology in her home; founder N.Y. Med. Coll. and Hosp. for Women, 1863; reorganized coll., became dean and prof. gynecology and obstetrics, 1867-88; mem. Nat. Working Women's League, W.C.T.U., N.Y.C. Suffrage League (pres. 13 years), Nat. Woman's Suffrage Assn. (pres. 5 years). Died N.Y.C., Apr. 26, 1888.

LUCAS, Edward, congressman; b. nr. Shepherdstown, Va. (now W.Va.), Oct. 20, 1780; grad. Dickinson Coll., Carlisle, Pa., 1809; studied law. Served as 1st lt. and acting capt. during War of 1812; admitted to Va. bar, practiced in Shepherdstown, until 1818; engaged in merc. business; member Va. House of Dels., 1819-22, 30-31; member U.S. House of Reps. (Democrat) from Va., 23d-24th congresses, 1833-37; mil. storekeeper of ordnance Harpers Ferry (Va.; now W.Va.) Armory, 1847-58. Died Harpers Ferry, Mar. 4, 1858; buried Harper Cemetery, Harpers Ferry.

LUCAS, James H., railroad exec.; b. Pitts., Nov. 12, 1800; s. John and Anne (Sebin) L.; attended St. Thomas' Coll., Ky., 1814, Jefferson Coll., Pa.; m. Mary Desruisseaux, May 1832, some children. Mcht., plantation owner, Ark. Territory, 1823-36; moved to St. Louis to handle father's property which contained large land holdings, 1836; aided in creation Pacific R.R., 1849, dir., pres.; founder bank of Lucas, Simonds & Co.; a founder St. Louis Gas Co.; mem. Mo. Senate, 1844-48. Died St. Louis, Nov. 9, 1873.

LUCAS, John Baptiste Charles, congressman; b. Normandy, France, Aug. 14, 1758; s. Robert Edouard and Mrs. (de l'Arche) L.; grad. law dept. U. Caen (France), 1782; m. Ann Sebin, circa 1783, at least 3 children including Charles, James H. Came to U.S., 1784; mem. Pa. Ho. of Reps., 1792-98; judge Allegheny Dist. (Pa.) Ct. of Common Pleas, 1794; mem. U.S. Ho. of Reps. from Pa., 8th Congress, 1803-05; U.S. judge for No. dist. La., 1805-20; acting gov. Mississippi Territory, circa 1813. Died St. Louis, Aug. 17, 1842; buried Calvary Cemetery, St. Louis.

LUCAS, Johnathan, millwright; b. Cumberland, Eng., 1754; s. John and Ann (Noble) L.; m. Mary Cooke, May 22, 1774; m. 2d, Ann Ashburn, between 1783-86; 5 children including Jonathan. Moved to Charleston, S.C., 1790; 1st built pounding-mill driven by wind to remove husks from rice grain; built water mills for various plantations; also constructed tide-mills (operated automatically on movement of tides); made prodn. of rice much more profitable for South. Died Apr. 1, 1821; buried St. Paul's Churchyard, Charleston.

LUCAS, Jonathan, millwright, inventor; b. Eng., 1775; s. Jonathan and Mary (Cooke) L.; m. Sarah Lydia Simons, July 18, 1799, some children. Came (with father) to S.C., 1790; builder and operator of rice mill, Cannonborough, S.C., 1798-1801; operated new rice mill on Middleburg Plantation on Cooper River, 1801-22; devised and patented new type of machine to remove husks from rice; took machine to Eng. because it was not widely accepted by farmers in S.C., 1822; established rice cleaning mills, London, Liverpool (Eng.), also Copenhagen (Denmark), other European cities; lived in Surrey, Eng., 1827-32. Died Surrey, Dec. 29, 1832; buried Camberwell Ch., London.

LUCAS, Robert, gov. Ohio; b. Shepherdstown, Va. (now W.Va.), Apr. 1, 1781; s. William and Susannah (Barnes) L.; m. Elizabeth Brown, Apr. 4, 1810; m. 2d, Friendly Sumner, Mar. 7, 1816. Surveyor for Scioto County (O.), 1804-06, justice of peace, 1806; officer Va. Militia, attained rank maj. gen.; mem. lower house Ohio Legislature, 1808-09, 31-32, Ohio Senate, 1814-22, 24-28, 29-30; gov. Ohio, 1832-36; 1st gov., supt. Indian affairs Territory Iowa, 1838-41; mem. Ia. Constl. Conv., 1844. Died Iowa City, Ia., Feb. 7, 1853.

LUCAS, William, congressman; b. "Cold Spring" nr. Shepherdstown, Va. (now W.Va.), Nov. 30, 1800; grad. Tucker Law Sch., Winchester, Va., 1825. Admitted to Va. bar, 1825, began practice in Shepherdstown; moved to Charles Town, Va. (now W.Va.), 1830, practiced law, also engaged in horticulture; mem. Va. Ho. of Dels., 1838-39; mem. U.S. Ho. of Reps. (Democrat) from Va., 26th, 28th congresses, 1839-41, 43-45; del. Va. Constl. Conv., 1850-51. Died "Rion Hall," Jefferson County, W.Va., Aug. 29, 1877; buried Zion Episcopal Churchyard, Charles Town.

LUDELING, John Theodore, jurist; b. New Orleans, Jan. 27, 1827; s. John and Francoise (de Salnavo) L.; attended St. Louis U., 1839-43; studied law in office of Isaiah Garrett, Monroe, La.; m. Maria Copley. Admitted to La. bar; chief justice, La., 1868-77; supported Union cause; a founder, 1st pres. Vicksburg, Shreveport & Pacific R.R. Died nr. Monroe, Jan. 21, 1891; buried City Cemetery, Monroe.

LUDLOW, Daniel, mcht., banker; b. N.Y.C., Aug. 2, 1750; s. Gabriel and Elizabeth (Crommelin) L.; m. Arabella Duncan, Oct. 4, 1773; m. 2d, Mrs. Van Horne. In importing business (which his father founded), N.Y.C., 1770-82; partner (with Edward Gould) in importing firm, 1782-90; partner (with nephew) in Daniel Ludlow & Co., merc. trade, 1790-1808; a founder Manhattan Co., subsidiary Bank of Manhattan Co., 1799, pres., 1799-1808; Navy agt. from 1801; dir. Harlem Bridge Co.; moved to Skaneateles (N.Y.) following failure of banking firm, 1808. Died Skaneateles, Sept. 26, 1814.

LUDLOW, Fitz Hugh, author; b. N.Y.C., Sept. 11, 1836; s. Rev. Henry G. and Abby (Wills) L.; attended Coll. of N.J. (now Princeton), 1854; grad. Union Coll., 1856; studied law, N.Y.C.; m. Rosalie H. Osborne, June 1859; m. 2d, Maria O. Milliken, Dec. 1867. Taught sch., Watertown, N.Y., 1857-58; admitted to N.Y. bar, 1859; contbr. articles to Comml. Advertiser, the World, Evening Post, Home Journal, after 1860; contbd. story The Household Angel to Harper's Mag., 1868; wrote treatise on effects of opium, What Shall They Do To Be Saved, 1867; went to Switzerland to regain health, 1870. Author: The Hasheesh Eater, 1857; The Heart of the Continent, 1870. Died Geneva, Switzerland, Sept. 12, 1870; buried Poughkeepsie, N.Y.

LUDLOW, Gabriel George, Loyalist; b. N.Y.C., Apr. 16, 1736; s. Gabriel and Frances (Duncan) L.; m. Ann Ver Planck, Sept. 3, 1760. Gov., King's Coll. (now Columbia), N.Y.C.; col. N.Y. Militia; justice of peace Queens County, N.Y.; commanded 3d Battalion of De Lancey's L.I. Brigade of Loyal Americans in Revolutionary War, commd. col. at close of war; mem. 1st Council of New Brunswick, 1784-1808; mem. 1st City Council of St. John (N.B.), mayor, 1785-95; 1st judge Vice Admiralty Ct., 1787-1803; administered govt. as pres. His Majesty's Council and comdr. in chief Province of New Brunswick, 1803-08. Died Carleton, N.B., Feb. 12, 1808.

LUDLOW, George Duncan, jurist; b. 1734; s. Gabriel and Frances (Duncan) L.; studied law, before 1768; m. Frances Duncan Ludlow (a cousin), Apr. 22, 1758, 3 children. Practiced as an apothecary, before 1768; mem. N.Y. Gov.'s Council, 1768-78; judge N.Y. Supreme Ct., 1769-78; supt. of police for L.I., 1778; a Loyalist supporter during Am. Revolution, lost all property to confiscation activities of Revolutionaries, 1779; sailed for Eng., 1783; chief justice Province of New Brunswick, 1784-1808. Died Fredericton, N.B., Nov. 13, 1808.

LUDLOW, Noah Miller, actor, theatrical mgr.; b. N.Y.C., July 3, 1795; s. John and Phebe (Dunham) L.; m. Mary (Maury) Squires (or Squire), Sept. 1, 1817. Mem. Samuel Drake's theatrical company travelling in Ky., Pa., Tenn., 1815-17; with 2 other actors formed own company, 1817; gave performance in New Orleans (1st performance in English in that city), 1817; made debut in N.Y.C. at Chatham Theatre as Young Wilding in The Liar, 1826; asst. theatrical mgr. theatres in Mobile, Ala., St. Louis, Cincinnati, New Orleans, 1835-53. Author: Dramatic Life as I Found It, 1880; A Genealogical History of the Ludlow Family, 1844; Manatua, or the Spirit of the Glen (sketch). Died St. Louis, Jan. 9, 1886.

LUDLOW, Roger, colonial ofcl.; b. Eng., 1590; s. Thomas Ludlow; grad. Balliol Coll., Oxford (Eng.) U., 1612; m. Mary Ludlow. Assistant of Mass. Bay Co., 1630; a founder Dorchester (Mass.); a leader in early govt. of colony; dep. gov. Mass., 1634; presided over 1st ct. held in Conn., 1636; credited with drafting Fundamental Orders adopted by colony, 1638/39 (resulted in Code of 1650, known as "Ludlow's Code," 1st compilation and codification of Conn. laws); founder Fairfield (Conn.), 1639; elected as either magistrate or dep. gov. from Fairfield, annually 1639-54; commr. United Colonies of New Eng., 1651-53; returned to Eng. to serve under Cromwell. Died Dublin, Ireland, 1664.

LUDLOW, Thomas William, lawyer, financier; b. N.Y.C., June 14, 1795; s. Thomas and Mary Ludlow; grad. Columbia, 1811; studied law in office of Martin Wilkins, N.Y.; m. Frances W. Morris, 1828. Served in N.Y. Militia during War of 1812; practiced law briefly; became Am. rep. for Dutch banking house of Crommelin & Co.; promoter N.Y. Life Ins. & Trust Co., trustee, 1830-78; trustee Columbia, 1833-36; founder N.Y. Life Ins. Co., 1845; an incorporator, 1st pres. Panama R.R. Co., 1849; promoter Ill. Central R.R. Died Yonkers, N.Y., July 17, 1878.

LUDWELL, Philip colonial gov.; b. Bruton, Sommershire, Eng., circa 1660; s. Thomas and Jane (Cottington) L.; m. Lucy Higginson; m. 2d, Frances Culpeper; at least 1 child. Came to Va., 1660; mem. Va. Gov.'s Council, 1674-79, 80-87, sec. to gov. for short time; mem. Va. Ho. of Burgesses, 1688; gov. Carolina, 1689-91-94. Died Eng., circa 1704; buried Stratford-le-Bow, Eng.

LUDWICK, Christopher, baker; b. Giessen, Heese (formerly Hesse-Darmstadt), Germany, Oct. 17, 1720; m. Mrs. Catharine England, 1755; m. 2d, Mrs. Sophia Binder, 1798. Fought in German Army against turks, 1737-40; fought in Prussian Army, 1741; went to London, became baker on East India ship, 1741-45; as sailor on English ship made voyages to West Indies and European ports, 1745-52; started his own bakery, Phila., circa 1754; supported Revolutionary War; apptd. by Congress as supt. bakers and dir. bakers in Continental Army, 1777-83; bequeathed fortune to various churches in Phila. and fund providing for free edn. of poor children. Died Phila., June 17, 1801; buried Trinity Lutheran Ch., Germantown, Phila.

LUELLING, Henderson, nurseryman; b. Randolph County, N.C., Apr. 23, 1809; s. Meshach Luelling; m. Elizabeth Presnell, Dec. 30, 1830 (dec. 1854), 8 children including Oregon Columbia. Operated tree nursery with his brother, Salem, Ia., 1837-47; went to Willamette Valley Ore. with his family and a group of settlers, brought with him nursery to be transplanted, 1847; set up nursery (including pears, apples, cherries, grapes) nr. present site of Milwaukie, Ore.; moved part of his nursery to Oakland, Cal., 1854; moved to Honduras, 1859, later returned to Cal. Died San Jose, Cal., Dec. 28, 1878; buried Mountain View Cemetery, Oakland.

LUERS, John Henry, clergyman; b. Luetten, Germany, Sept. 29, 1819; brought to U.S., 1831; attended St. Francis Xavier Sem., Ohio. Ordained priest Roman Catholic Ch., Cincinnati, 1846; did parish work in Cincinnati, 1846-56; apptd. 1st bishop of Ft. Wayne (Ind.), 1857; attended 2d Plenary Council, Balt., 1866. Died Cleve., June 29, 1871.

LUKENS, Rebecca Webb Pennock, iron mfr.; b. Coatesville, Pa., Jan. 6, 1794; d. Isaac and Martha (Webb) Pennock; m. Charles Lloyd Lukens, 1813, 3 children. Became mgr. Brandywine Rolling Mill (started by her father), Brandywine, Pa., after her husband's death, 1825; 1st Am. Woman to engage in iron industry; enlarged business after overcoming transp. difficulties; name of mills changed to Lukens Mills in her honor, upon her death. Died Coatesville, Dec. 10, 1854.

LULL, Edward Phelps, naval officer; b. Windsor, Vt., Feb. 20, 1836; s. Martin Lull; grad. U.S. Naval Acad., 1855; m. Elizabeth F. Burton, circa 1863; m. 2d, Emma Gillingham Terry, Nov. 5, 1873. Served as midshipman U.S. Navy in ships Congress (1855-58), Colorado, Roanoke; promoted warranted master, 1858; prof. English, ethics, fencing U.S. Naval Acad., 1860-61, prof. mathematics, Spanish, 1866-69; promoted lt., 1860, lt. comdr., 1862, master of ship John Adams, 1863; promoted comdr., 1870; commanded ship Guard on Darien Surveying Expdn., 1870-71; headed Nicaragua Exploring Expdn., 1872-73; hydrographic insp. Coast and Geodetic Survey, 1875-80; promoted capt., 1881; served duty at Boston and Pensacola navy yards. Author: History of the United States Navy-Yard at Gosport, Virginia, 1874. Died Mar. 5, 1887.

LUMBROZO, Jacob, physician, mcht.; b. Lisbon, Portugal; m. Elizabeth Lumbrozo, circa 1663, 1 son John. One of 1st Jews to settle in Md., 1656; practiced medicine in colony, often suffered verbal abuse because of his religion; commd. by some London mchts. to trade with Indians, 1665. Flourished 1656-65.

LUMPKIN, John Henry, congressman; b. Lexington, Ga., June 13, 1812; attended Franklin Coll. (now U. Ga.); attended Yale, 1830-32; studied law. Pvt. sec. to Gov. Wilson Lumpkin of Ga. (his uncle); admitted to Ga. bar, 1834, began practice in Ga.; mem. Ga. Ho. of Reps., 1835; solicitor gen. Cherokee Circuit, 1838; mem. U.S. Ho. of Reps. (Democrat) from Ga., 28th-30th, 34th congresses, 1843-49, 55-57; judge Ga. Superior Ct. for Rome circuit, 1850-53; unsuccessful candidate for gov. Ga., 1857; del. Dem. Nat. Conv., Charleston, S.C., 1860. Died Rome, July 10, 1860; buried Oak Hill Cemetery, Rome.

LUMPKIN, Joseph Henry, jurist; b. Oglethorpe County, Ga., Dec. 23, 1799; s. John and Lucy (Hopson) L.; grad. with honors, Coll. of N.J. (now Princeton), 1819, LL.D. (hon.), 1851; m. Callender Greve, Feb. 1821. Admitted to Ga. bar, 1820; mem. Ga. Legislature, 1824-26; assisted in framing Ga. Penal Code, 1833; justice 1st Supreme Ct. of Ga., 1845-67; chancellor U. Ga., 1860. Died Athens, Ga., June 4, 1867.

LUMPKIN, Wilson, senator, gov. Ga.; b. Pittsylvania County, Va., Jan. 14, 1783; s. John and Lucy (Hopson) L.; grad. U. Ga.; m. Elizabeth Walker, Nov. 20, 1800; m. 2d, Annis Hopkins, Jan. 1, 1821; 12 children. Admitted to Ga. bar, 1804; mem. Ga. Ho. of Reps., 1804-14, 19-21; mem. U.S. Ho. of Reps. from Ga., 14th Congress, 1815-17, 20th-21st congresses, 1827-31; apptd. commr. of lands ceded by Creek Indians to Ga., 1818; Indian commr., 1821; commd. to fix Ga.-Fla. boundary, 1823; mem. Bd. of Public Works created by Ga. Legislature to inaugurate system of internal improvements; gov. Ga., 1831-35; Cherokee Indian commr., 1836-37; mem. U.S. Senate from Ga., 1837-41; del. So. Comml. Conv., Montgomery, Ala., 1858. Died Athens, Ga., Dec. 28, 1870; buried Oconee Cemetery, Athens.

LUNA, Tranquilino, congressman; b. Los Lunas, N.M., Feb. 25, 1849; grad. U. Mo. Engaged in stock raising; del. Republican nat. convs., 1880, 88; del. U.S. Congress from Territory of N.M., 1881-84; sheriff of Valencia County (N.M.), 1888-92. Died Peralta, N.M., Nov. 20, 1892; buried Los Lunas Cemetery.

LUNA Y ARELLANO, Tristan de, see de Luna y Arellano, Tristan.

LUNDY, Benjamin, abolitionist; b. Sussex County, N.J., Jan. 4, 1789; s. Joseph and Eliza (Shotwell) L.; m. Esther Lewis, 1815. Apprenticed to a saddler, Wheeling, Va., 1808-15; organized Union Humane Soc. (anti-slavery group), St. Clairsville, O., 1815; organized several anti-slavery groups in Ohio, 1816-19, contbd. articles to The Philanthropist; agitated for free slave movement, St. Louis, 1819-21; organized more anti-slavery groups from Canada to Balt., 1821-35; began publishing Nat. Enquirer and Constl. Advocate of Universal Liberty, Phila., 1835; published pamphlet The War in Texas, 1836; began publishing The Genius, Phila., 1838; interested in Negro colonization, visited Haiti, Tex., Can. to consider possibilities of colonies in these places. Died Hennepin, Ill., Aug. 22, 1839; buried Friends Graveyard, Clear Creek, Ill.

LUNT, George, journalist, author; b. Newburyport, Mass., Dec. 31, 1803; s. Abel and Phoebe (Tilton) L.; grad. Harvard, 1824; m. Sarah Miles Greenwood, Oct. 25, 1834; m. 2d, Emily Ashton, Dec. 4, 1845; m. 3d, Adeline Parsons, 1864. Prin. of high sch., Newburyport, 1824-27; admitted to Mass. bar, 1831; mem. Mass. Senate, 1835-36, Mass. Ho., 1837, 41, 47; U.S. atty. for Dist. of Mass., 1848-53; engaged in gen. practice law, 1853-57; supported Whig Party; editor Boston Daily Courier, 1857-63; devoted himself to literature, after 1863. Author: Poems, 1839; The Age of Gold and Other Poems, 1843; The Dove and the Eagle, 1851; Eastford; or Household Sketches, 1855; The Union, 1860; The Origin of the Late War, 1866. Died May 16, 1885.

LUNT, Orrington, philanthropist; b. Bowdoinham, Me., Dec. 24, 1815; s. William Webb and Ann Matilda (Sumner) L.; m. Cornelia A. Gray, Jan. 16, 1842, 4 children. Partner father's store, 1837; clk., treas. Bowdoinham, 1838; moved to Chgo., 1842; a founder Galena & Chgo. Union R.R. (1st railroad built from Chgo.), v.p., 2 years; trustee Chgo. YMCA; pres. Chgo. Bible Soc.; a founder, sec.-treas. bd. trustees Northwestern U., Garrett Bibl. Inst.; trustee Clark St. Methodist Episcopal Ch.; Orringotn Av. (Evanston, Ill.) and Orrington Lunt Library, (Northwestern U.) named for him. Died Evanston, Apr. 6, 1897.

LUSK, William Thompson, obstetrician; b. Norwich, Conn., May 23, 1838; s. Sylvester Graham and Elizabeth Freeman (Adams) L.; attended Yale, 1855, Heidelberg (Germany) U., 1858-60, U. Berlin, 1860-61; grad. Bellevue Hosp. Med. Coll., 1864; m. Mary Hartwell Chittenden, May 4, 1864; m. 2d, Matilda Myer Thorn, 1876. Served with 79th N.Y. Inf. Highlanders, 1861-63; gen. practice medicine, Bridgeport, Conn., 1865-66; practiced medicine (in partnership with Benjamin Fordyce Barker), N.Y.C., 1866-73; prof. physiology and microscopic anatomy L.I. Coll. Hosp., 1868-71; editor (with Dr. J. B. Hunter) N.Y. Med. Journal, 1871-73; prof. obstetrics Bellevue Hosp. Med. Coll., 1871-97; pres. Am. Gynecol. Soc., 1894; Known Mainly for book: The Science and Art of Midwifery, 1882. Died June 12, 1897.

LUTHER, Seth, reformer; b. Providence, R.I.; flourished 1817-46. Traveled in Western states and Can., 1817; began work as carpenter in Providence area, 1830; supported laborers' cause; sec. Gen. Trades Conv., Boston, 1834; addressed Nat. Trades Union Conv. on condition of working women, 1835. Author: An Address to the Working Men of New England, 1832; An Address on the Right of Free Suffrage, 1833.

LUTTRELL, John King, congressman; b. nr. Knoxville, Tenn., June 27, 1831; attended common schs., Tenn.; studied law, Cal. Mem. surveying crew St. Joseph & Hannibal R.R. (Mo.); taught sch.; clk. merc. bus., St. Joseph; moved to Cal., 1852, engaged in mining, farming, teaming; admitted to Cal. bar, began practice in Oakland, 1856; justice of peace, Brooklyn (now part of Oakland), Cal., 1856-57; rancher, nr. Fort Jones, Siskiyou County, Cal., 1858; sgt. at arms Cal. Assembly, 1865-66; mem. Cal. Ho. of Reps., 1871-72; mem. U.S. Ho. of Reps. (Democrat) from Cal., 43d-45th congresses, 1873-79; mem. bd. dirs. Cal. State Prison, 1887-89; U.S. commr. of fisheries, spl. agt. U.S. Treasury for Alaska, 1893. Died Sitka, Alaska, Oct. 4, 1893; buried Fort Jones Cemetery.

LYLE, Aaron, congressman; b. Mount Bethel, Pa., Nov. 17, 1759; attended common schs. Engaged in farming; served in Revolutionary War; mem. Pa. Ho. of Reps., 1797-1801, Pa. Senate, 1802-04; commr. Washington County (Pa.), 1806-09; mem. U.S. Ho. of Reps. (Democrat) from Pa., 11th-14th congresses, 1809-17; trustee Jefferson (later Washington and Jefferson) Coll., 1802-22. Died Cross Creek, Pa., Sept. 24, 1825; buried Old Cemetery, Cross Creek.

LYMAN, Chester Smith, astronomer, physicist; b. Manchester, Conn., Jan. 13, 1814; s. Chester and Mary (Smith) L.; grad. Yale, 1837; attended Union Theol. Sem., 1839-40; m. Delia Williams Wood, June 20, 1850. Pastor, 1st Ch. (Congregational), New Britain, Conn., 1843-45; traveled, pursued varied occupations including surveyor in Hawaii, gold digger in Cal., 1845-50; helped prepare definitions for Webster's Dictionary, 1850-circa 1855; prof. indsl. mechanics and physics Sheffield Scientific Sch. of Yale, 1859-71, prof. astronomy and physics, 1871-84, prof. astronomy, 1884-90; made 1st satisfactory observation of planet Venus, 1866; v.p. A.A.A.S., 1874; pres. Conn. Acad. Arts and Science, 1859-77; inventions include: 1st combined transit and zenith instrument for determining latitude; an apparatus for demonstrating wave motion; improvements in clock pendulums. Died New Haven, Conn., Jan. 29, 1890.

LYMAN, Joseph, congressman; b. Lyons, Mich., Sept. 13, 1840; attended Ia. Coll.; studied law. Served with Ia. Volunteer Cavalry during Civil War, 1861; adj. 29th Regt., Ia. Volunteer Inf., 1862-65, commd. maj., 1865; admitted to Ia. bar, 1866, began practice in Council Bluffs; dep. collector internal revenue for 5th Ia. Dist., 1867-70; judge circuit ct., 1884; mem. U.S. Ho. of Reps. (Republican) from Ia., 49th-50th congresses, 1885-89. Died Council Bluffs, July 9, 1890; buried Fairview Cemetery, Council Bluffs.

LYMAN, Joseph Bardwell, agriculturalist; b. Chester, Mass., Oct. 6, 1829; s. Timothy and Experience (Bardwell) L.; grad. Yale, 1850; grad. law dept. U. La., 1856; m. Laura Elizabeth Baker, July 14, 1858, 6 children. Taught sch., Cromwell, Conn., also in Miss., 1850-53; practiced law, New Orleans, 1856-61; mem. 1st La. Cavalry, 1861-63, taken prisoner at Loudon, Tenn., 1863, released when he took oath to U.S.; agrl. editor N.Y. World, 1867-68; mng. editor Hearth and Home, 1868-69; agrl. editor N.Y. Weekly Tribune, 1870-72. Author: Resources of Pacific States, 1865. Died Richmond Hill, L.I., N.Y., Jan. 28, 1872.

LYMAN, Joseph Stebbins, congressman; b. Northfield, Mass., Feb. 14, 1785; grad. Dartmouth, 1806; studied law. Admitted to N.Y. bar, began practice in Cooperstown; mem. U.S. Ho. of Reps. from N.Y., 16th Congress, 1819-21. Died Cooperstown, Mar. 21, 1821; buried Greenfield, Mass.

LYMAN, Phineas, colonial legislator, army officer; b. Durham, Conn., 1715; s. Noah and Elizabeth Lyman; grad. Yale, 1738; m. Eleanor Dwight, Oct. 1742. Tutor, Yale, 1738-42; dep. from Suffield in Conn. Colonial Assembly, 1749-52, also 2 terms, circa 1772, assistant, 1752-59; provincial gen. Conn. in Northern colonies during 7 Years War; served as maj. gen., 2d in command of Lake George Expdn., 1755; served in battles of Crown Point, Ticonderoga, Montreal and in expdn. against Havana. Died Natchez, Miss., Sept. 10, 1774.

LYMAN, Samuel, congressman; b. Goshen, Conn., Jan. 25, 1749; attended Goshen Acad.; grad. Yale,

1770; studied law, Litchfield, Conn. Admitted to Conn. bar, 1773, began practice in Hartford; moved to Springfield, Mass., 1784; mem. Mass. Ho. of Reps., 1786-88, Mass. Senate, 1790-93; justice Hampshire County (Mass.) Ct. of Common Pleas, 1791-1800; mem. U.S. Ho. of Reps. from Mass., 4th-6th congresses, 1795-Nov. 6, 1800. Died Springfield, June 5, 1802; buried Goshen.

LYMAN, Theodore, mayor Boston; b. Boston Feb. 20, 1792; s. Theodore and Lydia (Williams) L.; grad. Harvard, 1810; m. Mary Elizabeth Henderson, 1821, at least 1 child. Studied and traveled for literary career, 1810-19; mem. Mass. Ho. of Reps., 1820-25; supported Andrew Jackson for Pres. U.S., 1828; mayor Boston, 1833-35; contbd. to several philanthropic causes, including $10,000 to start sch. for juvenile offenders, Westborough, Mass., 1846. Author works including: A Short Account of the Hartford Conventions, 1826; The Diplomacy of the United States, 2 vols., 1828. Died July 18, 1849.

LYMAN, Theodore, zoologist, congressman; b. Waltham, Mass., Aug. 23, 1833; s. Theodore and Mary Elizabeth (Henderson) L.; A.B., Harvard, 1855, B.S., 1858; m. Elizabeth Russell, Nov. 28, 1856. Studied zoology under Louis Agassiz at Lawrence Scientific Sch., joined Agassiz' scientific expdn. in Fla., 1855-58; elected as original mem. Museum of Comparative Zoology at Harvard, 1859; collected scientific data on the ophiuridae in Europe, 1861-63; served under Gen. Meade in Civil War, 1863-65; chmn. Fisheries Commn. of Mass., 1866; pres. Am. Fish Cultural Assn., 1884; overseer Harvard, 1868; mem. Am. Acad. Arts and Scis., mem. U.S. Ho. of Reps. from Mass, 48th Congress, 1883-85. Died Nahant, Mass., Sept. 9, 1897; buried Mt. Auburn Cemetery, Cambridge, Mass.

LYMAN, William, congressman, diplomat; b. Northampton, Mass., Dec. 7, 1755; grad. Yale, 1776. Served as aide to Gen. Shepard with rank of maj. during Shays' Rebellion; served in Revolutionary War; mem. Mass. Ho. of Reps., 1787; Mass. Senate, 1789; mem. U.S. Ho. of Reps. (Democrat) from Mass. 3d-4th congresses, 1793-97; brig. gen. Mass. Militia, 1796-1800; U.S. consul at London, Eng., 1805-11. Died Cheltenham, Gloucestershire, Eng., Sept. 2, 1811; buried in cathedral at Gloucester, Eng.; meml. monument erected in Old Cemetery, Northampton.

LYNCH, Charles, legislator; b. Chestnut Hill, Va., 1736; s. Charles and Sarah (Clark) L.; m. Anna Yerrell, Jan. 12, 1755. Justice of peace Bedford County, Va., 1766; mem. Va. Ho. of Burgesses, 1769-76; del. Va. Constl. Conv., 1776; helped mobilize Va. for Revolutionary War, 1776-89; mem. Va. Senate, 1784-89; presided over extra legal courts established in Bedford County during Am. Revolution, sentenced 2 mems. of a loyalist conspiracy (discovered 1780) to death (Lynch exonerated for this; term "Lynch law" derives from incident). Died Va., Oct. 29, 1796.

LYNCH, John, congressman; b. Portland, Me., Feb. 18, 1825; grad. Portland High Schs., 1842. Engaged in merc. bus.; mgr. Portland Daily Press, 1862; mem. Me. Ho. of Reps., 1862-64; mem. U.S. Ho. of Reps. (Republican) from Me., 39th-42d congresses, 1865-73; moved to Washington, D.C., established Washington Daily Union, 1877; mfr. bricks and drain pipes, Washington. Died Portland, July 21, 1892; buried Evergreen Cemetery, Portland.

LYNCH, John Joseph, clergyman; b. Clones, Monaghan, Ireland, Feb. 6, 1816; studied in Dublin, Ireland, Paris, France. Joined Lazarist order, Roman Catholic Ch., became tchr. and missionary in Ireland; came to U.S., taught and did missionary work in Tex. and Mo.; pres. Lazarist coll. in Mo.; founder-rector sem. of Our Lady of the Angels, Niagara Falls, N.Y.; apptd. titular bishop of Aechinas, also coadjutor of Toronto (Ont., Can.), 1859; became bishop Ont. (Can.), 1860; attended 3d, 4th provincial councils of Que., also Vatican Council of 1869-70; became 1st archbishop Toronto, 1870. Died Toronto, May 12, 1888.

LYNCH, Patrick Neeson, clergyman; b. Clones, Ireland, Mar. 10, 1817; s. Conlan and Eleanor (McMahon) L.; ed. Coll. of Propaganda, Rome, Italy, D.D. (hon.). Came to Am., 1819; ordained priest Roman Catholic Ch., 1840; asst. priest Cathedral of St. Finbar, 1840-45; rector St. Mary's Ch., Charleston, S.C., 1845; prin. Collegiate Inst., Charleston, 1847; vicar gen. Charleston Diocese, 1850, adminstr., 1855-58; bishop at Charleston, 1858-82; attended 9th Council of Province of Balt., 1858; del. Vatican Council, Rome, 1869; editor United States Catholic Miscellany. Died Charleston, S.C., Feb. 26, 1882.

LYNCH, Thomas, planter, Continental congressman; b. Berkeley County, S.C., 1727; s. Thomas and Sabena (Vanderhorst) L.; m. Elizabeth Allston, Sept. 5, 1745; m. 2d, Hannah Motte, Mar. 1755; 4 children including Thomas, Elizabeth. Mem. S.C. Ho. of Commons from St. James Parish, Santee, 1761-63, 65, 68, 72; rep. from S.C. to Stamp Act Congress, 1765; chmn. com. which drafted petition for repeal of Stamp Act to Ho. of Commons; mem. S.C. Gen. Com., 1769-74; mem. Continental Congress (selected by popular conv. in Charleston), 1774-76; del. 1st, 2d S.C. provincial congresses, 1775, 76; mem. 1st S.C. Gen. Assembly, 1776. Died Annapolis, Md., Dec. 1776; buried St. Anne's Churchyard, Annapolis.

LYNCH, Thomas, Continental congressman; b. Prince George's Parish, Winyaw, S.C., Aug. 5, 1749; s. Thomas and Elizabeth (Allstoh) L.; grad. Eton Coll., and Cambridge (Eng.) U.; m. Elizabeth Shubrick, May 14, 1772. Admitted to Middle Temple; practiced law, 1764-72; mem. 1st, 2d S.C. provincial congresses, 1774-76; mem. S.C., Constl. Com., 1776; served as capt. 1st S.C. Regt., then part of Continental Army, 1775-76; mem. 1st S.C. Gen. Assembly, 1776; mem. 2d Continental Congress, 1776-77, signer Declaration of Independence; went on voyage to West Indies and France because of illness, ship never heard from again. Presumed lost at sea, 1779.

LYNCH, William Francis, naval officer; b. Norfolk, Va., Apr. 1, 1801; m. Virginia Shaw, 2 children. Became midshipman U.S. Navy, 1819; promoted lt., 1828, commander, 1849; served in Gulf during Mexican War; explored by ship Jordan River and Dead Sea in Middle East, 1848; promoted capt., 1856; served as capt. Confederate Navy, 1861-65, commanded ship North Carolina, also ironclad Raleigh. Died Balt., Oct. 17, 1865.

LYNDE, Benjamin, jurist; b. Salem, Mass., Oct. 5, 1700; s. Benjamin and Mary (Browne) L.; grad. Harvard, 1718; m. Mary Bowes, Nov. 1, 1731. Naval officer at Salem, 1721-28; mem. council of Gen. Ct. of Mass., 1737-52; agt. to settle boundary dispute between N.H. and Mass., 1737, between R.I. and Mass., 1739; asso. justice Mass. Superior Ct., 1746-71, chief justice, 1771-72. Died Salem, Oct. 5, 1781.

LYNDE, William Pitt, congressman; b. Sherburne, N.Y., Dec. 16, 1817; attended Hamilton Coll., Clinton, N.Y.; grad. Yale, 1838; attended law dept. N.Y.U., 1 year; grad. Harvard Law Sch., 1841. Admitted to N.Y. bar, 1841; moved to Milw., 1841; atty. gen. of Wis., 1844; U.S. dist. atty. for Wis., 1845; mem. U.S. Ho. of Reps. (Democrat) from Wis., 30th, 44th-45th congresses, June 5, 1848-49, 75-79; mayor of Milw., 1860; mem. Wis. Assembly, 1866, Wis. Senate, 1869-70. Died Milw., Dec. 18, 1885; buried Forest Home Cemetery, Milw.

LYNDS, Elam, prison adminstr.; b. Litchfield, Conn., 1784. Served with Adam Yates' Regt. from Rensselaer County in N.Y. Militia, 1808-13; capt. 29th Inf., U.S. Army, 1813-15; prin. keeper Auburn State Prison, 1817-25; supervised constrn. Mt. Pleasant State Prison (now Sing-Sing), N.Y., 1834-38; creator of "Auburn system" of treatment of inmates, employing such measures as solitary confinement, labor in silence. Died South Brooklyn, N.Y., Jan. 8, 1855.

LYON, Asa, congressman; b. Pomfret, Conn., Dec. 31, 1763; grad. Dartmouth, 1790; studied theology, Somers, Conn.; studied law, South Hero, Vt. Ordained pastor Congregational Ch., Sunderland, Mass., 1792; moved to South Hero, 1794; mem. Vt. Ho. of Reps. from South Hero, 1799-1802, 04-06, 08, Vt. Exec. Council, 1808; pastor, South Hero, 1802-40; chief judge Grand Isle County (Vt.) Cts., 1805-09, 13-14; mem. Vt. Ho. of Reps. from Grand Isle, 1810-14; mem. U.S. Ho. of Reps. (Federalist) from Vt., 14th Congress, 1815-17. Died South Hero, Apr. 4, 1841; buried Grand Isle Cemetery.

LYON, Caleb, territorial congressman; b. Lyonsdale, N.Y., Dec. 8, 1821; s. Caleb and Mary (de Pont) L.; grad. Norwich U., Northfield, Vt., 1841, LL.D. (hon.), 1851; m. Anna Lyon, 1842. Apptd. U.S. consul at Shanghai, 1847, never reached China, resigned; asst. sec. Cal. Constl. Conv., 1849; credited with designing state seal of Cal., 1849; mem. N.Y. State Assembly, 1850, N.Y. State Senate, 1851; mem. U.S. Ho. of Reps. (Whig) from N.Y., 33d Congress, 1853-55; apptd. territorial gov. of Ida., 1864-66; supt Indian affairs of Ida. Died S.I., N.Y., Sept. 7, 1875; buried Greenwood Cemetery, Bklyn.

LYON, Francis Strother, congressman; b. Stokes County, N.C., Feb. 25, 1800; s. James and Behethe-land (Gaines) L.; m. Sarah Serena Glover, Mar. 4, 1824. Admitted to Ala. bar, 1821; sec. Ala. Senate, 1822-30, mem., 1833-36, 76-82, pres., 1834, 76; mem. U.S. Ho. of Reps. from Ala., 24th-25th congresses, 1835-39; commr. to adjust claims of Ala. state banks, 1845-53; chmn. Ala. Democratic Com., also del. Charleston Conv., 1860; mem. Ala. Ho. of Reps., 1861-62; mem. 1st-2d provisional congresses of Confederacy, 1862-65; del. Ala. Constl. Conv., 1875. Died Demopolis, Ala., Dec. 31, 1882; buried Old Glover Vault, Demopolis.

LYON, James, clergyman; b. Newark, N.J., July 1, 1735; s. Zopher and Mary Lyon; grad. Coll. of N.J. (now Princeton), 1759; m. Martha Holden, Feb. 18, 1768; m. 2d, Sarah Skillen, Nov. 24, 1793. Ordained to ministry Presbyn. Ch., 1764; pastor, Halifax, N.S., 1764-71, Machias, Me., 1772, 74-83, 85-94; ran a salt distillery to supplement his meager income. Author: Urania, 1761; The Lawfulness, Excellency and Advantages of Instrumental Musick in the Public Worship of God, 1763. Died Machias, Oct. 12, 1794.

LYON, Lucius, senator, congressman; b. Shelburne, Vt., Feb. 26, 1800; attended common schs. Moved to Bronson, Mich., 1821; land surveyor; del. U.S. Congress from Territory of Mich., 1833-35; mem. Mich. Constl. Conv., 1835; mem. U.S. Senate (Democrat) from Mich., Jan. 26, 1837-39; mem. bd. regents U. Mich., 1837-39; moved to Grand Rapids, Mich., 1839; apptd. Indian commr., La Pointe, Wis., 1839; mem. U.S. Ho. of Reps. from Mich., 28th Congress, 1843-45; surveyor gen. for Ohio, Ind. and Mich. (apptd. by Pres. Polk), 1845-50; del. Dem. Nat. Conv., Balt., 1848. Died Detroit, Sept. 24, 1851; buried Evergreen Cemetery, Detroit.

LYON, Mary, educator; b. Buckland, Mass., Feb. 28, 1797; s. Aaron and Jemima (Shephard) L.; attended seminary, Byfield, Mass., 1821. Tchr. at several acads. in Mass., 1823-36; interested in establishing coll. for women, founded Mt. Holyoke Sem., South Hadley, Mass., 1837. Died Mar. 5, 1849.

LYON, Matthew, congressman, army officer; b. County Wicklow, Ireland, July 14, 1750; m. Miss Hosford, 1771; m. 2d, Beulah Chittenden, 1783; 1 dau., Elizabeth A. Roe. Came to Am., 1765; organized co. Vt. Militia, 1774, aided in capture of Ft. Ticonderoga; served as adjutant Col. Seth Warner's Regt., Can., 1775; 2d lt. Green Mountain Boys, 1776. capt. and paymaster Vt. Militia, 1776; guide to Gen. Arthur St. Clair on march to Ft. Edward, 1777; moved to Arlington, Vt., 1777; mem. Vt. Ho. of Reps., 1779-83, 83-96; founder Town of Fair Haven (Vt.), 1783; built and operated various mills, including plant for mfg. paper from wood pulp; established printing office, 1793, published Farmer's Library (later Fair Haven Gazette); mem. U.S. Ho. of Reps. from Vt., 5th-6th congresses, 1797-1801, from Ky., 8th-11th congresses, 1803-11; moved to Caldwell (now Lyon) County, Ky., 1801; mem. Ky. Ho. of Reps., 1802-03; govt. contractor to build gunboats for War of 1812; apptd. U.S. factor to Cherokee Nation, Ark. Territory, 1820. Died Spadra Bluff, Ark., Aug. 1, 1822; buried Spadra Bluff Cemetery, reinterred Eddyville Cemetery, Lyon County, Ky., 1833.

LYON, Nathaniel, army officer; b. Ashford, Conn., July 14, 1818; s. Amasa and Keziah (Knowlton) L.; grad. U.S. Mil. Acad., 1841. Commd. 2d lt. inf. U.S. Army, assigned to 2d Regt du.ring Seminole War, 1841; served in Mexican War, 1846-48, distinguished himself at battles of Vera Cruz, Cerro Gordo, Contreras and Churubusco; commd. capt., 1851; commd. brig. gen. in supreme command U.S. Army forces in St. Louis, 1861; brig. gen. 1st brigade U.S. Mo. Volunteers, 1861; captured Jefferson City and Boonville, 1861. Killed in battle at Wilson's Creek, Mo., Aug. 10, 1861.

LYONS, Peter, jurist; b. Cork County, Ireland, circa 1734; s. John and Catherine (Power) L.; read law with James Power; m. Mary Power; m. 2d, Judith Bassett. Admitted to Va. bar, 1756; plaintiff's atty. in famous Parsons' Case, 1758; inactive during Am. Revolution; judge of Gen. Ct., also Vt. Ct. of Appeals, 1779; pres. Va. Ct. of Appeals, 1803-07. Died Hanover County, Va., July 30, 1809.

LYSTER, Henry Francis Le Hunte, physician; b. Sander's Court, Ireland, Nov. 8, 1837; s. Rev. William N. and Ellen Emily (Cooper) L.; grad. U. Mich., 1858, M,D., 1860; m. Winifred Lee Brent, Jan. 30, 1867, 5 children. Came with family to U.S., 1838; served as surgeon 5th Mich. Voluntary Inf., then with Army of Potomac, during Civil War, 1861-65; lectr. on surgery U. Mich., 1868-70, prof. theory and practice of medicine, 1888-90; a founder Mich. Coll. of Medicine; prof. practice of medicine Detroit Coll. of Medicine, 1885-93. Died Oct. 3, 1894.

LYTLE, Robert Todd, congressman; b. Williamsburg, Ohio, May 19, 1804; attended Cincinnati Coll.; studied law, Louisville, Ky. Admitted to Ky. bar, 1824, began practice in Cincinnati, O.; county pros. atty.; mem. Ohio Ho. of Reps., 1828-29; mem. U.S. Ho. of Reps. (Jacksonian Democrat) from Ohio, 23d Congress, 1833-Mar. 10, 1834, Dec. 27, 1834-35 (re-elected fo fill vacancy caused by his own resignation); surveyor gen. pub. lands N.W. Territory, 1836; commd. maj. gen. Ohio Militia, 1838. Died New Orleans, Dec. 22, 1839; buried Spring Grove Cemetery, Cincinnati.

LYTLE, William Haines, army officer, poet; b. Cincinnati, Nov. 2, 1826; s. Robert and Elizabeth (Haines) L.; grad. Cincinnati Coll., 1842. Served from 1st lt. to capt., 2d Ohio Inf., Mexican War; mem. Ohio Legislature (Democrat), 1852-54, speaker house; apptd. maj. gen. in command 1st div. Ohio Militia, 1857; commd. col. 10th Ohio Inf., 1861; in command 17th Brigade, 3d Div.,

U.S. Army under Gen. Buell, Huntsville, Ala., 1862; commd. brig. gen., 1863. Author poetry, including Antony and Cleopatra (best known lyric); works collected in Poems of William Haines Lytle, published 1894, 1912. Killed in Battle of Chickamauga (Tenn.), Sept. 20, 1863; buried Cincinnati.

LYTTLELTON, William Henry, colonial gov.; b. Eng., Dec. 24, 1724; s. Sir Thomas and Christian (Temple) L.; ed. Eton Coll., St. Mary's Hall, Oxford (Eng.) U.; m. Mary Macartney, June 2, 1761; m. 2d, Carolina Bristow, Feb. 19, 1774; 2 children. Admitted to Middle Temple, 1748; rep. borough of Bewdley (Worcestershire) in Parliament, 1748-55; gov. S.C., 1755-60; sailed to become gov. Jamaica, 1760; Brit. ambassador to Portugal, 1766-71. Author: Trifles in Verse, 1808. Died Hagley, Eng., Sept. 14, 1808.

M

MACALESTER, Charles, financier, philanthropist; b. Phila, Feb. 17, 1798; s. Charles and Ann (Sampson) M.; m. Eliza Lytle, 1824; m. 2d, Susan Wallace, 1841; 2 children. Apptd. govt. dir. 2d Nat. Bank of U.S., 1834, 35, 37; a founder Phila. Presbyn. Hosp; gave piece of property in Mpls. for establishment of instn. of higher learning (named Macalester Coll.), 1873; dir. Fidelity Ins. Trust & Safe Deposit Co.; mgr., contbr. to to Phila. Orthopaedic Hosp.; pres. St. Andrew's Soc., 1864-73. Died Phila., Dec. 9, 1873.

MACALESTER, Charles, mcht.; b. Campbeltown, Scotland, Apr. 5, 1765; s. Charles and Isabella (MacQuarrie) M.; m. Ann Sampson, several children including Charles. Came to Am., circa 1784; naturalized, 1786; settled in Phila., commanded mcht. ships; bought his own ship, soon became prosperous mcht.; pres. Ins. Co. of State of Pa., 1825-32; dir. Bank of N.Am.; a founder Mariner's Ch. of Phila., Marine Bible Soc.; v.p. St. Andrew Soc., 1813-25. Died Aug. 29, 1832.

MACDONALD, Moses, congressman; b. Limerick, Me., Apr. 8, 1815; studied law. Admitted to Me. bar, 1837, began practice in Biddeford; mem. Me. Ho. of Reps., 1841-42, 45, speaker, 1845; mem. Me. Senate, 1847; treas. State of Me., 1847-50; mem. U.S. Ho. of Reps. (Democrat) from Me., 32d-33d congresses, 1851-55; collector of customs, Portland, Me., 1857-61. Died Saco, Me., Oct. 18, 1869; buried Laurel Hill Cemetery, Saco.

MacDONALD, Ranald, adventurer; b. Ft. George, Wash., Feb. 3, 1824; s. Archibald and Princess (Sunday) MacDonald. Left bank bookkeeping to run away to sea, 1841; traveled around world, 1841-48; imprisoned in Japan, 1848-49, taught English to Japanese who negotiated with Americans in Treaty of 1854; rescued by Commodore James Glynn of Am. sloop-of-war Preble, 1849; later adventures took him to Australian gold fields and to Brit. Columbia during "gold rush" of 1860's; returned to Colville, Stevens County, Wash. Died Toroda Post Office, Ferry County, Wash., Aug. 26, 1894.

MacDONOUGH, Thomas, naval officer; b. The Trap (now Macdonough), Del., Dec. 31, 1783; s. Maj. Thomas and Mary (Vance) McDonough; m. Lucy Shaler, Dec. 12, 1812, children include Charles S. Commd. midshipman U.S. Navy, 1800; served on ships Philadelphia and Enterprise against Tripoli; cited for bravery for participation in recapture of Philadelphia, Feb. 16, 1804; commd. 1st lt., 1805, received permanent appointment as lt., 1807; joined Episcopal Ch., 1807; commanded Naval Station, Portland, Me., 1812, fleet on Lake Champlain, 1812; received gold medal from U.S. Congress for victory at Plattsburg (victory left Gt. Britain no claim of territorial adjustments at Treaty of Ghent); given land overlooking fight scene by N.Y. and Vt.; master-comdt., 1813; comdt. Portsmouth (N.H.) Navy Yard, 1815-18; comdr. Mediterranean squadron, 1824. Died at sea, Nov. 10, 1825; buried Middletown, Conn.

MacDOWELL, Katherine Sherwood Bonner, (pen name: Sherwood Bonner), author; b. Holly Spring, Miss., Feb. 26, 1849; d. Charles and Mary (Wilson) Bonner; m. Edward MacDowell, 1871, 1 child. First published story in Mass. Ploughman, 1864; contbd. articles, letters and verses to Boston Times, Memphis Avalanche, other newspapers; stories collected in Dialect Tales, 1883, Suwanee River Tales, 1884; published novel Like unto Like, 1878; published "The Volcanic Interlude" in Lippincotts' Mag., Apr. 1880 (caused more attention than any of her other stories); belonged to local color sch. of Am. writing. Died Holly Springs, Miss., July 22, 1883.

MACE, Daniel, congressman; b. Pickaway County, O., Sept. 5, 1811; attended pub. schs.; studied law. Admitted to Ind. bar, 1835, practiced in LaFayette; mem. Ind. Ho. of Reps., 1836, clk., 1837; U.S. atty. for Ind., 1849-53; mem. U.S. Ho. of Reps. from Ind., as Democrat, 32d-33d congresses, 1851-55, as Republican, 34th Congress, 1855-57; postmaster of LaFayette, 1866-67. Died LaFayette, July 26, 1867; buried Greenbush Cemetery, LaFayette.

MACFARLANE, Robert, dyer, editor; b. Rutherglen, Scotland, Apr. 23, 1815; m. Anna Garth Macfarlane. Learned art of dyeing in his father's works in Scotland; came to U.S., 1835; settled in Albany, N.Y., 1840; published (with Joel Munsell) Mechanic's Mirror, 1846-48; editor Scientific American, 1848-65; became an authority on mech. devices. Author: A Practical Treatise on Dyeing and Calico-Printing, 1860. Died Bklyn., Dec. 20, 1883.

MacGAHAN, Januarius Aloysius, war correspondent; b. Perry Co., O., June 12, 1874; s. James and Esther (Dempsey) MacG.; m. Barbara Nicholauna Elagin, 1872, 1 child. Special corr. for N.Y. Herald in Franco-Prussian War, 1871-72; defied Russian embargo on newspapermen to find expdn. sent out under Gen. Kauffmann to reduce Khanate of Khiva (now part of U.S.S.R.), 1873, for these adventures became popular hero, remained through campaign with Khiva and war with the Turkomans; correspondent in Spain following operations of Carlist insurrections, 1874-75; sent on independent investigation by London (Eng.) Daily News, he wrote on bashi-bazouk massacres (atrocities) in Bulgaria, did much to produce polit. reaction which made war between Russia and Turkey inevitable. Author: Campaigning on the Oxus and the Fall of Khiva, 1874; Under the Northern Lights, 1876; The Turkish Atrocities in Bulgaria, 1876; War Correspondence of the Daily News, 1877-78. Died Pera, Bulgaria, June 9, 1878; buried New Lexington, O.

MacGILLIVRAY, William, ornithologist; b. Scotland; assisted John James Audubon with tech. details of book Ornithological Biography; MacGillivray's warbler named in his honor (also known as Tolmie's warbler).

MACHEBEUF, Joseph Projectus, clergyman; b. Riom, Auvergne, France, Aug. 11, 1812; s. Michael Anthony and Gilberte (Plauc) M.; attended Sulpician Sem. of Montferrand. Ordained priest Roman Catholic Ch., 1836; curate, Cendre, France, 1836; began missionary work in Ohio, 1839; established a colony of Ursuline nuns and the 1st Am. group of sisters of Notre Dame de Namur, 1844; pastor Adobe Cathedral of Santa Fe; attended missions at Arroyo Hondo and Taos (N.M.) where with Kit Carson's aid he suppressed uprising led by a Mexican priest; built chs. in Denver, Central City, Golden City (Colo.); established a dozen chapels, stations in mining towns and new agrl. villages, under his direction the Sisters of Charity erected hosps. in Denver and Pueblo, Colo., also Sisters of Loretto founded St. Mary's Acad.; vicar apostolic with title of Bishop of Epiphania, 1868, consecrated titular bishop in Cincinnati, 1868, consecrated bishop, 1887. Died July 10, 1889.

MACHEN, Willis Benson, senator; b. Caldwell (now Lyon) County, Ky., Apr. 10, 1810; attended Cumberland Coll., Princeton, Ky. Engaged in farming, nr. Eddyville, Ky.; del. Ky. Constl. Conv., 1849; mem. Ky. Senate, 1854, Ky. Ho. of Reps., 1856, 60; mem. 1st and 2d Confederate congresses; mem. U.S. Senate (Democrat) from Ky., Sept. 27, 1872-73. Died Hopkinsville, Ky., Sept. 29, 1893; buried Riverview Cemetery, Eddyville.

MACHIR, James, congressman; b. Va. Mem. Va. Ho. of Dels., 1793-96, 1818-21; mem. U.S. Ho. of Reps. from Va., 5th Congress, 1797-99. Died June 25, 1827.

MACKAY, James, explorer; b. Kildonan, County Sutherland, Scotland, 1759; s. George and Elizabeth (McDonald) M.; m. Isabella Long, Feb. 24, 1800. Came to Canada, 1776, explored for British, then went to La.; dir. 3d expdn. sent by Spanish Comml. Co. to explore country on both sides of Missouri River and across continent to Pacific Ocean; constructed forts for protection of Spanish trade, resulting in peace among Indian tribes and between Indians and Spanish; took possession of Brit. fort at the Mandan village, prepared map of region explored; dep. surveyor for Spanish traders in Am., 1797; capt. St. Louis County (Mo.) Militia, comdt. of San Andres, Mo.; judge Ct. of Quarter Sessions, Mo. Territory, 1804; mem. Mo. Territorial Legislature, 1816; maj. militia; maps of his explorations later used by Lewis and Clark, 1804-06. Died Mar. 16, 1822.

MacKAYE, James Morrison Steele (stage name Steele MacKaye), dramatist, actor, inventor; b. Buffalo, N.Y., June 6, 1842; s. James Morrison and Emily (Steele) McKay; ed. École des Beaux-Arts, Paris, 1858-59; m. Jennie Spring, June 30, 1862; m. 2d, Mary Medbery, June 6, 1865; several children, including Percy. Made 1st stage appearance as Hamlet in a regtl. performance during Civil War, 1862; inventor "photo-sculpture," launched company to commercialize it; made début in Monaldi, N.Y.C., 1872; played Hamlet, Paris, 1872, 1st Am. to play role in Eng., London, 1873; opened an acting sch., N.Y.C., 1875; wrote Won at Last, acted at Wallacks, 1877; opened Madison Square Theatre (one of earliest small theatres), 1879; wrote Hazel Kirke (his most notable play), 1880, ran for over a year; built Lyceum Theatre, N.Y.C., established 1st dramatic sch. in Am. (later Am. Acad. Dramatic Arts); inventor mech. and elec. stage devices; 1st to light N.Y. theatre entirely by electricity, 1884; began erection of unsuccessful Spectatorium (vast auditorium) at Chgo. World's Fair, 1892. Died Timpas, Colo., Feb. 25, 1894.

MACKELLAR, Patrick, mil. engr.; b. Argyllshire, Scotland, 1717. Served as engr. Brit. Army, 1742-51; accompanied Gen. Braddock to Am., 1754; considered most competent engr. in Am. as early as 1756; sub-dir., maj. in capacity of engring., in charge siege of Louisbourg under Gen. Amherst; chief engr. under Wolfe at capture of Quebec; organized tng. sch. for engrs., 1760; chief engr. under Monckton in capture of Martinique, 1762; lt. col., chief engr. under Albemarle at siege of Havana, 1763; col., dir. defenses at Minorca, Balearic Islands, West Mediterranean, 1777. Died Minorca, Oct. 22, 1778.

MacKELLAR, Thomas, printer; b. N.Y.C., Aug. 12, 1812; s. Archibald and Harriet (Andrews) MacK.; m. Eliza Ross, Sept. 27, 1834, 10 children. Printer, John and James Harper, publishing house, N.Y.C., 1826-33; proofreader Lawrence, Johnson and George F. Smith, type foundry, Phila., 1833-45; partner (with 2 sons of George F. Smith), 1845-60; in printing business (with Smith bros. and Peter A. Jordon), 1860-99; editor Typog. Advertiser, 1855-84; published The Am. Printer, 1866; began writing poems in 1840's, including Droppings from the Heart, 1844, Rhymes Atween Times, 1873, Faith, Hope Love, These Three, 1893; pres. Type Founders Assn. of U.S., Phila. Book Trade Assn. Died Dec. 29, 1899.

MACKENZIE, Alexander Slidell, naval officer; b. N.Y.C., Apr. 6, 1803; s. John and Margaret (Mackenzie) Slidell; m. Catherine Robinson, Oct. 1, 1835, children—Ranald Slidell, Alexander S. Entered U.S. Navy as midshipman, 1815; aided in suppression of piracy in West Indies, 1824; promoted lt., 1825, served in Mediterranean, West Indian, Brazilian waters, also Pacific Ocean; became comdr. of brig Somers, 1841; made spl. mission to Gen. Santa Anna at Havana, Cuba, 1844; rep. from U.S. Navy at surrender of Veracruz; comdr. steamer Mississippi, 1847-48. Author: A Year in Spain, 1829; The American in England, 1835; Spain Revisited, 1836; Life of Commodore Oliver Hazard Perry, 1840. Died Tarrytown, N.Y., Sept. 13, 1848.

MACKENZIE, Donald, fur trader, colonial gov.; b. Scotland, June 15, 1783; m. Adelgonde Humbert-Droze, Aug. 1825; 13 children. Fur trader for N.W. Co. in Can., 1800-10; entered partnership with John Jacob Astor in Pacific Fur Co., 181C, sold out to N.W. Co., 1814; trader and explorer for N.W. Co. (merged into Hudson Bay Co., 1822), 1816-33, developed rich fur trade of So. Ida.; established Chesterfield House, fur trading post on Hudson Bay, 1822; chief factor at Ft. Garry (in what is now Winnipeg, Can.), apptd. councilor of gov., 1824; gov. Red River Colony, circa 1825-33; many of his adventures recorded by Washington Irving in Astoria, 1836, The Adventures of Captain Bonneville, 1837. Died Mayville, N.Y., Jan. 20, 1851.

MACKENZIE, George Henry, chess player; b. Belfield House, North Kessock, Scotland, Nov. 24, 1837; s. John and Ann (Douglass) M. Served from ensign to lt., 60th Scottish Rifles; sold his commn., 1861; defeated Anderssen (foremost European chess player) in London handicap tournament, 1862; came to N.Y., 1863; served to capt. Co. F, 83d N.Y. Inf., 1863-64, became profl. chess player, won 1st prize in tournaments of N.Y. Chess Club, 1865-68; won 1st prize in 2d Am. Chess Congress, 1871, also in 3d and 5th; in internat. tournaments won 4th place in Paris, 1878, tied for 4th-5th in Vienna, 1882, tied for 5th-6th at London, 1883, 7th at Hamburg, 1885, 1st in Frankfurt, 1887. Died Apr. 14, 1891.

MACKENZIE, Kenneth, fur trader, mcht.; b. Shire of Ross and Cromarty, Scotland, Apr. 15, 1797; s. Alexander and Isabella (Mackenzie) M.; m. Mary Marshall, June 26, 1842. Went to Can. in employ of North West Co., 1816; organized Columbia Fur Co., St. Louis, 1822; gained control of the Upper Missouri area in amalgamation of Columbia and Am. fur companies, 1827, built Fort Union (best equipped fort West of the Mississippi); joined firm Chouteau & Mackenzie, commn. and forwarding agts., 1834-41; commn. mcht. and importer fgn. liquors until 1854; known as "Emperor Mackenzie" in his fur-trading days. Died Apr. 26, 1861.

MACKENZIE, Ranald Slidell, army officer; b. Westchester County, N.Y., July 27, 1840; s. Alexander Slidell and Catherine (Robinson) M.; grad. U.S. Mil. Acad., 1862. Served as 1st lt. corps engrs. Army of Potomac, 1863, participated in Md. campaign, Rappahannock campaign (battles of Fredericksburg, Chancellorsville, 1863), Pa. campaign (Battle of Gettysburg), Rapidan campaign, 1863-64; commd. capt., comdr. engr. co. in battles of the Wilderness and Spottsylvania, 1863; took part in siege of Petersburg, 1864; commd. col. 2d Conn. Heavy Arty. Volunteers, 1864, brevetted col., brig. gen. U.S. Army; commd. maj. gen. U.S. Volunteers; commd. col. 4th Cavalry, participated in campaigns of early 1870's against marauding Indians in W. Tex., along Rio Grande River; as a result of his army services large areas were opened to permanent settlement; held brevet rank of maj. gen. U.S. Volunteers, from 1865; ret. from U.S. Army, 1884, with rank brig. gen. Died New Brighton, Staten Island, N.Y., Jan. 19, 1889.

MACKENZIE, Robert Shelton, author, journalist; b. Drew's Court, County Limerick, Ireland, June 22, 1809; s. Capt. Kenneth and Maria (Shelton) M.; m. Georgiana Dickinson, 1851; m. 2d, Adelheid Zwissler, 1858; 4 children. Taught sch., Fremoy, Ireland, 1825-26; editor county jour., Hanley, Staffordsville, Eng., 1829-30; wrote biographies for Georgian Era, 1830-31; editor Derbyshire Courier, 1831-33; English corr. for N.Y. Evening Star, 1834-51; came to N.Y., 1852; editor Sunday Paper, N.Y.C., 1852-57; literary and fgn. editor Phila. Press, 1857-77; an organizer Phila. Dental Coll. (now part Temple U.), 1862. Author: Lays of Palestine, 1828; A Romance of Venice, 1843; Bits of Blarney, 1854; Noctes Ambrosianae, 1854; Life of Charles Dickens, 1870; Sir Walter Scott: The Story of His Life, 1871. Died Nov. 21, 1881.

MACKENZIE, William, bibliophile; b. Phila., July 30, 1758; probably son of Kenneth and Mary (Thomas) M.; never married. Entered counting-house of John Ross, Phila., at early age, learned of merc. and shipping affairs; after inheriting sufficient income, spent life in scholarship and collection of books; acquired over 7,000 books, distributed them among libraries in Phila. area. Died Phila., July 23, 1828.

MACKEY, Albert Gallatin, physician, lodge ofcl.; b. Charleston, S.C., Mar. 12, 1807; s. John Mackey; grad. S.C. Med. Coll., Charleston, 1832; m. Sarah Pamela Hubbell, Dec. 27, 1836. Demonstrator of anatomy S.C. Med. Coll.; apptd. collector Port of Charleston by Pres. Johnson, 1865; mem. St. Andrew's Masonic Lodge No. 10, Charleston, 1841, Solomon's Lodge No. 1, Charleston, 1842, grand sec. Grand Lodge, grand high priest Grand Chpt., grand master Grand Council, gen. grand high priest Gen. Grand Chpt. of U.S., sec. gen. Supreme Council 33d Degree. Author: A Lexicon of Freemasonry, 1845; Mystic Tie, 1849; Principles of Masonic Law, 1856; Manual of the Lodge, 1862; Encyclopaedia of Freemasonry (most important work), 1874; Masonic Parliamentary Law, 1875; editor several Masonic mags. Died Old Point Comfort, Va., June 20, 1881; buried Glenwood Cemetery, Washington, D.C.

MACKEY, Edmund William McGregor, congressman; b. Charleston, S.C., Mar. 8, 1846. Apptd. asst. assessor internal revenue S.C., 1865; del. S.C. Constl. Conv., 1867; admitted to S.C. bar, 1868, practiced law; sheriff of Charleston County (S.C.), 1868-72; alderman Charleston, 1868, 73, 75; mem. S.C. Ho. of Reps., 1873, 77, speaker, 1877; del. Republican Nat. Conv., Phila., 1872, Chgo., 1880; asst. U.S. atty. for S.C., 1878-81; mem. U.S. Ho. of Reps. (Independent Republican), 44th Congress, 1875-July 19, 1876 (seat declared vacant), 47th Congress (contested election), May 31, 1882-83, 48th Congess, 1883-84. Died Washington, D.C., Jan. 27, 1884; buried Glenwood Cemetery, Washington.

MACKEY, Levi Augustus, congressman; b. Whitedeer Twp., Union County, Pa., Nov. 25, 1819; grad. Union Coll., Schenectady, N.Y., 1837; studied law Dickinson Coll., Carlisle, Pa. Admitted to Pa. bar, 1840; practiced law, Lock Haven, Pa., 1841-55; elected pres. Lock Haven Bank, 1855; del. Whig Nat. Conv., Balt., 1852, Democratic Nat. Conv., Balt., 1872; mayor of Lock Haven, 1870; pres. Bald Eagle Valley R.R. Co., other cos.; trustee normal sch., Lock Haven, 1870-89; mem. U.S. Ho. of Reps. (Democrat) from Pa., 44th-45th congresses, 1875-79. Died Lock Haven, Feb. 8, 1889; buried Highland Cemetery, Lock Haven.

MACLAY, Samuel, senator; b. Lurgan Twp., Pa., June 17, 1741; s. Charles and Eleanor (Query) M.; m. Elizabeth Plunket, Nov. 10, 1773, 6 sons, 3 daus. Justice Pa. Ct. Quarter Sessions, 1775; mem. Pa. Com. of Correspondence; served as lt. col. Pa. Militia; del. conv. of "Associators", Lancaster, Pa., 1776; mem. lower house Pa. Legislature, 1791, 97; mem. U.S. Ho. of Reps. (Republican) from Pa., 4th Congress, 1795-97; mem. Pa. Senate, 1798-1802, speaker, 1801-02; mem. U.S. Senate from Pa., 1803-09. Author: Journal of Samuel Maclay, 1790. Died Buffalo Valley, Pa., Oct. 5, 1811.

MACLAY, William, senator; b. New Garden Twp., Pa., July 27, 1734; s. Charles and Eleanor (Query) M.; m. Mary McClure Harris, Apr. 11, 1769, 9 children. Lt. with Gen John Forbes' expdn. to Ft. Duquesne, 1758; admitted to York County (Pa.) bar, 1760; surveyor in the employ of William Penn family, 1760; participated in Col. Henry Bouquet's expdn. against Indians, 1763-64; treas., clk. Northumberland County (Pa.) Ct., 1772; laid out town of Sunbury, Pa., 1772, moved to Harrisburg, Pa., 1786; commissar Continental Army during Revolutionary War; mem. Md. Legislature, 1781-85, 95, 03, mem. Supreme Exec. Council, 1786; mem. commns. to examine the navigation of Susquehanna, 1783, to deal with Indians for the purchases of lands, 1784-85; judge Pa. Ct. Common Pleas, dep. surveyor, 1788; mem. U.S. Senate from Pa., 1789-91; kept pvt. journal while serving in this 1st congress (only continuous report of the pvt. debates of that period), published as Sketches of Debates in the First Senate of the U.S., in 1789-90-91, 1880; asso. judge Dauphin County (Pa.), 1801-03; possibly the 1st Jeffersonian Democrat as revealed by his notes. Died Harrisburg, Apr. 16, 1804; buried Old Paxtong Churchyard, Harrisburg.

MACLAY, William, congressman; b. Lurgan Twp., Franklin County, Pa., Mar. 22, 1765; studied law. Admitted to Pa. bar, 1800, began practice in Chambersburg; commr. Franklin County, 1805-06; mem. Pa. Ho. of Reps., 1807-08; asso. judge Cumberland dist., 1809; mem. U.S. Ho. of Reps. from Pa., 14th-15th congresses, 1815-19. Died Lurgan, Pa., Jan. 4, 1825; buried Middle Springs Cemetery, Lurgan.

MACLAY, William Brown, congressman; b. N.Y.C., Mar. 20, 1812; s. Rev. Archibald and Mary (Brown) M.; grad. U. City of N.Y. (now N.Y.U.), 1836; m. Antionette Walton, Aug. 22, 1838, 3 children including Mark, Archibald. Temporary prof. latin langs. and lit. U. City of N.Y., 1836, trustee 1838-82; asso. editor N.Y. Quarterly Review, 1836; admitted to N.Y. bar, 1839; mem. N.Y. State Assembly, 1839-42, responsible for legislation reorganizing N.Y. Superior Ct. and Ct. of Common Pleas of City and County of N.Y., also mem. com. on colls., acads. and common schs., obtained passage of act which gave N.Y.C. full benefit of the state law providing for publicly supported and controlled schs.; mem. U.S. Ho. of Reps. (Democrat) from N.Y., 28th-30th, 35th-36th congresses, 1843-49, 1857-61, favored bill to aid Samuel F. Morse's practical demonstration of the telegraph as a utility, favored annexation of Tex. and Mexican War, advocated reduction of postal rates, favored homestead legislation instead of govt. sale of land to pvt. speculators, introduced unsuccessful bill for relief of heirs of John Paul Jones; pres. Am. Bible Union, 1855-56. Died N.Y.C., Feb. 19, 1882; buried Greenwood Cemetery, Bklyn.

MACLAY, William Plunkett, congressman; b. nr. Lewisburg, Pa., Aug. 23, 1774; attended common schs. Prothonotary of Mifflin County (Pa.), 1808-14; mem. Pa. Ho. of Reps.; mem. U.S. Ho. of Reps. (Democrat) from Pa., 14th-16th congresses, Oct. 8, 1816-21; mem. Pa. Constl. Conv., 1837; surveyor, farmer. Died Milroy, Pa., Sept. 2, 1842; buried Milroy Presbyn. Ch.

MACLEAN, John, educator; b. Glasgow, Scotland, Mar. 1, 1771; s. John and Agnes (Lang) M.; grad. U. Glasgow, 1791; M.D., U. Aberdeen, 1797; m. Phebe Brainbridge, Nov. 7, 1798, 2 daus., 4 sons including John. Came to U.S., 1795; prof. chemistry and natural history Coll. of N.J. (now Princeton), 1795-1812, also prof. mathematics and natural philosophy, 1797-1812; became mem. Am. Philos. Soc., 1805; became naturalized Am. citizen, 1807; prof. natural philosophy and chemistry Coll. William and Mary, Williamsburg, Va., 1813; returned to Princeton, 1814. Author: Two Lectures on Combustion: Supplementary to a Course of Lectures on Chemistry Read at Nassau Hall; Containing an Examination of Dr. Priestley's Considerations on the Doctrine of Phlogiston, and the Decomposition of Water, 1797. Died Princeton, N.J., Feb. 17, 1814; buried Coll. Cemetery, Princeton.

MacLEAN, John, coll. pres.; b. Princeton, N.J., Mar. 3, 1800; s. John and Phebe (Bainbridge) M.; grad. Coll. of N.J. (now Princeton), 1816; attended Princeton Theol. Sem., 1817-18. tutor Princeton Theol. Sem., 1818-22; ordained to ministry Presbyn. Ch., 1828; prof. mathematics Coll. of N.J., 1823, prof. ancient langs. and lit., 1830, prof. Greek, 1847, became v.p., 1829, responsible for building of East Coll., 1832, West Coll., 1836, also reformation of coll. calendar, pres., 1835-68, prof. Biblical instrn., 1866-68, established several scholarship funds for needy students; founder Alumni Assn. of Nassau Hall, 1826. Author: History of the College of New Jersey, 2 vols., 1877. Died Princeton, Aug. 10, 1886.

MaCLURE, William, geologist; b. Ayr, Scotland, Oct. 17, 1763; s. David and Ann (Kennedy) McC. Became partner Miller, Hast & Co., London, Eng., 1782; came to Am. 1796; apptd. a commr. to settle spoliation claims between Am. and France, 1803; made geol. map of U.S. (1st of its kind); an original mem. Acad. Natural Scis., 1812, pres., 1817-40, supr. publication of 1st vols. of Acad.'s Journal; visited West Indies, studied volcanic phases of geology, 1816-17; founder sch., New Harmony, Ind., 1824, New Harmony Working Men's Inst., 1838; pres. Am. Geol. Soc., several years. Author: Observations on the Geology of the U.S., 1817; Opinions on Various Subjects, Dedicated to the Industrious Producer, 2 vols., 1831-37. Died San Angel, Mexico, Mar. 23, 1840.

MacNEVEN, William James, physician; b. County Galway, Ireland, Mar. 21, 1763; s. James and Rosa (Dolphin) MacN.; studied medicine U. Prague; M.D., U. Vienna, 1784; m. Jane Riker, 1810, 3 children. Participated in Irish Revolution, 1797-98, polit. prisoner, 1798-1802; served with Irish brigade French Army, 1804-05; came to N.Y. C., 1805; elected prof. obstetrics Coll. Physicians and Surgeons, 1808, prof. chemistry, 1812, taught materia medica, 1816-20; established 1st chem. lab. in N.Y.C.; co-editor N.Y. Med. and Philos. Jour. and Review; elected mem. Am. Philos. Soc., 1823; with colleagues founded med. sch. affiliated with Rutgers Coll., 1826-30; established employment bur. to find positions for Irish immigrants; organizer, 1st pres. Friends of Ireland, 1828-29. Author: Rambles through Switzerland in the Summer and Autumn of 1802, published 1803; Pieces of Irish History, 1807; Expositions of the Atomic Theory, 1819. Editor: Brandes Chemistry, 1821. Died N.Y.C., July 12, 1841.

MACOMB, Alexander, army officer; b. Detroit, Apr. 3, 1782; s. Alexander and Catharine (Navarre) M.; grad. U.S. Mil. Acad., 1802; m. Catherine Macomb, July 23, 1803; m. 2d, Harriet Balch, 1826; numerous children. Sec. to commr. apptd. to treat with Indians of S.E., 1801-02; commd. 1st lt. Corps Engrs., U.S. Army, 1802, capt., 1805; chief engr. charge coast fortifications in Carolinas and Ga., 1807-12; promoted maj., 1808, lt. col., 1810, adj. gen., 1812; transferred to arty.; commd. col., 1812; sent to N.Y. to raise regt. brig. gen., 1814; defeated British at Battle of Plattsburg; breveted maj. gen., 1819; head Corps Engrs., 1821; sr. maj. gen. and commanding gen. U.S. Army, 1828-41; partly responsible for abolition of whiskey ration in army, 1830, Author Treatise on Martial Law and Court Martials, 1809; The Practice of Court Martial, 1840. Died Washington, D.C., June 25, 1841.

MACON, Nathaniel, senator, congressman; b. Edgecomb (later Bute, now Warren) County, N.C., Dec. 17, 1758; s. Gideon and Priscilla (Jones) M.; attended Coll. of N.J. (now Princeton), 1774-76; m. Hannah Plummer, Oct. 9, 1783, 3 children. Served in N.J. Militia during Revolutionary War, left army, 1777; returned to N.C., studied law, 1777; served as pvt. in Battle of Camden, 1780; mem. N.C. Senate, 1780-82, 84-85, N.C. Ho. of Commons, 1790; mem. U.S. Ho. of Reps. (Republican) from N.C., 2d-14th congresses, 1791-Dec. 13, 1815, speaker, 1801-07; supported continuation of treaty with France, opposed Jay Treaty, Alien and Sedition Acts, supported La. Purchase, (1803), urged Thomas Jefferson to purchase Fla.; chmn. fgn. relations com., 1809, Macon's Bill No. 1, No. 2 named for him (not author of these, opposed to 2d which gave Pres. power to suspend intercourse with either France or Gt. Britain because of interference with U.S. commerce), 1810, favored War of 1812, opposed conscription; mem. U.S. Senate (Republican) from N.C., Dec. 13, 1815-Nov. 14, 1828, pres. pro tem., 1826-28, participated in Mo. debate, opposed to compromise, defended slavery; Macon County (N.C.) named for him, 1828; opposed nullification, 1832; pres. N.C. Constl. Conv., 1835, declined to vote for amended constn. Died Warren County, N.C., June 29, 1837; buried at home, Bucks Creek, N.C.

MacSPARRAN, James, clergyman; b. probably Dungiven, Ireland, Sept. 10, 1693; M.A., U. Glasgow (Scotland), 1709; Ph.D. in Sacred Theology (hon.), Oxford (Eng.) U.; m. Hannah Gardiner, May 22, 1722. Received credentials as licentiate of Presbytery of Scotland; visited Boston and Bristol, Mass., 1718, invited to become pastor Congregational Ch. at Bristol (pastorate withdrawn due to Cotton Mather); returned to Eng.; ordained Anglican priest, 1720, sent by Soc. for Propagation of Gospel in Fgn. Parts to parish of St. Paul, Narragansett County, R.I., remained until 1757; instrumental in establishing Episcopal ch., New London, Conn., 1725; made trips to Eng., 1736-37, 54-56, consecrated bishop on latter visit; his diary kept during 1743-45, 51 was published in 1899. Author: The Sacred Dignity of Christian Priesthood Vindicated, 1752; America Dissected, 1753. Died South Kingston, R.I., Dec. 1, 1757.

MacWHORTER, Alexander; b. New Castle County, Del., July 15, 1735; s. Hugh and Jane MacWhorter; grad. Coll. of N.J. (now Princeton), 1757; studied theology under Rev. William Tennent, Freehold, N.J.; D.D. (hon.), Yale; m. Mary Cumming, Oct. 1759. Licensed to preach by Presbytery of New Brunswick, 1758; ordained to ministry Presbyn. Ch., 1759; pastor ch., Newark, N.J., 1759-1807; commd. by Continental Congress to go to N.C. to win over Loyalists, 1775; present at Gen.

George Washington's council which recommended crossing Delaware River, 1778; chaplain Gen. Henry Knox's brigade, 1778-79; forced to flee from British on many occasions because of his patriotic activities; helped frame constn. of Presbyn. Ch. in U.S., charter trustee of its gen. assembly, until 1803. Author: A Series of Sermons upon the Most Important Principles of Our Holy Religion, 1803; A Century Sermon, 1807. Died July 20, 1807.

MACY, John B., congressman; b. Nantucket, Mass., Mar. 25, 1799. Moved to N.Y.C., later to Buffalo, N.Y., 1826, to Cincinnati, 1842; a founder Toledo (O.); a propr. Rock River Valley R.R.; moved to Fond du Lac, Wis., 1845, engaged as realtor; moved to Empire, Wis., 1850; mem. U.S. Ho. of Reps. (Democrat) from Wis., 33d Congress, 1853-55. Died in burning of steamer Niagara on Lake Michigan, Sept. 24, 1856.

MACY, Josiah, sea capt., mcht.; b. Nantucket, Mass., Feb. 25, 1785; s. Jonathan and Rose (Pinkham) M.; m. Lydia Hussey, Feb. 6, 1805, 3 children including William H. Engaged in coastwide trade (with his father), became ship master in his early twenties; made his 1st transoceanic voyage to Cadiz, Gibralter and Lisbon, 1807; sailed in brig. Little William in Mediterranean, 1810-12; bought ship Prudence, 1812; accepted Brit. letters of protection in order to procure supplies for Nantucket, during War of 1812; after war bought ship Edward and entered N.Y.-Liverpool trade until his retirement in 1827; founded (with his son William H.) shipping and commn. house of Josiah Macy & Son, 1828; retired to Rye, N.Y., 1853. Died May 15, 1872.

MADISON, Dorothea (Dolly) Payne Todd, first lady; b. Guilford County, N.C., May 20, 1772; d. John and Mary (Coles) Payne; m. John Todd, Jr., Jan. 7, 1790 (died 1793); m. 2d, James Madison, Sept. 15, 1794 (died June 1836); 3 children including John Payne Todd. Lived with mother after death of her 1st husband until she met James Madison (through Senator Aaron Burr); unofcl. first lady to Pres. Thomas Jefferson (a widower) as wife of Sec. State Madison, 1801-09; ofcl. first lady as wife of Pres. Madison, 1809-17; her popularity is credited as a factor in Madison's re-election; noted for removing portrait of George Washington during burning of White House (by British), 1814; moved back to Washington (D.C.) after death of Madison, popular figure in Washington until death. Died Washington, July 12, 1849; buried Congressional Cemetery, Washington, later re-interred "Montpellier," Va.

MADISON, James, clergyman, coll. pres.; b. Staunton, Va., Aug. 27, 1749; s. John and Agatha (Strother) M.; grad. Coll. William and Mary, 1771; D.D., U. Pa., 1785; m. Sarah Tate, 1779, 2 children. Admitted to Va. bar; prof. natural philosophy and mathematics Coll. William and Mary, Williamsburg, Va., 1773-89, pres., 1777-1812, prof. natural and moral philosophy, 1784; ordained to ministry Ch. of Eng. (Protestant Episcopal Ch.), 1776; commd. capt. of a militia co., 1777; mem. commn. to define boundaries between Va. and Pa., 1779; prominent in formation Diocese of Va.; pres. 1st Conv. of Ch., 1785; elected 1st bishop Protestant Episcopal Ch. in Va., 1790. Author: A Map of Virginia formed from Actual Surveys, 1807. Died Mar. 6, 1812; buried Chapel, Coll. of William and Mary.

MADISON, James, 4th Pres. U.S.; b. Port Conway, Va., Mar. 16, 1751; s. James and Eleanor (Conway) M.; A.B., Coll. of N.J. (now Princeton), 1771; m. Dolly Payne Todd, Sept. 15, 1794, no children. A founder Am. Whig Soc. (debating club) at Coll. of N.J.; admitted to Va. bar; mem. Com. of Safety for Orange County (Va.), 1774; del. to Williamsburg (Va.) Conv., 1776, mem. com. which framed constn. and declaration of rights for Va.; mem. 1st Gen. Assembly of Va., 1776, Va. Exec. Council, 1778; mem. Continental Congress from Va., 1780-83, 86-88, kept notes on debates of Congress from 1782-83 (useful as supplement to ofcl. Journal), advocated fed. revenue to be raised on imports for 25 years; wrote instrns. to John Jay (U.S. minister to Spain) concerning U.S. rights to navigation of Mississippi River, 1780; proposed "3/5 Compromise" before Congress to break deadlock on changing basis of state contbns. from land values to population by counting 5 slaves as 3 free people; returned to Va., 1783, began study of law and natural history of U.S.; mem. Va. Ho. of Dels. from Orange County, 1783-86, completed disestablishment of Anglican Ch. in Va. (begun by Thomas Jefferson), 1779, favored admission of Ky. to statehood, inaugurated series of surveys for improvement of transmountain communications, urged power to be granted Congress to regulate commerce, leader in effecting a series of interstate confs.; del. from Va. to Annapolis Conv., 1786; published "Vices of the Political System of the United States"; made proposals incorporated in Virginia or Randolph Plan (drafted by Edward Randolph), including change in principle of representation to give larger states more influence, uniform nat. laws, a fed. veto on state legislation, extension of nat. authority to a judiciary dept., a 2 house fed. legislature with differing terms of office, a nat. exec., an article guaranteeing defense of states by fed. govt., ratification of amendments to U.S. Constn. by people as well as legislature; described as "the master-builder of the constitution;" del. from Va., chief recorder U.S. Constl. Conv., 1787, kept records published in Journal of the Federal Constitution, 1840; asso. with Alexander Hamilton and John Jay in writing essays known as The Federalist (published under signature Publius), 1788, described constl. system of govtl. checks and balances, emphasized protection of pvt. property; largely responsible for ratification of U.S. Constn. by Va., 1788; mem. U.S. Ho. of Reps. from Va., 1st-4th congresses, 1789-97, participated in passage of revenue legislation, creation of exec. depts., framing of Bill of Rights; a leader of Democratic-Republic Party which opposed creation of U.S. Banks and pro-British sympathies; published series of letters under name "Helvidius" in Gazette of the United States, Aug. 24-Sept. 18, 1793, criticized George Washington's neutrality proclamation; declined mission to France and post of U.S. sec. of state, 1794; wrote Va. Resolutions against Alien and Sedition Acts, exprsesed opinion that states could declare acts of Congress unconstl.; U.S. sec. of state under Pres. Jefferson, 1801-09, faced with problems of Anglo-French war, sought peace with both countries, protested against impressment of U.S. sailors by Eng., supported Jefferson's Embargo Act of Dec. 22, 1807, repealed, Mar. 1, 1809; elected 4th Pres. U.S. (Democratic-Republic; defeated Charles Cotesworth Pinckney), 1808, inaugurated, Mar. 4, 1809, re-elected, 1812; authorized by Congress to revive non-intercourse with either Eng. or France, tricked by Napoleon Bonaparte, proclaimed non-intercourse against Gt. Britain, Nov. 2, 1810; involved in feud with Sec. State Robert Smith, Apr. 1811, dismissed him and apptd. James Monroe; advised declaration of war against Gt. Britain because of continued impressment of seamen, interference in U.S. trade, incitement of Indians on U.S. borders, June 1, 1812, declared war, June 18, 1812; accepted offer of mediation by Russian Czar, Mar. 1813 (rejected by Eng.); forced to flee White House when British invaded and burned much of Washington, D.C., 1812; instructed U.S. Commrs. at Ghent to seek only surrender to U.S. territory occupied by Brit., 1814 (Treaty of Ghent signed Dec. 24, 1814); signed bill providing for 2d Bank of U.S., 1816, Tariff Act of 1816; enrolled in soc. for encouragement of Am. mfrs., 1816; left office, Mar. 3, 1817; became rector U. Va. (succeeded Jefferson), 1826; del. Va. Constl. Conv., 1829; ret. to "Montpellier," Orange County. Died "Montpellier," June 28, 1836; buried "Montpellier."

MAFFITT, David, privateersman; m. Mrs. Elizabeth B. Myers, July 21, 1819. In command in Atlas (one of 1st privateers to search for enemy vessels), captured Tulip, Pursuit and Planter, brought them safely to Phila., summer 1812; captured aboard Atlas by Brit. squadron at Ooracoke Inlet, N.C., 1813, released later that year; given command in Rattlesnake, made voyage to Brit. Isles capturing 3 ships, 12 brigs and 3 sloops, most of which reached port safely before he was captured by frigate Hyperion at La Rochelle, France, 1814; master warden Port of Phila. circa 1819-38. Died May 1, 1838.

MAFFITTZ, John Newland, naval officer; b. at sea in the Atlantic Ocean, Feb. 22, 1819; s. John Newland and Ann (Carnic) M. (adopted by uncle Dr. William Maffitt); m. Mary Florence Murrell, Nov. 17, 1840; m. 2d, Caroline Laurens Read, Aug. 3, 1852; m. 3d, Emma Martin, Nov. 23, 1870; 7 children. Commd. lt. U.S. Navy, 1843; served on coast survey for 16 years; apptd. lt. Confederate States Navy, 1861; served 3 tours of duty as capt. blockade-running service; engr. officer on staff of Gen. Robert E. Lee, 1861-62; promoted comdr., 1863; captured 22 merchantmen; commanded Brit. S.S. Widgeon, 1865-67; in command Cuban Revolutionists' cruiser Cuba, 1870. Died Wilmington, N.C., May 15, 1886.

MAGEE, John, congressman; b. Easton, Pa., Sept. 3, 1794; attended common schs. Served in War of 1812; moved to Bath, N.Y., 1812, constable, 1818-20; apptd. sheriff of Steuben County (N.Y.), 1821; mem. U.S. Ho. of Reps. (Democrat) from N.Y., 20th-21st congresses, 1827-31; declined appointment as mem. cabinet of Pres. Jackson; del. N.Y. Constl. Conv., 1867; engaged in banking, railroad bldg., mining. Died Watkins, N.Y., Apr. 5, 1868; buried Glenwood Cemetery, Watkins.

MAGELLAN, Ferdinand, (Fernão de Magalhães), navigator; b. Sabrosa, Portugal, circa 1480; son of Pedro de Magalhães; m. dau. of Diogo Barbosa, circa 1517. In Portuguese service in India and East Indies, 1505-12; served in Morocco, 1513-14; fell out of favor with Portuguese king; entered service of Spain, 1517, proposed to reach Spice Islands and China by traveling West; also hoped to clarify Spanish claims under line of demarcation drawn by Pope Alexander VI in 1493; left Spain with expdn. of 5 ships, Sept. 20, 1519; reached Rio de la Plata (in what is now Brazil), Jan. 20, 1520, briefly explored region; stayed for some months in Patagonia; put down a mutiny, lost 1 of ships in wreck while on scouting expdn.; entered Straits of Magellan (which he named Strait of All Saints), Oct. 21, 1520; 1 of his ships deserted and returned to Spain; entered Pacific Ocean (so named by Magellan), Nov. 28, 1520; discovered only 2 uninhabited islands in 98 days of sailing; finally reached Guam, Mar. 6, 1521; landed in Philippine Islands later in month; killed in fight with natives on Mactan Island, Apr. 27, 1521; 1 of his ships (the Victoria with crew of 18) returned to Spain, Sept. 6, 1522, completing 1st circumnavigation of globe.

MAGOFFIN, Beriah, gov. Ky.; b. Harrodsburg, Ky., Apr. 18, 1815; s. Beriah and Jane (McAfee) M.; grad. Centre Coll., 1835; grad. Law Dept., Transylvania U., 1838; m. Anna Shelby, Apr. 1840; 10 children. Practiced law, 1839-49; owned large farm nr. Harrodsburg; reading clk. Miss. Senate, 1839; police judge, Harrodsburg, 1840; Democratic presdl. elector, 1844, 48, 52, 56; mem. Ky. Senate, 1850; gov. Ky., 1859-62; refused both Lincoln's and Jefferson Davis' calls for troops, 1861; unable to preserve Ky.'s neutrality because of conflict between his Confederate sentiments and legislature's Unionist sympathies; resigned as gov. when legislature demanded removal of Confederate troops from Ky. (over his veto); mem. Ky. Legislature from Mercer County, 1867-69; hon. commr. Paris Exposition, 1878. Died Harrodsburg, Feb. 28, 1885.

MAGOFFIN, James Wiley, trader, diplomat; b. Harrodsburg, Ky., 1799; s. Beriah and Jane (McAfee) M.; m. Mary Gertrude Valdez, 1830, several children including Joseph, Samuel. Trader in Mexico, 1825, became 1st Am. consul at Santillo; went to Mo., 1844; was commd. col. in Gen. Stephen Kearney's expdn. during Mexican War, in advance of expdn. induced Mexicans to retire from Santa Fe, made it possible for Kearney to take possession of Dept. of Mexico without bloodshed; attempted same thing in Chihuahua, imprisoned; settled in Tex. after war, built up town of Magoffinsville (now part of El Paso); helped supply the Confederacy during Civil War. Died San Antonio, Tex., Sept. 27, 1868.

MAGOON, Henry Sterling, congressman; b. Monticello, Wis., Jan. 31, 1832; grad. Western Mil. Coll., Drennon, Ky., 1853; attended Montrose Law Sch., Frankfort, Ky. Admitted to Wis. bar, 1857, began practice in Shullsburg; prof. ancient langs. Nashville (Tenn.) U., 1855-57; practiced law, Darlington, Wis.; elected dist. atty., 1858; mem. Wis. Senate, 1871-72; mem. U.S. Ho. of Reps. (Republican) from Wis., 44th Congress, 1875-77; resumed practice of law, Milw.; regent U. Wis. Died Darlington, Mar. 3, 1889; buried Union Grove Cemetery, Darlington.

MAGOUN, George Frederic, clergyman, coll. pres.; b. Bath, Me., Mar. 29, 1821; s. David Crooker and Hannah (Webb) M.; grad. Bowdoin Coll., 1841; attended Yale Divinity Sch., Andover Theol. Sem.; m. Abby Anne Hyde, 1847; m. 2d, Elizabeth E. Earle, 1870. Ordained to ministry Congregational Ch., Shullsburg, Wis., 1848, founded ch. there; pastor 2d Presbyn. Ch., Galena, Ill., 1848-51; served Congl. chs., Davenport, Lyons, Ia., 1851-55; trustee Ia. Coll., Davenport, 1856 (coll. moved to Grinnell, 1859), pres., 1862-84, also taught, preached and wrote articles, taught mental and moral philosophy after his retirement until 1890; del. to peace confs. in Europe 3 times; lectr. Andover Theol. Sem., 1877-79. Author: The Past of Our College, 1895. Died Jan. 30, 1896.

MAGRATH, Andrew Gordon, gov. S.C.; b. Charleston, S.C., Feb. 8, 1813; s. John and Maria (Gordon) M.; grad. S.C. Coll., 1831; attended Harvard Law Sch.; m. Emma C. Mikell, Mar. 8, 1843; m. 2d, Mary McCord, circa 1865; 5 children. Mem. S.C. Ho. of Reps., 1835; judge U.S. Dist. Ct. for S.C., 1856-60; del. secession conv., active in withdrawal of S.C. from Union, 1860; sec. of state S.C., 1860; judge Confederate Dist. Ct., S.C., 1861; gov. S.C., 1864-65, took extreme states rights position, issued proclamation advising submission to fed. authorities, 1865. Died Charleston, Apr. 9, 1893.

MAGRUDER, Allan Bowie, senator; b. Ky., 1775; attended common schs.; studied law. Admitted to Ky. bar, 1795, practiced in Lexington; moved to La., practiced law; mem. La. Ho. of Reps.; mem. U.S. Senate (Democrat) from La., Sept. 3, 1812-13; resumed law practice. Died Opelousas, La., Apr. 16, 1822.

MAGRUDER, John Bankhead, army officer; b. Winchester, Va., Aug. 15, 1810; s. Thomas and Elizabeth (Bankhead) M.; grad. U.S. Mil. Acad., 1830. commd. 1st lt. U.S. Army, 1836, advanced to lt. col. during Mexican War, 1848; commd. col. Confederate Army, comdr. troops on Va. Peninsula, 1861; won Battle of Big Bethal, (one of 1st battles of Civil War), 1861; brig. gen. in command all forces on Va. Peninsula, with hdqrs. at Yorktown; commd. maj. gen., distinguished himself at Malvern Hill, also all of Seven Days' battles before Richmond, 1861; transferred to command Dist. of Tex., 1862, later N.M., Ariz.; served as maj. gen. under Prince Maximilian in Mexico; returned to U.S., settled in Tex., 1869. Died Houston, Tex., Feb. 18, 1871.

MAGRUDER, Patrick, congressman, govt. ofcl.; b. "Locust Grove" nr. Rockville, Md., 1768; attended Princeton; studied law. Admitted to Md. bar, practiced law; mem. U.S. Ho. of Reps. from Md., 9th Congress, 1805-07, clk., 1807-15; librarian of Congress, 1807-15. Died Petersburg, Va., Dec. 24, 1819; buried family burying ground "Sweden" nr. Petersburg.

MAHAN, Asa, clergyman, coll. pres.; b. Vernon, N.Y., Nov. 9, 1799; s. Capt. Samuel and Anna (Dana) M.; grad. Hamilton Coll., 1824, Andover Theol. Sem., 1827; D.D. (hon.), Hillsdale Coll., 1858, LL.D. (hon.), 1877. m. Mary Dix, May 9, 1828; m. 2d, Mrs. Mary E. Chase, 1866. Adopted doctrine of full moral freedom, 1817; active participant in revivals, 1824-32; ordained pastor Congl. Ch., Pittsford, N.Y., 1829; trustee Lane Theol. Sem.; 1st pres. Oberlin Coll., 1835-50, established theol. dept., 1st coll. pres. to award degrees to women under same conditions as men; resumed pastoral work, 1855; prof., later pres. Adrian Coll., 1860-71. Editor monthly mag. The Divine Life. Died Eastbourne, Eng., Apr. 4, 1889.

MAHAN, Dennis Hart, army officer, engr., educator; b. N.Y.C., Apr. 2, 1802; s. John and Mary (Cleary) M.; grad. U.S. Mil. Acad., 1824; A.M., Brown U., 1837, LL.D., 1852; A.M., Princeton, 1837; LL.D., Coll. William and Mary, 1852, Dartmouth, 1867. m. Mary Okill, June 25, 1839; 5 children including Alfred Thayer. Asst. prof. mathematics U.S. Mil. Acad., 1824-25, asst. prof. engring., 1825-26, asst. prof. civil and mil. engring, 1829-32, prof., 1832-71, dean faculty, 1838, sr. mem. academic bd.; sent by War Dept. to Europe to study pub. works, mil. instns., attended Sch. Application for Engrs. and Arty., Metz, France; an original incorporator Nat. Acad. Scis., 1863; commr. on bd. engrs. to find route for Wheeling & B. & O. R.R., 1850; mem. Geog. Soc. of Paris (France); overseer Thayer Sch. of Engring; Dartmouth, 1871. Died N.Y.C., Sept. 16, 1871; buried West Point, N.Y.

MAHAN, Milo, clergyman; b. Suffolk, Va., May 24, 1819; son of John Mahan; attended St. Paul's Coll., L.I., N.Y.; m. Mary Griffiths (Fisher) Lewis, Aug. 23, 1853. Tchr. Greek, Episcopal High Sch., Alexandria, Va., 1836; ordained deacon Protestant Episcopal ch., New Canaan, Conn., 1845, priest, Ch. of Holy Communion, N.Y., 1846; asst. at Ch. of Annunciation, N.Y.; rector Grace Ch., Jersey City, N.J., 1848-circa 1850; asst. St. Mark's Ch., Phila., circa 1850; prof. eccles. history Gen. Theol. Sem., N.Y., 1851-64; editor Ch. Jour., 1853; rector St. Paul's Ch., Balt., 1864. Author: The Exercise of Faith in Its Relation to Authority and Private Judgment, 1851; The Spiritual Point of View; or the Glass Reversed, an Answer to Bishop Colenso, 1863; Palmoni: or, the Numerals of Scripture a Proof of Inspiration, 1863; Church History of the First Seven Centuries, 1872. Died Sept 3, 1870.

MAHONE, William, army officer, senator, state polit. leader; b. Southampton County, Va., Dec. 1, 1826; s. Fielding Jordan and Martha (Drew) M.; grad. Va. Mil. Inst., 1847; m. Ortelia Butler, Feb. 1855, 3 children. Operated mail route from Jerusalem (now Courtland) to Hill's Ford (now Emporia), Va.; tchr. Rappahannock Mil. Acad., 2 years; civil engr., constructor Norfolk & Petersburg R.R., pres., chief engr., supt., 1861; served as q.m. gen., lt. col. and col. 6th Va. Regt., Confederate States Army, during Civil War; commanded Norfolk (Va.) Dist. until evacuation, 1862, sent to Drewry's Bluff defenses of James River; promoted brig. gen., maj. gen., 1864; mem. N.C. Senate, 1863-65; pres. Atlantic, Miss. & Ohio R.R., 1867-73; organizer, took command "Readjustors" (advocated reducing Va.'s debt, also popular, social and econ. legislation), 1879; mem. U.S. Senate (Republican) from Va., 1881-87; "Anti-Bourbon," defended Negroes rights; boss of Va. Rep. Party until 1882 (temporarily broke "Solid South"); monument to him erected by Daus. of Confederacy, Petersburg, Va. Died Washington, D.C., Oct. 8, 1895; buried Blandford Cemetery, Petersburg.

MAHONEY, Peter Paul, congressman; b. N.Y.C., June 25, 1848; attended common schs.. N.Y.C. Engaged in dry goods bus.; moved to Bklyn., sold liquor; mem. U.S. Ho. of Reps. (Democrat) from N.Y., 49th-50th congresses, 1885-89; became ill while attending inauguration of Benjamin Harrison, 1889. Died Washington, D.C., Mar. 27, 1889; buried Calvary Cemetery, Long Island City, N.Y.

MAIN, William, engraver; b. N.Y.C.; studied with Mauro Gandolfi, Italy, 1817, under Raphael Morghen, 1817-20. Returned to N.Y.C., 1820, opened studio; a founder N.A.D., 1826, mem., 1826-36, asso., 1837-38; left N.Y.C, circa 1833, engraved, until circa 1837. Died N.Y.C., 1876.

MAISCH, John Michael, pharmacist; b. Hanau, Hesse, Germany, Jan. 30, 1831; son of Conrad Maish; m. Charlotte Justine Kuhl, 1859, 5 sons, 2 daus. Came to U.S., 1849; with pharmacies in Balt., Washington, D.C., N.Y.; employed by Robert Shoemaker's wholesale drug and pharm. mfg. co., Phila.; prof. botany and materia medica N.Y. Coll. Pharmacy, 1861-63; in charge of U.S. Army Lab., Phila., 1863-65; prof. pharmacy Phila. Coll. Pharmacy, 1866-93; sec. Am. Pharm. Assn., 1865-93; chem., bot. and pharm. editor Nat. Dispensatory, 1879-84; editor Am. Jour. of Pharmacy, 1871-93. Author: A Manual of Organic Materia Medica, 1882. Died Sept. 10, 1893.

MAJOR, William Warner, artist; b. Bristol, Eng., Jan. 27, 1804. Joined Ch. of Jesus Christ of Latter-day Saints, 1842; came to Am., 1844; exhibited painting of assassination of Joseph Smith, Nauvoo, Ill., 1845; painted series to illustrate sufferings of Mormons; accompanied Mormon trek to Utah, 1846-48, sketched Indians, Western scenery; worked in Salt Lake City, 1843-53; returned to Eng., 1853. Died Eng., Sept. 2, 1854.

MAKEMIE, Francis, clergyman; b. nr. Rameltom, Donegal County, Ireland, 1658; grad. U. Glasgow; m. Naomi Anderson, before 1698, 2 children. Ordained to ministry Presbyn. Ch. as missionary to Am., 1682; arrived in Md., 1683; evangelist in N.C., Va., Md., Barbados; published catechism popularizing tenets of The Westminister Confession; 1st dissenting minister licensed to preach in Va. under Toleration Act; persuaded Presbyn. and independent ministers of London (Eng.) to send 2 Presbyn. ministers to Am.; founder, 1st moderator Am. Presbytery; persecuted by Gov. Cornbury of N.Y.; wrote A Narrative of a New and Unusual American Imprisonment of Two Presbyterian Ministers and Prosecution of Mr. Frances Makemie, 1707; chief founder Presbyn. Ch. in Am. Died Va., 1708.

MALBONE, Edward Greene, miniature painter; b. Newport, R.I., Aug. 1777; s. John and Patience (Green) M.; Moved to Providence, R.I., 1794; opened miniature portrait shop, Providence, 1794-96; moved to Boston, 1796, to Charleston, S.C., 1800; visited London, Eng., painted The Hours, 1801. Died Savannah, Ga., May 7, 1807; buried Colonial Cemetery, Savannah.

MALBONE, Francis, senator, congressman; b. Newport, R.I., Mar. 20, 1759. Mcht., Newport; col. Newport Arty., 1792-1809; mem. U.S. Ho. of Reps. (Federalist) from R.I., 3d-4th congresses, 1793-97; mem. R.I. Ho. of Reps., 1807-08; mem. U.S. Senate from R.I., 1809. Died on steps of Capitol, Washington, D.C., June 4, 1809; buried Congressional Cemetery, Washington.

MALCOLM, Daniel, mcht., sea capt., patriot; b. Georgetown, Me., Nov. 29, 1725; s. Michael and Sarah Malcolm; m. Ann Fudge, several children. Sea capt., owner several vessels; warden Christ Ch., Boston; leader Sons of Liberty, most active antagonist of customs authorities; presided at meeting of mchts. of Boston, 1768, entered agreement not to import any British goods for 18 months (1st movement of mchts. against Acts of Parliament); led patriots in 1st clash with Brit. armed forces, 1768. Died Boston, Oct. 23, 1769; buried Copp's Hill, Boston.

MALCOLM, James Peller, line-engraver, author; b. Phila., Aug. 1767; s. Moses and Mary (Peller) M.; attended Royal Acad., London, Eng., 3 years. Engraved frontispiece for Col. John Park's Lyric Works of Horace, 1786; lived in Eng., circa 1789-1815. Author, illustrator: Anecdotes of the Manners and Customs of London, During the Eighteenth Century, 1807; An Historical Sketch of the Art of Caricaturing, 1813. Died London, Apr. 5, 1815.

MALCOM, Howard, clergyman, coll. pres.; b. Phila., Jan. 19, 1799; s. John J. and Deborah (Howard) M.; ed. Dickinson Coll.; A.M. (hon.), 1842; D.D. (hon.), U. Vt., Union Coll. m. Lydia Morris Shields, May 1, 1820; m. 2d, Ruth Dyer, June 26, 1838; 5 children. Licensed to preach, 1818; ordained to ministry Baptist Ch., 1820; pastor Bapt. Ch., Hudson, N.Y., 1820; field worker Am. Sunday Sch. Union; sent abroad by Am. Bapt. Fgn. Missionary Union to visit missionary stations in India, Burma, China; pres. Georgetown (Ky.) Coll. 1840-49, Lewisburg U. (now Bucknell U.), 1851-57, Hahnemann Med. Coll. 1874-79; pres. Am. Bapt. Hist. Soc., Am. Peace Soc., Pa. Bapt. Ednl. Soc.; a founder Am. Tract Soc. Author: Nature and Extent of the Atonement, 1829; Christian Rule of Marriage, 1830; A Dictionary of Important Names, Objects and Terms Found in the Holy Scriptures, 1830; Travels in South-Eastern Asia, 1839. Died Phila., Mar. 25, 1879.

MALLARY, Rollin Carolas, congressman; b. Cheshire, Conn., May 27, 1784; s. Daniel and Martha (Dutton) M.; grad. Middlebury (Vt.) Coll., 1805; m. Ruth Stanley, Oct. 29, 1806; 3 children. Moved to Poultney, Vt., 1795; admitted to Rutland County (Vt.) bar, 1807; trustee Rutland County Grammar Sch., 1807; sec. to Gov. Vt., mem. Vt. Council, 1807, 09-12, 15-19; state's atty. for Rutland County, 1811-13, 15-16; mem. U.S. Ho. of Reps. (Republican) from Vt., 16th-22d congresses, Jan. 13, 1820-31, opposed admission of Mo. as a slave state, advocated protective tariff, chmn. com. on manufacture, responsible for Tariff of Abominations (1828), a high protective tariff which led to the Nullification Movement; trustee Middlebury Coll., 1825-31. Died Balt., Apr. 16, 1831; buried East Poultney (Vt.) Cemetery.

MALLERY, Garrick, army officer, ethnologist; b. Wilkes-Barre, Pa., Apr. 23, 1831; s. Garrick and Catherine (Hall) M.; grad. Yale, 1850; m. Helen W. Wyckoff, Apr. 14, 1870. Admitted to Pa. bar, 1853; capt. 71st Pa. Inf., 1861; wounded at Battle of Peach Orchard, Va., 1862; lt. col. 13th Pa. Cavalry, 1863, honorably discharged, 1864; brevetted col. U.S. Volunteers, 1865; capt. 43d Inf., U.S. Army, 1866; brevetted lt. col. U.S. Army, 1867; signal officer of meteorol. observations Signal Service Bur., U.S. Army, 1870-76; articles "The Former and Present Number of Our Indians" appeared in Proceedings of A.A.A.S., 1877, "A Calendar of the Dakota Nation" appeared in Bulletin of Geol. and Geog. Survey, 1877; retired from Army, 1879; mem. Bur. Ethnology, Smithsonian Instn., Washington, D.C., 1879-94; his article "Sign Language Among North American Indians Compared with that of Other Peoples and Deaf Mutes" appeared in 1st Annual Report of Bur. of Am. Ethnology, 1881, "Picture Writings of the North American Indians" appeared in 10th Annual Report of Bus. Am. Ethnology, 1893. Author: Introduction to the Study of Sign Language among the North American Indians as Illustrating the Gesture Speech of Mankind, 1880. Died Oct. 24, 1894.

MALLINCKRODT, Pauline, founder religious order; b. Minden, Westphalia, Germany, June 3, 1817. Established homes for the blind and infants, Paderborn, Westphalia; founder, 1st superior Congregation of Sisters of Christian Charity (also called Daus. of Immaculate Conception), 1849; forced into exile by Kulturkampf, 1873, came to U.S., founded provincial house, Wilkes-Barre, Pa.; returned to Europe to establish mother house nr. Brussels, Belgium; visited N. and S. Am. in later years. Died Paderborn, Apr. 30, 1881.

MALLORY, Francis, congressman; b. "Poplars" nr. Hampton, Va., Dec. 12, 1807; attended Hampton Acad.; studied law; grad. in Medicine, U. Pa., 1831. Served as midshipman U.S. Navy, 1822-28; practiced medicine, Norfolk, Va.; farmer, Elizabeth City County, Va.; mem. U.S. Ho. of Reps. (Whig) from Va., 25th, 26th-27th congresses, 1837-39, Dec. 18, 1840-43; del. So. Comml. Conv., Richmond, Va., 1838; naval agt., Norfolk, 1850-53; mem. Va. Ho. of Dels., 1853-55, 57-58; mem. Norfolk Common Council; pres. Norfolk & Petersburg R.R. Co., 1853-59. Died Norfolk, Mar. 26, 1860; buried Elmwood Cemetery, Norfolk.

MALLORY, Meredith, congressman; b. Conn.; attended common schs. Supr., Town of Benton (N.Y.), 1820; moved to Hammondsport, N.Y., owner and operator mill for grinding wheat and plaster, also a sawmill; held local offices; mem. N.Y. Assembly, 1835; justice of peace, 1838; mem. U.S. Ho. of Reps. (Democrat) from N.Y., 26th Congress, 1839-41.

MALLORY, Robert, congressman; b. Madison Court House, Va., Nov. 15, 1815; grad. U. Va., 1827; studied law. Farmer, La Grange, Ky.; admitted to Ky. bar, 1837, began practice in New Castle; mem. U.S. Ho. of Reps. (Union Democrat) from Ky., 36th-38th congresses, 1859-65; del. Union Nat. Conv., Phila., 1866; a v.p. Centinnial Exhbn. Phila., 1876; resumed farming. Died nr. La Grange, Aug. 11, 1885; buried family cemetery at Spring Hill, Ky.

MALLORY, Stephen Russell, senator; b. Trinidad, W.I., 1812; attended schs., Mobile, Ala., and Nazath, Pa.; studied law. Came to U.S., 1820; apptd. istoms insp., Key West, Fla., 1833; admitted to a. bar, 1840; practiced law, Key West, 1840-3; county judge Monroe County (Fla.), 1837-45; ptd. collector Port of Key West, 1845; served in eminole War; mem. U.S. Senate (Democrat) from a., 1851-Jan. 21, 1861; sec. of navy Confederate ates Am.; moved to Lagrange, Ga., 1865; moved Pensacola, Fla., 1866, practiced law. Died Pensa-la, Nov. 9, 1873; buried St. Michael's Cemetery, ensacola.

MANGIN, Joseph François, engr., architect; b. ance; flourished 1794-1818; married. Asst. to ief engr. of fortifications N.Y.C., became chief gr., 1795; freeman of N.Y.C., 1795; surveyor .Y.C., 1795, prepared map of city, published 1803; esigned N.Y. State Prison, Park Theatre (1795-8), St. Patrick's Cathedral (1809-15); probably esigned N.Y. City Hall.

MANGUM, Willie Person, senator; b. Orange ounty, N.C., May 10, 1792; s. William Person d Catharine (Davis) M.; B.A., U. N.C., 1815; ad law under Judge Duncan Cameron; m. arity Cain, Sept. 30, 1819, 1 child. Admitted N.C. bar, 1817; mem. N.C. Ho. Commons, 1818,); elected judge N.C. Superior Ct., 1819; mem. .S. Ho. of Reps. from N.C., 18th-19th congress-, 1823-Mar. 18, 1826; apptd. to fill vacancy as dge N.C. Superior Ct., 1826, re-elected, 1828; em. U.S. Senate from N.C., 1831-Nov. 26, 1837, ov. 25, 1840-53, pres. protem, 1842-45, acted vice pres. U.S. at death of William Henry arrison. Died Red Mountain, N.C., Sept. 14, 1861; uried Walnut Hill, nr. Red Mountain.

MANIGAULT, Arthur Middleton, army officer; Charleston, S.C., Oct. 26, 1824; s. Joseph and harlotte (Drayton) M.; m. Mary Huger, Apr. 8, 1851, 5 children. Became sgt. maj. of local ompany S.C. Militia; served as 1st lt. company , Palmetto Regt.; fought in Mexican War; elected apt. North Santee Mounted Rifles, 1860; became d.c. (volunteer) on staff Gen. Beauregard, 1861; ommd. lt. col.; assigned to do duty as adjutant nd insp. gen. on Beauregard's staff; elected col. 0th S.C. Volunteers 1861; became comdr. 1st il. dist. of S.C.; later ordered to Corinth (Miss.); romoted brig. gen., 1863; became adjutant and isp. gen. S.C., 1880. Died South Island, Georgetown County, S.C., Aug. 16, 1886.

MANIGAULT, Gabriel, planter; b. Charleston, .C., Apr. 21, 1704; s. Pierre and Judith Giton Royer) M.; m. Ann Ashby, Apr. 29, 1730, 1 on, Peter. Mem. S.C. Ho. of Commons; treas. S.C., 735-43; v.p. Charleston Library Soc.; one of wealth-est planters in S.C. Died Charleston, June 5, 1781.

MANIGAULT, Gabriel, architect; b. 1758. First rchitect to practice in the South (although he id not call himself an architect); designed several ublic bldgs. in Charleston (S.C.), including a ranch of U.S. Bank (now City Hall), 1802; cred-ted with design of Soc. Hall, Orphan's Home Chapel (built 1802), also several of earliest mansions in Charleston, including residence of James Manigault. Died Nov. 4, 1809.

MANIGAULT, Peter, legislator, planter; b. Charleston, S.C., Oct. 10, 1731; s. Gabriel and Ann (Ashby) M.; entered Inner Temple, London, Eng., 1752; m. Elizabeth Wragg, June 8, 1755, 7 children. Called to English bar, 1754; returned to S.C., 1754; mem. S.C. Colonial Assembly, 1755-72, speaker, 1765-72, opposed Stamp Act; took over mgmt. plantations of Ralph Izard in addition to own, 1763; returned to Eng. because of illness. Died London, Eng., Nov. 12, 1773; buried Charleston.

MANIGAULT, Pierre, mcht.; b. La Rochelle, France; s. Gabriel and Marie Manigault; m. Judith (Giton) Royer, 1699, 2 children. Came to Charles-ton, S.C., 1695, received land grant; became vic-tualler; later became extremely successful mcht. and distiller, conducting bus. directly with Eng. Died Charleston, Dec. 1729; buried French Churchyard, Charleston.

MANLEY, John, naval officer; b. Boston, circa 1734; m. Hannah Cheevers, Feb. 26, 1763; m. 2d, Friswith Arnold, Dec. 14, 1791. Master of ship Little Forteseue, 1768-69; commd. capt. Con-tinental Army to command schooner Lee against British, 1775; captured several valuable prizes, pro-moted to comdr. of fleet and master of schooner Hancock, 1776; commd. capt. Continental Navy, 1776; commanded frigate Hancock, was captured and imprisoned by English, 1777-78; entered pri-vateer service, in command of ships Marlborough and Cumberland; captured by British and escaped, 1779; captured for 3d time aboard ship Jason, im-prisoned 2 years; returned to Navy for last success-ful voyage in ship Hague, 1783. Died Boston, Feb. 14, 1793; buried with mil. honors, Boston.

MANLY, Basil, clergyman, coll. pres.; b. Pitts-boro, N.C., Jan. 29, 1798; s. Basil and Elizabeth (Matthias) M.; attended coll., Beaufort, S.C.; grad. S.C. Coll., 1821; m. Sarah Murray Rudulph, Dec. 23, 1824, 5 children. Convert to Baptist Ch., 1816; licensed to preach by Rocky Spring Ch., 1818; pas-tor, Edgefield and Stevens Creek (S.C.), 1822; or-dained to ministry Bapt. Ch. 1822; sec. of state Bapt. conv.; mem. founding com. Furman Acad. and Theol. Inst. (now Furman U.); pastor 1st Bapt. Ch., Charleston, S.C., 1826-37; pres. S.C. Coll., 1837-55; a founder Ala. Hist. Soc., Judson, Howard, Central colls.; pastor Wentworth Street Bapt. Ch.; pres. So. Bapt. Theol. Sem. Conv., 1856, 57, 58; chaplain at inauguration of Jefferson Davis. Died Greenville, N.C., Dec. 21, 1868.

MANLY, Basil, clergyman, coll. pres.; b. Edge-field, S.C., Dec. 19, 1825; s. Basil and Sarah Mur-ray (Rudulph) M.; grad. U. Ala., 1843; attended Newton Theol. Inst.; grad. Princeton Theol. Sem., 1847; m. Charlotte Elizabeth Whitfield, Apr. 28, 1852; m. 2d, Henrietta Summers Hair, June 10, 1869. Licensed to preach, 1844; ordained to ministry Baptist Ch., Tuscaloosa, Ala., 1848; pastor Bapt. Ch., Providence, Ala., 1848-49, 1st Bapt. Ch., Rich-mond, Va., 1850-54; pres. Richmond Female Inst., 1854-59; prof. So. Bapt. Theol. Sem., 1859-61, 65-71, 77-92; pres. Georgetown (Ky.) Coll., 1871-77. Author: The Bible Doctrine of Inspiration, 1888. Died Louisville, Ky., Jan. 31, 1892.

MANN, Abijah, Jr., congressman; b. Fairfield, N.Y., Sept. 24, 1793; s. Abijah Mann; attended common schs. Engaged in merc. bus.; justice of peace; postmaster of Fairfield, 1830-33; mem. N.Y. Assembly, 1828-30, 38; mem. U.S. Ho. of Reps. (Democrat) from N.Y., 23d-24th congresses, 1833-37; moved to N.Y.C.; unsuccessful candidate for atty. gen. N.Y., 1855; del. N.Y. Republican Conv., 1856. Died Auburn, N.Y., Sept. 6, 1868.

MANN, Ambrose Dudley, diplomat; b. Hanover Court House, Va., Apr. 26, 1801; studied U.S. Mil. Acad., 3 years. Apptd. U.S. consul, Bremen, Ger-many, 1842; spl. commr. to German states, given dipolmatic powers for purpose of negotiating comml. treaties, 1846; spl. U.S. agt. to Kossuth's govt. in Hungary, 1849; asst. sec. of state U.S., 1853-56; Confederate commr. to Europe, active in gaining favorable press for So. cause in Eng. and France, and in trying to get Pope to check number of Euro-pean Catholics who were enlisting in U.S. Army; remained in France after Civil War. Died Paris, France, Nov. 1889.

MANN, Horace, congressman, reformer, coll. pres.; b. Franklin, Mass., May 4, 1796; s. Thomas and Rebecca (Stanley) M.; grad. Brown U., 1819; m. Charlotte Messer, Sept. 12, 1830; m. 2d Mary Tyler Peabody, May 1, 1843; 3 children. Taught Latin and Greek, Brown U., 1820-21; admitted to Norfolk County (Mass.) bar, 1823; practiced law, 1823-37; mem. Mass. Ho. of Reps., 1827-32, Mass. Senate, 1835-37, pres., 1836-37; moved to Boston, 1833; commr. for revision of Mass. statutes, 1835; 1st sec. Mass. Bd. Edn., 1837-48; editor semi-monthly mag. Common Sch. Jour., 1838-48; responsible for establishing minimum 6 month sch. year, 1839, Am.'s 1st 3 state normal schs. (Mass.), 1839-40; spent more than $2,000,000 for schoolhouses and equipment, increased salaries for tchrs., established 50 new high schs.; went to Europe for health reasons and to compare U.S. and European schs., 1843; fought for establishment of state hosps. for insane, restriction of slavery, lotteries, liquor traffic; mem. U.S. Ho. of Reps. from Mass., 30th-32d congresses, Apr. 13, 1848-53; influenced by writings of Ralph Waldo Emerson and George Combe; pres. Antioch Coll., Yellow Springs, O., 1852-59. Author: Lectures on Education, 1845; A Few Thoughts for a Young Man, 1850; Slavery: Letters and Speeches, 1851; Powers and Duties of Woman, 1853. Died Yellow Springs, Aug. 2, 1859; buried North Burial Ground, Providence, R.I.

MANN, James, physician; b. Wrentham, Mass., July 22, 1759; s. David and Anna Mann; grad. Harvard, 1776; M.D. (hon.), Brown U., 1815; studied with Dr. S. Danforth; m. Martha Tyler, Dec. 12, 1788, 5 children. Served as surgeon with Col. W. Shepard's 4th Mass. Regt., 1779-82, im-prisoned by British, 2 months, 1781; practiced medicine, N.Y.C.; head of med. dept. U.S. Army on No. frontier during War of 1812; sr. hosp. sur-geon, Detroit, 1816-18; post surgeon, 1818-21, asst. surgeon, 1821-32. Author: Medical Sketches of the Campaigns of 1812, 13, 14, to Which are Added Surgical Cases, Observations on Military Hos-pitals; and Flying Hospitals Attached to a Moving Army, Also an Appendix . . ., 1816. Died Nov. 7, 1832.

MANN, James, congressman; b. Gorham, Me., June 22, 1822. Mem. Me. Ho. of Reps., 1848-50, Me. Senate, 1851-53; treas. Cumberland County (Me.), 1862-63; customhouse officer, Portland, Me.; served as paymaster with rank of maj. U.S. Army, during Civil War; agt. U.S. Treasury for La., 1867-68; mem. U.S. Ho. of Reps. (Democrat) from La., 40th Congress, July 18-Aug. 26, 1868. Died New Orleans, Aug. 26, 1868; buried Eastern Cemetery, Gorham, Me.

MANN, Job, congressman; b. Bethel Twp., Bed-ford (now Fulton) County, Pa., Mar. 31, 1795; at-tended Bedford Acad.; studied law. Clk. bd. county commrs. Bedford County, 1816, register, recorder, county clk., 1818-35; mem. U.S. Ho. of Reps. (Democrat) from Pa., 24th, 30th-31st congresses, 1835-37, 47-51; admitted to Pa. bar, 1839, began practice in Bedford; treas. State of Pa., 1842-48; mem. Pa. Ho. of Reps. Died Bedford, Oct. 8, 1873; buried Bedford Cemetery.

MANN, Joel Keith, congressman; b. Cheltenham Twp., Montgomery County, Pa., Aug. 1, 1780; at-tended common schs. Engaged in farming; mem. Pa. Ho. of Reps., 1817-20, Pa. Senate, 1824-29; mem. U.S. Ho. of Reps. (Democrat) from Pa., 22d-23d congresses, 1831-35. Died Jenkintown, Pa., Aug. 28, 1857; buried Presbyn. Cemetery, Abingdon, Pa.

MANN, Mary Tyler Peabody, author; b. Cam-bridge, Mass., Nov. 16, 1806; d. Nathaniel and Elizabeth (Palmer) Peabody; m. Horace Mann, May 1, 1843, 3 sons. Made trip to Cuba, 1832-35; col-laborated with her husband on many of his intellectu-al pursuits. Author: The Flower People, 1838; Chris-tianity in the Kitchen: A Physiological Cook Book, 1857; Juanita: A Romance of Real Life in Cuba Fifty Years Ago, 1887. Editor: Life and Works of Horace Mann, 3 vols., 1865-68. Died Jamaica Plain, Feb. 11, 1887.

MANN, William Julius, clergyman; b. Stuttgart, Württemberg, May 29, 1819; s. Johann Georg and Auguste Friederike (Gentner) M.; attended U. Tübingen, 1837-41; m. Margaretta Catherine Rom-mel, 1849, 1 son, 3 daus. Sch. tchr. and asst. pastor in So. Germany; came to Pa., 1845; taught sch., Mercersburg, Pa.; ordained to ministry, 1846; asst. pastor Salem German Reformed Ch., Mercers-burg; asst. pastor St. Michael's and Zion's congrega-tion, 1850-54, became pastor, 1854; prof. German, Phila. Lutheran Theol. Sem., 1864-84, housefather, 1872-84; pres. Ministerium of Pa., 1860-62, 80. Author: Die Ansiedler in Amerika, 1845; A Plea for the Augsburg Confession in Answer to the Objec-tions of the Definite Platform, 1856; Heilbotschaft, 1881. Died Boston, June 20, 1892; buried West Laurel Hill Cemetery, Phila.

MANNING, Daniel, sec. of treasury; b. Albany, N.Y., May 16, 1831; s. John and Eleanor Manning; m. Mary Little; m. 2d, Mary Margaret-ta Fryer, 1884. Apptd. page N.Y. Assembly, 1841, served 2 sessions; reporter N.Y. Assembly proceed-ings for Asso. Press, 1863, later legislative corr. Bklyn. Eagle; reporter N.Y. Senate proceedings for Albany Argus, 1858-71, became part owner, bus. mgr. Argus Co., 1865, pres., 1873; mem. N.Y. State Democratic Com., 1874-84, chmn., 1881-84; leader N.Y. State Dem. Party, 1877; del. to Nat. Dem. Conv., 1876, 80, 84; U.S. sec. of treasury un-der Pres. Cleveland, 1885-87; pres. Western Nat. Bank of N.Y., 1887. Died Albany, Dec. 24, 1887.

MANNING, James, clergyman, coll. pres.; b. Piscataway, N.J., Oct. 22, 1735; s. James and Grace (Fitz-Randolph) M.; grad. Coll. of N.J. (now Prince-ton), 1762; D.D. (hon.), U. Pa., 1785; m. Marga-ret Stites, Mar. 23, 1763. Licensed to preach by Scotch Plains Baptist Ch., 1763; ordained to min-istry Bapt. Ch., 1763; in charge of founding Bapt.-directed instn. in R.I., 1763, a founder R.I. Coll. (now Brown U.), 1763, granted charter by R.I. As-sembly, 1765, 1st pres., prof. languages, 1765-91; pastor 1st Bapt. Ch., Providence, R.I., 1771; re-presented R.I. in Congress of Confederation, 1786; mem. Providence Sch. Com.; drew up report re-commending establishment of free public schs., 1791. Died Providence, July 29, 1791.

MANNING, Richard Irvine, gov. S.C.; b. Cam-den Dist., S.C., May 1, 1789; s. Laurence and Susannah (Richardson) M.; grad. S.C. Coll. (now U.S.C.), 1811; m. Elizabeth Richardson (his cousin), 1814, 5 sons including Richard I. and John L., 4 daus. Served as capt. S.C. Militia, War of 1812; mem. S. C. Ho. of Reps., 1822; gov. S. C., 1824-26; mem. S.C. Nullification Conv. (1 of few Unionists elected), 1832; a vice pres. Union Conv., Columbia, S.C., 1832; mem. com. chosen to consider mediation of Va.'s agt. Benjamin Watkins Leigh, 1833; mem. U.S. Ho. of Reps. from S.C., 23d-24th congresses, 1833-36. Died Phila., May 1, 1836; buried Trinity Churchyard, Columbia.

MANNING, Robert, pomologist; b. Salem, Mass., July 18, 1784; s. Richard and Miriam (Lord) M.; m. Rebecca Dodge Burnham, Dec. 20, 1824. Operat-ed family stage coach lines; began raising fruits, 1817, developed large pomological garden with many varieties of fruit (including over 1000 varieties of pears) from European and Am.; a founder Mass. Hort. Soc. Author: Book of Fruit, 1838. Died Oct. 10, 1842.

MANNING, Thomas Courtland, jurist, diplomat; b. Edenton, N.C., Sept. 14, 1825; s. Joseph and

Sarah (Houghton) M.; ed. U. N.C., LL.D. (hon.), 1878; m. Mary Blair, Jan. 18, 1848. Admitted to N.C. bar, 1848; mem. La. Secession Conv., 1861; lt. of a Confederate mil. co. raised in Rapides Parish, 1861; aide-de-camp on staff Gov. Thomas D. Moore, 1861-63; apptd. adj. gen. La. with rank of brig. gen.; asso. justice La. Supreme Ct., 1864-65, 82-86, chief justice, 1877-80; del. to La. Democratic Conv., 1872; v.p. Nat. Dem. Conv., 1876; U.S. minister to Mexico (apptd. by Pres. Cleveland), 1886-87; mem. Peabody Ednl. Fund. Died N.Y.C., Oct. 11, 1887.

MANNING, Vannoy Hartrog, congressman; b. nr. Raleigh, N.C., July 26, 1839; attended U. Nashville (Tenn.); studied law, Ark. Admitted to Ark. bar, 1861, began practice in Hamburg; served as capt., later col. Ark. troops, Confederate Army, during Civil War; captured at Battle of Wilderness, imprisoned until 1865; resumed practice of law, Holly Springs, Miss.; mem. U.S. Ho. of Reps. (Democrat) from Miss., 45th-47th congresses, 1877-83, lost seat in 48th Congress as result of contested election; resumed law practice, Washington, D.C., 1883. Died Branchville, Md., Nov. 3, 1892; buried Glenwood Cemetery, Washington.

MANSFIELD, Edward Deering, editor; b. New Haven, Aug. 17, 1801; s. Jared and Elizabeth (Phipps) M.; grad. U.S. Mil. Acad., 1819, Coll. of N.J. (now Princeton), 1822; attended Litchfield (Conn.) Law Sch., 1823-25; m. Mary Wallace Peck, Apr. 24, 1839; m. 2d, Margaret Worthington. Admitted to Conn. bar, 1825; practiced law, Cincinnati, 1825-26; editor Cincinnati Chronicle, Mirror, Atlas, also Cincinnati Daily Gazette, 1826-80; editor Railroad Record, 1853-71; prof. constl. law and history Cincinnati Coll.; a founder coll. for tchrs., Cincinnati; Ohio commr. of statistics, 1858-68. Author: Cincinnati in 1826; published 1826; The Political Grammar, 1834; The Legal Rights, Liabilities and Duties of Women, 1845; The Utility of Mathematics, 1854. Died Oct. 27, 1880.

MANSFIELD, Jared, U.S. surveyor gen., educator; b. New Haven, Conn., May 23, 1759; s. Stephen and Hannah (Beach) M.; grad. Yale, 1777, A.M., 1787, LL.D. (hon.), 1825; m. Elizabeth Phipps, Mar. 2, 1800, 1 son, Edward Deering. Rector, Hopkins Grammar Sch., New Haven, 1786; apptd. capt. Engrs. Corps, U.S. Army by Pres. Jefferson, 1802; acting prof. mathematics U.S. Mil. Acad., 1802-03; apptd. surveyor gen. U.S. with rank of lt. col. to survey Ohio and N.W. Territory, 1803-12; promoted maj., 1805, lt. col., 1808;prof. natural and exptl. philosophy U.S. Mil. Acad. 1812-28; Mansfield (O.) named for him. Author: Essays, Mathematical and Physical, 1801; Essays on Mathematics, 1802. Died New Haven, Conn., Feb. 3, 1830; buried Grove Cemetery, New Haven.

MANSFIELD, Joseph King Fenno, army officer; b. New Haven, Conn., Dec. 22, 1803; s. Henry and Mary (Fenno) M.; grad. U.S. Mil. Acad., 1822; m. Louise Mather, Sept. 25, 1838, 4 children. Commd. 2d lt. Corps Engrs., U.S. Army, 1822, 1st lt., 1832, capt., 1838; served in Mexican War, 1846-48; chief engr., brevetted maj., then lt. col., col.; capt. in constrn. coast defenses until 1853; col., insp. gen., 1853; commd. brig. gen. U.S. Army, assigned to command Dept. Washington (D.C.), including capitol and surrounding territory, 1861; commd. maj. gen. U.S. Volunteers, 1862. Died Battle of Antietam (Va.), Sept. 18, 1862.

MANSFIELD, Richard, clergyman; b. New Haven, Oct. 1, 1723; s. Jonathan and Sarah (Alling) M.; grad. Yale, 1741, D.D., 1792; m. Anna Hull, Oct. 10, 1751, 13 children. Rector, Hopkins Grammar Sch., 1742-47; ordained deacon and priest Episcopal Ch. in Eng., 1748; missionary and rector to Derby, Conn., 1748-1820; Royalist during Am. Revolution, but remained in Am. Died Derby, Apr. 12, 1820; buried Derby.

MANSON, Mahlon Dickerson, congressman; b. Piqua, O., Feb. 20, 1820; attended common schs.; attended Ohio Medical College, Cincinnati. Taught schools, Montgomery County, Indiana; served as captain volunteers during Mexican War, 1847-48; member Indiana House of Reps., 1851-52; retail druggist, Crawfordsville, Ind.; served as capt., maj. and col. 10th Regt., Ind. Volunteer Inf. during Civil War, 1861; brig. gen. U.S. Volunteers, 1862-64; mem. U.S. Ho. of Reps. (Democrat) from Ind., 42d Congress, 1871-73; auditor State of Ind., 1878, lt. gov., 1884; collector of internal revenue 7th Ind. Dist., 1886-89. Died Crawfordsville, Feb. 4, 1895; buried Oak Hill Cemetery, Crawfordsville.

MANSON, Otis Frederick, physician; b. Richmond, Va., Oct. 10, 1822; s. Otis and Sarah Dews (Ferrill) M.; attended Hampden-Sydney Coll.; m. Mary Ann Spottswood Burwell; m. 2d, Helen (Gray) Watson, 1881. Practiced medicine, Granville County, N.C.; served as maj. Confederate Army, established Vet's Hosp., Richmond, 1862; prof. pathology and physiology Med. Coll. of Va., 1869-82, prof. emeritus, 1882-88; asso. editor Va. Clin. Record. 1871-72; mem. Med. Soc. N.C.; mem. Va. Bd. Med. Examiners, 1870-88; pres. Richmond City Council. Author: Remittent Fever, 1881; Physiological and Therapeutic Action of Sulphate of Quinine, 1882. Died Richmond, Jan. 25, 1888; buried Richmond.

MANSUR, Charles Harley, congressman; b. Phila., Mar. 6, 1835; attended Lawrence Acad., Groton, Mass.; studied law. Admitted to Mo. bar, 1856; practiced law, Chillicothe, Mo.; mem. Chillicothe Bd. Edn., 8 years; mem. Democratic Central Com., 1864-68; del. Dem. Nat. Conv., N.Y.C., 1868; pros. atty. Livingston County (Mo.), 1875-79; del. at large Dem. Nat. Conv., Chgo., 1884; mem. U.S. Ho. of Reps. (Democrat) from Mo., 50th-52d congresses, 1887-93; 2d comptroller U.S. Treasury, 1893-94, asst. comptroller, 1894-95. Died Washington, D.C., Apr. 16, 1895; buried Sunny Slope Cemetery, Richmond, Mo.

MANUCY, Dominic, clergyman; b. Mobile, Ala., Dec. 20, 1823; studied at Spring Hill. Ordained priest Roman Catholic Ch., Mobile, 1850, did parish work, Mobile Diocese, 1850-74; named titular bishop of Dulma, also vicar apostolic of Brownsville (Tex.), 1874, transferred to Mobile, 1884, reapptd. to Brownsville, 1885; attended 3d Plenary Council of Balt., 1884; named titular bishop of Maronea, 1885. Died Mobile, Dec. 4, 1885.

MAPES, James Jay, agriculturist; b. Maspeth, L.I., May 29, 1806; s. Jonas and Elizabeth (Tylee) M.; m. Sophia Furman, 1827, 5 daus., 1 son, Charles V. Mcht., 1827-32; invented sugar refining process, 1832; became patent cons., analytical chemist; prof. chemistry and natural philosophy of colors Nat. Acad. Design, 1835-38; editor Am. Repertory of Arts, Sciences and Manufactures, 1840-42; asso. editor Jour. of Franklin Inst., 1842-43; pres. Mechanics Inst. City of N.Y., 1845; v.p. Am. Inst. City of N.Y., 1847; founder Franklin Inst. of Newark (N.J.); became farmer, 1847, purchased old N.J. farm, converted it into show-place by using advanced scientific agrl. methods; founder, editor The Working Farmer, 1849-63. Died N.Y.C., Jan. 10, 1866.

MAPPA, Adam Gerard, land agt., type-founder; b. Delft, Holland, Nov. 25, 1754; m. Anna Adriana Passpoort, 3 children. Army officer, owner of type-foundry, mem. unsuccessful patriot movement, Netherlands, 1780's; exile in France, 2 years; came to Am., established 1st type-foundry in N.Y.C., 1789; became agt. for Holland Land Co., asst. land agt. at Olden Barneveld (Trenton), Oneida County, N.Y., 1794-97, head agt., 1797-1818. Died N.Y., Apr. 15, 1828.

MARABLE, John Hartwell, congressman; b. nr. Lawrenceville, Va., Nov. 18, 1786; studied medicine, Phila. Practiced medicine, Phila., later in Yellow Creek, Tenn.; mem. Tenn. Senate, 1817-18; mem. U.S. Ho. of Reps. (National-Republican) from Tenn., 19th-20th congresses, 1825-29; resumed practice of medicine. Died Montgomery County, Tenn., Apr. 11, 1844; buried Marable Cemetery, nr. Clarksville, Tenn.

MARBLE, Danforth, actor; b. East Windsor, Conn., Apr. 27, 1810; s. William and Mary Marble; m. Anne Warren. Trained as silversmith, Hartford; became silversmith, N.Y.C., also did acting; mem. local thespian soc.; played his 1st important role, 1831; developed skill in mimicking Yankee accent; appeared as Sam Patch in upper N.Y. State, Cleve., Cincinnati, late 1830's, became nationally renowned; appeared in London, 1844. Died Louisville, Ky., May 13, 1849; buried Louisville.

MARCH, Alden, physician; b. Sutton, Mass., Sept. 20, 1795; s. Jacob and Eleanor (Moore) M.; M.D., Brown U., 1820; m. Joanna P. Armsby, 1824. Ran his father's farm, 1814-17; taught sch., 1817; practiced medicine, operated pvt. sch. of anatomy, Albany, N.Y., 1820-38; prof. anatomy and physiology Vt. Acad. of Medicine, Castleton, 1824-38; founder, mem. faculty Albany Med. Coll., 1830-34, prof. surgery, 1839 (merged with Fairfield Med. Sch. to become Albany City Hosp.), prof. surgery Albany City Hosp., until 1869; pres. A.M.A., 1863. Author: (pamphlet) Coxalgia or Hip Disease, 1853. Died Albany, June 17, 1869.

MARCHAND, Albert Gallatin, congressman; b. nr. Greensburg, Pa., Feb. 27, 1811; s. David Marchand; attended common schs.; studied law. Admitted to Pa. bar, 1833, began practice in Greensburg; mem. U.S. Ho. of Reps. (Democrat) from Pa., 26th-27th congresses, 1839-43; resumed law practice. Died Greensburg, Feb. 5, 1848; buried Greensburg Cemetery.

MARCHAND, David, congressman; b. nr. Irwin, Pa., Dec. 10, 1776; studied medicine; children include Albert Gallatin Marchand. Practiced medicine, Westmoreland County, Pa.; maj. gen. 13th Div., Pa. Militia, 1812-14; mem. U.S. Ho. of Reps. from Pa., 15th-16th congresses, 1817-21; elected prothonotary Westmoreland County, 1821; resumed practice of medicine. Died Greensburg, Pa., Mar. 11, 1832; buried Greensburg Cemetery.

MARCHAND, John Bonnett, naval officer; b Greensburg, Pa., Aug. 27, 1808; s. David an Catherine (Bonnett) M.; m. Margaret Thorton 1856/57. Commd. midshipman U.S. Navy 1828 student Norfolk Naval Sch; passed midshipman 1834; served in ship Potomac, them the Joh Adams, Mediterranean Squadron, 1834-37; commd lt., 1840; served in war against Seminol Indians while in command ship Van Buren, 1841 promoted to comdr. 1855, capt. 1862; assigne to blockade duty in Gulf of Mexico during Civi War; commanded Phila. Navy Yard; commd. com modore, 1866, ret., 1870. Died Carlisle, Pa., Apr 13, 1875.

MARCHANT, Edward Dalton, artist; b. Edgartown, Mass., Dec. 16, 1806; at least 1 son, Henry A. Advertised as portrait painter, Charleston, S.C., 1827-28; exhibited at N.A.D., 1832, maintained studio, N.Y.C.; visited New Orleans and Ohio, circa 1838-39; returned to N.Y.C., later moved to Nashville, Tenn.; worked in N.Y.C., 1850-52, Phila., 1854-60; asso. N.A.D., 1833-87. Died Asbury Park, N.J., Aug. 15, 1887.

MARCHANT, Henry, Continental congressman, jurist; b. Martha's Vineyard, Mass., Apr. 9, 1741; s. Hexford Marchant; attended Coll. of Phila. (now U. Pa.), 1756-59, A.M.; read law under Edmund Trowbridge; m. Rebecca Cooke, Jan. 8, 1765, 1 son, William. Admitted to R.I. bar, circa 1767, practiced law in Newport; atty. gen. R.I., 1771-77; appeared before Privy Council in Eng. on pvt. legal bus., designated joint colonial agt. to obtain compensation for expenses in Crown Point campaign (1756), 1771-72; companion of Benjamin Franklin on visit to Scotland; friend of radicals and nonconformists in Gt. Britain (called "Friends of Am."); returned to U.S., suspected of accepting a retainer from custom's collector; mem. R.I. Com. of Correspondence, 1773; mem. com. to instruct dels. to 1st Continental Congress, 1774; mem. Continental Congress from R.I., 1777-79, mem. standing coms. on marine, appeals, treasury, So. dept.; mem. R.I. Gen. Assembly from Newport, 1784-90; signer minority protest against abstention of R.I. from Phila. Conv., 1787; mem. R.I. Conv. which ratified U.S. Constn., 1790; judge U.S. Dist. Ct. for R.I., 1790-96. Died Newport, Aug. 30, 1796; buried Common Burial Ground, Newport.

MARCOU, Jules, geologist; b. Salins, France, Apr. 20, 1824; attended Coll. of St. Louis 1842-44; m. Jane Belknap, 1850, 2 sons. Prof. mineralogy Sorbonne, 1846-48; traveling geologist for Jardin des Plantes, 1848-50; collected for Paris museums in North Am., especially in Lake Superior region, until 1854; prof. paleontology École Polytechnique, Zurich, 1856-60; returned to Am., 1860; geologist Mus. of Comparative Zoology, Harvard, 1862-64, made several field trips to Western U.S. Author: Lettres sur les Roches du Jura, 1857-60; Geology of North American, 1858; also produced Geological Map of the World, 1862. Died Apr. 17, 1898.

MARCY, Daniel, congressman; b. Portsmouth, N. H., Nov. 7, 1809; attended common schs. Engaged in shipbldg.; mem. N.H. Ho. of Reps., 1854-57, N.H. Senate, 1857-58, 71-72; mem. U.S. Ho. of Reps. (Democrat) from N.H., 38th Congress, 1863-65. Died Portsmouth, Nov. 3, 1893; buried Proprietors' Burying Ground, Portsmouth.

MARCY, Randolph Barnes, army officer; b. Greenwich, Mass., Apr. 9, 1812; s. Laban and Fanny (Howe) M.; grad. U.S. Mil. Acad., 1832; m. Mary Mann, 1833. Brevetted 2d lt., 5th Inf., U.S. Army 1832, commd. 2d lt., 1835, 1st lt., 1837, capt., 1846; acting insp. gen. Dept. of Utah, 1856; commd. maj., apptd. paymaster, 1859, served in N.W. until 1861, then chief-of-staff to Gen. George B. McClellan (his son-in-law); commd. col., insp. gen., 1861; temporary brig. gen., 1861-63, served with Army of Potomac in Md. campaign, 1862-63; participated in cavalry charge at Brandy Stations in Pa. campaign, 1863; distinguished himself at Battle of Gettysburg, in central Va. operations and actions at Rapidan, Auburn and New Hope Ch.; insp. in various depts., 1863-78; in charge 2d cavalry div. Army of Potomac in Richmond campaign, 1864-65; apptd. insp. gen. with rank brig. gen. U.S. Army, 1878. Died West Orange, N.J.,Nov. 22, 1887.

MARCY, William Learned, senator, cabinet officer; b. Sturbridge (now Southbridge), Mass., Dec. 12, 1786; s. Jedediah and Ruth (Learned) M.; grad. Brown U., 1808; m. Dolly Newell, Sept. 27, 1812; m. 2d, Cornelia Knower, circa 1825; 6 children. Made speech before Tammany Soc. in N.Y. defending policies of Thomas Jefferson against attacks of Stephen C. Carpenter published as "Oration on the Three Hundred and Eighteenth Anniversary of the Discovery of America," 1808 (1st of his literary works to be printed); admitted to N.Y. bar, 1811; served with 155th N.Y. Regt. during War of 1812, promoted ensign, 1812; 1st recorder of Troy (N.Y.), 1816-18, mayor, 1816-18, 21-23; partner (with acob L. Lane) firm Marcy & Lane, 1818-23; edited eeekly Troy Budget; wrote "Considerations in Favor f the Appointment of Rufus King to the Senate of ie United States" (pamphlet which led to restoral f Rufus King to Senate), 1820; comptroller N.Y. tate, 1823-29; asso. justice N.Y. State Supreme t., 1829-31; mem. U.S. Senate from N.Y., 1831, an. 1, 1833; mem. finance com., chmn. judiciary om.; introduced phrase "spoils system" in defending Martin Van Buren and his patronage system, 1832; gov. N.Y. State, 1833-39, organized 1st geol. urvey of 56 counties of N.Y., highest peak in Adironacks named for him, settled N.J. boundary dispute; iem. Mexican Claims Commn., 1840-42, secured bout $2,400,000 of Am. claims; U.S. sec. of war, 845-49, used diplomatic powers in settlement Ore. oundary question, 1846, advocated tariff of 1846; .S. sec. of state, 1853-57, responsible for numerous eaty negotiations, including Gadsden Treaty with Iexico, 1853, Reciprocity Treaty with Gt. Britain, 854, treaty with Netherlands, 1855, Denmark reaty, 1857; sec. during signing of Ostend Maniesto, 1855; dismissed Brit. minister and 3 Brit. onsuls from U.S. because of their attempts to enlist .S. recruits for Crimean War. Died Ballston Spa, .Y., July 4, 1857; buried Albany (N.Y.) Rural emetery.

MARDIS, Samuel Wright, congressman; b. Fayetteville, Tenn., June 12, 1800; studied law. Admited to Ala. bar, began practice in Montevallo, 1823; nem. Ala. Ho. of Reps., 1823-25, 28, 30; mem. J.S. Ho. of Reps. (Democrat) from Ala., 22d-3d congresses, 1831-35; moved to Mardisville, la., 1835, practiced law. Died Talladega, Ala., Nov. 14, 1836; buried Oak Hill Cemetery, Talladega.

MARÉCHAL, Ambrose, clergyman; b. Orléans, France, Aug. 28, 1764; ed. Sulpician Sem., Orléans. Ordained priest Roman Catholic Ch., 1792, sent to Am., assigned to missions in Md.; taught at Georgetown Coll., St. Mary's Sem.; went back to France, 1805-12; Returned to teach at St. Mary's Sem., 1812-17; named titular bishop and coadjutor of Balt., 1817, archbishop, 1817-28. Died Balt., Jan. 29, 1828; buried Balt.

MARENO, Francisco Ildefonse, see Antoine, Pére.

MAREST, Pierre Gabriel, clergyman; b. Laval, France, 1662. Ordained priest Roman Catholic Ch., ordered to Can., 1694; mem. Iberville's expdn. to Hudson's Bay, 1694-95; captured and imprisoned by English; aided Father Jacques Gravier in work in Ill. Missions, 1698-1714. Died Ill., Sept. 15, 1714; buried Kaskaskia, Ill.

MARETZEK, Max, opera impresario; b. Brünn, Moravia, June 28, 1821. Began composing music in his youth, wrote opera Hamlet (produced when he was 20 years old); moved to Paris, France, then to London, Eng.; composed ballets, songs, conducted various orchs., London; came to N.Y.C. as condr. Italian Opera Co., 1848, took over as impresario-condr. (when co. failed), 1849-79; played mainly in N.Y.C., made occasional tours in U.S. and Europe. Author: Sleepy Hollow (opera); Crotchets and Quavers: or, Revelations of an Opera Manager in America, 1855. Died Pleasant Plains, S.I., N.Y., May 14, 1897; buried N.Y.

MARGIL, Antonio, missionary; b. Valencia, Spain, Aug. 18, 1657. Joined Franciscan Order, Roman Catholic Ch., Valencia, 1673; went as missionary to Mexico City, Mexico, 1683, preached to Indians of Central Am., 1683-1726; apptd. guardian of mission coll. of Guadalupe, 1706; founded missions of Guadalupe, Tex., 1716; called "Apostle of Guatemala." Died Mexico City, Aug. 6, 1726.

MARIGNY, Bernard, planter; b. New Orleans, Oct. 28, 1785; s. Pierre Enquerrand Philippe de Meadville, Ecuyer (sieur de Marigny, Chevalier de St. Louis) and Jeanne Marie L'Estréhan; m. Mary Ann Jones, May 28, 1804, 2 sons; m. 2d, Anne Mathilde Morales, 2 sons, 3 daus. Son of richest man in La.; made trip to Eng., later introduced game of "craps" to Am., circa 1800; became known throughout La. Territory for his extravagance and dissipations; mem. La. Territorial Legislature, 1810-38; mem. La. Constl. Conv., 1812, Constl. Modifying Conv., 1845; registrar of conveyances, 1847-53; squandered huge fortune, died in poverty. Author: Réflexions sur La Campaigne du General André Jackson en Louisiane, 1848; Thoughts Upon the Foreign Policy of the United States, 1854. Died La., Feb. 3, 1868.

MARION, Francis, army officer; b. Berkeley County, S.C., 1732; s. Gabriel and Esther (Cordes) M.; m. Mary Videau, 1786. Owner plantation, nr. Eautaw Springs, S.C., 1759-95; served as lt. Royal Scots Regt. in campaigns against Cherokee Indians, 1761; mem. S.C. Provincial Congress from St. John's Parish, 1775; commd. capt. 2d S.C. Regt., served at occupation of Ft. Johnson, 1775; commd. lt. col. Continental Army, 1776, brig. gen. S.C. Militia, 1780; commanded only Revolutionary forces in S.C., 1780-81; continually disrupted Brit. communication and prevented orgn. of Loyalist forces by guerilla warfare tactics; nicknamed "Swamp Fox" by Brit. Gen. Tarlton because of tactics, hid in swamps between attacks; served at Battle of Eutaw Springs, 1781; mem. S.C. Senate, 1781, 82, 84; attended S.C. Constl. Conv., 1790; elected to fill unexpired term in S.C. Senate, 1791. Died St. John's Parish, S.C., Feb. 27, 1795; buried Belle Isle, St. Stephen's Parish, Berkeley County.

MARION, Robert, congressman; b. Berkeley Dist., S.C.; grad. U. Pa., 1784; mem. U.S. Ho. of Reps. from S.C., 9th-11th congresses, 1805-Dec. 4, 1810 (resigned).

MARKELEY, Philip Swenk, congressman; b. Skippack, nr. Norristown, Pa., July 2, 1789; studied law. Admitted to Pa. bar, 1810, began practice in Norristown; dep. state's atty. for Pa., 1819-20; mem. Pa. Senate, 1820-23; mem. U.S. Ho. of Reps. (Democrat) from Pa., 18th-19th congresses, 1823-27; apptd. naval officer of Phila. by Pres. Jackson; atty. gen. Pa., 1829. Died Norristown, Sept. 12, 1834; buried St. John's Episcopal Ch. Cemetery, Norristown.

MARKELL, Henry, congressman; b. Stone Arabia, N.Y., Feb. 7, 1792; s. Jacob Markell; attended common schs.; studied law. Admitted to the bar, practiced law; mem. U.S. Ho. of Reps. (Democrat) from N.Y., 19th-20th congresses, 1825-29. Died Palatine, N.Y., Aug. 30, 1831; buried St. Johnsville, N.Y.

MARKELL, Jacob, congressman; b. Schenectady County, N.Y., May 8, 1770; attended common schs.; children include Henry. Moved to Manheim, N.Y., 1790, engaged in farming; justice of peace; supr. Town of Manheim, 1797-1819, 24-29; mem. U.S. Ho. of Reps. (Federalist) from N.Y., 13th Congress, 1813-15; mem. N.Y. Assembly from Herkimer County, 1820. Died Manheim, Nov. 26, 1852; buried Snells Bush Cemetery, Manheim.

MARKHAM, William, colonial gov.; b. Eng., circa 1635; s. William Markham; m. Johannah, 1 dau. Received commn. as dep. gov. Pa. from cousin William Penn, 1681; presided over 1st Pa. Provincial Council, 1681, reorganized Upland (now Chester, Pa.) ct.; joined Nathaniel Allen and John Bezar in selecting site for City of Phila., 1681; became ordinary mem. Pa. Provincial Council upon arrival of William Penn in Pa., 1682; sec. Province of Pa., 1685-91; dep. gov. lower counties (now Del.), 1691-93; gov. Province of Pa., also lower counties, 1693-99; apptd. register gen. Pa., 1703. Died Phila., June 1, 1704.

MARKOE, Abraham, planter; b. St. Croix, W.I., July 2, 1727; s. Pierre and Elizabeth (Farrell) M.; m. Elizabeth Kenny, 1751; m. 2d, Elizabeth Baynton, Dec. 16, 1773; children—Peter, Abraham. Son of wealthy West Indian mcht. and planter; came to Phila., 1770; founder, capt. Phila. Light Horse (1st volunteer mil. assn. in Am.), 1774-76; built huge mansion in Phila., lived there on profits from his West Indian plantation. Died Phila., Aug. 28, 1806; buried Christ Ch. Graveyard, Phila.

MARKOE, Peter, poet, dramatist; b. Santa Cruz, W.I., circa 1752; s. Abraham and Elizabeth (Kenny) M. Admitted to bar at Lincoln's Inn, Eng., 1775; capt. Phila. Militia, 1775-76; resident of Phila. until 1792; landowner in Northumberland County, Pa. from 1785; poems include The Algerine Spy in Pennsylvania, 1787, The Storm, a Poem, 1788, The Times, 1788. Author: (play) The Patriot Chief, 1784; (poetry) Miscellaneous Poems, 1787. Died Phila., Jan. 30, 1792; buried Christ Ch. Cemetery, Phila.

MARKS, Elias, physician, educator; b. Charleston, S.C., Dec. 2, 1790; s. Humphrey and Frances Marks; grad. Coll. Phys. and Surg., N.Y.C., 1815; m. Jane Barham, 1817; m. 2d, Julia Warne, 1833. Moved to Columbia, 1817, practiced medicine, operated Columbia Female Acad.; owner, operator S.C. Female Inst., Barhamville, S.C., 1828-61, changed name to Female Collegiate Inst. 1835, provided instrn. at coll. devel from 1835, established reputation for broad curriculum and new teaching methods; lived in Washington, D.C., 1861-86. Author: Elfreide of Guldal, a Scandinavian Legend and Other Poems, 1850. Died Washington, June 22, 1886; buried Washington.

MARKS, William, senator; b. nr. "Fogg's Manor," Chester County, Pa., Oct. 13, 1778; studied law. Learned tanner's trade; admitted to Pa. bar, began practice in Pitts.; coroner Allegheny County (Pa.); mem. Pa. Ho. of Reps., 1810-19, speaker, 1813-19; comdr. Pa. Militia, 1814; mem. Pa. Senate, 1820-25; mem. U.S. Senate (Democrat) from Pa., 1825-31; resumed practice of law, Pitts.; moved to Beaver, Pa., 1850. Died Beaver, Apr. 10, 1858; buried old cemetery on Buffalo St., Beaver.

MARLING, James H., architect; b. Toronto, Can., 1857; ed., Toronto. Came to U.S., became partner (with James A. Johnson) in Marling & Johnson, archtl. firm, Buffalo, N.Y.; a designer Saturn Club, numerous residences, several bldgs. for Indsl. Expn. of 1889 (all Buffalo); pres. Buffalo chpt. A.I.A. Died May 24, 1895.

MARLING John Leake, editor, diplomat; b. Nashville, Tenn., Dec. 22, 1825; s. Samuel and Charlotte (Leake) M.; m. Mary March, May 16. 1850, 2 children. Admitted to Tenn. bar, 1850; editor, part-owner Nashville Daily Gazette, 1850-51, Nashville Daily Union, 1851-53; founder, editor Union and American, 1863-54; apptd. resident U.S. minister to Guatamala by Pres. Pierce, 1854. Died Nashville, Oct. 16, 1856.

MARMADUKE, John Sappington, army officer, gov. Mo.; b. nr. Arrow Rock, Mo., Mar. 14, 1833; s. Meredith Miles and Lavinia (Sappington) M.; grad. U.S. Mil. Acad., 1857. Commd. 2d lt. U.S. Army, 1857, assigned to 7th Inf. Regt.; served in Mormon War, 1858-60; became col. Mo. Militia, Confederate Army; commd. 1st lt. Confederate Army, 1861, then lt. col., fought at Battle of Shiloh; commd. brig. gen., 1863 (as of 1862), in command cavalry in Ark. and Mo.; promoted maj. gen., 1864; editor St. Louis Journal of Agr., 1871-74; mem. Mo. Ry. Commn., 1880-85; gov. Mo., 1884-87. Died Jefferson City, Mo., Dec. 28, 1887.

MARQUETT, Turner Mastin, ry. atty., legislator; b. Clark County O., July 9, 1829; s. John T. and Julia (Wright) M.; grad. Ohio U., Athens, 1855; m. Harriett Borders, 1861; m. 2d, Mrs. Aseneth Stetson, 1885; 4 children. Admitted to Neb. bar, 1857; mem. Neb. Territorial Ho. of Reps., 1857-60, Council of Neb. Territory, 1860-64; prominent in Neb. statehood movement; elected to U.S. Ho. of Reps. from Neb., June 1866 (in the event that Neb. was granted statehood), took office when Neb. became state Mar. 2, 1867, with only 2 days remaining in term; gen. atty. Missouri River and Burlington R.R. Co., 1869-94. Died Tampa, Fla., Dec. 22, 1894; buried Lincoln, Neb.

MARQUETTE, Jacques, explorer, missionary; b. Laon, France, June 1, 1637; s. Nicolas and Rose (de la Salle) M.; studied for novitiate, Nancy, France, circa 1655; studied philosophy, Pont-a-Mousson, 1656-57. Came to Am. 1666; became Roman Catholic missionary among Ottawa Indians in French colony of Que.; also active among Huron and Illinois tribes, 1666-71; wintered among Indians at Sault Ste. Marie, 1668-69; founded mission of St. Ignace on Straits of Mackinac, 1671; explored Mississippi River with Louis Joliet as far South as mouth of Arkansas River (named it Riviere de la Conception), 1672-73; at mission of St. Francis Xavier at De Pere, 1673-74; moved to Kaskaskia, Ill., 1675; died on way back to Sault Ste. Marie by way of East shore of Lake Michigan; several cities and counties, a railroad, a diocese, and univ. named in his honor. Died nr. mouth Marquette River, May 18, 1675; buried St. Ignance mission on No. shore of Straits of Mackinac.

MARR, Alem, congressman; b. Upper Mount Bethel, Pa., June 18, 1787; grad. Princeton, 1807; studied law. Admitted to Pa. bar, 1813, began practice in Danville; mem. U.S. Ho. of Reps. (Democrat) from Pa., 21st Congress, 1829-31. Died nr. Milton, Pa., Mar. 29, 1843; buried Milton Cemetery.

MARR, George Washington Lent, congressman; b. nr. Marrs Hill, Va., May 25, 1779; attended U. N.C. Atty. gen. for West Tenn., 1807-09, for 5th Tenn. Dist., 1809-13; served in Creek War, wounded in battle; mem. U.S. Ho. of Reps. from Tenn., 15th Congress, 1817-19; engaged in planting; moved to Obion County, Tenn., 1821; mem. Tenn. Constl. Conv., 1834; joined Whig Party. Died Island No. 10 (now washed away) in Mississippi River, nr. New Madrid, Mo., Sept. 5, 1856; buried Troy (Tenn.) Cemetery.

MARSH, Charles, congressman; b. Lebanon, Conn., July 10, 1765; grad Dartmouth, 1786; attended Litchfield (Conn.) Law Sch.; children include George Perkins. Admitted to the bar, 1788; began practice in Woodstock, Vt., 1788; U.S. dist. atty. for Vt. (apptd. by Pres. Washington), 1797-1801; mem. U.S. Ho. of Reps. (Federalist) from Vt., 14th Congress, 1815-17; founder Am. Colonization Soc., Washington, D.C.; resumed practice of law, Woodstock; trustee Dartmouth, 1809-49. Died Woodstock, Jan. 11, 1849; buried River St. Cemetery, Woodstock.

MARSH, George Perkins, diplomat; b. Woodstock, Vt., Mar. 15, 1801; s. Joseph and Susan (Perkins) M.; grad. Dartmouth, 1820, LL.D. (hon.), 1886; LL.D. (hon.), Harvard, 1856; m. Harriet Buell, Apr. 10, 1828; m. 2d, Caroline Crane, 1839; 2 children. Admitted to Vt. bar, 1825; mem. Vt. Gov.'s Council, 1835; mem. U.S. Ho. of Reps. (Whig) from Vt., 28th-31st congresses, 1843-49, opposed slavery, Mexican War; U.S. minister to Turkey, 1849-53, aided Sir Stratford Canning with refugees of East European Revolution; spl. agt. to investigate case of Jonas

King (an Am. missionary), Athens, Greece, 1852; recalled to Constantinople to settle case of Martin Koszta; fish commr. State of Vt., 1857-59; lectr. on English philosophy and etymology Columbia, Lowell Inst.; 1st U.S. minister to Italy, 1861-82; an authority on languages. Author: A Compendious Grammar of the Old-Northern or Icelandic Language, 1838; The Camel: His Organization, Habits and Uses, Considered with Reference to His Introduction into the United States, 1856; Lecture on the English Language, 1860; The Origin and History of the English Language, 1862; Man and Nature or Physical Geography as Modified by Human Action, 1864; contbr. to Oxford Dictionary, published 1880. Died Vallombrosa, Italy, July 23, 1882; buried Protestant Cemetery, Rome, Italy.

MARSH, James, coll. pres.; b. Hartford, Vt., July 19, 1794; s. Daniel and Marion (Harper) M.; grad. Dartmouth, 1817, Andover Theol. Sem., 1822; m. Lucia Wheelock, 1824. Prof. Oriental langs. Hampden-Sydney (Va.) Coll., 1824; ordained to ministry Congregational Ch., 1824; pres. U. Vt., Burlington, 1826-33, liberalized entrance requirements and curriculum, prof. philosophy, 1833-42; contbr. articles on edn. to Vt. Chronicle; adherent of romanticism, his writings influenced transcendentalist movement. Editor: Aid to Reflection (Coleridge), 1829, Selections from the Old English Writers on Practical Theology, 1830. Translator: The Spirit of Hebrew Poetry (Herder), 1833, Introduction to Historical Chronology (Hegewisch), 1837. Died Burlington, July 3, 1842; buried Burlington.

MARSH, John, clergyman; b. Wethersfield, Conn., Apr. 2, 1788; s. John and Ann (Grant) M.; grad. Yale, 1804. Licensed to preach in Congregational Ch., 1809; preached in several Conn. chs., 1809-18; ordained to ministry Congl. Ch., 1818; pastor Congl. ch., Haddam, Conn., 1818-33; active in temperance movement; sec., gen. agt. Conn. Temperance Soc., 1829; del. 1st Nat. Temperance Conv., Phila., 1833, sec. to that body; agt. Pa. Temperance Soc., 1833-36; editor Jour. of Am. Temperance Union, Phila., 1837-65 (later called Youth's Temperance Advocate, N.Y.C.). Author: An Epitome of General Ecclesiastical History from the Earliest Period to the Present Time, 1827; Autobiography, 1866. Died Bklyn., Aug. 4, 1868; buried Wethersfield.

MARSH, John, physician, land owner; b. South Danvers, Mass., June 5, 1799; s. John and Mary (Brown) M.; grad. Phillips' Andover Acad., 1819, Harvard, 1823; m. Marguerite Decouteaux, circa 1825, 1 son. Tutor to children at Ft. St. Anthony (now St. Paul, Minn.), 1822-23; apptd. sub-agt. to Sioux Indians at St. Peter (now in Minn.), 1824; sub-agt. for Indian affairs in Mich. Territory, 1826; justice of peace Prairie du Chien until 1833, while there wrote dictionary of Sioux lang.; participated in Black Hawk War on side of Sioux, 1832; in retail trade bus., Independence, Mo., 1833-35; went to Cal., 1836; practiced medicine, became land owner in San Joaquin Valley (including ranch nr. Antioch, Cal.), publicized advantages of settlement there among prospective immigrants in East. Died Martinez, Cal., Sept. 24, 1856.

MARSH, Othniel Charles, paleontologist; b. Lockport, N.Y., Oct. 29, 1831; s. Caleb and Mary (Peabody) M.; grad. Phillips Andover Acad., 1856, Yale, 1860; postgrad. Heidelberg, Berlin (both Germany), 1862-65. Prof. paleontology Yale, 1866-99; made many trips to Western U.S. to collect materials, from 1866; organized 1st Yale Scientific Expdn., 1870, explored Pliocene deposits of Neb. and Miocene deposits in No. Colo.; 1st to describe fossil serpents and flying reptiles of Western U.S.; apptd. vertebrate paleontologist to U.S. Geol. Survey, 1882; pres. Nat. Acad. Scis., 1883-95. Author: Dinocerata; A Monograph on the Extinct Toothed Birds of North America, 1880; Introduction and Succession of Vertebrate Life in America, 1877. Died New Haven, Conn., Mar. 18, 1899.

MARSH, Sylvester, inventor; b. Compton, N.H., Sept. 30, 1803; s. John and Mehitable (Percival) M. Owner meat packing business, Ashtabula, O., 1828-33; operated beef marketing firm, Chgo., 1833-37; in grain bus., Chgo., 1837-55, invented more efficient grain dryers and mfg. process for meal; used process to produce Marsh's Caloric Dry Meal, exported product, largely to W.I.; originated plan to build railroad up Mt. Washington, N.H. (railroad completed 1869); lived in Littleton, N.H., 1865-79; patented locomotive engines designed to ascend grades, cog rail for railroads, atmospheric brake for railroad cars; lived in Concord, N.H., 1879-84. Died Concord, Dec. 30, 1884; buried Concord.

MARSHALL, Alexander Keith, congressman; b. Buck Pond, nr. Versailles, Ky., Feb. 11, 1808; grad. med. dept. U. Pa., 1844. Practiced medicine, Nicholasville, Ky.; mem. Ky. Constl. Conv., 1849; mem. U.S. Ho. of Reps. (Am. Party rep.), 34th Congress, 1855-57; engaged in farming, Fayette County, Ky. Died nr. East Hickman, Ky., Apr. 28, 1884; buried Lexington (Ky.) Cemetery.

MARSHALL, Alfred, congressman; b. N.H., circa 1797. Mem. Me. Ho. of Reps., 1827-28, 34-35; served as gen. Me. Militia; mem. U.S. Ho. of Reps. (Democrat) from Me., 27th Congress, 1841-43; collector, Belfast, Me., 1846-49. Died China, Me., Oct. 2, 1868; buried Village Cemetery, China.

MARSHALL, Benjamin, mcht., mfr.; b. Huddersfield, Eng., 1782; m. Niobe Stanton, 1813, 1 son. Came to Am., 1803; became partner (with Francis Thompson) in cotton importing firm, N.Y.C.; founder (with 4 others) Black Ball Line, sailing packets monthly between N.Y.C. and Liverpool (Eng.), 1817; established (with Benjamin Walcott) cotton mfg. plant, nr. Utica, N.Y., 1824; built Hudson Print Works, cotton cloth mfg. firm, nr. Stockport, N.Y., 1827; sold out his interests in N.Y.C. enterprises, 1833, moved to Troy, N.Y.; managed textile mills, Troy, until 1858; pres. Troy & Schenectady R.R.; founder Marshall Infirmary, Troy, 1850. Died Troy, Dec. 2, 1858; buried Troy.

MARSHALL, Charles Henry, shipping exec.; b. Nantucket Island, Apr. 8, 1792; s. Charles and Hepzibah (Coffin) M.; m. Fidelia Wellman, 1822. Capt. ship Julius Caesar, running between Charleston and Liverpool (Eng.), 1816; capt. of packets of Black Ball Line, between N.Y.C. and Liverpool, 1822-34, gen. agt. Black Ball Line, 1834-36, mng. partner, 1836-65; built steamship United States, 1848; commr. of immigration, 1851-55; mem. Whig Party, later became a Republican; active in Union Defense Com., N.Y.C., during Civil War. Died N.Y.C., Sept. 23, 1865; buried N.Y.C.

MARSHALL, Christopher, pharmacist; b. Dublin, Ireland, Nov. 6, 1709; married twice; m. 2d, Abigail, 1782. Came to Am., 1727, became pharmacist in Phila.; supported colonial cause from 1773; active in enforcement of non-importation agreements and obtaining supplies for mil. forces, 1774-75; del. Provincial Congress in Phila., 1775; mem. Com. of Safety, Lancaster, Pa., 1777-80; kept diary which is important hist. source for Revolutionary period, portions published as Extracts from the Diary of Christopher Marshall, 1877. Died Phila., May 4, 1797; buried Phila.

MARSHALL, Daniel, clergyman; b. Windsor, Conn., 1706; s. Thomas and Mary (Drake) M.; m. Hannah Drake, Nov. 11, 1742; m. 2d, Martha Stearns, June 23, 1747; 3 children. Converted by George Whitefield, 1744, became preacher to Mohawk Indians in upper Susquehanna River region, 1747-48; preacher in Baptist sect in No. Va., 1748; became pracher of Separate Baptists, Sandy Creek Ch., Guilford County, N.C., 1755; ordained pastor Abbot's Creek (N.C.) Separate Bapt. Ch., 1758; became pastor Separate Bapt. Ch. nr. Ga. line in S.C., circa 1763; founded 1st Bapt. Ch. in Ga., nr. Kiokee Creek, 1772, remained there rest of life; an organizer Ga. Assn. of Baptists, 1784. Died Ga., Nov. 2, 1784.

MARSHALL, Edward Chauncey, congressman; b. Woodford County, Ky., June 29, 1821; attended Centre Coll., Danville, Ky.; grad. Transylvania U., Lexington, Ky.; attended Washington Coll. (now Washington and Lee U.), 1832-33; studied law. Admitted to the bar; moved to San Francisco, later to Sonora, Cal., practiced law; served in Mexican War; mem. U.S. Ho. of Reps. (Democrat) from Cal., 32d Congress, 1851-53; settled in Marysville, Cal., Practiced law; unsuccessful candidate for U.S. Senate, 1856; moved to Ky., practiced law, 21 years; returned to San Francisco, 1877, practiced law; atty. gen. Cal., 1883-86. Died San Francisco, July 9, 1893; buried Mountain View Cemetery, Oakland, Cal.

MARSHALL, Humphrey, botanist; b. Chester County, Pa., Oct. 10, 1722; s. Abraham and Mary (Hunt) M.; m. Sarah Pennock, Sept. 16, 1748; m. 2d, Margaret Minshall, Jan. 10, 1788. Engaged in farming, Chester County, Pa., from 1748; built 1st conservatory for plants in area, circa 1768; constructed hot house and bot. garden with collection of fgn. and domestic plants, at his home, Marshallton, Pa.; corresponded with Dr. John Fothergill and Peter Collinson in Eng.; mem. Am. Philos. Soc. Author: Arbustrum Americanum, the American Grove (list of native forest trees and shrubs), 1785. Died Marshallton, Nov. 5, 1801.

MARSHALL, Humphrey, senator; b. Orlean, Va., 1760; s. John and Mary (Quisenberry) M.; m. Anna Maria Marshall, Sept. 18, 1784, 3 children including Thomas Alexander, John Jay. Served in Am. Revolution, 1778-81, rose to rank capt.-lt. Va. Arty., 1781; moved to Ky., 1782; dep. surveyor Fayette County (Ky.), 1782; received gift of 4000 acres of land from Va. for his Revolutionary services, 1782; del. Danville Conv. to consider separation of Ky. from Va., 1787; mem. Va. Conv. (from Ky.) to ratify U.S. Constn., 1788; moved to Woodford County (Ky.), became county surveyor; mem. Ky. Ho. of Reps., 1793, 94, 1807, 08, 09, 23; mem. U.S. Senate from Ky., 1795-1801, voted for Jay Treaty, became disliked by people of Ky.; instrumental in exposing conspira of Aaron Burr, 1806; wrote articles in paper Western World under name "Observer" to expo U.S. conspirators with Spain, 1860; wounded in du with Henry Clay, 1809; established Am. Repu lic (only Federalist newspaper in Ky.), 181 changed name to Harbinger, sold it, 1825; Au thor: The History of Kentucky (1st history Ky.), 1 vol., 1812, 2 vols., 1824. Died Lexingto Ky., July 1, 1841; buried "Glen Willis," Lee town, Ky.

MARSHALL, Humphrey, diplomat, congres man; b. Frankfort, Ky., Jan. 13, 1812; s. Joh Jay and Anna (Birney) M.; grad. U.S. Mil. Acad 1832; m. Frances McAllister, Jan. 23, 183 6 children. Served as lt. Mounted Rangers, Bla Hawk expdn., 1832-33; admitted to Ky. bar, 183 practiced law, Frankfort, 1833-34, Louisville, Ky 1834-36, 67-72; mem. Frankfort City Counci 1836; commd capt. Ky. Militia, 1836, maj., 183 lt. col., 1841; col. 1st Ky. Cavalry, Mexican Wa 1846; mem. U.S. Ho. of Reps. from Ky., 31st 32d, 34th-35th congresses, 1849-Aug. 4, 1852 1855-59; U.S. minister to China, 1852-54; serve as brig. gen. Confederate Army, Civil War, 1861 63; moved to Richmond, Va., 1863; mem. 2 Confederate Congress, 1864-65; moved to New Or leans, 1865, until disfranchise removed by Con gress. Died Louisville, Mar. 28, 1872; buried Stat Cemetery, Frankfort.

MARSHALL, James Markham, landowner; b. Fau quier County, Va., Mar. 12, 1764; s. Thomas an Mary (Keith) M.; ed. privately; m. Hester Morris Apr. 1795, 6 children. Served with 1st Va. Arty. Va. Militia, 1779-82; moved to Ky., 1788, becam active in politics as a Federalist; worked for Ky statehood; returned to Va., circa 1793; purchase (with his brother John, also Raleigh Colston an Henry Lee) Fairfax lands in Va. (approximatel 180,000 acres), 1794-95; asst. judge of D.C., 1801 02; practiced law, Winchester, Va., from 1802 also engaged in mgmt. of lands. Died Winchester Apr. 26, 1848.

MARSHALL, James Wilson, discoverer Cal. gold b. Hunterdon County, N.J., Oct. 8, 1810; s. Phili and Sarah (Wilson) M. Settled nr. Ft. Leavenworth Kan., circa 1838, engaged in farming; became ranch er in Sacramento Valley, Cal., 1844; served wit John C. Fremont's Co. in Bear Flag War, 1846 erected sawmill in partnership with John A. Sutter nr. Sutter's fort, 1847-48, discovered gold (whil building mill), Jan. 24, 1848; his claims wer ignored by masses of gold seekers in following year failed in his sawmill operation, moved to Caloma, Cal., became a gardener. Died nr. Caloma, Aug. 10, 1885.

MARSHALL, John, chief justice U.S. Supreme Ct.; b. Germantown, Va., Sept. 24, 1755; s. Thomas and Mary (Keith) M.; attended Coll. William and Mary, May-June 1780; m. Mary Willis Ambler, Jan. 3, 1783, 10 children including Thomas. Influenced by writings of Alexander Pope, Adam Smith and Edmund Burke in early life; served in Revolutionary War, 1775-81, lt., then capt. 3d Va. Regt. (became part of 11th Va. Regt.), 1777, fought in battles of Brandywine, Germantown, Monmouth and at Valley Forge; admitted to bar, Fauquier County, Va., 1780; joined Continental Army under Von Steuben, resigned, 1781; del. Va. Ho. of Burgesses, 1780, 82-88; mem. Va. Exec. Council, 1782-95; presented by father with Fauquier County estate; city recorder Richmond (Va.), 1783-85; del. Va. Conv. to ratify U.S. Constn., 1788; commd. to purchase Fairfax estate, 1793-94; declined post of atty. gen. U.S., 1795; defended Jay Treaty, 1795-96; argued his only case before U.S. Supreme Ct. (Ware vs. Hylton), 1796; declined post of minister to France, 1796; mem. spl. commn. to France to demand redress and reparation for hostile actions (XYZ Affair), 1797-98 (mission failed when French agts. asked for bribes); declined seat on U.S. Supreme Ct., 1798; mem. U.S. Ho. of Reps. (Federalist) from Va., 6th Congress, 1799-June 7, 1800, successfully defended John Adams on charge of usurping judicial powers; declined post of U.S. sec. of war, 1800; U.S. sec. of state, 1800-01; chief justice U.S. Supreme Ct., 1801-35; reformed ct. system as result of case Talbot vs. Seeman (I Cranch, 1) by use of "the unanimous court" or the ct. speaking through chief justice, 1801; declared "doctrine of judicial review" in case Marbury vs. Madison (I Cranch, 137); presided in trial of Aaron Burr for treason, 1807, saved Burr from hanging; ruled that the obligation of contract held even when it involved a dishonest act in Fletcher vs. Peck (6 Cranch, 87), 1810; asserted power of Supreme Ct. over state cts. whenever fed. rights were involved in Martin vs. Hunter's Lessee (1816), Cohens vs. Virginia (1821); maintained a charter of incorporation as a contract within meaning of Constn. in Dartmouth College vs. Woodward, 1819; stated that State of Md. could not tax Balt. br. Bank of U.S., asserted supremacy of fed. govt. over states in McCulloch vs. Maryland, 1819; issued 519 decisions out of 1,215 cases; mem. Va. Constl. Conv., 1829.

Author: The Life of George Washington, 5 vols., 1804-07; prepared autobiography for Delaplaine's Repository, 1818. Died Phila., July 6, 1835; buried New Burying Ground, Richmond, Va.

MARSHALL, Louis, physician, educator; b. Fauquier County, Va., Oct. 7, 1773; s. Thomas and Mary (Keith) M.; studied at U. Edinburgh (Scotland), 1794-95; studied medicine, Paris, France, 1795; m. Agatha Smith, 1800, 6 children. Began practice of medicine, Woodford County, Ky., 1799; conducted classical sch. for boys at his home, nr. Frankfort, Ky., circa 1800-30; pres. Washington Coll. (now Washington and Lee U.), Lexington, Va., 1830-34, during his adminstrn. abandoned conventional sysetm of classes and all disciplinary rules; conducted sch. for boys, Frankfort, 1834-38; prof. langs. Transylvania U., Ky., 1838-44, acting pres., 1838-40; taught sch. irregularly after 1844, lived mainly in Covington, Ky. Died "Buck Pond," Woodford County, Apr. 1866; buried Frankfort.

MARSHALL, Samuel Scott, congressman; b. nr. Shawneetown, Ill., Mar. 12, 1821; attended Cumberland Coll., Ky.; studied law. Admitted to the bar, 1845, began practice in McLeansboro, Ill.; mem. Ill. Ho. of Reps., 1846-47; state's atty. for 3d Ill. Jud. Circuit, 1847-48; circuit ct. judge, 1851-54, 61-64; del. Democratic nat. convs., 1860, 64, 80; del. Union Nat. Conv., Phila., 1866; mem. U.S. Ho. of Reps. (Dem.), 34th-35th, 39th-43d congresses, 1855-59, 65-75, candidate for speaker, 1867; unsuccessful candidate for U.S. Senate, 1861; pres. bd. mgrs. Hamilton Coll., 1875-80. Died McLeansboro, July 26, 1890; buried Odd Fellows Cemetery, McLeansboro.

MARSHALL, Thomas, surveyor; b. Westmoreland County, Va., Apr. 2, 1730; s. John and Elizabeth (Markham) M.; m. Mary Keith, 1754, 15 children including Chief Justice John, James Markham, Louis. Began farming, Prince William County, Va., 1754; became land surveyor, friend of George Washington; helped survey Fairfax lands, Va.; justice of peace, county surveyor Fauquier County, Va., 1759-61; lived at "Oak Hill" plantation, Fauquier County, 1773-83; mem. Va. Ho. of Burgesses, 1761-67, 69-73, 75; sheriff Fauquier County, 1767-69; served as maj. 3d Va. Regt., 1776, as col. Va. Arty. regt. in battles of Brandywine Creek and Trenton, 1777-81; surveyor Ky. lands for State of Va., 1781-83; moved to Woodford County, Ky., 1783, purchased large tracts of land there; surveyor of revenue for Dist. of Ohio, circa 1787-97. Died Woodford County, June 22, 1802.

MARSHALL, Thomas Alexander, congressman; b. Versailles, Ky., Jan. 15, 1794; s. Humphrey and Mary Marshall; grad. Yale, 1815; m. Eliza Price, Nov. 26, 1816. Admitted to Ky. bar, 1817; moved to Paris, Ky., 1819; mem. Ky. Ho. of Reps., 1827-28, 63-65; mem. U.S. Ho. of Reps from Ky., 22d-23d congresses, 1831-35, active in tariff debates, advocating higher rates, 1832; judge Ky. Ct. of Appeals, 1835-56, chief justice, 1847-51, 66-67; prof. law Transylvania Coll., Lexington, Ky., 1836-49; moved to Louisville, Ky., 1859. Died Louisville, Apr. 17, 1871; buried Lexington (Ky.) Cemetery.

MARSHALL, Thomas Francis, congressman; b. Frankfort, Ky., June 7, 1801; studied law. Admitted to Ky. bar, began practice in Versailles, 1828; mem. Ky. Ho. of Reps., 1832-36, 38-39, 54; moved to Louisville, Ky., 1833; mem. U.S. Ho. of Reps., 27th Congress, 1841-43; served as capt. volunteers during Mexican War; moved to Chgo., 1856; returned to Ky., practiced law. Died nr. Versailles, Sept. 22, 1864; buried State Cemetery, Frankfort.

MARSHALL, William Rainey, army officer, gov. Minn.; b. Boone County, Mo., Oct. 17, 1825; s. Joseph M. and Abigail (Shaw) M.; m. Abby Langford, 1854. Surveyor govt. lands in Wis., 1847; mem. Wis. Legislature, 1848; established gen. store, East Minneapolis, Minn., 1849; leader movement for devel. of Minn. Territory; mem. 1st Minn. Territorial Legislature, 1849; chmn. conv. which organized Republican Party in Minn.; founder St. Paul Daily Press, 1861; commd. lt. col. 7th Minn. Inf., fought against Sioux outbreaks, 1862, promoted col., 1863, brevetted brig. gen., 1864; gov. Minn., 1867-69; 1st railroad and warehouse commr. in Minn., 1874-82; pres. Minn. Hist. Soc., 1868, sec., 1893-94. Died Pasadena, Cal., Jan. 8, 1896.

MARSIGLIA, Gherlando, artist; b. Italy, 1792. Came to Am., 1817, settled in N.Y.C.; began exhibiting at Am. Acad., 1824; a founder, charter mem. N.A.D., 1826, frequent exhibitor, until 1850; exhibited at Boston Athenaeum, Pa. Acad. Died N.Y.C., Sept. 4, 1850.

MARSTON, Gilman, senator, congressman; b. Oxford, N.H., Aug. 20, 1811; grad. Dartmouth, 1837, law dept. Harvard, 1840. Admitted to N.H. bar, began practice in Exeter, 1841; mem. N.H. Ho. of Reps., 1845-49, 72-73, 76-78; del. N.H. constl. convs., 1850, 76; mem. U.S. Ho. of Reps. (Republican) from N.H., 36th-37th, 39th congresses, 1859-63, 65-67; served as col. 10th Regt., N.H. Volunteer Inf., U.S. Army, during Civil War, 1861; brig. gen. U.S. Volunteers, 1862-65; declined appointment as gov. Ida. Territory, 1870; mem. U.S. Senate (filled vacancy), Mar. 4-June 18, 1889. Died Exeter, July 3, 1890; buried Exeter Cemetery.

MARTIN, A.C., architect; b. 1835; grad. Harvard Scientific Sch., 1856; studied architecture under Arthur Gilman, also traveled and studied in Europe. Practiced architecture, Boston; credited with design of many hotels, chs., pvt. homes in Boston area; mem. A.I.A.; a founder Boston Soc. Architects. Died 1879.

MARTIN, Alexander, senator, gov. N.C.; b. New Haven County, N.J., 1740 s. Hugh and Jane M.; A.B., Coll. of N.J. (now Princeton), 1756; never married. Moved to Salisbury, N.C., mcht., justice of peace, 1764, dep. King's atty., 1766, judge, 1774-75; admitted to N.C. bar, 1772; mem. N.C. Ho. of Commons, 1773-74, 2d, 3d, N.C. provincial congresses, 1775; commd. lt. col. 2d N.C. Regt., Continental Army, 1775, col., 1776, participated in defense of Charleston, S.C.; served under Washington in battles of Brandywine and Germantown, arrested for cowardly behavior at Battle of Germantown, court-martialed, acquitted, resigned commn., 1777; mem. N.C. Senate, 1778-82, 85, 87-88, 1804-05, speaker, 1778-82, 85; 1805; mem. N.C. Bd. War then N.C. Council Extraordinary, 1780-81; acting gov. N.C., 1781-82; gov., 1782-84, 89-92, advocated clemency for Tories, encouraged edn., more power for Continental Congress, growth of agr., commerce and mfg., internal improvements by convict labor. mem. Continental Congress from N.C., 1786; mem. N.C. Conv. which ratified U.S. Constn., 1787; trustee U. N.C., 1790-1807, pres. bd., 1792-93; mem. U.S. Senate (Republican)from N.C., 1793-99 (not re-elected because he voted for Alien and Sedition Acts). Died estate "Danbury" nr. Crawford (now Danbury), N.C., Nov. 2, 1807; buried "Danbury."

MARTIN, Auguste Marie, clergyman; b. St. Malo, France, Feb. 1, 1803. Ordained priest Roman Catholic Ch., Rennes, France, 1828; did parish work, also taught at Collège Royal, 1828-39; vicar gen. Vincennes, circa 1839-45; came to U.S., 1845; became vicar gen. New Orleans, 1849-53; apptd. 1st vicar Diocese of Natchitoches (now Alexandria), La., 1853; attended 2d Plenary Council of Balt., 1866, Vatican Council, 1869-70. Died Natchitoches, Sept. 29, 1875.

MARTIN, Barclay, congressman; b. Edgefield Dist., S.C., Dec. 17, 1802; studied law, Columbia, Tenn. Admitted to Tenn. bar, practiced law; mem. Tenn. Ho. of Reps., 1839-40, 47-49, 51-53; Tenn. Senate, 1841-43; mem. U.S. Ho. of Reps. (Democrat) from Tenn., 29th Congress, 1845-47; trustee Columbia Athenaeum, 1852-90. Died Columbia, Nov. 8, 1890; buried Zion Cemetery, Columbia.

MARTIN, Benjamin Franklin, congressman; b. nr. Farmington, Va. (now W.Va.), Oct. 2, 1828; grad. Allegheny Coll., Meadville, Pa., 1854; studied law. Taught schs., Fairmont, Va. (now W.Va.); admitted to the bar, began practice of law, 1856; mem. W.Va. Constl. Conv., 1872; del. Democratic Nat. Conv., Balt., 1872; mem. U.S. Ho. of Reps. (Dem.) from W.Va., 45th-46th congresses, 1877-81; Dem. presdl. elector, 1884; del. at large Dem. Nat. Conv., St. Louis, 1888; resumed practice of law, Grafton, W.Va. Died Grafton, Jan. 20, 1895; buried Woodlawn Cemetery, Fairmont.

MARTIN, Edward Livingston, congressman; b. Seaford, Del., Mar. 29, 1837; attended Del. Coll.; grad. U. Va., 1859, studied law, 1866. Clk., Va. Senate, 1863-65; del. Dem. nat. convs., 1864, 72, 76, 80, 84; admitted to Del. bar, 1866; practiced law, Dover, Del., 1866-67; engaged in farming and horticulture, Seaford; dir. Del. Bd. Agr.; pres. Peninsula Hort. Soc.; lectr. Del. Grange; commr. to settle boundary dispute between Del. and N.J., 1873-75; mem. U.S. Ho. of Reps. (Dem.) from Del., 46th-47th congresses, 1879-83; resumed hort. pursuits; twice unsuccessful candidate for U.S. Senate. Died Seaford, Jan. 22, 1897; buried St. Luke's Episcopal Churchyard, Seaford.

MARTIN, Elbert Sevier, congressman; b. nr. Jonesville, Va., 1829; attended Emory and Henry Coll., 1845-48. Engaged in merc. bus., Jonesville; mem. U.S. Ho. of Reps. (Am. Party rep.) from Va., 36th Congress, 1859-61; served as capt. of a volunteer co. formed in Jonesville during Civil War; moved to Dallas, Tex., 1870, engaged in newspaper publishing. Died Dallas, Sept. 3, 1876.

MARTIN, Francois-Xavier, jurist, author; b. Marseilles, France, Mar. 17, 1762; LL.D. (hon.), Harvard, 1841, also U. Nashville. Settled at New Bern, N.C., 1786; admitted to N.C. bar, 1789; compiled revision of Laws of the State of North Carolina; borough mem. N.C. Ho. of Commons, 1806, U.S. judge Miss. Territory, 1809, Territory of Orleans, 1810-13; 1st atty. gen. La., 1813-15; judge La. Supreme Ct., 1815-37, chief justice, 1837-45. Author: A General Digest of the Territorial and State Laws of Louisiana, 1816; History of Louisiana, 1827; History of North Carolina, 1829. Died New Orleans, Dec. 10, 1846.

MARTIN, Frederick Stanley, congressman; b. Rutland County, Vt., Apr. 25, 1794; attended local schs., New Hartford, N.Y. Employed in merc. bus., Whitehall, Vt., 1810; became steward on U.S. Govt. boat on Lake Champlain; sailor on board a merchantman; settled in Olean, N.Y., 1818, operated a hotel, engaged in lumber bus.; entered merc. bus., 1831; mem. bd. suprs. of Olean, 1830-31, 36, 38; apptd. maj. 226th Regt., N.Y. Militia, 1826, promoted lt. col., 1830, resigned, 1833; postmaster of Olean, 1830-39; judge county cts., 1840-45; involved in constrn. Genesee Valley Canal; mem. N.Y. Senate, 1847-49; N.Y. Assembly, 1850-51; mem. U.S. Ho. of Reps. (Whig) from N.Y., 32d Congress, 1851-53. Died Olean, June 28, 1865; buried Oak Lawn Cemetery, reinterred Mt. View Cemetery, Olean, 1896.

MARTIN, Henry Austin, surgeon; b. London, Eng., July 23, 1824; s. Henry James Martin; grad. Harvard Med. Sch., 1845; m. Frances Coffin Crosby, 1848, 5 children including Stephen Crosby, Francis Coffin. Practiced medicine, Roxbury, Mass.; apptd. surgeon U.S. Army, 1861, served at Ft. Monroe, later in Mo.; became med. dir. at Norfolk, Portsmouth and Newbern, Va.; apptd. surgeon-in-chief 1st Div., II Corp., Army of Potomac, circa 1864; brevetted lt. col., 1865, ret., 1865; introduced smallpox vaccine produced from cowpox (together with innoculation method) to U.S., 1870; develped use of rubber bandage for ulcers of leg, tracheotomy operation without tube. Died Boston, Dec. 7, 1884.

MARTIN, Henry Newell, physiologist; b. Newry, County Down, Ireland, July 1, 1848; B.Sc., Cambridge (Eng.) U.; M.B., U. London (Eng.); m. Hetty Pegram, 1878. Fellow, Trinity Coll., Cambridge U., 1874-76; came to U.S., 1876; prof. biology Johns Hopkins U., 1876-93, specialized in study of cardiac physiology; discovered method of studying isolated mammalian heart; founder, editor Johns Hopkins U. Studies from Biol. Lab., 1877-93; Croonian lectr. Royal Soc. London, 1883; returned permanently to Eng., 1893. Author: (with Julian Huxley) A Course of Practical Instruction in Elementary Biology, 1875; The Human Body, 1881; Physiological Papers, 1895. Died Burley-in-Wharfedale, Yorkshire, Eng., Oct. 27, 1896.

MARTIN, Homer Dodge, painter; b. Albany, N.Y., Oct. 28, 1836; s. Homer and Sarah (Dodge) M.; m. Elizabeth Gilbert Davis, June 21, 1861, several children including Ralph. Itinerant landscape painter, upper N.Y. State, until 1865; maintained studio, N.Y.C., 1865-82, in France, 1882-86; illustrator for mags., N.Y.C., for a time; exhibited for 1st time at N.A.D., 1857, became asso., 1868; became mem. Century Club, N.Y.C., 1866; his talent not recognized until after his death. Paintings include: Lake Sanford; Andante, Fifth Symphony; The Church at Criqueboeuf; Mussel Gatherers; Low Tide—Villerville; Ontario Sand Dunes; Blossoming Trees; The Sun Worshippers; Westchester Hills; Hanfleur Light; Old Manor; View on the Seine; Normandy Farm; Adirondack Scenery. Died St. Paul, Minn., Feb. 12, 1897.

MARTIN, James Green, army officer; b. Elizabeth City, N.C., Feb. 14, 1819; s. William and Sophia (Dauge) M.; grad. U.S. Mil. Acad., 1840; m. Marian Read, July 12, 1844; m. 2d, Hetty King, Feb. 8, 1858; at least 4 children. Fought in battles of Monterey, Vera Cruz, Churubusco and Contreras during Mexican War; commd. 1st lt. U.S. Army, 1847, capt., 1847; brevetted maj., 1847; adjutant gen. 10 regts. of N.C. Militia, 1861, commd. maj. gen. in command all state forces, supr. entire defense of state, 1861; commd. brig. gen. Confederate States Army, 1862; in command N.C. dist. 1862; command West dist. N.C., 1864-65. Died Asheville, N.C., Oct. 4, 1878.

MARTIN, John Alexander, journalist, army officer, gov. Kan.; b. Brownsville, Pa., Mar. 10, 1839; s. James and Jane (Crawford) M.; m. Ida Challiss, June 1, 1871, 8 children. Purchased newspaper Atchison-Kansas (renamed Freedom's Champion) 1858, publisher 1858-89; chmn. Atchison com. Central Republican Com., 1859-84 (except for period during Civil War); sec. Wyandotte Constl. Conv.; mem. 1st Kan. Senate from Atchison and Brown dists., 1858; del. to territorial conv., Lawrence, Kan., 1860; commd. lt. col. 8th Kan. Volunteer Inf., U.S. Army, 1861, col., 1862; provost marshal of Leavenworth (Kan.), 1861, Nashville (Tenn.), 1862-63, later brigade comdr.; retired from U.S. Army, 1864; mayor Atchison, 1865; mem. Nat. Rep. Com., 1868-84; mem. Kan. Rep. Com., 1870; gov. Kan., 1884-88, enforced prohibition law, successful in dealing with railroad labor troubles, 1885-88. Author: Military History of the Eighth Kansas Veteran Volunteer Infantry, 1869. Died Atchison, Oct. 2, 1889.

MARTIN, John Blennerhasset, artist; b. Bandon, County Cork, Ireland, Sept. 5, 1797; studied engraving, N.Y.C. Came to Am., circa 1815; moved to Richmond, Va., circa 1817; engraver and lithographer; specialized in portrait painting; visited other cities to obtain commns.; ruling elder Presbyn. Ch., Richmond, 1834-57. Died Richmond, Oct. 22, 1857.

MARTIN, John Preston, congressman; b. nr. Jonesville, Va., Oct. 11, 1811. Moved to Prestonsburg, Ky., 1828; mem. Ky. Ho. of Reps., 1841-43; mem. U.S. Ho. of Reps. (Democrat) from Ky., 29th Congress, 1845-47; mem. Ky. Senate, 1855-59; del. Dem. Nat. Conv., Cincinnati, 1856. Died Prestonburg, Dec. 23, 1862; buried May Cemetery, Prestonsburg.

MARTIN, Joshua Lanier, gov. Ala., congressman; b. Blount County, Tenn., Dec. 5, 1799; attended country schs.; studied law, Maryville, Tenn. and Russellville, Ala.; children include John Mason. Admitted to Ala. bar, practiced in Athens; mem. Ala. Ho. of Reps., 1822-28, 53; state solicitor, 1827-31; judge circuit ct., 1834; chancellor of Middle Ala., 1841; mem. U.S. Ho. of Reps. (Democrat) from Ala., 24th-25th congresses, 1835-39; gov. Ala., 1845-47; resumed practice of law, Tuscaloosa. Died Tuscaloosa, Nov. 2, 1856; buried Evergreen Cemetery, Tuscaloosa.

MARTIN, Josiah, colonial gov.; b. Antigua, B.W.I., Apr. 23, 1737; s. Col. Samuel and Sarah (Wyke) M.; m. Elizabeth Martin, 1761, 8 children. Commd. royal gov. N.C., 1771, in controversy with legislature (which formed own govt. 1774) throughout adminstrn., forced to flee, 1775; formulated plan for subjugation of So. colonies, approved by Brit. Govt., but not carried out; served in Brit. Army during Am. Revolution. Died London, Eng., July 1786.

MARTIN, Luther, Continental congressman, state ofcl.; b. New Brunswick, N.J., Feb. 9, 1744; s. Benjamin and Hannah M.; grad. Coll. of N.J. (now Princeton), 1766; m. Maria Cresap, Dec. 25, 1783; children—Maria, Eleanora. Taught sch., Queenstown, Md., 1766-69; moved to Somerset County, Md., studied law, 1769; supt. grammar sch., Onancock, Va., 1770; admitted to Va. bar, 1771; mem. Annapolis Conv. which drafted protests of Md. to British, 1774; published To the Inhabitants of the Peninsula between the Delaware River and the Chesapeake to the Southward of the British Lines reply to appeal by Lord William Howe, 1777; 1st atty. gen. Md., 1778-1805; mem. Continental Congress from Md., 1785; mem. U.S. Constl. Conv., Phila., 1787, opposed strong central govt.; mem. Md. Conv. which ratified U.S. Constn., 1788; wrote and published letters in Balt. newspapers defending Capt. Michael Cresap (his father-in-law) charged with murdering family of an Indian chief, 1797-98; wrote pamphlet Modern Gratitude (includes autobiog. sketch of his early life), 1802; Federalist counsel for Judge Samuel Chase in his impeachment trial, 1804; a counsel in treason trial of Aaron Burr, 1807; chief justice Ct. Oyer and Termines for City and County of Balt., 1813-16; atty. gen. Md., 1818-22, involved in case of McCulloch vs. State of Md., 1819, favored states rights but Chief Justice John Marshall declared taxing a U.S. Bank unconstl.; suffered paralytic stroke 1820; Md. Legislature passed act requiring every lawyer of state to pay annual license tax of $5.00 to be turned over to trustees for Martin's use, 1821, repealed, 1823; spent rest of life in home of Aaron Burr, N.Y.C. Died N.Y.C., July 10, 1826; buried Trinity Cemetery, N.Y.C.

MARTIN, Morgan Lewis, congressman, businessman; b. Martinsburg, N.Y., Mar. 31, 1805; grad. Hamilton Coll., Clinton, N.Y., 1824; studied law, Lowville, N.Y. Admitted to Mich. bar, 1827, began practice in Detroit; moved to Green Bay, Mich. Terr. (now Wis.), 1827; mem. Mich. Terr. Legislature, 1831-35; organized (with M. Strong) Democratic party in Wis., 1838; mem. upper ho. Wis. Terr. Legislature, 1838-44, pres., 1842-43; territorial del. Congress, 1845-47; pres. 2d Wis. State Constl. Conv., 1847-48; mem. Wis. State Assembly, 1855, 74, Wis. Senate, 1858-59; served as maj., paymaster in Civil War, 1861-65; chief promoter Fox-Wisconsin River improvement projects, circa 1829-79; purchased much of land that was to become Milw., (with S. Juneau) mapped out city, erected many early bldgs.; prominent in banking and ry. activities; U.S. Indian agt., 1866-69; judge Brown County (Wis.), 1875-87. Died Green Bay, Dec. 10, 1887; buried Woodlawn Cemetery, Green Bay.

MARTIN, Robert Nicols, congressman; b. Cambridge, Md., Jan. 14, 1798; attended pub. schs.; studied law. Admitted to Md. bar; practiced law, Princess Anne, Md., 1819-27; mem. U.S. Ho. of Reps. (Democrat) from Md., 19th Congress, 1825-27; practiced law, Balt.; chief justice Western Jud. Dist. of Md., 1845-51; judge Balt. Superior Ct., 1859-67; prof. internat. law U. Md., 1867-70. Died Saratoga Springs, N.Y., July 20, 1870; buried Christ Protestant Episcopal Ch. Cemetery, Cambridge, Md.

MARTIN, William Dobbin, congressman; b. Martintown, S.C., Oct. 20, 1789; attended Litchfield (Conn.) Law Sch. Admitted to S.C. bar, 1811, began practice in Edgefield; moved to Coosawhatchie, S.C., 1813; mem. S.C. Ho. of Reps. for St. Luke's Parish, 1816-18; clk. S.C. Senate, 1818-26; mem. U.S. Ho. of Reps. (Democrat) from S.C., 20th-21st congresses, 1827-31; judge circuit cts. of law and appeal, 1831-33. Died Charleston, S.C., Nov. 17, 1833; buried St. Michael's Ch. Cemetery, Charleston.

MARTINDALE, Henry Clinton, congressman; b. Berkshire County, Mass., May 6, 1780; grad. Williams Coll., 1800; studied law. Admitted to N.Y. bar; practiced law, Sandy Hill, N.Y., 1801-60; surrogate Washington County (N.Y.), 1816-19, dist. atty., 1821-28; mem. U.S. Ho. of Reps. (Whig) from N.Y., 18th-21st congresses, 1823-31; canal appraiser State of N.Y., 1840-43. Died Sandy Hill, Apr. 22, 1860; buried Kingsbury (N.Y.) Cemetery.

MARTINDALE, John Henry, lawyer, army officer; b. Hudson Falls, N.Y., Mar. 20, 1815; s. Henry C. Martindale; grad. U.S. Mil. Acad., 1835; m. Emeline Holden, June 16, 1840, 5 children. Admitted to N.Y. bar, 1838; organizer volunteer regts. in Civil War; commd. gen. U.S. Volunteers, 1861, served at battles of Yorktown, Mechanicsville, Gaine's Mill, Malvern Hill, Cold Harbor, Bermuda Hundred; mil. gov. D.C.; brevetted maj. gen. volunteers, 1865; atty. gen. N.Y., 1866-68; v.p. bd. mgrs. Nat. Asylum of Disabled Volunteer Soldiers, 1868-79. Died Nice, France, Dec. 13, 1881.

MARTINEAU, Harriet, English author; b. Norwich, Eng., June 12, 1802; d. Thomas and Elizabeth (Rankin) Martineau. Came to U.S. on visit, 1834-39; became asso. with new Abolitionist Party in U.S.; wrote article The Martyr Age of the United States in Westminster Rev. Author: Society in America, 1837; Retrospect of Western Travel, 1838. Died Ambleside, Eng., June 27, 1876.

MARTY, Martin, missionary; b. Schwyz, Switzerland, Jan. 12, 1834; s. Jacob Alois and Elizabeth (Reichlin) M. Took Benedictine vows, 1854; ordained priest Roman Catholic Ch., 1856; came to U.S., 1860; with monastery, St. Meinrad, Ind., 1860-73, apptd. prior, 1866, 1st mitred abbot of St. Meinrad, 1870; became missionary to Sioux Indians in Dakotas, 1873; apptd. vicar apostolic Dakota Territory, with hdqrs. Yankton (now S.D.), 1879; attended Council of Balt., 1884; 1st bishop Sioux Falls, S.C., 1890-95; bishop St. Cloud, Minn., 1895-96; known as Angel of West for his extensive missionary efforts. Author: Dr. Johann Martin Henni, 1888; Katolik Wocekiye (revision of Cath. ritual in Siouan lang.), 1890. Died St. Cloud, Sept. 19, 1896.

MARTYN, Sarah Towne Smith, author; b. Hopkinton, N.H., Aug. 15, 1805; d. Ethan and Bathsheba (Sanford) Smith; m. Job H. Martyn, Mar. 1841, 4 children including William Carlos. Mem. Female Moral Reform Soc., N.Y.C., edited soc.'s jour. Advocate of Moral Reform, 1836-45; editor Olive Plant and Ladies' Temperance Advocate, 1842, The True Advocate, 1846; editor, publisher White Banner (later called Ladies' Wreath), 1846-50. Author: (children's books) Margaret, the Pearl of Navarre, 1867; The English Exile, or William Tyndale at Home and Abroad, 1867; Daughters of the Cross, 1868; Women of the Bible, 1868. Died N.Y.C., Nov. 22, 1879; buried Cheshire, Conn.

MARVIN, Dudley, congressman; b. Lyme, Conn., May 9, 1786; s. Elisha and Elizabeth (Selden) M.; m. Mary Whalley, Jan. 31, 1818, 1 child. Admitted to Conn. bar, 1811; served as lt. col., brig. gen., maj. gen. N.Y. Militia in War of 1812; mem. U.S. Ho. of Reps. from N.Y., as Democrat, 18th-20th congresses, 1823-29, Whig 30th Congress, 1847-49; active in temperance movement, supported indsl. interests, advocated protective tariff and limitation of slavery. Died Ripley, Chawtauqua County, N.Y., June 25, 1852; buried East Ripley Cemetery, Ripley.

MARVIN, Enoch Mather, clergyman; b. Warren County, Mo., June 12, 1823; s. Wells and Mary (Davis) M.; m. Harriet Clark, 1845, 5 children. Licensed to preach, admitted on trial in Mo. Methodist Conf., 1841; chaplain to regts. in Ark. and Tex., 1862; chosen bishop Meth. Episcopal Ch., South, by Gen. Conf., 1866; missionary to Indians after Civil War; missionary in charge of ordaining native preachers in China, 1876-77. Author: To the East by Way of the West, 1878; Lectures, 1860; The Work of Christ, or the Atonement Sermons, 1876. Died St. Louis, Nov. 26, 1877.

MARVIN, Richard Pratt, congressman; b. Fairfield, N.Y., Dec. 23, 1803; attended pub. schs. studied law. Admitted to N.Y. bar, 1829, began practice in Jamestown; mem. N.Y. Assembly, 1836-37; mem. U.S. Ho. of Reps. (Whig) from N.Y. 1837-41; del. N.Y. Constl. Conv., 1846; judge 8th N.Y. Jud. Circuit, 1847-71. Died Jamestown, Jan. 11, 1892; buried Lakeview Cemetery, Jamestown.

MARWEDEL, Emma Jacobina Christiana, educator; b. nr. Göttingen, Germany, Feb. 27, 1818; d. Heinrich Ludwig and Jacobina (Brokmann) Marwedel; never married. Mem. of assn. for promotion public edn., Leipzig, Germany, 1864; mem. 1st German assn. for advancement of women, 1865; directress Girls' Indsl. Sch., also a kindergarten, Hamburg Germany, 1867-68; came to U.S., 1869; conducted kindergarten, Brentwood, L.I., N.Y., 1870; an early advocate of Froebelian kindergarten principles in U.S.; conducted sch. for indsl. arts, kindergarten also kindergarten normal sch., Washington, D.C., 1870-74; founded, conducted Pacific Kindergarten Normal Sch. (1st of its type in Cal.), Los Angeles, 1876, moved sch. to Oakland, Cal., 1878, to Berkeley, Cal., 1879, finally to San Francisco, 1880, founder Silver Street Kindergarten, San Francisco, 1878; founder, 1st pres. Cal. Kindergarten Union, 1879. Author: Warum bedürfen wir weibliche Gewerbeschulen? und wie sollen sie angelegt sein, 1868; Conscious Motherhood, or the Earliest Unfolding of the Child in the Cradle, Nursery and Kindergarten, 1887; The Connecting Link, to Continue the Three-Fold Development of the Child from the Cradle to the Manual-Labor School, 1891; An Appeal to Justice for Childhood; Games and Studies in Life Forms and Colors of Nature for Home and School. Died San Francisco, Nov. 17, 1893; buried Mountain View Cemetery, Oakland.

MARX, Karl (Heinrich Karl), social philosopher, economist; b. Treves, Rhenish Prussia, Germany, May 5, 1818; s. Heinrich (Hirschel) M., a lawyer; studied law at U. Bonn, history and philosophy at U. Berlin; Ph.D., U. Jena, 1841; m. Jenny von Westphalen, 1843; six children (3 reached maturity). Editor Radical newspaper, Rheinische Zeitung, Cologne, 1842-43; went to Paris, 1843; briefly coedited a review there, studied reformist writings, met Friedrich Engels; with Engels, acquired a workers' weekly in Brussels, Belgium; joined "League of the Just," wrote (with Engels) Communist Manifesto, pub. 1848, presenting view of history as class struggle, and exhorting working class to unite and take over means of production; expelled from Paris and Germany; lived in London, Eng., 1849-83; correspondent N. Y. Tribune (staff of which included Fourierists), wrote on Crimean War, Eastern Question, Am. Civil War; most prominent figure in Internat. Workingmen's Assn., 1864-76. Author: The Poverty of Philosophy, 1847 (a reply to Proudhon's The Philosophy of Poverty); The Civil War in France, 1852; The Eighteenth Brumaire of Louis Bonaparte, 1852; Critique of Political Economy, 1859; Value, Land and Profit, 1865; Das Kapital, Vol. I, 1867; Vols. II and III, ed. by Engels, 1885-95; Critique of the Gotha Program, 1875. Died London, Mar. 14, 1883; buried Highgate Cemetery, London.

MASON, Abraham John, engraver; b. London, Eng., Apr. 4, 1794. Established himself as wood engraver, London, circa 1820; gave series of public lectures on wood engraving, 1829; came to Am., 1829, established himself as wood engraver, N.Y.C.; elected asso. N.A.D., 1830, lectr., 1831-32, apptd. prof. wood engraving, 1832; wrote treatise on wood engraving published in Dunlap's History of the Arts of Design, 1834.

MASON, Armistead Thomson, senator; b. Louisa County, Va., Aug. 4, 1787; s. Stevens Thomson Mason; grad. Coll. William and Mary, 1807. Engaged in farming; served as col. Va. Volunteers during War of 1812, later commd. brig. gen. Va. Militia; mem. U.S. Senate from Va. (Democrat), Jan. 3, 1816-17; unsuccessful candidate for U.S. Congress, 1816, campaign resulted in several duels, one of which caused his death. Killed in a duel with John Mason McCarty (his brother-in-law), Bladensburg, Md., Feb. 6, 1819; buried Episcopal Churchyard, Leesburg, Va.

MASON, Charles, jurist; b. Pompey, N.Y., Oct. 24, 1804; s. Chauncey and Esther (Dodge) M.; grad. U.S. Mil. Acad., 1829; m. Angelica Gear, Aug. 1, 1837, 3 children. Asst. prof. engring. U.S. Mil. Acad., 1830-31; admitted to N.Y. bar, 1832; apptd. aide and public prosecutor Des Moines County, Wis., Territory, 1837; chief justice Supreme Ct. Territory Iowa, 1838-47; mem. commn. to draft 1st Code of Iowa, 1851; judge Des Moines County, 1851-52; U.S. commr. patents, 1853-57; mem. 1st Ia. State Bd. Edn., 1857; chmn. Democratic Nat. Central Com., 1864, del. to nominating convs., 1868, 72. Died Burlington, Ia., Feb. 25, 1882.

MASON, Claibourne Rice, railroad contractor; b. Chesterfield County, Va., Nov. 28, 1800; s. Rev. Peter and Elizabeth Mason; m. Drucilla W. Boxley, Mar. 13, 1838, 11 children. Contractor asso. with constrn. Midlothian R.R. of Va., 1829; began and superintended Louisa R.R. (now C.&O. R.R.) 1836; contractor Va. Central R.R.; raised and captained volunteers co., 1861, his co. built many bridges for Gen. Jackson; returned to railroad contracting, after Civil War. Died Va., Jan. 12, 1885; buried Va.

MASON, Francis, clergyman; b. York, Eng., Apr. 2, 1799; s. Thomas Mason; attended Newton Theol. Inst., 1828-29; m. Lucinda Gill, 1825; m. 2d, Helen Maria Griggs, May 23, 1830; m. 3d, Mrs. Ellen Huntly Bullard, 1847. Came to U.S., 1818, traveled and worked around country until 1824; cobbler, Randolph, Mass., 1825-27; licensed to preach by Canton Baptist Ch., 1827; ordained to ministry Bapt. Ch., 1830; missionary and evangelist Rangoon, Burma, 1831-53; made trip to Eng., 1854-57; returned to missionary work in Rangoon, 1857-65, broke with mission and formed own cult, 1865-71, reinstated to mission, 1871-74. Author: The Karen Apostle, or Memoir of Kothah-byu; Synopsis of a Grammar of the Karen Language, 1846; The Story of a Working Man's Life, 1870; also wrote a Karen version of Gospel of Matthew, 1837. Died Rangoon, Mar. 3, 1874; buried Rangoon.

MASON, George, planter; b. Eng., circa 1629; m. Mary, at least 1 son, George. Took land patent in Westmoreland County, Va., 1655; secured more land, 1664, 69; sheriff Stafford County, 1669; clk. Stafford County Ct., 1673; mem. Va. Ho. of Burgesses, 1676; county lt. Stafford County; his blunder of attacking Suspuehannock Indians resulted in Indian war which ended in Bacon's Rebellion; fought under Bacon until he discovered Bacon's progressive politics. Died Va., circa 1686; buried Va.

MASON, George, legislator; b. Doeg's Neck (now Mason's Neck), Va., 1725; s. George and Ann (Thompson) M.; m. Anne Eilbeck, Apr. 4, 1750; m. 2d, Sarah Brent, Apr. 11, 1780; 9 children. Trustee of Alexandria, Va., 1754-79; treas. Ohio Co., 1752-73; author paper Extracts from the Virginia Charters, with Some Remarks upon Them, 1773; mem. Va. Ho. of Burgesses, 1759; wrote Fairfax Resolves of July 18, 1774; mem. 1st Va. Conv., 1775, 5th Va. Conv., 1776; mem. Va. Council on Safety, 1775; framed Declaration of Rights and major part of Va. Constn., 1776; active organizer mil. affairs, particularly in West; partially responsible for fixing Brit-Am. boundary at Gt. Lakes rather than at Ohio River, in Peace Treaty 1783; Va. del. Mt. Vernon Meeting, 1785; mem. Va. Assembly, 1786; mem. U.S. Constl. Conv., 1787, became anti-ratification leader in Va., refused to sign U.S. Constn., wrote "Objections to the Federal Constitution" (insisting upon inclusion of Bill of Rights and condemnation of slavery, 1787. Died Gunston Hall, Va., Oct. 7, 1792.

MASON, George Champlin, architect; b. Newport, R.I., 1820. Practiced architecture, Newport, until 1880's, designed business bldgs., pvt. homes; moved to Phila., mid-1880's, practiced architecture in assn. with his son, George Champlin, Jr., for a few years; editor Newport Mercury, for a time; devoted later life to literary pursuits. Died 1894.

MASON, Henry, organ mfr.; b. Brookline, Mass., Oct. 10, 1831; s. Lowell and Abigail (Gregory) M.; attended univs. Göttingen, Paris, Prague; m. Helen Augusta Palmer, 1857, at least 1 son, Henry Lowell. Joined music firm of S.B. Pond, N.Y.C.; established (with E. Hamlin) Mason & Hamlin Organ Co., Boston, 1854 (became Am. Cabinet Organ, 1861), expanded into manufacture of pianos, 1882. Died Boston, May 15, 1890.

MASON, James Brown, congressman; b. Thompson, Conn., Jan. 1775; grad. Brown U., 1791; studied medicine. Practiced medicine, Charleston, S.C., 1795-98; returned to Providence, R.I., engaged in merc. bus., 1798-1819; mem. R.I. Ho. of Reps., 1804-14, speaker, 1812-14; mem. U.S. Ho. of Reps. (Federalist) from R.I., 14th-15th congresses, 1815-19; trustee Brown U., 1804-19. Died Providence, Aug. 31, 1819; buried North Burial Ground, Providence.

MASON, James Murray, senator, diplomat; b. Georgetown, D.C., Nov. 3, 1798; s. John and Anna Maria (Murray) M.; grad. U. Pa., 1818, Coll. William and Mary Law Sch., 1820; m. Elizabeth Margaretta Chew, July 25, 1822, 8 children. Admitted to Va. bar, 1820; practiced law, Winchester, Va.; mem. Va. Ho. of Dels., 1826-27, 28-32; presdl. elector from Va., 1832; mem. U.S. Ho. of Reps. (Democrat) from Va., 25th Congress, 1837-39; mem. U.S. Senate from Va., Jan. 21, 1847-Mar. 28, 1861, drafted fugitive slave law of 1850; chmn. Senate fgn. relations com., 1851-61; advocate of secession; del. from Va. to Provisional Congress of Confederacy, 1861; Confederate diplomatic commr. to Eng., 1861-65; seized (with colleague John Slidell) by U.S. Navy while enroute to Eng. on Brit. ship Trent, Nov. 1861, imprisoned until Jan. 1862 (incident almost caused war between Am. and Eng.); tried in vain to secure English recognition of Confederacy; lived in Can. (to escape U.S. arrest), 1866-68; returned to Va. after Pres. Andrew Johnson's 2d proclamation of amnesty. Died "Clarens," nr. Alexandria, Va., Apr. 28, 1871; buried St. Paul's Cemetery, Alexandria.

MASON, Jeremiah, senator; b. Lebanon, Conn., Apr. 27, 1768; s. Col. Jeremiah and Elizabeth (Fitch) M.; grad. Yale, 1788; m. Mary Means, Nov. 1799, 8 children. Admitted to Vt. bar, 1791; moved to N.H., practiced in Westmoreland, 1791-94, Walpole, 1794-97, Portsmouth, 1798-1832; atty. gen. N.H., 1802-05; friend of Daniel Webster, from 1807; mem. U.S. Senate from N.H., 1813-17; provided some of arguments used by Daniel Webster in Dartmouth Coll. Case, 1819; mem. N.H. Ho. of Reps., 1820, 21, 24, helped revise N.H. legal code; pres. Portsmouth br. U.S. Bank, 1825-29; moved to Boston, 1832. Died Boston, Oct. 14, 1848; buried Mt. Auburn Cemetery, Cambridge, Mass.

MASON, John, colonial ofcl.; b. Eng., circa 1600; m. Anne Peck, July 1639, 8 children. Came to Mass. 1630; commd. capt. Mass. Militia, 1633; leader migration to found Town of Windsor on Connecticut River, 1635; leader in breaking power of Pequot Indians, 1637; commd. maj. Conn. Militia, after 1637; mem. Conn. Gov.'s Council, 1637-42, magistrate, 1642-60, dep. gov., 1660-69, assistant, 1669-72; a founder Town of Norwich (Conn.), 1660. Author: A Relation of the Troubles That Have Happened in New England (history of Pequot War), 1677. Died Norwich, Jan. 30, 1672.

MASON, John Calvin, congressman; b. nr. Mount Sterling, Ky., Aug. 4 1802; attended Mount Sterling Law Sch., Lexington, Ky.; grad. Transylvania U., Lexington, 1823. Admitted to Ky. bar, practiced in Mount Sterling; iron mfr.; mem. Ky. Ho. of Reps., 1839, 44, 48; served in Mexican War, 1846-47; wounded in Battle of Monterey; sent with dispatches to Pres. Polk, Washington, D.C.; apptd. q.m. with rank of maj. by Pres. Polk, 1847; moved to Owingsville, Ky., 1847; mem. U.S. Ho. of Reps. (Jacksonian Democrat) from Ky., 31st-32d, 35th congresses, 1849-53, 57-59; del. Dem. Nat. Conv., Charleston, S.C., 1860; Dem. presdl. elector, 1860; served with Tex. troops Confederate Army, during Civil War, 1863. Died on a steamer on Mississippi River on the way from Tex. to Ky., Aug. 1865; buried State Cemetery, Frankfort, Ky.

MASON, John Mitchell, clergyman; b. N.Y.C., Mar. 19, 1770; s. Rev. John and Catharine (Van Wyck) M.; grad. Columbia, 1789; attended U. Edinburgh; m. Ann Lefferts, May 13, 1793, 5 sons including Ebenezer, 3 daus. Licensed to preach and ordained to ministry, 1793; established theol. sem. to educate Scotch Presbyterians (later became Union Theol. Sem.), N.Y.C., 1804; founder, editor Christian's Mag., 1806; trustee Columbia, 1795-1811, 1812-24, provost, 1811-16; pres. Dickinson Coll., Carlisle, Pa., 1821-24. Author: A Plea for Sacramental Communion on Catholic Principles, 1816. Died Dec. 26, 1829.

MASON, John Thomson, congressman; b. "Montpelier" nr. Hagerstown, Md., May 9, 1815; grad. Princeton, 1836; studied law. Admitted to Md. bar, began practice in Hagerstown, 1838; mem. Md. Ho. of Reps., 1838-39; mem. U.S. Ho. of Reps. (Democrat) from Md., 27th Congress, 1841-43; collector of customs, Balt., 1857-61; moved to Annapolis, Md. Died Annapolis, Mar. 28, 1873; buried Rose Hill Cemetery, Hagerstown.

MASON, John Young, cabinet officer, diplomat; b. Hicksford, Va., Apr. 18, 1799; s. Edmunds and Frances (Young) M.; A.B., U. N.C., 1816; attended Litchfield (Conn.) Law Sch.; m. Mary Ann Fort, Aug. 9, 1821, 8 children. Admitted to Va. bar, 1819; mem. Va. Ho. of Reps., 1823-27, Va. Senate, 1827-31; mem. Va. Constl. Conv., 1829, 30, opposed extended suffrage; presiding officer Va. Constl. Conv., 1850-51; mem. U.S. Ho. of Reps. (Democrat) from Va., 22d-24th congresses, 1831-37, chmn. com. fgn. affairs, refused to vote for rechartering of U.S. Bank, introduced bill for recognition of Tex. independence; U.S. dist. judge for Eastern Va., 1837; U.S. sec. navy, 1844-45, 46-49, opposed incorporation of Mexico by U.S., favored treaty with Mexico signed by Nicholas P. Trist; U.S. atty. gen., 1845-46; practiced law, Richmond, Va., 1849-54; pres. James River & Kanawha Co., 1849; mem. Va. Dem. Central Com., 1852; U.S. minister to France, 1854-59, signed Ostend Manifesto (with James Buchanan and Pierre Soulé) which advocated purchase or acquisition of Cuba by U.S., 1854. Died Paris, France, Oct. 3, 1859; buried Hollywood Cemetery, Richmond.

MASON, Jonathan, senator; b. Boston, Sept. 12, 1756; s. Jonathan and Miriam (Clark) M.; A.B., Coll. of N.J. (now Princeton); read law with John Adams in office of Josiah Quincy; m. Susannah Powell, 1779, 6 children. Admitted to Mass. bar, 1779; delivered annual oration commemorating Boston Massacre, 1780; mem. Mass. Ho. of Reps., 1786-96, 1805-08; established (with Harrison Gray Otis, Joseph Woodward and Charles Ward Apthorp) real estate syndicate, Boston, purchased southwestern slope of Beacon Hill, 1795, turned it into fashionable residential dist.; mem. Mass. Exec. Council, 1797-98, Mass. Senate, 1799-1800, 03-04; mem. U.S. Senate (Federalist) from Mass., Nov. 14, 1800-03, took part in debates on repealing Judiciary Act of 1801; moved to request Pres. Thomas Jefferson to remove Embargo (motion carried) at spl. meeting, Boston, 1808; mem. U.S. Ho. of Reps. (Federalist) from Mass., 15th-16th congresses, 1817-May 15, 1820; mem. South Boston Assn.; dir. Boston br. of U.S. Bank. Died Boston, Nov. 1, 1831; buried Mt. Auburn Cemetery, Cambridge, Mass.

MASON, Lowell, musician, educator; b. Medfield, Mass., Jan. 8, 1792; s. Johnson and Catharine (Hartshorn) M.; m. Abigail Gregory, 1817; children—William, Henry, Daniel, Lowell. Taught singing, played ch. organ, Savannah, 1812-27; pres. Handel and Haydn Soc., Boston, 1827-32; founded Boston Acad. Music, 1833; helped introduce music classes into Boston Public Schs., became roving music tchr. to public schs., 1838-41; collected large musical library, particularly hymns. Author: The Boston Handel and Haydn Society's Collection of Church Music, 1822; Manual of Instruction, 1834; Sabbath-School Songs, 1836; The Psaltery, 1845. Died Orange, N.J., Aug. 11, 1872.

MASON, Luther Whiting, educator; b. Turner, Me., Apr. 3, 1828; s. Willard and Mary (Whiting) M. Became supt. musical edn. in public schs., Louisville, Ky., 1853, later Cincinnati; became head of musical edn. system, Boston, 1865; toured Japan organizing musical tng., 1870's-82. Author: (with G. A. Veazie) The National Music Course, 4 vols., 1887-97. Died Buckfield, Me., July 14, 1896.

MASON, Moses, Jr., congressman; b. Dublin, N.H. June 2, 1789; s. Moses Mason; attended common schs., Bethel, Me.; studied medicine. Began practice of medicine, Bethel, 1813; 1st postmaster of Bethel, 1815-33; justice of peace, 1821-66; county commr., 1831-34; mem. U.S. Ho. of Reps. (Democrat) from Md., 23d-24th congresses, 1833-37; mem. Me. Exec. Council, 1843-45; trustee Me. State Insane Hosp., 1844; selectman of Bethel, 14 years; pres. Gould's Acad., 1854-56. Died Bethel, June 25, 1866; buried Woodlawn Cemetery, Bethel.

MASON, Richard Barnes, army officer; b. Fairfax County, Va., Jan. 16, 1797; s. George and Eleanor (Patton) M. Commd. 2d lt. 8th Inf., U.S. Army, 1817, capt. 1st Inf., 1819; served in Black Hawk War, 1832; commd. maj. 1st Dragoons (later became 1st Regt. U.S. Cavalry), 1833, lt. col., 1836, col., 1846; served with Gen. Kearny in Mexican War, occupied Los Angeles, 1847, became mil. comdr. of region, authorized to establish temporary civil govt. in Cal., served as acting gov., 1847-49; brevetted brig. gen., 1848. Died St. Louis, July 25, 1850; buried Jefferson Barracks, Mo.

MASON, Samson, congressman; b. Fort Ann, N. Y., July 24, 1793; attended common schs., Onendaga, N.Y.; studied law. Admitted to the bar; began law practice, Springfield, O., 1819; pros. atty. Clark County (O.), 1822; mem. Ohio Senate, 1829-31, 62-64; pres. judge Ohio Ct. of Common Pleas, 1834; mem. U.S. Ho. of Reps. (Whig) from Ohio, 24th-27th congresses, 1835-43; mem. Ohio Ho. of Reps., 1845-46; U.S. atty. for Ohio, 1850-53; del. Ohio Constl. Conv., 1850; served from capt. to maj. gen. Ohio Militia. Died Springfield, Feb. 1, 1869; buried Ferncliff Cemetery, Springfield.

MASON, Samuel, outlaw; b. Va., circa 1750; 4 sons. Served as capt. Ohio County (Va.) Militia during Revolutionary War; became outlaw, E. Tenn., later Russellville and Henderson, Ky.; operated with band including his sons from Cave-In-Rock, attacked and robbed passing Mississippi River men, 1797; continued his activities on lower Mississippi River; captured (with his band) by Spanish ofcls. in Mo., escaped; killed by his own robber friends, 1803 (who then attempted to collect reward, were recognized and killed by U.S. ofcls., Old Greenville, Miss., 1804). Died July 1803.

MASON, Stevens Thomson, senator; b. Stafford County, Va., Dec. 29, 1760; s. Thomas and Mary King (Barnes) M.; attended Coll. William and Mary; m. Mary Elizabeth Armistead, children—Armistead, John. Staff aid to Gen. Washington during Revolutionary War; mem. Va. Ho. of Dels., 1783-87, Va. Senate, 1787; mem. Va. Conv. to ratify U.S. Constn., 1788; mem. U.S. Senate (Democrat) from Va., 1794-1803. Died Phila., May 10, 1803; buried "Raspberry Plain," Loudoun County, Va.

MASON, Stevens Thomson, gov. Mich.; b. Loudoun County, Va., Oct. 27, 1811; s. John Thomson and Elizabeth (Moir) M.; ed. Transylvania U.; m. Julia Phelps, Nov. 1, 1838, 3 children. Sec., Mich. Territory, 1831-34; acting gov. Mich., 1834; 1st gov. Mich., 1836-38. Died Jan. 4, 1843; buried Capitol Sq., Detroit.

MASON, Thomson, legislator; b. Prince William County, Va., 1733; s. Col. George and Ann (Thomson) M.; m. Mary Barnes, 1758; m. 2d, Elizabeth Westwood. Admitted to Middle Temple, London, Eng., 1751; mem. Va. Assembly from Stafford County, 1758-61, 65-72, from Loudoun County, 1772-74, 77-78, from Elizabeth City County, 1779, 1783; chmn. com. on cts. of justice, author and chief supporter bill by which Assembly organized Northwest as county of Ill., 1778; wrote series of pamphlets signed "A British American," urging open resistance to Eng., 1774; judge Va. Gen. Ct., 1778. Died Va., Feb. 26, 1785.

MASON, William, congressman; b. Lebanon, Conn., Sept. 10, 1786; studied medicine and surgery, Vt. Practiced medicine, Preston, N.Y.; served as surgeon Chenango County Co., N.Y. Volunteers, 1812; clk. Chenango County, 1820-21; mem. N.Y. Assembly, 1821-22; mem. U.S. Ho. of Reps. (Democrat) from N.Y., 24th Congress, 1835-37; Dem. presdl. elector, 1844. Died Norwich, N.Y., Jan. 13, 1860; buried Mt. Hope Cemetery, Norwich.

MASON, William, inventor, mfr.; b. Mystic, Conn., Sept. 2, 1808; s. Amos and Mary (Holdredge) M.; m. Harriet Augusta Metcalf, June 10, 1844, at least 2 sons, 1 dau. Apprentice in cotton factory, 1822-28; patented power loom to make diaper cloth (1st in U.S.), began mfg. looms, 1832-33; developed ring frame for textile work, 1834, produced ring frames, Taunton, Mass., 1835-37; patented self-acting mule for spinning, 1840, improvement on it, 1846; engaged in textile mfg., 1842-83, expanded his firm's operations to include locomotive mfg., 1853, later made railroad wheels and arms; founder, pres. Machinists' Nat. Bank, Taunton, 1847-57. Died Mass., May 21, 1883.

MASON, William Sanford, artist; b. Providence, R.I., 1824; s. Sanford Mason. Began artistic career, Phila., 1843; best known for paintings with themes from ancient and modern literature; exhibited at Artists' Fund Soc., Pa. Acad., Am. Art-Union, Boston Athenaeum; Died Phila., 1864.

MASQUERIER, Lewis, reformer; b. Paris, Ky., Mar. 14, 1802; s. Lewis and Sarah (Hicklin) M.; m. Anna Taber, circa 1840. Employed in printing shop, Paris; admitted to Ill. bar, practiced law, Quincy, Ill., for a time; became land speculator; developed phonetic alphabet with 11 vowels, 22 consonants, moved to N.Y.C. to propagandize his alphabet; proponent of doctrines of George H. Evans, wrote treatise on anarchy; lectured and wrote in support of idea of agrarian anarchistic Utopia. Author: The Phonotypic Spelling and Reading Manual, 1867; Sociology, or the Reconstruction of Society, Government and Property, 1884.

MASSASSOIT (also known as "Great Chief," Ousamequin, "Yellow Feather"), Indian chief; children include Metacomet (later called King Philip). Chief of Wampanoag Indians, made main home at Pokanoket (Mt. Hope), nr. Bristol, R.I.; negotiator peace treaty and amity treaty with whites, Plymouth, Mass., Mar. 22, 1621, peace treaty with Roger Williams, 1635. Died 1661.

MAST, Phineas Price, businessman; b. Lancaster County, Pa., Jan. 3, 1825; s. John and Elizabeth (Trego) M.; grad. Ohio Wesleyan U., 1849; m. Anna M. Kirkpatrick, Jan. 4, 1850. Tchr., rural sch., nr. Urbana, Ill.; became partner (with J. H. Thomas) in cider-mill mfg. co., Springfield, O., 1856, expanded firm to produce various farm implements, became sole owner (changed firm name to P. P. Mast & Co.), 1871; organized Mast, Foos & Co., lawn mowing equipment firm, also Mast Buggy Co.; publisher Farm and Fireside, 1879-98, also Woman's Home Companion; pres. Springfield Nat. Bank; mem. Springfield City Council, 22 years. Died Springfield, Nov. 20, 1898.

MASTERS, Josiah, congressman; b. Woodbury, Conn., Nov. 22, 1763; grad. Yale, 1783; studied law. Admitted to N.Y. bar, began practice in Schaghticoke; mem. N.Y. Assembly, 1792, 1800, 01; supr. of Schaghticoke, 1796; justice of peace, Rensselaer County, N.Y., 1801-05; trustee Lansingburgh Acad.; sch. commr. Schaghticoke; mem. U.S. Ho. of Reps. (Democrat) from N.Y., 9th-10th congresses, 1805-09; founder Schaghticoke Powder Co.; judge Rensselaer County Ct. of Common Pleas, 1808-22. Died Fairfield, Conn., June 30, 1822; buried Masters Cemetery, nr. Schaghticoke.

MASTIN, Claudius Henry, surgeon; b. Huntsville, Ala., June 4, 1826; s. Francis Turner and Ann Elizabeth Caroline (Levert) M.; attended U. Va.; M.D., U. Pa., 1849; studied medicine with Dr. J. Y. Bassett, Huntsville; attended U. Edinburgh, Royal Coll. Surgeons, U. Paris; m. Mary Eliza McDowell, Sept. 20, 1848, at least 2 sons. Practiced medicine briefly, then went to Europe for further edn.; began practice medicine specializing in genito-urinary surgery, Mobile, Ala., 1854; asso. with U.S. Marine Hosp. Service, Mobile, 1854-57; surgeon Mobile Hosp., 1855; med. dir. on staffs of Generals Polk, Bragg, G. T. Beauregard, 1861-65; a founder Congress Am. Physicians and Surgeons; fellow Am. Surg. Assn., pres., 1890-91; mem. So. Surg. and Gynecol. Assn.; founder Am. Genito-Urinary Assn., pres., 1895-96; wrote many articles published by various orgns. to which he belonged. Died Oct. 3, 1898.

MASURY, John Wesley, mfr.; b. Salem, Mass., Jan. 1, 1820; s. John and Priscilla (Carroll) M.; m. Laura A. Carlton, Oct. 15, 1844; m. 2d, Grace Harkins. Began as clk. in paint store, Bklyn.; became partner in dye mfg. firm Prince, Masury & Weeks (became Masury & Whiton, 1857, Masury & Son, 1871); patented metallic paint canister, 1857, improved models, 1859, 73. Author: House-Painting, Carriage-Painting and Graining, 1881. Died N.Y., May 14, 1895; buried Center Moriches, L.I.

MATELIGER, Jan Ernst, inventor; b. Dutch Guiana, 1852. Apprenticed in machine shop, Dutch Guiana, circa 1862-72; came to U.S., 1872, worked in various machine shops, 1872-77; patented shoe lasting machine, 1883; a founder Consolidated Hand Method Lasting Machine Co., Lynn, Mass. Died Lynn, 1889.

MATHER, Cotton, clergyman, author; b. Feb. 23, 1663; s. Increase and Maria (Cotton) M.; A..B, Harvard, 1678, M.A., 1681; D.D. (hon.), U. Glasgow (Scotland), 1710; m. Abigail Phillips, 1686; m. second, Elizabeth (Clark) Hubbard; m. third, Lydia George; fifteen children including Samuel. Ordained to ministry in the Congregational Ch., 1684; teacher at the Second Congregational Ch. of Boston, 1685-1723; wrote against govt. of Sir Edmund Andros in The Declaration of the Gentlemen, Merchants, and Inhabitants of Boston, 1689; fellow Harvard, 1690-1703; wrote statement on witch trial evidence condemning reliance on "spectral" evidence, 1692; defended Salem witch trials in book Wonders of the Invisible World, 1693 (later attacked by Robert Calef in his book More Wonders of the Invisible World); a founder Yale Coll., refused to become its pres.; became 1st Am.-born mem. Royal Soc., 1713, contbd. many articles to its Proceedings; informed Dr. Zabdiel Boyleston of process of inoculation for smallpox, supported the radical idea financially and by his influence during smallpox epidemic of 1721; minister 2d Congregational Ch. of Boston, 1723-28; a leader in Boston charities, ednl. and social improvement plans; campaigned against intemperance, mistreatment of slaves. Author over 450 books including: A Family Well-Ordered, 1699; Magnalia Christi Americana: or the Ecclesiastical History of New England from its First Planting (most famous work), 1702; Some Few Remarks upon a Scandalous Book. . .by one Robert Calef, 1704; The Good Education of Children, 1708; Essays to do Good, 1710; Christian Philosopher, 1721; An Account. . .of Inoculating the Small-Pox, 1722. Died Boston, Feb. 24, 1728; buried Copp's Hill Burying Ground, Boston.

MATHER, Increase, clergyman, coll. pres.; b. Dorchester. Mass., June 21, 1639; s. Richard and Katherine (Holt) M.; A.B., Harvard, 1656; M.A., Trinity Coll., Dublin, Ireland, 1658; m. Maria Cotton, Mar. 1662, 10 children including Cotton; m. 2d, Ann Lake, 1715. Del. to Eccles. Synod from Dorchester; pastor North Ch., Boston, 1664, tchr. 2d Ch., Boston, 1664; apptd. a licenser of press, 1674; apptd. fellow Harvard, 1674, acting pres., 1685, pres., 1686-1701; chosen to take petitions from Congregational chs. in colony to King James II, 1688; agt. for Mass. in Eng., 1690, accepted charter from King William III. Author: Cases of Conscience Concerning Evil Spirits; A Brief History of the War with the Indians, 1676; A Relation of the Troubles Which Have Happened in New England by Reason of the Indians There, 1677; Life and Death of That Reverend Man of God, Mr. Richard Mather, 1670; also sermons: The Great Blessing of Primitive Counsellours," 1693; "The Surest Way to the Greatest Honour," 1699. Died Boston, Aug. 23, 1723.

MATHER, Richard, clergyman; b. Lowton, Lancashire, Eng., 1596; s. Thomas and Margaret Mather; privately educated; m. Katherine Holt, 1624; m. 2d, Sarah (Hawkridge) Cotton, circa 1657; 6 children including Samuel, Nathaniel, Eleazar, Increase. Ordained to ministry Anglican Ch., 1620; preached in Liverpool and Toxteth area (Eng.), 1618-33, became a leading Puritan; forbidden to preach, 1634; came to Boston, 1635; minister Congregational Ch., Dorchester, Mass., 1636-69; became leading ch. writer of his day; defended Congregational chs. in Church Government and Church-Covenant Discussed, 1643; wrote most of "Cambridge Platform" defining ch.'s govt. and role in society; a prin. backer of Half-Way Convenant doctrine established by ch. in 1662; a translator of edit. of Psalms known as Bay Psalm Book, 1640. Author: A Catechism, 1650; A Defence of the Answer . . . of the Synod, 1662. Died Dorchester, Apr. 22, 1669; buried Old Burial Ground, Dorchester.

MATHER, Samuel, clergyman; b. Boston, Oct. 30, 1706; s. Cotton and Elizabeth (Clark) M.; A.B., Harvard, 1723, D.D. (hon.), 1773; M.A. (hon.), U. Glasgow (Scotland), 1731; D.D. (hon.), U. Aberdeen (Scotland), 1762; m. Hannah Hutchinson, Aug. 23, 1733, children—Hannah, Samuel, Thomas, Increase. Chaplain of Castle William, Boston Harbor, 1724-32; minister 2d Congregational Ch., Boston, 1732-41; dismissed by ch., established (with minority of his old parishioners) a new ch., served as minister until death. Author: Life of the Very Reverend and Learned Cotton Mather, 1729; Attempt to Show that America Must be Known to the Ancients, 1773; The Sacred Minister, 1773. Died Boston, June 27, 1785; buried Copp's Hill Burying Ground, Boston.

MATHER, Samuel Holmes, banker; b. Washington, N.H., Mar. 20, 1813; s. Dr. Ozias and Harriet (Brainard) M.; grad. Dartmouth, 1834; m. Emily W. Gregory, May 9, 1842, at least 2 children. Admitted to Ohio bar, 1836; practiced law, Cleve., from 1836; a founder Soc. for Savings, 1849, sec., 1849-84, pres., 1884-94; mem. Cleve. Bd. Edn., 1854-57. Died Jan. 14, 1894.

MATHER, Samuel Livingston, businessman; b. Middletown, Conn., July 1, 1817; s. Samuel and Catherine (Livingston) M.; grad. Wesleyan U., 1835; m. Georgiana Pomeroy Woolson, Sept. 24, 1850; m. 2d, Elizabeth Lucy Gwin, June 11, 1856; children—William, Samuel. Worked for his father, Middletown; in commn. bus., N.Y.C., until 1843; became land agt. for father's huge holdings in Western Reserve, moved to Cleve.; an organizer Cleve. Iron Mining Co., circa 1850, became sec.-treas., 1853, pres.-treas., 1869-90, expanded co. holdings to include railroads and shipping; officer of Marquette Iron Co., Bancroft Iron Co., Cleve. Boiler Plate Co., Am. Iron Mining Co. Died Cleve., Oct. 8, 1890.

MATHER, William Williams, geologist; b. Brooklyn, Conn., May 24, 1804; s. Eleazar and Fanny (Williams) M.; grad. U.S. Mil. Acad., 1828; m. Emily Maria Baker, 6 children; m. Mary Harry, Aug. 1857, 1 son. Brevetted 2d lt. U.S. Army, 1828; professor of chemistry and mineralogy at U.S. Military Academy, West Point, N.Y., 1829-35; also prof. chemistry, mineralogy and geology Wesleyan U.; promoted 1st lt., 1834; aided G. W. Featherstonhaugh in survey of Green Bay (Wis.) region, 1835; resigned commn., 1836; prof. chemistry U. La., 1836; geologist for 1st Dist., N.Y. State, 1836-44; dir. Ohio Geologic Survey, 1837-38; state geologist Ky., 1838-39; prof. natural science Ohio U., Athens, 1842-45, acting pres. univ., 1845-47. Author: Elements of Geology for the Use of Schools, 1833. Died Columbus, O., Feb. 26, 1859.

MATHEWS, Alfred E., artist; b. Bristol, Eng., 1831; brought to U.S., 1833; self-taught artist. Became tchr. in rural sch., Ala.; served with U.S. Army during Civil War, made sketches of battles, army life, painted panorama of Civil War battles; moved to Neb., 1865, made sketches for lithograph co., Nebraska City, Neb.; went to Denver, 1865, painted scenery in Colo. Died Longmont, Colo., 1874.

MATHEWS, Cornelius, author; b. Port Chester, N.Y., Oct. 28, 1817; s. Abijah and Catherine (Van Cott) M.; attended Columbia Coll., 1830-32; grad. U. City N.Y., 1834. Admitted to N.Y. bar, 1837; contbd. to Am. Monthly Mag., N.Y. Review, Knickerbocker Mag. Author: Behemoth: A Legend of the Mound Builders, 1839; Poems on Man in his Various Aspects under the American Revolution, 1843; (plays) The Politicians, 1840, Jacob Leisler, 1848, False Pretences, 1855. Compiler: The Enchanted Moccassins (H. R. Schoolcraft's material), 1855. Died N.Y.C., Mar. 25, 1889.

MATHEWS, George, gov. Ga., army officer; b. Augusta County, Ga., Sept. 10, 1739; s. John Mathews; m. Miss Woods; m. 2d, Mrs. Reed; m. 3d, Mrs. Flowers) 6 children. Commanded co. Ga. Volunteers against Indians, 1757; served in Battle of Point Pleasant, Oct. 10, 1774; served as col. 9th Va. Regt. at battles of Brandywine and Germantown, Revolutionary War, wounded and captured; exchanged, 1781, joined Gen. Nathan Greene as col. 3d Va. Regt.; farmer, Oglethorpe County, Ga., 1785; brig. gen. Ga. Volunteers, 1785; gov. Ga., 1787, 93-96; mem. U.S. Ho. of Reps. from Ga., 1st Congress, 1789-91; employed U.S. Govt. on recommendation of Wilɑm H. Crawford to persuade Spanish gov. of W. ła. to turn over his province to U.S., 1810, ᵼilled; brig. gen. Ga. Militia in expdn. to capɪre W. Fla., 1811, captured Fernadina, Fla., 812. Died Augusta, Ga., Aug. 30, 1812; buried ᵼ. Paul's Churchyard, Augusta.

MATHEWS, Henry Mason, gov. W.Va.; b. Greenɾiar County, Va. (now W.Va.), Mar. 29, 1834; Mason and Eliza (Reynolds) M.; A.B., U. Va., 855, A.M., 1856; m. Lucy Fry, Nov. 24, 1857, daus., 1 son. Admitted to Va. bar, 1857; served ı Civil War; mem. W.Va. Constl. Conv., 1872; ᵼtty. gen. W.Va., 1872-76, gov. (Democrat), 876-81. Died Lewisburg, W.Va., Apr. 28, 1884.

MATHEWS, James, congressman; b. Liberty, O., ɯne 4, 1805; attended common schs.; studied law. dmitted to Ohio bar, 1830, began practice in oshocton; mem. Ohio Ho. of Reps., 1838-39; mem. ᴉ.S. Ho. of Reps. (Democrat) from Ohio, 27th-8th congresses, 1841-45, moved to Knoxville, Ia., 855; pros. atty. Marin County (Ia.), 1857-59; erved as dist. provost marshal during Civil War, 861-65; postmaster of Knoxville, 1869-70; prof. omology Ia. State Coll., 1870-74. Died Knoxville, lar. 30, 1887; buried Graceland Cemetery, Knoxɪlle.

MATHEWS, John, gov. S.C.; b. Charlestown now Charleston), S.C., 1744; s. John and Sarah Gibbes) M.; m. Mary Wragg, Dec. 1766; m. 2d, arah Rutledge, May 5, 1799. Served as Ensign, ɦen lt. in expdn. against Cherokee Indians, 1760; dmitted to Middle Temple, London, Eng., 1764; dmitted to S.C. bar, 1766; mem. 1st, 2d S.C. rovincial congresses from St. George's, Dorcheser, 1775; elected asso. justice S.C. Ct. Gen. Sessions, 1776; speaker S.C. Gen. Assembly under emporary constn. of 1776; 1st speaker S.C. Ho. f Reps. under Constn. of 1778; mem. Continental ongress from S.C., 1778-82, signer Articles of Confederation; gov. S.C. (elected in Jonesborugh Assembly), 1782-83; apptd. a judge S.C. t. of Chancery, 1784; judge S.C. Ct. Equity (after rgn. cts. of law and equity), 1791; an original ustee Coll. of Charleston. Died Charleston, Oct. 6, 1802.

MATHEWS, Samuel, planter, colonial gov.; b. ɪng., 1600; m. Frances Hinton, 1629. Came to ʼa., 1622, became owner of large plantation at Blunt Point, Va.; mem. Va. Assembly, comdr. xpdn. against Pamunkeys; became mem. Va. Gov.'s Council, 1622, served intermittently until 1658; commr. apptd. by Royal Privy Council to nvestigate conditions in Va., 1624; agt. to recover Md. to Va., in Eng., 1652-57; became gov. Va., 1658, dissolved Ho. of Burgesses for refusing to eat him and his councilors, Burgesses refused to disperse, declaring themselves true reps. of peoɔle; reelected (with councilors) as responsible only to the Ho. of Burgesses. Died Jan. 1660.

MATHEWS, Vincent, congressman; b. "Matthews Field" nr. Newburgh, N.Y., June 29, 1766; attended Noah Webster's Sch., Goshen, N.Y., acad., Hackensack, N.J.; studied law, N.Y.C. Admitted to N.Y. bar, 1790, began practice in Elmira; mem. N.Y. Assembly, 1794, 1826, N.Y. Senate, 1796, 97, 1809; bounty land claims commr., 1798; served as brig. gen. and comdr. cavalry N.Y. Militia; mem. U.S. Ho. of Reps. (Federalist) from N.Y., 11th Congess, 1809-11; dist. atty. 7th N.Y. Dist., 1813-15; moved to Bath, N.Y., later to Rochester, N.Y., 1821; dist. atty. Monroe County (N.Y.), 1831; resumed law practice, Rochester. Died Rochester, Aug. 23, 1846; buried Mt. Hope Cemetery, Rochester.

MATHEWS, William T., artist; b. Bristol, Eng., May 7, 1821. Came to Am., 1833; began artistic career, Ohio, circa 1840; went to N.Y.C., circa 1850, maintained studio, until circa 1860; painted numerous portraits in Washington, D.C., including those of Lincoln, Hayes, Garfield, Harrison, McKinley. Died Washington, Jan. 11, 1905.

MATHEWSON, Elisha, senator; b. Scituate, R.I., Apr. 18, 1767. Justice of peace, Scituate; engaged in farming; mem., speaker R.I. Ho. of Reps., 1821; mem. R.I. Senate, 1822; mem. U.S. Senate (Democrat) from R.I., Oct. 26, 1807-11; resumed farming. Died Scituate, Oct. 14, 1853; buried Scituate.

MATHIOT, Joshua, congressman; b. Connellsville, Pa., Apr. 4, 1800; studied law, Newark, O. Admitted to Ohio bar, practiced in Newark; pros. atty., 1832-36; mayor of Newark, 1834; mem. U.S. Ho. of Reps. (Whig) from Ohio, 27th Congress, 1841-43; grand worth patriarch Ohio Sons of Temperance; contracted cholera while attending a temperance conv., Sandusky, O. Died Newark, July 30, 1849; buried Cedar Hill Cemetery, Newark.

MATIGNON, Francis Anthony, clergyman; b. Paris, France, Nov. 10, 1753; B.D., Sem. of St. Sulpice; Ph.D. in Divinity, Sorbonne, 1785. Ordained priest Roman Catholic Ch., 1778; curate, 1778-82; prof. theology Coll. of Navarre, 1785-89; came to Balt., 1792; pastor in Boston, 1792-1818; active in raising funds for Holy Trinity Ch., Franklin Square, Boston. Died Boston, Sept. 19, 1818; buried St. Augustine's Cemetery, Boston.

MATLACK, James, congressman; b. Woodbury, N. J., Jan. 11, 1775; attended common schs. Owner extensive land holdings; justice of peace, 1803, 09, 13, 16, 20, surrogate, 1815, chmn. twp. com.; judge Gloucester County (N.J.) Ct. of Common Pleas, 1806-17; mem. bd. freeholders Gloucester County, 1812-15, 19-21, 28; mem. N.J. Senate, 1817-18; mem. U.S. Ho. of Reps. from N.J., 17th-18th congresses, 1821-25; joined Whig Party. Died Woodbury, Jan. 16, 1840; buried Eglington Cemetery, Clarksboro, N.J.

MATLACK, Timothy, Continental congressman; b. Haddonfield, N.J., circa 1733; s. Timothy and Martha (Burr) M.; m. Ellen Yarnall, Oct. 5, 1758; m. 2d, Elizabeth Claypoole, Aug. 17, 1797; 5 children. Asst. to Charles Thomson, sec. of Continental Congress, 1775; mem. Provincial Conf., Carpenter's Hall, Phila., 1775; joined Phila. Associators, 1775, commanded battalion in Revolutionary War, served in Battle of Princeton, 1776; mem. Pa. Constl. Conv., 1776; mem. Pa. Com. of Safety, 1776; keeper of Great Seal of Pa., 1777; sec. Supreme Exec. Council, Pa., 1777-82; trustee U. Pa., 1779; mem. Continental Congress from Pa., 1780-81; mem. Am. Philos. Soc., 1780-1829; an original dir. Bank of N.Am., 1781; a founder Soc. of Free Quakers, 1781; a commr. to inspect navigable waters of Pa., assigned to Delaware River, 1789; master of rolls Pa., 1800-09; alderman Phila., 1813-18; treas. U.S. Dist. Ct., Phila., 1817. Died Holmesburg, Pa., Apr. 14, 1829; buried Free Quaker Burial Ground, Phila., reinterred Matson's Ford, opposite Valley Forge, Pa., 1905.

MATSON, Aaron, congressman; b. Plymouth, Mass., 1770. Moved to Cheshire County, N.H.; judge of probate of Cheshire County; mem. N.H. Ho. of Reps., 1806-09, 10-14, 17-18, 27-28; N.H. Exec. Council, 1819-21; mem. U.S. Ho. of Reps. from N.H., 17th-18th congresses, 1821-25. Died Newport, Vt., July 18, 1855.

MATTESON, Joel Aldrich, gov. Ill.; b. Watertown, N.Y., Aug. 2, 1808; s. Elnathan and Eunice (Aldrich) M.; m. Mary Fish, Oct. 7, 1832, 3 sons, 4 daus. Mem. Ill. Senate (Democrat), 1842-48, chmn. com. on finance; gov. Ill., 1853-57; lessee and pres. Chgo. & Alton R.R. for many years; major stockholder several Ill. banks. Died Chgo., Jan. 31, 1873.

MATTESON, Orsamus Benajah, congressman; b. Verona, N.Y., Aug. 28, 1805; attended common schs.; studied law, Utica, N.Y. Admitted to N.Y. bar, 1830, began practice in Utica, city atty. Utica, 1834, 36; commr. N.Y. Supreme Ct.; mem. U.S. Ho. of Reps. (Whig) from N.Y., 31st, 33d-34th, 35th congresses, 1849-51, 53-Feb. 27, 1857, 57-59; involved in scheme for constrn. of St. Mary's Ship Canal; engaged in lumbering, iron mfg., acquiring large tracts of land. Died Utica, Dec. 22, 1889; buried Forest Hill Cemetery, Utica.

MATTESON, Tompkins Harrison, painter; b. Peterboro, N.Y., May 9, 1813; m. Elizabeth Merrill, 1839, several children. Painted from early youth; opened studio, N.Y.C., circa 1834, later moved to Geneva, N.Y., then back to N.Y.C., until 1850; painted primarily hist. scenes, including Spirit of Seventy-Six, Signing the Compact on the Mayflower; asso. N.A.D.; mem. N.Y. State Legislature. Died Sherburne, N.Y., Feb. 2, 1884.

MATTHEWS, Claude, stock-breeder, gov. Ind.; b. Bethel, Ky., Dec. 14, 1845; s. Thomas A. and Eliza (Fletcher) M.; grad. Centre Coll., Danville, Ky., 1867; m. Martha Whitcomb, Jan. 1, 1868. Became grain and stock raiser, Vermillion County, Ind., 1868; organizer 1st breeders livestock assn. in U.S.; an organizer Nat. Assn. Breeders Shorthorn Cattle of U.S. and Can.; mem. Ind. Legislature, 1876; sec. of state Ind., 1890, gov., 1893-97. Died Indpls., Aug. 28, 1898.

MATTHEWS, John, mfr.; b. London, Eng., 1808; m. Elizabeth Chester, 1830, at least 2 sons. Apprenticed in machineshops, then worked as machinist; came to U.S. (N.Y.C.), 1832; ran a machine shop; produced soda water by English Bramah System; improved on soda water machinery, but never applied for patents; became one of world's largest soda mfrs. Died Bklyn., Jan. 12, 1870; buried Bklyn.

MATTHEWS, Stanley, asso. justice U.S. Supreme Ct.; b. Cincinnati, July 21, 1824; s. Thomas Johnson and Isabella (Brown) M.; grad. Kenyon Coll., Gambier, O., 1840; studied law, Cincinnati, 1840-42; m. Mary Ann Black, Feb. 1843; m. 2d, Mrs. Mary Theaker, 1887; 8 children. Assisted Rev. John Hudson at Union Sem., Maury County, Tenn., 1842; admitted to Tenn. bar, 1842; editor weekly paper Tenn. Democrat, circa 1843; returned to Cincinnati, became asst. pros. atty. and editor Cincinnati Morning Herald, 1844; clk. Ohio Ho. of Reps., 1848-49; judge Ct. of Common Pleas for Hamilton County (O.), 1851-53; mem. Ohio Senate, 1855-58; U.S. atty. for So. Ohio, 1858-61, prosecuted W.B. Connelly (a reporter) under Fugitive Slave Act for aiding 2 Negro slaves to escape; served as lt. col. 23d Ohio Inf., col. 51st Ohio Volunteers during Civil War; judge Superior Ct. of Cincinnati, 1863-65; counsel before Electoral Commn. in Hayes-Tilden presdl. dispute, 1877; mem. U.S. Senate (Republican) from Ohio, 1877-79, introduced "Matthews resolution" which called for payment of interest and prin. of U.S. bonds in silver and making silver legal tender, Jan. 25, 1878; asso. justice U.S. Supreme Ct., 1881-89, decisions include those in cases Nat. Bank vs. Ins. Co. (a depositing trustee is not responsible for debts owed a bank by the depositor), Bowman vs. Chgo. & Northwestern R.R. Co. (state laws prohibiting carrying intoxicating liquor into the state by common vehicles are regulating interstate commerce and unconstl.), Yick Wo vs. Hopkins (a law which is apparently impartial and fair is against the 14th Amendment if carried out in a way that unjustly discriminates). Died Washington, D.C., Mar. 22, 1889; buried Spring Grove Cemetery, Cincinnati.

MATTHEWS, William, congressman; b. Cecil County, Md., Apr. 26, 1755. Judge, Cecil County Ct., 1778, 80, 82-86; mem. Md. Gen. Assembly, 1786-89; presdl. elector when George Washington was unanimously elected U.S. Pres., 1788; mem. U.S. Ho. of Reps., 5th Congress, 1797-99.

MATTHEWS, William, bookbinder; b. Aberdeen, Scotland, Mar. 29, 1822; married, 2 sons including Alfred, 3 daus. Apprenticed to bookbinder; established his own bindery, N.Y.C., 1846; won Gold medal for bindery Internat. Crystal Palace Exhibition, 1853; head of bindery D. Appleton & Co., 1853-90; pres. Flatbush Water Works Co.; mem. Grolier Club; wrote on bookbinding for Appletons' Am. Cyclopaedia. Author: (with N. L. Andrews) A Short Historicial Sketch of the Art of Bookbinding, 1895. Died Brooklyn Heights, N.Y., Apr. 15, 1896.

MATTISON, Hiram, clergyman; b. Norway, N.Y., Feb. 8, 1811; s. Solomon and Lydia W. Mattison; m. Melinda Griswold, 4 children; m. 2d, Elizabeth S. Morrison, 5 children. Ordained to ministry Methodist Ch., 1836; rep. Am. Bible Soc. in N.J., 1840-41; editor, publisher Primitive Christian (also called Tracts for the Times, The Conservative), 1841-46; tchr. astronomy at sem., Fulton, N.Y., 1850-51; supply pastor for N.Y. chs., 1852-58; pastor, Adams and Syracuse, N.Y., 1858-60; founder St. John's Independent Meth. Ch., N.Y.C., circa 1860; rejoined main body of Meth. Ch. (after it took stand against slavery), 1865; pastor, Jersey City, N.J., 1865-68. Author: A Scriptural Defense of the Doctrine of the Trinity; or a Check to Modern Arianism, 1846; Popular Amusements, 1867. Died N.J., Nov. 24, 1868.

MATTOCKS, John, gov. Vt.; b. Hartford, Conn., Mar. 4, 1777; s. Samuel Mattocks; m. Esther Nowell, Sept. 4, 1810, 4 children. Admitted to Vt. bar, 1797; moved to Peacham, Vt., 1800; dir. Vt. State Bank, 1806; mem. Vt. Ho. of Reps., 1807, 15, 16, 23, 24; served as brig. gen. Vt. Militia, War of 1812; mem. U.S. Ho. of Reps. from Vt., 17th, 19th, 27th congresses, 1821-23, 25-27, 41-43; judge Vt. Supreme Ct., 1833-34; del. Vt. Constl. Conv., 1836; gov. Vt., 1843-44. Died Peacham, Aug. 14, 1847; buried Peacham Cemetery.

MATTOON, Ebenezer, congressman; b. North Amherst, Mass., Aug. 19, 1755; grad. Dartmouth, 1776. Served to maj. Continental Army; taught sch.; engaged in farming; mem. Mass. Ho. of Reps., 1781, 1812; justice of peace, 1782-96; presdl. elector, 1792, 96, 1820, 28; mem. Mass. Senate, 1795-96; served to maj. gen. 4th Div., Mass. Militia; sheriff of Hampshire County (Mass.), 1796-1816; mem. U.S. Ho. of Reps. (Federalist) from Mass., 6th-7th congresses, Feb. 2, 1801-03; maj. gen. Mass. Militia, 1799-1816, adj. gen., 1816-18; became blind, 1818, del. Mass. Constl. Conv., 1820. Died Amherst, Mass., Sept. 11, 1843; buried West Cemetery, Amherst.

MATTOON, Stephen, clergyman; b. Champion, N. Y., May 5, 1816; s. Gershom and Anna Nancy (Sayre) M.; grad. Union Coll., 1842, Princeton Theol. Sem., 1846; m. Mary Lowrie, at least 1 dau. Ordained to ministry by Troy Presbytery, 1846; missionary (with Dr. S. R. House) in Siam, 1847-65; pastor 1st Presbyn. Ch., Bangkok; 1st Am. consul to Siam, 1856-59; returned to U.S., 1866; pastor Ballston Spa Presbyn. Ch., 1867-69; pres. Biddle Inst., 1870-85. Died Marion, O., Aug. 15, 1889.

MATTSON, Hans, settler, diplomat; b. Önnestad Parish, Skane, Sweden, Dec. 23, 1832; s. Matts and Elna (Larson) M.; m. Cherstin Peterson, Nov. 23, 1855. Came to U.S., 1851; settled briefly (with his family) in Moline, Ill., 1852; led group of Swedish pioneers to Minn. Territory, 1853, settled nr. Red Wing, Minn.; raised and served as col. of regt. for U.S. Army, during Civil War; spl. emigration agt. to gov. Minn., 1866; mem. Minn. Bd. Immigration, 1867-72; sec. of state Minn., 1870-72, 87-91;

agt. in Sweden for N.P. R.R., also land speculators and Canadian Govt., at various times; founder Minn. Stats Tidning, 1877-81; U.S. consul gen. to India, 1881-83. Author: Reminiscences: The Story of an Emigrant, 1891. Died Minn., Mar. 5, 1893.

MAURICE, James, congressman; b. N.Y.C., Nov. 7, 1814; attended Broad St. Acad., N.Y.C.; studied law. Became clk. law office, 1826; admitted to N.Y. bar, 1835, practiced in Maspeth; apptd. master in chancery, 1843; mem. N.Y. Assembly, 1850; del. N.Y. State Democratic convs., 1851, 53, 56; mem. U.S. Ho. of Reps. (Dem) from N.Y., 33d. Congress 1853-55; declined appointment as justice N.Y. Supreme Ct., 1865; mem. N.Y. Assembly (Republican), 1866. Died Maspeth, Aug. 4, 1884; buried Mt. Olivet Cemetery, Maspeth.

MAURY, Francis Fontaine, surgeon; b. Danville, Ky., Aug. 9, 1840; grad. Center Coll., 1860; attended U. Va., 1860-61; M.D., Jefferson Med. Coll., 1862. Resident intern, Phila., 1862-63; asst. surgeon U.S. Army at South Street Gen. Hosp., Phila., 1863-65; clin. asst. to Prof. S. D. Gross, Jefferson Med. Coll., 1863-64, chief of surgeons, 1865; became mem. Am. Dermatological Assn., Pathological Assn. of Phila. (1865), Coll. of Physicians (1866), Acad. of Natural Scis. (1868), Phila. County Med. Soc. (1877); co-editor Photographic Review of Medicine and Surgery, 1870-72. Died Phila., June 4, 1879.

MAURY, Matthew Fontaine, naval officer; b. Fredericksburg, Va., Jan. 14, 1806; s. Richard and Diana (Minor) M.; LL.D. (hon.), Cambridge; m. Ann Hall Herndon, July 15, 1834, 5 daus., 3 sons. Became midshipman U.S. Navy, 1825, promoted lt., 1836; on surveying duty in harbors of S.E. U.S.; contbd. many articles on U.S. Navy to newspapers and periodicals, 1838-42; supt. depot of charts and instruments Navy Dept., 1842-55, 58-61, developed wind and current charts; promoted comdr., 1858; served as comdr. Confederate States Navy, 1861-65; spl. agt. of Confederacy in Eng.; imperial commr. of immigration to emperor of Mexico, 1865-66; lived in Eng., 1866-68; prof. meteorology Va. Mil. Inst., Lexington, 1868. Author: Wind and Current Chart of the North Atlantic, 1847; Abstract Log for the Use of American Navigators, 1848; The Physical Geology of the Sea, 1855; First Lessons in Geography, 1868. Died Feb. 1, 1873; buried Hollywood Cemetery, Richmond, Va.

MAVERICK, Peter, engraver; b. N.Y.C., Oct. 22, 1780; s. Peter Rushton and Anne (Reynolds) M.; m. Matilda Brown, 1828, children—Peter, Augustus, Maria, Emily. Apprenticed to engraver A. B. Durand, Newark; became gen. engraver, copperplate printer; a founder N.A.D. Died N.Y.C., June 7, 1831.

MAVERICK, Samuel, colonizer; b. Eng., circa 1602; son of Rev. John M. Maverick; m. Amias Cole, 1628, 2 sons, 1 dau. Came to Am. in connection with Gorges scheme of colonization; owned land in Me.; constructed fortified house, Mass. Bay, circa 1625; ran trading vessels; became freeman Mass. Bay Colony, 1632; in Va., 1635-36; returned to Eng., 1650; royal commr., 1664-67. Author: A Briefe Discription of New England and the Severall Townes Therein, 1660. Died circa 1676.

MAXCY, Jonathan, clergyman, coll. pres.; b. Attleborough, Mass., Sept. 2, 1768; s. Levi and Ruth (Newell) M.; grad. R.I. Coll. (now Brown U.), 1787; D.D. (hon.), Harvard, 1801; m. Susan Hopkins, Aug. 22, 1791, 6 children. Tutor, R.I. Coll., 1787-90, 1st prof. divinity, 1791, trustee, 1791, 2d pres. pro tem, 1792-1804; licensed to preach by Baptist Ch., 1790, ordained to ministry, 1791; pastor 1st Bapt. Ch., Providence, R.I.; pres. Union Coll., Schenectady, N.Y., 1804; 1st pres. U. S.C., 1804-20. Died Columbia, S.C., June 4, 1820.

MAXCY, Virgil, diplomat; b. Attleborough, Mass., May 5, 1785; s. Levi and Ruth (Newell) M.; A.B., A.M., Brown U., 1804; studied law under Robert Goodloe Harper, Balt.; m. Mary Galloway. Admitted to Md. bar; mem. Md. Exec. Council, 1815; mem. Md. Ho. of Reps. and Senate, circa 1815-circa 1830; a leader in calling and transacting Md. Jacksonian Conv. (1st held in U.S.), 1827; 1st U.S. solicitor of treasury, 1830-37; charge d'affaires, Brussels, Belgium, 1837-42, unsuccessful in negotiating U.S.-Belgian comml. treaty and in securing payment of Am. mchts'. claims for goods destroyed in Antwerp, Belgium during 1830 revolution. Author: The Laws of Maryland, with The Charter, The Bill of Rights, The Consitution of The State and Its Alterations... 1692-1809, 3 vols., 1811. Died aboard ship Princeton, Potomac River, Feb. 28, 1844; buried "Tulip Hill." Annapolis, Md.

MAXEY, Samuel Bell, senator, army officer; b. Tompkinsville, Ky., Mar. 30, 1825; s. Rice and Mrs. (Bell) M.; grad. U.S. Mil. Acad., 1846; m. Marilda Cassa Denton, July 19, 1853. Commd. 2d lt. 7th Inf., U.S. Army, 1846; brevetted 1st lt. after serving at battles of Contreras and Churubusco; served in capture of Mexico City, resigned, 1849; admitted to Ky. bar, 1850; clk. of county and circuit cts., also master chancery for Ky., 1852-56; moved to Paris, Tex., 1857; dist. atty. Lamar County, Tex., 1858-59; served as col., raised 9th Regt., Tex. Inf., Confederate Army; commd. brig. gen., 1862, maj. gen., 1864; commander Indian Territory Mil. Dist., also supt. Indian affairs, 1863-65; served until surrender of Trans-Miss. Dept., May 1865; declined appointment as judge 8th Dist. Tex., 1873; mem. U.S. Senate from Tex., 1875-1887. Died Eureka Springs, Ark., Aug. 16, 1895; buried Evergreen Cemetery, Paris, Tex.

MAXIMILIAN (Ferdinand Maximillian Joseph), Emperor of Mexico; b. Schönbrunn Palace, Heitzing dist., Vienna, Austria, July 6, 1832; son of Archduke Francis Charles; m. Princess Carlotta (or Charlotte), 1857. Rear adm. Austrian Navy, 1854; viceroy of Austria's Lombardo-Venetian possessions, 1857-59; travelled in Brazil, 1859; became choice of Napoleon III of France and group of Mexican exiles to take Mexican throne in French attempt to build overseas empire (France had already intervened in Mexico with Spain and Eng. to collect debts, but Spain and Eng. withdrew); insisted upon gaining approval of people before taking throne, secured this approval through plebiscites in areas controlled by French troops; accepted Mexican throne, Apr. 10, 1864; arrived at Mexico City, June 12, 1864; offended both Mexican and U.S. govts. by actions including refusal to restore confiscated lands to clergy, inquiries into land titles, and choice of ex-Confederates from U.S. as colonists to be encouraged and subsidized; his position became increasingly precarious when Napoleon III came to recognize that his Mexican policy was a failure and that events in Europe required his concerted efforts, and when U.S. (now free from Civil War) repeated its earlier demands, in accordance with Monroe Doctrine, that Maximilian leave; opposition to his reign was led by Benito Juarez (who was receiving unofcl. aid from U.S.); planned to abdicate (after French promised to leave Mexico in 18 months, 1866), but was persuaded to remain with his troops; took refuge in Querétaro, Mexico, surrounded by Juaristos; captured, court-martialled and executed (though several govts. pleaded with Juarez for his safe release). Died Querétaro, June 19, 1867; buried Vienna.

MAXWELL, David Hervey, physician, state legislator; b. Garrard County, Ky., Sept. 17, 1786; s. Bazaleel and Margaret (Anderson) M.; m. Mary Dunn, 1809, at least 1 child, James Darwin. Served as mil. surgeon in War of 1812; del. to Ind. constl. Conv., 1816; mem. bd. trustees state sem., pres. bd., many years; mem. Ind. Ho. of Reps., 1821, 23-25, speaker 8th session; mem. Ind. Senate, 1826-29; unanimously elected to Ind. Bd. of Internal Improvements, 1836; twice postmaster of Bloomington (Ind.); intrested primarily in devel. of higher edn. in Ind. Died Bloomington, May 24, 1854.

MAXWELL, George Clifford, congressman; b. Sussex County, N.J., May 31, 1771; grad. Coll. of N.J. (now Princeton), 1792; studied law; children include John Patterson Bryan. Admitted to the bar, 1797; practiced law, Hunterdon County, N.J.; mem. U.S. H. of Reps. from N.J., 12th Congress, 1811-13; resumed law practice, Flemington, N.J. Died Flemington, Mar. 16, 1816; buried Pleasant Ridge Cemetery, Raritan Twp., Hunterdon County.

MAXWELL, George Troup, physician; b. Bryan County, Ga., Aug. 6, 1827; s. John Jackson and Mrs. (Baker) M.; M.D., U. City N.Y., 1848; m. Augusta Jones, 1848. Practiced medicine, Tallahassee, Fla., 1848-57; surgeon Marine Hosp., Key West, Fla., 1857-60; prof. obstetrics and diseases of women and children Oglethorpe Med. Coll., Savannah, Ga., 1860-61; served to col. Confederate Army, 1861-62, imprisoned, 1863-65; mem. Fla. Legislature, 1866; practiced medicine, Jacksonville, Fla., 1866-71, New Castle, Del., 1871-76; v.p. Del. Med. Soc., 1874, sec., 1875-76; prof. State Agrl. Coll., Lake City, Fla.; pres. Fla. Med. Assn. Died Jacksonville, Sept. 2, 1897.

MAXWELL, Hugh, lawyer; b. Paisley, Scotland, 1787; son of William Maxwell; grad. Columbia, 1808, A.M., 1816; m. Agnes Stevenson, 4 children. Came to N.Y.C., circa 1790; asst. judge advocate gen. U.S. Army, 1814-17; dist. atty. N.Y. County, 1817-29; collector Port of N.Y., 1849-53. Died N.Y.C., Mar. 31, 1873.

MAXWELL, John Patterson Bryan, congressman; b. Flemington, N.J., Sept. 3, 1804; s. George Clifford Maxwell; grad. Princeton, 1823; studied law. Admitted to N.J. bar, 1827, began practice in Newark; moved to Belvidere, N.J.; editor Belvidere Apollo; mem. U.S. Ho. of Reps. (Whig) from N.J., 25th, 27th congresses, 1837-39, 41-43; trustee Princeton, 1842-45. Died Belvidere, Nov. 14, 1845; buried Belvidere Cemetery.

MAXWELL, Lewis, congressman; b. Chester County, Pa., Apr. 17, 1790; studied law, Va. Admitted to Va. bar, began practice in Weston, Va. (no W.Va.); mem. Va. Ho. of Dels., 1821-24; mem U.S. Ho. of Reps. (National-Republican) from Va. 20th-22d congresses, 1827-33; resumed law practice surveyor and land patentee. Died West Union, Dodd ridge County, Va. (now W.Va.), Feb. 13, 1862 buried Odd Fellows Cemetery, West Union.

MAXWELL, Lucien Bonaparte, land owner; b Kaskaskia, Ill., Sept. 14, 1818; s. Hugh B. an Marie Odille (Menard) M.; married. Traveled t N.M.; scout for Ft. St. Vrain, 1840-41; hunter o Frémont's 1st expdn., 1845-46; managed his fa ther-in-law's huge land holdings in N.M.; founde 1st Nat. Bank of N.M., 1870; sold out his entir holdings (almost 2,000,000 acres), 1871; a founde Silver City (N.M.). Died N.M., July 25, 1875 buried Ft. Sumner, N.M.

MAXWELL, Thomas, congressman; b. Tioga Poin (now Athens), Pa., Feb. 16, 1792; studied law Apptd. q.m. of a cavalry regt. during War of 1812 never called into active service; clk. Tioga County (N.Y.), 1819-29; mem. U.S. Ho. of Reps. (Demo crat) from N.Y., 21st Congress, 1829-31; prosecu tor of pension claims; admitted to practice in Tiog County Ct. of Common Pleas, 1832; editor Elmir (N.Y.) Gazette, 1834-36; postmaster of Elmira 1834-39; dep. clk. Chemung County (N.Y.), 1835 treas., 1836-43; v.p. N.Y. & Erie R.R. Co., 1841 commr. of loans of U.S. deposit and of N.Y. State funds, 1843; moved to Geneva, N.Y., circa 1845 apptd. dep. clk. N.Y. Supreme Ct. Died Elmira, Nov. 4, 1864; buried Woodlawn Cemetery, Elmira.

MAXWELL, William, army officer, legislator; b. Ireland, 1733; s. John and Ann Maxwell. Came to Am., 1747; served from ensign to col. Colonial Army, French and Indian Wars, fought at battles of Ft. Duquesne, Ticonderoga; mem. N.J. Provincial Congress from Sussex County, 1775; chmn. N.J. Com. of Safety, 1775; commd. col. 2d N.J. Regt., 1775, fought at Battle of Three Rivers; commd. brig. gen., 1776, served at battles of Brandywine, Germantown, Monmouth, 1777-78; ret., 1780; mem. N.J. Assembly, 1783. Died Lansdown, N.J., Nov. 4, 1796.

MAXWELL, William, publisher; b. N.Y., circa 1755; son of William Maxwell; m. Nancy Robbins, 8 children. Printer, Lexington, Ky., 1792-93; founded Centinel of N.W. Territory, Cincinnati, 1793-96; postmaster Cincinnati; published Laws of the Territory of the United States Northwest of the Ohio (1st book published in N.W. Territory), 1796; moved to Dayton, later to Hamilton County, 1799; mem. 1st Ohio Legislature, 1803; 1st asso. judge of Greene County, 1803; sheriff Greene County, 1803-07; capt. Ohio Militia, 1804-06, col., 1806. Died Greene County, 1809; buried on his farm, Greene County.

MAXWELL, William, lawyer, coll. pres.; b. Norfolk, Va., Feb. 27, 1784; s. James and Helen (Calvert) M.; grad. Yale, 1802; LL.D. (hon.), Hampden-Sydney Coll., 1836; m. Mary Robertson. Admitted to Norfolk bar, 1808; elected editor New York Jour. of Commerce, 1827; mem. Va. Ho. of Dels., 1830-32; mem. Va. Senate, 1832-38; published A Memoir of Rev. John H. Rice, D.D. his most ambitious literary work, 1835; elected trustee Hampden-Sydney Coll., pres., 1838-44; reestablished Va. Hist. Soc., librarian; edited Virginia Hist. Register, 1848-53; mem. Va. Bible Soc., Va. Colonization Soc.; elder Presbyn. Ch. Died nr. Williamsburg, Va., Jan. 10, 1857; buried Hollywood Cemetery, Richmond, Va.

MAY, Edward Harrison, painter; b. Croydon, Eng., 1824; son of Rev. Edward Harrison May; came to U.S., 1834; studied under Daniel Huntington, N.Y.C. Lived most of life in Paris; painted hist. and genre works; did portraits of Americans including Anson Burlingame, William Lewis Dayton; paintings including Mary Magdalen, The Brigand, now in museums in U.S.; served as capt. Am. ambulance corps during Franco-Prussian War, 1870-71. Died Paris, May 17, 1887.

MAY, Edwin, architect; b. 1824. Awarded contract for constrn. Court House, Franklin, Ind., 1849; designed Court House, Brookfield, Ind., 1852; commd. architect several govt. bldgs. including Greensburg Court House, court houses, Sullivan, Vincennes, Ft. Wayne (all Ind.), also a bldg. for Hosp. of Insane, Indpls., 1852-62; later established archtl. office, Indpls.; prepared plans for Ind. State Capitol (completed after his death by Adolph Scherrer). Died Feb. 20, 1880.

MAY, Henry, congressman; b. Washington, D.C., Feb. 13, 1816; attended Columbian Coll. (now George Washington U.), Washington, D.C.; studied law. Admitted to the bar, 1840, practiced law; sent by Pres. Pierce to investigate Galpin frauds in Mexico; moved to Balt., 1850; mem. U.S. Ho. of Reps. (Democrat) from Md., 33d, 37th congresses, 1853-55, 61-63. Died Balt., Sept. 25, 1866; buried Cathedral Cemetery, Balt.

MAY, Samuel Joseph, clergyman; b. Boston, Sept. 12, 1797; s. Col. Joseph and Dorothy (Sewall) M.;

rad. Harvard, 1817; studied theology under Norton Ware; m. Lucretia Flagge Coffin, June 1, 1825. Asst. o William Ellery Channing in his parish, Boston; ordained to ministry Unitarian Ch., 1822; pastor, Brooklyn, Conn., 1822-36, South Scituate, Mass., 1836-42, Syracuse, N.Y., 1845-67; organizer Windham County (Conn.) Peace Soc., 1826; advocate of temperance, women's rights; prin. Normal Sch., Lexington, Mass., 1842-44; made his home a link n Underground R.R. Died July 1, 1871.

MAY, William L., congressman; b. Ky., circa 1793; attended common schs.; studied law. Moved o Ill.; apptd. justice of peace Madison County Ill.), 1817; served as capt. Ill. Militia, 1822; justice of peace Morgan County (Ill.), 1827-29; mem. Ill. Ho. of Reps., 1828; receiver pub. moneys U.S Land Office, Springfield, Ill.; admitted to Ill. bar, practiced law; operated a ferry across Illinois River at Peoria; organizer Peoria Bridge Co. to erect bridge across Illinois River, 1849; mem. U.S. Ho. of Reps. (Democrat) from Ill., 23d-24th congresses, Dec. 1, 1834-39; moved to Peoria, practiced law; mayor of Springfield, 1841; went to Cal. during gold rush. Died Sacramento, Cal., Sept. 29, 1849.

MAYALL, Samuel, congressman; b. North Gray, Me., June 21, 1816; attended pub. schs. Moved to Gray, Me.; mem. Me. Ho. of Reps., 1845, 47-48, Me. Senate, 1847-48; mem. U.S. Ho. of Reps. (Democrat) from Me., 33d Congress, 1853-55; del. Republican Nat. Conv., Phila., 1856; moved to St. Paul, Minn., 1857, became owner extensive land holdings; commd. capt. at beginning of Civil War, wounded twice, imprisoned several times. Died St. Paul, Sept. 17, 1892; buried Oakland Cemetery, St. Paul.

MAYER, Alfred Marshall, scientist; b. Balt., Nov. 13, 1836; s. Charles F. and Eliza (Blackwell) M.; attended St. Mary's Coll.; attended U. Paris, 1863-65; Ph.D., U. Pa., 1865; m. Katherine Duckett Goldsborough, 1865; m. 2d, Louisa Snowden, 1869; children including Alfred. Asst. prof. chemistry and physics U. Md., 1856-58, Westminster Coll., Fulton, Mo., 1858-63; prof. phys. science Pa. Coll., Gettysburg, 1865-67, prof. physics and astronomy, 1867-71; prof. Stevens Inst. Tech., 1871-97; mem. Nat. Acad. Scis. Author: The Earth a Great Magnet, 1872, Sound, 1878; co-author: Light, 1877; also contbr. many articles to scientific jours. Died July 13, 1897.

MAYER, Brantz, lawyer; b. Balt., Sept. 27, 1809; s. Christian and Anna Katerina (Baum) M.; attended St. Mary's Coll., U. Md.; m. Mary Griswold, Sept. 27, 1835, 5 daus.; m. 2d, Cornelia Poor, 3 daus. Made trip to China and India, circa 1827; admitted to Md. bar, 1832; sec. U.S. legation to Mexico, 1841-44; a founder Md. Hist. Soc.; pres. Library Co. of Balt.; practiced law, Balt., 1844-45; chmn. Md. Union Central Com., 1861; served as brig. gen. Md. Volunteers, 1862-63, paymaster, 1863-65; major, paymaster U.S. Army, 1865, brevetted lt. col., 1866, ret. as col., 1875. Author: Mexico as It Was and as It Is, 1844; Mexico, Aztec, Spanish and Republican, 2 vols., 1851; Capt. Canot; or Twenty Years of an African Slaver, 1854; Outlines of Mexican Antiquities, 1858; Memoir of Jared Sparks, 1867. Editor: Journal of Charles Carroll, during His Visit to Canada in 1776, 1845. Died Feb. 23, 1879.

MAYER, Francis Blackwell, artist; b. Balt., Dec. 27, 1827; studied in Paris, France. Painted colonial subjects; best remembered as painter of Plains Indians; visited Minn., 1851, made sketches; published With Pen and Pencil on the Frontier; lived in Paris, 1864-70; worked in Balt. and Annapolis (Md.). Died Annapolis, July 28, 1899.

MAYER, Lewis, clergyman; b. Lancaster, Pa., Mar. 26, 1783; s. George Ludwig and Maria Barbara (Haller) M.; studied divinity with Rev. Daniel Wagner; m. Catharine Line, Nov. 5, 1809, 1 son, 3 daus.; m. 2d, Mary Gonder. Licensed to preach German Reformed Ch., 1807, ordained to ministry, 1808; pastor, Shepherdstown, Martinsburg, Smithfield, Va. (now W.Va.), 1808-21; pastor, York, Pa., 1821-25; conducted German Reform Sem., Carlisle, Pa., 1825-29, moved sch. to York, 1829-35, to Mercersburg, Pa., 1835, prof. until 1839. Author: The Sin against the Holy Ghost 1867. Editor: Mag. of German Reformed Ch., 1827-35. Died York, Aug. 25, 1849.

MAYER, Philip Frederick, clergyman; b. N.Y.C., Apr. 1, 1781; s. George Frederick and Mary Magdalene (Kammerdiener) M.; grad. Columbia, 1799, D.D. (hon.); D.D. (hon.), U. Pa.; m. Lucy W. Rodman, May 24, 1804, 8 children including Mary. Licensed to preach, 1802, ordained to ministry Lutheran Ch.; pastor Loonenburg (Athens), N.Y., 1803-06; pastor St. John's Ch., Phila., 1806-58; a founder Pa. Bible Soc.; trustee U. Pa.; pres. Phila. Dispensary, Pa. Inst. for Deaf and Blind. Editor: Dr. Martin Luther's Catechism Translated from the German, 1804. Died Apr. 16, 1858.

MAYES, Joel Bryan, Indian chief; b. Old Cherokee nation nr. Cartersville, Ga., Oct. 2, 1833; s. Samuel and Nancy (Adair) M.; grad. seminary nr. Tahlequah, Okla., 1855; m. Martha Candy, 1857; m. 2d, Martha McNair; m. 3d, Mary Vann. Enlisted as pvt. in 1st Confederate Indian Brigade, promoted to paymaster; held office in Cherokee Nation as judge Northwestern circuit, clk. dist. ct., clk. commrs. ct., mem. nat. council, asso. justice, chief justice Cherokee Supreme Ct., elected prin. chief, 1887, reelected, 1891. Died Cherokee Reservation, Ga., Dec. 14, 1891.

MAYHEW, Experience, clergyman; b. Chilmark, Mass., Feb. 5, 1673; s. John and Elizabeth (Hilliard) M.; A.M. (hon.), Harvard, 1720; m. Thankful Hinkley, 1695; m. 2d, Remember Bourne, 1711; at least 1 son, Jonathan. Preached to Indians, 1694-98; tchr., English Ch., Tisbury, Mass.; minister for Soc. for Propagation of Gospel in New Eng., 1694-1758; translated Psalms into Indian dialects, 1709. Author: Indian Converts, 1727; Grace Defended, 1744. Died Mass., Nov. 29, 1758.

MAYHEW, Jonathan, clergyman; b. Chilmark, Mass., Oct. 8, 1720; s. Experience and Remember (Bourne) M.; grad. with honors Harvard, 1747; D.D. (hon.), Aberdeen (Scotland) U., 1749; m. Elizabeth Clarke, Sept. 2, 1756, 2 daus. Pastor, West Ch., Boston, 1747-66; Dudleian lectr. Harvard, 1765. Author: A Letter of Reproof to Mr. John Cleaveland, 1764; The Snare Broken, 1766. Died Boston, July 9, 1766.

MAYHEW, Thomas, colonial gov., missionary; b. Tisburg, Wiltshire, Eng., Mar. 1592; s. Matthew and Alice (Barter) M.; m. 2d, Jane Gallion, 1635; 5 children. Admitted as freeman to Mass. Bay Colony, 1634; dep. from Medford to Mass. Gen. Ct., 1636, from Watertown, 1637-44; also selectman and commr. Watertown; built bridge over Charles River; purchased Martha's Vineyard, Nantucket and Elizabeth islands, 1641, secured under Gorges patent more valid claim to Vineyard; magistrate Martha's Vineyard, from 1646, commd. gov. for life, 1671; organized Indian Ch., Martha's Vineyard, 1670, preached to Indians of Nantucket and Vineyard. Died Martha's Vineyard, Mar. 25, 1682.

MAYHEW, Thomas, clergyman; b. Eng., circa 1621; s. Gov. Thomas Mayhew; m. Jane Paine, 3 sons, including John, Thomas. Came to Am., 1631; granted (with his father) land patent to Martha's Vineyard, Nantucket and Elizabeth Island; pastor Edgartown Ch.; converted Indians of islands to Christianity; opened Indian sch., 1652. Died at sea, 1657.

MAYLATH, Heinrich, musician; b. Vienna, Austria, Dec. 4, 1827; studied music with his father. Went on tours, 1863-65; in Russia, until 1867; came to Am., 1867, settled in N.Y.C. as music tchr.; composed instructive piano music and concert pieces, also numerous transcriptions. Died N.Y.C., Dec. 31, 1883.

MAYNARD, Edward, dentist, inventor; b. Madison, N.Y., Apr. 26, 1813; s. Moses and Chloe (Butler) M.; attended U.S. Mil. Acad.; m. Ellen Sophia Doty, 1839; m. 2d, Nellie Long, 1869; 8 children including George W. Practiced dentistry, Washington, D.C., 1836-91; 1st dentist to fill teeth with gold foil, 1838; co-editor Am. Journal of Dental Science, 1843-46; patented firearm priming system, 1845; prof. theory and practice Balt. Coll. of Dental Surgery, 1857-91; developed and patented Maynard carbine (1 of 1st breech-loading rifles in Am.); court dentist to Emperor Nicholas I of Russia; named chevalier of mil. order of Red Eagle of Prussia; prof. dental theory and practice Nat. U., Washington, 1887-91; hon. mem. Am. Acad. Dental Scis. Died Washington, May 4, 1891.

MAYNARD, Horace, U.S. postmaster gen., congressman; b. Westboro, Mass., Aug. 30, 1814; s. Ephraim and Diana (Gogswell) M.; grad. Amherst Coll., 1838; m. Laura Washburn, Aug. 30, 1840, 7 children. Instr., prof. mathematics U. E. Tenn., 1839-41; admitted to Tenn. bar, 1844, practiced in Knoxville; mem. U.S. Ho. of Reps. from Tenn., 35th-37th congresses, 1857-63, 39th-43d congresses, 1866-75; atty. gen. Tenn., 1863-65; del. So. Loyalist Conv., Phila., 1866; minister to Turkey, 1875-80; U.S. postmaster gen., 1880-81. Died Knoxville, Tenn., May 3, 1882; buried Old Gray Cemetery, Knoxville.

MAYNARD, John, congressman; b. Whitestone, N.Y.; grad. Union Coll., Schenectady, N.Y., 1810; studied law. Admitted to N.Y. bar, began practice in Seneca Falls; clk. Seneca County (N.Y.), 1821-22; mem. N.Y. Assembly, 1822; mem. U.S. Ho. of Reps. (Whig) from N.Y., 20th, 27th congresses, 1827-29, 41-43; mem. N.Y. Senate, 1838-41; moved to Auburn, N.Y.; judge 7th dist. N.Y. Supreme Ct., 1847-50. Died Auburn, Mar. 24, 1850.

MAYO, Frank, actor; b. Boston, Apr. 18, 1839; married, 3 children. Played his 1st role in play Raising the Wind, San Francisco, 1856; acted in Cal., 1856-65; performed. primarily in Am. character roles, on East Coast; made European tour, 1879-80; adapted Puddin' Head Wilson (Mark Twain) for stage, 1895. Co-author: Nordeck, 1883. Died Grand Island, Neb., June 8, 1896; buried West Laurel Hill Cemetery, Phila.

MAYO, Robert, physician, author; b. Powhatan County, Va., Apr. 25, 1784; s. Joseph and Martha (Tabb) M.; grad. Coll. William and Mary, 1803; M.D., U. Pa., 1808; m. Eliza Harbaugh, July 11, 1831; children—Martha, Robert. Began practice medicine, Richmond, Va., 1808; devoted career to writing, from circa 1820; editor Jacksonian Democrat, newspaper, Richmond, 1828; with civil service, Washington, D.C., 1830-64. Author: An Epitome of Ancient Geography and History, 1815; New System of Mythology, 1815-19; Political Sketches of Eight Years in Washington, 1839. Died Washington, Oct. 1, 1864; buried Washington.

MAYO, Robert Murphy, congressman; b. Hague, Va., Apr. 28, 1836; attended Coll. William and Mary; grad. Va. Mil. Inst., 1858; attended Lexington Law Sch. (now Washington and Lee U.), 1858-59. Instr. mathematics Mt. Pleasant Mill. Acad., Sing Sing (now Ossining), N.Y., later at Va. Mil. Inst.; served from maj. to col. 47th Va. Regt., Confederate Army; admitted to Va. bar, began practice in Hague, 1865; mem. Va. Ho. of Dels., 1881-82, 85-88; mem. U.S. Ho. of Reps. (Readjuster) from Va., 48th Congress, 1883-Mar. 20, 1884 (lost seat as result of a successfully contested election); resumed law practice. Died Hague, Mar. 29, 1896; buried Yeocominco Cemetery, Tucker Hill, Westmoreland County, Va.

MAYO, Sarah Carter Edgarton, author; b. Shirley, Mass., Mar. 17, 1819; d. Joseph and Mehitable (Whitcomb) Edgarton; m. Rev. Amory Dwight Mayo, July 28, 1846, 1 dau. Began writing, circa 1836; contbd. to The Universalist and Ladies Repository, became asso. editor, 1839-42; editor The Rose of Sharon: A Religious Souvenir (Universalist annual), 1840-48. Author: The Palfreys; Ellen Clifford; Poems; The Flower Vase (1843); The Floral Fortune Teller (1846). Died July 9, 1848.

MAYO, William, surveyor; b. Eng., circa 1684; s. Joseph and Elizabeth (Hooper) M.; m. Frances Gould, 4 children; m. 2d, Anne Perratt, 4 children. Surveyed Island of Barbados, circa 1712; came to Va., circa 1723; justice of peace, county surveyor Goochland County (Va.), 1728; surveyed Va.-N.C. boundary line, 1728, boundary line between Goochland and Hanover counties, 1731, site of Richmond (Va.), 1733. Died circa 1744.

MAYO, William Kennon, naval officer; b. Drummondtown, Va., May 29, 1829; s. Peter Poythress and Leah Curtis (Upshur) M.; attended U.S. Naval Acad., Annapolis, 1847-48; m. Virginia Kendall; m. 2d, Nannie Glover; no children. Became midshipman U.S. Navy, 1841; did 1st duty aboard United States, 1842; served in ship St. Mary's during blockades of Tampico and Vera Cruz during Mexican War; passed midshipman, 1847; instr. seamanship and gunnery, 1854; instr. ethics and English, U.S. Naval Acad., 1859-60; promoted lt., 1855; served aboard St. Mary's, Pacific Squadron, 1860-62; exec. officer in ship Housutonic, 1862; promoted lt. comdr., 1862; commander ship Kanawha, W. Gulf Squadron, 1862-63; comdr. Nahant, 1864-65; ordnance officer S. Atlantic Blockading Squadron, 1865; commd. comdr., 1866; commanded ships Tuscarora, Congress, N. Atlantic Squadron, 1870-71; comdr. ship Omaha, 1872-74, Hartford, 1877-79; commandant Norfolk Navy Yard, 1882-85; promoted commodore, 1882, ret., 1886. Died Washington, D.C., Apr. 9, 1900.

MAYO, William Starbuck, physician, author; b. Ogdensburg, N.Y., Apr. 15, 1811; s. Obed and Elizabeth (Starbuck) M.; grad. Coll. Physicians and Surgeons, N.Y.C., 1832; m. Helen Stuyvesant, 1851. Traveled to Spain and Barbary States, circa 1835; settled in N.Y.C. Author: Kaloolah, or Journeyings to the Djebél Kumri, 1849; The Berber; or, the Mountaineer of the Atlas, 1850; Romance Dust from the Historic Placer, 1851; Never Again, 1873. Died N.Y.C., Nov. 22, 1895.

MAYRANT, William, congressman; b. S.C. Mem. U.S. Ho. of Reps. from S.C., 14th Congress, 1815-Oct. 21, 1816 (resigned); unsuccessful candidate for reelection.

MAZUREAU, Étienne, lawyer; b. France, 1777. Served in ships L'Entreprenant and Le Formidable, French Navy, 1793-94; insp. of agr., French Guiana, 1799, imprisoned for making remark against Napoleon; came to N.Y., 1803, to New Orleans, 1804; admitted to La. bar, circa 1804; became partner (with Edward Livingston) in law firm; atty. gen. La., 1815; prosecutor in The State vs. Hypolite Truette case, enforcing new law prohibiting dueling. Died New Orleans, May 25, 1849.

MAZZEI, Philip, wine mcht.; b. Poggio-a-Caiano, Italy, Dec. 25, 1730; s. Domenico and Elisabetta Mazzei; studied medicine at Santa Maria Nuova; m.

Marie Martin, 1774; m. 2d wife, 1796, 1 child. Went to London, Eng., 1755; wine mcht., London, 1755-73; came to Va. to introduce culture of grapes, 1773; agt. to secure money for Va. from Grand Duke of Tuscany, during Revolutionary War, 1779-84; "intelligencer" to King of Poland, 1788, pvt. adviser to Stanislas II of Poland, 1792. Author: Recherches historiques et politiques sur les États-Unis de l'Amérique septentrionale, 4 vols., 1788; Memorie della Vita e delle Pere grinazioni del Fiorentino Filippo Mazzei, 1813. Died Pisa, Mar. 19, 1816.

MAZZUCHELLI, Samuel Charles, clergyman, architect; b. Milan, Italy, Nov. 4, 1806; s. Luigi and Rachele (Merlini) M. Novice, Dominican Order, Rome, Italy, 1823; came to Am., 1828; ordained priest Roman Catholic Ch., Cincinnati, 1830; missionary to N.W. Territory, circa 1830; printed prayerbook and catechism in Winnebago lang., 1833; built 1st ch. in area of Prairie du Chien, Wis., 1835; vicar gen. and missioner extraordinary Dubuque Diocese, 1837-circa 1843; mem. 5th Provincial Council, Balt., 1843; visited Italy, 1844, returned to Am., 1845; built Sinsinawa Mound Coll., 1845; founded Dominican Congregation of the Most Holy Rosary (Teaching nuns), 1847; designed county court house, Galena, Ill., also 1st capital of Ia. at Ia. City. Died Feb. 23, 1864.

McAFEE, John Armstrong, clergyman, coll. pres.; b. Marion County, Mo., Dec. 12, 1831; s. Joseph and Priscilla (Armstrong) McA.; grad. Westminster Coll., Fulton, Mo., 1859, D.D. (hon.); m. Anna W. Bailey, Aug. 23, 1859, 6 children. Worked on father's farm and in other jobs to pay his way through coll.; taught sch., Ashley, Mo., for a time; taught at Pardee Coll., Louisiana, Mo., 1867-70, Highland (Kan.) Coll., 1870-75; a founder Park Coll. (specialized in missionary tng.), 1875, pres., 1875-90; ordained to ministry Presbyn. Ch. Died June 12, 1890.

McAFEE, Robert Breckinridge, state ofcl., diplomat; b. Salt River, Ky., Feb. 18, 1784; s. Robert and Anne (McCoun) McA.; attended Transylvania Sem.; m. Mary Cardwell, Oct. 1807. Admitted to Ky. bar, 1891; commd. capt. Ky. Militia; served from pvt. to 2d lt. U.S. Army, War of 1812; mem. Ky. Ho. of Reps., 1819, 30-33, Ky. Senate, 1821, 41; lt. gov. Ky., 1824-28; mem. 1st nat. Democratic Conv., 1832; U.S. charge d' affaires at Bogata, New Granada (now Colombia), 1833-37; pres. bd. visitors U.S. Mil. Acad., 1842-45; mem. Royal Antiquarian Soc. of Denmark; hon. mem. Ky. Hist. Soc. Author: History of the War of 1812, published 1816. Died Salt River, Mercer County, Ky., Mar. 12, 1849.

McALLISTER, Archibald, congressman; b. Fort Hunter, Pa., Oct. 12, 1813; attended Dickinson Coll., Carlisle, Pa. Engaged in mfg. charcoal iron, Springfield Furnace (now Royer), Blair County, Pa.; mem. U.S. Ho. of Reps. (Democrat) from Pa., 38th Congress, 1863-65. Died Royer, July 18, 1883; buried Mountain Cemetery, Royer.

McALLISTER, Hall, lawyer; b. Savannah, Ga., Feb. 9, 1826; s. Mathew Hall and Louisa Charlotte (Cutler) McA.; attended Yale, 1846-47; studied law privately; m. Louisa Clemence Hermann, 4 children. Admitted to Ga. bar, 1849; moved to San Francisco, 1849; formed law firm with his father and brother, 1850; became 2d lt. Cal. Guards (orgn. to enforce law and order); had large law practice, said to have tried and won more cases than any other Cal. lawyer of the time; McAllister Street (San Francisco) named for him. Died on estate "Miramonte," Ross Valley, Cal., Dec. 1, 1888; buried San Francisco.

McALLISTER, Matthew Hall, jurist; b. Savannah, Ga., Nov. 26, 1800; s. Matthew and Hannah (Gibbons) McA.; grad. Princeton; LL.D. (hon.), Columbia, 1860; m. Louisa Charlotte Cutler, 6 children including Hall, Ward, Cutler, Julian. Admitted to Ga. bar, 1820, practiced law in Savannah, 1820-49; apptd. U.S. dist. atty. for So. Ga., 1827; mem. Ga. Senate, 1834-37; mayor of Savannah, several terms; opposed nullification; del.-at-large Dem. Nat. Conv., 1848; declined election as a Ga. del. to Nashville Conv., 1850; apptd. 1st U.S. circuit judge in Cal., 1855-62. Author: Eulogy on President Jackson. Died San Francisco, Dec. 19, 1865.

McALLISTER, Samuel Ward, lawyer, society leader; b. Savannah, Ga., Dec. 1827; s. Matthew Hall and Louisa (Cutler) McA.; m. Sarah Gibbons, 1853, 3 children. Admitted to Ga. bar, 1848-49; partner (with father and brother, Hall) in law firm, San Francisco, 1850-52; made a fortune by 1852; ret. from practice to devote himself to social life; organized "Patiarchs" (a group of old N.Y. families to pass approval on social aspirants); originated term "Four Hundred" for top N.Y. socialites as a result of cutting Mrs. William Astor's guest list down for a small ball; symbol of N.Y. soc. for generations. Author: Society As I Have Found It. Died N.Y.C., Jan. 31, 1895.

McALPINE, William Jarvis, civil engr.; b. N.Y.C., Apr. 30, 1812; s. John and Elizabeth (Jarvis) McA.; m. Sarah Learned, Feb. 24, 1841. Asso. with John B. Jervis in constrn. Carbondale R.R., 1827-36; chief engr. eastern div. Erie Canal, 1836-44; chief engr. govt. dry dock, Bklyn., 1845-49; designer and builder Albany (N.Y.) Water Works, 1850-51; state engr., ry. commr. State of N.Y., 1852-57; chief engr. Erie R.R., 1856-57, Chgo. & Galena (later Northwestern) R.R., 1857, Ohio & Miss. R.R., 1861-64; chief engr. 3d Av. drawbridge over Harlem River, N.Y.C., 1860-61; chief or cons. engr. for many gt. bridge projects including Eads Bridge over the Mississippi at St. Louis, 1865, Clifton Suspension Bridge at Niagara, 1868, Washington Bridge, N.Y.C., 1885-88; supt. constrn. N.Y. State Capitol, Albany; engr. for N.Y.C. parks, built Riverside Dr.; pres. Am. Soc. C.E., 1870, named hon. mem.; 1889; 1st Am. elected mem. Instn. Civil Engrs. (Gt. Britain); recipient Telford medal for paper "The Supporting Power of Piles." Died New Brighton, R.I., Feb. 16, 1890.

McANALLY, David Rice, clergyman, educator; b. Grainger County, Tenn., Feb. 17, 1810; s. Charles and Elizabeth (Moore) McA.; m. Maria Thompson; m. 2d, Julia Reeves. Admitted on trial to Holston conf., Methodist Episcopal Ch., 1829; pastor various chs., Tenn., N.C., Va., 1829-43; pres. E. Tenn. Female Inst., 1843-51; editor St. Louis Christian Advocate, 1851-95; a founder Central Coll., Fayette, Mo., 1852; placed under arrest for a time because of alleged Confederate sympathies, 1861; del. Methodist Episcopal Conf., 5 times. Author: History of Methodism in Missouri, 1881. Died July 11, 1895.

McARTHUR, Duncan, gov. Ohio; b. Dutchess County, N.Y., June 14, 1772; s. John and Margaret (Campbell) McA.; m. Nancy McDonald, Feb. 1796, at least 1 dau., Effie. Moved nr. Pitts., 1780; served with Harmar's campaign against Indians, 1790, in Battle of Captina, 1792; settled nr. Chillicothe, O., 1796; mem. Ohio Ho. of Reps., 1804-05, 15-16, 17-18, 26-27, speaker, 1817-18; mem. Ohio Senate, 1805-14, 21-22, 22-23, 29-30, speaker, 1809-10; commd. col. regt. under Brig. Gen. William Hull, Ohio Militia, 1806; served as brig. gen. Ohio Volunteers in defense of Ft. Meigs, 1813, in command of troops at Sacketts Harbor on Lake Ontario, then in command U.S. Army in N.W., 1814; mem. several treaty-making commns. with Indians after war, 1816; mem. U.S. Ho. of Reps. from Ohio, 18th Congress, 1823-25; gov. Ohio, 1830-32. Died Chillicothe, Apr. 29, 1839; buried Grandview Cemetery, Chillicothe.

McARTHUR, John, architect; b. Bladenock, Scotland, May 13, 1823; attended drawing and design classes Franklin Inst., Phila.; m. Matilda Prevost, 4 children. Came to Am. in youth; apprenticed to his uncle (a carpenter), Phila.; won competition for design House of Refuge, Phila., 1848; designed, constructed various mansions, public bldgs., Phila.; architect naval hosps. during Civil War; designed Phila. City Hall. Died Phila., Jan. 8, 1890.

McARTHUR, William Pope, hydrographer, naval officer; b. St. Genevieve, Mo., Apr. 2, 1814; s. John and Mary (Linn) McA.; m. Mary Stone Young, May 3, 1838. Apptd. midshipman U.S. Navy, 1832; served in Seminole War of 1837-38; took part in Gulf Coast Survey, 1840; promoted lt., 1841; in command of hydrographic party that made 1st survey of Pacific Coast, 1848. Died on ship Oregon while returning from coast survey duties, Panama, Dec. 23, 1850.

McAULEY, Thomas, clergyman, educator; b. Ireland, Apr. 21, 1778; s. Thomas and Eliza J. (Warden) McA.; grad. Union Coll., Schenectady, N.Y., 1804; LL.D. (hon.), Dublin U. Frontier missionary before entering coll.; tutor Union Coll., 1805-06; lectr. in mathematics and natural philosophy, 1806-14, prof. mathematics and natural philosophy, 1814-22; ordained to ministry Presbyn. Ch. by Presbytery of Albany, 1819; pastor Rutgers Street Ch., N.Y.C., 1822-27; moderator Presbyn. Gen. Assembly, 1826; pastor 10th Presbyn. Ch., Phila., 1827-33; pastor, N.Y.C., 1833-45; a leader of "New Sch." movement in Presbyn. Ch.; a founder Union Theol. Sem., 1835, 1st pres., 1836-40. Died May 11, 1862.

McBEAN, Thomas, architect; designer St. Paul's Chapel (1st ch. of authentic Gothic design erected in N.Y.C.), 1764.

McBRYDE, Archibald, congressman; b. Wigtownshire, Scotland, Sept. 28, 1766; studied law. Came to U.S. with his parents, settled in Carbonton, N.C.; admitted to N.C. bar, practiced law; engaged in farming; clk. Moore County (N.C.) Superior Ct., 1792-1816; mem. U.S. Ho. of Reps. (Democrat) from N.C., 11th-12th congresses, 1809-13; mem. N.C. Senate, 1813-14; resumed law practice. Died Carbonton, Feb. 15, 1816; buried Farrar Cemetery, Carbonton.

McBURNEY, Robert Ross, assn. exec.; b. Castle-Blayney, Ireland, Mar. 31, 1837; never married. Came to Am., 1854; clk. in hat shop, N.Y.C 1854-61; led noon prayer meetings North Dutc Ch., N.Y.C.; became only paid officer YMCA, 186 helped obtain funds for YMCA bldg., N.Y.C., 186 metropolitan sec. YMCA, N.Y.C., 1887-98, orgn. both city and nat. level grew under his guidanc Died Clifton Springs, N.C., Dec. 27, 1898.

McCABE, James Dabney, clergyman, editor; Richmond, Va., Apr. 15, 1808. Ordained to mini try Methodist Episcopal Ch., 1829; pastor several chs Va., 1830's; joined Protestant Episcopal Ch., cir 1840, ordained to ministry, 1845; rector Episcop chs., Abingdon, East Wheeling, Va., 1845-56; ass rector St. Paul's Parish, Balt., 1856-75; editor Oli Branch, mag., 1850's-60's, also Odd Fellows Mag Balt. Author: Masonic Text Book. Died Balt., Aug. 1875; buried Balt.

McCABE, John Collins, clergyman; b. Richmon Va., Nov. 12, 1810; s. William and Jane (Collins McC.; m. Emily Hardaway; m. 2d, Eliza Gord (Taylor) Smith, Aug. 7, 1839; at least 1 son, Wi liam Gordon. Clk. for a time in Farmer's Bank Richmond; ordained to ministry Episcopal Ch., 184 served in various pastorates in Va., 1848-56; rect Ch. of Ascension, Balt., 1856-59; chaplain 32d V Regt., Confederate Army, 1861-62; chaplain ge Confederate mil. prisons, 1862-65; resumed preac ing in various locations after war; contbr. to S Literary Messenger; wrote monographs on coloni ch. history. Author: Scraps, 1835. Died Chamber burg, Va., Feb. 26, 1875.

McCAFFREY, John, clergyman, educator; b. Em mitsburg, Md., Sept. 6, 1806; attended Mt. S Mary's Coll., Emmitsburg. Ordained deacon Roma Catholic Ch., 1831, priest, 1838; with Mt. St Mary's Coll., 1838-72, began as tchr. in prep. sch. later became mem. seminary governing bd. and re tor, 1838-72; declined various bishoprics, preferrin to remain at the Coll. Author: A Catechism o Christian Doctrine. Died Emmitsburg, Md., Sept 26, 1881; buried Mt. St. Mary Coll. Cemetery Emmitsburg.

McCAINE, Alexander, clergyman; b. Ireland 1768; at least 1 child. Came to Am., circa 1788 settled in Charleston, S.C.; admitted on trial t Methodist Conf., 1797, full mem., 1799; sec. Meth Gen. Conf., 1820; mem. of the "reform" segmer of the ch. in regard to election of ch. elders an greater lay representation. Author: The History an Mystery of Methodist Episcopacy, 1827; A Defenc of the Truth, 1829; Letters on the Organizatio and Early History of the Methodist Episcopa Church, 1850; Slavery Defended from the Scriptur Against the Attacks of the Abolitionists (pam phlet), 1842. Died Augusta, Ga., June 1, 1856

McCALEB, Theodore Howard, jurist, educator; b Pendleton Dist., S.C., Feb. 10, 1810; s. David an Matilda (Farrar) McC.; attended Yale; studied la with Rufus Choate, Salem, Mass.; m. Agnes Bullitt 1832, 6 children. Practiced law, New Orleans; judg U.S. Dist. Ct. of La., 1841-46; U.S. Dist. Ct. fo Eastern La., 1846-61; prof. admiralty and internat law Tulane U., 1847-64, mem. coll. faculty, 1850 62. Died "Hermitage Plantation," Miss., Apr. 29 1864; buried "Hermitage Plantation."

McCALL, Edward Rutledge, naval officer; b Beaufort, S.C., Aug. 6, 1790; s. Hext and Eliza beth (Pickering) McC.; m. Harriett McKnights Apptd. midshipman U.S. Navy, 1808; acting lt. o Enterprise, 1812, in command of ship when it de feated Brit. ship Boxer, off Me.; promoted lt., 1813 recipient gold medal from Congress, 1814; serve in Mediterranean Squadron, 1815-17, various shor duty posts, 1817-25; promoted to master comdt. 1825; in command of the Peacock in West India Squadron, 1830-31; promoted capt., 1835. Die Bordentown, N.J., July 31, 1853.

McCALL, Peter, lawyer, mayor Phila.; b. Trenton N.J., Aug. 31, 1809; s. Peter and Sarah (Gibson McC.; grad. Princeton, 1826; m. Jane Mercer, 1846 8 children. Admitted to bar, 1830, practiced law Phila., 1830-80; mem. Phila. City Council, severa terms, 1840's-50's, mayor Phila., 1844; chancello Phila. Bar Assn., 1873-80; lectr. in pleading an evidence Pa. State U. Law Sch.; mem. Phila. Hist. Soc., Law Acad. Phila., Am. Philos. Soc. Died a residence Overbrook, nr. Phila., Oct. 30, 1880.

McCALLA, William Latta, clergyman; b. Jessa mine County, Ky., Nov. 25, 1788; s. Dr. Andrew and Martha (More) McC.; m. Martha Ann Finley Mar. 30, 1813. Examined for licensing by Wes Lexington Presbytery, 1813, licensing delayed (prob ably due to polit. differences resulting from War o 1812); served as chaplain Ohio Militia, 1816-18 Presbyn. pastor, Augusta, Ky., 1819-23; pasto Scots' Ch., Phila., 1824-35; pastor Assembly Ch. Phila. (formed as result of split in Fourth Ch congregation), 1836-42; pastor Union Ch., Phila. 1850-54; engaged in numerious theol. controversies throughout life; missionary in South in later life

Author: An Argument for Cleansing the Sanctuary, . . . Being in Opposition to the Prevailing System of Allowing Ungodly and Irresponsible Trustees to Manage Church Property, and Non-Communicants to Vote at Church Elections, 1853; Adventures in Texas, Chiefly in the Spring and Summer of 1840, published 1841. Died La., Oct. 12, 1859.

McCALLUM, Daniel Craig, mil. engr.; b. Johnston, Scotland, Jan. 21, 1815; m. Mary McCann, 3 children. Originator, patentee a type of bridge, 1851; gen. supt. N.Y. & Erie Ry., 1855-56; pres. McCallum Bridge Co., 1858-59; cons. engr. Atlantic & Gt. Western Ry.; apptd. mil. dir., supt. all U.S. railroads, 1862, commd. col. U.S. Army, apptd. aide-de-camp to comdr.-in-chief; brevetted brig. gen., 1864, maj. gen., 1865. Author: The Water Mill and Other Poems, 1870. Died Bklyn., Dec. 27, 1878; buried Mt. Hope Cemetery, Rochester, N.Y.

McCARROLL, James, journalist; b. Lanesboro, Ireland, Aug. 3, 1814. Went to Canada, 1831; became editor, owner Peterborough Chronicle, 1845; surveyor Port of Toronto; taught music, became music critic for Toronto Leader and Toronto Colonist; went to N.Y.C.; mem. editorial staff The People's Cyclopedia of Universal Knowledge, The American Cyclopedia; contbr. articles to Belford's Magazine; worked on fire-proof wire gauze and improved elevator. Author: The Adventures of a Night, 1865, Almost a Tragedy, a Comedy, 1874 (both plays); Terry Finnegan Letters, 1864; Madeline and Other Poems, 1889. Died N.Y.C., Apr. 10, 1892.

McCARTEE, Divie Bethune, missionary, diplomat, educator; b. Phila., Jan. 13, 1820; s. Robert and Jessie (Bethune) McC.; attended Columbia; M.D., U. Pa., 1840; m. Joanna M. Knight, 1853. Apptd. missionary to China by Presbyn. Bd., 1843; founded, ran mission in Ningpo, China, 1844-62, also Am. consul, Ningpo, 1857; vice consul, Chefoo, Japan, 1862-65; became interpreter to consul staff, Shanghai, China, 1872; prof. law and science Tokyo Imperial U., 1872-77, also curator Bot. Gardens; became sec. to Chinese legation in Japan, 1877; counselor to Japanese legation, Washington, D.C., 1885-87. Died San Francisco, July 17, 1900.

McCARTHY, Dennis, congressman, state ofcl.; b. Salina, N.Y., Mar. 19, 1814; attended Valley Acad., Salina. Engaged in salt mfg.; mem. N.Y. Assembly, 1846; mayor of Syracuse (N.Y.), 1853; mem. U.S. Ho. of Reps. (Republican) from N.Y., 40th-41st congresses, 1867-71; mem. N.Y. Senate, 1876-85, pres. pro tem, 1885; 1st gov. N.Y., 1885-86. Died Syracuse, Feb. 14, 1886; buried Oakwood Cemetery, Syracuse.

McCARTNEY, Mary Elizabeth Maxwell, artist; b. probably N.J., Apr. 21, 1814; m. Washington McCartney. Painted numerous views in and around Easton, Pa. (now owned by Northampton County Hist. and Geneal. Soc.), some of which were used to illustrate History of Easton (Condit), 1885. Died 1893.

McCARTNEY, Washington, educator, mathematician, lawyer; b. Westmoreland County, Pa., Aug. 24, 1812; grad. Jefferson Coll., Canonsburg, Pa., 1834; m. Mary E. Maxwell, Apr. 18, 1839. Admitted to bar, 1838; prof. mathematics Lafayette Coll., 1835-36, prof. mathematics, modern lang., 1836-37, prof. mathematics, philosophy, astronomy, 1837-46, trustee of coll., 1847-52, prof. philosophy, 1849-52; dep. atty. gen. Northampton County, Pa., 1846-48; founded, conducted Union Law Sch., 1854-56; pres. judge 3d Pa. Jud. Dist., 1851; mem. Easton (Pa.) Sch. Bd. Author: The Principles of the Differential and Integral Calculus, 1844; Origin and Progress of the United States, 1847. Died July 15, 1856.

McCARTY, Andrew Zimmerman, congressman; b. Rhinebeck, N.Y., July 14, 1808; studied law. Admitted to N.Y. bar, 1831, began practice in Pulaski; clk. Oswego County (N.Y.), 1840-43; mem. N.Y. Assembly, 1846-47; mem. U.S. Ho. of Reps. (Whig) from N.Y., 34th Congress, 1855-57; resumed practice of law; register of bankruptcy, 1875-79. Died Pulaski, Apr. 23, 1879; buried Pulaski Cemetery.

McCARTY, Johnathan, congressman; b. Culpeper County, Va., Aug. 3, 1795; attended pub. schs., Va. Engaged in merc. bus., Franklin County, Ind.; mem. Ind. Ho. of Reps., 1818; moved to Connersville, Ind.; clk. Fayette County (Ind.) Ct., 1819-27; mem. U.S. Ho. of Reps. (Whig) from Ind., 22d-24th congresses, 1831-37; Whig presdl. elector, 1840. Died Keokuk, Ia., Mar. 30, 1852; buried Oakland Cemetery, Keokuk.

McCARTY, Richard, congressman; b. Coeymans, N.Y., Feb. 19, 1780; attended common schs. Clk., Greene County (N.Y.), 1811-13; flour insp. State of N.Y.; mem. U.S. Ho. of Reps. (Democrat) from N.Y., 17th Congress, 1821-23; pres. Lafayette Bank, N.Y.C.; mem. com. apptd. to receive Gen. Lafayette on his visit to U.S., 1824-25. Died N.Y.C., May 18, 1844; buried Adams Cemetery, Coxsackie, N.Y.

McCARTY, William Mason, congressman; b. "Cedar Grove," Fairfax County, Va., circa 1789; attended Coll. William and Mary, 1813-14; studied law. Admitted to Va. bar, practiced law; mem. Va. Senate, 1823, 30-39; moved to Fla. Territory; mem. commn. to select site for Fla. capitol, 1824; apptd. sec. Territory of Fla. by Pres. John Quincy Adams, 1826; gov. Territory of Fla., 1827; returned to Va., 1830, settled in Loudoun County, practiced law; mem. U.S. Ho. of Reps. (Whig) from Va., 26th Congress, Jan. 25, 1840-41. Moved to Richmond, Va., 1852. Died Richmond, Dec. 20, 1863; buried Shockoe Hill Cemetery, Richmond.

McCAULEY, Charles Stewart, navy officer; b. Phila., Feb. 3, 1793; s. John and Sarah (Stewart) McC.; m. Leila Dickens, Oct. 25, 1831. Apptd. midshipman U.S. Navy, 1809, acting lt., 1813, lt., 1814, master comdr., 1831; commanded ship St. Louis of West India Squadron, 1834; promoted capt., 1839; comdt. Washington (D.C.) Navy Yard, 1846-49; comdr.-in-chief Pacific Squadron, 1850-53; capt., in command of South Atlantic Squadron, 1855, sent by Pres. Pierce to protect Am. interests at Cuba; comdt. Norfolk (Va.) Navy Yard, 1860-61, destroyed guns and ships there to prevent their capture by Confederate forces, 1861; ret. as capt., 1862, promoted to commodore on ret. list, 1867. Died Washington, Mar. 21, 1869.

McCAULEY, Edward Yorke, naval officer; b. Phila., Nov. 2, 1827; s. Daniel Smith and Sarah (Yorke) McC.; L.L.D. (hon.), Hobart Coll., 1892; m. Josephine Berkeley, Jan. 28, 1858, 1 son, Carter Nelson Berkeley. Commd. midshipman U.S. Navy, 1841, served in ship Constitution, 1846-48, passed midshipman, 1847; lt. in ship Niagara, assisted in laying Atlantic Cable, 1858, then stationed U.S. Naval Observatory; resigned, 1858, became businessman, St. Paul, Minn.; volunteered for service at outbreak Civil War; commd. lt. comdr. U.S. Navy, 1862; promoted comdr., 1866, fleet capt. N. Atlantic Squadron at Portsmouth and Boston navy yards, 1867-68; head French dept. U. S. Naval Acad., Annapolis, Md.; comdr. ship Lackawanna in Pacific; supt. Naval Asylum, Phila.; commd. capt., 1872, commodore, 1881, rear adm., 1885, ret., 1887; elected to Am. Philos. Soc., Phila., 1881. Author: A Manual for the Use of Students of Egyptology, 1883. Died Canonicut Island, Narragansett Bay, R.I., Sept. 14, 1894.

McCAULEY, Jeremiah, criminal, mission worker; b. Ireland, circa 1839; m. Maria. Came to Am., circa 1852; criminal in N.Y.C., arrested, convicted of robbery, sent to Sing Sing Prison for 15 years, 1858, pardoned, 1864, resumed criminal activities, never caught, but became reformed; opened mission on Water St., N.Y.C., 1872, became inc. as McAuley Water Street Mission, 1876; founder, operator Cremorne Mission, N.Y.C., 1882-84; publisher Jerry McAuley's Newspaper, 1883-84. Author: Transformed, or the History of a River Thief, 1876. Died N.Y.C., Sept. 18, 1884; buried Woodlawn Cemetery, N.Y.C.

McCAULEY, Mary Ludwig Hays (Molly Pitcher), Revolutionary heroine; b. Trenton, N.J., Oct. 13, 1754; d. John George Ludwig Hass; m. John Caspar Hays, July 24, 1769; m. 2d, George McCauley, after 1789. On field at Battle of Monmouth (N.J.), June 28, 1778, carried water in a pitcher back and forth from a well to the exhausted and wounded, received nickname Molly Pitcher; took her 1st husband's place when he was overcome by heat, served at a cannon for remainder of the battle; granted relief by an act of Pa. Legislature, 1822. Died Jan. 22, 1832.

McCAUSLEN, William Cochran, congressman; b. nr. Steubenville, O., 1796; attended pub. schs.; studied law. Admitted to Ohio bar, practiced in Steubenville; law partner of Sec. of War Stanton; mem. Ohio Ho. of Reps., 1829-30, 32-33; owner, editor Democratic newspaper, Steubenville; mem. U.S. Ho. of Reps. (Dem.) from Ohio, 28th Congress, 1843-45; served as capt. and commissary of subsistence 3d Regt., Ohio Inf. during Mexican War, 1846-47. Died Steubenville, Mar. 13, 1863; buried Union Cemetery, Steubenville.

McCAWLEY, Charles Grymes, marine officer; b. Phila., Jan. 29, 1827; s. Capt. James and Mary (Holt) McC.; m. Elizabeth Colegate, Mar. 1863; m. 2d, Elise Hender, 1870; 2 children. Served at Battle of Chapultepec and capture of Mexico City in Mexican War; apptd. 2d lt. Marine Corps, 1847; brevetted 1st lt., 1847, promoted 1st lt., 1855, capt., 1861, brevetted maj., 1863; present at Morris Island (S.C.) during bombardment and destruction of Ft. Sumter and capture of Fts. Wagner and Gregg, 1863; promoted maj., 1864, lt. col., 1867; ordered to command Marine Barracks, Washington, D.C., also to superintend recruiting, 1871; col.-comdt. Marine Corps, 1876. Died Phila., Oct. 13, 1891; buried Abington, Pa.

McCAY, Charles Francis, educator, ins. co. exec.; b. Danville, Pa., Mar. 8, 1810; s. Robert and Sarah (Read) McC.; grad. Jefferson Coll., 1829; m. Narcissa Williams, Aug. 11, 1840. Tchr. mathematics, natural philosophy and astronomy Lafayette Coll., Easton, Pa., 1832-33, U. Ga., Athens, 1833-53; actuary, life dept. So. Mut. Ins. Co., Athens, 1848-55; agt. Mut. Life Ins. Co. of N.Y., 1846-53; became prof. mathematics S.C. Coll., 1853, pres., 1855-57; devised So. Mut. Mortality Table, proposed bill to Ga. Legislature to make it effective for valuation purposes in Ga., 1859, bill passed, (became 1st adoption of life ins. valuation table by any state); prepared 1st select and ultimate table of life ins. mortality in U.S., 1887. Died Baltimore, O., Mar. 13, 1889.

McCLAMMY, Charles Washington, congressman; b. Scotts Hill, Pender County, N.C., May 29, 1839; grad. U. N.C., 1859. Taught sch., 1859-61; served to maj. 3d N.C. Cavalry Regt., Confederate Army, during Civil War; engaged in farming, Scotts Hill; mem. N.C. Ho. of Reps., 1866, N.C. Senate, 1871; Democratic presdl. elector, 1884; mem. U.S. Ho. of Reps. (Dem.) from N.C., 50th-51st congresses, 1887-91. Died Scotts Hill, Feb. 25, 1896; buried family cemetery, Scotts Hill.

McCLEAN, Moses, congressman; b. Gettysburg, Pa., June 17, 1804; studied law. Admitted to Pa. bar, 1825, began practice in Gettysburg; mem. U.S. Ho. of Reps. (Democrat) from Pa., 29th Congress, 1845-47; mem. Pa. Ho. of Reps., 1855. Died Gettysburg, Sept. 30, 1870; buried Evergreen Cemetery, Gettysburg.

McCLEERY, James, congressman; b. Mecca Twp., Trumbull County, O., Dec. 2, 1837; attended Oberlin Coll., 1859-60. Served to maj. Co. A, 41st Regt., Ohio Volunteer Inf., during Civil War, 1861-65; lost right arm at Battle of Shiloh; wounded at Battle of Stone River, 1862; commd. capt. 45th Inf., U.S. Army, 1866, later brevetted maj. and brig. gen. U.S. Volunteers; ret., 1870, settled in St. Marys Parish, La.; purchased a plantation, practiced law, asso. with Freedman's Bur., N.C. and La.; moved to Shreveport, La.; supt. pub. edn.; mem. U.S. Ho. of Reps. (Republican) from La., 42d Congress, 1871. Died N.Y.C., Nov. 5, 1871; buried Christian Ch. Cemetery, Cortland, O.

McCLELLAN, Abraham, congressman; b. "White Top," Sullivan County, Tenn., Oct. 4, 1789; grad. Washington (Tenn.) Coll. Engaged in farming; mem. Tenn. Ho. of Reps., 1823-25; Tenn. Senate, 1829-33; mem. Tenn. Constl. Conv., 1834; served with Tenn. Mounted Volunteer Militia during Seminole War, 1836-37; mem. U.S. Ho. of Reps. (Democrat) from Tenn., 25th-27th congresses, 1837-43. Died "White Top," May 3, 1866; buried Weavers Cemetery, nr. Bristol, Tenn.

McCLELLAN, Carswell, civil engr.; b. Phila., Dec. 3, 1835; s. Samuel and Margaret (Carswell) McC.; grad. Williams Coll., 1855. Enlisted in 32d N.Y. Regt., 1862, served in Battle of Malvern Hill; served as topog. asst. to Gen. Andrew Humphreys, Army of Potomac, served in battles of Gettysburg, Chancellorsville, Fredericksburg; taken prisoner, Aug. 1864, paroled and resigned from U.S. Army, Nov. 1864; engr. in charge of constrn. for several railroads including N.P. R.R., St. Paul & Pacific R.R., 1867-81; U.S. asst. civil engr., 1881-92. Died St. Paul, Minn., Mar. 6, 1892; buried St. Paul.

McCLELLAN, George, anatomist, surgeon; b. Woodstock, Conn., Dec. 23, 1796; s. James and Eunice (Eldredge) McC.; grad. Yale, 1816; grad. in medicine U. Pa., 1819; m. Elizabeth Brinton, 1829, 3 children including Gen. George B., John Hill Brinton. Founder Jefferson Med. Coll. (series of pvt. lectures on anatomy and surgery resulted in charter), 1825, prof. surgery, 1825-39, prof. anatomy, 1827-30; a leading opthalmic surgeon, 1st to remove lens of an eye; obtained charter for Pa. Coll. Med. Sch., 1838, lectr., 1839-43; Author: Principles and Practice of Surgery (completed by son, John Hill Brinton), 1848; editor: Theory and Practice of Physic, (Eberle), 1840. Died Phila., May 9, 1847.

McCLELLAN, George Brinton, army officer, gov. N.J.; b. Phila., Dec. 3, 1826; s. Dr. George and Elizabeth (Brinton) McC.; attended U. Pa., 1840-42; grad. U.S. Mil. Acad., 1846; m. Ellen Marcy, 1860, 2 children. Commd. 2d lt. Corps Engrs., U.S. Army, 1846, brevetted 1st lt., 1847; promoted capt., 1847, served in Mexican War; asst. instr. in practical mil. engring. U.S. Mil. Acad., 1848-51; asst. engr. for constrn. of Ft. Delaware, 1851; chief engr. on staff Gen. Persifor F. Smith, 1852; apptd. capt. U.S. Cavalry, 1855; resigned to become chief engr. I.C. R.R., 1857, v.p. in charge operations in Ill., 1858-60; became pres. Ohio & Miss. R.R., 1860; apptd. maj. gen. Ohio Militia, 1861; apptd. maj. gen. U.S. Army, May 1861, placed in command of Dept. of Ohio (including Ohio, Ind., Ill.); comdr. Division of Potomac, July 1861; became comdr.-in-chief U.S. Army, Nov. 1861; reorganized and retrained Army of Potomac, finally (after prodding from Pres. Lincoln) took offense in Peninsular Campaign, Mar.-Aug. 1862; advanced very slowly, fighting at Yorktown, Seven Pines, Fair Oaks; was stopped at Gaines' Mill, June, 1862; pushed back in Seven Days' Battle; stopped Lee's invasion of North at Battle of Antietam, but did not pursue Lee; replaced by Gen. Burnside, Nov. 7, 1862; Democratic candidate for Pres. U.S., 1864, defeated by Lincoln; chief engr. Dept. of Docks, N.Y.C., 1870-72; gov. N.J., 1878-81. Author: McClellan's Own Story, 1887. Died Orange, N.J., Oct. 29, 1885.

McCLELLAN, Robert, scout, trader; b. Mercersburg, Pa., 1770; s. Robert McClellan. Joined U.S. Army as spy, 1790; served as scout under Gen. Anthony Wayne in expdn. against Indians, 1794-95; commd. lt., 1795; began trading with Indians in West, 1801; traded with Sioux on Upper Missouri River, 1809-11; employed by Pacific Fur Co., 1811-12; imprisoned for debt, 1813; operated store, Cape Girardeau, Mo., 1814. Died nr. St. Louis, Nov. 12, 1815; buried on Gen. William Clark's farm, nr. St. Louis.

McCLELLAN, Robert, congressman; b. Livingston, N.Y., Oct. 2, 1806; grad. Williams Coll., 1825; studied law. Admitted to N.Y. bar; practiced law, Middleburg, N.Y., 1828-43; mem. U.S. Ho. of Reps. (Democrat) from N.Y., 25th, 27th congresses, 1837-39, 41-43. Died Greenpoint, Bklyn., June 28, 1860; buried Greenwood Cemetery, Bklyn.

McCLELLAND, Robert, gov. Mich.; b. Greencastle, Pa., Aug. 1, 1807; s. Dr. John and Eleanor (McCulloh) McClellan; grad. Dickinson Coll., 1829; m. Sarah Sabine, 1837, at least 1 child. Admitted to bar, Chambersburg, Pa., 1831; moved to Monroe, Mich., 1833; mem. Mich. Constl. Conv., 1835, 50, 67; bd. regents U. Mich., 1837, 50; mem Mich. Legislature, 1838-43; mayor Monroe (Mich.), 1841; mem. U.S. Ho. of Reps. from Mich., 28th-30th congresses, 1843-49; del. Nat. Democratic convs., 1848, 52, 68; chief Mich. campaign lt. for U.S. presdl. candidate Lewis Cass, also aided nat. campaign; gov. Mich., 1851-53; U.S. sec. of interior, 1853-57; practiced law, Detroit, 1857-80. Died Detroit, Aug. 30, 1880; buried Elmwood Cemetery, Detroit.

McCLELLAND, William, congressman; b. Mount Jackson, Pa., Mar. 2, 1842; attended Westminster Coll., Allegheny Coll.; studied law. Served in Civil War; admitted to Pa. bar, began practice in Mount Jackson, 1870; mem. U.S. Ho. of Reps. (Democrat) from Pa., 42d Congress, 1871-73; resumed law practice. Died Harrisburg, Pa., Feb. 7, 1892; buried Allegheny Cemetery, Pitts.

McCLENACHAN, Blair, congressman; b. Ireland. Came to U.S., settled in Phila.; engaged in merc. bus., banking, shipping; a founder, mem. 1st Troop of Phila. Cavalry during Revolutionary War; contbr. considerable money to aid Am. forces, donated money and credit to Continental Congress, 1780; mem. Pa. Ho. of Reps., 1790-95; mem. U.S. Ho. of Reps. from Pa., 5th Congress, 1797-99. Died Phila., May 8, 1812; buried St. Paul's Cemetery, Phila.

McCLENE, James, Continental congressman; b. New London, Pa., Oct. 11, 1730. Moved to Antrim Twp., Cumberland (now Franklin) County, Pa., 1754; del. Pa. constl. convs., 1776, 89-90; mem. Pa. Ho. of Reps., 1776-77, 90, 91, 93, 94; mem. Pa. Supreme Exec. Council, 1778-79; mem. Continental Congress from Pa., 1779-80. Died Antrim Twp., Mar. 13, 1806.

McCLOSKEY, John, clergyman; b. Bklyn., Mar. 10, 1810; s. Patrick and Elizabeth (Harron) McC.; grad. Mt. St. Mary's Coll., Emmittsburg, Md., 1828. Ordained priest Roman Catholic Ch., 1834; selected as assistant in cathedral and chaplain in Bellevue Hosp., N.Y.C.; teaching rector St. John's Coll., Fordham U., 1841; named titular bishop of Axiern with right of succession to N.Y., 1843; consecrated bishop at St. Patrick's, N.Y.C., 1844, given charge of See of Albany, 1847; became archbisnop of N.Y., 1864; attended 2d Plenary Council, Balt., 1866; introduced religious orders (Jesuits, Oblates, Franciscans, Capuchines, Augustinians, Sisters of Mary, Ladies of Sacred Heart, Sisters of Charity, Sisters of St. Joseph); founded theol. sem., Troy, N.Y.; erected St. Mary's Cathedral, Albany; became 1st Am. cardinal, 1875. Died N.Y.C., Oct. 10, 1885.

McCLURE, Alexander Wilson, clergyman; b. Boston, May 8, 1808; s. Thomas and Mary (Wilson) McC.; grad. Amherst Coll., 1827, Andover Sem., 1830; m. Mary Gould, 8 children. Ordained to ministry Presbyn. Ch., 1832; pastor 1st Congregational Ch., Malden, Mass., 1830-43, 48-51, Dutch Reformed Ch., Jersey City, N.J., 1851-65; editor Christian Observatory, Boston, 1847-50; sec. Am. and Fgn. Christian Union, 1855-57, pastor of Rome chapel maintained by orgn., 1855; editor Christian World, 1855-57. Author: The Life Boat; an Allegory; Lives of the Chief Fathers of New England, 2 vols., 1846. Died Canonsburg, Pa., Sept. 1865.

McCLURE, Charles, congressman; b. Willow Grove farm, nr. Carlisle, Pa., 1804; grad. Dickinson Coll., Carlisle; studied law. Admitted to Pa. bar, 1826, practiced law; mem. Pa. Ho. of Reps., 1835; mem. U.S. Ho. of Reps. (Democrat) from Pa., 25th, 26th congresses, 1837-39, Dec. 7, 1840-41; sec. of state Pa., 1843-45; promoted pub. sch. system of Pa. Died Allegheny, Pa., Jan. 10, 1846; buried Allegheny Cemetery, Pitts.

McCLURE, George, army officer; b. Londonderry, Ireland, 1770; s. Finla McClure; m. Eleanor Bole, Aug. 20, 1795; m. 2d, Sarah Welles, 1808. Mcht., Bath, Steuben County, N.Y., 1793-1812; served as brig. gen. N.Y. Militia; in command detachment at Ft. George, Can. on Niagara River, 1813; abandoned fort in face of superior enemy forces, burned Newark (once capital of Upper Can.); British burned Buffalo and Black Rock (N.Y.) in retaliation; sheriff Steuben County, 1815; mem. N.Y. Legislature from Steuben County, 3 terms. Died Elgin, Ill., Aug. 16, 1851.

McCLURG, James, physician, army officer; b. Hampton, Va., circa 1746; s. Dr. Walter McClurg; grad Coll. William and Mary, 1762; M.D., U. Edinburgh (Scotland), 1770; m. Elizabeth Selden, May 22, 1779. Published Experiments upon The Human Bile and Reflections upon the Biliary Secretions, 1772; Served as surgeon Va. Militia; physician-gen. and dir. hosps. Va.; prof. anatomy and medicine Coll. William and Mary, 1779-83; del. to U.S. Constl. Conv., Phila., 1787; mem. Va. Exec. Council, 1790; pres. Va. Med. Soc., 1820, 21. Died Richmond, Va., July 9, 1823.

McCLURG, Joseph Washington, gov. Mo., congressman; b. St. Louis County, Mo., Feb. 22, 1818; s. Joseph and Mary (Brotherton) McC.; attended Miami U., Oxford, O.; m. Mary C. Johnson, 1844. Taught sch., La., Miss., 1835, 36; moved to Tex., 1839; admitted to Tex. bar; clk. circuit ct., 1840; dep. sheriff St. Louis County, 1841-44; col. 8th Cavalry, Mo. Militia during Civil War; mem. U.S. Ho. of Reps. from Mo., 38th-40th congresses, 1865-68 (resigned); gov. Mo., 1869-71. Died London, Mo., Dec. 2, 1900; buried Lebanon Cemetery, London.

McCOMAS, William, congressman; b. nr. Pearisburg, Va., 1795; attended Emory and Henry Coll., Emory, Va. Engaged in farming, practiced law; Methodist minister; mem. Va. Senate, 1830-33; mem. U.S. Ho. of Reps. (Whig) from Va., 23d-24th congresses, 1833-37; del. Va. Secession Conv., 1861, voted against secession; judge U.S. Dist. Ct., during Civil War. Died on his farm nr. Barboursville, Va. (now W.Va.), June 3, 1865; buried family cemetery.

McCOMB, Eleazer, Continental congressman. Served as capt. Del. Militia, during Revolutionary War; apptd. mem. Del. Privy Council, 1779; mem. Continental Congress from Del., 1783-84; mem. commn. to confer concerning Chesapeake and Del. Canal, 1786; auditor accounts State of Del., 1787-93; moved from Dover to Wilmington, Del., circa 1792; engaged in shipping, Wilmington; dir. Bank of Del., 1795. Died Wilmington, Dec. 1798.

McCOMB, John, architect; b. Princeton, N.J.; son of James McComb; married, at least 2 sons, Isaac, John Jr. Credited with building old Brick Ch., 1767, North Dutch Ch., 1769, N.Y. Hosp., 1773 (all N.Y.C.); served with Continental Army during Revolutionary War; resumed practice architecture, N.Y.C., 1793; apptd. city surveyor N.Y.C., 1794. Died 1811.

McCOMB, John, architect; b. N.Y.C., Oct. 17, 1763; s. John and Mary (Davis) McC.; m. Elizabeth Glean, Dec. 15, 1792; m. 2d, Mrs. Rebecca Rockwell, June 24, 1821; 1 son, 1 dau. Designed facade of Govt. House in N.Y.C., (his 1st significant work), 1790; architect to superintend constrn. N.Y. City Hall, 1802-12; designed (in partnership with brother Isaac), St. John's Chapel, Varick St., N.Y.C. (his most important ch. design); designed "The Grange" for Alexander Hamilton; street commr. N.Y.C., 1813-21; became academician Am. Acad. Fine Arts, 1816; pres. Gen. Soc. of Mechanics and Tradesmen, 1818; trustee Brick Presbyn. Ch., deacon, 1827-53; also designed lighthouses, schs., pvt. homes. Died May 25, 1853.

McCONNEL, John Ludlum, lawyer, author; b. Morgan County (now Scott County), Ill., Nov. 11, 1826; s. Murray and Mary (Mapes) McC.; grad. Transylvania Law Sch., 1843; m. Eliza Deniston, 1847, 2 children. Served as 1st lt. 1st Ill. Volunteers, Mexican War, promoted capt., 1847; practiced law, Jacksonville, Ill. Author: Grahame: On Youth and Manhood, 1850; Talbot and Vernon, 1850; The Glenns: A Family History, 1851; Western Characters: Or Types of Border Life in the Western States, 1853. Died Jacksonville, Ill., Jan. 17, 1862.

McCONNELL, Felix Grundy, congressman; b. Nashville, Tenn., Apr. 1, 1809; studied law, Ala. Became a saddler; moved to Talladega, Ala., 1834; admitted to Ala. bar, 1836, began practice in Talladega; mem. Ala. Ho. of Reps., 1838, Ala. Senate, 1838-43; mem. U.S. Ho. of Reps. (Democrat) from Ala., 28th-29 congresses, 1843-46. Died Washington, D.C., Sept 10, 1846; buried Congressional Cemetery, Washington.

McCORD, Andrew, congressman; b. in what is no Stony Ford, N.Y., circa 1754; attended Newburg (N.Y.) Acad. Del. conv. to choose deps. to 2 N.Y. Provincial Congress, New Paltz, N.Y., 1775 commd. q.m. Ulster County (N.Y.) Militia, 1787 served as capt. until 1798; mem. N.Y. Assembly 1795-96, 98, 1800, 02, 07, speaker, 1807; mem U.S. Ho. of Reps. from N.Y., 8th Congress, 1803 95; engaged in farming. Died Stony Ford, 1808 buried family burying ground nr. Stony Ford.

McCORD, David James, editor; b. St. Matthew' Parish, S.C., Jan. 1797; s. Russell and Hanna (Turquand) M.; attended S.C. Coll. (now U. S.C.) 1810-14; m. Emmeline Wagner; m. 2d, Louisa Susanna Cheves, May 2, 1840. Admitted to S.C. bar 1818; partner (with H. J. Nott) in law firm 1818-21, (with W. C. Preston), 1822; became editor Columbia Telescope, 1823; mem. S.C. Legislature, 1832-39; pres. Columbia br. S.C. State Bank 1839-41; intendent City of Columbia; trustee S.C Coll., State Hosp. for Insane. Author: Reports c Cases . . . in the Constitutional Court, 2 vols. 1820-21. Editor: Statutes at Large of South Carolina, vols. 6-10, 1842. Died May 12, 1855.

McCORD, Louisa Susanna Cheves, nurse, author b. Charleston, S.C., Dec. 3, 1810; d. Langdon an Mary (Dulles) Cheves; m. David James McCord, Ma 2, 1840; 1 son, Capt. Langdon Cheves. Pres. Soldier' Relief Assn. and Lady's Clothing Assn., 1861; nurs in mil. hosp. of S.C. Coll., Columbia. Author: M Dreams; translator: Sophismes Économiques, 1848 Died Charleston, Nov. 23, 1879; buried Magnoli Cemetery, Charleston.

McCORKLE, Joseph Walker, congressman; b. Piqua, O., June 24, 1819; attended Kenyon Coll., Gambier, O.; studied law. Admitted to Ohio bar, circ 1842, began practice in Dayton; postmaster of Dayton, 1845-49; moved to San Francisco, 1849; mem Cal. Assembly, 1850-52; mem. U.S. Ho. of Reps (Democrat) from Cal., 32d Congress, 1851-53 moved to Marysville, Cal.; judge 9th Jud. Dist., 1853 57; unsuccessful candidate for U.S. Senate, 1855 resumed law practice, San Francisco; moved to Virginia City, Nev., 1860, practiced law; moved to Washington, D.C., 1870, practiced before Mexican Claim Commn. Died Branchville, Md., Mar. 18, 1884; burie Forest Hill Cemetery, Piqua.

McCORMICK, Cyrus Hall, mfr.; b. Walnut Grove Va., Feb. 15, 1809; s. Robert and Mary (Hall) McC.; m. Nancy Fowler, Jan. 26, 1858, 7 children Invented and patented hillside plough, 1831; patented reaping machine, 1834, began mfg. machin commercially, 1837; erected factory in Chgo., 1847 built up nat. business for McCormick Harvestin Machine Co., by 1850; added mowing attachment t reaper, 1850's, also developed self-raking device hand-binding harvester, wire-binder, twine-binder 1860's; introduced reaper in Europe in London Eng., 1851; awarded Council medal London World' Fair, 1851; won major prizes at world fairs, Paris London, Hamburg, Lille, Vienna, Phila., Melbourne 1855-80; named chevalier by France, later office Legion of Honor; elected mem. French Acad. o Scis., 1879; pioneer in creation of modern busines methods, among 1st to use field trials, guarantees testimonials in advt., cash and deferred payment for merchandise; owner Presbyn. Expositor, newspaper, 1860; endowed 4 professorships in Presbyn Theol. Sem. of N.W., 1859; The Interior (Presbyn newspaper, later named Continent), 1872-84; became owner Chgo. Times, 1860, publisher, 1860-61 chmn. Democratic State Central Com., 1872, 76 dir. U.P. R.R.; an organizer Mississippi Valley Soc. benefactor Union Theol. Sem., Hampden-Sydney, Va. also Washington Coll., Lexington, Va.; pres. Va Soc. in Chgo., 1880. Died Chgo., May 13, 1884.

McCORMICK, James Robinson, congressman; b. nr Irondale, Mo., Aug. 1, 1824; attended Transylvania U., Lexington, Ky.; grad. Memphis (Tenn.) Med. Coll., 1849. Began practice of medicine, Wayne County, Mo.; moved to Perry County, Mo., 1850, practiced medicine; del. Mo. Constl. Conv., 1861; served as surgeon 6th Regt., Mo. Volunteer Inf., Union Army, during Civil War; mem. Mo. Senate, 1862, 66-67; commd. brig. gen. Mo. Militia, 1863; resumed practice of medicine, Arcadia, Mo.; mem. U.S. Ho. of Reps. (Democrat) from Mo., 40th-42d congresses, Dec. 17, 1867-73; moved to Farmington, Mo., 1874, engaged in drug bus., practiced medicine. Died Farmington, May 19, 1897; buried Masonic Cemetery, Farmington.

McCORMICK, Robert, inventor; b. Rockbridge County, Va., June 8, 1780; s. Robert and Martha (Sanderson) McC.; m. Mary Ann Hall, Feb. 11, 1808; several children including Cyrus Hall, William S., Leander James. Inventor several farm implements (none were practical or commercially valuable); inventor and patentee hempbrake, gristmill, hydraulic machine and blacksmith's bellows, 1830-31 nventor threshing machine, 1834; experimenter with grain reapers, 1809-31; built an iron furnace, 1836; mfr. reaper invented by son Cyrus, 1837-45. Died Rockbridge County, July 4, 1846.

McCORMICK, Stephen, inventor, mfr.; b. Auburn, Va., Aug. 26, 1784; s. John and Elizabeth (Morgan) McC.; m. Sarah Barnett, Feb. 1807, 3 children; m. 2d, Elizabeth M. Benson, Feb. 29, 1816, 9 children. Improved shape of nether millstone on water-power grist mill; invented, manufactured, put into use a cast-iron plow with replaceable parts and adjustable wrought-iron point, by 1816, patented 1819, 26, 37, manufactured on farm Auburn; manufactured plows in factories, Leesburg and Alexandria, Va., circa 1826-50, plows widely-used in Va., less so in other So. States; responsible (with Jethro Wood) for introducing cast-iron plows in U.S. Died Auburn, Aug. 28, 1875.

McCOSH, James, coll. pres.; b. Aryshire, Scotland, Apr. 1, 1811; s. Andrew and Jean (Carson) McC.; attended U. Glasgow (Scotland), 1824-29; M.A. U. Edinburgh (Scotland), 1833; m. Isabella Guthrie, Sept. 29, 1845, 1 son, Andrew James. Licensed preacher Established Ch. of Scotland, 1834; a founder Free Ch. of Scotland; prof. logic and metaphysics Queen's Coll., Belfast, 1852-68; pres. Coll. of N.J. (now Princeton), 1868-88, restored coll. to ante-bellum status, more than doubled size and facilities of univ., also prof. psychology and history of philosophy, 1868-88, prof. emeritus, 1888; made most conspicuous contbns. to philos. thought in connection with subject of evolution (which he believed to be manifestation of wonder and mystery of God). Author: The Medhod of the Divine Government, Physical and Moral, 1850; (presented fundamental doctrines of Scottish sch.) The Intutions of the Mind Inductively Investigated, Being a Defense of Fundamental Truth, 1866; The 1860; An Examination of Mr. J.S. Mill's Philosophy: Laws of Discursive Thought: Being a Text-book of Formal Logic, 1870; Christianity and Positivism, 1871; Realistic Philosophy Defended in a Philosophic Series, 1887. Died Princeton, N.J., Nov. 16, 1894.

McCOY, Henry Kent, army officer, lawyer; b. Northumberland County, Pa., Jan. 8, 1820; s. Robert and Sarah (Read) McC.; grad. Coll. of N.J. (now Princeton), 1839); studied law under Joseph Henry Lumpkin; m. Catherine Hanson, 1842. Admitted to Ga. bar, 1842; practiced in partnership with George H. Dudley, Americus, Ga., 1842-49, with Willis A. Hawkins, 1849-61; mem. Ga. Democratic Conv., 1860; commd. 2d lt. 12th Ga. Regt., Confederate Army, 1861, promoted capt., asst. q.m., 1862, resigned, 1862; mem. Ga. Constl. Conv., 1868; asso. justice Ga. Supreme Ct., 1868-75; practiced in Atlanta, Ga., 1875-82; judge U.S. Dist. Ct. for Northern Ga., 1882-86. Died Atlanta, July 30, 1886.

McCOY, Isaac, Indian agt., missionary; b. Fayette County, Pa., June 13, 1784; s. William McCoy; m. Christiana Polke, 1803, 13 children. Converted to Baptist faith, 1801; licensed to preach by Bapt. Ch., 1805; apptd. missionary to Wabash Valley Indians, 1817; apptd. mem. commn. to move Ottawa and Miami Indians westward, 1828; published Remarks on the Practicability of Indian Reform, 1827; apptd. as surveyor and agt. to assist Indians in migration westward, 1830; aided Indians in selecting new reservations in West, surveyed their boundaries and helped them move to new homes; published Annual Register of Indian Affairs within the Indian Territory, 1835-38; 1st corr. sec., gen. agt. Indian Mission Assn., Louisville, Ky., 1842. Died Louisville, June 21, 1846.

McCOY, Robert, congressman; b. Carlisle, Pa.; attended common schs. Prothonotary of Cumberland County (Pa.); served as brig. gen. Pa. Militia; canal commr. State of Pa.; mem. U.S. Ho. of Reps. from Pa., 22d Congress, Nov. 22, 1831-33. Died Wheeling, Va. (now W.Va.), June 7, 1849.

McCOY, William, congressman; b. nr. Warrenton, Va. Mem. Va. Ho. of Dels., 1798-1804; del. Va. Constl. Conv. 1829-30; mem. U.S. Ho. of Reps. (Democrat) from Va., 12th-22d congresses, 1811-33. Died Charlottesville, Va., 1864; buried U. Va. Cemetery, Charlottesville.

McCRARY, George Washington, congressman; b. Evansville, Ind., Aug. 29, 1835; s. James and Matilda (Forest) McC.; m. Helen Gelatt, 1857, at least 1 child. Admitted to Ia. bar, 1856; mem. Ia. Legislature, 1857, Ia. Senate, 1861-65; mem. U.S. Ho. of Reps. from Ia., 41st-44th congresses, 1869-77, mem. com. investigating Credit Mobilier scandal, helped create Electoral Commn.; U.S. sec. of war, 1877-79, withdrew support of fed. troops from remaining carpet-bag govs. in S.C. and La., used fed. troops in Railroad Strike of 1877, ordered troops across Mexican border to pursue marauding Mexicans; fed. judge 8th Jud. Circuit, 1879-84; gen. counsel A., T. & S.F. R.R., 1884-90; mem. law firm Pratt, McCrary, Hagerman & Pratt, Kansas City, Mo., 1884-90. Author: A Treatise on the American Law of Elections, 1875; McCrary's Reports, 5 vols., 1881-84. Died St. Joseph, Mo., June 23, 1890; buried Oakland Cemetery, Keokuk, Ia.

McCRATE, John Dennis, congressman; b. Wiscasset, Me., Oct. 1, 1802; grad. Bowdoin Coll., 1819; studied law. Admitted to Me. bar; practiced law, Damariscotta, Me., 1823-35, Wiscasset, 1835-50; mem. Me. Ho. of Reps., 1831-35; customs collector, 1836-41; mem. U.S. Ho. of Reps. (Democrat) from Me., 29th Congress, 1845-46; resumed law practice, Wiscasset; moved to Boston, practiced law until 1852; moved to Sutton, Mass., 1852, engaged in farming. Died Sutton, Sept. 11, 1879; buried Ancient Cemetery, Wiscasset.

McCREARY, John, congressman; b. nr. Fishing Creek, S.C., 1761; educated privately. Became a surveyor; engaged in farming; served in Am. Revolution; mem. S.C. Ho. of Reps., S.C. Senate; sheriff Chester Dist. (now Chester County), S.C.; mem. U.S. Ho. of Reps. from S.C., 16th Congress, 1819-21. Died S.C., Nov. 4, 1833; buried Richardson Ch. Cemetery, Chester County.

McCREERY, Charles, physician; b. nr. Winchester, Ky., June 13, 1785; s. Robert and Mary (McClanahan) McC.; m. Ann Wayman Growe, 1811, 7 children. Settled in Hartford, Ky., 1810, practiced medicine, 1810-26; performed complete extirpation of clavicle (1st operation of kind performed in U.S.), 1813. Died West Point, Ky., Aug. 27, 1826; buried Hartford.

McCREERY, Thomas Clay, senator; b. nr. Owensboro, Ky., Dec. 12, 1816; grad. Centre Coll., Danville, Ky., 1837; studied law. Admitted to Ky. bar, practiced in Frankfort, 2 years; Democratic presdl. elector, 1852, 56, 60; mem. U.S. Senate (Dem.) from Ky., Feb. 19, 1868-71, 73-79. Died Owensboro, July 10, 1890; buried Elmwood Cemetery, Owensboro.

McCREERY, William, congressman; b. Province of Ulster, Ireland, 1750. Came to U.S., settled in Md.; engaged in farming; mem. U.S. Ho. of Reps. from Md., 8th-10th congresses, 1803-09; mem. Md. Senate, 1811-14. Died "Clover Hill" nr. Reisterstown, Md., Mar. 8, 1814.

McCREERY, William, congressman; b. Omagh, County Tyrone, Ireland, May 17, 1786. Came to U.S., 1791, settled nr. Fairfield, Pa.; moved to Paris, Pa., 1812, engaged in farming; mem. Pa. Ho. of Reps., 1824-27, 33-36; constructor Pa. State Canal, Pa. State Hwy., 1826-31; mem. U.S. Ho. of Reps. (Democrat) from Pa., 21st Congress, 1829-31; collector internal revenue, Pitts., 1831-33; supt. Pa. State Canal, 1835; acting pres. Pa. Bd. Canal Appraisers, until 1841. Died Fairfield, Sept. 27, 1841; buried Up-the-Valley United Presbyn. Ch. Cemetery, Fairfield.

McCULLAGH, Joseph Burbridge, journalist; b. Dublin, Ireland, Nov. 1842; s. John and Sarah (Burbridge) McC. came to N.Y., 1853; joined staff St. Louis Democrat, 1859, assigned to report proceedings of Mo. Gen. Assembly, 1859-60; reporter Cincinnati Daily Gazette, 1860, later war corr.; served as lt. in Benton Cadets, U.S. Army, 1861; Washington (D.C.) corr. Cincinnati Comml., 1863; Senate reporter for N.Y. Asso. Press; mng. editor Cincinnati Enquirer, 1868; in charge of Chgo. Republican, 1869-71; editor St. Louis Democrat, 1871; founded St. Louis Daily Globe, 1873-75 (merged with Democrat, 1875); editor St. Louis Globe-democrat, 1875-96; Republican. Died St. Louis, Dec. 31, 1896.

McCULLOCH, Ben, army officer; b. Ruthford County, Tenn., Nov. 11, 1811; s. Maj. Alexander and Frances (LeNoir) McC. Mem. Tex. Congress, 1834; organizer company of mounted men known as McCulloch's Tex. Rangers, 1846; commd. maj., 1848; marshal for coast dist. of Tex., 1853-59; a commr. to conciliate Mormons in Utah, 1858; col. in command of Tex. troop that received surrender of Gen. Twiggs at San Antonio, 1861; commd. brig. gen. Confederate Army, in command of troops in Ark. Died in Battle of Elkhorn Tavern, nr. Elkhorn, W. Va., Mar. 7, 1862.

McCULLOCH, George, congressman; b. Maysville, Ky., Feb. 22, 1792, Ironmaster, Center County, Pa.; mem. Pa. Senate, 1835-36; a propr. Hannah Furnace, 1836-50; mem. U.S. Ho. of Reps. (Democrat) from Pa., 26th Congress, Nov. 20, 1839-41. Died Port Royal, Pa., Apr. 6, 1861; buried Church Hill Cemetery, nr. Port Royal.

McCULLOCH, Hugh, govt. ofcl.; b. Dennebunk, Me., Dec. 7, 1808; s. Hugh and Abigail (Perkins) McC.; ed. Bowdoin Coll., A.M. (hon.), 1863, LL.D. (hon.), 1889; m. Susan Mann, 1838, 4 children. Admitted to Mass. bar, 1832; cashier, mgr. Ft. Wayne br. State Bank of Indiana, 1835-56, pres. State Bank of Ind., 1856-63; U.S. comptroller currency, launched "greenback" or nat. banking system, 1863-65; U.S. sec. treasury, 1865-69, recommended retirement U.S. notes and return to gold standard; partner for several years in London banking house Jay Cooke, McCulloch & Co. (reorganized as McCulloch & Co.); U.S. sec. treasury under Pres. Arthur, 1884-85. Author: Men and Measures of Half a Century, 1888. Died "Holly Hill," Prince George's County, Md., May 24, 1895.

McCULLOCH, John, congressman; b. McCulloch Mills, Pa., Nov. 15, 1806; grad. Jefferson Coll., Canonsburg, Pa., 1825; grad. med. dept. U. Pa., 1829, Began practice of medicine, Green Tree, Pa.; moved to Petersburg, Pa., 1830, practiced medicine, 1830-52; mem. U.S. Ho. of Reps. (Whig) from Pa., 33d Congress, 1853-55; resumed practice of medicine, Huntingdon, Pa.; joined Republican Party, 1856; mem. Pa. Constl. Conv., 1874. Died Huntingdon, May 15, 1879; buried Riverside Cemetery, Huntingdon.

McCULLOCH, Oscar Carleton, clergyman; b. Fremont, O., July 2, 1843; s. Carleston B. and Harriet (Pettibone) McC.; grad. Chgo. Theol. Sem., 1870; m. Agnes Buel, Sept. 8, 1870; m. 2d, Alice Barteau, May 8, 1878; 5 children. Ordained to ministry Congregational Ch., 1870; pastor Congregational Ch., Sheboygan, Wis., 1870-77, Plymouth Ch., Indpls., 1877-91; organizer Charity Orgn. Soc., 1878-79, Children's Aid Soc., 1881, Summer Mission for Sick Children, 1890. Died Indpls., Dec. 10, 1891; buried Crown Hill Cemetery, Indpls.

McCULLOGH, Thomas Grubb, congressman; b. Greencastle, Pa., Apr. 20, 1785; studied law. Admitted to Franklin County (Pa.) bar, 1806; served as pvt., later q.m. during War of 1812; mem. U.S. Ho. of Reps. from Pa., 16th Congress, Oct. 17, 1820-21; mem. Pa. Ho. of Reps., 1831-35; 1st pres. Cumberland Valley R.R. Co.; mgr., editor Franklin Repository; pres. Bank of Chambersburg (Pa.), until 1848. Died Chambersburg, Sept. 10, 1848.

McCULLOGH, Welty, congressman; b. Greensburg, Pa., Oct. 10, 1847; attended Washington and Jefferson Coll.; grad. Princeton, 1870; studied law. Served as 2d clk. under provost marshal 21st Dist. of Pa., during Civil War; admitted to Pa. bar, 1872, began practice in Greensburg; asst. solicitor Balt. & Ohio R.R.; mem. U.S. Ho. of Reps. (Republican) from Pa., 50th Congress, 1887-89. Died Greensburg, Aug. 31, 1889; buried new St. Clair Cemetery, Greensburg.

McCULLOUGH, Hiram, congressman; b. nr. Elkton, Md., Sept. 26, 1813; attended Elkton Acad.; studied law. Admitted to Md. bar, 1837, practiced in Elkton; mem. Md. Senate, 1845-51; apptd. a codifier of laws of Md., 1840; mem. U.S. Ho. of Reps. (Democrat) from Md., 39th-40th congresses, 1865-69; resumed law practice; counsel Phila., Wilmington & Balt. R.R., many years; del. Democratic Nat. Conv., Chgo., 1864, N.Y.C., 1868; mem. Md. Ho. of Dels., 1880-81, speaker, 1880. Died Elkton, Mar. 4, 1885; buried Presbyn. Cemetery, Elkton.

McCULLOUGH, John, actor; b. Coleraine, Londonderry, Ireland, Nov. 14, 1832; m. Letitia McClain, Apr. 8, 1849, 2 children. Came to U.S., 1847; trained for acting profession, Phila.; made 1st dramatic appearance in The Belle's Stratagem, Phila., 1857; engaged by Edward L. Davenport in Hovard Athenaeum, Boston, 1860-61; actor Edwin Forrest's Co., 1861-65; started co. of actors with Lawrence Barrett in Cal., 1865-70; mgr. Cal. Theatre, 1870-75; toured country in acting roles, 1873-84. Died Phila., Nov. 8, 1885.

McDANIEL, William, congressman. Mem. Mo. Senate, 1838-40; pres. bank, Palmyra, Mo., 1840; mem. U.S. Ho. of Reps. (Democrat) from Mo., 29th Congress, Dec. 7, 1846-47; operated an agy. for location of land claims, Palmyra, 1847. Died circa 1854.

McDEARMON, James Calvin, congressman; b. New Canton, Va., June 13, 1844; attended Andrew Coll., Trenton, Tenn., 1858-61; studied law. Served with Army of Tenn., Confederate Army, during Civil War; wounded at battles of Murfreesboro, Franklin; surrendered with army at Greensboro, Tenn., 1865; admitted to Tenn. bar, 1867, began practice in Trenton; mem. U.S. Ho. of Reps. (Democrat) from Tenn., 53d-54th congresses, 1893-97. Died Trenton, July 19, 1902; buried Oakwood Cemetery, Trenton.

McDILL, Alexander Stuart, congressman; b. nr. Meadville, Pa., Mar. 18, 1822; attended Allgeheny Coll.; grad. Cleve. Med. Coll., 1848. Practiced medicine, Crawford County, Pa., 1848-56; moved to Plover, Wis., 1856; mem. Wis. Assembly, 1862; bd. mgrs. Wis. State Hosp. for Insane, 1862-68, med. supt., 1868-73, 75; mem. Wis. Senate, 1863-64; Republican presdl. elector, 1864; mem. U.S. Ho. of Reps. (Rep.) from Wis., 43d Congress, 1873-75. Died nr. Madison, Wis., Nov. 12, 1875; buried Forest Hill Cemetery, Madison.

McDILL, James Wilson, senator; b. Monroe, O., Mar. 4, 1834; s. Rev. John and Frances (Wilson) McD.; grad. Miami U., Oxford, O., 1853; m. Narcissa Fullenwider, Aug. 1857, 5 children including Mrs. Elmer Bradford. Admitted to Ohio bar, 1856;

practiced law, Afton, Ia., 1857-60, 66-85; supt. Union County (Ia.), 1859, county judge, 1860-62; clk. Office of 3d Auditor of U.S. Treasury, Washington, D.C., 1862-65; circuit judge 2d dist. 3d Jud. Circuit Ia., 1868-71; dist. judge 3d Jud. Dist. Ia., 1871-73; mem. U.S. Ho. of Reps. from Ia., 43d-44th congresses, 1873-77; mem. Ia. Bd. of R.R. Commrs., 1878-81, 83-86; mem. U.S. Senate from Ia. (filling vacancy left by Samuel J. Kirkwood), 1881-83; testified in Senate investigation of regulation of freight and passenger transportation, calling for fed. commn. to lower exorbitant transp. rates, resulted in creation of ICC; mem. ICC, 1892-94. Contbr. "The Making of Iowa" to Ia. Hist. Record, 1891. Died Creston, Ia., Feb. 28, 1894; buried Graceland Cemetery, Creston.

McDONALD, Charles James, gov. Ga., jurist; s. Charles and Mary Glas (Burn) McD.; grad. S.C. Coll., 1816; m. Ann Franklin, 1819; m. 2d, Mrs. Ruffin; 5 children. Admitted to Ga. bar, 1817; solicitor gen. Flint Circuit, 1822-25, judge, 1825-30; mem. Ga. Gen. Assembly, 1830, Ga. Senate, 1834-37; gov. Ga., 1839-43, devised means for financially rehabilitating state, empowered to issue $1,000,000 in state bonds for redemption state bank notes; justice Supreme Ct. Ga., 1857-60; leader Ga. delegation to Nashville Conv.,1850, v.p. 1st session, pres. 2d session. Died Maietta, Ga., Dec. 16, 1860.

McDONALD, Edward Francis, congressman; b. Ireland, Sept. 21, 1844; attended pub. schs., Newark, N.J. Came to U.S., 1850; served as sgt. in command of a co. N.J. Volunteer Inf. during Civil War, 1861-62; became a skilled mechanic; moved to Harrison, N.J., 1874; mem. N.J. Assembly, 1874; dir. at large Bd. Chosen Freeholders of Hudson County (N.J.), 1877-81; elected to N.J. Senate, 1890; treas. of Harrison, 1881; mem. U.S. Ho. of Reps. (Democrat) from N.J., 52d Congress, 1891-92. Died Harrison, Nov. 5, 1892; buried Holy Sepulchre Cemetery, Newark.

McDONALD, Joseph Ewing, senator; b. Butler County, O., Aug. 29, 1819; s. John and Eleanor (Piatt) McD.; grad. Asbury Coll. (now De Pauw U.), 1840; m. Nancy Ruth Buell, Dec. 25, 1844; m. 2d, Araminta Vance, Sept. 15, 1874; m. 3d, Mrs. Josephine F. Bernard, Jan. 12, 1880; 4 children. Moved to Montgomery County, Ind., 1826; admitted to Ind. bar, 1843; pros. atty. LaFayette (Ind.) Circuit, 1843-47; practiced law, Crawfordsville, Ind., 1847-59; mem. U.S. Ho. of Reps. from Ind., 31st Congress, 1849-51; atty. gen. Ind., 1856, 58; chmn. Ind. Democratic State Com., 1874; mem. U.S. Senate from Ind., 1875-81, mem. spl. com. to investigate frauds in So. states that occasioned Hayes-Tilden election dispute. Died Indpls., Ind., June 21, 1891; buried Crown Hill Cemetery, Indpls.

McDONNOUGH, James, engraver, painter. Prominent banknote engraver, N.Y.C., 1845-96; pres. Am. Bank Note Co., 1887-96; exhibited landscapes at N.A.D., Am. Art-Union, 1849-51, including a Nicaraguan coastal scene.

McDONOGH, John, mcht., philanthropist; b. Balt., Dec. 29, 1779; s. John and Elizabeth (Wilkins) McD. Apprenticed to William Taylor, mcht., Balt., sent to New Orleans on bus., 1800, became successful mcht.; dir. La. State Bank, 1806; unsuccessful candidate for U.S. Senate, 1818; planned to use his money to emancipate his slaves by giving them opportunity to work their way gradually, and to educate youth of New Orleans and Balt. Died Oct. 26, 1850.

McDOUGAL, David Stockton, naval officer; b. Chillicothe, O., Sept. 27, 1809; s. Dr. John and Margaret (Stockton) McD.; m. Caroline Sterrett, 1833, at least 1 child, Charles J. Served as midshipman U.S. Navy in ship Natchez, West India Squadron, 1828-31, in Brandywine, Mediterranean Squadron, 1832-35; passed midshipman, 1834; served at Bklyn. Navy Yard, 1835-36; with West India Squadron, 1837-39; on coast survey, 1840-43; commd. lt., 1841; served at Battle of Veracruz, Mexican War; promoted comdr., 1857; in command of ship Wyoming, 1863, attacked Japanese force at Shimonoseki, destroyed ships and did much damage to batteries; commd. capt., 1864, comdt., 1864, rear adm., 1873; comdt. South Pacific Squadron, 1870-72. Died San Francisco, Aug. 7, 1882.

McDOUGALL, Alexander, Continental congressman, army officer; b. Islay, Inner Hebrides, Scotland, July/Aug. 1732; s. Ronald and Elizabeth McDougall; m. Hannah Bostwick, 1767, 3 children including Elizabeth. Came to Am., 1783; commanded privateers Tyger and Barrington, 1756-83; author of written attack addressed "to the Betrayed Inhabitants of the City and Colony of New York," signed "A Son of Liberty," 1769; arrested and imprisoned, 1770-71; mem. N.Y. Com. of 51, 1774-75; col. 1st Regt., N.Y. Militia, 1775; comm brig. gen. Continental Army, 1776, maj. gen., 1777, served in battles of Chatterton's Hill, Germantown and White Plains; commanding officer Highlands of the Hudson; took command of West Point after discovery of Arnold's treason, 1780; arrested and courtmartialed for insubordination, 1782; mem. Continental Congress from N.Y., 1781-82, 84-85; mem. N.Y. Senate, 1783-86; an organizer, 1st pres. Bank of N.Y.; pres. N.Y. Soc. of Cincinnati. Died N.Y.C., June 9, 1786; buried family vault 1st Presbyn. Ch., N.Y.C.

McDOUGALL, James Alexander, senator, congressman; b. Bethlehem, N.Y., Nov. 19, 1817; attended pub. schs., Albany, N.Y.; studied law. Admitted to Ill. bar, began practice in Cook County, 1837; atty. gen. Ill., 1842-46; explored Southwestern U.S.; settled in San Francisco; atty. gen. Cal., 1850-51; mem. U.S. Ho. of Reps. (Democrat) from Cal., 33d Congress, 1853-55; mem. U.S. Senate from Cal., 1861-67; del. Dem. Nat. Conv., Chgo., 1864, Union Nat. Conv., Phila., 1866. Died Albany, Sept. 3, 1867; buried Lone Mountain (later Calvary) Cemetery, San Francisco.

McDOUGALL, John Alexander, artist; b. Livingston, N.Y., 1810/11. Worked in Newark, N.J., Charleston, S.C., Saratoga Springs, N.Y.; maintained studio, N.Y.C., during 1840's and 1850's; exhibited at N.A.D., Am. Art-Union, Artists' Fund Soc.; recipient 1st prize for miniatures Am. Inst., 1845, 47, 48. Died 1894.

McDOWELL, Charles, army officer; b. Winchester, Va., 1743; s. Joseph and Margaret (O'Neal or O'Neil) McD.; m. Grace or Grizel (Greenlee) Bowman, circa 1780. Served as capt. of a militia regt. in backwater region of South, commd. lt. col., 1776, comdr. a rear guard of Continental Army; helped to bring about 1st Continental victory in the South after Gate's defeat; served as brig. gen in command expdn. against Cherokee Indians, 1782; mem. N.C. Senate, 1778, 82-88; commr. for settling boundary between Tenn. and N.C., 1797. Died Burke County, N.C., Mar. 31, 1815.

McDOWELL, Ephraim, physician; b. Rockbridge County, Va., Nov. 11, 1771; s. Samuel and Mary (McClung) McD.; attended med. lectures Med. Sch., U. Edinburgh (Scotland), 1793-94; M.D., U. Md., 1825; m. Sarah Shelby, 1802, 6 children. Most noted surgeon West of Phila.; pioneer in abdominal surgery; performed 1st ovariotomy in U.S., 1809, had performed 12 with only one death by 1824; repeatedly performed radical operative cures for nonstrangulated hernia, at least 32 operations for stones in bladder, without a death; used lateral perineal incision; performed considerable work for charity; helped found, gave ground for Episcopal Ch., Danville, Ky.; a founder, 1st trustee Centre Coll., Danville; received diploma of membership Med. Soc. Pa., 1817. Died Danville, June 25, 1830; buried Danville.

McDOWELL, Irvin, army officer; b. Columbus, O., Oct. 15, 1818; s. Abram Irvin and Eliza Shelden (Lord) McD.; grad. College de Troyes (France) U.S. Mil. Acad., 1838; m. Helen Burden, 1849, 4 children. Commd. 1st lt. U.S. Army, 1842; aide-de-camp to Gen. Wool during Mexican War, also in Army of Occupation, 1848, adj. gen.; brevetted capt., 1847; commd. maj., 1856; brig. gen. in command Army of Potomac, also Dept. of Northeastern Va., 1861, commanded 1st Battle of Bull Run; commd. maj. gen. U.S. Volunteers in command I Corps, Army of Potomac, 1862; commanded troops Army of Rappahannock, territorial dept. of Rappahannock, relieved of command after 2d Battle of Bull Run (where he lost again), held territorial command San Francisco, 1864; commanded Dept. of East, 1868, Dept. of South, 1872; commd. maj. gen. U.S. Army, 1872; ret., 1882; park commr. San Francisco, circa 1882-85; planned park improvements of Presido reservation, laid out roads overlooking Golden Gate Bridge. Died San Francisco, May 4, 1885; buried San Francisco.

McDOWELL, James, gov. Va.; b. Rockbridge County, Va., Oct. 13, 1796; s. Col. James and Sarah (Preston) McD.; grad. Princeton, 1816; m. Susanna Preston, Sept. 7, 1818, 10 children including James. Admitted to Va. bar, but did not practice law; mem. Va. Ho. of Dels., 1830-35, 38; gov. Va., 1842-46; mem. U.S. Ho. of Reps. from Va., 29th-31st congresses, 1846-51, delivered meml. tribute to John Quincy Adams, also 2 speeches against Wilmot Proviso (among his best speeches). Author: Speech of James McDowell, Jr.,. . . on the Slave Question, 2d edit., 1832; Address Delivered before the Alumni Association of the College of New Jersey, delivered 1838, published, 1839. Died Lexington, Va., Aug. 24, 1851; buried Presbyn. Cemetery, Lexington.

McDOWELL, James Foster, congressman; b. Mifflin County, Pa., Dec. 3, 1825; attended pub. schs., Ohio; studied law. Employed in a printing office; admitted to Ohio bar, 1846, practiced law; pros. atty. Darke County (O.), 1848; moved to Marion, Ind., 1851, practiced law; founder Marion Jour., 1851; Democratic presdl. elector, 1852, 60; mem. U.S. Ho. of Reps. (Dem.) from Ind., 38th Congress, 1863-65; del. Dem. Nat. Conv., St. Louis, 187 Died Marion, Apr. 18, 1887; buried Odd Fellow Cemetery, Marion.

McDOWELL, John, coll. pres.; b. Peters Twp. Cumberland (now Franklin) County, Pa., Feb. 1 1751; s. William and Mary (Maxwell) McD.; gra Coll. of Phila., 1771. Tutor, Coll. of Phila., 1771-82 joined Capt. Samuel Patton's Co., 1777; admitte to Pa. bar, 1782; pres. St. John's Coll., 1790-180 mem. bd. visitors, bd. govs., 1810-18; prof. natur philosophy, provost U. Pa., 1806-10. Died De 22, 1820.

McDOWELL, John, clergyman; b. Bedminste Somerset County, N.J., Sept. 10, 1780; s. Matthe and Elizabeth (Anderson) McD.; grad. Coll. of N. (now Princeton), 1801; studied theology under mi isters H. W. Hunt and John Woodhull; m. Henriett Kollock, Feb. 5, 1805. Ordained to ministry b Presbytery of N.Y., 1804; pastor Presbyn. Ch., Eliz abethtown, N.J., 1804-32, Central Ch., Phila., 1833 45, Presbyn. Spring Garden Ch., Phila., 1845-6 Author: The New Jersey Preacher (contains som of his sermons), 1813; Questions on the Bible f the Use of Schools, 1820; Theology, In a Seri of Sermons in the Order of the Westminster Short Catechism, 2 vols., 1825-26. Died Feb. 13, 1863

McDOWELL, Joseph, congressman, army offi cer; b. Winchester, Va., Feb. 15, 1756; s. Josep and Margaret (O'Neal or O'Neil) McD.; m. Mar garet Moffett, 8 children including Joseph Jeff erson. Served with Charles McDowell (his brother Regt., N.C. Militia during Revolutionary Wa took part in Rutherford expdn. against Cheroke Indians, 1776, also numerous battles against Loya ists in N.C., including Ramsour's Mill, 1780; pr moted maj. McDowell Regt., in command a Battle of King's Mountain, 1780; commande detachment of riflemen from Burke County N.C. in Battle of Cowpens, 1781; attacked Chero kee Indians, 1781; commanded McDowell Regt during brother's expdn. against Cherokees, 1782 mem. N.C. Ho. of Commons, 1785-88, N.C. Senate 1791-95; mem. N.C. convs. to ratify U.S. Constn. 1788, 89, mem. U.S. Ho. of Reps. from N.C., 5t Congress, 1797-99. Died Feb. 5, 1801; burie "Quaker Meadows," nr. Morgantown, N.C.

McDOWELL, Joseph (P G), congressman; b "Pleasant Gardens" nr. Morganton, N.C., Feb. 25 1758; attended schs., Winchester, Va.; studied law Commd. maj. during Am. Revolution, participate in Battle of Kings Mountain; commd. gen. N.C Militia; admitted to N.C. bar, 1791, practiced i Burke (now McDowell), Rowan and Rutherford coun ties, 1785-92; mem. U.S. Ho. of Reps. from N.C. 3d Congress, 1793-95; resumed law practice, als engaged in farming; mem. commn. to settle bound ary between N.C. and Tenn., 1796. Died "Pleasan Gardens," Mar. 7, 1799; buried Round Hill "Pleasant Gardens."

McDOWELL, Joseph Jefferson, congressman; b Burke (now McDowell) County, N.C., Nov. 13 1800; studied law. Engaged in farming, August County, Va.; moved to Highland County, O., 1824 continued farming; moved to Hillsboro, O., 1829 engaged in merc. bus.; mem. Ohio Ho. of Reps. 1832, Ohio Senate, 1834; admitted to Ohio bar 1835, began practice in Hillsboro; mem. U.S. Ho of Reps. (Democrat) from Ohio, 28th-29th congresses, 1843-47. Died Hillsboro, Jan. 17, 1877 buried Hillsboro Cemetery.

McDUFFIE, George, senator, gov. S.C.; b Columbia County, Ga., Aug. 10, 1790; s. John an Jane McDuffie; grad. S.C. Coll., 1813; m. Mar Singleton, 1829, 1 child. Admitted to S.C. bar, 1814 mem. lower house S.C. Legislature, 1818-20; autho newspaper article Defence of a Liberal Constru tion of the Powers of Congress, 1821; mem. U.S Ho. of Reps. from S.C., 17th-23d congresses, 1821-34, chmn. ways and means com., 1825-29; presente banks meml. for recharter, 1832; developed forty-bale theory on influence of protective tariff, 1832 del. S.C. Nullification Conv., 1832, author nulli fication address to people of U.S.; gov. S.C., 1834-36; mem. U.S. Senate from S.C, 1842-46. Died Sumter dist., S.C., Mar. 11, 1851.

McDUFFIE, John Van, congressman; b. Addison, N.Y., May 16, 1841; attended Luther Coll., Decorah, Ia.; studied law, Ala. Served with Ia. Volunteer Cavalry during Civil War; settled in Lowndes County, Ala., engaged in planting; admitted to Ala. bar, began practice in Hayneville; judge of probate, 1868-80; elected mem. Ala. Constl. Conv., 1875, did not serve; del. Republican Nat. Conv., Phila., 1872, Cincinnati, 1876; mem. U.S. Ho. of Reps. (contested election) from Ala., 51st Congress, June 4, 1890-91; engaged in merc. bus. Died Hayneville, Nov. 18, 1896; buried Pines Cemetery, Hayneville.

McELRATH, Thomas, publisher; b. Williamsport, Pa., May 1, 1807; m. Elizabeth Price, 1833. Admitted to N.Y.C. bar, 1828; mem. bd. trustees N.Y.C. Pub. Sch. Soc., 1834; elected to N.Y. Assembly (Whig), 1838; master of chancery for N.Y.C.,

1840; N.Y. State dir. Bank of Am., 1841; partner (with Horace Greely) in firm Greely & McElrath, publishers N.Y. Tribune, also bus. mgr.; alderman N.Y.C., 1845-46; U.S. appraiser gen. N.Y. dist., 1861; custom house officer, 1866; U.S. commr. to Paris Exposition, 1867; supt. Am. exhbns. Vienna Exposition, 1873; sec., exec. officer N.Y. State Commn. at Centennial Exposition, Phila., 1876; commr. World's Fair, N.Y.C., 1884. Author: A Dictionary of Words and Phrases Used in Commerce, 1871. Died N.Y.C., June 6, 1888.

McELROY, John, clergyman; b. Enniskillen, Ireland, May 14, 1782. Came to Am. 1803; lay-brother Soc. of Jesus, 1806; ordained Roman Catholic Ch., 1817; pastor Frederick, Md., 1822-46; built ch., Libertyville, Md., 1828; built orphanage under Sisters of Charity, also new ch. of St. John, Frederick; founded St. John's Literary Inst., 1829; served as chaplain U.S. Army, 1846; 1st Jesuit pastor in Boston, circa 1848, made St. Mary's a city ch., introduced Sisters of Notre Dame into the diocese, 1849; donated first retreat for Hartford diocesan clergy, 1854; purchased site for Ch., of Immaculate Conception, 1859, Boston Coll., 1860. Died Frederick, Sept. 12, 1877.

McENTEE, Jervis, painter; b. Rondout, N.Y., July 4, 1828; s. James S. and Sarah (Goetcheus) McE.; m. Gertrude Sawyer, 1854. Opened studio in N.Y.C., 1854; elected asso. N.A.D.,1860; commanded co. of 20th N.Y. Militia, 1861; elected to Nat. Acad. Design, 1861; exhibited Paris Exposition, 1867, Centennial Exposition, Phila., 1876, Paris Exposition, 1878; works include Melancholy Days (willed to Nat. Acad. Design), 1860, Indian Summer, 1861, Venice, 1870, Autumn, 1874, Clouds, 1889, November, 1880, Wintry River, 1883, A Cliff in the Catskills, 1888. Died Rondout Jan. 27, 1891.

McFADDEN, Obadiah Benton, congressman; b. West Middletown, Pa., Nov. 18, 1815; attended McKeever Acad., West Middletown; studied law. Admitted to Pa. bar, 1843, practiced law; mem. Pa. Ho. of Reps., 1843; prothonotary of Washington County (Pa.); apptd. asso. justice Supreme Ct. of Territory of Ore., 1853; asso. justice Supreme Ct. of Territory of Wash., 1854-58, chief justice, 1858-61; mem. Wash. Territorial Legislative Council, pres., 1861; resumed law practice, Olympia, Wash., also engaged in farming; del. U.S. Congress from Territory of Washington, 1873-75. Died Olympia, June 25, 1875; buried Masonic Cemetery, Olympia.

McFARLAN, Duncan, congressman; b. Laurel Hill, N.C.; attended common schs. Engaged in farming; mem. N.C. Ho. of Commons, 1792, N.C. Senate, 1793, 95, 1800, 1807-09; mem. U.S. Ho. of Reps. from N..C, 9th Congress, 1805-07. Died Laurel Hill, Sept. 7, 1816; buried Laurel Hill Cemetery.

McFARLAND, Francis Patrick, clergyman; b. Franklin, Pa., Apr. 16, 1819; studied at Mt. St. Mary's Coll., Md. Taught at Mt. St. Mary's Coll.; ordained priest Roman Catholic Ch., N.Y., 1845; taught at Fordham U., N.Y.C., 1 year; became pastor, Watertown and Utica (N.Y.); declined appointment as vicar apostolic of Fla., 1857; apptd. bishop of Hartford (Conn.), 1858, resided in Providence, R.I. until diocese was divided in 1872, then moved to Hartford; attended Vatican Council, 1869-70. Died Oct. 12, 1874.

McFARLAND, Samuel Gamble, clergyman; b. Washington County, Pa., Dec. 11, 1830; s. William and Mary (McKenahan) McF.; A.B., Washington and Jefferson Coll., 1857; attended Western Theol. Sem., 1857-60; m. Jane E. Hays, May 3, 1860, 4 children including George B. Ordained to ministry Presbyn. Ch., Washington, Pa., 1860; sent to Siam, 1860, assigned to open 1st sta. outside capital at Petchaburi, trained 1st Siamese to be licensed preachers, published 1st Siamese hymnbook to include tunes, 1876, prin. royal sch., 1878, laid foundations for system universal compulsory edn. Author: An English-Siamese Dictionary, 1865. Died Canonsburg, Pa., Apr. 25, 1897.

McFERRIN, John Berry, clergyman; b. Rutherford County, Tenn., June 15, 1807; son of James McFerrin; m. Almyra Avery Probart, 1833; m. 2d, Cynthia Tennessee McGavock, 1855; at least 4 children. Admitted on trial to Tenn. Conf. of Methodist Ch., 1825, circuit rider, 1825-27; missionary and elder to Cherokee Indians in territory around Ft. Oglethorpe, 1827-40; editor Southwestern Christian Advocate, Nashville, Tenn., 1840-58; del. Gen. Methodist Conf., 1844; del. Louisville Conv. which organized Methodist Episcopal Ch. South, 1845; book agt. for Methodist Ch., 1858-66; in charge of Methodist missionary work in Army of Tenn., 1861-66; dir. domestic and fgn. missions Methodist Ch., 1866-78; book agt. Methodist publishing house, 1878-87. Author: History of Methodism in Tennessee, 3 vols., 1869-73. Died May 10, 1887.

McGAUGHEY, Edward Wilson, congressman; b. nr. Greencastle, Ind., Jan. 16, 1817; attended pub. schs.; studied law. Dep. clk. Putnam County (Ind.); admitted to Ind. bar, 1835, began practice in Greencastle; mem. Ind. Ho. of Reps., 1839-40, Ind. Senate, 1842-43; mem. U.S. Ho. of Reps. (Whig) from Ind., 29th, 31st congresses, 1845-47; 49-51; nominated by Pres. Taylor as gov. Minn. Territory, 1849, nomination not confirmed by Senate; moved to Cal., 1852. Died San Francisco, Aug. 6, 1852; buried Yerba Buena Cemetery, San Francisco.

McGEE, Milton, pioneer guide; horseman with Chiles' party, 1843; led a party to Cal., 1849.

McGEE, Thomas D'Arcy, editor; b. Carlingford, Louth, Ireland, Apr. 13, 1825. Came to U.S., 1842, became an editor Boston Pilot; returned to Ireland, 1845, became mem. editorial staff Freeman's Journal and Nation, Dublin; arrested for his activities in Irish revolt, 1848, escaped to N.Y.; established paper The Nation, N.Y.C., became involved in disputes with Archbishop Hughes, moved paper to Boston, then to Buffalo, then (under title Am. Celt) back to N.Y.C.; founded paper The New Era, Montreal, Can.; became mem. Canadian Parliament, prominent in establishing Dominion of Can. Author: History of the Irish Settlers in North America, Catholic History of North America, History of Ireland, Poems. Assassinated by a Fenian, Ottawa, Can., Apr. 7, 1868.

McGIFFIN, Philo Norton, naval officer; b. Washington, Pa., Dec. 13, 1860; s. Col. Norton and Sarah (Quail) McG.; grad. U.S. Naval Acad., 1882. Served in Pacific Squadron, 1882, honorably discharged from U.S. Navy, 1884; served in Chinese Navy, 1885; prof. seamanship, gunnery Naval Coll., Tien-tsin, China; naval constructor; chiefly responsible for Chinese naval victory in Sino-Japanese War fought off of Yalu River, 1894, severly wounded, burned, suffered both physically and mentally. Committed suicide N.Y.C., Feb. 11, 1897.

McGILL, John, clergyman; b. Phila., Nov. 4, 1809; s. James and Lavenia (Dougherty) McG.; grad. St. Joseph's Coll., Ky., 1828; studied law under Gov. Charles A. Wickliffe; studied theology at St. Mary's, Balt. Ordained priest Roman Catholic Ch., 1835; pastor St. Peter's Ch., Lexington, Ky., 1835-50, also editor Catholic Advocate; bishop Diocese of Richmond, 1850-72; attended Vatican Council, Rome, Italy, 1869. Died Jan. 14, 1872.

McGILLIVRAY, Alexander, Indian chief; b. 1759; s. Lachlan and Sehoy (Marchand) McG.; children include Alexander, Elizabeth. Chief of Upper Creek Indian tribe; Brit. agt. among Southern Indians during Am. Revolution; connected with Loyalist trading firm Panton, Leslie & Co.; his property confiscated by Ga. because of his Loyalist activities; aligned with Spain after 1784 in attempt to separate area west of Alleghanies from U.S.; made constant raids on Am. frontier settlements, 1786-90; apptd. Spanish commissary to enforce Spain's monopoly of trade with Creeks, 1784; signed Treaty of N.Y. with U.S. (by which Creeks were given large areas of land), 1790; his property in Ga. was returned; apptd. brig. gen. U.S. Army; signed convention (which repudiated Treaty of N.Y., re-affirmed allegiance to Spain) with Francisco Carondelet, Spanish gov. Fla., 1792; began making plans for unified effort of all So. Indians to drive out Americans, died before completion. Died Pensacola, Fla., Feb. 17, 1793.

McGIVNEY, Michael Joseph, clergyman; b. Waterbury, Conn., Aug. 12, 1852; s. Patrick and Mary (Lynch) McG.; grad. Niagara U., 1873; theol. student St. Mary's Sem., Balt. Ordained priest Roman Catholic Ch., 1877; asst. to Father Murphy of St. Mary's Ch., New Haven, Conn.; organizer parochial total abstinence soc.; founder (with 9 lay assos.) Knights of Columbus, 1882, nat. chaplain, mem. supreme council. Died Thomaston, Conn., Aug. 14, 1890.

McGOWAN, Samuel, jurist; b. Laurens Dist., S.C., Oct. 9, 1819; s. William and Jeannie (McWilliams) McG.; grad. S.C. Coll., 1841; m. Susan Caroline Wardlaw, 7 children. Admitted to S.C. bar, 1842; mem. S.C. Ho. of Reps., 1852-65; served as capt. Palmetto Regt. during Mexican War, 1846-48; served as col. S.C. regt., Civil War, 1861-66; mem. S.C. Constl. Conv., 1865; mem. S.C. Ho. of Reps., 1878-79; judge S.C. Supreme Ct., 1878-93. Died Abbeville, S.C., Aug. 9, 1897; buried Long Cane Cemetery, Abbeville.

McGRATH, James, clergyman; b. County Tipperary, Ireland, June 26, 1835; attended U. Dublin; studied theology U. Ottawa (Can.), 1855-58. Curate, St. Patrick's Ch., Ottawa, 1859-61; missionary in Tex., 1861-64; constructed Ch. of Immaculate Conception, Ottawa, 1864-65; preached in N.Y. and New Eng. area, 1864-70; pastor St. John's Ch., Lowell, Mass., 1870-83; elected 1st provincial Oblate Community over Lowell, Buffalo, N.Y., also Tex. and Mexico, 1883-98. Died Albany, N.Y., Jan. 12, 1898.

McGREADY, James, clergyman; b. Western Pa., circa 1758. Licensed to preach by Presbytery of Redstone, Pa., 1788; pastor ch. in Orange County, N.C., 1790; had 3 small congregations in Logan County, Ky., 1796; responsible for revivals, 1797, 98, 99 (forerunners Gt. Revival of 1800); allied with Cumberland Presbytery, 1800; restored to Orthodox Transylvania Presbytery; pioneer preacher, founding chs. in So. Ind., 1811. Author: A Short Narrative of the Revival of Religion in Logan County in the State of Kentucky, and the Adjacent Settlements in the State of Tennessee, from May 1797 until September 1800. Died Henderson County, Ky., Feb. 1817.

McGROARTY, Susan (Sister Julia), educator; b. County Donegal, Ireland, Feb. 13, 1827; d. Neil and Catherine (Bonner) McGroarty. Came with her family to Quebec, 1831, then to Cincinnati; became postulant, 1846, professed as Sister Julia, 1848; mistress of boarders Acad. Notre Dame, Roxbury, Mass., 1854-60; built sch., Rittenhouse Square, Phila., 1867; operated free sch. for Negroes, 1877-82; mother superior in Cincinnati, 1787; built large convent and sch. at Summit, Cincinnati, 1889, Novitiate at Waltham, Mass., also many other founds.; took over mgmt. of Notre Dame schs. on Pacific Coast, 1892; founded instn. for orphans, San Jose, Cal.; founded Trinity Coll., 1899-1900. Died Peabody, Mass., Nov. 12, 1901; buried in community chapel at Summit, Cincinnati.

McGUFFEY, William Holmes, univ. pres.; b. Claysville, Washington County, Pa., Sept. 23, 1800; s. Alexander and Anna (Holmes) McG.; grad. Washington Coll., 1826; hon. degree U. Ind.; m. Harriet Spinning, 1827; m. 2d, Laura Howard, 1857; 6 children. Taught in one-room sch.; prof. langs. Miami U., Oxford, O., 1826-32, head dept. mental philosophy and philology, 1832; his wife ran exptl. elementary sch. in their home; licensed to preach in Presbyn. Ch., 1829; an organizer Coll. of Tchrs., 1831; pres. Cincinnati Coll., 1836-39, Ohio U., 1839-43; prof. Woodward Coll., 1843-45; prof. moral philosophy U. Va., 1845-73, twice offered univ. presidency, but declined. Author 1st, 2d Eclectic Readers, published 1836, 3d, 4th, published 1837 (over 140 million copies sold, also popular in France, Eng., Japan). Died Charlottesville, Va., May 4, 1873.

McGUIRE, Charles Bonaventure, clergyman; b. Dungannon, County Tyrone, Ireland, Dec. 16, 1768; attended Louvain U., Belgium. Ordained friar Franciscan Order; left France during Revolution; traveled in Europe conducting confidential work for his order, before 1817; came as missionary to Pa., 1817; assigned to western missions of Pa., 1817-20; pastor St. Patrick's Ch., Pitts., 1820-33; laid cornerstone for St. Paul's Ch., Pitts. (then 1 of largest chs. in Am.), 1829. Died Pitts., July 17, 1833; buried St. Paul's Ch., Pitts.

McHATTON, Robert Lytle, congressman; b. Fayette County, Va. (now Ky.), Nov. 17, 1788; attended common schs. Engaged in farming; mem. Ky. Ho. of Reps., 1814-16; served as maj. 77th Regt., Ky. Militia, 1816; mem. U.S. Ho. of Reps. (Jacksonian Democrat) from Ky., 19th-20th congresses, Dec. 7, 1826-29. Died Marion County, Ind., May 20, 1835; buried Old Cemetery, Georgetown, Ky.

McHENRY, Henry Davis, congressman; b. Hartford, Ky., Feb. 27, 1826; s. John Hardin McHenry; grad. law dept. Transylvania U., Lexington, Ky., 1845. Admitted to Ky. bar, 1845, began practice in Hartford; mem. Ky. Ho. of Reps., 1851-53, 65-67, Ky. Senate, 1861-65; mem. Democratic Nat. Conv., 1872-90; mem. U.S. Ho. of Reps. (Dem.) from Ky., 42d Congress, 1871-73; del. Ky. Constl. Conv., 1890. Died Hartford, Dec. 17, 1890; buried Oakwood Cemetery, Hartford.

McHENRY, James, U.S. sec. of war; b. Ballymena, County Antrim, Ireland, Nov. 16, 1753; s. Daniel and Agnes McHenry; m. Margaret Allison Caldwell, Jan. 8, 1784, at least 3 children including John. Came to Phila., 1771; became surgeon Col. Robert Magaw's 5th Pa. Battalion, 1776, sr. surgeon Flying Hosp., Valley Forge, 1778; sec. to George Washington, 1778-80; mem. staff Gen. Jean Lafayette, 1780; commd. maj., 1781; mem. Md. Senate, 1781-86, 91-96; mem. Continental Congress 1783-86; del. from Md. to U.S. Constl. Conv., 1787; U.S. sec. of war, 1796-1800; pres. 1st Bible soc. founded in Balt., 1813; published a Balt. directory, 1807; Ft. McHenry (Md.) named for him. Author: A Letter to the Honourable Speaker of the House of Representatives of the United States (speech in defense of actions as sec. of war) 1803. Died Balt., May 3, 1816; buried Westminster Churchyard, Balt.

McHENRY, James, author; b. Larne, County Antrim, Ireland, Dec. 20, 1785. Came to U.S., 1817, lived in Pitts., 1817-24; prominent as a physician, mcht., editor and poet in Phila., 1824-42; founder Am. Monthly Mag., 1824; apptd. to consulate, Londonderry, Ireland, 1843-45. Author: The Pleasures of Friendship (vol. of verse), 1822; The Wilderness; or

The Youthful Days of Washington (1st novel), 1823; The Spectre of the Forest, 1823; O'Halloran, or the Insurgent Chief, 1823; The Usurper (play), 1827. Died Larne, July 21, 1845.

McHENRY, John Hardin, congressman; b. nr. Springfield, Ky., Oct. 13, 1797; studied law; children include Henry Davis. Admitted to Ky. bar, 1818, began practice in Leitchfield; apptd. postmaster of Leitchfield, 1819; maj. 87th Regt., Ky. Militia, 1821; moved to Hartford, Ky., 1823; apptd. commonwealth atty., 1831, reapptd., 1837; commd. col. Ky. Militia, 1837; mem. Ky. Ho. of Reps. from Ohio County, 1840; apptd. mem. bd. Transylvania U., 1843; mem. U.S. Ho. of Reps. (Whig) from Ky., 29th Congress, 1845-47; mem. Ky. Constl. Conv., 1849; moved to Owensboro, Ky., 1854; judge circuit ct. of several counties, 1854. Died Owensboro, Nov. 1, 1871; buried Elmwood Cemetery, Owensboro.

McILVAINE, Abraham Robinson, congressman; b. Ridley, Pa., Aug. 14, 1804; attended common schs. Engaged in farming, Chester County, Pa.; mem. Pa. Ho. of Reps., 1836-37; Whig presdl. elector, 1840; mem. U.S. Ho. of Reps. (Whig) from Pa., 28th-30th congresses, 1843-49; resumed farming, also engaged in iron bus. Died "Springton Farms," Chester County, Aug. 22, 1863; buried Caln Orthodox Quaker Meeting Burial Ground, nr. Downington, Pa., reinterred Northwood Cemetery, Downington.

McILVAINE, Charles Pettit, clergyman; b. Burlington, N.J., Jan. 18, 1799; s. Joseph and Maria (Reed) McI.; grad. Coll. of N.J. (now Princeton), 1816; m. Emily Coxe, Oct. 8, 1822. Pastor, Christ Ch., Georgetown, D.C., 1820-24; ordained to ministry Episcopal Ch., 1823; chaplain U.S. Senate, 1821-22; chaplain, prof. geography and ethics U.S. Mil. Acad., 1825-27; rector St. Ann's, Bklyn., 1827-33; prof. evidences of Christianity, U. City N.Y., 1828-32; consecrated bishop Episcopal Ch., 1832; resided in Gambier, O., 1833-46, Clifton, O., after 1846; visited England on request of Pres. Lincoln to establish better relations with Eng. after Trent affair. Author: The Evidences of Christianity in their External Division, 1832; Oxford Divinity Compared with that of the Romish and Anglican Churches, 1841. Died Florence, Italy, Mar. 13, 1873; buried Clifton.

McILVAINE, Joseph, senator; b. Bristol, Pa., Oct. 2, 1769; studied law. Admitted to bar Supreme Ct. of N.J., 1790; began practice of law, Burlington, N.J., 1791; clk. Burlington County (N.J.), 1796-1800; clk. county ct., 1800-23; U.S. atty. for N.J., 1801-20; declined appointment as judge N.J. Superior Ct., 1818; mem. U.S. Senate (Democrat) from N.J., Nov. 12, 1823-26. Died Burlington, Aug. 19, 1826; buried St. Mary's Cemetery, Burlington.

McILVAINE, William, artist; b. Phila., June 5, 1813; s. Joseph Bloomfield McIlvaine; grad. U. Pa., 1832. Toured Europe; in bus. with father, Phila.; began painting professionally, circa 1845; visited gold fields in Cal., 1849; published Sketches of Scenery and Notes of Personal Adventures in California and Mexico, 1850; moved to N.Y.C., circa 1856; served with 5th N.Y. Volunteer Rgt., U.S. Army, during Civil War. Died Bklyn., June 16, 1867.

McINDOE, Walter Duncan, congressman; b. Dumbartonshire, Scotland, Mar. 30, 1819. Came to U.S., 1834; engaged in bus., N.Y.C., Charleston, S.C., St. Louis; settled in Wis., 1845, engaged in lumber bus.; mem. Wis. Assembly, 1840, 54-55; unsuccessful candidate for gov. Wis., 1857; provost marshal of Wis. during Civil War; Republican presdl. elector, 1856, 60, 72; mem. U.S. Ho. of Reps. (Republican) from Wis., 37th-39th congresses, Jan. 26, 1863-67. Died Wausau, Wis., Aug. 22, 1872; buried Pine Grove Cemetery, Wausau.

McINTIRE, Samuel, architect; b. Salem, Mass., Jan. 1757; s. Joseph and Sarah (Ruck) McI.; m. Elizabeth Field, 1778; 1 son, Samuel Field. Designer many colonial houses, chs., pub. bldgs., Old Salem, Mass., designer great house built by Jerathmeel Peirce (his 1st important archt. endeavor); designer house on Salem Common (built 1782-89), Assembly House, 1782, Washington Hall, 1785, Salem Ct. House, Nathan Read house, 1793, Theadore Lyman house, Waltham, Mass., Derby Mansion, 1795, several other houses for mem. of Derby family; remodeled great parlor of Peirce house, 1801; designed a Cook, Gardner houses (among his finest works), 1804; later works comprised hotels, bus. bldgs. of larger scale, including the Archer (now Franklin) Bldg. (his most extensive undertaking) Salem, 1809-10; pioneer in sculpture, furniture design; carved several bas-reliefs for gates of Boston Common; noted for mantelpieces, cornices; his interiors are exhibited in Met. Mus., N.Y.C., Boston Mus. Fine Arts, Essex Inst., Salem. Died Salem, Feb. 6, 1811.

McINTOSH, John Baillie, army officer; b. Tampa Bay, Fla., June 6, 1829; s. Col. James Simmons and Eliza (Matthews) Shumate McI.; m. Amelia Stout, 1850. Commd. 2d lt. cavalry U.S. Army, 1861, served in Peninsular Campaign; in temporary command 95th Pa. Regt., 1862; brevetted maj., 1862; col. 3d Pa. Cavalry, commanded a brigade at battles of Chancellorsville and Gettysburg, 1862; distinguished in Wilderness campaign, battles of Osequan, White Oak Swamp, Ashland, and Winchester, 1861-65; received brevets from maj. to maj. gen.; commd. lt. col. U.S. Army, 1865; comd. 42d Inf., 1866-67; dep. gov., then gov. Soldiers' Home, Washington, D.C., 1867-68; supt. Indian affairs in Cal., 1869-70; ret. with rank of brig. gen., 1870. Died New Brunswick, N.J., June 29, 1888.

McINTOSH, Lachlan, army officer, Continental congressman; b. Raits in Badenoch, Scotland, Mar. 17, 1725; s. John Mohr and Marjory (Fraser) McI.; m. Sarah Threadcraft. Came to Am., 1736; mem. Provincial Congress of Ga., from Parish of St. Andrew 1775; col. of a bn. Ga. Militia, 1776; commanded Western Dept., 1778; commanded 1st, 5th S.C. regts. in attack on Savannah, Ga., 1779; brevetted maj. gen., 1783; charter mem. Ga. br. Soc. of Cincinnati, 1784; del. Continental Congress, 1784, never attended sessions; twice commr. to adjust boundary dispute between Ga. and S.C.; commr. of Congress to deal with So. Indians, 1785-86. Died Savannah, Feb. 20, 1806; buried Colonial Cemetery, Savannah.

McINTOSH, William, Indian chief, army officer; b. Carroll County, Ga., 1775; s. William McIntosh; several Indian wives. Leader of Lower Creek Indians, friendly to Americans in War of 1812; commd. brig. gen. U.S. Army, served with Gen. Andrew Jackson in campaigns against Seminoles, 1817-18; influenced treaties between Lower Creeks and Ga.; expelled from Cherokee country as a renegade, 1824; signer treaty of cession of Indian lands to State of Ga., 1825, killed by Upper Creek Indians who opposed treaty. Died Ga., May 1, 1825.

McINTYRE, Rufus, congressman; b. York, Mass. (now Me.), Dec. 19, 1784; grad. Dartmouth, 1809; studied law. Admitted to the bar, began practice in Parsonfield, Me., 1812; served in War of 1813; mem. Me. Ho. of Reps., 1820; pros. atty. York County (Me.), 1820-43; mem. boundary commn. to settle N. and N.E. boundaries of Me., 1820; mem. U.S. Ho. of Reps. (Jacksonian Democrat) from Me., 20th-23d congresses, Sept. 10, 1827-35; land agt. State of Me., 1839-40; apptd. U.S. marshal for Me., 1845; surveyor of customs Port of Portland (Me.), 1853-57. Died Parsonfield, Me., Apr. 28, 1866; buried Middleroad Cemetery, Parsonfield.

McKAY, Donald, shipbuilder; b. Shelbourne County, N.S., Can., Sept. 14, 1810; s. Hugh and Ann (McPherson) McK.; m. Albenia Martha Boole, 1833; m. 2d, Mary Cressy Lightfield, 1849; 15 children. Came to N.Y., 1827; became apprentice ship carpenter; formed partnership as master shipbuilder with William Currier, 1841; chosen to design and build ship Joshua Bates for Boston-Liverpool Line, 1844; established shipyard, East Boston, 1844; designed, built Stag Hound (his 1st clipper ship; 1,534 tons), 1850, became greatest clipper ship builder, ships broke many speed records; converted to use of steam, steel-clad ships (realized wooden ships were obsolete), designs for some Union warships were not accepted (which caused his decline). Died Hamilton, Mass., Sept. 20, 1880.

McKAY, James Iver, congressman; b. Bladen County, N.C., July 17, 1792; s. John and Mary (Salter) McK.; m. Eliza Ann Harvey, Dec. 3, 1818, 1 child. Admitted to N.C. bar; mem. N.C. Senate, 1815-19, 22, 26, 29, 30; U.S. dist. atty. for N.C., 1817; mem. U.S. Ho. of Reps. from N.C. (Democrat), 22d-30th congresses, 1831-49; responsible for establishment of Ft. Caswell on Cape Fear and an arsenal at Fayetteville, N.C.; wrote a report on tariff (an important state paper), 1844; helped prepare, introduced Walker Tariff Bill. 1846. Died Goldsboro, N.C., Sept. 14, 1853; buried "Belfont," N.C.

McKEAN, James Bedell, congressman; b. Bennington, Vt., Aug. 5, 1821; attended schs., N.Y.; studied law. Taught in dist. schs.; prof. Jonesville (N.Y.) Acad.; supt. common schs., Half Moon, N.Y., 1842; elected col. 144th Regt., N.Y. Militia, 1844; admitted to N.Y. bar, 1849, began practice in Ballston Spa; moved to Saratoga Springs, N.Y., 1851; judge Saratoga County (N.Y.), 1854-58; mem. U.S. Ho. of Reps. (Republican) from N.Y., 26th-27th congresses, 1859-63; organizer, col. 77th Regt., N.Y. Volunteers during Civil War, 1861-63; apptd. treaty commr. to Honduras, 1865; declined appointment as U.S. consul to Santo Domingo; chief justice Utah Territorial Supreme Ct. (apptd. by Pres. Grant), 1870-75. Died Salt Lake City, Utah, Jan. 5, 1879; buried Mt. Olivet Cemetery, Salt Lake City.

McKEAN, Joseph Borden, jurist; b. New Castle, Del., July 28, 1764; s. Thomas and Mary (Borden) McK.; grad. U. Pa., 1782; m. Hannah Miles, Apr. 13, 1786. Admitted to Phila. bar, 1785; atty. gen. Pa., 1800-08, asso. judge for City and County of Phila., 1817-25, pres. judge, 1825-26; trustee U. Pa., 1796-1826. Died Phila., Sept. 3, 1826.

McKEAN, Samuel, senator; b. Huntingdo County, Pa., Apr. 7, 1787; s. James and Jane (Scott McK.; m. Julia McDowell, Jan. 7, 1812. Count commr. Bradford County (Pa.), 1814; found (with other Republicans) Bradford Gazette, T wanda, Pa.; mem. Pa. Ho. of Reps., 1815-19; mem U.S. Ho. of Reps. from Pa., 18th-20th congresses 1823-29; mem. Pa. Senate, 1829-30; sec. Commor wealth of Pa., 1829-33, drafted bill providing f taxation of all property for free sch. purposes Democratic persdl. elector, 1832; mem. U.S. Senat from Pa., 1833-39, supported Jackson's attack o U.S. Bank, 1834. Served as maj. gen. Pa., Militi Died West Burlington, Pa., Dec. 14, 1841; burie Old Church Cemetery, West Burlington.

McKEAN, Thomas, gov. Pa., Continental congress man; b. New London Twp., Pa., Mar. 30, 1735 s. William and Letitia (Finney) M.; studied la Middle Temple, London, Eng., 1758; m. Mary Bor den, July 21, 1763; m. 2d, Sarah Armitage, Sept. 3 1774; 11 children including Joseph. Dep. prothono tary, register for probate of wills for New Castl County, Del., 1752; admitted to Del. bar, 1755 practiced law, New Castle, Del., later Phila.; dep atty. gen. for Sussex County, Del., 1756-58; mem Del. Ho. of Assembly, 1762-75, speaker, 1772; trus tee for loan office New Castle County, 1764-76 mem. Stamp Act Congress, 1765; apptd. sole notar for lower counties of Del., justice of peace, judge Ct of Common Pleas and Quarter Sessions, judge Or phans' Ct. for New Castle County, 1765; collecto Port of New Castle, 1771; mem. Continental Con gress from Del., 1774-83, pres., 1781; signed Dec laration of Independence, circa 1777 (1st to correc popular impression that Declaration was signed Jul 4, 1776, later proved that no one signed on tha date); mem. Del. Constl. Conv., 1776; mem. Del Ho. of Reps., 1776-77, speaker, 1777; pres. of Del. 1777; chief justice of Pa., 1777-99; mem. Pa Conv. that ratified U.S. Constn., 1787; mem. Pa Constl. Conv., 1789-90; gov. Pa., 1799-1808, intro duced polit. "spoils system" on large scale in Pa Died Phila., June 24, 1817; buried Laurel Hil Cemetery, Phila.

McKEAN, William Wister, naval officer; b Phila., Sept. 19, 1800; s. Judge Joseph Borden an Hannah (Miles) McK.; m. Davis Rosa Clark, Aug 25, 1824, 12 children. Commd. midshipman U.S Navy, 1814, lt., 1825, comdr., 1841, capt., 1855 commodore, 1862; in charge of Naval Asylum Phila., 1843-44; mem. bd. which recommende locating regular naval sch. at Annapolis (Md.) commanded ship Niagara, carried Japanese em bassy staff home to Japan, 1860; in charge o the Gulf Blockading Squadron, occupied Hea of the Passes of the Mississippi River, 1861. Die "The Moorings," Binghamton, N.Y., Apr. 22, 1865; buried Spring Forest Cemetery, Binghamton.

McKEE, George Colin, congressman; b. Joliet, Ill., Oct. 2, 1837; attended Knox Coll., Lombard Coll. (both Galesburg, Ill.); studied law. Admitted to Ill. bar, 1858, began practice in Centralia; city atty. of Centralia, 1858-61; served with Ill. Volunteer Inf. during Civil War; commd. brig. gen. U.S. Volunteers; resumed law practice, Vicksburg, Miss.; engaged in planting, Hinds County, Miss.; apptd. register in bankruptcy, 1867; mem. Miss. Constl. Conv., 1868; mem. U.S. Ho. of Reps. (Republican) from Miss., 41st-43d congresses, 1869-75; postmaster of Jackson (Miss.), 1881-85, receiver of pub. moneys, 1889-90. Died Jackson, Nov. 15, 1890; buried Greenwood Cemetery, Jackson.

McKEE, John, Indian agt., congressman; b. Rockbridge County, Va., 1771; s. John (or James) and Esther (Houston) McK.; attended Liberty Hall Acad. (now Washington and Lee U.); m. an Indian woman, 1 son. Commr. to Cherokee Indians to agree on line designated in Treaty of Holston, 1792; apptd. by Gov. William Blount to try to conciliate the Cherokee, sent to accompany a deputation of Chickasaws to visit Pres. U.S., 1793; temporary agt. of Cherokee, 1794; active in persuading other tribes to remain at peace with U.S. during Creek War; led expdn. of about 600 Choctaw and Chickasaw Indians to Black Warrior River, 1814; one of 1st settlers of Tuscaloosa County (Ala.), in charge of land office; mem. U.S. Ho. of Reps. from Ala., 18th-20th congresses, 1823-29; a commr. to negotiate Treaty of Dancing Rabbit Creek whereby Choctaw Indians ceded all claims to land East of the Mississippi. Died Boligee, Ala., Aug. 12, 1832.

McKEE, Samuel, congressman; b. nr. Lexington, Va., Oct. 13, 1774; grad. Liberty Hall Acad. (now Washington and Lee U.), Lexington, 1794; studied law. Admitted to Va. bar, 1800; began practice of law, Somerset, Ky.; surveyor of Pulaski County (Ky.); moved to Lancaster, Ky., 1807, practiced law; mem. Ky. Ho. of Reps., 1802-08; mem. U.S. Ho. of Reps. (Democrat) from Ky., 11th-14th congresses, 1809-17; served on staff of Gen. Harrison during War of 1812; mem. commn. apptd. by Pres. Monroe to clear Ohio and Mississippi rivers of obstructions, until 1826. Died Hickman County,

Ky., Oct. 16, 1826; buried Frankfort (Ky.) Cemetery.

McKEEN, Joseph, clergyman; b. Londonderry, N.H., Oct. 15, 1757; s. John and Mary (McKeen) McK.; grad. Dartmouth, 1774; attended Harvard, 1782-circa 1783; m. Alice Anderson, 1785, 5 children. Tutored in Londonderry, 1774-82; licensed to preach by Londonderry Presbytery; ordained to ministry Presbyn. Ch., 1785; pastor Congregational Ch., Beverly, Mass., 1785-1802; pres. Bowdoin Coll., 1802-07. Died Brunswick, Me., July 15, 1807.

McKEIGHAN, William Arthur, congressman; b. Millville, N.J., Jan. 19, 1842; attended common schs., Fulton County, Ill. Served with Ill. Volunteer Cavalry during Civil War; settled nr. Pontiac, Ill., engaged in farming; moved to Neb., 1880, resumed farming nr. Red Cloud; an organizer Farmers' Alliance; probate judge Webster County (Neb.), 1885-87; mem. U.S. Ho. of Reps. (Democrat) from Neb., 52d-53d congresses, 1891-95. Died Hastings, Neb., Dec. 15, 1895; buried Red Cloud Cemetery.

McKENDREE, William, clergyman; b. William City, Va., July 6, 1757; s. John and Mary McK. Served as adj. during Revolutionary War; converted to Methodism, 1787; became preacher, 1788, ordained deacon, 1790, elder, 1791; attended Gen. Conf. of Meth. Ch., Balt., 1792; presiding elder Richmond (Va.) dist., 1796-99; put in charge missionary work in Western Va., Ohio, Ky., sects. of Ill., Tenn. Miss.; elected bishop at Gen. Conf. (1st Am.-born bishop of Meth. Episcopal Ch.), 1808; inaugurated practice of consultation with presiding elders in making of appointments; gave 480 acres of land to Lebanon (Ill.) Sem. Died Gallatin, Tenn., Mar. 5, 1835; buried Sumner County, Tenn.; reinterred on campus of Vanderbilt U., Nashville, Tenn.

McKENNAN, Thomas McKean Thompson, congressman, railroad pres.; b. Dragon Neck, New Castle County, Del., Mar. 31, 1794; s. Col. William and Elizabeth (Thompson) McK.; grad. Washington (Pa.) Coll., 1810; studied law in office of Parker Campbell, Washington, Pa.; m. Matilda Bowman, Dec. 6, 1815, 8 children. Admitted to bar, 1814; dep. atty. gen. for Washington County (Pa.), 1815-17; mem. Washington Town Council, 1818-31; mem. U.S. Ho. of Reps. (Whig) from Pa., 22d-25th, 27th congresses, 1831-39, May 30, 1842-43; became an ofcl. Washington & Pitts. R.R. Co., 1831; presdl. elector, 1840, 48; U.S. sec of interior under Pres. Fillmore, 1850; 1st pres. Hempfield R.R., 1851; trustee Washington Coll., 1818-52. Died Reading, Pa., July 9, 1852; buried Washington (Pa.) Cemetery.

McKENNEY, Thomas Loraine, govt. ofcl.; b. Hopewell, Md., Mar. 21, 1785. U.S. supt. of Indian trade, 1816-22; publisher, editor Washington (D.C.) Republican and Congressional Examiner, 1822-23; in charge Bur. of Indian Affairs, U.S War Dept., 1824-30, instrumental in obtaining annual $10,000 appropriation for civilizing Indian tribes adjoining frontier settlements; negotiator treaty with Chippewa, Menominee and Winnebago Indians, 1827; helped influence Chickasaw and Creek Indians to agree to migrate west of Mississippi River; negotiator agreement with Creek Indians, 1827. Author: Essays on the Spirit of Jacksonism as Exemplified in its Deadly Hostility to the Bank of the United States, 1835. Died N.Y.C., Feb. 20, 1859.

McKENTY, Jacob Kerlin, congressman; b. Douglassville, Pa., Jan. 19, 1827; grad. Yale, 1848, grad. in law, 1851. Admitted to Pa. bar, 1851, began practice in Reading; pros. atty. Berks County, 1856-58; mem. U.S. Ho. of Reps. (Democrat) from Pa., 36th Congress, Dec. 3, 1860-61; resumed law practice, Reading. Died Douglassville, Jan. 3, 1866; buried St. Gabriel's Episcopal Ch. Cemetery, Douglassville.

McKENZIE, Lewis, congressman; b. Alexandria, Va., Oct. 7, 1810. Engaged in shipping and merc. bus.; mem. Alexandria City Council, 1855-59, 63-66, 68-70, 87-91; mayor of Alexandria, 1861-63; mem. U.S. Ho. of Reps. from Va., as Unionist, 37th Congress, Feb. 16-Mar. 3, 1863, as Union Conservative, 41st Congress, Jan. 31, 1870-71; pres. Washington & Ohio R.R. Co.; apptd. postmaster of Alexandria, 1878. Died Alexandria, June 28, 1895; buried Presbyn. Cemetery, Alexandria.

McKEON, John, congressman; b. Albany, N.Y., Mar. 29, 1808; grad. law dept. Columbia, 1828. Admitted to N.Y. bar, 1828, practiced in N.Y.C.; mem. N.Y. Assembly, 1832-34; mem. U.S. Ho. of Reps. (Democrat) from N.Y., 24th, 27th congresses, 1835-37, 41-43; dist. atty. N.Y. County, 1846-50, 81-83; U.S. dist. atty. for So. N.Y., 1854-58. Died N.Y.C., Nov. 22, 1883; buried family vault under St. Patrick's Cathedral, N.Y.C.

McKIBBIN, Joseph Chambers, congressman; b. Chambersburg, Pa., May 14, 1824; attended Princeton, 1840-42; studied law, Cal. Admitted to Cal. bar, 1852, practiced in Downieville; mem. Cal. Senate, 1852-53; mem. U.S. Ho. of Reps. (Democrat) from Cal., 35th Congress, 1857-59; served with U.S. Army during Civil War, one of 1st cavalry officers apptd. by Pres. Lincoln; served as col. and a.d.c. on staffs of maj. gens. Halleck and Thomas; settled in Washington, D.C. after Civil War, engaged as gen. contractor. Died Marshall Hall, Md., July 1, 1896; buried Arlington (Va.) Nat. Cemetery.

McKIM, Alexander, congressman; b. Brandywine, Del., Jan. 10, 1748. Moved to Balt.; mem. Md. Ho. of Dels., 1778; served with Balt. Independent Cadets and 1st Balt. Cavalry during Am. Revolution; fought under Lafayette in Va. campaign of 1791; mem. Md. Senate, 1806-10; mem. U.S. Ho. of Reps. (Democrat) from Md., 11th-13th congresses, 1809-15; engaged in merc. bus.; justice ct. quarter sessions; presiding judge Baltimore County Orphans' Ct., until 1832. Died Balt., Jan. 18, 1832; buried Greenmount Cemetery, Balt.

McKIM, Baltimore, mcht., congressman; b. Phila., July 21, 1775; s. John and Margaret (Duncan) Mc.K; m. Ann Bowly, Dec. 21, 1808. Began partnership with father in shipping and importing firm as John McKim & Son, 1796, became full dir., 1801; a.d.c. to Gen. Samuel Smith (comdr. forces defending Balt.); built large steam flour mill, 1822; built copper rolling and refining works; said to be largest copper importer and mfr. in U.S.; an organizer B. & O. R.R., mem. 1st bd. dirs., 1827-31; planned and built Ann McKim (fastest mcht. ship afloat, design anticipated clipper ships); with brother established free co-ednl. sch., 1821; charter mem. Protective Soc. of Md. (to protect liberty of free Negroes); elected to Md. Senate (Democrat), 1821-23; mem. U.S. Ho. of Reps. from Md., 17th, 23d, 25th congresses, 1823-25, 33-38. Died Washington, D.C., Apr. 1, 1838; buried Balt.

McKIM, Isaac, congressman, mcht.; b. Phila., July 21, 1775; s. John and Margaret (Duncan) McK.; m. Ann Bowly, Dec. 21, 1808. Partner (with father) John McKim & Son, importers, 1796-1801, made it successful business, 1801-38; a.d.c. to Gen. Samuel Smith who commanded forces defending Balt., 1812-14; organizer, dir. B.&O. R.R., 1827-31; established free co-ednl. sch., Balt., 1821; charter mem. Protective Soc. of Md. to protect liberty of free slaves, 1816; mem. Md. Senate, 1821-23; built steam flour mill, 1822; mem. U.S. Ho. of Reps. from Md., 17th, 23d-25th congresses, Jan. 8, 1823-25, 33-Apr. 1, 1838; built copper rolling and refining works, circa 1825; originated large sailing vessel that anticipated Yankee Clipper, circa 1832. Died Washington, D.C., Apr. 1, 1838; buried St. Paul's Churchyard, Balt.

McKIM, James Miller, abolitionist, clergyman; b. Carlisle, Pa., Nov. 14, 1810; s. James and Catharine (Miller) McK.; grad. Dickinson Coll., 1828; attended Princeton Theol. Sem., 1831, Andover Theol. Sem., 1832-33, U. Pa. Med. Sch., 1838-39; m. Sarah Allibone Speakman, Oct. 1, 1840; children—Charles Follen, Lucy. Represented Carlisle Negroes in Am. Anti-Slavery Soc., Phila., 1833; ordained to ministry Presbyn. Ch., Wilmington, Pa., 1835; 1st pastor Presbyn. ch., Womelsdorf, Pa., circa 1835-circa 1837; editor Pa. Freeman (organ Pa. Anti-Slavery Soc.), Phila., circa 1840; accompanied Mrs. John Brown to Harpers Ferry to receive John Brown's body, 1859; organizer Phila. Port Royal Relief Com. which provided for freed slaves, 1862; corr. sec. Pa. Freedman's Relief Assn., 1863, Am. Freedman's Union Commn. (agy. to promote edn. among Negroes), N.Y.C., 1865-69. Died Llewellyn Park, Orange, N.J., June 13, 1874.

McKINLEY, John, asso. justice U.S. Supreme Ct.; b. Culpeper County, Va., May 1, 1780; s. Andrew and Mary (Logan) McK.; m. Juliana Bryan; m. 2d, Elizabeth Armistead. Admitted to Ky. bar; moved to Ala., circa 1818; mem. Ala. Legislature, 1820; mem. U.S. Senate from Ala., Nov. 27, 1826-1831; mem. U.S. Ho. of Reps. from Ala., 23d congresses, 1833-35; asso. justice U.S. Supreme Ct., 1837-52. Died Louisville, Ky., July 19, 1852; buried Cave Hill Cemetery, Louisville.

McKINLEY, William, congressman; b. Va. Mem. Va. Ho. of Dels. from Ohio County, 1798-1804, 06-07, 20-21, 24-26; mem. U.S. Ho. of Reps. (Democrat) from Va., 11th Congress, Dec. 21, 1810-11.

McKINLY, John, army officer, pres. Del.; b. North Ireland, Feb. 24, 1721; m. Jane Richardson, circa 1761. Came to Del., 1743; served as lt. Del. Militia, 1747-48, commd. maj. New Castle County Regt., 1756; sheriff of New Castle County, 1757-60; chief burgess Borough of Wilmington (Del.), 1759-74 (except for 3 years); mem. Del. Assembly, 1771; chmn. Del. Com. of Correspondence, 1773; col. New Castle County Regt., 1775, brig. gen. of 3 bns., 1775; elected mem. 1st Del. Legislature, also speaker lower house, 1776; pres. Del. Council of Safety, 1776; chosen 1st pres., comdr.-in-chief of Del., 1777; a founder 1st med. soc. in Del., 1789; trustee 1st Presbyn. Ch., Wilmington, 1789. Died Wilmington, Aug. 31, 1796.

McKINSTRY, Alexander, army officer, state ofcl.; b. Augusta, Ga., Mar. 7, 1822; s. Alexander and Elizabeth (Thompson) McK.; m. Virginia Thompson Dade, Mar. 20, 1845, 11 children. Admitted to Ala. bar, 1855; commd. col. 32d Regt., Ala. Inf., Confederate Army; provost marshal gen. Army of Tenn., 1863; commd. col. cavalry, 1864; served on ct. of mil. justice Nathan B. Forrest's Div., presiding judge until end of Civil War; mem. Ala. Legislature (Radical), 1865, 67, largely instrumental in securing adoption of Ala. Code of 1867; elected lt. gov. Ala., 1872, presiding officer Ala. Senate. Died Mobile, Ala., Oct. 9, 1879.

McKINSTRY, Elisha Williams, jurist; b. Detroit, Apr. 11, 1825; s. David Charles and Nancy Whiting (Backus) McK.; attended Kenyon Coll., Gambier, O.; m. Annie L. Hedges, July 27, 1863, 4 children. Admitted to N.Y. bar, 1847; arrived in San Francisco, 1849; practiced in Sacramento, Cal., 1850; mem. Cal. Legislature, 1850; moved to Napa, Cal., 1851; dist. judge Napa County, 1852-62; unsuccessful candidate for lt. gov. Cal., 1862; moved to Nev., 1863; unsuccessful candidate for Nev. Supreme Ct., 1864; returned to San Francisco, 1867; county judge San Francisco, 1868-69; judge 12th Dist. Ct. of Cal., 1869-73; justice Cal. Supreme Ct., 1873-88; prof. municipal law Hasting's Coll. Law, San Francisco, 1888-90; resumed pvt. practice law, 1890. Died San Jose, Cal., Nov. 1, 1901.

McKISSOCK, Thomas, congressman; b. Montgomery, N.Y., Apr. 17, 1790; studied medicine and law. Admitted to N.Y. bar, began practice in Newburgh; apptd. justice N.Y. Supreme Ct., 1847; mem. U.S. Ho. of Reps. (Whig) from N.Y., 31st Congress, 1849-51. Died St. Andrews, N.Y., June 26, 1866; buried Oldtown Cemetery, Newburgh.

McKNIGHT, Robert, trader, miner; b. Augusta County, Va., circa 1789; s. Timothy and Eleanor (Griffin) McK.; 2 daus., 1 son. Moved to St. Louis, 1809; mem. trading expdn. under Capt. Zebulon M. Pike to Santa Fe, 1812-22 (expdn. captured by Spanish upon arrival at Santa Fe); imprisoned in Durango, Mexico, 1812-21; mem. unsuccessful trading expdn. from St. Louis to mouth Canadian River, 1822-24; renounced his allegiance to U.S. because of govt.'s neglect of him while imprisoned in Mexico; moved to Mexico; owner Santa Rita del Cobre copper mine, Chihuahua, Mexico, 1828-46. Died Mar. 1846.

McKNIGHT, Robert, congressman; b. Pitts., Jan. 20, 1820; grad. Princeton, 1839; studied law. Admitted to Pa. bar, 1842, began practice in Pitts.; mem. Pitts. City Council, 1847-49; mem. U.S. Ho. of Reps. (Republican) from Pa., 36th-37th congresses, 1859-63. Died Pitts., Oct. 25, 1885; buried Allegheny Cemetery, Pitts.

McLANAHAN, James Xavier, congressman; b. nr. Greencastle, Pa., 1809; grad. Dickinson Coll., Carlisle, Pa. 1827; studied law. Admitted to Pa. bar 1837, began practice in Chambersburg; mem. Pa. Senate, 1842-44; mem. U.S. Ho. of Reps. (Democrat) from Pa., 31st-32d congresses, 1849-53. Died N.Y.C., Dec. 16, 1861; buried 1st Presbyn. Ch. Cemetery, N.Y.C.

McLANE, Allan, army officer; b. Phila., Aug. 8, 1746; m. Rebecca Wells, 1769. Toured Europe, 1767; settled in Kent County, Del., 1774; served as adj. Caesar Rodney's Volunteer Regt., 1775; commd. capt. Col. John Patton's Additional Continental Regt., 1777; in command of dismounted dragoons under Maj. Henry Lee, 1779; mem. Del. Ho. of Reps., 1785-91; in charge of defenses of Wilmington, Del., during War of 1812. Died May 22, 1829.

McLANE, Louis, senator, cabinet officer; b. Smyrna, Del., May 28, 1786; s. Allan and Rebecca (Wells) McL.; attended Newark (Del.) Coll.; read law under James A. Bayard; m. Catherine Mary Milligan, 1812, 1 son, Robert Milligan. Served as midshipman U.S. Navy on U.S.S. Philadelphia under Commodore Stephen Decatur, 1798-99, left navy, 1801; admitted to Del. bar, 1807, practiced law in Smyrna; served in War of 1812; mem. U.S. Ho. of Reps. (Republican) from Del., 15-19th congresses, 1817-27, refused to obey Del. Legislature in voting against admission of Mo. as slave state on grounds that he was an officer of U.S., not of state; mem. U.S. Senate from Del., 1827-Apr. 16, 1829; U.S. minister to Eng., 1829-31, 45-46, secured trade agreement regarding West Indies, conducted negotiations on Ore.; U.S. sec. of treasury, 1831-33, advocated rechartering of Bank of U.S. (unsuccessful); U.S. sec. of state 1833-34, advocated war with France because of failure to pay claims; pres. Morris Canal & Banking Co. (N.Y.); moved to Balt., 1837; pres. B. & O. R.R., 1837-47; mem. Md. Constl. Conv., 1850. Died Balt., Oct. 7, 1857; buried Greenmount Cemetery, Balt.

McLANE, Robert, Milligan, gov. Md., diplomat; b. Wilmington, Del., June 23, 1815; s. Louis and Catherine (Milligan) McL.; grad. U.S. Mil. Acad., 1837; m. Georgine Urquhart, 1841. Commd. 2d lt. arty. U.S. Army, 1837; participated in Seminole War in Fla., 1837-38; served with Corps Topog. Engrs., 1838-43, studied dikes and drainage in Europe, 1841; admitted to D.C. bar, 1840, Balt. bar, 1843; practiced law in Balt.; mem. Md. Ho. of Dels., 1845; mem. U.S. Ho. of Reps. (Democrat) from Md., 30th-31st congresses, 1847-51, 46th-47th congresses, 1879-83, chmn. com. on commerce, 1849; counsel in contest of possession rights of quicksilver mine in Santa Clara Valley, 1851; won 2 cases for Cornelius Vanderbilt (possession of steamship Pacific and transit route across Nicarague), also counsel to Western Pacific R.R. Co.; U.S. minister to China, 1853-54, accredited as minister to Japan, Siam, Korea, Cochin China, tried to renew comml. treaty with China, 1854; del. from Md. to Nat. Dem. Conv., Cincinnati, 1856, St. Louis, 1876; U.S. minister to Republic of Mexico, 1859-60, recognized Benito Juarez, signed treaty of transit and commerce with Juarez govt. (not ratified by U.S. Senate), 1859; mem. Md. Senate, 1877-78; gov. Md., 1883-85; U.S. minister to France, 1885-89, dealt with problem of rights of U.S. naturalized citizen, born in France and compelled to serve in French Army. Author: Reminiscences, 1827-97, privately printed, 1903. Died Paris, France, Apr. 16, 1898; buried Greenmount Cemetery, Balt.

McLAWS, Lafayette, army officer; b. Augusta, Ga., Jan. 15, 1821; s. James and Elizabeth (Huquenin) McL.; grad. U.S. Mil. Acad., 1842; m. Emily Taylor, circa 1842. Served as 1st lt. in Scott's Army during Mexican War; acting asst. adj. gen. Dept. of N.M.; mem. Utah expdn. of 1858; participated in campaign against Navajo Indians, 1859-60; commd. maj. Confederate Army, 1861; commd. col. 10th Ga. Regt., brig. gen., 1861, maj. gen., 1862; teamed with Stonewall Jackson in capture of Harpers Ferry, 1862; in command Dist. of Ga., also defenses of Savannah (Ga.); fought in battles of Antietam, Fredericksburg, Gettysburg, Chickamauga; collector of internal revenue, postmaster of Savannah, 1875-76. Died Savannah, July 24, 1897.

McLEAN, Alney, congressman; b. Burke (now McDowell) County, N.C., June 10, 1779; studied law, Ky. Apptd. surveyor of Muhlenberg County (Ky.), 1799; elected trustee of Greenville (Ky.); admitted to Ky. bar, began practice in Greenville, circa 1805; mem. Ky. Ho. of Reps., 1812-13; served as capt. during War of 1812; mem. U.S. Ho. of Reps. from Ky., 14th, 16th congresses, 1815-17, 19-21; judge 14th Ky. Dist., 1821-41; presdl. elector, 1824, 32. Died nr. Greenville, Dec. 30, 1841; buried Old Caney Station Cemetery, nr. Greenville.

McLEAN, Finis Ewing, congressman; b. nr. Russellville, Ky., Feb. 19, 1806; attended Lebanon Acad., Logan County, Ky.; studied law. Admitted to Ky. bar, began practice in Elkton, 1827; engaged in farming; mem. Ky. Ho. of Reps., 1837; Whig presdl. elector, 1848; mem. U.S. Ho. of Reps. (Whig) from Ky., 31st Congress, 1849-51; moved to Andrew County, Mo., 1860, farmer, 1860-65; moved to Greencastle, Ind., 1865. Died Greencastle, Apr. 12, 1881; buried Forest Hill Cemetery, Greencastle.

McLEAN, James Henry, congressman; b. Ayrshire, Scotland, Aug. 13, 1829; grad. St. Louis Med. Coll., 1863. Came to U.S., 1842, settled in Phila.; clk. drug store; moved to St. Louis, 1849, New Orleans, 1850; in charge of financial operations of Lopez expdn. to Cuba; returned to St. Louis, 1851; practiced medicine, St. Louis; mem. U.S. Ho. of Reps. (Republican) from Mo., 47th Congress, Dec. 15, 1882-83. Died Dansville, N.Y., Aug. 12, 1886; buried Bellefontaine Cemetery, St. Louis.

McLEAN, John, asso. justice U.S. Supreme Ct.; b. Morris County, N.J., Mar. 11, 1785; s. Fergus and Sophia (Blockford) McL.; m. Rebecca Edwards, 1807; m. 2d, Sarah Bella Ludlow, 1843; 7 children. Admitted to Ohio bar, 1807; founder paper Western Star, Lebanon, 1807; mem. U.S. Ho. of Reps. from Ohio, 13th-14th congresses, 1813-Oct. 1816; asso. judge Ohio Supreme Ct., 1816-22; commr. U.S. Gen. Land Office, 1822-23; U.S. postmaster gen., 1825-29; asso. justice U.S. Supreme Ct., assigned to 7th Circuit, 1829-61, rendered dissenting opinion that slavery had origin in force and was contrary to right in Dred Scott Case, 1856-57. Died Cincinnati, Apr. 4, 1861; buried Spring Grove Cemetery, Cincinnati.

McLEAN, John, senator, congressman; b. nr. Guklford Court House (now Greensboro), N.C., Feb. 4, 1791; studied law. Moved to Ill. Territory; admitted to the bar, began practice in Shawneetown; mem. U.S. Ho. of Reps. (Democrat) from Ill., 15th Congress, Dec. 3, 1818-19; mem. Ill. Ho. of Reps., 1820, 26, 28, speaker; mem. U.S. Senate from Ill., Nov. 23, 1824-25, 29-30. Died Shawneetown, Oct. 14, 1830; buried Westwood Cemetery, nr. Shawneetown.

McLEAN, Samuel, congressman; b. Summit Hill, Pa., Aug. 7, 1826; attended Lafayette Coll., Easton, Pa.; studied law. Admitted to Pa. bar, 1848, began practice in Mauch Chunk; pros. atty. Carbon County (Pa.), 1855-60; atty. gen. Provisional Territory of Jefferson (now Colo.), 1860; moved to Bannock, Mont., 1862; del. U.S. Congress (Democrat) from Territory of Mont., 1865-67; pres. McLean Silver Mining Co., 1870; moved to Va., settled on plantation nr. Burkeville, 1870. Died Burkeville, July 16, 1877; buried Presbyn. Churchyard, Burkeville.

McLEAN, William, congressman; b. Mason County, Ky., Aug. 10, 1794; attended common schs.; studied law. Admitted to Ohio bar, 1814, began practice in Cincinnati; moved to Piqua, O., 1820; receiver pub. moneys, Piqua; responsible for obtaining subsidy for bldg. Ohio Canal from Cincinnati to Cleve.; mem. U.S. Ho. of Reps. from Ohio, 18th-20th congresses, 1823-29; engaged in merc. bus., law practice, Cincinnati. Died Cincinnati, Oct. 12, 1829; buried Catharine St. Burying Ground, reinterred Spring Grove Cemetery, Cincinnati, 1863.

McLEES, Archibald, engraver; b. Eng., circa 1817; s. John McLees. Came to U.S., circa 1841; worked in N.Y.C., circa 1841-60; mem. original group of engravers Bur. Engraving and Printing, Washington, D.C., 1863. Died Rutherford, N.J., Feb. 11, 1890.

McLENE, Jeremiah, congressman; b. Cumberland County, Pa., 1767; attended common schs. Served as maj. gen. Pa. Militia, during Revolutionary War; moved to Ohio, settled in Chillicothe; mem. Ohio Ho. of Reps., 1807-08; sec. of state Ohio, 1808-31; moved to Columbus, O., 1816; mem. U.S. Ho. of Reps. (Democrat) from Ohio, 23d-24th congresses, 1833-37. Died Washington, D.C., Mar. 19, 1837; buried Congressional Cemetery, Washington.

McLEOD, Alexander, clergyman; b. Mull Island, Hebrides, June 12, 1774; s. Neil and Margaret (McLean) McL.; grad. Union Coll., 1798; m. Maria Anne Agnew, 1805. Came to U.S., 1792; joined Reformed Presbyn. Ch., 1793, licensed to preach, 1799; pastor 1st Reformed Presbyn. Ch., N.Y.C., 1800; responsible for his Presbytery's rule forbidding communicants to hold slaves; an organizer Am. Colonization Soc.; editor Christian Expositor, 2 years; mem. N.Y.C. Hist. Soc.; an organizer Am. Soc. for Meliorating the Condition of Jews, N.Y. Soc. for Instrn. of Deaf and Dumb. Author: Ecclesiastical Catechism, 1806; The Life and Power of True Godliness, 1816. Died N.Y.C., Feb. 17, 1833.

McLEOD, Hugh, army officer; b. N.Y.C., Aug. 1, 1814; grad. U.S. Mil. Acad., 1835; m. Rebecca Lamar, 1842, 1 son, Cazneau. Adjutant-gen. Tex. Army, 1837-41, 45-46; played important part in Indian wars until 1841; apptd. by Republic of Tex. Pres. Lamar as mil. head expdn. sent to Santa Fe to open trade route and to extend (peacefully) Tex. jurisdiction to Rio Grande, 1841; captured by Mexican troops, imprisoned in Mexico, 1841-42; commd. brig. gen. Tex. Army 1841; mem. Republic of Tex. Congress; mem. Tex. State Legislature: mem. company organized to construct Buffalo, Bayon, Brazos and Colo. R.R. (1st railroad in Tex.); enlisted in Confederate Army, commd. lt. col.; assisted in taking over U.S. forts on Rio Grande; commd. col. 1st Tex. Inf. Died Dumfres, Va., Jan. 2, 1862; buried Tex.

McLEOD, Martin, fur trader; b. L'Orignal, nr. Montreal, Que., Can., Aug. 30, 1813; s. John and Janet McL.; m. Mary E. Ortley, circa 1838, several children. Mem. filibustering expdn. of "Gen." James Dickson, who attempted to create "Indian Empire" in West, 1836; fur trader in Minn., 1837-58, became very influential with Indians, especially Sioux (largely responsible for treaty with Sioux favorable to traders, 1851); mem. Minn. Territorial Council, 1849-53, pres. during last term; author bill laying foundation of Minn. Sch. System; a founder Glemcoe (Minn.); McLeod County (Minn.) named after him. Died Ft. Snelling, Minn., Nov. 20, 1860.

M'CLINTOCK, John, clergyman, coll. pres.; b. Phila., Oct. 27, 1814; s. John and Martha (M'Mackin) M'C.; grad. U. Pa., 1835; m. Caroline A. Wakeman, 1837; m. 2d, Catharine W. Emory, Oct. 1851; 1 son, Emory. Admitted on trial to Phila. Conf. of Methodist Episcopal Ch., 1835, ordained elder, 1840; pastor in Jersey City, N.J., 1835-36, St. Paul's Ch., N.Y.C., 1856-60, Am. Chapel, Paris, France, 1860-64; asst. prof. mathematics Dickinson Coll., Carlisle, Pa., 1836-37, prof., 1837-40, prof. classical langs., 1840-48; editor Methodist Quarterly Review, 1848-56; pres. Wesleyan U., 1851-55, Troy U., 1855-62; del. Brit. Wesleyan Conf., London, also conf. of Evangelical Alliance, Berlin, Germany, 1856; chmn. planning com. for centennial celebration Am. Methodism, 1864-66; 1st pres. Drew Theol. Sem., 1867-70. Author: A First Book in Latin, 1846; A First Book in Greek, 1848; A Second Book in Greek, 1850; A Second Book in Latin, 1853; Sketches of Eminent Methodist Ministers, 1854; The Temporal Power of the Pope, 1855; Cyclopedia of Biblical, Theological, and Ecclesiastical Literature, 1867. Died Mar. 4, 1870.

McLOUGHLIN, John, businessman; b. La Riviere du Loup, Que., Can., Oct. 19, 1784; studied in Can., Scotland. Became a physician, gave up practice of medicine to become a partner in North-West Co. remained in charge at Ft. William on Lake Superior when N.W. Co. merged with Hudson's Bay Co., 1821 chief factor at hdqrs., Ft. Vancouver, Ore. Territory, 1824-46; fed, clothed and supplied immigrants to Ore., 1843-45; founded Oregon City; lost most of his property in law suit brought against him by Methodist missionary group. Died in poverty, Sept. 3, 1857.

McMAHON, Bernard, horticulturist; b. Ireland, 1775. Came to U.S., 1796; established nurseries, greenhouses, exptl. gardens nr. Germantown turnpike between Phila. and Nicetown; established seed and gen. nursery business, Phila. (one of largest in U.S. at time); published seed catalogue, 1804, Author: The American Gardener's Calendar (1st notable hort. book in Am.), 1806. Died Sept. 18, 1816.

McMAHON, John Van Lear, state polit. leader; b. Cumberland, Md., Oct. 18, 1800; s. William McMahon; grad. Coll. of N.J. (now Princeton), 1817; LL.D. (hon.), St. John's Coll., Annapolis ,Md., 1869; 1 illegitimate son, John A. Admitted to Md. bar, 1819; mem. Md. Ho. of Dels. from Allegheny County, 1823-25, from Balt., 1827-28; apptd. mem. com. to consider project for constrn. B. & O. R.R., 1827, later drafted charter which contributed to success of undertaking, also served as model for other railroad corps.; leader Jacksonian Democrats in Md. during presdl. campaign of 1829; polit. leader of Md., 1828-57, but declined all offices including two offers of cabinet posts from Presidents Harrison and Tyler. Author: Historical View of the Government of Maryland, 1831. Died Cumberland, June 15, 1871.

McMAHON, Lawrence Stephen, clergyman; b. St. Johns, N.B., Can., Dec. 26, 1835; studied at Holy Cross and St. Mary's, Balt., also in Montreal (Can.), France, Italy. Ordained priest Roman Catholic Ch., Rome, Italy, 1860; served as chaplain 28th Mass. Regt. during Civil War; pastor, Bridgewater, New Bedford (both Mass.); became vicar gen. of Providence (R.I.), 1872, bishop of Hartford (Conn.), 1879; finished building St. Joseph's Cathedral, Hartford. Died Lakeville, Conn., Aug. 21, 1893.

McMANES, James, polit. boss; b. County Tyrone, Ireland, Apr. 13, 1822; s. James and Rebecca (Johnson) McM.; m. Catherine. Came to Phila., 1830, became naturalized citizen U.S., 1844; mem. 17th Ward Sch. Bd., Phila., 1852; trustee Phila. municipal gas works, 1865-85; prothonotary Dist. Ct. of Phila., also mem. Phila. Bd. Edn., 1866-81; polit. boss of Phila., 1866-81. Died Phila., Nov. 23, 1899.

McMANUS, William, congressman; b. Brunswick, N.Y., 1780; studied law. Admitted to N.Y. bar, 1817, began practice in Troy; surrogate of Rensselaer County (N.Y.), 1815-18, dist. atty., 1818-21; mem. U.S. Ho. of Reps. from N.Y., 19th Congress, 1825-27; resumed law practice; moved to Tex., 1833, returned to Brunswick, 1834. Died Brunswick, Jan. 18, 1835.

McMASTER, Guy Humphreys, jurist, poet; b. Clyde, N.Y., Jan. 31, 1829; s. David and Adeline (Humphreys) McM.; m. Amanda Church, 1853, 4 children. Admitted to N.Y. bar, 1852; county judge and surrogate, 1863-83. Author: Carmen Bellicosum (lyric poem, published in Knickerbocker), 1849; The Northern Lights (poem, pub. in Am. Whig Review), 1851; Dream of Thanksgiving Eve (pub. in Hartford Courant), 1864; History of the Settlement of Steuben County, 1853. Died Sept. 13, 1887.

McMASTER, James Alphonsus, journalist; b. Duanesburg, N.Y., Apr. 1, 1820; s. Rev. Gilbert and Jane (Brown) McM.; attended Union Coll., Union Theol. Sem.; m. Miss Letterman, 1850, 3 daus. and 1 son, Alphonsus. Became a Catholic after visit to John Newman (late Cardinal), 1845, acquired vast knowledge Cath. theology; writer for N.Y. Tribune; writer for Freeman's Jour., N.Y.C., became part-owner, 1847, editor, until 1886, caused it to become an outstanding Cath. organ; imprisoned for outspoken views during Civil War, 1861-62. Died Dec. 29, 1886.

McMICHAEL, Morton, editor, mayor Phila.; b. Burlington, N.J., Oct. 20, 1807; s. John and Hannah (Masters) McM.; LL.D., U. Pa., 1877. m. Mary Estell, 1831, 8 children. Admitted to Pa. bar, 1827; editor Saturday Evening Post, 1826-31; editor-in-chief Saturday Courier, 1831-founder (with 2 partners) Saturday News and Literary Gazette, 1836; editor Neal's Saturday Gazette, 1844-47; joint owner Phila. North Amercan, 1847, sole owner, 1854; became leading Whig journalist in U.S.; sheriff Phila., 1843-46; largely responsible for ultimate passage Consolidation Act of 1854; mayor Phila., 1866-69; a founder Union League, pres., 1870-74; pres. Fairmount Park Commn., 1867-79; temporary chmn. Republican Nat. Conv., 1872; del.-at-large Pa. Constl. Conv., 1873; apptd. mem. bd. mgrs. Centennial Exposition, 1875. Died Phila., Jan. 6, 1879; buried Phila.

McMILLAN, Alexander, congressman. Mem. N.C. Senate, 1810-12; mem. U.S. Ho. of Reps. from N.C., 15th Congress, 1817. Died 1817.

McMILLAN, Samuel James Renwick, senator; b. Brownsville, Pa., Feb. 22, 1826; grad. Duquesne Coll., Pitts., 1846; studied law. Admitted to Pa. bar, 1848, began practice in Pitts.; moved to St. Paul, Minn., 1852, to Stillwater, Minn., 1854, practiced law; returned to St. Paul, 1856; judge 1st Minn. Jud. Dist., 1858-64; served as 2d lt. Stillwater Frontier Guards during war with Indians, 1862; asso. justice Minn. Supreme Ct., 1864-74, chief justice, 1874-75; mem. U.S. Senate (Republican) from Minn., 1875-87. Died St. Paul, Oct. 3, 1897; buried Oakland Cemetery, St. Paul.

McMILLAN, William, congressman; b. nr. Abingdon, Va., Mar. 2, 1764; grad. Coll. William and Mary; studied law. Moved to Ft. Washington (now Cininnati), O., 1787; admitted to the bar, 1788, began practice in Cincinnati; 1st justice Ct. of Gen. Quarter Sessions, 1790; mem. Territorial Ho. of Reps., 1799-1800; del. U.S. Congress from Territory N.W. of Ohio River, 1800-01; apptd. U.S. dist. atty. for Ohio, 1803, did not serve due to ill health. Died Cincinnati, May 1804; buried Spring Grove Cemetery, Cincinnati.

McMINN, Joseph, gov. Tenn.; b. Marlborough Twp., Pa., June 22, 1758; s. Robert and Sarah (Harlan) McM.; m. Hannah Cooper, May 9, 1795; m. 2d. Nancy Williams, Jan. 5, 1812. Mem. Tenn. Territorial Legislature, 1794; mem. Tenn. constl. conv., 1796; mem. Tenn. Legislature, 1796-1804, speaker 3 times; gov. Tenn., 1815-21; apptd. U.S. agt. to Cherokee Indians, 1823-24; negotiated treaty by which Cherokees cede vast tracts in Eastern Tenn.; McMinn County, Town of McMinnville (both Tenn.) named for him. Died at Cherokee Agy., Tenn., Nov. 17, 1824.

McMULLEN, Fayette, territorial gov., congressman; b. Estellville (now Gate City), Va., May 18, 1805; attended pvt. schs. Mem. Va. Senate, 1839-49; mem. U.S. Ho. of Reps. (Democrat) from Va., 21st-34th congresses, 1849-57; del. Dem. Nat. Conv., Balt., 1852, Cincinnati, 1856; gov. Wash. Territory, 1857-61; mem. 2d Confederate Congress from Va., until 1865; engaged in farming, banking. Killed by a train, Wytheville, Va., Nov. 8, 1880; buried Round Hill Cemetery, Marion, Va.

McMULLEN, John, clergyman; b. Ballynahinch, Down, Ireland, Jan. 8, 1832.; studied at St. Mary of the Lake, Chgo., also the Propaganda, Rome, Italy. Ordained priest Roman Catholic Ch., 1858; parish priest, Chgo., 1858-61, 66-81; rector St. Mary of the Lake, 1861-66; became vicar gen. of Chgo., 1877, adminstr. of see, 1879-80; founder Catholic Montly Mag., 1865; consecrated 1st bishop of Davenport (Ia.), 1881; founded St. Ambrose Coll., 1882. Died July 4, 1885.

McMURTRY, John, architect; b. 1812. Became builder, architect (in assn. with Thomas Lewinski), 1832; credited with design of mansion-type houses including "Loudon" (Gothic style), 1850, "Ingleside" (most important work), 1852, "Lyndhurst" (Tuscan style), 1861 (all Lexington, Ky.). Died 1890.

McNAIR, Alexander, gov. Mo.; b. Mifflin (now Juniata) County, Pa., May 5, 1775; s. David and Ann (Dunning) McN.; attended Phila. Coll. (now U. Pa.); m. Marguerite de Reilhe, Mar. 1805, 10 children. Commd. 1st lt. U.S. Army 1799; asso. judge Ct. Common Pleas, St. Louis, 1805; trustee City of St. Louis; sheriff St. Louis County; col., adj., insp. Mo. Territorial Militia, 1812; U.S. marshal; register St. Louis Land Office; fed. agt. to Osage Indians; mem. Mo. Constl. Conv.; 1st gov. Mo., 1821-24; Mason. Died St. Louis, Mar. 18, 1826.

McNAIR, John, congressman; b. Bucks County, Pa., June 8, 1800. Taught sch.; established a boys' sch., Abington, Pa.; prin. Loller Acad., Hatboro, Pa., 1825; clk. of cts. Montgomery County (Pa.), 1845-48; moved to Norristown, Pa.; mem. U.S. Ho. of Reps. (Democrat) from Pa., 32d-33d congresses, 1851-55; moved to a plantation, Prince William County, Va. Died Evansport, Va., Aug. 12, 1861.

McNEILL, Archibald, congressman; b. Moore County, N.C. Mem. N.C. Ho. of Commons, 1808-09, N.C. Senate, 1811-13, 20-21; mem. U.S. Ho. of Reps. from N.C., 17th, 19th congresses, 1821-23, 25-27; moved to Tex., 1836; organizer, capt. of a band of men who left for Cal. when gold was discovered, 1849. Died in a sandstorm in a desert in what is now Ariz.

McNEILL, Daniel, naval officer, privateer; b. Charlestown, Mass., Apr. 5, 1748; s. William and Catherine (Morrison) McN.; m. Mary Cuthbertson, Feb. 10, 1770; m. 2d, Abigail Harvey, circa 1772; 10 children including Daniel. Served as comdr. privateers during Am. Revolution, comdr. ship Hancock, 1776, also ships America, Eagle, Ulysses, Wasp and General Mifflin; commd. capt. U.S. Navy, 1798; commanded ship Portsmouth; commanded frigate Boston, 1801; served in undeclared naval war against France, also against Barbary States. Died 1833.

McNEILL, Hector, naval officer, privateer; b. County Antrim, Ireland, Oct. 10, 1728; s. Malcolm and Mary (Stuart) McN.; m. Mary Wilson, Nov. 12, 1750; m. 2d, Mary Watt, Dec. 26, 1770; 5 children. Came with family to Am., 1737; served in French and Indian War; apptd. capt. Continental Navy, 1776; in command frigate Boston; mem. privateer fleet, 1777, court martialed and dismissed or suspended from service on charge of not coming to rescue of sister ship in trouble; commanded 2 privateers later in Revolutionary War. Died at sea, Dec. 25, 1785.

McNEILL, John Hanson, stock raiser, army officer; b. Hardy County, Va., June 12, 1815; s. Strother McNeill; m. Jemima Cunningham, Jan. 1837, at least 1 child, Jesse. Went to Mo., 1848, became one of state's best stock raisers and cattle exhibitors; urged Mo. to join Confederacy; commd. capt. Confederate Army, 1861; returned to Va. to organize McNeill Partisan Rangers, 1862; fatally wounded in a foray into the Shenandoah Valley, 1864. Died Harrisonburg, Va., Nov. 10, 1864.

McNEILL, William Gibbs, civil engr.; b. Wilmington, N.C., Oct. 3, 1801; s. Dr. Charles Donald and Mrs. (Gibbs) McN.; grad. U.S. Mil. Acad., 1817; m. Maria Matilda Comman, 7 children. Aide-de-camp to Gen. Andrew Jackson, during Seminole War in Fla., 1819; transferred to Corps Topog. Engrs., 1823; mem. bd. of engrs. B. & O. R.R.; went to Europe to examine pub. works, especially railroads, 1828; became joint engr. (with George W. Whistler) for majority of new railroads in Eastern U.S.; brevetted maj. of engrs., 1834, resigned, 1837; became engr. State of Ga., 1837; served as maj. gen. R.I. Militia, 1842-45; helped to quell Dorr Rebellion; chief engr., prepared plans for Bklyn. dry dock; elected mem. Instn. Civil Engrs. (Gt. Britain) (1st Am. to be elected), 1857. Died Bklyn., Feb. 16, 1853.

McNEIRNY, Francis, clergyman; b. N.Y.C., Apr. 25, 1828; attended Montreal (Can.) Coll., Grand Sem., Montreal. Ordained priest Roman Catholic Ch., N.Y.C., 1854; parish priest, N.Y.; apptd. chancellor Archdiocese of N.Y., 1857, sec. to Archbishop Hughes, 1859; apptd. titular bishop of Rhesaina, coadjutor of Albany (N.Y.), 1871, adminstr., 1874, bishop, 1877. Died Albany, Jan. 2, 1894.

McNUTT, Alexander, colonizer; b. Londonderry, Ireland, circa 1725; s. Alexander and Jane McNutt. Came to Am., settled nr. Staunton, Va., before 1753; served as officer in militia commanded by Maj. Andrew Lewis, 1756; capt. Mass. Militia, 1760; rep. of Apthrop and Hancock of Boston to promote settlers for Nova Scotia, 1758-61; granted 1,745,000 acres of land in N.S. to promote immigration, 1765; moved to Jamaica Plain, Mass., 1778; urged Continental Congress to draw N.S. into Revolutionary War, 1778-81. Died circa 1811.

McPHERSON, Edward, editor, congressman; b. Gettysburg, Pa., July 31, 1830; s. John Bayard and Katharine (Lenhart) McP.; grad. Pa. (now Gettysburg) Coll., 1848; m. Anne Dods Crawford, 1862. Became editor Harrisburg American, 1851; author Political Manual published annually, 1866-69, Handbook of Politics published biennially, 1868-94; mem. U.S. Ho. of Reps. (Republican) from Pa., 36th-37th congresses, 1859-63, clk. house, 1863-75, 81-13, 89-91; mem. Republican Nat. Com., 1860; permanent pres. Rep. Nat. Conv., 1876; sec. Rep. Congl. Com., 1880; chief Bur. Engraving and Printing, 1877-78; bought, edited Gettysburg Star and Sentinel, 1879; editor N.Y. Tribune Almanac and Political Register, 1877-95; Am. editor Almanach de Gotha. Author: Political History of the United States During the Period of Reconstruction, 1871; Political History of the United States During The Great Rebellion, 1864; Died N.Y.C., Dec. 14, 1895.

McPHERSON, James Birdseye, army officer; b. Green Creek Twp., O., Nov. 14, 1828; s. William and Cynthia (Russell) McP.; grad. U.S. Mil. Acad., 1853. Served as engr. U.S. Army, 1853-58, commd. 1st lt., 1858, capt., 1861, lt. col., later col., camp to Maj. Gen. Halleck; asst. engr. Dept. of Mo.; chief engr. to Gen. Grant, 1862; promoted brig. gen. U.S. Volunteers, 1862; apptd. mil. supt. rys. Dist. of Western Tenn.; commd. maj. gen. U.S. Volunteers, 1862, commanded right wing of Grant's army at Battle of Vicksburg; commanded 2d div. Dept. of Tenn.; received command XVII Army Corps, 1863; commd. brig. gen. U.S. Army, 1863; took command Sherman's Army of Tenn., Huntsville, Ala., 1864. Killed at Atlanta, Ga., July 22, 1864.

McPHERSON, John Rhoderic, senator; b. York, N.Y., May 9, 1833; attended common schs. Moved to Jersey City, N.J., 1859; engaged in farming, livestock dealing; alderman, Jersey City, 1864-70, pres. bd., 3 years; mem. N.J. Senate, 1871-73; Democratic presdl. elector, 1876; mem. U.S. Senate (Dem.) from N.J., 1877-95; del. Dem. nat. convs., 1884, 88, 92. Died Jersey City, Oct. 8, 1897; buried Oak Hill Cemetery, Washington.

McQUEEN, John, congressman; b. Queensdale, N.C., Feb. 9, 1804; grad. U. N.C.; studied law. Admitted to the bar, 1828; began practice of law, Bennettsville, S.C.; served with S.C. Militia, 1833-37; mem. U.S. Ho. of Reps. (Democrat) from S.C., 32d-36th congresses, Feb. 12, 1849-Dec. 21, 1860; mem. 1st Confederate Congress from S.C. Died Society Hill, S.C., Aug. 30, 1867; buried Episcopal Cemetery, Society Hill.

McQUILLEN, John Hugh, dentist, editor; b. Phila., Feb. 12, 1826; s. Hugh and Martha (Scattergood) Mc.Q; M.D., Jefferson Med. Coll., 1852; D. D.S., Phila. Coll. Dental Surgery, 1853; m. Amelia D. Schellenger, 1852, 5 children. Mem. Pa. Assn. Dental Surgeons, later pres.; an editor Dental Cosmos, 1859; editor-in-chief, 1865-72; prof. operative dentistry and dental pathology Pa. Coll. Dental Surgery, 1857-62; founder Phila. Dental Coll., 1863, dean and prof. anatomy, physiology and hygiene, 1863-79; an organizer Am. Dental Assn., 1859, pres., 1865; an organizer, 1st corr. sec. Odontographic Soc. of Phila., 1863, pres., 1868-70; 1st corr. sec. Assn. Colls. Dentistry, 1866; one of 1st in Am. to demonstrate importance of microscopical knowledge of human teeth in health and disease; mem. Acad. Natural Science at Phila., founder biol. and microscopical sect. Died Phila., Mar. 3, 1879; buried Phila.

McRAE, Duncan Kirkland, diplomat, lawyer; b. Campbelltown (now Fayetteville), N.C., Aug. 16, 1820; s. John and Margaret (Kirkland) McR.; attended Coll. William and Mary, U. N.C.; m. Louise Virginia Henry, 1845. Admitted to N.C. bar, 1841; mem. N.C. Legislature, 1842; practiced law, Raleigh, N.C., 1844-51; U.S. consul to Paris, France, 1853-57; bearer of Ostend Manifesto from London to Washington; unsuccessful candidate for gov. N.C., 1858; served as col. 5th N.C. Regt., 1861; led charge at Williamsburg, Va.; wounded at Sharpsburg, 1862; envoy to Southern Europe from N.C. to secure market for Southern cotton, 1863; editor Confederate, Raleigh, 1864-65; practiced in Memphis, Tenn., 1865-80. Died Bklyn., Feb. 12, 1888.

McRAE, John Jones, senator, gov. Miss.; b. Sneedsboro, (now McFarian), N.C., Jan. 10, 1815; grad. Miami U., Oxford, O., 1834; studied law, Pearlington, Miss. Admitted to Miss. bar, practiced law; founder Eastern Clarion, Paulding, Miss.; mem. Miss. Ho. of Reps., 1848-50, speaker, 1850; mem. U.S. Senate (Democrat) from Miss., Dec. 1, 1851-52; gov. Miss., 1854-58; mem. U.S. Ho. of Reps. (States Rights Democrat) from Miss., 35th-36th congresses, Dec. 7, 1858-Jan. 12, 1961; mem. Confederate Congress from Miss., 1862-64; went to Brit. Honduras, 1868. Died Belize, Brit. Honduras, May 31, 1861; buried Belize.

McROBERTS, Samuel, senator; b. nr. Maeystown, Ill., Apr. 12, 1799; grad. law dept. Transylvania U., Lexington, Ky. Admitted to the bar, 1821; began practice of law, Monroe County, Ill.; clk. Circuit Ct. of Monroe County, 1819-21; judge Ill. Circuit Ct., 1824-27; mem. Ill. Senate, 1828-30; U.S. dist. atty., 1830-32; apptd. receiver U.S. Land Office, Danville, Ill., 1832; solicitor Gen. Land Office, Washington, D.C., 1839-41; mem. U.S. Senate from Ill., 1841-43. Died Cincinnati, Mar. 27, 1843; buried Moore Cemetery, Waterloo, Ill.

McSHERRY, James, congressman; b. Littlestown, Pa., July 29, 1776; attended Lancaster (Pa.) Acad. Engaged in merc. bus.; mem. Pa. Ho. of Reps., 1807-12, 24-30, 34-35, Pa. Senate, 1813; served in War of 1812; del. Pa. Constl. Conv., 1837-38; mem. U.S. Ho. of Reps. from Pa., 17th Congress, 1821-23. Died Littlestown, Feb. 3, 1849; buried St. Aloysius' Catholic Cemetery, Littlestown.

McSHERRY, Richard, physician; b. Martinsburg, W.Va., 1817; studied at Georgetown (D.C.) and in Md.; M.D., U. Pa., 1841. Served with Med. Corps, U.S. Army, 1838-40; served as an asst. surgeon U.S. Navy, 1843-56; began practice of medicine in Balt., 1856; 1st pres. Balt. Acad. of Medicine. Died Balt., Oct. 7, 1885.

McTYEIRE, Holland Nimmons, clergyman; b. Barnwell County, S.C., July 28, 1824; s. John and Elizabeth (Nimmons) McT.; grad. Randolph-Macon Coll. (Va.), 1844; m. Amelia Townsend, Nov. 9, 1847. Admitted on trial to Va. Conf. of Methodist Episcopal Ch. South, 1845, ordained deacon, 1848, elder, 1849; mem. Ala. Conf. Meth. Episcopal Ch., 1848-49, 62-66, La. Conf., 1849-58; founder New Orleans Christian Advocate, 1851, editor, 1851-58; pastor, Montgomery, Ala., 1862-66; elected bishop at Gen. Conf., 1866; a chief commr. in formation Colored Methodist Episcopal Ch. (as distinct eccles. body), 1870; a chief promotor of fgn. missionary enterprise of Meth. Ch. prin. founder Vanderbilt U., Nashville, Tenn., pres. bd. trustees, 1873-89. Author: Duties of Christian Masters, 1859; Catechism on Bible History, 1869; Manual of Discipline, 1870; A History of Methodism (his most important work). 1884. Died Vanderbilt U., Nashville, Tenn., Feb. 15, 1889; buried Vanderbilt U. campus.

McVEAN, Charles, congressman; b. nr. Johnstown, N.Y., 1802; studied law. Admitted to N.Y. bar, began practice in Johnstown; newspaper editor, Canajoharie, N.Y., 1827-31; mem. U.S. Ho. of Reps. (Democrat) from N.Y., 23d Congress, 1833-35; dist. atty. Montgomery County (N.Y.), 1836-39; moved to N.Y.C., 1839; surrogate N.Y. County, 1844-48; U.S. atty. for So. N.Y., 1848. Died N.Y.C., Dec. 22, 1848; buried St. Andrew's Cemetery, N.Y.C.

McVICKAR, John, clergyman, economist; b. N.Y.C., Aug. 10 1787; s. John and Anna (Moore) McV.; grad. Columbia, 1804, A.M. (hon.), 1818, S.T.D. (hon.), 1825; m. Eliza Bard, Nov. 12, 1809. Ordained deacon Protestant Episcopal Ch., 1811, priest, 1812; rector St. James Protestant Episcopal Ch., Hyde Park, N.Y., until 1817; prof. moral philosophy Columbia, 1817-57, one of 1st tchrs. polit. economy in U.S., prof. evidences of natural and revealed religion, 1857-64, acting pres. coll., 42; chaplain army post at Ft. Columbia, N.Y. Harbor, 1844-62; founder Chapel of St. Cornelius the Centurion, Ft. Columbia; helped establish St. Stephen's Coll. (tng. coll. for Episcopal clergy), Annandale - on - Hudson, 1860. Author: Outlines of Political Economy, 1825; Hints on Banking, 1827 (partially responsible for establishing free banking system in N.Y. and elsewhere); The Early Life and Professional Years of Bishop Hobart, 1838. Died N.Y.C., Oct. 29, 1868.

McVICKER, James Hubert, actor, theatrical exec.; b. N.Y.C., Feb. 14, 1822; s. James and Nancy McV.; m. Annie Levering; m. 2d, Mrs. Runnion; 1 adopted dau., Mary. Printer, St. Louis Republican, 1837; made debut as old servant in The Honeymoon, St. Charles Theatre, New Orleans; took collection of original Yankee comedies to Europe, 1852; mgr. People's Theatre, St. Louis; superintended constrn. New Chgo. Theatre (opened 1857); assembled a company; built 2d theatre, 1871, 3d theatre, 1872, last theatre, 1891; produced elaborate revivals of The School for Scandal, A Midsummer Night's Dream, The Tempest. Died Chgo., Mar. 7, 1876.

McWILLIE, William, gov. Miss., congressman; b. Kershaw Dist., S.C., Nov. 17, 1795; grad. S.C. Coll., 1817; studied law. Served as adj. during War of 1812; admitted to S.C. bar, 1818, began practice in Camden; pres. Camden Bank, 1836; mem. S.C. Senate, 1836-40; moved to Madison County, Miss., 1845, engaged in planting; mem. U.S. Ho. of Reps. (Democrat) from Miss., 31st Congress, 1849-51; gov. Miss., 1858-60. Died "Kirkwood," Madison County, Miss., Mar. 3, 1869; buried St. Philip's Churchyard, Madison County.

MEACHAM, James, congressman; b. Rutland, Vt., Aug. 15, 1810; grad. Middlebury (Vt.) Coll., 1832; attended Andover (Vt.)Theol. Sem. Taught in sem., Castleton, Vt., acad., St. Albans, Vt.; ordained to ministry Congregational Ch., 1838; pastor, New Haven, Vt., 1839-46; tutor, prof. Middlebury Coll. 1846-50; mem. U.S. Ho. of Reps. (Whig) from Vt., 31st-34th congresses, Dec. 3, 1849-56. Died Rutland, Aug. 23, 1856; buried West Cemetery, Middlebury.

MEAD, Cowles, congressman; b. Va., Oct. 18, 1776; studied law, Ga. Admitted to Ga. bar, practiced law; mem. U.S. Ho. of Reps. from Ga., 9th Congress, Mar. 4-Dec. 24, 1805 (lost seat as result of successfully contested election); sec. Miss. Territory (apptd. by Pres. Jefferson), 1806-07; acting gov., 1806-07; mem. Miss. Ho. of Reps., 1807, 22-23; del. 1st Miss. Constl. Conv., 1817; mem. Miss. Senate, 1821; unsuccessful candidate for gov. Miss., 1825. Died "Greenwood" nr. Clinton, Miss., May 17, 1844; buried "Greenwood."

MEADE, Edwin Ruthven, congressman; b. Norwich, N.Y., July 6, 1836; studied law. Admitted to N.Y. bar, 1858, began practice in Norwich; moved to N.Y.C., 1872, practiced law; mem. U.S. Ho. of Reps. (Democrat) from N.Y., 44th Congress, 1875-77. Died N.Y.C., Nov. 28, 1889; buried Greene (N.Y.) Cemetery.

MEADE, George, mcht.; b. Phila., Feb. 27, 1741; s. Robert and Mary (Stretch) M.; m. Henrietta Constantia Worsam, May 5, 1768, 10 children. Founder firm Garrett and George Meade, Phila.; signed Non-Importation Resolutions, 1765; served with 3d Phila. Battalion, 1775-76; mem. Public Defense Assn.; mem. Phila. Common Council, 1789-91; chmn. bd. of mgmt. of prisons, 1792. Died Phila., Nov. 9, 1808.

MEADE, George Gordon, army officer; b. Cadiz, Spain, Dec. 31, 1815; s. Richard Warsam and Margaret (Butler) M.; grad. U.S. Mil. Acad., 1835; m. Margaretta Sergeant, 1840, 6 children. Commd. 2d lt. 3d Arty., U.S. Army, resigned, 1836; became asst. engr. Ala., Fla. & Ga. R.R.; prin. asst. engr. on survey mouths of Mississippi River, 1839; an asst. to joint commn. to establish boundaries between U.S. and Tex., 1840; apptd. 2d lt. Topog. Engrs., U.S. Army, 1842; served in Mexican War at battles of Palo Alto, Monterey, Vera Cruz, brevetted 1st lt., 1846; 1st lt. Topog. Engrs., 1851, capt., 1856, in charge No. Lake Surveys, 1857-61; commd. brig. gen. U.S. Volunteers, 1861, aided in defense of Washington, (D.C.), served in battles of Mechanicsville, Gaine's Mill and New Market Cross Rd., wounded at Glendale; maj. Topog. Engrs, 1862, served at 2d Battle of Bull Run; comdr. Pa. Reserves at battles of South Mountain, Fredricksburg; maj. gen. volunteers, 1862; in command 5th Corps at Battle of Chancellorsville, May 24, 1863; in command Army of Potomac, 1863; promoted brig. gen. U.S. Army, 1863, repulsed Confederate Army under Gen. Lee at Battle of Gettysburg, 1863; commd. maj. gen., serving under Grant, 1864; in command Dept. of East, 1867, 3d Mil. Dist. of South (Ga., Ala., Fla.), 1868, Mil. Div. of Atlantic, 1869-72. Died Pa., Nov. 6, 1872.

MEADE, Richard Kidder, army officer; b. Nansemond County, Va., July 14, 1746; s. David and Susannah Meade; m. Jane Randolph, 1765; m. 2d, Mary Fitzhugh Grymes, 1780; 4 sons, 4 daus. Served as capt. under Col. Woodford at Battle of Great Bridge, 1775; lt. col., aide-de-camp to Gen. Washington, 1777; operated "Lucky Hit" farm, Frederick County, Va., after Revolutionary War. Died Frederick County, Feb. 9, 1805.

MEADE, Richard Kidder, congressman; b. nr. Lawrenceville, Va., July 29, 1803; studied law. Admitted to Va. bar, began practice in Petersburg; mem. Va. Senate, 1835-38; mem. U.S. Ho. of Reps. (Democrat) from Va., 30th-32d congresses, Aug. 5, 1847-53; declined appointment as chargé d'affaires to Sardinia, 1853; minister to Brazil (apptd. by Pres. Buchanan), 1857-61. Died Petersburg, Apr. 20, 1862; buried Old Blandford Cemetery, Petersburg.

MEADE, Richard Worsam, naval officer; b. Cadiz, Spain, Mar. 21, 1807; s. Richard Worsam and Margaret (Butler) M.; grad. St. Mary's Coll., Balt.; m. Clara Forsyth Meigs, Dec. 5, 1836, 5 children including Richard Worsam, Henry Meigs, Robert Leamy, 2 daus. Became midshipman U.S. Navy, 1826; served 1st duty aboard Brandywine in Pacific Ocean, 1827-30; served in ship St. Louis, W.I., 1833-35; commd. lt., 1837; commander of ship Massachusetts, 1853-55; relieved of duty during overhaul of naval personnel, 1855, reinstated with rank of commander (from 1855), 1857; promoted capt., 1862; commander of ship San Jacinto, E. Gulf Squadron, 1864, grounded San Jacinto on No Name Key, Bahama Islands, 1865, suspended from duty for 3 years, 1866; ret. because of illness, 1867. Died Apr. 16, 1870.

MEADE, Richard Worsam, naval officer; b. N.Y.C. Oct. 9, 1837; s. Richard Worsam and Clara (Meigs) M.; grad. U.S. Naval Acad., 1856; m. Rebecca Paulding, June 6, 1865, 1 son, 4 daus. Commd. lt. U.S. Navy, 1858; ordnance instr. to receiving ship Ohio, Boston, 1861; commd lt. comdr., 1862, in command ship Louisville on Mississippi River, 1862; head seamanship dept. U.S. Naval Acad., 1865-68; commd. comdr., 1868; prepared Manual of the Boat Exercise of the U.S. Naval Acad., 1868, A Treatise on Naval Architecture, 1868; commd. capt., 1880; comdt. Washington Navy Yard, 1887-90; commd. commodore, 1892, naval rep. at World's Columbian Expn., Chgo.; commd. rear adm., 1894, in command N. Atlantic Squadron; ret., 1895. Died Washington, D.C., May 4, 1897; buried Arlington (Va.) Nat. Cemetery.

MEADE, William, clergyman; b. Frederick County, Va., Nov. 11, 1789; s. Col. Richard Kidder and Mary Fitzhugh (Grymes) M.; grad. Coll. of N.J., 1808; studied theology under Rev. Walter Addison; m. Mary Nelson, Jan. 31, 1810; m. 2d, Thomasia Nelson, Dec. 2, 1820. Ordained deacon Episcopal Ch., 1811, priest, 1814; assigned to Episcopal Ch. of Va., 1814; elected asst. bishop Va., 1829; bishop Diocese of Va., 1841-62; established Am. Colonization Soc., circa 1850; presiding officer of conv. which formulated constn. of Gen. Council of Protestant Episcopal Ch. in Confederate States Am., Columbia, S.C., 1861. Author: Family Prayers Collected from Sacred Scriptures, the Book of Common Prayer and the Works of Bishop Wilson, 1834; Lectures upon the Pastoral Office, 1849; Old Churches, Ministers and Families of Virginia, 2 vols., 1857; The Bible and the Classics, 1861. Died Mar. 14, 1862; buried Theol. Sem., Alexandria, Va.

MEAGHER, Thomas Francis, army officer, temporary gov. Mont.; b. Waterford, Ireland, Aug. 3, 1823; s. Thomas and Miss (Quan) M.; grad. Stonyhurst Coll., Preston, Eng., 1843; m. Miss Bennett, Feb. 22, 1851; m. 2d, Elizabeth Townsend, Nov. 14, 1855. Joined "Young Ireland" party, 1846; banished for Irish revolutionary activities, came to U.S., 1853; admitted to N.Y. bar, 1855; joined 69th N.Y. Regt., U.S. Volunteers, 1861, comdr. N.Y.C. Irish Brigade, 1862; served as acting maj. during 1st Battle of Bull Run; apptd. brig. gen. Irish brigade, 1863, served in 2d Battle of Bull Run, battles of Fredericksburg and Antietam; commanded Dist. of Etowah, 1864; apptd. territorial sec. Mont., 1865; temporary gov. Mont., 1865-66; Author: Speeches on the Legislative Independence of Ireland, 1852. Died Ft. Benton, Mont., July 1, 1867.

MEARNS, Edgar A., physician, naturalist; lt. col. Med. Corps, U.S. Army; collector animals and plants; Mearns' quail named in his honor.

MEARS, John William, clergyman; b. Reading, Pa., Aug. 10, 1825; grad. Del. Coll., 1844; attended Yale Scientific Sch., 1846-48, Yale Divinity Sch., 1848-49; m. Phebe A. H. Tatem, Sept. 2, 1852. Ordained minister Presbyn. Ch., 1852; pastor Presbyn. Ch., Camden, N.J., 1852-53, Elkton, Md., 1854-57, Milford, Del., 1857-60; editor Am. Presbyn. Phila., 1860-65, publisher, 1865-70; Albert Barnes prof. intellectual and moral philosophy Hamilton Coll., Clinton, N.Y., 1871-81. Author: The Bible in the Workshop, 1857; The Martyrs of France, 1860; The Story of Madagascar, 1873; Brief English-French Compend of the Grammar of the French Language. 1879. Died Nov. 10, 1881.

MEASE, James, physician; b. Phila., Aug. 11, 1771; s. John and Esther (Miller) M.; grad. U. Pa., 1787, M.D., 1792; m. Sarah Butler, July 3, 1800, 2 children. Did research and writing in field of diseases produced by animal bites, 1792-1812; served as surgeon U.S. Army, 1814-15; curator Am. Philos. Soc., 1824-30, councilor, 1832-36. Author: Geological Account of the United States, 1807; Thermometrical Observations as Connected with Navigation, 1841; Archives of Useful Knowledge, 2 vols., 1811-12. Editor: The Surgical Works of the Late John Jones, M.D., 1795. Died Phila., May 14, 1846; buried 3d Presbyn. Ch. Cemetery, Phila.

MEASON, Isaac, iron mfr.; b. Va., 1742; m. Catharine Harrison, Apr. 28, 1778, 4 children. Moved to Pa., before 1771, purchased land which he named "Mt. Pleasant"; served under Gen. Anthony Wayne in Continental Army, 1776; mem. Pa. Assembly, 1779; mem. Supreme Exec. Council Pa., 1783; founded Union Furnace, 1st successful iron works West of Alleghanies, 1791; became partner Meason, Dillon & Co., 1793; financed mill for Thomas C. Lewis, 1816, thus was influential in devel. of manufacture of rolling bar iron in Am. Died Jan. 23, 1818.

MEBANE, Alexander, congressman; b. Hawfields, N.C., Nov. 26, 1744; attended common schs., Orange County, N.C. Del., N.C. Provincial Congress, 1776; justice of peace, 1776; sheriff of Orange County, 1777; auditor Hillsboro (N.C.) Dist., 1783-84; mem. Hillsboro Conv., 1788, Fayetteville Conv., 1789; mem. N.C. Ho. of Commons, 1787-92; mem. U.S. Ho. of Reps. from N.C., 3d Congress, 1793-95. Died Hawfields, July 5, 1795.

MECOM, Benjamin, printer; b. Boston, Dec. 29, 1732; s. Edward and Jane (Franklin) M. Mgr., Antigua Gazette (owned by Benjamin Franklin), 1752-57; owner printing firm, Boston, 1757-63, printed edits. of The New England Primer Enlarged (1757), The New England Psalter (1758); established unsuccessful printing office, N.Y., 1763-65; publisher Conn. Gazette, 1765-68; founded, published Penny Post, Phila., 1768-70; last heard of in letter from William Smith to Benjamim Franklin, 1776. Died sometime after 1776.

MEDARY, Samuel, editor, territorial gov.; b. Montgomery County, Pa., Feb. 25, 1801; m. Eliza Scott, 12 children. Sch. trustee, surveyor Clermont County, Batavia, O., 1827, later county auditor; mem. Ohio Legislature, 1834-37; Ohio supr. public printing (elected by Democrats), 1837; editor Ohio Statesman, Columbus; chmn. Ohio delegation Democratic Nat. Conv., Balt., 1844; supported adoption of new Ohio Constn., 1851; temporary chmn. Nat. Dem. Conv., 1856; gov. Minn. Territory, 1857-58, Kan. Territory, 1858; dep.

postmaster Columbus (O.), 1858; a framer Minn. Constn.; founder, editor Crisis (1st number published Jan. 31, 1861), Columbus, 1860. Died Columbus, Nov. 7, 1864.

MEDILL, Joseph, journalist, mayor Chgo.; b. St. John, N.B., Can., Apr. 6, 1823; son of William Medill; m. Katharine Patrick, Sept. 2, 1852, 3 children. Admitted to Ohio bar, 1846; owner, mgr. Coshocton Whig (renamed Republican), 1849-51; established Cleve. (O.) Leader, 1851; active in formation of Republican Party, believed to have been 1st to name the party "Republican"; part owner Chgo. Tribune, 1854-74, majority stockholder, 1874-99, editorially supported Lincoln; mem. Ill. Constl. Conv., 1869; mayor Chgo., 1871-75. Died Mar. 16, 1899.

MEDILL, William, gov. Ohio, congressman; b. New Castle County, Del., 1802; grad. Newark (Del.) Acad. (later Del. Coll.), 1825; studied law. Admitted to the bar; began practice of law, Lancaster, O., 1830; mem. Ohio Ho. of Reps., 1835-38, speaker, 1836-37; mem. U.S. Ho. of Reps. (Democrat) from Ohio, 26th-27th congresses, 1839-43; 2d asst. postmaster gen. U.S., 1845; U.S. commr. of Indians affairs, 1845-50; pres. Ohio Constl. Conv., 1850; lt. gov. Ohio, 1852-53, acting gov., 1853, gov., 1853-55; 1st comptroller U.S. Treasury, 1857-61. Died Lancaster, Sept. 2, 1865; buried Elmwood Cemetery, Lancaster.

MEDLEY, Mat, see Aston, Anthony.

MEECH, Ezra, congressman; b. New London, Conn., July 26, 1773; attended common schs., Hinesburg, Vt. Engaged in fur trading, ship-timber contracting; engaged in farming and stock raising, Shelburne, Vt.; mem. Vt. Ho. of Reps., 1805-07; mem. U.S. Ho. of Reps. (Democrat) from Vt., 16th-19th congresses, 1819-21, 25-27; del. Vt. constl. convs., 1822, 26; chief justice Chittenden County (Vt.) Ct., 1822-23; mem. unsuccessful candidate for gov. Vt., 1830, 31, 32, 33; Whig presdl. elector, 1840; resumed farming. Died Shelburne, Sept. 23, 1856; buried Shelburne Cemetery.

MEEK, Alexander Beaufort, state legislator; b. Columbia, S.C., July 17, 1814; s. Samuel Mills and Anna (McDowell) M.; grad. U. Ala., 1833; m. Emma Donaldson Slatter, 1856; m. 2d, Mrs. Eliza Jane Cannon, 1864. Admitted to Ala. bar, 1835; served as non-commd. officer in Seminole War in Fla., 1836; apptd. atty. gen. Ala., 1836; apptd. to fill out term as probate judge Tuscaloosa County (Ala.), 1842; with U.S. Treasury Detp., 1845-47; apptd. U.S. atty. So. dist. Ala., 1847; mem. editorial staff Flag of the Union and Southern; contbr. to The Southwest, 1840, Romantic Passages in Southwestern History, 1857; mem. Ala. Legislature, 1853, chmn. com. on edn., became speaker, 1859; del. to Charleston Secession Conv., 1860; trustee U. Ala., 1862-64. Author lyrics, best known for "The Red Eagle" and "Balaklava;" contbr. to Songs and Poems of the South, 1857; A Supplement to Aiken's Digest of the Laws of Alabama, 1836-41, 1841. Died Columbus, Miss., Nov. 1, 1865.

MEEK, Fielding Bradford, paleontologist; b. Madison, Ind., Dec. 10, 1817. Interested in geology; asst. to David Dale Owen, head of U.S. Geol. Survey of Ia., Wis. and Minn., 1848-49; asst. to James Hall, paleontologist, Albany, N.Y., 1852-58; took up residence in Smithsonian Instn., Washington, D.C., 1858-76; wrote over 100 publs.; most important publ.; Report on the Invertebrate Cretaceous and Tertiary Fossils of the Upper Missouri Country. Died Dec. 21, 1876.

MEEK, Joseph L., trapper, farmer; b. Washington County, Va., 1810; married 3 times (Indian wives). Set out from Va. for the West, 1828; trapped and hunted in wide areas in West, 1829-40; settled (with friend Robert Newell) on farm in Ore., 1840; sheriff Ore. Territory, 1843-46; mem. Ore. Territory Legislature, 1846-47; travelled to Washington, D.C. to ask for protection after Whitman massacre, 1848; U.S. marshall Ore. Territory, 1848-52; served as maj. in Indian War, 1855-56; farmer, Hillsboro, Ore., 1856-75. Died Hillsboro, June 20, 1875.

MEEKER, James Rusling, artist; b. Newark, 1827; student N.A.D., N.Y.C.; studied portrait painting with Charles Loring Elliott. Lived in Louisville, 1952-57, settled in St. Louis, 1859; served as paymaster in U.S. Navy during Civil War, stationed in La., active in St. Louis, also Wis., after Civil War; known for his landscape paintings of La. bayous. Died St. Louis, 1887.

MEEKER, Jotham, missionary, printer; b. Hamilton County, O., Nov. 8, 1804; m. Eleanor Richardson, Sept. 1830, 3 children. Learned printing trade, Cleve.; missionary to Potawatomi, Ottawa Indians at missions in Mich., 1825-33; established mission among Shawnee Indians in what is now Mich., 1833-37, printed some 65 works for the Indians in their own lang.; tchr. and preacher among Ottawas in Kan., 1837-49; moved printing equipment to Ottawa, Kan., produced code of Ottawa tribal laws, 1849-55. Died Ottawa, Jan. 12, 1855.

MEEKER, Moses, lead miner; b. New Haven, N.J., June 17, 1790; s. Jonathan and Rachel (Denham) M.; m. Mary R. Henry, 1813; m. 2d, Eliza P. Shakelton, 1837; 8 children. Moved to Cincinnati, 1817, engaged in manufacture of white lead; owned lead mining bus., Ill., 1822-37; served as capt. in Black Hawk War; moved to lead mining dist., Ia. County, Wis., 1837, built largest blast-furnace in area; mem. Wis. Territorial Legislature, 1842-44; mem. Wis. State Constl. Conv., 1846; became corresponding mem. Wis. Hist. Soc., 1854. Author: Early History of the Lead Region of Wisconsin, 1857. Died Shullsburg, Wis., July 7, 1865; buried Galena, Ill.

MEEKER, Nathan Cook, journalist, social reformer; b. Euclid, O., July 12, 1817; s. Enoch and Lurana (Hulbert) M.; m. Arvilla Delight Smith. Journalist, tchr., dry-goods store mgr., various locations, 1835-70; joined Trumbull Phalanx (where Fourierism was being practiced), Braceville, O., 1844-49; opened store, Euclid, 1849-57; mem. staff N.Y. Tribune, 1865-78, learned much about Mormons' coop. living plans while on newspaper assignment in Utah; organized and ran Union Colony in Colo. (compound of people cooperating in econ. and social endeavors but recognizing pvt. property), 1869-78; published 1st issue Greeley Tribune, Colo., 1870; Indian agt. White River Reservation, 1878-79. Killed by Ute Indians, White River Reservation, Sept. 29, 1879.

MEGAPOLENSIS, Johannes, clergyman; b. Holland, 1603; m. Machtelt Steengen, at least 4 children. Relinquished membership in Roman Catholic Ch., 1626, became minister Reformed Dutch Ch.; pastor several parishes, Holland, 1634-42; came to New Amsterdam, 1642, assigned to colony of Rensselaerswyck; minister to New Amsterdam at request of Gov. Stuyvesant, 1649-70. Died 1670.

MEIGGS, Henry, railroad builder; b. Catskill, N. Y., July 7, 1811; s. Elisha and Fanny (Williams) M.; m. Gertrude Burns, Apr. 9, 1832; m. 2d, Caroline Doyle, 1837; 2 children. In lumber trade, Catskill, Boston, N.Y.C.; opened lumber yard, Williamsburg, N.Y., 1837-42; invested heavily in San Francisco during gold rush, 1848-54, left city secretly, owing $800,000; fugitive from justice, 1854-61; negotiated with Chilean Govt. to build railroad, 1861, built it at $1,000,000 profit; built railroads in Peru and Bolivia, 1861-77; his best known constrn. was Callao, Lima & Oroya R.R. (highest in world). Died Sept. 29, 1877.

MEIGS, Charles Delucena, physician; b. St. George, Bermuda, Feb. 19, 1792; s. Josiah and Clara (Benjamin) M.; grad. U. Ga., 1809, U. Pa. Sch. of Medicine, 1817; m. Mary Montgomery, Mar. 15, 1815, 10 children. Came with family to New Haven, Conn., 1796; moved to Athens, Ga., 1801; practiced medicine, Augusta, Ga., 1814-17, Phila., 1817-61; prof. obstetrics and diseases of women Jefferson Med. Coll., Pa., 1841-61; lived in retirement, Hamanassett County, Pa., 1861-69. Author: Elementary Treatise on Midwifery, 1838. Died June 22, 1869.

MEIGS, Henry, congressman; b. New Haven, Conn., Oct. 28, 1782; grad. Yale, 1799; studied law. Admitted to the bar; began practice of law, N.Y.C.; served as adj. during War of 1812; mem. N.Y. Assembly, 1818; mem. U.S. Ho. of Reps. (Democrat) from N.Y., 16th Congress, 1819-21; pres. bd. aldermen N.Y.C., 1832-33; judge of a city ct., N.Y.C.; clk. N.Y.C. Ct. Gen. Sessions; recording sec. Am. Inst., 1845-61; sec. Farmers' Club. Died N.Y.C., May 20, 1861; buried St. Anne's Churchyard, Perth Amboy, N.J.

MEIGS, James Aitken, physician, educator; b. Phila., July 31, 1829; s. John G. and Mary A. Meigs; grad. Jefferson Med. Coll., 1851; never married. Practiced medicine, Phila., 1851-54; prof. climatology and physiology Franklin Inst., 1854-62; physician of pulmonary diseases Howard Hosp. and Infirmary for Incurables, 1855-68; librarian Acad. Natural Scis. of Phila., 1856-59; prof. insts. of medicine, 1857-59; prof. Pa. Med. Coll., 1859-60; prof. medicine and med. jurisprudence Phila. County Med. Soc., 1868-79; trustee Poly. Coll. State of Pa., several years. Died Nov. 9, 1879.

MEIGS, John Forsyth, physician; b. Phila., Oct. 3, 1818; s. Charles D. and Mary (Montgomery) M.; grad. U. Pa., 1838; m. Ann Wilcocks Ingersoll, Oct. 17, 1844, 8 children. Resident physician Pa. Hosp., 1838-40, mem. staff, 1859-81; took up his father's med. practice in Phila., 1841-82; taught obstetrics and practice of medicine Phila. Assn. for Med. Instrn., 1843-54. Author: A Practical Treatise on the Diseases of Children, 1848. Died Phila., Dec. 16, 1882.

MEIGS, Josiah, lawyer, editor, educator; b. Middletown, Conn., Aug. 21, 1757; s. Return and Elizabeth (Hamlin) M.; grad. Yale, 1778; m. Clara Benjamin, Jan. 21, 1782, 2 children. Elected tutor Yale, 1781; admitted to Conn. bar, 1783; city clk. New Haven (Conn.), 1784-89; opened printing office, established New Haven Gazette, 1784; prof. mathematics and natural philosophy Yale, 1794-1800; pres., prof. U. Ga., 1800; apptd. surveyor-gen. U.S., 1812; commr. Gen. Land Office U.S., Washington, D.C., 1814; pres. Columbian Inst., 1819-22; an original corporator and trustee Columbian Coll. (now George Washington U.). Died Washington, Sept. 4, 1822.

MEIGS, Montgomery Cunningham, army officer, engr.; b. Augusta, Ga., May 3, 1816; s. Dr. Charles Delucena and Mary (Montgomery) M.; grad. U.S. Mil. Acad., 1836; m. Louisa Rodgers, 1841, 7 children. Engaged in fed. engring. surveying projects, 1836; commd. capt. U.S. Army, 1853, col. 11th Inf., 1861, planner, organizer expdn. which saved Ft. Pickens and won harbor Pensacola for U.S., 1861; brig. gen., 1861; q.m. Army throughout Civil War; served at battles of Bull Run and Chattanooga; brevetted maj. gen., 1864; supr. plans for new War Dept. Bldg., 1866-67, Nat. Mus., 1876, Washington Aqueduct extension, 1876, Hall of Records, 1878; regent Smithsonian Instn.; mem. Am. Philos. Soc.; an early mem. Nat. Acad. Scis. Died Washington, D.C., Jan. 2, 1892; buried Arlington (Va.) Nat. Cemetery.

MEIGS, Return Jonathan, Jr., army officer, Indian agt.; b. Middletown, Conn., Dec. 17, 1740; s. Return Jonathan and Elizabeth (Hamlin) M.; m. Joanne Winborn, Feb. 14, 1764; m. 2d, Grace Starr, Dec. 22, 1774. Commd. lt. 6th Conn. Regt., 1772, capt., 1774; maj., with Arnold at Quebec (recorded campaign in Jour.), captured by British in Can.; commd. col. 6th Conn. Inf. (Leather-Cap Regt.), Peekskill, N.Y., 1777; apptd. a surveyor Ohio Co.; landed (with other New Englanders) at mouth of Muskingum River, 1788; drew up code of rules adopted by colony; apptd. Indian agt. to Cherokees, 1801, commd. to negotiate treaties 1805, 05, 07, given authority to negotiate conv. between Tenn. and Cherokees, 1808. Died Cherokee Agy., Tenn., Jan. 28, 1823.

MEIGS, Return Jonathan, Jr., senator, U.S. postmaster gen.; b. Middletown, Conn., Nov. 16, 1764; s. Return Jonathan and Joanna (Winborn) M.; grad. Yale, 1785; m. Sophia Wright, 1788, 1 dau., Mary. Admitted to Conn. bar, circa 1786; moved to Marietta, O., 1788; judge Ohio Territorial Govt., 1798; mem. Ohio Territorial Legislature, 1799; 1st chief justice Ohio Supreme Ct.; 1801-04; brevetted col. U.S. Army, commanded St. Charles (La.) Dist., 1804-06; judge La. Supreme Ct., 1805-06, transferred to Mich. Territory, 1806; judge U.S. Dist. Ct., Mich. Territory, 1807-08; mem. U.S. Senate from Ohio, Dec. 12, 1808-May 1, 1810; gov. Ohio, 1810-14; U.S. postmaster gen., 1814-23. Died Marietta, Mar. 29, 1824; buried Mound Cemetery, Marietta.

MEIGS, Return Jonathan, lawyer; b. Winchester, Ky., Apr. 14, 1801; s. John and Parthenia (Clendinen) M.; m. Sally Keyes Love, Nov. 1, 1825, 5 children. Admitted to Ky. bar, 1822; practiced law, Athens, Tenn., 1825-35; atty. gen. Tenn., also reporter decisions Supreme Ct., 1838-39; U.S. atty. for Middle Tenn. Dist., 1841-42; Whig mem. Tenn. Senate, 1847-48; Unionist during Civil War, moved to N.Y., 1861; clk. Supreme Ct. of D.C., 1863-91. Author: Digest of All the Decisions of the Former Superior Courts of Law and Equity and of the Present Supreme Court of Errors and Appeals in the State of Tennessee, 2 vols., 1848-50; (with William F. Cooper) Code of Tennessee, 1858. Died Oct. 19, 1891.

MELCHER, Joseph, clergyman; b. Vienna, Austria, Mar. 19, 1806; studied at sem., Modena, Italy. Ordained priest Roman Catholic Ch., Modena, 1830; came to U.S., after 1831, became pastor in Little Rock, Ark. and St. Louis; declined appointment as bishop of Quincy (Ill.), 1855; apptd. 1st bishop of Green Bay (Wis.), 1868. Died Green Bay, Dec. 20, 1873.

MELISH, John, geographer; b. Methuen, Perthshire, Scotland, June 13, 1771; attended Glasgow U.; m. Isabella Moncrieff. Apprenticed to cotton factor, Glasgow; voyaged to W.I., 1798; sailed to Savannah, Ga., 1806, established merc. firm; in Scotland, 1808-10; settled in Phila., 1811; published and printed maps, Phila., 1812-22. Works include: Travels in the United States of America in the Years 1806, 1807 and 1809, published 1812; A Statistical Account of the United States, 1813; A Geographical Description of the United States, Showing the Boundary Proposed by the British Commissioners of Ghent, 1814; The State Map of Pennsylvania, 1822. Died Phila., Dec. 30, 1822; buried Free Quakers Cemetery.

MELL, Patrick, H., clergyman, univ. chancellor; b. Walthourville, Liberty County, Ga., July 19, 1814; s. Benjamin and Cynthia (Sumner) M.; attended Amherst Col., 1833-35; m. Lurene Howard Cooper, June 29, 1840; m. 2d, Eliza Elizabeth Cooper, Dec. 24, 1861; 14 children. Sch. tchr., West Springfield, Conn., 1835-36; prin. high sch., East Hartford, Conn., 1836-37; tchr., Perry's Mill in Tatnall County, Ryall's in Montgomery County (both Ga.), 1837-39; prin. classical and English sch., Oxford, 1839-41; joined Baptist Ch., 1832, licensed to preach, 1839; prof. ancient langs. Mercer Coll., 1841-55; in charge of Bapt. congregation, Greensboro, Ga., 1842-52, Bairdstown, Ga., 1852-62, Antioch, Ga., 1862-88; prof. ancient langs. U. Ga., 1856-60, vice chancellor 1860-72, chancellor, 1878-88; served as volunteer in Confederate Army. Died Jan. 26, 1888.

MELLEN, Grenville, author; b. Biddleford, Me., June 19, 1799; s. Prentiss and Sarah (Hudson) M.; grad. Harvard, 1818, attended Harvard Law Sch., 1818-20; m. Mary King Southgate, Sept. 9, 1824. Settled at North Yarmouth, Me., 1823; contbr. (with Henry W. Longfellow) poems, prose, sketches and tales to U.S. Literary Gazette, Atlantic Souvenir, Legendary; editor Portland Advertiser, 1829. Author: The Martyr's Triumph; Buried Valley, and Other Poems, 1833; A Book of the United States, 1838. Died Sept. 5, 1841.

MELLEN, Prentiss, senator; b. Sterling, Mass., Oct. 11, 1764; s. Rev. John and Rebecca (Prentiss) M.; grad. Harvard, 1784; m. Sarah Hudson, May 5, 1795, 6 children including Grenville. Admitted to Taunton (Mass.) bar, 1788; practiced law, Bridgewater, Mass., 1789-91, Dover, N.H., 1791-92, Biddleford, Me., 1792-1806, Portland, Me., 1806-40; mem. Mass. Exec. Council, 1808, 09, 17; trustee Bowdoin Coll., Brunswick, Me., 1817-36; mem. U.S. Senate from Mass., June 5, 1818-May 15, 1820; 1st chief justice Me. Supreme Ct., 1820-34 chmn commn. to revise and codify public statutes of Me., 1838-40. Died Portland, Dec. 31, 1840; buried Western Cemetery, Portland.

MELLETTE, Arthur Calvin, gov. S.D.; B. Henry County, Ind., June 23, 1842; s. Arthur Calvin and Mary (Moore) M.; A.B., Ind. U., 1864, LL.D. 1866; m. Margaret Wylie, May 29, 1866. Served as pvt. until end of Civil War mem. Ind. Ho. of Reps. 1872,, 73, largely responsible for Ind. twp. sch. system; register U.S. Land Office, Dakota Territory; mem. 1st Dakota Constl. Conv., 1883; provisional gov. "State of Dakota," 1885-88 (regarded as territory and not recognized by fed. govt.); gov. Dakota Territory, 1888; 1st gov. S.D., 1889-93. Died Pittsburgh, Kan., May 25, 1896; buried Watertown, S.D.

MELLISH, David Batcheller, congressman; b. Oxford, Mass., Jan. 2, 1831; attended pub. schs. Engaged as printer, Worcester, Mass.; taught schs., Mass., Md. and Pa.; proofreader, N.Y.C.; reporter N.Y. Tribune; stenographer N.Y.C. Police Bd., 10 years; apptd. asst. appraiser mdse. Port of N.Y., 1871; mem. U.S. Ho. of Reps. (Republican) from N.Y., 43d Congress, 1873-74. Died Washington, D.C., May 23, 1874; buried Hillside Cemetery, Auburn, Mass.

MELSHEIMER, Friedrich Valentin, clergyman; b. Negenborn, Germany, Sept. 25, 1749; s. Joachim Sebastian and Clara Margaretha Melsheimer; attended U. Helmstedt; m. Mary Agnes Man, Jan. 18, 1779. Apptd. chaplain Dragoon Regt. of Brunswick Auxiliaries hired by Brit. Crown to suppress rebellious Am. colonies, 1776; wounded and captured at Battle of Bennington, 1777; pastor of 5 small Lutheran chs., Dauphin County, Pa., 1779-83; pastor, Manheim, Pa., 1784-86; prof. Greek, Latin and German, Franklin Coll., 1786-87, worked to keep coll. in existence, 1787-89; pastor St. Matthew's, Hanover, Pa., 1789-1814. Author: Catalogue of Insects of Pennsylvania, 1806. Died June 30, 1814.

MELVILLE, David, pewter maker, inventor; b. Newport, R.I., Mar. 21, 1773; s. David and Elizabeth (Thurston) M.; apprenticed to a pewterer; m. Patience S. Sherman, Mar. 4, 1812, 7 children. Established as pewterer, Newport, by 1803; developed method for producing illuminating gas, succeeded in lighting his own house with coal gas, 1806, obtained 1st U.S. patent for apparatus for making coal gas, 1813; unsuccessfully attempted (with Winslow Lewis) to influence U.S. Govt. to use coal gas for light houses. Author: An Exposé of Facts Respectfully Submitted to the Government of the United States Relating to the Conduct of Winslow Lewis, 1819. Died Newport, Sept. 3, 1856.

MELVILLE, Herman, author; b. N.Y.C., Aug. 1, 1819; s. Allan and Maria (Gansevoort) M.; m. Elizabeth Shaw, Aug. 4, 1847. Clk., N.Y. State Bank, 1834; decided to go to sea, 1837, became cabin boy in ship Highlander, bound for Liverpool, Eng. (described in book Redburn, 1849); mem. crew of whaling ship Acushnet, 1841-42 (recreated in Moby Dick, 1851); jumped ship at Marquesas Island, July 1842, lived among cannibals (described in Typee, 1846); escaped island aboard Australian ship Lucy Ann, then jumped ship in Tahiti, Sept. 1842 (described in Omoo, 1847); returned to Boston in U.S. frigate United States, Oct. 14, 1844 (described in White-Jacket or The World in a Man-of-War, 1850); his books Typee and Omoo were successful as travel books, created controversy in their description of effects of Christian missionaries on natives; went to Paris, 1849, later used city as setting for part of book Israel Potter (1855); moved to "Arrowhead," Pittsfield, Mass., made friends with Hawthorne, to whom he dedicated Moby Dick (finished in 1851); his books Moby Dick and Pierre: or the Ambiguities (1852) did not meet critical approval, did not sell well; wrote The Piazza Tales (contained short story Benito Cereno), 1856, The Confidence Man, 1857; moved to N.Y.C., 1863; apptd. outdoor customs insp., 1866-85; wrote his last novel Billy Budd, 1891 (not published until 1924); wrote poetry including Battle-Pieces and Aspects of the War (1866), Clarel (1876), John Marr and Other Sailors (1888), Timoleon (1891); his fame rests on his fiction, especially Moby Dick. Died in poverty and obscurity, N.Y.C., Sept. 28, 1891; buried Woodlawn Cemetery, N.Y.C.

MEMBRÉ, Zenobius, missionary; b. Bapaume, France, 1645. First novice in newly created Franciscan dept. of At. Anthony (Recollect Order), circa 1669; sent to Can., 1675-78; accompanied LaSalle's men on expdn. down to Illinois River to build Ft. Crêvecoeur, 1678-80; accompanied LaSalle on expdn. which claimed Mississippi Valley for France, 1681-82; missionary on LaSalle's expdn. to Tex., 1685-87, settled on Garcitas River (whole colony perished after LaSalle's departure). Died circa 1687.

MEMMINGER, Christopher Gustavus, legislator, Confederate govt. ofcl.; b. Nayhingen, Wurtemberg, Germany, Jan. 9, 1803; s. Christopher Godfrey and Eberhardina (Kohler) M.; grad. S.C. Coll., 1819; m. Mary Wilkinsan, 1832; m. 2d, Sarah Wilkinson, 1878; 8 children. Opponent of nullification, wrote satiric Book of Nullification, 1830; mem. S.C. Ho. of Reps., 1836, chmn. com. finance; commr. schs. Charleston (S.C.), 1855; mem. bd. S.C. Coll., 32 years; commr. to address Va. Legislature on necessity for joint defense measures, 1860; sec. Confederate Treasury, resigned, 1864. Died Flat Rock, N.C., Mar. 7, 1888.

MENARD, Michel Branamour, fur trader, pioneer; b. Laprairie, Lower Can., Dec. 5, 1805; s. Michel B. and Marguerite (deNoyer) M.; m. Marie Anne Leclere, 1832; m. 2d, Mary Riddle; m. 3d, Mrs. Rebecca Bass. Lived among Shawnee Indians, adopted, elected chief; founder sawmill on Menard Creek, 1833; located claim to approximately 6 sq. miles land on Galveston Island, Tex., 1834, organized Galveston City Co. (group settlers), 1838, founded Galveston, Tex., lived to see population approach 7,000; signer Tex. Declaration of Independence, 1836; mem. com. drafting constn. Republic Tex.; mem. 5th Tex. Congress from Galveston County, 1840-42; authority on Tex. land titles; Menard County (created 1858) named for him. Died Sept. 2, 1856; buried Catholic Cemetery, Galveston.

MENARD, Pierre, fur trader, legislator; b. St. Antoine, Que., Can., Oct. 7, 1766; s. Jean Baptiste and Marie (Ciree) M.; m. Therese Godin, June 13, 1792; m. 2d, Angelique Saucier, Sept. 22, 1806; 10 children. Went to Vincennes, Ind. to become fur trader, circa 1787; apptd. maj. Randolph County Regt., Ind. Militia, 1795, recommd., 1800, apptd. lt. col., comdg. officer, 1806; judge Ct. of Common Pleas, 1801-11; an organizing partner St. Louis Mo. Fur Co.; capt. inf. on expdn. of fur co. which restored Mandan chief Big White to his people, 1809; elected to 1st Ill. Senate, 1812, 1st pres., 1812-18; 1st lt. gov. Ill., 1818; served on commn. to treat with Winnebagos at Prairie du Chien (Wis.), 1828; served on commn. to treat witn other tribes of region, 1829. Died June 13, 1844.

MÉNARD, René, missionary; b. Paris, France, Sept. 7, 1605; attended Jesuit sems., Paris, La Flèche, Bourges, Rouen. Instr. at Orleans, France, 1629-32, at Moulins, 1636-39; sent as missionary of Soc. of Jesus to Can., 1640; worked among Huron and Algonquin Indians, 1641-49; established colony among Iroquois Indians, 1649-56; unsuccessfully attempted to conduct mission in Ottawa country, 1661. Died Aug. 1661.

MENEELY, Andrew, bell mfr.; b. West Troy, N.Y., May 19, 1802; s. Andrew and Eleanor (Cobb) M.; m. Philena Hanks, circa 1826. Apprenticed to bell-maker Benjamin Hanks, 1819-21; owner bell foundry, West Troy, 1826-51, acquired great precision in constrn. of his bells; pres. Village of West Troy, 1839, 43. Died Oct. 14, 1851.

MENEFEE, Richard Hickman, congressman; b. Owingsville, Ky., Dec. 4, 1809; grad. Transylvania U., Lexington, Ky.; studied law. Admitted to Ky. bar, 1830, began practice in Mount Sterling; apptd. commonwealth atty., 1832; mem. Ky. Ho. of Reps., 1836-37; mem. U.S. Ho. of Reps. (Whig) from Ky., 25th Congress, 1837-39; resumed practice of law, Lexington; Whig presdl. elector, 1840. Died Frankfort, Ky., Feb. 21, 1841; buried pvt. cemetery, Fayette County, Ky., reinterred Cave Hill Cemetery, Louisville, 1893.

MENÉNDEZ Pedro de Avilés, naval officer; b Spain, Feb. 15, 1519; m. Ana Mariá de Solís. Bega sea career at early age; distinguished himself fightin pirates off French coast, 1549; apptd. capt. ger Spanish Indies Fleet, 1554; made 3 voyages to Ne World, 1555-63; selected by Philip II to resis French influence in Fla., 1565; explored Fla. coas (at his own expense), expelled non-Spanish explo ers; captured and destroyed French fleet under Jea Ribaut, 1556; attempted to explore and coloniz Fla. for Spain, until 1574. Died Sept. 17, 1574 buried Avilés, Spain.

MENETREY, Joseph, missionary; b. Freiburg Switzerland. Joined Soc. of Jesus, 1836, ordaine priest Roman Catholic Ch., 1846; came to Am. a Jesuit missionary to Ore., 1847; missionary amor various Indian tribes in Northwest, 1847-54, calle "Pel Leméné" by Indians; founder Mission of St Ignatius, Ida., 1854; built ch., Helena, Mont. 1874, St. Patrick's Hosp. and St. Francis Xavie Ch., Missoula, Mont., 1877. Died St. Ignatius Mis sion, Apr. 27, 1891.

MENEWA, Indian chief (called Hothlepoya, "th crazy war hunter" in his younger days); probabl born circa 1766. A scourge of the Tenn. frontie adapted to ways of white men, became a trade known as Menewa (the great warrior) during th rise of Tecumseh 2d chief Oakfuskee Creek Indian in Ala.; against ceding tribal lands to the whit man; defeated by Andrew Jackson at Battle o Horseshoe Bend, 1814; mem. delegation sent t Washington to protest treaty signed by Willia McIntosh, 1826; when some of Creeks joined Sem inole Indians during Seminole War, 1835, h fought on side of white man with the promise tha he could remain on his native land to die, promis later broken, sent with rest of his tribe to Okla reservation. Died 1835.

MENGARINI, Gregory, missionary; b. Rome, Ita ly, July 21, 1811; attended Jesuit sems., Rome Modena and Reggio (all Italy). Missionary of Ro man Catholic Ch., came to U.S. as missionary t Flathead Indians, St. Mary's Mission in Mo., 1840 50; wrote Kalispel Indian-English dictionary; worke in Santa Clara (Cal.) mission, 1852-88; a founde Coll. of Santa Clara. Died Sept. 23, 1886.

MENKEN, Adah Isaacs, actress, poet; b. nr. Ne Orleans, June 15, 1835; m. Alexander Isaac Menke Apr. 3, 1856; m. 2d, John Carmel Heenan, Jul 1859; m. 3d, Robert Henry Newell, Sept. 24, 1861 m. 4th, James Barkley, Aug. 19, 1866. Played Paul ine in The Lady of Lyons, James Charles' theatre Shreveport, La., 1857; regular contbr. to Israelite Cincinnati, 1857-59; played Widow Cheerly in Th Soldier's Daughter, Purdy's Nat. Theatre, N.Y.C. 1859; appeared at Green Street Theatre, Albany N.Y., 1861, Tom Maguire's Opera House, San Fran cisco, 1863; played in Mazeppa at Astley's Theatre London, Eng., 1864; appeared in Child of the Sur London, 1865; starred in Les Pirates de la Savane Théatre de la Gaité, Paris, France, 1866; made las appearance at Sadler's Wells Theatre, London, 1868 Author: Infelicia (edited by John Thomson, 1868) Died Paris, Aug. 10, 1868; buried Montparnasse.

MENZIES, John William, congressman; b. Bry ants Station, Ky., Apr. 12, 1819; grad. U. Va. 1840; studied law. Admitted to Ky. bar, bega practice in Covington, 1841; mem. Ky. Ho. of Reps. 1848, 55; mem. U.S. Ho. of Reps. (Unionist) fror Ky., 37th Congress, 1861-63; del. Democratic Nat Conv., Chgo., 1864; judge Ky. Ct. of Chancery 1873-93. Died Falmouth, Ky., Oct. 3, 1897; burie Linden Grove Cemetery, Covington.

MERCER, Charles Fenton, congressman; b. Fred ericksburg, Va., June 16, 1778; s. James an Eleanor (Dick) M.; grad. Coll. of N.J. (no Princeton), 1797, postgrad. in law, 1797-1800 Admitted to Va. bar, 1802; mem. Va. Ho. of Dels. 1810-17, advocated increased banking capital o Va., founding of new bank, colonization of fre U.S. Negroes in Africa, building of roads an canals, author unsuccessful bill providing for pub lic edn. from common sch. through univ., 1817 author act granting sword and pension to Georg Rogers Clark; served as lt. col. of a Va. regt., ma in command of Norfolk (Va.), during War o 1812, apptd. insp. gen., 1814, aide-de-camp t Gov. Barbour, brig. gen. in command 2d Va. Bri gade; mem. U.S. Ho. of Reps. from Va., 15th-26t congresses, 1817-Dec. 26, 1839, chmn. com. o canals and roads, com. on D.C., gave speech a tacking Andrew Jackson's maneuvers in Seminol War, 1819; 1st pres. Chesapeake & Ohio Cana Co., 1828-33; mem. Va. Constl. Conv., 1829-30 advocated male suffrage, popular election of im portant officers, equal representation; an originat plan for establishing Free State of Liberia; v.p Va. Colonization Soc., 1836, Nat. Soc. Agr., 1842 original grantee, agt., partner Tex. Assn. (paid i land by Republic of Tex. in return for bringing settlers; colonization contracts declared unconstl. 1845); travelled in Europe, 3 years. Author: A xposition of the Weakness and Inefficiency of the overnment of the United States, 1845. Died oward, Va., May 4, 1858; buried Union Cemeery, Leesburg, Va.

MERCER Hugh, army officer; b. Aberdeenshire, cotland, circa 1721; s. Rev. William and Anna Munro) M.; ed. Aberdeen U.; m Isabella Gordon, sons, 1 dau. Asst. surgeon Prince Charles Edward's rmy at Battle of Culloden, 1745; served as capt. n French and Indian War, 1755-56; participated n Battle of Monongahela, 1755; commd. maj., ater lt. col., 1758; col. 3d Battalion, 5th Pa. egt., 1759; apptd. comdt. Ft. Pitt; elected col. f Va. Minutemen for Caroline, Stafford, King George, potsylvania counties, 1775; organized, elected ol. 3d Va. Regt., 1776, brig. gen., 1776; served in attles of Trenton, 1776, Princeton, 1777. Died an. 12, 1777; buried Christ Churchyard, Phila., einterred Laurel Hill Cemetery, Phila., 1840.

MERCER, James, Continental congressman; b. Mar. 8, 1737; s. John and Catherine (Mason) M.; n. Eleanor Dick, June 4, 1772, 3 children including harles Fenton, Mary Eleanor Dick. Served as apt. Va. Militia, French and Indian War; comdr. t. Loudoun, Winchester, Va., 1756; mem. Va. Io. of Burgesses from Hampshire County (now V.Va.), 1762-76; mem. Va. revolutionary convs., 1774, 75, 76; apptd. mem. Com. of Correspondnce, 1774; mem. 1st Va. Com. of Safety, 1775; nem. Va. Constl. Conv., 1776; mem. Continental ongress from Va., 1779, 80; mem. Va. Gen. Ct., 779; trustee, pres. Fredericksburg Acad., 1786-0; judge Va. Ct. of Appeals, 1789-93. Died Richnond, Va., Oct. 31, 1793; buried St. John's hurchyard, Richmond.

MERCER, Jesse, clergyman; b. Halifax County, N.C., Dec. 16, 1769; son of Silas Mercer; m. Sabrina Chivers, Jan. 31, 1788, 2 daus.; m. 2d, Nancy (Mills) Simonds, Dec. 11, 1827. Ordained to ministry Baptist Ch., at Phillips' Mill (Ga.) Ch., 1789; pastor, Sardis, Ga., 1790; pastor chs., Phillips' Mill, Bethesda, Powelton (all Ga.), 1796; clk. Ga. Bapt. Assn., 1795-1816, moderator, 1816-39; moderator Gen. Bapt. Assn. State of Ga., 1822-41; editor Christian Index, Washington, D.C., 1833-40; Mercer U. (Greensboro, Ga.) named for him. Died Butts County, Ga., Sept. 6, 1841.

MERCER, John Francis, gov. Md.; b. Stafford County, Va., May 17, 1759; s. John and Ann (Roy) M.; grad. Coll. William and Mary, 1775; studied law under Thomas Jefferson, Williamsburg, Va., 1779-80; m. Sophia Sprigg, 1785, 1 dau., Margaret. Commd. lt., 3d Va. Regt., Continental Army, 1776, capt., 1777, aide-de-camp to Gen. Charles Lee, 1778, resigned, 1779; commd. lt. col. Va. Cavalry, Continental Army, 1780, raised corps of militia grenadiers, 1781, served at Yorktown, witnessing surrender of Gen. Charles Cornwallis; mem. Va. Ho. of Dels., 1782, 85-86; mem. Continental Congress from Va., 1782, 83; mem. U.S. Constl. Conv. from Md., 1787; mem. Md. Ho. of Dels., 1788-89, 91-92, 1800-01, 03-06; mem. U.S. Ho. of Reps. from Md., 2d-3d congresses, 1791-Apr. 1794; gov. Md., 1801-03. Died Phila., Aug. 30, 1821; buried St. Peter's Ch., Phila., reinterred pvt. cemetery, Cedar Park, West River, Md.

MERCER, Margaret, anti-slavery worker, educator; b. Annapolis, Md., July 1, 1791; d. John Francis and Sophia (Sprigg) Mercer. Active mem. Am. Colonization Soc. (orgn. for purpose of sending free Negroes to Liberia, with idea of eventually ending slavery); conducted girls boarding sch., Leesburg, Va. Author: Studies for Bible Classes, circa 1841; Popular Lectures on Ethics or Moral Obligation for the Use of Schools, 1837. Died Va., Sept. 17, 1846.

MERCIER, Charles Alfred, author; b. nr. New Orleans, June 3, 1816; s. Jean and Eloise (Le Duc) M.; attended Collège Louis-le-Grand, France, circa 1833; studied medicine, Paris, 1855; m. Virginie Vezian, May 10, 1849, at least 3 children. Returned to La., 1838, went to Boston, then to Paris, circa 1840; toured Europe, circa 1843; practiced medicine, New Orleans, 1855-59, also after circa 1866; visited Paris, 1859; founder Athénée Louisianais (orgn. to promote French lang. in La.), 1876; awarded Palmes academiques, 1885. Author: La Rose de Smyrne; L'Ermite du Niagara; Erato Labitte (1840); Biographie de Pierre Soulé (1848); Du Pan-Latinisme-Necessité d'une Alliance entre la France et la Confédération du Sud; La Fille du Prêtre (1877); Réditus et Ascalaphos (1890); Johnelle (1891). Died La., May 12, 1894; buried Metairie Cemetery, New Orleans.

MERCUR, Ulysses, congressman; b. Towanda, Pa., Aug. 12, 1818; s. Henry and Mary (Watts) M.; grad. Washington & Jefferson Coll., 1842; m. Sarah Davis, Jan. 12, 1850. Admitted to bar, Bradford County, Pa., 1843; del. Republican Nat. Conv., Phila., 1856; presiding judge 13th dist. Pa., 1860-65; mem. U.S. Ho. of Reps. from Pa., 39th-42d congresses, 1865-Dec. 2, 1872, Radical Reconstructionist; asso. justice Pa. Supreme Ct., 1872-83, chief justice, 1883-87. Died Wallingford, Pa., June 6, 1887; buried Oak Hill Cemetery, Towanda.

MEREDITH, Samuel, treas. U.S.; b. Phila., 1741; s. Reese and Martha (Carpenter) M.; m. Margaret Cadwalader, May 19, 1772, 7 children. Signed non-importation resolutions, Phila., 1765; mem. Provincial Conv., 1775; served as maj., lt. col. 3d Battalion Associators (known as Silk Stocking Co.) in battles of Trenton, Princeton; promoted brig. gen. Pa. Militia for gallantry at battles of Brandywine and Germantown, 1777; resigned from army, 1778; mem. Pa. Colonial Assembly, 1778-79, 81-83; mem. Congress of Confederation, 1786-88; surveyor Port of Phila., 1789; treas. of U.S., 1789-1801. Died "Belmont," Mt. Pleasant, Pa., Feb. 10, 1817.

MEREDITH, William Morris, sec. of treasury; b. Phila., June 8, 1799; s. William and Gertrude (Ogden) M.; grad. U. Pa., 1812; m. Catherine Keppele, June 17, 1834. Admitted to Pa. bar, 1817; mem. Pa. Legislature, 1824-28; pres. Select Council of Phila., 1834-49; apptd. U.S. atty. for Eastern Dist. Pa., 1841-42; U.S. sec. of treasury, 1849-50; del. to Peace Conv., Washington, D.C., 1861; atty. gen. Pa., 1861-67; 1st pres. Union League Club of Phila.; a counsel for U.S. in Ala. claims case; pres. Pa. Constl. Conv., 1872-73. Died Phila , Aug. 17, 1873.

MERGENTHALER, Ottmar, inventor; b. Aachtel, Germany, May 11, 1854; s. Johann George and Rosina (Achermann) M.; m. Emma Frederica Lachenmayer, Sept. 11, 1881, at least 4 children. Watch-maker's apprentice, Bietigheim, Württemberg, Germany, 1868-72; came to Balt., 1872; with August Hahl's scientific instrument shop, Washington, D.C., 1872-76; moved to Balt., 1876, formed partnership with Hahl, Balt., 1880; patented linotype machine, 1884. Died Oct. 28, 1899.

MERGLER, Marie Josepha, physician; b. Mainstockheim, Bavaria, May 18, 1851; d. Dr. Francis R. and Henriette (von Ritterhausen) Mergler; grad. Women's Med. Coll., Chgo., 1879; studied medicine, Zurich, Switzerland, 1880. Came to Ill., 1853; tchr. Englewood (Ill.) High Sch., 1871-75; began practice medicine, Chgo., 1881; adj. prof. gynecology Women's Med. Coll., Chgo. (became Northwestern U. Women's Med. Sch., 1892), 1881-90; prof. gynecology, 1890; sec. of faculty, 1881-99, dean, 1899-1901; attending gynecologist Wesley Meml. Hosp., 1890; head physician-surgeon Women's and Children's Hosp. of Chgo., 1895-97; prof. gynecology Post-Grad. Med. Sch., Northwestern U., 1895-1901. Author: A Guide to the Study of Gynecology, 1891. Died Los Angeles, May 17, 1901.

MERIWETHER, David, congressman; b. Clover Field, nr. Charlottesville, Va., Apr. 10, 1755; children include James. Served as lt. during Am. Revolution; served with Va. troops at siege of Savannah (Ga.); settled in Wilkes County, Ga., 1785; commd. brig. gen. Ga. Militia, 1797; mem. Ga. Ho. of Reps., speaker, 1797-1800; mem. U.S. Ho. of Reps. (Democrat) from Ga., 7th-9th congresses, Dec. 6, 1802-07; apptd. commr. to Creek Indians, 1804; Dem. presdl. elector, 1816, 20. Died nr. Athens, Ga., Nov. 16, 1822; buried on his plantation.

MERIWETHER, David, senator; b. Louisa County, Va., Oct. 30, 1800; attended common schs., Jefferson County, Ky.; studied law. Fur trader, nr. what is now Council Bluffs, Ia., 1818; farmer, Jefferson County; admitted to Ky. bar, began practice of law; mem. Ky. Ho. of Reps., 1832-45, 58-85, speaker, 1859; del. Ky. Constl. Conv., 1849; sec. of state Ky., 1851; mem. U.S. Senate (Democrat; filled vacancy left by death of Henry Clay) from Ky., July 6-Aug. 31, 1852; gov. Territory of N.M. (apptd. by Pres. Pierce), 1853-55. Died nr. Louisville, Ky., Apr. 4, 1893; buried Cave Hill Cemetery, Louisville.

MERIWETHER, James, congressman; b. nr. Washington, Ga., 1789; s. David Meriwether; grad. U. Ga., 1807; studied law. Admitted to Ga. bar, practiced law, engaged in farming; instr. U. Ga., 1 year; served in war against Creek Indians, 1813; U.S. commr. to Cherokee Indians; trustee U. Ga., 1816-31; mem. Ga. Ho. of Reps., 1821-23; mem. U.S. Ho. of Reps. from Ga., 19th Congress, 1825-27. Died nr. Memphis, Tenn., 1854; buried on his plantation, nr. Athens, Ga.

MERIWETHER, James A., congressman; b. nr. Washington, Ga., Sept. 20, 1806; grad. U. Ga., 1826; studied law. Admitted to Ga. bar, began practice in Eatonton; engaged in farming; mem. Ga. Ho. of Reps., 1831-36, 38, 43, 51-52, speaker, 1852; del. Ga. Internal Improvement Conv., Eatonton, 1839; judge Ga. Superior Ct. for Eatonton dist., 1845-49; mem. U.S. Ho. of Reps. (Whig) from Ga., 27th Congress, 1841-43. Died Eatonton, Apr. 18, 1852; buried Union Cemetery, Eatonton.

MERRIAM, Augustus Chapman, philologist, archeologist; b. "Locust Grove," Leyden, N.Y., May 30, 1843; s. Ela and Lydia (Sheldon) M.; grad. Columbia, 1866; m. Louise Oley, July 23, 1869. Tchr., Columbia Grammar Sch., N.Y.C., circa 1867; tutor Greek & Latin, Columbia Coll., N.Y.C., 1868-76, adj. prof. Greek, 1880, prof. Greek archeology and epigraphy, 1890; pres. Am. Philol. Assn., 1886-87; became dir. Am. Sch. Classical Studies, Athens, Greece, 1886; made successful excavations at Sicyon and Dionyso, found birthplace of Thespis (founder Greek tragedy), 1887-88; pres. N.Y. Soc. of Archaeological Inst. Am., 1891-94. Author: The Phaeacian Episode of the Odyssey, 1880; The Greek and Latin Inscriptions on the Obelisk-Crab in the Metropolitan Museum, N.Y., 1884; The Sixth and Seventh Books of Herodotus, 1885; Classical Studies in Honor of Henry Drisler, 1894. Died Athens, Jan. 19, 1895.

MERRIAM, Charles, publisher; b. West Brookfield, Mass., Nov. 31, 1806; s. Dan and Thirza (Clapp) M.; m. Sophia Eleanor Warriner, Aug. 11, 1835, 3 daus., 2 sons; m. 2d, Rachel White (Capen) Gray, May 9, 1860, 1 dau. Printer's apprentice, Hartford, Conn., 1820-23; journeyman, foreman T. R. Marvin's print shop, Boston; established G. & C. Merriam, printing house and bookshop, Springfield, Mass., 1832; bought rights to publish Noah Webster's American Dictionary of the English Language, 1843; ret. from publishing, 1876. Died July 9, 1887.

MERRICK, Frederick, clergyman, coll. pres.; b. Wilbraham, Mass., Jan. 29, 1810; s. Noah and Statira (Hays) M.; attended Wesleyan U., Middletown, Conn., circa 1834; m. Sarah Fidelia Griswold, 1836. Joined Methodist Soc., 1829; prin., tchr. Amenia Sem., N.Y., 1834-38; prof. natural science Ohio U., Athens, 1838; joined Ohio Conf., Meth. Ch., 1841; pastor Meth. Ch., Marietta, O., 1842-43; ordained elder Meth. Ch., 1843; prof. natural science Ohio Wesleyan U., 1845-51, became prof. moral philosophy, 1851, pres. univ., 1860-73; del. Meth. Gen. Conf., 1860, 64, 76. Author: Formalism in Religion, 1865. Died Delaware, O., Mar. 5, 1894.

MERRICK, Pliny, jurist; b. Brookfield, Mass., Aug. 2, 1794; s. Pliny and Ruth (Cutler) M.; grad. Harvard, 1814; studied law under Levi Lincoln, Worcester, Mass.; m. Mary Rebecca Thomas, May 23, 1821, no children. Admitted to Mass. bar, 1817; mem. Mass. Legislature, 1827; dist. atty. Worcester and Norfolk counties, Mass., 1832-43; editor Nat. Aegis, Worcester, Mass.; judge Mass. Ct. of Common Pleas, 1843-48, 51-53; pres. Worcester Nashua R.R., 1848-50; defense counsel for Prof. John White Webster, tried for murder of Dr. George Parkman, 1850; judge Mass. Supreme Ct., 1853-64. Died Jan. 31, 1867.

MERRICK, Samuel Vaughan, mfr., railroad exec.; b. Hallowell, Me., May 4, 1801; s. John and Rebecca (Vaughan) M.; m. Sarah Thomas, Dec. 25, 1823, 6 children. Formed Merrick & Agnew, fire engine mfg. firm, 1820; a founder Franklin Inst. of Pa., 1824, pres., 1842-54; mem. Phila. City Council, circa 1834-37, brought about use of gas street lighting in Phila.; established Southwark Foundry, 1836 (became Merrick & Son, 1852); 1st pres. Pa. R.R. Co., 1847-49; pres. Sunbury & Erie R.R., 1856-57. Died Phila., Aug. 18, 1870.

MERRICK, William Duhurst, senator; b. Annapolis, Md., Oct. 25, 1793; grad. Georgetown U., Washington, D.C.; studied law; children include William Matthew. Served in War of 1812; register of wills Charles County (Md.), 1825-32; admitted to Md. bar, began practice in Port Tobacco; mem. Md. Ho. Dels., 1832-38, 56-57; mem. U.S. Senate (Whig) from Md., Jan. 4, 1838-45; mem. Md. Constl. Conv., 1850. Died Washington, Feb. 5, 1857; buried Mt. Olivet Cemetery, Washington.

MERRICK, William Matthew, congressman; b. nr. Faulkner, Md., Sept. 1, 1818; s. William Duhurst Merrick; grad. Georgetown U., Washington, D.C.; studied law U. Va. Admitted to Md. bar, 1839, began practice in Frederick, 1844; dep. atty. gen. for Frederick County, 1845-50; moved to Washington, 1854; asso. justice U.S. Circuit Ct. for D.C., 1954-63; resumed practice of law, Md.; prof. law Columbian Coll. (now George Washington U.), Washington, 1866-67; del. Md. Constl. Conv., 1867; mem. Md. Ho. of Dels., 1870; mem. U.S. Ho. of Reps. (Democrat) from Md., 42d Congress, 1871-73; asso. judge Supreme Ct. of D.C., 1885-89. Died Washington, Feb. 4, 1889; buried Mt. Olivet Cemetery, Washington.

MERRILL, Daniel, clergyman; b. Rowley, Mass., Mar. 18, 1765; s. Thomas and Sarah (Friend) M.; grad. Dartmouth, 1789; studied theology under Dr. Spring, Newburyport; m. Joanna Colby, Aug. 14, 1793; m. 2d, Susanna Gale, Oct. 14, 1794, 13 children. Served as pvt. 3d Mass. Inf., during Revolutionary War; licensed to preach, 1791; ordained to ministry Congregational Ch., Sedgewick, Me. 1793; converted to Baptist Ch., 1805; ordained to ministry Bapt. Ch., 1805; mem. Mass. Gen. Assembly, circa 1813; a founder Waterville (now Colby) Coll.,

1813; lived in Nottingham West (now Hudson), N.H., 1814-21; pastor Bapt. Ch., Sedgewick, 1821-33. Author: The Mode and Subjects of Baptism Examined, 1805; Eight Letters on Open Communion, 1805; Balaam Disappointed, 1815. Died June 3, 1833.

MERRILL, Orsamus Cook, congressman; b. Farmington, Conn., June 18, 1775; studied law, Bennington, Vt. Admitted to Vt. bar, 1804; served as maj. and lt. col. 11th Inf. Regt., also lt. col. 26th Inf. Regt., U.S. Army, during War of 1812; register of probate, 1815, 41-47; clk. of cts., 1816; mem. U.S. Ho. of Reps. (Democrat) from Vt., 15th-16th congresses, 1817-Jan. 12, 1820 (lost seat as result of contested election); del. Vt. Constl. Conv., 1822; mem. Vt. Ho. of Reps., 1822; judge Vt. Probate Ct., 1822-23; state's atty., 1823-25; mem. Vt. Exec. Council, 1824-27; mem. Vt. Senate, 1836; postmaster of Bennington, several years; resumed law practice, Bennington. Died Bennington, Apr. 12, 1865; buried Old Cemetery, Bennington.

MERRILL, Samuel, legislator; b. Peacham, Vt., Oct. 29, 1792; s. Jesse and Priscilla (Kimball) M.; m. Lydia Anderson, Apr. 12, 1818; m. 2d, Elizabeth Young; 10 children. Admitted to Ind. bar, 1817; tax assessor Switzerland County (Ind.); mem. Ind. Gen. Assembly from Switzerland County, 1819-22; treas. Ind., 1822-34; capt. 1st Ind. Mil. Co.; commr. for erection Ind. State Capitol Bldg.; an early pres. Temperance Soc., Indpls.; mgr. Ind. Colonization Soc.; trustee Wabash Coll.; pres. Ind. Hist. Soc., 1835-48; elected pres. State Bank of Ind., 1834; pres. Madison & Indpls. R.R., 1844-48. Died Indpls., Ind., Aug. 24, 1855; buried Greenlawn Cemetery, Indpls., reinterred, Crown Hill Cemetery, Indpls.

MERRILL, William Emery, army officer; b. Ft. Howard, Wis., Oct. 11, 1837; s. Capt. Moses E. and Virginia (Slaughter) M.; grad. U.S. Mil. Acad., 1859; m. Margaret Spencer, Jan. 1873, at least 2 sons. Commd. lt. Corps Engrs., U.S. Army, 1859; captured during W.Va. campaign, 1861, held prisoner until Feb. 1862; brevetted capt. after being wounded, Yorktown, Va., 1862; promoted capt., 1863; brevetted maj., lt. col., col. for services in battles of Chickamauga, Lookout Mountain, Missionary Ridge; chief engr. Army of Cumberland, 1864-65; chief engr. Div. of Mo., under Gen. Sherman, 1867-70; originator, chief engr. of canalization of Ohio River from Pitts. to its mouth, 1879-85; U.S. del. Congress of Engrs., Paris, France, 1889. Author: Iron Truss Bridges for Railroads, 1870. Died Dec. 14, 1891.

MERRIMAN, Truman Adams, congressman; b. Auburn, N.Y., Sept. 5, 1839; attended Auburn Acad.; grad. Hobart Coll., Geneva, N.Y., 1861; studied law. Organizer, capt. of co. 92d Regt., N.Y. Volunteer Inf., U.S. Army, 1861, mustered out as lt. col., 1864; admitted to N.Y. bar, 1867; became journalist, N.Y.C., 1871; pres. N.Y. Press Club, 1882-84; mem. U.S. Ho. of Reps. (Democrat) from N.Y., 49th-50th congresses, 1885-89. Died N.Y.C., Apr. 16, 1892; buried Fort Hill Cemetery, Auburn.

MERRIMON, Augustus Summerfield, senator; b. Cherryfields, N.C., Sept. 15, 1830; s. Branch H. and Mary (Paxton) M.; m. Margaret Baird, 1852. Admitted to N.C. bar, 1853; county atty. Buncombe County (N.C.), 1853-60; mem. N.C. Ho. of Commons, 1860; commd. capt. Confederate Army, 1861; apptd. solicitor Western Dist., 1861-65; judge N.C. Superior Ct., 1865-67; chmn. exec. com. Conservative Party; counsel of bd. mgrs. in impeachment trial of Gov. Willam Woods Holden of N.C., 1871; mem. U.S. Senate from N.C., 1873-79; asso. justice N.C. Supreme Ct., 1883-89, chief justice, 1889-92. Died Raleigh, N.C., Nov. 14, 1892; buried Oakwood Cemetery, Raleigh.

MERRY, Ann Brunton, actress; probably born London, Eng., May 30, 1769; dau. of John Brunton; m. Robert Merry, Aug. 1791; m. 2d, Thomas Wignell, Jan. 1, 1803, 1 child; m. 3d, William Warren, Aug. 15, 1806. Began acting career, Bath, Eng., 1785; played at Covent Garden, 1786, acted in London, 1786-92; retired from stage following her 1st marriage; returned to acting, Phila., 1796; became a great favorite in N.Y.C., Phila.; managed Wignell's theatre, Phila. (after his death), 1803-06. Died Alexandria, Va., June 28, 1808.

MERVINE, William, naval officer; b. Phila., Mar. 14, 1791; s. John and Zibia (Wright) M.; m. Amanda Crane, Jan. 12, 1815. Apptd. midshipman U.S. Navy, 1809, served on Gt. Lakes during War 1812; became acting lt., 1813, lt., 1815; master comdt., 1834, commanded ship Natchez, 1836-37; capt. 1841, on sea service in command ship Cyane, 1845-46, ship Savannah, 1846-47; mil. comdt. Monterey (Cal.); apptd. to command Gulf Blockading Squadron, 1861; promoted commodore, 1862, rear adm., 1866. Died Utica, N.Y., Sept. 15, 1868.

MERWIN, Orange, congressman; b. Merryall, Conn., Apr. 7, 1777; attended common schs. Engaged in farming; mem. Conn. Ho. of Reps., 1815-20, del. Conn. Constl. Conv., 1818; mem. Conn. Senate, 1821-25; mem. com. to draft Conn. Constn.; mem. U.S. Ho. of Reps. from Conn., 19th-20th congresses, 1825-29; unsuccessful candidate for lt. gov. Conn., 1831. Died New Milford, Conn., Sept. 4, 1853; buried Cedar Cemetery, New Milford.

MESERVE, Nathaniel, army officer; b. Newingham, N.H., circa 1705; s. Clement and Elizabeth (Jones) M.; m. Jane Libby, 1725; m. 2d, Mary (Odiorne) Jackson, June 18, 1747; 11 children. Served as lt. col. Moore's N.H. Regt. in seige of Louisbourg, 1745; built Brit. frigate America, 1749; served as col. N.H. Regt. at Ft. Edward, 1756; built barracks and storehouses, Halifax, 1757. Died of smallpox, Louisbourg, N.H., June 28, 1758.

MESSER, Asa, educator, coll. pres.; b. Methuen, Mass., May 31, 1769; s. Asa and Abiah (Whittier) M.; grad. R.I. Coll. (now Brown U.), 1790, D.D. (hon.), 1806; LL.D. (hon.), U. Vt., 1812; D.D. (hon.), Harvard, 1820; m. Deborah Angell, May 11, 1797, 4 children. Elected tutor R.I. Coll., 1791, prof. learned langs., 1798, prof. natural philosophy, 1799, pres. pro tem, 1802, pres. 1804-26; licensed to preach, 1792; ordained to ministry Baptist Ch., 1801; patentee "Flumes for Mill," 1822, "Waterwheel and Flume," 1826; alderman Providence (R.I.), many years; unsuccessful candidate for gov. R.I., 1830. Died Providence, Oct. 11, 1836.

MESSLER, Thomas Doremus, railroad exec.; b. Somerville, N.J., May 9, 1833; s. Rev. Abraham and Elma (Doremus) M.; m. Maria Remsen Varick, June 3, 1857, 3 sons. With auditor's office N.Y. & Erie R.R. Co. (now Erie R.R.), 1853; sec., auditor Pitts., Ft. Wayne & Chgo. Ry. Co., Pitts., 1856-69; developed Messler System of railroad accounting; comptroller Pa. R.R. Co., 1871, became 3d v.p., 1876. Died Cresson, Pa., Aug. 11, 1893.

METCALF, Arunah, congressman; b. Aug. 15, 1771; attended common schs. Moved from Conn. to N.Y., settled in Otsego (now Cooperstown), 1802; mem. U.S. Ho. of Reps. (Democrat) from N.Y., 12th Congress, 1811-13; mem. N.Y. Assembly, 1814-16, 28; pres. Otsego County Agrl. Soc., 1818. Died Cooperstown, Aug. 15, 1848.

METCALF, Theron, jurist; b. Franklin, Mass., Oct. 16, 1784; s. Hanan and Mary (Allen) M.; grad. Brown U., 1805; studied law under Seth Hastings, Mendon, Mass.; m. Julia Tracy, 1809. Admitted to Mass. bar, 1807; county atty. Dedham, Mass.; editor Dedham Gazette, 1813-19; opened law sch., 1828; mem. Mass. Legislature, 1833-34, Mass. Senate, 1835; reporter Mass. Supreme Jud. Ct., 1840-47, judge, 1848-65. Author: Reports of Cases Argued and Determined in the Supreme Judicial Court of Massachusetts, 13 vols., 1841-50; Law of Contracts, 1867. Died Nov. 13, 1875.

METCALFE, Henry Bleecker, congressman, jurist; b. Albany, N.Y., Jan. 20, 1805; studied law. Admitted to N.Y. bar, began practice in N.Y.C., 1826; pros. atty. Richmond County (N.Y.), 1826-32, county judge, 1840-41, 47-75; mem. U.S. Ho. of Reps. (Democrat) from N.Y., 44th Congress, 1875-77. Died Richmond, N.Y., Feb. 7, 1881; buried Moravian Cemetery, New Dorp, S.I., N.Y.

METCALFE, Samuel Lytler, physician, chemist; b. Winchester, Va., Sept. 21, 1798; s. Joseph and Rebecca (Littler or Sittler) M.; M.D., Transylvania U., Lexington, Ky., 1823; studied chemistry and biology in Eng., 1831; married twice; m. 2d, Ellen Blondel, 1846. Practiced medicine in Ind., Miss., Tenn., 1823-30; contbd. scientific articles to Knickerbocker Mag., 1833-35; went to Eng. to do research in chemistry and geology, 1835. Author: The Kentucky Harmonist, 1820; A Collection of Some of the Most Interesting Narratives of the Indian Warfare in the West, 1821; A New Theory of Terrestial Magnetism, 1833; Caloric: Its Mechanical, Chemical and Vital Agencies in the Phenomena of Nature, 1843. Died Cape May, N.J., July 17, 1856.

METCALFE, Thomas, senator, gov. Ky.; b. Fauquier County, Va., Mar. 20, 1780; s. John and Sally Metcalfe; m. Nancy Mason. Moved to Nicholas County, Ky., 1784; became stone mason; mem. Ky. Ho. of Reps., 1812-16; raised co. of Ky. Volunteers, War of 1812, served at Battle of Ft. Meigs; mem. U.S. Ho. of Reps. from Ky., 16th-20th congresses, 1819-June 1, 1828, advocated 2/3ds vote of U.S. Supreme Ct. necessary to declare unconstitutionality of state law, favored protective tariffs, internal improvements; gov. Ky., 1829-33; mem. Ky. Senate, 1834-38; pres. Ky. Bd. of Internal Improvements; del. Whig Nat. Conv., 1839; mem. U.S. Senate from Ky., June 23, 1848-49, denounced secession, declared that Ky. would uphold Union. Died Nicholas County, Aug. 18, 1855; buried family burial ground "Forest Retreat," Nicholas County.

METTAUER, John Peter, physician; b. Prince Edward County, Va., 1787; s. Francis Joseph and Jemimah (Gaulding) M.; M.D., U. Pa., 1809; r Mary Woodard; m. 2d, Margaret Carter, Apr. 1 1825; m. 3d, Louisa Mansfield, 1833; m. 4th, Ma E. Dyson; at least 10 children. Practiced medicin Prince Edward County, 1809-34, 37-55; prof. su gery Washington Med. Coll., Balt., 1835-36; pione in genito-urinary surgery; developed use of le sutures for treating vesico-vaginal fistula; establish Prince Edward Med. Inst. (became med. dep Randolph-Macon Coll.), 1837. Author: Continu Fever in Middle Southern Virginia from 1816 1829, published 1843. Died Nov. 22, 1875; buri College Ch. Cemetery, Hampden-Sydney, Va.

METZ, Christian, founder religious community; Neuwied, Prussia, Dec. 30, 1794. Leader of Comm nity of True Inspiration in Prussia, 1823-42; can to Am., 1842; organized Inspiration community, n Buffalo, N.Y., 1842-54; established Amana comm nity, Ia., 1854 (became Amana Soc., 1859). Di Amana, Ia., July 27, 1867.

MEY, Cornelius Jacobsen, Dutch explorer, s capt.; sailed into Delaware River, 1614; set up F Nassau, 1st white settlement on east bank of riv nr. present site of Gloucester, 1623 (10 years lat the 24 colonists had disappeared, area repossessed Indians); sailed by, claimed, and named Cape Ma early 1620's.

MEYER, Julius Eduard, musician; b. Altenburg Germany, Sept. 5, 1822; studied music with Schu mann, Moscheles, Hauptmann and David, Leipzig Germany. Became vocal tchr. at suggestion of Mer delssohn; came to Am., 1852, settled in Bklyn.; re fused offers of a vocal professorship at Leipzig Cor servatory. Died Bklyn., Sept. 20, 1899.

MIANTONOMO, (also spelled Miantunnomah) Indian chief; s. Mascus; m. Wawaloam. Sum moned to Boston to answer charges of murder English colonists, 1632, cleared; chief Narragar sett tribe, 1635; aided colonists in Pequot Wa 1637; signed peace treaty with English and Unca (chief Mohican tribe), Sept. 21, 1638; deede Island of R.I. to Richard Coddington; capture and executed by Uncas, 1643. Died Sachem' Plain, nr. what is now Norwich, Conn., 1643.

MICHAELIUS, Jonas, clergyman; b. Grootebroek Holland, 1584; grad. theol. coll., Leyden, 1605 married, at least 3 children. Minister in Brabar and Holland, 1605-25; set out for Brazil, Mar 1625, landed at Guinea, W. Africa (because shi changed course), Nov. 1625; returned to Holland 1627; came to New Amsterdam, 1628; founder Col legiate Ch., N.Y.C., and Reformed Ch. in Am., circ 1628; returned to Holland, 1632. Died sometim after 1637.

MICHAUX, André, explorer, botanist; b. Ver sailles, France, Mar. 7, 1746; studied botany unde Bernard de Jussieu; m. Cécile Claye, Oct. 1769, son, François André. Explored Tigris and Euphrate rivers region, 1782-85; came to U.S. to study fores trees of N.Am. for French Govt., 1785; establishe nursery, Hackensack, N.J.; went to Charleston, S.C. 1787; explored for bot. specimens in Appalachia Mountains, 1788; went to Bahama Islands, 1789 studied bot. species, Can., 1792; explored Am. Mid west, 1793-96; returned to Paris, 1796; naturalis on Capt. Nicolas Baudin's expdn., 1800. Author Flora Boreali-Americana, sistens caracteres Plantarur quas in America Septentrionali collegit et detexi Andreas Michaux, 1803. Died of tropical fever Madagascar, Nov. 1802.

MICHAUX, François André, botanist; b. Ver sailles, France, Aug. 16, 1770; s. André and Cécil (Claye) M.; married. Came to Am., 1785-90; agt for French Govt. regarding tree plantations in U.S. 1801-03; returned to U.S., 1806, traveled and mad bot. studies along Atlantic coast, 1806-09. Author Voyage à l'ouest des monts Alléghanys dans le e'tats de l'Ohio, et du Kentucky, et du Tennessée et retour à Charleston par les Hautes-Carolines 1804; The North American Sylva, or a Descriptior of the Forest Trees of the United States, Canada and Nova Scotia, Considered Particularly with Re spect to their Use in the Arts and their Introduc tion into Commerce, 3 vols., 1818-19. Died Oct. 23 1855.

MICHEL, William Middleton, physician; b Charleston, S.C., Jan. 22, 1822; s. Dr. William and Eugenia (Fraser) M.; M.D., École de Medicine, Paris, 1845; M.D., Med. Coll. of S.C., 1846; m. Cecilia S. Inglesby, Apr. 1866, 4 children. Founded Summer Med. Inst. of Charleston, lectured on anatomy, physiology and obstetrics, 1847-60; head of Confederate hosp., Manchester, Va., 1862; edited Confederate Med. and Surg. Jour., 1863-64; prof. physiology and histology Med. Coll. of S.C., 1868-94; mem. Charleston Bd. of Health, 1880-94; pres. Med. Soc. of S.C., 1880-83; mem. Acad. of Scis. of Phila., Imperial Soc. of Natural History of Paris; asso. editor Charleston Med. Journal and Review, Boston Med. Journal. Died June 4, 1894.

MICHENER, Ezra, physician; b. Chester County, a., Nov. 24, 1794; s. Mordecai and Alice (Dunn) I.; M.D., U. Pa., 1818; m. Sarah Spencer, Apr. 5, 1819; m. 2d, Mary S. Walton, 1844. Practiced edicine, Chester County; hon. mem. Med. Soc. of a.; correspondent Acad. Natural Scis.; a founder hester County Med. Soc.; made large natural his- ory and herbarium collections; a founder Guardian oc. for Preventing Drunkenness. Author: The Chris- an Casket, 1869; Manual of Weeds, 1872; Hand- ook of Eclampsia, 1883. Died Toughkenamon, Pa., une 24, 1887.

MICHI KINI KWA, see Little Turtle.

MICHLER, Nathaniel, army officer; b. Easton, a., Sept. 13, 1827; s. Peter S. and Miss (Hart) I.; attended Lafayette Coll., 1841-44; grad. U.S. il. Acad., 1848; m. Fannie Kirkland; m. 2d, Sal- e Hollingsworth, Feb. 12, 1861. Brevetted 2d lt., opog. Engrs., U.S. Army, made surveys and re- onnaissances in Tex., N.M., 1848-51; commd. 2d ., 1854, 1st lt., 1856; chief topog. engr. in charge f surveys for a canal extending from Gulf of arien to Pacific Ocean, 1857-60; in charge of inning boundary line between Md. and Va., 1858- 1; became capt. with armies of Ohio and Cum- erland, 1861-63; then on survey of Harpers Fer- y; attached to Army of the Potomac, 1863-65, i charge of topog. dept., engaged in making arious reconnaissances and bldg. of defensive orks connected with battles of Wilderness, potsylvania, Cold Harbor, Petersburg; commd. aj. Corps. Engr., 1864, brevetted lt. col., 1864, revetted col. for services at Battle of Peters- urg, brig. gen. for services during Civil War, 865; engaged in selecting site for presdl. man- ion and public park, preparing plans for new Var Dept. bldg., 1866-67; supt. public bldgs. and rounds, 1867-71, had charge of survey of Poto- ac River and repairing Fort Foote, Md.; light- ouse engr. on Pacific Coast, 1871-76; proposed anal connecting Coquille River with Coos Bay Ore.); superintended river and harbor improve- ents on Lake Erie, 1876-78; mil. attache of U.S. egation, Vienna, Austria, 1879; engaged in river nd harbor work for N.Y. and N.J., 1880-81. Died aratoga Springs, N.Y., July 17, 1881; buried Eas- on.

MIDDLESWARTH, Ner, congressman; b. Glas- ow, Scotland, Dec. 12, 1783. Came to U.S., 1792, ettled in N.J.; moved to Beavertown, Pa., 1792; erved as capt. during War of 1812; mem. Pa. Io. of Reps., 1815-41, speaker, 2 terms; mem. Pa. enate, 1853-55; mem. U.S. Ho. of Reps. (Whig) rom Pa., 33d Congress, 1853-55; engaged in farm- ing; pres. Beaver Furnace Co., Snyder County, Pa.; sso. judge Snyder County, 1858. Died Beavertown, une 2, 1865; buried Union Cemetery, Beavertown.

MIDDLETON, Arthur, colonial gov.; b. harlestown (now Charleston), S.C., 1681; s. Ed- ard and Sarah (Fowell) M.; m. Sarah Armory, 707; m. 2d, Sarah (Wilkinson) Morton, Aug. 3, 723; 1 child. Mem. S.C. Ho. of Commons, 1706- 0; dep. to Lord Casteret; mem. S.C. Council, 711-17; left council for House of Commons, 1716; ecame pres. of conv. into which Assembly re- olved self when dissolved by gov.; helped over- hrow proprietary control, 1719; administered ovt. after new Crown gov. sailed for Eng., 1725- 1; mem. and pres. gov.'s council, 1731-37. Died harleston, Sept. 7, 1737.

MIDDLETON, Arthur, Continental congress- man; b. Charleston, S.C., June 26, 1742; s. Henry and Mary (Williams) M.; m. Mary Izard, Aug. 19, 1764, 9 children including Isabella, Henry, John Izard. Admitted to Middle Temple, London, Eng., 1757-63; justice of peace, S.C., 1764; mem. S.C. Ho. of Assembly, 1764-68, 72; went to Eu- rope with family, 1768-71; mem. 1st S.C. Provin- cial Congress, mem. gen. com., secret com. of 5 which arranged and directed action of 3 parties of citizens who seized powder and weapons from public storehouses, Apr. 21, 1776, mem. spl. com. of May 5, 1772 (apptd. after receiving letter from Arthur Lee in London mentioning possibility of Brit. instigation of slave insurrections in colon- ies); mem. 1st S.C. Council of Safety, 1772; mem. Council of Safety in 2d S.C. Provincial Congress, 1775; mem. com. of 11 to prepare S.C. Constn., 1776; mem. Continental Congress, 1776; signer Declaration of Independence; served with S.C. Militia at seige of Charleston, taken prisoner, sent to St. Augustine (Fla.), 1780, exchanged, 1781; engaged as planter, after Revolutionary War; mem. racing and hunting clubs, St. George's Parish, S.C.; an original trustee Coll. of Charles- ton. Died Goose Creek, S.C., Jan. 1, 1787; buried family mausoleum at "Middleton Place" nr. Charles- ton.

MIDDLETON, George, congressman; b. Phila., Oct. 14, 1800; attended pub. schs., Burlington, N.J. Tanner, Burlington; moved to Allentown, N.J., held several local offices; mem. U.S. Ho. of Reps. (Democrat) from N.J., 38th Congress, 1863-65; resumed tanning bus. Died Allentown, Dec. 31, 1888; buried Crosswicks (N.J.) Community Ceme- tery.

MIDDLETON, Henry, Continental congress- man; b. Charlestown (now Charleston) S.C., 1717; s. Arthur and Sarah (Amory) M.; m. Mary Wil- liams, 1741; m. 2d, Maria Bull, 1762; m. 3d, Lady Mary Mackenzie, Jan. 1776; 12 children including Arthur, Thomas, Henrietta, Sarah. One of great- est landowners in S.C.; justice of peace; mem. S.C. Ho. of Commons, 1742-55, speaker, 1747, 54, 55; commr. Indian affairs, 1755; mem. His Maj- esty's Council for S.C., 1755-70; mem. Continental Congress from S.C., 1774-76, pres., Oct. 1774- May 1775; pres. S.C. Congress, mem. Council of Safety, after Nov. 1775; apptd. mem. com. to frame temporary S.C. Constn., 1776; mem. legis- lative council; mem. newly created S.C. Senate, 1779. Died Charleston, June 13, 1784; buried Church of St. James' Parish, Berkeley County, S.C.

MIDDLETON, Henry, gov. S.C., diplomat; b. London, Eng., Sept. 28, 1770; s. Arthur and Mary (Izard) M.; m. Mary Hering, Nov. 13, 1794, 12 children. Mem. lower house S.C. Legislature, 1801-10; mem. S.C. Senate, 1810; gov. S.C., 1810- 12; mem. U.S. Ho. of Reps. from S.C., 14th-15th congresses, 1815-19; U.S. minister to Russia, 1820-30; del. to anti-tariff conv., Phila., 1831; a vice pres. conv. at Columbia, S.C., 1832; apptd. to solicit Tenn. Legislature to attend a conv. Died Charleston, S.C., June 14, 1846.

MIDDLETON, John Izard, archeologist; b. Charleston, S.C., Aug. 13, 1785; s. Arthur and Mary (Izard) M.; attended Cambridge U.; m. Eliza Au- gusta Falconet, June 11, 1810, 3 children. Settled in Italy, lived on his mother's fortune; became a painter and amateur archeologist; active in society. Author: Grecian Remains in Italy, a Description of Cyclopian Walls and of Roman Antiquities with Topographical and Picturesque Views of Ancient Latium, 1812. Died Paris, Oct. 5, 1849; buried "Middleton Place," S.C.

MIDDLETON, Nathaniel Russell, coll. pres.; b. Charleston, S.C., Apr. 1, 1810; s. Arthur and Alicia (Russell) M.; grad. Coll. of Charleston, 1828; m. Margaret Emma Izard, Jan. 18, 1832, 3 sons; m. 2d, Anna Elizabeth de Wolf, Sept. 20, 1842, 4 daus., 1 son. Made trip to Europe, 1828-31; managed fa- ther's plantation, until 1852; treas. N.E. R.R. Co.; treas. City of Charleston; pres. Charleston Bible Soc.; pres. Coll. of Charleston, 1857-80. Died Charleston, Sept. 6, 1890.

MIDDLETON, Peter, physician; b. Eng.; M.D., U. St. Andrews, Scotland, 1752; m. Susannah Nicholls, Nov. 1766, 1 dau., Susannah Margaret. Made 1 of 1st recorded human dissections in Am. (with Dr. John Bard), 1752; served as surgeon gen. Crown Point expdn. in French and Indian War; a founder St. Andrew's Soc. of N.Y., pres., 1767-70; prof. physiology and pathology King's Coll. (now Colum- bia) Med. Sch., 1767-70, also prof. materia medica, 1770-73, gov. of coll., 1773; mem. staff N.Y. Hosp., 1774. Author: A Medical Discourse; or an Historical Inquiry into the Ancient and Present State of Medi- cine. Died Jan. 9, 1781.

MIFFLIN, Thomas, army officer, gov. Pa.; b. Phila., Jan. 21, 1745; s. John and Elizabeth (Bag- nell) M.; grad. Coll. of Phila. (now U. Pa.), 1760; m. Sarah Morris, Mar. 4, 1767. In Europe, 1764- 65; mcht. in partnership with brother George, 1765; mem. Am. Philos. Soc., 1765-99; mem. Pa. Provincial Assembly, 1772-76, 78-79, 82-84. pres., 1783-84, opposed Stamp Act; mem. Continental Congress from Pa., 1774-76; commd. maj. Con- tinental Army, 1775, chief a.d.c. to George Wash- ington, 1775, q.m. gen., 1775-77, promoted brig. gen., 1776, served as maj. gen., 1777-79; mem. U.S. Bd. War, 1777-78; involved in cabal to oust Washington as comdr.-in-chief, 1777; trustee Coll. of Phila., 1778-91; mem. spl. bd. of Continental Congress to seek ways of reducing expenses, 1780; mem. U.S. Constl. Conv., 1787; pres. Pa. Supreme Exec. Council, 1788-90; pres. Pa. Constl. Conv., 1789-90; gov. Pa., 1790-99, favored war with Eng. and alliance with France, 1793, helped suppress Whiskey Rebellion, 1794. Died Lancaster, Pa., Jan. 20, 1800; buried Lutheran Graveyard, Lancaster.

MILBERT, Jacques Gérard, artist; b. Paris, France, Nov. 18, 1766. Mem. several sci. expdns. sponsored by French Govt.; came to Am. with an expdn., 1815, headquartered in N.Y.C.; exhibited several landscapes and figure paintings at Am. Acad.; returned to France, 1824; wrote and illustrated Pic- turesque Views of North America, 1825; Inineraire Pittoresque du Fleuve Hudson et des Parties Later- ales, 1828-29. Died Paris, June 5, 1840.

MILES, Frederick, congressman; b. Goshen, Conn., Dec. 19, 1815; attended common schs. Engaged in merc. bus., Goshen, until 1858; moved to Twin- lakes, Conn., later to Salisbury, Conn., engaged in iron mfg.; mem. Conn. Senate, 1877-79; mem. U.S. Ho. of Reps. (Republican) from Conn., 46th-47th, 51st congresses, 1879-83, 89-91. Died nr. Salisbury, Nov. 20, 1896; buried Salisbury Cemetery.

MILLARD, Harrison, musician; b. Boston, Nov. 27, 1830; studied in Italy, 1851-54. Sang in ch. choir; sang with chorus of Handel and Haydn Soc. at age 10; became tenor concert singer; toured Gt. Britain with Catherine Hayes; returned to Boston, 1854; settled in N.Y.C. as singer, composer, vocal instr., 1856. Died Boston, Sept. 10, 1895.

MILLEDGE, John, senator, gov. Ga.; b. Savan- nah, Ga., 1757; s. Capt. John and Mrs. (Robe) M.; m. Martha Galphin; m. 2d, Ann Lamar; 4 children. Served with Continental Army in de- fense of Savannah, seige of Atlanta and assault to retake Savannah during Revolutionary War; atty. gen. Ga., 1780; mem. Ga. Gen. Assembly; mem. U.S. Ho. of Reps. from Ga., 3d-5th, 7th congresses, 1793-99, 1801-02; mem. com. to choose site for U. Ga., 1800 (site chosen outside of state grant, Milledge bought it for $400,000 and gave to Univ.); gov. Ga., 1802-06; mem. U.S. Senate from Ga., 1806-09, pres. pro tem, 1809; Milledge- ville (Ga. capitol 1805-68) named for him, also principal residence street in Athens, Ga., and Milledge Street, Sand Hills, Augusta, Ga.; Mil- edge Chair of Ancient Langs., U. Ga., also named for him. Died Feb. 9, 1818; buried Summerville Cemetery, Augusta.

MILLEDOLER, Philip, clergyman, coll. pres.; b. Rhinebeck, N.Y., Sept. 22, 1775; s. John and Anna (Mitchell) M.; grad. Columbia, 1793; studied re- ligion under John D. Gros; m. Susan Lawrence Ben- son, Mar. 29, 1796; m. 2d, Margaret Steele, Nov. 4, 1817; 10 children. Ordained to ministry by Ger- man Reformed Synod, Reading, Pa., 1794; pastor German Reformed Ch., Rhinebeck, 1795-1800; pastor Pine Street Presbyn. Ch., Phila., 1800-05, Rutgers Street Presbyn. Ch., N.Y.C., 1805-13, Collegiate Dutch Reformed Ch., N.Y.C., 1813-52; a founder Am. Bible Soc., Soc. for Evangelizing the Jews; prof. theology Dutch Reformed Ch. Sem., Brunswick, N.J., 1825; pres. Rutgers Coll., 1825-40. Died Staten Island, N.Y., Sept. 22, 1852.

MILLEN, John, congressman; b. Savannah, Ga., 1804; studied law. Admitted to Ga. bar, practiced in Savannah; mem. Ga. Ho. of Reps., 1828, 34-35, 39-40; mem. U.S. Ho. of Reps. (Democrat) from Ga., 28th Congress, 1843. Died Savannah, Oct. 15, 1843; buried Laurel Grove Cemetery, Savannah.

MILLER, Alfred Jacob, artist; b. Balt., Jan. 2, 1810; studied with Thomas Sully, 1831-32, in Europe, 1833-34. Worked in Balt.; moved to New Orleans, 1837; artist on Capt. William Drummond Stewart's expdn. to Rocky Mountains; made sketches of In- dian life, later elaborated on these in his studio; visited Scotland, 1840-42; successful portrait painter, Balt., after 1842. Died Balt., June 26, 1874.

MILLER, Daniel Fry, congressman; b. Cumber- land, Md., Oct. 4, 1814; attended pub. schs., Wayne County, O.; studied law. Taught sch.; journalist, Wooster, O.; moved to Pitts., 1830, employed as retail clk.; admitted to the bar, 1839, began prac- tice in Fort Madison, Ia.; mem. Ia. Territorial Ho. of Reps., 1840; mem. U.S. Ho. of Reps. (Whig) from Ia., 31st Congress, Dec. 20, 1850-51; resumed law practice; mayor Fort Madison, 1859; moved to Keokuk, Ia., practiced law; elected mayor of Keo- kuk, 1873; mem. Ia. Ho. of Reps., 1894; moved to Omaha, Neb., 1895. Died Omaha, Dec. 9, 1895; buried St. Peter's Cemetery, Keokuk.

MILLER, Daniel H., congressman; b. Phila. Mem. U.S. Ho. of Reps. (Jacksonian Democrat) from Pa., 18th-21st congresses, 1823-31. Died Phila., 1846.

MILLER, Elihu Spencer, lawyer; b. Princeton, N.J., Sept. 3, 1817; s. Samuel and Sarah (Ser- geant) M.; grad. Princeton, 1836; m. Anna Emlen, 1853. Admitted to bar, Balt., 1842; practiced law, Phila., from 1843; active in reform movements, Phila.; expert in tax and equity cases; prof. law U. Pa., 1852-72; active Unionist during Civil War, com- manded arty. co. of militia, helped raise bounty funds for Pa.; vice provost Law Acad. of Phila. Author: A Treatise on the Law of Partition by Writ in Pennsylvania, 1847. Editor: Treatise on the Lien of Mechanic and Material Men in Pennsylvania (Sergeant), 1846. Died Phila., Mar. 6, 1879.

MILLER, Ezra, state senator, inventor; b. Pleasant Valley, N J., May 12, 1812; s. Ezra Wil- son and Hannah (Ryerson) M.; m. Amanda Mil- ler, May 1841, 5 children. Enlisted in 2d N.Y. Militia, 1833-43, adj. gen., 1839, lt. col., 1840, col., 1842; went to Rock County, Wis., 1848; justice of peace, Magnolia, Wis., 1848; col. 8th Regt., Wis. Militia, 1851; mem. Wis. Senate from Rock County; perfected a car coupler, obtained patent, 1863, improved basic idea; granted patent for combined railroad-car platform, coupler and buf- fer, 1865; dep. postmaster Janesville (Wis.), 2 years; mem. N.J. Senate, 1883-85; candidate for U.S. Ho. of Reps., several times. Died Mahwah, N.J., July 9, 1885.

MILLER, George Funston, congressman; b. Chil- lisquaque Twp., Pa., Sept. 5, 1809; attended Kirkpatrick's Acad., Milton, Pa.; studied law. Taught sch.; admitted to Union County (Pa.) bar, 1833, began practice in Lewisburg, Pa.; mem. bd. curators of univ. at Lewisburg (now Bucknell U.), 1846-82, scribe, 1847-51, sec. bd. trustees, 1848-64; mem. U.S. Ho. of Reps. (Republican) from Pa., 39th-40th congresses, 1865-69; 1st pres. Lewisburg, Centre & Spruce R.R.; dir. Northumberland Bank, Lewisburg Nat. Bank. Died Lewisburg, Oct. 21, 1885; buried Lewisburg Cemetery.

MILLER, George M., artist; b. Scotland; married. Came to U.S., circa 1798; modelled wax portrait of George Washington, Phila., 1798; worked in Balt., 1810-12; returned to Phila., circa 1813; exhibited at Pa. Acad., 1813-15; known works include a bust of Bishop White (exhibited posthumously by his widow, 1821), wax portrait of Jefferson, a wax Venus. Died 1819.

MILLER, Homer Virgil Milton, senator; b. Pendleton Dist., S.C., Apr. 29, 1814; grad. Med. Coll. of S.C., 1835; studied medicine, Paris, France. Began practice of medicine, Cassville, Ga., 1838; served as surgeon 8th Ga. Inf., Confederate Army, during Civil War, later brigade and div. surgeon in Va., med. dir. surgeon of posts, insp. of hosps., Ga.; resumed practice of medicine, Rome, Ga.; mem. Ga. Reconstrn. Conv., 1867; mem. faculty Atlanta (Ga.) Med. Coll.; mem. U.S. Senate (Democrat) from Ga., Feb. 24-Mar. 3, 1871; trustee U. Ga. Died Atlanta, May 31, 1896; buried Myrtle Hill Cemetery, Rome.

MILLER, Jacob Welsh, senator; b. German Valley, N.J., Aug. 29, 1800; attended pub. schs.; studied law. Admitted to N.J. bar, 1823, practiced in Morristown; mem. N.J. Gen. Assembly, 1832, N.J. Council, 1838-40; mem. U.S. Senate (Whig) from N.J., 1841-53. Died Morristown, Sept. 30, 1862; buried St. Peter's Parish Churchyard, Morristown.

MILLER, Jesse, congressman; b. nr. Landisburg, Pa., 1800; attended common schs.; children include William Henry. First clk. to county commr. Perry County (Pa.), 1820-23; sheriff of Perry County, 1823-26; mem. Pa. Ho. of Reps., 1826-28; mem. U.S. Ho. of Reps. (Democrat) from Pa., 23d-24th congresses, 1833-Oct. 30, 1836; 1st auditor U.S. Dept. Treasury (apptd. by Pres. Jackson), 1836-42; canal commr. of Pa., 1844-45, sec. of state, 1845-48. Died Harrisburg, Pa., Aug. 20, 1850; buried Harrisburg Cemetery.

MILLER, John, congressman; b. Amenia, N.Y., Nov. 10, 1774; studied medicine U. Pa. Began practice of medicine, Washington County, N.Y., 1798; moved to Fabius (now Truxton), N.Y., 1801; coroner of Cortland County (N.Y.), 1802; postmaster of Truxton, 1805-25; organizer Cortland County Med. Soc., 1st v.p., 1808; justice of peace, 1812-21; mem. N.Y. Assembly, 1817, 20, 45; judge county ct., 1817-20; mem. U.S. Ho. of Reps. from N.Y., 19th Congress, 1825-27; del. N.Y. Constl. Conv., 1846. Died Truxton, Mar. 31, 1862; buried City Cemetery, Truxton.

MILLER, John, gov. Mo.; b. Berkeley County, Va. (now W. Va.), Nov. 25, 1781. Moved to Steubenville, O., 1803; editor and publisher Western Herald and Steubenville Gazette, 1803; served as gen. Ohio Militia, before War of 1812; commd. col. 19th Inf., U.S. Army, War of 1812, commanded sortie from Ft. Meigs which drove British from batteries, 1813, resigned, 1818; register Land Office, Franklin, Howard County, Mo., 1821-25; gov. Mo., 1825-32, advocated well-organized and trained militia, withdrawal of state paper money from circulation, state and fed. protection of trade and travel on Santa Fe trail, establishment of state library and coll., exclusion by fed. govt. of all Brit. traders from fur-trading region of Rocky Mountains; mem. U.S. Ho. of Reps. from Mo., 25th-27th congresses, 1837-43. Died Florissant, St. Louis County, Mo., Mar. 18, 1846; buried Col. John O'Fallon's pvt. vault, O'Fallon's farm, reinterred Bellefontaine Cemetery, St. Louis.

MILLER, John, clergyman; b. Princeton, N.J., Apr. 6, 1819; s. Rev. Samuel and Sarah (Sergeant) M.; grad. Princeton, 1836, D.D., 1841; m. Margaret Benedict, Sept. 24, 1844; m. 2d, Sally Campbell Preston McDowell, Nov. 3, 1856. Asst. to Prof. Joseph Henry at Princeton; ordained to ministry Presbyn. Ch., 1843; pastor Presbyn. Ch., Frederick, Md., 1844-50, West Arch Street Presbyn. Ch., Phila., 1850-55; served as capt. Confederate Arty., 1861-62; pastor 2d Presbyn. Ch., Petersburg, Va., 1863-71; suspended by Presbytery of New Brunswick, 1887; founded independent Presbyn. Ch., 1880-95. Author: Church Creed, 1879; Commentary on Romans, 1887. Died Princeton, Apr. 14, 1895.

MILLER, John Franklin, senator; b. South Bend, Ind., Nov. 21, 1831; s. William and Mary (Miller) M.; grad. N.Y. State Law Sch., Ballston Spa, N.Y., 1852; m. Mary Chess, 1857, 2 children. Admitted to N.Y. bar, 1852; settled at Napa, Cal., 1853; mem. Ind. State Senate, 1860; commd. col. 29th Ind. Volunteer Inf., 1861, participated in battles of Stone River, Liberty Gap, Nashville, Tenn.; commd. brig. gen. U.S. Volunteers at Nashville, 1864, brevetted maj. gen., 1865; collector Port of San Francisco, 1865-69; pres. Alaska Comml. Co.; Republican candidate for presdl. elector, 1872, 76, 80; mem. Cal. Constl. Conv.; mem. U.S. Senate from Cal. (Republican), 1881-86, chmn. com. on fgn. relations. Died Washington, D.C., Mar. 8, 1886; buried Laurel Hill Cemetery, San Francisco, removed to Arlington (Va.) Cemetery, 1913.

MILLER, John Gaines, congressman; b. Danville, Ky., Nov. 29, 1812; grad. Centre Coll., Danville; studied law. Admitted to Ky. bar, 1834; moved to Boonville, Mo., 1835; mem. Mo. Ho. of Rep., 1840; mem. U.S. Ho. of Reps. (Whig) from Mo., 32d-34th congresses, 1851-56. Died nr. Marshall, Mo., May 11, 1856; buried Mt. Olive Cemetery, nr. Marshall.

MILLER, John Krepps, congressman; b. Mount Vernon, O., May 25, 1819; grad. Jefferson Coll., Canonsburg, Pa., 1838; studied law. Admitted to Ohio bar, 1841, began practice in Mount Vernon; del. Democratic Nat. Conv., Balt., 1844; mem. U.S. Ho. of Reps. (Dem.) from Ohio, 30th-31st congresses, 1847-51; declined appointment as chief justice Wash. Territory, 1853. Died Mount Vernon, Aug. 11, 1863; buried Mound View Cemetery, Mount Vernon.

MILLER, Jonathan Peckham, army officer; b. Randolph, Vt., Feb. 24, 1796; s. Heman and Deimia (Walbridge) M.; attended Dartmouth, U. Vt.; m. Sarah Arms, June 26, 1828, 1 dau. Apprentice tanner, farmer; mem. Randolph Volunteers; served as pvt. U.S. Army, 1817-19; served as col. under Gen. George Jarvis in war to liberate Greece, 1824-26; agt. N.Y. Greek Com., 1827; admitted to Vt. bar; mem. Vt. Legislature, 1831-33; del. World's Anti-Slavery Conv., London, 1840. Died Feb. 17, 1847.

MILLER, Joseph, congressman; b. Va., Sept. 9, 1819; grad. Miami U., Oxford, O., 1839; studied law. Admitted to Ohio bar, 1841, began practice in Chillicothe; pros. atty. Ross County (O.), 1844-48; mem. Ohio Ho. of Reps., 1856; mem. U.S. Ho. of Reps. (Democrat) from Ohio, 35th Congress, 1857-59; apptd. U.S. judge for Neb. Territory, 1859. Died Cincinnati, May 27, 1862; buried Grandview Cemetery, Chillicothe.

MILLER, Josiah, newspaperman; b. Chester dist., S.C., Nov. 12, 1828. Established (with Elliott) Kan. Free State newspaper, Lawrence, 1855. Claimed to have authored state seal motto: Ad astra per aspera. Died Lawrence, Kan., July 7, 1870.

MILLER, Lewis, mfr.; b. Greentown, O., July 24, 1829; son of John Miller; m. Mary Valinda Alexander, Sept. 16, 1852, 11 children. Taught sch., also Sunday Sch.; became partner Ball, Aultman & Co., 1852 (became Aultman, Miller & Co., 1863); aided in devel. various agrl. machinery; trustee Mt. Union Coll. (O.), 1865-99; advocated (with J. H. Vincent) adult edn. at Lake Chautauga Inst., N.Y. Died N.Y.C., Feb. 17, 1899.

MILLER, Morris Smith, congressman; b. N.Y.C., July 31, 1779; grad. Union Coll., Schenectady, N.Y., 1798; studied law; children include Rutger Bleecker. Admitted to N.Y. bar; pvt. sec. to Gov. Jay of N.Y.; began practice of law, Utica, N.Y., 1806; pres. Village of Utica, 1808; judge Oneida County (N.Y.) Ct. of Common Pleas, 1810-24; mem. U.S. Ho. of Reps. (Federalist) from N.Y., 13th Congress, 1813-15; rep. of U.S. Govt. at negotiation of treaty between Seneca Indians and proprs. of Seneca Reservation, Buffalo, N.Y., 1819. Died Utica, Nov. 15, 1824; buried Rural Cemetery, Albany, N.Y.

MILLER, Nathan, Continental congressman; b. Warren, R.I., Mar. 20, 1743; attended pvt. sch. Mcht., shipbuilder; dep. to R.I. Gen. Assembly, 1772-74, 80, 82, 83, 90; served to brig. gen. R.I. Militia from Newport and Bristol counties, 1772-78; dep. R.I. Assembly, 6 years; mem. Continental Congress from R.I., 1786, reelected but did not take seat; mem. R.I. Constl. Conv., 1790. Died Warren, May 20, 1790; buried Kickamuet Cemetery, Warren.

MILLER, Pleasant Moorman, congressman; b. Lynchburg, Va. Moved to Rogesville, Tenn., 1796, to Knoxville, Tenn., 1800; a commr. for govt. of Knoxville, 1801-02; mem. U.S. Ho. of Reps. from Tenn., 11th Congress, 1809-11; moved to West Tenn., circa 1824, chancellor, 1836-37. Died 1849; buried Trenton, Tenn.

MILLER, Rutger Bleecker, congressman; b. Lowville, N.Y., July 28, 1805; s. Morris Smith Miller; attended Catholic Coll., Montreal, Que., Can., also Yale; grad. Litchfield (Conn.) Law Sch., 1824; Admitted to N.Y. bar, practiced law, Utica, N.Y., 1829-31; trustee Village of Utica, 1829-31, mem. 1st bd. aldermen; mgr. Utica Wilberforce Soc., 1829; engagd in banking, railroad promotion, 1832-33; mem. N.Y. Assembly, 1832; clk. U.S. Dist. Ct., 1833-34; mem. U.S. Ho. of Reps. (Democrat) from N.Y., 24th Congress, Nov. 9, 1836-37; engaged i bldg. and railroad constrn., later managed his farm Boonville, N.Y. Died Utica, Nov. 12, 1877; burie Forest Hill Cemetery, Utica.

MILLER, Samuel Franklin, congressman; b. Franklin, N.Y., May 27, 1827; grad. Delaware Lit. Inst. grad. Hamilton Coll., Clinton, N.Y., 1852; studie law. Admitted to N.Y. bar, 1853; engaged in farming and lumbering; mem. N.Y. Assembly, 1854 served as col. N.Y. Militia; mem. U.S. Ho. of Reps (Republican) from N.Y., 38th Congress, 1863-65 mem. N.Y. Constl. Conv., 1867; dist. collector of internal revenue, 1869-73; mem. N.Y. State Bd. c Charities, 1869-77; mem. U.S. Ho. of Reps., 44t Congress, 1875-77. Died Franklin, Mar. 16, 1892 buried Ouleout Valley Cemetery, Franklin.

MILLER, Samuel Freeman, asso. justice U.S Supreme Ct.; b. Richmond, Ky., Apr. 5, 1816; s Frederick and Patsy (Freeman) M.; M.D., Transylvania U., 1838; m. Lucy Ballinger, circa 1839 m. 2d, Elizabeth Winter, 1857. Justice of peac and mem. county court; admitted to Knox Count (Ky.) bar, 1847; chmn. dist. Republican Com. a Keokuk; apptd. asso. justice U.S. Supreme Ct. 1862, wrote opinion in Loan Assn. vs. Topek banning public taxation for support of privat corps. which did not have public representation wrote opinion on Slaughter House Case limitin interpretation of "due process" clause of 14th Amendment; one of majority in Electora Commn., 1876. Died Washington, D.C., Oct. 13, 1890.

MILLER, Smith, congressman; b. nr. Charlotte, N.C., May 30, 1804. Engaged in farming, Patoka, Ind.; mem. Ind. Ho. of Reps., 1835-39, 46, Ind. Senate, 1841-44, 47-50; mem. U.S. Ho. of Reps. (Democrat) from Ind., 33d-34th congresses, 1853-57; del. Dem. Nat. Conv., Charleston, S.C., 1860. Died nr. Patoka, Mar. 21, 1872; buried Robb Cemetery, Patoka.

MILLER, Stephen Decatur, senator, congressman; b. Lancaster Dist., S.C., May 8, 1787; s. William and Margaret (White) M.; grad. S.C. Coll., 1808; m. Miss Dick, circa 1814; m. 2d, Mary Boykin, May 1819; 7 children. Admitted to S.C. bar, 1811; mem. U.S. Ho. of Reps. from S.C., 14th-15th congresses, 1815-19; mem. S.C. Senate from Sumter Dist., 1822-28; gov. S.C., 1828-30; mem. U.S. Senate (Nullifier) from S.C., 1831-33; mem. S C. Nullification Conf., 1832-33. Died Raymond, Miss., Mar. 8, 1838.

MILLER, William, religious leader; b. Pittsfield, Mass., Feb. 15, 1782; s. Capt. William and Paulina (Phelps) M.; m. Lucy P. Smith, June 29, 1803. Farmer in Vt.; justice of peace, dep. sheriff, Poultney, Vt.; served as capt. U.S. Army during War of 1812; converted from deism to militant fundamentalism, circa 1843, believed Christ would soon return to earth; licensed to preach Baptist Ch., 1833; became founder, spiritual leader of Adventist movement; prophesied 2d coming of Christ, 1843, 44, and ½ million of his followers prepared themselves to meet their end; became pres. Adventist Ch. (formed by Millerites), 1845. Author: Evidence from Scripture and History of the Second Coming of Christ, about the Year 1843, Exhibited in a Course of Lectures, 1836. Died Hampton, Vt., Dec. 20, 1849.

MILLER, William Henry, congressman; b. Landisburg, Pa., Feb. 28, 1829; s. Jesse Miller; grad. Franklin and Marshall Coll., Lancaster, Pa., 1846; studied law. Admitted to Pa. bar, 1846; practiced in Harrisburg, Pa., 1846-49, New Bloomfield, Pa., 1849-54; returned to Harrisburg; clk. Pa. Supreme Ct., 1854-63, Pa. Senate, 1858-59; mem. U.S. Ho. of Reps. (Democrat) from Pa., 38th Congress, 1863-65; resumed practice of law, also engaged in journalism. Died Harrisburg, Sept. 12, 1870; buried Harrisburg Cemetery.

MILLER, William Rickarby, artist; b. Staindrop, County Durham, Eng., May 20, 1818; s. Joseph Miller. Came to Am., circa 1844, settled in N.Y.C.; painted Am. views in watercolors and oils; did many illustrations for books and periodicals; engaged in making pen and ink sketches for collection to be titled 1,000 Gems of Am. Landscape (never published), after 1873. Died N.Y.C., July, 1893.

MILLER, William Starr, congressman; b. Wintonburg (now Bloomfield), Conn., Aug. 22, 1793. Alderman, N.Y.C., 1845; mem. U.S. Ho. of Reps. from N.Y., 29th Congress, 1845-47, unsuccessful candidate for reelection, 1846. Died N.Y.C., Nov. 9, 1854; buried Greenwood Cemetery, Bklyn.

MILLIGAN, John Jones, congressman; b. Bohemia Manor, Md., Dec. 10, 1795; attended St. Mary's Coll., Balt.; grad. Princeton, 1814; studied law. Admitted to the bar; began practice of law, New Castle County, Del., 1818; mem. U.S. Ho. of Reps. (Whig) from Del., 22d-25th congresses, 1831-39; judge Del. Superior Ct., 1839-64. Died Phila., Apr. 20,

875; buried Wilmington and Brandywine Cemery, Wilmington, Del.

MILLIKEN, Seth Llewellyn, congressman; b. Montlle, Me., Dec. 12, 1831; attended Waterville Coll.; rad. Union Coll., Schenectady, N.Y., 1856; studied w. Mem. Me. Ho. of Reps., 1857-58; clk. Me. upreme Jud. Ct., 1859-71; admitted to Me. bar, 871, did not practice; del. Republican Nat. Conv., incinnati, 1876, Chgo., 1884; Rep. presdl. elector, 876; mem. U.S. Ho. of Reps. (Rep.) from Me., 8th-55th congresses, 1883-97. Died Washington, .C., Apr. 18, 1897; buried Grove Cemetery, Belst, Me.

MILLS, Benjamin, legislator, jurist; b. Worcester ounty, Md., Jan. 12, 1779. Head, Washington cad. (now Washington and Jefferson Coll.); em. Ky. Ho. of Reps., 1806-16; apptd. judge Iontgomery (Ky.) Circuit Ct., 1817; asso. justice Ky. Ct. of Appeals, declared unconstitutional elief laws passed by legislature to aid those ho had suffered by collapse of state banks, 823, resigned, 1828; a founder Am. Bible Soc. ied Dec. 6, 1831.

MILLS, Clark, sculptor; b. Onondaga County, N. ., Dec. 13, 1810; 2 sons including Theodore Auustus, 1 step-dau. Carved a bust of John C. Caloun in Carolina marble, bought by City Council f Charleston (S.C.), won gold medal, 1846; deigned equestrian monument of Gen. Andrew Jackon, finished full sized plaster model, 1850; cast ackson statue in bronze (the largest bronze cast in .S. at that time); statue of Jackson dedicated, 853, now stands in Lafayette Square, Washington, .C.; New Orleans (La.) replica of Jackson dediated, 1856; cast Liberty (statue on Capitol Bldg. Vashington), 1863. Died Jan. 12, 1883.

MILLS, Cyrus Taggart, missionary, educator; b. aris, N.Y., May 4, 1819; s. William Mills; grad. William Coll., 1844; grad. Union Theol. Sem., 847; m. Susan Tolman, Sept. 11, 1848. Ordained y Third Presbytery of N.Y., 1848; sailed soon fter ordination to India under appointment Am. d. Commrs. of Fgn. Missions; took charge of atticetta Sem., Ceylon, 1848-59; went to Hawaian Islands where he took charge Oahu Coll., r. Honolulu, 1860-64, put coll. on self-supporting basis; established Mills Sem. in Cal., 1871; ormed Pomona Land & Water Co., 1882, pres. 882-84. Died Oakland, Cal., Apr. 20, 1884.

MILLS, Elijah Hunt, senator; b. Chesterfield, Mass., Dec. 1, 1776; s. Rev. Benjamin and Mary (Hunt) M.; grad. Williams Coll., 1797; m. Sarah Hunt, 1802; m. 2d Harriette Blake, 1804; children—George Francis, Helen Sophia, Harriette Blake, Sarah, Benjamin Pierce, William Kilby, Charles Henry. Admitted to Northampton (Mass.) bar, 1803; town clk. Northampton, 1804-14; an active Federalist leader in Western Mass.; mem. Mass. Senate, 1811-14, 19-20, speaker, 1820; mem. U.S. Ho. of Reps. from Mass., 14th-15th congresses, 1815-19; mem. U.S. Senate from Mass., June 12, 1820-27. Author: Address of the House of Representatives to the People of Mass., 1812. Died Northampton, May 5, 1829; buried Bridge St. Cemetery, Northampton.

MILLS, Robert, architect, engr.; b. Charleston, S.C., Aug. 12, 1781; s. William and Anne (Taylor) M.; attended Coll. of Charleston; m. Eliza Smith, 1808, 4 children including Sarah, Mary. Studied under Thomas Jefferson; designed Congregational Ch. (the "circular ch."), 1804; supervised erection Bank of Phila.; adopted for 1st time in Am. the auditorium type of plan suited for preaching a service; designed Washington Hall, 1809; rebuilt for municipal offices some wings of Old State House (Independence Hall, Phila.), 1812; designed Brockenbrough house in Richmond, Va. which became "White House of Confederacy"; designed important pub. monument to Washington in Balt., 1814; made pres., chief engr. Balt. Waterworks Co.; returned to Charleston, 1820, became mem. Bd. Pub. Works; pub. bldgs. erected by him (on plans either made or revised by him) in Charleston include: fire-proof record bldg., begun 1822, State Hosp. for Insane at Columbia, S.C.; designed Potomac Bridge, circa 1830; apptd. by Fed. govt. as "architect of pubilc bldgs.," 1836-51, designed Treasury, Patent Office, Post Office, Washington, D.C.; main archtl. achievement was victory in competition for design of Washington Monument, at capital, completed in 1884; mem. Soc. of Artists organized in Phila., 1810, 1st sec. Author: Treatise on Inland Navigation, 1820; Guide to the Capitol of the U.S., 1832 (appeared 1834). Died Mar. 3, 1855.

MILLS, Robert, mcht., banker; b. Todd County, Ky, Mar. 9, 1809; s. Adam and Janet (Graham) M.; attended Cumberland Coll. (now George Peabody Coll. for Tchrs.), Nashville, Tenn., 1826-27; m. Elizabeth McNeel, 1 child. Joined an elder brother, Andrew G., in merchandizing at Brazoria, Tex., 1830; fought in Battle of Velasco, 1832; took over bus. (after brother's death) under name R. & D. G. Mills, 1835, moved firm to Galveston, Tex., 1849 (in absence of banks, co. counter-signed questionable notes of No. Bank of Miss. at Holy Springs, between $25,000 and $500,000 of this money circulated, resulting in co. bankruptcy, 1873); became partner Mills, McDowell & Co., N.Y., also McDowell and Mills & Co., New Orleans, 1850. Died Galveston, Apr. 13, 1888; buried Trinity Ch., Galveston.

MILLS, Samuel John, clergyman, missionary; b. Torringford, Conn., Apr. 21, 1783; s. Rev. Samuel John and Esther (Robbins) M.; grad. Williams Coll., 1809, Andover Theol. Sem., 1812. Led religious revival at Williams Coll., 1806; partly responsible for founding Am. Bd. Commrs. for Fgn. Missions, circa 1810; licensed to preach, 1812; missionary preacher from Conn. and Mass. to West, 1812, 14-15; ordained to ministry Congregational Ch., 1815; instigator, chief organizer Am. Bible Soc., United Fgn. Mission Soc., a sch. for tng. Negro preachers, 1816; despatched to Africa to find suitable territory for purchase by Am. Colonization Soc.; called "father of foreign missionary work in Christian America". Died on return voyage from Africa, June 16, 1818; buried Atlantic Ocean.

MILLSON, John Singleton, congressman; b. Norfolk, Va., Oct. 1, 1808; studied law. Admitted to Va. bar, 1829, began practice in Norfolk; Democratic presdl. elector, 1844, 48; mem. U.S. Ho. of Reps. (Dem.) from Va., 31st-36th congresses, 1849-61. Died Norfolk, Mar. 1, 1874; buried Cedar Grove Cemetery, Norfolk.

MILLWARD, William, congressman; b. Phila., June 30, 1822; attended pub. schs. Engaged in leather mfg.; mem. U.S. Ho. of Reps. (Whig) from Pa., 34th, 36th congresses, 1855-57, 59-61; U.S. marshal for Eastern Pa., 1861-65; apptd. dir. U.S. Mint, 1866, appointment not confirmed by Senate. Died Kirkwood, Del., Nov. 28, 1871; buried Laurel Hill Cemetery, Phila.

MILMORE, Martin, sculptor; b. Sligo, Ireland, Sept. 14, 1844; ed. Lowell Inst.; studied sculpture in Rome, 1870-75. Came to U.S., 1851; executed "Phosphor" and "Devotion", 1863; commd. to execute 3 granite figures for Boston Hort. Hall, "Ceres", "Flora", "Pomona", 1864-66; design accepted by City of Boston for Roxbury Soldiers Monument, Forest Hills Cemetery, 1867; most significant undertaking was Soldiers' and Sailors' Monument erected Boston Commons, 1877; executed busts of Pope Pius IX, Wendell Phillips, Ralph Waldo Emerson, Rome, 1870-75; other busts include Abraham Lincoln, Gen. Grant, Daniel Webster, Gen. Ticknor; executed (with brother Joseph) granite Sphinx commemorating Union dead, Mt. Auburn Cemetery, Cambridge, Mass.; other works include statue of Gen. Sylvanus Taylor, "Weeping Lion". Died Boston Highlands, Mass., July 21, 1883; buried Forest Hills Cemetery, Roxbury, Mass.

MILNER, John Turner, businessman, legislator; b. Pike County, Ga., Sept. 29, 1826; s. Willis Jay and Elizabeth (Turner) M.; attended U. Ga., 1843-46; m. Flora J. Caldwell, Dec. 30, 1855, 4 children. Gained practical insight into railroad constrn. in youth from his father; prin. asst. in building Macon & Western R.R., 1848; went to Cal. during gold rush, 1849; became city surveyor San Jose (Cal.), circa 1850; returned to Ga., 1854, built Montgomery & West Point R.R.; granted subsidy (with Frank Gilmer) by Confederate Govt. to erect Oxmoor (Ala.) furnaces to provide war materials, during Civil War; asso. with S.& N. Ala. R.R.; formed Elyton Land Co. (which founded Birmingham, Ala.), 1871; organized Newcastle Coal & Iron Co., 1873, Milner Coal & R.R. Co., 1879; mem. Ala. Senate from Jefferson County, 1888-96. Died Newcastle, Ala., Aug. 18, 1898.

MILNER, Moses Embree (known as California Joe), scout, soldier; b. Stanford, Ky., May 8, 1829. Went to Cal., 1849, later to Ore.; served in Berdan's Sharpshooters, U.S. Army during Civil War; scout under Gen. George Custer, 7th Cavalry, 1868; served in Washita expdn., other Indian campaigns, later in Black Hills Expdn., 1875; joined 5th Cavalry as guide, 1876; shot in the back by Tom Newcombe (an old enemy), 1876. Died Camp Robinson, S.D., Oct 29, 1876.

MILNES, William, Jr., congressman; b. Yorkshire, Eng., Dec. 8, 1827; s. William Milnes; attended pub. schs. Came to U.S., 1829, settled in Pottsville, Pa.; engaged in mining and shipping coal; moved to Va., 1865, settled in Shanandoah; engaged in iron bus.; mem. Va. Ho. of Dels., 1870-71; mem. U.S. Ho. of Reps. (Conservative) from Va., 41st Congress, Jan. 27, 1870-71. Died Shenandoah, Aug. 14, 1889; buried Old Cemetery, Shenandoah.

MILNOR, James, congressman, clergyman; b. Phila., June 20, 1773; attended Phila. Grammar Sch., U. Pa.; studied law and theology. Admitted to Pa. bar, 1794, began practice in Norristown; moved to Phila., 1797, practiced law; mem. Phila. Common Council, 1800; mem. Select Council, 1805-10, pres. 1808-09; mem. U.S. Ho. of Reps. (Federalist) from Pa., 12th Congress, 1811-13; ordained to ministry Protestant Episcopal Ch.; apptd. asst. minister St. Peter's Ch., Phila., 1814; rector St. George's Ch., N.Y.C., 1816-44. Died N.Y.C., Apr. 8, 1844; buried Greenwood Cemetery, Bklyn.

MILNOR, William, congressman, mayor Phila.; b. Phila., June 26, 1769. Engaged in merc. bus., Phila.; mem. U.S. Ho. of Reps. (Federalist) from Pa., 10th-11th, 14th, 17th congresses, 1807-11, 15-17, 21-May 8, 1822 (resigned); mayor Phila., 1829-30. Died Burlington, N.J., Dec. 13, 1848; buried St. Mary's Churchyard, Burlington.

MILROY, Robert Huston, army officer, Indian agt.; b. Washington County, Ind., June 11, 1816; s. Samuel and Martha (Huston) M.; B.A., Master of Mil. Science, Norwich U., Vt., 1843; LL.B., Ind. U., 1850; m. Mary Armitage, May 17, 1849, 7 children. Served in Mexican War; admitted to Ind. bar, 1850; elected del. to 2d Ind. Constnl. Conv., 1850; organized volunteer company in Rennselaer, Ind., made capt.; commd. col. 9th Regt. Ind. Volunteers, 1861; promoted brig. gen. U.S Volunteers, 1861, maj. gen., 1862; served under Gens. McClellan and Rosecrans in Western Va., under Gen. Fremont in Shenandoah Valley, as maj. gen. commanded 2d div. VIII Army Corps; a trustee Wabash and Erie Canal; became supt. Indian affairs for Wash., 1872; Indian agt. with hdqrs. at Olympia, Wash., 1875-85. Died Olympia, Mar. 29, 1890.

MILTON, John, gov. Fla.; b. Jefferson County, Ga., Apr. 20, 1807; s. Homer Virgil and Elizabeth (Robinson) M.; m. Susan Cobb, Dec. 9, 1826; m. 2d, Caroline Howze, 1840. Admitted to Ga. bar; capt. Mobile Volunteers in Seminole War; Democratic elector for Fla., 1848; mem. Fla. Senate, 1848-49; gov. Fla., 1861-65, did utmost to raise troops for Confederacy and to keep them supplied with clothing and hosp. supplies, vigorously used militia for defense of state with result that Fla. capitol was only So. state capitol remaining uncaptured at end of war; took his own life at fall of Confederacy. Died Marriana, Fla., Apr. 1, 1865.

MINER, Ahiman Louis, congressman; b. Middletown, Vt., Sept. 23, 1804; attended Castleton (Vt.) Acad.; studied law, Poultney and Rutland, Vt. Admitted to the bar, 1832; practiced law, Wallingford, Vt., 1833-36; moved to Manchester, Vt., 1836, practiced law; clk. Vt. Ho. of Reps., 1836-37, mem., 1838-39, 46, 54; mem. Vt. Senate, 1840; state's atty. for Bennington County (Vt.), 1843-44; register of probate, 7 years; judge of probate, 1846-49; justice of peace, 1846-86; mem. U.S. Ho. of Reps. (Whig) from Vt., 32d Congress, 1851-53. Died Manchester, July 19, 1886; buried Dellwood Cemetery, Manchester.

MINER, Alonzo Ames, clergyman, coll. pres ; b. Lempster, N.H., Aug. 17, 1814; s. Benjah and Amanda (Carey) Ames; S.T.D. (hon.), Harvard, 1863; LL.D. (hon.), Tufts, 1875; m. Maria S. Perley, Aug. 24, 1836. Asso. prin. of an acad., Cavendish, Vt., 1834; head acad., Unity, N.Y., 1835-39; ordained Universalist preacher, 1839; pastor School St. Ch., 2d Universalist Soc. of Boston, 1848; pres. Tufts, 1862-74, also trustee; active in promoting devel. Dean Acad., Mass., Goddard Sem., Vt. Author: Bible Exercises; Old Forts Taken. Died Boston, June 14, 1895.

MINER, Charles (pen name: John Harwood), editor, congressman; b. Norwich, Conn., Feb. 1, 1780; s. Seth and Anna (Charlton) M.; m. Letitia Wright, Jan. 16, 1804, 10 children. Published (with brother Asher) Luzerne Federalist and Susquehannah Intelligencer, Wilkes-Barre, Pa., 1802, sole propr., publisher, 1804-09, 10-11; published journal Gleaner and Luzerne Intelligencer, 1811-16; wrote and published "The Ballad of James Bird;" mem. Pa. Ho. of Reps., 1807-09, 12; mem. firm Hillhouse, Miner and Cist, responsible for sending 1st boatload of anthracite coal down Schuylkill River to Phila.; went to Phila., 1816, became editor and part owner The American; bought Chester and Del. Federalist, West Chester, Pa., changed name to Village Record, 1817, published, 1817-32; mem. U.S. Ho. of Reps. from Pa., 19th-20th congresses, 1825-29, offered series of resolutions in favor of abolishing slavery in Washington (D.C.), and its eventual extinction in U.S., 1826, drew up and introduced to Congress 1st resolutions on silk culture; wrote History of Wyoming, 1845; originated phrase "to have an axe to grind." Died Wilkes-Barre, Pa., Oct. 26, 1865; buried Hollenback Cemetery, Wilkes-Barre.

MINER, Myrtilla, educator; b. Brookfield, N.Y., Mar. 4, 1815; attended Newton Inst., Miss., 2 years. Opened normal sch. for free colored girls, Washington, D.C., 1851, often attacked, threatened, but persevered, sch. placed under bd. trustees, 1856, incorporated by U.S. Congress as Inst. for Edn. of Colored Youth in Washington, 1863. Died Washington, Dec. 17, 1864; buried Georgetown, D.C.

MINER, Phineas, congressman; b. Winchester, Conn., Nov. 27, 1777; studied law. Admitted to Conn. bar, 1797, began practice in Winchester; elected justice of peace, 1809; mem. Conn. Ho. of Reps., 1809, 11, 13, 14, 16, 23, 27, 29, 35; moved to Litchfield, Conn., 1816; mem. Conn. Senate, 1830-31; mem. U.S. Ho. of Reps. (Whig) from Conn., Dec. 1, 1834-35; elected judge of Conn. Probate Ct. for Litchfield dist., 1838. Died Litchfield, Sept. 15, 1839; buried East Burying Ground, Litchfield.

MINOR, John Barbee, lawyer, educator; b. "Minor's Folly," Louisa County, Va., June 2, 1813; s. Lancelot and Mary Overton (Tompkins) M.; attended Kenyon Coll., Gambier, O., 1831; grad. U. Va., 1834; m. Martha Macon Davis; m. 2d, Anne Jacqueline Fisher Colston; m. 3d, Ellen Temple Hill; 8 children. Admitted to Va. bar, circa 1834, began practice of law, Buchanan; prof. law U. Va., 1845-95, raised sch.'s standards and increased enrollment, after Civil War, borrowed money on his personal credit to prepare for session of 1865-66. Author: The Virginia Report 1799-1800, published 1850; Institutes of Common and Statute Law, 1875-95; Exposition of the Law of Crimes and Punishments, 1894. Died July 29, 1895.

MINOR, Lucian, temperance advocate; b. Louisa County, Va., Apr. 24, 1802; s. Lancelot and Mary (Tompkins) M.; grad. Coll. William and Mary, 1823; m. Lavinia Price, May 4, 1846, 4 children. Commonwealth's atty. for Louisa County, 1828-52; author "Letters from New England," publishd in So. Lit. Messenger, Nov. 1834-Apr. 1835, also "Address of Education . . before the Institute of Education at Hampden-Sydney College," 1835; mem. conv. temperance advocates, Charlottesville, Va., 1834; officer, lectr., editorial supr. Sons of Temperance of U.S.; chmn. central com. Va. prohibition movement, prepared its legislative papers; published "The Temperance Reformation in Virginia" in So. Lit. Messenger, July 1850; became prof. law Coll. William and Mary, 1855. Author: Reasons for Abolishing the Liquor Traffic, 1853. Died Williamsburg, Va., July 8, 1858.

MINOR, Virginia Louisa, suffragette; b. Goochland County, Va., Mar. 27, 1824; d. Warner and Maria (Timberlake) Minor; m. Francis Minor, Aug. 31, 1843; 1 son, Francis Gilmer. Active in welfare and relief work among sick and wounded in St. Louis area hosps. during Civil War; launched woman-suffrage movement in Mo., 1866; took leading part in organizing Woman Suffrage Assn. of Mo., 1867, elected pres.; made unsuccessful attempt to register to vote, 1872; with husband tried unsuccessfully to sue for damages in Circuit Ct. of St. Louis; appeared before Senate Com. on Woman Suffrage to reiterate arguments, 1889; 1st woman in U.S. to claim suffrage as a right and not a favor; hon. v.p. Interstate Woman Suffrage Conv., Kansas City, 1892. Died St. Louis, Aug. 14, 1894.

MINOT, George Richards, jurist; b. Boston, Dec. 22, 1758; s. Stephen and Sarah (Clark) M.; grad. Harvard, 1778, M.A., 1781; m. Mary Speakman, 1783, 2 children, including George Richards. Admitted to Mass. bar; clk. Mass. Ho. of Reps., 1781; sec. Mass. Conv. to adopt U.S. Constn., 1787; apptd. judge probate Suffolk County (Mass.), 1792; mem. Amicable Fire Soc.; pres. Mass. Charitable Fire Soc.; an original mem. Mass. Hist. Soc., librarian, 1793-95, treas., 1796-99. chief justice Mass. Ct. Common Pleas, 1799; judge Municipal Ct. of Boston, 1800. Author: The History of the Insurrection in Massachusetts in the Year Seventeen Hundred and Eighty-Six and the Rebellion Consequent Thereon, 1788; Continuation of the History of the Province of Massachusetts Bay from the Year 1748, published 1798. Died Boston, Jan. 2, 1802.

MINTO, Walter, mathematician; b. Cowden Knowes, Merse, Scotland, Dec. 5, 1753; grad. U. Edinburgh (Scotland); LL.D. (hon.), U. Aberdeen, 1787; m. Mary Skelton. Wrote Researches into Some Parts of the Theory of the Planets, 1783; came to Am., 1786; became prin. Erasmus Hall, Flatbush, L.I., N.Y.; became prof. mathematics and natural philosophy Coll. of N.J. (now Princeton), 1787, treas. coll. Author: Inaugural Oration on the Progress and Importance of the Mathematical Sciences, 1788. Died Princeton, N.J., Oct. 21, 1796; buried Princeton Cemetery.

MINTURN, Robert Bowne, mcht.; b. N.Y.C., Nov. 16, 1805; s. William and Sarah (Bowne) M.; m. Anna Wendell, June 2, 1835. Sr. partner firm Grinnell, Minturn & Co. by 1832; one of greatest Am. shipowners of his day; commr. of emigration to improve condition of incoming foreigners; helped found Assn. for Improving Condition of Poor and St. Luke's Hosp.; 1st pres. Union League Club, N.Y.C. Died N.Y.C., Jan. 9, 1866.

MINUIT, Peter, colonial gov.; b. Wesel, Dutchy of Cleves (Germany), 1580. Dir.-gen. New Netherlands, 1626-31; purchased Manhattan Island from Indian sachems for trinkets valued at $24; made New Amsterdam the rallying point of isolated settlements North and South of Manhattan; started diplomatic relations with Gov. Bradford, opened trade with Plymouth colonists, 1627; commd. by West India Co. to establish Swedish colony on Delaware Bay; as gov. group arrived at mouth of South River, or Delaware; concluded contract with Indian chiefs purchasing tract of land on right bank of Delaware (now Trenton, N.J.); gave country name New Sweden; built Ft. Christina on site of present Wilmington, Del. Lost at sea, 1638.

MIRANDA, Francisco de, see De Miranda, Francisco.

MIRO, Esteban Rodriquez, colonial gov.; b. Catalonia, Spain, 1744; m. Celeste Macarty. In campaign against Portugal, 1762; col. and comdr. of regular La. Regt. during Am. Revolution; made acting Spanish gov. of La., 1782, appointment made permanent, 1785; promoted to brig. gen., 1789; intendency combined with governorship, 1788, had duties of both offices until 1791; encouraged fgn. immigration and partial opening of the Mississippi River to Western Americans; notorious for his intrigue with James Wilkinson who conspired with Miro to gain trade monopolies for himself and, it is said, to separate Ky. region from U.S. and turn it over to Spain; however Miro in most instances was merely following orders from Madrid. Died Spain, 1795.

MITCHEL. Charles Burton, senator; b. Gallatin, Tenn., Sept. 19, 1815; grad. U. Nashville (Tenn.), 1833, Jefferson Med. Coll., Phila., 1836. Moved to Washington, Ark., practiced medicine, 25 years; mem. Ark. Ho. of Reps., 1848; receiver of public moneys, 1853-56; mem. U.S. Senate from Ark., Mar. 4-July 11, 1861; mem. Confederate Senate from Ark., 1861-64. Died Little Rock, Ark., Sept. 20, 1864; buried Presbyn. Cemetery, Washington, Ark.

MITCHEL, Ormsby MacKnight, astronomer, army officer; b. Morganfield, Ky., July 28, 1809; s. John and Elizabeth (MacAlister) M.; grad. U.S. Mil. Acad., 1829; LL.D. (hon.), Harvard, 1851, Washington Coll., 1853, Hamilton Coll., 1856; m. Louisa (Clark) Trask, 1831. Asst. prof. mathematics U.S. Mil. Acad., 1829; chief engr. Rittle Miami R.R., 1836-37; prof. mathematics, philosophy, astronomy Cincinnati Coll., 1836-46; putlished mag. Sidereal Messenger, 1846-1848; adj. gen. Ohio, 1848; inventor chronograph, 1848; chief engr. Ohio & Miss. R.R., 1848-53; dir., largely responsible for erection Cincinnati Observatory; largely responsible for erecting 2d largest telescope, and largest on Western continent under auspices of Cincinnati Astron. Soc., 1845; made approximately 50,000 observations of faint stars between 1854-59; discovered the duplicity of stars (e.g. Antares); dir. Dudley Observatory, Albany, N.Y., 1859; apptd. brig. gen. U.S. Volunteers, 1861; assigned to command Dept. of Ohio; brevetted maj. gen. volunteers, 1862; surprised and captured Huntsville, Ala. without firing a gun, thus obtained control of Memphis & Charleston R.R ; promoted maj. gen. volunteers; transferred to command Dept. of South and X Army Corps, Sept. 17, 1862. Author: Planetary and Stellar Worlds, 1848; Popular Astronomy, 1860. Died Beaufort, S.C., Oct. 30, 1862.

MITCHELL, Alexander, congressman, financier; b. Ellon, Aberdeenshire, Scotland, Oct. 18, 1817; s. John and Margaret (Lendrum) M.; m. Martha Reed, Oct. 7, 1841, 1 son, John L. Came to Am., 1839; sec. Wis. Marine and Fire Ins Co. (later became state bank), Milw., 1839, pres., 1853, principal owner, 1854; 1st pres. Wis. Bankers Assn.; 1st mem. Milw. Debt Commn., 1861; restored and enlarged Milw. & St. Paul R.R. Co., became pres., 1865; pres. C. & N.-W. Ry.; also N.W. Ins. co., 1869; mem. U.S. Ho. of Reps. from Wis., 42d-43d congresses, 1871-75; del.-at-large Nat. Democratic Conv., 1876; declined Dem. nomination for gov. Wis., 1877. Died N.Y.C., Apr. 19, 1887; buried Forest Home Cemetery, Milw.

MITCHELL, Anderson, congressman; b. nr. Milton, N.C., June 13, 1800; grad. U. N.C., 1821; studied law. Admitted to N.C. bar, began practice in Morganton, 1830; moved to Jefferson, N.C., 1831; clk. Ashe County (N.C.) Superior Ct., moved to Wilkesboro, N.C., 1835, practiced law; mem. U.S. Ho. of Reps. (Whig) from N.C., 27th Congress, Apr. 27, 1842-43; mem. N.C. Senate, 1860; del. N.C. Secession Conv., 1861, voted against secession; judge N.C. Superior Ct., 1865-75. Died Statesville, N.C., Dec. 24, 1876; buried Presbyn. Cemetery, Statesville.

MITCHELL, Charles F., congressman; b. N.Y.C., circa 1808; attended pub. schs. Moved to Lockport, N.Y., 1829; apptd. fireman, Lockport, 1829; engaged in milling bus., 1835; mem. U.S. Ho. of Reps. (Whig) from N.Y., 25th-26th congresses, 1837-41; engaged in milling in the West.

MITCHELL, Charles Le Moyne, congressman; b. New Haven, Conn., Aug. 6, 1844; grad. Cheshire Acad., 1863. Traveled in Europe, Asia, Africa; engaged in mfg. silver-plated ware and brass, New Haven; mem. Conn. Ho. of Reps., 1877; mem. U.S. Ho. of Reps. (Democrat) from Conn., 48th-49th congresses, 1883-87; moved to N.Y.C., 1886. Died N.Y.C., Mar. 1, 1890; buried Evergreen Cemetery, New Haven.

MITCHELL, David Brydie, gov. Ga., Indian agt.; b. Muthill, Perthshire, Scotland, Oct. 22, 1766; s. John Mitchell. Came to Savannah, Ga., 1783; elected atty. gen. Ga., 1795; mem. Ga. Ho. of Reps., 1796; commd. maj. gen. Ga. Militia, 1804; gov. Ga., 1809-13, 15-17, liberal supporter of internal improvements, edn., road bldg., especially frontier defense, signer 1st Ga. law against dueling; apptd. U.S. Indian agt. to Creek Nation, 1817, concluded treaty in which Creeks ceded 1,500,000 acres of land to Ga., 1818, agy. terminated on charge that he was smuggling African slaves into the vicinity,, 1821, (charge upheld by Pres. Monroe). Died Milledgeville, Ga., Apr. 22, 1837.

MITCHELL, David Dawson, fur-trader, army officer, supt. Indian affairs; b. Louisa County, Va., July 31, 1806; m. Martha Berry, 1840, 6 children. Entered employ of Am. Fur. Co., St. Louis, 1828; built Ft. Mackenzie, 1832; supt. Indian affairs Central Div., 1841-53; lt. col. 2d Mo. Regt., 1846; promoted orgn. of corp. known as Mo. & Cal. Overland Mail & Transp. Co., 1855, pres.; helped supply mules to U.S. for Utah Expdn., 1858. Died May 23, 1861.

MITCHELL, Elisha, geologist, botanist; b. Washington, Conn., Aug. 19, 1793; s. Abner and Phoebe (Eliot) M.; grad. Yale, 1813; attended Andover Theol. Sem., 1817-18; D.D. (hon.), U. Ala., 1838; m. Maria Sybil North, Nov. 19, 1819, 7 children. Tutor, Yale, 1816-17; prof. mathematics and natural philosophy, U. N.C., 1818-25, prof. chemistry, mineralogy and geology, 1825-57; licensed to preach, 1817; ordained to ministry Presbyn. Ch., 1821; made geol. and bot. excursions throughout N.C.; contbd. articles to Am. Journal of Sci., also other publs.; 1st to measure height of highest mountain in U.S. East of Rockies, Black Mountain (now called Mitchell's Peak), N.C. Author: Elements of Geology, 1842. Killed by fall during storm while exploring Black Mountain, June 27, 1857; buried Asheville, N.C.; reinterred top of Black Mountain, 1858.

MITCHELL, George Edward physician congressman, army officer; b. Head of Elk (now Elkton), Md., Mar. 3, 1781; s. Abraham and Mary (Thompson) M.; grad. med. dept. U. Pa., 1805. Practiced medicine, Elkton, 1806-12; mem. Md. Ho. of Dels., 1808-09; pres. Md. Exec. Council, 1809-12; recruited co. of volunteers from Cecil County (Md.); commd. lt. col. 3d Md. Arty., 1813; brevetted col., 1814; mem. U.S. Ho. of Reps. (Democrat) from Md., 18th-19th, 21st-22d congresses, 1823-27, 29-32, wrote and introduced resolution inviting Lafayette to Am., 1824. Died Washington, D.C., June 28, 1832; buried Congressional Cemetery, Washington.

MITCHELL, Henry, congressman; b. Woodbury, Conn., 1784; grad. med. dept. Yale, 1804. Practiced medicine, Norwich, N.Y.; mem. N.Y. Assembly, 1827; mem. U.S. Ho. of Reps. (Jacksonian Democrat) from N.Y., 23d Congress, 1833-35. Died Norwich, Jan. 12, 1856; buried Mt. Hope Cemetery, Norwich.

MITCHELL, Isaac, editor; b. nr. Albany, N.Y., circa 1759. Editor, Am. Farmer and Dutchess County Advertiser, Poughkeepsie, N.Y., 1799-1801; became editor the Guardian, Poughkeepsie, 1801, owner (renamed paper Polit. Barometer), 1802; editor Republican Crisis, Albany, 1806-12; became owner Rep. Herald, Poughkeepsie, 1812, also began publishing Northern Politician. Author: The Asylum or Alonzo and Melissa (completely plagiarized by Daniel Jackson, Jr., 1811, reprinted by Jackson, 1824, became best seller), 1811. Died Nov. 26, 1812.

MITCHELL, James Coffield, congressman; b. Staunton, Va., Mar. 1786; attended common schs.; studied law. Admitted to Va. bar, practiced law; moved to Rhea County, Tenn.; solicitor gen. 2d Dist. of Tenn., 1813-17; moved to Athens, Tenn., 1817; mem. U.S. Ho. of Reps., 19th-20th congresses, 1825-29; judge 11th Tenn. Circuit, 1830-36; moved to Hinds County, Miss.; settled nr. Jackson, Miss., circa, 1837, engaged in farming; unsuccessful Whig candidate for gov. Miss. Author: Mitchell's Justice. Died nr. Jackson, Aug. 7, 1843.

MITCHELL, James S., congressman; b. nr. Rossville, Pa., 1784; attended common schs. Mem. Pa. Ho. of Reps., 1812-14; mem. U.S. Ho. of Reps. (Democrat) from Pa., 17th-19th congresses, 1821-27; moved to Jefferson County, O., 1827, later to Belleville, Ill. Died Belleville, 1844; buried Dillsburg, Pa.

MITCHELL, John, physician, map maker; probably born Brit. Isles; ed. U. Edinburgh (Scotland). Came to Va., 1725; justice of peace Middlesex County (Va.), 1738; practiced medicine in Va., circa 1725-46; went to Eng., 1746; elected fellow Royal Soc., 1747; made Map of the British & French Dominions in North America with the Roads, Distances, Limits, and Extent of the Settlements, published, London, Eng., 1755 (most important map in Am. history, used in various treaties, border adjustments up to 1932, basis for Webster Ashburton Treaty, 1842, Wis.-Mich. boundary dispute, 1926, others). His method of treating yellow fever thought to have saved more than 6,000 lives in Phila. during epidemic of 1793. Died, 1768.

MITCHELL, John, congressman; b. nr. Newport, Pa., Mar. 8, 1781; attended common schs. Moved to Bellefonte, Pa., 1800, clk. in ironworks; elected sheriff Centre County (Pa.), 1818; engr., surveyor; laid out Centre and Kishacoquillas Turnpike, 1821; constructed numerous turnpikes in Pa.; mem. Pa. Ho. of Reps., 1822-23; mem. U.S. Ho. of Reps. (Democrat) from Pa., 19th-20th congresses, 1825-29; surveyor of proposed canal routes between Susquehanna and Potomac rivers, 1826; engr. Erie Canal extension, 1827; canal commr. Pa., 1829; Dem. presdl. elector, 1826; moved to Bridgewater, Pa., 1842, engaged in civil engring., iron mfg.; mem. Canal Survey Commn., 1845-49. Died Bridgewater, Aug. 3, 1849; buried Old Beaver Cemetery, Bridgewater.

MITCHELL, John, journalist; b. Camnish, County Londonderry, Ireland, Nov. 3, 1815; s. Rev. John and Mary (Haslett) M.; grad. Trinity Coll., Dublin, Ireland, 1834; m. Jane Verner, Feb. 3, 1837. Practiced law, Newry, Ireland, 1840-45; joined nationalist movement Young Ireland, 1845; mem. editorial staff of Nation, Newry, 1845-47; founded, edited United Irishman, Newry, advocated armed resistance to Eng., 1847-48; banished from Ireland for 14 years for revolutionary activities, 1848; in Bermuda, 1848-49, Van Diemen's Land, 1851-53; came to U.S., 1853; published Citizen, N.Y.C., 1854-55; advocated Irish independence and carried on debate with abolitionists; published Southern Citizen, Knoxville, Tenn., 1857-59; correspondent for several Am. newspapers, Paris, France, 1860-62; editor Richmond (Va.) Enquirer, 1863-65, Irish Citizen, N.Y.C., 1867-72; returned to Ireland, 1875. Author: Jail Journal, 1854; The Last Conquest of Ireland (Perhaps), 1861; History of Ireland from the Treaty of Limerick, 1868. Died Cork, Ireland, Mar. 20, 1875.

MITCHELL, John Kearsley, physician, chemist; b. Shepherdstown, Jefferson County, Va. (now W. Va.), May 12, 1793; s. Alexander and Elizabeth (Kearsly) M.; grad. U. Edinburgh (Scotland); M.A., U. Pa., 1819; m. Sarah Matilda Henry, 1822, 9 children including Silas Weir. Ship's surgeon on voyages to China and East Indies, 1819-21; prof. medicine and physiology Phila. Med. Inst., 1824; lectr. chemistry Franklin Inst., 1833-38; prof. medicine Jefferson Med. Coll., Phila., 1841-58. Author: Indecision, a Tale of the Far West and Other Poems, 1839; On the Cryptogamous Origin of Malarious and Epidemical Fevers, 1849. Died Phila., Apr. 4, 1858.

MITCHELL, Jonathan, clergyman; b. Halifax, Eng., 1624; s. Matthew and Susan (Butterfield) M.; grad. Harvard, 1647; m. Margaret (Boradel) Shepard, Nov. 19, 1650. Came to Am., 1635; ordained to ministry Congregational Ch., 1650; pastor ch., Cambridge, Mass., 1650-68; became life fellow of Harvard, 1650; leading advocate of Half-way Covenant adopted by Synod of 1662 (most outstanding achievement); published sermons A Discourse of the Glory to Which God Hath Called Believers by Jesus Christ, 1677; other writings include: Letter of Counsel, 1664, An Election Sermon, 1667, A Letter Concerning the Subjects of Baptism, 1675. Died Cambridge, July 9, 1668.

MITCHELL, Lucy Myers Wright, art historian; b. Urumiah, Persia, Mar. 20, 1845; d. Rev. Austin Hazen and Catherine (Myers) W.; ed. Mt. Holyoke Sem.; m. Samuel S. Mitchell, 1867. Family returned to Am., 1860; missionary (with husband) to Syria; prepared manuscript of modern Syriac; in Rome, 1876-78; gave parlor lectures to ladies on Greek and Roman sculpture; made regular mem. Imperial German Archeol. Inst.; Author: A History of Ancient Sculpture, 1883; Selections from Ancient Sculpture (plates to accompany above vol.). Died Lausanne, Switzerland, Mar. 10, 1888.

MITCHELL, Maria, astronomer, educator; b. Nantucket Island, Mass., Aug. 1, 1818; d. William and Lydia (Coleman) Mitchell; LL.D. (hon.), Hanover Coll., 1882, Columbia, 1887. Assisted father in his chronometer ratings during her youth; apptd. librarian Town of Atheneum, Nantucket Island, Mass., 1836; discovered new comet, Oct. 1847; recipient gold medal from King of Denmark; 1st woman elected to membership Am. Acad. Arts and Scis., hon. mem., 1848, later fellow; apptd. computer Am. Ephemeric and Nautical Almanac; 1st prof. astronomy Vassar Coll., 1865-88; elected mem. Am. Philos. Soc., 1869. Died Lynn, Mass., June 28, 1889.

MITCHELL, Nahum, jurist, congressman; b. East Bridgewater, Mass., Feb. 12, 1769; s. Cushing and Jennet (Orr) M.; A.B., Harvard, 1789; m. Nabby Lazell, 1794, 2 sons, 3 daus. Admitted to Mass. bar, 1792; mem. Mass. Ho. Reps., 1798-1802, 09-10, 12-13, 39-40; mem. U.S. Ho. of Reps. from Mass., 8th Congress, 1803-05; mem. Mass. Senate, 1813-14; mem. Mass. Gov.'s Council, 1814-20; treas. Mass., 1821-26; justice Mass. Circuit Ct. of Common Pleas, 1811-21, chief justice, 1819-21; chosen chmn. commrs. in charge of route for Boston & Albany R.R., 1827; helped found, endow Plymouth County Acad., 1799, trustee, 54 years; pres. Bridgewater's 1st lyceum, 1827; mem. Mass. Hist. Soc., 1818, librarian, 1835-36, treas., 1839-44. Assisted in compiling: The Columbian and European Harmony: or Bridgewater Collection of Sacred Music, 1802; History of the Early Settlement of Bridgewater, in Plymouth County, Mass., 1840. Died East Bridgewater, Aug. 1, 1853; buried Old Central St. Cemetery, East Bridgewater.

MITCHELL, Nathaniel, gov. Del., army officer; b. Laurel, Del., 1753; s. James and Margaret (Dogworthy) M.; m. Hannah Morris, 1 son, Theodore. Commd. capt. Continental Army, transferred to Col. Samuel Patterson's Del. Battalion of "Flying Camp."; transferred to Col. William Grayson's Additional Continental Regt., 1777, promoted maj., 1777; brigade maj. and insp. to Gen. Peter Muhlenberg, 1779; captured by British, imprisoned, then paroled, 1781; mem Congress of Confederation from Del., 1786-88; treas. Sussex County (Del.), 1788-1805; gov. Del., 1804-08; mem. Del. Ho. of Reps., 1808-10, Del. Senate, 1810-12. Died Laurel, Feb. 21, 1814; buried Broad Creek Episcopal Graveyard, Christ Church, Del.

MITCHELL, Robert, congressman; b. Westmoreland County, Pa., 1778; attended common schs.; studied medicine. Moved to Ohio, 1807; practiced medicine, Zanesville, O.; clk. to commrs. of Muskingum County (O.), 1811-12; county collector, 1812-13; served in War of 1812; mem. Ohio Ho. of Reps., 1815-16; judge ct. of common pleas, 1818; commd. brig. gen. Ohio Militia, 1822; mem. U.S. Ho. of Reps. (Democrat) from Ohio, 23d Congress, 1833-35. Died Zanesville, Nov. 13, 1848; buried Greenwood Cemetery, Zanesville.

MITCHELL, Robert Byington, territorial gov.; b. Mansfield, O., Apr. 4, 1823; m. Jennie St. John, 1855. Admitted to Ohio bar; served in Mexican War; Democratic mayor Mt. Gilead (O.), 1855; mem. lower house Kan. Territorial Legislature, 1857-59; del. to Leavenworth (Kan.) Constl. Conv., 1858; treas. Kan. Territory, 1859-61; del. to Charleston (S.C.) Conv., 1860; commd. col. 2d Kan. Volunteer Inf., brig. gen., 1862; chief of cavalry Army of Cumberland; apptd. to command Dist. of Kan., 1865; gov. N.M. Territory, 1866-69. Died Washington, D.C., Jan. 26, 1882.

MITCHELL, Samuel Augustus, geographer, publisher; b. Bristol, Conn., Mar. 20, 1752; s. William and Mary (Alton) M.; m. Rhoda Ann Fuller, Aug. 1815. Prepared textbooks, maps, geog. manuals, including Mitchell's Geographic Reader 1840; Map of the United States and Territories, 1861; published A New American Atlas, 1831; Mitchell's Traveller's Guide Through the United States, 1832; published successful series of sch. geography books; began series of Tourist's Pocket Maps of different states, 1834; published A New Universal Atlas, 1847; an outstanding figure in devel. of Am. geography. Died Phila., Dec. 18, 1868.

MITCHELL, Stephen Mix, senator; b. Wethersfield, Conn., Dec. 9, 1743; s. James and Rebecca (Mix) M.; grad. Yale, 1763, postgrad. (Berkeley scholar), 1763-66, LL.D. (hon.), 1807; m. Hannah Grant, Aug. 2, 1796, 6 sons, 5 daus. Tchr., Yale, 1766-69; admitted to Conn. bar, 1770; mem. Conn. Gen. Assembly, 1778-84; asso. judge Hartford County (Conn.) Ct., 1779-90, presiding judge, 1790-93; mem. Congress of Confederation, 1783-85; mem. Conn. Conv. which ratified U.S. Constn., 1788; mem. U.S. Senate from Conn., 1793-95; judge Conn. Supreme Ct., 1795-1807, chief justice, 1807-14; mem. Conn. Constl. Conv., 1818 Died Wethersfield, Sept. 30, 1835; buried Wethersfield Cemetery.

MITCHELL, Thomas Daché, physician; b. Phila., 1791; grad. U. Pa., 1812. Prof. animal and vegetable physiology St. John's Coll., Phila., 1812; physician Phila. Lazaretto, 1813-16; practiced medicine, Frankfort, Pa., 1822-31; prof. chemistry Miami U., Oxford, O., 1831, Med. Coll. of Ohio, 1832; coeditor Western Med. Gazette, 1832-33; prof. chemistry Med. Inst., Louisville, Ky., 1837; prof. chemistry Transylvania U., Lexington, Ky., 1837-39, prof. materia medica and therapeutics, 1839-49; prof. medicine, obstetrics, med. jurisprudence Phila. Coll. of Medicine, 1849-57; prof. materia medica Jefferson Med. Coll., 1857-65. Author: Elements of Chemical Philosophy, 1832; Hints on the Connexion of Labor with Study, as a Preventive of Diseases Peculiar to Students, 1832; Materia Medica and Therapeutics, 1850. Died May 13, 1865.

MITCHELL, Thomas Rothmaler, congressman; b. Georgetown, S.C., May 1783; grad. Harvard, 1802; studied law. Admitted to S.C. bar, 1808, began practice in Georgetown; mem. U.S. Ho. of Reps. from S.C., 17th, 19th-20th, 22d congresses, 1821-23, 25-29, 31-33. Died Georgetown, Nov. 2, 1837.

MITCHELL, William, banker, astronomer; b. Nantucket, Mass., Dec. 20, 1791; s. Pelez and Lydia (Cartwright) M.; M.A. (hon.), Brown U., 1848, Harvard, 1860; m. Lydia Coleman, Dec. 10, 1812, 10 children including Maria, Henry. Del. to Mass. Constl. Conv., 1820; master 1st free school of Nantucket, 1827; sec. Phoenix Marine Ins. Co., 1830; cashier Pacific Bank, 1837-61; mem. Mass. Senate, 1845; mem. council of Gov. George Briggs, 1848-49; pursued astronomy as hobby; pres. Nantucket Atheneum for 30 years; made observations of sta. positions for U.S. Coast Survey; mem. vis. com. Harvard Coll. Observatory, 1848-65; overseer Harvard, 1857-65; fellow Am. Acad. Arts and Scis.; mem. A.A.A.S. Died Poughkeepsie, N.Y., Apr. 1, 1869.

MITCHELL, William, actor, theater mgr.; b. Billquay, Eng., 1798. Came to U.S., 1836; made Am. debut as Grimes in The Man with the Carpet Bag and as Fern Baggs in The Wandering Minstrel, Nat. Theatre, N.Y.C., 1836; actor, N.Y.C., 1836-39; mgr. Olympic Theatre on Broadway, N.Y.C., 1839-59, produced some of most amazing series of seasons in history Am. stage, burlesque of Hamlet among most sensational prodns. Died N.Y.C., May 11, 1856.

MITCHELL, William, jurist; b. N.Y.C., Feb. 24, 1801; s. Edward and Cornelia (Anderson) M.; grad. Columbia Coll., 1820; m. Mary Berrien, June 2, 1841. Admitted to N.Y. bar, 1823; master in chancery, 1840; judge N.Y. Supreme Ct., 1849-54, chief justice, 1854-57; v.p. N.Y. Bar Assn. Died Morristown, N.J., Oct. 6, 1886.

MITCHELL, William, congressman; b. Root, N.Y., Jan. 19, 1807; attended pub. schs.; studied law. Admitted to the bar, 1836; moved to Kendallville, Ind., practiced law; 1st postmaster of Kendallville, 1836-46; mem. Ind. Ho. of Reps., 1841; justice of peace; mem. U.S. Ho. of Reps. (Republican) from Ind., 37th Congress, 1861-63; engaged in cotton bus. Died Macon, Ga., Sept. 11, 1865; buried Lake View Cemetery, Kendallville.

MITCHILL, Samuel Latham, physician, senator; b. North Hempstead, L.I., Aug. 20, 1764; s. Robert and Mary (Latham) M.; M.D., U. Edinburgh (Scotland), 1786; m. Catherine Akerly, June 23, 1799. Mem. N.Y. Legislature, 1791, 98, 1810; prof. natural history, chemistry, agr. Columbia, 1792, asso. prof. botany, 1793-95; gave mineral collection to Columbia museum for use of future tchrs.; a founder Soc. for Promotion of Agr., Arts and Manufactures; made mineral exploration of banks of Hudson River, 1796; a founder Medical Repository, 1797, editor, 23 years; mem. U.S. Ho. of Reps. from N.Y. (Democrat), 7th, 9th, 12th congresses, 1801-03, 05-07, 11-13; mem. U.S. Senate (Democrat) from N.Y., 1804-09; commd. to supervise constrn. of a steam war-vessel during War of 1812; prof. chemistry Coll. Physicians and Surgeons, N.Y.C., 1807, prof. natural history, 1808-20, prof. botany and materia medica, 1820-26; an organizer Rutgers Med. Coll., v.p., 1826-30; a founder N.Y. Lit. and Philos. Soc., 1814; prin. founder Lyceum of Natural History, 1817; surgeon gen. N.Y. State Militia, 1818. Author: Explanation of the Synopsis of Chemical Nomenclature and Arrangement, 1801; A Sketch of the Mineralogical History of N.Y., 1797, 1800, 02; most notable contbns. include papers on the fishes of N.Y., the origin of Indians, Indian poetry, Indian antiquities. Died Bklyn., Sept. 7, 1831; buried Greenwood Cemetery, Bklyn.

MIX, Edward Townsend, architect; b. New Haven, Conn., May 13, 1831; studied architecture, New Eng., 1848-55; m. Mary Hayes. Moved to Milw., 1856; state architect of Wis., 1874-79; mem. N.Y. State Inst. Architects; pres. Wis. State Archtl. League, 1888-90. Prin. works include: C. of C. Bldg., St. Paul's Ch., Mitchell's Bank (all Milw.); St. Paul R.R. Depot; St. Grace's Ch. (Mpls.). Died Mpls., Sept. 23, 1890.

MOFFAT, James Clement, church historian; b. Glencoe, Scotland, May 30, 1811; s. David Douglas and Margaret (Clement) M.; grad. Princeton, 1835; D.D. (hon.) Miami U., Oxford, O., 1853; m. Ellen Stewart, Oct. 13, 1840; m. 2d, Mary Matthews, Dec. 26, 1850; 8 children including Edward Stewart. Came to N.Y., 1833; prof. Latin and Greek, Lafayette Coll., 1839; prof. Latin and esthetics Miami U., 1841-52; licensed to preach, 1851, ordained, 1851; prof. Latin and history, then prof. Greek Princeton (N.J.), 1853-61; prof. ch. history Princeton Theol. Sem., 1861-78. Author: A Rhyme of the North Countrie, 1847; Life of Dr. Thomas Chalmers, 1853; Introduction to the Study of Aesthetics, 1856; Alwyn: A Romance of Study (poem), 1875; A Comparative History of Religions, 2 vols., 1871-73; Outlines of Church History, 1875; The Church in Scotland, 1882. Died Princeton, June 7, 1890.

MOFFATT, Seth Crittenden, congressman; b. Battle Creek, Mich., Aug. 10, 1841; grad. law dept. U. Mich., 1863. Admitted to Mich. bar, began practice in Traverse City; pros. atty. for Grand Traverse and Leelanaw counties (Mich.), 10 years; mem. Mich. Senate, 1871-72; del. Mich. Constl. Conv., 1873; register U.S. Land Office, Traverse City, 1874-78; mem. Mich. Ho. of Reps., 1881-82, speaker; del. Republican Nat. Conv., 1884; mem. U.S. Ho. of Reps. (Rep.) from Mich., 49th-50th congresses, 1885-87. Died Washington, D.C., Dec. 22, 1887 buried Oakwood Cemetery, Traverse City.

MOFFET, John, congressman; b. County Antrim, Ireland, Apr. 5, 1831; studied medicine U. Pa. Came to U.S., settled in Phila.; became an apothecary, 1853, also practiced medicine; mem. U.S. Ho. of Reps. (Democrat) from Pa., 41st Congress, Mar. 4-Apr. 9, 1869 (lost seat as result of contested election); del. Dem. nat. convs. Died Phila., June 19, 1884; buried Laurel Hill Cemetery, Phila.

MOFFITT, Hosea, congressman; b. Stephentown, N.Y., Nov. 17, 1757. Served from ensign to lt. 4th Regt., Albany County (N.Y.) Militia, during Revolutionary War; justice of peace, 1791; town clk., 1791, 97; mem. N.Y. Assembly, 1794-95, 1801; apptd. brig. gen. N.Y. Militia, 1806; supr. Town of Stephentown, 1806-09; sheriff Rensselaer County (N.Y.), 1810-11; mem. U.S. Ho. of Reps. (Federalist) from N.Y., 13th-14th congresses, 1813-17; mem. bd. mgrs. Rensselaer County Bible Soc., 1815. Died Stephentown, Aug. 31, 1825; buried Old Presbyn. Cemetery, Stephentown.

MOISE, Pennina, civic worker, poet; b. Charleston, S.C., Apr. 23, 1797; d. Abraham and Sarah Moise. Active in religious and welfare work; founded a small sch. for Jewish girls, Charleston; wrote poetry exclusively, after 1830; contbd. poems to mags. Occident, Am. Jewish Advocate, Godey's Lady's Book, Home Journal; work is characterized by 18th Century English classicism and romanticism; works include Fancy's Sketchbook, 1833; Hymns Written for the Use of Hebrew Congregations (best known work), 1856. Died Sept. 13, 1880.

MOLLENHAUER, Henry, cellist; b. Erfurt, Germany, Sept. 10, 1825; children include Henry, Adolph. Mem. Royal Orchestra, Stockholm, Sweden, 1853; toured U.S. with Thalberg, Gottschalk, Carlotta Patti, 1856-58; settled in Bklyn. as tchr. and concert cellist, founder Henry Mollenhauer Conservatory, 1868. Died Bklyn., Dec. 28, 1889.

MOLONY, Richard Sheppard, congressman; b. Northfield, N.H., June 28, 1811; grad. Dartmouth Med. Sch., 1838. Began practice of medicine, Belvidere, Ill., del. Democrat nat. convs., Balt., 1852, Chgo., 1884; mem. U.S. Ho. of Reps. (Dem.) from Ill., 32d Congress, 1851-53; moved to Humboldt, Neb., engaged in farming, 1866-91; declined Dem. nomination for U.S. sneator from Neb., 1882. Died Humboldt, Dec. 14, 1891; buried Belvidere Cemetery.

MOLYNEUX, Robert, clergyman, educator; b. Formby, Lancashire, Eng., July 24, 1738. Joined Soc. of Jesus, 1757; arrived in Md., 1771; appt. pastor St. Mary's Ch., Phila., 1773; pastor St. Joseph's Ch., Phila.; opened parochial sch., 1782; vicar gen. So. Dist. Md., circa 1782; participant diocesan synod, 1791; pres. Georgetown Coll., circa 1791-96; became Am. superior Soc. of Jesus, 1806. Author: Sermon on the Death of Father Farmer (one of 1st Catholic publs. in U.S.), 1786. Died Dec. 9, 1808.

MONCKTON, Robert, army officer, colonial gov.; b. England, June 24, 1726; s. John and Lady Elizabeth (Manners) M.; 4 children. Served with English Army at Flanders and Germany, 1742-43; commd. capt., 1744; served in campaign of 1745; commd. maj., 1747, served in 3d Foot Guard; lt. col. 47th Foot Guard, 1751; mem. Parliament from Pontefract, 1751-52, 71; apptd. provincial councillor for N.S., 1753; lt. gov. Annapolis Royal, 1754; commanded capture of Beausejour and other French ports, 1755; lt. gov. N.S., 1756; apptd. col. comdt. 2d Battalion 60th Royal Am. Regt., 1757; gov. N.S., 1758; 2d in command Quebec expdn. with temporary rank brig. gen., 1759; col. 17th Regt., 1759; commanded So. dist., 1760; maj. gen. and comdr.-in-chief expdn. against Martinque, 1761, effected surrender of Island by Feb. 5, 1761; gov. Province of N.Y., 1761-63; gov. Berwick-on-Tweed and Holy Island, 1765; commd. lt. gen., 1770; gov. Portsmouth (Eng.), 1779, 82. Died Eng., May 21, 1782.

MONCURE, Richard Cassius Lee, judge; b. Stafford County, Va., Dec. 11, 1805; s. John M. and Alice (Gaskins) M.; m. Mary Conway, Dec. 29, 1825. Admitted to Va. bar, 1825; state's atty. for Stafford County, 1826; mem. Va. Ho. of Dels., 1827-28, 47-49; mem. Va. Constl. Conv., 1850; judge Va. Supreme Ct. of Appeals, 1851-64, 66, 70-82. Died on his farm Glencairne, Stafford County, Aug. 24, 1882.

MONELL, Robert, congressman; b. Columbia County, N.Y., 1786; studied law. Admitted to N.Y. bar, 1809, began practice in Binghamton; moved to Greene, N.Y., 1811, practiced law; mem. N.Y. Assembly, 1814-15, 25-26, 28; mem. U.S. Ho. of Reps. (Democrat) from N.Y., 16th, 21st congresses, 1819-21, 1829-Feb. 21, 1831; dist. atty. Chenango County (N.Y.), 1827; circuit judge, 1831-45; clk. N.Y. State Supreme Ct., 1846. Died Greene, Nov. 29, 1860; buried Hornby Cemetery, Greene.

MONETTE, John Wesley, physician, historian; b. Shenandoah Valley, Va., Apr. 5, 1803; s. Samuel and Mary (Wayland) Monett; M.D., Transylvania U., Lexington, Ky., 1825; m. Cornelia Newman, Dec. 10, 1828, 10 children. Practiced medicine; 1st to suggest quarantine as means of preventing spread of yellow fever; mayor, councilman Washington (Miss.). Author: An Account of the Epidemic of Yellow Fever that Occurred in Washington, Mississippi, in the Autumn of 1825, 1827; Observations on the Epidemic of Yellow Fever of Natchez and the Southwest, 1842; Oil of Turpentine as an External Irritant, 1827; History of the Discovery and Settlement of the Valley of the Mississippi by the Three Great European Powers, Spain, France, and Great Britain, and the Subsequent Occupation, Settlement, and Extension of Civil Government by the United States until the Year 1816, 2 vols., 1846. Died Mar. 1, 1851; buried Washington.

MOÑINO y REDONDO, José, see Floridablanca, conde de.

MONIS, Judah, Hebrew scholar, educator; b. Algiers or Italy, Feb 4, 1683; M.A., Harvard, 1720; m. Abigail Masrett, Jan. 1723/24. Made free citizen in N.Y.C., 1715; converted to Christianity, 1722; instr. of Hebrew, Harvard, 1722-60; 1st Jew to receive degree from Harvard, 1st tchr. at Harvard to hold title of instr.; Author: Dickdook Leshon Gnebreet: A Grammar of the Hebrew Tongue (1st Hebrew grammar published in Am.), 1735. Died Apr. 25, 1764.

MONROE, James, 5th Pres. U.S.; b. Westmoreland County, Va., Apr. 28, 1758; s. Spence and Elizabeth (Jones) M.; attended Coll. William and Mary, 1774-76; studied law under Thomas Jefferson, 1780-83; m. Eliza Kortright, Feb. 1786, 2 children, Eliza, Maria. Commd. lt. 3d Va. Regt., Continental Army, 1776; served at battles of Harlem, White Plains and Trenton; promoted maj., 1777; aide to Earl of Stirling, 1777-78; served at battles of Brandywine, Germantown and Monmouth; as mil. commr. for Va. with rank of lt. col. visited Southern army, 1780; mem. Va. Assembly, 1782, 86, 1810-11; mem. Continental Congress from Va., 1783-86; admitted to Va. bar, 1786; attended Annapolis Conv., 1786; mem. Va. Conv. to ratify U.S. Constn., 1788; mem. U.S. Senate from Va., Nov. 9, 1790-May 27, 1794, mem. senatorial com. to investigate Alexander Hamilton's handling of public funds, 1792; U.S. minister plenipotentiary to France, 1794-96, unable to establish friendly Franco-Am. relations due to French anger over Jay Treaty of 1794; gov. Va., 1799-1802, 11; U.S. minister to France to arrange terms for La. Purchase, 1803; U.S. minister to Eng., 1803-07; U.S. envoy to Spain, 1804; U.S. sec. of state under Pres. James Madison, 1811-17, gave tacit approval to Gen. George Mathews' plans to invade Fla., 1811, withdrew support, 1812; U.S. sec. of war, 1814-15; Pres. of U.S. (Democrat), 1817-25; signed treaty with Spain by which U.S. received Fla., 1819, signed Mo. Compromise Bill, 1820; with Sec. of State John Quincy Adams drew up Monroe Doctrine, 1823, declaring that new world was no longer open to European colonization; mem. bd. visitors U. Va., 1828-31; pres. Va. Constl. Conv., 1829. Died N.Y.C., July 4, 1831; buried Marble Cemetery, N.Y.C.; reinterred Hollywood Cemetery, Richmond, Va., 1858.

MONROE, James, army officer, congressman; b. Albemarle County, Va., Sept. 10, 1799; grad. U.S. Mil. Acad., 1815. Assigned to Arty. Corps., U.S. Army; served under Stephen Decatur in war with Algiers, wounded, 1815; served as aide to Gen. Winfield Scott, 1817-22; commd. 2d lt. 4th Arty., 1821, served on garrison and commissary duty, 1821-32 aide to Gen. Scott on Black Hawk expdn., 1832; resigned commn., moved to N.Y.C., 1832; asst. alderman N.Y.C., 1832, alderman, 1833-35, pres. bd., 1834; declined appointment as aide to Gov. William L. Marcy of N.Y., 1836; mem. U.S. Ho. of Reps. (Whig) from N.Y., 26th Congress, 1839-41; mem. N.Y. State Senate, 1852-55. Died Orange, N.J., Sept. 7, 1870; buried Trinity Cemetery, N.Y.C.

MONTAGUE, Henry James, actor; b. England, Jan. 20, 1843. Active on English stage, 1863-74; came to U.S., 1874; appeared at Wallack's Theater as Tom Gilroy in Partners for Life, N.Y.C; toured U.S. with Wallack's Theater, 1874-78. Died Aug. 11. 1878; buried Greenwood Cemetery, Bklyn.

MONTEFIORE, Joshua, army officer, lawyer; b. London, Eng., Aug. 17, 1762; s. Moses Haim and Esther (Racah) M.; m. twice; 7 children. Admitted as atty. in chancery, England, 1704; led attempt to colonize Bulama Island (off Africa), 1792; paymaster Brit. Army, 1807-12; came to U.S., 1812; practiced law. Author: An Account of the Late Expedition to Bulam, 1794; also books on comml. law. Died St. Albans, Vt., June 26, 1843; buried St. Albans.

MONTEZ, Lola (Marie Dolores Eliza Rosanna Gilbert), dancer, adventuress; b. Limerick, Ireland, 1818; m. Capt. Thomas James, 1837 (div. 1842); m. 2d, Lt. George Heald, 1849; m. 3d, Patrick Purdy Hall. Dau. of Brit. army officer, spent most of girlhood in India; eloped with Capt. James, 1837; made unsuccessful dancing debut, London, Eng., 1843; a very beautiful woman, had no difficulty in finding dancing engagements in Europe, took name Lola Montez at this time; made unsuccessful debut in Paris, France, 1844; appeared in Munich, 1846, became mistress of King Ludwig of Bavaria; created countess of Lansfield by king (who also built her a castle); became very influential in directing govt. policies of Bavaria, forced to flee during revolution, 1848; married and soon left her 2d husband; toured U.S. in play Lola Montez in Bavaria, 1851-53; toured and lived in Australia for a time; lectr. on fashion and beauty in U.S., 1857-61. Author: The Art of Beauty, 1858. Died Astoria, N.Y., Jan. 17, 1861.

MONTEZUMA II (Xocoyotzin), emperor of Aztecs; b. in what is now Mexico, 1466; son of Axayacatl and Xochicueitl; at least 2 children, Ucuauhtemotzin (son), Tecuichpotzin (dau., later baptized as Isabella). Succeeded to Aztec throne upon death of his uncle, Ahuitzotl, Sept. 1502; his reign noted for much warfare and cruelty, as he attempted to bring all Indian tribes of Mexico under his rule; his warring attempts at unity took him as far South as Guatemala, Nicaragua and Honduras; feared that an ancient prophecy of new conquerors from the East had been fulfilled when Cortez arrived, 1518-19, attempted to bribe Cortez to leave; the emperor's harsh policies enabled Cortez to get Indian allies against him; captured by Cortez, who attempted to use him as puppet ruler, 1519. Killed in Aztec uprising against Spaniards, June 1520.

MONTGOMERIE, John, colonial gov.; b. Scotland. Served as officer Brit. Army, also mem. Parliament, before coming to Am.; gov. N.Y. and N.J., 1728-31; avoided controversies with legislature and thus easily gained several supplies needed from them; author of many N.Y.C. charters, signed charter of Aug. 13, 1730. Died probably of smallpox, N.Y.C., July 1, 1731.

MONTGOMERY, Daniel, Jr., congressman; b. Londonderry, Pa., Oct. 30, 1765; s. Daniel Montgomery. Moved to Danville, Pa.; elected to Pa. Ho. of Reps., 1800; commd. lt. col. 81st Regt., Pa. Militia, 1805, apptd. maj. gen. 9th Div., Militia, 1809; mem. U.S. Ho. of Reps. (Democrat) from Pa., 10th Congress, 1807-09; apptd. canal commr. Pa., 1828. Died Danville, Dec. 30, 1831.

MONTGOMERY, George Washington, translator, diplomat; b. Alicante, Spain, 1804; s. John Montgomery; attended Exeter Sch., Eng. Created, published 1st Spanish version of writings of Washington Irving, including Taseas de un Solitario, 1829; Gronica de la Conquista de Granada, 1831; El Bastardo de Castilla, 1832; apptd. U.S. consul, San Juan, P.R., 1835, consul to Guatemala, 1838, later consul at Tampico. Author: Narrative of A Journey to Guatemala. Died Washington, D.C., June 5, 1841.

MONTGOMERY, James, army officer; b. Ashtabula County, O., Dec. 22, 1814; m. Moved to Ky, 1837, became Campbellite minister; moved to Kan., 1852; organized anti-slavery men in his area to fight slavery supporters, raided into Mo., 1857; mem. Kan. Senate under Topeka Constn., 1859; commd. col. 3d Kan. Volunteers, 1861, led raids which resembled robbery and looted towns in Mo.; carried on similar activities in South with Colored troops, 1864. Died Mound City, Kan., Dec. 6, 1871.

MONTGOMERY, John, congressman, mayor Balt.; b. Carlisle, Pa., 1764; studied law. Admitted to Md. bar, 1791, began practice in Harford County; mem. Md. Ho. of Dels., 1793-98, 1819; state's atty., 1793-96; mem. U.S. Ho. of Reps. (Democrat) from Md., 10th-12th congresses, 1807-Apr. 29, 1811; moved to Balt., 1811; atty. gen. Md., 1811-

18; apptd. capt. Balt. Union Arty., 1814, participated in Battle of North Point; mayor Balt., 1820-26. Died Balt., July 17, 1828; buried Methodist Episcopal Ch. cemetery, Bel Air, Md.

MONTGOMERY, John Berrien, naval officer; b. Allentown, N.J., Nov. 17, 1794; s. Dr. Thomas West and Mary (Berrien) M.; m. Mary Henry, Aug. 1820, 9 children. Apptd. midshipman U.S. Navy, 1812, lt., 1818; served on African Coast, 1818-20; exec. officer frigate Constitution, 1835; promoted comdr., 1839; in command ship Portsmouth in Sloat's Squadron on West Coast during Mexican War; raised Am. flag at San Francisco and near-by settlements, 1846; commd. capt., 1853; commanded Pacific Squadron, 1861; promoted to commodore (ret.), 1862; commanded Charlestown (Mass.) Navy Yard, 1862-63, Washington Navy Yard, 1863-65; commd. rear adm. (ret.), 1866. Died Carlisle, Pa., Mar. 25, 1873; buried Oak Hill Cemetery, Washington, D.C.

MONTGOMERY, John Gallagher, congressman; b. Northumberland, Pa., June 27, 1805; grad. Washington (now Washington and Jefferson) Coll., 1824; studied law. Admitted to Pa. bar, 1827, began practice in Danville; mem. Pa. Ho. of Reps., 1855; mem. U.S. Ho. of Reps. (Democrat) from Pa., 35th Congress, Mar. 4-Apr. 24, 1857. Died (probably) as a result of poison in food served at a banquet in Washington (D.C.) during inauguration of Pres. Buchanan, Danville, Apr. 24, 1857; buried Episcopal Cemetery, Danville.

MONTGOMERY, Joseph, Continental congressman; b. Paxtang, Pa., Sept. 23, 1733; grad. Coll. of N.J. (now Princeton), 1755; studied theology. Licensed to preach by Presbytery of Phila., 1759; ordained to ministry Presbyn. Ch., 1761; pastor, 1761-77; del. Pa. Gen. Assembly, 1780-82; mem. Continental Congress from Pa., 1783-84; recorder of deeds and register of wills Dauphin County (Pa.), 1785-94; justice Ct. of Common Pleas, 1786-94. Died Harrisburg, Pa., Oct. 14, 1794; buried Lutheran Ch. Cemetery, Harrisburg.

MONTGOMERY, Richard, army officer; b. Swords, Ireland, Dec. 2, 1738; s. Thomas and Mary M.; ed. St. Andrews and Trinity Coll., Dublin, Ireland; m. Janet Livingston, July 24, 1773. Ensign, 17th Inf., Brit. Army at seige of Louisbourg, 1757, commd. capt., 1762; mem. N.Y. Provincial Congress from Dutchess County, 1775; brig. gen. in command Schuyler's expdns. in Que. and Montreal (Can.), 1775, captured fts. Chambly and St. Johns, also Montreal. Killed during siege of Que., Dec. 31, 1775; buried St. Paul's Ch., N.Y.C.

MONTGOMERY, Thomas, congressman; b. in what is now Nelson County, Va., 1779; studied law. Admitted to the bar; began practice of law, Stanford, Ky.; judge Lincoln County (Ky.) Circuit Ct.; mem. Ky. Ho. of Reps., 1811; mem. U.S. Ho. of Reps. (Democrat) from Ky., 13th, 16th-17th congresses, 1813-15, Aug. 1, 1820-23. Died Stanford, Apr. 2, 1828.

MONTGOMERY, William, congressman; b. Londonderry Twp., Chester County, Pa., Aug. 3, 1736. Served as col. 4th Battalion, Chester County (Pa.) Militia, during Revolutionary War (his regt. known as Flying Camp after Battle of L.I.); del. Pa. provincial convs., 1775, 76; elected to Pa. Assembly from Northumberland County, 1779, reelected several times; sent to Wyoming, Pa. to settle boundary disputes, 1783; apptd. pres. judge Northumberland and Luzerne counties, 1785, justice of peace for Northumberland County, 1791; mem. U.S. Ho. of Reps., from Pa., 3d Congress, 1793-95; served as maj. gen. Pa. Militia, 1793-1816; asso. judge Northumberland County, 1801-13; 1st postmaster Danville (Pa.), 1801-03; Dem. presdl. elector, 1808. Died Danville, May 1, 1816.

MONTGOMERY, William, congressman; b. Guilford County, N.C., Dec. 29, 1789; studied medicine. Practiced medicine, Albrights, N.C; mem. N.C. Senate, 1824-27, 29-34; mem. U.S. Ho. of Reps. (Democrat) from N.C., 24th-26th congresses, 1835-41. Died Albrights, Nov. 27, 1844.

MONTGOMERY, William, congressman; b. Canton Twp., Washington County, Pa., Apr. 11, 1818; grad. Washington (now Washington and Jefferson) Coll., 1839; studied law. Admitted to Pa. bar, 1841, began practice in Washington; dist. atty., 1845; mem. U.S. Ho. of Reps. (Democrat) from Pa., 35th-36th congresses, 1857-61. Died Washington, Pa., Apr. 28, 1870; buried Washington Cemetery.

MONTRESOR, James Gabriel, mil. engr.; b. Ft. William, Scotland, Nov. 19, 1702; s. James Gabriel and Nanon (de Hautville) Le Tresor; m. Mary Haswell, June 11, 1735; m. 2d, Henrietta Fielding, Aug. 25, 1766; m. 3d, Frances Nicholls; 1 son, John. Served as matross in Royal Arty., Minorca, 1727; commd. as practitioner engr., Gibralter, 1731, chief engr. by 1754; commd. lt. 14th Foot Inf.; served as chief engr. under Gen. Braddock in Am., 1754; promoted maj., 1757; became dir. Corps of Engrs. and lt. col., 1758, planned and directed considerable building in No. N.Y.; in charge of rebldg. Ft. George at lower end Lake George, 1759; returned to Eng., 1760; designer, supt. constrn. of powder magazines at Purfleet; chief engr. at Chatham, Eng.; commd. col., 1772. Died Jan. 6, 1776.

MONTRESOR, John, mil. engr.; b. Gibraltar, Apr. 6, 1736; s. James Gabriel and Mary (Haswell) M.; m. Frances Tucker, Mar. 1, 1764. Came to Am., 1754; served as lt. Brit. Army under Gen. Braddock, 1755; engr. in French and Indian War, 1755-63; engr. extraordinary, capt.-lt. with a commn. as barracks master for the ordnance in N. Am.; improved fortifications or repaired barracks at N.Y., Boston, Phila., the Bahamas; bought Montresor's (now Randall's) Island, N.Y.; commd. chief engr. in Am. with rank of engr. in ordinary and capt. Brit. forces, 1775; chief engr. at Battle of Brandywine; returned to Eng., 1778. Died London, Eng., June 26, 1799.

MOOD, Francis Asbury, clergyman, coll. pres.; b. Charleston, S.C., June 23, 1830; s. John and Catherine (McFarlane) M.; grad. Coll. of Charleston, 1850, M.A., 1852; m. Sue Logan, 1858, 9 children. Licensed to ministry in S.C. Conf. of Methodist Episcopal Ch., 1850; served as Confederate chaplain in army hosps., Charleston, 1863; founded Record, weekly newspaper, 1865; pres. Soule U., Chappell Hill, Tex., 1868-73; pres. Southwestern U., Georgetown, Tex., 1873-82. Author: Methodism in Charleston, S.C., 1856. Died Waco, Tex., Nov. 12, 1884.

MOODY, James, Brit. spy, loyalist; b. N.J., 1744; at least 3 children. Farmer at outbreak Am. Revolution; objected to N.J. law requiring oath of allegiance; enlisted in loyal brigade under command Gen. Courtland Skinner, 1777, commd. ensign 1779; ordered arrested on sight by N.J. govt., 1777, his property confiscated by N.J., 1778; spied on troop movements of Washington, Sullivan and Gates; captured at Englishtown, N.J., 1780, escaped; promoted lt., 1781; planned other activities such as capture of Continental Congress papers (plans revealed by his confederates before he could undertake them); went to Eng., 1782, granted pension of 100 pounds a year; went to N.S., 1786; col. N.S. Militia, 1786-1809. Author: Narrative, 1783. Died Weymouth, N.S., Apr. 6, 1809.

MOODY, Paul, inventor; b. Byfield Parish, Newbury, Mass., May 21, 1779; s. Capt. Paul and Mary Moody; m. Susannah Morill, July 13, 1800, 3 children. Established (with Francis C. Lowell) cotton mill and other machinery plant, Waltham, Mass.; secured patent for mechanism to wind yarn from bobbins or spools, 1816; perfected soapstone rollers, doubled efficiency of Horrock's dressing machine, 1818; granted patents for machines to make cotton roping, also to rope and spin cotton, 1821; supt. cotton mills, East Chelmsford (now Lowell), Mass., 1823; under his direction the manufacture of cotton machinery was continued and improved designs of machinery were perfected at Lowell Machine Works, 1825. Died Lowell, July 8, 1831.

MOONEY, William, polit. leader; b. N.Y.C., 1756. Upholsterer, dealer in wall paper, N.Y.C., 1780-1821; a founder N.Y. Soc. of Tammany, 1786, elected grand sachem, 1789, reelected 1811; dir. museum established for preservation hist. objects; supt. alms house, 1808-09. Died Nov. 27, 1831.

MOOR, Wyman Bradbury Seavy, senator; b. Waterville, Me., Nov. 11, 1811; grad. Waterville Coll.; attended Dane Law Sch., Cambridge, Mass. Taught sch., St. Stephen's, N.B., Can., 1 year; admitted to Me. bar, 1835, began practice in Waterville; mem. Me. Ho. of Reps., 1839; atty. gen. State of Me., 1844-48; moved to Bangor, Me., 1847, practiced law; mem. U.S. Senate (Democrat) from Me., Jan. 5-June 7, 1848; supt. constrn. of railroad from Waterville to Bangor; returned to Waterville, 1852, practiced law; one of those who became ill as result of poison in food served at banquet during inauguration of Pres. Buchanan, 1857; resumed practice of law, Bangor; consul gen. to Brit. N.Am. Provinces (apptd. by Buchanan), 1859-61; purchased estate nr. Lynchburg, Va., 1868, operated an iron furnace. Died Lynchburg, Mar. 10, 1869; buried Pine Grove Cemetery, Waterville.

MOORE, Alfred, army officer, asso. justice U.S. Supreme Ct.; b. New Hanover County, N.C., May 21, 1755; s. Judge Maurice and Anne (Grange) M.; m. Susanna Eagles, Sept. 1, 1775. Licensed to practice law, 1775; capt. 1st N.C. Regt., Continental Army, until 1777; col. Brunswick County Regt., N.C. Milita; participated in battles of Guilford Ct. House, Wilmington (Del.); mem. N.C. Senate from Brunswick County, 1782; atty. gen. N.C., 1782-91; trustee state univ., 1789-1807; a Federalist; mem. N.C. Ho. of Commons, 1792; elected judge N.C. Superior Ct., 1798; apptd. asso. justice U.S. Supreme Ct., 1799. Died Bladen County, N.C., Oct. 15, 1810.

MOORE, Andrew, senator, congressman; b. "Cannicello," Rockbridge County, Va., 1752; s. David and Mary (Evans) M.; ed. Washington and Lee U.; read law under George Wythe; m. Sarah Reid, circa 1782, a son, Samuel McDowell. Admitted to Va. bar, 1774, head of co. 9th Va. Regt., continental Army, served as lt. under Gen. Gates at Battle of Saratoga, present at surrender of Burgoyne, rose to maj. gen. Va. Militia; mem. Va. Ho. of Dels., 1780-83, 85-88, 1799-1800; trustee, largely responsible for permanent establishment of Washington and Lee U., 1782-1821; mem. Va. Privy Council, 1788; del. Va. Conv. which ratified U.S. Constn., 1788; mem. U.S. Ho. of Reps. from Va., 1st-4th, 8th congresses, 1789-97, Mar. 5-Aug. 11, 1804; mem. Va. Senate, 1800-01; apptd. U.S. marshal for Western Dist. Va., 1801; mem. U.S. Senate from Va., Aug. 11, 1804-09. Died Lexington, Va., Apr. 14, 1821; buried Lexington Cemetery.

MOORE, Bartholomew Figures, state ofcl.; b. Halifax County, N.C., Jan. 29, 1801; s. James and Sally Lowe (Lewis) M.; grad. U. N.C., 1820; m. Louisa Boddie, Dec. 2, 1828; m. 2d, Lucy Boddie, Apr. 19, 1835. Admitted to N.C. bar, 1823; mem. N.C. Ho. of Commons, 1836, 40, 42, 44; atty-gen. N.C., 1848-51; one of commrs. to revise statute law of N.C., reported in The Revised Code of North Carolina . . . 1854, published 1855; mem. N.C. Bd. of Claims during Civil War; mem., leader N.C. Conv. of 1865, drew ordinance declaring the ordinance of secession null and void from the beginning; served on commn. to suggest such changes in laws as were made necessary by emancipation and wrote report later adopted by state legislature which recognized citizenship of the freedmen; mem. N.C. Conv. of 1866 which drew up new constn., induced conv. to adopt it and submit it to people, unsuccessful in urging its ratification. Died Raleigh, N.C., Nov. 27, 1878.

MOORE, Benjamin, bishop, coll. pres.; b. Newton, L.I., N.Y., Oct. 5, 1748; s. Samuel and Sarah (Fish) M.; grad. at head of his class, Kings Coll. (now Columbia) 1768; m. Charity Clarke, Apr. 20, 1778; 1 son, Clement Clarke. Received deacon's and priest's orders from Bishop of London, 1774; pres. pro tem Kings Coll., 1775-84, prof. rhetoric and logic Columbia, 1784-86, pres., 1801-11; became rector Trinity Ch., N.Y.C., 1800; Protestant Episcopal bishop of N.Y. Died Greenwich, nr. N.Y.C., Feb. 27, 1816.

MOORE, Clement Clarke, scholar, writer; b. N.Y.C., July 15, 1779; s. Rev. Benjamin and Charity (Clarke) M.; grad. Columbia, 1798; m. Catharine Taylor, Nov. 20, 1813. Gave 60 lots in N.Y.C. to make possible Gen. Theol. Sem., 1819, became prof. Oriental and Greek lit., 1823, Author: A Compendious Lexicon of the Hebrew Language: In Two Volumes, 1809; A Visit from St. Nicholas, or Twas the Night Before Christmas, When All Through the House, 1822; Poems, 1844; George Castriot, Surnamed Scanderberg, King of Albania, 1850. Died Newport, R.I., July 10, 1863.

MOORE, Edwin Ward, naval officer; b. Alexandria, Va., June 1810; m. Emma (Stockton) Cox, 1849. Commd. midshipman U.S. Navy, 1825, lt., 1835, resigned 1839; accepted command Navy of Republic of Tex., 1839; commd. post capt., commanding with court sy title commodore, 1842; destroyed Mexican commerce from the Gulf of Mexico, entered into de facto alliance with Yucatan rebels, and captured town of Tabasco, 1841; surveyed, charted Tex. coast, saved federalist Yucatecans from hasty peace with Centralist Santa Anna, continuing an alliance with Texas; agreed with Yucatan authorities, in consideration of a money payment sufficent to finish refitting the fleet, to attack the Mexican Squadron blockading the Yucatan Coast; received a proclamation from Houston declaring him guilty of "disobedience, contumacy, and mutiny", and suspended from command; tried by ct. martial, found not guilty on 18 counts, guilty on 4. Author: To The People of Texas (best collection of source materials on Texan Navy), 1843. Died N.Y.C., Oct. 5, 1865.

MOORE, Ely, congressman, labor leader; b. Belvidere, N.J., July 4, 1798; s. Moses and Mary (Coryell) M.; m. Emma Contant; m. 2d, Mrs. Clara Baker; 6 children. Elected 1st pres. Gen. Trades Union, N.Y..C, editor Nat. Trades' Union (ofcl. organ), chmn., 1834; mem. U.S. Ho. of Reps. (Democrat elected with Tammany support), 24th-25th congresses, 1835-39; surveyor Port of N.Y., 1839; U.S. marshal for So. Dist. of N.Y., 1845; published and edited Warren Journal; agt. for Miami and other Indian tribes, 1853; register U.S. Land Office, Lecompton, Kan., 1855-60. Died Jan. 27, 1860.

MOORE, Gabriel, senator, gov. Ala.; b. Stokes County, N.C., 1785; s. Matthew and Letitia (Dalton) M.; m. Miss Callier. Practiced law in Miss. Territory, 1810-17; mem. Miss. Territorial Legislature, 1817, became speaker Ala. Territorial Ho. of Reps. (after division into Ala. and Miss. territories 1817); mem. Ala. Constl. Conv., 1817; mem. Ala. Senate, 1819-20, speaker, 1820; mem. U.S. Ho. of Reps. (Republican) from Ala., 17th-20th congresses, 1821-29; gov. Ala., 1829; mem. U.S. Senate (Rep.) from Ala., 1831-37, voted against confirmation of Martin Van Buren as minister to Ct. of St. James (Eng). Died Caddo, Tex., June 9, 1845.

MOORE, George Fleming, jurist; b. Elbert County, Ga., July 17, 1822; s. William H. and Mary Garland (Marks) M.; attended U. Ala., U. Va. law school (did not graduate); m. Susan Spyker, 1846, 7 children. Admitted to Ala. bar, 1844; sr. mem. firm Moore & Walker, Austin, Tex., firm was reporter for Tex. Supreme Court, published volumes 22-24 of Texas Reports, 1860-61; served as col. 17th Regiment, Tex. Cavalry during Civil War, 1860-61; elected to Tex. Supreme Ct., 1862, chief justice, 1866-67, 78-81, asso. justice, 1874-78; upheld power of Confederate Congress to raise army by draft in "Ex parte F.H. Coupland" (26 Texas Reports 38T); gave opinion in Jacob Kuechler vs. George Wright which established rule in effect that all exec. officers (except gov.) are subject to control by writ of mandamus. Died Washington, D.C., Aug. 30, 1883; buried Austin, Tex.

MOORE, George Henry, bibliographer, historian; b. Concord, N.H., Apr. 20, 1823; s. Jacob Bailey and Mary Adams (Hill) M.; grad. U. City N.Y., 1842; m. Mrs. Mary Howe (Givan) Richards, Oct. 21, 1850, 2 children. Asst. librarian N.Y. Hist. Soc., 1841-48, sec. exec. com., 1848-91, librarian, 1849-76; sec. Mexican Boundary Commn., 1850; sec. bd. trustees Lenox Library, N.Y.C., 1876-92. Author: Mr. Lee's Plan—March 29, 1777: The Treason of Charles Lee, 1860; Notes on the History of Slavery in Massachusetts, 1866; Notes on the History of Witchcraft in Massachusetts, 1883-85; Libels on Washington, 1889; also many bibliog. and hist. monographs. Died N.Y.C., May 5, 1892.

MOORE, Heman Allen, congressman; b. Plainfield, Vt., Aug. 27, 1809; studied law, Rochester, N.Y. Admitted to the bar; began practice of law, Columbus, O.; mem. U.S. Ho. of Reps. (Democrat) from Ohio, 28th Congress, 1843-44. Died Columbus, Apr. 3, 1844; buried Green Lawn Cemetery, Columbus.

MOORE, Sir Henry, colonial gov.; b. Vere, Jamaica, B.W.I., Feb. 7, 1713; s. Samuel and Elizabeth (Lowe) M.; ed. Eton Coll., Eng.; U. Leyden (Netherlands); m. Catharine Maria Long, 1 child. Mem. Legislative Assembly of Jamaica, mem. council, also sec. of island became lt. gov. Jamaica, 1755, acting gov., 1756-62; created baronet, 1864; apptd. gov. N.Y., arrived at time of Stamp Act controversy, 1765; failed to receive support of his council; refused to permit cts. to function, denied vessels permission to sail, but on the whole pursued a conciliatory policy; devoted much effort to settlement of boundary disputes with neighboring provinces; made 2 trips to Country of the 5 Nations; prorogated N.Y. Assembly, because of failure to pass quartering act, 1766, (led to signing of restraining act by King George, 1767). Died Sept. 11, 1769.

MOORE, Henry Dunning, congressman; b. Goshen, N.Y., Apr. 13, 1817; attended pub. schs., N.Y. C. Engaged as tailor, N.Y.C.; moved to Phila., 1844, engaged in mahogany and marble bus.; mem. U.S. Ho. of Reps. (Whig) from Pa., 31st-32d congresses, 1849-53; unsuccessful candidate for mayor Phila., 1856; treas. State of Pa., 1861-63, 64-65; collector Port of Phila., 1869-71; traveled in Europe, resided in St. Petersburg, Russia, 1870-77; mgr. silver mines called "The Daisy" nr. Leadville, Colo., 1885-87. Died nr. Leadville, Aug. 11, 1887; buried Monument Cemetery, Phila.

MOORE, Jacob Bailey, journalist, printer; b. Andover, N.H., Oct. 31, 1797; s. Jacob Bailey and Mary (Eaton) M.; m. Mary Adams Hill, Aug. 28, 1820, 6 children including Frank, George Henry. Apprentice to Isaac Hill, owner, editor New Hampshire Patriot, 1813-19, partner, 1819-23; owned printing business; a founder N.H. Hist. Soc., 1st librarian, 1823-30, 37-39; started N.H. Journal, Concord, 1826; sheriff Merrimack County (N.H.), 1828-33, justice of peace, 1825-35; went to N.Y. C., 1839; editor N.Y. Daily Whig, 1839-40; chief clk. U.S. Post Office Dept., 1841-45; librarian N. Y. Hist. Soc., 1848-49; dep. postmaster, San Francisco, 1850-53. Co-author: Collections, Historical and Miscellaneous, 3 vols., 1822-24; author: A Gazeteer of the State of New Hampshire, 1823. Died Bellows Falls, Vt., Sept. 1, 1853; buried Bellows Falls.

MOORE, James, colonial gov.; b. Ireland; m. Margaret Berringer. Came to Am., 1675; participated in overthrow of Gov. Colleton of S.C., 1690; active in protests against quit rents, 1693-94; gov. S.C., 1700-03; engaged in cattle trading; caused bill to be introduced in Assembly which would give him a monopoly of Indian trade, dissolved assembly when bill was defeated; prorogued new Assembly; led unsuccessful force against St. Augustine during Queen Anne's War, besieged city, 1702; gathered army of whites and Indians at Okmulgee, made successful raid against Apalachees, 1704; advocated trip to explore Mississippi River (nothing resulted from the idea). Died Charlestown (now Charleston), S.C., 1706.

MOORE, James, army officer; b. New Hanover County, N.C., 1737; s. Maurice and Mary (Porter) M.; m. Ann Ivie, 4 children. Served as capt. during French and Indian War; mem. N.C. Provincial Ho. of Commons, 1764-71, 73; a leader Cape Fear mob which marched to Brunswick to prevent enforcement of Stamp Act in N.C., 1766; served as col. arty., 1768, 71; mem. N.C. Assembly, 1773; 1st signer circular letter of com. which called 1st Revolutionary Provincial Congress, 1774; del. from New Hanover County to 3rd Provincial Congress, Hillsboro, N.C., 1775; commd. col. 1st N.C. Continental Regt., 1775, apptd. brig. gen. in command N.C. Militia, 1776. Died Wilmington, Del., Apr. 1777.

MOORE, James, clergyman, coll. pres.; b. Va., 1764. Received as candidate by Transylvania Presbytery, Apr. 27, 1792; ordained to ministry Episcopal Ch., 1794; apptd. prin. or dir. Transylvania Sem., 1st public ednl. instn. in area, circa 1792-1794; prin. Ky. Acad., 1796, pres. Transylvania U., 1797, acting pres., prof. logic metaphysics, moral philosophy and belles-lettres, 1799-1804; organized Episcopalian Ch. in Ky., 1809, 1st Episcopalian rector in Ky. Died Lexington, Ky., June 22, 1814.

MOORE, Jesse Hale, clergyman, congressman; b. nr. Lebanon, Ill., Apr. 22, 1817; grad. McKendree Coll., Lebanon, 1842; studied theology. Taught schs., Nashville, Ill., 1842-44, Georgetown, Ill., 1844-48; ordained to ministry, Methodist Ch., 1849; served as col. 115th Regt., Ill. Volunteer Inf., during Civil War, 1862-65; brevetted brig. gen. U.S. Volunteers, 1865; presiding elder Decatur dist. Ill. Conf., Meth. Ch., 1868; mem. U.S. Ho. of Reps. (Republican) from Ill., 41st-42d congresses, 1869-73; U.S. pension agt., Springfield, Ill., 1873-77; pastor Mechanicsburg (Ill.) Meth. Ch.; U.S. consul at Callao, Peru (apptd. by Pres. Arthur), 1881-83. Died Callao, July 11, 1883; buried Callao, reinterred Greenwood Cemetery, Decatur.

MOORE, John, colonial ofcl.; b. Eng., circa 1659; s. Sir Francis Moore; m. Rebecca Axtell, 1685, at least 7 children including William. Came to S.C., 1680; became provincial sec., Province of S.C., receiver-gen. 1682-83; dep. to Sir Peter Colleton, a lord proprietor of S.C., 1684; apptd. advocate Ct. Vice Admiralty for Pa., also lower counties (now Del.), and West Jersey, 1698; leader (with Robert Quarry) in Anglican Party in efforts to enforce acts of trade and navigation; king's atty. gen., also register-gen. Province of Pa., 1700-04; dep. judge Admiralty Ct., 1704-circa 1713; collector Port of Phila., 1704-28; dep. register-gen. Phila., 1724-26; dep. collector Phila., 1728-32. Died Phila., Dec. 2, 1732; buried Christ Church, Phila.

MOORE, John, congressman; b. Berkeley County, Va. (now W.Va.), 1788. Moved to Franklin, La.; mem. La. Ho. of Reps., 1825-34; mem. U.S. Ho. of Reps. (Whig) from La., 26th-27th, 32d congresses, Dec. 17, 1840-43, 51-53; moved to New Iberia, La.; Whig presdl. elector, 1848; del. La. Secession Conv., 1861. Died Franklin, June 17, 1867; buried "The Shadows" nr. New Iberia.

MOORE, John Weeks, editor; b. Andover, N.H., Apr. 11, 1807; s. Jacob Bailey and Mary (Eaton) M.; m. Emily Jane Eastman, Sept. 17, 1832. Apprentice printer New Hampshire Patriot; editor, publisher Androscoggin Free Press (weekly Me. newspaper), 1827-38; editor Bellows Falls (Vt.) Gazette, 1838-55; began editing and publishing musical journals, 1840; editor World of Music and Musical Library, for a time; editor A Dictionary of Musical Information, 1876. Author: Puritanism of Music in America; Complete Encyclopedia of Music, Elementary, Technical, Historical, Biographical, Vocal and Instrumental (editor, collector), 1854; Songs and Song Writers of America, 1859-80; Musical Record, 5 vols., 1867-70; Moore's Historical, Biographical and Miscellaneous Gatherings . . . Relative to Printers, Printing, Publishing, and Editing . . . from 1420 to 1886 (chief work), 1886. Died Manchester, N.H., Mar. 23, 1889.

MOORE, Laban Theodore, congressman; b. Wayne County, Va. (now W.Va.), Jan. 13, 1829; grad. Marietta Coll., O.; attended Transylvania Law Coll., Lexington, Ky. Admitted to the bar, 1849; began practice of law, Louisa, Ky.; mem. U.S. Ho. of Reps. (National American) from Ky., 36th Congress, 1858-61; organizer, col. 14th Regt., Ky. Volunteer Inf., during Civil War, 1861-62; moved to Catlettsburg, Ky., practiced law; became Democrat after Civil War; mem. Ky. Senate, 1881; del. Ky. Constl. Conv., 1890-91. Died Catlettsburg, Nov. 9, 1892; buried Ashland (Ky.) Cemetery.

MOORE, Maurice, jurist; b. New Hanover County, N.C., 1735; s. Maurice and Mary (Porter) M.; m. Anne Grange, 1 son, Alfred. Became an asso. judge N.C. Cts., 1758; mem. N.C. Ho. of Commons, 1757-60, 62, 64-71, 73-74; mem. Gov.'s Council, 1760-61, 68-73; asso. judge Province of N.C. until 1765; a leader in Regulator Movement; col. in Gov. Tryon's 1st armed expdn.; judge at Hillsboro (N.C.) Trial of 1768, at spl. ct. in Hillsboro that sentenced 12 Regulators to death on treason charges, 1771; mem. com. to try to induce Regulators to support patriotic cause, 1775, became more lenient towards the insurgents; mem. N.C. provincial congresses from Brunswick. Died Wilmington, N.C., Apr. 1777.

MOORE, Nathaniel Fish, coll. pres.; b. Newtown, L.I., N.Y., Dec. 25, 1782; s. William and Jane (Fish) M.; grad. Columbia, 1802, LL.D. (hon.) 1825. Admitted to N.Y. bar, 1805; adj. prof. Greek and Latin, Columbia, 1817, prof., 1820-35, sold his library (about 1,000 vols.) to Columbia, 1837; librarian Columbia, 1838-39; pres., 1842-49. Author: Remarks on the Prounciation of the Greek Language, 1819; Ancient Mineralogy: or, An Inquiry Respecting Mineral Substances Mentioned by the Ancients, 1834; An Historical Sketch of Columbia College, 1846. Died Highlands of the Hudson, Apr. 27, 1872.

MOORE, Orren Cheney, congressman; b. New Hampton, N.H., Aug. 10, 1839; attended pub. schs. Journalist; mem. N.H. Ho. of Reps., 1863, 64, 75, 76, 78, 87; established Nashua (N.Y.) Daily Telegraph, 1869; mem. N.H. Tax Commn., 1878; mem. N.H. Senate, 1879-81; chmn. N.H. R.R. Commn., 1884-88; mem. U.S. Ho. of Reps. (Republican) from N.H., 51st Congress, 1889-91. Died Nashua, May 12, 1893; buried Woodlawn Cemetery, Nashua.

MOORE, Oscar Fitzallen, congressman; b. Lagrange, O., Jan. 27, 1817; grad. Washington (now Washington and Jefferson) Coll., 1836; studied law. Admitted to Ohio bar, 1838, began practice in Portsmouth, 1839; mem. Ohio Ho. of Reps., 1850-51, Ohio Senate, 1852-53; mem. U.S. Ho. of Reps. (Republican) from Ohio, 34th Congress, 1855-57; served as lt. col., later col. 33d Regt., Ohio Volunteer Inf., during Civil War. Died Waverly, O., June 24, 1885; buried Greenlawn Cemetery, Portsmouth.

MOORE, Richard Channing, bishop; b. N.Y.C., Aug. 21, 1762; s. Thomas and Elizabeth (Channing) M.; ed. King's Coll. (now Columbia); studied medicine under Dr. Richard Bayley, religion under Bishop Samuel Provoost D.D. (hon.), Dartmouth, 1805; m. Christian Jones, 1784; m. 2d, Sarah Mersereau, Mar. 23, 1797; 3 children including David. Ordained deacon Protestant Episcopal Ch., 1787, priest, 1787; rector St. Andrew's Parish, S.I., N.Y., 1789-1809; dep. at Gen. Conv., 1808; rector St. Stephens Ch., N.Y.C., 1809-14, Monumental Ch., Richmond, Va., 1814; consecrated bishop of Va., 1814, active in restoring discipline, reestablishing chs., increasing number of clergy; founder Va. Theol. Sem.; a leader in reconstrn. Episcopal Ch. in U.S. Author: The Doctrines of the Church (discourse delivered to Gen. Conv., 1820). Died Lynchburg, Va., Nov. 11, 1841; buried Richmond.

MOORE, Robert, congressman; b. nr. Washington, Pa., Mar. 30, 1778; attended Washington (now Washington and Jefferson) Coll.; studied law. Admitted to Pa. bar, 1802, began practice in Beaver; treas. Beaver County (Pa.), 1805-11; served with Pa. Militia during War of 1812; mem. U.S. Ho. of Reps. from Pa., 15th-16th congresses, 1817-21; mem. Pa. Ho. of Reps., 1830-31. Died Beaver, Jan. 14, 1831; buried Beaver Cemetery.

MOORE, Samuel, congressman; b. Deerfield (now Deerfield Street), Cumberland County, N.J., Feb. 8, 1774; grad. U. Pa., 1791; studied medicine. Instr., U. Pa., 1792-94; practiced medicine, Dublin, Pa. and Greenwich, N.J.; engaged in East Indian trade; purchased, operated grist and oil mills, Bridge Point (now Edison), Pa., 1808, later built and operated sawmill and woolen factory; mem. U.S. Ho. of Reps. (Democrat) from Pa., 15th-17th congresses, Oct. 13, 1818-May 20, 1822; dir. U.S. Mint, 1824-35; moved to Phila., involved in mining and marketing of coal; pres. Hazleton Coal Co. until 1861. Died Phila., Feb. 18, 1861; buried Woodland Cemetery, Phila.

MOORE, Samuel McDowell, congressman; b. Phila., Feb. 9, 1796; s. Andrew Moore; attended Washington Coll. (now Washington and Lee U.), Lexington, Va. Settled in Lexington; mem. Va. Ho. 23d Congress, 1833-35; mem. Va. Senate, 1845-47;

of Dels., 1825-33, 36-37; mem. Va. Constl. Conv., 1829; mem. U.S. Ho. of Reps. (Whig) from Va., del. Va. Secession Conv., 1861; served in Confederate Army during Civil War. Died Lexington, Sept. 17, 1875; buried Lexington Cemetery.

MOORE, Samuel Preston, surgeon gen. Confederate Army; b. Charleston, S.C., 1813; s. Stephen West and Eleanor Screven (Gilbert) M.; grad. Med. Coll. S.C., 1834; m. Mary Augusta Brown, 1845. Commd. asst. surgeon U.S. Army, 1835, surgeon with rank of maj., 1849-61; surgeon gen. Confederate Army; established examining bds. to weed out unfit, introduced orgn. and methods of med. dept. U.S. Army into Confederate Army; organizer, pres. Assn. Army and Navy Surgeons of Confederate States; mem. Richmond (Va.) Sch. Bd., 1877-89, also Va. Agrl. Soc. Died May 31, 1889.

MOORE, Sydenham, army officer, congressman; b. Rutherford County, Tenn., May 25, 1817; attended U. Ala., 1833-36; studied law. Admitted to Ala. bar, began practice in Greensboro; judge Greene County (Ala.) Ct., 1840-46, 48-50; judge circuit ct., 1857; served as capt. Ala. Inf. during Mexican War, 1846-47; elected brig. gen. Ala. Militia; mem. U.S. Ho. of Reps. (Democrat) from Ala., 35th-36th congresses; 1857-Jan. 21, 1861; served as col. 11th Ala. Regt., Confederate Army, during Civil War; fatally wounded in Battle of Seven Pines, Va. Died Richmond, Va., May 31, 1862; buried City Cemetery, Greensboro.

MOORE, Thomas, congressman; b. Spartanburg Dist., S.C., 1759. Served in Revolutionary War, participated in Battle of Cowpens; served as brig. gen. during War of 1812; engaged as planter; a founder 1st high sch. in Spartanburg Dist.; mem. U.S. Ho. of Reps. from S.C., 7th-12th, 14th congresses, 1801-13, 15-17; resumed planting. Died nr. Moores Station, Spartanburg County, S.C., July 11, 1822; buried Moore's Burying Ground.

MOORE, Thomas Love, congressman; b. nr. Charles Town, Va. (now W.Va.); studied law. Practiced law; mem. U.S. Ho. of Reps. from Va., 16th-17th congresses, Nov. 13, 1820-23; resumed practice of law, Warrenton, Va.; gave prin. speech at visit of Gen. Lafayette to Warrenton, 1825. Died Warrenton, 1862; buried Warrenton Cemetery.

MOORE, Thomas Overton, gov. La.; b. Sampson County, N.C., Apr. 10, 1804; s. John and Jean (Overton) M.; m. Bethiah Leonard, Nov. 30, 1830, 5 children. Came to La., 1829; became an important sugar planter; mem. La. Ho. of Reps., 1848, La. Senate, 1856; gov. La., 1860-62; on his recommendation the legislature called a state conv. at Baton Rouge to decide on La.'s response to Abraham Lincoln's election, 1861; ordered La. troops to take Ft. Jackson, Ft. Philip, which commanded Mississippi below New Orleans, also Ft. Pike and barracks and arsenal at Baton Rouge; took lead in making La. a mem. Confederacy; organized local companies for defense, established supply depots on Red River, built packing plants to feed soldiers; continued to act as gov. over No. La. until 1864, despite U.S. Govt. appointment of George Shepley (who could only control Union area); fled to Havana, Cuba, 1865, later pardoned, returned to La. Died Rapides Parish, nr. Alexandria, La., June 25, 1876.

MOORE, William, jurist; b. Phila., May 6, 1699; s. John and Rebecca (Axtell) M.; grad. Oxford (Eng.) U., 1719; m. Williamina Wemyss, circa 1722, 12 children. Col. of a regt. in Chester County (Pa.) Militia during French and Indian War; mem. Provincial Assembly, 1733-40; justice of the peace, 1741-83; presiding judge of Chester County Ct. during most of period 1750 to 1776; 28 petitions were presented to Assembly in 1757 urging his removal as presiding judge, but he denied jurisdiction of Assembly; arrested for libel and imprisoned, Phila., 1758. Died Moore Hall, Chester County, May 30, 1783; buried Radnor (Pa.) Churchyard.

MOORE, William, patriot, jurist; b. Phila.; circa 1735; s. Robert Moore; m. Susan Lloyd, Dec. 13, 1757, 3 children including Elizabeth Moore de Barbe Marbois. Mem. Pa. Council of Safety, 1776, mem. Bd. of War, 1777; mem. Pa. Supreme Exec. Council, 1779-82, v.p., 2 years, pres., 1 year; judge Pa. High Ct. Errors and Appeals, 1781-84; mem. Pa. Assembly, 1784; dir. Bank of Pa.; trustee U. State Pa., 1784-89; important mem. St. Tammany Soc. Died July 24, 1793.

MOORE, William, congressman; b. Norristown, Pa., Dec. 25, 1810; attended pvt. schs. Engaged in merc., later ironworks bus.; moved to Weymouth, N.H., 1845, engaged in iron bus.; also interested in bldg. and sailing ships, devel. of banks and other financial instns.; judge Atlantic County (N.J.) Ct. of Common Pleas, 1855-65; a founder Republican Party; del. Rep. Nat. Conv., Phila., 1856; moved to Mays Landing, N.J., 1865, engaged in shipbldg., banking, iron bus.; mem. U.S. Ho. of Reps. (Rep.) from N.J., 40th-41st congresses, 1867-71; mem. N.J. Senate, 1872-75. Died Mays Landing, Apr. 26, 1878; buried Union Cemetery, Mays Landing.

MOORE, William Sutton, congressman; b. nr. Amity, Pa., Nov. 18, 1822; grad. Washington (now Washington and Jefferson) Coll., 1847; studied law. Admitted to Pa. bar, 1848; began practice in Washington; prothonotary of Washington County (Pa.), 1854-57; del. Republican Nat. Conv., Phila., 1856; editor, part owner of the Reporter, 1857; treas. Washington County, 1863-66; mem. U.S. Ho. of Reps. (Rep.) from Pa., 43d Congress, 1873-75. Died Washington, Pa., Dec. 30, 1877; buried Washington Cemetery.

MOORE, Zephaniah Swift, clergyman, coll. pres.; b. Palmer, Mass., Nov. 20, 1770; s. Judah and Mary (Swift) M.; grad. Dartmouth, 1793, D.D., 1815; m. Phoebe Drury, Feb. 21, 1799. Licensed to preach, 1796, pastor 1st Congl. Ch., Leicester,, Mass., 1797-1811; trustee Leicester Acad., prin. preceptor, 1806-07; prof. learned langs. (Latin, Greek, Hebrew) Dartmouth, 1811-15; pres. Williams Coll., 1815; 1st pres. Amherst (Mass.) Coll., May 8, 1821. Died June 30, 1823.

MOORHEAD, James Kennedy, congressman, telegraph co. exec.; b. Halifax, Pa., Sept. 7, 1806; s. William and Elizabeth (Kennedy Young) M.; m. Jane Logan, Dec. 17, 1829, 5 children. Offered low bid, obtained contract for constrn. Susquehanna br. Pa. Canal, then became supt. Juniata div.; 1st to run passenger packet on canal; adjutant gen. Pa., 1838; with Monongahela Navigation Co., Pitts., 1839, pres., 1846; established Union Cotton Factory, Pitts., 1840; owned part interest in Novelty Works, Pitts.; largely responsible for establishment of telegraph lines between Pitts. and Phila., from 1853; pres. Atlantic & Ohio Telegraph Co. (later became Western Union Telegraph Co.), pres. various other cos. owning lines to Cincinnati and Louisville; active Democrat, left party, aided in formation Republican Party, 1854-58; mem. U.S. Ho. of Reps. from Pa., 36th-40th congresses, 1859-69; del. Rep. Nat. Conv., Chgo., 1868; pres. Pitts. C. of C., 1877-84; del. to Pan-Presbyn. Council, 1884. Died Pitts., Mar. 6, 1884; buried Allegheny Cemetery, Pitts.

MOOSER, William, architect; b. Switzerland, 1834; at least 2 sons including William. Came to U.S., 1852; pioneer architect, San Francisco; designed and built Met. Hall, Cosmos Club (San Francisco), French Hosp. (Richmond, Cal.), McDonough Theatre (Oakland, Cal.), Woolen Mills (North Beach, Cal.); became partner (with his 2 sons) firm William Mooser & Sons. Died Nov. 17, 1896.

MOOSMÜLLER, Oswald William, clergyman; b. Aidling, Bavaria, Germany, Feb. 26, 1832. Entered novitiate Benedictine order; sent to U.S., 1852; ordained priest Roman Catholic Ch., 1856; missionary to Brazil, 1859-61; superior of Benedictine monastery, Sandwich, Ont., Can., 1861-63; prior St. Mary's Ch., Newark, N.J., 1863-66; procurator Am. Congregation, also dir. St. Elizabeth Sem., Rome, Italy, 1866-72; prior, treas. St. Vincent Abbey; superior St. Benedict Abbey, Atchison, Kan., 1874-77, also acted as Army chaplain and missionary to Indians; founder agrl. school for Negroes in Ga.; organized, headed monastery of Cluny, Wetang, Ill., 1892-1901; contbr. articles to Am. and German lang. newspapers; wrote on Benedictine order in U.S. Author: St. Vincenz in Pennsylvanien, 1873; Bonifax Wimmer Erzalt von St. Vincent in Pennsylvanien, 1891. Died Cluny Monastery, Jan. 10, 1901.

MORAIS, Sabato, clergyman, educator; b. Leghorn, Italy, Apr. 13, 1823; s. Samuel and Bjonina (Wolf) M.; LL.D. (hon.), U. Pa., 1887; m. Clara Esther Weil, 1855, 7 children. Hebrew master of orphan school in Bevis Marks, London, Eng., 1846; came to U.S., 1851; minister Mikueh Israel Congregation, Phila., 1851-97; hon. mem. Union League Club, Phila., circa 1865; procured fund for settlement of immigrants from Russia in agrl. colonies in N.J.; prof. Bible and Bibl. lit. Maimonides Coll., 1867-73; a founder Jewish Theol. Sem., N.Y.C., 1886, pres. faculty, prof. Bible, 1886-97; most important articles reprinted as Italian Hebrew Literature, 1926. Died Phila., Nov. 11, 1897.

MORAN, Benjamin, diplomat; b. West Marlborotownship, Pa., Aug. 1, 1820; s. William Moran. Spent most of life in Eng.; pvt. sec. to James Buchanan, minister to Gt. Britain, 1854; asst. sec. to U.S. legation, Eng. 1857-64, sec. 1864-74, often acting charge d'affaires on absence of minister; U.S. minister to Portugal, 1874-76; U.S. charge d'affaires, Lisbon, Portugal, 1876-82. Wrote a history of Am. literature in Trubner's Bibliographical Guide to American Literature, 1859. Died Braintree, Essex County, Eng., June 20, 1886.

MORAN, Edward, painter; b. Bolton, Eng., Aug. 19, 1829; s. Thomas and Mary (Higson) M.; m. 2d, Annette Parmentier, 1869. Came to U.S., 1844; worked as hand-loom weaver as youth; later went to Phila., engaged in various jobs; noticed by Paul Weber, landscape painter of local repute, studied painting under Weber and James Hamilton; specialized in marine painting, became associate Nat. Acad.; went to Eng. to study at Royal Acad., London, 1862; exhibited paintings in Phila., 1871; went to N.Y.C., 1872; lived in Paris, 1879-80; most important work: series 13 marine paintings depicting scenes from Am. history, 1st exhibited N.Y.C., 1904, now in Pa. Mus. Art, Phila. Died N.Y.C., June 9, 1901.

MORDECAI, Alfred, army officer, engr.; b. Warrenton, N.C., Jan. 3, 1804; s. Jacob and Rebecca (Myers) M.; grad. U.S. Mil. Acad., 1823; m. Sara Hays, 6 children including Alfred. Commd. 2d lt. Corps Engrs., U.S. Army, 1823; asst. prof. engring. U.S. Mil. Acad., 1823-25; asst. engr. in charge of constructing Ft. Monroe, Va., 1825-28; commd. capt. Ordnance Dept., U.S. Army, 1832; commanded 1st Washington (D.C.) Arsenal, then Frankford (Pa.) Arsenal, 1833-38; asst. to chief of ordnance, 1838-42; commanded Washington Arsenal during Mexican War, brevetted maj.; commd. maj. Ordnance Dept., 1854; mem. U.S. Mil. Commn. to Crimea War, 1855-57; resigned from Army at outbreak of Civil War; tchr. mathematics, Phila., 1861-63; asst. engr. Mexico & Pacific R.R., 1863-66; sec., treas. Pa. R.R., 1867-87. Author: A Digest of Laws Relating to the Military Establishment of the United States, 1833; Artillery for the United States Land Service, 1849. Died Phila., Oct. 23, 1887.

MORDECAI, Moses Cohen, shipowner, legislator; b. Charleston, S.C., Feb. 19, 1804; s. David Cohen and Rinah (Cohen) M.; m. Isabel Rebecca Lyons, Feb. 20, 1828. Founder Mordecai & Co., shipowners, extensive importers Mediterranean fruits, Cuban sugar and tobacco, Brazilian coffee; established line of steamers between Charleston and Havana (Cuba); made Charleston his port of entry, brought large amount of business to city, moved base of operation to Balt., 1865, started steamer line between Charleston and Balt.; del., Augusta Conv., 1838; mem. S.C. Ho. of Reps., 1845-46; founder newspaper Southern Standard, Charleston, 1851; mem. S.C. Senate, 1855-58; pres. synagogue Beth Elohim, 1857-61; his ship Isabel became famous blockade runner during Civil War. Died Dec. 30, 1888.

MORE, Nicholas, jurist; b. Eng.; m. Mary More, before 1682, 4 children. Pres. Free Soc. of Traders, 1682; came to Pa., 1682; sec. Pa. Provincial Council, 1683; mem. Pa. Assembly, 1684-85, speaker, 1684; presiding judge Phila., County Cts. 1683-84, prior judge or chief justice Province of Pa. and lower counties (now Del.), 1684, 1st impeachment trial in Am. history conducted against him, 1685, expelled from Assembly and suspended from judicial position, but Council refused to sanction impeachment proceedings. Died Phila., 1689.

MOREAU de SAINT MERY, Mederic-Louis-Elie, publisher, historian; b. Ft. Royal, Martinique, Jan. 13, 1750; s. Bertrand-Mederic and Marie-Rose (Beeson) M. de S.-M.; married, at least 2 children. Admitted to bar, Paris, France, 1777; discovered tomb of Columbus, restored it at his own expense in Santo Domingo; a founder Mus. of Paris, pres., 1787; pres. Electors of Paris, 1789, persuaded Electors to place Lafayette in command of Nat. Guard; escaped to Am., 1794; founder bus. as bookseller, printer and stationer, 1794, which became rendezvous of French emigres; non-resident mem. Am. Philos. Soc., 1789, resident mem., 1795; printer and publisher A. E. Van Braam Houckgeest's Voyage de l' Ambassade de la Compagnie des Indes Orientales Hollandaises, ver l' Empereur de la Chine, en 1794-95, 1797; one of best early Am. printers and publishers; returned to France, 1798, became historiographer at Ministry of Marine, Paris; councillor of state, 1800; resident to Duke of Parma, 1801; adminstr. Parma, Piacenza. and Guastalla, 1802-06. Author: Description topographique et politique de la partie Espagnole de l'ile de Saint Dominique, 2 vols., 1797, 98; Loix et Constitutions des Colonies francais de l'amerique sous le Vent, 1784-90. Died Paris, Jan. 28, 1819.

MOREAU-LISLET, Louis Casimir Elisabeth, lawyer; b. Cap Francais, Santo Domingo, 1767; ed. in France; m. Anne Philipine de Peters, 1 dau. Came to New Orleans, circa 1800, became noted lawyer; partly responsible for insuring recognition of Roman civil law in La. (Napoleon Code); atty. gen. La., 1817; mem. La. Senate; opposed nullification theory of John Calhoun; helped prepared revised code Civil Code of the State of Louisiana, 1825. Author: Explication des Lois Criminelles du Territoire d'Orleans, 1806; co-author: Digeste des Lois Civiles Maintenant en Vigueur dans le Territoire d'Orleans, 1808 (published both in English and French). Died New Orleans, Dec. 3, 1832.

MOREHEAD, Charles Slaughter, gov. Ky., congressman; b. Nelson County, Ky., July 17, 1802; s. Charles and Margaret (Slaughter) M.; grad. Transylvania U., 1820, LL.B., 1822. Mem. Ky. Legislature, 1828-29, 38-45, 53-54, speaker, 1840-42, 44-45; mem. U.S. Ho. of Reps. (Whig) from Ky., 30th-31st congresses, 1847-51, chmn. Ho. Ways and Means Com. which opposed Pres. James Polk's fiscal policies; gov. Ky., 1855-59, campaigned during serious anti-fgn. riots called Bloody Monday, Louisville, Ky.; denounced No. "nullification of Fugitive Slave Act," maintained slaves could be taken to any territory; mem. Washington (D.C.) Peace Conf., 1861; accused U.S. Sec. of War William Seward of trying to cut off trade from South; arrested Sept. 1861, imprisoned at Ft. Lafayette in N.Y. Harbor, later at Ft. Warren in Boston Harbor; released through influence of Sen. John Crittenden of Ky., Jan. 1862; fled to Can., then to Mexico, to avoid arrest for not signing oath of allegiance to Union; returned to 1 of his plantations, Greenville, Miss. Author: A Digest of the Statute Laws of Kentucky, 1834. Died Greenville, Dec. 21, 1868; buried Frankfort (Ky.) Cemetery.

MOREHEAD, James Turner, senator, gov. Ky.; b. nr. Shepherdsville, Ky., May 24, 1797; s. Armistead Morehead; attended Transylvania U., 1813-15; studied law under Judge H. P. Broadnax and John J. Crittenden; m. Susan A. Roberts, May 1, 1823. Admitted to Ky. bar, 1818, began practice law, Bowling Green; mem. Ky. Ho. of Reps., 1828-31, 37-38, 39-40, mem. com. on internal improvements, arranged for return of fugitive slaves; del. from Ky. to Nat. Republican Conv. which nominated Henry Clay, Balt., 1831; lt. gov. Ky., 1831-34; gov. Ky., 1834-36; favored jud. reform and popular edn., denounced abolitionists; ex officio 1st pres. permanent Ky. Bd. of Internal Improvements, then acting pres., 1836-37; mem. U.S. Senate (Whig) from Ky., Feb. 20, 1841-47, supported Henry Clay and Nat. Bank Bill, opposed annexation of Tex., but voted to declare war against Mexico. Author: An Address in Commemoration of the First Settlement of Kentucky, 1840; Practice in Civil Action and Proceeding at Law, 1846. Died Covington, Ky., Dec. 28, 1854; buried Frankfort (Ky.) Cemetery.

MOREHEAD, James Turner, congressman; b. Rockingham County, N.C., Jan. 11, 1799; grad. U. N.C., 1819; studied law. Admitted to N.C. bar, began practice in Greensboro; commr. of Greensboro, 1832, 34-35; mem. N.C. Senate, 1835-36, 38, 40, 42; trustee U. N.C., 1836-68; mem. U.S. Ho. of Reps. (Whig) from N.C., 32d Congress, 1851-53; resumed law practice, also engaged in farming, operating an iron works. Died Greensboro, May 5, 1875; buried Presbyn. Cemetery, Greensboro.

MOREHEAD, John Motley, gov. N.C.; b. Pittsylvania County, Va., July 4, 1796; s. John and Obedience (Motley) M.; grad. U. N.C., 1817; m. Ann Lindsay, Sept. 6, 1821, 8 children. Mem. N.C. Ho. of Commons, 1821, 26-27, 38; gov. N.C., 1841-45; established a state instn. for deaf, Raleigh, N.C.; pres. N.C. R.R.; promoter Atlantic & N.C. R.R., Western N.C. R.R.; del. from N.C. To Nat. Peace Conf., Washington, D.C., 1861, mem. Confederate Provisional Congress. Died Alum Springs, Va., Aug. 27, 1866.

MORELL, George Webb, army officer, lawyer; b. Cooperstown, N.Y., Jan. 8, 1815; s. Judge George and Maria (Webb) M.; grad. U.S. Mil. Acad., 1835; m. Catherine Schermerhorn Creighton, 1866. Constrn. engr. Charleston & Cincinnati R.R., 1837; admitted to N.Y. bar, 1842; commd. maj. 4th N.Y. Volunteers, 1846; commd. maj., div. engr. N.Y. Militia, 1849, col., 1852-61; commr. U.S. Circuit ct. for So. dist. N.Y., 1954-61; col., q.m. chief of staff to Maj. Gen. Sanford in organizing regts. in N.Y.C., 1861; commd. brig. gen. U.S. Volunteers, 1861, maj. gen., 1862; on duty guarding approaches to Washington D.C., 1861-62; in command of draft rendezvous in Indpls., 1863-64. Died Feb. 11, 1883.

MOREY, Frank, congressman; b. Boston, July 11, 1840; attended pub. schs.; studied law, Ill. Served as capt. 33d Regt., Ill. Volunteer Inf., U.S. Army, during Civil War, 1861-65; settled in La., 1866, engaged in cotton planting, ins. bus.; mem. La. Ho. of Reps., 1868-69; apptd. commr. to revise statutes and codes of La.; commr. to Vienna Expn., 1873; mem. U.S. Ho. of Reps. (Republican) from La., 41st-44th congresses, 1869-June 8, 1876 (lost seat as result of contested election); moved to Washington, D.C. Died Washington, Sept. 22, 1889; buried Congressional Cemetery, Washington.

MOREY, Samuel, inventor; b. Hebron, Conn., Oct. 23, 1762; s. Israel and Martha (Palmer) M.; m. Hannah Avery, 1 child. Participated in constrn. Conn. River locks between Windsor (Conn.) and Okott Falls, engr. in charge, Bellows Falls, Vt.; obtained 1st patent for steam-operated spit, 1793; patented rotary steam engine, 1795; patented windmill, water wheel, steam pump; built stern wheel steamboat, ran from Hartford, Conn. to N.Y.C., 1794; attempted to persuade Robert Fulton to adopt his steamboat model, claimed his ideas were stolen by Fulton; patented internal combustion engine, 1826; propelled boat Aunt Sally by a vapor engine on Fairlee (Vt.) Pond (now known as Lake Morey), 1820. Died Fairlee, Apr. 17, 1843.

MORFIT, Campbell, chemist; b. Herculaneum, Mo., Nov. 19, 1820; s. Henry Mason and Catherine (Campbell) M.; attended Columbian Coll. (now George Washington U.); m. Maria Clapier Chancellor, Apr. 13, 1854, 1 dau. Left sch. to go to pvt. chemistry lab. of James Curtis Booth, Phila.; became indsl. chemist, owner of business in Phila.; prof. applied chemistry U. Md., 1854-58, offered to set up chemistry dept. in conjunction with med. sch. (offer rejected); published his research in various scientific journals; prepared (with Booth) Encyclopedia of Chemistry, 1850; went to Eng., 1861. Author: A Treatise on Chemistry Applied, 1856; Chemical and Pharmaceutical Manipulations, 1857. Died South Hampstead, Eng., Dec. 8, 1897.

MORFORD, Henry, journalist, author; b. New Monmouth, N.J., Mar. 10, 1823; s. William and Elizabeth (Willett) M. Established N.J. Standard, Matawan, 1852, editor, mgr., 1852-54, 55; clk. N.J. Ct. Common Pleas, 1862-68; mem. editorial staff N.Y. Atlas; author Sprees and Splashes, 1863; Morford's Short-Trip Guide to Europe, 1868; Morford's Short-Trip Guide to America, 1872; established, edited Bklyn, News Monthly Mag., Jan. 1880-81; author The Rest of Don Juan (best of his poetical work), 1846; also several novels. Died Aug. 4, 1881.

MORGAN, Abel, clergyman, Biblical scholar; b. Cardiganshire, South Wales, Eng., 1673; s. Morgan ap Rhyddergh ap Dafydd ap Gruffyd; m. Priscilla Powell; m. 2d, Martha Burrows; m. 3d, Judith (Griffiths) Gooding; 6 children. Arrived in Phila., 1712; in charge of Pennepek Baptist Ch., Phila., 1712-22; one of Bapt. leaders of Pa.; established churches in Del. and N.J.; author Cyd Goriad . . . (2d Welsh book published in Am., 1st real concordance to Welsh Bible). Died Phila., Dec. 16, 1722.

MORGAN, Charles, shipping and railroad magnate, b. Killingworth (now Clinton), Conn., Apr. 21, 1795; s. George and Elizabeth (Redfield) M.; m. Emily Reeves, Dec. 20, 1817; m. 2d, Mary Jane Sexton, June 24, 1852; 5 children. Ran line of sailing vessels to West Indies, had regular line of mail steamers plying between New Orleans and Galveston, Tex., circa 1835; provided service from Galveston to Indianola, Corpus Christi and Vera Cruz, from New Orleans to Mobile, also another on Lake Pontchartrain (La.); established Tex. & New Orleans Mail Line, Mexican Ocean Mail & Inland Co.; agt. in N.Y. for Vanderbilt's Nicaragua Transit on the Atlantic, pres., 1853; secured control of T.F. Secor marine engine works in N.Y., 1850, became Morgan Iron Works, 1850; started Morgan Line from N.Y. to New Orleans, 1870; largest shipowner in U.S.; purchased New Orleans, Upelousas & Great Western R.R., 1869, became Morgan's La. & Tex. R.R.; held virtual monopoly of transp. in region from N.Y. to Tex.; secured control of Houston & Tex. Central R.R., 1877; organizer; chmn. bd. Morgan's La. & Tex. R.R. and S.S. Co. Died N.Y.C., May 8, 1878.

MORGAN, Christopher, congressman; b. Aurora, N.Y., June 4, 1808; grad. Yale, 1830; studied law. Admitted to N.Y. bar, began practice in Aurora; mem. U.S. Ho. of Reps. (Whig) from N.Y., 26th-27th congresses, 1839-43; moved to Auburn, N.Y., practiced law; sec. of state N.Y., 1847-51; supt. N.Y. Pub. Schs., 1848-52; mayor Auburn, 1860, 62; trustee State Lunatic Asylum, Utica, N.Y. Died Auburn, Apr. 3, 1877; buried Fort Hill Cemetery, Auburn.

MORGAN, Daniel, congressman, army officer; b. Hunterdon County, N.J. or Bucks County, Pa., 1736; s. James and Eleanora Morgan; m. Abigail Bailey, children—Nancy, Betty. Worked in Bucks County (where his father was ironmaster Durham Iron Works); quarrelled with father, moved to Shenandoah Valley, Va., transported supplies to frontier points of Va.; served as lt. in Pontiac's War, 1774, accompanied Lord Dunmore's expdn. to Western Pa.; commd. capt. co. of riflemen from Va., 1775, accompanied Benedict Arnold in assault of Quebec, was captured, 1775; commd. col. 11th Va. Regt., 1776; commd. brig. gen. Continental Army, 1780, joined Gen. Nathaniel Gates; defeated British at Battle of Cowpens (N.C.), 1781, awarded Gold medal by Continental Congress; retired to estate in Va. after Revolutionary War; commanded Va. Militia ordered by Pres. Washington to suppress Whiskey Rebellion in Pa., 1794; mem. U.S. Ho. of Reps. from Va., 5th Congress, 1797-99. Died Winchester, Va., July 6, 1802; buried Mt. Hebron Cemetery, Winchester.

MORGAN, Edwin Barber, congressman; b. Aurora, N.Y., May 2, 1806; s. Christopher and Nancy (Barber) M.; m. Charlotte Fidelia Wood, Sept. 27, 1829, 2 children. Mcht. (took over father's bus.), Aurora, N.Y., 1827-81; became pres. Wells Fargo & Co. Express, Aurora, 1852; a founder U.S. Express Co., 1854, owner, 1854-81; made fortune operating gypsum beds, Grand Rapids, Mich.; mem. U.S. Ho. of Reps. (Republican) from N.Y., 33d-35th congresses, 1853-59; trustee Cornell U., 1865-74; pres. bd. trustees Wells Coll., Aurora, N.Y., 1878-81; bought enough stock in N.Y. Times to prevent William Marcy Tweed from gaining control (thus maintaining paper's anti-Tweed editorial policy), 1871. Died Aurora, Oct. 13, 1881; buried Oak Glen Cemetery, Aurora.

MORGAN, Edwin Denison, senator, gov. N.Y.; b. Washington, Berkshire County, Mass., Feb. 8, 1811; s. Jasper Avery and Catherine (Copp) M.; m. Eliza Matilda Waterman, 1833, 5 children. Partner in grocery store, Hartford, Conn., 1831-36; mem. Hartford City Council, 1832; partner (with Morris Earle) in firm Morgan & Earle, wholesale grocers, N.Y.C., 1836-37; established E. D. Morgan & Co., 1837-83; alderman City of N.Y., 1849; mem. N.Y. State Senate, 1850-55, introduced bill establishing Central Park, N.Y.C.; N.Y. commr. immigration, 1855-58; v.p. Republican Nat. Conv., Phila., 1856, chmn. Rep. Nat. Com., 1856-64, 72-76; gov. State of N.Y., 1859-62; chmn. Union Congressional Com., 1864; served as maj. gen. U.S. Volunteers, 1861-63, commanded Dept. of N.Y., 1861-63; mem. U.S. Senate from N.Y., 1863-69; left estate valued at 10 million dollars at time of death, made gifts to Williams Coll., Union Theol. Sem., Women's Hosp., Presbyn. Hosp., Eye and Ear Hosp. (all N.Y.C.). Died N.Y.C., Feb. 14, 1883; buried Cedar Hill Cemetery, Hartford.

MORGAN, Eliot S. N., territorial ofcl.; b. Pitts., Jan. 1832. Mem. Pa. Ho. of Reps. from Lawrence County, 1873-76; sec. Wyo. Territory, 1880-87; acting gov. Wyo. Territory, 1885, 86-87; admitted to Wyo. bar, 1887; mem. Wyo. Constl. Conv., 1889. Died Cheyenne, Wyo., Apr. 20, 1894.

MORGAN, George, land speculator, Indian agent; b. Phila., Feb. 14, 1743; s. Evan and Joanna (Biles) M.; m. Mary Baynton, Oct. 21, 1764, 11 children. Apprentice firm Baynton & Wharton, mchts., Phila., circa 1756, became full partner, 1763, went to Ill., country in effort to find trading opportunities for firm, 1764, firm went into receivership but its assets included grant of land approximately 2,800 acres in what is now W.Va. by treaty of Ft. Stanwix with Six Nations, 1768; became sec.-gen. and supt. newly formed Indiana company, 1776, Va. opposed claims of Ind. Co., prevented from furthering his claim by adoption of 11th Amendment, 1798; held rank of col. with duties as Indian agt. and dep. commissary gen. for purchases during Revolutionary War; resigned from Continental Army, 1779; became farmer and land owner, N.J.; wrote scientific articles for various publications; helped found Colony of New Madrid in Spanish La. (now Mo.); declined Aaron Burr's attempt to enlist him in his Western project. Died on his farm nr. Washington, Pa., Mar. 10, 1810.

MORGAN, George Washbourne, organist; b. Gloucester, Eng., Apr. 9, 1823. Sang in Gloucester Philharmonic Chorus, 1834, condr., circa 1845; articled to John Amott; organist in several chs.; came to Am., 1853, settled in N.Y.C.; organist St. Thomas' Ch., 1854-55, Grace Ch., 1855-68, St. Anne's Roman Catholic Ch., 1868-69, St. Stephen's Roman Catholic Ch., 1869-70, Bklyn. Tabernacle, 1870-82, Dutch Reformed Ch., 1886-88 (all N.Y. C.). Died Tacoma, Wash., July 1892.

MORGAN, George Washington, congressman, army officer; b. Washington County, Pa., Sept. 20, 1820; s. Thomas and Katherine (Duane) M.; attended Washington Coll., Chestertown, Md., 1835-36, U.S. Mil. Acad., 1841-42; studied law under J. K. Miller, Mt. Vernon, O.; m. Sarah H. Hall, Oct. 7, 1851, 2 children. Served as capt. in co. raised by his brother, Thomas Jefferson Morgan, in Texan War of Independence, 1836; admitted to Ohio bar, 1843, became pros. atty. Knox County; served as col. 2d Ohio Volunteers in Mexican War, 1846; commd. col. 15th U.S. Inf., 1847, brevetted brig. gen., 1848; U.S. minister to Lisbon, Portugal, 1858-61; commd. brig. gen. U.S. Army, 1861, commanded 7th div. Army of Ohio under Gen. Don Carlos Buell, 1861-63; commanded battalion under Gen. William Tecumseh Sherman at Vicksburg (Miss.), resigned because he did not agree with Sherman's policy of using Negro troops, 1863; del. from Ohio to Nat. Democratic Conv., 1864, defended Gen. George B. McClellan against charges of defeatism; mem. U.S.

Ho. of Reps. (Democrat) from Ohio, 40th, 41st-42d congresses, 1867-June 3, 1868, 1869-73, opposed harsh measures favored by radical Republicans; del. Nat. Dem. Conv., 1876. Died Fortress Monroe, Va., July 26, 1893; buried Mt. Vernon, O.

MORGAN, James, congressman; b. Amboy, N.J., Dec. 29, 1756; attended pub. schs. Served as officer, N.J. Regt., Continental Army, during Revolutionary War; rep. Gen. Assembly, Phila., 1794-99; mem. U.S. Ho. of Reps. (Federalist) from N.J., 12th Congress, 1811-13; engaged in farming; commd. Nov. 11, 1822; buried Morgan (N.J.) pvt. ceme-maj. gen. N.J. Militia. Died South Amboy, N.J., tery.

MORGAN, James Bright, congressman; b. nr. Fayetteville, Tenn., Mar. 14, 1833; studied law, Miss. Admitted to Miss. bar, 1857, began practice in Hernando; probate judge De Soto County, 1857-61; served from pvt. to col. Confederate Army, during Civil War; mem. Miss. Senate, 1876-78; del. all Miss. convs., 1876-90; chancellor 3d Chancery Dist., 1878-82; mem. U.S. Ho. of Reps. (Democrat) from Miss., 49th-51st congresses, 1885-91. Died nr. Horn Lake, Miss., June 18, 1892; buried Baptist Cemetery, Hernando.

MORGAN, James Dada, army officer, businessman; b. Boston, Aug. 1, 1810; s. James and Martha (Patch) M.; m. Jane Strachan (dec. 1855); m. 2d, Harriet Evans, June 14, 1869; at least 2 children. Helped organize the Quincy (Ill.) Grays, later the Quincy Riflemen; entered Mexican War as capt. 1st Ill. Volunteer Inf., 1846, promoted maj. at Battle of Buena Vista; brig. gen. U.S. Volunteers, 1862, brevetted maj. gen. 1865; treas. Ill. Soldiers and Sailors Home, 1887; v.p. Soc. of Army of Cumberland; mcht. and banker. Died Quincy, Sept. 12, 1896.

MORGAN, John, physician; b. Phila., June 10, 1735; s. Evan and Joanna (Biles) M.; grad. Coll. of Phila. (now U. Pa.), 1757; M.D., U. Edinburgh (Scotland), 1763; m. Mary Hopkinson, Sept. 4, 1765. Admitted to Academie Royal de Chirurgie de Paris (France), 1764, mem. Royal Soc. London (Eng.) Belles-Lettres Soc. of Rome (Italy); licentiate Royal Coll. Physicians, London and Edinburgh; established med. sch. in connection with U. Pa., 1765, apptd. prof. theory and practice of physic; author oration A Discourse upon the Institution of Medical Schools in America, 1765; published Four Dissertations on The Reciprocal Advantages of a Perpetual Union between Great Britain and her American Colonies (won a gold medal), 1766; dir. gen. hosps. Continental Army, 1775, physician in chief, 1775, dir. hosps. East of Hudson River, 1776-77; physician Pa. Hosp.; mem. Am. Philos. Soc.; Phila. Coll. Physicians was an outgrowth of his suggestion (organized 1787). Author: A Recommendation of Inoculation, According to Baron Pimsdale's Method, 1776. Died Phila., Oct. 15, 1789.

MORGAN, John Hunt, army officer; b. Huntsville, Ala., June 1, 1825; s. Calvin Cogswell and Henrietta (Hunt) M.; m. Rebecca Bruce, circa 1848; m. 2d, Miss Ready, Dec. 14, 1862. Served as enlisted man during Mexican War; organized Lexington Rifles, 1857; scout Confederate Army, 1861, commd. capt., 1862; began raids in Ky., Ohio, Ind., harassed Federals; commd. col., 1862, headed brigade which raided extensively in Ky.; captured Fed. force, Hartsville, Tenn., took over 1,700 prisoners, 1862, for which action he was commd. brig. gen. in command cavalry div.; a raid of Ky. and Ohio resulted in his surrender, 1863, however he saved E. Tenn. for the Confederacy for several months; escaped, 1863; commanded Dept. of S.W. Va., 1864. Killed in action, Greenville, Tenn., Sept. 4, 1864; buried Lexington, Ky.

MORGAN, John Jordan, congressman; b. Queens County, N.Y., 1770; attended pub. schs. Mem. N.Y. Assembly, 1819, 36, 40; mem. U.S. Ho. of Reps. (Democrat) from N.Y., 17th-18th, 23d congresses, 1821-25, Dec. 1, 1834-35. Died Port Chester, N.Y., July 29, 1849; buried Trinity Churchyard, N.Y.C.

MORGAN, John Paul, organist; b. Oberlin, O., Feb. 13, 1841. Organist, N.Y.C., many years; made 1st English translation of Richter's Manual of Harmony, 1867. Died Oakland, Cal., Jan. 1879.

MORGAN, Junius Spencer, internat. banker; b. West Springfield, Mass., Apr. 14, 1813; s. Joseph and Sarah (Spencer) M.; m. Juliet Pierpont, May 2, 1836, 5 children including John Pierpont. One of the chief links in financial relationship between Gt. Britain and U.S. in middle half of 19th century; joined banking house of Morgan, Ketchum & Co., N.Y.C., 1834; became jr. partner dry goods firm Howe, Mather & Co., 1835, sr. partner, 1850; became a partner J.M. Beebe, Morgan & Co., Boston; became partner George Peabody & Co., internat. banking firm, London, Eng., 1854, firm name changed to J. S. Morgan & Co., 1864, head firm, 1864-90; most important event of career was placing of $50,000,000 loan at 6% to France in 1870 during war with Prussia, which (besides assisting France) placed J.S. Morgan & Co. in front rank of issuing houses in London; gave $100,000 to establish a free library, Hartford, Conn.; gave substantial gifts to Hartford Orphan Asylum, Guy's Hosp. in London, Nat. Nurses Pension Fund (Eng.), Trinity Coll., Wadsworth Atheneum, Hartford, also to Yale for establishment of a professorship in law dept. Died Monte Carlo, Monaco, Apr. 8, 1890.

MORGAN, Justin, musician, horse breeder; b. West Springfield, Mass., 1747; m. Martha Day, 1774, children—Emily, Nancy, Justin, Polly. Tchr. music and penmanship, also tavern keeper, at various times, moved to Randolph, Vt., 1788, became lister, 1789, town clk., 1790-93; received 2 horses in payment for debt, circa 1795 (1 was small, but extremely strong); may have furthered this breed by certain mating process (known as Morgan Horse, became very popular after Morgan's death, especially in West); cross-breeding with other horses almost killed off original Morgan Horse, but small band was gathered to save them from extinction and they thrive today. Composer numerous tunes, including hymn tune "Amanda" (basis for fantasy by 20th century composer Thomas Canning), "Montgomery" (printed in Antiquarian by Leonard Marshall, 1849), Judgement Anthem. Died Mar. 22, 1798.

MORGAN, Lewis Henry, anthropologist; b. Aurora, N.Y., Nov. 21, 1818; s. Jedediah and Harriet (Steele) M.; grad. Union Coll., 1840, LL.D. (hon.), 1873; m. Mary Elizabeth Steele, Aug. 13, 1851. Admitted to N.Y. bar; legal adviser of a railroad under constrn. between Marquette, Mich. and Lake Superior iron region, 1855; mem. N.Y. State Assembly, 1861-68, N.Y. State Senate, 1868-69; known as "father of Am. anthropology"; leading mem. The Grand Order of the Iroquois (chief purposes were to study and perpetuate Indian lore, to educate Indians, reconcile them to conditions imposed on them by civilization); succeeded in defeating ratification of a fraudulent treaty by which the Seneca would have given up their lands to Ogden Land Co.; adopted by Hawk clan of Seneca, 1847, given name Tayadawahkugh; entrusted by Univ. State N.Y. with executing the enlargement of its Indian collection, for which an appropriation had been made, 1849; author League of the Ho-de-no-sau-nee, or Iroquois (1st sci. account of an Indian tribe), 1851; published Laws of Consanguinity and Descent of the Iroquois, 1859; Systems of Consanguinity and Affinity of the Human Family; Ancient Society or Researches in the Lines of Human Progress, 1877; studied various ruins, visited some of existing pueblos, 1878; wrote On the Ruins of a Stone Pueblo on the Animas River in New Mexico, 1880; Houses and House-Life of the American Aborigines, 1881; The American Beaver and His Works, 1868; instrumental in organizing anthropology sect. A.A.A.S., 1875, 1st chmn.; mem. Nat. acad. Scis.; pres. A.A.A.S., 1879. Died Rochester, N.Y., Dec. 17, 1881.

MORGAN, Louis M., artist; b. Mt. Pleasant, Pa., Nov. 21, 1814. Began portrait painting, Pitts., circa 1830; commd. to paint portrait of Simon Kenton of Ohio for Nat. Portrait Gallery; worked in Ky., circa 1840-50. Died Montgomery County, Tenn., 1852.

MORGAN, Matthew Somerville, cartoonist; b. London, Eng., Apr. 27, 1839; s. Matthew and Mary (Somerville) M.; married twice; 16 children. Artist for Illustrated London News, drew pictures of Austro-Italian War, 1859; artist for Fun, drew cartoons about Am. Civil War, 1862-67; owner, illustrator Tomahawk, 1867; came to U.S., 1870; worked on Frank Leslie's Illustrated Newspaper in 1870's; mgr. Strobridge Lithographing Co., Cincinnati, 1880; founder Morgan Art Pottery Co., in 1880's; art editor Collier's Mag., 1888-90; painted large backdrops for Buffalo Bill's Wild West Show, 1889. Died N.Y.C., June 2, 1890.

MORGAN, Philip Hicky, jurist, diplomat; b. Baton Rouge, La., Nov. 9, 1825; s. Judge Thomas and Eliza (McKennan) M.; studied law, Paris, France; m. Beatrice Ford, May 22, 1852, 5 children. Lt., La. Volunteers during Mexican War, 1848; admitted to La. bar; judge 2d Dist. Ct. of La., circa 1854; supported Union during Civil War, fled La.; acting U.S. dist. atty. for La., 1866-67, dist. atty., 1869-72; judge La. Supreme Ct., 1873-76; judge Internat. Ct. in Egypt, 1877-80; U.S. minister to Mexico under Pres. Hayes, 1880-85. Died N.Y.C., Aug. 12, 1900; buried Allegheny Cemetery, Pitts.

MORGAN, Thomas, actor. Purchased (with Noah Miller Ludlow and John Vaughn) keel boat in Nashville, Tenn., 1817, traveled (with their wives) to Natchez, Miss. where they gave 1st theatrical performance in history of city; traveled with same troupe by steamboat to New Orleans, 1818, performed for 4 months at Theatre St. Philippe (1st performances ever given in English in the city), made $5,000 for each man.

MORGAN, William, mem. fraternal orgn.; b. Culpeper County, Va., Aug. 1774; m. Lucinda Pendleton, circa 1819. Moved to Batavia (N.Y.) as brick mason, 1825; rose to rank of Royal Arch Mason in Masonic orders, 1825; planned to publish book Illustrations of Masonry, 1826; arrested for petty theft and taken to jail, Canandaigua, N.Y., 1826, never seen again although his body is said to have been found shortly afterwards in area; supposedly killed by Masons to stop him from publishing secrets of the order; mystery and sensation of his disappearance caused formation of Anti-Masonic Party (against secret orgns., later dissolved into other more important polit. parties). Died circa 1826.

MORGAN, William Stephen, congressman; b. Monongalia County, Va. (now W.Va.), Sept. 7, 1801; attended pub. schs. Engaged in farming, White Day, Va.; mem. U.S. Ho. of Reps. (Democrat) from Va., 24th-25th congresses, 1835-39, clk., 1840; clk. Va. Legislature; mem. Va. Ho. of Dels., 1841-44; presdl. elector, 1844; clk. U.S. Treasury Dept., 1845-61; employed in Smithsonian Instn., 1861-63; moved to Rivesville, W.Va., Died Washington, D.C., Sept. 3, 1878; buried Congressional Cemetery, Washington.

MORIARITY, Patrick Eugene, clergyman, coll. pres.; b. Dublin, Ireland, July 4, 1804; attended Carlow Coll.; studied with Order of the Hermits of St. Augustine, 1820; studied philosophy and theology in Augustinian colls. of Lucca, Perugia, Rome; awarded doctorate in divinity by Pope Gregory XVI, 1839; Ordained priest Roman Catholic Ch., 1828; volunteered for East Indian Missions, 1834, sec., vicar gen. of Bishop O'Connor, Madras, India, 1834-39, assisted in establishing Madras Expositor; came to Am. as superior or commissary Augustinian missions, landed in Phila., 1839; became temperance reformer, established St. Augustine's Cath. Total Abstinence Soc., 1840, Cath. Temperance Beneficial Soc. of Phila., 1840; founder Villanova (Pa.) Coll., 1842, prof. sacred eloquence, 1851-57, pres., 1854; asst. gen. Augustinian Order, 1847, commissary gen., 1851-57; inaugurated Augustinian mission, Lansingburg, N.Y.; aided Sisters of St. Joseph in establishing their mother house in his parish, 1858; attended Councils of Balt. Author: Life of St. Augustine, Bishop, Confessor, Doctor of the Church, 1873; address "What Right has England to rule Ireland?" Died Villanova, July 10, 1875.

MORPHY, Paul Charles, chess player; b. New Orleans, June 22, 1837; s. Alonzo and Thelcide (Le Carpentier) M.; grad. Spring Hill Coll., Ala., 1854, U. La. Law Sch., 1857. Childhood chess star in La., defeated J. J. Löwenthal, 1850; admitted to La. bar, 1858; starred at 1st Am. Chess Congress, 1857; gave public exhbns. and played multiple matches, sometimes playing blindfolded during late 1850's; toured Europe giving exhbns., also defeated many of Europe's most famous players in matches; claimed world chess championship; wrote Articles for Chess Monthly and New York Ledger, 1859-60; ret., 1860, lived with his family in New Orleans. Died New Orleans, July 10, 1884.

MORRELL, Benjamin, sealing capt., explorer; b. Rye, N.Y., July 5, 1795; s. Benjamin Morrell; married twice; m. 2d, Abby Wood 1824; 2 children. Capt. on sealing voyages into South Seas in ships Wasp, 1822-24, Tartar, 1824-26, Antarctic, 1828-29, 29-31, believed to have been 1st Am. sealing capt. to penetrate Antarctic Circle. Author: A Narrative of Four Voyages to the South Sea (vivid 1st hand description of certain parts of South Seas, best obtainable information at the time), 1832. Died Mozambique, S.E. Africa, 1839.

MORRELL, Daniel Johnson, congressman; b. North Berwick, Me., Aug. 8, 1821; attended pub. schs. Moved to Phila., 1836; clk. counting room, later engaged in merc. bus.; moved to Johnstown, Pa., 1855, became gen. mgr. Cambria Iron Co.; pres. local gas and water co., Johnstown, 1860-84, 1st Nat. Bank of Johnstown, 1863-84; pres. Johnstown City Council, many years; mem. U.S. Ho. of Reps. (Republican) from Pa., 40th-41st congresses, 1867-71; commr. to Paris Expn., 1878. Died Johnstown, Aug. 20, 1885; buried Grandview Cemetery, Johnstown.

MORRIL, David Lawrence, senator, gov. N.H.; b. Epping, N.H., June 10, 1772; s. Samuel and Anna (Lawrence) M.; studied medicine, N.H.; studied for ministry under Rev. Jesse Remington, Candia, N.H., 1800-02; hon. degree, Dartmouth, 1821; LL.D. (hon.), U. Vt., 1825; m. Jane Wallace, Sept. 25, 1794; m. 2d, Lydia Poore, Aug. 3, 1824; 4 children. Practiced medicine, Epsom, N.H., 1793-1800, 1807-30; pastor Presbyn. Ch., Goffstown, N.H., 1802-11; mem. N.H. Ho. of Reps., 1808-17, speaker, 1816; mem. U.S. Senate (Adams Democrat) from N.H., 1817-23; mem. N.H. Senate, 1823-24; gov. N.H., 1824-27 moved to Concord, N.H., 1831; editor newspaper N.H. Observer, 1831-33; v.p. Am. Bible Soc., Sunday Sch. Union. Died Concord, Jan. 28, 1849; buried Old North Cemetery, Concord.

MORRILL, Anson Peaslee, gov. of Me., congressman; b. Belgrade, Me., June 10, 1803; s. Peaslee and Nancy (Macomber) M.; m. Rowena Richardson, 1827, 2 children. Owner gen. stores, successively Dearborn, Madison, Readfield, Me.; bought wool mill, Readfield, 1844; pres. Me. Central R.R., 1871-87; postmaster, Dearborn, 1825-41; mem. Me. Ho. of Reps., 1833, 80; sheriff, Somerset County, Me., 1839; land agt. for State of Me., 1850-53; 1st gov. of Me. (Republican, apptd. to office when none of 4 candidates received majority of votes), 1855; del. to Rep. Nat. Conv., 1856; mem. U.S. Ho. of Reps. from Me., 37th Congress, 1861-63. Died Augusta, Me., July 4, 1887; buried Forest est Grove Cemetery, Augusta.

MORRILL, Justin, senator, congressman; b. Strafford, Vt., Apr. 14, 1810; s. Nathaniel and Mary (Hunt) M.; m. Ruth Barrell Swan, Sept. 17, 1871, 2 children. Engaged in merchandising, Portland, Me., 1828-31; owner, operator (with Jedediah H. Harris) village store, Strafford, 1831-48; mem. Whig Nat. Conv., 1842; mem. U.S. Ho. of Reps. from Vt., 34th-39th congresses, 1854-66, mem. Ho. Ways and Means Com.; author Morrill Tariff Act (highly protectionist), 1861; proposed Land-Grant College Act, 1857 (vetoed by Pres. James Buchanan, 1859, passed by Pres. Abraham Lincoln, 1862); mem. U.S. Senate (Republican) from Vt., 1866-98, mem. finance com., 1871-79, 81-93, 95-98; author 2d Morrill Act which provided for allotment of $25,000 from U.S. Govt. for all land grant colls., 1890; served 44 consecutive years in U.S. Congress (2d longest consecutive term of service in U.S. history). Author: Self-Consciousness of Noted Persons, 1882. Died Washington, D.C., Dec. 28, 1898; buried City Cemetery, Strafford.

MORRILL, Lot Myrick, senator, gov. of Me.; b. Belgrade, Me., May 3, 1812; s. Peaslee and Nancy (Macomber) M.; attended Waterville (now Colby) Coll., 1830-31; m. Charlotte Holland Vance, 1845, 4 children including Anne Morrill Hamlin. Admitted to Me. bar, 1839, practiced law at Augusta, Me.; mem. Me. Senate, 1854, 56, pres. 1856; gov. State of Me., 1858-60; mem. U.S. Senate (Republican) from Me., Jan. 17, 1861-69, Oct. 30, 1869-July 7, 1876; mem. peace conv., Washington, D.C., 1861; U.S. sec. of the treasury, 1876-77 (under Grant and Hayes); U.S. collector of customs, Portland, Me., 1877-83. Died Augusta, Jan. 10, 1883; buried Forest Grove Cemetery, Augusta.

MORRILL, Samuel Plummer, congressman; b. Chesterville, Me., Feb. 11, 1816; attended Farmington (Me.) Acad.; studied theology. Ordained to ministry, pastor, Farmington, 1848-53; register of deeds Franklin County (Me.), 1857-67; mem. U.S. Ho. of Reps. (Republican) from Me., 41st Congress, 1869-71; minister, East Dixfield, Me., 1877-79; moved to Vienna, Me., 1885, ret. from ministry, 1886. Died Chesterville, Me., Aug. 4, 1892; buried Chesterville Hill Cemetery.

MORRIS, Anthony, mayor Phila.; b. London, Eng., Aug. 23, 1654; s. Anthony and Elizabeth (Senior) M.; m. Mary Jones, Mar. 30, 1676; m. 2d, Mrs. Agnes Bom, 1689; m. 3d, Mrs. Mary Coddington, 1693; m. 4th, Elizabeth Watson, 1700; 15 children. Came to Burlington, West Jersey, 1683; clk. Phila. Yearly Meeting, 1687; mem. Quarterly Meeting of Phila., 1688; mem. 1st bd. overseers William Penn Sch.; justice Ct. of Common Pleas for City and County of Phila., 1691, presiding justice, 1693-98; commd. asso. justice Provincial Supreme Ct. Pa., 1694-98; one of 6 alderman, when Phila. was inc., 1691; elected mem. Pa. Provincial Council, 1695, 96; mem. Phila. Assembly, 1698-1704; mayor Phila., 1703-04. Died Phila., Oct. 23, 1721.

MORRIS, Anthony, mcht.; b. Phila., Feb. 10, 1766; s. Samuel and Rebecca (Wister) M.; grad. U. Pa., 1783; m. Mary Pemberton, May 13, 1790; 4 children. Admitted to Pa. bar, 1787; mcht. in East India trade; speaker Pa. Senate, 1793-94; dir. Bank of N.Am., 1800-06; unofcl. rep. of U.S. to Spain, 1810-14, attempted to obtain treaty for purchase of East and West Fla. when in Spain; trustee U. Pa., 1806-17; founder agrl. sch., Bucks County, Pa., 1830. Died nr. Georgetown, D.C., Nov. 3, 1860.

MORRIS, Cadwalader, mcht., congressman; b. Phila., Feb. 19, 1741; s. Samuel and Hannah (Cadwalader) M.; m. Ann Strettell, Apr. 8, 1779, 5 children. Served as mem. 1st Troop, Phila. City Cavalry during Revolutionary War; a founder, insp. Bank of Pa., 1780; founder, dir. Bank of N. Am., 1781-87; Pa. del. to Continental Congress, 1783-84; mem. Democratic Soc. of Phila.; operated an iron furnace; engaged in merc. pursuits. Died Phila., Jan. 25, 1795.

MORRIS, Calvary, congressman; b. Charleston, Va. (now W.Va.), Jan. 15, 1798; attended common schs. Moved to Athens, O., 1819; sheriff of Athens County, 1823-27; mem. Ohio Ho. of Reps., 1835-36; mem. U.S. Ho. of Reps. (Whig) from Ohio, 25th-27th congresses, 1837-43; engaged in wool growing; moved to Cincinnati, 1847, engaged in merc. bus.; returned to Athens; elected probate judge Athens County, 1854. Died Athens, Oct. 13, 1871; buried Athens Cemetery.

MORRIS, Caspar, physician; b. Phila., May 2, 1805; s. Israel Westar and Mary (Hollingsworth) M.; M.D., U. Pa., 1826; m. Anne Cheston, Nov. 11, 1829. Apptd. physician Phila. Dispensary, 1828; founder House of Refuge, physician, 1830-34; helped establish Pa. Instn. for Instrn. of Blind, mgr., physician, 1833-84; published an article which resulted in movement to establish Episcopal Hosp., became mgr. hosp.; wrote Appeal on Behalf of the Sick, 1851;"Five Essays Relating to the Construction, Organization and Management of Hospitals" published in Hospital Plans, 1875; mem. Nat. Acad. Scis., 1829-38, Am. Philos. Soc., 1851-60; fellow Coll. of Physicians; aided in founding Phila. Med. Inst., 1838; one of 5 selected to submit ideas for bldg. of Johns Hopkins Hosp. in Balt. Died May 17, 1884.

MORRIS, Charles, naval officer; b. Woodstock, Conn., July 26, 1784; s. Charles and Miriam (Nichols) M.; m. Harriet Bowen, Feb. 1, 1815; 10 children, including Charles, George. Apptd. midshipman U.S. Navy, 1799; on board the Constitution during war with Tripoli, 1803-05; lt. during Mediterranean cruise on ship Hornet, 1807; 1st lt. under Isaac Hull in Constitution at outbreak of War of 1812; promoted to capt. over grade of muster commandant, 1812; on ship Congress, comdg. forces in Carribean while on diplomatic missions to Haiti and Venezuela, 1814-17; mem. Bd. Navy Commrs., 1823-24, 27; commanded ship Brandywine in which Lafayette returned to France, 1825-26; commanded Boston Navy Yard, 1827-32; commanded Brazil and Mediterranean squadrons, 1841-44; head Bur. Constrn., later Bur. Ordnance until 1856. Died Washington, D.C., Jan. 27, 1856.

MORRIS, Daniel, congressman; b. Fayette, N.Y., Jan. 4, 1812; attended Canandaigua Acad.; studied law. Admitted to N.Y. bar, 1845, began practice in Penn Yan; dist. atty. Yates County (N.Y.), 1847-50; mem. N.Y. Assembly, 1859; mem. U.S. Ho. of Reps. (Republican) from N.Y., 38th-39th congresses, 1863-67. Died Penn Yan, Apr. 22, 1889; buried Lake View Cemetery, Penn Yan.

MORRIS, Edmund, editor; b. Burlington, N.J., Aug. 20, 1804; s. Richard and Mary (Smith) M.; m. Mary Jenks, Dec. 27, 1827, 4 children. Editor (with S. R. Kramer) Bucks County (Pa.) Patriot and Farmers' Advertiser, 1824-27; editor Burlington Gazette, 1846-48, Daily State Gazette, Trenton, N.J., 1854-56; mem. staff N.Y. Tribune during and after Civil War; wrote on agrl. and anti-slavery subjects. Author: Ten Acres Enough for Intensive Gardening, 1844; How To Get a Farm and Where To Find One, 1864. Died May 4, 1874.

MORRIS, Edward Joy, diplomat, congressman; b. Phila., July 16, 1815; attended U. Pa.; grad. Harvard, 1836; m. Elizabeth Gatliff Ella, July 15, 1847; m. 2d, Susan Leighton, Oct. 1876; at least 2 children. Admitted to Pa. bar, 1842; mem. Pa. Assembly, 1841-43; mem. U.S. Ho. of Reps. (Whig) from Pa., 28th, 35th-37th congresses, 1843-45, 1857-June 8, 1861; U.S. charge d'affaires to Kingdom of Two Sicilies (now part of Italy), 1850-53; bd. dirs. Gerard Coll., Phila., 1853; U.S. minister to Turkey, 1861-70, negotiated comml. treaty with Turkey which was approved by Senate. Author: The Turkish Empire: Its Historical, Statistical and Religious Condition, 1854. Translator (from German) Corsica, Picturesque, Historical and Social (Ferdinand Gregorovius), 1855. Died Phila., Dec. 31, 1881; buried Laurel Hill Cemetery, Phila.

MORRIS, Elizabeth, actress (stage name Mrs. Owen Morris); b. Eng., circa 1753; m. Owen Morris. First definitely known stage appearance was at Southwark Theatre, Phila., 1772; performed with American Co., Charleston, S.C., 1773; made N.Y.C. debut, 1773; participated in 1st theatrical season in Boston, 1792 (against law, arrested); asso. mainly with Chestnut St. Theatre, Phila., 1794-1810; regarded as greatest attraction on Am. stage after Am. Revolution, particularly in high comedy roles. Died Apr. 17, 1826.

MORRIS, George Pope, journalist, poet; b. Phila., Oct. 10, 1802; m. Mary Hopkins; several children. Helped found N.Y. Mirror, 1823, Ladies Lit. Gazette, 1823; the gazette afforded medium of pub. expression for the early knickerbocker sch. until 1842; editor New Mirror, 1843-44 (carried on same journalistic tradition), Evening Mirror, 1844; founded weekly Nat. Press (name changed to Home Journal, 1846), 1845, editor, 1845-64; Chatham Theatre produced his drama Brier Cliff, 1826; poems include Woodman, Spare that Tree, Near the Lake; prose and humourous sketches include The Little Frenchman and his Water Lots; songs include "Near the Lake Where Drooped the Willow", "Long Long Ago", "My Mother's Bible". Died N.Y.C., July 6, 1864.

MORRIS, George Sylvester, educator, philosopher; b. Norwich, Vt., Nov. 15, 1840; s. Sylvester and Susanna (Weston) M.; grad. Dartmouth, 1861; attended Union Theol. Sem.; attended U. Halle and U. Berlin (Germany), 1866-68; m. Victoria Celle, 1876, 2 children. Became prof. Modern languages U. Mich., 1870, head philosophy dept., 1885; translated Friedrich Ueberweg's History of Philosophy, published 1871-73; champion idealistic movement initiated by Kant and advanced by Hegel. Author: British Thought and Thinkers 1880; Kant's Critique of Pure Reason, 1882; Philosophy and Christianity, 1883; Hegel's Philosophy of the State and of History, 1887. Died Ann Arbor, Mich., Mar. 23, 1889.

MORRIS, Gouverneur, senator, diplomat; b. Morrisiania, N.Y., Jan. 31, 1752; s. Lewis and Sarah (Gouverneur) M.; grad. Kings Coll. (now Columbia), 1768; studied law under William Smith; m. Anne Carey Randolph, Dec. 25, 1809, 1 child. Admitted to N.Y. bar, 1771; mem. N.Y. Provincial Congress from Westchester County, 1775-77; held conservative position between radicals (who wished "reign of terror" against Loyalists) and staunch Loyalists (who wished to remain united with Eng.); mem. Constl. Conv. from N.Y., July 1775, drafted (with John Jay and Robert R. Livingston) Articles of Confedn., secured provision of elected gov. rather than exec. bd.; a signer Articles of Confedn., 1775; mem. com. to organize new govt. N.Y. State; mem. 1st N.Y. Council of Safety; mem. Continental Congress from N.Y., 1777-78, drafted instrn. to Benjamin Franklin (1st U.S. minister to France); not reelected to Continental Congress because of refusal to support Gov. George Clinton and N.Y.'s claims to Vt.; moved to Pa., practiced law, Phila.; contbd. essays on finance (signed "An American") to Pa. Packet, Feb.-Apr. 1780; U.S. asst. supt. finance under Robert Morris, 1781-85; del. from Pa. to U.S. Constl. Conv., Phila., 1787, favored strong centralized govt. controlled by rich and well-born, a pres. elected for life, and a senate apptd. for life by pres.; noted for his cynical contempt for democracy; went to France as agt. of Robert Morris, 1789, assisted in opening tobacco trade on better terms for America, and selling of Am. lands; engaged in plot to rescue Louis XVI from Tuleries; apptd. U.S. minister to France by Pres. George Washington, 1792-94, only fgn. minister to remain in Paris during Reign of Terror; traveled throughout Europe, 1794-98; mem. U.S. Senate (Federalist) from N.Y., Apr. 3, 1800-03, supported Jefferson's La. Purchase; ret. to Morrisania, 1803-16; denounced Jefferson's Embargo Acts, War of 1812; approved Hartford Conv. Died Morrisania, Nov. 6, 1816; buried St. Anne's Episcopal Churchyard, Bronx, N.Y.

MORRIS, Isaac Newton, congressman; b. Bethel, O., Jan. 22, 1812; s. Thomas Morris; attended Miami U., Oxford, O.; studied law. Admitted to Ill. bar, 1835, began practice in Warsaw, 1836; moved to Quincy, Ill., 1838, practiced law; declined appointment as sec. of state Ill., 1840; pres. Ill. & Mich. Canal Co., 1841; mem. Ill. Ho. of Reps., 1846-48; promoted constrn. of No. Cross R.R.; mem. U.S. Ho. of Reps. (Democrat) from Ill., 35th-36th congresses, 1857-61; apptd. commr. for Union Pacific R.R. by Pres. Grant, 1869. Died Quincy, Oct. 29, 1879; buried Woodland Cemetery, Quincy.

MORRIS, John Gottlieb, clergyman; b. York, Pa., Nov. 14, 1803; s. John and Barbara (Myers) M.; grad. Dickinson Coll., 1823; attended Princeton Theol. Sem., 1825-26, Gettysburg Theol. Sem., 1826-27; m. Eliza Hay, Nov. 21, 1827. Ordained to ministry Lutheran Ch., 1827; pastor 1st English Luth. Ch., Balt., 1827-60; librarian Peabody Inst., 1860-65; pastor 3d Ch., 1864-73; founder Lutheran Observer, 1831; often pres. Md. Synod; pres. Gen. Synod, 1843, 83; dir. Gettysburg Sem., also trustee Gettysburg Coll., more than 60 years; attended 1st conv. Evang. Alliance, London, Eng., 1846; a founder Lutherville, Md. (a Balt. suburb), 1851; a founder Luth. Hist. Soc.; pres. entomol. sect. A.A.A.S., many years; Author: Synopsis of the Described Lepidoptera of the United States, 1862; Bibliotheca Lutherana, 1876, Died Lutherville, Oct. 10, 1895.

MORRIS, Jonathan David, congressman; b. Columbia, O., Oct. 8, 1804; s. Thomas Morris; attended pub. schs.; studied law. Admitted to Ohio bar, began practice in Batavia; clk. of cts. Clermont County (O.); mem. U.S. Ho. of Reps. (Democrat) from Ohio, 30th-31st congresses, 1847-51. Died Connersville, Ind., May 16, 1875; buried Citizens Cemetery, Batavia.

MORRIS, Joseph, congressman; b. Greene County, Pa., Oct. 16, 1795; attended pub. schs.; children include James Remley. Sheriff of Greene County,

1824; moved to Woodsfield, O., 1829, engaged in merc. bus.; mem. Ohio Ho. of Reps., 1833-34; treas. Monroe County (O.); mem. U.S. Ho. of Reps. (Democrat) from Ohio, 28th-29th congresses, 1843-47. Died Woodsfield, Oct. 23, 1854; buried Morris Cemetery, nr. Woodsfield.

MORRIS, Lewis, jurist, colonial gov.; b. N.Y.C., Oct. 15, 1671; s. Richard and Sarah (Pole) M.; m. Isabella Graham, Nov. 3, 1691; children—Lewis, Robert Hunter. First Lord of Manor of Morrisania, N.Y.; judge Ct. Common Rights of East Jersey, 1692; mem. N.J. Gov. Council, 1692-98, 1702-07, 10-33; vestryman Trinity Ch., 1697-1700; elected to N.J. Assembly (a bitter opponent of Gov. Edward Cornbury), 1707; apptd. chief justice N.Y. Supreme Ct., 1715; elected to N.J. Assembly, 1733, presented assembly's grievances against Gov. William Cosby in London, Eng., 1734; became gov., councilor N.J., at the time when the polit. connection between N.Y. and N.J. was severed, 1738, his adminstrn. was marked by bitter quarrels with the assembly over taxation, support of militia, issuance of bills, credit, validity of land titles. Died Trenton, N.J., May 21, 1746; buried Morrisania, N.J.

MORRIS, Lewis, Continental congressman; b. Morrisania, N.Y., Apr. 8, 1726; s. Lewis and Tryntje (Staats) M.; A.B., Yale, 1746; m. Mary Walton, Sept. 24, 1749, 10 children. Became 3d and last lord of the manor of Morrisania, 1762; mem. N.J. Provincial Assembly, 1769; chmn. delegation N.Y. Provincial Conv., N.Y.C., 1775; mem. Continental Congress, 1775-77, mem. com. of ways and means to supply army, com. of Indian affairs; brig. gen. in command Militia of Westchester County (N.Y.); mem. 4th Provincial Congress at White Plains, 1776; signer Declaration of Independence, July 20, 1776; judge Westchester County (N.Y.), 1777-78; mem. bd. regents U. State N.Y., 1784-98; mem. N.Y. Senate, 1777-81, 84-88; mem. Council of Appointment, 1786. Died Morrisania, Jan. 22, 1798; buried St. Anne's Episcopal Churchyard, Bronx, N.Y.

MORRIS, Lewis Richard, congressman; b. Scarsdale, N.Y., Nov. 2, 1760; s. Richard and Sarah (Ludlow) M.; m. Mary Dwight, 1786; m. 2d, Theodora Olcott; m. 3d, Ellen Hunt. Sec. to U.S. sec. of fgn. affairs (Robert R. Livingston), 1781-83; mem. Springfield (Vt.) Meeting House Com., 1785, tax collector, 1786-87, selectman, 1788, town treas., 1790-94; clk. county ct., 1789-96, judge, 1796-1801; clk. Vt. Ho. of Reps., 1790, 91; sat in Bennington (Vt. Conv. to ratify U.S. Constn. 1791; one of 2 commrs. to Congress to arrange Vt.'s admission to the Union, 1791; sec. Vt. Constl. Conv. at Windsor, 1793; 1st U.S. marshal Vt. Dist., 1791-1801; mem. Vt. Assembly, 1795, 96, 1803, 05, 06, 08, speaker, 1795, 96; brig. gen. Vt. Militia, 1793-95, promoted maj. gen. 1795-1817; mem. U.S. Ho. of Reps. (Federalist) from Vt., 5th-7th congresses, 1797-1803. Died Springfield, Vt., Dec. 29, 1825; buried Forrest Cemetery, Charlestown, N.H.

MORRIS, Luzon Burritt, gov. Conn.; b. Newtown, Conn., Apr. 16, 1827; s. Eli Gould and Lydia (Bennett) M.; A.B., Yale, 1858; m. Eugenia Tuttle, June 15, 1856, 6 children, including Helen, Robert T. Admitted to Conn. bar, 1856; judge of probate New Haven (Conn.), 1857-63; mem. lower house Conn. Legislature, 1855-56, re-elected, 1870, 76, 80, 81; mem. Conn. Senate, 1874, pres. pro tem; mem. commn. which settled old boundary dispute between Conn. and N.Y.; officer Conn. Savs. Bank, New Haven; dir. N.Y., N.H. & H. R.R. Co.; mem. commn. to revise Conn. laws; gov. Conn., 1893-95. Died Aug. 22, 1895.

MORRIS, Mathias, congressman; b. Hilltown, Pa., Sept. 12, 1787; attended common schs., Newtown and Doylestown, Pa.; studied law. Admitted to Pa. bar, 1809, began practice in Newtown; dep. atty. gen., 1819; mem. Pa. Senate, 1828-33; mem. U.S. Ho. of Reps. (Whig) from Pa., 24th-25th congresses, 1835-39. Died Doylestown, Nov. 9, 1839; buried Hilltown Baptist Ch. Cemetery.

MORRIS, Richard, jurist; b. N.Y.C., Aug. 15, 1730; s. Lewis and Tryntje (Staats) M.; grad. Yale, 1748; m. Sarah Ludlow, June 13, 1759; children—Mary, Lewis Richard, Robert. Admitted to N.Y. bar, 1752; judge Vice-admiralty ct. with jurisdiction over N.Y. State, Conn., N.J., 1762-75; mem. N.Y. State Senate, 1778-80; chief justice N.Y. State Supreme Ct., 1779-90; mem. N.Y. County delegation to Poughkeepsie Conv. of 1788. Died Scarsdale, N.Y., Apr. 11, 1810; buried Trinity Churchyard, N.Y.C.

MORRIS, Richard Valentine, naval officer; diplomat; b. Morrisania, N.Y., Mar. 8, 1768; s. Lewis and Mary (Walton) M.; m. Anne Walton, Jan. 24, 1797, 4 children. Commd. capt. U.S. Navy, 1798; commanded a naval squadron sent to operate against Tripoli, 1802, later superintended all U.S. negotiations with Tripoli, Tunis, Algiers, Morocco, unable to conclude peace on favorable terms, commn. revoked, 1803. Author: A Defence of the Conduct of Commodore Morris During His Command in the Mediterranean (pamphlet), 1804. Died May 13, 1815.

MORRIS, Robert, Continental congressman, financier; b. Liverpool, Eng., Jan. 31, 1734; s. Robert Morris; ed. by pvt. tutor, Phila.; m. Mary White, 1773, 7 children. Went to Md., circa 1747; mem. firm Willing, Morris & Co., shipping mchts., Phila., 1754; signed Non-Importation Agreement of 1765; warden Port of Phila., 1766; mem. Pa. Council of Safety, 1775; a secret com. of Continental Congress contracted with Willing & Morris for importation of arms and ammunition, 1775; mem. last Pa. Assembly held under colonial charter 1775; mem. Com. of Correspondence; del. to Continental Congress, 1774, 75, mem. secret com. for procuring munitions, 1775, mem. com. of secret correspondence which drew up instructions to Silas Deane, envoy to France, 1776; signed Declaration of Independence, Aug. 1776; chosen to 1st Pa. Assembly under new constn., 1776-77; mem. Com. of Secret Correspondence (later Com. of Fgn. Affairs, then Com. of Commerce), 1777; signed Articles of Confederation for Pa., 1778; mem. Pa. Assembly, 1778, 80-81; supt. of finance under Articles of Confederation, 1781; accused in press of fraudulent comml. ventures with Silas Deane but was cleared of all charges, 1778-79; authorized to fit out and employ ships of U.S., 1781; assumed task of buying supplies for the armies; reorganized civil adminstrn.; he paid off money owed Continental soldiers by securing loans from France, 1781, Netherlands, 1783-84; mem. Gen. Assembly of Pa. for spl. purpose of defending Bank of N.Am., 1785-86; made contract with French Farmers-General which gave him monopoly of Am. tobacco trade with France, 1785; mem. Annapolis Conv., 1786; mem. U.S. Senate (Federalist) from Pa., 1789-95; mem. U.S. Constl. Conv., 1787; his fortunes collapsed through large land speculations in N.Y. and elsewhere, 1798; arrested, spent over 3 years in debtors prison and died in near poverty circumstances. Died Phila., May 8, 1806; buried Christ Church, Phila.

MORRIS, Robert, judge; b. New Brunswick, N.J., circa 1745; s. Chief Justice Robert Hunter Morris. Admitted to bar, 1770; licensed as counselor, 1773; chief justice N.J. Supreme Ct., 1777-79; judge N.J. dist. U.S. Cts., 1789-1814. Died New Brunswick, June 2, 1815.

MORRIS, Robert, coll. pres., assn. ofcl.; b. Boston, Aug. 31, 1818; m. Charlotte Mendenhall, Aug. 26, 1841, 6 children. Principal, Mount Sylvan Acad., Oxford, Miss.; pres. Masonic Coll., La Grange, Ky.; sec. Am. Assn. Numismatics; master Mason, Oxford (Miss.) Lodge No. 33, 1846, grand master Grand Lodge of Ky., 1858-59; founder Order of Eastern Star; published Universal Masonic Library, 30 vols.; pres. Oldham Coll., La Grange, Ky., 1856. Author: The Lights and Shadows of Freemasonry, 1852; A Code of Masonic Law, 1856; The Dictionary of Freemasonry, 1867; Freemasonry in the Holy Land, 1872; The Poetry of Freemasonry, 1884; The Level and the Square (most famous poem). Died La Grange, Ky., July 31, 1888.

MORRIS, Robert Hunter, jurist, gov. Pa.; b. Morrisania, N.Y., circa 1700; s. Lewis and Isabella (Graham) M.; never married; at least 3 children, including Robert. Chief justice of N.J., 1738-54, 56-57, 58-64; became mem. Council of Proprs. for East Jersey, 1742; active in protecting interests of N.J. landholders; gov. Pa., 1754-56, failed to secure adequate support for militia; Died Shrewsbury, N.J., Jan. 27, 1764.

MORRIS, Roger, army officer; b. Netherby, Eng., Jan. 28, 1727; s. Roger and Mary (Jackson) M.; m. Mary Philipse, Jan. 1758, 4 children. Served as capt. 48th Regt., Brit. Army; in Braddock campaign in French and Indian Wars, 1755-63; promoted maj., 1757, at battles of Quebec and Montreal; made lt. col. 47th Regt., 1760; retired from Brit. Army, 1764; mem. N.Y. Council, 1765-76; a leading Loyalist, had his property (over 51,000 acres in N.Y. State) confiscated; moved to Yorkshire, Eng. Died York, Eng., Sept. 13, 1794; buried St. Savioursgate Churchyard, York.

MORRIS, Samuel Wells, congressman; b. Phila., Sept. 1, 1786; attended Princeton; studied law. Admitted to Pa. bar, began practice in Wellsboro; judge dist. ct.; 1st treas. Wellsboro County (Pa.); mem. Pa. Ho. of Reps.; mem. U.S. Ho. of Reps. (Democrat) from Pa., 25th-26th congresses, 1837-41. Died Wellsboro, May 25, 1847.

MORRIS, Thomas, congressman; b. Phila., Feb. 26, 1771; s. Robert Morris; attended sch., Geneva, Switzerland, 1781-86, U. Leipsig (Germany), 1786-88; studied law, Phila. Admitted to the bar; began practice of law, Canandaigua, N.Y.; mem. N.Y. Assembly, 1794-96; mem. U.S. Ho. of Reps. from N.Y., 7th Congress, 1801-03; resumed practice of law, N.Y.C., 1803; apptd. U.S. marshal for So. N.Y., 1816, 20, 25, 29. Died N.Y.C., Mar. 12, 1849.

MORRIS, Thomas, senator, abolitionist; b. Berks County, Pa., Jan. 3, 1776; m. Rachel Davis, Nov. 19, 1797, 11 children including Isaac Newton, Jonathan David. Moved to Columbia (now part of Cincinnati), O., 1795, clerked in store for Rev. John Smith; admitted to Ohio bar, 1804; mem. Ohio Legislature from Clermont County, 1806-33; founder (with Samuel Medary) publ. Ohio Sun to support Andrew Jackson; mem. U.S. Senate (Democrat) from Ohio, 1833-39, denounced nullification and secession; an expansionist and abolitionist; opposed extension of slavery into the territories, favored abolition of slavery in D.C.; ostracized by people of Ohio, but went on anti-slavery campaign throughout state, 1840-41; unsuccessful Liberty Party candidate for vice pres. U.S., 1844. Died Bethel, O., Dec. 7, 1844; buried 1st Bethel Cemetery.

MORRIS, William Hopkins, army officer; b. N.Y. C., Apr. 22, 1827; s. George and Mary (Hopkins) M.; grad. U.S. Mil. Acad., 1851; m. Catharine (Hoffman) Hyatt, 1870. Commd. 2d lt. 2d Inf., U.S. Army, 1851, resigned commn., 1854; invented repeating carbine with Charles Brown, 1859, patented, 1860; reenlisted as capt. U.S. Volunteers, 1861, promoted brig. gen., 1862; fought at battles of Fair Oaks, Bristol, Wilderness; commd. maj. gen., U.S. Volunteers, 1865; commd. col. N.Y. Nat. Guard, 1866, brig. gen., 1869; mem. N.Y. Constl. Conv., 1867. Author: Field Tactics for Infantry, 1864. Died Long Branch, N.J., Aug. 26, 1900.

MORRIS, William V., artist. Came from Wales to Utah, 1852; opened 1st art store in Utah Territory; did art work for Brigham Young's Bee-Hive and Lion houses; 1st scene painter Salt Lake Theater; a founder Deseret Acad. Arts, circa 1860; painted frescoes for Assembly Hall, 1880. Died before 1887.

MORRISON, George Washington, congressman; b. Fairlee, Vt., Oct. 16, 1809; attended Thetford (Vt.) Acad.; studied law. Taught sch.; admitted to Vt. bar, 1835, began practice in Manchester, 1836; mem. Vt. Ho. of Reps., 1840-41; solicitor Hillsborough County (Vt.), 1845-49; mem. Vt. Senate, 1849-50; mem. U.S. Ho. of Reps. (Democrat) from Vt., 31st, 33d congresses, Oct. 8, 1850-51, 53-55; practiced law, Manchester, until 1872. Died Manchester, Dec. 21, 1888; buried Valley Cemetery, Manchester.

MORRISON, James Lowery Donaldson, congressman; b. Kaskaskia, Ill., Apr. 12, 1816; studied law. Served as midshipman U.S. Navy, 1832-39; admitted to Ill. bar, began practice in Belleville; mem. Ill. Ho. of Reps., 1844; organizer, lt. col. of a volunteer co. during Mexican War, 1846-47; presented a sword by Ill. Legislature for services at Battle of Buena Vista; mem. Ill. Senate, 1848; mem. U.S. Ho. of Reps. (Democrat) from Ill., 34th Congress, Nov. 4, 1856-57; unsuccessful Dem. candidate for gov. Ill., 1860. Died St. Louis, Aug. 14, 1888; buried Calvary Cemetery, St. Louis.,

MORRISON, John Irwin, educator; b. Chambersburg, Pa., July 25, 1806; s. Robert and Ann (Irwin) M.; A.B., Miami U., Oxford, O., 1828; m. Catherine Morris, 1832. In charge Salem (Ind.) Grammar Sch., 1825-27, Washington County (Ind.) Sem., 1828; established Salem (Ind.) Female Inst., 1835-39; mem. Ind. Ho. of Reps., 1839-40; prof. ancient langs. Ind. U., 1840-43, trustee, 1846-49, 50-55, pres. bd., 1854-55, 75-78; mem. Ind. Senate, 1847-50; senatorial del. to Ind. Constl. Conv., 1850-51, drafted article on edn.; author Sect. 8 of law which created office of state supt. pub. instrn., 1852; helped secure passage of laws which provided for establishment of tchrs. inst., 1865; responsible for passage of law which created office of county supt. schs., 1873; treas. Washington County (Ind.), 1856-60; purchased Washington Republican which he renamed Washington Democrat, 1847; became editor Salem Times, 1861, renamed it Union Advocate; apptd. commr. of enrollment by Pres. Lincoln in 1863; state treas. Ind., 1865-67; pres. sch. bd., 1874-77. Died Knightstown, Ind., July 17, 1882.

MORRISON, William, mcht.; b. Doylestown, Pa., Mar. 14, 1763; s. John and Rebecca (Bryan) M.; m. Catherine Thoumur, circa 1794; m. 2d, Euphrosine Huberdeau, Nov. 27, 1798; m. 3d, Elisa Bissell, July 20, 1812. Moved to Kaskaskia, Ill., mem. firm Bryan & Morrison, mcht. firm, 1790; opened store, Cahokia, Ill., 1800; traveled as far West as Santa Fe, N.M., interested in fur trade; an organizer St. Louis Mo. Fur. Co., 1807. Died Kaskaskia, Apr. 19, 1837.

MORRISSEY, John, congressman, gambler, prizefighter; b. Templemore, Ireland, Feb. 12, 1831; s. Timothy Morrissey; m. Sarah Smith, 1 child. Came to Canada, circa 1835, then to U.S.; defeated Yankee Sullivan at Boston Four Corners, Oct. 12, 1853, gave him claim on heavyweight championship; defeated John C. Heenan, Long Point, Can., Oct. 20, 1858, retained his title; mem. U.S. Ho. of Reps. (Democrat) from N.Y., 40th-41st congresses, 1867-71; had gambling house in Saratoga, N.Y., 1862, opened new clubhouse there, 1870; mem. N.Y. State Senate, 1875, 77; part owner gambling casino at Saratoga, race track and buildings by 1878; made and lost several fortunes on Wall Street. Died Troy, N.Y., May 1, 1878.

MORROW, Jeremiah, senator, gov. Ohio; b. Gettysburg, Pa., Oct. 6, 1771; s. John and Mary (Lockart) M.; m. Mary Parkhill, Feb. 19, 1799, 6 children. Moved to N.W. Territory (now Ohio), 1795; mem. Ohio Territorial Ho. of Reps., 1801-02, mem. Ohio Senate, 1803, 27; mem. U.S. Ho. of Reps. from Ohio, 8th-12th, 26th-27th congresses, 1803-13, 40-43; mem. Ohio Ho. of Reps., 1829, 35; mem. U.S. Senate from Ohio, 1813-19; Ohio canal commr., 1822; gov. Ohio, 1822-26; became pres. Little Miami R.R. Co., 1836. Died Twenty-Mile-Stand, O., Mar. 22, 1852; buried Union Cemetery, Warren County, O.

MORROW, John, congressman. Mem. U.S. Ho. of Reps. from Va., 9th-10th congresses, 1805-09.

MORROW, Thomas Vaughan, pioneer in eclectic medicine; b. Fairview, Ky., Apr. 14, 1804; s. Thomas and Elizabeth (Vaughan) M.; attended Transylvania U., Reformed Med. Coll. of N.Y.; m. Isabel Greer. Pres., dean, prof. materia medica, obstetrics, theory and practice of medicine Reformed Med. Coll. of Ohio, 1830-39; organized Reformed Med. Sch. of Cincinnati, 1842, became Cincinnati Eclectic Med. Inst., 1845, dean, treas., prof. physiology, pathology and theory and practice, 1845-50; advocated the eclectic system of medicine, founder of 1st schs. of that cult in West; pres. Nat. Eclectic Med. Assn., 1848; wrote articles, editorials for Western Med. Reformer and Eclectic Med. Jour. Died Cincinnati, July 16, 1850; buried Wesleyan Cemetery, Cincinnati.

MORSE, Alpheus, architect; b. 1818. Practiced architecture, Providence, R.I., more than 30 years; works include Mchts. Bank Bldg. (with G. A. Hall), circa 1855, Chem. Lab. at Brown U., 1862, R.I. Hosp., 1866, Trinity Ch. (with Hall), 1868, Sayre Hall at Brown U., 1881 (all Providence); built number of residences, 1850's; mem. A.I.A., 1st pres. R.I. chpt., 1875. Died Nov. 25, 1893.

MORSE, Freeman Harlow, congressman, diplomat; b. Bath, Me., Feb. 19, 1807; s. William and Eliza (Harlow) M.; m. Nancy Leavitt, Apr. 21, 1834, 2 children. Employed as ship-carver, Bath; mem. Me. Ho. of Reps. (Whig), 1840, 41, 43, 53, 56; mem. U.S. Ho. of Reps. from Me., 28th, 35th-36th congresses, 1843-45, 57-61; mayor Bath, 1849, 50, 55; attended Peace Conv., Washington, D.C., 1861; U.S. consul, London, Eng., 1861-69, consul gen., 1869-70; became Brit. citizen. Died Surbiton, Surrey, Eng., Feb. 5, 1891; buried St. Mary's, Long Ditton, Surrey, Eng.

MORSE, Henry Dutton, diamond cutter; b. Boston, Apr. 20, 1826; s. Hazen and Lucy (Cary) M.; m. Ann Hayden, May 22, 1849; 4 children. Partner in retail firm Crosby, Hunnewell & Morse, Boston, until 1875; organized Morse Diamond Cutting Co., 1877; 1st Am. to learn technique of diamond-cutting, made improvements which revolutionized the art; invented labor-saving machinery for sawing and polishing stones; cut 1st modern brilliants with 56 facets and powers of refraction; cut Dewey diamond, 1859; cut Tiffany No. 2 diamond, 125 carats, reduced to 77 carats in cutting (largest diamond ever handled in U.S.). Died Jamaica Plains, Mass.. Jan. 2, 1888.

MORSE, Isaac Edward, congressman; b. Attakapas, La., May 22, 1809; attended Norwich (Vt.) Mil. Acad.; grad. Harvard, 1829; studied law. Admitted to La. bar, practiced in New Orleans and St. Martinsville, 1835-42; mem. La. Senate, 1842-44; mem. U.S. Ho. of Reps. (Democrat) from La., 28th-31st congresses, Dec. 2, 1844-51; del. Dem. Nat. Conv., Balt., 1848; atty. gen. La., 1853-55; apptd. a spl. commr. to New Granada to negotiate transit of citizens and officers of U.S. across Isthmus of Panama. Died New Orleans, Feb. 11, 1866; buried Washington Cemetery, New Orleans.

MORSE, Jedidiah, clergyman, geographer; b. Woodstock, Conn., Aug. 23, 1761; s. Jedidiah and Sarah (Child) M.; grad. Yale, 1783; studied theology, New Haven, Conn., 1783-85; S.T.D. (hon.), U. Edinburgh (Scotland), 1794; m. Elizabeth Breese, May 14, 1789, 11 children including Samuel Finley Breese, Sidney Edwards, Richard. Licensed to preach Congregational Ch., 1785, ordained to ministry, 1786; pastor 1st Congregational Ch., Charlestown, Mass., 1789-1819; proponent of orthodox Congl. views; mem. bd. overseers Harvard; assisted in founding The Mercury and New England Palladium, 1801; founder, editor The Panoplist, 1805-10; a founder, Gen. Assn. of Mass., Andover Theol. Sem., 1808, Park St. Ch., Boston, 1809, New Eng. Tract Soc., 1814, Am. Bible Soc., 1816; mem. Am. Bd. Commrs. for Fgn. Missions, 1811-19; commd. by sec. war to study conditions of the Indian nations, 1820, published report, 1822; mem. Phi Beta Kappa; known as "father of American Geography." Author: Geography Made Easy, 1784 (1st published Am. geography); The American Geography, 1789; The American Universal Geography; Elements of Geography, 1795; The American Gazeteer, 1797; A New Gazeteer for the Eastern Continent, 1802; co-author A Compendious History of New England, 1804; True Reasons on which The Election of a Hollis Professor of Divinity in Harvard College Was Opposed by the Board of Overseers, 14 February, 1805, 1805; A Report to the Secretary of War—On Indian Affairs, Comprising A Narrative of a Tour Performed in the Summer of 1820, 1822. Died New Haven, June 9, 1826.

MORSE, Leopold, congressman; b. Wachenheim, Bavaria, Aug. 15, 1831; attended common schs., Wachenheim. Came to U.S., 1849, settled in Sandwich, N.H.; moved to Boston, employed in a clothing store, later became owner; del. Democratic nat. convs., St. Louis, 1876, Cincinnati, 1880; mem. U. S. Ho. of Reps. (Dem.) from Mass., 45th-48th, 50th congresses, 1877-85, 87-89; elected pres. Post Publishing Co., 1884. Died Boston, Dec. 15, 1892; buried Mt. Auburn Cemetery, Cambridge, Mass. ,

MORSE, Oliver Andrew, congressman; b. Cherry Valley, N.Y., Mar. 26, 1815; grad. Hamilton Coll., Clinton, N.Y., 1833; studied law. Admitted to N.Y. bar, began practice in Cherry Valley; mem. U.S. Ho. of Reps. (Republican) from N.Y., 35th Congress, 1857-59; writer, translator. Died N.Y.C., Apr. 20, 1870; buried Cherry Valley Cemetery.

MORSE, Samuel Finley Breese, inventor, artist; b. Charlestown, Mass., Apr. 27, 1791; s. Rev. Jedidiah and Elizabeth (Breese) M.; grad. Yale, 1810, LL.D. (hon.); attended Royal Acad., London, Eng., 1811-15; m. Lucretia Walker, Sept. 29, 1818; m. 2d, Sarah Griswold, Aug. 9, 1848; 8 children. Painter in Eng.; noteworthy works include: Hercules, 1812 (recipient gold medal), The Dying Hercules, 1813, The Judgment of Jupiter, 1815; engaged in portrait painting in U.S., 1815-29, best-known were two portraits of Lafayette, 1821, 22, also The Old House of Representatives; a founder N.A.D., 1st pres., 1826-42, also pres., 1861; made trip to Europe for artistic study, 1829-31; prof. painting, sculpture N.Y.U., 1832; invented electro-magnetic recording telegraph; invented sending and receiving apparatus, code (Morse Code), by 1832; worked out system of electro-magnetic relays to be placed in the telegraph line weak points, 1836; Congress voted $30,000 for an exptl. line from Washington, D.C. to Balt., 1843, line completed, May 24, 1844; Morse's rights to profits from his invention were upheld in the courts; electrician for Cyrus W. Field's Co., engaged in laying Transatlantic Cable, 1857-58; a founder Vassar Coll., 1861. Died N.Y.C., Apr. 2, 1872; buried Greenwood Cemetery, Bklyn.

MORSE, Sidney Edwards, editor, inventor; b. Charlestown, Mass., Feb. 7, 1794; s. Jedidiah and Elizabeth (Breese) M.; A.B., Yale, 1811; attended Litchfield (Conn.) Law Sch., then Andover Theol. Sem., 1817-20; m. Catharine Livingston, Apr. 1, 1841, 2 children. A founder, Recorder (1st religious newspaper in Boston), 1816; a founder N.Y. Observer, 1823, sr. editor, propr., 1823-58; editor (with father) A New System of Modern Geography . . . Accompanied by an Atlas, 1822; patentee (with brother Samuel) flexible piston pump; inventor process "cerography" (map of Conn. was first example), 1839; patentee (with son) bathometer, 1866. Author: The New States, or a Comparison of the . . . Northern and Southern States: With a View to Expose the Injustice of Erecting New States at the South (collection of reprinted articles), 1813; An Atlas of the United States, 1823; Cerographic Atlas of the United States, 1842-45; A System of Geography for the Use of Schools, 1844. Died Dec. 23, 1871.

MORTIMER, Mary, educator; b. Trowbridge, Eng., Dec. 2, 1816; d. William and Mary (Pierce) Mortimer; attended Geneva (N.Y.) Sem., 1838-40. Came to U.S. with family, 1821; pioneer in higher edn. of women in period before and after Civil War; inaugurated (with Catharine Beecher) a college system of instrn. for young women, Milw., 1st prin. Milw. Female Coll. (merged with Downer Coll. to form present-day Milw. Downer Coll., 1895); 1851, head coll., 1850-57, 66-64; formed (with Catharine Beecher) Am. Woman's Ednl. Assns. at home of Harriet Beecher Stowe; prin. sem. Baraboo, Wis., 1857-66; initiated and organized Woman's Club of Wis. Died Milw., July 14, 1877

MORTON, Charles, clergyman, educator; b. Pendavy, Eng., 1627; s. Rev. Nicholas and Francis (Kestell) M.; B.A., Wadham Coll., Oxford, 1649, M.A., 1662; m. Joan Morton, 1 child. Set up Newington Green, most famous of Dissenter's academies nr. London, 1666; landed in Boston, July 1686; minister, Charlestown, Mass.; fellow Harvard, 1692, 1st v.p., 1697; wrote Compendium Physicae and System of Logic, used as textbooks at Harvard into 18th century; best known work The Spirit of Man..., 1693; founded assn. of 22 leading ministers from Boston vicinity, 1690; 1st minister in New Eng. to perform marriages; began ceremony of "installation" among Congregationalists. Died Apr. 11, 1698.

MORTON, George, colonist; b. nr. Scrooby, Eng., 1585; s. Anthony Morton; m. Juliana Carpenter, July 23, 1612, 4 children including Nathaniel. Converted to Puritanism as a youth by William Brewster; became financial mainstay of Pilgrims while at Leyden, circa 1612-23; went as agt. to London to negotiate with mchts. for a charter for colonization, 1619; an organizer of voyage of ships Anne and Little James on which he came with wife and children to Am., 1623; published 1st writings sent from Am. under title A Relation or Journal of the Beginnings and Proceedings of the English Plantation Settled at Plimoth in New England... London, printed for John Bellamie, 1622, Died June 1624.

MORTON, George, architect; b. Edinburgh, Scotland, 1790; ed. Edinburgh. Came to U.S., circa 1815, settled in Pitts.; moved to St. Louis, 1823, became partner (with Joseph Laveille) in archtl. firm Morton & Laveille. Works include (with Laveille): 1st Court House (no longer standing), 1825; old Jefferson Barracks, 1825; Episcopal Ch., 1825; Roman Catholic Cathedral (Greek Revival style, most noteworthy work), 1834 (all St. Louis). Died 1865.

MORTON, Jackson, senator; b. nr. Fredericksburg, Va., Aug. 10, 1794; grad. Washington Coll. (now Washington and Lee U.), Lexington, Va., 1814, Coll. William and Mary, 1815. Moved to Pensacola, Fla., 1820, engaged in lumber bus.; mem. Fla. Legislative Council, 1836-37, pres., 1837; del. Fla. Constl. Conv., 1838; Navy agt. at Pensacola, 1841-45; Whig presdl. elector, 1848; mem. U.S. Senate (Whig) from Fla., 1849-55; dep. to Provisional Congress of Confederate States Am., 1861; mem. Confederate Congress from Fla., 1862-65. Died "Mortonia" nr. Milton, Fla., Nov. 20, 1874; buried "Mortonia."

MORTON, James St. Clair, army officer, engr., author; b. Phila., Sept. 24, 1829; s. Dr. Samuel George and Rebecca Grellet (Pearsall) M.; grad. U.S. Mil. Acad., 1851. Asst. engr. in constrn. defenses of Charleston harbor, S.C., 1851-52; commd. 2d lt., 1854, asst. prof. engring. U.S. Mil. Acad.; promoted 1st lt., 1856; charge Potomac Water Works, 1859-60; engr. in charge Chiriqui Expdn. to C.Am. of Washington Aqueduct, 1860-61; capt. engrs., 1861; chief engr. Army of the Ohio, 1862; brig. gen. U.S. Volunteers, 1862; chief engr. Army of the Cumberland, 1862-63; brevetted lt. col. engrs. in regular army, 1863; maj. Corps Engrs., 1863; brevetted col., 1863; supt. defenses of Nashville, Murfreesboro, Clarksville, Ft. Donelson, 1863-64; asst. to chief engr., Washington, D.C., 1864; brevetted brig. gen., 1864. Author: Memoir on the Dangers and Defences of New York City, 1858; Memoir on American Fortification, 1859. Died Petersburg, Va., June 17, 1864; buried Laurel Hill Cemetery, Phila.

MORTON, Jeremiah, congressman; b. Fredericksburg, Va., Sept. 3, 1799; attended Washington Coll. (now Washington and Lee U.), 1814-15; grad. Coll. William and Mary, 1819; studied law. Admitted to Va. bar, practiced in Raccoon Ford; engaged in farming; mem. U.S. Ho. of Reps. (Whig) from Va., 31st Congress, 1849-51; trustee Theol. Sem. of Va., Alexandria; mem. Va. Secession Conv., 1861. Died "Lessland," Orange County, Va., Nov. 28, 1878; buried "Morton Hall," Orange County.

MORTON, John, Continental congressman; b. Ridley, Pa., circa 1724; s. John and Mary (Archer) M.; m. Anne Justice, 1754, 8 children. Surveyor of land, Delaware County, Pa., before 1757; justice of peace, Delaware County, 1757-67; mem. Pa. Gen. Assembly; 1756-66, 69-75, speaker, 1771-75; mem. Stamp Act Congress, 1765; high sheriff Delaware County, 1766-70; judge Delaware County Ct. Common Pleas, 1770-74; asso. judge Supreme Ct. Appeals of Pa., 1774; mem. Continental Congress from Pa., 1774-77, cast deciding vote for Declaration of Independence, also signer. Died Ridley Park, Delaware County, Apr. 1777; buried St. Paul's Churchyard, Chester, Pa.

MORTON, Marcus, gov. Mass., congressman; b. Freetown, Mass., Feb. 19, 1784; s. Nathaniel and Mary (Cary) M.; grad. Brown U., 1804; attended Litchfield, (Conn.) Law Sch.; m. Charlotte Hodges, Dec. 23, 1807, 12 children including Marcus. Admitted to Mass. bar, 1806; clk. Mass. Senate, 1811; mem. U.S. Ho. of Reps. (Democrat) from Mass., 15th-16th, 18th congresses, 1817-21, 24-25; lt. gov. Mass., 1823; judge Mass. Supreme Ct., 1825-40; gov. Mass., 1840, 41, 43, 44; collector of customs, Boston, 1845-49; del. Mass. Constl. Conv., 1853; mem. Mass. Ho. of Reps., 1858. Died Taunton, Mass., Feb. 6, 1864; buried Mt. Pleasant Cemetery, Taunton.

MORTON, Marcus, jurist; b. Taunton, Mass., Apr. 8, 1819; s. Marcus and Charlotte (Hodges) M.; grad. Brown U., 1838, Harvard Law Sch., 1840; m. Abby B. Hoppin, Oct. 19, 1843, 6 children. Admitted to Suffolk (Mass.) bar, 1841; mem. Mass. Constl. Conv., 1853; mem. Mass. Ho. of Reps., 1858; judge Superior Ct. of Suffolk County, 1858;

an original mem. Mass. Superior Ct., 1859-69; justice Mass. Supreme Jud. Ct., 1869, chief justice, 1882-90. Died Andover, Mass., Feb. 10, 1891.

MORTON, Nathaniel, colonist, author; b. Leyden, The Netherlands, 1613; s. George and Juliana (Carpenter) M.; m. Lydia Cooper, Apr. 29, 1635; m. 2d, Ann (Pritchard) Templar, 1674. Came to Plymouth, Mass., 1623; sec. of colony, keeper of records, Plymouth, 1647-85, entrusted with most of routine work of govt., drafted most of laws of colony, statute book probably largely his work, tax collector, assessor, constantly mem. coms. to survey land, determine boundaries, lay out roads, settle disputes; mem., sec. council of war to conduct campaigns against King Philip, 1671; town clk. of Plymouth, 1674-79; sec., compiler records, prominent mgmt. and affairs of Pilgrim Ch.; prepared New Englands Memorial, painted Cambridge, Eng., 1669, which remains only authority for list of signers of the Compact in 1620, for the name of Speedwell, also for many minor biog. details, and period after 1646; author Symposium of Church History of Plymouth, 1680; also some of earliest verse in Am. Died Plymouth, June 16, 1685.

MORTON, Oliver Hazard Perry, senator, gov. Ind.; b. Salisbury, Ind., Aug. 4, 1823; s. James Throck and Sarah (Miller) M.; grad. Miami U., Oxford, O., 1845; m. Lucinda Burbank, May 15, 1845, 5 children. Admitted to Ind. bar, 1847; practiced in Centerville, Ind., 1847-60; judge 6th jud. circuit of Ind., 1852; lt. gov. Ind., 1860-61; gov. Ind., 1861-67, an active supporter of Civil War efforts, dissolved state legislature after Peace Democrats won control in 1862 elections, ran state without calling legislature, 1863-65; del. from Ind. to Nat. Rep. Conv., 1872, 76; mem. U.S. Senate from Ind., 1867-77, a radical reconstructionist in Senate, largely responsible for ratification 15th Amendment which prohibits laws against suffrage because of race; mem. Electoral Commn. apptd. to determine outcome contested presdl. election in several states, 1876. Died Indpls., Nov. 1, 1877; buried Crown Hill Cemetery, Indpls.

MORTON, Samuel George, physician, naturalist; b. Phila., Jan. 26, 1799; s. George and Jane (Cummings) M.; M.D., U. Pa., 1820; M.D., U. Edinburgh, 1823; m. Rebecca Pearsall, Oct. 23, 1827, 7 children including James St. Clair. Became mem. Acad. Natural Scis. Phila. circa 1820, recording sec., 1825-29, corr. sec., 1831, v.p., 1840, pres., 1849-51; prof. anatomy Pa. Med. Coll., 1839-43; collected large number human skulls for comparative study, concluded that races of man were of diverse origin; credited with describing new species of hippopotamus. Author: Synopsis of the Organic Remains of the Cretaceous Group of the U.S., 1834; Illustrations of Pulmonary Consumption, 1834; Crania Americana, 1839; Crania Egyptiaca, 1839; Human Anatomy, Special, General and Microscopic, 1849. Died Phil.., May 15, 1851.

MORTON, Sarah Wentworth Apthorpe (pseudonym Philenia), poetess; b. Boston, Aug. 1759; d. James and Sarah (Wentworth) Apthorp; m. Perez Morton, Feb. 24, 1781, 5 children. Contbr. to Massachusetts Mag., 1789-93; enjoyed great popularity in her time, style widely copied and imitated; there is some question as to whether she authored earliest Am. novel, The Power of Sympathy; works include: Quabi, or the Virtues of Nature, an Indian Tale, pub. Boston, 1790; The African Chief (verses), 1792; Beacon Hill, a Local Poem, Historical and Descriptive, 1797. Died Quincy, Mass., May 14, 1846.

MORTON, Thomas, pioneer; b. England. Came to Am. for a year, 1622, returned, 1625, settled nr. Quincy, Mass.; moved to Merry Mount, Mass., became fur trader; sold guns to Indians; chastized by Pilgrims who cut down his maypole, 1627, captured by Capt. Miles Standish, 1628, sent to Eng. to be tried; returned to Am., 1629, tried to reestablish fur trade; captured by Puritans (who burned his trading post), sent to Eng. for trial; returned to Plymouth, again banished, 1643; arrested and held prisoner in Boston, 1644-45; moved to Me. Author: New English Canaan, 1637. Died Me.

MORTON, William Thomas Green, dentist; b. Charlton, Mass., Aug. 9, 1819; s. James and Rebecca (Needham) M.; studied dentistry Coll. Dental Surgery, Balt., 1840-42; also studied dentistry Harvard Med. Sch.; M.D. (hon.), Washington U. of Medicine, Balt.; m. Elizabeth Whitman, May 1844, 4 children including William James. While experimenting with mesmerism and nostrums became involved with sulfur ether which he later connected and linked to use in dental anaesthesia; used ether in drops as local anaesthetic during filling of a tooth, 1844, extracted a tooth with this method, 1846; etherized a patient from whom Dr. John Warren removed vascular tumor from left side of neck, 1846; applied for patent to protect his rights, received patent for 14 years, 1846; issued weekly circular Morton's Letheon, 5 editions, under his direction, 1846; awarded Montyon prize of 5,000 francs from French Acad. Medicine, 1847; although he was not only discoverer of anaesthesia he convinced surg. world of value of discovery of a surg. anaesthetic; during Civil War worked in various hosps.; made many improvements on crude methods of attaching false teeth. Author: Remarks on the Proper Mode of Administering Sulphuric Ether by Inhalation, 1847; On the Loss of the Teeth and the Modern Way of Restoring Them, 1848; On the Physiological Effects of Sulphuric Ether, and Its Superiority to Chloroform, 1850. Died N.Y.C., July Mass.

MORWITZ, Edward, physician, publisher; b. Danzig, Prussia, June 11, 1815; studied Semetic languages, Oriental literature and theology at U. Halle (Germany); M.D., U. Berlin, 1841; 1 son, Joseph. First asst. Hufeland Clinic, Berlin, 1841-43; opened, financed hosp. for sick poor, Konitz, Germany; wrote Geschichte der Medicin (History of Medicine), 1848-49; invented breech-loading mechanism for field guns; came to U.S., 1850; established German dispensary for poor, Phila.; contbr. articles to Phila. Demokrat, bought controlling interest in paper, 1853; published polit. weekly Die Vereinigte Staaten Zeitung, 1855; started Sunday literary paper Die Neue Welt, 1856; purchased newspaper Pennsylvanian, sold it, 1860; issued Abendpost, 1866; leader in orgn. a German Press Assn. of Pa.; organized Newspaper Union; published Uncle Sam's Almanac, 1873; established Jewish Record, 1875-86; purchased newspaper, The Age, 1874-75; published New American Pocket Dictionary of the English and German Languages, 1883. Died Phila., Dec. 13, 1893.

MOSCOSO de ALVARADO, Luis de, see de Moscoso de Alvarado, Luis.

MOSELEY, Jonathan Ogden, congressman; b. East Haddam, Conn., Apr. 9, 1762; grad. Yale, 1780; studied law. Admitted to Conn. bar, began practice in East Haddam; mem. Conn. Ho. of Reps., 1794-1804; justice of peace of East Haddam, 1794-1817; state's atty. Middlesex County, 1801-05; col. 24th Regt., Conn. Militia, 1802; mem. U.S. Ho. of Reps. (Federalist) from Conn., 9th-16th congresses, 1805-21; moved to Saginaw, Mich., practiced law. Died Saginaw, Sept. 9, 1838.

MOSELEY, William Abbott, congressman; b. Whitesboro, N.Y., Oct. 20, 1798; grad. Yale, 1816; studied medicine and law. Practiced medicine; admitted to N.Y. bar, practiced in Buffalo; mem. N.Y. Assembly, 1835, N.Y. Senate, 1838-41; mem. U.S. Ho. of Reps. (Whig) from N.Y., 28th-29th congresses, 1843-47. Died N.Y.C., Nov. 19, 1873; buried Forest Lawn Cemetery, Buffalo.

MOSENTHAL, Joseph, musician; b. Cassel, Germany, Nov. 30, 1834; studied music with his father and Ludwig Spohr. Leader of 2d violins in Ct. Orch. under Spohr, 4 years; came to Am., 1853; organist and choirmaster Calvary Ch., N.Y.C., 1860-87; condr. N.Y. Mendelssohn Glee Club, 1867-96; played with 1st violins in Philharmonic Orch., N.Y.C., 40 years, 2d violin Mason and Thomas Quartet. Died N.Y.C., Jan. 6, 1896.

MOSS, John Calvin, photoengraver; b. Bentleyville, Pa., Jan. 5, 1838; s. Alexander J. and Mary (Calvin) M.; m. Mary Bryant, 1856. Publisher, Colleague, Washington, Pa., 1859; a founder Actinic Engraving Co., N.Y.C., 1871; founder Photoengraving Co., N.Y.C., 1872, Moss Engraving Co., N.Y.C., 1881; 1st to establish photoengraving as comml. bus. in U.S.; developed Moss Process. Died N.Y.C., Apr. 8, 1892.

MOTLEY, John Lothrop, historian, diplomat; b. Dorchester, Mass., Apr. 15, 1814; s. Thomas and Anna (Lothrop) M.; grad. Harvard, 1831; student U. Berlin and U. Gottingen (Germany); m. Mary Benjamin, Mar. 2, 1837, 4 children. Mem. Mass. Ho. of Reps., 1849, chmn. com. on edn.; sec. legation at St. Petersburg, 1841; U.S. minister to Austria, 1861-67, to Gt. Britain, 1869. Author: Morton's Hope, 1839; Merry Mount: A Romance of the Massachusetts Colony, 1849; The Rise of the Dutch Republic, 3 vols., 1856; The History of the United Netherlands, 1860; also contbr. articles to N.Am. Review, Atlantic Monthly. Died Dorsetshire, Eng., May 29, 1877; buried Kensal Green Cemetery, London.

MOTT, Gershom, army officer; b. Lamberton, N.J., Apr. 7, 1822; s. Gershom and Phoebe (Scudder) M.; m. Elizabeth Smith, Aug. 8, 1849, 1 child. Enlisted for service in war with Mexico, 1846; commd. 2d lt. 10th U.S. Inf.; worked for Bordentown (N.J.) Bank, 1855-61; lt. 5th Regt., N.J. Volunteers, 1861, col. 6th Regt., 1862; served in 2d battle of Bull Run; brevetted maj. gen. U.S. Volunteers, 1864; commd. maj. gen. of volunteers, 1865; paymaster Camden & Amboy R.R., 1866; maj. gen. N.J. Militia, 1873; treas. of N.J., 1875; keeper N.J. State Prison, 1876-81; mem. Riparian Com. of N.J., 1882-84; mem. firm Thompson & Mott, iron foundry, 1873-76; dir. Bordentown Banking Co.; maj. gen. N.J. Nat. Guard, 1873-84. Died N.Y.C., Nov. 29, 1884.

MOTT, Gordon Newell, congressman; b. Zanesville, O., Oct. 21, 1812; studied law. Admitted to Ohio bar, began practice in Zanesville; moved to Tex., served as volunteer; moved to Cal., 1849; judge Sutter County (Cal.), 1850; dist. judge, 1851-54; moved to Nev., 1861; asso. justice Supeme Ct. of Nev. Territory, 1861-63; del. U.S. Congress from Territory of Nev., 1863-64. Died San Francisco, Apr. 27, 1887; buried Laurel Hill Cemetery, San Francisco.

MOTT, James, congressman; b. nr. Middletown, N.J., Jan. 18, 1739; ed. privately. Engaged in farming; capt. 2d Regt., Monmouth County (N.J.) Militia, 1775; mem. N.J. Ho. of Assembly, 1776-79; treas. State of N.J., 1783-99; mem. U.S. Ho. of Reps. (Democrat) from N.J., 7th-8th congresses, 1801-05; Dem. presdl. elector, 1808. Died nr. Middletown, Oct. 18, 1823; buried Middletown Baptist Churchyard.

MOTT, James, abolitionist; b. North Hempstead, N.Y., June 20, 1788; s. Adam and Anne (Mott) M.; m. Lucretia Coffin, Apr. 10, 1811, 5 children. Engaged in commission bus., Phila., 1822-30, dealt mainly in cotton; left this field because of its connection with slavery; mem. newly-founded Am. Anti-Slavery Soc., 1833; del. (with his wife) to World Anti-Slavery Conv., London, Eng., 1840; believed in greater rights for women; a founder Swarthmore Coll., 1864. Author: Three Months in Great Britain, 1841. Died Bklyn., Jan. 26, 1868.

MOTT, Lucretia Coffin, reformer; b. Nantucket, Mass., Jan. 3, 1793; d. Thomas and Anna (Folger) Coffin; m. James Mott, Apr. 10, 1811, 6 children. Became speaker at Quaker meetings, 1817; spoke for temperance, peace, women's rights, anti-slavery; attended Am. Anti-Salvery Conv., 1833, organizer, pres. Phila. woman's br.; denied membership in World Anti-Slavery Conv., London; Eng., because she was a woman; helped organize (with Elizabeth Cady Stanton) 1st Woman's Rights Conv., 1848, active in movement until 1880. Died Nov. 11, 1880.

MOTT, Richard, congressman; b. Mamaroneck, N.Y., July 21, 1804; attended Quaker Sem., Dutchess County, N.Y.; banker, N.Y.C.; moved to Toledo, O., 1836, egaged in real estate and other businesses; mayor of Toledo, 1845-46; mem. U.S. Ho. of Reps. (Republican) from Ohio, 34th-35th congresses, 1855-59; chmn. Citizens' Mil. Com. during Civil War. Died nr. Toledo, Jan. 22, 1888; buried Mt. Hope Cemetery, Rochester, N.Y.

MOTT, Valentine, surgeon; b. Glen Cove, L.I., N.Y., Aug. 20, 1785; s. Henry and Jane (Way) M.; M.D., Columbia, 1806; M.D. (hon.), U. Edinburgh (Scotland); LL.D. (hon.), Univ. State N.Y., 1851; m. Louisa Mums, 1819, 9 children. Prof. surgery Columbia, 1811-13; prof. surgery Coll. Physicians and Surgeons, 1813-26, 30-35, mem. staff during 1850's; a founder Rutgers Med. Coll.; a founder med. dept. Univ. State N.Y., 1840, prof. surgery and anatomy until 1850; 1st to tie innominate artery with aim of preventing death from subclavian aneurism, 1818; successfully tied common iliac artery for an aneurism of external iliac, to perform successful amputation of hip joint, 1824; a pioneer in vein surgery; hon. fellow Imperial Acad. Medicine of Paris (France); mem. Paris Clin. Soc. Author: Pain and Anaesthetics, 1862. Co-editor Medical Mag., 1814-15, Medical and Surgical Reporter, 1818-20. Died N.Y.C., Apr. 26, 1865.

MOTTE, Isaac, Continental congressman; b. Charleston, S.C., Dec. 8, 1738. Apptd. ensign His Majesty's 60th Royal Am. Regt., 1756, promoted lt., 1759; served in Canada during French and Indian, War, 1756, resigned, returned to Charleston, 1766; mem. S.C. Ho. of Commons, 1772; del. S.C. provincia congresses, 1774, 75, 76; commd. lt. col. 2d S.C. Regt., Continental Army, 1775, participated in defense of Ft. Moultrie, promoted col., 1776; mem. S.C. Privy Council, 1779; mem. S.C. Assembly from Charleston, 1779; mem. Continental Congress from S.C., 1780-82; mem. S.C. Conv. which ratified U.S. Constn., 1788; apptd. naval officer for Port of Charleston by George Washington. Died Charleston, May 8, 1795; buried St. Philip's Churchyard, Charleston.

MOULD, Jacob Wray, architect; b. Eng., 1825; ed., Eng.; studied architecture under Owen Jones. Accompanied Jones to Spain to gather material for book Alhambra, later illustrated book; collaborator (with Jones) Grammar of Ornament; moved to N.Y.C., 1853; commd. to design All Saints Ch., N.Y.C., 1853; architect several other noteworthy chs., including 2d Unitarian, Bklyn.; designed numerous country homes; asst. to chief architect of pub. parks, N.Y.C., 1867-70, apptd. chief architect, 1870. Died June 14, 1884.

MOULTON, Mace, congressman; b. Concord, N.H., May 2, 1796; attended pub. schs. Sheriff of Hillsborough County (N.H.), 1845; mem. U.S. Ho. of Reps. (Democrat) from N.H., 29th Congress, 1845-47; mem. N.H. Council, 1848-49; engaged in banking. Died Manchester, N.H., May 5, 1867; buried Valley Cemetery, Manchester.

MOULTRIE, John, physician, colonial ofcl.; b. Charleston, S.C., Jan. 18, 1729; s. Dr. John and Lucretia (Cooper) M.; M.D., U. Edinburgh (Scotland), 1749; m. Dorothy (Dry) Morton, Apr. 30, 1753; m. 2d, Eleanor Austin, Jan. 5, 1762; 7 children. Maj. in militia, 1761; served in campaign against Cherokees; mem. James Grant's council on East Fla., 1764; lt. gov. East Fla., 1771; Loyalist, went to England, 1784. Died St. Andrews Parish, Shifnal, Eng., Mar. 19, 1798; buried St. Andrews Parish.

MOULTRIE, William, army officer, gov. S.C.; b. Charlestown (now Charleston), S.C., Nov. 23, 1730; s. Dr. John and Lucretia (Cooper) M.; m. Elizabeth Damares de St. Julien, Dec. 10, 1749; m. 2d, Hannah (Motte) Lynch, Oct. 10, 1779. Mem. S.C. Assembly, 1751-71; commanded a light inf. co. in Cherokee fighting, 1761; mem. S.C. Provincial Congress at Charleston, 1775; S.C. legislative council, S.C. Senate, 1775-80; col. 2d Regt., Continental Army, 1776, promoted to brig. gen., 1777, maj. gen., 1782; mem. S.C. Ho. of Reps., 1783; lt. gov. S.C., 1784, gov., 1785-87, 92-94; pres. S.C. br. Soc. of Cincinnati. Died Charleston, Sept. 27, 1805.

MOUNT, William Sidney, painter; b. Setauket, L.I., N.Y., Nov. 26, 1807; s. Thomas Shepard and Julia (Hawkins) M. Mem. N.A.D., 1832; works include Raffling for the Goose (in Met. Mus. of Art, N.Y.C.), The Long Story (in Corcoran Gallery of Art, Washington, D.C.), Coming to the Point (in N.Y. Pub. Library), The Truant Gamblers, The Fortune Teller, Bargaining for a Horse (all at N.Y. Hist. Soc.), also Farmers Nooning, Men Husking Corn, Walking the Crack, The Courtship, Sportsman's Last Visit. Died Setauket, Nov. 19, 1868.

MOUTON, Alexander, senator; b. Attakapas County (now Lafayette Parish), La., Nov. 19, 1804; s. Jean and Marie (Bordat) M.; grad. Georgetown (D.C.) Coll.; m. Zelia Rousseau, 1826; m. 2d, Emma Gardner, 1842; 10 children including Jean Jacques. Admitted to La. bar, 1825; owned sugar plantation nr. Vermillionville (now Lafayette), La.; mem. La. Ho. of Reps., 1827-32, 36, speaker, 1831-32; mem. U.S. Senate (Democrat) from La., 1837-42; gov. La., 1842-46; pres. Southwestern R.R. Conv., New Orleans, 1852; pres. Attakapas County vigilance committee to rid area of bandits, 1858; del. from La. to Nat. Dem. Conv., Cincinnati, 1856, Charleston, S.C., 1860; pres. La. Secession Conv., 1861. Died Vermillionville, Feb. 12, 1885; buried St. John's Cemetery, Vermillionville.

MOWATT, Anna Cora Ogden, writer, actress; b. Bordeaux, France, Mar. 5, 1819; d. Samuel Gouverneur and Eliza (Lewis) Ogden; m. James Mowatt, Oct. 6, 1834; m. 2d, William Ritchie, June 6, 1854. Wrote under pseudonym Helen Berkley for Godey's Lady's Book, Graham's, other mags.; wrote plays Armand; or the Peer and the Peasant, 1849; Fashion; or, Life in New York, 1850; made debut as actress as Pauline in The Lady of Lyons at the Park Theatre, N.Y.C., 1845; published novel Autobiography of an Actress; or Eight Years on the Stage, 1854; other works include: Mimic Life, 1855, Twin Roses, 1857, Fairy Fingers, 1865 (plays); The Fortune Hunter, 1842, Evelyn, 3 vols., 1845, The Mute Singer, 1866, The Clergyman's Wife and Other Sketches, 1867 (novels). Died Twenkenham, Eng., July 21, 1870.

MOWBRAY, George Mordey, oil refiner, inventor; b. Brighton, Eng., May 5, 1814; m. Annie Fade. Came to U.S., 1854; producer 1st refined oil in Tutsville, Pa. (after Edwin L. Drake had drilled 1st successful well); 1st oilman to use nitroglycerin (which he called tri-nitro-glycerin) in shooting dormant wells; only Am. mfr. producing nitroglycerin in quantity; supplier explosives for Hoosac Tunnel, 1868, also for building of C.P. Ry.; developer method of diluting nitroglycerin with finely divided scales of mica; a developer of zylonite; tech. mgr. Am. Zylonite Co., 1881-91; contracted with Maxim-Nordenfeldt Guns and Ammunition Co. to turn over all patents for smokeless powder that might result from his researches. Died North Adams, Mass., June 21, 1891.

MOWER, Joseph Anthony, army officer; b. Woodstock, Vt., Aug. 22, 1827; s. Nathaniel and Sophia (Holmes) M.; attended Norwich (Vt.) U., 1843-45; m. Betsey Bailey, June 6, 1851. Served as enlisted man in Mexican War; commd. 2d lt., U.S. Army, 1855, 1st lt., 1857; commd. capt. U.S. Volunteers, 1861, maj., 1862, lt. col., 1862, col. 1863, distinguished himself at Battle of Vicksburg; with Gen. Sherman in march from Atlanta to sea; commd. brig. gen. U.S. Volunteers, 1865, maj. gen., 1865; col. U.S. Army; in command Dept. La. received many commendations from superiors during Civil War. Died New Orleans, Jan. 6, 1870.

MOWRY, Daniel Jr., Continental congressman; b. Smithfield, R.I., Aug. 17, 1729; s. Daniel Mowry. Learned cooper's trade. Town clk. Smithfield, 1760-80, mem. R.I. Gen. Assembly, 1766-76; judge Ct. of Common Pleas, 1776-81; mem. Continental congress from R.I., 1780-82; engaged in farming. Died Smithfield, July 6, 1806; buried family cemetery, North Smithfield, R.I.

MOYLAN, Stephen, army officer; b. Cork, Ireland, 1734; s. John Moylan; m. Mary Van Horn, Sept. 12, 1778. Came to Phila., 1768; organizer Friendly Sons of St. Patrick, 1771, pres., 1771, 96; became army muster-master gen., 1775, q.m. gen., 1776; recruiter 1st Pa. Regt. of Cavalry, 1776, commd. col.; served at Valley Forge, 1777-78; brevetted brig. gen., 1783; U.S. commr. loans, Phila., 1793. Died Phila., Apr. 13, 1811.

MOZIER, Joseph, sculptor; b. Burlington, Vt., Aug. 22, 1812. Entered merchandising bus., N.Y., 1831; gave up bus. to devote himself completely to sculpture, 1845; lived in Rome, 1845-70; best known works include: Wept of Wish-ton-Wish; Il Penseroso; Prodigal Son; Undine (won grand prize in Rome, 1867). Died Faido, Switzerland, Oct. 3, 1870.

MUDGE, Enoch, clergyman, legislator; b. Lynn, Mass., June 28, 1776; s. Enoch and Lydia (Ingalls) M.; m. Mrs. Jerusha Hinckley, Nov. 29, 1797. First native of New Eng. to become Methodist minister, 1793, ordained elder, 1796; settled in Orrington, Mass. (now Me.), 1797; mem. Mass. Ho. of Reps. from Orrington, 1811-12, 15-16, helped pass religious freedom bill which took away old privileges of established church granted to Puritan churches; entered travelling ministry, 1817; incorporator Wilbraham Acad., 1824; port chaplain, New Bedford, Me., 1831-44. Died Lynn, Apr. 2, 1850.

MUELLER, Alfred, architect; born Germany, Sept. 10, 1853; ed., Berlin, Germany. Practiced as architect, Berlin; came to U.S., settled in Washington, D.C.; moved to Galveston, Tex., practiced as architect, 1886-96; designed City Hall, Williams Bldg., Orphans' Home, Letitia Rosenberg Home for Women, Marwitz Bldg., also numerous pvt. residences, Galveston; remodeled Tremont Opera House, Galveston; planned several bldgs. in other cities, including Sam Houston Normal Sch., Huntsville, Ala. Died June 29, 1896.

MUHLENBERG, Francis Swaine, congressman; b. Phila., Apr. 22, 1795; s. John Peter Gabriel Muhlenberg; attended Dickinson Coll., Carlisle, Pa.; studied law. Admitted to Pa. bar, 1816, began practice in Reading; pvt. sec. to Gov. Hiester of Pa., 1820-23; moved to Pickaway County, O.; mem. Ohio Ho. of Reps., 1827; mem. U.S. Ho. of Reps. (National Republican) from Ohio, 20th Congress, Dec. 19, 1828-29; engaged in real estate bus., Ohio and Ky. Died Pickaway County, Dec. 17, 1831; buried Protestant Cemetery, Circleville, O.

MUHLENBERG, Frederick Augustus Conrad, clergyman, congressman; b. Trappe, Pa., Jan. 1, 1750; s. Henry Melchior and Anna Maria (Weiser) M.; attended U. Halle (Germany); m. Catherine Schaefer, Oct. 15, 1771, 7 children including William Augustus. Ordained minister of Lutheran Ch. by ministerium of Pa., 1770; pastor, Stouchsburg, Lebanon, Pa., 1770-74, Christ Ch., N.Y.C., 1774-76, churches of Hanover, Oley, New Goshenhoppen, Pa., 1776-79; mem. Continental Congress from Pa., 1779-80; member Pa. Ho. of Reps., 1780-83, also speaker; mem. Pa. Conv. to ratify U.S. Constn., 1787; mem. U.S. Ho. of Reps. from Pa., 1st-4th congresses, 1789-97, 1st speaker of Ho. of Reps., also speaker in 3d Congress; pres. Pa. Council of Censors, 1783-84; justice of peace, 1784; registrar of wills and recorder of deeds for Montgomery County, Pa., 1784; receiver gen. of Pa. Land Office, 1800-01; partner firms Muhlenberg & Wegmann, importers, Muhlenberg and Lawersweiler, sugar refiners, both Phila. Died Lancaster, Pa., June 4, 1801; buried Woodward Hill Cemetery, Lancaster.

MÜHLENBERG, Gotthilf Henry Ernest, clergyman, coll. pres., b. Trappe, Pa., Nov. 17, 1753; s. Henry Melchior and Anna Maria (Weiser) M.; attended U. Halle (Germany); M.A. (hon.), U. Pa., 1780; D.D., Princeton, 1787; m. Mary Hall, July 26, 1774. Ordained to ministry Lutheran Ch., 1770; pastor, Phila., 1774-79, Lancaster, Pa., 1779-1815; sec. or pres. at various times of Ministerium of Pa.; 1st pres. Franklin Coll. 1787; studied botany independently and contributed descriptions of over 100 species and varieties flora. Author: Index Flora Lancastriense; co-author: English-German and German-English Dictionary, 2 vols., 1812. Died Lancaster, May 23, 1815; buried Lancaster.

MUHLENBERG, Henry Augustus, congressman; b. Reading, Pa., July 21, 1823; s. Henry Augustus Philip Muhlenberg; grad. Dickinson Coll., Carlisle, Pa., 1841; studied law; Admitted to Pa. bar, 1844, began practice in Reading; mem. Pa. Senate, 1849-52; mem. U.S. Ho. of Reps. (Democrat) from Pa., 33d Congress, 1853-54. Died Washington, D.C., Jan. 9, 1854; buried Charles Evans Cemetery, Reading.

MUHLENBERG, Henry Augustus Philip, clergyman, congressman, diplomat; b. Lancaster, Pa., May 13, 1782; s. Gotthilf H. E. and Mary (Hall) M.; m. Mary Hiester, 1805; m. 2d, Rebecca Hiester, 1808. Pastor, Trinity Ch., Reading, Pa., 1803-28; ordained to ministry Lutheran Ch., Easton, Pa., 1804; sec., pres. Luth. Ministerium; mem U.S. Ho. of Reps. from Pa., 21st-26th congresses, 1829-Feb. 9, 1838; 1st U.S. minister to Austria, 1838-40. Died Reading, Aug. 11, 1844; buried Charles Evans Cemetery, Reading.

MÜHLENBERG, Henry Melchior, clergyman; b. Einbeck, Hanover, Sept. 6, 1711; s. Nicolaus Melchoir and Anna Marie (Kleinschmid) M.; attended U. Göttingen, 1735-38; m. Anna Maria Weiser, Apr. 22, 1745, 6 sons, 5 daus. Apptd. tchr. in Waisenhaus at Halle, 1738; came to Phila. to prevent union of Lutherans of the United Congregations (Phila., New Providence, New Hanover) with other German Protestants in Pa., 1742; organized 1st Lutheran Synod in Am., 1748; visited Lutheran congregations throughout New Eng.; recognized as virtual founder of Lutheran Ch. in Am. Died Oct. 7, 1787; buried New Providence, N.J.

MUHLENBERG, John Peter Gabriel, congressman; b. Trappe, Pa., Oct. 12, 1746; s. Henry Melchoir and Anna Maria (Weiser) M.; attended U. Halle (Germany), 1763-66; m. Anna Barbara Meyer, Nov. 6, 1770, 6 children. Ordained pastor by ministerium of Lutheran Ch. in Pa., 1768; pastor, Bedminster, New Germantown, Pa., 1769-71, Woodstock, Va., 1771-76; ordained priest Episcopal Ch., London, Eng., 1772; mem. Va. Ho. of Burgesses, 1774; chmn. com. of safety for Dunmore County, Va., 1774; col. 8th Va. Regt., Continental Army, 1776-83, promoted brig. gen., 1777, brevetted maj. gen., 1783; returned to Pa.; mem. Supreme Exec. Council of Pa., 1784; v.p. of Pa., 1785-87; mem. Pa. Constl. Conv., 1790; mem. U.S. Ho. of Reps. from Pa., 1st, 3d, 6th congresses, Congress, 1789-91, 93-95, 1799-1801; elected to U.S. Senate, 1801, resigned before taking seat; supr. revenue for Pa., 1801; collector customs, Phila., 1802-07; pres. German Soc. of Pa., 1788, 1801-07. Died Phila., Oct. 1, 1807; buried Augustus Lutheran Ch. Cemetery, Trappe.

MUHLENBERG, William Augustus, clergyman; b. Phila., Sept. 16, 1796; s. Henry William and Mary (Sheaff) M.; grad. U. Pa., 1815. Ordained deacon Episcopal Ch., 1817, priest, 1820; founder, headmaster Flushing (L.I., N.Y.) Inst., 1828; established St. Paul's Coll., L.I., 1838; rector Ch. of Holy Communion, N.Y.C., 1846; a founder Sisterhood of the Holy Communion, 1852; a founder St. Luke's Hosp., N.Y.C.; became leader Meml. Movement, 1853, drafted meml. presented to the House of Bishops which proved to have an enduring influence on Episcopal thought; a founder St. Johnsland, 1870. Author: Christian Education, 1831; Letters on Protestant Sisterhood, 1853; Family Prayers, 1861; Evangelical Catholic Papers, Addresses, Lectures and Sermons, 2 vols., 1875-77; (hymns) "I Would Not Live Away," "Like Noah's Weary Dove," "Shout the Glad Tidings." Died N.Y.C., Apr. 8, 1877; buried St. Johnsland.

MULEY SOLIMAN, emperor of Morocco; b. Morocco; s. Sidi Muhammed. Became emperor of Morocco after struggle with other claimants to throne, circa 1793; renewed treaty of 1786 with U.S. (made by his father), 1795; relations between U.S. and Morocco gradually worsened; declared War on U.S., 1802, peace was restored before any fighting took place; aided Tripoli at various times during the latter's war with U.S., 1801-05; troubled with internal disturbances in Morocco, hence was not as troublesome to Am. shipping as other Barbary leaders.

MULFORD, Elisha, clergyman; b. Montrose, Pa., Nov. 19, 1833; s. Silvanus Sandford Mulford; grad. Yale, 1855; m. Rachel Price Carmalt, Sept. 17, 1862. Ordained deacon Episcopal Ch., 1861, priest, 1862; retired as active minister because of deafness, 1864; lectr. theology and apologetics Episcopal Theol. Sch., Cambridge, Mass., 1881-85. Author: The Nation, 1870; The Republic of God, 1880. Died Cambridge, Dec. 9, 1885; buried Sleepy Hollow Cemetery, Concord, Mass.

MULFORD, Prentice, journalist; b. Sag Harbor, L.I., N.Y., Apr. 5, 1834; s. Ezekiel and Julia (Prentice) M.; m. 1873. Crewman in Wizzard, 1856, sailed from Sag Harbor to San Francisco; began career as comic lectr., 1865, contributed poems and essays under pen-name Dogberry to Union Democrat, Sonora, Cal.; worked for several newspapers including

Dramatic Chronicle, 1866-71; editor Stockton Gazette, 1868; wrote column "The History of a Day" in Daily Graphic, N.Y.C., circa 1875-81; published 1st of philos. essays known as "Your Forces and How To Use Them," 1886. Author: The Swamp Angel, 1888; Prentice Mulford's Story, 1889. Died circa May 27, 1891.

MULLANPHY, John, businessman; b. nr. Enniskillen, Fermanagh, Ireland, 1758. Went to France, 1778, served in Irish Brigade; returned to Ireland at outbreak of French Revolution; came to U.S., 1792, lived in Phila., Balt., then Frankfort, Ky., 1792-1804; settled in St. Louis, 1804, became real-estate investor; served under Andrew Jackson at New Orleans in War of 1812; made a fortune in cotton speculation during and after the war; made many contbns. to philanthropic causes during last years of life. Died St. Louis, Aug. 29, 1833.

MULLANY, James Robert Madison, naval officer; b. N.Y.C., Oct. 26, 1818; s. Col. James R. and Maria (Burger) M.; m. twice. Apptd. midshipman U.S. Navy, 1832, lt., 1844; attached to Coast Survey, 1844-46, 48-61; served as officer Home Squadron during Mexican War, participated in attack and capture of Tabasco, 1846; commanded ships Wyandotte and Supply, Pensacola, Fla., 1861; became comdr., 1861; in command ship Bienville in North Atlantic and West Gulf squadrons, 1862-65; capt., 1866; commanded ship Richmond, 1868-70; commd. commodore, 1870, served with Mediterranean Squadron, 1870-71; rear adm., 1874, in North Atlantic Squadron, 1874-76; gov. Naval Asylum, Phila., 1876-79; ret., 1879. Died Bryn Mawr, Pa., Sept. 17, 1887.

MULLANY, Patrick Francis (pen name Brother Azarias), educator, author; b. County Tipperary, Ireland, June 29, 1847; s. Thomas and Margaret (Ryan) M.; ed. Christian Bros. Acad. Apptd. prof. mathematics and lit. Rock Hill Coll., Ellicott City, Md., 1866, pres., 1879; prof. rhetoric De La Salle Inst., N.Y.C., 1889. Author: An Essay Contributing to a Philosophy of Literature, 1874; The Development of Old English Thought, 1879; Aristotle and the Christian Church, 1888. Died Plattsburg, N.Y., Aug. 20, 1893.

MULLIN, Joseph, congressman, jurist; b. Dromore, County Down, Ireland, Aug. 6, 1811; attended pub. schs.; grad. Union Coll., Schenectady, N.Y., 1833; studied law. Came to U.S., 1820, settled in Watertown, N.Y.; prin. Union Acad.; tchr. Watertown Acad.; admitted to N.Y. bar, 1837; apptd. examiner of chancery, supreme ct. commr., commr. in bankruptcy State of N.Y., 1841; pros. atty. Jefferson County (N.Y.), 1843-49; mem. U.S. Ho. of Reps. (Republican) from N.Y., 30th Congress, 1847-49; pres. Village of Watertown, 1853-54; asso. justice N.Y. Supreme Ct., 1857-81, served as presiding justice. Died Saratoga Springs, N.Y., May 17, 1882; buried Brookside Cemetery, Watertown.

MULLINS, James, congressman; b. Bedford County, Tenn., Sept. 15, 1807. Millwright's apprentice; col. Tenn. Militia, 1831; sheriff of Bedford County, 1840-46; fled from Tenn. because of Union sympathies, 1862; served with U.S. Army during Civil War, 1862-64; mem. Tenn. Ho. of Reps., 1865, speaker; mem. U.S. Ho. of Reps. (Republican) from Tenn., 40th Congress, 1867-69. Died Shelbyville, Tenn., June 20, 1873; buried Arnold Graveyard, nr. Shelbyville.

MUMFORD, George, congressman; b. Rowan County, N.C.; attended common schs. Mem. N.C. Ho. of Commons, 1810-11; mem. U.S. Ho. of Reps. (Democrat) from N.C., 15th Congress, 1817-18. Died Washington, D.C., Dec. 31, 1818; buried Congressional Cemetery, Washington.

MUMFORD, Gurdon Saltonstall, congressman; b. New London, Conn., Jan. 29, 1764; attended common schs. Pvt. sec. to Benjamin Franklin in Paris, France; returned to Am., 1785, settled in N.Y.C.; asso. with his brothers in commn. bus., 1791; mem. U.S. Ho. of Reps. (Federalist) from N.Y., 9th-10th congresses, 1805-11; presdl. elector, 1812; elected dir. Bank of N.Y., 1812; opened broker's office, Wall St., N.Y.C., 1813; a founder N.Y. Exchange. Died N.Y.C., Apr. 30, 1831; buried Old Collegiate Dutch Ch. Cemetery, N.Y.C.

MUNDY, Johnson Marchant, artist; b. May 13, 1831. Apprenticed to Henry Kirke Brown; opened studio, Rochester, N.Y., engaged primarily in portrait painting; moved to Tarrytown, N.Y.; best known for statue of Washington Irving. Died Tarrytown, 1897.

MUNFORD, Robert, army officer, dramatist; b. Prince George County, Va.; s. Robert and Anna (Bland) M.; m. Anne Beverley. Served as capt. 2d Va. Regt., French and Indian War; mem. Va. Ho. of Burgesses, 1765-75, Gen. Assembly, 1779, 80-81; signer Williamsburg Assn. (non-importation agreement), June 22, 1770; served to maj., Revolutionary War. Writings collected in Collection of Plays and Poems, published posthumously 1798. Died 1784.

MUNFORD, William, legislator, writer; b. Mecklenburg County, Va., Aug. 15, 1775; s. Col. Robert and Anne (Beverly) M.; attended Coll. William and Mary; m. Sally Redford, 1802. Mem. Va. Ho. of Dels. from Mecklenburg County, 1797-98, 1800-02; mem. Va. Senate, 1802-06; clk. Va. Ho. of Dels., 1811-25; sec., treas. Conv. of Diocese of Va. (Episcopalian), 1815-24. Author: Poems and Compositions in Prose on Several Occasions, 1798. Translator: Iliad, 1846. Compiler: (with W. W. Hening) Reported Decisions of the Virginia Supreme Court of Appeals, 1806-10, published 1808-11; Munford's Reports 1810-21, published 1821. Died June 21, 1825.

MUNGEN, William, congressman; b. Balt., May 12, 1821; attended common schs., Ohio; studied law. Taught sch.; editor, publisher Findlay (O.) Democratic Courier; auditor Hancock County (O.), 1846-50; mem. Ohio Senate, 1851-52; admitted to Ohio bar, 1853, began practice in Findlay; del. Dem. Nat. Conv., Cincinnati, 1856; served as lt. col. and col. 57th Regt., Ohio Volunteer Inf., U.S. Army, during Civil War, 1851-53; mem. U.S. Ho. of Reps. (Dem.) from Ohio, 40th-41st congresses, 1866-71. Died Findlay, Sept. 9, 1887; buried Maple Grove Cemetery, Findlay.

MUNRO, George, publisher; b. West River, N.C., Can., Nov. 12, 1825; m. Catherine Forrest, 2 sons, 2 daus. Tchr. mathematics, headmaster Free Ch. Acad., Halifax, N.S.; left for N.Y., 1856; worked for Beadle & Adams, publishers dime novels, 1863-66; established publishing firm, 1866, began publication of Fireside Companion (inexpensive family paper), 1867; published Old Sleuth the Detective by H. P. Halsey, 1872; became wealthy by reprinting English novels in inexpensive pamphlets (led to promulgation of internat. copyright law); benefactor Dalhousie U., Halifax, N.S., U. City of N.Y. Died Apr. 23, 1896.

MUNRO, Henry, clergyman; b. Scotland, 1730; s. Robert and Anne Munro; B.A., M.A., St. Andrews, Scotland; studied divinity U. Edinburgh (Scotland); M.A. (hon.), King's Coll. (now Columbia), 1773; married 3 times; m. 2d, Miss Stockton; m. 3d, Eve Jay, Mar. 31, 1766; 1 child. Ordained to ministry Ch. of Scotland, 1757, became chaplain 77th Regt. of Highlanders which came to Am., 1757; accompanied regt. on expdns. against Ft. Duquesne, 1758, fts. Ticonderoga and Crown Point, 1759, Montreal, 1760; went to N.Y., 1762; returned to Eng., 1764, became mem. Ch. of Eng.; ordained to ministry Anglican Ch., 1765; returned to Am., 1765, missionary to Philipsburgh, N.Y.; apptd. rector St. Peter's Ch., Albany, N.Y., 1768; active missionary on N.Y. frontier, 1768-76; supported Brit. position during Am. Revolution, imprisoned at Albany, 1776, escaped to Can., became chaplain to Brit. forces; returned to Eng., 1778; lived in Scotland, 1783-1801. Died Edinburgh, May 30, 1801.

MUNSELL, Joel, printer, author; b. Northfield, Mass., Apr. 14, 1808; s. Joel and Cynthia (Paine) M.; m. Jane C. Bigelow, June 17, 1834; m. 2d, Mary Anne Reid, Sept. 11, 1856. Established himself as printer, Albany, N.Y., 1827; asst. editor Microscope, 1827; edited N.Y. State Mechanic, Mechanics Jour., Lady's Mag., Am. Literary Mag., Northern Star and Freeman's Advocate, Webster's Calendar, The Spectator, Unionist, N.Y. Teacher, The Morning Express, New Eng. Hist. and Geneal. Register; a founder Albany Inst. Author: Outline of the History of Printing, 1839; The Every Day Book of History and Chronology, 1843; Annals of Albany, 10 vols., 1850-59; Chronology of Paper and Paper Making. Died Albany, Jan. 15, 1880.

MURAT, Achille Napoléon (christened Charles Louis Napoléon Achille), author; b. Paris, France, Jan. 21, 1801; s. Joachim (King of Naples) and Caroline Maria Annunciata Carolina (Buonaparte) (sister of Napoleon I) M.; m. Catherine Willis Gray, July 12, 1826. Came to U.S., 1823; alderman Tallahassee (Fla.), 1824, mayor, 1825, postmaster, 1826-35; accompanied Lafayette throughout U.S.; admitted to bar, 1828; active in promoting Fla. Inst. Agr.; commd. col. in command of frontier during Seminole War. Author: Lettres d'un Citoyen des Etats-Unis à Ses Amis d'Europe, Paris, 1830; Esquisses Morales et Politiques sur les Etats-Unis d'Amerique, 2 vols., Paris, 1838. Died Wacissa, Jefferson County, Fla., Apr. 15, 1847; buried Episcopal Cemetery, Tallahassee.

MURCH, Thompson Henry, congressman; b. Hampden, Me., Mar. 29, 1838; attended common schs. Went to sea; engaged as stonecutter, 18 years; became editor and publisher Granite Cutters' Internat. Jour., 1877; sec. Granite Cutter's Internat. Assn. Am., 1877-78; mem. U.S. Ho. of Reps. (Greenback Labor Reformer) from Me., 46th-47th congresses, 1879-83; engaged in merc. bus. Died Danvers, Mass., Dec. 15, 1886; buried Hampden Cemetery.

MURDOCH, Frank Hitchcock, playwright; b. Chelsea, Mass., Mar. 11, 1843; s. George Frank and Mary (Murdoch) Hitchcock; m. Jennie Workman. Adopted his actor uncle James Edward Murdoch's last name for his stage career; joined and acted with theater company of Louisa Drew, 1861-72. Author: (plays) The Keepers of Lighthouse Cliff; Only a Few, 1873; Bohemia or the Lottery of Art, 1872; Davy Crockett, 1872 (most famous). Died Phila., Nov. 13, 1872.

MURDOCH, James Edward, actor; b. Phila., Jan. 25, 1811; s. Thomas and Elizabeth Murdoch; m. Eliza Middlecott, 1831. Toured U.S. as actor, 1830-42; lectr. on theater in East, 1842-45; returned to acting, became star, toured U.S. and appeared for long stand in Haymarket Theater, London, Eng., 1845-60; entertained Federal troops during Civil War; retired to farm outside Cincinnati. Author: Orthophony, or Vocal Culture in Elocution, 1845; Recollections of Actors and Acting, 1880. Died May 19, 1893.

MURDOCK, James, clergyman; b. Westbrook, Conn., Feb. 16, 1776; s. Abraham and Hannah (Lay) M.; grad. Yale, 1797; D.D. (hon.), Harvard, 1819; m. Rebecca Atwater, Oct. 8, 1799, 10 children. Licensed to preach in Congregational Ch., 1801; pastor Congl. ch., Princeton, Mass., 1802-05; prof. ancient languages U. Vt., 1815-19, also taught mathematics and natural philosophy; prof. sacred rhetoric and eccles. history Andover Theol. Sem., 1819-28; pres. Conn. Acad. Arts and Scis.; v.p. Conn. Philol. Soc.; mem. Am. Oriental Soc. Author: Sketches of Modern Philosophy, 1842. Translator: Mosheim's Institutes of Ecclesiastical History, 3 vols., 1832; The Literal Translation of the Whole New Testament from the Ancient Syriac Version, 1851. Died Columbus, Miss., Aug. 10, 1856; buried New Haven, Conn.

MURFREE, William Hardy, congressman; b. Hertford County, N.C., Oct. 2, 1781; grad. U. N.C., 1801; studied law. Admitted to N.C. bar, began practice in Edenton; mem. N.C. Ho. of Reps., 1805, 12; Democratic presdl. elector, 1812; mem. U.S. Ho. of Reps. (Dem.) from N.C., 13th-14th congresses, 1813-17; moved to Williamson County, Tenn., 1823. Died Williamson County, Jan. 19, 1827; buried Murfree Cemetery nr. Franklin, Tenn.

MURPHEY, Archibald De Bow, judge; b. Caswell County, N.C., 1777; s. Archibald and Jane (De Bow) M.; grad. U. N.C., 1799; m. Jane Scott, Nov. 5, 1801, 5 children. Admitted to N.C. bar, 1802; mem. N.C. Senate, 1812-18; editor Reports of Cases in the North Carolina Supreme Court 1804 to 1819, 3 vols., 1821-26; judge N.C. Superior Ct., 1818-20; advocated internal improvements, public schs., abolishment debtors prisons. Author: Memoir on the Internal Improvements, 1819. Died Feb. 1, 1832.

MURPHEY, Charles, congressman; b. nr. Anderson, S.C., May 9, 1799; attended country schs.; studied law. Admitted to the bar, 1825; began practice of law, Decatur, Ga.; clk. Superior Ct. of De Kalb County (Ga.), 1825-27; mem. Ga. Ho. of Reps., 1839-41, Ga. Senate, 1842, 45, 49-50, 55-56; mem. U.S. Ho. of Reps. (Democrat) from Ga., 32d Congress, 1851-53; del. Dem. Nat. Conv., Balt., 1860. Died Decatur, Jan. 16, 1861; buried Decatur City Cemetery.

MURPHY, Henry Cruse, congressman, diplomat, editor; b. Bklyn., July 5, 1810; s. John G. and Clarissa (Runyon) M.; grad. Columbia, 1830; m. Amelia Greenwood, July 29, 1833, 2 children. Admitted to N.Y. bar, 1830; city atty. Bklyn., 1834; mayor Bklyn., 1842; mem. U.S. Ho. of Reps. from N.Y. (Democrat), 28th, 30th congresses, 1843-45, 47-49; U.S. minister to Netherlands, 1857-61; mem. N.Y. Senate, 1861-73; chief editorial writer Bklyn. Advocate; propr., asso. editor Bklyn. Eagle; a founder L.I. Hist. Soc., Bklyn. City Library; translator various jours. and hist. tracts from the Dutch; owner one of finest collections early Americana of his time. Author: Henry Hudson in Holland, 1859; The First Minister of the Dutch Reformed Church in the U.S., 1857. Died Bklyn., Dec. 1, 1882.

MURPHY, Isaac, gov. Ark.; b. nr. Pitts., Oct. 16, 1802; s. Hugh and Jane (Williams) M.; m. Angelina Hockhart, July 31, 1830; 6 children, including Matilda, Mary. Admitted to Ark. bar, 1835; mem. Ark. Legislature, 1848-49; conducted Huntsville (Ark.) Female Acad., 1854-56; mem. Ark. Senate, 1856; Union del. to Secession Conv., only del. to vote against secession, 1861; served as maj. 1st Ark. Inf., U.S. Army, 1862; provisional gov. Ark., 1864; gov. Ark., 1864-69. Died Huntsville, Sept. 8, 1882.

MURPHY, Jeremiah Henry, congressman; b. Lowell, Mass., Feb. 19, 1835; attended Appleton (Wis.) U.; grad. U. Ia., 1857; studied law. Admitted to Ia. bar, 1858, began practice in Marengo; elected alderman Marengo, 1860; del. Democratic nat. convs., Chgo., 1864, N.Y.C., 1868; moved to Davenport, Ia., 1867, practiced law; elected mayor of Davenport, 1873, 78; mem. Ia. Senate, 1874-78; Dem. presdl. elector, 1880; mem. U.S. Ho. of Reps. (Dem. from Ia., 48th-49th congresses, 1883-87. Died Washington, D.C., Dec. 11, 1893; buried St. Marguerite's Cemetery, Davenport.

MURPHY, John, gov. Ala., congressman; b. Columbia, N.C., 1786; grad. S.C. Coll. (now U. S.C.), 1808; studied law. Clk., N.C. Senate, 1810-17; moved to Ala., 1818; del. Ala. Constl. Conv., 1819; admitted to Ala. bar; mem. Ala. Senate, 1822; gov. Ala., 1825-29; mem. U.S. Ho. of Reps. (Democrat) from Ala., 23d Congress, 1833-35. Died nr. Gosport, Ala., Sept. 21, 1841; buried nr. Gosport.

MURPHY, John, publisher; b. Omagh, Ireland, Mar. 12, 1812; s. Bernard and Mary (McCullough) M.; m. Margaret O'Donnoghue, 1852, 6 children including Frank K. Came to U.S., 1822; became printer in Phila.; established printing shop, Balt., 1835, specialized in Catholic books; published sch. textbooks, Bibles and theol. works; printed mag. The Religious Cabinet, 1842-43, The U.S. Catholic Mag., 1843-48, The Metropolitan; A Monthly Mag., 1853-54, The Catholic Youth's Mag., 1857-61; also published Catholic Almanac; received papal medal of merit for his publication Definition of the Dogma of the Immaculate Conception, 1855; given honorary title of printer to pope for his Acts and Decrees of the Second Plenary Council of Baltimore, 1866; published The Maryland Code of Public General Laws, 2 vols., 1860, also supplements; mem. Md. Hist. Soc. Died Balt., May 27, 1880.

MURPHY, John W., bridge engr.; b. New Scotland, N.Y., Jan. 20, 1828; grad. Rensselaer Poly. Inst., 1847; married twice, 2 children. Builder of the levees on Alabama River, 1851-52; chief engr. Montgomery (Ala.), 1860-61; builder Union Hall, Phila., 1864; initiator use of pin connections, metal bridge constrn., 1859; designer (for Lehigh Valley R.R.) pin connected bridge with all wrought iron members (1st bridge of kind in U.S.), 1863; builder Broad Street Bridge, Phila. Died Phila., Sept. 27, 1874.

MURPHY, William Sumter, diplomat; b. S.C., 1796; m. Lucinda Sterret, 1821. Practiced law; mem. Ohio Boundary Com., 1835; brig. gen. Ohio Militia; apptd. by Pres. Tyler as charg d'affaires to Tex., 1843, aided in carrying out annexation diplomacy but treaty offered in 1844 to U.S. Senate voted down, his appointment not approved in same month. Died Galveston, Tex., July 13, 1844.

MURPHY, William Walton, diplomat; b. Ernestown, Can., Apr. 3, 1816; m. Ellen Beaumont, 1849. Clk., U.S. Land Office, Monroe, Mich., 1835-37; operated real estate office, Jonesville, Mich., 1837-61; founded local newspaper Jonesville Telegraph; partner in local bank; prosecutor Hillsdale County (Mich.), 1843; mem. Mich. Ho. of Reps., 1844; v.p. Mich. Republican Conv., 1854; consul gen. to Frankfort-on-Main, Germany, (apptd. by Pres. Lincoln), 1861-69, active in writing propaganda which hurt Confederate chances of getting financial aid in Europe and which kept Germany open for purchase of U.S. bonds; financial agt. for many Am. railroads in Heidelberg, Germany, 1869-86. Died June 8, 1886.

MURRAY, Alexander, naval officer; b. Chestertown, Md., July 12, 1754; s. Dr. William and Ann (Smith) M.; m. Mary Miller, June 18, 1782, 1 son, Alexander M. commd. lt. Continental Army during Revolutionary War, capt., 1776-77, participated in battles of White Plains and Flatbush; Am. privateer for a time; commd. lt. U.S. Navy, 1781, capt., 1798; comdr. ships Insurgent and Constellation during naval war with France, 1798; commanded Constellation against Barbary pirates in Mediterranean Sea, 1803; commanded ship Adams, 1805; commanding naval officer, Phila., 1808-21, had been ranking Am. naval officer since 1811. Died Phila., Oct. 6, 1821.

MURRAY, Ambrose Spencer, congressman; b. Wallkill, N.Y., Nov. 27, 1807; attended common schs. Clk. merc. establishment, Middletown, N.Y., 1824-31; moved to Goshen, N.Y., engaged in banking; treas. Orange County (N.Y.), 1851-54; mem. U.S. Ho. of Reps. (Republican) from N.Y., 34th-35th congresses, 1855-59; del. Rep. Nat. Conv., Chgo., 1860. Died Goshen, Nov. 8, 1885; buried St. James' Cemetery, Goshen.

MURRAY, James Ormsbee, clergyman, educator; b. Camden, S.C., Nov. 27, 1827; s. James Syng and Aurelia (Pearce) M.; grad. (valedictorian) Brown U., 1850, LL.D. (hon.), 1865; grad. Andover Theol. Sem., 1854; D.D. (hon.), Princeton, 1867, M.A. (hon.), 1896; m. Julia Richards Haughton, Oct. 22, 1856, 5 children. Instr. in Greek, Brown U., 1851; pastor Congregational Ch., Peabody, Mass., 1854-61, Brick (Presbyn.) Ch., N.Y.C., 1873-75; Holmes prof. belle lettres and English lang. and lit. Coll. of N.J. (now Princeton), 1875-99, became 1st dean faculty, 1833; trustee Princeton Theol. Sem., 1867-74, 83, pres. bd., 1889. Author: Life of Francis Wayland, 1891; George Ide Chase, A Memorial, 1886; joint editor, compiler The Sacrifice of Praise. Died Princeton, N.J., Mar. 27, 1899.

MURRAY, John (4th earl Dunmore, viscount Fincastle, baron Blair, Moulin and Tillymont), colonial gov.; b. 1732; s. William and Catherine (Nairne) M.; m. Lady Charlotte Stewart, 1759. One of 16 reps. of Scotland to Brit. Ho. of Lords, 1761-69; Scottish peer in Parliament, 1768; gov. royal colony of N.Y., 1770; gov. Va., Sept. 1771, refused to recognize Va. Ho. of Burgesses, in reaction Ho. held secret meeting (May 29, 1774) at which circular was issued calling assembly of deputies to meet in conv. in Williamsburg (first public revolutionary assemblage), Aug. 1, 1774; gov. Bahamas, 1787-96. Died Ramsgate, Eng., Mar. 5, 1809.

MURRAY, John, mcht., philanthropist; b. Lancaster, Pa., 1737; s. John Murray; m. Hannah Lindley, Dec. 1766. Mem. N.Y.C. C. of C., 1779-1806, pres., 1798-1806; dir. Bank of N.Y., 1789; dir. ins. co.; mem. commn. to build one of state prisons in N.Y.C., 1796; dir. Humane Soc.; a founder of a soc. for free edn. of poor children; Quaker. Died N.Y.C., Oct. 11, 1808.

MURRAY, John, clergyman; b. Alton, Eng., Dec. 10, 1741; m. Eliza Neale, before 1770; m. 2d, Judith (Sargent) Stevens, Oct. 1788. Excommunicated by Methodist Ch. after accepting teachings of Universalism as taught by John Relly in Eng.; came to Am., 1770; roving preacher for 4 years; settled, Gloucester, Mass., 1774; served as chaplain R.I. troops, 1775; organized 1st Universalist ch. in Am., 1779; pastor Universalist Soc. of Boston, 1793. Author: Letters and Sketches, 1812; Autobiography, 1813. Died Boston, Sept. 3, 1815; buried Mt. Auburn Cemetery, Cambridge, Mass.

MURRAY, John, congressman; b. nr. Potts Grove, Northumberland County, Pa., 1768; attended pvt. schs. Engaged in farming; mem. Pa. Ho. of Reps., 1807-10; mem. U.S. Ho. of Reps. from Pa., 15th-16th congresses, Oct. 14, 1817-21. Died East Chillisquaque Twp., Northumberland County, Mar. 7, 1834; buried Chillisquaque Cemetery, nr. Ports Grove.

MURRAY, John L., congressman; b. Wadesboro, Ky.; studied law. Admitted to Ky. bar, began practice in Wadesboro; held several local offices; mem. U.S. Ho. of Reps. (Democrat) from Ky., 25th Congress, 1837-39.

MURRAY, John O'Kane, physician; b. Antrim, Ireland, Dec. 12, 1847; brought to U.S., 1856; attended Fordham Coll. Became a physician, also wrote books on ch. history, saints' lives, Irish poetry, English literature and history. Died Chgo., July 30, 1885.

MURRAY, Joseph, lawyer; b. Queens County, Ireland, 1694; s. Thomas Murray; m. Grace (Cosby) Freeman, 1738. Admitted to Middle Temple, London, Eng., 1725, N.Y. bar, 1728; del. 2d Colonial Congress, Albany, N.Y., 1754; mem. 1st bd. trustees N.Y. Soc. Library, also gov.; gov. King's Coll. (now Columbia); councilor attending conf. with Indians, Albany, 1744; politically aligned against Clinton family; bequeathed his library to Columbia. Died N.Y.C., Apr. 28, 1757.

MURRAY, Judith Sargent Stevens, author; b. May 1, 1751; d. Capt. Winthrop and Judith (Sanders) Sargent; m. Capt. John Stevens, Oct. 3, 1769; m. 2d, Rev. John Murray, Oct. 6, 1788. Contributed poems, essays and stories to local newspapers; wrote essays under heading "The Gleaner" for Mass. Mag., 1792-94; edited and completed her husband's autobiography Letters, Sketches of Sermons and Autobiography of Rev. John Murray, 3 vols., 1812-13. Author: The Gleaner (collection of her early works), 3 vols., 1798. Died Natchez, Miss., July 6, 1820.

MURRAY, Lindley, grammarian; b. Swatara Creek, Dauphin County, Pa., June 7, 1745; s. Robert and Mary (Lindley) M.; attended Friends' Sem., N.Y.C.; m. Hannah Dobson, June 22, 1767. Admitted to N.Y.C. bar; became mcht., 1779, retired, 1783; minister Soc. of Friends. Author: English Grammar, 1795; English Exercises, 1797; A Key to the Exercises, 1797; An English Grammar, 1818; (religious tracts) The Power of Religion on the Mind in Retirement, Sickness and Death, 1787; Selections from Bishop Home's Commentaries on the Psalms, 1812; Biographical Sketch of Henry Tuke, 1815; Compendium of Religious Faith and Practice, 1815; On the Duty and Benefit of a Daily Perusal of the Scriptures, 1817. Died Holdgate, York, Pa., Jan. 16, 1826.

MURRAY, Nicholas, clergyman; b. Westmeath County, Ireland, Dec. 25, 1802; grad. Williams Coll., 1826, Princeton Theol. Sem., 1829. Came to Am., 1818; clk. Harper Bros., publishing co., N.Y.C., until 1821; ordained to ministry Presbyn. Ch., 1829, became pastor, Wilkes Barre, Pa.; pastor Presbyn. Ch., Elizabethtown, N.J., 1835-61; gen. agt. Bd. Fgn. Missions, circa 1840. Author: Notes Historical and Biographical Concerning, Elizabethtown; Men and Things As I Saw Them in Europe in 1853, published 1854. Died Elizabethtown, Feb. 4, 1861; buried Elizabethtown.

MURRAY, Robert, mcht.; b. Scotland, 1721; son of John Murray; m. Mary Lindley, 1744, at least 1 child. Came (with father) to Am., 1732; operated flour mill, Dauphin County, Pa., before 1750; lived in N.C., 1750-53; engaged in gen. trade, operating from N.Y., 1753-67, from Eng., 1767-75; supported British during Revolutionary War; returned to Am., 1775, continued in trading activities, 1775-86. Died July 22, 1786.

MURRAY, Thomas, Jr., congressman; b. nr. Potts Grove, Northumberland County, Pa., 1770; attended pvt. schs. Engaged in farming; mem. Pa. Ho. of Reps., 1813, Pa. Senate, 1814; mem. U.S. Ho. of Reps. (Democrat) from Pa., 17th Congress, Oct. 9, 1821-23. Died East Chillisquaque Twp., Northumberland County, Aug. 26, 1823; buried Chillisqueque Cemetery, nr. Potts Grove.

MURRAY, William, congressman; b. nr. Middletown, N.Y., Oct. 1, 1803; attended common schs. Clk. merc. establishments, Middletown and N.Y. C.; engaged in merc. bus.; moved to Goshen, N.Y., 1841; mem. U.S. Ho. of Reps. (Dem.) from N.Y., 32d-33d congresses, 1851-53; engaged in farming; an organizer Republican Party, 1856; pres. Goshen Bank, 1857-75. Died Goshen, Aug. 25, 1875; buried St. James' Cemetery, Goshen.

MURRAY, William Vans, diplomat, congressman; b. Cambridge, Md., Feb. 9, 1760; s. Dr. Henry and Rebeckah (Orrick) M.; studied law in Middle Temple, London, Eng., 1784-87; m. Charlotte Hughins, before 1787. Admitted to Md. bar, 1791; mem. Md. Ho. of Reps., 1791; mem. U.S. Ho. of Reps. from Md., 2d-4th congresses, 1791-97; minister resident to The Netherlands, 1797-1801; apptd. (with Oliver Ellsworth and Gov. W. R. Davie) minister plenipotentiary to France to negotiate with French govt. over question of denial of diplomatic recognition to Charles Cotesworth Pinckney by French Fgn. Minister Talleyrand in 1796, 1799, obtained recognition and French-Am. agreement resulted in Treaty of Morfontaine (which released U.S. from any defensive Alliance with France), 1800; minister to France, 1800-01; returned to farm nr. Cambridge, Md. Died nr. Cambridge, Dec. 11, 1803; buried Christ Protestant Episcopal Ch. Cemetery, Cambridge.

MURRELL, John A., outlaw; b. Tenn., 1804. Led life characterized by stealing and gen. illegal activities before 1826; leader of a large band of outlaws who terrorized Southwest territories, 1826-34; especially known for his acts of Negro stealing for which he was caught by Virgil A. Stewart, 1834; sentenced to 10 years in Nashville (Tenn.) Penitentiary; subject of a biography written by Stewart (contains most what little information is available on Murrell). Died of consumption, Pikesville, Tenn., circa 1846.

MURRIETA, Joaquin, outlaw; b. Sonora, Mexico, circa 1832. Arrived in Cal., 1849; leader band of outlaws in gold mining area; pursued by Capt. Harry S. Love (dep. sheriff of Los Angeles County) under authorization of Cal. Legislature, 1853. Killed by rangers, Los Angeles County, July 25, 1853.

MUSSEY, Reuben Dimond, surgeon, educator; b. Pelham, N.H., June 23, 1780; s: John and Beulah (Butler) M.; A.B., Dartmouth, 1803, M.B., Med. Dept., 1805, LL.D. (hon.), 1854; M.D., U. Pa., 1809; m. Mary Sewell, before 1807; m. 2d, Mehitable Osgood, 1813; 9 children including William Hand Francis. Taught theory and practice of medicine, materia medica, obstetrics Dartmouth, 1814-20, prof. anatomy and surgery, 1822-38; proved union was possible in cases of intra-capsular fracture, 1830; 1st to tie both carotid arteries successfully; lectr. on anatomy and surgery Coll. Physicians and Surgeons, Fairfield, N.Y., 1836-38; prof. surgery Med. Coll. Ohio, 1838; founder Miami Med. Coll., prof. surgery, 1852-57; fellow Med. Coll., Phila.; mem. A.M.A. (pres. 1850), N.H. Med. Soc. (pres.), Mass. Med. Soc., Am. Acad. Arts and Scis. Died Boston, June 21, 1866.

MUSTAPHA II, dey of Algiers. Succeeded to deyship of Algiers, 1798; successful in obtaining Am. tribute of money and naval stores; offered to go to war against Tunis for America, but outcome of war was inconclusive; refused to be bound by Algerine-Am. treaty which had been concluded with his predecessor (1796). Died 1805.

MUTCHLER, William, congressman; b. Palmer Twp., Northampton County, Pa., Dec. 21, 1831; attended Vandeveer's Acad., Easton, Pa.; studied law. Admitted to Pa. bar, began practice in Easton; sheriff of Northampton County, 1854-60, prothonotary, 1861-67; adj. 38th Regt., Pa. Volunteers, 1863; apptd. assessor of internal revenue, 1867-69; chmn. Pa. Democratic Com., 1869-70; del. Dem. nat. convs., 1876-93; mem. U.S. Ho. of Reps. (Dem) from Pa., 44th, 47th-48th, 51st-53d congresses, 1875-77, 81-85, 89-93. Died Easton, June 23, 1893; buried Easton Cemetery.

MUYBRIDGE, Eadweard, photographer; b. Kingston-on-Thames, Eng., Apr. 9, 1830; s. John and Susannah Muggeridge; never married. Photographer on U.S. Coast and Geodetic Survey, Pacific coast, 1872; engaged by Leland Stanford to ascertain whether at any point a running horse has all 4 feet off ground, May 1872, used camera operated by string stretched across horse's path, definitely proved that all 4 feet are off the ground at certain times; performed series of experiments designed to make more detailed study of moving horse, 1872-78; continued experiments, using men, dogs and birds, 1878-81; developed zoopraxiscope (machine which reproduced moving figures on screen), 1879; worked on animal motion studies with Dr. E. J. Marey, Paris, France, 1881-82; did series of electro-photographic experiments in animal movement under sponsorship of U. Pa., 1884-86; lectured at World's Columbian Expn., Chgo., 1893. Author: The Horse in Motion, 1878; Animal Locomotion; An Electro-Photographic Investigation of Consecutive Phases of Animal Movements, 1872-85, 11 vols., published 1887; Descriptive Zoopraxography, 1893; The Human Figure in Motion, 1901. Died May 8, 1904.

MYER, Albert James, army officer; b. Newburgh, N.Y., Sept. 20, 1829; s. Henry Beekman and Eleanor Pope (McLannan) M.; A.B., Hobart Coll, 1847; M.D., Buffalo Med. Coll., 1851; m. Catherine Walden, 6 children. Saw the possibilities of visual signals while serving in Tex.; became signal officer, 1860; organized, commanded Signal Corps, U.S. Army, 1861; furnished plans for naval signaling; promoted lt. col., 1862, col., 1862; col. and chief signal officer, 1863-64; signal officer Div. of West Miss., 1864 to end of Civil War; brevetted brig. gen., 1865; commd. col., chief signal officer U.S. Army, 1866; established, supervised U.S. Weather Bur., 1870. U.S. rep. at meteorol. congresses in Vienna, 1873, Rome, 1879; promoted brig. gen., 1880; army camp Ft. Myer (Va.) named for him. Died Buffalo, N.Y., Aug. 24, 1880.

MYER, Henry, architect; b. Buffalo, N.Y., Oct. 16, 1837. Practiced architecture, Cleve., 1860-81, credited with designs of many bldgs. in Cleve., N.Y. and Pa.; built county court houses, Canton, O., 1869-70, Mansfield, O., 1870-73, Zanesville, O., 1874-77. Died Mar. 10, 1881.

MYERS, Abraham Charles, army officer; b. Georgetown, D.C., 1811; s. Abraham Meyers; grad. U.S. Mil. Acad., 1833; m. Marion Twiggs. Served in Seminole War in Fla.; served as capt. Q.M. Dept., 1839; brevetted maj., then col.; chief q.m. U.S. Army of Mexico, 1848; commd. lt. col. Q.M. Gen.'s Dept., Confederate Army, 1861, became 1st q.m. gen., 1861, col., 1862, removed by Jefferson Davis, 1863, as result never reconciled to Davis. Died Washington, D.C., June 20, 1889.

MYERS, Amos, congressman; b. Petersburg, Pa., Apr. 23, 1824; grad. Meadville Coll., 1843; studied law. Admitted to Pa. bar, 1846, began practice in Clarion; held several local offices; apptd. dist. atty. Clarion County, 1847; mem. U.S. Ho. of Reps. (Republican) from Pa., 38th Congress, 1863-65; moved to Ky.; ordained to ministry Baptist Ch.; preached in Ky., Pa. and N.Y. Died East Carleton (now Kent), N.Y., Oct. 18, 1893; buried Crown Hill Cemetery, Indpls.

MYERS, John J., trapper, mountain guide; mem. Chiles' party of 1843; officer Fremont's battalion, 1847; guide with Hudspeth's party, 1849; discovered gold at Rich Bar, July 1850; known as the great desert god.

MYLES, John, clergyman; b. Eng., circa 1621; son of Walter Myles; ed. Brasenose Coll., U. Oxford (Eng.); m. Anne (Humphreys) Palmer; 1 son, Samuel. A founder, pastor Baptist Ch. (one of earliest in Wales), Ilston, Wales; an organizer of an assn. of Welsh Baptist Chs.; ejected from his church after the Restoration, came to New Eng.; arrived at Rehoboth, Plymouth Colony, 1663, organized Baptist Ch.; ejected (with congregation) by Gen. Ct. of Plymouth Colony, 1667, moved to Wannamoisett region, built Town of Swansea (Mass. Bay Colony); pastor 1st Baptist Ch., Boston, for a time after King Phillip's War; later resumed ministerial duties, Swansea. Died Swansea, Feb. 3, 1683.

N

NABERS, Benjamin Duke, congressman; b. Franklin, Tenn., Nov. 7, 1812; attended common schs.; studied law. Moved to Hickory Flat, Miss., engaged as commn. mcht.; mem. U.S. Ho. of Reps. (Unionist) from Miss., 32d Congress, 1851-53; admitted to Tenn. bar, 1860, began practice in Memphis; Constitutional-Union presdl. elector, 1860; returned to Miss., settled in Holly Springs, 1860; chancery clk., 1870-74; mem. bd. govs. Miss. State Penitentiary, Jackson, 2 years. Died Holly Springs, Miss., Sept. 6, 1878; buried Hill Crest Cemetery, Holly Springs.

NACK, James M., poet; b. N.Y.C., Jan. 4, 1809; m. Martha W. Simon, 1838. Lost hearing, later speech as result of childhood accident, 1817; inmate N.Y. Deaf and Dumb Asylum, 1818-23; began writing at age 12; began to publish through influence of Abraham Asten; works include: The Legend of the Rocks and Other Poems, 1827; Ode on the Proclamation of President Jackson, 1833; Earl Rupert and Other Tales and Poems, 1839; The Immortal, A Dramatic Romance, 1850. Died Sept. 23, 1879.

NAHL, Charles Christian, artist; b. Cassel, Germany, Oct. 13, 1818. Came to Am., 1849; went to Cal., 1850, worked in gold fields; resumed career as artist, San Francisco, 1850; worked with brother Hugo as photographer and comml. artist; painted hist. subjects; obtained patronage of Judge E. B. Crocker, 1867, painted several large paintings; considered a leading painter of pioneer life in Cal. Died Mar. 1, 1878.

NAHL, Hugo Wilhelm Arthur, artist; b. Cassel, Germany; studied in Paris, France. Came to Am., 1849; went to Cal., 1850, worked in gold fields; resumed a career as artist, San Francisco, 1850; worked with brother Charles as photographer and comml. artist; frequent exhibitor at San Francisco Art Assn.; won silver medal at Cal. State Fair for pictures in crayon and charcoal; designed Cal. State Seal. Died San Francisco, Apr. 1, 1881.

NAIRNE, Thomas, Indian agt.; b. Scotland; m. Elizabeth Quintine, 1 child. Employed by S.C. Assembly to regulate traders among Yamasee Indians, 1702; became 1st provincial Indian agt. (diplomatic agt.) by Indian Act of 1707; mem. S.C. Assembly, 1707-08; judge advocate of S.C., 1710. Killed by an Indian (during uprising of 1712-15), Apr. 1715.

NANCRÉDE, Paul Joseph Guérard de, see de Nancréde, Paul Joseph Guérard.

NAPTON, William Barclay, jurist; b. Princeton, N.J., Mar. 23, 1808; s. John and Susan (Hight) N.; grad. Coll. N.J. (now Princeton), 1826; grad. dept. law U. Va., 1830; m. Malinda Williams, 1838, 10 children. Sec., Mo. Senate, 1836; atty. gen. Mo., 1836-39; judge Mo. Supreme Ct., 1839-51, chief justice, 1845-51, primary author Jackson Resolution (famous instructions to Senator Thomas H. Benton to uphold pro-slavery program in Congress), 1847, judge 1857-61 (resigned rather than take required loyalty oath 1861), 1873-80. Died Elk Hill, Mo., Jan. 8, 1883.

NARVAEZ, Panfilo, see de Narváez, Panfilo.

NASH, Abner, gov. N.C., Continental congressman; b. Templeton Manor, Prince Edward County, Va., Aug. 8, 1740; s. John and Ann (Owen) N.; m. Justina (Davis) Dobbs; m. 2d, Mary Whiting Jones, 1774. Mem. Va. Ho. of Burgesses, 1761, 62; mem. N.C. Ho. of Commons, 1764, 65, 70-71, 78, 82, 84, 85, speaker 1777; brigade maj. N.C. Militia, 1768; del. to 5 N.C. provincial congresses, 1774-76; mem. N.C. Provincial Council, 1775, 76, agt. of council, 1776; speaker N.C. Senate, 1779-80; gov. N.C., 1780-81; mem. Continental Congress from N.C., 1782, 83, 84, 85, 86; elected to Annapolis Conv., 1786, did not attend. Died N.Y.C., Dec. 2, 1786; buried "Pembroke" nr. New Bern, N.C.

NASH, Albert C., architect; b. 1826. Practiced architecture, Cincinnati; designed chs. including Cath. Ch. of Assumption, Walnut Hills, O., Presbyn. Ch., Clinton, O., Presbyn. Ch., Pine Hills, O.; pres. local chpt. A.I.A., 1873-76, 82-89. Died 1890.

NASH, Daniel, clergyman; b. Mass., May 28, 1763; s. Jonathan and Anna Maria (Spoor) N.; grad. Yale, 1785; studied Episcopalian theology under Rev. John Croes; m. Olive Susk, Jan. 1796, at least 1 child. Tchr., Pittsgrove, N.J., Swedesboro, N.J., 1785-94; head of acad., New Lebanon Springs, N.Y., 1794-97; ordained deacon Episcopal Ch., 1797; missionary in Western N.Y., 1797-1836; rector Christ Ch., Cooperstown, N.Y., 1811-36. Died Burlington, N.Y., June 4, 1836; buried Christ Ch. Churchyard, Cooperstown.

NASH, Francis, army officer; b. Templeton Manor, Prince Edward County, Va., 1742; s. John and Ann (Owen) N.; m. Sarah Moore; at least 2 children. Justice of peace, clk. N.C. Ct. Pleas and Quarter Sessions, 1763; mem. N.C. Ho. of Commons, 1764, 65, 71, 73-75; served as capt. Brit. Army, participated in battle of Alamanance against the Regulators, 1771; mem. N.C. Provincial Congress, 1775; col. N.C. Militia; lt. col., then col. 1st N.C. Regt., Continental Army, 1775, brig. gen., 1777, led a brigade at Germantown, Pa., wounded, 1777. Nash County, N.C., Nashville, Tenn. named in his honor. Died Kulpsville, Pa., Oct. 7, 1777.

NASH, Frederick, jurist; b. New Bern, N.C., Feb. 19, 1781; s. Abner and Mary (Jones) N.; grad. Coll. of N.J. (now Princeton), 1799; LL.D. (hon.), U. N.C., 1853; m. Mary G. Kollock, Sept. 1, 1803. Mem. N.C. Ho. of Commons, 1804-05, 14-17, 28-29, speaker, 1814; judge N.C. Superior Ct, 1818-26, 36-44; became judge N.C. Supreme Ct., 1844, chief justice, 1852-58; trustee U. N.C., 1807. Died Hillsboro, N.C., Dec. 4, 1858.

NASH, Simeon, jurist; b. South Hadley, Mass., Sept. 21, 1804; s. Simeon and Amy (White) N.; grad. Amherst Coll., 1829; m. Cynthia Smith, Dec. 16, 1831; 7 children. Admitted to Ohio bar, 1833; mem. Ohio Senate, 1838-43; became judge Ohio Ct. Common Pleas, 1851. Author: A Digest of Decisions of the Supreme Court of Ohio, 1853; Pleadings and Practice under the Civil Code, 1856; Morality and the State, 1859; Pleadings and Practice, 1875; Crime and the Family, 1876. Died Gallipolis, O., Jan. 17, 1879.

NASON, Elias, clergyman; b. Wrentham, Mass., Apr. 21, 1811; s. Levi and Sarah (Newton) N.; grad. Brown, 1835; m. Myra Bigelow, Nov. 28, 1836; 6 children. Prin. various high schs., acads., including high sch., Milford, Mass., 1849; minister Congl. Ch., 1852. Author: Songs for the School Room, 1842; Christomathie Francaise, 1849; Memoir of Rev. Nathaniel Howe, 1851; Thou Shalt Not Steal, 1852; Strength and Beauty of the Sanctuary, 1854; Our Obligations to Defend our Country, 1861; Songs for Social and Public Worship, 1862; Eulogy on Sir Charles Henry Frankland, 1865; Eulogy on Abraham Lincoln, 1865; Gazetteer of Massachusetts, 1872. Editor New England Historical and Genealogical Register, 1866, 67, Congregational Hymn Book, 1857. Died North Billerica, Mass., June 17, 1887.

NASON, Henry Bradford, educator, chemist; b. Foxboro, Mass., June 22, 1831; s. Elias and Susanna (Keith) N.; grad. Amherst, 1855; Ph.D., U. Gottingen, 1855-57; M.D., Union Coll., 1880; LL.D., Beloit Coll.; m. Frances Townsend; 2 children. Prof. natural history Rensselaer Poly. Inst., 1858-66, prof. chemistry and natural sci., 1866-95; prof. natural history Beloit (Wis.) Coll., 1858-66; chem. adviser Standard Oil Co., 1880-90; insp. petroleum oils N.Y. State Bd. of Health, 1881; rep. U.S. at Paris Exposition of 1878; prominent in orgn. Geol. Soc. Am., Am. Chem. Soc. (pres. 1889-90). Fellow A.A.A.S., London Chem. Soc., Soc. Chem. Industry; mem. Gen. Alumni Assn. Rensselaer Poly Inst. (sec. 1872-86) Am. Chem. Soc. Died Jan. 18, 1895.

NAST, William, clergyman, coll. pres.; b. Stuttgart, Wurttemberg, Germany, June 15, 1807; s. Johann and Eliza (Boehm) Wilhelm; attended U. Tubingen (Germany) 2 years; D.D. (hon.), McKendree Coll., 1836; m. Margaret Eliza McDowell, Aug. 1, 1836, 5 children. Came to Am., 1828; librarian, instr. German, U.S. Mil. Acad., 1830-32; taught Hebrew, Greek, Kenyon (O.) Coll., 1832-35; missionary to Cincinnati, 1835; largely responsible for the founding of German Methodism; organized 1st German Meth. Ch. in U.S., Cincinnati, 1838; editor Der Christliche Apologate, 1838-92; started German Meth. Christian literature in Am.; founder, pres. German Wallace Coll., Berea, O. Author: Das Leben und Wirken des Johannes Wesley und Seiner Haupt-mitarbeiter, 1852; Die Aufgabe der Christlichen Kirche im neunzehnten Jahrhundert, 1857. Died Cincinnati. May 16, 1899.

NAUDAIN, Arnold, senator; b. nr. Dover, Del., Jan. 6, 1790; grad. Princeton, 1806, med. dept. U. Pa., 1810. Began practice of medicine, Dover; surgeon gen. Del. Militia during War of 1812; mem. Del. Ho. of Reps., 1823-27, speaker, 1826; unsuccessful candidate for gov. Del., 1832; mem. U.S. Senate from Del., Jan. 13, 1830-June 16, 1836; resumed practice of medicine, Wilmington, Del.; mem. Del. Senate, 1836-39; collector Port of Wilmington, 1841-45; moved to Phila., 1845, practiced medicine. Died Odessa, Del., Jan. 4, 1872; buried Old Drawyer's Presbyn. Churchyard, Odessa.

NAVARRO, José Antonio, army officer; b. San Antonio, Tex., 1795. Advocate of Tex. independence from Mexico (despite Mexican background); land title commr. Bexar Dist., Tex., 1834-35; a signer Tex. Declaration of Independence, 1836; served in Republic of Tex. Congress, various times; imprisoned by Mexicans in Santa Fe, N.M., 1841-43; mem. Tex. State Constl. Conv., 1845; Navarro County (Tex.) named for him. Died 1870.

NAYLOR, Charles, congressman; b. Philadelphia County, Pa., Oct. 6, 1806; studied law. Admitted to Pa. bar, 1828, began practice in Phila.; mem. U.S. Ho. of Reps. (Whig) from Pa., June 29, 1837-41; organized a volunteer co. known as Phila. Rangers, during Mexican War, served as capt.; settled in Pitts. after Mexican War, practiced law; returned to Phila. Died Phila., Dec. 24, 1872; buried South Laurel Hill Cemetery, Phila.

NEAGLE, John, painter; b. Boston, Nov. 4, 1796; m. Mary Sully, May 1826. Began to paint portraits, Lexington, Ky., 1818; travelled extensively; returned to Phila.; painted portrait of Washington (now in Independence Hall, Phila.), painting of Pat Lyon, the Blacksmith (replica hangs in Boston Athenuem); portrait of Coll. Richard Johnston (now in Corcoran Galley); other portraits include William Russell Birch, Matthew Carey, Thomas Pym Cope, Dr. William Gibson, William Short, Gilbert Stuart; dir. Pa. Acad. Fine Arts, 1830-31; 1st pres. Artists Fund of Phila., 1835-44. Died Phila., Sept. 17, 1865.

NEAL, John, author, editor; b. Portland, Me., Aug. 25, 1793; s. John and Rachel (Hall) N.; M.A. (hon.), Bowdoin Coll., 1836; m. Eleanor Hall, Oct. 12, 1828, 5 children. Editor Balt., Telegraph and Portico; editor Portland (Me.) Yankee, 1828-29. Author: (poems) "Men of the North," "Music of the Night"; (best novel) Seventy-Six, 1821; Battle of the Niagara, 1819; Goldau, 1819; Logan, 1821; Errata, 1822; Randolph, 1823; Brother Jonathan, 1825; Rachel Dyer, 1828; Bentham's Morals and Legislation, 1830; Downeasters, 1833; One Word More, 1854; True Womanhood, 1859; Wandering Recollections of A Somewhat Busy Life, 1869; Great Mysteries and Little Plagues, 1870. Died Portland, Me., June 20, 1876.

NEAL, John Randolph, congressman; b. nr. Clinton, Tenn., Nov. 26, 1836; attended Hiwassee Coll., Tenn.; grad. Emory and Henry Coll., 1858; studied law. Admitted to Tenn. bar, 1859, began practice in Athens; served as capt. Tenn. Cavalry Confederate Army, during Civil War, later promoted lt. col.; taught sch.; settled in Rhea Springs, Tenn., practiced law; mem. Tenn. Ho. of Reps., 1874; mem. Tenn. Senate, 1878-79, presiding officer, 1879; Democratic presdl. elector, 1880; mem. U.S. Ho. of Reps. (Dem.) from Tennessee ,49th-50th congresses, 1885-59. Died Rhea Springs, Mar. 26, 1889; buried W. F. Brown family cemetery, Post Oak Springs, Tenn.

NEAL, Joseph Clay, journalist, humorist; b. Greenland, N.H., Feb. 3, 1807; s. Rev. James A. and Christina (Palmer) N.; m. Emily Bradley, 1846. Editor, The Pennsylvanian; established Saturday News and Literary Gazette (later Neal's Saturday Gazette), Lady's Literary Museum, 1836; published Charcoal Sketches: or Scenes in a Metropolis, 1838; editor Democratic Review; 1st humorous sketches published under title City Worthies. Author: In Town and About, 1843; Peter Ploddy and Other Oddities, 1844. Died Phila., July 17, 1847.

NEALE, Leonard, clergyman, coll. pres.; b. Port Tobacco, Md., Oct. 15, 1746; s. William and Anne (Brooke) N.; attended Jesuit Coll. of St. Omer, Flanders, Belgium, circa 1758-62, Bruges (Belgium) Coll., 1762-66, Soc. of Jesus Sem., Ghent, Belgium, 1767-77. Missionary in Eng., 1777-79, Demerara, Brit. Guiana, 1779-83; arrived in Md., 1783; stationed at St. Thomas Manor, Md., 1783-93; participated in 1st Diocesan Synod of Balt., 1791; pastor St. Mary's Ch., Phila., 1793-99, also vicar gen. Phila. area; pres. Georgetown Coll., Md., 1799-1806; bishop coadjutor of Balt., 1800-15, archbishop, 1815-17. Died Md., June 18, 1819; buried Visitation Chapel, Georgetown Coll.

NEALE, Raphael, congressman; b. St. Marys County, Md. Mem. U.S. Ho. of Reps. from Md., 16th-18th congresses, 1819-25. Died Leonardtown, Md., Oct. 19, 1833.

NECKERE, Leo Raymond De, see De Neckere, Leo Raymond.

NEEDHAM, James, explorer; possibly son of George and Barbara (Fitch) N. Arrived in S.C. settlement from Barbados, 1670; mem. of exploring co. in Va., 1671-72; commd. by Col. Abraham Wood to attempt to find water passage to Southwest and to trade with Indians, 1673 (venture unsuccessful). Died Sept. 1673.

NEEF, Francis Joseph Nicholas, educator; b. Soultz, Alsace, Dec. 6, 1770; s. Francis Joseph and Anastasia (Ackerman) N.; m. Elosia Buss, July 5, 1803. Tchr. langs. under Johann Heinrich Pestalozzi, Burghdorf, Switzerland, 1803-05; came to U.S., 1806; founder 1st Pestalozzian sch. in U.S., Schuylkill, Pa., 1808-12, removed sch. to Village Green, Pa., 1813; elected corr. mem. Acad. Natural Scis., Phila., 1812; condr. sch., Louisville, Ky., 1814-26; in charge (with wife) ednl. program under Robert Owen, New Harmony, Ind., 1826-28. Author: Method of Instructing Children Rationally in the Arts of Writing and Reading, 1813. Died New Harmony, Apr. 6, 1854.

NEGLEY, Daniel, businessman; b. Pitts., Apr. 10, 1802; son of Jacob Negley. Successfully engaged in merc. bus., brick mfg., coal and transp. enterprises; a developer East Liberty sect. of Pitts.; mem. Pa. Legislature (Republican), 1858-60. Died Pitts., Dec. 4, 1867.

NEIDHARD, Charles, pioneer homeopathist, physician; b. Bremen, Germany, Apr. 19, 1809; s. Friedrich Neidhard; grad. Leipzig Med. Soc.; grad. Allentown Homeopathic Med. Coll., 1837; M.D. (hon.), Hahnemann Med. Coll. of Chgo., 1862; m. Isabella Taylor, 5 children. Family emigrated to U.S., 1825; an organizer, incorporator, prof. clin. medicine Hahnemann Med. Coll. of Pa., 1839, charter mem. Am. Inst. Homeopathy, 1844; prof. clin. medicine Homepathic Med. Coll. of Pa., 1849-53. Asso. editor American Journal of Homeopathy, 1838; co-editor North American Journal of Homeopathy, 1862-68. Died Phila., Apr. 17, 1895.

NEIGHBORS, Robert Simpson, Indian agt.; b. Va., Nov. 3, 1815; married, 2 children. Commd. lt. Tex. Army, 1840, capt., 1841; sub-agt. for Tex. to Lipan, Tonkawa Indians, 1845; state commr. (to make treaty with Comanches and other plains Indians), 1846; commd. spl. agt. of U.S. for all Tex. Indians, 1847-53, succeeded in getting some Comanches to the Indian Territory; mem. Tex. Legislature, 1851; Assassinated by an outlaw, Tex., Sept. 14, 1859.

NEILL, Edward Duffield, clergyman, coll. pres., diplomat; b. Phila., Aug. 9, 1823; s. Dr. Henry and Martha (Duffield) N.; grad. Amherst, 1842; studied at Andover Theol. Sem.; m. Nancy Hall, Oct. 4, 1847, 5 children. Licensed to preach by Presbyn. Ch., 1847, ordained to ministry, 1848; founder 1st Presbyn. Ch. St. Paul, Minn. Territory, 1849, pastor, 1849-54; pastor House of Hope Presbyn. Ch., 1855-60; sec. Minn. Hist. Soc., 1851-63; a founder St. Paul pub. sch. system; 1st supt. instrn. Minn. Territory, 1851-53; founder, pres. Baldwin Sch. and Coll. St. Paul; chancellor U. Minn., 1858-61; state supt. pub. instrn. Minn., 1860-61; chaplain 1st Minn Inf., 1861-62; hosp. chaplain U.S. Army, Phila., 1862-64; asst. sec. to presidents Lincoln and Johnson; U.S. consul in Dublin, Ireland; founder Minn. Jesus Coll., 1872; pres. Macalester Coll., 1874-84, prof. history, English lit. and polit. economy, 1885. Author: A History of Minnesota, 1858; Terra Mariae; or Threads of Maryland Colonial History, 1867; Virginia Carolorum, 1886; Concise History of Minnesota, 1887. Died St. Paul, Sept. 26, 1893.

NEILL, John, surgeon; b. Phila., July 9, 1819; s. Dr. Henry and Martha R. (Duffield) N.; B.A., U. Pa., 1837, M.D., 1840; m. Anna Maria Hollingsworth, Sept. 24, 1844. Demonstrator anatomy Med. Dept., U. Pa., 1845, prof. surgery 1854-59, prof. clin. surgery, 1874-75; surgeon Pa. Hosp., 1852-59; med. dir. 1st U.S. Mil. Hosp., Phila., 1861; med. dir. Pa. Militia, 1863; inventor apparatus for the treatment of leg fractures; co-compiler An Analytical Compendium of the Various Branches of Medical Science, 1848. Died Phila., Feb. 11, 1880.

NEILL, Thomas Hewson, army officer; b. Phila., Apr. 9, 1826; s. Dr. Henry and Martha (Duffield) N.; grad. U.S. Mil. Acad., 1847; m. Eva Looney, Nov. 20, 1873, 3 children. Commd. 2d lt. 5th Inf., U.S. Army, 1847; asst. prof. of drawing U.S. Mil. Acad., 1853-57; served as capt. in Utah expdn. and in N.M., 1857-61; commd. col. 23d Pa. Volunteers, 1862, served at siege of Yorktown; brevetted maj., 1862, promoted brig. gen. U.S. Volunteers, 1862, brevetted lt. col., then col., 1863; brevetted brig. gen. U.S. Army, 1865, maj. gen. U.S. Volunteers; insp. gen. U.S. Army, 1867-69 with hdqrs. at New Orleans; commd. lt. col., 1869; comdt. of cadets U.S. Mil. Acad., 1875-79; known as Beau Neill. Died Phila., Mar. 12, 1885.

NEILL, William, clergyman, coll. pres.; b. McKeesport, Pa., Apr. 25, 1778; s. William and Jane (Snodgrass) N.; grad. Coll. of N.J. (now Princeton), 1803; D.D. (hon.), Union Coll., 1812; m. Elizabeth Van Dyke, Oct. 5, 1805; m. 2d, Frances King, Feb. 25, 1811; m. 3d, Sarah Elmer, Apr. 15, 1835; 7 children. Tutor, Coll. of N.J., circa 1803; licensed to preach by Presbyn. Ch., Cooperstown, N.Y., 1805; pastor 1st Ch., Albany, N.Y., 1809; moderator Presbyn. Gen. Assembly, 1815; pastor 6th Ch., Phila., 1816-24; pres. Dickinson Coll., 1824-29; sec. Bd Edn. of Presbyn. Ch., 1829-31; pastor Germantown (Pa.) Ch., 1829-40; an organizer Am. Bible Soc.; dir. Princeton Theol. Sem. Author: Lectures on Biblical History, 1846; Exposition of the Epistle to the Ephesians, 1850; editor Presbyterian. Died Phila., Aug. 8, 1860.

NEILSON, John, army officer, Continental congressman; b. Raritan Landing,, N.J., Mar. 11, 1745; s. Dr. John and Joanna (Coejeman) N.; attended U. Pa.; m. Catherine Voorhees, Dec. 31, 1768, 11 children including James. Commd capt. during Revolutionary War; made col. by Pa. Provincial Congress, 1775; commd. col. 2d Regt., Middlesex Militia, 1776; commd. brig. gen. N.J. Militia, 1777; mem. Continental Congress from N.J., 1778-79; in command N.J. Militia at Elizabethtown and Newark, 1779; dep. q.m. gen. for N.J., 1780-83; mem. N.J. Conv. which ratified U.S. Constn., 1790; judge N.J. Ct. of Common Pleas, 1795-98; mem. N.J. Assembly, 1800-01; register-recorder New Brunswick (N.J.), 1796-1821; elder, trustee 1st Presbyn. Ch. of New Brunswick; truste Rutgers Coll., 1782-1833; presented with a swor by Lafayette, 1824. Died New Brunswick, Mar 3, 1833; buried Van Liew Cemetery, New Brunswick.

NELL, William Cooper, writer; b. Boston, Dec 20, 1816; s. William G. and Louisa M. Nell; studie law office William I. Bowditch, Boston; married Head of several coms. in Mass. for equal rights fo Negro; petitioned Mass. Legislature to allow Negroes into public schs.; assisted Frederick Douglas in publication of North Star, 1851; clk. U.S. Pos Office, Boston, (1st Negro to hold post in Fed. govt.), 1861-74. Author: Services of Colored Americans in the Wars of 1776 and 1812 (pamphlet), 1851; The Colored Patriots of the American Revolution, 1855. Died May 25, 1874.

NELSON, David, clergyman; b. Jonesboro, Tenn., Sept. 24, 1793; s. Henry and Anna (Kelsey) N.; grad. Washington Coll., 1809; studied medicine under Dr. Ephraim McDowell; m. Miss Deaderick, 1815. Served as surgeon in Can. invasion and Fla. during War of 1812; ordained to ministry Presbyn. Ch., 1825; editor Calvinistic Mag., 1827-29; founder, pres. Marion Coll., Palmyra, Mo., 1831-35; became agt. for Am. Anti-Slavery Soc., 1835. Author: The Cause and Cure of Infidelity, 1836. Died Oakland, Ill., Oct. 17, 1844.

NELSON, Homer Augustus, congressman; b. Poughkeepsie, N.Y., Aug. 31, 1829; studied law. Admitted to N.Y. bar, began practice in Poughkeepsie; judge Dutchess County (N.Y.), 1855-62; col. 159th Regt., N.Y. Volunteer Inf., during Civil War; mem. U.S. Ho. of Reps. (Democrat) from N.Y., 38th Congress, 1863-65; del. N.Y. Constl. Conv., 1867; sec. of state N.Y., 1867-70; mem. N.Y. Senate, 1882-83; apptd. mem. commn. to revise judiciary article of N.Y. State Constn., 1890. Died Poughkeepsie, Apr. 25, 1891; buried Poughkeepsie Rural Cemetery.

NELSON, Hugh, congressman; b. Yorktown, Va., Sept. 30, 1768; s. Gov. Thomas and Lucy (Grymes) N.; grad. Coll. William and Mary, 1790; m. Eliza Walker, Apr. 28, 1799, 9 children. Del., Va. Assembly, 1805-09; judge Gen. Ct. of Va., 1809-11; mem. U.S. Ho. of Reps. from Va., 12th-17th congresses, 1811- Jan 14, 1823. U.S. minister plenipotentiary to Spain, from Episcopal Ch. of Va. to Gen. Conv. Protestant Episcopal Ch. in U.S. Died "Belvoir," Albemarle County, Va., Mar. 18, 1836; buried Belvoir Cemetery, Cismont, Albemarle County.

NELSON, Jeremiah, congressman; b. Rowley, Mass., Sept. 14, 1769; grad. Dartmouth, 1790. Engaged in merc. bus., Newburyport, Mass.; mem. Mass. Gen. Ct., 1803-04; mem. U.S. Ho. of Reps. (Federalist) from Mass., 9th, 14th-18th, 22d congresses, 1805-07, 15-25, 31-33; chmn. bd. selectmen Newburyport, 1811; pres. Newburyport Mut. Fire Ins. Co., 1829; engaged in shipping bus. Died Newburyport, Oct. 2, 1838; buried Oak Hill Cemetery, Newburyport.

NELSON, John, mcht.; b. England, 1654; s. Robert and Mary (Temple) N.; m. Elizabeth Tailer, 6 children. Came to Boston, 1670; inherited claims of his uncle (Sir Thomas Temple) to land and trade in Nova Scotia, 1674; managed bus. interests in Canada, 1682; joined in overthrow of Randolph and Andros in Boston, 1689; commd. by Mass. Colony to make expdn. to N.S., 1691, captured by French, prisoner, 1 year; prisoner in Bastille, 1692-94; while in French custody entered into discussions with French ofcls. to secure neutrality of America in war with England; released after Peace of Ryswick, 1697, continued to agitate for removal of French influence from Am.; commr. of Indians in Mass., 1697-1734. Died Nov. 15, 1734.

NELSON, John, congressman, diplomat; b. Frederick, Md., June 1, 1794; s. Roger Nelson; grad. Coll. William and Mary, 1811; studied law. Admitted to Md. bar, 1813, began practice in Md.; mem. U.S. Ho. of Reps. (Democrat) from Md., 17th Congress, 1821-23; chargé d'affaires to Two Sicilies (apptd. by Pres. Jackson), 1831-32; U.S. atty. gen. and sec. of state ad interim under Pres. Tyler, 1843-45. Died Balt., Jan. 18, 1860; buried Greenmount Cemetery, Balt.

NELSON, Reuben, clergyman, educator; b. N.Y.C., Dec. 16, 1818; s. Abraham and Huldah Nelson; attended Hartwick Sem., Otsego County, N.Y.; m. Jane Scott Eddy, 1842. Licensed as exhorter Methodist Episcopal Ch., N.Y.C., 1833, licensed to preach, 1834, ordained deacon, Aug. 10, 1842, elder, 1846; apptd. 3d preacher Otsego circuit by Oneida Conf. of Meth. Episcopal Ch., N.Y.C., 1840; apptd. to Westford circuit, N.Y., 1841; prin. Otsego Acad., Cooperstown, N.Y., 1842-44, Wyoming Sem., Kingston, Pa., 1844-71; publishing agt. Meth. Book Concern, N.Y., 1872-79; treas. Missionary Soc. of Meth. Episcopal Ch., 1872-79. Died N.Y.C., Feb. 20, 1879; buried Forty Fort, Pa.

NELSON, Roger, army officer, congressman; b. Frederick County, Md., 1759; s. Dr. Arthur and Lucy (Waters) N.; attended Coll. William and Mary; m. Mary Brooke Sim, 1787; m. 2d, Eliza Harrison, Feb. 2, 1797; 8 children. Commd. lt. Md. Militia, 1780, advanced to brig. gen.; admitted to Md. bar, 1785; mem. Md. Ho. of Dels., 1795, 1801, 02; mem. U.S. Ho. of Reps. from Md., 8th-11th congresses, Nov. 6, 1804-May 14, 1810; asso. judge 6th Jud. Circuit of Md., 1810-15. Died Frederick, Md., June 7, 1815; buried Mt. Olivet Cemetery, Frederick.

NELSON, Samuel, justice U.S. Supreme Ct.; b. Hebron, N.Y., Nov. 10, 1792; s. John Rogers and Jane (McCarter) N.; grad. Middlebury Coll., 1813; m. Pamela Woods, 1819; m. 2d, Catherine Ann Russell, 1825; 4 children including Rensselaer Russell Nelson. Admitted to N.Y. bar, 1817; postmaster Cortland, N.Y., 1820; judge 6th Circuit of N.Y., 1823-31; asso. justice N.Y. State Supreme Ct., 1831-37, chief justice, 1837; asso. justice U.S. Supreme Ct., 1845-72, wrote preliminary majority opinion in Dred Scott case; apptd. mem. Joint High Commns. to negotiate settlements of Ala. claims. Died Cooperstown, Dec. 13, 1873.

NELSON, Thomas, gov. Va., Continental congressman; b. Yorktown, Va., Dec. 26, 1738; s. William and Elizabeth (Burwell) N.; grad. Trinity Coll., Cambridge (Eng.) U., 1761; m. Lucy Grymes, July 29, 1762, 11 children including Hugh. Mem. His Majesty's Council of Va., 1764; mem. Va. Ho. of Burgesses, 1774; del. 1st Va. Provincial Conv., Williamsburg, 1774; del. from Va. to Continental Congress, 1775-77, attended 3d Va. Conv., Richmond, 1776 (where Va. Resolutions were drawn which evolved into Declaration of Independence); signer of Declaration of Independence; brig. gen., comdr.-in-chief Va. Militia, 1778; mem. Continental Congress from Va.; financier, gov., comdr. Va. Militia; mem. Va. Assembly 1779, 80; gov. Va., 1781; took part in Yorktown campaign as head of Va. Militia, 1781; statue of him located in Capital Park, Richmond. Died Hanover County, Va., Jan. 4, 1789; buried Old Churchyard, Yorktown.

NELSON, Thomas, diplomat; b. Maysville, Ky., circa 1823; s. Dr. Thomas W. and Frances (Doniphan) N.; m. Elizabeth Key, 1844, 6 children. A founder Republican Party in Middle West; U.S. minister to Chile, 1861-66, to Mexico, 1869-73; practiced law, Terre Haute, Ind. Died Terre Haute, Mar 14, 1896.

NELSON, Thomas Amos Rogers, congressman; b. Kingston, Tenn., Mar. 19, 1812; grad. East Tenn. Coll., 1828; studied law. Admitted to Tenn. bar, 1832, began practice in Washington County; atty. gen. 1st Tenn. Jud. Circuit, 2 terms; Whig presdl. elector, 1844, 48; diplomatic commr. to China, 1851; mem. U.S. Ho. of Reps. (Unionist) from Tenn., 36th Congress, 1859-61, reelected to 37th Congress, arrested by Confederate scouts en route to Washington, D.C., taken prisoner, paroled; moved to Knoxville, Tenn., 1868; del. Union Nat. Conv., Phila., 1866, Democratic Nat. Conv., N.Y.C., 1868; a counsel for Pres. Johnson during his impeachment trial, 1868; judge Tenn. Supreme Ct., 1870-71. Died Knoxville, Aug. 24, 1873; buried Gray Cemetery, Knoxville.

NELSON, Thomas Maduit, congressman; b. Oak Hill, Va., Sept. 27, 1782; attended common schs. Commd. capt. 10th Inf. Regt., later maj. 30th and 18th inf. regts., during War of 1812; reduced to capt. after war, resigned commn., 1815; mem. U.S. Ho. of Reps. (Democrat) from Va., 14th-15th congresses, Dec. 4, 1816-19. Died nr. Columbus, Ga., Nov. 10, 1853; buried Linwood Cemetery, Columbus.

NELSON, William, mcht., planter, colonial legislator; b. Yorktown, Va., 1711; s. Thomas and Margaret (Reade) N.; m. Elizabeth Burwell, 1738, 6 children, including Thomas. Sheriff, York County, (Va.), 1738; rep. from York County to Va. Ho. of Burgesses, 1742-44; mem. Va. Council, 1744-72, served pres.; ex officio acting gov. Va., 1770-71; mem. Com. of Correspondence of Va. Assembly; mem. bd. visitors Coll. William and Mary; helped form Piswal Swamp Co. (to drain Piswal swamp), 1763. Died Yorktown, Nov. 19, 1772; buried churchyard at Yorktown.

NELSON, William, congressman; b. Hyde Park, N.Y., June 29, 1784; grad. Poughkeepsie (N.Y.) Acad.; studied law. Admitted to N.Y. bar, began practice in Peekskill, 1807; dist. atty. for Putnam, Rockland and Westchester counties (N.Y.), 30 years; mem. N.Y. State Assembly, 1820-21, N.Y. State Senate, 1824-27; judge Ct. for Correction of Errors, 1824-27; mem. U.S. Ho. of Reps. (Whig) from N.Y., 30th-31st congresses, 1847-51. Died Peekskill, Oct. 3, 1869; buried Hillside Cemetery, Peekskill.

NELSON, William, naval officer, army officer; b. Maysville, Ky., 1825; s. Dr. Thomas W. and Frances (Doniphan) N.; Commd. midshipman U.S. Navy, 1840, passed midshipman, 1846; served in Mexican War; commd. master, 1854, lt, 1855; Union supporter, sent by Pres. Lincoln to help organize Loyalist, 1861; established Camp Dick Robinson; commd. brig. gen. U.S. Army, 1861, commanded 4th div. Dept. of Ohio; commd maj. gen. U.S. Volunteers, 1862; commanded Louisville, Ky. Shot in altercation with Brig. Gen. Jeff C. Davis, Louisville, Sept. 29, 1862.

NEPOMUK, Felix Constatin Alexander Johann, see Salm-Salm, Prince.

NERAZ, John Claudius, clergyman; b. Anse, Rhone, France, Jan. 12, 1828; attended St. Jodard Sem., Anse, also Aix Sem., Grand Sem. at Lyons. Ordained priest Roman Catholic Ch., Galveston, Tex., 1853; did missionary work in Tex.; apptd. 1st vicar gen. of San Antonio (Tex.), 1870, adminstr. of see, 1880-81, bishop, 1881. Died San Antonio, Nov. 15, 1894.

NERINCKX, Charles, missionary; b. Herffelingen, Belgium, Oct. 2, 1761; s. Dr. Sebastian and Petronilla (Langendries) N.; attended Louvain (Belgium) U. Joined Soc. of Jesus, 1785; curate at St. Rumoldus, Mechlin, Belgium, 1785-94; pastor of Fuerberg-Murbeke, 1794-96; lived in seclusion avoiding French Directory, 1796-1803; arrived in Balt., 1804; missionary to Ky. area, 1805-24; founded Sisters of Loretto at Foot of Cross, 1812; missionary to The Barrens, Mo., 1824-27. Died Ste. Genevieve, Mo., Aug. 12, 1824; buried Loretto (Ky.) Cemetery.

NES, Henry, congressman; b. York, Pa., May 20, 1799; grad. Princeton; studied medicine. Practiced medicine, York; mem. U.S. Ho. of Reps. (Independent) from Pa., 28th, 30th-31st congresses, 1843-45, 47-50. Died York, Sept. 10, 1850; buried Prospect Hill Cemetery, York.

NESBITT, John Maxwell, merchant; b. Loughbrickland, County Down, Ireland, 1730; s. Jonathan Nesbitt. Came to Am., 1747; partner Conygham & Nesbitt, Phila., 1756; mem. Com. of Correspondence, 1774; paymaster Pa. State Navy, 1775; treas. Pa. Council of Safety, 1776; insp. Pa. Bank, 1780; mem. 1st troop Phila. City Cavalry, 1776; dir. Bank of N.Am., 1781-92; mem. organizing com. Ins. Co. of N.Am., 1st pres., 1792-96; a warden Port of Phila., 1788, alderman, 1790; an original mem. Friendly Sons of St. Patrick, v.p., 1771- 73, pres. 1773-74, 82-96. Died Phila., Jan. 22, 1802.

NESBITT, Wilson, congressman; attended S. C. Coll. (now U. S.C.), 1805-06. Engaged in farming; operated an iron foundry; justice of quorum Spartanburg County (S.C.), 1810; mem. S.C. Ho. of Reps., 1810-14; mem. U.S. Ho. of Reps. (Democrat) from S.C., 15th Congress, 1817-19; moved to Ala. Died Montgomery, Ala., May 13, 1861; buried Oakwood Cemetery, Montgomery.

NESMITH, James Willis, army officer, senator; b. New Brunswick, Can., July 23, 1820; s. William Morrison and Harriet (Willis) N.; m. Pauline Goff, 1846. Went to Ohio, 1838; among 1st settlers to Ore., 1843; judge Provisional Govt. of Ore. Territory, 1845; commd. capt. Volumteers in Cayuse War, 1848; U.S. marshal for Ore., 1853-55; in Yakima War of 1855-56; supt. Indian affairs for Ore. Territory, 1857-59; mem. U.S. Senate from Ore., 1861-67; mem. bd. visitors U.S. Mil. Acad., 1866; road supr. Polk County (Ore.), 1868; mem. U.S. Ho. of Reps. from Ore., 43d Congress, Dec. 1, 1873-1875. Died Rickreall, Ore., June 17, 1885.

NESMITH, John, realtor, mfr., inventor; b. Londonderry, N.H., Aug. 3, 1793; s. John and Lucy (Martin) N.; m. Mary Ann Bell, June 1825; m. 2d, Eliza Thorn Bell, 1831; m. 3d, Harriet Rebecca Mansur, Oct. 1840; 9 children. Real estate dealer, Lowell, Mass., 1831; inventor machines for shawl fringing, weaving wire fences; a founder Lawrence, Mass.; mem. N.H. Legislature, 1 term; lt. gov. Mass., 1862; presdl. elector Republican party, 1860, 64; collector internal revenue Mass., 1863-69; v.p. Mass. State Temperance Soc. Died Lowell, Mass., Oct. 15, 1869.

NETTLETON, Asahel, evangelist; b. Killingworth, Conn., Apr. 21, 1783; s. Samuel and Anne (Kelsey) N.; grad. Yale, 1809; never married. Preacher in Western Assn. of New Haven, 1811-17; evangelist for Consociation of Litchfield County, Conn., 1817-22; said to have converted thousands to Calvinist faith; preached and wrote tracts, Conn., 1822-27; lived in Va., 1827-29, in Eng., 1831-32; a founder Theol. Inst. of Conn., East Windsor Hill, 1834. Died May 16, 1844.

NETTLETON, Edwin S., civil and irrigation engr.; b. Medina, O., Oct. 22, 1831; s. Lewis Baldwin and Julia (Baldwin) N.; attended Oberlin (O.) Coll., 1853-54; m. Lucy F. Grosvenor, Oct. 17, 1861, 4 children. Engr. of Union or Greeley colony on its way to Colo., 1870; surveyed present site of Greeley (Colo.), laid out irrigation ditches (46 miles long) used by farmers; built for Larimer and Weld Canal between Ft. Collins and Greeley Colo. Mortgage and Investment Co. (also known as English co.); surveyed sites of Colorado Springs, 1871, Manitou, 1872, South Pueblo (now Pueblo), 1873; engr. State of Colo., 1883-87; chief engr. in project diverting Yaqui River (Mexico) for irrigation purposes; U.S. cons. engr., 1889-93; a founder, one of 1st trustees Colo. Coll., Colorado Springs; established weather bur. on Pike's Peak, Colo. Died Denver, Apr. 22, 1901; buried Forest Hill Cemetery, Kansas City, Mo.

NEUENDORFF, Adolph Heinrich Anton Magnus, musician; b. Hamburg, Germany, June 13, 1843; m. Georgine von Januschowsky. Came to U.S., 1854; concert pianist, made debut, 1859; concert-master orch., Stadt Theatre, N.Y.C., 1860, dir., chorus-master, 1867; musical dir. German Theatre, Milw., 1864-65; condr. at Acad. Music, N.Y.C., 1872; mgr. Germania Theatre, N.Y.C., 1872-74; dir., condr. Wagner Festival, N.Y.C., 1877,; condr. N.Y. Philharmonic Soc., 1878-79, Promenade Concerts, Boston, 1884-89, Emma Fuch Opera Co., 1889-91, English Grand Opera, N.Y.C., 1892, Vienna-Hofoper, 1893-95; dir. music Temple Emanu-El, 1896; condr. Met. Opera House, 1897; composer symphonies, overtures, cantatas, comic operas including: The Ratcharmer of Hamelin, 1880; Don Quixote, 1882; Prince Waldmeister, 1887; The Minstrel, 1892. Died N.Y.C., Dec. 4, 1897.

NEUMANN, John Nepomucene, clergyman; b. Prachatitz, Bohemia, Mar. 28, 1811; s. Philip and Agnes (Lebisch) N. Ordained priest Roman Catholic Ch. by Bishop Dubois, Diocese of N.Y., 1836; worked in mission, Williamsville, N.Y., 1836-40; took vows in Congregation of Redemptorist Fathers, 1840; did mission work in N.Y., Pa., Va., Md., Ohio, 1840-44; superior Am. Redemptorist Community, 1844-47; vice provincial, 1847-51; pastor St. Alphonsus Ch., Balt., 1851-52; ordained bishop by Archbishop Kendrick, 1852; bishop Phila., 1852-60; declared venerable by commn. in Rome, 1866. Died Phila., Jan. 5, 1860; buried St. Peter's Ch., Phila.

NEUPERT, Edmund, musician; b. Christiania, Norway, Apr. 1, 1842; attended Kullak's Acad., Berlin, Germany, 1858. Tchr. Kullak's Acad., Stern Conservatory; became pianoforte tchr. Copenhagen (Denmark) Conservatory, 1868; became prin. pianoforte tchr. Moscow (Russia) Conservatory, 1881; came to Am., 1883, settled in N.Y.C.; wrote instructive pieces for piano, including: Technical Studies; Concert-Études; Octave Studies; Studies in Style; Poetical Études; Poetiske Etuder; Exercises for the Various Hand Movements and Modes of Touch. Died N.Y.C., June 2, 1888.

NEVILLE, John, army officer; b. Occoquan River, Va., July 26, 1731; s. George and Ann (Burroughs) N.; m. Winifred Oldham, Aug. 24, 1754, a son, Col. Presley Neville. Served under Washington in Gen. Braddock's expdn. against Ft. Duquesne, 1755; sheriff Winchester (Va.); comdr. Ft. Pitt; commd. lt. col. Continental Army, 1776, col., 1777; served in battles of Trenton, Germantown, Princeton, Monmouth; brevetted brig. gen., 1783; mem. Supreme Exec. Council of Pa.; mem. Pa. Conv. to ratify U.S. Constn.; mem. Pa. Constl. Conv., 1789-90; insp. survey for collection of whiskey tax in Western Pa., 1792-95, participated in Whiskey Rebellion, 1794; fed. agt. for sale pub. lands N.W. of Ohio, 1796. Died Montour's Island, Pa., July 29, 1803.

NEVILLE, Joseph, congressman; b. 1730. Mem. Va. Ho. of Burgesses for Hampshire County, 1773-76; mem. convs. of Dec. 1, 1775, and May 6, 1776; served with Continental Army during Revolutionary War; mem. Va. Ho. of Dels., 1777, 80, 81; involved in settling Pa.-Md. boundary dispute, 1782; mem. U.S. Ho. of Reps. from Va., 3d Congress, 1793-95. Died Hardy County, Va., Mar. 4, 1819.

NEVIN, Alfred, clergyman; b. Shippensburg, Pa., Mar. 14, 1816; s. Maj. David and Mary (Peirce) N.; attended Jefferson Coll.; grad. law dept. Dickinson Coll., 1837, Western Theol. Sem., 1840; m. Sara Jenkins, 1841. Admitted to bar, 1837; licensed to preach by Carlisle (Pa.) Presbytery, 1840; organizer, pastor Alexander Presbyn. Ch., Phila., 1857-61; became editor The Standard, 1861; editor Presbyn. Weekly; editor-in-chief Presbyn. Jour.; served as army chaplain during Civil War; mem. 1st bd. trustees Presbyn. Hist. Soc.; mem. Pa., Wis. hist. socs. Author over 20 books including: Churches of the Valley, 1852; Parables of Jesus, 1881. Died Sept. 2, 1890.

NEVIN, Edwin Henry, clergyman, coll. pres.; b. Shippensburg, Pa., May 9, 1814; s. Maj. David and Mary (Peirce) N.; grad. Jefferson Coll., 1833, Princeton Theol. Sem., 1836; D.D. (hon.), Franklin Coll., Columbus, Ohio, 1870; m. Ruth C. Little, 1837. Licensed as minister by 1st Presbytery of Phila., 1836; pastor, Poland, Pa., 1839-40; pres. Franklin Coll.. 1840-44; ret. from active ministry,

1875; mem. Victoria Philos. Soc. of Gt. Britain. Author: Mode of Baptism, 1847; Warning Against Popecy, 1851; Faith in God, the Foundations of Individual and National Greatness, 1852; The Man of Faith, 1856; The City of God, 1868; History of All Religions, 1872; The Ministers' Handbook, 1872; Humanity and Its Responsibilities, 1872; Thoughts About Christ, 1882. Died June 2, 1889.

NEVIN, John Williamson, theologian, coll. pres.; b. Strasburg, Pa., Feb. 20, 1803; s. John and Martha (McCracken) N.; grad. Union Coll., 1821, LL.D. (hon.), 1873; grad. Princeton Theol. Sem., 1826; D.D. (hon.), Jefferson Coll., 1839; m. Martha Jenkins, 1835, 7 children. Temporary prof. Bibl. and oriental lit. Princeton Theol. Sem., 1826; prof. Biblical lit. Western Theol. Sem., 1830-40; prof. Mercersburg (Pa.) Sem., 1840-53; founder Mercersburg Review, 1849, editor 1849-53; acting pres. Marshall Coll., 1841-53 (merged with Franklin Coll., 1853), prof. history and aesthetics Franklin and Marshall Coll., 1861-66, pres., 1866-76; a developer "Mercersburg theology." Died Lancaster, Pa., June 6, 1886.

NEVIUS, John Livingston, clergyman, missionary; b. Ovid, N.Y., Mar. 4, 1829; s. Benjamin Hageman and Mary (Denton) N.; grad. Union Coll., 1848, Princeton Theol. Sem., 1853; m. Helen Coan, June 1853. Ordained to ministry Presbyn. Ch., sent as missionary to China, 1853, missionary at Ningpo, 1853-60; sent to open missions in Japan by Presbyn. Bd. Fgn. Missions, 1860-61; Am. chmn. 2d Missionary Conf., Shanghai, China, 1890; for a time the "Nevius method" was accepted method of tng. missionaries. Author: China and Chinese; Demon Possession and Allied Themes; also at least 16 tracts, books, translations in Chinese. Died "San-lou," Chefoo, China, Oct. 19, 1893.

NEW, Anthony, congressman; b. Gloucester County, Va., 1747; studied law. Admitted to Va. bar, practiced law; served as col. Continental Army during Revolutionary War; mem. U.S. Ho. of Reps. (Democrat) from Va., 3d-8th congresses, 1793-1805; moved to Elkton, Ky.; mem. U.S. Ho. of Reps. (Dem.) from Ky., 12th, 15th, 17th congresses, 1811-13, 17-19, 21-23; engaged in farming. Died "Dunheath" nr. Elkton, Mar. 2, 1833; buried "Dunheath."

NEW, Jeptha Dudley, congressman; b. Vernon, Ind., Nov. 28, 1830; grad. Bethany (W.Va.) Coll.; studied law. Admitted to Ind. bar, 1851; practiecd law, Vernon, 1851-64; mayor of Vernon, 1852-54; pros. atty. Jennings County (Ind.), 1860-64; judge Dist. Ct. of Common Pleas, 1864-68; resumed law practice, Vernon; mem. U.S. Ho. of Reps. (Democrat) from Ind., 44th, 46th congresses, 1875-77, 79-81; judge 6th Ind. Jud. Circuit, 1883-88; appellate judge, 1891. Died Vernon, July 9, 1892; buried Vernon Cemetery.

NEWBERRY, John Stoughton, railroad exec., congressman; b. Sangerfield, N.Y., Nov. 18, 1826; s. Elihu and Rhoda (Phelps) N.; grad. U. Mich., 1847; m. Harriet Newell Robinson, 1855; m. 2d, Helen Parmllee Handy, Oct. 6, 1859. Civil engr. with Mich. Central R.R., 1848-51; admitted to Mich. bar, 1853; provost marshall (with rank of capt.) of Mich., 1862-64; elected to Bd. of Edn., 1862; founder Mich. Car Co. (made railroad cars for Union Army), 1863, pres., 1863-80; organized (with James McMillin) Detroit, Mackinac and Marquette R.R., 1878; mem. U.S. Ho. of Reps. from Mich., 46th Congress, 1879-81. Died Detroit, Jan. 2, 1887; buried Elmwood Cemetery, Detroit.

NEWBERRY, John Strong, geologist; b. Windsor, Conn., Dec. 22, 1822; s. Henry and Elizabeth (Strong) N.; grad. Western Res. Coll., 1846, LL.D. (hon.), 1867; grad. Cleve. Med. Sch., 1848; m. Sarah Brownell Gaylord, Oct. 22, 1848, 6 children. Asst. surgeon, geologist on expdn. from San Francisco Bay to Columbia River, May 1855; prof. geology Columbian U. (now George Washington U.), 1856-57; physician, naturalist on mil. exploration expdn. of Colorado River, 1857-58; an organizer, prof. geology and paleontology Sch. of Mines, Columbia, 1866, pres. A.A.A.S., 1862; geologist State of Ohio, 1869-74; incorporator, mem. Nat. Acad. Scis.; recipient Murchison medal Geol. Soc. of London, 1888; v.p. Internat. Geol. Congress, 1891. Author: Report on the Colorado River of the West, Explored (1857-58), 1861; Report of the Exploring Expedition from Santa Fe to the Junction of the Grand and Green Rivers, 1876. Died New Haven, Conn., Dec. 7, 1892.

NEWBERRY, Oliver, steamship exec.; b. East Windsor, Conn., Nov. 17, 1789; s. Amasa and Ruth (Warner) N. served in War of 1812; became agt. Am. Fur Co. at Detroit, 1826; builder steamship the Michigan, 1833; founder regular steamship service between Detroit and Chgo., 1835; builder 1st lightship at Strait of Mackinac; instrumental in opening Chicago River to large ships; a stockholder, later dir. Detroit & St. Joseph R.R. Died Detroit, July 30, 1860.

NEWBERRY, Walter Loomis, philanthropist, banker, mcht.; b. East Windsor (now South Windsor), Conn., Sept. 18, 1804; s. Amasa and Ruth (Warner) N.; m. Julia Butler Clapp, Nov. 22, 1842, 4 children. Adj. gen. Territory of Mich., 1829-31; alderman City of Detroit, 1832; head Newberry & Burch, banking house; founder, dir. Mchts. Loan & Trust Co., 1857; dir. Galena & Chgo. Union R.R. Co., 1857, pres., 1859; mem. Chgo. bd. Health, 1843; city comptroller, acting mayor, Chgo., 1851; founder, 1st pres. Young Men's Library Assn., 1841; mem. Chgo. Bd. Edn., 1859-63, pres., 1863; mem. Chgo. Hist. Soc., 1857, v.p., 1858-60, pres., 1860-68; half of his estate used to found Newberry Library (independent free pub. library), Chgo. Died Nov. 6, 1868, at sea; buried Graceland Cemetery, Chgo.

NEWBOLD, Thomas, congressman; b. Springfield Twp., Burlington County, N.J., Aug. 2, 1760. Engaged in farming; sole owner League Island, Phila.; mem. N.J. Gen. Assembly, 1797, 1820-22; presdl. elector, 1804; banker; mem. U.S. Ho. of Reps. (Democrat) from N.J., 10th-12th congresses, 1807-13. Died Springfield Twp., Dec. 18, 1823; buried Old Upper Springfield Friends Burying Ground.

NEWBROUGH, John Ballou, dentist, religious leader; b. Springfield, O., June 5, 1828; s. Jacob and Mary N.; grad. from a Cincinnati dental coll., 1849; m. Rachel Turnbull, 1860; m. 2d, Frances Van de Water; 2 children. Went to Cal. during Gold Rush, 1849; went to Australia in search of gold, 1851; practiced dentistry, Phila., 1860-62, N.Y.C., 1862-84; became interested in spiritualism, typed out a Bible supposedly inspired by angels, 1881, this Bible inspired him to establish community in Sholam (N.M.) for foundlings and orphans; also established home for infants, castaways and orphans, New Orleans; Mason (33°). Author: A Catechism on Human Teeth, 1865; Oahspe: A New Bible, 1882. Died Apr. 22, 1891; buried Masonic Burial Ground, Las Cruces, N.M.

NEWCOMB, Harvey, clergyman, editor; b. Thetford, Vt., Sept. 2, 1803; s. Simon and Hannah (Curtis) N.; m. Alithea A. Wells, May 19, 1830, 4 children. Owner, editor Western Star, Westfield, N.Y., 1826-28; editor Buffalo (N.Y.) Patriot, 1828-30, Christian Herald, Pitts., 1830-31; prepared books for Am. Sunday Sch. Union, 1831-41; ordained to ministry Congregational Ch., 1842; in charge of Congregational Ch., West Roxbury, Mass.; asst. editor Boston Traveller, 1849, New York Observer, 1850-51; regular contbr. to Boston Recorder and Youth's Companion. Author children's books: Manners and Customs of North American Indians, 1835; Young Lady's Guide, 1839; How To Be a Man, 1846; How To Be a Lady, 1846; Cyclopaedia of Missions, 1854. Died Bklyn., Aug. 30, 1863.

NEWCOMB, Josephine Louise Le Monnier, philanthropist; b. Balt., Oct. 31, 1816; d. Alexander Louis and Mary (Waters) Le Monnier; m. Warren Newcomb, 2 children including Harriet Sophie. Inherited large fortune from her husband, 1866; gave her fortune to woman's coll. in memory of her deceased daughter (H. Sophie Newcomb Meml. Coll. in Tulane U. of La.), made 1st gift of $100,000, 1886, left $2,700,000 to coll. in her will; donated money to bldg. a meml. chapel to Robert E. Lee in Lexington, Ky.; gave gifts to Confederate Orphan's Home, Charleston, S.C. Died N.Y.C., Apr. 7, 1901; buried Greenwood Cemetery, Bklyn.

NEWCOMER, Christian, clergyman; b. Lancaster County, Pa., Feb. 1, 1750; s. Wolfgang and Elizabeth (Weller) N.; m. Elizabeth Baer, Mar. 31, 1770. Entered ministry, 1777; a leader in founding Ch. of United Brethren in Christ, especially active in missionary work West of Alleghenies; bishop, 1813-29. Author: Newcomer's Journal (diary; contains much of early history of ch.). Died Mar. 12, 1830.

NEWELL, Robert, trapper, pioneer; b. Muskingum County, O., Mar. 30, 1807; m. a Nez Perce Indian; m. 2d, Rebecca Newman, 1846; m. 3d, Mrs. Ward, June 1869; several, children. Trapper in Northwest, 1829-40; settled in Willamette Valley, Ore., 1840, participated in formation of Ore. Provisional Govt., 1843, mem. ho. of reps., speaker for 2 sessions; commanded a company of scouts in Northwest Indian troubles, 1855-56; elected to Ore. State Legislature, 1860. Died Lewiston, Ida., Nov. 1869.

NEWHALL, John Bailey, artist; b. Lynn, Mass., 1806. Settled in Burlington, Ia., circa 1830; visited Nauvoo (Ill.), 1843, made drawing of Mormon Temple which he exhibited with a lecture to promote emigration to Nauvoo, Salem, Mass.; visited Europe to promote emigration, 1843-44; published A Glimpse of Iowa in 1846; continued to lecture and exhibit paintings. Died of cholera, Independence, Mo., May 7, 1849.

NEWHARD, Peter, congressman; b. Allentown, Pa., July 26, 1783; attended pvt. sch., Allentown. Opened 1st hardware store in Allentown, 1812; street commr. Borough of Allentown, 1812; coroner Lehigh County (Pa.), 1816-17; mem. Pa. Ho. of Reps. 1817-19, 24-25, 29; chmn. Allentown Town Council, 1824, 37; mem. U.S. Ho. of Reps. (Democrat) from Pa., 26th-27th congresses, 1839-43; trustee Allentown Acad., 1822, 26, 43, burgess, 1843 Died Allentown, Feb. 19, 1860; buried City Cemetery, Allentown.

NEWKIRK, Matthew, businessman; b. Pittsgrove, N.J., May 31, 1794; m. Jane Reese Stroud, May 1817; m. 2d, Margaret Heberton, July 1821; m. 3d, Hetty Smith, July 1846; 8 children. Mem. Washington Guards to protect Phila. from threats of English fleet, 1815-16; operated small dry goods store, Phila., 1816-39; assisted Nicholas Biddle as dir. Bank of U.S., circa 1828-29; 1st pres. Phila., Wilmington & Balt. R.R., introduced personal baggage checking system, 8-wheel passenger car; connected with Cambria Iron Works, Johnstown, Pa., from 1854; pres. Female Med. Coll., Pa.; trustee Coll. of N.J. (now Princeton), 34 years; trustee Gen. Assembly of Presbyn. Ch., treas. for 12 years. Died May 31, 1868.

NEWMAN, Alexander, congressman; b. nr. Orange, Va., Oct. 5, 1804. Held several local offices; mem. Va. Ho. of Dels., 1836-38, Va. Senate, 1841-46; postmaster of Wheeling, Va. (now. W. Va.), 1846-49; mem. U.S. Ho. of Reps. (Democrat) from Va., 31st Congress, 1849. Died Pitts., Sept. 8, 1849; buried Old First St. Cemetery, Moundsville, W.Va.

NEWMAN, Henry, philanthropist; b. Rehoboth, Mass., Nov. 20, 1670; s. Rev. Noah and Joanna (Flynt) N.; A.B., Harvard, 1687, A.M., 1690. Librarian, Harvard, 1690's; went to London, 1703; corr. mem. Soc. for Promoting Christian Knowledge, 1703, sec., 1708-43; agt. for Harvard; a commr. for Relief of Poor Proselytes; agt. of N.H., intermittently 1709-20, became permanent agt., 1720. Author: Harvard's Ephemeris, 1690; News from the Stars, 1691. Died June 26, 1743.

NEWMAN, John Philip, clergyman; b. N.Y.C., Sept. 1, 1826; s. Philip and Mary D'orfey (Allen) N.; ed. Cazenovia (N.Y.) Sem.; D.D. (hon.), U. Rochester, 1863; LL.D. (hon.), Otterbein U., 1881, Grant Meml. U., 1881; m. Angeline Ensign, 1855. Ordained to ministry Methodist Episcopal Ch., 1849; studied in, visited Europe, Syria, Egypt, 1860; re-established Meth. Episcopal Ch. in S.W., New Orleans, 1864-69, established 3 confs., 2 colls., a ch. jour.; del. Gen. Conf., Meth. Episcopal Ch., 1868, 72, 80; organizer Met. Meml. Ch., Washington, D.C., 1869, pastor, 1869. 76-79; chaplain U.S. Senate, 1869-74; insp. U. S. consulates in Asia, 1874; pastor Central Ch., N.Y.C., 1879-82, Madison Av. Congl. Ch., N.Y. C., 1882-84; missionary sec., 1880, with offices in Omaha, Neb., 1888-96, San Francisco, 1896-99; spiritual adviser to Gen. Grant during his terminal illness, 1884; elected, consecrated bishop, 1888. Author: From Dan to Beersheba, 1864; Babylon and Nineveh, 1875; Christianity Triumphant, 1884; America for Americans, 1887. Died Saratoga, N.Y., July 5, 1899.

NEWMAN, Samuel Phillips, clergyman, educator; b. Andover, Mass., June 6, 1797; s. Rev. Mark and Sarah (Phillips) N.; grad. Harvard, 1816; attended Andover Theol. Sem., 1818; m. Caroline Kent, May 31, 1821, 5 daughters. Tutor, Bowdoin Coll., 1818, prof. Greek and Latin, 1819, prof. rhetoric and oratory, 1824, lectr. civil polity and political economy, 1824-39, acting pres., 1830-33; became head newly established State Normal Sch., Barre, Mass., 1839. Author: A Practical System of Rhetoric or the Principals and Rules of Style (textbook), 1827; Elements of Political Economy, 1835. Died Andover, Feb. 10, 1842.

NEWNAN, Daniel, congressman; b. Salisbury, N. C., circa 1780; attended U. N.C., 1796-97. Commd. ensign and 2d lt. 4th inf., U.S. Army, 1799, promoted to 1st lt., 1799, resigned commn., 1801; engaged in planting; comdr. Ga. Volunteers during Creek War, 1812-14; commd. maj. gen. 3d div. Ga. Militia, 1817; supt. Ga. State Penitentiary, 1823-25; sec. of state Ga., 1825-27; City of Newnan (Ga.) named for him, 1828; mem. U.S. Ho. of Reps. (State Rights Democrat) from Ga., 22d Congress, 1831-33. Died nr. Rossville, Ga., Jan. 16, 1851; buried Newnan Springs (Ga.) Churchyard.

NEWPORT, Christopher, mariner; b. England; m. Katharine Procter, Oct. 10, 1584; m. 2d, Ellen Ade, Jan. 29, 1590; m. 3d, Elizabeth Glanfield, Oct. 1, 1595; 4 children including John. Served with Sir Francis Drake in Cadiz expdn. of 1587; comdr. of privateers in West Indies against Spanish colonies, 1592; made trips to N.Am., 1603, 05; given command on early trips of Va. Co. to Am., founded Jamestown on 1st trip, 1606-07; returned to Eng. with promise of return to Va., 1607; returned to Jamestown, 1608, found only 40 of 104 settlers alive; managed to save Capt. John

Smith from being hanged by community; returned to Eng., 1608, made 3 voyages, 1608-11, shipwrecked in Bermudas, 1609, brought some 300 colonists; joined East India Co., made 3 voyages for it, 1613-16. Died Bantom, Java, Aug. 1617.

NEWSAM, Albert, lithographer; b. Steubenville, O., May 20, 1809; s. William Newsam; attended Asylum for Deaf and Dumb, Phila., 1820-26, Pa. Acad. Fine Arts; m. Rosanna Edgar, Mar. 26, 1834. Apprentice to Col. Cephas G. Childs, engraver, Phila., 1827-31; interested in being lithographer instead of engraver, became best lithographer of his time; designed monument to Thomas H. Gallaudet, Hartford, Conn., 1853. Died Wilmington, Del., Nov. 20, 1864; buried Laurel Hill Cemetery, Phila.

NEWTON, Eben, congressman; b. Goshen, Conn., Oct. 16, 1795; attended common schs.; studied law, Ohio. Engaged in farming, Portage County, O., 1814; admitted to Ohio bar, 1823, began practice in Canfield; mem. Ohio Senate, 1842-51, 62-64; pres. judge Ct. of Common Pleas, 1844-51; mem. U.S. Ho. of Reps. (Whig) from Ohio, 32d Congress, 1851-53; pres. Ashtabula & New Lisbon R.R., 1856-59; resumed law practice and farming. Died Canfield, Nov. 6, 1885; buried Canfield Village Cemetery.

NEWTON, Henry Jotham, inventor, mfr.; b. Hartleton, Pa., Feb. 9, 1823; s. Sr. Jotham and Harriet (Wood) N.; m. Mary Gates, 1850, 3 children. Partner piano firm Lights, Newton & Bradbury, 1853; pres. Henry Bonnard Bronze Co., 1884; interested in photography, improved the dry-plate process, pioneered in preparation of ready-sensitized paper credited with paraffin paper process; treas. photog. sect. Am. Inst. City N.Y., chmn., after 1873; effected 1st scientific cremation of human body in Am.; pres. 1st Soc. Spiritualists, N.Y.; founder, treas. Theosophical Soc., 1875. Died Dec. 23, 1895.

NEWTON, Hubert Anson, mathematician; b. Sherburne, N.Y., Mar. 19, 1830; s. William and Lois (Butler) N.; grad. Yale, 1850; LL.D. (hon.), U. Mich., 1868; m. Anna C. Stiles, Apr. 14, 1859. Tutor, Yale, July 1852, became head mathematics dept., 1853, prof. mathematics, 1855-90; mem. Nat. Acad. Scis.; mem., recipient Lawrence-Smith medal for meteoric studies Am. Philos. Soc.; elected to Royal Astron. Soc., London, 1872; v.p. A.A.A.S., 1875, pres., 1885; pres. Conn. Acad. Arts and Scis.; a founder Am. Metrol. Soc.; asso. editor Am. Jour. of Sci. Author: Investigations on the Construction of Certain Curves by Points; Certain Transcendental Curves . . . ; The Metric System of Weights and Measures (advocating adoption of metric system), 1868. Died New Haven, Conn., Aug. 12, 1896.

NEWTON, Isaac, naval architect; b. Schodack, N.Y., Jan. 10, 1794; s. Abner and Alice (Baker) N.; m. Hannah Humphreys Cauldwell, 10 children including Henry, Isaac. Founder, People's Line Assn., steamboat line between Albany, N.Y. and N.Y.C., built approximately 80 steamboats; designer boats North America, 1840, South America, 1841; introduced burning of anthracite coal; designer boats Hendrick Hudson, 1845, Isaac Newton, 1846, New World, 1847; introduced grand saloon; president Mohawk & Hudson R.R., 1846; designer boats Western World, Plymouth Rock, 1854; a projector N.Y. Central, Lake Shore and Mich. So. rys. Died N.Y.C., Nov. 23, 1858.

NEWTON, Isaac, govt. ofcl.; b. Burlington County, N.J., Mar. 31, 1800; s. Isaac and Mary (Newton) N.; m. Dorothy Burdsall, Oct. 18, 1821; Early active mem. Pa. U.S. agrl. socs.; supt. agrl. div. U.S. Patent Office, 1861; 1st commr. U.S. Dept. Agr., 1862. Author: Circular on the Present Agricultural, Mineral and Manufacturing Condition and Resources of the U.S., 1862. Died Washington, D.C., June 19, 1867.

NEWTON, John, army officer, engr.; b. Norfolk, Va., Aug. 24, 1823; s. Thomas and Margaret (Jordan) Pool N.; grad. U.S. Mil. Acad., 1842; LL.D., St. Francis Xavier Coll., 1886; m. Anna M. Starr, 1848, 6 children. Commd. 2d lt. Corps Engrs., 1842; asst. to Bd. of Engrs.; asst. prof. engring. U.S. Mil. Acad.; 1st lt., 1852, capt., 1856; chief engr. Utah Expdn., 1858; chief engr. Dept. of Pa. and Dept. of Shenandoah; commd. brig. gen. U.S. Volunteers, 1861; constructed Ft. Lyon; commanded brigade at West Point, Va., also at battles of Gaines' Mill, Glendale, South Mountain, and Antietam, 1862; maj. gen.; brevetted lt. col., col., brig. gen., maj. gen. of volunteers, 1863-64; maj. gen. U.S. Army; lt. col. engrs., 1865, col., 1879, brig. gen. and chief engrs., 1884; commr. public works of N.Y.C., 1886; pres. Panama R.R. Co., 1888-95; mem. Nat. Acad. Scis.; hon. mem. Am. Soc. C.E. Died N.Y.C, May 1, 1895; buried Post Cemetery, N.Y.

NEWTON, Richard, clergyman, author; b. Liverpool, Eng., July 26, 1812; s. Richard and Elizabeth (Cluett) N.; grad. U. Pa., 1836; attended Gen. Theol. Sem., N.Y.C., 1836-39; m. Lydia Greatorex, July 31, 1839, 2 children—Richard Heber, William Wilberforce. Arrived in U.S. with parents, 1824; ordained deacon Protestant Episcopal Ch., 1839, ordained priest, 1840; rector Holy Trinity Ch., West Chester, Pa., 1840, St. Paul's Ch., Phila., 1840-62, Ch. of Epiphany, Phila., 1862-81, Ch. of Covenant, Phila., 1882-87. Author: The King's Highway, 1861; Bible Jewels, 1867; The Life of Jesus Christ for the Young, 1876. Died Phila., May 25, 1887.

NEWTON, Robert Safford, physician, editor; b. Gallipolis, O., Dec. 12, 1818; s. John Newton; grad. Louisville Med. Coll., 1841; m. Mary M. Hoy, Sept. 14, 1843, 1 son, Robert Safford, Jr. Prof. surgery Memphis Inst., 1849; prof. surgery Eclectic Med. Inst. of Cincinnati, 1851, prof. med. practice and pathology, 1853-62; condr. Newton's Clin. Inst.; founder Eclectic Med. Jour., 1852, editor, 1852-62; co-editor Western Med. News of Cincinnati, 1851-59, Am. Eclectic Med. Rev., N.Y,. 1866-72, Am. Eclectic Register, N.Y. 1868; founder Eclectic Med. Soc. of State N.Y., pres., 1863-66; a founder Eclectic Med. Coll. of City N.Y., 1665, also prof. surgery. Died N.Y.C., Oct. 9, 1881.

NEWTON, Thomas, colonial ofcl.; b. Eng., June 10, 1660; ed. in Eng.; m. Christian Phillips; children—Hibbert, Elizabeth, Christian, Hannah. Came to Am. before 1688; atty. for Crown during Salem (Mass.) Witch Trials, 1692; sec. N.H., 1692; mem. N.H. Council, 1698; dep. judge Admiralty Ct. for Mass. Bay, R.I. and N.H. colonies, 1702; atty. gen. Mass. Bay Colony, 1720-21; mem. Ancient and Honorable Arty. Co., 1702. Died Portsmouth, N.H., May 28, 1721.

NEWTON, Thomas, congressman; b. Norfolk, Va., Nov. 21, 1768; s. Thomas and Martha (Tucker) N.; m. Mrs. Myers; m. 2d, Margaret Pool; 10 children including John Newton. Admitted to Va. bar, circa 1795; mem. Va. Ho. of Reps., 1796-99; mem. U.S. Ho. of Reps. from Va., 7th-20th congresses, 1801-29, 21st Congress, 1829-30 (term completed by George Loyall who contested election), 22d Congress, 1831-33; practiced law, Norfolk, 1833-47. Died Norfolk, Aug. 5, 1847; buried St. Paul's Cemetery, Norfolk.

NEWTON, Thomas Willoughby, congressman; b. Alexandria, Va., Jan. 18, 1804; attended local schs., Alexandria. Moved to Little Rock, Ark., 1820; clk. of ct. Pulaski County (Ark.), 1825-29; moved to Shelby County, Ky.; returned to Little Rock, 1837, employed as bank cashier; mem. Ark. Senate, 1844-48; mem. U.S. Ho. of Reps. (Whig) from Ark., 29th Congress, Feb. 6-Mar. 3, 1847. Died N.Y.C., Sept. 22, 1853; buried Mt. Holly Cemetery, Little Rock.

NEWTON, Willoughby, congressman; b. "Lee Hall" nr. Hague, Va., Dec. 2, 1802; attended Coll. William and Mary; studied law. Admitted to Va. bar, began practice in Westmoreland County; mem. Va. Ho. of Dels., 1826-32, 61-63; mem. U.S. Ho. of Reps. (Whig) from Va., 28th Congress, 1843-45; engaged in farming; pres. Va. Agrl. Soc., 1852. Died "Linden," Westmoreland County, May 23, 1874; buried "Linden."

NEZ COUPE, see Rose, Edward.

NIBLACK, Silas Leslie, congressman; b. Camden County, Ga., Mar. 17, 1825; attended common schs.; studied law. Admitted to the bar, circa 1851; began practice of law, Lake City, Fla.; judge Columbia County (Fla.) Probate Ct.; mem. U.S. Ho. of Reps. (Democrat; successfully contested election) from Fla., 42d Congress, Jan. 29-Mar. 3, 1873; mem. Fla. Senate, 1879; engaged in farming. Died Lake City, Feb. 13, 1883; buried Old Cathey Cemetery, Lake City.

NIBLACK, William Ellis, congressman; b. Dubois County, Ind., May 19, 1822; s. John and Martha (Hargrave) N.; attended Ind. U.; m. Belvina Reily, Jan. 1848 (dec. Apr. 1849); m. 2d, Eliza Ann Sherman, Oct. 4, 1849, 5 children including Albert Parker. Admitted to bar, 1845; mem. Ind. Ho. of Reps., 1849, Senate, 1850; circuit judge, 1854; mem. U.S. Ho. of Reps. from Ind., 35-36th congresses, 1857-61, 39th-43d congresses, 1864-75; mem. Ind. Legislature, 1862, Democratic Nat. Com., 1864-72; judge Supreme Ct. of Ind., 1876. Died May 7, 1893.

NIBLO, William, hotel, theatre mgr.; b. Ireland, 1789; m. Martha King. Conducted Bank Coffee House, N.Y.C.; leased Colombian Gardens located at Broadway and Prince, N.Y.C., also Sans Souci Theatre, 1823, reopened as Niblo's Garden, 1829; purchased Am. history library which he presented to N.Y. Hist. Soc., also gave a library to YMCA; retired, 1861. Died N.Y.C., Aug. 21, 1878.

NICHOLAS, George, state ofcl.; b. Williamsburg, Va., 1755; s. Robert Carter and Anne (Cary) N.; grad. Coll. William and Mary, 1772; m. Mary Smith, circa 1778; Served as maj. 2d Va. Regt., 1777, later col.; mem. Va. Ho. of Dels., 1787; mem. Va. Conv. which ratified U.S. Constn., 1788; mem. 1st Ky. Constl. Conv., 1792; 1st atty. gen. Ky.; helped to frame, advocate Thomas Jefferson's Ky. Resolutions of 1798 in response to Alien and Sedition Acts of 1798. Died June 1799.

NICHOLAS, John, congressman; b. Williamsburg, Va., 1756; s. Robert Carter and Anne (Cary) N.; attended Coll. William and Mar- m. Anne Lawson, 11 children. Practiced law, Williamsburg, Va.; mem. U.S. Ho. of Reps. from Va., 3d-6th congresses, 1793-1801; moved to Geneva, Ontario County, N.Y.; mem. N.Y. State Senate, 1806-09; judge N.Y. Ct. of Common Pleas, 1806-19. Died Geneva, Dec. 31, 1819; buried Glenwood Cemetery, Geneva.

NICHOLAS, Philip Norborne, banker, jurist; b. Williamsburg, Va., circa 1775; s. Robert Carter and Anne (Cary) N.; ed. Coll. William and Mary; m. Mary Spear; m. 2d, Maria Carter Byrd. Atty. gen. Va., 1800; pres., dir. 1st bank to be established in Richmond, Va., 1804, pres. Farmer's Bank; dir. Richmond br. Bank of U.S., 1817; judge Gen. Ct. Va., 1823-49; mem. Va. Constl. Conv., 1829; influential in forming Jackson wing of Democratic party in Va. Died Aug. 18, 1849.

NICHOLAS, Robert Carter, colonial ofcl., b. Hanover, Va., Jan. 28, 1728; s. Dr. George and Elizabeth (Carter) Burwell N.; ed. Coll. William and Mary; m. Anne Cary, 1751, children—George, John, Wilson Cary, Philipe Norborne, Elizabeth. Mem. Va. Ho. of Burgesses, 1756-77; opposed Patrick Henry's Stamp Act Resolves, 1765; treas. Va., 1766-77; gradually came to favor Am. cause in pre-Revolutionary struggle; mem. Com. of Correspondence, 1773; opposed assertion in Declaration of Independence that all men are by nature equally free and independent, but was often placed on coms. to execute resolves of patriots; mem. Va. Ho. of Dels., 1777-79; judge Va. High Ct. Chancery, 1779. Died Hanover County, Va., Sept. 8, 1780.

NICHOLAS, Robert Carter, senator; b. Hanover, Va., 1793; attended Coll. William and Mary, 1816-17. Served as capt. and maj. during War of 1812; moved to La., became sugar planter, Terrebonne Parish, 1820; mem. U.S. Senate (Democrat) from La., Jan. 13, 1836-41; sec. of state La., 1843-46. Died Terrebonne Parish, Dec. 24, 1857; buried St. Louis Cemetery, New Orleans.

NICHOLAS, Wilson Cary, senator, gov. Va.; b. Williamsburg, Va., Jan. 31, 1761; s. Robert Carter and Anne (Cary) N.; grad. Coll. William and Mary, 1774; m. Margaret Smith, circa 1781, 4 children. Served in Continental Army, mem. George Washington's Life Guard, until 1783; mem. Va. Ho. of Reps., 1784-88; del. to Va. Constl. Conv. which ratified U.S. Constn., 1788; mem. U.S. Senate from Va., 1799-Mar. 22, 1804; collector Port of Norfolk, 1804-07; mem. U.S. Ho. of Reps. from Va., 10th-11th congresses, 1807-Nov. 27, 1809; gov. Va., 1814-17. Died "Tufton," nr. Charlottesville, Va., Oct. 10, 1820; buried "Monticello," Charlottesville.

NICHOLLS, John Calhoun, congressman; b. Clinton, Ga., Apr. 25, 1834; grad. Coll. William and Mary, 1855; studied law. Admitted to Ga. bar, 1855, practiced in Clinch and Ware counties; engaged in planting; served as capt. Co. I, 4th Regt., Ga. Cavalry, Confederate Army during Civil War; mem. Ga. Constl. Conv., 1865; del. Democratic nat. convs., Cincinnati, 1866, St. Louis, 1876; Dem. presdl. elector, 1868; mem. Ga. Senate, 1870-75; mem. U.S. Ho. of Reps. (Dem.) from Ga., 46th, 48th congresses, 1879-81, 83-85; resumed law practice, Blackshear, Ga. Died Blackshear, Dec. 25, 1893; buried Blackshear Cemetery.

NICHOLLS, Richard, colonial gov.; b. Ampthill, Bedfordshire, Eng., 1624; s. Francis and Margaret (Bruce) N.; LL.D., Oxford (Eng.) U., commanded expdn. against New Netherlands, 1664; 1st English gov. Province of N.Y., 1664-68; changed name of New Amsterdam to N.Y.C.; determined Eastern boundary of N.Y.; issued legal code known as "Duke's Laws" (prepared with Matthias Nicolls) drawn mainly from laws in effect in Mass. and New Haven (Conn.). Killed at Battle of Sole Bay (Eng.), May 28, 1672; buried Ampthill Ch.

NICHOLS, Charles Henry, psychiatrist; b. Vassalboro, Me., Oct. 19, 1820; s. Caleb Nichols; M. D., U. Pa., 1843; m. Ellen Maury, 1860; m. 2d, Sallie Lathrop Garlio, 1872; 2 children. First supt. St. Elizabeth's Hosp. (govt. hosp. for insane), Washington, D.C., 1852-77; became supt. Bloomingdale Asylum, N.Y.C., 1877; pres. Assn. Am. Supts. of Instns. for the Insane; hon. mem. Medico-Psychol. Assn. of Gt. Britain; foremost forensic psychiatrist of his time, appeared in many causae celebre; a witness for Charles J. Guiteau, (who assassinated Pres. Garfield) in U.S. vs. Charles J. Guiteau. Died Washington, D.C., Dec.

16, 1889; buried Congessional Cemetery, Washington.

NICHOLS, Clarina Irene Howard, social reformer; b. Townshend, Vt., Jan. 25, 1810; d. Chapin and Birsha (Smith) Howard; m. Justin Carpenter, Apr. 21, 1830; m. 2d, George Nichols, Mar. 6, 1843. Founder young ladies' sem., Herkimer, N.Y., 1835; took financial and editorial control of husband's paper Windham County Democrat, 1843-53, advocated women's right in its columns; writer series of articles dealing with women's legal disabilities for Herald of Freedom, Lawrence, Kan., 1856; mem. Kan. Constl. Conv., helped frame constn. giving all citizens legal equality; mem. 1st Kan. Legislature (representing Kan. Women's Rights Assn.), Topeka, 1860; matron home for Negro orphans, Washington, D.C., 1863-66. Died Potter Valley, Cal., Jan. 11, 1885.

NICHOLS, George Ward, army officer, coll. pres.; b. Mt. Desert, Me., June 21, 1831; s. John and Esther (Ward) N.; m. Maria Longworth, May 6, 1868. Art editor and critic N.Y. Evening Post, 1859; commd. capt. U.S. Army, 1862, aide-de-camp on Gen. Sherman's staff, 1864, resigned as brevet lt. col. U.S. Volunteers; a founder Sch. of Design of U. Cincinnati; pres. Harmonic Soc. Cincinnati; head May Festival Assn. of Cincinnati, 1872-80; founder, also a financial backer Coll. Music of Cincinnati, 1879, became 1st pres. Author: The Story of the Great March; 1865; Art Education Applied to Industry, 1877. Died Cincinnati, Sept. 15, 1885.

NICHOLS, Ichabod, clergyman; b. Portsmouth, N.H., June 5, 1784; s. Ichabod and Lydia (Ropes) N.; grad. Harvard, 1802, D.D., 1831; m. Dorothea Folsom, May 15, 1810; m. 2d, Martha Salisbury. Tutor in mathematics Harvard, 1802-09; asso. pastor 1st Unitarian Ch., Portland, Me., 1809-14, pastor, 1814-55; trustee Bowdoin Coll., from 1821; v.p. Am. Acad. Arts and Scis.; pres. Am. Unitarian Assn., circa 1835. Author: A Catechism of Natural Theology, 1830; Remembered Words, 1860. Died Cambridge, Mass., Jan. 5, 1859; buried Cambridge.

NICHOLS, James Robinson, chemist; b. West Amesbury, Mass., July 18, 1819; s. Stephen and Ruth (Sargent) N.; M.D., Yale, 1867, M.A. (hon.); m. Harriet Porter, 1844; m. 2d, Margaret Gale, 1851; 1 child. Founder J.R. Nichols & Co:, 1857; inventor soda-water apparatus, carbonic-acid fire extinguisher, improved hot-air furnace; founder Boston Jour. of Chemistry and Pharmacy (1st U.S. publ. devoted to chemistry in popular manner), 1866, merged into Popular Science News and Boston Jour. of Chemistry, 1881, editor-in-chief, 1881-88; founder Merrimac Pub. Library, 1877; mem. Mass. Bd. Agr., 1878; pres. Vt. & Can. R.R., 1873-78; dir. Boston & Me. R.R., 1873-88; trustee George Peabody Fund. Author: Chemistry of the Farm and Sea, 1867; From Whence, What, Where?, 1882. Died Haverhill, Mass., Jan. 2, 1888.

NICHOLS, Mary Sargeant Neal Gove, reformer, author; b. Goffstown, N.H., Aug. 10, 1810; d. William and Rebecca Neal; m. Hiram Gove, 1831; m. 2d, Thomas Low Nichols, July 29, 1848; 2 children. Editor periodical Health Jour. and Advocate of Physiol. Reform, Worcester, Mass., 1840-44; advocated dress reform, spiritualism, Fourierism, temperance; taught (with husband) water-cure practitioners, N. Y.C., 1851-53; editor (with husband) Nichols' Journal, monthly mag., Cincinnati, 1853. Author: Lectures to Women on Anatomy and Physiology, 1846; Experience in Water-Cure, 1849; (with Thomas Low Nichols) Marriage: Its History, Character, and Results, 1854; Mary Lyndon; or Revelations of a Life, 1855. Died London, Eng., May 30, 1884.

NICHOLS, Matthias H., congressman; b. Sharptown, N.J., Oct. 3, 1824; attended common schs.; studied law, Lima, O. Admitted to Ohio bar, 1849, began practice in Lima; pros. atty. Allen County (O.), 1851-52; mem. U.S. Ho. of Reps. (Whig) from Ohio, 33d-35th congresses, 1853-59; resumed law practice. Died Cincinnati, Sept. 15, 1862; buried Old Cemetery, Lima, reinterred Woodlawn Cemetery, Lima.

NICHOLSON, Alfred Osborn Pope, senator; b. nr. Franklin, Tenn., Aug. 31, 1808; grad. U. N.C., 1827; studied law. Admitted to Tenn. bar, 1831, began practice in Columbia; editor Western Mercury, Columbia, 1832-35; mem. Tenn. Ho. of Reps., 1833-39; mem. U.S. Senate (Democrat) from Tenn., Dec. 25, 1840-42, 59-61; mem. Tenn. Senate, 1843-45; editor Nashville (Tenn.) Union, 1844-46; dir. Bank of Tenn., later pres., 1846-47; chancellor middle div. of Tenn.; declined a cabinet appointment offered by Pres. Pierce, 1853; editor Washington Union, 1853-56; chief justice Tenn. Supreme Ct., 1870-76. Died Columbia, Mar. 23, 1876; buried Rose Hill Cemetery, Columbia.

NICHOLSON, Eliza Jane Poitevent Holbrook, author; b. Hancock County, Miss., Mar. 11, 1849; d. William J. and Mary (Russ) P.; grad. Amite (La.) Female Sem., 1867; m. Col. A. M. Holbrook, May 18, 1872; m. 2d, George Nicholson, June 27, 1878; 2 children. Contbd. poetry to local newspapers and mags., especially her husband's newspaper New Orleans Picayune, 1869-76; carried on newspaper after husband's death, 1876, with aid of bus. mgr. George Nicholson (whom she later married). Author: Lyrics by Pearl Rivers, 1873. Died New Orleans, Feb. 15, 1896.

NICHOLSON, Francis, colonial gov.; b. Downhame Parke, Eng., Nov. 12, 1655; probable son of Francis Nicholson. Began career in English Army, 1679; mem. Council for Dominion of New Eng., 1686; commd. lt. gov. N.Y., 1688; lt. gov. Va., 1890-92; a founder Coll. William and Mary; gov. Md., 1694-98, largely responsible for moving Md. capital to Annapolis, Md.; a founder King William's Sch. (now St. John's Coll.), Annapolis; gov. Va., 1698-1705, largely responsible for moving Va. capitol to Williamsburg; elected fellow Royal Soc., 1706; commd. brig. gen., comdr. in chief expdn. to reduce Port Royal, N.S., Can., 1710; commd. lt. gen. in Am., 1711; gov. N.S., 1713-17; gov. S.C., 1721-25. Author: Journal of an Expedition . . . For the Reduction of Port Royal, 1711. Died London, Eng., Mar. 5, 1728.

NICHOLSON, James, naval officer; b. Chestertown, Md., 1737; s. Joseph and Hannah (Smith) Scott; m. Frances Wilter, Apr. 30, 1763, 8 children including Hannah (Mrs. Albert Gallatin). In command of ship Defence, 1775; apptd. by Congress as capt. Continental Navy, 1776; comdr. ship Virginia, 1777; sr. officer Continental Navy, 1777; comdr. frigate Trumbull, 1779; commanded fleet including ship Nesbit, 1781; an active Republican in N.Y.C.; commr. of loans for N.Y., 1801. Died N.Y.C., Sept. 2, 1804.

NICHOLSON, James Bartram, bookbinder; b. St. Louis, Jan. 28, 1820; s. John W. and Eliza (Lowry) N.; m. Adelaide Broadnix, Oct. 5, 1841, 3 children. Apprentice bookbinder with firm Weaver & Warnick, Phila.; founder (with James Pawson) bookbinding firm Pawson & Nicholson, 1848-90; grand sec. Grand Lodge of Pa., Independent Order of Odd Fellows, 1866, grand scribe of Grand Encampment, 1869-1901. Author: A Manual of the Art of Bookbinding, 1856; I.O.O.F.; The Story of '65, 1896. Died Phila., Mar. 4, 1901; buried Odd Fellows Cemetery, Phila.

NICHOLSON, James William Augustus, naval officer; b. Dedham, Mass., Mar. 10, 1821; s. Nathaniel Dowse and Hannah (Gray) N.; m. Mary Heap, at least 1 child. Apptd. midshipman U.S. Navy, 1838, 1st active service on Levant of West Indies Squadron; passed midshipman, 1844, ordered to vessel Princeton; promoted lt., 1852; served on Vandalia, 1853; received 1st command Isaac Smith, 1861; participated in Battle of Mobile Bay in ship Manhattan, 1862; commanded Mohongo, 1865-66; promoted capt., 1866, commodore, 1873; comdt. N.Y.C. Navy Yard, 1876-80; commanded European station as acting rear adm., 1881, commended by several countries for aid and other duties rendered during Brit. bombardment of Alexandria, Egypt, 1881; ret. as rear adm., 1883. Died N.Y.C., Oct. 28, 1887.

NICHOLSON, John, state ofcl.; b. Wales; survived by 8 children. Came to Am. before Revolution; a commr. of accounts Pa., 1781-82, commn. abolished, 1782; became comptroller gen. Pa., 1782, receiver gen. taxes, 1785; escheator gen. to liquidate estates of those attainted of treason. 1787, impeached by Pa. Ho. of Reps. for redeeming certain of his own state certificates instead of funding them into fed. certificates, acquitted by Pa. Senate, resigned, 1794; partner firm Morris & Nicholson, 1780; a founder N.Am. Land Co., 1795; promoter Pa. Population Co., 1794, Territorial Co., 1795; editor The Supporter or Daily Repast (after being sent to debtors' prison). Died Dec. 5, 1800.

NICHOLSON, John, congressman; b. Herkimer, N.Y., 1765; studied law. Admitted to N.Y. bar, practiced law; held local offices; mem. U.S. Ho. of Reps. (Democrat) from N.Y., 11th Congress, 1809-11. Died Herkimer, Jan. 20, 1820.

NICHOLSON, Joseph Hopper, congressman, jurist; b. Chestertown, Md., May 15, 1770; s. Joseph, Jr. and Elizabeth (Hopper) N.; studied law in Md.; m. Rebecca Lloyd, Oct. 10, 1793, 6 children. Practiced law, Queen Annes County, Md., before 1796; mem. Md. Ho. of Dels., 1796-98; mem. U.S. Ho. of Reps. from Md., 6th-9th congresses, 1799-1806, although ill during 1801-02, had himself carried into the House for 17 successive days so as to register his vote for Thomas Jefferson over Aaron Burr in U.S. presdl. contest; judge 6th Jud. Circuit for Md., 1806-17; 1st pres. Comml. and Farmers' Bank of Balt., 1810-12; raised (at own expense) and commanded arty. co. in War of 1812. Died Balt. County, Md., Mar. 4, 1817; buried "Wye House," nr. Easton, Md.

NICHOLSON, Samuel, naval officer; b. Chestertown, Md., 1743; s. Joseph and Hannah Smith (Scott) N.; m. Mary Dowse, Feb. 9, 1780, at least 4 children. Commd. capt. Continental Navy 1776, secured English cutter Dolphin for U.S. commanded frigate Deane, 1778; commd. capt U.S. Navy, 1794; supt. bldg. of frigate Constitution; 1st supt. Charlestown (Mass.) Navy Yard 1801; torpedoship Nicholson named for him, 1901 Died Charleston, Dec. 29, 1811.

NICHOLSON, William Thomas, inventor, mfr. b. Pawtucket, R.I., Mar. 22, 1834; s. William and Eliza (Forrestell) N.; m. Elizabeth Gardiner 1857, at least 5 children. Machinist apprentice at 14, later worked in various machine shops patented spirit level, egg beater, 1860, manufactured both in his Providence (R.I.) shop; demand for war materials during Civil War gave him opportunity to manufacture spl. machinery for prodn. of small arms; obtained 2 patents for file-cutting machine, 1864; organized Nicholson File Co., Providence, 1864, devised over 400 different kinds of files, pres., gen. mgr.; city alderman Providence; trustee Providence Pub. Library, dir. several pub. utilities, banks, R.I.; mem. Am. Soc. M.E. Died Providence, Oct. 17, 1893

NICOLA, Lewis, patriot; b. France, 1717. Came to Phila. from Dublin, Ireland, circa 1766; editor American Magazine or Gen. Repository; wholesale mcht.; propr. circulating library, Phila.; elected mem. one of Phila.'s 2 scientific socs., 1768, negotiated merger by which Am. Philos. Soc. was formed, often served as curator; a justice Northampton County (Pa.), 1774; published 3 mil. manuals during Revolutionary War; apptd. barrack master Phila., 1776; town maj., commanding Home Guards, 1776-82; col. Invalid Regt., 1777, commandant, 1788; brevetted brig. gen., 1783; a proponent of crowning George Washington "King of America." Author: A Treatise of Military Exercise, 1776. Died Alexandria, Va., Aug. 9, 1807.

NICOLET, Jean, explorer; b. Cherbourg, France, 1598; s. Thomas and Marguerite (de la Mer) N.; m. Marguerite Couillard, Oct. 7, 1637. Came to New France (now Can.) with Samuel de Champlain, 1618; lived among Indians on Allumette Island, upper Ottowa River; ofcl. interpreter among Nipissing Indians, 1624; returned to Can., 1633, became ofcl. interpreter for colony at Three Rivers; 1st known white man to discover Lake Michigan and Wis., 1634, hoped to find Chinese, instead found Winnebago Indian tribe; called Manitou-iriniou the "wonderful man" by Indians. Drowned in storm on St. Lawrence River, Nov. 1, 1642; buried Que., Can.

NICOLL, Henry, congressman; b. N.Y.C., Oct. 23, 1812; grad. Columbia, 1830; studied law. Admitted to N.Y. bar, 1835, began practice in N.Y.C.; del. N.Y. Constl. Conv., 1847; mem. U.S. Ho. of Reps. (Democrat) from N.Y., 30th Congress, 1847-49. Died N.Y.C., Nov. 28, 1879; buried family burying ground, Mastic, L.I., N.Y.

NICOLLET, Joseph Nicolas, explorer, mathematician; b. Cluses, Savoy France, July 24, 1786; ed. Coll. of Cluses. Discovered comet in constellation Pegasus, 1821; apptd. astron. asst. French Bur. of Longitude, 1822; prof. mathematics Coll. Louis-le-Grand; came to U.S., 1832; made 1st expdn. (an ascent up Mississippi River to find its source), 1836; head ofcl. expdn. for survey of upper Missouri River, 1838, head 2d expdn., 1839. Author: Report Intended to Illustrate A Map of the Hydrographical Basin of the Upper Mississippi (a map of region N.W. of the Mississippi), 1843. Died Sept. 11, 1843, Washington, D..C,

NICOLLS, Matthias, mayor N.Y.C.; b. Plymouth, Eng., Mar. 29, 1626; s. Rev. Matthias and Martha (Oakes) N.; m. Abigail Johns, at least 2 children. Admitted to Lincoln's Inn, 1649; sec. to royal commr. investigating conditions in New Eng., 1663; sec. Province of N.Y., 1664-73, 74-80; presiding judge N.Y. Ct. Assizes; mayor N.Y.C., 1671-72, 74-75; judge N.Y. Ct. of Oyer and Terminer, 1683-87; speaker 1st N.Y. Provincial Assembly, 1683; prin. author "Duke's Laws," 1665. Died N.Y.C., circa 1688.

NICOLLS, Richard, colonial gov. N.Y.; b. Bedfordshire, Eng., 1624; s. Francis and Margaret (Bruce) N.; LL.D., Oxford U., 1663; took command Royalist horse troop against Parilamentary army, 1643; followed Stuarts into exile; served under Duke of York in French Army, gaining rank of col.; became groom of bedchamber to Duke of York upon Restoration; apptd. gov. Dutch colony of New Netherland and lands between Connecticut and Delaware Rivers by Duke of York (upon whom Charles II conferred the terr. in anticipation of acquiring it), 1664; also named prin. mem. commn. to investigate conditions in New Eng.; blockaded New Amsterdam with 4 vessels and 3 companies of troops, Aug. 18, 1664, obtained surrender of Peter Stuyvesant, Dutch ir. gen., without bloodshed, Aug. 29; gradually nstituted English system of local govt. (while balancing interests of English and Dutch); issued legal ode known as Duke's laws, 1664-65; frustrated by heocratic leaders of Mass. in his efforts as commr. or New Eng.; resigned as gov., 1668, resumed post as groom of bedchamber to Duke of York in Eng.; killed in Battle of Solebay, Third Dutch War. Died May 28, 1672; buried Ampthill Ch., Bedfordshire Eng., beneath monument enclosing part of fatal cannon ball.

NICOLLS, William, colonial legislator; b. Eng., 1657; s. Matthias and Abigail (Johns) N.; m. Anne Van Rensselaer, 1693, 9 children. Came to Am., 1664; returned to Eng., served 2 years in Brit. Army, 1677; clk. Queen's County (N.Y.), 1683-87; atty. gen. N.Y. State, 1687; N.Y. Provincial agt. to Eng. to discuss colony's defenses, 1695; mem. N.Y. Assembly from Suffolk County, 1702, dep., speaker, 1702-18; a noted anti-Leislerian, served as one of prosecutors who obtained a conviction for treason against Jacob Leisler (who had led a revolt against the aristocratic ruling families of the colony), 1691. Died L.I., N.Y., May 1723.

NIERENSEE, John R., architect; b. Vienna, Austria, 1831; ed. Vienna; studied architecture, Balt.; married, at least 1 son, Frank. Became draftsman B. & O. R.R., Balt.; became partner (with J. C. Neilson) in archtl. firm, Balt., designed number of bldgs. in Balt. before Civil War; apptd. supervising architect State Capitol, Columbia, S.C., early 1860's (bldg. uncompleted at start of Civil War, badly damaged during Sherman's occupation), called back to complete Capitol Bldg., early 1880's, died before completion; mem. A.I.A. Died Apr. 7, 1885.

NILES, Hezekiah, editor; b. Jefferis' Ford, Pa., Oct. 10, 1777; s. Hezekiah and Mary (Way) N.; m. Ann Ogden, May 17, 1798; m. 2d, Sally Warner, 1826; 20 children. Editor, Balt. Evening Post, 1805; editor, publisher Niles' Weekly Register, 1811-36; wrote Principles and Acts of Revolution in America, 1822; town clk. Wilmington (Del.), asst. burgess, 2 terms, mem. 1st branch of Balt. City Council, 2 terms; elected grand high priest Masonic Order in Md., 1818-19; a leader Balt. Typog. Soc.; favored nat. industry protection, also Am. system of Henry Clay; towns of Niles (Mich. and O.) named for him. Died Wilmington, Apr. 2, 1839.

NILES, Jason, congressman; b. Burlington, Vt., Dec. 19, 1814; grad. U. Vt., 1837; studied law. Taught sch., Ohio and Tenn.; admitted to the bar, 1851; began practice of law, Kosciusko, Miss.; del. Miss. constl. convs., 1851, 65, 68; mem. Miss. Ho. of Reps., 1870; circuit judge 13th Miss. Jud. Dist., 1871-72; mem. U.S. Ho. of Reps. (Republican) from Miss., 43d Congress, 1873-75; editor Kosciusko Chronicle, 1876-80. Died Kosciusko, July 7, 1894; buried City Cemetery, Kosciusko.

NILES, John Milton, senator; b. Windsor, Conn., Aug. 20, 1787; s. Moses and Naomi (Marshall) N.; studied law, Hartford, Conn.; m. Sarah Robinson, June 17, 1824; m. 2d, June Pratt, Nov. 26, 1845; no children. Admitted to Conn. bar, 1817; founded Hartford Weekly Times, 1817; judge Hartford County Ct., 1821-29; mem. Conn. Ho. of Reps., 1826-27; postmaster Hartford, 1829-36; mem. U.S. Senate (Democrat) from Conn., 1835-39, 43-49; postmaster gen. U.S. under Pres. Martin Van Buren, 1840-41. Author: A Gazetteer of the States of Connecticut and Rhode Island, 1819; The Life of Oliver Hazard Perry, 1820. Died Hartford, May 31, 1856; buried Old North Cemetery, Hartford.

NILES, Nathaniel, congressman; b. South Kingston, R.I., Apr. 3, 1741; s. Samuel and Sarah (Niles) N.; grad. Coll. of N.J. (now Princeton), 1766; A.M. (hon.), Harvard, 1772, Dartmouth, 1791; m. Nancy Lathrop, circa 1775; m. 2d, Elizabeth Watson, Nov. 22, 1787; 9 children. Invented process for making wire, erected mills in Norwich and Torrington, Conn.; mem. Conn. Legislature, 1779-81; one of 1st settlers, West Fairlee, Vt., circa 1782; speaker lower house Vt. Legislature, 1784; judge Vt. Supreme Ct., 1784-88; mem. Vt. Council, 1785-87; mem. U.S. Ho. of Reps. (Jefferson Democrat) from Vt., 2d-3d congresses, Oct. 17, 1791-95; a leading mem. Vt., Conv. to ratify U.S. Constn., 1791; trustee Dartmouth, 1793-1820; mem. Gov.'s Council, Vt., 1803-09; presdl. elector, 1804, 13; active in revising fundamental laws of Vt., 1814; del. Vt. Constl. Conv., 1814; an itinerant lay preacher. Author: The American Hero (ode). Died West Fairlee, Vt., Oct. 31, 1828; Oct. 31, 1828; buried West Fairlee Center Cemetery,

NILES, Nathaniel, diplomatic agt.; b. Dec. 27, 1791; s. Nathaniel and Elizabeth (Watson) N.; grad. Harvard Med. Sch., 1816; m. Rosella Sue. Sec., Am. legation, Paris, France, 1830-33; apptd. spl. diplomatic agt. to Austria-Hungary, 1837; charge d'affaires to Sardinia, 1848-50. Died N.Y.C., Nov. 16, 1869.

NILES, Samuel, clergyman; b. Block Island, R.I., May 1, 1674; s. Nathaniel and Sarah (Sands) N.; A.B., Harvard, 1699; A.M. (hon.), Harvard, 1759; m. Elizabeth Milton, May 29, 1701; m. 2d, Ann Coddington, Nov. 22, 1716; m. 3d, Elizabeth (Adams) Whiting, Dec. 22, 1737. Missionary at Kingstown, R.I., 1702-10; ordained minister, 2d Ch., Braintree, Mass., 1711; moderator of assn. of ministers (which attacked George Whitefield) at Weymouth, Mass., 1744; refused to permit new way of singing from notes to be introduced into his church. Author: A Summary Historic Narrative of the Wars in New England with the French and the Indians. Died Braintree, May 1, 1762.

NISBET, Charles, clergyman, coll. pres.; b. Haddington, Scotland, Jan. 21, 1736; s. William Nisbet; grad. U. Edinburgh (Scotland), 1754, grad. Theol. Course, 1760; D.D., Coll. of N.J. (now Princeton), 1783; m. Anne Tweedie, 1766; 4 children. Licensed by Presbytery of Edinburgh, 1760; ordained, became pastor, Montrose (Scotland), 1764; came to Am., 1785; 1st pres. Dickinson Coll., Carlisle, Pa., 1785-1804; co-pastor Presbyn. Ch., Carlisle. Died Carlisle, Jan. 18, 1804; buried Old Graveyard, Carlisle.

NISBET, Eugenius Aristides, congressman, jurist; b. Greene County, Ga., Dec. 7, 1803; s. James and Penelope (Cooper) N.; grad. U. Ga., 1821; m. Amanda Battle, Apr. 12, 1825, 12 children. Admitted to Ga. bar, 1821; mem. Ga. Ho. of Reps., 1827-29, Ga. Senate, 1829-32, 34-35; mem. U.S. Ho. of Reps. from Ga., 26th-27th congresses, 1838-42; judge Ga. Supreme Ct., 1845-53; mem. Ga. Secession Conv., 1861, favored secession; practiced law, Macon, Ga., 1861-71. Died Macon, Mar. 18, 1871; buried Rose Hill Cemetery, Macon.

NITSCHMANN, David, clergyman; b. Zauchtenthal, Germany, Dec. 27, 1696; son of George Nitschmann; m. Rosina Schindler, Nov. 12, 1726; m. 2d, Mary Leinbach Martin. Joined Ancient Brethren's Ch. on estate of Count Zinzendorf, 1724, became missionary for ch. in Germany; a founder Moravian Ch., 1727, did evang. work in various European countries; missionary St. Thomas, W.I., 1732; became bishop Moravian Ch., 1735; organized 1st Moravian settlement in Savannah, Ga., 1735; organized settlement at Bethlehem, Pa., 1740, directed immigration and govt. of town, 1740-44; made many trips between Am. and Europe in work of Moravian Ch., 1744-55; ret. in Bethlehem, 1755. Died Bethlehem, Oct. 8, 1772.

NIVEN, Archibald Campbell, congressman; b. Newburgh, N.Y., Dec. 8, 1803. Surrogate of Sullivan County (N.Y.), 1828-40; adj. gen. N.Y. State 1844; mem. U.S Ho. of Reps. (Democrat) from N.Y., 29th Congress, 1845-47; dist. atty. Sullivan County, 1847-50; mem. N.Y. Senate, 1864-65. Died Monticello, N.Y., Feb. 21, 1882; buried Rock Ridge Cemetery, Monticello.

NIXON, John, army officer; b. Framingham, Mass., Mar. 1, 1727; s. Christopher and Mary (Seaver) N.; m. Thankful Berry, Feb. 7, 1754; m. 2d, Hannah (Drury) Gleason, Feb. 5, 1778; 5 sons, 5 daus. Served in expdn. against Louisbourg, 1745; commd. lt. Continental Army, 1755, capt., 1775; capt. of a co. Col. Ruggles' Regt., Half Moon, N.Y., 1758; commanded a co. of minute-men, Lexington and Concord (Mass.) Apr. 19, 1775; col. 4th Inf., Continental Army, 1776, elected brig.-gen., 1776, resigned, 1780. Died Middlebury, Vt., Mar. 24, 1815.

NIXON, John, army officer, financier; b. Phila., 1733; s. Richard and Sarah (Bowles) N.; m. Elizabeth Davis, Oct. 1765, 4 daus., 1 son. Lt., Dock Ward Co. (home guard orgn.), 1756; apptd. warden Delaware River Port, 1766; a signer Pa. paper money, 1767; mem. 1st Com. of Correspondence, 1774; dep. to Gen. Conf. Province of Pa., 1774; del. Pa. Provincial Conv., 1775; an organizer, lt. col. 3d Battalion of Assos., 1775; mem. Pa. Com. of Safety, 1775, pres. pro tem; comdr. defenses Delaware River at Ft. Island, 1776, Phila. City Guard, 1776; mem. Continental Navy Bd.; leader Phila. Guard in defense of Perth Amboy (N.J.) and Battle of Princeton, 1777; mem. com. to settle and adjust accounts of Pa. Com. and Council of Safety, 1778; an organizer, dir. Bank of Pa., formed to aid in supplying Continental Army, 1780; dir. Bank of N.Am., 1784, pres., 1792; alderman Phila., 1789-96; bd. mgrs. Pa. Hosp., 1768-72; trustee Coll. Phila., 1789-91. Died Phila., Dec. 31, 1808; buried St. Peter's Church Yard, Phila.

NIXON, John Thompson, congressman, jurist; b. Fairton, N.J. Aug. 31, 1820; s. Jeremiah S. and Mary Shaw (Thompson) N.; grad. Coll. of N.J. (now Princeton), 1841; m. Mary H. Elmer, Sept. 24, 1851. Taught language Coll. of N.J., circa 1841-43; tutor in family of Judge Isaac S. Pennybacker, Staunton, Va., 1843; admitted to Va. bar, 1844, N.J. bar, 1845; became partner (with Charles E. Elmer) in law firm, assisted in publ. of Elmer's Digest, a compendium of a Digest of the Laws of New Jersey; mem. N.J. Assembly, 1849-50; mem. U.S. Ho. of Reps. from N.J., 36th-37th congresses, 1859-63; apptd. U.S. judge for Dist. N.J., 1870; trustee Princeton Theol. Sem., 1883-89. Died Stockbridge, Mass., Sept. 28, 1889; buried City Cemetery, Bridgeton, N.J.

NIZA, Marcos de, see de Niza, Marcos.

NOAH, Mordecai Manuel, journalist; b. Phila., July 19, 1785; s. Manuel M. and Zipporah (Phillips) N.; m. Rebecca Jackson, 1826; 6 sons, 1 dau. Reporter at sessions of Pa. Legislature, 1800; appt. U.S. consul to Tunis with spl. mission to Algiers, 1813; editor National Advocate, 1817; apptd. sheriff of N.Y.C., 1822; admitted to N.Y. bar, 1823; established N.Y. Enquirer 1826 (merged with Morning Courier to form Morning Courier and N.Y. Enquirer), 1829; appt. surveyor Port of N.Y., 1829, resigned, 1833; founded Evening Star, 1834; asso. judge N.Y. Ct. of Sessions, 1841-42; successively edited Union, Noah's Times, Weekly Messenger. Author: She Would Be a Soldier, 1822; Gleanings from a Gathered Harvest, 1845; also various patriotic plays. Died N.Y.C., Mar. 22, 1851.

NOAILLES, Louis Marie (Vicomte de Noailles), army officer; b. Paris, France, Apr. 17, 1756; son of Philippe, duc de Mouchy; m. Louise de Noailles (cousin), Sept. 19, 1773, at least 2 children. Served with French Army during Am. Revolution; col. Royal-Soissonais Regt. at battles of Savannah and Yorktown; rep. French Army at surrender negotiations; mem. French Estates-General, leader in nobles' renunciation of ancient privileges, 1789; fled France, 1792; became partner Bingham & Co., banking firm, Phila., 1793; speculated in Pa. lands; served as mil. officer in French West Indies during Napoleonic Wars. Died of wounds received in naval battle off Havana, Cuba, Jan. 5, 1804.

NOBILI, John, missionary, coll. pres.; b. Rome, Italy, Apr. 8, 1812. Entered Soc. of Jesus, 1826; ordained priest Roman Catholic Ch., 1843, went to Ore. as missionary and superior Oregon-Rocky Mountain missions; baptized over 1500 Indians; assigned to San Francisco, 1849; pastor mission of Santa Clara (Cal.), 1851; founder Coll. of Santa Clara, 1852, pres., 1855. Died Santa Clara, Mar. 1, 1856.

NOBLE, David Addison, congressman; b. Williamstown, Mass., Nov. 9, 1802; grad. Williams Coll., 1825; studied law, Albany, N.Y., and N.Y.C. Admitted to N.Y. bar, 1831, began practice in N.Y.C.; moved to Monroe, Mich., 1831, practiced law; city recorder Monroe, 1838-39, 44-50, mayor, 1852, alderman, 2 terms; mem. Mich. Ho. of Reps., 1847-48; pros. atty. and probate judge Monroe County (Mich.); mem. U.S. Ho. of Reps. (Democrat) from Mich., 33d Congress, 1853-55; mgr. Louisville, New Albany & Chgo. R.R., 1858-62; del. Dem. Nat. Conv., Chgo., 1864. Died Monroe, Oct. 13, 1876; buried Woodlawn Cemetery, Monroe.

NOBLE, James, senator; b. Clarke County, Va., Dec. 16, 1783; s. Thomas and Elizabeth Claire (Sedgwick) N.; studied law under Richard Southgate, Newport, Ky.; m. Mary Lindsey, Apr. 7, 1803. Moved to Ky., circa 1800, to Ind., circa 1809; admitted to Ind. bar, began practice law, Lawrenceburg; pros. atty. Franklin County (Ind.), 1810; commd. lt. col. Ind. Militia, 1811; operated ferry across Ohio River from Switzerland County, Ind., 1815; apptd. to Ind. 3d Dist. Ct. by Gov. Thomas Posey, 1815; mem. Ind. Constl. Conv. from Franklin County, 1816, mem. coms. on legislative dept., elections, banks and militia; mem. 1st Ind. Ho. of Reps., 1816; mem. U.S. Senate from Ind., Dec. 11, 1816-Feb. 26, 1831, worked for internal improvements and devel. of West. Died Washington, D.C., Feb. 26, 1831; buried Congressional Cemetery, Washington.

NOBLE, Samuel, ironmaster; b. Cornwall, Eng., Nov. 22, 1834; s. James and Jenifer (Ward) N.; m. Christine Stoeckel, 1861, 1 son, 3 daus. Came to Am., 1837; became leader James Noble & Sons, 1855; sec.-treas., gen. mgr. Woodstock Iron Co., 1872; founded town of Anniston (Ala.), 1873; an organizer Clifton Iron Co., 1880-85; iron master Anniston Pipe Works Co., organized 1887; founded Weekly Hot Blast (Anniston's 1st newspaper); built Episcopal Ch., Anniston. Died Aug. 14, 1888.

NOBLE, William Henry, congressman; b. New Milford, Conn., Sept. 22, 1788. Engaged as tanner and farmer; mem. N.Y. State Assembly, 1828-30; affiliated politically with so-called "Bucktail" wing; mem. U.S. Ho. of Reps. (Democrat) from N.Y., 25th Congress, 1837-39; insp. Auburn (N.Y.) Prison, 1843-45. Died Rochester, N.Y., Feb. 5, 1850.

NOEGGERATH, Emil Oscar Jacob Bruno, physician; b. Bonn, Germany, Oct. 5, 1827; s. Jacob John Noeggerath, attended U. Bonn; M.D., U. Berlin (German), 1853; m. Rolanda Noeggerath, 4 children. Came to Am., 1857; a founder Am. Gynecol. Soc., N.Y. Obstet. Soc.; prof. obstetrics and gynecology N.Y. Med. Coll.; considered one of most talented physicians of his time, believed in conservative treatment of disease, one of earliest to be interested in bacteriology; developed a surg. aseptic technique which was better than Joseph Lister's. Author: Die Latente Gonorrhae in Weiblichen Geschlecht (greatest work), 1872. Died Germany, May 3, 1895.

NOELL, John William, congressman; b. Bedford County, Va., Feb. 22, 1816; attended rural schs.; studied law, Mo.; children include Thomas Estes. Engaged in milling and storekeeping, Perryville, Mo.; admitted to Mo. bar, 1843, began practice in Perryville; clk. Circuit Ct. for Perry County, 1841-50; mem. Mo. Senate, 1851-55; mem. U.S. Ho. of Reps. (Democrat) from Mo., 36th-38th congresses, 1859-63. Died Washington, D.C., Mar. 14, 1863; buried St. Mary's Cemetery, Perryville.

NOELL, Thomas Estes, congressman; b. Perryville, Mo., Apr. 3, 1839; s. John William Noell; attended pub. schs.; studied law. Admitted to Mo. bar, 1858, began practice in Perryville; apptd. mil. commr. during Civil War, 1861; served as maj. Mo. Militia, 1861-62; capt. Co. C, 19th Inf., U.S. Army, 1862-65; mem. U.S. Ho. of Reps. (Radical) from Mo., 39th-40th congresses, 1865-67. Died St. Louis, Oct. 3, 1867; buried St. Mary's Cemetery, Perryville.

NOLAN, Philip, trader; b. circa 1771; m. Frances Lintot, Dec. 19, 1799, 1 child. Tobacco agt. for Gen. James Wilkinson in New Orleans, 1790; trader in furs and horses (bulk of business was illegal), 1791-1801; suspected of being an Am. spy in employ of Gen. Wilkinson; his license from Spanish govt. revoked. Shot for horse trading without a license, Tex., Mar. 21, 1801.

NORHEIMER, Isaac, Hebrew scholar; b. Nemelsdorf, Bavaria, 1809; s. Meyer and Esther (Strauss) N.; Ph.D., U. Munich (Germany), 1834; never married. Came to N.Y., 1835; instr. Union Theol. Sem., 1838; prof. Hebrew, Univ. City N.Y., 1839-40, prof. German and Oriental langs., 1840-42; considered most brilliant Semitic grammarian of 19th century Am. Author: A Critical Grammar of the Hebrew Language, 2 vols., 1838-41; A Grammatical Analysis of Selections from the Hebrew Scriptures, 1838. Died Nov. 3, 1842; buried Jewish Cemetery, 21st St., N.Y.C.

NORMAN, John, engraver, publisher; b. Eng., 1748. Came to Am., circa 1774; very few facts known about his life; in 1789 engraved portrait of Gen. Washington which appeared in Phila. Alamnack for the Year of Our Lord 1780; printed at intervals Geographical Gazetteer of Mass.; made plates for An Impartial History of the War in America between Great Britain and the United States, 2 vols., 1781-82; published Wetherwise's Federal Almanack for the Year of Our Lord 1790. began publishing The American Pilot, 1791; published A Map of the Present Seat of the War, 1776; 1st Boston Directory, 1789. Died Boston, June 8, 1817; buried Copp's Hill, Boston.

NORRIS, Benjamin White, congressman; b. Monmouth, Me., Jan. 22, 1819; grad. Waterville (now Colby) Coll., 1843; studied law, Skowhegan, Me. Tchr., Kents Hill Sem.; engaged in grocery bus., Skowhegan; del. Free-Soil Conv., Buffalo, 1848; went to Cal., 1849, returned to Skowhegan, 1850; admitted to Somerset County (Me.) bar, 1852, began practice in Somerset County; land agt. State of Me., 1860-63; cmmr. for Me., Soldiers' Nat. Cemetery, Gettysburg, Pa., 1863; del. Republican. Nat. Conv., Balt., 1864; served as paymaster Union Army during Civil War, 1864-65; apptd. maj. and additional paymaster Bur. of Freedmen and Abandoned Lands, 1865; mem. Ala. Constl. Conv., 1868; mem. U.S. Ho. of Reps. (Rep.) from Ala., 40th Congress, 1868-69. Died Montgomery, Ala., Jan. 26, 1873; buried South Cemetery, Skowhegan.

NORRIS, Edward, clergyman; b. Gloucestershire, Eng., 1584; s. Edward Norris; attended Balliol Coll., Oxford (Eng.) U.; B.A., Magdalen Hall, 1606/07; m. Eleanor. Tchr., minister, Gloucestershire; involved in theol. dispute with John Traske over interpretation of the Gospel; sailed to Am. with his congregation, 1636; mem. Boston Ch., 1639; tchr. Salem Ch., 1639; named 1st of 7 mininsters commd. to draw up a confession of faith; opposed accusations of witchcraft; opposed violent persecution of Quakers. Author: Reply to John Traske's "True Gospel Vindicated," 1638; The New Gospel not the True Gospel, 1638. Died Dec. 23, 1659.

NORRIS, George Washington, surgeon; b. Phila., Nov. 6, 1808; s. Joseph Parker and Elizabeth (Fox) N.; A.B., U. Pa., 1827, M.D., 1830; m. Mary Fisher, 1838, at least one son William Fisher. Resident physician Pa. Hosp., 1830-33, surgeon, 1836-63; elected prof. clin. surgery U. Pa., 1848, resigned, 1857, mem. bd. trustees, 1857; mem. Am. Philos. Soc.; pres. Hist. Soc. Pa., 1858-60; v.p. Phila. Med. Soc., 1859; mem. Acad. Natural Scis. Phila., censor Coll. Physicians of Phila., 1848-75, v.p., 1864; mem. Phila. Library Co.; v.p. A.M.A., 1850-57; cons. surgeon Children's Hosp. of Phila., pres. bd. mgrs; cons. surgeon Phila. Orthopaedic Hosp., 1868-75; wrote essay On the Occurrence of Non-union after Fractures; its Causes and Treatment, 1842. Died Phila., Mar. 4, 1875.

NORRIS, Isaac, mayor Phila.; b. London, Eng., July 26, 1671; s. Thomas and Mary (Moore) N.; m. Mary Lloyd, Mar. 7, 1694, 14 children including Isaac. Came to Pa., 1693; mem. Pa. Assembly, 1699-1703, 1705, 10-13, 15-16, 18-20, 34; mayor Phila., 1724; mem. Pa. Gov.'s Council, 1709-35; a rescuer of William Penn from debtors' prison in Eng., between 1706-08, later named trustee Province of Pa. by Penn; justice Phila. County Cts., 1715-35; apptd. commr. in Pa.-Md. boundary dispute, 1734; strong advocate of English proprietary interests in Pa.; Norristown (Pa.) named for him. Died Germantown, Pa., June 4, 1735.

NORRIS, Isaac, mcht. legislator; b. Phila., Oct. 23, 1701; s. Isaac and Mary (Lloyd) N.; m. Sarah Logan, June 6, 1739; children—Mary, Sarah. Mem. Common Council of Phila., 1727-30, alderman, 1730-42; mem. Pa. Assembly, 1734-66, speaker, 1750-64; rep. from Pa. to Indian confs., Albany, N.Y., 1745, 54; trustee Acad. and Coll. of Phila. (now U. Pa.), 1751-55; apptd. commr. (with Benjamin Franklin) to Eng., did not go, 1757; opposed petition sent to King to have Pa. changed from a proprietary to royal govt., 1764; leader polit. power group of Pa. Quakers. Died Phila., July 13, 1766.

NORRIS, Moses, Jr., senator, congressman; b. Pittsfield, N.H., Nov. 8, 1799; grad. Dartmouth, 1828; studied law. Admitted to N.H. bar, 1832, began practice in Barnstead; returned to Pittsfield, 1834; mem. N.H. Ho. of Reps., 1837-40, 42, 47-48, served as speaker; mem. N.H. Council, 1841-42; mem. U.S. Ho. of Reps. (Democrat) from N.H., 28th-29th congresses, 1843-47; mem. U.S. Senate from N.H., 1849-55. Died Washington, D.C., Jan. 11, 1855; buried Floral Park Cemetery, Pittsfield.

NORRIS, William, locomotive builder; b. July 2, 1802; s. William and Mary (Schaefer) N.; grad. St. Mary's Coll.; m. May Ann Heide, 1825, 1 child. Built and demonstrated steam carriage with upright boiler in Phila.; organized (with Col. Stephen Long) Am. Steam Carriage Co., 1832; constructed engine "Black Hawk," 1833, used on Phila. & Columbia R.R., later on Phila. & Germantown R.R.; attained fame through constrn. of another engine "George Washington," sold it to various countries, including England, France, Austria, Germany; chief engr. Eastern div. Panama R.R., 1846. Died Jan. 5, 1867.

NORTH, Elisha, physician; b. Goshen, Conn., Jan. 8, 1771; s. Joseph and Lucy (Cowles) N.; M.D. conferred by Conn. Med. Soc., 1813; m. Hannah Beach, 1797, 8 children. Instigated 1st use of Kine-pox for vaccination purposes in N.Y. C.; established 1st eye dispensary, New London, Conn., 1812. Author: A Treatise on a Malignant Epidemic Commonly Called Spotted Fever, 1811. Died Dec. 29, 1843.

NORTH, Frank Joshua, scout, plainsman; b. Ludlowville, N.Y., Mar. 10, 1840; s. Thomas Jefferson and Jane (Townley) N.; m. Mary Smith, Dec. 25, 1865, 1 dau. Moved with family to Neb. Territory, 1856; clk.-interpreter at Pawnee reservation on Loup River, Neb., 1861; commd. capt. of scouts, 1864, took part in Powder River Indian Expdn., other expdns.; commd. maj. of 4 Pawnee battalions for protection of U.P. R.R. during constrn., 1867; guide-interpreter at Ft. D.A. Russell (Wyo.) and Sidney Barracks (Neb.); leader Pawnee scouts in expdn. against the Cheyennes, 1876; elected to Neb. Legislature, 1882; mem. William F. Cody's Wild West Show; known as leading plainsman of his time; good pistol shot, beat James Butler ("Wild Bill") Hickok in competition, 1873. Died Columbus, Neb., Mar. 14, 1885.

NORTH, Orlando, businessman, territorial ofcl. Became store mgr., Evanston, Wyo., 1871; became dir. Mut. Exchange Bank (1st bank in Evanston), 1873; territorial auditor Wyo., 1875-77. Died 1896.

NORTH, Simeon, mfr.; b. Berlin, Conn., July 13, 1763; s. Jedediah and Sarah (Wilcox) N.; m. Lucy Savage, 1786; m. 2d, Lydia Huntington, Mar. 2, 1812; 9 children including Simeon, Reuben. Opened scythe mill, 1795; received U.S. Govt. contract for 500 pistols, 1799, one of 1st to use interchangeable parts in mfg., manufactured pistols, carbines, rifles for U.S. govt. until 1852; lt. col. 6th Conn. Regt., 1811-13; a founder Berlin Acad. Died Aug. 25, 1852.

NORTH, Simeon, clergyman, coll. pres.; b. Berlin, Conn., Sept. 7, 1802; s. Simeon and Lucy (Savage) N.; grad. Yale (valedictorian), 1825, attended Divinity Sch., 1825-27; LL.D. (hon.), Western Res. U., 1842; S.T.D. (hon.), Wesleyan Coll., 1849; m. Frances Hubbard, Apr. 21, 1835, 1 son. Apptd. tutor Yale, 1827; prof. ancient langs. Hamilton Coll., Clinton, N.Y., 1829-39, pres., 1839-57, trustee until 1884; trustee Auburn Theol. Sem., 1840-49; ordained to ministry by Oneida Assn. Congregational Chs., 1842; a founder Maynard Professorship of Law and History. Author: The American System of Collegiate Education, 1839; The Weapons in Christian Warfare, 1849. Died Clinton, Feb. 9, 1884.

NORTH, William, senator, army officer; b. Ft. Frederic, Pemaquid, Me., 1755; s. John and Elizabeth (Pitson) N.; m. Mary Duane, Oct. 14, 1787, 6 children. Moved to Boston after father's death, 1763; became 2d lt. in Col. Thomas Craft's train of arty., 1776; apptd. aide-de-camp to Baron von Steuben, 1779 (mil. relationship grew into close friendship), wrote biog. sketch of Von Steuben; served as insp. of army with rank of maj., after war; mem. commn. to strengthen defenses of N.Y.State, 1794; speaker N.Y. Assembly, 1795, 96, 1810; mem. U.S. Senate (Federalist) from N.Y., May 5, 1798-Aug. 17, 1798, voted for Alien and Sedition Acts; commd. brig. gen., served as adjutant gen. of provisional army, 1798-1800; mem. commn. to report on possibility of canal between lakes Erie and Ontario and Hudson River, 1810. Died Duanesburg, N.Y., Jan. 3, 1836; buried Christ Episcopal Ch., Duanesburg.

NORTHEN, William Ezra, civil engr.; b. Amesbury, Mass., Mar. 14, 1819; s. Ezra and Mary (Currier) W.; grad. Harvard, 1838; m. Margaret Hobbs. Engr., Albany & West Stockbridge R.R., 1840-42, worked under George Whistler; partner with Whistler in engring. company, 1842-49; a specialist in water problems, dams, floating docks and pumping machinery; v.p., engr. N.Y. and New Haven R.R., 1854-66; san. engr. N.Y. Met. Bd. Health, 1866-69; chief engr. Chgo. Main Drainage Canal, 1890-91; pres. Am. Soc. C.E., 1887. Author: First Lessons in Mechanics, 1862. Died Apr. 2, 1897.

NORTHEND, Charles, educator; b. Newbury (now Newburyport), Mass., Apr. 2, 1814; s. John and Anna (Titcomb) N.; attended Amherst Coll.; m. Lucy Ann Moody, Aug. 18, 1834, 3 sons. Instr. Dummer Acad., South Byfield, Mass., 1831; prin. 1st grammar sch., Danvers, Mass., 1836; in charge Epes Grammar Sch., Salem, Mass., 1841-52; Pres. Essex County Tchrs. Assn., 1846, 47, 48; supt. pub. schs. Danvers, 1852-55; sch. visitor New Britain, Conn., 1855-56; editor Conn. Common Sch. Jour., 1856-66; asso. editor New Eng. Jour. of Edn. (later Jour. of Edn.), 1878; elected pres. Am. Inst. Instrn., 1863-64; mem. New Britain Sch. Bd., 1872, sec., 1873; supt. schs., New Britain, 1879-80. Died Aug. 7, 1895.

NORTHROP, Birdsey Grant, educator; b. Kent, Conn., July 18, 1817; s. Thomas Grant and Aurelia (Curtiss) N.; grad. Yale, 1841, Yale Theol. Sem., 1845; m. Harriette Chichester, Feb. 18, 1846, 5 children. Ordained to ministry Congregational Ch.; pastor Congregational Ch., Saxonville, Mass., 1846-56; agt. Mass. Bd. Edn., 1857-67; apptd. sec. Conn. Bd. Edn., 1867, resigned, 1883; original trustee Smith Coll.; trustee Hampton Inst.; founder Arbor Day; known as "father of the village improvement society." Author: Education Abroad; Forestry in Europe; Lessons from European Schools. Died Clinton, Conn., Apr. 27, 1898.

NORTHROP, Lucius Bellinger, army officer; b. Charleston, S.C., Sept. 8, 1811; s. Amos Bird and Claudia (Bellinger) N.; grad. U.S. Mil. Acad., 1831; m. Maria de Bernabeu, 1841. Brevetted 2d lt. inf., U.S. Army, 1831; transferred to 1st Dragoons, 1833; commd. 1st lt., 1834, capt., 1839; col. and commissary gen. Confederate Army, 1861; responsible for feeding of Confederate troops and Northern war prisoners; unpopular among many Confederate gens., some of whom (Lee, Johnston, Beauregard) pressed for his removal. Died Pikeville, Md., Feb. 9, 1894.

NORTON, Andrews, educator; b. Hingham, Mass., Dec. 31, 1786; s. Samuel and Jane (Andrews) N.; grad. Harvard, 1804; m. Catharine Eliot, May 21, 1821, 6 children including Charles Eliot, Grace. Tutor, Bowdoin Coll., 1809; apptd. tutor mathematics Harvard, 1811, librarian, 1813, Dexter lectr. on Bible, 1813, Dexter prof. sacred lit. Harvard Div. Sch., 1819-30; founder, editor, contbr. to General Repository and Review, 1812-13, Author: Evidences of the Genuineness of the Gospels, Vol. I., 1837, Vols. II, III, 1844; Tracts Concerning Christianity, 1852; A Translation of the Gospels with Notes, 1856; also some verse. Died Newport, R.I., Sept. 18, 1853.

NORTON, Daniel Sheldon, senator; b. Mount Vernon, O., Apr. 12, 1829; grad. Kenyon Coll., Gambier, O.; studied law. Served in Mexican War; admitted to Ohio bar, began practice in Mount Vernon, 1852; moved to St. Paul, Minn., 1855, Winona, Minn., 1856; practiced law; mem. Minn. Ho. of Reps., 1857-60, Minn. Senate, 1861-64; mem. U.S. Senate (Union Conservative) from Minn., 1865-70.

Died Washington, D.C., July 13, 1870; buried Greenmount Cemetery, Balt.

NORTON, Ebenezer Foote, congressman; b. Goshen, Conn., Nov. 7, 1774; studied law. Admitted to Conn. bar, practiced law; moved to Buffalo, N.Y., 1815; atty. Niagara Bank; held local offices; an organizer Buffalo Harbor Co., 1819, petitioned state legislature for a loan to be used for harbor improvement; mem. U.S. Ho. of Reps. (Democrat) from N.Y., 21st Congress, 1829-31. Died Buffalo, May 11, 1851.

NORTON, Jesse Olds, congressman; b. Bennington, Vt., Dec. 25, 1812; grad. Williams Coll., 1835; studied law, Ill. Admitted to Ill. bar, 1840, began practice in Joliet; mem. Ill. Constl. Conv., 1847; mem. Ill. Ho. of Reps., 1851-52; mem. U.S. Ho. of Reps. (Republican) from Ill., 33d-34th, 38th congresses, 1853-57, 63-65; judge 11th Ill. Jud. Dist., 1857-62; del. Union Nat. Conv., Phila., 1866. Died Chgo., Aug. 3, 1875; buried Oakwood Cemetery, Joliet.

NORTON, John, clergyman; b. Hertfordshire, Eng., May 6, 1606; s. William and Alice (Browest) N.; B.A., Peterhouse Coll., Cambridge (Eng.) U., 1624, M.A., 1627; m. 2d, Mary Norton, July 23, 1656. Chaplain to Sir William Masham, circa 1630; came to Mass., 1635, tchr. Congregational Ch., Ipswich; admitted freeman of Mass., 1637; participant in Ann Hutchinson's trial, 1637; ordained pastor Ipswich ch., 1638-56; mem. Cambridge Synod which drew up Cambridge Platform, 1648; overseer Harvard, 1654; pastor 1st Ch. of Boston, 1656-63; Mass. agt. to Charles II of England, 1662. Author: The Orthodox Evangelist, 1654; The Heart of New England Rent at the Blasphemies of the Present Generation, 1659. Died Apr. 5, 1663.

NORTON, John Nicholas, clergyman; b. Waterloo, N.Y., 1820; s. George and Maria (Gault) N.; grad. Geneva (now Hobart) Coll., 1842; attended Gen. Theol. Sem., N.Y.C. 1842-45; m. Mary Sutton, 1855. Ordained to ministry Protestant Episcopal Ch., 1845; rector Ch. of Ascension, Frankfort, Ky., 1847-70; asso. rector Christ Ch., Louisville, Ky., 1870, aided devel. Negro Episcopal Ch., Louisville. Author: The Boy Who Was Trained Up To Be a Clergyman, 1853; Pioneer Missionaries, 1859; The Lay Reader, 1870; The King's Ferry Boat, 1876; Old Paths, 1880. Died Louisville, Jan. 18, 1881.

NORTON, John Pitkin, educator, agrl. chemist; b. Albany, N.Y., July 19, 1822; s. John Treadwell and Mary (Pitkin) N.; m. Elizabeth Marvin, Dec. 15, 1847, 2 sons. Studied chemistry with various tchrs., various places; apptd. prof. agrl. chemistry Yale, 1846, helped to found dept. scientific edn. which later became Sheffield Scientific Sch. Author: Elements of Scientific Agriculture, 1850; also numerous papers, particularly in field of chemistry of corps. Died Farmington, Conn., Sept. 5, 1852.

NORTON, Nelson Ira, congressman; b. nr. Salamanca, N.Y., Mar. 30, 1820. Engaged in farming; supr. Cattaraugus County (N.Y.), 1860, 65-67; justice of peace, 1852-70; mem. N.Y. State Assembly, 1861-62; Republican presdl. elector, 1872; mem. U.S. Ho. of Reps. (Republican) from N.Y., 44th Congress, Dec. 6, 1875-77. Died Hinsdale, N.Y., Oct. 28, 1887; buried Maplehurst Cemetery, Hinsdale.

NORVELL, John, senator; b. Danville, Va. (now Ky.), Dec. 21, 1789; attended common schs.; studied law. Newspaper editor, Hagerstown, Md.; admitted to Md. bar, 1814, began practice in Balt.; served as pvt. during War of 1812; editor of an Anti-Federalist newspaper, Phila., 1816-32; moved to Mich. Territory; postmaster of Detroit, 1831-36; del. Mich. Constl. Conv., 1837; mem. U.S. Senate (Democrat) from Mich., Jan. 26, 1837-41; resumed practice of law, Detroit; mem. Mich. Ho. of Reps., 1842; U.S. dist. atty. for Mich., 1846-49. Died Detroit, Apr. 24, 1850; buried Elmwood Cemetery, Detroit.

NOTMAN, John, architect; b. 1810. Practiced architecture, specializing in eccles. work; credited with design of chs. including: St. Mark's (Gothic style), 1847-49, St. Clements, 1859, Ch. of Holy Trinity (Gothic), circa 1859 (all Phila.); Ch. of St. James-the-less, Falls of Schuykill, Pa.; St. Peter's Episcopal Ch. (Gothic), Pitts.; Immanuel Ch., Newcastle, Del.; Episcopal Ch. of St. Thomas (Gothic), Glassboro, N.J.; a founder Pa. Inst. Architects (now Phila. chpt. A.I.A.), 1861. Died 1865.

NOTT, Abraham, congressman, jurist; b. Saybrook, Conn., Feb. 5, 1768; s. Josiah and Zerviah (Clark) N.; grad. Yale, 1787; m. Angelica Mitchell, Aug. 1794; children—Henry Junius, Josiah Clark. Admitted to S.C. bar, 1791; mem. U.S. Ho. of Reps. from S.C., 6th Congress, 1799-1801; judge S.C. Circuit Ct., 1810-24; elected head S.C. Circuit Ct. of Appeals, 1824, declared it unconstl. for S.C. Legislature to determine time and meetings of S.C. Constl. Conv. Died Fairfield, S.C., June 19, 1830; buried 1st Presbyn. Church Yard, Columbia, S.C.

NOTT, Eliphalet, clergyman, coll. pres.; b. Ashford, Conn., June 25, 1773; s. Stephen and Deborah (Selden) N.; M.A., R.I. Coll. (now Brown U.), 1795, LL.D. (hon.), 1828; D.D. (hon.), Coll. of N.J. (now Princeton), 1805; m. Sarah Benedict, July 4, 1796; m. 2d, Gertrude (Peebles) Tibbitts, Aug. 3, 1807; m. 3d, Urania Sheldon, Aug. 8, 1842. Ordained, installed pastor 1st Presbyn. Ch., Albany, N.Y., 1798; became trustee Union Coll., Schenectady, N.Y., 1800, pres. (taking office at crucial period and financially strengthening coll.), 1804-66; pres. Am. Assn. for Advancement Edn., 1850; temperance advocate. Died Schenectady, Jan. 29, 1866.

NOTT, Henry Junius, educator; b. Union Dist., S.C., Nov. 4, 1797; s. Judge Abraham and Angelica (Mitchell) N.; grad. S.C. Coll. (now U.S.C.), 1814; read law under William Harper; 1 dau. Admitted to S.C. bar, 1818; prof. logic S.C. Coll., 1824-37, chmn. faculty, 1835. Author: Novellettes of a Traveller, 2 vols., 1834. Died at sea on trip to N.Y., Oct. 9, 1837.

NOTT, Josiah Clark, physician, author; b. Columbia, S.C., Mar. 31, 1804; s. Abraham and Angelica (Mitchell) N.; grad. S.C. Coll (now U.S.C.), 1824; studied medicine under Dr. James Davis, Columbia; attended Coll. Physicians and Surgeons, N.Y.C., 1825; M.D., U. Pa., 1827; m. Sarah Deas, 1832, 8 children. Demonstrator anatomy U. Pa., 1827-29; practiced medicine, Columbia, 1829-35; an organizer Mobile (Ala.) Med. Soc., 1841; prof. anatomy U. La., 1857-58; a founder Med. Coll. of Ala., 1858, prof. surgery, 1858-61; served in Confederate Army during Civil War; mem. N.Y. Obstet. Soc., 1868; best known for his conclusions on yellow fever (believed it was living organism and had nothing to do with atmospheric conditions). Author: (with George R. Gliddon) Types of Mankind, 1854, Indigenous Races of the Earth, 1857; Contributions to Bone and Nerve Surgery, 1866; contbr. paper on anatomy to New Orleans Med. Jour., 1844. Died Mobile, Mar. 31, 1873.

NOTT, Otis Fessenden, physician; b. Ballston Springs, Saratoga County, N.Y., Mar. 6, 1825; s. Oran Gray and Lucy (Kingman) O.; A.M. (hon.), Union Coll., 1851; grad. N.Y. Med. Coll., 1852; m. Frances Helen Cooke, 1867. Took up landscape painting, 1843, also taught landscaping; ship surgeon in Panama and Pacific service; practiced medicine, N.Y.C., 1860; police surgeon for N.Y.C., 1861-71; pres. med. bd. N.Y. Police Dept., 1869-71; lectr. Coll. Physicians and Surgeons, N.Y.C., 1871-90; 1st man to cure stricture in male urethra. Author: Essays Lessons in Landscape, 1856; Stricture of the Male Urethra: Its Radical Cure, 1878; Classroom Lectures on Syphilis and the Genito-Urinary Disease, 1878; Clinical Lectures on the Physiological Pathology of Syphilis and Treatment of Syphilis, 1881. Died New Orleans, May 24, 1900.

NOTT, Samuel, clergyman; b. Saybrook (now Essex), Conn., Jan. 23, 1754; s. Stephen and Deborah (Selden) N.; studied under Rev. Daniel Welch, Mansfield, Conn., 1774-76; grad. Yale, 1780; m. Lucretia Taylor, Feb. 14, 1782, 11 children. Blacksmith's apprentice in Conn., 1762-66; licensed to preach by New Haven Assn. of Ministers, 1781; ordained to Ministry Congregational Ch., Conn., 1782; pastor 2d Parish Congl. Ch., Norwich (now Franklin), Conn., 1782-1852; dir. Missionary Soc. of Conn., 18 years; pres. Conn. Bible Soc., Norwich Fgn. Missionary Soc. Author: The Sixtieth Anniversary Sermon (considered his best work), 1842. Died Franklin, May 26, 1852.

NOURSE, Amos, senator; b. Bolton, Mass., Dec. 17, 1794; grad. Harvard, 1812; studied medicine. Postmaster of Hallowell (Me.), 1822-41; moved to Bath, Me., 1841; collector of customs, Bath, 1845-46; began practice of medicine, Bath; med. lectr., prof. obstetrics Bowdoin Coll., Brunswick, Me., 1846-53; mem. U.S. Senate from Me., Jan. 16-Mar. 3, 1857; judge of probate Sagadohoc County (Me.). Died Bath, Apr. 7, 1877; buried Hallowell Cemetery.

NOYAN, Pierre-Jacques Payende, see de Noyan, Pierre-Jacques Payen.

NOYES, Edward Follansbee, gov. Ohio, diplomat; b. Haverhill, Mass., Oct. 3, 1832; s. Theodore and Hannah (Stevens) N.; grad. Dartmouth, 1857; grad. Law Sch., Cincinnati Coll., 1858; m. Margaret Proctor, Feb. 15, 1863, 1 son. Served as maj. 39th Ohio Inf., U.S. Army, 1861; became col.; commanded Camp Dennison, O.; brevetted brig. gen.; resigned, 1865; city solicitor in Hamilton County, O., 1865; probate judge Hamilton County; gov. Ohio, 1872-74; chmn. Ohio delegation Republican Nat. Conv., 1876; U.S. minister to France, 1877-81; elected judge Superior Ct. at Cincinnati, 1889. Died Sept. 4, 1890.

NOYES, George Rapall, clergyman, educator; b. Newburyport, Mass., Mar. 6, 1798; s. Nathaniel and Mary (Rapall) N.; grad. Harvard, 1818, grad. Harvard Divinity Sch., 1822, D.D. (hon.), 1839; m. Eliza Buttrick, May 8, 1828, at least 5 children. Ordained to ministry Unitarian Ch., 1827; pastor Unitarian Ch., Brookfield, Mass., 1827-34; Hancock prof. Hebrew and Oriental langs. Dexter lectr. Bibl. lit. and theology Harvard Divinity Sch., 1827-34. Author: An Amended Version of the Book of Job, 1827; The Psalms, 1827; The Prophets, 1843; Theological Essays, 1856; translator Old and New Testaments. Died Cambridge, Mass., June 3, 1868.

NOYES, John, congressman; b. Atkinson, N.H. Apr. 2, 1764; grad. Darthmouth, 1795; studied theology. Tutor, Chesterfield (N.H.) Acad., 1795-97, Dartmouth, 1797-99; moved to Brattleboro, Vt., 1800, engaged in merc. bus.; mem. Vt. Ho. of Reps., 1808-10, 12; moved to Dummesston, Vt., 1812, resumed merc. bus.; held local offices; mem. U.S. Ho. of Reps. (Federalist) from Vt., 14th Congress, 1815-17; ret. from merc. bus., 1819. Died nr. Putney, Vt., Oct. 26, 1841; buried Maple Grove Cemetery, Putney.

NOYES, John Humphrey, social reformer; b. Brattleboro, Vt., Sept. 3, 1811; s. John and Polly (Hayes) N.; grad. Dartmouth, 1830; studied law under Larkin G. Mead, Chesterfield, N.H.; attended Andover (Mass.) Theol. Sem., 1831, Yale Theol. Dept., 1831-34; m. Harriet A. Holton, 1838. Organized free church with others at Yale as reaction against Calvinism, requested to leave Yale and refused license to preach because of his radical beliefs, 1834; began a Bible sch., Putney, Vt., 1836; promoted free love and promiscuity in his community, 1846; arrested on charge of adultery, broke bail, escaped to N.Y.; his community followed him and he established Oneida (N.Y.) Community, 1848; forced birth control and stirpiculture on members; Community became incorporated, 1881. Author: The Berean, 1847; Bible Communism, 1848; Male Continence, 1848; Scientific Propagation, circa 1873. Died Niagra Falls, Ont., Can., Apr. 13, 1886.

NOYES, Joseph Cobham, congressman; b. Portland, Me., Sept. 22, 1798; atended common schs. Moved to Eastport, Me., 1819; ship chandler and shipper of mdse., Eastport; mem. Me. Ho. of Reps., 1833; mem. U.S. Ho. of Reps. (Whig) from Me., 25th Congress, 1837-39; collector of customs for Passamaquoddy (Me.) Dist., 1841-43; moved to Portland, engaged in flour and commn. bus.; treas. Portland Co., locomotive works, 1859; a founder Portland Savs. Bank, 1852, treas., 1859-68. Died Portland, July 28, 1868; buried Evergreen Cemetery, Portland.

NOYES, William Curtis, lawyer; b. Schodack, N.Y., Aug. 19, 1805; s. George and Martha (Curtis) N.; LL.D. (hon.), Hamilton Coll., circa 1856; m. Anne Tracy, 3 children; m. 2d, Julia Tallmadge, 2 children. Admitted to N.Y. bar as atty., 1827, as counselor, 1830; dist. atty. Oneida County (N.Y.), circa 1834; bequeathed his library (over 7,000 books) to Hamilton Coll.; famous cases include: Huntington Case, Rose Will Case (4 Abbott's Court of Appeals Decision, 108), achieved his greatest victory in suit of Mechanics' Bank vs. N.Y. & New Haven R.R. Co. (13 N.Y. Reports, 599); del. to Peace Conf., Wash., Washington, D.C., 1861; gave address "One Country! One Constitution! One Destiny!" (in support of Emancipation Proclamation), 1861; mem. exec. com. Am. Temperance Union; pres. New Eng. Soc., 1864. Died N.Y.C., Dec. 25, 1864.

NUCKOLLS, Stephen Friel, congressman; b. Grayson County, Va., Aug. 16, 1825. Moved to Linden, Mo., 1846; engaged in merc. bus., Linden, 1847-53; moved to Territory of Neb., 1854; founder Nebraska City; held local offices; established Platte Valley Bank, 1855; mem. Neb. Territorial Legislature, 1859; moved to Territory of Colo., 1860, engaged in banking and mining; moved to N.Y.C., 1864; moved to Territory of Dakota, 1867, settled in Cheyenne, engaged in merc. bus.; del. U.S. Congress (Democrat) from Territory of Wyo., 1869-71; mem. presiding officer 2d Wyo. Legislative Council, 1871; del. Dem. nat. convs., Balt., 1872, St. Louis, 1876; moved to Salt Lake City, Utah, 1872, engaged in milling. Died Salt Lake City, Feb. 14, 1879; buried Mt. Olivet Cemetery, Salt Lake City.

NUGEN, Robert Hunter, congressman; b. nr. Hallidays Cove, Washington County, Pa., July 16, 1809. Engaged in farming and contracting, Tuscarawas County, Ohio, 1828; held local offices; del. Democratic Nat. Conv., Charleston, S.C., 1860; mem. U.S. Ho. of Reps. (Dem.) from Ohio, 37th Congress, 1861-63; supt. Ohio Canal, until 1872. Died Newcomerstown, O., Feb. 28, 1872; buried Newcomerstown Cemetery.

NUÑEZ, Alvar Cabeza de Vaca, explorer; b. Jerez de la Frontera, Spain, circa 1490; s. Fransisco de Vera and Theresa Cabeza de Vaca (carried last name of a maternal ancestor). Served in war against Italy, 1511-12; appt. treas. of expdn. under Pánfilo de Narváez to conquer Fla., 1527, later became adm. of expdn. fleet; reached an island off coast of what is now Tex. after encountering difficulties, captured and enslaved by Indians; escaped and lived dangerous existence as a trader on the mainland, 1530; started overland journey to Mexico City (with 4 others from group), their ability to kill Indians saved them from capture and enslavement, 1535; reached Mexico City, 1536; returned to Spain, 1537; apptd. head of expdn. to Rio de la Plata Region, S.Am., 1540; mem. group of 1st white men to reach falls of the Ig Uazú, in what is now Paraguay; arrested and sent back to Spain after successful rebellion in his expdn., 1544; imprisoned, Seville, Spain, 1545-51; pardoned by royal govt., granted an estate in Spain, 1556. Author: La Relacion que Dio Alvar Núñez, Cabesa de Vaca de lo Acaescido enlos Indias (described various N.Am. animals such as oppossum and bison, also various Indian tribes of Southwest; largely cause of Coronado's expdn. into what is now Southwestern U.S.), 1552. Died probably Seville, circa 1557.

NURSE, Rebecca, witchhunt victim; b. Yarmouth, Eng., 1621; d. William and Joanna (Blessing) Towne; m. Francis Nurse, 8 children. Involved in local arguments during period of witchcraft frenzy, Salem Village (now Danvers), Mass.; accused of being witch, arrested and indicted, found guilty by jury of women, 1692. Executed, Salem Village, July 19, 1692.

NUTE, Alonzo, congressman; b. Milton, N.H., Feb. 12, 1826; attended common schs. Engaged in mfg. boots and shoes, Farmington, N.H.; served with 6th Regt., N.H. Volunteer Inf., Union Army during Civil War, mem. staffs of generals Griffin and Rush Hawkins; mem. N.H. Ho. of Reps., 1886, N.H. Senate, 1867-68; del. Republican Nat. Conv., Cincinnati, 1876; mem. U.S. Ho. of Reps. (Rep.) from N.H., 51st Congress, 1889-91. Died Farmington, N.H., Dec. 24, 1892; buried Pine Grove Cemetery, Farmington.

NUTHEAD, William, printer; b. England, 1654; m. Dinah Nuthead. Set up printing press, Jamestown, Va. (1st press South of Mass.); forbidden to continue printing by Va. Council because he had printed account of Va. Assembly of 1682 without license, 1683; operated press, St. Mary's, Md., 1686-95, printed documents for Md. Assembly. Died 1695.

NUTTALL, Thomas, naturalist; b. Settle, Eng., Jan. 5, 1786; s. Jonas Nuttall. Came to U.S. (Phila.), 1808; investigated flora up Missouri River, 1809-11; went along Arkansas and Red rivers in Ark., La., Indian territories, 1818-20; with Wyeth Expdn. to mouth of Columbia River, 1834-35; fellow Linnaean Soc. of London, 1813; mem. Am. Philos. Soc.; contributed many articles to Jour. of Acad. of Natural Scis., Transactions of Am. Philos. Soc., and others; curator Bot. Garden of Harvard, 1822-33; delivered paper to Phila. Acad. Natural Scis. entitled "Observations on the Geological Structure of the Valley of the Mississippi" (1st attempt in America to correlate by means of fossils geog. formations widely separated geographically; mem. Phila. Acad. Natural Sciences, Phila. Author: The Genera of North American Plants, and a Catalogue of the Species, to the Year 1817, 1818; A Journal of Travels into the Araknsas Territory during the Year 1819, 1821; A Manual of the Ornithology of the United States and Canada, 1832; An Introduction to Systematic and Physiological Botany; wrote supplement to Michaux's North American Sylva, 3 vols., 1846. Died Liverpool, Eng., Sept. 10, 1859.

NUTTING, Newton Wright, congressman; b. West Monroe, N.Y., Oct., 22, 1840; studied law. Admitted to N.Y. bar, practiced in Oswego; mem. Oswego County Sch. Com., 1864-67; dist. atty. Oswego County, 1869-72, county judge, 1878-83; mem. U.S. Ho. of Reps. (Republican) from N.Y., 48th, 50th-51st congresses, 1883-85, 87-89. Died Oswego, Oct. 15, 1889; buried Riverside Cemetery, Oswego.

NYE, Edgar Wilson (Bill Nye), writer; b. Shirley, Me., Aug. 25, 1850; s. Franklin and Elizabeth (Loring) N.; m. Clara Smith, Mar. 7, 1877, 4 children. Admitted to Wyo. Territory bar, 1876; justice of peace, wrote for various Western jours.; with Judge Jacob Blair started Laramie (Wyo.) Boomerang, 1878; postmaster Laramie, 1882-83; moved East, 1886, became mem. staff N.Y. World; appeared as lectr. with James Whitcomb Riley, 1886-90; helped make Am. humor a distinct branch of nat. literature. Author: Bill Nye and the Boomerang, 1881; The Forty Liars, 1883; Nye and Riley's Railway Guide, 1888; Bill Nye's History of the U.S., 1894; Bill Nye's History of England, 1896; also plays The Cadi, The Stag Party. Died Arden, N.C., Feb. 22, 1896.

NYE, James Warren, senator, territorial gov.; b. De Ruyter, N.Y., June 10, 1815; s. James and Thankful (Crocker) N.; studied law, Troy, N.Y.; m. Elsie Benson, 2 children. Admitted to N.Y. bar, circa 1838; dist. atty. N.Y. State, 1839; judge Madison County (N.Y.), 1840-48; practiced law, Syracuse, N.Y., 1847-57; 1st pres. Met. Bd. of Police, N.Y.C., 1857-60; gov. Nev. Territory (apptd. by Pres. Lincoln), 1861-64; mem. U.S. Senate (Republican) from Nev., 1864-73; returned to N.Y., 1875. Died White Plains, N.Y., Dec. 25, 1876; buried Woodlawn Cemetery, N.Y.C.

O

OAKES, Urian, clergyman, coll. pres.; b. Eng., 1631; s. Edward and Jane O.; B.A., Harvard, 1694. Came to Am., 1640; named fellow Harvard Coll., 1650; returned to Eng., circa 1653, to Am., 1671; pastor Congregational Ch., Cambridge, Mass., 1671; acting pres. Harvard, 1675-80, pres., 1680-81; a censor of Mass. press; published one poem Elegie. Died Cambridge, Mass., July 25, 1681.

OAKLEY, Thomas Jackson, jurist, congressman; b. Beekman, N.Y., Nov. 10, 1783; s. Jesse and Jerushah O.; grad. Yale, 1801; m. Lydia S. Williams, 1808; m. 2d, Matilda Caroline Cruger, Mar. 29, 1831; at least 4 children. Surrogate of Dutchess County, N.Y., 1810-11; mem. U.S. Ho. of Reps. from N.Y., 13th, 20th congresses, 1813-15, 27-28; mem. N.Y. State Assembly, 1816, 18-20; atty. gen. N.Y. State, 1819; judge Superior Ct. of N.Y., 1828-47. Died N.Y.C, May 11, 1857; buried Trinity Churchyard, N.Y.C.

O'BRIEN, Fitz-James, journalist; b. County Limerick, Ireland, 1828; never married. Came to U.S., 1852; exhausted his inheritance through extravagant living in Bohemian circles, N.Y.C.; contbr. poems and short stories to N.Y.C. newspapers and Harper's Weekly, Vanity Fair, Atlantic Monthly; joined 7th Regt., N.Y. Nat. Guard, 1861. Works collected as: Poems and Stories of Fitz-James O'Brien, Collected and Edited with a Sketch of the Author by William Winter, 1881. Died of tetanus after improper treatment of shoulder wound, Cumberland, Md., Apr. 6, 1862.

O'BRIEN, Jeremiah, naval officer; b. Kittery, Me., 1744; s. Morris and Mary (Hutchins) O.; m. Elizabeth Fitzpatrick, no children. Led group of volunteers in seizure of Brit. sloops Unity and Margaretta (1st naval engagement of Am. Revolution), 1775, commd. capt. Unity (renamed Machias Liberty) and Diligent (1st ships of Mass. Navy), 1775-76; privateer, 1777-80; captured by British, 1780, escaped, 1781; commanded privateers Hibernia and Tiger, 1781; U.S. collector customs for Machias dist. of Me., 1811-18. Died Sept. 5, 1818.

O'BRIEN, Jeremiah, congressman; b. Machias, Me., Jan. 21, 1778; attended common schs. Engaged in lumber mfg., shipping; mem. Me. Senate, 1821-24; mem. U.S. Ho. of Reps. (Democrat) from Me., 18th-20th congresses, 1823-29; mem. Me. Ho. of Reps, 1832-34. Died Boston, May 30, 1858; buried O'Brien Cemetery, Machias.

O'BRIEN, John, see Raymond, John T.

O'BRIEN, Matthew Anthony, clergyman; b. Bawn, County Tipperary, Ireland, May 1804; s. John and Grace (Meagher) O. Came to U.S., 1826; tutor St. Mary's Coll., Marion County, Ky., 1829-35; took final vows of Dominican Order, Roman Catholic Ch., 1837, ordained priest, 1839; master of novices St. Rose's Dominican Sem., Springfield, Ky., 1839-42, St. Joseph's House of Studies, Perry County, O., 1842-44; pastor St. Patrick's Ch., Perry County, 1844-50; Am. provincial of Dominican Order, 1850-54; pastor, prior St. Rose's Ch., Springfield, 1854-61; vis. preacher, N.Y. and Ky., 1863-71. Died Louisville, Ky., Jan. 15, 1871; buried St. Rose's Ch. Cemetery.

O'BRIEN, Richard, mariner, diplomat; b. Me., 1758; s. William and Rebecca (Crane) O'Bryen; m. Elizabeth Robeson, Mar. 25, 1799. Became mariner; served as Am. privateer during Revolutionary War; master brig Dauphin, circa 1781; captured by Algerine pirates and became interested in Algiers-Am. relations; apptd. to conclude treaty of peace with Tripoli, 1797; consul gen. to Algiers, 1797-1803; mem. Pa. Legislature, 1808. Died Washington, D.C., Feb. 14, 1824.

O'BRIEN, William Shoney, financier; b. Queen's County, Ireland, 1826; never married. Became U.S. citizen, 1845; worked as miner and mcht. in Cal., 1849-54; partner (with James C. Flood) Auction Lunch Saloon, San Francisco, 1854-66; invested heavily in mines in Grass Valley region of Cal.; brought Hale & Norcross Mine on Comstock Lode, Nev., 1865, bought Consol. Va. & Cal. Mines, 1868; established Nev. Bank of San Francisco, 1875; mem. Soc. Cal. Pioneers. Died San Rafael, Cal., May 2, 1878; buried Calvary Cemetery, San Francisco.

O'CALLAGHAN, Edmund Bailey, physician, historian; b. Mallow, Ireland, Feb. 28, 1797; m. Charlotte Crampe; m. 2d, Ellen Hawe, May 9, 1841; 2 children. Admitted to med. practice in Can., 1823; editor Vindicator, Montreal, 1834; mem. Canadian Parliament, 1836; participated in Louis Joseph Papineau's Revolution, 1837; moved to Albany, N.Y., 1837; treas. Albany County Med. Soc.; contbr. poetry to The Northern Light, 1842-44; editor The Documentary History of the State of New York, 1849-51; Documents Relative to the Colonial History of the State of New vols. 1-11, 1853-61; Laws and Ordinances of New Netherland, 1638-74, 1868. Author: History of New Netherland, 2 vols., 1846-48; Jesuit Relations, 1847; Remonstrances of New Netherland, 1856; "Orderly Books" of Commissary Wilson, 1857. Died N.Y.C., May 29, 1880.

O'CALLAGHAN, Jeremiah, clergyman; b. County Cork, Ireland, 1780; s. Jeremiah and Mary (Twohig) O'C.; Ordained priest Roman Catholic Ch., 1805; came to U.S., 1823; travelling preacher in Vt., 1830-59; established 1st Cath. ch. in Vt., Burlington; founder, pastor St. Jerome's Ch., Holyoke, Mass., 1854-61; fanatically denounced usury throughout his career. Author: Usury, 1824; The Creation and Offspring of the Protestant Church, 1837; Banks and Paper Money, 1852; Exposure of the Vermont Banking Companies, 1854. Died Holyoke, Feb. 23, 1861; buried St. Jerome's Ch. Cemetery.

OCCOM, Samson, Indian clergyman; b. Mohegan, Conn., 1723; studied theology under Rev. Eleazar Wheelock, 1743-47; m. Mary Fowler, 1751, 10 children, Tchr., minister to Montauk tribe on L.I., 1749-64; ordained to ministry by L.I. Presbytery, 1759; missionary to Oneida tribe, 1761, 63; went to England to raise funds for Eleazar Wheelock's Indian Charity Sch., 1765-68; itinerant preacher in New Eng., 1768-89; founder Indian settlement, Brotherstown, N.Y., 1784, pastor, 1789-92. Author: Sermon Preached at the Execution of Moses Pacel, an Indian, 1772; A Choice Selection of Hymns, 1774. Died July 14, 1792.

OCHS, Julius, mcht.; b. Furth, Germany, June 29, 1826; s. Lazarus and Nannie (Wetzler) O.; m. Bertha Levy, Feb. 28, 1855, 6 children including Adolph Simon, Milton Barlow. Came to U.S., 1845; served in various capacities during Civil War; treas. Chattanooga (Tenn.) Times, 1878; justice of peace, also judge Knox County (Tenn.) Ct., 1868-72; a commr. to build 1st bridge accross Tennessee River at Knoxville; organizer 1st 2 humane socs. at Chattanooga; a founder Erlanger Hosp.; proficient in 4 langs.; author light operas including The Megilah; or The Story of Esther. Died Chattanooga, Oct. 26, 1888.

O'CONNELL, Mary, see Anthony, Sister.

O'CONNELL, Eugene, clergyman; b. Kingscourt, Meath, Ireland, June 18, 1815; studied at Navan Sem., also St. Patrick's, Maynooth. Ordained priest Roman Catholic Ch., Maynooth, 1842; taught at Navan Sem., until 1851; apptd. head of Santa Inez Coll., Cal., 1851, dir. St. Thomas Sem., San Francisco, 1852; returned to Ireland as dean All Hallows Coll., 1854; consecrated titular bishop of Flaviopolis, also vicar apostolic of Marysville (West of Colorado River in Northwestern U.S.), 1861; 1st bishop Diocese of Grass Valley, 1868-84; apptd. titular bishop of Joppa, 1884. Died Los Angeles, Dec. 4, 1891.

O'CONNER, William Douglas, govt. ofcl., author: b. Boston, Jan. 2, 1832; m. Ellen M. Tarr, 1856, 2 children. Reporter, Boston Commonwealth, 1853, Saturday Evening Post, Phila., 1854-59; corr. clk. Light House Bd., 1861-73, chief clk., 1873-74; librarian Treasury Dept., 1874-75; asst. gen. supt. Life Saving Service, 1878-79; befriended Walt Whitman, 1860, aided him until his death. Author: Harrington (abolitionist novel), 1860. Died Washington, D.C., May 9, 1889.

O'CONNOR, James, bishop; b. Queenstown, Cobh, Ireland, Sept. 10, 1823; studied theology, Rome, Italy. Came to U.S., circa 1838; ordained Roman Catholic Ch., Mar. 25, 1848; vicar gen., 1859-60; rector Sem. of St. Charles Borromeo, 1862-72; apptd. 2d vicar-apostolic of Neb., 1876; 1st bishop Omaha (Neb.) (newly formed see), 1885; founder coll. (now Creighton U.), Omaha, 1879, Sisters of Divine Providence, 1889; an organizer Cath. Mut. Relief Soc. of Am.; dir. Irish Cath. Colonization Assn. Died Omaha, May 27, 1890.

O'CONNOR, Michael, clergyman; b. nr. Cork, Ireland, Sept. 27, 1810; attended Propaganda, Rome, Italy. Ordained priest Roman Catholic Ch., 1833; transferred to U.S., 1839; vicar gen., rector St. Paul's Ch., Pitts.; founded a Cath. literary inst., 1843; named 1st bishop of Pitts., consecrated by Cardinal Franzoni, 1843; built cathedral, Pitts., 1855, established Passionist Order in U.S.; resigned bishopric, entered Jesuit novitiate at Gorheim, Germany, 1860, took vows, Boston, 1862; tchr. Boston Coll., 1863; socius to Jesuit provincial of Md., 1864; founded St. Francis Xavier Ch., Balt.;

travelled throughout U.S. as Jesuit missionary, did much work among Negroes. Died Woodstock, Md., Oct. 18, 1872; buried Community Cemetery; Woodstock.

O'CONNOR, Michael Patrick, congressman; b. Beaufort, S.C., Sept. 29, 1831; grad. St. John's Coll., Fordham, N.Y., 1850; studied law. Admitted to S.C. bar, 1854, began practice in Charleston; mem. S.C. Ho. of Reps., 1858-66; served as lt. Lafayette Arty. during Civil War; del. Democratic nat. convs., Balt., 1872, St. Louis, 1876; mem. U.S. Ho. of Reps. (Dem.) from S.C., 46th Congress, 1879-81. Died Charleston, Apr. 26, 1881; buried St. Lawrence Cemetery, Charleston.

O'CONOR, Charles, lawyer; b. N.Y.C., Jan. 22, 1804; s. Thomas and Margaret (O'Connor) O'Conor; m. Cornelia Livingston McCraken, 1854. Admitted to bar, 1824, became a leader in N.Y. State bar, specializing in law of trusts and corps., 1824-44; also active in Democratic Party in N.Y.; mem. N.Y. Constl. Conv., 1846; won fame in Edwin Forrest divorce case, 1852; U.S. dist. atty. for So. Dist. of N.Y., 1853; counsel for Jefferson Davis, 1866-67; pres. N.Y. Law Inst., 1869; spl. dep. atty. gen. of N.Y. to assist in prosecution of Tweed Ring, 1871-74; nominated for Pres. U.S. by faction of Dem. Party at Louisville Conv. (had close ties with So. Democrats because of sympathy for slavery and right of secession), 1872; counsel in Hayes-Tilden election controversy, 1877. Died Nantucket, Mass., May 12, 1884.

OCONOSTOTA, Indian chief; at least 1 child, Tuksi. Chief, Cherokee Indians; sided with British during French and Indian War; made repeated attacks on frontier settlement when some of his warriors were killed by Americans after they had helped them in attack on Ft. Duquesne, 1759; massacred inhabitants of Ft. Loudoun after they had surrendered to him, 1760; went to England, 1762; signed peace treaty with Iroquois, 1768; fought against Americans during Revolutionary War; resigned chieftainship after signing peace treaties with Am. states, 1782. Died 1785.

ODDIE, Walter M., artist; b. circa 1808. Worked in N.Y.C. and Long Island, N.Y.; painted landscapes of L.I., Hudson Valley, and New Eng.; exhibited frequently at N.A.D., Apollo Assn., Am. Art-Union, N.Y.C., also in Phila., Boston, Washington, D.C.; asso. N.A.D. Died 1865.

ODELL, Jonathan, clergyman, Loyalist; b. Newark, N.J., Sept. 25, 1737; s. John and Temperance (Dickinson) O.; grad. Coll. of N.J. (now Princeton), 1759; also studied medicine; m. Anne DeCou, May 6, 1772, 3 children including William Franklin. Ordained deacon Ch. of Eng., 1766, priest, 1767; minister St. Anne's (Anglican) Ch., Burlington, N.J., 1767-76; remained loyal to Eng. at outbreak of Am. Revolution, became chaplain of reg. of Pa. Loyalists; wrote bitterly satirical verse opposing Am. cause, became influential Loyalist publicist; wrote essays and verse published in such papers as Rivington's Gazette; played asst. sec. to comdr.-in-chief of Brit. Forces in N. Am., 1783; returned to Eng., 1783-84; settled in New Brunswick, Can., 1784-1818, clk. of province, mem. N.B. Exec. Council, 1784-1818. Poetry published in The Loyal Verses of Joseph Stansbury and Jonathan Odell, 1860. Died Fredericton, N.B., Nov. 25, 1818.

ODELL, Moses Fowler, congressman; b. Tarrytown, N.Y., Feb. 24, 1818. Apptd. entry clk. N.Y. Customhouse, 1845, rose to pub. appraiser; mem. U.S. Ho. of Reps. (Democrat) from N.Y., 37th-38th congresses, 1861-65; Navy agt. N.Y.C., 1865-66. Died Bklyn., June 13, 1866; buried Greenwood Cemetery, Bklyn.

ODENHEIMER, William Henry, clergyman, author; b. Phila., Aug. 11, 1817; s. John W. and Henrietta (Burns) O.; grad. U. Pa., 1835; grad. Gen. Theol. Sem., N.Y.C., 1838; m. Anne D.R. Shaw, 2 children. Ordained deacon Protestant Episcopal Ch., 1838, priest, 1841; asst. rector St. Peter's Ch., Phila., 1841-59; bishop of N.J., 1859-74; bishop of Northern Diocese of N.J., 1874-79. Author: Thoughts on Immersion, 1843; The Private Prayer Book, 1851; Jerusalem and Its Vicinity, 1855; Canon Law, 1868. Died Aug. 14, 1879.

ODIN, John Mary, clergyman; b. Ambierle, France, Feb. 25, 1807; s. Jean and Claudine (Seyrole) O.; attended Sem. of Barrens, nr. St. Louis. Came to U.S., 1822; ordained priest Roman Catholic Ch., 1824; missionary to Ark. and Mo., dir. Sem. of Barrens, 1824-33, 36-40; went to Europe to seek money and recruits for missionary work, 1833-35; vice prefect of Tex., 1840-42, vicar apostolic, 1842-47; 1st bishop of Galveston (Tex.), 1847-61; founder Coll. of Immaculate Conception, Galveston, 1857; made annual visit through his territory preaching to both Indians and settlers; archbishop of New Orleans, 1867-70; attended Vatican Council, Rome, 1869. Died Ambierle, May 25, 1870.

ODIORNE, Thomas, poet, businessman; b. 1769; grad. Dartmouth Coll., 1791. Mfr. of nails, owner hardware bus., Boston. Author: The Progress of Refinement, 1792; Moral Evil No Accident, 1821; Ethic Strains on Subjects Sublime and Beautiful, 1821. Died 1851.

O'DWYER, Joseph, physician; b. Cleve., Oct. 12, 1841; grad. Coll. physicians and Surgeons, N.Y.C., 1866; m. Catherine Begg, 8 children. First physician to successfully employ intubation for asphyxia in diptheria, and to use diptheria serum; apptd. to staff N.Y. Foundling Asylum, 1872. Died N.Y.C., Jan. 7, 1898.

OEMLER, Arminus, agriculturist; b. Savannah, Ga., Sept. 12, 1827; s. Augustus Gottlieb and Mary Ann (Shad) O.; grad. with honors Dresden Technische Bildungsanstalt, 1848; M.D., U. City N.Y., 1856; m. Elizabeth P. Heyward, Apr. 10, 1856, 6 children. Joined Confederate Army, commd. capt. 2d Company, deKalb Riflemen; made 1st map of Chatham County (Ga.); founder 1st comml. oyster packing plant in South, Wilmington Island, Ga.; discoverer presence of nitrogen-fixing bacteria in nodules of leguminous plants, 1886, discouraged from further research by U.S. Dept. of agr. (actual discovery made in Germany 2 years later). Died Savannah, Aug. 8, 1897; buried Wilmington Island.

OERTEL, John James Maximilian, journalist; b. Ansbach, Bavaria, Germany, Apr. 27, 1811; attended U. Erlangen. Ordained to ministry Lutheran Ch.; came to N.Y., 1837; after involvement in denominational disputes, converted to Roman Catholic Ch., 1840; taught German at Fordham Coll.; editor of German Catholic weekly, Cincinnati; founder Kirchenzeitung, Balt., 1836, developed it into leading German paper in U.S., moved paper to N.Y., 1851; published Altes und Neues, 1869. Died Jamaica, N.Y., Aug. 21, 1882.

O'FALLON, Benjamin, Indian agt.; b. Ky., Sept. 20, 1793; s. Dr. James and Frances Eleanor (Clark) O'F.; m. Sophia Lee, Nov. 1823, 6 children. indian agt., Prairie du Chien (in present-day Wis.), made treaties between U.S. and Otos and Poncas Indians, 1817; apptd. Indian agt. for the Upper Missouri, 1819, signed 15 treaties between U.S. and Indian tribes, 1825, resigned, 1827; a prin. mem. Mo. Fur Co. Died Dec. 17, 1842.

O'FALLON, James, army officer; b. Ireland, Mar. 11, 1749; s. William and Anne (Eagan) O'F.; attended U. Edinburgh (Scotland); m. Frances Clark, Feb. 1791; children—John, Benjamin. Came to Am., 1774; served as surgeon U.S. Army during Am. Revolution; mem. Charleston (S.C.) Marine Anti-Britannic Soc., 1785; gen. agt. S.C. Yazoo Co., 1790; intrigued with Spain and France in role of mil. leader; Pres. Washington issued public proclamation against Am. support for his plans, 1791; served as officer under George Rogers Clark, 1791. Died circa 1794.

O'FALLON, John, philanthropist; b. Louisville, Ky., Nov. 17, 1791; s. Dr. James and Frances Eleanor (Clark) O'F.; m. Harriet Stokes, 1821; m. 2d, Ruth Caroline Sheets, Mar. 15, 1827; 5 children. Served from 2d lt. to capt. in War of 1812, acting dep. adj. gen. at Ft. Meigs; pres. St. Louis br. U.S. Bank, Miss. & Ohio R.R., N. Mo. R.R.; liberal contbr. to O'Fallon Poly. Inst., St. Louis U., Washington U. Died St. Louis, Dec. 17, 1865.

O'FARRELL, Michael Joseph, clergyman; b. Limerick, Ireland, Dec. 2, 1832; attended All Hallows Coll., Dublin, Ireland; studied at St. Sulpice, Paris, France. Joined Sulpician Order; ordained priest Roman Catholic Ch., Limerick, 1855; sent to teach at Grand Sem., Montreal, Can.; left Sulpician Order; became rector of St. Peter's N.Y.; consecrated 1st bishop of Trenton (N.J.), 1881; attended 3d Plenary Council of Balt., 1884. Died Trenton, Apr. 2, 1894.

OFFLEY, David, mcht., diplomat. Went to Smyrna, Turkey, 1811; opened 1st Am. comml. house there; had much to do with opening of Am.-Turkish trade; a favorite at Turkish court; consular comml. agt., Smyrna, 1823-32, consul, 1832-38. Died Oct. 4, 1838.

OGDEN, Aaron, senator, gov. N.J.; b. Elizabeth, N.J., Dec. 3, 1756; s. Robert and Phebe (Hatfield) O.; grad. Coll. of N.J. (now Princeton), 1773; m. Elizabeth Chetwood, Oct. 27, 1787, 7 children. Tchr., Barber's Grammar Sch., Elizabeth, 1773-75; served to brig. maj. 1st Regt., N.J. Militia 1776-83; admitted to N.J. bar, 1784; commanded N.J. 15th Inf., 1797-1800, also lt. col. 11th Inf.; mem. U.S. Senate (Federalist, filled vacancy), from N.J., 1801-03; mem. N.Y.-N.J. Boundary Commn., 1807; built steamer Sea Horse to run between Elizabethtown and N.Y.C., 1811; gov. N.J,. 1812-13; applied to N.J. Legislature for monopoly of steamboat navigation between Elizabethtown and N.Y.C., 1815 (monopoly granted); litigant famous U.S. Supreme Ct. case, Gibbons vs. Ogden, 1824 (John Marshall gave ct. decision that there could be no monopolies in interstate commerce); apptd. collector of customs Jersey City (N.J.), 1829. Died Elizabeth, Apr. 19, 1839; buried 1st Presbyn. Ch. Burial Ground, Elizabeth.

OGDEN, David, jurist; b. Newark, N.J., 1707; s. Josiah and Catharine (Hardenbroeck) O.; grad. Yale, 1728; m. Gertrude Gouverneur, 11 children including Samuel, Nicholas, Sarah, Isaac. Mem. His Majesty's Council for Province of N.J, 1751-74; a leading lawyer of N..J and N.Y.; apptd. del. to Stamp Act Congress, 1765, disagreed with its recommendations; asso. justice N.J. Supreme Ct., 1772-76, deprived of position because of Loyalist leanings, escaped to N.Y.; property confiscated by rebels; mem. Bd. Refugees, N.Y.C.; went to Eng., 1783, returned to Am. 1790. Died Whitestone. L.I., N.Y., 1798.

OGDEN, David A., congressman; b. Morristown, N.J., Jan. 10, 1770; attended King's Coll. (now Columbia); studied law. Admitted to N.J. bar, 1791, began practice in Newark; became counselor at law, N.J., 1796; moved to Hamilton (now Waddington), N.Y., practiced law; asso. judge St. Lawrence County (N.Y.) Ct. of Common Pleas, 1811-15; mem. N.Y. State Assembly, 1814-15; mem. U.S. Ho. of Reps. (Federalist) from N.Y., 15th Congress, 1817-19; judge Ct. of Common Pleas, 1820-24, 25-29; a commr. to settle boundary dispute between Can. and U.S. Died Montreal, Que, Can., June 9, 1829; buried Brookside Cemetery, Waddington.

OGDEN, David Bayard, lawyer; b. Morrisania, N.Y., Oct. 31, 1775; s. Samuel and Euphemia (Morris) O.; A.B., U. Pa., 1792; m. Margaretta Ogden, 8 children. Admitted to N.J. bar, 1796; a Federalist, later became a Whig; mem. N.Y. Assembly, 1814, 38; trustee Columbia many years; surrogate N.Y. County, 1840-44; atty., argued many cases before U.S. Supreme ct., (upheld greater jurisdiction of ct., expounded nationalist position); cases include Cohens vs. Va., 1821, Sturges vs. Crowninsfield, 1819, Bank of Augusta vs. Earle, 1839. Died Staten Island, N.Y., July 16, 1849.

OGDEN, Francis Barber, engr., diplomat; b. Boonton, N.J., Mar. 3, 1783; s. Gen. Matthias and Hannah (Dayton) O.; m. Louisa Pawnall, 1837. Aide-de-camp under Gen. Andrew Jackson in Battle of New Orleans, 1815; built 1st low pressure condensing engine with 2 cylinders, Leeds, Yorkshire, Eng., 1817; apptd. U.S. consul, Liverpool, Eng., 1830; consul, Bristol, Eng., 1840-57; helped make John Ericssen (inventor of Monitor) known in U.S. Died Bristol, July 4, 1857.

OGDEN, Peter Skene, fur trader, explorer; b. Que., Can., 1794; s. Isaac and Sarah (Hanson) O.; m. 2 Indian wives. With Hudson Bay Co., from circa 1854, head bus. in Columbia Dist.; pioneer explorer in Gt. Salt Lake region, also Humboldt River valley in No. Nevada; City of Ogden (Utah) named in his honor; in charge New Caledonia dist. on Fraser River, 1836-42; stationed at Ft. Vancouver (now in Wash.), 1844, later in command; familiar with regional Indian langs. and customs. Author: Traits of American Indian Life and Culture, published London, Eng., 1853. Died Oregon City, Ore., Sept. 1854.

OGDEN, Samuel, mfr.; b. Newark, N.J., Dec. 9, 1746; s. David and Gertrude (Gouverneur) O.; m. Euphemia Ogden, Feb. 5, 1775, 12 children including David. Mfr. iron used as ammunition during Am. Revolution, Boonton, N.J., mfr. nails and other iron products after war; invested in land in upper N.Y. State; founder Town of Ogdensburg (N.Y.). Died Dec. 1, 1810.

OGDEN, Thomas Ludlow, lawyer; b. Morristown, N.J., Dec. 12, 1773; s. Abraham Ogden; grad. Columbia, 1792; m. Martha Hammond, Jan. 23, 1796, 11 children. Admitted to N.Y. bar, 1796; practiced law in partnership with his brother David, later with Alexander Hamilton; a leading trust and corp. lawyer in N.Y.C.; vestryman Trinity Ch., N.Y.C.; 1807-44; trustee Columbia, 1817-44, Gen. Theol. Sem.; Federalist. Died Dec. 17, 1844.

OGDEN, Uzal, clergyman; b. Newark, N.J., 1744; s. Uzal and Elizabeth Charlotte (Thebaut) O.; D.D. (hon.), Princeton, 1795; m. Mary Gouverneur, 1776, 6 children. Went to Eng., ordained to ministry Episcopal Ch. by Bishop of London, 1773; preached occasionally at Trinity Ch., Newark, asked to become rector, did not accept until 1788; elected 1st bishop of N.J., 1798, (was refused consecration by Gen. Conv., N.J. did not actually have bishop for 14 years); had reputation for doctrinal laxity; suspended because of controversy with his congregation, 1805; became mem. N.Y. Presbytery. Author: Antidote to Deism, 2 vols., 1795. Died Newark, Nov. 4, 1822.

OGDEN, William Butler, railroad exec., mayor Chgo., coll. pres.; b. Walton, N.Y., June 15, 1805; s. Abraham and Abigail (Weed) O.; m. Maryanne T. Arnat, Feb. 9, 1875. Mem. N.Y. Legislature, 1834; 1st mayor Chgo., 1837, councilman for many years; became pres. Galena & Chgo. Union R.R., 1846; became dir. Pitts., Ft. Wayne & Chgo. R.R. Co., 1853, apptd. gen. receiver, 1859; presided over Nat. Ry. Conv., 1850; dir. Mchts. Loan & Trust Co., 1857; pres. Chgo., St. Paul and Fon-du-Lac R.R., 1857, merged into C.& N.W. Ry., pres. 1859-68; mem. Ill. Senate, 1860-63; 1st pres. U.P. R.R., 1862; pres. Ill. & Wis. R.R., Buffalo & Miss. R.R., Wis. & Superior Land Grant R.R.; 1st pres. Rush Med. Coll.; pres. bd. trustees U. Chgo.; charter mem. Chgo. Hist Soc.; Ogden Avenue (Chgo.) named for him. Died High Bridge, N.Y., Aug. 3, 1877.

OGILVIE, James, educator; b. Aberdeen, Scotland. Came to Am., opened acad., Milton, Va., moved sch. to Richmond, Va., closed sch., 1809; became public lectr.; toured Am. advocating free lecture halls and coll. courses in rhetoric; lectr. S.C. Coll. (now U. S.C.), 1815; left for Scotland to claim title as earl of Findlater, 1820. Author: Philosophical Essays, 1816. Died Aberdeen, Sept. 18, 1820.

OGILVIE, John, clergyman; b. N.Y.C., 1724; grad. Yale, 1748; m. Susanna Symes, 1755; m. 2d, Margaret (Marston) Philipse, Apr. 17, 1769; 2 children including George. Ordained to ministry Episcopal Ch., 1749; missionary to Indians in Albany (N.Y.) area, 1750-56; chaplain Royal Am. Regt., Brit. Army, 1756-63; asst. minister Trinity Ch., N. Y.C., 1764. Translator (into Mohawk): The Order for Morning and Evening Prayer. Died N.Y.C., Nov. 26, 1774.

OGLE, Alexander, congressman; b. Frederick, Md., Aug. 10, 1766; children include Charles. Moved to Somerset, Pa., 1795; mem. Pa. Ho. of Reps., 1803-04, 07-08, 11, 19-23; served as maj. gen. Pa. Militia; prothonotary, recorder of deeds, clk. of cts., 1812-17; mem. U.S. Ho. of Reps. (Democrat) from Pa., 15th Congress, 1817-19; mem. Pa. Senate, 1827-28. Died Somerset, Oct. 14, 1832; buried Union Cemetery, Somerset.

OGLE, Andrew Jackson, congressman; b. Somerset, Pa., Mar. 25, 1822; attended Jefferson Coll., Canonsburg, Pa.; studied law. Admitted to Pa. bar, 1843, began practice in Somerset; prothonotary Somerset County, 1845; mem. U.S. Ho. of Reps. (Whig) from Pa., 31st Congress, 1849-51; apptd. U.S. chargé d'affaires to Denmark, 1852, did not assume post. Died Somerset, Oct. 14, 1852; buried Union Cemetery, Somerset.

OGLE, Charles, congressman; b. Somerset, Pa., 1789; s. Alexander Ogle; studied law. Admitted to Pa. bar, 1822, began practice in Somerset; mem. U.S. Ho. of Reps. (Whig) from Pa., 25th-27th congresses, 1837-41. Died Somerset, May 10, 1841; buried Union Cemetery, Somerset.

OGLE, Samuel, colonial gov.; b. Northumberland County, Eng., circa 1702; s. Samuel and Ursula (Markam) O.; m. Anne Tasker, 1741, 5 children including Benjamin. Proprietary gov. Province of Md., 1731-32, gov. (one of ablest colonial govs. Md.), 1732-42, 1747-circa 1752; an organizer Md. Jockey Club. Died Annapolis, Md., May 3, 1752.

OGLESBY, Richard, senator, gov. Ill.; b. Oldham County, Ky., July 25, 1824; s. Jacob and Isabella (Watson) O.; studied law under Silas W. Robbins, Springfield, Ill.; m. Anna White, 1859; m. 2d, Emma Keyes, 1873. Moved to Decatur, Ill., after death of parents, 1833; admitted to Ill. bar, 1845, started practice of law, Sullivan, Ill.; served as 1st lt. 4th Ill. Volunteers in Mexican War, 1846; went to prospect for gold, Cal., 1849-51; mem. Ill. Senate, 1860; served as col. 8th Ill. Volunteers, 1861-64, served under Ulysses S. Grant at forts Henry and Donelson, promoted maj. gen., 1863; gov. Ill., 1865-69, 73, 85-89, supported Lincoln's war policies, later denounced Andrew Johnson and sent formal demand that action be taken against him to Washington, D. C.; mem. U.S. Senate from Ill., 1873-79, chmn. coms. on public lands and Indian affairs. Died Elkart, Ill., Apr. 24, 1899; buried Elkart Cemetery.

OGLETHORPE, James Edward, founder Ga.; b. London, Eng., Dec. 22, 1696; s. Sir Theophilus and Lady Eleanor (Wall) O.; ed. Eton, Corpus Christi Coll., Oxford (Eng.) U.; m. Elizabeth Wright, Sept. 15, 1744. Mem. Parliament from Haslemere, 1722-54; author pamphlet The Sailor's Advocate, based on reports to Parliament concerning penal conditions (especially debtors' prisons), 1729-30; conceived idea of sending newly freed and unemployed debtors to Am.; received (with 19 assos.) charter creating them "Trustees for establishing the colony of Georgia in America," 1732, largely responsible for obtaining proper publicity and adequate revenues for venture; wrote A New and Accurate Account of the Provinces of South Carolina and Georgia, 1732; landed at Charleston, 1733; founded Savannah (Ga.), 1733; returned to Eng., 1734, largely responsible for enacting important measures prohibiting sale of rum, negro slavery, and providing for regulation of peaceful dealings with Indians by means of licensing system; returned to Ga., 1735, administered colony's affairs, 1735-43; spent great deal of personal fortune on devel. of Ga.; brought before court martial by a subordinate because of Ga. policies, 1743, acquitted; founded Frederica on Altamaha River as So. outpost against Spaniards, circa 1736; repulsed Spanish attack, 1742; surrendered Ga. Charter to Brit. govt., 1752; led campaign against Young Pretender, 1745, court martialed, acquitted; commd. lt. gen. Brit. Army, 1746, gen., 1765. Died Essex, Eng., June 30, 1785.

O'HARA, James, army officer, mfr.; b. Ireland, 1752; s. John O'Hara; ed. Sem. of St. Sulpice, Paris, France; m. Mary Carson, circa 1782, 6 children. Came to Am., settled in Phila., 1772; became govt. agt. among Indians, circa 1774; capt. Revolutionary Army, 1775; became commissary at gen. hosp., stationed Carlisle, Pa., circa 1780; asst. q.m. for Gen. Nathaniel Greene, 1780-83; apptd. q.m. U.S. Army by Pres. Washington, 1792; govt. contractor, 1796-1802; founder (with Maj. Isaac Craig) 1st glassworks in Pitts., (1st plant of its kind to use coal for fuel, 1st successful product was bottles) circa 1800; a pioneer in exporting cotton to Liverpool, Eng., built vessels for the purpose; dir., pres. Pitts. br. Bank of Pa.; partner (with John Henry Hopkins) in iron works, Ligionier, Pa. Died Dec. 16, 1819; buried 1st Presbyn. Ch., Pitts.; reinterred Allegheny Cemetery, Pitts.

O'HARA, Theodore, editor, army officer; b. Danville, Ky., Feb. 11, 1820; s. Kean O'Hara; grad. st. Joseph's Coll., Bardstown, Ky., 1839. Admitted to Ky. bar, 1842; served as capt. and asst. q.m. Ky. Volunteers, Mexican War, 1846-48, brevetted maj., 1847; capt. Ky. Regt. in Narciso Lopez's expdn. to "liberate" Cuba, winter 1849-50; an editor Louisville (Ky.) Times, 1852-55; capt. 2d Cavalry, U.S. Army, 1855-56; editor Mobile (Ala.) Register, 1856-61; seized Ft. Barrancas in Pensacola Harbor, 1861; col. 12th Ala. Inf., circa 1861; became cotton mcht., Columbus, Ga., circa 1865. Author poetry: "The Old Pioneer" (poetic elegy); "The Bivouac of the Dead" (in memory of heroic dead at Battle Buena Vista, 1847). Died nr. Guerryton, Ala., June 6, 1867; reinterred State Mil. Cemetery, Frankfort, Ky., 1874.

O'HIGGINS, Bernardo, Chilean revolutionist; b. Chillán, Chile, Aug. 20, 1778; son of Ambrosio O'Higgins; educated in Eng. Joined Chilean revolutionists, 1810; supreme comdr. Chilean Army, 1813; led unsuccessful attack against Spanish, Rancagua, 1814; fled to Argentina after defeat; returned to Chile as chief lt. of José de San Martín, 1817; engaged in Battle of Chacabuco, Feb. 1817; dictator of Chile, circa 1817-23, declared Chilean independence, drove out Spanish; deposed by aristocratic party, 1823; lived in retirement, Lima, Peru, 1823-42. Died Lima, Oct. 24, 1842.

O'KELLY, James, clergyman; b. circa 1735; m. Elizabeth Meeks, 1760. Methodist preacher, Va. and N.C., 1778-84; elder and mem. ruling council Meth. Episcopal Ch., 1784-92; left Meth. Episcopal Ch., 1792, established Republican Meth. Ch., 1793, head, 1793-1822. Author: Essay on Negro Slavery, 1784; The Christian Church, 1801; Letters from Heaven Consulted, 1822. Died Oct. 16, 1826.

OKEY, John Waterman, jurist; b. Woodsfield, O., Jan. 3, 1827; s. Cornelius and Hannah (Weir) O.; m. May Jane Bloor, 1849, 4 children. Admitted to Ohio bar, 1849; apptd. probate judge Monroe County (O.), 1853, elected, 1854; judge Ohio Ct. Common Pleas, 1856-65; published (with William Yates) Digest of Ohio Reports, 1867, (with S.A. Miller) The Municipal Code of Ohio, 1869; apptd. mem. commn. to revise and consolidate laws of Ohio, 1875; judge Ohio Supreme Ct., 1877-85. Died Columbus, O., July 25, 1885.

OLCOTT, Simeon, senator; b. Bolton, Conn., Oct. 1, 1735; grad. Yale, 1761; studied law. Admitted to N.H. bar, began practice in Charlestown; selectman Charlestown, 1769-71; judge of probate for Cheshire County (N.H.), 1773; mem. N.H. Provincial Gen. Assembly, 1772-73; apptd. chief justice N.H. Ct. of Common Pleas, 1784; apptd. judge N.H. Superior Ct., 1790, chief judge, 1795; mem. U.S. Senate (Federalist) from N.H., June 17, 1801-05. Died Charlestown, Feb. 22, 1815; buried Forest Hill Cemetery, Charlestown.

OLDEN, Charles Smith, gov. N.J.; b. Princeton, N.J., Feb. 19, 1799; s. Hart and Temperance (Smith) O.; m.. Phoebe Ann Smith, 1832, adopted dau. Businessman in New Orleans, 1826-32; became dir. Trenton Banking Co., 1842; mem. N.J Senate from Mercer County, 1844-50; gov. N.J., 1859-63; judge N.J. Ct. of Errors and Appeals, mem. Ct. of Pardons, 1868-73; riparian commr. (rivers and waterways), 1869-75; head N.J. electors in presdl. election 1872; treas. Coll. N.J. (now Princeton), 1845-69, trustee, 1863-75. Died Princeton, Apr. 7, 1876; buried old Friends Burying Ground, Princeton.

OLDHAM, John, colonist, trader; b. Lancashire, Eng., circa 1600. Came to Am., 1623; religious agitator, united with Rev. John Lyford and other malcontents, 1624, established (with Lyford) own church, brought to trial and sentenced to banishment; settler at Nantasket, Mass., then at Cape Anne, Mass.; trader, engaged in bus. between Mass. and Va., also extensive trade with Indians; returned to Eng., 1628; proposed comml. scheme to Mass. Bay Co. in Eng., circa 1628, failed in negotiations, forbidden to trade with Indians, grantee (with Richard Vines) tract of land on south side Saco River (Me.) by Council for New Eng., 1629-30; settler at Watertown, Mass.; took oath as freeman, 1631; rep. to Mass. Gen. Ct., 1632-36; an overseer powder and shot for Colony, 1634; Murdered by Pequot Indians (an episode leading to Pequot War), Block Island, R.I., July 1636.

OLDHAM, Williamson Simpson, Confederate senator, jurist; b. Franklin County, Tenn., June 19, 1813; s. Elias and Mary (Bratton) O.; m. Mary Vance McKissick, Dec. 12, 1837; m. 2d, Mrs. Anne S. Kirk, Dec. 26, 1850; m. 3d, Agnes Harper, circa 1858; 5 children. Admitted to Tenn. bar, 1836; moved to Fayetteville, Ark., 1836, became successful lawyer; mem. Ark. Gen. Assembly from Washington County, 1838; speaker Ark. Ho. of Reps., 1842; presdl. elector, 1844; asso. justice Ar. Supreme Ct., 1844-48; an editor Tex. State Gazette (Democratic organ, became State Gazette 1855), 1854-57; mem. Provisional Congress; del. to Confederate Senate from Tex., 1862; fled to Mexico, later to Can., circa 1865-66; allowed to return to Tex.; refused to be pardoned. Author: (with aid of George W. White) A Digest of the General Statute Laws of the State of Texas, 1859. Died Houston, Tex., May 8, 1868.

OLDS, Edson Baldwin, congressman; b. Marlboro, Vt., June 3, 1802; grad. med. dept. U. Pa., 1824. Taught sch., Ohio; began practice of medicine, Kingston, Pa., 1824; moved to Circleville, O., 1828, practiced medicine, 1828-37; engaged in gen. produce and merc. bus., 1837; mem. Ohio Ho. of Reps., 1842-43, 45-46; mem. Ohio Senate, 1846-48, presiding officer, 1846-47; mem. U.S. Ho. of Reps. (Democrat) from Ohio, 31st-33d congresses, 1848-55; moved to Lancaster, O., 1857; arrested for disloyalty and imprisoned in Ft. Lafayette, 1862; elected to Ohio Ho. of Reps. (while in prison), 1862, mem., 1862-66; resumed merc. bus. Died Lancaster, Jan. 24, 1869; buried Forest Cemetery, Circleville.

OLDSCHOOL, Oliver, see Sargent, Nathan.

OLIN, Abram Baldwin, congressman; b. Shaftsbury, Vt., Sept. 21, 1808; s. Gideon Olin; grad. Williams Coll., 1835; studied law. Admitted to the bar, 1838; began practice of law, Troy, N.Y.; recorder City of Troy, 1844-52; mem. U.S. Ho. of Reps. (Republican) from N.Y., 35th-37th congresses, 1857-63; asso. justice D.C. Supreme Ct. (apptd. by Pres. Lincoln), 1863-79. Died nr. Sligo, Md., July 7, 1879; buried Danforth family lot adjacent to West Lawn Cemetery, Williamstown, Mass.

OLIN, Gideon, congressman; b. East Greenwich, R.I., Nov. 2, 1743; children include Abram Baldwin. Engaged in farming; moved to Shaftsbury, Vt., 1776; del. Windsor Conv., 1777; mem. Vt. Ho. of Reps., 1778, 80-93, 99, speaker, 1788-93; served as maj. during Revolutionary War; asst. judge Bennington County (Vt.) Ct., 1781-98, chief judge, 1807-11; del. Vt. Constl. Conv., 1791; mem. Vt. Gov.'s Council, 1793-98; mem. U.S. Ho. of Reps. (Democrat) from Vt., 8th-9th congresses, 1803-07; resumed farming. Died Shaftsbury, Jan. 21, 1823; buried Shaftsbury Center.

OLIN, Henry, congressman; b. Shaftsbury, Vt., May 7, 1768; attended common schs.; studied law. Admitted to Vt. bar, practiced law; moved to Leicester, Vt., 1788; mem. Vt. Ho. of Reps., 1799-1804, 06-15, 17-19, 22-24; del. Vt. constl. convs., 1814, 22, 28; asso. judge, later chief judge Addison County (Vt.) Ct., 1801-24; mem. Vt. Exec. Council, 1820-21; mem. U.S. Ho. of Reps. (Jeffersonian Democrat) from Vt., 18th Congress, Dec. 13, 1824-25; lt. gov. Vt., 1827-30. Died Salisbury, Vt., Aug. 16, 1837; buried Brookside Cemetery, Leicester.

OLIN, Stephen, clergyman, coll. pres.; b. Leicester, Vt., Mar. 2, 1797; s. Henry and Lois (Richardson) O.; grad. Middlebury (Vt.) Coll.,

1820, D.D. (hon.), 1832; D.D. (hon.), U. Ala., 1834, Wesleyan U., 1834; LL.D. (hon.), Yale, 1845; m. Mary Ann Aliza Bostick, Apr. 10, 1827; m. 2d, Julia M. Lynch, Oct. 18, 1843; 1 son. Instr., Tabernacle Acad., S.C., 1820; admitted on trial as preacher to S.C. Conf., Methodist Episcopal ch., 1824; prof. ethics and belles-lettres Franklin Coll., Athens, Ga., 1826-33; ordained elder Meth. Episcopal Ch., 20, 1828; 1st pres. Randolph-Macon Coll., 1834-37; pres. Wesleyan U., Middletown, Conn., 1842-51; contbr. articles to Christian Advocate and Jour.; del. Gen. Conf. from N.Y., 1844; mem. com. apptd. to find basis of agreement for pro-slavery and anti-slavery groups; instrumental in organizing Evang. Alliance, rep. from N.Y., New Eng. confs. at meeting, London, Eng., 1846. Author: Travels in Egypt, Arabia Petracea, and the Holy Land, 2 vols., 1843; works published posthumously include: The Works of Stephen Olin, 1852, Life and Letters, 1853, Greece and the Golden Horn, 1854, College Life and Practice, 1867. Died Middlebury, Conn., Aug. 16, 1851.

OLIVER, Andrew, colonial ofcl.; b. Boston, Mar. 28, 1706; s. Daniel and Elizabeth (Belcher) O.; grad. Harvard, 1724; m. Mary Fitch, June 20, 1728; m. 2d, Mary Sanford, Dec. 19, 1734; 17 children including Andrew. Mem. Mass. Gen. Ct. from Boston, 1743-45; commr. (with Thomas Hutchinson) at meeting for negotiations with the Six Nations, Albany, N.Y. 1748; mem. Provincial Council, 1746-65; sec. Province of Mass., 1756-71; apptd. distbr. stamps after passage of Stamp Act, 1765, agreed not to serve after mob attacked his home; lt. gov. Mass. (commd. by King, 1770), 1771-74, identified with Hutchinson Tory faction; wrote letters to English gov. describing unsettled conditions in colonies and advising remedies, 1768-69 (letters obtained by Benjamin Franklin and forwarded to popular party in Boston, causing great unpopularity among colonists). Died Boston, Mar. 3, 1774; buried Boston.

OLIVER, Andrew, jurist, scientist; b. Boston, Nov. 13, 1731; s. Andrew and Mary (Fitch) O.; grad. Harvard, 1749; m. Mary Lynde, May 28, 1752. Judge of Inferior Ct. Common Pleas for Essex County (Mass.), 1761-75; mem. Mass. Gen. Ct. from Salem, 1762-67; apptd. a mandamus councilor, 1774, refused to serve; founder Am. Acad. Arts and Scis.; elected mem. Am. Philos. Soc., 1773. Author: An Essay on Comets, in Two Parts, 1772, reprinted, 1811; Elegy on the late Professor Winthrop, 1st published in Independent Chronicle, 1779. Died Salem, Dec. 6, 1799.

OLIVER, Andrew, congressman; b. Springfield, N.Y., Jan. 16, 1815; grad. Union Coll., Schenectady, N.Y., 1835; studied law. Admitted to N.Y. bar, began practice in Penn Yan, 1838; judge Ct. of Common Pleas, 1843-47; county judge and surrogate, 1846, 72-77; mem. U.S. Ho. of Reps. (Democrat) from N.Y., 33d-34th congresses, 1853-57; unsuccessful Am. Party candidate, 1856; engaged in farming and practice of law. Died Penn Yan, Mar. 6, 1889; buried Lake View Cemetery, Penn Yan.

OLIVER, Fitch Edward, physician; b. Cambridge, Mass., Nov. 25, 1819; s. Daniel and Mary Robinson (Pulling) O.; grad. Dartmouth, 1839; studied medicine Dartmouth, Med. Coll. Ohio, also under Oliver Wendell Holmes; M.D., Harvard, 1843; m. Susan Lawrence Mason, July 17, 1866, at least 6 children. Mem. staff Boston City Hosp.; instr. materia medica Harvard Med. Sch., 1860-70; editor Boston Med. and Surg. Jour., 1860-64; cabinet keeper Mass. Hist. Soc., 1880-92; published A Selection of Ancient Psalm Melodies, Adapted to the Canticles of the Church in the United States of America, 1852, also an arrangement of De Profundis. Translator: (with W.W. Marland) Elements of General Pathology, (A.F. Chomel), 1848. Author: (paper) The Health of Boston, 1875; (paper) The Use and Abuse of Opium; A Sketch of the History of the Parish of the Advent in the City of Boston 1844-94, published 1894. Editor The Diaries of Benjamin Lynde and of Benjamin Lynde, Jr., 1880; (with P. O. Hutchinson.) The Diary and Letters of His Excellency Thomas Hutchinson, Esq. Died Dec. 8, 1892.

OLIVER, Henry Kemble, educator, state ofcl., musician; b. Beverly, Mass., Nov. 24, 1800; s. Rev. Daniel and Elizabeth (Kemble) O.; grad. Dartmouth, 1818, Mus. D. (hon.), 1883; A.B., A.M. (as of 1818), Harvard, 1862; m. Sarah Cook, Aug. 30, 1825, 7 children. Became 1st master Salem (Mass.) High Sch., 1827; founded and conducted acad. for boys, Salem, 1830-35; entered Salem Light Inf., 1821; lt. col. 6th Mass. Inf., 1832; adj. gen. Mass. Militia, 1844-48; capt. Ancient and Hon. Arty. of Boston, by 1846; supt. Atlantic Cotton Mills, 1848-58; treas. State of Mass., 1860-65; organist various chs., Salem, 1823-59; founder Salem Oratorio Soc.; attended Peace Jubilee, Boston, 1872; organizer, developer Mass. Bur. Statistics of Labor (1st of its kind in U.S.), 1870, 1st chief, 1870-73; mayor Salem, 1877-80. Author: Original Hymn Tunes, 1875. Died Salem, Aug. 12, 1885.

OLIVER, Peter, Loyalist; b. Boston, Mar. 26, 1713; s. Daniel and Elizabeth (Belcher) O.; grad. Harvard, 1730; D.C.L. (hon.), Oxford U.; m. Mary Clarke, July 5, 1733, 6 children. Judge, Inferior Ct. of Common Pleas, Plymouth County (Mass.), 1747-56; judge Superior Ct., 1756, chief justice, 1771-74 (grand juries of Worcester and Suffolk County refused to serve under him because of his acceptance of an independent salary from Brit. Crown, 1774); apptd. a mandamus councillor, 1774; a signer of address to Gen. Gage, 1775; left with Brit. forces for Halifax when they evacuated Boston, 1776; lived in Birmingham, Eng., until death. Author: The Scripture Lexicon, 1787. Died Birmingham, Oct. 1791.

OLIVER, William Morrison, congressman; b. Londonderry, N.H., Oct. 15, 1792; studied law, Penn Yan, N.Y. Admitted to N.Y. bar, began practice in Penn Yan; judge Ct. of Common Pleas for Yates County (N.Y.), 1823-28, 38-45; mem. N.Y. Senate, 1827-30; lt. gov. N.Y., 1830; mem. U.S. Ho. of Reps. (Democrat) from N.Y., 27th Congress, 1841-43; clk. N.Y. Supreme Ct., circa 1844; pres. Yates County Bank, until 1857. Died Penn Yan, July 21, 1863; buried Lake View Cemetery, Penn Yan.

OLMSTED, Denison, scientist, educator; b. nr. East Hartford, Conn., June 18, 1791; s. Nathaniel and Eunice (Kingsbury) O.; A.B., Yale, 1813, M.A., 1816; m. Eliza Allyn, 1818; m. 2d, Julia Mason, 1831; 7 children. Tchr. Union Sch., New London, Conn., 1813-15; apptd. tutor Yale, 1815; prof. chemistry U. N.C., 1817; apptd. state geologist and mineralogist N.C., 1822, made 1st survey of and reports on state's natural resources; prof. mathematics, natural philosophy Yale, 1825, prof. natural philosophy and astronomy, 1836-59. Author: Introduction to Natural Philosophy, 2 vols., 1831-32; Compendium of Natural Philosophy, 1833 (100 edit.); Introduction to Astronomy, 1839; A Compendium of Astronomy (for schs.), 1839; Letters on Astronomy Addressed to A Lady, 1840; Rudiments of Natural Philosophy and Astronomy, 1844 (also pub. in raised letters for the blind); also papers dealing with meteoric showers of Nov. 13, 1833, study of hailstorms; invented a gas process called gas light from cotton seed, patented, 1827, also a lubricant for machinery made from lard and rosin. Died New Haven, Conn., May 13, 1859.

OLMSTED, Gideon, naval officer; b. East Hartford, Conn., Feb. 12, 1749; s. Jonathan and Hannah (Meakins) O.; m. Mabel Roberts, 1777. Master sloop Seaflower, 1776-78; capt. French ship Polly, captured as privateer, taken prisoner, 1778; captured sloop Active with support of other Am. prisoners, sailed to America; served as privateer around N.Y. harbor, 1779-82; served as French privateer, 1793-95; mcht., East Hartford. Died East Hartford, Feb. 8, 1845.

OLNEY, Jesse, educator, state ofcl.; b. Union, Conn., Oct. 12, 1798; s. Eziekiel and Lydia (Brown) O.; m. Elizabeth Barnes, 1829, 6 children including Ellen Warner. Prin., Stone Sch., Hartford, Conn., 1821-33; became mem. Conn. Legislature from Southington, 1835, served 8 terms; comptroller pub. accounts State of Conn., 1867-68; supported movement which culminated in orgn. of Conn. Bd. Commrs. Pub. Schs., 1838. Author: A Practical System of Modern Geography, 1828; A New and Improved School Atlas, 1829; also other text-books for elementary students. Died Stratford, Conn., July 30, 1812.

OLYPHANT, David Washington Cincinnatus, mcht., philanthropist; b. Newport, R.I., Mar. 7, 1789; s. David and Ann (Vernon) O.; m. Mrs. Ann Archer; at least 1 son, Robert Morrison. Started career in counting room of cousin Samuel King, sr. partner of King & Talbot, N.Y.C., circa 1806; businessman in Balt., during War of 1812; asso. with George W. Talbot, 1817; with Thomas H. Smith, mchts. in China trade, 1818, agt., Canton, China, 1820-circa 1823; formed (with G.W. Talbot) Talbot, Olyphant & Co., N.Y.C., circa 1827; mem. Am. Bd. Commrs. for Fgn. Missions; mem. exec. com. Presbyn. Bd. Fgn. Missions; sent 1st Am. Protestant missionary to China, 1830; provided (with partners) free passage to China for many missionaries; underwrote Chinese Repository. Died Cairo, Egypt, June 10, 1851.

O'MAHONY, John, revolutionist; b. Mitchelstown, Ireland, 1816; son of Daniel O'Mahony; attended Trinity Coll., Dublin, Ireland. Mem. Young Ireland nat. revolutionary movement; took part in abortive insurrection, 1848, escaped to France; came to N.Y., 1853; an organizer Emmet Monument Assn. to turn Britain's difficulties in Crimean War into advantages for Ireland, 1854; founder and head of Fenians (Am. br. of Irish Revolutionary Brotherhood), 1858; raised and served as col. 99th Regt., N.Y. Nat. Guard, 1854; became pres. Fenian Brotherhood at Fenian Congress (which also adopted constn. for group), Phila., 1865; forced to resign after consenting to an abortive demonstration against Campobello Island, 1866; again leader of Fenians, 1872-77. Died Feb. 6, 1877; buried Glasnevin Cemetery, Dublin.

OMAR, dey of Algiers. Became dey after palace revolution, 1815; concluded peace treaty with U.S., 1815; refused to recognize terms of treaty, 1816; seized an Am. ship; forced by Stephen Decatur (who had arrived with an Am. naval force) to sign treaty ending Am. tribute and abolishing enslavement of Christians in Algiers (marked end of Barbary pirate trouble), 1817. Assassinated 1817.

OÑATE, Juan de, see de Oñate, Juan.

ONDERDONK, Benjamin Tredwell, clergyman; b. N.Y.C., July 15, 1791; s. Dr. John and Deborah (Ustick) O.; grad. Columbia Coll., 1809; m. Eliza Moscrop, 1813. Ordained deacon Protestant Episcopal Ch., St. Paul's Chapel, N.Y.C., 1812, priest, Trinity Ch., N.Y.C., 1813-30; sec. N.Y. Dioceson Conv., 1816-30; prof. eccles. history Gen. Theol. Sem., N.Y.C., also prof. nature, ministry and polity of ch., 1821-61; consecrated bishop N.Y. in St. John's Chapel, 1830; tried on charge of immorality and impurity (1st trial of bishop ever held under Canons of Episcopal Ch.), 1844, suspended from office of bishop and from all functions of sacred ministry; trustees of Gen. Theol. Sem. Did not remove him from professorship; various Gen. Convs. were petitioned in effort to remove suspension, but not acted upon by time of his death. Died N.Y.C., Apr. 30, 1861.

ONDERDONK, Henry, educator, historian; b. Manhasset, N.Y., June 11, 1804; s. Joseph and Dorothy (Monfoort) Onderdonck; grad. Columbia, 1827; m. Maria Hegeman Onderdonk, Nov. 28, 1828. Prin., Union Hall Acad., Jamaica, N.Y.; writings include: Documents and Letters Intended to Illustrate the Revolutionary Incidents of Queens County, 1846; Revolutionary Incidents of Suffolk and Kings Counties, 1849; The Bibliography of Long Island, 1866; History of the First Reformed Dutch Church of Jamaica, Long Island, 1884. Died June 22, 1886.

ONDERDONK, Henry Ustick, clergyman; b. N.Y.C., Mar. 16, 1789; s. Dr. John and Deborah (Ustick) O.; grad. Columbia, 1805, S.T.D. (hon.), 1827; M.D., U. Edinburgh (Scotland); m. Eliza Carter, Apr. 15, 1811. Asso. editor N.Y. Med. Mag., 1814-15; ordained priest Protestant Episcopal Ch. in Trinity Ch., N.Y.C., 1815; elected rector St. Ann's Ch., Bklyn., 1820; elected asst. bishop Pa.; became 2d bishop Pa., 1836, resigned jurisdiction after confessing habitual use intoxicating liquor, 1844, suspended by Ho. of Bishops from all offices of the ministry; restored to Active ministry by Ho. of Bishops, 1856; an outstanding theol. scholar of his day. Author: Episcopacy Listed by Scriptures, 1830; Episcopacy Examined and Re-examined, 1835; Sermons and Charges, 1851. Died Phila., Dec. 6, 1858.

O'NEAL, Edward Ashbury, gov. Ala., Confederate soldier; b. Madison County, Ala., Sept. 21, 1818; s. Edward and Rebecca (Wheat) O'N.; grad. La Grange Coll., 1836; m. Olivia Moore, Apr. 12, 1838; Admitted to Ala. bar, 1840; solicitor 4th dist. Ala., 1841-45; one of leaders of secession in Northern Ala.; commd. maj. 9th Ala. Inf., Confederate Army, 1861, lt. col., 1861; promoted to col., assigned to 26th Ala. Inf., 1862; fought in battles of Chancellorsville and Gettysburg; acted as brig.-gen., 1864-65; leader Democratic party in N. Ala. during reconstruction period; mem. Ala. Constl. Conv., 1875; gov. Ala., 1882-86, responsible for ednl. and prison reform, establishing normal schs., bd. convict insps. Died Nov. 7, 1890; Florence, Ala.

O'NEALE, Margaret (Peggy), wife U.S. Sec. of War Eaton; b. Washinton, D.C., 1796; d. William and Rhoda (Howell) O'Neale; ed. Mrs. Hayward's Sem., Washington; m. John B. Timberlake (dec. 1828), 1 son, 2 daus.; m. 2d, John H. Eaton, Jan. 1, 1829; m. 3d, Antonio Buchignani circa 1857. Wife of John H. Eaton (apptd. U.S. sec. of war 1829), socially rejected by other cabinet members' wives, forcing (despite Pres. Jackson's intervention) Eaton's resignation, 1831; accompanied Eaton when apptd. gov. Fla., 1834, also when apptd. minister to Spain, Madrid, 1836-40; lost fortune at hands of 3d husband, early 1860's. Died in poverty, Washington, Nov. 8, 1879.

O'NEALL, John Belton, jurist; b. Bush River, Newberry Dist., S.C., Apr. 10, 1793; s. Hugh and Anne (Kelly) O'N.; grad. S.C. Coll., 1812; m. Helen Pope, June 25, 1818. Admitted to bar, 1814; entered S.C. Militia, rose to maj. gen. by 1825; became mem. in S.C. Legislature from Newberry Dist., 1816, speaker of ho., 1822-28; elected S.C. circuit judge, 1828; mem. S.C. Ct. Appeals, 1830-35; mem. S.C. Ct. Law Appeals, circa 1835-03; pres. Ct. Law Appeals and Ct. of Errors, 1850; chief justice S.C., 1859; pres. S.C. Temperance Soc., 1841; became mem. Sons of Temperance, 1849, state pres., 1850, nat. pres., 1852; wrote column Drunkard's Looking Glass in S.C. Temperance Advocate; pres. Columbia and Greenville R.R.; pres. Newberry Agrl. Soc.; trustee S.C. Coll., 40 years; pres. Newberry Baptist Bible Soc. Author: The Negro Law of South Carolina, 1848; Annals of Newberry, 1858; The Biographical Sketches of the Bench and Bar of South Carolina, 2 vols., 1859. Died "Springfield," Newberry, Dec. 27, 1863.

O'NEILL, Charles, congressman; b. Phila., Mar. 21, 1821; grad. Dickinson Coll., Carlisle, Pa., 1840; studied law. Admitted to Pa. bar, 1843, began practice in Phila.; mem. Pa. Ho. of Reps., 1850-52, 60, Pa. Senate, 1853; mem. U.S. Ho. of Reps. (Republican) from Pa., 38th-41st, 43d-53d congresses, 1863-71, 73-93. Died Phila., Nov. 25, 1893; buried West Laurel Hill Cemetery, Montgomery County, Pa.

O'NEILL, John, army officer; b. Drumgallon, parish of Contibret, County Monaghan, Ireland, Mar. 8, 1834; m. Mary Crow, 1864. Came to Am., 1848; served with 2d U.S. Dragoons in Mormon War, 1857; served wtih 1st Cav. in Cal., became sgt. by 1861; commd. 2d lt. 5th Ind. Cav., U.S. Army, 1862, 1st lt., 1863, resigned, 1864, apptd. capt. 17th U.S. Colored Inf.; a Fenian organizer in his dist., led detachment from Nashville to attack Can., 1866, led raid from Buffalo into Can., occupied Canadian village Ft. Erie, 1866; apptd. insp. gen. Irish Republican Army in U.S., late 1866; attempted another raid on Can., 1870, arrested and jailed, made another attack on Can., 1871, seized Hudson's Bay post, Pembina; agt. for land speculators desiring Irish settlers for tract of land in Holt County, Neb., in 1870's. Died Omaha, Neb., Jan. 7, 1878.

OPDYKE, George, mcht., mayor N.Y.C.; b. Kingwood Twp., Hunterdon County, N.J., Dec. 7, 1805; s. George and Mary (Stout) O.; m. Elizabeth Hall Stryker, Sept. 26, 1829, 6 children. Established clothing factory, N.Y.C., 1832, became retailer dealing principally in rough clothing for plantation hands, later opened branch stores, Memphis, Tenn. and Charleston, S.C.; owner import and wholesale dry goods bus., 1846-96; del. Free-Soil Party Conv., Buffalo, N.Y., 1848; a millionaire, by 1853; became Republican, 1854; mem. N.Y. Assembly, 1859; del. Rep. Nat. Conv., 1860; manufactured uniforms and arms for U.S. Govt., 1861-65; mayor N.Y.C., 1862-63, proposed many reforms, restored order during draft riots of July 1863 without compromising with rioters; mem. N.Y. Constl. Conv., 1867-68; mem. N.Y. Constl. Commn., 1872-73. Author: Treatise on Political Economy, 1851; Report on the Currency, 1858. Died N.Y.C., June 12, 1880.

OPTIC, Oliver, see Adams, William Taylor.

ORCUTT, Hiram, educator; b. Acworth, N.H., Feb. 3, 1815; s. John and Hannah (Currier) O.; grad. Dartmouth, 1842; m. Sarah Cummings, Aug. 15, 1842; m. 2d, Ellen Dana, Apr. 8, 1865; at least 1 son, William. Prin., Hebron Acad., N.H., 1842, Thetford Acad., Vt., 1843-55, Ladies Sem., North Granville, N.Y., 1855-60; supt. Brattleboro (Vt.) and Lebanon (N.H.) schs., 1860-66; ed. Vt. Sch. Jour., 1861-65; mem. N.H. Gen. Ct., 1870-72; sec. bd. trustees Vt. State Normal Sch., 1870-76; mgr. New Eng. Bur. Edn., 1875-98. Author: Methods of School Discipline, 1871. Died Apr. 17, 1899.

ORD, Edward Otho Cresap, army officer; b. Cumberland, Md., Oct. 18, 1818; s. James Ord; grad. U.S. Mil. Acad., 1839; m. Mary Mercer Thompson, Oct. 14, 1854, 3 children. Commd. 1st lt. U.S. Army, circa 1840, served in Seminole War; sent in ship Lexington from N.Y., around Cape Horn to Cal., 1847; capt., 1850; served in expdn. suppressing John Brown's raid at Harper's Ferry, 1859; promoted brig. gen. U.S. Volunteers, 1861, commanded brigade defending Washington, D.C., 1861-62; leader attack against Confederate Army under Gen. J.E.B. Stuart, Dranesville, Va., 1861; brevetted lt. col. U.S. Army; maj. gen. U.S. Volunteers, 1862; commanded left wing Army of Tenn., Aug.-Sept., 1862, brevetted col. U.S. Army, 1862; commanded 13th Corps, Army of Tenn. in Vicksburg campaign, June-Oct. 1863; served in capture of Jackson, Miss., 1863; served with Gen. George Crook, 1864, directed campaign against Staunton, Va.; in command 8th Army Corps, 1864, later of 18th Army Corps, in operations before Richmond; assumed command Army of the James and Dept. N.C., 1865; brevetted maj. gen. U.S. Army, 1865; maj. gen. on ret. list, 1881. Died Havana, Cuba, July 22, 1883; buried Arlington (Va.) Nat. Cemetery.

ORD, George, naturalist, philologist; b. Phila., Mar. 4, 1781; s. George and Rebecca (Lindemeyer) O.; m. 1815, 2 children including Joseph Benjamin. Employed in father's ship chandler and rope making business, 1806-29; completed book by friend Alexander Wilson, American Ornithology or, the Natural History of Birds of the United States, 9 vols., 1808-14, edited vol. 8, wrote entire text vol. 9, published another edit. of work with much additional material, 1824-25; attempted (with Charles Waterton) to discredit Audubon, circa 1824; accompanied Thomas Say, Titian Peale and William Maclure on extensive field trip to Ga. and Fla., 1818; prepared memoirs of Say and C.A. Lesueur; prepared anonymous account of zoology of N. Am. for 2d Am. edit. New Geographical and Commercial Grammar (William Guthrie), 1815; disposed of manuscripts on philology to Latham of London who used them in compilation new edit. Johnson's Dictionary, circa 1860; mem. Am. Philos. Soc.; pres. Phila. Acad. Scis., 1851-58; contbd. personal library to Coll. Physicians Phila., $16,000 to Pa. Hosp. Died Phila., Jan. 24. 1866.

ORDWAY, John, explorer; b. Bow, N.H., 1775; s. John and Hannah (Morse) O.; married. Enlisted in U.S. Army, circa 1800; sgt. in Capt. Russell Bissell's Co., 1st Inf., Kaskaskia, Ill., 1803 with Lewis and Clark expdn., 1803-06, apptd. to keep the rosters and orderly books, frequently in charge of the detachment during absence of Lewis and Clark (his jour. covering period July 13-19, 1806 is sole record of that portion of expdn.); established plantation in New Madrid Dist., Mo., 1807. Died New Madrid Dist., 1817.

O'REGAN, Anthony, clergyman; b. Lavalleyroe, Mayo, Ireland, 1809; studied at Maynooth. Ordained priest Roman Catholic Ch., 1834; taught theology and scripture St. Jarlath's Coll., Tuam, became pres. coll., 1844; came to U.S., 1849; became head of sem., St. Louis, 1849; consecrated bishop of Chgo., 1854, after many difficulties with clergy of the see, resigned 1858; apptd. titular bishop of Dora, 1858. Died London, Eng., Nov. 13, 1866.

O'REILLY, Alexander, army officcer; b. Baltrasna, County Meath, Ireland, 1722; s. Thomas Reilly; m. Rosa de las Casas, at least 2 children. Became cadet Hibernia regt. Spanish Army, 1732; leader in Spanish Army reform; maj. gen., 1763, lt. gen., 1767, sent to take formal possession province of La., punish rebels and assimilate govt. to that of other Spanish dominions in Am., 1768-69; insp. gen., inf., 1770, in charge sch. for officers; given title Count, 1771; mil. gov. Madrid (Spain), circa 1773; leader unsuccessful expdn. against Algiers, 1775; participant in intrigues against Jose conde de Floridablanca, which later led to banishment to Province of Galicia; recalled to take command army in Catalonia, 1794. Died Bonete, nr. Chincilla, Murcia, Spain, Mar. 23, 1794.

O'REILLY, Bernard, clergyman; b. Cunnareen, Longford, Ireland, 1803; came to U.S., 1825; studied at Grand Sem., Montreal, Can., also St. Mary's, Balt. Ordained priest Roman Catholic Ch., Phila., 1831; clergyman in Bklyn., 1831, Rochester, N.Y., 1832-47; apptd. vicar gen. of Rochester, also rector of diocesan sem., 1847; apptd. titular bishop of Pompeiopolis, coadjutor of Hartford (Conn.), 1850, bishop, 1852; founder St. Mary's Sem., Providence, R.I., 1851. Died at sea, Jan. 23, 1856.

O'REILLY, Henry, editor, telegraph pioneer; b. Carrickmacross, Province of Ulster, Ireland, Feb. 6, 1806; s. Alicia (Ledbetter) O'Reilly; m. Marcia Brooks, 1 son, Henry Brook. Came (with family) to U.S., 1816, settled in N.Y.; asst. editor N.Y. Patriot, (organ of People's Party), 1823; editor Rochester (N.Y.) Daily Advertiser, 1826; became chief polit. opponent of Thurlow Weed, 1826-27; began agitation for rebuilding and enlargement of Erie canal, 1833; entered into contract with S.F.B. Morse and Amos Kendall to raise capital for constrn. of telegraph lines from Eastern Pa. to St. Louis and Great Lakes, 1845, erected about 8,000 miles of line but broke terms of contract; gave his collection of hist. manuscripts to N.Y. Hist. Soc., 1859. Author: Sketches of Rochester, with Incidental Notices of Western New York, 1838. Died Aug. 17, 1886.

O'REILLY, John Boyle, poet, editor; b. Castle Dowth, nr. Drogheda, Ireland, June 28, 1844; s. William David and Eliza (Boyle) O'R.; LL.D. (hon.), U. Notre Dame, 1881, Georgetown U., 1889; m. Mary Murphy, Aug. 15, 1872. Enlisted in 10th Husars, Brit. Army, 1863; joined Fenian Order, tried and court martialed, 1866, sentenced to death as conspirator to levy war against the Queen, sentence commuted to 20 years penal servitude; one of 63 polit. prisoners deported to Australia (1st company sent there since uprising of 1848), arrived 1868; escaped, came to Phila., 1869; employed by Boston Pilot (most influential Irish-Am. paper), 1869, covered Fenian Raid into Can. from St. Albans (Vt.) as war correspondent, 1870, became co-owner (with Catholic archbishop of Boston), 1876, editor, 1876-90; became ardent advocate of Irish Home Rule; Irish leader in New Eng.; lectured throughout country; 1st rec. sec. Catholic Union of Boston, 1873. Author: Songs from Southern Seas, 1873; Songs, Legends and Ballads, 1878; The Statues in the Block, 1881; In Bohemia, 1886; Moondyne; Athletics and Manly Sport. Died Hull, Mass., Aug. 10, 1890.

ORMSBY, Stephen, congressman; b. County Sligo, Ireland, 1759; studied law. Came to U.S., settled in Phila.; admitted to the bar, 1786; began practice of law, Danville, Ky.; dep. atty. gen. Jefferson County (Ky.), 1787; served in Indian wars as brig. gen. under Gen. Josiah Harmar in campaign of 1790; judge Jefferson County Dist. Ct., 1791; presdl. elector, 1796; judge circuit ct., 1802-10; mem. U.S. Ho. of Reps. (Democrat) from Ky., 12th, 13th-14th congresses, 1811-13, Apr. 20, 1813-17; 1st pres. Louisville (Ky.) br. U.S. Bank, 1817. Died nr. Louisville, 1844; buried Ormsby Burial Ground, Lyndon, Ky.

ORMSBY, Waterman Lilly, engraver; b. Hampton, Conn., 1809; studied Nat. Acad. Design, N.Y.C., 1829. Settled in N.Y., became propr. N.Y. Note Co.; a founder Continental Bank Note Co.; inventor engraving machinery including ruling machines, transfer presses and grammagraph; designer bank notes which were widely used by govt. by 1861. Author several pamphlets including Cycloidal Configurations, or the Harvest of Counterfeiters; A Description of the Present System of Bank Note Engraving, 1852. Died Bklyn., Nov. 1, 1883.

ORR, Alexander Dalrymple, congressman; b. Alexandria, Va., Nov. 6, 1761; attended local schs. Moved to Bourbon County, Ky. (then part of Va.), circa 1782, later to a plantation nr. Maysville, Ky.; engaged in farming; mem. Va. Ho. of Dels., 1790; Va. Senate, 1792; mem. U.S. Ho. of Reps. from Ky., 2d-4th congresses, Nov. 8, 1792-97. Died Paris, Ky., June 21, 1835; buried Paris Cemetery.

ORR, Benjamin, congressman; b. Bedford, N.H., Dec. 1, 1772; grad. Dartmouth, 1798; studied law. Apprenticed as carpenter; taught sch., Concord and New Milford, N.H.; admitted to the bar, 1801; began practice of law, Brunswick, Mass. (now Me.); moved to Topsham, Mass. (now Me.), 1801, practiced law; overseer Bowdoin Coll., Brunswick, trustee, 1814-28, treas., 1815-16; mem. U.S. Ho. of Reps. (Federalist) from Mass., 15th Congress, 1817-19; resumed practice of law, Topsham; returned to Brunswick, 1822, practiced law. Died Brunswick, Sept. 3, 1828; buried Pine Grove Cemetery, Brunswick.

ORR, Gustavus John, educator; b. Orrville, Anderson County, S.C., Aug. 9, 1819; s. James and Anne (Anderson) O.; grad. Emory Coll., Oxford, Ga., 1844; m. Eliza Caroline Anderson, 1847, 10 children. Prof. mathematics Emory Coll., 1848-58; apptd. Ga. commr. to settle boundary dispute with Fla., 1859; pres. So. Masonic Female Coll., Covington, Ga., 1867-70; prof. mathematics Oglethorpe Coll., Atlanta, Ga., 1870; Ga. sch. commr., 1872-87; v.p. N.E.A., 1881, pres., 1882; agt. Peabody Fund in Ga. Died Atlanta, Dec. 11, 1887.

ORR, Hugh, inventor, firearms mfr.; b. Lochwinnoch, Renfrewshire, Scotland, Jan. 2, 1715; s. Robert Orr; m. Mary Bass, Aug. 4, 1742, 10 children including Robert. Came to America, 1740; employed by a scythe-maker, East Bridgewater, Mass., 1741, became owner of shop, circa 1745; inventor trip-hammer (said to have been 1st in colonies); became mfr. firearms, made 500 muskets (believed to be 1st made in colonies), 1748; inventor machine to clean flaxseed, 1753; began producing muskets again, 1775, built foundry for casting cannon, Bridgewater, Mass.; built machines for carding and roping wool in own shop with mechanic from Scotland, 1785-87; mem. Mass. Senate, 1786, obtained state grants for encouragement of textile industry; brought various European mechanics to U.S., also introduced new types of machinery. Died Bridgewater, Dec. 6, 1798.

ORR, James Lawrence, diplomat, congressman; b. Craytonville, S.C., May 12, 1822; s. Christopher and Martha (McCann) O.; grad. U. Va., 1842; m. Mary Jane Marshall, 1844. Admitted to S.C. bar, 1842; mem. S.C. Ho. of Reps., 1844-48; mem. U.S. Ho. of Reps. from S.C., 31st-35th congresses, 1849-59, speaker, 1858-59; mem. So. Rights Conv., Charleston, S.C., 1851; mem. Democratic Nav. Conv., 1860; mem. Secession Conv., 1860; one of 3 reps. sent to Washington (D.C.) to ask for surrender of Union forts in Charleston Harbor, S.C., 1860; mem. Confederate Congress, 1861; served with Confederate Army during Civil War; spl. commr. to Pres. Andrew Johnson to negotiate a provisional gvt. for S.C., 1865; mem. S.C. Constl. Conv., 1865; gov. S.C., 1866-68; pres. S.C. Conv., 1866; del. Union Nat. Conv., Phila., 1866; judge 8th S.C. Jud. Circuit, 1868-70; mem. S.C. Republican Conv., 1872, del. Rep. Nat. Conv., Phila., 1872; U.S. minister to Russia (apptd. by Pres. Grant), 1872-73. Died St. Petersburg, Russia, May 5, 1873; buried Presbyn. Cemetery, Anderson, S.C.

ORR, John William, engraver; b. Ireland, Mar. 31, 1815; studied with William Redfield, N.Y.C., 1836. Established himself as wood engraver, Buffalo, N.Y., 1837; moved to Albany, N.Y., 1842; settled in N.Y.C., 1844; in bus. with his brother as J. W. & N. Orr, N.Y.C., 1844-46, illustrated books and mags., had one of largest engraving plants in N.Y.C.; editor and publisher American Odd Fellow, 1862-71. Died Jersey City, N.J., Mar. 4, 1887.

ORR, Robert, businessman; b. Derry County, Ireland, Jan. 20, 1814. Came to U.S., 1831, entered dry goods bus., Phila.; employed by G. R. White, Pitts., 1834-41; head of straw millinery firm John Orr & Co., 1841-61; mem. firm White, Orr & Co., 1861-73; dir. Citizen's Bank of Pitts.; mem. Prison Reform Assn. Died Aug. 2, 1873.

ORR, Robert, Jr., congressman; b. nr. Hannastown, Pa., Mar. 5, 1786; s. Robert Orr. Attended pub. schs. Dep. sheriff Armstrong County (Pa.), 1805; apptd. dep. dist. surveyor; served to col. during War of 1812; mem. Pa. Ho. of Reps., 1817-20, Pa. Senate, 1821-26; mem. U.S. Ho. of Reps. (Democrat) from Pa., 18th-20th congresses, Oct. 11, 1825-29; rose to rank of gen.; became holder of extensive lands. Died Kittanning, Pa., May 22, 1876; buried Kittanning Cemetery.

ORTH, Godlove Stein, congressman; b. Lebanon, Pa., Apr. 22, 1817; attended Pa. Coll., Gettysburg; studied law under James Cooper in Pa.; m. Sarah Elizabeth Miller, Oct. 1840; m. 2d, Mary A. Ayres, Aug. 28, 1850. Moved to Lafayette, Ind., 1839; admitted to Ind. bar, 1839; mem. Ind. Senate, 1843-48, pres., 1845; presdl. elector for Taylor, 1848; joined Know-Nothing Party, 1850, pres. Ind. Know-Nothing Party, 1854-55; an organizer Republican Party in Ind.; mem. Washington (D.C.) Peace Conf., 1861; mem. U.S. Ho. of Reps. from Ind., 38th-41st, 43d, 46th-47th congresses, 1862-70, 73-75, 79-82; favored strong war policy during Civil War and strong reconstrn. measures; framed Orth Bill which made changes in diplomatic and consular services, 1868; minister to Austria-Hungary, 1875-76. Died Lafayette, Dec. 16, 1882; buried Springvale Cemetery, Lafayette.

ORTHWEIN, Charles F., grain mcht.; b. nr. Stuttgart, Wurttemberg, Germany, Jan. 28, 1839; s. Charles C. Orthwein; m. Caroline Nulsen, 1866, 9 children. Came to U.S., 1854; with Eggers & Co., wholesale grocery and commn. house, St. Louis, circa 1860; became partner in grain commn. firm Haenschen & Orthwein, circa 1862 (warehouse became base of supplies for Union Army during Civil War), eventually made St. Louis dominant grain center of Mississippi Valley; sent 1st grain shipment to Europe by way of Mississippi River, 1866; instrumental in putting petition before U.S. Congress for river and harbor improvements; owned grain elevators and mills, St. Louis, Kansas City, other Am. and European cities; pres. So. Electric Ry. Co., Mchts. Exchange; dir. German Savs. Bank of St. Louis. Died St. Louis, Dec. 28, 1898.

ORTON, Harlow South, jurist; b. Madison County, N.Y., Nov. 23, 1817; s. Harlow N. and Grace (Marsh) O.; attended Madison U. (now Colgate U.), 1835-37; LL.D. (hon.) U. Wis., 1869; m. Elizabeth Cheney, July 5, 1839. Admitted to Ind. bar, 1838; independent Democrat after 1854; apptd. probate judge Porter County by gov. Ind., 1843; pvt. sec. to gov. of Wis., Leonard G. Farwell, 1853; mem. Wis. Assembly, 1854-71; retained as consul in case of atty. gen. ex rel. Bashford vs. Bastow, 1855; retained in so-called Granger case, atty. gen. vs. Railroad Cos.; judge 9th Wis. Jud. Circuit, 1859-65; elected mem. Wis. Legislature, 1869, 71; mem. com. which compiled Revised Statutes of State of Wis., 1878; dean law sch. U. Wis., 1869-74; elected justice Wis. Supreme Ct., 1878, chief justice, 1894-95. Died Madison, Wis., July 4, 1895.

ORTON, James, educator, explorer; b. Seneca Falls, N.Y., Apr. 21, 1830; s. Rev. Azariah Giles and Minerva (Squire) O.; grad. Williams Coll., 1855, Andover Theol. Sem., 1858; m. Ellen Foote, 1859. Ordained to ministry Presbyn. Ch., 1860; instr. natural history U. Rochester N.Y., 1866; prof. natural history Vassar Coll., 1869-77; explored on 3 expdns. to S. Am., explored Equatorial Andes and Amazon regions, 1867, 73, 76 (collections of 3d expdn. taken over by Peruvian govt.). Author: The Miner's Guide and Metallurgist's Directory, 1849; Comparative Zoology, Structural and Systematic, 1876; Underground Treasures, How and Where to Find Them, 1872; The Liberal Education of Women, the Demand and the Method, 1873. Died Lake Titacaca, Peru, Sept. 25, 1877; buried by the lake.

ORTON, William, telegraph exec.; b. Cuba, Allegheny County, N.Y., June 14, 1826; s. Horatio Woodruff and Sarah (Carson) O.; grad. Albany (N.Y.) Normal Sch., 1846; m. Agnes Johnston Gillespie, 1850, 8 children. Became partner publishing firm Derby, Orton & Mulligan, Buffalo, N.Y., 1852; moved to N.Y.C., 1856; became mem. N.Y. Common Council, 1861, leader Republican minority; admitted to N.Y. bar, 1867; apptd. collector internal revenue N.Y. by Pres. Lincoln, 1862; apptd. commr. internal revenue Washington, D.C. by Pres. Johnson, 1865; became pres. U.S. Telegraph Co., 1865 (merged with Western Union, 1866), v.p. Western Union Telegraph Co., then pres., 1867 (after merger Am. Telegraph Co. into Western Uinon, 1866) suspended dividends, encouraged invention, stimulated scientific standards in telegraph engring.; opponent of govt. ownership, operation or legislation for telegraph cos. Died N.Y.C., Apr. 22, 1878.

OSBORN, Charles, abolitionist; b. Guilford County, N.C., Aug. 21, 1775; s. David and Margaret (Stout) O.; m. Sarah Newman, Jan. 11, 1798; m. 2d, Hannah Swain, Sept. 26, 1813; 19 children. Became Quaker preacher, circa 1794; active minister, preached in numerous meetings throughout U.S., Can., Gt. Britain; founder Tenn. Manumission Soc., 1814-15, founder similar socs., Guilford County, N.C., 1816; published The Philanthropist (paper partially devoted to anti-slavery agitation, denounced Am. Soc. Colonizing Free People of Colour of U.S.), Mt. Pleasant, O., 1817-18; founder Free Produce Assn. of Wayne County (Ind.), Free Labor Advocate and Anti-Slavery Chronicle (propagandist newspaper); participated in formation Ind. Yearly Meeting of Anti-Slavery Friends, 1843. Died Porter County, Ind., Dec. 29, 1850.

OSBORN, Henry Stafford, clergyman; b. Phila., Aug. 17, 1823; s. Rev. Truman and Eliza (Paget) O.; grad. U. Pa., 1841, Union Theol. Sem., 1845; m. Pauline Courson, 1860, 1 child. Ordained to ministry Presbyn. Ch., 1848; pastor in Richmond, Va., 1849-53, Liberty, Va., 1853-58, Belvidere, N.J., 1859-65; prof. chemistry Lafayette Coll., 1866-70; prof. natural scis. Miami U., Oxford, O., 1870-73, practiced in ministry, lectr., wrote on sciences, Oxford, 1873-94. Author: Palestine Past and Present, 1859; Metallurgy, Iron and Steel, 1869; New Descriptive Geography of Palestine, 1877. Died Feb. 2, 1894.

OSBORN, Laughton, poet, dramatist; b. N.Y.C. circa 1809; grad. Columbia, 1827. Traveled in Europe, 1827-28; author: Sixty Years of the Life of Jeremy Levis, 1831; The Dream of Alla-Ad-Deen, 1835; The Confessions of a Poet, 1835; A Handbook of Young Artists and Amateurs in Oil Painting, 1845; tragedies and comedies The Heart's Sacrifice, Matilda of Denmark, Bianco Capello, A Tragedy of Jewish History. Died N.Y.C., Dec. 13, 1878.

OSBORN, Selleck, journalist; b. Trumbull, Conn., circa 1782; s. Nathaniel Osborn; m. Mary Hammond, 1810, 2 children. Apprenticed to printer at early age; editor Suffolk County Herald, Sag Harbor, N.Y., 1802-03, The Witness, Litchfield, Conn., 1805-08; supported Pres. Jefferson against Federalists at Litchfield, sued for libel by Federalist Justice Julius Deming, convicted, spent several months in jail; volunteered for U.S. Army, 1808, promoted capt., 1811; served in War of 1812 in 1st regt. of cavalry troops, discharged 1814; owner, editor American Watchman, Wilmington, Del., 1817-20; editor New York Patriot, 1823-24, supported John C. Calhoun for president; lived in Phila., 1824-26. Died Phila., Oct. 1826.

OSBORN, Thomas Andrew, gov. Kan., diplomat; b. Meadville, Pa., Oct. 26, 1836; s. Carpenter and Elizabeth (Morris) O.; m. Julia Delahay, 1870, 1 child. Admitted to bar, Pontiac, Mich., 1857; compositor, acting editor Kan. Herald of Freedom, Lawrence; mem. Kan. State Legislature, 1859-62, 88-90. Republican, Free-Stater; pres. pro tem, Kan. Senate, 1862; lt. gov. Kan., 1862; U.S marshal Kan., 1864-67; gov. Kan., 1873-77, under his adminstrn. efficient relief measures taken during Grasshopper Year 1874, Kan. settlement progressed rapidly, many new counties organized; U.S. minister to Chile, 1877, to Brazil, 1881; dir. A. T. & S.F. Ry., 1894-98. Decorated Grand Cross of Order of Rose (Brazil). Died Meadville, Feb. 4, 1898.

OSBORN, William Henry, railroad exec.; philanthropist; b. Salem, Mass., Dec. 21, 1820; s. William and Anna Henfield (Bowditch) O.; m. Virginia Reed Sturges, Dec. 14, 1853, 4 children. Entered East India House of Peale, Hubbell & Co., Boston, 1833, co. rep., Manila, P.I., 1836-53; pres. Ill. Central R.R., 1855-65, dir., 1854-76; pres. Chgo., St. Louis & New Orleans R.R., 1877-82; ret. from bus., 1882, supported many philanthropic activities. Died N.Y.C., Mar. 2, 1894.

OSBORNE, John, physician; b. Sandwich, Mass., 1713; s. Samuel Osborne; grad. Harvard, 1735; studied for ministry, 1735-37; m. Miss Doane, 1738, 6 children. Failed to receive ordination to ministry Congregatonal Ch., 1737; then prepared for medical career, began practice medicine, Middletown, Conn., circa 1739; wrote poetry dealing mainly with maritime themes. Best known poems include: A Whaling Song; An Elegiac Epistle on the Death of a Sister. Died Middletown, May 31, 1753; buried Middletown.

OSBORNE, Thomas Burr, congressman; b. Weston (now Easton), Conn., July 8, 1798; grad. Yale, 1817; studied law. Admitted to Conn. bar, 1820, began practice in Fairfield; clk. county and superior cts., 1826-39; mem. Conn. Ho. of Reps., 1836, 50; mem. U.S. Ho. of Reps. (Whig) from Conn, 26th-27th congresses, 1839-43; mem. Conn. Senate, 1844; apptd. judge Fairfield County (Conn.) Ct., 1844; judge of probate for Fairfield Dist., 1851; moved to New Haven, Conn., 1854; prof. Yale Law Sch., 1855-65. Died New Haven, Sept. 2, 1869; buried Evergreen Cemetery, New Haven.

OSCEOLA (known as Powell), Indian chief; b. nr. Tallapoosa River, Ga., circa 1800. Fought against Andrew Jackson in War of 1812, also in 1818; opponent of Treaty of 1832 at Payne's Landing, rejected Treaty of 1833 at Ft. Gibson, again rejected Payne's Landing treaty at meeting of chiefs called by Wiley Thompson, 1835; arrested and imprisoned, 1835; gathered opposition forces, murdered Wiley Thompson and Charley Emalthla, precipitating 2d Seminole War; led warriors to harass U.S. army after hiding women and children in swamps; seized on order of Gen. Thomas S. Jesup when he came for interview, 1837, taken to Ft. Marion at St. Augustine, Fla., later removed to Ft. Moultrie, Charleston, S.C. Died Ft. Moultrie, Jan. 30, 1838.

OSGOOD, Frances Sargent Locke (pen name: Carol, Kate), poet; b. Boston, June 18, 1811; d. Joseph and Mary (Ingersoll) Locke; m. Samuel Stillman Osgood, Oct. 7, 1835; children—Ellen Frances, May Vincent, Fanny Fay. Contbr. (under pseudonym Florence) to Juvenile Miscellany, edited by Mrs. Child; friend of Edgar Allan Poe, a cause of quarrels leading to Poe's libel suit against Thomas Dunn English. Published works include: The Casket of Fate (miniature vol.); A Wreath of Wild Flowers from New England (vol. poetry); The Poetry of Flowers and the Flowers of Poetry, 1841; Puss in Boots, 1844; Poems, 1846. Died N.Y.C., May 12, 1850; buried Mt. Auburn Cemetery, Cambridge, Mass.

OSGOOD, Gayton Pickman, congressman; b. Salem, Mass., July 4, 1797; grad. Harvard, 1815; studied law. Admitted to Mass. bar, began practice in Salem; moved to North Andover, Mass., 1819; mem. Mass. Ho. of Reps., 1829-31; mem. U.S. Ho. of Reps. (Democrat) from Mass., 23d Congress, 1833-35; engaged in farming. Died Andover, Mass., June 26, 1861; buried Old North Parish Burying Ground, North Andover.

OSGOOD, Jacob, founder religious sect; b. South Hampton, N.H., Mar. 16, 1777; s. Philip and Mehitable (Flanders) O.; m. Miriam Stevens, 1797, 8 children. Converted to Christianity (to no particular sect), 1802; preached in N.H. area, 1805-12; started sect called Osgoodites, 1812, held that anything established by law was from devil, alleged to have caused numerous miracles through his prayers. Died Nov. 29, 1844.

OSGOOD, Samuel, Continental congressman; b. Andover, Mass., Feb. 3, 1748; s. Capt. Peter and Sarah (Johnson) O.; grad. Harvard, 1770; m. Martha Brandon, Jan. 4, 1775; m. 2d, Maria Bowne Franklin, May 26, 1786. Mem. Essex Conv. (opposed to more radical element of Am. Revolution), 1774; served as maj., later col. as aide-de-camp to Gen. Artemas Ward, Continental Army, 1775; became mem. Mass. Provincial Congress, 1775; del. Mass. Constl. Conv., 1779, del. to conv. for the limitation of prices, Phila., 1780; mem. Continental Congress, 1780-84; apptd. a dir. Bank of N. Am., 1781; largely responsible for commissioning of U.S. Treasury, 1784, 1st commr. U.S. Treasury, 1785-89; postmaster-gen. U.S. under Pres. Washington, 1789-91; speaker N.Y. Assembly, 1800; supt. internal revenue for Dist. of N.Y., 1801-02; naval officer Port of N.Y., 1803-13; organizer and incorporator Soc. for Establishment of Free School for Edn. of Poor Children; a founder Am. Acad. Fine Arts. Died N.Y.C., Aug. 12, 1813; buried Brick Presbyn. Ch., N.Y.C.

OSGOOD, Samuel Stillman, artist; b. June 9, 1808; studied painting, Boston; m. Frances S. Locke, 1835 (dec. 1851); married a 2d time. Went to Europe; returned to Am., 1839; settled in N.Y.C.; made trips to Europe and New Orleans after 1st wife's death; moved to Cal., after 1869; asso. mem. N.A.D.; exhibited frequently in N.Y.C., Boston, Phila. Died Cal., 1885.

OSTENACO, see Outacity.

O'SULLIVAN, Jeremiah, clergyman; b. Kanturck, Cork, Ireland, Feb. 6, 1842; came to U.S., 1863; attended St. Charles Coll., St. Mary's Sem. (Md.). Ordained priest Roman Catholic Ch., Balt., 1868; consecrated bishop of Mobile (Ala.), 1885. Died Mobile, Aug. 10, 1896.

O'SULLIVAN, John Louis, editor, diplomat; b. Harbor of Gibraltar, Nov. 1813; s. John O'Sullivan; A.B., Columbia, 1831, A.M., 1834; m. a dau. of Dr. Kearney Rodgers, 1846. A backer of Narciso Lopez in filibustering expdns. against Cuba, 1849-51, twice indicted for violating neutrality laws; founder (with S.D. Langtree) U.S. Mag. and Democratic Review, mouthpiece for period's nationalism (phrase "manifest destiny" was 1st used in article in this mag., 1845), 1837-46; a founder N.Y. Morning News, 1844, editor, 1844-46; mem. N.Y. Legislature, 1841; bd. regents U. State N.Y., 1846-54; charge d'affaires in Portugal, 1854, U.S. minister resident, 1854-58; Confederate sympathizer, lived abroad during Civil War. Died N.Y.C., Feb. 24, 1895.

OTERMÉN, Antonio de. see de Otermén, Antonio.

OTERO, Miguel Antonio, congressman; b. Valencia, N.M., June 21, 1829; attended St. Louis U.; grad. Pingree's Coll., Fishkill, N.Y.; studied law. Admitted to N.M. bar, 1851, began practice in Albuquerque; declined appointment by Pres. Pierce as U.S. dist. atty.; mem. N.M. Territorial Ho. of Reps., 1852-54; atty. gen. Territory of N.M., 1854; del. U.S. Congress (Democrat) from Territory of N.M., 1856-61; del. Dem. Nat. Conv., Charleston, S.C., 1860; declined appointment by Pres. Lincoln as minister to Spain; 1861; apptd. sec. and acting gov. Territory of N.M., 1861; engaged in merc. bus., Westport Landing (now Kansas City), Mo., 1861-64, elsewhere in West until 1877; railroad ofcl.; engaged in banking; unsuccessful candidate for election to U.S. Congress, 1880. Died Las Vegas, N.M., May 30, 1882; buried Riverside Cemetery, Denver, Colo.

OTEY, James Hervey, clergyman, univ. chancellor; b. Bedford County, Va., Jan. 27, 1800; s. Isaac Otey; B. Belles-lettres, U. N.C., 1820; m. Eliza Pannill, Oct. 13, 1821, 9 children. Instr. Greek and Latin, U. N.C.; ordained deacon Protestant Episcopal Ch., 1825, priest, 1827; founder sch., Franklin, Tenn., pastor, missionary, 8 years; elected 1st Protestant Episcopal bishop Tenn., 1833, consecrated, Phila., 1834; originator idea, a founder U. of South, Sewanee, Tenn., elected chmn., 1857, later chancellor; Whig. Author: Doctrine, Discipline and Worship of the American Branch of the Catholic Church, Explained and Unfolded in Three Sermons, 1852. Died Memphis, Tenn., Apr. 23, 1863; buried Ashwood, Tenn.

OTIS, Bass, portrait painter; b. Bridgewater, Mass., July 17, 1784; s. Dr. Josiah and Susanna (Orr) O.; m. Alice Pierie, 1819, more than one child. Apprenticed to scythe-maker, Bridgewater; while working for coach painter became interested in painting; had established reputation as painter, N.Y. by 1808; had studio, Phila., 1812-45; painted portraits of Thomas Jefferson, James Madison, Joseph Hopkinson and others for Delaplaine's Repository of the Lives and Portraits of Distinguished American Characters; sent Interior of an Iron Foundry to Phila. Exhbn. (only known composition), 1819; made 1st lithograph in Am., 1818; painted in N.Y.C., 1845-59, Phila., 1859-61. Died Phila., Nov. 3, 1861; buried Christ Ch. Burial Ground, Phila.

OTIS, Elisha Graves, mfr., inventor; b. Halifax, Vt., Aug. 3, 1811; s. Stephen and Phoebe (Glynn) O.; m. Susan Houghton, June 2, 1834; m. 2d, Mrs. Elizabeth Boyd; at least 2 children including Charles R., Norton P. Mfr. wagons and carriages in Vt., 1838-45; constructed and invented a turbine water-wheel, Albany, N.Y.; with bedstead factory, Bergen, N.J., master mechanic, 1851; in charge of erection and installation of machinery in new factory, Yonkers, N.Y.; devised, incorporated unique features into the elevator (1st one with safety features); established own shop, Yonkers (thought to be the beginning of elevator bus.); demonstrated his safety elevator at Am. Inst. Fair, N.Y., 1854; patented railroad car trucks and brakes, 1852; patented steam plow, 1857, bake oven, 1858; established The Otis Elevator Co., after invention, patenting of steam elevator, 1861. Died Yonkers, Apr. 8, 1861.

OTIS, George Alexander, mil. surgeon; b. Va., Nov. 12, 1830; s. George Alexander and Anna Marie (Hickman) O.; grad. Princeton, 1849, A.M., 1851; grad. U. Pa. Sch. Medicine, 1851; m. Pauline Clark Baury, 2 children. Practiced gen. surgery, Paris, France, 1851-52; founded Va. Med. and Surg. Jour., 1852; gen. practice medicine, Springfield, Mass., 1854-61; apptd. surgeon 27th Mass. Volunteers, 1861, served in Md., Va., S.C.; asst. surgeon U.S. Volunteers, 1864, surgeon, 1864-81; asst. surgeon U.S. Army, 1866; invalid due to stroke, 1877-81. Author: Report of Surgical Case Treated in the Army of the United States from 1865-1871, 1871; A Report on a Plan for Transporting Soldiers by Railway in Time of War, 1875. Died Feb. 23, 1881.

OTIS, Harrison Gray, senator, congressman; b. Boston, Oct. 8, 1765; s. Samuel Allyne and Elizabeth (Gray) O.; grad. Harvard, 1783; m. Sally Foster, May 31, 1790, 11 children. Admitted to Boston bar, 1786; mem. Mass. Gen. Ct. from Boston, 1795-96; U.S. atty. for Mass., 1796-97; mem. U.S. Ho. of Reps. from Mass., 6th-7th congresses, 1797-1801, supported Pres. John Adams; mem. Mass. Ho. of Reps., 1802-05, 13-14, speaker, 1803-05; mem. Mass. Senate, 1805-13, 14-17, pres., 1805-06, 08-11; overseer Harvard, 1810-23; a leading supporter and mem. Hartford Conv. (New Eng. states' rights movement against War of 1812), 1814; judge Mass. Ct. Common Pleas, 1814-18; mem. U.S. Senate from Mass., 1817-22 (resigned); unsuccessful candidate for mayor Boston, 1823 (defeated by William Eustis, spelling end of Federalist Party); mayor Boston, 1829-32; owned mfg. stock, 1820's; became supporter of Henry Clay. Author: Letters Developing the Character and Views of the Hartford Convention, 1820; Otis' Letters in Defense of the Hartford Convention, 1824. Died Boston, Oct. 28, 1848; buried Mt. Auburn Cemetery, Cambridge, Mass.

OTIS, James, lawyer, colonial legislator; b. West Barnstable, Mass., Feb. 5, 1725; s. James and Mary (Allyne) O.; grad. Harvard, 1743; m. Ruth Cunningham, 1755, 3 children. Admitted to Plymouth County (Mass.) bar, 1748; practiced law, Boston, 1750; published The Rudiments of Latin Prosody . . . and the Principles of Harmony in Poetic and Prosaic Composition, 1760; king's atty., 1754; served as king's adv. gen. of vice admiralty ct., Boston; opposed issuance of Brit. writs of assistance; argued (in collaboration with Oxenbridge Thacker) illegality of writs before Mass. Superior Ct., 1761, based argument on natural law, lost case; active mem. Sons of Liberty; mem. Mass. Gen. Ct., 1761-69, 71, speaker, 1766; directed majority in Gen. Ct. (with Samuel Adams and Joseph Hawley); prepared rough draft of state papers that issued from Gen. Ct.; helped draw up Mass. circular letter adopted by House, 1768; lapses of sanity lessened his influence after 1769. Author: (pamphlets which laid broad basis for Am. polit. theory on natural law) A Vindication of the Conduct of the House of Representatives, 1762; The Rights of the British Colonies Asserted and Proved, 1764; Considerations on Behalf of the Colonists, In a Letter to a Noble Lord; A Vindication of the British Colonies; Brief Remarks on the Defence of the Halifax Libel on the British-American Colonies. Died Andover, Mass., May 23, 1783.

OTIS, John, congressman; b. Leeds, Me., Aug. 3, 1801; grad. Bowdoin Coll., Brunswick, Me., 1823; studied law. Admitted to Me. bar, began practice in Hallowell, 1826; mem. Me. Ho. of Reps., 1841, 46-47; apptd. mem. Northeastern Boundary Commn., 1842; mem. Me. Senate, 1842; mem. U.S. Ho. of Reps. (Whig) from Me., 31st Congress, 1849-51. Died Hallowell, Oct. 17, 1856; buried Hallowell Cemetery.

OTIS, Samuel Allyne, Continental congressman; b. Barnstable, Mass., Nov. 24, 1740; grad. Harvard, 1759. Engaged in merc. bus., Boston; mem. Mass. Ho. of Reps., 1776; mem. Bd. of War, 1776; collector of clothing for Continental Army, 1777; mem. Mass. Constl. Conv.; mem. Mass. Ho. of Reps., 1784-87, speaker, 1784; mem. Continental Congress from Mass., 1787-88; sec. U.S. Senate, 1789-1814. Died Washington, D.C., Apr. 22, 1814; buried Congressional Cemetery, Washington.

OTTENDORFER, Anna Behr Uhl, journalist, philanthropist; b. Wurzburg, Germany, Feb. 13, 1815; d. Eduard Behr; m. Jacob Uhl., 1838; m. 2d, Oswald Ottendorfer, July 23, 1859; 6 children. Came to U.S., 1836 or 37; purchased (with husband) German job-printing, book, newspaper publishing bus. of Julius Botticher, N.Y.C., 1844; compositor, sec., gen. mgr. New-Yorker Staats-Zeitung, organ of large German population in N.Y.C., sole mgr., 1852-59; founder Isabella Home for Aged Women, Astoria, L.I., N.Y., 1875; established Hermann Uhl Meml. Fund for German-Am. ednl. purposes, N.Y.C. and Milw., 1881; decorated for charitable activities by Empress Augusta of Germany, 1883. Died N.Y.C., Apr. 1, 1884.

OTTER, Thomas, artist; lived in Phila.; known only by 2 paintings: Moonlight, 1860, now in Wilstach Collection, Phila. Mus., and On the Road, now in William Rockhill Nelson Gallery Art, Kansas City.

OTTERBEIN, Philip William, clergyman; b. Dillenburg, Germany, June 3, 1726; s. Johann Daniel and Wilhelmina Henrietta (Hoerlen) O.; attended Reformed Sem., Herborn, Germany; m. Susan LeRoy, Apr. 19, 1762. Ordained as vicar German Reformed Ch., 1749; came to Am. (N.Y.), 1752; pastor German Reformed congregations, Lancaster, Pa., 1752-58, Tulpehocken, Pa., 1758-60, Frederick, Md., 1760-65, York, Pa., 1765-74, 2d Evang. Reformed Ch., Balt., 1774-1813; formed orgn. which was basis of United Brethren Ch., 1789, held 1st annual conf. nr. Frederick, 1800. Author: Die Heilbringende Menschwerdung und der Herrliche Sieg Jesu Christi, 1763. Died Balt., Nov. 17, 1813.

OTTO, Bodo, surgeon; b. Hanover, Germany, 1711; s. Christopher and Maria (Nienecken) O.; m. Elizabeth Sanchen, 1736; m. 2d, Catharina Dahncken, 1742; m. 3d, Maria Paris, 1766; at least 3 children, including John Conrad. Mem. Coll. of Surgeons, Luneburg; chief surgeon for dist. of Schartzfels, Germany, 1749; came to Am., 1755; del. Pa. Provincial Congress, 1776; apptd. sr. surgeon middle div. Continental Hosps., 1776; ordered by Continental Congress to establish mil. hosp. for treatment of smallpox, Trenton, N.J., 1777; in charge hosps., Yellow Springs, Pa., spring 1778; selected for hosp. dept., 1780; mem. Am. Philos. Soc. Died Reading, Pa., June 12, 1787; buried Trinity Luth. Churchyard, Reading.

OTTO, John Conrad, physician; b. nr. Woodbury, N.J., Mar. 15, 1774; s. Dr. Bodo and Catherine (Schweighauser) O.; grad. Coll. of N.J. (now Princeton), 1792, U. Pa., 1796; m. Eliza Tod, 1802; 9 children including William Tod. Physician, Phila. Dispensary, 1798-1803; physician Orphan Asylum, Magdalen Asylum, many years; most important contbn. to med. sci. was description of hemophilia in paper An Account of an Hemorrhagic Disposition Existing in Certain Families, (pub. in Med. Repository, vol. VI, 1803, reprinted in London Med. and Phys. Jour., 1808); physician Pa. Hosp., 1813-34; mem. com. of 12 leading physicians appt. to deal with cholera epidemic in Phila., 1832; mem. Phila. Coll. of Physicians, 1819, censor, many years, v.p., 1840-44. Died Phila., June 26, 1844; buried Woodlands Cemetery, West Phila.

OURAY, Indian chief; b. Colo., circa 1833; m. Chepeta, 1859. Became chief Uncompahgre Utes, 1860; apptd. interpreter Los Pinos Agy., So. Colo., 1862; visited Washington, D.C., on behalf of tribe, 1862; signer, as head chief of Western Utes, treaty at Conejos, 1863; served with Kit Carson in suppressing uprising of Ute Sub-chief Kaniatse, 1867; a negotiator Treaty of 1868, Washington; accepted compromise relinquishing certain Ute lands to fed. govt., 1873; became Methodist, 1878. Died Los Pinos Agy., Aug. 24, 1880.

OURY, Granville Henderson, congressman; b. Abingdon, Va., Mar. 12, 1825; studied law, Bowling Green, Mo. Admitted to Mo. bar, 1848; moved to San Antonio, Tex., 1848, to Marysville, Cal., 1849; engaged in mining; went to Tucson, Ariz., 1856, began practice of law; chosen capt. of a party sent from Tucson to relief of Crabbe Expdn. besieged at Caborca, Sonora, Mexico, 1857; presiding judge Dist. Ct. for Ariz. and N.M., Misilla, N.M.; del. from Ariz. to Confederate Congress, 1862; served as capt. Herbert's Bn., Ariz. Cavalry, Confederate Army, 1862; col. on staff of Gen. Sibley in Tex. and La., 1862-64; resumed practice of law, Tucson; mem. Ariz. Territorial Ho. of Reps., 1866, 73, 75, speaker, 1866; apptd. atty. gen. Ariz. Territory, 1869; moved to Phoenix, Ariz., 1870; dist. atty. Maricopa County (Ariz.), 1871-73; dist. atty. Pinal County (Ariz.), 1879, 89-90; del. U.S. Congress from Ariz. Territory, 1881-85; del. Dem. Nat. Conv., 1884; resumed law practice, Florence, Ariz., 1885. Died Tucson, Jan. 11, 1891; buried Masonic Cemetery, Florence.

OUTACITY (known as Ostenaco, Mankiller, also other names), Indian chief; probably born in Tenn., flourished 1756-77. Cherokee Indian, took active part in uprising led by Oconostota, 1757; visited Eng. under guidance of Henry Timberlake, 1762, had an audience with King George III (in order to increase Timberlake's reputation of influence over Indians); fought on side of Gt. Britain during Am. Revolution. Died circa 1777.

OVERMAN, Frederick, metallurgist; b. Elberfeld, Germany, circa 1803; s. Johann and Maria Catherina (Ruhl) Overmann; studied metallurgy Royal Poly. Inst., Berlin, Germany. Apprenticed to cabinet maker in Germany; became authority in iron metallurgy before age of 40; came to U.S., 1842, engaged in writing technol. works; died after inhaling arsenic gas in laboratory. Author: The Manufacture of Iron 1850; The Manufacture of Steel, 1851; Practical Mineralogy, Assaying and Mining, 1851; A Treatise on Metallurgy, 1851. Died Phila., Jan. 7, 1852.

OVERSTREET, James, congressman; b. nr. Barnwell Court House, Barnwell Dist., S.C., Feb. 11, 1773; attended common schs.; studied law. Admitted to S.C. bar, 1798, began practice in Barnwell Dist.; held local offices; mem. U.S. Ho. of Reps. from S.C., 16th-17th congresses, 1819-22. Died China Grove, N.C., May 24, 1822; buried Savitz Cemetery at Mt. Zion Reformed Ch., China Grove.

OVERTON, John, judge; b. Louisa County, Va., Apr. 9, 1766; s. James and Mary (Waller) O.; studied law, Ky.; m. Mary McConnell White. Practiced law in Nashville, Tenn., 1788; asso. with Andrew Jackson in purchase of Rice Tract of land, 1794, founder (with Jackson) Memphis (Tenn.) on that site, 1819; judge Tenn. Superior Ct., 1804-10; mem. Tenn. Supreme Ct., 1811-16; supported candidacy of Andrew Jackson for U.S. Pres., 1821-28. Author: Tennessee Reports, 2 vols., 1813-17. Died Nashville, Apr. 12, 1833.

OVERTON, Walter Hampden, congressman; b. nr. Louisa Court House, Va., 1788; attended common schs., Tenn. Commd. 1st lt. 7th Inf. Regt., U.S. Army, 1808, promoted capt., 1810, maj. 3d Rifles, 1814, transferred to Arty. Corps, 1815; brevetted lt. col. for gallant conduct at Battle of New Orleans, 1814, comdr. forts Jackson and St. Phillip; resigned commn., 1815; commd. maj. gen. La. Militia; settled nr. Alexandria, La.; mem. Ct. House Bldg. Commn., 1820-21; mem. Commn. on Navigation of Bayou Rapides, 1824; engaged in planting; mem. U.S. Ho. of Reps. (Democrat) from La., 21st Congress, 1829-31. Died nr. Alexandria, Dec. 24, 1845; buried McNutt Hill Cemetery, nr. Alexandria.

OWEN, Allen Ferdinand, congressman; b. Wilkes County, N.C., Oct. 9, 1816; grad. Franklin Coll., Athens, Ga.; grad. Yale, 1837, Dane Law Sch. of Harvard, 1839. Admitted to the bar, Boston, 1839; began practice of law, Talbotton, Ga., 1840; mem. Ga. Ho. of Reps., 1843-47, clk., 1849; del. Whig Nat. Conv., 1848; mem. U.S. Ho. of Reps. (Whig) from Ga., 31st Congress, 1849-51; became Democrat; U.S. consul at Havana (Cuba), 1851. Died Upatoi, Ga., Apr. 7, 1865; buried Oak Hill Cemetery, Talbotton.

OWEN, David Dale, geologist; b. New Lanark, Scotland, June 24, 1807; s. Robert and Ann (Dale) O.; attended ednl. inst. of Phillip Emanuel von Fellenberg, Berne, Switzerland, 1824-27; M.D., Ohio Med. Coll., Cincinnati, 1836; m. Caroline Neef, Mar. 23, 1837; 4 children. Came to Am., 1827; state geologist Ind., 1837-38; made survey of Dubuque (Ia.) and Mineral Point (Wis.) dists. under U.S. appointment, 1838 (report published as House Document 239, 1840); U.S. geologist to survey Chippewa Land Dist., 1847-52; published Report of a Geological Exploration of a Part of Iowa, Wisconsin and Minnesota and, Incidentally, a Portion of Nebraska Territory, 1852; state geologist Ky., 1854-59, Ark., 1857-60; apptd. state geologist Ind., 1860, died before taking office; 1st to point out rich mineral nature of Ia., Wis. lands, also that lead and zinc ores were limited to the magnesian limestone; 1st to give name sucarboniferous to beds underlying Ind. coal; published Geological Survey of Kentucky, 4 vols., 1856-61; The Report of a Geological Reconnaissance of Indiana Made During the Years 1859 and 1860 Under the Direction of the Late D. D. Owen, published by Richard Owen, 1862. Died New Harmony, Ind., Nov. 13, 1860.

OWEN, George Washington, congressman; b. Brunswick County, Va., Oct. 20, 1796; grad. U. Nashville (Tenn.); studied law. Admitted to Ala. bar, 1816, began practice in Claiborne; mem. Ala. Ho. of Reps., 1819-21, speaker, 1821; mem. U.S. Ho. of Reps. from Ala., 18th-20th congresses, 1823-29; collector Port of Mobile (Ala.), 1828-36; mayor of Mobile, 1836-37. Died nr. Mobile, Aug. 18, 1837; buried Old Church St. Cemetery, Mobile.

OWEN, Griffith, colonial leader, clergyman, surgeon; b. Wales, 1647; s. Robert and Jane Vaughan) O.; m. 2d, Sarah Saunders, 1704; at least 3 children. Came to U.S., 1684; mem. Pa. Colonial Assembly, 1686-90; mem. Pa. Provincial Council, 1690-1717; one of foremost Friends in public service; apptd. mem. most important coms. of Phila. Yearly Meeting, usually chmn.; one of outstanding Quaker preachers in Colony of Pa.; main' drafter of tract Our Ancient Testimony Renewed (attempted to explain Quaker position in Colony of Pa. theologically), 1695; founder (with William Penn, Thomas Story, others) Meeting of Ministers of Phila., Sept. 1701. Died Phila., Aug. 19, 1717.

OWEN, James, congressman; b. nr. Wilmington, N.C., Dec. 7, 1784; ed. Bingham's Acad., Pittsboro, N.C. Engaged in farming; mem. N.C. Ho. of Commons, 1808-11; pres. Wilmington & Raleigh R.R. Co.; mem. U.S. Ho. of Reps. (Democrat) from N.C., 15th Congress, 1817-19. Died Wilmington, Sept. 4, 1865; buried Oakdale Cemetery, Wilmington.

OWEN, John, trader; one of earliest settlers in Mont.; bought bldgs. from Roman Catholic Ch. at St. Mary's Mission, Bitter Root area, added other bldgs., 1850; remained in Mont. throughout gold rush, his fort becoming most important travel and trading center in area nr. Florence, Mont. Author: Journals of Major Owen, pub. 1927.

OWEN, Robert, reformer; b. Newtown, Montgomeryshire, Wales, May 14, 1771; s. Robert and Anne (Williams) O.; self-educated; m. Anne Dale, Sept. 30, 1799; 3 sons including Robert Dale. Became asst. in sadlery at age 11, mgr. cotton mill in Manchester at age 19; formed Chorlton Twist Co., 1794-95; moved to New Lanark, Scotland, 1799, became part owner of father-in-law's cotton mills, set up modern indsl. community; inspired passage of ill-fated Factory Act of 1819; campaigned unsuccessfully for widespread establishment of communities on New Lanark model; founded exptl. Community of Equality, New Harmony, Ind., 1825, admitted its failure, 1827; returned to Britain, promoted various assns., including Equitable Labor Exchange; again resident in Am., 1844-47; advocated unification of labor and coop. movements; was converted from agnosticism to spiritualism late in life; convened Congress of the Advanced Minds of the World, 1857. Author: New View of Society, or Essays on the Principle of the Formation of the Human Character, 1813-16; Report to County of Lanark, 1821; Book of the New Moral World, 1826-44; Revolution in Mind and Practice, 1849; Letters to the Human Race, 1850; autobiography, 1857-58. Died Newtown, Nov. 17, 1858; buried St. Mary's Church, Newtown.

OWEN, Robert Dale, reformer, congressman, diplomat; b. Glasgow, Scotland, Nov. 9, 1801; s. Robert and Ann (Dale) O.; ed. instn. of Philipp Emanuel von Fellenberg, Hofwyl, Switzerland, 4 years; m. Mary Robinson, Apr. 12, 1832; m. 2d, Lottie Walton Kellog, June 23, 1876. On return from sch. took charge of the community founded by his father at New Lanark, Scotland; came to U.S., where his father wanted to found new type of community, New Harmony, Ind., 1825; taught sch., 1825-27; edited New Harmony Gazette (name changed to Free Enquirer 1829); influenced by social reformer Frances Wright; went to N.Y.; a founder Assn. for Protection of Industry and for Promotion of Nat. Edn.; mem. Ind. Legislature, 1836-38, secured for pub. schs. one half of excess funds allocated by U.S. Govt.; mem. U.S. Ho. of Reps. (Democrat) from Ind., 28th-29th congresses, 1843-47, introduced bill establishing Smithsonian Instn.; mem. Ind. Constl. Conv., 1850; charge d'affaires, Naples, Italy, 1853-58; became an emancipation advocate; commd. by Ind. to purchase arms for state troops in Europe; Author: An Outline of the System of Education at New Lanark, 1824; Hints on Public Architecture, 1849; The Wrong of Slavery (written after having served as chmn. com. to investigate condition of freedmen 1863), 1864. Died Lake George, N.Y., June 24, 1877.

OWENS, George Welshman, congressman; b. Savanah, Ga., Aug. 29, 1786; attended sch., Harrow, Eng.; grad. Cambridge (Eng.) U.; studied law, London, Eng. Admitted to the bar, practiced law; mem. U.S. Ho. of Reps. (Unionist) from Ga., 24th-25th congresses, 1835-39. Died Savannah, Mar. 2, 1856; buried Laurel Grove Cemetery, Savannah.

OWENS, John Edmond, actor; b. Liverpool, Eng., Apr. 2, 1823; s. Owen Griffith and Mary (Anderton) Owen; m. Mary C. Stevens, Apr. 19, 1849. Came to U.S. with family, 1828; made debut on stage, 1840; acquired reputation as comedian, 1841-51; famous for his impersonations, including Toodles, Dr. Pangloss in The Heir at Law and Dr. Ollapod in The Poor Gentleman. Died Dec. 7, 1886.

OWSLEY, Bryan Young, congressman; b. nr. Crab Orchard, Ky., Aug. 19, 1798; attended common schs., Lincoln County, Ky.; studied law. Admitted to Ky. bar; moved to Jamestown, Ky.; clk. circuit ct., 1827; Whig presdl. elector, 1840; mem. U.S. Ho. of Reps. (Whig) From Ky., 27th Congress, 1841-43; register U.S. Land Office, Frankfort, Ky., 1845-49. Died Frankfort, Oct. 27, 1849.

OWSLEY, William, gov. Ky., jurist; b. Va., 1782; s. William and Catherine (Bolin) O.; m. Elizabeth Gill, circa 1804, 5 children. Mem. Ky. Legislature, 1809-11; judge Ct. of Appeals, 1812-28, important decisions included Commonwealth vs. James Morrison, Blair et al. vs. Williams; mem. Ky. Ho. of Reps., 1831, Ky. Senate, 1832-34; Clay presdl. elector, 1833; sec. of state Ky., 1834-36, gov., 1844-48. Died Dec. 9, 1862.

P

PACA, William, gov. Md., Continental congressman; b. Abingdon, Md., Oct. 31, 1740; s. John and Elizabeth (Smith) P.; grad. Coll. of Phila., 1759; studied law, Inner Temple, London, Eng.; m. Mary Chew, May 26, 1763; m. 2d, Anne Harrison, 1777; 5 children. Admitted to practice before Mayor's Ct., Phila., 1761, to Md. Provincial Ct. bar, 1764; mem. Md. Provincial Legislature, 1768, mem. com. that directed constrn. of state house, Annapolis; mem. Md. Com. of Correspondence; mem. Continental Congress, 1774-79, mem. com. of 13 for Fgn. Affairs; signed Declaration of Independence; mem. Md. Constl. Conv., 1st Md. Senate; chief judge Md. Gen. Ct., 1778; apptd. chief justice Ct. of Appeals in Admiralty and Prize Cases, 1780; gov. Md., 1782-83, 84-85; raised subscriptions for Washington Coll.; hon. mem. Soc. of Cincinnati. Died Abingdon, Oct. 13, 1799; buried family burial grounds, Abingdon.

PACHELBEL, Carl Theodorus, musician; b. Stuttgart, Germany, Nov. 24, 1690; s. Johann Pachelbel. Came to Boston, circa 1730; assisted in erection of organ Trinity Ch., Newport, R.I., 1733, organist, circa 1 year; gave concerts in N.Y.C., 1736; moved to Charleston, S.C., became organist of St. Philip's Ch.; gave public concert, Charleston, 1737; composed Magnificat (only known composition; now in Royal Library, Berlin, Germany); name also appears as Perchival. Died Charleston, Sept. 1750.

PACKARD, Alpheus Spring, educator; b. Chelmsford, Mass., Dec. 23, 1798; s. Hezekiah and Mary (Spring) P.; grad. Bowdoin Coll., 1816; m. Frances Elizabeth Appleton, 1827; m. 2d, Mrs. Caroline W. (Bartelles) McLellan, 1844; 6 children. Taught at various Me. academies, 1816-19; taught Latin, Greek, rhetoric, natural and revealed religion Bowdoin Coll., 1819-84, among his students were Henry Wadsworth Longfellow and Nathaniel Hawthorne. Editor: Zenophon's Memorabilia of Socrates, with English Notes, 1839. Died Squirrel Island, Me., July 13, 1884.

PACKARD, Frederick Adolphus, editor; b. Marlboro, Mass., Sept. 26, 1794; s. Rev. Asa and Nancy (Quincy) P.; grad. Harvard, 1814; m. Elizabeth Hooker, 4 children including Lewis Richard, John Hooker. Owner and editor Hampshire Federalist (became Hampden Federalist), 1819; supt. Sunday Sch., 1st Congregational Ch., Springfield, Mass., 1827; del. to 4th Anniversary of Sunday Sch. Union, 1828; mem. Mass. Legislature, 1828-29; editorial sec. Am. Sunday Sch. Union (continuously edited all weekly and monthly periodicals of Union as well as all books with its imprint), 1828-58; dir. Girard Coll. for Orphans; mgr. Ho. of Refuge; editor Jour. of Prison Discipline, 21 years; editor Sunday Sch. Jour., Advocate of Christian Religion, Youth's Penny Gazette. Author: Life of Robert Owen, 1866. Died Nov. 11, 1867.

PACKARD, Lewis Richard, educator; b. Phila., Aug. 22, 1836; son of Frederich Adolphus Packard; grad. Yale, 1856, Ph.D., 1863; Ph.D., U. Berlin (Germany). Tutor, Yale, 1859-63, prof. Greek, 1866-83; pres. Am. Philol. Assn., 1880-81; in charge of Am. Archaeological Sch., Athens, Greece, 1883. Author: Studies in Greek Thought, 1886. Died New Haven, Conn., Oct. 26, 1884.

PACKARD, Silas Sadler, educator; b. Cummington, Mass., Apr. 28, 1826; s. Chester and Eunice (Sadler) P.; m. Marion Crocker, Mar. 6, 1850. With Niagara River Pilot, a weekly in Tonawanda, N.Y., 1853; pioneer bus. educator, promoted (with Henry Bryant and Henry Stratton) a chain of bus. colls., 1856; founded Packard's Bus. Coll., N.Y.C., 1858; assisted in compiling Bryant and Stratton's National Bookkeeping; publisher Packard's Monthly, 1868-70; promoted the tng. of young women for office work and in convincing employers of their capability; active in Ohio Soc. Died N.Y.C., Oct. 27, 1898.

PACKER, Asa, congressman, railroad exec.; b. Mystic, New London County, Conn., Dec. 29, 1805; son of Elisha Packer, Jr.; m. Sarah M. Blakeslee, Jan. 23, 1828, 3 children. Apprenticed to carpenter, Pa., 1822; became owner and master of canal boat which carried coal from Mauch Chunk (Pa.) to Phila., 1823; operator (with brother R. W. Packer) store and boatyard, 1831, took contract for constrn. of canal locks on upper Lehigh River, Pa. (completed constrn. 1837); mem. Pa. Ho. of Reps., 1842-43; asso. judge Carbon County (Pa.), 1843-44; built Lehigh Valley R.R., 1852, operated line until 1879; mem. U.S. Ho. of Reps. (Democrat) from Pa., 33d-34th congresses, 1853-57; built Lehigh U. (chartered by Pa. Legislature), 1866. Died Phila., May 17, 1879; buried Mauch Chunk Cemetery.

PACKER, John Black, congressman; b. Sunbury, Pa., Mar. 21, 1824; attended Sunbury Acad.; studied law. Mem. corps engrs. employed in survey and constrn. of pub. improvements State of Pa., 1839-42; admitted to Pa. bar, 1844, began practice in Sunbury; engaged in banking; dep. atty. gen., 1845-47; mem. Pa. Ho. of Reps., 1850-51; an organizer Susquehanna R.R. Co., 1851; mem. U.S. Ho. of Reps. (Republican) from Pa., 41st-44th congresses, 1869-77; declined appointment as postmaster gen. under Pres. Grant, 1874. Died Sunbury, July 7, 1891; buried Pomfret Manor Cemetery, Sunbury.

PACKER, William Fisher, gov. Pa.; b. Howard Twp., Pa., Apr. 2, 1807; s. James and Charity (Bye) P.; m. Mary Vanderbelt, Dec. 24, 1828, 6 children. In fall of 1827 became asso. with Lycoming (Pa.) Gazette, 1827-36, sole owner, publisher 1829-36; del. Democratic Nat. Conv., Balt., 1835; supt. West Branch div. Pa. Canal, 1832-35; helped publish Keystone (organ of Pa. Dem. Party), Harrisburg, 1836-41; a canal commr. State of Pa., 1839-41; auditor-gen. Pa., 1842-45; speaker Pa. Ho. of Reps., 1847, 48; mem. Pa. Senate, 1849; responsible for passage of bill to incorporate Susquehanna R.R. Co., pres. railroad, 1852-54; mem. bd. dirs. No. Central Ry. Co., 1859; gov. Pa. (Democrat), 1857-61. Died Williamsport, Pa., Sept. 27, 1870.

PADDOCK, Algernon Sidney, senator; b. Glens Falls, N.Y., Nov. 9, 1830; s. Ira A. and Lucinda (Wells) P.; attended Union Coll., Schenectady, N.Y.; m. Emma Mack, Dec. 22, 1859, 5 children. Admitted to Neb. bar, 1857; contbr. strong anti-slavery editorials to Neb. Republican; del. 1st Neb. Territorial Conv., 1859; del. Republican Nat. Conv., 1860, 64; sec. Territory of Neb., 1861-67; mem. U.S. Senate from Neb., 1875-81, 87-93; mem. fed. commn. which had jurisdiction over elections in Neb. Territory, 1882-86. Died Beatrice, Neb., Oct. 17, 1897; buried Prospect Hill Cemetery, Omaha, Neb.

PADDOCK, Benjamin Henry, clergyman; b. Norwich, Conn., Feb. 29, 1828; s. Rev. Seth Birdsey and Emily (Flagg) P.; grad. Trinity Coll., 1848; grad. Gen. Theol. Sem., N.Y.C., 1852; m. Caroline Cooke, May 1853; m. 2d, Anna Sanger, 1863. Ordained deacon Protestant Episcopal Ch., 1852, priest, 1853; rector St. Luke's Ch., Portland, Me., 1853, Trinity Ch., Norwich, 1853, Christ Ch., Detroit, 1860-68, Grace Ch., Bklyn., 1869-73; bishop of Mass., 1873-91 (policies resulted in reconciliation of high and low factions in Mass). Author: The First Century of the Protestant Episcopal Church in the Diocese of Mass., 1885. Died Boston, Mar. 9, 1891.

PADDOCK, John Adams, clergyman; b. Norwich, Conn., Jan. 19, 1825; s. Rev. Seth Birdsey and Emily (Flagg) P.; grad. Trinity Coll., 1845; grad. Gen. Theol. Sem., 1849; m. Ellen M. Jones, June 1, 1850; m. 2d, Frances Chester Fanning, Apr. 23, 1856. Ordained deacon, Protestant Episcopal Ch. 1849, priest, 1850; in charge of St. Peter's Ch., Bklyn., 1855-80; active in administration of diocese of L.I.; became missionary bishop of Wash. Territory, 1880; a founder Tacoma (Wash.) Gen. Hosp, 1882; raised $50,000 in East to insure conditional gift of land and money for establishment of Anna Wright Sem. and Wash. Coll. at Tacoma; missionary-bishop of Olympia, 1892. Author: The Modern Manifestations of Superstition and Skepticism, 1870. Died Santa Barbara, Cal., Mar. 4, 1894; buried Vancouver, B.C., Can.

PADILLA, Juan de, see de Padilla, Juan.

PAGE, Charles Grafton, inventor; b. Salem, Mass., Jan. 25, 1812; s. Jeremiah Lee and Lucy (Lang) P.; grad. Harvard, 1832; m. Priscilla Webster, Sept. 23, 1844, at least 5 children. Devised self-acting circuit breaker, (probably 1st to apply it to produce extreme alterations necessary in induction machines), circa 1837; his inventions incorporated in a coil machine by Daniel Davis, Jr., 1838; an examiner in U.S. Patent Office, 1841-52; prof. chemistry med. dept. Columbian Coll. (now George Washington U.), 1844-49; completed small reciprocating electro-magnetic engine by 1846; developed induction apparatus (which in principle is modern induction coil); granted spl. Congressional appropriation to continue work on larger scale, 1849; built several large stationary reciprocating electro-magnetic engines of both vertical and horizontal type; established (with J.J. Greenough and Charles L. Fleischmann) Am. Poly. Journal of Science, Washington, D.C., 1852; patented design of reciprocating electro-magnetic engine, 1854; examiner of patents U.S. Patent Office, 1861-68. Author: Psychomancy, Spirit-Rappings and Table-Tippings Exposed, 1853; History of Induction: The American Claim to the Induction Coil and its Electrostatic Developments, 1867. Died Washington D.C., May 5, 1868.

PAGE, David Perkins, educator; b. Epping, N.H., July 4, 1810; m. Susan Maria Lunt, Dec. 16, 1832. Opened sch., Newburyport, N.H., 1829; asso. prin. Newburyport High Sch., 1831-43; prin. new normal sch. established in Albany by N.Y. State Legislature, 1844-48. Author: The Theory and Practice of Teaching or the Motives and Methods of Good School Keeping, 1847. Died Jan. 1, 1848.

PAGE, Horace Francis, congressman; b. nr. Medina, N.Y., Oct. 20, 1833; attended Millville Acad.; studied law. Taught sch., La Porte County, Ind., until 1854; moved to Cal., engaged in sawmill bus. nr. Colfax; moved to Placerville, Cal., engaged in livery-stable bus., mining, mail contracting; state propr.; admitted to Cal. bar, began practice; served as maj. Cal. Militia; mem. U.S. Ho. of Reps. (Republican) from Cal., 43d-47th congresses, 1873-83; del. Rep. Nat. Conv., Chgo, 1884; resumed practice of law, Washington, D.C. Died San Francisco, Aug. 23, 1890; buried Mountain View Cemetery, Oakland, Cal.

PAGE, John, gov. Va., congressman; b. Gloucester County, Va., Apr. 17, 1744; s. Mann and Alice (Grymes) P.; grad. in philosophy Coll. William and Mary, 1763; m. Frances Burwell, circa 1765; m. 2d, Margaret Lowther, 1789; 20 children. Early interest in astronomy; mem. Va. Constl. Conv., 1776; lt. gov. Va., 1776-78; mem. Va. Ho. of Reps., 1781-83, 85-88, 97-98, 1800-01; lay del. from Va. to Anglican Ch. Conv., N.Y., 1785; mem. U.S. Ho. of Reps. from Va., 1st-4th congresses, 1789-97; presdl. elector from Va., 1800; gov. Va., 1802-05; U.S. commr. of loans for Va., during last years of life. Died Richmond, Va., Oct. 11, 1808; buried St. John's Churchyard, Richmond.

PAGE, John, senator, gov. N.H.; b. Haverhill, N.H., May 21, 1787; attended pub. schs. Engaged in farming; served as lt. during War of 1812; asst. U.S. tax assessor, 1813, assessor, 1815; mem. N.H. Ho. of Reps., 1818-20, 35; register of deeds for Grafton County, 1827, 29-35; selectman Haverhill, 14 terms; town clk.; mem. N.H. Gov.'s Council, 1836, 38; mem. U.S. Senate (Democrat) from N.H., June 8, 1836-37; gov. N.H., 1840-42. Died Haverhill, Sept. 8, 1865; buried Ladd St. Cemetery, Haverhill.

PAGE, Mann, planter, miner; b. Va., 1691; s. Matthew and Mary (Mann) P.; grad. St. John's Coll., Oxford, Eng.; m. Judith Wormeley, 1712; m. 2d, Judith Carter, 1718; 9 children. Mem. Va. Council, 1714-30; inherited large estates in Va. from father and maternal grandfather (John Mann); became 2d largest landowner in Va.; partner (with father-in-law Robert Carter) Frying Pan Co., mining copper in what is now Fairfax and Loudoun counties (Va.). Died Jan. 24, 1730.

PAGE, Mann, Continental congressman; b. "Rosewell," Gloucester County, Va., 1749; grad. Coll. William and Mary, studied law. Admitted to Va. bar, practiced law; managed a large estate; mem. Va. Ho. of Burgesses; moved to Spotsylvania County, Va.; mem. Continental Congress from Va., 1777. Died "Mansfield" nr. Fredericksburg, Va., 1781; buried nr. Fredericksburg.

PAGE, Robert, congressman; b. "North End," Gloucester (now Matthews) County, Va., Feb. 4, 1765; attended Coll. William and Mary; studied law. Served as capt. during Am. Revolution; admitted to Va. bar, practiced in Frederick (now Clarke) County; mem. Va. Council of State; mem. Va. Ho. of Dels., 1795; mem. U.S. Ho. of Reps. (Federalist) from Va., 6th Congress, 1799-1801. Died "Janesville," Clarke County, Va., Dec. 8, 1840; buried Old Chapel Cemetery, nr. Millwood, Va.

PAGE, Sherman, congressman; b. Cheshire, Conn., May 9, 1779; attended common schs.; studied law. Taught sch., Coventry, N.Y., 1799; admitted to N.Y. bar, 1805, began practice in Unadilla; mem. N.Y. Assembly, 1827; judge Otsego County (N.Y.) Ct. of Common Pleas; mem. U.S. Ho. of Reps. (Jacksonian Democrat) from N.Y., 23d-24th congresses, 1833-37. Died Unadilla, Sept. 27, 1853; buried St. Matthews's Cemetery, Unadilla.

PAGE, Thomas Jefferson, naval officer; b. Matthews County, Va., Jan. 4, 1808; s. Mann and Elizabeth (Nelson) P.; m. Benjamina Price, 1838, 7 children. Apptd. midshipman U.S. Navy, 1827; participated in coast survey work, 1833-42; promoted lt., 1837; on voyages to Mediterranean and Brazil, 1842-44; attached to U.S. Naval Observatory, 1844-48; commanded brig Dolphin in Far East, 1848-51; commanded steamer Water Witch in exploration of Paarara, Paraguay, La Plata rivers, 1853-55, 59-60; resigned commn., 1861, joined Confederate Navy; in charge of various shore defenses, 1861-63; commanded ironclad Stonewall, 1864-65; never saw action; rancher, shipbuilder, Argentina, 1865-80. Author: La Plata: The Argentine Confederation and Paraguay, 1859. Died Rome, Italy, Oct. 26, 1899.

PAGE, William, painter; b. Albany, N.Y., Jan. 1811; s. Levi and Tamer (Gale) Dunnel P.; m. Lavinia Twibill, circa 1832; m. 2d, Sara Dougherty, circa 1844; m. 3d, Sophia Hitchcock, 1858; 9 children. Recipient prize for sepia drawing from Am. Inst., 1822; pupil of S.F.B. Morse at N.A.D., 1826, became mem., 1836, pres., 1871-73, recipient silver medal for drawing; portraits include John Quincy Adams, William Lloyd Garrison (both in Boston Art Mus.), Ruth and Naomi (at N.Y. Hist. Soc.), The Young Merchants (in Pa. Acad. Fine Arts), also James Russell Lowell, Charles Sumner, Wendell Phillips; lived in Italy, 1849-60, N.Y.C., 1860-85; considered leading Am. painter of the time; among most important hist. pieces was Farragut's Triumphal Entry into Mobile Bay (presented to Grand Duke Alexis of Russia), 1871. Author: New Geometrical Method of Measuring the Human Figure, 1860. Died Staten Island, N.Y., Sept. 30, 1885.

PAIN, Philip, poet; wrote Daily Meditations: Or Quotidien Preparations for, and Considerations of, Death and Eternity, Begun July 19, 1666, pub. 1668; described in that publ. as having drowned in shipwreck; has been called author of "the earliest known specimen of original Am. verse printed in the English Colonies."

PAINE, Bryon, jurist; b. Painesville, O., Oct. 10, 1827; s. James H. and Marilla (Paine) P.; LL.D. (hon.), U. Wis., 1869; m. Clarissa Wyman, Oct. 7, 1854, 4 sons. Went to Wis. Territory, 1845; admitted to Milw. bar, 1849; counsel for Sherman Booth in famous fugitive slave law case before Wis. Supreme Ct., won writ of habeas corpus with his defense attacking constitutionality of law; became famous among anti-slavery proponents; judge Milw. County Ct., 1856-59; asso. justice Wis. Supreme Ct., 1859-64, 67-71; apptd. lt. col. 43d Wis. Volunteers, 1864. Died Madison, Wis., Jan. 13, 1871.

PAINE, Charles, woolen mfr., railroad promoter, gov. Vt.; b. Williamstown, Vt., Apr. 15, 1799; s. Elijah and Sarah (Porter) P.; grad. Harvard, 1820. Managed father's woolen-mills, Northfield, Vt., was a financial success; mem. Vt. Ho. of Reps., 1828-29; gov. Vt., 1841-42, introduced more thorough system of accounting by state officers; became pres. bd. dirs. Vt. Central R.R. Co., 1845, built railroad, 1845-49; donated equipment to Northfield Acad., land for Elmwood Cemetery, Northfield. Died while on inspection tour for a proposed Pacific route through the S.W., Waco, Tex., July 6, 1853.

PAINE, Elijah, senator; b. Brooklyn, Conn., Jan. 21, 1757; s. Seth and Mabel (Tyler) P.; grad. Harvard, 1781, LL.D. (hon.), 1812; A.B. (hon.), Dartmouth, 1786; LL.D. (hon.), U. Vt., 1825; m. Sarah Porter, June 7, 1790, 8 children including Charles, Martyn, Elijah. Admitted to Vt. bar, 1784; founded Town of Wiliamstown (Vt.), 1784; bought large farm and established grist mill and saw mill at nearby Northfield, Vt.; sec. Vt. Constl. Conv. 1786; mem. Vt. Ho. of Reps., 1787-90; asso. justice Vt. Supreme Ct., 1791-95; mem. U.S. Senate from Vt., 1795-1801; U.S. dist. judge for Vt., 1801-42; co-founder, pres. Bank of Montpelier (Vt.), 1825-42; postmaster, Williamstown, 1815-42; developed large flock of sheep, built woolen mill, Northfield, 1812; trustee U. Vt., Middleburg Coll., Dartmouth. Died Williamstown, Apr. 28, 1842; buried Old Williamstown Cemetery.

PAINE, Ephraim, Continental congressman; b. Canterbury, Conn., Aug. 19, 1730; studied medicine. Practiced medicine, Amenia, N.Y.; del. N.Y. Provincial Congress, 1775; county judge, 1778-81; mem. Council of Appointment, 1780; supr. of Amenia, 1782-83; mem. N.Y. State Senate, 1789-84; mem. Continental Congress from N.Y., 1784-85. Died Amenia, Aug. 10, 1785; buried Red Meeting House Cemetery, nr. Amenia.

PAINE, Henry Warren, lawyer; b. Winslow, Me., Aug. 30, 1810; s. Lemuel and Jane (Warren) P.; grad. Waterville (now Colby) Coll., 1830; attended Harvard Law Sch., 1832-33; m. Lucy Coffin, May 1, 1837, 1 child. Admitted to Kennebec County (Me.) bar, 1834; practiced in Hallowell, Me., 1834-54; mem. Me. Ho. of Reps., 1837, 53; atty. for Kennebec County, 1834-39; trustee Waterville (Me.) Coll., 1849-62; practiced in Boston, 1854-85; lectr. real property law Boston U. Law Sch., 1872-85; unsuccessful Democratic candidate for gov. Mass., 1863-64. Died Cambridge, Mass., Dec. 26, 1893.

PAINE, Martyn, physician, educator; b. Williamstown, Vt., July 8, 1794; s. Elijah and Sarah (Porter) P.; A.B., Harvard, 1813, M.D., 1816; LL.D., U. Vt., 1854; m. Mary Ann Weeks, 1825, 1 dau., 2 sons. A promoter of med. coll. U. City N.Y., 1841-67, prof. insts. of medicine, 1841-50, prof. therapeutics and materia medica, after 1850; leading prof. of therapeutics in nation sent by faculty colleagues to Albany to use influence for passage of legislation permitting dissections in N.Y. (act passed, 1854); mem. Royal Soc. Prussia, Med. Soc. Sweden, Soc. Naturalists and Physicians of Dresden, Med. Soc. Leipzig. Author: On the Cholera Asphyxia as It Appeared in the City of N.Y in 1832; Medical and Physiological Commentaries, 1840-44; Essays on the Philosophy of Vitality and on the Modus Operandi of Remedial Agents, 1842; Institutes of Medicine, 1847; Materia Medica and Therapeutics, 1848. Died N.Y.C., Nov. 10, 1877.

PAINE, Robert, clergyman, coll. pres.; b. Person County, N.C., Nov. 12, 1799; s. James and Nancy (Williams) P.; m. Susanna Beck, 1824; m. 2d, Amanda Shaw, 1837; m. 3d, Mary Millwater, 1839; 9 children. Admitted on trial to Tenn. Conf. of Methodist Episcopal Ch., 1818, ordained deacon, 1821, elder, 1823; del. to Gen. Conf., 1824-44; 1st pres. LaGrange Coll., Franklin County, Ala., 1830-46; chmn. com. preparing Plan of Separation for peaceable division of the Church, 1844; attended conv. where Methodist Episcopal Ch. of

South was formally organized, Louisville, Ky., 1845, bishop, 1846-82; preached in Confederate camps; secured chaplains for Confederate Army; largely responsible for prosperity of church immediately after Civil War; trustee Southern U., Vanderbilt U. Author: Life and Times of William McKendree, 1869. Died Aberdeen, Miss., Oct. 19, 1882.

PAINE, Robert Treat, Continental congressman; jurist; b. Boston, Mar. 11, 1731; s. Thomas and Eunice (Treat) P.; grad. Harvard, 1749; m. Sally Cobb, Mar. 15, 1770, 8 children including Robert Treat Paine. Served as chaplain on the Crown Point Expdn. during French and Indian War, 1755; admitted to Mass. bar, 1757; asso. pros. atty. in "Boston Massacre" trial, 1768; mem. Mass. Provincial Assembly, 1773-75, 77-78, speaker, 1777-78; del. to Provincial Congress, 1774, 75; mem. Continental Congress, 1774-78; signer Declaration of Independence, 1776; signed "Olive Branch" petition and declaration to King George III; sent with commr. to negotiate treaty with Indians of Upper N.Y.; 1st atty-gen. Mass., 1777-90; mem. com. to prepare draft of Mass. Constn., 1778; mem. Mass. Gov.'s Council, 1779, 80; a founder Am. Acad. Arts and Scis., 1780; judge Mass. Supreme Ct., 1790-1804; a counselor Commonwealth of Mass., 1804. Died Boston, May 12, 1814; buried Old Granary Burial Ground, Boston.

PAINE, Robert Treat, poet; b. Taunton, Mass., Dec. 9, 1773; s. Robert Treat and Sally (Cobb) P.; grad. Harvard, 1792; m. Eliza Baker, Feb. 1795. Founded Federal Orrery (satirical attacks on contemporaries), 1794-96; important poems include: The Invention of Letters, 1795; The Ruling Passion, 1796; Adams and Liberty, 1798; much of his poetry had patriotic bent; admitted to Boston bar, 1802; led erratic life and died in poverty. Died Boston, Nov. 13, 1811.

PAINE, Robert Treat, congressman; b. Edenton, N.C., Feb. 18, 1812; grad. Washington (now Trinity) Coll., Hartford, Conn.; studied law. Admitted to the bar, practiced law; held local offices; engaged in shipping bus., owner shipyards; mem. N.C. Ho. of Commons, 1838, 40, 44, 46, 48; served as col. of a N.C. regt. during Mexican War; war gov. of Monterey (Mexico), 1846; mem. Mexican Claims Commn.; mem. U.S. Ho. of Reps. (Am. Party rep.) from N.C., 34th Congress, 1855-57; moved to Austin County, Tex., 1860, engaged in farming. Died Galveston, Tex., Feb. 8, 1872; buried Brenham (Tex.) Cemetery.

PAINE, Thomas, polit. writer; b. Thetford, Norfolk, Eng., Jan. 29, 1737; s. Joseph and Frances (Cocke) P.; m. Mary Lambert, Sept. 27, 1759; m. 2d, Elizabeth Ollive, Mar. 26, 1771. Excise officer, Eng., chosen as agt. for excisemen to agitate for higher pay, 1772; left for Phila. after meeting Benjamin Franklin in Eng., 1774; edited, contributed to Robert Aitken's Pa. Mag., 1775; pioneer in movement for abolition of Negro slavery; published pamphlet Common Sense, Phila., Jan. 10, 1776, urged immediate declaration of independence; ex panded ideas in Common Sense in Public Good, 1780; edited Crisis, 12 issues, 1776-83, supported colonial cause; sec. to com. on fgn. affars Continental Congress, 1777-79; published Dissertations on Government, the Affairs of the Bank and Paper Money, 1786; went to Eng., 1787; defended measures taken in revolutionary France and urged Eng. to overthrow monarchy and establish Republic; published 1st part of Rights of Man, 1791, 2d part, 1792; popular with English radicals; suppressed by William Pitt, outlawed and tried for treason; went to France as French citizen, 1792; elected to Nat. Conv. of France; deprived of citizenship when Robespierre came to power, 1793, arrested and imprisoned, 1793-94; wrote 1st part of Age of Reason, 1794, 2d part, 1796; released from prison at request of Am. minister James Monroe; seat in Nat. Conv. restored, 1795; wrote Dissertation on the First Principles of Government, 1795, Letter to George Washington, 1796 (both undermined his reputation in Am.); returned to U.S., 1802. Died N.Y.C., June 8, 1809; buried New Rochelle, N.Y., remains taken to Eng. for burial, 1819, later lost.

PAINE, William Wiseham, congressman; b. Richmond, Va., Oct. 10, 1817; attended sch., Mount Zion, Ga.; studied law, Washington, Ga. Served in Seminole War, 1836; admitted to Ga. bar, 1838; moved to Telfair, Ga., 1840, began practice of law; mem. Ga. Constl. Conv., 1850; pvt. sec. to Gov. Howell Cobb of Ga., 1851-52; mem. Ga. Senate, 1857-60; served as capt. 1st Ga. Regt., Confederate Army, during Civil War; moved to Savannah, Ga., practiced law; mem. U.S. Ho. of Reps. (Democrat) from Ga., 41st Congress, Dec. 22, 1870-71; mem. Ga. Ho. of Reps., 1877-79; curator Ga. Hist. Soc. Died Savannah, Aug. 5, 1882; buried Bonaventure Cemetery, Savannah.

PAINTER, Gamaliel, army officer, legislator; b. New Haven, Conn., May 22, 1743; s. Shubael and Elizabeth (Dunbar) P.; m. Abigail Chipman, Aug. 20, 1767; m. 2d, Victoria Ball, 1795; m. 3d, Mrs. Ursula Bull, 1807; 3 children. Served as lt. in Seth Warner's Additional Continental Regt., 1776; capt. Baldwin's Arty. Artificer Regt.; attended Windsor Conv. which formed Vt. Constn., 1777; bought part of site of future village of Middlebury, Vt., 1787, layed out village streets, sold lots, erected gristmill; asst. judge Addison County, 1785-86, 87-95; mem. lower house Vt. Legislature, various times, 1786-1810; mem. Gov.'s Council sharing exec. power with gov. Vt., 1813-14; a Federalist; a founder Middlebury Coll., 1800, fellow. 1800-19. Died Middlebury, May 22, 1819.

PALEN, Rufus, congressman; b. Palenville, N.Y., Feb. 25, 1807. Engaged in leather mfg.; held local offices, Fallsburg, N.Y.; mem. U.S. Ho. of Reps. (Whig) from N.Y., 26th Congress, 1839-41. Died N.Y.C., Apr 26, 1844; buried Old Cemetery, Palenville.

PALFREY, John Gorham, congressman; b. Boston, May 2, 1796; s. John and Mary (Gorham) P.; grad. Harvard, 1815; LL.D., St. Andrews' Coll., Scotland; m. Mary Ann Hammond, Mar. 11, 1823, 6 children including John Carver. Ordained to ministry Unitarian Ch., 1818; pastor ch., Brattle Square, Boston, 1818-31; became owner, editor N. Am. Review, Boston, 1835; mem. Mass. Legislature, 1842-43; sec. Commonwealth of Mass., 1844-47; mem. U.S. Ho. of Reps. from Mass., 31st Congress, 1847-49; postmaster Boston, 1861-67; mem. Mass. Hist. Soc., Am. Antiquarian Soc. Author: Academical Lectures on the Jewish Scriptures and Antiquities, 4 vols., 1838-52; History of New England, 4 vols., 1858-75. Died Cambridge, Mass., Apr. 26, 1881; buried Mt. Auburn Cemetery, Cambridge.

PALMER, Alonzo Benjamin, physician, educator; b. Richfield, N.Y., Oct. 6, 1815; s. Benjamin and Anna (Layton) P.; grad. Coll. Physicians and Surgeons, Fairfield, N.Y., 1839; LL.D. (hon.), U. Mich., 1881; m. Caroline Wright, July 19, 1843; m. 2d, Love Root, 1867. City physician Chgo., 1852-55, became ofcl. med. adviser to city health officer; prof. materia medica, therapeutics and diseases of women and children U. Mich., 1854, prof. pathology and practice of medicine, 1860-87, dean med. dept., 1875-87; prof. pathology and practice medicine Berkshire Med. Instn., Pittsfield, Mass., 1864-67; prof. practice medicine Bowdoin Coll., 1869-79; served as surgeon 2d Mich. Inf., 1861; editor Peninsular Jour. of Medicine and the Collateral Scis., also Peninsular and Independent Med. Jour., 1853-60; pres. Mich. State Med. Soc., 1872-73. Author: Observations on the Cause, Nature, and Treatment of Epidemic Cholera, 1854; Treatise on the Science and Practice of Medicine, or the Pathology and Treatment of Internal Diseases, 2 vols., 1882; A Treatise on Epidemic Cholera, 1885; The Temperance Teachings of Science, 1886. Died Ann Arbor, Mich., Dec. 23, 1887.

PALMER, Beriah, congressman; b. Bristol County, Mass., 1740; attended common schs.; studied law, Cornwall, N.Y. Admitted to N.Y. bar, practiced law; engaged in surveying and farming, nr. Burnt Hills, N.Y.; moved to Ballston Spa, N.Y., 1774; served with 12th Regt., N.Y. Militia, during Am. Revolution; assessor, 1779; commr. roads Ballston Dist., 1780, 83-84; postmaster, 1784; mem. Albany County (N.Y.) Com. of Safety, supr. Saratoga County (N.Y.), 1790-91, 99; apptd. judge Ct. of Common Pleas, 1791; moderator 1st bd. suprs. Saratoga County, 1791; mem. N.Y. State Assembly, 1792-95; del. N.Y. Constl. Conv., 1801; mem. U.S. Ho. of Reps. from N.Y, 8th Congress, 1803-05; surrogate Saratoga County, 1808-12. Died Ballston Spa, May 20, 1812; buried Village Cemetery, Ballston Spa.

PALMER, Elihu, deist; b. Canterbury, Conn., Aug. 7, 1764; s. Elihu and Lois (Foster) P.; grad. Dartmouth, 1787; m. 2d, Mary Powell, 1803; several children. Pastor, Presbyn. Ch., Newtown, L.I., N.Y., 1788-89, Universalist Ch., Phila., 1789; discharged from both for radical deist beliefs; scoffed at organized religion, divinity of Bible and immortality of Christ; believed all organized religions were primary cause of world's evils; blinded by yellow fever, 1793; established Philos. Soc. (deist orgn.), N.Y.C., 1794, later known as Theistical Soc. and Soc. of Columbia Illumiate (similar orgns. established later in Phila. and Balt.); publisher The Prospect, deist weekly, N.Y.C., 1803-05. Author: The Examiners Examined: Being a Defense of the Age of Reason, 1794; An Enquiry Relative to the Moral and Political Improvement of the Human Species, 1797; Principles of Nature; or, a Development of the Moral Causes of Happiness and Misery among the Human Species, 1802. Died Phila., Apr. 7, 1806.

PALMER, Frances Flora Bond, artist; b. Leicester, Eng., 1812; m. Edward S. Palmer. Came to U.S. with husband and her brother and sister, Robert and Maria Bond, early 1840's; began working as artist and colorist for M. Currier, lithographer, N.Y.C., 1840's, became 1 of Currier and Ives' best known artists, specializing in landscapes, railroad, Mississippi and sporting subjects, continued working with firm until her death. Died N.Y.C., 1876.

PALMER, Innis Newton, army officer; b. Buffalo, N.Y., Mar. 30, 1824; s. Innis Bromley and Susan (Candee) P.; grad U.S. Mil. Acad., 1846; m. Catharine Jones, 1853, 4 children. Apptd. brevet 2d lt. U.S. Army, 1846; served at battles of Cerro Gordo, Contreras, Churubusco, Chapultepec and Mexico City during Mexican War; brevetted capt., 1848; served in cavalry in Western U.S., 1848-61; promoted maj., 1861; brevetted lt. col. regular army and promoted brig. gen. U.S. Volunteers, 1861; served at battles of Bull Run, Fair Oaks, Glendale and Malvern Hill during Civil War; brevetted col. 2d Cavalry, promoted maj. gen. U.S. Volunteers, 1865; commanded 2d Cavalry in West, 1865-79; promoted col., 1868, ret., 1879. Died Chevy Chase, Md., Sept. 9, 1900.

PALMER, James Croxall, naval surgeon; b. Balt., June 29, 1811; s. Edward and Catherine (Croxall) P.; grad. Dickinson Coll., 1829, med. course U. Md., 1833; m. Juliet Gittings, May 22, 1837, 2 children. Commd. asst. surgeon U.S. Navy, 1834; served in Wilkes' Antarctic exploring expdn., 1838-42; promoted to surgeon, 1842, in charge hosp. Washington (D.C.) Navy Yard; served on steam frigate Niagara (employed in laying 1st Atlantic cable), 1857; in charge med. service Naval Acad., Newport, R.I., 1861-62; fleet surgeon West Gulf Blockading Squadron under Adm. Farragut, 1863-65; in charge Naval Hosp., Bklyn., 1866-69, med. dir., 1871; surgeon gen. U.S. Navy, 1872-73. Author: The Antarctic Mariner's Song (poem), 1868. Died Washington, D.C., Apr. 24, 1883.

PALMER, James Shedden, naval officer; b. N.J., Oct. 13, 1810. Became midshipman U.S. Navy, 1825; lt., 1838; commanded schooner Flirt, during Mexican War; made unsuccessful attempt to capture Confederate raider Sumter, 1861; sent by David Farragut to take possession of Baton Rouge (La.) and Natchez (Miss.), 1862; commanded ship Hartford; succeeded Farragut in command on Mississippi River; commd. commodore, 1863; commanded West Gulf Squadron, 1864; commanded West India Squadron in ship Susquehanna, 1865; commd. rear adm., 1866. Died of yellow fever in W.I., Dec. 7, 1867; buried N.Y.C.

PALMER, Joel, legislator; b. Ontario, Can., Oct. 4, 1810; s. Ephraim and Hannah (Phelps) P.; m. Catherine Caffee, 1830; m. 2d, Sarah Derbyshire; 7 children. Came to Am., 1812; mem. Ind. Legislature, 1843-45; commissary-gen. of volunteer forces during Cayuse War; laid out Town of Dayton, (Ore.); supt. Indian affairs for Ore. Territory, 1853-57; negotiator of 9 treaties of cession, 1854-55; opened a route to Brit. Columbia gold mines from Ore.; dir., pres. Oregon City Mfg. Co.; speaker Ore. Ho. of Reps., 1862; mem. Ore. Senate, 1864-66. Author: Journal of Travels over the Rocky Mountains, 1847. Died Dayton, June 9, 1881.

PALMER, John, congressman; b. Hoosick, N.Y., Jan. 29, 1785; grad. Williams Coll.; studied law. Admitted to N.Y. bar, began pratcice in Plattsburg, 1810; served as paymaster 8th Regt., N.Y. Militia, 1812; mem. U.S. Ho. of Reps. (Democrat) from N.Y., 15th, 25th congresses, 1817-19, 37-39; dist. atty., 1818-32; mem. N.Y. State Assembly, 1832; judge Clinton County (N.Y.), 1832-37; Died St. Bartholomew, French West Indies, Dec. 8, 1840; buried St. Bartholomew Cemetery.

PALMER, Joseph, mfr., army officer; b. Higher Abbotsrow, Shaugh Prior, Devonshire, Eng., Mar. 31, 1716; s. John and Joan (Pearse) P.; m. Mary Cranch, 1745, 3 children. Came to Am., 1746; erected (with brother-in-law Richard Cranch) glass manufactory in Germantown (now part of Quincy), Mass., 1752; mem. Mass. Provincial Congress, 1774-75; mem. Cambridge Com. of Safety; commd. col. 5th Suffolk Regt., Mass. Militia, 1776; chosen brig. gen. for Suffolk County, 1776, apptd. brig. gen. to command forces on a secret expdn. to attack enemy at Newport, R.I., 1777, expdn. failed; started salt factory, Boston Neck, Mass., circa 1784. Died Dorchester, Mass., Dec. 25, 1788.

PALMER, Nathaniel Brown, explorer; b. Stonington, Conn., Aug. 8, 1799; s. Nathaniel and Mercy (Brown) P.; m. Eliza Babcock, Dec. 7, 1826. Discovered mainland of Antarctica at Orleans Channel, during a sealing expdn. in sloop Hero, 1820; explored the region more thoroughly in ship James Monroe, 1822, discovered (with an Englishman) South Orkney Islands; made several voyages to Caribbean with ships Cadet and Tampico transporting troops and supplies to Simon Bolivar; became packet capt., 1834; captained clippers Hougna, Samuel Russell, Oriental; took steamship United States to Bremen; superintended rebuilding of the Great Republic; dir. Fall River Line; became mem. N.Y. Yacht Club, 1845. Died San Francisco, June 21, 1877.

PALMER, Ray, clergyman, hymn-writer; b. Little Compton, R.I., Nov. 12, 1808; s. Thomas and Susanna Palmer; grad. Yale, 1830; D.D. (hon.), Union Coll., 1852; m. Ann Maria Wand, Oct. 3, 1832. Licensed to preach, Conn., 1832; ordained and installed as pastor Congregational Ch., Bath, Me., 1835; 1st pastor 1st Congregational Ch., Albany, N.Y., 1850-66; corr. sec. Am. Congregational Union, 1866-78; wrote hymns including My Faith Looks up to Thee, Away from Earth my Spirit Turns, Take Me, O Take Me; asso. pastor Bellevue Av. Ch., Newark, N.J., 1881-84. Author: Spiritual Improvement; or, Aid to Growth in Grace, 1839; Closet Hours, 1851; Remember Me, 1855; Hymns and Sacred Pieces, 1865; Home; or, the Unlost Paradise, 1868; Complete Poetical Works, 1876; Voices of Hope and Gladness, 1880. Died Newark, Mar. 29, 1887.

PALMER, William Adams, senator, gov. Vt.; b. Hebron, Conn., Sept. 12, 1781; s. Stephen and Susannah (Sawyer) P.; m. Sarah Blanchard, Sept. 1813, 7 children. Admitted to Vt. bar, 1802; clk. Caledonia County (Vt.) Ct., 1807-15; farmer nr. Danville, Vt.; probate judge Caledonia County, 1807-08, 11-17; mem. Vt. Ho. of Reps., 1811-12, 18, 25-26, 29; justice Vt. Supreme Ct., 1816-18; mem. U.S. Senate from Vt., Oct. 20, 1818-25; asst. judge Caledonia County, 1826-28; gov. Vt. (Anti-Masonic), 1831-35; mem. Vt. Senate, 1836-37; del. Vt. Constl. Conv., 1826, 36, 50. Died Danville, Dec. 3, 1860; buried Green Cemetery, Danville.

PALMER, William Henry, magician; b. England, 1830; m. Annie Maria Kieckhoefer, 1855, 3 children. Came to U.S., circa 1853; toured U.S., England, Australia, appeared primarily in N.Y.C., Phila.; one of 1st magicians to use electric devices; employed comical approach to his act with great success. Died Phila., Nov. 28, 1878.

PALMERSTON, 3d viscount, see Temple, Henry John.

PALOU, Francisco, missionary; b. Mallorca, circa 1722; entered U. of Lulliam of Monastary of San Francisco at Palma; became pupil of Junipero Serra (founder of Franciscan missions in Cal.), 1740; accompanied Serra to Mexico, 1749; became Franciscan missionary in Sierra Gorda, northeast of Querétaro at Jalpan, 1750, pres. of mission, 1760; mem. band of Franciscans who replaced Jesuits when they were expelled from Baja Cal., 1767; pres. of mission, Baja Peninsula, Cal., 1769-73; marked boundary between Upper and Lower Cal., 1773; founded Dolores Mission in San Francisco, 1776, headed mission until 1785; pres. Coll. of San Fernando, Mexico, 1785-89. Author: Relación Historica de la Vida y Apostólicas Tareas del Venerable Fray Junípero Serra, 1787. Died circa 1789.

PANCOAST, Joseph, anatomist, surgeon; b. nr. Burlington, N.J., Nov. 23, 1805; s. John and Ann (Abbott) P.; M.D., U. Pa., 1828; m. Rebecca Abbott, June 2, 1829, 1 son, William Henry. Conducted Phila. Sch. Anatomy, 1831-38; elected physician to Phila. Hosp., 1835; vis. surgeon, 1838-45; prof. surgery Jefferson Med. Coll., 1838, prof. anatomy, 1841-74; mem. staff Pa. Hosp., 1854-64; prin. achievements in surgery include operation for remediation of exstrophy of bladder by plastic abdominal flaps, for soft and mixed cataracts, for correction of occlusion of nasal duct; originated an abdominal tourniquet; mem. Am. Philos. Soc., Phila. County Med. Soc., Med. Soc. Pa. Author: Treatise on Operative Surgery, 1st edit., 1844, 3d edit., 1852. Died Phila., Mar. 7, 1882.

PANCOAST, Seth, physician, cabalist; b. Darby, Pa., July 28, 1823; s. Stephen and Anna (Stroud) P.; M.D., U. Pa., 1852; m. Sarah Osborn; m. 2d, Susan Osborn; m. 3d, Carrie Fernald; some children. Prof. anatomy Female Med. Coll. Pa., 1853; prof. anatomy Pa. Med. Coll., 1854-59, prof. emeritus, 1859; built what was probably largest library dealing with occult scis. ever assembled in U.S. Author: Ladies Medical Guide, 1858; Boyhold's Perils, 1860; The Kabbala; or the True Science of Light; an Introduction to the Philosophy and Theosophy of the Ancient Sages (1st book written in English to explain the "Ten Sepheroth," and gave mystical interpretation of Holy Scriptures as contained therein), 1877; Blue and Red Light. . ., 1877; Bright's Disease, 1882. Died Phila., Dec. 16, 1889.

PANTON, William, trader; b. Aberdeenshire, Scotland, 1742; s. John and Barbara (Wenys) P.; never married. Came to Am., circa 1770; mem. mcht. firm Moore & Panton, Savannah, Ga., 1770-75; established firm Panton, Forbes & Co. for trade with Creek Indians in E. Fla., 1775-84; head of firm Panton, Leslie & Co., 1784-1801, held exclusive charter from Spain for trade with Indians in W. Fla.; established many trading posts, dealt with Choctaw, Creek, Cherokee, Chickasaw Indians. Died at sea, Feb. 26, 1801; buried Great Harbours, Berry Islands.

PAQUET, Anthony C., engraver; b. Hamburg, Germany, 1814. Came to Am., 1848; worked in Phila., 1850-55, N.Y.C., 1856-58; asst. engraver U.S. Mint, Phila., 1857-64; engraved 1st Congressional Medal of Honor; exhibited medals at Pa. Acad. during Civil War. Died Phila., 1882.

PARDEE, Ario, engr., businessman; b. Chatham, N.Y., Nov. 19, 1810; s. Ariovistus and Eliza (Platt) P.; m. Elizabeth Jacobs, 1838; m. 2d, Anna Maria Robison, Aug. 29, 1848; 14 children. Engr. on constrn. of Del. and Raritan Canal, 1830-32; chief engr. on constrn. Beaver Meadow R.R. in Pa., 1832-36; chief engr. Hazelton R.R. & Coal Co.,1836-40; founded firm Pardee, Miner & Co., 1840 (became largest anthracite coal producer in Pa.); owner several mining cos., iron works, also had large lumber holdings; contbd. over $500,000 to Lafayette Coll., Easton, Pa., trustee, 1865-82, chmn. bd., 1882-92; presdl. elector for Pa., 1876; chmn. bd. commrs. for 2d Pa. Geol. Survey. Died Ormond, Fla., Mar. 26, 1892.

PARISH, Elijah, clergyman, author; b. Lebanon, Conn., Nov. 7, 1762; s. Elijah and Eunice (Foster) P.; B.A., Dartmouth, 1785, M.A., 1788; m. Mary Hale, Nov. 7, 1796, 5 children. Pastor, Congregational Ch., Byfield, Mass., 1787-1825. Author: (with Jedediah Morse) A New Gazetteer of the Eastern Continent, 1802, A Compendious History of New England, 1804; New System of Modern Geography, 1810; (with David McClure) Memoirs of the Rev. Eleazar Wheelock, D.D., Founder and President of Dartmouth College and Moore's Charity School, 1811; Sacred Geography; or, A Gazeteer of the Bible, 1813. Died Oct. 15, 1825.

PARK, James, iron and steel mfr.; b. Pitts., Jan. 11, 1820; s. James and Margaret (McCurdy) P.; m. Sarah Gray, 7 children. Partner (with brother David E.) firm Park, Brother & Co., 1840, became James Park, Jr. and Co., 1843; founded Lake Superior Copper Works for manufacture of sheathing copper, 1857, had partial control his whole life; encouraged introduction new indsl. processes; instrumental in increasing tariff schedule which entrenched steel in position of special privilege; established Black Diamond Steel Works, 1862; incorporated (with others) Kelly Pneumatic Process Co., 1863, made 1st steel in U.S. by complete Bessemer process, 1864; 1st to introduce Siemens gas furnace into U.S. for metal conversion (1st Siemens furnace completed by Park, McCurdy & Co., 1863); v.p. Am. Iron and Steel Assn., 1873-83; had great influence in securing final result as embodied in tariff bill approved 1883. Died Allegheny, Pa., Apr. 21, 1883.

PARK, Linton, artist; b. 1826. Engaged as lumberman; painted logging and farm scenes in Clearfield and Indiana counties (Pa.), circa 1850-60; painted flax-scutching party on a Western Pa. farm (one of best known Am. primitives), circa 1860.

PARK, Roswell, educator, clergyman; b. Lebanon, Conn., Oct. 1, 1807; s. Avery and Betsey (Meech) P.; attended Hamilton Coll., 1826-27; grad. U.S. Mil. Acad., 1831; A.B., Union Coll., Schenectady, N.Y., 1831; m. Mary Brewster, Dec. 28, 1836; m. 2d, Eunice Elizabeth Niles, Apr. 25, 1860. Commd. brevet 2d lt. Corps Engrs., U.S. Army, 1831, resigned, 1836; prof. chemistry and natural philosophy U. Pa., 1836-42, ordained deacon Protestant Episcopal Ch., 1843, priest, 1844; rector Christ Ch., Pomfret, Conn., 1843-52; headmaster Christ Ch. Hall, Pomfret, 1845-52; founder, 1st pres. Racine (Wis.) Coll., 1852-59, chancellor, 1859-63; pastor St. Luke's Ch., Racine, 1856-63; founded and conducted Immanuel Hall (pvt. sch.), Chgo., 1863-69; mem. A.A.A.S. Author: Selections of Juvenile and Miscellaneous Poems, 1836; A Sketch of the History and Topography of West Point and of the United States Military Academy, 1840; Pantology; or, A Systematic Survey of Human Knowledge, 1841; Handbook for American Travellers in Europe, 1853. Died July 16, 1869.

PARK, Trenor William, legislator, railroad promoter; b. Woodford, Vt., Dec. 8, 1823; s. Luther and Cynthia (Pratt) P.; m. Laura Hall, Dec. 15, 1846; m. 2d, Ella Nichols, May 30, 1882; 3 children. Admitted to Vt. bar, 1844; jr. partner in Cal. firm Halleck, Peachy, Billings & Park, 1852; local mgr. Mariposa estate of Gen. John C. Fremont; established 1st Nat. Bank of Bennington (Vt.); assisted in reorgn. Vt. Central R.R.; purchased Western Vt. R.R.; began constrn. Lebanon Central R.R.; mem. Vt. Legislature, 1865-68; del. Republican Nat. Conv., 1868; acquired controlling interest in Emma mine, Utah, 1871; went to London, Eng., 1871, formed English co. to take over mine, sued for fraud, acquitted; dir. Pacific Mail S.S. Lines, 1875-82; bought controlling interest in Panama R.R., pres., 1875-82, sold to De Lesseps Panama Canal Co., 1881; bequeathed $5,000 toward establishment Bennington Pub. Library; trustee U. Vt., donated art gallery. Died at sea, Dec. 13, 1882.

PARKE, Benjamin, territorial del. to Congress, jurist; b. N.J., Sept. 22, 1777; m. Eliza Barton, 2 children. Moved to Lexington, Ky., 1797; admitted to Ky. bar, circa 1800; moved to Vincennes, Ind. Territory, 1804-08; elected to 1st Ind. Territorial Legislature, 1805; 1st del. to U.S. Congress from Ind. Territory, Dec. 12, 1805-Mar. 1, 1808; mem. staff Gov. William Henry Harrison; territorial judge, 1808-17; del. Ind. Constl. Conv., 1816, responsible for adoption provisions which became basis of state pub. sch. system, 1816; served with Ind. Militia, 1801-11, raised a dragoon (cavalry) company which saw action at Battle of Tippecanoe, 1811; became maj. of cavalry; served as Indian agt. and U.S. commr. in drawing up land treaties with Indians, especially St. Marys (O.) Treaty deeding central Ind. to White settlement, 1818; judge U.S. Dist. Ct., 1817-35; 1st pres. Ind. Hist. Soc.; chmn. bd. trustees Vincennes U. Died Salem, Ind., July 12, 1835; buried Crown Hill Cemetery, Salem.

PARKE, John, army officer, poet; b. Dover, Del., Apr. 7, 1754; s. Thomas Parke; A.B., Coll. of Phila. (now U. Pa.), 1771, A.M., 1775. Apptd. asst. q.m. gen. Continental Army, Cambridge, Mass., 1775, lt. col. artificers, N.Y.C., 1776. Author: The Lyric Works of Horace, Translated into English Verse: to Which Are Added, a Number of Original Poems, by a Native of America, 1786. Died Kent County, Del., Dec. 11, 1789.

PARKER, Amasa Junius, congressman, jurist; b. Sharon, Conn., June 2, 1807; s. Rev. Daniel and Anna (Fenn) P.; B.A., Union Coll., 1825; LL.D. (hon.), Geneva Coll., 1846; m. Harriet Langdon Roberts, Aug. 1834, 4 children. Principal, Hudson (N.Y.) Acad., 1823-27; admitted to N.Y. bar, 1828; rep. N.Y. Assembly, 1833, 34; dist. atty., Delaware County, N.Y., 1834-36; regent U. State N.Y., 1835-44; mem. U.S. Ho. of Reps. from N.Y., 25th Congress, 1837-39; circuit judge, vice chancellor 3d Circuit N.Y., 1844-47; justice Supreme Ct., 3d Circuit N.Y., 1847-55; chmn. Democratic and Constl. Unionist Conv., Albany, N.Y., 1861; a founder Albany Law Sch., 1851, lectr., 10 years, spl. lectr., 10 years; trustee Albany Female Acad., Union Coll., Cornell U.; trustee State Hosp. for Insane, Poughkeepsie, N.Y., circa 1866-81; del. to N.Y. State Constl. Conv., 1867, 68. Editor: Reports of Decisions in Criminal Cases—State of N.Y., 1823-68, 6 vols., 1855-68; (with others) The Revised Statutes of the State of N.Y., 1859. Died Albany, May 13, 1890; buried Albany Rural Cemetery.

PARKER, Andrew, congressman; b. Cumberland County, Pa., May 21, 1805; grad. Dickinson Coll., Carlisle, Pa., 1824; studied law, Carlisle. Admitted to Pa. bar, 1826, began practice in Lewiston; apptd. dep. atty. gen. Mifflin County (Pa.); moved to Mifflintown, Pa., 1831, practiced law; mem. U.S. Ho. of Reps. (Democrat) from Pa., 32d Congress, 1851-53. Died Mifflintown, Jan. 15, 1864; buried Presbyn. Cemetery, Mifflintown.

PARKER, Edwin Wallace, clergyman; b. St. Johnsbury, Vt., Jan. 21, 1833; s. Quincy B. and Electa (McGaffy) P.; grad. Meth. Bibl. Inst., Concord, N.H., 1858; m. Lois Lee, 1856. Admitted on trial to Vt. Conf., Methodist Episcopal Ch., 1857, ordained pastor and missionary, 1859; missionary in No. India, with base at Morabadad, 1859-1901; 1st presiding elder India Conf., Meth. Episcopal Ch., 1864-1900; in U.S., 1868-70; organized Women's Fgn. Missionary Soc., Boston; del. Gen. Conf. Meth. Ch., 1884, 92, 96, 1900; missionary bishop, 1900-01. Died Naini Tal, India, June 4, 1901.

PARKER, Ely Samuel, (Indian name: Do-ne-ho-ga-wa, or Keeper of the Western Door of the Long House of the Iroquois) Indian chief; b. Indian Falls, Pembroke, N.Y., 1828; s. William and Elizabeth Parker (Indian names: Jo-no-es-do-wa and Ga-ont-gwut-turus); attended Rensselaer Poly. Inst.; m. Minnie Sackett, Dec. 25, 1867. Represented his people in prosecuting Indian claims, Washington, D.C.; chief of Seneca Indian tribe, 1852; gave Lewis Morgan important help in preparing 1st sci. study of Indian tribe, published as League of the Ho-de-no-sau-nee Iorquois, 1851; supt. constrn. for govt. works, Galena, Ill., 1857-62; commd. capt. of engrs., 1863; div. engr. 7th Div., 17th Corps, U.S. Army; commd. lt. col. and Grant's mil. sec., 1864; transcribed ofcl. copies of document ending Civil War; commd. brig. gen. U.S. Volunteers, 1865; brevetted capt., maj., lt. col., col., brig. gen., 1867; commr. Indian affairs, commd. by Grant, 1869; tried by U.S. Ho. of Reps. on charges of defrauding govt., acquitted, 1871. Died Fairfield, Conn., Aug. 31, 1895; buried Forest Lawn Cemetery, Buffalo, N.Y.

PARKER, Foxhall Alexander, naval officer; b. N.Y.C., Aug. 5, 1821; s. Foxhall Alexander and Sarah (Bogardus) P.; m. Mary Greene, Feb. 10, 1846; m. 2d, Lydia Mallory, Nov. 2, 1853; m. 3d, Caroline Donaldson, Oct. 20, 1863; 10 children. Apptd. midshipman U.S. Navy, 1839, commd. lt., 1850; exec. officer Washington (D.C.) Navy Yard, 1861; manned Ft. Ellsworth, Alexandria, for defense of Washington, 1861; comdr., 1862; commanded ship Mahaska, sr. officer in operation against Matthews Court House, 1862; commd. capt., 1866; commanded ship Franklin, European Squadron, 1870-71; chief of staff North Atlantic Fleet, 1872, drew up new signal code for steam tactics; commd. commodore, 1872; chief signal officer, 1873-76; in charge of Boston Navy Yard, 1876-78; supt. Naval Acad.; chmn. com. organizing U.S. Naval Inst., 1873, pres., 1878. Author: Squadron Tactics under Steam, 1864; Fleet Tactics under Steam, 1870; The Naval Howitzer Ashore, 1865; The Naval Howitzer Afloat (latter two used as textbooks), 1866. Died Annapolis, Md., June 10, 1879.

PARKER, Isaac, congressman, jurist; b. Boston, June 17, 1768; s. Daniel and Margaret (Jarvis) P.; grad. Harvard, 1786, LL.D. (hon.), 1814; m. Rebecca Hall, June 19, 1794, 8 children. Mem. U.S. Ho. of Reps. from Mass., 5th Congress, 1797-99; U.S. marshal for Me. Dist. (apptd. by Pres. John Adams), 1799-1803; judge Mass. Supreme Ct., 1806-14, chief justice, 1814-30; 1st Royal prof. law at Harvard, 1815-27, submitted plan for law sch. at Harvard, 1817 (plan adopted and sch. established); overseer Harvard, 20 years; trustee Bowdoin Coll., 11 years; pres. Mass. Constl. Conv., 1820; consolidated reforms in Mass. jud. system. Author: Oration on Washington, 1800; Sketch of the Character of Chief Justice Parsons, 1813. Died Boston, July 26, 1830; buried Copps Hill Cemetery.

PARKER, Isaac Charles, congressman, jurist; b. Belmont County, O., Oct. 15, 1838; s. Joseph and Jane (Shannon) P.; m. Mary O'Toole, Dec. 12, 1861, 2 children. City atty., St. Joseph, Mo., 1860-64; presdl. elector, 1864; judge 12th Circuit, Mo., 1868-70; mem. U.S. Ho. of Reps. from Mo., 42d-43d congresses, 1871-75, mem. com. on territories; judge Western Dist. of Ark., 1875-96, restored law and order, had reputation for severity outside of the dist., was known as "the hanging judge"; drew up bill for donating U.S. Reservation in Ft. Smith, Ark. to schs. of the city instead of to a railroad. Died Nov. 17, 1896; buried Nat. Cemetery, Fort Smith.

PARKER, James, printer, journalist; b. Woodbridge, N.J., circa 1714; s. Samuel and Janet (Ford) P.; m. Mary Ballareau; children—Samuel Franklin, Jane. In printing business (with Benjamin Franklin as silent partner), N.Y.C., 1742-48; financial auditor Franklin & Hall of Phila.; public printer of N.Y., 1743-circa 1760; founder, publisher N.Y. Weekly Post-Boy), (later called N.Y. Gazette or Weekly Post-Boy), 1743-73; librarian Library of Corp. of City of N.Y., 1746; established (with John Holt as mgr. and silent partner) Conn. Gazette, New Haven, 1755; comptroller, sec. gen. of post offices of Brit. Colonies, 1756; judge Ct. of Common Pleas, Middlesex County, N.J., 1764; compiled and printed Conductor Generalis (designated duties and powers of justices), 1764; public printer N.J.; printer to Yale; set up 1st permanent printing office of N.J. at Woodbridge, issued Constl. Courant (1st newspaper in N.J.), 1765; published periodicals including Independent Reflector (1752-53), Occasional Reverberator (Sept. Oct. 1753), John Englishman (Apr.-July 1755), Instructor (1755), New Am. Mag. (1758-60). Died Burlington, N.J., July 2, 1770; buried Woodbridge.

PARKER, James, congressman; b. Boston, 1768; studied medicine. Began practice of medicine, Gardiner, Mass. (now Me.); mem. Mass. Senate, 1811-12; mem. U.S. Ho. of Reps. (Democrat) from Mass., 13th, 16th congresses, 1813-15, 19-21. Died Gardiner, Nov. 9, 1837: buried Oak Grove Cemetery, Gardiner.

PARKER, James, congressman; b. Bethlehem Twp., N.J., Mar. 3, 1776; s. James and Gertrude (Skinner) P.; grad. Columbia, 1793; m. Penelope Butler, Jan. 5, 1803; m. 2d, Catherine Ogden, Sept. 20, 1827; at least 1 child. Mem. N.J. Assembly, 1806, 10, 12, 13, 15, 16, 18, 27, promoted constrn. of canal between Delaware and Raritan rivers, 1827; Democratic presdl. elector, 1824; commr. to fix boundary line between N.J. and N.Y., 1827-29; collector Port of Perth Amboy (N.J.), 1829-30; dir. Delaware & Raritan Canal Co., circa 1830-68; mayor Perty Amboy, 1815, 50; mem. U.S. Ho. of Reps. from N.J., 23d, 24th congresses, 1833-37; registrar bd. of proprs. of East Jersey; influential in N.J. Constl. Conv., 1844; trustee Rutgers Coll., Coll. of N.J. (now Princeton); pres. N.J. Hist. Soc., 1864-68; mem. Protestant Episcopal Conv. of N.J. from St. Peter's Ch., Perth Amboy. Died Perth Amboy, Apr. 1, 1868; buried St. Peter's Churchyard, Perth Amboy.

PARKER, Joel, jurist; b. Jaffrey, N.H., Jan. 25, 1795; s. Abel and Edith (Jewett) P.; grad. Dartmouth, 1811, LL.D. (hon.), 1837; LL.D. (hon.), Harvard, 1848; m. Mary Parker, Jan. 20, 1848. Admitted to N.H. bar, 1817; mem. N.H. Legislature, 1824, 25, 26; asso. judge N.H. Superior Ct., 1833, chief justice, 1838-48; Rayall prof. law Harvard, 1847-68; del. from Cambridge to Mass. Constl. Conv., 1853; commr. to revise Statutes of Mass.; Whig. Author: Daniel Webster as a Jurist, 1853; A Charge to the Grand Jury on the Uncertainty of Law, 1854; The Non-Extension of Slavery, 1856; Personal Liberty Laws and Slavery in the Territories, 1861; The Right of Secession, 1861; Constitutional Law, 1862; Habeas Corpus and Martial Law, 1862; The War Powers of Congress and the President, 1863; The Three Powers of Government, 1869; Conflict of Decisions, 1875. Died Cambridge, Mass., Aug. 17, 1875.

PARKER, Joel, clergyman; b. Bethel, Vt., Aug. 27, 1799; grad. Hamilton Coll., 1824; attended Auburn (N.Y.) Theol. Sem., 1824-26; m. Harriet Phelps, May 9, 1826. Founder, pastor 3d Presbyn. Ch., Rochester, N.Y., 1827-30; pastor 1st Free Presbyn. Ch. of N.Y.C., 1830-33, 1st Presbyn. Ch., New Orleans, 1833-38, Tabernacle Ch., N.Y.C., 1838-40; pres., prof. sacred rhetoric Union Theol. Sem., 1840-42, dir., 1857-69; pastor Clinton Street Presbyn. Ch., Phila., 1842-52, Bleecker Street Ch., N.Y.C., 1852-62, Park Street Ch., Newark, N.J., 1862-68. Author: Lectures on Universalism, 1830; The Pastor's Initiatory Catechism, 1855. Editor: Sermons on Various Subjects (John Watson Adams), 1851. Died N.Y.C., May 2, 1873.

PARKER, Joel, gov. N.J., jurist; b. Freehold, N.J., Nov. 24, 1816; s. Charles and Sarah (Coward) P.; grad. Coll. of N.J. (now Prineton), 1839; LL.D. (hon.), Rutgers Coll., 1872; m. Maria Gummere, 1843, at least 3 children. Admitted to N.J. bar, 1842; mem. N.J. Legislature (Democrat) from Monmouth County, 1847-51; pros. atty., 1852-57; brig. gen. N.J. Militia, 1857; Dem. presdl. elector, 1860; gov. N.J., 1863-66, opposed move in Congress to secure use of roadway of Raritan & Delaware Bay R.R. for War Dept., helped supply troops for Civil War, sponsored establishment of sinking fund for redemption of war loans; gov. N.J., 1872-75; atty. gen. N.J., Jan.-Apr. 1875; judge N.J Supreme Ct., 1880-88. Died Phila., Jan. 2, 1888.

PARKER, John, army officer; b. Lexington, Mass., July 13, 1729; s. Josiah and Anna (Stone) P.; m. Lydia Moore, May 25, 1755, 7 children. Engaged in farming; served at battles of Louisburg and Quebec during French and Indian War; capt. co. of Mass. Minutemen at outbreak of Revolutionary War; assembled group of 130 men to defend the house in which John Hancock and Samuel Adams were staying, Lexington (8 Americans were killed, 10 wounded when British attacked), Apr. 1775; led force in pursuit of British as far as Concord, Mass.; became too ill to serve in Battle of Bunker Hill. Died the following autumn, Sept. 17, 1775.

PARKER, John, Continental congressman; b. Charleston, S.C., June 24, 1759; grad. Middle Temple, London, Eng. Admitted to S.C. bar, 1785, began practice in Charleston, engaged in rice planting; mem. Continental Congress from S.C., 1786-88; executor large rice estates. Died nr. Charleston, Apr. 20, 1832; buried family burying ground at "Hayes" nr. Charleston.

PARKER, John Mason, congressman; b. Granville, N.Y., June 14, 1805; attended Granville Acad.; grad. Middlebury (Vt.) Coll., 1828; studied law. Admitted to N.Y. bar, began practice in Owego, 1833; mem. U.S. Ho. of Reps. (Whig) from N.Y., 34th-35th congresses, 1855-59; justice N.Y. Supreme Ct., 1859-73, justice gen. term of 3d dept., 1867-73; mem. Ct. of Appeals. Died Owego, Dec. 16, 1873; buried Evergreen Cemetery, Owego.

PARKER, Josiah, congressman; b. Isle of Wight County, Va., May 11, 1751; s. Nicholas and Ann (Copeland) P.; m. Mary (Pierce) Bridger, 1773. Mem. local com. of safety, 1775; mem. Va. Revolutionary Conv., 1775; commd. maj., 1776, served as lt. col. 5th Va. Regt. at Battle of Trenton, 1776, promoted col., 1777; mem. Va. Ho. of Dels., 1780-81; naval officer Port of Norfolk (Va.), 1786-88; an anti-Federalist; mem. U.S. Ho. of Reps. from Va., 1st-6th congresses, 1789-1801. Died Isle of Wight County, Mar. 18, 1810.

PARKER, Julia Evelina Smith (Mrs. Amos G. Parker), see Smith, Julia Evelina.

PARKER, Nahum, senator; b. Shrewsbury, Mass., Mar. 4, 1760. Served in Continental Army during Am. Revolution; settled in Fitzwilliam, N.H., 1786, selectman, 1790-94, clk. and town treas., 1792-1815; mem. N.H. Ho. of Reps., 1794-1804, 06-07; mem. N.H. Gov.'s Council, 1804-05; mem. U.S. Senate from N.H., 1807-June 1, 1810; justice Ct. of Common Pleas for Cheshire and Sullivan counties (N.H.), 1807-13; asso. justice Western circuit, 1813-16; judge Cheshire County Ct. of Sessions, 1821, Hillsborough County (N.H.) Ct. of Common Pleas, 1822; mem. N.H. Senate, pres. 1828. Died Fitzwilliam, Nov. 12, 1839; buried Town Cemetery, Fitzwilliam.

PARKER, Peter, med. missionary, diplomat; b. Framingham, Mass., June 18, 1804; s. Nathan and Catherine (Murdock) P.; grad. Yale, 1831, M.D., 1834; m. Harriet Colby Webster, Mar. 29, 1841; 1 son. Ordained to ministry Presbyn. Ch., Phila., 1834; sailed to Canton as 1st Protestant med. missionary to China, 1834; opened hosp., Canton, began giving med. instrn. to Chinese, 1835; accompanied Morrison expdn. to Japan which tried to repatriate 7 shipwrecked Japanese sailors, 1835; an organizer Med. Missionary Soc. in China, 1838; opened hosp. in Macao, 1838; U.S. agt. in China, 1842-55; a sec. to Caleb Cushing in negotiation of 1st treaty between U.S. and China, 1844; sec. Am. legation, during interims between commrs. was chargé d'affaires, 1845; Am. commr., minister to China, 1855-57; elected regent Smithsonian Instn., 1868. Died Washington, D.C., Jan. 10, 1888.

PARKER, Richard, congressman, jurist; b. Richmond, Va., Dec. 22, 1810; studied law. Admitted to Va. bar, began practice in Berryville; held local offices; mem. U.S. Ho. of Reps. (Democrat) from Va., 31st Congress, 1849-51; judge 13th Va. Jud. Circuit, 1851-69; pronounced death sentence on John Brown, 1859; resumed law practice, Winchester, Va. Died Winchester, Nov. 10, 1893; buried Mt. Hebron Cemetery, Winchester.

PARKER, Richard Elliot, senator, jurist; b. Rock Spring, Westmoreland County, Va., Dec. 27, 1783; s. William Harwar and Mary (Sturman) P.; attended Washington Coll. (now Washington and Lee U.), 1800-03; studied law; m. Elizabeth Foushee, at least 1 son, Richard. Admitted to Va. bar, 1804; mem. Va. Ho. of Dels., 1807-09; served as lt. col., later col. 35th Va. Regt., 1812-14; judge Gen. Ct. Va., 1817-36; 1st judge Ct. Law and Chancery of Frederick County (Va.), 1831; mem. U.S. Senate from Va., Dec. 12, 1836-Mar. 13, 1837; asso. judge Va. Supreme Ct. of Appeals, 1837-40; declined appointment as U.S. atty. gen. by Pres. Van Buren, 1840. Died "The Retreat," nr. Snickersville (now Bluemont), Loudoun County, Va., Sept. 6, 1840; buried family cemetery nr. Warsaw, Richmond County, Va.

PARKER, Richard Green, educator; b. Dec. 25, 1798; s. Rev. Samuel and Anne (Cutler) P.; A.B., Harvard, 1817; m. Mary Davis, Apr. 20, 1820; m. 2d, Catherine Hall, circa 1848; 5 children. Acquired outstanding reputation as tchr. in Boston Public Sch. System; wrote textbooks of great popularity; collaborated (with James M. Watson) on Nat. Series of Readers. Author: Progressive Exercises in English Composition, 1832; The Boston School Compendium of Natural and Experimental Philosophy 1837; Tribute to the Life and Character of Jonas Chickering, 1854. Died Boston, Sept. 25, 1869; buried Old Trinity Ch., Boston.

PARKER, Samuel, missionary; b. Ashfield, Mass., Apr. 23, 1779; s. Elisha and Thankful (Marchant) P.; grad. Williams Coll., 1806, Andover Theol. Sem., 1810; married 3 times; m. N. Sears; m. 2d, Jerusha Lord, 1815. Missionary in Western N.Y., 1810-12; ordained to ministry Congregational Ch., 1812; pastor Congregational Ch., Danby, N.Y., 1812-27; agt. Auburn Theol. Sem., N.Y., 1827-30; preacher, Apulia, N.Y., 1830-32, Middlefield, Mass., 1832-33; did missionary work among Indian tribes in St. Louis area, 1834; began trips into Ore. Territory, 1835, spent winters of 1835, 36 at Ft. Vancouver; explored many interior parts of Ore. Territory. Author: Journal of an Exploring Tour Beyond the Rocky Mountains, 1838. Died Mass., Mar. 21, 1866.

PARKER, Samuel Wilson, congressman; b. nr. Watertown, N.Y., Sept. 9, 1805; grad. Miami U., Oxford, O., 1828; studied law. Admitted to Ind. bar, 1831, began practice in Connersville; pros. atty. Fayette County (Ind.), 1836-38; mem. Ind. Ho. of Reps., 1839, 43, Ind. Senate, 1841-43; mem. U. S. Ho. of Reps. (Whig) from Ind., 32d-33d congresses, 1851-55. Died nr. Sackets Harbor, N.Y., Feb. 1, 1859; buried nr. Sackets Harbor.

PARKER, Severn Eyre, congressman; b. nr. Eastville, Va., July 19, 1787; attended common schs.; studied law. Admitted to the bar, practiced law; held local offices; mem. Va. Ho. of Dels., 1809-12, 28-29, 34-36; dep. clk. Northampton County

(Va.), 1813; served as capt. of a rifle co., 1814; mem. Va. Senate, 1817-20; mem. U.S. Ho. of Reps. from Va., 16th Congress, 1819-21. Died Northampton County, Oct. 21, 1836; buried nr. Eastville.

PARKER, Theodore, clergyman; b. Lexington, Mass., Aug. 24, 1810; s. John and Hannah Stearns) P.; student Harvard Div. sch., 1834-36; M.A. (hon.), Harvard, 1840; m. Lydia (Dodge) Cabot, Apr. 20, 1837. Co-editor Scriptural Interpreter, Harvard, 1834-36; ordained to ministry Unitarian Ch., 1837; caused great controversy in Boston religious circles with sermon, The Transient and Permanent in Christianity, 1841; mem. Boston Assn. of Ministers; traveled in Europe, 1843-44, became convinced of mission to spread enlightened liberalism; ostracized by Boston churchmen, 1844; installed as minister of new 28th Congregational Soc. of Boston, 1845; a Transcendentalist; leader of vigilance com. active in escape of fugitive slaves, William and Ellen Craft, 1850; supported New Eng. Emigrant Aid Soc., also Mass. Kan. Com.; mem. of secret com. that abetted John Brown's plan of foray in mountains of Va.; bequeathed his library of nearly 16,000 vols. to Boston Public Library. Author: (series of lectures) A Discourse on Matters Pertaining to Religion, 1842; A Letter to the People of the United States Touching the Matter of Slavery, 1848; (collection of writings pub. after death) Theodore Parker's Works, 14 vols., 1863-70. Died while on European trip for his health, Florence, Italy, May 10, 1860.

PARKER, Thomas, clergyman; b. Stanton St. Bernard, Wilts, Eng., June 8, 1595; s. Rev. Robert and Dorothy (Stevens) P.; attended Trinity Coll., Dublin, Ireland, 1610, then Magdalen Coll., Oxford (Eng.) U., U. Leyden (Netherlands), 1614; M. Philosophy, U. Franeker, 1617. Came to Mass., 1634; founder (with cousin James Noyes) church at Newbury, Mass., circa 1635; ordained minister Congregationalist Ch.; orthodox Calvinist, argued for Presbyterianism at New Eng. Ch. Synods, 1643, 62; admitted the unconverted to communion; condr. free sch. to prepare boys for Harvard. Author: A Letter on Church Government, 1644; The Prophesies of Daniel Expounded, 1649; Methodus Gratiae Divinae, 1657. Died Newbury, Apr. 24, 1677.

PARKER, Willard, surgeon, educator; b. Lyndeborough, N.H., Sept. 2, 1800; s. Jonathan and Hannah (Clark) P.; A.B., Harvard, 1826, M.D., 1830; M.D., Berkshire Med. Instn.; LL.D. (hon.), Princeton, 1870; m. Caroline Stirling, June 21, 1831; m. 2d, Mary Bissell, May 25, 1844; 5 children. Prof. anatomy and surgery Clin. Sch. Medicine, Woodstock, Vt., 1830-33; prof. surgery Berkshire Med. Instn., 1833-36; prof. anatomy, Geneva, N.Y., 1834-36; prof. surgery, Cincinnati, 1836-37; prof. principles and practice of surgery Coll. of Physicians and Surgeons, N.Y.C., 1839-70, emeritus prof. surgery, 1870; performed cystotomy for irritable bladder, 1850; tied subclavian artery for aneurism on 5 occasions, 1864; 1st American to operate successfully on abscessed appendix; pres. N.Y. Acad. Medicine, 1856; Willard Parker Hosp. (N.Y.C.) named in his honor. Author (med. monograms) Cystotomy, 1850; spontaneous Fractures, 1852; Concussion of Nerves, 1856; Ligature of the Subclavian Artery, 1864; Cancer, 1873. Died N.Y.C., Apr. 25, 1884.

PARKER, William Harwar, naval officer; b. N.Y.C., Oct. 8, 1826; s. Foxhall Alexander and Sara (Bogardus) P.; grad. (1st in class) U.S. Naval Acad., 1848; m. Margaret Griffin, Dec. 14, 1853. Served from midshipman to lt. U.S. Navy, 1841-61; served in Mexican War; instr. U.S. Naval Acad., Annapolis, Md., 1853-57, 60-61; translated Tactique Navale from French; joined Confederate Navy, took command gunboat Beaufort Roanoke Island, 1862; exec. officer in ironclad Palmetto State at Charleston, winter 1862-63; promoted capt. 1863; organizer, supt. Confederate Naval Acad., 1863-65 (on evacuation of Richmond, Va. he and his cadets were given charge of govt. archives and treasure); capt. Pacific mail steamer between Panama and San Francisco, 1865-74; pres. Md. Agrl. Coll., 1875-83; U.S. minister to Korea in Cleveland's adminstrn., 1886. Author: Instructions for Light Naval Artillery, 1862; Elements of Seamanship, 1864; Remarks on the Navigation of the Coasts between San Francisco and Panama, 1871; Recollections of a Naval Officer 1841-65, published 1883. Died Washington, D.C., Dec. 30, 1896; buried Norfolk, Va.

PARKMAN, Francis, educator, author; b. Boston, Sept. 16, 1823; s. Rev. Francis and Caroline (Hall) P.; grad. Harvard, 1844, LL.B., 1846; m. Catherine Bigelow, May 13, 1850, 3 children. Traveled along Ore. Trail, 1846; partially disabled by nervous disorder, 1853, 58; pres. Mass. Hort. Soc., 2 years; bd. overseers Harvard, 1868-71, 74-76, apptd. prof. hort., 1871, fellow corp., 1875-88; a founder Archeol. Inst. Am., 1879; a founder (gave financial assistance) Am. Sch. of Classical Studies, Athens, Greece; mem. Phi Beta Kappa; instrumental in publication series of documents edited by Pierre Margry, Decouvertes et Etablissements des Francais dan L'guest et dan le Sud de L'Amerique Septentrionale, 1876-786. Author: The California and Oregon Trail, 1849; History of the Conspiracy of Pontiac, 2 vols., 1851; Pioneers of France in the New World, 1865; The Jesuits in North America, 1867; The Discovery of the Great West, 1869; The Old Regime in Canada, 1874; Count Frontenac and New France Under Louis XIV, 1877; Montcalm and Wolfe, 2 vols., 1884; A Half-Century of Conflict, 2 vols., 1892. Died Nov. 8, 1893.

PARKS, Gorham, congressman; b. Westfield, Mass., May 27, 1794; grad. Harvard, 1813; studied law. Admitted to Mass. bar, 1819, practiced law; moved to Bangor, Me., 1823, practiced law; mem. U.S. Ho. of Reps. (Democrat) from Me., 23d-24th congresses, 1833-37; U.S. marshal for Me., 1838-41, U.S. atty., 1843-45; U.S. consul at Rio de Janeiro, Brazil, 1845-49. Died Bay Ridge, N.Y., Nov. 23, 1877; buried Greenwood Cemetery, Bklyn.

PARKS, William, printer, publisher; b. Shropshire, Eng., 1698; m. Eleanor, at least 1 child. Established Ludlow (Eng.) Post-Man, 1719, Reading (Eng.) Mercury, 1723 (1st journals to be published in those towns); came to Annapolis, 1725/26; Md. established Md. Gazette (1st newspaper in country south of Pa., 1727; apptd. public printer of Md., 1727-37; established a press, Williamsburg, Va., 1730; public printer of Va., until 1750; began to edit Va. Gazette, 1736; built 1st paper mill south of Pa., circa 1743; a pioneer of newspaper advt. Publisher: A Collection of All the Acts of the Assembly Now in Force in the Colony of Virginia, 1733; The History of the First Discovery and Settlement of Virginia (William Stith), 1747; (earliest Am. sporting book) A Compleat System of Fencing (Edward Blackwell), 1734; (1st Am. cook book) The Compleat Housewife (E. Smith), 1742. Died on voyage to Eng., Apr. 1, 1750.

PARKYNS, George Isham, artist; b. Nottingham, Eng., circa 1749. Exhibited at exhbns., London, Eng., 1772-1813; came to U.S., circa 1794; proposed to issue a series of aquatints showing prin. cities and scenery of U.S. in assn. with James Harrison. Author: Monastic Remains and Ancient Castles in Great Britain. Died circa 1820.

PARLEY, Peter, see Goodrich, Samuel Griswold.

PARMENTER, William, congressman; b. Boston, Mar. 30, 1789; attended Boston Latin Sch. Mem. Mass. Ho. of Reps., 1829, Mass. Senate, 1836; selectman of Cambridge (Mass.), 1836; a pioneer in glass industry, East Cambridge, Mass.; mgr., agt. New Eng. Crown Glass Co., 1824-36; pres. Middlesex Bank; mem. U.S. Ho. of Reps. (Democrat) from Mass., 25th-28th congresses, 1837-45; naval officer Port of Boston, 1845-49. Died East Cambridge, Feb. 25, 1866; buried Cambridge Cemetery.

PARMENTIER, Andrew, horticulturist, landscape gardener; b. Enghien, Belgium, July 3, 1780; s. Andre Joseph P.; m. Sylvia Marie Parmentier, before 1814, 5 children including Adele Bayer. Came to Am., 1824; purchased 24 acre triangular tract of land to establish bot. gardens and nursery, Bklyn., 1825, enclosed area with high stone wall, collected fgn. and domestic plants; introduced black beech tree, several species vegetables, shrubs and vines to U.S.; contbd. to New Eng. Farmer and N.Y. Farmer; earliest profl. landscape gardener in U.S., laid out grounds and gardens for clients from Can. to the Carolinas. Died Nov. 26, 1830.

PARMLY, Eleazar, dentist coll. pres.; b. Braintree, Vt., Mar. 13, 1797; s. Eleazar and Hannah (Spear) P.; D.D.S., Am. Soc. Dental Surgeons; D.D.S. (hon.), Balt. Coll. Dental Surgery, 1842; m. Anna Smith, June 17, 1827, 9 children including Julia. Compositor, reporter Canadian Courant, 1810-12; practiced as an intinerant dentist on Mississippi, Ohio rivers, 1817-19; studied with J.F.C. Maury, Paris, France, 1819; entered partnership with brother Levi, London, Eng., 1819; practiced dentistry, N.Y.C., 1821-66, specialist in operative dentistry; leader in early opposition to use of amalgam for filling teeth; became 1st pres. Soc. Surgeon Dentists of City and State of N.Y., 1834; a founder 1st dental periodical Am. Jour. Dental Sci.; 2d v.p. Am. Soc. Dental Surgeons when organized, 1840, 1st v.p., 1841-44, pres., 1844-53; provost Balt. Coll. Dental Surgery, 1848-52; opened Parmly House (a hotel), Painesville, O., 1861; 1st pres. N.Y. Coll. Dentistry, 1866, prof. emeritus insts. of dentistry until 1869. Author: The Babe of Bethlehem, 1861; Thoughts in Rhyme, 1867. Died N.Y.C., Dec. 13, 1874; buried Rumson (N.J.) Burying Ground.

PARRETT, William Fletcher, congressman; b. nr. Blairsville, Ind., Aug. 10, 1825; attended Ind. Asbury (now De Pauw) U., Greencastle, Ind.; studied law. Admitted to Ind. bar, practiced in Evansville, until 1852; moved to Ore., practiced law, 1852-54; returned to Evansville, 1854, moved to Boonville, Ind., 1855; Democratic presdl. elector, 1856; mem. Ind. Ho. of Reps., 1858; judge 15th Ind. Circuit, 1859-65, 65-71, 1st Ind. Circuit, 73-88; mem. U.S. Ho. of Reps. (Dem.) from Ind., 51st-52d congresses, 1889-93. Died Evansville, June 30, 1895; buried Oak Hill Cemetery, Evansville.

PARRIS, Albion Keith, senator, gov. Me., govt. official; born in Hebron, Massachusetts (now Maine), on January 19th, 1788; son of Samuel and Sarah (Pratt) P.; grad. Dartmouth, 1806; m. Sarah Whitman, 1810, 5 children. Admitted to Cumberland (Mass.) bar, 1809; pros. atty. Oxford County (Mass.), 1811; mem. Mass. Ho. of Reps., 1813-14, Mass. Senate, 1814-15; mem. U.S. Ho. of Reps. from Mass., 14th-15th congresses, 1815-Feb. 3, 1818; judge U.S. Dist. Ct. for Me., 1818; mem. Me. Conv., 1819, mem. com. which drafted new constn., treas. conv.; judge probate Cumberland County (Me.), 1820-21; gov. Me., 1822-27; mem. U.S. Senate from Me., 1827-Aug. 26, 1828; asso. justice Me. Supreme Ct., 1828-36; comptroller U.S. Treasury, 1836-50; mayor Portland (Me.), 1852-54. Died Portland, Feb. 22, 1857; buried Western Cemetery, Portland.

PARRIS, Alexander, architect; b. Hebron, Me., Nov. 24, 1780; s. Matthew and Mercy (Thompson) P.; m. Silvina Stetson, Apr. 19, 1801. Served as capt. of a company artificers (engrs.) during War of 1812; architect, Boston, designed David Sears House, 1816, St. Paul's Ch., 1819; cons. engr. in building of masonry dry dock at Charlestown Navy Yard; supt. for Charles Bulfinch in constrn. Mass. Gen. Hosp., completed 1823; architect for Market Hall and bldgs. of Faneuil Hall Market, 1825; designer Marine Hosp., Chelsea, Boston; civil engr. Navy Yard, Portsmouth, N.H., 1847-52. Died Pembroke, Mass., June 16, 1852; buried Briggs Cemetery, North Pembroke, Mass.

PARRIS, Samuel, clergyman; b. London, Eng., 1653; s. Thomas Parris; ed. Harvard; m. Elizabeth; m. 2d, Dorothy; 5 children. Came to Am. before 1674; pastor, Salem, Mass., 1689-96; believed that Satan was attacking his flock, that as a faithful pastor he must fight back, 1692; accepted spectral evidence contrary to the advice of Boston ministers; during witchcraft trials sometimes acted as ct. clk., also a witness; read sermon Meditations for Peace to his congregation in which he acknowledged his error in countenancing spectral evidence, begged forgiveness, 1694, congregation vindicated him, but required him to leave village, left, 1697. Died Sudbury, Mass., Feb. 17, 1719/20.

PARRIS, Virgil Delphini, congressman; b. Buckfield, Me., Feb. 18, 1807; attended Hebron (Me.) Acad., Colby Coll., Waterville, Me.; grad. Union Coll., Schenectady, N.Y., 1827; studied law. Admitted to Me. bar, 1830, began practice in Buckfield; asst. sec. Me. Senate, 1831; mem. Me. Ho. of Reps., 1832-37; mem. U.S. Ho. of Reps. (State Rights Democrat) from Me., 25th-26th congresses, May 29, 1838-41; mem. Me. Senate, 1842-43, served as pres. pro tem and acting gov. Me.; U.S. marshal for Me., 1844-48; spl. mail agt. for New Eng., 1853; apptd. naval storekeeper Kittery Navy Yard, 1856; del. Dem. nat. convs., Balt., 1852, 72. Died Paris, Me., June 13, 1874; buried Old Cemetery, Paris.

PARRISH, Anne, philanthropist; b. Phila., Oct. 17, 1760; d. Isaac and Sarah (Mitchell) P. Founded Aimwell Sch. (for girls in needy circumstances), Phila., 1796, Home of Industry (for employment of poor women), Phila., 1795 (incorporated 1815). Died Phila., Dec. 26, 1800.

PARRISH, Charles, coal operator, banker; b. Dundaff, Pa., Aug. 27, 1826; s. Archippus and Phebe (Miller) P.; m. Mary Conyngham, June 21, 1864, 4 children. Founded Kembleton Coal Co., 1856, originated important plans in fields of mining and transp.; pres. Phila. Coal Co. which operated Empire Mine; organizer Lehigh & Wilkes-Barre Coal Co. (Pa.), pres. 20 years; an organizer Lehigh & Susquehanna R.R., Sunbury & Wilkes-Barre R.R., Lehigh Coal Navigation Co. (dir. 30 years); a dir. Jersey Central R.R.; pres. First Nat. Bank of Wilkes-Barre 20 years; organized troops, contbd. money to Union cause, early in Civil War; elected mem. Wyoming (Pa.) Hist and Geol. Soc., 1885, life mem., 1889. Died Phila., Dec. 27, 1896.

PARRISH, Edward, pharmacist, coll. pres.; b. Phila., May 31, 1822; s. Dr. Joseph and Susanna (Cox) P.; grad. Phila. Coll. Pharmacy, 1842; m. Margaret Hunt, 1848, 5 children. Propr. drugstore, nr. U. Pa., Phila., 1843-50, conducted practical pharmacy sch. in rear of store, 1849-64;

prof. materia medica Phila. Coll. Pharmacy, 1864-67, prof. theory and practice of pharmacy, 1867-72; a founder (secured passage of incorporation act) Swarthmore Coll., sec. bd. mgrs., 1864-68, pres. coll., 1868-71; mem. Phila. Coll. Pharmacy, 1843, mem. bd. trustees, 1845, sec. trustees, 1845-52, sec. coll., 1854-64; a founder Am. Pharm. Assn., 1852, recording sec., 1853. 1st v.p., 1866, pres., 1868; del. to Internat. Pharm. Conv., London, Eng., 1860; mem. commn. in Phila. to carry into effect Pharmacy Act of 1872; apptd. peace commr. by U.S. Govt. to visit Indian tribes in Okla., 1872. Author: (textbook) An Introduction to Practical Pharmacy, 1855; Summer Medical Teaching in Philadelphia, 1857; contbr. papers to Proceedings of Am. Pharm. Assn. and Am. Jour. Pharmacy. Died Ft. Sill, Indian Territory (now Okla.), Sept. 9, 1872.

PARRISH, Isaac, congressman; b. nr. St. Clairsville, O., Mar. 1804; studied law. Admitted to Ohio bar, practiced law; pros. atty. Guernsey County (O.), 1833; mem. Ohio Ho. of Reps., 1837; mem. U.S. Ho. of Reps. (Democrat) from Ohio, 26th, 29th congresses, 1839-41, 45-47; resumed law practice and bus. activities, Sharon, O.; engaged in real estate bus., steamboat freighting; established Harrison County Flag, Calhoun, Ia. Died Parrish City, Ia., Aug. 9, 1860; buried Calhoun Cemetery.

PARRISH, Isaac, physician, reformer; b. Phila., Mar. 19, 1811; s. Isaac Parrish; grad. U. Pa., 1832; m. Sarah Redwood Longstreth, 1834. Practiced medicine, Phila.; surgeon Wills Hosp., Phila., 1834-52, gave 1st instrn. in opthalmic surgery, 1839; mem. Phila. Soc. for Relieving Miseries of Prisons; toured prisons of Md., R.I., N.Y., 1846-47, advocated equal treatment for all prisoners, regardless of race. Died July 31, 1852.

PARRISH, Joseph, physician, b. Phila., Sept. 2, 1779; s. Isaac and Sarah (Mitchell) P.; M.D., U. Pa., 1805; m. Susanna Cox, Oct. 20, 1808, 11 children including Isaac, Joseph, Edward. Resident physician to emergency hosp. established by Bd. Health during yellow fever epidemic, Phila., 1805; gave course of popular lectures on chemistry, 1808; mem. staff, mgr. Phila. Dispensary, physician Phila. Almshouse, 1807-11, mem. surg. staff, 1811-21; mem. staff Pa. Hosp., 1816-29; pres. bd. mgrs. Wills Eye Hosp., 1833-40; v.p. Coll. Physicians of Phila., Phila. Med. Soc.; in charge of cholera hosp. during epidemic, Phila., 1832; pres. Pa. Abolition Soc. Author: Practical Observations on Strangulated Hernia, and Some of the Diseases of the Urinary Organs, 1836. Died Phila., Mar. 18, 1840.

PARROTT, Enoch Greenleafe, naval officer; b. Portsmouth, N.H., Nov. 17, 1815; s. Enoch Greenleafe and Susan (Parker) P. Commd. lt. U.S. Navy, 1841; in frigate Congress accompanied Fremont's expdn. from Monterey to Los Angeles, 1846-48; promoted comdr., 1861; commanded ship Perry, captured the Savannah (1st privateer captured), June 1861; sr. officer in steamer Augusta, off Charleston; 1862; commanded Monadnock in 2 attacks on Ft. Fisher, 1864-65, and in blockade of Charleston; commd. capt., 1866, commodore, 1870, rear adm., 1873; comdr. of receiving ship, Boston, 1865-68, Portsmouth Navy Yard, 1869; comdt. Mare Island Yard, 1871-72; commanded Asiatic Squadron, 1872-74. Died N.Y.C., May 10, 1879; buried St. John's Episcopal Ch., Portsmouth, N.H.

PARROTT, John Fabyan, senator, congressman; b. Portsmouth, N.H., Aug. 8, 1767; attended common schs. Mem. N.H. Ho. of Reps., 1809-14; held local offices; mem. U.S. Ho. of Reps. (Democrat) from N.H., 15th Congress, 1817-18; mem. U.S. Senate from N.H., 1819-25; postmaster of Portsmouth, 1826; mem. N.H. Senate, 1830-31. Died Greenland, N.H., July 9, 1836; buried family burying ground, Greenland.

PARROTT, Marcus Junius, congressman; b. Hamburg, S.C., Oct. 27, 1828; grad. Dickinson Coll., Carlisle, Pa., 1849; studied law Cambridge (Eng.) U. Admitted to Ohio bar, began practice in Dayton; mem. Ohio Ho. of Reps., 1853-54; moved to Leavenworth, Kan., 1855; ct. reporter 1st session Kan. Territorial Supreme Ct., 1855; del. Kan. Constl. Conv., 1855; del. U.S. Congress (Republican) from Territory of Kan., 1857-61; engaged in farming, nr. Leavenworth. Died Dayton, Oct. 4, 1879; buried Woodland Cemetery, Dayton.

PARROTT, Robert Parker, ordnance inventor, manufacturer; b. Lee, N.H., Oct. 5, 1804; s. John Fabyan and Hannah (Parker) P.; grad. U. S. Mil. Acad., 1824; m. Mary Kemble, 1839, 1 adopted son. Asst. prof. natural and experimental philosophy U.S. Mil. Acad., 1824-29; commd. 1st lt., 1831; promoted capt. of ordnance, 1836, went to Washington (D.C.) as asst. to bur. of ordnance; resigned from army to become supt. West Point Foundry, Cold Spring, N.Y., 1836, became lessee of foundry, 1839, directed bus. until 1877; bought 7,000 acre tract of land, built Greenwood Iron Furnace (ran with his brother), 1839-77; patented design for strengthening cast-iron cannon with a wrought-iron hoop shrunken on the breech, also an improved expanding projectile for rifled ordnance, 1861; received large orders for guns and projectiles in Civil War; began (with brother) 1st comml. prodn. of slag wool in U.S., 1875; 1st judge Ct. of Common Pleas for Putnam County, N.Y., 1844-47. Died Cold Spring, Dec. 24, 1877.

PARRY, Charles Christopher, botanist; b. Admington, Eng., Aug. 28, 1823; s. Joseph and Eliza (Elliott) P.; A.B., Union Coll., 1842; M.D., Columbia Coll., 1846; m. Sarah M. Dalzell, 1853; m. 2d, Emily R. Preston, 1859. Came to U.S., 1832; botanist under David Dale Owen in geol. survey of Wis., Ia. and Minn., 1848; apptd. botanist to U.S. and Mexican boundary survey, 1849; author intro. "Botany of the Boundary" for Report on the U.S. and Mexican Boundary Survey, 2 vols. in 3, 1857-59; botanical explorer of western states and territories, 1850-79; 1st botanist in U.S. Dept. Agr.; organized plant collections brought back by govt. scientists and surveying expdns. at Smithsonian Instn., 1869-71; discoverer Picea Engeimannii spruce, new species Cal. manzanitas, lilium Parryi of So. Cal. mountains, lote bush of Colorado Desert, Ensenada Buckeye, many others; 1st investigator of these groups to study living plants in the field in connection with specimens in herbarium. Died Davenport, Ia., Feb. 20, 1890.

PARRY, Charles Thomas, locomotive builder; b. Phila., Sept. 15, 1821; s. Samuel and Mary (Hoffline) P.; married, 3 children. Gen. supt. in charge of locomotive constrn. Baldwin Locomotive Works, 1855; mem. firm M. Baird & Co. (became Burnham, Parry, Williams & Co. 1873), 1867, installed labor saving devices, began practice of having complete drawings of locomotives prepared in advance of constrn., primarily responsible for introduction of piece-work system; a founder of Beach Haven (N.J.); supervised Russian locomotive constrn., 1877; mem. Franklin Inst. (mem. bd. mgrs. for 1 year); dir. Nat. Bank of the Republic. Died Beach Haven, July 18, 1887.

PARRY, John Stubbs, physician; b. Drumore Twp., Pa., Jan. 4, 1843; s. Seneca and Priscilla P. M.D., U. Pa., 1865; m. Rachel Sharpless, Apr. 5, 1866. Apptd. dist. physician to Phila. Dispensary; became vis. obstetrician to Phila. Hosp., 1867, reorganized obstet., gynecol. depts.; physician for diseases peculiar to women Phila. Presbyn. Hosp., 1872; a founder State Hosp. for Women and Infants, 1872; mem. council Phila. Coll. Physicians; pres. Phila. Obstet. Soc.; v.p. Path. Soc. of Phila. Author: Extra-Uterine Pregnancy, 1876; contbr. 28 articles to med. jours., primarily on obstetrics and children's diseases; wrote on rachitis (proved prevalence of this "disease" in Phila.), 1870. Died Jacksonville, Fla., Mar. 11, 1876.

PARSONS, Albert Richard, socialist anarchist; b. Montgomery, Ala., June 24, 1848; s. Samuel and Elizabeth (Tompkins) P.; attended Waco (Tex., now Baylor) U.; m. Lucy Eldine Gonzalez, June 10, 1871, at least 2 children. Enlisted in Confederate army at age 13, 1861; started weekly newspaper Spectator, Waco, 1868; traveling correspondent Daily Telegraph, 1869; with U.S. Internal Revenue Bur., 1869-71; moved to Chgo., 1871, joined Typographical Union, became a socialist; became editor The Alarm, 1884, presented his strong views on labor rights in this publ.; spoke at protest meeting in front of Haymarket, May 4, 1886 (he was protesting actions of previous night in which police had fired into crowd of strikers); convicted (with 7 others) of murder of policeman who was killed by bomb at the meeting; his conviction affirmed by Ill. Supreme Ct.; granted sympathy because of his general reputation, refused clemency unless others were similarly treated (they were not). Hung (along with 3 others), Nov. 11, 1887.

PARSONS, Edward Young, congressman; b. Middletown, Ky., Dec. 12, 1842; grad. U. Louisville (Ky.), 1861, Louisville Law Sch., 1865. Taught sch., Louisville, 3 years; admitted to Ky. bar, began practice in Henderson; moved to Louisville, 1865, practiced law; mem. U.S. Ho. of Reps. (Democrat) from Ky., 44th Congress, 1875-76. Died Washington, D.C., July 8, 1876; buried Cave Hill Cemetery, Louisville.

PARSONS, Lewis Eliphalet, provisional gov. Ala.; b. Lisle, Broome County, N.Y., Apr. 28, 1817; s. Erastus Bellamy and Jennette (Hepburn) P.; attended pub. schs., N.Y.C.; read law in N.Y. and Pa.; m. Jane Ann Chrisman, Sept. 16, 1841, 7 children. Settled in Talladega, Ala., 1840; practiced law in partnership with Alexander White; mem. Ala. Legislature, 1859; del. Nat. Democratic Conv., Balt., 1860; provisional gov. Ala. (apptd. by Pres. Andrew Johnson), 1865, recognized all local and judicial offcls. who had been in office during Confederacy, permitted them to perform duties of office if they took oath of allegiance to U.S., obtained pardons for those exempted from gen. amnesty, reorganized civil govt., supervised framing of new constn.; elected to U.S. Senate, 1865, denied seat by Republican majority; del. Nat. Union Conv., Phila., 1866; leader movement which resulted in Ala.'s rejection of 14th Amendment; said to have originated "the white man's movement" against ratification of Ala. Constn. of 1867; mem., speaker Ala. Legislature, 1872-72. Died Talladega, June 8, 1895.

PARSONS, Samuel Holden, Revolutionary patriot; b. Lynne, Conn., May 14, 1737; s. Jonathan and Phebe (Griswold) P.; grad. Harvard, 1756, Master's Degree, 1759; m. Mehetable Mather, Sept. 1761, 8 children. Admitted to Conn. bar, 1759; mem. Conn. Gen. Assembly, 1762-74; active Conn. Com. of Correspondence; commd. col. 6th Regt., Conn. Militia, 1775, served in taking of Ft. Ticonderoga; commd. brig. gen. Continental Army, 1776, was depended upon for defense of Conn.; in charge of important secret service post; promoted comdr. Conn. div., 1779, maj. gen., 1780; on Sept. 22, 1785 Congress named him commr. to deal with Indian claims to territory N.W. of Ohio River; became a promoter, dir. Ohio Co., 1787; apptd. 1st judge of Northwest Territory, 1787. Author: (essay) Antiquities of the Western States. Drowned in Big Beaver River, O., Nov. 17, 1789.

PARSONS, Theophilus, jurist; b. Byfield, Mass., Feb. 24, 1750; s. Rev. Moses and Susan (Davis) P.; grad. Harvard, 1769; LL.D. (hon.), Brown U., 1809; m. Elizabeth Greenleaf, Jan. 13, 1780, 12 chldren including Theophilus. Began practice law, Falmouth, Mass. (now Portland, Me.), 1774; dominant mem. Essex County Conv., opposed to proposed Mass. Constn. of 1778, wrote conv. report The Essex Result (exposing weakness of exec. under that constn. and outlining main principles for govt. later adopted by federalists), 1778; del. to Mass. Conv. ratifying U.S. Constn., 1788; mem. Mass. Legislature, 1787-91, 1805; popular lawyer, Boston, 1800-06; chief justice Supreme Jud. Ct. of Mass., 1806-13, insisted upon speedy trials; formed law of new Commonwealth of Mass., and indirectly that of other states; established rules of gen. application derived from English law, unwritten colonial law, principles of bus. embodied in usages as rules of law; decisions particularly useful in field of shipping and insurance; developed improved method of lunar observation adopted in New American Practical Navigator (Nathaniel Bowditch), 1802; prin. founder Boston Athenaeum, Social Law Library; fellow Harvard Coll., 1806; fellow Am. Acad. Arts and Scis. Died Boston, Oct. 30, 1813.

PARSONS, Theophilus, lawyer, educator; b. Newburyport, Mass., May 17, 1797; s. Theophilus and Elizabeth (Greenleaf) P.; grad. Harvard, 1815, LL.D. (hon.), 1849; m. Catherine Chandler, 1823, 3 sons, 4 daus. Began practice law, 1822; editor U.S. Literary Gazette; joint editor Taunton Free Press and New Eng. Galaxy; Dane prof. Harvard Law Sch., 1848-69; fellow Harvard Coll.; mem. Mass. Hist. Soc.; Swedenborgian. Author: The Law of Contracts, 2 vols., 1853-55; The Elements of Mercantile Law, 1856, 62; Laws of Business for Business Men, 1857; A Treatise on Maritime Law, 2 vols., 1859; The Constitution, 1861; Deus Horis, 1867; A Treatise on the Law of Shipping, 2 vols., 1869; The Infinite and the Finite, 1872; Outlines of the Religion and Philosophy of Swedenborg, 1875. Died Cambridge, Mass., Jan. 26, 1882.

PARSONS, Thomas William, dentist, poet; b. Boston, Aug. 18, 1819; s. Thomas William and Asenath (Read) P.; attended Harvard Med. Sch.; studied in Europe, 1836; m. Anna (or Hannah) Allen, 1857. Became dentist, 1844; translator Dante's Inferno, published with Dore's illustrations, Boston, 1865; translator part of Dante's Purgatorio, published in The Catholic World, 1879-83; best known poems include: On a Bust of Dante, published 1841; Paradisi Gloria. author volumes of verse: Ghetto di Roma, 1854; The Magnolia, 1866; The Shadow of the Obelisk, London, 1872; The Old House at Sudbury, 1870. Died Scituate, Mass., Sept. 3, 1892; buried Mt. Auburn Cemetery, Cambridge, Mass.

PARSONS, Usher, surgeon; b. Alfred, Me., Aug. 18, 1788; s. William and Abigail (Blunt) P.; studied medicine under various physicians; M.D., Harvard Med. Coll., 1818; m. Mary Holmes, Sept. 23, 1822; 1 child. Licensed to practice medicine by Mass. Med. Soc., 1812; commd. surgeon's mate, 1812; in charge of sick and wounded at Black Rock, 1812-13; served with Perry at Battle of Lake Erie, 1813, distinguished self at battle with operations on and treatment of wounded; promoted surgeon,

1814; published Surgical Account of the Naval Battle of Lake Erie in New Eng. Jour. of Medicine and Surgery, 1818; became prof. anatomy and surgery Dartmouth, 1820; appt. prof. anatomy and surgery Brown U., 1822; apptd. prof. obstetrics Jefferson Med. Coll., Phila., 1831; pres. R.I. Med. Soc., several times an organizer A.M.A., v.p., 1853; a founder R.I. Hosp.; recipient Boylston prize 4 times; papers collected and published in Boylston Prize Dissertations, 1839; recipient Fiske Fund prize, 1842; summary of larger surg. operations pub. in Am. Jour. of Med. Scis., 1848. Author: (med. guide for use on mcht. vessels) The Sailor's Physician, 1820. Died Providence, R.I., Dec. 19, 1868.

PARTON, James, author; b. Canterbury, Eng., Feb. 9, 1822; s. James and Ann (Leach) P.; m. Sarah Payson Willis, Jan. 5, 1856; 1 stepdau., Ellen Eldredge (whom he later married); m. 2d, Ellen Eldredge, Feb. 3, 1876; 2 children and 1 adopted child. Came to N.Y., 1827; wrote The Life of Horace Greeley, 1855; The Legend and Times of Aaron Burr, 1857, enlarged edit., 2 vols., 1864; Life of Andrew Jackson, 3 vols., 1859-60; General Butler in New Orleans, 1863; Life and Times of Benjamin Franklin, 2 vols., 1864; Life of John Jacob Astor, 1865; Famous Americans of Recent Times, 1867; Life of Thomas Jefferson, 1874; Life of Voltaire, 2 vols., 1881; life-long contbr. to N.Y. Ledger, Youth's Companion and others; most famous and important biographer of his time. Died Newburyport, Mass., Oct. 17, 1891.

PARTON, Sara Payson Willis (pseudonym Fanny Fern), author; b. Portland, Me., July 9, 1811; d. Nathaniel and Hannah (Parker) Willis; attended Catharine Beecher's Sch., Hartford, Conn.; m. Charles Eldridge, 1837; m. 2d, Samuel Farrington, Jan. 15, 1849; m. 3d, James Parton, Jan. 5, 1856; 2 children. Contbr. to periodical Youth's Companion; writer weekly article for N.Y. Ledger, 1856-72; wrote novel Ruth Hall, 1855; other works include: Little Ferns for Fanny's Little Friends, 1854; The Play-Day Book: New Stories for Little Folks, 1857; A new Story Book for Children, 1864. Died N.Y.C., Oct. 10, 1872.

PARTRIDGE, Alden, educator; b. Norwich, Vt., Feb. 12, 1785; s. Samuel and Elizabeth (Wright) P.; attended Dartmouth, 1802-05, U.S. Mil. Acad., 1805-06; m. Ann Swasey, 1837, 2 sons. Commd. 1st lt. Corps Engrs., U.S. Army, 1806, promoted capt., 1810; assigned to duty as instr. U.S. Mil. Acad., became prof. mathematics, 1813, prof. engring., 1813, acting supt., 2 years, tried by court martial on numerous charges of neglect of duty and insubordination, sentenced to be cashiered, 1817, punishment remitted; resigned 1818; established Am. Lit., Scientific and Mil. Acad., Norwich, 1819, (chartered as Norwich U., 1834), pres. until 1843; opened and ran mil. prep. sch., Norwich, 1827-29; established young ladies sem., Norwich, 1835; founded mil. prep. schs. in Va., Pa., Del., N.H., 1839-53; founder system of mil. acads. of elementary and secondary grades; surveyor gen. Vt., 1822-23; mem. Vt. Legislature, 1833, 34, 37, 39. Died Norwich, Jan. 17, 1854.

PARTRIDGE, George, congressman; b. Duxbury, Mass., Feb. 8, 1740; grad. Harvard, 1762; studied theology. Taught sch., Kingston, Mass.; del. Mass. Provincial Congress, 1774-75; mem. Mass. Ho. of Reps., 1775-59, 88; sheriff of Plymouth County (Mass.), 1777-1812; mem. Continental Congress from Mass., 1779-82, 83-85; mem. U.S. Ho. of Reps. from Mass., 1st Congress, 1789-90; endowed Partridge Sem., Duxbury. Died Duxbury, July 7, 1828; buried Mayflower Cemetery, Duxbury.

PARTRIDGE, James Rudolph, diplomat; b. Balt., 1823; s. Eaton R. and Susan (Crook) P.; A.B., Harvard, 1841, LL.B., 1843; m. Mary Baltzell, Oct. 21, 1847, 2 children. Elected to Md. Legislature, 1856; sec. of state Md., 1858; apptd. commr. Exhbn. of Industries of All Nations, 1862; U.S. minister resident to Honduras, 1862-63, Salvador, 1863-66; minister to Venezuela, 1869-70, Brazil, 1871-77; arbitrator of claims of Lord Dundonald against Govt. of Brazil; apptd. to diplomatic mission in Peru, 1882, served 1 year. Died by own hand, Alicante, Spain, Feb. 24, 1884.

PARTRIDGE, Richard, mcht., colonial agt.; b. Portsmouth, N.H., Dec. 9, 1681; s. William and Mary (Brown) P. Colonial agt. in Eng., 1701-59, agt. for R.I., 1715-59, agt. for N.Y., 1731, for the Jerseys, 1733, for Mass., 1737, for Pa. Assembly, 1740; for Conn. 1750-59; conducted lengthy appeals to the Crown, fought detrimental imperial legislation, tried to keep in check plans of aggressive neighboring colonies; succeeded in establishing boundaries for R.I. which brought Narragansett County and Narragansett Bay within its borders; responsible for softening some features objectionable to northern colonies in Molasses Act, 1730-33; acted as rep. for Gov. Belcher as Parliamentary agt. for London Meeting for Sufferings to ease the hardships of the Quakers. Died Eng., Mar. 6, 1759.

PARVIN, Theophilus, obstetrician, gynecologist; b. Buenos Aires, Argentina, Jan. 9, 1829; s. Theophilus and Mary (Rodney) P.; grad. Ind. U., 1847; studied Hebrew at Princeton Theol. Sem.; doctorate in medicine U. Pa., 1852; m. Rachel Butler, 1853, 3 children. Elected pres. Ind. Med. Soc., 1861; prof. materia medica Med. Coll. of Ohio, 1864-69; prof. obstetrics Louisville (Ky.) U., 1869; transferred to Ind. Med. Coll., 1872; pres. A.M.A., 1879; prof. obstetrics and gynecology Jefferson Med. Coll., Phila., 1883-98; co-editor Cincinnati Jour. of Medicine, 1866-67; editor Western Jour. Medicine, 1867-69; co-editor Am. Practitioners, 1869-83; pres. Am. Med. Journalists Assn., Am. Acad. Medicine, Am. Gynecol. Soc., Phila. Obstet. Soc.; hon. pres. obstet. sect. Internat. Med. Congress, Berlin, Germany, 1890; pres. Periodic Internat. Congress of Gynecology and Obstetrics, Brussels, Belgium, 1892; mem. Am. Philos. Soc.; hon. mem. Washington (D.C.) Obstet. and Gynecol. Soc.; hon. fellow Edinburgh (Scotland) Obstet. Soc. Author: Science and Art of Obstetrics, 1886. Died Phila., Jan. 29, 1898.

PASCALIS-OUVRIERE, Felix, (known as Felix Pascalis after 1801), physician; b. in Southern France, circa 1750; M.D., Montpellier U. Came to Am., 1793, settled in Phila.; v.p. Chem. Soc. of Phila., 1801; mem. editorial staff Medical Repository, N.Y.C., 1813-20; a founder, pres. N.Y. br. Linnaean Soc., of Paris, 1 term. Author: The Medico-Chymical Dissertations on the Causes of the Epidemic Called Yellow Fever, and on the Best Antimonial Preparations for the Use of Medicine, by a Physician, Practitioner in Philadelphia, 1796; An Account of the Contagious Epidemic Yellow Fever, Which Prevailed in Philadelphia in the Summer and Autumn of 1797, 1798; An Exposition of the Dangers of Internment in Cities, 1823. Died N.Y.C., July 29, 1833.

PASCHAL, George Washington, jurist, journalist; b. Skull Shoals, Ga., Nov. 23, 1812; s. George and Agnes (Brewer) P.; ed. Athens (Ga.) Acad.; LL.D. (hon.), Georgetown U., 1875; m. Sarah Ridge, 1835; m. 2d, Marcia Duval, 1 dau., Betty; m. 3d, Mrs. Mary Scoville Harper, Admitted to Ga. bar, 1832; ordered to New Echota, Ga., as aide-de-camp to Gen. John E. Wool in forcible removal of Cherokees to Indian Territory, 1835; justice Ark. Supreme Ct., 1842-43; assisted in adoption of treaty of amnesty with Cherokees, 1846; admitted to Tex. bar; editor semi-weekly Southern Intelligence, Austin, Tex., late 1850's; head Union Party in Tex., 1860; prepared for publ. Digest of the Laws of Texas, 1866, The Constitution of the United States Defined and Carefully Annotated, 1868; edited as reporter 28-31 Texas Reports: compiled A Digest of decisions Comprising Decisions of the Supreme Courts of Texas and of the United States upon Texas Law, 3 vols., 1872-75; a founder, lectr. Law Dept., Georgetown U. Died Washington, D.C., Feb. 16, 1878; buried Rock Creek Cemetery, Washington.

PASKO, Wesly Washington, printer; b. Waterloo, N.Y., Jan. 4, 1840; s. Jeremiah and Martha (Van Osdol) P.; m. Elizabeth Theresa Jarrett, Oct. 21, 1860, 3 children including Rev. Edgar W. Printer's apprentice, Utica, N.Y., 1855; with N.Y. Tribune, 1859; served as pvt. 16th Regt., N.Y. Heavy Arty., during Civil War; assisted in preparing codification of laws in regard to public schs., N.Y., 1867; editor N.Y. Albion; editor in publishing house, Cincinnati; invented Pasko Press, printing press using cylinder principle, 1886; librarian Typothetae (master printer's soc.), 1885; del. United Typothetae, Cincinnati, 1891. Author: Men Who Advertise, 1870; History of Printing in New York from its Beginning to the Present Time; Biographical History of Indiana, 1881. Died 1897.

PASQUIN, Anthony, see Williams, John.

PASSAVANT, William Alfred, clergyman, editor; b. Zelienople, Pa., Oct. 9, 1821; s. Philip Louis and Zelie (Basse) P.; grad. Jefferson Coll., Canonsburg, Pa., 1840; grad. Gettysburg (Pa.) Theol. Sem., 1842; m. Eliza Walter, May 1, 1845, 5 children including William Alfred. Licensed by Mo. Synod, Lutheran Ch., 1842; ordained to ministry Luth. Ch., 1843; published Luth. Almanac, 1842, 43; mem. staff Benjamin Kurtz's Luth. Observer, 1842-48; a founder Conservative Gen. Council of Evang. Luth. Ch. in N.Am., 1867; pastor 1st English Luth. Ch., Pitts., 1845-53; established Missionary (monthly periodical, to promote Luth. conservatism and strengthen missionary movement), 1848; became weekly publ., 1856, merged with publ. Lutheran, Phila., 1861; established, edited Workman, 1881-94; opened small hosp., Pitts., 1848; founded hosps. in Milw., Chgo., Jacksonville, Ill.; founded orphanages in Rochester, Zelienople, Mt. Vernon (N.Y.), Germantown (Pa.), Boston; a founder Chgo. Luth. Theol. Sem., also Thiel Coll., Greenville, Pa. Died Pitts., June 3, 1894.

PASTORIUS, Francis Daniel, lawyer; b. Sommerhausen, Franconia, Germany, Sept. 26, 1651; s. Melchior Adam and Magdalena (Dietz) P.; J.D., U. Altdorf, 1676; attended Univs. Strasbourg, Basel, Jena; m. Ennecke Klostermanns, Nov. 6, 1688, 2 sons. Agt. for group of Frankfurt Quakers who proposed to buy land in Penn's grant, arrived in Phila., Aug. 1683, completed negotiations for 15,000 acres; laid out settlement of Germantown, Pa., Oct. 1683, became 1st mayor (bailiff), then served continuously as mayor, clk, or keeper of records until 1707; agt. Frankfurt Land Co. until 1700; mem. Pa. Provincial Assembly, 1687, 91, signed protest against practice of keeping slaves (1st protest of its kind in English colonies), 1688. Author: (largest most important non-published work) Beehive; (important published works) Umstandige Geographische Beschreibung Der zu Allerletzt erfundenen Provintz Pensylvanice; A New Primmer or Methodical Directions to Attain the True Spelling, Reading and Writing of English (1st sch. book written in Pa.); also verse in German, Latin, English. Died Germantown, Sept. 27, 1719.

PATCH, Sam, stunt diver; b. R.I., circa 1807. Cottonspinner, Hamilton Mills, Paterson, N.J., in early years; dived from Chasm Bridge into Passaic River (N.J.), 1827; traveled from town to town, diving from any reasonable platform; became nat. celebrity after diving into Niagara Falls, 1829. Died while attempting 125-foot dive into Genesee Falls between U.S. and Can., Nov. 13, 1829.

PATERSON, John, army officer, congressman, landowner; b. Newington Parish, Wethersfield, Conn., 1744; s. John and Ruth (Bird) P.; grad. Yale, 1762; m. Elizabeth Lee, June 2, 1766. Practiced law in Conn.; moved to Lenox, Mass., 1774; elected mem. Berkshire County Conv. which adopted "Solemn League and Covenant" (boycotting Englishmade products), 1774; rep. from Lenox to 1st, 2d Mass. provincial congresses, 1774, 75; raised a regt. Mass. Militia, 1775, commd. col., 1775; commd. col. 15th Inf., Continental Army, 1776; served in rear position at Battle of Bunker Hill; ordered to relief of Am. troops in Can., on retreat through Crown Point and Ticonderoga, served in battles of Trenton and Princeton; commd. brig. gen., 1777; participated in capture of Gen. Burgoyne at Battle of Saratoga; wintered at Valley Forge, 1777-78; served in Battle of Monmouth; mem. court martial which tried Maj. Andre; brevetted maj. gen., 1783; comdr. Mass. Militia in suppression of Shays' Rebellion, 1787; moved to Lisle (now Whitneys Point), Broome County, N.Y., 1790, an owner land co. with extensive holdings in N.Y. State; mem. N.Y. State Assembly, 1792-93; mem. N.Y. Constl. Conv. from Broome County, 1801; mem. U.S. Ho. of Reps. from N.Y., 8th Congress, 1803-05; apptd. judge Broome and Tioga counties (N.Y.), 1798, 1807; an organizer Soc. of Cincinnati, Ohio Co. Died Lisle, July 19, 1808; buried Lenox Cemetery.

PATERSON, William, asso. justice U.S. Supreme Ct., senator, gov. N.J.; b. County Antrim, Ireland, Dec. 24, 1745; s. Richard and Mary Paterson; grad. Coll. of N.J. (now Princeton), 1763; studied law under Richard Stockton; m. Cornelia Bell, Feb. 9, 1779; m. 2d, Euphemia White, 1785; 3 children including Cornelia. A founder Well Meaning Soc. (literary soc., now called Cliosophic Soc.), Princeton, 1765-68; admitted to N.J. bar, 1768, began practice law, New Bromley, N.J., returned to Princeton, 1772; mem. N.J. Provincial Congress from Somerset County, 1775-76, sec. 1776; atty. gen. State of N.J., 1776-83; mem. N.J. Senate, 1776-77; del. N.J. State Constl. Conv., 1776; purchased farm on Raritan River, nr. New Brunswick, N.J., 1779; del. from N.J. to U.S. Constl. Conv., Phila., 1787, introduced N.J. Plan which sought establishment of fed. govt. with unicameral legislature representing states, not populations (dispute between N.J. and Va. plans resulted in compromise creating Senate giving equal representation to states, and Ho. of Reps. where mems. were chosen on basis of population); signed U.S. Constn., advocated its adoption in N.J.; mem. U.S. Senate (Democrat) from N.J., 1789-Nov. 13, 1790; gov. N.J., 1790-93, revised all Pre-Revolutionary English laws still in force in N.J.; asso. justice U.S. Supreme Ct., 1793-1806, presided over treason trials of participants in Whiskey Rebellion (notably over Matthew Lyon, accused of violation of Sedition Laws of 1798), also presided at trial of Samuel Odgen and William Smith for violation of Neutrality Laws in giving aid to S.Am.

patriot Francisco Miranda; City of Paterson (N.J.) named for him. Died Albany, N.Y., Sept. 9, 1806; buried Van Rensselaer Manor House vault, nr. Albany.

PATILLO, Henry, clergyman; b. Scotland, 1726; m. Mary Anderson, July 12, 1758. Licensed to preach by Presbytery of Hanover (Va.), 1757; pastor churches, Willis Creek, Byrd and Buck Island, Va., 1758-62, Hawkfields and Little River, N.C., 1764-74, Grassy Creek, N.C., 1774-1801. Author: On the Divisions Among Christians, 1788; Geographical Catechism, 1796. Died Dinwiddie County, Va., 1801.

PATRICK, Marsena Rudolph, army officer, agriculturist; b. Jefferson County, N.Y., Mar.11, 1811; s. John and Miriam (White) P.; grad. U.S. mil. Acad., 1835; m. Mary McGulpin, 1836. Served in Seminole War and Gen. Wool's Mexican expdn.; served as capt. in Mexican War, 1846-48; brevetted maj., by 1850, resigned; pres. N.Y. State Agrl. Coll., 1859; insp. gen. N.Y. Volunteers, 1861; commd. brig. gen. U.S. Volunteers, 1862; appted. provost marshal-gen. Army of Potomac, 1862; designated by Grant as provost marshal-gen. all armies operating against Richmond, 1864; brevetted maj. gen. U.S. Volunteers, 1865; commanded dist. of Henrico (including Richmond), 1865; pres. N.Y. State Agrl. Soc., 1867-68; pioneered for conservation and reforestation; gov. central br. Nat. Home for Disabled Volunteer Soldiers, Dayton, O., 1880-88. Died Dayton, July 27, 1888.

PATTEN, John, congressman; b. Kent County, Del., Apr. 26, 1746; attended common schs. Engaged in farming; served from lt. to maj. Continental Army, participated in all battles from Long Island to Camden during Revolutionary War; mem. Continental Congress from Del., 1785-86; mem. U.S. Ho. of Reps. from Del., 3d, 4th congresses, 1793-Feb. 14, 1794, 95-97; engaged in farming. Died "Tynhead Court" nr. Dover, Del., Dec. 26, 1800; buried Presbyn. Churchyard, Dover.

PATTERSON, Daniel Todd, naval officer; b. L.I., N.Y., Mar. 6, 1786; s. John and Catherine (Livingston) P.; m. George Ann Pollock, 1807, 5 children including Carlile Pollock, George Ann (Mrs. David D. Porter), Thomas Harman. Commd. midshipman U.S. Navy, 1800, lt., 1808; semi independent command 12 gunboats, La., 1810-11; promoted master comdt., 1813; commanded New Orleans (La.) station, 1813; captured 6 schooners and other small vessels of pirate Jean Lafite, 1814; caused enemy delay by gunboat action on Lake Borgne, aiding Gen. Andrew Jackson's final victory, 1815; commd. capt., 1815; fleet capt., comdr. flagship Constitution, Mediterranean Squadron, 1824-28; mem. Bd. of Navy Commrs., 1828; commanded Mediterranean Squadron, 1832-36; comdt. Washington (D.C.) Navy Yard, 1836-39. Died Washington Navy Yard, Aug. 25, 1839; buried Congressional Cemetery, Washington, D.C.

PATTERSON, David Trotter, senator; b. Cedar Creek, Tenn., Feb. 28, 1818; attended Greeneville (Tenn.) Coll., 2 years; studied law. Admitted to Tenn. bar, 1841, began practice in Greeneville; engaged in mfg.; judge 1st Tenn. Circuit Ct., 1854-63; mem. U.S. Senate (Democrat) from Tenn., July 24, 1866-69; managed his extensive agrl. interests. Died Afton, Tenn., Nov. 3, 1891; buried Andrew Johnson Nat. Cemetery, Greeneville.

PATTERSON, George Washington, congressman; b. Londonderry, N.H., Nov. 11, 1799; grad. Pinkerton Acad. Moved to Genesee County, N.Y., 1818; engaged in mfg. farm implements; settled in Leicester, N.Y., 1825, engaged in farming, mfg. farm implements; commr. of hwys., Leicester; justice of peace; mem. N.Y. State Assembly, 1832, 33, 35-40, speaker, 1839-40; basin commr., Albany, N.Y., 1839-40; took charge of Chautauqua Land Office, Westfield, N.Y., 1841; del. N.Y. Constl. Conv., 1846; elected lt. gov. N.Y., 1848; chmn. N.Y.C. Harbor Commn., 1855-57; quarantine commr. Port of N.Y., 1859; supr., pres. N.Y.C. Bd. Edn., many years; del. Republican nat. convs., Phila., 1856, Chgo., 1860; mem. U.S. Ho. of Reps. (Republican) from N.Y., 45th Congress, 1877-79. Died Westfield, Oct. 15, 1879; buried Westfield Cemetery.

PATTERSON, James Willis, senator, educator; b. Henniker, N.H., July 2, 1823; s. William and Frances Mary (Shepard) P.; grad. Dartmouth, 1848; attended Theol. Sem., New Haven, Conn.; LL.D. (hon.), Ia. Coll., 1868; m. Sarah Parker Wilder, Dec. 24, 1854, 1 son, George W. Tchr., then prin. Woodstock (Conn.) Acad., 1848-51; tutor Dartmouth, 1852, prof. mathematics, 1854-65, prof. astronomy and meteorology, 1859-65, prof. rhetoric, 1893; sch. commr. Grafton County (N.H.), 1858-62; mem. N.H. Ho. of Reps. (Republican), 1862, 77-78; mem. U.S. Ho. of Reps. from N.H., 38th-39th congresses, 1863-67; mem. U.S. Senate from N.H., 1867-73, recommended for expulsion by Senate investigating com. because of involvement in Credit Mobilier scandal; supt. pub. instrn. State of N.H., 1881-93; regent Smithsonian Instn.; pres. Am. Inst. Instrn. Died Hanover, N.H., May 4, 1893; buried Dartmouth Cemetery, Hanover.

PATTERSON, John, congressman; b. Little Britain Twp., Lancaster County, Pa., Feb. 10, 1771; attended common schs., Pattersons Mills, Pa. Moved to St. Clairsville, O.; engaged in merc. bus.; 1st mayor of St. Clairsville, 1807-08; mem. Ohio Ho. of Reps., 1807-08, Ohio Senate, 1815-18; asso. judge Belmont County (O.) Ct. of Common Pleas, 1810-15; mem. U.S. Ho. of Reps. (Democrat) from Ohio, 18th Congress, 1823-25; engaged in hardware bus., farming. Died St. Clairsville, Feb. 7, 1848; buried Union Cemetery, St. Clairsville.

PATTERSON, Morris, mcht., philanthropist; b. Phila., Oct. 26, 1809; s. John and Rachel (Cauffman) P.; m. Mary Strom, Apr. 8, 1846, 3 children. Worked in his father's grocery store, 1819-30; operated own grocery store, 1830-40; pioneer in anthracite coal mining in Pa.; became partner (with Benjamin Junney, Jr.) in wholesale grocery bus., 1840; partner (with Joseph Bailey) in plate iron mfg. firm, Douglasville, Pa., 1845; dir. Western Nat. Bank, Montgomery Iron Co.; founder Pa. Working Home for Blind Men; connected with many charitable orgns. Died Oct. 23, 1878.

PATTERSON, Robert, educator; b. Hillsborough, County Down, Ireland, May 30, 1743; s. Robert Patterson; LL.D. (hon.), U. Pa., 1819; m. Amy Ewing, May 9, 1774, 8 children including Robert M. Came to U.S., 1768; prin. of acad., Wilmington, Del., 1772-75; served as brigade maj. in Revolutionary War; prof. math. U. Pa., 1779-1814, vice provost, 1810-13; mem. Select Council of Phila., pres., 1799; dir. Phila. mint (apptd. by Pres. Jefferson), 1805; elected mem. Am. Philos. Soc., 1783, pres., 1819-24. Author: Lectures on Select Subjects in Mechanics, 2 vols., 1806, Newtonian System of Philosophy, 1808, A Treatise of Practical Arithmetic, 1818. Died Phila., July 22, 1824.

PATTERSON, Robert, army officer, industrialist; b. County Tyrone, Ireland, Jan. 12, 1792; s. Francis and Ann (Graham) P.; m. Sarah Engle, 1817, 11 children including Francis Engle. Came to Am., 1799; served as capt., lt. col., col. Pa. Militia in War of 1812; commd. lt. 22d U.S. Inf., then capt. and dep q.m. 32d Inf., mustered out as capt., 1815; mem. Pa. Democratic-Republican Conv., Harrisburg, 1824; commr. internal improvements Pa., 1827; presdl. elector twice; commd. maj. gen. Volunteers, 1847, took Jalapa, Mexico; prominent in sugar industry in La.; owned 30 cotton mills in Pa.; commanded div. Pa. Militia, 1833-67; an original trustee Lafayette Coll., 1825-35, 74-81, pres. bd., 1876-81; commd. maj. gen. Volunteers in command of mil. dept. of Pa., Del., Md., D.C., 1861; failed to give battle to Joseph E. Johnston and to cooperate with McDowell at Bull Run (claimed Gen. Scott did not send him orders to attack.) Author: A Narrative of the Campaign in the Valley of the Shenandoah in 1861, 1865. Died Phila., Aug. 7, 1881; buried Laurel Hill Cemetery, Pa.

PATTERSON, Thomas, congressman; b. Little Britain Twp., Lancaster County, Pa., Oct. 1, 1764; attended schools, Patterson Mills, Pa. Engaged in farming, operated a flour mill; served as maj. gen. Pa. Militia, War of 1812; Democratic presdl. elector, 1816; mem. U.S. Ho. of Reps. (Dem.) from Pa., 15th-18th congresses, 1817-25. Died nr. Pattersons Mills, Nov. 16, 1841; buried West Middletown (Pa.) Cemetery.

PATTERSON, Thomas Harman, naval officer; b. New Orleans, May 10, 1820; s. Daniel Todd and George Ann (Pollock) P.; m. Maria Wainwright, Jan. 5, 1847, 5 children. Commd. midshipman U.S. Navy, 1836, lt., 1849; commanded ship Chocura in naval force which cooperated with McClellan during Peninsular Campaign, 1862; promoted comdr., 1862; sr. officer in York and Pamunkey rivers, 1862, offshore blockade, Charleston, S.C., 1864-65; commd. capt., 1866, commodore, 1871; rear adm., 1877; commanded flagship Brooklyn, Brazil Squadron, 1865-67; comdt. Washington (D.C.) Navy Yard, 1873-76; commanded Asiatic Squadron, 1878-80. Died Washington, Apr. 9, 1889.

PATTERSON, Thomas J., congressman; b. N.Y. State, circa 1808; attended pub. schs. Mem. U.S. Ho. of Reps. (Whig) from N.Y., 28th Congress, 1843-45; land agt., Rochester, N.Y.

PATTERSON, Walter, congressman; b. Columbia County, N.Y. Mem. N.Y. State Assembly, 1818; supr. Town of Ancram (N.Y.), 1821-23; mem. U.S. Ho. of Reps. from N.Y., 17th Congress, 1821-23; moved to Livingston, N.Y.; supr. Town of Livingston, 1826-28; asso. justice Columbia County Ct., 1828-30.

PATTERSON, William, mcht.; b. Fanad, County Donegal, Ireland, Nov. 1, 1752; s. William and Elizabeth (Peoples) P.; m. Dorcas Spear, 13 children including Elizabeth Patterson Bonaparte. Came to Phila., 1766; accumulated a fortune of $60,000 voyages to France and French and Dutch West Indies (his 1st shipping venture), 1775-78; prospered as mcht., Balt.; 1st pres. Bank of Md.; an organizer Mcht.'s Exchange, Balt., 1815; an incorporator, 1st dir. B. & O. R.R., 1827; an incorporator Canton Co., 1828; v.p. of a meeting of Balt. citizens which condemned nullification ordinance of S.C., 1832. Died July 7, 1835.

PATTERSON, William, congressman; b. Londonderry, N.H., June 4, 1789; attended common schs. Moved to Rensselaerville, N.Y., 1815, to Lyons, N.Y., 1816; engaged in mfg. and selling fanning mills; engaged in farming nr. Warsaw, N.Y., 1822; settled in Warsaw, 1837, held local offices; mem. U.S. Ho. of Reps. (Whig) from N.Y., 25th Congress, 1837-38. Died Warsaw, Aug. 14, 1838; buried Warsaw Town Cemetery.

PATTERSON, William, congressman; born Md., 1790; studied law, Mansfield, O. Admitted to Ohio bar, practiced law; held local offices; asso. judge Ct. of Common Pleas, 1820, 27; mem. U.S. Ho. of Reps. (Democrat) from Ohio, 23d-24th congresses, 1833-37. Died Van Wert, O., Aug. 17, 1868; buried Mansfield Cemetery.

PATTIE, James Ohio, trapper; b. Bracken County, Ky., 1804; s. Sylvester Pattie; attended Augusta Coll. Joined his father in Sylvestre Pratt's expdn. to Santa Fe, 1824, was apparently arrested and imprisoned by Mexican Govt. in Cal. (cannot be verified with Mexican documents); joined gold rush to Cal., 1849. Author: Personal Narrative (written largely by Timothy Flint), 1831. Died 1850.

PATTISON, Granville Sharp, anatomist; b. nr. Glasgow, Scotland, 1791; s. John Pattison; attended U. Glasgow. Prof. anatomy, physiology, surgery in Andersonian Instn. (U. Glasgow); came to U.S., 1819; became mem. Medico-Chirurg. Soc. of London also fellow Royal Coll. Surgeons, 1819; gave a series pvt. lessons in anatomy in Phila., 1819-20; prof. anatomy, physiology, surgery U. Md., Balt., 1820-26; editor: Observations on the Surgical Anatomy of the Head and Neck (Allen Burn), 1824; prof. anatomy U. London, 1828-31; prof. anatomy Jefferson Med. Coll., Phila., 1832-41; prof. anatomy U. City of N.Y., 1841-51; editor of Register and Library of Medicine and Surgical Science, Washington, 1833-36; co-editor American Medical Library and Intelligencer, Phila., 1836. Author: Experimental Observations on the Operation of Lithotomy, 1820; "A Refutation of Certain Calumnies" in pamphlet Correspondence Between Mr. Granville Sharp Pattison and Dr. Nathaniel Chapman, 1821. Died N.Y.C., Nov. 12, 1851.

PATTISON, Thomas, naval officer; b. Troy, N.Y., Feb. 8, 1822; s. Elias and Olivia (Gardiner) P.; m. Serafina Catalina Webster, July 1, 1850, 1 dau., Maria Webster. Apptd. midshipman U.S. Navy, 1839; served in Mexican War; sailing master on ship Portsmouth, China Sta., circa 1852, promoted to lt. while on cruise; escorted 1st Am. minister to Japan from Simoda to Tokyo, 1858 (became 1st Am. naval officer to enter Tokyo); exec. of sloop Perry which captured privateer Savannah (1st privateer taken), off Charleston, N.C., 1861; in command steamer Sumter on S.E. coast blockade, 1861; sr. officer at Fernandina, Fla., summer and autumn 1862; comdt. naval. sta. established at former Confederate base, Memphis, Tenn., 1863-65; commd. lt. comdr., 1862, comdr., 1865, capt., 1870, commodore, 1877, rear adm., 1883; commanded naval sta. Port Royal, S.C., 1878-80, Washington Navy Yard, 1880-83. Died New Brighton, S.I., N.Y., Dec. 17, 1891.

PATTON, Abigail Hutchinson, singer; b. Milford, N.H., Aug. 29, 1829; d. Jesse and Mary (Leavitt) Hutchinson; attended Edes Sem., Plymouth, Mass., circa 1842; m. Ludlow Patton, Feb. 28, 1849. A contralto, sang with Hutchinson Quartet (led by her brother Adoniram) on tours of New Eng. and N.Y., from 1841; sang at many abolitionist convs., 1840's; made appearances on behalf of slave emancipation during Civil War. Composer vocal and instrumental music including songs: Kind Words Can Never Die, Ring Out Wild Bells. Author: (collection of prose and poetry) A Handful of Pebbles, 1891. Died N.Y.C., Nov. 24, 1892; buried N.Y.C.

PATTON, John, congressman; b. Covington, Pa., Jan. 6, 1823; attended pub. schs., Curwensville, Pa.; children include Charles Emory, John. Engaged in merc. and lumber bus., 1844-60.; organizer 1st Nat. Bank of Curwensville, 1864, elected pres.; organizer, pres. Curwensville Bank; del. Whig Nat.

Conv., Balt., 1852, Republican Nat. Conv., Chgo., 1860; mem. U.S. Ho. of Reps. (Rep.))from Pa., 37th, 50th congresses, 1861-63, 87-89; Rep. presdl. elector, 1864. Died Phila., Dec. 23, 1897; buried Oak Hill Cemetery, Curwensville.

PATTON, John Mercer, congressman; b. Fredericksburg, Va., Aug. 10, 1797; s. Robert and Ann Gordon (Mercer) P.; attended Princeton, 1 year; grad. in medicine, U. Pa., 1818; studied law, Fredericksburg; m. Margaret French Williams, Jan. 8, 1824, at least 6 children. Never practiced medicine; admitted to bar, began practice of law; mem. U.S. Ho. of Reps. from Va. 21st-25th congresses, Nov. 25, 1830-Apr. 7, 1838; mem. Va. Exec. Council, 1838-42; acting gov. Va., 1841; practiced law, Richmond, Va., 1842-58, became leading lawyer revised Civil Code of Va., 1846, Va. Criminal Code, 1847; published (with Conway Robinson) The Code of Virginia, 1849; mem. bd. visitors Med. Coll. of Ga., 1854. Died Richmond, Oct. 29, 1858; buried Shockee Cemetery, Richmond.

PATTON, William, clergyman, author; b. Phila., Aug. 23, 1798; s. Col. Robert and Cornelia (Bridges) P.; grad. Middlebury Coll., 1818; attended Princeton Theol. Sem., 1819-20; m. Mary Weston, 1819; m. 2d, Mary Bird, 1860; m. 3d, Emily Trowbridge Hayes, 1864; 10 children. Ordained to ministry by Congl. Assn. of Vt., 1820; sec. Central Am. Ednl. Soc., 1833-37; successful in revival work in N.Y.; 1st to propose establishment of a Presbyn. theol. sem., N.Y.C.: became one of 4 ministerial founders of Union Sem. 1836, dir., 1836-49, instr. or prof. extraordinary for 3 years; revised Cottage Bible and Family Expositor (Thomas Williams), 1834; published (with Thomas Hastings) The Christian Psalmist (a hymn book), 1839; in London, published pamphlet The American Crisis; or The True Issue, Slavery or Liberty; proposed and attended London meeting which organized Evangelical Alliance, 1846; mem. exec. com. Am. Home Missionary Soc., 1830-70. Died New Haven, Conn., Sept. 9, 1879.

PATTON, William Weston, clergyman, coll. pres.; b. N.Y.C., Oct. 19, 1821; s. William and Mary (Weston) P.; grad. U. City of N.Y., 1839, LL.D. (hon.), 1882; grad. Union Theol. Sem., 1842; D.D. (hon.) Ind. Asbury (now DePauw) U., 1862; m. Sarah Jane Mott, Jan. 11, 1843; m. 2d, Mary Boardman Smith, 1851; 9 children. Ordained to ministry Congregational Ch., 1843; pastor Phillips Ch., South Boston, Mass., 1843-46, 4th Ch., Hartford, Conn., 1846-57, 1st Ch., Chgo., 1857-67; editor Chgo. Advance, 1867-72; Western sec. Am. Missionary Assn., 1873-74; lectr. U. Chgo., Oberlin Coll., 1874-77; pres. Howard U., Washington, D.C., 1877-89; mem. Am. Bd. Commrs. for Fgn. Missions, 1869-89. Author: The American Board and Slave-Holding, 1846; Conscience and Law, 1850; Spiritual Victory, 1871. Died Westfield, N.J., Dec. 31, 1889.

PAUGHER, Adrien de, see de Paugher, Adrien.

PAUL, Gabriel, architect; b. Santo Domingo, 1781; ed. in France; m. Louise Choteau, at least 3 children. Came to U.S., settled in Balt., early 1800's; moved to St. Louis, 1817; his most important archtl. work was 1st Cathedral in St. Louis (no longer standing), 1818; built number of brick mansions, St. Louis, including Berthold house, 1821. Died 1845; buried Calvary Cemetery.

PAUL, Jeremiah, Jr., artist; b. probably Phila. A founder Columbianum, Phila., 1795; became mem. firm Pratt, Rutter & Co., Phila., 1796, later Paul, Rutter & Clarke; painted miniatures, traced profiles, Charleston, S.C., 1803; worked in Balt., 1806-08; exhibited Venus and Cupid, Phila., 1811; painted portraits and signs, Pitts., 1814; painted theatrical scenery in West. Died nr. St. Louis, July 13, 1820.

PAULDING, Hiram, naval officer; b. Westchester County, N.Y., Dec. 11, 1797; s. John and Esther (Ward) P.; grad. Capt. Alden Partridges Mil. Acad., Norwich, Vt., 1823; m. Ann Kellogg, 1828, 6 children. Apptd. midshipman U.S. Navy, 1811; served as acting lt. in Ticonderoga in Battle of Lake Champlain, 1813, commended by U.S. Congress; commd. lt., 1816; 1st lt. in Dolphin, 1825, pursued mutineers from whaleship Globe during cruise in South seas; capt., in ship on China cruise, Vincennes 1844-47; in command of frigate St. Lawrence (1st Am. warship to reach Bremen, Germany), 1848; in charge of Washington (D.C.) Navy Yard, 1849-53; command of Home Squadron, seized Gen. William Walker and about 150 filibusterers who had landed in defiance of U.S. sloop Saratoga at Grey Town, Nicaragua, 1855-58; Apptd. head Bur. of Detail, 1861; led expdn. which evacuated Norfolk Navy Yard, 1861; head N.Y. Navy Yard, 1861-65; retired as rear adm., 1861; gov. U.S. Naval Asylum, Phila., 1866-69; port admiral of Boston, 1869-70, Author: Journal of a Cruise of the United States Schooner Dolphin, 1831. Died L.I., N.Y., Oct. 20, 1878.

PAULDING, James Kirke, author, sec. of navy; b. Putnam County, N.Y., Aug. 22, 1778; s. William and Catharine (Ogden) P.; m. Gertrude Kemble, Nov. 15, 1818, several children including William. Mem. Calliopean Soc. (one of earliest literary socs. in N.Y.); collaborated with Washington Irving in periodical Salmagundi, 1807-08; wrote against Brit. criticism in his work, The United States and England, 1814; sec. Bd. Navy Commrs., 1815-23; navy agt. for N.Y., 1823-38; U.S. sec. of navy under Van Buren, 1838-41, sent South Sea Exploring Expdn. on its 4 year cruise to Ore. coast and Antarctic. Author: The Diverting History of John Bull and Jonathan Brother, 1812; (poem) The Lay of the Scottish Fiddle; A Tale of Havre de Grace, 1813; Letters from the South, by a Northern Man, 1817; (chief poetical work) "The Backwards Man," 1818; (second series) Salmagundi, 1819; (1st novel) Koningsmark, or The Long Finne, 1823; (contbns. to so-called literary war between Eng. and Am.) A Sketch of Old England, 1822, John Bull in America, 1825; New Mirror for Travelers, 1828; The Dumb Girl, 1830; (best novel) The Dutchman's Fireside, 1831; Westward Ho!, 1832; A Life of Wasington, 1835; (lesser known works) The Merry Tales of the Three Wise Men of Gotham, 1826; Tales of the Good Woman, 1829; The Lion of the West, 1831; The Book of St. Nicholas, 1837; A Gift from Fairy Land, 1838; American Comedies, 1847. Died Apr. 6, 1860; buried Greenwood Cemetery, Bklyn.

PAULDING, William, Jr., congressman, mayor N.Y.C.; b. Phillipsburgh (now Tarrytown), N.Y., Mar. 7, 1770; s. William Paulding; studied law. Admitted to N.Y. bar, began practice in N.Y.C.; mem. U.S. Ho. of Reps. (Democrat) from N.Y., 12th Congress, 1811-13; served as brig. gen. N.Y. Militia during War of 1812; del. N.Y. Constl. Conv., 1821; adj. gen. State of N.Y.; mayor N.Y.C., 1824-26. Died Tarrytown, Feb. 11, 1854; buried Old Dutch Burying Ground at Sleepy Hollow, Tarrytown.

PAVY, Octave, physician, explorer; b. New Orleans, June 22, 1844; attended U. Paris, 1866; m. Lilla Stone, 1878. Organized (with Lt. Beauregard) equipped and financed independent Zouave corps; surgeon and naturalist on H.W. Hawgate's expdn. to Greenland, 1800-81, sailed in ship Gulnare, explored country, collected specimens for Smithsonian Instn.; commd. surgeon of Lady Franklin Bay expdn. under Lt. A.W. Greely, 1881, naturalist and surgeon in Artic region, 1881-84; discovered Pavy Valley and Pavy River between Cape Baird and Cape Ritter Bay. Died just before rescue ship arrived, Cape Sabine, Arctic, June 6, 1884.

PAWLING, Levi, congressman; b. Fatland, nr. Norristown, Pa., July 25, 1773; grad. U. Pa.; studied law, Norristown. Admitted to Pa. bar, 1795, practiced in Norristown and Phila.; trustee of lands for U. Pa.; apptd. chmn. commn. to raise funds for lock navigation on Schuylkill River, 1816; mem. U.S. Ho. of Reps. (Democrat) from N.Y., 15th Congress, 1817-19; elected burgess of Norristown, 1818; pres. bd. dirs. Bank of Montgomery County. Died Norristown, Sept. 7, 1845; buried St. John's Protestant Episcopal Cemetery, Norristown.

PAXTON, Philip, see Hammett, Samuel Adams.

PAYEN de NOYLAN, Gilles-Augustin, army officer; b. France, 1697; s. Pierre and Catherine Jeanne (Le Moyne) P. de N.; m. Jeanne Faucon Du Manoir, May 1, 1735, at least 2 children including Jean Baptiste. Came to La. as lt. in French Army, 1717-18; engaged in capture of Pensacola (Fla.) from Spanish, 1719; in command of New Orleans and an inf. co., 1720; dismissed from army, 1726; adjutant of Mobile (Ala.), 1732, New Orleans, 1733; acted as diplomatic agt. to Choctaw Indians and commanded several raids against them; wounded, 1736; sent on unsuccessful expdn. up Mississippi River to prepare sites for battle against Chickasaw Indians by a combined French and Indian army, 1739; made lieutenant du roi, 1741; mem. La. Supreme Council; acting gov. La., 1748. Died Feb. 26, 1751.

PAYERAS, Mariano, missionary; b. Inca, Marjorca, 1739. Joined Franciscan Order, Parma, Italy, 1784; sent as missionary to Mexico, 1793; did missionary work among Indians in Monterey and Cal., became pres. of missions, 1815-20; vicar to bishop of Sonora; later visited all missions in Cal.; honored for his work and reports of explorations by Spanish monarch, 1819. Died Apr. 28, 1823.

PAYNE, Daniel Alexander, clergyman, coll. pres.; b. Charleston, S.C., Feb. 24, 1811; s. London and Martha P.; LL.D. (hon.), Lincoln U., 1879; m. Julia (Becraft) Ferris, 1847; m. 2d, Mrs. Eliza J. Clark, 1853. Born of free persons of color; joined Meth. Episcopal Ch., 1826; opened sch. for colored children, Charleston, 1829-34; entered Lutheran Theol. Sem., Gettysburg, Pa., 1835; licensed to preach, 1837; ordained by Franckean Synod, Luth. Ch., 1839; joined African Meth. Episcopal Ch., 1841; received as preacher at Phila. Conf. of A.M.E. Ch., 1842; historiographer A.M.E. Ch., 1848, elected bishop, 1852; promoted formation of ch. lit. socs., debating lyceums; purchased Wilberforce U. (an Ohio instn. established by Meth. Episcopal Ch. for edn. colored youth, 1856), pres. until 1869; del. 1st Ecumenical Conf., Meth. Episcopal Ch., London, Eng., 1881; attended Parliament of Religions During World's Columbian Exposition, Chgo., 1893. Author: The Semi-Centenary . . . of the African Methodist Episcopal Church in the United States of America, 1866; A History of the African Methodist Episcopal Church from 1816-1856, published 1865; Recollections of Men and Things, 1877; Domestic Education, 1886. Died Wilberforce, Nov. 29, 1893.

PAYNE, Henry B., senator; b. Hamilton, N.Y., Nov. 30, 1810; s. Elisha and Esther (Douglass) P.; grad. Hamilton Coll., 1832; m. Mary Perry, 1836, 5 children including Flora, Oliver H., Nathan. Admitted to Cleve. (O.) bar, 1834; city clk. Cleve., 1836; mem. 1st Cleve. Water Works Commn.; Democratic presdl. elector, 1848; sinking fund commr. Cleve., 1862-96; reformed city finances; a founder Cleve. and Columbus R.R., 1849, pres., 1851-54; mem. Ohio Senate, 1849-51; chmn. Ohio delegations at Dem. convs., Cincinnati, 1856, Balt., 1860, 72; mem. U.S. Ho. of Reps. from Ohio, 44th Congress, 1875-77, chmn. com. on electoral count at Tilden's request, helped in passage legislation providing for the electoral commn. (of which he became a mem.); mem. U.S. Senate (Democrat) from Ohio, 1885-91. Died Cleve., Sept. 9, 1896; buried Lake View Cemetery.

PAYNE, John Howard, actor, playwright; b. N.Y. C., June 9, 1791; s. William and Sarah (Isaacs) P.; attended Union Coll., Schenectady, N.Y., 1806-09; never married. Made acting debut as Norval in John Home's play Douglas, N.Y.C., 1809; 1 of most popular actors in Am., 1809-10; went to Eng., 1813, worked as actor, playwright, theater sec.; amassed huge debts, held in Fleet Street Debtors' Prison, London, Eng., 1820-21; published Opera Glass, weekly theatrical paper, London, 1826-27; returned to U.S., 1832; U.S. consul at Tunis, 1842-45, 51-52. Author: (plays) Julia, or the Wanderer, 1806; The Maid and the Magpie, 1814; Brutus, or the Fall of Tarquin, 1818; Thérèse, the Orphan of Geneva, 1821; Clari, or the Maid of Milan (operetta, including song Home, Sweet Home), 1823; Romulus the Shepherd King, 1839; (with Washington Irving) Charles the Second, 1824, Richelieu, A Domestic Tragedy, 1826. Died Tunis, Apr. 9, 1852; buried Oak Hill Cemetery, Washington, D.C.

PAYNE, Lewis Thornton Powell, conspirator; probably b. Fla., 1845. Joined Confederate Army, 1861; wounded and captured at Battle of Gettysburg, 1863; became acquainted with John Wilkes Booth, Mar. 1865, agreed on plot to kidnap Pres. Lincoln (plot never materialized); entered into assassination plot, assigned to murder Sec. of State William Seward; succeeded in entering Seward's home (Washington, D.C.), wounded Seward and 3 persons who attempted to capture him; managed to escape, but was captured (Apr. 17, 1865) when he returned to boarding house of Mary Surratt (where plot had been formulated), Washington; tried, convicted and sentenced to death for his part in assassination of Lincoln. Hung, Washington, July 17, 1865.

PAYNE, William Winter, congressman; b. "Granville" nr. Warrenton, Va., Jan. 2, 1807; studied law. Moved to Franklin County, Ala., 1825, engaged in planting; mem. Ala. Ho. of Reps., 1831, 34-38, 40; moved to Sumter County, Ala.; mem. U.S. Ho. of Reps. (Democrat) from Ala., 27th-29th congresses, 1841-47; returned to Va., 1847, engaged in planting nr. Warrenton; chmn. Va. Dem. Conv., 1859. Died Warrenton, Sept. 2, 1874; buried City Cemetery, Warrenton.

PAYNTER, Lemuel, congressman; b. Lewes, Del., 1788; attended common schs. Moved to Phila.; served as maj. and lt. col. 93d Regt., Pa. Militia during War of 1812; mem. and pres. bd. commrs. Southwark dist. of Phila.; mem. guardians of poor, sch. dir.; mem. Pa. Senate, 1833; mem. U.S. Ho. of Reps. (Democrat) from Pa., 25th-26th congresses, 1837-41. Died Phila., Aug. 1, 1863; buried Union Sixth St. Cemetery, Phila.

PAYSON, Edward, clergyman; b. Rindge, N.H., July 25, 1783; s. Seth and Greta P.; grad. Harvard, 1803; studied theology, Rindge; m. Anna Louise Shipman, May 8, 1811, 8 children. Prin. of an acad., Portland, Me., 1803-06; licensed to preach in Congregational Ch., 1807, ordained to ministry, 1807; pastor 2d Congregational Ch., Portland, 1811-27. Author: The Bible Above all Price, 1814; Address to Seamen, 1821. Died Oct. 22, 1827.

PAYSON, Seth, clergyman; b. Walpole, Mass., Sept. 30, 1758; s. Rev. Phillips and Kezia (Bullen) P.; grad. Harvard, 1777; m. Grata Payson,

1782, 7 children. Ordained to ministry Congregational Ch., 1782, pastor, Rindge, N.H., 1782-1820; v.p. N.H. Bible Soc., several years; rep. from N.H. in Gen. Assembly Presbyn. Ch., Phila., 1815; mem. N.H. Senate, 1802-06. Author: Proofs of the Real Existence and General Tendency of Illuminism, 1802. Died Feb. 26, 1820.

PEABODY, Andrew Preston, clergyman; b. Beverly, Mass., Mar. 19, 1811; s. Andrew and Mary (Rantoul) P.; grad. Harvard, 1826, Harvard Divinity Sch., 1832; m. Catherine Whipple Roberts, Sept. 12, 1836. Prin. acad., Portsmouth, N.H., 1828; ordained to ministry Unitarian Ch., 1833; pastor South Parish Unitarian Ch., Portsmouth, 1833-59; editor N.Am. Review, 1853-63; acting pres. Harvard, 1862, 68-69, overseer, 1883-93. Author 120 books and pamphlets including: Conversation: Its Faults and Graces, 1856; A Manual of Moral Philosophy, 1873; Building a Character, 1886. Died Mar. 10, 1893.

PEABODY, Elizabeth Palmer, educator; b. Billerica, Mass., May 16, 1804; d. Nathaniel and Elizabeth (Palmer) Peabody. Conducted pvt. sch., Lancaster, Mass., 1820-22, Boston, 1822-23; pvt. governess, Me., 1823-25; sec. to William Ellery Channing, 1825-34; asst. at Bronson Alcott's sch., Boston, 1834-36; joined Ralph Waldo Emerson's Transcendental Club, 1836; operated bookshop, Boston, 1839-42; contbd. articles to Dial (Transcendental organ), 1842-43; advocated advancement of study of history in public schs., 1850-60; opened 1st Am. kindergarten, Boston, 1860; published Kindergarten Messenger, 1873-75; mem., lectr. Alcott's Concord Sch. of Philosophy, 1879-84; became interested in Indian edn., 1880. Author: Record of a School, 1835; A Last Evening with Allston, 1886. Died Jamaica Plain, Mass., Jan. 3, 1894; buried Concord, Mass.

PEABODY, George, mcht., philanthropist; b. South Danvers (now Peabody), Mass., Feb. 18, 1795; s. Thomas and Judith (Dodge) P.; D.C.L. (hon.), Oxford U., 1867; never married. Partner (with Elisha Riggs) in wholesale dry goods bus., Balt., 1814-37; an incorporator, pres. Eastern R.R., 1836-37; owner George Peabody & Co., firm dealing in fgn. exchange and Am. securities, London, Eng., 1837-69; negotiated loan from Eng. for State of Md., 1835; financed Am. display at Crystal Palace, London, 1851; financed expdn. to search for Arctic explorer Sir John Franklin, 1852; established Peabody Inst. (including free library, art gallery, acad. of music, endowment for lectures), Balt., also Peabody (Mass.) Inst. (including free library, lecture endowment); founded Peabody Mus. of natural history and natural science Yale, Peabody Mus. of archeology and ethnology Harvard; established Peabody Acad. of Sci., Salem, Mass., Peabody Edn. Fund for edn. in South; constructed tenements for workingmen of London. Died London, Nov. 4, 1869; buried Peabody.

PEABODY, Joseph, privateersman, mcht.; b. Middleton, Mass., Dec. 12, 1757; s. Francis and Margaret (Knight) P.; m. Catherine Smith, Aug. 28, 1791; m. 2d, Elizabeth Smith, Oct. 24, 1795; 7 children. Served in Revolutionary War; served in privateers Bunker Hill, Pilgrim; captured in privateer Fish Hawk, imprisoned at St. John's, Newfoundland, then exchanged; became 2d officer on letter-of-marque Ranger, wounded in skirmish with Loyalists; purchased schooner Three Friends, used ship for trading in Europe and W.I. for several years; established mcht. business, Salem, Mass., 1791, traded with Baltic, Mediterranean, W.I., China, India; believed to have employed 6,000 to 7,000 men, amassed great fortune, Died Salem, Jan. 5, 1844.

PEABODY, Nathaniel, Continental congressman, army officer, physician; b. Topsfield, Mass., Mar. 12, 1742; s. Jacob and Susanna (Rogers) P.; studied medicine privately with father; m. Abigail Little, Mar. 1, 1763. Began practice of medicine, N.H., 1761; justice of peace Rockingham County N.H.), 1771; commd. lt. col. Brit. Army, resigned to enter Continental Army, 1774; a leader at capture Ft. William and Mary, New Castle, N.H., (one of 1st open acts of Am. Revolution), 1774; mem., later chmn. N.H. Com. of Safety, 1776; mem. N.H. Ho. of Reps., 1776-79, 81-85, 87-90, 93-96, speaker, 1793; adjutant gen. N.H. Militia, 1777, participated in R.I. expdn., 1778; del. from N.H. to Continental Congress, 1779-80; mem. N.H. constl. convs., 1781-83, 91-92, chmn. com. to draft N.H. Constn., 1782-83; mem. N.H. Senate, 1785, 86, 90-93, chosen to serve as councilor (mem. Gov.'s Council) from N.H. Ho. of Reps., 1784, from N.H. Senate, 1785; an organizer N.H. Med. Soc., 1791; maj. gen. N.H. Militia, 1793-98; spent last 20 years of life in debtor's prison. Died Exeter, N.H., June 27, 1823; buried Old Cemetery, Exeter.

PEABODY, Oliver William Bourn, state legislator, clergyman; b. Exeter, N.H., July 9, 1799; s. Oliver and Frances (Bourn) P.; grad. Harvard, 1816, LL.D., Harvard Law Sch., 1822. Admitted to N.H. bar, 1822; mem. N.H. Legislature, 1824-31; editor Rockingham Gazette and Exeter News Letter; asso. with Alexander Hill Everett (his brother-in-law) on N.Am. Review, Boston, 1830; supervised preparation of Dramatic Works of William Shakespeare, published by Hilliard, Gray & Co., 1836; mem. Mass. Legislature, 1834-36; register probate ct. for Suffolk County, Mass., 1836-42; prof. English literature Coll. of Jefferson, Convent, La., 1842; licensed to preach by Boston Assn. of Congregational Ministers, 1844; pastor Unitarian Ch., Burlington, Vt., 1845-48. Died Burlington, July 5, 1848; buried Burlington.

PEABODY, William Bourn Oliver, clergyman; b. Exeter, N.H., July 9, 1799; s. Oliver and Frances (Bourn) P.; grad. Harvard, 1816; studied theology, 1818-20; m. Elizabeth Amelia White, Sept. 8, 1824; 5 children. Taught at Phillips Exeter Acad., 1817; ordained to ministry Unitarian Ch., 1820; pastor 3d Congregational (Unitarian) Ch., Springfield, Mass., 1820-47. Author: Poetical Catechism, 1823; Springfield Collection of Hymns for Sacred Worship, 1835; A Report on the Ornithology of Massachusetts, 1839. Died Springfield, May 28, 1847; buried Springfield Cemetery.

PEALE, Anna Claypoole, artist; b. Phila., Mar. 6, 1791; d. James and Mary (Claypoole) Peale; studied oil painting with father; m. Dr. William Stoughton, 1829; m. 2d, Gen. William Duncan, 1841; no children. Exhibited her 1st picture, Phila., 1811; specialized in miniatures, painted extensively, 1820-40; most famous miniatures include those of Andrew Jackson (1819), Commodore William Bainbridge, Pres. James Monroe. Died Dec. 25, 1878.

PEALE, Charles Willson, painter; b. Queen Anne County, Md., Apr. 15, 1741; s. Charles and Margaret (Triggs Matthews) P.; m. Rachel Bruner, Jan. 12, 1762; m. 2d, Elizabeth De Peyster, 1791; m. 3d, Hannah Moore, 1805; 12 children including Raphael, Rembrandt, Titian, Rubens, Franklin, Titian Ramsay. Apprenticed to saddler, Nathan Walters, 1754-61; began painting portraits, 1762; gained recognition which prompted several men to pay for his visit and study in Eng., 1766; studied under American portrait painter Benjamin West; returned to Annapolis, Md., 1769, moved to Phila., 1776; active in recruiting for Continental Army during Revolutionary War; commd. capt. 4th Battalion after serving in battles of Trenton and Princeton, 1777; mem. Pa. Gen. Assembly, 1779-80; painted miniature portraits, 1780-90; established Phila. Mus.; largely responsible for establishment Pa. Acad. Fine Arts, 1805; painted approximately 60 portraits of George Washington (including the 1st, done in 1772). Author: An Essay on Building Wooden Bridges, 1797; Introduction to a Course of Lectures on Natural History, 1800; An Epistle to a Friend on the Mean of Preserving Health, 1803. Died Phila., Feb. 22, 1827; buried St. Peter's Churchyard, Phila.

PEALE (Benjamin) Franklin, medallist; s. Charles Willson Peale; b. Phila., Oct. 15, 1795. Operated cotton mill, nr. Phila., after War of 1812; assisted father and bros. at Peale Mus., mgr., until 1833; employed by U.S. Mint, Phila., 1833-54, chief coiner, 1840-54; executed Pres. Polk's Indian medal; pres. Hazelton Coal and R.R. Co., Musical Fund Soc., Pa. Instn. for Instrn. Blind. Died Phila., May 5, 1870.

PEALE, James, painter; b. Chestertown, Md., 1749; s. Charles and Margaret (Triggs Matthews) P.; m. Mary Claypoole, 1785, 6 children. Learned saddlery trade from his brother, Charles Willson Peale, 1762-70; began to study painting, 1770; served with Continental Army, 1776-79, commd. capt. 1st Md. Inf. Regt., 1778; moved to Phila., 1785, began painting in earnest; concentrated on still lifes, landscapes and hist. figures; famous for miniatures of George Washington. Works include: Ramsay-Polk Family; The View of the Battle of Princeton; A View of Belfield Farm near Germantown. Died May 24, 1831.

PEALE, Raphael, painter; b. Annapolis, Md., Feb. 17, 1774; s. Charles Willson and Rachel (Brewer) P.; studied painting under his father; m. Martha McGlathery, May 25, 1797, at least 7 children. Moved with family to Phila., 1776; worked in mediums including oils, water color, paper vellum, ivory; worked with his brother Rembrandt to establish portrait gallery of distinguished persons, Balt., 1790-99; established as profl. miniature painter, by 1799; painted still lifes, after 1815. Died Mar. 4, 1825.

PEALE, Rembrandt, painter; b. Richboro, Pa., Feb. 22, 1778; s. Charles Willson and Rachel (Brewer) P.; attended sch. of design established by his father, Phila., 1795; studied under Benjamin West, Eng., 1802-03; m. Eleanora Mary Short, 1798; m. 2d, Harriet Caney; 9 children. Began painting hist. portraits, including George Washington, Gens. Gadsden and Sumter, 1795; attempted to establish gallery of hist. portraits, Balt., 1796-99; exhibited 2 portraits Royal Acad., London, Eng., 1803; established painting room in State House, Phila., 1804, hired by his father to paint portraits of Pres. Thomas Jefferson, other govt. ofcls.; a founder Pa. Acad. Fine Arts, 1805; commd. by father to go to Paris, 1808-10, painted portraits of Bernardin de St. Pierre, Count Rumford, Abbe Huay, others; returned to Phila., 1810, painted large equestrian picture of Napoleon; exhibited painting The Court of Death (measured 24' by 13'), 1820; pres. Am. Acad. Fine Arts, 1825-26; wrote numerous articles relating to art, 1830-60. Author: Notes on Italy, 1831; Graphics: A Manual of Drawing and Writing, 1835; Portfolio of an Artist, 1839. Died Oct. 3, 1860.

PEALE, Sarah Miriam, painter; b. Phila., May 10, 1800; d. James and Mary (Claypoole) P.; studied painting; never married. Exhibited a portrait at Pa. Acad. Fine Arts, 1818, elected academician, 1824-25, exhibited miniatures, 1826; painted portrait of Marquis de Lafayette (who gave her 4 sittings), 1825; lived and painted in Balt., 1831-47, St. Louis, 1847-77, Phila., 1877-85. Died Phila., Feb. 4, 1885.

PEALE, Titian Ramsay, naturalist, artist; b. Phila., Nov. 17, 1799; s. Charles Willson and Elizabeth (De Peyster) P.; studied anatomy U. Pa.; m. Eliza Cecilia La Forgue, 1822; m. 2d, Lucy Mullen; 6 children. Apprenticed to spinning machine mfr., 1814; worked with his brother Rubens (curator of mus., Phila.), 1816-18; joined William MacLure and Thomas Say in expdn. to coasts of Ga. and Fla. to study and collect fauna specimens, 1818-19; asst. naturalist under Stephen H. Long on U.S. Army expdn. to Upper Missouri, 1819-20; asst. mgr. Phila. Mus., 1821-24; exhibited 4 water color paintings Pa. Acad. Fine Arts, 1822; sent to Fla. by Charles Lucien Bonaparte to collect specimens and make drawings for book American Ornithology, 1824; mem. civil staff U.S. exploring expdn. to South Seas under Charles Wilkes, 1838-42, made drawings which appeared in published accounts of expdn.; examiner U.S. Patent Office, Washington, D.C., 1849-72. Died Mar. 13, 1885.

PEARCE, Dutee Jerauld, congressman; b. Island of Prudence, R.I., Apr. 3, 1789; grad. Brown U., 1808; studied law. Admitted to R.I. bar, began practice in Newport; held local offices; atty. gen. R.I., 1819-25; Dem. presdl. elector, 1820; U.S. dist. atty., 1824-25; mem. R.I. Ho. of Reps.; mem. U.S. Ho. of Reps. (Dem.) from R.I., 19th-24th congresses, 1825-37. Died Newport, May 9, 1849; buried Common Burial Ground, Newport.

PEARCE, James Alfred, senator; b. Alexandria, Va., Dec. 14, 1805; s. Gideon and Julia (Dick) P.; grad. Coll. of N.J. (now Princeton), 1822; studied law under Judge John Glenn, Balt.; m. Martha Laird, Oct. 6, 1829; m. 2d, Mathilda Cox, Mar. 22, 1847; 4 children. Admitted to Md. bar, 1824; mem. Md. Legislature, 1831-35; mem. U.S. Ho. of Reps. (Whig) from Md., 24th-25th, 27th congresses, 1835-39, 41-43; mem. U.S. Senate from Md. (Whig), 1843-61, (Democrat), 1861-62. Died Chestertown, Md., Dec. 20, 1862; buried New Chester Cemetery, Chestertown.

PEARCE, Stephen Austen, musician; b. Brompton, Kent, Eng., Nov. 7, 1836; s. Stephen and Elizabeth (Austen) P.; Mus.B., Oxford, 1859, Mus.D., 1864. Came to U.S., 1872; organist for several chs., N.Y.C.; instr. in vocal music Columbia, 1878-79; lectr. on harmony N.Y. Coll. of Music, Gen. Theol. Sem., Peabody Inst., Johns Hopkins U.; gave numerous organ recitals, N.Y.C.; considered by many to be best organist of his time; musical editor N.Y. Evening Post, 1874-1900. Composer: La Belle Americaine (3 act opera), Celestial Visions (dramatic oratorio), The Psalm of Praise (ch. cantata). Died Jersey Heights, N.J., Apr. 8, 1900.

PEARSON, Eliphalet, educator; b. Newbury, Mass., June 11, 1752; s. David and Sarah (Danforth) P.; grad. Harvard, 1773; m. Priscilla Holyoke, July 17, 1780; m. 2d, Sarah Bromfield, Sept. 29, 1785; 5 children. Taught grammar sch., Andover, Mass., 1775-78; 1st prin. Phillips Acad., Andover, 1778-86; Hancock prof. Hebrew and Oriental langs. Harvard, 1786-1806, acting pres., 1804; a founder Andover Theol. Sem., 1807, pres. bd. trustees, 1807-21, prof. sacred theology, 1808-09; pres. bd. trustees Phillips Acad., 1802-21. Died Greenland, N.H., Sept. 12, 1826.

PEARSON, John James, congressman; b. nr. Derby, Pa., Oct. 25, 1800; attended pvt. schs., Mercer, Pa.; studied law. Admitted to Pa. bar, 1822, began practice in Mercer County; mem. U.S. Ho. of Reps. (Whig) from Pa., 24th Congress, Dec. 5, 1836-37; mem. Pa. Senate, 1838-42; pres. judge Dauphin and Lebanon counties (Pa.), 1849-82. Died Harrisburg, Pa., May 30, 1888; buried Mt. Kalmia Cemetery, Harrisburg.

PEARSON, Joseph, congressman; b. Rowan County, N.C., 1776; studied law. Admitted to N.C. bar, began practice in Salisbury; mem. N.C. Ho. of Commons; mem. U.S. Ho. of Reps. (Federalist) from N.C., 11th-13th congresses, 1809-15; fought a duel with John George Jackson (congressman from Va.). Died Salisbury, Oct. 27, 1834.

PEARSON, Richmond Mumford, jurist; b. Rowan County, N.C., June 28, 1805; s. Richmond and Elizabeth (Mumford) P.; grad. U. N.C., 1823, LL.D. (hon.), 1853; m. Margaret Williams, June 12, 1831; m. 2d, Mary (McDowell) Bynum, 1859; 10 children. Admitted to N.C. bar, 1826; elected mem. N.C. Ho. of Commons, 1829, served 4 successive terms, elected judge N.C. Superior Ct., 1836; elected asso. justice N.C. Supreme Ct. by N.C. Legislature, 1848, became chief justice, 1858, reelected 1868-78; stayed with N.C. during Civil War, but made decisions in various conscription cases which were looked on unfavorably by Confederate authorities. Died Winston, N.C., Jan. 5, 1878.

PEASE, Alfred Humphreys, musician; b. Cleve., May 6, 1838; s. Sheldon and Marianne (Humphreys) P.; studied piano under Theodor Kullak, Berlin, Germany; studied composition under Wüerst, orchestration under Wieprecht. Returned to Am., circa 1862, went on tour of major cities, playing classical piano. Compositions include: Hush Thee, My Baby; When Sparrows Build, 1864; Stars of the Summer Night, 1864; Tender and True, Adieu, 1864. Died July 13, 1882.

PEASE, Calvin, jurist; b. Suffield, Conn., Sept. 9, 1776; s. Joseph and Mindwell (King) P.; m. Laura Risley, June 1804, 7 children. Admitted to Conn. bar, 1798; clk. Ct. Common Pleas, Youngstown, O.; 1st postmaster, Youngstown, 1800; presiding judge of a circuit Ct. Common Pleas, 1803-10, impeached by Ohio Legislature for holding an act granting jurisdiction in civil suits to the amount of $50 to justices of the peace to be unconstl.; mem. Ohio Senate, 1812-13; chief justice Ohio Supreme Ct., 1821-30; mem. Ohio Ho. of Reps., 1831-32. Died Warren, O., Sept. 17, 1839.

PEASE, Elisha Marshall, gov. Tex.; b. Enfield, Conn., Jan. 3, 1812; s. Lorrain Thompson and Sarah (Marshall) P.; m. Lucadia Niles, Aug. 1850, 3 children. Moved to Tex., 1835; sec. provisional govt. of Tex. (established by consultation held at San Felipe), 1835-36; chief clk. of navy and treasury depts. Republic of Tex., also sec. of treasury short time; clk. judiciary com. of Congress, 1836; admitted to bar, 1837; dist. atty. for Republic of Tex.; mem. Tex. Ho. of Reps., 1845-47, Tex. Senate, 1849; gov. Tex., 1853-57; v.p. Southern Unionist Conv., Phila., 1866; candidate for gov., 1866; apptd. provisional gov., 1867, resigned, 1869; represented Tex. in Liberal Republican Conv., Cincinnati, 1872; collector Port of Galveston (Tex.), 1879. Died Lampasas, Tex., Aug. 26, 1883.

PEASE, Joseph Ives, engraver; b. Norfolk, Conn., Aug. 9, 1809; s. Earl P. and Mary (Ives) P.; apprenticed to line-engraver Oliver Pelton, Hartford, Conn.; m. Mary Spencer, Dec. 8, 1841. Line-engraver, Hartford, 1830-35, Phila., 1835-50; illustrated several annuals published in Phila., including The Gift; engraved fashion plates for Godey's Lady's Book, 1848-50; engraved banknotes, Stockbridge, Mass., 1850. Died Twin Lakes, Conn., July 2, 1883.

PEASLEE, Charles Hazen, congressman; b. Gilmanton, N.H., Feb. 6, 1804; grad. Dartmouth, 1824; studied law. Admitted to N.H. bar, 1828, began practice in Concord; mem. N.H. Ho. of Reps., 1833-37; adj. gen. N.H. Militia, 1839-47; mem. U.S. Ho. of Reps. (Democrat) from N.H., 30th-32d congresses, 1847-53; collector Port of Boston, 1853-57; moved to Portsmouth, N.H., 1860. Died St. Paul, Minn., Sept. 18, 1866; buried Harmony Grove Cemetery, Portsmouth.

PEASLEE, Edmund Randolph, physician; b. Newton, N.H., Jan. 22, 1814; s. James and Abigail (Chase) P.; grad. Dartmouth, 1836; attended Dartmouth Med. Sch., 1837-39; M.D., Yale, 1840; m. Martha Kendrick, 1841, 2 children. Prof. anatomy and physiology Dartmouth, 1842-69, lectr. on diseases of women, 1868-70, prof. obstetrics and diseases of women, 1870-73, prof. gynecology, 1873-78, trustee, 1860-78; prof. surgery and anatomy Med. Sch. of Me., 1843-60; prof. pathology and physiology N.Y. Med. Coll., 1852-56; prof. obstetrics, 1856-60; lectr. obstetrics Albany Med. Coll., 1872-74, prof. gynecology, 1874-78; prof. gynecology Bellevue Hosp. Med. Coll., 1874-78; attending physician Demilt Dispensary, N.Y.C., 1858-65; pvt. practice medicine, N.Y.C., 1858-78. Author: Necroscopic Tables for Postmortem Examinations, 1851; Human Histology in Its Relations to Descriptive Anatomy, Physiology, and Pathology, 1857; Ovarian Tumors; Their Pathology, Diagnosis, and Treatment, Especially by Ovariotomy, 1872. Died N.Y.C., Jan. 21, 1878.

PEAVEY, Frank Hutchinson, businessman; b. Eastport, Me., Jan. 18, 1850; s. Albert D. and Mary (Drew) P.; m. Mary Wright, 1872, 3 children including George W. Partner in implement firm Booge, Smith & Peavey, Sioux City, Ia., 1870-71; partner firm Evans & Peavey (dealers in implements, grain, grain elevators), 1871-75, sole owner, 1875-81; established F. H. Peavey & Co., Mpls., 1881; became owner of more elevators than any other man in world, also invested in land, railroads, banking cos., piano cos. established Peavey S.S. Co. to carry freight on Great Lakes, 1899. Died Chgo., Dec. 30, 1901.

PECK, Erasmus Darwin, congressman; b. Stafford, Conn., Sept. 16, 1808; grad. med. dept. Yale, 1829. Moved to Portage County, O., 1830, practiced medicine; moved to Perrysburg, O., 1834, practiced medicine; mem. Ohio Ho. of Reps., 1856-59; mem. U.S. Ho. of Reps. (Republican) from Ohio, 41st-42d congresses, Apr. 23, 1870-73. Died Perrysburg, Dec. 25, 1876; buried Fort Meigs Cemetery, Perrysburg.

PECK, George, clergyman; b. Otsego County, N.Y., Aug. 8, 1797; s. Luther and Annis (Collar) P.; m. Mary Myers, June 10, 1819, at least 1 child, Mary Helen (Peck) Crane. Admitted on trial as pastor Genesee Conf., Methodist Episcopal Ch., 1816, ordained deacon, 1818, elder, 1820; circuit preacher in N.Y., 1820-35; prin. Cazenovia (N.Y.) Acad., 1835-38; del. to all 13 gen. confs., 1824-72; editor Methodist Quarterly Review, 1840-48, Christian Advocate, N.Y.C., 1848-52; del. to world conv. Methodist Episcopal Ch., London, Eng., 1846; pastor, presiding elder Wyoming Conf., Pa., 1852-73. Author: The Scripture Doctrine of Christian Perfection, Stated and Defended, 1842; An Answer to the Question, Why Are You a Wesleyan Methodist, 1847; Slavery and the Episcopacy, 1845; Formation of a Manly Character, 1853; Our Country; Its Trial and Triumph, 1865. Died Scranton, Pa., May 20, 1876; buried Forty Fort, Pa.

PECK, George Washington, journalist; b. Reheboth, Mass., Dec. 4, 1817; s. George Washington and Hannah (Carpenter) P.; grad. Brown U., 1837; read law under Richard Henry Dana; never married. Admitted to Mass. bar, 1843; practiced law, Boston, 1843-47; music and drama critic for Boston Post; published Boston Musical Review, 1845; contbr. articles on music and literature to various papers and mags., N.Y.C., 1847-54. Author: Aurifodina, 1849; Melbourne and the Chincha Islands; with Sketches of Lima and a Voyage Round the World, 1854. Died Boston, June 6, 1859.

PECK, James Hawkins, jurist; b. N.C. (now Jefferson County, Tenn.), 1790; s. Adam and Elizabeth (Sharkey) P.; never married. Admitted to Tenn. bar; served with Tenn. Militia during War of 1812; judge U.S. Dist. Ct. at St. Louis, 1818-32, impeached for convicting lawyer Luke Lawless of contempt (after which Lawless published articles criticizing an opinion rendered by Peck), 1830, acquitted by U.S. Ho. of Reps., 1831 (U.S. Congress passed act clarifying definition of circumstances under which courts may punish for contempt as result of this case). Died St. Charles, Mo., Apr. 29, 1836.

PECK, Jared Valentine, congressman; b. Port Chester, N.Y., Sept. 21, 1816; attended common schs. Engaged in lumber, brick, hardware, bldg. material bus.; auditor Town of Rye (N.Y.), 1844-45; mem. N.Y. State Assembly, 1848; mem. U.S. Ho. of Reps. (Democrat) from N.Y., 33d Congress, 1853-55; Republican presdl. elector, 1856; warden Port of N.Y., 1859-65; a founder Union League Club, N.Y.C.; mem. bd. auditors Town of Rye; donated Brundage Bldg. for use as pub. library, Port Chester. Died "The Cedars," Rye, Dec. 25, 1891; buried Greenwood Union Cemetery, Rye.

PECK, Jesse Truesdell, clergyman; b. Middlefield, N.Y., Apr. 4, 1811; s. Luther and Annis (Collar) P.; m. Persis Wing, Oct. 13, 1831, no children. Admitted on trial to Oneida Conf., Methodist Episcopal Ch., 1832, ordained deacon, 1834; ordained elder in Black River Conf., 1836; prin. high sch., Gouverneur, N.Y., 1837-40, Troy Conf. Acad., Poultney, Vt., 1841-48; del. Gen. Conf., 1844; pres. Dickinson Coll., Carlisle, Pa., 1848-52; pastor Foundry Ch., Washington, D.C., 1852-54; sec. Tract Soc. of Methodist Ch., 1854-56; pastor Green Street Ch., N.Y.C., 1856-58; pastor, presiding elder at San Francisco and Sacramento, Cal., 1858-66; pastor Hudson Street (now 1st) Ch., Albany, N.Y., 1867-70; pastor Methodist Ch., Syracuse, N.Y., 1870-72; a founder Syracuse U.; elected bishop, 1872; attended 1st Ecumenical Methodist Conf., London, 1881. Author: The Central Idea of Christianity, 1856; The History of the Great Republic Considered from a Christian Standpoint, 1868. Died May 17, 1883.

PECK, John James, army officer; b. Manlius, N.Y., Jan. 4, 1821; s. John Wells and Phoebe (Raynor) P.; grad. U.S. Mil. Acad. 1843; m. Robie Loomis, Nov. 20, 1850, 6 children. Served with U.S. Army in battles of Palo Alto, Resaco de la Palma, Contreras, Churubusco, Maleria del Rey, during Mexican War; resigned from U.S. Army, 1853; treas. N.Y., Newburgh & Syracuse R.R. Co.; pres. Syracuse (N.Y.) Bd. Edn., 1859-61; v.p. Franklin Inst., Syracuse; del. Democratic Nat. Conv., 1856, 60; twice nominated for U.S. Congress; commd. brig. gen. U.S. Volunteers, 1861, maj. gen., 1862; served in defenses of Washington, D.C., 1861-62; given command on Canadian frontier, 1864; organizer N.Y. State Life Ins. Co., 1867, pres. Died Syracuse, Apr. 21, 1878.

PECK, John Mason, clergyman; b. Litchfield, Conn., Oct. 31, 1789; s. Asa and Hannah (Farnum) P.; m. Sarah Paine, May 8, 1809, 10 children. Licensed to preach Baptist Ch., 1811, ordained pastor, 1813; founded, operated mission, St. Louis, 1817-20; missionary Mass. Baptist Missionary Soc., travelled in Ill., Ind. and Mo., made his home at Rock Spring, Ill., 1822-58; founder Rock Spring Sem. (now Shurtleff Coll.), 1827, trustee, 1827-58; editor Pioneer (religious mag.), 1829-39; agt. Western Baptist Publ. Soc., 1841-42; sec. Am. Bapt. Publ. Soc., 1943-46; pastor, St. Louis, 1849, Covington, Ky., 1854. Author: Guide for Emigrants 1831; Gazetteer of Illinois, 1834; The Traveller's Directory for Illinois, 1840; Life of Daniel Boone, 1847; Father Clark or the Pioneer Preacher, 1855. Died Rock Spring, Mar. 14, 1858.

PECK, Lucius Benedict, congressman; b. Waterbury, Vt., Nov. 17, 1802; attended U.S. Mil. Acad., 1 year; studied law. Admitted to Vt. bar, began practice in Barre, 1825; mem. Vt. Ho. of Reps., 1831; moved to Montpelier, Vt., 1832, practiced law; mem. U.S. Ho. of Reps. (Democrat) from Vt., 30th-31st congresses, 1847-51; unsuccessful candidate for gov. Vt., 1850; U.S. dist. atty. for Vt., 1853-57; pres. Vt. & Can. R.R., 1859-66. Died Lowell, Mass., Dec. 28, 1866; buried Green Mount Cemetery, Montpelier.

PECK, Luther Christopher, congressman; b. Conn., Jan. 1800; studied law. Admitted to Conn. bar, practiced law; moved to Allegheny County, Pa., later to Pike, N.Y., practiced law; held local offices; mem. U.S. Ho. of Reps. (Whig) from N.Y., 25th-26th congresses, 1837-41; joined Republican Party; moved to Nunda, N.Y., practiced law. Died Nunda, Feb. 5, 1876; buried Oakwood Cemetery, Nunda.

PECK, Thomas Ephraim, clergyman; b. Columbia, S.C., Jan. 29, 1822; grad. Coll. of S.C., 1840; studied theology under Rev. James Henley Thornwell; m. Ellen Church Richardson, Oct. 28, 1852, 7 children. Licensed to preach by Charleston Presbytery, 1844; pastor 2d Presbyn. Ch., Balt., 1845-46, Broadway Street Ch., Balt., 1846-57, Central Presbyn. Ch., Balt., 1857-60; published Presbyn. Critic and Monthly Review, 1855-56; prof. eccles. history and ch. govt. Union Theol. Sem., Va., 1860-83, prof. theology, 1883-93; moderator Gen. Assembly of Presbyn. Ch. in U.S., 1878. Author: Notes on Ecclesiology, 1892; Miscellanies of Rev. Thomas E. Peck (edited by T. C. Johnson, 3 vols.), 1895-97. Died Oct. 2, 1893.

PECK, William Dandridge, naturalist; b. Boston, May 8, 1763; s. John and Hannah (Jackson) P.; B.A., Harvard, 1782; never married. Lived with father on farm at Kittery, Me., 1785-1805, engaged in botanical and zoological studies; 1st prof. natural history Harvard, 1805-22; established Botanic Garden, Cambridge, Mass.; 1st tchr. of entymology in U.S.; a founder Am. Antiquarian Soc., 1812; recipient Gold medals from Mass. Agrl. Soc. for article The Description and History of the Canker-Worm, 1795, also for book Natural History of the Slug Worm, 1799; 1st to discover and describe an egg parasite in U.S. Died Oct. 3, 1822.

PECK, William Guy, educator, mathematician; b. Litchfield, Conn., Oct. 16, 1820; grad. U.S. Mil. Acad., 1844; A.M., Trinity Coll., 1853, LL.D., 1863; Ph.D., Columbia Coll., 1877; m. Miss Davis. Mem. survey of mil. fortifications of Portsmouth, N.H.; brevetted 2d lt. Topog. Engrs., U.S. Army; mem. John C. Fremont's 3d expdn. to Rocky Mountains; promoted lt. Topog. Engrs.; asst. prof. philosophy and mathematics U.S. Mil. Acad., 1846-55; prof. physics and civil engring. U. Mich., 1855-57; prof. mathematics Columbia, 1857-61; mem. bd. visitors U. S. Mil. Acad., 1868. Author: Elementary Mechanics, 1859; Manual of Arithmetic, 1874; Popular Astronomy, 1883. Died Greenwich, Conn., Feb. 7, 1892.

PECKHAM, Mary Chace, reformer; b. Nantucket, Mass., July 15, 1839; d. Charles Miller and Adriana (Fisher) Peck; m. Stephen F. Peckham, June 13, 1865, at least 2 children. Ministered to soldiers in hosp., Providence, R.I., during Civil War; worked for women's rights in East, 1866-73; lived in Mpls., 1873-80; mem. R.I. Woman Suffrage Assn., also Assn. for Advancement of Women, 1880-92. Author: Father Gabriel's Fairy, 1873; Windfalls Gathered Only for Friends (collected posthumously), 1894. Died Ann Arbor, Mich., Mar. 20, 1892.

PECKHAM, Rufus Wheeler, congressman; b. Rensselaerville, N.Y., Dec. 20, 1809; grad. Union Coll., Schenectady, N.Y., 1827; studied law. Admitted to N.Y. bar, 1830, began practice in Albany; dist. atty. Albany County, 1838-41; mem. U.S. Ho. of Reps. (Democrat) from N.Y., 33d Congress, 1853-55; justice N.Y. Supreme Ct. for 3d jud. dist., 1861-69; asso. judge N.Y. Ct. of Appeals, 1870-73. Lost at sea in a ship collision, Nov. 22, 1873.

PEDDER, James, agriculturist; b. Newport, Isle of Wight, Eng., July 29, 1775; m. Eliza. Asst. to chemist Dr. Samuel Parks, London, Eng., 1809-19; in charge of various large estates, Eng., 1819-32; came to U.S., 1832; employed by Phila. Beet Sugar Soc. to study French methods of mfg. beet sugar, 1832-33; editor Farmers' Cabinet, Phila., 1840-43; mem. Phila. Soc. for Promoting Agr., librarian, 1842; corr. editor Boston Cultivator, 1844-48, resident editor, 1848-59. Author: The Yellow Shoestrings, or The Good Effects of Obedience to Parents, 1814; Report Made to the Beet Sugar Society on the Culture in France of the Beet Root, 1836; The Farmer's Land Measurer, or Pocket Companion, 1842. Died Roxbury (now part of Boston), Aug. 27, 1859; buried Forest Hills Cemetery, Jamaica Plain, Mass.

PEDDIE, Thomas Baldwin, congressman; b. Edinburgh, Scotland, Feb. 11, 1808; attended elementary schs. Came to U.S., 1833, settled in Newark, N.J.; engaged in mfg. traveling bags and trunks; mem. N.J. Ho. of Assembly, 1864-65; mayor of Newark, 1866-69; pres. Newark Bd. of Trade, 1873; mem. U.S. Ho. of Reps. (Republican) from N.Y., 45th Congress, 1877-79; v.p. Essex County Nat. Bank; pres. Security Savs. Bank of Newark. Died Newark, Feb. 16, 1889; buried Mt. Pleasant Cemetery, Newark.

PEEK, Harmanus, congressman; b. Albany, N.Y., June 24, 1782; grad. Union Coll., Schenectady, N.Y., 1804; studied law. Admitted to N.Y. bar, began practice in Schenectady; mem. N.Y. State Assembly, 1816-17; mem. U.S. Ho. of Reps. from N.Y., 16th Congress, 1819-21. Died Schenectady, Sept. 27, 1838; buried Dutch Ch. Cemetery, reinterred Vale Cemetery, Schenectady.

PEERS, Benjamin Orrs, educator; b. Loudoun County, Va., Apr. 20, 1800; son of Valentine Peers; grad. Transylvania U., 1821; attended Princeton Theol. Sem., 1822-23; grad. Theol. Sem. of Protestant Episcopal Ch., Alexandria, Va., 1826. Ordained deacon P.E. Ch., 1826; established, conducted Mechanics' Inst., Lexington, Ky., 1829-30; established, operated Eclectic Inst., Lexington, 1830-33; prof. moral theology, proctor Morrison Coll., also acting pres. Transylvania U., 1833-34; established boys' sch., also served as rector St. Paul's Episcopal Ch., Louisville, Ky., 1835-38; editor Journal of Christian Edn., N.Y.C., 1838-42. Author: Christian Education, 1836. Died Louisville, Aug. 20, 1842.

PEERSON, Cleng, colonizer; b. Tysvaer parish, Stavanger amt, Norway, 1783; son of Peder Hesthammer; m. Catherine; m. 2d, Charlotte Marie, 1847. Came to U.S., 1821; led Norwegian immigrants in establishing settlements nr. Rochester, N.Y., 1825, at Fox River, Ill. (1st Norwegian settlement in West), 1834, in Shelby County, Mo., 1837, Sugar Creek, Ia., 1840, Dallas County, Tex., 1850; visited Norway to encourage immigration to U.S., 1824, 42-43; travelled almost constantly throughout West and S.W. in search of sites for colonies. Died Bosque County, Tex., Dec. 16, 1865.

PEERY, William, Continental congressman; studied law. Engaged in farming; organizer, commd. capt. of an independent co. during Revolutionary War, 1777; mem. Del. Ho. of Reps., 1782, 84, 87, 93, 94; admitted to the bar, 1785; began practice of law, Sussex County, Del.; mem. Continental Congress from Del., 1785-86; treas. Sussex County, 1785-96; apptd. mem. commn. to purchase land and build a ct. house and prison for Sussex County, 1791. Died Cool Spring, Del., Dec. 17, 1800; buried Cool Spring Presbyn. Churchyard.

PEET, Harvey Prindle, educator; b. Bethlehem, Conn., Nov. 19, 1794; s. Richard and Johannah (Prindle) P.; grad. Yale, 1822; m. Margaret Maria Lewis, Nov. 27, 1823; m. 2d, Sarah Ann Smith, 1835; m. 3d, Louisa Hotchkiss, Jan. 15, 1868; 3 children including Isaac Lewis. Tchr., Am. Sch. for Deaf, Hartford, Conn., 1822-31; prin. N.Y. Instn. of Instrn. of Deaf and Dumb, 1831-67, made sch. largest and best equipped of its type in U.S. Author: Course of Instruction for the Deaf and Dumb, 3 vols., 1844-49. Died N.Y.C., Jan. 1, 1873.

PEET, Isaac Lewis, educator; b. Hartford, Conn., Dec. 4, 1824; s. Harvey Prindle and Margaret (Lewis) P.; grad. Yale, 1845, Union Theol. Sem., 1849; m. Mary Toles, 1854, 4 children. Instr., later vice prin. N.Y. Instn. for Instrn. of Deaf and Dumb, 1845-67, prin., 1867-92, prin. emeritus, 1892-98; mem. Conf. of Supts. and Prins. of Am. Schs. for Deaf, pres., 1896; mem. exec. com. Conv. of Am. Instrs. of Deaf, 1868-96; pres. Medico-Legal Soc. of N.Y.C. Author: Monograph on Decimal Fractions, 1866; Language Lessons, Designed to Introduce Young Learners, Deaf Mutes and Foreigners to a Correct Understanding of the English Language on the Principle of Object Teaching, 1875. Died N.Y.C., Dec. 27, 1898.

PEGRAM, John, congressman; b. "Bonneville," Danville County, Va., Nov. 16, 1773; attended common schs. Held local offices; mem. Va. Ho. of Dels., 1797-1801, 13-15, Va. Senate, 1804-08; served as maj. gen. Va. Militia during War of 1812; mem. U.S. Ho. of Reps. from Va., 15th Congress, Apr. 21, 1818-19; apptd. U.S. marshal for Eastern Va., 1821. Died in a burning boat on the Ohio River, Apr. 8, 1831.

PEIRCE, Benjamin, mcht., librarian; b. Salem, Mass., Sept. 30, 1778; s. Jerethmiel and Sarah (Ropes) P.; grad. Harvard, 1801; m. Lydia Ropes, Dec. 11, 1803; children—Charlotte, John, Benjamin, Charles. Became asso. with his father's trading firm, specializing in Far Eastern trade, Boston, 1801; mem. Mass. Gen. Ct., 1811-circa 1816; became known for his knowledge of classics in Latin and Eng.; librarian Harvard, 1826-31, issued 1st published catalogue of library, completed most of research for history of coll. (later published by Dr. John Pickering). Died Cambridge, Mass., July 26, 1831; buried Cambridge.

PEIRCE, Benjamin, mathematician, astronomer; b. Salem, Mass., Apr. 4, 1809; s. Benjamin and Lydia (Nichols) P.; grad. Harvard, 1829; m. Sarah Hunt Mills, July 23, 1833, 5 children including Charles S., James Mills, Herbert Henry Davis. Instr., Round Hill Sch., Northampton, Mass., 1829-31; tutor mathematics Harvard, 1831-33, prof. astronomy and mathematics, 1833-42, Perkins prof. mathematics and astronomy, 1842-80, largely responsible for establishment of Harvard Observatory, 1843; founder, editor Cambridge Miscellany of Mathematics, Physics, and Astronomy, 1842-43; cons. astronomer for Am. Nautical Almanac, 1849-67, renamed Astronomical Almanac for the Use of Navigators, 1860; mem. Am. Philos. Soc., 1842-80; asso. mem. Royal Astron. Soc., 1850-80; pres. A.A.A.S., 1853; fellow Am. Acad. Arts and Scis., 1858-80; hon. fellow U. St. Vladimir, Kiev, Russia, 1860-80; corr. mem. Brit. Assn. for Advancement Science, 1861-80, Royal Soc. Sciences, Göttingen, Germany, 1867-80; hon. fellow Royal Soc. Edinburgh, 1867-80; an organizer Smithsonian Instn., 1847; dir. longitude determinations of U.S. Coast Survey, 1852-67, supt., 1867-74, cons. geometer, 1874-80, directed Am. expdn. to Sicily to observe eclipse of sun, 1870; a founder Nat. Acad. Scis., 1863, chmn. mathematics and physics class; asso. editor Am. Jour. of Mathematics, 1878; proved there is no odd perfect number having fewer than 4 prime factors, 1832; computed gen. perturbations of Uranus and Neptune; formulated "Peirce's criterion," object of which was to solve practically important problem of probabilities in connection with series of observations. Author: An Elementary Treatise on Sound, 1836; An Elementary Treatise on Algebra, 1837; An Elementary Treatise on Plane and Solid Geometry, 1837; An Elementary Treatise on Plane and Spherical Trigonometry, 1840; An Elementary Treatise on Curves, Functions, and Forces, vol. I, 1841, vol. II, 1846; Tables of the Moon, 1853; A System on Analytic Mechanics, 18550 Tables of the Moon's Parallax, 1856; Linear Associative Algebra, 1870. Died Oct. 6, 1880.

PEIRCE, Benjamin Mills, mining engr.; b. Cambridge, Mass., Mar. 19, 1844; s. Benjamin and Sarah Hunt (Mills) P.; grad. Harvard, 1865; post-grad. Sch. of Mines, Paris, France, 1865-67, U. Freiburg (Germany), 1867. Worked in Iceland and Greenland, 1867-68, wrote U.S. Govt. report on mineral resources and conditions there (his most noted work); mining engr. in Mich., 1868-70. Died Ishpeming, Mich., Apr. 22, 1870.

PEIRCE, Bradford Kinney, clergyman; b. Royalton, Vt., Feb. 3, 1819; s. Thomas C. and Sally (Kinne) P.; grad. Wesleyan U., 1841; m. Harriet W. Thompson, Aug. 5, 1841, 4 children. Admitted on trial to New Eng. Conf. of Methodist Episcopal Ch., 1842, ordained deacon, 1844, elder, 1846; editor Sunday Sch. Tchr., Sunday Sch. Messenger, 1847-50; agt. for Am. Sunday Sch. Union, 1850-56; mem. Mass. Senate, 1855; a founder, trustee, supt., chaplain Mass. Indsl. Sch., Lancaster, 1856-62; chaplain House of Refuge, Randall's Island, N.Y., 1863-72; editor Zion's Herald, Meth. weekly, Boston, 1872-89; trustee Boston U., Wellesley Coll. Author: The Eminent Dead, or the Triumphs of Faith in the Dying Hour, 1846; Notes on the Acts of the Apostles, 1848; Life in the Woods, or the Adventures of Audubon, 1863; Trials of an Inventor; Life and Discoveries of Charles Goodyear, 1866; The Word of God Opened, 1868; A Half Century with Juvenile Delinquents, 1869. Died Apr. 19, 1889.

PEIRCE, Cyrus, educator; b. Waltham, Mass., Aug. 15, 1790; s. Isaac and Hannah (Mason) P.; grad. Harvard, 1810, Div. Sch., 1815; m. Harriet Coffin, Apr. 1, 1816. Taught pvt. sch., Nantucket, R.I., 1815-18, 31-37, North Andover, Mass., 1827-31, West Newton, Mass., 1850-60; ordained pastor Congregational Ch., North Reading, Mass., 1819-27; prin. Nantucket High Sch., 1837-39; prin. 1st Mass. State Normal Sch., 1839-42, 44-49; del. from Am. Peace Soc. to World's Peace Congress, Paris, France, 1849. Died West Newton, Apr. 5, 1860.

PEIRCE, Henry Augustus, mcht., diplomat; b. Dorchester, Mass., Dec. 15, 1808; s. Joseph Hardy and Frances (Cordis) P.; m. Susan Thompson, July 3, 1838. Partner (with brother) in shipping trade between Mexico and Alaska, 1824-28; partner (with James Hunnewell) trading between Pacific Islands and New Eng., Honolulu, Hawaii, 1828-33; traded with China, Hawaii and Siberia, 1833-43; in shipping business, Boston, 1843-66; served as Hawaiian consul for New Eng.; lost large part of his mcht. fleet during Civil War; U.S. minister to Hawaiian Kingdom, 1869-77, called Am. Marines to Honolulu to restore order during riots brought on by election of King Kalakaua, 1874, concluded U.S-Hawaiian reciprocity treaty, 1876; Hawaiian minister for fgn. affairs, 1878. Died San Francisco, July 29, 1885.

PEIRCE, Joseph, congressman; b. Portsmouth, N.H., June 25, 1748; attended sch., Portsmouth. Served with Col. Pierce Long's regt. during Revolutionary War, 1775-76; mem. N.H. Ho. of Reps., 1788-89, 92-95, 1800-01; town clk., 1789-94; mem. U.S. Ho. of Reps. from N.H., 7th Congress, 1801-02 (resigned); engaged in farming. Died Alton, N.H., Sept. 12, 1812.

PEIRCE, William, shipmaster; b. England, 1590; m. Jane Peirce, 3 children. Shipmaster carrying goods and emigrants between England, Va. and New Eng., circa 1623-24; explored Nantucket Island and shores of Narragansett Bay, 1634; commr. mil. affairs of Mass. Bay Colony, 1635-36; granted land and started fishery, Cape Ann, Mass., 1637; carried cargoes of Indian and Negro slaves, cotton, tobacco between New Eng. and West Indies; brought 1st Negroes to New Eng., 1638. Author: An Almanac for the Year of Our Lord (1st almanac in English America), 1639. Killed by Spanish while trying to take colony of Providence in Caribbean, 1641.

PEIXOTTO, Benjamin Franklin, diplomat, journalist; b. N.Y.C., Nov. 13, 1834; s. Daniel C. M. and Rachel (Seixas) P.; m. Hannah Strauss, 1858, at least 1 son, George. Editor, Cleve. Plain Dealer; grand master Ind. Order B'nai B'rith, 1863-66; a founder Cleve. Orphan Home; apptd. U.S consul to Bucharest in attempt to retard anti-Semitic movement in Rumania, 1870-76; U.S. consul to Lyons, France, 1877-81; founded, edited The Menocah, A Monthly Magazine, N.Y.C., 1886-90 (at that time only English Jewish monthly in U.S.). Died N.Y.C., Sept. 18, 1890.

PELHAM, Henry, artist, cartographer; b. Boston, Feb. 21, 1749; s. Peter and Mary (Singleton) Copley P.; m. Catherine Butler, 2 children, Peter, William. Worked as portraitist in miniatures, Boston, until 1776; went to England because of extreme Loyalist sympathies, 1776, worked as civil engr., cartographer, artist; paintings include The Finding of Moses, 1777; map of Plan of Boston, 1777. Drowned in River Kenmare, Ireland, 1806.

PELHAM, John, army officer; b. Benton (now Calhoun) County, Ala., Sept. 14, 1838; s. Atkinson and Martha (McGehee) P.; attended U.S. Mil. Acad., 1856-61; never married. Commd. lt. Confederate States Army, 1861; promoted capt. in charge of Stuart Horse Arty. under Gen. J. E. B. Stuart, 1861, unit became famous for its mobility, effectiveness and recklessness; promoted maj., 1862; active in battles of Seven Days, 2d Manassas, Antietam, Stuart's raid on Loudoun County, battles of Port Royal and Fredericksburg. Killed in action at Battle of Kelly's Ford (Va.), Mar. 17, 1863.

PELHAM, Peter, engraver; b. England, 1695; s. Peter Pelham; m. Martha Pelham; m. 2d, Margaret Lowrey, Oct. 15, 1734; m. 3d, Mary (Singleton) Copley, May 22, 1748; several children including George, Henry. Came to Am., circa 1728; one of 1st to use mezzotint technique of engraving; besides engraving portraits conducted small sch. and tobacco shop, Boston; portrait subjects included Queen Anne, King George I, Gov. Samuel Shute of Mass., Rev. Cotton Mather, John Smibert. Died Boston, Dec. 1751.

PELL, Philip, Continental congressman; b. Pelham Manor, N.Y., July 7, 1753; grad. King's Coll. (now Columbia), 1770; studied law. Admitted to

N.Y. bar, practiced in N.Y.C. and Westchester County; served as lt. N.Y. Volunteers, 1776; dep. judge adv. Continental Army, 1777; mem. N.Y. State Assembly, 1779-81, 84-86; judge adv. gen. U.S. Army, 1781-83; mem. staff of Gen. Washington at evacuation of N.Y.C., 1783; regent Univ. State N.Y., 1784-87; surrogate Westchester County, 1787-1800; mem. Continental Congress from N.Y., 1788-89. Died Pelham Manor, N.Y., May 1, 1811; buried St. Paul's Churchyard, Eastchester (now Bronx), N.Y.

PELLEW, George, author; b. Cowes, Isle of Wight, Eng., 1859; grad. Harvard, 1880, Cambridge Law Sch., 1883. Admitted to N.Y., Mass. bars. Author: In Cabin and Castle, 1888; Women and the Commonwealth, 1888; Life of John Jay, 1890; Poems, 1892. Died Feb. 18, 1892; buried N.Y.C.

PELLICER, Anthony Dominic, clergyman; b. St. Augustine, Fla., Dec. 7, 1824; attended Spring Hill Coll., St. Vincent de Paul Sem., New Orleans. Ordained priest Roman Catholic Ch., Mobile, Ala., 1850; parish priest, Mobile, then vicar gen., 1867-74; apptd. 1st bishop of San Antonio (Tex.), 1874. Died San Antonio, Apr. 14, 1880.

PELTON, Guy Ray, congressman; b. nr. Great Barrington, Mass., Aug. 3, 1824; attended Conn. Lit. Inst., Suffield; studied law. Taught sch.; admitted to N.Y. bar, began practice in N.Y.C., 1851; held local offices; mem. U.S. Ho. of Reps. (Whig) from N.Y., 34th Congress, 1855-57; resumed practice of law, Great Barrington. Died in attempt to climb Mary's Mountain, Yellowstone Nat. Park, Wyo., July 24, 1890; buried Mahaiwe Cemetery, Great Barrington.

PEMBERTON, Israel, mcht., philanthropist; b. Phila., May 21, 1715; s. Israel and Rachel (Read) P.; m. Sarah Kirkbride, Apr. 6, 1737; m. 2d, Mary Stanbury, Dec. 21, 1747. Made fortune in father's merc. bus., Phila.; mem. Pa. Assembly, 1750-56, 66; mgr. Pa. Hosp., Phila., 1751-79, contributed large sums for its support; mem. Friendly Assn. for Regaining and Preserving Peace with the Indians by Pacific Measures; mem. Am. Philos. Soc., 1768-79; signed Non-Importation Agreement, 1765; refused to take oath of allegiance to Pa. during Revolution because of Quaker faith, imprisoned by Pa. Legislature, 1777-78. Died Apr. 22, 1779.

PEMBERTON, James, mcht., philanthropist; b. Phila., Sept. 6, 1723; s. Israel and Rachel (Read) P.; m. Hannah Lloyd, Oct. 15, 1751; m. 2d, Sarah Smith, Mar. 22, 1768; m. 3d, Phoebe (Lewis) Morton, July 12, 1775. Made fortune in Phila. merc. bus. (with father and brother Israel); mem. Meeting for Sufferings (exec. body of Soc. of Friends), 1756-1808; mem., financial supporter Friendly Assn. for Regaining and Preserving Peace with the Indians by Pacific Measures; a founder, contbr. to Soc. for Relief of Free Negroes, 1775, name changed to Pa. Soc. for Promoting the Abolition of Slavery, 1787, v.p., 1787-90, pres., 1790-1803; mem. bd. mgrs. Pa. Hosp., Phila., 1751-72, sec., 1759-72; mem. Pa. Assembly, 1750-56, 65-69; signer Non-Importation Agreement, 1765; refused to support violence of Revolution; imprisoned by Pa. Legislature, 1777-78. Died Feb. 9, 1809.

PEMBERTON, John, clergyman; b. Phila., Dec. 7, 1727; s. Israel and Rachel (Read) P.; m. Hannah Zane, May 8, 1766. Quaker preacher, missionary in Pa., N.J., Del., Va.; made preaching tours of Eng., Scotland, Ireland, 1750-53, 81-86, Holland, Germany, 1794-95; mem. Friendly Assn. for Regaining and Preserving Peace with the Indians by Pacific Measures; imprisoned by Pa. Legislature because of refusal to sign oath of allegiance 1777-78; opposed violence in Am. Revolution. Died Prymont, Westphalia (now Germany), Jan. 31, 1795.

PEMBERTON, John Clifford, army officer; b. Phila., Aug. 10, 1814; s. John and Rebecca (Clifford) P.; grad. U.S. Mil. Acad., 1837; m. Martha Thompson, Jan. 18, 1848, 5 children. Served as 2d lt. arty. in Seminole War, 1837-39; commd. 1st lt., 1842; brevetted capt., 1846, maj., 1847, for services in Mexican War; commd. capt., 1850; served in operations against Mormons in Utah, 1858; commd. lt. col. Confederate Army, 1861, then col., brig. gen., 1861, maj. gen. and lt. gen., 1862; surrendered to Grant at Vicksburg; somewhat suspect throughout South because of No. birth. Died "Penllyn," Pa., July 13, 1881; buried Laurel Hill Cemetery, Phila.

PENALOSA BRICENO, Diego Dioniso de, see de Penalosa Briceno, Diego Dioniso.

PEÑALVER Y CARDENAS, LUIS IGNATIUS, clergyman; b. Havana, Cuba, Apr. 3, 1749; attended St. Ignatius Coll., St. Jerome U. (both Havana). Ordained priest Roman Catholic Ch., Havana, 1772; vicar gen. of Santiago, 1773-79; named titular bishop of Tricca, apptd. adminstr. of La. and Two Flas., 1793; traveled throughout area which later comprised La. Purchase; archbishop of Guatemala, 1801-06, resigned, returned to Havana. Died July 17, 1810.

PENDER, William Dorsey, army officer; b. Edgecombe County, N.C., Feb. 6, 1834; s. James and Sarah (Routh) P.; grad. U.S. Mil. Acad., 1854; m. Mary Shepperd, Mar. 3, 1859; children—Turner, William D., Stephen Lee. Brevetted 2d lt., 2d Arty. U.S. Army, 1854, promoted 1st lt., 1858; apptd. adjutant 1st Dragoons, 1860-61; commd. capt. arty. Confederate Army, placed in charge of recruiting, Balt.; elected col. 3d N.C. Volunteers, then transferred to command 6th N.C. Regt., 1861; served in Battle of Fair Oaks, 1862; promoted to brig. gen., served with Jackson at battles of Cedar Run, Fredericksburg, Chancellorsville; commd. maj. gen., 1863. Died as result of wounds received at Battle of Gettysburg, Staunton, Va., July 18, 1863.

PENDLETON, Edmund, Continental congressman, jurist; b. Caroline County, Va., Sept. 9, 1721; s. Henry and Mary (Taylor) P.; studied law under clk. Caroline County Ct.; m. Elizabeth Roy, 1742 (dec. 1742) m. 2d, Sarah Pollard, June 20, 1743; no children. Clk., Caroline County Ct., 1740; admitted to practice at local bar, 1741, before Va. Gen. Ct., 1745; justice of peace, Caroline County, 1751; mem. Va. Ho. of Burgesses, 1752-74; mem. Com. of Correspondence, 1773; mem. Va. Conv.; mem. 1st Continental Congress from Va., 1774; mem. all revolutionary convs. in Va.; pres. Va. Com. of Safety (in effect gov. of state), 1774-76; lt. Caroline County; mem. Va. Ho. of Dels., 1776-77, speaker, 1776; pres. Va. Conv. called after passage of Boston Port Act, 1776, drew up resolution instructing Va. dels. to Continental Congress to propose independence; presiding judge 1st Va. Ct. of Chancery; pres. 1st Va. Supreme Ct. of Appeals, 1779-1803; pres. Va. Conv. to ratify U.S. Constn., 1788. Died Richmond, Va., Oct. 23, 1803; buried Brutton Parish Church Cemetery, Williamsburg, Va.

PENDLETON, Edmund Henry, congressman; b. Savannah, Ga., 1788; studied law. Admitted to N.Y. bar, practiced in Hyde Park; judge Dutchess County (N.Y.), 1830-40; mem. U.S. Ho. of Reps. (Whig) from N.Y., 22d Congress, 1831-33. Died N.Y.C., Feb. 25, 1862; buried St. James' Churchyard, Hyde Park.

PENDLETON, Edmund Monroe, physician, chemist; b. Eatonton, Ga., Mar. 19, 1815; s. Coleman and Martha (Gilbert) P.; grad. Med. Coll. of S.C., Charleston, 1837; m. Sara Jane Thomas, Nov. 27, 1838, 11 children. Practiced medicine, Warrenton, Ga., 1837-38, Sparta, Ga., 1838-67; owned large plantation nr. Sparta; organized fertilizer mfg. firm Pendleton & Dozier, Augusta, Ga., 1867, 1st to use cotton seed in manufacture of fertilizer; taught agr. U. Ga., 1872-76. Author: Text Book of Scientific Agriculture, 1875. Died Jan. 26, 1884.

PENDLETON, George Hunt, senator, diplomat; b. Cincinnati, O., July 19, 1825; s. Nathaniel Greene and Jane (Hunt) P.; attended Heidelberg (Germany) U.; m. Alice Key, 1846, 3 children. Admitted to Cincinnati bar, 1847; mem. Ohio Senate (Democrat), 1854-56; mem. U.S. Ho. of Reps. from Ohio, 35th-38th congresses, 1857-65, mem. judiciary com., ways and means com., mem. com. of mgrs. in impeachment of U.S. Judge West H. Humphreys of Tenn.; nominated for vice pres. U.S. on Nat. Dem. ticket with McClellan, 1864; del. to Nat. Union Conv., Phila., 1866; pres. Ky. Central R.R., 1869-79; mem. U.S. Senate from Ohio, 1879-85, chmn. com. on civil service, 1883; E.E. and M.P. to Germany, 1885-89. Died Brussels, Belgium, Nov. 24, 1889; buried Spring Grove Cemetery, Cincinnati.

PENDLETON, James Madison, clergyman; b. Spotsylvania County, Va., Nov. 20, 1811; s. John and Frances (Thompson) P.; m. Catherine Stockton Garnett, Mar. 13, 1838, 4 children. Licensed to preach, Baptist Ch., 1831, ordained to ministry Bapt. Ch., 1833; pastor, Bowling Green, Ky., 1837-57; editor So. Bapt. Review Eclectic, 1855-61; pastor and prof. theology Union U., Murfreesboro, Tenn., 1857-62; pastor, Hamilton, O., 1862-65, Upland, Pa., 1865-83; trustee Crozer Theol. Sem., Upland, 1868-83. Author: Three Reasons Why I Am a Baptist, 1853; Church Manual, 1867; A Treatise on the Atonement of Christ, 1869; Christian Doctrines, 1878; Reminiscenses of A Long Life, 1891. Died Bowling Green, Mar. 4, 1891.

PENDLETON, James Monroe, congressman; b. North Stonington, Conn., Jan. 10, 1822; attended sch., North Stonington and Suffield, Conn. Moved to Westerly, R.I., engaged in merc. and ins. bus., banking; mem. R.I. Senate, 1862-65; del. Republican Nat. Conv., Chgo., 1868; Rep. presdl. elector, 1868; mem. U.S. Ho. of Reps. (Rep.) from R.I., 42d-43d congresses, 1871-75; mem. R.I. Ho. of Reps., 1879-84; chmn. R.I. Bd. Charities and Corrections, 1884-89. Died Westerly, Feb. 16, 1889; buried River Bend Cemetery, Westerly.

PENDLETON, John B., lithographer; b. N.Y.C., 1798; s. William Pendleton; m. Eliza Matilda Blydenburgh, 1830; m. 2d, Hester Travis, 1846. Copper plate engraver, Pitts., 1820-23, Boston, 1824-25; brought one of 1st lithographic machines to U.S., 1825; partner brother in firm W. S. & J. B. Pendleton, lithographers, Boston, 1825-30; head firm Pendleton, Kearny & Childs, lithographers, Phila., 1830; established own firm, N.Y.C., 1832-66. Died N.Y.C., Mar. 10, 1866.

PENDLETON, John Strother, congressman, diplomat; b. nr. Culpeper, Culpeper County, Va., Mar. 1, 1802; s. William and Nancy (Strother) P.; m. Lucy Ann Williams, 1824. Admitted to Va. bar, 1824; mem. Va. Ho. of Dels., 1830-33, 36-39; U.S. charge d'affaires in Chile, 1841-44; mem. U.S. Ho. of Reps. (Whig) from Va., 29th-30th congresses, 1845-49; charge d'affaires Argentine Confederation, 1851-54; authorized with Robert C. Schenck (Am. minister to Brazil) to negotiate treaty of commerce with Paraguay and Uruguay which also provided for unhampered use of internat. waterways, 1852. Died Culpeper County, Nov. 19, 1868; buried "Redwood," Culpeper.

PENDLETON, Nathanael Greene, congressman; b. Savannah, Ga., Aug. 25, 1793; grad. Columbia, 1813; studied law. Admitted to N.Y. bar; served in War of 1812; moved to Cincinnati, 1818, practiced law; mem. Ohio Senate, 1825-29; mem. U.S. Ho. of Reps. (Whig) from Ohio, 27th Congress, 1841-43. Died Cincinnati, June 16, 1891; buried Spring Grove Cemetery, Cincinnati.

PENDLETON, William Kimbrough, clergyman, coll. pres.; b. Yanceyville, Va., Sept. 8, 1817; s. Edmund and Unity Yancey (Kimbrough) P.; grad. U. Va., 1840; m. Lavinia Campbell, Oct. 1840; m. 2d, Clarinda Campbell, July 1848; m. 3d, Catherine Huntington King, Sept. 19, 1855; 7 children. Admitted to Va. bar, 1840; baptized into Disciples of Christ by Alexander Campbell, 1840; prof. natural philosophy Bethany Coll. (founded by father-in-law Alexander Campbell), v.p. coll., 1845-66, pres., 1866-86; asso. editor Millenial Harbinger, 1846-56; editor in chief, 1856-70; mem. editorial staff Christian Quarterly, 1869-76; del. W.Va. Constl. Conv., 1872; supt. W.Va. Public Schs., 1873-80; founder Disciples of Christ Ch., Eustis, Fla. Died during commencement period at Bethany Coll., Sept. 1, 1899.

PENDLETON, William Nelson, clergyman, army officer; b. Richmond, Va., Dec. 26, 1809; s. Edmund and Lucy (Nelson) P.; grad. U.S. Mil. Acad., 1830; m. Anzolette Elizabeth Page, July 15, 1831, several children including Alexander, Susan (Pendleton) Lee. Apptd. 2d lt. 4th Arty. Regt., U.S. Army, 1830, resigned, 1833; prof. mathematics Bristol Coll., Pa., 1833-37, Del. Coll., Newark, 1837-39; ordained deacon Protestant Episcopal Ch., 1837, priest, 1838; prin. Episcopal High Sch. of Va., Alexandria, 1839-44; taught pvt. sch., pastor 2 chs., Balt., 1844-47; rector All Saints Ch., Frederick, Md., 1847-53, Grace Ch., Lexington, Va., 1853-61, 65-83; dep. to Gen. Conv. Protestant Episcopal Ch., 1856; commd. capt. Rockbridge Arty., Confederate States Army, 1861, promoted col., 1861, brig. gen., 1862; chief of arty. Army of Northern Va., 1863-65. Died Lexington, Va., Jan. 15, 1883.

PENDLETON, William S., engraver; b. N.Y.C., Jan. 27, 1795. Installed gas fixtures Peale Museums, Phila. and Balt., 1816, exhibited Rembrant Peale's Court of Death in various cities and towns; engraver in partnership with Abel Bowen, Boston, circa 1825, later with his brother John; lithographer, Boston, until 1836; bank note engraver, engaged in hardware bus., Phila., after 1836; settled in Staten Island, N.Y., after Civil War. Died S.I., Jan. 22, 1879.

PENHALLOW, Samuel, mcht., jurist; b. St. Mabyn, County Cornwall, Eng., July 13, 1665; s. Chamond and Ann (Tamlyn) P.; m. Mary Cutt, July 12, 1687; m. 2d, Abigail Atkinson, Sept. 19, 1714; 14 children. Came to Am., 1686; mcht., Portsmouth, N.H., 1687-1726; justice of peace Portsmouth; speaker N.H. Gen. Assembly, 1699; treas. N.H., 1699-1726; recorder and privy councillor of N.H., 1702, 19-22; justice N.H. Superior Ct., 1714-17, chief justice, 1717-26. Author: The History of the Wars of New England with the Eastern Indians, or a Narrative of Their Continued Perfidy and Cruelty from the 10th of August 1703 to the Peace Renewed the 13th of July 1713, and from the 25th of July 1722 to Their Submission 15 December 1725. Died Dec. 13, 1726.

PENINGTON, Edward, pamphleteer, colonial ofcl.; b. Amersham, Bucks County, Eng., Sept. 14, 1667; s. Isaac and Mary (Proude) P.; m. Sarah Jennings, Nov. 27, 1699, 1 son, Isaac. Prolific Quaker pamphleteer in England; came to Am., 1698; surveyor gen. Colony of Pa., 1698-1701; apptd. atty. to dispose of property of Letitia Penn, 1701. Author pamphlets: The Discoverer Discovered, 1695; Rabshakeh Rebuked, and his Railing Accusations Refuted, 1695; A Reply to Thomas Crisp, 1695; Some Brief Observations upon George Keith's Earnest Expostulation, 1696. Died Phila., Nov. 22, 1701.

PENN, Alexander Gordon, congressman; b. nr. Stella, Va., May 10, 1799; attended Emory and Henry Coll. Engaged in planting, nr. Covington, La., 1821; mem. La. Ho. of Reps.; postmaster of New Orleans, 1843-49; del. Democratic nat. convs., 1844, 52, 56, 60; mem. U.S. Ho. of Reps. (Dem.) from La., 31st-32d congresses, Dec. 30, 1850-53; engaged in planting, operating lumber mill, nr. Covington. Died Washington, D.C., May 7, 1866; buried Glenwood Cemetery, Washington.

PENN, John, colonial govt. ofcl.; b. London, Eng., July 14, 1729; s. Richard and Hannah (Lardner) P.; attended U. Geneva, 1747-51; m. Miss Cox; m. 2d, Ann Allen, May 31, 1766. Mem. Pa. Provincial Council, 1752-55; commr. Indian rights, Albany, N.Y., 1754; commd. by proprs. as lt. gov. Pa., 1763-77 (except for brief period during which his brother Richard held office, 1771-73); in office when proprietary rule was abolished, had boundary, frontier, Indian troubles throughout his tenure. Died Bucks County, Pa., Feb. 9, 1795; buried Christ Ch., Phila.

PENN, John, Continental congressman; b. nr. Port Royal, Caroline County, Va., May 17, 1741; s. Moses and Catherine (Taylor) P.; read law privately; m. Susannah Lyme, July 28, 1763, 3 children. Licensed to practice law, Bowling Green, Va., 1762; moved to Granville County, N.C., 1774; mem. N.C. Provincial Congress, 1775; mem. Continental Congress, 1775-80; signed Declaration of Independence, 1776; mem. N.C. Bd. of War, 1780; a rep. from N.C. to ratify Articles of Confederation; apptd. N.C. receiver of taxes for the Confederation, 1784. Died nr. Williamsburg, N.C., Sept. 14, 1788; buried Guilford Battle Grounds, Greensboro, N.C.

PENN, Richard, colonial govt. ofcl.; b. Eng., 1735; s. Richard and Hannah (Lardner) P.; ed. St. Johns Coll., Cambridge (Eng.) U.; m. Mary Masters, May 21, 1772, 5 children including William, Richard. Came to Am., 1763; lt. gov. Pa., 1771-73, superseded by his brother John; returned to Eng., entrusted by Continental Congress with last conciliation offer made to King George III, 1775; returned 4 times to Parliament while in Eng., once for Appleby, 1784-90, twice for Haslemere, 1790, 1806, once for Lancaster, 1796-1802. Died Richmond, Surrey, Eng., May 27, 1811.

PENN, Thomas, colonial propr.; b. Bristol, Eng., Mar. 20, 1703; s. William and Hannah (Callowhill) P.; m. Lady Juliana Fermor, Aug. 22, 1751, 8 children including Juliana, John, Granville, Sophia Margaretta. Inherited a quarter of the proprietorship of Pa. from mother, 1727, inherited another half from brother John, 1746; mgr. proprietary affairs of Pa., Phila., 1632-41; returned to England, 1741; purchased Forks of Delaware River from Indians, 1737; managed property through correspondence; made large fortune by selling parts of property to immigrants. Died Mar. 21, 1775.

PENN, William, colonizer; b. London, Eng., Oct. 14, 1644; s. Sir William and Margaret (Jasper) P.; attended Christ Coll., Oxford (Eng.) U., 2 years; m. Gulielma Springett, Apr. 4, 1672; m. 2d, Hannah Callowhill, Jan. 1696; 4 sons, including John, Thomas, Richard. Imprisoned for writing The Sandy Foundation Shaken, 1669; completed 1st draft of No Cross, No Crown in prison; a defendant in "Bushell's Case" which resulted in a victory for freedom of English juries from dictates of the judges, 1670; chief author Concessions and Agreements for Government, West Jersey, 1677; granted a tract of land North of Md. (now Pa.) by King of Eng. as payment for debt owed his father, 1681; framed 1st govt. for Province of Pa., dated Apr. 25, 1682, proprietary gov., 1682-92, 94-1718; superintended laying out of Phila.; returned to Eng. because of renewal of persecution of Quakers there, 1684; forfeited governership of Pa., 1692-94, later restored; involved in boundary dispute with Md. not settled in his lifetime, also had troubles with colonial assembly; a founder N.J. and Del.; best known for fair and just treatment of Indians. Died Ruscombe, Berkshire, Eng., July 30, 1718.

PENNIMAN, Ebenezer Jenckes, congressman; b. Lansingburgh, N.Y., Jan. 11, 1804; attended common schs. Apprenticed as printer; moved to N.Y.C., 1822, later to Orwell, Vt., engaged as dry-goods mcht.; moved to Plymouth, Mich., 1840; supr. Plymouth Twp.; mem. bd. to locate state reform sch., 1849; mem. U.S. Ho. of Reps. (Whig and Free-Soiler) from Mich., 32d Congress, 1851-53; became pres. 1st Nat. Bank of Plymouth, 1871; mem. conv. which organized Republican Party in Mich., 1854. Died Plymouth, Apr. 12, 1890; buried Riverside Cemetery, Plymouth.

PENNINGTON, Alexander Cumming McWhorter, congressman; b. Newark, N.J., July 2, 1810; attended U.S. Mil. Acad., 1826-28; studied law. Admitted to N.J. bar, 1833, began practice in Newark; mem. N.J. Gen. Assembly, 1837-38; alderman Newark, 1837-40; mem. U.S. Ho. of Reps. (Whig) from N.J., 33d-34th congresses, 1853-57. Died N.Y.C., Jan. 25, 1867; buried Mt. Pleasant Cemetery, Newark.

PENNINGTON, Edward, Continental congressman, mcht.; b. Bucks County, Pa., Dec. 15, 1726; s. Isaac and Ann (Biles) P.; m. Sarah Shoemaker, Nov. 26, 1754. Mcht., banker, Phila.; mem. Pa. Assembly, 1761; judge Pa. Ct. Common Pleas, 1761-circa 1774; trustee Pa. State House and Grounds, 1761; mgr. Pa. Hosp., Phila., 1773-79; pres. Phila. Com. of Correspondence, 1774; mem. Continental Congress from Pa., 1774; Quaker, opposed to revolution; arrested and exiled to Va., 1777-78; mem. Phila. City Council, 1790; mem. Am. Philos. Soc., 1768-96; treas. Soc. for Cultivation of Silk. Died Phila., Sept. 30, 1796.

PENNINGTON, James W. C., clergyman; b. Eastern Shore, Md., 1809. Escaped from slavery on Md. plantation, 1830; aided by Quakers in Pa.; taught in Negro schs., Newtown, L.I., N.Y., New Haven, Conn., 1835-37; pastor African Congregational Ch., Newtown, 1838-40, Hartford, Conn., 1840-47; pres. Hartford Central Assn. Congl. Ministers for 2 terms; del. from Conn. to World's Anti-Slavery Conv., London, Eng., 1843; del. Am. Peace Conv. to World's Peace Soc., London, 1843; 1st pastor First Shiloh Presbyn. Ch., N.Y.C., 1847-55; in Europe to escape Fugitive Slave Law, 1850-51, purchased manumission, 1851; became alcoholic in later years. Author: Text Book of the Origin and History of the Coloured People, 1841; Covenants Involving Moral Wrong Are Not Obligatory upon Man: A Sermon, 1842; The Fugitive Blacksmith, 1849; The Reasonableness of the Abolition of Slavery, 1856. Died Jacksonville, Fla., Oct. 1870.

PENNINGTON, William, gov. N.J., congressman; b. Newark, N.J., May 4, 1796; s. William Sandford and Phoebe (Wheeler) P.; grad. Coll. N.J. (now Princeton), 1813; m. Caroline Burnet, circa 1835. Became licensed atty., 1817, counselor, 1820; clk. dist. and circuit cts., 1815-26; mem. N.J. Assembly from Essex County, 1828; gov. and chancellor N.J., 1837-43; mem. U.S. Ho. of Reps. from N.J., 36th Congress, 1859-61, speaker. Died Newark, Feb. 16, 1862; buried Mt. Pleasant Cemetery.

PENNINGTON, William Sandford, gov. N.J.; b. Newark, N.J., 1757; s. Samuel and Mary (Sandford) P.; m. Phoebe Wheeler, circa 1786; m. 2d, Elizabeth Pierson. Became sgt. 2d Regt. of Arty., Continental Army, 1777, commd. 2d lt., 1778-1780, mustered out as brevet capt.; mem. N.J. Assembly, 1797, 98, 99, N.J. Council, 1801, 02; licensed as atty.-at-law, 1803; clk. Essex County (N.J.), 1803; elected to fill vacancy in N.J. Supreme Ct., 1804, justice, recorder, 1806-13; gov. and Chancellor N.J., 1813-15; judge U.S. Dist. Ct. for N.J., 1815-26. Died Newark, Sept. 17, 1826.

PENNOCK, Alexander Mosley, naval officer; b. Norfolk, Va., Oct. 1, 1814; s. William Pennock; m. Margaret Loyall. Apptd. midshipman U.S. Navy, 1828, passed midshipman, 1834; commd. lt., 1840, served ship Decatur, Brazil Squadron, 1843-46, store-ship Supply during Mexican War; served 1st extended shore duty as lighthouse insp., 1853-56; commanded steamer Southern Star in Paraguay Expdn.; became fleet capt. in charge of flotilla equipment, 1862; commanded naval base, Cairo, Ill., 1862-64; promoted capt., 1863, commodore, 1868; commanded European Squadron, 1868-69; commandant Portsmouth Navy Yard, 1870-72; rear adm., 1872, in command of Pacific Squadron, 1874-75. Died Portsmouth, N.H., Sept. 20, 1876; buried Norfolk, Va.

PENNYBACKER, Isaac Samuels, senator, congressman; b. Pine Forge, Va., Sept. 3, 1805; attended Winchester Law Sch. Admitted to Va. bar, began practice in Harrisonburg; mem. U.S. Ho. of Reps. (Democrat) from Va., 25th Congress, 1837-39; judge U.S. Dist. Ct. for Western Va., 1839-45; declined appointment by Pres. Van Buren as U.S. atty. gen.; mem. U.S. Senate from Va., Dec. 3, 1845-47; mem. bd. regents Smithsonian Instn., 1846-47. Died Washington, D.C., Jan. 12, 1847; buried Woodbine Cemetery, Harrisonburg.

PENNYPACKER, Elijah Funk, reformer; b. Schuylkill Twp., Chester County, Pa., Nov. 29, 1804; s. Joseph and Elizabeth (Funk) P.; m. Sarah W. Coates, 1831; m. 2d, Hannah Adamson, 1843; 9 children. Mem. Pa. Ho. of Reps., 1831-35; sec. Pa. Bd. Canal Commrs., 1836-77, mem. bd., 1838; joined Soc. of Friends, 1841; became abolitionist, used his home for station of Underground R.R.; v.p. Pa. Mut. Fire Ins. Co., 1869-79, pres., 1879-87; unsuccessful Prohibitionist candidate for treas. Pa., 1875. Died Jan. 4, 1888.

PENROSE, Charles Bingham, govt. ofcl., lawyer; b. Phila., Oct. 6, 1798; s. Clement Biddle and Anne (Bingham) P.; m. Valeria Fullerton Biddle, Mar. 16, 1824, 6 children including Richard Alexander Fullerton, Clement Biddle. Admitted to Pa. bar, 1821; collaborator on reports of cases adjudged in Supreme Ct. Pa., 1831-33; mem. Pa. Senate, 1833-41, served as speaker, reelected 1856; solicitor U.S. Treasury, 1841-45. Died Apr. 6, 1857, Harrisburg, Pa.

PEPPER, George Seckel, philanthropist; b. Phila., June 11, 1808; s. George and Mary (Seckel) P.; never married. Admitted to Pa. bar, 1830; inherited large fortune from father; bd. dirs. Pa. Acad. Fine Arts, 1850-84, pres. bd., 1884-90; contbr. funds to build Am. Acad. Music, Phila., 1853, chmn. exec. com., 1857-70; founder, trustee Henry Seybest Fund for Care Indigent Children; provided in his will for founding of free public library, Phila., other beneficiaries included 10 Phila. hosps., Franklin Inst., Zool. Soc., Pa. Museum and Sch. Indsl. Art, Rittenhouse Club, U. Pa. Died Phila., May 2, 1890.

PEPPER, William, physician; b. Phila., Jan. 21, 1810; s. George and Mary (Seckel) P.; grad. Coll. of N.J. (now Princeton), 1828, U. Pa. Med. Sch., 1832; studied medicine under Pierre Louis and Guillame Dupuytren, Paris, France; m. Sarah Platt, 1840, 7 children including George, William. Physician, Phila. Dispensary, 1833-39, Wills Eye Hosp., 1839-41, Inst. for Instrn. of Blind, 1841-42, Pa. Hosp., 1842-58 (all Phila.); prof. medicine U. Pa., 1860-64. Died Oct. 15, 1864.

PEPPER, William, physician; b. Phila., Aug. 21, 1843; s. William and Sarah (Platt) P.; grad. U. Pa., 1862, Med. Dept., 1864; m. Frances Sergeant Perry, June 25, 1873, 4 children. Resident physician Pa. Hosp., Phila., 1864-65; pathologist, vis. physician Pa. Hosp., Phila. Hosp., 1865-68; lectr. morbid anatomy U. Pa., 1868-70, prof. clin. medicine, 1876-84, provost, 1880-94, prof. theory and practice of medicine, 1884-98, founder Univ. Hosp. (1st hosp. in U.S. directly associated with and staffed by faculty of univ. med. sch.), 1874, founded nurses' tng. sch., 1887, as provost founded Wharton Sch. Finance, vet., hygiene, biol. and archtl. schs., univ. extension lectures, Bennett Sch. (for grad. instrn. of women); med. dir. Phila. Centennial Exhbn., 1875-76; founder Am. Climatol. Soc., 1884, pres., 1886; pres. Am. Clin. Assn., 1886, Assn. Am. Physicians, 1891; founded Coll. Assn. of Pa., 1886; mem. exec. com. A.M.A.; pres. 1st Pan-Am. Med. Congress, 1893; founded, endowed William Pepper Lab. of Clin. Medicine, U. Pa. (1st lab. in U.S. devoted to advanced clin. studies of causes of disease), 1894; directed establishment of 1st Phila. Free Library (endowed by his uncle George S. Pepper), 1890; founded Archaeol. Assn. of U. Pa., 1892, founded Univ. Museum. Author: The Morphological Changes of the Blood in Malarial Fever, 1867; A Practical Treatise on the Diseases of Children, 1870; Higher Medical Education, the True Interest of the Public and the Profession, 1877, 94; A System of Practical Medicine, 5 vols., 1885-86; Textbook of the Theory and Practice of Medicine, 2 vols., 1893-94. Died Pleasanton, Cal., July 28, 1898.

PEPPERRELL, Sir William, army officer; b. Kittery Point, Me., June 27, 1696; s. William and Margery (Bray) P.; m. Mary Hirst, Mar. 16, 1723; 4 children including Elizabeth, Andrew. Col. in command all militia in Province of Me., 1726; mem. Mass. Gen. Ct. from Kittery, 1726; became mem. Council, 1727, pres., 18 years; apptd. chief justice 1730; col., 1745; created baronet, 1746; mem. Council, Boston, 1746; a commr. to negotiate treaty with Me. Indians, 1753; maj. gen., 1755; de facto gov. Mass.; apptd. comdr. in-chief Castle William and all mil. forces Me. Colony, strategy led to tremendous Am. victory at French ft. at Louisburg, N.S., Can.; commd. lt. gen. Brit. Army, 1759. Died Kittery, July 6, 1759.

PERALTA, Pedro de, see de Peralta, Pedro.

PERCHE, Napoleon Joseph, clergyman; b. Angers, France, Jan. 10, 1805; grad. Sem. of Beaupréau (France). Ordained priest Roman Catholic Ch., 1829; came to U.S., 1837; missionary in Ky., 1837-42; almoner Ursuline Convent, New Orleans, 1842-70; editor French weekly La Propagateur Catholique, 1842-57; coadjutor to Archbishop John Mary Odin, New Orleans, 1870; archbishop of New Orleans, 1870-83, introduced Carmelite Order of nuns into his diocese, 1872. Died Dec. 27, 1883.

PERCIVAL, James Gates, poet, geologist; b. Kensington, Conn., Sept. 15, 1795; s. James and Elizabeth (Hart) P.; grad. Yale, 1815, Med. Instn., 1820; attended U. Pa. Med. Sch., 1818-19; never married. Apptd. asst. surgeon U.S. Army and prof. chemistry U.S. Mil. Acad., 1824; surgeon recruiting offices, Boston, 1824-25; editor Am. Atheneum, N.Y.C., 1825; Phi Beta Kappa poet Harvard, 1824; Phi Beta Kappa orator Yale, 1825; assisted Noah Webster in editing An American Dictionary of the English Language, 1827-28; state geologist of Conn., 1835-42; surveyor Am. Mining Co., Ill. and Wis., 1853; state geologist of Wis., 1854-56. Author:

Zamor, 1815, Prometheus, 1821 (both single poems); Poems, 1821; Clio I and II, 1822; Prometheus Part II with Other Poems, 1822; Poems, 1823; Clio Number III, 1827; The Dream of a Day, and Other Poems, 1843; Report on the Geology of the State of Connecticut, 1842; editor: Elegant Extracts (Vicesimus Knox), 6 vols., 1825; System of Universal Geography (Malte-brun), 3 vols., 1827-34. Died Hazel Green, Wis., May 2, 1856.

PERCIVAL, John, naval officer; b. West Barnstable, Mass., Apr. 5, 1779; s. John and Mary (Snow) P.; m. Maria Pinkerton, 1823, no children. Sailed on ships in Atlantic trade, 1793-97; impressed into Brit. Navy, 1797, escaped, 1799; warranted midshipman U.S. Navy, 1800, discharged, 1801; mate and master in mcht. trade, 1801-09; known as "Mad Jack" or "Roaring Jack"; sailing master U.S. Navy, 1809; captured Brit. tender Eagle, 1813; promoted lt., 1814; served against pirates in West Indies; commanded schooner Dolphin (1st Am. warship to visit H.I.) in pursuit of mutineers aboard Globe in Pacific, 1825-26; court-martialed for violating Hawaiian anti-prostitution ordinances, acquitted because he had helped to quell riot his libertine action had instigated; promoted comdr., 1831, capt., 1841; commanded Cyane in Mediterranean, 1838-39, Constitution on voyage around world, 1844-46; put on reserve list, 1855. Died Sept. 17, 1862.

PERCY, George, colonial gov.; b. Northumberland County, Eng., Sept. 4, 1580; s. Henry and Catherine (Neville) P. Served with Brit. Army in Dutch wars; joined Va. expdn. of 1606; became a trusted leader of 1st colonization effort; gov. Va. at Jamestown succeeding John Smith, 1609-11, gov. during "starving time" of the colony, was himself very ill, became counciliar, comdt., dep. gov. Va. Colony, 1611-12; left Va., returned to service in Brit. Army, 1612. Author: Discourse of the Plantation of the Southern Colonie in Virginia; A Trewe Relacyon of the Proceedings and Ocurrentes of Momente wch have Hapnd in Virginie. Died Eng., Mar. 1632.

PERELLI, Achille, artist; b. Milan, Italy; attended Acad. of Arts, Milan. Served with Garibaldi; came to Am., settled in New Orleans; 1st sculptor in bronze in La.; also painted fish and game. Died New Orleans, Oct. 9, 1891.

PEREZ de VILLAGRÁ, Gaspar, explorer; b. Pueblo de los Angeles, Spain, 1555; s. Henan Perez de Villagrá; Litt.B., U. Salamanca; m. Catalina de Soto, 2 children. Came to Mexico; procurador gen., capt. of cavalry, mem. council of war in Oñate expdn. to N.M.; 1596-98; capt. Tepehaunes Indians, 1603-05; mayor Guanecevi, Durango, N.M.; returned to Spain, 1608/09; published Historia de la Nueva Mexico (epic poem of 34 cantos) at Alcalá de Henares, 1610; put on trial on charges of being too severe on deserters, N.M., 1613, banished from N.M. for 6 years, from Mexico City for 2 years; died on way to become mayor Zapotitlan, Guatemala. Died at sea, 1620.

PERHAM, Josiah, railroad exec.; b. Wilton, Me., Jan. 31, 1803; s. Josiah and Elizabeth (Gould) P.; m. Esther Sewell. Storekeeper, woollen mfr., Wilton, until 1842; mcht., Boston, 1842-49; set up moving panorama of Great Lakes, Melodeon Hall, Boston, 1850; made considerable fortune, later lost fortune; organized 1st excursion trains in U.S., featured cheap round-trip fares for sight-seers; secured charter, 1st pres. N.P. R.R., 1864-65. Died East Boston, Mass., Oct. 4, 1868.

PERKINS, Bishop, congressman; b. Becket, Mass., Sept. 5, 1787; grad. Williams Coll., 1807; studied law. Admitted to the bar, 1812, began practice in Lisbon, N.Y.; moved to Ogdensburg, N.Y., practiced law; clk. bd. suprs. St. Lawrence County (N.Y.), 1820-52; dist. atty. St. Lawrence County, 1821-40; mem. N.Y. State Constl. Conv., 1846; mem. N.Y. State Assembly, 1846-47, 49; mem. U.S. Ho. of Reps. (Democrat) from N.Y., 33d Congress, 1853-55. Died Ogdensburg, Nov. 20, 1866; buried Ogdensburg Cemetery.

PERKINS, Bishop Walden, senator, congressman; b. Rochester, O., Oct. 18, 1841; attended Knox Coll., Galesburg, Ill.; studied law. Prospector, Cal. and N.M., 1860-62; served as sgt. 83d Regt., Ill. Volunteer Inf., later adj. and capt. 16th Regt., U.S. Colored Inf., Union Army, during Civil War; admitted to the bar, 1867, began practice in Princeton, Ind.; moved to Oswego, Kan., practiced law; county atty. Mo., Kan. & Tex. R.R., 2 years; pros. atty. Labette County (Kan.), 1869; judge Labette County Probate Ct., 1870-82; editor Oswego Register, 1873; mem. U.S. Ho. of Reps. (Republican) from Kan., 48th-51st congresses, 1883-91; mem. U.S. Senate from Kan., Jan. 1, 1892-93; resumed law practice, Washington, D.C. Died Washington, June 20, 1894; buried Rock Creek Cemetery, Washington.

PERKINS, Charles Callahan, cultural leader; b. Boston, Mar. 1, 1823; s. James and Eliza (Callahan) P.; grad. Harvard, 1843; m. Frances D. Bruen, June 12, 1855. Inherited fortune from father; studied and painted in Europe, 1843-50, 65-69; pres. Handel and Haydn Soc., Boston, 1850-51, 75-86; contbd. funds to build Boston Music Hall, Boston Museum of Fine Arts; lectr. painting Trinity Coll., Hartford, Conn., 1857-58, later gave public lectures in Boston; founder Mass. Normal Art Sch. (now Mass. Sch. Art); mem. Boston Sch. Com., 1870-83; pres. Boston Art Club, 1869-79. Author: Tuscan Sculptors, 1864; Italian Sculptors, 1868; Art in Education, 1870; Raphael and Michaelangelo, 1878; Historical Handbook of Italian Sculpture, 1883; Ghiberti et Son École, 1886; History of the Handel and Haydn Society of Boston, Massachusetts, 1886. Died nr. Windsor, Vt., Aug. 25, 1886.

PERKINS, Elias, congressman; b. Newent Society (now Lisbon), Conn., Apr. 5, 1767; grad. Yale, 1786; studied law. Admitted to Conn. bar, began practice in New London; mem. Conn. Ho. of Reps., 1795-1800, 1814-15, speaker, 1798, 1815; asst. judge New London County Ct., 1799, chief justice, 1807-25; mem. U.S. Ho. of Reps. (Federalist) from Conn., 7th Congress, 1801-03; mem. Conn. Senate, 1817-22; mayor of New London, 1829-32. Died New London, Sept. 27, 1845; buried Cedar Grove Cemetery, New London.

PERKINS, Elisha, physician; b. Norwich, Conn., Jan. 27, 1742; s. Joseph and Mary (Bushnell) P.; attended Yale; m. Sarah Douglass, Sept. 23, 1762, 10 children including Benjamin Douglas. Practiced medicine, Plainfield, Conn.; incorporator Conn. Med. Soc., 1792; chmn. Windham County (Conn.) Med. Soc.; invented "tractor" (U-shaped piece of metal which when applied to affected parts of body eased pain and cured disorders), patented, 1796, popular in U. S., England, parts of Europe, until 1800; expelled from Conn. Med. Soc., 1798; devised remedy composed of vinegar and muriate of soda; went to N.Y.C. during yellow fever outbreak to test remedy, 1799. Died of yellow fever, N.Y.C. Sept. 6, 1799.

PERKINS, Frederic Beecher, librarian, editor: b. Hartford, Conn., Sept. 27, 1828; s. Thomas Clap and Mary (Beecher) P.; attended Yale, 1846-48, M.A. (hon.), 1860; studied law under his father; m. Mary Anne Westcott, May 21, 1857; m. 2d, Frances (Johnson) Beecher, May 1894; 4 children including Charlotte (Perkins) Gilman. Admitted to Conn. bar, 1851; editor N.Y. Tribune, 1854-57; asst. editor Am. Jour. of Edn., 1857-circa 1861; librarian Conn. Hist. Soc., 1857-61; mem. editorial staff Galaxy, Independent, Christian Union, all Hartford; editor Old and New, Boston, 1870-73; sec. Boston Pub. Library, 1874-79; chief librarian San Francisco Pub. Library, 1880-87; asso. editor Library Jour., 1877-80. Author: Charles Dickens, 1870; The Best Reading, 1872; Check List for American Local History, 1876; Devil-Puzzlers and Other Studies, 1877; Scrope; or, the Lost Library (novel), 1879. Died Morristown, N.J., Jan. 27, 1899.

PERKINS, George Hamilton, naval officer; b. Hopkinton, N.H., Oct. 20, 1836; s. Hamilton Eliot and Clara (George) P.; grad. U.S. Naval Acad., 1855; m. Anna Minot Weld, July 25, 1870, 1 dau. Isabel (Perkins) Anderson. Apptd. midshipman U.S. Navy, 1855; acting master ship Sumter in suppression of African slave trade, 1859-61; promoted lt., 1861; served in West Gulf Blockading Squadron, 1861-65; with Capt. Theodorus Bailey entered city of New Orleans, walked unarmed through hostile mob, accepted surrender of city, 1862; commanded ships Sciota in blockade of Tex. coast and Chickasaw on lower Mississippi River; promoted comdr., 1871, commanded ships Ashuelot, Asiatic Station, 1877-79, Hartford off South America, 1884-85; promoted capt., 1882; ret., 1891; promoted commodore ret., 1896. Died Boston, Oct. 28, 1899.

PERKINS, Jacob, inventor; b. Newburyport, Mass., July 9, 1766; s. Matthew and Jane (Noyes) Dole P.; m. Hannah Greenleaf, Nov. 11, 1790, 6 children. Apprenticed to goldsmith, Ipswich, Mass., 1779-81; Operated own goldsmith shop, Ipswich, 1781-87; employed by State of Mass. in manufacture of dies for copper coins, 1787-90; owned mfg. company making nails and tacks using machine he had invented, 1790-95; published series of school books (in partnership with Gideon Fairman) entitled Perkins and Fairman's Running Hand (using 1st steel plates in Am.), 1809-10; worked in bank-note improvements, 1814-17; began firm Perkins, Fairman & Heath, printers, 1819-40; began work in expts. in steam boilers, 1823; patented steam-pressure boiler for steam vessel. Died July 30, 1849.

PERKINS, James Handasyd, editor; b. Boston, July 31, 1810; s. Samuel G. and Barbara (Higginson) P.; m. Sarah H. Elliott, Dec. 17, 1834, at least 2 children including Charles Elliott. Employed in uncle's import business, Boston, England, W.I., 1828-31; admitted to Ohio bar, 1834; editor, publisher Saturday Evening Chronicle, Cincinnati 1834, merged with Cincinnati Mirror, 1834, editor, 1834-35; gardener, Cincinnati, 1837-49; editor Western Messenger (Unitarian monthly), 1839; minister at large to 1st Congregational Soc. of Cincinnati, 1838-49; pres. Cincinnati Relief Union, 1841-49, Cincinnati Hist. Soc., 1844-47; 1st v.p. Hist. and Philos. Soc. of Ohio, 1849. Author: Digest of the Constitutional Opinions of Chief Justice John Marshall, 1838; Annals of the West, 1846. Committed suicide by drowning in Ohio River, Cincinnati, Dec. 14, 1849.

PERKINS, Jared, congressman; b. Unity, N.H., Jan. 5, 1793; attended common schs., Unity and Clarement, N.H.; studied theology. Ordained to ministry, 1824; mem. N.H. Council, 1846-48, N.H. Ho. of Reps., 1850; mem. U.S. Ho. of Reps. (Whig) from N.H., 32d Congress, 1851-53; nominated for gov. N.H., 1854; justice of peace, 1854. Died Nashua, N.H., Oct. 15, 1854; buried West Unity Cemetery, Unity.

PERKINS, John, Jr., congressman; b. Natchez, Miss., July 1, 1819; s. John Perkins; grad. Yale, 1840, law dept. Harvard, 1842. Admitted to La. bar, 1843, began practice in New Orleans; engaged in cotton planting; traveled in Europe; apptd. judge circuit ct. for dist. of Tensas and Madison parishes (La.), 1851; mem. U.S. Ho. of Reps. (Democrat) from La., 33d Congress, 1853-55; chmn. La. Secession Conv., 1861; mem. Confederate Senate from La., 1862-65; traveled in Mexico and Europe until 1878. Died Balt., Nov. 28, 1885; buried Natchez Cemetery.

PERKINS, Justin, missionary; b. West Springfield (now Holyoke), Mass., Mar. 5, 1805; s. William and Judith (Clough) P.; grad. Amherst, 1829; attended Andover Theol. Sem., 1830-32; m. Charlotte Bass, July 21, 1833, 7 children. Ordained to ministry Congregational Ch., 1833; missionary under auspices of Am. Bd. Commrs. for Fgn. Missions, assigned to Nestorian Christians in Northwestern Persia, 1833-69; established missionary center, Urumiah, Persia, 1835; established 1st Lancasterian sch. in Central Asia, Urumiah; 1st to reduce Nestorian vernacular (modern Syriac) to writing; established printing press, 1840; editor Rays of Light, 1840-69; translated New Testament into Syriac, 1846, Old Testament, 1852. Author: Residence of Eight Years in Persia, 1843; Missionary Life in Persia, 1861; Historical Sketch of the Mission to the Nestorians, 1862. Died Chicopee, Mass., Dec. 31, 1869.

PERKINS, Samuel Elliott, jurist; b. Brattleboro, Vt., Dec. 6, 1811; s. John T. and Catherine (Willard) P.; m. Amanda Juliet Pyle; m. 2d, Lavinia M. Pyle; 13 children. Admitted to Ind. bar, 1837; justice Ind. Supreme Ct., 1847-64; prof. law Northwestern Christian (now Butler) U., 1857, Ind. U., 1870-73; judge Marion County (Ind.) Superior Ct., 1872-76. Author: A Digest of the Decisions of the Supreme Court of Indiana, 1858; Pleading and Practice in the Courts of Indiana, 1859. Died Dec. 17, 1879.

PERKINS, Thomas Handasyd, mcht., philanthropist; b. Boston, Dec. 15, 1764; s. James and Elizabeth (Peck) P.; m. Sarah Elliot, Mar. 25, 1788, 7 children. Partner with brothers in merc. firm trading between U.S. and Santo Domingo, 1785-92; partner with brother James in firm J. & T. H. Perkins, Boston, 1792-1822, traded with China, chief partner, 1822-38; mem. Mass. Senate, 8 terms, Mass. Ho. of Reps., 3 terms; presdl. elector from Mass., 1816, 32; diplomatic courier to France for U.S. ministry at London, Eng., 1811-12; col. Mass. Militia; pres. Boston br. of U.S. Bank; contbd. to Mass. Gen. Hosp., Boston Athenaeum, Bunker Hill and Nat. Monument assns., New Eng. (later Perkins) Asylum for Blind. Died Boston, Jan. 11, 1854.

PERLEY, Ira, jurist; b. Boxford, Mass., Nov. 9, 1799; s. Samuel and Phoebe (Dresser) P.; LL.D. (hon.), Dartmouth, 1852; m. Mary Nelson, June 11, 1840. Tutor, Dartmouth, 1823-25, treas., 1830-35; admitted to N.H. bar, 1827; asso. justice N.H. Superior Ct., 1850-52; chief justice Supreme Jud. Ct. N.H., 1855-59, 64-69; mem. N.H. Legislature from Hanover, 1 term, from Concord, 1839-40, 70-71. Died Concord, Feb. 26, 1874.

PERRILL, Augustus Leonard, congressman; b. nr. Moorefield, Va. (now W.Va.), Jan. 20, 1807; attended schs., Madison Twp., O. Taught sch., nr. Circleville, O., later engaged in farming; apptd. dep. sheriff, 1833, sheriff, 1834-37; mem. Ohio Ho. of Reps., 1839-41, 65-67; U.S. Ho. of Reps. (Democrat) from Ohio, 29th Congress, 1845-47; mem. Ohio Senate, 1858-63. Died nr. Circleville, June 2, 1882; buried Forest Cemetery, Circleville.

PERRINE, Henry, botanist; b. Cranburg, N.J., Apr. 5, 1797; s. Peter and Sarah (Rozengrant)

P.; m. Ann Fuller Townsend, Jan. 8, 1822, 3 children. Practiced medicine, Ripley, Ill., 1819-24, Natchez, Miss., 1824-27; U.S. consul at Campeche, Mexico, 1827-37; made bot. collections in Mexico; introduced useful tropical plants to Fla. including henequen and sisal; built nursery, Indian Key, Fla., 1833; received grant of land in Fla. from Congress, 1838. Killed by Seminole Indians, Aug. 7, 1840.

PERROT, Nicholas, explorer; b. France, 1644; m. Marie Madeleine Raclot, 1671, several children. Served with Sulpicians and Jesuit missionaries in Canada; engaged in fur trade with Ottawa Indians in Lake Superior region, 1663; one of 1st French traders to Algonquian Indians, Green Bay, Wis., 1667; interpreter for expdn. which took possession of West for France, 1670-71; led Western tribes in French and Indian expdns. against Iroquois, 1684, 87; commandant of La Baye and its dependencies, 1685-96; explored and claimed regions of upper Mississippi River for France; built Ft. St. Nicholas, 1685, Ft. St. Antoine, 1686; initiated French trade with Sioux, 1686; discovered lead mine in what is now Southwestern Wis., 1690; interpreter at French-Indian peace conf., 1701. Died 1718.

PERRY, Aaron Fyfe, congressman; b. Leicester, Vt., Jan. 1, 1815; attended Yale Law Sch. Admitted to Conn. bar, 1838, Ohio bar, 1840; began practice of law, Columbus, O.; mem. Ohio Ho. of Reps., 1847-48; moved to Cincinnati, O., 1854, practiced law; declined appointment by Pres. Lincoln as asso. justice U.S. Supreme Ct., 1861; del. Republican Nat. Conv., Balt., 1864; mem. U.S. Ho. of Reps. (Rep.) from Ohio, 42d Congress, 1871-72; apptd. chief counsel for U.S. Govt. in Credit Mobiliér case, 1873; mem. bd. of sinking-fund trustees of Cincinnati, 1877-92, pres., 1884-92; became mem. 3d class Mil. Order of Loyal Legion of U.S. (for distinguished civilian services), 1889. Died Cincinnati, Mar. 11, 1893; buried Spring Grove Cemetery, Cincinnati.

PERRY, Benjamin Franklin, gov. S.C.; b. Pendleton, dist., S.C., Nov. 20, 1805; s. Benjamin and Anne (Foster) P.; m. Elizabeth McCall, 1837. Admitted to S.C. bar, 1827; elected to Nullification Conv. of 1832 as Unionist, voted against nullification; became editor Greenville (S.C.) Mountaineer (a Union paper), 1832; mortally wounded Turner Bynum (another editor) in a duel over polit. differences; mem. S.C. Ho. of Reps., 1836-44, S.C. Senate, 1844-46; established So. Patriot (only Union newspaper in S.C.), 1850; elected to Conv. of 1852; mem. Conv. of 1860, Unionist in sentiment but followed his state into Confederacy; Confederate commr., 1862; dist. atty., 1863; dist. judge, 1864; apptd. provisional gov. by Andrew Johnson, 1865; del. Nat. Union Conv., 1866; elected to U.S. Senate, 1865, denied seat. Died Greenville, Dec. 3, 1886.

PERRY, Christopher Raymond, naval officer; b. South Kingstown, R.I., Dec. 4, 1761; s. Freeman and Mercy (Hazard) P.; m. Sarah Wallace Alexander, Aug. 1784, 8 children including Oliver Hazard, Matthew Calbraith, Ann Maria. Served in several Continental privateers during Am. Revolution; present at siege of Charleston (S.C.); served in Trumbull during Trumbull-Watt battle; captured by British, 4 times; capt. in mcht. service, 1784-98; commd. capt. U.S. Navy, 1798; commanded ship General Greene in suppression of pirates of Cuba and escorting mcht. vessels to U.S. during naval war with France; re., 1801; comdt. Charlestown (Mass.) Naval Yard, 1812. Died Newport, R.I., June 1, 1818.

PERRY, Edward Aylesworth, gov. Fla.; b. Richmond, Mass., Mar. 15, 1831; s. Asa and Philura (Aylesworth) P.; attended Yale, 1850-51; m. Wathen Taylor, Feb. 1, 1859, 5 children. Practiced law, Pensacola, Fla., 1857-61, 65-84; commd. capt. 2d Fla. Inf., Confederate Army, 1861, promoted col., brig. gen., 1862; served at battles of Frayser's Farm, Chancellorsville and Wilderness; gov. Fla., 1885-87. Died Kerrville, Tex., Oct. 15, 1889; buried Pensacola.

PERRY, Eli, congressman; b. Cambridge, N.Y., Dec. 25, 1799; attended common schs. Businessman, Albany, N.Y., 1827-52; mem. bd. aldermen Albany, 2 years; mem. N.Y. State Assembly, 1851; mayor Albany, 1851-53, 56-60, 62-66; mem. U.S. Ho. of Reps. (Democrat) from N.Y., 42d-43d congresses, 1871-75. Died Albany, May 17, 1881; buried Albany Rural Cemetery.

PERRY, John Jasiel, congressman, lawyer; b. Portsmouth, N.H., Aug. 2, 1811; attended Me. Wesleyan Sem. Dep. sheriff Oxford County (Me.); mem. Me. Ho. of Reps., 1840, 42-43, 72, clk., 1854; admitted to bar, 1844, began practice of law, Oxford, Me.; mem. Me. Senate, 1846-47; mem. U.S. Ho. of Reps. (Republican) from Me., 34th, 36th congresses, 1855-57, 59-61; mem. Washington (D.C.) Peace Conv., 1861; editor Oxford Democrat, 1860-75, correspondent for other newspapers; mem. Me. Exec. Council, 1866-67; practiced law, Portland, Me., 1875-97. Died Portland, May 2, 1897; buried Evergreen Cemetery.

PERRY, Matthew Calbraith, naval officer; b. Newport, R.I., Apr. 10, 1794; s. Christopher Raymond and Sarah (Alexander) P.; m. Jane Slidell, Dec. 24, 1814, 10 children including Carline Slidell. Commd. midshipman U.S. Navy, 1809, lt., 1813; held 1st command in ship Shark, 1821; exec. officer in ship North Carolina, 1825-26; master comdt., 1826; comdr. ship Brandywine, 1832; 2d officer N.Y. Navy Yard, 1833; mem. bd. examiners preparing 1st course of instrn. for U.S. Naval Acad., Annapolis, Md., 1845; leader in organizing U.S. Naval Lyceum to promote diffusion of knowledge among naval officers, 1833, 1st curator, v.p., 1836, later pres.; commd. capt., 1837, in command ship Fulton; comdt. N.Y. Navy Yard, 1841; in command African Squadron, 1843; 1st comdr. ship Mississippi; 2d officer in command of squadron operating on East coast of Mexico, later comdr.-in-chief; selected to negotiate treaty with Japan (at that time sealed against intercourse with Western countries), 1852, treaty of peace, amity and commerce signed between U.S. and Japan, Mar. 31, 1854. Author: Narrative of the Expedition of an American Squadron to the China Seas and Japan, published by U.S. Govt., 1856. Died N.Y.C., Mar. 4, 1858.

PERRY, Nehemiah, congressman, businessman; b. Ridgefield, Conn., Mar. 30, 1816; ed. Wesleyan Sem., Ridgefield. Clk. in stores, Norwalk, Conn., also N.Y.C.; moved to Newark, N.J., 1836; entered textile mfg. and clothing businesses; mem. N.J. Ho. of Assembly, 1850, 56, speaker, 1856; mem. Common Council, 1852; mem. U.S. Ho. of Reps. (Constl.-Union Party) from N.J., 37th-38th congresses, 1861-65; mayor Newark, 1873. Died Newark, Nov. 1, 1881; buried Mt. Pleasant Cemetery.

PERRY, Nora, author; b. Dudley, Mass., 1831; d. Harvey and Sarah (Benson) Perry; never married. Boston corr. for Chgo. Tribune and Providence (R.I.) Journal; contbr. stories and articles to Harper's Mag., Atlantic Monthly, National Era; stories written primarily for young girls. Author: After the Ball, and Other Poems, 1875; Her Love's Friend, and Other Poems, 1880; The Tragedy of the Unexpected, and Other Stories, 1880; A Book of Love Stories, 1881; For a Woman, a Novel, 1885; New Songs and Ballads, 1887; A Flock of Girls, 1887; The Youngest Miss Lorton, and Other Stories, 1889; Brave Girls, 1889; Lyrics and Legends, 1891; Hope Benham, a Story for Girls, 1894; Cottage Neighbors, 1899; That Little Smith Girl, 1899; May Bartlett's Stepmother, 1900. Died Dudley, May 13. 1896.

PERRY, Oliver Hazard, naval officer; b. South Kingstown, R.I., Aug. 20, 1785; s. Christopher Raymond and Sarah (Alexander) P.; m. Elizabeth Mason, May 5, 1811; 5 children. Apptd. midshipman U.S. Navy, 1799; promoted acting lt., 1803, lt., 1807; commanded schooner Revenge, 1809; master commandant, 1812; in charge Am. fleet on Lake Erie, defeated British in battle, Sept. 9, 1813 (enabled Americans to make a strong claim to N.W. at peace negotiations in Ghent, Belgium); after this battle sent message "we have met the enemy and they are ours"; commended by U.S. Congress, received gold medal; commd. capt., 1813; aide-de-camp to comdr.-in-chief in Battle of Thames; took command ship Java, 1814. Died Angostura, Venezuela, Aug. 23, 1819; buried Port of Spain, Trinidad; reinterred Newport, R.I., 1826.

PERRY, Rufus Lewis, clergyman; b. Smith County, Tenn., Mar. 11, 1834; s. Lewis and Maria P.; grad. Kalamazoo (Mich.) Theol. Sem.; Ph.D. (hon.), Ky. State U., Louisville, 1887; m. Charlotte Handy, 7 children. Escaped from slavery in Tenn., 1852; ordained pastor 2d Baptist Ch., Ann Arbor, Mich., 1861, later pastor St. Catharine's Ch., Ont., Can., Buffalo, N.Y.; founder, pastor Messiah Bapt. Ch., Bklyn., 1887; editor Sunbeam and People's Jour.; co-editor Am. Baptist, 1869-71; joint editor, later editor-in-chief Nat. Monitor, 1872-95; corr. sec. Consol. Am. Bapt. Missionary Conv. of Am. Ednl. Assn. and of Am. Bapt. Free Mission Soc. Author: The Cushite; or the Descendants of Ham as Seen by Ancient Historians, 1893. Died Bklyn., June 18, 1895.

PERRY Stuart, inventor; b. Newport, N.Y., Nov. 2, 1814; grad. Union Coll., 1837; m. Amy Jane Carter, 1837; m. 2d, Jane W. Maxson, 1873; 1 child. In partnership with brother in wholesale dairy products business, Newport, 1840-60; invented internal combustion gas engine, patented, 1844; patented lock, key, and safe bolt, 1857, combination lock, 1858; also invented milk cooler, stereopticon, velocipede, hay tender and improved sawmill machinery. Died Feb. 9, 1890.

PERRY, Thomas Johns, congressman, jurist; b. Cumberland, Md., Feb. 17, 1807; studied law. Admitted to bar, 1828, began practice of law, Cumberland; mem. Md. Ho. of Dels., 1834-36; mem. U.S. Ho. of Reps. (Democrat) from Md., 29th Congress, 1845-47; asso. judge 6th Jud. Dist. of Md., 1851-61, 64-71; del. Md. Constl. Conv., 1867. Died Cumberland, June 27, 1871; buried Rose Hill Cemetery.

PERRY, William, physician, mfr.; b. Norton, Mass., Dec. 20, 1788; s. Nathan and Phebe (Braman) P.; grad. Harvard, 1811, M.D., 1814; m. Abigail Gilman, Apr. 8, 1818, 5 children including Caroline Frances (Perry) Jewett. Practiced medicine, Exeter, N.H., 1814-80; prin. founder 1st N.H. State Insane Asylum, Concord; lectr. Bowdoin Coll. Med. Sch., 1836-37; devised means of using potato starch to replace Brit. gum (expensive product used as sizing agent in mfg. cotton cloth), manufactured starch, 1824-30. Died Jan. 11, 1887.

PERRY, William Stevens, clergyman, coll. pres.; b. Providence, R.I., Jan. 22, 1823; s. Stephen and Katharine (Stevens) P.; grad. Harvard, 1854; attended theol. sem., Va.; m. Sarah Abbott Woods Smith, Jan. 15, 1862. Ordained deacon Protestant Episcopal Ch., 1857, priest, 1858; rector St. Luke's Ch., Nashua, N.H., 1858-61, St. Stephen's Ch., Portland, Me., 1861-63, St. Michael's Ch., Litchfield, Conn., 1864-69, Trinity Ch., Geneva, N.Y., 1869-76; prof. history Hobart Coll., Geneva, 1871-74, pres., 1876; served as either asst. sec. or sec. to Gen. Conv. of Episcopal Ch., 1865-76; apptd. historiographer of Episcopal Ch., 1868; bishop of Ia., 1876-98; founder St. Katharine's Hall for Girls and Kemper Hall for Boys, Davenport, Ia. Author: Historical Collections Relating to the American Colonial Church, 5 vols., 1870-78; The History of the American Episcopal Church, 1587-1883, 2 vols., 1885; The Men and Measures of the Massachusetts Conventions of 1784-85, 1885; A Missionary Apostle, 1887; The Christian Character of George Washington, 1891; The Episcopate in America, 1895; The Alleged "Toryism" of the Clergy of the United States at the Breaking out of the War of the Revolution, 1895; The Faith of the Signers of the Declaration of Independence, 1896. Died May 13, 1898.

PERSICO, E. Luigi, artist; b. Naples, Italy, 1791. Came to Am., 1818; worked in Lancaster, Harrisburg (both Pa.), 1819-20, Phila., 1819-20, 24-25; commd. to execute several pieces of sculpture for U.S. Capitol, Washington, D.C., completed War and Peace, 1834; work exhibited at Boston Athenaeum and Artists' Fund Soc., 1834-55. Died Marseilles, France, 1860.

PERSON, Thomas, state legislator; b. (probably) Brunswick County, Va., Jan. 19, 1733; s. William and Ann P.; m. Johanna Thomas, 1760. Justice of the peace, 1756, 76, sheriff, 1762; mem. N.C. Assembly, 1764, head of Granville delegation in all N.C. provincial congresses from 1774; mem. com. which proposed Halifax Resolution of Apr. 12, 1776 (instructing dels. to Continental Congress to vote for a declaration of independence); mem. com. which drafted bill of rights for N.C.; mem. com. which drew up N.C. Constn. of 1776; elected to N.C. Council, 1775, N.C. Council of Safety, 1776; gen. N.C. Militia, 1776; mem. N.C. Council of State; elected to Continental Congress, 1784, never served; mem. N.C. House of Commons, 1777-86, 88-91, 93-95, 97; mem. N.C. Senate, 1787, 91; chief commr. to settle N.C. accounts with U.S., 1787; del. to Fayetteville (N.C.) Conv., 1789, opposed ratification of U.S. Constn.; apptd. charter trustee N.C. State U., 1789, generous benefactor, 1789-95. Died Franklin County, N.C., Nov. 16, 1800; buried Personton, N.C.

PETER, George, congressman; b. Georgetown, Md. (now D.C.), Sept. 28, 1779; grad. Georgetown Coll. Entered army as 2d lt. 9th Inf., 1799, later transferred to Arty.; organized and commanded 1st light battery of arty in country, 1808; engaged in agriculture, after 1809; served as maj. Volunteers in War of 1812; mem. U.S. Ho. of Reps. (Democrat, filled vacancy) from Md., 14th-15th, 19th congresses, Oct. 7, 1816-19, 25-27; mem. Md. Ho. of Dels., 1819-23; commr. public works of Md., 1855. Died nr. Darnestown, Montgomery County, Md., June 22, 1861; buried Oak Hill Cemetery, Georgetown.

PETER, Hugh, clergyman; b. England, 1598; s. Thomas and Martha (Treffry) Dirkwood (father changed name to Peter); B.A., Trinity Coll., Cambridge, Eng., 1618, M.A., 1622; m. Elizabeth (Cooke) Reade, 1624; m. 2d, Deliverance Sheffield, 1639; 1 dau., Elizabeth (Peter) Barker. Ordained deacon Ch. of Eng., 1621, priest, 1623, left Eng. to preach to English Puritans on Continent, 1829; came to Am., 1635; pastor at Salem, Mass., 1636-41; admitted as freeman of Mass. Bay Colony, 1636; mem. coms. to draft code of laws for Mass. Bay Colony, 1636, 38; a founder Harvard, 1637, overseer, 1640; returned to Eng. to aid Puritan movement and to act as agt. of Mass. Bay Colony, 1641; chaplain to Cromwell's forces during Puritan Revolution. Executed after Royalists returned to power, Charing Cross, London, Eng., Oct. 16, 1660.

PETER, John Frederick, musician; b. Herrndyck, Holland, May 19, 1746; s. John Frederick and Susanna P.; m. Catharine Leinbach. Came to Am., 1769; tchr., ch. organist, accountant, Bethlehem, Pa., 1770-86, 93-1813; dir. Bethlehem Collegium Musicium; directed 1st Am. performance of Haydn's Creation, Bethlehem, 1811; 1st Am. composer of serious music. Died Bethlehem, July 19, 1813.

PETER, Robert, physician, chemist; b. Launceston, Cornwall, Eng., Jan. 21, 1805; s. Robert and Johanna (Dawe) P.; attended Rensselaer Sch. (now Rensselaer Poly. Inst.), Troy, N.Y.; M.D., Transylvania U., 1834; m. Frances Paca Dellam, Oct. 6, 1835, 11 children including Alfred M. Came to U.S., 1817, naturalized, 1826; lectr. chemistry Western U. of Pa., 1830-31; mem. Hesperian Soc., Pitts. Philos. Soc.; prof. chemistry Morrison Coll., Lexington, Ky., 1833-38; editor Transylvania Jour. of Medicine and Asso. Scis., 1837; prof. chemistry and pharmacy med. dept. Transylvania U., Lexington, 1838-57, dean med. faculty, 1847-57; prof. chemistry and toxicology Ky. Sch. Medicine, Louisville, 1850-53; chemist to geol. surveys of Ky., 1854, Ark., Ind.; 1st to note that richness of bluegrass soils of Ky. is caused by high phosphorous content; acting asst. surgeon in charge of U.S. mil. hosps., Lexington, 1861-65; prof. chemistry and exptl. philosophy Agrl. and Mech. Coll. of Ky. U., 1865-78; asst. editor Farmer's Home Jour., 1867-68; prof. chemistry Ky. Agrl. and Mech. Coll. (now separate instns.), 1878-87, prof. emeritus, 1887-94. Author: Chemical Examination of the Urinary Calcali in the Museum of the Medical Department of Transylvania University, 1846. Died Winton, Ky., Apr. 26, 1894.

PETER, Sarah Worthington King, philanthropist; b. Chillicothe, O., May 10, 1800; d. Thomas and Eleanor (Van Swearingen) Worthington; m. Edward King, 1816; m. 2d, William Peter, Oct. 1844; 2 children. Helped found 1st Episcopal ch., Chillicothe, 1820; a founder Protestant Orphan Asylum, Cincinnati; organized Phila. Sch. of Design for Women; financed constrn. of Quaker's Rosina House for Magdalens, Phila.; founded Women's Museum Assn., Cincinnati; became Roman Catholic, 1855; brought Sisters of Good Shepherd to Cincinnati, 1857, Sisters of Mercy, 1857, Franciscan Sisters, 1858, Sisters of Poor, 1869; founded hosps., Cincinnati, 1859, Covington, Ky., 1861; worked in U.S. war prisons during Civil War. Died Cincinnati, Feb. 6, 1877; buried St. Joseph's Cemetery, Cincinnati.

PETERS, Absalom, clergyman; b. Wentworth, N. H., Sept. 19, 1793; s. Absalom and Mary (Rogers) P.; grad. Dartmouth, 1816, Princeton Theol. Sem., 1819; m. Harriet Hinckley Hatch, Oct. 25, 1819, 7 children. Pastor, 1st Congregational Ch., Bennington, Vt., 1819-25; ordained pastor by Troy Presbytery, 1820; sec. United Missionary Soc. of N.Y., 1825-26, corr. sec., 1826-37; editor Home Missionary and Pastor's Jour., 1828-36; sided with New Sch. in schism of Presbyn. Ch.; a founder Union Theol. Sem., 1836, dir., 1836-42, financial agt., prof. extraordinary homiletics, pastoral theology and ch. govt., 1842-44; editor Am. Bibl. Repository, 1838-41; founder, editor Am. Eclectic, 1841-42; pastor 1st Congl. Ch., Williamstown, Mass., 1844-57; trustee Williams Coll., 1845-69; editor Am. Jour. of Edn. and Coll. Review, 1856-69. Author: Sprinkling the Only Mode of Baptism and the Scripture Warrant for Infant Baptism, 1848; Life and Time, a Birthday Memorial of Seventy Years, 1866. Died N.Y.C., May 18, 1869.

PETERS, Christian Henry Frederick, astronomer; b. Coldenbüttel, Schleswig, Germany, Sept. 19, 1813; Ph.D., U. Berlin (Germany), 1836. With expdn. surveying Mt. Etna, 1838-43; dir. trigonometrical survey in Sicily, 1843-48; came to U.S., 1854; with U.S. Coast Survey, 1854-58; dir. observatory Hamilton Coll., 1858-67, Litchfield prof. astronomy, dir. Litchfield Observatory, 1867-90; led expdn. to observe solar eclipse, Des Moines, Ia., 1869; led U.S. expdn. to New Zealand to observe transit of Venus, 1874; described apparent division of sun spots by bridges of luminous gas; discovered 48 new asteroids, 2 comets, 1846, 57; revised Ptolemy's Almagest, catalogue stars' positions; mem. Nat. Acad. Scis.; fgn. asso. Royal Astron. Soc. Author: Celestial Charts, 1882; Heliographic Positions of Sun Spots, Observed at Hamilton College from 1860 to 1870 (edited by E. B. Frost), published 1907; articles "Contributions to the Atmospherology of the Sun" in Proceedings of A.A.A.S., Vol. IX, 1856, "Corrigenda in Various Star Catalogues" in Memoirs of Nat. Acad. Sciences, Vol. III, part 2, 1886. Died July 19, 1890.

PETERS, John Charles, physician; b. N.Y.C., July 6, 1819; m. Georgina Snelling, May 16, 1849. Licensed to practice medicine, 1842; practiced medicine, N.Y.C., 1842-93; founder N.Y. Path. Soc., 1844, Med. Library and Jour. Soc.; joint editor North Am. Jour. of Homeopathy, 1855-61; pres. New York County Med. Soc., 1866-67. Author: The Science and Art or the Principles and Practice of Medicine, 4 parts, 1858-59; A Review of Some of the Late Reforms in Pathology and Therapeutics, 1860. Died Williston, L.I., N.Y., Oct. 21, 1893.

PETERS, Richard, clergyman; b. Liverpool, Eng., 1704; s. Ralph and Esther (Preeson) P.; studied law Inner Temple, London, Eng.; D.D. (hon.), Oxford (Eng.) U., 1770; m. 2d, Miss Stanley. Ordained deacon Ch. of Eng., 1730, priest, 1731; came to Am., 1735; asst. rector Christ Ch., Phila., 1736-37, rector, 1762-75; sec. land office Province of Pa., 1737-60; admitted to Phila. bar, 1737; provincial sec., pvt. sec. for proprietaries and clk. of council, 1743-62; mem. Pa. Council, 1749-76; made frequent missionary trips to Indians; rector St. Peter's Ch., Phila., 1762-75; trustee Phila. Acad., pres. bd. trustees, 1756-64; a founder Library Co. of Phila., Pa. Hosp. Author: A Sermon on Education, 1751; A Sermon Preached in the New Lutheran Church of Zion, in the City of Philadelphia, 1769, 1769. Died Phila., July 10, 1776.

PETERS, Richard, Continental congressman, jurist, agriculturist; b. Phila., June 22, 1743; s. William and Mary (Breintnall) P.; grad. Coll. of Phila. (now U. Pa.), 1761; studied law; m. Sarah Robinson, Aug. 1776, 6 children. Admitted to bar, 1763; commr. Indian Conf., Ft. Stanwix, 1768; register of admiralty, Phila., 1771-76; commd. capt. Pa. Militia, 1775; sec. bd. war Continental Congress, 1776-81, mem. from Pa., 1782-83; mem. Pa. Assembly, 1787-90, speaker, 1788-90; trustee U. Pa., 1788-91; speaker Pa. Senate, 1791-92; judge U.S. Dist. Ct. for Pa., 1792-1828; 1st pres. Phila. Soc. for Promotion of Agr.; published several volumes and more than 100 papers on agr.; specialist in maritime law; published Admiralty Decisions in the District Court of the United States for the Pennsylvania District, 1780-1807; Died Phila., Aug. 22, 1828; buried St. Peter's Churchyard, Phila.

PETERS, Richard, railroad exec.; b. Germantown, Pa., Nov. 10, 1810; s. Ralph and Catherine (Conyngham) P.; m. Mary Jane Thompson, Feb. 18, 1848, 9 children. Asst. engr. in location and constrn. of Ga. R.R., 1835-37, supt., 1837-46; established stage line from Madison (Ga.) to Montgomery (Ala.), 1844, later ran between Montgomery and Mobile, Ala., circa 1847-61; bought large plantation, Gordon County, Ga., 1847, imported horses, cattle and goats, promoted sorghum crops and silk culture; built largest flour mill in Ga., 1856; pres. Ga. Western R.R., 1860-65; dir. Atlanta and West Point R.R., 1865-89, Western and Atlantic Ry., 1870-89; established street ry., Atlanta, Ga., 1871; mem. Atlanta City Council; commr. Gordon County. Died Atlanta, Feb. 6, 1889.

PETERS, Samuel Andrew, clergyman; b. Hebron, Conn., Nov. 31, 1735; s. John and Mary (Marks) P.; B.A., Yale, 1757, M.A., 1760; m. Hannah Owen, Feb. 14, 1760; m. 2d, Abigail Gilbert, June 25, 1769; m. 3d, Mary Birdseye, Apr. 21, 1773; at least 2 children. Ordained deacon and priest Anglican Ch., 1759; rector Anglican Ch., Hebron, 1760-74, preached against Revolutionary activities; fled to Eng. after 2 attacks by mobs of Sons of Liberty, 1774; elected bishop of Vt., 1794, not allowed to take office because Parliament had prohibited Archibishop of Canterbury from consecrating Am. bishops; returned to U.S. as land agt. for heirs of Jonathan Carver, 1805. Author: A General History of Connecticut, 1781; A Letter to the Rev. John Tyler, A.M.; Concerning the Possibility of Eternal Punishments, and the Improbability of Universal Salvation; A History of the Reverend Hugh Peters, A.M., 1807. Died N.Y.C., Apr. 19, 1826; buried Hebron.

PETERS, William Cumming, musician; b. Woodbury, Devonshire, Eng., Mar. 10, 1805. Taught music, Pitts., 1825-28; established music store, Louisville, Ky., 1829, opened branch in Cincinnati, 1839, Balt., 1849; edited the Olio (musical mag.), Balt., 1849-50; published 3 songs by Stephen Foster, "Susanna," "Louisiana Belle," "Old Uncle Ned," from which he made great profits (Foster received almost nothing). Author: "Sweet Memories of Thee," 1839; "Kind, Kind and Gentle is She," 1840; "Citizens Guards' March," 1841; Peters' Catholic Harmonist, 1848; Eclectic Piano Instructor, 1855; Catholic Harp, 1862. Died Cincinnati, Apr. 20, 1866.

PETERSON, Charles Jacobs, journalist; b. Phila., July 20, 1819; s. Thomas P. and Elizabeth (Jacobs) P.; attended U. Pa.; m. Sarah Powell Howard, 1 child. Editor, Atkinson's Casket (later Graham's Mag.), 1839-40; editor, co-publisher Saturday Evening Post, 1840-43; founder, editor Lady's World (name changed to Ladies' Nat. Mag. 1843, to Peterson's Mag. 1848), 1840-87; also mem. editorial staffs Saturday Gazette, Phila. Bulletin, Public Ledger. Author: The Military Heroes of the Revolution, with a Narrative of the War of Independence, 1848; Grace Dudley, or Arnold at Saratoga, 1849; The Naval Heroes of the United States, 1850; A History of the U.S. Navy, 1852; Kate Aylesford, a Story of the Refugees, 1855; The American Navy, Being an Authentic History, 1856; Mabel, or Darkness and Dawn, 1857; The Old Stone Mansion, 1859. Died Phila., Mar. 4, 1887.

PETERSON, Henry, journalist; b. Phila., Dec. 7, 1818; s. George and Jane (Evans) P.; m. Sarah Webb, Oct. 28, 1842. Editor, Saturday Evening Post, 1846-74, partner in ownership (with Edmund Deacon) 1848-73; also publisher The Lady's Friend. Author (poetry) Poems, 1863, The Modern Job, 1869, Fairmount, 1874, Poems: Second Series, 1883, Columbus, 1893; (dramatic works) Helen, or One Hundred Years Ago, 1876, Caesar: a Dramatic Study, 1879; (novels) Pemberton, 1873, Confessions of a Minister, 1874, Bessie's Lovers, 1877. Died Germantown, Pa., Oct. 10, 1891.

PETERSON, Robert, publisher, editor; b. Phila., Nov. 12, 1815; M.D., U. Pa., 1862; m. Hannah Mary Bouvier; m. 2d, Blanche Gottschalk, 1872; m. 3d, Clara, 1879. Admitted to Pa. bar, 1843; a founder Childs & Peterson, publishing house; editor Bacon's Abridgement of the Law, 1850, Familiar Science, 1850. Author: The Roman Catholic Church, not the Only True Church; not an Infallible Church, 1869. Translator: Notes of a Pianist (Gottschalk), 1881. Died Asbury Park, N.J., Oct. 30, 1874.

PETIGRU, James Louis, legislator; b. Abbeville Dist., S.C., May 10, 1789; s. William and Louise (Gilbert) Pettigrew; A.B., S.C. Coll., 1809; m. Jane Postell, Aug. 17, 1816. Admitted to bar, 1812; elected solicitor Abbeville County, S.C., 1816; atty. gen. S.C., 1822; unsuccessful Union candidate for S.C. Senate, 1830, elected to fill vacancy in lower house, 1830, became leader of anti-nullificationists; U.S. dist. atty., 2 years; S.C. code commr., 1859-63. Died Charleston, S.C., Mar. 9, 1863.

PETRIE, George, congressman; b. Little Falls, N.Y., Sept. 8, 1793; attended common schs. Mem. U.S. Ho. of Reps. (Republican) from N.Y., 30th Congress, 1847-49; with Post Office Dept., Washington, D.C., 1869-75. Died Little Falls, May 8, 1879; buried Church Street Cemetery.

PETRIKIN, David, congressman, physician; b. Bellefonte, Centre County, Pa., Dec. 1, 1788; studied medicine. Practiced medicine, Danville, Pa.; served as surgeon 2d Regt., Pa. Riflemen during War of 1812; built and operated woolen mill, after War of 1812; elected prothonotary Columbia County (Pa.), 1821; mem. Pa. Ho. of Reps.; postmaster Danville, 1834-37; mem. U. S. Ho. of Reps. (Democrat) from Pa., 25th-26th congresses, 1837-41. Died Catawissa, Columbia County, Pa., Mar. 1, 1847; buried Petrikin Cemetery (later converted into meml. park), Danville.

PETTIGREW, Charles, clergyman; b. Chambersburg, Pa., Mar. 31, 1744; s. James and Mary (Cochrane) P.; m. Mary Blount, Oct. 28, 1778; m. 2d, Mary Lockhart, June 12, 1794; 2 children including Ebenezer. Ordained deacon Protestant Episcopal Ch., 1774, priest, 1775; rector St. Paul's Ch., Edenton, N.C., 1776-1807; reestablished orgn. of Episcopal Ch. in N.C. after Revolutionary War; called Gen. Conv., 1792; 1st bishop-elect Episcopal Ch. in N.C., 1795 (never consecrated); a founder U. of N.C., 1789, trustee, 1790-93. Died "Bonarva," Tyrrell County, N.C., Apr. 7, 1807.

PETTIGREW, Ebenezer, congressman; b. nr. Plymouth, Tyrrell County, N.C., Mar. 10, 1783; attended U. N.C. at Chapel Hill. Became a planter; mem. N.C. Senate, 1809-10; mem. U.S. Ho. of Reps. (Whig) from N.C., 24th Congress, 1835-37. Died Magnolia plantation, Tyrrell County, July 8, 1848; buried family cemetery.

PETTIGREW, James Johnston, lawyer, army officer; b. "Bonarva," Tyrell County, N.C., July 4, 1828; s. Ebenezer and Ann (Shepard) P.; grad. U. N.C., 1847. Asst. prof. U.S. Naval Observatory, Washington, D.C., 1847-49; practiced law, Charleston, South Carolina, 1850-61; mem. S.C. Gen. Assembly, 1856; col. 1st Regt. of Charleston Rifles; commd. col. 12th Regt., Hamptons Legion, Confederate Army, 1861, promoted brig. gen., 1861; served in Peninsular Campaign, battles at Blount's Creek and Gettysburg. Mortally wounded during retreat from Gettysburg, died Raleigh, N.C., July 17, 1863; buried Raleigh, reinterred "Bonarva," 1866.

PETTIS, Spencer Darwin, congressman, lawyer; b. Culpeper County, Va., 1802; studied law. Admitted to bar, circa 1824, began practice of law, Fayette, Mo.; held various local offices; sec. of state, 1826-28; mem. U.S. Ho. of Reps. (Democrat) from Mo., 21st-22d congresses, 1829-31; duelled with Maj. Thomas Biddle as result of quarrel regarding U.S. bank issue in campaign of 1830, both fell mortally wounded. Died St. Louis on day following duel, Aug. 28, 1831; buried Old City Cemetery, St. Louis.

PETTIT, Charles, Continental congressman, businessman; b. nr. Amwell, Hunterdon County,

N.J., 1736; s. John Pettit; pvt. classical edn.; m. Sarah Reed, Apr. 5, 1758, 4 children including Elizabeth, Theodosia. Apptd. a N.J. provincial surrogate, 1767; surrogate, keeper and register of records Province of N.J., 1769-78; clk. N.J. Gov.'s Council, also clk. N.J. Supreme Ct., 1769-71; admitted to N.J. bar as atty., 1770, as counselor, 1773; dep. sec. Province of N.J.; lt. col. N.J. Militia, aide to Gov. William Franklin, 1771; 1st sec. of state N.J., 1776-78; col., aide to Gov. William Livingston, 1776; asst. q.m. gen. (under Gen. Nathanael Greene) Continental Army, 1778-81; became importer in Phila.; mem. Pa. Assembly, 1783-84; chmn. com. of mchts. to promote nat. commerce, 1784; mem. Continental Congress, 1785-87; recognized fiscal expert, established Pa.'s funding system; delegated to present Pa.'s Revolutionary War claims against fed. govt. to Congress, 1790- 91; original dir. Ins. Co. of N.Am., pres., 1796-98, 99-1806; trustee U. Pa., 1791-1802; mem. Am. Philos. Soc. Died Phila., Sept. 4, 1806.

PETTIT, John, senator, congressman; b. Sackets Harbor, N.Y., June 24, 1807; studied law. Admitted to bar, 1831; began practice of law, LaFayette, Ind., 1838; mem. Ind. Ho. of Reps., 1838-39; U.S. dist. atty., 1839-43; mem. U.S. Ho. of Reps. (Democrat) from Ind., 28th-30th congresses, 1843-49; del. Ind. Constl. Conv., 1850; Dem. presdl. elector, 1852; mem. U.S. Senate (filled vacancy) from Ind., Jan. 11, 1853-55; chief justice U.S. Cts. in Kan. Territory, 1859-61; judge Ind. Supreme Ct., 1870-77. Died LaFayette, Jan. 17, 1877; buried Greenbush Cemetery.

PETTIT, John Upfold, congressman, lawyer; b. Fabius, Onondaga County, N.Y., Sept. 11, 1820; attended Hamilton Coll., Clinton, N.Y.; grad. Union Coll., Schenectady, N.Y., 1839; studied law. Admitted to bar, 1841, began practice of law, Wabash, Ind.; Am. consul to Maranham, Brazil, 1850-53; mem. U.S. Ho. of Reps. (Republican) from Ind., 34th-36th congresses, 1855-61; speaker Ind. Ho. of Reps., 1865; judge 27th Jud. Dist. of Ind., 1872-80. Died Wabash, Mar. 21, 1881; buried Falls Cemetery.

PETTIT, Thomas McKean, jurist; b. Phila., Dec. 26, 1797; s. Andrew and Elizabeth (McKean) P.; grad. U. Pa., 1815; studied law under Jared Ingersoll, Phila.; m. Sarah Barry Dale, Feb. 7, 1828, 7 children. Admitted to Pa. bar, 1818, began practice of law, Phila.; sec. Phila. Bd. of Public Edn., 1819, 21; city solicitor, 1820-23; dep. atty. gen. Pa., 1824-30; mem. Pa. Ho. of Reps., 1830; mem. Phil. Select Council, 1831; asso. judge Pa. Dist. Ct. for City and County of Phila., 1833-35, presiding judge, 1835-45; mem. bd. visitors U.S. Mil. Acad., 1839; U.S. dist. atty. for Eastern Pa. Dist., 1845-49; supt. U.S. Mint at Phila., Mar.-May, 1853; mem. Hist. Soc. of Pa. Died Phila., May 30, 1853.

PETTY, William (Lord Shelburne, 1st marquis Lansdowne), Brit. govt. ofcl.; b. Dublin, Ireland, May 20, 1737; s. Hon. John Fitzmaurice (assumed name Petty 1751); attended Christ Ch., Oxford (Eng.) U., 1754-55; m. Lady Sophia Carteret, Feb. 3, 1765; m. 2d, Lady Louisa Fitzpatrick, July 9, 1779. Served with 20th Regt. of Foot in expdn. to Rochefort, 1757-58; served with 3d Regt. Foot Guards, 1758-60; mem. Ho. of Commons from High Wycombe, 1760-62; pres. Bd. of Trade in Grenville's cabinet, 1763-66; sec. of state in William Pitt's cabinet, 1766-68, resigned because his conciliatory policies toward Am. colonies were not supported by King and Parliament; head of ministry of King's friends, 1782-83; concluded Treaty of Paris, which granted independence to Am., 1783; driven from office by coalition of Tories under Lord North and Whigs under Charles James Fox, 1783; created marquis Lansdowne, 1784. Died 1805.

PEYTON, Balie, congressman, diplomat; b. nr. Gallatin, Tenn., Nov. 26, 1803; studied law. Admitted to bar, began practice of law, Gallatin, 1824; mem. U.S. Ho. of Reps. (Whig) from Tenn., 23d-24th congresses, 1833-37; U.S. atty. for Eastern Dist. La., New Orleans, 1841-45; served as aide-de-camp on Gen. W. J. Worth's staff during Mexican War, voted a sword by La. Legislature for gallantry; U.S. minister to Chile (apptd. by Pres. Taylor), 1849-53; moved to San Francisco, 1853, continued practice of law; pros. atty. San Francisco, 1853-59; resumed practice of law, Gallatin, 1859; Constl.-Union ticket presdl. elector, 1860; mem. Tenn. Senate, 1869-70. Died on his farm nr. Gallatin, Aug. 1878; buried family burying ground.

PEYTON, John Lewis, lawyer; b. nr. Staunton, Va., Sept. 15, 1824; s. John Howe and Anne (Lewis) P.; grad. U. Va., 1844; m. Henrietta E. Washington, Dec. 17, 1855, 1 child. Practiced law, Staunton, 1844-52, 56-61; sent by Pres. Willard Fillmore on secret mission to Eng., France and Austria, 1852; European agt. for State of N.C., 1861-65; mem. Royal Geog. Soc.; returned to U.S., 1876. Author: A Statistical View of the State of Illinois, 1855; The American Crisis; or Pages from the Notebook of a State Agent during the Civil War in America, 2 vols., 1867; Over the Alleghanies and Across the Prairies, 1869; Memoir of William Madison Peyton, 1873; History of Augusta County, Virginia, 1882; Rambling Reminiscenses of a Residence Abroad, 1888; Memoirs of John Howe Payton, 1894. Died "Steephill," nr. Staunton, May 21, 1896.

PEYTON, Joseph Hopkins, congressman, physician; b. nr. Gallatin, Tenn., May 20, 1808; grad. coll., 1837; studied medicine. Practiced medicine; held various local offices; mem. Tenn. Senate, 1840; mem. U.S. Ho. of Reps. (Whig) from Tenn., 28th-29th congresses, 1843-45. Died nr. Gallatin, Nov. 11, 1845; buried family burying ground nr. Gallatin.

PEYTON, Samuel Oldham, congressman, physician; b. Bullitt County, Ky., Jan. 8, 1804; grad. med. dept. Transylvania U., Lexington, Ky., 1827. Began practice of medicine, Hartford, Ky.; mem. Ky. Ho. of Reps., 1835; mem. U.S. Ho. of Reps. (Democrat) from Ky., 30th, 35th-36th congresses, 1847-49, 57-61. Died Hartford, Jan. 4, 1870; buried Oakwood Cemetery.

PFEIFFER, Carl, architect; b. Germany, 1838; studied architecture, engring, Germany. Came to U. S., 1863, began practice architecture, N.Y.C.; architect of N.J. State Hdqrs. of Phila. Centennial Expn., 1876; designed several noteworthy chs., including Fifth Ave. Presbyn. Ch.; other works include: Roosevelt Hosp. and Asylum for Colored Children, N.Y.C.; many residences in Washington Heights dist.; Yorkshire Apts. (last bldg. constructed from his plans); fellow A.I.A., sec., 1871-73. Died Apr. 25, 1888.

PHELAN, James, businessman; b. Queen's (now Leix) County, Ireland, Apr. 23, 1824; m. Alice Kelly, May 12, 1859, 3 children including James Duval. Owner gen. merchandising bus., N.Y.C., until 1848; went as mcht. to San Francisco, 1849; partner (with brother Michael) in firm J. & M. Phelan, 1849-58, expanded activities to include trade in liquor, grain, wool, real estate; obtained charter for 1st Nat. Gold Bank, San Francisco (1st bank in Cal.), 1870, 1st pres., later dir.; built Phelan Bldg., San Francisco, 1881-82; a founder Firemen's Fund Ins. Co., Western Fire & Marine Ins. Co., Mutual Savs. Bank (San Francisco); v.p. Am. Contracting and Dredging Co. (for dredging French Panama Canal). Died San Francisco, Dec. 23, 1892; buried Holy Cross Cemetery, San Mateo County, Cal.

PHELAN, James, congressman; b. Aberdeen, Miss., Dec. 7, 1856; s. James and Eliza Jones (Moore) P.; Ph.D., Leipzig, 1878; m. Mary Early, 3 children. Became owner Memphis (Tenn.) Avalanche, 1881; admitted to Tenn. bar, 1881; mem. U.S. Ho. of Reps. (Democrat) from Tenn., 50th-51st congresses, 1887-91. Author: History of Tennessee, 1888. Died Nassau, New Providence, Bahama Islands, Jan. 20, 1891; buried Memphis.

PHELPS, Almira Hart Lincoln, educator; b. Berlin, Conn., July 15, 1793; d. Samuel and Lydia (Hinsdale) Hart; m. Simeon Lincoln, 1817; m. 2d, John Phelps, 1831; 5 children including Charles E. Phelps. Acting prin. Troy (N.Y.) Female Sem., 1823-31; prin. West Chester (Pa.) Young Ladies' Sem., 1838; later taught at Rahway, N.J.; tchr. Patapsco Female Inst., Ellicott City, Md., 1841-56; mem. A.A.A.S., Md. Acad. of Sci. Author: Familiar Lectures on Botany, 1829; Dictionary of Chemistry (translated from French of L. N. Vauguelin), 1830; Caroline Westerly, 1833; Lectures to Young Ladies, 1833; Botany for Beginners, 1833; Geology for Beginners, 1834; Chemistry for Beginners, 1834; Natural Philosophy for Beginners, 1836; Lectures on Natural Philosophy, 1836; Lectures on Chemistry, 1837; Christian Households, 1858; Hours With My Pupils, 1859; Our Country in its Relation to Past, Present, and Future, 1864. Died Balt., July 15, 1884.

PHELPS, Anson Greene, mcht., philanthropist: b. Simsbury, Conn., Mar. 24, 1781; s. Thomas and Dorothy (Woodbridge) P.; m. Olivia Eggleston, Oct. 26, 1806, 8 children. Began career as saddle mfr.; asso. of Elisha Peck in metals merchandising and importing firm Phelps, Peck, and Co., 1812-28; asso. of William Earl Dodge in copper mfg. and mining firm Phelps, Dodge, & Co., 1832-53; dir. Ansonia Mfg. Co. (later called Ansonia Brass and Copper Co.); mining and factory town of Ansonia (Conn.) named in his honor; contributed materially to American Bible Society, American Bd. Commrs. for Fgn. Missions, Am. Home Missionary Soc., N.Y. Inst. for Edn. of Blind, Colonization Soc. of State of Conn. Died N.Y.C., Nov. 30, 1853.

PHELPS, Austin, clergyman; b. West Brookfield, Mass., Jan. 7, 1820; s. Eliakim and Sarah (Adams) P.; grad. U. Pa., 1837; attended Union Theol. Sem., Yale Divinity Sch.; m. Elizabeth Stuart, Sept. 1842; m. 2d, Mary Stuart, Apr. 1854; m. 3d, Mary A. Johnson, June 1858; 3 children including Elizabeth Stuart Phelps Ward. Licensed to preach by 3d Presbytery of Phila., 1840; pastor Pine Street Congregational Ch., Boston, 1842-48; prof. sacred rhetoric and homiletics Andover Theol. Sem., 1848-79, chmn. faculty, 1869-79, prof. emeritus, 1879-90. Author: (with E. A. Park and Lowell Mason) The Sabbath Hymn Book; for the Service of Song in the House of the Lord, 1858; (with E. A. Park and D. L. Furber) Hymns and Choirs, 1860; The Still Hour; or Communion with God, 1860; The New Birth, or the Work of the Holy Spirit, 1867; Sabbath Hours, 1875; The Theory of Preaching; Lectures on Homiletics, 1881; Men and Books; or Studies in Homiletics, 1882; My Study and Other Essays, 1886; My Notebook; Fragmentary Studies in Theology and Subjects Adjacent Thereto, 1891; Rhetoric; Its Theory and Practise, 1895. Died Bar Harbor, Me., Oct. 13, 1890.

PHELPS, Darwin, congressman; b. East Granby, Conn., Apr. 17, 1807; attended Western U., Pitts.; studied law, Pitts. Admitted to bar, began practice of law, Kittanning, Pa., 1835; mem. bd. trustees Kittanning Acad.; member town council, 1841, 48, burgess, 1844-45, 49, 52, 55, 58-59, 61; Whig presdl. elector, 1852; del. Republican Nat. Conv., Chgo., 1860; commd. maj. 22d Regt., Pa. Volunteer Militia, 1862; mem. Pa. Ho. of Reps., 1865; mem. U.S. Ho. of Reps. (Rep.) from Pa., 41st Congress, 1869-71. Died Kittanning, Dec. 14, 1879; buried Kittanning Cemetery.

PHELPS, Elisha, congressman, lawyer; b. Simsbury, Conn., Nov. 16, 1779; grad. Yale, 1800, Litchfield (Conn.) Law Sch.; at least 1 son, John Smith Phelps. Admitted to bar, 1803, began practice of law, Simsbury; mem. Conn. Ho. of Reps., 1807, 12, 14-18, 21, 29, 35, speaker, 1821, 29; mem. U.S. Ho. of Reps. (Democrat) from Conn., 16th, 19th-20th congresses, 1819-21, 25-29; mem. Conn. Senate, 1822-24; apptd. commr. to revise and codify Conn. laws, 1835. Died Simsbury, Apr. 6, 1847; buried Hop Meadow Cemetery.

PHELPS, Guy Rowland, ins. co. exec.; b. Simsbury, Conn., Apr.1, 1802; s. Noah Amherst and Charlotte (Wilcox) P.; grad. Med. Instn. of Yale, 1825; m. Hannah Latimer, Mar. 20, 1833, 4 children. Wrote charter for Conn. Mut. Life Ins. Co. (fought through 2 legislative sessions to have it granted, 1846), sec. of co., 1846-66, pres., 1866-69; did much to popularize system of mutual type insurance; mem. city council, 1846-47, alderman, 1856-59. Died Mar. 18, 1869.

PHELPS, James, congressman, lawyer; b. Colebrook, Conn., Jan. 12, 1822; s. Lancelot Phelps; attended Trinity Coll., Hartford, Conn., also law dept. Yale. Admitted to bar, 1845, began practice of law, Essex, Conn.; mem. Conn. Ho. of Reps., 1853-54, 56, Conn. Senate, 1858-59; judge Conn. Superior Ct., 1867-73, 85-92, Conn. Supreme Ct. of Errors, 1873-75; mem. U.S. Ho. of Reps. (Democrat) from Conn., 44th-47th congresses, 1875-83; engaged in banking; del. to various state convs. Died Essex, Conn., Jan. 15, 1900; buried River View Cemetery.

PHELPS, John Smith, gov. Mo., congressman, army officer; b. Simsbury, Conn., Dec. 22, 1814; s. Elisha and Lucy (Smith) P.; A.B., Washington (now Trinity Coll.), Hartford, Conn., 1859; m. Mary Whitney, Apr. 30, 1837, 5 children. Admitted to Mo. bar, 1835; mem. Mo. Ho. of Reps., 1837, 40; mem. U.S. Ho. of Reps. (Democrat) from Mo., 29th-37th congresses, 1845-63; enlisted as pvt. Capt. Coleman's Mo. Inf., later organized Phelps Regt., during Civil War; promoted lt. col., 1861, col., 1861; apptd. mil. gov. Ark. by Pres. Lincoln, 1862; resumed law practice after Civil War; gov. Mo., 1877-81; again resumed law practice. Died St. Louis, Nov. 20, 1886; buried Hazelwood Cemetery, Springfield, Mo.

PHELPS, Lancelot, congressman; b. Windsor, Conn., Nov. 9, 1784; attended common schs.; studied medicine, at least 1 son, James. Practiced medicine, Colebrook, Conn.; farmer and mcht., Hitchcockville (now Riverton), Conn., for a time; held various local offices; mem. Conn. Ho. of Reps., 1817, 19-21, 24, 27-28, 30; mem. U.S. Ho. of Reps. (Democrat) from Conn., 24th-25th congresses, 1835-39. Died Colebrook, Sept. 1, 1866; buried Center Cemetery, Winsted, Conn.

PHELPS, Oliver, congressman; b. Poquonock, Conn., Oct. 21, 1749; s. Thomas and Ann (Brown) P.; m. Mary Seymour, Dec. 16, 1773; children—Oliver Leicester, Mary. In merc. bus., Granville, Mass., 1770-75; Mass. supt. of army supply purchases, 1777-81; mem. Mass. Gen. Ct., 1778-80; mem. Mass. Constl. Conv., 1779-80; mem. Mass. Senate, 1785, Mass. Gov.'s Council, 1786; went heavily into debt when land speculation schemes in Western Mass., lower Mississippi Valley and Western Reserve failed; mem. U.S. Ho. of Reps. from Mass., 8th Congress, 1803-05. Died Canandaigua, Mass., Feb. 21, 1809.

PHELPS, Samuel Shethar, senator; b. Litchfield, Conn., May 13, 1793; grad. Yale, 1811; studied law. Admitted to bar, began practice of law, Middlebury, Vt., 1812; served as paymaster in War of 1812; mem. Vt. Ho. of Reps., 1821-32; judge Vt. Supreme Ct., 1832-38; mem. Vt. Senate, 1838-39; mem. U.S. Senate (Whig) from Vt., 1839-51, (filled vacancy), Jan. 17, 1853-Mar. 16, 1854. Died Middlebury, Mar. 25, 1855; buried West Cemetery.

PHELPS, Timothy Guy, congressman, businessman; b. Chenango County, N.Y., Dec. 20, 1824; studied law. Engaged in business, N.Y.C.; moved to San Francisco, 1849; engaged in mining, Tuolumne County; returned to San Francisco; entered real estate business, 1853; mem. Cal. Assemly, 1855-57, Cal. Senate, 1858-61; unsuccessful candidate for gov. Cal., 1861, 75; mem. U.S. Ho. of Reps. (Republican) from Cal., 37th Congress, 1861-63; collector of customs Port of San Francisco, 1870-72, 90-93; engaged in agriculture; moved to San Mateo County, Cal.; regent U. Cal. at Berkeley, 1880-99; chmn. bd. regents Lick Observatory, 19 years. Died nr. San Carlos, Cal., June 11, 1899; buried Cypress Lawn Meml. Park Cemetery, Lawndale, San Mateo County.

PHELPS, William Wallace, congressman, lawyer; b. Oakland County, Mich., June 1, 1826; grad. U. Mich. at Ann Arbor, 1846; studied law. Admitted to bar, 1848, began practice of law; register U.S. Land Office, Red Wing, Minn.; mem. U.S. Ho. of Reps. (Democrat) from Minn., 35th Congress, May 11, 1858-59. Died Spring Lake, Ottawa County, Mich., Aug. 3, 1873; buried Oakwood Cemetery, Red Wing, Minn.

PHELPS, William Walter, congressman, diplomat; b. Dandoff, Pa., Aug. 24, 1839; s. John Jay and Rachel (Phinney) P.; grad. Yale, 1860; LL.B., Sch. Law, Columbia, 1863; m. Ellen Maria Sheffield, June 26, 1860, 3 children. Legal rep. numerous corps., N.Y.C.; moved to Englewood, N.J., 1869; mem. U.S. Ho. of Reps. (Republican) from N.J., 43d, 48th-50th congresses, 1873-75, 83-89; del. Rep. Nat. Conv., 1880, 84; apptd. U.S. minister to Austria-Hungary, 1881, to Germany, 1889; commr. Internat. Congress on Samoan Question (apptd. by Pres. Harrison), 1889; apptd. judge N.J. Ct. Errors and Appeals, 1893. Died June 17, 1894; buried City Cemetery, Simsbury, Conn.

PHILE, Philip, musician; b. Germany. Came to Phila., before 1784; appeared in concert and theatre orchs., Phila. and N.Y.C.; apptd. orch. leader Old Am. Co. of Comedians, circa 1785; credited with authorship of President's March (to which Hail Columbia was set, 1798); composed concerto of harmonial music, also piece called Harmony Music; name also appears as Fyles, Pfeil, Phyla. Died Phila., 1793.

PHILENIA, see Morton, Sarah Wentworth Apthorpe.

PHILIP (Indian names: Pometacom, Metacom or Metacomet), Indian sachem; m. Wootonekanuske, at least 1 child. Became hereditary sachem Wampanoag Indian tribe, 1662; called King Philip by white settlers; honored peace treaty signed by his father until 1771, when he was fined and disarmed by colonists for plotting against them; King Philip's War (1675-76) started when 3 of his warriors were executed for murdering an Indian who had betrayed Philip's plans for revolt to settlers; supported in war (which killed several thousand settlers in Mass. and Conn.) by Nipmuck Indians; defeated after English began capturing Indian women and children and offering pardon to those who would betray Philip. Killed while hiding in a swamp nr. Mt. Hope (now Bristol, R.I.) by an Indian in service of the English, Aug. 23, 1676; later drawn and quartered; his head exhibited at Plymouth (Mass.) for many years.

PHILIPS, Martin Wilson, planter; b. Columbia, S.C., June 17, 1806; grad. med. dept. U. Pa., 1829; m. Mary Montgomery, 1829; m. 2d, Rebecca Tillinghast Wade. Became owner plantation "Log Hall," Hinds County, Miss., 1836, raised fruit trees and cotton, bred stock (plantation destroyed by U.S. Army 1863); later owner of nursery bus., Magnolia, Miss.; 1st prof. agr., supt. univ. farm at U. Miss., 1872-75, proctor, 1875-80; contbr. to all major U.S. farm journals; editor South-Western Farmer, Raymond, Miss., 1843-45, Philips' Southern Farmer, Memphis, Tenn., 1867-73; treas. Miss. Baptist State Conv.; a founder Central Female Inst. (now Hillman Coll.), Clinton, Miss., 1853, mem. 1st bd. trustees; trustee Miss. Coll. Died Oxford, Miss., Feb. 26, 1889.

PHILIPSE, Frederick, mcht.; b. Friesland, Holland, Nov. 17, 1626; s. Frederick and Margaret (Dacres) P.; m. Margaret Hardenbrook, Dec. 1662; m. 2d, Catharine Van Cortlandt Dervall, Nov. 30, 1692. Came to Am., 1647; traded with East and West Indies, Madagascar, also with local Indians; manufactured wampum; mem. Council of N.Y., 1675-98, removed from council after being convicted of trading with pirate Capt. William Kidd; his various land acquisitions consolidated in Royal Patent of Philipsburgh, 1693. Died 1702.

PHILLIPS, George, clergyman; b. South Rainham, Norfolk, Eng., 1593; son of Christopher Phillips; B.A., Cambridge (Eng.) U., 1613, M.A., 1617; m. Miss Sergeant; m. 2d, Elizabeth Welden, 1630; 9 children including Samuel. Came to Am., 1629; a founder Watertown (Mass.), 1630; drafted covenant of Watertown Ch., pastor until 1644; 1st minister in Mass. to use congregational form of ch. polity; led protest against arbitrary tax levied on Watertown by Mass. gov., 1632 (protest led to agreement of taxation by representation in Gen. Ct.). Died Watertown, July 12, 1644.

PHILLIPS, Henry, philologist; b. Phila., Sept. 6, 1838; s. Jonas Altamont and Frances (Cohen) P.; grad. U. Pa., 1856; never married. Admitted to Pa. bar, 1859; became mem. Am. Philos. Soc., 1877, apptd. mem. com. to judge scientific value of Volapük, 1877, curator, 1880-84, sec., 1884-85, librarian, 1885-95; treas. Am. Folk-Lore Soc.; treas. Numis. and Antiquarian Soc. of Phila., 1862-68, sec., 1868; Belgian vice consul for Phila., 1892-95. Translator: Faust (Adalbert von Chamisso), 1881; La Patria dell'Italiano (Antonio Gazzaletti), 1887; Attempts Toward an International Language (L. L. Zamenhof), 1889; also works of Alexander Petofi, Hermann Rollet, Fray Louis Ponce de Leon. Died June 6, 1895.

PHILLIPS, Henry Myer, congressman, lawyer; b. Phila., June 30, 1811; attended Franklin Inst.; studied law. Admitted to bar, 1832, began practice of law, Phila.; clk. Phila. Ct. of Common Pleas; mem. U.S. Ho. of Reps. (Democrat) from Pa., 35th Congress, 1857-59; trustee Jefferson Med. Coll., 1862; apptd. mem. Bd. of Fairmount Park Commrs., 1867, pres., 1881; became mem. Bd. of City Trusts, 1869, v.p., 1870-78, pres., 1878-82; became dir. Acad. of Music, 1870, pres., 1872-84; mem. commn. to supervise erection of Phila. municipal bldgs., 1870-71; dir. Pa. R.R. Co., 1874. Died Phila., Aug. 28, 1884; buried Mt. Sinai Cemetery, Phila.

PHILLIPS, John, educator; b. Andover, Mass., Dec. 27, 1719; s. Rev. Samuel and Hannah (White) P.; M.A. (salutatorian), Harvard, 1735; LL.D. (hon.), Dartmouth, 1777; m. Sarah (Emery) Gilman, Aug. 4, 1743; m. 2d, Mrs. Elizabeth Hale, Nov. 3, 1767. Mem. Mass. Gen. Ct., 1771-73; moderator town meeting, 1778-79; founder Phillips Acad. (incorporated as Phillips Exeter Acad.) Exeter, Mass., 1781, 1st pres. bd. trustees; trustee Phillips Andover Acad., pres., 1791-94; contbr. liberal gifts to Dartmouth, trustee, 1773. Died Exeter, Apr. 21, 1795.

PHILLIPS, John, congressman; b. Chester County, Pa. Mem. U.S. Ho. of Reps. (Federalist) from Pa., 17th Congress, 1821-23.

PHILLIPS, Philip, congressman, lawyer; b. Charleston, S.C., Dec. 13, 1807; studied law. Admitted to bar, began practice of law, Charleston, 1828; mem. S.C. Constl. Conv., 1832; mem. S.C. Ho. of Reps., 1833-34; moved to Mobile, Ala.; mem. Ala. Ho. of Reps., 1844, 51; del. Democratic Nat. Conv., Balt., 1852; mem. U.S. Ho. of Reps. (Democrat) from Ala., 33d Congress, 1853-55; practiced law, Washington, D.C., until 1884. Died Washington, Jan. 14, 1884; buried Laurel Hill Cemetery, Savannah, Ga.

PHILLIPS, Philip, musician; b. Cassadaga, N.Y., Aug. 13, 1834; s. Sawyer and Jane (Parker) P.; m. Odlie M. Clarke, Sept. 27, 1860, at least 1 son, Philip. Organized singing sch., Alleghany, N.Y., 1853 later partner (with D. S. Cook) in musical instrument store, Fredonia, N.Y.; joined music firm of William Summer and Co., Cincinnati, 1862 (became Philip Phillips and Co., 1863); appeared as Methodist musical evangelist in all major Northern cities; as music editor Methodist Book Concern, 1867; made singing tour of Eng., 1868, Sandwich Islands, Australia, New Zealand, Palestine, Egypt, India and Europe, 1875. Author: Early Blossoms, 1860; Musical Leaves, 1862; The Singing Pilgrim, 1866; New Hymn and Tune Book, 1867; American Sacred Songster, 1868; The Gospel Singer, 1874; Song Ministry, 1874; Song Pilgrimage Round the World, 1882; Gem Solos, 1887. Died Delaware, O., June 25, 1895.

PHILLIPS, Samuel, legislator, educator; b. North Andover, Mass., Feb. 5, 1752; s. Samuel and Elizabeth (Barnard) P.; grad. Harvard, 1771, LL.D. (hon.), 1793; m. Phoebe Foxcroft, July 6, 1773, 2 children including John. Del. to Mass. Provincial Congress, 1775-80, to Mass. Constl. Conv., 1779-80; mem. Mass. Senate, 1780-1801, pres., 1785; justice Ct. Common Pleas, Essex County, 1781; founder Phillips Acad., Andover, Mass., 1778, mem. original bd. trustees, pres., 1796; lt. gov. Mass.; 1801. Died Andover, Feb. 10, 1802; buried South Ch., Andover.

PHILLIPS, Stephen Clarendon, congressman, businessman; b. Salem, Mass., Nov. 4, 1801; grad. Harvard, 1819. Engaged in business, Salem; mem. Mass. Ho. of Reps., 1824-29, Mass. Senate, 1830; mem. U.S. Ho. of Reps. (Whig, filled vacancy) from Mass., 23d-25th congresses, Dec. 1, 1834-Sept. 28, 1838 (resigned); mayor Salem, 1838-42; unsuccessful Free-Soil candidate for gov. Mass., 1848, 49; in lumber bus., Can. Died in burning of steamer Montreal on St. Lawrence River, June 26, 1857.

PHILLIPS, Wendell, reformer; b. Boston, Nov. 29, 1811; s. John and Sarah (Walley) P.; grad. Harvard 1831, attended Harvard Law Sch.; m. Ann Terry Greene, Oct. 12, 1837, no children. Admitted to Suffolk County (Mass.) bar, 1834; practiced in Boston; joined Mass. Anti-Slavery Soc., 1837; made nation-wide tours lecturing on abolition; del. from Mass. to World's Anti-Slavery Conv., London, Eng. 1840; pres. Am. Anti-Slavery Soc., 1865; also active in movements for prohibition, penal reform, female suffrage, and unity in labor; unsuccessful Labor Reform and Prohibitionist candidate for gov. Mass. 1870; presided over Labor Reform Conv., Worcester, Mass., 1871. Died Boston, Feb. 2, 1884; buried Granary Burying Ground, Boston.

PHILLIPS, Willard, lawyer; b. Bridgewater, Mass. Dec. 19, 1784; s. Joseph and Hannah (Egerton) P. grad. Harvard, 1810; s. Hannah Brackett Hill, 1833 m. 2d, Harriet Hill. Tutor, Harvard, 1811-15; contbd. articles and editorials to Gen. Repository and Review, N.Am. Review, Am. Jurist; admitted to Mass. bar, 1818; practiced in Boston; mem. Mass Legislature, 1825-26; publisher New Eng. Galaxy 1828-34; chmn. commn. to codify criminal law of Mass., 1837-42; probate judge for Suffolk County 1839-47; pres. New Eng. Mut. Life Ins. Co., 1847-circa 1870; mem. Am. Acad. Arts and Scis. Author A Treatise on the Law of Insurance, Vol. I, 1823 Vol. II, 1834; Manual of Political Economy, 1828 The Inventor's Guide, 1837; The Law of Patents for Inventions, 1837; Propositions Concerning Protection and Free Trade, 1850. Died Cambridge, Mass., Sept. 9, 1873.

PHILLIPS, William, banker, state ofcl.; b. Mar. 19, 1750; s. William and Abigail (Bromfield) P. m. Miriam Mason, Sept. 13, 1774, 7 children. Became pres. Mass. Bank, 1804; mem. Mass. Gen. Ct., 1805-12; lt. gov. Mass. (Federalist), 1812-22; presdl. elector at large, 1816, 20; del. to Mass. Constl. Conv., 1820; mem. Mass. Senate, 1823; bd. trustees Phillips Acad., Andover, 1791, pres., 1821; original incorporator Am. Bd. Fgn. Missions; pres. Am. Bible Soc. Mass. Gen. Hosp., Am. Edn. Soc., Soc. for Propagating Gospel. Died May 26, 1827.

PHILLIPS, William, businessman; b. nr. Pitts., circa 1814. Mem. glass-making firm Whitehead, Ihmsen & Phillips; founder (with his brother) R. B. & W. Phillips, glass works; a builder of rolling mill, Kittanning, Pa.; retired from active business pursuits, 1862; pres. pro tem, later pres. Allegheny R.R., from 1862. Died Apr. 14, 1874.

PHILLIPS, William Addison, journalist, congressman; b. Paisley, Scotland, Jan. 14, 1824; s. John Phillips; studied law; m. Carrie Spillman, 1859; m. 2d, Anna Stapler, 1885; 4 children. Newspaper correspondent, 1845-62, corr. N.Y. Tribune, 1855, famous anti-slavery journalist; admitted to Ill. bar, 1852; moved to Lawrence, Kan., 1855, began practice of law; a founder Town of Salina (Kan.), 1858; 1st justice Kan. Supreme Ct. under Leavenworth Constn., 1857; raised some of 1st troops in Kan. during Civil War, served as officer U.S. Army, prominent as comdr. Cherokee Indian Regt. in Indian Territory and Ark., left army as col. 3d Indian Regt., 1865; pros. atty. Cherokee County (Kan.), 1865; mem. Kan. Legislature, 1865; mem. U.S. Ho. of Reps. from Kan., 43d-45th congresses, 1873-79, chiefly interested in land legislation; pres. Kan. Hist. Soc. Author: The Conquest of Kansas by Missouri and her Allies (an anti-slavery polit. tract supporting Fremont), 1856; Labor, Land and Law, A Search for the Missing Wealth of the Working People, 1888. Died Ft. Gibson, Muskogee County, Ind., Nov. 30, 1893; buried Gypsum Hill Cemetery, Salina.

PHILSON, Robert, congressman; b. County Tyrone, Ireland, 1759. Came to U.S., settled in Berlin, Pa., 1785; engaged in agriculture; held various local offices; asso. judge Somerset County, 20 years; commd. brig. gen. 2d Brigade, 10th Div., Pa. Militia, 1800; served as brig. gen. 2d Brigade, 12th Div., Pa. Volunteers, during War of 1812; mem. U.S. Ho. of Reps. from Pa., 16th Congress, 1819-21. Died Berlin, June 25, 1831; buried Reformed Church Cemetery.

PHINIZY, Ferdinand, mcht., financier; b. Bowling Green (now Stephens), Ga., Jan. 20, 1819; s. Jacob and Matilda (Stewart) P.; grad. U. Ga., 1838; m. Harriet H. Bowdre, 1849; m. 2d, Anne S. Barrett, Aug. 11, 1865; 11 children. Mem. cotton trading firm of Phinizy and Clayton, Augusta, Ga., later mem. firm Phinizy & Co.; made large fortune; served as Confederate fiscal agt. selling bonds and running cotton through blockade during Civil War; also served as dir. Ga. R.R. and Banking Co., Augusta & Savannah R.R., Atlanta & West Point R.R., Northeastern R.R. of Ga., Augusta Factory; dir. So. Mut. Ins. Co., Bank of the Univ., Athens, Ga.; trustee U. Ga. Died Athens, Oct. 20, 1889.

PHIPS, Sir William, colonial gov.; b. Woolwick, Me., Feb. 2, 1651; s. James Phips; m. Mary (Spencer) Hull, circa 1673. Created Knight for raising sunken treasure off coast of Haiti, 1687; provost marshal gen. Boston, 1687; 1st native American to be knighted, 1687; elected magistrate Mass. Provincial Govt., 1690; fought against French in Nova Scotia, Can., 1st royal gov. Mass.; helped to bring an end to witchcraft trials, 1692. Died while being investigated on charges of maladministration, London, Eng., Feb. 18, 1695.

PHISTER, Elijah Conner, congressman, lawyer; b. Maysville, Ky., Oct. 8, 1822; attended Sem. of Rand and Richardson, Maysville; grad. Augusta Coll., Ky., 1840; studied law. Admitted to bar, began practice of law, 1844; mayor Maysville, 1848; circuit judge, 1856-62; mem. Ky. Ho. of Reps., 1867-71; mem. U.S. Ho. of Reps. (Democrat) from Ky., 46th-47th congresses, 1879-83. Died Maysville, May 16, 1887; buried City Cemetery.

PHOENIX, Jonas Phillips, congressman; b. Morristown, N.J., Jan. 14, 1788; became a mcht., N.Y. C.; alderman of 1st ward, 1840, 42, 47; Whig presdl. elector, 1840; apptd. commr. Croton Aqueduct Works, 1842; mem. U.S. Ho. of Reps. (Whig) from N.Y., 28th, 31st congresses, 1843-45, 49-51. Died N.Y.C., May 4, 1859; buried Presbyn. Cemetery, Morristown.

PHYFE, Duncan, cabinet maker; b. Loch Fannich, nr. Inverness, Scotland, 1768; m. Rachel Lowzade, Feb. 17, 1793, 7 children including James D., Michael. Came to Am., circa 1783; his 1st shop (a joiner's shop) located at 2 Broad St., N.Y.C., 1792, called Duncan Phyfe & Sons by 1837; noted for excellence of his furniture, mastery of proportion, line, detail; worked primarily with mahogany; work may be divided into periods, including Adam-Sheraton influence, 1795-1802, Sheraton Directoire, 1802-18, American Empire, 1818-30, so called butcher furniture, 1830-47; works before 1825 are more notable (catered to taste of masses after 1825), executed his best works before 1814; ret., 1847. Died Bklyn., Aug. 16, 1854; buried Greenwood Cemetery, Bklyn.

PHYSICK, Philip Syng, surgeon; b. Phila., July 7, 1768; s. Edmund and Abigail (Syng) P.; grad. U. Pa., 1785; studied medicine Windmill St. Sch., London, Eng., 1788. M.D., U. Edinburgh (Scotland), 1792; m. Elizabeth Emlen, Sept. 18, 1800, 7 children. House surgeon St. George's Hosp., London, 1790; physician during yellow fever epidemics, Phila., 1793, 98; clin. tchr. on staff Pa. Hosp., 1794-1816; surgeon Almshouse Infirmary, 1800; became lectr. U. Pa., circa 1800, prof. surgery, 1805-19; called father of Am. surgery; responsible for many surg. advances including: manipulation instead of mech. traction in reduction of dislocations, new methods in treatment of hip-joint disease by immobilization, use of animal ligatures (including catgut) in surgery and leaving them in tissues to become absorbed, notable work in urinary tract and bladder-stone operations; a pioneer in use of stomach tube; peformer successful operation on arteriovenous aneurism, 1804; inventor guillotine tonsillotome, needle forceps, snare for use in tonsillectomy, new type of catheters; elected mem. English and French med. socs., Am. Philos. Soc.; 1st pres. Acad. Medicine. Died Phila., Dec. 15, 1837.

PIATT, Donn, journalist; b. Cincinnati, June 29, 1819; s. Judge Benjamin and Elizabeth (Barnett) P.; ed. St. Xavier Coll., Cincinnati; m. Louise Kirby, 1847; m. 2d, Ella Kirby, 1866. Began to publish Democratic Club, West Liberty, O., 1840; judge Ct. Common Pleas, Hamilton County, O., 1852-53; sec. to Am. legation, France, 1853-55; commd. capt. 13th Ohio Inf. during Civil War, 1861, maj., 1862, lt. col., 1863; elected to Ohio Legislature, 1865; Washington corr. Cincinnati Comml., 1868; editor Club Room column of Galaxy, 1871; co-editor, founder weekly Capital, 1871-80; printed editorial The Beginning of the End (interpreted as a threat to assassinate Pres. Hayes), Feb. 18, 1877; indicted on charge of inciting rebellion, insurrection and riot, prosecution dropped; introduced term "twisting the British lion's tail". Author: Memories of the Men Who Saved the Union, 1887; The Lone Grave of the Shenandoah and Other Tales, 1888; Rev. Melanchthon Poundex, 1889. Died West Liberty, Nov. 12, 1891.

PICKENS, Andrew, army officer; b. Paxton, Pa., Sept. 19, 1739; s. Andrew and Nancy Pickens; m. Rebecca Calhoun, Mar. 19, 1765, at least 4 children. fought against Cherokee Indians, 1761; served as capt. S.C. Militia in 1st fight at Ninetysix fort, 1775; commd. col., circa 1777, brigadier, circa 1780; mem. S.C. Ho. of Reps., 1781-94, 1800-12; mem. S.C. Constl. Conv., 1790; mem. U.S. Ho. of Reps. from S.C., 3d Congress, 1793-95; maj. gen. S.C. Militia, circa 1795; served in War of 1812. Died Pendleton Dist., S.C., Aug. 11, 1817; buried Old Stone Ch.. nr. Pendleton Dist.

PICKENS, Francis Wilkinson, gov. S.C., congressman; b. St. Paul's Parish, Colleton Dist., S.C., Apr. 7, 1805; s. Andrew and Susannah (Wilkinson) P.; attended Franklin Coll. (now part of U. Ga.), S.C. Coll. (now U. S.C.); studied law, Edgefield, S.C.; m. Margaret Simkins, 1828, 8 children; m. 2d, Marion Antoinette Dearing, 1858, 1 child; m. 3d, Lucy Holcombe, 1 child. Admitted to S.C. bar, 1828; mem. S.C. Ho. of Reps., 1832-34, 44-46; mem. U.S. Ho. of Reps. from S.C., 23d-27th congresses, Dec. 8, 1834-Mar. 3, 1844; del. Nashville Conv., 1850; presiding officer S.C. Conf. of 1852, drafted ordinance advocating secession; chmn. S.C. Conv. to choose dels. to Nat. Democratic Conv. which nominated Buchanan, 1856, chosen del.; U.S. minister to Russia, 1858-60; gov. S.C., 1860-62, declared in inaugural address that S.C. would not compromise with Pres. Lincoln and must secede, responsible for firing opening guns of Civil War, ordered Charleston Batteries to fire on steamer Star of the West, carrying supplies for Ft. Sumter, Jan. 9, 1861. Died Edgefield, Jan. 25, 1869; buried Edgefield Cemetery.

PICKENS, Israel, senator, gov. Ala.; b. Concord, N.C., Jan. 30, 1780; s. Capt. Samuel and Jane (Carrigan) P.; grad. Jefferson Coll. (now Washington and Jefferson Coll.), Canonsburg, Pa., 1802; m. Martha Lenoir, June 9, 1814. Admitted to N.C. bar; mem. N.C. Senate, 1808-09; mem. U.S. Ho. of Reps. from N.C., 12th-14th congresses, 1811-17; register land office, St. Stephens, Miss. Territory (now Ala.), 1817-21; pres. Tombeckbee Bank of St. Stephens, 1818; rep. from Washington County to Ala. Constl. Conv., 1819; gov. Ala., 1821-25, established 1st state-owned, state-operated bank in Ala.; 1st ex-officio pres. bd. trustees U. Ala.; mem. U.S. Senate from Ala., Feb. 17-Nov. 27, 1826. Died nr. Matanzas, Cuba, Apr. 24, 1827; buried family cemetery nr. Greensboro, Hale County, Ala.

PICKERING, Charles, physician, naturalist; b. Susquehanna, County, Pa., Nov. 10, 1805; s. Timothy Pickering, Jr. and Lurena (Cole) P.; M.D., Harvard, 1826, A.B. (as of 1823), 1849; m. Sarah Hammond, 1851. Physician; active mem. Am. Philos. Soc., Phila., 1827; mem. Acad. Natural Scis., 1827, librarian, 1828-33, curator, 1833-37; chief zoologist U.S. Exploring Expdn. which sailed to South Seas, 1838, Author: Races of Men and Their Geographical Distribution, 1848; The Chronological History of Plants: Man's Record of His Own Existence Illustrated Through Their Names, Uses and Companionship, 1879; Essay on the Invention of the Art of Writing; Notes on the Stinging Power of the Physalia; Geographical Distribution of Plants. Died Boston, Mar. 17, 1878.

PICKERING, John, jurist, b. Newington, N.H., Sept. 22, 1737; s. Joshua and Mary (Smithson) P.; grad. Harvard, 1761; LL.D. (hon.), Dartmouth, 1792; m. Abigail Sheafe. Mem. N.H. constl. convs., 1781, 91-92; mem. N.H. Legislature from Portsmouth, 1783-87; influential mem. N.H. Constl. Conv. to ratify U.S. Constn., 1788; presdl. elector, 1788, 92; mem. N.H. Senate and Council; chief justice Superior Ct. of Judicature, 1790-1795; judge U.S. Dist. Ct. for N.H., 1795-1804, impeached by U.S. Ho. of Reps., convicted by U.S. Senate, 1804, removed from office. Died Portsmouth, Apr. 11, 1805.

PICKERING, John, lawyer, philologist; b. Salem, Mass., Feb. 7, 1777; s. Timothy and Rebecca (White) P.; grad. Harvard, 1796, LL.D. (hon.), 1835; LL.D. (hon.), Bowdoin Coll., 1822; m. Sarah White, Mar. 3, 1835, 2 sons, 1 dau. Sec. to William Smith, Am. minister to Portugal, 1779-99; sec. to Rufus King, Am. minister to Eng., 1799-1801; admitted to Essex County (Mass.) bar, 1804; solicitor City of Boston, 1829; mem. Mass. Gen. Ct. from Salem, 1812, 14, 26; mem. Mass. Gov.'s. Council, 1818, Mass. Senate, 1829; mem. commn. to revise and prepare Mass. statutes, prepared part entitled Of the Internal Administration of Government, 1833; a pioneer Am. philologist, knew most of Western European langs., also Arabic, Hebrew, Turkish, Chinese, classical langs.; expert on Am. Indian langs.; mem. bd. overseers Harvard, 1818-24; a founder, pres. Am. Oriental Soc., Am. Acad. Arts and Sci.; author legal articles, numerous philological works. Author: A Vocabulary or Collection of Words and Phrases which Have Been Supposed To Be Peculiar to the United States of America, 1816; On the Adoption of a Uniform Orthography for the Indian Languages of North America, 1820; A Comprehensive Lexicon of the Greek Language, 1826; Remarks on the Indian Languages of North America, 1836; Memoir on the Language and Inhabitants of Lord North's Island, 1845. Died Boston, May 5, 1846; buried Salem.

PICKERING, Timothy, senator, cabinet officer; b. Salem, Mass., July 17, 1745; s. Timothy and Mary (Wingate) P.; grad. Harvard, 1763; studied law; m. Rebecca White, Apr. 5, 1776, 10 children including John, Timothy. Clk., Office of Register of Deeds for Essex County, Salem, 1763; admitted to Mass. bar, 1768; selectman, town clk., assessor, Salem, 1772-77; rep. Mass. Gen. Ct.; register of deeds Salem, 1775; judge Maritime Ct. of Province of Mass., 1775-76, Essex County Ct. of Common Pleas, 1775; commd. lt. Essex County Militia, 1776; elected to Mass. Legislature, 1776; commd. col. Continental Army, 1776, apptd. adj. gen. by Gen. Washington, 1777; elected to Bd. of War by Continental Congress, 1777; q.m. gen. Continental Army, 1780-83; moved to Phila., then to Wyoming County (Pa.), 1787, organized Luzerne County, 1787; rep. from Luzerne County to Pa. Conv. which ratified U.S. Constn., 1789; mem. Pa. Constl. Conv., 1789-90; went on mission to Seneca Indians to prevent an Indian war, 1790; postmaster gen. U.S. (apptd. by Pres. Washington), 1791-95, sec. of war, 1795; U.S. sec. of state, 1795-1800, actions in preparing for war with France ("Quasi-War"), 1797-98, support of Britain, and intrigues against John Adams resulted in his removal from office; reentered local politics, Mass.; mem. U.S. Senate from Mass., 1803-11; mem. U.S. Ho. of Reps. (Federalist) from Mass., 13th-14th congresses. 1813-17; bitterly opposed War of 1812; a scientific farmer in Mass.; Author of a widely used drill manual, also numerous articles and letters on politics and farming. Died Salem, Jan. 29, 1829; buried Broad Street Cemetery, Salem.

PICKET, Albert, educator, coll. pres.; b. Apr. 15, 1771; m. Esther Rockwell Hull, May 8, 1791, 5 children including John. Taught sch. for girls, N.Y.C., 1794-1826; pres. Incorporated Soc. of Tchrs.; editor, publisher bi-monthly The Academician; established girls sch., Cincinnati, 1826; mem. Cincinnati Bd. Edn.; trustee Cincinnati Coll.; founder Western Literary Inst. and Coll. of Profl. Tchrs., 1829, pres., 1829-40 (orgn. played major part in establishing state sch. system). Died Aug. 3, 1850.

PICKETT, Albert James, historian; b. Anson County, N.C., Aug. 13, 1810; s. William Raiford and Frances (Dickson) P.; m. Sarah Harris, Mar. 20, 1832, 12 children. Interested in experiments for improving agr.; wrote for The Southern Cultivator; a Jacksonian Democrat; published History of Alabama and Incidentally of Georgia and Mississippi from the Erliest Period (his chief work), 2 vols., 1851; left papers which comprise one of most valuable collections in Ala. State Dept. of History and Archives. Died Montgomery, Ala., Oct. 28, 1858.

PICKETT, George Edward, army officer; b. Richmond, Va., Jan. 25, 1825; s. Col. Robert and Mary (Johnston) P.; grad. U.S. Mil. Acad., 1846; m. Sally Minge, Jan. 1851; m. 2d, La Salle Corbell, Sept. 15, 1863; 2 children. Served in Mexican War; commd. 2d lt. 2d Inf., U.S. Army, 1847, brevetted 1st lt., 1847; served frontier duty in Tex., commd. capt., 1855; served on Indian duty in Northwest, 1856-61; seized control of San Juan Island in Puget Sound under orders (during Brit.-Am. controversy over control); resigned commn., 1861; commd. col. Confederate Army, 1861, brig. gen., 1862; served in battles of Williamsburg, Gaines Mills, Seven Pines; commd. maj. gen., 1862; served in Battle of Fredericksburg; most famous as leader Pickett's charge during Battle of Gettysburg, 1863; commanded Dept. of Va. and N.C., 1864; saw action at Battle of Petersburg; after war refused offer of Khedive of Egypt of commn. in Egyptian Army; in charge Va. agency Washington Life Ins. Co. Died Norfolk, Va., July 30, 1875; buried Hollywood Cemetery, Richmond,

PICKETT, James Chamberlayne, diplomat; b. Fauquier County, Va., Feb. 6, 1793; s. John and Elizabeth (Chamberlayne) P.; m. Ellen Desha, Oct. 6, 1818, 2 children. Served as 3d lt. 2d U.S. Atry., 1813-15, as capt. and asst. dep. q.m.-gen., 1818-June 1821; mem. Ky. Legislature, 1822; sec. of state Ky., 1825-28; became sec. legation in Colombia, 1829; supt. U.S. Patent Office for 3 months, 1835; apptd. 4th auditor Treasury Dept., 1836; charge d'affaires of U.S. to treat with Peru-Bolivian Confedn. and Republic of Ecuador, 1838; editor Daily Globe, Washington, D.C., 1848-53. Died Washington, July 10, 1872.

PICKMAN, Benjamin, Jr., congressman, businessman; b. Salem, Mass., Sept. 30, 1763; grad. Harvard, 1784; studied law, Newburyport, Mass. Admitted to bar, practiced law for short time, then engaged in business; mem. Mass. Ho. of Reps., 1797-1802, 12-13, Mass. Senate, 1803; mem. Mass., Executive Council, 1805, 08, 13-14, 19-21, drafted answers of House to Governor's speeches in several sessions; member U.S. House of Representatives 13-14, 19-21, drafted answers of Ho. to Gov.'s speeches in several sessions; mem. U.S. Ho. of Reps. from Mass., 11th Congerss, 1809-11; mem. Mass.

Constl. Conv., 1820; overseer Harvard, 1810-18; pres. bd. dirs. Theol. Sch. at Cambridge; active in many religious and ednl. socs. Died Salem, Aug. 16, 1843; buried Broad Street Cemetery.

PICKNELL, William Lamb, painter; b. Hinesburg, Vt., Oct. 23, 1853; s. Rev. William Lamb and Ellen (Upham) P.; m. Gertrude Powers, Apr. 18, 1889. Worked under J. L. Gerome at Ecole des Beaux-Arts, Paris; painted Road to Concarneau (now in Corcoran Gallery, Washington, D.C.), also En Provence, circa 1880; painted Morning on the Loing at Moret, Sand Dune of Essex (both in Boston Mus. of Fine Arts); Morning on the Mediterranean Antibes (in Luxembourg Mus., Paris); asso. N.A.D., mem. Soc. Am. Artists (N.Y.C.), Soc. Brit. Artists (London); recipient numerous medals, also Walter Lippincott prize Phila. Acad. Fine Arts, 1896. Died Marblehead, Mass., Aug. 8, 1897.

PICQUET, Francois, missionary; b. Bourg, Bresse, France, Dec. 4, 1708; studied at Lyons (France Sem., also St. Sulpice, Paris, France; doctoral degree Sorbonne (U. Paris). Joined Sulpician Order, ordained priest Roman Catholic Ch., 1734; sent to Can., 1734, became missionary to Algonquin and Iroquois Indians, kept them neutral in French and English War, 1743-48; founder Ft. Presentation (now Ogdensburg, N.Y.), 1749, developed St. Presentation and Oka into centers for Cath. Indians; returned to France to discuss ways of strengthening the colony, came back to Can. and led Indians against the British, 1754-60; returned to France, pastor in Paris until 1772; canon Bourg Cathedral. Died Verjon, France, 1781.

PICTON, Thomas (real name Thomas Picton Milner), journalist; b. N.Y.C., May 16, 1822; grad. N.Y. U., 1840; m. Miss Gardner, 1860. Admitted to N.Y. bar, 1843; served as officer in French army, circa 1845-48; fought in revolutionary army of Narcisco Lopez in Cuba, 1850; published newspaper The Ear, N.Y.C., 1850; editor The Sachem, 1851; later founder, editor True American; officer in William Walker's army in attempt to take over Nicaragua, 1855-60; organized 38th N.Y. Inf., U.S. Volunteers, 1861, did not serve himself; connected with fire dept., N.Y.C., also asst. cashier Nassau Bank, after war; contbr. to various sports jours. Author: (under pseudonym Paul Preston) Paul Preston's Book of Gymnastics: or Sports for Youth; Acrostics from Across the Atlantic (poems), 1869; The Fireside Magician, 1870; A Tempest in a Teapot (play), 1871; There's No Smoke without Fire (play), 1872; Rose Street, Its Past, Present, and Future, 1873. Died N.Y.C., Feb. 20, 1891; buried Cypress Hills Cemetery, N.Y.C.

PIERCE, Benjamin, gov. N.H.; b. Chelmford, Mass., Dec. 25, 1757; s. Benjamin and Elizabeth (Merrill) P.; m. Elizabeth Andrews, May 24, 1787; m. 2d, Anna Kendrick, Feb. 1, 1790; 9 children including Franklin (14th pres. U.S.). Served as pvt. in Mass. Militia, then became lt. in command of a co.; brigade-major, apptd. to organize Hillsborough County (N.H.) Militia, 1786-1807, became brig. gen., 1805; mem. N.H. Ho. of Reps., 1789-1802; mem. N.H. Constl. Conv., 1791; mem. N.H. Gov.'s Council, 1803-09, 14; apptd. sheriff Hillsborough County, 1809-12, 18-27; elected gov. N.H., 1827, 29; Democratic elector in 1832. Died Hillsborough, N.H., Apr. 1, 1839.

PIERCE, Edward Lillie, lawyer; b. Stoughton, Mass., Mar. 29, 1829; s. Jesse and Elizabeth (Lillie) P.; grad. Brown U., 1850, Harvard Law Sch., 1852; m. Elizabeth H. Kingsbury, Apr. 19, 1865; m. 2d, Maria L. Woodhead, Mar. 8, 1882; 8 children. Sec. to Salmon P. Chase in Cincinnati, also Washington, D.C., 1852-55; practiced law, Boston, 1855; del. Nat. Republican Conv., 1860; U.S. collector internal revenue, Boston, 1864-66; dist. atty. Norfolk and Plymouth counties (Mass.), 1866-70; sec. Mass. Bd. State Charities, 1870-74; mem. Mass. Legislature, 1875-76, 97; moderator Milton (Mass.) Town Meeting, 1888-93, 95-97; lectr. Boston Law Sch. Author: A Treatise on American Railroad Law, 1857; Index of the Special Railroad Laws of Massachusetts, 1874; Memoir and Letters of Charles Sumner, Vols. I and II, 1877, Vol. III, 1893; A Treatise on the Law of Railroads, 1881; Major John Lillie, 1755-1801, publishd 1896; Enfranchisement and Citizenship; Addresses and Papers, 1896. Died Paris, France, Sept. 5, 1897.

PIERCE, Franklin, 14th Pres. U.S.; b. Hillsborough, N.H., Nov. 23, 1804; s. Benjamin and Anna (Kendrick) P.; grad. Bowdoin Coll., 1824; studied law under Levi Woodbury, Portsmouth, N.H.; m. Jane Means Appleton, Nov. 18, 1834, 3 children. Admitted to Hillsborough County (N.H.) bar, 1827, practiced law, Hillsborough; mem. N.H. Ho. of Reps., 1829-33, speaker, 1832-33; mem. U.S. Ho. of Reps. (Democrat) from N.H., 23d-24th, congresses, 1833-37; mem. U.S. Senate from N.H., 1837-42; resumed practice law, Concord, N.H., 1842; leader Dem. Party politics in N.H., 1842-47; declined appointment as U. S. atty. gen., 1845; commd. col. 9th Regt., N.H. Inf., 1846; apptd. brig. gen. U.S. Volunteers, 1847, served in battles of Contreras and Churubusco, resigned from service, 1847; pres. N.H. Constl. Conv., 1850; nominated for Pres. U.S. as compromise candidate on 49th ballot at Dem. Nat. Conv., Balt., 1852; Pres. U.S., 1853-57; sent James Gadsden to Mexico to purchase land for Southern railroad to Pacific, 1853; believed continued existence of slavery guaranteed by U.S. Constn.; approved Kan.-Neb. Bill, 1854; sought to restore order under legal, pro-slavery govt. when civil war broke out in Kan.; attempted to purchase Cuba, 1854; toured Europe, 1857-60; resumed practice law, Concord. Died Concord, Oct. 8, 1869; buried Minat Inclosure Cemetery, Concord.

PIERCE, George Foster, clergyman, coll. pres.; b. Greene County, Ga., Feb. 3, 1811; s. Lovick and Ann (Foster) P.; grad. Franklin Coll., Athens, Ga., 1829; m. Ann Maria Waldron, Feb. 4, 1834, 7 children. Admitted on trial to Ga. Conf. of Methodist Episcopal Ch., 1831; pastor at Augusta, Ga., Savannah, Ga., Charleston, S.C., 1831-36; presiding elder Augusta Dist., 1836-38; pres. Ga. Female Coll. (now Wesleyan Coll.), Macon, 1838-40, financial agt., 1840-42; editor So. Ladies' Book (monthly), 1840; itinerant minister in Ga., 1840-48; del. gen. confs. of M.E. Ch., 1840, 44; mem. conv. which organized M.E. Ch. of South, 1845; del. to gen. confs., 1846, 50, 54; pres. Emory Coll., Oxford, Ga., 1848-54; elected bishop, 1854. Author: (collected writings): Incidents of Western Travel (edited by T. O. Summers), 1857; Bishop Pierce's Sermons and Addresses (edited by A. G. Haygood), 1886. Died Sunshine, nr. Sparta, Ga., Sept. 3, 1884.

PIERCE, Henry Lillie, congressman; b. Stoughton, Mass., Aug. 23, 1825; s. Jesse and Elizabeth (Lillie) P. Worked for sch. com., Stoughton, 1848 supported Free-Soil Party in nat. elections; moved to Dorchester, Mass., 1849; worked in cocoa factory of Walter Baker (his uncle), leased plant from trustees after death of Baker, 1854, products won Gold medal at Paris (France) Exposition, 1867; mem. Mass. Ho. of Reps., 1860-62, 66; alderman Boston, 1870-71; mayor Boston, 1873, 78, placed various depts. of city govt. under adminstrv. bds. responsible to mayor; mem. U.S. Ho. of Reps. (Republican) from Mass. 43d-44th congresses, Dec. 1, 1873-77, one of 2 Republicans in House who voted to throw out La. electoral vote counted in favor of Rutherford Hayes; refused to support James G. Blaine in presdl. election, 1884, from that time on voted with Democrats; pres. Mass. Tariff Reform League, 1887. Died Boston, Dec. 17, 1896; buried Dorchester Burying Ground.

PIERCE, John Davis, clergyman, educator; b. Chesterfield, N.H., Feb. 18, 1797; s. Gad and Sarah (Davis) P.; grad. Brown U., 1822; attended Princeton Theol. Sem., 1823; m. Millicent Estabrook, Feb. 1, 1825; m. 2d, Mary Ann Cleveland, Oct. 28, 1829; m. 3d, Harriet Reed, 1833; 4 children. Ordained pastor, 1825; pastor Congregational Ch., Sangerfield, N.Y., 1825-30; established 1st ch., Marshall, Mich., pastor, 1831-36, 41-50; 1st supt. public instrn. State of Mich., 1836-41; published Jour. of Edn. (1st ednl. paper in Northwest Territory), 1838-40; mem. Mich. Ho. of Reps., 1847; mem. com. to draft new constn. for Mich., 1850. Died Medford, Mass., Apr. 5, 1882; buried Marshall.

PIERCE, William, Continental congressman; b. Ga., 1740. Served as aide-de-camp to Gen. Nathanael Greene, Continental Army, during Revolutionary War; presented with sword by Congress for conduct at Battle of Eutaw Springs; became a mcht., Savannah, Ga.; mem. Ga. Ho. of Reps., 1786; mem. Continental Congress from Ga., 1786-87; del. from Ga. to U.S. Constl. Conv., Phila., 1787; an original mem., v.p. Soc. of Cincinnati; trustee Chatham County Acad. Died Savannah, Dec. 10, 1789.

PIERCE, William Leigh, army officer, Continental congressman; b. Ga., 1740; m. Charlotte Fenwick, circa 1783, 2 sons including William Leigh. Served as aide-de-camp to Gen. Nathanael Greene during Revolutionary War; presented with sword by Continental Congress for conduct at Battle of Eutaw Springs; left army as brevet maj., 1783; became head mcht. house William Pierce and Co.; mem. Continental Congress, 1787, concurrently mem. U.S. Constl. Conv. of 1787, wrote notes on proceedings; original mem., v.p. Soc. of Cincinnati; trustee Chatham County Acad. Died Savannah, Ga., Dec. 10, 1789.

PIERPONT, Francis Harrison, gov. Va.; b. Monongalia County, Va., Jan. 25, 1814; s. Francis and Catherine (Weaver) Pierpoint; B.A., Allegheny Coll., Meadville, Pa., 1839; m. Julia Augusta Robertson, 1854, at least 1 child. Admitted to Va. bar, 1842; practiced in Fairmont, Va. (now W.Va.); atty. B.& O. R.R., 1848-53; presdl. elector from Va., 1848; called conv. at Wheeling which declared acts of secessionist ofcls. unconstl. and elected him provisional gov. Va., 1861-63; organized rump legislature which established separate state of W.Va. 1861; gov. "restored" Va. (those counties not in W.Va., but controlled by U.S.), 1861-65; apptd. gov. of all Va., 1865-68; mem. W.Va. Ho. of Reps., 1870; U.S. collector internal revenue, 1881. Died Pitts., Mar. 24, 1899; buried Fairmont.

PIERPONT, James, clergyman; b. Roxbury, Mass., Jan. 4, 1660; s. John and Thankful (Show) P.; grad. Harvard, 1681; m. Abigail Davenport, Oct. 27, 1691; m. 2d, Sarah Haynes, May 30, 1694 m. 3d, Mary Hooker, July 26, 1698; 2, daus. including Sarah. Invited to preach as candidate for pastorate 1st Ch. of New Haven (Conn.), 1684, ordained pastor, 1685, served until 1714; a founder Collegiate Sch. of Conn. (beginning of Yale Coll.), chartered 1701, an original trustee, primarily responsible for directing sch. through critical opening years; mem. Saybrook Synod of 1708. Died New Haven, Nov. 22, 1714.

PIERPONT, John, clergyman, poet; b. Litchfield, Conn., Apr. 6, 1785; s. James and Elizabeth (Collins) P.; grad. Yale, 1804, Litchfield Law Sch., 1812, Harvard Divinity Sch., 1818; m. Mary Sheldon Lord, Sept. 23, 1810; m. 2d, Harriet Louise (Campbell) Fowler, Dec. 8, 1857; 6 children including William Alston. Admitted to Mass. bar, 1812; practiced in Newburyport, Mass., 1812; in dry goods business, Boston, 1814-15; ordained pastor Hollis Street (Unitarian) Ch., Boston, 1819-45; pastor 1st Unitarian Soc., Troy, N.Y., 1845-49, 1st Congregational (Unitarian) Ch., West Medford, Mass., 1849-58; active in movements for temperance, spiritualism and abolition of slavery, imprisonment for debt, and state militia; clk. U.S. Treasury Dept., Washington, D.C., 1861-66. Author: (poems) The Portrait, 1812, Airs of Palestine, 1816, Airs of Palestine, and Other Poems, 1840, The Anti Slavery Poems of John Pierpont, 1843. Editor: (sch. readers) The American First Class Book, 1823, The National Reader, 1827. Died Medford, Mass., Aug. 27, 1866.

PIERREPONT, Edwards, atty. gen., diplomat; b. North Haven, Conn., Mar. 4, 1817; s. Giles and Eunice (Munson) Pierpont; grad. Yale, 1837; m. Margaretta Willoughby, May 27, 1846. Admitted to Conn. bar, 1840; tutor Yale, 1840-41; judge N.Y.C. Superior Ct., 1857; mem. Union Defense Com.; asst. U.S. dist. atty. in prosecution of John H. Surrat for complicity in assasination of Abraham Lincoln, 1867; U.S. dist. atty., 1869-70; U.S. minister to Gt. Britain, 1876-77; mem. N.Y. Constl. Conv., 1867-68; mem. Com. of 70, to help free N.Y.C. from "Tweed Ring", 1870. Died N.Y.C., Mar. 6, 1892.

PIERSON, Abraham, clergyman; b. Yorkshire, Eng., 1609; A.B., Trinity Coll., Cambridge, Eng., 1632; at least 1 son, Abraham. Ordained deacon Ch. of Eng., Southwell, Nottingham, Eng., 1632; came to Am., 1640; founded 1st ch. at Southampton, L.I., N.Y., 1640, pastor, 1640-47; founded 1st ch., Branford, New Haven Colony (now Conn.), 1647, pastor, 1647-67; employed as missionary to Indians by Commrs. of United Colonies; learned several Indian langs.; established 1st ch. at Newark, N.J., 1667, pastor, 1667-78. Author: Some Helps for the Indians Shewing Them How To Improve Their Natural Reason, To Know the True God, and the True Christian Religion, 1658 (written in Quiripi dialect). Died Newark, Aug. 9, 1678.

PIERSON, Abraham, clergyman; b. Southampton, L.I., N.Y., 1645; son of Abraham Pierson; grad. Harvard, 1668; m. Abigail Clark, 1673. Asst. pastor Congregational Ch., Newark, N.J., 1669-72, co-pastor, 1672-78, pastor, 1678-92; preached (but not installed as pastor) at ch. at Greenwich, Conn., 1692-94; pastor in Killingworth (now Clinton), Conn., 1694-1707; a founder Collegiate Sch. of Conn. (later Yale), 1701, trustee, rector, 1701-07. Died Mar. 5, 1707.

PIERSON, Hamilton Wilcox, clergyman, coll. pres.; b. Bergen, N.Y., Sept. 22, 1817; s. Josiah and Rebecca (Parmele) P.; grad. Union Coll., 1843, Union Theol. Sem., N.Y.C., 1848; never married. Agt. for Am. Tract Soc., Va., 1843-45, Washington, D.C., 1861-63, for Am. Bible Soc. in Dominican Republic, 1848-50, Ky., 1853-58; ordained pastor by Presbytery of N.Y., 1853; pres. Cumberland Coll., Princeton, Ky., 1858-61; sec. Christian Commn., Toledo, O., 1861-63; preached to freedmen in Va., Ga., 1863-69; state librarian of Ohio, 1885-86; mem. N.Y. Hist. Soc. Author: American Missionary Memorial, Including Biographical and Historical Sketches, 1853; Jefferson at Monticello: The Private Life of Thomas Jefferson, 1862; In the Brush; or, Old-Time Social, Political and Religious Life in the Southwest, 1881. Died Bergen, Sept. 7, 1888.

PIERSON, Isaac, congressman, physician; b. Orange, N.J., Aug. 15, 1770; grad. Princeton, 1789, Coll. of Physicians and Surgeons, N.Y.C. Began practice of medicine, Orange; assessor of Orange, 1807; pres. N.J. Med. Soc., 1827; sheriff Essex County (N.J.), 1807-09; mem. U.S. Ho. of Reps. (Whig) from N.J., 20th-21st congresses, 1827-31. Died Orange, Sept. 22, 1833; buried Old Burying Ground; reinterred Rosedale Cemetery, 1840.

PIERSON, Jeremiah Halsey, congressman, businessman; b. Newark, N.J., Sept. 13, 1766; studied law. Admitted to bar, practiced law, Mass.; moved to Ramapo, N.Y., 1795, practiced law, engaged in merc. activities; built dam on Ramapo River; mfr. files and wood screws; justice of peace, 1800-11; asso. justice Ct. of Common Pleas, 1808; instrumental in constrn. of Erie R.R.; mem. U.S. Ho. of Reps. (Federalist) from N.Y., 17th Congress, 1821-23; del. Nat.-Republican Conv., Balt., 1831. Died Ramapo, Dec. 12, 1855; buried Ramapo Cemetery.

PIERSON, Job, congressman, lawyer; b. East Hampton, N.Y., Sept. 23, 1791; grad. Williams Coll., 1811; studied law, Salem and Schaghticoke. Admitted to bar, 1815, began practice of law, Rensselaer County, N.Y.; dist. atty., 1824-33; mem. U.S. Ho. of Reps. (Democrat) from N.Y., 22d-23d congresses, 1831-35; surrogate Rensselaer County, 1835-40; del. Democratic nat. convs., 1848, 52, 56. Died Troy, N.Y., Apr. 9, 1860; buried Oakwood Cemetery.

PIERZ, Franz, missionary; b. Kamnik, Carniola, Austria, Nov. 20, 1785. Ordained priest Roman Catholic Ch., 1813; came to U.S. as missionary to Chippewa Indians, supported by Leopoldinen-Stiftung mission bd. in Vienna (Austria), 1835; worked at Sault Ste. Marie, established missions on Lake Superior, 1835-39, Arbre Croche (now Harbor Springs), Mich., 1839-52; worked in Upper Miss. region, 1852-73; returned to Austria, 1873; encouraged Austrian emigration to U.S. Author: Die Indianer in Nord-Amerika, 1855. Died Austria, Jan. 22, 1880.

PIGGOT, Robert, engraver, clergyman; b. N.Y.C., May 20, 1795. Apprenticed to David Edwin, engraver, Phila., 1812-16; partner (with Charles Goodman) in engraving business, Phila., 1816; later owned bookstore, Phila.; ordained deacon Protestant Episcopal Ch., 1823, priest, 1825; rector St. Matthews Ch., Phila., 1824-25, Holy Trinity parish, Sykesville, Md., 1869-87; served various chs. as missionary for Soc. for Advancement Christinity in Pa.; later pastor in Md. Died Sykesville, Md., July 23, 1887.

PIGGOTT, James, pioneer ofcl. in Ill.; b. Conn., circa 1739; married twice; m. 2d, Francies James; 8 children. Commd. capt. from Westmoreland County in Pa. Militia, served undler Gen. Arthur St. Clair, 1776-77; had command of Ft. Jefferson, nr. mouth Ohio River, during seige of Chickasaw Indians, 1780; a leader against French in area, 1787, signed contract appointing Bartholomew Tardiveau as agt. to U.S. Congress; apptd. capt. Ill. Territorial Militia, also justice of peace at Cahokia, Ill., circa 1790; judge of common pleas Cahokia, 1795, judge of quarter sessions, 1796; proclaimed opening of Orphans' Ct.; started ferry service and bldgs. (nucleus of present-day East St. Louis), Ill. Died Kaskaskia, Ill., Feb. 20, 1799.

PIKE, Albert, lawyer; b. Boston, Dec. 29, 1809; s. Benjamin and Sarah (Andrews) P.; A.M. (hon.), Harvard, 1859; m. Mary Ann Hamilton, Oct. 10, 1834, 6 children. Tchr. various schs. in East; went to St. Louis, 1831; became fur trader; owner, editor Ark. Advocate, 1835; licensed to practice law, 1837; asst. clk. Ark. Territorial Legislature; 1st reporter Ark. Supreme Ct., work appears in 1st 5 vols. of Reports, 1840-45; admitted to practice before Ark. Supreme Ct., 1842; served in Mexican War; commr. to negotiate treaties with Indian tribes west of Ark., 1861; commd. brig. gen. Confederate Army with orders to recruit Indians, had troubles with his superiors, once arrested as being hostile to Confederate cause; Mason (sovereign grand comdr. Supreme Grand Council, So. Jurisdiction of U.S., 1859). Author: Morals and Dogma of the Ancient and Accepted Scottish Rite of Freemasonry (several edits.); Prose Sketches and Poems Written in the Western County, 1839. Died Washington, D.C., Apr. 2, 1891; buried Oak Hill Cemetery, Washington.

PIKE, Austin Franklin, senator, congressman; b. Hebron, N.H., Oct. 16, 1819; studied law. Admitted to Merrimack County (N.H.) bar, 1845; mem. N.H. Ho. of Reps., 1850-52, 65-66, speaker, 1865-66; del. Republican Nat. Conv., Phila., 1856; mem. N.H. Senate, 1857-58, pres., 1858; chmn. N.H. Republican Com., 1858-60; mem. U.S. Ho. of Reps. (Rep.) from N.H., 43d Congress, 1873-75; mem. U.S. Senate (Rep.) from N.H., 1883-86. Died Franklin, N.H., Oct. 8, 1886; buried Franklin Cemetery.

PIKE, Frederick Augustus, congressman, lawyer; b. Calais, Me., Dec. 9, 1816; attended Washington Acad., East Machias, Me.; grad. Bowdoin Coll., Brunswick, Me., 1837; studied law. Admitted to bar, began practice of law, Calais, 1840; mayor Calais, 1852-53; mem. Me. Ho. of Reps., 1858-60, 70-71, speaker, 1860; mem. U.S. Ho. of Reps. (Republican) from Me., 37th-40th congresses, 1861-69. Died Calais, Dec. 2, 1886; buried Calais Cemetery.

PIKE, James, congressman, clergyman; b. Salisbury, Essex County, Mass., No. 10, 1818; studied theology Wesleyan U., Conn., 1837-39. A minister, 1841-54; moved to Pembroke, N.H., 1854; mem. U.S. Ho. of Reps. (Am. Party) from N.H., 34th-35th congresses, 1855-59; served as col. 16th Regt., N.H. Volunteer Inf., 1862-63; unsuccessful candidate for gov. N.H., 1871; became presiding elder Dover dist.; ret. from preaching, 1886. Died Newfields, N.H., July 26, 1895; buried Locust Cemetery.

PIKE, James Shepherd, journalist; b. Calais, Me., Sept. 8, 1811; s. William and Hannah (Shepherd) P.; m. Charlotte Grosvenor, 1837; m. 2d, Elizabeth Ellicott, 1855. Editor Boundary Gazette and Calais Advertiser, 1835-36; corr. Portland (Me.) Advertiser, also Boston Courier, 1840-50; invited by Horace Greeley to be regular corr. N.Y. Tribune, 1850, Washington corr., 1850-60, became asso. editor, 1852; minister resident to The Hague, The Netherlands, 1861-66; supported Horace Greeley for Pres. U.S., 1872; went to S.C. (1872) to collect material for The Prostrate State: South Carolina under Negro Government, published 1874. Author: The Restoration of the Currency, 1868; The Financial Crisis, 1869; Horace Greeley in 1872, 1873; The New Puritan, 1878; First Blows of the Civil War, 1879. Died Calais, Nov. 29, 1882.

PIKE, Nicolas, educator; b. Somersworth, N.H., Oct. 17, 1743; s. James and Sarah (Gilman) P.; grad. Harvard, 1766; m. Hannah Smith; m. 2d, Eunice Smith, Jan. 9, 1779; 6 children. Master, Newburyport (Mass.) Grammar Sch., 1773-circa 1800; taught pvt. schs., Newburyport, 1774-83; justice of peace; wrote 1st popular arithmetic text books in Am.; mem. Am. Acad. Arts and Scis., 1788-1819. Author: New and Complete System of Arithmetick, Composed for the Use of the Citizens of the United States, 1788; Abridgement of the New and Complete System of Arithmetick, 1793. Died Dec. 9, 1819.

PIKE, Robert, colonial ofcl.; b. Whiteparish, Wiltshire, Eng., 1616; s. John and Dorothy (Daye) P.; m. Sarah Sanders, Apr. 3, 1641; m. 2d, Martha (Moyce) Goldwyer, Oct. 30, 1684; 8 children including John. Arrived in Boston, 1635; was part of colony which founded Salisbury (Mass.); took oath as freeman, 1637; elected to Gen. Ct. of Mass., 1648, reelected; served as maj. during Indian Wars; elected a magistrate, 1688-89; mem. Mass. Gov.'s Council, 1689-96; mem. group which bought Island of Nantucket from Thomas Mayhew, 1659; a leader in fight for civil and religious liberties. Died Dec. 12, 1708.

PIKE, Zebulon Montgomery, explorer, army officer; b. Lamberton (now part of Trenton), N.J., Feb. 5, 1779; s. Zebulon and Isabella (Brown) P.; m. Clarissa Brown, Mar. 1801, several children. Commd. 1st lt., 1st Regt., U.S. Inf., 1799; led exploring party to mouth of Mississippi River; at head of company of 20 set out for St. Louis, Aug. 9, 1805; explored headwaters of Arkansas and Red Rivers, 1806, discovered Pike's Peak (named for him) in Colo.; commd. capt., 1806; explored South Park and head of Arkansas River; commd. maj., 1808, col. of inf., 1810; promoted brig. gen., 1813; killed in War of 1812. Died York (now Toronto), Can., Apr. 27, 1813.

PILAT, Ignaz Anton, landscape gardener; b. St. Agatha, Austria, June 27, 1820; grad. U. Vienna (Austria); m. Clara L. Rittler, 5 children including Oliver I. Layed out part of Prince Metternich, Vienna; came to U.S., 1848, worked as landscape architect in South; landscape architect, N.Y.C., 1856-70; worked primarily on executing designs for Central Park prepared by Frederick Olmsted and Calvert Vaux; also designed parks for William Cullen Bryant, Cyrus Field and Mass. Agrl. Coll. Died N.Y.C., Sept. 17, 1870.

PILCHER, Joshua, fur trader, Indian agt.; b. Culpeper County, Va., Mar. 15, 1790; s. Joshua and Nancy Pilcher; never married. Partner with N. S. Anderson in fur trade, St. Louis, later with Thomas F. Riddick in firm Riddick & Pilcher; dir. Bank of St. Louis; made yearly expdns. into Indian country to collect furs; dir. Mo. Fur Co., 1819, pres., 1820-31; served in campaign against Arikara Indians, 1823; in charge of post at Council Bluffs (now Ia.), 1831-43; Indian agt. for Upper Missouri River tribes, 1837-39; supt. Indian affairs, 1839-41. Died St. Louis, June 5, 1843.

PILE, William Anderson, congressman, gov. N.M.; b. nr. Indpls., Feb. 11, 1829; studied theology. Ordained to ministry Methodist Episcopal Ch., became mem. Mo. Conf.; commd. chaplain 1st Regt., Mo. Light Arty., U.S. Army, 1861; promoted lt. col. 33d Regt., Mo. Inf., 1862, then col., 1862; commd. brig. gen. Volunteers, 1863; brevetted maj. gen., 1865; mem. U.S. Ho. of Reps. (Republican) from Mo., 40th Congress, 1867-69; gov. N.M., 1869-70; minister resident to Venezuela, 1871-74. Died Monrovia, Cal., July 7, 1889; buried Live Oak Cemetery.

PILLING, James Constantine, ethnologist; b. Washington, D.C., Nov. 16, 1846; s. James and Susan (Collins) P.; grad. Gonzaga Coll., Washington; m. Minnie L. Harper, 1888, 1 child. Joined geol. survey of Rocky Mountains under John W. Powell, 1875; collected ethnol. material concerning Am. Indians, 1875-80; chief clk. U.S. Ethnol. Bur., 1880-95. Author: Proof-sheets of a Bibliography of the Languages of the North American Indians, 1885; also bibliographies of Eskimo (1887), Siouan (1887), Iroquoian (1888), Muskhogean (1889), Athapascan (1892) (all published in U.S. Bur. Ethnology Bulls.). Died Olney, Md., July 26, 1895.

PILLOW, Gideon Johnson, army officer; b. Williamson County, Tenn., June 8, 1806; s. Gideon and Anne (Payne) P.; grad. U. Nashville, 1827; m. Mary Martin, 10 children. Admitted to Tenn. bar; practiced in partnership with James K. Polk in Columbia, Tenn.; apptd. brig. gen. U.S. Volunteers, 1846, promoted maj. gen. due to friendship of Pres. Polk, 1846; served at battles of Vera Cruz, Cerro Gordo, Contreras and Chapultepec; mem. So. Conv., Nashville, 1850; apptd. sr. maj. gen. Provisional Army of Tenn., later brig. gen. Confederate Army, 1861; served at Battle of Belmont (Mo.), 1861; practiced law in partnership with Isham G. Harris, Memphis, Tenn., after 1865. Died Helena, Ark., Oct. 8, 1878.

PILLSBURY, Charles Alfred, flour mill exec.; b. Warner, N.H., Dec. 3, 1842; s. George Alfred and Margaret (Carlton) P.; grad. Dartmouth, 1863; m. Mary A. Stinson, Sept. 12, 1866, 4 children including John S., Charles S. Bought flour mill, Mpls., 1869; one of 1st to make use of flour purifier invented by Edmond La Croix; organized firm C. A. Pillsbury and Co., 1872 (became world's largest flour milling firm), sold firm to English syndicate, 1889, remained as mng. dir., 1889-99; organized Millers' Assn. and Mpls. C. of C. in order to concentrate grain trade at Mpls.; a builder Mpls., Saulte Ste. Marie & Atlantic Ry.; initiated one of 1st employee profit-sharing plans; mem. Minn. Senate, 1878-85. Died Mpls., Sept. 17, 1899.

PILLSBURY, Parker, reformer; b. Hamilton, Mass., Sept. 22, 1809; s. Oliver and Anna (Smith) P.; grad. Gilmanton Theol. Sem., 1838; attended Andover Theol. Sem., 1839-40; m. Sarah H. Sargent, Jan. 1, 1840, 1 dau., Helen Buffam. Abolitionist in New Eng., 1840; editor Herald of Freedom, 1840, 45-46, National Anti-Slavery Standard, 1866; became advocate of woman's rights; joint editor (with Elizabeth Cady Stanton) of Revolution, 1868-69. Author: Acts of the Anti-Slavery Apostles, 1883. Died Concord, N.H., July 7, 1898.

PILMORE, Joseph, clergyman; b. Tadmouth, Yorkshire, Eng., Nov. 11, 1739; m. Mary (Benezet) Wood, 1790, 1 child. Lay asst. of John Wesley, Eng.; lay missionary in Am., 1769-74, in Eng., 1774-84; returned to U.S., 1784; ordained deacon and priest Protestant Episcopal Ch., 1785; rector United Parish of Trinity, All Saints', St. Thomas's, Phila., 1785-93; del. Gen. Conv., 1789; rector Christ Ch., N.Y.C., 1793-1804, St. Paul's Ch., Phila., 1804-25. Died Phila., July 24, 1825.

PILSBURY, Amos, prison adminstr.; b. Londonderry, N.H., Feb. 8, 1805; s. Moses Cross and Lois (Cleaveland) P.; m. Emily Heath, 1826, 5 children. Guard, N.H. State Prison, 1824-25, dep. warden, 1825-26; dep. warden Conn. State Prison, 1826-30, warden, 1830-45; supt. Albany County (N.Y.) Penitentiary, 1845-55, 60-73, N.Y.C. prisons, Ward's Island, 1855-59; gen. supt. N.Y.C. police, 1859-60; one of 1st prison wardens in U.S. to operate instns. to make financial profit for state; a founder Nat. Prison Assn. of U.S. (now Am. Prison Assn.), 1870; del. from N.Y. to Internat. Penitentiary Congress, London, Eng., 1872. Died July 14, 1873.

PILSBURY, Timothy, congressman; b. Newburyport, Mass., Apr. 12, 1789; attended common schs. Worked in a store, then became a sailor; commanded privateer Yankee during War of 1812; engaged in shipping, settled in Eastport, Me.; mem. Me. Ho. of Reps., 1825-26, Me. Exec. Council, 1827-36; moved to Ohio, then to New Orleans, later to Brazoria, Tex.; mem. Republic of Tex. Ho. of Reps., 1840-41, Senate, 1842, 45; chief justice of county ct.; judge of probate Brazoria County; mem. U.S. Ho. of Reps. (Calhoun Democrat) from Tex., 29th-30th congresses, Mar. 30, 1846-49. Died Henderson, Tex., Nov. 23, 1858; buried City Cemetery.

PINCKNEY, Charles, senator, gov. S.C.; b. Charleston, S.C., Oct. 26, 1757; s. Col. Charles and Frances (Brewton) P.; m. Mary Laurens, Apr. 27, 1788, 3 children. Admitted to S.C. bar, 1779; enlisted in Charleston Regt.; S.C. Militia, 1779, taken prisoner by British, 1780; mem. S.C. Ho. of Reps., 1779-84, 86-89, 92-96, 1805-06, 10-14; mem. Continental Congress, 1784-87; mem. U.S. Constl. Conv., 1787, submitted proposed draft of fed. constn. (many provisions of which were incorporated into U.S. Constn.); pres. S.C. Constl. Conv. that ratified U.S. Constn., 1788; pres. S.C. State Constl. Conv., 1790; gov. S.C., 1789-92, 96-98, 1806-08; mem. U.S. Senate (Democrat) from S.C., Dec. 6, 1798-1805; U.S. minister to Spain, 1801-04; mem. U.S. Ho. of Reps. from S.C., (Democrat) 16th Congress, 1819-21. Died Charleston, Oct. 29, 1824; buried St. Philip's Churchyard, Charleston.

PINCKNEY, Charles Cotesworth, diplomat, army officer; b. Charlestown (now Charleston), S.C., Feb. 25, 1746; s. Charles and Elizabeth (Lucas) P.; matriculated at Christ Ch. Coll., 1764; m. Sarah Middleton, Sept. 28, 1773; m. 2d, Mary Stead, June 23, 1786; 3 children. Admitted to Middle Temple, 1764, English bar, 1769, S.C. bar, 1770; mem. S.C. Provincial Assembly, 1769, 75; acting atty. gen. for Camden, Georgetown and the Cherows, 1773; mem. lower house S.C. Legislature, 1778, 82; pres. S.C. Senate, 1779; ranking capt. 1st Regt., S.C. Militia, 1775, apptd. col., 1776; aide to George Washington, served at battles of Germantown and Brandywine, 1777; commanded his regt. at seige of Savannah, commanded Ft. Moultrie at attacks on Charlestown; taken prisoner by British when Charlestown fell, exchanged, 1782; apptd. brig. gen. Continental Army, 1783; del. U.S. Constl. Conv., 1787; mem. S.C. Conv. to ratify U.S. Constn., 1788; mem. S.C. Constl. Conv., 1790; apptd. U.S. minister to France, 1796 (French Directory refused to recognize his status due to reaction over Jay Treaty), left Paris for Amsterdam (Holland); apptd. rep. of Am. (with John Marshall, Elbridge Gerry) to France to negotiate situation (series of letters between Talleyrand's ministers and the 3 Americans precipitated the XYZ affair); left Paris, 1798, apptd. (by Washington) comdr. all forces and posts South of Md.; Federalist candidate for U.S. Pres., 1800, 04; 1st pres. Charleston Bible Soc., 1810. Died Charleston, Aug. 16, 1825.

PINCKNEY, Elizabeth Lucas, planter; b. Antigua, B.W.I., 1722; dau. of George Lucas; m. Charles Pinckney, May 27, 1744 (dec. 1758), at least 3 children, Charles Cotesworth, Thomas, Mrs. Daniel Horry. Came to Am., 1738; took over mgmt. father's 3 plantations in S.C., 1739; 1st to successfully raise indigo in S.C., 1741-44; revived silk culture in S.C. on husband's plantation; after husband's death owned and managed several plantations in S.C. Died Phila., May 26, 1793; buried St. Peter's Churchyard, Phila.

PINCKNEY, Henry Laurens, congressman; b. Charleston, S.C., Sept. 24, 1794; s. Charles and Mary Eleanor (Laurens) P.; grad. S.C.Coll. (now U.S.C.), 1812; studied law; m. Rebecca Elliot; m. 2d, Sabina Ramsay; 3 children. Admitted to S.C. bar, 1813; mem. S.C. Ho. of Reps., 1816-32; founder Charleston Mercury, 1819, editor, 1819-34; mem. U.S. Ho. of Reps. (Democrat) from S.C., 23d-24th congresses, 1833-37; mayor Charleston, 1829, 31-32, 37-40, converted Coll. of Charleston into 1st municipal coll. in U.S., 1837; collector Port of Charleston, 1841-42; tax collector St. Philip's and St. Michael's parishes, Charleston, 1845-63. Died Charleston, Feb. 3, 1863; buried Circular Congregational Ch. Burying Ground, Charleston.

PINCKNEY, Thomas, gov. S.C., diplomat; b. Charleston, S.C., Oct. 23, 1750; s. Charles and Elizabeth (Lucas) P.; grad. Oxford (Eng.) U.; studied Middle Temple, London, Eng., 1768; m. Elizabeth Motte, July 22, 1779; m. 2d, Frances Motte, Oct. 19, 1797; 4 children. Admitted to English bar, 1774, S.C. bar, 1774; served as capt. 1st Regt., S.C. Militia, 1775, promoted maj., 1778; mil. aide to Count d'Estaing at Savannah, Ga.; served under marquis de Lafayette at Yorktown; gov. S.C., 1787-88; pres. S.C. Conv. to ratify U.S. Constn, 1788; mem lower house S.C. Legislature, 1791; U.S. minister to Eng., 1791-95; spl. commr. to Spain, 1795, determined So. boundary of U.S. and navigational arrangements for Mississippi River in Treaty of San Lorenzo el Real (Pinckney Treaty), 1795; unsuccessful Federalist Party candidate for vice pres. U.S., 1796; mem. U.S. Ho. of Reps. from S.C., 5th-6th congresses, 1797-1801; maj. gen. U.S. Volunteers in command of dist. extending from N.C. to Mississippi River, 1812; neogtiated Treaty of Ft. Jackson with Creek Indian Nation ending the Creek War, 1814. Died Charleston, Nov. 2, 1828; buried St. Philip's Churchyard, Charleston.

PINDALL, James, congressman, lawyer; b. Monongahela County, Va. (now W.Va.), circa 1783; attended common schs.; studied law. Admitted to bar, 1803, practiced law, Morgantown, then in Clarksburg, Va. (now W.Va.); held various local offices; mem. Va. Senate, 1808-12; served as col. militia; mem. U.S. Ho. of Reps. (Federalist) from Va., 15th-16th congresses, 1817-July 26, 1820 (resigned). Died Clarksburg, Nov. 22, 1825; buried Clarksburg.

PINE, Robert Edge, painter; b. London, Eng., 1730; s. John Pine; 2 children. Portrait artist in London; mem. Soc. for Encouragement Arts, Royal Acad.; came to U.S., 1784, settled in Phila.; subjects include David Garrick, King George II, John Wilkes, Francis Hopkinson, 1785, George Washington and his family, 1785, Robert Morris, Benjamin Franklin; other paintings include The Surrender of Calais, 1760, Canute Rebuking his Courtiers, 1763, The Congress Voting Independence. Died Phila., Nov. 19, 1788.

PINKERTON, Allan, detective; b. Glasgow, Scotland, Aug. 25, 1819; son of William Pinkerton; m. Joan Carfrae, 1842, at least 2 children. Apprenticed to cooper, Glasgow, 1831-39; came to U.S., 1842; cooper, Dundee, Ill., 1842-50; dep. sheriff Kane County, Ill., 1846; operated sta. of Underground R.R. at his home; 1st detective Chgo. police force, 1850-51; established Pinkerton Detective Agy., Chgo. (one of 1st pvt. detective agys. in U.S.), 1850; established Pinkerton's Preventive Watch (one of 1st corps of night-watchmen in U.S.), 1860; discovered and squelched plan to assassinate Pres. Lincoln, 1861; organized 1st secret service div. of U.S. Army, 1861; toured Tenn., Ga., Miss. as a spy, 1861; 1st chief U.S. Secret Service, 1861-62; head secret service Dept. of Gulf, 1862-65; worked under name Maj. E. J. Allen during Civil War; important cases solved include $40,000 robbery of Bank of Carbondale, Pa., 1866, $700,000 train robbery of Adams Express Co., 1866, $300,000 robbery of express car on Hudson River R.R. Author: 15 books narrating his experiences including: The Molly Maguires and the Detectives, 1877; Criminal Reminiscences, 1878; The Spy of the Rebellion, 1883; Thirty Years a Detective, 1884. Died July 1, 1884.

PINKERTON, Lewis Letig, clergyman, editor; b. Baltimore County, Md., Jan. 28, 1812; s. William and Elizabeth (Letig) P.; m. Sarah A. Bell, Mar. 19, 1833. Practiced medicine, Carthage, O., 1834-39; pastor chs. of Disciples of Christ at New Union, later at Lexington, Ky., 1839-44, Midway, Ky., 1844-60; established Baconian Inst. for Girls, Midway; a founder Ky. Female Orphan Sch., 1847; published mag. Christian Mirror, 1848; edited Christian Age, 1853-54, The New Era (temperance paper), 1854; prof. English, Ky. U., 1860-62, 63-66; commd. surgeon 11th Ky. Cavalry, U.S. Volunteers, 1862; agt. Freedman's Bur., Fayette County, Ky., 1866; edited Independent Monthly, 1869; spl. U.S. mail agt., 1873-74; pastorates closed to him after war because of Union sympathies and because of liberal theol. convictions; opposed conformity to prescribed doctrines and ritual. Author: A Discourse Concerning Some of the Effects of the Late Civil War on Ecclesiastical Matters in Kentucky, 1866. Died Jan. 28, 1875.

PINKHAM, Lydia Estes, patent medicine mfr.; b. Lynn, Mass., Feb. 9, 1819; d. William and Rebecca (Chase) Estes; m. Isaac Pinkham, Sept. 8, 1843, 4 sons, 1 dau. Mem. Female Anti-Slavery Soc. of Lynn; commercially sold herb medicine she had devised as remedy for "woman's weakness," 1875 (became most widely advertised merchandise in the country by 1898). Died May 17, 1883.

PINKNEY, Edward Coote, poet; b. London, Eng., Oct. 1, 1802; s. William and Ann Maria (Rodgers) P.; attended St. Mary's Coll., Balt.; m. Georgiana McCausland, Oct. 12, 1824, 1 child. Commd. midshipman U.S. Navy, 1815; served in Mediterranean, later against pirates in West Indies; left active duty, 1822, resigned, 1824; admitted to Md. bar, 1822; practiced law, Balt.; editor bi-weekly The Marylander, Balt., 1827-28; best known poems include "A Health," "Serenade." Author: Look out upon the Stars, My Love: A Serenade Written by a Gentleman of Baltimore, 1823; Rodolph, A Fragment, 1823; Poems, 1825. Died Balt., Apr. 11, 1828; buried Unitarian Cemetery, Balt.; reinterred Greenmount Cemetery, Balt., 1872.

PINKNEY, Ninian, naval surgeon; b. Annapolis, Md., June 7, 1811; s. Ninian Hobbs and Amelia (Grason) P.; grad. St. John's Coll., Annapolis, 1830, LL.D. (hon.), 1873; M.D., Jefferson Med. Coll., 1833; m. Mary Sherwood Hambleton, 1 dau., Amelia. Commd. asst. surgeon U.S. Navy, 1834; served in S.Am. and Mediterranean; stationed Phila. Naval Hosp., 1838-39; promoted surgeon, 1841; served at Callao, Peru, 1841-44; on blockade duty during Mexican War; apptd. instr. U.S. Naval Acad., 1852; fleet surgon Miss. Squadron, 1863-65; established naval hosp., Memphis, Tenn., 1863 (named Pinkney Hosp. in his honor); apptd. med. dir. with rank of commodore, 1871; retired 1873. Died Easton, Md., Dec 15, 1877.

PINKNEY, William, senator, diplomat; b. Annapolis, Md., Mar. 17, 1764; s. Jonathan and Ann (Rind) P.; studied law under Samuel Chase, 1783-86; m. Ann Maria Rodgers, Mar. 16, 1789, 10 children including Edward Coote, Frederick. Admitted to Md. bar, 1786; practiced law in Hartford County, Md., later developed 1 of nation's most lucrative law practices, Balt.; del. Md. Conv. to ratify U.S. Constn., 1788; mem. Md. Ho. of Dels., 1788-92; mem. Md. Exec. Council, 1792-95; elected to U.S. Ho. of Reps., 1792, refused to serve; commr. under Jay Treaty in Eng. to adjust Am. claims for maritime losses, 1796-1804; atty. gen. of Md., 1805-06; joint commr. with James Monroe to treat with Eng. on subjects of violation of rights of neutrals and impressment, 1807; U.S. minister to Eng., 1807-11; mem. Md. Senate, 1811; U.S. atty. gen., 1811-14; served as maj. Md. Militia in War of 1812, wounded at Battle of Bladensburg, 1814; mem. U.S. Ho. of Reps. from Md., 14th Congress, 1815-Apr. 18, 1816; U.S. minister to Russia and spl. envoy to Naples, 1816-18; mem. U.S. Senate from Md., 1819-22. Died Washington, D.C., Feb. 25, 1822; buried Congressional Cemetery, Washington.

PINNER, Max, pianist; b. N.Y.C., Apr. 14, 1851; attended Leipzig (Germany) Conservatory, 1865-67; studied with Tausig and Weitzmann, Berlin, Germany, 1867-69. Made long pianistic tours; settled in N.Y.C., 1877; became noted tchr. and pianist. Died Davos, Switzerland, May 10, 1887.

PINNEY, Norman, clergyman, educator; b. Simsbury, Conn., Oct. 21, 1804; s. Butler and Eunice (Griswold) P.; grad. Yale, 1823; never married. Tutor, Washington (now Trinity) Coll., Hartford, Conn., 1826-28, adjunct prof. ancient langs., 1828-31; ordained to ministry Protestant Episcopal Ch., 1831; rector Christ Ch., Mobile, Ala., 1831-36; founded, conducted Mobile Inst. for Boys, 1836-62. Author: The Principles of Education as Applied in the Mobile Institute, 1836; Practical French Teacher, 1847; First Book in French, 1848; The Progressive French Reader, 1850; The Practical Spanish Teacher, 1855; French Grammar, 1861. Died New Orleans, Oct. 1, 1862.

PINTARD, John, mcht.; b. N.Y.C., May 18, 1759; s. John and Mary (Cannon) P.; A.B., Coll. of N.J. (now Princeton), 1776; LL.D. (hon.), Allegheny Coll., 1822; m. Eliza Brashear, Nov. 12, 1784, 2 children. Dep. to commr. of prisoners at N.Y.; book auctioneer and editor Daily Advertiser; sec. N.Y. Fire Ins. Co., later pres.; known as father of hist. socs. in Am.; an organizer Mass. Hist. Soc., 1789; alderman N.Y.C., 1788-89; mem. N.Y. State Legislature, 1790; organized hist. museum under auspices of Tammany Soc. 1791, 1st sagamore, later grand sachem; an organizer N.Y. Hist. Soc., 1804, sec. several years, clk. of corp., 1804-10; city insp. of N.Y.C., 1804-10; a founder Gen. Theol. Sem.; sec., v.p. Am. Bible Soc.; sec., reviver N.Y. City C. of C., 1817-27; organized 1st savings bank, N.Y.C., 1819, pres., 1828-41. Died N.Y.C., June 21, 1844.

PINTARD, Lewis, mcht.; b. N.Y.C., Oct. 12, 1732; s. John and Catherine (Carré) P.; m. Susan Stockton, several children. Inherited father's shipping and commn. business with Eng. and East Indies, N.Y.C., 1748; commissary for Am. prisoners in N.Y.C. during Brit. occupation in Revolutionary War; responsible for administering relief funds provided by Continental Congress; became chief Am. importer of Madeira wines and chief exporter of flaxseed, after war; later engaged in sugar and molasses trade with West Indies; sch. commr. New Rochelle (N.Y.), 1797. Died Princeton, N.J., Mar. 25, 1818.

PINTO, Isaac, mcht., translator; b. Portugal, June 23, 1720; never married. Became wealthy in import export business, N.Y.C.; wholesale wine mcht., Charlestown (now Charleston), S.C., 1760-62; taught Spanish privately, N.Y.C., 1790-91. Translator: (into English) The Form of Prayer for a General Thanksgiving for the Reducing of Canada, 1760; Evening Service of Roshashanah and Kippur (1st Jewish prayer book printed in Am.) 1761; Prayers for Shabbath, Rosh-Hashannah, and Yom Kippur, 1766. Died N.Y.C., Jan. 17, 1791; buried Spanish and Portuguese Burial Ground, N.Y.C.

PIPER, William, congressman; b. Bloody Run (now Everett), Bedford County, Pa., Jan. 1, 1774. Commanded a regt. during War of 1812; adj. gen. Pa., after the war; mem. U.S. Ho. of Reps. from Pa., 12th-14th congresses, 1811-17. Died nr. Everett, 1852; buried Piper Cemetery on his farm nr. Everett.

PIQUENARD, Alfred H., architect; b. France. came from Havre to Am., 1848; submitted winning design in competition for constrn. of State Capitol Bldg., Des Moines, Ia., served as architect of structure, 1871-74; also identified (with John C. Cochrane of Chgo.) with design and constrn. of Ill. Capitol, Springfield, circa 1867. Died Nov. 22, 1876.

PIRCE, William Almy, congressman; b. Hope, Providence County, R.I., Feb. 29, 1824; attended Smithville Sem. (now Lapham Inst.). Became a school tchr.; mgr. of store and counting room of his father's cotton mill, Simmons Upper Village, R.I., 10 years; mfr. of cotton goods, 1854-63; mem. R.I. Senate, 1855, 82; mem. R.I. Ho. of Reps., 1858, 62, 79-81; assessor internal revenue for 2d Dist. R.I., 1862-73; apptd. paymaster with rank of maj. R.I. Militia, 1863; chmn. R.I. delegation to Republican Nat. Conv., Chgo., 1880; mem. Rep. Nat. Com., 1880, 84; mem. U.S. Ho. of Reps. (Rep.) from R.I., 49th Congress, 1885-Jan. 25, 1887; justice of peace, assessor of taxes, Johnston, R.I. Died Johnston, Mar. 5, 1891; buried Swan Point Cemetery, Providence, R.I.

PIRSSON, James W., architect; b. Dec. 15, 1833; son of James Pirsson. Became a musician and artist; later practiced architecture as mem. firm Hubert Pirsson & Co., N.Y.C.; his firm pioneered planning and constrn. of "modern" apt. houses including Chelsea and Central Apts., N.Y.C.; mem. A.I.A. Died Mar. 24, 1888.

PISE, Charles Constantine, clergyman, author; b. Annapolis, Md., Nov. 22, 1801; s. Louis and Marguerite (Gamble) P.; grad. Mt. St. Mary's Coll., Emmitsburg, Md., 1821. Ordained priest Roman Catholic Ch., 1825; tchr. rhetoric Mt. St. Mary's Coll.; curate, Balt.; later asst. curate St. Patrick's Ch., Washington, D.C.; visited Europe, 1832, 42; 1st American to become Knight of Sacred Palace and Count Palatine, 1832; 1st Roman Cath. to serve as chaplain U.S. Senate, 1832; pastor at Annapolis, 1833, St. Joseph's Ch., N.Y.C., 1834-40, St. Charles Borromeo Ch., Bklyn., 1849-66; asst. pastor St. Peter's Ch., N.Y.C., 1840-49; founder The Cath. Expositor and Literary Mag., 1841. Author: History of the Church from Its Establishment to the Present Century, 5 vols., 1827-30; Father Rowland (novel), 1829; The Indian Cottage, a Unitarian Story, (novel), 1829; The Pleasures of Religion and Other Poems, 1833; Aletheia, or, Letters on the Truth of Catholic Doctrine, 1843; St. Ignatius and his First Companions, 1845; Lectures on the Invocation of the Saints, Veneration of Sacred Images, and Purgatory, 1845; Zenosius or the Pilgrim Convert, 1845; Christianity and the Church, 1850. Died Bklyn., May 26, 1866.

PITCAIRN, John, army officer; b. Dysart, Scotland, 1722; s. David and Katherine (Hamilton) P.; m. Elizabeth Dalrymple, several children including Robert, David. Commd. capt. Royal Marines, 1756, promoted maj., 1771; came to Am., 1774; stationed at Boston; with detachment ordered to destroy rebel stores, Concord, Mass., 1775; in command of advance forces which fought battle with minutemen on Lexington Common, 1775; insisted that Americans fired first; mortally wounded in Battle of Bunker Hill. Died Boston, June 1775; buried Christ Ch., Boston; reinterred Ch. of St. Bartholomew the Less, London, Eng.

PITCHER, Molly, see McCauley, Mary Ludwig Hays.

PITCHER, Nathaniel, congressman; b. Litchfield, Conn., 1777; studied law. Moved to Sandy Hill, N.Y.; supr., 1804-10; mem. N.Y. State Assembly, 1806, 15-17; assessor Kingsbury, 1812; surrogate Washington County (N.Y.), 1812-13; town clk. Kingsbury, 1813-14, also justice of peace; admitted to bar, practiced law; del. N.Y. Constl. Conv., 1821; lt. gov. N.Y., 1826, acting gov., 1827-29; mem. U.S. Ho. of Reps. (Democrat) from N.Y., 16th-17th, 22d congresses, 1819-23, 31-33. Died Sandy Hill (now Hudson Falls), N.Y., May 25, 1836; buried Wright Cemetery.

PITCHER, Zina, physician, naturalist, mayor Detroit; b. Washington County, N.Y., Apr. 12, 1797; s. Nathaniel and Margaret (Stevenson) P.; M.D., Middlebury (Vt.) Coll., 1822; m. Anne Sheldon, 1824; m. 2d, Emily L. (Montgomery) Backus, 1867. Apptd. asst. surgeon U.S. Army, 1822; served on posts in Mich., 1822-30; in Indian Territory, 1830-36; resigned, 1836; made extensive studies of natural history of regions in which he served; practiced medicine; mem. staff St. Mary's Hosp., Detroit, 1836-71; mem. 1st Mich. Bd. Regents, 1837-52; mayor of Detroit, 1840-42, 43-44; founder med. dept. U. Mich., 1850; served as city physician, county physician, mem. city bd. health, surgeon to Govt. Marine Hosp.; pres. Mich. Territorial Med. Soc., 1838-51, Mich. Med. Soc., 1855-56, A.M.A., 1856; a founder Detroit Sydenham Soc.; a founder Mich. Hist. Soc., 1822; librarian, 1836; a founder Peninsular Jour. Medicine, 1853, co-editor, 1855-58; asso. editor Richmond and Louisville Med. Jour. Died Detroit, Apr. 5, 1872.

PITCHLYNN, Peter Perkins, Indian chief; b. Noxubee County, Miss., Jan. 30, 1806; s. John and Sophia (Folsom) P.; m. Rhoda Folsom; m. 2d, Caroline (Eckloff) Lombardy. Mem. Choctaw tribe (father was interpreter for U.S. Govt.); established school in Ky. for Indian children, supported by funds from Choctaw govt.; led Indian delegation sent by U.S. Govt. into Osage country on peace-making and exploring expdn., 1828; moved to Indian Territory after Choctaw Treaty of 1830; signed treaty of Dancing Rabbit Creek, 1830, Treaty of 1855; prin. chief of Choctaws, 1860, witnessed treaty of Washington (D.C.) in 1866; represented tribe in Washington; influential in getting Choctaws to abandon polygamy and stop liquor traffic. Died Washington, D.C., Jan. 17, 1881; buried Congressional Cemetery.

PITKIN, Frederick Walker, gov. Colo.; b. Manchester, Conn., Aug. 31, 1837; s. Eli and Hannah (Torrey) P.; grad. Conn. Wesleyan U., 1858, Albany (N.Y.) Law Sch., 1859; m. Fidelia M. James, July 17, 1862. Began practice of law, Milw., 1859; went to Colo., 1874; gov. Colo. (Republican), 1878-83, largely responsible for removal Ute Indians from Colo.; town and county of Pitkin (Colo.) are named for him. Died Pueblo, Colo., Dec. 18, 1886.

PITKIN, Timothy, congressman; b. Farmington, Conn., Jan. 21, 1766; s. Rev. Timothy and Temperance (Clap) P.; grad. Yale, 1785, LL.D. (hon.), 1829; m. Elizabeth Hubbard, June 6, 1801, 6 children. Taught Latin and Greek, Plainfield (Conn.) Acad., 1785; admitted to Conn. bar, 1788; mem. Conn. Ho. of Reps., 1790, 92, 94-1805, 19-30, clk., 1800-02, speaker 1803-05; mem. U.S. Ho. of Reps. (Federalist) from Conn., 9th-14th congresses, 1805-19, author of a plan for progressive emancipation of slaves in border states; del. Conn. Constl. Conv., 1818; resumed law practice, engaged in writing, after 1830; awarded membership in Societe Francaise de Statisstique Universaille for contbns. in field of statistics, 1837. Author: Statistical View of the Commerce of the United States, 1813; A Political and Civil History of the United States, 1828. Died New Haven, Conn., Dec. 18, 1847; buried Grove Street Cemetery, New Haven.

PITKIN, William, lawyer; b. Marylebone, Eng., 1635; s. Roger Pitkin; m. Hannah Goodwin, several children. Came to Am., 1659; tchr., Hartford (Conn.) sch., 1660; practiced law, Hartford; apptd. Conn. atty. for prosecution of delinquents, 1664; mem. spl. ct. to try witches, Fairfield, Conn., 1693, secured reprieve for only woman convicted; asst. for Conn., mem. Ct. of Assts., 1690-94; a leader movement to keep Conn. independent of Eng.; one of largest landowners in Conn. Died Hartford, Dec. 15, 1694; buried churchyard of 1st Ch. of Hartford.

PITKIN, William, colonial gov., jurist; b. Hartford, Conn., Apr. 30, 1694; s. William and Elizabeth (Stanley) P.; m. Mary Woodbridge, May 7, 1724. Rate collector Hartford, 1715; capt. train band, 1730; del. Conn. Assembly, 1732-34; commr. to treat with Indians; judge Hartford County Ct., 1735-52; served as maj., then col. 1st Conn. Regt., 1739; judge Conn. Superior Ct., 1741, chief judge, 1742-54; dep. gov. Conn., 1754-66, gov., 1766-69. Died Conn., Oct. 1, 1769.

PITKIN, William, jurist, mfr.; b. Hartford, Conn., 1725; s. William and Mary (Woodbridge) P.; m. Abigail Church. Owner various power sites and mills; commd. capt. 3d Militia Co. of Hartford, 1756; became maj.-comdr. 1st Regt. Conn. Militia, 1758, lt. col., 1762; asst. to Conn. Gov.'s Council, 1766-85; mem. Council of Safety during Am. Revolution; elected to U.S. Congress, 1784, but did not serve; del. from East Hartford to Conn. Conv. to ratify U.S. Constn.; judge Superior Ct., 1769-89, chief justice, 1788-89. Died Hartford, Dec. 12, 1789.

PITT, William (1st earl Chatham), statesman; b. Westminster, Eng., Nov. 15, 1708; s. Robert and Harriet (Villiers) P.; attended Trinity Coll., Oxford (Eng.) U.; m. Hester Grenville, Nov. 16, 1754; children—John, William (the Younger), James, Hester, Harriet. Mem. English Ho. of Commons, 1735-66; apptd. joint vice-treas. of Ireland, paymaster-gen. Brit. Army, mem. Privy Council, 1741-55; sec. of state for So. Dept. (included Am. colonies), 1756-60, led England during 1st 4 years of Seven Years War; placed major English war effort in French colonial holdings, letting allies fight European war supported mainly by English subsidies (under plan Eng. captured Ft. Duquesne, Louisburg, Quebec, thus established control over Canada); Eng. received Can. by Treaty of Paris (1763), thus eliminating French influence on Am. continent; lord privy seal, 1766-68, created 1st earl of Chatham, 1766; leader in Ho. of Lords against English colonial policies (despite his poor health), 1766-78; attacked Parliament's right of taxation in colonies, fought for repeal of Stamp Act; introduced bill (in conjunction with Benjamin Franklin) aimed at reconciliation between Eng. and colonies, 1775; protested use of Indians against colonists, 1777; made last appearance in Ho. of Lords to speak against Am. independence, but for polit. compromise; Pittsburgh (Pa.) named for him. Died Hayes Place, Kent, Eng., May 11, 1778; buried Westminster Abbey.

PITTMAN, Charles Wesley, congressman; b. N.J.; grad. Dickinson Coll., Carlisle, Pa., 1838. Conducted Pottsville (Pa.) Acad.; mem. U.S. Ho. of Reps. (Whig) from Pa., 31st Congress, 1849-51; later became a Republican; engaged in lumber business; sheriff Schuylkill County (Pa.), 1871. Died Pottsville, June 8, 1871; buried Presbyn. Cemetery.

PITTS, Hiram Avery, inventor; b. 1800; s. Abial and Abiah Pitts; m. Leonora Hosley, 4 children. Blacksmith, Winthrop, Me., 1825-27; developed improved chain type of hand pump; invented chain band for horse-power treadmill, patented, 1834, manufactured this invention in partnership with brother John; built portable combined threshing and fanning mill, 1834, patented, 1837; carried on business alone, 1840-47; manufactured threshers, Alton, Ill., 1847-52, Chgo., 1852-60; invented machine for breaking hemp and separating stalk from fiber, also several corn and cob mills. Died Chgo., Sept. 19, 1860.

PIZARRO, Francisco, conquistador; b. Trujillo, Spain, circa 1475; son of Gonzalo Pizarro. Mem. Ojeda expdn. to Columbia coast, 1509; mem. Balboa's expdn. which discovered Pacific ocean, 1513; settled in Panama, 1519; having heard tales of Inca Empire in S.Am., formed partnership with Diego de Almargo to conquer Peru, 1522; made 1st attempt, 1524-25, had to turn back after reaching Columbia; received financial aid from mayor of Panama, undertook 2d expdn. (which proved existence of Inca Empire), 1526-28; went to Spain for aid, 1528, received funds and charter of conquest from Charles V; conquered Peru (aided by use of horses and cannon, and fact that Inca Empire was split by civil war), 1531-33; executed the Inca, Atahualpa, Aug. 15, 1533; seized Cuzco, Nov. 1533; founded Lima (Peru) as capital of his domains, 1535; a harsh ruler over both Spaniards and Indians; engaged in war with his partner Almagro over division of spoils, 1537-38, executed Almagro, 1538. Attacked and killed by Almagro's followers, Lima, June 26, 1541.

PLACIDE, Alexander, actor, dancer, mgr.; b. France; m. Charlotte Sophia Wrighten, June 28, 1796, children—Henry, Thomas, Jane, Elizabeth, Caroline. Made Am. debut with his troupe of ballet dancers and tight rope walkers at John Street Theatre. N.Y.C., 1792; appeared as ballet star New Exhbn. Room, Boston, 1792; bought and remodeled bldg. for theatrical use (with Joseph Harper), presented plays, operettas, pantomimes, Newport (R. I.) Theatre, 1793; mgr. French Theatre, Charleston, S.C., 1794; moved co. to Charleston Theatre, 1800, managed co. until 1812; managed co. for summers at Vaux-Hall Gardens, Charleston, 1800-12; set up seasons and travelled with company to Richmond, Va., Savannah, Ga., Augusta, Ga., 1801-12; mgr. (with Twaits and Breschard) Olympic Theatre, N.Y. C., 1812. Died 1812.

PLACIDE, Henry, actor; b. Sept. 8, 1799; s. Alexander and Charlotte (Wrighten) P. Made acting debut at age 9, Augusta, Ga.; appeared at Park Theatre, N.Y.C., 1823-43, mgr. for short time; at Burton's Theatre, N.Y.C., 1843-65; made several nationwide tours; roles include Zekiel Homespun in The Heir at Law, Sir Benjamin Backbite, Crabtree and Sir Peter Teazle in The School for Scandal, Dogberry in Much Ado about Nothing, Capt. Cuttle in Dombey and Son. Died Babylon, N.Y., Jan. 23, 1870.

PLAISTED, Harris Merrill, gov. Me., congressman; b. Jefferson, N.H., Nov. 2, 1828; s. William and Nancy (Merrill) P.; grad. Waterville (now Colby) Coll., 1853, Albany (N.Y.) Law Sch., 1855; m. Sarah Mason, Sept. 21, 1858; m. 2d, Mabel Hill, Sept. 27, 1881; 4 children. Supt. schs., Waterville, Me., 1850-53; admitted to Me. bar, 1856; apptd. by Gov. Washburn to raise mil. co. in Bangor for U.S. Army; became lt. col. 11th Me. Regt., 1861, promoted col., 1862; brevetted brig. gen. Me. Volunteers, 1865, maj. gen., 1865; mem. Me. Legislature, 1867-68; del. at large Republican Nat. Conv., 1868; elected atty. gen. Me., 1873; mem. U.S. Ho. of Reps. (Rep.) from Me., 44th Congress, 1875-76; gov. Me., 1880-82; editor The New Age, 1883-98; supporter of William Jennings Bryan. Died Bangor, Me., Jan. 31, 1898; buried Mt. Hope Cemetery, Bangor.

PLANT, David, congressman, lawyer; b. Stratford, Conn., Mar. 29, 1783; attended Episcopal Acad., Cheshire, Conn.; grad. Yale, 1804; attended Litchfield (Conn.) Law Sch. Admitted to bar, 1804, began practice of law, Stratford; judge probate ct. Fairfield County; mem. Conn. Ho. of Reps., 1817-20, served as speaker; mem. Conn. Senate, 1821-22; lt. gov. Conn., 1823-27; mem. U.S. Ho. of Reps. (Nat.-Republican) from Conn., 20th Congress, 1827-29. Died Stratford, Oct. 18, 1851; buried Congregational Burying Ground.

PLANTS, Tobias Avery, congressman, lawyer; b. Sewickley, Pa., Mar. 17, 1811; apprenticed to saddler at age 12; attended Beaver Coll., Meadville, Pa., a short time; studied law with Edwin M. Stanton in Judge David Powell's office, Steubenville, O. Taught sch.; admitted to bar, began practice of law, Athens, O., 1846, then practiced in Pomeroy, O.; mem. Ohio Ho. of Reps., 1858-61; owner, publisher Pomeroy Weekly Telegraph, circa 1860; mem. U.S. Ho. of Reps. (Republican) from Ohio, 39th-40th congresses, 1865-69; judge Megis County Ct. of Common Pleas, 1873-75; pres. 1st City Bank of Pomeroy, 1878-87. Died Pomeroy, June 19, 1887; buried Beech Grove Cemetery.

PLASSMANN, Ernst, sculptor; b. Sondern, Westphalia, Germany, June 14, 1823. Came to Am., 1853; conducted art sch., N.Y.C., 1854-77; executed statues and monuments for public and pvt. patrons. Author: Modern Gothic Ornaments, 1875; Designs for Furniture, 1877. Died N.Y.C., Nov. 28, 1877.

PLATER, George, gov. Md., Continental congressman; b. "Sotterly" nr. Leonardtown, St. Mary's County, Md., Nov. 8, 1735; s. George and Rebecca Addison (Bowles) P.; grad. Coll. William and Mary, 1753; m. Hannah Lee, Dec. 5, 1762; m. 2d, Elizabeth Rousby, July 19, 1764; 6 children. Del. lower house Md. Assembly, 1758-66; justice of peace St. Mary's County, 1757-71; naval officer Patuxent Dist., 1767-71; judge Md. Provincial Ct., 1771-73; mem. Md. Exec. Council, 1773, 74; collector (apptd. by Md. Council of Safety) to obtain money for mil. operations against Can., 1776; mem. Md. Council of Safety, 1776; mem. com. to draft declaration of rights and form a govt. for Md., 1776; rep. from St. Mary's County to Annapolis Conv.; mem. Continental Congress from Md., 1778-81; mem. Md. Senate from St. Mary's County after Am. Revolution; pres. Md. Conv. which ratified U.S. Constn., 1788; presdl. elector, 1789; gov. Md., 1791-92, negotiations for establishment of District of Columbia (partly on Md. land) completed during his term. Died Annapolis, Feb. 10, 1792; buried "Sotterly."

PLATER, Thomas, congressman, lawyer; b. Annapolis, Md., May 9, 1769; son of George Plater; attended Coll. William and Mary, Williamsburg, Va.; studied law. Admitted to bar, practiced law; served as lt. col. Md. Militia during Whisky Insurrection, 1794; held several local offices; mem. U.S. Ho. of Reps from Md., 7th-8th congresses, 1801-05. Died Poolesville, Montgomery County, Md., May 1, 1830.

PLATT, James Henry, Jr., congressman, businessman; b. St. John's, Can., July 13, 1837; grad. med. dept. U. Vt. at Burlington, 1859. Joined U.S. Army as 1st sgt. 3d Regt., Vt. Volunteer Inf., during Civil War; served as capt. and lt. col.; settled in Petersburg, Va., 1865; mem. Va. Constl. Conv., 1867; mem. city council, 1867-68; moved to Norfolk, Va.; mem. U.S. Ho. of Reps. (Republican) from Va., 41st-43d congresses, Jan. 26, 1870-75; moved to N.Y., 1876, manufactured oil products; engaged in insurance bus., paper mfg. and mining, Denver, Colo., from 1887. Drowned in Green Lake, nr. Georgetown, Colo., Aug. 13, 1894; buried Fairmont Cemetery, Denver.

PLATT, Jonas, congressman, lawyer; b. Poughkeepsie, N.Y., June 30, 1769; son of Zephaniah Platt; attended French acad., Montreal, Can.; studied law. Admitted to bar, 1790, practiced law, Poughkeepsie; clk. Herkimer County, 1791-98, Oneida County, 1798-1802; mem. N.Y. State Assembly, 1796; mem. U.S. Ho. of Reps. (Federalist) from N. Y., 6th Congress, 1799-1801; served as cavalry gen. N.Y. Militia; unsuccessful candidate for gov. N.Y., 1810; mem. N.Y. Senate, 1810-13; mem. council of appointment, 1813; asso. justice N.Y. Supreme Ct., 1814-21; del. N.Y. Constl. Conv., 1821. Died Peru, N.Y., Feb. 22, 1834; buried Riverside Cemetery, Plattsburg, N.Y.

PLATT, Zephaniah, Continental congressman, lawyer; b. Huntingdon, L.I., N.Y., May 27, 1735; received thorough English edn.; studied law; at least 1 son, Jonas. Admitted to bar, began practice of law, Poughkeepsie, N.Y.; mem. Provincial Congress, 1775-77; mem. Council of Safety, 1777; mem. N.Y. Senate, 1777-83; mem. Continental Congress from N. Y., 1784-86; mem. council of appointment, 1778, 81; judge Dutchess County, 1781-95; founder Town of Plattsburg (N.Y.), 1784; del. N.Y. Constl. Conv., 1788; regent of state univ., 1791-1807; a projector of Erie Canal. Died Plattsburg, Sept. 12, 1807; buried Riverside Cemetery.

PLEASANTS, James, senator, gov. Va.; b. Goochland County, Va., Oct. 24, 1769; s. James and Anne (Randolph) P.; grad. Coll. William and Mary; m. Susanna Rose, 8 children including John Hampden. Admitted to Va. bar, 1791; mem. Va. Ho. of Dels., 1797-1802, clk., 1803-11; mem. U.S. Ho. of Reps .from Va., 12th-16th congresses, 1811-19; mem. U.S. Senate from Va., 1819; gov. Va., 1822-25; mem. Va. Constl. Conv., 1829, 30. Died "Contention," Goochland County, Nov. 9, 1836; buried "Contention."

PLEASANTS, John Hampden, journalist; b. Goochland County, Va., Jan. 4, 1797; s. James and Susanna (Rose) P.; grad. Coll. William and Mary, 1817; m. Ann Irving; m. 2d, Mary Massie; children—James, Ann Eliza. Editor, Lynchburg (Va.) Virginian, 1823; founder, editor Richmond (Va.) Whig (became daily newspaper 1841, leading Whig exponent in Va.), 1824-46; established (with Edward W. Johnston and John Woodson) Washington (D.C.) Independent, 1841. Killed in duel with editor of a rival newspaper, Richmond, Feb. 27, 1846.

PLEASONTON, Alfred, army officer; b. Washington, D.C., June 7, 1824; s. Stephen and Mary (Hopkins) P.; grad. U.S. Mil. Acad., 1844. Commd. 2d lt. 2d Dragoons, U.S. Army, 1845; brevetted 1st lt. for bravery in Mexican War, 1846; promoted 1st lt., 1849, capt., 1855; led march of 2d Cavalry from Utah to Washington, D.C., Sept.-Oct. 1861; commd. maj. 2d Cavalry, 1862; served in Peninsular campaign, promoted brig. gen. U.S. Volunteers, 1862; commanded cavalry div. of Army of Potomac which pursued Lee's forces into Md., Sept.-Nov. 1862; served in battles of S. Mountain, Antietam, Fredericksburg; brevetted lt. col., 1862; helped check advance of Stonewall Jackson's forces against Hooker at Chancellorsville, 1863; promoted maj. gen. U.S. Volunteers, 1863; commanded cavalry at Gettysburg, brevetted col. U.S. Army; transferred to Mo., 1864, campaigned against Gen. Sterling Price; defended Jefferson City, 1864, routed Price nr. Marais des Cygnes River, Kan.; brevetted brig. gen., also maj. gen., Mar. 13, 1865; resigned commn., 1868; collector internal revenue 4th Dist. N.Y., 1869-70, 32d Dist., 1870; commr. internal revenue, 1870-71; pres. Cincinnati & Terre Haute R.R., 1872-74; commd. maj. on retired list, 1888. Author: The Successes and Failures of Chancellorsville, published in Battles and Leaders of the Civil War, Volume 3, 1888. Died Feb. 17, 1897; buried Congressional Cemetery, Washington.

PLEASONTON, Augustus James, lawyer, army officer; b. Washington, D.C., Aug. 18, 1808; s. Stephen Pleasonton; grad. U.S. Mil. Acad., 1826. Served at arty. sch., Fortress Monroe, Va., 1826-30; resigned from U.S. Army, 1830; admitted to bar, began practice of law, Phila., 1832; commd. maj. Pa. Militia, 1833, col., 1835, brig. gen. in charge of organizing defense of Phila., 1861-65; pres. Harrisburg, Portsmouth, Mountjoy & Lancaster R.R., 1839-40; originated "Blue-glass" theory of beneficial effects of sun's rays. Author: Influence of the Blue Ray of the Sunlight . . . in Developing Animal and Vegetable Life, 1876. Died Phila., July 26, 1894.

PLUMB, Preston B., senator, editor; b. Berkshire, O., Oct. 12, 1837; s. David and Hannah (Bierce) P.; m. Caroline (Carrie) A. Southwick, Mar. 8, 1867, 6 children. Co-founder Xenia (O.) News, 1854, editor, 1854-56; became mcht., transported arms and munitions to Kan. Territory, 1856; founder Kan. News (vigorous advocate of free-state cause). Emporia, 1857; sec. Kan. Free-State Conv., 1857; mem. Leavenworth Constl. Conv., 1859; admitted to Ohio bar, 1861; 1st reporter Kan. Supreme Ct., 1861; mem. Kan. Ho. of Reps., 1862, 67-68, speaker, 1867; commd. maj. 11th Kan. Cavalry, U.S. Army, 1862, apptd. chief-of-staff and provost marshal, 1863, partially cleared Dist. of the Border of guerrilla fighters, promoted lt. col., 1864; founder Emporia Nat. Bank (Kan.), 1865, pres., 1873; mem. U.S. Senate (Republican), 1877-91, made greatest contbn. in Land Law of 1891, repealing timber-culture and preemption acts and inaugurating reclamation and conservation projects. Died Washington, D.C., Dec. 20, 1891; buried Maplewood Cemetery, Emporia.

PLUMBE, John, railroad exec., photographer; b. Wales, July 1809. Came to U.S., 1821; became supt. ry. from Richmond to Roanoke River, N.C., 1832; 1st responsible and effective advocate of ry. to Pacific; secured $2000 appropriation for survey of route from Milw. to Sinipee, Wis. (on Mississippi River above Dubuque, Ia.), 1832; surveyor and register of Squatter Assn.; a prominent photographer of time, devised Plumbeotype reproduction on paper of daguerreotype; started weekly Popular Mag., 1846 (became a monthly, The Plumbe Popular Mag). Author: A Faithful Translation of the Papers Respecting the Grant Made by Gov. Alvarado to Mr. J.A. Sutter, 1850, Sketches of Iowa and Wisconsin Taken During A Residence of Three Years in Those Territories, 1839; Memorial Agaist Mnr. Asa Whitney's Railroad Scheme, (publ. which exposed scheme as land-grab), 1851. Died Dubuque, July 1857.

PLUMER, Arnold, congressman; b. nr. Cooperstown, Pa., June 6, 1801; ed. privately. Sheriff of Venango County, 1823; prothonotary Venango County, 1829, clk. of cts., recorder, 1830-36; mem. U.S. Ho. of Reps. (Democrat) from Pa., 25th Congress, 1837-39; marshall of Western Dist. Pa. (apptd. by Pres. Van Buren), 1839-41, also 1847-48; state treas. Pa., 1848; engaged in mining and banking; declined appointment as postmaster gen. under Pres. Buchanan. Died Franklin, Pa., Apr. 28, 1869; buried Franklin Cemetery.

PLUMER, George, congressman; b. nr. Pitts., Dec. 5, 1762. Mem. Pa. Ho. of Reps., 1812-15, 17; mem. U.S. Ho. of Reps. (Democrat) from Pa., 17th-19th congresses, 1821-27; engaged in agriculture. Died nr. West Newton, Pa., June 8, 1843; buried Old Sewickley Presbyn. Ch. Cemetery.

PLUMER, William, senator, gov. N.H.; b. Newburyport, Mass., June 25, 1759; s. Samuel and Mary (Dole) P.; read law under Joshua Atherton, 1784-87; m. Sally Fowler, Feb. 12, 1788, 6 children. Elected selectman, Epping (N.H.), 1783; admitted to N.H. bar, 1787; mem. N.H. Legislature, 1785-86, 88, 90-91, 97-1800, speaker, 1791, 97; mem. N.H. Constl. convs. of 1791, 92; mem. U.S. Senate (Federalist) from N.H., June 17, 1802-1807, wrote William Plumer's Memorandum of Proceedings of the United States Senate 1803-07 (edited by E.S. Brown, 1923); became Republican, circa 1808; pres. N.H. Senate, 1810, 11; gov. N.H., 1812-13, 16-19; supported War of 1812; recommended alterations in charter of Dartmouth Coll., started action which led to Dartmouth Coll. case; founder, 1st pres. N.H. Hist. Soc. (his sketches of Am. biography now in their possession). Died Epping, N.H., Dec. 22, 1850; buried nr. Epping.

PLUMER, William, Jr., congressman, lawyer; b. Epping, Rockingham County, N.H., Feb. 9, 1789; attended Phillips Exeter (N.H.) Acad.; grad. Harvard, 1809; studied law. Admitted to bar, 1812, began practice of law, Epping; engaged in polit. and hist. investigations; U.S. commr. of loans, 1816-17; mem. N.H. Ho. of Reps., 1818; mem. U.S. Ho. of Reps. (Democrat) from N.H., 16th-18th congresses, 1819-25; mem. N.H. Senate, 1827-28; mem. N.H. Constl. Conv., 1850. Author: biography of his father William Plumer. Died Epping, Sept. 18, 1854; buried family burial ground on father's estate nr. Epping.

PLUMER, William Swan, clergyman, educator; b. Griersburg, Pa., July 26, 1802; s. William and Catherine (McAllister) P.; grad. Washington Coll. (now Washington and Lee U.), Lexington, Va., 1824; grad. Princeton Theol. Sem., 1826, D.D. (hon.), 1838; D.D. (hon.), Lafayette Coll., Washington Coll., 1838; LL.D. (hon.) U. Miss., 1857; m. Eliza (Garden) Hasell, 1829, 2 children. Licensed to preach, 1826; ordained to ministry Presbyn. Ch., 1827; did evangelistic work in N.C., and Va.; pastor chs. in Va. and Md. including 1st Presbyn. Ch., Richmond, Va., 1834-46; outstanding Old Sch. leader and debater in Old Sch., New School Controversy, 1837; elected moderator Old School Gen. Assembly, 1838; prof. didactic and pastoral theology Western Theol. Sem., Allegheny, Pa., 1854-62; prof. Columbia (S.C.), Theol. Sem., 1867-80; moderator Gen. Assembly Presbyn. Ch. in U.S., 1871; founded The Watchman of the South, religious paper, 1864, sole editor for 8 years; attended Pan-Presbyn. Alliance, Edinburgh, Scotland, 1877. Author: Studies of the Book of Psalms, Being A Critical and Expository Commentary, 1866; The Law of God as Contained in the Ten Commandments, 1864. Died Balt., Oct. 22, 1880; buried Hollywood Cemetery, Richmond.

PLUMMER, Franklin E., congressman, lawyer; b. Mass.; studied law. Taught sch., Copiah County, Miss.; admitted to bar, began practice of law, Westville, Miss.; held several local offices; mem. Miss. Ho. of Reps.; founded town of Pittsburg (now part of Grenada); mem. U.S. Ho. of Reps. from Miss., 22d-23d congresses, 1831-35. Died Jackson, Miss., Sept. 24, 1847.

PLUMMER, Henry, bandit; b. circa 1837; m. Electa Bryan, June 20, 1863. Marshal, Nevada City, Cal., 1856-58, murdered man named Vedder (carried on intrigue with Vedder's wife); sentenced (after 2 trials) to 10 years in Yarba County (Cal.) Penitentiary; pardoned on assumption he was dying of Tb by Gov. John P. Weller; left for Walla Walla, Wash. Territory, 1861; sent back to Cal. newspapers plausible account of his having been lynched, then proceeded to Lewiston, Ida., accompanied by wife of a citizen of Walla Walla; organized bandit gang which controlled routes from Lewiston to mining camps by 1862; crossed Continental Divide into what is now Mont., 1862, stayed 2 months in Sun River as guest of J. A. Vail, supt. of govt. sch. for Blackfoot Indians; arrived in Bannack, Mont., Dec. 1862, killed Jack Cleveland (a former companion, only man in Bannack who knew of his past), Jan. 1863, tried and acquitted; pressured sheriff of territory into leaving, then was himself elected sheriff, May 1863; organized and directed gang which robbed or murdered 102 men in a few months; captured by com. of vigilantes formed to drive the outlaws away. Hanged on same gallows he had erected as sheriff, Jan. 10, 1864.

PLUMMER, Jonathan, trader, preacher; b. Newbury, Mass., July 13, 1761; s. Jonathan and Abigail (Greenleaf) P. Became a trader, country sch. tchr., itinerant preacher; his success as a trader permitted him to print and peddle his sermons; decided to marry for money, 1786, but after being rejected 9 times in 2 months, vowed celibacy; employed by self-styled "Lord" Timothy Dexter as his post-laureate, 1793-1806. Author: more than 30 broadsides and pamphlets including The Author's Congratulatory Address to Citizen Timothy Dexter on His Attaining an Independent Fortune, 1793; Sketch of the History of the Life of Jonathan Plummer, circa 1797. Died Sept. 13, 1819.

POCAHONTAS (Mataoha), Indian princess; b. Va., circa 1595; d. Powhatan; m. John Rolfe, Apr. 1614. Dau. of head of Powhatan Confederacy in Va.; saved Capt. John Smith from being executed by Powhatan, 1608; captured by Capt. Samuel Argall as security for English men and goods held by her father, 1613; taken to Jamestown, baptized "Rebecca"; marriage to John Rolfe regarded as bond of friendship between Indians and Whites; travelled to Eng., received as a princess, 1616. Died Gravesend, Eng., Mar. 1617; buried Gravesend Ch.

POE, Edgar Allan, author; b. Boston, Jan. 19, 1809; s. David and Elizabeth (Arnold) P.; attended U. Va., 1826; attended U.S. Mil. Acad., 1830-31 (dismissed); m. Virginia Clemm (his cousin), May 1836. Grew up in household of foster-father John Allan, ran away from home, 1827; published Tamerlane and Other Poems (1st vol. of verse), Boston, 1827; enlisted in U.S. Army, 1827, became regimental sgt.-maj., Jan. 1829, discharged (through Allan's influence), Apr. 1829; published Al Aaraaf, Tamerlane, and Minor Poems, 1829, Poems by Edgar A. Poe, 1831; resided with Mrs. Clemm and dau., Balt., 1831-35; won prize for best short story submitted to Balt. Saturday Visitor with story MS. Found in a Bottle, 1833; gained patronage of John P. Kennedy; mem. staff So. Literary Messenger, Richmond, Va., 1835-37, asst. editor, 1836-37; moved to Phila., 1838; co-editor Burton's Gentleman's Mag., 1839-40; contbd. many famous stories to Burton's, including Fall of the House of Usher, Tales of the Grotesque and Arabesque; literary editor Graham's Lady's and Gentleman's Mag., 1841-42; perfected mystery story technique, 1842, 43, in stories including Murders in the Rue Morgue, Mystery of Marie Rogêt, The Gold Bug (won $100 prize when published in Dollar Newspaper, 1843); moved to N.Y.C., 1844; 1st published poem The Raven anonymously in N.Y. Evening Mirror, 1845, became famous as result of its enormous success; editor Broadway Journal, 1845, owner, 1845-46; influenced Am. literature by the strength of his individuality which broke traditional limits. Best known single poems include: To Helen, The Bells, For Annie, Ulalume, Annabel Lee, El Dorado; short stories include: The Masque of the Red Death, The Black Cat, The Purloined Letter, The Cask of Amontillado, The Pit and the Pendulum; critical works include: The Philosophy of Composition, The Poetic Principle. Died Balt., Oct. 7, 1849; buried Westminster Presbyn. Churchyard, Balt.

POE, Elizabeth Arnold, actress; b. London, Eng.; d. Henry and Elizabeth (Smith) Arnold; m. C. D. Hopkins, 1802 (dec. 1805); m. 2d, David Poe, 1805 (dec. 1810); children—William Henry Leonard, Edgar Allan Poe, Rosalie. Brought to Boston by widowed mother, 1796; made debut as entr'acte singer at Fed. Street Theatre, Boston, 1796; played Biddy Bellaire in play Miss in Her Teens in theater set up by Charles Tubbs (her stepfather), Portland, Me., 1796; left an orphan, 1798; mem. Chestnut Street Theatre company, Phila., 1798-1802; acted with David Poe at Fed. Street Theatre, 1808-09; made last appearance in Richmond, Va., 1811; a comedienne. Died Richmond, Dec. 8, 1811; buried St. John's Churchyard, Richmond.

POE, Orlando Metcalfe, army officer; b. Navarre, O., Mar. 7, 1832; s. Charles and Susanna (Warner) P. grad. U.S. Mil. Acad., 1856; m. Eleanor Brent, Mar. 17, 1861, 4 children. Asst. topog. engr. on survey northern lakes, 1856-61; commd. 1st lt. U.S. Army, 1860; assisted in organizing Ohio Volunteers, 1861; col. 2d Mich. Volunteers, 1861; brig. gen. Volunteers, 1862; chief engr. 23d Army Corps in march on Knoxville, Tenn., 1863; chief engr. Army of Ohio; brevetted maj., 1864; asst. engr. Mil. Div. of Mississippi, 1863; chief engr. to Gen. Sherman, 1864; brevetted lt. col., then col., 1864; brevetted brig. gen. U.S. Army, 1865; engr. sec. Lighthouse Bd., 1865-70; maj. Corps Engrs., 1867; engr. Upper Lakes Lighthouse Dist., also supt. river and harbor work in Lake region, 1870; built Spectacle Reef Light, Lake Huron; col., aide-de-camp to Gen. Sherman, 1873-84; lt. col. Corps Engrs., 1882, col., 1888; superintending engr. of improvement rivers and harbors on lakes Superior and Huron, also St. Mary's Falls, Can., 1883. Died Detroit, Oct. 2, 1895; buried Arlington (Va.) Nat. Cemetery.

POINDEXTER, George, senator, gov. Miss., congressman; b. Louisa County, Va., 1779; s. Thomas and Lucy (Jones) P.; m. Lydia Carter; m. 2d, Agatha Chinn; 2 children. Admitted to Va. bar, 1800; atty. gen. Miss. Territory, 1803; mem. Miss. Territorial Assembly, 1805; del. to U.S. Ho. of Reps. from Miss. Territory, 10th-12th congresses, 1807-13; U.S. dist judge Miss. Territory, 1813-17; mem. conv. which framed 1st Miss. Constn., 1817; mem. U.S. Ho. of Reps. from Miss., 15th Congress, 1817-19; gov. Miss., 1819-21; codified laws of state in Revised Code of the Laws of Mississippi, 1824; mem. U.S. Senate from Miss., Oct. 15, 1830-35. Died Jackson, Miss., Sept. 5, 1853; buried Jackson Cemetery.

POINSETT, Joel Roberts, sec. of war, diplomat; b. Charlestown (now Charleston), S.C., Mar. 2, 1779; s. Dr. Elisha and Ann (Roberts) P.; attended med. sch. of St. Paul's Sch., Edinburgh, Scotland, 1796-1800; LL.D. (hon.), Columbia, 1825; m. Mary (Izard) Pringle, Oct. 24, 1833. U.S. spl. agt. in Rio de la Plata and Chile, 1810-14; mem. S.C. Ho. of Reps., 1816-20; chmn. S.C. Bd. Pub. Works, 1818-20; mem. U.S. Ho. of Reps. from S.C., 17th-18th congresses, 1821-25; made spl. mission to Mexico, 1822-23; 1st Am. minister to Mexico, 1825-30; unsuccessful leader Unionist party in S.C., 1830-33; largely responsible for raising S.C. Militia to defend Unionist cause; U.S. sec. of war, 1837-41, improved status of U.S. Army, proposed plan for universal mil. tng. and frontier def., organized gen. staff, improved arty., strengthened U.S. Mil. Acad., removed more than 40,000 Indians to territory West of Mississippi River, directed war against Seminole Indians in Fla.; a foundeer Nat. Inst. for Promotion of Sci. and Useful Arts, 1840; developed poinsettia from a Mexican flower. Author: Notes on Mexico, 1824. Died Statesburg, S.C., Dec. 12, 1851; buried Ch. of Holy Cross, Statesburg.

POINT, Nicholas, clergyman, artist. Went West, 1841; designed and built mission among Coeur d'Alene Indians, 1842; founded mission among Blackfeet Indians, 1845; made many sketches owned by Jesuit Provincial House, St. Louis; made sketches which formed basis for lithographs illustrating Oregon Missions and Travels over the Rocky Mountains in 1845-46 (written by Father de Smet with whom he travelled).

POINT DU SABLE, Jean Baptiste, reputed 1st settler Chgo.; b. San Domingo; of African descent. Lived and traded among Peoria Indians; settled in cabin on N. shore Chgo. River, before 1778, was harried out, 1779; fled to Rivière du Chemin, Ind.; taken into custody by English because of his French sympathies, sent to Mackinac, later released; returned to cabin and trading post in Chgo., remained there until selling out to French trader LeMai, 1796; went back to Peoria to live with countryman named Glamorgan. Died Peoria, Ill., circa 1800.

POLAND, Luke Potter, senator, jurist; b. Westford, Vt., Nov. 1, 1815; s. Luther and Nancy (Potter) P.; m. Martha Smith Page, Jan. 12, 1838; m. 2d, Adelia Page, 1854; 3 children. Admitted to Vt. bar, 1836; register of probate, 1838, 40; mem. Vt. Constl. Conv., 1843; pros. atty., 1844; judge Vt. Supreme Ct., 1848-65, chief justice, 1860-65; mem. U.S. Senate (Republican) from Vt., Nov. 21, 1865-67; mem. U.S. Ho. of Reps. from Vt., 40th-43d 48th congresses, 1867-75, 83-85, chmn. com. to investigate Ku Klux Klan in South, 1871; chmn. com. to investigate activities of Credit Mobilier Co., 1872, chmn. com. to investigate affairs in Ark., 1874, chmn. com. on revision of laws (resulting in Revised Statutes of the United States in Force Dec. 1, 1873); chmn. N.J. delegation to Rep. Nat. Conv., 1876; mem. Vt. Ho. of Reps., 1878, 86; trustee U. Vt., State Agrl. Coll.; pres. 1st Nat. Bank of St. Johnsbury (Vt.) 20 years. Died Waterville, Vt., July 2, 1887; buried Mt. Pleasant Cemetery, St. Johnsbury.

POLE, Elizabeth, colonist; b. Devonshire, Eng., Aug. 25, 1588; d. Sir William and Catherine (Popham) Pole. Came to Am., circa 1636; became large land owner in area of Cohaunet, Mass.; owned area which included what is now Taunton, Mass., actively promoted settlement of area; an incorporator of Taunton, 1639-40. Died Taunton, May 21, 1654; buried Taunton.

POLK, Charles Peale, artist; b. Md., Mar. 17, 1767. Advertised as portrait painter, Balt., 1785, 91-93, as house, ship and sign painter Phila., 1787; painted portraits of Washington, Franklin, Lafayette, sold copies of these; worked at Richmond, Va., 1799-1800; painted portrait of Jefferson; became clk. U.S. Govt., Washington, D.C. Died 1822.

POLK, James Knox, 11th Pres. U.S.; b. Mecklenburg County, N.C., Nov. 2, 1795; s. Samuel and Jane (Knox) P.; grad. U. N.C., 1818; read law under Felix Grundy; m. Sarah Childress, Jan. 1, 1824. Admitted to Tenn. bar, 1820; chief clk. Tenn. Senate, 1821-23; mem. Tenn. Ho. of Reps., 1823-25; mem. U.S. Ho. of Reps. (Jacksonian Democrat) from Tenn., 19th-25th congresses, 1825-39, mem. ways and means com. (placed there to lead fight against U.S. Bank), 1832, chmn., 1833, speaker of house, 1835-39; gov. Tenn., 1838-41; nominated for U.S. Pres. by Dem. Party largely through support of Andrew Jackson and because of his stand on so-called reannexation of Tex. and Ore., 1844, elected under slogan "Fifty-four forty or fight;" inaugurated Pres. U.S., Mar. 4, 1845; success of his programs caused further conflict between North and South and directly influenced Civil War; reduced tariff by Walker Tariff Law, 1846, angered North; signed Independent Treasury Bill of 1846, antagonized supporters of nat. bank; compromised on annexation of Ore. in treaty with Gt. Britain, 1846; made unsuccessful attempt to buy Cal. from Mexico, used skirmish on Tex.-Mexican border as grounds for war; declared war on Mexico, 1846; received Cal. and N.M. in treaty with Mexico, 1848; opposed Wilmot Proviso (attempt to exclude slavery from territory acquired in war), 1848; did not receive nomination for reelection, left office, 1849. Died Nashville, Tenn., June 15, 1849; buried Tenn. Capitol Grounds, Nashville.

POLK, Leonidas, clergyman, army officer; b. Raleigh, N.C., Apr. 10, 1806; s. Col. William and Sarah (Hawkins) P.; grad. U.S. Mil. Acad., 1827; ed. Va. Theol. Sem.; m. Frances Ann Devereux, May 1830, 8 children. Ordained deacon Protestant Episcopal Ch., 1830, priest, 1831; missionary bishop of S.W., 1838; bishop of La., 1841; chiefly responsible for founding U. of South, 1860; commd. maj. gen. Confederate Army, 1861; in charge of defending Mississippi River, 1861-62; his troops 1st to violate neutrality of Ky. at Columbus, 1861; defeated Grant at Belmont, Mo., 1861; commd. lt. gen., 1862; fought at battles of Shiloh, Murfreesboro, Chickamauga. Died Pine Mountain nr. Marietta, Ga., June 14, 1864.

POLK, Leonidas Lafayette, editor, agriculturist; b. Anson County, N.C., Apr. 24, 1837; s. Andrew and Serena (Autry) P.; m. Sarah P. Gaddy, 1857, 7 children. Mem. N.C. Legislature, 1860, 64-65; 1st commr. N.C. Dept. Agr., 1877-80; editor Raleigh (N..C.) News, 1880-81; published Progressive Farmer, 1886; established N.C. State Coll. of Agr. and Mechanic Arts (now N.C. State Coll. Agr. and Engring.), nat. v.p. Southern Alliance, 1887, pres., 1889; joined People's Party, circa 1890; presided over Indsl. Conf., St. Louis, 1892. Died June 11, 1892.

POLK, Lucius Eugene, army officer; b. Salisbury, N.C., July 10, 1833; s. Dr. William Julius and Mary Rebecca (Long) P.; attended U. Va., 1850-51; m. Sallie Moore Polk, Aug. 19, 1863, 5 children including Rufus. Commd. col., then brig. gen. Confederate Army, 1862, commanded Cleburne's brigade; fought at battles of Shiloh, Murfreesboro, Chickamanga, Kenesaw Mountain; del. to Democratic Conv., Chgo., 1884; mem. Tenn Senate, 1887. Died Maury County, Tenn., Dec. 1, 1892.

POLK, Sarah Childress, 1st lady; b. 1803; dau. of wealthy planter nr. Murfreesboro, Tenn.; educated by the Moravians; m. James Knox Polk, Jan. 1, 1824, no children. A Methodist, prohibited liquor and dancing in the White House.

POLK, Thomas, army officer, Continental congressman; b. Cumberland County, Pa., circa 1732; s. William and Margaret (Taylor) P.; m. Susan Spratt, 1755, 9 children including William. Led in War of Sugar Creek, 1760; commr. and 1st treas. Charlotte (N.C.), 1768; mem. N.C. Ho. of Commons, 1766-71, 73-74; served as capt. N.C. militia, 1758-71, fought against Regulators; surveyor in running N.C.-S.C. boundary line, 1772; mem. Mecklenburg Com., 1775; mem. N.C. Provincial Congress, 1775; col. N.C. Militia, 1775; commd. col. 4th N.C. Continental Regt., 1776; served in battles of Brandywine and Valley Forge; commissary gen. of provisions N.C., 1780; commissary of purchases Continental Army; commd. col. comdt., 1781; councilor of N.C., 1783-84; del.

to Continental Congress, 1786; promoter, trustee Queen's Coll., Charlotte, 1771, Liberty Acad., 1777, Salisbury Acad., 1784. Died Charlotte, Jan. 26, 1794.

POLK, Trusten, senator, gov. Mo.; b. Sussex County, Del., May 29, 1811; s. William Nutter and Lavenia (Causey) P.; grad. Yale, 1831, postgrad. in law 1832-34; m. Elizabeth Skinner, Dec. 26, 1837, 5 children. Admitted to bar, 1835; counselor of St. Louis, 1843; St. Louis del. to conv. to revise Mo. constn., 1845; gov. Mo., 1857, resigned to become mem. U.S. Senate from Mo., 1857-62; commd. col. Confederate Army, 1861; presiding mil. judge Dept. of Miss., 1864, 65. Died St. Louis, Apr. 16, 1876; buried Bellefontaine Cemetery.

POLK, William, army officer; b. Charlotte, N.C., July 9, 1758; s. Thomas and Susan (Spratt) P.; studied Queen's Coll.; m. Grizelda Gilchrist, Oct. 15, 1789; m. 2d, Sarah Hawkins, Jan. 1, 1801; 14 children. Maj. 9th Regt. of N.C. Militia, 1776; served in battles of Brandywine and Germantown (1776), Camden, Guilford Ct. House; lt. col. comdt. 4th S.C. Cavalry, circa 1782; surveyor gen. N.C. Land Office, 1783; mem. N.C. Ho. Commons, 1785-86, 87, 90; supr. internal revenue for N.C., 1791-1808; pres. N.C. State Bank, 1811-19; pres. Neuse River Navigation Co.; trustee U. N.C., 1790-1834, pres. bd. trustees, 1802-05; grand master Masons for N.C. and Tenn., 1799-1802; managed Jackson's campaign in N.C., 1824, 28. Counties in Tenn., N.C. named after him. Died Raleigh, N.C., Jan. 14, 1834.

POLK, William Hawkins, congressman, lawyer; b. Maury County, Tenn., May 24, 1815; attended U. N.C. at Chapel Hill, 1832-33; grad. U. Tenn. Knoxville; studied law. Admitted to bar, 1839, began practice of law, Columbia, Tenn.; mem. Tenn. Ho. of Reps., 1842-45; minister to Kingdom of Naples, 1845-47; served as maj. 3d Dragoons in Mexican War, 1847-48; mem. U.S. Ho. of Reps. (Democrat) from Tenn., 32d Congress, 1851-53. Died Nashville, Tenn., Dec. 16, 1862; buried Greenwood Cemetery, Columbia.

POLLARD, Edward Alfred, journalist; b. "Alta Vista," Albemarle County, Va., Feb. 27, 1831; s. Richard and Paulina Cabell (Rives) P.; attended Hampden-Sydney Coll., circa 1846, U. Va., 1847-49; m. 1st wife, circa 1852-55; m. 2d, Marie Antoinette Nathalie (Granier) Dowell, 1866. Clk. judiciary com. U.S. Ho. of Reps., circa 1857-61; editor Daily Richmond Examiner, 1861-67; captured while running the blockade in steamer Greyhound, 1864; owned weekly newspaper So. Opinion, 1867-69; founded The Polit. Pamphlet, 1868. Author: The Southern Spy, or Curiosities of Negro Slavery in the South, 1859; Letters of the Southern Spy, in Washington and Elsewhere, 1861; Southern History of the War, 1866; Lee and His Lieutenants, 1867; The Key to the Ku Klux Klan; The Lost Cause Regained; Life of Jefferson Davis, with the Secret History of the Southern Confederacy, 1869; The Virginia Tourist, 1870. Died Lynchburg, Va., Dec. 16, 1872.

POLLOCK, James, gov. Pa., congressman; b. Milton, Pa., Sept. 11, 1810; s. William and Sarah (Wilson) P.; grad. Princeton, 1831, LL.D. (hon.), 1858; LL.D. (hon.), Jefferson Coll., Pa., 1857; m. Sarah Hepburn, Dec. 19, 1837. Admitted to Pa. bar, 1833; dep. atty. gen. Northumberland County (Pa.), 1835-38; mem. U.S. Ho. of Reps. from Pa., 28th-30th congresses, 1844-49; pres. judge 8th Jud. Dist., 1851-55; gov. Pa., 1855-58; dir. U.S. Mint, Phila., 1861-66, 69-73, supt., 1873, originated use of phrase "In God We Trust" on U.S. coinage; naval officer of customs, Phila., 1879-83; trustee Lafayette Coll., 1855-76; pres. bd. trustees Pa. Mil. Coll., 1862-90. Died Lock Haven, Pa., Apr. 20, 1890; buried Milton (Pa.) Cemetery.

POLLOCK, Oliver, trader, planter, financier; b. Coleraine, No. Ireland, 1737; s. Jaret Pollack; m. Margaret O'Brien, 1770; m. 2d, Mrs. Winifred Deady, Nov. 2, 1805; 8 children. Came to Carlisle, Pa., circa 1760; mcht. in trade between Boston and Cuba, 1760-68; moved to New Orleans, 1768; granted freedom of trade in La. by Gen. Alexander O'Reilly for services to his army, 1769; supplied ammunition and information during Am. Revolution to Am. forces; comml. agt. for U.S. in La., 1778-83, was responsible for George Rogers Clark's ability to finance his western conquest, U.S. drew supplies on his credit in excess of $300,000 during war; comml. agt. for U.S. in Havana, 1783-circa 1796, debts caused by his work as comml. agt. U.S. Govt., returned to Va., circa 1796, purchased an estate. Died Pinckneyville, Miss., Dec. 17, 1823.

POLSLEY, Daniel Haymond, congressman, lawyer; b. Palatine, nr. Fairmont, Va. (now W.Va.), Nov. 28, 1803; studied law. Admitted to bar, 1827, began practice of law, Wellsburg, Va. (now W.Va.); editor Western Transcript, 1833-45; farmed, practiced law, Mason County, from 1845; mem. Wheeling loyal convs., 1861; lt. gov. of "restored govt." of Va., 1861; judge 7th Jud. Dist W.Va., 1863-66; mem. U.S. Ho. of Reps. (Republican) from W.Va., 40th Congress, 1867-69. Died Point Pleasant, W. Va., Oct. 14, 1877; buried Lone Oak Cemetery.

POMAREDE, Leon, artist; b. Tarves, France, circa 1807. Came to Am., 1830, settled in New Orleans; moved to St. Louis, 1832, painted view of town, decorated the cathedral; returned to New Orleans, opened studio, 1837; painted religious pictures for St. Patrick's Ch., New Orleans, 1841; went into partnership with T. E. Courtenay, St. Louis, 1843; collaborated with Henry Lewis on panorama of the Mississippi River, collaboration dissolved and each painted his own panorama; exhibited Panorama of the Mississippi River and Indian Life, St. Louis, 1849, later shown in New Orleans and on East Coast, destroyed by fire, Newark, N.J., 1850; reopened studio, St. Louis, 1850, painted religious and genre pictures, murals for chs., theaters, public bldgs. Died from injuries received in a fall from a scaffolding, St. Louis, 1892.

POMEROY, Charles, congressman; b. Meriden, New Haven County, Conn., Sept. 3, 1825; studied law. Practiced law; moved to Ia., 1855, became a farmer; Republican presdl. elector, 1860; receiver U.S. Land Office, Ft. Dodge, Ia., 1861-69; mem. U.S. Ho. of Reps. (Republican) from Ia., 41st Congress, 1869-71; claim agt., Washington, D.C., until 1891. Died Washington, Feb. 11, 1891; buried Oak Hill Cemetery.

POMEROY, John Norton, lawyer, educator; b. Rochester, N.Y., Apr. 12, 1828; s. Enos and Sarah Strong (Norton) P.; grad. Hamilton Coll., 1847, LL.D. (hon.), 1865; m. Ann Rebecca Carter, Nov. 21, 1855, 4 children. Admitted to N.Y. bar, 1851; mem. law faculty N.Y.U., 1864-70; mem. faculty Hastings (Cal.) Coll. of Law, 1878, prin. instr., 1878-80, tchr., 1880-85; editor West Coast Reporter, established early 1880's. Author: An Introduction to Municipal Law, 1864; An Introduction to the Constitutional Law of the United States, 1868; Remedies and Remedial Rights According to the Reformed American Procedure, 1876; Treatise on the Specific Performance of Contract, 1879; A Treatise on Equity Jurisprudence, 1883; A Treatise on the Law of Riparian Rights, 1884. Died San Francisco, Feb. 15, 1885.

POMEROY, Marcus Mills, editor, publisher, author; b. Elmira, N.Y., Dec. 25, 1833; s. Hunt and Orlina (White) P.; m. Anna Amelia Wheeler, Jan. 26, 1854; m. 2d, Mrs. Louise M. Thomas, 1872; m. 3d, Emma Stimson, Sept. 2, 1876. Established 1st paper the Sun, Corning, N.Y., 1854; established, edited Argus, Horicon, Wis., 1857-60; editor Democrat, La Crosse, Wis., 1860-68; published Democrat, N.Y.C., 1868, sold, 1870; published mag. Pomeroy's Democrat; published Democrat, Chgo., 1873; engaged in orgn. work for Greenback cause, composed about 4000 clubs, 1876-80; organized, promoted Atlantic-Pacific Ry. tunnel in Colo., pres. 1890; published gen. news Advance Thought, N.Y.; most popular books include Sense, 1868, Nonsense, 1868; Our Saturday Nights, 1870; Gold Dust, 1871; Brick-Dust, 1871; Home Harmonics, 1876. Died Bklyn., May 30, 1896.

POMEROY, Samuel Clarke, senator; b. Southampton, Mass., Jan. 3, 1816; s. Samuel and Dorcas (Burt) P.; attended Amherst Coll., 1836-38; m. Annie Pomeroy; m. 2d, Lucy Ann Gaylord, Apr. 23, 1846; m. 3d, Mrs. Martha Whitin. Mem. Mass. Ho. of Reps., 1852, 53; financial agt. New Eng. Emigrant Aid Co., 1854, accompanied 2d party of settlers to Kan. Territory; chmn. Kan. Com. of Public Safety; del. to Republican Nat. Conv., Phila., 1856, Chgo., 1860; Kan. free-state advocate; mayor Atchison (Kan.), 1858-59; head relief com. for drought and famine in Kan., 1860-61; mem. U.S. Senate from Kan., 1861-73. Died Whitinsville, Mass., Aug. 27, 1891; buried Forest Hills Cemetery, Boston.

POMEROY, Seth, army officer; b. Northampton, Mass., May 20, 1706; s. Ebenezer and Sarah (King) P.; m. Mary Hunt, Dec. 14, 1732; 9 children. Commd. capt. Mass. Militia, 1744; served as maj. 4th Mass. Regt. in expdn. against French fortress at Louisbourg, 1745; an organizer opposition to pastor of Northampton Ch. (Jonathan Edwards), 1750; commd. lt. col. Continental Army, fought at Battle of Lake George, 1775; head West Mass. dist. Mass. Militia, in command forts along Mass. frontier, late 1775; mem. Northampton Com. of Safety, 1774; rep. 1st, 2d Mass. provincial congresses; mil. commander Province of Mass.; raised and drilled troops in West Mass., 1775-76; 1st brig. gen. Contitnental Army, 1775; fought at Battle of Bunker Hill; gunsmith in spare time. Died Peekskill, N.Y., Feb. 19, 1777.

PONCE de LEÓN, Juan, explorer; b. San Servos, Spain, circa 1460; married, survived by 2 children. Served in war against Moors in Granada, Spain thought to have accompanied Columbus on 2d voyag to Am.; served under Nicolas de Ovando in conques of Higuey, Hispaniola, 1502-04; gov. Higuey, circ 1504-08; explored, conquered Island of Borique (Puerto Rico) in hope of finding gold, 1508-09 Spanish gov. P.R., 1509-12 (office contested b Diego, son of Christopher Columbus); commd. b King Ferdinand of Spain to find Island of Bimir (which Indians described as having much gold and fountain of youth), Feb. 23, 1512; landed on Fla coast, Apr. 2, 1513, searched for Bimini arroun the coast of Fla.; visited Bahamas, 1813; returne to P.R., disappointed in not having found fountai of youth, 1514; returned to colonize Fla., 1521 mortally wounded in Indian attack, taken immediate ly to Cuba on his flagship. Died on return to Cuba 1521; buried Dominican Ch., San Juan, P.R.

POND, Enoch, clergyman, educator; b. Wrentham, Mass., July 29, 1791; s. Elijah and Mary (Smith) P.; grad. Brown U. (valedictorian), 1813 D.D. (hon.), Dartmouth, 1835. m. Wealthy Ann Hawes, Aug. 28, 1814; m. 2d, Julia Ann Maltby May 17, 1825; m. 3d, Mrs. Ann (Mason) Pearson July 9, 1839; 14 children. Ordained to ministry Congregational Ch., 1815; editor Spirit of the Pilgrims (periodical opposing Unitarianism) 1828-32; with Bangor (Me.) Theol. Sem., 1832 82, prof. theology, 1832-56, prof. history, 1832-70 pres. faculty, 1856-82; exponent of the New Eng Theology. Author: The Young Pastor's Guide 1844; Lectures on Pastoral Theology, 1866; Lectures on Christian Theology, 1868; A History of God's Church, 1870; The Seals Opened, 1871. Died Bangor, Jan. 21, 1882.

POND, Peter, fur trader, explorer; b. Milford, Conn., Jan. 18, 1740; s. Peter and Mary (Hubbard) P.; m. Susanna Newell, between 1761-65, at least 2 children. Sergeant in N.Y. regt. from Suffolk County in French and Indian Wars, 1759, commd. officer under Gen. Amherst at Montreal, 1760; in Western fur trade, 1765-88, Detroit base, 1765-70, Mackinac base, 1770-75; explored Athabaska River, Can., opened rich fur region; trader with N.W. Co., 1775-85, shareholder, 1883-85; presented to Congress a map of his voyages (copied for archives of Gt. Britain and France); prepared another map for Empress of Russia. Died Boston, 1807.

POND, Samuel William, missionary; b. Litchfield County, Conn., Apr. 10, 1808; s. Elnathan J. and Sarah (Hollister) P.; m. Cordelia Eggleston, 1838; 4 children; m. 2d, Rebecca Smith, 1852. Became missionary to Dakota (Sioux) Indians in Minn., 1834; helped establish mission, Lake Harriet, Minn., 1835; published spelling book (1st work ever printed in Dakota lang.), 1836; ordained missionary to Sioux Indians, Congregational Ch., 1837; took charge Lake Harriet station, 1839; joined Indians at Oak Grove, Minn., 1843; established mission at Shakopee (which he renamed Prairieville), Minn. 1847, conducted mission, 1847-53; pastor to incoming White settlers, Prairieville, 1853-66. Author: The Dakotas or Sioux in Minnesota as They Were in 1834; (with brother) The History of Joseph, in the Language of the Dakota or Sioux Indians, 1839; Wowapi-inonpa . . . The Second Dakota Reading Book, 1842, Dakota Wiwangapi Wowapi: Catechism in the Dakota or Sioux Language, 1844. Died Sahkopee, Dec. 12, 1891.

POND, Silvanus Billings, music publisher; b. nr. Worcester, Mass., 1792; children include William A. Piano mfr., Albany, N.Y.; became partner publishing house Mechan & Pond, Albany, 1820; moved firm to N.Y.C. under name Firth, Hall-Pond & Co., 1832, reorganized as Firth, Pond & Co., 1848, firm purchased by son William A., circa 1856, since known as William A. Pond & Co., firm one of prin. publishers of songs of Stephen Foster; prominent musician; condr. N.Y. Sacred Musical Soc., N.Y. Acad. Sacred Music; composed Sunday sch. and secular songs; editor, publisher The United States Psalmody, 1841. Died N.Y.C., 1871.

PONT-au-SABLE, Jean Baptiste, see Point du Sable, Jean Baptiste.

PONTIAC, Indian chief; b. nr. Maumee River, 1720; s. an Ojibwa woman. Led Indian band in attempt to surprise by treachery garrison commanded by Maj. Henry Gladwin at Detroit, 1763-64, regarded as greatest local menace in long siege which followed; most popular knowledge about him probably fiction, probably did not start uprising to which Parkman gave name Pontiac's Conspiracy (merely took up opposition at Detroit), was not necessarily chief of Ottawa Indians in 1763; attended conf. at Ft. Ontario, 1766, made peace with English and abided by it; Pontiac (Mich.) named for him. Died 1769.

POOL, John, senator; b. Pasquotank County, N.C., June 16, 1826; s. Solomon and Martha (Gaskins) P.; grad. U. N.C., 1847; m. Narcissa Sawyer; m. 2d, Mollie McBane. Admitted to N.C. bar, 1847; mem. N.C. Senate, 1856, 58, 64, 65, introduced peace resolutions providing for appointment of peace commrs. by state; mem. N.C. Constl. Conv., 1865-66; elected to U.S. Senate, 1865, not seated; mem. N.C. Republican Conv., 1867, introduced resolutions (voted down) demanding universal suffrage, restriction on taxing power of Legislature and immediate removal all disabilities; mem. U.S. Senate from N.C., July 4, 1868-1873; apptd. supt. public instrn. N.C., 1876; joined labor orgn., 1876. Died Washington, D.C., Aug. 16, 1884; buried Oak Hill Cemetery, Washington.

POOL, Maria Louise, author; b. Rockland Mass., Aug. 20, 1841; d. Elias and Lydia (Lane) Pool. Contributed local color sketches of New Eng. life to Boston and N.Y. papers, 1891; author: Dally, 1891; Against Human Nature, 1895; In Buncombe County, 1896; chief and best works include: Roweny in Boston, 1892; In a Dike Shanty, 1896; Boss and Other Dogs, 1896. Died Rockland, May 19, 1898.

POOL, Walter Freshwater, congressman, lawyer; b. "Elm Grove," nr. Elizabeth City, N.C., Oct. 10, 1850; attended public sch. conducted by his family and U. N.C. at Chapel Hill; studied law. Admitted to bar, 1873, began practice of law, Elizabeth City; mem. U.S. Ho. of Reps. (Republican) from N.C. 48th Congress, 1883. Died Elizabeth City, Aug. 25, 1883; buried Pool Cemetery, nr. Elizabeth City.

POOLE, Fitch, journalist; b. South Danvers (now Peabody), Mass., June 13, 1803; s. Fitch and Elizabeth (Cutler) P.; m. Mary Ann Poor, July 8, 1824, 9 children. Mem. com. Essex Agrl. Soc.; wrote "Lament of the Bats Inhabiting the Old South Church in Danvers" for Salem Register, 1836; an editor Danvers Courier, 1846; made the Wizard, South Danvers, famous with his witty articles and poems on politics, people and local affairs, 1859-69; wrote satirical attacks on Mexican War, "The House that Zack Built," "Mr. Polk's Bridge of Sighs"; wrote "The Political John Gilpins," 1852; librarian Peabody Inst., South Danvers. Died Peabody, Aug. 19, 1873.

POOLE, William Frederick, librarian, historian; b. Peabody, Mass., Dec. 24, 1821; s. Ward and Eliza (Wilder) P.; grad. Yale, 1849; LL.D. (hon.), Northwestern U., 1882; m. Fanny Gleason, Nov. 22, 1854, 7 children. Librarian of literary soc., The Brothers in Unity, 1848-49; began Poole's Index to Periodical Literature, 1st edit., 1848, 2d edit., 1853, 3d edit., 1882; asst. at library Boston Athenaeum, 1851, librarian, 1856-69; librarian Boston Merc. Library Assn., 1852-56, Cincinnati Library, 1871-73; served as library expert in organizing new libraries including U.S. Naval Acad. (organized 1869), 1871-73; librarian Chgo. Pub. Library, 1874-87; organized new reference library The Newberry Library, Chgo., 1887, librarian, 1887-94; attended 1st conf. of Am. librarians in N.Y.C., 1853; an organizer A.L.A., 1876, pres., 1885-87; v.p. Internat. Conf. of Librarians, London, Eng., 1877; mem. Phi Beta Kappa; pres. Am. Hist. Assn., 1888. Author: Cotton Mather and Salem Witchcraft, 1869; The University Library and the University Curriculum, 1894; contbr. several papers to Public Libraries in the United States, Their History, Condition and Management, 1876. Died Evanston, Ill., Mar. 1, 1894.

POOR, Charles Henry, naval officer; b. Cambridge, Mass., June 9, 1808; s. Moses and Charlotte (White) P.; m. Mattie Stark, May 13, 1835, 8 children. Commd. lt. U.S. Navy, 1835, comdr., 1855; commanded ship St. Louis of the Home Squadron, 1860-61; commanded landing party of soldiers, marines, sailors sent ashore to reinforce garrison of Ft. Pickens, Fla. 1861; ordnance officer North Atlantic Blockading Squadron stationed at Ft. Monroe, 1862; commd. capt., 1862, commodore, 1863; commanded naval sta. Mound City, Ill., 1865-68; commd. rear adm., 1868; head Washington (D.C.) Navy Yard, 1869; commanded North Atlantic Squadron, 1869-70. Died Washington. D.C., Nov. 5, 1882; buried Oak Hill Cemetery, Washington.

POOR, Daniel, clergyman, missionary; b. Danvers, Mass., June 27, 1789; s. Joseph and Mary (Abbott) P.; grad. Dartmouth, 1811, D.D. (hon.), 1835; grad. Andover Theol. Sem., 1814; m. Susan Bulfinch, Oct. 9, 1815; m. 2d, Ann Knight, Jan. 21, 1823; 3 children. Ordained to Ministry Presbyn. ch., Newburyport, Mass., June 21, 1815; sent (with others) by Am. Bd. of Missions to Colombo, Ceylon, 1816; missionary to Tillypally, Ceylon, 1816-23; missionary to Batticotta, Ceylon, 1823-35, founded boys' boarding sch., 1823, Missionary Scientific Sem., 1826 (important ednl. center for entire region); missionary and founder schs. Madura, India, 1835-41; visited U.S., 1848-50; kept jour. from which extracts were published in Panoplist and Missionary Herald, Boston, 1817-55. Died Manepy, Ceylon, Feb. 3, 1855.

POOR, Enoch, army officer; b. Andover, Mass., June 21, 1736; s. Thomas and Mary (Adams) P.; m. Martha Osgood, 1760. Fought in French and Indian War in Nova Scotia, 1755; twice mem. N.H. Provincial Congress; commd. col. 2d N.H. Regt. of foot soldiers, 1775; took part in battles of Trenton, Princeton, Saratoga, Monmouth; commd. brig. gen. Continental Army, 1777; accompanied Gen. John Sullivan in expdn. against Six Nations, 1779. Died Paramus, N.J., Sept. 8, 1780.

POOR, John, educator; b. Plaistow, N.H., July 8, 1752; s. Daniel and Anna (Merrill) Poore; grad. Harvard, 1775; m. Sarah Folson, Nov. 2, 1777; m. 2d, Jane Neely, Jan. 7, 1789, 10 children including Charles M. Poore. Head of Young Ladies' Acad., Phila., 1787-1809, largely responsible for obtaining state charter, 1792 (1st encouragement of the sort given to girls' edn. in U.S.); conducted young ladies' sch., New Hope, Pa., from 1815. Died York Haven, Pa., Dec. 5, 1829.

POOR, John Alfred, lawyer, railroad exec.; b. Andover, Me., Jan. 8, 1808; s. Dr. Silvanus and Mary (Merrill) P.; m. Elizabeth Adams Hill, July 8, 1833; m. 2d, Elizabeth Orr; m. 3d, Mrs. Margaret Barr Gwynne, July 19, 1860; 4 children. Admitted to Me. bar, 1832; mem. Me. Whig Com.; a founder Bangor Lyceum and Bangor Social Library; announced plan for two railroad lines, from Halifax, N.S. to Portland, Me. and from Portland to Montreal, Can., 1844, granted charter for both railroads, 1845; bd. dirs. Atlantic & St. Lawrence R.R. Co., 1845-49; purchased Am. R.R. Jour., N.Y.C., 1849; pres. Gas Light Co., Portland, circa 1850-52; helped secure charter for European & No. Am. Ry. Co. 1850; became pres. York and Cumberland R.R., 1851; established newspaper The State of Maine, Portland, 1853-59; pres. Portland, Rutland, Oswego & Chgo. Ry., 1871; became mem. Me. Hist. Soc., 1846. Author: Commrcial Railways and Shipbuilding Statistics of the City of Portland and the State of Maine, 1855. Died Sept. 5, 1871.

POORE, Benjamin Perley, writer, editor; b. Indian Hill Farm, Newburyport, Mass., Nov. 2, 1820; s. Benjamin and Mary Perley (Dodge) P.; m. Virginia Dodge, June 12, 1849. Editor Southern Whig (paper his father purchased for him) Athens, Ga., 1839-41; attaché Am. legation in Belgium, 1841; agt. for Mass. Legislature in Paris, France, to secure copies of documents in French archives relating to Am. history, 1844, published material under title, Collection de Manuscrits Contenant Lettres, Mémoirs, et Autre Documants Historiques Relatifs à la Nouvelle-France, 1883-85; regular contbr. to Boston Atlas, fgn. corr., Paris, 1844; editor Daily Bee, Boston, 1848, American Sentinel, Phila.; Washington corr. Boston-Journal, 1854, became famous as columnist "Perley"; served briefly as Maj. 6th Mass. Regt., 1861; Sec. U.S. Soc. Agr., editor its Journal of Agr. 1857-62; editor of 1st issue Congressional Directory, 1865; clk. Senate com. on printing public records, responsible for A Descriptive Catalogue of the Government Publications of the U.S., Sept. 5, 1774-Mar. 4, 1881, published 1885, The Federal and State Constitutions, Colonial Charters and other Organic Laws of the U.S., 2 vols., 1877, The Political Register and Congressional Directory, 1776-1878, published 1878. Author: Life of General Zachary Taylor, 1848; Rise and Fall of Louis Philippe, 1848, Early Life and First Campaigns of Napoleon Bonaparte, 1851; Agricultural History of Essex County, Massachusetts, 1865; The Conspiracy Trial for the Murder of Abraham Lincoln, 1865; Life of Burnside, 1882; Perley's Reminiscences of Sixty Years in the National Metropolis, 1886. Died Washington, D.C., May 29, 1887.

POPE, Franklin Leonard, electrician, inventor; b. Great Barrington, Mass., Dec. 2, 1840; s. Ebenezer and Electa (Wainwright) P.; attended Amherst Acad.; m. Sarah Amelia Dickinson, Aug. 6, 1873, 5 children. Edited and published small newspaper, Great Barrington; operator for Am. Telegraph Co., Great Barrington, 1857-59; asst. engr. Am. Telegraph Co., serving as circuit mgr. Boston & Albany R.R. telegraph lines, Springfield, Mass., 1862; reestablished communication between N.Y.C. and Boston during draft riots, 1863; asst. to the chief engr. Russo-Am. Telegraph Co., 1864-66, made preliminary exploration and survey of Brit. Columbia and Alaska; N.Y. editor The Telegrapher, 1867-68; made valuable improvements in stock ticker, 1869; partner firm Pope, Edison & Co., 1869-70; devised system which made practicable the automatic electric block signal for railways (invented by Thomas S. Hall); in charge all patent interests of Western Union Telegraph Co., 1875-81; editor Electrician and Elec. Engineer and Engrng. Mag., 1884-93; cons. engr. Great Barrington Electric Light Co., converted plant from steam to water power, 1893-95; charter mem. Am. Inst. E.E., an original v.p., pres., 1886-87. Author: Modern Practice of the Electric Telegraph, 1869; The Telegraphic Instructor, 1871; Life and Work of Joseph Henry, 1879; Evolution of the Electric Incandescent Lamp, 1889, 94. Died Great Barrington, Oct. 13, 1895.

POPE, John, senator, congressman; b. Prince William County, Va., 1770; studied law. Admitted to bar, practiced law, Washington, Shelby and Fayette counties (Ky.); Democratic presdl. elector, 1800; mem. Ky. Ho. of Reps., 1802, 06-07; mem. U.S. Senate (Democrat) from Ky., 1807-13, pres. pro tem, Feb. 23, 1811; mem. Ky. Senate, 1825-29; gov. Ark. Territory, 1829-35; mem. U.S. Ho. of Reps. (Democrat) from Ky., 25th-27th congresses, 1837-43. Died Springfield, Ky., July 12, 1845; buried Springfield.

POPE, John, artist; b. Gardiner, Me., Mar. 2, 1820; studied painting, Boston, circa 1836. Exhibited at Boston Athenaeum, 1843; went to Cal., during Gold Rush, 1849; returned to Boston, later went to Europe; maintained studio, N.Y.C., 1857-80; became asso. N.A.D., 1859; best known for full length portrait painted for Town of Charlestown (Mass.; now part of Boston). Died N.Y.C., Dec. 29, 1880.

POPE, John, army officer; b. Louisville, Ky., Mar. 16, 1822; s. Nathaniel and Lucretia (Backus) P.; grad. U.S. Mil. Acad., 1842; m. Clara Pomeroy Horton, Sept. 15, 1859, 4 children. Brevetted 1st lt. U.S. Army, 1846, served under Gen. Taylor in Mexican War; commd. capt., 1847; chief topog. engr. Dept. of N.M., 1851-53; commd. 1st lt., 1853, capt., 1856; mustering officer at Chgo., 1861; promoted brig. gen. U.S. Volunteers, 1861; commanded Army of the Mississippi for opening of river 1862; maj. gen. U.S. Volunteers, 1862; organized and concentrated all separate forces in region of Rappahannock and Shenadoah into Army of Va.; commd. brig. gen. U.S. Army, 1862; defeated in 2d Battle of Manassas, relieved of command, 1862; brevetted maj.-gen. U.S. Army, 1865; commanded 3d Mil. Dist. (Ga., Ala., Fla.), 1867, Dept. of the Lakes, 1868-70, Dept. of Miss., 1870-83, Dept. of Cal. and Div. of Pacific, 1883-86; commd. maj. gen., 1882. Died Sandusky, O., Sept. 23, 1892.

POPE, Nathaniel, jurist, territorial del.; b. Louisville, Ky., Jan. 5, 1784; s. William and Penelope (Edwards) P.; attended Transylvania U.; m. Lucretia Backus, 6 children including John. Admitted to Ky. bar, circa 1808; sec. Ill. Territory, 1809-16, orgainzed territory in absence of gov., revised and digested Laws of the Territory of Illinois, 1815; territorial del. to U.S. Congress from Ill., 1816-18; register land office, Edwardsville, Ill., 1818-19; responsible for present Ill. boundary giving outlet on Lake Michigan, 1818; largely responsible for educational provisions of creating state of Ill.; U.S. dist. judge for Ill., 1819-50. Died St. Louis, Jan. 22, 1850; buried Col. O'Fallon Burying Ground, St. Louis.

POPE, Patrick Hamilton, congressman, lawyer; b. Louisville, Ky., Mar. 17, 1806; grad. St. Joseph Coll., Bardstown, Ky.; studied law. Admitted to bar, 1827, began practice of law, Louisville; mem. U.S Ho. of Reps. (Democrat) from Ky., 23d Congress, 1833-35; mem. Ky. Ho. of Reps., 1836. Died Louisville, May 4, 1841; buried Cave Hill Cemetery.

POPHAM, George, colonial gov.; b. Somersetshire, Eng., 1550; s. Edward and Jane (Norton) P. Capt. in Robert Dudley's expdn. to Guiana and West Indies, 1594-95; among those who petitioned King James for patent for lands in Am., among those named in Va. Co. Patent, 1606; mem. governing council of North Va.; commanded vessels Gift of God and Mary and John, 1607, reached Me., July 1607; gov. of colony; Popham (Me.) named after him. Died Me., Feb. 5, 1608.

POPOV-VENIAMINOV, Joann, missionary; b. Aginskoe, Siberia, Aug. 26, 1797; s. Esveil Popov; m. Ekaterina Sharina. Russian Orthodox missionary to Unalaska, 1823; bishop of Kamchatka, Karile and Aleutian Islands, 1841-50; established sem., Novo-Arkhangel'sk, 1845; archbishop for Alaska and Amur region, 1850-68; built chs. and schs. in Amur region; metropolitain of Russia, 1868-79. Died Mar. 31, 1879.

PORCHER, Francis Peyre, physician, botanist; b. St. John, S.C., Dec. 14, 1825; s. Dr. William and Isabella (Peyre) P.; A.B., S.C. Coll., 1844; grad. Med. Coll. S.C., 1847; m. Virginia Leigh; m. 2d, Margaret Ward. Established Charleston (S.C.) Prep. Med. Sch.; mem. Charleston Bd. of Health; surgeon, physician marine and city hosps.; prof. clin. medicine, materia medica, therapeutics Med. Coll. State S.C.; opened hosp. for Negroes, 1855; surgeon Holcombe Legion, also naval hosp., Norfolk, Va., S.C. Hosp., Petersburg, Va., during Civil

War; asso. fellow Coll. of Physicians of Phila.; mem. S.C. Med. Assn. (pres. 1872), Elliot Soc. Natural History, A.M.A. (v.p. 1879), 10th Internat. Med. Congress, Berlin, 1890, Pan. Am. Congress (pres. sect. on gen. medicine 1892); editor Charleston Med. Jour. and Review, 1853-58, 73-76; authority on diseases of the heart and chest. Author: A Medico-Botanical Catalogue of the Plants and Ferns of St. John's Berkely, S.C., 1847; A Sketch of the Medical Botany of South Carolina, 1849; The Medicinal, Poisonous and Dietetic Properties of the Cryptogamic Plants of the United States, 1854; Illustrations of Disease with the Microscope, and Clinical Investigations aided by the Microscope and by Chemical Reagents, 1861; The Resources of the Southern Fields and Forests, 1863. Died Nov. 19, 1895.

PORMORT, Philemon, schoolmaster; b. Grimsby, Lincolnshire, Eng., 1595; s. Thomas and Dorothy (Dawson) P.; m. Susanna Bellingham, Oct. 11, 1627; m. 2d, Elizabeth, circa 1643; children—Elizabeth, Martha, Maria, Pedajah. Came to Boston, 1634; schoolmaster, 1st pub. sch. in Boston, 1635-38; a founder Exeter (N.H.), 1638. Died Boston, 1656.

PORTER, Albert Gallatin, gov. Ind., congressman; b. Lawrenceburg, Ind., Apr. 20, 1824; s. Thomas and Miranda (Tousey) P.; grad. Asbury Coll. (now DePauw U.), 1843; read law under John C. Spooner; m. Minerva Brown, Nov. 30, 1846; m. 2d, Cornelia Stone, Jan. 5, 1881; 5 children. Admitted to Ind. bar, 1845; wrote digests of supreme ct. opinions for Indpls. Journal; atty. of Indpls., 1851-53; reporter Ind. Supreme Ct., 1853-56; city councilman Indpls., 1857-59; mem. U.S. Ho. of Reps. from Ind., 36th-37th congresses, 1859-63; head law firm including Fishback and Benjamin Harrison, 1863-77; 1st comptroller of U.S. Treasury (apptd. by Pres. Hayes), 1878-80; gov. Ind., 1881-85; nominated Benjamin Harrison for Pres. U.S., Republican Nat. Conv., Chgo., 1888; U.S. minister to Italy, 1889-91. Died Indpls., May 3, 1897.

PORTER, Alexander, senator; b. Armagh, County Donegal, Ireland, 1786; s. James and Anna (Knox) P.; 2 children. Came to U.S., 1801; admitted to Tenn. bar, 1807; mem. La. Constl. Conv., 1811-12; mem. La. Ho. of Reps., 1816-18; asso. justice La. Supreme Ct., 1821-33; established "Oakland" plantation (La.), raised cane sugar, imported cattle, maintained race course and stables; mem. U.S. Senate (Whig) from La., Dec. 19, 1833-37, re-elected, 1842, did not serve due to ill health. Died Attakapas, La., Jan. 13, 1844, buried "Oakland."

PORTER, Andrew, army officer, surveyor; b. Montgomery County, Pa., Sept. 24, 1743; s. Robert Porter; m. Elizabeth McDowell, Mar. 10, 1767; m. 2d, Elizabeth Parker, May 20, 1777; 13 children. In charge of an English and math. sch. Phila., 1767-76; commd. capt. of Marines, 1776; fought at Trenton, Princeton, Brandywine, Germantown; joined Sullivan's expdn. against Indians of Central N.Y., 1779; supervised manufacture ammunition at Phila. for siege of Yorktown, 1781; 1t col., also col. 4th (Pa.) Arty., 1782; commissary for commn. which surveyed southwestern bundary of Pa., 1784, assisted in determining Western termination of Mason-Dixon line; commr. to run Western and No. boundaries of Pa., 1785-87; commd. brig. gen. Pa. Militia, 1800, later maj. gen.; surveyor gen. Pa., 1809-13. Died Harrisburg, Pa., Nov. 16, 1813.

PORTER, Augustus Seymour, senator, lawyer; b. Canandaigua, N.Y., Jan. 18, 1798; attended Canandaigua Acad.; grad. Union Coll., Schenectady, N.Y., 1818; studied law. Admitted to bar, began practice of law, Detroit; recorder Detroit, 1830, mayor, 1838; mem. U.S. Senate (Whig) from Mich., 1839-45; moved to Niagara Falls, N.Y., 1848; del. Union Nat. Conv., Phila., 1866. Died Niagara Falls, Sept. 18, 1872; buried Oakwood Cemetery.

PORTER, Charles Howell, congressman, lawyer; b. Cairo, Greene County, N.Y., June 21, 1833; grad. law univ., Albany, N.Y., 1853. Admitted to bar, 1854, began practice of law, Ashland, N.Y.; served with 1st Regt., N.Y. Mounted Rifles during Civil War, was in Fortress Monroe (Va.) during battle between Monitor and Merrimac; moved to Norfolk, Va.; city atty., 1 year; commonwealth atty., 1863-67; moved to Richmond, Va., 1867; mem. Va. Constl. Conv., 1867-68; mem. U.S. Ho. of Reps. (Republican) from Va., 41st-42d congresses, Jan. 26, 1870-73; practiced law, N.Y.C., also Beacon, N.Y. Died Cairo, July 9, 1897; buried Cairo Cemetery.

PORTER, David, naval officer, diplomat; b. Boston, Feb. 1, 1780; s. David and Rebecca (Gay) P.; m. Evelina Anderson, Mar. 10, 1808, 10 children including David Dixon, William D., 1 adopted son, David Glasgow Farragut. Commd. 1t., 1799; comdr. ship Enterprise during Tripolian War, captured with ship Philadelphia, imprisoned; commd. master comdt., 1806; commanded New Orleans Naval Sta., 1809-11; comdr. Essex raiding English commerce during War of 1812, 1811, took Essex to Pacific (1st U.S. naval vessel in that ocean); commd. capt., 1812; renamed one of Marquesas islands Madison Island, 1813, took possession on behalf of U.S., erected Ft. Madison and Village of Madison; commr. Navy Bd., 1815-23; comdr.-in-chief West India Squadron, 1823-25; recalled by sec. of navy and ct. martialled for retaliatory action against Spanish authorities in P.R., 1825; resigned from Navy, 1826; comdr.-in-chief Mexican Navy with rank of gen. of marine, 1826-29; U.S. consul gen. to Algiers, 1830-36; chargé d'affaires to Turkey, 1836-43, minister, 1839. Author: Journal of a Cruise Made to the Pacific Ocean, 1815; Guide-Book to Constantinople, circa 1842. Died Pera, Constantinople, Mar. 3, 1843; buried Woodlands Cemetery, Phila.

PORTER, David Dixon, naval officer; b. Chester, Pa., June 8, 1813; s. David and Evelina (Anderson) P.; m. George Ann Patterson, Mar. 10, 1839, 10 children. Commd. lt. U.S. Navy, 1841; commanded landing party of 70 seamen, captured fort, Tabasco, Mexico, 1847; commanded mcht. steamer Panama, 1849, made voyage through Straits of Magellan to Pacific; commanded privately owned mail steamer Georgia, 1850-52, made regular trips between N.Y.C., Havana, Chagres; capt. ship Golden Age between Melbourne and Sydney for Australian S.S. Co., 1852-circa 1855; 1st lt. Portsmouth (Va.) Navy Yard, 1857-60, took prominent part in preliminary planning of New Orleans expdn.; in command mortar flotilla under Adm. Farragut, New Orleans and on Mississippi River, 1862; commanded fleets below fts. St. Philip and Jackson, demanded and accepted their surrender (on favorable terms), 1862; served as acting rear adm., comdr. Mississippi Squadron, 1862, aided U.S. Army in capture of Ark. Post, cooperated with Grant in assault on Vicksburg, 1863; commd. rear adm., 1863, took charge of lower Mississippi River as far down as New Orleans; commanded naval force cooperating with army in Red River expdn., 1864; commanded naval forces attacking Ft. Fisher, 1864-65; with Gen. Terry captured defenses of Wilmington, N.C.; commanded N. Atlantic Blockading Squadron, 1864; supt. U.S. Naval Acad., 1865-69, improved curriculum and instrn. methods; conducted unsuccessful diplomatic mission to Santo Domingo to secure cession or lease of Samana Bay, 1866-67; apptd. adviser to Sec. of Navy Adolph Borie by Pres. Grant, 1869-70, instituted reform policy, organized bds. to inspect fleets and navy yards, began to repair many vessels; promoted adm., 1870; chosen to command fleet assembled at Key West, 1873; head Bd. of Inspection, 1877-91. Author: Memoir of Commodore David Porter, 1875. Died Washington, D.C., Feb. 13, 1891; buried Arlington (Va.) Nat. Cemetery.

PORTER, David Rittenhouse, gov. Pa., iron mfr.; b. Norristown, Pa., Oct. 31, 1788; s. Andrew and Elizabeth (Parker) P.; m. Josephine McDermott, 1820; at least 1 child, Horace. Owner (with Edward Patton) Sligo Iron Wroks (Pa.), 1814-19; mem. Pa. Ho. of Reps., 1819, 20, 22; apptd. prothonotary and clk. Huntingdon County (Pa.) Cts., 1823; apptd. recorder of deeds and register of wills, 1827; elected to Pa. Senate, 1836; gov. Pa. (Democrat) 1839-45, upheld state credit, forced state banks to resume specie payments, 1840. suppressed anti-Catholic riots in Phila., 1844, abolished imprisonment for debt; built anthracite iron furnace, Harrisburg, Pa. (one of 1st in that part of state, used as model for other furnaces). Died Harrisburg, Aug. 6, 1867.

PORTER, Ebenezer, clergyman, educator; b. Cornwall, Conn., Oct. 5, 1772; s. Thomas and Abigail (Howe) P.; grad. Dartmouth, 1792, D.D. (hon.), 1814; A.M. (hon.), Yale, 1795; m. Lucy Merwin, May 1797. Ordained to ministry Congregational Ch., 1796; Bartlet prof. pulpit eloquence Andover (Mass.) Theol. Sem., 1812-27, pres., 1827-34; a founder Monthly Concert for Prayer, Am. Tract Soc.; active in furthering interests of home and fgn. missions, Am. Ednl. Soc., temperance movement. Author: The Young Preacher's Manual, 1819; An Analysis of the Principles of Rhetorical Delivery, 1827; Lectures on Revivals of Religion, 1832; Lectures on Homiletics, Preaching and Public Prayer, 1834. Died Andover, Apr. 8, 1834.

PORTER, Gilchrist, congressman, jurist; b. Windsor, nr. Fredericksburg, Va., Nov. 1, 1817; studied law. Admitted to bar, began practice of law, Bowling Green, Mo.; mem. U.S. Ho. of Reps. (Whig) from Mo., 32d, 34th congresses, 1851-53, 55-57; circuit judge, 1866-80. Died Hannibal, Mo., Nov. 1, 1894; buried Riverside Cemetery.

PORTER, James, congressman, lawyer; b. Williamstown, Mass., Apr. 18, 1787; grad. Williams Coll., Williamstown, 1810; studied law. Admitted to bar, began practice of law, Skaneateles, N.Y.; mem. N.Y. State Assembly, 1814-15; mem. U.S. Ho. of Reps. (Democrat) from N.Y., 15th Congress, 1817-19; surrogate Onondaga County, 1822-24; moved to Albany, N.Y.; register Ct. of Chancery, until 1839. Died Albany, Feb. 7, 1839; buried Greenwood Cemetery, Bklyn.

PORTER, James Madison, sec. of war, railroad pres.; b. nr. Norristown, Pa., Jan. 6, 1793; s. Gen. Andrew and Elizabeth (Parker) P.; m. Eliza Michler, Sept. 18, 1821. Raised volunteer company, Phila., 1813, commd. 2d lt. (co. served as garrison until relieved by Pa. Militia); continued mil. service in Pa. Militia, reached rank of col.; admitted to Pa. bar, 1813; a founder Lafayette Coll. (chartered 1826), Easton, Pa., pres. bd. trustees, 1826-52, prof. jurisprudence and polit. econ., 1837-52; mem. Pa. Constl. Conv., 1838; pres. judge 12th Jud. Dist., 1839-40; U.S. Sec. of War ad interim, 1843-44 (Senate refused to ratify his nomination); elected to Pa. Legislature, 1849; pres. judge 22d Jud. Dist., 1853-55; 1st pres. Delaware, Lehigh, Schuylkill & Susquehanna R.R. (chartered 1847), name changed to L V. R.R., 1853, pres., 1853-56; pres. Belvidere Delaware R.R: Mason. Died Easton, Nov. 11, 1862.

PORTER, John, congressman; b. Pa. Mem. U.S. Ho. of Reps. (filled vacancy) from Pa., 9th-11th congresses, Dec. 8, 1806-Mar. 4, 1811.

PORTER, John Addison, chemist; b. Catskill, N.Y., Mar. 15, 1822; s. Addison and Ann (Hogeboom) P.; grad. Yale, 1842, M.D. (hon.), 1854; m. Josephine Sheffield, July 16, 1855, 2 sons. Prof. rhetoric Delaware Coll., Newark, N.J., 1844-47; studied agrl. chemistry, Germany, 1847-50; prof. chemistry applied to the arts Brown U., 1850-52; prof. analytical, agrl. chemistry Yale (later Sheffield) Scientific Sch., 1852-56, prof. organic chemistry, 1856-64, 1st dean Sheffield Sci. Sch., Yale, consolidated depts. of instrn., established and extended courses of study which emphasized science, made available reliable, useful information about agr. and nutrition; a founder Scroll and Key of Yale, 1842. Author: Plan of an Agricultural School, 1856; Principles of Chemistry, 1856; First Book of Chemistry and Allied Sciences, 1857; Outlines of the First Course of Yale Agaricultural Lectures, 1860. Died New Haven, Conn., Aug. 25, 1866.

PORTER, John Luke, naval constructor; b. Portsmouth, Va., Sept. 19, 1813; s. Joseph and Frances (Pritchard) P.; m. Susan Buxton, 1834, 6 children. Designed, built steam-tug Water Witch, Washington, D.C., 1843-44; as acting constructor, superintended bldg. of ship Alleghany, 1846-47, in Pitts.; 1st pres. Portsmouth Common Council, 1852; superintended constrn. naval steam sloops Seminole and Pensacola, 1858-59; commd. naval constructor Pensacola Navy Yard, 1859; commd. naval constructor Confederate Navy, 1862; (with Lt. J. M. Brooke and W. P. Williamson) reconstructed ship Merrimac (renamed C.S.S. Virginia), 1861; chief constructor Confederate Navy, Richmond, Va., circa 1862, designed ships North Carolina, Charleston, Columbia, Savannah; mgr. naval dept. Atlantic Works, Norfolk, Va., 1865; supt. Norfolk and Portsmouth ferries; Died Portsmouth, Dec. 14, 1893.

PORTER, Noah, clergyman, coll. pres.; b. Farmington, Conn., Dec. 14, 1811; s. Noah and Mehetabel (Meigs) P.; grad. Yale, 1831; studied U. Berlin, (Germany) 1853; D.D. (hon.), U. City N.Y., 1858, Edinburgh (Scotland) U., 1886; LL.D. (hon.), Western Res. Coll., 1870, Trinity Coll., 1871; m. Mary Taylor, Apr. 13, 1836. Rector, Hopkins Grammar Sch., New Haven, Conn., 1831-33; ordained to ministry Congregational Ch., 1836; pastor 2d Congregational Ch., Springfield, Mass., 1843-46; Clark prof. moral philosophy and metaphysics Yale, 1846-92, pres., 1871-86. Author: The Human Intellect (chief work), 1868; The American Colleges and the American Public, 1870; The Christian College; An Address Delivered at Wellesley College, 1880. Editor: Noah Webster's American Dictionary of the English Language of 1864; Webster's International Dictionary of the English Language, 1890. Died Farmington, Mar. 4, 1892.

PORTER, Peter Buell, congressman, sec. of war; b. Salisbury, Conn., Aug. 14, 1773; s. Joshua and Abigail (Buell) P.; grad. Yale, 1791; attended Litchfield (Conn.) Law Sch.; m. Letitia Breckenridge, 1818. Admitted to bar; began practice law, Canandaigua, N.Y., 1795; clk. Ontario County (N.Y.), 1797-1804; mem. N.Y. State Legislature, 1801-02; mem. firm Porter, Barton & Co. (which acquired monopoly of transp. bus. on portage between Lewiston and Schlosser); mem. U.S. Ho. of Reps. from N.Y., 11th-12th, 14th congresses, 1809-13, 1815-Jan. 23, 1816, leader "War Hawks"; mem. N.Y. Canal Commn., 1810; q.m.

gen. N.Y. Militia, 1812; authorized by War Dept. to raise, command brigade of volunteers militia, 1813, instructed to incorporate them with "corps" from Six Nations Indians, commanded both, 1813; 14; commd. maj. gen. N.Y. Militia, 1814; voted gold medal by Congress, 1814; sec. state N.Y., 1815, 16, U.S. commr. to determine internat. boundary from St. Lawrence to Lake of Woods, 1816-22; regent U. State N.Y., 1824-30; U.S. sec. of war, 1828-29; Whig presdl. elector, 1840. Died Niagara Falls, N.Y., Mar. 20, 1844; buried Oakwood Cemetery, Niagara Falls.

PORTER, Rufus, inventor, editor; b. Boxford, Mass., May 1, 1792; s. Tyler and Abigail (Johnson) P.; at least 1 child. Served as pvt. Me. Militia, War of 1812; invented cameraobscura (produced portraits in 15 minutes), 1820, cord-making machine, 1825; founder, editor Am. Mechanic (1st scientific mag. of its kind), circa 1840; established publ. Scientific American, 1845; published Aerial Navigation, 1849; other inventions include: horse-drawn flat boat, clock carriage, washing machine, fire alarm, portable house, revolving rifle, rotary plow, reaction wind wheel. Died New Haven, Conn., Aug. 13, 1884.

PORTER, Sarah, educator; b. Farmington, Conn., Aug. 16, 1813; d. Rev. Noah and Mehetabel (Meigs) P.; attended Mr. Hart's Acad., Farmington, circa 1830-31; attended Sch. of Prof. Andrews, New Haven, Conn., 1832. At Prof. Andrew's Sch. became acquainted with mems. Yale faculty, 1832; tchr., Springfield, Mass., Phila., Buffalo, N.Y., circa 1832-circa 1842; opened Miss Porter's Sch., Farmington, 1843, tchr. Greek, Latin, French, literature, history, philosophy, mathematics, 1843-1900; cultivated friendship of distinguished authors, intellectuals of time including John Fiske, Prof. George Trumbull Ladd of Yale. Died Farmington (probably), Feb. 17, 1900.

PORTER, Timothy H., congressman; b. New Haven, Conn. Moved to Cattaraugus County, N.Y.; mem. N.Y. State Assembly, 1816-17, 38, 40; judge Cattaraugus County, 1817-30; admitted to bar of Tioga and Cattaraugus counties, 1819, began practice of law, Olean, N.Y.; 1st judge Ct. of Common Pleas, 1819; dist. atty. for Cattaraugus County, 1819-20, 24; mem. N.Y. Senate, 1823, 28-31; presdl. elector, 1824; mem. U.S. Ho. of Reps. from N.Y., 19th Congress, 1825-27. Died nr. Oleon, circa 1840; buried Mt. View Cemetery, Olean.

PORTER, William Trotter, journalist; b. Newbury, Vt., Dec. 24, 1809; s. Benjamin and Martha (Olcott) P.; attended Dartmouth. In charge of Farmer's Herald, St. Johnsbury, Vt., 1829; asso. editor Norwich (Vt.) Enquirer, 1830-31, owner, editor, 1831-32, 35-42; established Spirit of the Times (1st journal in U.S., renamed Porter's Spirit of the Times at time of sale) 1831, editor, 1831-32, 35-56, asso. editor, 1856-58; connected editorially with New Yorker, The Constellation, N.Y. Atlas Mag., 1831-35; owner, editor Am. Turf Register and Sporting Mag., 1839-44; founder N.Y. Cricket Club, 1852. Published: Colonial Peter Hawker's Instructions to Young Sportsmen; with additions relative to North American hunting and shooting, 1846. Editor: The Big Bear of Arkansaw and Other Tales, 1835; A Quarter Race in Kentucky and Other Sketches, 1846. Died N.Y.C., July 19, 1858.

PORTIER, Michael, clergyman; b. Montbrison, Lyons, France, Sept. 2, 1795; attended Sem. of Lyons; grad. St. Mary's Sem., Balt. Ordained priest Roman Catholic Ch., St. Louis, 1818; a founder Catholic schs., New Orleans; vicar-apostolic of Fla. and Ala., 1825-59; consecrated 1st Roman Catholic bishop of Mobile (Ala.), 1826; founder Spring Hill Coll., 1830; erected Cath. acad., Mobile, 1833, also orphanages. Died Mobile, May 14, 1859.

PORTOLA, Gaspar de, see de Portolá, Gaspar.

PORY, John, geographer, colonial ofcl.; b. Thompston, Norfolk, Eng., 1572; s. William Pory; B.A., Gonville and Caius Coll., Cambridge (Eng.) U., 1591-92, M.A., 1595; M.A., Oxford (Eng.) U., 1610. Translated and published A Geographical Historie of Africa, Written in Arabicke and Italian by John Leo, A More, 1600; came to Va., 1619; sec. Va. Colony; speaker Va. Ho. of Burgesses, mem. Gov.'s Council, 1619; made exploratory trading voyage along New Eng. Coast, 1622; returned to Eng., 1623; chosen by Privy Council to publish their recent orders in Va., 1623, apptd. mem. of investigating commn. of conditions in colony; mem. Va. Commn., 1624; mem. in Eng. of Council for Va. Died Sutton St. Edmund, Eng., Sept. 1635.

POSEY, Thomas, army officer, senator; b. Fairfax County, Va., July 9, 1750; m. Martha Matthews; m. 2d, Mary (Alexander) Thornton; 1 dau., Mary. Served with Va. militia against Indian tribes on Western frontier, 1774; mem. Va. Com. of Correspondence; commd. maj. 7th Va. Regt. during Revolutionary War; promoted lt. col., 1782, brig. gen., 1793; moved to Ky., 1794; mem. Ky. Senate, presiding officer, 1805, 06; lt. gov. Ky., 1805-09; commd. maj. gen. U.S. Volunteers, 1809; moved to Attakapas, La.; mem. U.S. Senate from La., Oct. 1812-Feb. 1813; gov. Ind. Territory, 1813-16; Indian agt. Ill. Territory, 1816-18. Died Shawneetown, Ill.; buried Westwood Cemetery, Shawneetown.

POST, Christian Frederick, missionary; b. Conitz, East Prussia, circa 1710; m. Rachel, 1743; m. 2d, Agnes, 1747; m. 3d, Mary Stadelman, Aug. 27, 1763. Came to Bethlehem, Pa., 1742; itinerant Moravian missionary to various German groups; began missionary work among Indians in area between N.Y. and Conn., 1743; Indian wars of 1744 forced him to leave, went to live in Iroquois Country among the Six Nations; with Isaac Stille held conf. on Ohio River with mems. of Delaware, Shawnee, other tribes, persuaded Indians to ally with British forcing French to abandon Fort Duquesne, 1758; founded a settlement nr. Bolivay in Ohio country, 1759. Died May 1, 1785.

POST, Isaac, reformer; b. Westbury, L.I., N.Y., Feb. 26, 1798; s. Edmund and Catherine (Willets) P.; m. Hannah Kirby, circa 1823; m. 2d, Amy Kirby, Sept. 18, 1828; 4 children. Pioneer in anti-slavery reform; his house was a well-known sta. Underground R.R.; converted to spiritualism by Margaret Fox (among earliest converts), 1848, furthered spiritualist movement. Author: Voices from the Spirit World, being Communications from Many Spirits, by the hand of Isaac Post, Medium, 1852. Died Rochester, N.Y., May 9, 1872.

POST, Jotham, Jr., congressman, businessman; b. nr. Westbury, Nassau County, N.Y., Apr. 4, 1771; grad. Columbia, 1792; studied medicine. Became drug importer, N.Y.C.; mem. bd. aldermen; mem. N.Y. State Assembly, 1795, 1805-08; dir. N.Y. Hosp., 1798-1802; mem. U.S. Ho. of Reps. (Federalist) from N.Y., 13th Congress, 1813-15. Died N.Y.C., May 15, 1817.

POST, Philip Sidney, congressman, diplomat; b. Florida, Orange County, N.Y., Mar. 19, 1833; grad. Union Coll. Schenectady, N.Y., 1855; attended Poughkeepsie Law Sch. Admitted to bar, Ill., 1856; commd. 2d lt. 59th Regt., Ill. Inf., 1861, 1st lt., adj., 1861, maj., col., 1862; brevetted brig. gen. U.S. Volunteers for service in Battle of Nashville (Tenn.), 1864; decorated Congressional Medal of Honor, 1893; apptd. consul to Vienna, 1866, promoted consul gen. to Austria-Hungary, 1874-79; comdr. dept. of Ill., Grand Army of Republic, 1886; mem. U.S. Ho. of Reps. (Republican) from Ill., 50th-54th congresses, 1887-95. Died Washington, D.C., Jan. 6, 1895; buried Hope Cemetery, Galesburg, Ill.

POST, Truman Marcellus, clergyman, educator; b. Middlebury, Vt., June 3, 1810; s. Martin and Sarah (Hulburd) P.; grad. Middlebury Coll., 1829, D.D. (hon.), 1855; m. Frances Henshaw, Oct. 5, 1835, 5 children. Prin., Castleton (Vt.) Sem., 1829-30; prof. ancient langs. and ancient history Ill. Coll., circa 1833-47; ordained pastor Congregational Ch., 1840; pastor 3d Presbyn. Ch. (became a Congl. ch. 1851), St. Louis, 1847-82; Author: Skeptical Era in Modern History, 1856; History as a Teacher of Social and Political leader in advancement of Congl. Ch. in Mo.; non-resident lectr. on eccles. history Chgo. Theol. Sem. Science, 1870. Died St. Louis, Dec. 31, 1886.

POST, Wright, surgeon; b. North Hempstead, L.I., N.Y., Feb. 19, 1766; s. Jotham and Winifred (Wright) P.; studied at London Hosp.; M.D. (hon.) regents U. State N.Y., 1814; m. Mary Magdalen Bailey, 1790. Prof. surgery med. dept. Columbia, 1792-1813, created anatomical mus.; prof. anatomy and physiology Coll. Physicians and Surgeons, 1813, pres., 1821-26; attending surgeon N.Y. Hosp., 1792-1821, consulting surgeon, 1821; ligated the subclavian outside scaleni muscles, 1817; helped introduce Hunterian principles of surg. thought and procedure in Am.; 1st in U.S. to perform operation for case of false aneurism of femoral artery. Died Throgg's Neck, N.Y., June 14, 1828.

POSTL, Karl Anton, see Sealsfield, Charles.

POSTON, Charles Pebrille, congressman; b. Hardin County, Ky., Apr. 20, 1825; s. Temple and Judith (Dubrill) P.; m. Margaret John Haycraft, 1848, 1 dau. Clk., Supreme Ct. at Nashville, Tenn.; moved to Cal., 1850; clk. San Francisco Customs House, 1850-53; explored east coast Cal. for harbors, So. Ariz. for mineral deposits, 1854; supt. Indian affairs, Ariz. Territory, 1863; del. from Ariz. Territory to Congress, 38th Congress, 1864-65; admitted to bar, 1867; recipient hon. commn. to study irrigation and immigration in Asia, 1868; fgn. corr. N.Y. Tribune, 1870; register U.S. Land Office, Florence, Ariz., 1878. Author: Europe in the Summer Time, 1868; Apache Land, 1878. Died Phoenix, Ariz., June 24, 1902; buried Florence.

POTT, John, colonial ofcl.; b. Eng.; s. Henry and Grace Pott; m. Elizabeth Pott. Apptd. physician gen. by Va. Co., came to Va., 1621; mem. Va. Council, 1621-24, 26-30; dep. gov. Va., 1629-30; arrested and convicted of felony, 1630, pardoned by King, 1631; leader revolt against royal gov., Sir John Harvey, 1635. Died Va., circa 1642.

POTTER, Allen, congressman, businessman; b. Galloway, Saratoga County, N.Y., Oct. 2, 1818; attended common schs.; learned tinsmith's trade, Mich. In retail hardware bus., Kalamazoo, Mich., 1845-58; then engaged in banking, gas mfg.; mem. Mich. Ho. of Reps., 1857; pres. village council, 1859, 63, 70, 72; mem. bd. edn., 1867, 69, 71, pres., 1869; mem. bd. water commrs., 1872; mem. U.S. Ho. of Reps. (Independent) from Mich., 44th Congress, 1875-77; engaged in railroad and Colo. mining enterprises; mem. sewer commn., 1880-83; 1st mayor Kalamazoo, 1884; treas. state asylum for insane. Died Kalamazoo, May 8, 1885; buried City Cemetery.

POTTER, Alonzo, clergyman, educator; b. Beekman, N.Y., July 6, 1800; s. Joseph and Anne (Knight) P.; grad. Union Coll., 1818, LL.D. (hon.), 1846; D.D. (hon.), Kenyon Coll., 1834, Harvard, 1843; m. Sarah Nott, 1824; m. 2d, Sarah Benedict, 1841; m 3d, Frances Seaton, 1865; at least 3 children, Robert Brown, Henry Codman, Eliphalet Nott. Prof. mathematics and natural philosophy Union Coll., Schenectady, N.Y., 1822-26, prof. moral and intellectual philosophy and polit. economy, 1831-38, v.p., 1838-45; ordained deacon Protestant Episcopal Ch., 1822, priest, 1824; bishop of Pa., 1845-65; revived Protestant Episcopal Acad., 1846, established Episcopal Hosp., 1860, instituted system of convocations, founded Divinity Sch. of Protestant Episcopal Chs., Phila., 1863; Author: Church Comprehension and Church Unity in Memorial Papers, 1857; Political Economy, 1840; The School and the Schoolmaster, 1842; Religious Philosophy; or Nature, Man and the Bible Witnessing to God and to Religious Truth, 1872. Died San Francisco Bay, Cal., July 4, 1865.

POTTER, Clarkson Nott, congressman, lawyer; b. Schenectady, N.Y., Apr. 25, 1825; grad. Union Coll., Schenectady, 1842, Rensselaer Poly. Inst., 1843; studied law. Surveyor in Wis., 1843; admitted to bar, 1846, began practice of law, N.Y.C., 1847; mem. U.S. Ho. of Reps. (Democrat) from N.Y., 41st-43d, 45th congresses, 1869-75, 77-79; pres. Mich. Democratic convs., 1875, 77; del. Dem. nat. convs., 1872, 76; trustee Union Coll., 1863-82; pres. Am. Bar Assn., 1881-82. Died N.Y.C., Jan. 23, 1882; probably buried Vale Cemetery, Schenectady.

POTTER, Elisha Reynolds, congressman, lawyer; b. Little Rest (now Kingston), R.I., Nov. 5, 1764; learned blacksmith's trade; attended Plainfield Acad.; studied law. Served as pvt. in Revolutionary War; admitted to bar, circa 1789, began practice of law, South Kingstown Twp., R.I.; mem. R.I. Ho. of Reps., 1793-96, 98-1808, 1816-17, 19-35, speaker, 1795-96, 1802, 06-08; mem. U.S. Ho. of Reps. (Federalist, filled vacancy) from R.I., 4th-5th, 11th-13th congresses, Nov. 15, 1796-97 (resigned), 1809-15; unsuccessful candidate for gov. R.I., 1818. Died South Kingston, R.I., Sept. 26, 1835; buried family burial ground, Kingston.

POTTER, Elisha Reynolds, congressman, jurist; b. South Kingston, R.I., June 20, 1811; s. Elisha Reynolds and Mary (Mawney) P.; grad. Harvard, 1830; read law under Nathaniel Searle. Admitted to R.I. bar, 1832; adjutant gen. R.I., 1833-37; mem. R.I. Gen. Assembly, 1838-40; mem. RI. Constl. Conv., 1841-42; mem. U.S. Ho. of Reps. from R.I., 28th Congress, 1843-45; mem. R.I. Senate, 1847-52, 61-63; commr. R.I. Public Schs., 1849-54; publisher R.I. Ednl. Magazine, 1852, editor until 1853; asso. justice R.I. Supreme Ct., 1868-82. Author: The Early History of Narragansett, 1835. Died Kingston, R.I., Apr. 10, 1882; buried family burial ground.

POTTER, Emery Davis, congressman, lawyer; b. Providence, R.I., Oct. 7, 1804; attended acad., Herkimer County, N.Y.; studied law, Cooperstown, N.Y. Admitted to N.Y. bar at Utica, 1833, began practice of law, Cooperstown; moved to Toledo, O., 1834; judge Circuit Ct. for No. Counties of Ohio; pres. judge Ct. of Common Pleas, 1834-43; mem. U.S. Ho. of Reps. (Democrat) from Ohio, 28th, 31st congresses, 1843-45, 49-51; mayor Toledo, 1846-48; mem. Ohio Ho. of Reps., 1848-50; city solicitor Toledo, 1861-62; mem. bd. edn., 1864-65; mem. Ohio Senate, 1874-76, pres. Died Toledo, Feb. 12, 1896; buried Forest Cemetery.

POTTER, Horatio, clergyman; b. Beekman, N.Y., Feb. 9, 1802; s. Joseph and Anne (Knight) P.; A.B., Union Coll. 1826; m. Mary Jane Tomlinson, Sept. 22, 1827; m. 2d, Margaret Atcheson Pollock; 6 children. Ordained deacon Protestant Episcopal Ch., 1827, priest, 1828; prof. mathematics and natural philosophy Trinity Coll., Hartford, Conn., 1828-33; rector St. Peter's Ch., Albany, N.Y., 1833-54; provisional bishop Diocese of N.Y., 1854-61, bishop, 1861-87; partly responsible for return of bishops from the South to their seats in Gen. Conv., Protestant Episcopal Ch. Died N.Y.C., Jan. 2, 1887; buried Poughkeepsie N.Y.

POTTER, James, army officer, farmer; b. County Tyrone, Ireland, 1729; s. John Potter; m. Elizabeth Cathcart; m. 2d, Mary (Patterson) Chambers; 7 children. Came to Am., 1741; served as capt. under Gen. Armstrong in victorious Kittanning campaign, 1755; served as maj., then lt. col. fighting French and Indians, 1763-64; commr. to induce settlers in western Pa. to withdraw from Indian lands under Treaty of 1768; col., battalion of associators, 1776; mem. Constl. Conv., Phila., 1776; commd. brig. gen., 1777, fought at Trenton, Princeton, Brandywine, Germantown; mem. Supreme Exec. Council Pa. (Constitutionalist), 1780-81, v.p., 1781; commd. maj. gen. Pa. Militia, 1782; mem. Council of Censors, 1784; dep. surveyor for Pa. in Northumberland County, also supt. devel. of land schemes in Penn's Valley for land speculation co., 1785-89; a commr. rivers and streams, 1785. Died Centre Point, Pa., Nov. 1789.

POTTER, Nathaniel, physician; b. Easton, Md., 1770; s. Dr. Zabdiel and Lucy (Bruff) P.; M.D., U. Pa., 1796; m. Miss Ford, 2 children. Physician, Balt. Gen. Dispensary, 1803; prof. theory and practice of medicine Med. Coll. of Md. (now U. Md. Sch. of Medicine), 1807-43; sec. Med. and Chirurgical Faculty of Md., 1801-09; dean faculty physic U. Md., 1812-14; pres. Balt. Med. Soc., 1812. Med. Soc. of Md., 1817; established non-contagiousness of yellow fever. Author: An Essay on the Medicinal and Deleterious Qualities of Arsenic, 1796; Memoir on Contagion, 1818; Some Account of the Rise and Progress of the University of Maryland, 1838; editor Balt. Med. and Philos. Lycaeum, 1811; co-editor Md. Med. and Surg. Jour., 1840-43. Died Balt., Jan. 2, 1843; buried Greenmount Cemetery, Balt.

POTTER, Orlando Brunson, congressman, lawyer; b. Charlemont, Mass., Mar. 10, 1823; attended Williams Coll., Williamstown, Mass., also Dane Law Sch., Cambridge, Mass. Admitted to bar, 1848, began practice of law, Boston; engaged in mfg., agriculture; moved to N.Y., 1853; mem. U.S. Ho. of Reps. (Union Democrat) from N.Y., 48th Congress, 1883-85; mem. Rapid Transit Commn., N.Y.C., 1890-94. Died N.Y.C., Jan. 2, 1894; buried Greenwood Cemetery.

POTTER, Platt, jurist; b. Galway, N.Y., Apr. 6, 1800; s. Restcone and Lucinda (Strong) P.; grad. Acad. of Schenectady (N.Y.), 1820; LL.D. (hon.), Union Coll., 1867; m. Antoinette (Paige) Smith, June 15, 1836. Admitted to N.Y. bar; mem. N.Y. Supreme Ct., 1825; mem. N.Y. Legislature, 1831, responsible for legislation providing asylum for insane at Utica (1st state asylum in N.Y.); master and examiner of chancery, 1828-47; dist. atty. Schenectady County, 1835-47; justice N.Y. Supreme Ct., 1857-73; judge Ct. of Appeals; trustee Union Coll., 1865; v.p. N.Y. Bar Assn.; pres. Mohawk Nat. Bank of Schenectady; caused arrest of Henry Ray (mem. N.Y. Assembly who refused to answer a subpoena), accused of high breach of privilege for this action, published winning argument for this case (won him much fame). Author: A General Treatise of Statutes, 1871, Treatise on the Law of Corporation, 1879. Died Schenectady, Aug. 11, 1891.

POTTER, Robert, congressman; b. Granville County, N.C., circa 1800; m. Miss Pelham; m. 2d, Mrs. Harriet A. Page. Became a lawyer, Halifax, N.C.; mem. N.C. Ho. of Commons, 1826-28, 34-35, introduced bill to organize state instn. to train poor boys for public service, expelled for fighting, 1835; mem. U.S. Ho. of Reps. (Democrat), from N.C. (21st-22d congresses, 1829-Nov. 1831, offered bill to destroy banks, also bill to sell public lands and divide the proceeds among the states, resigned from Ho. of Reps. to serve jail term for his part in a riot; went to Tex., became del. to Tex. Conv., 1835-36, signed Tex. Declaration of Independence, 1836; sec. of navy Tex.; mem. Tex. Senate, 1842. Died in polit. feud (shot while trying to escape from another senator), Lake Caddo, Tex., Mar. 2, 1842.

POTTER, Robert Brown, lawyer, army officer; b. Schenectady, N.Y., July 16, 1829; s. Bishop Alonzo and Sarah Maria (Nott) P.; attended Union Coll.; m. Frances Paine Tileston, Apr. 14, 1857; m. 2d, Abby Austin Stevens, Sept. 29, 1865; at least one child. Admitted to N.Y. bar; commd. maj. Scott Rifles, 1861; commd. lt. col. 51st Regt. N.Y. Volunteers, 1861, col., 1862, fought in Battle at Antietam; commanded 51st Regt. at Battle of Fredericksburg, 1862; brig. gen. U.S. Volunteers, 1863; commanded 2d Div. participating in capture of Vicksburg, 1863; maj. gen. U.S. Volunteers, 1864-65; receiver for Atlantic and Gt. Western R.R., 1866-69. Died Newport, R.I., Feb. 19, 1887.

POTTER, Samuel John, senator; b. South Kingston Twp., R.I., June 29, 1753; studied law. Admitted to bar, practiced law; dep. gov. R.I., 1790-1803; presdl. elector, 1792, 96; mem. U.S. Senate from R.I., 1803-04. Died Washington, D.C., Oct. 14, 1804; buried family burial ground, Kingston, R.I.

POTTER, William James, clergyman, editor; b. North Dartmouth, Mass., Feb. 1, 1829; s. William and Anna (Aiken) P.; attended State Normal Sch., Bridgewater, Mass.; attended Harvard Divinity Sch., 1856-57, U. Berlin (Germany), 1857-58; m. Elizabeth Claghorn Babcock, Nov. 26, 1863, 2 children. Ordained to ministry Unitarian ch., 1859; minister 1st Congl. Soc. of New Bedford, Mass., 1859-93; drafted into U.S. Army, 1863, served as insp. mil. hosps., later chaplain to convalescent camp, Alexandria, Va.; organized Free Religious Assn., circa 1867, sec., 1867-82, pres., 1882-92. Author: Twenty-five Sermons of Twenty-five Years, 1885; editor Free Religious Index, circa 1885-86. Died Boston, Dec. 21, 1893.

POTTER, William Wilson, congressman, lawyer; b. Potters Mills, Pa., Dec. 18, 1792; grad. Dickinson Coll., Carlisle, Pa.; studied law. Admitted to bar, 1814, practiced law; mem. U.S. Ho. of Reps. (Democrat) from Pa., 25th-26th congresses, 1837-39. Died Bellefonte, Pa., Oct. 28, 1839; buried Union Cemetery, Bellefonte.

POTTLE, Emory Bemsley, congressman, lawyer; b. Naples, N.Y., July 4, 1815; attended Penn Yan (N.Y.) Acad.; studied law. Admitted to bar, N.Y.C., 1838, began practice of law, Springfield, O.; returned to Naples, continued practice of law; mem. N.Y. State Assembly, 1847; mem. U.S. Ho. of Reps. (Republican) from N.Y., 35th-36th congresses, 1857-61; apptd. by Pres. Lincoln mem. of commn. which prepared bill for tariff on wool. Died Naples, Apr. 18, 1891; buried Rose Ridge Cemetery.

POTTS, Benjamin Franklin, army officer, territorial gov.; b. Carroll County, O., Jan. 29, 1836; s. James and Jane (Maple) P.; ed. Westminster Coll., 1854-55; m. Angeline Jackson, May 28, 1861. Admitted to Ohio bar, 1859, and began practice law; del. Balt. Democratic Conv., 1860; commd. capt. Co. F, 32d Ohio Volunteers, U.S. Army, 1861, lt. col., then col., 1862, fought at Memphis, Vicksburg, Atlanta, Savannah, brig. gen., 1865, ret., 1866; mem. Ohio Senate (Republican), 1868; territorial gov. Montana, 1870-83, wrote Report of the Governor of Montana . . . to the Secretary of the Interior . . . 1878-79; under his administrn., territorial debt almost paid off, legislation passed to modernize civil and criminal laws and procedures; mem. Mont. Territorial Legislature, 1884. Died Helena, Mont., June 17, 1887.

POTTS, David, Jr., congressman, iron co. exec.; b. Warwick Furnace, nr. Pottstown, Pa., Nov. 27, 1794. Became an ironmaster, owner and mgr. Warwick Furnace; mem. Pa. Ho. of Reps., 1824-26; mem. U.S. Ho. of Reps. (Whig) from Pa., 22d-25th congresses, 1831-39. Died Warwick Furnace (now Warwick), June 1, 1863; buried Coventry Cemetery, nr. Warwick.

POTTS, Jonathan, physician; b. Colebrookdale, Berks County, Pa., Apr. 11, 1745; s. John and Ruth (Savage) P.; M.B., Coll. of Phila. Med. Sch. (now U. Pa.), 1768, M.D., 1768; m. Grace Richardson, May 5, 1767, 5 sons, 2 daus. Began practice of medicine, Reading, Pa., 1768; del. to provincial meeting of deputies, Phila., 1774; mem. Provincial Congress, Phila., 1775; dep. dir. gen. hosps. of No. Dept., Continental Army, 1777, dep. dir. gen. Middle Dept., 1778. Died Reading, Oct. 1781.

POTTS, Richard, senator, jurist; b. Upper Marlborough, Md., July 19, 1753; s. William and Sarah (Lee) P.; read law under Judge Samuel Chase; m. Elizabeth Hughs, Apr. 15, 1779; m. 2d, Eleanor Murdoch, Dec. 19, 1799; 13 children. Mem. com. of observation Frederick County (Md.), 1776; clk. Frederick County Ct., 1777-78; aide to Gov. Thomas Johnson in Md. Militia, 1777; mem. Md. Ho. of Dels., 1779-80, 87-88; del. to Continental Congress, 1781, 82; Md. pros. atty. for Frederick, Montgomery and Washington counties, 1784; mem. Md. ratifying conv., Annapolis, 1788; U.S. atty. for Md. dist., 1789-91; chief judge 5th Jud. Dist., 1791-92, 96-1801; mem. U.S. Senate from Md., 1793-Oct. 24, 1796; judge Md. Ct. of Appeals, 1801-04. Died Frederick, Md., Nov. 26, 1808; buried Mt. Olivet Cemetery, Balt.

POUILLY, Jacques Nicholas Bussiere de, see de POUILLY.

POUILLY, Joseph de, see de Pouilly, Joseph.

POULSON, Zachariah, editor, publisher, b. Phila., Sept. 5, 1761; s. Zachariah and Anna Barbara (Stollenberger) P.; m. Susanna Knorr, Apr. 23, 1780. Studied printing under Christopher Sower (publisher 1st German Edit. of Bible in U.S.); librarian Phila. Library Co., 21 years, treas. 6 years, dir. 32 years; published Poulson's Town and Country Almanac, 1788-1801; published Jours. of Gen. Convs. of Delegates from Abolition Socs. of U.S., 1794-1801; mem. Pa. Constl. Conv., 1789; printer to Pa. Senate, 1789; editor, publisher Poulson's Am. Daily Advertiser (Whig journal), 1800-39; founder, pres. Phila. Soc. for Ameliorating the Miseries of Public Prisons; mgr. Pa. Hosp.; dir. Phila. Contributionship for Insurance of Homes from Loss by Fire, 35 years. Died Phila., July 31, 1844.

POUND, Thomas, cartographer, naval officer; b. Eng., circa 1650; m. Elizabeth. Apptd. pilot on ship Rose by gov. Mass., 1687; pirate along Atlantic Coast of Am., captured and condemned to hang, 1689, reprieved, 1690; capt. frigate Sally Rose of Royal Navy, 1691; produced 1st engraved map of Boston Harbor, 1691-92; served as capt. Brit. Navy, in Europe, 1692-95, off Ireland, 1698-97, off Am., 1697-98. Died Middlesex, Eng., 1703.

POURTALES, Louis François de, see de Pourtales, Louis Francois.

POWEL, John Hare, legislator, agriculturist; b. Phila., Apr. 22, 1786; s. Robert and Margaret (Willing) Hare; ed. Coll. of Phila., 1800-03; m. Julia DeVeaux, Oct. 20, 1817, 9 children. Sec. U.S. legation under William Pinkney, London, Eng., 1809-11; commd. brig. maj. U.S. Volunteers, 1812; commd. insp. gen. with rank of col., 1814; livestock breeder, introduced improved Durham Short Horn cattle from Eng., also Southdown breed of sheep; an organizer Pa., Agr. Soc., sec., 1823; mem. Pa. Senate, 1827-30. Contbr. to agrl. periodicals including Am. Farmer, Memoirs of Pa. Agrl. Soc. Author: Hints for American Husbandmen, 1827. Died Newport, R.I., June 14, 1856.

POWELL, see Osceola.

POWELL, Alfred H., congressman, lawyer; b. Loudoun County, Va., Mar. 6, 1781; grad. Princeton; studied law. Admitted to bar, began practice of law, Winchester, Va., 1800; mem. Va. Senate, 1812-19; mem. U.S. Ho. of Reps. from Va., 19th Congress, 1825-27; del. Va. Constl. Conv., 1830. Died Loudoun County, 1831.

POWELL, Charles Stuart, theatrical mgr.; b. in England. Came to Am., 1792, joined with number of actors in campaign to bring theater to Boston, where theatrical performances had been illegal since 1750; performed at New Exhibition Room, Boston, 1792; after public opinion had been aroused in favor of theater and anti-theater law repealed, set out for Eng. to assemble theatrical co. for Boston, 1793; mgr. (with Baker) Federal Street Theatre, Boston, 1794; promoted building of Haymarket Theatre, Boston, 1796, managed theatre, 1796-97.

POWELL, Cuthbert, congressman, lawyer; b. Alexandria, Va., Mar. 4, 1775; son of Levin Powell; studied law. Admitted to bar, practiced law, Alexandria; mayor Alexandria; moved to Loudoun County, Va., engaged in agriculture; held various local offices; mem. Va. Senate, 1815-19; mem. Va. Ho. of Dels., 1828-29; mem. U.S. Ho. of Reps. (Whig) from Va., 27th Congress, 1841-43. Died "Llangollen," Loudoun County, May 8, 1849; buried pvt. cemetery at "Llangollen."

POWELL, Lazarus Whitehead, senator, gov. Ky.; b. Henderson County, Ky., Oct. 6, 1812; s. Lazarus and Ann (McMahon) P.; grad. St. Joseph's Coll., Bardstown, Ky., 1833; studied law Transylvania U.; m. Harriet Ann Jennings, Nov. 8, 1837, 3 children. Admitted to Ky. bar, 1835; mem. Ky. Assembly, 1836; gov. Ky., 1851-55; commr. to Utah to compromise difficulties with Mormons, 1858; mem. U.S. Senate from Ky., 1859-65, author resolutions providing for com. of 13, chmn. com., 1861; opposed fed. govt. policy of polit. arrests and mil. interference with elections; Powell County (Ky.) named for him. Died Henderson, Ky., July 3, 1867; buried Fernwood Cemetery, Henderson.

POWELL, Levin, congressman; b. nr. Manassas, Prince William County, Va., 1737; attended pvt. schs.; at least 1 son, Cuthbert. Dep. sheriff Prince William County; moved to Loudoun County, 1763, engaged in merc. activities; served as maj. Continental Army in Revolutionary War, 1775, lt. col. 16th Regt., 1777-78; mem. Va. Ho. of Dels., 1779, 87-88, 91-92; del. Va. Conv. which ratified U.S. Constn., 1788; presdl. elector, 1796; mem. U.S.

Ho. of Reps. (Federalist) from Va., 6th Congress, 1799-1801; a builder of turnpike from Alexandria, Va. to upper country. Died Bedford, Pa., Aug. 23, 1810; buried Old Presbyn. Graveyard.

POWELL, Paulus, congressman; b. Amherst County, Va., 1809; attended Amherst (Va.) Coll. Held various local offices; mem. Va. Ho. of Dels., 1843-49, 63-64; mem. U.S. Ho. of Reps. (Democrat) from Va., 31st-35th congresses, 1849-59. Died Amherst, Va., June 10, 1874; buried pvt. burying ground at "Kenmore," nr. Amherst.

POWELL, Samuel, congressman, jurist; b. Norristown, Pa., July 10, 1776; attended Phila. Coll.; studied law. Admitted to bar, Norristown, before 1800; moved to Blountville, Tenn., 1800; established 1st law sch. in Tenn. in his home; moved to Rogersville, Tenn., 1805, practiced law; mem. Superior Ct. of Law and Equity, 1807-09; judge 1st Circuit Ct, of Tenn., 1812-13, 19-41; mem. U.S. Ho. of Reps. from Tenn., 14th Congress, 1815-17. Died Rogersville, Aug. 2, 1841; buried Old Presbyn. Cemetery.

POWELL, Snelling, actor; b. Carmarthen, Wales, 1758; son of S. Powell; m. Elizabeth Harrison, 1794, 8 children including Elizabeth. Came to U.S., 1793; made Am. debut as actor in Gustavus Vasa, the Deliverer of His Country, 1794; joined company at Haymarket Theatre, Boston, 1796; joint lessee of Boston Theatre, 1806, asso. with theatre in Boston for rest of his life. Died Apr. 8, 1821.

POWELL, Thomas, editor, author; b. London,, Eng., Sept. 3, 1809. An editor The Poems of Geoffrey Chaucer Modernized, 1841; published poems, plays, frequent contbr. to London periodicals; came to U.S., 1849; mem. editorial staff Frank Leslie Publishing House, 1849-87; 1st editor Frank Leslie's Illustrated Newspaper (established 1855), also Frank Leslie's New Family Mag. editor Lantern, Figaro, N.Y. Reveille; author The Living Authors of England, 1849, The Living Authors of America, 1850, Pictures of Living Authors of Great Britain, 1851, Leaves from My Life (describes London literary life in 1830's). Died Newark, N.J., Jan. 14, 1887.

POWELL, William Byrd, educator, eclectic physician; b. Bourbon County, Ky., Jan. 8, 1799; med. degree, Transylvania U., 1826; studied phrenology, 1825; attended lectures U. Pa. Announced theory that human character could be read from examination of cranial structure, 1836; toured among western Indian tribes to add to his collection of human crania, 1843-46; prof. chemistry Med. Coll. La., 1835-38; obtained univ. charter from Tenn. Legislature for Memphis Inst., 1847, opened sch., 1849, prof. cerebral physiology, med. geology in its sch. eclectic medicine, 1849-51; prof. cerebral physiology Eclectic Med. Inst. of Cincinnati, 1856-58; co-editor Jour. Human Science, 1860. Author: Natural History of the Human Temperaments, 1856; (with Robert S. Newton) The Eclectic Practice of Medicine, 1854, The Eclectic Practice of Medicine (Diseases of Children), 1858. Died Covington, Ky., May 13, 1866.

POWELL, William Henry, painter; b. N.Y.C., Feb. 14, 1823; s. William Henry and Mary (Cowing) P.; married, 1842, 5 children. Painter The Discovery of the Mississippi River by DeSoto, completed 1853, hung in rotunda of U.S. Capitol, Washington, D.C.; commd. by Ohio to paint Oliver Hazard Perry at the Battle of Lake Erie for Ohio Capitol Bldg., 1863, enlarged replica ordered for U.S. Capitol; portraits include Albert Gallatin, Washington Irving, Gen. George B. McClellan. Died N.Y.C., Oct. 6, 1879.

POWER, John, clergyman; b. Roscarberry, County Cork, Ireland, June 19, 1792; took courses in philosophy and theology at Maynooth. Came to N.Y.C. as pastor St. Peter's Ch., 1819; adminstr. (on Bishop Connolly's death), N.Y.C., 1825; mem. 1st Provincial Council of Balt., 1829; a founder mag. The Truth Teller; consulting theologian 2d Provincial Council of Balt., 1833; founded orphan asylum; constructed New St. Peter's Ch.; promoter Irish Emigrant Sco.; vicar-gen. N.Y. under Bishop Connolly, circa 1819-25, Bishop Dubois, circa 1825-39, Bishop Hughes, 1839-circa 1849. Editor: (pioneer publ. of its type) Laity's Dictionary, 1822. Compiler: The New Testament by Way of Question and Answer, 1824; (manual of prayers) True Piety, 1832. Died Apr. 14, 1849.

POWERS, Daniel William, banker, philanthropist; b. Batavia, N.Y., June 14, 1818; s. Asahel and Elizabeth Powers; m. Lucinda Young; m. 2d, Helen M. Craig, 1856; 6 children. Started brokerage, 1850, became leading financier of Western N.Y.; established private bank, 1850 (survived panic of 1857, later incorporated, then merged with another instn. 1890); won suit in N.Y. State courts to establish legality of payment for debt in Treasury notes made legal tender by Act of Congress, 1862; completed office bldg. (1 of earliest large fireproof bldgs. west of N.Y.C.), Rochester, N.Y., 1870 (contained Roscoe Conkling's Law Library of 6,000 volumes for tenants' use); started art gallery, acquired one of largest and most valuable art collections in U.S.; erected fireproof hotel, 1883; established Rochester park system; dir. (representing Rochester) Genesee Valley Ry.; pres. bd. trustees of city hosp. and home for friendless; trustee of indsl. sch. and house of refuge. Died Rochester, Dec. 11, 1897.

POWERS, Gershom, congressman, lawyer; b. Croydon, Sullivan County, N.H., July 11, 1789; grad. law sch., 1810. Taught sch., Sempronius, N.Y.; admitted to bar, 1810, began practice of law, Auburn, N.Y.; apptd. supt. Auburn prison, 1820, insp., 1830-31; 1st judge Cayuga County (N.Y.) Ct. of Common Pleas, 1823-28; mem. U.S. Ho. of Reps. (Jackson Democrat) from N.Y., 21st Congress, 1829-31. Died Auburn, June 25, 1831; buried North Street Cemetery.

POWERS, Hiram, sculptor; b. Woodstock, Vt., July 29, 1805; s. Stephen and Sarah (Perry) P.; m. Elizabeth Gibson, 1832, at least 4 children including Longworth, Preston. With waxworks dept. Dorfeuille's Western Museum, Cincinnati; employed in portraiture, made busts of Chief Justice Marshall, John Quincy Adams, Levi Woodbury, Martin Van Buren, Andrew Jackson, John C. Calhoun, Daniel Webster, Washington, D.C., 1834; established studio, Florence, Italy, 1837; important works include Eve Before the Fall, Greek Slave (most celebrated single statue of the day); 1843, Fisher Boy, 1846, California, 1858, The Last of the Tribe, 1872; statues of Franklin and Jefferson in Capitol Building, Washington, 1863; statue of Webster, 1859, in front Boston State House. Followed Swedenborgian religion. Died Florence, June 27, 1873; buried Protestant Cemetery, Florence.

POWERS, Horatio Nelson, clergyman, poet; b. Amenia, N.Y., Apr. 30, 1826; grad. Union Coll., 1850, D.D. (hon.), 1867; grad. Gen. Theol. Sem., N.Y.C., 1855; m. Clemence Emma Fauvel-Gouraud, 1857, 5 children including Edward Fauvel. Ordained to ministry Congregational Ch., 1855; asst. to rector St. James Ch., Lancaster, Pa., 1855-57; pastor ch., Davenport, Ia., 1857-68; rector St. John's Ch., Chgo., 1868-75, Christ Ch., Bridgeport, Conn., 1875-86; lived in Piermont-on-the-Hudson, N.Y., 1886-90; contbr. to various publs. including Harper's Monthly and Century Mag.; a founder Chicago Literary Club. Author: (poetry) Early and Late, 1876, Ten Years of Song, 1887. Died Piermont-on-the-Hudson, Sept. 5, 1890.

POWHATAN (personal name Wa-hun-sen-a-cawh or Wa-hun-son-a-cock), Indian chief; father of Pocahontas. Chief or emperor of Powhatan federation which extended over Tidewater Va., conquered other tribes, increased empire inherited from his father; crowned under orders from Christopher Newport, agent of Va. Co., 1609; harassed English with ambushes, murders and cruelties; concluded a peace when daughter married Englishman, John Rolfe. Died Powhatta, Va., Apr. 1618.

POWNALL, Mrs., actress; b. Eng.; 2 daus., Charlotte Sophia Wrighten, Mary Wrighten. Known on London stage as Mrs. Wrighten; made Am. debut at Southwark Theatre, Phila., 1792; engaged by John Joseph Leger Sollee to perform at Church Street Theater, Charleston, S.C., 1795, became popular actress in Charleston. Died suddenly after dau. Charlotte eloped with Alexander Placide, Charleston, 1796.

POWNALL, Thomas, colonial gov.; b. Lincoln, Eng., 1722; s. William and Sarah (Burniston) P.; B.A., Trinity Coll., Cambridge (Eng.) U., 1743; m. Harriet (Churchill) Fawkener, Aug. 1765; m. 2d, Hannah (Kennett) Astell, Aug. 2, 1784. Came to N.Y. as sec. to colonial gov., 1753; attended Gen. Braddock's council of govs., Alexandria, Va., 1755; lt. gov. N.J., 1755-57; sec. extraordinary to comdr.-in-chief Lord Loudoun, 1756; gov. Mass., 1757-60; cultivated "anti-prerogative" party; upheld constl. authority of the civil govt. against war-powers claimed by the military; led expdn. to build fort on Penobscot, 1759; urged vigorous measures towards driving French from Am.; col., 1st commissary-gen. to the British-Hanoverian army on the Rhine, 1761-63; published The Administration of the Colonies (proposals of reorgn. in adminstrn., in law, and in the status of the colonies that were necessary to form permanently the Am. colonies into one unit); mem. English Ho. of Commons, 1767-80; fellow Soc. of Antiquaries, Royal Soc. Author: Colonial Constitutions, 1764, Principles of Polity, 1752, The Demonstration of the Colonies, 1764, Letters Advocating Free Trade, 1795; contbr. to Gentleman's Mag. Died Bath, Eng., Feb. 25, 1805; buried Walcot Church, Bath.

POYDRAS, Julien de Lallande, congressman, philanthropist; b. Nantes, France, Apr. 3, 1746; s. Francois and Magdelaine (Simon) P. Served in French Navy; captured by British, taken to Eng., 1760, escaped on board West Indian mcht. marine ship to San Domingo; came to new Orleans, 1768; wrote La Prise du Morne du Baton Rouge (poem to celebrate French capture of English fort at Baton Rouge, La.), 1779; mcht., traded as far as Tex.; civil comdt. at Pointe Coupee, 1804; pres. 1st legislative council Territory of Orleans, 1804; territorial del. to 11th U.S. Congress, 1809-11; pres. 1st constl. conv. of La., 1812; pres. La. Senate, 1812-13, 20-21; contbr. large sums to Charity Hosp., Poydras Female Orphan Asylum (founder), 130,000 to Pointe Coupee Parish (La.) for founding of acad. of coll., $930,000 to parishes of Pointe Coupee and West Baton Rouge to provide dowries for poor girls. Died Pointe Coupee Parish, June 14, 1824; buried St. Francis Ch., reinterred Poydras High Sch. grounds, New Roads, La.

POZNANSKI, Gustavus, clergyman; b. Storchnest, Poland, 1804; s. Joseph and Sarah Poznanski; m. Hetty Barrett, Dec. 5, 1838. Came to Am., 1831; rabbi Congregation Beth Elohim, Charleston, S.C. (one of wealthiest and most cultured Jewish communities in Am. at the time), 1836-47; developed into an extreme radical, installed organ in the synagogue (which caused dissention in the congregation and subsequent schism between mems.), late 1830's recommended alterations in the Jewish ritual and observances, 1843; one of earliest Reform Jewish leaders in Am. Died N.Y.C., Jan. 7, 1879.

PRATT, Charles, oil mcht., philanthropist; b. Watertown, Mass., Oct. 2, 1830; s. Asa and Elizabeth (Stone) P.; m. Lydia Richardson, Dec. 1854; m. 2d, Mary Richardson, Sept. 1863; 8 children. Became partner Raynolds, Devoe & Pratt, paint and oil firms; 1854; established Charles Pratt & Co., crude oil refining firm, Greenpoint, L.I., N.Y., 1867, produced Pratt's Astral Oil (illuminating oil), merged into Rockefeller's Standard Oil combination, 1874, became important exec. in Standard Oil; erected model tenement for workingmen The Astral, nr. Greenpoint; pres. bd. trustees Adelphia Acad., Bklyn.; contbr. large sums to Amherst Coll., U. Rochester; founded Pratt Inst. for training of skilled artisans, foremen, designers, and draftsmen, Bklyn., 1887; established Pratt Inst. Free Library (1st free public library in either Bklyn. or N.Y.C.); organized The Thrift (savs. and loan assn.), 1888; financially responsible for erection Emanuel Baptist Ch., Bklyn.; wealthiest man in Bklyn. at time of death. Died N.Y.C., May 4, 1891.

PRATT, Daniel, industrialist, state legislator; b. Temple, N.H., July 20, 1799; s. Edward and Asenath (Flint) P.; received Master of Mechanic and Useful Arts (hon.), U. Ala., 1846; m. Elizabeth Ticknor, circa 1831, 3 children including Ellen, Daniel. In charge of cotton gin factory owned by Samuel Griswold, Clinton, Ga., became partner, 1832; established Prattville (Ala.), 1838, erected grist mill, lumber and shingle mill, added a cotton-gin plant (made town the indus. center of Ala.), later built cotton and woolen mills, foundry, carriage factory, tinshop, and a merc. establishment; mem. Ala. Ho. of Reps., 1860-65; organized, equipped "Prattville Dragoons" for Confederate Army; dir. North and South Ry.; controlled Oxmoor Iron Furnaces, Bimingham, Ala. Died Ala., May 13, 1873.

PRATT, Daniel, vagrant; b. Chelsea, Mass., Apr. 11, 1809; s. Daniel and Mary (Hall) P. Wandered across U.S. from Me. to Dakotas; fancied himself to be the Great Am. Traveler, insisted upon title of General; under the delusion that he had been elected Pres. U.S. and was being prevented from taking office by his rivals; widely known and admired among students of New Eng. colls.; addressed students on such subjects as The Harmony of the Human Mind, The Solar System, The Vocabulaboratory of the Human Mind; received unofcl. hon. degree, C.O.D. from Dartmouth. Died Boston, June 20, 1887.

PRATT, Daniel Darwin, senator; b. Palermo, Me., Oct. 26, 1813; attended Cazenovia Sem.; grad. Hamilton Coll., Clinton, N.Y., 1831. Became sch. tchr. in Ind., 1832; with office of sec. of state, Indpls., 1834; admitted to bar, began practice of law, Logansport, Ind., 1836; mem. Ind. Ho. of Reps., 1851, 53; sec. Republican Nat. Conv., Chgo., 1860; mem. U.S. Senate from Ind., 1869-75; commr. of internal revenue (apptd. by Pres. Grant), 1875-76. Died Logansport, June 17, 1877; buried Mt. Hope Cemetery.

PRATT, Enoch, bus. exec., philanthropist; b. North Middleborough, Mass., Sept. 10, 1808; s. Isaac and Naomi (Keith) P.; m. Maria Hyde, Aug. 1, 1837. Established E. Pratt & Co., dealers in iron and steel products, Balt., 1831; obtained controlling interest in Md. Steamboat Co., 1872, greatly improved service to Chesapeake Bay and river wharves; dir. Susquehanna Canal Co.; v.p. Phila., Wilmington & Balt. R.R., 27 years; dir. Nat. Farmers and Planters Bank of Balt., nearly

60 years, pres., 1860-96; pres. Balt. Clearing House, Md. Bankers Assn.; finance commr. Balt., 1877; established Enoch Pratt Free Library, Balt., 1886, endowed it with $833,000; founded House of Reformation and Instrn. for Colored Children, Cheltenham, Md., Md. Sch. for the Deaf and Dumb, Frederick; donated bldg. to Md. Acad. Sciences; mem. Am. Colonization Soc.; helped establish asylum for treatment of nervous and mental diseases. Died Balt., Sept. 17, 1896.

PRATT, Henry Cheever, artist; b. Orford, N.H., June 13, 1803. Obtained patronage of S. F. B. Morse, circa 1817; established studio, Boston, 1827; moved to Wakefield, Mass., 1860; went on painting expdn. to Me., 1845; accompanied John Russell Bartlett's expdn. to explore Mexican boundary, 1851-53. Died Wakefield, Nov. 27, 1880.

PRATT, James Timothy, congressman; b. Cromwell, Conn., Dec. 14, 1802; attended common schs. Engaged in business and agriculture, Hartford, Conn.; joined "Horse Guard," 1820; maj. 1st Regt. of Cavalry, 1834, col., 1836, brig. gen., 1837-39, maj. gen., 1839-46, adj. gen., 1846; ret. from business, settled in Rocky Hill, Conn.; mem. Conn. Ho. of Reps., 1847-48, 50, 57, 62, 70-71; mem. Conn. Senate, 1852; mem. U.S. Ho. of Reps. (Democrat) from Conn., 33d Congress, 1853-55; unsuccessful candidate for gov. Conn., 1858, 59; mem. Washington (D.C.) Peace Conv., 1861; engaged in farming. Died Wethersfield, Conn., Apr. 11, 1887; buried Indian Hill Cemetery, Middletown, Conn.

PRATT, Matthew, portrait painter; b. Phila., Sept. 23, 1734; s. Henry and Rebecca (Claypoole) P.; studied under Benjamin West in Eng., 1764; m. Elizabeth Moore, Dec. 11, 1756. Opened portrait painting shop in Phila., 1768; clientele included the Penns, Dickinsons, Willings, other prominent families; resorted to sign-painting for taverns and shops, circa 1775-81, including sign of hist. significance, The Representation of the Constitution (containing portraits of 38 mems. of Constl. Conv.); most familiar work: The American School (at Met. Mus. of Art, N.Y.C.); portraits include Benjamin West and wife (owned by Pa. Acad. Fine Arts, Phila.), Benjamin Franklin. Died Phila., Jan. 9, 1805; buried Christ Church Cemetery, Phila.

PRATT, Orson, clergyman; b. Hartford, N.Y., Sept. 19, 1811; s. Jared and Charity (Dickinson) P.; married several wives (polygamously) including Sarah Bates, July 4, 1836; 45 children. Converted to Mormonism, ordained elder, 1830, high priest, 1832; mem. High Council of Ch., 1834; ordained one of the 12 apostles, 1835; accompanied Mormons on trek to Salt Lake Valley, Utah, 1847; determined longitude and latitude of Salt Lake City, Utah, assisted in laying out street pattern; head of Mormon mission in Eng., 1848-50; missionary in U.S. and Europe, 1852-72; apptd. historian and gen. recorder Ch. of Jesus Christ of Latter-day Saints, 1874; speaker Utah Territorial Ho. of Reps., 7 terms; an inventor. Deseret Alphabet (a phonetic lang.). Died Salt Lake City, Oct. 3, 1881.

PRATT, Parley Parker, clergyman; b. Burlington, N.Y., Apr. 12, 1807; s. Jared and Charity (Dickinson or Dickison) P.; m. Thankful Halsey, Sept. 1827; m. 2d, Mary Ann Frost, 1837; 1 child. Converted and ordained elder Ch. of Jesus Christ of Latter-day Saints, 1830; ordained high priest, 1831, one of 12 apostles, 1835; designated "The Archer of Paradise"; preached in Can., N.Y., Mo.; went to London, Eng. as missionary, 1840-46; published Millennial Star (Latter-Day Saints' publ.), Manchester, Eng., 1840; accompanied Mormon migration to Great Salt Lake, spring 1847; helped frame constn. of State of Deseret; missionary to Chile, S.Am., 1851-52; pres. Eastern branches of church; built road in Parley's Canon; Parley's Peak also named for him. Author: The Voice of Warning, 1838; Key to the Science of Theology; Immorality of the Body. Murdered, Utah, May 13, 1857.

PRATT, Thomas George, senator, gov. Md.; b. Georgetown, D.C., Feb. 18, 1804; s. John Wilkes and Rachel (Belt) P.; attended Georgetown U., Princeton; m. Adeline McCubbin Kent, Sept. 1, 1835, 6 children. Mem. Md. Ho. of Dels., 1832-35, Md. Electoral Coll., 1836; apptd. pres. Md. Exec. Council, 1836; mem. Md. Senate, 1838-43; gov. Md., 1844-47; mem. U.S. Senate from Md., 1850-57. Died Balt., Nov. 9, 1869; buried St. Anne's Cemetery, Annapolis, Md.

PRATT, Thomas Willis, civil engr., inventor; b. Boston, July 4, 1812; s. Caleb and Sally (Willes or Willis) P.; attended Rensselaer Poly. Inst.; m. Sarah Bradford, 1835, 2 children. Engring. asst. with U.S. Govt. on constrn. dry docks, Charleston, S.C., also Norfolk, Va., 1830; division engr. on constrn. of Norwich & Worcester Ry. and supt. of road, 1835; engr. and supt. Providence & Worcester Ry., 1845-47, Hartford & New Haven Ry., 1847-50; chief engr. Middletown Branch R.R.; chief engr., supt. N.Y. & Boston R.R.; chief engr., supt. Conway & Great Falls br. Eastern Ry., 1871-75; built number of important bridges, largest over Merrimac River at Newburyport, Mass.; invented Pratt Truss (bridge and roof truss), patented 1844; patented improved type of combined timber and steel truss, 1873; invented new method of hull constrn. and proplusion for ships, 1875. Died Boston, July 10, 1875.

PRATT, Zadock, leather mfr., congressman; b. Stephenstown, N.Y., Oct. 30, 1790; s. Zadock and Hannah (Pickett) P.; m. Beda Dickerman; m. 2d, Esther Dickerman; m. 3d, Abigail Watson; m. 4th, Mary Watson; at least 2 children Served as sgt. cavalry N.Y. Militia, 1819, commd. capt. 5th Arty., then col. 116th Inf.; built extensive tannery and founded village of Prattsville (N.Y.), 1824; mem. U.S. Ho. of Reps. from N.Y., 25th, 28th congresses, 1837-39, 43-45; presdl. elector, 1852; a founder Bur. of Statistics and Commerce, Washington, D.C., circa 1844/45; del. of Mechanics' Inst. (N.Y.C.) to World's Fair, London, Eng., 1851; recipient 2 medals for excellence in tanning of leather from Am. Inst. Died Bergen N.J. Apr. 6, 1871; buried City Cemetery, Prattsville.

PRATTE, Bernard, mcht., fur trader; b. Ste. Genevieve, Mo., June 11, 1771; s. Jean Baptiste and Marie Anne (Lalumandiere) P.; m. Emilie Sauveur Labbadie, May 13, 1794, 7 children including Bernard. Mcht. on Mississippi River, 1793-1816; commd. capt. Mo. Militia, 1807; mem. Com. of Safety, St. Louis, Mo., circa 1812; entered fur trade as partner Cabanne & Co., 1816-30 (firm later called Berthold, Chouteau & Pratte, reorganized as Bernard Pratte & Co., 1823); mem. 1st St. Louis Grand Jury, 1804; judge Territory of Mo., 1807; treas. Dist. of St. Louis, trustee, 1808-20; mem. Mo. Constnl. Conv., 1820; U.S. receiver of public monies, 1825. Died Apr. 1, 1836.

PRAY, Isaac Clark, journalist, dramatist; b. Boston, May 15, 1813; s. Isaac and Martha (Haggens) P.; attended Harvard, 1829; grad. Amherst Coll., 1833; m. Sarah Henry, 2 children. Edited Boston Pearl, other papers during 1830's; mgr. Nat. Theatre, N.Y.C., 1836; editor Sunday Morning News, N.Y., Dramatic Guardian and the Ladies Companion; appeared successfully as actor in Eng., 1846-47; mgr. Theatre Royal, Cork, Ireland, circa 1847, Beach Street Museum, Boston, 1849; music and dramatic critic Herald, N.Y.C., 1850; editor Phila. Inquirer, 1859-60; tutored students for theatre in N.Y.C., 1850-60. Author: (dramas) Medea, Orestes, Virginius, The Hermit of Malta; Prose and Verse, 1835, The Old Cock (farce, played N.Y.), 1836; Poems, 1837, Book of the Drama, 1851, Memoirs of James Gordon Bennett, 1855. Died N.Y.C., Nov. 28, 1869.

PREBLE, Edward, naval officer; b. Falmouth, Me., Aug. 15, 1761; s. Gen. Jedidiah and Mehitable (Bangs) Roberts P.; m. Mary Deering, Mar. 17, 1801. Served in ship Winthrop (a captured, armed English brig of superior force), until 1783; lt. in command brig Pickering, West Indies, 1798; capt. frigate Essex, 1799, (1st Am. warship to sail flag beyond Cape of Good Hope, 1800-02); protected Am. trade from French privateers in East Indies; commd. commodore, in command 3d squadron sent to Mediterranean, 1803; made 1st assault on Tripoli, 1804, made 4 subsequent attacks, failed to capture Tripoli; built gunboats for navy, circa 1805-07. Died Portland, Me., Aug. 25, 1807.

PREBLE, George Henry, naval officer, author; b. Portland, Me., Feb. 25, 1816; s. Enoch and Sally (Cross) P.; m. Susan Cox, Nov. 18, 1845, 4 children. Served as midshipman U.S. Navy, 1835-41; commanded 1st Am. armed landing force in China, Canton, 1844; blockade service in Mexican War on schooner Petrel and siege of Veracruz, 1846-47; accompanied Perry's mission to Japan in ship Macedonian, 1853-56; prepared surveys and sailing directions for Wu-Song River leading to Shanghai, 1855; exec. officer Narragansett in Pacific, 1858-61; in command of gunboat Katahdin during Civil War, 1861; fought at battles of New Orleans, Vicksburg; promoted comdr., 1862; allowed Confederate cruiser Oreto to break through blockade of Mobile Bay, dismissed from service; restored to previous rank, 1863; comdr. fleet brigade of Southeastern Am. coast, 1864; commanded ship State of Ga., protected comml. interests at Panama, 1865; commd. capt., 1867, comdr., 1871; chief of staff in Pacific, circa 1868-74; promoted rear adm., 1876, commanded South Pacific Squadron, 1876. Author: Our Flag: Origin and Progress of the Flag of the United States of America..., 1872, other books and articles. Died Boston, Mar. 1, 1885.

PREBLE, William Pitt, diplomat, jurist, railroad pres.; b. York, Me., Nov. 27, 1783; s. Esaias and Lydia (Ingrahan) P.; grad. Harvard, 1806; LL.D. (hon.) Bowdoin Coll., 1829; m. Nancy Gale Tucker, Sept. 1810; m. 2d, Sarah Forsaith, 1852; 4 children. Opened law office, York, 1811; county atty. in Me.; U.S. dist. atty., 1814; mem. Brunswick Conv. (an attempt to separate Mass. from Me.), 1816; aided in separation of Me. from Mass., 1820; justice Me. Supreme Judicial Ct., 1820-28; minister at court of King of Netherlands to protect U.S. interests in Northeastern boundary case for which King was arbitrator, 1830-31; helped build Atlantic & St. Lawrence R.R., 1845-48, 1st pres. Canadian branch. Died Portland, Me., Oct. 11, 1857.

PRENTICE, George Dennison, journalist; b. New London County, Conn., Dec. 18, 1802; s. Rufus and Sarah (Stanton) Prentice; grad. Brown U., 1823; m. Henrietta Benham, Aug. 18, 1835, 2 children. Admitted to Conn. bar, circa 1825; editor paper, New London, Conn., 1827; 1st editor New Eng. Review, a Hartford weekly, 1828; mgr., editor Louisville, (Ky.) Daily Jour., 1830-circa 1868, made it most influential Whig paper in South and West. Author: A Biography of Henry Clay, 1831; (collection of editorial paragraphs) Prenticeana, 1860. Died Jan. 22, 1870.

PRENTISS, Elizabeth Payson, author; b. Portland, Me., Oct. 26, 1818; d. Rev. Edward and Ann (Shipman) Payson; m. Rev. George Lewis Prentiss, Apr. 1845, at least 1 child. Taught sch. in her mother's home, Portland, 1838-39; moved to New Bedford, Mass., 1845. Author: The Flower of the Family, 1854; Stepping Heavenward, 1869; Golden Hours, 1873. Died Dorset, Vt., Aug. 13, 1878.

PRENTISS, John Holmes, congressman, journalist; b. Worcester, Mass., Apr. 17, 1784; attended local and pvt. schs. Became foreman N.Y. Evening Post, 1808; moved to Cooperstown, N.Y., 1808, founder, editor Freeman's Journal, 1808; apptd. col. N.Y. Militia, served as div. insp. on staff of comdr. in chief; postmaster Cooperstown, 1833-37; vice pres. N.Y. Democratic Conv., Albany; mem. U.S. Ho. of Reps. (Democrat) from N.Y., 25th-26th congresses, 1837-41; pres. Bank of Cooperstown. Died Cooperstown, June 26, 1861; buried Lakewood Cemetery.

PRENTISS, Samuel, senator; b. Stonington, Conn., Mar. 31, 1782; s. Samuel and Lucretia (Holmes) P.; m Lucretia Houghton, Oct. 3, 1804, 12 children. Admitted to Vt. bar, 1802; mem. Vt. Ho. of Reps., 1824-25; chief justice Vt. Supreme Ct., 1825-29; mem. U.S. Senate from Vt., 1831-42, sponsored law forbidding dueling in D.C., presiding judge U.S. Dist. ct. for Vt., 1842-57. Died Montpelier, Vt., Jan. 15, 1857; buried Green Mount Cemetery, Montpelier.

PRENTISS, Seargent Smith, congressman, orator; b. Portland, Me., Sept. 30, 1808; s. William and Abigail (Lewis) P.; grad. Bowdoin Coll., 1826; m. Mary Jane Williams, 1842, 4 children. Admitted to Miss. bar, circa 1829; mem. lower house Miss. Legislature, 1835; gave speech before U.S. Congress which contested the election of John F.H. Claiborne to 25th Congress (election was set aside by Ho. of Reps.); mem. U.S. Ho. of Reps. (Whig) from Miss., 25th Congress, May 30, 1838-39; campaigned in behalf of William Henry Harrison throughout Eastern part of U.S., 1840, made many speeches for Whig Party; gave speech in defense of Nicos Lopez (Cuban revolutionist), New Orleans, 1850. Died "Longwood," nr. Natchez, Miss., July 1, 1850; buried pvt. burying ground, "Longwood."

PRESCOTT, George Bartlett, telegraph engr.; b. Kingston, N.H., Sept. 16, 1830; s. Mark Hollis and Priscilla (Bartlett) P.; m. Eliza Curtis Parsons, Dec. 9, 1857, 1 dau., Mrs. Philip V.R. Van Wyck, Jr. Joined N.Y. & New Eng. Telegraph Co., 1850, in Boston, 1850-52; mgr. N.Y. & Boston (or Comml.) Telegraph Co., Springfield, Mass., 1852; mgr. submarine telegraph cos. along Eastern coast; gen. mgr. Am. Telegraph Co., 1859, supt. all lines in Eastern N.Y., Conn., Vt., 1861; apptd. electrician Western Union Telegraph Co., 1866; an original mem. bd. dirs. Am. Speaking Telephone Co.; v.p., dir. Gold & Stock Telegraph Co., 1878-81. Author: History, Theory, and the Practice of the Electric Telegraph, 1860; Electricity and the Electric Telegraph, 1877; The Speaking Telephone, 1878; Dynamo-Electricity, 1884; Bell's Electric Speaking Telephone: Its Invention, Construction, Application, Modification, and History, 1884; The Electric Telephone, 1890. Died N.Y.C., Jan. 18, 1894.

PRESCOTT, Mary Newmarch, author; b. Calais, Me., Aug. 2, 1849; d. Joseph N. and Sarah (Bridges) Prescott. Leading contbr. to mags., including Harper's Mag. Author: Matt's Follies, 1873. Died Amesbury, Mass., June 14, 1888.

PRESCOTT, Oliver, physician; b. Groton, Mass., Apr. 27, 1731; s. Benjamin and Abigail (Oliver) P.; grad. Harvard, 1750, M.D. (hon.), 1791; studied medicine under Dr. Ebenezer Robie; m. Lydia Baldwin, Feb. 19, 1756. Commd. brig. gen. Middlesex County (Mass.) Militia, 1775, maj. gen. Mass. Militia, 1778; mem. Mass. Com. of Correspondence, mem. supreme exec. council, 1777-80; judge of probate Middlesex, 1799-1804; trustee, 1st pres. bd. Groton Acad.; an original incorporator Mass. Med. Soc.; mem. N.H. Med. Soc.; pres. Middlesex Med. Soc., also Western Soc. of Middlesex Husbandmen; fellow Am. Acad. Arts and Scis., 1780. Died Groton, Nov. 17, 1804.

PRESCOTT, Samuel, physician, patriot; b. Concord, Mass., Aug. 19, 1751; s. Dr. Abel and Abigail (Brigham) P.; Successfully completed the midnight ride of warning after Paul Revere was captured, Apr. 18, 1775, reached Concord where his warning enabled Minute Men to assemble and to hide most of mil. stores before British arrived; in service at Fort Ticonderoga, 1776; captured by British, 1777. Died Halifax, Nova Scotia, circa 1777.

PRESCOTT, William, army officer; b. Groton, Mass., Feb. 20, 1726; s. Benjamin and Abigail (Oliver) P.; m. Abigail Hale, Apr. 13, 1758, at least 1 child, William. Served as lt. in French and Indian War, 1758; col. of regt. of Minute Men, 1775; mem. Council of War, Cambridge, Mass.; in direct charge of fortifying Breed's Hill, 1775, co-comdr. at Battle of Bunker (Breed's) Hill, 1775; served in Long Island Campaign and at surrender of Burgoyne, 1777. Died Pepperell, Mass., Oct. 13, 1795.

PRESCOTT, William Hickling, historian; b. Salem, Mass., May 4, 1796; s. William and Catherine Green (Hickling) P.; grad. Harvard, 1814; D.C.L. (hon.), Oxford (Eng.) U., 1850; m. Susan Amory, May 4, 1820, 3 children. Contbr. review of Byron's Letters on Pope to North Am. Review (his 1st contbn.), 1821; devoted himself to study and writing of Spanish history despite almost total blindness; became corr. mem. Royal Acad. of Berlin, 1845; Institut de France; his histories were and are still very popular; works include The History of the Reign of Ferdinand and Isabella the Catholic, 3 vols., 1838; History of the Conquest of Mexico, 3 vols., 1843; Biographical and Critical Miscellanies (essays), 1845; History of the Conquest of Peru, 2 vols., 1847; History of the Reign of Philip the Second, 3 vols., 1855. Died Boston, Jan. 28, 1859.

PRESTON, Ann, physician; b. Westgrove, Pa., Dec. 1, 1813; d. Amos and Margaret (Smith) Preston; grad. Female Med. Coll. of Pa., Phila., 1852 (one of 1st grads.). Sec., Clarkson Anti-Slavery Soc.; sec. temperance conv. of women, Chester County, Pa., 1848; published Cousin Ann's Stories for Children, 1848; prof. physiology and hygiene Female Med. Coll. of Pa., 1853; prin. founder Woman's Hosp. of Phila., 1861, mem. bd. mgrs., cons. physician, corr. sec., 1st dean, 1866; wrote article in reply to resolution of Philadelphia County Med. Soc. expressing its disapproval of women in med. profession, 1867. Died Phila., Apr. 18, 1872.

PRESTON, Francis, congressman, lawyer; b. Greenfield, Va., Aug. 2, 1765; grad. Coll. William and Mary, Williamsburg, Va., 1783; studied law. Admitted to bar, practiced law, Montgomery and Washington counties; mem. Va. Ho. of Dels., 1788-89, 1812-14; mem. U.S. Ho. of Reps. from Va., 3d-4th congresses, 1793-97; practiced law, Abingdon, Va.; served as col. Volunteers in War of 1812; mem. Va. Senate, 1816-20. Died at brother's home, Columbia, S.C., May 26, 1836; buried Aspinvale Cemetery, nr. Seven Mile Ford, Va.

PRESTON, Jacob Alexander, congressman, physician; b. Bel Air, Harford County, Md., Mar. 12, 1796; grad. med. dept. U. Md. at Balt., 1816. Practiced medicine, also farmed, Harford, Baltimore and Cecil counties; served as lt. of a Md. regt. in War of 1812; mem. U.S. Ho. of Reps. (Whig) from Md., 28th Congress, 1843-45. Died Perryman, Md., Aug. 2, 1868; buried St. George's Churchyard, Spesutia Island, Md.

PRESTON, John Smith, army officer; b. Abingdon, Va., Apr. 20, 1809; s. Francis Smith and Sarah Buchanan (Campbell) P.; attended Hampden-Sydney Coll., 1823-25, U. Va., 1825-27; studied law at Harvard; m. Caroline Hampton, Apr. 28, 1830. Admitted to Va. bar, circa 1827; owned large sugar plantation "The Homus" in La., circa 1840-50; mem. S.C. Senate, 1848-56; chmn. S.C. delegation Democratic Nat. Conv., Charleston, S.C., 1860; commr. to visit Va. and urge secession, 1861; commd. asst. adjutant with rank lt. col., 1861; participated in 1st battle of Bull Run, 1861; command prison camp at Columbia, Ga., 1862; supt. Bur. of Conscription, Confederate Govt., 1863-65; commd. col. Confederate Army, 1863, given control of conscription in West, 1863, promoted brig. gen., 1864; spent rest of life defending Confederacy and principles of state's rights. Died Columbia, S.C., May 1, 1881.

PRESTON, Jonas, physician; b. Chester, Pa., Jan. 25, 1764; s. Jonas and Mary (Yarnall) P.; grad. U. Pa., 1784; m. Orpah Reese, 1794; m. 2d, Jane Thomas, Aug. 19, 1812. Practiced medicine; mem. Pa. Ho. of Reps., 1794-1800, Pa. Senate, 1808-11; dir. Bank of Pa., Schuylkill Navigation Co. Died Apr. 4, 1836.

PRESTON, Jonathan, architect; b. 1801. Practiced architecture, Boston, 50 years; designer old Mass. Inst. Tech. (no longer standing), Natural History Bldg.; designed (with Edward C. Cabot) old Boston Theatre; ret., 1875. Died 1888.

PRESTON, Margaret Junkin, author; b. Milton, Pa., May 19, 1820; d. Rev. George and Julia (Miller) Junkin; m. John T. L. Preston, 1857, 2 sons. Author: Silverwood, a Book of Memories, 1856; Beechenbrook, a Rhyme of the War, 1865; Old Songs and New (poetry), 1875; Cartoons, 1875. Died Mar. 28, 1897; buried Lexington, Va.

PRESTON, Paul, see Picton, Thomas.

PRESTON, Thomas Scott, clergyman; b. Hartford, Conn., July 23, 1824; s. Zephaniah and Ann (Canfield) P.; grad. Trinity Coll., Hartford, 1843, Gen. Theol. Sem., N.Y.C., 1846. Ordained deacon Protestant Episcopal Ch., 1846, priest, 1847; entered Roman Catholic Ch., 1849, ordained priest, 1850; chancellor Diocese of N.Y., 1855, vicar gen., 1873-91, sole vicar gen. administering the diocese, 1890; organized House of the Holy Family (a refuge for children and young girls); founder Sisterhood of the Divine Compassion, 1873; apptd. domestic prelate to His Holiness, by Pope Leo XIII, 1881, prothonetary apostolic, 1888; Author: Life of St. Mary Magdalene, 1860; The Purgatorial Manual, 1866; The Catholic View of the Public School Question, 1870. Died N.Y.C., Nov. 4, 1891.

PRESTON, William, diplomat, congressman; b. Louisville, Ky., Oct. 16, 1816; s. William and Caroline (Hancock) P.; attended Yale, 1835; LL.B., Harvard, 1838; m. Margaret Wickliffe, 1840, 6 children. Admitted to Louisville bar, circa 1838; served as lt. col. 4th Ky. Inf., Mexican War, 1846-48; del. from Louisville to Ky. Constl. Conv., 1849 mem. Ky. Ho. of Reps., 1850, 68-69; mem. U.S. Ho. of Reps. (Whig) from Ky., 32d-33d congresses, 1852-55; U.S. minister to Spain, 1858-61; commd. col. Confederate Army, 1861, brig. gen., 1862, maj. gen., 1864; apptd. Confederate minister to Maximilian, Emperor of Mexico, 1864. Died Louisville, Sept. 21, 1887; buried Cave Hill Cemetery, Louisville.

PRESTON, William Ballard, congressman, sec. of navy; b. "Smithfield," Montgomery County, Va., Nov. 25, 1805; s. James Patton and Ann (Taylor) P.; grad. Coll. William and Mary, 1823; postgrad. U. Va., 1825; m. Lucinda Redd, Nov. 21, 1839. Admitted to Va. bar, 1826; mem. Va. Ho. of Dels., 1830-32, 44, 45, Va Senate, 1840-44; mem. U.S. Ho. of Reps. (Whig) from Va., 30th Congress, 1847-49; U.S. sec. of navy, 1849-50; went on unsuccessful mission to France to negotiate establishment of steamship line from Norfolk, Va. to LeHavre, France, 1858; mem. Va. Secession Conv., 1861; met Lincoln informally, 1861, heard him read statement of policy and reported it to conv.; mem. Confederate Senate, 1861-62. Died Nov. 16, 1862; buried "Smithfield."

PRESTON, William Campbell, senator; b. Phila., Dec. 27, 1794; s. Francis Smith and Sarah Buchanan (Campbell) P.; A.B., S.C. Coll., 1812; studied law, Edinburgh, Scotland; m. Maria Coalter, 1822; m. 2d, Louise Davis, 1831; 1 child. Admitted to Virginia bar, 1820; moved to South Carolina, 1824, member S.C. House of Reps., 1828-34; member U.S. Senate from S.C., 1833-42, advocated annexation of Tex., 1836; an anti-Jackson Democrat, later a. Whig; pres. S.C. Coll., 1845-51, trustee, 1851-57, founder Columbia Lyceum, pres. bd. dirs. Died Columbia, S.C., May 22, 1860; buried Trinity Churchyard, S.C.

PRÉVOST, Eugéne-Prosper, musician; b. Paris, France, Aug. 23, 1809; studied at Paris Conservatory. Recipient Grand Prix de Rome for cantata Bianca Capello, 1831; condr., Le Havre, 1835-38; came to Am., 1838; condr., singing tchr., New Orleans, until 1862; condr. Niblo's Garden, N.Y.C., 1842; chef d'orchestre Bouffes-Parisiens, later of Champs Élysées concerts, Paris, 1862-67; returned to New Orleans, 1867; produced several operas, Paris, also opera Blanche et René, New Orleans; composed oratorios and masses. Died New Orleans, Aug. 30, 1872.

PREVOST, Francois Marie, surgeon; b. Pont-de-Ce, France, circa 1764; s. Jean Pierre and Maria Anne (Kenotaire) P.; grad. in medicine U. Paris; m. Marie Therese Burrychon, Dec. 13, 1799; m. 2d, Victorine Castellain, May 29, 1838; at least 2 children, Jean Louis and adopted son, John Robertson. Came to U.S., 1800; practiced medicine, Donaldsonville, La., 1800-42; saved 7 out of 8 lives in 4 operations by Caesarian section on Negro slave mothers, 1822-31; thought to be 2d U.S. physician to perform Caesarian section. Died Donaldsonville, May 18, 1842.

PRIBER, Christian, reformer; probably born in Saxony. Forced to flee from Saxony to Eng. because of his radical ideas; came to S.C., 1734; went to live among Cherokee Indians in the mountains, 1736; wanted to organize commonwealth of So. Indians, forming them into independent confedn.; founded communistic community at Cusawatee (intended to serve as a model for France), based this state on principles of liberty, equality, community of goods and property (corresponded to ideals of 18th century "socialism"); jailed as polit. prisoner by British, 1743. Died Ft. Frederica, Ga., circa 1745.

PRICE, Eli Kirk, lawyer; b. East Bradford, Pa., July 20, 1797; s. Philip and Rachel (Kirk) P.; m. Anna Embree, 1828, 3 children including Rebecca. Admitted to Pa. bar, 1822; published Digest of the Acts of Assembly and of the Ordinances of the Inhabitants and Commissioners of the District of Spring Garden, 1822; Institutes of Morality for the Instruction of Youth, 1838; mem. Pa. bd. Revenue Commrs., 1845-48; mem. Pa. Senate, 1854-56, introduced bill which became new charter of City of Phila., 1854; established Fairmount Park, Phila., 1867, chmn. park governing commn., 1867-84; prepared and secured passage of "An Act Relating to the Sale and Conveyance of Real Estate," 1853, act broadening law of aescent, 1855, "An Act for the Greater Security of Title," 1856; wrote bill supplementary to statute of limitations, 1859; wrote Of the Limitation of Actions, and of Liens, against Real Estate, in Philadelphia, 1874; The Act for the Sale of Real Estate in Philadelphia, 1874; trustee U. Pa.; pres. Univ. Hosp.; pres. Preston Retreat; pres. Pa. Colonization Soc.; v.p. Am. Philos. Soc.; pres. Numismatical and Antiquarian Soc.; mem. Pa. Hist. Soc. Died Phila., Nov. 15, 1884.

PRICE, Rodman McCamley, gov. N.J.; b. Sussex County, N.J., May 5, 1816; s. Francis and Anne (McCamley) P.; attended Coll. of N.J. (now Princeton); m. Matilda Trenchard. Served as purser U.S. Navy in ship Cyane with Commodore Sloat's squadron on West coast of Mexico, 1846; read proclamation of annexation of Cal. from custom house, Monterey, Cal., 1846; perfect and alcade of Monterey (1st American to exercise judicial functions in Cal.), 1846; naval agt. to facilitate transmissions of funds and prevent gold shipments to Eng. during Gold Rush, 1849; mem. 1st San Francisco Municipal Council; mem. Cal. Constl. Conv., 1849; mem. U.S. Ho. of Reps. from Cal., 32d Congress, 1851-53; gov. N.J., 1854-57, originated pub. sch. system of N.J., established state geol. survey, improved system of road constrn.; assisted bldg. of Nassau Hall, Princeton; N.J. del. to Washington (D.C.) Peace Conf., 1861; Copperhead throughout Civil War, started successful ferry from Weehawken, N.J. to 42d St., N.Y.C.; involved in quarrying bus., reclamation of lands on Hackensack River; commr. N.Y. & N.J. Bridge Co. Died Sussex County, June 7, 1894; buried Reformed Cemetery, Mahwah, N.J.

PRICE, Samuel, senator, lawyer; b. Fauquier County, Va., July 28, 1805; studied law. Admitted to bar, 1832, began practice of law, Nicholas and Braxton counties; clk. Nicholas County, 1830; pros. atty., 1833; mem. Va. Ho. of Dels., 1834-36, 47-50, 52; moved to Wheeling, Va. (now W.Va.), 1836, to Lewisburg, Va. (now W.Va.), 1838; pros. atty. for Braxton County, 1836-50; del. constl. convs., 1850, 51, 61; lt. gov. Va., 1863 until close of Civil War; pres. W.Va. Constl. Conv., 1872; mem. U.S. Senate (filled vacancy) from W.Va., Aug. 26, 1876-Jan. 26, 1877. Died Lewisburg, Feb. 25, 1884; buried Stuart Burying Ground, Stuart Manor, nr. Lewisburg.

PRICE, Stephen, theatrical mgr.; b. Sept. 25, 1782; s. Michael and Helena (Cornell or Cornwell) P.; grad. Columbia, 1799. Practiced law in N.Y.C., 1805; purchased share of Park Theatre, N.Y.C., 1808, became co-mgr., sole lessee and mgr., 1815, took Edmund Simpson into partnership, circa 1818-40, added a dramatic and equestrian co., 1823; lessee of Drury Lane Theatre, London, Eng. season 1826-27; became 1st Am. theatre magnate by founding system of importing Brit. stars to U.S. and sending them on tours to various U.S. cities; (system had harmful effect on Am. actors as it forced them to play subordinate roles to support fgn. notables) imported and managed such celebrities as Edmund Kean, Tyrone Power, Fanny Kemble, Ellen Tree. Died Jan. 20, 1840.

PRICE, Sterling, gov. Mo., army officer; b. Prince Edward County, Va., Sept. 20, 1809; s. Pugh Williamson and Elizabeth (Williamson) P.; attended Hampden-Sydney Coll., 1826-27; m. Martha Head, May 14, 1833. Moved to Mo., 1831; mem. Mo. Ho. of Reps., 1836-38, 40-45, speaker, 1840-44; mem. U.S. Ho. of Reps. from Mo., 29th Congress, 1845-Aug. 12, 1846; served as col. 2d Mo. Inf., Mexican War, 1846-48, promoted brig. gen., mil. gov. Chihuahua; gov. Mo., 1853-57, reorganized public sch. system; bank commr. Mo., 1857-61; pres. Mo. Democratic Conv., 1860; in command Mo. Militia, circa 1860; collected and trained approximately 5,000 troops, united forces with smaller Confederate army of Gen. Ben McCulloch; defeated U.S. Army in Battle of Wilson's Creek, 1861, captured 3,000 fed. troops, Lexington, Ky., 1861; officially joined Confederate Army, Ark., 1862; retreated to Tex. plains, 1864-65; resided in Mexico until fall of Maximilian's Empire, 1866. Died St. Louis, Sept. 29, 1867; buried Bellefontaine Cemetery, St. Louis.

PRICE, Thomas Lawson, congressman, mayor; b. Danville, Va., Jan. 19, 1809; s. Maj. and Mrs. (Lawson) Price; m. Lydia Bolton, 1828; m. 2d, Caroline V. Long, Apr. 20, 1854; at least 2 children. Organized merc. and trading bus., Jefferson City, Mo., 1831; established 1st stage-line between St. Louis and Jefferson City, 1838, controlled all stage-line bus. in Mo.; 1st mayor Jefferson City, 1839-42; organized Capitol City Bank, Jefferson City; brevetted maj. gen. 6th Div., Mo. Militia, 1847; lt. gov. (Democrat) Mo., 1849-52; mem. Mo. Ho. of Reps., 1860-62; served as brig. gen. in charge Mo. Militia, U.S. Army, 1861; mem. U.S. Ho. of Reps. (War Democrat) from Mo., 37th Congress, Jan. 21, 1862-63, instrumental in defeat of compensated emancipation for Mo. slaves by fed. appropriation; a reorganizer Democratic Party in Mo., circa 1865. Died Jefferson City, July 15, 1870; buried Riverview Cemetery, Jefferson City.

PRICE, William Thompson, congressman, lawyer; b. Huntingdon County, Pa., June 17, 1824; attended common schs.; studied law. Clk. in store, Hollidaysburg, Pa.; moved to Mt. Pleasant, Ia., 1845, to Black River Falls, Wis., circa 1846; engaged in lumbering and farming; dep. sheriff Crawford County, 1849; mem. Wis. Assembly, 1851, 82; admitted to bar, 1852, practiced law; moved to La Crosse, Wis., 1854, operated stage line between La Crosse and Black River Falls; practiced law, Black River Falls, until 1857; judge Jackson County, 1854, 59; under sheriff Crawford County, 1855; county treas., 1856-57; mem. Wis. Senate, 1857, 70, 78-81, pres., 1879; collector of internal revenue, 1863-65; Republican presdl. elector, 1868; mem. U.S. Ho. of Reps. (Republican) from Wis., 48th-49th congresses, 1883-86. Died Black River Falls, Dec. 6, 1886; buried Riverside Cemetery.

PRIESTLEY, James, educator; b. Rockbridge County, Va.; probably son of William Pressley, Sr.; attended Liberty Hall Acad. until 1782; married, 4 children. Principal, Salem Acad., Bardstown, Ky., 1788-92, developed sch. into a foremost instn. of learning in that region; prin. classical sch., Georgetown, D.C., 1792-95; prin. male dept. Balt. Acad., 1796-98; organized, conducted acad. in Paul's Lane, Balt., 1798-1803; formed (with Bishop John Carroll), Md. Soc. for the Promotion of Useful Knowledge, 1800; prin. Cumberland Coll. (now George Peabody Coll. for Tchrs.), Nashville, Tenn., 1809-16, 20-21. Died Nashville, Feb. 6, 1821.

PRIESTLEY, Joseph, scientist, educator, writer b. Fieldhead Leeds, Yorkshire, Eng., Mar. 13, 1733; s. Jonas and Mary (Swift) P.; attended Daventry Acad., Eng., 1751-54; LL.D. (hon.), U. Edinburgh (Scotland), 1765; m. Mary Wilkinson, June 23, 1762; children—Joseph, Sarah, William, Henry. Pastor, Needham Market, Surrey, Eng., 1755; ordained to ministry Congregational Ch., 1762; tutor belles-lettres Warrington Acad. until 1767; preached, wrote, taught history, anatomy, botany, astronomy; pastor Mill Hill Ch., Leeds, Eng., 1767-72; librarian to Lord Shelburne, 1772-80; minister New Meeting, Birmingham, Eng., 1780-91; made citizen of France for Revolutionary sympathies, 1792; pastor, Hackney, Eng., 1792-94; came to U.S., 1794; settled in Northumberland, Pa.; made many notable experiments in chemistry; 1st to isolate and describe oxygen, nitrous oxide, nitric oxide, nitrogen peroxide, ammonia, silicon flouride, sulphur dioxide, hydrogen sulphide and carbon monoxide; chief early proponent of Unitarianism in U.S. Author: History and Present State of Electricity, 1767; Essay on the First Principles of Government, 1768; The History and Present State of Discoveries Relating to Vision, Light and Colours, 1772; Experiments and Observations on Different Kinds of Air, 3 vols., 1774, 75, 77; An History of the Corruptions of Christianity, 1782; A General History of the Christian Church, 4 vols., 1790-1802; Unitarianism Explained and Defended, 1796; The Doctrine of Phlogiston Established, 1803. Died Northumberland, Feb. 6, 1804.

PRIME, Benjamin Youngs, physician, balladist; b. Huntington, L.I., N.Y., Dec. 20, 1733; s. Rev. Ebenezer and Experience (Youngs) P.; grad. Coll. of N.J. (now Princeton) 1751; A.M. (hon.), Yale, 1760; M.D., U. Leyden (Holland), 1764; m. Mary (Wheelwright) Greaton, Dec. 18, 1774, 5 children including Ebenezer, Nathaniel Scudder. Tutor Coll. of N.J., 1756-57; practiced medicine, Easthampton, L.I. Author: The Patriot Muse, or Poems on Some of the Principal Events of the Late War . . by an American Gentleman, 1764; A Song for the Sons of Liberty in New York circa 1767; Columbia's Glory or British Pride Humbled . . . a Poem on the American Revolution, 1791; upheld Am. cause in colonial Conflict. Died Huntington, L.I., Oct. 31, 1791.

PRIME, Edward Dorr Griffin, clergyman; b. Cambridge, Washington County, N.Y., Nov. 2, 1814; s. Rev. Nathaniel Scudder and Julia Ann (Jermain) P.; grad. Union Coll., 1832; grad Princeton Theol. Sem., 1838; D.D. (hon.). Jefferson Coll., 1857; m. Maria Darlington Wilson, Sept. 26, 1839; m. 2d, Abbie Davis Goodell, June 14, 1860. Ordained to ministry Presbyn. Ch., 1839; pastor Scotchtown ch. in N.Y., 1847-51; asso. editor, contbr. N.Y. Observer, 1854-85, editor, 1853, 85-86; served as chaplain U.S. diplomatic mission, Rome, Italy, traveled in Europe, 1845-55. Author: Calvinism and Missions: An Address before the Synod of New York; Jan. 1853; Around the World: Sketches of Travel through Many Lands and Over Many Seas, 1872. Died N.Y.C., Apr. 7, 1891.

PRIME, Nathaniel Scudder, clergyman; b. Huntington, L.I., N.Y., Apr. 21, 1785; grad. Coll. of N.J. (now Princeton), 1804; m. Julia Jermain, July 5, 1808. Licensed to preach by Presbyn. Ch., 1805; preacher, Cutchogue, L.I., 1805-06, Sag Harbor, L.I., 1806-08; ordained to ministry Presbyn. Ch., 1809; pastor ch., Smithtown, L.I., 1809-11, Cambridge, N.Y., 1813-30; head of Washington Acad., Cambridge, 1821-30; ardent temperance advocate; trustee Middlebury (Vt.) Coll., 1822-26, Williams Coll., Mass., 1826-31; pastor Presbyn. Ch., Sing Sing, N.Y., also headmaster Mt. Pleasant Acad., Sing Sing, 1830-35. Author: History of Long Island. Died Mamaroneck, N.Y., Mar. 27, 1856.

PRIME, Samuel Irenaeus, clergyman, editor; b. Ballston, N.Y. Nov. 4, 1812; s. Nathaniel Scudder and Julia Ann (Jermain) P. grad. Williams Coll., 1830; attended Princeton Theol. Sem., 1832-33; D.D. (hon.), Hampden-Sydney Coll.; m. Elizabeth Thornton Kemeys, Oct. 15, 1833; m. 2d, Eloisa L. Williams, Aug. 17, 1835. Ordained to ministry Presbyn. Ch., 1835; asst. editor N.Y. Observer, 1840-49, editor, 1851-85; wrote weekly essays Irenaeus Letters; wrote "Editor's Drawer" in Harper's Mag., 1853-85. Author: The Old White Meeting House, 1845; Travels in Europe and the East, 1855; The Power of Prayer, 1859; Thoughts on the Death of Little Children. Died N.Y.C., July 18, 1885.

PRINCE, Oliver Hillhouse, senator, journalist; b. Montville, Conn., 1787; studied law. Became a newspaperman, Ga.; admitted to bar, 1806, began practice of law, Macon, Ga.; a commr. to lay out Town of Macon, 1824; mem. Ga. Senate, 1824; mem. U.S. Senate (filled vacancy) from Ga., Nov. 7, 1828-29; author and editor in Macon; presided at 1st railroad conv. in Ga.; an original stockholder and dir. Ga. R.R. Co.; editor Ga. Journal, 1830-35. Died in wreck of packet ship Home nr. Ocracoke Inlet, N.C., Oct. 9, 1837.

PRINCE, Thomas, clergyman; b. Sandwich, Mass., May 15, 1687; s. Samuel and Mercy (Hinckley) P.; grad. Harvard, 1709; m. Deborah Denny, Oct. 30, 1719, 5 children including Thomas, Jr. Ordained pastor Old South Ch., Boston, 1718, pastor, 1718-58; preached and published many funeral sermons; bibliophile, acquired large library, most of which is now in Boston Public Library. Author: Sermon on the Death of Cotton Mather, 1728; A Chronological History of New England in the Form of Annals, 1736; The Christian History (accounts of revivals of 1743-44), 1744-45; Earthquakes of New England, 1755; The New England Psalm-book Revised and Improved, 1758. Died Boston, Oct. 22, 1758.

PRINCE, William, horticulturist; b. Flushing, L. I., N.Y., circa 1725; s. Robert and Mary (Burgess) P.; m. Anne Thorne, 13 children including William, Benjamin. Pioneer Am. horticulturist, 1 of 1st to sell budded or grafted stock and to attempt to breed new varieties; established Prince's Nursery, developed Prince's Gage plum, raised fruits, trees and shrubs; thousands of his cherry trees made into barrel hoops during Revolutionary War. Died Flushing, 1802.

PRINCE, William, horticulturist; b. Flushing, L.I., N.Y., Nov. 10, 1766; s. William and Ann (Thorne) P.; m. Mary Statton, 4 children including William Robert. Founder Linnaean Botanic Garden and Nurseries, 1793, imported and introduced many varieties of fruits and plants, also exported Am. plants and trees to Europe; introduced Isabella grape (which he renamed), 1816; standardized name of Bartlett pear, others; mem. N.Y. Hort. Soc., Mass. Hort. Soc., Linnaean Soc. of Paris, Hort. Soc. of London and Paris, Imperial Soc. of the Georgofili, Florence, Italy. Author: A Short Treatise on Horticulture, 1828; (with son William Robert) A Treatise on the Vine, 1830, The Pomological Manual, 1831. Died Flushing, Apr. 9, 1842.

PRINCE, William, congressman; b. Ireland, 1772; studied law. Came to U.S., settled in Ind.; mem. Ind. Senate, 1816; del. Ind. Constl. Conv., 1816; served as capt. at Battle of Tippecanoe; mem. Ind. Ho. of Reps., 1821-22; mem. U.S. Ho. of Reps. from Ind., 18th Congress, 1823-24. Died nr. Princeton, Ind., Sept. 8, 1824; buried Old Cemetery, nr. Princeton.

PRINCE, William Robert, horticulturist; b. Flushing, L.I., N.Y., Nov. 6, 1795; s. William and Mary (Stratton) P.; m. Charlotte Goodwin Collins, Oct. 2, 1826, 4 children including LeBaron Bradford. Botanized entire range of Atlantic states; importer 1st merino sheep to U.S., 1816; became mgr. (with brother) Linnaean Botanic Garden and Nurseries, circa 1835; pioneer (with father) in introducing silk culture, 1837; importer mulberry Morus multicaulis (became very popular.); from Tarascon, France; introduced culture of osiers and sorghum, 1854-55; importer Chinese yam, 1854; corr. mem. Mass. Hort. Soc., 1829; mem. Am. Pomological Soc.; greatest contbn. to Am. horticulture: advancement of grape-growing. Author: Prince's Manual of Roses, 1846; (with father) Treatise on the Vine, 1830; The Pomological Manual, 1831. Contbr. many short articles and arguments to Gardeners' Monthly and Rural New Yorker. Died Flushing, Mar. 28, 1869.

PRINDLE, Elizur H., congressman, lawyer; b. Newtown, Conn., May 6, 1829; attended acad., Homer, N.Y.; studied law. Admitted to bar, 1854, practiced law; moved to Norwich, N.Y.; dist. atty. Chenango County (N.Y.), 1859-63; mem. N.Y. State Assembly, 1863; mem. N.Y. Constl. Conv., 1867-68; mem. U.S. Ho. of Reps. (Republican) from N.Y., 42d Congress, 1871-73. Died Norwich, Oct. 7, 1890; buried Mt. Hope Cemetery.

PRING, Martin, explorer, naval officer; b. Eng., circa 1580; s. John Pring; m. Elizabeth, 6 children. Sent on expdn. to No. Va., 1603; in command of ships Speedwell and Discoverer, sighted land at Penobscot Bay, drifted westward into Cape Cod Bay, landed at Plymouth Harbor (naming it Whitson Bay); built a barricade; sent on expdn. to join Challons on coast of Va.; explored the coast, made chart and report; employed to survey Bristol Channel, 1610; master in service of East India Co., 1613, comdr. naval forces of co., 1619; launched policy of friendship with Dutch in order to secure monopoly against the Spanish and Portuguese; became mem. Mcht. Venturers Soc. of Bristol, 1623, a warden of soc., 1625; took command of 300-ton privateer, Charles, 1626. Died 1626; buried St. Stephen's Ch., Bristol, Eng.

PRINGLE, Benjamin, congressman, jurist; b. Richfield Springs, N.Y., Nov. 9, 1807; studied law. Admitted to bar, 1830, practiced law for number of years; pres. bank, Batavia, N.Y.; judge Genesee County (N.Y.) Ct., 1841-46; mem. U.S. Ho. of Reps. (Whig) from N.Y., 33d-34th congresses, 1853-57; mem. N.Y. State Assembly, 1863; apptd. by Pres. Lincoln judge of ct. of arbitration, Cape Town, Africa (under treaty with Gt. Britain for suppression of African slave trade), 1863; apptd. mem. bd. trustees State Instn. for Blind, 1873. Died Hastings, Minn., June 7, 1887; buried Old Cemetery, Batavia.

PRINGLE, John Julius, state legislator; b. Charleston, S.C., July 22, 1753; s. Robert and Judith Mayrant (Bull) P.; grad. Coll. of Pa., 1771; m. Susannah Reid, Jan. 1, 1784, 10 children. Admitted to Middle Temple, London, Eng., 1773; sec. to Ralph Izard (commr. to Ct. of Tuscany, France), 1778-79; admitted to Charleston bar, 1781; mem. S.C. Ho. of Reps., 1785, 86-88, speaker, 1787, 88; mem. S.C. Conv. to ratify U.S. Constn. 1788, S.C. Constl. Conv. 1790; U.S. dist. atty., 1789-92; atty. gen. S.C., 1792-1808; trustee Coll. of Charleston, 1796-1824, pres. bd., 1811-15; pres. Charleston Library Soc., 1812-16; chmn. vestry St. Michael's Ch.. several years. Died Charleston, Mar. 17, 1843.

PRINTZ, Johan Bjornsson, colonial gov.; b. Bottnarydl, Smaland, Sweden, July 20, 1592; s. Rev. Bjorn Hansson and Gunilla Svensdotter (adopted grandfather's name Printz); studied theology at univs. Leipzig, Wittenberg, Helmstedt and Jena; m. Elizabeth von Boche, 1622; m. 2d, Maria (von Linnestau) von Stralendorff, 1642, 6 children including Gustaf. Commd. lt. col. Swedish Army, 1638; in command of Chemnitz, 1639; created knight by Queen Christina, 1642; gov. New Sweden on Delaware River, 1643-53; began constrn. Ft. Elfsborg at Varkenskill; assigned land to settlers for farming, maintained peaceful relations with Indians, sent agt. to trade at New Amsterdam, built block-house, church, wharf, grist mill, brewery; 1st American yachtsman; comdr. Jonkoping Castle, 1657; gov. Jonkoping Lan, Sweden, 1658. Died Sweden, May 3, 1663.

PRIOR, William Matthew, artist; b. Bath, Me., May 16, 1806; children included Gilbert, Matthew. Maintained studio, Boston, 1841-46, East Boston, after 1846; itinerant painter in New Bedford (Mass.), Newport (R.I.), Balt.; copied Stuart's portrait of Washington on glass; wrote several religious books. Died Boston, Jan. 1873.

PROCTOR, Joseph, actor; b. Marlboro, Mass., May 7, 1816; s. Nicholson Broughton and Lucy (Bond) P.; m. Hester (Warren) Willis, 1835; m. 2d, Elizabeth Wakeman, Feb. 1851; 1 dau., Anna E. Made 1st appearance as Damon in play Pythias at Warren Theatre, Boston, 1833; acted leading roles in Phila., 1837; most famous part: prin. character in Nick of the Woods, or the Renegade's Daughter, Bowery Theatre, N.Y.C., 1839; played in all major U.S. cities and numerous small towns in Shakespearean and contemporary roles, 1837-88; made acting tour of London, other cities of U.K. and Europe, 1859-61, tour of U.S., 1861; made last profl. appearance in Macbeth at benefit performance, Globe Theatre, Boston, 1890; profl. instr. for stage, Boston, 1890's. Died Oct. 2, 1897.

PROCTOR, Lucien Brock, lawyer; b. Hanover, N.H., Mar. 6, 1823; s. Jonathan and Ruth (Carter) P.; m. Araminta D. Whitney, Jan. 1843; m. 2d, Margaret Scott Wylie. Admitted to N.Y. bar, 1852; a founder Livingston County Hist. Soc.; sec. N.Y. Bar Assn., 1889-97. Author: The Bench and Bar of New York, 1870; The Civil, Political, Professional and Ecclesiastical History . . . of the County of Kings and the City of Brooklyn, New York, from 1683 to 1884, published 1884; William H. Seward as a Lawyer, 1887. Died Apr. 1, 1900.

PROCTER, William, pharmacist, educator; b. Balt., May 3, 1817; s. Isaac and Rebecca (Farquhar) P.; grad. Phil. Coll. Pharmacy, 1837; m. Margaretta Bullock, Oct. 1849; m. 2d, Catherine Parry, 1864. Owned, operated drugstore, Phila., 1844-74; prof. theory and practice of pharmacy Phila. Coll. Pharmacy, 1846-66; editor Am. Jour. of Pharmacy, 1850-71; published Am. edition of Practical Pharmacy (Mohn and Redwood); mem. Phila. Coll. Pharmacy, 1850, trustee, 1851-53, corr. sec., 1855, 1st v.p., 1867; del. to conv. of pharmaceutists to fix standards for use of customs ofcls. in inspection of drugs N.Y.C., 1851; a founder Am. Pharm. Assn., 1852, corr. sec., 1852-57, 1st v.p., 1859, pres., 1862. Died Phila., Feb. 9, 1874.

PROFFIT, George H., congressman, lawyer; b. New Orleans, Sept. 7, 1807; studied law. Moved to Petersburg, Ind., 1828; engaged in merc. activities, Petersburg, also Portersville, Ind.; admitted to bar, began practice of law, Petersburg; mem. Ind. Ho. of Reps., 1831-32, 36-38; mem. U.S. Ho. of Reps. (Whig) from Ind., 26th-27th congresses, 1839-43; minister to Brazil (apptd. by Pres. Tyler, but not confirmed by U.S. Senate), 1843-44. Died Louisville, Ky., Sept. 7, 1847; buried Walnut Hills Cemetery, Petersburg.

PROUD, Robert, educator, b. "Low Foxton," Yorkshire, Eng., May 10, 1728; s. William and Ann Proud. Came to Phila., 1759; operated a sch. for boys, 1759-70; master Friends Public Sch., 1761-70, 80-90. Author: The History of Pennsylvania, in North America, from the Original Institution and Settlement of that Province . . . in 1681, till after the Year 1770 (included chpt. covering 1760-70), 2 vols., 1797-98. Died Phila., July 5, 1813.

PROUDFIT, David Law, author; b. Newburgh-on-the-Hudson, N.Y., Oct. 27, 1842; m. Frances Marian Dodge, July 8, 1868, 3 children. Served from pvt. to maj. 1st N.Y. Mounted Rifles, 1861-65, served at Richmond and Petersburg. Author: Love among the Gamins, 1877; From the Chapparal to Wall Street; or a Man from the West, 1891. Died N.Y.C., 1897.

PROVOOST, Samuel, clergyman; b. N.Y.C., Mar. 9, 1743; s. John and Eve (Rutgers) Provost; grad. King's Coll. (now Columbia), 1758; fellow-commoner St. Peter's Coll., Cambrdge (Eng.) U., 1761; D.D. (hon.), U. Pa., 1786; m. Maria Bousfield, June 8, 1766, 4 children. Ordained deacon Protestant Episcopal Ch., 1766, priest, 1776; asst. minister Trinity Ch., N.Y.C., circa 1771; accepted invitation to officiate at St. Paul's and St. George's chapels Trinity Parish, N.Y., 1784; apptd. regent U. State N.Y., 1784; chaplain Continental Congress, 1785; elected 1st bishop N.Y.C., 1786, consecrated by Archbishop of Canterbury, 1787; officiated at confirmation service at St. Peter's Ch., Perth Amboy, 1st held in N.J., 1788; conducted service at St. Paul's Chapel following Washington's inauguration, 1789; chaplain U.S. Senate, 1789; chmn. com. which drafted constn. of Church, responsible for necessary changes in prayer book following establishment of the Church as Am. entity; presided over Episcopal Gen. Conv., 1801. Died N.Y.C., Sept. 6, 1815; buried Trinity Churchyard, N.Y.C.

PROVOST, Etienne, trapper, guide; b. circa 1782; s. Albert and Marianne (Menard) P.; m. Marie Sallé dit Lajoie, Aug. 14, 1829, 1 dau., Marie. Traveled from St. Louis to Colorado River, 1823; 1 of 1st white men to see Great Salt Lake; fur trapper, guide, 1822-47; guide on Audubon's expdn. to upper Western country, 1843. Died July 3, 1850.

PRUD'HOMME, John Francis Eugene, engraver; b. St. Thomas, W.I., Oct. 4, 1800. Came to U.S., 1807; engraved number of plates for Nat. Portrait Gallery of Distinguished Americans, 1831, important portraits were of Henry Clay, De-Witt Clinton, Oliver Cromwell, Stephen Decatur, Alexander Hamilton, John Paul Jones, Dolly Madison, George Washington; curator Nat. Acad. of Design, 1834-53; designer-engraver of decorative work for banknote engraving firm. N.Y., 1852-69; with Bur. Engraving and Printing, Washington, D.C., 1869-85; designer of the ornamentation of bank notes and securities. Died Georgetown, D.C., June 27, 1892.

PRUYN, John Van Schaick Lansing, congressman, univ. chancellor; b. Albany, N.Y., June 22, 1811; s. David and Hybertje (Lansing) P.; grad. Albany Acad., 1826; studied law in office of James King; M.A. (hon.), Rutgers U., 1835, Union Coll., 1845; LL.D. (hon.), U. Rochester; m. Harriet Corning Turner, Oct. 22, 1840; m. 2d, Anna Fenn Parker, Sept. 7, 1865. Admitted to N.Y. bar, 1831; examiner in chancery, 1833-36, master, 1836-46; atty., counselor U.S. Supreme Ct., 1848; dir. Mohawk & Hudson R.R. Co., 1835-38, 43-45, atty. and counsel, 1843; drew up consolidation agreement, became sec., treas., gen. counsel. N.Y. Central R.R., 1863-66; trustee Mut. Life Ins. Co.; dir. Union Trust Co. of N.Y.; mem. N.Y. State Senate, 1861-63; mem. U.S. Ho. of Reps. from N.Y., 38th, 40th congresses, Dec. 7, 1863-65, 67-69; regent Univ. State N.Y., 1844-62, chancellor, 1862-77; pres. bd. trustees St. Stephen's Coll., Annandale, N.Y.; a founder N.Y. State Bd. Charities, pres. 1866-77; mem. Assn. Codification of Law of Nations; pres. bd. N.Y. State Survey. Died Clifton Springs, N.Y., Nov. 21, 1877; buried Albany Rural Cemetery.

PRUYN, Robert Hewson, diplomat; b. Albany, N.Y., Feb. 14, 1815; s. Casparus F. and Anne (Hewson) P.; A.B., Rutgers Coll., 1833, A.M., 1836; m. Jane Anne Lansing, Nov. 9, 1814, 2 sons. Admitted to N.Y. bar, 1836; atty. and counsel to city corp. Albany, 1836-39, mem. municipal council, 1839; judge adv. gen. N.Y. Militia, 1841-46, 51-53; mem. N.Y. Assembly (Whig), 1845-50, 54, speaker; adj. gen. N.Y., 1855-57; commd. U.S. minister resident to Japan, 1861-65; instrumental in persuading Japanese to pay indemnity claims to European powers, 1862; helped strengthen authority of central Japanese govt., 1863; largely responsible for keeping Japanese ports open to Western trade; concluded a conv. reducing tariff on Am. manufactured goods, 1864; largely responsible for joint action on Straits of Shimonoseki which broke power of one of leading opponents of fgn. penetration; presided over N.Y. Commn. to draft amendments to state constn. for submission to popular vote, 1872; pres. Albany Nat. Comml. Bank, 1880-82; trustee Met. Trust Co., N.Y.C. Died Albany, Feb. 26, 1882.

PRYOR, Nathaniel, army officer; b. Amherst County, Va. (probably), circa 1775; m. an Osage Indian, circa 1820. Enlisted with Lewis and Clark expdn., Louisville, Ky., 1803; apptd. sgt., 1804; ensign 1st Inf., U.S. Army, 1807; resigned from army, 1810; reentered army as 1st lt., 1813; promoted capt., 1814; fought with distinction in Battle of New Orleans; honorably discharged, 1815; apptd. sub-agt. Osage Indians, 1831. Died June 10, 1831.

PUENTE, Giuseppe Del, baritone; b. Naples, Italy, Jan. 30, 1841; studied at Naples Conservatory; m. Helen Dudley Campbell. Made operatic debut at Jassy; engaged for Teatro San Carlo, Naples; made appearances in France, Germany, Russia, Spain and Eng. (Covent Garden, 1873); made 1st Am. appearances under Strakosch at N.Y. Acad. Music, 1873-74, reappeared, 1878; became mem. 1st Met. Opera House Co., appeared as Valentin in 1st performance of Faust, 1883; returned to N.Y. Acad. Music, 1885, took part in Am. premiere of Manon; mem. opera troupes of Patti, Hinrichs; sang in Am. premiere of Cavalleria Rusticana, 1891; appeared in music festivals and as orchestral soloist. Died Phila., May 25, 1900.

PUGET, Peter Richings (see Richings, Peter).

PUGH, Ellis, clergyman; b. Parish of Dolgelley, Merionethshire, North Wales, June 1656. Converted to Quakerism by John ap John, 1674; approved as a Quaker minister, 1680; settled nr. Phila., 1687. Author: Annerch ir Cymru (a salutation to the Britains), 1721. Died Oct. 3, 1718.

PUGH, Evan, chemist, coll. pres.; b. Jordan Bank, E. Nottingham Twp., Pa., Feb. 29, 1828; s. Lewis and Mary (Hutton) P.; studied U. Leipzig (Germany), 1853-54; Ph.D. in Chemistry, U. Gottingen (Germany), 1856; m. Rebecca Valentine, Feb. 4, 1864. Researcher at labs. Sir John Bennett Lawes and Sir Joseph Henry Gilbert, Rothamsted, Eng.; laid down principles of plant growth, 1859; pres. Agrl. Coll. Pa., 1856-64, (now Pa. State Coll.); helped push Land-Grant Coll. Act through Congress, 1862. Author: On a New Method for the Quantative Estimation of Nitric Acid., 1860; On the Sources of the Nitrogen of Vegetation, 1862; A Report Upon a Plan for the Organization of Colleges for Agriculture and the Mechanic Arts, with Especial Reference to the . . . Agricultural College of Pennsylvania . . . in View of the Endowment of this Institution by the Land Script Fund, 1864. Died Bellefonte, Pa., Apr. 19, 1864.

PUGH, George Ellis, senator; b. Cincinnati, Nov. 28, 1822; s. Lot and Rachel (Anthony) P.; grad. Miami U., Oxford, O., 1840; m. Theresa Chalfant, 4 children. Admitted to Ohio bar, 1843; served as capt. 4th Ohio Inf., Mexican War, 1848-50; mem. Ohio Ho. of Reps. (Democrat), 1848-50; city solicitor Cincinnati, 1850; atty. gen. Ohio, 1852-54; mem. U.S. Senate from Ohio, 1855-61, advocated congressional non-intervention in slavery question in territories, opposed proslavery Lecompton Constn. for Kan., 1858; head of Ohio delegation to Dem. Conv., Charleston, S.C., 1860; del. Dem. Nat. Conv., Balt., 1860; unsuccessful candidate for lt. gov. Ohio on Vallandigham ticket, 1863; assisted Charles O'Conor as counsel for defendant in treason trial of Jefferson Davis, 1866-67. Died Cincinnati, July 19, 1876; buried Spring Grove Cemetery, Cincinnati.

PUGH, John, congressman; b. Bucks County, Pa., June 2, 1761; attended common schs. Served from pvt. to capt. Continental Army, during Revolutionary War; engaged in farming and merc. activities; justice of peace; mem. Pa. Ho. of Reps., 1800-04; mem. U.S. Ho. of Reps. (Democrat) from Pa., 9th-10th congresses, 1805-09; register of wills, recorder of deeds Bucks County, 1810-21. Died Doylestown, Pa., July 13, 1842; buried Presbyn. Churchyard.

PULASKI, Casimir, army officer; b. Podolia, Poland, Mar. 4, 1748; s. Count Joseph Pulaski. Joined in active rebellion to combat fgn. domination of Poland through Stanislaus II, 1768; fled to Turkey, 1772, tried to incite Turkey to attack Russia, 1772-75; arrived in Boston, 1776; served as volunteer in battles of Brandywine and Germantown; commanded cavalry at Trenton, winter 1777, later at Flemington; commd. by Congress to organize independent cavalry corps, 1778; ordered to support of Gen. Lincoln in S.C., 1779. Died of wounds suffered at Battle of Charleston (S.C.), on board the Wasp, off Charleston, Oct. 11, 1779.

PULLMAN, George Mortimer, inventor, railroad car mfr.; b. Brocton Chautauqua County, N.Y., Mar. 3, 1831; s. James Lewis and Emily Caroline (Minton) P.; m. Harriet Sanger, June 13, 1867, 4 children. Contractor in Chgo., 1855-59, successful in raising the level of some bldgs. and streets; store-keeper in mining town, Colo., 1859-63; contracted with Chgo & Alton R.R. to remodel 2 day coaches into sleeping cars (incorporating his basic idea of upper berth hinged to side of car), 1858, constructed a 3d car, 1859; patentee (with friend Ben Field) folding berth, 1864, lower berth, 1865; completed 1st car The Pioneer, 1865, constructed number of other cars modeled after The Pioneer; organized Pullman Palace Car Co., 1867 (grew to be greatest car bldg. orgn. in world); established 1st mfg. plant at Palmyra, N.Y., then moved to Detroit; built Town of Pullman (Ill.) for accomodation of employees, completed 1881; responsible for combined sleeping and restaurant car, 1867, dining car, 1868, chair car, 1875, vestibule car, 1887; owner Eagleton Wire Works, N.Y.; pres. Met. Elevated R.R., N.Y.; contbd. bequest of $1,200,000 for establishment free manual tng. sch. at Pullman. Died Chgo., Oct. 19, 1897.

PULTE, Joseph Hippolyt, homeopathic physician; b. Meschede, Prussia, Oct. 6, 1811; s. Dr. Herman Pulte; M.D., U. Hamburg (Germany); m. Mary Jane Rollins, 1840. Came to U.S., 1834; joined Northampton County (Pa.) Homeopathic Med. Soc., 1834; practiced in Allentown, Pa., 1834-40; opened pvt. dispensary, Cincinnati, 1840; founder (with others) Am. Inst. Homeopathy,

N.Y.C., 1844; lectr. obstetrics and clin. medicine Cleve Homeopathic Med. Coll. Author: Organon der Weltgeschichte, 1856; Homeopathic Domestic Physician, 1850; A Reply to Dr. Metcalf, 1851; The Science of Medicine, 1852; Woman's Medical Guide, 1853; Civilization and its Heroes; an Oration, 1855; co-editor American Mag. Devoted to Homeopathy and Hydropathy, 1851-54; editor Quarterly Homeopathic Mag., 1854; translator Diseases of Children (Teste), 1857. Died Cincinnati, Feb. 25, 1884.

PURCELL, John Baptist, clergyman, educator; b. Mallow, Ireland, Feb. 26, 1800; s. Edmond and Johanna (O'Keefe) P.; attended Mt. St. Mary's Coll., 1820-23; studied under Sulpicians in Paris, France. Ordained priest Roman Catholic Ch. at Notre Dame, Paris, 1826; prof. moral philosophy Mt. St. Mary's Coll., Emmitsburg, Md., 1826-29, pres., 1829; consecrated bishop of Cincinnati, 1832; went to Europe to obtain missionaries and financial aid, 1838-39, brought Sisters of Notre Dame de Namur, also Ursulines and Sisters of Charity to Cincinnati; a founder St. Francis Xavier Coll., 1841; encouraged Fathers of the Precious Blood to enter Am. mission field and establish their seminary and coll. at Carthagena; brought Sisters of Mercy of Kinsdale, Sisters of Francis of Cologne, Sisters of the Good Shepherd, and Little Sisters of the Poor to Cincinnati; began erection of new Mt. St. Mary's of the West Sem., Price Hill, Cincinnati, 1847; during Civil War encouraged enlistments, made provisions for prisoners, sent Sisters of Charity as war nurses, maintained Catholic Telegraph (Unionist organ); archbishop of Cincinnati, 1850; held 1st series of provincial councils (acts and decrees of which were largely responsible for the eccles. orgn. of arch-diocese), 1855; retired to convent of Brown County Ursulines, 1879, because of embarrassment caused by brother's failure to protect savings of parishioners entrusted to him during and after panic of 1873. Died Brown County, O., July 4, 1883.

PURDUE, John, mcht., philanthropist; b. Huntingdon County, Pa., Oct. 31, 1802; s. Charles and Mary (Short) P. Settler, Lafayette, Ind., 1839, became a comml. leader of region; partner in successful commission house, N.Y.C., during 1850's; purchaser newspaper Lafayette Jour., 1866; contbr. $150,000 to Indiana Agrl. Coll. (supplementing $50,000 and land and bldgs. already donated by citizens of county) with specification that instn. bear his name, became life trustee Purdue U. Died Lafayette, Sept. 12, 1876; buried Purdue U., West Lafayette, Ind.

PURDY, Smith Meade, congressman, lawyer; b. North Norwich, N.Y., July 31, 1796; attended common schs.; studied law. Admitted to bar, began practice of law, Sherburne, N.Y., 1819; moved to Norwich, N.Y., 1827; judge Ct. of Common Pleas, also surrogate Chenango County (N.Y.), 1833-37; mem. U.S. Ho. of Reps. (Democrat) from N.Y., 28th Congress, 1843-45; declined appointment as atty. gen. U.S. under Pres. Polk, 1844; judge and surrogate Chenango County 1847-51. Died Norwich, Mar. 30, 1870; buried Mt. Hope Cemetery.

PURNELL, William Henry, state ofcl., coll. pres.; b. Worcester County, Md., Feb. 3, 1826; s. Moses and Maria (Bowen) P.; grad. Del. Coll. (now U. Del.), 1846; read law with Judge John R. Franklin; m. Margaret Neill Martin, June 13, 1849, 5 children including Caroline. Admitted to Md. bar, 1848; pros. atty. Worcester County (Md.), 1850-53; dep. atty. gen. Md., 1853-55; comptroller Md. Treasury, 1855-61; dep. postmaster Balt., 1861; organized "Purnell Legion," 1861, commd. col., resigned command, 1862; pres. Del. Coll., 1870-75, instr. elocution and oratory, 1897-1902; prin. Frederick Female Sem,, 1885. Died Annapolis, Md., Mar. 30, 1902.

PURRY, Jean Pierre, colonist; b. Neuchatel, Switzerland, circa 1675; s. Henry and Marie (Ersel) de Purry; m. Lucrece de Chaillet, 3 children including Charles, David. Proposed that Dutch East India Co. establish a colony in South Australia, 1717; urged England to settle persecuted Protestants in an area South and West of S.C. to be called "Georgia", 1724; selected site for Settlement on Savannah River, 1730; brought 150 Swiss to S.C., founder Town of Purrysburg, 1732. Died July 1736.

PURSH, Frederick (Friedrich Traugott Pursch) botanist; b. Grossenhain, Saxony, Germany, Feb. 4, 1774; studied in Royal Botanic Gardens, Dresden, Germany. Came to Am., 1799; mgr. bot. garden nr. Balt., 1799-1802; in charge bot. garden of William Hamilton, nr. Phila., 1802-05; explorer on bot. expdn. from Western Md. through mountains to border of N.C. and back along coast, 1806; made 2d expdn. across Pocono region of Pa. to central N.Y., then east to Green Mountains of Vt.; in charge Hosack Garden, 1807-10. Author: Flora Americae Septentrionalis (1st complete flora of America N. of Mexico), 1814; Journal of a Botanical Excursion in the Northeastern Parts of the State of Pennsylvania and New York, 1869. Died Montreal, Can., July 11, 1820; buried Mt. Royal Cemetery.

PURVIANCE, David, clergyman, legislator; b. Iredell County, N.C., Nov. 14, 1766; s. John and Jane (Wasson) P.; m. Mary Ireland, 1789, at least 1 child. Leader of farmer mems. in Ky. Legislature, 1797-circa 1800; licensed by Presbytery as exhorter, 1801; withdrew from Ky. Synod, circa 1802, ordained to ministry Presbyn. Ch. by Springfield Presbytery, became co-pastor congregations of Cane Ridge and Concord, Ky.; renounced all man-made creeds, 1804; 1st of seceders to repudiate infant baptism and insist on immersion as form required by New Testament; made preaching tours through N.C., Tenn., Ohio; established ch. at New Paris, Preble County, O.; mem. Ohio Ho. of Reps., 1809, 26, Ohio Senate, 1810-16; trustee Miami U., Oxford, O., sometimes pres. pro tem; a founder of "Christian denomination". Died Preble County, Aug. 19, 1847.

PURVIANCE, Samuel Anderson, congressman, lawyer; b. Butler, Pa., Jan. 10, 1809; studied law. Admitted to bar, 1827, began practice of law, Butler, Pa.; pros. atty. Warren County, 2 years; del. Pa. Constl. Conv., 1837, 38; mem. Pa. Ho. of Reps., 1838-39; del. Whig Nat. Conv., Balt., 1844, Republican Nat. Conv., Phila., 1856; Whig presdl. elector, 1848, 52; mem. U.S. Ho. of Reps. (Whig) from Pa., 34th-35th congresses, 1855-59; practiced law, Pitts., 1859-76; del. Rep. nat. convs., 1860, 64, 68; atty. gen. Pa., 1861; mem. nat. exec. com. Rep. Party, 1864-68; mem. Pa. Constl. Conv., 1872. Died Allegheny (now part of Pitts.), Feb. 14, 1882; buried Bellevue (now Highwood) Cemetery.

PURVIANCE, Samuel Dinsmore, congressman; b. Masonboro Sound at Castle Fin House, nr. Wilmington, N.C., Jan. 7, 1774; attended pvt. sch.; studied law. Admitted to bar, practiced law, Fayetteville, N.C.; owner, operator of large plantation; mem. N.C. Ho. of Commons, 1798-99; mem. N.C. Senate, 1801; trustee Fayetteville Acad., 1803; mem. U.S. H. of Reps. (Federalist) from N.C., 8th Congress, 1803-05. Died while on exploring expdn. into the West, on Red River, circa 1806.

PURYEAR, Richard Clauselle, congressman, planter; b. Mecklenburg County, Va., Feb. 9, 1801. Became a planter, nr. Huntsville, N.C.; Served as col. of militia; magistrate Surry County (N.C.); mem. N.C. Ho. of Commons, 1838, 44, 46, 52; mem. N.C. Senate; mem. U.S. Ho. of Reps. (Whig) from N.C., 33d-34th congresses, 1853-57; del. Confederate Provisional Congress, Richmond, 1861; del. Peace Congress, Phila., after Civil War. Died on his plantation "Shallow Ford," Yadkin County, N.C., July 30, 1867, buried family burial ground.

PUSEY, Caleb, miller, colonial ofcl.; b. Berkshire, Eng., circa 1650; s. William Pusey; m. Anne Worley, 1681, 2 daus. Joined Soc. of Friends; settled in Chester County, Pa., 1682; mgr. Chester Mills, 1682-1717; mem. Pa. Provincial Assembly, intermittently, 1686-1713; mem. Pa. Gov.'s Council, 1695, 97, 99-1715; founded and presided over "Peacemakers" (an informal ct. to settle controversies between Quakers). Author (abbreviated titles): Satan's Harbinger Encountered, 1700; The Bomb search'd and found stuff'd with False Ingredients . . . , 1705. Died Mar. 8, 1727.

PUSHMATAHAW (The Eagle), Indian chief; b. Noxubee County, Miss., circa 1765. Elected chief of Choctaw Indians 1805; signer Treaty of Mt. Dexter, providing for cession large tract of land in Ala. and Miss., 1805; opposed efforts of Tecumseh to form Indian Confederacy against westward thrust of white settlement; leader (with John Pitchlynn) in persuading Choctaws to join U.S.; leader band of some 500 warriors in Andrew Jackson's forces in War of 1812; signed treaties of cession, 1816, 20. Died Washington, D.C., Dec. 24, 1824; buried Congressional Cemetery, Washington.

PUTNAM, George Palmer, publisher; b. Brunswick, Me., Feb. 7, 1814; s. Henry and Catherine Hunt (Palmer) P.; m. Victorine Haven, Mar. 13, 1841, 11 children including Mary Corinna (Putnam) Jacobi, Ruth, George Haven. Author hist. manual Chronology, or an Introduction and Index to Universal History, 1833; employee firm of Wiley & Long, 1833, became Wiley & Putnam, 1840; settled in London, Eng.. 1841-48, opened agency for sale of Am. books in Eng. in Paternoster Row, London; compiler volume of American Facts (designed to improve Anglo-Am. relations), 1845; corr. for N.Y. newspapers, New World, Comml. Advertiser and Evening Post, 1841-48; began publication Putnam's Monthly Mag., 1853-57, 68-70, merged with Scribner's Monthly, 1870; collector internal revenue 8th dist. N.Y., circa 1861-66; established firm G.P. Putnam & Son, 1866, G.P. Putnam & Sons, 1870; sec. of an internat. copyright assn., 1837; campaigner for internat. copyright agreements, 1837-72. Died N.Y.C., Dec. 20, 1872.

PUTNAM, Gideon, pioneer; b. Sutton, Mass., Apr. 17, 1763; s. Stephen and Mary (Gibbs) P.; m. Doana Risley. Settled in Saratoga Springs, N.Y., 1789, laid foundation of town, built sawmill; began bldg. hotel Union Hall, 1802; laid out a village, enclosing several springs; began erection Congress Hall, 1811. Died Dec. 1, 1812.

PUTNAM, Harvey, congressman, lawyer; b. Brattleboro, Vt., Jan. 5, 1793; attended common schs.; studied law. Admitted to bar, 1816, began practice of law, Attica, N.Y., 1817; held several local offices; mem. U.S. Ho. of Reps. (Whig, filled vacancy) from N.Y., 25th, 30th-31st congresses, Nov. 7, 1838-39, 47-51; surrogate of Genessee County, then of Wyoming County, 1840-42. Died Attica, Sept. 20, 1855; buried Forest Hill Cemetery.

PUTNAM, Israel, army officer; b. Salem Village (now Danvers), Mass., Jan. 7, 1718; s. Joseph and Elizabeth (Porter) P.; m. Hannah Pope, July 19, 1739; m. 2d, Deborah (Lothrop) Gardiner, June 3, 1767; 10 children. Commd. 2d lt. Conn. Militia, 1754, capt., 1755, maj., 1758; lt. col., 1759; served in French and Indian Wars; maj., then lt. col. Conn. Militia, 1764, served in Pontiac's War; an organizer Sons of Liberty, del. to warn Gov. Fitch of Conn. that he could not enforce Stamp Act; mem. exploration expdn. to discover possible values of West Fla., cruised through W.I., Gulf of Mexico, up to Mississippi River 1773; lt. col. 11th Regt., Conn. Militia, brig. gen., 1775; maj. gen. Continental Army, 1775; a leader in planning for Battle of Bunker Hill; chief in command of N.Y. before Washington arrived, 1776; in charge of removal of all troops and stores from N.Y.C. after retreat, 1776, then had command of Phila.; command in the Highlands (upper N.Y. State), delayed twice in obeying orders from Gen. Washington, acquitted of charges of refusing to obey orders by ct. of inquiry; in charge recruiting service in Conn., 1778-79. Author: Two Putnams—in the Havana Expedition 1762 and in the Mississippi River Exploration 1772-73, published 1931. Died Brooklyn, Conn., May 29, 1790.

PUTNAM, Rufus, army officer, pioneer; b. Sutton, Mass.. Apr. 9, 1738; s. Elisha and Susanna (Fuller) P.; m. Elizabeth Ayres, Apr. 6, 1761; m. 2d, Persis Rice, Jan. 10, 1765; 10 children. served as ensign during French and Indian Wars, 1757-60; mem. com. to explore and survey lands on Mississippi River which were claimed as bounties for veterans of French and Indian Wars, 1773; commd. lt. col. Continental Army, 1775; took charge defensive works around Boston and N.Y.C., 1775-76; chief engr. with rank of col., 1776; served under Gates in campaign against Burgoyne; rebuilt fortifications at West Point, 1779; commd. brig. gen., 1783; chmn. of an officers' orgn., framed Newburgh Petition (on behalf of land bounties for revolutionary vets.), 1783; undertook survey and sale of lands in Me. belonging to Mass.; surveyor of Western lands, 1785; an organizer of Ohio Co., purpose to colonize on North bank of Ohio River, led colony to Marietta, O., 1788, laid out town, 1st organized territory of N.W.; judge of N.W. Territory, 1790-96; commd. brig. gen. U.S. Army, 1792; made treaty at Vincennes with lower Wabash Indian tribes, 1792; took charge important surveys in neighborhood of Marietta, circa 1794; surveyor gen. U.S., 1796-1803; del. to Ohio Constl. Conv., 1802. Died Marietta, O., May 4, 1824.

PYNCHON, John, mcht.; b. Chelmsford, Essex, Eng., circa 1626; s. William and Anna (Andrew) P.; m. Amy Willys, Oct. 20, 1645; children—Joseph, John, Mary, William and Mehitable (both died in infancy). Inherited profitable business from father (founder Springfield, Mass.), 1652, extended family fur monopoly; assistant upper house Mass. Legislature, 1662-1701; lt. Train Band, 1653, promoted capt., 1657; built 1st brick house in the valley, 1662; established friendly relations with Mohawk Indians, 1680; apptd. to establish boundary line between Mass. and Conn., 1680. Died Jan. 28, 1703.

PYNCHON, William, colonial ofcl., trader, b. Eng., 1590; s. John and Frances (Brett) P.; m. Anna Andrew; m. 2d, Frances Sanford; at least 3 children. Came to Am. in Winthrop fleet, 1630, settled 1st, Dorchester, Mass.; started fur trading operations, Roxbury, Mass.; an original patentee Mass. Bay Colony, asst. treas., 1630-36, treas., 1632-34; commr. to govern new settlement of Conn., 1636; one of 1st settlers, Spring field, Conn.; magistrate of Conn., 1636-38; mem.

Mass. Bd. of Assistants, 1642-51; author The Meritorius Price of Our Redemption (attacking current orthodox view of atonement), 1650, denounced heretic by colonial church authority as a result of this tract; sailed for Eng., 1652. Died Wraysbury, nr. Windsor, Eng., Oct. 29, 1662.

Q

QUACKENBUSH, Stephen Platt, naval officer; b. Albany, N.Y., Jan. 23, 1823; s. John N. and Nancy (Smith) Q.; m. Cynthia Herrick Wright, Jan. 18, 1849, 3 children. Commd. midshipman U.S. Navy, 1840, passed midshipman, 1846; served in Mexican War, then in various squadrons and posts throughout world; commd. lt., 1855, at Phila. Naval Yard, 1857-58, commanded gunboat Delaware, 1861; commd. lt. comdr., 1862, engaged in blockade duty and coastal operations against Confederate forts, lost right leg in patrol action on James River, Va., 1864; on duty with Atlantic Squadron, 1866-72; commanded ship New Hampshire, 1873-75; commanded Pensacola (Fla.) Naval Sta., 1880-82; commd. comdr., 1866, commodore, 1880, rear adm., 1884, ret., 1885. Died Washington, D.C., Feb. 4, 1890; buied Oak Hill Cemetery, Washington.

QUANTRILL, William Clarke, outlaw; b. Canal Dover, O., July 31, 1837; s. Thomas Henry and Caroline (Clark) Q. Settled in Kan., 1857; travelled to Utah with an army provision train, 1858; gambled under name Charley Hart, Salt Lake City, Utah; taught sch., Kan., 1859-60; fled when accused of murder and horse theft; betrayed plot of 5 abolitionists to seize and free slaves, 3 were killed; connected with Confederate Army during Civil War; chief of a band of guerrillas which plundered Unionist communities in Mo. and Kan.; part of Confederate force which captured Independence (Mo.), 1862; commd. capt. Confederate Army; pillaged Lawrence (Kan.) with a force of 450 men, killed about 150 people, 1863; defeated a body of Union cavalry, killed 17 musicians and non-combatants; fatally wounded, Taylorsville, Ky., May 10, 1865. Died Louisville, Ky., June 6, 1865.

QUARLES, Tunstall, congressman, lawyer; b. King William County, Va., circa 1770; attended local schs.; studied law. Admitted to bar, practiced law; mem. Ky. Ho. of Reps., 1796, 1811-12, 28, speaker, 1828; moved to Somerset, Pulaski County, Ky.; armed and equipped at his own expense a company of 2d Regt. Ky. Militia, also in command; apptd. circuit judge by Ky. gov.; mem. U.S. Ho. of Reps. (Democrat) from Ky., 15th-16th congresses, 1817-June 15, 1820 (resigned); apptd. receiver public moneys for Cape Girardeau Land District, Jackson, Mo., 1821-24; returned to Somerset, practiced law, became farmer; Dem. presdl. elector, 1829; mem. Ky. Senate, 1840. Died Somerset, Jan. 7, 1855; buried old Baptist Cemetery.

QUARTER, William, clergyman; b. Kings County, Killurine, Ireland, Jan. 21, 1806; s. Michael and Ann (Bennet) Q.; ed. Mt. St. Mary's Coll., Emmitsburg, Md. Came to U.S., 1822; ordained priest Roman Catholic Ch., 1829; pastor St. Mary's Ch., N.Y.C., 1833; 1st Roman Cath. bishop of Chgo., 1844-48, established U. of St. Mary's of Lake, introduced Sisters of Mercy of Pitts. as tchrs. for parochial schs. and orphanages, built several chs. including St. Peter's and St. Joseph's; obtained legislative enactment which incorporated bishops of Chgo. as corporation to hold diocesan properties; inaugurated 1st diocesan theol. confs. in U.S. Died Chgo., Apr. 10, 1848.

QUARTLEY, Arthur, artist; b. Paris, France, May 24, 1839; s. Frederick W. and Ann (Falkard) Q.; m. Laura Delamater, 3 children. Came to Peekskill, N.Y., 1851; began Eemmart & Quartley, sign painting firm, Balt., 1862; opened an art studio, NY.C., 1875; became asso. N.A.D., 1879, academician, 1886; paintings include: Morning Effect, North River, 1877; Queen's Birthday, 1883; Dignity and Impudence. Died N.Y.C., May 19, 1886.

QUEEN, Walter, naval officer; b. Washington, D.C., Oct. 6, 1824; s. John W. and Mary (Wells) Q.; m. Christiana Crosby, Commd. midshipman U.S. Navy, 1841; served in West India Squadron, 1841-43, East India Squadron, 1843-45; fought in battles of Palo Alto, Tampico and Vera Cruz during Mexican War; promoted lt., 1855; participated in bombardment of Ft. Jackson, Ft. St. Phillip, Vicksburg, capture of New Orleans, during Civil War; promoted lt. comdr., 1862; ordnance insp. Scott Foundry, Reading, Pa., 1865-67; promoted comdr., 1866, capt., 1874, commodore, 1884, rear adm., 1886; ret., 1886. Died Washington, Oct. 24, 1893; buried Arlington (Va.) Nat. Cemetery.

QUELCH, John, pirate; b. London, Eng., circa 1665, Chosen capt. by mutinous crew of brigantine Charles, 1703; captured and looted 9 Portuguese ships, 1703-04; brought to trial in Boston as a pirate, 1704. Hung on the gallows, Boston, June 30, 1704.

QUESNAY, Alexandre-Marie, army officer; b. Saint-Germain-en-Viry, France, Nov. 23, 1755; s. Blaise and Catherine (Deguillon) Q.; m. Catherine Cadier, 1 son. Arrived in Va., 1777; served as capt. Continental Army, 1777-78; conducted a sch., Phila., 1780-84; produced 1st French play in Am. (Beaumarchais's Eugenie); returned to France, 1786; proposed an Acad. of U.S.A., including an extensive system of schs. and univs. and a learned soc. for advancement of art and science at Richmond (Va.), plan rejected by Pres. Jefferson who felt that the U.S. was too poor to support such a program. Died St. Maurice, France, Feb. 8, 1820.

QUIDOR, John, artist; b. Tappan, N.Y., Jan. 26, 1801; s. Peter and Maria (Smith) Q. Moved to N.Y.C., 1826; decorated stage coaches and fire engines; exhibited paintings in N.A.D., 1828-39; painted scenes from books by Washington Irving; paintings include: Peter Stuyvesant's Journey up the Hudson; Ichabod Crane Pursued by the Headless Horseman; The Return of Rip Van Winkle. Died Jersey City, N.J., Dec. 13, 1881.

QUIMBY, Phineas Parkhurst, mental healer; b. Lebanon, N.H., Feb. 16, 1802; s. Jonathan and Susannah (White) Q.; m. Susannah Haraden, 4 children. Apprenticed as a clockmaker; became interested in mesmerism, 1838; abandoned clockmaking to give public exhbns. of mesmerism; gave up mesmerism to devote himself to mental healing, 1847; believed all disease was on mental orgin; one of his patients was Mary Baker Eddy (founder Christian Science), 1862, 64; his theories strongly influenced her and served as the basis for her doctrine. Died Jan. 16, 1866.

QUINAN, John Russell, physician, educator; b. Lancaster, Pa., Aug. 7, 1822; s. Rev. Thomas Henry and Eliza (Hamilton) Q.; attended Marietta (O.) Coll.; M.D., Jefferson Med. Coll., Phila., 1844; m. Elizabeth Lydia Billingsley, Aug. 31, 1845, 10 children. Supt. schs. Calvert County (Md.), 1860-65; mem. Med. and Chirurg. Faculty of Md., both v.p. and pres., 1884; lectr. on med. jurisprudence Women's Med. Coll., Balt., 1883-85. Author: Medical Annals of Baltimore from 1608 to 1880 (most important work), 1884; also articles for An Illustrated Encyclopaedic Medical Dictionary, 4 vols., 1888-94. Died Nov. 11, 1890.

QUINBY, Isaac Ferdinand, army officer, educator; b. Morris County, N.J., Jan. 29, 1821; s. Isaac and Sarah (De Hart) Q.; grad. U.S. Mil. Acad., 1843; m. Elizabeth Gardner, Oct. 6, 1848, 13 children. Instr. mathematics U.S. Mil. Acad., 1845, asst. prof. natural philosophy, 1845-47; prof. mathematics, natural and exptl. philosophy U. Rochester (N.Y.), 1851-61, 1861-62, 69-77; raised 13th N.Y. Volunteer Regt., 1861, 1st U.S. force to enter Balt. after attack on 6th Mass. Regt., reestablished order in Balt.; led regt. in Battle of Bull Run, 1861; brig. gen. U.S. Volunteers, 1862, command Dist. of the Miss., later 7th Div., Army of Tenn.; commanded Yazoo Pass expdn., 1863; provost marshal 28th Congl. Dist. in N.Y., 1864-65; U.S. marshal for No. Dist. of N.Y., 1869; surveyor City of Rochester, 1885-89; trustee Soldiers Home, Bath, N.Y., v.p., 1879-86. Died Rochester, Sept. 18, 1891.

QUINCEY, Josiah, lawyer, patroit; b. Boston, Feb. 23, 1744; s. Josiah and Hannah (Sturgis) Q.; B.A., Harvard, 1763, M.A., 1766; m. Abigail Phillips, Oct. 26, 1769, 2 children including Josiah. Wrote several essays on the Non-importation Agreement and other questions on strongly patriotic aide, including "An Address of the Merchants, Traders and Freeholders of the Town of Boston; signed his articles "An Independent" or "An Old Man"; with John Adams undertook task of defending British soldiers accused of Boston Massacre, 1770; became one of the leaders of patriot cause; went on mission to Eng. to argue cause of the colonies, 1774-75. Author: Observations of the Act of Parliament Commonly Called the Boston Port Bill with Thoughts on Civil Society and Standing Armies (his chief polit. work). 1774; Reports of Cases . . . In the Superior Court of Judicature of the Province of Massachusetts Bay between 1761 and 1772, printed in 1865. Died at sea, Apr. 26, 1775.

QUINCY, Edmund, reformer, editor, author; b. Boston, Feb. 1, 1808; s. Josiah and Eliza Susan (Morton) Q.; grad. Harvard, 1827, M.A., 1830; m. Lucilla P. Parker, Oct. 14, 1833. Mem. Mass. Anti-Slavery Soc., 1837, corr. sec., 1844-53; mem. Am. Anti-Slavery Soc., 1838, v.p., 1853, 56-59; prominent mem. Non-Resistance Soc., 1839; asso. (with William Lloyd Garrison and Maria Weston Chapman) in conducting newspaper Non Resistant, 1839-42; editor Abolitionist, 1839; contbr. to Liberty Bell Mag., 1839-56; editor Anti-Slavery Standard, 1844; conducted Liberator, 1843, 46, 47; fellow Am. Acad. Arts and Scis.; rec. sec. Mass. Hist. Soc.; mem. Am. Philos. Soc.; bd. overseers Harvard Coll. Author: Wensley, a Story Without a Moral, 1854; The Haunted Adjutant and Other Stories (some of his best short stories), 1885; co-author Life of Josiah Quincy, 1867, Editor: Speeches Delivered in the Congress of the United States: by Josiah Quincy, 1874. Died Dedham, Mass., May 17, 1877.

QUINCY, Josiah, congressman, coll. pres.; b. Boston, Feb. 4, 1772; s. Josiah, Jr. and Abigail (Phillips) Q.; grad. Harvard, 1790; M.A., Princeton, 1796; m. Eliza Susan Morton, June 6, 1797, 5 children. Admitted to Boston bar, 1793; mem. Mass. Senate, 1804-05, 13-20; mem. U.S. Ho. of Reps. (Federalist) from Mass., 9th-12th congresses, 1805-13, minority leader, opposed Embargo and non-intercourse system; opposed admission of La. to Union, 1811; mem. Mass. Ho. of Reps., 1821-22, speaker, 1822; judge Boston Municipal Ct., 1822; mayor Boston, 1823-29, during his adminstrn. Faneuil Hall Market was built, water and sewer systems introduced, fire dept. reorganized; pres. Harvard, 1829-45. Author: The History of Harvard University, 1840; A Municipal History of the Town and City of Boston, 1852. Died Quincy, Mass., July 1, 1864; buried Mt. Auburn Cemetery, Cambridge, Mass.

QUINLAN, John, clergyman; b. Cloyne, Cork, Ireland, Oct. 19, 1826; came to U.S., 1844; attended Mt. St. Mary's Coll., Emmitsburg, Md. Ordained priest Roman Catholic Ch., Cincinnati, 1853; pastor and missionary in Cincinnati area; rector Mt. St. Mary of the West Sem., 1854-59; consecrated bishop of Mobile (Ala.), 1859. Died Mobile, Mar. 9, 1883.

QUINN, Terence John, congressman; b. Albany, N.Y., Oct. 16, 1836; ed. pvt. sch., Boy's Acad., Albany. In brewery business with his father, became sr. mem. of firm; 2d lt. Company B, 25th Regt., N.Y. State Militia Volunteers at outbreak Civil War, ordered to defense of Washington, D.C., 1861, assigned to duty at Arlington Heights; credited with having captured 1st prisoner in war; mem. Albany Common Council, 1869-72; mem. N.Y. State Assembly, 1873; mem. U.S. Ho. of Reps. (Democrat) from N.Y., 45th Congress, 1877-78. Died Albany, June 18, 1878; buried St. Agnes' Cemetery.

QUINTARD, Charles Todd, physician, clergyman; b. Stamford, Conn., Dec. 22, 1824; s. Isaac and Clarissa (Hoyt) Shaw Q.; M.D., U. Med. Coll. (now part of N.Y.U.), 1847; D.D. (hon.), Columbia, 1866; LL.D. (hon.), Cambridge (Eng.) U., 1868; m. Katherine Hand, 3 children. Prof. physiology and path. anatomy Memphis, (Tenn.) Med. Coll., 1851; an editor Memphis Medical Recorder, circa 1851; ordained deacon Episcopal Ch., 1855; priest and rector Calvary Ch., Memphis, 1856; served as chaplain 1st Tenn. Regt., 1861; bishop of Tenn., 1865-98; adherent of Oxford movement; attended every Pan-Anglican Conf., 1867-97; chaplain Order Knights St. John of Jerusalem, assisted in installing Prince of Wales as grand prior, 1888; 2d founder U. of South at Sewanee (had been ruined during Civil War), elected vice chancellor, opened coll. to students, 1868, managed it until 1872. Died Feb. 15, 1898.

QUITMAN, John Anthony, gov. Miss., congressman; b. Rhinebeck, N.Y., Sept. 1, 1798; s. Rev. Frederick Henry and Anna (Hueck) Q.; grad. Hartwick Sem., 1816; m. Eliza Turner, Dec. 24, 1824, 4 children. Instr., Mt. Airy Coll., Pa., 1818; admitted to bar, 1821, moved to Natchez, Miss.; mem. Miss. Ho. of Reps., 1826-27; grand master Miss. Masons, 1826-38, 40, 45; chancellor Miss., 1828-35; supporter of nullification, 1834; mem. Miss. Senate, 1835-36, became pres., Dec. 1835; acting gov. Miss., 1835-36; served as brig. gen. Volunteers, participated in Battle of Monterey, promoted maj. gen. U.S. Army, 1847; gov. Miss., 1850-51; mem. U.S. Ho. of Reps. from Miss., 34th-35th congresses, 1855-58. Died "Monmouth," nr. Natchez, July 17, 1858; buried Natchez City Cemetery.

R

RADCLIFF, Jacob, jurist, mayor N.Y.C.; b. Rhinebeck, N.Y., Apr. 20, 1764; s. William and Sarah (Kip) R.; grad. Princeton, 1783; m. Juliana Smith, 2 daus. Admitted to N.Y. bar, 1786; mem. N.Y. Assembly, 1794-95; asst. atty. gen. N.Y., 1796-98; justice N.Y. Supreme Ct., 1798-04; codified (with James Kent) Laws of the State of New York, 2 vols., 1802; founder (with Anthony Dey and Richard Varick) Jersey City, 1804; mem. N.Y. Com. of Correspondence of Federalist party, 1808, 12; mayor N.Y.C., 1810-11, 15-18, commr. to decide question of land for Bklyn. Navy Yard; granted certificates of freedom to many Negroes; del. from N.Y.C. to N.Y. State Constl. Conv., 1821; trustee Columbia Coll., 1805-17; practiced law while not holding public office. Died Troy, N.Y., May 6, 1844.

RADFORD, William, congressman, mcht.; b. Poughkeepsie, N.Y., June 24, 1814; had limited schooling. Moved to N.Y.C., 1829, became mcht.; mem. U.S. Ho. of Reps. (Democrat) from N.Y., 38th-39th congresses, 1863-67. Died Yonkers, N.Y., Jan. 18, 1870; buried Old Presbyn. Cemetery, Westfield, Union County, N.J.

RADFORD, William, naval officer; b. Fincastle, Va., Sept. 9, 1809; s. John and Harriet (Kennerly) R.; m. Mary Elizabeth Lovell, Nov. 21, 1848, 6 children. Apptd. midshipman U.S. Navy, 1825, commd. lt., 1837, comdr. 1855, commodore, 1863, rear adm. 1866; served in various capacities in West Indies, Mediterranean and Pacific; participated in Mexican War; lighthouse insp. at N.Y., 1858-59, 61-62; comdr. steam sloop Dacotah, (1st Am. naval expdn. up Yangtse River to Hankow), 1860; comdr. Cumberland at Hampton Roads, 1862; exec. N.Y. Navy Yard, 1862-64; comdr. New Ironsides (leader ironclads in attacks on Ft. Fisher), 1864, 1865; comdr. Atlantic Squadron, 1865, Washington (D.C.) Navy Yard and European Squadron, 1869-70. Died Washington, D.C., Jan. 8, 1890.

RADISSON, Pierre Esprit, explorer; b. probably Lyons, France, circa 1636; s. Pierre Esprit and Madeline (Hainault) R.; m. Miss Kirke, 1672. Arrived in Canada, 1651; captured by Iroquis Indians, 1862; entered Minn. region (with brother-in-law Médard Chouart, 1st white men to do so), 1659-60, entered service of the English, circa 1661; made report of expdn. to entrance of Hudson's Straits (led to founding of Hudson Bay Co., 1670); visited Hudson's Bay, 1670, 72; made several more voyages for Hudson Bay Co., circa 1684. Author: Voyages of Peter Esprit Radisson, published 1885. Died 1710.

RAE, John, physician, economist; b. Footdee, Aberdeen, Scotland, June 1, 1796; s. John and Margaret (Cuthbert) R.; M.A., Marischal Coll., 1815; studied medicine U. Edinburgh (Scotland). Came to Can., 1821; conducted pvt. sch., Williamstown, Can., circa 1821-31; headmaster Gore Dist. Grammar Sch., Hamilton, Ont., Can., circa 1834-36, 39-48; came to U.S., circa 1848; sailed as ship's doctor in ship Brutus from Panama to Cal., circa 1848; taught sch., Sutter's Creek, Cal., 1849-51; went to Sandwich Islands, 1851, became med. agt., later dist. justice Island of Maui; economist, worked out time discount theory of interest. Author: Statement of Some New Principles on the Subject of Political Economy, Exposing the Fallacies of the System of Free Trade, and of Some Other Doctrines Maintained in the "Wealth of Nations," 1834. Died Staten Island, N.Y., July 14, 1872.

RAFFEINER, John Stephen, clergyman; b. Walls, Austrian Tyrol, Dec. 26, 1785. Ordained priest Roman Catholic Ch., 1825; arrived in N.Y.C. 1833; served as vicar gen. for German immigrants under Bishop Hughes of N.Y., until 1853; built St. Nicholas Ch., N.Y.C., 1836; organized parishes, Roxbury, Mass., 1835, also Boston; instrumental in building St. John's Ch., N.Y.C., also Holy Trinity, Williamsburg, L.I., N.Y.; organizer 1st German congregations in Rochester, Utica, Inama and Buffalo (all N.Y.); vicar gen. Bklyn. under Bishop John Loughlin, 1853-61. Died July 16, 1861.

RAFINESQUE, Constantine Samuel, naturalist; b. Galata, Constantinople, Turkey, Oct. 22, 1783; s. G.F. Rafinesque; m. Josephine Vaccaro, 1809, 2 children including Emily. Came to U.S., 1802; collected bot. specimens, So. N.J. and Dismal Swamp of Va., 1804; went to Palermo, Sicily, 1805; sec., chancellor to Am. consul, Palermo, for a while; exporter squills, medicinal plants, Palermo, 1808; returned to U.S., 1815; explored Hudson Valley, Lake George, L.I. and other regions, 1815-18; prof. botany, natural history, modern langs. Transylvania U., 1818-26; advocated Jussieu's method of classification. Wrote and published books and articles on botany, ichthyology, banking, econs. and other topics, including: Icthyologia Ohioensis, 1820; Medical Flora of the United States, 1828-30; (autobiography) A Life of Travels aand Researches in North America and South Europe, 1836. Died Phila., Sept. 18, 1840.

RAGUET, Condy, editor, economist; b. Phila., Jan. 28, 1784; son of Paul Claudius Raguet. Raised and commanded a company stationed nr. Wilmington, Del., during War of 1812; admitted to Pa. bar, 1816; mem. Pa. Senate, 1816; consul to Rio de Janeiro, Brazil, 1822-27; founded Free Trade Advocate and Jour. of Polit. Economy, 1829 (became Banner of the Constn., 1830-33, succeeded by The Examiner and Journal of Polit. Economy, 1833-35); propr. Phila. Gazette, 1835; founded Financial Register of the U.S., 1837-38; mem. Am. Philos. Soc. of Phila.; pres. Phila. C. of C., 1842. Author: The Principles of Free Trade, 1835; A Treatise on Currency and Banking, 1839, 40. Died Phila., Mar. 21, 1842.

RAINEY, Joseph Hayne, congressman; b. Georgetown, S. C., June 21, 1832. Born a slave, freedom purchased while still a child by his father; became a barber, Charleston, circa 1861; mem. exec. com. of newly formed Republican Party of S.C., 1867; del. from Georgetown to S.C. Constl. Conv., 1868; mem. S.C. Senate, 1869-70; mem. U.S. Ho. of Reps. (1st Negro mem.) from S.C., 41st-45th congresses, 1870-79, gave speeches in favor of legislation to enforce 14th Amendment, against Ku Klux Act, and for Civil Rights Bill; demanded that Negro be given all civil rights and admitted to all public places; most notable speech: eulogy of Charles Sumner at his death; spl. internal revenue agt. U.S. Treasury Dept. for S.C., 1879-81. Died Georgetown, Aug. 2, 1887; buried Baptist Cemetery, Georgetown.

RAINS, Gabriel James, army officer; b. Craven County, N.C., June 4, 1803; s. Gabriel M. and Hester (Ambrose) R.; grad. U.S. Mil. Acad., 1827; m. Mary Jane McClellan, 6 children. Commd. capt. U.S. Army, 1839; took part in Seminole War, 1839-42; brevetted maj., 1842; served in Mexican War; took part in 2d Seminole War, 1849-50; promoted lt. col., 1860; commd. brig. gen. Confederate States Army, 1861; in command at Yorktown, mined nearby waters, 1861-62; withdrew from Yorktown, 1862, left shells with percussion fuses in the road; employed early land mines at Battle of Williamsburg; in charge of Bur. of Conscription, Richmond, Va., 1863; given series of defense missions, 1863, let to assignment as supt. Torpedo Bur., Confederacy, 1864-65; arranged demolitions, mines and torpedo protection for Richmond, Mobile, Charleston, the James River; two of his operations blew up two U.S. barges and an ammunition warehouse, City Point, Va., 1864; clk. U.S. Quartermaster Dept., Charleston, S.C., 1877-80. Died Aiken, S.C., Aug. 6, 1881.

RAINS, George Washington, army officer, educator; b. Craven County, N.C., 1817; s. Gabriel M. and Hester (Ambrose) R.; grad. (1st in science studies), U.S. Mil. Acad., 1842; M.D. (hon.), Med. Coll. Va., 1867; m. Frances Josephine Ramsdell, Apr. 23, 1856. With Corps Engrs. U.S. Army, 1842, 4th Arty., 1843; asst. prof. chemistry, geology, mineralogy U.S. Mil. Acad., 1844-46; 1st lt. Mexican War; brevetted capt., 1847, maj., 1848; resigned 1856; pres. Washington Iron Works and Highland Iron Works, Newburgh, N.Y., 1856-61; commd. maj. Corps Arty., Confederate Army, 1861; lt. col., 1862, col., 1863; initiated wholesale collection of nitre from limestone caves in Tenn., Ala., Ga., N.C.; improvement in gunpowder plant efficiency patented in Confederate States Patent Office, 1864; in charge all munitions operations in Augusta, 1862, commanding officer troops at Augusta, 1864; prof. chemistry Med. Coll. Ga., 1866-94, dean, circa 1868-83, prof. emeritus, 1894-98; regent Acad. of Richmond County, 1867. Author: pamphlet Notes on Making Saltpetre from the Earth of the Caves, circa 1862; History of the Confederate Powder Works, 1882. Died nr. Newburgh, N.Y., Mar. 21, 1898.

RALE, Sébastien, clergyman; b. Pontarlier, France, circa 1654. Entered Jesuit order, 1675; instr. at Carpentras and Nîmes, 1677-84; came to do missionary work in Can., 1689, succeeded Marquette at Illinois mission; sent to Abnaki mission in what is now Me., 1693; converted entire tribe of Malecites; hostilities between France and Eng. led to Brit. agitation for his removal. Shot by British, Aug. 23, 1724.

RALEIGH, Sir Walter, statesman; b. Eng., circa 1552; attended Oxford (Eng.) U., circa 1570-72; m. Elizabeth Throckmorton. Served with Huguenot Army in France, 1569-70; served as statesman in Ireland, 1579-82; returned to Eng., 1582, became favorite of Queen Elizabeth; created knight, 1583; warden to Stanneries, 1585-87; capt. Queen's Guard, 1587-89; conceived and organized colonizing expdns. to Am. which ended with "lost colony" on Roanoke Island; recalled from privateering expdn. and imprisoned, 1592, won his liberty by quelling riots in Dartmouth, Eng.; mem. Parliament, 1592-95; attempted (with scholar Laurence Hemys) to find fabled El Dorado, 1595-96; made gov. of Jersey, 1600; imprisoned on treason charge, circa 1614-16; made another search for gold to the Orinoco, 1616-18; introduced tobacco into Eng.; executed upon demand of Spanish ambassador who claimed he had interferred with Spanish shipping. Author: (works including) Discovery of Guiana, 1596; History of the World (incomplete). Died Eng., 1618.

RALPH, James, author; b. N.J., 1695; m. Rebekah Ogden, before 1724, 1 dau., Mary. Went to Eng. with Benjamin Franklin, 1724; wrote The Tempest & Night, 1727; wrote original ballad opera The Fashionable Lady, (1st play by an American produced on London stage), 1730; wrote The Touchstone, 1728; Fielding's asst. in mgmt. Little Theatre, Haymarket, Eng., 1735-37; asst. editor (with Fielding) the Champion, 1739; employed by George Bubb Dodington, Eng., wrote several long polit. pamphlets, also editor Old England & The Remembrancer, 1742-circa 1751; wrote The History of England, 2 vols., 1744, 46; founded the Protester (in service of Duke of Bedford), 1753; joined staff of Monthly Review, 1756; wrote The Case of Authors by Profession, 1758; helped Benjamin Franklin prepare An Historical Review of the Constitution and Government of Pennsylvania, 1759; wrote for side which paid the most. Died Chiswick, Eng., Jan. 24, 1762.

RALSTON, William Chapman, banker, steamship owner; b. Wellsville, O., June 12, 1826; s. Robert and Mary (Chapman) R.; m. Elizabeth Fry, May 20, 1858, 4 children. Panama City agt. Garrison & Morgan steamship co., 1850-54, partner, 1854; instrumental in establishing banking firm Garrison, Morgan, Fretz & Ralston, 1856; organized (with D. O. Mills) Bank of Cal., 1864, pres., promoted unwarranted speculative schemes with bank's funds; owned interest in Comstock Lode, bank handled all Comstock Lode business; purchased (with assos.) additional mines, 1875; bank survived panic of 1873 but collapsed in 1875 because of his corrupt use of bank's money for personal profit; James G. Flood demanded $6,000,000, Aug. 1875; interested in building of railroads, established woolen mills, sugar refineries, silk factories, steamship lines to Australia and China; unsuccessful investor in Palace, Grand hotels. Died San Francisco, Aug. 27, 1875.

RAMAGE, John, painter; probably born Dublin, Ireland, circa 1748; attended sch. of Dublin Soc. of Art, circa 1763; m. Maria Victoria Ball, Mar. 8, 1776; m. 2d, Mrs. Taylor, circa 1777; m. 3d, Catharine Collins, Jan. 29, 1787. A goldsmith and miniature painter, Boston, 1775; commd. 2d lt. Loyal Irish Volunteers, 1776; leading miniature painter in N.Y.C., 1777-94, painted miniature of Washington, 1789; moved to Montreal, Can., because of debts contracted in N.Y., 1794. Died Montreal, Oct. 24, 1802; buried Christ Ch. Cemetery, Montreal.

RAMEE, Joseph Jacques, architect, landscape architect; b. Charlemont, Ardennes, France, Apr. 18, 1764; at least 1 child, Daniel. Inspector bldgs. at court Count of Artois, 1780-92; served as maj. French Army of Charles Dumouriez, 1792; architect, landscape designer in northeastern Germany and Denmark, 1794-1811; architect Hamburg (Germany) Bourse, designer Chateau of Sophienholm (Denmark); worked in Am., 1811-16, Belgium and Germany, 1816-23, France, 1823-42; most important work in Am. was layout and 1st bldgs. for Union Coll., Schenectady, N.Y. (1st coll. in Am. to be built from an architect's carefully studied and composed plan;. Author: (collection of his designs) Parcs et Javdins composees et Executees dans Differens Countrées de l'Europe et des États Unis d'Amerique, par Joseph Ramée, arthitecte (Parks and Gardens Designed and Executed in Different Countries of Europe and the United States of America, by Joseph Ramée, architect). Died Beaurains nr. Noyon, France, May 18, 1842.

RAMSAY, Alexander, anatomist; b. Edinburgh, Scotland, circa 1754; studied anatomy under Cruikshank, Baille and Munroe; M.D. (hon.), U. St. Andrews, 1805. Began teaching anatomy, Edinburgh, 1790, founded an anat. soc.; came to U.S., circa 1801, settled in Fryeburg, Me., founded unsuccessful sch. of anatomy; practiced medicine and lectured on anatomy in region, 1801-08; lectr. Dartmouth Med. Sch., 1808; lectured in Europe, 1810-16; lectured on natural philosophy in U.S., 1816-24. Author: Anatomy of the Heart, Cranium, and Brain, 1812. Died Parsonfield, Me., Nov. 24, 1824; buried Fryeburg.

RAMSAY, David, Continental congressman, physician, historian; b. Drumore Twp., Lancaster County, Pa., Apr. 2, 1749; s. James and Jane (Montgomery) R.; grad. Princeton, 1765; M.D., Coll. of Pa., 1772; m. Sabina Ellis, Feb. 1775; m. 2d, Frances Witherspoon, 1783; m. 3d, Martha Laurens, Jan. 23, 1787. Mem. S.C. Legislature, 1776-80, 81-82, 84-90; del. to Continental Congress, 1782-85; mem. S.C. Senate, 1792, 94, 96, pres. 3 terms. Author: Review of the Improvements, Progress, and State of Medicine in the XVIIIth Century; History of The Revolution of S.C., 2 vols., 1785; History of the American Revolution, 2 vols., 1789; History of S.C., 2 vols., 1809; The History of the United States, 3 vols., 1816-17. Died Charleston, S.C., May 8, 1815.

RAMSAY, George Douglas, army officer; b. Dumfries, Va., Feb. 21, 1802; s. Andrew and Catherine (Graham) R.; grad. U.S. Mil. Acad., 1820; m. Frances Whetcroft Munroe, Sept. 23, 1830; m. 2d, Eliza Hennen Gales, June 28, 1838; 6 children including Francis Monroe. Commd. 1st lt., 1st Arty., 1826, adjutant to regt., 1833; commd. capt. of ordnance, 1835-61, commanded arsenals in Washington, D.C., N.Y., Pa., N.J., Ga., 1835-45; brevetted maj. for distinguished service at Battle of Monterey, 1847; chief of ordnance, 1847 48; maj. 1861, lt. col., 1861, col. ordnance, 1863, brig. gen. and chief of ordnance U.S. Army, 1864; insp. of arsenals, 1864-66; brevetted maj. gen., 1865 Died May 23, 1882.

RAMSAY, Nathaniel, army officer, Continental congressman; b. Lancaster County, Pa., May 1, 1741; s. James and Jane (Montgomery) R.; grad. Coll. of N.J. (now Princeton), 1767; m. Mary Jane Peale, 1771; m. 2d, Charlotte Hall, 1792; 3 children. Del to Md. Conv., 1775, signer Md. Declaration of Freemen; mem. Continental Congress from Md., 1775, 85-87; capt. Smallwood's Md. Regt., 1776; commd. lt. col. 3d Md. Regt., Continental Army, 1776-81; served at Battle of Monmouth, 1778, helped check retreat begun by Gen. Charles Lee; U.S. marshal. Dist. of Md., 1790-98; naval officer Port of Balt., 1794-1817. Died Balt., Oct. 24, 1817; buried 1st Presbyn. Ch., Balt.

RAMSEUR, Stephen Dodson, army officer; b. Lincolnton, N.C., May 31, 1837; s. Jacob A. and Lucy M. (Wilfong) R.; grad. U.S. Mil. Acad., 1860; m. Ellen E. Richmond, Oct. 22, 1863, 1 child. Served from lt. arty. to capt. N.C. battery in Confederate Army, 1861; commd. col. 49th N.C. Inf., 1863; commd. brig. gen.; served in battles of Gettysburg, Wilderness, Spotsylvania; promoted maj. gen., 1864. Died of wound received at Cedar Creek, Va., Oct. 20, 1864.

RAMSEY, James Gettys McGready, physician; railroad promoter; b. Knoxville, Tenn., Mar. 25, 1797; s. Francis Alexander and Peggy (Alexander) R.; B.A., Washington Coll. in Tenn., 1816; studied medicine U. Pa.; M.D. (hon.), Med. Coll. S.C., 1831; m. Margaret Barton Grozier, 1821, 11 children. Began med. practice, Knoxville, 1820; advocated establishment of railroad between Tennessee River and S. Atlantic seaboard; a dir. Louisville, Cincinnati & Charleston R.R.; agt. for Tenn. in financing completion of East Tenn. & Ga. R.R.; pres. Knoxville branches Southwestern R.R. Bank and Bank of Tenn.; supported Confederacy, slavery and African slave trade; pres. Tenn. Hist. Soc., 1874-84. Author: The Annals of Tennessee to the End of the Eighteenth Century, 1853. Died Knoxville, Apr. 11, 1884.

RAMSEY, Robert, congressman; b. Warminster Twp., Bucks County, Pa., Feb. 15, 1780; attended public schs., Hartsville, Pa. Mem. Pa. Ho. of Reps., 1825-31; mem. U.S. Ho. of Reps. (Whig) from Pa., 23d, 27th congresses, 1833-35, 41-43; became farmer. Died Warwick, Bucks County, Dec. 12, 1849; buried Neshaminy Cemetery.

RAMSEY, William, congressman, lawyer; b. Sterretts Gap, Cumberland County, Pa., Sept. 7, 1779; attended public schs.; studied law. Apptd. surveyor Cumberland County, 1803; clk. Cumberland County Orphans Ct.; admitted to bar, practiced in Carlisle, Pa.; mem. U.S. Ho. of Reps. (Democrat) from Pa., 20th-22d congresses, 1827-31. Died Carlisle, Sept. 29, 1831; buried Ashland Cemetery.

RAMSEY, William Sterrett, congressman; b. Carlisle, Cumberland County, Pa., June 12, 1810; classical studied in U.S., Europe. Attaché, Am. legation, London, Eng.; mem. U.S. Ho. of Reps. (Democrat) from Pa., 26th Congress, 1829-40. Died Balt., Oct. 17, 1840; buried Ashland Cemetery, Carlisle.

RAND, Addison Crittenden, mfr.; b. Westfield, Mass., Sept. 17, 1841; s. Jasper and Lucy (Whipple) R. Took over his father's whip-mfg. bus., 1865; moved to N.Y., founded (with his brother) Laflin & Rand Powder Co., 1871; organizer, pres. Rand Drill Co., 1871; substituted rock drill for the hammer and chisel in mining operations; a founder, 1st treas. Engrs. Club of N.Y. Died N.Y.C., Mar. 9, 1900.

RAND, Edward Sprague, mcht., wool mfr., legislator; b. Newburyport, Mass., June 23, 1782; s. Edward and Ruth (Sprague) R.; m. Hannah Pettingill, Apr. 6, 1807, 3 children. Started bus. as East India mcht. and gen. freighter, 1814; pres. Mechanics Bank of Newburyport, 1825-27; purchased (with others) woolen mill, became pres., 1821, developed it into Salisbury Mills; selectman Newburyport, 1813-15; mem. lower br. Mass. Legislature, 1815-16, 19, Mass. Senate, 1822; del. gen. convs. Protestant Episcopal Ch. Died Oct. 22, 1863.

RAND, John Goffe, artist; b. Bedford, N.H., 1801. Began portrait painting, circa 1825; exhibited at Boston Athenaeum, 1828-29; worked in Charleston, S.C., 1831; moved to N.Y.C., 1833; exhibited at N.A.D., elected asso. mem., 1833; lived in London Eng., exhibited at Royal Acad., 1840; developed screw-top compressible paint tube; made 2d visit to Eng., in 1840's; established himself as portrait painter, N.Y.C., circa 1848. Died Roslyn, L.I., N.Y., Jan. 21, 1873.

RANDALL, Alexander, congressman, lawyer; b. Annapolis, Md., Jan. 3, 1803; grad. St. John's Coll., Annapolis, 1822; studied law. Admitted to bar, practiced in Annapolis, 1824; mem. U.S. Ho. of Reps. (Whig) from Md., 27th Congress, 1841-43; became banker, Annapolis; auditor Md. High Ct. of Chancery, 1844-48; del. Md. Constl. Conv., 1850; atty. gen. Md., 1864-68. Died Annapolis, Nov. 21, 1881; buried St. Anne's Cemetery.

RANDALL, Alexander Williams, gov. Wis.; b. Ames Montgomery County, N.Y., Oct. 31, 1819; s. Phineas and Sarah (Beach) R.; m. Mary C. Van Vechten, 1842; m. 2d, Helen M. Thomas, 1863. Admitted to bar, 1840; formerly a Whig, became Democrat by 1845; del. Wis. Constl. Conv., 1846, successfully supported resolution submitting separately question of Negro suffrage; mem. Wis. Assembly (Democrat), 1848; asso. justice Milw. Circuit Ct., 1855-57; gov. Wis. (Republican), 1857-61; enlisted militia regt., 1861; enthusiastically supported Pres. Lincoln and his calls for mobilization of nat. resources; minister to Rome, 1862-63; 1st asst. postmaster-gen., 1863-65, head U.S. Post Office Dept., 1865-69. Died Elmira, N.Y., July 26, 1872.

RANDALL, Benjamin, religious leader; b. New Castle, N.H., Feb. 7, 1749; s. Capt. Benjamin and Margaret (Mordantt) R.; m. Joanna Oram, Nov. 28, 1771, 9 children. Converted to Methodism, 1770; united with Congregational Ch. at New Castle, 1772-75; asso. with small Baptist group, New Lights, 1775; adopted believer's immersion, 1776; publicly ordained to work of an evangelist, 1780; drew up covenant which became known as Freewill Baptist (later Free Baptist, renewal of Great Awakening), 1870; itinerant minister and missionary preaching, baptizing, establishing chs. throughout New Eng., 1780-1808; devised system of quarterly meetings, 1783, also yearly meeting, 1792; important effect of his work was modification of Northern Baptists' Calvinism. Died New Durham,N.H., Oct. 22, 1808.

RANDALL, Benjamin, congressman, lawyer; b. Topsham, Me. (then Mass.), Nov. 14, 1789; grad. Bowdoin Coll., 1809; studied law. Admitted to bar, 1812, practiced in Bath, Me.; served in Col. Reed's Regt., Me. Militia, stationed at Coxes Head, 1814; mem. Me. Senate, 1833, 35, 38; mem. U.S. Ho. of Reps. (Whig) from Me., 26th-27th congresses, 1838-43; apptd. collector of customs Port of Bath, 1849-59. Died Bath, Oct. 11, 1859; buried Maple Grove Cemetery.

RANDALL, David Austin, clergyman; born Colchester, Connecticut, January 14, 1813; son of James and Joanna (Pemberton) R.; Doctor of Divinity, Denison University, 1870; m. Mary Ann Witter, Mar. 3, 1837; m. 2d, Mrs. Harriet Bronson, June 6, 1843. Licensed to preach Baptist Ch., Gorham, N.Y., 1838; pastor Richfield (O.) Bapt. Ch., 1839, Medina (O.) Bapt. Ch., 1840-45; active in temperance movement, 1840's; editor Christian Journal (Bapt. organ), Columbus, O., 1845-58; chaplain Ohio Hosp. for Insane, 1862-66; pastor, Columbus, O., 1885-66; partner Randall & Aston, book dealers, Columbus; v.p. 1st Nat. Bank, Columbus. Author: The Wonderful Tent, 1885. Died Columbus, June 27, 1884; buried Columbus.

RANDALL, Henry Stephens, agriculturist, educator; b. Brookfield, Madison County, N.Y., May 3, 1811; s. Roswell and Harriet (Stephens) R.; grad. Union Coll., 1830; m. Jane Rebecca Polhemus, Oct. 4, 1834, 3 children. Admitted to bar, 1834; youngest regular del. to Democratic Nat. Conv., 1835; supt. schs. Madison County (N.Y.), 1843-47; sec. state N.Y., also ex officio supt. public instrn., 1851-53; responsible for creation of a separate dept. public instrn. State of N.Y.; mem. Nat. Dem. Com. at Charleston, 1860; mem. N.Y. Legislature, 1871; corr. sec. N.Y. State Agrl. Soc.; proposed the N.Y. State Fair; editor sheep husbandry dept. Moore's Rural New Yorker, 1864-67. Author: The Life of Thomas Jefferson (the most detailed biography of Jefferson), 3 vols., 1858; The Practical Shepherd, 1863 (originally written as "Fine Wool Sheep Husbandry"). Died Cortland, N.Y., Aug. 14, 1876.

RANDALL, Robert Richard, privateer, mcht., philanthropist; b. N.J., 1750; s. Thomas and Gertrude (Crooke) R. Became mem. Marine Soc. in N.Y., 1771; privateer for Continental Army in Revolutionary War; partner (with father) in firm Randall, Son & Stewart, 1781; mem. N.Y. C. of C., 1788; following war Randall family bought several pieces of land in various parts N.Y.C., property willed to him by father; he in turn willed most of fortune to trust to provide asylum and hospital for aged, decrepit and worn-out seamen to be called Sailors' Snug Harbor. Died N.Y.C., June 1801.

RANDALL, Samuel, jurist; b. Sharon, Mass., Feb. 10, 1778; s. Joseph and Esther (Fisher) R.; grad. R.I. U. (now Brown U.), 1804; studied law, Providence, 1804-05; m. Patty Maxwell, 1809, 6 children. Taught at Warren (R.I.) Acad., 1805; justice of peace, postmaster Warren; a Republican; published the Telescope, the Telegraph, 1813-26; judge Bristol County (R.I.) Ct. of Common Pleas, 1822-24; justice R.I. Supreme Ct., 1824-33. Author: (plays) The Miser, The Sophomore. Died Mar. 5, 1864.

RANDALL, Samuel Jackson, congressman, state polit. leader; b. Phila., Oct. 10, 1828; s. Josiah and Ann (Worrell) R.; attended Univ. Acad., Phila.; m. Fannie Agnes Ward, June 24, 1851, 3 children. Mem. Phila. Common Council, 1852-55; mem. Pa. Senate, 1858-59; served with 1st Troop of Phila., U.S. Army, 1861, promoted capt., 1863; served as provost marshall, Battle of Gettysburg; mem. U.S. Ho. of Reps. from Pa. (Democrat), 38th-51st congresses, 1863-90, speaker, 1875-81, conducted filibusters against Civil Rights and Force bills, 1875, helped institute investigations of Credit Mobilier, Sanborn contracts and Pacific Mail subsidy, chmn. com. on appropriations, reduced total appropriations by $30,000,000, 1876, codified rules of Ho. of Reps:, 1880, strengthened speaker's power; del. to Nat. Dem. Conv., 1884, responsible for non-committal tariff plank; lost control of Dem. orgn. in Pa., 1887. Died Washington, D.C., Apr. 13, 1890; buried Phila.

RANDALL, Samuel Sidwell, ednl. adminstr.; b Norwich, N.Y., May 27, 1809; s. Perez and Betsey (Edmunds) R.; attended Hamilton Coll., 1824-circa 1826; m. Lucy Ann Breed, Oct. 29, 1829; m. 2d, Sarah Hubbell; 4 children. Admitted to N.Y. bar, 1830; clk. in dept. of common schools, 1837-41, gen. dep. supt., 1841-46, 49-52; frequent contbr. to Dist. Sch. Journal, editor for a time; asso. editor Am. Journal of Edn. and Coll. Review; commr. to embody in a single act and to report to legislature a common school code of state, made his report, 1852 (recommendations adopted by N.Y. Legislature, 1854-67; supt. Bklyn. Public Schs., 1853-54; supt. N.Y.C. Public Schools, 1854-70. Author: A Digest of the Common School System of the State of New York, 1844; History of the Common School System of the State of N.Y., 1871. Died N.Y.C., June 3, 1881.

RANDALL, William Harrison, congressman, lawyer; b. nr. Richmond, Madison County, Ky., July 15, 1812; studied law. Admitted to bar; practiced in London, Laurel County, Ky., 1835; clk. Laurel County circuit ct. and county ct., 1836-44; mem. U.S. Ho. of Reps. (Republican) from Ky., 38th-39th congresses, 1863-67; judge Ky. 15th Dist., 1870-80. Died London, Aug. 1, 1881; buried family cemetery, London.

RANDOLPH, Beverley, gov. Va.; b. Henrico County, Va., 1754; s. Col. Peter and Lucy (Bolling) R.; grad. Coll. William and Mary, 1771. Mem. Va. Gen. Assembly, various times during Revolutionary War; bd. visitors Coll. William and Mary, 1784; pres. Va. Exec. Council, 1787-88; 1st gov. State of Va. (under U.S. Constn.), 1788-91; his term marked by Indian trouble on Va. frontier and controversy with Pa. over state boundary. Died "Green Creek," Cumberland County, Va., 1797.

RANDOLPH, Edmund, lawyer; b. Richmond, Va., June 9, 1819; s. Peyton and Maria (Ward) R.; grad. Coll. William and Mary, 1836; studied law U. Va.; m. Thomassa Meaux, 2 daus. Practiced law, New Orleans; clk. U.S. Circuit Ct. for La.; moved to San Francisco, 1849; mem. Cal. Ho. of Reps. from San Francisco, 1849; asso. editor San Francisco Herald, 1850; partner (with R. A. Lockwood, Frank Tilford) in law firm, 1851; involved with William Walker in attempt to conquer Nicaragua, 1855-56. Died Sept. 8, 1861.

RANDOLPH, Edmund Jennings, sec. of state, gov. Va.; b. "Tazewell Hall" Williamsburg, Va., Aug. 10, 1753; s. John and Ariana (Jenings) R.; ed. Coll. William and Mary; m. Elizabeth Nicholas, Aug. 29, 1776, 4 children including Peyton, Edmund, Lucy (Randolph) Daniel. Served as a.d.c. to Washington, 1775-76; youngest mem. Va. Constl. Conv., 1776; atty. gen. Va., until circa 1782; mayor Williamsburg, 1776; mem. Continental Congress, 1779-82; gov. Va., 1786-88; del. to Annapolis Conv. and to Fed. Conv. of 1787, proposed Virginia Plan; declined to sign U.S. Constn. because feared danger of monarch in exec. dept.; advocated ratification of U.S. Constn. in Va. Conv. of 1788; atty. gen. of U.S., 1789-94; U.S. sec. of state, 1795, got rid of offensive French minister Edmond Charles Genet, advised Monroe on his negotiations with French govt.; conflict of opinion with U.S. envoys to Eng. (Jay, Hamilton) and envoy to France (Monroe) resulted in ineffectual term as sec. of state; wrote A Vindication of Mr. Randolph's Resignation, 1795; sr. counsel for Aaron Burr in treason trial. Died Clarke County, Va., Sept. 12, 1813.

RANDOLPH, Edward, colonial govt. ofcl.; b. Canterbury, Eng., July 9, 1632; s. Dr. Edmund and Deborah (Master) R.; studied Queens' Coll., Cambridge (Eng.) U.; m. Jane Gibbon, before 1660;

m. 2d, Grace Grenville, after 1679; m. 3d, Sarah (Backhouse) Platt, after 1682; 5 children. Carried royal instructions to Mass. requiring colonial govt. to send agts. to Eng. to answer complaint of Mason and Gorges heirs, 1675-76, made complete report of conditions in colony; arrived Boston and investigated conditions in N.H., Me., and Plymouth, wrote report to King denouncing colonists, 1676; wrote "Representation of Ye Affaires of New England" (attacked legality of Mass. charter), 1677; collector of customs throughout New Eng., 1678-89; landed in N.Y., 1679, inaugurated new govt. of N.H.; largely responsible for Mass. charter being declared forfeited, 1684; commd. sec. and register for dominion of New Eng., 1685-87; councilor in new royal govt., 1685-89; commd. sec. of enlarged jurisdiction after N.Y. and the Jerseys were added to Dominion of New Eng.; arrested Apr. 1689 after rebellion overthrew govt. of Dominion, freed in Eng., late 1689; surveyor gen. of customs for all N.Am. in all colonies, 1692-97, quarrelled constantly with authorities because of his attempts to enforce trade laws; imprisoned in Bermuda, 1699-1700; went to Eng. to attack colonies in Parliament; returned to Am., 1702. Died Apr. 1703.

RANDOLPH, George Wythe, Confederate sec. of war, army officer; b. "Monticello," Va., Mar. 10, 1815; s. Gov. Thomas Mann and Martha (Jefferson) R.; attended U. Va., 1837-39; m. Mary E. (Adams) Pope, circa 1852. Practiced law in Richmond, Va., 1849-61; organized Richmond Howitzers (arty. co.), 1861; peace commr. from Va. to U.S. Govt., 1861; secessionist to Va. Conf. of 1861; commd. col., 1861, promoted to chief of arty. under Magruder; promoted brig. general, 1862; sec. of war Confederate States Am., Mar. 22-Nov. 15, 1862. Died "Edgehill," Va., Apr. 3, 1867.

RANDOLPH, Jacob, physician; b. Phila., Nov. 25, 1796; s. Edward Fitz and Anna Julianna (Steel) R.; M.D., U: Pa., 1817; m. Sarah Emlen Physick, 1822. Practiced as surgeon, circa 1820-35; asst. in Almshouse Infirmary, Phila.; introduced new operation for removing stones from the bladder (lithotripsy), 1831; surgeon Pa. Hosp., 1835-48; prof. clin. surgery U. Pa., 1847-48; performed early radical operations, including amputation of the lower jaw for osteosarcoma, ligation of an external iliac aneurism. Author: A Memoir of the Life and Character of Philip Syng Physick, 1839; contbr. articles to Am. Jour. Med. Sci., N. Am. Med. and Surg. Jour., Med. Examiner. Died Phila., Feb. 29, 1848.

RANDOLPH, James Fitz, congressman; b. Middlesex County, N.J., June 26, 1791; had limited schooling; at least 1 son, Theodore Fitz. Learned printing trade. Editor New Brunswick (N.J.) Fredonian, 1812-42; U.S. collector internal revenue, 1815-46; clk. Ct. Common Pleas; mem. N.J. Ho. of Assembly, 1823-24; mem. U.S. Ho. of Reps. (filled vacancy) from N.J., 20th-22d congresses, Dec. 1, 1827-33; pres. bank, New Brunswick. Died Easton, Northampton County, Pa., Jan. 25, 1872; buried Easton Cemetery.

RANDOLPH, Sir John, colonial ofcl.; b. Turkey Island, Henrico County, Va., 1693; s. William and Mary (Isham) R.; attended Coll. William and Mary; studied law Gray's Inn, London, Eng., 1715-17; m. Susanna Beverly, before 1721, at least 2 children, John, Peyton. Admitted to English bar, 1717; clk. Va. Ho. of Burgesses, 1718-34, speaker, 1734-37; atty. gen Va., 1728; diplomat from Va. to London to obtain changes in tobacco trade laws, and in charter of Coll. William and Mary, 1728, 32; created knight, 1732; treas. Va., 1734-35. Author: Virginia Colonial Decisions, the Reports by Sir John Randolph and by Edward Barradall, 1728-1741, posthumously published 1909. Died Williamsburg, Va., Mar. 13, 1737.

RANDOLPH, John, colonial govt. ofcl.; b. "Tazewell Hall," Williamsburg, Va., 1727/28; s. Sir John and Susanna (Beverly) R.; grad. Coll. William and Mary; m. Ariana Jenings, circa 1752; children—Susanna, Ariana (Mrs. Wormley), Edmund Jennings. Admitted to bar, 1750; mem. Common Council of Williamsburg, Va., 1751; clk. Va. Ho. of Burgesses, 1752-56; Va. atty. gen. for the Crown, 1756-75; Loyalist during Revolution, fled to Eng., 1775; granted pension from Crown; headed movement of Loyalist refugees offering mil. service to King to defend Eng. against feared invasion by France. Author: A Treatise on Gardening (1st book on gardening published in colonies), 1793. Died Brompton, Eng., Jan. 31, 1784; buried Chapel of Coll. William and Mary, Va.

RANDOLPH, John (known as Randolph of Roanoke), senator, congressman, diplomat; b. Cawsons, Prince George County, Va., June 2, 1773; s. John and Frances (Bland) R.; attended Coll. of N.J. (now Princeton), 1787-88, Columbia, 1788-89, Coll. William and Mary, 1792-93. Mem. U.S. Ho. of Reps. from Va., 6th-12th, 14th, 16th-18th, 20th congresses, 1799-1813, 15-17, 19-25, 27-29. Jeffersonian leader Ho. of Reps., 1800-05, chmn. ways and means com., 1800-07, supervised passage of the Louisiana Purchase; manager unsuccessful impeachment proceedings against Justice Samuel Chase, 1804; broke with Jefferson, 1805, leading exponent States Rights doctrines, 1805-29; mem. U.S. Senate from Va., 1825-29; mem. Va. Constl. Conv., 1829-30; U.S. minister to Russia, 1830-31; suffered from periodical insanity, after 1818. Died Phila., May 24, 1833; buried Roanoke, Va., reinterred on capitol grounds, Richmond, Va.

RANDOLPH, Joseph Fitz, congressman, lawyer; b. N.Y.C., Mar. 14, 1803; had pvt. tutors, pvt. schs.; studied law. Admitted to bar, 1825, practiced in Freehold, N.J.; pros. atty. Monmouth County, circa 1836; mem. U.S. Ho. of Reps. (Whig) from N.J., 25th-27th congresses, 1837-43; moved to New Brunswick, N.J., 1843, practiced law; del. N.J. Constl. Conv., 1844; mem. com. apptd. by gov. to revise N.J. statutes, 1845; asso. justice N.J. Supreme Ct., 1845-52; del. Washington (D.C.) Peace Conv., 1861; moved to Jersey City, N.J., 1864; Democratic presdl. elector, 1868. Died Jersey City, Mar. 20, 1873; buried Easton (Pa.) Cemetery.

RANDOLPH, Peyton, pres. Continental Congress; b. "Tazewell Hall," Williamsburg, Va., Sept. 1721; s. Sir John and Susanna (Beverly) R.; grad. Coll. William and Mary, 1742; m. Elizabeth Harrison, Feb. 1746. Admitted to Middle Temple, London, Eng., 1739, Va. bar, 1744; King's atty. for Va., 1748-66; mem. Va. Ho. of Burgesses, 1748-75, speaker, 1766-75, sent to England to oppose gov.'s policy and to secure withdrawal of land fee; chmn. Va. Com. of Correspondence, 1773; presided over revolutionary convs. of Va., 1774, 75; pres. Continental Congress, 1774, 75; most popular leader in Va. decade before Revolution; mem. bd. visitors Coll. William and Mary; provincial grand master Masonic Order, Williamsburg. Died Phila., Oct. 22, 1775; buried beneath chapel of Coll. William and Mary.

RANDOLPH, Theodore Fitz, senator, gov. N.J.; b. New Brunswick, N.J., June 24, 1826; s. James Fitz R.; m. Fannie Coleman, 1852. Mcht., Vicksburg, Miss., 1840-50; mem. N.J. Assembly, 1858-61; mem. N.J. Senate, 1862-63; del. Democratic Nat. Conv., 1864-72, chmn. exec. com., 1872; pres. Morris & Essex R.R., 1867; gov. N.J., 1869-72, secured repeal of so-called Camden & Amboy R.R. "monopoly tax," also responsible for adoption of laws against bribery at elections, plan to make prison self-supporting, plan for establishment of insane asylum, Morristown, N.J.; mem. U.S. Senate (Dem.) from N.J., 1875-81, mem. coms. on mines and mining, mil. affairs and commerce; invented ditching machine and steam typewriter; trustee Rutgers Coll. Died Morristown, Nov. 7, 1883; buried Woodlawn Cemetery, Morristown.

RANDOLPH, Thomas Jefferson, banker, legislator; b. "Monticello," Albemarle County, Va., Sept. 11, 1792; s. Thomas Mann and Martha (Jefferson) R.; m. Jane Nicholas, 1815. Mgr., Thomas Jefferson's financial affairs, 1816-26; chief executor Jefferson's estate, 1826; mem. bd. visitors U. Va., 1829-60, rector, 7 years; mem. Va. Ho. of Dels., 1831; mem. Va. Constl. Conv., 1850-51; Secession Conv., Montgomery, Ala., 1861; commd. col. Confederate Army; chmn. Nat. Democratic Conv., 1872; mem. Albemarle Agrl. Soc.; pres. Farmers' Bank of Charlottesville (Va.). Author: Memoir, Correspondence, and Miscellanies from the Papers of Thomas Jefferson, 4 vols., 1829; Sixty Years' Reminiscences of the Currency of the United States. Died "Edgehill," Albemarle County, Oct. 7, 1875; buried "Monticello."

RANDOLPH, Thomas Mann, gov. Va., congressman; b. Tuckahoe, Va., Oct. 1, 1768; s. Thomas Mann and Anne (Cary) R.; attended Coll. William and Mary, U: Edinburgh (Scotland), 1785-88; m. Martha Jefferson (dau. Thomas Jefferson), Feb. 23, 1790, 10 children including Thomas Jefferson, George Wythe. Claimed to have originated practice of transverse rather than horizontal plowing on hillsides; mem. Va. Senate, 1793-94; mem. U.S. Ho. of Reps. from Va., 7th-9th congresses, 1803-07; col. 1st light corps of 20th U.S. Inf., 1812; mem. Va. Ho. of Dels., 1819, 20, 23-25; gov. Va., 1819-22; noted botanist. Died "Monticello," Albemarle County, Va., June 20, 1828; buried family burial ground.

RANDOLPH, William, planter, colonial ofcl.; b. Warwickshire, Eng., 1651; s. Richard and Elizabeth (Ryland) R.; m. Mary Isham, circa 1685, 9 children including William, Thomas, Isham, Sir John, Richard, Henry, Edward. Came to Va., 1673; purchased "Turkey Island," 1684; became one of largest planters in Va., by 1705; lt. col. of militia, 1699; rep. Va. House of Burgesses many times, speaker, 1696, 98, clk., 1699-1702; escheater gen. for lands on South side of James River; atty. gen. for the Crown in Va., 1694-98; a founder, an original trustee Coll. William and Mary. Died "Turkey Island," Va., Apr. 11, 1711.

RANKIN, Christopher, congressman, lawyer; b. Washington County, Pa., 1788; had prep. studies Canonsburg, Pa.; studied law. Taught village sch., Ga.; admitted to bar, 1809, practiced in Liberty, Amite County, Miss.; mem. Miss. Territorial Legislature, 1813; moved to Natchez, Miss., 1816, practiced law; mem. Miss. Constl. Conv., 1817; held several local offices; mem. U.S. Ho. of Reps. (Democrat) from Miss., 16th-19th congresses, 1819-26. Died Washington, D.C., Mar. 14, 1826; buried Congressional Cemetery.

RANKIN, John, clergyman, abolitionist; b. Jefferson County, Tenn., Feb. 4, 1793. Pastor Presbyn. ch., Carlisle, Ky., 1817-21; founded local anti-slavery soc., Carlisle, 1818; pastor 1st and 2d Presbyn. chs., Ripley, O., 1821-65; an organizer N.Y.C. Anti-Slavery Soc., also Am. Anti-Slavery Soc.; contbr. to Liberator (William L. Garrison's anti-slavery paper); mem. exec. com. Am. Anti-Slavery Soc., 1835; founded Am. Reform Book and Tract Soc. of Cincinnati; assisted in escape of slave and her son who were originals for Eliza and her son in Uncle Tom's Cabin. Author: The Covenant of Grace, 1869. Died Ironton, O., Mar. 18, 1886.

RANKIN, Joseph, congressman; b. Passaic, N.J., Sept. 25, 1833; had academic course. Moved to Mishicott, Manitowoc County, Wis., 1854, became mcht.; mem. Manitowoc County Bd., 1859; mem. Wis. Assembly, 1860, 71-74; enlisted in Union Army in Civil War, 1862, chosen capt. Company D, 26th Regt., Wis. Volunteer Infantry; settled in Manitowoc, Wis., after war; clk. City of Manitowoc, 1866-71; mem. Wis. Senate, 1877-82; mem. U.S. Ho. of Reps. (Democrat) from Wis., 48th-49th congresses, 1883-86. Died Washington, D.C., Jan. 24, 1886; buried Evergreen Cemetery, Manitowoc.

RANNEY, Henry Joseph, civil engr.; b. Middletown, Conn., circa 1800; s. Moses and Elizabeth (Gilchrist) R.; grad. Norwich U., 1828. Asst. engr. B&O. R.R., 1831; chief engr. Lexington & Ohio R.R., Ky., 1832-35; chief engr. New Orleans & Nashville R.R., 1835-42; cons. engr., New Orleans, from circa 1842; pres. New Canal & Shell Rd. Co., New Orleans, circa 1850; Whig, became active in local politics, 1850's; mem. La. Legislature from New Orleans, 1850's; a promoter New Orleans, Jackson & Gt. Northern R.R., 1858-62. Died Lewisburg, La., May 1, 1865.

RANNEY, Rufus Percival, jurist; b. Blanford, Mass., Oct. 30, 1813; s. Rufus and Dolly (Blair) R.; attended Western Reserve Coll., 1833-34; read law in office of Joshua R. Giddings and Benjamin F. Wade, Jefferson, O.; m. Adaline Warner, May 1, 1839, 6 children. Admitted to Ohio bar, 1836; partner (with B. F. Wade) in law firm, 1838-45; del. from Trumbull County to 2d Ohio Constl. Conv., 1850; mem. Ohio Supreme Ct., 1851-56, 62-64; resumed practice of law, Cleve., 1856-62, 65-81; 1st pres. Ohio Bar Assn., 1881. Died Dec. 6, 1891.

RANNEY, William Tylee, artist; b. Middletown, Conn., May 9, 1813; s. William and Clarissa (Gaylord) R.; m. Margaret Agnes O'Sullivan, 1848, several children. Portrait painter, N.Y.C., 1843-47; served as pvt. U.S. Army under Gen. Zachary Taylor, 1847; had studio, West Hoboken, N.J., 1848-57; painted hist. and frontier scenes; mem. N.A.D., 1850-57; paintings include: Duck Shooters (1849), On the Wing, The Old Oaken Bucket, Wild Horses, Washington on His Mission to the Indians (1847), The Sale of Manhattan by the Indians. Died West Hoboken, Nov. 18, 1857.

RANSIER, Alonzo Jacob, congressman; b. Charleston, S.C., Jan. 3, 1834; son of free Negroes; had limited schooling. Shipping clk., 1850; mem. conv. of Friends of Equal Rights, Charleston, 1865; mem. S.C. Constl. Conv., 1868, 69; Republican presdl. elector, 1868; lt. gov. S.C., 1870; pres. Southern States Conv., Columbia, 1871; del. Nat. Rep. Conv., Phila., 1872; mem. U.S. Ho. of Reps. (Rep.) from S.C., 43d Congress, 1873-75; U.S. internal revenue collector S.C. 2d Dist., 1875-76. Died Charleston, Aug. 17, 1882; buried United Friendship Cemetery.

RANSOM, Thomas Edward Greenfield, army officer; b. Norwich, Vt., Nov. 29, 1834; s. Truman Bishop and Margaret Morrison (Greenfield) Ransome; completed civil engring. course Norwich U., 1851. Raised a company which was incorporated into 11th Ill. Inf., 1861; maj., then lt. col. in command of a regt.; volunteer aide in surprise of Confederate Army at Charleston, 1861; col., serving at Newbern, Beaufort, Goldsboro, Kingston (all N.C.), 1861-62; brig. gen. in command of a brigade in Vicksburg campaign, 1863; in charge expdn. against Natchez, Miss., 1863; joined Tex. expdn., 1863; conducted successful operations along the Gulf Coast; commanded XIII Corps, U.S. Army, 1864; assigned to command XVI Corps, 1864, participated in siege of Atlanta (Ga.); brevetted maj. gen. U.S. Volunteers, 1864, assigned to command XVII Corps; fought at Ft. Donelson, Shiloh, Corinth. Died nr. Rome, Ga., Oct. 29, 1864; buried Rosehill Cemetery, Chgo.

RANTOUL, Robert, reformer; b. Salem, Mass., Nov. 23, 1778; s. Robert and Mary (Preston) R.; m. Joanna Lovett, June 4, 1801, 7 children including Robert. Owner apothecary shop, Beverly, Mass., 1796-1858; overseer of poor, Beverly, 1804; mem. Mass. Gen. Ct., 1809-20, 23-33, Mass. Senate, 1808-58; mem. Mass. constl. convs., 1820, 53; co-founder 1st Sunday Sch. in U.S. at Unitarian Ch. of Beverly, 1810; mem. Mass. Temperance Soc., 1813-58, mem. Mass. Peace Soc., 1814; mem. Mass. Gen. Ct. com. to consider subject of capital punishment, advocated its abolition, 1831. Died Beverly, Oct. 24, 1858.

RANTOUL, Robert, congressman, lawyer; b. Beverly, Mass., Aug. 13, 1805; s. Robert and Joanna (Lovett) R.; grad. Harvard, 1826; m. Jane Elizabeth Woodbury, Aug. 3, 1831, 2 children. Admitted to bar, 1829, began practice of law, Salem, Mass., 1829; mem. Mass. Ho. of Reps., 1834-39, advocated abolition of death penalty; mem. commn. to revise Mass. laws; mem. Mass. Bd. of Edn., did much to popularize tax-supported public schs., 1837-42; customs collector Boston, 1843; U.S. dist. atty., Mass., 1845-49; supported 15 gallon liquor law, advocated furtherance of temperance by edn., moral pursuasion; instrumental in defeating petition of Boston bankers and mchts. for chartering of $10,-000,000 bank; drew up liberal charter for I.C. R.R., responsible for its passage in Ill. Legislature; mem. U.S. Senate from Mass. (filled vacancy caused by Daniel Webster's resignation), Feb. 1-Mar. 3, 1851, mem. U.S. Ho. of Reps. (Democrat) from Mass., 32d Congress, 1851-52. Editor: Workingmen's Library; Common School Library. Died Washington, D.C., Aug. 7, 1852; buried Central Cemetery, Beverly.

RAPHALL, Morris Jacob, clergyman; b. Stockholm, Sweden, Oct. 3, 1798; s. Jacob Raphall; attended U. Giessen, Ph.D. (hon.), 1840; Ph.D., U. Erlangen; m. Rachel Goldstein, 1825, 6 children. Profl. lectr., 1832; sec. to chief rabbi Solomon Hirschell, 1840; became rabbi, preacher, master Hebrew Sch., Birmingham (Eng.) Hebrew Congregation, 1841; contributed to Jewish battle for equal rights in Eng.; came to N.Y.C., 1849, lectr., preacher Congregation B'nai Jeshurun, 1849-65; rabbi emeritus, 1865-68; 1st rabbi in N.Y.C. to preach regular weekly English sermons; 1st Jew to be invited to open a session of U.S. Ho. of Reps. with prayer, 1860; active charitable activities, including gathering funds for relief of distressed Jews in the Holy Land, and elsewhere; defended orthodox Judaism in Am. Author: Festivals of the Lord, 1839; Devotional Exercises for the Daughters of Israel, 1852; Post Biblical History of the Jews, 2 vols., 1855; The Path of Immortality, 1859; The Bible View of Slavery, 1861; co-translator Eighteen Treatises from the Mishnah, 1845; founder, editor Hebrew Review, or Magazine of Rabbinical Literature (1st Jewish weekly in Gt. Britain), 1834-36. Died N.Y.C., June 23, 1868.

RAPIER, James Thomas, congressman; b. Florence, Lauderdale County, Ala., Nov. 13, 1837; had pvt. tutors, Ala., Canada; studied law. Admitted to bar; taught sch.; returned to South; traveled as corr. for Northern newspaper; became cotton planter, Ala., 1865; apptd. notary public by Ala. gov., 1866; mem. 1st Republican Conv. held in Ala., mem. of com. that framed platform; mem. Ala. Constl. Conv., Montgomery, 1867; apptd. assessor internal revenue, 1871; apptd. Ala. commr. to Vienna Expn. by gov., 1873; U.S. commr. to World's Fair, Paris, France; mem. U.S. Ho. of Reps. (Rep.) from Ala., 43d Congress, 1873-75; collector internal revenue Ala. 2d Dist., 1878-83. Died Montgomery, May 31, 1883; buried Calvary Cemetery, St. Louis.

RAPP, George, religious leader; b. Iptingen, Oberamt Maulbronn, Württemberg, Nov. 1, 1757; s. Hans Adam and Rosine (Berger) R.; m. Christine Benzinger, 1783; 2 children including John. Leader of a group of separatists in Europe; came to U.S., 1803; bought land in Butler County, Pa., sent for his people who crossed the Atlantic Ocean, 1804; built town of Harmony, Pa., 1804; founder Harmony Soc. (a communistic theocracy), 1805; community established in Wabash Valley at Harmony, Ind., 1814-24; established 3d community, Economy, Pa., 1825; sect. known as Harmonists, or Harmonites. Author: The Destinies of Humanity, 1824. Died Economy, Aug. 7, 1847; buried Economy.

RAPPE, Louis Amadeus, clergyman; b. Andrehem, France, Feb. 2, 1801; attended Boulogne Coll. Ordained priest Roman Catholic Ch., Arras, France, 1829; came to U.S., 1840, became missionary, Diocese of Cincinnati; consecrated 1st bishop of Cleve., 1847, established diocesan sem., 1848, held 5 diocesan synods, finished building cathedral, 1852, resigned, 1870; did missionary work in Vt., 1870-77. Died St. Albans, Vt., Sept. 8, 1877.

RAREY, John Solomon, horse tamer; b. Groveport, O., Dec. 6, 1827; s. Adam and Mary (Pontius) R.; never married. Began giving lessons in horse tng., 1852; gave instrn. to Queen Victoria and her family in Eng., 1857; travelled throughout Europe and Middle East teaching methods of horse taming, 1858-60; gave public exhbns. in U.S., 1860-62. Author: The Modern Art of Taming Wild Horses, 1856. Died Groveport, Oct. 4, 1866.

RARIDEN, James, congressman, lawyer; b. nr. Cynthiana, Harrison County, Ky., Feb. 14, 1795; had limited schooling; studied law. Moved to Brookville, Ind., later to Salisbury, Ind.; dept. clk. of court; admitted to bar, 1818; practiced in Centerville, Ind., 1820; pros. atty., 1822-25; mem. Ind. Senate, 1823; mem. Ind. Ho. of Reps., 1829, 30, 32, 33; mem. U.S. Ho. of Reps. (Whig) from Ind., 25th-26th congresses, 1837-41; moved to Cambridge City, Ind., 1846; del. Ind. Constl. Conv., 1850. Died Cambridge City, Oct. 20, 1856; buried Riverside Cemetery.

RATCLIFFE, John, colonial gov.; born in Eng.; flourished 1606-10. Believed to have changed his original surname to Ratcliffe; sailed in ship Discovery to Va., 1606; mem. 1st Va. Council, 1606-07; headed (with John Smith) faction which deposed Edward M. Wingfield (1st gov. Va.); chosen gov. Va., 1607-08; returned to Eng., 1608; went back to Va. with supplies for colonists, 1609, deposed John Smith (who had replaced him as gov.), and sent him back to Eng. Believed to have been killed by Indian chief Powhaten, Va. Colony, winter 1609-10.

RATHBONE, Justus Henry (Henry Edwin Dwight Rathbone), assn. founder; b. Deerfield, Oneida County, N.Y., Oct. 29, 1839; s. Justus Hull and Sarah (Dwight) R.; m. Emma Sanger, Aug. 11, 1862; 5 children. Clk., Treasury Dept., 1865-69; employed by Independent News Co. of Boston and N.Y.C., 1869-73; clk. War Dept., 1874-89; organizer (with Robert Allen Champion) Washington (D.C.) Lodge No. 1, mother lodge of Order Knights of Pythias, 1864, worthy chancellor, 1864, supreme lectr. of the order, 1877. Died Lima, O., Dec. 9, 1889; buried Utica, N.Y.

RATHBUN, George Oscar, congressman; b. Scipioville, nr. Auburn, Cayuga County, N.Y., 1803; grad. Hamilton Coll.; studied law. Admitted to bar, practiced in Auburn; mem. N.Y. State Assembly; mem. U.S. Ho. of Reps. (Democrat) from N.Y., 28th-29th congresses, 1843-47. Died Auburn, Jan. 5, 1870; buried Ft. Hill Cemetery.

RAU, Charles, archaeologist, mus. curator; b. Verviers, Belgium, 1826; attended U. Heidelberg (Germany); Ph.D. (hon.), U. Freiburg (Baden, Germany), 1882. Came to Am., 1848; resident collaborator in ethnology U.S. Nat. Mus., 1875, curator dept. archeology, 1881-87; assisted in preparation for Centennial Exposition of 1876; made contbns. to process of classification; 1st Am. to recognize importance of study of aboriginal technology. Author: The Archeological Collection of the United States National Museum; Early Man in Europe, 1876; Prehistoric Fishing in Europe and North America, 1885. Translator: Account of the Aboriginal Inhabitants of the California Peninsula (Jacob Buegert), 1863. Died Phila., July 25, 1887.

RAUCH, Frederick Augustus, philosopher, coll. pres.; b. Kirchbracht, Prussia (Germany), July 27, 1806; s. Heinrich and Friederike (Haderman) R.; Ph.D., Marburg U., 1827; studied Giessen U., also U. Heidelberg; m. Phebe Bathiah Moore, 1833. Made a pub. expression of sympathies for the polit. fraternities which the German Govt. was attempting to suppress, 1831; privat docent, later prof. extraordinarius Giessen U.; came to Am., 1831; prof. German, Lafayette Coll.; prin. Hochshule connected with the German Reformed Ch., York, Pa., 1832; ordained to ministry German Reformed Ch., 1832; elected prof. bibl. lit. in seminary, York; organizer, 1st pres. Marshall Coll. (now Mercersburg Acad.), Pa., 1836; started doctrinal system known as Mercersburg Theology. Author: Vorlesungen über Goethes Faust, 1830; Psychology or a View of the Human Soul, including Anthropology (1st attempt to unite German and Am. mental philosophy), 1840; The Inner Life of the Christian, 1856. Died Mercersburg, Mar. 2, 1841; buried Lancaster, Pa.

RAUCH, John Henry, physician; b. Lebanon, Pa., Sept. 4, 1828; s. Bernard and Jane (Brown) R.; grad. Med. Sch., U. Pa., 1849. Joined Ia. Med. Soc., 1850, 1st del. to A.M.A., 1852, published article in Proceedings "Report on the Medical and Economical Botany of Iowa," 1851; effected establishment of marine hosps., Galena, Ill., and Burlingame, Ia.; mem. Ia. Hort. Soc., Ia. Hist. Soc., Ia. Geol. Soc.; made a natural history collection from the upper Mississippi and Missouri rivers, 1855-56; aided in effecting passage of a bill providing for a geol. survey of Ia., 1856; prof. materia medica Rush Med. Coll., Chgo., 1857-58; founder Chgo. Coll. Pharmacy, 1859, 1st prof. materia medica; served as surgeon during Civil War; helped reorganize Chgo. Bd. Health, 1867; made collections in Venezuela, 1870; a founder Am. Public Health Assn., treas., 1872, pres., 1876; 1st pres. Ill. Bd. Health, 1877-91, superintended adminstrn. of Med. Practice Act; assisted in establishing a quarantine sta. for cholera cases and suspects, 1892; editor public health dept. Jour. of A.M.A., 1894, made nation-wide study of prevalence and control of smallpox published as "The Smallpox Situation in the United States"; mem. bd. trustees A.M.A. Died Lebanon, Mar. 24, 1894.

RAUE, Charles Gottlieb, physician; b. Nieder Cunnersdorf, Saxony, Germany, May 11, 1820; s. Hans Gottlieb and Christine (Seiler) R.; ed. Tchrs. Coll., Bantren, Germany, 1837-41; grad. Phila. Coll. Medicine, 1850; m. Philippina Welsling; M: 2d, Mathilda Germine Jurgerich; 2 children. Came to Am., 1848; prof. pathology and diagnosis in homeopathic Med. Coll. Pa., 1864; prof. practice of medicine, spl. pathology and therapeutics Hahnemann Med. Coll., Phila., 1867-71. Author: Die Neue Seelen Lehre Beneckes (1st work on psychology), 1847; Special Pathology and Diagnostics, 1867; Psychology as a Natural Science as Applied to the Solution of Occult Psychic Phenomena, 1889; published Annual Record of Homeopathic Literature, 1870-75. Died Phila., Aug. 21, 1896.

RAVALLI, Antonio, missionary; b. Ferrara, Italy, May 16, 1811. Entered Soc. of Jesus, 1827; ordained priest, 1843; arrived in Vancouver, B.C., Can. 1844; asst. to Father Adrian Hoecken at St. Ignatius among the Kalispel Indians, Mont., 1844; ordered to St. Mary's Mission, Mont., circa 1845-50; assigned to work with the Coer d'Alene Indians of No. Ida., circa 1850-57, built a flour mill, improvised sawmill, built ch.; largely responsible for No. tribe's quiet days of Yakima outbreak of 1856-57; missionary to Colville Indians, 1857-60; master of novices Santa Clara Coll., 1860; returned to Mont., 1863, priest and physician to Indian tribes and isolated whites. Died Hell Gate, Mont., Oct. 2, 1884.

RAVENEL, Edmund, physician, naturalist; b. Charleston, S.C., Dec. 8, 1797; s. Daniel and Catherine (Prioleau) R.; M.D., U. Pa., 1819; m. Charlotte Ford; m. 2d, Louisa Ford; at least 1 son. Prof. chemistry 1st faculty Med. Coll. of S.C., 1824-35; corr. mem. Acad. Natural Scis. of Phila., 1832; published a catalogue of shells, 1834; bought The Grove (plantation on Cooper River, S.C.), 1835; v.p. Elliot Soc. of Natural History, 1853; purchased patent rights in Sawyer's brick-making machine for S.C., 1836, similar rights in Brown's machine, 1838; in charge of hosp. at Ft. Moultrie; chmn. polit. meeting in St. Thomas's Parish which endorsed secession, 1860; remains of his collection now in Charleston Mus. Author: Echinidae, Recent and Fossil of South Carolina, 1848. Died Summerton Plantation, Berkley County, S.C., July 27, 1871.

RAVENEL, Henry William, botanist, agrl. writer; b. "Pooshee", Berkely, S.C., May 19, 1814; s. Henry and Catherine (Stevens) R.; grad. S.C. Coll., 1832; LL.D., U. N.C., 1886; m. Elizabeth Gaillard Snowden, 1835; m. 2d, Mary Huger Dawon, 1858; 10 children. Given plantation and slaves by his father, became planter, circa 1832-65; elected correspondent Acad. Natural Science, Phila., 1849; published best known of his botanical works The Fungi Cardiniani Exsiccati, 5 vols., 1853-60 (1st published series of named specimans of Am. fungi); published (with English botanist Prof. M. C. Cooke) 2d series Fungi Americani Exsiccati, 8 parts, 1878-82; sent by U.S. Govt. to Tex. to aid in investigation of a cattle disease, 1869 (investigation proved disease not due to eating of poisonous fungus); agrl. editor Weekly News and Courier, 1882-87; collected and classified herbarium and fungi, mosses and lichens, later sold to Brit. Mus. and Converse Coll., Spartanburg, S.C.; became mem. Zoölogische Botanische Gesellschaft, Vienna, 1884. Died Aiken, S.C., July 17, 1887.

RAVENEL, St. Julien, physician, agrl. chemist; b. Charleston, S.C., Dec. 19, 1819; s. John and Anna Elizabeth (Ford) R.; grad. Charleston Med. Coll., 1840; studied medicine in Phila. and Paris, France; m. Harriett Horry Rutledge, Mar. 20, 1851, 9 children. Established 1st stone lime works in S.C. at Stoney Landing on Cooper River, 1857; surgeon in charge Confederate hosp., Columbia, S.C., also in charge Confederate lab. (where much of medicine used for Confederate Army was made) during Civil War; designer torpedo cigarboat Little David; originated a process which rendered phosphate rocks readily soluble, produced an ammoniated fertilizer, produced phosphate fertilizer without the use of ammonia (acid fertilizer), developed process of adding marl to acid fertilizers to counteract free acid; chemist Charleston Agrl. Lime Co.; discovered that lanting and plowing of leguminous plants restored to the worn out soil properties which made it produce larger crops; proposed artesian well system for Charleston. Died Charleston, Mar. 17, 1882.

RAVENSCROFT, John Stark, clergyman; b. Petersburg, Va., May 17, 1772; s. John and Lillias (Miller) R.; studied law Coll. William and Mary; m. Anne Spotswood Burwell, Sept. 29, 1792; m. 2d, Sarah Buford, 1818; 2 adopted children. Planter until 1817; decided to join Episcopal Ch., also to become clergyman, 1812; ordained to ministry Episcopal Ch., Va., 1817; minister St. James Ch., Mecklenburg County, N.C., 1817-23; 1st Episcopal bishop of N.C., 1823-28, sought to impress his interpretation of Episcopal doctrines upon people, greatly increased membership in Episcopal Ch.; rector small ch, Williamsboro, N.C. until 1830. Died Raleigh, N.C., Mar. 5, 1830.

RAWLE, Francis, legislator, polit. economist; b. Plymouth, Eng., 1662; s. Francis and Jane Rawle; m. Martha Turner, Oct. 18, 1689, 10 children. Came to Am., 1686; a mcht.; became justice of peace and judge county ct., Plymouth Twp., Pa., 1689; alderman Phila., 1691; dep. register wills, 1692; mem. Pa. Assembly, 1704-09, 19-27; leader anti-proprietary party; 1st Am. writer on polit. economy and its application to local conditions; leading mem. Pa. com. which drafted The Paper Money Act of 1723. Author: Some Remedies Proposed for the Restoring the Sunk Credit of the Province of Pennsylvania, 1721; Ways and Means for the Inhabitants of Delaware to Become Rich, 1725. Died Phila., Mar. 5, 1726/27.

RAWLE, William, lawyer; b. Phila., Apr. 28, 1759; s. Francis and Rebecca (Warner) R.; studied law Middle Temple, London, Eng., 1781-82; m. Sarah Coates Burge, Nov. 13, 1783, 12 children, including William. Admitted to Phila. bar, 1783; mem. Am. Philos. Soc., 1786; mem. Pa. Legislative Assembly, 1789; mem. Soc. Polit. Inquiries; U.S. atty. for Pa., 1791-99; prosecuted authors of Whiskey Rebellions, 1794, 99; hon. mem. Md. Soc. for Promoting Abolition of Slavery, 1792, pres., 1818-36; trustee U. Pa., 1795-1835; joined Phila. Soc. for Promoting Agr., 1805; a founder Pa. Acad. Fine Arts, 1805; hon. mem. Linnaean Soc., 1807; dir. Library Co. of Phila.; founder Soc. for Promotion of Legal Knowledge and Forensic Elegance, 1820; chancellor Soc. Asso. Mems. of the Bar, 1822; 1st pres. Hist. Soc. of Pa. (founded 1825); mem. commn. to revise, collate and digest the statutes of Pa. Author: View of the Constitution of the United States, 1825. Died Phila., Apr. 12, 1856.

RAWLE, William Henry, lawyer, ednl. adminstr.; b. Phila., Aug. 31, 1823; s. William and Mary Anna (Tilghman) R.; grad. U. Pa., 1841; m. Mary Cadwalader, Sept. 13, 1849; m. 2d, Emily Cadwalader, Oct. 7, 1869; 3 children. Admitted to Pa. bar, 1844; practiced law, Phila., 1844-62, 65-89; served as pvt. U.S. Army, 1862-65; vice provost Phila. Law Acad., 1865-73; vice chancellor Phila. Law Assn., 1885-89. Author: A Practical Treatise on the Law of Covenants for Title, 1852; Equity in Pennsylvania, 1868; Some Contrasts in the Growth of Pennsylvania and English Law, 1881. Died Phila., Apr. 19, 1889.

RAWLINS, John Aaron, army officer, U.S. sec. of war; b. Galena, Ill., Feb. 13, 1831; s. James Dawson and Lovisa (Collier) R.; attended Rock River Sem., Mt. Morris, Ill.; m. Emily Smith, June 5, 1856; m. 2d, Mary Hurlburt, Dec. 23, 1863; 3 children. Admitted to Ill. bar, 1854; city atty., Galena, 1857; participated in orgn. 45th Ill. Inf., became maj., 1861; aide de camp to Gen. Grant; lt., Aug. 1861; capt., asst. adj. gen. U.S. Volunteers as mem. Grant's staff, Aug. 30, 1861; verified, edited, finalized Grant's papers; promoted maj., then lt. col., 1862, brig. gen. U.S. Volunteers, 1863; brig. gen., chief of staff Army, 1865; promoted maj. gen. U.S. Army, 1865; U.S. sec. of war, 1869. Died Washington, D.C., Sept. 6, 1869.

RAY, Charles Bennett, journalist, clergyman; b. Falmouth, Mass., Dec. 25, 1807; s. Joseph Aspinwall and Annis (Harrington) R.; attended Wesleyan Sem., Wilbraham, Mass., also Wesleyan U., Middletown, Conn., until 1832; m. Henriette Regulus, 1834; m. 2d, Charlotte Augusta Burroughs, 1840; 8 children. Mem. Negro race; joined Anti-Slavery Soc., 1833; ordained to ministry Methodist Ch., 1837; apptd. gen. agt. The Colored American, 1837, part owner paper, 1838, subsequently sole owner, editor, 1839-42; participated in activities Underground Railroad to further escape of runaway slaves; corr. sec. N.Y. State Vigilance Com., 1843, mem. exec. com., 1850; pastor Bethesda Congregational Ch, N.Y.C., 1846; city missionary, N.Y.C., 1846-86; helped organize several temperance socs., 1847-48. Died Aug. 15, 1886.

RAY, Charles Henry, editor; b. Norwich, N.Y., Mar. 12, 1821; s. Levi and Bertha (Cornwall) R.; attended N.Y.U.; m. Jane Yates, 1849; m. 2d, Julia Clark, Sept. 5, 1864; children—Maria, Francis Perlee, Charles Paul, Edmond Gilbert, Bertha Cornwall, Julia Lincoln. Granted license to practice medicine, 1844; moved to Galena, Ill., 1851, became editor Galena Jeffersonian; purchased interest in Chgo. Tribune, 1855, represented Tribune in conv. opposed to slavery, Decatur, Ill., 1856; apptd. to Republican Nat. Conv., 1856; succeeded John Scripps as editor Chgo. Tribune, 1860-63, 65-57, supported Lincoln for Pres. U.S.; became editor Chgo. Evening Post, 1867; 1st sec. Chgo. Hist. Soc., 1857. Died Chgo., Sept. 23, 1870.

RAY, Isaac, hosp. adminstr., psychiatrist; b. Beverly, Mass., Jan. 16, 1807; s. Isaac and Lydia (Simonds) Rea; M.D., Med. Dept., Bowdoin Coll. (Med. Sch. of Me.), 1827; m. Abigail May Frothingham, 1831; 2 children, including Dr. B. Lincoln Ray. Supt., Me. Insane Hosp., 1841-45; physician-in-chief, supt. Butler Hosp. (hosp. for mental diseases), Providence, R.I., 1845-66; visited European hosps., asylums, 1845-46; pres. R.I. Med. Soc., 1856-58; a founder Assn. Med. Supts. of Am. Instsn. for Insane, 1844, pres., 1855-59; bequeathed $75,000 to Butler Hosp. Author: A Treatise on the Medical Jurisprudence of Insanity, 1838; Observations on the Principal Hospitals for the Insane in Great Britain, France, and Germany, 1846; Mental Hygiene, 1863; Contributions to Mental Pathology, 1873; Ideal Character of the Officers of a Hospital for the Insane, 1873. Died Phila., Mar. 31, 1881.

RAY, Joseph, educator; b. Va., Nov. 25, 1807; attended Washington Coll., Athens Coll. (now Ohio U.); M.D., Ohio Med. Coll. Prof. mathematics Woodward Coll., 1834-51; pres. bd. dirs. Cincinnati Ho. of Refuge, from circa 1849. Died Cincinnati, Apr. 17, 1865.

RAY, Ossian, congressman, lawyer; b. Hinesburg, Chittenden County, Vt., Dec. 13, 1835; attended common schs., academy, Derby, Vt.; studied law, Irasburg, Lancaster, N.H. Moved to Lancaster, 1854; admitted to bar, 1857; practiced in Essex and Coos counties, N.H.; solicitor Coos County, 1862-72; mem. N.H. Ho. of Reps., 1868-69; del. Nat. Republican Conv., Phila., 1872; U.S. atty. for N.H. Dist., 1879-80, resigned; mem. U.S. Ho. of Reps. (Rep., filled vacancy) from N.H., 46th-48th congresses, Jan. 8, 1881-85. Died Lancaster, Coos County, Jan. 28, 1892; buried Summer Street Cemetery.

RAY, William Henry, congressman, mcht.; b. Amenia, Dutchess County, N.Y., Dec. 14, 1812; attended common schs. Moved to Rushville, Schuyler County, Ill., 1834, became mcht., interested in banking; mem. 1st Ill. Bd. of Equalization, 1867-69; mem. U.S. Ho. of Reps. (Republican) from Ill., 43d Congress, 1873-75. Died Rushville, Jan. 25, 1881; buried Rushville Cemetery.

RAYMOND, Benjamin Wright, mcht., mayor Chgo., univ. pres.; b. Rome, N.Y., Oct. 23, 1801; s. Benjamin and Hannah (Wright) R.; m. Amelia Porter, Jan. 12, 1884, 2 chidren, including George Lansing. Mcht., Norfolk, St. Lawrence County, N.Y., 1820; obtained financial backing of S. Newton Dexter, agt. Oriskany Mfg. Co. of N.Y., 1831; conducted wool buying enterprise, East Bloomfield, N.Y., 1832-36; with B.W. Raymond & Co., Chgo., 1836-43; mayor Chgo. (1839), (Democrat 1842); an organizer 2d Presbyn. Ch. of Chgo., 1842; started Chgo. park system; active in promotion Galena & Chgo. Union R.R., 1846, mem. 1st bd. dirs.; laid out Town of Lake Forest (Ill.); pres. Lake Forest U., 12 years; trustee Beloit (Wis.) Coll., Rockford (Ill.) Female Sem; bought half interest in Town of Elgin (Ill.; built (for partner Dexter) 1st woolen mill in Ill., 1844; organizer Nat. Watch Co. (later became Elgin Nat. Watch Co.), Elgin, Ill., 1st pres., dir., until 1878. Died Chgo., Apr. 5, 1883.

RAYMOND, Daniel, polit. economist; b. New Haven, Conn., 1786; m. Eliza Amos; m. 2d, Delia Matlock, 1837; 8 children. Admitted to bar, Balt., 1814; practiced law in Balt., 1814-40, Cincinnati, 1840-49; rebelled against dominant European classical economists, advocated strict govt. control of trade and prodn., advocated abolition of slavery. Author: Thoughts on Political Economy. 1829; The Missouri Question, 1819; The American System, 1828; Elements of Constitutional Law, 1840. Died 1849.

RAYMOND, Henry Jarvis, congressman, editor; b. Lima, N.Y., Jan. 24, 1820; s. Jarvis and Lavinia (Brockway) R.; grad. U. Vt., 1840; m. Juliette Weaver, Oct. 24, 1843, 7 children. Staff, New Yorker, 1840; chief asst. N.Y. Tribune, 1841-43; staff Morning Courier and N.Y. Enquirer, 1843; mem. N.Y. Assembly (Whig), 1849-51, speaker, 1851; mng. editor Harper's New Monthly Mag., 1850-56; with George Jones established N.Y. Daily Times (name changed to N.Y. Times, 1857), 1851, editor, 1851-69; del. Whig. Nat. Conv., 1852; advocated in Daily Times that free-soilers remain with Whigs, active in Anti-Neb. movement, 1854; lt. gov. N.Y., 1854-55; attended Pitts. meeting founding Nat. Republican Party, 1856, wrote statement of party principles; went to Italy to report Franco-Austrian War, 1859; del. Rep. Nat. Conv., Chgo., 1860; speaker N.Y. Assembly, 1862; wrote most of platform for Rep. Nat. Conv., Balt., 1864; chmn. Rep. Nat. Com., 1864; mem. U.S. Ho. of Reps. from N.Y., 39th Congress, 1865-67, adminstrv. leader in House; attended Nat. Union Conv., Phila., 1866; attended Phila. Rep. Conv., 1866; expelled from Nat. Rep. Com., 1866; began attacks on "Tweed Ring" in Times; advocated tariff reduction, sound money, civil service reform; contributions to journalism include substitution of decency for personal invective and fairness for partisan techniques, eye-witness battle pictures of Solferino and Bull Run in Times; at his best in Disunion and Slavery, 1860; an example of rivalry with H. Greeley is Association Discussed; or, the Socialism of the Tribune Examined, 1847. Author: A Life of Daniel Webster, 1853; A History of the Administration of President Lincoln, 1864. Died N.Y.C., June 18, 1869; buried Greenwood Cemetery, Bklyn.

RAYMOND, John Baldwin, congressman; b. Lockport, Niagara County, N.Y., Dec. 5, 1844; attended public schs., Poughkeepsie (N.Y.) Bus. Coll., 1865-66. Enlisted as pvt. 31st Regt., Ill. Infantry in Civil War, 1861, promoted capt. Company E after siege of Vicksburg, 1863, served through war; settled in Miss.; publisher Miss. Pilot (Jackson) during reconstruction of Miss., until 1877; asst. treas. Miss., 1873-75; apptd. U.S. marshal of Dakota Territory, headquarters at Yankton, later Fargo, 1877-82; mem. U.S. Congress (Republican) from Dakota Territory, 48th Congress, 1883-85; became wheat grower. Died Fargo, Dak. (now N.D.), Jan. 3, 1886; buried public vault in Rock Creek Cemetery, Washington, D.C.

RAYMOND, John Howard, coll. pres.; b. N.Y.C., Mar. 7, 1814; s. Eliakim and Mary (Carrington) R.; attended Columbia Coll., 1828; grad. Union Coll., Schenectady, N.Y., 1832, Bapt. Theol. Sem., Colgate U., 1838; m. Cornelia Morse, May 12, 1840, 9 children. Prof., Colgate U., 1838-50; an organizer U. Rochester (N.Y.). 1850, prof. belles-lettres, 1850-55; 1st pres. Bklyn. Collegiate and Poly. Inst., 1855, responsible for plan of orgn. and policy of govt., used honor system; mem. 1st bd. trustees Vassar Coll., 1861, pres., 1864-78, responsible for entire internal orgn., selection of faculty and making of curriculum. Died Poughkeepsie, N.Y., Aug. 14, 1878; buried Greenwood Cemetery, Bklyn.

RAYMOND, John T. (John O'Brien), actor; b. Buffalo, N.Y., Apr. 5, 1836; ed. public schs.; m. Marie Gordon, 1863; m. 2d, Rose Barnes, Apr. 11, 1881. Made debut as Lopez in The Honeymoon, June 27, 1853; relied on facial and physical subtilities to obtain effects; mem. Laura Keene's co., N.Y., 1861; played Asa Trenchard in Our American Cousin, 1866, Tony Lumpkin in She Stoops To Conquer, Crabtree in The School for Scandal; gave operatic performances in co. of which Caroline Richings was leading mem., season 1861; 1st acted Col. Mulberry Sellers in The Guilded Age (his most famous role), 1873; played Mr. Posket in Pinero's The Magistrate; legally changed name from O'Brien to his stage name John T. Raymond, 1881. Died Evansville, Ind., Apr. 10, 1887.

RAYMOND, Miner, clergyman, educator; b. N.Y.C., Aug. 29, 1811; s. Nobles and Hannah (Wood) R.; grad. Wesleyan Acad., Wilbraham, Mass., 1831 (studied for ministry); M.A. (hon.), Wesleyan U., 1840, D.D. (hon.), 1854; LL.D., Northwestern U., 1884; m. Elizabeth Henderson, Aug. 20, 1837; m. 2d, Isabella Hill, July 28, 1879; 5 children. Joined Methodist Ch., 1828; tchr. English, later mathematics Wesleyan Acad., circa 1831-40; prin., 1848-64; ordained minister Meth. Episcopal Ch., 1838; served in chs., Worcester, Mass., Westfield, Mass., Boston, 1840-48; prof. systematic theology Garrett Bibl. Inst., Evanston, Ill., 1864-95; leader anti-slavery movement. Author Systematic Theology, 3 vols., 1877. Died Nov. 25, 1897.

RAYNER, Kenneth, congressman; b. Bertie County, N.C., June 20, 1808; s. Amos Rayner; m. Susan Polk. Mem. N.C. Constnl. Conv., 1835; mem. N.C. House of Commons, 1836-40, 46-52; mem. U.S. Ho. of Reps. (Democrat) from N.C, 26th-28th congresses, 1839-45; Whig presdl. elector, 1848; mem. N.C. Senate, 1854; mem. grand council Am. (Know-Nothing) Party; wrote, secured adoption 3d (or Union) degree (which was designed to protect, maintain, defend Union under all circumstances), 1855; mem. Secession Conv., 1861; secretly joined peace movement led by William J. Holden, 1863; advocated Pres. Andrew Johnson's reconstrn. policy, 1865; judge of the Ala. Claims Commn., 1874-77; solicitor U.S. Treasury, 1877-84. Author: Life and Times of Andrew Johnson, published anonymously, 1866. Died Washington, D.C., Mar. 5, 1884; buried Old City Cemetery, Raleigh, N.C.

REA, John, congressman; b. Rea's Mansion, nr. Chambersburg, Pa., Jan. 27, 1755; completed prep. studies. Served as lt. and capt. with Cumberland

County (Pa.) Militia, during Revolutionary War; commd. 1st coroner Franklin County, Pa., 1784; mem. Pa. Ho. of Reps., 1785, 86, 89-90, 92-93, 1801-02; county auditor, 1793, 94; mem. U.S. Ho. of Reps. (Democrat, filled vacancy) from Pa., 8th-11th, 13th congresses, 1803-11, May 11, 1813-15; served as maj. gen. 11th Div. of Militia during War of 1812; mem. Pa. Senate, 1823-24. Died Chambersburg, Feb. 26, 1829; buried Rocky Spring Churchyard, nr. Chambersburg.

READ, Almon Heath, congressman; b. Shelburne, Chittenden County, Vt., June 12, 1790; grad. Williams Coll., 1811; studied law. County clk., 1815-20; admitted to bar, 1816; practiced in Montrose, Susquehanna County, Pa.; mem. Pa. Ho. of Reps., 1827-32; mem. Pa. Senate, 1833-37; treas. Pa., 1840; mem. U.S. Ho. of Reps. (Democrat, filled vacancy) from Pa., 27th-28th congresses, Mar. 18, 1842-44. Died Montrose, June 3, 1844; buried Montrose Cemetery.

READ, Charles, jurist, iron mfr.; b. Phila., Feb. 1, 1715; s. Charles and Anne (Bond) R.; m. Alice Thibou, at least 2 children, Jacob, Charles. Clk. Burlington (N.J.), 1739; collector Port of Burlington, circa 1739; surrogate, Burlington; apptd. clk. N.J. Circuit Cts., 1739, sec. Province of N.J., 1744; mem. Burlington City Assembly, 1757-60, speaker, 1751-54; mem. N.J. Gov.'s Council, 1758-74; Indian commr., 1755, 58, instrmental in setting aside Indian reservation in So. Burlington County; apptd. asso. justice N.J. Supreme Ct., 1749, chief justice, 1764; admitted to bar, 1753; land speculator on large scale; experimented to improve farm practices; began mfg. iron from bog ore, 1765, established iron furnaces at Taunton, Etna, Atsion, Batsto, (all N.J.), circa 1765-68; served as col. Burlington County Militia in French and Indian Wars. Author: Charles Read's Notes on Colonial Agriculture most fruitful known source of information on agr. in Am. colonies, edited by C.R. Woodward, now in Rutgers U. Library). Died Martinburg, N.C., Dec. 27, 1774.

READ, Charles William, naval officer; b. Yazoo County, Miss., May 12, 1840; grad. U.S. Naval Acad., 1860. Served as midshipman U.S. Navy aboard Pawnee and Powhatan, 1860-61, resigned, 1861; apptd. midshipman Confederate States Navy, 1861, promoted lt. Confederate Provisional Navy, 1862; in action at Ship Island, Head of the Passes, and Island No. 10, 1862; promoted 2d lt. Regular Navy, 1863; given command of brig. Clarence with orders to raid U.S. coast, 1863; captured 21 prizes, 1863; captured in attack on revenue cutter Caleb Cushing in harbor of Portland (Me.), 1863; promoted 1st lt. Provisional Navy, 1864; exchanged, 1864; commanded torpedo boat div. on James River, 1865; captured again in attempt to run blockade on Mississippi River, Apr. 1865, released, July, 1865; became mcht., New Orleans, after Civil War; later harbor master Port of New Orleans. Died Meridian, Miss., Jan. 25, 1890.

READ, Daniel, musician; b. Attleboro, Mass., Nov. 16, 1757; s. Daniel and Mary (White) R.; m. Jerusha Sherman, 1785; 4 children. Served for short periods in Sullivan's expdn. to R.I. during Revolutionary War, 1777, 78; a stockholder New Haven City Bank (Conn.); dir. library, New Haven; mem. Gov.'s Guards; published 1st music book The American Singing Book, 1785; editor The Am. Musical Mag. (1st periodical of its kind in Am.), 1 year, circa 1786; one of earliest Am. psalmodists, hymn-tune writers; other works include: An Introduction to Psalmody, 1790; 1st number The Columbian Harmonist, published 1793; The New Haven Collection of Sacred Music, 1818; best known tunes include: "Lisbon," "Sherburne," "Windham." Died New Haven, Dec. 4, 1836.

READ, Daniel coll. pres.; b. nr. Marietta, O., June 24, 1805; s. Ezra Read; grad. Ohio U., 1824; m. Alice Brice, 1826, at least 5 children, including Theodore. Admitted to Ohio bar; preceptor Ohio U., 1824, prof. ancient langs., polit. economy, constl. and pub. law, 1836-43, v.p.; sec. bd. visitors U.S. Mil. Acad., 1840; prof. langs. Ind. State U., 1843-56, pres., 1853-54; mem. Ind. Constl. Conv., 1850, presented legislature with plan for edn., organized, instructed class for tng. tchrs.; prof. mental and moral philosophy U. Wis., 1856-67; pres., prof. mental, moral and polit. philosophy, U. Mo., 1867, under his direction sch. became a univ. with profl. divs., including normal, agrl., mech., law, med. colls., analytical and applied chemistry dept., became pres. emeritus, 1876. Contbr. articles to Merwin's Jour. of Edn. Died Keokuk, Ia., Oct. 3, 1878.

READ, George, pres. Continental Congress, senator; b. North East, Md., Sept. 18, 1733; s. John and Mary (Howell) R.; m. Gertrude (Ross) Till, Jan. 11, 1763, 1 dau., 4 sons including John. Admitted to Phila. bar, 1753; atty. gen. Lower Counties, Del., 1763-74, protested Stamp Act; mem. Del. Provincial Assembly, 1765-77; aided in obtaining adoption of Non-Incorporation Agreement in New Castle County, Del., 1769; helped secure relief for Boston, 1774; an organizer, mem. 1st-2d Continental congresses, 1774-77; signer Declaration of Independence; presiding officer Del. Constl. Conv., 1776; mem. Del. Legislative Council, 1776, 82-88, speaker and v.p. Del.; became pres. Continental Congress when Pres. John McKinley was imprisoned by British, 1777-78; mem. Del. Ho. of Reps., 1779, 80, mem. assembly drafting act authorizing Del. congressional dels. to sign Articles of Confederation, 1779; elected judge Admiralty Ct., 1782; apptd. by N.Y. and Mass. as a commr. to adjust boundary dispute, 1784; rep. to Annapolis Conv., 1786; del. to U.S. Constl. Conv., Phila., 1787; mem. U.S. Senate (Federalist) from Del., 1789-93; chief justice of Del., 1793-98. Died New Castle, Del., Sept. 21, 1798; buried Immanuel Churchyard, New Castle.

READ, George Campbell, naval officer; b. Ireland, 1787; s. Benjamin Read. Entered U.S. Navy as midshipman from Pa., 1804, commd. lt., 1810; served in battle between ships Constitution and Guerriere in War of 1812, participated in her escape from Sir Philip Broke's squadron, July 1812, won victory over Guerriere, Aug. 1812; on ship United States in action with Macedonian, Oct. 1812; commanded ship Chippewa in William Bainbridge's squadron against Algiers, 1815; on ship Hornet in West Indies, 1818-21, then on 2 voyages to Spain during treaty negotiations, 1819; commd. comdr., 1816, capt., 1825; commanded Constitution, 1826, Constellation, 1832-34; received much publicity due to difficulties with refractory officers, requested court martial, Balt., 1835, sentenced to year's suspension; best known service on flagship Columbia and John Adams; sailed for Orient on expdn. to punish Sumatrans and obtain restitution for capture of schooner Eclipse, 1838, bombarded Quallah Battoo, Sumatra, landed 350 men at town of Muckie, 1839, razed villages and secured pledge of restitution and friendship for local rajah; acting pres. of midshipmen's examining bd., 1845; commanded African Squadron, 1846-49; served at Phila. Navy Yard until 1853; on reserved list, 1855; gov. Phila. Naval Asylum, 1861-62; ret. with rank of rear adm. 1862. Died Phila., Aug. 22, 1862; buried Phila. Naval Asylum.

READ, Jacob, army officer, Continental congressman, senator; b. Christ Church Parish, S.C., 1752; s. James and Rebecca (Bond) R.; m. Catherine Van Horne, Oct. 13, 1785, 4 children. Admitted to Ga. bar, 1773; admitted to Gray's Inn, Eng., 1773; a signer of petition of Americans in London protesting against Mass. Govt. Acts, 1774; capt. S.C. Militia, 1776; speaker S.C. Ho. of Reps., 1781, 82, 89-94; Charleston rep. to Jacksonborough Assembly of 1782; mem. S.C. Privy Council, 1783; mem. S.C. Legislative Council, 1783, 84, also justice of quorum; del. Continental Congress from S.C., 1783-86; charter mem. co. to build canal from Ashley to Edisto rivers, S.C., 1787; mem. S.C. conv. to ratify U.S. Constn., 1788; admitted to S.C. bar, 1799; mem. U.S. Senate (Federalist) from S.C., 1795-1801; comdg. officer 7th brigade S.C. Militia, 1808-16, brig. gen., 1808-16. Died Charleston, July 16, 1816; buried Family Cemetery, Hobcaw, S.C.

READ, John, colonial ofcl.; b. Fairfield, Conn., Feb. 9, 1680; s. William and Deborah (Baldwin) R.; grad. Harvard, 1697; m. Ruth Talcott, several children. Preacher, Waterbury, East Hartford and Stratford (all Conn.), 1698-1706; admitted to Conn. bar, 1708; atty. gen. for the Crown in Conn., 1712-circa 1715; commr. for Conn. in boundary disputes with N.Y., Mass., R.I., and N.H., 1719-20; moved to Boston, 1721; atty. gen. Mass., 1723, 26, 34; mem. Mass. Gen. Ct. from Boston, 1738; mem. Mass. Gov.'s Council, 1741-42. Died Feb. 18, 1750.

READ, John, lawyer; b. New Castle, Del., July 17, 1769; s. George and Gertrude (Ross) R.; A.B., Princeton, 1787; m. Martha Meredith, June 25, 1796, 5 children including John Meredith. Admitted to bar at Phila., 1792; agent gen. U.S. to act upon Am. claims under Jay's Treaty of 1794 for compensation for slaves carried off by British during Revolutionary War, 1797-1809; mem. Phila. City Council, 1809-15; mem. Pa. Assembly, 1815-16, mem. Pa. Senate, 1817-18; pres. Phila. Bank, 1819-41; city solicitor Phila., 1818; active nat. councils Episcopal Ch., sr. warden Christ Ch., Phila., 1801-17, St. James Ch., Phila., 1817-41. Died Trenton, N.J., July 13, 1854.

READ, John Meredith, jurist; b. Phila., July 21, 1797; s. John and Martha (Meredith) R.; grad. U. Pa., 1812; LL.D. (hon.), Brown U., 1860; m. Priscilla Marshall, Mar. 20, 1828; m. 2d, Amelia Thompson, July 26, 1855; 5 children. Admitted to Pa. bar, 1818; city solicitor Phila., 1830-31; mem. Pa. Legislature from Phila., 1823-25; U.S. dist. atty. for Eastern Pa., 1837-44; atty. gen. Pa., 1846; judge Pa. Supreme Ct., 1858-73, became chief justice, 1872; participated in creation of Free Soil Party at Pa. State Conv., 1849; an early adherent Republican Party; delivered speech On the Power of Congress over the Territories and in Favor of Free Kansas, Free White Labor, and of Fremont and Dayton, Delivered . . . Sept. 30, 1856, at Philadelphia. Author: Views, Sustained by Facts, on the Suspension of the Privilege of the Writ of Habeas Corpus, Jan. 1863. Died Phila., Nov.29, 1874.

READ, John Meredith, diplomat; b. Phila., Feb. 21, 1837; s. John Meredith and Priscilla (Marshall) R.; grad. Brown U., 1858, Albany Law Sch., 1859; m. Delphine Pumpelly, Apr. 7, 1859, at least 4 children. Admitted to Phila. bar, 1859; served as adj. gen. with rank brig. gen. N.Y. Volunteers, 1860-61, directed mil. efforts of N.Y. State in opening months of Civil War; consul gen. at Paris, France, 1869; counsul gen. to Germany during Franco-Prussian War, 1870-72; minister resident in Greece, 1873; secured revocation of order against sale of translations of Bible and other religious works circulated by Brit. and Am. bible societies; for purposes of economy. U.S. Congress reduced his rank to chargé d'affaires, 1876, cut off all appropriations for the legation, 1878; he served at post without compensation until Sept. 1879; received highest Greek decoration. Author: A Historical Inquiry Concerning Henry Hudson, 1866; Historic Studies in Vaud, Berne, and Savoy: From Roman Times to Voltaire, Rousseau, and Gibbon, 1897. Died Paris, Dec. 27, 1896.

READ, Nathan, iron mfr., inventor; b. Warren, Mass., July 2, 1759; s. Rueben and Tamsin (Meacham) R.; grad. Harvard, 1781; m: Elizabeth Jeffrey, Oct. 20, 1790. Tchr., Beverly and Salem, Mass., 1781-83; tutor Harvard, 1783-87; devised double-acting steam engine, 1788; invented manually-operated paddle-wheel propelled boat, 1789; granted patents, on portable multitubular boiler, improved double-acting steam engine, chain wheel method of propelling boats 1791; organized Salem Iron Factory, 1796-1807; patented rail cutting and heading machine, 1798; mem. U.S. Ho. of Reps. (Federalist) from Mass., 6th-7th congresses, 1800-03; apptd. spl. justice Ct. of Common Pleas for Essex County (Mass.), 1803; chief justice Hancock County (Me.) Ct. of Common Pleas, 1807; mem. Am. Acad. Arts and Scis., 1791; hon. mem. Linnaean Soc. New Eng., 1815. Died Belfast, Me., Jan. 20, 1849.

READ, Thomas, naval officer; b. New Castle County, Del., 1740; s. John and Mary (Howell) R.; m. Mary Peele, circa 1782. Served as commodore Delaware River defense flotilla in Am. Revolution; became 2d in rank, Pa. State Navy, 1775 with command of brig Montgomery; resigned for captaincy in Continental Navy; ordered to protect Chesapeake Bay, Feb. 1779; apptd. to frigate Bowbon, Sept., 1779; made voyage on frigate Alliance to China by new route east of Dutch Indies and through Solomon Islands, discovered 2 islands which were thought to be Ponape and another of the Carolines, renamed islands Morris and Alliance. Died Fieldsboro, N.J., Oct. 26, 1788.

READ, Thomas Buchanan, painter, poet; b. Corner Ketch, Pa., Mar. 12, 1822; m. Mary J. Pratt, 1843; m. 2d, Harriet Denison Butler, 1856; at least 3 children. Published novelette Paul Redding: A Tale of the Brandywine, 1845; compiled anthology The Female Poets of America, 1849; best known painting is Sheridan's Ride; primarily portrait painter; had studio in Boston, 1841-46; moved to Phila., 1846, spent remainder of life there except for brief periods in Europe; author: Poems, 1847; Lays and Ballads, 1849; Poems, 1854, 56; The New Pastoral, 1855; House by the Sea, 1855; Rural Poems, 1857; Sylvia, or the Last Shepard, 1857; The Wagoner of the Alleghanies, 1862; A Summer Story, Sheridan's Ride, and Other Poems, 1865; Poetical Works, 1866. Died Astor House, N.Y.C., May 11, 1872; buried Central Laurel Hill Cemetery, Phila.

READ, William Brown, congressman, lawyer; b. Hardin County, nr. Hodgenville, Ky., Dec. 14, 1817; completed prep. studies; studied law. Admitted to bar, practiced in Hodgenville, 1849; mem. Ky. Senate, 1857-65; unsuccessful candidate for lt. gov. Ky., 1863; del. Nat. democratic convs., Charleston, Balt., 1860, Chgo., 1864; mem. Ky. Ho. of Reps., 1867-69; mem. U.S. Ho. of Reps. (Dem.) from Ky., 42d-43d congresses, 1871-75. Died Hodgenville, Aug. 5, 1880; buried Red Hill Cemetery.

READE, Edwin Godwin, congressman, jurist; b. Mt. Tirzah, N.C., Nov. 13, 1812; s. Robert R. and Judith (Gooch) R.; m. Emily Moore; m. 2d, Mrs. Mary E. Parmele, 1871. Admitted to N.C. bar, 1835; a Whig until he joined Am. Party, 1855; mem. U.S. Ho. of Reps. from N.C., 34th Congress, 1855-57; elected judge N.C. Superior Ct., 1863; mem. Confederate Senate, Jan-Feb. 1864; pres. Johnson or Reconstrn. Conv., 1865; asso. justice

N.C. Supreme Ct., 1865-79; important opinions include those issued in cases Jacob vs. Smallwood, and Hill vs. Kessler (63 N.C.), People vs. McKee (68 N.C.), State vs. Parrott (71 N.C.); pres. Nat. Bank, Raleigh, N.C., 1879-94. Died Raleigh, Oct. 18, 1894.

READING, John Roberts, congressman, physician; b. Somerton, Philadelphia County, Pa., Nov. 1, 1826; completed prep. studies; grad. Jefferson Med. Coll., 1847; grad. Hahnemann Coll. Practiced medicine, Somerton; practiced homeopathy. Mem. U.S. Ho. of Reps. (Democrat, contested election) from Pa., 41st Congress, 1869-Apr. 13, 1870. Died Phila., Feb. 14, 1886; buried William Penn Cemetery, Somerton.

READY, Charles, congressman, lawyer; b. Readyville, Rutherford (now Cannon) County, Tenn., Dec. 22, 1802; grad. Greenville (Tenn.) Coll.; studied law Admitted to bar, 1825, practiced in Murfreesboro, Tenn.; mem. Tenn. Ho. of Reps., 1835; mem. U.S. Ho. of Reps. (Whig) from Tenn., 33d-35th congresses, 1853-59. Died Murfreesboro, June 4, 1878; buried Evergreen Cemetery.

REALF, Richard, abolitionist, poet; b. Framfield, Sussex, Eng., June 14, 1834; s. Richard and Martha (Highland) R.; m. Sophia Emery Graves, 1865; m. 2d, Catherine Cassidy, 1867; married a 3d time; 4 children. Came to U.S., 1854; newspaper correspondent in Kan., 1856-58; asso. with John Brown; apptd. sec. of state in govt. which Brown planned to set up in Kan., 1858; served as pvt. 88th Ill. Regt., 1862-65; worked on newspaper, Pitts., 1872-77. Author: Guesses at the Beautiful, 1852; Poems by Richard Realf, Poet, Soldier, Workman, published posthumously, 1898. Died Oakland, Cal., Oct. 28, 1878; buried Lone Mountain Cemetery, Oakland.

RECTOR, Henry Massey, gov. Ark.; b. Louisville, Ky., May 1, 1816; s. Elias and Fannie (Thruston) R.; m. Jane Elizabeth Field, Oct. 1838; m. 2d, Ernestine Flora Linde, Feb. 1860; 7 children. U.S. marshal in Ark., 1842-48; mem. Ark. Senate, 1848-52, Ark. Ho. of Reps., 1855-59; asso. justice Ark. Supreme Ct., 1859-60; gov. Ark., 1860-62; mem. Ark. Constl. Conv., 1874. Died Aug. 12, 1899.

RED EAGLE, see Weatherford, William.

REDFIELD, Isaac Fletcher, jurist; b. Weathersfield, Vt., Apr. 10, 1804; s. Dr. Peleg and Hannah (Parker) R.; grad. Dartmouth, 1825; m. Mary Ward Smith, Sept. 28, 1836; m. 2d, Catherine Blanchard Clark, May 4, 1842; number of children uncertain, none survived him. Admitted to bar, Orleans County, Vt., 1827; states atty. Orleans County, 1832-35; justice Vt. Supreme Ct., 1835-60, chief justice, 1852-60; prof. med. jurisprudence Dartmouth, 1858-61; apptd. spl. counsel for U.S. to prosecute claims in Brit. Cts. for property held by Confederates and for losses caused by privateers fitted out in Eng., 1867-69; published Practical Treatise upon the Laws of Railways, 1858; published Reading American Railway Cases, 1870, added 2d vol., 1872; prepared edits. of Conflict of Laws and Equity Pleading (Joseph Story), published 1865, 70, Greenleaf's Evidence, published 1866; New Eng. editor Am. Law Register, 1862-76; published (posthumously) Law of Wills, 3d edit., 3 vols., 1864. Died Charlestown, Mass., Mar. 23, 1876; buried Windsor, Vt.

REDFIELD, Justus Starr, publisher, diplomat; b. Wallingford, Conn., Jan. 2, 1810; s. William and Sarah (Dejean) R.; m. Elizabeth Hall, 1835; m. 2d, Elizabeth Jones; 5 children. Printer, N.Y.C., 1827-34; publisher Family Mag., N.Y.C., 1834-41; owner bookstore, printing and publishing house, N.Y.C., 1841-60; published complete works of Edgar Allan Poe, 1850; dir. Nassau Bank, N.Y.C.; U.S. consul at Otranto, Italy, 1861-64, Brindisi, Italy, 1864-66. Died Florence, N.J., Mar. 24, 1888.

REDFIELD, William C., saddle and harness maker, meteorologist; b. Middletown, Conn., Mar. 26, 1789; s. Peleg and Elizabeth (Pratt) R.; m. Abigail Wilcox, Oct. 15, 1814; m. 2d, Lucy Wilcox, Nov. 23, 1820; m. 3d, Jane Wallace, Dec. 9, 1828; 4 children, including Charles Bailey. Apprenticed to saddle and harness maker, Upper Middletown, Conn., 1804; introduced correct and fundamental concept. of hurricanes in article "Remarks on the Prevailing Storms of the Atlantic Coast of the North American States", published in Am. Jour. Sci. and Arts, Apr. 1831, published meteorol. classic "Observations on the Hurricanes and Storms of the West Indies and the Coast of the United States", Oct. 1833; devised set of practical rules by which mariners could know their position during hurricanes; published pamphlet on proposed railroad to connect the Hudson and Mississippi rivers; a founder A.A.A.S., pres. 1848. Died N.Y.C., Feb. 12, 1857.

REDING, John Randall, congressman; b. Portsmouth, N.H., Oct. 18, 1805; attended common schs. Apprentice in printer's trade, became editor; mem. U.S. Ho. of Reps. (Democrat) from N.H., 27th-28th congresses, 1841-45; naval storekeeper, Portsmouth, 1853-58; mayor Portsmouth, 1860; mem. N.H. Ho. of Reps., 1867-70. Died Portsmouth, Oct. 8, 1892; buried Haverhill (N.H.) Cemetery.

RED JACKET (Sagoyewatha), Indian chief; b. Seneca County, N.Y., 1758; married twice. Chief of Seneca Indians; advocated war at Indian council at mouth of Detroit River, 1786; tried to make peace with U.S. and avoid being used as foil of Brit. diplomacy after 1791; protested at Washington (D. C.) against Pa. frontiersmen, 1801; strove to preserve right of separate Iroquois customs and jurisdiction, 1821; best known for opposition to white civilization, although sanctioned moves toward bringing white culture to Iroquois, 1792; opposed all changes in language, creed, blood by 1805; opposed establishment of missions; at height of his power tried to drive all white men from reservations; obtained law protecting reservations, 1821, insisted on law's enforcement for removal of missionaries, 1824; deposed as chief, circa 1827. Died Seneca Village, N.Y., Jan. 20, 1830; buried Christian cemetery on reservation's mission, Buffalo, N.Y.

REDMAN, John, physician; b. Phila., Feb. 27, 1722; s. Joseph and Sarah Redman; M.D., U. Leyden, July 15, 1748; m. Mary Sobers; at least 3 children. Strenuously advocated saline purgatives as opposd to emetics and bleeding in yellow fever epidemics in Phila., 1762, 93; a founder Coll. of Physicians, Phila., 1786; educated young physicians including John Morgan, Benjamin Rush, Caspar Wistar; cons. physician Pa. Hosp., 1751-80; 1st pres. Coll. of Physicians, Phila., 1786-1804; trustee Coll. of N.J. (now Princeton), Coll. of Phila.; elder Presbyn. Ch.; mem. Phila. Common Council, 1751; mem. Am. Philos. Soc. Author: A Defense of Inoculation (advocating direct inoculation for smallpox), 1759. Died Phila., Mar. 19, 1808.

REDPATH, James, journalist, booking agt.; b. Berwick-on-Tweed, Scotland, 1833; s. James and Marie (Davidson) R.; m. Mrs. Caroline Chorpenning, 1858. Staff mem. N.Y. Tribune, 1850, became an editor, 1853; an abolitionist, made visits to Kan., traveled through South writing on slavery, 1854-60; apptd. commr. of emigration in U.S. by pres. of Haiti, 1859; founded Haitian Emigrant Bur., Boston and N.Y.C.; sent several thousand ex-slaves to Haiti; Haitian consul in Phila., instrumental in making U.S. Govt. recognize Haitian independence; correspondent with U.S. Army during Civil War; supt.of edn. Charleston (S.C.), circa 1865, reorganized Colored schools; founded Colored orphan asylum; established 1st regular decoration of soldiers graves, Charleston, 1865; organized agy. for booking of lectures (early clients included Emerson, Greeley, Beecher, Thoreau, Sumner, Wendell Phillips, Julia Ward Howe.), booked humorists Mark Twain, Josh Billings, also poets, magicians, musical soloists, quartettes; finally organized small opera companies; edited North Am. Review, 1886-88. Author: The Roving Editor; or Talks with Slaves in the Southern States, 1859; A Handbook to Kansas Territory, 1859; Echoes of Harpers Ferry, 1860; The John Brown Invasion, 1860; Life of John Brown, 1860; John Brown the Hero, 1862; Talks about Ireland, 1881. Died N.Y.C., Feb. 10, 1891.

RED WING, (Indian name Tantagamini), Indian chief; b. probably Red Wing, Minn., circa 1750. Chief, Khemnichan band of Mdewakanton Sioux; most powerful leader among Mdewakanton Sioux; had reputation as seer; aided British in War of 1812; participated in attack on Ft. Sandusky (O.), 1813, probably in battle on Mackinac Island, in capture of Ft. Shelby, Prairie du Chien, Wis., 1814; later noted for his friendship to whites. Died circa 1825.

REDWOOD, Abraham, mcht., philanthropist; b. Island of Antigua, B.W.I., Apr. 15, 1709; s. Abraham and Mehetable (Langford) R.; m. Martha Coggeshall, Mar. 6, 1726, 6 children. Emigrated to U.S., 1711; developed one of 1st bot. gardens in Am. at Portsmouth, R.I.; mem. Philos. Soc., Newport, R.I.; financial contbr. to founding Redwood Library (one of earliest in U.S. whose building was designed by Peter Harrison), Newport; helped establish Friends sch., Newport; left 500 pounds in his will for founding of a coll. in R.I. Died Newport, Mar. 8, 1788.

REED, Charles Manning, congressman, mcht.; b. Erie, Pa., Apr. 3, 1803; grad. Washington (Pa.) Coll.; studied law. Admitted to Phila. bar, 1824, did not practice; in business with his father (owner vessels on Great Lakes), Erie; apptd. col. of militia, 1831, brig. gen. at end of his commn.; mem. Pa. Ho. of Reps., 1837, 38; mem. U.S. Ho. of Reps. (Whig) from Pa., 28th Congress, 1843-45; engaged in banking, mcht. activities, railroad business, shipping on Great Lakes, 1846-49. Died Erie, Dec. 16, 1871; buried Erie Cemetery.

REED, David, clergyman, editor; b. Easton, Mass., Feb. 6, 1790; s. William and Olive (Pool) R.; grad. Brown U., 1810; m. Mary Ann Williams, May 2, 1836, 3 children. Prin., Plymouth Acad., Bridgewater, Mass., 1810-13; licensed to preach by Unitarian Ch., 1814, itinerant preacher in New Eng., 1814-21; founder, editor Christian Register (a Unitarian weekly), 1821-66; co-founder Am. Anti-Slavery Soc., 1828. Died June 7, 1870.

REED, Edward Cambridge, congressman, lawyer; b. Fitzwilliam, N.H., Mar. 8, 1793; grad. Dartmouth, 1812; studied law, Troy, N.Y. Served under Gov. Marcy in War of 1812; admitted to bar, 1816, practiced in Homer, N.Y.; sec. bd. trustees Cortland Acad., Homer, 1822-70; dist. atty. Cortland County, 1827-36, 56; admitted to Ct. of Chancery, 1830; mem. U.S. Ho. of Reps. (Democrat) from N.Y., 22d Congress, 1831-33; asso. judge Cortland County Ct. Common Pleas, 1836-40; moved to Ithaca, N.Y., 1875, practiced law. Died Ithaca, May 1, 1883; buried Glenwood Cemetery, Homer.

REED, Henry Hope, literary critic, educator; b. Phila., July 11, 1808; s. Joseph and Maria (Watmaugh) R.; grad. U. Pa., 1825; m. Elizabeth Bronson, 1834; 6 children. Admitted to Pa. bar, 1829, practiced in Pa.; became asst. prof. English literature U. Pa., 1831, also prof. rhetoric, 1835-54; mem. Am. Philos. Soc., 1838; 1st Am. exponent of Wordsworth, prepared Am. editor Wordsworth's Complete Works, 1837; published critique of Wordsworth in N.Y. Review, 1839; prepared Reid's Dictionary of the English Language, 1845; Graham's English Synonymes (for which he supplied quotations from Shakespeare, Milton, Wordsworth), 1847; prepared Gray's Poetical Works; published Memoirs of William Wordsworth, 1851. Author: Lecture on the Literary Opportunities of Men of Business, 1838; other lectues published posthumously. Died in wreck of ship Arctic in Atlantic Ocean, Sept. 27, 1854.

REED, Isaac, congressman, ship builder; b. Waldoboro, Me., Aug. 22, 1809; attended Bloomfield Acad. Became mcht. ship builder, also banker; clk. Town of Waldoboro, 1836-38; mem. Me. Senate, 1839-40, 50, 63; mem. Me. Ho. of Reps., 1842-43, 46, 70, 71; pres. town board, 1843-68, selectman, 1849-53, 55-56; mem. Me. Bd. Agr.; trustee Me. Insane Hosp.; mem. U.S. Ho. of Reps. (Whig, filled vacancy) from Me., 32d Congress, June 25, 1852-53; unsuccessful candidate for gov. Me., 1854, 55; treas. Me., 1856; became Democrat at dissolution Whig Party. Died Waldoboro, Sept. 19, 1887; buried Central Cemetery.

REED, James, army officer; b. Woburn, Mass., Jan. 8, 1724; s. Thomas and Sarah (Sawyer) R.; m. Abigail Hinds, 1745; m. 2d, Mary Farrar, 1791; 2 children. Served as capt. during French and Indian War; went with expdn. of 1775 to Crown Point; served under Gen. Abercromby, 1758; raised troops after Battle of Lexington; commd. col. 3d N.H. Regt., 1775; served at Battle of Bunker Hill; commd. col. 2d Regt., Continental Army, 1776, while in Canada promoted to brig. gen. by Act of Congress, Aug. 1776; retired, Sept. 1776. Died Fitchburg, Mass., Feb. 13, 1807.

REED, John, congressman, clergyman; b. Framingham, Mass., Nov. 11, 1751; grad. Yale, 1772; studied theology; at least 1 son, John. Ordained to ministry Congregational Ch., 1780; chaplain U.S. Navy for 2 years; moved to West Bridgewater, Mass., 1780; pastor First Congrl. Soc., 1780-1831; mem. U.S. Ho. of Reps. (Federalist) from Mass., 4th-6th congresses, 1795-1801. Died West Bridgewater, Feb. 17, 1831; buried Old Graveyard.

REED, John, miner; b. Hesse-Cassel, Germany, Jan. 6, 1757; m. Sarah Kisor, 8 children. Served as mercenary for British during Am. Revolution; became farmer, Cabarrus County, N.C., 1784; discovered gold on his property, 1802; began mining operations, 1803; mine had produced over $10,000,000 worth of gold by his death; as result of his discovery gold mining became 2d only to agr. in econ. importance to N.C.; bought large plantation, Cabarrus County. Died Cabarrus County, Mar. 28, 1845.

REED, John congressman; b. West Bridgewater, Mass., Sept. 2, 1781; son of John Reed; grad. Brown U., 1803; studied law. Tutor languages Brown U. for 2 years; prin. Bridgewater (Mass.) Acad., 1806-07; admitted to bar, practiced in Yarmouth, Mass.; mem. U.S. Ho. of Reps. (Federalist) from Mass., 13th-14th, (Whig) 17th-26th congresses, 1813-17, 21-41; lt. gov. Mass., 1845-51; retired from public life. Died West Bridgewater, Nov. 25, 1860.

REED, Joseph, Continental congressman; b. Trenton, N.J., Aug. 27, 1741; s. Andrew and Theodosia (Bowes) R.; B.A., Coll. of N.J. (now Princeton), 1757; studied Middle Temple, London, Eng. 2 years; m. Ester de Berdt, May 22, 1770; Admitted to N.J. bar, 1763; apptd. dep. sec. Colony of N. J., 1767; apptd. mem. Com. of Correspondence for

Phila., 1774; pres. 2d N.J. Provincial Congress, 1775; apptd. lt. col. Pa. Asso. Militia, 1775, became mil. sec. to Gen. Washington; mem. Pa. Com. of Safety, 1775; mem. Continental Congress from Pa., 1775, 77-78; adj. gen. Continental Army with rank of col., 1775, participated in L.I. campaign, promoted brig. gen., 1777; served at battles of Brandywine, Germantown, Monmouth, Portsmouth; pres. Supreme Exec. Council Pa., 1778-81; responsible for abolition of slavery in Pa.; prosecuted Benedict Arnold, a founder U. Pa., trustee, 1782-85. Died Phila., Mar. 5, 1785; buried Arch St. Presbyn. Ch. Cemetery, Phila.

REED, Luman, mcht., art patron; b. Austerlitz, N.Y., June 4, 1787; s. Eliakim and Rebecca (Fitch) R.; m. Mary Baker, 3 children. Served as supercargo on sloop carrying farm produce on Hudson River; became clerk in grocery business of Roswell Reed, N.Y.C., partner 1815-36; an art patron, supported many artists (including George Flagg, Thomas Cole, William Sydney Mount) paid their expenses for European study; owned personal gallery in N.Y.C., collection given to N.Y. Hist. Soc. after his death; mem. Sketch Club, N.Y.C. Died June 7, 1836.

REED, Philip, senator, congressman; b. nr. Chestertown, Kent County, Md., 1760; completed prep. studies. Served in Revolutionary Army, attained rank capt. of Infantry; mem. Md. Ho. of Dels., 1787; sheriff Kent County, 1791-94; mem. Exec. Council, 1805, 06, resigned. Mem. U.S. Senate (filled vacancy) from Md., Nov. 25, 1806-13; lt. col. 21st Regt., Md. Militia in War of 1812, lt. col. commandant of 1st Regt., 1814, defeated British in Battle of Caulk's Field, made brig. gen. Md. Militia in recognition of his service; mem. U.S. Ho. of Reps. (contested election) from Md., 15th, 17th congresses, 1817-19, Mar. 19, 1822-23. Died Huntingtown, Kent County, Nov. 2, 1829; buried cemetery of Christ Ch., nr. Chestertown.

REED, Robert Rentoul, congressman, physician; b. Washington, Pa., Mar. 12, 1807; grad. Washington (Pa.) and Jefferson Coll., 1824; grad. med. dept. U. Pa., 1829. Practiced medicine, Washington; mem. U.S. Ho. of Reps. (Whig) from Pa., 31st Congress, 1849-51; mem. Pa. Ho. of Reps., 1863-64. Died nr. Washington, Dec. 14, 1864; buried Washington Cemetery.

REED, Sampson, businessman, author; b. West Bridgewater, Mass., June 10, 1800; s. John and Hannah (Sampson) R.; grad. Harvard, 1818, M.A., 1821; attended Harvard Divinity Sch.; m. Catharine Clark, Dec. 25, 1832, at least 4 children including James. Built one of largest wholesale drug establishments in New Eng.; a chief supporter of New Jerusalem Mag., from 1828, became one of its editors, 1854; founded New Church Mag. for Children, 1843; (called Children's New-Church Mag. after 1860); a Swedenborgian writer. Author: Observations on the Growth of the Mind, 1826; The Correspondence of the Sun, Heat and Light, 1862; A Biographical Sketch of Thomas Worcester, D.D., 1880. Died Boston, July 8, 1880.

REED, Simeon Gannett, mcht., steamboat operator; b. East Abington, Mass., Apr. 23, 1830; s. Simeon Gannet and Rachel (Burgess) R.; m. Amanda Wood, Oct. 17, 1850. Invested in 3 steamers on Columbia River 1858; organizer (with J.C. Ainsworth and Robert Thompson) Ore. Steam Navigation Co., 1860, brought railroad from the Columbia River to Walla Walla, Wash.; developed valuable mines in Eastern Ore.; owner Bunker Hill Mine in No. Ida., 1887; bequeathed entire fortune to wife to give some portion "to development of the fine arts of said city of Portland (Ore.)," resulted in founding of Reed Coll. (opened 1911). Died Nov. 7, 1895.

REED, Thomas Buck, senator; b. nr. Lexington, Ky., May 7, 1787; attended Princeton; studied law. Admitted to bar, practiced in Lexington, 1808; moved to Natchez, Miss., 1809; city clk., 1811; atty. gen. Miss., 1821-26; mem. Miss. Ho. of Reps., 1825, did not take seat; mem. U.S. Senate (Democrat, filled vacancy) from Miss., Jan. 28, 1826-27, Mar. 4-Nov. 26, 1829. Died Lexington, Nov. 26, 1829; buried Old Baptist Cemetery.

REED, Walter, physician; b. Belroi, Gloucester County, Va., Sept. 13, 1851; s. Lemuel Sutton and Pharaba (White) R.; M.D., U. Va., 1869, Bellevue Hosp. Med. Coll., N.Y.C., 1870; A.M. (Hon.), Harvard, 1902; LL.D. (hon.), U. Mich., 1902; m. Amelia Laurence, 1876, 2 children. Commd. asst. surgeon with rank of lt., M.C., U.S. Army, 1875; stationed at Ft. Lowell, Ariz., 1876-87; attending surgeon and examiner of recruits, Balt., 1890-93; promoted maj., 1893; curator Army Med. Museum, prof. bacteriology and clin. microscopy Army Med. Sch., Washington, D.C., 1893-1902; made extensive studies of bacteriology of erysipelas and diptheria; apptd. chmn. com. to study typhoid fever among U.S. soldiers in Cuba, 1898, proved that disease transmitted by dust and flies; head commn. to study yellow fever, Cuba, 1900, discovered disease transmitted by mosquito Aëdesoegypti; prof. pathology and bacteriology Columbian U., Washington, 1901-02; died of appendicitis, 1902. Author: The Contagiousness of Erysipelas, 1892. Died Washington, Nov. 22, 1902; buried Arlington Nat. Cemetery.

REED, William, congressman, mcht.; b. Marblehead, Essex County, Mass., June 6, 1776. Became mcht.; mem. U.S. Ho. of Reps. (Federalist) from Mass., 12th-13th congresses, 1811-15; mem. bd. Andover Theol. Sem.; trustee Dartmouth. Died Marblehead, Feb. 18, 1837; buried pvt. burying ground on Harris St.

REED, William Bradford, diplomat, author; b. Phila., June 30, 1806; s. Joseph and Maria (Watmaugh) R.; grad. U. Pa., 1822; m. Louisa Whelan; m. 2d, Mary Ralston; at least 3 children. Admitted to Pa. bar, 1826; mem. Pa. Assembly (Whig), 1834-35; atty. gen. of Pa., 1838; mem. Pa. Senate, 1841-42; elected dist. atty. of Phila., 1850-56; parttime prof. Am. history U. Pa., 1850-56; joined Democratic Party, 1856; apptd. to Chinese mission, circa 1857, arrived China, Nov. 1857, concluded Treaty of Tientsin, 1858; supported James Buchanan and Democratic Party on his return to U.S., 1860; Am. corr. London Times; wrote for Am. Quar. Review, The N.Am. Review; began contributing to N.Y. world, 1870. Author: Life and Correspondence of Joseph Reed, 1847; The Life of Esther De Berdt, Afterwards Esther Reed of Pennsylvania, 1853; Pres. Reed of Pa., a Reply to Mr. George Bancroft and Others, 1867. Died N.Y.C., Feb. 18, 1876.

REEDER, Andrew Horatio, territorial gov.; b. Easton, Pa., July 12, 1807; s. Absalom and Christiana (Smith) R.; m. Amelia Hutter, 1831, 8 children. Admitted to N.J. bar, 1828; apptd. Democratic gov. Kansas Territory, 1854, removed from office at request of legislature, 1855; attended Big Springs conv., wrote report of resolutions com. attacking legislature, circa 1855; indicted for treason, but escaped by way of Missouri River (disguised as Irish laborer), arrived in Ill., 1856; kept diary from May 5-31, 1856 (printed in Transactions of the Kansas State Hist. Soc.); presided at Cleve. Conv. for Kansas aid, 1856; participated in Fremont presdl. campaign; chmn. Pa. delegation to Rep. Nat. Conv., Chgo., 1860, Balt., 1864. Died Easton, July 5, 1864.

REES, James, steamboat builder, inventor; b. Wales, Dec. 25, 1821; s. Thomas and Mary (Bowen) R.; m. Mary Morris, 10 children. Came to Am., 1828; foreman Snowden & Co., Brownsville, Pa., also Stackhouse & Thompson; supervised constrn. engines for revenue cutter Lake Michigan, 1843; in charge shop Rowe & Davis, which he subsequently leased and operated; bought establishment of Robert Whiteman; in early 1850's, started passenger and freight steamer line on Allegheny River (his vessels being important factors in oil-carrying trade); popularized "sternwheeler" in U.S.; had orders from South Am. countries, also built boats for carrying trade on Volga and Dneiper rivers; inventor hot die press for making nuts and bolts; improved steamboat constrn., especially protection of working parts; introduced 10-hour day in his shops; mem. Pitts. City Council. Died Sept. 12, 1889.

REESE, David Addison, congressman, physician; b. Charlotte, N.C., Mar. 3, 1794; studied medicine; grad. Jefferson Med. Coll. Practiced medicine, Elberton, Ga.; moved to Monticello, Ga., practiced medicine; mem. Ga. Senate, 1829-30, 34-36; trustee U. Ga. for 25 years; mem. U.S. Ho. of Reps. (Whig) from Ga., 33d Congress, 1853-55; moved to Auburn, Ala., practiced medicine. Died Auburn, Dec. 16, 1871; buried Hopewell Cemetery, West Point, Troup County, Ga.

REESE, John James, physician, toxicologist; b. Phila., June 16, 1818; s. Jacob and Leah (James) R.; A.B., U. Pa., 1836, A.M., M.D., 1839; m. Sallie Gibson, several children. Lectr. on materia medica and therapeutics Phila. Med. Inst.; prof. med. chemistry med. dept. Pa. Coll., 1852-59; prof. med. jurisprudence and toxicology U. Pa., 1865-91; mem. firm Booth, Reese & Camac, analytic chemists, Phila.; commd. asst. surgeon U.S. Army during Civil War, head Christian Street Hosp., Phila.; treas. Phila. County Med. Soc.; pres. Med. Jurisprudence Soc. of Phila., 1886-87; gave expert testimony on toxicology in ct., expecially in trial of Mrs. Warton (J.T. Morse, Jr. in Am. Law Rev. July 1872). Author: The American Medical Formulary, 1850; Syllabus of a Course of Lectures on Medical Chemistry, 1857; Manual of Toxicology, 1874. Died Atlantic City, N.J., Sept. 4, 1892.

REEVE, Tapping, jurist, educator; b. Brookhaven, L.I., N.Y., Oct. 1744; s. Abner Reeve; grad. Coll. of N.J. (now Princeton), 1763; m. Sally Burr; married second to his former housekeeper, 1799; 1 son, Aaron Burr Reeve. Tutor, Coll. of N.J., 1769-70; admitted to Conn. bar, 1772; apptd. mem. com. to arouse interest in Revolution by Conn. Assembly, 1776; state's atty. Conn., 1788; mem. Conn. Legislature, Conn. Council; Federalist; frequent contbr. to Litchfield (Conn.) Monitor, using nom de plume Phocion or Asdrubal; indicted by fed. grand jury for libelling Pres. Jefferson in the Monitor, 1806; founder Litchfield Law Sch. (1st ind. law sch.), 1784, sole tchr., 1784-98; judge Conn. Superior Ct., 1798-1814; agt. in Litchfield for Conn. Bible Soc.; chmn. of meeting to found soc. for suppression of vice and promotion of good morals, New Haven, Conn., 1812; chief justice Conn. Supreme Ct. of Errors, 1814-16. Author: The Law of Baron and Femme . . ., 4 edits., 1816; A Treatise on the Law of Descents in the Several United States of America, published 1825. Died Litchfield, Dec. 13, 1823.

REEVES, Arthur Middleton, philologist, historian; b. Cincinnati, Oct. 7, 1856; s. Mark Ewen and Caroline (Middleton) R.; grad. Cornell U., 1878. Established thriving printing business, 1872 (later consolidated with Palladium); learned German, Swedish, Icelandic, French, Italian, Danish, Spanish, langs.; became philological authority; traveled in Iceland with Prof. Fiske, 1879; examined Old Norse manuscripts in Copenhagen. Translator Lad and Lass (Thoroddsen), 1890; The Finding of Wineland the Good (saga dealing with Norse discoveries of Am., posthumously reproduced in The Norse Discovery of America, 1906), 1890. Died Hagerstown, Ind., Feb. 25, 1891.

REICH, Johann (John) Mathias, medallist; b. Furth, Bavaria, 1768; s. Johann Christian Reich. Came to Phila., circa 1800; executed several medals for U.S. Govt., 1801-13; apptd. asst. engraver U.S. Mint, 1807; a founder Soc. of Artists, 1811, Pa. acad., 1812; went West, after 1813. Died Albany, N.Y., 1833.

REICHEL, Charles Gotthold, educator; clergyman; b. Hermsdorff, Silesia, July 14, 1751; s. Carl Rudolph and Eleanore (Müller) R.; theol. degree, Barby, Saxony; D.D., U. N.C.; m. Anna Maass, Oct. 2, 1780; m. 2d, Catharina Fetter, July 31, 1809, 10 children. Tchr., Niesky, Prussia, 1774, 78-80; ednl. work, Barby, 1775-77; sec. to governing bd. of ch., 1780-84; came to Am., 1784; 1st prin. (insp.) acad., Nazareth, Pa.; consecrated bishop Moravian Ch., Bethlehem, Pa., 1801; supr. So. province, Salem, N.C.; head No. province, Bethlehem, 1811; sent to Gen. Synod, Herrnhut, Saxony, 1818. Author: Geographie aum Gebrauch der Schulen in den Evangelischen Brüdergemeinen (geog. textbook), 2 vols., 1785; editor (for Am. use) Lesebuch für Deutsche Schulkinder, 1795. Died Niesky, Apr. 18, 1825.

REICHEL, William Cornelius, educator, historian; b. Salem, N.C., May 9, 1824; s. Gotthold Benjamin and Henrietta (Vierling) R.; B.A., Moravian Coll. and Theol. Sem., Bethlehem, Pa., 1844; m. Mary Jane Gray, 1852; m. 2d, Addie Harkins, Oct. 27, 1867; 2 children. Tchr. drawing and Latin, Nazareth Hall, Salem, 1844-52, Boy's Sch., Bethlehem, 1852-58; prof. classical langs. Moravian Coll., 1858-62; prin. Linden Hall Sch. for Girls, Lititz, Pa., 1862-70; engaged in hist. research, taught drawing and painting at Bethlehem Sem. for Young Ladies, 1870-76. Author: A History of the Rise, Progress, and Present Condition of the Bethlehem Female Seminary, 1858; Memorials of the Moravian Church, 1870; A Red Rose from the Olden Time, 1872; The Old Sun Inn at Bethlehem, 1873. Died Bethlehem, Oct. 25, 1876.

REID, David Boswell, chemist, educator, engr.; b. Edinburgh, Scotland, June 1805; s. Peter and Christian (Arnot) R.; M.D., U. Edinburgh, 1830; m. Elizabeth Brown, 1834; at least 5 children. Pvt. lectr. on chemistry and sanitation in his own pvt. sch. (contained lab. larger than any in Eng.); circa 1833; tested principles of ventilation and acoustics in "1st systematic plan of ventilation ever carried out in any public building," in Temporary Ho. of Parliament Bldg., 1835; arranged and superintended ventilation and lighting of new Houses of Parliament, London, Eng., 1840; came to U.S., 1855; prof. physiology and hygiene, dir. Museum Practical Scis., U. Wis., 1859-60; inspector mil. hosps. throughout U.S., 1863. Author: Introduction to the Study of Chemistry, 1832; Rudiments of the Chemistry of Daily Life, 1836; Outlines for the Ventilation of the House of Commons, 1837; Illustrations of the Theory and Practice of Ventilation, 1844. Died Washington, D.C., Apr. 5, 1863.

REID, David Settle, senator, gov. N.C.; b. Rockingham County, N.C., Apr. 19, 1813; s. Reuben and Elizabeth (Settle) R.; m. Henrietta Settle, circa 1834. Admitted to N.C. bar, 1833; mem. N.C. Senate (Democrat), 1835-42; mem. U.S. Ho. of Reps. (Democrat) from N.C., 28th-29th congresses, 1843-47; gov. N.C., 1850-54; mem. U.S. Senate (Democrat) from N.C., 1850-54; mem. Washington (D.C.) Peace Conv., 1861; mem. N.C. Secession Conv., 1861; del. N.C. Constl. Conv., 1875. Died Reidsville, N.C., June 19, 1891; buried Greenwood Cemetery, Reidsville.

REID, James Randolph, Continental congressman; b. Phila., Aug. 11, 1718; had academic tng.; studied law. Admitted (or readmitted) to bar, 1781; mem. Continental Congress from Pa., 1787-89.

REID, John Morrison, clergyman, coll. pres., editor; b. N.Y.C., May 30, 1820; s. John and Jane (Morrison) R.; grad. U. City of N.Y., 1839; attended Union Theol. Sem., N.Y.C., 1839-41; A.M. (hon.), Wesleyan U., 1852; D.D. (hon.), N.Y.U., 1858; LL.D. (hon.), Syracuse U., 1881; m. Anna Mason, Nov. 14, 1844; m. 2d, Caroline Fanton, May 10, 1848; 1 dau., Annie M. Licensed to preach 1838; as Methodist Episcopal Minister; taught at Mechanics Inst. Sch., N.Y.C., 1841-44; entered N.Y. Conv., 1844; ordained to ministry Methodist Ch., 1846; pastor chs. in Conn. and N.Y., 14 years; abolitionist; mem. Gen. Conf., Meth. Ch., 1856-88; pres. Genesee Coll. (now Syracuse U.), Lima, N.Y., 1858-64; editor Western Christian Advocate, 1864, Northwestern Christian Advocate, 1868; corr. sec. Methodist Missionary Soc., 1872-88, hon. sec., 1888; contbr. to endowment of Syracuse U. Author: Missions and Missionary Society of the Methodist Episcopal Church, 1879; Doomed Religions, 1883. Died N.Y.C., May 16, 1896.

REID, John William, congressman, lawyer; b. nr. Lynchburg, Va., June 14, 1821; attended common schs.; studied law. Moved to Mo., 1840; taught sch.; admitted to bar, practiced in Jefferson City, Mo., 1844; served as capt. in Mexican War; mem. Mo. Ho. of Reps., 1854-56; mem. U.S. Ho. of Reps. (Democrat) from Mo., 37th Congress, Mar. 4-Aug. 3, 1861 (withdrew); served as volunteer aide to Gen. Price in Confederate Army in Civil War; apptd. commr. to adjust claims against Confederate Govt.; settled in Kansas City, Mo., practiced law, became banker. Died Lees Summit, Jackson County, Mo., Nov. 22, 1881; buried Elmwood Cemetery, Kansas City.

REID, Robert Raymond, congressman, Fla. territorial gov.; b. Prince William Parish, Beaufort Dist., S.C., Sept. 8, 1789; attended S.C. Coll., Columbia; studied law. Moved to Augusta, Ga.; admitted to bar, began practice of law, 1810; elected judge Ga. Superior Ct., 1816-19; mem. U.S. Ho. of Reps. (Democrat, filled vacancy) from Ga., 15th-17th congresses, Feb. 18, 1819-23; judge Ga. Middle Circuit Ct., 1823-25, Augusta City Ct., 1827-32; Dem. presdl. elector, 1828; U.S. judge East Fla. Dist., 1832-39; gov. Fla. Territory, 1839-41; pres. Fla. Constl. Conv. Died Blackwood, nr. Tallahassee, Fla., July 1, 1841.

REID, Samuel Chester, sea capt.; b. Norwich, Conn., Aug. 25, 1783; s. Lt. John and Rebecca (Chester) R.; m. Mary Jennings, June 8, 1813, 8 children, including Samuel Chester, Mary Isabel, Louise Gouvernour. Master of brig Merchant, 1803; commanded privateer General Armstrong during War of 1812, in Fayal harbor in the Azores repulsed 3 attacks from Brit. warships, scuttled his ship to escape capture; harbor master of N.Y.C., improved pilot-boat service, pub. signal code for Am. vessels, secured lightship off Sandy Hook; devised system of rapid signaling on land, demonstrated that message could be sent from N.Y.C. to New Orleans in 2 hours; designer of an Am. flag, proposed 13 stripes and 1 star for each state with stars in parallel rows for mil. use and 1 great star for other purposes; flag adopted by U.S. Congress, 1818, 1st flag made by his wife, hoisted on Capitol Bldg., Apr. 12, 1818; sailing master in U.S. Navy, 1843. Died Jan. 28, 1861; buried Franklin Square, N.Y.C.

REID, Thomas Mayne, author; b. Ballyroney, County Down, Ireland, Apr. 4, 1818; s. Thomas Mayne and Miss (Rutherford) R.; m. Elizabeth Hyde, 1853; at least 1 child. Came to New Orleans, circa 1838; published early verse in Pitts. Morning Chronicle under penname The Poor Scholar, 1842, also poems in Godey's Lady's Book; wrote 5-act tragedy Love's Martyr produced at Walnut Street Theatre, Oct. 23, 1848; became society corr. for N.Y. Herald at Newport, R.I., summer 1846; wrote for Spirit of the Times, fall 1846; served from 2d lt. to 1st lt., 1st N.Y. Volunteers in Mexican War, 1846-48, served at Veracruz, Battle of Chapultepec; published Little Times (evening daily), London, Eng., 1866; returned to Am., 1867; published mag. Onward, 1869-circa 1870. Author of more than 90 books including books for boys and nearly 70 novels, novels include The Rifle Rangers, 1850, The Quadroon, 1856, The Child Wife, 1868. Died London, Oct. 22, 1883.

REID, William Shields, clergyman, coll. pres.; b. Chester County, Pa., Apr. 21, 1778; s. Adam and Martha (Shields) R.; grad. Princeton, 1802; m. Clemintina Venable, Dec. 12, 1807, 12 children. Tutor, Hampden-Sydney Coll., 1804-06, pres., 1807; licensed to preach by Winchester Presbytery, 1806; conducted boarding sch., Lynchburg, Va., 1808-48; pastor Presbyn. Ch., Lynchburg, 1822-48. Died Lynchburg, June 23, 1853.

REIERSEN, Johan Reinhart, immigrant leader, editor; b. Vestre Moland, Norway, Apr. 17, 1810; s. Ole and Kirsten (Gjerulfsdatter) R.; m. Henrietta Waldt, Aug. 5, 1836; m. 2d, Ouline Orbek; 8 children. Edited several Danish mags., Copenhagen, Denmark, 1830's; published nearly 20 vols. of translations (mostly English, French, Spanish works including George Sand's Valentine); established publ., Christianssandsposten, in Norway, 1839; pictured Am. favorably and argued for emigration; came to U.S. in behalf of group of prospective emigrants, 1843; published Pathfinder for Norwegian Emigrants to the United North American States and Texas (most comprehensive book about Am. published in Norway at that time, had marked influence on Norwegian emigrants), 1844; led small group of emigrants to Tex., Spring 1845, established Brownsboro (1st Norwegian settlement in Tex.); founded monthly mag., Norway and America, 1845-47; founded 2d Norwegian settlement in Tex. at Prairieville, 1848. Died Prairieville, Sept. 6, 1864.

REILLY, Wilson, congressman, lawyer; b. Waynesboro, Franklin County, Pa., Aug. 8, 1811; attended common schs.; studied law. Became a hatter, Waynesboro, Chambersburg, Pa.; admitted to bar, 1837, practiced in Chambersburg; pros. atty. Franklin County, 1842-45; mem. U.S. Ho. of Reps. from Pa., 35th Congress, 1857-59; capt. McClure Rifles which joined Pa. Reserve Corps at Camp Curtin, Harrisburg, Pa. Died Chambersburg, Aug. 26, 1885; buried Falling Spring Cemetery.

REILY, Luther, congressman, physician; b. Myerstown, Pa., Oct. 17, 1794; completed prep. studies; studied medicine. Practiced medicine, Harrisburg, Pa.; held various local offices; served as pvt. in Capt. R. M. Crane's company of Pa. Volunteers in War of 1812, 1814, surgeon's mate in Maj. Gen. R. Watson's company, 1814; mem. U.S. Ho. of Reps. (Democrat) from Pa., 25th Congress, 1837-39. Died Harrisburg, Feb. 20, 1854; buried Harrisburg Cemetery.

REINAGLE, Alexander, musician, composer; b. Portsmouth, Eng., Apr. 1756; son of Joseph Reinagle; married twice; m. 2d, Anna Duport, Sept. 20, 1803; children—Thomas, Hugh, Georgianna. Performed in Lisbon, Portugal, Jan. 1785 (once for royal family); came to Am., 1786; worked on series of city concerts, Phila., 1786-94; composed 4 piano sonatas which are finest surviving Am. instrumental prodns. of 18th Century; superintended constrn. New Theatre, Phila., opened for concert series, Feb. 1793, active with theatre until 1809; elected hon. mem. St. Andrew's Soc. of Pa., 1794. Composer: Twenty-Four Short and Easy Pieces for the Pianoforte, circa 1774; original incidental music for: Slaves in Algiers, 1794, Columbus, 1797, The Savoyard, 1797, Pizarro, 1800, The Castle Spectre, 1800; (entire score for operas) The Sicilian Romance, 1795, The Volunteers, 1795; (songs) "The Federal March," "America, Commerce and Freedom," "The Tars of Columbia." Died Balt., Sept. 21, 1809.

REINHART, Benjamin Franklin, artist; b. Waynesburg, Pa., Aug. 29, 1829; s. Joseph and Sarah (Smith) R.; studied at N.A.D., N.Y.C., 1847-50, Paris, France, Rome, Italy, 1850-53. Genre and portrait painter, N.Y.C., 1853-61, London, Eng., 1861-68, N.Y.C., 1868-85; mem. N.A.D., 1871-85; portraits include Thomas Carlyle, Alfred Lord Tennyson, James Buchanan, Winfield Scott, Stephen A. Douglas, and Samuel Houston; genre paintings include Cleopatra, 1865, Evangeline, 1877, Pride of the Village, 1884. Died May 3, 1885.

REINHART, Charles Stanley, genre painter, illustrator; b. Pitts., May 16, 1844; s. Aaron Grantley and Catherine (McHenry) R.; studied Atelier Suisse, Paris, 1867, Royal Acad., Munich, Germany, 1868-70; m. Emily Varet, 1873, 3 children. Telegraph operator U.S. R.R. Corps, br. of Q.M.'s Dept., Army of Potomac, 1861-64; went to Paris, 1867; illustrator for Harper & Bros. (drew for firm exclusively), 1870-77; worked for Scribner, Appleton, Osgood; did drawings for G. P. Lathrop's Spanish Vistas, 1883; his large painting "Washed Ashore" exhibited in Paris Salon of 1887, "High Tide at Gettysburg" in Salon of 1900; made series of drawings for C. D. Warner's Their Pilgrimage, 1887; sold picture "Rising Tide" to French Govt., 1890. Oils include "In a Garden," 1883, "Mussel Fisherwoman," 1884, "Fla at Villerville," 1884, "Sunday," 1885, "English Garden," "Fisherman of Villerville," 1886, "Awaiting the Absent," 1888; water colors include "Gathering Wood," 1877, "Close of Day," 1877, "At the Ferry;" "Spanish Barber," 1884; awarded 1st gold medal and silver medal Paris Expn., 1889. Died N.Y.C., Aug. 30, 1896.

REITZEL, Robert, writer, critic; b. Weitenau, Amt Schopfheim, Baden, Germany, Jan. 27, 1849; s. Reinhard and Katharina (Uehline) R.; m. Anna Martin, 1872, 8 children. Came to U.S., 1870; pastor 1st German Reformed Ch., Washington, D.C., 1871; started "free ch." (no dogmatic restraints on the speaker), circa 1873; launched weekly Der Arme Teufel, Detroit, 1884 (became most popular German-Am. publ. outside ch. circles); Arme Teufel Klubs were organized in many cities; literary critic, favorite subjects were Shakespeare, Lessing, Goethe, Schiller, Hawthorne, Thoreau, Whitman; wrote only in German; published verses Des Arme Teufel. Died Detroit, Mar. 31, 1898.

RELFE, James Hugh, congressman, physician; b. Va., Oct. 17, 1791; studied medicine. Practiced medicine, Caledonia, Mo.; apptd. mem. commn. to adjust Spanish land claims; mem. Mo. Ho. of Reps., 1835-44; served in Black Hawk War; apptd. U.S. marshal for Mo. Dist., 1841; mem. U.S. Ho. of Reps. (Democrat) from Mo., 28th-29th congresses, 1843-47. Died Caledonia, Sept. 14, 1863; buried Methodist Cemetery.

REMANN, Frederick, congressman; b. Vandalia, Ill., May 10, 1847; attended Miffin (Pa.) Acad.; grad. Iron City Bus. Coll., Pitts., 1865; grad. Ill. Coll., Jacksonville, 1868. Served as cpl. Company E, 143d Regiment, Ill. Volunteer Infantry in Civil War; returned to Vandalia, became mcht.; supt. Fayette County, Ill.; alderman, Vandalia; del. numerous Ill. Republican convs.; mem. Ill. Ho. of Reps., 1877, 78; mem. U.S. Ho. of Reps. (Rep.) from Ill., 54th Congress, Mar. 4-July 14, 1895. Died Vandalia, July 14, 1895; buried South Hill Cemetery.

REMINGTON, Eliphalet, mfr.; b. Suffield, Conn., Oct. 27, 1793; s. Eliphalet and Elizabeth (Kilbourn) R.; m. Abigail Paddock, May 12, 1814, at least 5 children, including Philo, Samuel, Eliphalet. Made gun barrel out of scrap metals, subsequently received orders for gun barrels; was forging barrels and rifling, stocking, lock fitting for guns, by 1828; erected new gunshop, 1828; purchased entire gun-finishing machinery of Ames & Co., Springfield, Mass., 1845, assumed unfinished contract for several thousand carbines for U.S. Govt.; procured contract in own right for 5,000 Harper's Ferry rifles; marketed Remington pistol, 1847; began mfg. agrl. implements, beginning with cultivator tooth, later plows, mowing machines, wheeled rakes, horse hoes; received large contract from U.S. Govt. for rifles, carbines, pistols during Civil War; 1st pres., one of 1st dirs. Ilion Bank (N.Y.). Died Ilion, Aug. 12, 1861.

REMINGTON, Philo, mfr.; b. Litchfield, N.Y., Oct. 21, 1816; s. Eliphalet and (probably) Abigail (Paddock) R.; ed. Cazenovia Sem.; m. Caroline Lathrop, Dec. 28, 1841; at least 2 children. Took charge of father's factory, 1861, reorganized firm, separating agrl. implements from armory; manufactured and aided in developing over 50 types of pistols; then manufactured Remington Breechloader rifle; organized armory as E. Remington & Sons, pres. until 1889; manufactured sewing machines (1st marketed), 1870; sole owner Sholes & Glidden typewriter after 1873; began manufacturing Remington typewriter, 1873 (introduced to public at Centennial Exhbn., Phila., 1876). Died Silver Springs, Fla., Apr. 4, 1889; buried Ilion, N.Y.

REMOND, Charles Lenox, anti-slavery advocate; b. Salem, Mass., Feb. 1, 1810; s. John and Nancy Remond; (mulatto, free born; father former slave). Gifted orator, made frequent speeches at anti-slavery meetings; apptd. agt. Mass. Anti-Slavery Soc., 1838; named a del. to represent Am. Anti-Slavery Soc. at World's Anti-Slavery Conv., London, Eng., May, 1840; recruiting officer for 54th Mass. Inf. (1st regt. of colored troops to be sent into action from any Northern state during Civil War); apptd. light insp., clk. in a custom house, Boston, circa 1868-73. Died Dec. 22, 1873.

RÉMY, Henri, (full name Charles Henri Rémy Carrete), editor; b. Agen Department of Lot-en-Gáronne, France, 1811; m. Louise Chapdu, circa 1840. Exiled from France for Republican polit. beliefs, 1830; came to U.S., 1836, landed in New Orleans; began teaching French and Italian, New Orleans; admitted to La. bar, 1840, began practice of law; apptd. notary, circa 1840; wrote 5 essays on history of La. published in La. Courier, 1843; editor St. Michel: Journal Hebdomadaire, Littéraire et Politique (French newspaper), St. Michel, La., 1844-54; joined William Walker in seizing Nicaragua by force, 1854-57. Author: Tierra Colunte (collection of impressions of Mexico), 1859. Died New Orleans, Feb. 21, 1867.

RENCHER, Abraham, gov. N.M., congressman; b. nr. Raleigh, N.C., Aug. 12, 1798; attended Pittsboro (N.C.) Acad.; grad. U. N.C., 1822; studied law. Admitted to bar, 1825, practiced in Pittsboro, Chatham County; mem. U.S. Ho. of Reps. (Democrat) from N.C., 21st-25th, 27th congresses, 1829-39, 41-43; minister to Portugal, 1843-47; Dem. presdl. elector, 1852; declined position sec. of navy under Pres. Buchanan; apptd. gov. N.M. by Pres. Buchanan, 1857-61; became farmer, businessman. Died Chapel Hill, N.C., July 6, 1883; buried St. Bartholomew's Protestant Episcopal Churchyard, Pittsboro.

RENICK, Felix, cattleman; b. Hardy County, Va., Nov. 5, 1770; son of William Renick; m. Hannah See, circa 1795, 9 children. Founder, 1st pres. Logan Hist. Soc.; contbr. to Am. Pioneer; outstanding agrl. leader in Central Ohio; 1st cattleman (with his brother) to make long overland drives of fat cattle to market; imported English cattle for the Ohio Co.; brought 19 head of shorthorn cattle to Am., 1834. Died nr. Chillicothe, O., Jan. 27, 1848; buried in family cemetery.

RENO, Jesse Lee, army officer; b. Wheeling, Va. (now W. Va.), June 20, 1823; s. Louis and Rebecca (Quinby) R.; grad. U.S. Mil. Acad., 1846; m. Mary Cross, Nov. 1, 1853. Brevetted 2d lt. of ordnance U.S. Army, 1846; brevetted for gallant and meritorious conduct at Cerro Gordo in Mexican War; brevetted capt. for actions at Chapultepec; asst. prof. mathematics U.S. Mil. Acad., 1849; sec. bd. on heavy arty. technique, 1849-50; asst. to ordnance bd. Washington (D.C.) Arsenal, 1851-52; on border and coast surveys, 1853-54; in command of arsenal, Mt. Vernon, Ala., 1859-61, Leavenworth, Kan. until fall 1861; commd. 1st lt., 1853, capt., 1860; brig. gen. U.S. Volunteers, 1861, commanded brigade in Gen. Ambrose Burnside's expdn. to N.C.; commanded div. in Dept. of N.C., 1862, took part in movement to Newport News, Va., and the Rappahannock; commd. maj. gen., 1862; commanded IX Corps of Burnside's right wing in August campaign in Va. and took part in Battle of Manassas, Aug. 1862; served at Battle of Chantilly, Sept. 1862; Reno (Nev.) named in his honor. Killed in Battle of South Mountain (Md.), Sept. 14, 1862; buried Trinity Ch., Boston.

RENWICK, Henry Brevoort, engr., patent expert; b. N.Y.C., Sept. 4, 1817; s. James and Margaret Anne (Brevoort) R.; grad. Columbia, 1833; m. Margaret Janney, June 22, 1852, at least 2 children. Studied engring., 1835-37; entered U.S. Govt. service as asst. engr., 1837, took part in bldg. breakwaters at Sandy Hook and Egg Harbor, N.J.; asso. with U.S. Boundary Commn., 1840-47; became examiner U.S. Patent Office in charge of divisions of metallurgy, steam engines, navigation, civil engring., ordnance, 1847; 1st U.S. insp. steam vessels Port of N.Y., 1853; took part in great patent litigations, 1870-95, including cases involving the sewing machine, McCormick reaper, Bell telephone; sr. warden St. Mark's Protestant Episcopal Ch., N.Y.C. Author: (with father) The Lives of John Jay and Alexander Hamilton, 1840. Died N.Y.C., Jan. 27, 1895.

RENWICK, James, engr., educator; b. Liverpool, Eng., May 30, 1792; s. William and Jane (Jeffery) R.; grad. Columbia, 1807, A.M., 1810, LL.D. (hon.), 1829; m. Margaret Anne Brevoort, 1816; 4 children—Henry Brevoort, Edward Sabine, James, Laura K. Brought to U.S. as child; lectured on natural philosophy Columbia, 1812, trustee, 1817-20, prof. natural philosophy and exptl. chemistry, 1820-53, 1st emeritus prof., 1853-63; topog. engr. with rank of maj. U.S. Army, 1814; commd. col. of engrs. N.Y. Militia, 1817; authority in every branch of engring. of his day; his suggestions for uniting Hudson and Delaware rivers resulted in Morris Canal, a system of inclined planes or railways for transporting canal boat in cradle up or down the incline (awarded medal from Franklin Inst. for cradle innovation, 1826); commd. to test "the usefulness of inventions to improve and render safe the boilers of steam-engines against explosions," 1838; a commr. to survey Northeastern boundary of disputed territory between U.S. and New Brunswick, 1840; Author: Outlines of Natural Philosophy (1st extensive treatise on subject from Am. writer), 2 vols., 1822-23; Treatise on the Steam Engine, 1830; Applications of the Science of Mechanics to Practical Purposes, 1840. Editor: (Am. editions with notes) Rudiments of Chemistry (Parke), 1824, Chemical Philosophy (Daniell), 2 vols., 1840. Translator: (from French) Treatise on Artillery (Tallemand), 2 vold., 1820. Contbd. biographies including David Rittenhouse (1839), Robert Fulton (1845), Count Rumford (1848) to Sparke's Library of American Biography. Died N.Y.C., Jan. 12, 1863.

RENWICK, James, architect; b. Bloomingdale, N.Y., Nov. 1, 1818; s. James and Margaret Anne (Brevoort) R.; grad. Columbia Coll., 1836; m. Anna Lloyd Aspinwall, Dec. 16, 1861. Joined engineering staff Erie R.R., 1836; mem. engring. staff Croton Aqueduct, supt. for building of distbg. reservoir that stood between 40th and 42d sts. on Fifth Av.; architect of New Grace Ch., 1843, Cavalry Ch., Ch. of the Puritans on Union Square, both 1846, St. Stephen's and St. Bartholomew's, 1872, St. Patrick's Cathedral, opened 1879 (all N.Y.C.); designed fountain for Bowling Green, 1843; architect for New Smithsonian Instn., Washington, D.C., 1846; designed hotels including Clarendon, Albemarle and St. Denis; designed Fulton Bank, Bank of State of N.Y., N.Y.C., new facade for N.Y. Stock Exchange; residences in N.Y. for Charles Morgan and Courtlandt Palmer; architect on Bd. Govs. Charities and Correction of N.Y.C.; designed Work House, Smallpox Hosp. on Blackwell's Island, Inebriate and Lunatic asylums on Ward's Island, Children's Hosp. on Randall's Island; designed Vassar Coll., Poughkeepsie, N.Y., 1865, Booth's Theatre, N.Y.C., Corcoran Gallery (example of French Renaissance), Washington, D.C., tchr. of apprentices and draftsmen; favored Gothic and Romanesque styles. Died N.Y.C., June 23, 1895; buried Greenwood Cemetery, Bklyn.

REQUIER, Augustus Julian, Confederate govt. ofcl., author; b. Charleston, S.C., May 27, 1825; m. Mary Elizabeth Evans. Admitted to bar, Charleston, 1844; editor Marion (S.C.) Star; U.S. dist. atty. for Ala., 1853-61; dist. atty. Confederate States Am., 1861-65; asst. dist. atty. N.Y.C., circa 1863. Author: (plays) The Spanish Exile, 1842; (prose narrative) The Old Sanctuary: A Romance of the Ashley, 1846; Poems, 1860; Ode to Shakespeare, 1862; The Legend of Tremaine, 1864; Crystalline (longest and most ambitious poem); Ashes of Glory (best known poem). Died N.Y.C., Mar. 19, 1887.

RESE, Frederick, clergyman; b. Weinenburg, Hanover, Germany, Feb. 6, 1791; s. John Gotfried and Caroline (Alrutz) Reese; grad. Coll. of the Propaganda, Rome, Italy, 1815. Joined a cavalry regt., fought during War of Liberation until Battle of Waterloo, 1813; ordained priest Roman Catholic Ch., 1822; missionary in Africa, 1822-24; came to U.S., 1824, 1st German priest in N.W.; went abroad, 1829 to enlist German priests for the Middlewest, 1829; a founder Leopoldine Soc. of Vienna; 1st bishop of Detroit, 1833-37; established St. Philips Coll., Hamtramck, Wis.; introduced Sisters of St. Clare, circa 1833-37; established several Indian schs.; built Holy Trinity Ch., Detroit. Died Hildesheim, Germany, Dec. 30, 1871.

REVELS, Hiram Rhoades, senator, clergyman; b. Fayetville, N.C., Sept. 1822; attended Knox Coll., Nashville, Tenn.; m. Phoebe Bass, 2 children. Ordained to ministry African Methodist Ch., 1854; itinerant preacher among Negroes in Ohio, Ill., Ind., Kan., Mo., Ky., Tenn., 1854-61; pastor Negro Meth. Ch., Balt., 1861; organized 2 volunteer Negro regt. in Md., U.S. Army, 1861; established school for freedmen, St. Louis, 1863-64; organized Negro churches in Miss., Ky., Kan., 1864-66; settled at Natchez, Miss., 1866; joined Meth. Episcopal Ch. 1868; alderman Natchez, 1868; mem. Miss. Senate from Adams County, 1869; mem. U.S. Senate (Republican) from Miss., Jan. 1870-Mar. 4, 1871. Died Aberdeen, Miss., Jan. 16, 1901.

REVERE, Joseph Warren, naval officer; b. Boston, May 17, 1812; s. John and Lydia LeBaron (Goodwin) R.; m. Rosanna Duncan, Oct. 4, 1842; 5 children. Became midshipman U.S. Navy, 1828; made Pacific cruise in ship Guerriére, 1828-31, China cruise, 1838-40; promoted lt., 1841; assigned to Cal. coast, 1845, in command of landing party from the Portsmouth; raised flag at Sonoma, 1846; served in conquest of Cal., 1846-48; participated in subsequent naval activities on Mexican west coast; resigned from Navy, 1850; organizer artillery of Mexican army, col., 1851; commd. col. 7th N.J. Volunteers, 1861; fought in Peninsular Campaign, battles of Seven Pines and Antietam in Civil War; promoted brig. gen., 1862, led 2d Brigade, 2d Div., III Corps, at Fredericksburg; led Excelsior Brigade, 2d Div., at Chancellorsville; court martialed and dismissed for withdrawal of orders at Chancellorsville (decision revoked); resigned, Sept. 1864. Author: A Tour of Duty in California, 1849; A Retrospect of Forty Years of Military and Naval Service, 1872. Died Hoboken, N.J., Apr. 20, 1880.

REVERE, Paul, silversmith, patriot; b. Boston, Jan. 1, 1735; s. Paul and Deborah (Hichborn) R.; m. Sarah Orne, Aug. 17, 1757; m. 2d, Rachel Walker, Oct. 10, 1773; 16 children. Applied silverwork techniques to copper plate, 1765; did engravings for Royal Am. Magazine; manufactured artificial dental devices; participated in Boston Tea Party; ofcl. courier for Mass. Provincial Assembly to Continental Congress, 1774; rode to Concord, Mass., to warn patriots to move mil. stores, Apr. 16, 1775; made ride to warn countryside that Brit. troops were marching, also to warn John Hancock and Samuel Adams that they were in danger of being captured, Apr. 18, 1775; completed mission to Lexington, Mass., but was stopped by Brit. en route to Concord; designed, printed 1st Continental money; made 1st ofcl. seal for colonies; designed Mass. State Seal; directed manufacture of gunpowder, Canton, Mass.; mem. Com. of Correspondence, 1776; discovered process for rolling sheet copper. Died Boston, May 10, 1818.

REY, Anthony, clergyman; b. Lyons, France, Mar. 19, 1807; studied at Fribourg. Joined Soc. of Jesus, 1827; taught at Fribourg and Sion; came to U.S., 1840, became prof. philosophy Georgetown (D.C.) U., became v.p. of univ., 1845; pastor in Phila. for a time; served as army chaplain in Mexican War, 1846-47. Killed by Mexican guerilla fighters, Ceralvo, Mexico, Jan. 19, 1847.

REYNOLDS, Alexander Welch, army officer; b. Clarke Co., Va., Aug. 1817; grad. U.S. Mil. Acad., 1838; 1 son, Frank. Served in Seminole War, 1838-40; commd. 1st lt., 1839; frontier duty in Ia., Wis., Mo., 1841-46; asst. q.m. with staff rank of capt., 1847; went to Mexico, 1848-52; joined Confederacy, commd. col. 50th Va. Inf., 1861; served in W.Va. under Gen. John Floyd, 1861-62; captured in defense of Vicksburg, later exchanged; commd. brig. gen., 1863, served in Atlanta campaign; col. in forces of Ismail Pasha during Abyssinian War, Egypt, 1869. Died Alexandria, Egypt, May 26, 1876.

REYNOLDS, Charles Alexander, guide, scout; b. Stephensburg, Ky., Mar. 20, 1842; s. Joseph Boyer and Phoebe (Buah) R.; never married. Pvt., U.S., Army, 1861-64; became hunter in Dakotas, 1867-73; scout for Yellowstone expdn. under Col. David Stanley, 1873; guide for Black Hills expdn. under Col. George A. Custer, 1874; partly responsible for capture of Chief Rain-in-the-Face, 1876; scout for Big Horn expdn. under Custer, 1876. Killed in Battle of Little Big Horn, nr. junction of Big Horn and Little Big Horn Rivers, Mont., June 25, 1876; buried Custer Field, Mont.

REYNOLDS, Gideon, congressman, farmer; b. Petersburg, N.Y., Aug. 9, 1813; ed. pvt. schs. Became farmer, Hoosick, Rensselaer County, N.Y.; mem. N.Y. State Assembly, 1839; sheriff Rensselaer County, 1843-46; mem. U.S. Ho. of Reps. (Whig) from N.Y., 30th-31st congresses, 1847-51; del. Republican nat. convs., Phila., 1856, Chgo., 1860; mem. N. Y. state Rep. Central Com.; apptd. internal revenue collector N.Y. State 15th Dist., 1862-65; mem. Hoosick Bd. Suprs., 1875. Died Hoosick, July 13, 1896; buried Hoosick Rural Cemetery.

REYNOLDS, Igantius Aloysius, clergyman; b. Bardstown, Ky., Aug. 22, 1798; attended St. Thomas Sem., Bardstown, also St. Mary's Sem., Balt. Ordained priest Roman Catholic Ch., 1823; tchr., later pres. St. Joseph's Coll., Bardstown; also taught at St. Thomas Sem., until 1830; went into missionary work, 1830, served as superior Sisters of Charity of Nazareth, 1833-34; vicar gen. of Bardstown, 1841-44; consecrated bishop of Charleston (S.C.), 1844. Editor: Works of Bishop John England of Charleston, 1849. Died Charleston, Mar. 6, 1855

REYNOLDS, James B., congressman, lawyer; b. County Antrim, Ireland, 1779; attended common schs.; studied law. Came to U.S., settled in Clarksville, Tenn.; admitted to bar, 1804, practiced law; mem. U.S. Ho. of Reps. (Democrat) from Tenn., 14th, 18th congresses, 1815-17, 23-25. Died Clarksville, June 10, 1851; buried City Cemetery.

REYNOLDS, John, colonial gov.; b. Eng., 1713; several children. Served in Brit. Navy, in command of ship Arundel, 1746; 1st royal gov. Ga., 1754-55, organized courts, encouraged new settlements, strengthened local defenses, suppressed Edmund Grey's conspiracy for protection of liberties endangered by royal govt.; accused by Ga. Council, later by Ga. Assembly of incompetence, 1755-56, dissolved Assembly, recalled, 1756; capt. ship Firm, Brit. Navy, 1759; acted as commodore of a cruising squadron in Hawke's fleet; rear adm. of the Blue, 1775, adm., 1787. Died Eng., Feb. 3, 1788.

REYNOLDS, John, gov. Ill.; b. Montgomery County, Pa., Feb. 26, 1789; s. Robert and Margaret (Moore) R.; m. Catherine (Dubuque) La Croix Manegee, 1817; m. 2d, Sarah Wilson, 1836; no children. Admitted to Tenn. bar, 1812; began practice law, Cahoka, Ill., 1814; asso. justice Ill. Supreme Ct., 1818-25, also judge circuit ct.; supported attempt to revise Ill. Constn. to establish slavery in Ill., 1824; mem. Ill. Gen. Assembly, 1826, 28; mem. Ill. Ho. of Reps., 1827-29, 46, speaker, 1852; gov. Ill., 1830-34; called Ill. militia during Black Hawk War, helped U.S. Army defeat Indians; mem. U.S. Ho. of Reps. from Ill., 24th, 26th-27th congresses, 1835-37, 39-43; chief constructor 1st railroad in Mississippi Valley, 1837; Ill. financial commr., visited Europe to sell bonds for Ill. and Mich. Canal; mem. Ill. Legislature, 1846-48, 52-54; attended Democratic Nat. Conv., Charleston, S.C., 1860. Author: My Own Times, 1855; The Pioneer History of Illinois, 1852. Died Belleville, Ill., May 8, 1865.

REYNOLDS, John Fulton, army officer; b. Lancaster, Pa., Sept. 20, 1820; s. John and Lydia (Moore) R.; grad. U.S. Mil. Acad., 1841. Commd. 1st lt. U.S. Army, accompanied Gen. Taylor to Mexico, 1846; fought at battles of Monterey and Buena Vista; brevetted capt. U.S. Army, 1846, maj., 1847, promoted capt., 1855; comdt. of cadets U.S. Mil. Acad., 1860-61, instr. arty., cavalry and inf. tactics; commd. lt. col., 1861; commd. brig. gen. U.S. Volunteers, 1861; mil. gov., Fredericksburg (Va.), 1862; returned to Army of Potomac in command I Army Corps, 1862; commd. maj. gen. U.S. Volunteers, 1862; commd. col U.S.

Army, 1863; fought at Battle of Gettysburg (Pa.), 1863, in command of I, III and XI Corps, Army of Potomac. Killed at Battle of Gettysburg, July 1, 1863; buried Lancaster, Pa.

REYNOLDS, John Hazard, congressman, lawyer; b. Moriah, N.Y., June 21, 1819; attended public schs., Sandy Hill (now Hudson Falls), N.Y., Bennington, Vt.; grad. Kinderhook Acad., 1840; studied law. Became civil engr.; admitted to bar, practiced in Kinderhook, Columbia County, N.Y. ,1843; moved to Albany, N.Y., 1851, practiced law; mem. U.S. Ho. of Reps. (Republican) from N.Y., 36th Congress, 1859-61; apptd. judge N.Y. State Commn. of Appeals, 1873-75. Died Kinderhook, Sept. 24, 1875; buried Kinderhook Cemetery.

REYNOLDS, Joseph, congressman; b. Easton, Washington County, N.Y., Sept. 14, 1785; completed academic studies. Moved to Virgil, N.Y., 1809, became farmer; organizer company of riflemen for War of 1812; maj., col., brig. gen. N.Y. State troops; justice of peace, 1815-37; mem. N.Y. State Assembly, 1818; judge Cortland County, N.Y.. 1821-39; supr. Town of Cortlandville, 1825-35; Democratic presdl. elector, 1832; mem. U.S. Ho. of Reps. (Dem.) from N.Y., 24th Congress, 1835-37; 1st pres. Village of Cortland (N.Y.), 1864. Died Cortland, Sept. 24, 1864; buried Cortland Rural Cemetery.

REYNOLDS, Joseph Jones, army officer; b. Flemingsburg, Ky., Jan. 4, 1822; s. Edward and Sarah (Longley) R.; grad. U.S. Mil. Acad., 1843; m. Mary Elizabeth Bainbridge, Dec. 3, 1846, 4 children. Brevetted 2d lt. 4th Arty., U.S. Army, 1843, promoted 2d lt., 1846; tchr. U.S. Mil. Acad., 1846-55; resigned from Army, 1857; prof. mechanics and engring. Washington U., St. Louis, 1857-60; partner with brother in grocery business, Lafayette, Ind., 1860-62; apptd. col., then brig. gen. Ind. Volunteers, U.S. Army, 1861; maj. gen. U.S. Volunteers, 1862; commanded Cheat Mountain Dist., 1861-62; commanded division in Army of Cumberland, 1862; served at battles of Hoover's Gap and Chickamauga; chief staff of Army of Cumberland, 1863-64, at battles of Chattanooga and Missionary Ridge; commanded Dept. of Ark., 1864-66; became col. 26th Inf., U.S. Army, 1866; commanded successively Dist. of Tex., 5th Mil. Dist. of U.S. and Dept. of Tex.; brevetted brig. gen. for service at Chickamauga and maj. gen. for service at Missionary Ridge, both 1867; transferred to cavalry, 1872; commanded various posts in Indian Territory, 1872-76; retired, 1877. Died Washington, D.C., Feb. 25, 1899.

REYNOLDS, Samuel Godfrey, inventor; b. Bristol, R.I., Mar. 9, 1801; s. Greenwood and Mary (Caldwell) R.; m. Elizabeth Anthony, 1823; m. 2d, Catherine Ann Hamlin, Nov. 18, 1845; 5 children. Invented machine for making wrought-iron nails and rivets, patented 1829, improvements to original machine patented, 1835; patented a spike-making machine, went directly to Eng., secured financial backing for manufacture of machines from Coates & Co., bankers, also obtained patents in Eng., Holland, Belgium, France; patented machinery for heading and pointing pins, 1845; returned to U.S. in 1850; invented horse-nail machinery, patented 1852, patented improvements, 1866, 67; perfected steam plow, invented a rotary plow. Died Bristol, R.I., Mar. 1, 1881.

REYNOLDS, William, naval officer; b. Lancaster, Pa., Dec. 18, 1815; s. John and Lydia (Moore) R.; m. Rebecca Krug. Became midshipman U.S. Navy, 1833; sent with Lt. Charles Wilkes on exploring expdn. to South Seas, 1838, discovered a mountain peak in Antarctic; became lt., 1838; retired, 1855; naval storekeeper, Honolulu, Hawaii, 1857-61; commd. comdr. on U.S. Navy reserve list, given command naval depot, Port Royal, S.C., 1862-65; became commodore, 1866, rear admiral, 1873; chief bur. equipment and recruiting, 1870-75, had condensers for distilling fresh water and ovens for baking fresh bread installed for the 1st time on all naval vessels; commanded Asiatic Sta., 1875-77; did much to promote friendly relations between U.S. and Far East; retired, 1877. Died Nov. 5, 1879, Washington, D.C.

REZANOV, Nikolai Petrovich, diplomat; b. St. Petersburg, Russia, Apr. 8, 1764; m. Miss Shelekov, 1795. Came to Siberia on spl. mission relating to expansion of empire in Northwestern Am., 1793-94; largely responsible for formation Russian-Am. Co., granted right to trade in Alaska; sailed from Kronstadt to visit new territory, investigate resources and needs, to inspect co. offices, revise its bus. methods and policies, 1803; sent to Japan as minister plenipotentiary to open gates of empire to Russian trade, jailed, held virtual prisoner at Nagasaki through winter 1804-05; landed at New Archangel (Sitka) on Baranov Island, Aug. 1805; compiled dictionary of local Indian tongue, 1805; reached port of San Francisco early 1806. Died Krasnoyarsk, Siberia, Mar. 13, 1807.

RHEA, John, congressman; b. County Donegal, Ireland, 1753; s. Joseph and Elizabeth (McIlwaine) R.; grad. Princeton, 1780. Came to U.S., 1769; mem. N.C. Ho. of Commons, 1785-90; mem. N.C. Conv. for ratification U.S. Constn.; incorporator or trustee Washington Coll., Greenville (now Tusculum) Coll., Blount Coll. (now U. Tenn.); del. 1st Tenn. Constl. Conv., 1796; mem. Tenn. Legislature, 1796, 97; mem. U.S. Ho. of Reps. from Tenn., (Democrat.) 8th-13th, 15th-17th congresses, 1803-15, 17-23; U.S. commr. signed treaty with Choctaw Indians, 1816; Rhea County (Tenn.) named for him. Died Blountville, Tenn., May 27, 1832.

RHEES, John Morgan, clergyman; b. Glamorganshire, Wales, Dec. 8, 1760; s. John and Elizabeth Rhys; attended Bristol Coll., Aug. 1776; m. Ann Loxley, Feb. 22, 1796; children—John, Benjamin Rush, Mary, Morgan John, Eliza. Ordained to ministry baptist Ch., Nov. 17, 1785; pastor Penygarn Bapt. Ch., Pontypool, Monmouthshire, Eng.; interested in results of French Revolution, went to Paris, 1792, preached, distbd. Bibles; published quarterly (in Welsh) devoted to civil and religious liberty, 1793-94; came to N.Y.C., 1794; formed soc. for benefit of immigrants; influential in movements on behalf of missions, evangelism, civil and religious liberty; published The Good Samaritan: An Oration in Behalf of the Philadelphia Society for the Information and Assistance of Persons Emigrating from Foreign Countries, 1796; justice of peace, asso. judge (1799), clk. quarter sessions, recorder deeds (1800), all Somerset, Pa. Died Somerset, Sept. 17, 1804.

RHETT, Robert Barnwell, senator, congressman; b. Beaufort, S.C., Dec. 21, 1800; s. James and Marianna (Gough) Smith (family name legally changed from Smith to Rhett, 1837); m. Elizabeth Washington Burnet, 1827; m. 2d, Catharine Herbert Dent, circa 1853. Admitted to S.C. bar, 1822; mem. S.C. Ho. of Reps., 1826; accepted Calhoun theory of peaceful constl. nullification by 1830, later more radical in his politics and largely split from Calhoun; S.C. atty. gen., 1832; mem. U.S. Ho. of Reps. from S.C., 24th-30th congresses, 1837-49; led Bluffton movement for separate state action on tariff, 1844; important supporter of Polk's adminstrn., 1845-49; attended and wrote address for Nashville Conv., 1850-52; began campaign for secession of S.C. from U.S., 1850; mem. U.S. Senate from S.C., 1850-52; largely responsible for S.C.'s secession, 1860 (called father of secession); del. Confederate Provisional Congress, 1861, Southern Congress at Montgomery, 1861; joined his son on Charleston Mercury where he continued attack on Confederate adminstrn. for failure to gain independence, 1861; only man in S.C. who ever defied Calhoun without sacrificing his polit. career; del. Democratic Nat. Conv., N.Y.C., 1868. Died St. James Parish, La., Sept. 14, 1876; buried Magnolia Cemetery, Charleston, S.C.

RHIND, Alexander Colden, naval officer; b. N.Y. C., Oct. 31, 1821; s. Charles and Susan (Fell) R.; attended Naval Sch., Phila., 1844-45. Became midshipman U.S. Navy, 1838; served at capture of Alvarado and Tabasco during Mexican War; promoted lt., 1854; commanded ship Crusader in S. Atlantic Blockading Squadron, 1861; commanded ship Seneca, 1862; commd. lt. comdr., 1862; commanded iron clad Keokuk, 1862-63; comdr. Paul Jones and flagship Wabash, took part in attacks on Ft. Wagner and other Charleston defenses; promoted comdr., 1863; light house insp., 1880-82; commd. rear adm., 1883. Died N.Y.C., Nov. 8, 1897; buried Coldenham, N.Y.

RHIND, Charles, mcht., diplomat; b. Aberdeen, Scotland, flourished 1810-45; probably son of Alexander Rhind; m. Susan Fell, between 1804-08, 10 children including Alexander Colden. Came to U.S. by 1810; became agt. North River Steam Boat Co., 1822; served as adm. N.Y.C. Fleet during the festivities which accompanied opening of Erie Canal, 1825; made 1st consul at Odessa, Russia, 1829; mem. commn. (with David Offley and Commodore James Biddle) to renew negotiations with Ottoman Porte for treaty of commerce and navigation which had been begun by Offley in 1828; arrived in Constantinople, Feb. 1830, signed treaty May 1830 (treaty included secret article authorizing the Porte to obtain materials for naval constrn. in U.S.; U.S. Senate ratified treaty but excepted secret article, Feb. 1831); sailed to Constantinople, Nov. 1831; returned to N.Y.C., resumed bus. activities, 1832.

RHOADS, James, coll. pres.; b. Marple, Delaware County, Pa., Jan. 21, 1828; s. Joseph and Hannah (Evans) R.; M.D., U. Pa., 1851; m. Margaret Wilson Ely, Mar. 21, 1860, 3 children. Resident physician Pa. Hosp., 1852-54; gen. practice medicine, Germantown, Pa., 1854-62; became sec. exec. com. of central orgn. Soc. of Friends, 1870, in charge of ednl. and missionary affairs on Indian reservation; pres. Indian Rights Assn., many years; editor Friends' Review, 1876-84; an original trustee Bryn Mawr (Pa.) Coll., 1st pres., 1883-94. Died Bryn Mawr, Jan. 2, 1895.

RHOADS, Samuel, Continental congressman, mayor Phila.; b. Phila., 1711; had limited schooling. Became carpenter and builder; mem. Phila. City Council, 1741; mem. Pa. Provincial Assembly, 1761-64, 71-74; commr. to conf. of Western Indians and Six Nations, Lancaster, Pa., 1761; mem. Continental Congress from Pa., 1774-75; mayor Phila., 1774; founder, bd. mgrs. Pa. Hosp., 1751-81; bd. dirs. Phila. Library. Died Phila., Apr. 7, 1784.

RIBAUT, Jean, colonist; b. Dieppe, France, 1520. Became capt. in French Navy; apptd. to establish colony of New France on coast of Fla., 1562; arrived in Am., 1562, established colony called Charlesfort (now Port Royal, S.C.); returned to France for supplies for new colony but unable to return because of civil war which had broken out between Catholics and Huguenots (colony abandoned when he failed to return); fled to Eng. because of Huguenot beliefs after capture of Dieppe by Catholics in 1562; imprisoned in London (Eng.) for refusing to aid English in establishing colony in New World, 1562-65; commanded fleet sent to reinforce new French colony of Ft. Caroline, 1565; engaged in skirmish with Spanish fleet sent to destroy Ft. Caroline; his fleet wrecked by storm while pursuing the Spanish; (Spanish marched overland and killed most of colonists at Ft. Caroline); captured (with other survivors of storm). Executed by Spanish for Huguenot convictions, Oct. 23, 1565.

RICAUD, James Barroll, congressman, lawyer; b. Balt., Feb. 11, 1808; grad. Washington Coll., Chestertown, Md., 1828; studied law. Admitted to bar, 1829, practiced in Chestertown; mem. Md. Ho. of Dels., 1834; mem. Md. Senate, 1836-44; Whig presdl. elector, 1840, 44; mem. U.S. Ho. of Reps. (Am. Party) from Md., 34th-35th congresses, 1855-59; apptd. asso. judge 2d Md. Jud. Dist., 1864. Died Chestertown, Jan. 24, 1866; buried St. Paul's Ch. Cemetery.

RICE, Alexander Hamilton, mfr., gov. Mass.; b. Newton, Mass., Aug. 30, 1818; s. Thomas and Lydia (Smith) R.; grad. Union Coll., 1844; m. Augusta E. McKim, Aug. 19, 1845; m. 2d, Angie Erickson Powell; 4 children. Joined Merc. Library Assn., 1838; head paper mfg. concern which became known as Rice-Kendall Co., 1889; mem. Boston Sch. Com., also Bd. Pub. Instns., 1851; dir. Montague Paper Co.; Whig mem. Common Council of Boston, 1853, 54, pres., 1854; an organizer Republican Party in Mass.; 1st Rep. mayor Boston, 1856, 57, made improvements in Back Bay sect., established city hosp., organized city's pub. instns.; mem. U.S. Ho. of Reps. (Rep.) from Mass., 36-39th congresses, 1859-67; del. to Phila. Union Conv., 1866; del. Rep. Nat. Conv., Chgo., 1868; gov. Mass., 1876-78; pres. Keith Paper Co., Turner Falls, Mass., Am. Sulphate Pulp Co. Died Melrose, Mass., July 22, 1895; buried Newton Cemetery.

RICE, Charles, chemist, philologist; b. Munich, Bavaria, Germany, Oct. 4, 1841; never married. Came to U.S., 1862; served as surgeon's steward U.S. Navy, 1862-65; chief chemist dept. of public charities and correction City of N.Y., 1865; supt. gen. drug dept. Bellevue Hosp., N.Y.C. until 1901; trustee, librarian Coll. of Pharmacy of City of N.Y., 1870-1901; chmn. com. of revision of U.S. Pharmacopoeia, 1880-1901; a leading Sanskrit scholar in U.S., also spoke or read 12 other langs. including Greek, Arabic, Chinese. Died May 13, 1901.

RICE, Charles Allen Thorndike, journalist; b. Boston, June 18, 1851; s. Henry Gardner and Elizabeth (Thorndike) R.; B.A., Christ Church, Oxford (Eng.) U., 1874, M.A., 1878; studied Columbia Law Sch., N.Y., 1879. Bought and edited quarterly N. Am. Review, 1876, (became popular through his editorship), moved Review from Boston to N.Y.C., changed it to a monthly publ.; induced Pierre Lorillard and French Govt. to finance Charnay Expdn. to study Mayan ruins in C. Am. and Mexico, 1879. acquired interest in Le Matin, Paris, 1884; edited Reminiscences of Abraham Lincoln, 1886. Died N.Y.C., May 16, 1889.

RICE, Dan (real name McClaren), clown; b. N. Y.C., Jan. 25, 1823; s. Daniel and Elizabeth (Crum) McClaren; m. 3 times. Was successively part owner of trained pig, singer, circus strong man, then press agt. for Mormon prophet Joseph Smith, 1841-44; appeared as clown with various circuses, 1844-85; his act included trained horses Excelsior and Excelsior Jr.; owned several river-boat circuses; candidate for Republican nomination for Pres. U.S., 1868; forced to retire due to chronic alcoholism, 1885. Died Long Branch, N.J., Feb. 22, 1900.

RICE, David, clergyman; b. Hanover County, Va., Dec. 29, 1733; s. David Rice; grad. Coll. of N.J. (now Princeton), 1761; m. Mary Blair, 1763, 11 children. Licensed to preach by Hanover Presbytery, 1762, ordained, 1763; pastor, Hanover, Va., 1763-68; missionary in Bedford County, Va.. 1769-83; co-founder Hampden-Sydney Coll., 1775, Transylvania U., Lexington, Ky., 1780; itinerant preacher organizing churches in Ky. and Ohio, 1783-98; mem. Ky. Constl. Conv., 1792; pastor in Green County, Ky., 1798-1816; largely responsible for establishment Presbyterianism in Ky.; gave sermon at founding Presbyn. Synod of Ky., 1802. Author: An Essay on Baptism, 1789; Slavery Inconsistent with Justice and Good Policy, 1792; An Epistle to the Citizens of Kentucky Professing Christianity, 1805; a Second Epistle, 1808. Died June 18, 1816.

RICE, Edmund, railroad pres., congressman; b. Waitsfield, Vt., Feb. 14, 1819; s. Edmund and Ellen (Durkee) R.; m. Anna M. Acker, Nov. 28, 1848, 11 children. Register ct. of chancery also clk. Mich. Supreme Ct., 1841; admitted to Mich. bar, 1842; master in chancery, 1845; commd. 1st lt. U.S. Army, served in Mexican War, 1847; sr. mem. law firm Rice, Hollinshead & Becker, St. Paul, Minn., 1849-56; clk. Minn. Supreme Ct., 3d Circuit, 1849; mem. Territorial Ho. of Reps., 1851; elected commr. Ramsey County, 1856; leader railroad movement in Minn., 1850's; dir. Minn. & Northwestern R.R. Co.; pres. Minn. & Pacific, St. Paul & Pacific, St. Paul & Chgo. railroads; mem. Minn. Senate, 1864-66, 74-76; mem. Minn. Ho. of Reps., 1867, 72, 77-78; mayor St. Paul, 1881-83, 85-87; mem. U.S. Ho. of Reps. from Minn., 50th Congress, 1887-89. Died White Bear Lake, Minn., July 11, 1889; buried Oakland Cemetery, St. Paul.

RICE, Edward Young, congressman, lawyer; b. nr. Russellville, Logan County, Ky., Feb. 8, 1820; studied law. Admitted to bar, 1844; moved to Montgomery County, Ill., practiced in Hillsboro; elected county recorder, 1847; mem. Ill. Ho. of Reps., 1848, 50; judge Montgomery County Ct., 1851-52; master in chancery, 1853-57; elected judge Ill. 18th Circuit, 1857, 61, 67; mem. Ill. Constl. Conv., 1869, 70; mem. U.S. Ho. of Reps. (Democrat) from Ill., 42d Congress, 1871-73; practiced in Hillsboro, Springfield, Ill. Died Hillsboro, Apr. 16, 1883; buried Oak Grove Cemetery.

RICE, Fenelon Bird, music tchr.; b. Greensburg, O., Jan. 2, 1841; s. David Lyman and Emily (Johnson) R.; attended Hillsdale (Mich.) Coll., 1858-61; grad. Boston Music Sch., 1863; studied piano in Europe, 1867-69; m. Helen Maria Libby, Sept. 26, 1863; 1 son, Louis M. Instr. music Hillsdale Coll., 1863-67, Oberlin (O.) Coll., 1869-71; dir. Oberlin Conservatory of Music, 1871-1901 (when Conservatory became part of Oberlin Coll., 1885, he retained title of dir. and became prof. of music); dir. Oberlin Musical Union, 1871-1901; pres. Music Tchrs. Nat. Assn., 1880-81. Died Oberlin, Oct. 26, 1901.

RICE, Henry Mower, senator; b. Waitsfield, Vt., Nov. 29, 1817; s. Edmund and Ellen (Durkee) R.; m. Matilda Whitall, Mar. 29, 1849, 9 children. Surveyor in Mich., 1835; fur trader with Winnebago and Miss. Chippewa Indians, 1847-52; made U.S. treaty with Ojibway Indians for land, 1847; del. U.S. Congress from Territory of Minn., 33d-34th congresses, 1853-57; obtained extension of the preemption right over unsurveyed rights in Minn., established post office, land offices, extension of territorial roads, helped to obtain land grant of 1857 for aid Minn. railroads, helped obtain passage of Minn. Enabling Act; one of 1st mems. U.S. Senate from State of Minn., 1858-63; del. to Phila. Nat. Union Conv., 1866; mem. U.S. Chippewa Commn. to carry out provisions of Act of 1889 for relief and civilization of Chippewas in Minn.; mem. bd. regents U. Minn.; pres. Minn. Hist. Soc.; pres. Bd. Pub. Works; treas. Ramsey County (Minn.), 1878-84. Died San Antonio, Tex., Jan. 15, 1894.

RICE, John Birchard, congressman, physician; b. Fremont, Sandusky County, O., June 23, 1832; attended Oberlin College; graduate medical department University Michigan, 1857; postgraduate course Jefferson Medical College, Bellevue Hospital, New York City, 1859. Lectr. mil. surgery and obstetrics Charity Hosp. Med. Coll., med. dept. U. Wooster, Cleve.; served on med. staff during Civil War as asst. surgeon 10th Regt., Ohio Volunteer Infantry, as surgeon 22d Regt.; surgeon in chief division in 15th Army Corps and Dist. of Memphis; apptd. trustee State Hosp., Toledo; mem. Fremont Bd. Health; mem. U.S. Ho. of Reps. (Republican) from Ohio, 47th Congress, 1881-83; practiced medicine, Fremont. Died Fremont, Jan. 14, 1893; buried Oakwood Cemetery.

RICE, John Blake, congressman, mayor Chgo.; b. Easton, Talbot County, Md., May 28, 1809; had limited schooling. On stage in N.Y., 1839; moved to Chgo., 1847, mgr. of theater; also managed theaters, Bangor, Me., Buffalo, N.Y., Milw.; retired from stage, 1857, from theatrical mgmt., 1861; mayor Chgo., 1865-69; mem. U.S. Ho. of Reps. (Republican) from Ill., 43d Congress, 1873-Dec. 17, 1874. Died Norfolk, Va., Dec. 17, 1874; buried Rosehill Cemetery, Chgo.

RICE, John Holt, clergyman, educator; b. Bedford, Va., Nov. 28, 1777; s. Benjamin and Catherine (Holt) R.; D.D. (hon.), Princeton, 1819; m. Anne Smith Morton, July 9, 1802; Tutor, Hampden-Sydney (Va.) Coll., 1801; licensed to preach by Hanover Presbytery, 1803, ordained, 1804; pastor Cub Creek Presbyn. Ch., Charlotte County, Va., 1804; agt. for Presbytery of Hanover to raise funds for theol. school to be established at Hampden-Sydney, 1806-08; founder, pastor First Presbyn. Ch., Richmond, Va., 1812-23; organized Va. Bible Soc., 1813; a founder Am. Bible Soc., 1816; edited religious newspaper Christian Monitor, 1815-17, formed co. for publn. of its literature, until 1818; editied monthly The Va. Evang. and Literary Mag., 1818-28; organized Young Men's Missionary Soc., Richmond; elected moderator of Gen. Assembly of Presbyn. Ch., 1819; prof. theology at theol. sem., Hampden-Sdyney, 1824; organized Presbyn. Bd. Fgn. Missions. Author: Historical and Philosophical Considerations on Religion: Addressed to James Madison Esq., Late President of the United States, 1832. Died Hampden-Sydney, Sept. 3, 1831.

RICE, John McConnell, congressman, lawyer; b. Prestonsburg, Floyd County, Ky., Feb. 19, 1831; grad. law sch., Louisville, Ky., 1852; Admitted to bar, 1853, practiced in Pikeville, Ky.; supt. schs. Pike County, 1854; elected pros. atty. Pike County, 1856; mem. Ky. Ho. of Reps., 1858, 61; moved to Louisa, Lawrence County, Ky., 1860; mem. U.S. Ho. of Reps. (Democrat) from Ky., 41st-42d congresses, 1869-73; practiced in Louisa; apptd. judge Lawrence County Criminal Ct., 1883, elected, 1884, 90-95. Died Louisa, Sept. 18, 1895; buried Pine Hill Cemetery.

RICE, Luther, clergyman; b. Northboro, Mass., Mar. 25, 1783; s. Capt. Amos and Sarah (Graves) R.; grad. Williams Coll., 1810; attended Andover Theol. Sem., 1810-12. Ordained for missionary service of Congregational Ch., 1812; arrived in Calcutta, India, Aug. 1812; immersed, thus serving Congregational affiliation, Nov. 1812; went to Boston to obtain discharge from further obligations to Am. Bd. Commrs. Fgn. Missions, devoted himself to organizing Baptist of Am. for missionary and ednl. work, 1813-26; largely responsible for establishment of nat. Bapt. orgn. for fgn. missionary endeavor; as result of his activities Triennial Conv. organized; a founder and developer Columbia Coll. (later George Washington U.), ; 1821; established numerous Baptist ednl. instns. throughout U.S.; a founder Columbian Star (religious weekly); organized Am. Baptist Home Mission Soc. and Am. Baptist Publication Soc. Died Sept. 25, 1836.

RICE, Nathan Lewis, clergyman, coll. pres.; b. Garrard County, Ky., Dec. 29, 1807; s. Gabriel and Phebe (Harrett) R.; attended Centre Coll. Danville, Ky., 1826-28, Princeton Theol. Sem., 1828-30; m. Catherine P. Purch, Oct. 3, 1832. Licensed to preach by Transylvania Presbytery, 1828; ordained to ministry Presbyn. Ch., 1833; edited paper Western Protestant, 1833, merged into Presbyn. Herald, Louisville, Ky.; pastor Presbyn. Ch., Bardstown, Ky., 1833-41, founded school for boys, another for girls; pastor, Woodford and Paris, Ky., 1841-44, Central Presbyn. Ch., Cincinnati, 1845-53, Second Presbyn. Ch., St. Louis, 1853-58, North Presbyn. Ch., Chgo., 1858-61, Fifth Av. Presbyn. Ch., N.Y.C., 1861-67; prof. theology Theol. Sem. of N.W., Chgo., 1858-61; pres. Westminster Coll., Fulton, Mo., 1869-74; prof. theology Danville (Ky.) Theol. Sem., 1874-77; debated with Alexander Campbell on meaning and mode of baptism, Lexington, Ky., 1843, printed A Debate Between Rev. A. Campbell and Rev. N.L. Rice on Christian Baptism, 1844; elected moderator Gen. Assembly of Presbyn. Ch., 1855. Author: Romanism the Enemy of Free Institutions and Christianity, 1851; Baptism, the Design, Mode and Subjects, 1855; Signs of the Times, 1855; Lectures on Slavery, 1860; The Pulpit: Its Relations to our National Crisis, 1862; Immortality, 1871. Died Chatham, Ky., June 11, 1877; buried Fulton, Mo.

RICE, Theron Moses, congressman, lawyer; b. Mecca, Trumbull County, O., Sept. 21, 1829; attended academy, Chester, O. for 4 years; studied law. Taught dist. sch. in winter months; admitted to bar, 1854, practiced law, Mahoning County, O. about 3 years; moved to California, Moniteau County, Mo., 1858; served with U.S. Infantry Volunteer Service from Mo. during Civil War, 1861-65, promoted from 1st lt. to col.; returned to Mo., 1866, practiced in Tipton, Moniteau County; circuit judge, 1868-74 mem. U.S. Ho. of Reps. (Nat. Greenbacker) from Mo., 47th Congress, 1881-83; practiced in Boonville, Mo. Died Boonville, Nov. 7, 1895; buried Tipton Cemetery.

RICE, Thomas, congressman, lawyer; b. Pownalborough (now Wiscasset), Me. (then Mass.), Mar. 30, 1768; grad. Harvard, 1791; studied law. Admitted to Suffolk County (Mass.) bar, 1794; practiced in Winslow, Kennebec County, Me., 1795; apptd. an examiner of counselors and attys. for Kennebec County by Me. Supreme Jud. Ct., 1807; mem. Me. Ho. of Reps., 1814; mem. U.S. Ho. of Reps. from Mass., 14th-15th congresses, 1815-19. Died Winslow, Aug. 25, 1854; buried Pine Grove Cemetery, Waterville, Me.

RICE, Thomas Dartmouth, entertainer; b. N.Y.C., May 20, 1808; m. Charlotte B. Gladstone, June 18, 1837, several children. Introduced song and dance number "Jim Crow," 1828; appeared at Columbia Theatre, Cincinnati, 1828-29; repeated his success as impersonator of "Jim Crow," Pitts., 1829-30; made 1st appearance in N.Y.C. in role of "Jim Crow," 1832; also visited Phila., Boston, Washington, D.C.; played Surrey Theatre in London, 1836, was tremendous success; wrote many Negro extravaganzas, helped create what was known as "Ethiopian Opera" in which he introduced old Negro songs into his own libretto; most popular pieces were a Negro burlesque of Othello, "Bone Squash Diavolo," "Jumbo Jum," "Ginger Blue," and "Jim Crow in London;" his success brought a vogue for minstrels; known as "father of Am. minstrelsy." Died N.Y.C., Sept. 19, 1860; buried Greenwood Cemetery, Bklyn.

RICE, Victor Moreau, educator; b. Mayville, N.Y., Apr. 5, 1818; s. William and Rachel (Waldo) R.; grad. Alleghany Coll., Meadville, Pa., 1841; m. Maria L. Winter, Nov. 26, 1846. Admitted to N.Y. bar, 1845; tchr. Buffalo (N.Y.) high school, 1843-46; editor Cataract, Buffalo, 1846-48; supt. schs. of Buffalo, 1852-54; pres. N.Y. State Tchrs. Assn., 1853; N.Y. State supt. of public instrn., 1854-60, 62-68, procured legislation which established free schs. throughout N.Y.; mem. N.Y. State Assembly, 1860; pres. Am. Popular Life Ins. Co., 1868-69, Met. Bank of N.Y.C., 1869. Died N.Y.C., Oct. 18, 1869.

RICE, William Marsh, businessman; b. Springfield, Mass., Mar. 14, 1816; s. David and Patty (Hall) R.; m. Margaret Bremond, 1850; m. 2d, Elizabeth (Baldwin) Brown, June 26, 1867; no children. Partner firm Rice & Nichols, Exporters, Importers, and Wholesale Grocers of Houston, Tex., 1838-61; founded stage line from Houston to Austin, also railroad line from Houston to Dallas (Tex.); in import-export business, Matamoras, Mexico, 1861-65; became financial and purchasing agt. for Houston and Tex. Central R. R., N.Y.C., 1865; Rice Inst. (Houston) endowed and founded by provisions of his will, 1912. Murdered by Charles F. Jones (his valet), N.Y.C., Sept. 23, 1900.

RICE, William Whitney, congressman, lawyer; b. Deerfield, Franklin County, Mass., Mar. 7, 1826; attended Gorham Acad., Me.; grad. Bowdoin Coll., 1846; studied law, Worcester, Mass. Preceptor, Leicester Acad., Mass., 1847-51; admitted to bar, 1854, practiced in Worcester; apptd. judge of insolvency Worcester County, 1858; mayor Worcester, 1860; dist. atty. Middle Dist. Mass., 1869-74; mem. Mass. Ho. of Reps., 1875; mem. U.S. Ho. of Reps. (Republican) from Mass., 45th-49th congresses, 1877-87. Died Worcester, Mar. 1, 1896; buried Rural Cemetery.

RICH, Charles, congressman; b. Warwick, Hampshire County, Mass., Sept. 13, 1771; had limited schooling. Moved to Shoreham, Addison County, Vt., 1787; mem. Vt. Ho. of Reps., 1800-11; county judge for 6 years; mem. U.S. Ho. of Reps. (Dem.) from Vt., 13th, 15th-18th congresses, 1813-15, 17-24. Died Shoreham, Oct. 15, 1824; buried family vault on his farm nr. Shoreham.

RICH, Isaac, mcht., philanthropist; b. Wellfleet, Mass., Oct. 24, 1801; s. Robert and Eunice (Harding) R.; m. Sarah Andrews, 1822, 4 children. Opened oyster stall in Faneuil Hall Market, Boston, 1820, built one of largest fish businesses in Boston; turned from shipping to real estate during Civil War, 1861; contbr. over $50,000 to Wesleyan Acad., Wilbraham, Mass., trustee, contbr. to Wesleyan U., bequeathed $150,000 to Rich Hall; left partically his entire estate ($700,-000) to Boston U. Died Jan. 13, 1812.

RICH, Obadiah, bibliographer; b. Truro, Mass., 1783; s. Obadiah and Salome (Lombard) R.; m. Ann Montgomery, 6 children. Am. consul at Valencia, Spain, 1816-29; took charge of archives of legation, Madrid, Spain, 1823; moved to London, Eng., 1829; Am. consul at Port Mahon in Balearic Islands, 1834-45; became mem. Mass. Hist. Soc., 1805; charter mem. Boston Athenaeum, 1807; elected to Am. Antiquarian Soc., 1834; also mem. other hist. societies; owned most remarkable collection of rare Americana up to that time; for years acted as agt. of Am. libraries and collectors; chiefly remembered for bibliographies and manuscripts relating to America; prin. works include A Catalogue of Books, Relating Principally to America, Arranged under the Years They were Printed, 1832; Bibliotheca Americana Nova; or a Catalogue of Books in Various Languages Relating to America, Printed Since the Year 1700, 2 vols., 1835-46; Catalogue of a Collection of Manuscripts, Principally in Spanish, Relating to America, in the Possession of O. Rich. Author: A General View of the United States of America (little gazetteer), pub. London, 1833. Died London, Jan. 20, 1850.

RICH, Sir Robert (2d earl Warwick), statesman; b. 1587; s. Robert and Penelope (Devereux) R.; attended U. Cambridge (Eng.). Mem. English Ho. of Commons, 1610; became 2d earl Warwick, 1619; mem. Ho. of Lords, 1619-49; a leading Puritan in Eng.; secured patent for Mass. Bay Colony, 1628; leading mem. Saybrook Corp. (composed of leading English Puritans) to establish colony in Conn., 1621; managed Bermudas Co. (Puritan venture to settle Bermuda); mem. council New Eng. Co.; lord high adm. English Navy, 1643-49; head of commn. for govt. of colonies, 1643-49, aided in incorporation of Providence Plantation (now R.I.). Died 1658.

RICHARD, Gabriel, missionary, educator; b. Saintes, France, Oct. 15, 1767; s. Francis and Genevieve (Bossuet) R.; ed. Coll. of Saintes, and Sulpician seminaries at Angers and Issy. Ordained Sulpician priest Roman Catholic Ch., 1790; came to U.S., arrived in Baltimore, O., June 24, 1792; worked among French, half-breeds and Indians with missionary centers at Prairie du Rocher, Kaskaskia and Cahokia; pastor St. Anne's Ch., 1800, became vicar-gen. of whole region of Detroit; opened primary sch., Detroit, 1802, acad. for young ladies, 1804; a founder 6 primary schs., 2 acads.; established 1st printing press in Ill. Territory, printed Essai du Michigan ou Observateur Impartial (1st paper printed in Detroit), 1809; edited child's spelling book, several devotional books, volume of selections from French poets, Bible for Indians, laws of Mich.; held by British until his release was demanded by Tecumseh during War of 1812; one of founder of Catholepistemiad or U. Michigania, 1817, v.p., also trustee, 1821; del. U.S. Congress from Territory of Mich., 1823-25, presented petitions relative to sch. grants, streets in Detroit, Western roads; charter mem. Mich. Hist. Soc., 1832. Died Detroit, Sept. 13, 1832; buried cemetery St. Anne Roman Catholic Ch., Detroit.

RICHARD(S), John H., engraver; b. Germany, circa 1807. Experimented with lithotinting, produced Grandpapa's Pet (1st true lithotint produced in Am., published in Miss Leslie's Mag., 1843); engraver, Phila., 1843-44; employed at U.S. Mint, 1851-52; artist with Smithsonian Instn., 1852-55 made drawings of various wild life specimens, engravings published in ofcl. reports, 1855-60; contbr. drawings for a series of turtle prints, also for Treatise on Some of the Insects Injurious to Vegetation (T.W. Harris), 1862.

RICHARD, Matthias, congressman, b. nr. Pottstown, New Hanover Twp., Montgomery County, Pa., Feb. 26, 1758; prep. studies under pvt. tutoring. Served as pvt. in Col. Daniel Udree's 2d battalion, Berks County (Pa.) Militia in Revolutionary War, 1777-78; participated in battles of Brandywine and Germantown; maj. 4th Battalion, Philadelphia County Militia, 1780; apptd. justice of peace, 1788, held office 40 years; judge Berks County Ct., 1791-97; insp. customs, 1801-02; mem. U.S. Ho. of Reps. from Pa., 10th-11th congresses, 1807-11; apptd. collector revenue Pa. 9th Dist., 1813; clk. Berks County Orphans Ct., 1823; asso. judge Berks County Cts.; became mcht., Reading, Pa. Died Reading, Aug. 4, 1830; buried Charles Evans Cemetery.

RICHARDS, Jacob, congressman; b. nr. Chester, Delaware County, Pa., 1773; grad. U. Pa., 1794; studied law. Admitted to bar, 1795, practiced in Phila.; mem. U.S. Ho. of Reps. (Democrat) from Pa., 8th-10th congresses, 1803-09; commd. col. militia in Delaware County; practiced in Chester. Died Chester, July 20, 1816.

RICHARDS, John, congressman, mcht.; b. New Hanover, Phila. County, Pa., Apr. 18, 1753; ed. by pvt. tutors. Served as magistrate during Revolutionary War; justice of peace Philadelphia County, 1777-1822; judge Montgomery County Ct., Common Pleas, 1784; mem. U.S. Constl. Conv., 1787; mem. U.S. Ho. of Reps. from Pa., 4th Congress, 1795-97; became ironmaster, mcht., farmer; mem. Pa. Senate, 1801-07. Died New Hanover, Nov. 13, 1822; buried Faulkner Swamp (Lutheran) Ch. Cemetery.

RICHARDS, John, congressman; b. Wales, Apr. 13, 1765. Came to U.S., settled in Johnsburg, Warren County, N.Y.; mem. N.Y. State Assembly, 1811; surveyor N.Y. State, 1810-12 del. N.Y. State Constl. Conv., 1821; mem. U.S. Ho. of Reps. from N.Y., 18th Congress, 1823-25. Died Lake George, Warren County, Apr. 18, 1850.

RICHARDS, Mark, congressman; b. Waterbury, Conn., July 15, 1760. Served at Stony Point, Monmouth, Red Bank, Valley Forge, during Revolutionary War, settled in Boston after Revolution, became mcht.; moved to Westminster, Vt., 1796; mem. Vt. Ho. of Reps., 1801-05, 24-26, 28, 32-34; sheriff Windham Co., 1806-10; Democratic presdl. elector, 1812; mem. Vt. Gov.'s Council, 1816; mem. U.S. Ho. of Reps. (Democrat) from Vt., 15th-16th congresses, 1817-21; lt. gov. Vt., 1830-31. Died Westminster, Aug. 10, 1844; buried Bradley tomb, Old Cemetery.

RICHARDS, William, missionary, diplomatic agt., govt. ofcl.; b. Plainfield, Mass., Aug. 22, 1793; s. James and Lydia (Shaw) R.; grad. Williams Coll., 1819, Andover Theol. Soc., 1822; m. Clarissa Lyman, Oct. 30, 1822, at least 6 children. Ordained missionary Congregational Ch., 1822; stationed at Lahaina, Main Island, Hawaii, 1822-25; served as preacher, tchr., physician, artisan; visited U.S. to rouse enthusiasm for world evangelization as agt. Sandwich Islands Mission, 1837; returned to Islands, 1838; entered service of kings and chiefs as advisor, interpreter, chaplain, tchr.; Republican teachings influenced character of Hawaiian bill of rights, 1839, constn. of 1840, laws passed, 1838-42; sent on diplomatic mission to secure recognition of Hawaiian govt. by U.S., Gt. Britain, France, also to negotiate more favorable treaties, 1842; pres. bd. commrs. to quit land titles, 1848; 1st minister pub. instrn., 1848. Author: Memoir of Keopuolani, Late Queen Sandwich Islands, 1825; edited and translated Constitution and Laws of Hawaiian Islands, 1842; translated 13 books of Bible into Hawaiian. Died Honolulu, Hawaii, Nov. 7, 1847.

RICHARDS, Zalmon, educator; b. Cummington, Mass., Aug. 11, 1811; s. Nehemiah and Betsey Richards; grad. Williams Coll., 1836; m. Minerva Todd, 1836; m. 2d, Mary Mather, Aug. 19, 1874; 1 child. Prin., Cummington Acad., 1836-39, Stillwater (N.Y.)Acad., 1839-49; prin. prep. dept. Columbian Coll., Washington, D.C., 1849-52; founded Columbian Tchrs. Assn., 1849; established and conducted Union Acad., Washington, 1852-61; founder Washington YMCA, 1852; mem. Christian Commn. for D.C., 1861-65; clk. U.S. Bur. Statistics, Washington, 1862-67; mem. common council of Washington, 1867-69; largely responsible for passage of act which created nat. dept. of edn., 1867, mem. dept., 1867-69; 1st supt. public schs. Washington, 1869-70; auditor for D.C., 1871-74; co-founder, 1st pres. Nat. Tchrs. Assn. (now N.E.A.), 1857. Author: Teachers' Manual, 1880; The Natural Arithmetic, 1885. Died Washington, Nov. 1, 1899.

RICHARDSON, Albert Deane, jooournalist; b. Franklin, Mass., Oct. 6, 1833; s. Elisha and Harriet (Blake) R.; m. Mary Louise Pease, Apr. 1855; m. 2d, Abbie Sage McFarland, 1869; 5 children. Corr., Boston Journal in Leavenworth, Lawrence and Topeka, Kan., 1857-59; served as adj. gen., of territory sec. of legislature territory of Kansas; accompanied Horace Greeley and Henry Villard to Pike's Peak journalistic expdn., 1859-60; with N.Y. Herald Tribune, 1860-69, secret correspondent in New Orleans, 1861, became chief war correspondent, 1862; captured by Confederates (with Junius Henri Browne), 1863, escaped, 1864; went to Cal. as correspondent for N.Y. Tribune, 1865. Author: The Secret Service, the Field, the Dungeon, and the Escape, 1865; Beyond the Mississippi, 1866; Personal History of Ulysses S. Grant, 1868; Garnered Sheaves (published posthumously by his widow), 1871. Died N.Y.C., Dec. 2, 1869.

RICHARDSON, Edmund, cotton planter and mfr.; b. Caswell County, N.C., June 28, 1818; s. James and Nancy Payne (Ware) R.; m. Margaret Elizabeth Patton, May 1848; 7 children. Jr. mem. Thornhill & Co., factorage business, New Orleans, 1852-67; owner 5 plantations, 1861; established factorage firm Richardson and May, New Orleans, 1867; leased Miss. Penitentiary, employed convicts on his plantation, 1868-73; purchased plantations in Miss., La. and Ark.; held largest cotton plantation holdings in world; bought controlling interest in cotton mills, Wesson, Miss., 1873, pres., until 1886; controlled Refuge Oil Mill, Vicksburg, Miss., also Vicksburg, Shreveport & Pacific R.R.; apptd. commr. from cotton states at Phila. Centennial Expn. of 1876; elected v.p. Atlanta Cotton Expn. of 1881; apptd. by Pres. Arthur as commr. World's Indsl. and Cotton Centennial Expn., New Orleans, 1884, pres. bd. mgmt. Died Jackson, Miss., Jan. 11, 1886.

RICHARDSON, Henry Hobson, architect; b. St. James Parish, La., Sept. 29, 1838; s. Henry Dickenson and Caroline (Priestley) R.; attended U. La.; grad. Harvard, 1859; attended Ecole des Beaux Arts, Paris, France, 1860-62, 62-65; m. Julia Hayden, Jan. 3, 1867, 6 children. Settled in N.Y.C., 1865; won archtl. competitions for 1st Unitarian Ch., Springfield, Mass., Episcopal Ch., West Medford, Mass., 1866; Brattle Street Ch., Boston, 1870, Trinity Ch., Boston, 1872; partner with Charles D. Gambrill, 1867-78; apptd. (with Leopold Eidlitz and Frederick Law Olmstead) to complete bldg. and grounds N.Y. State Capitol, 1876; moved office to Brookline, Mass., 1878; prin. works include: shingled summer cottage of Rev. P. Browne, Marion, Mass. (best domestic work), 1881; library, Quincy, Mass., 1880, Sever Hall, Harvard, 1878, Austin Hall, Harvard, 1881, Cincinnati C. of C. Bldg., 1885, Marshall Field Bldg., Chgo., 1885, series of stations for Boston & Albany R.R., from Auburndale to Wellesley Hills, Mass., 1885, Billings Library, U. Vt., Burlington, 1833, Conversse Library, Malden, Mass., 1883, Baptist Ch., Newton, Mass., 1884, Bagley Meml. Fountains, Detroit, Glessner home, Chgo., homes of Henry Adams and John Hay, Washington, D.C.; fellow A.I.A., Am. Acad. Arts and Scis., Archeol. Inst. Am.; elected hon. and corresponding mem. Royal Inst. Brit. Architects, 1885; set Eastern Architectural fashions, 1880-93, style lost precedence after "renaissance" of classicism began, 1893. Died Brookline, Apr. 27, 1886.

RICHARDSON, Israel Bush, army officer; b. Fairfax, Vt., Dec. 26, 1815; s. Israel Putnam and Susan (Holmes) R.; grad. U.S. Mil. Acad., 1841; m. Rita Stevenson, Aug. 3, 1850; m. 2d, Francis A. Traver, May 29, 1861; 1 child. Commd. brevet 2d lt. 3d Inf., U.S. Army, 1841, promoted 2d lt., 1841; in Seminole Indian War in Fla., 1841-42; commd. 1st lt., 1846; at battles of Resaca-de-la-Palma, Monterrey, Cerro Gordo, Palo Alto, Vera Cruz and Mexico City in Mexican War; brevetted capt. and maj., 1848; promoted capt., 1851; resigned from army, 1855; farmer in Mich., 1855-61; apptd. col. 2d Mich. Volunteer Regiment, U.S. Army, 1861; at Battle of Bull Run; promoted brig. gen. of Volunteers, 1861, maj. gen., 1862; mortally wounded in battle of Antietam, 1862. Died Sharpsburg, Md., Nov. 3, 1862.

RICHARDSON, John Peter, gov. S.C., congressman; b. Hickory Hill, S.C., Apr. 14, 1801; grad. S.C. Coll. at Columbia, 1819; studied law. Admitted to bar, practiced in Fulton, Sumter County, S.C.; mem. S.C. Ho. of Reps.; judge circuit ct.; mem. U.S. Ho. of Reps. (State Rights Democrat, filled vacancy) from S.C., 24th-25th congresses, Dec. 19, 1836-39; gov. S.C., 1840-42. Died Fulton (later Pinewood), Jan. 24, 1864.

RICHARDSON, John Smythe, congressman, lawyer; b. Bloomhill plantation, nr. Sumter, S.C., Feb. 29, 1828; grad. S.C. Coll. (now U. S.C.), 1850; studied law. Admitted to bar, 1852, practiced in Sumter; entered Confederate Army as capt. of Infantry during Civil War, served under Gen. Joseph Brevard Kershaw until after 1st Battle of Manassas where he was wounded; later promoted adjutant 23d Regt., S.C. Infantry, served until 1865; mem. S.C. Ho. of Reps., 1865-67; apptd. agt. State of S.C. to apply for and receive land script donated by S.C. to Congress, 1866; del. Nat. Democratic Conv., St. Louis, 1876; mem. U.S. Ho. of Reps. (Democrat) from S.C., 46th-47th congresses, 1879-83; master in equity for Sumter County, 1884-93. Died at his country home Shadyside, nr. Sumter, Feb. 24, 1894; buried Sumter Cemetery.

RICHARDSON, Joseph, silversmith; b. Phila., Sept. 28, 1711; s. Francis and Elizabeth (Growdon) R.; m. Hannah Worrell, Aug. 24, 1741; m. 2d, Mary Allen; 6 children including Joseph, Nathaniel. Inherited his father's silversmith shop, Phila., 1829; one of leading silversmiths in Phila.; helped organize Friendly Assn. for Regaining and Preserving Peace with Indians, Phila., 1756; presented silver jewelry to Indian leaders; mem. bd. Pa. Hosp., Phila., 1756-70. Died Dec. 3, 1784.

RICHARDSON, Joseph, congressman, clergyman; b. Billerica, Mass., Feb. 1, 1778; grad. Dartmouth, 1802; studied theology. Tchr., Charlestown, 1804-06; ordained to ministry Unitarian Ch.; assigned to 1st parish of Unitarian Ch., Hingham, Plymouth County, Mass., 1806; del. Mass. Constl. Conv., 1820; mem. Mass. Ho. of Reps., 1821-22; mem. Mass. Senate, 1823-24, 26; mem. U.S. Ho. of Reps. from Mass., 20th-21st congresses, 1827-31. Died Hingham, Sept. 25, 1871; buried Old Ship Cemetery.

RICHARDSON, Robert, physician, educator; b. Pitts., Sept. 25, 1806; s. Nathaniel and Julia (Logan) R.; attended Sch. Medicine, U. Pa., 1826-27; A.M., Jefferson Coll., 1829; m. Rebecca Encell, Apr. 10, 1831, 10 children. Confirmed in Episcopal Ch., 1824; baptized as follower Disciples of Christ, 1829; preached, evangelized, made several converts, 1829-30; practiced medicine, 1829-76; co-editor Millenial Harbinger, 1848-52, contbd. to publ., 1830-60; when he became mem. 1st faculty Bethany (W. Va.) Coll., 1841, prof. chemistry, physiology, botany, rhetoric, 1841-50, lectr. on Bible, 1865-67; v.p. Ky. U., Harrodsburg, 1859-65, pioneer in agrl. experiment. Author: The Principles and Objects of Religious Formation, 1853; A Scriptural View of the Office of the Holy Spirit, 1873. Died Bethany, Oct. 22, 1876.

RICHARDSON, Tobias Gibson, surgeon, educator; b. Lexington, Ky., Jan. 3, 1827; M.D., U. Louisville (Ky.), 1848; m. Ida Ann Slocum, Nov. 12, 1868; 3 children including Sarah Short. Demonstrator of anatomy U. Louisville, 1848-56; published Elements of Human Anatomy, 1854; co-editor Louisville Med. Review, 1856; prof. anatomy Med. Dept. of Pa. Coll., Phila., 1856-58; prof. anatomy U. La. (now Tulane), New Orleans, 1858-62, 65-72, prof. surgery, 1872-89, dean of coll., 1865-85; asst. med. dir. Army of Tenn., 1862-63, med. insp., 1862, med. dir. to Gen. Braxton Bragg, 1865; volunteer visiting surgeon to Charity Hosp. of New Orleans, 28 years; pres. A.M.A., 1877; urged appointment of nat. sec. of health, pleaded for appropriations from fed. govt. to promote research for investigation and prevention of disease, 1878; a founder Orleans Parish Med. Soc., 1877, La. State Med. Assn., 1878, Am. Surg. Assn., 1880; an original mem. New Orleans Auxiliary Sanitary Assn., 1878; mem. Am. Pub. Health Assn.; fellow Coll. of Pharmacy and Acad. Phys. Scis. of Phila.; adminstr. of fund established by Paul Tulane for benefit of U. La., 1884; ruling elder First Presbyn. Ch. of New Orleans, 1860-92; gave $150,000 to Tulane Med. Sch. Died New Orleans, May 26, 1892.

RICHARDSON, Willard, journalist; b. Mass., June 24, 1802; B.A., S.C. Coll., Columbia, S.C., 1828; m. Louisa Blanche Murrell, 1849, 1 child. Moved to Tex., 1837; opened sch. for young men, Houston, Tex., 1837; editor Houston Telegraph, 1842; temporary editor Galveston (Tex.) News, 1843, editor, 1843-75, directed efforts toward annexation of Tex. to U.S. became owner, 1845, under his control paper became most widely circulated, infuential, wealthiest jour. in Tex.; pioneer in South in field of nonpolit. independent journalism; 1st published Texas Almanac, 1857, became important factor in immigration movement to Tex.; influential in one and only defeat in Tex. of Sam Houston as candidate for gov., 1857; paper maintained continuous publication during Civil War. Died Galveston, July 26, 1875.

RICHARDSON, William Adams, jurist, sec. of treasury; b. Tyngsborough, Mass., Nov. 2, 1821; s. Daniel and Mary (Adams) R.; grad. Harvard, 1843, LL.B., 1846, LL.D. (hon.); LL.D. (hon.), Columbian U., Washington, D.C., Dartmouth Coll., Georgetown Coll., Washington; m. Anna Marston, Oct. 29, 1849, 1 child. Admitted to Mass. bar, 1846; apptd. (with Joel Parker) to consolidate and rearrange statute law of Mass., 1855; prepared Richardson's supplements to congressional legislation, 1874-95; judge probate for Middlesex County (Mass.), 1856-58, held combined office of judge of probate and insolvency, 1858-72; pres. Lowell (Mass.) Common Council, 1860; became asst. sec. of U.S. Treasury, 1869, managed Treasury's funding operations, London, Eng., 1871-72, sec. of treasury, 1873-74, arranged for receipt of $15,500,000 Geneva Award through simultaneous retirement of U.S. bonds held in Europe (so that no gold movement was entailed); apptd. to U.S. Ct. of Claims, 1874, chief justice, Jan. 1885; taught at Georgetown Law Sch., 1879-94; mem. bd. overseers Harvard, 1863-75. Author: Banking Laws of Massachusetts, 1855; Practical Information Concerning the Public Debt of the United States, 3d edit., 1873; History, Jurisdiction and Practice of the Court of Claims, 1882; edited supplement to revised statutes of U.S., 1881. Died Washington, Oct. 19, 1896.

RICHARDSON, William Alexander, senator, congressman; b. nr. Lexington, Ky., Jan. 16, 1811; attended coll., Walnut Hill, Ky., also Centre Coll., Danville, Ky., Transylvania U., Lexington; studied law. Taught sch.; admitted to bar, 1831, practiced in Shelbyville, Ill.; state's atty., 1834, 35; mem. Ill. Ho. of Reps., 1836-38, 44-46, speaker, 1844; mem. Ill. Senate, 1838-42; Democratic presdl. elector, 1844; enlisted as capt. during Mexican War, promoted maj.; moved to Quincy, Ill., 1849; mem. U.S. Ho. of Reps. (Democrat, filled vacancy) from Ill., 30th-34th, 37th congresses, Dec. 6, 1847-Aug. 25, 1856 (resigned), 61-Jan. 29, 1863 (resigned); mem. U.S. Senate (filled vacancy) from Ill., Jan. 30, 1863-65; del. Nat. Dem. Conv., Charleston, S.C., 1860, N.Y.C., 1868; engaged in newspaper work. Died Quincy, Dec. 27, 1875; buried Woodland Cemetery.

RICHARDSON, William Merchant, congressman, jurist; b. Pelham, Hillsboro County, N.H., Jan. 4, 1774; s. Capt. Daniel and Sarah (Merchant) R.; grad. Harvard, 1797; LL.D., Dartmouth; m. Betsy Smith, Oct. 7, 1799, 7 children including Anne. Prin., Groton (Mass.) Acad., circa 1799; admitted to bar, began practice law, Groton, circa 1802; mem. U.S. Ho. of Reps. from Mass., 11th-12th congresses, Nov. 14-1811-Apr. 18, 1814; U.S. atty. for N.H., 1814-16; chief justice N.H. Superior Ct., 1816-38, responsible for establishing N.H. laws of practice, wrote opinion in case Trustees of Dartmouth Coll. vs. William H. Woodward that charter of coll. was not a contract and legislature might add new members without consulting old corp., decision reversed in U.S. Supreme Ct. by Chief Justice John Marshall; in Britton vs. Turner (1834) held that an employee under a definite term of service might recover earned wages even though he left employment without just cause; chmn. commn. to revise statutes of N.H., 1826. Author: (legal works) The New Hampshire Justice of the Peace, 1824, The New Hampshire Town Officer, 1829, co-editor: New Hampshire Superior Ct. Cases, 11 vols., 1819-44. Died Chester, N.H., Mar. 23, 1838.

RICHINGS, Peter (real name Peter Richings Puget), actor; b. London, Eng., May 19, 1798; s. Peter and Hannah Puget; m. 1818, 1 adopted dau., Mary Caroline Reynoldson Richings. Came to U.S., 1821; made acting debut as Henry Bertram in Guy Mannering, N.Y.C., 1821; on stage, N.Y.C., 1821-40; appeared as Marcus in The Green-eyed Monster, as Sir Benjamin Backbite in The School for Scandal, as Bill Sikes in Oliver Twist; in Phila., 1840-58; mgr. Walnut Street and Chestnut Street theaters, Phila.; managed English opera company on tour of U.S., 1866; retired from theater, 1867. Died Media, Pa., Jan. 18, 1871.

RICHMOND, (Elkanah) Dean, railroad exec., polit. leader; b. Barnard, Vt., Mar. 31, 1804; s. Hathaway and Rachel (Dean) R.; m. Mary Elizabeth Mead, Feb. 19, 1833, 8 children. Moved to Buffalo, N.Y., 1842, engaged in grain forwarding business, ran fleet of steam and sailing vessels on Gt. Lakes; mem. Utica Conv., 1848; del. to Buffalo Free Soil Conv., 1848; chmn. N.Y. State Democratic Com., 1850-66; headed N.Y. delegation at Dem. Nat. Conv., Charleston, S.C., Balt., 1860; secured nomination and election of Seymour as gov. N.Y., 1862; helped arrange Nat. Union Conv., Phila., 1866; originator and dir. Buffalo & Rochester R.R.; formed N.Y. Central from 7 separate corps., 1853, mem. com. which drafted plans for consolidation, v.p., 1853, pres., 1864; organizer, dir. Buffalo & State Line R.R., pres., 1866. Died N.Y.C., Aug. 27, 1866.

RICHMOND, Hiram Lawton, congressman, lawyer; b. Chautauqua, N.Y., May 17, 1810; studied medicine with father 2 years; attended Allegheny Coll., Meadville, Pa., 1834-35; studied law. Admitted to bar, 1838, practiced in Meadville; began as Whig but united with Republican Party at its organization; mem. U.S. Ho. of Reps. (Rep.) from Pa., 43d Congress, 1873-75; trustee Allegheny Coll. many years. Died Meadville, Feb. 19, 1885; buried Greendale, Cemetery.

RICHMOND, John Lambert, clergyman, physician; b. nr. Chesterfield, Mass., Apr. 5, 1785; s. Nathaniel and Susanna (Lambert) R.; Med. Diploma, Med. Coll. of Ohio, 1822; m. Lorna Sprague Patchin, Nov. 23, 1806, 10 children. Ordained to ministry Baptist Ch., 1816, served as minister until 1842; performed 1st successful Caesarian operation to be reported in med. press. of U.S., 1827. Died Covington, Fountain County, Ind., Oct. 12, 1855.

RICHMOND, John Wilkes, physician, publicist; b. Little Compton, R.I., Sept. 25, 1775; s. Dr. Benjamin and Sarah (Church) R.; grad. R.I. Coll. (now Brown U.), 1794; m. Mary Sheffield, Nov. 1804; m. 2d, Henrietta (Shaw) Bours, Apr. 1815. Endeavored to secure payment of Revolutionary debt of R.I. through petitions to R.I. Legislature and pamphlets to the public. Author: The History of the Registered State Debt of Rhode Island, 1848; Rhode Island Repudiation of History of the Revolutionary Debt of Rhode Island, 1855. Died Phila., Mar. 4, 1857; buried Stonington, Conn.

RICHMOND, Jonathan, congressman; b. Dartmouth, Mass., July 31, 1774; completed prep. studies. Moved to Western N.Y., 1813, settled in Aurora, Cayuga County; sheriff Cayuga County, 1808-12; U.S. internal revenue collector; mem. U.S. Ho. of Reps. from N.Y., 16th Congress, 1819-21. Died Aurora, July 28, 1853; buried Aurora Cemetery.

RICKETSON, Daniel, author; b. New Bedford, Mass., July 30, 1813; s. Joseph and Anna (Thornton) R.; m. Maria Louisa Sampson, June 27, 1834, 4 children including Anna, Walton; m. 2d, Angeline Standish Gidley, Nov. 10, 1880. Personal friend of Henry Thoreau, Ralph Waldo Emerson, Amos Bronson Alcott, other writers, humanitarians; abolitionist, aided in escape of runaway slaves, works include: History of New Bedford, 1858; The Autumn Sheaf, a Collection of Miscellaneous Poems (1st book of verse), 1869; The Factory Bell and Other Poems, 1873. Died New Bedford, July 16, 1898.

RICKETTS, James Brewerton, army officer; b. N.Y.C., June 21, 1817; s. George R.A. and Mary (Brewerton) R.; grad. U.S. Mil. Acad., 1839; m. Harriet Josephine Pierce, 1840; m. 2d, Frances Lawrence, 1856; 6 children. Commd. 2d lt. U.S. Army, 1839, 1st lt., 1846; served at battles of Monterey and Buena Vista during Mexican War, in Seminole War in Fla., 1852; promoted capt., 1852; commanded battery U.S. Army under Gen. McDowell, 1861; commd. brig. gen. U.S. Volunteers, 1861; assigned to command div. in Gen. McDowell's Corps, 1862, fought at battles of Cedar Mountain and Manassas, in Joseph Hooker's Corps at Battle of Antietam; court martial duty, 1862-64; joined army under Gen. Philip Sheriden in Shenandoah Valley, at Battle of Cedar Creek, 1864; temporarily in command VI Corps; discharged as brig. gen. volunteers, reverted to rank maj. U.S. Army, 1866; ret. as maj. gen., 1867. Died Washington, D.C., Sept. 23, 1887.

RICORD, Frederick William, mayor, author; b. Island of Guadeloupe, B.W.I., Oct. 7, 1819; s. Jean Baptiste and Elizabeth (Stryker) R.; attended Geneva (now Hobart) Coll., Rutgers Coll.; m. Sophia Bradley, 1843, 4 children. Librarian, Newark (N.J.) Library Assn., 1849-69; mem. 1st Newark Bd. Edn., 1853-69, pres., 1867-69, served many terms as sec.; N.J. supt. schs., 4 years; published Youth's Grammar, 1853, 3 textbooks of Roman history; sheriff Essex County (N.J.), 1865; lay judge Essex County Ct. Common Pleas; mayor of Newark, 1870-74; treas., librarian N.J. Hist. Soc., 1881-97, also 1st regular librarian; translated fgn. works; published English Songs from Foreign Tongues, 1879, The Self-Tormentor, 1885. Died Newark, Aug. 12, 1897; buried Mt. Pleasant (N.J.) Cemetery.

RICORD, Philippe, physician; b. Balt., Dec. 10, 1800; M.D. from med. sch. Paris, France, 1826. Became surgeon to Central Bur., Paris, 1828; surgeon-in-chief for syphilis Hopital du Midi, 1831-61; established a rational therapy of syphilis and gave laws of transmission of disease in precise terms, 1834; demonstrated that gonorrhea is entirely distinct from syphilis; received Monthyon prize for devising a new method of curing varicocele and a spl. technique in urethroplasty; became mem. Acad. Medicine in Paris, 1850, pres., 1868; became ofcl. surgeon to Prince Napoleon, 1852, later to Emperor Napoleon III; of cons. surgeon to imperial troops; dir. Lazaretto (instn. for care of needy and ailing poor) during Siege of Paris; decorated officer Legion d'Honneur by Thiers (1st pres. 3d Republic of France). Author: De la Blennorrhagie de la Femme, 1834; Monographic du Chancre, 1837; Traite pratique maladies veneriennes (treatise on venereal disease) 1838; Lettress sur la Syphillis, 1851; Lecons sur le Chancre, 1857. Died Paris, Oct. 22, 1889.

RIDDELL, John Leonard, physician, scientist; b. Leyden, Mass., Feb. 20, 1807; s. John and Lephe (Gates) R.; grad. Rensselaer Sch., Troy, N.Y., 1829; M.D., Cincinnati Med. Coll., 1836; Adjunct prof. chemistry and botany Cincinnati Med. Coll., 1835-36; published Synopsis of the Flora of the Western States, 1835; prof. chemistry Med. Coll. of La., 1836-65; published Catalogus Florae Ludovicianae (catalogue of La. plants), 1852; apptd. by Pres. Van Buren as melter and refiner in branch of U.S. Mint, 1838/39-49; mem. commn. to devise means of protection for New Orleans against Mississippi River, 1844; later discovered microscopial characteristics of blood and black vomit in yellow fever; devised binocular microscope, 1851, instrument finished and sent to him, 1854; active mem. 1st La. State Med. Soc. (founded 1849), New Orleans Physico-Medico Soc. Died New Orleans, Oct. 7, 1865.

RIDDLE, George Read, senator, congessman; b. New Castle, Del., 1817; attended Del. Coll.; studied civil engring. and law. Engaged in constrn. railroads and canals; admitted to bar, 1848, practiced in Wilmington, Del., 1848; commr. to retrace Mason and Dixon line, 1849; del. to several Nat. Democratic Convs.; dep. atty. gen., 1849, 50; mem. U.S. Ho. of Reps. (Dem.) from Del., 32d-33d congresses, 1851-55; mem. U.S. Senate (filled vacancy) from Del., Feb. 2, 1864-Mar. 29, 1867. Died Washington, D.C., Mar. 29, 1867; buried Wilmington and Brandywine Cemetery.

RIDDLE, Haywood Yancey, congressman, lawyer; b. Van Buren, Hardeman County, Tenn., June 20, 1834; grad. Union U., Murfreesboro, Tenn., 1854; grad. law dept. Cumberland U., Lebanon, Tenn., 1857. Adjunct prof. mathematics and langs. Union U. for 15 months; admitted to Ripley (Miss.) bar, 1857; moved to Smith County, Tenn., 1858, became farmer; enlisted as pvt. in Confederate Army during Civil War, 1861, served throughout war, during last year of war on staffs Brig. Gens. Wright and Mackall; moved to Lebanon, Wilson County, Tenn., 1865; dep. clk. Chancery Clk's. Office for 5 years, apptd. clk., 1870-75; mem. U.S. Ho. of Reps. (Democrat, filled vacancy) from Tenn., 44th-45th congresses, Dec. 14, 1875-79. Died Lebanon, Mar. 28, 1879; buried Cedar Grove Cemetery.

RIDDLEBERGER, Harrison Holt, senator, lawyer; b. Edinburg, Shenandoah County, Va., Oct. 4, 1844; attended common schs.; studied law. Served as 2d and 1st lt. of Infantry and capt. of Cavalry in Confederate Army during Civil War for 3 years; returned to Edinburg, became editor Tenth Legion Banner; admitted to bar, practiced in Woodstock, Va.; mem. Va. Ho. of Dels., 1871-75; commonwealth atty. of Shenandoah County, 1876-80; mem. Va. Senate, 1879-82; editor Shenandoah Democrat, later Virginian, Woodstock; mem. Va. Conservative Party Com. until 1875; Democratic presdl. elector, 1876; Readjuster presdl. elector, 1880; mem. U.S. Senate (Readjuster) from Va., 1883-89. Died Woodstock, Jan. 24, 1890; buried Cedarwood Cemetery, Edinburg.

RIDGAWAY, Henry Baseom, clergyman, coll. pres.; b. Talbot County, Md., Sept. 7, 1830; s. James and Mary (Jump) R.; grad. Dickinson Coll., Carlisle, Pa., 1849; m. Rosamund Caldwell, 1855. Admitted on trial to Balt. Conf., Methodist Episcopal Ch., 1850, ordained deacon, 1853, elder, 1855; served in Md. chs., 1855-60, Chestnut St. Ch., Portland, Me., 1861-62, various N.Y. chs., 1862-76; minister Meth. Ch., Cincinnati, 1876-81; prof. hist. theology Garret Bibl. Inst., Evanston, Ill., 1882-89, prof. practical theology, 1884-95, pres., 1885-92; visited English Wesleyan Conf., 1870; del. Gen. Conf., Meth. Episcopal Ch., 1872, 92; fraternal del. gen. Conf., Meth. Ch. South, 1882; attended Centennial Conf., Balt., 1884. Author: The Lord's Land, 1876; Outlines of Theological Encyclopedia, 1889. Died Evanston, Mar. 30, 1895.

RIDGE, Major, Indian chief; b. Hiwassee (now Polk) County, Tenn., 1771; at least 1 son, John. Held rank of maj. in Cherokee forces allied with Americans in Creek War, 1814; speaker Cherokee Council; partner in trading ventures of George Lavender; without tribunal authority signed a treaty to cede all Cherokee lands East of Mississippi River, also to remove to other side of the river, Dec. 29, 1835. Attacked and killed nr. Van Buren, O. (Cherokee Reservation), June 22, 1839.

RIDGELEY, Henry Moore, senator, congressman, lawyer; b. Dover, Del., Aug. 6, 1779; studied law. Admitted to bar, 1802, practiced in Dover; sec. of state Del., 1817-27; mem. U.S. Ho. of Reps. (Federalist) from Del., 12th-13th congresses, 1811-15; mem. U.S. Senate (filled vacancy) from Del., Jan. 12, 1827-29. Died Dover, Aug. 6, 1847; buried Episcopal Cemetery.

RIDGELY, Charles Goodwin, naval officer; b. Balt., July 21, 1784; s. Dr. Lyde and Abigail (Levy) G.; m. Cornelia L. Livingston, 1822, 3 children. Commd. lt. U.S. Navy, 1807; comdr., 1813, master-comdt., 1813; commanded brig Jefferson on Lake Ontario, 1814, sloop-of-war Erie, Independence in Bainbridge's squadron during and after Algerian war, circa 1815-17; promoted capt., 1815; commanded naval sta., Balt., 1820; in command flagship sloop-of-war Natchez, West India Squadron, 1827-circa 1829; comdr. N.Y.C. Navy Yard, 1834-39; served in command Brazil Squadron with flagship frigate Potomac, 1840-41; took command naval sta., Balt., 1842-43. Died Balt., Feb. 4, 1848.

RIDGELY, Daniel Bowly, naval officer; b. nr. Lexington, Ky., Aug. 1, 1813; s. Daniel Bowly and Jane (Price) R.; m. Johanna M. Clemm, Oct. 11, 1837; m. 2d, Elizabeth Dulany Rogers, Feb. 8, 1858; 2 children including Dr. Nicholas. Commd. lt. U.S. Navy, 1840; served as 1st lt. on ship Albany, participated in bombardment and capture of Vera Cruz, taking of Tuspan, Alvarado, Tampico, during Mexican War, 1846-48; became comdr., 1855; held 1st command, steamer Atalanta, dispatched to demand satisfaction from govt. of Paraguay for an insult to U.S. flag and injuries to Am. citizens, 1857-58; commanded steamer Santiago de Cuba, 1861-62, cruised in Gulf of Mexico, West Indian waters, capturing several blockade runners; commd. capt., 1862; commanded steam sloop Shenandoah, N. Atlantic Blockading Squadron, 1863, then cruised independently in West Indian waters, participated in blockade of Wilmington and New Inlet (N.C.); commd. commodore, 1866, mem. Naval Examining Bd. in Phila., 1868. Died Balt., May 5, 1868; buried Greenmount Cemetery, Balt.

RIDGELY, Nicholas, jurist, legislator; b. Dover, Del., Sept. 30, 1762; s. Dr. Charles Greenberry and Mary (Wynkoop) R.; m. Mary Brereton, May 20, 1806. Del. from Kent County to Del. Conv. which ratified U.S. Constn., 1787, to conv. forming Del. Contsn., 1792; mem. Del. Legislative Council, 1788, 89, 90; atty. gen. Del., 1791-1801; del. from Kent County to 2d State Constl. Conv., 1791-92; elected mem. 1st Del. Ho. of Reps., 1792, reelected, 1796, 97, 99, 1800, 01; chancellor Del., 1802-30; dep. 2d session of conv. which organized Protestant Episcopal Ch. in U.S., Phila., 1786. Died Dover, Apr. 1, 1830; buried Christ Churchyard, Dover.

RIDGELY, Richard, Continental congressman, lawyer; b. Queen Caroline Parish, Anne Arundel County, Md., Aug. 3, 1755; attended St. John's Coll., Annapolis, Md.; studied law. Asst. clk. Council of Safety, 1776, later clk.; admitted to bar, 1780, practiced in Balt.; advocate Md. Ct. of Chancery; mem. Continental Congress from Md., 1785-86, declined to serve latter year; mem. Md. Senate, 1786-91; apptd. judge county ct., 1811-24. Died Howard County, Md., Feb. 25, 1824; buried Dorsey Hall estate, nr. Columbia, Howard County.

RIDGWAY, Joseph, congressman; b. Staten Island, N.Y., May 6, 1783; attended public schs. Learned carpenter's trade; moved to Cayuga County, N.Y., 1811, manufactured plows; settled in Columbus, O., 1822, established iron foundry; mem. Ohio Ho. of Reps., 1828-32; mem. U.S. Ho. of Reps. (Whig) from Ohio, 25th-27th congresses, 1837-43; mem. Ohio Bd. Equalization; dir. Clinton Bank for 20 years; mem. City Council. Died Columbus, Feb. 1, 1861; buried Green Lawn Cemetery.

RIDGWAY, Robert, congressman; b. Lynchburg, Va., Apr. 21, 1823; attended Emory and Henry Coll.; grad. U. Va.; studied law. Admitted to bar, practiced in Liberty (now Bedford), Va., 1853; editor Richmond Whig until outbreak of Civil War when he retired to Amherse, Va.; mem. U.S. Ho. of Reps. (Conservative) from Va., 41st Congress, Jan. 27-Oct. 16, 1870. Died Cool Well, Amherst County, Va., Oct. 16, 1870; buried family cemetery, Amherst.

RIED, William Wharry, surgeon; b. Argyle, N.Y., 1799; A.B., Union Coll., Schenectady, N.Y., 1825; studied medicine under Dr. A. G. Smith, Rochester, N.Y., 1826-28; m. Elizabeth Manson, Oct. 4, 1830. Practiced medicine, Rochester, 1828-64, N.Y.C., 1864-66; pres. Monroe County (N.Y.) Med. Soc., 1836, 49; 1st to perfect and publish flexion method of reducing hip dislocations "Dislocation of the Femur on the Dorsum Ilis Reducible without Pulleys or any other Mechanical Means," printed in Buffalo Med. Journal, 1851. Died N.Y.C., Dec. 9, 1866; buried Framingham, Mass.

RIEGER, Johann Georg Joseph Anton, clergyman; b. Aurach, Bavaria, Germany, Apr. 23, 1811; m. Minette Schemel, 1839; m. 2d, Henrietta Wilkins, Apr. 15, 1845; 11 children. Chosen as German missionary to Am., 1836, among 1st German missionaries to introduce English into Evang. service; missionary, Alton, Ill., 1836-37, Beardstown, Ill., 1837-39; returned to Germany, 1839, to U.S., 1840; one of dominating figures in Evang. movement called Deutsche Evangelische Synode von Nord-Amerika; sold literature for Bible and Tract Soc. of N.Y., circa 1845-47; established Evang. Sem., Marthasville, Mo., 1850; a trustee Lincoln Inst. (coll. for Negroes); worked among prisoners in Mo. State Penitentiary. Died Jefferson City, Mo., Aug. 20, 1869.

RIEL, Louis, Canadian insurgent leader; b. St. Boniface, Assiniboia (now Man.), Oct. 23, 1844; ed. Coll. de Montreal. Of metis (mixed French and Indian) background; became leader metis protest against transfer Hudson's Bay Co. terr. to Can., autumn 1869; became pres. metis provisional govt.; negotiated with Canadian govt., entered Assiniboia into Canadian fedn. as Province of Man., 1870; gov. Man. until Aug. 1870, when he fled arrival of Canadian armed force; elected M.P. for dist. Provencher, 1873, 74, but expelled from seat and banished for 5 years, 1875; committed to asylums of Longue Pointe, Beauport (Que.), 1876-78; spent brief period in Keeseville, N.Y., then settled in Mont, to teach at mission sch., became naturalized Am. citizen; returned to N.W. Can. at invitation to head polit. protest against fed. govt.'s treatment of local populace, 1884; broke with Catholic Ch. when protest grew into rebellion, Mar. 1885, organized provisional govt. and appealed to Indians; surrendered when revolt was suppressed by Canadian troops, May 1885, convicted of treason and hanged; his execution caused repercussions in Que. and Ont., and he remained symbol of Can.'s Franco-English ethnic problems. Died Regina, Sask., Can., Nov. 16, 1885.

RIGDON, Sidney, religious leader; b. Piny Fork, Pa., Feb. 19, 1793; s. William and Nancy (Gallaher) R.; m. Phoebe Brooks, June 1820, at least 1 dau., Nancy. Worked on father's farm until 1817; licensed to preach, 1819; took charge small Baptist congregation, Pitts., 1820; in tanning bus. in Ohio, Aug. 1824-26; definitely allied with Cambellite movement, by 1828; credited with rewriting, expanding a novel by Solomon Spaulding, palmed off as Book of Mormon, denied authorship; became an enthusiastic Mormon, 1830; involved in land speculation with Joseph Smith, Kirtland, O.; fled to Mo. to escape mob violence, jud. action over debacle of Kirtland Safety Soc. Anti-BANKing Co. (which had unloaded illegal bank notes on creditors and gen. public), 1838; imprisoned following clash between Mormons and non-Mormons, 1838; city councilman, postmaster, trustee, city atty. Nauvoo (Ill.); prof. ch. history Univ. City of Nauvoo; excommunicated after he aspired to leadership of sect (Brigham Young was preferred by 12 apostles), 1844; collected small number of Pitts. Mormons, elected 1st pres., prophet, seer, revelator, translator, trustee, New Ch. of Christ, which denied connection with Western Mormons, 1845; wrote Lectures on Faith (a basic Mormon document); carried Campbellite ideas into Mormonism, stimulated practice of healing, visions; supported a communistic order at one time Died Friendship, N.Y.. July 14, 1876.

RIGGS, George Washington, banker; b. Georgetown, D.C., July 4, 1813; s. Elisha and Alice (Lawrason) R.; entered Yale, 1829, did not graduate; m. Janet Madeleine Cecilia Shedden, June 23, 1840, 9 children. Employed by father's merc. firm Riggs, Taylor & Co., N.Y.C.; partner banking firm Corcoran & Riggs, Washington, D.C., 1840-48, firm took up loans required by U.S. Govt. to finance Mexican War, bought Corcoran's interest, 1854, firm became known as Riggs & Co. (Riggs Nat. Bank since 1896), dir, until 1881; mem. bd. aldermen D.C.; chmn. of com. to present to U.S. Congress a petition for an investigation into the conduct of the Bd. Pub. Works, 1873; built and owned Riggs House (hotel); an organizer Washington and Georgetown R.R. Co.; trustee Corcoran Gallery of Art, Peabody Edn. Fund; treas. Mt. Vernon Ladies' Assn. of the Union. Died Prince George's County, Md., Aug. 24, 1881; buried St. Aloysius Ch., Washington, D.C.

RIGGS, Jetur Rose, congressman, physician; b. nr. Drakesville (now Ledgewood), Morris County, N.J., June 20, 1809; grad. N.Y. Coll. Physicians and Surgeons, 1837. Practiced medicine, Newfoundland, N.J.; mem. N.J. Gen. Assembly, 1836; a founder Dist. Med. Soc. of Passaic County, N.J., 1844, pres., 1846-48; moved to Cal., 1849, in charge of hosp. at Sutters Fort; returned to N.J., settled in Paterson, 1852; mem. N.J. Senate, 1855-58; mem. U.S. Ho. of Reps. (Democrat) from N.J., 36th Congress, 1859-61; moved to Drakesville. Died Drakesville, Nov. 5, 1869; buried Presbyn. Cemetery, Succasunna, Morris County.

RIGGS, John Mankey, dentist; b. Seymour, Conn., Oct. 25, 1810; s. John and Mary (Beecher) R.; A.B., Trinity Coll., Hartford, Conn., 1837; attended Jefferson Med. Coll., Phila. Prin., Brown Sch. (now 1st Dist. Sch. of Hartford), circa 1837-39; studied dentistry with Dr. Horace Wells, began practice circa 1840; extracted a tooth from a patient who was under influence of nitrous oxide gas (laughing gas) (becoming one of pioneers in use of modern anesthesia), 1844; interested in scientific agr., spoke at agrl. soc. meetings; strong advocate of hygienic care of mouth; specialist in treatment of pyorrhea alreolaris which he first demonstrated at conv. Am. Dental Assn., 1865; joined Conn. Valley Dental Assn., 1865, pres. 1871-72; pres. Conn. State Dental Assn., 1867, mem. com. of Conn. State Dental Assn. that succeeded in having statue of Horace Wells erected at Hartford, 1874; mem. Am. Dental Assn.; attended 7th Internat. Med. Congress, London, Eng., 1881. Died Nov. 11, 1885.

RIGGS, Lewis, congressman, physician; b. Norfolk, Conn., Jan. 16, 1789; studied medicine, Torringford, Litchfield County, Conn., diploma, 1812; attended med. lectures U. Pa., 1812. Apprenticed to carpenter's trade; practiced medicine in East Winsted, Conn., Vernon, Oneida County, N.Y., 1813, Homer, Cortland County, N.Y.; became retail druggist, dry goods, mcht., 1828; sec. Cortland County Med. Soc., 1820-23, pres., 1825-26; apptd. postmaster of Homer by Pres. Jackson, 1829-39; mem. U.S. Ho. of Reps. (Democrat) from N.Y., 27th Congress, 1841-43; practiced medicine, operated flour mill. Died Homer, Nov. 6, 1870; buried Glenwood Cemetery.

RIGGS, Stephen Return, missionary; b. Steubenville, O., Mar. 23, 1812; s. Stephen and Anna (Baird) R.; grad. Jefferson Coll., 1834, LL.D. (hon.), 1873; attended Western Theol. Sem.; D.D. (hon.), Beloit (Wis.) Coll., 1873; m. Mary Longley, Feb. 16, 1837; m. 2d, Mrs. Annie Ackley, 1872; 9 children. Licensesd to preach by Chillicothe (O.) Presbytery, 1836; preacher, Hawley, Mass., 1836-37; began missionary work among Sioux Indians, Lacqui Parle (Upper Minnesota River), 1837, stationed at Traverse Des Sioux, 1843-46; stationed at Hazelwood, 1854-62, founder sch. for Indian children; published (or helped to publish) The Dakota First Reading Book, 1839; published Wowapi Mitawa: Tamakoce Kaga (a primer), 1842; The Book of Genesis, part of Psalms, 1842; Book of Revelation, 1843; Grammar and Dictionary of the Dakota Language, 1852; Pilgrim's Progress, 1857; Dakota Wiwicawangapi Kin (catechism), 1864; published entire New Testament in Dakota, 1865; The Gospel Among the Dakotas, 1869; Dakota Wowapi Wakon: The Holy Bible in the Language of the Dakotas, 1880; Mary and I: Forty Years with the Sioux,

1880; Protestant Missions in the Northwest; Dakota-English Dictionary appeared after his death in Contributions to North American Ethnology. Died Beloit, Aug. 24, 1883.

RIKER, Samuel, congressman; b. Newtown, L.I., N.Y., Apr. 8, 1743; attended common schs. Mem. Newtown Com. of Corr., 1774; supr. Suffolk County, 1783; lt. of Light Horse in Revolutionary War; mem. N.Y. State Assembly, 1784; mem. U.S. Ho. of Reps. (filled vacancy) from N.Y., 8th, 10th congresses, Nov. 5, 1804-05, 07-09. Died Newtown, May 19, 1823; buried Dutch Reformed Cemetery.

RILEY, Bennet, army ofcl., govt. ofcl.; b. Nov. 27, 1787; s. Bennet and Susanna (Drury) R.; m. Arabella, 5 children. Entered U.S. Army as ensign of riflemen, 1813; fought at Sacketts Harbor (N.Y.) in War of 1812; regtl. adj., 1816-17; promoted capt., 1818; served with inf. 1821-46; brevetted maj. for distinguished service in battle with Ark. Indians in Dakota Territory, 1823; fought in Black Hawk War, 1831-32; commd. maj., 1837, lt. col., 1839; fought in Seminole War in Fla., 1839-42; brevetted col.; commanded 2d Inf. during Mexican War; adviser to commander of brigade; brevetted brig. gen. at Battle of Cerro Gordo, brevetted maj. gen. at Battle of Contreras, 1847; served in La. and Mo., until 1848; commanded Dept. of Pacific, became ex officio provisional gov. Cal., circa 1848; convened constituent assembly at Monterey which drew up 1st constn, of Cal. and applied for admission to Union, 1849; promoted to col. 1st Inf., 1850. Died Buffalo, N.Y., June 9, 1853.

RILEY, Charles Valentine, entomologist; b. Chelsea, London, Eng., Sept. 18, 1843; s. Charles and Mary (Valentine) R.; took incompleted course U. Bonn (Germany); Ph.D. (hon.), Washington U., St. Louis, Mo. State U.; A.M. (hon.), Kan. State Agrl. Coll.; m. Emilie Conzelman. Reporter, artist, editor entomological dept. of Prairie Farmer, Chgo., 1864; served with U.S. Army during latter part of Civil War; founder (with B.D. Walsh) journal Am. Entomologist, 1868; entomologist state of Mo., 1868-77, published 9 annual reports (considered the beginning of science of econ. entomology); influential in securing passage of bill creating U.S. Entomol. Commn., 1877, 1st chief, 1877-78; entomologist to U.S.Dept. Agr. (post grew in size and importance in his adminstrn.), 1878-79, 81-94, began publishing Insect Life, 1889-94; decorated by French Govt. for work on grapevine Phylloxera; hon. mem. Entomol. Soc. of London; 1st pres. Entomol. Soc. of Washington; held honorary position in Nat. Museum. Compiler: bibliography of 1657 individual titles; co-compiler (with Walsh) 479 titles, (with L.O. Howard) 364 titles. Died Sept. 14, 1895.

RIMMER, William, sculptor; b. Liverpool, Eng., Feb. 20, 1816; s. Thomas and Mary Rimmer; studied medicine independently, received M.D.; m. Mary Peabody, 1840, at least 1 child. Moved to Nova Scotia, 1818; went to Boston, 1826, had studio in School St., produced religious paintings for Endicott Street Catholic Ch.; moved to Chelsea, Mass., 1855, practiced medicine; moved into granite dist., East Milton, Mass., taught anatomy privately, 1861, at Lowell Inst., 1863; head of successful pvt. art sch., 2 years; dir., chief instr. Sch. of Design for Women, Cooper Inst., N.Y.C., 1866-70; lectured at Worcester, Mass., also Yale; lectr., Providence, R.I., 1871-73; taught at Mass. Normal Art Sch., 1875-76; instr. anatomy, school of Boston Mus. of Fine Arts, circa 1877-79; prin. works include: granite head St. Stephen, life-size clay statue Falling Gladiator (highly praised), 9-foot granite statue Alexander Hamilton, 3 over-life-size statues of Chaldean Shepherd, Endymion, Osiris. Author: Elements of Design, 1864; Art Anatomy, 1877. Died Aug. 20, 1879.

RINDISBACHER, Peter, artist; b. Berne, Switzerland, 1806. Came to U.S., 1821; self-taught as artist; began painting scenery in Manitoba, Can.; settled in St. Louis, 1829; illustrator for Am. Turf Register; 1st artist to paint Am. Indian in his daily pursuits, and wild animals in natural habitat West of Mississippi River. Died St. Louis, 1834.

RINEHART, William Henry, sculptor; b. nr. Union Bridge, Md., Sept. 13, 1825; s. Israel and Mary (Snader) R.; ed. Calvert Coll., New Windsor, Md. Apprenticed to Baughman & Bevan, stonecutters, Balt., 1846, foreman, 1848; recipient gold medal from Md. Inst. for stone copy of Tenier's Smokers, 1851; executed reclining figure Faith, circa 1853; stonecutter, Florence, Italy, circa 1855; returned to Am. with 4 marble bas-reliefs, 1857; went to Rome, Italy, 1858; executed caryatid for clock in U.S. Ho. of Reps., bronze door for Capitol Bldg., Washington, D.C.; recipient award of Taney Commn., 1866; executed Latona and Her Children (now in Met. Mus. N.Y.C.), circa 1872-78; executed Clytie (considered his masterpiece; now Peabody Inst.); neo-classical in style; executed monumental statue of Chief Justice Taney; left estate which established Rinehart Sch. Sculpture at Md. Inst.; other works include: Hero, Day, Night, Strewing Flowers (all in Corcoran Gallery, Washington, D.C.); The Sleeping Children, Love Reconciled with Death. Died Rome, Oct. 28, 1874; buried Balt.

RINGGOLD, Cadwalader, naval officer; b. Washington County, Md., Aug. 20, 1802; s. Samuel and Maria (Cadwalader) R. Apptd. midshipman U.S. Navy, 1819, commd. lt., 1828, comdr., 1829; commanded schooner Weasel against West Indian pirates; cruised in ship Vandalia in Pacific, 1828-32, in ship Adams in Mediterranean Sea, 1834-35; comdr. Porpoise in Wilkes Antarctic Exploring Expdn., 1838-42, commanded North Pacific surveying and exploring expdn., left Norfolk, June 1853, reached China, Mar. 1854; declared insane, made inactive, 1854, recovered, commd. capt. on active list with promotion to date from Apr. 2, 1856; commanded sail-frigate Sabine during Civil War; commd. commodore, 1862, ret., 1864, commd. rear adm. (ret.), 1866. Author: A Series of Charts, with Sailing Directions ... to the Bay of San Francisco, 1851; Correspondence to Accompany Maps and Charts of California. Died N.Y.C., Apr. 29, 1867; buried Greenmount Cemetery, Balt.

RINGGOLD, Samuel, congressman, farmer; b. Chestertown, Md., Jan. 15, 1770; had limited schooling. Moved to Washington County, Md., settled at Fountain Rock, nr. Hagerstown, became farmer and large landowner; mem. Md. Ho. of Dels., 1795; mem. Md. Senate, 1801-06; judge Washington County Levy Ct., 1806-10, 22-26; apptd. brig. gen. Md. Militia, 1810; mem. U.S. Ho. of Reps. (Democrat, filled vacancy) from Md., 11th-13th, 15th-16th congresses, Oct. 15, 1810-15, 17-21; served in War of 1812. Died Frederick, Md., Oct. 18, 1829; buried Fountain Rock Cemetery.

RIPLEY, Eleazar Wheelock, congressman, army officer; b. Hanover, N.H., Apr. 15, 1782; s. Sylvanus and Abigail (Wheelock) R.; grad. Dartmouth, 1800; m. Love Allen, 1811; m. 2d, Mrs. Smith; 2 children. Mem. Mass. Legislature, 1807-11, speaker, 1811; mem. Mass. Senate, 1812; commd. lt. col. to rank, 1812; commanded 21st Infantry or regular army; took part in Gen. William Wilkinson's unsuccessful invasion of Canada, 1813; commd. col. U.S. Army, 1813; in attack on York (now Toronto), Ont., Can., 1813; commd. brig. gen. U.S. Army, 1814, brevetted maj. gen., 1814, commanded brigade; fought at battles of Ft. Erie, Chippewa, Lundy's Lane, 1814; received gold medal from Congress for gallantry and good conduct in battle, 1814; resigned from army, 1820; practiced law, New Orleans; mem. La. Senate, 1832; mem. U.S. Ho. of Reps. from La., 23d-25th congresses, 1835-39. Died West Feliciana, La., Mar. 2, 1839; buried St. Francisville, La.

RIPLEY, Ezra, clergyman; b. Woodstock, Conn., May 1, 1751; s. Noah and Lydia (Kent) R.; grad. Harvard, 1776, D.D. (hon.), 1818; m. Phoebe Bliss, 3 children. Ordained, installed pastor 1st Ch., Concord, Mass., 1778, pastor, 1778-1814; mem. sch. com. Concord; drew up constn. for Concord Library, 1784; gave land for battle monument, 1836; established one of 1st temperance socs.; mem. Mass. Temperance Soc. Author: History of the Fight at Concord, 1827; Half Century Discourse Delivered November 16, 1828. Died Concord, Sept. 21, 1841.

RIPLEY, George, editor, reformer; b. Greenfield, Mass., Oct. 3, 1802; s. Jerome and Sarah (Franklin) R.; grad. Harvard, 1823, Harvard Divinity Sch., 1826; m. Sophia Willard Dana, Aug. 1827; m. 2d, Mrs. Louisa Schlossberger, 1865. Taught mathematics Harvard, 1824; ordained to ministry Unitarian Ch., 1826; minister Purchase St. Ch., Boston; editor Christian Register; wrote 10 articles for Christian Examiner, including blast against conservatism in review of Martineau's Rationale of Religious Enquiry (Nov. 1836); began editing (with F.H. Hedge) Specimins of Foreign Standard Literature, 1st 2 vols., 1838, continued until 14 vols. had been issued; published Letters on the Latest Form of Infidelity (in answer to attacks on his Discourses on the Philosophy of Religion published 1836), 1840; mem. Transcendental Club; a founder, editor, contbr. The Dial; took charge of orgn. Brook Farm Colony (called Brook Farm Inst. of Agr. and Edn.), 1841, pres., 1841-46; editor mag. Harbinger, also a Fourierite jour., 1845-49; moved to Flatbush, L.I., 1847; lit. critic N.Y. Tribune, 1849-80 (recognized importance of Hawthorne's Scarlet Letter, Darwin's Origin of Species), pres. Tribune Assn., 1872-80; a founder Harper's New Monthly Mag., 1850, editor lit. dept., until 1854; editor (with B. Taylor) American Cyclopedia, 16 vols., 1858-63. Died N.Y.C., July 4, 1880; buried Woodlawn Cemetery, nr. N.Y.C.

RIPLEY, James Wheelock, congressman, lawyer; b. Hanover, N.H., Mar. 12, 1786; attended Fryeburg (Me.) Acad.; studied law. Admitted to bar, practiced in Fryeburg (until 1820 part of Mass.); served in War of 1812; mem. Mass. Ho. of Reps., 1814-19; mem. U.S. Ho. of Reps. (Democrat, filled vacancy) from Me., 19th-21st congresses, Sept. 11, 1826-Mar. 12, 1830, resigned; collector customs Passamaquoddy Dist. Me., 1830-35. Died Fryeburg, June 17, 1835; buried Village Cemetery.

RIPLEY, James Wolfe, army officer; b. Windham County, Conn., Dec. 10, 1794; s. Ralph and Eunice (Huntington) R.; grad. U.S. Mil. Acad., 1814; m. Sarah Denny, Aug. 11, 1824, 9 children. Commd. 2d lt. arty. U.S. Army, 1814, ordered to duty at Sacketts Harbor, N.Y.; served in garrisons, circa 1814-17; commd. 1st lt. during Seminole War; asst. commr. under James Gadsden to run boundaries of Indian reservations of Fla., 1823-24; commd. capt., stationed in Charleston, S.C. when state threatened secession; assigned to command arsenal, Kennebec, Me., 1833-41; promoted maj., 1838; commanded armory, Springfield, Mass., 1841-54, arsenal, Watertown, Mass., 1824; commd. lt. col., 1854; chief of ordnance Pacific Dept., Cal., 1855-59, insp. arsenals, 1857; spl. duty in Japan, 1860; chief of ordnance with rank of col., 1861; commd. brig. gen., 1861, ret., 1863; insp. armaments, until 1869; brevetted maj. gen., 1865. Died Hartford, Conn., Mar. 15, 1870; buried Springfield Cemetery, Hartford.

RIPLEY, Roswell Sabine, army officer; b. Worthington, O., Mar. 14, 1823; s. Christopher and Julia (Caulkins) R.; grad. U.S. Mil. Acad., 1843; m. Alicia Burroughs, Dec. 22, 1852. Brevetted 2d lt., assigned to 3d Arty., U.S. Army; served at Ft. McHenry, Md., Ft. Johnston, N.C., Augusta (Ga.) Arsenal, 1843-46; asst. prof. mathematics U.S. Mil. Acad.; served on Coast Survey, 1846; commd. 2d lt. 2d Arty., 1846; served in Mexican War under gens. Taylor and Pillow; commd. 1st lt., then maj., 1847; took part in battles from Monterey to taking of Mexico City; brevetted capt. and maj. for gallantry at battles of Cerro Goredo and Chapultepec; resigned, 1853; officer S.C. Militia, 1853-60, apptd. maj. ordnance, 1860; commd. lt. col. Confederate Army, brig. gen. in command S.C., 1860, maj., 1860; directed firing on Ft. Sumter, 1861; served in defense of Charleston, 1863; served under Gen. Lee to end of war; poem in his honor written by Timrod. Author: History of the War with Mexico, 2 vols., 1849; Correspondence Relating to Fortification of Morris Island (pamphlet), 1878. Died N.Y.C., Mar. 29, 1887.

RIPLEY, Thomas C., congressman; b. Schaghicoke, N.Y.; had limited schooling; studied law. Admitted to bar, practiced in Harts Falls, N.Y.; mem. U.S. Ho. of Reps. (filled vacancy) from N.Y., 29th Congress, Dec. 7, 1846-47.

RISING, Johan Classon, colonial gov.; b. Risinge Parish, Ostergotland, Sweden, 1617; s. Clas Botvidi; received doctor's degree U. Upsala, 1640; studied at U. Leyden (Holland). Tutor to Count Clas Akessen Tott, 1646-48; 1st Swede to publish writings of any importance in polit. economy; apptd. sec. Comml. Coll., 1651; knighted by Queen Christina; came to Ft. Elfsburg on the Delaware River; gov. New Sweden, 1654-55; expelled Dutch garrison from Ft. Casimer, forced Dutch settlers to take oath of allegiance to Sweden, succumbed to mil. conquest of Gov. Peter Stuyvesant of New Amsterdam; returned to Sweden; in Swedish Customs Service, stationed at Elbing, East Prussia. Author: Itt Uthtogh om Kiop-Handelen aller Commerciern, 1669; Een Landbook, 1671. Died Sweden, Apr. 1672.

RISLEY, Elijah, congressman, mcht.; b. Conn., May 7, 1787; completed prep. studies. Moved to Fredonia, Chautauqua County, N.Y., 1807, became mcht.; sheriff Chautauqua County, 1825-28; supr. Town of Pomfret, 1835; raised garden seeds, 1833-53; mem. U.S. Ho. of Reps. (Whig) from N.Y., 31st Congress, 1849-51; maj. gen. N.Y. State Militia Died Fredonia, Jan. 9, 1870; buried East Main Street Cemetery.

RITCHEY, Thomas, congressman; b. Bedford County, Pa., Jan. 19, 1801; attended common schs. Became farmer, Somerset, Perry County, O.; treas. Perry County, 1835, 37, 39; mem. U.S. Ho. of Reps. (Democrat) from Ohio, 30th, 33d congresses, 1847-49, 53-55. Died Somerset, Mar. 9, 1863; buried Zion Methodist Episcopal Cemetery, Perry County.

RITCHIE, Alexander Hay, artist; b. Glasgow, Scotland, Jan. 14, 1822; studied drawing under Sir William Allan, Edinburgh, Scotland. Came to U.S., 1841; gen. engraver, N.Y.C., 1847; exhibited N.A.D., 1848, became asso., 1863, academician, 1871. Works include: The Death of Lincoln; portrait of Dr. James McCosh; engravings (after his own paintings) The Death of Lincoln, Washington and His Generals, Mercy Knocking at the Gate; painted Lady Washington's Reception; engraved Felix O.C. Darley's hist. pictures The First Blow for Liberty, 1858; Washington Entering New York; The Class of 1863 (at Yale); Authors of the United States, 1866. Died New Haven, Conn., Sept. 19, 1895.

RITCHIE, David, congressman, lawyer; b. Canonsburg, Washington County, Pa., Aug. 19, 1812; grad. Jefferson Coll., Canonsburg, 1829; grad. U. Heidelberg (Germany); studied law. Admitted to bar, 1835, practiced in Pitts.; mem. U.S. Ho. of Reps. (Republican) from Pa., 33d-35th congresses, 1853-59; apptd. asso. judge Allegheny County Ct. Common Pleas, 1862, served 9 months. Died Pitts., Jan. 24, 1867.

RITCHIE, John, congressman, lawyer; b. Frederick, Md., Aug. 12, 1831; completed prep. studies Frederick Acad.; studied medicine; grad. law dept. Harvard. Admitted to bar, practiced in Frederick, 1854; capt. Jr. Defenders (militia), ordered by Pres. Buchanan to John Brown's raid, Harpers Ferry; Democratic presdl. elector, 1860; state's atty. for Frederick County, 1867-71; mem. U.S. Ho. of Reps. (Democrat) from Md., 42d Congress, 1871-73; chief judge 6th Jud. Circuit and asso. justice Md. Ct. Appeals, 1881-87. Died Frederick, Oct. 27, 1887; buried Mt. Olivet Cemetery.

RITCHIE, Thomas, journalist; b. Tappahannock, Va., Nov. 5, 1778; s. Archibald and Mary (Roane) R.; m. Isabella Foushee, Feb. 11, 1807, 12 children. Owner paper Enquirer (became Richmond (Va.) Enquirer), 1804-45; sec. Richmond mass meeting promoted by Enquirer, in protest against Brit. outrages, 1807; served briefly in War of 1812; apptd. state printer by Va. Legislature, 1814-33, 35-39; sec. Jefferson Republican (became Democratic Party) Central Com.; editor; publisher Debates of Va. Constl. Conv., 1829; published another Richmond newspaper Crisis, 1840; conducted The Washington Union (nat. adminstrn. organ established at request of Pres. Polk), 1845-51. Died Washington, D.C., July 3, 1854.

RITNER, Joseph, gov. Pa.; b. Berks County, Pa., Mar. 25, 1780; s. Michael Ritner; m. Susan Alter, 1802. Served as pvt. during War of 1812; mem. Pa. Assembly, 1821-26, speaker, 1825-26; gov. Pa. (Anti-Mason), 1835-39 (during time of Buckshot War); presdl. elector, 1840; dir. U.S. Mint, Phila., 1849; mem. Pa. delegation to conv. which nominated Fremont for Pres. U.S., 1856; insp. ednl. instns. during Civil War, Erie, Pa., 1865. Died Carlisle, Pa., Oct. 16, 1869.

RITTENHOUSE, David, inventor, astronomer, mathematician; b. Paper Mill Run, nr. Germantown, Pa., Apr. 8, 1732; s. Matthias and Elizabeth (Williams) R.; m. Eleanor Colston, Feb. 20, 1766; m. 2d, Hannah Jacobs, 1772; 3 children. Conducted boundary survey for William Penn to settle dispute with Lord Baltimore, 1763-64; designed his orrery (represents motions of bodies of the solar system and illustrates solar and lunar eclipses and other phenomena for a period of 5000 years either forward or back), 1767; experimented on compressibility of water; invented metallic thermometer; published article Easy Method of Deducing The True Time of the Sun's Passing the Meridian, 1770; presented calculations on the transit of Venus that was to occur (1769) to Am. Philos. Soc., 1768; said to have made 1st telescope in Am.; invented collimating telescope (introduced spider threads in eyepiece), 1785; measured grating intervals, deviations of several orders of spectra; experimented on magnetism and electricity; measured barometric effect on a pendulum clock rate and expansion of wood by heat; constructed compensating pendulum, wooden hygrometer; solved math. problem of finding the sum of the several powers of the sines, 1792; published papers Method of Raising the Common Logorithm of any Number, 1795, To Determine the True Place of a Planet, in an Elliptical Orbit, 1796; engaged in boundary surveys and commns. involving Pa., Del., Md., Va., N.Y., N.J., Mass.; conducted canal and river surveys; served on coms. to test specimens of flint glass, to inspect the 1st steam-engine in U.S.; supervised casting of cannon, manufacture of saltpeter; engr. Council of Safety, 1775, v.p., 1776, pres., 1777; mem. Pa. Gen. Assembly, Pa. Constl. Conv., 1776; trustee loan fund (Pa. loan to Continental Congress); mem. Bd. of War created by Continental Congress; treas. State of Pa.; prof. astronomy, trustee U. Pa.; mem. commn. to organize U.S. Bank; 1st dir. U.S. Mint (apptd. by George Washington), 1792-95; curator, librarian, sec., v.p., pres. (1791-96) Am. Philos. Soc.; fgn. mem. Royal Soc. of London (Eng.). Died Phila., June 26, 1796.

RITTENHOUSE, William, clergyman, paper mfr.; b. Mulheim-am-Ruhr, Rhenish Prussia, 1644; s. George and Maria (Hagerhoffs) Rittenhausen; children—Klaas, Gerhard, Elizabeth. Came to Am., 1688; 1st minister Mennonite Ch., Germantown, Pa., circa 1688; bishop 1st Mennonite Ch. in Am., 1703, refused to exercise functions as bishop because he was not properly installed; formed co. to build paper mill, Germantown, circa 1688; built Paper Mill Run, nr. Wissahickon Creek, Pa., (1st paper mill in colonies), 1690, became propr. with son, 1705/06. Died Germantown, Feb. 17, 1708.

RITTER, Burwell Clarke, congressman; b. nr. Russellville, Barren County, Ky., Jan. 6, 1810. Mem. Ky. Ho. of Reps., 1842, 50; Democratic presdl. elector, 1864; mem. U.S. Ho. of Reps. (Conservative) from Ky., 39th Congress, 1865-67; became farmer. Died Hopkinsville, Christian County, Ky., Oct. 1, 1880; buried Hopewell (later named Riverside) Cemetery, Hopkinsville.

RITTER, Frederic Louis, composer, educator; b. Strasbourg, Germany, June 22, 1834; D. Mus., Univ. State N.Y., 1878; m. Frances Raymond. Prof. music Protestant Sem., Fenestrange, Lorraine, France, 1852; came to Am., 1856; founder Cecilia (choral) Soc., Philharmonic Orch. of Cincinnati (promoted mus. appreciation in his part of Middle West); conductor Sacred Harmonic Soc., Arion (male chorus) Soc., N.Y.C.; prof. music Vassar Coll., 1862-91; compositions include: 3 symphonies; Stella (a concert overture); Othello; organ fantasia and fugue; choral settings for Psalms 4, 23, 46, 95; more than 100 songs. Author: History of Music, 2 vols., 1870-74; Manual of Musical History, 1886. Died July 6, 1891.

RITTER, John, congressman; b. Exeter, Pa., Feb. 6, 1779. Apprenticed as printer; mem. Pa. Constl. Conv. 1836; mem. U.S. Ho. of Reps. (Democrat) from Pa., 28th-29th congresses, 1843-47; editor, publisher Adler (German newspaper), Reading, Pa. Died Reading, Nov. 24, 1851; buried Charles Evans Cemetery.

RIVERS, Thomas, congressman, lawyer; b. Franklin County, Tenn., Sept. 18, 1819; attended La Grange Coll., Ala.; studied law. Admitted to bar, 1839, practiced in Somerville, Tenn.; served in Tenn. Militia many years, brig. gen.; mem. U.S. Ho. of Reps. (Am. Party) from Tenn., 34th Congress, 1855-57. Died on his plantation nr. Somerville, Mar. 18, 1863; buried Somerville Cemetery.

RIVES, Francis Everod, congressman; b. Prince George County, nr. Petersburg, Dinwiddie County, Va., Jan. 14, 1792; completed prep. studies. Became planter, engaged in building and mgmt. of railroads in Va. and N.C.; mem. Va. Ho. of Dels., 1821-31; mem. Va. Senate, 1831-36, 48-51; mem. U.S. Ho. of Reps. (Democrat) from Va., 25th-26th congresses, 1837-41; became developer internal improvements in Va.; mayor Petersburg, 1847-48. Died Petersburg, Dec. 26, 1861; buried Blandford Cemetery.

RIVES, John Cook, journalist; b. Franklin County, Va., Mar. 24, 1795; probably s. George Rives; m. 1833, 7 children including Franklin, Jefferson. Admitted to Ill. bar, circa 1824; worked in office U.S.Telegraph; clk. 4th auditor's office U.S. Treasury Dept., circa 1829-32; employee Washington Daily Globe, circa 1832; Democrat; gave $17,000 to widows and orphans during 1 year in D.C.; founder, publisher Congressional Globe to report congl. debates impartially (succeeded by Congressional Record 1873), 1833-64. Died Prince George's County, Md., Apr. 10, 1864.

RIVES, William Cabell, senator, diplomat; b. Amherst County, Va., May 4, 1792; s. Robert and Margaret (Cabell) R.; attended Hampden-Sydney Coll.; grad. Coll. William and Mary, 1809; m. Judith Walker, Mar. 24, 1819, at least 2 children including Amelie. Admitted to Va. bar, circa 1814; aide to Gen. John H. Cocke, 1814; represented Nelson County in Va. Constl. Conv., Staunton, 1816; mem. Va. Ho. of Dels. from Albemarle County, 1822; mem. U.S. Ho. of Reps. from Va., 18th-20th congresses, 1823-29; U.S. minister to France, 1829-32, 49-53, handled negotiations which led to indemnity trial, 1831; mem. U.S. Senate from Va., 1832-34, 36-39 (replaced John Tyler), 41-45; mem. Peace Conv., Washington, D.C., 1861; mem. Va. Conv. to decide position in Civil War, 1861; mem. Confederate Provisional Congress from Va., Montgomery, Ala.; mem. 1st Confederate Congress, 1861-62. Author: Discourse . . . on the Ethics of Christianity, 1855; Discourse on the Character and Services on John Hampden, 1855; History of the Life and Times of James Madison (prin. lit. work), 3 vols., 1859-68. Died Albermarle County, Apr. 25, 1868; buried pvt. burial plot at "Castle Hill," Albemarle County.

RIVINGTON, James, bookseller, journalist; b. London, Eng., 1724; s. Charles and Eleanor (Pease) R.; m. Elizabeth Minshull, Sept. 14, 1752; m. 2d, Elizabeth Van Horne, Mar. 1769; 4 children. Partner (with James Fletcher), publisher Smollett's History of England; came to Am., 1760, opened bookstore, Market St., Phila.; opened bookstore, Hanover Square, N.Y., 1760, moved store to Wall St., 1768; became partner (with Samuel Brown) in merchandise and bookselling firm, 1761, in picture gallery, 1763; extended chain of stores to Boston, 1762; propr. Md. Lottery, Annapolis, 1766; published poetical works of Charles Churchill; became freeman City of N.Y., 1769; began publishing newspaper Rivington's N.Y. Gazetteer, 1773, maintained open policy which became offensive to Sons of Liberty; his printing plant ruined by Sons of Liberty from Conn., 1775; went to London, 1776; returned to N.Y. as King's printer, circa 1778; resumed publication of newspaper in Loyalist interest, 1777-83; established with other N.Y. newspapers a mutual daily gazette (1st daily newspaper in Am.), 1783; in debtor's prison, 1797; Rivington Street (N.Y.) named for him. Died N.Y.C., July 4, 1802.

ROACH, John, ironmaster, shipbuilder; b. Mitchelstown, County Cork, Ireland, Dec. 25, 1813; s. Patrick and Abigail (Meany) Roche; m. Emeline Johnson, 1836, 9 children. Came to U.S., 1829; naturalized, 1842; purchased (with others) small iron works, circa 1841, became sole owner, obtained contract for constructing iron drawbridge over Harlem River, N.Y.C., 1860, had one of best-equipped foundries in U.S. by end of Civil War; carried out plans for devel. iron shipbldg. industry in U.S., 1868, purchased small marine-engine plants in nr. N.Y.C., consolidated then with Morgan Iron Works; transferred hdqtrs. to Chester, Pa., 1871; produced City of Peking, City of Tokio (iron vessels for fgn. service), Pacific Mail S.S. Co., 1874; authorized by Dept. of Navy to install compound engine in ram Tennessee; built sloops of war Alert and Huron for U.S. Govt., launched, 1874; built sectional dry dock, Pensacola, Fla.; obtained contracts for monitors Miantonomoh, and Puritan; built Dolphin, cruisers Atlanta, Boston, Chicago; launched 126 iron vessels 1872-86. Died N.Y.C., Jan. 10, 1887.

ROANE, Archibald, gov. Tenn.; b. Derry Twp., Tenn., circa 1759; s. Andrew and Margaret (Walker) R.; m. Anne Campbell. Signed petition (with Andrew Jackson and others) requesting N.C. to grant independence to people of Western part, 1887; granted permission to practice law before ct. of Washington County, N.C. (now East Tenn.), 1788; atty.-gen. Hamilton (Tenn.) dist., 1790 mem. Tenn. Constl. Conv., 1796; judge Tenn. Supreme Ct. Errors and Appeals; gov. Tenn., 1801-03; circuit judge, 1811-15; judge Tenn Supreme Ct., 1815-19. Died Jan. 4, 1819.

ROANE, John, congressman; b. Uppowac, King William County, Va., Feb. 9, 1766; completed prep. studies; at least 1 son, John Jones. Washington presdl. elector; mem. Va. Ho. of Dels., 1788-90, 92; mem. Va. Constl. Conv., 1788; mem. U.S. Ho. of Reps. (Democrat) from Va., 11th-13th, 20th-21st, 24th congresses, 1809-15, 27-31, 35-37; became farmer. Died at his home Uppowac, Nov. 15, 1838; buried old family burying ground, Rumford, Va.

ROANE, John Jones, congressman; b. Essex County, Va., Oct. 31, 1794; s. John Roane; attended Rumford Acad., King William County, also Princeton. Became farmer; served in War of 1812 as pvt. 4th Regt., Va. Militia; mem. Va. Ho. of Dels., 1820-23; mem. U.S. Ho. of Reps. (Democrat) from Va., 22d Congress, 1831-33; clk. U.S. Patent Office, 1836-51; spl. agt. Treasury Dept., 1855-67. Died Washington, D.C., Dec. 18, 1869; buried Glenwood Cemetery.

ROANE, John Selden, lawyer, army officer, gov. of Alabama; born in Wilson County, Tennessee, Jan. 8, 1817; s. Hugh and Hannah (Calhoun) R.; ed. Cumberland Coll., Princeton, Ky.; m. Mary K. Smith, July 5, 1855, 4 children. Admitted to the bar, 1842; pros. atty. 2d Judicial Dist. 1840; mem. Ark. Legislature, elected speaker; served as lt. col. Archibald Yell's Regt. during Mexican War, took over command at Battle of Buena Vista when Col. Yell was killed; gov. Ala., 1849-52; favored geol. survey, use of land granted by Congress for internal improvements to promote railroad building and edn.; endorsed Memphis as starting point proposed Pacific R.R.; opposed secession, 1861; volunteered, then commd. brig. gen. Confederate Army, 1862; chief in command of Ark. at Battle of Prairie Grove. Died Pine Bluff, Ark., Apr. 8, 1867; buried Oakland Cemetery, Little Rock, Ark.

ROANE, Spencer, jurist; b. Essex County, Va., Apr. 4, 1762; s. William Roane; ed. Coll. William and Mary; m. Anne Henry, Sept. 7, 1786; m. 2d, Elizabeth Hoskins, after 1799; 9 children. Admitted to Va. bar, 1782; mem. Va. Ho. of Dels., 1783, 84, Va. Council of State, 1784, Va. Senate, 1788-89; adviser to Gov. Henry of Va.; judge Va. Gen. Ct., 1789, Supreme Ct. Appeals, 1794-1821; upheld right of Gen. Ct. to declare void an unconstl. act of the legislature, 1793; approved manumission of slaves according to the policy of the country; strict constructionist; refused in Fairfax Case to execute fed. ct. order, 1815; founder (with Thomas Ritchie) Richmond Enquirer, contbd. articles attacking U.S. Supreme Ct. under John Marshall, signed Amphictyon, Hampden, Algernon Sidney, 1819, 21; mem. Phi Beta Kappa. Died Warm Springs, Va., Sept. 4, 1822.

ROANE, William Henry, senator, congressman; b. Va., Sept. 17, 1787; completed prep. studies. Mem. Va. Ho. of Dels., 1812-15; mem. U.S. Ho. of Reps. (Democrat) from Va., 14th Congress, 1815-17; mem. Va. Exec. Council; mem. U.S. Senate (filled vacancy) from Va., Mar. 14, 1837-41; became farmer. Died Tree Hill, nr. Richmond, Va., May 11, 1845 buried Lyons Family pvt. cemetery, Hanover County, Va.

ROBB, James, banker, railroad exec.; b. Brownsville, Pa., Apr. 12, 1814; m. Louisa Werninger, June 14, 1856; m. 2d, Mrs. Craig; m. 3d, Mrs. Stannard; a son, James Hampden. Established pvt. bank The Bank of James Robb, New Orleans; pres. New Orleans Gas, Light & Banking Co., 1842; head New Gas Light Co. of Havana, Cuba, 1844-54; prominent in New Orleans comml., ry. convs. of early 1850's, pres. of a conv., 1851; interested in projecting 1st rail connections from New Orleans northward; pres. New Orleans, Jackson & Gt. No. R.R. Co., 1852; receiver St. Louis, Alton & Chg. R.R. Co. (reorganized as Chgo. & Alton R.R. Co. 1862), pres. 1862-64; pres. Dubuque & Sioux R.R. Co., circa 1864-65; established La. Nat. Bank, New Orleans, 1866, pres., 1866-69; mem. La. Senate, 1 session; mem. New Orleans City Council. Died Cheviot (now part of Cincinnati), O., July 30, 1881.

ROBBINS, Asher, senator; b. Wethersfield, Conn., Oct. 26, 1757; grad. Yale, 1782; studied law. Tutor, R.I. Coll. (now Brown U.), 1782-90; admitted to bar, 1792, practiced law, Providence, R.I.; moved to Newport, R.I., 1795; apptd. U.S. dist. atty., 1812; mem. R.I. Assembly, 1818-25, 40-41; mem. U.S. Senate (Whig, filled vacancy) from R.I., Oct. 31, 1825-39; postmaster Newport, 1841-45. Died Newport, Feb. 25, 1845; buried Burial Ground Common.

ROBBINS, Chandler, clergyman; b. Lynn, Mass., Feb. 14, 1810; s. Peter Gilman and Abba (Dowse) R.; grad. Harvard, 1829, Harvard Divinity Sch., 1833; m. Mary Frothingham, Dec. 12, 1833; m. 2d, Sarah Fiske, June 1874; 10 children. Ordained to ministry Unitarian Ch., 1833; pastor 2d Ch., Boston, 1833-74; editor Christian Register, 1837-39; mem. exec. com. Am. Unitarian Assn., 1837-39; chaplain Mass. Senate, 1834, Mass. Ho. of Reps., 1845; a founder Children's Hosp., 1869, mem. bd. mgrs., 1869-82; became mem. Mass. Hist. Soc., 1845, mem. standing com., 1854-57, corr. sec., 1864-77, recording sec., 1857-64, contbr. to its Proceedings; delivered lecture The Early History of Massachusetts, published under title The Regicides Sheltered in New England, 1869; chmn. of com. which published The Mather Papers; mem. Am. Antiquarian Soc., Am. Acad. Arts and Scis. Author: A History of the Second Church, or Old North, in Boston, 1852; Hymn Book for Christian Worship, 1854; hymn Lo, the day of rest declineth; editor The Works of Henry Ware, Jr., D.D., 4 vols., 1846-47. Died Weston, Mass., Sept. 11, 1882.

ROBBINS, George Robbins, congressman, physician; b. nr. Allentown, Monmouth County, N.J., Sept. 24, 1808; grad. Jefferson Med. Coll., 1837. Practiced medicine, Falsington, Bucks County, Pa., then in Hamilton Square, Mercer County, N.J.; mem. U.S. Ho. of Reps. (Whig) from N.J., 34th-35th congresses, 1855-59. Died Hamilton Square, Feb. 22, 1875; buried Presbyn. Ch. Cemetery.

ROBBINS, John, congressman, steel mfr.; b. Bustleton (now part of Phila.), 1808; attended Gunmere Acad., Burlington, N.J. Moved to Phila., 1836, manufactured steel; mem. bd. commrs. Kensington Dist., pres. several years; mem. U.S. Ho. of Reps. (Democrat) from Pa., 31st-33d, 44th congresses, 1849-55, 75-77; unsuccessful candidate for mayor Phila., 1862; held several municipal offices; mem. bd. edn., pres. many years; pres., dir. Kensington Nat. Bank. Died Phila., Apr. 27, 1880; buried Laurel Hill Cemetery.

ROBBINS, Thomas, clergyman, antiquarian; b. Norfolk, Conn., Aug. 11, 1777; s. Rev. Ammi Ruhamah and Elizabeth (Le Baron) R.; attended Yale, Williams Coll.; studied theology under several New Eng. clergyman, 1796-98; D.D. (hon.) Harvard, 1838. Licensed to preach by Litchfield Northern Assn. of Congregational Ministers, 1798; made missionary tour to Vt., circa 1798; tchr. acad., Danville, Conn., 1799-1802; made missionary tour of newly settled dists. of N.Y., 1801-02; apptd. by Missionary Soc. Conn. missionary to Western Res. U., Cleveland, O., 1803-06; ordained at Norfolk, Conn., 1803; pastor in what is now South Windsor, Conn., 1809-27; pastor, Stratford, Conn., 1830-31, Mattapoisett, Mass., 1832-44; original mem. Mass. Bd. Edn.; mem. corp. Williams Coll., 1842-53; a founder Conn. Hist. Soc., Hartford, 1825, which later received his library, librarian, 1844-54. Delivered and published: An Oration Occasioned by the Death of Gen. George Washington, 1800; A Century Sermon . . . Jan. 1, A.D., 1801. Author: An Historical View of the 1st Planters of New Eng., 1815 (written as series of biog. articles for Conn. Evange. Mag., 1811-15); Diary Thomas Robbins, D.D., 1796-1854, published 1886-87; editor 1st Am. edition of Magnalia Christi Americana (Cotton Mather), 1820. Died Colebrook, Conn. Sept. 13, 1856; buried Hartford.

ROBERDEAU, Daniel, Continental congressman; b. St. Christopher, B.W.I., 1727; s. Isaac and Mary (Cunyngham) R.; m. Mary Bostwick, Oct. 3, 1761; m. 2d, Jane Milligan, Dec. 2, 1778; at least 9 children including Isaac. Successful mcht. engaged largely in W.I. trade, until Am. Revolution; warden of Phila.; mem. Pa. Provincial Assembly, 1756-61; mgr. Pa. Hosp., 1756-58, 66-76; mem. Pa. Com. of Safety; chmn. Phila. mass meeting, 1776; helped unite city and back country groups which facilitated drafting new state constn.; offered (in Congress) to build lead mine at own expense in Western Pa., 1778, built Ft. Roberdeau to protect mine; col. 2d Battalion, Pa. Militia, 1775, brig. gen., 1776, mem. Continental Congress, 1777-79, mem. fgn. affairs com.; Freemason. Died Winchester, Va., Jan. 5, 1795.

ROBERDEAU, Isaac, civil and mil. engr.; b. Phila., Sept. 11, 1763; s. Daniel and Mary (Bostwick) R.; studied engring. London, Eng., 1785-87; m. Nov. 7, 1792, 3 children. Employed with U.S. Topog. Engrs. to lay out new City of Washington (D.C.), 1791-92; most important work was canal to connect Schuylkill and Susquehanna rivers; mem. Topog. Engrs. U.S. Army in war with Great Britain, 1813-15, commd. maj. 1813; assigned to duty at Ft. Mifflin; employed on fortification work; charged with survey of No. boundary which he carried westward to Sault St. Marie; reinstated as maj., 1816; stationed at U.S. Mil. Acad., until 1818; became chief Topog. Bur., Washington, 1818; brevetted lt. col., 1823. Author: Observations of the Survey of the Seacoast of the U.S., 1827; Mathematics and Treatise on Canals; An Oration upon the Death of Gen. George Washington (delivered at Trenton, N.J. Feb. 22, 1800), published 1800. Died Georgetown, D.C., Jan. 15, 1829.

ROBERT, Christopher Rhinelander, mcht., philanthropist; b. Brook Haven, Suffolk County, L.I., N.Y., Mar. 23, 1802; s. Daniel and Mary Tangier (Smith) R.; m. Anna Maria Shaw, 1830. Established firm Robert & Williams, importers sugar, cotton, tea, 1835-62; pres. Del., Lackawanna & Western R.R. Co., 1858-63; supt. Sunday Sch., elder Laight St. Presbyn. Church, 1834-62; financially supported a German congregation; influential in establishing 1st ch. in Northern Ill., Galena, mem. exec. com. after 1838, treas., 1855-70; made substantial anonymous gifts to Beloit and Hamilton colls., also Auburn Theol. Sem.; bought hosp. bldgs. on Lookout Mountain, Tenn. from U.S. Govt. at close of Civil War to establish coll. there for poor whites, abandoned experiment; responsible for purely secular coll. at Bebek, a suburb of Constantinople, Turkey; opened Robert Coll., 1863; left it 1/5 of his estate. Died Paris, France, Oct. 27, 1878.

ROBERTS, Anthony Ellmaker, congressman, mcht.; b. nr. Barneston Station, Chester County, Pa., Oct. 29, 1803; had limited schooling. Became mcht., New Holland, Lancaster County, Pa., 1816-39; moved to Lancaster, Pa., 1839; sheriff Lancaster County, 1839-42; apptd. U.S. marshal Eastern Dist. of Pa., 1850-53; mem. U.S. Ho. of Reps. (Whig) from Pa., 34th-35th congresses, 1855-59; active in organization Republican Party in Pa.; operated his real estate holdings, Lancaster, executor for various estates. Died Lancaster, Jan. 25, 1885; buried Lancaster Cemetery.

ROBERTS, Benjamin Stone, army officer, engr.; b. Manchester, Vt., Nov. 18, 1810; s. Gen. Martin and Betsey (Stone) R.; grad. U.S. Mil. Acad., 1835; m. Elizabeth Sperry, Sept. 18, 1835, 3 children. Chief engr. Champlain & Ogdensburg R.R., 1839; geologist N.Y. State, 1841; assisted in constrn. of ry. in Russia from St. Petersburg to Moscow, 1842-43; began practice of law, Des Moines, Ia., 1843; lt. col. Ia. Militia, 1844-46; commd. lt. U.S. Army, 1846, capt., 1847; brevetted maj. for gallantry at Battle of Chapultepec, 1847, lt. col. for gallantry nr. Matamoras, 1847; received sword of honor from State of Ia.; maj. 3d Cavalry, 1861, commanded Southern mil. dist. of N.M.; active in battles at Ft. Craig, Albuquerque, Valverde, Peralta; brevetted col., 1862; promoted brig. gen. U.S. Volunteers, 1862, brig. gen., maj. gen., 1865; in command 1st Div., XIX Army Corps in La., 1864; chief cavalry Dept. of Gulf, until 1865; lt. col. 3d Cavalry, 1866; served in N.M., 1867-68; prof. tactics in mil. science Yale, 1868-70; ret. from active service, 1870; practiced law and prosecution of claims before govt., Washington, D.C. Author: Description of Newly Patented Solid Shot and Shells for Use in Rifled Ordnance, 1864; Lt. Gen. U.S. Grant, an address delivered at Yale, 1864. Died Washington, Jan. 29, 1875.

ROBERTS, Benjamin Titus, clergyman; b. Gowanda, N.Y., July 25, 1823; s. Titus and Sally (Ellis) R.; grad. Conn. Wesleyan U., 1848; m. Ellen Stowe, May 3, 1849, 7 children. Admitted on trial to Genesee Conf., Methodist Episcopal Ch., 1848, ordained deacon, 1850, elder, 1852; pastor several chs. in Western N.Y., 1850-58; wrote article called New School Methodism, published in No. Independent, Aurora, N.Y., on basis of which was convicted of unchristian and unmoral conduct at annual meeting of conf., 1857, because of republishing and recirculating article was expelled at conf., 1858; organized Free Meth. Ch., Pekin, N.Y., 1860, 1st gen. supt., 1860-93; established Earnest Christian, 1860, publisher, editor, 1860-93; editor Free Methodist, 1886-90; a founder Chili Sem., North Chili, N.Y., prin., 1866. Author: Fishers of Men, or Practical Hints to Those Who Would Win Souls, 1878; Why Another Sect, 1879; First Lessons in Money, 1886; Ordaining Women, 1891. Died Catharugus, N.Y., Feb. 27, 1893.

ROBERTS, Edmund, mcht., diplomat; b. Portsmouth, N.H., June 29, 1784; s. Capt. Edmund and Sarah (Griffiths) R.; m. Catherine Langdon, Sept. 1808. Owner large fleet of ships, trading mostly with Far East; sailed in ship Mary Ann to Zanzibar, 1827; an intimate of the sultan, a friendship which developed into treaty relations with U.S.; spl. agt. of U.S. to negotiate treaties with Muscat, Siam, and Cochin, China; negotiated with Japan, 1832; instructed to investigate operations of Brit. East India Co. (secret mission); sailed for Bangkok, concluded a treaty of amity and commerce with Siam (freeing Am. trade with Siam from governmental monopoly and from all export and import duties), Mar. 1833; signed treaty of amity and commerce with Sultan of Muscat granted Am. consul extraterritorial powers, fixed duties at five percent, contained a most-favored nation clause), Sept. 1833; proceeded to Muscat and Siam to exchange the ratifications of the treaties he had negotiated, 1834. Died Macao, China, June 12, 1836.

ROBERTS, George Brooke, railroad ofcl.; b. "Pencoed," Montgomery County, Pa., Jan. 15, 1833; s. Isaac Warner and Rosalinda Evans (Brooke) R.; grad. Rensselaer Poly. Inst., Troy, N.Y., 1849; m. Sarah Lapsley Brinton, 1868; m. 2d, Miriam P. Williams, 1874; at least 6 children. Asst. engr. Sunbury & Erie R.R., 1852; asst. to pres. in full charge of building lines for Pa. R.R., 1862, dir., 1869, 4th v.p., 1869, then 2d v.p., 1st v.p., 1874, pres., 1880-97; frequent chmn. bd. of presidents Trunk Line Assn.; encouraged formation and devel. of railroad depts. YMCA; dir. Free Pub. Library of Phila.; v.p. Fairmount Park Art. Assns. Died Bala, Pa., Jan. 30, 1897.

ROBERTS, Issachar Jacob, missionary; b. Sumner County, Tenn., Feb. 17, 1802; attended Furman Theol. Instn., S.C.; m. Jan. 4, 1830; m. 2nd, 1849; at least 2 children. Organized Roberts Fund and China Mission Soc., sailed for China under this fund, 1836, arrived, 1837, began missionary work at Macao; joined Baptist Mission, 1841, transferred to So. Bapt. Conv. after its founding, 1846; reverted to completely independent status, 1852; helped open Bapt. Mission at Hong Kong, 1842; moved to Canton, leased a lot and built a chapel, 1844; for two months taught Tien Wang (became leader of Taiping Rebellion), joined rebellion, became asst. to chief minister of state, 1860, minister of fgn. affairs, 1862; accused Kanwang of murdering his servant, fled to Shanghai; returned to U.S., 1866. Died Upper Alton, Ill., Dec. 28, 1871.

ROBERTS, Job, agriculturist; b. Whitpain, Pa., Mar. 23, 1756; s. John and Jane (Hunk) R.; m. Mary Naylor, May 22, 1781; m. 2d, Sarah (Williams) Thomas, Oct. 12, 1820; at least 2 children. Began experimenting in better farming methods, 1785; published results of experiments as The Pennsylvania Farmer, 1804; experimented with fertilizers, use of lime, plaster, various barnyard manures, deep ploughing of land; built improved harrow, devised new roller, 1792; attached water wheel to dairy churn making it possible to churn 150 pounds of butter a week, 1797; invented machine for planting corn, 1815; advanced growing season of corn by soaking before planting; introduced Merino sheep into Pa.; interested in cultivation of mulberry for silk culture; substituted green fodder for his cattle for grazing;

apptd. justice of peace, 1791; called Squire Job Roberts. Died Whitpain, Aug. 20, 1851.

ROBERTS, Jonathan, senator; b. Norristown, Pa., Aug. 16, 1771; s. Jonathan and Anna (Thomas) R.; m. Eliza Hite Bushby, 1813, 9 children. Mem. lower house Pa. Assembly, 1799-1800, Pa. Senate, 1807-11; mem. U.S. Ho. of Reps. from Pa., 12th-13th congresses, 1811-14, one of "War Hawks"; mem. U.S. Senate from Pa., 1814-21; mem. Pa. Ho. of Reps., 1826; mem. Francis Biddle's Bank Bd., 1836; nominated Tyler for vice pres. U.S. at Harrisburg Conv., 1839; collector Port of Phila., 1841-42. Died Montgomery County, Pa., July 24, 1854; buried nr. Norristown.

ROBERTS, Joseph Jenkins, pres. Liberia; b. Petersburg, Va., Mar. 15, 1809; s. "Aunty Robos;" m. Jane Waring, 1836. Went to Liberia with brother and mother, 1829; became 1st Negro gov. Liberia, 1842; began buying land from natives and negotiating treaties; visted U.S. in unsuccessful effort to secure U.S. support of Liberian policy of imposing import duties, 1844; Am. Colonization Soc. gave up all claims upon the colony, 1844; returned to Liberia, continued his purchase of lands from native chiefs; called conf. at which new Republic of Liberia was proclaimed, 1847; 1st pres. Liberia, 1847-55, 71-76; signed comml. treaty with Gt. Britain which recognized Liberia as independent nation and gave Englishmen freedom of domicile, 1849; 1st pres. New Coll. of Liberia, 1856-76; Belgian consul in Liberia, 1862; addressed annual meeting of African Colonization Soc., Washington, D.C., 1869. Died Monrovia, Liberia, Feb. 24, 1876.

ROBERTS, Marshall Owen, financier; b. N.Y.C., Mar. 22, 1814; s. Owen Roberts; m. C.D. Amerman; m. 2d, Caroline D. Smith, 1847; m. 3d, Susan Lawrence Endicott, after 1874. An original promoter, dir. Erie R.R.; original promoter Lackawanna R.R.; came into prominence through connection with govt. subsidy of mail steamships, 1847; joint trustee (with George Law and others), took over contract awarded to Albert G. Sloo which granted $290,000 annually for fortnightly N.Y. to New Orleans service, with branch line from Havana to connect with Pacific Mail S.S. Co.; 1st ship sailed, 1848; organized (with assos.) U.S. Mail S.S. Co., 1850, pres., 1854; chartered and sold steamships during Civil War; a leading contbr. to Republican Party, del. to 1st Rep. Nat. Conv., 1856, helped finance senatorial election of R.E. Fenton; pres. North River Bank; a financial backer Cyrus W. Field's 1st cable venture, 1854; owned personal art collection appraised at half-million dollars. Died Saratoga Springs, N.Y., Sept. 11, 1880.

ROBERTS, Nathan Smith, civil engr.; b. Piles Grove, N.J., July 28, 1776; s. Abraham Roberts; m. Lavinia White, Nov. 4, 1816, at least 1 son, Nathan Smith. Tchr., Oriskany, N.Y., 1804-06; prin. acad. Whitesboro, N.Y., 1806-16; bought farm nr. Lenox (N.Y.) 1816; asst. engr. in constrn. of middle sect. of Erie Canal, 1816-22, in charge of constrn. Western sect., 1822-25; cons. engr. for Chesapeake and Del. Canal, 1825-26; made survey for ship canal around Niagara Falls, 1826; chief engr. for Western end Pa. State Canal, 1826-28; mem. bd. engrs. Chesapeake & Ohio Canal Co., 1828-30; made survey for ship canal around Muscle Shoals in Ala., circa 1830; made surveys to estimate expenses of enlarging Erie Canal, 1835, chief engr. for enlargement, 1839-41. Died nr. Lenox, Nov. 24, 1852.

ROBERTS, Oran Milo, gov. Tex.; b. Laurens Dist., S.C., July, 1815; s. Obe and Margaret (Ewing) R.; grad. U. Ala., 1836; m. Frances W. Edwards, Dec. 1837; m. 2d, Mrs. Catherine E. Border, Dec. 1887; 7 children. Admitted to the bar; practiced law, Talladega, then Ashville, Ala., 1837-41; served one term in Ala. Legislature; moved to Tex., 1841; made extensive circuit of Eastern Tex. counties along with dist. judge, other lawyers; U.S. dist. atty., 1844-46, dist. judge, 1846-51; asso. justice Supreme Ct. Tex., 1857, chief justice, 1864-65, 74; pres. Tex. Secession Conv., 1861; raised 11th Tex. Inf. Regt., col., 1862-64; conducted law sch. at Gilmer; gov. Tex., 1878-82 (adopted as his motto "Pay as you go"), establishment of U. Tex. achievement of his adminstrn.; prof. law U. Tex., 1883-93. Author: A Description of Texas, Its Advantages and Resources, 1881; The Elements of Texas Pleading, 1890; Our Federal Relations from a Southern View of Them, 1892. Died Austin, Tex., May 19, 1898.

ROBERTS, Robert Richford, clergyman; b. Frederick County, Md., Aug. 2, 1778; s. Robert Morgan and Mary (Richford) R.; m. Elizabeth Oldham, Jan. 1799. Licensed to preach, 1802; admitted on trial to Balt. Conf., Methodist Episcopal Ch., 1802; ordained deacon, 1804, elder, 1806; spent 1st years of ministry in Pa., Md., Va.; attended Gen. Conf., Meth. Ch., 1808; minister at Balt., 1808, Alexandria, Va., 1811, Georgetown, D.C., 1812, Phila., 1813-14; presiding elder Schuylkill (Pa.) dist., 1815; presiding officer Phila. Conf., 1816; elected bishop Meth. Ch. by No. Confs. and Gen. Conf., 1816. Died Lawrence County, Ind., Mar. 26, 1843; buried Indiana Asbury U., Greencastle.

ROBERTS, Robert Whyte, congressman, lawyer; b. Kent County, Del., Nov. 28, 1784; had liberal edn.; studied law. Admitted to bar; moved to Tenn., elected circuit judge; moved to Limestone County, Ala., 1822, to Scott County, Miss., 1826, settled nr. Hillsboro; became farmer; practiced law, Hillsboro; circuit judge Scott County, 1830-38; mem. Miss. Ho. of Reps., 1838-44, speaker, 1842, 43; mem. U.S. Ho. of Reps. (Democrat) from Miss., 28th-29th congresses, 1843-47; became planter. Died on his plantation Long Avenue, nr. Hillsboro, Jan. 4, 1865; buried pvt. cemetery on Roberts plantation.

ROBERTS, Solomon White, civil engr., transp. exec.; b. Phila., Aug. 3, 1811; s. Charles and Hannah (White) R.; m. Anna Smith Rickey. Asst. engr. for State of Pa. in constrn. of canal on Conemaugh River, 1829-31; prin. asst. engr. Allegheny Portage R.R., resident engr., supt. transp. until 1836; designed, supervised constrn. masonry railroad viaduct over Conemaugh River; went to Eng. to procure and superintend manufacture of iron rails for several railroads, 1836-38; chief engr. Catowissa R.R., 1838-41; pres. Phila., Germantown & Norristown R.R. Co., 1842, Shuylkill Navigation Co., 1843-45; mem. Pa. Ho. of Reps., 1848; chief engr. Ohio & Pa. R.R., 1848, gen. supt. chief engr., gen. supt. North Pa. R.R., 1856-79; mem. Am. Philos. Soc. Author: Reminiscenses of the First Railroad over the Allegheny Mountain; The Destiny of Pittsburgh and the Duty of Her Young Men, 1850. Died Atlantic City, N.J., Mar. 22. 1882.

ROBERTS, William Milnor, civil engr.; b. Phila., Feb. 12, 1810; s. Thomas Pascal and Mary Louise (Baker) R.; m. Annie Gibson, June 1837; m. 2d, Adeline Beelen, Nov. 1868; at least 9 children. Assistant in survey and constrn. Lehigh Canal between Mauch Chunk and Phila., 1826; sr. asst. engr. for proposed Allegheny Portage R.R., 1831-34, gen. mgr., 1834-35; chief engr. Lancaster & Harrisburg R.R., 1836-37; greatest engring. accomplishments include constrn. of two-level lattice-truss bridge across Susquehanna River at Harrisburg, 1837; in charge of extensions of Pa. state canals, 1838-40; built Bellefontaine & Ind., Allegheny Valley, The Atlantic & Miss., Iron Mountain railroads; chmn. commn. to consider reconstrn. of Allegheny Portage R.R.; constructed railroads in Mid-West, 1855-57; contracted to build Dom Pedro Segundo R.R., Brazil, 1865; proposed improvements of Mississippi River at Keokuk, Ia., 1866; U.S. engr. in charge of improvement of navigation of Ohio River; asso. chief engr. in constrn. Eads Bridge across Mississippi River at St. Louis, 1868; chief engr. No. Pacific R.R., 1869-79; mem. Mississppi River Jetty Commn.; chief engr. all pub. works in Brazil, 1879-81; v.p. Am. Soc. C.E. 1873-78, pres., 1878. Died Soledade, Brazil, July 14, 1881.

ROBERTS, William Randall, congressman, diplomat; b. Mitchelstown, County Cork, Ireland, Feb. 6, 1830; s. Randall and Mary (Bishop) R.; 1 child. Came to Am., 1849; active in Irish socs., N.Y.C., during Civil War; pres. Knights of St. Patrick, 1865; joined Ferian Brotherhood, 1863, pres. senate, 1865-67, met with Brit. reps. of brotherhood for purposes of cooperation between groups, Paris, France, 1867; mem. U.S. Ho. of Reps. (Democrat) from N.Y., 42d-43d congresses, 1871-75; mem. bd. aldermen, N.Y.C., 1878, 79, pres., 1878; U.S. minister to Chile, 1885-89. Died Bellevue Hosp., N.Y.C., Aug. 9, 1897; buried Calvary Cemetery, Long Island City, N.Y.

ROBERTSON, Archibald, painter; b. Monymusk, Scotland, May 8, 1765; s. William and Jean (Ross) R.; attended King's Coll., Aberdeen, Scotland; m. Eliza Abramse, 1794, 10 children including Anthony Lispenard. Portraitist, conducted drawing acad. at Aberdeen, circa 1780-91; came to U.S., 1791; painted miniatures of Pres. Washington and his wife, Martha, 1791; established and conducted Columbian Acad. of Painting, N.Y.C., 1792-1828; painted portraits, miniatures and water-color views of N.Y.C.; mem. Am. Acad. Fine Arts, 1817-35, displayed works in Acad.'s annual exhibitions, dir., 1817-33; designed medal used in celebration of opening of Erie Canal, 1825. Author: Elements of the Graphic Arts, 1802. Died Dec. 6, 1835.

ROBERTSON, Edward White, congressman; b. nr. Nashville, Tenn., June 13, 1823; attended prep. dept. Centenary Coll., Jackson, La.; attended Augusta Coll., Ky., 1842; studied law Nashville U., 1845; grad. law dept. U. La., 1850; at least 1 son, Samuel Matthews. Served as orderly sgt. 2d Regt., La. Volunteers in Mexican War, 1846; mem. La. Ho. of Reps., 1847-49, 53; admitted to bar, 1850, practiced law, Iberville and East Baton Rouge parishes; La. auditor public accounts, 1857-62; entered Confederate service as capt. of company which he had raised for 27th Regt., La. Infantry in Civil War; practiced in Baton Rouge, La.; mem. U.S. Ho. of Reps. (Democrat) from La., 45th-47th, 50th congresses, 1877-83, Mar. 4-Aug. 2, 1887. Died Baton Rouge, Aug. 2, 1887; buried Magnolia Cemetery.

ROBERTSON, George, congressman; b. Harrodsburg, Mercer County, Ky., Nov. 18, 1790; s. Alexander and Margaret (Robinson) R.; attended Transylvania U., Rev. Samuel Finley's Classical Sch.; LL.D. (hon.), Centre Coll., Danville, Ky., Augusta Coll., Bracken County, Ky.; m. Eleanor Bainbridge, Nov. 28, 1809. Admitted to Ky. bar, 1809; licensed to preach, 1809; mem. U.S. Ho. of Reps. from Ky., 15th-16th congresses, 1817-21, introduced, helped pass bill organizing Ark. Territory, initiated legislation changing land system reducing minimum land purchase to 80 acres and price to $1.25 per acre (passed 1820); mem. lower house Ky. Legislature from Garrard County, 1822-27, from Fayette County, 48-51, 52, speaker, 1823, 25, 26, 51-53, chmn. edn. com., 1823; sec. of state Ky., 1828; asso. justice Ky. Ct. of Appeals, 1829, chief justice, 1829-34; lectr. Law Sch., Transylvania U., 1834-57; supported Union in Civil War; judge Ct. Appeals for 2d Dist. Ky., 1864-71; chief justice, 1870-71; Robertson County (Ky.) named for him. Author: Memoir of. Hon. John Boyle, 1838; An Address Delivered at Camp Madison on the Fourth of July, 1843, published 1843; Scrapbook on Law and Politics, Men, and Times, 1856. Died Lexington, Ky., May 16, 1874; buried Lexington Cemetery.

ROBERTSON, James, printer, journalist; b. Scotland, 1740; m. Amy. Published (with brother Alexander) N.Y. Chronicle, 1769; began printery, 1771, issued The Albany Gazette, (1st newspaper printed in N.Y. province outside N.Y.C.); formed partnership with John Trumbull of Norwick, Conn. as gen. printers and publishers of Norwich Packet and the Conn., Mass., N.H. & R.I. Weekly Advertiser (a Royalist paper), 1773-76; publisher Royal Am. Gazette, N.Y.C., 1777-78; opened printing office and established Royal Pa. Gazette, Phila., 1778; opened new printing bus. at 857 Hanover Sq., N.Y.C., 1778; began Royal S.C., Gazette, Charleston, S.C., 1780, sole propr., publisher until 1782; moved to Nova Scotia, 1782, published Royal Am. Gazette, 1782-86. Died circa 1812.

ROBERTSON, James, pioneer; b. Brunswick County, Va., June 28, 1742; s. John and Mary (Gower) R.; m. Charlotte Reeves, Oct. 20, 1768, 11 children. Crossed Blue Ridge Mountains with Daniel Boone, 1769; mem. ct. created by Watauga Assn., N.C.; participated in Lord Dunmore's War at Battle Point Pleasant, 1774; agt. to Cherokee Indians for N.C. and Va.; conducted defense of Watauga Ft. against Cherokee, 1777, held rank of capt.; apptd. agt. by N.C. Assembly to reside permanently among Cherokee, 1778, resigned, 1779; explored Cumberland Valley, 1779; led group of settlers to present site of Nashville (Tenn.), 1780, adopted Cumberland Compact as basis of govt.; served as presiding officer of ct.; made alliance with Chickasaw Indians, 1781; col. regional militia; trustee U. Nashville, 1785; county rep. in N.C. Assembly, 1785; led Coldwater Expdn. against Indians, 1787; brig. gen. Territorial Govt. S.W. of Ohio, until 1794; aided Blount in negotiating Holston Treaty, 1791; mem. Tenn. Constl. Conv. from Davidson County, 1796; served in Tenn. Senate, 1798; rep. from Tenn. at 1st treaty of Tellico between U.S. and Cherokee, 1798. Died Chickasaw Bluffs, Tenn., Sept. 1, 1814; buried Old City Cemetery, Nashville.

ROBERTSON, Jerome Bonaparte, physician, army officer; b. Woodford County, Ky., Mar. 14, 1815; s. Cornelius and Clarissa (Hill) R.; grad. in medicine Transylvania U., 1835; m. Mary Elizabeth Cummins, May 4, 1838; m. 2d, Mrs. Harriet Hendly Hook, 1879; at least 3 children. Raised company of volunteers for Tex. Revolution; arrived in Tex., 1836, mustered out, 1837; began practice of medicine, Washington, Tex.; took active part in campaigns against Vasquez and Wohl; held numerous civil offices, including coroner Washington County; mem. Tex. Senate from Washington County; mem. conv. which passed ordinance of secession in 1861; one of 1st in Tex. to raise a company for service in Civil War; served as capt. 5th Tex. Inf., Confederate Army, later brig. gen. Hood's Brigade, 1862, fought in more than 40 battles; supt. Tex. Bur. Immigration, 1874; active promoter railroad bldg. in West Tex., 1881-91. Died Jan. 7, 1891.

ROBERTSON, John, congressman, jurist; b. Petersburg, Va., Apr. 13, 1787; s. William and Elizabeth (Bolling) R.; grad. Coll. William and

Mary; m. Anne Trent. Admitted to Va. bar, 1803; mem. Va. Legislature, 1816-19; atty. gen. Va., 1823; mem. U.S. Ho. of Reps. (Whig) from Va., 24th-26th congresses, 1835-41; judge (adminstr. chancery) 21st Va. Jud. Circuit, 1841-51; judge Circuit Ct. Richmond and Henrico County (Va.), 1851-61; commr. from Va. to urge So. states not to secede pending proposed peace conv., 1861; mem. Va. Senate, 1861-63. Author: Riego, or the Spanish Martyr, 1850; Opuscula (book of verse), 1872. Died "Mt. Athos," nr. Lynchburg, Va., July 5, 1873; buried pvt. cemetery at "Mt. Athos."

ROBERTSON, Thomas Austin, congressman, lawyer; b. Hodgenville, Larue County, Ky., Sept. 9, 1848; grad. Cecilian Coll.. law dept. U. Louisville. Admitted to bar, 1871, practiced law, Hodgenville; atty. Larue County, 1874-77; mem. Ky. Ho. of Reps., 1877-78; Commonwealth atty. 18th Jud. Dist., 1878-83; mem. U.S. Ho. of Reps. (Democrat) from Ky., 48th-49th congresses, 1883-87; practiced in Elizabethtown, Ky. Died Elizabethtown, July 18, 1892; buried Red Hill Cemetery, Hodgenville.

ROBERTSON, Thomas Bolling, gov. La.; b. Petersburg, Va., Feb. 27, 1779; s. William and Elizabeth (Bolling) R.; attended Coll. William and Mary; m. Lelia Skipwith. Admitted to Va. bar, 1806; atty. gen. Territory of Orleans, sec. of territory with power of sucession to governorship, 1807-11; mem. U.S. Ho. of Reps. (Democrat) from La., 12th-15th congresses, 1812-18; wrote series of letters which appeared in Richmond Inquirer, 1815; gov. La., 1820-24, responsible for legislation for benefit of parish schs. and hwy. improvement; U.S. dist. judge for La., 1824-28. Author: Events in Paris, 1816. Died White Sulphur Springs, Va., Oct. 5, 1828, buried Copeland Hills Cemetery, White Sulphur Springs.

ROBERTSON, Thomas James, senator; b. nr. Winnsboro, Fairfield County, S.C., Aug. 3, 1823; grad. S.C. Coll. (now U. S.C.), 1843. Became planter; mem. S.C. Constl. Conv., 1865; mem. U.S. Senate (Republican) from S.C., July 15, 1868-77; retired from public life and business because of poor health. Died Columbia, S.C., Oct. 13, 1897; buried Elmwood Cemetery.

ROBERTSON, Walter, artist; b. Dublin, Ireland, circa 1750. Worked in Dublin, circa 1765-84, London, Eng., 1784-92; came to Am. with Gilbert Stuart, 1793; lived in N.Y.C., later moved to Phila.; made miniatures of Stuart portraits, also painted miniatures of George Washington from life; went to India, 1795. Died Futtehpore, India, 1802.

ROBERTSON, William Henry, congressman; b. Bedford, Westchester County, N.Y., Oct. 10, 1823; s. Henry and Hulduh (Fanton) R.; m. Mary Ballard, 1865. Supt. schs., Bedford; served 4 terms as supr. Westchester County; admitted to N.Y. bar, 1847; mem. N.Y. State Assembly, 1849, 50; mem. N.Y. Senate, 1854-55; county judge, Westchester County, 1855-67; presdl. elector, 1860; county draft commr. during Civil War; insp. 7th Brigade, N.Y. State Militia, 1860-66; leader Westchester County Republican party; mem. U.S. Ho. of Reps. from N.Y., 40th Congress, 1867-69; mem. N.Y. Senate, 1871-81, 87, pres. pro tem, 1874-81; collector Port of N.Y., 1881-85; del. N.Y. Rep. conv., 1896. Died Katonah, N.Y., Dec. 7, 1898; buried Union Cemetery, Bedford.

ROBERTSON, William Joseph, lawyer; b. Culpeper County, Va., Dec. 30, 1817; s. John and Sarah (Brand) R.; grad. Law Sch. U. Va., 1842; m. Hannah Gordon, Aug. 16, 1842; m. 2d, Alice (Watts) Morris, July 16, 1863, 14 children. Began law practice at Louisa County (Va.) Ct. House, 1842; commonwealth atty. Albemarle County (Va.) 1852; mem. bd. visitors U. Va., 1853-59; atty. U. Va.; judge Supreme Ct. Appeals of Va., 1859-65; corp. lawyer in Va. after Civil War; gen. counsel C. & O. Ry., N. & W. R.R.; greatest victories before U.S. Supreme Ct. include Samuel Miller Will case, Gilbert vs. R.R. Co., Arlington cases including U.S. vs. Lee, Kaufman vs. Lee; 1st pres. Va. Bar Assn., 1888. Died Charlottesville, N.C., May 27, 1898.

ROBERTSON, William Schenck, educator; b. Huntington, L.I., N.Y., Jan. 11, 1820; s. Rev. Samuel and Dorcas (Platt) R.; grad. Union Coll., 1842; m. Ann Eliza Worcester, Apr. 15, 1850, at least 2 children including Alice Mary. Offered services to Presbyn. Bd. Fgn. Missions, requested assignment among Indians; prin. tchr. manual labor boarding sch. among Creek Indians in Indian Territory (later known as Tullahassee Mission), 1849, mission closed at outbreak of Civil War; tchr., Mattoon, Ill., 1862-63, Centralia, Ill., 1863-64; in charge of orphan inst., Highland, Kan., 1864-66; ordained to ministry by Presbytery of Highland, 1866; sent by mission bd. to reopen Tullahassee; published, distributed newspaper Our Monthly (in Creek lang.), 4 years; in charge of ednl. exhibit Phila. Centennial Exhbn., 1876; began translation of New Testament into Creek lang. based on earlier work of Robert Loughbridge, issued in parts, 1875-86, complete edition finished by his wife and published as Pu Pucase Momet Pu Hesayeev Cesus Klist in Testement Mucvsat, 1887. Died June 16, 1881.

ROBERTSON, Wyndham, gov. Va.; b. Richmond, Va., Jan. 26, 1803; s. William and Elizabeth (Bolling) R.; attended Coll. William and Mary; m. Mary T. Smith. Admitted to Richmond bar, 1824; mem. Exec. Council of Va., 1830, 33, sr. mem., 1836; active part in devel. of internal improvements in Va., including orgn. of James River and Kanawha Canal Co.; Whig gov. Va., 1836-37; mem. Va. Ho. of Dels., 1838-41, 59-65; capt. of a company of homeguards organized in Richmond, Va.; opposed secession, author of a resolution adopted by Va. Legislature declaring against separation but stating that Va. would join South if coercion were attempted against states that had seceded, 1861. Author: Pocahontas, alias Matooka and her Descendants through her Marriage...with John Rolfe (most important work), 1887. Died Abingdon, Va., Feb. 11, 1888.

ROBESON, George Maxwell, congressman, sec. of navy; b. Oxford Furnace, N.J., Mar. 16, 1829; s. William Penn and Ann (Maxwell) R.; grad. Princeton, 1847; m. Mary (Ogston) Aulick, 1872. Admitted to N.J. bar, 1850; licensed as counselor, 1854; prosecutor Camden County (N.J.), 1859; served as brig. gen. Union Army during Civil War, active in organizing N.J. troops, commanded camp of volunteers, Woodbury, N.J.; U.S. sec. of navy, 1869-77; atty. gen. N.J., 1867; instrumental in securing fed. appropriation for ill-fated North Polar Expdn., 1871; mem. U.S. Ho. of Reps. (Republican) from N.J., 46th-47th congresses, 1878-82. Died Trenton, N.J., Sept. 27, 1897; buried Belvidere, N.J.

ROBIDON, Antoine, trapper, trader; b. St. Louis, Sept. 24, 1794; s. Joseph and Catherine (Rollet) R.; m. Carmel Benavides, 1828, 1 adopted child. One of 1st fur traders in region of Taos, N.M., 1822-28; built trading post on Gunnison River (now Colorado), 1828, one in Vinta Valley of Utah, 1832; travelled between these 2 posts and his N.M. home until 1845; Ute Indians destroyed Vinta post and killed its residents, 1844; moved to St. Joseph, Mo., 1845; interpreter for Gen. Stephen W. Kearny's New Mexican expdn., wounded at battle of San Pascual, 1846; became blind, 1852. Died St. Joseph, Aug. 29, 1860.

ROBIE, Reuben, congressman, mcht.; b. Corinth, Orange County, Vt., July 15, 1799; attended common schs. Moved to Bath, Steuben County, N.Y., became mcht., 1822; town clk., 1825-30, supr., 1831-32; apptd. postmaster, 1837, held office 4 years; treas. Steuben County, 1844-47; mem. U.S. Ho. of Reps. (Democrat) from N.Y., 32d Congress, 1851-53. Died Bath, Jan. 21, 1872; buried Grove Cemetery.

ROBINSON, Beverly, Loyalist; b. Middlesex County, Va., Jan. 11, 1722; s. John and Catherine (Beverly) R.; m. Susanna Philipse, July 7, 1748, 7 children. Raised co. for expdn. intended against Can., ordered to N.Y., 1746; raised Loyal Am. Regt., became col.; col., dir. Loyal Guides and Pioneers; constantly on various bds. and coms.; furnished information as to terrain rds. and disposition of people, directed spies and messengers, active in cases of defection from Am. side; banished from N.Y. State, 1779, property confiscated; moved to Eng. Died Thornbury, Eng., Apr. 9, 1792; buried St. James Church, Bath, Eng.

ROBINSON, Charles, gov. Kan., pioneer; b. Hardwick, Mass., July 21, 1818; s. Jonathan and Holdah (Woodward) R.; student Amherst Coll., 1 year; LL.D. (hon.), U. Kan.; m. Sarah Adams, 1842; m. 2d, Sara Lawrence, Oct. 30, 1851. Opened hosp. (with Josiah G. Holland), Springfield, Mass., 1845; started restaurant, Sacramento, Cal., 1849; pres. of a squatters' assn. in Cal.; co-editor Settler and Miners Tribune, Sacramento; held anti-slavery position, supported Frémont for U.S. Senate in Cal. Assembly; editor Fitchburg News, 1852-54; Kan. resident of New Eng. Emigrant Aid Co., 1854; conducted three parties of emigrants to Kan.; chmn. Free State exec. com. at Lawrence Conv., 1855; del. Free-State Constl. Conv., 1855, influenced conv. to refuse to endorse principle of popular sovereignity; comdr.-in-chief during Wakarusa War; 1st gov. Kan., 1856, organized legislature at Topeka, resigned, 1856, again gov., 1861; impeached and acquitted, 1862; mem. Kan. State Senate, 1874, 76; obtained passage of comprehensive law regulating pub. sch. system; regent U. Kan., 1864-74, 93-94; supt. Haskell Inst., 1887-89; pres. Kan. Hist. Soc., 1879-80. Author: The Kansas Conflict, 1892. Died Lawrence, Kan., Aug. 17, 1894.

ROBINSON, Charles Seymour, clergyman, hymnologist; b. Bennington, Vt., Mar 31, 1829; s. Henry and Martha (Haynes) R.; grad. Williams Coll., 1849, Princeton Theol. Sem., 1855; m. Harriet Reed Church, 1858. Ordained to ministry Presbyn. Ch., 1855; pastor Park Presbyn. Ch., Troy, N.Y., 1855-60, First Presbyn. Ch., Bklyn., 1860-68, Am. Chapel, Paris France, 1868-70, Eleventh (later Madison Av.) Presbyn. Ch., N.Y.C., 1870-87; edited Illustrated Christian Weekly, 1876-77, Every Thursday, 1890-99; pastor N.Y. Presbyn. Ch. on 128th St., 1892-98. Author: Hymns of the Church, 1862, Songs for the Sanctuary, 1865, Psalms and Hymns, 1875, Selection of Spiritual Songs, 1878; Sabbath Evening Sermons, 1887; The Pharoahs of the Bondage and the Exodus, 1887; Simon Peter, His Early Life and Times, 1889. Died N.Y.C., Feb. 1, 1899; buried Bennington.

ROBINSON, Christopher, congressman, diplomat; b. Providence, R.I., May 15, 1806; s. Benjamin and Ann (Pitts) R.; grad. Brown U., 1825; m. Mary Tillinghast; m. 2d, Mary Jencks; m. 3d, Louisa Aldrich; 5 children. Admitted to R.I. bar, 1833; atty. gen. R.I., 1854-55; mem. U.S. Ho. of Reps. from R.I., 6th Congress, 1859-61, mem. judiciary com., select com. "state of the union"; U.S. minister to Peru, 1861-65; del. Loyalist's Conv., Phila., 1866; practiced law, Woonsocket, R.I. Died Woonsocket, Oct. 3, 1889; buried Oak Hill Cemetery, Woonsocket.

ROBINSON, Conway, lawyer; b. Richmond, Va., Sept. 15, 1805; s. John and Agnes Conway (Moncure) R.; m. Mary Susan Leigh, July 14, 1836, at least 7 children. Admitted to the bar, 1827, U.S. Supreme Ct. bar, 1839; clk. Va. Gen. Ct., 1828-31; assisted in founding Va. Hist. and Philos. Soc., 1831; pres. Richmond, Fredericksburg & Potomac R.R. Co., 1836-38; ofcl. reporter Va. Ct. of Appeals, 1842; revised civil code of Va., 1846, criminal code, 1847; mem. Va. Legislature, assisted in adapting these codes to new Va. Constn., 1852; practiced law before Va. Ct. Appeals, 1866-78, before U.S. Supreme Ct., 1866-84. Author: An Account of Discoveries in the West Until 1519, and of Voyages to and along the Atlantic Coast of North America, from 1520 to 1573, published 1848; Practice in the Courts of Law and Equity in Virginia, vol. I, 1832, vol. II, 1835, vol. III, 1839; Virginia Reports, 2 vols., 1842; Practice in the Courts of Justice in England and the United States, 7 vols., 1854-74; History of the High Court of Chancery and Other Institutions of England, 1st vol. published 1882. Died Phila., Jan. 30, 1884.

ROBINSON, Edward, philologist, geographer, educator; b. Southington, Conn., Apr. 10, 1794; s. William and Elizabeth (Norton) R.; studied at Hamilton Coll., 1816, univs. of Göttingen, Halle, Berlin (Germany), 4 years; m. Eliza Kirkland, Sept. 3, 1818; m. 2d, Therese A. L. von Sakob, 1828. Tutor mathematics and Greek, Hamilton Coll., Clinton, N.Y., 1818; went to Andover (Mass.) to check printing of certain portions of the Iliad which he edited with Latin introduction and notes, 1822; licensed to preach by Hartford South Assn., 1822; instr. Hebrew, Andover Theol. Sem., 1823-26, prof. bibl. literature, librarian, 1830-33; assisted Stuart in Greek Grammar of the New Testament (a transl. from the German by G. B. Winer), 1825; founded Am. Bibl. Repository, 1831-35, editor, 1843; founded Bibliotheca Sacra, 1843; chmn. bibl. literature Union Theol. Sem., N.Y.C., 1837-63; traveled in Sinai, Palestine, So. Syria, 1838. Author: Biblical Researches in Palestine, Mt. Sinai and Arabia Petraea, 3 vols., London, 1841; Later Biblical Researches in Palestine and the Adjacent Regions, 1856; Memoir of Rev. William Robinson, 1859; A Greek and Eng. Lexicon of the New Testament, 1836; edited Iliad Libri Novem Priores Librique XVIII et XXII, 1822; translated Wahl's Clavis Philological Novi Testamenti, 1825; A Hebrew and Eng. Lexicon of the Old Testament (a transl. of Gesenius' work with additions and alterations), 1836. Died N.Y.C., Jan. 27, 1863.

ROBINSON, Edward, congressman, mcht.; b. Cushing, Me., Nov. 25, 1796; self-educated. In seafaring activities; became mcht., Thomaston, Knox County, Me., 1837; mem. Me. Senate, 1836, 37; mem. U.S. Ho. of Reps. (Whig, filled vacancy) from Me., 25th Congress, Apr. 28, 1838-39; Whig presdl. elector, 1840; also engaged in banking, shipbuilding, Thomaston. Died Thomaston, Feb. 19, 1857; buried Thomaston Cemetery.

ROBINSON, Edward Mott, mcht.; b. Phila., Jan. 8, 1800; s. James and Mary (Attmore) R.; m. Abby Howland, Dec. 29, 1833, 1 dau., Hetty Howland (Robinson) Green. Mem. firm Isaac Howland, Jr., and Co., whaling mchts., New Bedford, Mass., 1830-61; pres. Bedford Comml. Bank, New Bedford; partner firm William T. Coleman & Co., operators packet line to Cal., N.Y.C., 1861-65; left estate of over $5,000,000 to his dau. Died N.Y.C., June 14, 1865.

ROBINSON, Ezekial Gilman, clergyman, univ. pres.; b. South Attleboro, Mass., Mar. 23, 1815; s. Ezekial and Cynthia (Slack) R.; grad. Brown U., 1838, D.D. (hon.), 1853; grad. Newton Theol. Instn., 1842; LL.D. (hon.), Harvard, 1866; m. Harriet Richards Parker, Feb. 21, 1844. Licensed to preach before 1838; represented Am. Tract Soc. among churches of Hartford County, Conn.; pastor Cumberland St. Baptist Ch., Norfolk, Va.; ordained to ministry Bapt. Ch., 1842; chaplain U. Va., 1843-44; pastor Old Cambridge (Mass.) Bapt. Ch., Oct. 1845-Sept. 1846; prof. Bibl. interpretation Western Bapt. Theol. Inst., Covington, Ky., circa 1846-48; pastor 9th St. Bapt. Ch., Cincinnati, 1848-53; became prof. Bibl. theology Rochester (N.Y.) Theol. Sem., 1853; gave lectures published in Christian Theology, 1894; pres., 1860-72; pres. Brown U., 1872-89; prof. ethics and apologetics U. Chgo., 1892. Author: The Relation of Church to the Bible, 1866; Yale Lectures on Preaching, 1883; Principles and Practice of Morality, 1888, 91, 96; Lectures on Christian Evidence, 1895; editor Christian Review, 1859-64. Died Boston, June 13, 1894; buried Rochester.

ROBINSON, George Dexter, gov. Mass., congressman; b. Lexington, Mass., Jan. 20, 1834; attended Lexington Acad., Hopkins Classical Sch., Cambridge, Mass.; grad. Harvard, 1856; studied law. Prin. tchr. Chicopee (Mass.) High Sch., 1856-65; admitted to Cambridge bar, 1866, practiced law, Chicopee; mem. Mass. Ho. of Reps., 1874, Mass. Senate, 1876; mem. U.S. Ho. of Reps. (Republican) from Mass., 45th-48th congresses, 1877-Jan. 7, 1884 (resigned); gov. Mass., 1884-87; practiced law, Springfield, Mass. Died Chicopee, Feb. 22, 1896; buried Fairview Cemetery.

ROBINSON, Henry Cornelius, state legislator, mayor; b. Hartford, Conn., Aug. 28, 1832; s. David Franklin and Anne (Seymour) R.; grad. Yale, 1853; m. Eliza Trumbull, Aug. 28, 1862, 5 children. Admitted to Conn. bar, 1855; partner in law practice with brother, 1858-61, Hartford, practiced alone, 1861-88; fish commr. of Vt., 1866-68; mayor of Hartford, 1872-74; mem. Vt. Ho. of Reps., 1879, chmn. judiciary committee; del. Nat. Republican Conv., Chgo., 1880; dir. N.Y., N.H. & H. R.R. Died Hartford, Feb. 14, 1900.

ROBINSON, James Carroll, congressman, lawyer; b. nr. Paris, Edgar County, Ill., Aug. 19, 1823; studied law. Became farmer; served as cpl. during Mexican War; admitted to bar, 1850, practiced in Marshall, Clark County, Ill.; mem. U.S. Ho. of Reps. (Democrat) from Ill., 36th-38th, 42-43 congresses, 1859-65, 71-75; unsuccessful candidate for gov. Ill., 1864; moved to Sangamon County, Ill., 1869, practiced law in Springfield; apptd. mem. Ill. Bd. Livestock Commrs., 1886. Died Springfield, Nov. 3, 1886; buried Oak Ridge Cemetery.

ROBINSON, James Sidney, congressman; b. nr. Mansfield, Richland County, O., Oct. 14, 1827; attended common schs.; learned printing. Moved to Kenton, O., 1845; editor, publisher Kenton Republican; chief clk. Ohio Ho. of Reps., 1856; enlisted in Co. G, 4th Regt., Ohio Volunteer Infantry in Civil War, 1861, 1st lt., capt., 1861, apptd. maj. 82d Regt., 1861, lt. col., col., 1862, brevetted brig. gen., 1864, became brig. gen., 1865, brevetted maj. gen., 1865; chmn. Ohio Republican Exec. Com., 1877-79; apptd. commr. railroads and telegraphs in Ohio, 1880; mem. U.S. Ho. of Reps. (Rep.) from Ohio, 47th-48th congresses, 1881-Jan. 12, 1885 (resigned); sec. State of Ohio, 1885-89. Died Kenton, Jan. 14, 1892; buried Grove Cemetery.

ROBINSON, John, clergyman; b. Nottinghamshire, Eng., 1575; M.A., Corpus Christi Coll., Cambridge (Eng.) U., 1599; 2 children. Favored Puritan religion; formally separated from Ch. of Eng., 1604; one of ministers at Scrooby, Nottinghamshire, led congregation to Leyden, Holland; leader in plan to emigrate to Am., never actually came to Am. Author (among other works): A Justification of Separation from the Church of England Against Mr. Bernard's Invective Entitled The Separatist's Schism, 1610; Observations Divine and Moral, 1625. Died Leyden, Mar. 3, 1625.

ROBINSON, John colonial ofcl.; b. Feb. 3, 1704; s. John and Catherine (Beverley) R.; attended Coll. William and Mary; m. Mary Storey; m. 2d, Lucy Moore; m. 3d, Susanna Chiswell. Mem. Va. Ho. of Burgesses from County of King and Queen, 1736, speaker, 1738-66; treas. Colony of Va., 1738-66; guilty of breach of trust, accused but not clearly guilty of a plan to defraud the public. Died May 11, 1766.

ROBINSON, John Cleveland, army officer; b. Binghamton, N.Y., Apr. 10, 1817; s. Dr. Tracy and Sarah (Cleveland) R.; grad. U.S. Mil. Acad., 1838; m. Sarah Pease, May 15, 1842, 9 children. Commd. 2d lt. 5th Inf., U.S. Army, 1839; served as regtl. and brigade q.m. during Mexican War; fought in battles of Pato Alto, Resaca de la Palma, siege of Monterey; commd. capt., 1850; foguht in Seminole War, 1856-57; commd. col., 1861, brig. gen. U.S. Volunteers, 1862; brevetted for actions at battles of Gettysburg, Wilderness; served with Army of Potomac until Battle of Spotsylvania; commanded mil. dist. of N.Y.; brevetted maj., 1864; mil. comdr., commr. Bur. Freedmen, N.C.; comdr. Dept. of South, 67, Dept. of Lakes, 1868; lt. gov. N.Y., 1872-74; comdr.-in-chief G.A.R., 1877-78; pres. Soc. Army of Potomac, 1887; recipient Congressional Medal of Honor for gallantry, Laurel Hill, Va., 1894; statue dedicated to him, Gettysburg, Pa., 1917. Died Binghampton, Feb. 18, 1897.

ROBINSON, John Larne, congressman; b. nr. Maysville, Mason County, Ky., May 3, 1813; attended public schools. Moved to Rush County, Ind.; became mcht., Milroy, Ind.; clk. Rush County, 1841-45; mem. U.S. Ho. of Reps. (Democrat) from Ind., 30th-32d congresses, 1847-53; apptd. by Pres. Pierce as U.S. marshal for Ind. Southern Dist., 1853, reapptd. by Pres. Buchanan, 1858-60; apptd. brig. insp. 4th Mil. Dist. of Ind., 1854; trustee Ind. U., 1856-59. Died Rushville, Ind., Mar. 21, 1860; buried East Hill Cemetery.

ROBINSON, John McCracken, senator, lawyer; b. nr. Georgetown, Scott County, Ky., Apr. 10, 1794; grad. Transylvania U., Lexington, Ky.; studied law. Admitted to bar, practiced in Carmi, Ill., 1818; judge Ill. Supreme Ct.; served as gen. Ill. Militia; mem. U.S. Senate (Democrat, filled vacancy) from Ill., Dec. 11, 1830-41; elected asso. justice Ill. Supreme Ct., 1843. Died Ottawa, Ill., Apr. 25, 1843; buried Old Graveyard, Carmi.

ROBINSON, John Mitchell, jurist; b. Caroline County, Md., Dec. 6, 1827; s. Peter and Sarah (Mitchell) R.; grad. Dickinson Coll., 1847; m. Marianna Emory, Nov. 19, 1857, 6 children. Admitted to Md. bar, Nov. 1849; apptd. dep. atty. gen. for Queen Anne's and Kent counties (Md.), 1851; Md. atty. for Queen Anne's County, 1851-55; elected judge of circuit comprising Kent, Queen Anne's counties, 1864; elected to Md. Ct. Appeals, 1867, chief judge, 1893-96; delivered over 400 opinions, most important decision concerned validity of a tax imposed upon gross receipt of railroad cos. (The State of Maryland vs. the Philadelphia, Wilmington & Baltimore R.R. Co., 45 Md., 361, 1876; State vs. Baltimore & Ohio R.R. Co., 48 Md., 49, 1878). Died Annapolis, Md., Jan. 14, 1896; buried Waverly, on Chester River, Md.

ROBINSON, Jonathan, senator, jurist; b. Hardwick, Mass., Aug. 11, 1756; had limited schooling; studied law. Admitted to bar, 1796, practiced in Bennington, Vt.; town Clk., 1795-1801; mem. Vt. Ho. of Reps., 1789-1802, 18; judge Vt. Probate Ct., 1795-98, 15-19; chief justice Vt. Supreme Ct., 1801-07; mem. U.S. Senate (filled vacancy) from Vt., Oct. 10, 1807-15. Died Bennington, Nov. 3, 1819; buried Old Cemetery, Old Bennington, Vt.

ROBINSON, Milton Stapp, congressman, jurist; b. Versailles, Ripley County, Ind., Apr. 20, 1832; studied law. Admitted to bar, 1851, practiced in Anderson, Ind.; Republican presdl. elector, 1856; apptd. dir. Ind. State Penitentiary, Michigan City, 1861, resigned after few months; entered Union Army as lt. col. 47th Regt., Ind. Volunteer Infantry in Civil War, 1861, promoted col. 75th Regt., 1862-64, resigned; brevetted brig. gen., 1865; mem. Ind. Senate, 1866-70; del. Nat. Rep. Conv., Phila., 1872; mem. U.S. Ho. of Reps. (Rep.) from Ind., 44th-45th congresses, 1875-79; apptd. asso. justice Ind. Appellate Ct., 1891, later apptd. chief justice. Died Anderson, July 28, 1892; buried Maplewood Cemetery.

ROBINSON, Moncure, civil engr.; b. Richmond, Va., Feb. 2, 1802; s. John and Agnes (Moncure) R.; m. Charlotte Taylor, Feb. 2, 1835, 10 children. Accompanied topographic survey from Richmond (Va.) to Ohio River, 1818; attended lectures in mathematics and science in France, studied public works in France, England, Wales, The Low Countries, 1825-28; made surveys for Pottsville & Danville Ry. (Pa.), 1828 (1st railroad constructed in U.S.); apptd. to make surveys for Allegheny Portage R.R.; built Petersburg & Roanoke, Richmond and Petersburgh, Winchester and Potomac railroads; began building Phila. & Reading R.R., 1834; locomotive Gowan and Mary built in Phila. from his plans; mem. commn. which recommended Wallabout Bay as site for drydock to be constructed in N.Y. Harbor; ret. from profl. activity, 1847; mem. Am. Philos. Soc., 1833; hon. mem. Am. Soc. C.E. Died Phila., Nov. 10, 1891.

ROBINSON, Moses, senator, gov. Vt,; b. Hardwick, Mass., Mar. 26, 1742; s. Samuel and Mercy (Lennard or Leonard) R.; m. Mary Fay; m. 2d, Susana Howe; 6 children. Town clk., Bennington, Vt., 1762; admitted to Vt. bar by spl. act of legislature, 1777; col. Vt. Militia during Revolutionary War, head of regt. on Mt. Independence when Ft. Ticonderoga was evacuated by Gen. Edmund St. Clair, 1777; mem. Vt. Council of Safety; mem. conv. which declared independence of Vt., 1777; mem. Vt. Gov.'s Council, 1778-85; 1st chief justice Vt. Supreme Ct., 1778-81, 82-84, 85-89; del. from Vt. to Continental Congress to join articles of union and confederation with U.S., 1779; served on commn. authorized to agree upon terms for admission of Vt. to Union, 1782; Vt. agt. to Continental Congress in adjustment of boundary dispute with N.Y.; mem. 3d Council of Censors (supervised constn., legislative, exec. depts. of Vt.); gov. Vt., 1789, 90; mem. Vt. Conv. which ratified U.S. Constn., 1791; mem. U.S. Senate from Vt., Oct. 17, 1791-Oct. 17, 1796; opposed Jay Treaty, 1794; mem. Vt. Gen. Assembly from Bennington, 1802. Died Bennington, May 26, 1813; buried Old Bennington Cemetery.

ROBINSON, Orville, congressman; b. Richfield, Oswego County, N.Y., Oct. 28, 1801; completed prep. studies; studied law. Admitted to bar, 1827, practiced in Mexico, N.Y.; justice of peace, Mexico, 1828; town clk., 1829, surrogate Oswego County, 1830-38; mem. N.Y. State Assembly, 1834, 36-37, 56, speaker, 1856; dist. atty. Oswego County, 1841-43; supr. Town of Mexico, 1843; mem. U.S. Ho. of Reps. (Democrat) from N.Y., 28th Congress, 1843-45; moved to Oswego, N.Y., 1847; recorder, Oswego, 1853; collector customs Dist. of Oswego, 1858-60. Died Oswego, Dec. 1, 1882; buried Riverside Cemetery.

ROBINSON, Solon, agriculturist, writer; b. Tolland, Conn., Oct. 21, 1803; s. Jacob and Salinda (Ladd) R.; m. Mariah Evans, Oct., 1828; m. 2d Mary Johnson, June 30, 1872, 5 children. Formed Squatter's Union, Ind., 1836; known as "king of the squatters"; county clk., justice of peace, register of claims, postmaster (all Lake County, Ind.); pub. intermittently a small news sheet, Crown Point, Ind.; began contbg. articles on aspects of frontier to Albany Cultivator, 1837; prominent participant Log Cabin Conv., Lafayette, Ind., 1840; delivered address, later published as "History of Lake County," 1847; a founder U.S. Agrl. Soc., 1852; contbd. travel sketches and observations to Cultivator, Am. Agriculturist, Prairie Farmer (articles from a valuable hist. record of rural soc. of time); agrl. editor N.Y. Tribune, 1853; conducted exptl. farm, Westchester, N.Y.; played influential role in establishment Dept. of Agr., 1862; pub. Florida Republican, Jacksonville, Fla. Author: The Will: A Tale of the Lake of Red Cedars & Shabbona, 1841; Hot Corn (novel), 153; Life Scenes in N.Y., Tales of Slum Life, 1854; How to Live; or Domestic Economy Illustrated, 1860; Facts for Farmers: Also for the Family Circle, 1864; A Tale of Frontier Life and Indian Character, 1867; Mewonitac, 1867. Died Jacksonville, Fla., Nov. 3, 1880.

ROBINSON, Stuart, clergyman, editor; b. Strabane, County Tyrone, Ireland, Nov. 14, 1814; son of James and Martha (Porter) R.; grad. Amherst Coll., 1836; attended Union Theol. Sem. in Va., 1837, Princeton Theol. Sem., 1839-40; m. Mary Brigham, Sept. 1841, 8 children. Taught at acad., Charleston, S.C., 1838-39; licensed by Greenbriar Presbytery, 1841; ordained to ministry Presbyn. Ch., Oct. 8, 1842; pastor, Malden, W. Va., 1842-47, conducted a sch.; pastor Presbyn. Ch., Frankfort, Ky., June 8, 1847-Sept. 2, 1852, Fayette St. Ch. (Independent), Balt., circa 1852-53; organizer Central Presbyn. Ch., Balt., pastor, until 1856; prof. ch. govt. and pastoral theology Danville (Ky.) Theol. Sem., 1856; pastor 2d Presbyn. Ch., Louisville, Ky., 1858-81; published (with Thomas E. Peck) Presbyterian Critic and Review Monthly, Balt., 1855-56; editor Louisville True Presbyterian; suspected of disloyalty during Civil War, sought refuge in Toronto, Ont., Can., 1862, preached, lectured, wrote, aided So. refugees; resumed publication of True Christian under name Free Christian Commonwealth, (previously True Presbyterian), Louisville, 1866; commr. Presbyn. Gen. Assembly of 1866, St. Louis; led main part of Ky. Synod to unite with Gen. Assembly of So. Presbyn. Ch., 1869, moderator of assembly, 1869; through his influence the So. ch. became constituent mem. Alliance of Presbyn. and Reformed Chs. throughout the World, 1875. Author: The Churches of God, an Essential Element of the Gospel, 1858; The Infamous Perjuries of the 'Bureau of Military Justice' Exposed, 1865. Died Louisville, Oct. 5, 1881.

ROBINSON, Theodore, painter; b. Irasburg, Vt., June 3, 1852; s. Elijah and Ellen (Brown) R.; attended N.A.D., 1874. Organizer (with fellow students) Art Students League of N.Y.; studied 1st in artelier of Carolus-Duran, later under Jean-Leon Gerome; mem. Soc. Am. Artists, 1881, received Webb prize for landscape, 1890, Shaw prize for figure, 1892; went to Paris, 1884, under influence of French impressionists; returned to Am., 1892; asst. of John La Farge on mural decorations for Vanderbilt House, N.Y.C., circa 1892; with firm Prentice Treadwell of Boston, circa 1893-96; an art critic; important in Am. impressionist movement;

pioneer in realism; paintings include: Valley of the Seine from Giverny Heights. Contbr. essay on Claude Monet to Century mag., 1892; poem A Normandy Patoral to Scribner's mag., 1897. Died Apr. 2, 1896.

ROBINSON, Therese Albertine Louise von Jakob, philologist; b. Halle, Prussian Saxony, Jan. 26, 1797; d. Ludwig Heinrich von Jakob; m. Edward Robinson, Aug. 7, 1828, at least 2 children. Mastered classical langs., Anglo-Saxon, Scandinavian, English, French, Spanish; translated, published Old Morality, also The Black Dwarf (Sir Walter Scott) under name Ernst Berthold, 1821; used pseudonym Talvj after 1825; published 3 edits. Volkslieder der Serben, 1825-26; translated Essay on ... The Indian Languages of North America (John Pickering) into German, 1834; Published Historical View of the Slavic Language (her 1st literary work in English), 1834; published several essays in North American Review, 1836; published essays and other writings in Versuch einer Geschichtlichen Charakteristik der Volkslieder germanischer Nationen; Die Unachteit der Lieder Ossians und des Mephersonschen Ossians ins besondere, 1840; articles accepted by Putnams' Monthly Magazine, Atlantic Monthly, Westermann's Monatshefte; best known novels include: Heloise, 1850; Die Auswandere (in English The Exiles or Woodhill), 1853. Died Hambrug, Germany, Apr. 13, 1870.

ROBINSON, Thomas, Jr., congressman; b. Georgetown, Sussex County, Del., 1800; grad. Princeton; studied law. Admitted to bar, 1823, practiced in Georgetown; treas. Sussex County, 1825; commr. Levy Ct., 1831-32; mem. U.S. Ho. of Reps. (Democrat) from Del., 26th Congress, 1839-41. Died Georgetown, Oct. 28, 1843; buried Old Cemetery of St. George's Chapel.

ROBINSON, William, businessman; b. Pa., Dec. 17, 1785; son of James Robinson; grad. Princeton; studied law with James Ross; m. Mary Parker, July 3, 1810. Admitted to Pa. bar, never practiced law; commd. officer Pa. Militia, became known as General; donated land, invested heavily in bldg. of canals, also Ohio & Pa. R.R.; supported constrn. of 1st iron mill in Pitts., also 1st suspension bridge in West; pres. Exchange Bank of Pitts.; mem. Pa. Legislature; 1st mayor Allegheny City (Pa.). Died Feb. 25, 1868.

ROBINSON, William Erigena, journalist, congressman; b. Unagh, County Tyrone, Ireland, May 6, 1814; s. Thomas and Mary (Sloss) R.; grad. Yale, 1841, attended Yale Law Sch., 1842-43; m. Helen Dougherty, 1853, 6 children. Came to N.Y.C., 1836; founder Yale Banner, Yale chpt. Psi Upsilon frat.; spoke for Henry Clay in polit. campaign of 1844; became asst. editor N.Y. Tribune, 1843, contbd. Washington (D.C.) dispatches under signature "Richelieu," 1844-48; contbr. to publs. Whig, Boston Atlas, Louisville Jour.; editor Buffalo Daily Express, 1846; supporter Young Ireland Rebellion of 1848; a founder The People, 1849; editor Newark Daily Mercury, 1850-53; weigher N.Y. Custom House, until 1853; admitted to N.Y. bar, 1854; assessor internal revenue (apptd. by Pres. Lincoln) for 3d Dist. N.Y., 1862-67; mem. U.S. Ho. of Reps. (Democrat) from N.Y., 40th, 47th-48th congresses, 1867-69, 81-85; chiefly responsible for bill which established right to expatriation; mem. editorial bd. Irish World, 1871; published Shamrock (weekly newspaper), Bklyn., 1872. Author (treatise) "Origin and Source of the American People." Died Bklyn., Jan. 23, 1892; buried Greenwood Cemetery, Bklyn.

ROBINSON, William Stevens, journalist; b. Concord, Mass., Dec. 7, 1818; s. William and Martha (Cogswell) R.; m. Harriet Hanson, Nov. 30, 1848, 4 children. Joined brother in office Norfolk Advertiser, Dedham, Mass., 1837; editor Yeoman's Gazette, 1839, later The Republican, (a Whig paper) Concord, Mass.; del. Whig Conv., Balt., 1840; asst. editor, Washington, (D.C.) correspondent Lowell Courier 1842-48; editor The American Manchester, N.H., 1845; editor Boston Daily Whig, later Boston Daily Republican, 1848; sec. Worchester (Mass.) Free-Soil Conv., 1848; started Lowell American became most radical Mass. anti-slavery journalist, circa 1850-54; served in Mass. Legislature, 1852-53; clk. Mass. Constl. Conv., 1853; mem. editorial staff The Commonwealth, Boston Telegraph, 1854; contbd. letters on Mass. politics and politicians to Springfield Republican (signed Warrington), N.Y. Tribune (signed Gilbert), 1856; clk. Mass. Ho. Reps., 1862-73; sec. Mass. Republican Com., 1863-68; successfully led opposition against Benjamin F. Butler's bid for Mass. governorship. Author: Warrington's Manual (a handbook of parliamentary law), 1875. Died Malden, Mass., Mar. 11, 1876.

ROBISON, David Fullerton, congressman, lawyer; b. Antrim Twp., nr. Greencastle, Franklin County, Pa., May 28, 1816; attended public schs.; studied law. Taught sch.; admitted to Franklin County bar, 1843, practiced in Chambersburg, Pa.; mem. U.S. Ho. of Reps. (Whig) from Pa., 34th Congress, 1855-57; presumably poisoned at banquet in Washington (D.C.) during Pres. Buchanan's inauguration. Died Chambersburg, June 24, 1859; buried Cedar Hill Cemetery, Greencastle.

ROBOT, Isidore, clergyman, missionary; b. Tharoiseau, Burgundy, France, July 18, 1837; entered Benedictine Preachers of the Monastery of Pierre-Qui-Vire, 1857. Ordained priest Roman Catholic Ch., 1862; came to New Orleans, 1871; founder monastery Benedictine Congregation Casinese of the Primitive Observance (elevated to an Abbey by Pope Pius IX, 1877) Sacred Heart, Okla., 1875; became (with other Benedictines) 1st resident priest in Indian Territory, founded 1st Cath. missions for Choctaw Indians, Atoka, McAllister, Caddo (all Okla.); founded coll. for boys, Sacred Heart, also an acad. for girls, Indian agrl. and missionary schs.; a leader in deliberations in 3d Plenary Council of Balt., pleaded cause of Indian missionaries. Died Dallas, Tex., Feb. 15, 1887; buried monastic cemetery, Sacred Heart Abbey.

ROBYN, Edward, artist; b. Emmerich, Prussia, 1820. Lithographer, Phila., 1848-50; moved to St. Louis, 1850, in lithographing bus. with brother Charles, until 1857; painted self portrait, panorama of Eastern and Western Hemispheres (owned by Mo. Hist. Soc.). Died nr. Hermann, Mo., 1862.

ROCHAMBEAU, comte de, see Vimeur, Jean Baptiste Donatien de.

ROCHESTER, Nathaniel, mcht.; b. Westmoreland County, Va., Feb. 21, 1752; s. John and Hester (Thrift) R.; m. Sophia Beatty, 1788, 9 children. Mem. Revolutionary Com. Safety for Orange County, (N.C.), 1775; attended 2 N.C. provincial convs., 1775-76; commd. maj. N.C. Militia, lt. col., 1776, dep. commissary gen. stores and clothing; apptd. a commr. to establish and superintend arms manufactory, Hillsboro, S.C., 1777; served in S.C. Assembly, 1777; went into bus. with Col. Thomas Host, Hillsboro, then Hagerstown, Md., 1778; mem. Md. Legislature, 1 term: pres. Hagerstown Bank, 1807; a founder Monroe County (N.Y.), county clk., 1821; founder City of Rochester (N.Y.); organized bank, Rochester, 1824. Died Rochester, May 17, 1831.

ROCHESTER, William Beatty, congressman; b. Hagerstown, Md., Jan. 29, 1789; grad. Charlotte Hall, St. Marys County, Md.; studied law. Aide-de-camp to Gen. McClure in War of 1812; admitted to bar, practiced in Bath, N.Y.; moved to Angelica, N.Y.; mem. N.Y. State Assembly, 1816-18; Democratic presdl. elector, 1821; mem. U.S. Ho. of Reps. from N.Y., 17th-18th congresses, 1821-23 (resigned); circuit judge N.Y. 8th Circuit, 1823-26; unsuccessful Dem. candidate for gov. N.Y., 1826; sec. to spl. E. E. and M. P., Colombia, 1826; chargé d'affaires to Central America, 1827; settled in Buffalo, N.Y., 1828; branch pres. Bank of U.S., Buffalo; pres. Bank of Pensacola (Fla.); dir. Ala. & Fla. R.R. Co., 1837-38. Died in wreck of steamer Pulaski off coast of N.C., June 14, 1838.

ROCKHILL, William, congressman, farmer; b. Burlington, N.J., Feb. 10, 1793; attended public schs. Moved to Ft. Wayne, Ind., 1822, became farmer; commr. Allen County, Ind., 1825, justice of peace; mem. 1st Ft. Wayne City Council, also assessor; mem. Ind. Ho. of Reps., 1834-37; mem. Ind. Senate, 1844-47; mem. U.S. Ho. of Reps. (Democrat) from Ind., 30th Congress, 1847-49. Died Ft. Wayne, Jan. 15, 1865; buried Lindenwood Cemetery.

ROCKINGHAM, Charles Watson-Wentworth, prime minister Eng.; b. Eng., 1730; attended St. John's Coll., Cambridge (Eng.) U. Entered Ho. of Lords after father's death, 1750; formed coalition govt. in Eng., 1765, repealed Stamp Act, began reconciliation with Am.; again became prime minister of Eng., 1782. Died July 1, 1782.

ROCKWELL, John Arnold, congressman, lawyer; b. Norwich, Conn., Aug. 27, 1803; grad. Yale, 1822; studied law. Admitted to bar, practiced in Norwich; mem. Conn. Senate, 1839; judge county ct.; mem. U.S. Ho. of Reps. (Whig) from Conn., 29th-30th congresses, 1845-49; practiced before U.S. Ct. of Claims, Washington, D.C. until 1861. Died Washington, Feb. 10, 1861; buried Yantic Cemetery, Norwich.

ROCKWELL, Julius, senator, congressman; b. Colebrook, Conn., Apr. 26, 1805; grad. Yale, 1826; studied law. Admitted to bar, practiced in Pittsfield, Mass., 1830; mem. Mass. Ho. of Reps., 1834-38, 58, speaker various times; Mass. bank commr., 1838-40; mem. U.S. Ho. of Reps. (Whig) from Mass., 28th-31st congresses, 1843-51; del. Mass. Constl. Conv., 1853; mem. U.S. Senate (filled vacancy) from Mass., June 3, 1854-Jan. 31, 1855; Republican presdl. elector, 1856; judge Mass. Superior Ct., 1859-86. Died Lenox, Mass., May 19, 1888; buried Lenox Cemetery.

RODDEY, Philip Dale, army officer, mcht.; b. Moulton, Ala., 1820; m. Margaret McGaughey, 4 children. Formed cavalry troop, elected capt. during Civil War, 1861; became col., 1862; organizer, comdr. 4th Ala. Cavalry, 1862-65; defended banks of Tennessee river; executed successful raid towards Corinth, Miss., 1862; called Swamp Fox of Tennessee Valley; operated in Miss., Tuscumbia, Ala., Columbia, Tenn., 1863; comd. brig. gen.; active in Atlanta campaign, Hood's campaign in Tenn.; entered commission bus. in N.Y.C. after Civil War. Died London, Eng., Aug. 1897.

RÖDER, Martin, musician; b. Berlin, Germany, Apr. 7, 1851; attended Royal Hochschule, Berlin, 1870-71. Chorusmaster, Teatro dal Verme, Milan, Italy, 1873-80; organized Societá del Quartetto Caale, 1875; conducted opera in various cities; singing tchr., Berlin, 1880-81; taught at Scharwenka's Conservatory, 1881-87; became prof. Royal Acad. Music, Dublin, Ireland, 1887; became dir. vocal dept. New Eng. Conservatory, Boston, 1892; author and contbr. to various profl. publs. Died Boston, June 7, 1895.

RODES, Robert Emmett, army officer; b. Lynchburg, Va., Mar. 29, 1829; s. David and Martha (Yancey) R.; grad. Va. Mil. Inst., 1848; m. Virginia Woodruff, Sept. 10, 1857, 2 children. Became civil engr., 1851; chief engr. N.E. & S.W. Ala .R.R., 1858; capt. Mobile (Ala.) Cadets, 1861; volunteered, became col. 5th Ala. Inf., 1861; commd. brig. gen. in Manassas campaign, 1861; commanded brigade at Battle of Fair Oaks (Va.); served in Battle of Gaines' Mill; fought at battles of Bloody Lane, Antietam; given command of Daniel Hill's division, 1863; with Stonewall Jackson led van of flank march at Battle of Chancellorsville; apptd. maj. gen., 1863; served in Battle of Gettysburg; stopped Union advance in Battle of Wilderness, 1864; in action at Battle of Spotsylvania; took part in raid Washington, D.C. Killed in action at Winchester, Va., Sept. 19, 1864.

RODGERS, Christopher Raymond Perry, naval officer, ednl. adminstr.; b. Bklyn., Nov. 14, 1819; s. George Washington and Ann (Perry) R.; m. Jane Slidell, July 7, 1845, 5 children. Commd. midshipman U.S. Navy, 1833; served at N.Y. Navy Yard, 1836-37; on a cruise on ship Fairfield in Brazil Squadron during Seminole War, 1839-42, served on board ships Flirt, Wave; comdr. ship Phoenix, passed midshipman, 1839, lt., 1844; with ship Saratoga in African Squadron, 1842-43; Cumberland, Mediterranean Squadron, 1843-45, acting master on both ships; served at Veracruz during Mexican War, 1846-48; served with ship Constitution of African Squadron, 1852-53, Wabash, Mediterranean Squadron, 1858-59; comdt. of midshipmen U.S. Naval Acad., 1860-61, played active part in moving acad. to Newport, R.I.; ordered to take command of ship Wabash, 1861, commanded vessel as flagship at Battle of Port Royal; promoted comdr., 1861; fleet capt. South Atlantic Blockading Squadroon, 1862-63; served on ship New Ironsides during Battle of Charleston, 1863; commd. capt., 1866, commodore, 1870; rear adm., 1874; chief Bur. of Yards and Decks, 1871-74; acting chief Bur. of Equipment; supt. U.S. Naval Acad., 1874-78; comdr. in chief Pacific Squadron, 1878-80; pres. U.S. Naval Inst., 1875-78, 82-83; pres. Internat. Meridian Conf., 1884. Contbr. article "DuPont's Attack at Charleston" to Battles and Leaders of the Civil War, 1887-88. Died Washington, D.C., Jan. 8, 1892; buried Annapolis, Md.

RODGERS, George Washington, naval officer; b. Cecil County, Md., Feb. 22, 1787; s. John and Elizabeth (Reynolds) R.; m. Ann Perry, July 5, 1815, at least 3 children, including George Washington, Christopher Raymond Perry, Alexander P. Commd. midshipman U.S. Navy, 1804; acting lt., served on ship United States, 1809; commd. lt., 1810; served on ship Wasp during War of 1812; voted silver medal by U.S. Congress for services in engagement with ship Frolic; commanded ship Firefly, 1815; commd. master comdt., 1816; comdr. ship Peacock, Mediterranean Squadron, 1816-19; with N.Y. Navy Yard, 1819-25, comdt. part of this period; commd. capt., 1825; served on Naval Bd. Examiners; commanded Brazil Squadron, 1831-32. Died Buenos Aires, Argentina, May 21, 1832; buried New London, Conn.

RODGERS, George Washington, naval officer; b. Bklyn., Oct. 20, 1822; s. George Washington and Ann (Perry) R.; m. Kate Lane, Aug. 21, 1842. Commd. midshipman U.S. Navy, 1836, passed midshipman, 1842; served with Col. Herney, then in ship John Adams in the Gulf of Mexico, 1846-48; promoted lt., 1850; commanded ship Constitution, 1860; comdt. midshipman, 1861; commd. comdr., 1862; appointed chief of staff, 1863; commanded Catskill in attack on Charleston (S.C.), 1863. Killed in attack on Charleston., Aug. 17, 1863.

RODGERS, John, clergyman, univ. ofcl.; b. Boston, Aug. 5, 1727; s. Thomas and Elizabeth (Baxter) R.; D.D. (hon.), U. Edinburgh (Scotland), 1768; m. Elizabeth Bayard, Sept. 19, 1752; m. 2d, Mary (Antrobus) Grant, Aug. 15, 1764; 5 children. Licensed to preach by Presbytery of New Castle (Del.), 1747; ordained to ministry Presbyn. Ch., 1749; pastor, Saint Georges, New Castle County, Del., 1749-65; trustee Coll. of N.J. (now Princeton), 1765-circa 1785; pastor, N.Y.C., 1765-1810; chaplain in Gen. Heath's brigade, 1776; chaplain N.Y. Council of Safety; chaplain 1st N.Y. State Legislature; mem. com. revising standards of Presbyn. Ch., 1788; moderator 1st Gen. Assembly, Phila., 1789; vice chancellor U. State of N.Y., 1784-1811. Died N.Y.C., May 7, 1811.

RODGERS, John, naval officer; b. Lower Susquehanna Ferry, Md., 1773; s. John and Elizabeth (Reynolds) R.; m. Minerva Denison, Oct. 21, 1806, 11 children including John, Louisa. Apptd. 2d lt. U.S. Navy on board Constellation by Pres. Adams, 1798, exec. officer (capt.), 1799; participated in capture of frigate Insurgenta; at end of war honored by being selected to convey John Dawson (bearer of French-Am. treaty) to France; in mcht. service, 1801; recalled to U.S. Navy, 1802; forced Tripoli to sign treaty to end slavery of Christians, 1805; in command N.Y. flotilla and naval station, 1807; had duty enforcing Embargo in waters between The Delaware and Passamaquddy Bay, 1808; commanded Northern div. of ships for protection of Am. coast with frigate President, 1810; in active service War of 1812; in command of Del. flotilla and ship Guerriere, 1814; chosen by Pres. Madison to head newly created Bd. of Navy Commrs., 1815-24, 27-37; sr. officer in navy, 1821; served as sec. of navy ad interim, 1823; commanded Am. Squadron, 1825-27. Died Naval Asylum, Phila., Aug. 1, 1838; buried Congressional Cemetery, Washington, D.C.

RODGERS, John, naval officer; b. Sion Hill, Md., Aug. 8, 1812; s. Capt. John and Minerva (Denison) R.; attended U. Va. one year; m. Ann Hodge, Nov. 27, 1857, 3 children. Apptd. midshipman U. S. Navy, 1828, passed midshipman, 1834; comdr. in Wave, then Jefferson in Seminole War; commd. lt., 1840; commanded ship Boxer of Home Squadron, 1842-44; ordered to duty with North Pacific Surveying Expdn., 1852, 2d in rank commanding ship John Hancock; surveyed Liu-Kius, Ladrones and other islands, Hawaiian and Society Islands; promoted comdr., 1855; in charge of office in Washington (D.C.) preparing results of expdn. for publication, 1856; commanded ship Flag, 1861; aide to Rear Adm. Samuel Du Pont at Battle of Point Royal (S.C.); commanded ship Galena, 1862; commd. capt., 1862; served in attack on Ft. Sumter, 1863; promoted to commodore by Congress, 1863; served in ships Dictator, 1864, Monadnock, 1866-67; comdt. Boston Navy Yard, 1866-69; commd. rear adm., 1869; commanded Asiatic Squadron as rear adm., 1870-72; pres. Naval Examining and Retiring bds., 1872-73; comdt. Mare Island (Cal.) Navy Yard, 1873-77; supt. Naval Observatory, 1877-82; chmn. Light House Board, 1878-82; pres. U.S. Naval Inst., Transit of Venus Commn., 1st Naval Adv. Bd., Jeannette Relief Bd.; charter mem. Nat. Acad. Scis. Died Washington, May 5, 1882.

RODMAN, Isaac Peace, state legislator, army officer; B. South Kingston, R.I., Aug. 18, 1822; s. Samuel and Mary (Peckham) R.; m. Sally Arnold, June 17, 1847, 7 children. Pres., South Kingston Town Council; dir. Wakefield Bank; mem both branches R.I. Legislature; commd. capt. 2d R.I. Inf., 1861; served in 1st Battle of Bull Run; commd. lt. col., then col., 1861; at Battle of New Bern, South Mountain, 1862; promoted brig. gen., 1862; fatally wounded in Battle of Antietam. Died Hagerstown, Md., Sept. 30, 1862; buried South Kingston, R.I.

RODMAN, Thomas Jackson, inventor, army officer; b. Salem, Ind., July 30, 1815; s. James and Elizabeth (Burton) R.; grad. U.S. Mil. Acad., 1841; m. Martha Black, 1843, 7 children. Commd. capt. U.S. Army, 1855, lt. col., 1867; had original idea of casting guns upon hollow core, cooling inner surface by flow of waters; did experiments resulting in successful manufacture of so-called mammoth and perforated-cake, or prismatic gun powder; inventions approved and adopted by govt., 1859; methods utilized by Russia, Gt. Britain, Prussia; commanded arsenal at Watertown, Mass.; supervised casting of smooth bores and rifled guns during Civil War; brevetted lt. col., col., brig. gen., 1865; comd. Rock Island (Ill.) Arsenal, 1865. Died Rock Island Arsenal, June 7, 1871.

RODMAN, William, congressman; b. Bensalem Twp., nr. Bristol, Pa., Oct. 7, 1757; completed prep. studies. Served as pvt., later brigade q.m. during Revolutionary War; commanded company during Whisky Insurrection, 1794; justice of peace, 1791-1800; mem. Pa. Senate, 1804-08; presdl. elector, 1809; mem. U.S. Ho. of Reps. (Democrat) from Pa., 12th Congress, 1811-13. Died Flushing, nr. Bristol, July 27, 1824; buried Episcopal Cemetery (later known as St. James Burying Ground).

RODNEY, Caesar, congressman; b. Dover, Del., Oct. 7, 1728; s. Caesar and Elizabeth (Crawford) R. High sheriff, Kent County, Del., 1755-58; register of wills, recorder of deeds, clk. of orphans' ct., clk. of peace, justice of peace (all Kent County); capt. Del. Militia, 1756; judge, 1758; supt. printing of Del. currency, 1759; co-trustee Kent County Loan Office, 1769, sole trustee, 1775-84; apptd. 3d justice Supreme Ct. for Three Lower Counties, 1769, 2d justice, 1773; elected Kent County del. to Del. Colonial Legislature, 1758, mem. legislature, 1761-76 (except 1771), speaker 1769, 73, 74, 75; Kent County rep. Stamp Act Congress, 1765; mem. Com. of Correspondence; helped draw up address to King objecting to Townshend Act, 1768; mem. Continental Congress, 1774-76, 77-78; col. "upper" regt. Kent County Militia, 1775; brig. gen. Kent County Militia and western bn. of Sussex County; speaker regular session of assembly, 1775; presided over colonial assembly at New Castle, 1776; voted for adoption, signed Declaration of Independence, 1776; chmn. Kent County br. Council of Safety, 1776; recruited Kent County men for Continental Army; brig. gen. in command Del. Militia when British invaded Del., 1777; maj. gen. del. Militia, 1777; judge of admiralty, 1777; pres. of Del., 1778-81, Del.'s war exec. until 1781; mem. upper house Del. Legislature, 1783, speaker. Died Dover, Del., June 29, 1784; buried Christ Episcopal Churchyard, Dover.

RODNEY, Caesar Augustus, senator, diplomat; b. Dover, Del., Jan. 4, 1772; s. Thomas and Elizabeth (Fisher) R.; grad. U. Pa., 1789; studied law with Joseph McKean, Phila.; m. Susan Hunn, 15 children. Admitted to Del. bar, 1793; mem. Del. Ho. of Reps. from New Castle County, 1796-1802; mem. U.S. Ho. of Reps. from Del., 8th Congress, 1803-05, a mgr. to conduct impeachment proceedings against John Pickering (judge U.S. Dist. Ct. for N.H.), 1804, for impeachment proceedings against Justice Samuel Chase, 1804; U.S. atty. gen., 1807-11; active in defense of Del., War of 1812, capt. 2d Arty. Co., 1813, mem. Del. Com. of Safety, 1813, maj. bn. of arty., 1815; mem. Del. Senate, 1815, 16; mem. Pres. Monroe's commn. to determine polit. status of new S. Am. republics, 1817; mem. U.S. Ho. of Reps. from Del., 17th Congress, 1821-22; mem. U.S. Senate from Del., Jan. 24, 1822-Jan. 29, 1823; E..E and M.P. (apptd. by Pres. Monroe) to Argentine Republic, 1823-24. Died Buenos Aires, Argentina, June 10, 1824; buried English Churchyard, Buenos Aires.

RODNEY, Daniel, senator, gov. Del., congressman; b. Lewes, Sussex County, Del., Sept. 10, 1764. Became mcht.; asso. judge Ct. Common Pleas, 1793-1806; Federalist presdl. elector, 1808; gov. Del., 1814-17; mem. U.S. Ho. of Reps. (Federalist, filled vacancy) from Del., 17th Congress, Oct. 1, 1822-23; mem. U.S. Senate (filled vacancy) from Del., Nov. 8, 1826-Jan. 12, 1827. Died Lewes, Sept. 2, 1846; buried St. Peter's Churchyard.

RODNEY, George Brydges, congressman, lawyer; b. Lewes, Del., Apr. 2, 1803; grad. Princeton, 1820; studied law. Register in chancery and clk. Sussex County Orphans Ct., 1826-30; admitted to bar, 1828, practiced law, New Castle, Del.; mem. U.S. Ho. of Reps. (Whig) from Del., 27th-28th congresses, 1841-45; del. Washington (D.C.) Peace Conv., 1861. Died New Castle, June 18, 1883; buried Immanuel Churchyard.

RODNEY, Thomas, Continental congressman, jurist; b. Sussex County, Del., June 4, 1744; s. Caesar and Elizabeth (Crawford) R.; m. Elizabeth Fisher, Apr. 8, 1771, at least 3 children including Caesar Augustus. Justice of peace, Kent County, Del., 1770-74; mem. Colonial Assembly of Govt. of Three Lower Counties (New Castle, Kent, Sussex) from Kent County, 1775; mem. Council of Safety, also Com. of Observation, Kent County, 1775; organized, became col. of a volunteer militia, 1775; mem. Del. Assembly to elect dels. to Continental Congress, 1774; chief justice Kent County Ct., 1778; register of wills, 1779; judge Del. Admiralty Ct., 1778-85; mem. Continental Congress 1781-83, 85-87; mem. lower house Del. Gen. Assembly, 1786, 87, speaker, 1787; supt. Kent County Almshouse, 1802; asso. justice Del. Supreme Ct., 1802; U.S. judge for Miss. Territory (apptd. by Pres. Jefferson), 1803-11. Died Natchez, Miss., Jan. 2, 1811.

ROE, Azel Stevens, author; b. N.Y.C., Aug. 16, 1798. Author: James Montjoy; or, I've Been Thinking, 1850; To Love and Be Loved, 1852; Time and Tide; or, Strive and Win, 1852; A Long Look Ahead, 1855; How Could He Help It?, 1860; Woman Our Angel, 1866; True Love Rewarded, 1877. Died East Windsor Hill, Conn., Jan. 1, 1886.

ROE, Edward Payson, clergyman, author; b. New Windsor, N.Y., Mar. 7, 1838; s. Peter and Susan (Williams) R.; attended Williams Coll., 2 years, Auburn Theol. Sem., 1 year; m. Anna Sands, Nov. 24, 1863, at least 5 children. Ordained by North River Presbytery, Somers, N.Y., 1862; chaplain 2d N.Y. Cavalry, hosp. at Fortress Monroe, Va., until 1865; pastor Highland Falls (N.Y.) Presbyn. Ch., 1865-74; published mag. serial and book Barriers Burned Away (about Chgo. fire 1871), 1872, novel Opening a Chestnut Burr, 1874; author of 17 best-selling novels, including Near to Nature's Heart, 1876; A Knight of the Nineteenth Century, 1877; Without a Home, 1881; He Fell in Love with His Wife, 1886; The Earth Trembled, 1887; helped to dispel lingering Am. prejudice against novel; other works include Play and Profit in my Garden, 1873, A Manual on the Culture of Small Fruits (brochure), 1876, Success with Small Fruits, 1880, Nature's Serial Story, 1885, The Home Acre, 1889 (all based on his avocation, horticulture); host to Author's Club of N.Y. Died Cornwall, N.Y., July 19, 1888.

ROEBLING, John Augustus, civil engr., bridge builder, mfr.; b. Mühlhausen, Thuringia, Germany, June 12, 1806; s. Christoph Polycarpus and Friederike (Mueller) R.; studied architecture, engring, bridge constrn., hydraulics, langs., also philosophy (under Hegel) Royal Poly. Inst., Berlin, Germany, civil engr. degree, 1826; m. Johanna Herting, May 1836; m. 2d, Lucia Cooper; 9 children including Washington Augustus, Ferdinand W., Josephine. Roadbuilder for Prussian govt. in Westphalia, 1826-29; made spl. study of chain suspension bridge, Bamberg, Bavaria; came to U.S., 1831, naturalized, 1837; engr. working on constrn. dams and locks on Beaver River, Pa., 1837; conceived idea of twisted wire rope (to replace hempen cables), devised equipment to manufacture wire rope, produced 1st wire rope made in U.S. in his factory, Saxonburg, Pa., 1841; built wooden aqueduct for Pa. Canal, 1844-45; completed hwy. bridge over Monongahela River at Pitts. (his 1st suspension bridge), 1846; constructed 4 suspension aqueducts for Del. and Hudson Canal; built pioneer railroad suspension bridge at Niagara Falls, 1851-55; built suspension bridge over Ohio River between Cincinnati and Covington, Ky. (completed 1867), bridge over Allegheny River at Pitts., 1858-60; apptd. chief engr. for bridge over East River between Lower Manhattan and Bklyn., drew up plans (approved 1869), died before constrn. started on Bklyn. Bridge (completed by his son Washington Augustus, 1883); an early advocate of railroad transp., trans-Atlantic telegraph. Author: Diary of My Journey from Mühlhausen in Thuringia via Bremen to the United States of North America in the Year 1831, Written for My Friends, published 1931; Long and Short Span Railway Bridges, 1869. Died Bklyn., July 22, 1869.

ROEMER, (Karl) Ferdinand, geologist; b. Hildesheim Hanover, Germany, Jan. 5, 1818; s. Friedrich and Charlotte (Lüntzel) R.; student law at U. Göttingen, Germany, 1836-39; doctor's degree in science, U. Berlin (Germany), May 10, 1842; m. Katharina Schäfer, spring 1869. Contbr. to Neues Jahrbuch fur Mineralogie Geologie und Palaeontologie, until circa 1887; sailed for Am. on funds provided by Soc. for the Protection of German Emigrants in Tex. and Berlin Acad. Science, 1845, undertook mission to study conditions of colonists in Tex. and to report on natural resources of country; became privat-docent in mineralogy and paleontology at U. Bonn (Germany), 1848; became dir. mineral cabinet at U. Breslau (Germany), 1855, also prof. geology and paleontology; recipient Murchison medal Geol. Soc. London, 1855. Author: Texas—Mit besonderes Rücksicht auf deutsche Auswandesung und die physischen Verhältnisse des Lands nach eigener Beobachtung geschildert, 1849, Die Kreidbildungen von Texas und ihre organischen Einschlüsse, 1852, Die Silurische fauna des Westlichen Tennessee, 1860; Geologie von Oberschlesien, 3 vols. with maps and plates, 1870. Died Breslau, Dec. 14, 1891.

ROETTER, Paulus, artist; b. Jan. 4, 1806. Painted miniature landscapes for tourists, taught sch., Switzerland, 1825-45; came to Am. in order to found communistic colony, 1845; settled in St. Louis, became minister, sch. tchr.; 1st instr. drawing Washington U., St. Louis; illustrated Engelmann's the Cactaceae of the Boundary in Report of the U.S. and Mexican Boundary Survey, 1859; served with Home Guard, during Civil War; asso. with Louis Agassiz at Harvard, until 1884. Died St. Louis, 1894.

ROGERS, Charles, congressman; b. Northumberland, Saratoga County, N.Y., Apr. 30, 1800; attended Granville Acad.; grad. Union Coll., Schenectady, N.Y., 1818; studied law. Admitted to bar, did not have extensive practice; mem. N.Y. State Assembly, 1833, 37; mem. U.S. Ho. of Reps. (Whig) from N.Y., 28th Congress, 1843-45; retired from public life; became affiliated with Republican Party.

Died Sandy Hill (now Hudson Falls), Washington County, N.Y., Jan. 13, 1874; buried Union Cemetery, nr. Sandy Hill.

ROGERS, Edward, congressman, lawyer; b. Cornwall, Conn., May 30, 1787; grad. Williams Coll., 1809; grad. Yale; studied law. Admitted to bar, practiced law, Madison, N.Y.; del. N.Y. State Constl. Conv. 1822; judge Madison County Ct. Common Pleas; mem. U.S. Ho. of Reps. (Democrat) from N.Y., 26th Congress, 1839-41; engaged in literary activities. Died Galway, Saratoga County, N.Y., May 29, 1857; buried Madison Cemetery.

ROGERS, Edward Standiford, horticulturist; b. Salem, Mass., June 28, 1826; s. Nathaniel Leverett and Harriet (Wait) R.; never married. Worked in counting room of his father's firm until 1858; devoted himself to horticulture, expecially experiments in grape hybridization, Salem, 1858-99; succeeded in crossing Am. grape Vitis labrusca with European wine grape Vitis vinifera; produced 45 varieties of grapes, of which Agawam is the only one still grown. Died Peabody, Mass., Mar. 29, 1899.

ROGERS, Henry Darwin, geologist, educator; b. Phila., Aug. 1, 1808; s. Patrick Kerr and Hannah (Blythe) R.; LL.D. (hon.), U. Dublin, 1857; m. Elza Lincoln, Mar. 1854, 1 child. Lectr. in chemistry Md. Inst., Balt., 1828; prof. chemistry and natural philosophy Dickinson Coll., 1830-31; accompanied socialist Robert Dale Owen to London, Eng., 1832; became asso. Geol. Soc. of London; lectr. geology Franklin Inst., Phila., circa 1833-35; prof. geology and mineralogy U. Pa., 1835-46; dir. N.J. Geol. Survey, 1835-38, Pa. Geol. Survey, 1836-42; Regius prof. natural history U. Glasgow (Scotland), circa 1855-66; published Geology of Pennsylvania, 2 vols., 1858 (a report on the Pa. Geol. Survey which was one of the most important geol. documents of its time in Am.); advanced noteworthy ideas regarding structures of Appalachian Mountains. Author: Description of the Geology of New Jersey, 1840. Died Glasgow, May 29, 1866.

ROGERS, Henry J., telegraph pioneer, inventor; b. Balt., Mar. 10, 1811; s. John H. Rogers; attended St. Mary's Coll., Balt; m. Miss McGlennan, 4 children. Employed by Samuel F. B. Morse in constrn. of demonstration telegraph line between Balt. and Washington, D.C., 1843, apptd. telegraph operator when Balt. office opened for pub. business; an incorporator Magnetic Telegraph Co., 1845; joined N. Am. Telegraph Co., 1846, supt., 1848-52; supt. House Printing Telergaph Co. (organized 1852), 1852-55; patented marine signaling system using flags, 1844, system adopted by U.S. Navy, 1846; at outbreak of Civil War established field telegraph lines for Army of Potomac; sec. Potomac flotilla; navigation officer Washington (D.C.) Navy Yard; patented semaphore telegraph system at Washington, 1864; supt. Bankers' & Brokers' Telegraph Line, 1865-67; with So. & Atlantic Telegraph Line, 1867-73; devised flare signal code for use at night; patented insulation system for telegraph lines, 1872. Died Balt., Aug. 20, 1879.

ROGERS, Isaiah, architect; b. Marshfield, Mass., Aug. 17, 1800; s. Isaac and Hannah (Ford) R.; m. Emily Tobey, 1823, at least 2 children. Started archtl. practice, circa 1826; 1st large commn. was Tremont Hotel, Boston (1st example of luxurious, elaborately planned Am. hotel with extensive plumbing), opened 1829; architect New Astor House, N.Y.C., opened 1836; called father of the modern hotel; archtl. works include: Bank of N.Y. at Wall and William sts., Mchts. Bank, Lafayette Pl. Reformed Dutch Ch. (1836), Astor Pl. Opera House, Mchts. Exchange (1836-42) (all N.Y.C.); Bangor (Me.) House, Exchange Hotel, Richmond, Va., Battle House, Mobile, Ala., Charleston (S.C.) Hotel, 2d St. Charles Hotel, New Orleans (circa 1851), 2d Galt House, Louisville, Ky. (circa 1865), Maxwell House, Nashville, Tenn.; Protestant Episcopal Ch., Longview Insane Asylum (Cincinnati), alterations on Ohio State Capitol, Columbus; Egyptian Judah Touro meml. gate to Jewish Cemetery, Newport, R.I.; patented 3 improvements in iron bridge design, also burglar-proof safe, 1841-63; supervising architect Dept. Treasury, Washington, D.C., 1862-65 (and nominally until 1868). Died Apr. 13, 1869.

ROGERS, James, congressman; b. in what is now Goshen Hill Twp., Union County, S.C., Oct. 24, 1795; grad. S.C. Coll. (now U. S.C.), 1813; studied law. Admitted to bar, practiced in Yorkville (now York), S.C.; held various local offices; mem. U.S. Ho. of Reps. (Democrat) from S.C., 24th, 26th-27th congresses, 1835-37, 39-43. Died S.C., Dec. 21, 1873; buried in what was formerly called Irish Graveyard at Kings Creek A.R.P. Ch., nr. Newberry, S.C.

ROGERS, James Blythe, chemist, educator; b. Phila., Feb. 11, 1802; s. Patrick Kerr and Hannah (Blythe) R.; attended Coll. William and Mary, 1820-21; M.D., U. Md., 1822; m. Rachel Smith, 1830, 3 children. Supt. chemical works of Tyson and Ellicott, 1827; prof. chemistry Washington Med. Coll., Balt., circa 1827; lectured at Md. Inst.; wrote with George W. Andrews and William R. Fisher) "Minutes of an Analysis of Soup Containing Arsenic" for Jour. of Phila. Coll. of Pharmacy, 1834; wrote (with James Green) "Experiments with the Elementary Voltaic Battery" published in Am. Jour. Science and Arts, 1835; prof. chemistry med. dept. Cincinnati Coll., 1835-39; worked on Va. survey with his brother William, 1837; helped brother Henry who was conducting Pa. Geol. Survey; prof. chemistry Med. Inst. of Phila., 1841, Franklin Inst., Phila., 1844; mem. Am. Philos. Soc., 1846; became prof. chemistry U. Pa., 1847; published (with brother Robert(A Text Book on Chemistry, 1846, article "On the Alleged Insolubility of Copper in Hydrochloric Acid . . ." in Am. Jour. Science and Arts, 1848. Died Phila., June 15, 1852.

ROGERS, John, founder religious sect.; b. Milford, Conn., Dec. 12, 1648; s. James and Elizabeth (Rowland) R.; m. Elzabeth Lyme, 1670; m. 2d, Mary Ransford, 1699; m. 3d, Sarah Cole, 1714; 3 children. Became mem. 7th Day Baptists of Newport, R.I., 1674; opposed salaried clergy, use of meeting houses, ch. ritual and connections between ch. and state, slavery, use of medicines; disowned by Baptists for unorthodox doctrine, founder new sect called Rogerenes; travelled throughout New Eng. in attempt to make converts, had little success; constantly persecuted by Conn. authorities for religious beliefs; often fined, publicly whipped twice, served total of 15 years in prison. Died New London, Conn., Oct. 28, 1721.

ROGERS, John, Continental congressman; b. Annapolis, Md., 1723; had liberal schooling; studied law. Admitted to bar, practiced law; mem. Com. of Safety, 1774, 75; mem. Md. Provincial Convs., 1774-76; trustee Lower Marlboro Acad., 1775; 2d maj. of battalion Prince George's County, Md.; mem. Continental Congress from Md., 1775-76; judge Ct. of Admiralty, 1776; mem. exec. council of Md. Govt., 1777; presdl. elector, 1788, voted for Washington and Adams; chancellor Md., 1778-89. Died Upper Marlboro, Prince Georges County, Sept. 23, 1789.

ROGERS, John, congressman, mfr.; b. Caldwell, N.Y., May 9, 1813; completed prep. studies. Moved to Black Brook, Clinton County, 1832, became iron mfr.; supr. Town of Black Brook for 10 years, also held other local offices; mem. U.S. Ho. of Reps. (Democrat) from N.Y., 42d Congress, 1871-73. Died Rogers Place, nr. Ft. Edward, Washington County, N.Y., May 11, 1879; buried family burial ground on his estate at Moreau, nr. Ft. Henry, N.Y.

ROGERS, Moses, steamboat capt.; b. New London, Conn., 1779; s. Amos and Sarah (Phillips) R.; m. Adelia Smith, Feb. 18, 1804, 5 children. Commanded steamer Phoenix from Sandy Hook and Cape May to Delaware River (earliest ocean voyage of a steam vessel), 1809; commanded Eagle on 1st voyage of a steamer from N.Y.C. to Balt., 1815; obtained patents for horsepower ferryboat, 1814, 15; persuaded shipping firm Scarborough & Isaacs, Savannah, Ga., to purchase vessel Savannah 1818, superintended conversion of ship to steamer, made 1st transatlantic steamship voyage (to Liverpool, Eng.), 1819; superintended constrn. of steamer Peedee, 1820. Died Georgetown, S.C., Oct. 15, 1821; buried Georgetown.

ROGERS, Randolph, sculptor; b. Waterloo, N.Y., July 6, 1825; s. John and Sara (McCarthy) R.; m. Rosa Gibson, 1857, 9 children. Worked at Acad. of St. Mark under Lorenzo Bastolini, Florence, Italy, 1848-51; sculpted bust Night, kneeling figure Ruth; returned to Am., 1853; commn. for statue of John Adams for Mt. Auburn Cemetery, Cambridge, Mass.; received commn. for bronze doors to face corridor leading from Statuary Hall to New House wing of Capitol, Washington, D.C.; sculpted The Angle of the Resurrection, 1862, mil. monuments The Soldier of the Line, soldier's monument, Worcester, Mass., seated Lincoln, Fairmount Park, Phila. Seward, Madison Square, N.Y.C., Lost Pleiad, Genius of Conn. for state Capitol, Hartford, Conn., Nydia, Lost Arrow; forwarded most of casts representing his life work to Mus. Art and Architecture, U. Mich., Ann Arbor, Mich., 1886-88; prof. sculpture Acad. of St. Luke, Rome, Italy, 1873, councilor, 1875; decorated order of Cavaliere della Corona D' Italia, 1884; exhibited works at Centennial Exhbn., Phila., 1876; work Nydia now at Chgo. Art Inst., Lost Pleiad at art museum, San Francisco, Ruth at Met. Mus., N.Y.C.; his best work represented by Michigan and Emancipation, (figures on Detroit monument). Died Rome, Jan. 15, 1892; buried San Lorenzo Cemetery, Rome.

ROGERS, Robert, army officer; b. Methuen, Mass., Nov. 7, 1731; s. James and Mary R.; m. Elizabeth Browne, June 30, 1761, 1 child. Entered N.H. Regt., 1755; capt. William Johnson's Crown Point Expdn.; scouted enemy forces and positions; apptd. capt. of an independent co. of rangers, 1756; served with generals Loudon at Halifax, 1757, Abercombie at Ticonderoga, 1758, Amherst at Crown Point, 1759; destroyed St. Francis Indians in raid, Crown Point; in final campaign about Montreal, 1760; served as capt. of an independent co. against Cherokee Indians in S.C., 1761; supt. So. Indians; capt. of a N.Y. independent co., 1763; aided in defense of Detroit against Pontiac; involved in illicit trading with Indians; sailed for Eng. to solicit preferment, 1765; apptd. to command Ft. Michilimackinac; arrested on charge of treasonable dealings with French, acquitted for lack of evidence; returned to Eng., put in debtors prison, rescued by brother, 1769; returned to Am., 1775; imprisoned as spy by George Washington, 1776; escaped to British; fled to Eng., 1780; kept jour. from Sept. 21, 1766-July 3, 1767 printed by William L. Clements in Proceedings of the Am. Antiquarian Soc., Oct. 1918. Died London, Eng., May 18, 1795; buried St. Mary's, Newington, Eng.

ROGERS, Robert Empie, chemist, educator; b. Balt., Mar. 29, 1813; s. Patrick Kerr and Hannah (Blythe) R.; M.D., U. Pa., 1836; m. Fanny Montgomery, Mar. 13, 1843; m. 2d, Delia Saunders, Apr. 30, 1866. Connected with ry. surveying parties in New Eng., 1831-32; chemist 1st Pa. Geol. Survey; made independent analysis of limestones (with Martin H. Boye); prof. gen. and applied chemistry U. Va., 1842; devised (with brother William) new process for preparing chlorine; improved processes for making formic acid, and aldehyde, perfected method of determining carbon in graphite, studied volatility of potassium and sodium carbonates, decomposition of rocks by meteoric water, absorption of carbon dioxide by liquids; studied (with brother James) alleged insolubility of copper in hydrochloric acid; published Textbook on Chemistry, 1846; prof. chemistry Med. Sch., U. Pa., 1852, dean, 1856; asst. surgeon West Phila. Mil. Hosp.; made study of petroleum, circa 1864; investigated waste silver in Phila. mint, made suggestions about refining, 1872; prepared plans for equipment of refinery of mint, San Francisco, 1875; prof. med. chemistry and toxicology Jefferson Med. Coll., Phila., 1877-circa 1884; an original mem. Nat. Acad. Scis.; an organizer Assn. Am. Geologists and Naturalists (now A.A.A.S.). Died Phila., Sept. 6, 1884.

ROGERS, Sion Hart, congressman; b. nr. Raleigh, N.C., Sept. 30, 1825; grad. U. N.C., 1846; studied law. Admitted to bar, 1848, practiced in Raleigh; mem. U.S. Ho. of Reps. (Whig) from N.C., 33d, (Democrat) 42d congresses, 1853-55, 71-73; solicitor Raleigh dist. Superior Ct.; served as lt. 14th Regt., N.C. State Troops in Confederate Army during Civil War, 1861, col. 47th N.C. Infantry, 1862-63; elected atty. gen. N.C., 1863-66. Died Raleigh, Aug. 14, 1874; buried City Cemetery.

ROGERS, Stephen, surgeon; b. Tyre, N.Y., Jan. 1826; M.D., N.Y. Med. Coll., 1856; M.D. (hon.), U. Havana (Cuba), 1857, U. Chile, 1857; m. Miss Haveland, 1857. Surgeon in constrn. Panama R.R., 1849-55, So. R.R. of Chile, 1856-65; practiced medicine, N.Y.C., 1865-75; U.S. commr. Internat. Exhbn. of Chile, 1875; practiced medicine, Santiago, Chile, 1875-78; mem. Medico-Legal Soc. of N.Y. (pres. 1871), N.Y. Acad. Medicine, Obstet. Soc. of Berlin (Germany); described symptoms of ruptured extra-uterine pregnancy and surg. treatment for the condition (his most important med. contbn.). Died Valparaiso, Chile, May 23, 1878.

ROGERS, Thomas, locomotive mfr.; inventor; b. Groton, Conn., Mar. 16, 1792; s. John and Mary (Larrabee) R.; m. Marie Small, 5 children. Organizer (with John Clark) firm Clark & Rogers, 1819, began mfg. new loom, spinning of cotton; completed textile machine mfg. plant, Patterson, N.J., known as Jefferson Works, 1832; organizer, pres. Rogers, Ketchum & Grosvenor Machine Works, began mfg. railroad car wheels, boxes, other railroad castings, 1832, constructed locomotives, 1836, sold 1st locomotive to (given name Sandusky: 1st locomotive West of Allegheny Mountains); to Mad River & Lake Erie R.R.; credited with shifting link valve motion on locomotives in U.S.; 1st to apply wagon top boiler; initiated use of two pairs of coupled driving wheels. Died N.Y.C., Apr. 19, 1856.

ROGERS, Thomas Jones, congressman; b. Waterford, Ireland, 1781; brought to U.S., 1784; at least 1 son, William Findlay. Learned printing trade; editor, owner Northampton Farmer, 1805-14; mem. U.S. Ho. of Reps. (Democrat, filled vacancy) from Pa., 15th-18th congresses, Mar. 3, 1818-Apr. 20, 1824 (resigned); trustee Lafayette Coll., 1826-32; register and recorder of deeds Northampton County (Pa.), 1828-30; served as brig. gen. Pa. Militia; U.S. naval officer Port of Phila. Died N.Y.C., Dec. 7, 1832; buried graveyard of New Market Street Baptist Ch., Phila.; reinterred Glenwood Cemetery, 1851.

ROGERS, William Augustus, mathematician, astronomer, physicist; b. Waterford, Conn., Nov. 13, 1832; s. David Potter and Mary (Rogers) R.; M.A., Brown U., 1857; m. Rebecca Titsworth, 1857, 3 children. Instr. and tutor in mathematics Alfred Acad., 1857; prof. mathematics Alfred U., 1859, prof. indsl. mechanics, 1860-circa 1870, built and equipped astron. observatory, 1865; pursued advanced mechanics Yale; studied practical astronomy under Prof. Bond at Harvard Observatory; served with U.S. Navy 14 months at close of Civil War; asst. Harvard Observatory, 1870, asst. prof. astronomy, 1877-86; prof. physics and astronomy Colby U., 1886-98; sent to Europe by Am. Acad. Arts and Scis. to obtain copies of imperial yard and French meter; organized physical lab. with model for accurate measurements Colby U.; contbr. scientific papers to 10 vols. of Harvard Annals; did research on value of yard and meter, his changes therein among most important ever made; hon. fellow Royal Soc. of London; fellow Royal Micros. Soc., A.A.A.S.; mem. Am. Micros. Soc., pres., 1887; mem. Am. Acad. Arts and Scis., Nat. Acad. Scis. Died Waterville, Me., Mar. 1, 1898.

ROGERS, William Barton, geologist, coll. pres.; b. Phila., Dec. 7, 1804; s. Patrick Kerr and Hannah (Blythe) R.; grad. Coll. William and Mary, 1822; LL.D. (hon.), Harvard, 1866; m. Emma Savage, June 20, 1849. Conducted sch. (with brother Henry), Windsor, Md.; lectr. Md. Inst., 1827; prof. natural philosophy and chemistry Coll. William and Mary, 1828-35; prof. natural philosophy U. Va., 1835; state geologist Va., 1835-48; state insp. gas meters Mass., 1861; responsible for act incorporating Mass. Inst. Tech., 1861, 1st pres., 1862-70, pres., 1878-81; prof. emeritus of geology and physics, 1878-82; noted for work (with brother Henry) on structure of Appalachian Mountain chain. Chmn. Assn. Am. Geologists and Naturalists, 1845, 47; corr. sec. Am. Acad. Arts and Scis., 1863-69; an original mem. Nat. Acad. Scis., pres., 1878-82. Author: A Reprint of Annual Reports and Other Papers on the Geology of the Virginias. Died Boston, May 30, 1882.

ROGERS, William Crowninshield, clipper-ship capt.; b. Salem, Mass., July 26, 1823; s. Richard Saltonstall and Sarah (Crowninshield) R.; attended Harvard, A.B. (hon.), 1865; m. Mary Bowditch, July 6, 1871, 1 son, William Bowditch. Commanded ship Thomas Perkins, made passage from N.Y.C. to San Francisco in 126 days, 1849; took command clipper Witchcraft, 1851; made passage frim Rio de Janerio to San Francisco in record time of 62 days; enlisted in U.S. Navy in Civil War, assigned to command clipper barque William G. Anderson, with rank of volunteer lt.; promoted volunteer lt. comdr., 1864, resigned, 1866; instrumental in bringing about consolidation of several small lines to form Eastern R.R. Co. Died London, Eng., July 2, 1888.

ROLETTE, Jean Joseph, fur trader, jurist; b. Canada, Sept. 23, 1781; s. Jean Joseph and Angelique (Lortie) R.; m. Marguerite Dubois, 1807; m. 2d, Jane Fisher, 1819; 3 children. Partner with Murdoch Cameron in fur trade on upper Mississippi River, 1806-12; served on side of British in War of 1812; present when Brit. captured Mackinac (1812) and Prairie du Chien (1814); imprisoned by U.S. at Ft. Crawford, Prairie du Chien, Wis., 1815; agt. Am. fur Co., 1820-42; naturalized 1823; chief justice Crawford County (Wis.), 1830-42. Died Dec. 1, 1842.

ROLFE, John, colonist; b. England, 1585; s. John and Dorothea (Mason) R.; m., 1608; m. 2d, Pocahontas, Apr. 1614; m. 3d, Jane Pierce (or Pyers); 3 children. Sailed for Va. in ship Sea Adventure, 1609; began successful experimenting with Va. native tobacco, 1612; his marriage to Pocahontas brought peace with Indians for 8 years; wrote description of Va. in England for King and Sir Robert Rich (number 208 Duke of Manchester's manuscripts in Public Record Office, London); sec., recorder colony of Va., 1614-19; influential in establishing England's 1st permanent settlement in Am.; apptd. to Va. Council of State, 1621; Killed in Indian massacre. Bermuda Hundred, Va., 1622.

ROLLINS, Alice Marland Wellington, author; b. Boston, June 12, 1847; d. Ambrose and Lucy (Kent) Wellington; attended Lasell Sem.; m. Daniel M. Rollins, 1876, at least 1 son. Reviewer for N.Y. Critic; published My Welcome Beyond and Other Poems (1st published work), 1877; published volume of verse The Ring of Amethyst, 1878; books for children include: The Story of a Ranch, 1885; All Sorts of Children, 1886; The Three Tetons: A Story of the Yellowstone, 1887; The Finding of the Gentian, 1895; wrote novel Uncle Tom's Tenement (credited with some reform influence), 1888; wrote From Snow to Sunshine (volume of verse), 1889, Aphorisms for the Year, 1894, wrote Unfamiliar Quotations, 1895; stories published in Ladies Home Journal, 1897-98; published last poem Vita Benefica in Century Magazine, Feb. 1898; contbr. prose and verse to Harper's, Scribner's, and other mags.; mem. Barnard Club, Wednesday Club, Nineteenth Century Club. Died Bronxville, N.Y., Dec. 5, 1897.

ROLLINS, Edward Henry, senator; b. Rollinsford, N.H., Oct. 3, 1824; s. Daniel and Mary (Plumer) R.; m. Ellen West, Feb. 13, 1849, at least 4 children including Frank. In drug bus., Concord, N.H., 1847-61; N.H. committeeman Whig Party, 1850-53; mem. lower house N.H. Legislature, 1855-57, speaker, 1856-57; aided in merger of Know-Nothings, Free Soilers, Whigs, Anti-Slavery Democrats into Republican party; chmn. N.H. Republicans, 1856-61; chmn. N.H. delegation Rep. Nat. Conv., Chgo., 1860; mem. U.S. Ho. of Reps. (Rep.) from N.H., 37th-39th congresses, 1861-67; N.H. del. to Union Nat. Conv., Phila., 1866; mem. N.H. Rep. Com., 1868-72; asst. treas., sec. bd. dirs. U.P. R.R., 1869, became treas., 1871; mem. U.S. Senate from N.H., 1877-83; founder banking firm E.H. Rollins & Sons, Boston, 1st Nat. Bank, Concord; pres. Boston, Concord & Montreal R.R.; Died Isles of Shoals, N.H., July 31, 1889; buried Blossom Hill Cemetery, Concord.

ROLLINS, James Sidney, congressman, state polit. leader; b. Richmond, Ky., Apr. 19, 1812; s. Anthony Wayne and Sallie (Rodes) R.; attended Centre Coll., Danville, Ky., Washington Coll.; grad. Ind. U.; completed legal edn. Transylvania U., 1834; m. Mary Hickman, June 6, 1837, 11 children. Admitted to Mo. bar, 1834; practiced law, Columbia, Mo.; served as maj. during Black Hawk War; editor Columbia Patriot; mem. Mo. Ho. of Reps., 1838-40, 54, 67; interested in edn. and pub. improvements, sponsored legislation founding U. Mo., Columbia, 1839; del. Whig Nat. Conv., Balt., 1844; supported Henry Clay; mem. Mo. Senate, 1846-48; leader Whig Party in Mo., by 1848; mem. U.S. Ho. of Reps. from Mo., 37th-38th congresses, 1861-65; Whig del. to Phila. Union Conv., 1866; mem. Mo. Legislature, 1866-72, sponsored 5 statutes relating to U. Mo. and Coll. of Agr., 1867-72, known as "father of U. Mo." Died Columbia, Jan. 9, 1888; buried Columbia Cemetery.

ROLLINSON, William, engraver; b. Dudley, Worcester, Eng., Apr. 15, 1762; s. Robert and Mary (Hill) R.; m. Mary Johnson, May 10, 1782, 1 child. Came to Am., 1789; became engraver, N.Y.C., made silver ornaments, engraved portraits, bookplates, maps, certificates; made portraits of George Washington (1790) and Alexander Hamilton (1804); became banknote engraver, developed method of ruling lines by machine to prevent counterfeiting; Mason; mem. Soc. Mechanics and Tradesmen; served as lt. arty. N.Y. Militia. Died Sept. 21, 1842.

ROMAN, André Bienvenu, gov. La.; b. St. Landry Parish, La., Mar. 5, 1795; s. Jacques and Marie (Patin) Etienne; grad. St. Mary's Coll., Balt., 1815; m. Aimée Parent, 1816, 8 children. mem. La. Ho. of Reps., 1818-22, served as speaker; judge St. James Parish (La.), 1826-28; gov. La., 1831-35, 39-43, effected creation of board of public works, fund for internal improvements, used and threatened to use veto power against plunging state into debt by unsound railroad legislation, insisted on La.'s paying her bonds, 1839-43; pres. New Orleans Drainage Co., circa 1843, planned system of drainage to relieve New Orleans of swamp behind city; founded Jefferson Coll., St. James Parish 1831; responsible for constrn. of state penitentiary based on modern ideals of prison mgmt., Baton Rouge, La., endorsed incorporation New Orleans C. of C., 1834, a founder La. State Agrl. Soc., became pres.; mem. La. constl. convs., 1845, 52; sent to Europe as agt. for 2 banks to obtain extension of time for interest and renewal of bonds, 1848; Whig; del. La. Secession Conv., 1861; mem. commn. to confer with U.S. for peaceable separation, 1861; apptd. recorder of deeds and mortgages in New Orleans, 1866. Died New Orleans, Jan. 28, 1866.

ROMAN, James Dixon, congressman, lawyer; b. Chester County, Pa., Aug. 11, 1809; attended common schs., pvt. sch., West Nottingham (now Nottingham); studied law, Frederick, Md. Admitted to bar, 1834, practiced in Hagerstown, Md.; mem. Md. Senate, 1847; mem. U.S. Ho. of Reps. (Whig) from Md., 30th Congress, 1847-49; Whig presdl. elector, 1848; Democratic presdl. elector, 1856; pres. Old Hagerstown Bank, 1851-67; del. Washington (D. C.) Peace Conv., 1861. Died nr. Hagerstown, Jan. 19, 1867; buried Rose Hill Cemetery.

ROMANS, Bernard, civil engr., naturalist; b. Netherlands, 1720; m. Elizabeth Whiting, Jan. 28, 1779, at least 1 child, Hubertus. Sent to N. Am. by Brit. Govt. for engring. work, 1757; apptd. dep. surveyor Ga., 1766; went to East Fla. to survey Lord Edgmont's estates on Amelia Island and St. John's River; apptd. prin. dep. surveyor Fordham dist.; explored Fla. and Bahama banks, and West Coast as far as Pensacola, Fla.; assisted in survey of West Fla., also in map preparation, circa 1771; made bot. discoveries, became king's botanist in Fla.; elected mem. N.Y.C. Marine Soc., 1773, Am. Philos. Soc., 1774; contbd. article on Indigo to Royal American Magazine, 1774; mem. Conn. com. to take possession of Ticonderoga and its outposts, 1775; with N.Y. Com. of Safety to construct fortifications on the Hudson nr. West Point, N.Y., 1775; gave allegiance to N.Y. Provincial Congress, 1775; commd. capt. of a co. of Pa. arty., 1776; ordered to join So. Army at S.C., circa July 1780, captured and taken to Montigo Bay, Jamaica, B.W.I. Author: A Concise Natural History of East and West Florida, vol. I, 1775; The New American Military Pocket Atlas, 1776; Annals of the Troubles in the Netherlands, vol. I, 1778, vol. 2, 1782; also author printed maps, including plans of Pensacola Harbor, Mobile Bay, Tampa Bay. Died at sea, 1784.

ROMAYNE, Nicholas, physician; b. N.Y.C., Sept. 1756; s. John and Julia (McCarty) Romeyn; entered Med. Sch., King's Coll. (now Columbia), 1774; M.D., U. Edinburgh (Scotland), 1780; m. Susan Van Dam. An original mem. bd. regents Univ. State N.Y., 1784-87; prof. of practice of physic Med. Sch., Columbia, 1785-87, an original trustee Columbia, 1787-93; instructed pvt. classes, after 1787; licentiate Royal Coll. Physicians (London, Eng.); fellow Royal Coll. Physicians (Edinburgh); speculated in Western land, implicated in Blount Conspiracy of 1797, left U.S. briefly; 1st pres. Med. Soc. of City and County N.Y., 1806; founded Coll. of Physicians and Surgeons (became Columbia Coll. Phys. and Surg. 1807), pres., trustee, from 1807, prof. insts. of medicine, 1808, lectr. in anatomy, 1807-08, gave Address Delivered at the Commencement of the Lectures, published 1808; prof. insts. medicine and forensic medicine Queen's (now Rutger's) Coll., 1812-16. Died N.Y.C., July 21, 1817.

ROOSEVELT, Hilborne Lewis, organ builder, inventor; b. N.Y.C., Dec. 21, 1849; s. Silas Weir and Mary (West) R.; m. Kate Watson, Feb. 1, 1883. Pioneer in devel. of electric organ and in application of new elec. devices to organ mfg.; took out 1st patent for electric organ action, 1869; operated own factory, N.Y.C., 1872, added factories in Phila. and Balt., constructed some of largest church organs then known in U.S., including those at Grace Ch. and Trinity Ch., N.Y.C.; constructed organ for main bldg. of Phila. Centennial Exhbn., 1876 (1st electric action organ built in Am.); interested in Bell Telephone Co., invented several telephone devices including automatic switch-hook. Died N.Y.C., Dec. 30, 1886.

ROOSEVELT, James I., congressman, lawyer; b. N.Y.C., Dec. 14, 1795; grad. Columbia Coll., N.Y. C., 1815; studied law; studied fgn. law in courts England, Holland, France. Admitted to bar, 1818, practiced in N.Y.C.; councilman; mem. N.Y. State Assembly, 1835, 40; mem. U.S. Ho. of Reps. (Democrat) from N.Y., 27th Congress, 1841-43; justice N. Y. State Supreme Ct., 1851-59; ex officio judge N.Y. State Ct. Appeals, 1859; apptd. U.S. dist. atty. for Southern N.Y. by Pres. Buchanan, 1860, 61; became farmer. Died N.Y.C., Apr. 5, 1875; buried Greenwood Cemetery, Bklyn.

ROOSEVELT, Nicholas J., inventor, engr.; b. N.Y.C., Dec. 27, 1767; s. Jacobus and Annetje (Bogard) R.; m. Lydia Latrobe, Nov. 15, 1808, 9 children. Dir., N.J. (Schuyler) Copper Mine Assn., 1793; interested in steam engines and their manufacture, succeeded in inducing his assos. to purchase land in Belleville (N.J.) and erect metal foundry and shop; entered into agreement with Robert R. Livingston and John Stevens to build steamboat, engines for which were to be constructed at his foundry, circa 1797, exptl. boat Polacca attained speed equivalent to 3 miles an hour in still water; became associated with Robert Fulton in introduction of steamboats in Western Rivers, 1809, built steamboat New Orleans at Pitts., 1811; granted patent for use of vertical paddle wheels, Dec. 1, 1814. Died Skaneateles, N.Y., July 30, 1854.

ROOT, Elisha King, mechanic, inventor; b. Ludlow, Mass., May 10, 1808; s. Darius and Dorkas (Sikes) R.; m. Charlotte Chapin, Oct. 16, 1832; m. 2d, Matilda Colt, Oct. 7, 1845, 4 children. Employed by Collins Co., mfg. axes, 1832-49, supt., 1845-49, his inventions and improvements in axe mfg. machinery and methods converted co. into a modern factory; supt. Colt Armory, Hartford, Conn., 1849, designed, built factory, most of machinery, 1849-54; pres., 1862-65; adopted principle of interchangeable parts, automatic machinery was widely used; patented a drop hammer, 1853; invented machines for boring and rifling gunbarrels, for stock-turning, for splinting; patented a cam pump to raise water from Connecticut River to a reservoir in the workmen's village, 1856; trained many of Am.'s tool builders. Died Hartford, Aug. 31, 1865.

ROOT, Erastus, congressman; b. Hebron, Conn., Mar. 16, 1773; s. William and Zerviah (Baldwin) R.; grad. Dartmouth, 1793; m. Elizabeth Stockton, Oct. 4, 1806, 5 children. Mem. N.Y. State Assembly, 1798-1802, 18-22, 30; mem. U.S. Ho. of Reps. (Democrat) from N.Y., 8th, 11th, 14th, 22nd congresses, 1803-05, 09-11, 15-17, 31-33; mem. N.Y. State Senate, 1812-15, 40-44; del. N.Y. Constl. Conv. from Delaware County, 1821; lt. gov. N.Y., 1823-24; served to maj. gen. N.Y. Militia. Author: An Introduction to Arithmetic for the Use of Common Schools (first sch. book to teach decimal system of coinage), 1796. Died N.Y.C., Dec. 24, 1846.

ROOT, George Frederick, musician, educator; b. Sheffield, Mass., Aug. 30, 1820; s. Frederick Ferdinand and Sarah (Flint) R.; m. Mary Woodman, Aug. 1845, children include eldest dau., Mrs. Clara Louisa Burnham. Asst. organist Winter and Park St. churches, Boston; singing tchr. Abbotts Sch. for Young Ladies, N.Y.C., 1844; organist Mercer St. Presbyn. Ch.; singing tchr. Rutgers Female Inst., Miss Haines' Sch. for Young Ladies, Union Theol. Sem., N.Y. State Instn. for Blind; a founder N.Y. Normal Inst., 1853; trained music tchrs. in latest methods of class singing instrn. (one of most important contbns. to mus. devel. in Am.); with Root & Cady, music publishing house, Chgo., 1859-71; held classes in bldg. at U. Chgo.; author songs (under pseudonym Wurzel) Hazel Dell, Rosalee, The Prairie Flower, The Flower Queen, 1851; (under own name) The Shining Shore, The Battle Cry of Freedom, Tramp, Tramp, Tramp, the Boys are Marching, 1853-55; more than 200 other songs, 70 collections. Died Aug: 6, 1895.

ROOT, Jesse, Continental congressman, jurist; b. Coventry, Conn., Jan. 8, 1737; s. Ebenezer and Sarah (Strong) R.; grad. Princeton, 1756; LL.D., Yale; m. Mary Banks, May 18, 1758, 9 children. Licensed to preach by Hartford South Assn., 1757; admitted to Conn. bar, 1763; mem. Conn. Council of Safety; commd. capt. Conn. Militia, 1776, lt. col., adj. gen:, 1777; mem. Continental Congress, 1778-83; chmn. Conn. Council, 1780-89; state's atty., 1785-89; asst. judge Conn. Superior Ct., 1789, chief justice, 1796-1807; mem. Conn. Ho. of Reps., 1807, 09; presdl. elector, 1808; del. Conn. Constl. Conv., 1818; sch. visitor, Coventry, Conn.; mem. Am. Acad. Arts and Scis. Author: Reports of Cases Adjudged in the Superior Court and Supreme Court of Errors of Connecticut, 1789-93, published, 1798. Died Coventry, Mar. 29, 1822; buried Nathan Hale Meml. Cemetery, South Coventry, Conn.

ROOT, John Wellborn, architect; b. Lumpkin, Stewart County, Ga., Jan. 10, 1850; s. Sidney and Mary (Clark) R.; attended Oxford (Eng.) U., 1866; grad. Univ. City N.Y., 1869; m. Mary Louise Walker, 1880; m. 2d, Dora Louise Monroe, Dec. 12, 1882; 3 children. Head draftsman firm Carter, Drake, & Wight, Chgo., 1871; formed partnership with Daniel H. Burnham, 1873, firm became well known after 1875; 1st outstanding work was a house for John B. Sherman, 1874; devised system of grillage foundations which largely replaced the more expensive cut stone foundations; designer Monadnock Bldg.; cons. architect World's Columbian Exposition, Chgo., 1890, credited with final choice of a lakeside site, settlement of basic plan; organizer Western Assn. Architects; sec. A.I.A. Author: (with Russell Sturgis, Bruce Price, Donald G. Mitchell and others) Homes in City and Country (to which he contributed The City House in the West), published 1893. Died Chgo., Jan. 15, 1891.

ROOT, Joseph Mosley, congressman, lawyer; b. Brutus, Cayuga County, N.Y., Oct. 7, 1807; classical studies; studied law, Auburn, N.Y. Moved to Ohio, 1829; admitted to bar, 1830, practiced in Norwalk, Huron County, O.; elected pros. atty. Huron County, 1837; mem. Ohio Senate, 1840-41, 69; mem. U.S. Ho. of Reps. (Whig) from Ohio, 29th-31th congresses, 1845-51; assisted in organization of Republican Party; Rep. presdl. elector, 1860; apptd. U.S. atty. for No. Dist. Ohio, 1861; Dem. del. Ohio Constl. Conv., 1873. Died Sandusky, O., Apr. 7, 1879; buried Oakland Cemetery.

ROOT, Joseph Pomeroy, physician, diplomat; b. Greenwich, Mass., Apr. 23, 1826; s. John and Lucy (Reynolds) R.; grad. Berkshire Med. Coll., Pittsfield, Mass., 1850; m. Frances Evaline Alden, Sept. 1851, 5 children. Elected as Whig to Conn. Legislature, 1855; moved to Kan., 1856; chmn. Free-State Exec. Com.; elected to Kan. Senate under Topeka constn., 1857; one of pioneer corps who located public road from Topeka to Nebraska City; editorial contbr. to Wyandotte (Kan.) papers, Register, 1857, Gazette, 1858; elected Republican lt. gov. Kan., 1859; chosen an officer of 1st annual meeting of Kan. Temperance Soc., 1861; surgeon 2d Kan. Cavalry during Civil War, med. dir. Army of Frontier; presided over Kan. Rep. Conv., 1866; by Pres. Grant apptd. as minister to Chile, 1870-73, undertook on his own account to have Chile establish system of towboats in Straits of Magellan, helped during smallpox epidemic, 1872, served on Santiago (Chile) Bd. of Health, contributed his services to hosps. and private patients, laboring to improve sanitary treatment of the disease; Calle de Root (street in Santiago) named for him; elected v.p. Temperance conv., 1874; published Catechism of Money (advocating greenbackism), 1876; mem. Chilean Centennial Commn., 1876; del. Rep. Nat. Conv., 1884; mem. staff sanitarium at Clifton Srpings, N.Y., 1877-79; interested in Kan. Hist. Soc., contbd. several manuscript writings to its archives, among them a memoir of his experiences in Kan. in 1856; surgeon gen. of Kan., 1874; Mason; mem. Grand Army of Republic. Died Wyandotte, Kan., July 20, 1885.

ROOTS, Logan Holt, congressman, banker; b. nr. Tamaroa, Perry County, Ill., Mar. 26, 1841; grad. Ill. State Normal U., 1862. Assisted in recruiting 81st Ill. Volunteers; held various responsible positions in Army until end of Civil War; settled in Ark., became planter and trader; mem. U.S. Ho. of Reps. (Republican) from Ark., 40th-41st congresses, June 22, 1868-71; became banker; pres. First Nat. Bank of Little Rock (Ark.) until 1893. Died Little Rock, May 30, 1893; buried Oaklawn Cemetery.

ROPES, Joseph, mcht., privateer; b. Salem, Mass., Dec. 15, 1770; s. David and Ruth (Hathorne) R.; m. Sarah Burchmore, Feb. 3, 1801, 2 children. Commanded ship Recovery, 1794, ship John, 1797; made many voyages to China, East Indies, Arabia, France; took command of ship America (one of fastest of her time), 1809; made voyage to the Mediterranean Sea, 1st Am. mcht. to visit Constantinople, received by the Sultan who wished to negotiate a comml. treaty with the U.S.; the ship America was converted into a privateer during War of 1812, commanded 1st cruise; sailed from Salem, 1812; captured 6 prizes during the cruise valued at $158,000; chosen capt. of a co. of sea fencibles (arty. force for coastal defense); selectman Town of Salem; mem. Mass. Legislature, several terms; dir. bank, ins. co., a founder East India Marine Soc. Died Sept. 29, 1850.

RORER, David, lawyer; b. May 12, 1806; s. Abraham Rorer; m. Martha (Daniel) Martin, 1827; m. 2d, Delia Maria Viele, 1839; at least 6 children. Admitted to Va. bar, 1825; moved to Little Rock, Ark., 1826, practiced law, investigated condition of Indians, supervised constrn. mil. hwy.; pros. atty. Little Rock, resigned, 1835; moved to Burlington, Mich. Territory (now Ia.), 1836; plotted town of Burlington, drafted charter and some of ordinances. 1836-39; suggested nickname Hawkeyes for people of Ia.; admitted to Ia. bar, 1838, mem. 40 years; abolitionist, freed his own slaves; successfully defended Negro by arguing that Ia. (by the Ordinance of 1787 and the Mo. Compromise) was free territory, and that prohibition of slavery annihilated slave property, 1839; railroad atty. Burlington & Mo. River R.R. Co. (later became Chgo., Burlington & Quincy R.R.). Author: A Treatise on the Law of Judicial and Execution Sales, 1873; American Inter-State Law, 1879; A Treatise on the Laws of Railways, 1884. Died Burlington, July 7, 1884.

ROSATI, Joseph, clergyman; b. Sora (in Kingdom of Naples), Italy, 1789; completed classical studies Diocesan Sem., 1807. Received clerical tonsure, 1801, entered Congregation of the Mission in Rome, Italy, 1807, took vows, 1808; ordained priest Roman Catholic Ch., 1811; arrived in Balt. with 6 companions, July 26, 1816; arrived in Bardstown, Ky., 1816; prof. theology St. Thomas' Sem., Ky., 1817-18; opened St. Mary's Sem., Perryville, Mo. (1st instn. of classical and theol. learning West of the Mississippi River), 1818, planned and supervised constrn. of the instn. while teaching most important courses and acting as Catholic pastor in the area; became superiorship of his congregation in Am., 1820; apptd. bishop of Tenagra, vicar apostolic of Miss. and Ala., 1822; apptd. co-adjutor to bishop of La., by Pope Pius VII, 1823; received episcopal consecration, Donaldson, La., 1824; administered dioceses of New Orleans, and St. Louis, 1826-27, continued to administer Lower La. until 1830; partly responsible for establishment of the Ladies of the Sacred Heart, St. Louis, 1827, bldg. of St. Mary's Coll. at "The Barrens," 1827, opening of St. Louis Hosp. by the Sisters of Charity from Emmitsburg, Md., 1828, erection of St. Louis Coll. by Jesuits, 1829; erected Cathedral of St. Louis, 1831-34; attended Provincial Council of Balt., 1840; apostolic del. to negotiate an arrangement between the Haytian Republic and the Holy See, 1840. Died Rome, Sept. 25, 1843.

ROSE, Aquila, poet; b. England, 1695; m. Maria, 1 son, Joseph. Came to Am., before 1717; became compositor in printing office of Andrew Bradford, Phila.; obtained franchise on ferry service on Schuylkill River, Phila.; clk. Pa. Assembly, 1722; poems published posthumously as Poems on Several Occasions, 1740. Died Phila., 1723.

ROSE, Chauncey, railroad builder, philanthropist; b. Wethersfield, Conn., Dec. 24, 1794; s. John and Mary (Warner) R. Opened grist and sawmill, Rosedale, Ind., 1818; established as mcht., farmer, contractor, Terre Haute, Ind., 1825; interested in securing railroad facilities for Terre Haute, succeeded in diverting a railroad there, financed bldg. operations by pvt. subscription; pres. Terre Haute & Richmond R.R. (later became Terre Haute & Indpls. R.R.), 1847-53; promoted bldg. of other railroads through Terre Haute, including Evansville & Crawfordsville R.R., Crawfordsville br. (or Logansport div.) Terre Haute & Indpls. R.R., Terre Haute & Chgo. R.R.; directed preliminary surveys of St. Louis, Vandalia & Terre Haute R.R.; donated to Ind. State Normal Sch., Wabash Coll.; largest gifts in Terre Haute were to Providence Hosp., Rose Ladies Aid Soc., Rose Dispensary, Chauncey Rose Sch., Rose Poly. Inst. Died Terre Haute, Aug. 13, 1877.

ROSE, Edward, guide. Born of Cherokee Indian, Negro and white extraction; raised among Cherokees; became interpreter to William H. Ashley of Rocky Mountain Fur Co., 1823; made an ensign U.S. Army in action against Arikara Indians; interpreter to Gen. Henry Atkinson on treaty-making expd. up the Missouri River; at conf. with Crow Indians personally restored order after dangerous brawl; ranked as chief in a Crow village, had 4 wives; helped Zenas Leonard and other trappers recover some stolen horses, 1832; nicknamed Nez Coupe (from a scar); strengthened Crows against Blackfoot Indians, established tradition of friendship for whites. Died 1834; buried on the banks of the Missouri River nearly opposite mouth of Milk River.

ROSE, Ernestine Louise Siismondi Potowski, reformer; b. Potrkow, Russian Poland, Jan. 13, 1810; m. William E. Rose, 1829. Presided at orgn. Assn. All Classes of All Nations, Eng., 1835; came to N.Y., 1836; traveled through Eastern states. lectr. on religion, free schs., science of govt., abolition, woman's rights; worked with Women's Nat. Loyal League during Civil War; spl. interest was in obtaining justice for women; campaigned for married women's property bill in N.Y. State, 1837-48; attended nearly every N.Y. State and nat. Conv. relating to woman's rights, 1850-69, Author: Speech of Mrs. Rose . . . at the Anniversary Paine Celebration, 1850; An Address on Woman's Rights, delivered before the People's Sunday Meeting in Cochituate Hall . . . Oct. 19, 1851, published 1851. Died Brighton, Eng., Aug. 4, 1892.

ROSE, Robert Lawson, congressman; b. Geneva, N.Y., Oct. 2, 1804; s. Robert Selden Rose. Moved to Allens Hill, N.Y., became farmer; held several local offices; mem. U.S. Ho. of Reps. (Whig) from N.Y., 30th-31st congresses, 1847-51; moved to Pleasant Grove, nr. Funkstown, Washington County, Md., 1868; paper mfr., until 1877. Died Pleasant Grove, Mar. 14, 1877; buried Rose Hill Cemetery, Hagerstown, Md.

ROSE, Robert Selden, congressman, farmer; b. Amherst County, Va., Feb. 24, 1774; attended common schs.; at least 1 son, Robert Lawson. Moved to Seneca County, N.Y., 1803, settled at Fayette, nr. Geneva, became farmer; mem. N.Y. State Assembly, 1811, 20-21; mem. N.Y. State Constl. Conv., Albany, 1821; mem. U.S. Ho. of Reps. from N.Y., 18th-19th, 21st congresses, 1823-27, 29-31; became affiliated with Whig Party. Died Waterloo, Seneca County, Nov. 24, 1835; buried Old Pulteney Street Cemetery; reinterred Glenwood Cemetery, Geneva.

ROSECRANS, Sylvester Horton, clergyman; b. Homer, O., Feb. 5, 1827; s. Crandall and Jemima (Hopkins) R.; attended Kenyon Coll.; grad. St. John's Coll., 1846; attended Mt. St. Mary's Sem. of West; Doctorate in Divinity, Coll. Propaganda, Rome, Italy, 1852. Ordained priest Roman Catholic Ch., 1852; curate St. Thomas' Ch., also Cathedral, Cincinnati; tchr., rector collegiate dept. Archdiocesan Sem.; asso. editor Cath. Telegraph; named titular bishop of Pompeiopolis and coadjutor of Cincinnati by Pope Pius XI; published The Divinity of Christ, 1866; given pastorate St. Patrick's Ch., Columbus, O., 1867; elevated to new See of Columbus, 1868-78; established Cath. Columbian, 1875, regular contbr.; fostered religious confraternities; instituted St. Aloysius Sem., 1871; twice pres. Alumni Assn. St. John's Coll.; assisted in building St. Joseph's Cathedral, Columbus. Died Columbus, Oct. 21, 1878.

ROSECRANS, William Starke, army office., diplomat; b. Kingston Twp., Delaware County,

O., Sept. 6, 1819; s. Crandall and Jemima (Hopkins) R.; grad. U.S. Mil. Acad., 1842; m. Ann Eliza Hegeman, Aug. 24, 1843, 8 children. Brevetted 2d lt. of engrs., 1842; served as 2d lt. on the fortifications of Hampton Roads, Va., 1843-47; asst. prof. natural and exptl. philosophy dept. engring. U.S. Mil. Acad.; supt. repairs at Ft. Adams, Mass., also in charge of various govt. surveys and improvements, 1847-53; promoted 1st lt., 1853, resigned commn., 1854; architect and civil engr., Cincinnati; pres. Coal River Navigation Co., Kanawha County, Va. (now W. Va.), 1856; organizer Preston Coal Oil Co., mfrs. kerosene, 1857; became volunteer a.d.c. to Gen. George B. McClellan in Ohio, 1861; made col., chief engr. Dept. of Ohio, U.S.Army, 1861; apptd. col. 23d Ohio Volunteer Inf., 1861; commd. brig. gen. U.S. Army, 1861; commanded brigade, won Battle of Rich Mountain, 1861; succeeded McClellan as comdg. gen. Dept. of Ohio, 1861; chief new dept. of western Va., 1861, expelled Confederates, making formation of W.Va. possible; promoted maj. gen. U.S. Volunteers, 1862; succeeded Gen. John Pope in command Miss. Army, involved in successful engagements at Iuka and Corinth, 1862; commanded Army of the Cumberland; defeated at Battle of Chickamauga, 1863, relieved of command; commanded Dept. of Mo., 1864; brevetted maj. gen. for services at Murfreesboro, 1865; resigned from U.S. Army, 1867; U.S. minister to Mexico, 1868, 69; engaged in mining operations, Mexico, later Cal.; pres. Safety Powder Co., Los Angeles, Cal., 1875; mem. U.S. Ho. of Reps. from Cal., 47th-48th congresses, 1881-85, chmn. com. on mil. affairs; commd. brig. gen. on ret. list U.S.Army, 1889; register of the treasury, 1885-93. Died Mar. 11, 1898; buried Arlington (Va.) Nat. Cemetery.

ROSELIUS, Christian, state ofcl., univ. adminstr.; b. Bremen, Germany, Aug: 10, 1803; s. Johann Conrad and Anna (Wacker) R.; studied law under Auguste D'Avezac, New Orleans, 1826-28; married, 3 children. Came to U.S., 1823; published and edited The Halcyon (1st lit. jour. in La.), New Orleans, 1825-26; admitted to La. bar, 1828; practiced law in New Orleans, 1828-73; mem. La. Ho. of Reps., 1840; atty. gen. La., 1841-43; mem. La. Constl. Conv., 1845; mem. bd. adminstrs. U. La. (now Tulane U.), 1847-55, prof. civil law, 1850-73, dean law dept., 1865-72. Died New Orleans, Sept. 5, 1873; buried St. Louis Cemetery, New Orleans.

ROSENBERG, Henry, businessman, diplomat, philanthropist; b. Bilten, Canton Glarus, Switzerland, June 22, 1824; s. Johan Rudolph and Waldburg (Blum) Rosenberger; m. Letitia Cooper, June 11, 1851; m. 2d, Mary Ragan Macgill, Nov. 13, 1889. Came to Galveston, Tex., 1843; owner largest retail drygoods store in Galveston, 1859; organized Galveston Bank & Trust Co., 1874, sole owner, 1882-93; asso. with First Nat. Bank, Galveston City Ry. Co., Gulf, Colo. & Santa Fe Ry. Co.; founder Rosenberg Bank, 1874, pres., 1874-77; pres. Bd. of Harbor Improvements, 1869-73; alderman Galveston, 1871-71, 85-87; donated Rosenberg Sch. to City of Galveston, 1886; bd. dirs. Galveston Orphans' Home; vestryman Trinity Episcopal Ch.; contributed about half cost of Eaton Chapel, 1882; vice consul for Switzerland, 1866-69, consul, 1869-93; bequests to Galveston include: bldgs. for Island City Protestant and Israelitish Orphans' Home, Grace Episcopal Ch., sites and bldgs. for Letitia Rosenberg Woman's Home, YMCA, charity fund for German Lutheran Ch., 17 drinking fountains for men and beasts, $50,000 for Tex. Heroes' Monument, a residuary legacy provided for endowment of free public library (Rosenberg Library opened, 1904, bronze statue of him placed in front of library, 1906). Died Balt., May 12, 1893; buried Loudon Park Cemetery, Balt.

ROSS, Abel Hastings, clergyman; b. Winchendon, Mass., Apr. 28, 1831; s. Phineas and Betsey (Marshall) R.; grad. Oberlin Coll., 1857, Andover Theol: Sem., 1860; m. Mary Maria Gilman, Oct. 15, 1860. Ordained to ministry Congregational Ch., Boylston, Mass., 1861, pastor, 1861-66; pastor First Ch., Springfield, O., 1866-73, Plymouth Ch., Columbus, O., 1873-75, Port Huron, Mich., 1876-93; lectr. on ch. polity Oberlin Theol. Sem., 1871-91; Southworth lectr. on Congregationalism at Andover Theol. Sem., 1882-86; an authority on history and polity of Congl. denomination, one of its most influential leaders; advocated an advisory ecumenical Congl. council, wrote "An Ecumenical Council of the Congregational Churches," published Congl. Quarterly, 1874; had important role in Internat. Congl. Council, London, 1891. Author: The Ohio Manual; Statement of the Historical, Doctrinal and Ecclesiastical Position of the Congregational Churches, 1877; The Church of God; a Catechism, 1881; Sermons for Children, 1887; Church-Kingdom, 1887; Pocket Manual of Congregationalism, 1889; Immanuel Catechism for Infant Classes, 1893. Died Port Huron, Mich., May 13, 1893.

ROSS, Alexander, fur trader, explorer; b. Nairnshire, Scotland, May 9, 1783; s. Alexander Ross; m. "Granny Ross". Came to Can., 1804; as part of John Jacob Astor expdn. to Ore. aided in bldg. Ft. Astoria, later Ft. Okanogan, 1810-12; joined North West Co., 1814; 2d in command at Ft. George, 1816; mem. expdn. that founded Ft. Nez Perces (known as Fort Walla Walla), 1818-23; mem. Hudson's Bay Co., 1821; led an expdn. into Snake River country, 1824; penetrated Ida. as far north as mouth of Boise River, 1824; 1st sheriff Colony of Winnipeg (Man., Can.); only first-hand authority for early history of white man's occupation of Ore. Author: Adventures of the First Settlers on the Oregon or Columbia River, 1849; The Fur Hunters of the Far West, 1855; The Red River Settlement, 1856. Died Winnipeg, Oct. 23, 1856.

ROSS, Alexander Coffman, jeweler; b. Zanesville, O., May 31, 1812; s. Elijah and Mary (Coffman) R.; m. Caroline Granger, Apr. 2, 1838, 3 children. A jeweler; took what he believed to be 1st daguerreotype taken west of N.Y.; wrote Tippecanoe and Tyler, Too (to tune of Little Pigs). Died Zanesville, Feb. 26, 1883.

ROSS, Bernard Rogan, factor Hudson Bay Co.; correspondent Smithsonian Instn., shipped many specimens No. birds and mammals to instn.; little snow goose, Chen rossi, named in his honor, 1861.

ROSS, Betsy, seamstress; b. Phila., Jan. 1, 1752; d. Samuel and Rebecca (James) Griscom; m. John Ross, Nov. 4, 1773; m. 2d, Joseph Ashburn, June 15, 1777; m. 3d, John Claypoole, May 8, 1783; at least 7 children. Ran upholsterer's shop, Phila.; credited with making 1st stars-and-stripes at request of George Washington, Robert Morris and George Ross (based on family tradition 1st made public by her grandson William Canby in paper before Pa. Hist. Soc., 1870); Pa. State Navy Board ordered payment for "making ships' colours, etc.," May 29, 1777, other documentary evidence has not been found; stars-and-stripes adopted as nat. flag by resolution of Continental Congress, June 14, 1777. Died Phila., Jan. 30, 1836; buried Mt. Moriah Cemetery, Phila.

ROSS, David, Continental congressman; b. Prince Georges County, Md., Feb. 12, 1755; studied law. Apptd. by Gen. Washington as maj. of Grayson's additional Continental Regt., 1777, resigned; managed large estate of his father after his death; admitted to bar, 1783, practiced in Frederick, Md.; mem. Continental Congress from Md., 1786-88. Died Frederick County, Md., 1800.

ROSS, George, Continental congressman, jurist; b. Newcastle, Del., May 10, 1730; s. Rev: George and Catherine (Van Gezel), R.; m: Anne Lawler, Aug. 17, 1751, 3 children. Admitted to Pa. bar, 1750; prosecutor for crown, Cumberland County, Pa., 12 years; mem. Pa. Provincial Congress, Phila., 1774-77; mem. Pa. Assembly, Pa. Com. of Safety, 1775; mem. Continental Congress, 1774-77; signer Declaration of Independence; assisted in negotiating a treaty to pacify Indians of N.W. Pa.; 1776; v.p. Pa. Constl. Conv., 1776, aided in drafting declaration of rights; mem. Continental Congress, 1776-77; commd. judge Pa. Admiralty Ct., 1779. Died Lancaster, Pa., July 14, 1779; buried Christ Churchyard, Phila.

ROSS, Henry Howard, congressman, lawyer; b. Essex, N.Y., May 9, 1790; grad. Columbia Coll., N.Y.C., 1808; studied law. Admitted to bar, practiced in Essex; served as 2d lt. and adjutant 37th Infantry Regt., N.Y. State Militia in War of 1812, at battles of Boquet River (Willsboro, N.Y.) and Plattsburgh (N.Y.), rose to rank maj. gen.; mem. U.S. Ho. of Reps. (Whig) from N.Y., 19th Congress, 1825-27; judge Essex County, 1847-48; Whig presdl. elector, 1848. Died Essex, Sept. 14, 1862; buried in vault on his family place Hickory Hill, Essex.

ROSS, James, senator; b. nr. Delta, York County, Pa., July 12, 1762; s. Joseph and Jane (Graham) R.; m. Ann Woods, Jan. 13, 1791, at least 1 child. Tchr. Latin and Greek, McMillan's Acad., nr. Canonsburg (now Washington), Pa.. 1780-82; admitted to bar, 1784; atty. for Pres. Washington's estates in Western Pa.; mem. Pa. Constl. Conv., 1789-90; Federalist; apptd. fed. commr. to treat with insurgents in Whiskey Rebellion by Pres. Washington, 1794, largely responsible for peaceful settlement of uprising; mem. U.S. Senate (Federalist) from Pa., 1794-1803, pres. pro tem, 1799, defended Federalist legislation against Jeffersonian attacks, notably Excise Law and Judiciary Act of 1801, introduced series of resolutions which demanded immediate seizure of mouth of Mississippi River and fortification of its banks, 1803; pres. Pitts. Select Council, 1816-33. Died Allegheny City (now part of Pitts.), Nov. 27, 1847; buried Allegheny Cemetery, Pitts.

ROSS, John, congressman, lawyer; b. Solebury, Bucks County, Pa., Feb. 24, 1770; studied law, West Chester, Pa.; at least 1 son, Thomas. Admitted to bar, 1792, practiced in Easton, Pa.; mem. Pa. Ho. of Reps., 1800; clk. and recorder Orphans Ct., 1800-03; county register, 1800-09; burgess of Easton, 1804; mem. U.S. Ho. of Reps. from Pa., 11th, 14th-15th congresses, 1809-11, 15, Feb. 24, 1818 (resigned); pres. judge Pa. 7th Jud. Dist., 1818-30; transferred to Pa. Supreme Ct., 1830-34. Died Easton, Jan. 31, 1834; buried pvt. cemetery on family estate Ross Common, Ross Twp., Pa.

ROSS, John, (Indian name Caaweescoowe or Kooweskowe), Indian chief; b. nr. Lookout Mountain, Tenn., Oct. 3, 1790; s. David and Mary (McDonald) R.; m. Quatie, 1813; m. 2d, Mary Bryan Stapler, 1845; 1 son, William R. Sent by U.S. Indian agent on mission to Western Cherokee of Ark., 1809; adjutant of Cherokee regiment in army of Andrew Jackson, fought in battle of Horseshoe Bend against Creeks, 1812-14; mem. nat. council of Cherokee, 1817, pres., 1819-26; helped draft Cherokee constn., of 1827, elected asst. chief, 1827; elected prin. chief Eastern Cherokee, 1828-39; leader Cherokee party opposed to westward removal; led his people to new home in what is now Okla., 1838-39, helped to make constn. of 1839, united Eastern and Western Cherokee under one govt.; chief of united Cherokee Nation, 1839-66; signed treaty of alliance with Confederacy, 1861, repudiated, 1863. Died Washington, D.C., Aug. 1, 1866.

ROSS, Lawrence Sullivan, army officer, gov. Tex.; b. Bentonsport, Ia., Sept. 27, 1838; s. Capt. Shapely P. and Catherine (Fulkerson) R.; grad. Wesleyan U., Florence, Ala., 1859; m. Elizabeth Finsley, 1859, 6 children. Served as capt. of a co. of rangers, assigned to guard border and to defeat Comanche Indians, 1859; aide-de-camp with rank of col., circa 1860; commd. maj. 6th Tex. Cavalry, 1861; promoted col., May 1862; promoted brig. gen., 1864; sheriff McLennan County (Tex.), 1873-75; mem. Tex. Constl. Conv. of 1875; mem. Tex. Senate, 1881-85; gov. Tex., 1887-91, led legislature in passing laws prohibiting dealing in cotton futures, stopped sale of pub. land to corps., increased powers of land commn.; pres. Tex. A. and M. Coll., College Station, 1891-98; apptd. railroad commr., 1895, accepted, then declined. Died Waco, Tex., Jan. 3, 1898.

ROSS, Lewis Winans, congressman, lawyer; b. nr. Seneca Falls, N.Y., Dec. 8, 1812; attended Ill. Coll., Jacksonville, 1837; studied law. Admitted to bar, 1839, practiced in Lewistown, Ill.; mem. Ill. Ho. of Reps., 1840-41, 44-45; Democratic presdl. elector, 1848; mem. Ill. constl. convs., 1861, 70; mem. U.S. Ho. of Reps. (Dem.) from Ill., 38th-40th congresses, 1863-69. Died Lewistown, Oct. 20, 1895; buried Oak Hill Cemetery.

ROSS, Martin, clergyman; b. Martin County, N.C., Nov. 27, 1762; s. William Ross; m. Deborah (Clayton) Moore, 1783; m. 2d, Mary Harvey, 1806; several children. Became mem. Baptist Flat Swamp Ch., Martin County, 1782; licensed to preach, 1784; pastor, Skewarkey, N.C., 1787-96, Yoppim, N.C., 1796-1806, Bethel, N.C., 1806-27; founder Philanthropic Missionary Soc. of Kehukee Assn. Bapt. Ch., 1805; started movement which led to formation of N.C. Bapt. Conv. (1830), died before completion of orgn. Died 1827.

ROSS, Sobieski, congressman; b. Coudersport, Potter County, Pa., May 16, 1828; attended Coudersport Acad. Became civil engr., also engaged in real estate business and farming; apptd. asso. judge, 1852; mem. U.S. Ho. of Reps. (Republican) from Pa., 43d-44th congresses, 1873-77. Died Coudersport, Oct. 24, 1877; buried Eulalia Cemetery.

ROSS, Thomas, congressman, lawyer; b. Easton, Pa., Dec. 1, 1806; s. John Ross; grad. Princeton, 1823; studied law. Admitted to bar, 1829, practiced in Doylestown, Pa.; apptd. dep. atty. gen. of Pa. for Bucks County, 1829; frequently candidate on Democratic and Anti-Masonic Party tickets; mem. U.S. Ho. of Reps. (Dem.) from Pa., 31st-32d congresses, 1849-53. Died July 7, 1865; buried Doylestown Cemetery.

ROSS, Thomas Randolph, congressman, lawyer; b. New Garden Twp., Chester County, Pa., Oct. 26, 1788; completed prep. studies; studied law. Admitted to bar, practiced in Lebanon, O., 1810; mem. U.S. Ho. of Reps. (Democrat) from Ohio, 16th-18th congresses, 1819-25; lost eyesight, 1866. Died on his farm, nr. Lebanon, June 28, 1869; buried Lebanon Cemetery.

ROSSITER, Thomas Prichard, painter; b. New Haven, Conn., Sept. 29, 1818; s. Harry Caldwell and Charlotte (Beers) R.; m. Anna Ehrick Parmly, Oct. 15, 1851, 3 children. Studied and painted in

Europe, 1840-46; exhibited Salon of 1855, Paris, France, received gold medal; elected to N.A.D., 1849; noted for hist. paintings, including Washington and Lafayette at Mount Vernon, 1776, painted 1859 (now in Met. Mus. Art, N.Y.C.), The Prince of Wales and President Buchanan with Other Dignitaries at the Tomb of Washington (Nat. Gallery of Art, Washington, D.C.); made a number of large Bibl. illustrations, including Rebecca at the Well (Corcoran Gallery of Art, Washington). Died Cold Springs, N.Y., May 17, 1871.

ROTCH, Arthur, architect; b. Boston, May 13, 1850; s. Benjamin Smith and Annie Bigelow (Lawrence) R.; grad. Harvard, 1871; attended Sch. Architecture, Mass. Inst. Tech., 1871-73; attended Ecole des Beaux Arts, Paris, France, 1873; m. Lissette de Wolf Colt, Nov. 16, 1892. In charge of part of restoration and redecoration Chateau of Chenonceaux, late 1870's; formed partnership with George J. Tilden, 1880, built large houses in Boston, Washington, D.C., Bar Harbor, Me., churches of Messiah and Ascension, Boston, Ch. of Holy Spirit, Mattapan, Mass., art museum at Wellesley Coll., public libraries, Bridgewater and Groton, Mass., Eastport, Me.; trustee Boston Museum of Fine Arts; a founder Rotch Traveling Scholarship (endowed by his father, 1884) to enable draftsmen or architects to study abroad; furnished archtl. library of Mass. Inst. Tech.; financed entire 1st of Harvard Sch. Architecture (founded 1893); he left $25,000 Boston Mus. Fine Arts, $40,000 to Sch. Architecture, Mass. Inst. Tech. Died Beverly, Mass., Aug. 15, 1894.

ROTCH, William, mcht.; b. Nantucket, Mass., Dec. 15, 1734; s. Joseph and Love (Macy), R.; m. Elizabeth Barney, Oct. 31, 1754. Joined his father in whale fishery, New Salem, Mass., continued in business until 1785; owner 1st ship (the Bedford) to enter a British port flying the American flag, 1783; established whaling business, Dunkirk, France, 1785-94. Died New Bedford, Mass., May 16, 1828.

ROTHERMEL, Peter Frederick, artist; b. Luzerne County, Pa., July 8, 1817; son of Peter Rothermel; attended Pa. Acad. Fine Arts, 1840; m. Caroline Goodhart, 3 children. Dir. Pa. Acad. Fine Arts, 1847-55; active in promotion Artists' Fund Soc.; traveled and painted in Europe, 1856-59; exhbtd. Salon of Paris, 1859; contbd. to Centennial Exhbn. at Phila., 1876. Paintings include: The Battle of Gettysburg (in Hall of Trophies, Capitol Bldg., Harrisburg, Pa.), De Soto Discovering the Mississippi; (European paintings) King Lear, St. Agnes, Rubens and Van Dyck. Died at country home, Montgomery County, Pa., Aug. 15, 1895.

ROTHWELL, Gideon Frank, congressman, lawyer; b. nr. Fulton, Callaway County, Mo., Apr. 24, 1836; grad. U. Mo.; studied law. Admitted to bar, 1864, practiced in Huntsville, Mo.; mem. U.S. Ho. of Reps. (Democrat) from Mo., 46th Congress, 1879-81; practiced in Moberly, Mo.; Dem. presdl. elector, 1884; apptd. mem. bd. curators U. Mo., 1889, pres. bd. curators, 1890-94. Died Moberly, Jan. 18, 1894; buried Oakland Cemetery.

ROULSTONE, George, printer, state ofcl.; b. Boston, Oct. 8, 1767; m. Miss Gilliam. Employed as printer for Gazette (later N.C. Chronicle), Fayetteville, 1786-91; founder and publisher Knoxville Gazette (1st newspaper in Tenn.), 1791-1804; territorial printer of Tenn., 1791-96; public printer State of Tenn., 1796-1804; clk. Tenn. Legislative Council; city commr., postmaster City of Knoxville; trustee Blount Coll. (now U. Tenn.). Died Knoxville, 1804.

ROUQUETTE, Adrien Emmanuel, clergyman, poet; b. New Orleans, Feb. 13, 1813; s. Dominique and Louise (Cousin) R.; attended Transylvania U., also College Royal, Nantes, France; grad. Coll. of Rennes, Brittany, France, 1833. Ordained priest Roman Catholic Ch., 1846, preached in St. Louis Cathedral, New Orleans; preached series of anti-slavery sermons during late 1850's; missionary to the Choctaw Indians. Published Les Savanes (a collection of his poems), 1841; author book La Thebaide en Amerique, ou Apologie de la Vie Solitaire et Contemplative, 1852; published Wild Flowers: Sacred Poetry (in English), 1848; published volume of mystical verse L'Antoniade, ou la Solitude avec Tieu, 1860; other works include: Poemes Patriotiques, 1860; Catherine Tegehkivitha, 1873, La Nouvelle Atala, 1879; Critical Dialogue between Aboo and Caboo on a New Book, or a Grandissime Ascension. Died Hotel-Dieu, New Orleans, July 15, 1887.

ROUQUETTE, Francois Dominique, poet; b. Bayou Lacombe, New Orleans, Jan. 2, 1810; s. Dominique and Louise (Cousin) R.; grad. Royal Coll. of Nantes, Brittany, France, 1828; m. Laura Verret, 1846, 2 children. Opened boys sch., New Orleans, operated until 1849; opened another sch., Ft. Smith, Ark., failed opened sch., Bonfouca, La., 1852. Author (vol. of poems) Meschaeebeenes, Paris, France, (an immediate success) 1839; Flerus d'Amerique, 1856; translator The Arkansas (J.B. Bossu), (his only work in English), 1850; contbr. poems and articles to L'Abeille, also Le Propagatuer Catholique. Died Bonfouca, May 1890.

ROUSSEAU, Lovell Harrison, congressman; b. nr. Stanford, Lincoln County, Ky., Aug. 4, 1818. Admitted to bar, Bloomfield, Ind., 1841; Whig mem. Ind. Ho. of Reps., 1844-45; commd. capt. 2d Ind. Inf., 1846; capt. 2d. Ind. Regt. Volunteers, Mexican War, received spl. mention for gallantry at Battle of Buena Vista, 1847; mem. Ind. Senate, 1847-49, Ky. Senate, 1860-61; organized 5th Regt., Ky. Militia, 1861; credited with preventing sucession of Ky. from Union; commd. col. 3d Ky. Inf., 1861, brig. gen. U.S. Volunteers, 1861; served in battles of Shiloh and Perryville; promited to maj. gen. Volunteers, 1862; mem. U.S. Ho. of Reps. from Ky., 39th Congress, 1865-67; brig. gen. with brevet rank of maj. gen. U.S. Army, 1867, in charge of Dept. of La., 1868. Died New Orleans, Jan. 7, 1869; buried Arlington (Va.) Nat. Cemetery.

ROWAN, John, senator; b. nr. York, Pa., July 12, 1773; s. William and Eliza (Cooper) R.; m. Annie Lyttle, 8 children. Admitted to Ky. bar, 1795; Nelson County rep. in 2d Ky. Constl. Conv., 1799; sec. state of Ky., 1804-06; mem. U.S. Ho. of Reps. (Republican) from Ky., 10th Congress, 1807-09, obtained passage of resolutions to investigate alleged Spanish intrigues of U.S. Judge Harry Innes of Ky.; mem. Ky. Ho. of Reps. from Nelson County, 1813-17, from Jefferson County, 1822-24; judge Ky. Ct. of Appeals, 1819-21; apptd. by legislature (with John J. Crittenden) to settle boundary dispute with Tenn., 1820, apptd. (with Henry Clay) to protect state's interests in complicated dispute with Va. over occupying claimants laws, 1823; mem. U.S. Senate from Ky., 1825-31, took part in Webster-Hayne debate; under Conv. of Washington apptd. mem. commn. to adjust claims against Mexico, 1839; pres. Ky. Hist. Soc., 1838-43. Rowan County (Ky.) named for him. Died Louisville, Ky., July 13, 1843; buried family cemetery nr. Bardstown, Ky.

ROWAN, Stephen Clegg, naval officer; b. nr. Dublin, Ireland, Dec. 25, 1808; s. John Rowan; m. Mary Stark, at least 1 child, Maj. Hamilton Rowan. Came to U.S., 1818; promoted to lt., 1837; served in ship Delaware in Brazil and Mediterranean stations, 1841-44; became exec. officer ship Cyane, Pacific Station, 1845; helped retake Los Angeles during Mexican War; served 2tours of duty as ordnance insp. N.Y. Navy Yard; commd. comdr., 1855; in command steam sloop Pawnee which supplied chief defense of Washington (D.C.) during Lincoln's inauguration, 1861; directed 1st shot fired from naval vessel in Civil War against batteries at Aquia Creek, 1861; cooperated with Gen. Burn side in capture of Roanoke Island and destruction of Confederate gunboat, 1862; attacked Cable's Point on Pasquotank River, destroyed fort and captured or routed Confederate squadron, 1862; assisted army to capture New Bern, 1862; promoted capt. and commodore, 1862; commanded New Ironsides in Charleston Harbor, 1863; detached to command all naval forces in N.C. Sound, 1864; promoted rear adm., 1866; in command Norfolk (Va.) Navy Yard, 1866-67, Asiatic Squadron, 1867-70, N.Y. Navy Yard, 1872-76; gov. Naval Asylum, Phila., 1881; supt. Naval Observatory, 1882; commd. vice adm., 1870; retired, 1889. Died Washington, D.C., Mar. 31, 1890; buried Oak Hill Cemetery, Washington.

ROWE, Peter, congressman; b. Crescent, Saratoga County, N.Y., Mar. 10, 1807; grad. Schenectady (N.Y.) Acad. Became mcht.; chief auditor N.Y. Central R.R.; mayor Schenectady, 1846-50; mem. U.S. Ho. of Reps. (Democrat) from N.Y., 33d Congress, 1853-55. Died Schenectady, Apr. 17, 1876; buried Vale Cemetery.

ROWLANDS, William, clergyman, editor; b. London, Eng., Oct. 10, 1807; s. Thomas and Mary (Jones) R.; attended Ystradmeurig and Llangeitho schs. in Wales for 4 years; m. Ann Jacob, Aug. 25, 1829; m. 2d, Catherine Parry, May 17, 1838; 14 children. Taught sch. in Wales at Merthyr Tidfil and Pontypool, 1824-29; ordained to ministry Calvinistic Methodist Ch., 1832; published, edited a monthly Sunday Sch. paper, 1829-33; arrived in N.Y.C., 1836; preached to Welsh communities of N.Y.C. and Oneida County, N.Y., 1836-66; pastor, Scranton, Pa., 1856-58; began publ. monthly periodical Y Cyfaill (The Friend), 1838; Democrat, joined Republican Party, 1861; life mem. Am. Tract Soc., 1851; life dir. Am. Bible Soc., 1852. Author: Dammeg y Rab. Afradlon (vol. of sermons), 1860. Died Utica, N.Y., Oct. 27, 1866.

ROWLANDSON, Mary White, author; b. England (probably), 1635; d. John White; m. Joseph Rowlandson, circa 1656; 4 children. Captured by Indians during King Philip's War, 1675-76, returned, 1676; family moved to Wethersfield, Conn., 1677, voted an allowance of 30 pounds per year by Town of Wethersfield when her husband died; published The Soveraignty & Goodness of God, Together with the Faithfulness of His Promise Displayed; Being a Narrative of the Captivity and Restauration of Mrs. Mary Rowlandson, Cambridge (one of most widely-read pieces of 17th century prose), 1682. Died Wethersfield, 1678.

ROWSE, Samuel Worcester, artist; b. Bath, Me., Jan. 29, 1822; s. Edward and Mercy (Blake) R.; never married. Lithographer, portrait artist, Boston, circa 1840-80, N.Y.C., 1880-1901; did portraits mostly in crayon; portraits include Nathaniel Hawthorne, Ralph Waldo Emerson, James Russell Lowell; visited England, 1872. Died Morristown, N.J., May 24, 1901.

ROWSON, Susanna Haswell, novelist, actress, educator; b. Portsmouth, Eng., 1762; d. Lt. William and Susanna (Musgrave or Musgrove) Haswell; m. William Rowson, 1787, childless, adopted at least 1 daughter. Published 1st novel Victoria, 1786; produced novel Charlotte, a Tale of Truth (better known as Charlotte Temple), 1791, Rebecca, or the Fille de Chambre, 1792; appeared on stage in Edinburgh, Scotland, other cities, 1792-93; acted in Phila., Balt., Annapolis, Md., 1793-96; began conducting select school for young ladies in or nr. Boston, 1797; editor Boston Weekly Mag., 1802-05; published novel Charlotte's Daughter, or The Three Orphans (better known as Lucy Temple), 1828; pres. Boston Fatherless and Widows Soc. Died Boston, Mar. 2, 1824.

ROYALL, Anne Newport, traveler, author; b. Md., June 11, 1769; d. William Newport; m. William Royall, 1797. Began traveling in U.S. and publishing accounts of her journeys, 1824; tried and convicted on charge of being a common scold, Washington, D.C., 1829; propr. and editor of Paul Pry (small, independent newspaper), Washington, 1831-36, The Huntress, 1836-54, tried to uncover graft in any dept. of government; published 10 volumes of travels between 1826-31, including Sketches of History, Life and Manners in the United States, by a Traveller (1st and best), 1826; works considered valuable sources of study of social history of United States; other writings include: The Tennessean, a Novel Founded on Facts, 1827; The Black Book, or a Continuation of Travels in the U. S., Washington, 1828; The Black Book, or Sketches of History, Life and Manners in the United States, 3 vols., 1829; Letters from Alabama, 1830. Died Washington, Oct. 1, 1854; buried Congressional Cemetery, Washington.

ROYCE, Homer Elihu, congressman, jurist; b. East Berkshire, Franklin County, Vt., June 14, 1819; attended local acads. of St. Albans and Enosburg, Vt.; studied law. Admitted to bar, practiced in East Berkshire, 1844; mem. Vt. Ho. of Reps., 1846-47; Vt. pros. atty., 1848; mem. Vt. Senate, 1849-51, 61, 68; mem. U.S. Ho. of Reps. (Republican) from Vt., 35th-36th congresses, 1857-61; elected asso. justice Vt. Supreme Ct., 1870, apptd. chief justice, 1882-90 (resigned). Died St. Albans, Vt., Apr. 24, 1891; buried Calvary Cemetery, East Berkshire.

ROYCE, Sarah Eleanor Bayliss, pioneer; b. Stratford-on-Avon, Eng., 1819; came to U.S., circa 1820; acad. edn.; m. Josiah Royce, Sr., before 1847; children—Ruth, Mary, Harriet, Josiah. Moved with husband from N.Y. State to Ia., 1848, then to Salt Lake City, 1849; traveled to Cal., 1849, arrived in San Francisco, Jan. 1850; moved with family to Grass Valley, Nevada County, 1855, there organized and taught sch. in her home; returned to San Francisco, 1866; a Puritan mystic. Author: A Frontier Lady (edited by R.H. Gabriel, pub. 1932).

ROYE, Edward James, pres. Republic of Liberia; b. Newark, O., Feb. 3, 1815; s. John Roye. Went to Liberia with stock of goods, 1846, became leading mcht. in country, exported African products to England and U.S., considered richest man in Liberia, 1870; speaker Liberian Ho. of Reps., 1849; chief justice of Liberia, 1865-68; inaugurated 5th pres. Republic of Liberia, 1871; went to England to settle boundary dispute and conducted negotiations for the loan, agreeing to rectification of boundary that practically gave back to England land that Liberia had bought; accused of embezzling some money from English loan to Liberia; deposed from office, 1871, summoned to trial before supreme court but escaped. Died nr. Monrovia, Liberia, Feb. 12, 1872.

RUBLEE, Horace, diplomat, journalist; b. Berkshire, Vt., Aug. 19, 1829; s. Alvah and Martha (Kent) R.; attended U. Wis., circa 1850; m. Kate Hopkins, 1856/57, at least 2 children. Reported session of Wis. State Legislature for Madison (Wis.)

Argus, 1852; became editorial writer Wis. State Journal, 1853, owner half-interest, 1854-69; a sec. 1st Wis. Republican Conv., 1854; state librarian Wis., 1856-57; chmn. Wis. Rep. Com., 1859-69, 77; del. Rep. Nat. Conv., 1868; U.S. minister to Switzerland (apptd. by Pres. Grant, 1869-77; temporary ed. Daily Advertiser, Bos., 1879; organized co. to purchase Daily Milw. News (a Democratic morning paper), became editor under new name Republican and News; co. bought Milw. Sentinel, 1882, editor, editorial writer, 1883-89. Died Milw., Oct. 19, 1896.

RUCKER, D.H., army officer; b. Mich.; married, at least 1 child, Irene (wife of Gen. P.H. Sheridan). Commd. 2d lt. First Dragoons, 1837; served in Mexican War; trans. to Q.M.'s Dept., 1849, became q.m.-gen. U.S. Army; comd. govt. relief party on Feather River in No. Cal., supplying food to emigrants, including J.G. Bruff; kept a jour., Report.

RUDERSDORFF, Hermine, soprano; b. Ivanovsky, Ukraine, Dec. 12, 1822; studied in Paris, France, Milan, Italy; m. Dr. Küchenmeister, 1844 (div.); m. 2d, Maurice Mansfield, 1850, 1 son, Richard M. Made 1st appearances in concerts in Germany, 1840; sang in opera at Karlsruhe, then at Frankfort and Breslau, Germany, 1841-52, Friedrich Wilhelmstädtisches Theatre, Berlin, Germany, 1852-54, Drury Lane Theatre, London, Eng., 1854-65; came to Am. to participate in Boston Jubilees of 1871-72; settled in Boston, became known as tchr. Died Boston, Feb. 26, 1882.

RUFFIN, Edmund, agriculturist, publisher; b. Prince George County, Va., Jan. 5, 1794; s. George and Jane (Lucas) R.; attended Coll. William and Mary, 1810; m. Susan Travis, 1813, 11 children. Assumed charge of Coggin's Point farm, 1813; mem. Va. Senate (1st as Whig, then Democrat), 1824-27; published essay "Calcareous Manures," 1832; published and edited Farmers Register (an agrl. jour. which helped arouse interest in farming), 1833-43; early advocate of fertilizing and crop rotation; a founder Prince George Soc. in Va., a leader in move to form local socs. to oppose protective tariffs; apptd. mem., 1st corr. sec., 1st Va. State Bd. Agr., 1841, agrl. surveyor of S.C., 1842; published Report of the Commencement and Progress of the Agricultural Survey of South Carolina, 1843; pres. Va. State Agrl. Soc., 1852-54, commr., 1854; wrote and spoke much on agrl. improvement for newspapers, farm jours., agrl. socs., including Address on the Opposite Results of Exhausting and Fertilizing Systems of Agriculture, 1853, Premium Essay on Agricultural Education, 1853; one of 1st secessionists in Va.; wrote pamphlet The Political Economy of Slavery, probably 1858; advocate of direct trade with Europe, attended 3 So. comml. convs., served as chmn. Va. delegation at conv. held in Montgomery, Ala., 1858; originated League of United Southerners; served as volunteer with Palmetto Guard of Charleston, 1861-65, fired 1st shot from Morris Island against Ft. Sumter. Committed suicide after fall of Confederacy, Redmoor, Amelia County, Va., June 18, 1865; buried Marlbourne, Hanover County, Va.

RUFFIN, Thomas, jurist; b. "Newington," King and Queen County, Va., Nov. 17, 1787; s. Sterling and Alice (Roane) R.; grad. Coll. of N.J. (Princeton), 1805; m. Anne Kirkland, Dec. 9, 1809, 14 children. Admitted to N.C. bar, 1808; rep. from Borough of Hillsboro to N.C. House of Commons (Jeffersonian Republican), 1813, 15, 16, speaker, 1816; judge Superior Ct. of N.C., 1817-19, 25-28, 58; reporter N.C. Supreme Ct., 1820-21; pres. State Bank, 1828; asso. justice N.C. Supreme Ct., 1829-33, chief justice, 1833-52; represented N.C. at Washington (D.C.) Peace Conf., 1861; del. to N.C. Secession Conv., 1861, offered a compromise between ordinance of revolution and outright secession; responsible for 2 important departures in equity from English precedents, the rejection of doctrine of part performance as a basis for decreeing the specific execution of a verbal contract for sale of land, also the discarding of the doctrine of vendor's lien upon land sold upon credit; trustee U. N.C., 1813-31, 42-68; pres. N.C. Agrl. Soc., 1854-60. Died Hillsboro, N.C., Jan. 15, 1870.

RUFFIN, Thomas, congressman; b. Louisburg, Franklin County (formerly part Edgecombe County), N.C., Sept. 9, 1820; grad. law dept. U. N.C., 1841. Admitted to bar, 1841, practiced in Goldsboro, N.C.; circuit atty. Mo. 7th Jud. Dist., 1844-48; returned to Goldsboro, 1850; mem. U.S. Ho. of Reps. (Democrat) from N.C., 33d-36th congresses, 1853-61; del. Confederate Provisional Congress, Richmond, 1861; col. 1st N.C. Cavalry in Confederate Army in Civil War; mortally wounded in action at Bristoe Station, nr. Alexandria, Va. Died while prisoner of war at Alexandria, Oct. 13, 1863; buried pvt. cemetery on Ruffin homestead, nr. Louisburg.

RUFFNER, Henry, clergyman, coll. pres.; b. Shenandoah County, Va., Jan. 16, 1790; s. David and Ann (Brumbach) R.; grad. Washington Coll., Lexington, Va., 1813, LL.D. (hon.), 1849; D.D. (hon.), Princeton, 1838; m. Sarah Lyle, Mar. 31, 1819, 4 children including Henry. Pastor, Timber Ridge Presbyn. Ch., Lexington, 1819-31; tchr. Washington Coll., 1819-48, pres., 1836-48; submitted plan for orgn. entire ednl. system of pub. instrn. at ednl. conv., Lexington, 1842; argued for confinement of slavery to region East of Blue Ridge. Author: Early History of Washington College, Vol. I; A Discourse on the Duration of Future Punishment, 1823 Against Universalism, 1833; (pamphlet) Address to the People of West Virginia. . . Showing that Slavery is Injurious to the Public Welfare, and that it May be Gradually Abolished, without Detriment to the Rights and Interests of Slave Holders, by a Slaveholder of West Virginia, 1847; The Fathers of the Desert, 2 vols., 1850. Died Malden, Kanawha County, Va., Dec. 17, 1861.

RUGGLES, Benjamin, senator, lawyer; b. Abington, Windham County, Conn., Feb. 21, 1783; completed prep. studies; studied law. Admitted to bar, practiced in Marietta, O., 1807; moved to St. Clairsville, Belmont County, O.; pres. judge Ct. Common Pleas for 3d Jud. Circuit, 1810-15; mem. U.S. Senate (Democrat) from Ohio, 1815-33; Whig presdl. elector, 1836; also became farmer. Died St. Clairsville, Sept. 2, 1857; buried Union Cemetery.

RUGGLES, Charles Herman, congressman, lawyer; b. New Milford, Conn., Feb. 10, 1789; completed prep. studies; studied law. Admitted to bar, practiced in Kingston, N.Y.; mem. N.Y. State Assembly, 1820, also at later date; mem. U.S. Ho. of Reps. from N.Y., 17th Congress, 1821-23; circuit judge, vice chancellor N.Y. State 2d Jud. Dist., 1833-46; moved to Poughkeepsie, N.Y.; mem. N.Y. State Constl. Conv., 1846; judge Dutchess County (N.Y.) Ct.; judge Ct. Appeals, 1847-55. Died Poughkeepsie, June 16, 1865.

RUGGLES, John, senator, lawyer; b. Westboro, Mass., Oct. 8, 1789; grad. Brown U., 1813; studied law. Admitted to bar, practiced in Skowhegan, Me., 1815; moved to Thomaston, Me., 1817; mem. Me. Ho. of Reps., 1823-31, speaker, 1825-29, 31; justice Me. Supreme Jud. Ct., 1831-34; mem. U.S. Senate (Democrat, filled vacancy) from Me., Jan. 20, 1835-41, framed bill for reorgn. U.S. Patent Office, 1836; became inventor, orator, writer. Died Thomaston, June 20, 1874; buried Elm Grove Cemetery.

RUGGLES, Nathaniel, congressman; b. Roxbury, Mass., Nov. 11, 1761; grad. Harvard, 1781; studied law. Admitted to bar, practiced in Roxbury; apptd. judge of gen. sessions, 1807; Mass. chief justice, 1808; mem. U.S. Ho. of Reps. (Federalist) from Mass., 13th-15th congresses, 1813-19. Died Roxbury, Dec. 19, 1819.

RUGGLES, Samuel Bulkley, lawyer; b. New Milford, Conn., Apr. 11, 1800; s. Philo and Ellen (Bulkley) R.; grad. Yale, 1814, LL.D. (hon.), 1859; m. Mary Rosalie Rathbone, May 25, 1822, 3 children. Admitted to N.Y. bar, 1821; practiced in N.Y.C.; bought land and converted it into residential dist., Gramercy Park, 1831; active in promoting creation of Union Square; a commr. Croton Aqueduct; elected to lower house N.Y. State Legislature, 1838, chmn. ways and means com.; wrote Report upon Finances and Internal Improvements of the State of New York, 1838; a founder of Bank of Commerce, N.Y., 1839; canal commr. N.Y. State, 1839-58, pres. commn., 1840; had part in building of N.Y. & Erie R.R.; U.S. del. to Internat. Statis. Congress, Berlin, Germany, 1863, The Hague, Netherlands, 1869, Internat. Monetary Conf., Paris, France, 1867; trustee Columbia, 1836-81, a founder Sch. Polit. Science; trustee Astor Library; mem. N.Y. State C. of C.; mem. gen. conv. of Protestant Episcopal Ch. Author: The Duty of Columbia College to the Community, 1854; also reports Internationality and International Congresses, 1869, International Coinage, 1867, International Coinage: Supplemental Report, 1870. Died Fire Island, N.Y., Aug. 28, 1881.

RUGGLES, Timothy, army officer; b. Rochester, Mass., Oct. 20, 1711; s. Rev. Timothy and Mary (White) R.; grad. Harvard, 1732; m. Bathsheba Bourne, 1736; 7 children including Bathsheba. Mem. Mass. Gen. Ct., 1736; mem. Mass. Legislature, 1739-52, almost continuously until 1770, speaker, 1762-63; became justice of peace, circa 1753; commd. col. of a regt. Mass. Militia, 1755, brig. gen., 1758, took part in invasion of Can.; apptd. judge of common pleas for Worcester County (Mass.), 1757, chief justice, 1762-75; elected pres. at Stamp Act Congress of 1765, refused to sign petitions drawn up; mem. Council by the King's Mandamus, 1774; attempted to form an assn. of Loyalists pledged not to "acknowledge or submit to authority of any congress, com. of correspondence or any other unconstl. assemblies of men"; apptd. by Gen. Howe to command 3 cos. of volunteers to be called Loyal Am. Associates; banished from Mass. and his lands confiscated by Act of 1778; moved to an estate in Wilmot, N.S., Can., 1783. Died Wilmot, Aug. 4, 1795.

RUMFORD, Count, see Thompson, Benjamin.

RUMSEY, Benjamin, Continental congressman, jurist; b. Bohemia Manor, Cecil County, Md., Oct. 6, 1734; attended Princeton. Mem. Md. Conv., 1775; mem. com. to prepare instructions to Md. dels. in Congress; mem. com. to raise supplies for provincial forces; apptd. col. Lower Battalion of Harford County by Provincial Conv., 1776; mem. Council of Safety, 1776; mem. Continental Congress from Md., 1776-78; chief justice Md. Ct. Appeals, 1778-1805. Died Joppa, Hartford County, Md., Mar. 7, 1808; buried Old St. John's Cemetery.

RUMSEY, David, congressman, lawyer; b. Salem, Washington County, N.Y., Dec. 25, 1810; attended Hobart Coll.; studied law. Admitted to bar, 1831, practiced in Bath, Steuben County, N.Y.; surrogate Steuben County, 1840-44; held many local offices; mem. U.S. Ho. of Reps. (Whig) from N.Y., 30th-31st congresses, 1847-51; del. N.Y. State Constl. Conv., 1867; mem. commn. to propose amendments to .Y. State Consn., 1872; became asso. justice N.Y. State Supreme Ct., 1873. Died Bath, Mar. 12, 1883; buried pvt. cemetery on Rumsey place.

RUMSEY, Edward, congressman, lawyer; b. Botecourt County, Va., Nov. 5, 1796; completed prep. studies, Hopkinsville; studied law. Admitted to bar, practiced law, Greenville, Ky.; held several local offices; mem. Ky. Ho. of Reps., 1822; Whig presdl. elector, 1836; mem. U.S. Ho. of Reps. (Whig) from Ky., 25th Congress, 1837-39. Died Greenville, Apr. 6, 1868; buried Old Caney Station Cemetery, nr. Greenville.

RUMSEY, James, inventor; b. Bohemia Manor, Cecil County, Md., Mar. 1743; s. Edward and Anna (Cowman) R.; 1st wife unknown; m. 2d, Mary Morrow; 3 children. Began operating grist mill, Sleepy Creek, Md., 1782; opened (with a friend) gen. store, engaged in bldg. trade, Bath (now Berkley Springs), W. Va., 1783-84; accepted position as supt. constrn. of canals Potomac Navigation Co., 1785; began to experiment with steam engine, 1785, experimented in bldg. steamboat, 1783; exhibited boat propelled by streams of water forced out through stern, steam engine being employed to operate the force pump on Potomac River, nr. Sherpherdstown, W. Va., 1787; Rumseian Soc. formed to promote Rumsey's projects which included improved saw mill, improved grist mill, improved steam boiler, 1781; sent by Rumseian Soc. to Eng. to patent his improvements and to interest English capital; secured English patents on boiler and steamboat, 1788, secured U.S. patents 1791. Died (shortly before his 2d steamboat was completed) London, Eng., Dec. 20, 1792; buried St. Margaret's Churchyard, nr. Westminster, Eng.

RUNK, John, congressman, mcht.; b. Milltown (now Idell), Hunterdon County, N.J., July 3, 1791; attended dist. schs. Took charge mills and gen. store on his father's property, Milltown; mem. Bd. Chosen Freeholders from Kingwood, 1825-33; high sheriff Hunterdon County, 1836-38; Whig presdl. elector, 1840, 48; mem. U.S. Ho. of Reps. (Whig) from N.J., 29th Congress, 1845-47; unsuccessful candidate for gov. N.J., 1850; moved to Lambertville, Hunterdon County, 1854, became mcht., in milling business. Died Lambertville, Sept. 22, 1872; buried Rosemont (N.J.) Cemetery.

RUPP, Israel Daniel, educator, historian; b. East Pennsboro (now Hampden) Twp., Cumberland County, Pa., July 10, 1803; s. George and Christina (Boeshor) R.; m. Caroline Aristide, July 19, 1827, 8 children. Opened subscription sch. at Silver Spring, Pa., 1825, then at Mechanicsburg, Pa.; sch. master Cumberland, Dauphin, Lancaster counties, Pa., 1827-60; published Geschichte der Martyrer, nach dem. Ausfuhrlichen original des Ehrw. Johann Fox und anderer kurz gefasst, besonders fur den gemeinen deutschen Mann in den Uer. Staaten von Nord-America aus dem Englischen ubersetzt, 11 works inclusive, 1830; editor Carlisle (Pa.) Herald, 1833, Practical Farmer, 1837. Author: History of Religious Denominations of the United States, 1844; The Geographical Catechism of Pennsylvania and the Western States, 1836; The Farmer's Complete Farrier, 1843; Events in Indian History, 1842; Early History of Western Pennsylvania, 1846; Collection of Names of Thirty Thousand German and Other Immigrants to Pennsylvania from 1727-1776, 1856; Genealogy of the Descendants of John Jonas Rupp, 1874, also numerous histories of counties in Pa. Died Phila., May 31, 1878.

RUSH, Benjamin, physician, Continental congressman, humanitarian; b. Phila., Jan. 4, 1746; s. John Harvey and Susanna (Hall) R.; A.B., Coll. of N.J. (now Princeton), 1760; studied medicine under Dr. John Redman, 1761-66; attended 1st lectures of Dr. William Shippen and Dr. John Morgan in Coll. of Phila.; M.D., U. Edinburgh (Scotland), 1768; m. Julia Stockton, Jan. 11, 1776, 13 children including James, Richard. Returned to Phila., 1769, began practice of medicine; prof. chemistry Coll. of Phila., 1769-91, also prof. theory and practice, 1789; published A Syllabus of A Course of Lectures on Chemistry (1st Am. text on chemistry), 1770, reissued 1773; published anonymously Sermons to Gentlemen upon Temperance and Exercise (one of 1st Am. works on personal hygiene) 1772; mem. Am. Philos. Soc.; published An Address to the Inhabitants of the British Settlements in America, upon Slave-Keeping, 1773; an organizer Pa. Soc. for Promoting the Abolition of Slavery, 1774, pres. 1803; elected to Pa. Provincial Conv., 1776; mem. Continental Congress, 1776-77, signer Declaration of Independence; apptd. surgeon gen. Armies of the Middle Dept. Continental Army, 1777; became lectr. U. State of Pa., 1780; mem. staff Pa. Hosp., 1783-1813; established 1st free dispensary in Am., 1786; recognized as the "instaurator" of the Am. temperance movement; persuaded the Presbyns. to found Dickinson Coll., 1783, served as trustee; mem. Pa. Conv. which ratified U.S. Constn. 1787, with James Wilson led successful fight for adoption; with James Wilson inaugurated a campaign which secured a more liberal and effective constn. for Pa., 1789; apptd. treas. U.S. Mint by Pres. John Adams, 1797-1813; became prof. the Institutes Medicine and Clin. Practice, U. Pa., 1792, prof. theory and practice, 1796; a founder Phila. Coll. Physicians, 1787; thought to be pioneer worker in exptl. physiology in U.S.; 1st Am. to write on cholera infantum, 1st to recognize focal infection of the teeth; greatly contributed to the establishment of Phila. as the leading Am. center of med. tng. during 1st half of 19th century. Author: Medical Inquiries and Observations, initial vol., 1789; An Account of the Bilious Remitting Yellow Fever, As It Appeared in the Essays, Literary, Moral and Philosophical, 1798; Medical Inquiries and Observations upon the Diseases of the Mind, 1812. Died Phila., Apr. 19, 1813; buried Christ's Church Graveyard, Phila.

RUSH, Jacob, jurist; b. Phila., Dec. 1746; grad. Princeton, 1765, LL.D., 1804. Judge, Ct. of Errors and Appeals, 1784-1806; pres. City Ct. of Common Pleas, 1806. Author: Charges on Moral and Religious Subjects, 1803; Christian Baptism, 1819. Died Phila., Jan. 5, 1820.

RUSH, James, physician, psychologist; b. Phila., Mar. 15, 1786; s. Dr. Benjamin and Julia (Stockton) R.; grad. Coll. of N.J. (now Princeton), 1805; M.D., U. Pa., 1809; postgrad. U. Edinburgh (Scotland); m. Phoebe Ridgway, Oct. 19, 1819. Began practice of medicine, Phila., 1811; concerned with devel. of psychology as an objective science; left his estate to Library Company of Phila. to establish Ridgway branch. Home: Chestnut St., Phila. (1869). Author: The Philosophy of the Human Voice, 1827; Hamlet, A Dramatic Prelude, 1834; Brief Outline of an Analysis of the Human Intellect, 2 vols., 1865; Rhymes of Contrast on Wisdom and Folly, 1869. Died Phila., May 26, 1869.

RUSH, Richard, cabinet officer; b. Phila., Aug. 29, 1780; s. Dr. Benjamin and Julia (Stockton) R.; grad. Coll. of N.J. (now Princeton), 1797; m. Catherine Eliza Murray, Aug. 29, 1809, 10 children. Admitted to Pa. bar, 1800; apptd. atty. gen. of Pa., 1811; Republican; became comptroller U.S. Treasury, 1811; U.S. atty. gen., 1814-17; U.S. sec. of state, 1817; U.S. minister to Gt. Britain, 1817-24, negotiated treaty of joint occupation of Oregon, sent dispatches which were an important factor in persuading James Monroe and John Quincy Adams to proclaim Monroe Doctrine, 1823; U.S. sec. of treasury, 1825-28; commd. (with Gen. Benjamin Chew Howard to settle boundary dispute between Ohio and Mich., 1835; U.S. agt. to secure Smithson bequest to U.S. (which established Smithsonian Instn., Washington, D.C.), 1836-38; U.S. minister to France, 1847-49, decided to recognize republic set up in 1848 without waiting for instructions from Washington; mem. Am. Philos. Soc. Author: John Randolph Abroad and at Home (under pseudonym Julius), 1828; Memoranda of a Residence at the Court of London, 1st edit., 1833, 2d edit., 1845; Occasional Productions, Political, Diplomatic, and zmiscellaneous, 1860; Washington in Domestic Life; editor The Laws of the United States, 5 vols., 1815. Died Phila., July 30, 1859.

RUSH, William, sculptor; b. Phila., July 4, 1756; s. Joseph and Rebecca (Lincoln) R.; m. Martha Wallace, Dec. 14, 1780. Renowned especially for figureheads carved to adorn prows of ships, including "America" for U.S. frigate America, "Nature" for the Constellation, "Genius of the United States" for the United States, "Indian Trader" for the William Penn, "River God" for the Ganges; carved life-size statue of Washington (now in Independence Hall, Phila.) originally intended as figurehead for a ship to be named Washington; his most notable work is the "Spirit of the Schuylkill" (1st public fountain figure erected in U.S.), the original wood carving was placed in Center Square (now Penn Square) to commemorate the founding of the Phila. water system; did a life-size group in work, "Liberty Crowning the Bust of Washington"; a founder Pa. Acad. Fine Arts (earliest orgn. of its kind in U.S.), 1805, a dir., 1805-33; 1st native Am. sculptor. Died Phila., Jan. 17, 1833.

RUSK, Jeremiah McLain, gov. Wis., cabinet officer; b. Morgan County, O., June 17, 1830; s. Daniel and Jane (Faulkner) R.; m. Mary Martin, Apr. 5, 1849; m. 2d, Elizabeth M. Johnson, Dec. 1856; 5 children. Held various jobs in Ohio and Wis., as constrn. foreman, tavern keeper, owner stageline, sheriff, coroner, until 1861; mem. Wis. Assembly, 1861-62; commd. maj. 25th Wis. Inf., 1862; took part in seige of Vicksburg, 1863; commd. lt. col. U.S. Volunteers, 1863, brevetted col. and brig. gen., 1865; bank controller State of Wis., 1865, 67-69; mem. U.S. Ho. of Reps. (Republican) from Wis., 42d-44th congresses, 1871-77; gov. Wis., 1882-89; U.S. sec. agr. under Benjamin Harrison, 1889-93, secured inspection of all Am. meat exports with consequent eradication of cattle and swine diseases, prepared way for European removal of restrictions on meat imports. Died Viroqua, Wis., Nov. 21, 1893; buried Viroqua Cemetery.

RUSK, Thomas Jefferson, senator; b. Pendleton Dist., S.C., Dec. 5, 1803; s. John and Mary (Sterritt) R.; m. Mary F. Cleveland, 1827, 7 children. Admitted to bar; began practice of law, Clarksville, Ga., 1825; became partner of John Cleveland in mere. bus., circa 1828; elected capt. of a co. of rangers, circa 1835, joined Stephen F. Austin, San Antonio, Tex.; apptd. col., authorized to raise men, arms, food in East Tex.; signer Declaration of Independence for Tex. in Conv. of 1836, aided in drafting and adoption of Constn. of Republic of Tex.; elected sec. of war Provisional Govt. of Tex., 1836; took command of Army Republic of Tex. after Battle of San Jacinto, 1836; apptd. sec. of war Republic of Tex. under Houston, 1837; mem. Ho. of Reps. in 2d Congress of Republic of Tex., 1838; elected maj. gen. Militia of Republic of Tex., 1838, cleared East Tex. of hostile Indian tribes, 1838-39, promoted brig. gen., maj. gen., 1843; chief justice Supreme Ct. of Republic of Tex., 1838-42; favored annexation of Tex. to U.S., pres. Tex. Conv. which confirmed annexation and formulated Constn. of 1845; mem. U.S. Senate from Tex., Feb. 21, 1846-July 29, 1857, supported adminstrn. in Mexican War, sponsored final settlement of Tex. debt, 1854, pres. pro tem, 1857. Committed suicide, Nacogdoches, Tex., July 29, 1857; buried Oak Grove Cemetery, Nacogdoches.

RUSS, John, congressman; b. Ipswich, Mass., Oct. 29, 1767; completed prep. studies. Moved to Hartford, Conn., became mcht.; mem. U.S. Ho. of Reps. (Democrat) from Conn., 16th-17th congresses, 1819-23; elected to Conn. Ho. of Reps., 1824; elected judge Hartford Probate Ct., 1824-30. Died Hartford, June 22, 1833; buried Old North Cemetery.

RUSS, John Denison, physician, educator of the blind, penologist; b. Essex, Mass., Sept. 1, 1801; s. Dr. Parker and Elizabeth (Cogswell) R.; grad. Yale, 1823, M.D., 1825; m. Eliza Phipps Jenkins, 1830; m. 2d, Elsie Birdsell, 1872. Began practice medicine, N.Y.C., 1826; sailed for Greece in charge of a shipload of food sent by Am. sympathizers, 1827, remained until 1830 as distbr. of food, organizer of hosps.; with Dr. Samuel Akerly and Samuel Wood established a sch. called N.Y. Instn. for the Blind, opened 1832, tchr., bus. mgr., 1832-35; an organizer Prison Assn. of N.Y., 1843-53, sec., 1845-53, also its investigator of conditions in city and state prisons; a corporator N.J. Juvenile Asylum (now Children's Village of Dobbs Ferry), 1851, supt., 1853-58; invented the phonetic alphabet. Home: Pompton, N.J. Died Pompton, Mar. 1, 1881; buried Essex, Mass.

RUSSELL, Benjamin, journalist; b. Boston, Sept. 13, 1761; s. John Russell; m. Esther Rice, Sept. 21, 1783; m. 2d, Guest Campbell, 1803; 3 children. With William Warden began publ. of Mass. Centinel and Republican Jour., 1784, became sole owner, editor, 1786-1828, title shortened to Mass. Centinel, later changed to Columbian Centinel, 1790; Federalist; leader among the Boston mechanics who influenced the Mass. Conv. in favor of ratification of U.S. Constn., 1789; denounced adminstrns. of Jefferson and Madison, pres. Printers' Mut. Protective Soc.; founder Charitable Mechanic Assn., 1795, pres., 1808-17; pres. Boston Bd. Health, mem. Sch. Com., Common Council, alderman (all Boston); mem. Mass. Ho. of Reps., 1828-35; mem. Mass. Senate from Suffolk County, 1822, 25, Mass. Exec. Council, 1836, 37. Died Boston, Jan. 4, 1845.

RUSSELL, Benjamin, artist; b. New Bedford, Mass., 1804. Went to sea on whaling ship, during 1840's; specialized in painting marine scenes in watercolor; painted panorama of a whaling voyage around the world, exhibited in Boston, 1849, later in Cincinnati, Louisville (Ky.), Balt., St. Louis, N.Y.C. Died circa 1870.

RUSSELL, David Abel, congressman, lawyer; b. Petersburg, N.Y., 1780; completed prep. studies; studied law. Admitted to bar, practiced in Salem, N.Y.; apptd. justice of peace,1807; admitted to practice as counselor, 1809; dist. atty. for N.Y. Northern Jud. Dist., 1813; mem. N.Y. State Assembly, 1816, 30, 33; mem. U.S. Ho. of Reps. (Whig) from N.Y., 24th-26th congresses, 1835-41. Died Salem, Nov. 24, 1861; buried Evergreen Cemetery.

RUSSELL, David Allen, army officer; b. Salem, N.Y., Dec. 10, 1820; s. David Abel and Alida (Lansing) R.; grad. U.S. Mil. Acad., 1845. Served in U.S. Army under Gen. Scott's Army during Mexican War; brevetted 1st lt., 1847; commd. 1st lt., 1848, capt., 1854; col. 7th Mass. Volunteers; commd. brig. gen. U.S. Volunteers, 1862; assigned to command of a brigade in VI Corps, Army of Potomac, 1862, participated in battles of Fredericksburg, 1862, Gettysburg, 1863, Rappahannock Station, Va., 1863; fought in all battles of Grant's campaign of 1864 from the Wilderness to Petersburg; brevetted maj. U.S. Army for gallantry at Battle of Williamsburg, brevetted full maj. 8th Inf. at Battle White Oaks, lt. col. for service in Peninsular Campaign, maj. gen., 1864. Killed in battle of Opequan, nr. Winchester, Va., Sept. 19, 1864.

RUSSELL, Irwin, poet; b. Port Gibson, Miss., June 3, 1853; s. Dr. William McNab and Elizabeth (Allen) R.; grad. St. Louis U., 1869. Admitted to Miss. bar, 1872; one of 1st to recognize literary possibilities of Negro dialect and character; with New Orleans Times, 1879. Author:(poem) Ships from the Sea (one of 1st poems in Negro dialect), in Port Gibson Standard, 1871; (poem) Uncle Cap Interviewed, pub. in Scribner's Monthly, 1876; also The Cemetery and many other poems, published in mags. including St. Nicholas, Appleton's Jour., Popular Science Monthly, Puck. Died New Orleans, Dec. 23, 1879.

RUSSELL, James McPherson, congressman, lawyer; b. York, Pa., Nov. 10, 1786; attended James Ross's classical acad., Chambersburg, Pa.; studied law; at least 1 son, Samuel Lyon. Admitted to Franklin County bar, 1807, Bedford County bar, 1808; practiced in Bedford, Pa.; 1st burgess Bedford Borough, 1818-19; mem. Pa. Constl. Conv., 1837; mem. U.S. Ho. of Reps. (Whig, filled vacancy) from Pa., 27th Congress, Dec. 21, 1841-43; trustee Bedford Acad.; sec. Chambersburg & Bedford Turnpike Co. Died Bedford, Nov. 14, 1870; buried Bedford Cemetery.

RUSSELL, Jeremiah, congressman, banker; b. Saugerties, N.Y., Jan. 26, 1786. Became mcht., also in real estate and banking; served several times as supr.; Democratic presdl. elector, 1836; mem. N.Y. State Ho. of Reps., 1842; mem. U.S. Ho. of Reps. (Democrat) from N.Y., 28th Congress, 1843-45; resumed banking. Died Saugerties, Sept. 30, 1867; buried Mountain View Cemetery.

RUSSELL, John, congressman; b. Branford, Conn., Sept. 7, 1772; attended public sch.; studied medicine. Practiced medicine short time, Cooperstown, N.Y.; clk. Otsego County (N.Y.), 1801-04; mem. U.S. Ho. of Reps. from N.Y., 9th-10th congresses, 1805;09; Clinton presdl. elector, 1812; became mcht. Died Cooperstown, Aug. 2, 1842; buried Christ Churchyard.

RUSSELL, John Henry, naval officer; b. Frederick, Md., July 4, 1827; s. Robert Grier and Susan Hood (Worthington) R.; grad. U.S. Naval Acad., 1848; m. Cornelia Pierpont Treadway, 1864, 3 children. Commd. midshipman U.S. Navy, 1841; assigned to North Pacific Exploring Expdn. as acting navigator and lt. in sloop Vincennes under Cadwalader Ringgold, 1853; commd. master, 1855, lt., 1855; ordnance duty Washington (D.C.) Navy Yard, 1857-61, 64; sent to Norfolk (Va.) Navy Yard to assist in saving Union Vessels from capture by Confederates, 1861; commanded boat expdn., destroyed privateer Gudah, Pensacola, Fla., 1861; given command of steamer Kennebec in Rear Adm. David Farragut's Squadron, 1861, participated in all operations of Farragut's squadron up Mississippi River to Vicksburg, 1861-62; commd. lt. comdr., 1862, commanded Kennebec in blockade of Mobile and Pontiac in South Atlantic Blockading Squadron; commanded ship Cyane, 1865; promoted comdr., 1867, capt., 1874, commodore, 1883, rear adm., 1886; rescued shipwrecked passengers and crew of steamer Continental in Gulf of California, 1869; command Mare Island Navy Yard, 1883-86. Died Washington, D.C., Apr. 1, 1897.

RUSSELL, Jonathan, congressman, diplomat; b. Providence, R.I., Feb. 27, 1771; s. Jonathan and Abigail (Russell) R.; grad. with highest honors, R.I. Coll. (now Brown U.), 1791; m. Sylvia Ammidon, Apr. 3, 1794; m. 2d, Lydia Smith, Apr. 21, 1817; 8 children. Engaged in merc. bus., 1791-1810; apptd. by Madison as chargé d'affaires Paris (France), 1810, chargé d'affaires London (Eng.), 1811; a peace commr. to negotiate and conclude treaty of peace with Gt. Britain; U.S. minister to Sweden and Norway, Stockholm, 1814-18, elected to Mass. Gen. Ct., 1820; mem. Mass., Constl. Conv., 1820; mem. U.S. Ho. of Reps. (Democrat) from Mass., 17th Congress, 1821-23. Died Boston, Feb. 17, 1832; buried Forest Hills, Mass.

RUSSELL, Joseph, congressman; b. N.Y.; had limited schooling. Sheriff, Warren County, N.Y., 1834-37; mem. N.Y. State Assembly, 1840; mem. U.S. Ho. of Reps. (Democrat) from N.Y., 29th, 32d congresses, 1845-47, 51-53.

RUSSELL, Joseph, whaler; b. Dartmouth (now New Bedford) Mass., Sept. 27, 1719; s. Joseph and Mary (Tucker) R.; m. Judith Howland, 1744, 11 children. Prominent in devel. whaling industry in New Eng.; owner ships which made whaling voyages and traded with West Indies, by 1775; a pioneer in mfg. spermaceti candles; supported Am. Revolution; most of his ships and bldgs. burned by Brit. when they raided New Bedford, 1778; his ship Rebecca made 1st whaling voyage around Cape Horn to the Pacific hunting grounds, 1791-93. Died Oct. 16, 1804.

RUSSELL, Mother Mary Baptist (baptized Katherine), founder Sisters of Mercy in Cal.; b. Newry, Ireland, Apr. 18, 1829; d. Authur and Margaret (Mullan) Russell; ed. schs., Killowen and Belfast, Ireland. Joined Inst. of Mercy, Kinsale, Ireland, 1848, took final vows, 1851; named superior of colony of 8 selected nuns and novices who enlisted for the archdiocese of San Francisco, 1854; arrived in San Francisco, 1854; established (with assistance of Archbishop Alemany) a convent and sch., 1855; given charge of county hosp. where cholera victims were isolated, 1855, bought bldg., named it St. Mary's Hosp., 1857; superior Sisters of Mercy in Cal., 1854-67, 70-76, guiding counselor to other superiors, established orphanages for boys and girls, a Magdalen Asylum, a home for destitute aged, a convent sch. and orphanage at Grass Valley (1863), St. Peter's and St. Anthony's Sch., Oakland, Cal., St. Hilary's Sanitarium, Marin County, Cal. (1897); supr. smallpox hosp. during epidemic of 1868; furnished nurses at the Presidio during Spanish Am. War, 1898; went to Ireland to obtain novices, 1878. Died San Francisco, Aug. 6, 1898.

RUSSELL, Osborne, pioneer, trapper; b. Hallowell, Me., June 12, 1814. Engaged with a fur co. operating in Wis. and Minn., circa 1830-33; joined Nathaniel J. Wyeth in his 2d expdn. to the Rocky Mountains, participated in bldg. of Ft. Hall, Ida., 1834; went to Ore. with Dr. Elijah White's emigrant party, 1842; chosen mem. exec. com. Ore. Provisional Govt., 1844; gold prospector, Cal., 1848-49; operated 2 trading vessels between Sacramento, Cal. and Portland, Ore., 1855. His jour. published as Journal of A Trapper or Nine Years in the Rocky Mountains, 1834-43, 1914. Died Placerville, Cal., 1865.

RUSSELL, Samuel Lyon, congressman; b. Bedford, Pa., July 30, 1816; s. James McPherson Russell; attended Bedford Acad.; grad. Washington Coll., Pa., 1834; studied law. Admitted to bar, 1837, practiced in Bedford; pros. atty. Bedford County, Pa. in 1840's; mem. U.S. Ho. of Reps. (Whig) from Pa., 33d Congress, 1853-55; became a Republican, 1856; mem. Pa. Constl. Conv., 1873; mem. town council and sch. bd.; trustee cemetery assn. Died Bedford, Sept. 27, 1891; buried Bedford Cemetery.

RUSSELL, William, congressman; b. Ireland, 1782. Came to U.S., settled in West Union, O.; held several local offices; mem. Ohio Ho. of Reps., 1809-10, 11-13, Ohio Senate, 1819-21; mem. U.S. Ho. of Reps. from Ohio (as Jackson Democrat), 20th-22d, (as Whig) 27th congresses, 1827-33, 41-43; moved to Portsmouth, Scioto County, O.; retired to his farm on Scioto Brush Creek. Died on his farm Scioto Brush Creek, Sept. 28, 1845; buried church burying ground, Rushtown, Scioto County.

RUSSELL, William, educator; b. Glasgow, Scotland, Apr. 28, 1798; s. Alexander and Janet (Jamieson) R.; attended U. Glasgow, 1811-15; m. Ursula Wood, Aug. 22, 1821. Sailed for Ga., 1817; conducted pvt. sch. in connection with Chatham Acad., Savannah, Ga., 1818-20, prin. acad., 1821-22; conducted sch. in New Twp. Acad. bldg., New Haven, Conn., 1822; became headmaster Hopkins Grammar Sch., 1825; 1st editor Am. Jour. Edn., 1826; established sch. for girls in connection with Germantown Acad., Phila., 1831; organized 1st tchrs.' assn. in Phila., 1831; founded Jour. of Edn., Phila., 1832; established, ran sch. for girls, Phila., 1833-38, with James E. Murdoch opened a sch. for speech, Boston, 1839; taught elocution, oratory Phillips Acad., Andover, Mass., Andover Theol. Sem. Abbot Acad., 1842-44; lectr. Theol. Inst., East Windsor, Conn., circa 1842-82; founder, condr. Merrimack (N.H.) Normal Inst. (pvt. normal sch.), 1849-52; opened New Eng. Normal Inst., Lancaster, Mass., 1853, closed 1855; an organizer Am. Inst. of Instrn. Author: Manual of Mutual Instruction, 1826; Lesson in Enunciation, 1830; Orthophony; or the Cultivation of the Voice, 1845. Died Lancaster, Aug. 16, 1873.

RUSSELL, William Eustus, gov. Mass.; b. Cambridge, Mass., Jan. 6, 1857; s. Charles Theodore and Sarah Elizabeth (Ballister) R.; grad. Harvard, 1877; grad. summa cum laude, Boston U. Law Sch., 1879; m. Margaret Manning Swan, June 3, 1885, 3 children. Admitted to Mass. bar, Apr. 1880; mem. Cambridge Common Council, 1881, alderman, 1882, 83, mayor, 1884-87; pres. alumni Boston Law Sch., 1884; gov. Mass., 1890-92 (1st gov. to campaign through the small towns); returned to pvt. law practice, 1894; del. Dem. Nat. Conv., Chgo., 1896. Died St. Adelaide, Que., Can., July 16, 1896; buried Cambridge.

RUSSELL, William Fiero, congressman, banker; b. Saugerties, Ulster County, N.Y., Jan. 14, 1812; completed prep. studies. Became mcht., banker; founder, pres. Saugerties Bank; postmaster Saugerties, 1836-41; mem. N.Y. State Assembly, 1851; mem. U.S. Ho. of Reps. (Democrat) from N.Y., 35th Congress, 1857-59; apptd. naval agt. for Port of N.Y.C., 1859. Died Saugerties, Apr. 29, 1896; buried Mountain View Cemetery.

RUSSELL, William Henry, diplomat; b. Nicholas County, Ky., Oct. 9, 1802; s. Robert Spottswood and Deborah (Allen) R.; m. Zanette Freeland, 1830. Mem. Ky. Legislature, 1830; U.S. marshall Dist. of Mo. (included Indian Country), 1841-45; joined wagon-train of Cal. emigrants, 1846, elected capt. of co., later displaced, left train with 8 others and followed John Fremont's track of 1845, arriving in Cal., late 1846; became maj. Fremont's Cal. Battalion; a peace commr. who framed Treaty of Cahuenga, Jan. 13, 1847; sec. of state Cal., Jan.-Mar. 1847; prin. witness for Fremont during his ct. martial, 1847; practiced law, San Jose, Cal., 1849-54; U.S. consul at Trinidad, Cuba, 1861-65. Died Washington D.C., Oct. 13, 1873; buried Oak Hill Cemetery, D.C.

RUSSELL, William Hepburn, founder Pony Express; b. Burlington, Vt., Jan. 31, 1812; s. William Eaton and Myrtella (Hepburn) R.; m. Harriet Elliot Warder, June 9, 1835, 5 children. Formed partnership with Alexander Majors and W.B. Waddell, 1854, firm became Majors, Waddell, 1858, operated freight bus. out of Leavenworth, Kan.; obtained contract to supply army ordered to Utah, 1857; with John S. Jones started a stage line from Leavenworth to Denver, 1859; pres. of co. chartered Central Overland Cal. and Pike's Peak Express Co., 1860-61; with Alexander Majors began operation of a Pony Express carrying mail between Sacramento, Cal. and St. Joseph, Mo. in 10 days, 1860; went to Washington to obtain funds for his venture, became involved in biggest financial scandal of the time by accepting $870,000 in bonds taken from the Indian Trust Fund by Sec. War John B. Floyd, indicted 1861, indictment dismissed; sold Pony Express Co., 1862; attempted new start, N.Y.C. Died Palmyra, Mo., Sept. 10, 1872.

RUSSWURM, John Brown, gov. Negro colony; b. Port Antonio, Jamaica, Oct. 1, 1799; son of white Am. father and Nergo mother; grad. Bowdoin Coll., 1826; m. dau. of Lt. Gov. McGill (of Monrovia); 4 children. Established Freedom's Jour. (one of 1st Negro papers in U.S.), N.Y.C., 1827; abolitionist; emigrated to Liberia, 1829,, became supt. schs.; editor, publisher Liberia Herald, 1830-34; gov. Md. colony established by Md. State Colonization Soc. at Palmas, Africa, 1836-51; instrumental in union of Liberia and the Md. colony; promoted trade, agriculture, took census (1843), established a ct. with presiding justices. Died Monrovia, Liberia, June 17, 1851.

RUST, Albert, congressman, lawyer; b. Va.; completed prep. studies; studied law. Admitted to bar, practiced in El Dorado, Ark.; mem. Ark. Ho. of Reps., 1842-48, 52-54; mem. U.S. Ho. of Reps. (Democrat) from Ark., 34th, 36th congresses, 1855-57, 59-61; brig. gen. Confederate Army during Civil War. Died El Dorado, Apr. 3, 1870; buried Old Methodist Cemetery.

RUTGERS, Henry, army officer, philanthropist; b. N.Y.C., Oct. 7, 1745; s. Hendrick and Catharine (dePeyster) R.; grad. King's Coll. (now Columbia), 1766. Supported Sons of Liberty; served as capt. 1st Regt., N.Y. Militia, Battle of White Plains, 1776, resigned command 1st Regt., 1795; mem. N.Y. Assembly, 1784, 1800; raised fund of $28,000 for constrn. 1st Great Wigwam of Tammany Hall, N.Y.C., 1811; gave land for 2d free sch. established for city's poor; pres. Free Sch. Soc., 1828-30; regent U. State N.Y., 1802-26; trustee Princeton, 1804-17; trustee Queen's Coll., 1816-21, also benefactor, name changed to Rutgers Coll. in his honor, 1825; pres. bd. corp. Dutch Reformed Ch.; gave land to Rutgers Street Presbyn. Ch., opened 1798. Died N.Y.C., Feb. 17, 1830.

RUTHERFORD, Robert, congressman; b. Scotland, Oct. 20, 1728; attended Royal Coll. of Edinburgh. Came to Am., settled in Berks County, Tenn., later moved to Va.; high sheriff Federick County (Va.), 1743-44; held several local offices; del. to convs. in Richmond, 1775, Williamsburg, 1776; mem. Va. Senate, 1776-90; mem. U.S. Ho. of Reps. from Va., 3d-4th congresses, 1793-97; settled on his estate Flowing Spring, nr. Charles Town, Va. (now W. Va.). Died Charles Town, Oct. 1803; buried Flowing Spring.

RUTHERFURD, John, senator; b. N.Y.C., Sept. 20, 1760; grad. Princeton, 1779; studied law. Admitted to bar, practiced law, N.Y.C., 1784; moved to farm, nr. Allamuchy, Warren County, N.J., 1787; presdl. elector, 1788; mem. N.J. Gen. Assembly, 1788-89; mem. U.S. Senate (Federalist) from N.J., 1791-Dec. 5, 1798 (resigned); pres. East Jersey Bd. Proprs., 1804-40; apptd. by N.Y. State Legislature as commr. to lay out area North of 14th St., N.Y.C., 1807-11; moved to farm (named Edgerston) on Passaic River (between Belleville and Passaic), 1808; apptd. by N.J. Legislature as commr. to determine route and cost of canal to connect Delaware and Raritan rivers, 1816; a commr. to determine boundary lines between N.J. and N.Y. State and N.J. and Pa., 1826-33; del. Anti-Masonic Conv., Balt., 1831. Died at his home Edgerston, N.J., Feb. 23, 1840; buried family vault in burying ground Christ Ch., Belleville, N.J.

RUTHERFURD, Lewis Morris, astrophysicist; b. Morrisania, N.Y. Nov. 25, 1816; s. Robert Walter and Sabina (Morris) R.; grad. Williams Coll., 1835; m. Margaret Stuyvesant Chamler, July 22, 1841, 7 children. Admitted to N.Y. bar, 1837; practiced law N.Y.C., 1837-49; began work in astronomical photography and spectroscopy, 1856; invented a photographic telescope, 1858; made his 1st attempt at classification of stellar spectra, 1862; made many photographs of sun and moon and various star fields; trustee Columbia, 1858-84, responsible for establishing dept. of geodesy and astronomy, 1881, donated all his equipment to Columbia. Died N.Y.C., May 30, 1892.

RUTLEDGE, Ann, probably born New Salem, Ill. Lived in New Salem at same time as Abraham Lincoln; engaged to John McNamar; became tentatively engaged to Lincoln during McNamar's long absence from New Salem, on condition that she receive honorable release from McNamar; died of brain fever before this occurred; her acquaintance with Lincoln became topic of many romantic and folk stories which distorted relationship and made legend of Lincoln's supposed "true love." Died New Salem, Aug. 25, 1835.

RUTLEDGE, Edward, gov. S.C.; b. Charlestown (now Charleston) or Christ Church Parish, S.C., Nov. 23, 1749; s. Dr. John and Sarah (Hext) R.; m. Henrietta Middleton, Mar. 1, 1774; m. 2d, Mary Shubrick Eveleigh, Oct. 28, 1792; 3 children including Henry Middleton. Admitted to Middle Temple, London, Eng., 1767, called to the English bar, 1772; returned to S.C. as a barrister, 1773; mem. Continental Congress, 1774-77, 79 (did not reach Phila. due to ill health, 1779), mem. 1st bd. of war, 1776, voted for resolution of independence, July 2, 1776, signed Declaration of Independence, 1776; member of the 1st, 2d S.C. provincial congresses, 1775-76; capt. S.C. Arty., 1776; fought at Beaufort, 1779, captured at fall of Charleston, imprisoned by British, 1780-81; one of the St. Augustine "exiles", Sept. 1780-July 1781; mem. S.C. Ho. of Reps., 1782, 86, 88-92, drew up bill proposing confiscation of Loyalist properties, 1782, author act abolishing law of primogeniture, 1791; investor in plantations as partner of brother-in-law Charles Cotesworth Pinckney; Federalist presdl. elector, 1788, 92, 96; mem. S.C. Senate from Charleston, 1796, 98; gov. S.C., 1798-1800. Died Charleston, Jan. 23, 1800.

RUTLEDGE, John, governor S.C., congressman; b. Charlestown (now Charleston), S.C., Sept. 1739; s. Dr. John and Sarah (Hext) R.; studied at Middle Temple, London, Eng.; m. Elizabeth Grimke, May 1, 1763, 10 children. Mem. S.C. Ho. of Commons, 1761-76; atty. gen. S.C. pro tem, 1764-65; mem. Stamp Act Congress, 1765, chmn. com. which wrote meml. and petition to Ho. of Lords; mem. Continental Congress from S.C., 1774-76, 82-83, led successful fight to eliminate rice from boycott list, advocated home rule in colonies; mem. S.C. Council of Safety, 1776; a writer S.C. Constn. of 1776; pres. S.C. Gen. Assembly, 1776-78, vetoed new S.C. Constn. which would substitute a senate elected by people instead of legislative council and resigned; gov. S.C., 1779-82, given emergency powers in times of invasion, 1780, restored civil govt., 1781; issued proclamation which suspended use of currency, forbade suits for debts, offered pardon to Brit. supporters on condition that they serve 6 months militia duty; mem. S.C. Ho. of Reps., 1781-82, 84-90; declined appointment as U.S. minister to Holland, 1783; judge S.C. Chancery Ct., 1784; mem. U.S. Constl. Conv., 1787, chmn. com. of detail; mem. S.C. Conv. to ratify U.S. Constn., 1788; sr. asso. justice U.S. Supreme Ct., 1789-91; chief justice

S.C. Supreme Ct., 1791-95; nominated chief justice U.S. Supreme Ct., 1795, served at Aug. term (Senate refused to confirm his appointment, 1795). Died Charleston, July 23, 1800; buried St. Michael's Cemetery, Charleston.

RUTLEDGE, John, Jr., congressman; b. Charleston, S.C., 1766; attended schs. in Charleston and Phila.; studied law with his father. Admitted to bar, circa 1787, practiced in Charleston; became planter; mem. S.C. Ho. of Reps., 1788-94, 1811; mem. U.S. Ho. of Reps. (Federalist) from S.C., 5th-7th congresses, 1797-1803; commanded company of 28th Regt., S.C. Militia, 1799, promoted maj., in command of regt., 1804, served as its comdr. in War of 1812; in command of 7th Brigade, 1816-19. Died Phila., Sept. 1, 1819.

RYALL, Daniel Bailey, congressman, lawyer; b. Trenton, N.J., Jan. 30, 1798; attended Trenton Acad.; studied law. Admitted to bar, 1820, practiced in Freehold, Monmouth County, N.J.; mem N.J. Gen. Assembly, 1831, 33-35, speaker, 1833-35; mem. U.S. Ho. of Reps. (Democrat) from N.J., 26th Congress, 1839-41. Died Freehold, Dec. 17, 1864; buried Maplewood Cemetery.

RYAN, Abram Joseph, clergyman, poet; b. Hagerstown, Md., Feb. 5, 1838; s. Matthew and Mary (Coughlin) R.; studied theology Niagara U. Entered novitiate of Vincentian Fathers, 1854; ordained priest Roman Catholic Ch., 1856; taught at Niagara U. and at diocesan sem., Cape Girardeau, Mo., circa 1857-62; chaplain Confederate Army, 1862-65; ministered to smallpox victims at Gratiot Prison, New Orleans; became recognized poet of the Confederacy with poems In Memory of My Brother, In Memoriam, The Conquered Banner, Sword of Robert E. Lee, The Lost Cause, Gather the Sacred Dust, March of the Deathless Dead; edited ephemeral Pacificator, Augusta, Ga.; edited The Banner of the South; edited Cath. weekly The Star, New Orleans; pastor St. Mary's Ch., Mobile, Ala., 1870-83; other poetical works include: Father Ryan's Poems, 1879; Poems, Patriotic, Religious and Miscellaneous, 1880; A Crown for Our Queen, 1882. Died Franciscan Monastery, Louisville, Ky., Apr. 22, 1886; buried Mobile.

RYAN, Dennis, actor, theatrical co. mgr.; b. Ireland. Made Am. debut at theater on East Baltimore St., Balt., 1782, mgr., 1783, toured with company to John Street Theatre, N.Y.C., 1783; presented 1st Am. profl. prodn. of Sheridan's School for Scandal, Bal., 1784; managed season in Charleston, S.C., 1785. Died 1786.

RYAN, Edward George, jurist; b. New Castle House, County Meath, Ireland, Nov. 13, 1810; s. Edward and Abby (Keogh) R.; ed. Clongowes Wood Coll., 7 years; m. Mary Graham, 1842; m. 2d, Caroline Willard Pierce, 1850; at least 3 children. Came to U.S., 1830; admitted to N.Y. bar, 1836; del. 1st Wis. Constl. Conv., 1846; partner law firm James G. Jenkins and Matthew H. Carpenter, in Wis.; chief justice Wis. Supreme Ct., 1874-80. Episcopalian. Author: Address Delivered Before the Law Class of the University of Wisconsin, 1873. Died Madison, Wis., Oct. 19, 1880.

RYAN, Stephen Vincent, clergyman; b. Lanark County, Ont., Can., Jan. 1, 1825; s. Martin and Catherine (McCarthy) R.; attended St. Mary's Sem. at the Barrens, Mo., 1844-49. Arrived in Pottsville, Pa., 1828; joined Congregation of the Mission (Lazarists, Vincentians), 1844; ordained priest Roman Catholic Ch., 1849; instr. St. Mary's Sem. at the Barrens, 1849-51; prof. and rector at Lazarist Coll. of SMT Vincent, Cape Girardeau, Mo.; elected visitor gen. of his order in Am. at a gen. synod in Paris, 1857; established a new motherhouse and novitiate of the order at Germantown, Pa., and St. John's Coll., Bklyn., 1867; consecrated bishop by Pope Pius IX, 1868; founder Cath. Union of Buffalo 1872 merged with Cath. Times of Rochester as Cath. Union and Times, 1881); tried to improve Our Lady of Angels Sem. at Niagara (N.Y.), to promote secondary schs., and to build parochial schs. Author: Claims of a Protestant Episcopal Bishop to Apostolic Succession and Valid Orders Disproved, 1880; Early Lazarist Missions and Missionaries, 1887. Died Buffalo, Apr. 10, 1896.

RYDER, Thomas Philander, organist; b. Cohasset, Mass., June 29, 1836; studied with Gustav Satter. Organist, Tremont Temple, Boston, many years; composer of light and popular piano music. Died Somerville, Mass., Dec. 2, 1887.

RYKEN, Theodore James, founder religious order; b. Elshout, Holland, Aug. 30, 1797. Became sec. to Le Sage-ten-Broek. 1822; made pilgrimage to Rome, Italy, 1826; decorated for his work during cholera epidemic in Groningen (Netherlands) by Pope Leo XII, 1826; joined Trappist Order, 1827; came to U.S., 1831-34; returned to Europe to establish teaching inst. to provide tchrs. for Roman Catholics in Am.; established Xaverian Brothers, Bruges, Belgium, 1839, served as superior gen. (as Brother Francis Xavier) until 1860. Died Bruges, 1871.

RYLAND, Robert, clergyman, coll. pres.; b. King and Queen County, Va., Mar. 14, 1805; s. Josiah and Catharine (Peachey) R.; grad. Columbian Coll., Washington, D.C., 1826; m. Josephine Howell, 1830; m. 2d, Betty Presley Thornton; 7 children. Ordained to ministry Baptist Ch., 1827; pastor Bapt. Ch., Lynchburg, Va., 1827-32; in charge of Va. Bapt. Sem., Richmond, 1832-40, chartered as Richmond Coll., 1840, pres., 1840-66; pastor 1st African Bapt. Ch. of Richmond, 1841-65; tchr. Nat. Theol. Sch., Richmond, 1866-68; pres. Shelbyville (Ky.) Female Coll., 1868-71, Lexington (Ky.) Female Inst., 1871-78; pres. of a sch. for girls, New Castle, Ky., 1878-81; chaplain S.W. Va. Inst., Bristol, Va., 1893-97. Author: Baptism for the Remission of Sins, 1836; A Scripture Catechism for the Instruction of Children and Servants, 1848; The American Union, 1857; Lectures on the Apocalypse, 1857. Died Apr. 23, 1899.

RYNNING, Ole, immigrant leader; b. Ringsaker, Norway, Apr. 4, 1809; s. Rev. Jens and Severine Catherine (Steen) R.; attended nat. univ., Christiana (now Oslo), Norway, 1830-33. Conducted pvt. sch., Snaasen, Norway, 1833-37; led a group of 84 colonists to U.S., 1837; founded Beaver Creek Colony in Iroquois County region of Ill., 1837; wrote A True Account of America for the Information and Help of Peasant and Commoner (became known as "America Book" and stimulated Norwegian immigration to U.S.), 1838; malaria killed most of colonsist, 1838-40, colony abandoned, 1840. Died Beaver Creek Colony, Ill., Sept. 1838.

S

SABIN, Alvah, congressman, clergyman; b. Georgia, Franklin County, Vt., Oct. 23, 1793; attended Burlington Coll.; studied theology, Phila.; grad. Columbian Coll. (now George Washington U.), 1821. Mem. Vt. Militia, served during War of 1812; ordained to ministry; pastor at Cambridge, Westfield, Underhill until 1825; returned to Georgia, 1825; pastor Georgia Baptist Ch. for more than 40 years; mem. Vt. Ho. of Reps., 1826-35, 38-40, 47-49, 51, 61-62; mem. Vt. Senate, 1841, 43, 45; sec. state Vt., 1841; mem. U.S. Ho. of Reps. (Whig) from Vt., 33d-34th congresses, 1853-57; del. 1st Anti-Slavery Nat. Conv.; commr. Franklin County, 1861-62; moved to Sycamore, Dekalb County, Ill., 1867, minister. Died Sycamore, Jan. 22, 1885; buried Georgia Plain (Vt.) Cemetery.

SABIN, Joseph, bibliographer; b. Northamptonshire, Eng., Dec. 6, 1821; m. Miss Winterborn, 1844, at least 2 children. Employed by Charles Richards, book dealer, Oxford, Eng., circa 1839, became mgr., in charge of book buying; partner (with Mr. Winterborn) as bookseller and auctioneer, 1842-48; came to N.Y.C., 1848; introduced halfbinding in calf and morocco in Am., circa 1848; went to Phila., employed by firm Cooley & Kesse, book auctioneers, 1850, later by successors Lyman & Rawdon; cataloguer of pvt. book collections Bangs, Brother & Co., 1851-56; operator book store, Phila., 1857-61; partner (with H.A. Jennings) in an auction room, N.Y.C., 1861-65; published mags. Sabin & Son's American Bibliopolist, Sabin's Reprints, circa 1869-72. Author: The Thirty-nine Articles of the Church of England, with Scripture Proof and References, 1844; Dictionary of Books Relating to America, from its Discovery to the Present Time (known also by fly-leaf title Bibliotheca Americana), 14 vols., 1868-84; Died Bklyn., June 5, 1881.

SABINE, Lorenzo, congressman, historian; b. Lisbon, N.H., July 28, 1803; s. Elijah R. and Ann (Clark) Sabin; A.M. (hon.), Bowdoin Coll., 1846, Harvard, 1848; m. Matilda F. Green, Nov. 20, 1825; m. 2d, Abby R.D. Deering, July 13, 1829; m. 3d, Elizabeth H. Deering, Sept. 17, 1837. Bank clerk, later in fishing business; mem. Me. Ho. of Reps., 1833, 34; dep. commr. of customs for Me.; edited Easport Sentinel short time; wrote articles in North American Review between 1843-46, including "Fisheries," 1843, "Our Commercial History and Policy," 1843, "American Fisheries," 1846; called to Washington, D.C., 1852-53, worked under direction Dept. of Treasury; mem. U.S. Ho. of Reps. (Whig) from Mass., 32d Congress, Dec. 13, 1852-53; sec. Boston Bd. of Trade, 1857; stayed in Boston until 1867; published Notes on Duels and Duelling...with a Preliminary Historical Essay, 1855. Author: The American Loyalists or Biographical Sketches of Adherents to the British Crown in the War of the Revolution, 1847; Biographical Sketches of Loyalists, 2 vols., 1864. Died Roxbury, Mass., Apr. 14, 1877; buried Hillside Cemetery, Washington County, Me.

SACAGAWEA (or Sacajawea) (Bird Woman), Indian guide; b. Shoshone Indian Village, probably nr. Lemhi, Ida., 1787; m. Toussaint Charbonneau, circa 1807; 2 children, Jean Baptist, Lizette. Captured by war party of Hidatsa Indians, 1800, sold to Toussaint Charbonneau, a French trader; 1807; employed (with her husband) as interpreter and guide by Meriwether Lewis and William Clark in their exploring expeditions of Far West, 1805-06, obtained aid from Shoshone Indians which helped make it possible for Lewis and Clark to continue West beyond the Rockies; family moved to St. Louis, 1809-11; returned to Hidatsa Indians, 1811. Died Ft. Manuel on Missouri River in Dakota Terrtiory, Dec. 20, 1812; buried Ft. Manuel.

SACKETT, William August, congressman, lawyer; b. Aurelius, nr. Auburn, N.Y., Nov. 18, 1811; attended Aurora Acad.; studied law. Admitted to bar, 1834, practiced in Seneca Falls, Seneca County, N.Y.; mem. U.S. Ho. of Reps. (Whig) from N.Y., 31st-32d congresses, 1849-53; moved to Saratoga Springs, N.Y., 1857; register in bankruptcy during term of 1867 bankruptcy law. Died Saratoga Springs, Sept. 6, 1895; buried Greenridge Cemetery.

SACKVILLE, Lord, see Germain, George.

SADLER, Thomas William, congressman, lawyer; b. nr. Russellville, Franklin County, Ala., Apr. 17, 1831; had academic edn.; studied law. Moved to Autauga County, Ala., 1855, became mcht.; volunteered and served in division of Confederate Army under command Gen. Joseph Wheeler in Civil War; became farmer; admitted to bar, 1867, practiced in Prattville, Autauga County; county supt. edn., 1875-84; Democratic presdl. elector, 1880; mem. U.S. Ho. of Reps. (Dem.) from Ala., 49th Congress, 1855-57. Died Prattville, Oct. 29, 1896; buried Oak Hill Cemetery.

SADLIER, Denis, publisher; b. Tipperary, Ireland, 1817; s. James Sadlier; m. Julia Browne, 1841. Arrived in N.Y.C., 1830; established (with brother James) book-binding bus. under name of D.&J. Sadlier & Co., N.Y.C., 1836, became prin. publishers of Catholic books in Am.; firm compiled ofcl., annual Sadlier's Cath. Dictionary, 1864-96, published The N.Y. Tablet, 1857-81; carried on publishing bus. alone from 1869; public sch. trustee of Harlem dist., N.Y.C.; Democrat; trustee Manhattan Coll. Died Wilton, Westchester County, N.Y., Feb. 4, 1885.

SADTLER, John Phillip Benjamin, clergyman, coll. pres.; b. Balt., Dec. 25, 1823; grad. Pa. Coll. (now Gettysburg Coll.), 1842, Theol. Sem., 1844, D.D. (hon.), 1867; m. Caroline Elizabeth Schmucker, Oct. 9, 1845, 9 children including Samuel Philip. Licensed to preach by Md. Synod of Lutheran Ch., 1844; pastor, Pine Grove, Pa., 1845-49, Shippensburg, Pa., 1849-53, Middletown, Pa., 1853-56, Easton, Pa., 1856-62; prin. Ladies' Sem., Lutherville, Md., 1862-75; pres. Muhlenberg Coll., Allentown, Pa., 1875-86; trustee Pa. Coll., 1862-77; pres. Soc. for History of Germans in Md. Died Atlantic City, N.J., Apr. 28, 1901.

SAENDERL, Simon, clergyman; b. Malgerzdorf, Lower Bavaria (now Germany), Sept. 30, 1800. Ordained priest Roman Catholic Ch., 1825; entered order of Redemptorists, 1829; arrived in Am. as 1st superior of order in U.S., 1832; ministered to French inhabitants and Menominee Indians, Green Bay, Wis., 1832-33; missionary to Ottawa Indians, Arbre Croche, Mich., 1833-35, 36-39; minister to German Catholics, Rochester, N.Y., 1841-43; had small mission, Toronto, Ont., Can., 1844-48; minister, Monroe, Mich.; suspended from Redemptorist Order, 1848; joined Trappist Order, 1852, professed vows on Easter 1853, made master of German novices; lived in Trappist monastary, Gethsemane, Ky., 1853-79. Died Gethsemane, Feb. 22, 1879.

SAGE, Bernard Janin, lawyer, naval officer; b. New Haven, Conn., Feb. 5, 1821; never married. Practiced law, New Orleans; owner large sugar plantation nr. New Orleans; master Confederate Navy, 1861-65; sent to Europe on spl. missions by Pres. Jefferson Davis; chosen one of counsel for defense in projected trial of Davis. Author: Davis and Lee (argued that primary allegiance was due to one's state, not to the Union), 1865. Died New Orleans, Sept. 2, 1902; buried Thibodaux, La.

SAGE, Ebenezer, congressman, physician; b. Chatham (now Portland), Conn., Aug. 16, 1755; grad. Yale, 1778; studied medicine. Practiced medicine, Easthampton. L.I., N.Y., 1784; moved to Sag Harbor, Suffolk County, N.Y., circa 1801, practiced medicine; mem. U.S. Ho. of Reps. (Democrat) from N.Y., 11th-13th congresses, 1809-15; del. N.Y. State Constl. Conv., 1821. Died Sag Harbor, Jan. 20, 1834; buried Old Burying Ground; reinterred Oakland Cemetery.

SAGE, Henry Williams, mcht., mfr., philanthropist; b. Middletown, Conn., Jan. 31, 1814; s. Charles and Sally (Williams) S.; m. Susan Elizabeth Linn. Entered employ of uncles, Williams & Bros., mchts., owners transp. lines, N.Y.C.,

1832, became propr., 1837; elected to N.Y. Legislature (Whig), 1847; bought large tract of timber land, Lake Simcoe, Can., 1854, manufactured lumber; trustee Plymouth Ch., Bklyn.; became mem. bd. trustees Cornell U., Ithaca, N.Y., 1870, chmn. 1875, offered to erect a coll. for women; 1870 (resulted in opening of Sage Coll., 1874), furnished funds for erection of chapel, dedicated 1875, established Sage Sch. of Philosophy, gave $560,000 to library and its endowment; founded Lyman Beecher Lectures on Preaching, Yale Divinity Sch., 1871. Died Sept. 18, 1897; buried Sage Chapel at Cornell U.

SAILLY, Peter, congressman; b. Lorraine, France, Apr. 20, 1754. Came to U.S., 1783, settled in Plattsburg, N.Y., became mcht., fur trader, potash mfr.; lumber shipper; asso. justice Ct. Common Pleas, 1788-96; commr. hwys., sch. commr., 1797-98; supr schs., 1799-1800; mem. N.Y. State Assembly, 1803 judge Clinton County, 1804-06; mem. U.S. Ho. o Reps. (Democrat) from N.Y., 9th Congress, 1805 07; collector customs at Plattsburg, 1807-26. Die Plattsburg, Mar. 16, 1826; buried Riverside Ceme tery.

SAINT-AULAIRE, Felix Achille, marine painter, lithographer; b. Vercelli, Piedmont, France, 1801; studied with Franc and Hippolyte Garnerey; works include Keelboat on the Mississippi, in collection City Art Mus. St. Louis.

SAINT-COSME, Jean Francois Buisson de, missionary; b. Quebec, Can.; attended Missions Etrangres Sem., Que. Ordained priest Roman Catholic Ch., 1690, served as missionary in Nova Scota and Ill.; established mission, Natchez, Miss., circa 1699; went to work with Indians along Mississippi River, 1704. Killed (with 4 companions) by Shetimasha Indians, 1707.

SAINT-MEMIN, Charles Bathazar Julien Fevret de, painter; b. Dijon, France, 1770; student Paris Mil. Sch., 1784-85. Joined French guards, 1788; went to Switzerland at outbreak of revolution, joined Army of the Princes, circa 1790; also painted monochrome miniatures during this period; came to Can., 1793, later settled in N.Y., made engravings of N.Y.; active in portraiture in N.Y., Phila., Balt., Annapolis, Washington, Richmond, Norfolk and Charleston, 1796-1810; made 1st portraits of Plains Indians in Washington; returned to France, 1810, became curator and restorer of museum in Dijon. 1817; perfected physionotrace for drawing accurate profile likenesses. Died Dijon, 1852.

SAINT-PALAIS, Jacques Maurice Landes de, clergyman; b. La Salvetat, Herault, France, Nov. 15, 1811; studied at St. Nicholas du Chartonet, also St. Sulipce, Paris. Ordained priest Roman Catholic Ch., 1836; came as missionary to U.S., apptd. vicar gen. of Vincennes (Ind.), 1847, bishop, 1848; also superior of St. Charles Sem., Vincennes, from 1847. Died St. Mary-of-the-Woods, Ind., June 28, 1875.

SALISBURY, Edward Elbridge, Orientalist; b. Boston, Apr. 6, 1814; s. Josiah and Abby (Breese) S.; grad. Yale, 1832; studied Oriental langs. in Europe, 1836-40, 42-43; m. Abigail Salisbury Phillips, 1836; m. 2d, Evelyn McCurdy. Prof. Arabic and Sanskrit, Yale, 1843-54, prof. Arabic, 1854-56; cofounder Am. Oriental Soc., 1842; mem. Sociéte Asiatique, 1838-1901, Imperial Acad. Scis. and Belles Lettres, Constantinople (now Istanbul), Turkey, 1855-1901, Deutsche Morgenandische Gesellschaft, 1859-1901. Author: Genealogical and Biographical Monographs, 1885; contbr. papers to Jour. of Am. Oriental Soc. including: Contributions from Original Sources to our Knowledge of the Science of Muslim Tradition, 1859, Materials for the History of the Muhammadan Doctrine of Predestination and Free Will, 1863, The Book of Sulaimân's First Ripe Fruit, Disclosing the Mysteries of the Nusairian Religion, 1864. Died Feb. 5, 1901.

SALM-SALM, Prince (Felix Constatin Alexander Johann Nepomuk), soldier of fortune; b. Anholt, Prussia, Dec. 25, 1828; m. Agnes Winona Leclercq Joy, Aug. 20, 1862. Became officer Prussian Cavalry, later joined Austrian Army; col. 8th N.Y. Volunteers, 1862-64, col., comdr. 68th N.Y. Volunteers, served under Gen. Sherman, 1864-65; brevetted brig. gen. U.S. Volunteers; mil. comdr. Dist. of Atlanta, 1865-66; went (with his wife) to Mexico, joined service of Maximilian, 1866, became chief aide to the emperor; captured by Mexicans at Battle of Queretaro, his life spared through efforts of wife; returned to Germany, became maj. Queen Augusta Regt., Prussian Army. Killed at Battle of Gravelotte during Franco-Prussian War, Aug. 18, 1870.

SALOMON, Haym, mcht., banker, Revolutionary financier; b. Lissa, Poland, circa 1740; m. Rachel Franks, Jan. 22, 1777. Fled Poland, 1772, came to N.Y., circa 1773, opened brokerage and commn. mcht.'s business; arrested by British as spy and imprisoned, 1776, used as interpreter by British; tried to induce Hessian mercenaries (employed by British) nr. N.Y.C. to resign or desert; resumed business as mcht., continued to act as undercover desertion agt. among Hessions; again arrested, 1778, charged with being accomplice in plot to burn King's fleet and destroy Brit. warehouses around N.Y., confined to prison and condemned to death; bribed jailer and escaped, went to Am. lines; opened office as dealer in bills of exchange and other securities, Phila., 1778-85; became leading broker in Phila., also subscriber and a major depositor in Bank of N. Am.; paymaster for French forces in Am.; contbd. much to maintain bankrupt U.S. Govt.'s credit, his financial aid justified title "The Financier of the Revolution"; died in debt, holding over $650,000 of U.S.A. debts which were unpayable due to financial situation. Died Jan. 6, 1785.

SALPOINTE, John Baptist, clergyman; b. St. Maurice de Poinsat, Puy-de-Dôme, France, Feb. 21/22, 1825; attended seminary in Clermont-Ferrand. Ordained priest Roman Catholic Ch., 1851; became parish priest; taught at Clermont-Ferrand prep. sem., 1855-59; came to U.S., became missionary in Diocese of Santa Fe (N.M.); apptd. vicar gen., 1860; consecrated titular bishop of Doryla and vicar apostolic of Ariz., 1869; opposed govt. practice of placing Roman Catholic Indians under Protestant missionaries; named titular archbishop of Anazarbus and coadjutor of Santa Fe, 1884-94; apptd. titular archbishop of Constantia (Tomi), 1894. Died Tucson, Ariz., July 15, 1898.

SALTONSTALL, Dudley, naval officer; b. New London, Conn., Sept. 8, 1738; s. Gen. Gurdon and Rebecca (Winthrop) S.; m. Frances Babcock, 1765, 7 children. Privateersman in French and Indian Wars; commanded fort at New London, 1775; given command in Alfred, flagship of Commodore Esek Hopkins, 1775; apptd. 4th on list of captains, 1776; commanded expdn. of Bagaduce (now Castine), in Penobscot Bay, arrived in Penobscot Bay, 1779, fled at arrival of Brit. fleet; dismissed from navy because two ships were taken by Brit., 1779; became successful privateer and mcht. Died Mole St. Nicolas, Haiti, 1796.

SALTONSTALL, Gurdon, clergyman, colonial gov.; b. Haverhill, Mass., Apr. 7, 1666; s. Nathaniel and Elizabeth (Ward) S.; grad. Harvard, 1684; m. Jerusha Richards; m. 2d, Elizabeth Rosewell; m. 3d, Mary Whittingham; 10 children. Ordained minister of Congregational (Puritan) Ch. at New London, Conn., 1691; became confidant and adviser John Winthrop; with Winthrop helped Conn. Assembly draft state papers and settle disputes within colony and with neighboring colonies, 1698-1707; gov. Colony of Conn., 1707-24; established system of eccles. discipline embodied by Synod at Saybrook in Saybrook Platform of 1708; the New London Press (which he had established) published his book, A Confession of Faith . . . by Delegation at Say-Brook, 1710; one of ministerial leaders in movement which led to chartering Collegiate Sch. (later Yale), 1701, influenced decision to permanently locate Yale at New Haven, Conn. Died New London, Conn., Oct. 1, 1724.

SALTONSTALL, Leverett, congressman; b. Haverhill, Mass., June 13, 1783; attended Phillips Exeter (N.H.) Acad.; grad. Harvard, 1802; studied law. Admitted to bar, practiced in Salem, Mass., 1805; del. Mass. Constl. Conv., 1820; mem. Mass. Ho. of Reps., 1813, 14, 16, 22, 29, 34, 44; mem. Mass. Senate, 1817-19, 31-32, pres., 1831-32; 1st mayor Salem, 1836-38; Whig presdl. elector, 1836; mem. U.S. Ho. of Reps. (Whig, filled vacancy) from Mass., 25th-27th congresses, Dec. 5, 1838-43; overseer Harvard, 1835-45. Died Salem, May 8, 1845; buried Harmony Grove Cemetery.

SALTONSTALL, Richard, colonist; b. Woodsome, Almondbury, Yorkshire, Eng., 1610; s. Sir Richard and Grace (Kaye) S.; m. Muriel Gurdon, July 4, 1633, 4 children including Nathaniel. Admitted as fellow commoner at Emmanuel Coll., Cambridge (Eng.) U., 1627; accompanied father to Mass. Bay where they established settlement of Watertown, 1630; admitted freeman, 1631; propr. only grist mill in town of Ipswich, Mass.; sojourned in Eng., 1649-63, 72-80, 86-94, apptd. commr. High Ct. of Justice to repress enemies of Commonwealth, 1650, trustee for settling sequestered estates in Scotland, 1654; an assistant in Mass., 1637-49, 64, 80-82; a magistrate, Ipswich, Newbury and Piscataqua, Mass.; served as sgt. maj. in Col. Endicott's Regts.; an alternate commr. of New Eng. Confederacy, 1644; substitute agt. of colony to Eng., 1660; condemned the proposed Life Council as sinful and contrary to the charter; petitioned the Confederacy against unneutral aid to LaTour as impolite and dishonorable, 1645; overseer Harvard, contbr. over 450 pounds. Died Hulme, Lancaster, Eng., Apr. 29, 1694.

SALVATIERRA, Juan Maria, missionary; b. Milan, Italy, Nov. 15, 1648; attended Jesuit Coll., Parma, Italy. Joined Soc. of Jesus, was sent to Mexico, 1675; taught at Puebla, 1675-80; missionary to Tarumari Indians of Chihuahua, 1680-90; apptd. visitor of Jesuit missions, 1690; went to So. Cal., 1697, explored region, founded several missions including Our Lady of Loreto at Concepcion Bay; apptd. Provincial of Mexico, 1704, returned to his missions, 1707. Died Guadalajara, Mexico, July 17, 1717.

SALZMANN, Joseph, clergyman; b. Münzbach, Austria, Aug. 17, 1819. Ordained priest Roman Catholic Ch., 1842; parish priest, Linz, Austria; came to U.S., 1847, became pastor of ch., Milw.; raised funds to open seminary, St. Francis, Wis., 1856; founder 1st Roman Catholic normal sch. in U.S., also Pio Nono Coll. Died St. Francis, Jan. 17, 1874.

SAMMONS, Thomas, congressman, farmer; b. Shamenkop, Ulster County, N.Y., Oct. 1, 1762; attended rural schs. Served as officer in Revolutionary War; became farmer; del. N.Y. State Constl. Conv., 1801; mem. Council of Appointment; served as lt., capt., maj. N.Y. State Militia; mem. U.S. Ho. of Reps. (Democrat) from N.Y., 8th-9th, 11th-12th congresses, 1803-07, 09-13. Died Sammons homestead, Montgomery County, nr. Johnstown, N.Y., Nov. 20, 1838; buried on homestead in Simeon Sammons Cemetery.

SAMPLE, Samuel Caldwell, congressman, lawyer; b. Elkton, Cecil County, Md., Aug. 15, 1796; attended rural sch.; studied law. Learned carpenter's trade; asst. to his father who was contractor; admitted to bar, 1833, practiced in South Bend, Ind.; elected pros. atty., 1834; judge 9th Jud. Circuit, 1836-43; 1st pres. First Nat. Bank of South Bend; mem. U.S. Ho. of Reps. (Whig) from Ind., 28th Congress, 1843-45. Died South Bend, Dec. 2, 1855; buried City Cemetery.

SAMPSON, Ezekiel Silas, congressman, lawyer; b. Huron County, O., Dec. 6, 1831; attended Howe's Acad., Mt. Pleasant, Ia., Knox Coll., Ill.; studied law. Admitted to bar, 1856, practiced in Sigourney, Keokuk County, Ia.; pros. atty., 1856-58; enlisted as capt. 5th Regt., Ia. Volunteer Infantry in Union Army during Civil War, 1861, promoted lt. col.; mem. Ia. Senate, 1866; judge Ia. 6th Dist., 1867-75; mem. U.S. Ho. of Reps. (Republican) from Ia., 44th-45th congresses, 1875-79. Died Sigourney, Oct. 7, 1892; buried West Cemetery.

SAMPSON, William, lawyer, Irish patriot; b. Londonderry, Ireland, Jan. 17, 1764; s. Rev. Arthur Samson and Anne (Wilson) S.; attended U. Dublin (Ireland); studied law Lincoln's Inn, London, Eng., 1790; m. Grace Clarke, 1790, 3 children. Admitted to Irish bar; became part of Irish nationalist movement; contbr. to nationalist newspapers, defended state prisoners, took oath of United Irishmen; presided over treasonable meeting, Belfast, Ireland, 1796; imprisoned without trial during Irish Rebellion, 1787, for collecting information regarding atrocities of English troops; exiled to Portugal, 1799, sent by Portugal to France; sent to Eng., 1806, then to U.S.; admitted to N.Y. bar, 1806; advocate of personal rights, defended organized labor (journeymen cordwainers), in its efforts to establish a closed shop, 1810; defended right of priest to hold in confidence secrets imparted during confession, 1813; lived in Georgetown. D.C., 1825-30; a chief advocate of codification of common law. Author: The Catholic Question in America, 1815; Memoirs of William Sampson (a denunciation of Brit. policy in Ireland), 1807; History of Ireland, 2 vols., 1833. Died N.Y.C., Dec. 28, 1836.

SAMPSON, Zabdiel, congressman; b. Plympton, Mass., Aug. 22, 1781; grad. Brown U., 1803; studied law. Admitted to bar, 1806, practiced in Plymouth, Mass.; mem. U.S. Ho. of Reps. (Democrat) from Mass., 15th-16th congresses, 1817-July 26, 1820 (resigned); apptd. collector customs at Plymouth, 1820-28. Died Plymouth, July 19, 1828; buried Burial Hill Cemetery.

SAMSON, George Whitefield, clergyman, coll. pres.; b. Harvard, Mass., Sept. 29, 1819; grad. Brown U., 1839, Newton Theol. Sem., 1843. Pastor, E Street Baptist Ch., Washington, D.C., 1843-circa 1850, 52-59; pastor, Jamaica Plain, Mass., 1850-52; pres. Columbian Coll., 1859-71, influenced reestablishment of Columbian Law Sch., 1865; pres. Rutgers Female Coll., N.Y.C., 1871-75, 86-circa 1896. Author: To Daimonion, or the Spiritual Medium, 1860; Physical Media in Spiritual Manifestations, 1868; The Atonement, 1878; Divine Law as to Wines, 1880; Guide to Self-Education, 1886; Idols of Fashion and Culture, 1888. Died 1896.

SAMUELS, Green Berry, congressman, lawyer; b. nr. Red Banks, Shenandoah County, Va., Feb. 1, 1806; had classical studies; studied law. Admitted to bar, 1827, practiced law. Lived in Woodstock, Shenandoah County; mem. U.S. Ho. of Reps. (Democrat) from Va., 26th Congress, 1839-41; mem. Va. Constl. Conv., 1850-51; elected judge Circuit Ct., 1850, Ct. Appeals, 1852. Died Richmond, Va., Jan. 5, 1859; buried Old Lutheran Graveyard, Woodstock.

SANBORN, Edwin David, educator; b. Gilmanton, N.H., May 14, 1808; s. David Edwin and Hannah (Hook) S.; grad. Dartmouth, 1832; attended Andover Theol. Sem., 1834-35; LL.D. (hon.), U. Vt., 1859; m. Mary Ann Webster, Dec. 11, 1837; m. 2d, Mrs. Sarah Fenton Clarke, 1868; 4 children including Edwin Webster, Katherine Abbot. In charge Deerfield (Mass.) Pub. Schs., 1825-27; prin. sch., Topsfield, Mass., 1832-33; preceptor Gilmanton Acad., 1933-34; prof. Latin and Greek, Dartmouth, 1836-59, prof. oratory and belles-lettres, 1863-80, Winkley prof. Anglo-Saxon and English lit. 1880-82; prof. Latin and Greek, Washington U., St. Louis, 1859-63; twice mem. N.H. Constl. Conv., 1850. Died N.Y.C., Dec. 29, 1885.

SANCHEZ, José Bernardo, missionary; b. Robledillo, Spain, Sept. 7, 1778. Joined Franciscan Order, 1794, sent to Mexico, 1803; sent to Cal., 1804, served the rest of his life in various missions in Cal.; pres. of missions and vicar of the bishop, 1827-31. Died San Gabriel Mission, Jan. 15, 1833.

SANDEMAN, Robert, promoter religious sect; b. Perth, Scotland, Apr. 29, 1718; s. David and Margaret (Ramsay) S.; attended U. Edinburgh (Scotland); m. Catherine Glas (Glass), 1737. Partner (with brother) in linen manufacture, 1736-44; became elder Glassite chs., 1744; served at Perth, Dundee, Scotland, Edinburgh, also London, Eng.; organizer London Congregation, 1760; came to U.S., 1764, established Glassite (called Sandemanian in U.S.) chs., Boston, Portsmouth, N.H., Taunton, Mass.; established residence and sect hdqrs., Danbury, Conn., 1767; Sandemanians rejected Covenant of Grace, believed in independence of ch. and state, practiced primitive Christian rites, preached that the mere acknowledgement of "the person and work of Jesus Christ" is all that is required for justification and regeneration. Author: Letters on Theron and Aspasia Addressed to the Author, 1757; Some Thoughts on Christianity, 1764. Died Danbury, Apr. 2, 1771.

SANDERS, Billington McCarter, clergyman, univ. pres.; b. Columbia County, Ga., Dec. 2, 1789; s. Ephraim and Nancy S.; grad. S.C. Coll., 1809; m. Martha Lamar, Mar. 17, 1812; m. 2d, Cynthia Halliday, Feb. 25, 1824; 22 children. Farmer, 1811-32; mem. lower house Ga. Legislature, 1817; joined Kiokee Baptist Ch., 1810; licensed to preach by Union Ch., Warren County, Ga.; ordained to ministry Baptist Ch., 1825; pastor Bapt. chs. in Ga.; 1st prin. Mercer Inst. (became Mercer U., 1839), Penfield, Ga., 1832-39, pres. Mercer U., 1839, trustee, 1839-54, sec., treas., several years; moderator Ga. Bapt. Assn., 9 years, clk., several years; pres. Bapt. State Conv., 6 years; editor Christian Index, 1 year; del. Triennial and So. Bapt. convs. Died Penfield, Mar. 12, 1854.

SANDERS, Charles Walton, educator; b. Newport, N.Y., Mar. 24, 1805; s. Jacob and Lydia (Martin) S.; m. Elizabeth Barker, Aug. 2, 1842, 3 children. Licensed to teach, Homer, Cortland County, N.Y., 1821; elected insp. common schs. Cortland County, 1829, served several years; began writing and compiling spellers and readers for elementary schs., 1837/38, sold 13,000,000 copies between 1838 and 1860; a founder N.Y. State Tchrs. Assn., 1845. Author: The Speller and Definer; Analysis; German and English Primer; High School Reader. Died N.Y.C., July 5, 1889.

SANDERS, Daniel Clarke, clergyman, coll. pres.; b. Sturbridge, Mass., May 3, 1768; s. Michael and Azubah (Clarke) S.; grad. Harvard, 1788, D.D. (hon.), 1809; m. Nancy Fitch, 1792, 8 children. Licensed to preach by Dedham Assn., 1790; ordained to ministry Congregational Ch., 1794; conducted pvt. sch., Burlington, Vt., 1799-1800; sec. corp. U. Vt., 1791, trustee, U. Vt., 1800, 1st pres., 1801, supervised part of constrn. of first bldg., dismissed when trustees suspended instrn., 1814; pastor, Burlington, 1799-1807, 1st Congl. Ch., Medfield, Mass., 1815-29; del. Mass. Constl. Conv., 1820-21; mem. Mass. Ho. of Reps. from Medfield dist., 1833-36; published numerous sermons, including A Sermon, Preached in Medfield . . . Near the 166th Anniversary of the Incorporation of the Town (1st hist. sketch of Medfield), 1817. Author: A History of the Indian Wars with the First Settlers of the United States, Particularly in New England, 1812 Died Medfield, Oct. 18, 1850.

SANDERS, Elizabeth Elkins, reformer, author; b. Salem, Mass., Aug. 12, 1762; d. Thomas and Elizabeth (White) Elkins; m. Thomas Sanders, Apr. 28, 1782, 5 children, including Charles. Contbr. articles to local newspapers encouraging prison reform, greater ednl. opportunities for the poor, health reform; published Conversations Principally on the Aborigines of North America, 1828, The First Settlers of New England, 1829 (2 books dealing with white man's inhumane and un-Christian treatment of Indians); opposed missionary aid to fgn. lands; other works include: A Tract on Missions, 1844; The Second Part of the Tract on Missions, 1845; Remarks on the Tour Around Hawaii by the Missionaries, Messrs. Ellis, Thurston, Bishop and Goodrich, in 1823, published 1848. Died Salem, Feb. 19, 1851.

SANDERS, George Nicholas, revolutionist; b. Lexington, Ky., Feb. 27, 1812; s. Lewis and Ann (Nicholas) S.; m. Anna Reid. Went to N.Y.C., 1845; involved in dubious polit. and financial ventures; made questionable personal profits as agt. to adjust claims for Hudson's Bay Co. in Ore.; worked for Eastern capitalists who were speculating in Chgo. real estate; became leader Young America movement, promoting European revolutionary causes in U.S.; bought U.S. Magazine and Democratic Review, changed name to Democratic Review, 1851; supported Stephen A. Douglas; apptd. U.S. consul London, Eng., 1853, left U.S. before appointment was confirmed by U.S. Senate; his home became hdqrs. of European revolutionary exiles; Senate refused to confirm appointment; apptd. navy agt., N.Y.C., 1857; Confederate agt. in Europe and Can.; mem. Niagara Peace Conf., 1864; lived in Europe, after Civil War. Died Aug. 12, 1873.

SANDERS, James Harvey, journalist; b. Union County, O., Oct. 9, 1832; m. Martha Rodgers. Published Sigourney (Ia.) News, 1863-69; founded and published Western Stock Jour. (1st periodical in U.S. devoted to animal husbandry), Sigourney, 1869, merged with Nat. Livestock Jour., Chgo., 1870; asso. editor Nat. Livestock Jour., 1870-73, publisher and editor, 1876-81; founded and published Breeders' Gazette, Chgo., 1881-88. Author: Norman Stud Book, 1876; Breeders' Trotting Stud Book, 1881; Horse-Breeding, 1885; The Breeds of Livestock and the Principles of Heredity, 1887. Died Memphis, Tenn., Dec. 22, 1899.

SANDERSON, George, banker, real estate developer; b. Boston, 1810; s. Jacob and Jarusha (Gardner) S.; m. Marion Kingsbury; children—Emily, James Gardner, Anna K., Marion, George. Universalist minister for a time; practiced law (in partnership with David Wilmot for a time), Towanda, Pa.; moved to Scranton, Pa., 1855; founder George Sanderson & Co., banking house (became Lackawanna Valley Safe Deposit Co.); a developer Green Ridge sect. of Scranton. Died Scranton, Apr. 1, 1886.

SANDERSON, Henry, artist; b. Phila., Aug. 24, 1808; studied in London, Eng., circa 1841. Settled in New Brunswick, N.J., circa 1830; exhibited at N.A.D., 1841-44; sold 10 paintings at auction, New Brunswick, 1868; painted copy of Washington Crossing the Delaware (Leutze; now at Rutgers U.); active in local affairs; mem. New Brunswick Bd. Edn.; postmaster of New Brunswick, 1853-61. Died New Brunswick, Dec. 23/24, 1880.

SANDERSON, John, educator, author; b. nr. Carlisle, Pa., 1783; s. William and Agnes McClellan (Buchanan) S.; m. Sophie Carre, circa 1810. Tchr., asst. prin. Clermont Acad., Phila., 1807-32; popular contbr. to several publs. including the Aurora, the Portfolio, the Knickerbocker; editor Aurora, 1822, bought an interest in the paper, 1822, sold to Richard Penn Smith, 1823; author (with brother Joseph M. Sanderson) 1st 2 vols. Biography of the Signers to the Declaration of Independence, 1820 (later completed in 7 additional vols. by Robert Waln, Jr., 1823-27); in Paris, France, 1835-36; published Sketches of Paris: in Familiar Letters to His Friends; by an American Gentleman in Paris, 1838, published in London, Eng. as The American in Paris, 2 vols., 1838; prof. Greek and Latin, assisted in dept. English and belles-lettres Central High Sch., Phila., 1840-44. Died Phila., Apr. 5, 1844.

SANDERSON, Robert, silversmith; b. Eng., 1608; m. Lydia; m. 2d, Mrs. Mary Cross, 1642; m. 3d, Elizabeth; 5 children. Learned, practiced trade of silversmith in Eng.; came to Am., circa 1635; among 1st settlers, Hampton, N.H., 1638; landholder, freeman, Watertown, Mass., 1639; probably 1st tchr. of John Hull; did much to establish New Eng. tradition of silverwork as exemplified in works of Jeremiah Dummer, John Coney, and the two Reveres; established (with John Hull) a mint in the colonies, 1652; became deacon First Ch., Boston, 1668. Died Boston, Oct. 7, 1693.

SANDFORD, James T., congressman; b. Va.; attended common schs. Moved to Columbia, Tenn., became farmer; mem. U.S. Ho. of Reps. from Tenn., 18th Congress, 1823-25; contbr. to establishment Jackson Coll., Columbia.

SANDFORD, Thomas, congressman; b. Westmoreland County, Va., 1762; had classical studies. Served in Revolutionary War; settled on highlands back of Covington, Ky., 1792, became farmer; del. Ky. Constl. Conv., 1799; mem. Ky. Senate, 1800-02; mem. Ky. Ho. of Reps., 1802; mem. U.S. Ho. of Reps. (Democrat) from Ky., 8th-9th congresses, 1803-07. Drowned in Ohio River, nr. Covington, Dec. 10, 1808; buried Highland Cemetery, Ft. Mitchell, nr. Covington.

SANDIDGE, John Milton, congressman; b. nr. Carnesville, Franklin County, Ga., Jan. 7, 1817. Moved to La., became planter; served as col. in Mexican War; mem. La. Ho. of Reps., 1846-55, speaker 2 years; del. La. Constl. Conv., 1852; mem. U.S. Ho. of Reps. (Democrat) from La., 34th-35th congresses, 1855-59; served as col. of Bossier Cavalry throughout Civil War; surrendered La. archives to U.S. authorities in absence of gov. Died Bastrop, Morehouse Parish, La., Mar. 30, 1890; buried Christ Ch. Cemetery.

SANDS, Benjamin Franklin, naval officer; b. Balt., Feb. 11, 1812; s. Benjamin and Rebecca (Hooks) Norris; m. Henrietta Maria French, Nov. 15, 1836, 8 children. Commd. lt. U.S. Navy, served in African Squadron as comdr. ship Porpoise, 1848-50; promoted comdr., chief Bur. of Constrn., 1858-61; sent with expdn. to evacuate Norfolk (Va.) Navy Yard, Apr. 1861, in charge of party which fired ships and ship-houses; commd. capt., 1862, served as sr. officer on Cape Fear River and Wilmington (Del.) blockade until late 1864; claimed to have originated idea of additional outer line of blockaders; participated in both attacks on Ft. Fisher, Dec. 1864, Jan. 1865; commanded 2d div. West Gulf Squadron, until July 1865; surrender of last Confederate troops occurred on his ship, Galveston, Tex., June 2, 1865; promoted commodore, 1866, rear adm., 1871; in charge of Naval Observatory, Washington, D.C., 1867-74. Author: From Reefer to Rear Admiral, 1899. Died Washington, June 30, 1883; buried Mt. Olivet Cemetery, Washington.

SANDS, Comfort, mcht., patriot; b. Sands' Point, L.I., N.Y., Feb. 26, 1748; s. John and Elizabeth (Cornell) S.; m. Sarah Dodge, June 3, 1769; m. 2d, Cornelia Lott, Dec. 5, 1797; 18 children including Robert Charles. Opened a store, Peck Slip, N.Y., 1769, mcht. in West Indian trade, 1769-76; participated in non-importation agreements; mem. several N.Y. provincial congresses and state assemblies; mem. N.Y. Com. of Public Safety, 1776, N.Y. Constl. Conv., 1777; mem. auditor gen. of N.Y. Province, later of N.Y. State, 1776-82; served on commn. to regulate price of labor and commodities for the army, New Haven, Conn., 1778; a founder, dir. Bank of New York (1st bank of N.Y.C.), 1784; pres. N.Y.C. C. of C., 1794-98; declared bankrupt, 1801. Died Hoboken, N.J., Sept. 22, 1834.

SANDS, David, clergyman; b. Cowneck, L.I., N.Y., Oct. 15, 1745; s. Nathaniel and Mercy Sands; m. Clementine Hallock, 1771. Established merc. business, Cornwall, N.Y., 1765; became minister in Soc. of Friends, 1775; itinerant preacher in New Eng., 1775-76, 77-79, 95; in Europe, 1795-1805; established several chs. in Kennebec River region of Me.; called founder of Quakerism in Me. Died Cornwall, June 4, 1818.

SANDS, Joshua, congressman; b. Cow Neck (now Sands Point), L.I., N.Y., Oct. 12, 1757. Served as capt. during Revolutionary War; became mcht.; mem. N.Y. State Senate, 1792-99; collector customs Port of N.Y., 1797; mem. U.S. Ho. of Reps. from N.Y., 8th, 19th congresses, 1803-05, 25-27; pres. bd. trustees Village of Bklyn., 1824. Died Bklyn., Sept. 13, 1835; buried St. Paul's Ch. Cemetery, Eastchester, N.Y.; reinterred Greenwood Cemetery, Bklyn., 1852.

SANDS, Joshua Ratoon, naval officer; b. Bklyn., May 13, 1795; s. Joshua and Ann (Ayscough) S.; m. Mary Steven, 1826; m. 2d, Henrietta Steven; m. 3d, Ellen Ann Crook, 1830; 4 children. Commd. midshipman U.S. Navy, 1812; served in War of 1812, distinguished in attack upon British ship Royal George, in capture of Toronto and Ft. George; commd. lt., 1818; fought 1st duel with Lt. T.S. Hamersley which led to ct. martial and long confinement, 1823; fought another duel killing opponent Surgeon H. Basset, exonerated, 1830; became comdr., 1841; commanded steamer Vixen participating in operations at Alvarado, Tabasco, Laguna, elsewhere during Mexican War, 1846-48; served as gov. Laguna (Mexico), circa 1846; commanded ship St. Lawrence carrying Am. exhibits to London (Eng.) World's Fair, 1851; promoted capt., 1854; assisted in Atlantic cable-laying operations in ship Susquehanna, 1857; commanded Brazil sta. in ship Congress, 1859-61; commd. commodore (ret.), 1862, rear adm., 1866; lighthouse insp. on lower Gt. Lakes, 1862-66; port adm., Norfolk, Va., 1869-72. Died Balt., Oct. 2, 1883; buried Greenwood Cemetery, Bklyn.

SANDS, Robert Charles, author, journalist; b. Flatbush, N.Y.C., May 11, 1799; s. Comfort and Cornelia (Lott) S.; attended Columbia, 1815; began study of law, 1815. Formed an assn. (with James Eastburn and 2 other friends) called Literary Confederacy, wrote and circulated The Aeronaut (a manuscript periodical); admitted to the bar, 1820; Literary Confederacy began to publish St. Tammany's Mag., 1821; editor Atlantic Mag., 1824; editor New York Review, 1825-26; mem. editorial staff New York Comml. Advertiser, 1827-32; joined Bryant and Gulian C. Verplanck in publ. of The Talisman (an annual), 1828. Author: "Historical Notice of Herman Cortes," 1828; "The Dream of the Princess Papantzin" pub. in The Talisman, 1829; "Life and Correspondence of Paul Jones," 1831; "Boyuca" (his best short story) published in Tales of Glauber-Spa, 1832. Died Hoboken, N.J., Dec. 17, 1832.

SANDYS, George, colonist, poet; b. Bishopsthorpe, nr. York, Eng., March 13, 1578; s. Edwin and Cicely (Wilford) S. Toured Middle East, 1610; shareholder in Va. Co. under its 3rd charter, also of Bermudas Co., 1611; came to Va. from Eng., 1621; treas. Va. Colony, 1621-28; commanded punitive force against Tappahannock Indians; built 1st water-mill in Am.; sponsored iron manufacture; engaged in making glass; introduced shipbldg. into the colony; apptd. mem. Va. Gov's. Council, 1624, reapptd., 1626, 28; mem. commn. for better plantation of Va., 1631; made a gentleman of the privy chamber to King Charles, circa 1632; acted as an unofcl. London rep. of colonial liberal party, 1630's; apptd. agt. Va. Colony in Eng., 1640, presented the Assembly's petition to Parliament (which renewed original charter). Author: A Relation of a Journey Begun Anno Domingo 1610, published 1615; Ovid's Metamorphosis Englished by G.S., 1626; A Paraphrase upon the Psalmes of David and upon the Hymnes Dispersed Throughout the Old and New Testaments, 1636; Christ's Passion (translated from Latin of Grotius), 1640; A Paraphrase upon the Song of Solomon, 1641. Died Boxley Abbey, Eng., Mar. 15, 1644; buried Boxley Church.

SANFORD, Giles, mcht.; b. New London County, Conn., Sept. 18, 1783; m. Laura Goodwin, Oct. 6, 1816. Moved to Herkimer County, N.Y., 1801, Erie, Pa., 1810; partner (with R. S. Reed) in merc. firm, 1814-24, became contractors for supplying mil. posts of Ft. Dearborn, Mackinaw, St. Mary, Ft. Howard, 1823. Died Feb. 13, 1866.

SANFORD, Henry Shelton, diplomat; b. Woodbury, Conn., June 15, 1823; s. Nehemiah Curtis and Nancy (Shelton) S.; attended Washington Coll. (now Trinity Coll.), Hartford, Conn., 1839-41; LL.D. (hon.), Heidelberg (Germany) U.; m. Gertrude E. duPuy, Sept. 21, 1864, 7 children. Attache, St. Petersburg, Russia, 1847; acting sec. of legation, Frankfort, Germany, 1848; sec. of legation, Paris, France, 1849-54, charge d'affaires, 1853-54; published The Different Systems of Penal Codes in Europe; also a Report on the Administrative Changes in France, 1854; minister resident to Belgium, 1861-69; bought large tract of land on St. John's River, Fla., 1870; built sawmill and store (beginnings of Town of Sanford); established colony of Swedish immigrants, New Upsala, Fla.; enlisted Brit. capital, formed company to promote devel. Sanford region, 1880; apptd. mem. exec. com. Internat. Assn. for Exploration and Civilization of Central Africa, 1876; del. from Am. Geog. Soc. to internat. congress of African Assn., 1877, through his exertions U.S. recognized the Assn. as friendly govt., 1884; decorated grand officer Order of Leopold by King Leopold of Belgium, 1878; del. from U.S. to Conf. of Berlin, 1884-85, signed Gen. Act of Conf. establishing status of Congo Free State, signed Gen. Act between U.S. and other powers for repression of slave trade and restriction of commerce in fire-arms and liquor in Africa, 1890. Died Healing Springs, Va., May 21, 1891.

SANFORD, John, congressman, mcht.; b. Roxbury, Conn., June 3, 1803; at least 1 son, Stephen. Moved to Amsterdam, N.Y., 1821; taught sch., Amsterdam, Mayfield; became mcht., Mayfield; returned to Amsterdam, mcht. until 1840; mem. U.S. Ho. of Reps. (Democrat) from N.Y., 27th Congress, 1841-43; founded largest carpet mfg. firm in N.Y., factory destroyed by fire, 1849, retired from active business. Died Amsterdam, Oct. 4, 1857; buried Green Hill Cemetery.

SANFORD, John W. A., congressman; b. nr. Milledgeville, Baldwin County, Ga., Aug. 28, 1798; attended Yale. Became farmer; mem. U.S. Ho. of Reps. (Union Democrat) from Ga., 24th Congress, Mar. 4-July 25, 1835, resigned to assist in removal Cherokee Indians; served as maj. gen. in Cherokee War, 1836; mem. Baldwin Blues (discharged on surgeon's certificate of disability due to wounds); elected to Ga. Senate, 1837, resigned before taking seat; sec. state Ga., 1841-43; mem. Ga. Conv., 1850. Died Milledgeville, Sept. 12, 1870; buried Milledgeville Cemetery.

SANFORD, Jonah, congressman; b. Cornwall, Vt., Nov. 30, 1790; attended dist. schs.; studied law. Moved to Hopkinton, St. Lawrence County, N.Y., 1811; enlisted as volunteer and participated in Battle at Plattsburg, 1814; apptd. justice of peace, 1818, served 22 years; admitted to bar, practiced in Franklin County; supr. Hopkinton, 1823-26; apptd. commr. to lay out Port Kent Road, 1827, later apptd. commr. to build road; commd. capt. Volunteer Cavalry, 1827, promoted lt. col., 1828, col., 1831, brig. gen. N.Y. State Militia, 1832-33; mem. N.Y. State Assembly, 1829-30; mem. U.S. Ho. of Reps. (Jackson Democrat, filled vacancy) from N.Y., 21st Congress, Nov. 3, 1830-31; judge Ct. Common Pleas, 1831-37; del. to conv. to revise N.Y. State Constn., 1846; became a Republican, 1856; raised regt. during Civil War, elected its col., acompanied regt. to James River (his ill health and age forced him to abandon field). Died Hopkinton, Dec. 25, 1867; buried Hopkinton Cemetery.

SANFORD, Nathan, senator; b. Bridgehampton, L.I., N.Y., Nov. 5, 1777; s. Thomas and Phebe (Baker) S.; attended Yale; m. Eliza Van Horne, May 9, 1801; m. 2d, Mary Isaacs, Apr. 14, 1813; m. 3d, Mary Buchanan; at least 3 children. Admitted to N.Y. bar., 1799; a leader Tammany faction of Jeffersonian Republican Party, 1802; U.S. commr. of bankruptcy, 1802; U.S. atty. for dist. N.Y., 1803-16; mem. N.Y. Assembly, 1810-11, speaker, 1811; mm. U.S. Senate from N.Y., 1815-21, Jan. 14, 1826-31, urged creation of Dept. of Interior, expansion of atty. gen.'s office into Dept. of Justice, also presented report on currency, 1830; mem. N.Y. Constl. Conv., 1821, introduced and promoted adoption of resolution abolishing property qualifications for suffrage; chancellor N.Y. State, 1823-26. Died Flushing, L.I., Oct. 17, 1838.

SANGER, George Partridge, jurist, editor; b. Dover, Mass., Nov. 27, 1819; s. Ralph and Charlotte (Kingman) S.; A.B., Harvard, 1840, LL.B., A.M., 1844; m. Elizabeth Sherburne Thompson, Sept. 15, 1846, 5 sons including Charles Robert. In charge of pvt. sch., Portsmouth, N.H., 1840-42; a proctor Harvard, 1842-48; admitted to Mass. bar, 1846; editor The American Almanac and Repository of Useful Knowledge, 1848-61, The Monthly Law Reporter, 1851-55; asst. U.S. atty. Suffolk dist. (Mass.), 1849-53, states atty., 1853-54; capt. Ancient and Honorable Arty. Co., 1853-54; capt. Charlestown (Mass.) Guards; judge Mass. Ct. Common Pleas, 1854-59; editor (with George Minot) vol. 11 of Statutes at Large of the United States of America (covering period 1855-59), became sole editor of series (12th-17th vols.); apptd. (with Judge William A. Richardson) to revise and edit The General Statutes of the Commonwealth of Massachusetts, 1859, supervised publication of annual supplements, 1860-81; elected to lower br. Mass. Gen. Ct., also apptd. U.S. atty. for Mass. by Pres. Grant, 1873; ret., 1886; 1st pres. John Hancock Mut. Life Ins. Co., 1863. Died July 3, 1890.

SANTA ANNA, Antonio López de, army officer, pres. Mexico; b. Jalapa, Mexico, circa 1795. Joined Mexican Army, circa 1810; took part in successful revolution against Spain, 1821; apptd. mil. comdr. Vera Cruz, 1822; led revolt against Pres. Augustin de Iturbide, 1823; supported Vincente Guerrero's claim for Mexican presidency, 1828; minister of war, comdr.-in-chief of fed. forces of Mexico, 1829; joined Anastasio Bustamante to overthrow Guerrero; led revolt against Bustamante, 1832; became pres. of Mexico, 1833, dictator of Mexico, 1835; attacked San Antonio (Tex.) during War of Tex. Independence, Feb. 1836; led successful attack on Alamo, Mar. 6, 1836; defeated and taken prisoner by Sam Houston at Battle of San Jacinto, Apr. 21, 1836, released after negotiating treaty which recognized independence of Tex.; lived in retirement, 1837; recalled to duty when Mexico was threatened by France, 1838; successfully defended Vera Cruz, Dec. 5, 1838, lost leg during battle; pres. of Mexico with dictatorial powers, 1841-44, overthrown in Revolution of 1844, taken prisoner and banished; recalled to duty at beginning of Mexican War, July 1846; provisional pres. Mexico, 1846-48; defeated at battles of Buena Vista and Cerro Gordo, during Mexican War, 1847; escaped after fall of Mexico City (Sept. 14, 1847), and carried on guerrilla warfare; lived in Venezuela, 1848-53; recalled, elected pres. Mexico, 1853, established himself as pres. for life, with right of choosing his successor, 1853; revolt against him began Mar. 1854, he fled to Cuba, Aug. 1855; convicted of treason, his property confiscated during his absence; returned to Mexico, 1864, was not allowed to stay; returned again, 1867, exiled to U.S., 1867-74; returned to Mexico, 1874. Author: Mi Historia Militar y Politica, published 1905. Died Mexico City, June 20, 1876.

SAPP, William Fletcher, congressman, lawyer; b. Danville, Knox County, O., Nov. 20, 1824; attended Martinsburg Acad.; studied law. Admitted to bar, 1850, practiced in Mt. Vernon, O.; elected pros. atty. Knox County, 1854, 56; moved to Omaha, Neb. Territory, 1861; mem. Neb. Territorial Legislative Council; entered Union Army as lt. col. 2d Neb. Cavalry during Civil War, 1862; moved to Council Bluffs, Ia., practiced law; mem. Ia. Ho. of Reps., 1865; U.S. dist. atty. for Ia., 1869-73; mem. U.S. Ho. of Reps. (Republican) from Ia., 45th-46th congresses, 1877-81; Rep. presdl. elector, 1884. Died Council Bluffs, Nov. 22, 1890; buried Mound View Cemetery, Mt. Vernon.

SAPP, William Robinson, congressman, lawyer; b. Cadiz, O., Mar. 4, 1804; attended public schs.; studied law. Admitted to bar, 1833, practiced in Millersburg, Holmes County, O.; pros. atty. Holmes County; Whig presdl. elector, 1844; moved to Mt. Vernon, Knox County, O., 1846; mem. U.S. Ho. of Reps. (Whig) from Ohio, 33d-34th congresses, 1853-57; assessor internal revenue for 13th dist., 1869-72; collector internal revenue, 1872-75. Died Mt. Vernon, Jan. 3, 1875; buried Mound View Cemetery.

SAPPINGTON, John, physician; b. Md., May 15, 1776; s. Mark Brown and Rebecca (Boyce) S.; attended course med. lectures U. Pa., 1814-15; m. Jane Breathitt, Nov. 22, 1804. Settled in Saline County, Mo. (Kan.), 1817; strong advocate use of quinine for malaria without recourse to treatment by bleeding, vomiting, purging; began wholesale distbn. Dr. John Sappington's Anti-Fever Pills, 1832. Author: Theory and Treatment of Fevers (perhaps 1st med. treatise written West of Mississippi River), 1844. Died Sept. 7, 1856.

SARGENT, Aaron Augustus, senator, diplomat; b. Newburyport, Mass., Sept. 28, 1827; s. Aaron Peaslee and Elizabeth (Stanwood) S.; m. Ellen Clark, Mar. 14, 1852, 3 children. Mem. staff Sacramento (Cal.) Placer Times, 1850; bought Whig Daily Journal, Nevada City, Cal., became editor and mgr., circa 1845; admitted to Cal. bar, 1854; active in orgn. of Republican party in Cal.; dist. atty. Nevada County (Cal.), 1855-56; mem. Cal. Senate, 1856; del., v.p. Rep. Nat. Conv., 1860; mem. U.S. Ho. of Reps from Cal., 37th, 41st-42d congresses, 1861-63, 69-73, started 1st Pacific R.R. act passed by Congress, 1861; mem. U.S. Senate from Cal., 1873-79; U.S. minister to Germany, 1882, became persona non grata to German Government, resigned, 1884; candidate for U.S. Senate, 1884. Died San Francisco, Aug. 14, 1887; buried Laurel Hill Cemetery.

SARGENT, Epes, journalist, author; b. Gloucester, Mass., Sept. 27, 1813; s. Epes and Hannah Dane (Coffin) S.; m. Elizabeth W. Weld, May 10, 1848. Mem. editorial staff Boston Daily Advertiser, early 1830's; mem. editorial staff, Washington (D.C.) corr. Boston Daily Atlas; author plays The Bride of Genoa, 1837; Velasco (best of his plays), produced in Boston, 1839; mem. staff N.Y. Mirror, later mem. staff New World, N.Y.C.; established, published Sargent's New Monthly Magazine, Jan.-June 1843; editor The Modern Standard Drama, 7 vols., 1846; editor Boston Transcript, 1847-53; proponent of spiritualism in later life; other works include verse Songs of the Sea with Other Poems, 1847, The Woman Who Dared, 1870; fiction Fleetwood, or the Stain of Birth, 1845; Peculiar, a Tale of the Great Transition, 1864; spiritualist tracts Planchette or the Despair of Science, 1869; The Proof Palpable of Immorality, 1875; The Scientific Basis of Spiritualism, 1880; editor poetry anthologies The Emerald, 1866; The Saphhire, 1867; Harper's Cyclopedia of British and American Poetry, 1881. Died Boston, Dec. 30, 1880.

SARGENT, Fitzwilliam, physician; b. Gloucester, Mass., Jan. 17, 1820; s. Winthrop and Emily (Haskell) S.; B.A., Jefferson Coll., Canonsburg, Pa., 1837; M.D., U. Pa., 1843; m. Mary Newbold Singer, June 27, 1850, 1 son, John Singer. Succeeded father in mgmt. large shipping interests belonging to family; resident physician Wills Eye Hosp. of Phila., 1842-43; attending physician, 1849-52, attending surgeon, resident physician 1852; Pa. Hosp., Phila., 1843-45; elected fellow Coll. of Physicians of Phila., 1852. Author: On Bandaging and Other Operations of Minor Surgery; editor Am. editions of The Principles and Practice of Modern Surgery (Robert Druitt), 1848, The Principles of Surgery (James Miller), 1852. Died Bournemouth, Eng., Apr. 25, 1889.

SARGENT, Henry, painter, army officer; b. Gloucester, Mass., Nov. 1770; s. Daniel and Mary (Turner) S.; M.A. (hon), Harvard; m. Hannah Welles, Apr. 2, 1807, 4 children including Henry Winthrop. Went to London, Eng., 1793, studied with Benjamin West; returned to Boston, 1799; joined Boston Light Inf., 1799, commd. 1st Lt., 1804, capt., 1807; apptd. aide-de-camp to gov. Mass. with rank of col., 1815; mem. Mass. Senate, 1812, 15, 16, 17;

painted Landing of the Pilgrims (now at Pilgrim Hall, Plymouth, Mass.), The Tea Party, The Dinner Party (both owned by Mus. of Fine Arts, Boston), altar painting The Christ Crucified (made for Ch. of Holy Cross, Boston); elected hon. mem. N.A.D., 1840; pres. Artists Assn. of Boston, 1845; other works include: Christ Entering into Jerusalem; The Starved Apothecary; The Tailor's News, Portrait of Peter Faneuil. Died Boston, Feb. 21, 1845.

SARGENT, Henry Winthrop, horticulturist; b. Boston, Nov. 26, 1810; s. Henry and Hannah (Welles) S.; grad. Harvard, 1830; m. Caroline Olmsted, Jan. 10, 1839, 3 children. Partner banking house of Gracie & Sargent, N.Y.C., 1831-41; ret. to estate nr. Fishkill-on-the-Hudson (now Beacon), N.Y., 1841, engaged in horticulture and landscape gardening; travelled in Europe to gather plants and study parks, 1847-49. Author: Skeleton Tours, 1870; also supplements for 2 books by Andrew Downing: A Treatise on the Theory and Practise of Landscape Gardening, 1841; Cottage Residences, 1842. Died Fishkill-on-the-Hudson, Nov. 11, 1882.

SARGENT, John Osborne, lawyer, journalist; b. Gloucester, Mass., Sept. 20, 1811; s. Epes and Hannah Dane (Coffin) S.; grad. Harvard, 1830; m. Georgiana Welles, Jan. 17, 1854, 1 dau. Admitted to Mass. bar, 1834; contbr. polit. articles to Boston Atlas, 1834-37; assisted in editing New Eng. Magazine, 1835; mem. lower house Mass. Legislature (Whig), 1836, 37; asso. editor Courier and Enquirer, N.Y.C., 1838-41; published A Lecture on the Lake Improvements in Steam Navigation, 1844; conducted a publ. supporting Taylor's candidacy, 1848; joint editor the Republic (ofcl. organ of the adminstrn.), Washington, D.C., 1849; published in Europe a translation of The Last Knight (A.A. von Auersperg) from the German, 1871; published Chapters for the Times (in opposition to Republican James Blaine), 1884; translations of Horace appeared in Horatian Echoes (his best work), 1893; elected to bd. overseers Harvard; 1880; offered prize of $100 for best translation from Horace by a Harvard or Radcliffe student, from 1886-87 on. Died Dec. 28, 1891.

SARGENT, Lucius Manlius, reformer, author; b. Boston, June 25, 1786; s. Daniel and Mary (Turner) S.; attended Harvard, 1804-circa 1807, A.M. (hon.), 1842; m. Mary Binney, Apr. 3, 1816; m. 2d, Sarah Cutler Dunn, July 14, 1825; 3 children. Published Translations from the Minor Latin Poets, 1807; The Culex of Virgil; with a Translation into English Verse, 1807; admitted to the bar, 1811; Hubert and Ellen, 1813; prominent leader in temperance movement; wrote Temperance Tales, 2 vols., 1848; began series of weekly articles entitled Dealings with the Dead in Boston Evening Transcript, 1848, published in book form, 1856; attacked coolie trade of British in India in Boston Evening Transcript, 1856; published The Ballad of the Abolition Blunderbuss, 1861. Died June 2, 1867.

SARGENT, Nathan, journalist; b. Putney, Vt., May 5, 1794; s. Samuel and Mary (Washburn) S.; m. Rosina (Hodgkinson) Lewis, Feb. 14, 1821, 4 children. Admitted to N.Y. bar, 1818; judge county and probate cts. Cahawba, Ala., circa 1820-25; estabished Comml. Herald (Whig newspaper), Phila., 1830; successful corr. U.S. Gazette, Phila., under pseudonym Oliver Oldschool, 1842; sgt.-at-arms U.S. Ho. of Reps., 1847-51; register gen. U.S. Land Office, 1851-53; U.S. commr. customs, 1861-71; pres. Washington (D.C.) Reform Sch., 1867-circa 1870; Whig. Author: Brief Outline of the Life of Henry Clay, 1844; Some Public Men and Events. Died Washington, Feb. 2, 1875.

SARGENT, Winthrop, lawyer, author: b. Phila., Sept. 23, 1825; s. George Washington and Margaret (Percy) S.; grad. U. Pa., 1845, Harvard Law Sch., 1847; m. Sarah Ellery Gray, Apr. 22, 1851, 1 child. Practiced law, Boston, 1847-51, N.Y.C., 1865-67; lived in Phila., 1851-60, New Orleans, 1860-65; author Life and Career of Major John Andre, 1861; edited (with notes) The History of an Expedition against Fort du Quesne in 1775, published 1855, The Loyal Verses of Joseph Stansbury and Doctor Jonathan Odell, 1860. Died Paris, France, May 18, 1870.

SARGENT, Winthrop, territorial gov.; b. Gloucester, Mass., May 1, 1753; s. Winthrop and Judith (Saunders) S.; grad. Harvard, 1771; m. Rowena Tupper, Feb. 9, 1789; m. 2d, Mary (McIntosh) Williams, Oct. 24, 1798; 3 sons. Joined Continental Army, 1775; brevetted maj., 1781; surveyor on Seven Ranges in Ohio, 1786; an original member Ohio Co., 1786, elected sec., 1787; a founder Marietta (O.), 1788; apptd. by Congress as sec. Territory N.W. of River Ohio, 1787-98; adj. gen. to Gen. Arthur St. Clair's expdn. against the Indians; acting gov. Territory N.W. of River Ohio, organized militia to repel anticipated Indian attacks, 1791; 1st gov. Miss. Territory, 1798-1801; mem. Am. Philos. Soc., Soc. of Cincinnati, Am. Acad. Arts and Scis., Mass. Hist. Soc.; published (with Benjamin Smith) Papers Relative to Certain American Antiquities; wrote poem entitled Boston, 1803; name possibly Sargeant. Died nr. New Orleans, June 3, 1820.

SARONY, Napoleon, artist; b. Que., Can., Mar. 9, 1821. Came to N.Y.C., circa 1836; lithographer with Henry R. Robinson and Nathaniel Currier; established (with Henry B. Major) firm Sarony & Major (later Sarony, Major & Knapp), N.Y.C., 1846, left firm, circa 1867; visited Cuba, travelled in Europe, did lithographic work in Germany, France and Eng.; opened photographic studio, Birmingham, Eng., noted for artistic photography; returned to N.Y.C., became successful photographer; did charcoal portraits. Died N.Y.C., Nov. 9, 1896.

SARPY, Peter A., fur trader; b. St. Louis, Nov. 3, 1805; s. Gregoire Berald and Palagie (L'Abadie) S.; m. Nicomi Sarpy.. Probably 1st White resident of Neb.; employed as clk. of John P. Cabanné (agt. for Mo. and Am. fur cos.), Council Bluffs, Ia., 1823, took charge of post established at Bellevue on West bank of Mississippi River; arrested Leclerc party, 1832; licensed fur trader at fork of Missouri and Platte rivers; played significant part in negotiation of land session treaties with Omaha and Oto Indians, 1854; helped Brigham Young and Mormon expdn. with supplies and by negotiating with Indians, early 1840's; made q.m. brigade of Neb. Volunteers to carry ferries over Missouri, Elkhorn and Loup rivers; introduced steam ferry service between St. Mary (Ia.) and Bellevue (Neb.); established post store at St. Mary; founder St. Mary Gazette; participated in laying out towns of Bellevue and Decatur (Neb.). Died Plattsmouth, Neb., Jan. 4 ,1865; buried St. Louis.

SARTAIN, John, engraver, publisher; b. London, Eng., Oct. 24, 1808; s. John and Ann (Burgess) S.; m. Susannah Longmate Swaine, Jan. 11, 1830 8 children including Samuel, William, Emily. Apprentice to William Young Ottley who was writing an hist. sketch of the early Florentin sch. of painters; executed 18 plates, left 14 plates unfinished, 1826; came to Am., 1830; held exhbn. Franklin Inst., 1830; executed plates for Gentleman's Magazine, the Casket, Godey's Lady's Book; mem. staf Graham's Magazine, 1841; introduced pictorial illustration as a distinctive feature of Am. periodicals; propr. Campbell's Fgn. Semi-Monthly Magazine, 1843; owner, editor quarto-volume The American Gallery of Art, 1847; held financial interest in Eclectic Mus.; purchased (with William Sloanaker) Union Magazine, 1848, changed name to Sartain's Union Magazine of Literature and Art, published with noted personages of the time as contbrs.), 1849-52; made engravings, vignettes for early bank notes; attended Internat. Exposition, Paris, France, 1855; delivered diplomas of hon. membership in Pa. Acad. of Fine Arts to European notables, 1862; became chief bur. art Centennial Exhbn., Phila., 1875; chief Am. art dept., collected pictures for London Exposition, 1886; made Freeman of London, circa 1890; v.p. Phila. Sch. Design for Women, 14 years; mem. Artists Fund Soc. (pres. 1844), Soc. St. George; responsible for unique arrangement of galleries and rooms at Pa. Acad. Fine Arts, dir., academician, 23 years; founder in Am. of br. of engraving on steel known as mezzo-tinto, circa 1831 (a copy of Neagle's painting Old Age); works Christ Rejected (after Benjamin West), The Iron-Worker and King Solomon (after Christian Schussele) were among largest and finest ever executed in Am. Author: Reminiscenses of a Very Old Man (autobiography). Died Phila., Oct. 25, 1897; buried Monument Cemetery, Phila.

SARTWELL, Henry Parker, physician, botanist; b. Pittsfield, Mass., Apr. 18, 1792; s. Levi and Eleanor (Crotut) S.; Ph.D. (hon.), Hamilton Coll., 1864; m. 4 times. Licensed to practice medicine by Oneida County (N.Y.) Med. Soc., Sept. 7, 1811; began practice of medicine, New Hartford, N.Y., 1811; served as surgeon U.S. Army during War of 1812; pres. Yates County (N.Y.) Med. Soc.; contbr. to Catologue of Plants Found in Oneida County and Vicinity (John Alsop Paine). 1865; his meteorol. observations now on reference at Smithsonian Instn.; an expert horticulturist; most valuable work is Carices Americae Septentrionalis Exsiccatae, 2 vols., 1848-50; his herbarium now forms part of collection of Hamilton Coll., Clinton, N.Y. Died Penn Yan, N.Y., Nov. 15, 1867.

SASSACUS, Indian chief; b. nr. what is now Groton, Conn., 1560; s. Wopigwooit. Chief sachem of Pequot Indians, 1633-37; involved in conflict with English settlers, 1633-36, became full scale war, 1636; attempted to persuade Narragansett Indians to ally with him; made frequent raids on Conn. settlements, 1636-37; an English force led by John Mason attacked and killed most of his tribe at camp on Mystic river in Conn., May 1637. Killed by Mohawk Indians while fleeing from English, June 1637.

SATTER, Gustav, musician; b. Vienna, Austria, Feb. 12, 1832; studied medicine, Paris, France. Became pianist, toured U.S. and Brazil, 1854-60; returned to Paris, resided successively in Vienna, Dresden, Hanover, Gothenburg, and Stockholm, later revisited Am.; toured So. states, after 1874, resided mainly in Ga. as tchr. and pianist. Died Savannah, Ga., 1879.

SATTERLEE, Richard Sherwood, army surgeon, physician; b. Fairfield, Herkimer County, N.Y., Dec. 6, 1798; s. William and Hanna (Sherwood) S.; attended Fairfield Acad.; m. Mary S. Hunt, June 1827. Licensed to practice medicine, 1818; entered U.S. Army as asst. surgeon, 1822; served with brigade of Col. Zachary Taylor during Seminole War in Fla., 1837; received ofcl. commendation for med. seervice at Battle of Okeechobee, 1837; with army at Veracruz and Mexico City during Mexican War, sr. surgeon Gen. William Worth's div. of regulars, dir. med. service of div. at battles of Cerro Gordo, Churubusco, Molino del Rey, Chapultepec; apptd. med. dir. on staff Gen. Scott, charged with establishment of gen. hosp. to care for bulk of army casualties; commd. maj., 1832; apptd. med. purveyor, 1853; brevetted lt. col., then brig. gen., 1866; apptd. chief med. purveyor with rank lt. col.; in charge of med. supply depot, N.Y.C., 1866-69. Died N.Y.C., Nov. 10, 1880.

SAUGRAIN DE VIGNI, Antoine Francois, physician; b. Paris, France, Feb. 17, 1763; s. Antoine and Marie (Brunet) Saugrain; m. Genevieve Rosalie Michau, Mar. 20, 1793, 6 children. Went to Mexico to examine mines and mineral prodn., 1785-86; sailed for U.S., 1787; taken captive by Indians in attack, escaped, 1788; apptd. post surgeon by Spanish lt. gov. Delassus, St. Louis, 1800; army surgeon (apptd. by Jefferson), 1805-11; only practicing physician in St. Louis when Upper Louisiana was transferred to U.S.; made and sold ink, thermometers, phosphoric lights for hunters, barometers; conducted experiments in electricity and had electric battery; introduced 1st smallpox vaccine virus brought to St. Louis and publicly offered to vaccinate free of charge all indigent persons, paupers and Indians, 1809. Died circa May 19, 1820.

SAULSBURY, Eli, senator; b. Kent County, Del., Dec. 29, 1817; s. William and Margaret (Smith) S.; attended Dickinson Coll., Carlisle, Pa. Represented Kent County in Del. Ho. of Reps., 1853, 54; admitted to Del. bar, 1857; del. to Democratic Nat. Conv., Chgo., 1864; mem. U.S. Senate from Del., 1871-89, made speech in favor of removal of political disabilities of former Confederates and against Civil Rights bill, 1872, opposed recognition La. state government, 1874, favored white supremacy, author resolution to inquire into conditions in Samoa, presented many petitions for legislation prohibiting liquor traffic. Died Dover, Del., Mar. 22, 1893; buried Silver Lake Cemetery, Dover.

SAULSBURY, Gove, gov. Del.; b. Kent County, Del., May 29, 1815; s. William and Margaret (Smith) S.; attended Del. Coll., Newark; M.D., U. Pa., 1842; m. Rosina Jane Smith, Nov. 1, 1848, 5 children. Joined Methodist Episcopal Ch., 1843; pres. bd. trustees Wilmington Conf. Acad.; del. Ecumenical Council of Methodism, London, Eng., Sept. 1881; del. Nat. Democratic Conv., 1856, 76, 80; mem. Del. Senate, 1862-65, became recognized Dem. leader, elected speaker, 1865; acting gov. Del., 1865, gov., 1866-71; opposed successively each of amendments to U.S. Constn. growing out of Civil War (each rejected by Del. Legislature). Died Dover, Del., July 31, 1881.

SAULSBURY, Willard, senator, jurist; b. Mispillion Hundred, Kent County, Del., June 2, 1820; s. William and Margaret (Smith) S.; attended Del. Coll., Newark, Dickinson Coll., Carlisle, Pa.; m. Annie Miby Ponder, May 11, 1850, 3 children including John P., Willard. Admitted to Del. bar, 1845; practiced in Georgetown, Del.; apptd. atty. gen. of Del., 1850-55; chosen del. democratic Nat. Conv., Cincinnati, 1856; mem. U.S. Senate from Del., 1859-71, proposed referendum on compensated emancipation in Mo., 1863; del. Dem. Nat. Conv., Chgo., 1864; chancellor of Del., 1873-92; his opinions published in 6 Delaware Chancery Reports (edited by his son Willard); notable opinion is Green vs. Saulsbury wherein he defined jurisdiction of Orphans' Ct. and traced its history from its establishment in 1683 at Phila. Died Dover, Del., Apr. 6, 1892; buried Christ Episcopal Churchyard, Dover.

SAUNDERS, Alvin, senator, territorial gov.; b. nr. Flemingsburg, Ky., July 12, 1817; s. Gunnell and Mary (Maury) S.; m. Marthena Barlow, Mar. 11, 1856, 2 children. Postmaster, Mt. Pleasant (Ia.), 1838-46; del. Ia. Constl. Conv., 1846; mem. Ia. Senate, 1854-61; mem. 1st Ia. Republican Conv.,

Iowa City, 1856; mem. Rep. Nat. Conv., 1860, 68; gov. Territory of Neb., 1861-67; mem. Neb. Bd. Edn., 1874; mem. U.S. Senate from Neb., 1877-83; founder, pres. State Bank of Neb., Omaha; founder, pres. Omaha Real Estate Exchange, 1886; incorporator Neb. Christian U. (later Cotner Coll.; now defunct), Bethany Heights, Neb. Died Omaha, Nov. 1, 1899; buried Forest Lawn Cemetery, Omaha.

SAUNDERS, Henry Dmochowski, sculptor; b. Vilna, Lithuania, Oct. 14, 1810; ed. Vilna; studied sculpture in Paris, France, circa 1846. Came to Am., added name Saunders to original name Dmochowski; lived in Phila., 1853-57, exhibited at Pa. Acad.; went to Washington, D.C., sold busts of Kosciuszko and Pulaski to U.S. Govt. (now in Capitol), 1857; returned to Poland. Died in fight for Polish liberation, 1863.

SAUNDERS, Prince, reformer, attorney-gen. Haiti; b. Thetford, Vt., 1775; s. Cuff and Phyllis Saunders; attended Moor's Charity Sch. at Dartmouth Coll., 1807-08. Tchr. in sch. for Negroes, Colchester, Conn., then in sch. for Negro children, Boston, 1809; founded Belles Lettres Soc. in Boston; sent from Boston to Eng. as del. of Masonic Lodge of Africans, circa 1813; sent with other tchrs. to Haiti to organize a sch. system on the English Lancastrian Plan and to aid in the changing of the religion of Haiti from Catholic to Protestant, circa 1814; under the direction of Wilberforce he introduced vaccination into Haiti, 1816; sent back to Eng. as messenger or envoy of Emperor Christophe of Haiti; published Haytian Papers (a translation of laws of Haiti and the Code Henri with his own comments), Eng., 1816, Am. edit. published by Bingham & Co., Boston, 1818; went back to Haiti, 1820; became atty. gen. Haiti by 1839. Author: An Address . . . before the Pennsylvania Augustine Society, 1818; A Memoir . . . to the American Convention for Promoting the Abolition of Slavery, 1818. Died Port-au-Prince, Haiti, Feb. 1839.

SAUNDERS, Romulus Mitchell, congressman, diplomat; b. Caswell County, N.C., Mar. 3, 1791; s. William and Hannah (Mitchell) S.; attended U. N.C., 1809-11; m. Rebecca Peine Carter, Dec. 22, 1812; m. 2d, Anna Heyes Johnson, May 26, 1823; 11 children. Admitted to Tenn. bar, 1812; mem. N.C. Ho. of Commons from Caswell County, 1815, 18-21, from Wake County, 1850-52, speaker, 1819-20, mem. N.C. Senate, 1816; mem. U.S. Ho. of Reps. from N.C., 17th-19th, 27th-28th congresses, 1821-27, 41-45; atty. gen. N.C., 1828-31; apptd. mem. commn. on French Spoliation claims, 1834; judge N.C. Superior Ct., 1835-40, 52-67; del. Democratic Nat. Conv., 1844, moved for adoption of 2/3 rule which helped defeat Van Buren and became permanent part of Dem. nominating conv. procedure; apptd. U.S. minister to Spain by Pres. Polk with spl. commn. to negotiate for purchase of Cuba for $100,000,000, 1846, broached Cuban question but encountered refusal to discuss matter, 1848, resigned, 1849; mem. Code Commn. to revise N.C. laws, 1852-54; trustee U. N.C., 1859-64. Died Raleigh, N.C., Apr. 21, 1867; buried Old City Cemetery, Raleigh.

SAUNDERS, William, horticulturist; b. St. Andrews, Scotland, Dec. 7, 1822; attended U. Edinburgh (Scotland); m. Martha Mildwaters, 1848. Came to U.S., 1848; in partnership with Thomas Meehan in landscape gardening, Phila., 1854-62; designed several parks and cemeteries including Rose Hill Cemetery, Chgo.; supt. exptl. gardens of U.S. Dept. Agr., 1862-1900; designed grounds of Dept. Agr. at Washington, D.C., nat. cemetery at Gettysburg, grounds for Lincoln monument in Springfield, Ill., and U.S. Dept. Agr. exhibits for Centennial Exhbn., Phila., 1876, New Orleans Expn., 1884, Paris Exhbn., 1889; established conservatories and greenhouses for study of economically important plants; mem. Parking Commn. of Washington, 1871; introduced Washington Navel orange from Brazil, 1871, several hundred varieties of Russian apples, 1870, eucaylptus globulus from Australia, 1866; co-founder Patrons of Husbandry, 1867, pres., 1867-73. Died Sept. 11, 1900.

SAUNDERS, William Laurence, editor, historian; b. Raleigh, N.C., July 30, 1835; s. Rev. Joseph Hubbard and Laura (Baker) S.; grad. U. N.C., 1854, LL.B., 1858, LL.D., 1889; m. Florida Cotten, Feb. 3, 1864. Licensed in law, 1856, began practice in Salisbury, N.C.; editor Salisbury Banner; served from pvt. to col. Confederate States Army, 1861-65, in command of 46th N.C. Regt. at Appomatox; assumed direction of the activities of the "Invisible Empire" or Ku Klux Klan, 1866 (although he was never a regular mem. of orgn. and bound by no oath); an editor Wilmington (N.C.) Jour., 1872-76; chief clk. N.C. Senate, 1870-74; moved to Raleigh, N.C., established (with Peter M. Hale) the Observer, editor, 1876-80; sec. of state N.C., 1879-91; played large part in the reopening of U. N.C., trustee, 1875-91, sec. bd. Author: The Colonial Records of North Carolina, 10 vols., 1886-90. Died Raleigh, Apr. 2, 1891.

SAVAGE, Edward, painter, engraver; b. Princeton, Mass., Nov. 26, 1761; s. Seth and Lydia (Craige) S.; m. Sarah Seaver, Oct. 13, 1794, 8 children. Commd. by pres. of Harvard to paint a portrait of Washington, 1789-90, picture delivered at Cambridge, Mass., Aug. 1790; received art instrn. from Benjamin West, London, Eng., 1791; in Phila., 1795, exhibited a panorama depicting London and Westminster in a circle; joined with Daniel Bowen in opening N.Y. Museum, 1801; painted Family Group at Mount Vernon (portraits of George and Martha Washington; now owned by Boston Museum of Fine Arts); made mezzotints of his own oil portraits of Gen. Anthony Wayne, Dr. Benjamin Rush, Thomas Jefferson and plates of "Liberty" and "The Washington Family;" became a partner Poignaud and Plantcotton Factory, Lancaster, Mass., 1809. Died July 6, 1817.

SAVAGE, James, antiquary; b. Boston, July 13, 1784; s. Habijah and Elizabeth (Tudor) S.; grad. Harvard, 1803, LL.D. (hon.), 1841; m. Elizabeth Otis (Stillman) Lincoln, Apr. 1823, 4 children. Admitted to Mass. bar, 1807; compiled an index of the Charters and General Laws of the Colony and Province of Massachusetts Bay, published by State of Mass., 1814; copied and annotated 3d vol. of History of New England (John Winthrop) for Mass. Hist. Soc., 1816; as a result of his persistence Provident Instn. for Savs. was incorporated (one of 1st savs. banks inc. in U.S.), 1816; elected to lower house Mass. Legislature, also to Mass. Senate, Mass. Exec. Council, several times; del. Mass. Constl. Conv., circa 1820; mem. Common Council, Bd. of Aldermen and Sch. Com., all Boston; mem. bd. overseers Harvard, 15 years; a founder Boston Athenaeum; pres. Mass. Hist. Soc. Author: The History of New England from 1630 to 1649, 2 vols., 1825-26, 3d vol., 1853; Genealogical Dictionary of the First Settlers of New England Showing Three Generations of Those Who Came before May 1692 on the Basis of the Farmer's Register, 4 vols., 1860-62. Died Boston, Mar. 8, 1873.

SAVAGE, John, congressman, jurist; b. Salem, Washington County, N.Y., Feb. 22, 1779; grad. Union Coll., Schenectady, N.Y., 1799; studied law. Admitted to bar, 1800, practiced in Salem; dist. atty. 4th N.Y. Dist., 1806-11, 12-13; mem. N.Y. State Assembly, 1814; mem. U.S. Ho. of Reps. (Democrat) from N.Y., 14th-15th congresses, 1815-19; dist. atty. Washington County, 1818-20; N.Y. State comptroller, 1821-23; chief justice N.Y. State Supreme Ct., 1823-26; apptd. treas. U.S., 1828 (did not accept office); Dem. presdl. elector, 1844. Died Utica, N.Y., Oct. 19, 1863; buried Forest Hill Cemetery.

SAVAGE, John, journalist, dramatist; b. Dublin, Ireland, Dec. 13, 1828; attended art school of Royal Dublin Soc.; LL.D. (hon.), St. John's Coll., Fordham, N.Y., 1875; m. Louise Gouverneur, Aug. 1854, 1 adopted dau. With J. DeC. Young issued Patriot, Apr. 1848; promoted Irish Tribune issued by "Students' Club;" fled from Dublin, 1848, came to N.Y.C.; became proof-reader N.Y. Tribune, 1848; literary editor Citizen, 1854-59; published '98 and '48: The Modern Revolutionary History and Literature of Ireland, 1856; went to Washington (D.C.), 1857, became editorial writer on the States, part owner by 1861; wrote mediocre tragedy Sybil, produced in various cities, 1858, published 1865; published The Life and Public Services of Andrew Johnson, 1866; joined 69th Regt. under Gen. Corcoran; wrote number of tuneful verses designed to inspirit Northern forces including "The Starry Flag" published in collection of verse by Savage entitled Faith and Fancy, 1864; editorial writer New Orleans Times, 1864-67; became chief exec. Fenian Brotherhood in Am., 1867, organizing Irish socs. and collection funds for Fenian cause; wrote Fenian Heroes and Martyrs, 1868; visited Cal., 1870; popular lectr. before Catholic colls. and fraternal orgns. Died Laurelside, Pa.,Oct. 9, 1888.

SAVAGE, John Simpson, congressman, lawyer; b. Clermont County, O., Oct. 30, 1841; attended public schs.; studied law. Taught sch.; admitted to bar, 1865, practiced in Wilmington, Clinton County, O., 1865; mem. U.S. Ho. of Reps. (Democrat) from Ohio, 44th Congress, 1875-77. Died Wilmington, Nov. 24, 1884; buried Sugar Grove Cemetery.

SAVAGE, Thomas Staughton, clergyman, physician, missionary; b. Middletown (now Cromwell), Conn., June 7, 1804; s. Josiah and Mary (Roberts) S.; grad. Yale, 1825, M.D., 1833; grad. Theol. Sem., Alexandria, Va., 1836; m. Susan Metcalf, June 2, 1838; m. 2d, Maria Chapin, Dec. 18, 1842; m. 3d, Elizabeth Rutherford, 1844. Ordained priest Protestant Episcopal Ch., 1836; 1st missionary sent to Africa by Protestant Episcopal Ch., arrived Cape Palmas, Liberia, 1836, established mission on Mt. Vaughan; returned to Am. due to health, 1838; returned to Cape Palmas, 1839; stationed at Fishtown, 1845-46; returned to U.S., 1847; wrote papers and articles on gorilla (previously unknown in U.S.), also on habits of chimpanzee, published in Boston Jour. of Natural History, also in Proceedings of Acad. of Natural Scis. of Phila., served in parishes in Miss., Ala., 1847-50; apptd. asso. sec. Episcopal Bd. Missions, 1868; rector Ch. of Ascension, Rhinecliff, N.Y., 1869-80. Died Rhinecliff, Dec. 29, 1880.

SAVERY, William, cabinet maker; b. 1721; m. Mary Peters, Apr. 19, 1746, 11 children including William. Assessor of central wards, Phila., 1754; agt., collector taxes for Guardians of the Poor, Phila., 1767; prosperous cabinet maker, his work responsible for reputation of Phila. furniture of colonial period as most elaborate and ornate of any Am. furniture; influenced by Thomas Chippendale and Robert Manwaring of Eng.; several pieces of his furniture now in Met. Museum of Art, N.Y.C. Died May 1787.

SAVERY, William, preacher; b. Phila., Sept. 3, 1750; s. William and Mary (Peters) S.; m. Sarah Evans, Nov. 19, 1778. Operated own tanneries, Phila.; was present with other mems. Soc. of Friends (Quakers) during treaty negotiations with Indians nr. Detroit, 1793, at Council of 1794 with Six Nations, Canandiagua, N.Y.; made reports on these activities which influenced Soc. of Friends of Phila. to establish extensive missionary work among Seneca Indians; made religious pilgrimage to Europe, 1796-98; outstanding event of his ministry was the conversion of Elizabeth (Gurney) Fry; became famous as preacher in Eng.; returned to Phila., resumed tanning bus., 1798. Died Phila., June 19, 1804.

SAWTELLE, Cullen, congressman, lawyer; b. Norridgewock, Me., Sept. 25, 1805; grad. Bowdoin Coll., 1825; studied law. Admitted to bar, 1828, practiced in Norridgewock until 1841; register of probate, 1830-38; mem. Me. Senate, 1842-44; mem. U.S. Ho. of Reps. (Democrat) from Me., 29th, 31st congresses, 1845-47, 49-51; atty., credit mgr. for several merc. firms, N.Y.C., 1852-82. Died Englewood, Bergen County, N.J., Nov. 10, 1887; buried Brookside Cemetery.

SAWYER, Frederick Adolphus, senator; b. Bolton, Worcester County, Mass., Dec. 12, 1822; grad. Harvard, 1844. Taught sch., Gardiner, Me., 1844-47, Wiscasset, Me., 1847-51, Lowell, Mass., Nashua, N.H., 1852, Wakefield, Mass., 1853-55, Boston, 1855-59; in charge of State Normal Sch., Charleston, S.C., 1859; allowed to return to North in Civil War, 1864; returned to Charleston, 1865, active in advancing reconstrn. measures; apptd. collector internal revenue 2d S.C. Dist., 1865; mem. U.S. Senate (Republican) from S.C., July 16, 1868-73; asst. sec. Treasury, 1873-74; with U.S. Coast Survey, 1874-80; spl. agt. War Dept., 1880-87; conducted prep. sch., Ithaca, N.Y.; gave pvt. instrn. to students Cornell U.; moved to Tenn., became pres. of company to promote sale agrl. lands, Cumberland Gap. Died suddenly in hotel at Shawnee, Caliborne County, Tenn., July 31, 1891; buried at Sawyer Heights on property of his land company, N.E. of Scott Cemetery, nr. East Cumberland Gap, Tenn.

SAWYER, Leicester Ambrose, clergyman; b. Pinckney, Lewis County, N.Y., July 28, 1807; s. Jonathan and Lucy (Harper) S.; grad. Hamilton Coll., 1828, Princeton Theol. Sem., 1831, m. Pamelia Bert Bosworth, Sept. 26, 1832, 10 children. Licensed to preach by Presbytery of Watertown (Conn.), 1831, ordained, 1832; pastor North (now United) Congregational Ch., New Haven, Conn., 1835-37; pastor Pack St. (now Dwight Pl.) Ch., New Haven, 1840-43; pres. Central Coll., Columbus, O., 1843-54, also pastor; pastor Presbyn. chs., Monroeville, O., then Sackets Harbor, N.Y., until 1854, Congl. Ch., Westmoreland, N.Y., 1854-59; retired as an independent Christian minister, 1859; night editor Utica (N.Y.) Morning Herald, 1868-83; translated entire Bible from original langs., stated that Old Testament contained no reference to Jesus as Messiah, believed Jesus was merely a social reformer. Author: Baptism by Affusion and Sprinkling, 1838; The Children of Believers Entitled to Baptism, 1839; A Critical Exposition of Mental Philosophy, 1839; The New Testament Translated from the Original Greek, 1858; The Holy Bible Translated and Arranged with Notes, 3 vols., 1860-62. Died Whitesboro, Onedia County, N.Y., Dec. 29, 1898.

SAWYER, Lemuel, congressman, author; b. Camden County, N.C., 1777; s. Lemuel and Mary (Taylor) S.; grad. U. N.C., 1799; attended U. Pa.; studied law, 3 years; m. Mary Snowden, Aug. 1810; m. 2d, Camilla Wertz, Dec. 24, 1820; m. 3d, Diana (Ropalye) Fisher, 1828. Admitted to N.Y. bar; mem. N.C. Ho. of Commons from Camden County, 1800-01; Republican presdl. elector, 1804; mem. N.C. Council of State, 1804; mem. U.S. Ho. of Reps. (Rep.) from N.Y., 10th-12th, 15th-17th, 19th-20th congreses, 1807-13, 17-23, 25-29, offered resolution designed to open trade with West Indies, 1808, proposed increase in size of U.S. Navy, 1812, proposed use of war vessel for exploration of polar regions of N. Am., 1825, 'acksonian Democrat, after 1824; departmental lk. U.S. Govt., Washington, D.C., 1850-52. Author: Blackbeard, A Comedy in Four Acts; 'ounded on Fact (staged, N.Y.C. 1833), 1824; The Wreck of Honor, A Tragedy, in Five Acts, irca 1826; A Biography of John Randolph of Roanoke, with a Selection from His Speeches, 1844; Autobiography, 1844. Died Washington, Jan. 9, 1852; buried Lambs Ferry, Camden County.

SAWYER, Lorenzo, jurist; b. Leray, Jefferson County, N.Y., May 23, 1820; s. Jesse and Elizabeth (Goodell) S.; grad. Western Res. Coll.; LL.D. (hon.), Hamilton Coll., 1877; m. Jennie M. Aldrich, Mar. 10, 1857, 3 children. Tchr., Latin and mathematics Central Coll., Columbus, O., admitted to Ohio bar, 1846; formed partnership with Lt. Gov. J. E. Holmes in Wis., circa 1848; arrived in Cal., 1850; moved to San Francisco, 1853; became city atty. San Francisco, 1854; apptd. judge dist. ct. 12th Jud. dist. Cal., 1862; elected to Cal. Supreme Ct., 1863, chief justice, 1868-70; U.S. circuit judge for 9th circuit, 1870, presiding judge Ct. of Appeals for 9th circuit, 1891; 1st a Whig, later mem. Am. Party, a Republican most of his life; 1st pres. bd. trustees Leland Stanford Junior U. Died San Francisco, Sept. 7, 1891.

SAWYER, Samuel Locke, congressman, lawyer; b. Mt. Vernon, N.H., Nov. 27, 1813; grad. Dartmouth, 1833; studied law. Admitted to Amherst (N.J.) bar, 1836; moved to Lexington, Mo., 1838, practiced law. Elected circuit atty. Mo. 6th Jud. Circuit, 1848, 52; del. Mo. Constl. Conv., 1861; del. Nat. Democratic Conv., N.Y.C., 1868; judge 24th Jud. Circuit, 1871-76; mem. U.S. Ho. of Reps. (Dem.) from Mo., 46th Congress, 1879-81; became banker. Died Independence, Mo., Mar. 29, 1890; buried Woodlawn Cemetery.

SAWYER, Samuel Tredwell, congressman, lawyer; b. Edenton, Chowan County, N.C., 1800; attended Edenton Acad., U. N.C.; studied law. Admitted to bar, practiced in Edenton; mem. N.C. Ho. of Reps., 1829-32; mem. N.C. Senate, 1834; mem. U.S. Ho. of Reps. (Democrat) from N.C., 25th Congress, 1837-39; moved to Norfolk, Va., practiced law; editor Norfolk Argus several years; apptd. collector of customs at Norfolk, 1853-58; moved to Washington, D.C.; apptd. commissary with rank of maj. in Confederate Army during Civil War, 1861-62. Died Bloomfield, N.J., Nov. 29, 1865.

SAWYER, Sylvanus, inventor; b. Templeton, Mass., Apr. 15, 1822; s. John Sawyer. Sent to work in gunsmith shop, Augusta, Me., 1839; invented several things, including a small railroad car operated by foot; employed in coppersmith's shop, Boston, 1844; employed by mfr. locks and house trimmings, 1845; patentee machinery for splitting and dressing rattan, 1849, for cutting rattan, 1851, additional rattan machinery, 1854, 55; supt. Am. Rattan Co., Fitchburg, Mass., circa 1852-55; patented improvements in rifled cannon and projectiles, 1855, dividers and calipers, 1867, steam generator, 1868, shoe-sole machine, 1876, centering lathe, 1882. Died Fitchburg, Oct. 13, 1895.

SAWYER, William, congressman; b. Montgomery County, O., Aug. 5, 1803. Apprenticed to blacksmith, 1818, worked in Dayton, O., also nr. Grand Rapids, Mich.; moved to Miamisburg, O., 1829; mem. Ohio Ho. of Reps., 1832-35, 56, speaker, 1835; moved to St. Marys, Auglaize County, O., 1843; mem. United States Ho. of Reps. (Dem.) from Ohio, 29th-30th congresses, 1845-49; de l.Ohio Constl. Conv., 1850-51; receiver of Land Office of Otter Trail dist. in Minn., 1855-61; trustee Ohio A. and M. Coll. (later Ohio State U.), 1870-74; mayor, justice of peace, St. Marys, 1870-77. Died St. Marys, Sept. 18, 1877; buried Elm Grove Cemetery.

SAXE, John Godfrey, journalist, poet; b. Highgate, Franklin County, Vt., June 2, 1816; s. Peter and Elizabeth (Jewett) S.; grad. Middletown Coll., 1839; LL.D. (hon.), Middlebury Coll., 1866; m. Sophia Newell Sollace, Sept. 9, 1841, 6 children including Charles. Admitted to Vt. bar, 1843; supt. common schs. Chittenden County (Vt.), 1847-48; states atty. Chittenden County, 1850-51; owner, editor weekly newspaper Burlington (Vt.) Sentinel, 1850-56. Author: Progress: A Satirical Poem, 1846; Humorous and Satirical Poems, 1850; Leisure-Day Rhymes, 1875; contbr. humorous poems to Knickerbocker mag.; works collected in Selections from the Poems of John Godfrey Saxe, published 1905. Died Albany, N.Y., Mar. 31, 1887.

SAXTON, Joseph, inventor; b. Huntington, Pa., Mar. 22, 1799; s. James and Hannah (Ashbaugh) S.; m. Mary Abercrombie, 1850, 1 child. Watchmaker, Phila., 1817-28; made clock for Belfry of Independence Hall; in England, 1828-37; invented magneto-electric machine, 1833, also invented a fountain pen, locomotive differential pulley; constructor and curator of standard weighing apparatus of U.S. Mint, Phila., 1837-43; designed standard balance used in govt. assay and coining offices; supt. weights and measures for U.S. Coast Survey, Washington, D.C., 1843-73; invented hydrometer, fusible metal seal, ever-sharp pencil; mem. Nat. Acad. Scis., Am. Philos. Soc. Died Oct. 26, 1873.

SAY, Benjamin, physician, congressman; b. Phila., Aug. 28, 1755; s. Thomas and Rebekah (Atkinson) Budd Say; M.D., U. Pa., 1780; m. Ann Bonsall, Oct. 1, 1776; m. 2d, Miriam Moore, Dec. 22, 1795; 7 children including Thomas. Conducted apothecary shop in connection with med. practice; a founder, jr. fellow Coll. of Physicians, Phila., signed coll. constn. at its adoption, 1787, treas., 1791-1809; an incorporator Pa. Humane Soc., pres., 1799; mem. Pa. Senate, 1799-1801; mem. U.S. Ho. of Reps. from Pa., 10th congress, Nov. 16, 1808-June 1809; mem. Pa. Prison Soc. Author: A Short Compilation of the Extraordinary Life and Writings of Thomas Say, 1796; An Annual Oration Pronounced before the Humane Society of Philadelphia, 1799. Died Phila., Apr. 23, 1813.

SAY, Lucy Way Sistare, artist; b. New London, Conn., Oct. 14, 1801; m. Thomas Say. Provided some of illustrations for American Conchology (Thomas Say); lived at New Harmony (Ind.), 1833-41; became 1st woman mem. Acad. Natural Scis. of Phila., 1841; lived in N.Y.C., Newburgh, N.Y., and West New Brighton, N.Y., after 1842. Died Lexington, Mass., Nov. 15, 1886.

SAY, Thomas, entomologist, conchologist; b. Phila., June 27, 1787; s. Benjamin and Ann (Bonsall) S.; m. Lucy Way Sistaire, Jan. 4, 1827. Called father of descriptive entomology in Am.; an original mem. Phila. Acad. Natural Scis., 1812; apptd. zoologist to accompany expdn. to Rocky Mountains under Maj. Stephen H. Long, 1819; accompainied Long's 2d expdn. which explored sources of the Minnesota River, 1823; curator Am. Philos. Soc., 1821-27; prof. natural history U. Pa., 1822-28; went to Ind. (with others) to Robert Owen's village, New Harmony (an attempt to establish an ideal community), 1825; fgn. mem. Linnaean Soc. of London; his collections and library went to the Phila. Acad. Natural Scis. after his death. Author: American Entomology; or Descriptions of the Insects of North America, 3 vols., 1824, 25, 28; American Conchology, 6 vols., 1830-34; prepared for publ. American Ornithology; or the Natural History of Birds Inhabiting the United States (Charles Bonaparte), 1825; works collected in The complete Writings of Thomas Say on the Conchology of the United States (W. G. Binney), 1858; The Complete Writings of Thomas Say on the Entomology of North America with a biographical memoir by George Ord (edited and published by J.L. LeConte), 2 vols., 1859. Died New Harmony, Oct. 10, 1834.

SAYLER, Milton, congressman, lawyer; b. Lewisburg, Preble County, O., Nov. 4, 1831; grad. Miami U., Oxford, O., 1852; studied law Cincinnati Law Sch. Admitted to bar, practiced in Cincinnati; mem. Ohio Ho. of Reps., 1862-63; mem. Cincinnati City Council, 1864-65; mem. U.S. Ho. of Reps. (Democrat) from Ohio, 43d-45th congresses, 1873-79, speaker pro tem, June 4, 1876; moved to N.Y.C., practiced law. Died N.Y.C., Nov. 17, 1892; buried Spring Grove Cemetery, Cincinnati.

SAYLES, John, lawyer; b. Ithaca, N.Y., Mar. 9, 1825; s. Welcome and Harriet Elizabeth (Sergeant) S.; grad. Hamilton Coll., 1845; m. Mary Elizabeth Gillespie, 1849, 6 children. Admitted to Tex. bar, 1846; partner firm Sayles & Bassett, 1856-86; mem. Tex. Legislature, 1853-55; mem. faculty Law Sch., Baylor U. (1st law sch. established in Tex.), 1857-60; commd. brig. gen. Tex. Militia during Civil War; Mason (grand master Tex.). Author: A Treatise on Practice of the District and Supreme Courts of the State of Texas, 1858; A Treatise on the Civil Jurisdiction of Justices of the Peace, 1867; A Treatise on the Principles of Pleading in Civil Actions in The Courts of Texas, 1872; Precedents and Rules of Pleading in Civil Actions in the County and District Courts of Texas, 1893; The Constitutions of the State of Texas, 1872. Died Abilene, Tex., May 22, 1897.

SAYRE, Stephen, banker, diplomatic agt.; b. Southampton, L.I., N.Y., June 12, 1736; s. John and Hannah (Howell) S.; grad. Coll. of N.J. (now Princeton, 1757; m. Elizabeth Noel, Feb. 18, 1775; m. 2d, Elizabeth Dorone, 1790. Went to Eng.; organizer banking house Stephen Sayre & Barth-Coote-Purdon, London, Eng., 1770; promoted cause of colonies in Eng.; sheriff of London, 1773; signer petition from Americans in London protesting closing of Port of Boston, 1774; arrested for polit. activities, charged with plotting to seize King and overthrow govt., released due to lack of evidence, 1775; sec. to Arthur Lee on diplomatic mission to Berlin for U.S., 1777; made unofcl. visit to Copenhagen, Denmark to propose comml. relations with U.S., 1777; posed as U.S. agt., Stockholm, Sweden, accomplished nothing, 1779; engaged in pvt. financial ventures in Russia, 1779-83; bought estate in N.J., 1793. Died Brandon, Middlesex County, Va., Sept. 27, 1818.

SCAEVA, see Stuart, Isaac William.

SCALES, Alfred Moore, gov. N.C., congressman; b. Reidsville, Rockingham County, N.C., Nov. 26, 1827; attended Caldwell Inst., Greensboro, N.C., U. N.C., 1845-46; studied law. Admitted to bar, 1851, practiced in Madison, N.C.; solicitor Rockingham County, 1853; mem. N.C. Ho. of Commons, 1852-53, 56, 57; mem. U.S. Ho. of Reps. (Democrat) from N.C., 35th, 44th-48th congresses, 1857-59, 75-Dec. 30, 1884 (resigned); Dem. presdl. elector, 1860; volunteered as pvt. in Confederate Army, served throughout Civil War, attained rank brig. gen.; practiced in Greensboro, Guilford County, N.C.; mem. N.C. Ho. of Reps., 1866-69; gov. N.C., 1884-88; became banker, Greensboro. Died Greensboro, Feb. 9, 1892; buried Green Hill Cemetery.

SCAMMAN, John Fairfield, congressman; b. Wells, Mass. (now Me.), Oct. 24, 1786; attended common schs. Became mcht.; mem. Mass. Ho. of Reps., 1817; mem. Me. Ho. of Reps., 1820-21; collector customs in Saco, Me., 1829-41; mem. U.S. Ho. of Reps. (Democrat) from Me., 29th Congress, 1845-47; mem. Me. Senate, 1855. Died Saco, May 22, 1858; buried Laurel Hill Cemetery.

SCAMMELL, Alexander, army officer; b. Mendon (now Milford), Mass., Mar. 27, 1747; s. Samuel Leslie and Jane (Libbey) S.; grad. Harvard, 1769. Went to Portsmouth, N.H., 1772, employed in surveying and exploring for lands and for royal navy timber; participated in capture of Ft. William and Mary, nr. Portsmouth, 1774; commd. brig. gen., 1775; brigade maj. Gen. John Sullivan's brigade, 1778, served in seige of Boston; participated in L.I. campaign as aide-de-camp to Sullivan; became brigade maj. in div. of Gen. Charles Lee, then col. 3d N.H. Bn., Continental Army, 1776; served with Gen. Arthur St. Clair at Ticonderoga, 1777; adj. gen. Continental Army, 1778-81; arrested his old gen., Charles Lee, after Battle of Monmouth; took charge of execution of Maj. John Andre, 1780; took command 1st N.H. Regt., led a party of continental light horse; captured at Battle of Yorktown, Sept. 30, 1781. Died from brutal handling, Williamsburg, Va., Oct. 6, 1781.

SCAMMON, Jonathan Young, banker; b. Whitefield, Me., July 27, 1812; s. Eliakin and Joanna (Young) S.; attended Waterville (now Colby) Coll., 1830-31, LL.D. (hon.), 1865; m. Mary Ann Haven Dearborn, 1837; m. 2d, Maria (Sheldon) Wright, 1867. Admitted to Me. bar, 1835; admitted to Ill. bar, circa 1836; dep. clk. Chgo.; atty. State Bank, Chgo., 1837; reporter Ill. Supreme Ct., 1839-45, compiled 4 volumes of its reports as Reports of Cases Argued and Determined in the Supreme Court of . . . Illinois (1840-44); founded Chgo. Jour., 1844; mem. Chgo. Bd. Edn., pres., 1845-48; Whig, later became Republican; del. Rep. Nat. Conv., 1864, 72; mem. Ill. Senate, 1861; a founder Chgo. Republican, 1865; began publication of Inter Ocean, 1872; responsible for reform of Ill. banking laws; founder, pres. Marine Bank, Chgo., 1851, Mechanics Nat. Bank, 1864; founder Chgo. Fire and Marine Ins. Co., pres., 1849; leader in devel. of Galena and Chgo. Union R.R. Co.; a founder numerous Chgo. socs. and charitable instns., including Chgo. Hist. Soc., Chgo. Acad. Scis., Hahnemann Med. Coll., Hahnemann Hosp., Old Ladies' Home, U. Chgo., Chgo. Astron. Soc.; Swedenborgian. Died Chgo., Mar. 17, 1890.

SCARBOROUGH, William Harrison, artist; b. Dover, Tenn., Nov. 7, 1812; studied medicine and art, Cincinnati; married, 1835. Worked as portraitist in Tenn.; moved to S.C., 1830; settled in Columbia, S.C., 1843; successful portrait and miniature painter in N.C. and S.C., made frequent visits to N.Y.C.; went to Europe, 1857. Died Columbia, Aug. 16, 1871.

SCARBROUGH, William, planter, businessman; b. S.C., Feb. 18, 1776; s. William and Lucy (Sawyer) S.; m. Julia Bernard, 1805, at least 3 children. Inherited large plantations, nr. Savannah, Ga.; obtained (with number of Savannah businessmen) incorporation of Savannah S.S. Co. from Ga. Legislature, 1818, became dir. of co. which purchased and equipped steamship Savannah in 1 of 1st attempts to establish trans-Atlantic steamship service, 1819 (venture unprofitable because ship could not carry both sufficient fuel and profitable amount of cargo); went bankrupt after yellow fever epidemic and fire and storm that almost destroyed city of Savannah, 1820. Died N.Y.C., June 11, 1838.

SCATTERGOOD, Thomas, clergyman, tanner; b. Burlington, N.J., Jan. 23, 1748; s. Joseph and Rebecca S.; m. Elizabeth Bacon, 1772; m. 2d, Sarah Hoskins, 1783; at least 1 child. Became a tanner, Phila., 1767; became itinerant Quaker minister, made religious journeys to Md., Va. Pa., 1778; active in religious services in Gt. Britain, Ireland, Orkney Islands, 1794-1800; founded Westtown Sch., also an asylum for the insane (now called Friend's Hosp.) Works published as Memoirs of Thomas Scattergood (edited by William and Thomas Evans in Friends' Library, vol. VIII), 1844, and separately, 1845. Died Phila., Apr. 24, 1814.

SCHAEFFER, Charles Frederick, clergyman; b. Germantown, Pa., Sept. 3, 1807; s. Frederick David and Rosina (Rosenmuller) S.; grad. U. Pa., 1827; m. Susanna Schmucker, Aug. 27, 1832, 5 children. Licensed to preach by Md. and Va. Synod, Lutheran Ch., 1829; ordained by West Pa. Synod, 1831; pastor, Carlisle, Pa., 1830-34, Hagerstown, Md., 1834-40; prof. English, Sem. of Joint Synod of Ohio at Columbus, 1840-43; prof. German, Gettysburg Theol. Sem., 1856; 1st prof., chmn. faculty Phila. Sem., 1864-78. Contbr. to Evang. Review, Bibliotheca Sacra; translator Manual of Sacred History (J. F. Kurtz), 1855; The Acts of the Apostles (G.V. Lechler and Charles Gerok), 1869; revised Philip Frederick Mayer's translation of Luther's Smaller Catechism (edited by C. F. Welden, A. T. Geissenhainer, B. M. Schmucker), 1854; composed a commentary on the Gospel according to St. Matthew published as vols. I and II of The Lutheran Commentary (H. E. Jacob); revised True Christianity (Johann Arndt), 1868. Died Phila., Nov. 23, 1879.

SCHAEFFER, Charles William, clergyman; b. Hagerstown, Md., May 5, 1813; s. Frederick Solomon and Catherine Elizabeth (Cremer or Graber) S.; grad. U. Pa., 1832, D.D. (hon.), 1879; attended Gettysburg Theol. Sem., 1833-35; LL.D. (hon), Thiel Coll, Greenville, Pa., 1887; m. Elizabeth Ashmead, 1837, 4 children. Licensed to preach by Ministerium of Pa., Lutheran Ch., 1835, ordained, 1836; pastor Barren Hill and Whitemarsh (formerly part of Germantown Parish), 1835-41; pastor Zion's Ch., Harrisburg, Pa., 1841-49, St. Michael's Ch., Germantown, Pa., 1849-75; pres. or treas. Ministerium of Pa., many years; pres. Gen. Synod, Luth. Ch., 1859, Gen. Council, 1868; trustee Pa. Coll., 1855-73, Muhlenberg Coll., 1868-76, U. Pa., 1859-96; asst. prof. Phila. Theol. Sem., 1864, Burkhalter prof. ch. history and pastoral theology, 1874, prof. emeritus, 1894, Author: Family Prayer for Morning and Evening and the Festivals of the Church Year, 1861; translator A Golden Treasury, 1858; The Life of Dr. Martin Luther (Wilhelm Wackernagel), 1883; Wittenberg Nightengale, 1883; Halle Reports, 1892; also numerous hymns included in Luth. Common Hymnal, published 1915; editor The Lutheran, The Foreign Missionary, The Philadelphian. Died Germantown, Mar. 15, 1896.

SCHAEFFER, David Frederick, clergyman; b. Carlisle, Pa., July 22, 1787; s. Frederick David and Rosina (Rosenumuller) S.; grad. U. Pa., 1807; D.D., St. John's Coll., 1836; m. Elizabeth Krebs, June 28, 1810, 6 children. Licensed to preach, 1808; called to Lutheran Ch., Frederick, Md., 1808; ordained to ministry Luth. Ch., 1812; an organizer Md. Synod; an organizer Gen. Synod, 1820, sec., 1821, 25, 27, 29, pres., 1831, 33; founder, conductor Lutheran Intelligencer (1st English Luth. ch. paper), 1826-31; trained candidates for the ministry. Died Frederick, May 5, 1837.

SCHAEFFER, Frederick Christian, clergyman; b. Germantown, Pa., Nov. 12, 1792; s. Frederick David and Rosina (Rosenmiller) S.; D.D. (hon.), Columbia, 1830. Licensed to preach, 1813; pastor Lutheran Ch., Harrisburg, Pa., 1812-15; established English services alongside the German; sole pastor United Congregations, N.Y.C., 1815-22, co-pastor in charge English speaking sect., 1822-26; pastor St. James' Ch., N.Y.C., 1826-31. Published sermons "The Blessed Reformation"; A Sermon . . . on Occasion of the Solemnization of the Third Centurial Jubilee in Commemoration of the Reformation (1817) and An Address pronounced at the laying of the corner stone of St. Matthew's Church, New York, October 22, 1821 (1822) Author: Parables and Parabolic Stories, 1829. Died N.Y.C., Mar. 25, 1831.

SCHAEFFER, Frederick David, clergyman; b. Frankfurt-am-Main, Germany, Nov. 15, 1760; s. Johann Jakob and Susanna Maria S.; D.D. (hon.), U. Pa., 1813; m. Rosina Rosenmuller, 1786, 8 children, including David Frederick, Frederick Christian, Charles Frederick, Frederick Solomon. Went to Pa., 1774; licensed by Ministerium of Pa., Lutheran Ch., 1786, ordained, 1788; pastor, missionary in York and Cumberland counties, Carlisle, Pa., 1786-90; founder Luth. congregation, Harrisburg, Pa., 1788; pastor St. Michael's Ch., Germantown, Pa., and affiliated chs., 1790-1812, St. Michael's and Zion's churches, Phila., 1812-34. Author: Antwort auf eine Vertheidigung der Methodisten, 1806. Died Frederick, Md., Jan. 27, 1836; buried Frederick.

SCHAFF, Philip, church historian; b. Switzerland, Jan. 1, 1819; s. Philip Schaf; grad. U. Tubingen, 1837, U. Halle, 1839; licentiate of theology, U. Berlin, 1841; LL.D. (hon.), Amherst Coll., 1876; D.D. (hon.), St. Andrew's Coll., Scotland; m. Mary Elizabeth Schley, Dec. 1845; 3 children. Published thesis Die Sunde wider den Heiligen Geist, 1841; privat-docent U. Berlin, 1842; ordained to ministry Reformed Ch., Elberfeld, Germany, 1844; tchr. (engaged by Eastern Synod of German Reformed Ch. 1843) Mercersburg (Pa.) Theol. Sem., 1844-65; founded, edited Der Deutsche Kirchenfreund (1st theol. jour. in German issued in U.S.), 1846-54; sec. N.Y. Sabbath Comm (group organized to preserve religious character of Sunday), 1864; became Presbyn., 1870; mem. faculty Union Theol. Sem., N.Y.C., 1870-93; a strong supporter of Evang. Alliance; a founder Alliance of Reformed Chs.; organizer, pres. Am. com. to revise English Bible, 1881-85. Author: The Principle of Protestantism (presented doctrine of hist. devel. describing Reformation as continuing devel. of good forces in Catholic Ch., which might eventually result in union of Protestantism and Catholicism), 1845; What Is Church History? A Vindication of the Idea of Historical Development, 1846; Geschichte der Apostolischen Kirche, 1851; History of the Christian Church 5th edit. revised and enlarged, 7 vols., 1882-92. Editor: A Commentary on the Holy Scriptures, 25 vols., 1865-80, Religious Encyclopedia, 3 vols., 1882-84, 3d edit., 4 vols., 1891. Died N.Y.C., Oct. 20, 1893.

SCHARF, John Thomas, army officer, historian; b. Balt., May 1, 1843; s. Thomas G. and Anna Maria (McNulty) S.; m. Mary McDougall, Dec. 2, 1869, 3 children. Enlisted in 1st Md. Arty., Confederate States Army, 1861; fought at 2d Battle of Bull Run and at Chancellorsville; commd. midshipman Confederate Navy, 1863; sent by war dept. on mission to Can., winter 1864, captured; pardoned by Pres. Johnson, 1865; served on editorial staffs of 3 Balt. papers Balt. News, Sunday Telegram, and Morning Herald; elected mem. Md. Ho. of Dels., 1877; commr. of Land Office, 1884-92; spl. insp. of Chinese immigration Port of N.Y., 1893-97; presented to Johns Hopkins U. Library a collection of Americana (one of most important Civil War collections in U.S., includes 50,000 pamphlets mostly on So. history, files of 15 or more Confederate newspapers for Civil War period and mass of ofcl. Md. records), 1891. Author: History of Maryland, 3 vols., 1879; The Chronicles of Baltimore, 1874; History of the Confederate States Navy, 1887. Died N.Y.C., Feb 28, 1898.

SCHAUFFLER, William Gottlieb, missionary; b. Stuttgart, Germany, Aug. 22, 1798; s. Philip Frederick and Caroline Henrietta (Schuckart) S.; attended Andover Theol. Sem., 1826-31; D.D. (hon.), U. Halle, 1867; LL.D. (hon.), Princeton, 1879; m. Mary Reynolds, Feb. 26, 1834, several children including Henry Albert. Arrived in Boston, 1826; ordained at Park Street Congregational Ch., Boston, 1831, commd. by Am. Bd. as missionary to Jews of Turkey; arrived in Constantinople, 1832, then transferred to Smyrna; engaged in missionary tours and Bible translation, 1834, completed new translation of Old Testament into Hebrew-Spanish (Sephardi), 1839; received grant from Missionary Soc. of Established Ch. of Scotland for work among Jews, 1843; chaplain Mission to German (Ashkenaz) Jews; missionary among Armenians and Turks under Turkey Mission of Am. Bd., after 1856; rep. Armenian missions at meeting of World's Evang. Alliance, pleading cause of religious liberty in Turkey, Paris, France, Aug. 1855; aided in revision of Turkish New Testament, 1856-57; visited America on behalf of Turkish missions, 1857; translated New Testament into Turkish, 1866; decorated by King of Prussia. Author: "Essay on the Right Use of Property," 1832; Meditations on the Last Days of Christ, 1837; contbr. article "What Drink Did Our Lord Jesus Christ Use at the Institution of the Eucharist?" to Biblical Repository and Quarterly Observer, Oct. 1836. Died N.Y.C., Jan. 26, 1883.

SCHELE de VERE, Maximilian, philologist; b. Wexio, Sweden, Nov. 1, 1820; attended U. Bonn (Germany); Ph.D., U. Berlin (Germany), 1841; Juris Utriusque Doctor, Greifswald U., 1842; m. Eliza Wydown Rives, July 25, 1849; m. 2d, Lucy Brown Rives, Mar. 21, 1860; at least 1 child. Came to Boston, 1843; prof. modern langs. U. Va., 1844-95, taught French, Spanish, Italian and German langs. and lits., also literary and polit. history of these nations; introduced systematic study Anglo-Saxon, pioneered courses in comparative philology; worked on Standard Dictionary, 1893-95. Author: Outlines of Comparative Philology, 1853; Studies in English, 1867; Americanisms; The English of the New World, 1871; Students of the University of Virginia, a Semi-Centennial Catalogue, 1878. Died Washington, D.C., May 12, 1898.

SCHELL, Augustus, lawyer, businessman; b. Rhinebeck, N.Y., Aug. 1, 1812; s. Christian and Elizabeth (Hughes) S.; grad. Union Coll., 1830; attended Tapping Reeve's Law Sch., Litchfield, Conn., 1830-31; m. Anna Fox, Mar. 1873. Admitted to bar, 1833; became corporate lawyer, friend, adviser to Cornelius Vanderbilt, Jay Gould and others; became dir. N.Y. and Harlem R.R., 1862, Hudson River R.R., 1864, N.Y.C. R.R., 1867, Lake Shore and Mich. So. R.R., 1869, later dir. C. & N.-W. Ry., U.P. R.R., others; dir. several banks and ins. cos.; v.p. Union Trust Co.; chmn. legal com., sr. v.p. Western Union Telegraph Co.; became chmn. Tammany Gen. Com., 1852; chmn. Democratic State Com., N.Y., 1853-55; apptd. collector Port of N.Y., 1857-61; grand sachem Tammany Hall, 1872-84, helped name Com. of 21 to reconstruct Tammany after William Tweed's downfall again, chmn. Tammany Gen. Com.; chmn. Nat. Dem. Com., 1872-76; opened Nat. Dem. Conv., St. Louis, 1876; chmn. exec. com. N.Y. Hist. Soc., 19 years, pres. twice; pres. N.Y. Instn. for Blind (his favorite charity), 1866-84. Died N.Y.C., Mar. 27, 1884.

SCHELL, Richard, congressman, mcht.; b. Rhinebeck, Rhinebeck County, N.Y., May 15, 1810; completed prep. studies. Became mcht.; moved to N.Y.C., 1830, became wholesale dry goods mcht.; mem. N.Y. State Senate, 1857; mem. U.S. Ho. of Reps. (Democrat, filled vacancy) from N.Y., 43d Congress, Dec. 7, 1874-75. Died N.Y.C., Nov. 10, 1879; buried Old Dutch Cemetery, Rhinebeck.

SCHEM, Alexander Jacob, editor, educator; b. Wiedenbruck, Westphalia, Germany, Mar. 16, 1826; s. Friedrich and Adolphine (von Felgenhauer) S.; student Catholic theology Bonn U., 1843-45; attended Tübingen U., 1845-46; m. Miss Gerhard, 1853. Ordained priest Roman Cath. Ch., 1849; left church, came to U.S., 1851; tchr. ancient and modern langs. Collegiate Inst., Mt. Holly, N.J., 1853-54; prof. Hebrew and modern langs. Dickinson Coll., 1854-60; fgn. news editor N.Y. Tribune, 1860-69; became editor-in-chief Deutsch-amerikanishes Conversations-lexicon (published in 2 vols. 1869-74), 1869; asst. supt. public schs. N.Y., 1874-81; contbr. numerous articles to New Am. Cyclopaedia (edited by C. S. Dana and George Ripley), 1858-63, also to Am. Eccles. Year-Book, 1860; editorial contbr. to The Methodist and The Methodist Quarterly Review; collaborator in preparing Tribune Almanac, Nat. Almanac, Am. Yearbook and Nat. Register. Author: (with George R. Crooks) A New Latin-English School-Lexicon, 1858; (with Henry Kiddle) The Cyclopaedia of Education, 1877; The War in the East, 1878; The American Ecclesiastical and Educational Almanac, 1869; Latin-English Dictionary, 1857; American Ecclesiastical Year-book, 1860. Died West Hoboken, N.J., May 21, 1881.

SCHENCK, Abraham Henry, congressman, mfr.; b. Matteawan, Dutchess County, N.Y., Jan. 22, 1775; had English edn. Became machinery mfr., furnished some parts for cannons built at old West Point Foundry, Cold Spring, N.Y.; mem. N.Y. State Assembly, 1804-06; mem. U.S. Ho. of Reps. (Democrat) from N.Y., 14th Congress, 1815-17; became mfr. cotton goods after passage non-intercourse act. Died Fishkill, Dutchess County, June 1, 1831; buried Dutch Reform Churchyard, Beacon (formerly Fishkill Landing), N.Y.

SCHENCK, Ferdinand Schureman, congressman, physician; b. Millstone, Somerset County, N.J., Feb. 11, 1790; completed prep. studies; grad. Coll. Physicians and Surgeons, N.Y., 1814. Practiced medicine, Six-Mile Run (now Franklin Park), N.J.; mem. N.J. Gen. Assembly, 1829-31; mem. U.S. Ho. of Reps. (Jackson Democrat) from N.J., 23d-24th congresses, 1833-37; trustee Rutgers Coll., 1841-61; mem. N.J. Constl. Conv., 1844; judge N.J. Ct. Errors and Appeals, 1845-57. Died Camden, N.J., May 16, 1860; buried pvt. cemetery, Pleasant Plains, nr. Franklin Park.

SCHENCK, James Findlay, naval officer; b. Franklin, O., June 11, 1807; s. William Cortenus and Elizabeth (Rogers) S.; attended U.S. Mil. Acad., 1822-24; m. Dorothea Ann Smith, July 27, 1829, 4 children. Apptd. midshipman U.S. Navy, 1825; commanded sloop Surprise in action against pirates in W.I., 1828; promoted lt., 1835; assigned to frigate Congress under Commodore Robert F. Stockton, 1845; active in campaign against California, 1846-49, present at capture of Santa Barbara, led landing party that captured San Pedro, participated in capture of Los Angeles, Guaymas, Mazatlan; commanded U.S. mail steamer Ohio, 1849-52; promoted comdr., 1855; in command of ship North Carolina, 1858-60; commanded brig Saginaw at East India station, 1860-62; on blockading duty Gulf of Mexico, 1862-64; promoted commodore, 1864; commanded 3d div. N. Atlantic Blockading Squadron, 1864; commanded naval sta., Mound City, Ill., 1866-68; promoted rear adm., 1868, ret., 1869. Died Dayton, O., Dec. 21, 1882.

SCHENCK, Robert Cumming, congressman, diplomat, army officer; b. Franklin, O., Oct. 4, 1809; s. William Cortenus and Elizabeth (Rogers) S.; grad. Miami U., Oxford, O., 1827; m. Rennelche W. Smith, Aug. 21, 1834, 6 children. Prof., Miami U., Oxford, O., 1827-29; admitted to Ohio bar, circa 1833; mem. Ohio Ho. of Reps., 1839-43; leader Whig Party in Ohio Ho. of Reps.; mem. U.S. Ho. of Reps. (Whig) from Ohio, 28th-31st congresses, 1843-51; U.S. minister to Brazil, 1851-53, negotiated comml. treaties with Uruguay, 1852, with

Paraguay, 1853 (treaties never proclaimed), 2 treaties with Argentine Confederation, 1853; apptd. brig. gen. U.S. Volunteers, 1861, promoted maj. gen., 1862; assigned to command in Balt., 1862; advocate of contraction of currency at end of Civil War; del. Phila. Loyalist Conv., 1866; apptd. mem. Joint High Commn. for Ala. Claims Commn., 1871; signed Treaty of Washington for U.S., 1871; minister to Gt. Britain, 1871-76, failed to conclude consular conv. with Gt. Britain and to persuade England to support U.S. in its demands on Spain for concessions in Cuban policy; made dir. Emma Silver Mine, Utah, used his name in sale of stock in Gt. Britain, 1871. Author: Draw Poker, 1880. Died Washington, D.C., Mar. 23, 1890; buried Woodland Cemetery, Dayton, O.

SCHERMERHORN, Abraham Maus, congressman; b. Schenectady, N.Y., Dec. 11, 1791; grad. Union Coll., Schenectady, 1810; studied law. Admitted to bar, 1812; moved to Rochester, N.Y., 1813, became banker; supr. Rochester, 1834, mayor, 1837; mem. N.Y. State Assembly, 1848; mem. U.S. Ho. of Reps. (Whig) from N.Y., 31st-32d congresses, 1849-53. Died Savin Rock, nr. New Haven, Conn., Aug. 22, 1855; buried Mt. Hope Cemetery, Rochester.

SCHILLING, Gustav, musician, writer; b. Schwiegershausen, nr. Hanover, Germany, Nov. 3, 1803; studied theology U. Göttingen (Germany); Ph.D., U. Halle (Germany). Dir., Stöpel Sch. Music, Stuttgart, Germany; came to N.Y.C., later went to Montreal, Que., Can., finally settled in Neb.; author many works in German concerning musical subjects, including: Enzyklopädie der gesammten musikalischen Wissenschaft oder Universal-Lexikon der Tonkunst, 6 vols., 1835-38; Franz Liszt, 1844; Der Pianist, 1854; revised edition of P. E. Bach's Versuch über die wahre Art, das Klavier zu spielen, 1857. Died Neb., Mar. 1881.

SCHIRMER, Gustav, music publisher; b. Konigsee, Saxony, Germany, Sept. 19, 1829; s. Ernest Rudolph and Wilhelmine (Dunkler) S.; m. Mary Fairchild, 7 children including Rudolph Edward. Came to U.S., 1840; with Scharfenberg and Luis, music firm, N.Y.C.; later with Kirksieg and Breusing, music dealers; became partner firm Beer and Schirmer, N.Y.C., 1861, became sole owner, changed name to G. Schirmer, music publisher, importer and dealer, 1866; publisher European and Am. works, encouraged Am. composers. Died Eisenach, Germany, Aug. 6, 1893.

SCHLATTER, Michael, clergyman, supt. schs.; b. St. Gall, Switzerland, July 14, 1716; s. Paulus and Magdalena (Zallikofer) S.; m. Maria Schleidorm, 9 children. Ordained to ministry German Reformed Ch., 1739; missionary in Pa., Md., Va., N.J., founded 46 congregations which he organized into 16 pastoral charges, 1746-51; supt. schs. Pa., 1754; chaplain Brit. Army, 1756; a chaplain Royal Am. Regt., 1757; pastor Reformed chs., Phila., 1759; chaplain 2d Pa. Bn., 1764; taken prisoner by Brit. at capture of Germantown during Revolutionary War, 1777, his property confiscated by Brit. because of his colonial sympathies. Died Phila., Oct. 31, 1790; buried Reformed Cemetery (now part of Franklin Sq.), Phila.

SCHLEICHER, Gustave, congressman; b. Darmstadt, Germany, Nov. 19, 1823; attended U. Giessen. Became civil engr.; employed in constrn. several European railroads; came to U.S., 1847, settled in San Antonio, Tex., 1850; mem. Tex. Ho. of Reps., 1853, 54; mem. Tex. Senate, 1859-61; mem. U.S. Ho. of Reps. (Democrat) from Tex., 44th-45th congresses, 1875-Jan. 10, 1879. Died Washington, D.C., Jan. 10, 1879; buried U.S. Nat. Cemetery, San Antonio.

SCHLEY, William, gov. Ga., congressman, coll. pres.; b. Frederick, Md., Dec. 15, 1786; attended acads., Louisville, Augusta, Ga.; studied law. Admitted to bar, practiced in Augusta, 1812, judge Superior Ct., 1825-28; mem. Ga. Ho. of Reps., 1830; mem. U.S. Ho. of Reps. (Democrat) from Ga., 23d-24th congresses, 1833-July 1, 1835 (resigned); gov. Ga., 1835-37; pres. Ga. Med. Coll., Augusta. Died nr. Augusta, Nov. 20, 1858; buried family burying ground at Richmond Hill, nr. Augusta.

SCHLIEMANN, Heinrich, archeologist; b. New Buckow, Mecklenburg-Schwerin, Germany, Jan. 6, 1822; m. Ekaterina Lishin, Oct. 12, 1852; m. 2d, Sophia Engastromenos, Sept. 24, 1869; several children. Apprentice in grocery bus., Furstenberg, 1836-41; employed in Amsterdam, 1842-46; founded own export-import bus., 1847, traveled extensively; was in Cal. when it was admitted to union, 1850, thus automatically became U.S. citizen; operated bank for gold prospectors, Sacramento, 1851-52; spent several years in Russia, primarily in St. Petersburg, made fortune as mil. contractor during Crimean War; ret. from bus. to pursue archeol. interests, 1863, went to visit Homeric sites in Greece; on basis of his faith in historicity of Homer's Iliad and his conviction of the existence of Priam's Troy, he theorized that Hissarlik, Turkey (not Bunarbashi) was its site; dug extensively at Hissarlik, discovering ruins on several strata, and treasure he assumed to be Priam's (Homeric Troy now believed to be several strata above that accepted as such by Schliemann); excavated and discovered graves at Mycenae (which he believed to contain remains of King Agamemnon, though proved to be earlier) containing important treasures, 1876; established at Mycenae the evidence of a culture as described by Homer, refuting belief it was a myth; later settled in Athens, resumed diggings at Hissarlik; cleared out tomb of Orchomenos, 1880-81; cleared upper stratum of rock of Tiryns, revealing entire floorplan of Pre-Homeric palace, 1885; also dug at Ithaca, Alexandria, Cythera. Author: Ithaka, der Peloponnes, und Troja, circa 1869; Troy and Its Remains, 1875; Mycenae (in English), 1877; Ilios, 1878; Troja, 1884; an autobiography, pub. 1892. Died Naples, Italy, Dec. 26, 1890.

SCHMUCKER, Beale Melanchthon, clergyman; b. Gettysburg, Pa., Aug. 26, 1827; s. Samuel Sion and Mary Catherine (Steenbergen) S.; grad. Pa. Coll. (later Gettysburg Coll.), 1844; grad. Gettysburg Theol. Sem., 1847; D.D. (hon.), U. Pa., 1870; m. Christiana M. Pretz, Mar. 6, 1860, 2 children. Licensed to preach by West Pa. Synod, Lutheran Ch., 1847, ordained by Va. Synod, 1849; pastor Martinsburg and Shepherdstown, Va. (now W.Va.), 1848-51, St. John's English Luth. Ch., Allentown, Pa., 1852-62, St. John's Ch., Easton, Pa., 1862-67, St. James Ch., Reading, Pa., 1867-81, Ch. of Transfiguration, Pottstown, W.Va., 1881-88; English sec., bd. dirs. Phila. Theol. Sem., 1864-88; sec. bd. fgn. missions Ministerium of Pa. and Gen. Council Evang. Luth. Ch. in Am. Author: A Liturgy for the Use of the Evangelical Lutheran Church, 1860, 68, 71; editor Hymns for the Use of the Evangelical Lutheran Church, 1865, 68. Died nr. Phoenixville, Pa., Oct. 15, 1888.

SCHMUCKER, John George, clergyman; b. Mickelstadt, Hesse, Germany, Aug. 18, 1771; s. John Christopher Schmucker; D.D. (hon.), U. Pa., 1825; m. Elizabeth Grass; m. 2d, Anna Hoffman, 1821; 18 children including Samuel Simon. Licensed to Lutheran ministry, 1793, ordained, 1800; pastor Luth. Ch., Hagerstown, Md., 1794-1809; pastor congregations, York, Pa., 1809-36; pres. Ministerium of Pa., 1820-21; a founder Gen. Synod of Luth. Ch., Gettysburg (Pa.) Theol. Sem. (now Gettysburg Coll.), Western Pa. Synod. Author: The Prophetic History of the Christian Religion, or Explanation of the Revelation of St. John, 2 vols., 1817-21. Died Williamsburg, Pa., Oct. 7, 1854; buried Christ Ch., York.

SCHMUCKER, Samuel Simon, clergyman, coll. pres.; b. Hagerstown, Md., Feb. 28, 1799; s. Rev. John George and Elizabeth (Grass) S.; grad. gratiae causa U. Pa., 1819, D.D. (hon.), 1830; grad. Princeton Theol. Sem., 1820; D.D. (hon.), Rutgers U., 1830; m. Elenora Geiger, Feb. 28, 1821; m. 2d, Mary Catherine Steenbergen, Oct. 12, 1825; m. 3d, Esther M. Wagner, Apr. 28, 1849; 13 children including Beale Melanchthon. Licensed to preach, 1820; ordained to ministry Lutheran Ch., 1821; a founder Gettysburg (Pa.) Theol. Sem., 1825, 1st prof., 1825-30; founder classical sch. 1827, which became Pa. Coll., 1832 (now Gettysburg Coll.), pres., 1832-34; an organizer Evangelical Alliance, 1846. Author: Elements of Popular Theology, 1834. Died Gettysburg, July 26, 1873.

SCHNAUFFER, Carl Heinrich, editor; b. Heimsheim, Germany, July 4, 1823; s. Johann Heinrich and Karoline (Hasenmaier) S.; entered U. Heidelburg (Germany), 1846; m. Wilhelmine Moos, May 1851, 2 children. Mem. staff of liberal Mannheimer Abendzeitung, Heidelburg, 1847; fought in uprising of South German liberals, 1848, taken prisoner at Mannheim, 1849, and transported to Prussia; escaped to Switzerland; deported by Swiss Govt., 1850, forced to leave for London, Eng., along with other revolutionary leaders; came to U.S., 1851; founder German daily, Balt. Wecker, which stood for popular edn., freedom and enlightenment, opposing current Know-Nothingness, 1851. Author: Todten Kranze, circa 1849; Koenig Karl I oder Cromwell und die englische Revolution (5-act drama), 1854; Lieder und Gedichte aus dem Nachlass von Carl Heinrich Schnauffer (collected poems), 1879. Died Balt., Sept. 4, 1854.

SCHNEIDER, Benjamin, missionary; b. New Hanover, Pa., Jan. 18, 1807; s. Henry and Mary (Noyce) S.; grad. Amherst, 1830, Andover Theol. Sem., 1833; m. Eliza Cheyney Abbott, Sept. 15, 1833; m. 2d, Susan Maria Abbott, 1858. Ordained to ministry Presbyn. Ch., 1833; missionary in Turkey apptd. by Am. Bd. Commrs. for Fgn. Missions, established mission, Smyrna, Turkey, 1834-49, worked primarily among Greeks and Armenians; missionary at Aintab, Turkey, 1849-66, at Brusa, Turkey, 1868-72; returned to U.S. for one year, 1858, 66-68; with theol. sem. in Marsovan (now Merzifan), Turkey, 1872-73; retired from missionary work, 1873, returned to U.S. Died Boston, Sept. 14, 1877.

SCHNEIDER, Theodore, clergyman; b. Gunsheim, Rhenish Palatinate, Germany, Apr. 7, 1703. Joined Soc. of Jesus, 1721; prof. philosophy and polemics Jesuit Coll. of Liege; rector Jesuit House of Studies at U. Heidelberg (Germany); rector magnificus U. Heidelberg, 1738; ordered by gen. of Soc. to go to Pa. missions, 1840, arrived in Phila., 1841; founder several chapels, large ch. at Goshenhoppen, Pa., schs. (taught children himself); preached throughout Pa., and N.J., 1741-64. Died July 10, 1764.

SCHNELLER, George Otto, inventor, mfr.; b. Nürnberg, Germany, Jan. 14, 1843; s. Henry and Elizabeth (Ruckert) S.; m. Clarissa Alling, May 1, 1873, 3 children. Came to U.S., 1860; cashier, accountant Osborne and Cheesman Co., brass manufactory, Ansonia, Conn.; returned to Germany, 1870, to U.S., 1872; obtained 4 patents on corset springs between 1872-73; bought spectacle factory, Shelton, Conn.; began mfg. brass corset eyelets; secured patents on die for making eyelets, eyelet machine, punch and die for eyelet machines, 1884; bought Osborne and Cheesman business, 1882, reorganized it as Ansonia Osborne and Cheesman Co., began manufacture of brass goods under his patent rights; revolutionized corset industry of world by his inventions; founder, treas. Union Fabric Co., Ansonia; invented and patented hook and eye, bustle, machine for covering dress stays, button press, button-fastening device; active in building electric street ry. system between Derby, Ansonia and Shelton, Conn.; mem. Ansonia Bd. Edn.; represented Ansonia in lower house of Conn. Legislature, 1891-93. Died Ansonia, Oct. 20, 1895.

SCHOLTE, Hendrick Peter, clergyman; b. Amsterdam, Netherlands, Sept. 25, 1805; s. Jan Hendrik and Johanna Dorothea (Roelofsz) S.; attended Amsterdam Athenaeum Illustre, 1827; Th.D., U. Leyden, 1832; m. Sara Maria Brand, Nov. 1832; m. 2d, M.H.E. Krantz, after 1842; at least 5 children. Leader of a group of clergymen who protested against secularism of State Ch. of Holland, seceded from ch., 1834, fined and imprisoned; editor dissenting periodical De Reformatie; urged emigration to escape religious persecution; pres. emigration assn., Utrecht, Holland, 1846; came to U.S., 1847, settled in Marion County, Ia.; founder Town of Pella (Ia.); a founder Central U. (later Central Coll.), Pella, 1853, pres. bd. trustees; preacher, farmer, atty., publisher and editor, mcht., banker, land agt.; del. at large from Ia. to Nat. Republican Conv., Chgo., 1860. Died Pella, Aug. 25, 1868.

SCHOOLCRAFT, Henry Rowe, explorer, ethnologist; b. Albany County, N.Y., Mar. 28, 1793; s. Lawrence and Margaret Anne Barbara (Rowe) S.; attended Union Coll. and Middlebury Coll.; LL.D. (hon.), U. Geneva, 1846; married, 1823; m. 2d, Mary Howard, 1847. Visited mineral regions in So. Mo., Ark., 1817-18; agt. on N.W. frontier; supt. Indian affairs for Mich., 1836-41, negotiated several treaties with Chippewa Indians, including treaty which gave U.S. parts of Mich., 1836; a founder Hist. Soc., 1828, Algic Soc. of Detroit, 1832; projected an Indian encyclopedia. Author: A View of the Head Mines of Missouri, 1819; Narrative Journals of Travels through the Northwestern Regions of the United States . . . to the Sources of the Mississippi River, 1821; Narrative of an Expedition through the Upper Mississippi to Itasca Lake, the Actual Source of the Mississippi, 1834; Algic Researches (concerning Indian mental characteristics), 2 vols., 1839; Oneonta (describing Indian history), 1844-45; Notes on the Iroquois, 1847; Personal Memories of . . . Thirty Years with the Indian Tribes, 1851; Historical and Statistical Information Respecting the History, Condition, and Prospects of the Indian Tribes of the United States, 6 parts, 1851-57; Grammatical Construction of the Indian Languages. Died Washington, D.C., Dec. 10, 1864.

SCHOOLCRAFT, John Lawrence, congressman, banker; b. Albany, N.Y., 1804. Became mcht.; mem. U.S. Ho. of Reps. (Whig) from N.Y., 31st-32d congresses, 1849-53; chosen pres. Comml. Bank, Albany, 1854-60; del. Nat. Republican Conv., Chgo. 1860. Died (while returning to his home), St. Catherines, Ont., Can., July 7, 1860; buried Rural Cemetery, Albany.

SCHOONMAKER, Cornelius Corneliusen, congressman; b. Shawangunk (now Wallkill), Ulster County, N.Y., June 1745. Became surveyor, farmer; mem. Coms. Vigilance and Safety during Revolutionary War; mem. N.Y. State Assembly, 1777-90, 95; mem. N.Y. State Conv. to ratify U.S. Const., 1788; mem. U.S. Ho. of Reps. from N.Y., 2d congress, 1791-93. Died Shawangunk, spring 1796; buried Old Shawangunk Churchyard at Bruynswick, Shawangunk.

SCHOPF, Johann David, physician, scientist; b. Wunsiedel, Germany, Mar. 8, 1752; studied medicine and natural sciences U. Erlangen (Germany), 1770-73, M.D., 1776. Served as surgeon in German regt. assigned to Brit. Army, N.Y., 1777-83; traveled throughout Eastern U.S. and Bahamas, 1783-84; pres. Ansbach Medicinal-Collegium, Prussia, 1795. Author: Beytrage zur Mineralogischen Kenntniss des Ostlichen Theils von Nordamerika und seiner Geburge (1st systematic work on Am. geology), 1787; Materia Medica Americana, Potissimum Regni Vegetabilis, 1787; Reise durch einige der mittlern and sudlichen vereinigten nordamerikanischen Staaten nach Ost-Florida und den Bahama-Inselen (his masterpiece), 2 vols., 1788; Historia Testiludinum, Iconibus Illustrata (Fasc. I-VI, Erlangen, 1792-1801;; wrote papers on Am. climate and diseases, also 1st papers ever written on Am. ichthyology, Am. frogs and turtles. Died Sept. 10, 1800.

SCHOULER, William, editor; b. Kilbarchan, Scotland, Dec. 31, 1814; s. James and Margaret (Clark) S.; m. Frances Eliza Warren, Oct. 6, 1835, 2 children including James. Contbr. polit. articles to Yeoman's Gazette, Concord, Mass.; editor and publisher Lowell (Mass.) Courier (later Lowell Courier-Citizen), 1841; mem. Mass. Ho. of Reps. (Whig), 1844, 45, 47; mem. Mass. Legislature from Boston, 1849-53, made famous speech repudiating polit. leadership of Daniel Webster, Mar. 7, 1850; became part owner Cincinnati Gazette, 1853; became editor Ohio State Jour., Columbus, 1856; del. to 1st Republican Nat. Conv., 1856; adj.-gen. Ohio; editor Boston Atlas and Daily Bee, 1858; adj.-gen. Commonwealth of Mass., 1860-66, gave warning of impending war that stirred Mass. toward preparation in Annual Report of 1860, made inspection of Mass. troops beyond the Potomac, 1862; mem. Mass. Legislature, 1868; contbr. "Political and Personal Recollections" to Boston Morning Jour., 1870. Author: A History of Massachusetts in the Civil War, 2 vols., 1868-71. Died West Roxbury, Mass., Oct. 24, 1872.

SCHRIECK, Sister Louise Van der, founder religious order; b. Bergen-op-Zoom, Holland, Nov. 14 1813; d. Joseph and Clara Maria (Weenen) Vander Schrieck; attended inst. of Sisters of Notre Dame at Namur. Devoted her spare time to religious missionary and social work among oppressed poor of Antwerp; entered novitiate of Notre Dame nuns at Namar, 1837, professed as Sister Louise, 1839; came to United States, arrived at Cincinnati, 1840; named superior of Notre Dame Convent, Cincinnati, 1845; superior-provincial with jurisdiction over area East of Rocky Mountains, 1848-86; founded 26 convents in Washington, D.C., Phila., Ohio and Mass.; provided nursing nuns for Ft. Denison, nr. Cincinnati, during Civil War. Died Cincinnati, Dec. 3, 1886.

SCHRIVER, Edmund, army officer; b. York, Pa., Sept. 16, 1812; s. Daniel and Rebecca (Zinn) S.; grad. U.S. Mil. Acad., 1833. Brevetted 2d lt. 2d Arty., U.S. Army, 1833, commd. 2d lt., 1834; asst. instr. inf. tactics U.S. Mil. Acad., 1834-35; served in office of adj. gen., 1835-41, asst. adj. gen., 1838-41; commd. 1st lt., 1836; brevetted capt., 1838; promoted capt., 1842; resigned, 1846; treas. Saratoga and Washington R.R., 1847-52, Saratoga, & Schenectady R.R. (both N.Y.C.), 1847-61; treas. Rensselaer & Saratoga R.R., 1847-61; pres. 1851-61; commd. lt. col. 11th U.S. Inf., 1861; chief of staff 1st Corps, Army of Potomac, 1862-63; commd. col., 1862; served at battles of Cedar Mountain, Chantilly and Manassas; insp. Army of Potomac, 1863-65; at battles of Chancellorsville and Gettysburg; active in Richmond campaign of 1865; brevetted brig. gen., 1864, maj. gen., 1865; in charge of inspector's bur., Washington, D.C., 1865-69, 71-76; insp. U.S. Mil. Acad., 1869-71; insp.-gen. Div. of Pacific, 1876-81; retired, 1881. Died Washington, Feb. 10, 1899; buried Oakwood Cemetery, Troy, N.Y.

SCHROEDER, John Frederick, clergyman, author; b. Balt., Apr. 8, 1800; s. Henry and Mary (Schley) S.; grad. with highest honors Coll. of N.J. (now Princeton), 1819, A.M., 1823; studied Oriental langs. under Phila. clergyman for 1 year; attended Gen. Theol. Sem., 1821; A.M., Yale, 1823; S.T.D., Trinity Coll., 1857; m. Caroline Maria Boardman, May 25, 1825, 8 children. Ordained deacon Episcopal Ch., Balt., 1823, priest, 1824; rector St. Michael's Parish, Md.; temporary asst. Trinity Ch., N.Y.C., 1823, asst. rector, circa 1824-39; became involved in dispute with vestry over question of precedence which led to his resignation, 1839; founder, operator St. Ann's Hall (girls sch.), Flushing, L.I., N.Y., 1839-57; rector Ch. of Crucifixion, N.Y., 1846-52, St. Thomas Ch., Bklyn., 1852-57. Author: The Intellectual and Moral Resources of Horticulture, 1828; A Plea for the Industrious Poor and Strangers in Sickness, 1830; Memoir of the Life and Character of Mrs. Mary Anna Boardman, 1849; Life and Times of Washington, 2 vols., 1857-61; frequent contbr. to religious and secular periodicals; edited collection of maxims of George Washington, 1855. Died Bklyn., Feb. 26, 1857.

SCHUNEMAN, Martin Gerretsen, congressman; b. Catskill, Albany (now Greene) County, N.Y., Feb. 10, 1764; ed. by father. Justice of peace, Albany County, 1792; became mcht.; owned inn, Madison, N.Y.; supr. for Catskill in Albany and Greene counties, 1797, 99, 1802; mem. N.Y. State Assembly from Ulster County, 1798-1800, from Greene County, 1803; del. from Greene County to N.Y. State Constl. Conv. which decided relative powers of gov. and council of appointment, 1801; mem. U.S. Ho. of Reps. (Democrat) from N.Y., 9th Congress, 1805-07. Died Catskill, Feb. 21, 1827; buried Old Cemetery, Madison (now Leeds).

SCHUREMAN, James, Continental congressman, senator; b. New Brunswick, N.J., Feb. 12, 1756; grad. Rutgers Coll., 1775. Became mcht.; served in Revolutionary Army; mem. N.J. Gen. Assembly, 1783-85, 88; del. N.J. Provincial Congress, 1786; mem. Continental Congress from N.J., 1786-87; mem. U.S. Ho. of Reps. (Federalist) from N.J., 1st, 5th, 13th congresses, 1789-91, 97-99, 1813-15; pres. New Brunswick, 1792; mem. U.S. Senate from N.J., 1799-Feb. 16, 1801 (resigned); mayor New Brunswick, 1801-13, 21-24; mem. N.J. State Council, 1808, 10. Died New Brunswick, Jan. 22, 1824; buried First Reformed Ch. Cemetery.

SCHUSSELE, Christian, painter, educator; b. Guebviller, Haut Rhin, Alsace, France, Apr. 16, 1826; m. Cecilia Muringer, 1849, 2 children. Entered art acad., Strasbourg, France, 1841; went to Paris, 1847, worked under Paul Delaroche; came to Phila., circa 1849; works include: The Artist's Recreation, 1851; Clear the Track, 1852; Franklin Before the Lords in Council, 1856, Men of Progress, 1857 (both now in Cooper Inst., N.Y.C.); Zeisberger Preaching to the Indians (painted for James Harrison), circa 1859; Washington at Valley Forge, 1862; Home on Furlough, 1863; McClellan at Antietam, 1863; Queen Esther Denouncing Haman to Ahasuerus, 1869; The Alsation Fair, 1870; many works popularized through John Sartain's engravings; among the 1st painters to bring to Am. talent trained in Paris art schs.; active local art affairs; mem. Phila. Sketch Club; pres. Artist's Fund Soc., several years; prof. drawing and painting Pa. Acad. Fine Arts, 1868-79. Died Merchantville, N.J., Aug. 21, 1879.

SCHUTTLER, Peter, wagonmaker; b. Wachenheim, Grand Duchy of Hesse Dormstadt, Germany, Dec. 22, 1812; m. Dorothy Gauch, 1838, 3 children including Peter. Came to U.S., 1834; worked in wagon shop, Buffalo, N.Y.; moved to Sandusky, O., 1838; established wagon shop, Chgo., 1843; in brewery bus. for short time; began mfg. buggies, carriages, harnesses, as well as wagons, 1849; Schuttler wagon. (stronger, lighter, larger capacity) helped displace old prairie schooner; traveled to Germany, 1855; owner finest mansion of the time in Chgo. Died Chgo., Jan. 16, 1865.

SCHUYLER, Eugene, diplomat; b. Ithaca, N.Y., Feb. 26, 1840; s. George Washington and Matilda (Scribner) S.; grad. Yale, 1859, Ph.D., 1861; grad. Columbia Law Sch., 1863; m. Gertrude Wallace King, July 1877. Admitted to N.Y. bar, 1863; U.S. consul, 1867-69; successively consul at Revel, sec. of legation at St. Petersburg, Russia, sec. of legation and consul gen. at Constantinople, Turkey, 1869-78; published The Turkish Atrocities in Bulgaria, London, 1876; recalled after Turkey protested his actions with Russians with whom he had discussed plans for setting up Bulgaria as independent nation, 1878; consul general in Rome, 1879-80; became 1st Am. diplomatic representative to Rumania, 1880-82; minister resident and consul gen. to Greece, Rumania and Serbia, 1882; made comml. treaty with Rumania, signed 1881 (did not take effect); signed comml. treaty and consular conv. with Serbia, 1881; returned to U.S. to lecture at Johns Hopkins and Cornell univs., 1884; accepted appointment to Cairo, Egypt, 1889; Author: Turkistan: Notes of a Journey in Russian Turkistan, Khokand, Bukhara, and Kuldja, 2 vols., 1876; Peter the Great, 2 vols., 1884; American Diplomacy and the Furtherance of Commerce, 1886; edited John A. Porter's Selections from the Kalevala, 1868; translated Fathers and Sons (Ivan Turgenev), published 1867, The Cossacks (Leo Tolstoi), 1878. Died Venice, Italy, July 16, 1890.

SCHUYLER, George Washington, state ofcl; b. Stillwater, N.Y., Feb. 2, 1810; s. John H. and Annatje (Fort) S.; B.A., Univ. City N.Y., 1837; studied theology Union Sem.; m. Matilda Scribner, Apr. 18, 1839, 5 children. Operated successful merc. and banking enterprises, Tompkins County, N.Y.; state treas. N.Y. (Republican ticket), 1863-65; supt. N.Y. Banking Dept., 1866-70; chmn. com. of banking N.Y. State Assembly, 1875; auditor N.Y. Canal Dept. 1876-80; treas. Cornell U., 1868-74, trustee, 1868-88; an anti-slavery Whig. Author: Colonial New York: Philip Schuyler and His Family, 2 vols., 1885. Died Ithaca, N.Y., Feb. 1, 1888.

SCHUYLER, Margurita, colonial hostess; b. 1701 d. Johannes and Elizabeth (Staats) Schuyler m. Philip Schuyler, Dec. 29, 1720. Settled with husband on Hudson River, North of Albany, N.Y. home became meeting place for provincial aristocracy, Brit. officers and trades; became an unofcl polit. and mil. adviser to English ofcls. Loyalist during Am. Revolution. Died Albany Aug. 1782.

SCHUYLER, Peter, army officer, colonial ofcl. b. Beverwyck (now Albany), N.Y., Sept. 17, 1657 s. Philip Pieterse and Margarita (Van Slichtenhorst) S.; m. Engeltie Van Schaick, 1681; m 2d, Maria Van Rensselaer, 1691; 8 children including Margarita, Philip. Served as lt. cavalry Albany Militia, 1684; 1st mayor Albany, also head Albany Bd. Indian Commrs., 1686, removed from office, 1690, reinstated as mayor, 1691; maintained friendly relations with Iroquois Indians apptd. judge N.Y. Ct. Common Pleas, 1691; led a co. of militia against French in Can., 1691 apptd. to N.Y. Gov.'s Council, 1692; defeated French and Indians in battle nr. Schenectady, N.Y., 1693; apptd. to announce terms of Treaty of Ryswick at Frontenac, France, which ended King William's War, 1698; visited Ct. of Queen Anne, taking along several Mohawk Indian chiefs; acting gov. N.Y., 1719-20. Died Albany, Feb. 19, 1724.

SCHUYLER, Philip Jeremiah, congressman, farmer; b. Albany, N.Y., Jan. 21, 1768; son of Philip John Schuyler; ed. by pvt. tutors. Engaged in agriculture, Dutchess County, N.Y.; mem. N.Y. State Assembly, 1798; mem. U.S. Ho. of Reps. from N.Y., 15th Congress, 1817-19. Died N.Y.C., Feb. 21, 1835; buried family burial grounds, nr. Rhinebeck, N.Y.; reinterred Poughkeepsie (N.Y.) Rural Cemetery.

SCHUYLER, Philip John, Continental congressman, senator, army officer; b. Albany, N.Y., Nov. 20, 1733; s. Johannes and Cornelia (Van Cortlandt) S.; m. Catherine Van Rensselaer, Sept. 17, 1755, 8 children including Elizabeth (wife of Alexander Hamilton). Commd. to raise and command company in Gen. William Johnson's expdn. against Crown Point, 1755; mem. forces under Col. John Bradstreet which carried provisions to Oswego and cleared Oneida portage of French raiders, spring 1756; dep. commissary with rank of maj. in Brit. Army under Lord George Howe, 1758; stationed at Albany in campaigns of 1759-60, collected and forwarded provisions to Amherst's forces; inherited his father's estate, 1763, large land holder in Mohawk Valley and along Hudson River; inherited additional land from uncle and developed waterpower for his sawmills and gristmills, built 1st water-driven flaxmill in N.Y., had fleet of 1 schooner and 3 sloops engaged in trade on Hudson; mem. boundary commn. to settle line between N.Y. and Mass., 1764; mem. N.Y. Assembly, 1768; mem. Continental Congress from N.Y., 1775, 78-81; one of 4 maj. gens. under Washington, 1775, assigned to command Northern Dept.; organized expdn. against Can. 1775-76; supported N.Y.'s claims to N.H. (later Vt.) Grants; reprimanded by Congress and relieved of command, 1777, later reinstated, 1777; superseded by Gen. Horatio Gates (by order of Congress) because of loss of Ft. Ticonderoga, 1777, charged with incompetence, acquitted by court martial, 1778; resigned from service, 1779; remained on Congressional Bd. Commrs. for Indian Affairs; chmn. com. at hdqrs. authorized to assist Washington in reorganizing staff depts. of army, 1780; mem. N.Y. State Senate, 1780-84, 86-90, 92-97; mem. U.S. Senate (Federalist) from N.Y., 1789-91, 97-98; mem. N.Y. Bd. Regents, promoted plan for establishment of Union Coll., Schenectady, N.Y., subscribed 100 pounds to endowment. Died Albany, Nov. 18, 1804; buried Albany Rural Cemetery.

SCHWARTZ, John, congressman; b. Sunbury, Pa., Oct. 27, 1793. Apprenticed to mcht., Reading, Pa., circa 1803, became partner upon expiration of apprenticeship; served as maj. in War of 1812; became mfr. of iron products; mem. U.S. Ho. of Reps. (Democrat) from Pa., 36th Congress, 1859-60. Died Washington, D.C., June 20, 1860; buried Charles Evans Cemetery, Reading.

SCHWARZMANN, Herman J., architect, engr.; b. Munich, Germany, 1843. Came to U.S., circa 1864, settled in Phila.; became asst. engr. on works in Fairmont Park, later chief engr. of design; architect-in-chief Centennial Expdn., Phila., 1876, identified especially with plans for Meml. Hall and Horticulture Bldg.; worked in assn. with Alfred Buchman, N.Y.C., from close of expdn. until 1890. Died Sept. 23, 1891.

SCHWATKA, Frederick, explorer; b. Galena, Ill., Sept. 29, 1849; s. Frederick Schwatka; attended Willamette (Ore.) U.; grad. U.S. Mil. Acad., 1871; M.D., Bellevue Hosp. Med. Coll., N.Y.C., 1876. Commd. 2d lt. 3d Cavalry, U.S. Army; admitted to Neb. bar, 1875; comdr. (with William Henry Gilder of N.Y. Herald) Arctic exploring expdn. sailing on ship Eothen from N.Y.C., 1878, they performed longest sledge journey then on record, 1879-80; resigned from U.S. Army, 1885; explored course of Yukon River; commanded Alaskan expdn. sponsored by N.Y. Times, 1886; established the fact that white men could exist and carry on useful scientific work in the Arctic. Author: Along Alaska's Great River, 1885; Nimrod in the North, 1885; The Children of the Cold, 1886; In the Land of Cave and Cliff Dweller, 1893. Died Portland, Ore., Nov. 2, 1892.

SCHWEINITZ, Edmund Alexander, see de Schweinitz, Edmund Alexander.

SCOFIELD, Glenni William, congressman, lawyer; b. Dewittville, Chautauqua County, N.Y., Mar. 11, 1817; learned printing trade; grad. Hamilton Coll., Clinton, N.Y., 1840; studied law. Taught sch. for a time; admitted to bar, 1842, began practice of law, Warren, Pa.; dist. atty., 1846-48; mem. Pa. Ho. of Reps., 1849-51; became a Republican, 1856; mem. Pa. Senate, 1857-59; apptd. pres. judge 18th Jud. Dist. Pa., 1861; mem. U.S. Ho. of Reps. (Rep.) from Pa., 38th-43d congresses, 1863-75; register of treasury (apptd. by Pres. Hayes); 1878-81; asso. justice U.S. Ct. of Claims, 1881-91. Died Warren, Aug. 30, 1891; buried Oakland Cemetery.

SCOTT, Charles, gov. Ky.; b. Goochland County, Va., 1739; m. Frances Sweeney, Feb. 25, 1762; m. 2d, Judith Cary (Bell) Gist, July 25, 1807. At beginning of Revolution raised 1st companies of volunteers South of James River; apptd. lt. col. 2d Va. Regt., 1776, later col. 3d Regt., 1776; commd. brig. gen. Continental Army, 1777, captured at Charleston, S.C., 1780; brevetted maj. gen., 1783; an original mem. Soc. of Cincinnati; rep. from Woodford County (Ky.) in Va. Assembly, 1789, 90; comdt. Ky. dist. with rank of brig. gen., 1791; conducted expdn. against Indians on Wabash River, 1791; Scott County (Ky.) named for him, 1792; fought against Indians with Gen. Anthony Wayne at battle of Fallen Timbers, 1794; chosen presdl. elector from Ky., 1793, 1801, 05, 09; gov. Ky., 1808-12. Died "Canewood", Clark County, Ky., Oct. 22, 1813; buried State Cemetery, Frankfort, Ky.

SCOTT, David, jurist, Elected mem. U.S. Ho. of Reps. from Pa., 15th Congress, but resigned before Congress assembled, 1817, to accept appointment as pres. and judge of ct. of common pleas.

SCOTT, Dred, b. Southampton County, Va., 1795; m. Harriet (slave woman), 1836, 2 children. A slave owned by Capt. Peter Blow on plantations in Va. and Mo. until 1831; owned by Elizabeth Blow, 1831-33; bought by John Emerson, surgeon U.S. Army, 1833, as Emerson's servant spent 3 years in Ill., 2 years in Wis. Territory; upon Emerson's death property of Irene Sanford Emerson St. Louis, hired out by her to various families in city, left behind in St. Louis when Mrs. Emerson moved tc Mass., circa 1845; sought freedom for himself and family in suits instituted by Henry T. Blow in state court, 1846 (suits based on grounds that having travelled in free territory with consent of his master he was legally free upon his return to Mo.), lost suit; took case to fed. courts, 1854-57, U.S. Supreme Ct. ruled that since he was not citizen of Mo. he could not bring suit in fed. courts, thus state decision upheld, 1857; (Supreme Ct. went out of way to declare Mo. Compromise unconstl. in hopes of preventing similar suits and North-South strife); bought by Taylor Blow who freed him, 1857; spent remainder of life as hotel porter, St. Louis. Died St. Louis, Sept. 17, 1858.

SCOTT, Gustavus, lawyer, Continental congressman; b. Prince William County, Va., 1753; s. James and Sarah (Brown) S.; m. Margaret Caile, Feb. 16, 1777, 9 children. Admitted to Middle Temple, London, Eng., 1771; admitted to English bar, 1772; del. Md. Conv., 1775; mem. Md. Constl. Conv., 1776 (drafted 1st state constn.); mem. Md. Ho. of Dels., 1780-91, 83-85, helped to draft bill for establishment of state univ.; elected del. to Continental Congress, 1784; apptd. by Pres. Washington mem. bd. commrs. Washington (D.C.), 1794. Died at home Rock Hill, Washington, D.C., Dec. 25, 1800; buried on his farm in Va.

SCOTT, Harvey David, congressman, lawyer; b. nr. Ashtabula, O., Oct. 18, 1818; attended Asbury (now De Pauw) U., Greencastle, Ind.; studied law. Admitted to Bar, began practice of law, Terre Haute, Ind.; held several local offices; mem. U.S. Ho. of Reps. (Republican) from Ind., 34th Congress, 1855-57; judge Vigo County Circuit Ct., 1881-84; moved to Cal., 1887. Died Pasadena, Cal., July 11, 1891; buried Mountain View Cemetery.

SCOTT, James Wilmot, journalist; b. Walworth County, Wis., June 26, 1849; s. David Wilmot Scott; attended Beloit (Wis.) Coll., 2 years; m. Carrie Green, 1873, 1 child. Became a drummer boy in recruiting duty in Ill., at outbreak of Civil War; started weekly paper in Prince Georges County, Md., 1872; founded (with his father) Indsl. Press, Galena, Ill.; went to Chgo., 1875; owner interest in Daily Nat. Hotel Reporter, 1875-78; organized Chgo. Herald Co., publishers Chgo. Herald, 1881; pres. Am. Newspaper Publisher's Assn., United Press; pres. Chgo. Press Club, 3 years; founder Chgo. Evening Post, 1890. Died N.Y.C., Apr. 14, 1895.

SCOTT, Job, clergyman; b. Providence, R.I., Oct. 18, 1751; s. John and Lydia (Comstock) S.; m. Eunice Anthony, June 1, 1780, 6 children. Conducted Quaker school, Providence, 1774-78; tchr., Smithfield, R.I., 1778-83; practiced medicine, Glocester, R.I., 1783-84; made preaching pilgrimages to Vt., N.Y., Pa., N.J., 1784-86; preached at Friend's meetings along Atlantic seaboard from R.I. to Ga., 1789; made preaching tour of England and Ireland, 1792-93; mystic, outstanding example of quietism, believed that by completely suspending all his natural powers divine spirit could work through him, that messages received from divine spirit within were more important than Scriptures; after separation of Quaker Ch. into Orthodox and Hicksite branches, 1727-28, Hicksites followed Scott's teachings. Died Ballitore, Ireland, Nov. 22, 1793.

SCOTT, John, adventurer; b. Kent, Eng., 1630; m. Deborah Rayner, Imprisoned by the Dutch, L.I., N.Y., 1654; posed as rep. Brit. govt. at L.I., apptd. mem. commn. to negotiate with Dutch on ownership of L.I. and New Amsterdam, 1663; pres. English settlers on L.I., declared their independence of Conn., 1663; imprisoned by Conn. after discovery of false credentials; participated in campaign that took New Amsterdam from Dutch, 1664; served in Brit. Army fighting French, 1665-66; went to Eng., 1667, apptd. royal geographer on strength of stolen manuscript of geography book describing Am. coast and islands (lost post when his deception was discovered); served as spy for various European govts.; appeared as witness in trial of Samuel Pepys, 1677, accused Pepys of being French spy and Roman Catholic, Pepys acquitted; went to Norway, returned to Eng., 1688. Died Eng., 1696.

SCOTT, John, congressman; b. Marsh Creek, nr. Gettysburg, Pa., Dec. 25, 1784. Moved to Alexandria, Pa., 1806, became tanner and shoemaker; served as maj. in War of 1812; mem. Pa. Ho. of Reps., 1819-20; mem. U.S. Ho. of Reps. from Pa., 21st Congress, 1829-31. Died Alexandria, Sept. 22, 1850; buried Alexandria Cemetery.

SCOTT, John, congressman; lawyer; b. Hanover County, Va., May 18, 1785; grad. Princeton, 1805; studied law. Admitted to bar, began practice of law, Ste. Genevieve, Mo., 1806; mem. U.S. Congress from Mo. Territory, 14th Congress Aug. 6, 1816-Jan. 13, 1817 (election declared illegal), 15th-16th congresses Aug. 4, 1817-21; mem. U.S. Ho. of Reps. from State of Mo., 17th-19th congresses, Aug. 10, 1821-27. Died Ste. Genevieve, Oct. 1, 1861.

SCOTT, John, senator, lawyer; b. Alexandria, Pa., July 24, 1824; son of John Scott; attended Marshall Coll., Chambersburg, Pa.; studied law. Admitted to bar, 1846, practiced law, Huntingdon, Pa., 1846-69; Pros. atty. 1846-49; mem. revenue commn., 1851; mem. Pa. Ho. of Reps., 1862; mem. U.S. Senate (Republican) from Pa., 1869-75; moved to Pitts., 1875; gen. counsel Pa. R.R., 1875-77, gen. solicitor, 1877-95. Died Phila., Nov. 29, 1896; buried Woodlands Cemetery.

SCOTT, John Guier, congressman; b. Phila., Dec. 26, 1819; grad. in civil engring. Bethlehem Acad., Pa. Moved to Mo., 1842; gen. mgr. Iron Mountain Co.; founded Irondale Iron Co., 1858; mem. U.S. Ho. of Reps. (Democrat, filled vacancy) from Mo., 38th Congress, Dec. 7, 1863-65; went into drug bus., St. Louis; resumed mining activities, built furnaces, Scotia, Mo., 1868, Nova Scotia, 1869; returned to St. Louis, 1870; moved to East Tenn., circa 1880. Died Oliver Springs, Tenn., May 16, 1892; buried Bellefontaine Cemetery, St. Louis.

SCOTT, John Morin, Continental congressman; b. N.Y.C., 1730; s. John and Marian (Morin) S.; grad. Yale, 1746; m. Helena Rutgers, 1752, 4 children. Admitted to N.Y. bar, 1752; Whig; wrote articles in behalf of Whig Presbyn. cause which appeared in Independent Reflector, N.Y.C., 1752-53, "Watch Tower" column of N.Y. Mercury, 1754-55; proposed bill for establishment of King's Coll. on non-sectarian principles, 1754; author essay against Stamp Act, signed "Freeman;" alderman N.Y.C., 1756-61; mem. N.Y. Gen. Com., 1775; a leader radical party in N.Y. provincial congresses, 1775-77; a leader democratic forces in N.Y. Constl. Conv., 1777; apptd. mem. N.Y. Council of Safety, 1777; one of 1st mems. Sons of Liberty; sec. of state N.Y., 1778-84; served as brig. gen. Continental Army in Battle of L.I., 1776; mem. N.Y. Senate, 1777-82; mem. Continental Congress, 1779-83; a del. from N.Y. to settle boundary dispute with Vt.; mem. N.Y. br. Soc. of Cincinnati. Died N.Y.C., Sept. 14, 1784; buried Trinity Ch., N.Y.C.

SCOTT, John Randolph, actor; b. Phila., Oct. 19, 1805. Made debut in Macbeth, Park Theatre, N.Y., 1829; appeared at Arch Street Theatre, Phila., 1831; went to Eng., 1847; gave last performance, Sandford's Opera House, Phila., 1856. Died Phila., Apr. 4, 1856.

SCOTT, Orange, clergyman; b. Brookfield, Vt., Feb. 13, 1800; s. Samuel and Lucy (Whitney) S.; m. Amy Fletcher, May 7, 1826; m. 2d, Eliza Dearborn, Oct. 6, 1835; 7 children. Became circuit preacher, 1821, fully ordained minister Methodist Episcopal Ch., 1825; pastor, Charlestown, Mass.; presiding elder, Springfield, Mass., 1832-34, Providence (R.I.) dist., 1834-35; del. to Gen. Conf., 1831; became ardent abolitionist, 1833, began contbg. anti-slavery articles to Zion's Herald, Meth. paper in Boston, 1834, and delivering public lectures on slavery in larger New Eng. cities; made address on slavery Gen. Conf., Cincinnati, 1836; because of abolition activity, refused reappointment to Providence dist. by bishop; speaker for Am. Anti-Slavery Soc. throughout New Eng. and N.Y., 1837-39; began publication (with Gothan Horton) Am. Wesleyan Observer to plead abolition cause, 1839; pastor St. Paul's Ch., Lowell, Mass.; left the church, 1842, agitated for withdrawal of all abolition Methodists to form new eccles. body; pres. Utica Conv. (anti-slavery conv. where Wesleyan Meth. Connection of Am. was formed), 1843. Author: The Grounds of Secession from the Methodist Episcopal Church: Being an Examination of her Connection with Slavery, and also of her Form of Government. Died Newark, N.J., July 31, 1847.

SCOTT, Robert Nicholson, army officer; b. Winchester, Tenn., Jan. 21, 1838; son of W. A. Scott. Accompanied father to Cal., 1854; commd. lt. 4th U.S. Inf., 1857; sent on duty with Army of Potomac as acting adjutant gen. 1st Brigade, U.S. Inf., 1861; promoted capt. U.S. Army, 1861, brevetted maj., 1862; sr. aide to Gen. Henry Halleck, 1863-64, 67-72; instr. mil. science Shattuck Sch., Faribault, Minn., 1872-73; comdr. of Ft. Ontario, N.Y., 1873-77; promoted maj. U.S. Army, 1879, lt. col. 1885; on duty with publications of U.S. Army, also mem. com. to reorganize Army for a time, 1877-87. Author: Digest of The Military Laws of the United States, 1872. Died Washington, D.C., Mar. 5, 1887.

SCOTT, Thomas, congressman, lawyer; b. Chester County, Pa., 1739; attended rural schs., Pa.; studied law. Admitted bar, practiced law; moved to Westmoreland County, 1770; justice of peace, 1773; mem. 1st Pa. Assembly, 1776, 91; mem. Supreme Council, 1777; prothonotary Washington County, 1781-89; commd. a justice Washington Co., 1786; mem. Pa. Conv. that ratified U.S. Constn., 1887; mem. U.S. Ho. of Reps. from Pa., 1st, 3d congresses, 1789-91, 93-95. Died Washington, Pa., Mar. 2, 1796; buried old graveyard on 1st Walnut St.; reinterred Washington Cemetery.

SCOTT, Thomas Alexander, railroad exec.; b. Ft. Loudon, Franklin County, Pa., Dec. 28, 1823; s. Thomas and Rebecca (Douglas) S.; m. Anna Margaret Mullison, 1847; m. 2d, Anna Dike Riddle, 1865; 6 children. Chief clk. Office Collector of Tolls, Phila., 1847-49; station agt. Pa. R.R., Duncansville, 1850, apptd. 3d asst. supt. in charge of division starting westward from Altoona (Pa.) with office at Pitts., 1852, gen. supt., 1858, 1st v.p., 1860; commd. col. U.S. Volunteers, 1861; apptd. asst. U.S. sec. of war to supervise all govt. rys. and transp. lines, 1861; given temporary appointment col. and asst. q.m. gen.; pres. Pennsylvania Co., 1870, U.P. R.R., 1871-72, T. & P. Ry., 1872-80, Pa. R.R. Co., 1874-80. Died "Woodburn," Darby, Pa., May 21, 1881.

SCOTT, Thomas Fielding, clergyman; b. Iredell County, N.C., Mar. 12, 1807; grad. Franklin Coll. (now U. Ga.), 1829, D.D. (hon.), 1853; m. Evelyn Appleby, 1830. Licensed to preach in Presbyn. Ch.; became Episcopalian, 1842; ordained deacon Protestant Episcopal Ch., St. Paul's Ch., Augusta, Ga., 1843, ordained priest, Christ Ch., Macon, Ga., 1844; rector St. James Ch., Marietta, Ga., Trinity Ch., Columbus, Ga.; 1st missionary bishop Diocese of N.W. (Ore. and Wash. Territory), 1853-66, administered Diocese of Cal. in addition, several times. Died of Panama fever en route to Gen. Conv. of 1868, N.Y.C., July 14, 1867; buried Trinity Cemetery, N.Y.C.

SCOTT, Walter, religious reformer; b. Moffat, Dumfriesshire, Scotland, Oct. 31, 1796; s. John and Mary (Innes) S.; grad. U. Edinburgh (Scotland), 1818; m. Sarah Whitsett, Jan. 3, 1828; m. 2d, Annie B. Allen, 1850; m. 3d, Mrs. Eliza Sandige, 1855; 6 children. Came to U.S., 1818; tchr. pvt. sch. operated by George Forrester, Pitts., 1819; converted from Presbyterianism to Haldaneanism, 1819; in charge of pvt. acad. and Haldanean Ch., Pitts., circa 1820-26; became a follower of Alexander Campbell (founder Disciples of

Christ), 1822; moved to Steubenville, O., 1826; evangelist Mahoning Baptist Assn., 1826-27; preached that salvation depended on faith in Christ as the Messiah, repentance of sins, baptism by immersion; established monthly mag. the Evangelist, Cincinnati; preached in Ohio, Ky., Va., Mo.; pastor, publisher weekly newspaper Protestant Unionist, Pitts., 1844; prin. of a female acad., Covington, Ky., 1850-54. Author: The Gospel Restored, 1836; The Messiahship, or the Great Demonstration, 1859. Died May's Lick, Mason County, Apr. 23, 1861.

SCOTT, William, jurist; b. Warrenton, Fauquier County, Va., June 7, 1804; m. Elizabeth Dixon, 1835, 6 children. Admitted to Va. bar, 1825; moved to Old Franklin, Mo., 1826; apptd. judge 9th circuit of Mo., 1835; asso. justice Mo. Supreme Ct., 1841-61, chief justice, 1854-61, wrote many opinions including Emerson vs. Harriet and Emerson vs. Dred Scott (1848, 11 Mo., 413), Scott, a Man of Color vs. Emerson (1852, 15 Mo., 576); pro-slavery Democrat; removed from office by Mo. State Conv. when he refused to take to loyalty oath to U.S., 1861. Died Jefferson City, Mo., May 18, 1862.

SCOTT, William Anderson, clergyman, educator; b. Rock Creek, Bedford County, Tenn., Jan. 31, 1813; s. Eli and Martha (Anderson) S.; grad. Cumberland Coll., Princeton, Ky., 1833; attended Princeton (N.J.) Theol. Sem.; D.D. (hon.), U. Ala., 1844; LL.D. (hon.), U. City N.Y., 1872); m. Ann Nicholson, Jan. 19, 1836. Licensed to preach, 1830, missionary, 1830-31, ordained by Presbytery of La., 1835, missionary in La. and Ark., 1835-36; prin. Female Acad., Winchester, Tenn., 1836-38; pres. Nashville Female Sem., 1838-40; pastor Tuscaloosa, Ala., 1840-42, 1st Presbyn. Ch., New Orleans, 1842-54; editor the Presbyterian, 1842-54; founder Calvary Ch., San Francisco, 1854, pastor, 1854-61; founder, editor religious publ., Pacific Epxositor; a southern sympathizer, departed for Eng., 1861; pastor 42d St. Ch., N.Y.C. (congregation of southern sympathizers), 1863-70; organizer St. John's Ch., San Francisco; a founder City Coll., San Francisco, 1856; board directors San Francisco Theological Sem. (now at San Anselmo, Cal.), 1871-85, 1st pres. bd., 1st elected prof. (to chair of logic and systematic theology); 1st faculty pres.; moderator Presbyn. Gen. Assembly (Old School), 1858. Author: Daniel: A Model for Young Men, 1854; The Wedge of Gold; or Achan in El Dorado, 1855; Trade and Letters, 1856; The Giant Judge, 1858; The Bible and Politics, 1859; The Church in the Army; or The Four Centurions, 1862; The Christ of the Apostles' Creed, 1867. Died San Francisco, Jan. 14, 1885.

SCOTT, William Lawrence, railroad and coal magnate, congressman; b. Washington, D.C., July 2, 1828; s. Robert James and Mary Ann (Lewis) S.; m. Mary Tracy, Sept. 19, 1853, at least 2 children. Became a partner coal firm John Hearn & Co., 1851; mfr. iron in Pa. and Mo., owner coal mines in Pa., Ill., Ia., Mo., coal distbg. cos. in Pa. and Middle West; opened Erie & Pitts. R.R., 1861, pres.; formed W.L. Scott Co., 1871; organizer extension of Chgo., Rock Island & Pacific R.R. from central Ia. to Missouri River; an organizer 1st elevated railroad in N.Y.C.; invested in Can. So., Union Pacific, Canadian Pacific rys.; a founder N.Y., Phila. & Norfolk R.R.; mayor Erie (Pa.), 1866, 71; del. Nat. Dem. Conv., 3 times; mem. U.S. Ho. of Reps. from N.Y., 49th-50th congresses, 1885-89; conservative "Gold" Democrat, opposed activities of unions in mining industry; invested heavily in U.S. bonds during Civil War; benefactor many local charities. Died Sept. 19, 1891; buried Erie Cemetery.

SCOTT, Winfield, army officer; b. Laurel Branch, Va., June 13, 1786; s. William and Ann (Mason) S.; attended Coll. William and Mary, 1805-06; m. Maria D. Mayo, Mar. 11, 1817, 7 children. Commd. lance cpl. in Petersburg (Va.) troop of cavalry, 1807; commd. capt. of light artillery U.S. Army, May 3, 1808; court martialled for criticizing superior officer Gen. James Wilkinson, 1809, suspended from Army for 1 year; served on staff brig. gen. Wade Hampton, New Orleans, 1811-12; promoted to lt. col., 1812; captured by British at battle of Queenstown, N.Y., Oct. 1812; paroled, Nov. 1812; promoted col., Mar. 1813; led forces which captured Ft. George and defeated British at Upholds Creek, N.Y.; promoted brig. gen., Mar. 9, 1814; led Am. troops at battle on Chippewa River at Lundy's Lane, N.Y.; directed writing of 1st standard set of drill regulations for army Rules and Regulations for the Field Exercise and Maneuvers of Infantry, 1815; head of board to determine which officers would be discharged from army after War of 1812; studied French mil. methods in Europe, 1815-16; early temperance leader, wrote scheme for Restricting the Use of Ardent Spirits in the United States, 1821; pres. boards of tactics, 1815, 21, 24, 26; revised and enlarged Infantry-Tactics for army, 1835; given command in Black Hawk War, 1832 (troops rendered inactive by cholera epidemic); sent by Pres. Jackson to S.C. during nullification troubles; sent to Fla. to conduct campaign against Creek and Seminole Indians, 1835; recalled by President Jackson, 1837, returned to command of Eastern Div. in N.Y., 1837; commd. to restore order on Canadian border in Caroline affair (in which U.S. citizens gave aid and sympathy to rebels in Canada who demanded more democratic govt.), 1838; transported 16,000 Cherokee Indians from Tenn. and S.C. to new lands west of Mississippi River, spring 1838; sent again to Canadian border to settle boundary dispute between Canada and Me., fall 1838; gen.-in-chief U.S. Army, 1841-61; dissatisfied with accomplishments of Gen. Zachary Taylor in Mexican War, personally led forces in Mexico; captured Vera Cruz, Mar. 26, 1847; led troops in victories at Cerro Gordo, Contreras, Churubusco, Molino del Rey and Chapultepec; occupied Mexico City, Sept. 14, 1847; Whig candiate for Pres. U.S., 1852, defeated by Franklin Pierce; lt. gen., 1855; settled Anglo-Am. dispute over possession of San Juan Island in Puget Sound, 1859; retired due to infirmities and age, Nov. 1, 1861; remained loyal to U.S. during Civil War, although Confederacy sought his services. Died West Point, N.Y., May 29, 1866; buried National Cemetery, West Point.

SCOVILLE, Jonathan, congressman, mfr.; b. Salisbury, Conn., July 14, 1830; attended scientific dept. Harvard. Became iron mfr. and mine owner, Canaan, Conn., 1854; established car-wheel foundry, Buffalo, N.Y., 1860, Toronto, Can., 1861; mem. U. S. Ho. of Reps. (Democrat, filled vacancy) from N.Y., 46th-47th congresses, Nov. 12, 1880-83; mayor Buffalo, 1884-85. Died N.Y.C., Mar. 4, 1891; buried Salisbury Cemetery.

SCOVILLE, Joseph Alfred, journalist, novelist; b. Woodbury, Conn., Jan. 30, 1815; s. Joseph and Caroline (Preston) S.; m. Caroline Schaub, 1 child. Instrumental in Northern publication of campaign biography Life of John C. Calhoun, 1843; editor newspaper Spectator, Washington, D.C., 1843, which supported Calhoun; became Calhoun's pvt. sec., circa 1845-50; editor New York Picayune, 1850-52; published, edited Pick, humorous newspaper, N.Y.C., 1852-55; edited Evening State Gazette, N.Y.C., 1857; disliked in North for Southern sympathies; published novel Vigor, 1864, attack on Am. bourgeois society; criticized Lincoln, the North, and Union war policies. Author: Adventures of Clarence Bolton; The Old Merchants of New York City, 5 series, 1863-66. Died N.Y.C., June 25, 1864.

SCRANTON, George Whitefield, iron mfr., congressman; b. Madison, Conn., May 11, 1811; s. Theophilus and Elizabeth (Warner) S.; m. Jane Hiles, 1835, at least 3 children. Purchased (with brother Selden) an iron furnace, Oxford, N.Y., 1839; founder City of Scranton (Pa.), 1840; developed (with partners) process for smelting iron with anthracite; opened rolling-mill for prodn. of railroad iron; mem. U.S. Ho. of Reps., 36th to 37th congresses (Rep.), 1859-61; instrumental in devel. of transp. facilities in Lackawanna Valley, including Northumberland div. Del., Lackawanna & Western R.R.; pres. Cayuga & Susquehanna R.R.; promoter 1st Nat. Bank of Scranton, Scranton Gas & Water Co. Died Scranton, Mar. 24, 1861; buried Dunmore Cemetery, Scranton.

SCRIBNER, Charles, publisher; b. N.Y.C., Feb. 21, 1821; s. Uriah Rodgers and Betsey (Hawley) S.; attended Univ. City N.Y., 1837-38; grad. Coll. of N.J. (now Princeton), 1840; m. Emma Elizabeth Blair, June 13, 1848; children—John Blair, Charles, Arthur Hawley. Partner publishing firm Baker & Schribner, N.Y.C., 1846-50, took over entire bus. after partner's death, 1850; formed partnership Scribner & Welford, book importers, 1857; established Charles Scribners & Sons, 1878, published writers including Archibald Alexander, James W. Alexander, Dwight Woolsey, Noah Porter, Johann Peter Lange, Joel T. Headley; established a liberal tradition in publishing; published mag. Hours at Home, 1865-70, 1st published Scribner's Monthly Mag., 1870 (became Century Illustrated Monthly Mag., 1881). Died Luzerne, Switzerland, Aug. 26, 1871.

SCRIPPS, John Locke, journalist; b. Jackson County, Mo., Feb. 27, 1818; attended McKendree Coll.; never married. Moved to Chgo., 1847, began practice law; purchased 1/3d interest in Chgo. Tribune, 1848, soon became sr. editor; sold interest to Whig syndicate, 1852; again became sr. editor, 1860; elected pres. Tribune Co. (upon incorporation by State of Ill.), 1861, sold stock to Horace White, ret. from paper, 1865; apptd. postmaster Chgo. by Abraham Lincoln, 1861. Died Mpls., Sept. 21, 1866.

SCUDDER, Henry Joel, congressman, lawyer; b. Northport, N.Y., Sept. 18, 1825; attended Huntington Acad.; grad. Trinity Coll., Hartford, Conn., 1846; studied law. Admitted to bar, 1848, practiced law, N.Y.C., commd. capt. 37th Regt., N.Y. Nat. Guard, 1862, served throughout Civil War; mem. U.S. Ho. of Reps. (Republican) from N.Y., 43d Congress, 1873-75; trustee Trinity Coll., more than 20 years. Died N.Y.C., Feb. 10, 1886; buried family cemetery, Northport.

SCUDDER, Isaac Williamson, congressman, lawyer; b. Elizabethtown (now Elizabeth), N.J., 1816; studied law. Admitted to bar, 1838, began practice of law, Elizabeth; moved to Jersey City; prosecutor of pleas of Hudson County, N.J., 1845-55; apptd. mem. 1st police commn. of Jersey City, 1866; became dir. and counsel N.J. R.R. & Transp. Co., 1866; dir. United N.J. R.R. & Canal Co., 1872; mem. U.S. Ho. of Reps. (Republican) from N.J., 43d Congress, 1873-75; apptd. solicitor Pa. R.R. Co. for Hudson County, 1875. Died Jersey City, Sept. 10, 1881; buried St. John's Churchyard, Elizabeth.

SCUDDER, John, missionary; b. Freehold, N.J., Sept. 3, 1793; s. Joseph and Maria (Johnston) S.; grad. Coll. of N.J. (now Princeton), 1811; grad. Coll. Physicians and Surgeons, N.Y.C., 1813; m. Harriet Waterbury, 14 children, including Joseph, Henry. Apptd. med. missionary Am. Bd. Commrs. for Fgn. Missions, 1819; stationed, Jaffna, Ceylon, 1819, began teaching, practice of medicine; ordained by Council of Missionaries, Dutch Reformed Ch., 1821; opened hosps., schs.; established mission with printing press, Madras, India, 1836; travelled throughout India; returned to Am. for reasons of health, promoted missionary causes, 1842-45; missionary in India, 1846-49, Madras, 1849-54, S.Am., 1854. Author religious tracts in Tamil lang., also English booklets and tracts published by Am. Tract Soc. Died Wynberg, S.Am., Jan. 13, 1855; buried Madras.

SCUDDER, John Anderson, congressman, physician; b. Freehold, Monmouth County, N.J., Mar. 22, 1759; grad. Princeton, 1775; studied medicine. Began practice of medicine, Monmouth County; served as surgeon's mate 1st Regt. of Monmouth County during Revolutionary War, 1777; sec. N.J. Med. Soc., 1788-89; mem. N.J. Gen. Assembly, 1801-07; mem. U.S. Ho. of Reps. (Democrat, filled vacancy) from N.J., Oct. 31, 1810-11; moved to Ky., after 1810, to Daviess County, Ind., 1819. Died Washington, Ind., Nov. 6, 1836; buried Old City Cemetery.

SCUDDER, John Milton, eclectic physician; b. Harrison, O., Sept. 8, 1829; s. John Scudder; grad. Eclectic Med. Inst., Cincinnati, 1856; m. Jane Hannah, Sept. 8, 1849; m. 2d, Mary Hannah, after 1861; at least 4 children. Prof. spl. and pathological anatomy Eclectic Med. Inst., 1857, dean, 1861, prof. diseases of women and children, 1858-60, prof. pathology and principles and practice of medicine, 1860-87, prof. hygiene and phys. diagnosis, 1887-94; edited Eclectic Med. Journal, 1861-94, Journal of Health, The Eclectic (literary journal); 1870-71. Author: Practical Treatise on the Diseases of Women, 1857; Materia Medica and Therapeutics, 1860; Eclectic Practise of Medicine, 1864; Domestic Medicine; or Home Book of Health, 20 editions, 1865; Principles of Medicine, 1867; Eclectic Practice in Diseases of Children, 1869; Familiar Treatise on Medicine, 1869; Specific Medication and Specific Medicines, 1870; Specific Diagnosis, 1874. Died Daytona, Fla., Feb. 17, 1894.

SCUDDER, Nathaniel, army officer, Continental congressman; b. Monmouth County, N.J., May 10, 1733; s. Jacob and Abia (Rowe) S.; grad. Coll. of N.J. (now Princeton), 1751; m. Isabella Anderson, Mar. 23, 1752, 5 children. Elder, Tennent Ch., nr. Freehold, N.J.; trustee Princeton, 1778-81; became mem. local com. of safety; del. to 1st N.J. Provincial Congress, New Brunswick, 1774; speaker N.J. Gen. Assembly, 1776; lt. col. 1st Monmouth County Regt., N.J. Militia, 1776; commd. col., 1781; del. Continental Congress, 1777-1779; present at Battle of Monmouth; his most important service was writing letter to John Hart (speaker N.J. Legislature), strongly urging that state's delegates to Congress be empowered to ratify and sign Articles of Confederation, 1778. Killed while resisting invading party of Brit. Army at Blacks Point nr. Shrewsbury, N.J., Oct. 16, 1781; buried Tennent Churchyard, Monmouth Battlefield, N.J.

SCUDDER, Tredwell, congressman; b. Islip, Suffolk County, N.Y., Jan. 1, 1778; attended public schs. Engaged in farming; town supr. Islip, 1795-96, 1804-15, 24-33; mem. N.Y. State Assembly, 1802, 10-11, 14-15, 22, 28; mem. U.S. Ho. of Reps. from N.Y., 15th Congress, 1817-19. Died Islip, Oct. 31, 1834; buried Islip.

SCUDDER, Zeno, congressman, lawyer; b. Osterville, Barnstable County, Mass., Aug. 18, 1807; studied law. Admitted to bar, 1836, began practice of law, Falmouth, Mass.; mem. Mass. Senate, 1846-48, served as pres.; mem. U.S. Ho. of Reps. (Whig) from Mass., 32d-33d congresses, 1851-Mar. 4, 1854 (resigned because of an accident). Died Barnstable, Mass., June 26, 1857; buried Hillside Cemetery, Osterville.

SCULL, John, newspaper editor; b. Reading, Pa., 1765; s. Jasper Scull; m. Mary Irwin, 1789, 3 children. Established (with Joseph Hall) Pitts. Gazette (1st newspaper West if Alleghenies), 1786, partner, 1786-1816; published 3d vol. of Modern Chivalry (Brackenridge), 1st book printed West of Alleghenies, 1793; helped secure post-route to Pitts., postmaster, 1789-96; mem. 1st council Borough of Pitts., 1804; pres. 2d bank established in Pitts., 1814-18; an incorporator Western U. Pa. (now U. Pitts.), 1819. Died Irwin, Pa., Feb. 8, 1828.

SCURRY, Richardson, congressman, lawyer; b. Gallatin, Tenn., Nov. 11, 1811; ed. by pvt. tutors; studied law. Admitted to bar, circa 1830, began practice of law, Covington, Tenn.; moved to Clarksville, Tex.; del. conv. which issued Tex. Declaration of Independence; pioneer in forming state govt. of Tex.; served in Texan War; mem. U.S. Ho. of Reps. (Democrat) from Tex., 32d Congress, 1851-53. Died Hempstead, Tex., Apr. 9, 1862; buried Hempstead Cemetery.

SEABURY, Samuel, clergyman; b. Groton, Conn., Nov. 30, 1729; s. Rev. Samuel and Abigail (Mumford) S.; B.A., Yale, 1748; attended U. Edinburgh (Scotland), 1752-53; D.D. (hon.), Oxford (Eng.) U.; m. Mary Hicks, Oct. 12, 1756, at least 6 children. Catechist, Huntington, L.I., N.Y., 1748-52; ordained deacon Protestant Episcopal Ch., 1753, licensed to preach by Bishop of London, 1754; missionary, New Brunswick, Can., 1754-57, transferred to Jamaica, L.I., 1767; rector, Westchester, N.Y., 1767; sec. Conv. of N.Y. (composed of Anglican clergy), 1766-67; wrote pamphlets urging colonies to remain loyal to Crown (most important pamphlets signed A.W. Farmer); entered Loyalists' campaign to prevent election of coms. and dels. to Provincial and Continental congresses, and to nullify the measures enacted by those bodies, 1775; went into hiding, Apr. 29, 1775, taken prisoner, Nov. 22, released, Dec. 23, 1775; apptd. chaplain Provincial Hosp. of N.Y., 1777; served as guide to Brit. Army, 1776; consecrated bishop by non-juring Scottish prelates, 1784; rector St. James' Ch., bishop of Conn. and R.I. (1st bishop Episcopal Ch. in Am.), 1785-96. Author collections of sermons: Discourses on Several Subjects, 2 vols., 1793; Discourses on Several Important Subjects, 1798. Died New London, Feb. 25, 1796; buried beneath altar of St. James' Ch., New London.

SEABURY, Samuel, clergyman; b. New London, Conn., June 9, 1801; s. Charles and Anne (Saltonstall) S.; m. Lydia Huntington Bill, May 17, 1829; m. 2d, Hannah Amelia Jones, Nov. 17, 1835; m. 3d, Mary Anna Jones, Oct. 17, 1854; 6 children including William. Ordained deacon Protestant Episcopal Ch., N.Y.C., 1826, priest, 1828; took charge of St. George's Ch., Hallet's Cove (now Astoria), N.Y.; became classical instr. at William Muhlenberg's sch., Flushing, N.Y., 1828; editor The Churchman (Episcopal weekly newspaper), 1833-35; taught evidences, Gen. Theol. Sem., N.Y.C., 1835-38, became prof. Bibl. learning, 1862; rector Ch. of Annunciation, N.Y.C., 1838-68; founder the Protestant Churchman, 1846. Author: The Joy of the Saints, 1844; The Continuity of the Church of England, 1853; American Slavery . . . Justified, 1861; Mary the Virgin as Commemorated in the Church of Christ, 1868; The Theory and Use of the Church Calendar, 1872; writings collected in Discourses Illustrative of the Nature and Work of the Holy Spirit, and Other Papers (edited and published by son William), 1874. Died Oct. 10, 1872.

SEALSFIELD, Charles (real name: Karl Anton Postl), author; b. Poppitz, Moravia, Mar. 3, 1793; s. Anton and Juliane (Rabel) Postl; attended Untergymnasium, Znaim, 1802-07; entered Coll. of the Kreuzherrenstift, Prague, 1808. Novice in monastery of Knight of Cross, Prague, 1813; fled monastery (because of Metternich system of religious censorship and conservatism) using name Charles Sealsfield, 1823; came to New Orleans; traveled through So. states, Mexican Province of Tex., probably also Mexico; in Europe, 1827; published 2 volumes of Die Vereinigten Staaten von Nordamerika, nach ihrem Politischen, Religiösen, und Gesellschaftlichen Verhältnisse Betrachtet by Charles Sidons (pseudonym which he never used again), this work appeared anonymously in English translation in 2 parts The United States as They Are, and The Americans as They Are; Described in a Tour through the Valley of the Mississippi. By the Author of Austria as it Is, 1828; wrote Austria as it Is; or Sketches of Continental Courts, by an Eyewitness; correspondent for German journals in Phila.; wrote novel Tokeah; or the White Rose, 2 vols., 1828 (published in German as Der Legitime and die Republikaner, 3 vols., 1833); active as journalist, 1828-32; conceived new type of fiction, the ethnographical novel using a whole people as his hero; all of his novels dealt with people of U.S. and Mexico; continued his anonymity until 1845; complete works published in 15 vols. under name of Charles Sealsfield, 1845-47; became U.S. citizen; retired to Switzerland. Other works include: Der Virey and die Aristokraten; oder Mexiko im Jahre 1812, 3 vols., 1834; Morton oder die Grosse Tour, 1835; Die Deutsch-amerikanischen Wahlverwandtschaften, 4 vols., 1839-40; Das Cajütenbach, oder Nationale Charakteristiken, 2 vols., 1841; Süden und Norden, 3 vols., 1842-43; Lebensbilder aus der Westlichen Hemisphäre, 5 vols., 1846. Died nr. Solothurn, Switzerland, May 26, 1864.

SEAMAN, Henry John, congressman; b. Marshland (now Greenridge), S.I., N.Y., Apr. 16, 1805. Engaged in farming; promoter Richmond village, 1836; mem. U.S. Ho. of Reps. (Am. Party candidate) from N.Y., 29th Congress, 1845-47; dir. S.I. R.R., 1851; sec. Plank Rd. Co., 1856; built bridge over Fresh Kills. Died S.I., May 3, 1861; buried Woodlawn Cemetery, N.Y.C.

SEARING, John Alexander, congressman; b. North Hempstead, N.Y., May 14, 1805. Sheriff, Queens County (N.Y.), 1843-46; mem. N.Y. State Assembly, 1854; mem. U.S. Ho. of Reps. (Democrat) from N.Y., 35th Congress, 1857-59. Died Mineola, Nassau County, N.Y., May 6, 1876; buried Greenfield Cemetery, Hempstead.

SEARLE, James, mcht., Continental congressman; b. N.Y.C., 1733; s. John and Catherine (Pintard) S.; m. Ann (or Nancy) Smith, 1762; m. 2d, Isabella West, 1785; several children. Employee, later mem. firm John Searle (his brother) & Co., Madeira, Spain, 1746-62, co. agt. in Phila., 1762-87; signer Non-Importation Agreement of 1765, participated in all later merc. protests against Gt. Britain; commd. lt. col. Pa. Militia, 1775; mgr. U.S. Lottery, 1776-78; mem. U.S. Naval Bd., 1778; mem. Continental Congress, 1778-80, served on many coms.; apptd. agt. for a Madeira firm (when his firm was on brink of bankruptcy) with salary and commns., 1787; trustee U. Pa., 1778-81; unsuccessful commr. to France and Holland to negotiate a loan for State of Pa., 1780-82. Died Phila., Aug. 7, 1797; buried St. Peter's Churchyard, Phila.

SEARS, Barnas, clergyman, univ. pres.; b. Sandisfield, Mass., Nov. 19, 1802; s. Paul and Rachel (Granger) S.; attended Brown U., 1825, Newton (Mass.) Theol. Sem., 2 years; m. Elizabeth Griggs Carey, July 6, 1830, 5 children. Ordained pastor First Baptist Ch., Hartford, Conn., 1827; prof. langs. Hamilton (N.Y.) Literary and Theol. Instn. (now Colgate U.), 1829-33; prof. Christian theology Newton Theol. Inst., 1836-48, pres., 1839-48; editor Christian Review, 1838-41; sec. Mass. Bd. Edn., 1848-55; pres. Brown U., 1855-67, prof. moral philosophy; gen. agt. Peabody Edn. Fund, Stauton, Va., 1867-80. Author: A Grammar of the German Language, 1842; Life of Luther, 1850; Objections to Public Schools Considered, 1875; prin. author Classical Studies: Essays on Ancient Literature and Art, 1843; editor Roget's Thesaurus of English Words and Phrases, 1873. Died Saratoga, N.Y., July 6, 1880; buried Walnut Street Cemetery, Brookline, Mass.

SEARS, Edmund Hamilton, clergyman; b. Sandisfield, Mass., Apr. 6, 1810; s. Joseph and Lucy (Sears) Smith; grad. Union Coll., Schenectady, N.Y., 1834; D.D. (hon.), 1871; grad. Harvard Divinity Sch., 1837; m. Ellen Bacon, Nov. 7, 1839, 4 children. Missionary, Am. Unitarian Assn., Toledo, O., 1837-39; ordained to ministry Unitarian Ch., Wayland, Mass., 1839; pastor, Lancaster, Mass., 1840-47, Wayland, 1848-65, Weston, Mass., 1866-76; an editor Monthly Religious Mag., 1859-71; wrote hymns Calm on the Listening Ear of Night, It Came upon a Midnight Clear. Author: Regeneration, 1853; Pictures of the Olden Times as Shown in the Fortunes of A family of Pilgrims, 1857; Genealogies and Biographical Sketches of the Ancestry and Descendants of Richard Sears, 1857; Athanasia: or Foregleams of Immortality, 1858; The Fourth Gospel, the Heart of Christ (most notable book), 1872. Died Weston, Jan. 16, 1876.

SEARS, Isaac, patriot, privateer; b. West Brewster, Mass., July 1, 1730; s. Joshua and Mary (Thacher) S.; m. Sarah Drake, 11 children. Commanded a trading sloop between N.Y.C. and Boston, 1752; privateer during French and Indian War; became leader in colonial resistance after the passage of Stamp Act; leader gen. populace, instigated demonstrations, mob violence, 1765-76; led Sons of Liberty in destroying cargo of tea ship in N.Y.C.; mem. several revolutionary coms.; led patriots in seizure of Brit. arms, after battles of Lexington and Concord, took command of N.Y.C.; recruiter for Continental Army in Conn., 1776; commd. to capture Brit. supplies for colonial forces; promoted privateering in Boston, 1877-83; returned to mdse. bus., N.Y.C., after Revolutionary War; elected to N.Y. State Assembly, 1784, 86; trustee, vestryman Trinity Ch., N.Y.C., 1784-86; v.p. N.Y. State C. of C., 1784; sailed to China on bus. venture, 1786. Died of fever, Canton, China, Oct. 28, 1786; buried French Island, Canton Harbor.

SEARS, Robert, publisher; b. St. John, N.B., Can., June 28, 1810; s. Thatcher and Abigail (Spurr) S.; m. Harriet Martin, 1832, 8 children. Went to N.Y.C. as journeyman printer, 1831; set up printing business, N.Y.C.; brought out 3-volume work Pictorial Illustrations of the Bible, 1840-41 (25,000 sets sold); published The Wonders of the World, in Nature, Art, and Mind, 1843, A New and Complete History of the Holy Bible, 1844; one of earliest of N.Y. publishers to try to serve all sections of country; edited, published New Pictorial Family Magazine, 1844-49; published The Pictorial History of the American Revolution, 1845, A New and Popular Pictorial Description of the United States, 1848, Pictorial Bible, 1858. Died Toronto, Ont., Can., Feb. 17, 1892.

SEATON, William Winston, journalist, mayor Washington (D.C.); b. Chelsea, King William County, Va., Jan. 11, 1785; s. Augustine and Mary (Winston) S.; m. Sarah Weston Gales, Mar. 30, 1809; 3 children, including Josephine. Asst. editor Virginia Patriot, Richmond; editor Republican, Petersburg, Va., also N.C. Jour., Halifax; served as pvt. Va. Militia during War of 1812; asso. editor Nat. Intelligence, Washington, D.C., 1812-26; exclusive reporter (with brother-in-law Joseph Gales) U.S. Congress, 1812-29, reports published as The Debates and Proceedings in the Congress of the United States (better known by the half-title Annals of Congress), 42 vols., 1834-56; published Register of Debates in Congress (covering years 1824-37), 14 vols., 1825-37, American State Papers,, 38 vols., 1832-61; alderman Washington (D.C.), 1819-31, mayor, 1840-50; led movement for Washington Monument; an organizer Smithsonian Instn., regent, treas., 1846-66; an ofcl. in Am. Colonization Soc., favored gradual emancipation, freed his own slaves; Whig, Unionist; Unitarian; Mason. Died Washington, June 16, 1885.

SEATTLE, Indian chief; b. nr. Seattle, Wash., 1786; s. Schweabe and Scholitza. Chief, Swamish, Suquamish and allied Indian tribes; befriended 1st white settlers in Seattle area, remained loyal to them during Indian raids of other tribes; signed Treaty of Point Ellicott, 1855, to provide for land cession to whites and agy. adminstrn.; became Roman Catholic, instituted custom of holding morning and evening services in his tribe; city of Seattle named for him. Died June 7, 1866.

SEAVER, Ebenezer, congressman; b. Roxbury, Mass., July 5, 1763; grad. Harvard, 1784. Engaged in farming; mem. Mass. Ho. of Reps., 1794-1802, 22-23, 26; mem. U.S. Ho. of Reps. (Democrat) from Mass., 8th-12th congresses, 1803-13; mem. Mass. Constl. Conv., 1820. Died Roxbury, Mar. 1, 1844.

SEBASTIAN, Benjamin, jurist; b. 1745; at least 1 child, Charles. Moved to Jefferson County, Ky., 1784; admitted to bar, Louisville, Ky., 1784, licensed as atty., 1786; mem. Polit. Club, Danville, Ky.; advocate of separation from Va. and establishment of Ky. as separate state; suspected of negotiating with Spanish to seek means to make Ky. a Spanish subject; apptd. judge Ky. Appellate Ct., 1792, continued correspondence with Spanish, received Spanish pension (Federalist faction in Ky. obtained petition asking legislature to investigate his activities with Spanish), resigned (making guilt certain), 1806; built saw-and-grist mill, engaged in gen. merchandising, Livingston, Ky., 1810. Died Mar. 1834.

SEBASTIAN, William King, senator; b. Centerville, Hickman County, Tenn., 1812; grad. Columbia Coll., Tenn., circa 1834; studied law. Admitted to bar, began practice of law, Helena, Ark., 1835; later became cotton planter; pros. atty., 1835-37; circuit judge, 1840-43; asso. justice Ark. Supreme Ct., 1843-45; pres. Ark. Senate, 1846-47; Democratic presdl. elector, 1846; mem. U.S. Senate (Democrat, filled vacancy) from Ark., May 12, 1848-July 11, 1861 (expelled; Senate revoked resolution of expulsion, paid full amount of his compensation to his children, 1877); practiced law, Helena, during Civil War, did not participate in Confederate movements; moved to Memphis, Tenn. (after U.S. troops occupied Helena), 1864. Died Memphis, May 20, 1865; buried Dunn family burying ground nr. Helena.

SECCOMB, John, clergyman; b. Medford, Mass., Apr. 25, 1708; s. Peter and Hannah (Willis) S.; grad. Harvard, 1728; m. Mercy Williams, Mar. 10, 1737, 4 children. Wrote poems while at Harvard which were published together in Boston, 1731, popular among several generations of New Englanders; ordained to ministry Congregational Ch., Harvard, Mass., 1733; pastor, Harvard, 1733-57; minister Congl. Ch., Chester, Nova Scotia, Can., 1763, wrote to Christian History describing increase in size of congregation (a part of the Great Awakening), 1743/44; an old-fashioned Calvinist. Died Chester, Oct. 27, 1792.

SECHER, Samuel, mcht.; b. Columbus, Burlington County, N.J., 1771; m. Elizabeth West, 1797. Moved to Phila., 1794; began business Archer & Newbold, 1797, later Samuel Archer & Co., 1804, then Archer & Bispham; engaged in retail drygoods bus., 1798, and importing bus., 1799; dealt primarily in Chinese and Indian imports, 1800-12; visited Europe to purchase goods, 1810-11; bulk of his fgn. trade cut off by War of 1812; after War began to export Am. fabrics to China (1st Am. mcht. to export Am.-made cotton goods to Asia); mem. Phila. Saving Fund Soc., 1816; dir. Ins. Co. of N.Am., 1816; presented lot upon which Phila. Orphan Asylum was built, 1817. Died Apr. 14, 1839; buried Friends' burial-ground, Phila.

SEDDON, James, congressman, Confederate sec. of war; b. Fredericksburg, Va., July 13, 1815; s. Thomas and Susan (Pearson) S.; grad. Law Sch., U. Va., 1835; m. Sarah Bruce, 1845. Admitted to bar, 1838; mem. U.S. Ho. of Reps. from Va., 29th, 31st congresses, 1845-47, 49-51, supported John Calhoun; mem. com. on resolutions Peace Conv., Washington, D.C., 1861, introduced minority report which recognized right of peaceful secession; elected to 1st Confederate Congress, 1861; sec. of war Confederate States Am., 1862-65, exerted considerable influence over Pres. Jefferson Davis until 1863, worked closely with Gen. Robert E. Lee, approved his movement to take offensive at Battle of Gettysburg, 1863, performed duties of office with tact, indecisive in settling adminstrv. problems, resigned at time of cabinet reorgn., 1865; ret. to estate "Sabot Hill," Goochland County, Va. Died "Sabot Hill," Aug. 19, 1880; buried Hollywood Cemetery, Richmond, Va.

SEDGWICK, Catharine Maria, author; b. Stockbridge, Mass., Dec. 28, 1789; d. Theodore and Pamela (Dwight) Sedgwick. Published anonymously 1st novel A New England Tale, 1822; published Redwood, 1824; The Travelers, 1825; Hope Leslie, 1827; Clarence; or a Tale of Our Own Times, 1830; The Linwoods; or "Sixty Years Since" in America, 1835; Letters from Abroad to Kindred at Home, 1841; published 2 biographical sketches, an account of Lucretia M. Davidson in Spark's The Library of American Biography, vol. VII, 1837, Memoir of John Curtis, a Model Man, 1858; author many short tales, books designed to be helpful to persons of less-favored class; participated in philanthropic activities; active Unitarian Ch., also Women's Prison Assn. of N.Y.; other works include: Home, 1835; The Poor Rich Man, and the Rich Poor Man, 1836; Live and Let Live; or Domestic Service Illustrated, 1837; Means and Ends; or Self-Training, 1839; Wilton Harvey, 1845; Morals of Manners, 1846; Facts and Fancies for School-Day Reading, 1848; Married or Single, 1857. Died West Roxbury, Mass., July 31, 1867.

SEDGWICK, Charles Baldwin, congressman, lawyer; b. Pompey, Onondaga County, N.Y., Mar. 15, 1815; attended Pompey Hill Acad., Hamilton Coll., Clinton, N.Y.; studied law. Admitted to bar, 1848, began practice of law, Syracuse, N.Y.; mem. U.S. Ho. of Reps. (Republican) from N.Y., 36th-37th congresses, 1859-63; spent 2 years codifying naval laws for Navy Dept., Washington, D.C. Died Syracuse. Feb. 3, 1883; buried Oakwood Cemetery.

SEDGWICK, Henry Dwight, lawyer; b. Sheffield, Berkshire County, Mass., Sept. 22, 1785; s. Theodore Sedgwick; grad. Williams Coll., 1804. Wrote articles advocating free trade for Banner and Constn.; contbr. N.Am. Review. Author: An Appeal to the City on the Proposed Alteration of its Charter; English Practice of the Common Law (1822). Died Stockbridge, Mass., Dec. 23, 1831.

SEDGWICK, John, army officer; b. Cornwall Hollow, Conn., Sept. 13, 1813; s. Benjamin and Olive (Collins) S.; grad. U.S. Mil. Acad., 1837. Served with arty. U.S. Army during Seminole War, assisted in moving Cherokee Indians West of the Mississippi River; served on No. frontier during Canadian border disturbances; joined Gen. Zachary Taylor's army on Rio Grande River, 1846; participated in all battles of Mexican War; brevetted capt. and maj. for services at battles of Churubusco and Chapultepec respectively; maj. 1st Regt. of Cavalry, 1855; participated in Utah Expdn., 1857-58, also in warfare with Kiowa and Comanche Indians, 1858-60; lt. col. 2d Cavalry, 1861; col. 1st Cavalry, U.S. Army, 1862; transferred to 4th Cavalry; commd. brig. gen. U.S. Volunteers, 1862; commanded div. of Sumner's 2d Corps. during Va. peninsular campaign of 1862, participated in siege of Yorktown, pursuing Confederate Army up the peninsula; distinguished at battles of Fair Oaks, Savage Station, Glendale, Antietam; apptd. maj. gen. U.S. Volunteers in command 9th Corps, 1862, transferred to command 6th Corps, 1863; distinguished in Rappahannock campaign, Pa. campaign of 1863, as comdr. right wing of U.S. Army in battles of Chancellorsville, Fredericksburg, Gettysburg; distinguished in battles of Wilderness and Spotsylvania in Richmond campaign, 1864. Killed at Battle of Spotsylvania (Va.), May 9, 1864; buried Cornwall Hollow.

SEDGWICK, Robert, colonist, army officer; b. Wobwen, Bedfordshire, Eng., 1613; s. William and Elizabeth (Howe) S.; m. Joanna Blake. One of 1st settlers of Charlestown (Mass.); chosen capt. Charlestown Militia, 1637; an organizer Military Co. of Mass., capt., 1640, 45, 48; granted (with 6 others) a monopoly of Indian trade of Mass. Colony, until 1665; elected maj. gen. Mass. Colony, 1652; given charge of 12 ships and 800 men, sent to reinforce expdn. of William Penn, operating against Spanish West Indies. Died Jamaica, B.W.I., May 24, 1656.

SEDGWICK, Theodore, senator, jurist; b. West Hartford, Conn., May 9, 1746; s. Benjamin and Ann (Thompson) S.; received degree from Yale, 1772 (as of 1765); m. Eliza Mason, 1768; m. 2d, Pamela Dwight, Apr. 17, 1774; m. 3d, Penelope Russell, 1808; 10 children including Theodore, Catharine Maria. Admitted to Berkshire County (Mass.) bar, 1766; clk. Berkshire County Conv. to consider resistance to Brit. taxation, 1774; mil. sec. to Gen. John Thomas, 1776; mem. Mass. Legislature, 1780, 82, 83, 87, 88, speaker, 1788; mem. Mass. Senate, 1784, 85; defended Negro slave Elizabeth Freeman, established illegality of slavery in Mass., 1783; staunch Federalist; mem. Continental Congress, 1785-88; active in suppressing Shays' Rebellion, 1787; mem. Mass. Conv. which ratified U.S. Constn., 1788; mem. U.S. Ho. of Reps. from Mass., 1st-4th, 6th congresses, 1789-June 1796, 1799-1801, speaker, 1799-1801; mem. U.S. Senate from Mass., June 11, 1796-99; judge Supreme Ct. of Mass., 1802-13; trustee Williams Coll., until 1813; corporate mem. Am. Acad. Arts and Scis. Died Boston, Jan. 24, 1813; buried family cemetery, Stockbridge, Mass.

SEDGWICK, Theodore, 2d, lawyer, b. Sheffield, Mass., Dec. 31, 1780; s. Judge Theodore and Pamela (Dwight) S.; grad. Yale, 1798; m. Susan Anne Livingston Ridley, Nov. 28, 1808, 2 children including Theodore 3d. Admitted to N.Y. bar, 1801; practiced in Albany, N.Y.; pres. Berkshire County Agrl. Soc.; mem. Mass. Legislature (Democrat), 1824-25, 27, introduced bill for constructing Boston & Albany R.R. at state expense, 1827; became power in Mass. Democratic Party: delivered address The Practicability of the Abolition of Slavery, 1831. Author: Hints to my Countrymen, 1826; Hints for the People, with Some Thoughts on the Presidential Election, by Rusticus, 1823; Private Economy, 3 vols., 1836-39 (most important work). Died Pittsfield, Mass., Nov. 7, 1839.

SEDGWICK, Theodore, lawyer; b. Albany, N.Y., Jan. 27, 1811; s. Theodore and Susan Anne Livingston (Ridley) S.; grad. Columbia, 1829; m. Sarah Morgan Ashburner, Sept. 28, 1835, 7 children including Arthur George, Susan. Admitted to N.Y. bar, 1833; attaché at U.S. legation in Paris, 1833; practiced in N.Y.C., 1834-50; pres. Assn. for Exhbn. of Industry of all Nations, 1852; U.S. dist. atty. for Southern Dist. N.Y., 1858-59. Author: A Memoir of the Life of William Livingston, 1833; What Is a Monopoly, 1835; A Statement of Facts in Relation to the Delays and Arrears of Business in the Court of Chancery of the State of New York, 1838; Review of the Memoirs of the Life of Sir Samuel Romilly, 1841; Constitutional Reform, 1843; Thoughts on the Proposed Annexation of Texas, 1844; The American Citizens, 1847; A Treatise on the Measure of Damages, or, an Inquiry into the Principles which Govern the Amount of Compensation Recovered in Suits of Law (most important work), 1847; A Treatise on the Rules which Govern the Interpretation and Application of Statutory and Constitutional Law, 1857. Contbr. to Harper's Weekly, Harper's Monthly, also (under pseudonym Veto) to N.Y. Evening Post. Died Stockbridge, Mass., Dec. 8, 1859.

SEELEY, Elias P., gov. N.J.; b. N.J., 1791; studied law with Daniel Elmer, Bridgeton, N.J. Admitted to N.J. bar, 1815; mem. N.J. Legislature, 1829; gov. of N.J. for a few months in 1833. Died 1846.

SEELEY, John Edward, congressman, lawyer; b. Ovid, N.Y., Aug. 1, 1810; attended Ovid Acad.; grad. Yale, 1835; studied law. Admitted to bar, began practice of law, Monroe, Mich.; returned to Ovid, 1839; supr. Ovid, 1842; county judge, surrogate Seneca County (N.Y.), 1851-55; del. Republican Nat. Conv., Phila., 1856; Rep. presdl. elector 1860, 64; mem. U.S. Ho. of Reps. (Rep.) from N.Y., 42d Congress, 1871-73. Died Ovid, Mar. 30, 1875; buried on his farm nr. Ovid.

SEELOS, Francis X., missionary; b. Füssen, Bavaria, Jan. 11, 1819; studied at Augsburg and Munich (Germany). Joined Congregation of Most Holy Redeemer; came to U.S., 1843; ordained priest Roman Catholic Ch., Balt., 1844; became superior, Pitts., 1851, spiritual dir. of professed Redemptorists, Balt., 1860; declined bishopric of Pitts., 1860, spent rest of life in missionary work. Died New Orleans, Oct. 4, 1867.

SEELYE, Julius Hawley, clergyman, coll. pres., congressman; b. Bethel, Conn., Sept. 14, 1824; s. Seth and Abigail (Taylor) S.; grad. Amherst Coll., 1849, Auburn Theol. Sem., 1852; studied philosophy U. Halle (Germany), 1 year; m. Elizabeth Tillman James, Oct. 23, 1854, 4 children. Ordained to ministry Reformed Protestant Dutch Ch., 1833; pastor 1st Dutch Reformed Ch., Schenectady, N.Y., 1853-58; prof. philosophy (expounded L.P. Hickok's transcendentalist views) Amherst (Mass.) Coll., 1858, pres., 1876-90; gave lectures in India, 1872; mem. Mass. commn. for revision of state tax laws; chmn. bd. visitors Andover (Mass.) Theol. Sem., 1887; mem. U.S. Ho. of Reps. from Mass., 44th Congress, 1875-77; translated History of Philosophy (Albert Schwegler), 1856; edited and revised System of Moral Science 1880, Empirical Psychology, 1882 (both L.P. Hickok. Died Amherst, May 12, 1895; buried Wildwood Cemetery, Amherst.

SEEVERS, William Henry, jurist; b. Shenandoah County, Va., Apr. 8, 1822; s. James and Rebecca (Wilkins) S.; m. Caroline Lee, Feb. 20, 1849, 5 children. Sheriff of Shenandoah County, 1843-44; admitted to Ia. bar, 1846; practiced in Oskaloosa, Ia., 1846-95; pros. atty. Mahoska County, Ia., 1848-50; judge 3d Jud. Dist. of Ia., 1852-56; mem. Ia. Ho. of Reps., 1857, 76; chmn. commn to codify statutes of Ia., 1871; judge Ia. Supreme Ct., 1876-83, chief justice, 1876, 82, 87-88. Died Oskaloosa, Mar. 24, 1895.

SEGAR, Joseph Eggleston, congressman, lawyer; b. King William County, Va., June 1, 1804; attended common schs.; studied law. Admitted to bar, practiced law; held several local offices; mem. Va. Ho. of Dels., 1836-38, 48-52, 55-61; mem. U.S. Ho. of Reps. (Unionist) from Va., 37th Congress, Mar. 15, 1862-63, elected to 38th, 41st congresses, but not allowed to take seat; elected to U.S. Senate from Va., not allowed to take seat. Died on steamer George Leary en route from Norfolk, Va. to Washington, D.C., Apr. 30, 1880; buried St. John's Cemetery, Hampton, Va.

SEGHERS, Charles Jean, clergyman, missionary; b. Ghent, Belgium, Dec. 26, 1839; s. Charles Frances and Pauline (Seghers) S.; attended Coll. of Ste. Barbe, Ghent, Am. Coll., Louvain, Belgium. Ordained priest Roman Catholic Ch., Mechlin, Belgium, 1863; began missionary work among Indians, hunters and settlers, Vancouver, B.C., Can., 1863; founded St. Joseph's Hosp., Victoria, B.C.; attended Vatican Council, 1869; became administrator of diocese, 1871; apptd. bishop, 1873; made 1st trip to Alaska, 1877; established mission, Wrangell, Alaska, 1878; apptd. coadjutor to archbishop of Portland, 1878; archbishop of Portland, 1879-84; visited Rome, 1883; took part in 3d Plenary Council, Balt., 1883; resigned to return to missionary work in B.C. and Alaska, 1884; established missions at Juneau and Sitka, Alaska; founded sch. and hosp., Juneau, 1885; introduced Jesuits to mission work in Alaska. Killed while trying to establish mission, Yessetlatoh, Alaska, Nov. 28, 1886; buried Victoria.

SEGUIN, Edouard, psychiatrist; b. Clamency, France, Jan. 20, 1812; s. T.O. Seguin; ed. Coll. of Auxerre, Lycee St. Louis, Paris, France; M.D. (hon.), Univ. City N.Y. (now N.Y.U.), 1861; m. 2d, Elsie Mead, 1880; at least 1 son, Edward Constant. Opened sch. for idiots in France, 1839; published chief work Traitement Moral, Hygiene et Education des Idiots, 1846; came to U.S., circa 1850; an organizer sch. for defectives, Randall's Island, N.Y.: published Idiocy and its Treatment by the Physiologic Method, 1866; interested in med. thermometry, Author: New Facts and Remarks Concerning Idiocy, 1869; Family Thermometry, 1873; The Clinical Thermoscope and Uniformity of Means of Observations, 1875; Medical Thermometry and Human Temperature, 1876. Died Mt. Vernon, N.Y., Oct. 28, 1880.

SEGUIN, Edward Constant, neurologist; b. Paris, France, 1843; s. Edouard Seguin; grad. Coll. Physicians and Surgeons, N.Y.C., 1764; m. Margaret Amidon, 3 children. Came to U.S., 1850; served with M.C., U.S. Army, 1864-69, asst. surgeon, Little Rock, Ark., 1864-65, post surgeon in N.M., 1865-69; published paper on use of thermometer containing 1st temperature chart used in U.S., 1866; wrote papers on subcutaneous injection of quinine in malarial fevers in which he emphasized importance of a sterile hypodermic needle, 1867; studied mental and nervous diseases in Paris, 1869; contributed to the recognition of functional and organic nervous diseases; one of leading neurologists in U.S.; lectr. on diseases of nervous system Coll. Physicians and Surgeons, 1868-73, clin. prof., 1873-87; founder, pres. Am. Neurol. Assn., N.Y. Neurol. Soc.; advocated use of drugs in mental and spinal diseases, developed treatment these diseases involving use of iodides. Author: Opera Minora, 1884. Died Feb. 19, 1898.

SEIDENBUSH, Rupert, clergyman; b. Munich, Bavaria, Germany, Oct. 13 (or 30), 1830; came to U.S.; attended St. Vincent's Coll., and sem., Beatty, Pa. Joined Benedictine Order, 1850, ordained priest Roman Catholic Ch., 1852; missionary in N.J. and Pa., 1852-62; elected prior of St. Vincent's, 1862; 1st abbot of St. Louis-on-the Lake, Collegeville, Minn., 1866-75; apptd. titular bishop of Halia, vicar apostolic of No. Minn., 1875-88. Died Richmond, Va., June 2, 1895.

SEIDENSTICKER, Oswald, historian; b. Gottingen, Hanover, May 3, 1825; s. Georg Freidrich Seidensticker; grad. U. Gottingen, 1846; m. Emma Logo, Dec. 30, 1858, 1 child. Came to U.S., 1846; conducted schs. at Bayridge, Mass., 1852-55, Bklyn., 1855-58, Phila., 1858-68; prof. German, U. Pa., 1867-94; studied German and Pa.-German history; founded Deutsche Pionier Gesellschaft of Pa. Author: Geschichte der Deutschen Gesellschaft von Pennsylvanien, 1876; Die Erste Deutsche Einwanderung in Amerika und die Grundung von Germantown in 1683, 1883; Bilder aus der Deutsche-pennsylvanischen Geschichte, 1885; The First Century of German Printing in America, 1728-1830, 1893. Died Phila., Jan. 10, 1894.

SEIDL, Anton, musician; b. Pest, Hungary, May 7, 1850; studied at Leipzig (Germany) Conservatorium, 1870; m. Auguste Kraus, Feb. 29, 1884, no children. Asst. to Richard Wagner, Bayreuth, Germany, 1872-78; made 1st copy of Nibelungen score and helped complete scores of Die Götterdämmerung and Parsifal; conductor Leipzig Opera House, 1879-82, Travelling Wagner Theatre in tour of Europe and Eng., 1882-83, Bremen (Germany) Opera House, 1884-85; came to U.S., 1885; conductor Met. Opera, N.Y.C., 1885-91, 95-97; became Am. citizen, 1891; conductor Philharmonic Soc. of N.Y., 1891-98; conducted many Am. premiers of Wagnerian operas, also premier Dvorak's New World Symphony. Editor-in-chief The Music of the Modern World, 2 vols., 1895-97. Died of ptomaine poisoning, N.Y.C., Mar. 28, 1898.

SEIXAS, Gershom Mendes, clergyman; b. N.Y.C., Jan. 15, 1746; s. Isaac Mendez and Rachel (Levy) S.; m. Elkaly Cohen, Sept. 6, 1775; m. 2d, Hannah Manuel, Nov. 1, 1789; 15 children. Chosen rabbi Shearith Israel Congregation (Spanish and Portuguese synagogue), N.Y.C., 1768; chief prof. Hebrew Lang., lit. and laws for the N.Y.C. Jewish community; a chief spokesmen for Am. Jewry; strictly orthodox; 1st rabbi to preach sermons in English in an American synagogue; a Revolutionary patriot; protested Pa. law which held that eligibility for an Assembly seat depended on recognition of divine origin of New Testament; founded Hebra Hased Va-Amet (one of N.Y.C.'s earliest charitable orgns.); regent, trustee Columbia, 1784-1815; published sermons Religious Discourse, Delivered in the Synagogue . . . The 26th November 1789, Agreeable to the Proclamation of the President . . . to be Observed as a Day of Public Thanksgiving, 1789; A Discourse Delivered . . . on the Ninth of May 1798, Observed as a Day of Humiliation, 1798. Died N.Y.C., July 2, 1816; buried New Bowery Cemetery of Shearith Israel Congregation, N.Y.C.

SEJOUR, Victor (christened Juan Victor Sejour Marcou et Ferrand), dramatist; b. New Orleans, June 2, 1817; illegitimate s. Francois Ferrand and Eloisa Phillipe Ferrand. Published heroic poem Le Retour de Napoleon, 1841; 1st play Diegarias, produced in Theatre Francais, 1844; wrote play La Chute de Sejan, 1849; 21 of his plays were produced in Paris, France; most successful plays include: Richard III, 1852; Les Nouces Venitiennes, 1855; Le Fils de la Nuit, 1856; Les Grands Vassaux, 1859; Les Fils de Charles Quint, 1864; Les Volontaires de 1814, 1862; Cromwell; Le Vampire. Died Paris, Sept. 21, 1874; buried Cemetery of Pere-Lachaise, Paris.

SELBY, William, composer; b. Eng., 1739; m. Susannah Parker, Jan. 7, 1792. Organist, King's Chapel, Boston, 1772-74, returned as organist, 1777; organist Trinity Ch., R.I., 1774; became intrested in choral singing; founder Mus. Soc. of Boston, 1785, composer much of music performed at Soc.'s concerts; composer songs including Ode in Honour of General Washington, 1786, On Musick, 1789, The Rural Retreat, 1789, Ptalaemon to Pastoca, 1789, Ode for the New Year, 1790, The Lovely Lass, 1790. Died Dec. 1798.

SELDEN, Dudley, congressman, lawyer; grad. Union Coll., Schenectady, N.Y., 1819; studied law. Admitted to bar, began practice of law, N.Y.C., 1831; mem. N.Y. State Assembly, 1831; mem. U.S. Ho. of Reps. (Democrat) from N.Y., 23d Congress, 1833-July 1, 1834 (resigned). Died Paris, France, Nov. 7, 1855; buried Greenwood Cemetery, Bklyn.

SELIGMAN, Jesse, banker, philanthropist; b. Baiersdorf, Bavaria, Aug. 11, 1827; s. David and Fanny (Steinhardt) S.; grad. Gymnasium of Erlangen (Bavaria); m. Henrietta Hellman, Oct. 18, 1854, 7 children. Joined his brothers in U.S., 1841; opened dry goods store, Watertown, N.Y., 1848; established dry goods bus., San Francisco, 1850; active mem. San Francisco Vigilance Com.; mem. San Francisco Com. of 21; moved to N.Y.C., 1857; organized banking firm J. & W. Seligman & Co., 1862, became head of firm, 1880-94; active in flotations of ry. securities in South and S.W.; head Am. Syndicate which handled Panama Canal shares, fiscal agt. U.S. Govt.; v.p. Union League Club of N.Y., resigned, 1893; pres. Hebrew Benevolent and Orphan Asylum of N.Y.C.; an original mem. bd. trustees Baron de Hirsch Fund, 1891. Died Coronado, Cal., Apr. 23, 1894.

SELIGMAN, Joseph, banker, civic leader; b. Baiersdorf, Bavaria, Nov. 22, 1819; s. David and Fanny (Steinhardt) S.; grad. Gymnasium of Erlangen, Bavaria; m. Babette Steinhardt, Oct. 26, 1848; 9 children. Came to U.S., 1837; became clothing mcht. (with his brothers), N.Y.C., 1848; operated clothing and importing firm, N.Y.C., 1857; pres. German Hebrew Orphan Asylum; organized internat. banking firm J. & W. Seligman & Co., N.Y.C., 1862, had branches in Frankfurt-am-Main, Germany, London, Eng., Paris, France, San Francisco, New Orleans; sold U.S. Bonds amounting to approximately $200,000,000 in Frankfurt during Civil War; cooperated with U.S. Treasury Dept. in handling conversions operations of U.S. Bonds, and resumption of specie payments, 1874-79; v.p. Union League Club of N.Y.; active mem. Com. of 70 which ousted Tweed Ring from control of N.Y.C.; a commr. rapid transit N.Y.C., chmn. of commn., laid out N.Y. elevated railroad system; active mem. N.Y. Bd. of Edn., 1873-75. Died New Orleans, Apr. 25, 1880.

SELIJNS, Henricus, clergyman; b. 1636; s. Jan Selijns and Janneken (de Marees) Hendrickszoon; studied for ministry U. Leyden (Holland); m. Machtelt Specht, July 9, 1662; m. 2d, Margaretha de Rumer, Jan. 10, 1694. Ordained to ministry Dutch Reformed Ch., 1660; arrived in New Amsterdam, 1660; had congregation at Breuckelen (now Bklyn.); returned to Holland, accepted parish of Waverveen in Province of Utrecht, 1664; accepted preaching post, N.Y.C., 1682; through his efforts the Dutch Reformed Ch. obtained 1st ch. charter granted in the Colony of N.Y., 1696. Died 1701.

SELLERS, Isaiah, steamboat pilot; b. Iredell County, N.C., 1802; m. Amanda. Engaged in commerce on lower Mississippi River, 1825-28, on boats Rambler, Gen. Carroll, President; introduced bell-tapping as pilot's signal to take soundings (on Gen. Carroll); piloted his 1st trip to upper Mississippi River on steamboat Jubilee; took charge of Prairie (1st boat with a stateroom cabin to visit St. Louis), Pitts., 1836; pilot of the J.M. White II, left New Orleans, May 4, 1844, brought ship to St. Louis in record time of 3 days, 23 hours, 9 minutes; introduced signal for meeting steamboats, 1857; his boat was the Aleck Scott; contbr. to New Orleans Daily Picayune under pseudonym Mark Twain (later used by Samuel Clemens). Died Memphis, Tenn., Mar. 6, 1864; buried Bellefontaine Cemetery, St. Louis.

SELYE, Lewis, congressman, businessman; b. Chittenango, N.Y., July 11, 1803; attended common schs.; learned blacksmith trade. Engaged in manufacture of iron, Rochester, N.Y., 1824; mem. bd. suprs. Monroe County, several terms; became alderman, 1841; mem. common council, 1843, 56, 71; treas. Monroe County, 1848-51, 54; mem. U.S. Ho. of Reps. (Independent) from N.Y., 40th Congress, 1867-69; founded Rochester Daily Chronicle, 1868, merged with Rochester Democrat and Chronicle, 1870; trustee Monroe County Savs. Bank. Died Rochester, Jan. 27, 1883; buried Mt. Hope Cemetery.

SEMMES, Alexander Jenkins, physician, clergyman, coll. pres.; b. Georgetown, D.C., Dec. 17, 1828; s. Raphael and Matilda (Jenkins) S.; A.B., Georgetown Coll., 1850; M.D., Med. Dept., Columbian Coll., D.C., 1851; attended Pio Nono Coll., nr. Macon, Ga., also Benedictine monastery of St. Vincent, Latrobe, Pa.; m. Sarah Berrien, Oct. 4, 1864. Resident physician Charity Hosp., New Orleans; surgeon 8th La. Inf., during Civil War; commd. surgeon Confederate Army; surgeon La. Brigade in Gen. Thomas J. (Stonewall) Jackson's corps Army of No. Va.; med. insp. Dept. No. Va., insp. hosps.; mem. exam. bds. La., Jackson, Stuart, Winder hosps. (all Richmond, Va.); prof. physiology Savannah (Ga.) Med. Coll., 1870-76; ordained priest Roman Catholic Ch., Macon, 1878; pres., lectr. English and Am. lit. and history Pio Nono Coll., 1886-91; chaplain of sch. and asylum of Sisters of St. Joseph, Sharon, Ga., 1891-95, Author: Report on the Medico-legal Duties of Coroners, 1857; contbr. articles to publs. including Poisoning by Strychnia—The Gardiner Case, published in Stethoscope, 1855; Reports of Cases of Gunshot Wounds, published in London Lancet, 1864. Died Hotel Dieu, New Orleans, Sept. 20, 1898.

SEMMES, Benedict Joseph, congressman; b. Charles County, Md., Nov. 1, 1789; attended med. coll., Phila.; grad. Balt. Med. Sch., 1811. Began practice of medicine, Piscataway, Prince Georges County, Md., later engaged in agriculture; mem. Md. Ho. of Dels., 1825-28, 42-43, served as speaker; mem. Md. Senate; mem. U.S. Ho. of Reps. (Democrat) from Md., 21-st-22d congresses, 1829-33. Died Oak Lawn, Prince Georges County, Feb. 10, 1863.

SEMMES, Raphael, naval officer; b. Charles County, Md., Sept. 27, 1809; s. Richard Thompson and Catherine (Middleton) S.; studied law; m. Anne Spencer, May 5, 1837, 6 children. Commd. midshipman U.S. Navy, 1826; served in Mediterranean Squadron, 1826; passed for promotion, 1823; commd. lt., 1837; admitted to Md. bar, 1834; practiced law, Md. and Ohio; held 1st command, spent time on survey duty on So. coast, Gulf of Mexico on ships Consor, Poinsett; commanded brig. Somers on blockade of the Eastern coast of Mexico, 1846; commd. comdr., 1855, resigned, 1861; became a comdr. from Ala. in Confederate States Navy, 1861; made chief Light House Bur. (Dept. Treasury), Apr. 4-18, 1861; given command of C.S.S. Sumter, 1861-62; promoted capt., voted thanks of Confederate Congress, 1862; commanded ship Alabama, 1862-64; sank U.S.S. Hateras, 1863; commd. rear adm. Confederate Navy, 1864; ship Alabama sunk by U.S. Kearsarge off Cherbourg, France, June 19, 1864; assigned as rear adm. to command James River Squadron, 1865; probate judge Mobile County, Ala., 1866; prof. moral philosophy and English literature La. State Sem. (now La. State U.), Baton Rouge, 1866-67; editor Memphis (Tenn.) Daily Bull.; practiced law Mobile, Ala., 1867-77. Author: Service Afloat and Ashore during the Mexican War, 1851; The Campaign of General Scott in the Valley of Mexico (an abridgement of his earlier work), 1852; Memoirs of Service, Afloat, during the War between the States, 1869; published his papers as The Cruise of the Alabama and the Sumter From the Private Journals and Other Papers of Commander R. Semmes, C.S.N. and Other Officers, 2 vols., 1864 (translated into French, 1864, Dutch, 1865). Died at home Point Clear, Mobile Bay, Ala., Aug. 30, 1877; buried Catholic graveyard, Mobile.

SEMMES, Thomas Jenkins, Confederate senator; b. Georgetown, D.C., Dec. 16, 1824; s. Raphael and Matilda (Jenkins) S.; grad. Georgetown Coll., 1842, Harvard Law Sch., 1845; m. Myra Knox, Jan. 8, 1850, 5 children. Admitted to La. bar, 1851; in partnership with Matthew C. Edwards, New Orleans, 1851-55; mem. La. Ho. of Reps., 1856; U.S. atty. for Eastern Dist. of La., 1857-58; atty. gen. of La., 1859-61; mem. La. Secession Conv. 1861 mem; Confederate States Senate from La., 1862-65; mem. La. Constl. Conv., 1879, 98, chmn. judiciary com., 1898; prof. civil law U. La. (now Tulane), 1873-79, circa 1881-99; pres. Am. Bar Assn., 1886; pres. New Orleans Sch. Bd. Died New Orleans, June 23, 1899.

SEMPLE, James, senator, diplomat; b. Green County, Ky., Jan. 5, 1798; attended common schs.; studied law, Louisville, Ky. Joined U.S. Army, 1814, served under Gen. Jackson; commd. ensign 81st Regt., Ky. Militia, 1816; moved to Ill., 1818, to Chariton, Mo., 1819; became businessman, Chariton; elected commr. of loan office; admitted to bar, began practice of law, Clinton County, Ky.; continued practice law, Edwardsville, Ill., 1827; mem. Ill. Ho. of Reps., 1828-33, speaker 4 years; served as pvt., adj., judge advocate during Black Hawk War; atty. gen. Ill., 1833; moved to Alton, Ill., 1837; chargé d'affaires to Colombia, 1837-42; judge Ill. Supreme Ct., 1842-43; mem. U.S. Senate (Democrat, filled vacancy) from Ill., Dec. 4, 1843-47; engaged in real estate business, Alton; moved to Jersey County, Ill., 1853, founded Town of Elsah; continued in real estate, also engaged in literary pursuits. Died Elsah, Ill., Dec. 20, 1866; buried Bellefontaine Cemetery, St. Louis.

SEÑAN, José Francisco de Paula, missionary; b. Barcelona, Spain, Mar. 3, 1760. Joined Franciscan Order, 1774; sent to San Fernando Coll., Mexico City, Mexico, 1784; stationed at San Carlos Mission, Cal., 1787-95; visited Mexico to report on Cal. missions; served at San Buenaventura Mission, Cal., 1798-1823; pres. of missions, 1812-15, 19-23. Died San Buenaventura Mission, Aug. 24, 1823.

SENER, James Beverley, congressman, lawyer; b. Fredericksburg, Va., May 18, 1837; grad. U. Va. at Charlottesville, 1859; grad. in law Washington Coll. (now Washington and Lee U.), Lexington, 1860. Admitted to bar, 1860, began practice of law, Fredericksburg; sheriff Fredericksburg, 1860; sergeant City of Fredericksburg, 1863-65; army correspondent So. Asso. Press with army of Gen. Robert E. Lee; became editor Fredericksburg Ledger, 1865; del. Republican Nat. Conv., Phila., 1872; mem. U.S. Ho. of Reps. (Rep.) from Va., 43d Congress, 1873-75; chief justice Wyo. Territory, 1878-82. Died Washington, D.C., Nov. 18, 1903; buried Citizens Cemetery, Fredericksburg.

SENEY, George Ingraham, banker, philanthropist; b. Astoria, N.Y., May 12, 1826; s. Robert and Jane (Ingraham) S.; grad. U. City of N.Y., 1846; m. Phoebe Moser, 1849, at least 9 children. Paying teller Met. Bank, N.Y.C., 1853, cashier, 1857, pres., late 1870's; financed constrn. of N.Y., C. & St. L. R.R.; financed East Tennessee, Va., Ga. R.R.; Met. Bank failed when road bankrupted, 1884, paid depositors out of his personal fortune; trustee Wesleyan U.; made large gifts to Wesleyan Emory Univs. contbr. funds to Methodist Hosp., Bklyn. and to construction fund for Washington Meml. Arch; gave many paintings from his pvt. collection to Met. Mus. of Art, N.Y.C. Died N.Y.C., Apr. 7, 1893.

SENEY, Joshua, Continental congressman; b. nr. Church Hill, Queen Annes County, Md., Mar. 4, 1756; grad. U. Pa. at Phila., 1773; studied law. Admitted to bar, practiced law; high sheriff Queen Annes County, 1779; mem. Md. Ho. of Dels., 1785-87; mem. Continental Congress from Md., 1787-88; engaged in agriculture; mem. U.S. Ho. of Reps. from Md., 1st-2d congresses, 1789-May 1, 1792 (resigned); chief justice 3d Jud. Dist. Md., 1792-96; presdl. elector for Washington and Adams, 1792. Died nr. Church Hill, Oct. 20, 1798; buried pvt. cemetery on Everett farm, between Church Hill and Sudlersville, Md.

SENNET, George Burritt, ornithologist, mfr.; b. Sinclairville, N.Y., July 28, 1840; s. Pardon and Mary (Burritt) S.; m. Sarah Essex, 1 child. Mfr. oil-well machinery, Meadville, Pa., 1865-95, Youngstown, O., 1895-1900; mayor of Meadville, 1877-81; made ornithol. expdn. to Western Minn., 1867; made expdns. to Rio Grande region of Southern Tex., 1877, 78, 82; contbd. collection of birds to Am. Museum Natural History, N.Y.C., 1883; discovered 10 new species of birds; 4 birds named in his honor. Author articles "Notes on the Ornithology of the Lower Rio Grande, Texas, from Observations Made During the Season 1877," published in Bulletin of the U.S. Geol. and Geog. Survey of the Territories, Vol. IV, 1878; "Descriptions of a New Species and Two New Subspecies of Birds from Texas," published in Auk, 1888. Died Mar. 18, 1900.

SENTER, William Tandy, congressman; b. Bean Station, Grainger County, Tenn., May 12, 1801; attended common schs. Held several local offices; engaged in farming; minister of Holston conf. Methodist Episcopal Ch. South; mem. Tenn. Constl. Conv., Nashville, 1834; mem. U.S. Ho. of Reps. (Whig) from Tenn., 28th Congress, 1843-45. Died Panther Springs, Hamblen County, Tenn., Aug. 28, 1848; buried Senter Meml. Ch. Cemetery.

SEQUOYAH (later took name George Guess), inventor Indian syllabary; b. Loudon County, Tenn., 1770; s. Nicholas Gist; married, several children. Hunter, fur trader, silversmith with Cherokee Indians in Ga., until 1821; completed a table of 86 characters representing the sounds of the Cherokee language, 1821; taught thousands of Indians to read and write their own language; introduced system to Cherokees in Ark., 1822, moved with them to Okla., 1828; began publishing weekly paper in Cherokee, 1828; visited Washington (D.C.) as envoy for his tribe, 1828; granted life-time pension by Cherokee Nat. Council, 1843; Sequoia redwood trees in Cal. named for him; statue of him placed in Statuary Hall of Nat. Capitol by State of Okla. Died Tamaulipas, Mexico (probably), Aug. 1843.

SERGEANT, John, missionary; b. Newark, N. J., 1710; s. Jonathan and Mary S.; grad. Yale (valedictorian), 1729; m. Abigail Williams, Aug. 16, 1739, at least 3 children including John. Tutor, Yale, 1731-35; erected sch. and ch. bldg. between two settlement of Housatonic Indians, circa 1734; returned to New Haven, Conn., completed year at Yale; entered permanent missionary work, 1735; ordained to ministry Congregational Ch., Deerfield, Mass., 1735; worked among Indians, Berkshire County, Mass., until 1749; translated prayers, portions of Bible, Watt's shorter catechism into their lang. Author: The Causes and Danger of Delusions in the Affairs of Religion Consider'd and Caution'd Against, with Particular Reference to the Temper of the Present Times (sermon), 1743; A Letter from the Revd. Mr. Sergeant of Stockbridge to Dr. Colman of Boston; Containing Mr. Sergeant's Proposal of a More Effectual Method for the Education of Indian Children, 1743. Died Stockbridge, Mass., July 27, 1749.

SERGEANT, John, congressman; b. Phila., Dec. 5, 1779; s. Jonathan Dickinson and Margaret (Spencer) S.; grad. Coll. of N.J. (now Princeton), 1795; m. Margaretta Watmough, June 23, 1813, 10 children. Admitted to Phila. bar, 1799; dep. atty. gen. for Chester County (Pa.) and Phila., 1800; commr. bankruptcy for Pa., 1801; mem. Pa. Legislature, 1808-10, chmn. com. on roads and inland navigation; mem. U.S. Ho. of Reps. from Pa., 14th-17th, 20th, 25th-26th congresses, Oct. 10, 1815-23, 27-29, 37-Sept. 15, 1841; gave important legal and polit. counsel to 2d Bank of U.S., undertook diplomatic mission to London bankers, 1816, influenced Biddle to apply for renewal of bank's charter, often represented bank before U.S. Supreme Ct.; pres. Pa. Bd. Canal Commrs., 1825-26; mem. Panama Congress of 1826; Nat.-Republican candidate for vice pres. U.S., 1832; pres. Pa. Constl. Conv., 1837-38; won cases including Girard Will Case; cases conducted before Supreme Ct. include Osborn vs. U.S. Bank, Worcester vs. Ga.; collected speeches into Select Speeches of John Sergeant of Pennsylvania, 1832. Died Phila., Nov. 23, 1852; buried Laurel Hill Cemetery, Phila.

SERGEANT, Jonathan Dickinson, Continental congressman; b. Newark, N.J., 1746; s. Jonathan and Abigail (Dickinson) S.; grad. Coll. of N.J. (now Princeton), 1762, U. Pa., 1763; m. Margaret Spencer, Mar. 14, 1775; m. 2d, Elizabeth Rittenhouse, Dec. 20, 1788; at least 11 children including John, Thomas. Admitted to the bar, 1767; surrogate Somerset County (N.J.), 1769; mem. Sons of Liberty; active in Stamp Act controversy; sec. 1st, 2d N.J. provincial congresses, 1774, 75, mem., 1776; mem. local coms. of correspondence, 1774, 75; treas. Province of N.J., 1775; del. Continental Congress from N.J., Feb-June 1776, Nov. 30, 1776-77; moved to Phila., 1776; atty. gen. Pa., 1777-80; known for extra-legal methods in prosecution of Loyalists; identified with McKean-Bryan "Constitutionalists," 1777; mem. Council of Safety, 1777; represented Pa. in Conn.-Pa. dispute arbitrated at Trenton, N.J., 1782; counsel for Pa. in Wyoming land controversy; defended Anti-Federalist editor Eleazar Oswald, 1788. Died Phila., Oct. 8, 1793; buried Laurel Hill Cemetery, Phila.

SERGEANT, Thomas, jurist; b. Phila., Jan. 14, 1782; s. Jonathan Dickinson and Margaret (Spencer) S.; grad. Coll. of N.J. (now Princeton), 1798; m. Sarah Bache, Sept. 14, 1812, 4 children. Admitted to Phila. bar, 1802; mem. Pa. Legislature, 1812, 13; asso. judge Dist. Ct. of Phila. 1814-17; sec. of commonwealth Pa., 1817-19; atty. gen. Pa., 1819-20; apptd. solicitor Philadelphia County, 1825; postmaster Phila., 1828-31; asso. justice Pa. Supreme Ct., 1834-46; trustee U. Pa., 1842-54; provost Law Acad. of Phila., 1844-55; pres. Hist. Soc. Pa.; mem. Am. Philos. Soc.; Author: A Treatise upon the Law of Pennsylvania Relative to the Proceeding by Foreign Attachment, 1811; Constitutional Law: Being a Collection of Points Arising upon the Constitution and Jurisprudence of the United States, Which Have Been Settled by Judicial Decision and Practise, 1822; Sketch of the National Judiciary Powers Exercised in the United States Prior to the Adoption of the Present Federal Constitution, 1824; View of the Land Laws of Pennsylvania, 1838. An editor: Reports of Cases Argued and Determined in the English Courts of Common Law, 1822-25. Died Phila., May 5, 1860.

SERRA, Junipero (Miguel Jose), missionary; b. Petra, Mallorca, Nov 24, 1713; s. Antonio and Margarita (Ferrer) S. Entered Franciscan Order, Palma, Spain, 1730; took name Junipero, 1731; joined Apostolic Coll. of San Fernando, Mexico City, Mexico, 1750; missionary to Indians of Sierra Gordo, Mexico, 1750-59; preacher, confessor, Mexico City, 1759-67; pres. missions in Cal., 1767-84; founded missions at San Diego, San Carlos, San Antonio, San Gabriel, San Luis Obispo, San Francisco de Assisi, San Juan Capistrano, Santa Clara, San Buenaventura; baptized over 6000 Indians by 1783. Died at mission of San Carlos nr. Monterey, Cal., Aug. 28, 1784.

SERVOSS, Thomas Lowery, mcht., shipowner; b. Phila., Oct. 14, 1786; s. Jacob and Isabella (Servass) S.; m. Elizabeth Courtney, Oct. 31, 1807; m. 2d, Louisa Pintard, Apr. 4, 1824; 5 children. Mcht., Natchez, Miss., 1810-16, 17-25, prin. dealings in cotton, operated new and larger cotton bus., 1817-25; lived in N.Y.C., 1816-17, 25-66; operated line of sailing packets between N.Y.C. and New Orleans; dir. N.Am. Trust & Banking Co.; trustee Chambers Street Bank for Savs.; mem. Am. Bible Soc. built St. Clements Episcopal Ch., N.Y.C. Died N.Y.C., Nov. 30, 1866.

SESSINGHAUS, Gustavus, congressman, businessman; b. Koela, Prussia, Nov. 8, 1838. Came to U.S., settled in St. Louis; served with Co. A, 5th Regt., U.S. Res. Corps, Mo. Volunteer Inf., during Civil War; mem. sch. bd., 1878-80; mem. U.S. Ho. of Reps. (Republican), contested election from Mo., 47th Congress, 2 days only, Mar. 2-3, 1883; engaged in milling business. Died St. Louis, Nov. 16, 1887; buried Bellefontaine Cemetery.

SESSIONS, Walter Loomis, congressman, lawyer; b. Brandon, Rutland County, Vt., Oct. 4, 1820; attended Westfield (N.Y.) Acad.; studied law. Admitted to bar, 1849, began practice of law, Panama Chautauqua County, N.Y.; also a tour.; commr. schs., several years; mem. N.Y. State Assembly, 1853-54; mem. N.Y. Senate, 1860-61, 66-67; supr. Town of Harmony (N.Y.), 1870-72; mem. U.S. Ho. of Reps. (Republican) from N.Y., 42d-43d, 49th congresses, 1871-75, 85-87; practiced law, Jamestown and Panama, N.Y.; apptd. N.Y. commr. to World's Columbia Exposition, Chgo., 1893. Died Panama, May 27, 1896; buried Forest Hill Cemetery.

SESTINI, Benedict, clergyman, educator; b. Florence, Italy, Mar. 20, 1816; studied philosophy and theology Roman Coll. Entered Soc. of Jesus, Rome, Italy, 1836; asst. astronomer Roman Observatory until 1848; came to U.S., circa 1848; taught mathematics and natural scis. Georgetown U., Washington, D.D., 1848-69, continued research at univ. observatory; made studies of sun's surface, 1850-69; organized expdn. to Denver (Colo.) to observe total eclipse of sun, 1874, wrote account appearing in Am. Catholic Quarterly Review, 1878; planned and supervised constrn. Holy Trinity and St. Aloysius churches, Washington, also Jesuit Sem., Woodstock, Md., 1869-83; published Messenger of the Sacred Heart, (came to have widest circulation of any Catholic mag. in U.S.), 1866-85; taught higher mathematics Gonzaga Coll., Washington; taught astronomy and geology Jesuit Sem., Woodstock, 1869-85. Author: Memoria Sopra; Colori delle Stelle del Catalogo di Baily Osservati, 1845; Memoria Seconda Intorno ai Colori delle Stelle, 1847; A Treatise of Analytical Geometry, 1852; Astronomical Observations Made During the Year 1847 at the National Observatory, Washington, vol. III, 1853; A Treatise on Alegebra, 2 credits, 1855, 57; Elements of Geometry and Trigonometry, 1856; Manual of Geometrical and Infinitestimal Analysis, 1871; Theoretical Mechanics, 1873; Animal Physics, 1874; Principles of Cosmography, 1878. Died Frederick, Md., Jan. 12, 1890.

SETON, Elizabeth Ann Bayley (known as Mother Seton), founder religious order; b. N.Y.C., Aug. 28, 1774; d. Dr. Richard and Catharine (Charlton) Bayley; m. William Magee Seton, Jan. 25, 1794, 5 children. Founder (with Isabella Marshall Graham and other leading women) Soc. for Relief of Poor Widows with Small Children (1st charitable orgn. in N.Y., probably 1st in U.S.), 1797; joined Roman Catholic Ch., N.Y., 1805; opened sch. for Roman Catholic girls, Balt., 1808; a founder, 1st mother superior Sisters of St. Joseph, Emmittsburg, Md., 1809, adopted rules of Daus. of Charity of St. Vincent de Paul, order known as Sisters of Charity of St. Joseph, after 1812; founded country's 1st Cath. orphanage, 1st Cath. hosp., 1st maternity hosp.; founder 1st Am. parish sch., Phila., 1818; Composer hymns including Jerusalem, My Happy Home; writings edited by grandson Robert Seton, published under title Memoirs, Letters, and Journal of Elizabeth Seton, 2 vols., 1869. Beatified by Pope John XXIII, Mar. 17, 1963 (1st native American to be beatified). Died Emmittsburg, Jan. 4, 1821.

SETTLE, Thomas, congressman, lawyer; b. nr. Reidsville, N.C., Mar. 9, 1789; ed. by pvt. tutors; studied law. Admitted to bar, 1812, began practice of law, Wentworth, N.C.; mem. N.C. Ho. of Commons, 1816, 26-27, speaker, 1827; mem. U.S. Ho. of Reps. (Democrat) from N.C., 15th-16th congresses, 1817-21; judge N.C. Superior Cts., 1832. Died Rockingham County, N.C., Aug. 5, 1857; buried Settle family graveyard, nr. Reidsille.

SETTLE, Thomas, jurist; b. Rockingham, N.C., Jan. 23, 1831; s. Thomas and Henrietta (Graves) S.; grad. U. N.C., 1830; m. Mary Glenn, circa 1854, 9 children, Admitted to N.C. bar, 1854. mem. N.C. Ho. of Commons (Democrat), 1854-59, speaker, 1858-59; presdl. elector, 1856; solicitor 4th Jud. Circuit N.C., 1861, then volunteered as capt. 3d N.C. Regt., Confederate Army, and resumed office as solicitor, 1862; del. N.C. Constl. Conv., 1865, also chmn. com. on abolition of slavery and N.C. debt, elected to N.C. Senate, 1865, chosen speaker; asso. justice N.C. Supreme Ct., 1868-71, 72-76; minister to Peru (apptd. by Pres. Grant), 1871-72. pres. Republican Nat. Conv., 1872; U.S. dist. judge for Fla., 1877-88. Died Dec. 1, 1808.

SEVERANCE, Luther, congressman; b. Montague, Mass., Oct. 26, 1797; attended common schs., N.Y.; learned printer's trade, Peterboro, N.Y. Founded Kennebec Journal, Augusta, Me., 1825; mem. Me. Ho. of Reps., 1829, 39-40, 42, 48, Me. Senate, 1835-36; mem. U.S. Ho. of Reps. (Whig) from Me., 28th-29th congresses, 1843-47; v.p. Whig Nat. Conv., Phila., 1848; U.S. commr. to Sandwich Islands, 1850-54. Died Augusta, Jan. 25, 1855; buried Forest Grove Cemetery.

SEVIER, Ambrose Hundley, senator; b. Greene County, Tenn., Nov. 10, 1801; s. John and Susannah (Conway) S.; m. Juliette Johnson, 1827, 5 children. Went to Ark., 1821; clk. Ark. Territorial Ho. of Reps., 1821, mem., 1823-27, speaker, 1827; del. to U.S. Congress from Territory of Ark., 1828-36; mem. U.S. Senate (Democrat) from Ark., Sept. 18, 1836-48, mem. com. on Indian affairs, urged creation of an Indian Territory out of region west of Mo. and Ark., chmn. com. fgn. relations, supported annexation of Tex. and Pres. Polk's Ore. policy, introduced "3 million dollar bill" to finance peace negotiations with Mexico, 1847; U.S. minister to Mexico, 1848. Died Pulaski County, Ark., Dec. 31, 1848; buried Mt. Holly Cemetery nr. Little Rock, Ark.

SEVIER, John, gov. Tenn., congressman, army officer. b. nr. New Market, Va., Sept. 23, 1745. s. Valentine and Joanna (Goade) S.; m. Sarah Hawkins, 1761; m. Catherine Sherill, Aug. 14, 1780, Served as capt. Va. Colonial Militia under Washington in Lord Dunmore's War, 1773-74; commr. Watauga Assn., Knoxville, N.C. (now Tenn.); mem. Knoxville Com. of Safety, 1776; elected rep. N.C. Provincial Congress, then apptd. lt. col. N.C. Militia; led 240 men to victory over British at Battle of King's Mountain, Oct. 7, 1780; made 3 raids against Indians, 1781-82; established (with William Blount) settlement at Muscle Shoals, Ala., circa 1783; elected gov. State of Franklin, 1785-88, regime collapsed following battle with Tipton faction, 1788; elected to N.C. Senate, 1789; mem. N.C. Conv. which ratified U.S. Constn., voted for ratification; commd. brig. gen. N.C. Militia, 1791; mem. U.S. Ho. of Reps. from N.C., 1st Congress, 1789-Sept. 24, 1791; active land speculator in West during 1790's; trustee Washington Coll. (Tenn.), Blount Coll. (now U. Tenn.); 1st gov. Tenn., 1796-1801, re-elected, 1803-09; mem. Tenn. Senate, 1809-11; mem. U.S. Ho. of Reps. from Tenn., 12th-13th congresses, 1811-15; apptd. mem. commn. to survey boundary of Creek Cession, 1815. Died Ala., Sept. 24, 1815; buried Knoxville.

SEWALL, Charles S., congressman; b. Queen Annes County, Md., 1779; attended common schs. Served with 42d Regt., Md .Militia, in War of 1812; mem. Md. Ho. of Dels., also Md. Senate; mem. U.S. Ho. of Reps. (filled vacancies) from Md., 22d, 27th congresses, Oct. 1, 1832-33, Jan. 2-Mar. 3, 1843; moved to Harford County, Md. Died Rose Hill, Md., Nov. 3, 1848.

SEWALL, Harriet Winslow, poet; b. Portland, Me., June 30, 1819; d. Nathan and Comfort (Hussey) Winslow; attended Friends' boarding sch., Providence, R.I.; m. Charles List, 1848; m. 2d, Samuel Sewall, 1856. Became interested in abolitionism, transcendentalism, 1840's; active in philanthropic work, women's suffrage movement, ednl. work; a founder New Eng. Women's Club; edited letters of her friend, Lydia Maria Child, 1833; wrote poetry which was collected and published by Ednah D. Cheyney, 1889. Died Wellesley, Mass., Apr. 19, 1889.

SEWALL, Jonathan, Loyalist; b. Boston, Aug. 17, 1728; s. Jonathan and Mary (Payne) S.; grad. Harvard, 1748; m. Esther Quincy, Jan. 21, 1764; children—Jonathan, Stephen. Taught Latin sch., Salme, Mass., 1748-56; began practice of law, Charlestown, Mass., 1756; solicitor gen. of Mass.; atty. gen. Mass., 1767-68; judge Vice Admiralty Ct. of Halifax (Nova Scotia, Can.), 1768-74; sailed to Eng., 1775; legally banished from Mass., property confiscated, 1778; returned to Halifax, 1788. Died St. John, New Brunswick, Can., Sept. 26, 1796

SEWALL, Jonathan Mitchell, lawyer, poet; b. Salem, Mass., 1748; s. Mitchell and Elizabeth (Prince) S. Admitted to bar, Portsmouth, N.H. register of probate Grafton County (N.H.), 1773; poetical works include: Versification of President Washington's excellent Farewell-Address, 1798; Eulogy on the Late General Washington, 1800; patriotic ballad War and Washington, 1801; Miscellaneous Poems, 1801; Epilogue to Cato. Died Pirtsmouth, Mar. 29, 1808.

SEWALL, Samuel, mcht., colonial magistrate; b. Bishopstoke, Eng., Mar. 28, 1652; s. Henry and Jane (Dummer) S.; A.B., Harvard, 1671; m. Hannah Hull, Feb. 28, 1676; m. 2d, Abigail Melyen, Oct. 29, 1719; m. 3d, Mary Shrimpton, Mar. 29, 1722; 14 children. Moved to New Eng., 1661; elected fellow Harvard, 1673; in charge of Mass. printing press, 1681-84; mem. Mass. Gen. Ct. from Westfield, Hampden County, 1683; mem. Mass. Gov.'s Council, ex-officio judge Mass. Superior Ct. 1684-86, named councilor in new charter of 1691, 1691-1725; apptd. a spl. commr. to try cases of witchcraft at Salem, 1692, made public confession of error while acting in that capacity, 1697; apptd. justice Mass. Superior Ct., 1692; commr. Soc. for Propagation of Gospel in New Eng., 1699, sec. and treas., circa 1700; probate judge for Suffolk County, (Mass.) 1715-18; chief justice Superior Ct. of Mass., 1718-28. Author: A Memorial Relating to the Kennebeck Indians, 1721; (with Edward Rawson) The Revolution in New England Justified, 1691; kept a diary published in 3 volumes by Mass. Hist. Soc., 1880. Died Boston, Jan. 1, 1730; buried Granary Burying Ground, Boston.

SEWALL, Samuel, congressman, jurist; b. Boston, Dec. 11, 1757; grad. Harvard, 1776; studied law. Admitted to bar, began practice of law, Marblehead, Mass.; mem. Mass. Ho. of Reps., 1783, 88-96; mem. U.S. Ho. of Reps. (filled vacancy) from Mass., 4th-6th congresses, Dec. 7, 1796-Jan. 10, 1800 (resigned), a mgr. apptd. by Ho. of Reps. to conduct impeachment proceedings against Senator William Blount from Tenn., 1798; asso. judge Mass. Supreme Ct., 1801-13, chief justice, 1813-14. Died Wiscasset, Me., June 8, 1814; buried Ancient Cemetery; reinterred family tomb, Marblehead.

SEWALL, Stephen, Hebraist; b. York, Me., Apr. 11, 1734; s. Nicholas and Mehitable (Storer) S.; grad. Harvard, 1761; m. Rebecca Wigglesworth, Aug. 9, 1763; married 2d time; 1 child. Instr. Hebrew, Harvard, 1761-64, 1st Hancock prof. Hebrew and Oriental langs., 1764-84, librarian, 1762-63; mem. Mass. Gen. Ct. (Whig) from Cambridge, 1777; original mem. Am. Acad. Arts and Scis., 1785. Author: An Hebrew Grammar Collected Chiefly from Those of Mr. Israel Lyons and the Rev. Richard Grey, 1763; The Scripture Account of the Schechinah, 1794; The Scripture History Relating to the Overthrow of Sodom and Gomorrah, 1796. Died July 23, 1804.

SEWARD, James Lindsay, congressman, lawyer; b. Dublin, Laurens County, Ga., Oct. 30, 1813; attended common schs.; studied law. Admitted to bar, 1835, began practice of law, Thomasville, Ga.; mem. Ga. Ho. of Reps., 1835-39, 47-48, 51-52; mem. U.S. Ho. of Reps. (Democrat) from Ga., 33d-35th congresses, 1853-59; resumed law practice, also engaegd in planting; del. Ga. Democratic convs. ,1858, 59, 60; mem. Ga. Senate, 1859-65; del. Dem. nat. convs., Charleston and Balt., 1860; mem. bd. trustees Young's Female Coll., 1860-86, U. Ga. at Athens, 1865-86; del. Reconstrn. Constl. Conv., 1865, Dem. Conservative Conv., 1870, Ga. Constl. Conv., 1877. Died Thomasville, Nov. 21, 1886; buried Laurel Hill Cemetery.

SEWARD, William Henry, senator, sec. of state; b. Florida, N.Y., May 16, 1801; s. Dr. Samuel S. and Mary (Jennings) S.; grad. Union Coll., 1820; LL.D. (hon.), Yale, 1854; m. Frances Miller, Oct. 10, 1824, 3 sons including Frederick William, 2 daus. Admitted to N.Y. bar, 1822; practiced law, Auburn, N.Y.; mem. N.Y. State Senate, 1830-34; unsuccessful Whig candidate for gov. N.Y., 1834, gov., 1838-42; mem. U.S. Senate as Whig, 1849-55, as Republican, 1855-61, used phrase "a higher law than the Constitution" in speech of Mar. 11, 1850, urging senators to consider moral as well as legal aspects of slavery; favored abolition only by constl. means; denounced Dred Scott decision; declared slavery an "irrepressible conflict" in speech, Rochester, N.Y., Oct. 25, 1858; aspired to Rep. nomination for U.S. Pres., 1860; U.S. sec. of state (apptd. by Pres. Lincoln), 1861-69; advocated war with Spain and France to solidify Union, flattered No. opinion to avoid war with Eng., freed James Mason and John Slidell (Confederate agts. illegally captured on English ship Trent, Nov. 18, 1861), protested against outfitting of Confederate privateers in Brit. ports (his protests of Alabama, an English built Confederate ship, laid basis for later settlement of "Alabama Claims"); secured promise of evacuation when French intervened in Mexico, negotiated purchase of Alaska from Russia for $7,200,000 against public opinion, 1867, became known as "Seward's Folly" and "Seward's Ice-box"; unsuccessful in endeavors to acquire 2 islands of Danish West Indies, to incorporate Dominican Republic, and obtain annexation of Hawaii; supported Pres. Andrew Johnson in conciliatory measures toward South. Author: Autobiography of William H. Seward, from 1801 to 1834, with a Memoir of His Life and Selections from His Letters, from 1831 to 1846, published 1877. Died Auburn, Oct. 15, 1872; buried Fort Hill Cemetery, Auburn.

SEXTON, Leonidas, congressman, lawyer; b. Rushville, Ind., May 19, 1827; grad. Jefferson Coll., Canonsburg, Pa., 1847; studied law, Rushville; attended Cincinnati Law Sch., 1848-49. Admitted to Ind. bar, 1850, began practice of law, Rushville; mem. Ind. Ho. of Reps., 1856; lt. gov. Ind., 1873-77; mem. U.S. Ho. of Reps. (Republican) from Ind., 45th Congress, 1877-79. Died Parsons, Kan., July 4, 1880; buried East Hill Cemetery, Rushville.

SEYBERT, Adam, congressman; b. Phila., May 16, 1773; s. Sebastian and Barbara Seybert; M.D., U. Pa., 1793; studied at London, Edinburgh, Gottingen, mineralogy at Ecole des Mines, Paris; m. Maria Sarah Pepper, 2 children including Henry. Became mem. Am. Philos. Soc., 1797, sec., 1799-1808, counselor, 1810-11; earliest Am. expert in mineral analysis; ran drug and apothecary shop, Phila., early 1800's, also lab. for mfg. chemicals (manufactured 1st mercurials in Am.); mem. U.S. Ho. of Reps. (Democrat) from Pa., 11th-13th, 15th congresses, 1809-15, 17-19; mem. Am. Med. Soc., Chem. Soc. of Phila., Royal Scientific Soc. of Gottingen. Author: (dissertation) An Attempt to Disprove the Doctrine of the Putrefaction of the Blood of Animals, 1793; Statistical Annals . . . . . of the United States, 1789-1818, 1818 (listing expenditures of depts. of govt.); (written for Am. Philos. Soc.) Experiments and Observations on Land and Sea Air; also The Atmosphere of Marshes. Died Paris, France, May 2, 1825; buried Pere La Chaise Cemetery, Paris.

SEYBERT, Henry, mineralogist, philanthropist; b. Phila., Dec. 23, 1801; s. Adam and Maria Sarah (Pepper) S.; ed. Ecole des Mines, Paris, France. Discoverer fluorine; mem. Am. Philos. Soc., 1822; contbr. numerous articles on mineralogy to Jour. Scis. and Art and other publs.; contbr. to various philanthropic projects, established chair of philosophy at U. Pa., bequeathed residue of estate to City of Phila. for assistance to poor children. Died Mar. 3, 1883.

SEYBERT, John, clergyman; b. Manheim, Lancaster County, Pa., July 7, 1791; s. Henry and Susan (Kreuger) S. Converted by Mathia Bentz, an Evangelical preacher, 1810, joined Evang. Assn., licensed as an exhorter, elected class-leader for Manheim and Mount Joy, Pa.; became itinerant preacher on N.Y. circuit, 1820, traveled Pa. and Ohio circuits; ordained deacon Evang. Ch., 1822, elder, 1824, elected presiding elder, 1825, assigned to Canaan dist., assigned to Salem dist., 1829-33; did missionary work in Northwestern counties of Pa., 1833; bishop Evang. Assn., 1839-60. Died Bellevue, O., Jan. 4, 1860; buried Flat Rock, O.

SEYFFARTH, Gustavus, archeologist; b. Uebigaunr. Torgau, Germany, July 13, 1796; s. Traugott August Seyffarth; Ph.D., U. Leipzig (Germany), 1819. Finished De Lingua et Literis Vetirum AEgyptiorum (F.A.W. Spohn), 1825-31; 1st prof. archeology U. Leipzig, 1830-54; came to U.S., 1856; tchr. Concordia Coll., St. Louis; minister Yorkville, N.Y. Author: Rudimenta Hieroglyphices, 1826; The Literary Life of Gustavus Seyffarth (autobiography), 1886; Clavis AEgyptiaca (translation of hieroglyphic inscriptions, argued that Egyptian literature was syllable writing). Died N.Y.C., Nov. 17, 1885.

SEYMORE, Truman, army officer; b. Burlington, Vt., Sept. 24, 1824; s. Truman and Ann (Armstrong) Seymour; grad. U.S. Mil. Acad., 1846; m. Louisa Weir, circa 1852. Brevetted 2d lt. U.S. Army, 1846; brevetted 1st lt., then capt. for bravery in Mexican War; asst. prof. drawing U.S. Mil. Acad., 1850-53; served in Seminole War, Fla., 1856-58; brevetted maj. for gallant conduct as arty. capt., Ft. Sumter, 1861; comdr. tng. camp, Harrisburg, Pa., served in defense of Washington, D.C., autumn 1861; commd. brig. gen. U.S. Volunteers, 1862, served with distinction at battles of Beaver Dam Creek, Malvern Hill and Antietam; brevetted lt. col. and col. U.S. Army for gallantry at Antietam; comdr. unsuccessful attack on Battery Wagner, Charleston Harbor, 1863, expdn. to Fla., 1864, defeated at Olustee Station; taken prisoner in Battle of Wilderness, exchanged, 1864; comdr. div. 6th Corps, Shenadoah Valley, late 1864; recipient 3 brevet commns. (maj. gen. Volunteers, brig. and maj. gen. U.S. Army), 1865; arty. maj. in coastal ports Ft. Warren (Mass.) and Ft. Preble (Me.), following Civil War; ret., 1876. Died Florence, Italy, Oct. 30, 1891.

SEYMOUR, David Lowrey, congressman, lawyer; b. Wethersfield, Conn., Dec. 2, 1803; grad. Yale, 1826; studied law. Tutor at Yale, 1828-30; admitted to bar, 1829, began practice of law, Troy, N.Y.; mem. N.Y. State Assembly, 1836; dist. atty. for Rensselaer County, 1839-42; master in chancery, 1839; mem. U.S. Ho. of Reps. (Democrat) from N.Y., 28th, 32d congresses, 1843-45, 51-53; mem. N.Y. Constl. Conv., 1867. Died Lanesboro, Mass., Oct. 11, 1867; buried Mt. Ida Cemetery, Troy.

SEYMOUR, Edward Woodruff, congressman, lawyer; b. Litchfield, Conn., Aug. 30, 1832; son of Origen Storrs Seymour; grad. Yale, 1853; studied law. Admitted to bar, 1856, practiced law, Litchfield and Bridgeport, Conn.; mem. Conn. Ho. of Reps., 1859-60, 70-71, Conn. Senate, 1876; mem. U.S. Ho. of Reps. (Democrat) from Conn., 48th-49th congresses, 1883-87; apptd. judge Conn. Supreme Ct., 1889. Died Litchfield, Oct. 16, 1892; buried East Cemetery.

SEYMOUR, Horatio, senator, jurist; b. Litchfield, Conn., May 31, 1778; grad. Yale, 1797; attended Litchfield Law Sch. Admitted to bar, 1800, began practice of law, Middlebury, Vt.; postmaster Middlebury, 1800-09; mem. Vt. Exec. Council, 1809-14; states atty. for Addison County (Vt.), 1810-13, 15-19; mem. U.S. Senate (Clay Democrat) from Vt., 1821-33; unsuccessful Whig candidate for gov. Vt., 1836; judge probate ct., 1847-56. Died Middlebury, Nov. 21, 1857; buried West Cemetery.

SEYMOUR, Horatio, gov. N.Y.; b. Pompey Hill, Onondaga County, N.Y., May 31, 1810; s. Henry and Mary Ledyard (Forman) S.; m. Mary Bleecker, May 31, 1835. Admitted to N.Y. bar, 1832; mil. sec. of Gov. William Marcy, 1833-39; mem. N.Y. Assembly, 1842, 44, speaker, 1845, instrumental in obtaining approval of legislature for Erie Canal; asso. with Hunker faction Democratic Party, but gained prominence through efforts to unite all factions of party; unsuccessful candidate for gov. N.Y., 1850; gov. N.Y., 1852-54, 62-64, vetoed Me. Law Bill (favoring prohibition), 1854; opponent of abolitionism, fed. interference with slavery, prohibitionism and nativism during 1850's; opponent of Emancipation Proclamation and war powers of adminstrn., but filled state's quotas in Union Army; criticized for role in draft riots, 1863; presiding officer Dem. convs., 1864, 68; Dem. candidate for Pres. U.S., 1868, defeated by Grant; aided reformers in expelling Tweed from N.Y. Dem. orgn., 1870's; refused nomination for gov. N.Y., 1876. Died Deerfield Hills, N.Y., Feb. 12, 1886.

SEYMOUR, Origen Storrs, congressman, jurist; b. Litchfield, Conn., Feb. 9, 1804; grad. Yale, 1824; studied law; at least 1 son, Edward Woodruff Seymour. Admitted to bar, 1826, began practice of law, Litchfield; county clk., 1836-44; mem. Conn. Ho. of Reps., 1842, 49-50, 80, speaker, 1850; mem. U.S. Ho. of Reps. (Democrat) from Conn., 32d-33d congresses, 1851-55; judge Conn. Superior Ct., 1855-63; unsuccessful Democratic candidate for gov. Conn., 1864, 65; became judge Conn. Supreme Ct., 1870, chief justice, 1873-74; chmn. commn. to settle boundary dispute between Conn. and N.Y., 1876. Died Litchfield, Aug. 12, 1881; buried East Cemetery.

SEYMOUR, Samuel, artist; b. Eng.; active as painter and engraver, Phila., by 1801; said to have executed 150 views while accompanying Stephen H. Long's expdn. up the South Platte, 1819-20 (6 used as illustrations in Edwin James' account of expdn., pub. 1823) accompanied Long on another expdn. into No. Minn. and Man., 1823, did the illustrations of landscapes and Indians for ofcl. Narrative of journey; 1st artist to paint landscape of the West; exhibited at Peale's Mus., Phila., 1832; his only paintings now extant are watercolors in Yale U. collection.

SEYMOUR, Thomas Hart, gov. Conn., congressman, diplomat; b. Hartford, Conn., Sept. 29, 1807; s. Henry and Jane (Ellery) S.; grad. Partridge's Mil. Acad., Middletown, Conn., 1829. Admitted to Conn. bar, 1833; probate judge Hartford Dist., 1836-38; comdr. Hartford Right Guard, 1837-41; editor The Jeffersonian, 1837-38; mem. U.S Ho. of Reps. (Democrat) from Conn., 28th Congress, 1843-45, declined renomination, 1844; commd. maj. Conn. Volunteers, sailed with Gen. Scott to Veracruz, Mexico, 1847; commd. maj. 9th Inf., U.S. Army, 1847, lt. col. 12th Inf., 1847; brevetted col. for service in Battle of Chapultepec, 1847; gov. Conn., 1850-53; U.S. minister to Russia, 1853-58. Died Hartford, Sept. 3, 1868; buried Cedar Hill Cemetery, Hartford.

SEYMOUR, William, congressman, jurist; b. Conn., circa 1780; attended public schs., N.Y. Admitted to bar, 1806, began practice of law, Binghamton, N.Y.; moved to Windsor, N.Y., 1807; justice of peace, 1812-28; apptd. 1st judge Broome County Ct. of Common Pleas, Binghamton, 1833, served intermittently until 1847; an original trustee Village of Binghamton; 1834; mem. U.S. Ho. of Reps. (Democrat) from N.Y., 24th Congress, 1835-37. Died Binghamton, Dec. 28, 1848; buried Binghamton.

SHABONEE, Indian chief; b. in Ottowa tribe, nr. Maumee River, O., circa 1775; m. dau. of Potawatomi chief. Became powerful as chief Potawatomi tribe upon father-in-law's death; became attached to Tecumseh, taking his side against whites in Battle of Thames, circa 1807; refused to participate in massacres of white settlements during War of 1812 saved many lives in Chgo. massacre, 1812; warned white settlers at Fox River and Indian Creek of Black Hawk war plans, 1832; a monument erected to him for his friendship to white settlers 1903, park established, 1906. Died Grundy County, Ill., July 1859.

SHACKELFORD, John Williams, congressman; b. Richlands, N.C., Nov. 16, 1844; attended Richlands Acad. Served to lt. Confederate Army, throughout Civil War; mem. N.C. Ho. of Reps., 1872-78, N.C. Senate, 1878-80; mem. U.S. Ho. of Reps. (Democrat) from N.C., 1881-83. Died Washington, D.C., Jan. 18, 1883; buried Wallace Graveyard, Richlands.

SHAFER, Helen Almira, coll. pres.; b. Newark, N.J., Sept. 23, 1839; d. Archibald and Almira (Miller) Shafer; grad. Oberlin Coll., 1863, A.M. (hon.), 1877, LL.D. (hon.), 1893. Prof. mathematics Wellesley (Mass.) Coll., 1877-88, pres., 1888-94, revamped curriculum, set new standards for admission, added 67 new courses (opening way to elective system), encouraged establishment of Greek letter socs. and periodicals. Died Wellesley, Jan. 20, 1894.

SHAFER, Jacob K., congressman, lawyer; b. nr. Broadway, Rockingham County, Va., Dec. 26, 1823; grad. Washington Coll., Lexington, Va., 1843; grad. L. P. Thompson's law sch., Staunton, Va., 1846. Admitted to bar, practiced law, Stockton, Cal.; dist. atty, 5th Jud. Dist. of Cal., 1850; mayor Stockton, 1852; judge San Joaquin County Ct., 1853-62; moved to what later became Ida. Territory, 1862; mem. U.S. Congress from Ida. Territory, 41st Congress, 1869-71; moved to Eureka, Nev. Died Eureka, Nov. 22, 1876; buried Masonic Cemetery.

SHAFFNER, Taliaferro Preston, inventor; b. Smithfield, Va., 1818. Admitted to bar, circa 1840; asso. of Samuel F. B. Morse in constrn. of early telegraph lines, supervised constrn. of line from Louisville to New Orleans, 1851, also line from St. Louis to Jefferson; a promoter N. Atlantic cable enterprise, 1856-58; received 12 patents for methods of blasting with nitro-glycerine. Author: Telegraph Manual, 1859; The Secession War in America, 1862; Odd Fellowship, 1875. Died Troy, N.Y., Dec. 11, 1881; buried Troy.

SHALER, William, diplomat; b. Bridgeport, Conn., 1773; s. Capt. Timothy and Sibbel (Warner) S. Sea capt., engaged in trading ventures in S.Am. and Pacific, 1800-04; aided Hawaiian king in negotiating annexation of an independent island, 1804; U.S. consul, Havana, Cuba, 1810, 30-33; U.S. Govt. rep. in La. to report on Mexican revolutionary activities. 1812: apptd. observer at Ghent Peace Conf. by Pres. Madison, 1814; commr. to negotiate settlement with Algiers, 1815, success led to appointment as U.S. consul gen. Algiers, 1816-21, 22-28. Died Havana, Mar. 29, 1833.

SHANANAN, Jeremiah Francis, clergyman; b. Silver Lake, Susquehanna, Pa., July 13, 1834; studied at St. Joseph's, Binghamton, N.Y., also St. Charles Borromeo, Phila. Ordained priest Roman Catholic Ch., 1859; head of prep. sem., Phila., from 1859; 1st bishop of Harrisburg (Pa.), 1868-86. Died Sept. 24, 1886.

SHANKLIN, George Sea, congressman, lawyer, b. Jessamine County, Ky., Dec. 23, 1807; attended pvt. sch., Nicholasville, Ky.; studied law. Admitted to bar, began practice of law, Nicholasville; mem. Ky. Ho. of Reps., 1838, 44, 61-65; apptd. commonwealth atty., 1854; Democratic presdl. elector, 1864; mem. U.S. Ho. of Reps. (Democrat) from Ky., 39th Congress, 1865-67. Died Jessamine County, Apr. 1, 1883; buried Lexington (Ky.) Cemetery.

SHANNON, Thomas, congressman, mcht.; b. Washington County, Pa., Nov. 15, 1786; attended public schs. Moved to Ohio, 1800, later engaged in agrl. pursuits, Belmont County, O.; moved to Barnesville, O., 1812, became mcht.; served as capt. Belmont County Co., Col. Delong's Regt. in War of 1812; mem. Ohio Ho. of Reps., 1819-22, 24-25; mem. U.S. Ho. of Reps. (Democrat, filled vacancy) from Ohio, 19th Congress, Dec. 4, 1826-27; became leaf-tobacco mcht., Barnesville; mem. Ohio Senate, 1829, 37-41. Died Barnesville, Mar. 16, 1843; buried Green Mount Cemetery.

SHANNON, Thomas Bowles, congressman, mcht.; b. Westmoreland County, Pa., Sept. 21, 1827; attended public schs. Moved to Ill., 1844, to Cal., 1849; engaged in merc. activities; mem. Cal. Assembly, 1859-60, 62, 71-72, speaker, 1871; mem. U.S. Ho. of Reps. (Republican) from Cal., 38th Congress, 1863-65; surveyor Port of San Francisco, 1865-69; collector of customs (apptd. by Pres. Grant), San Francisco, 1872-80. Died San Francisco, Feb. 21, 1897; buried Masonic Cemetery.

SHANNON, Wilson, gov. Ohio, territorial gov., diplomat; b. Mount Olivet, Ohio Territory, Feb. 24, 1802; s. George and Jane (Milligan) S.; attended Ohio U., Athens, 1820-22. Transylvania U., Lexington, Ky., 1823; m. Elizabeth Ellis; m. 2d, Sarah Osbun; at least 3 children. Admitted to Ohio bar, 1830, Kan. bar, circa 1856; gov. Ohio, 1839-41, 43-44; U.S. minister to Mexico, 1844-45; led expdn. of Forty-Niners from Eastern Ohio and Western Va. to Cal., 1844-45; mem. U.S. Ho. of Reps. from Ohio, 33d Congress, 1853-55; gov. Kan. Territory, 1855-56; presided at pro-slavery meeting which organized "Law and Order Party," Leavenworth, Kan., 1855; persuaded factions to disband during conflict between anti-slavery and pro-slavery forces, (known as Wakarusa War) 1855; refused to intervene when guerilla bands assembled, Lawrence, Kan., 1856; issued proclamation commanding that armed combinations organized to resist law disband, 1856, continued to attempt settlement between pro-slavery faction (in charge of govt.) and Freesoilers (who had set up own govt. in Topeka, Kan.) throughout term as gov., effected a settlement, Aug. 1856; del. Ohio and Nat. Democratic convs.; leading mem. Kan. bar. Died Lawrence, Aug. 30, 1877; buried Oak Hill Cemetery, Lawrence.

SHARKEY, William Lewis, provisional gov. Miss., jurist; b. Muscle Shoals, Tenn., July 12, 1798; s. Patrick and Mrs. (Rhodes) S.; m. Minerva (Hyland) Wren. Admitted to Miss. bar, 1822; mem. Miss. Ho. of Reps., 1828, 29, mem. judiciary com.; circuit judge of Miss., 1832; chief justice Miss. High Ct. of Errors and Appeals, 1832-57; pres. Nashville (Tenn.) Conv., 1850; mem. commn. to compile The Revised Code of the Statute Laws of Mississippi, 1857; charter mem. bd. trustees U. Miss., 1844-65; a state-rights Whig, became anti-secessionist by 1861; took oath of allegiance to Union, 1863; negotiated with Pres. Johnson concerning reconstrn. of Miss., 1865; provisional gov. Miss., 1865; elected to U.S. Senate, 1866, denied seat. Died Washington, D.C., Mar. 30, 1873; buried Greenwood Cemetery, Jackson, Miss.

SHARON, William, senator, businessman; b. Smithfield, Jefferson County, O., Jan. 9, 1821; attended Athens Coll.; studied law. Admitted to bar, practiced law; engaged in merc. activities, Carrollton, Ill.; became businessman, Sacramento, Cal., 1849, real estate dealer, San Francisco, 1850; became mgr. branch of Bank of Cal., Virginia City, Nev., 1864; engaged in silver mining; mem. U.S. Senate (Republican) from Nev., 1875-81. Died San Francisco, Nov. 13, 1885; buried Laurel Hill Cemetery.

SHARP, Daniel, clergyman; b. Huddersfield, Eng., Dec. 25, 1783; s. Rev. John Sharp; studied under Rev. William Staughton, Phila.; m. Ann Cauldwell, Jan. 1, 1818, 11 children. Apptd. Am. agt. of Yorkshire merc. firm, established residence in N.Y.C., 1805; also did lay preaching; ordained to ministry Baptist Ch., Newark; pastor 3d Baptist Ch., Boston, 1812-53; asked to preach election sermon before Mass. gov. and legislature, 1824. Author: Recognition of Friends in Heaven, 3d edit., 1844. Died Balt., June 23, 1853.

SHARP, John, Mormon pioneer; b. Clackmannanshire, Scotland, Nov. 9, 1820; s. John and Mary (Hunter) S.; m. Jean Patterson, 1839; m. Ann Wright Gibson and Sophie Smith, after 1850; 13 children. Arrived at Salt Lake City, Utah, 1850; supt. in ch. quarries, circa 1851; ordained by Brigham Young bishop of 20th Ward, Salt Lake City, 1856; maj. later col. in Nauvoo Legion (Mormon Militia); sponsor formation of local inst. of young people (later became Mut. Improvement Assn.), 1872; contractor with Young for both U.P. and Central Pacific railroads; asst. supt. Utah Central R.R., 1869, later supt, then pres., 1873; v.p. Utah Soc. Ry., 1871; brought to trial for polygamy, 1885, pleaded guilty, fined $300. Died Dec. 23, 1891.

SHARP, Solomon P., congressman, lawyer; b. Abingdon, Va., 1780; studied law. Engaged in agriculture, Ky.; admitted to bar, 1809, began practice of law, Russellville, Ky.; mem. Ky. Ho. of Reps., 1809-11, 17-18, 25; organized, served as capt. of company, during War of 1812, later commd. col. of militia; mem. U.S. Ho. of Reps. (Democrat) from Ky., 13th-14th congresses, 1813-17; moved to Frankfort, Ky., 1820; atty. gen. Ky., 1820-24. Assassinated in Frankfort, Nov. 7, 1825; buried State Cemetery.

SHARP, William, lithographer; b. Ramsey, nr. Peterborough, Eng., circa 1802; children include Philip T., George Henry. Lithographer, London, Eng., circa 1832-38; came to Am., circa 1838, settled in Boston; exhibited portraits and landscapes at Boston Athenaeum several times between 1839 and 1872; one of 1st Am. lithographers to expt. with color; noted for illustrations of fruit and flowers in Fruits of America, 1847-52; practiced in various partnerships, 1840-62, including with his sons.

SHARPE, Horatio, colonial gov.; b. Hull, Yorkshire, Eng., Nov. 15, 1718. Gov. Md., 1753-69, responsible for providing men and supplies for approaching French and Indian War; royal comdr.-in-chief during war, gathered supplies, inspected mil. posts, strengthened Ft. Cumberland, erected 4 small fts.; mem. mil. councils in N.Y. and Phila., 1755-57; in conflict with lower house about appropriation bills throughout term; in communication to Lord Baltimore outlined concise plan that is prototype of Stamp Act, 1754, warned ministry that Stamp Act could be enforced only by troops; arrived at boundary agreement between Md. and Va., 1760; returned to Eng., 1773. Died Eng., Nov. 9, 1790.

SHARPE, Peter, congressman; born N.Y. Became mem. Columbia County Med. Soc., 1807; mem. N.Y. State Assembly from York County, 1814-21, speaker, 1820-21; del. N.Y. Constl. Conv., 1821; mem. U.S. Ho. of Reps. from N.Y., 18th Congress, 1823-25.

SHARPE, William, Continental congressman; b. nr. Rock Church, Cecil County, Md., Dec. 13, 1742; studied law. Admitted to bar, began practice of law,

Mecklenburg County, N.C., 1763; also became a surveyor; moved to Rowan (now Iredell) County, N.C.; mem. Provincial Congress, 1775; aide to Gen. Rutherford in Indian campaign, 1776; a commr. apptd. by Gov. Caswell to treat with Indians, 1777; del. N.C. Constl. Conv., Halifax, 1776; mem. Continental Congress from N.C., 1779-82; mem N.C. Ho. of Reps., 1781-82. Died nr. Statesville, N.C., July 1, 1818; buried Snow Creek Graveyard.

SHARPLES, James, painter; b. Eng., 1751; m. 3d, Ellen Wallace; children—George, Felix Thomas, James, Rolinda. Exhibited paintings at Royal Acad., 1779; came to U.S. with family, 1793; portrait painter, toured country making portraits of famous personages including Washington; returned to Eng., 1801-09, to N.Y.C., 1809-11; copies of famous portraits were made by wife and 2 sons, all unsigned, leading to questions of authenticity; represented in collections of portraits at Royal West of Eng. Acad., Independence Hall, Phila. Died N.Y.C., Feb. 26, 1811.

SHARSWOOD, George, jurist, educator; b. Phila., July 7, 1810; s. George and Esther (Dunn) S.; grad. U. Pa., 1828; LL.D., (hon.), Columbia, 1856; m. Mary Chambers, Nov. 27, 1849, 1 child. Admitted to Pa. bar, 1831; vice provost Law Acad., Phila., 1835-53; mem. Pa. Legislature, 1837-38, 42-43; asso. judge Dist. Ct. Phila., 1845, pres. judge, 1848-67; asso. justice Supreme Ct. Pa., 1868-79, chief justice, 1879-82 (of some 4,000 cases, only 156 decisions appealed 32 reversed); prof. law U. Pa., 1850, dean, 1852-68, trustee 1872-83; pres. of an instn. for deaf and dumb; trustee Gen. Assembly of Presbyn. Ch.; mem. Am. Philos. Soc.; editor Am. Law Mag., 1843-46. Author: A Compendium of Lectures on the Aims and Duties of the Profession of Law, 1854; Lectures Introductory to the Study of Law, 1870; Died Phila., May 28, 1883.

SHATTUCK, George Cheyne, physician, philanthropist; b. Templeton, Mass., July 17, 1783; s. Dr. Benjamin and Lucy (Barron) S.; A.B., Dartmouth, 1803, M.B., 1806, M.D. (hon.), 1812, LL.D. (hon.). 1853; M.D., U. Pa., 1807; m. Dliza Cheever Davis, Oct. 3, 1811; m. 2d, Amelia H. Bigelow, Aug. 17, 1835; 6 children including George Cheyne. Leading physician in Boston from 1807; consulting physician to City of Boston for short period; pres. Mass. Med. Soc., 1836-40; pres. Am. Statis. Assn., 1845-51; contbd. toward building of astron. observatory Dartmouth Coll.; contbd. funds to Harvard (endowment now Chattuck Professorship of Path. Anatomy, Harvard Med. Sch.); gave grant to Mass. Med. Soc. for foundation of Shattuck lectures; financially assisted John James Audubon with Birds of America, 1827-38; founder Shattuck Sch., Faribault, Minn.; won Boylston med. prize 2 years in succession for essay series published in Boston, 1808; mem. N.H. Med. Soc., Am. Acad. Arts and Scis. Author: A Dissertation on the Uncertainty of the Healing Art, 1829; Died Boston, Mar., 18, 1854.

SHATTUCK, George Cheyne, physician, educator; b. Boston, July 22, 1813; s. George Cheyne and Eliza Cheever (Davis) S.; grad. Harvard, 1831, M. D., 1835; studied in Europe, 1835-40, under P. C. A. Louis, Paris, France; m. Anne Henrietta Brune, Apr. 9, 1840, 3 children. Translated Anatomical, Pathological and Therapeutic Researches on the Yellow Fever of Gibralter of 1828 (Louis), 1839; studied typhus fever at London Fever Hosp., Eng., read report in which he differentiated between typhus and typhoid fevers before Med. Soc. of Observation of Paris, 1838; began practice of medicine with father, Boston, 1840; founder (with Oliver Wendell Holmes, Henry Ingersol Bowditch, James Jackson) Boston Soc. Med. Observation; vis. physician Mass. Gen. Hosp., 1849-55; succeeded Jacob Bigelow as prof. clin. medicine Harvard Med. Sch., 1855-64, dean, 1864; founder St. Paul's Sch., Concord, N.H., 1855. Died Mar. 22, 1893.

SHATTUCK, Lemuel, statistician, genealogist; b. Ashby, Mass., Oct. 15, 1793; s. John and Betsy (Miles) S.; m. Clarissa Baxter, Dec. 1, 1825, 5 children. Organizer 1st Sunday Sch. in Mich., circa 1820; mcht., Concord Mass., 1823-34; mem. Concord Sch. Com., reorganized schs., introduced annual sch. reports; mem. Mass. Legislature, 1838; publisher and bookseller, Boston, 1836-39; a founder Am. Statis. Assn., 1839, New Eng. Historic Geneal. Soc., circa 1840; influenced passage of law requiring system of registration of births, marriages and deaths, 1842; active mem. Boston Common Council, 1837-41, induced Council to take census in 1845; chmn. commn. to make san. survey of Mass., 1849, wrote its Report, 1850, resulting in creation of Mass. Bd. of Health. Author: A History of the Town of Concord, 1835; Memorials of the Descendants of William Shattuck, 1855. Died Boston, Jan. 17, 1859.

SHAW, Aaron, congressman, lawyer; b. nr. Goshen, Orange County, N.Y., Dec. 19, 1811; attended Montgomery Acad., N.Y.; studied law, Goshen. Admitted to bar, 1833, began practice of law, Lawrenceville, Ill.; del. 1st Ill. Internal Improvement Conv.; elected states atty. by Ill. Legislature, 1842; mem. Ill. Ho. of Reps., 1850, 60; mem, U.S. Ho. of Reps. (Democrat) from Ill., 35th, 48th congresses, 1857-59, 83-85; circuit judge 4th Jud. Dist. Ill., 1863-69. Died Olney, Ill., Jan. 7, 1887; buried Haven Hill Cemetery.

SHAW, Elijah, clergyman; b. Kensington, Rockingham County, N.H., Dec. 19, 1793; s. Elijah and Deborah (Nudd) S.; m. Lydia True, July 16, 1818. Converted to movement for undenominational Christianity (Christian Connection), 1810, ordained minister, 1814; minister, Brutos, N.Y., 1818-26, Salisbury, Mass., 1828, Portland, Me., 1830; editor Christian Journal, 1835-40, contbr. until 1851; agt. to secure funds to found Durham (N.H.) Acad., 1842-43; held various pastorates, 1840-51; agt. New Eng. Missionary Soc., 1845; made missionary tour from Mass. to Mich. and back, 1850. Author: Sentiments of the Christians (history, beliefs and eccles, polity of Christian Connection), 1847. Died May 5, 1851.

SHAW, George Bullen, congressman, businessman; b. Alma, Allegany County, N.Y., Mar. 12, 1854; grad. Internat. Bus. Coll., Chgo., 1871. Engaged in lumer mfg. bus.; mem. Eau Claire (Wis.) Common Council, 1876-87; del. Republican Nat. Conv., Chgo., 1884; mayor Eau Claire, 1888-89; supreme chancellor Knights of Pythias of World, 1890-92; mem. U.S. Ho. of Reps. (Rep.) from Wis., 53d Congress, 1893-94. Died Eau Claire, Aug. 27, 1894; buried Lake View Cemetery.

SHAW, Henry, congressman, lawyer; b. nr. Putney, Windham County, Vt., 1788; son of Samuel Shaw; studied law. Admitted to bar, began practice of law, Albany, N.Y., 1810; moved to Lanesboro, Mass., 1813; mem. U.S. Ho. of Reps. (Federalist) from Mass., 15th-16th congresses, 1817-21; mem. Mass. Ho. of Reps., 1824-30, 33, Mass. Senate, 1835; Nat.-Republican presdl. elector, 1832; unsuccessful candidate for gov. Mass., 1845; moved to N.Y.C., 1848; mem. N.Y.C. Bd. Edn., 1849; mem. N.Y.C. Common Council, 1850-51; mem. N.Y. State Assembly, 1853; moved to Newburgh, N.Y., 1854. Died Peekskill, N.Y., Oct. 17, 1857; buried Lower Cemetery, Lanesboro.

SHAW, Henry, founder Mo. Bot. Garden; b. Sheffield, Eng., July 24, 1800; s. Joseph and Sarah (Hoole) S. Settled in St. Louis, 1819; owned hardware and cutlery business until retirement, 1840; established Mo. Botanical Garden (instn. for systematic study of plants), St. Louis, 1857, opened garden to public circa 1860, established trust for its maintenance; established one of best bot. libraries, also one of largst herbariums in U.S.; endowed Henry Shaw Sch. of Botany at Washington U., St. Louis. Died St. Louis, Aug. 25, 1889; buried Mo. Bot. Garden.

SHAW, Henry Marchmore, congressman, physician; b. Newport, R.I., Nov. 20, 1819; grad. med. dept. U. Pa. at Phila., 1838. Began practice of medicine, Indiantown, Camden County, N.C.; mem. U.S. Ho. of Reps. (Democrat) from N.C., 33d, 35th congresses, 1853-55, 57-59; served as col. Confederate Army during Civil War. Killed nr. New Bern, N.C., Nov. 1, 1864; buried Shawboro, N.C.

SHAW, Henry Wheeler (pseudonym Josh Billings), humorist; b. Lanesboro, Berkshire County, Mass., Apr. 21, 1818; s. Henry and Laura (Wheeler) S.; attended Hamilton Coll., 1832; m. Zilpha Bradford, Feb. 18, 1845, 2 children. Became real estate broker, Poughkeepsie, N.Y. circa 1860; earliest examples of humor which were based on rural dialects were printed in local newspapers under pseudonym Josh Billings, circa 1863; well-known lectr. around country in 1870's. Author: Josh Billings, His Sayings, 1865; Josh Billing's Farmers Allminax for Year of 1870, 1869-70 (published editions annually until 1880); Josh Billings Struggling with Things, 1881. Died Monterey, Cal., Oct. 14, 1885; buried Lanesboro, Mass.

SHAW, John, naval officer; b. Mountmellick, Queens County, Ireland, 1773; s. John and Elizabeth (Barton) S.; m. Elizabeth Palmer; m. 2d, Mary Breed, Oct. 13, 1820; 7 children. Came to N.Y.C., 1790; commd. lt. U.S. Navy, 1798; commanded the George Washington on mission to Algiers, 1801; promoted comdr., 1804, in command the John Adams, 1805; commd. capt., 1807, in charge Norfolk (Va.), Navy Yard, 1808-10, in command naval squadron blockaded by British nr. New London, Conn., 1814; joined Mediterranean Squadron, 1815, ordered to reach settlement with Algiers, remained in Algiers to protect Am. interests, until 1817; in charge of Boston Navy Yard, 1820's, later Naval Station, Charleston, S.C. Died Phila., Sept. 17, 1823.

SHAW, John, physician, poet; b. Annapolis, Md., May 4, 1778; grad. St. John's Coll., 1796; studied medicine U. Pa.; studied medicine U. Edinburgh (Scotland), 1801-03; m. Jane Selby (or Telby), Feb. 12, 1807. Studied medicine in Md., 1795-98; had post of surgeon on squadron to Algiers, 1798-1800; returned to Annapolis, 1805; practiced medicine, Balt., 1805-08; helped found Coll. of Medicine in Md., 1807, in charge chemistry work; John Elihutlall published Poems by the Late Doctor John Shaw, 1810. Died at sea between Charleston, S.C. and the Bahamas, Jan. 10, 1809.

SHAW, Joshua, artist, inventor; b. Bellingborough, Lincolnshire, Eng., circa 1777. Sign painter, Manchester, Eng.; became known as painter of portraits, flowers, still life, landscapes, cattlepieces; began exhibiting at Royal Acad., London, 1802; came to Am., 1817, settled in Phila.; travelled through South making sketches and taking subscriptions for series of Am. views, engraved and published, 1819-20; a founder Artists' Fund Soc.; exhibited frequently in Phila., N.Y.C., Boston and Balt.; made several important improvements in firearms for which he later received awards from U.S. and Russian govts.; moved to Bordentown, N.J., circa 1843; stricken with paralysis, 1853. Died Burlington, N.J., Sept. 8, 1860.

SHAW, Lemuel, jurist; b. Barnstable, Mass., Jan. 9, 1781; s. Oakes and Susanna B. Shaw; grad. Harvard, 1800, LL.D. (hon.), 1831; LL.D. (hon.), Brown U., 1850; m. Elizabeth Knapp, Jan. 6, 1818; m. 2d, Hope Savage, Aug. 29, 1827. Admitted to N.H. bar, 1804, also Plymouth County (Mass.) bar; practiced in Boston from 1804; rep. Gen. Mass. Court, 1811-14, 20, 29; mem. Mass. Senate, 1824-22, 28-29; mem. Mass. Constl. Conv., 1820; drew 1st charter of Boston, 1822; chief justice Mass. Supreme Ct., 1830-60, influenced comml. and constl. law throughout nation, demonstrated courage in refusal to release a fugitive slave on habeas corpus, 1851; fellow Harvard, 1834-61, overseer, 1831-53; Federalist and Whig; mem. Am. Acad. Arts and Scis., Mass. and New Eng. hist. socs. Died Boston, Mar. 30, 1861; buried Mt. Auburn Cemetery, Cambridge, Mass.

SHAW, Nathaniel, mcht., naval agt.; b. Dec. 5, 1735; s. Nathaniel and Temperance (Harris) S.; m. Lucretia (Harris) Rogers. Mcht. in West Indian trade, early 1760's; participated in various colonial actions against British restrictive measures, 1765-75; negotiator purchase of powder for Conn. Gen. Assembly, 1774; agt. for provisioning ships for Colony of Conn., 1775; apptd. by Continental Congress agt. in Conn. to supervise prize vessels and purchase stores, 1775, acted as agt. for exchange naval prisoners; apptd. by Conn. Gen. Assembly dir. of all armed ships belonging to Conn., 1778; dep. Conn. Assembly, 2 terms; his wharves and warehouses destroyed by Benedict Arnold's attack, New London, Conn., 1781. Died Conn., Apr. 15, 1782.

SHAW, Oliver, musician, composer; b. Middleboro, Mass., Mar. 13, 1779; s. John and Hannah (Heath) S.; attended Bristol Acad., Taunton, Mass.; studied with John L. Berkenhead, blind organist, Newport, R.I., studied under Johann Christian Graupner, Boston, clarinet from Thomas Granger, Boston; m. Sarah Jenckes, Oct. 20, 1812, 5 daus., 2 sons including Oliver J. Became blind, 1800; settled in Providence, 1807; organist 1st Congregational Ch., Providence, 1807-48 (until death); pvt. tchr. music; organizer Psallonian Soc. for performance choral works, 1809, gave annual concerts, 1809-32; composed numerous hymns including "Taunton" and "Bristol;" sacred songs included "Arrayed in Clouds of Golden Light" and "The Missionary Angel"; other compositions include: March (performed at Providence Centennial, 1832), For the Gentlemen (collection of tunes for 6 instruments), published, 1807, Died Providence, Dec. 31, 1848.

SHAW, Robert Gould, army officer; b. Boston, Oct. 10, 1837; s. Francis George and Sarah Blake (Sturgis) S.; student Harvard, 1856-59; m. Anna Kneeland Haggerty, May 2, 1863. Entered accounting room, N.Y.C., intending to become mcht.; enlisted in 7th Regt., Apr. 1861, promoted 1st lt. 2d Mass. Regt., July 1861, capt., Aug. 1862; apptd. col. 5th Mass. Regt. (1st Negro unit from free states), Feb. 1863; killed and buried with many of his men in assault on Ft. Wagner, Charleston, S.C. Sculpture meml. to him by Saint-Gaudens, on Boston Commons; his story was basis for William Vaughan Moody's An Ode in Time of Hesitation. Died July 18, 1863.

SHAW, Samuel, army officer, diplomat; b. Boston, Oct. 2, 1754; s. Francis and Sarah (Burt) S.; m. Hannah Phillips, Aug. 21, 1792. Commd. 1st lt. 3d Continental Arty., 1766; aide-de-camp to Gen. Knox, 1779; commd. capt., 1780; assisted in arranging disbandment of Continental Army; sec. com. of officers that formed Soc. of Cincinnati; held post on Empress of China, 1st Am.

vessel sent to Canton, 1784; 1st sec. (apptd. by Gen. Knox) War Dept., 1785-86; 1st Am. consul in China, 1786-89, 90-92. Died at sea, Cape of Good Hope, May 30, 1794.

SHAW, Samuel, congressman, physician; b. Dighton, Mass., Dec. 1768; studied medicine; at least 1 son, Henry. Began practice of medicine, Castleton, Vt., 1789; imprisoned for denouncing Pres. Adams, liberated by the people; mem. Vt. Ho. of Reps., 1800-07; mem. U.S. Ho. of Reps. (Democrat, filled vacancy) from Vt., 10th-12th congresses, Sept. 6, 1808-13; served as hosp. surgeon U.S. Army, 1813-15, post surgeon, 1818. Died Clarendon Springs, Vt., Oct. 23, 1827; buried Castleton Cemetery.

SHAW, Thomas, inventor; b. Phila., May 5, 1838; s. James and Catherine (Snyder) S.; m. Matilda Garber, 1 dau. Apprenticed to machinist, Phila.; patented a gas meter (1st invention), 1858; patented a press mold for glass, gas stove, sewing machine, 1859; supt. Cyclops Machine Works, Phila., circa 1860; supt. Midvale Steel Works, 1867; produced many inventions including a centrifugal shot making machine, a steam power hammer, spring-lock nut washer, 1867-70; established factory for mfg. his inventions, Phila., 1871; patented some 200 devices including pressure gauges, pile drivers, hydraulic pumps, a device to detect and measure presence of noxious gases in mines (adopted by several European govts.), 1871-1901. Died Hammonton, N.J., Jan. 19, 1901; buried Phila.

SHAW, Tristram, congressman; b. Hampton, Rockingham County, N.H., May 23, 1786. Held several offices, Exeter, N.H.; mem. U.S. Ho. of Reps. from N.H., 26th-27th congresses, 1839-43. Died Exeter, Mar. 14, 1843; buried Bride Hill Cemetery, Hampton.

SHAW, William Smith, librarian; b. Haverhill, Mass., Aug. 12, 1778; s. Rev. John and Elizabeth (Smith) S.; grad. Harvard, 1798. Pvt. sec. to Pres. Adams, 1798-1800; admitted to bar in Boston, circa 1804; a founder, treas. Anthology Soc. which took over the Monthly Anthology, 1805; clk. U.S. Dist. Ct. for Mass., 1806; librarian Boston Athenaeum, devoted time and effort to expansion of library collection, also collections of coins and manuscripts, 1807-22, sec. until 1823. Died Boston, Apr. 25, 1826.

SHAYS, Daniel, army officer, insurgent; b. Hopkinton, Mass., circa 1747; s. Patrick and Margaret (Dempsey) Shay (changed spelling); m. Abigail Gilbert, 1772. Served as ensign in battles of Bunker Hill, Ticonderoga, Saratoga, Stony Point; commd. capt. 5th Mass. Regt., 1777; mem. Pelham (Mass.) Com. of Safety, 1781, 82; prominent in insurrection in West Mass. known as Shays' Rebellion, (caused by econ. depression), demanded redress of grievances; chmn. com. which drew up resolutions that Mass. Supreme Ct. should be allowed to sit, provided it dealt with no case involving indictments of insurgents or debts; leader force of 1,000 insurgents, Wilbraham, Mass., 1787, attacked U.S. arsenal, Springfield, Mass. (protected by Gen. William Shepard), defeated by Mass. Militia, routed by Gen. Lincoln at Petersham; fled to Vt. after defeat; condemned to death, 1787; petitioned for pardon, 1788, pardon granted; ret. to Sparta, N.Y.; Shays' Rebellion took his name even though many others participated who were equally prominent. Died Sparta, Sept. 29, 1825.

SHEA, John Dawson Gilmary, historian, editor; b. N.Y.C., July 22, 1824; s. James and Mary Ann (Flannigan) S.; grad. Columbia Grammar Sch., 1837; studied St. John's Coll., Fordham, 1848-50, LL.D. (hon.); studied St. Mary's Coll., Montreal, Que., Can., 1850-52; LL.D. (hon.), St. Francis Xavier's Coll., Georgetown Coll.; m. Sophie Savage, 2 children. Admitted to N.Y. bar, 1846; mem. N.Y. Hist. Soc., 1846; joined Soc. of Jesus, 1848, decided not to become a priest, 1852; compiler A General History of Modern Europe (widely used in Cath. schs.), 1854; editor Sacllier's General Catholic Directory, 1858-90, Library of American Linguistics, 1860-74; founder U.S. Cath. Hist. Soc., editor, 1887-89, pres., 1890; compiler History of the Catholic Missions Among the Indian Tribes of the U.S., 1529-1854, 1854; editor Cath. News, 1889. Author: Discovery and Exploration of the Mississippi Valley, 1852; History of the Catholic Church in the United States, 4 vols., 1886-92. Died Elizabeth, N.J., Feb. 22, 1892.

SHEAFE, James, senator, congressman; b. Portsmouth, N.H., Nov. 16, 1755; grad. Harvard, 1774. Engaged in business; mem. N.H. Ho. of Reps., 1788-90, N.H. Senate, 1791, 93, 99; mem. Exec. Council, 1799; mem. U.S. Ho. of Reps. (Federalist) from N.H., 6th Congress, 1799-1801; mem. U.S. Senate from N.H., 1801-June 14, 1802 (resigned); unsuccessful candidate for gov. N.H., 1816. Died Portsmouth, Dec. 5, 1829; buried St. John's Ch. Cemetery.

SHECUT, John Linnaeus Edward Whitridge, physician; b. Beaufort, S.C., Dec. 4, 1770; s. Abraham and Marie (Barbary) S.; M.D., Coll. of Phila., 1791; m. Sarah Cannon, Jan. 26, 1792; m. 2d, Susanna Ballard, Feb. 7, 1805; 9 children. An early experimenter with use of electricity in treatment of yellow fever and crippled limbs, suggested that yellow fever was in part caused by lack of electricity in atmosphere; discouraged blood-letting and use of mercury as drug; organizer Antiquarian Soc. of Charleston (S.C.), 1813, incorporated as Literary and Philos. Soc. of S.C., 1814. Author: Flora Carolinaeensis (most thorough work on botany of S.C. then available), 1806. Died Charleston, June 1, 1836.

SHEDD, William Greenough Thayer, educator; b. Acton, Mass., June 21, 1820; s. Marshall and Eliza (Thayer) S.; grad. U. Vt., 1839, Andover Theol. Sem., 1843; m. Lucy Ann Myers, Oct. 7, 1845, 4 children. Ordained to ministry, 1844; prof. English lit. U. Vt., 1845-52; prof. sacred rhetoric Auburn Theol. Sem., 1852-54, prof. ch. history, 1854-62; prof. Union Theol. Sem., N.Y.C., 1862-93, prof. systematic theology (expounding an orthodox Calvinist theology), 1874-93. Author: Dogmatic Theology, 2 vols., 1888, 3 vols., 1894; Lectures Upon the Philosophy of History, 1856; translator (from German) Theremin's Outline of a Systematic Rhetoric, 1850; editor Coleridge's Collected Works, 1852; Manual of Church History, 1868; History of Christian Doctrine, 1863; Homiletics and Pastoral Theology, 1869; Sermons to the Natural Man, 1871; Theological Essays, 1877; Augustine on the Trinity, 1887. Died N.Y.C., Nov. 17, 1894.

SHEFFER, Daniel, congressman, physician; b. York, Pa., May 24, 1783; attended Harvard; studied medicine, Phila. Began practice of medicine, York Springs, Adams County, Pa.; asso. judge Adams County, 1813-37; Democratic presdl. elector, 1824; mem. U.S. Ho. of Reps. (Democrat) from Pa., 25th Congress, 1837-39; del. Dem. Nat. Conv., Balt., 1848. Died York Springs, Feb. 16, 1880; buried Old Lutheran Cemetery.

SHEFFEY, Daniel, congressman, lawyer; b. Frederick, Md., 1770; apprenticed as shoemaker in his father's shop; studied law, Wytheville, Va. Admitted to bar, 1802, began practice of law, Wytheville; later practiced in Abbeville, then Staunton, Va.; mem. Va. Ho. of Dels., 1800-04, 22-23, Va. Senate, 1804-08; mem. U.S. Ho. of Reps. (Federalist) from Va., 11th-14th congresses, 1809-17. Died Staunton, Dec. 3, 1830.

SHEFFIELD, Joseph Earl, financier, philanthropist; b. Southport, Conn., June 19, 1793; s. Paul King and Mabel (Thorp) S.; m. Maria St. John, Aug. 22, 1822, 9 children. Became partner in dry-goods firm, New Bern, N.Y., 1814; in cotton trade, Mobile, Ala., circa 1818-35, established connections in New Orleans, N.Y., Liverpool, Havre, became largest exporter of Mobile; moved to New Haven, Conn., 1835, helped finance completion of railroad from N.Y. to New Haven; undertook to complete unfinished part of Mich. So. R.R.; built 182 miles of Chgo. & Rock Island R.R., 1852-54; contbd. gifts and bequests of more than $1,000,000 to sci. dept. Yale (renamed Sheffield Scientific Sch.), 1861. Died New Haven, Feb. 16, 1882.

SHELBURNE, Lord, see Petty, William.

SHELBY, Evan, army officer, state senator; b. Tregaron, Cardiganshire, Wales, 1719; s. Evan and Catherine (Davies) S.; m. Laetitia Cox, 1744; m. 2d, Isabella Elliott, 1787; at least 1 son, Isaac. Came to Am., circa 1734, settled in Hagerstown, Md.; laid out part of road from Ft. Frederick to Ft. Cumberland in Gen. Braddock's campaign, 1755; commd. capt. of co. of rangers, also capt. Pa. Militia; served under Gen. John Forbes in capture of Ft. Duquesne, 1758; mgr. Potomac Co. for Md., 1762; moved to Va., 1773, became landowner, Fincastle County (Va.); commanded Fincastle Co., Va. Militia in Lord Dunmore's War, 1774; commd. maj. Va. Militia, 1776; col. Washington (Va.) Militia, 1776; led expdn. of 2000 men against Chickamauga Indian towns on lower Tenn. River, 1779; mem. N.C. Senate, 1781; brig. gen. Washington Dist. (N.C.) Militia, 1786-87; commr. for N.C. to negotiate temporary truce with Col. John Sevier, 1787; refused position of gov. State of Franklin, 1787; resigned as brig. gen., 1787. Died Bristol, Sullivan County, Tenn., Dec. 4, 1794; buried East Hill Cemetery, Bristol.

SHELBY, Isaac, army officer, gov. Ky.; b. North Mountain, Washington County, Md., Dec. 11, 1750; s. Evan and Laetitia (Cox) S.; m. Susannah Hart, Apr. 19, 1783, 11 children. Served as lt. Fincastle Company at Battle of Point Pleasant, 1774; commanded garrison Ft. Blair, 1774-75; attended proceedings of L.I. Treaty with Cherokee Indians; mem. Va. Legislature, 1779; col. Sullivan County (N.C.) Militia, 1780; organized a force, joined Gen. McDowell at Cherokee Ford (S.C.), 1780; captured Ft. Anderson on headwaters of Pacolet River, 1780; went to aid of Gen. Greene, 1781; mem. N.C. Legislature, 1781, 85; trustee Transylvania Sem. (now U.), 1783; mem. bd. War for Dist. of Ky., 1791; mem. Ky. Constl. Conv., 1792; 1st gov. Ky., 1792-96, 5th gov., 1812-16; assembled and led Ky. Volunteers to join Gen. Harrison in N.W. for invasion of Can.; apptd. (with Gen. Andrew Jackson) to make a treaty with Chickasaw Indians for purchase of lands west of Tennessee River; declined appointment as U.S. sec. of war, 1818; chmn. 1st bd. trustees Centre Coll., 1819-26; counties in 9 states named for him. Died July 18, 1826; buried "Traveller's Rest," nr. Stanford, Ky.

SHELBY, Joseph Orville, army officer; b. Lexington, Ky., Dec. 12, 1830; s. Orville and Anna M. (Boswell) S.; studied Transylvania U., 1846-49; m. Elizabeth N. Shelby, 1858, 7 children. Founder, rope factory, Waverly, Mo., 1852; commd. capt. Confederate Army, 1861; organizer cavalry brigade, 1862, became prominent cavalry comdr., invaded Mo. each year, 1862-64, held own against superior Union forces; brevetted brig. gen., 1864; crossed border to Mexico, 1865, his men voted to support Maximilian, who gave Shelby land upon which colony named Charlotta was formed; returned to Bates County, Mo., circa 1867; apptd. U.S. marshal for western dist. of Mo. by Pres. Cleveland, 1893. Died Adrian, Mo., Feb. 13, 1897; buried Forest Hill Cemetery, Kansas City, Mo.

SHELDON, David Newton, clergyman, coll. pres.; b. Suffield, Conn., June 26, 1807; s. David and Elizabeth (Hall) S.; grad. Williams Coll., 1830; attended Newton Theol. Instn., 1831-34; D.D., Brown U., 1847; m. Rachel Hobart Ripley, 1835, 4 sons, 1 dau. Ordained to ministry Baptist Ch., 1835; missionary to Paris, 1835-39; returned to Am., 1839, settled in Waterville, Me., 1842; pres. Waterville Coll., 1843-53; pastor Baptist Ch., Bath, Me., 1853-56; became a Unitarian, 1856, preacher in Bath, 1856-62; pastor Unitarian Ch., Waterville, 1862-78. Author: Sin and Redemption, 1856. Died Waterville, Oct. 4, 1889.

SHELDON, Edward Austin, educator; b. Perry Center, N.Y., Oct. 4, 1823; s. Eleazer and Laura (Austin) S.; attended Hamilton Coll., 1844-47, A.M., 1869; Ph.D., U. State N.Y., 1875; m. Frances Ann Bradford Stiles, May 16, 1849, at least 5 children including Mary Downing (Sheldon) Barnes. An organizer Orphan and Free Sch. Assn. of Oswego, N.Y., 1848-49; opened pvt. sch. for boys and girls, 1849; supt. pub. schs. Syracuse (N.Y.), circa 1851; established evening schs. and sch. libraries; sec. Oswego Bd. of Edn., 1853, head 1st system of free schs. there; pres. N.Y. State Tchrs. Assn., 1860; editor N.Y. Tchr., 1860; an organizer Oswego Primary Tchrs.' Training Sch. (1st city tng. sch. in U.S.), 1861, prin., 1862-97, secured state recognition and financial aid for sch., 1863, used Pestalozzian Ednl. Theory. Author: A Manual of Elementary Instruction, 1862; Teachers' Manual of Instruction in Reading, 1875. Died Oswego, Aug. 26, 1897.

SHELDON, William Evarts, educator; b. Dorset, Vt., Oct. 22, 1832; s. Julius King and Harriet (Newell) S.; grad. Burr Sem., Manchester, Vt., 1853; m. Mary Ames Soule, July 3, 1854, 1 dau. Prin., East Abington (Mass.) High Sch., 1853, effected reforms in adminstrn., established graded schs. in town; a founder, sec. Nat. Tchrs. Assn., Phila., 1857; prin. high sch., West Newton, Mass., 1858-64; pres. Mass. Tchrs. Assn., 1862-64; a founder Soc. of Arts, 1862; prin. Hancock Sch., Boston, also dir. primary schs., Boston, 1864, introduced Pestalozzian methods of instrn.; prin. Waltham Grammar Sch., 1869; bus. mgr. Boston Daily News, circa 1873; an organizer Jour. of Edn., 1875, advt. mgr., 1875-1900; sec. N.E.A., 1882-83, 85-86, pres., 1887. Died Apr. 16, 1900.

SHELEKHOV, Grigorii Ivanovich, trader, explorer; b. Rylsk, Russia, 1747; s. Ivan Shelekhov; m. Natalia Aleksieevna, 1781, at least 3 children including Ivan. Organizer (with others) fur trading and exploring expdn. to Alaska, Irkutsk, Siberia, 1783, set sail at head of expdn., 1783, reached Kodiak Island, Alaska, 1784; founder 1st Russian colony in Am.; named harbor The Three Saints; expanded activities and conquests to other islands and Alaskan mainland, 1784-86; returned to Siberia, 1788, given laudatory charter by Empress, but explicitly denied a monopoly; established hdqrs. in Irkutsk, organized several Russian fur trading cos., 1788, leading way for establishment Russian-Am. Co., 1799. Author: The Voyage of Grigorii Shelekhov . . . , 1791; A Sequel to the Voyage of Grigorii Shelekhov . . . in the Year 1788, 1792. Died Krkutsk, July 31, 1795.

SHELLABARGER, Samuel, congressman, lawyer; b. nr. Enon, Clark County, O., Dec. 10, 1817; grad. Miami U., Oxford, O., 1841; studied law. Admitted to bar, began practice of law, Springfield, O., 1846; mem. Ohio Ho. of Reps., 1852-53; mem. U.S. Ho. of Reps. (Republican) from Ohio, 37th, 39th, 40th, 42d congresses, 1861-63, 65-69, 71-73; minister to Portugal, 1869; mem. U.S. Civil Service Commn.,

1874-75. Died Washington, D.C., Aug. 7, 1896; buried Ferncliff Cemetery, Springfield.

SHELTON, Frederick William, clergyman, author; b. Jamaica, L.I., N.Y., May 20, 1815; s. Nathan and Eliza (Starman) S.; grad. Coll. of N..J (now Princeton), 1834; grad. Gen. Theol. Sem., N.Y.C., 1847; attended Union Hall Sem., Jamaica, N.Y.; m. Rebecca Conkling, circa 1836, 6 children. Ordained to ministry Episcopal Ch., N.Y.C., 1847; rector St. John's Ch., Huntington, L.I., 1848-52, Trinity Ch., Fishkill, N.Y., 1852-54, Christ Ch., Montpelier, Vt., 1854-66, St. Thomas Ch., East Somerville, Mass., 1866-67, St. Mark's Ch., Carthage Landing, N.Y., 1869-81. Author: The Trollopiad (satirical poem critical of English travelers in Am.), 1837; The Tinnecum Papers (sketches; best-known of works), 1838; contbr. to Knickerbocker mag.; published rural sketches, romances including "Crystalline, or The Heiress of Fall Down Castle" (best known), reprinted, 1854, 56, 82. Died Carthage Landing, June 20, 1881.

SHEPARD, Charles Biddle, congressman, lawyer; b. New Bern, N.C., Dec. 5, 1807; grad. U. N.C. at Chapel Hill, 1827; studied law. Admitted to bar, 1828, began practice of law, New Bern; mem. N.C. Ho. of Reps., 1831-32; mem. U.S. Ho. of Reps. (Democrat) from N.C., 25th-26th congresses, 1837-41. Died New Bern, Oct. 31, 1843; buried Cedar Grove Cemetery.

SHEPARD, Charles Upham, mineralogist; b. Little Compton, R.I., June 29, 1804; s. Rev. Mase and Deborah (Haskins) S.; grad. Amherst Coll., 1824, LL.D. (hon.), 1857; M.D. (hon.), Dartmouth, 1836; m. Harriet Taylor, Sept. 23, 1831, 3 children. Lectr. botany Yale, 1830-31, lectr. natural history, 1833-47; in charge of Brewster Scientific Inst., New Haven, Conn., 1831-33; prof. chemistry S.C. Med. Coll., 1834-60, 65-69; lectr. natural history Amherst Coll., 1844-77; visited all known mineral localities East of Mississippi River; discovered phosphate of lime, 1865; his collection of meteorites largest in America by 1886; wrote 40 papers for Am. Journ. of Science and Arts; mem. Imperial Soc. of Natural Science (St. Petersburg, Russia), Royal Soc. of Gottingen (Germany), Soc. of Natural Science (Vienna). Author textbook: Treatise on Mineralogy, 1832, (2d part 1835). Died Charleston, S.C., May 1, 1886.

SHEPARD, Thomas, clergyman; b. Towcester, Eng., Nov. 5, 1605; s. William and Miss (Bland) S.; B.A., Emmanuel Coll., Cambridge (Eng.) U., 1623, M.A., 1627; m. Margaret Tauteville, 1632; m. 2d, Joanna Hooker, 1637; m. 3d, Margaret Boradel, Sept. 8, 1647; 7 children including Thomas, Samuel, John, Jeremiah. Ordained deacon, then priest Ch. of Eng., 1627; came to Boston, 1635; pastor church at Newtown (now Cambridge), Mass., 1635; a founder Harvard, 1636; an active leader in Synod at Cambridge which condemned Antinomians, 1637; founded tradition of scholarships in U.S. through donations of food to students; initiated public confession of faith, also plan of ch. govt. (adopted in Synod of 1647) which became part of laws of Mass. and platform for Congregational churches in Am. Author: Three Valuable Pieces, Viz., Select Cases Resolved: First Principles of the Oracles of God; . . . And a Private Diary; Containing Meditations and Experiences Never Before Published, 1747 (edited and published by Nehemiah Adams as The Autobiography of Thomas Shepard, 1832. Died Cambridge, Aug. 25, 1649.

SHEPARD, William, army officer, congressman; b. Westfield, Mass., Dec. 1, 1737; s. John and Elizabeth (Noble) S.; m. Sarah Dewey, Jan. 31, 1760, 9 children. Served to capt. Provincial Army, French and Indian War, 1754-63 mem. Westfield Com. of Correspondence; lt. col. Mass. Regt., Continental Army, 1775, served through siege of Boston; lt. col. 3d Continental Inf., 1776, then col.; col. 4th Mass. Inf.; selectman Westfield, 1784-87; mem. lower house Mass. Legislature, 1785, 86; brig. gen. Mass. Militia, 1786, maj. gen., 1786; responsible for defense of fed. arsenal, and protection of fed. ct., Springfield, Mass. at time of Shays' Rebellion, repulsed Shays' attack on arsenal, 1787; mem. Mass. Exec. Council, 1788-90; presdl. elector, 1789; mem. Gov.'s Council, Mass., 1792-97; apptd. to treat with Penobscot Indians, 1796, with Six Nations, 1797; mem. U.S. Ho. of Reps. from Mass., 5th-7th congresses, 1797-1803. Died Westfield, Nov. 16, 1817; buried Mechanic Street Cemetery, Westfield.

SHEPARD, William Biddle, congressman, lawyer; b. New Bern, N.C., May 14, 1799; attended U. N.C. at Chapel Hill, 1813; grad. U. Pa. at Phila.; studied law. Admitted to bar, practiced law, Camden County, later in Elizabeth City, N.C.; also a banker; mem. U.S. Ho. of Reps. (Nat.-Republican) from N.C., 21st-24th congresses, 1829-37; mem. N.C. Senate, 1838-40, 48-50; mem. bd. trustees U. N.C., 1838-52. Died Elizabeth City, June 20, 1852; buried St. Paul's Churchyard, Edenton, N.C.

SHEPLER, Matthias, congressman; b. Westmoreland County, Pa., Nov. 11, 1790. Moved to Ohio, 1818, engaged in agriculture, Stark County; justice of peace, 30 years; county commr., 2 terms; mem. Ohio Ho. of Reps., 1829, Ohio Senate, 1832; mem. U.S. Ho. of Reps. (Democrat) from Ohio, 25th Congress, 1837-39; moved to Navarre, O., 1860. Died Navarre, Apr. 7, 1863; buried Shepler Church Cemetery, nr. Navarre.

SHEPLEY, Ether, senator; b. Groton, Mass., Nov. 2, 1789; s. John and Mary Gibson (Thurlow) S.; grad. Dartmouth, 1811, LL.D. (hon.), 1845; LL.D. (hon.), Waterville (now Colby) Coll., 1842; m. Anna Foster, June 10, 1816, 5 children including George Foster. Admitted to Mass. bar, 1814; practiced law, 1814-21; mem. Mass. Ho. of Reps., 1819; mem. Me. Constl. Conv., 1820; U.S. dist. atty. for Me., 1821-33; trustee Bowdoin Coll., 1829-66; mem. Me. Senate, 1833-36; mem. U.S. Senate from Me., 1833-36; asso. justice Me. Supreme Ct., 1836-48, chief justice, 1848-55; sole commr. to revise and print public laws of Me., 1856, published as The Revised Statutes of the State of Maine. Died Portland, Me., Jan. 15, 1877; buried Evergreen Cemetery, Portland.

SHEPLEY, George Foster, army officer, jurist; b. Saco, Me., Jan. 1, 1819; s. Ether and Anna (Foster) S.; grad. Dartmouth, 1837, LL.D. (hon.), 1878; m. Lucy A. Hayes, July 24, 1844; m. 2d, Helen Merrill, May 23, 1872; 2 children. Practiced law, Bangor, Me., 1839; U.S. dist. atty. for Me., 1848-49, 53-61; del. Democratic Nat. Conv., Charleston, 1860, and adjourned session in Balt.; commd. col. 12th Regt., 12th Me. Volunteers, 1861; mil. cmdt. of New Orleans, 1862, assigned to command of defenses of New Orleans; mil. gov. La., 1862-64; commd. brig. gen., 1862; in command of Dist. of Eastern Va. in XXV Army Corps under Gen. Weitzel, 1864; mil. gov. Richmond, 1865; circuit judge U.S. Court, specializing in equity and patent cases, 1869-78. Died Portland, Me., July 20, 1878.

SHEPPERD, Augustine Henry, congressman, lawyer; b. Rockford, N.C., Feb. 24, 1792; studied law. Admitted to bar, began practice of law, Surry County, N.C.; mem. N.C. Ho. of Reps., 1822-26; Democratic presdl. elector, 1824; mem. U.S. Ho. of Reps. from N.C., 20th-25th, 27th, 30th-31st congresses, 1827-39, 41-43, 47-51; Whig presdl. elector, 1844. Died "Good Spring," Salem (now Winston-Salem), N.C., July 11, 1864; buried Salem Cemetery.

SHERBURNE, John Samuel, congressman, jurist; b. Portsmouth, N.H., 1757; grad. Dartmouth, 1776; grad. law dept. Harvard. Admitted to bar, began practice of law, Portsmouth, 1776; served to rank brigade maj. of staff Continental Army during Revolutionary War, lost leg at Battle of Butts Hill (R.I.), 1778; mem. U.S. Ho. of Reps. from N.H., 3d-4th congresses, 1793-97; U.S. dist. atty. for N.H., 1801-04; judge U.S. Dist. Ct. for N.H., 1804-30. Died Portsmouth, Aug. 2, 1830.

SHEREDINE, Upton, congressman, jurist; b. nr. Balt., 1740. Del. Md. Constl. Conv., 1776; mem. Md. Ho. of Dels., 1777, Md. Senate, 1776-81; judge County Ct. of Appeals, 1777; mem. spl. ct. to try, convict and sentence Tories, 1781; judge Frederick County (Md.) Orphans Ct., many years from 1777; asso. judge 5th Jud. Dist., 1791; mem. U.S. Ho. of Reps. (Democrat) from Md., 2d Congress, 1791-93; apptd. commr. 4th Div. of Md. for valuation of land and houses and enumeration of slaves, 1798. Died "Midhill," nr. Liberty, Md., Jan. 14, 1800; buried pvt. cemetery at "Midhill."

SHERIDAN, George Augustus, congressman; b. Millbury, Mass., Feb. 22, 1840. Moved to Chgo., 1858; became a publisher; served as capt. Co. D, 88th Regt., Ill. Volunteer Inf. during Civil War; moved to New Orleans, 1866; served as brig. gen. militia on Gov. Warmouth's staff; sheriff Carroll Parish (La.), 1867; mem. U.S. Ho. of Reps. (Liberal) from La., 43d Congress, 1873-75; recorder of deeds for D.C., 1878-81. Died Nat. Soldiers' Home, Va., Oct. 7, 1896; buried Arlington (Va.) Nat. Cemetery.

SHERIDAN, Philip Henry, army officer; b. Albany, N.Y., Mar. 6, 1831; s. John and Mary (Meenagh) S.; grad. U.S. Mil. Acad., 1853; m. Irene Rucker, June 3, 1875. Served in Rio Grande and N.W., 1853-60; commd. capt. 13th Inf., U.S. Army, S.W. Mo., 1861, col. 2d Mich. Cavalry, 1862; commd. brig. gen. U.S. Volunteers, 1862, promoted maj. gen. (for saving Rosecrans at Stone River), 1862; won Battle of Cedar Creek, 1862; commanded the Twentieth Corps of the Army of the Cumberland at battles of Chickamauga and Chattanooga, 1863; given command of cavalry Army of Potomac by Gen. Grant, 1864, participated in battles of Spotsylvania Ct. House, Cold Harbor; raided Confederate supply lines nr. Richmond, destroyed railroads, 1864; commanded Army of Shenandoah, destroyed all supplies in Shenandoah Valley on which Confederate Army had depended, in the year 1864; commissioned major general of U.S. Army, 1864; led raid from Winchester to Petersburg, destroyed Confederate railroads and depots, inflicted further defeat upon Gen. Early at Waynesboro, 1865; position of his forces at Battle of Five Forks made possible the turning of Confederate flank, 1865, forced evacuation of Petersburg by Lee's Army, cut off Confederate retreat at Appomattox; cmdr. Div. of Gulf, 1865-67; mil. gov. 5th Mil. Dist. (comprised La. and Tex.), 1867; transferred to Dept. of Mo. by Pres. Johnson because of harshness of his adminstrn., settled hostile Indians on allotted reservations. 1867; promoted lt. gen., 1869; observed operations in Franco-Prussian War, 1870-71; commanded Western and Southwestern divs., 1878; became comdr. gen. U.S. Army, 1884; given rank of gen. by U.S. Congress, 1888. Author: Personal Memoirs, 2 vols., 1888. Died Nonquitt, Mass., Aug. 5, 1888; buried Arlington (Va.) Nat. Cemetery.

SHERMAN, John, clergyman; b. Dedham, Eng., Dec. 26, 1613; s. Edmund and Joan (Makin) S.; attended St. Catharine's Coll., Cambridge (Eng.) U. (completed all degree requirements not granted degree because of refusal to take religious test); married twice; m. 2d, Mary Launce, circa 1645, at least 13 children (according to Cotton Mather, 25 or 26 children). Came to Mass. Bay Colony, 1634, ordained to ministry Puritan Ch., became asso. minister, Watertown, Mass.; gentleman farmer nr. Milford, Conn., sometimes preached and taught in area, 1636-47; a founder of ch., Wethersfield, Conn., 1636; dep. to Gen. Ct. from Milford, 1643-47; became widely known as preacher in Conn. and Mass.; pastor ch., Watertown, 1647-85; lectr. mathematics Harvard, circa 1650-80, became overseer, 1672, mem. coll. corp., 1677; published math. lectures in An Almanack of Celestial Motions, 1674, 76, 77. Died Aug. 8, 1685.

SHERMAN, Judson W., congressman; b. N.Y., 1808. Held several local offices, Angelica, N.Y.; clk., Allegany County (N.Y.), 1831-37; dep. treas. N.Y., circa 1850; mem. U.S. Ho. of Reps. (Republican) from N.Y., 35th Congress, 1857-59; served as capt., commissary of subsistence of Volunteers, 1861. Died Angelica, Nov. 12, 1881; buried Until the Day Dawn Cemetery.

SHERMAN, Roger, Continental congressman, jurist; b. Newton, Mass., Apr. 19, 1721; s. William and Mehetabel (Wellington) S.; M.A. (hon.), Yale, 1768; m. Elizabeth Hartwell, Nov. 17, 1749; m. 2d, Rebecca (or Rebekah) Prescott, May 12, 1763; 15 children. Surveyor, New Haven County, Conn., 1745-52, Litchfield County, Conn.; 1752-58; published series of almanacs between 1750-61; admitted to Litchfield (Conn.) bar, 1754; mem. Conn. Gen. Assembly, 1755, 56, 58-61; 64-66; moved to New Haven, Conn., 1761; mem. Conn. Senate, 1766-85; judge Superior Ct. of Conn., 1766-67, 73-88; signer Articles of Association, 1774; mem. com. on declaration of rights 1st Continental Congress, 1774, mem. com. apptd. to draft Declaration of Independence; one of leading figures in shaping laws of Congress, 1774-81; mem. Continental Congress, 1783-84; mem. com. on Articles of Confederation, 1774; mem. Council of Safety of Conn., 1777-79, 82; with Richard Law revised statutory law of Conn., 1783; mayor New Haven, 1784-93; leading member of compromise group in U.S. Constl. Conv., Phila., 1787, introduced Conn. Compromise; mem. U.S. Ho. of Reps. from Conn., 1st Congress, 1789-91; mem. U.S. Senate from Conn., June 13, 1791-July 23, 1793; only member of Continental Congress who signed all 4 of great state papers, Declaration of 1774, Declaration of Independence, Articles of Confederation, U.S. Constitution. Died New Haven, July 23, 1793; buried Grove Street Cemetery, New Haven.

SHERMAN, Socrates Norton, congressman, physician; b. Barre, Vt., July 22, 1801; grad. Mt. Castleton Med. Coll., 1824. Began practice of medicine, Ogdensburg, N.Y., 1825; mem. U.S. Ho. of Reps. (Republican) from N.Y., 37th Congress, 1861-63; served as maj. and surgeon 34th Regt., N.Y. Volunteer Inf., during Civil War, brevetted lt. col. U.S. Volunteers. Died Ogdensburg, Feb. 1, 1873; buried Ogdensburg Cemetery.

SHERMAN, Thomas West, army officer; b. Newport, R.I., Mar. 26, 1813; s. Elijah and Martha (West) S.; grad. U.S. Mil. Acad., 1836; m. Mary Shannon, circa 1850, at least 1 child. Commd. 2d lt. U.S. Army, 1836; served in Cherokee Indian Territory during Fla. War, 1836-38; became q.m., 1846; served as capt. under Gen. Zachary Taylor, Mexican War, 1846; brevetted maj. for service in Battle of Buena Vista, 1848; commanded expdn. to Yellow River, Minn.; served in expdn. to Kettle Lake, Dakota, 1859; maj. and lt. col. U.S. Army, brig. gen. U.S. Volunteers, 1861; seized Bull's Bay, S.C. and Fernandina, Fla., 1861; commanded land forces Port Royal expdn., Oct. 1861-Mar. 1862, captured Port Royal; commanded div.

under Gen. Henry W. Halleck, 1862; col. 3d Arty., 1863; brevetted brig. gen. U.S. Army for gallant service at capture Port Hudson, 1864; successful in command of defenses of New Orleans, So. and Eastern Dists. of La.; maj. gen. U.S. Volunteers, circa 1865; ret. as maj. gen. U.S. Army, circa 1871. Died Newport, Mar. 16, 1879.

SHERMAN, William Tecumseh, army officer; b. Lancaster, O., Feb. 8, 1820; s. Charles Robert and Mary (Hoyt) S.; grad. U.S. Mil. Acad., 1840; m. Ellen Ewing, May 1, 1850, 8 children. Commd. 1st lt. U.S. Army, 1841; served in Ga., 1844-45; served as aide to Gen. Philip Kearny during Mexican War; resigned commn., 1853, entered banking bus., San Francisco; became supt. new mil. acad., Alexandria, La., 1859; pres. of a street ry. co., St. Louis, 1861; commd. col. 13th Inf., U.S. Army, commanding brigade under Gen. McDowell at 1st Battle of Bull Run; brig. gen. U.S. Volunteers, comdr. Dept. of Cumberland, 1861; served in Dept. of Mo., 1861-62; served with distinction under Gen. Grant at Shiloh for which promoted maj. gen. U.S. Volunteers, 1862; commanded Dist. of Memphis, 1862; promoted to brig. gen. U.S. Army for leadership XV Corps in advance on Vicksburg, 1863; comdr. Army of Tenn., participated in Chattanooga campaign, relieved Gen. A. E. Burnside of his command of Army of Potomac, Knoxville, 1863; supreme comdr. in West, led attack on Atlanta which fell by siege, 1864, for this victory given rank maj. gen. U.S. Army; his famed March to the Sea followed, for which he received harsh criticism (although the orders he gave in this campaign were to destroy mil. installations and mfg. facilities only, great destruction of pvt. property took place); his view held that the paralysis of the enemy and quick end of the war could best be accomplished by impressing civilian population with futility of resistance through destruction of property rather than lives; this policy of devastation continued with greater vigor in S.C., 1865, until surrender of Gen. Joseph Johnston, 1865; offered Johnston liberal terms (illustrating Sherman's understanding of conditions in South); received command Div. of Mississippi after Civil War, instrumental in constrn. transcontiental railroad; promoted lt. gen. U.S. Army, 1866; sent on diplomatic mission to Mexico, 1866; comdg. gen. U.S. Army, 1869-83; established mil. sch., Ft. Leavenworth (Kan.), 1881; ret. from active service, 1883. Author: Memoirs, 1875. Died N.Y.C., Feb. 14, 1891.

SHERRERD, William D., ins. broker; b. Phila., Apr. 11, 1816. Employed in counting house owned by Stephen Baldwin, 1832-37; bookkeeper, gen. clk. for agy. of Delaware County Ins. Co., 1838-43, elected sec., 1843-46, specialized in marine ins.; comml. agt., ins. broker, Phila.; sec. Merc. Mut. Ins. Co., 1850; v.p. Phila. Ins. Co., 1852-53. Died June 13, 1869.

SHERRILL, Eliakim, congressman; b. Greenville, Ulster County, N.Y., Feb. 16, 1813; attended public schs. Tanner and farmer; held several local offices; served as maj. N.Y. Militia; mem. U.S. Ho. of Reps. (Whig) from N.Y., 30th Congress, 1847-49; mem. N.Y. Senate, 1854; organized, served as col. 126th N.Y. Volunteer Regt. during Civil War, wounded at Harpers Ferry; commanded 3d Brigade, 3d Div., 2d Army Corps at Battle of Gettysburg. Mortally wounded at Gettysburg, July 3, 1863, died next day; buried Washington Street Cemetery, Geneva, N.Y.

SHERWIN, Thomas, educator; b. Westmoreland, N. H., Mar. 26, 1799; s. David and Hannah (Pritchard) S.; grad. Harvard, 1825; m. Mary King Gibbens, June 10, 1836, at least 3 children. Headmaster academy in Lexington, Mass., 1825-26; mathematics tutor Harvard, 1827; opened pvt. sch. for boys, Boston, 1828; submaster English High Sch. (1st sch. to be called high sch.), Boston, 1829, prin., 1837-69, made sch. the leading ednl. instn. of its grade in U.S., mem. Am. Acad. Arts and Sciences for achievements in high sch. instrn., 1836; a founder Am. Inst. Instrn., 1830, pres., 1853-54; a founder Mass. State Tchrs. Assn., 1845; an original editor Mass. Teacher, often mem. editorial bd.; founder Mass. Inst. Tech., dir. and counselor until 1869. Author: Elementary Treatise on Algebra, 1841; Common School Algebra, 1845. Died Dedham, Mass., July 23, 1869.

SHERWOOD, Adiel, clergyman, educator; b. Ft. Edwards, N.Y., Oct. 3, 1791; s. Adiel and Sarah S.; grad. Union Coll., 1817, LL.D. (hon.); attended Andover Theol. Sem., 1817-18; m. Anne Adams (Smith) Early, May 17, 1821; m. 2d, Emma Heriot, May 1824; 5 children including Thomas Adiel. Ordained to ministry Baptist Ch., 1820; itinerant preacher and organizer of churches in Ga., circa 1820-37; treas. Bapt. State Conv. of Ga. for many years; a founder Mercer Inst. (later Mercer U.), prof. sacred lit., 1838-41; prof. George Washington U., 1837-38; pres. Shurtleff Coll., Ill., 1841-46, Masonic Coll., Lexington, Mo., 1848-49, Marshall Coll., Griffin, Ga., 1857-61. Author several pamphlets and books including: Notes on the New Testament, 2 vols., 1856. Died St. Louis, Aug. 18, 1879.

SHERWOOD, Henry, congressman, lawyer; b. Bridgeport, Conn., Oct. 9, 1813; attended common schs., N.Y.; studied law. Served in Tex. Army under Sam Houston during Tex. War for Independence, 1836-37; moved to Wellsboro, Pa., 1840; admitted to bar, 1847, practiced law, Wellsboro; burgess Wellsboro; mem. U.S. Ho. of Reps. (Democrat) from Pa., 42d Congress, 1871-73; pres. Wellsboro & Lawrenceville R.R., also Pa. div. Pine Creek road. Died Wellsboro, Nov. 10, 1896; buried Wellsboro Cemetery.

SHERWOOD, Samuel, congressman, lawyer; b. Kingsbury, N.Y., Apr. 24, 1779; studied law, Kingston and Delhi, N.Y. Admitted to bar, 1800, practiced law, Delhi; mem. U.S. Ho. of Reps. (Federalist) from N.Y., 13th Congress, 1813-15; practiced law, N.Y.C., 1830-58. Died N.Y.C., Oct. 31, 1862; buried Woodlawn Cemetery, Delhi.

SHERWOOD, Samuel Burr, congressman, lawyer; b. Northfield Society (later Weston), Conn., Nov. 26, 1767; grad. Yale, 1786; studied law. Admitted to bar, began practice of law, Fairfield (now Westport), Conn.; mem. Conn. Ho. of Reps., 1809-15; mem. Conn. Senate, 1816; mem. U.S. Ho. of Reps. (Federalist) from N.Y., 15th Congress, 1817-19; ret. from practice law, 1831. Died Westport, Apr. 27, 1833; buried Evergreen Cemetery.

SHIEL, George Knox, congressman, lawyer; b. Ireland, 1825; came to U.S., lived in New Orleans, then in Ohio; studied law. Admitted to bar, practiced law; moved to Ore., 1854, began practice of law, Salem, Ore.; mem. U.S. Ho. of Reps. (Democrat, contested election) from Ore., 37th Congress, July 30, 1861-63; barred from practice of law for refusal to take oath of allegiance, lived in retirement. Accidentally killed, Salem, Dec. 12, 1893; buried Odd Fellows Cemetery.

SHIELDS, Benjamin Glover, congressman, diplomat; b. Abbeville, S.C., 1808; moved (with father) to Ala. Mem. Ala. Ho. of Reps., 1834; mem. U.S. Ho. of Reps. (Whig) from Ala., 27th Congress, 1841-43; U.S. chargé d'affaires to Venezuela (commd. by Pres. Polk), 1845-50; engaged in planting, Tex., until death.

SHIELDS, Ebenezer J., congressman, lawyer; b. Ga., Dec. 22, 1778; grad. U. Nashville (Tenn.), 1827; studied law. Admitted to bar, began practice of law, Pulaski, Tenn.; mem. Tenn. Ho. of Reps., 1833-35; mem. U.S. Ho. of Reps. (Whig) from Tenn., 24th-25th congresses, 1835-39; moved to Memphis, Tenn., 1844, continued practice of law. Died nr. La Grange, Tex., Apr. 21, 1846.

SHIELDS, James, congressman; b. Banbridge, County Down, Ireland, Apr. 13, 1762; grad. U. Glasgow (Scotland), 1786; attended med. coll., 2 years. Came to U.S., 1791, became sch. tchr., Frederick County, Va.; naturalized, 1804; moved to Ohio, 1807; mem. Ohio Ho. of Reps., 1806-27; Democratic presdl. elector, 1828; mem. U.S. Ho. of Reps. (Jackson Democrat) from Ohio, 21st Congress, 1829-31. Killed in stagecoach accident nr. Venice, O., Aug. 13, 1831; buried Venice Cemetery.

SHIELDS, James, senator; b. Altimore, County Tyrone. Ireland, May 10, 1810; s. Charles and Katherine (McDonnell) S.; m. Mary Ann Carr, 1861, at least 3 children. Came to N.Y.C., circa 1826; mem. Ill. Ho. of Reps., 1836; state auditor Ill., 1839, helped correct state's disordered finances; mem. Supreme Ct. Ill., 1843-45; commr. to gen. land office, Washington, D.C., 1845-47; served as brig. gen. Ill. Volunteers, brevetted maj. gen. for gallantry at Cerro Gordo, Mexican War, 1847; apptd. gov. Ore. Territory, 1849, resigned immediately to become mem. U.S. Senate from Ill., Oct. 27, 1849-55; settled in Minn. Territory, 1855, encouraged Irish immigration into region by organizing twps. of Shieldsville, Erin, Kilkenny, Montgomery; founded (with Alexander Faribault) Faribault Twp.; mem. U.S. Senate from Minn., May 11, 1858-59; went to San Francisco, 1859; mine mgr., Mazatlan, Mexico 1861; served as brig. gen. Ill. Volunteers in Shenandoah Valley campaign during Civil War, 1861-63; railroad commr. in Cal., 1863-66, moved to Mo., 1866; mem. Mo. Legislature, 1874, 79; adjutant gen. Mo., 1877; mem. U.S. Senate from Mo., Jan. 22, Mar. 3, 1879. Died Ore., June 1, 1879; buried St. Mary's Cemetery, Carrollton, Mo.

SHIKELLAMY, Indian chief; b. probably into Cayuga tribe, early adopted by Oneida tribe. Sent by the Six Nations to assert the right of Iroquois dominion over Delaware and Shawnee tribes and to prevent their selling land to white govts., circa 1728; kept English informed of French activity among Indians; negotiator treaties with Pa., 1736, with Md. and Va., 1744, in which Iroquois received indemnities and lands on lower Delaware River; baptized a Roman Catholic, later received into Moravian communion. Died Shamokin, Dec. 6, 1748.

SHILLABER, Benjamin Penhallow, editor, humorist; b. Portsmouth, N.H., July 12, 1814; s. William and Sarah (Sawyer) S.; m. Ann Tappan de Rochemont. Compositor, Royal Gazette of Brit. Guina, 1835-38; with Boston Post, 1838-50, 53-56, wrote about Mrs. Partington (whom he invented), 1847-50, local reporter, 1853-56; editor Pathfinder and Ry. Guide, 1850-51, The Carpet-Bag (humor mag. to which many famed writers contbd.), 1851-53; mem. staff Saturday Evening Gazette, 1856-66. Author: Rhymes with Reason and Without, 1853; Life and Sayings of Mrs. Partington, 1854. Died Chelsea, Mass., Nov. 25, 1890.

SHINN, Asa, clergyman; b. N.J., May 3, 1781; s. Jonathan and Mary (Clarke) S.; m. Phebe Barnes, 1807; m. 2d, Mary Bennington (Wrenshall) Gibson; 5 children. Convert to Methodist faith, 1798; circuit preacher, 1801-25, joined Balt. Conf., Meth. Episcopal Ch., 1801, transferred to Western Conf., 1803, returned to Balt. Conf., 1807, transferred to Pitts. Conf., 1825; experienced 4 periods of insanity, 1816, 20, 43; a voluminous and effective contbr. to The Mutual Rights of Ministers and Members of the Methodist Episcopal Church; a founder separate Meth. Protestant Ch., 1830; pres. newly-constituted Ohio Conf.; pres. Pitts. Conf., 1833; editor (with Nicholas Snethen) Mutual Rights and Methodist Protestant, Balt., 1834-36. Author theol. tracts including "An Essay On the Plan of Salvation," 1812; "On the Benevolence and Rectitude of the Supreme Being," 1840. Died Brattleboro, Vt., Feb. 11, 1853.

SHINN, William Norton, congressman, farmer; b. Burlington County, N.J., Oct. 24, 1782; attended public schs. Engaged in agriculture; sheriff Burlington County, 1825-28; mem. N.J. Gen. Assembly, 1828; mem. N.J. Council, 1829-31; chmn. N.J. Democratic Central Com., 1832; mem. U.S. Ho. of Reps. (Jackson Democrat) from N.J., 23d-24th congresses, 1833-37; pres. Burlington Agrl. Assn., 1853-54; dir. Camden & Amboy R.R. Co. Died Mt. Holly, N.J., Aug. 18, 1871; buried Mt. Holly Cemetery.

SHIPHERD, John Jay, missionary, coll. founder; b. West Granville, N.Y., Mar. 28, 1802; s. Zebulon Rudd and Elizabeth (Bull) S.; M.A. (hon.), Middlebury Coll., 1830; m. Esther Raymond, 1824, 7 children. Ordained as evangelist, 1827; published semi-annual The Sabbath School Guide; missionary in Elyria, O., 1830-32; collaborated with Philo P. Stewart to found Oberlin Coll., 1832; traveled through N.Y. and New Eng. securing money, tchrs., settlers, 1832-33, 1st settlement made in Ohio, 1833; presided at depts. of the Oberlin Collegiate Inst., 1833; Oberlin became center of reform and revival piety; secured firm establishment by bringing dissatisfied students as well as financial backing from Lane Sem., 1835; led small group of people who established colony and sch., Olivet, Mich., 1844. Died Olivet, Sept. 16, 1844.

SHIPHERD, Zebulon Rudd, congressman, lawyer; b. Granville, N.Y., Nov. 15, 1768; studied law. Admitted to bar, began practice of law, Granville; mem. U.S. Ho. of Reps. (Federalist) from N.Y., 13th Congress, 1813-15; trustee Middlebury (Vt.) Coll., 1819-41; moved to Moriah, Essex County, circa 1830. Died Moriah, Nov. 1, 1841; buried Moriah Corners Cemetery.

SHIPP, Albert Micajah, clergyman, coll. pres.; b. Stokes County, N.C., June 15, 1819; s. John and Elizabeth (Oglesby) S.; grad. U. N.C., 1840, A. M., 1845, LL.D. (hon.), 1883; D.D. (hon.), Randolph-Macon Coll.; m. Mary Gillepsie, several children. Admitted on trial to S.C. Conf. of Meth. Episcopal Ch., 1841, ordained deacon, 1843, elder, 1844; pres. Greensboro (N.C.) Female Coll., 1848-49; prof. history U. N.C., 1849-59; pres. Wofford Coll., Spartanburg, S.C., 1859-75; prof. exegetical theology Vanderbilt U., 1875-85. Author: The History of Methodism in South Carolina, 1883. Died Cleveland Springs, N.C., June 27, 1887.

SHIPPEN, Edward, mayor Phila.; b. Methley, Yorkshire, Eng., 1639; s. William and Mary (Nunes) S.; m. Elizabeth Lybrand, 1671; m. 2d, Rebecca (Howard) Richardson, Sept. 4, 1689; m. 3d, Esther (Wilcox) James, Aug. 1, 1706; 11 children including Joseph. Came to Boston, 1668; joined Soc. of Friends, 1671; moved to Phila., 1694; mem. Pa. Provincial Assembly, 1695, 1700-01, 05-06, speaker, 1695; elective mem. Pa. Provincial Council, 1696-1701, appointive mem., pres., 1702-12; presiding justice Phila. County Cts., 1698-1701; asso. justice Pa. Supreme Ct., 1699-1703; mayor Phila. (apptd. by William Penn), 1701-12; a proprietary commr. of property, 1701-12; acting gov. Pa., 1703-04. Died Phila., Oct. 2, 1712.

SHIPPEN, Edward, jurist; b. Phila., Feb. 16, 1729; s. Edward and Sarah (Plumley) S.; m. Margaret Francis, Nov. 29, 1753, 9 children including Margaret (Shippen) Arnold Called to English bar, 1750; admitted to Pa. Supreme Ct. bar, 1750; mem. Common Council of Phila., 1755-56, clk., 1758; clk. Phila. City Ct., 1758; prothonotary Pa.

Supreme Ct., circa 1762-78; mem. Pa. Provincial Council, 1770-75; wrote earliest published law reports of Pa. Supreme Ct.; judge Ct. of Vice Admiralty, 1752-76; moderate Loyalist during Am. Revolution; pres. Ct. of Common Pleas of Phila. County, 1784-91; justice of peace, 1785-86; pres. Pa. Ct. of Quarter Sessions of Peace, Oyer and Terminer, 1785-86; judge High Ct. of Errors and Appeals, 1784-91; asso. justice Pa. Supreme Ct., 1791-99, chief justice, 1799-1805; Federalist; impeached by Pa. Democratic Assembly, 1804, acquitted by Senate, 1805. Died Phila., Apr. 15, 1806.

SHIPPEN, William, Continental congressman, physician; b. Phila., Oct. 1, 1712; studied medicine. Practiced medicine, Phila.; a founder Public Acad., trustee 1749; a founder Coll. of Phila. (now U. Pa.), trustee, 1749-79; a founder Coll. of N.J. (now Princeton), trustee, 1765-96; mem. Am. Philos. Soc., v.p. many years from 1768; mem. Continental Congress from Pa., 1778-80. Died Germantown, Pa., Nov. 4, 1801; buried 1st Presbyn. Ch. Cemetery, Phila.

SHIPPEN, William, physician, educator; b. Phila., Oct. 21, 1736; s. William and Susannah (Harrison) S.; grad. Princeton, 1754; M.D., U. Edinburgh (Scotland), 1761; m. Alice Lee, 1760, 1 child. Pioneer in establishing courses in midwifery and anatomy using dissection, Phila., 1762; prof. anatomy and surgery med. school Coll. of Phila., 1765; chief physician, dir. gen. Continental Army hosp. in N.J., 1776; chief med. dept. Continental Army, 1777; submitted plan for reorgn. army med. dept. to Continental Congress, 1777 (adopted 1777); physician Pa. Hosp., 1778-79; prof. anatomy U. State of Pa., 1779; prof. anatomy, surgery and midwifery U. Pa., Phila., 1791; a founder Coll. of Physicians of Phila., pres., 1805-08. Died Phila., July 11, 1808.

SHIRLEY, William, colonial gov.; b. Preston, Sussex, Eng., Dec. 2, 1694; s. William and Elizabeth (Godman) S.; A.B., Pembroke Coll., Cambridge (Eng.) U., 1714-15; m. Frances Barker, circa 1718; m. 2d, Julie Shirley, circa 1751; 9 children including Thomas. Admitted to English bar, 1720; came to Boston, 1731; judge of admiralty, 1733; advocate gen., circa 1735; gov. Mass., 1741-49, 53-56, abolished land bank, 1741, stabilized paper currency, planned expdn. to Louisbourg (fortress captured largely through his efforts and administrn; 1745; used reimbursement from Parliament for Mass. war effort (1744-45) to retire paper currency and establish sound finances; commd. col. Brit. regt. to be raised from New Eng. provincial troops, 1746; mem. commn. in Paris to determine boundary line between French N.Am. and New Eng., 1749-53; maj. gen. at outbreak French and Indian Wars, 1755; one of 5 govs. who attended council of war with Gen. Braddock, Alexandria, Va., Apr. 1755; became comdr. all Brit. forces after Braddock's death, July 1755; failed in Niagara expdn. because of lack of supplies and troops, end of 1755, superseded as comdr.; went to Eng., 1756, malfeasance charges against him dropped; commd. lt. gen., 1757; gov. Bahama Islands, 1761-67. Died Shirley Place, Roxbury, Mass., Mar. 24, 1771.

SHOBER, Francis Edwin, congressman, lawyer; b. Salem (now Winston-Salem), N.C., Mar. 12, 1831; grad. U. N.C. at Chapel Hill, 1851; studied law; at least 1 son, Francis Emanuel. Admitted to bar, 1853, began practice of law, Salisbury, N.C., 1854; mem. N.C. Ho. of Commons, 1862, 64, N.C. Senate, 1865, 87; mem. U.S. Ho. of Reps. (Democrat) from N.C., 41st-42d congresses, 1869-73; del. N.C. Constl. Conv., 1875; judge Rowan County, 1877-78; apptd. chief clk. U.S. Senate, 45th Congress, acting sec., 47th Congress, Oct. 24, 1881-Mar. 3, 1883; del. Dem. nat. convs., 1880, 84. Died Salisbury, May 29, 1896; buried Oakdale Cemetery.

SHOEMAKER, Lazarus Denison, congressman; b. Kingston, Pa., Nov. 5, 1819; attended Nazareth (Pa.) Hall, also Kenyon Coll., Gambier, O.; grad. Yale, 1840; studied law. Admitted to bar, 1842, began practice of law, Wilkes-Barre, Pa.; mem. Pa. Senate, 1866-70; mem. U.S. Ho. of Reps. (Republican) from Pa., 42d-43d congresses, 1871-75; resumed practice of law, also a banker. Died Wilkes-Barre, Sept. 9, 1893; buried Forty Fort (Pa.) Cemetery.

SHOEMAKER, Robert, pharmacist; b. Shoemakertown, Pa., Feb. 1, 1817; s. Richard M. and Sarah (Cleaver) S.; M.A. (hon.), Phila. Coll. of Pharmacy, 1894; m. Elizabeth Moore, 1837; m. 2d, Ann Summers, 1858; 13 children including Richard M., Thomas E., Benjamin H. Became apprentice in drug store owned by William Scattergood, Phila., 1832, owner of store, 1837-56; founded (with his brother Benjamin) Robert Shoemaker & Co., wholesale drug firm, Phila., 1856; dir. various ins. cos., banks. Died Phila., Dec. 17, 1896.

SHOLES, Christopher Latham, editor, inventor; b. Mooresbury, Pa., Feb. 14, 1819; s. Orrin Sholes; m. Mary Jane McKinney, Feb. 4, 1841, 10 children. Editor, Wis. Enquirer, 1840, Southport (later Kenosha, Wis.) Telegraph, 1841-45; postmaster Southport, 1845; mem. Wis. Senate, 2 terms, Wis. Assembly, 1 term; editor Milw. News, 1860, then Milw. Sentinel; collector Port of Milw., circa 1862; patentee (with Samuel Soule) paging machine, 1864; patentee improvement on numbering machine, 1867; patentee (with Glidden and Soule) typewriter, 1868; patentee improvements, 1871, sold patents to Remington Arms Co., 1873. Died Milw., Feb. 17, 1890.

SHOONMAKER, Marius, congressman; b. Kingston, Ulster County, N.Y., Apr. 24, 1811; attended Kingston Acad.; grad. Yale, 1830. Admitted to bar, 1833, practiced law, Kingston; mem. N.Y. Senate, 1850-51; mem. U.S. Ho. of Reps. (Whig) from N..Y, 32d Congress, 1851-53; auditor canal dept. N.Y. State, 1854-55, supt. banking dept., 1854-56; pres. Kingston Bd. Edn. for 9 years; pres. Village of Kingston, 1866, 69-70; del. N.Y. State Constl. Conv., 1867; pres. bd. dirs. Kingston. Died Kingston, Jan. 5, 1894; buried Wiltwyck Rural Cemetery.

SHORT, Charles, educator; b. Haverhill, Mass., May 28, 1821; s. Charles and Rebecca (George) S.; grad. Harvard, 1846, A.M. (hon.), 1847; LL.D. (hon.), Kenyon Coll., 1868; m. Anne Jean Lyman, 1849, 4 children. Headmaster, Roxbury Latin Sch., 1848-53; head of own sch. in Phila., 1853-63; pres. Kenyon Coll., Gambier, O., 1863-67; prof. Latin Columbia, N.Y.C., 1867-86; mem. Am. Com. on Revision of Bible, 1872. Author monograph: The Order of Words in Attic Greek Prose, 1870; editor Schmitz and Zumpts' Advanced Latin Exercises; Mitchell's Ancient Geography. Died N.Y.C., Dec. 24, 1886; buried Sleepy Hollow Cemetery, N.Y.C.

SHORT, Charles Wilkins, physician, educator, botanist; b. "Greenfield," Woodford County, Ky., Oct. 6, 1794; s. Peyton and Maria (or Mary) (Symmes) S.; grad. Transylvania U., 1810; M.D., U. Pa., 1815; m. Mary Henry Churchill, Nov. 1815, 6 children. Prof. medicine and med. botany Transylvania U., 1825-38; initiated publication (with Dr. John Cooke) Transylvania Jour. Medicine and Associate Scis., 1828; with Robert Peter and H.A. Griswold wrote "A Catalogue of the Native Phaenogamous Plants and Ferns of Kentucky," 1833, prepared and distributed 25,000 specimens among correspondents in Europe and America within 5 years; prof. medicine Med. Inst. of Louisville (Ky.), 1838-48; valuable herbarium of over 15,000 species now belongs to Nat. Acad. Natural Scis., Phila. Died "Hayfield," nr. Louisville, Mar. 7, 1863; buried Cave Hill Cemetery, Ky.

SHORT, Sidney Howe, inventor; b. Columbus, O., Oct. 8, 1858; s. John and Elizabeth (Cowen) S.; grad. Ohio State U., 1880; m. Mary Morrison, July 26, 1881, 4 children. Prof. physics and chemistry U. Colo., also v.p. univ., 1880; patented several electric traction inventions, 1880-85; joined U.S. Electrical Co., Denver, Colo., 1885, developed improved electric arc-lighting, new electric motor for streetcars; formed (with Charles Brush) Short Electric Ry. Co. for mfg. electric railroad equipment, Cleve., O., 1889, sold co. to Gen. Electric Co., 1892; joined Walker Mfg. Co., Cleve., 1893, made further improvements in electric traction equipment; obtained around 500 patents on elec. inventions, gained internat. reputation for knowledge in elec. ry. operation; went to Eng. to arrange for production of his inventions in electric ry. field, 1898; became tech. supt. English Electric Mfg. Co., Ltd., 1900. Died in Eng., Oct. 21, 1902.

SHORT, William, diplomat; b. "Spring Garden," Surry County, Va., Sept. 30, 1759; s. William and Elizabeth (Skipwith) S.; grad. Coll. William and Mary, 1779. Mem. Exec. Council Va., 1783-84; sent by Jefferson, Adams and Franklin as rep. to negotiate comml. treaty between Prussia and U.S. with Prussian envoy, The Hague, Netherlands, 1783-84; pvt. sec. to Jefferson in Paris, France, circa 1786-89, later sec. of legation, charge d'affaires, 1789-92; U.S. minister at The Hague, 1792-93; a key figure in drawing up Pinckney Treaty of 1795 between Spain and U.S., 1793-95; apptd. U.S. minister to Russia, 1808, appointment rejected by Senate, 1809. Died Phila., Dec. 5, 1849.

SHORTER, Eli Sims, congressman, lawyer; b. Monticello, Ga., Mar. 15, 1823; grad. in law Yale, 1844. Admitted to bar, began practice of law, Eufaula, Ala., 1844; also engaged in agriculture; mem. U.S. Ho. of Reps. (Democrat) from Ala., 34th-35th congresses, 1855-59; served as col. 18th Regt., Ala. Volunteer Inf., Confederate Army, during Civil War. Died Eufaula, Apr. 29, 1879; buried Fairview Cemetery.

SHORTER, John Gill, gov. Ala., Confederate congressman; b. Monticello, Ga., Apr. 23, 1818; s. Reuben and Martha (Gill) S.; grad. U. Ga., 1837; m. Mary Jane Battle, Jan. 12, 1843, 1 child Admitted to Eufaula (Ala.) bar, 1838; solicitor of Ala., 1842-45; mem. Ala. Senate, 1845-47, Ala. Ho. of Reps., 1851-52; judge Ala. Circuit Ct., 1852-60; Ala. commr. to Ga. Secession Conv., 1860; Ala. del. to provisional Confederate Congress, aided in framing Confederate Constn.; gov. Ala., 1861-63, constructed necessary defenses, especially tried to defend port of Mobile, raised and equipped troops, cared for families of soldiers, strongly supported Davis govt. and such unpopular measures as conscription; defeated for reelection, 1863, retired from polit. life. Died Eufaula, May 29, 1872.

SHOUP, Francis Asbury, army officer, clergyman; b. Laurel, Ind., Mar. 22, 1834; s. George Grove and Jane (Conwell) S.; grad. U.S. Mil. Acad., 1855; m. Esther Habersham Elliott, 1870, 3 children. Admitted to Indpls. (Ind.) bar, 1860, St. Augustine (Fla.) bar, 1861; erected Confederate battery, Fernandina, Fla.; lt. arty.; maj., 1861; chief of arty. under Hardee, 1861, played important part in capture of Prentiss' command; commd. brig. gen., 1862; commanded La. brigade at Vicksburg; supr. works constructed at Chattahochee River, 1863-64; chief of staff under Hood, 1864-65; prof. applied mathematics U. Miss., Oxford, 1865-69, prof. mathematics, 1869-75; took orders in Episcopal Ch., 1868, rector chs. in Waterford, N.Y., Nashville, Tenn., Jackson, Miss., New Orleans, 1875-83; prof. metaphysics U. of South, Sewanee, Tenn., 1883-88, also chaplain, prof. engring. and physics, later prof. mathematics, until 1896. Author: Infantry Tactics, 1862; Artillery Division Drill, 1864; The Elements of Algebra, 1874; Mechanism and Personality, 1891. Died Columbia, Tenn., Sept. 4, 1896.

SHOWER, Jacob, congressman, physician; b. Manchester, Md., Feb. 22, 1803; grad. med. dept. U. Md. at Balt., 1825. Served as drummer boy in War of 1812; began practice of medicine, Carroll County, Md., circa 1825; charter mem. 1st Andrew Jackson Club in Md., 1824; mem. Md. Ho. of Dels. (Democrat), 1834-40; clk. Carroll County Circuit Ct., 1842-50; del. Md. Constl. Conv., 1851; mem. U.S. Ho. of Reps. (Independent) from Md., 33d Congress, 1853-55. Died Manchester, May 25, 1879.

SHREVE, Henry Miller, steamboat capt.; b. Burlington County, N.J., Oct. 21, 1785; s. Israel and Mary (Cokely) S.; m. Mary Blair, Feb. 28, 1811, 5 children. Became trader between St. Louis and Phila., by way of Pitts., 1807, took cargo of lead from Fevre (Galena) River to New Orleans, thus inaugurating lead trade, 1810; became stockholder in steamboat "Enterprise," one of 1st on Mississippi River, 1814, performed valuable service to Gen. Jackson by running the Brit. batteries to New Orleans and exchanging prisoners with Brit. fleet, 1814-15; ascended Mississippi and Ohio rivers to Louisville in "Enterprise," (1st steamboat to make the trip), 1815; established practicability of steam navigation on Mississippi and Ohio route with 2d steamboat "Washington" (which he built), 1816-17; opened navigation of Mississippi and tributaries to competitive enterprise by winning law suits against Fulton-Livingston interests; supt. western river improvements, 1827-41; designer 1st steam snagboat, Heliopolis. Died St. Louis, Mar. 6, 1851.

SHREVE, Thomas Hopkins, journalist; b. Alexandria, Va., Dec. 17, 1808; s. Thomas and Ann (Hopkins) S.; attended Alexandria Acad.; m. Octavia Bullit, Apr. 16, 1840, 3 children. Editor (with William Davis Gallagher) Cincinnati Mirror, 1831-36; owner firm T.H. Shreve & Co., published 1st 5 numbers of Unitarian mag. The Western Messenger, 1835; established Bowles, Shreve & Co., wholesale dry goods firm, Louisville, Ky., 1838; made his reputation as asst. editor Georg Dennison Prentice's newspaper Louisville Daily Journal, 1842-53; part of collection of his essays published in Knickerbocker, 1837-38; helped bring publicity to Western literary endeavors in early 19th century. Author: Betterton: A Novel (unpublished), and Drayton: A Story of American Life, 1851; contbr. many poems and essays to mags. including Western Messenger, Western Literary Journal and Monthly Magazine. Died Louisville, Dec. 22, 1853; buried Cave Hill Cemetery.

SHRYOCK, Gideon, architect; b. Lexington, Ky., son of Mathias Shryock; studied under William Strickland, Phila., circa 1823. Began practice architecture, Lexington, circa 1824, became leading exponent of Greek Revival movement in Ky.; designed many classical style houses for wealthy planters of Blue Grass region (Ky.). Works include: old State Capitol, Frankfort, Ky. (built in Greek temple form), circa 1828; Morrison Coll. bldg. (now on Transylvania Coll. campus), Lexington, 1830; old State Capitol, now State War Meml.) Little Rock, Ark., 1830's; Jefferson County Court House, So. Nat. Bank Bldg. (both Louisville, Ky.), mid-1830's. Died 1880.

SHUBRICK, John Templer, naval officer; b. Charleston, S.C., Sept. 12, 1788; s. Col. Thomas and Mary (Branford) S.; m. Elizabeth Matilda Ludlow, 1814, 1 son, Edward Templer. Commd. lt. U.S. Navy, 1812; served in ship Constitution during her victory over Guerriere, Aug. 1812, and defeat of Java, Dec. 1812; 1st lt. in Hornet in capture of Peacock, 1813; an outstanding young naval officer of War of 1812, received 3 medals from Congress; 1st lt. in Decatur's flagship Guerriere against Algiers, in capture of Algerian frigate Mashuda, 1815; given command of Epervier to carry home treaty of 1815, ship never heard of again. Lost at sea, July 1815.

SHUBRICK, William Branford, naval officer; b. "Belvidere," Bull's Island, S.C., Oct. 31, 1790; s. Thomas and Mary (Branford) S.; attended Harvard, 1805; m. Harriet Cordelia Wethered, Sept. 1815, 1 child. Commd. midshipman U.S. Navy, 1806, lt., 1813; served as 3d lt. in ship Constitution in capture of Cyane and Levant, 1815; decorated Congressional Medal, 1815; commd. capt., 1831; in command West Indies Squadron, 1838-40; in command Norfolk Navy Yard, also commanded adminstrn. Bur. Provisions and Clothing, 1845-46; in command Cal. coast, 1846-48; head Phila. Naval Yard, 1849, later head Bur. Constrn. and Repair; chmn. Lighthouse Bd., 1852-71; in command expdn. sent to settle comml. and other difficulties with Paraguay, 1858; commd. rear adm., ret., 1862. Died Washington, D.C., May 27, 1874.

SHUCK, Jehu Lewis, missionary; b. Alexandria, Va., Sept. 4, 1812; studied Va. Bapt. Sem., Richmond, 1832-35; m. Henrietta Hall, Sept. 8, 1835; m. 2d, Lizzie Sexton, Oct. 1846; m. 3d, Anna L. Trotti, June 5, 1854; several children. Missionary to Chinese under Am. Bapt. Bd. Fgn. Missions, sailed from Boston, 1835, lived in Singapore and Macao, 1836-42; became (with wife) 1st Bapt. missionary to reside in China; organizer 1st Bapt. Ch. in Hong Kong, 1842, Chinese Ch. in Sacramento, Cal., after 1852; pastor in S.C., 1861-63; author number of tracts in Chinese and in English, including Portfolio Chinensis, published Macao, 1840. Died Barnwell Court House, S.C., Aug. 20, 1863.

SHUFELDT, Robert Wilson, navy officer; b. Red Hook, N.Y., Feb. 21, 1822; s. George Adam and Mary (Wilson) S.; m. Sarah Abercrombie, Oct. 16, 1847, 6 children. Apptd. midshipman U.S. Navy, 1839, passed midshipman, 1845, chief officer mail steamers Atlantic and Georgia, 1849-51, lt., 1853, resigned, 1854; comdr. Collins Line steamer Liverpool, 1854-56; consul gen. to Cuba, until 1863; comdr. U.S. Navy, 1862, sr. naval officer in joint operations, St. Marks, Fla., 1865, capt., 1869, comdr. Miantonomah expdn. surveying Isthmus of Tehuantepec canal route, 1870-71; chief Bur. of Equipment and Recruiting, 1875-78, reorganized naval apprentice system; rep. U.S. and Britain in settlement of Liberian boundary dispute, 1878-79; naval attache in China, 1881, negotiated treaty of 1882 establishing diplomatic relations, extraterritoriality and trade privileges to Americans; pres. Naval Adv. Bd., 1882-84; supt. Naval Observatory; rear adm., 1883-84. Died Washington, D.C., Nov. 7, 1895; buried Arlington (Va.) Nat. Cemetery.

SHULZE, John Andrew, gov. Pa.; b. Tulpehocken, Berks County, Pa., July 19, 1775; s. Christopher and Eva (Muhlenberg) S.; m. Susan Kimmell, 2 children. Ordained, admitted to German Lutheran Synod of Eastern Pa., 1796; mem. Pa. Ho. of Reps., 1806-09, 21; became register and clk. Sessions Ct. of Lebanon County (Pa.), 1813; mem. Pa. Senate, 1822; gov. Pa. (Republican), 1823-29; del. to Pa. State Conv., Harrisburg, 1839; mem. Electoral Coll. Pa., 1840-52, pres. Died Lancaster, Pa., Nov. 18, 1852.

SHUNK, Francis Rawn, gov. Pa.; b. Trappe, Pa., Aug. 7, 1788; s. John and Elizabeth (Rawn) S.; m. Jane Findley, 1820, 1 child. Clk., office of Surveyor Gen. Pa., Harrisburg, 1812; admitted to Pa. bar, 1816; assistant, then prin. clk. Pa. Ho. of Reps., 1816-20; clk. Pa. Canal Commn., 1829; sec. Commonwealth of Pa., 1839; gov. Pa. (Democrat), 1844-48, improved state's financial affairs, opposed extension of spl. privilege. Died Harrisburg, July 30, 1848.

SHURTLEFF, Nathaniel Bradstreet, mayor Boston, antiquary; b. Boston, June 29, 1810; s Benjamin and Sally (Shaw) S.; grad. Boston Public Latin Sch., 1822; A.B., Harvard, 1831, M.D., 1834; m. Sarah Smith, 6 children Practiced medicine, Boston, 1834; mayor (Democrat) of Boston, 1868-70; mem. Mass. Hist. Soc., 1847; sec. to bd. overseers Harvard, 1854-74, mem. bd., 1852-61, 63-69; trustee Boston Public Library. Author: Epitome of Phrenology, 1835; Perpetual Calendar for Old and New Style, 1848; Passengers of the Mayflower in 1620, 1849; A Topographical and Historical Description of Boston (most important work); 1871. Editor: Records of the Governor and Company of the Massachussets Bay in New England, 5 vols. in 6, 1853-54, Records of the Colony of New Plymouth in New England, 8 vols., 1853-57; (with David Pulsifer) Decimal System for Libraries, 1856. Died Boston, Oct. 17, 1874.

SHUTE, Samuel, colonial gov. Mass.; b. London, Eng., Jan. 12, 1662; s. Benjamin and Caryl Shute; fellow commoner Christ's Coll. Cambridge (Eng.) U., 1683. Admitted to Middle Temple, 1683; lt. col. 3d Dragoon Guards, 1712; gov. Mass. Bay and N.H., 1716-27, engaged in continuous dispute with Assembly over his rights and powers; opposed issues of paper money but over-powered by Assembly; quarrelled with Assembly over his right to disapprove choice of speaker (was forced to accept explanatory charter defining this right of the gov., 1725); requested that Assembly provide fortifications as protection against Indians (assembly refused); made treaty of friendship with Indians at Arrowsick Island, 1717; went to England, 1723, presented grievances to Privy Council and attempted to collect salary in arrears; given pension following expiration of commn.,1727. Died Eng., Apr. 15, 1742.

SIBLEY, George Champlain, Indian agt., explorer; b. Great Barrington, Mass., Apr. 1, 1782; s. John and Elizabeth (Hopkins) S.; m. Mary B. Easton, Aug. 19, 1815. Clk. in Indian Bur., circa 1808; mem. mil. expdn. sent to Jackson County (Mo.) to construct Ft. Osage, 1808; explorer territory of Grand Saline in Okla., 1811; a commr. to lay out Santa Fe trail from Council Grove (Mo.) to Mexican border, 1825; founder Lindenwood Sch. for Girls (later Lindenwood Coll.) nr. St. Charles, Mo., 1827; del. to state and nat. Whig convs., 1844. Died St. Charles, Jan. 31, 1863.

SIBLEY, Henry Hastings, gov. Minn., congressman; b. Detroit, Feb. 20, 1811; s. Solomon and Sarah Whipple (Sproat) S.; m. Sarah Jane Steele, May 2, 1843, 9 children. Clk., Am. Fur Co., Mackinac, Mich., 1829-34; became partner in operating a co. post, Mendota, nr. Ft. Snelling, Minn., 1834, managed trade with Sioux Indians from Lake Pepin to Canadian boundary; mem. U.S. Congress from Territory of Wis., 30th Congress, Oct. 30, 1848-49; promoted orgn. of Minn. Territory, 1849; mem. U.S. Congress from Minn. Territory, 31st-32d congresses, July 7, 1849-53; 1st gov. Minn. (Democrat), 1858-60; regent Minn. State U., 1860-69, pres. bd., 1876-91; led volunteer mil. forces of Minn. against Indians in Sioux uprising in Minn., 1862; served as brig. gen. U.S. Volunteers in Civil War, 1862-63, 63-65; fought at Battle of Wood Lake, 1862; commanded expdns. against Sioux in Dakota region, 1863, 64; brevetted maj. gen. U.S. Volunteers, 1865; went to St. Paul, Minn., circa 1868; pres. St. Paul Gas Co., 1866, also insurance co. and bank in St. Paul; mem. Minn. Legislature, 1871; pres. Minn. Hist. Soc., 1879-91. Died St. Paul, Feb. 18, 1891; buried Oakland Cemetery, St. Paul.

SIBLEY, Hiram, telegraph co. exec.; b. North Adams, Mass., Feb. 6, 1807; s. Benjamin and Zilpha (Davis) S.; m. Elizabeth M. Tinker, 2 children. Sheriff, Monroe County (N.Y.), 1843; founder N.Y. & Mississippi Valley Printing Telegraph Co., 1851, founder (with Ezra Cornell) Western Union Telegraph Co., 1854, pres., 1856-66; began constrn. transcontinental telegraph line, 1860; ret., 1869, became large landowner, interested in agrl. experimentation; an incorporator Cornell U. Died Rochester, N.Y., July 12, 1888.

SIBLEY, John, physician, Indian agt.; b. Sutton, Mass., May 19, 1757; s. Timothy and Ann (Waite) S.; m. Elizabeth Hopkins, 1780; m. 2d, Mrs. Mary White Winslow, Nov. 10, 1791; m. 3d, Eudalie Malique, 1813; 1 son, George Champlain. Established Fayetteville (N.C.) Gazette, circa 1785; contract surgeon to U.S. Army in Orleans Territory, 1803; Indian agt. for Orleans Territory, 1805-14, (began gathering vocabulary of tribes within territory, his reports to Jefferson valuable source of knowledge about La. in this period; mem. La. Legislature many years; col. La. Militia, served with Col. James Long's raid on Tex., 1819; mem. supreme council governing Nacogdoches (mil. post), Tex., circa 1819; owned cotton plantation, Grand Encore, nr. Natchitoches, La. Died Apr. 8, 1837.

SIBLEY, John Langdon, librarian; b. Union, Me., Dec. 29, 1804; s. Dr. Jonathan and Persis (Morse) S.; grad. Harvard, 1825, Harvard Div. Sch., 1828; m. Charlotte Cook, May 20, 1866. Ordained minister Congregational Ch., 1829; pastor, Stow, Mass., 1829-33; asst. librarian Harvard, 1825-26, 41-56, librarian, 1856-77, greatly enlarged collection, introduced adminstrv. improvements, began public card catalogue indexed according to author and subject, 1861, prepared 12 triennial catalogues of Harvard, 1842-75, quinquennial catalogue, 1880, edited annual catalogues, 1850-70; editor of an illustrated monthly journal called Am. Mag. of Useful and Entertaining Knowledge, 1833-36; contbd. generously to charities, established scholarship fund at Phillips Exeter Acad. Author: Bibliographical Sketches of Graduates of Harvard University, 3 vols., 1873-85; A History of the Town of Union, Maine, 1851. Died Cambridge, Mass., Dec. 9, 1885.

SIBLEY, Jonas, congressman; b. Sutton, Mass., Mar. 7, 1762. Selectman, 1801-03, 19; town moderator, 1802-27; town treas., 1806-16; mem. Mass. Ho. of Reps., 1806-22, 27-29, Mass. Senate, 1826; Democratic presdl. elector, 1820; del. Mass. Constl. Conv., 1820; mem. U.S. Ho. of Reps. (Democrat) from Mass., 18th Congress, 1823-25; engaged in farming. Died Sutton, Feb. 5, 1834; buried Center Cemetery.

SIBLEY, Mark Hopkins, congressman, lawyer; b. Great Barrington, Mass., 1796; studied law. Admitted to bar, began practice of law, Canandaigua, N.Y., 1814; mem. N.Y. State Assembly, 1834-35; mem. U.S. Ho. of Reps. (Whig) from N.Y., 25th Congress, 1837-39; mem. N.Y. Senate, 1841; judge Ontario County, 1847-51. Died Canandaigua, Sept. 8, 1852; buried West Avenue Cemetery.

SIBLEY, Solomon, congressman, jurist; b. Sutton, Mass., Oct. 7, 1769; grad. Coll. of R.I., Providence, 1794; studied law; at least 1 son, Henry Hastings Sibley. Admitted to bar, 1795, began practice of law, Marietta, O.; moved to Detroit, 1797; mem. Northwest Territorial Legislature, 1799; mayor Detroit, 1806; pres. bd. trustees Detroit, 1815; auditor Mich. Territory, 1814-17; U.S. atty. Mich. Territory (apptd. by Pres. Madison), 1815-23; mem. U.S. Congress (filled vacancy) from Mich. Territory, 16th-17th congresses, Nov. 20, 1820-23; judge Supreme Ct. of Mich. Territory, 1824-37. Died Detroit, Apr. 4, 1846.

SICKELS, Frederick Ellsworth, inventor; b. Gloucester County, N.J., Sept. 20, 1819; s. John and Hester (Ellsworth) S.; m. Ranane Shreeves, 5 children. Perfected 1st successful drop cut-off for steam engines devised in U.S., 1841, patented, 1842; patent pended for steam-steering apparatus, 1849-60; completed construction of a full-size steam-steering unit, 1854, succeeded in having equipment installed on steamer Augusta, 1858, secured no purchaser for invention; made trip to Eng., 1860-67, found no buyer there; thereafter became civil engineer; cons. engr. Nat. Water Works Co. of N.Y., 1890, chief engr. its operations at Kansas City, Mo., 1891. Died Mar. 8, 1895; buried Paterson, N.J.

SICKLES, Nicholas, congressman, lawyer; b. Kinderhook, Ulster County, N.Y., Sept. 11, 1801; attended Kinderhook Acad.; studied law. Admitted to bar, 1823, began practice of law, Kingston, N.Y.; mem. U.S. Ho. of Reps. (Democrat) from N.Y., 24th Congress, 1835-37; pros. atty. Ulster County, 1836-37; surrogate Ulster County, 1844-45. Died Kingston, May 13, 1845; buried Houghtaling Burying Ground.

SIDELL, William Henry, army officer; b. N.Y.C., Aug. 21, 1810; s. John Sidell; grad. U.S. Mil. Acad., 1833. Brevetted 2d lt. U.S. Army, 1833, resigned, 1833; engr., various civil engring. posts, 1833-39; engr. with various railroads, U.S. and Mexico, 1840-60; acting asst. provost marshal gen. for Ky., also chief mustering and dlisbursing officer, Louisville, Ky., 1863-65; commd. lt. col. 10th Inf., 1864; brevetted col. and brig. gen., 1865, ret., 1870. Died N.Y.C., July 1, 1873.

SIDI MUHAMMED, emperor of Morocco; at least 1 son, Muley Soliman. Became emperor of Morocco, circa 1758; one of 1st rulers to recognize independence of Am.; stated that Am. vessels would not be harmed by Morocco, 1778; signed peace and trade treaty with Am., 1786 treaty cost America $5,000, but was the cheapest of all initial treaties concluded by America with Barbary states; promised to aid America in obtaining favorable treaties with other Barbary powers (but nothing came of the promise), 1786; never violated treaty throughout his lifetime. Died circa 1791.

SIENI, Cyril, clergyman; b. Catalonia, Spain; flourished 1772-99. Joined Capuchin Order; apptd. vicar gen. of New Orleans, 1772; made unsuccessful attempts to initiate eccles. reforms, thus incurring enmity of Dagobert (Capuchin superior) and Unzaga (gov.); apptd. titular bishop of Tricali and auxiliary of Santiago; ordered back to Spain, 1793, but was still in Havana, Cuba, 1799.

SIGOURNEY, Lydia Howard Huntley, author; b. Norwich, Conn., Sept. 1, 1791; d. Ezekiel and Zerviah (Wentworth) Huntley; m. Charles Sigourney, June 16, 1819, 2 children including Andrew. Conducted school, Norwich, 1811-13, small school for girls, Hartford, Conn., 1814-19; edited The Religious Souvenir, 1839, 40; contbd. verse and miscellaneous articles to many current periodicals including Ladies Companion and Southern Literary Messenger from 1830's; an editor Godey's Lady's Book; writing characterized by moralizing and sentimentality. Author: Moral Pieces, in Prose and Verse, 1815; Letters to Mothers, 1838; Scenes in My Native Land, 1844; Voice of Flowers, 1845; Letters to My Pupils, 1850; The Daily Counsellor, 1858; Letters of Life (autobiography), 1866. Died Hartford, June 10, 1865.

SIKES, William Wirt, journalist, diplomat; b. Watertown, N.Y., Nov. 23, 1836; s. Dr. William

Johnson and Meroe (Redfield) S.; m. Jeanette A. Wilcox, 1855; m. 2d, Olive Logan, Dec. 19, 1871. State canal insp. Ill., 1861-63; contbd. articles to many journals including Harper's, The Sun, 1860's; established Authors' Union, circa 1866; edited City and Country, Nyack, N.Y., 1868-circa 1872; edited Rockland County Journal, Piermont, N.Y.; devoted attention to conditions in city slums, published novels on subject; became interested in art, wrote sketch of Antoine Weirtz of Brussels, 1873; U.S. consul to Cardiff, Wales, 1876-83. Author: (2 novels) The World's Broad Stage, 1868; One Poor Girl, 1869; British Goblins: Welsh Folk-Lore, Fairy Mythology, Legends, and Traditions, 1880; Rambles and Studies in Old South Wales, 1881. Died Cardiff, Aug. 18, 1883; buried London, Eng.

SILL, Anna Peck, educator; b. Burlington, Otsego County, N.Y., Aug. 9, 1816; d. Abel Sill; attended Phipps Union Sem., circa 1836. Tchr., Phipps Union Sem., circa 1837-43; condr. sem. for young ladies, Warsaw, N.Y., 1843-46; head female dept. Cary Collegiate Inst., Oakfield, N.Y., 1846-49; founder Rockford (Ill.) Female Sem. (became Rockford Coll. 1892). 1849, dir., 1849-84, prin. emerita, 1884-89. Died Rockford, June 18, 1889.

SILL, Edward Rowland, (pseudonym: Andrew Hedbrooke), poet, educator; b. Windsor, Conn., Apr. 29, 1841; s. Theodore and Elizabeth Newberry (Rowland) S.; grad. Yale, 1861; attended Harvard Div. Sch., 1867; m. Elizabeth Newberry Sill (his cousin), 1867. Mem. editorial bd. Yale Literary Mag., 1860/61; mem. staff N.Y. Evening Mail, 1868; supt. schs. Cuyahoga Falls O., 1869-70; prof. English, U. Cal., 1874-82, one of finest teachers of era; contributed poetry to Atlantic Monthly under pseudonym Andrew Hedbrooke in 1880's; among better known poems are The Fool's Prayer, Opportunity (expressed humane idealism); essays collected as The Prose of Edward Rowland Sill, 1900; poetry collected as The Poems of Edward Rowland Sill, 1902. Author: The Hermitage and Other Poems, 1868; The Venus of Milo and Other Poems, published privately, 1883. Died Cleve., O., Feb. 27, 1887.

SILL, Thomas Hale, congressman, lawyer; b. Windsor, Conn., Oct. 11, 1783; grad. Brown U., Providence, R.I., 1804; studied law. Admitted to bar, 1809, began practice of law, Lebanon, O.; moved to Erie, Pa., 1813; mem. staff Gen. Wallace, also mem. Minute-men of Pa. Militia; dep. U.S. marshal, 1816-18; dep. atty. gen., 1819; mem. Pa. Ho. of Reps., 1823; mem. U.S. Ho. of Reps. (Nat.-Republican, filled vacancy), from Pa., 19th, 21st congresses, Mar. 14, 1826-27, 29-31; pres. U.S. branch bank, Erie, 1837; mem. Pa. Constl. Conv., 1837-38; postmaster, Erie, 1847-53; Whig presdl. elector, 1848; dir. Erie Acad., more than 30 years. Died Erie, Feb. 7, 1856; buried Erie Cemetery.

SILLIMAN, Augustus Ely, businessman; b. Newport, R.I., Apr. 11, 1807; son of Gold Selleck Silliman. Went into business, N.Y.C., at early age; established merc. clearing house, N.Y.C., 1853; pres. Mcht.'s Bank, 1857-68; ret. from bus., 1868, engaged in astron. studies, literary pursuits; mem. Century Club, R.I. Hist. Soc., Merc. Library Assn. N.Y. Author: A Gallop Among American Scenery, or Sketches of American Scenes and Military Adventures; Conversations with M. Ramsai on the Truth of Religion with His Letters on the Immortality of the Soul and Freedom of the Will. Died Bklyn., May 30, 1884.

SILLIMAN, Benjamin, educator, scientist, b. Trumbull, Conn., Aug. 8, 1779; s. Gold Selleck and Mary (Fish) S.; grad. Yale, 1796; M.D. (hon.), Bowdoin Coll., 1818; LL.D. (hon.), Middlebury (Vt.) Coll., 1826; m. Harriet Trumbull, Sept. 17, 1809; m. 2d, Sarah (McClellan) Webb, Sept. 17, 1851; 9 children including Benjamin. Admitted to Conn. bar, 1802; prof. chemistry, natural history Yale, 1802-53, gave 1st course of exptl. lectures ever given at Yale, 1804, largely responsible for Yale's acquisition of George Gibbs' mineral collection, began full course illustrated lectures in mineralogy, geology, 1813, instrumental in establishment Yale Med. Sch. (opened 1813), became prof. chemistry, induced Yale corp. to establish Dept. of Philosophy and the Arts, 1847, became prof. emeritus, 1853; founder, propr., 1st editor Am. Jour. of Science and Arts, 1818; experimented with Votiac current produced by powerful deflagrator (which he had developed with improvements along lines of one made earlier by Robert Hare), early 1800's; delivered series of geol. lectures before Boston Soc. Natural History, 1835 (acquiring reputation as lectr.); mem. Am. Philos. Soc., 1805; 1st pres. Assn. Am. Geologists, 1840; an original mem. Nat. Acad. Sciences, 1863. Author: Elements of Chemistry, 1830-31. Editor: Elements of Experimental Chemistry (of William Henry), 1814. Died New Haven, Conn., Nov. 24, 1864.

SILLIMAN, Benjamin, Jr., chemist, educator; b. New Haven, Conn., Dec. 4, 1816; s. Benjamin and Harriet (Trumbull) S.; grad. Yale, 1837; m. Susan Huldah Forbes, May 14, 1840, 7 children. Became asso. editor Am. Jour. of Science and Arts, 1838, editor, 1845-85; prof. practical chemistry Yale, 1846-53, founder Sch. Applied Chemistry in new Dept. of Philosophy and the Arts (later Sheffield Scientific Sch.), asso., 1847-69, prof. chemistry Yale Med. Sch. and Yale Coll., 1853-85; an original incorporator Nat. Acad. Scis., 1863; demonstrated that petroleum was essentially a mixture of hydrocarbons different in character from vegetable and animal oils and that it could be separated by distillation and simple means of purification into a series of distillates; identified what were to become major uses of petroleum for next 50 years, outlined principal methods of purifying those products; in charge chem. dept. World's Fair, N.Y.C., 1853. Author: First Principles of Chemistry, 1847; First Principles of Natural Philosophy, 1858. First Principles of Physics, 1859; Died New Haven, Jan. 14, 1885.

SILSBEE, Nathaniel, senator; b. Salem, Mass., Jan. 14, 1773; s. Nathaniel and Sarah (Becket) S.; m. Mary Crowninshield, Dec. 12, 1802, at least 4 children including Nathaniel. Took command ship Benjamin, 1793, made highly profitable voyage to Europe; mem. U.S. Ho. of Reps. from Mass., 15th, 16th congresses, Dec. 1, 1817-21; mem. Mass. Ho. of Reps., 1821-22; pres. Mass. Senate, 1823-26; mem. U.S. Senate from Mass., Dec. 4, 1826-35, chmn. commerce com., 1833-35; dir. Boston br. main div. Bank of U.S. in Phila., 1816-32; presdl. elector, 1824, 36; pres. Mass. Whig Conv., 1832. Died Salem, Mass., July 14, 1850; buried Harmon Grove Cemetery, Salem.

SILVER, Thomas, inventor; b. Greenwich, Cumberland County, N.J., June 17, 1813; m. Miss Bird, at least 1 child. Patentee governor for marine engines, 1855, governor installed on U.S. mail steamships, 1856, patented in Eng., 1857, adopted by French Navy, adopted by Brit. Navy, 1864; inventor hoisting apparatus, completely enclosed oil lamp; mem. Franklin Inst., Phila., 1855. Died N.Y.C., Apr. 12, 1888.

SILVESTER, Peter, congressman, lawyer; b. Shelter Island, L.I., N.Y., 1734; studied law. Admitted to bar, 1763, began practice of law, Albany, N.Y.; mem. Albany Common Council, 1772; mem. Com. of Safety, 1774; mem. 1st, 2d provincial congresses, 1775, 76; moved to Kinderhook, N.Y.; apptd. judge Ct. of Common Pleas Columbia County, 1786; regent U. State N.Y., 1787-1808; mem. U.S. Ho. of Reps. from N.Y., 1st-2d congresses, 1789-93; mem. N.Y. State Assembly., 1788, 1803-06, N.Y. Senate, 1796-1800. Died Kinderhook, Oct. 15, 1808; buried Old Van Schaack Cemetery (over which Reformed Dutch Ch. was built 1814).

SILVESTER, Peter Henry, congressman, lawyer; b. Kinderhook, N.Y., Feb. 17, 1807; attended Kinderhook Acad.; grad. Union Coll., Schenectady, N.Y., 1827; studied law. Admitted to bar, 1830, practiced law, Coxsackie, N.Y.; mem. U.S. Ho. of Reps. (Whig) from N.Y., 30th-31st congresses, 1847-51. Died Coxsackie, Nov. 29, 1882; buried Kinderhook Cemetery.

SIMKINS, Eldred, congressman, lawyer; b. Edgefield, S.C., Aug. 30, 1779; grad. S.C. Coll. (now U. S.C.) at Columbia; attended Litchfield (Conn.) Law Sch., 3 years. Admitted to bar, 1805, began practice of law, Edgefield, 1806; mem. S.C. Ho. of Reps.; mem. S.C. Senate, 1810-12; lt. gov. S.C., 1812-14; mem. U.S. Ho. of Reps. (Democrat, filled vacancy) from S.C., 15th-16th congresses, Jan. 24, 1818-21; resumed practice of law, also engaged in agriculture. Died Edgefield, Nov. 17, 1831; buried Cedar Fields (family burial ground), nr. Edgefield.

SIMMONS, George Abel, congressman, lawyer; b. Lyme, N.H., Sept. 8, 1791; grad. Dartmouth, 1816; studied law. Prin. of local acad., Lansingburg, N.Y.; admitted to bar, 1825, began practice of law, Keeseville, N.Y.; mem. N.Y. State Assembly, 1840-42; mem. N.Y. Constl. Conv., 1846; mem. U.S. Ho. of Reps. (Whig) from N.Y., 33d-34th congresses, 1853-57. Died Keeseville, Oct. 27, 1857; buried Evergreen Cemetery.

SIMMONS, James Fowler, senator, mfr.; b. nr. Little Compton, R.I., Sept. 10, 1795; attended pvt. sch., Newport, R.I. Moved to Providence, R.I., 1812; asso. with various mfg. firms, R.I. and Mass.; became yarn mfr., Simmonsville, N.H., 1822, Johnston, R.I., 1827; also engaged in agriculture; mem. R.I. Ho. of Reps., 1828-41; mem. U.S. Senate (Whig) from R.I., 1841-47, 57-62 (resigned). Died Johnston, July 10, 1864; buried North End Cemetery, Providence.

SIMMONS, Thomas Jefferson, jurist; b. Hickory Grove, Ga., June 25, 1837; s. Allen G. and Mary (Cleveland) S.; studied law under A. D. Hammond, Forsyth, Ga.; m. Pennie Hollis, 1859; m. 2d, Lucille Peck, 1867; m. 3d, Nannie R. Renfro, 1888; 3 children. Admitted to Ga. bar, 1857; commd. lt. 6th Ga. Inf., Confederate Army, 1861, lt. col., then col., 1862; served in Va. throughout Civil War, mainly in A.P. Hill's Div. of Gen. James Longstreet's Corps; del. Ga. Constl. Conv., to 1865; mem. Ga. Senate, 1865, 71-77, pres. 1875, chmn. com. on finance and bonds; judge Macon (Ga.) Circuit, 1878-87; judge Ga. Supreme Ct., 1887-1905, chief justice, 1894-1905. Died Sept. 12, 1905.

SIMMS, Jeptha Root, historian; b. Canterbury, Conn., Dec. 31, 1807; s. Joseph and Phebe (Fitch) S.; m. Catherine Sawyer, 1833, no children. With dry-goods house, N.Y.C., 1829-32; part-owner Pearl Street Dry-Goods House, N.Y.C., 1832-33; moved for health reasons to Schoharie, N.Y., 1833; did hist. research of Albany (N.Y.) area, 1833-83; toll collector Fultonville, N.Y. and Erie Canal; ticket agt. N.Y.C. R.R., Ft. Plain, N.Y., 9 years. Author: History of Schoharie County and Border Wars of New York, 1845; The American Spy, Nathan Hale, 1846; Frontiers of New York, 1882-83. Died Fort Plain, N.Y., May 31, 1883.

SIMMS, William Elliot, congressman; b. nr. Cynthiana, Harrison County, Ky., Jan. 2, 1822; s. William Marmaduke and Julia (Shropshire) S.; grad. law dept. Transylvania U., 1846; m. Lucy Ann Blythe, Sept. 27, 1866, 3 children. Began practice law, Ky., 1846; raised company of 3d Ky. Regt. of Inf. in Mexican War, 1846; mem. Ky. Ho. of Reps. (Democrat), 1849; editor Ky. State Flag, 1857; mem. U.S. Ho. of Reps. from Ky., 36th Congress, 1859-61, defeated for re-election, 1860; joined Confederate forces of Humphrey Marshall, 1861; col. Ky. Cavalry, served in eastern Ky. and western Va.; resigned from army to serve as mem. Confederate Senate, 1862. Died June 25, 1898.

SIMMS, William Gilmore, author; b. Charleston, S.C., Apr. 17, 1806; s. William Gilmore and Harriet Ann Augusta (Singleton) S.; m. Anna Malcolm Giles; m. 2d, Chevillette Roach; 9 children. Admitted to S.C. bar, 1827; editor Charleston City Gazette, circa 1828; opponent doctrine of nullification, 1832; friend of William Cullen Bryant in N.Y.C., 1833; became head of household upon marrying dau. of planter in Barnwell County, S.C., 1836; contbd. to So. apology for slavery, 1852; editor So. Quarterly Rev., 1849-56; a leading novelist and man of letters in ante-bellum South, reputation based on hist. romance novels; aspired to write epics dealing with life in Carolina from early times; writing known for realism in descriptions (at his best when describing color and vitality of frontier life) rather than for convincing characterization or original plotting; most famous of frontier sagas were Guy Rivers, 1834 and Beauchampe, 1842; most often read work, Yemasse, 1835, dealt with Yemasse War of 1715 and is representative of his hist. romances; other novels of Revolutionary era include The Partisan, 1835, Mellichampe, 1836, Katharine Walton, 1851; biographer of Francis Marion, 1844, Nathanael Greene, 1849; short stories include Carl Werner, 1838, The Wigwam and the Cabin, 1845; author History of South Carolina, 1840, geography of South Caroline, 1843, South Carolina in the Revolution, 1854; edited The War Poetry of the South, 1867. Died Charleston, June 11, 1870.

SIMOND, Louis, artist; b. France, 1767. Came to Am., 1792, settled in N.Y.C.; mcht., auctioneer, N.Y.C., 1792-1815; elected mem. N.Y. Hist. Soc., 1812; designed vignette of Hudson's Half Moon later engraved for soc.'s membership diploma; made drawing of Moses Rescued by Pharaoh's Daughter, engraved 1816; wrote 3 travel books on Eng., Switzerland, Italy, published 1815-28; noted amateur painter, art critic. Died Geneva, Switzerland, July 1831.

SIMONDS, William, author; b. Charlestown, Mass., Oct. 30, 1822. Editor, publisher Boston Saturday Rambler, 1846-50 (merged with New Eng. Farmer 1850), publisher, 1850-59; published Pictorial Nat. Library (monthly), 1848-49. Author: (children's books) The Pleasant Way, 1841; The Sinner's Friend, 1845; The Boy's Own Guide, 1852; The Boy's Book of Morals and Manners, 1855; The Aimwell Stories (under pseudonym Walter Aimwell, 6 vols., 1855-63. Died Winchester, Mass., July 7, 1859.

SIMONS, Samuel, congressman, physician; b. Bridgeport, Conn., 1792; studied medicine. Held several local offices; taught sch.; practiced medicine, Bridgeport; mem. Conn. Ho. of Reps., 1830; dir. Housatonic R.R.; trustee Bridgeport Savs. Bank; mem. U.S. Ho. of Reps. (Democrat) from Conn., 28th Congress, 1843-45. Died Bridgeport, Jan. 13, 1847; buried Mountain Grove Cemetery.

SIMONTON, James William, journalist; b. Columbia County, N.Y., Jan. 30, 1823; m. 2d, Minnie Bronson, 1881; 3 children. Congressional correspondent, 1844-50; a propr. N.Y. Times, 1851, Washington correspondent for Times and other newspapers, circa 1852, writer weekly letters

"The History of Legislation," 1855-58, exposed in the Times a congl. bill ostensibly granting public lands to the Pacific R.R., but actually surrendering territories of Minn., 1857; recalled to N.Y.C. as gen. agt. Asso. Press, 1867-81, exposed corruption in U.S. Grant's adminstrn. Died Napa, Cal., Nov. 2, 1882.

SIMONTON, William, congressman; b. West Hanover Twp., nr. Harrisburg, Pa., Feb. 12, 1788; grad. med. dept. U. Pa. at Phila., 1810. Practiced law; resided on farm nr. Hummelstown, Pa.; auditor Dauphin County (Pa.), 1823-26; an original supporter of free-sch. system established by act of 1834; mem. U.S. Ho. of Reps. (Whig) from Pa., 26th-27th congresses, 1839-43. Died South Hanover, Pa., May 17, 1846; buried Old Hanover Cemetery, nr. Shellsville, Pa.

SIMPSON, Edmund, actor, theatrical exec.; b. Eng., 1784; m. Julia Elizabeth Jones, Mar. 9, 1820, several children including Edward. Came to U.S., 1809; made Am. debut at Park Theatre, N.Y.C., 1809, became a success in comedy roles, 1809-33; introduced Italian opera to N.Y.C., 1825; mgr. Park Theatre, 1812-48. Died N.Y.C., July 31, 1848.

SIMPSON, Edward, naval officer; b. N.Y.C., Mar. 3, 1824; s. Edmund Shaw and Julia Elizabeth (Jones) S.; grad. U.S. Naval Acad., 1846; m. Mary Ann Ridgely, 1853, 5 children. Served in Mexican War, 1846-48; instr. in gunnery U.S. Naval Acad., 1853-54, in charge ordnance instrn., 1858-62, 1st head that dept., 1860, comdt. of midshipman, 1862; promoted to lt., 1855; commd. lt. comdr., 1862; in command ship Passaic in attacks on fts. Wagner and Sumter and in campaign off Charleston, S.C., 1863; commd. comdr., 1865; acted as fleet capt. under Rear Adm. Thatcher in operations below Mobile until after its capitulation, 1865; made reputation in area of naval ordnance; asst. chief Ordnance Bureau, 1869-70; commd. capt., 1870, commodore, 1878, rear adm., 1884; commanded New London (Conn.) Station, 1878-80, League Island Navy Yard, 1880-83; pres. gun foundry bd., 1883-84, naval adv. bd., 1884-85, bd. of inspection and survey, 1885-86; pres. U.S. Naval Inst., 1886-88. Author: Treatise on Ordnance and Naval Gunnery, 1859; Report on a Naval Mission to Europe Especially Devoted to the Material and Construction of Artillery, 1873. Died Washington, D.C., Dec. 1, 1888; buried Cypress Hills Cemetery, L.I., N.Y.

SIMPSON, James Hervey, army officer; b. New Brunswick, N.J., Mar. 9, 1813; s. John Neely and Mary (Brunson) S.; grad. U.S. Mil. Acad., 1832; m. Jane Champlin; m. 2d, Elizabeth (Borup) Champlin, 1871; 4 children. Served with Topog. Engrs., U.S. Army, on road constrn. in East and South, 1838-60; commd. capt., 1853, maj., 1861; chief Topog. Engrs. in Shenandoah and Ohio depts. 1861-63; in charge fortifications and projects in Ky., 1863-65; brevetted col. and brig. gen., 1865; chief engr. Dept. of Interior, 1865-67, in charge of direction of U.P.R.R. and govt. wagonroads; author reports including: The Shortest Route to California, 1869; Coronado's March in Search of the Seven Cities of Cibola, 1871. Died St. Paul, Minn., Mar. 2, 1883.

SIMPSON, Matthew, bishop, coll. pres.; b. Cadiz, O., June 21, 1811; s. James and Sarah (Tingley) S.; M.D., 1833; m. Ellen Holmes Verner, Nov. 3, 1835. Admitted to Pitts. Methodist Conf., 1834, gained frame rapidly in this sect; pres. Indiana Asbury (now De Pauw) U., 1839; editor Western Christian Advocate; elected bishop Meth. Ch., 1852; strong supporter of Union cause during Civil War; gave eulogy at Lincoln's funeral, Springfield, Ill. Author: Cyclopedia of Methodism, 1876. Died Phila., June 18, 1884.

SIMPSON, Michael Hodge, wool processing exec.; b. Newburyport, Mass., Nov. 15, 1809; s. Paul and Abigail Johnson (Hodge) S.; ed. Newburyport Acad.; m. Elizabeth Kilham, Dec. 24, 1832; m. 2d, Evangeline Mans, June 1, 1882; 4 children. Owner, wood importing bus., Newburyport, circa 1829-31; purchaser patents on wool burring machine, 1833, sold rights after making improvements, 1837; became part-owner mills, Saxonville, Mass., repurchasing interest after panic of 1837 and restoring operation's profits; builder carpet factory, Roxbury, Mass., 1854; philanthropist, donating to many activities including Wellesley Coll., Newburyport Public Library. Died Boston, Dec. 21, 1884.

SIMPSON, Richard Franklin, congressman, lawyer; b. Laurens, S.C., Mar. 24, 1798; grad. S.C. Coll. (now U. S.C.) at Columbia, 1816; studied law. Admitted to bar, 1819, began practice of law, Pendleton, S.C.; held several local offices; served as maj. during Seminole War, 1835; mem. S.C. Senate, 1835-41; mem. U.S. Ho. of Reps. (Democrat) from S.C., 28th-30th congresses, 1843-49; engaged in agriculture; mem. Secession Conv., 1860, signed secession ordiance. Died Pendleton, Oct. 28, 1882; buried family cemetery nr. Pendleton.

SIMPSON, Stephen, journalist; b. Phila., July 24, 1789; s. George Simpson. Founder, the Portico (miscellany), Balt., circa 1815, joint editor, 1816-17, co-propr. weekly paper Columbian Observer, Phila., 1822; 1st candidate for U.S. Congress on ticket of Workingman's Party of Phila. (1st polit. workers orgn. in U.S.), 1830. Author: The Working Man's Manual: A New Theory of Political Economy on the Principle of Production the Source of Wealth, Phila., 1831; Biography of Stephen Girard, 1832; The Lives of George Washington and Thomas Jefferson: with a Parallel, 1833. Died Phila., Aug. 17, 1854.

SIMPSON, William Dunlap, gov. S.C.; b. Laurens Dist., S.C., Oct. 27, 1823; s. John W. and Elizabeth (Saterwhite) S.; grad. S.C. Coll. (now U. S.C.), 1843; m. Jane Young, Mar. 1847, 8 children. Admitted to S.C. bar, 1846; mem. S.C. Legislature, circa 1850; served in siege of Ft. Sumter and 1st Battle of Manassas; maj., later lt. col. Confederate Army, circa 1862; mem. Confederate Congress from S..C, 1863-65; del. Nat. Democratic Conv., 1868; elected to U.S. Congress, 1868, denied seat; acting gov. S.C., 1878-79, gov., 1879-80; chief justice S.C., 1880-90. Died Dec. 26, 1890.

SIMS, Alexander Dromgoole, congressman, lawyer; b. nr. Randals Ordinary, Brunswick County, Va., June 12, 1803; attended U. N.C. at Chapel Hill; grad Union Coll., Schenectady, N.Y., 1823; read law with Gen. Dromgoole, Brunswick County. Admitted to S.C. bar, 1829, practiced law, Darling-S.C., 1826; in charge of Darlington Acad., 1827; admitted to X.C. bar, 1829, practiced law, Darlington; also engaged in literary pursuits; mem. S.C. Ho. of Reps., 1840-44; mem. U.S. Ho. of Reps. (Democrat) from S.C., 29th-30th congresses, 1845-48. Died Kingstree, S.C., Nov. 22, 1848; buried 1st Baptist Cemetery, Darlington.

SIMS, James Marion, gynecologist; b. Lancaster County, S.C., Jan. 25, 1813; s. John and Mahala (Mackey). S.; grad. S.C. Coll., 1832; studied Charleston Med. Sch., 1833; grad. Jefferson Med. Coll., 1835, LL.D. (hon.), 1881; m. Eliza Theresa Jones, Dec. 21, 1836, 9 children. Practiced medicine, Ala., 1835-50, performed unprecedented fistula operations with notable success, attracting wide attention; published history of vesicovaginal operations, on which he was recognized authority, 1852; founder Women's Hosp., N.Y.C., 1854; visitor to France and Eng. several times, 1861-82, consulting with gynecologists, lecturing, receiving honors in several nations; pres. A.M.A., 1876, Am. Gynecol. Soc., 1881; author several works including autobiography, published 1884. Died N.Y.C., Nov. 13, 1883.

SIMS, Leonard Henly, congressman, farmer; b. Burke County, N.C., Feb. 6, 1807; Engaged in agriculture, Rutherford County, Tenn., 1830-39, 47-59, Springfield, Mo., 1839-47; mem. Tenn. Ho. of Reps., 2 terms; mem. Mo. Ho. of Reps., 1842-46; mem. U.S. Ho. of Reps. (Democrat) from Mo., 29th Congress, 1845-47; settled on farm nr. Batesville, Ark., 1859, farmed and raised cotton; mem. Ark. Senate, 1866-70, 74-78. Died nr. Batesville, Feb. 28, 1886; buried family plot on his farm.

SINGER, Isaac Merrit, inventor, machinist; b. Oswego, N.Y., Oct. 27, 1811; m. Catherine Maria Haley, 1835; m. 2d, Isabella Summerville, 1865. Patented rock-drilling machine, 1839, wood and metal carving machine, 1849; received 1st patent on sewing machine (superior because it could do continuous stitching), 1851; organized sewing machine mfg. firm I.M. Singer & Co., 1851, reached commanding position in sewing machine industry by 1854, brought about pooling of patents in industry; received 20 patents for improvements on his machine, including continuous wheel feed and yielding presser foot, 1851-63; developed 1st practical domestic sewing machine brought into wide use; withdrew from active connection with co., 1863. Died Torquay, Eng., July 23, 1875.

SINGER, Otto, musician; b. Sora, Saxony, July 26, 1833; studied at Leipzig Conservatory, 1851-55, later under Franz Liszt; children include Otto. Taught in Leipzig and Dresden; came to N.Y.C., 1867; taught at Mason and Thomas Conservatory, 1867-73; asst. condr. 1st May Festival, Cincinnati, 1873; became tchr. pianoforte and theory Cincinnati Coll. Music, 1873-93; returned to N.Y.C., 1893; composer: 2 cantatas The Landing of the Pilgrim Fathers, 1876, Festival Ode, 1878, symphonies, symphonic fantasia, 2 piano concertos, violin sonata, piano sonata, other piano music. Died N.Y.C., Jan. 3, 1894.

SINGERLY, William Miskey, editor, publisher; b. Phila., Dec. 27, 1832; s. Joseph and Catherine (Miskey) S.; m. Pamelia Anna Jones, June 4, 1854; m. 2d, Mary Ryan, Aug. 12, 1872; 2 children. Purchased Phila. Public Record, 1877, changed name to Phila. Record, 1st morning daily in Phila., attacked monopoly and corruption in Phila., resulting in one instance in lower coal prices to consumers; leader Democratic Party in Pa., unsuccessful candidate for gov., 1894; owner several factories; pres. Chestnut Street Nat. Bank, 1891. Died Phila., Feb. 27, 1898.

SINGLETON, James Washington, congressman; b. Frederick County, Va., Nov. 23, 1811; s. Gen. James and Judith Throckmorton (Ball) S.; m. probably Catherine McDaniel; m. 2d, Ann Craig; m. 3d, Parthenia McDonald, 1844; 7 children. Admitted to Ill. bar, 1838; brig. gen. militia in "war" against Mormons in Ill., 1844; mem. Ill. Ho. of Reps. (Democrat), 1850-54, 60-62; mem. Ill. constl. convs., 1847, 62; mem. internat. commn. to investigate water communication between U.S. and Can., 1862; prominent "Peace" Democrat, attended Peace Convs. at Peoria and Springfield, 1864; mem. U.S. Ho. of Reps. from Ill., 46th-47th congresses, 1879-83; directed building of Quincy & Toledo R.R. (merged with the Wabash) and Quincy, Alton & St. Louis R.R. (absorbed by Chgo., Burlington & Quincy). Died Balt., Apr. 4, 1892.

SINGLETON, Otho Robards, congressman, lawyer; b. nr. Nicholasville, Ky., Oct. 14, 1814; grad. St. Joseph's Coll., Bardstown, Ky.; grad. law dept. U. Lexington. Admitted to bar, 1838, began practice of law, Canton, Miss.; mem. Miss. Ho. of Reps., 1846-47; mem. Miss. Senate, 1848-54; Democratic presdl. elector, 1852; mem. U.S. Ho. of Reps. (Democrat) from Miss., 33d, 35th-36th, 44th-49th congresses, 1853-55, 1857-Jan. 12, 1861 (withdrew), 1875-87; rep. from Miss. to Confederate Congress, 1861-65. Died Washington, D.C., Jan. 11, 1889; buried Canton Cemetery.

SINGLETON, Thomas Day, congressman; b. nr. Kingstree, S.C.; attended common schs. Held several local offices; mem. U.S. Ho. of Reps. (Nullifier) from S.C., 1833. Died (en route to Washington, D.C.), Raleigh, N.C., Nov. 25, 1833; buried Congressional Cemetery, Washington.

SINNICKSON, Thomas, congressman; b. nr. Salem, N.J., Dec. 21, 1744. A mcht.; served as capt. Continental Army; held several local offices; mem. N.J. Gen. Assembly, 1777, 82, 84-85, 87-88; mem. U.S. Ho. of Reps. from N.J., 1st, 5th congresses, 1789-91, 97-99; Federalist presdl. elector. Died Salem, May 15, 1817; buried St. John's Episcopal Cemetery.

SINNICKSON, Thomas, congressman, jurist; b. Salem, N.J., Dec. 13, 1786. Became a mcht.; judge N.J. Ct. of Errors and Appeals; mem. N.J. Gen. Assembly; judge Ct. of Common Pleas, 20 years; mem. U.S. Ho. of Reps. (filled vacancy) from N.J., Dec. 1, 1828-29. Died Salem, Feb. 17, 1873; buried St. John's Episcopal Cemetery.

SITGREAVES, Charles, congressman, businessman; b. Easton, Pa., Apr. 22, 1803; studied law. Admitted to bar, Easton, 1824, began practice of law, Phillipsburg, N.J.; mem. N.J. Gen. Assembly, 1831-33; maj. commandant N.J. Militia, 1828-38; mem. town council, 1834-35; mem. N.J. Senate, 1851-54; pres. Belvidere & Del. R.R. Co.; mayor Phillipsburg, 1861-62; pres. Nat. Bank of Phillipsburg, 1856-78; mem. U.S. Ho. of Reps. (Democrat) from N.J., 39th-40th congresses, 1865-69. Died Phillipsburg, Mar. 17, 1878; buried Seventh Street Cemetery, Easton.

SITGREAVES, John, Continental congressman; b. Eng., 1757; attended Eton Coll.; came to U.S., studied law. Admitted to bar, began practice of law, New Bern, N.C.; served to lt. during Revolutionary War, later served as mil. aide to Gen. Caswell; commr. in charge of confiscated property; clk. N.C. Senate, 1778-79; mem. Continental Congress from N.C., 1784-85; mem. N.C. Ho. of Commons, 1784, 86-89, speaker, 1787-88; U.S. dist. judge for N.C., 1789-1802. Died Halifax, N.C., Mar. 4, 1802; buried City Cemetery, Raleigh, N.C.

SITGREAVES, Samuel, congressman, lawyer; b. Phila., Mar. 16, 1764; studied law. Admitted to bar, Phila., 1783, began practice, Easton, Pa., 1786; del. Pa. Constl. Conv., 1790; mem. U.S. Ho. of Reps. (Federalist) from Pa., 4th-5th congresses, 1795-98 (resigned), a mgr. apptd. by Ho. of Reps. to conduct impeachment proceedings against Senator William Blount from Tenn., 1798; apptd. U.S. commr. to Gt. Britain under Jay Treaty, 1798; burgess of Easton, 1804-07; treas. Northampton County, 1816-19; pres. Easton Bank, 1815-27. Died Easton, Apr. 4, 1827; buried Easton Cemetery.

SITJAR, Buenaventura, missionary; b. Porrera, Majorca, Balearic Islands, Dec. 9, 1739. Joined Franciscan Order, 1758, ordained priest Roman Catholic Ch.; sent to San Fernando Coll., Mexico City, Mexico; apptd. by Junipero Serra 1st missionary in Cal., 1771, worked among and baptized some 3400 Indians; wrote grammar of Telame lang. Died Mission of San Antonio, Cal., Sept. 3, 1808.

SITTING BULL, Indian chief; b. Grand River, S.D., circa 1834; s. Sitting Bull. Medicine man, polit. leader Sioux, Arapaho, Cheyenne Indians, from circa 1870; became leader of war council of Sioux Confederacy by 1875 (camp attracted large number of disaffected warriors of the Sioux. Araphoe, Cheyenne Indians); did no fighting at Battle of Little Big Horn, 1876; took refuge in Can., circa 1876-circa 1881; surrendered to U.S. Army Ft. Byford, 1881; took active part in Messiah agitation, 1890; known as a stalwart antagonist of white rule and of settlement of Indians on reservations, used his position as a medicine man to gain influence among Indians. Arrested by Indian police, shot and killed S.D., Dec. 15, 1890; buried Mil. Cemetery, Ft. Yates, S.D.

SIZER, Nelson, phrenologist; b. Chester, Mass., May 27, 1812; s. Fletcher and Lydia (Bassett) S.; m. 2d, Sarah Remington, Mar. 12, 1843; 3 children. Lectr. in South and East, 1839-49; became examiner in phrenological cabinet of Orson Fowler and Samuel Wells, N.Y.C., 1849; editor Am. Phrenological Jour., 1859-63; pres. Am. Inst. Phrenology, 1866. Author: Heads and Faces, and How to Study Them, 1885; How to Study Strangers by Temperament, Face, and Head, 1895; Forty Years in Phrenology, 1882. Died Bklyn., Oct. 18, 1897.

SKANIADARIIO (also known as Ganiodaiio or Handsome Lake), Indian religious leader; b. village of Ganawaugus, west side Genesee River, 1735. Following severe illness in 1796, declared he had been informed by Creator of certain precepts that were to constitute new religion, Gaiwiio; gave a new faith based on abstention from witchcraft, drunkenness and infidelity to Iroquois, 1800-15; religion survived among Iroquois for several generations, weakening older tribal religion. Died Onondaga, N.Y., Aug. 10, 1815.

SKELTON, Charles, congressman, physician; b. Bucks County, Pa., Apr. 19, 1806; attended Trenton (N.J.) Acad.; grad. Jefferson Med. Coll., Phila., 1838. Became a mcht.; moved to Phila., 1835; began practice of medicine, Phila., circa 1838; returned to Trenton, 1841; supt. public schs. Trenton, 1848; mem. U.S. Ho. of Reps. (Democrat) from N.J., 32d-33d congresses, 1851-55; mem. common council, 1873-75. Died Trenton, May 20, 1879; buried City Cemetery, Hamilton Square, Mercer County, N.J.

SKENANDOA, Indian chief; b. 1706. Born into another tribe, adopted by Oneida Indians at early age; converted to Christianity by Samuel Kirkland, 1755; fought against French in French and Indian Wars; instrumental in keeping Oneida and Tuscarora Indians from joining rest of Iroquois Confedn. in fighting for British, 1775; persuaded Oneida Indians to remain neutral, 1775; influenced many Oneida and Tuscarora Indians to join Americans, 1775-76. Died nr. Oneida Castle, N.Y., Mar. 11, 1816; buried Clinton, N.Y., reinterred graveyard Hamilton Coll., Clinton.

SKILLIN, John, ship carver; b. 1746; s. Simeon Skillin. Worked as carver, Boston, 1767-1800; carved figurehead for Continental frigate Confederacy, 1778; in partnership with brother Simeon, after 1780. Died Boston, Jan. 24, 1800.

SKILLIN, Simeon, ship carver; b. 1716; children include Simeon, John Samuel, Active as ship carver, Boston, circa 1738-78; commd. to carve figurehead for brig Hazard (one of 1st armed ships of Revolutionary War), 1777. Died 1778.

SKILLIN, Simeon, Jr., ship carver; b. 1756/57; s. Simeon Skillin. Ship carver, Boston, circa 1776-1806; worked in partnership with brother John; carved 1st figurehead for frigate Constitution; carved bust of Milton, 4 figures for garden of Elias Hasket Derby, Salem, Mass., during 1790's. Died 1806.

SKINNER, Halcyon, inventor; b. Mantua, O., Mar. 6, 1824; s. Joseph and Susan (Eggleston) S.; m. Eliza Pierce, 2 sons and 3 daus.; m. 2d, Adelaide Cropsey. Designed hand loom to weave figured carpet, 1850; constructed and patented power loom to weave tufted carpet, 1856; invented power loom to weave ingrain carpets; patented power loom for weaving moquette carpets, 1877. Died Nov. 28, 1900.

SKINNER, John Stuart, editor; b. Calvert County, Md., Feb. 22, 1788; s. Frederick Skinner; m. Elizabeth G. Davies, Mar. 10, 1812, 3 children. Admitted to bar, 1809; insp. European mails, Annapolis, 1812; agt. for prisoners of war and purser in navy, 1814; postmaster Balt., 1816-37; founder and editor Am. Farmer (1st continuous agrl. periodical in U.S.), 1819-29, sold, 1830; founder Am. Turf Register and Sporting Magazine (1st of its kind in U.S.), 1829, sold, 1835; 3d asst. postmaster-gen. U.S., 1841-45; editor Farmer's Library and Monthly Jour. of Agr., 1845-48; founder periodical The Plough, the Loom and the Anvil, Phila., 1848. Author: The Dog and the Sportsman, 1845; editor many agrl. works. Died Balt., Mar. 21, 1851.

SKINNER, Richard, congressman, gov. Vt., lawyer; b. Litchfield, Conn., May 30, 1778; grad. Litchfield Law Sch. Admitted to the bar, 1800, began practice law, Manchester, Vt.; state's atty. for Bennington County, 1801-13, 19; judge of probate Manchester dist., 1806-13; mem. U.S. Ho. of Reps. (Democrat) from Vt., 13th Congress, 1813-15; asst. judge Vt. Supreme Ct., 1815-16; mem. Vt. Ho. of Reps., 1815, 18, speaker, 1818; gov. Vt., 1820-23; chief justice Supreme Ct. of Vt., 1823-28; pres. northeastern br. Am. Ednl. Soc.; trustee Middlebury (Vt.) Coll. Died Manchester, May 23, 1833; buried Dellwood Cemetery.

SKINNER, Thomas Harvey, clergyman, educator; b. Harvey's Neck, N.C., Mar. 7, 1791; s. Joshua and Martha Ann Skinner; grad. Princeton, 1809; studied theology under Pres. Samuel Stanhope Smith of Princeton after 1811; D.D. (hon.), Williams Coll., 1826, LL.D. (hon.), 1855; married, several children including Thomas Harvey. Ordained to ministry Presbyn. Ch., Phila., 1813; pastor 5th Presbyn. ch., Phila., 1816-32; prof. sacred rhetoric Andover Theol. Sem., 1832-35; pastor New Mercer Street Presbyn. Ch., N.Y.C 1835-circa 1847; a founder, dir. Union Theol. Sem.; moderator Presbyn. Gen. Assembly (New Sch.), 1854; prof. rhetoric, 1848-71. Author: Aids to Preaching and Hearing, 1839; Discussions in Theology, 1868. Died N.Y.C., Feb. 1, 1871.

SKINNER, Thomson Joseph, congressman; b. Colchester, Conn., May 24, 1752; prep. edn. Moved to Mass.; mem. Mass. Ho. of Reps., 1781, 85, 1789-1801; mem. Mass. Senate, 1786-88, 90-97, 1802-03; del. Mass. Conv. which ratified U.S. Constn., 1788; judge Ct. of Common Pleas, 1788-1807; presdl. elector for Washington and Adams, 1792; treas. State of Mass., 1806-07; mem. U.S. Ho. of Reps. (Democrat, filled vacancy) from Mass., 4th-5th, 8th congresses, Jan. 27, 1797-99, 1803-Aug. 10, 1804 (resigned). Died Boston, Jan. 20, 1809.

SKINNER, William, mfr.; b. London, Eng., Nov. 14, 1824; s. John and Sarah (Hollins) S.; m. Nancy Edward Warner, Apr. 12, 1842; m. 2d, Sarah Elizabeth Allen, May 15, 1856; 7 children. Came to Florence, Mass., offered position of foreman in dyeing factory by friend of his father's; took over bus. after employer failed, developed firm into Nonotuck Co.; started (with Joseph Warner) firm to manufacture sewing silk, 1848; built mill between Haydenville and Williamsburg (now Skinnerville; named for him), Mass., circa 1849; lost everything but his home in flood of 1874; settled in Holyoke, Mass., 1874, commd. by Holyoke Water Power Co. to set up a mill; formed partnership William Skinner & Sons, 1883; founder Holyoke City Hosp.; trustee Vassar Coll., Mt. Holyoke Coll. Died Feb. 28, 1902.

SLADE, Charles, congressman; born in Eng.; came to Am. with parents; attended pub. schs., Alexandria, Va. Moved to Carlyle. Ill., became a mcht.; held several local offices; mem. Ill. Ho. of Reps., 1820, 26; mem. U.S. Ho. of Reps. (Democrat) from Ill., 23d Congress, 1833-34. Died nr. Vincennes, Ind., July 26, 1834.

SLADE, Joseph Alfred, (Jack Slade), outlaw; b. Carlyle, Ill., circa 1824. Served with U.S. Army in N.M., 1847-48; freighter and wagon boss for Russell, Majors and Waddell, late 1850's, apptd. div. agt. in Julesburg, Colo. with instrns. to rid area of bandits who were preying on co. property, 1860; known to have worn the dried ears of his victims on his watch chain; transferred to Virginia Dale, Colo., 1862, discharged because of drunkeness; went to Mont. gold fields; worked for small freighting outfit in Mont., 1863, but again started drinking robustly; called in by Peoples Ct. in Virginia City, Mont., challenged and killed the judge with a revolver; a prominent figure in Mark Twain's Roughing It. Hung by Vigilantes of Virginia City (in reaction to his murder of judge), Mar. 10, 1864.

SLADE, William, gov. Vt., congressman; b. Cornwall, Vt., May 9, 1786; s. Capt. William and Rebecca (Plumb) S.; grad. Middlebury Coll., 1807; m. Abigail Foote, Feb. 5, 1810, 9 children. Admitted to Vt. bar, 1810; Democrat; helped found Columbian Patriot, weekly newspaper, 1813, became National Standard, 1815, editor and propr. circa 1814-17; sec. of state Vt., 1815; judge county court, Vt., 1816-22, then state's atty.; clk. Dept. of State, Washington, D.C., 1824-29; mem. U.S. Ho. of Reps. from Vt., 22d-27th congresses, Nov. 1, 1831-Mar. 3, 1843; joined Whig party; reporter Vt. Supreme Ct., 1843-44; gov. of Vt., 1844-46; corr. sec., gen. agt. of bd. of Nat. Popular Edn., 1846-59; published Vermont State Papers, 1823. Died Middlebury, Vt., Jan. 18, 1859; buried West Cemetery, Middlebury.

SLATER, John Fox, mfr., philanthropist; b. Slatersville, R.I., Mar. 4, 1815; s. John and Ruth (Bucklin) S.; m. Marianna L. Hubbard, May 13, 1844, 6 children. Partner (with brother William S. Slater) textile mfg. firm, Norwich, Conn., 1843-72; a founder, contbr. to endowment Norwich Free Acad., 1868; contbr. one million dollars for Negro Christian edn.; contbr. John F. Slater Fund (incorporated by N.Y. State, 1882, distributed over four million dollars for tng. tchrs. for Negroes). Died Norwich, May 7, 1884.

SLATER, Samuel, textile exec.; b. "Holly House," Belper, Derbyshire, Eng., June 9, 1768; s. William and Elizabeth (Fox) S.; m. Hannah Wilkinson, Oct. 2, 1791; m. 2d, Mrs. Esther Parkinson, Nov. 21, 1817; 9 children. Became thoroughly acquainted with cotton machinery as made by Arkwright, Hargreaves and Crompton in Eng., 1783-89; came to U.S., 1789; contracted with Moses Brown to reproduce cotton machinery, 1790; builder 1st factory of Almy, Brown & Slater, Pawtucket, R.I., 1793; became partner (with father-in-law and brothers-in-law) Samuel Slater & Co., erected textile plant nr. Pawtucket, 1798; builder mill, Amoskeag Falls, N.H. (beginning of indsl. center now located at Manchester, N.H.); founder Mfrs. Bank, Pawtucket, pres. 15 years; considered founder of Am. cotton textile industry. Died Webster, Mass., Apr. 21, 1835.

SLAUGHTER, Philip, clergyman; b. "Springfield," Culpeper County, Va., Oct. 26, 1808; s Philip and Elizabeth (Towles) S.; attended U. Va., 1825-28, Theol. Sem., Alexandria, Va., 1833-34; D.D. (hon.), Coll. William and Mary, 1874; m. Anne Sophia Semmes, June 20, 1834, 1 surviving child. Practiced law in Va., 1828-33; ordained deacon Episcopal Ch., 1834, priest, 1835; pastor in Va., 1835-47; founder and editor Va. Colonizationist, (advocated colonization of Negro slaves in Africa), 1850-55; publisher religious paper Army and Navy Messenger, circa 1861-65; elected historiographer Diocese of Va., 1879. Author: A History of Bristol Parish, 1846; A History of St. George's Parish, 1847; Man and Woman, 1860; Life of Hon. William Green, Jurist and Scholar, 1883; Views from Cedar Mountains, in Fiftieth Year of Ministry and Marriage, 1884. The Colonial Church in Virginia, 1885. Died June 12, 1890.

SLAYMAKER, Amos, congressman, businessman; b. London Lands, Lancaster County, Pa., Mar. 11, 1755. Became a farmer, builder, operator hotel on Lancaster and Phila. pike, also promoter; a propr. of stage line over the pike; served as ensign in co. of Capt. John Slaymaker during Revolutionary War; mem. assn. formed for suppression of Tory activities in Lancaster County; justice of peace Salisbury Twp.; county commr. Lancaster County, 1806-10; mem. Pa. Senate, 1810-11; mem. U.S. Ho. of Reps. from Pa. (filled vacancy), 13th Congress, Oct. 11, 1814-15. Died Salisbury, Pa., June 12. 1837.

SLEEPER, Jacob, mcht., philanthropist; b. Newcastle, Me., Nov. 21, 1802; s. Jacob and Olive (Dinsdale) S.; m. Eliza Davis, May 7, 1827; m. 2d, Maria Davis, Apr. 7, 1835; 4 children. Partner, Carney & Sleeper, clothiers, 1835-50; mem. Mass. Ho. of Reps., 1851-52. Mass. Gov.'s Council, 1859-61; alderman Boston 1852-53; dir. Bank of Commerce Boston, N. Am. Ins. Co.; mem. Bromfield Street Methodist Ch., Boston, supt. Sunday Sch. for 59 years, treas. bd. trustees for 46 years; original mem. Boston Wesleyan Assn., frequently pres.; pres. New Eng. Methodist Hist. Soc.; trustee Wesleyan U., 1844-78; overseer Harvard, 1856-68; a founder (donated half-million dollars) Boston U., 1869, treas., 1869-73, v.p. corp. 1875-89; an organizer New Eng. Edn. Soc., 1855; benefactor Boston YMCA; endowed Wesleyan Home for Orphans, Newton, Mass.; contbd: $10,000 to New Eng. Conservatory of Music; pres. Mass. Bible Soc. Died Boston, Mar. 31, 1889.

SLIDELL, John, senator, Confederate diplomat; b. N.Y.C., circa 1793; s. John and Margery (Mackenzie) S.; grad. Columbia, 1810; m. Mathilde Deslonde, 1835, 3 or 4 children. Admitted to bar, N.Y.C., circa 1815; dist. atty., New Orleans, 1829-30; mem. U.S. Ho. of Reps. (Democrat) from La., 28th Congress, 1843-45; U.S. commr. to Mexico to adjust Tex. boundary, to purchase N.M., Cal., 1845, did not accomplish goal, helped prepare Am. attitude for war; polit. boss. of La., during 1850's; mem. U.S. Senate from La., 1853-61; Buchanan's campaign mgr., 1856, instrumental in obtaining his nomination and election; presented resolution in Senate to grant Pres. limited authority to suspend neutrality laws, 1858; as chief power behind Buchanan adminstrn, managed redistbn. of fed. patronage in Ill.; apptd. Confederate commr. to France, 1861; removed (with John Mason) from Brit. mail steamer, Nov. 8, 1861, detained at Ft. Warren, Boston (caused crisis between Eng., U.S.);

arrived France, 1862, proposed recognition of independence and a Franco-Confederate treaty to admit French products duty free, provide cotton subsidy for naval convoys of mcht. vessels; Napoleon III proposed 6 months armistice, never recognized Confederacy because of English attitude); arranged (with James D. Bulloch) for constrn. of 2 ironclads, 4 corvettes in France, 1863 (ships never delivered); supported French puppet regime in Mexico (unable to obtain French diplomatic recognition in return); arranged Confederate bond issue by French bankers, 1863; lived in France until 1870. Died Cowes, Eng., July 29, 1871.

SLINGERLAND, John I., congressman, farmer; b. Jerusalem, Albany County, N.Y., Mar. 1, 1804; attended public schs. Became farmer; mem. N.Y. State Assembly, 1843-44, 60-61; mem. U.S. Ho. of Reps. (Republican) from N.Y., 30th Congress, 1847-49. Died Slingerland, N.Y., Oct. 26, 1861; buried Slingerland family mausoleum.

SLOAN, Andrew, congressman, lawyer; b. McDonough, Henry County, Ga., June 10, 1845; attended Marshall Coll., Griffin, Ga., also Bethany (W.Va.) Coll.; studied law. Admitted to bar, 1866, practiced law; solicitor Henry County, 1866; moved to Savannah, Ga.; dep. collector customs, 1867; asst. U.S. dist. atty., 1869; apptd. dist. atty. until 1872 (resigned); also local counsel for U.S. for cotton claims and with commn. on Brit. and Am. claims; mem. U.S. Ho. of Reps. (Republican, contested election) from Ga., 43d Congress, Mar. 24, 1874-75; moved to N.M., 1881, settled in Silver City. Died Silver City, Sept. 22, 1883; buried City Cemetery.

SLOAN, Andrew Scott, congressman, lawyer; b. Morrisville, Madison County, N.Y., June 12, 1820; attended Morrisville Acad.; studied law. Admitted to bar, 1842, practiced in Morrisville; clk. Madison County Ct., 1847-49; moved to Wis., 1854, settled in Beaver Dam, Dodge County, practiced law; mem. Wis. Assembly, 1857; mayor Beaver Dam, 1857-58, 79; apptd. judge 3d Dist. Circuit Ct., 1858; mem. U.S. Ho. of Reps. (Republican) from Wis., 37th Congress, 1861-63; clk. U.S. Dist. Ct. for Wis., 1864-66; judge Dodge County Ct., 1868-74; atty. gen. Wis., 1874-78; judge 13th Jud. Dist. Circuit Ct., 1882-95. Died Beaver Dam, Wis., Apr. 8, 1895; buried Oakwood Cemetery.

SLOAN, James, congressman; b. N.J. Became farmer; assessor Newton Twp. for several years; held several local offices; mem. U.S. Ho. of Reps. from N.J., 8th-10th congresses, 1803-09. Died Gloucester County, N.J., Nov. 1811.

SLOANE, John, U.S. treas., congressman; b. York, Pa., 1779; completed prep. studies. Mem. Ohio Ho. of Reps., 1803-05, 07; col. of militia in War of 1812; U.S. receiver public moneys, Canton, O., 1808-16, Wooster, O., 1816-19; mem. U.S. Ho. of Reps. (Whig) from Ohio, 16th-20th congresses, 1819-29; apptd. clk. Wayne County Ct. Common Pleas, 1831, served for several years; sec. state Ohio, 1841-44; treas. U.S., 1850-53. Died Wooster, May 15, 1856; buried Oak Hill Cemetery.

SLOANE, Jonathan, lawyer; b. Pelham, Mass., Nov. 1785; grad. Williams Coll., 1812; studied law. Admitted to bar, 1816, practiced in Ravenna, O.; gen. agt. of Tappan family for sale of lands; pros. atty. Portage County, O., 1819; mem. Ohio Ho. of Reps., 1820-22, Ohio Senate, 1826-27; mem. U.S. Ho. of Reps. (Whig) from Ohio, 23d-24th congresses, 1833-37; retired from business because of poor health. Died Ravenna, Apr. 25, 1854; buried Evergreen Cemetery.

SLOAT, John Drake, naval officer; b. Goshen, N.Y., July 26, 1781; s. Capt. John and Ruth (Drake) S.; m. Abby Gordon, Nov. 27, 1814, 3 children. Served as master U.S. Navy, 1812, commd. lt., 1813; received 1st naval command in schooner Grampus, 1823; cruised Windward Islands suppressing piracy, 1824-25; commd. master comdt., 1826, capt., 1837; comdt. Portsmouth (Va.) Navy Yard, 1840-44; comdr. Pacific Squadron, 1844-46, landed detachment of marines, took possession of Cal., 1846; sent one of officers to take possession of San Francisco, 1846; comdt. Norfolk (Va.) Navy Yard, 1848-51; on spl. duty with bur. Constrn. and Repair, 1852-51; on spl. duty with bur. Constrn. and Repair, 1852-55; promoted to commodore, 1862, rear adm., 1866 (both ret.). Died Staten Island, N.Y., Nov. 28, 1867; buried Greenwood Cemetery, Bklyn.

SLOCUM, Francis, Indian captive; b. Warwick, R.I., Mar. 4, 1773; d. Jonathan and Ruth (Tripp) Slocum; m. Little Turtle (Delaware Indian); m. 2d, Shepancanah (Miami Indian), 4 children. Moved with family to upper Susquehanna Valley, nr. Wyoming, Pa., 1777; captured when family was attacked by Delaware Indians, 1778, adopted by Delaware family and given name Weletawash; remained behind when her Delaware Indian husband went West, married a Miami Indian and settled in his village (now Peru, Ind.); Miami Nation confined to reservation on Wabash River by Treaty of St. Mary's, 1818; discovered by a chance traveler, 1837, visited by her white relatives; after treaty which sent Miami Nation West, 1840, remained with her Indian family, refused to return to white relatives on the Susquehanna. Died Mar. 9, 1847.

SLOCUM, Henry Warner, congressman, army officer; b. Delphi, Onondaga County, N.Y., Sept. 24, 1827; s. Matthew Barnard and Mary (Ostrander) S.; grad. U.S. Mil. Acad., 1852; m. Clara Rice, Feb. 9, 1854, 4 children. Commd. 1st lt. U.S. Army, 1855; admitted to N.Y. bar, 1858; mem. N.Y. State Assembly, 1859; col. 27th N.Y. Inf., 1861; commd. brig. gen. U.S. Volunteers, 1861, maj. gen., 1862, in command XII Army Corps; fought at Battle of Gettysburg, 1863; commanded dist. of Vicksburg, 1864 and participated in march through Ga. and Carolinas commanding XIV and XX Corps comprising left wing of Sherman's forces; command of Dept. of Miss., 1865; mem. U.S. Ho. of Reps. (Democrat) from N.Y., 41st-42d, 48th congresses, 1869-73, 83-85; commr. pub. works Bklyn., 1876. Died N.Y.C., Apr. 14, 1894.

SLOCUM, Joseph, mfr.; b. Wilkes-Barre, Pa., July 15, 1800; s. Ebenezer and Sarah (Davis) S.; m. Eldida Bingham, Dec. 22, 1830. Worked for his father's various business enterprises (including distilleries, saw mill, coal mines), took over mgmt. (with his brother) when father retired, 1828; twp. collector Slocum Hollow, 1833; burgess, city auditor Scranton (Pa.); owned over 600 acres of land in Scranton. Died June 22, 1890.

SLOCUM, Samuel, inventor, mfr.; b. Canonicut Island, Jamestown Twp., Newport County, R.I. Mar. 4, 1792; s. Peleg and Anne (Dyer) S.; m. Susan Stanton, 1817, 3 surviving children. Perfected, patented machine to make wrought-iron nails, London, 1835; invented, patented machine for making pins with solid heads, 1835; established pin mfg. firm Slocum & Jillson, Poughkeepsie, N.Y., by 1840, operated firm till 1846; patented machine for sticking pins on paper, 1841, developed in partnership with John Ireland House, 1841, sold his interest to Am. Pin. Co., 1846; received extension and reissue of his patented machine for sticking pins on paper, 1855. Died Pawtucket, R.I., Jan. 26, 1861.

SLOCUMB, Jesse, congressman; b. Spring Bank, Dobbs (later Wayne) County, N.C., 1780; completed prep. studies. Became farmer; held several local offices; mem. county ct. pleas and quarter sessions; register of deeds, 1802-08; mem. U.S. Ho. of Reps. (Federalist) from N.C., 15th-16th congresses, 1817-Dec. 20, 1820. Died Washington, D.C., Dec. 20, 1820; buried Congressional Cemetery.

SLOSS, James Withers, businessman; b. Mooresville, Ala., Apr. 7, 1820; s. Joseph and Clarissa (Wasson) S.; m. Mary Bigger, Apr. 7, 1842; m. 2d, Martha Lundie; 12 children. Bookkeeper for butcher in home town, 1835-42; opened gen. store, Athens, Ala., after 1842; opened branch stores, Northern Ala., purchased number of plantations nr. Decatur, Ala., by late 1850's; combined number of smaller railroads into Nashville and Decatur R.R., after Civil War, became pres. by 1867, later extended line to Montgomery and Birmingham, Ala.; founded (with Truman Aldrich and H. F. De Bardeleben) Pratt Coal and Coke Co., Birmingham, 1878, withdrew from co., 1879; bought into Eureka Mining Co. (1st co. in Birmingham dist. to make pig iron with coke instead of charcoal), 1879; organized Sloss Furnace Co. (later became Sloss-Sheffield Steel & Iron Co.), Birmingham, 1881. Died May 4, 1890.

SLOSS, Louis, businessman; b. Bavaria (now Germany), July 13, 1823; m. Sarah Greenebaum, July 19, 1855, 6 children. Came to U.S., 1845, opened country store, Mackville, Ky.; went to Cal. during gold rush, 1849; owner (with Lewis Gerstle) wholesale grocery bus. Louis Sloss and Co., Sacramento, Cal., 1852-61, moved firm to San Francisco, 1862; opened stock brokerage office, San Francisco, 1862, acquired seat on San Francisco Stock and Exchange Bd. by 1866; organized Alaska Comml. Co. (obtained exclusive rights to seal fishing on Pribilof Islands), 1870; contbd. much money to charities and to setting up worthy people in bus. Died San Rafael, Cal., June 4, 1902.

SMALL, Alvan Edmond, homeopathic physician; b. Wales, Me., Mar. 4, 1811; s. Joseph and Mary (Jackson) S.; grad. Pa. Med. Coll., 1841; m. Martha Mary Sloan, 1834, 4 children. Prof. physiology, pathology Homeopathic Med. Coll. of Pa., 1848-56; 1st dean Hahnemann Med. Coll., Chgo., 1859-65, prof. theory and practice medicine, 1860-69, pres., 1869-85 (or 86); elected life mem. Chgo. Hist. Soc., 1869; gen. sec. Am. Inst. of Homeopathy, 1849-50, pres. 1850; co-editor Phila. Jour. of Homeopathy, 1849-50. Author: Manual of Homeopathic Practice, 1854; Diseases of the Nervous System, 1856. Died Chgo., Dec. 31, 1886.

SMALL, William Bradbury, congressman, lawyer; b. Limington, Me., May 17, 1817; attended Phillips Exeter (N.H.) Acad.; studied law. Admitted to bar, 1846, practiced in Newmarket, N.H.; solicitor Rockingham County (N.H.); mem. N.H. Ho. of Reps., 1865; mem. N.H. Senate, 1870; mem. U.S. Ho. of Reps. (Republican) from N.H., 43d Congress, 1873-75; practiced law, also became banker. Died Newmarket, Apr. 7, 1878; buried Riverside Cemetery.

SMALLEY, Eugene Virgil, journalist; b. Randolph, O., July 18, 1841; s. Jared Frost and Cordelia (Lewis) S.; m. Josephine M. Conday, 1873, at least 2 children including a step-son. Learned printer's trade at age of 11; served with 7th Ohio Inf. from outbreak of Civil War until wounded; reporter Cleve. (O.) Herald, 1862; held minor clerkship in Treasury Dept., 1863-67; owner Mahoning Register, Youngstown, O., 1868; became free lance journalist, 1868; traveled in Europe, contbd. articles to N.Y. Tribune, 1869-70, became regular staff mem., 1871; founder, editor Northwest Illustrated Monthly Mag. 1883, moved to St. Paul, Minn., 1884; mem. St. Paul C. of C. Author: A Brief History of the Republican Party, 1884; American Journalism—An Appendix to the Encyclopaedia Britannica, 1884. Died Dec. 30, 1899.

SMALLWOOD, William, army officer, gov. Md.; b. Charles County, Md., 1732; s. Bayne and Priscilla (Heaberd) S. Mem. Md. Assembly, 1761; del. to Md. Conv. of 1775; joined Assn. of Freemen of Md., 1775; commanded a regt. Md. Militia, 1776; served in Battle of L.I.; commd. brig. gen. Continental Army, 1776; protected Gen. Washington's stores near head of Elk River, Wilmington, Del., suppressed Tory revolt on Eastern Shores of Md., 1778-79; commd. maj. gen., 1780; sent to Md. to obtain supplies and reinforcements, 1780-83; served as drill master, raised troops and supplies; gov. Md., 1785-88, called Md. Conv. which ratified U.S. Constn. Died Prince George's County, Md., Feb. 12, 1792; buried Charles County, Md.

SMART, Ephraim Knight, congressman, lawyer; b. Prospect (now Searsport), Me., Sept. 3, 1813; attended Me. Wesleyan Sem., Readfield; studied law. Admitted to bar, 1838, practiced in Camden, Knox County, Me.; apptd. postmaster Camden, 1838, 45; mem. Me. Senate, 1841-42, 62; apptd. a.d.c. with rank of lt. col. on staff Gov. Fairfield, 1842; moved to Mo., 1843, practiced law; returned to Camden, 1844; mem. U.S. Ho. of Reps. (Democrat) from Me., 30th, 32d congresses, 1847-49, 51-53; collector customs, Belfast, 1853-58; founded Me. Free Press, 1854, editor 3 years; mem. Me. Ho. of Reps., 1858; unsuccessful candidate for gov. Me., 1860; moved to Biddeford, York County, Me., 1869, founded Me. Democrat. Died Camden, Sept. 29, 1872; buried Mountain Street Cemetery.

SMELT, Dennis, congressman; b. nr. Savannah, Ga., circa 1750. Served in Revolutionary War; mem. U.S. Ho. of Reps. (filled vacancy) from Ga., 9th-11th congresses, Sept. 1, 1806-11.

SMET, Pierre-Jean de, see de Smet, Pierre-Jean.

SMIBERT, John, painter; b. Edinburgh, Scotland, 1688; s. John and Alison (Bell) S.; studied painting in Italy, 1717-20; m. Mary Williams, July 30, 1730, 9 children including Nathaniel. Came to Va., 1728; founder studio, Boston, 1730; portrait painter of eminent personages of Mass., including Sir William Essex Pepperrell (painted circa 1745, now in Essex Inst., Salem, Mass.); propr. store (in his house) for sale painting equipment and prints, Boston; designer Faneuil Hall, Boston, built 1742; profl. career ended, circa 1748. Died Boston, Apr. 2, 1751; buried Granary Burying Ground, Boston.

SMILIE, John, congressman; b. Ireland, 1741; attended public schs. Came to America, settled in Pa., 1760; served in Revolutionary War; moved to Fayette, Pa., 1780; mem. Pa. Ho. of Reps., 1784-86; mem. Pa. Constl. Conv., 1790; mem. Pa. Senate, 1790-93 (resigned); mem. U.S. Ho. of Reps. (Democrat) from Pa., 3d, 6th-12th congresses, 1793-95, 99-Dec. 30, 1812; Dem. presdl. elector, 1796. Died Washington, D.C., Dec. 30, 1812; buried Congressional Cemetery.

SMILLIE, James, engraver; b. Edinburgh, Scotland, Nov. 23, 1807; s. David and Elizabeth (Cummins) S.; m. Katharine Van Valkenbergh, 1832, 6 children including James David, George Henry, William Main. Settled in N.Y. as banknote engraver, 1830; engraved on steel works of some of leading figure painters and landscapists of period, especially successful as engraver of landscapes; supplied prints of sketches by Richards, Weir, Chapman and other artists; devoted time to engraving banknote vignettes, after 1861; asso. mem. N.A.D., 1832-51. Died Poughkeepsie, N.Y., Dec. 4, 1885.

SMITH, Abby Hadassah, suffragette; b. Glastonbury, Conn., June 1, 1797; d. Zephaniah and Hannah Hadassah (Hickock) H.; Took over family homestead after parents' death; became active (with her sister) in women's suffrage movement, Hartford, Conn.; attended Woman's Congress, N.Y.C., 1873; refused to pay taxes without a vote in town meeting, from 1873 until death; attended hearing on equal suffrage amendment before com. of U.S. Senate, 1878; annually petitioned Conn. Legislature for the vote. Died July 23, 1878.

SMITH, Abraham Herr, congressman, lawyer; b. nr. Millersville, Manor Twp., Lancaster County, Pa., Mar. 7, 1815; attended Prof. Beck's Acad., Lititz, Pa.; grad. Dickinson Coll., Carlisle, Pa., 1840; studied law. Admitted to bar, 1842, practiced in Lancaster, Pa.; mem. Pa. Ho. of Reps., 1843-44, Pa. Senate, 1845; mem. U.S. Ho. of Reps. (Republican) from Pa. 43d-48th congresses, 1873-85. Died Lancaster, Feb. 16, 1894; buried Woodward Hill Cemetery.

SMITH, Adrian W., architect; b. Cincinnati, Dec. 6, 1860; ed. in Cincinnati; studied architecture, Balt. Established archtl. office, Phila.; known for his design of Roman Catholic chs. and institutional bldgs., including Convent of Visitation, Wilmington, Del., Convent of Sacred Heart, Phila.; mem. A.I.A. Died Dec. 18, 1892.

SMITH, Albert, congressman, lawyer; b. Hanover, Mass., Jan. 3, 1793; grad. Brown U., 1813; studied law. Admitted to bar, practiced in Portland, Me., 1817; mem. Me. Ho. of Reps., 1820; U.S. marshal for Dist. of Me., 1830-38; mem. U.S. Ho. of Reps. (Democrat) from Me., 26th Congress, 1839-41; retired from public life. Died Boston, May 29, 1867; buried Mt. Auburn Cemetery, Cambridge, Mass.

SMITH, Albert, congressman, lawyer; b. Cooperstown, N.Y., June 22, 1805; completed prep. studies; studied law. Moved to Batavia, N.Y.; admitted to bar, practiced law; held several local offices; mem. N.Y. State Assembly, 1840; mem. U.S. Ho. of Reps. (Republican) from N.Y., 28th-29th congresses, 1843-47; moved to Milw., 1849, practiced law; justice of peace, 1851-59; judge Milwaukee County Ct., 1859-70. Died Milw., Aug. 27, 1870; buried Forest Home Cemetery.

SMITH, Albert Holmes, obstetrician, gynecologist; b. Phila., July 19, 1835; s. Moses B. and Rachel (Caote) S.; A.B., U. Pa., 1853, M.D., 1856; m. Emily Kaighn, June 5, 1860, 7 children. Asso. with Phila. Lying In Charity, Women's and Wills Ophthalmic hosps., 1860-82; developed, modified various instruments for practical obstetrics; advocated recognition of women in medicine; founder, pres. Phila. Obstet. Soc., 1874-76; founder Am. Gynaecol. Soc., 1880-81; mem. Am. Philos. Soc. Died Phila., Dec. 16, 1885.

SMITH, Andrew Jackson, army officer; b. Buckingham, Pa., Apr. 28, 1815; s. Samuel and Mrs. (Wilkinson) Smith; grad. U.S. Mil. Acad., 1838; m. Ann Mason Simpson. Served in expdn. to South Pass of Rocky Mountains, 1840; commd. 1st lt. U.S. Army, 1845, capt., 1847; maj. 1st Dragoons, 1861; col. 2d Cal. Cavalry, 1861; became chief of cavalry under Henry Wager Halleck, 1861, served in Corinth campaign, 1862; brig. gen. U.S. Volunteers, 1862, commanded div. in Vicksburg campaign, 1863; maj. gen. U.S. Volunteers, 1864, defeated Nathan Bedford Forrest at Tupelo, Miss., served in Battle of Nashville (Tenn.); commd. lt. col. U.S. Army, 1864; comdr. XVI Corps in Mobile campaign, 1865; col. 7th Cavalry, 1866; postmaster St. Louis, 1869, city auditor, 1877-89; commanded militia brigade during strikes in St. Louis, 1877; col. (ret.) U.S Army, 1889. Died St. Louis, Jan. 30, 1897.

SMITH, Arthur, congressman, lawyer; b. Windsor Castle, nr. Smithfield, Isle of Wight County, Va., Nov. 15, 1785; grad. Coll. William and Mary; studied law. Admitted to bar, 1808, practiced in Smithfield; also became farmer; served as col. in War of 1812; mem. Va. Ho. of Dels., 1818-20, 36-41; mem. U.S. Ho. of Reps. from Va., 17th-18th congresses, 1821-25. Died Smithfield, Mar. 30, 1853; buried family burying ground on Windsor Castle Estate.

SMITH, Asa Dodge, clergyman, coll. pres., b. Amherst, N.H., Sept. 21, 1804; s. Dr. Roger and Sally (Dodge) S.; grad. Dartmouth, 1830, Andover Theol. Sem., 1834; m. Sarah Ann Adams, Nov. 9, 1836. Pastor, Brainerd Presbyn. Ch., N.Y.C., 1834-63; trustee Union Theol. Sem.; mem. controlling bds. of several Presbyn. socs.; pres. Dartmouth Coll. (more than doubled student body, substantially increased scholarship funds, established Thayer Sch. of Engring. and N.H. Coll. of Agr., received large donations), 1863-77. Author many sermons published as pamphlets, also mag. articles. Died Hanover, N.H., Aug. 16, 1877.

SMITH, Ashbel, state ofcl.; b. Hartford, Conn., Aug. 13, 1805; s. Moses and Phoebe (Adams) S.; grad. Yale, 1824, M.D., 1828; studied medicine, Paris, France, 1831-32. Editor and part owner of nullification newspaper Western Carolinian, 1832; surgeon gen. Army of Republic of Tex., 1837; a commr. to negotiate treaty with Comanche Indians, 1838; Tex. minister to Eng. and France, 1842-44; sec. of state Republic of Tex., 1845, negotiated Smith-Cuevas Treaty by which Mexico recognized Tex. independence; mem. Tex. Legislature, 1855, 1866, 78, leader in movements for advancement of edn. in Tex.; served as capt. Bayland Guards, then lt. col. and col. 2d Tex. Volunteer Inf., Civil War; brevetted brig. gen., commanded forces at Matagorda Peninsula, later commanded defenses of Galveston (Tex.); pres. bd. trustees Galveston Med. Sch.; commr. to locate Agrl. and Mech. Coll. for colored youths; a founder, pres. bd. regents U. Tex.; mem. Phi Beta Kappa. Author: An Account of the Yellow Fever Which Appeared in the City of Galveston, 1839. Died Evergreen plantation, Tex., Jan. 21, 1886; buried State Cemetery, Austin, Tex.

SMITH, Azariah, clergyman, missionary; b. Manlius, N.Y., Feb. 16, 1817; s. Azariah and Zilpah (Mack) S.; grad. Yale, 1837; attended Geneva (N.Y.) Med. Coll., 1837-39; grad. Yale Divinity Sch., 1842; m. Corinth Sarah Elder, July 6, 1848, no children. Ordained to ministry Presbyn. Ch., Manlius, 1842, sailed for Constantinople as missionary of Am. Bd. Commrs. for Fgn. Missions; preached and practiced medicine among Gregorian, Armenian and Nestorian Christians throughout Turkey, 1843-45; assigned to Aintab, Turkey, 1847, practiced medicine, published tracts and preached to Christians; published description of 1st excavations in field of Assyriology at Botta in Am. Jour. of Arts and Scis., 1845; obtained recognition for separate civil community for Protestant Armenians in Aintab region from Turkish Govt., circa 1850. Died of typhoid fever while founding ch. at Arabkir, Aintab, June 3, 1851.

SMITH, Benjamin Mosby, clergyman, educator; b. Powhatan County, Va., June 30, 1811; s. Josiah and Judith Micheau (Mosby) S.; grad. Hampden-Sydney Coll., 1829; attended Union Theol. Sem. in Va., 1832-34; m. Mary Morrison, 6 children survived. Instr. Union Theol. Sem., 1834-36; ordained to ministry Presbyn. Ch., 1835; pastorates in Va. and Pa., 1838-54; prof. Oriental literature Union Theol. Sem., 1854-89, prof. emeritus, 1889; moderator Gen. Assembly of Southern Presbyn. Ch. (Presbyn. Ch. of U.S.), 1876; authored report on Prussian primary school system, 1839; county supt. of new board of education in Va., 1870-72; published Family Religion, 1859. Died Mar. 14, 1893.

SMITH, Bernard, congressman; b. Morristown, N.J., July 5, 1776; completed prep. studies. Collector of customs, 1809, 10; postmaster New Brunswick, N.J., 1810-19; mem. U.S. Ho. of Reps. from N.J., 16th Congress, 1819-21; apptd. register Land Office, Little Rock, Ark., 1821; settled in Ark.; sec. to Ark. gov., 1825-28; apptd. by Gov. Izard as subagent of Quapaw Indians, 1825-35. Died Little Rock, July 16, 1835; buried Mt. Holly Cemetery.

SMITH, Buckingham, lawyer, diplomat; b. Cumberland Island, Ga., Oct. 31, 1810; s. Josiah and Hannah (Smith) S.; attended Trinity Coll., Hartford, Conn., circa 1830-circa 1833; grad. Harvard Law Sch., 1836; m. Julia G. Gardner, Sept. 18, 1843. Mem. Fla. Territorial Legislature, 1841; sec. U.S. legation, Mexico City, 1850-52, sec. legation in Spain, 1855-58; del. Democratic Nat. Conv., Balt., 1864; tax commr. in Fla., 1868-70; bequeathed valuable papers to N.Y. Hist. Soc. Author: The Narrative of Alvar Nunez Cabeca de Vaca 1851; Narratives of the Career of Hernando de Soto in the Conquest of Florida, as told by A Knight of Elvas (his most important publ.), 1866. Died Bellevue Hosp., N.Y.C., Jan. 5, 1871; buried St. Augustine, Fla.

SMITH, Byron Caldwell, philologist; b. Island Creek, O., Aug. 28, 1849; s. George and Margaret (Caldwell) S.; attended prep. sch. Ill. Coll., Jacksonville, 1863-68; studied Greek philology U. Heidelberg (Germany), then in Vienna, Austria, 1868-72. Became instr. Greek, U. Kan., 1872, prof., 1873, resigned to go to Phila. for med. treatment, 1874; became engaged to Kate Stephens (his pupil), 1873; editorial writer Phila. Press, 1875-76; went to Boulder, Colo. for health, 1877; letters to parents published as A Young Scholar's Letters, 1897; letters to fiancee published as The Love Life of Byron Caldwell Smith, 1930. Died Boulder, May 4, 1877.

SMITH, Caleb Blood, cabinet officer, congressman; b. Boston, Apr. 16, 1808; attended Coll. of Cincinnati, 1823-25, Miami U., 1825-26; m. Elizabeth B. Walton, July 8, 1831, 3 children. Admitted to Ind. bar, began practice law, 1828; mem. Ind. Ho. of Reps. (Whig), 1832-37, 40-41, speaker, 1835-36, 36-37 co-owner editor Polit. Clarion (changed name to Ind. Sentinel), 1832, apptd. commr. to collect assets, adjust debts, Ind., 1837; mem. U.S. Ho. of Reps. from Ind., 28th-30th congresses, 1842-49; mem. bd. commrs. to adjust claims against Mexico, 1849-51; pres. Cincinnati & Chgo. R.R. Co., 1854-59; del. Republican Nat. Conv., Chgo., 1860; mem. Peace Conv., Washington, D.C., 1861; U.S. sec. of interior under Lincoln, 1861-62; judge U.S. Dist. Ct. of Ind., 1862-64. Died Indpls., Ind., Jan. 7, 1864.

SMITH, Charles Ferguson, army officer; b. Phila., Apr. 24, 1807; s. Samuel Blair and Mary (Ferguson) S.; grad. U.S .Mil. Acad., 1825; m. Fanny Mactier, 3 children. Instr. inf. tactics U.S. Mil. Acad., later adjutant, then comdr. of cadets, 1829-43; commd. 1st lt. 2d Arty., U.S. Army, 1832, capt., 1838; in command of battalion, distinguished in battles of Palo Alto and Resaca de la Palma (Tex.), 1846; brevetted maj. and lt. col. for service in Mexican campaign, 1846; brevetted col., 1847; commd. maj. 1st Arty., 1854; lt. col. 10th Inf., 1855; led expdn. to Red River of North, 1856; in command of Dept. of Utah, 1860-61; commd. brig. gen. U.S. Volunteers, also col. U.S. Army, 1861, commanded Dist. of W. Ky.; commanded 2d Div., Grant's Army, fts. Henry and Donelson (Tenn.) and Ft. Heiman (Ky.); commd. maj. gen. U.S. Volunteers, 1862. Died Savannah, Tenn., Apr. 25, 1862.

SMITH, Charles Perrin, editor; b. Phila., Jan. 5, 1819; s. George Wishart and Hannah (Carpenter) S.; ed. common schs., Salem County, N.J.; m. Hester Driver, circa 1842, 1 dau., Elizabeth A. Owner newspaper Nat. Standard (Whig Party organ), 1840-51, used influence on behalf of constrn. of railroad in Western N.J.; mem. N.J. Senate from Salem County, 1855-57; clk. N.J. Supreme Ct., 1857-72; mem. opposition faction of N.J. Republican Exec. Com., 1859-69; active in securing state cooperation with fed. govt. in war effort, during Civil War; supported nomination of Gen. Grant for Pres. U.S., in N.J., 1867-68. Author: Lineage of the Lloyd and Carpenter Families, 1870; also reminiscences, containing memoirs of years 1857-75 and genealogy of family (in manuscript of N.J. Hist. Soc.). Died Trenton, N.J., Jan. 27, 1883.

SMITH, Charles Shaler, bridge engr.; b. Pitts., Jan. 16, 1836; s. Frederick Rose and Mary Anne (Shaler) S.; m. Mary Gordon Gairdner, May 23, 1865, several children. Asst. engr. Louisville & Nashville R.R., 1855, resident engr. on Memphis br., 1856, supr. track and bridge constrn. for Memphis div., 1859; chief engr. of bldgs. and bridges Wilmington, Charlotte & Rutherford R.R. (N.C.), 1860-61; served as capt. engrs. Confederate Army in Civil War, built powder mill in Augusta dist.; partner (with Benjamin H. and Charles H. Latrobe) in Balt. Bridge Co., 1866; built series of iron trestles on Louisville, Cincinnati & Lexington R.R. and Elizabethtown & Paducah R.R.; 1st to use metal viaducts; built Ky. River Bridge for Cincinnati So. R.R. (his most notable structure), 1876-77; cantilever became dominant type for long-span constrn. as result of his work; most eminent bridge engr. in Am. Author: Comparative Analysis of the Fink, Murphy, Bollman and Triangular Trusses (treatise), 1865; Wind Pressure Upon Bridges (paper), 1881. Died St. Louis, Dec. 19, 1886.

SMITH, Chauncy, lawyer; b. Wailsfield, Vt., Jan. 11, 1819; s. Ithamar and Ruth (Barnard) S., studied U. Vt., 1845-47; m. Caroline E. Marshall, Dec. 10, 1856, 3 children. Admitted to Vt. bar, 1848; editor English Reports in Law and Equity, 40 vols., 1851-58; compiler Digest of the Decisions of the Courts of England, Contained in the English Law and Equity Reports, 1857; counsel to provost marshall in Washington (D.C.), 1861-63; a prominent lawyer of Bell Telephone Co. and successors in telephone litigation, 1878-96, in which Bell Telephone Co. sued various cos. infringing on Bell patents and won favorable decision from U.S. Supreme Ct., 1888. Died Cambridge, Mass., Apr. 5, 1895.

SMITH, Daniel, senator; b. Stafford County, Va., Oct. 28, 1748; s. Henry and Sarah (Crosby) S.; attended Coll. William and Mary; m. Sarah Michie, June 20, 1773, 2 children. Deputy surveyor, 1773; justice of peace, 1776; aided in orgn. Washington County, Va., 1777, became maj. county militia; a surveyor who extended boundary between Va. and N.C., 1779 (established disputed Walker's Line); high sheriff Augusta County, 1780; col. militia, 1781; moved to Cumberland Settlements (now part of Tenn.), 1783; dir. for laying out Town of Nashville (Tenn.), 1784; trustee Davidson Acad., 1785; brig. gen. Mero Dist. (N.C.) Militia, 1788; mem. N.C. Conv. that ratified U.S. Constn., 1789; sec. territory southwest of Ohio River, 1790; made 1st map Tenn., published 1794; mem. Tenn. Constl. Conv., 1796; mem. U.S. Senate from Tenn., 1798-99, 1805-09. Author: A Short Description of the Tennessee Government, 1793. Died "Rock Castle," Sumner County, Tenn., June 6, 1818.

SMITH, Daniel B., pharmacist, philanthropist, educator, coll. pres.; b. Phila., July 14, 1792; s.

Benjamin and Deborah (Morris) S.; m. Esther Morton, 1824, 1 child. Opened drug store in Phila., 1819-49; active Phila. Coll. of Pharmacy, pres., 1829-54; founder Franklin Inst., 1824 mem. Am. Philos. Soc., Acad. Nat. Scis., 1825; chemistry tchr. Haverford Sch. (later Coll.), 1834-46; contbr. original articles to Jour. of the Phila. Coll. of Pharmacy; 1st pres. Am. Pharm. Assn., 1852; published The Principles of Chemistry for the Use of Schools, Academies and Colleges, 1837. Died Germantown, Pa., Mar. 29, 1883.

SMITH, David H., artist; b. Nauvoo, Ill., Nov. 18, 1844; posthumous son of Joseph Smith. Made drawings of ruins of Nauvoo, circa 1853; painted idealized picture, 1863; became leader Reorganized Ch. of Jesus Christ of Latter-day Saints, Utah; well-known hymn writer. Died Elgin, Ill., Aug. 27, 1904.

SMITH, Delazon, senator; b. New Berlin, Chenango County, N.Y., Oct. 5, 1816; grad. Oberlin (O.) Coll., 1837; studied law. Admitted to bar; founder New York Watchman, Rochester, N.Y., 1838, editor 2 years; publisher, editor True Jeffersonian and Western Herald, Rochester, 1840; founder Western Empire, Dayton, O., 1841; spl. U.S. commr. to Quito, Ecuador, 1842-45; moved to Ia. Territory, 1846, entered ministry; moved to Ore. Territory, 1852; editor Ore. Democrat; mem. Ore. Territorial Ho. of Reps., 1854-56; del. Ore. Constl. Conv., 1857; mem. U.S. Senate (Democrat) from Ore., Feb. 14-Mar. 3, 1859. Died Portland, Ore., Nov. 19, 1860; buried City Cemetery, Albany, Ore.

SMITH, Edmund Kirby, army officer, educator, univ. pres.; b. St. Augustine, Fla., May 16, 1824; s. Joseph Lee and Frances (Kirby) S.; grad. U.S. Mil. Acad., 1845; m. Cassie Selden, Sept. 24, 1861, 11 children. Brevetted 2d lt. U.S. Infantry, 1845; brevetted for gallantry at Cerro Gordo and Contreras in Mexican War, 1846-48; asst. prof. mathematics U.S. Mil. Acad., 1849-52; promoted capt. 2d Cavalry, 1855, maj., 1860; commd. lt. col. of cavalry Confederate Army, 1861; brig. gen. in command 4th Brigade, Army of Shenandoah, 1861; commd. maj. gen., 1861; in command dept. of East Tenn., Ky., North Ga., Western N.C., 1862; lt. gen., 1862; in command Trans-Miss. dept., 1863; commd. gen., 1864; last Confederate officer to surrender his force; pres. insurance co.; pres. Atlantic & Pacific Telegraph Co., 1866-68; active layman Protestant Episcopal Ch.; pres. U. Nashville, 1870-75; prof. mathematics U. of South, Sewanee, Tenn., 1875-93; last surviving full general of either U.S. or Confederate Army. Died Sewanee, Mar. 28, 1893.

SMITH, Edward Delafield, lawyer; b. Rochester, N.Y., May 8, 1826; grad. N.Y. U., 1846; m. dau. of Rev. Dr. Gilbert Morgan, circa 1846. Admitted to N.Y. bar, 1848; practiced law (with Isaac P. Martin, Augustus F. Smith), from 1851; counsel of U.S., also dist. atty. for N.Y.C., 1861-65; corp. counsel N.Y.C., 1871-75; active mem. Republican Party. Died Shrewsbury, N.J., Apr. 13, 1878.

SMITH, Edward Henry, congressman, farmer; b. Smithtown, L.I., N.Y., May 5, 1809; attended pvt. schs. Became farmer; justice of peace Smithtown Twp., 1833-43, assessor, 1840-43, supr., 1856-60; mem. U.S. Ho. of Reps. (Democrat) from N.Y., 37th Congress, 1861-63. Died Smithtown, Aug. 7, 1885; buried St. James' Protestant Episcopal Cemetery, St. James, L.I.

SMITH, Eli, missionary; b. Northford, Conn., Sept. 13, 1801; s. Eli and Polly (Whitney) S.; grad. Yale, 1821; grad. Andover Theol. Sem., 1826; m. Sarah Lanman Huntington, July 21, 1833; m. 2d, Maria Ward Chapman, Mar. 9, 1841; m. 3d, Hetty Simpkins Butler, Oct. 23, 1846; 6 children including Benjamin Eli. Ordained to ministry Congregational Ch., 1826; apptd. by Am. Bd. Commrs. for Fgn. Missions as asso. editor publishing house at Malta, 1826; travelled through Asia Minor, Armenia, Georgia, into Persia with Harrison Gray Otis Dwight, 1830-31, their trip resulted in founding of important mission at Urumiah; began tour in Sinai Palestine and So. Syria, Cairo, 1838; devoted his life to translation of Bible into Arabic, 1847-57. Died Beirut, Lebanon, Jan. 11, 1857.

SMITH, Elias, clergyman; b. Lyme, Conn., June 17, 1769; s. Stephen and Irene (Ransom) S.; m. Mary Burleigh, Jan. 7, 1793; m. 2d, Rachel Thurber, 1814; several children. Joined Baptist Ch., 1789, began to preach, 1790, ordained evangelist, 1792; itinerant preacher, N.H. and Mass.; revolted against Baptists' Calvinistic system, repudiated doctrine of Trinity and all systems of church order not found in New Testament, circa 1800; moved to Portsmouth, N.H., circa 1800, founded church acknowledging no creed but the Bible, and having no denominational name but Christian; wrote several works setting forth his views; editor quarterly mag. The Christian's Mag. Reviewer and Religious Intelligencer, 1805-07; editor Herald of Gospel Liberty (1st weekly religious newspaper in U.S.), 1808, sold paper, 1818; became Universalist; asso. in med. practice with Dr. Samuel Thompson, Boston, 1818, established pvt. sanitarium, circa 1830; returned to Christian sect, 1823. Author: The New Testament Dictionary, 1812; (autobiography) The Life, Conversion, Preaching, Travels and Sufferings of Elias Smith, 1816; The People's Book, 1836. Died June 29, 1846.

SMITH, Elihu Hubbard, physician, editor; b. Litchfield, Conn., Sept. 4, 1771; s. Dr. Reuben and Abigail (Hubbard) S.; grad. Yale, 1786; studied medicine, Phila. Practiced Medicine, Wethersfield, Conn., 1791-93, N.Y.C., 1793-98; published 1st volume of American Poems (earliest anthology of Am. poetry), 1793; published Letters to William Buel on the Fever . . . in New York in 1795, 1795; active N.Y. Soc of Promoting Manumission of Slaves; organizer Am. Mineral. Soc., 1798; projected Medical Repository (1st Am. med. jour.); published Am. edition of The Botanic Garden (Erasmus Darwin), 1798. Died N.Y.C., Sept. 19, 1798.

SMITH, Elizabeth Oakes Prince, author, lectr., reformer; b. North Yarmouth, Me., Aug. 12, 1806; d. David and Sophia (Blanchard) Prince; m. Seba Smith, Mar. 6, 1823, 5 children. Author of novels, poems, sketches, contbr. to contemporary journals; social and moral issues dominated her work, especially that of woman's suffrage; wrote under pseudonym Ernest Helfenstein; Lyceum lectr., 1851-57; selections from her autobiography published 1924. Died Hollywood, S.C., Nov. 15, 1893; buried Patchogue, L.I., N.Y.

SMITH, Erasmus Darwin, jurist; b. De Ruyter, N.Y., Oct. 10, 1806; s. Hubbard and Eunice (Jones) S.; attended Hamilton Coll., 1826-29; m. Janet Morrison, 1831; m. 2d, Emilie (Perkins) Smith, June 6, 1879; several children. Admitted to N.Y. bar, 1830; held several positions in chancery ct.; polit. editor Rochester (N.Y.) Daily Advertiser, 1849; justice N.Y. Supreme Ct., 1855-77; judge N.Y. Ct. of Appeals, 1862, 70; important decisions include Clark vs. City of Rochester, Hague vs. Powers, and People vs. Albany and Susquehanna R.R., upheld principle of strong public authority in relation to pvt. rights and property. Died Rochester, Nov. 11, 1883.

SMITH, Erasmus Deshine, jurist; b. N.Y.C., Mar. 2, 1814; grad. Columbia Coll., 1832, Harvard Law Sch., 1835. Practiced law, Rochester, N.Y., 1835-50; prof. mathematics Rochester U., 1850-52; supt. public instrn. State of N.Y., 1853-57; reporter N.Y. Ct. of Appeals, 1857-64; U.S. commr. of emigration, Mar.-July, 1866; recommended by U.S. Sec. of State Hamilton Fish to be adviser to emperor of Japan in field of internat. law, 1871-76; introduced word "telegram" to English lang. Author: Manual of Political Economy, 1853. Died Rochester, Oct. 21, 1882.

SMITH, Erminnie Adelle Platt, geologist, ethnologist; b. Marcellus, N.Y., Apr. 26, 1836; d. Joseph Platt; grad. Troy (N.Y.) Female Sem., 1853; m. Simeon H. Smith, 4 children. Mem. staff Bur. of Am. Ethnology of Smithsonian Instn., Washington, D.C., 1880, studied culture of Iroquois Indians, 1880-82, compiled Iroquois-English Dictionary; wrote Myths of the Iroquois, published by Bur. of Ethnology, 1883; 1st woman elected fellow N.Y. Acad. Scis.; mem. A.A.A.S.; reflected deep interest in geology and botany; founder, 1st pres. Aesthetic Soc. of N.J. Died Jersey City, N.J., June 9, 1886.

SMITH, Francis Henney, army officer, educator; b. Oct. 18, 1812; s. Francis and Ann (Marsden) S.; grad. U.S. Mil. Acad., 1833; m. Sarah Henderson, 1834, 7 children. Tchr., geography, history and ethics U.S. Mil. Acad., 1835, resigned from U.S. Army, 1836; prof. mathematics Hampden-Sydney (Va.) Coll., 1836-39, prin. prof., 1839; supt. Va. Mil. Inst., Lexington, 1840-89, arranged system of instrn. exchange with Washington Coll. (now Washington and Lee U.), 1840-46, recommended expansion of Inst. into gen. scientific sch., 1859; founder Episcopal Ch., Lexington; col. Va. Militia, commanding officer at John Brown's execution; mem. Va. Gov.'s Adv. Bd., 1861; commd. maj. gen. Va. Volunteers, Confederate Army, 1861, in command Craney Island, Va.; returned to head Va. Mil. Inst., 1862, urged immediate rebuilding and reorgn. (after destruction of Inst. in Civil War), 1865, opposed classic edn. prevalent before war, emphasized program of practical studies. Author series of math. textbooks including An Elementary Treatise on Analytical Geometry, 1840. Died Lexington, Va., Mar. 21, 1890.

SMITH, Francis Ormand Jonathan, congressman, lawyer; b. Brentwood, N.H., Nov. 23, 1806; attended Phillips Exeter (N.H.) Acad.; studied law. Admitted to bar, practiced in Portland, Me., 1826; div. advocate 5th Div. Circuit Ct.-Martial in Me., 1829-34; mem. Me. Ho. of Reps., 1831, 63-64; pres. Me. Senate, 1833; mem. U.S. Ho. of Reps. (Democrat) from Me., 23d-25th congresses, 1833-39; assisted Morse in perfecting and introducing electric telegraph. Died Deering (later Woodfords), Me., Oct. 14, 1876; buried on his estate Forest Home; reinterred Evergreen Cemetery, Portland.

SMITH, George, congressman. Mem. U.S. Ho. of Reps. from Pa., 11th-12th congresses, 1809-13.

SMITH, George Luke, congressman, businessman; b. New Boston, Hillsboro County, N.H., Dec. 11, 1837; attended Union Coll., Schenectady, N.Y. Served in Union Army during Civil War; moved to Shreveport, La., became mcht.; held several local offices; mem. La. Ho. of Reps., 1870-72; propr. Shreveport Southwestern Telegram; pres. Shreveport Savs. Bank & Trust Co.; mem. U.S. Ho. of Reps. (Republican, filled vacancy) from La., 43d Congress, Nov. 24, 1873-75; collector of customs Port of New Orleans (apptd. by Pres. Hayes), 1878-79; moved to Hot Springs, Ark., engaged in real estate business. Died Hot Springs, July 9, 1884; buried West Street Cemetery, Milford, N.H.

SMITH, Gerrit, congressman, philanthropist reformer; b. Utica, N.Y., Mar. 6, 1797; s. Peter and Elizabeth (Livingston) S.; grad. Hamilton Coll., 1818; m. Wealthy Ann Backus, Jan. 11, 1819; m. 2d, Ann Carroll Fitzhugh, Jan. 3, 1822; 4 children. Del. to N.Y. State Convs., 1824, 28; experimented with systematic charity on large scale; attempted to colonize Negroes in Adirondack wilderness; anti-Mason; advocated vegetarianism and woman's suffrage cause; contributed to home and fgn. missions; v.p. Am. Peace Soc.; joined anti-slavery movement, 1835, became one of best-known abolitionists in U.S.; founder Liberty Party, 1840; a friend of William Lloyd Garrison; joined Kan. Aid Socs. in N.Y., 1855-57; mem. U.S. Ho. of Reps. from N.Y., 33d Congress, 1853-Aug. 17, 1854; aided John Brown with Harper's Ferry scheme, 1859; became affiliated with Republican Party in 1864 election. Author: Religion of Reason, 1864; Speeches of Gerrit Smith in Congress, 1856. Died N.Y.C., Dec. 28, 1874; buried Peterboro Cemetery, N.Y.C.

SMITH, Giles Alexander, army officer; b. Jefferson County, N.Y., Sept. 29, 1829; s. Cyrus and Laura (Wales) S.; m. Martha McLain, July 31, 1856. Commd. capt. 8th Mo. Volunteer Regt., 1861, lt. col., 1862, col., 1862; in command of brigade in Vicksburg campaign; commd. brig. gen. U.S. Volunteers, 1863; in command 2d div. XVII Corps, U.S. Army 1864; brevetted maj. gen. U.S. Volunteers 1865; mustered out, 1865; 2d asst. postmaster gen. U.S. 1869-72. Died Bloomington, Ill., Nov. 5, 1876.

SMITH, Green Clay, congressman, clergyman; b. Richmond, Madison County, Ky., July 4, 1826; s. John Speed Smith; grad. Transylvania U., Lexington, Ky., 1849; studied law. Served as 2d lt. 1st Regt. Ky. Volunteer Infantry in Mexican War, 1846-47; admitted to bar, 1852, practiced in Covington, Ky.; sch. commr., 1853-57; mem. Ky. Ho. of Reps., 1861-63; commd. col. 4th Regt., Ky. Volunteer Cavalry during Civil War, 1862; brig. gen. Volunteers, 1862, resigned, 1863; brevetted maj. gen. of Volunteers, 1865; mem. U.S. Ho. of Reps. (Union Party) from Ky., 38th-39th congresses, 1863-66 (resigned); gov. Mont. Territory (apptd. by Pres. Johnson), 1866-69; moved to Washington, D.C., ordained to ministry Baptist Ch.; became evangelist; Nat. Prohibition Party candidate for Pres. U.S., 1876; pastor Met. Bapt. Ch., Washington, 1890-95. Died June 29, 1895; buried Arlington (Va.) Nat. Cemetery.

SMITH, Gustavus Woodson, army officer, engr.; b. Georgetown, Scott County, Ky., Mar. 1822; s. Byrd and Sarah Hatcher (Woodson) S.; grad. U.S. Mil. Acad., 1842; m. Lucretia Bassett, Oct. 3, 1844. Instr. civil, mil. engring. U.S. Mil. Acad., 1844-46; brevetted 1st lt., then capt., maj. U.S. Army for services at Vera Cruz, Cerro Gordo, Contreras, Churubusco, Mexico City, 1846-48; asst. prof. engring. U.S. Mil. Acad., 1848-54; designated by Treasury Dept. to supervise repairs to the Mint, and constrn. Marine Hosp., New Orleans, 1855; chief engr. Trenton Iron Works, 1856-58; street commr., N.Y.C., 1858-61; commd. maj. gen. 2d Corps, Confederate Provisional Army, 1861; commanded a wing of Army of No. Va. until conclusion Peninsular Campaign; commanded sector from right of Lee's theatre of operations on the Rappahannock to Cape Fear River with hdqrs. Richmond, 1862; sec. of war Confederate States Am., 1862; resigned commn. as maj. gen. Confederate Army, 1862; commd. maj. gen. to command 1st Div., Ga. Militia, 1864, assigned a sector in Dept. of S.C., Ga., Fla.; surrendered 1865; gen. mgr. Southwestern Iron Co., Chattanooga, Tenn., 1866-70; 1st ins. commr., Ky., 1870-75. Author: Notes on Life Insurance, 1870; Confederate War Papers, 1884; The Battle of Seven Pines, 1891. Died N.Y.C., June 24, 1896.

SMITH, Hamilton, mining engr.; b. Louisville, Ky., July 5, 1840; s. Hamilton and Martha (Hall) S.; m. Mrs. Charles Congreve. Became head of engring. dept. at coal mine owned by father, Cannelton, Ind., circa 1858; supervised coal mines in Ky. and Ind., 1860's; became chief engr. Triunfo mine, Lower Cal., 1869; chief engr. mine in Nevada County, Cal., pioneered use of hydraulic power; supr. Rothschild mine, El Callao, in Venezuela, 1881-85; founder (with Edmund de Crano) Exploration Co., Ltd., London, Eng., 1886, developed many mines around the world; promoted Am. mining ventures in Eng., founded Fraser & Chalmers (mining machinery co.); consultant on orgn. of many mines; moved to N.Y., 1896, continued as consultant. Author: Treatise on Hydraulics, 1886; published article on costs of gold mining in Engring. and Mining Journal, 1886. Died Durham, N.H., July 4, 1900.

SMITH, Henry Boynton, clergyman, educator; b. Portland, Me., Nov. 21, 1815; s. Henry and Arixene (Southgate) S.; grad. Bowdoin Coll., 1834; attended Andover Theol., Sem., Bangor Sem., 1834-36, U. Halle and U. Berlin (Germany), 1837-40; D.D. (hon.), U. Vt., 1850; LL.D. (hon.), Princeton, 1869; m. Elizabeth Lee Allen, Jan. 5, 1843 4 children. Ordained to ministry Congregational Ch., 1842; prof. Hebrew and philosophy Amherst Coll., 1847-50; taught ch. history Union Theol. Sem., 1850-54, taught theology, 1859-74; a leader of New Sch. Presbyn. Ch. moderator Gen. Assembly, 1863, largely responsible for reunion 2 brs. Presbyn. Ch., 1869; editor Am. Theol. Review, 1859-74. Author: History of the Church of Christ in Chronological Tables, 1859; Apologetics, 1882; Introduction to Christian Theology 1883; System of Christian Theology, 1884; translated and revised Textbook of Church History (Johan K. L. Gieseler), 5 vols., 1855-79. Died N.Y.C., Feb. 7, 1877.

SMITH, Hezekiah, clergyman; b. Hempstead, L.I., N.Y., Apr. 21, 1737; s. Peter and Rebecca (Nichols) S.; grad. Princeton, 1762; m. Hephzibah Kimball, June 27, 1771, 6 children. Baptized into Baptist Ch., 1756, ordained, 1763; 1st pastor Bapt. Ch., Haverhill, Mass., 1766; a founder R.I. Coll. (now Brown U.), helped raise funds, 1769-70, one of 1st fellows; an organizer Warren Assn., 1767, worked to obtain separation of church and state in Mass.; served as regimental chaplain Continental Army, 1775-78, brigade chaplain, 1778-80. Died Jan. 24, 1805.

SMITH, Hezekiah Bradley, congressman, mfr.; b. Bridgewater, Windsor County, Vt., July 24, 1816; attended common schs. Learned cabinet-making trade; settled in Lowell, Mass., circa 1840, manufactured woodworking machinery; an inventor, received gold medal from Mass. Mech. Assn., received more than 40 patents for his inventions; moved to Smithville, Burlington County, N.J., 1865, manufactured woodworking machinery, also Star bicycle; made 1st steam-driven vehicle operated in N.J.; mem. U.S. Ho. of Reps. (Democrat, Greenbacker) from N.J., 46th Congress, 1879-81; mem. N.J. Senate, 1883-85. Died Smithville, Nov. 3, 1887; buried Pine Street Cemetery, Mt. Holly, Burlington County.

SMITH, Hiram, dairyman; b. Tinicum, Bucks County, Pa., Feb. 19, 1817; s. Jonas Smith; m. Catherine A. Conover, Mar. 20, 1845, 2 children. Owner dairy farm, Sheboygan Falls, Wis.; pres. Wis. Dairymen's Assn., 1875-76, v.p., 1878-90; a founder Dairy Bd. of Trade, Sheboygan Falls, 1872, pres., 1872, 89; mem. Wis. Legislature, 1871-72; regent U. Wis., 1877-90, largely responsible for establishment of Dairy Sch. (1st dairy sch. in U.S.). Died May 15, 1890.

SMITH, Hiram Ypsilanti, congressman, lawyer; b. Piqua, Miami County, O., Mar. 22, 1843; grad. Albany (N.Y.) Law Sch., 1866. Enlisted in Ia. Militia for service against Indians, 1861; apptd. clk. Post Office Dept., Washington, D.C., 1862-64; transferred to Treasury Dept., resigned 1865. admitted to bar, 1866, practiced in Des Moines, Ia.; dist. atty. 5th Jud. Dist. of Ia., 1875-79; mem. Ia. Senate, 1882-84; mem. U.S. Ho. of Reps. (Republican, filled vacancy) from Ia., 48th Congress, Dec. 2, 1884-85. Died Des Moines, Nov. 4, 1894; buried Woodland Cemetery.

SMITH, Horace, inventor, mfr.; b. Cheshire, Mass., Oct. 28, 1808; s. Silas and Phoebe Smith; m. Eliza Foster, 1836; m. 2d, Mrs. Eliza Hebbard Jepson, 1872; m. 3d, Mary Lucretia Hebbard, 1887. Self-employed gun mfr., 1846-49, improved breech-loading rifle, obtained 1st patent, 1851; formed partnership with Daniel Wesson to manufacture repeating rifle, Norwich, Mass., 1853, secured patent, 1854, sold business to Volcanic Arms Co., 1855; invented and patented (with Wesson) central-fire metallic cartridge, 1854, reestablished partnership (with Smith as exec. head 1857-73) to produce the new firearm and cartridge, Springfield, Mass., 1857, produced 1st revolvers, 1857, granted patents, 1859, 60 (revolver used by U.S. mil. authorities), built new plant, 1860; exhibited products at Internat. Expn., Paris, France, 1867, sold guns to many European nations; sold interest in co. to Wesson, 1873; pres. Chicopee Nat. Bank, 1893. Died Jan. 15, 1893.

SMITH, Horace Boardman, congressman, lawyer; b. Whittingham, Windham County, Vt., Aug. 18, 1826; grad. Williams Coll., 1847; studied law. Admitted to bar, 1850, practiced in Elmira, N.Y.; held several local offices; judge Chemung County, N.Y., 1859-60; mem. U.S. Ho. of Reps. (Republican) from N.Y., 42d-43d congresses, 1871-75; practiced in Elmira until 1883; justice N.Y. State Supreme Ct., 1883-88; retired to Elmira. Died Elmira, Dec. 26, 1888; buried Woodlawn Cemetery.

SMITH, Isaac, congressman; b. Trenton, N.J., 1740; grad. Princeton, 1755; studied medicine. Mem. faculty Princeton, 1755-58; practiced medicine, Trenton; col. Hunterdon County Militia, 1776-77; asso. justice N.J. Supreme Ct., 1777-1804; mem. U.S. Ho. of Reps. (Federalist) from N.J., 4th Congress, 1795-97; apptd. by Pres. Washington as commr. to treat with Seneca Indians, 1797; Democratic presdl. elector, 1800; 1st pres. Trenton Banking Co., 1805-07. Died Trenton, Aug. 29, 1807; buried First Presbyn. Churchyard.

SMITH, Isaac, congressman, farmer; b. Chester County, Pa., Jan. 4, 1761; attended common schs. Became farmer, nr. Level Corners, Lycoming County, Pa.; mem. Pa. Ho. of Reps., 1806-08; mem. U.S. Ho. of Reps. (Democrat) from Pa., 13th Congress, 1813-15; became millwright. Died on his farm, Level Corners, Apr. 4, 1834; buried Pine Creek Presbyn. Churchyard; reinterred Jersey Shore (Pa.) Cemetery, Lycoming County.

SMITH, Israel, senator, gov. Vt., congressman; b. Suffield, Conn., Apr. 4, 1759; s. Daniel and Anna (Kent) S.; grad. Yale, 1781; m. Abiah Smith between 1779-89, 2 children. Admitted to Vt. bar, 1783; served 4 terms in Vt. Legislature between 1785 and 1788-91; served in joint commn. for adjusting boundary and title disputes with N.Y. and Vt., 1789; took part in Vt. Conv. which ratified U.S. Constn., 1791; mem. U.S. Ho. of Reps. (Republican) from Vt., 2d, 7th congresses, Oct. 17, 1791-97, 1801-03; re-entered Vt. Legislature, 1797; chief justice of Vt., 1797-98; mem. U.S. Senate from Vt., 1803-Oct. 1, 1807; gov. Vt., 1807-08; Democratic presdl. elector, 1808. Died Rutland, Vt., Dec. 2, 1810; buried West Street Cemetery, Rutland.

SMITH, James, Continental congressman; b. No. Ireland, circa 1719; s. John Smith; attended Coll. of Phila.; m. Eleanor Armor, circa 1760, 5 children. Came to Pa., 1729; admitted to Pa. bar, 1745, only resident practicing lawyer in York, Pa., circa 1750-69; in iron mfg. bus., 1771-78; del. Pa. Provincial Conf., 1774; del. Pa. Provincial organized, became capt. co., 1774; del. Pa. Provincial Conv., Phila., 1775, Provincial Conf., 1776; sent to Pa. Constl. Conv., 1776, mem. com. to draft new frame of govt.; mem. Continental Congress, 1776, 78; signer Declaration of Independence; mem. Pa. Assembly, 1779; judge Pa. High Ct. of Errors and Appeals, 1780-81; brig. gen. Pa. Militia, 1782; counselor for Pa. in Wyoming controversy. Died York, July 11, 1806.

SMITH, James, pioneer, army officer, author; b. Conococheague Settlement, Franklin County, Pa., 1737; m. Anne Wilson, May 1763; m. 2d, Margaret (Rodgers) Irvin, 1785; 7 children. Frontier leader, settled Franklin County, Pa., 1760; leader "Black Boys" whose purpose was to defend frontier settlements, 1763, 65, 69; lt. in Bouquets' expdn. against Ohio Indians, 1764; served in militia to defend Pa. frontier from Indians, 1760's; mem. bd. commrs. Bedford County (Pa.), 1771, Westmoreland County (Pa.), 1773; active Westmoreland County govt., 1771-77; moved to Ky., 1788; mem. Ky. Constl. Conv., 1792; mem. Gen. Assembly of Ky.; An Account of the Remarkable Occurences in the Life and Travels of Col. James Smith, During his Captivity with the Indians in the Years, 1755-59, published 1799, also a pamphlet about Shakers, 1810. Died Washington County, Ky., 1813.

SMITH, James McCune, physician; b. N.Y.C., Apr. 18, 1813; student African Free Sch., N.Y.C.; B.A., U. Glasgow (Scotland), 1835, M.A., 1836, M.D., 1837; 5 children. Opened pharmacy on W. Broadway, N.Y.C. (1st in city to be operated by Negro), circa 1838; mem. med. staff Free Negro Orphan Asylum, 20 years; opponent of Am. Colonization Soc. plan to remove Negroes to Africa; prominent worker for Underground R.R. in N.Y.C.; editor Colored American, 1839; contbr. articles "Abolition of Slavery and the Slave Trade in the French and British Colonies" (1838), and "Freedom and Slavery for Africans" (1844) to N.Y. Tribune; apptd. prof. anthropology became partner, 1830, sole owner, 1837; partner sale mdse. bus., 1843-62; organizer James Y. Smith Wilberforce U., 1863; did not teach because of ill health. Died Williamsburg, L.I., N.Y., Nov. 17, 1865.

SMITH, James Strudwick, congressman, physician; b. nr. Hillsboro, Orange County, N.C., Oct. 15, 1790; grad. Jefferson Med. Coll., 1818. Practiced medicine, nr. Hillsboro, later nr. Chapel Hill, N.C.; mem. U.S. Ho. of Reps. (Democrat) from N.C., 15th-16th congresses, 1817-21; mem. N.C. Ho. of Commons, 1821, 22; del. N.C. Constl. Conv., 1835. Died nr. Chapel Hill, Aug. 1859; buried pvt. cemetery on his farm.

SMITH, James Youngs, mfr., gov. R.I.; b. Poquonoc village, Groton, Conn., Sept. 15, 1809; s. Amos Denison and Priscilla (Mitchell) S.; m. Emily Brown, Aug. 13, 1835. Joined Aborn & Smith' lumber dealers, Providence, R.I., 1826, became partner, 1830, sole owner, 1837; partner with brother Amos in cotton goods mfg. and wholesale mdse. bus., 1843-62; organizer James Y. Smith Mfg. Co., 1862; mayor Providence, 1855, 56; gov. R.I. (Republican), 1863-66, successfully raised troops for US. Govt. despite strong opposition; active in civic affairs, known for philanthropies. Died Providence, Mar. 26, 1876.

SMITH, Jedediah Kilburn, congressman, jurist; b. Amherst, N.H., Nov. 7, 1770; completed prep. studies; studied law. Admitted to bar, practiced in Amherst, 1800; mem. N.H. Ho. of Reps., 1803, N.H. Senate, 1804-06, 09; mem. U.S. Ho. of Reps. from N.H., 10th Congress, 1807-09; councilor, 1810-15; postmaster Amherst, 1819-26; asso. justice Ct. Common Pleas, 1816-21; asso. justice Ct. of Sessions, 1821-23, chief justice, 1823-25. Died Amherst, Dec. 17, 1828.

SMITH, Jedediah Strong, trader, explorer; b. Bainbridge, Chenango County, N.Y., June 24, 1798; s. Jedediah Smith. Trader in Rocky Mountains, 1826-30; entered Cal. from Mohave Desert, 1826, explored Cal. and Ore., 1826-30, (1st man to enter Cal. from East and exit from West; entered Santa Fe trade, 1831; 1st explorer of Gt. Basin. Died nr. Cimarron, N.M., May 27, 1831.

SMITH, Jeremiah, gov. N.H., jurist; b. Peterborough, N.H., Nov. 29, 1759; s. William and Elizabeth (Morison) S.; attended Harvard, 1777-79; grad. Queen's Coll. (now Rutgers), 1780; m. Eliza Ross, Mar 8, 1797; m. 2d, Elizabeth Hale, Sept. 20, 1831; 6 children including Jeremiah. Admitted to Amherst (N.H.) bar, 1786; mem. N.H. Ho. of Reps., 1788-91; mem. U.S. Ho. of Reps. from N.H., 2d-4th congresses, 1791-97; mem. N.H. Constl. Conv., 1791-92; U.S. dist. atty. for N.H. dist., 1797-1800; judge probate Rockingham County (N.H.), 1800-02; circuit judge of U.S., 1801-02; chief justice N.H. Supreme Ct., 1802-09, 13-16; presdl. elector, 1808; gov. N.H. Federalist, 1809, 10; asso. counsel (with Daniel Webster and Jeremiah Mason) in Dartmouth Coll. Case. Died Dover, N.H., Sept. 21, 1842; buried Winter St. Cemetery (also called Old Cemetery), Exeter, N.H.

SMITH, Job Lewis, physician; b. Onondaga County, N.Y., Oct. 15, 1827; s. Lewis and Chloe (Benson) S.; B.A., Yale, 1849; M.D., Coll. Physicians and Surgeons, N.Y.C., 1853; m. Mary Anne Hannah, Apr. 22, 1858, 7 children. Practiced medicine, N.Y.C., 1853-97; became one of leading pediatricians in U.S.; prof. anatomy Bellevue Hosp. Med. Coll., N.Y.C., 1871-72, clin. prof. diseases of children, 1876-96; a founder Am. Pediatric Soc., pres. 1890. Author: A Treatise on the Diseases of Infancy and Childhood (one of earliest Am. publs. dealing with diseases of children), 1869. Died N.Y.C., June 9, 1897.

SMITH John, adventurer, colonial gov. Va.; b. Willoughby, Lincolnshire, Eng., Jan. 1579; s. George and Alice S. Mil. adventurer in war against Turks, circa 1597-1604; a promoter and organizer Va. Company of London, 1606, arrived Jamestown; Va., May 1607, mem. governing council of colony; taken prisoner by Indians while on expdn. to obtain food, 1607, sentenced to death, according to legend saved by Pocahontas, dau. of Powhatan; returned to Jamestown, 1608, arrested and condemned to hang, but soon released and restored to place on council; explored Potomac and Rappahannock rivers and Chesapeake Bay, summer 1608; pres. council, gov. Va., 1608-09, saved settlers from starvation by getting corn from Indians; sailed for Eng., 1609; sailed to New Eng., 1614, explored coast, returned with cargo of furs and fish, pointing up value of trade and colonization. Author: A Map of Virginia, With a Description of the Country, the Commodities, People, Government and Religion, 1612; A Description of New England (containing highly useful map of New Eng.), 1616; New England Trials, 1620; The General Historie of Virginia, New England, and the Summer Isles, 1624; The True Travels, Adventures, and Observations of Captaine John Smith, in Europe, Asia, Affrica, and America, 1630; Advertisements for the Inexperienced Planters of New England (which offered advice on settlement in colonies based on experience as explorer), 1631. Died June 21, 1631.

SMITH, John, congressman, army officer, farmer; b. Shooter's Hill, nr. Locust Hill, Middlesex County, Va., May 7, 1750. Moved to Frederick County, Va., 1773, became planter at Hackwood, nr. Winchester, acquired large land holdings; commd. by gov. as one of King's justices, 1773; apptd. col. by Va. Council of Safety, 1776; promoted lt. of county militia by Gov. Patrick Henry, 1777; commd. lt. col. commandant by Gov. Henry Lee, 1793, brig. gen. by Gov. James Monroe, 1801, maj. gen. 3d Div., Va. Troops, 1811-36; served in Dunmore's War with Indians, 1774, Revolutionary War and War of 1812; mem. Va. Ho. of Dels., 1779-83; mem. Va. Senate, 1792-95, 96; mem. U.S. Ho. of Reps. (Democrat) from Va., 7th-13th congresses, 1801-15. Died at Rockville, nr. Middletown, Frederick County, Mar. 15, 1836; buried family burying ground at Hackwood; reinterred Mt. Hebron Cemetery, Winchester, 1890.

SMITH, John, senator, clergyman; b. Hamilton County, O., circa 1735. Minister to Baptist congregation, W. Va., 1790; mem. 1st Legislative Assembly of N.W. Territory, 1799-1803; mem. U.S. Senate from Ohio, Apr. 1, 1803-Apr. 25, 1809; his association with Aaron Burr (1805-06) resulted in suspicion of complicity with Burr, 1806; contributed provisions and credit to keep Ohio Militia in field when Burr's plans were threatened; able to explain most of charges acceptably but not to clear himself of suspicion of knowledge of Burr's plans; Senate censure of his activities failed to pass but he resigned seat. Died Hamilton County, circa 1824.

SMITH, John, senator, congressman; b. Mastic, L.I., N.Y., Feb. 12, 1752; completed prep. studies. Mem. N.Y. State Assembly, 1784-99; del. N.Y. State Conv. to ratify U.S. Constn., 1788; mem. U.S. Ho. of Reps. (Democrat, filled vacancy) from N.Y., 6th-8th congresses, Feb. 6, 1800-Feb. 23, 1804 (resigned); mem. U.S. Senate (filled vacancy) from N.Y., Feb. 23, 1804-13; U.S. marshal for Dist. of N.Y., 1813-15; maj. gen. N.Y. State Militia. Died Mastic, Aug. 12, 1816; buried Smiths Point, N.Y.

SMITH, John, educator, clergyman; b. Rowley, Essex County, Mass., Dec. 21, 1752; s. Joseph and Elizabeth (Palmer) S.; grad. Dartmouth, 1773; D.D., Brown U., 1803; m. Mary Cleaveland; m. 2d, Susan Mason; at least 2 children. Tutor, Moor's Charity Sch., Mass., 1774-78; pastor Congregational Ch. of West Hartford, Conn., 1778-1809; prof. classical langs. Dartmouth, 1778-1809, librarian, 1779-1809 trustee, 1788-1809; asso. preacher Dartmouth Coll. Ch., 1773-77. Author: Hebrew Grammar, 1802; Chaldee Grammar, 1802; Cicero de Oratore, 1804. Died Hanover, N.H., Apr. 30, 1809.

SMITH, John, congressman, lawyer; b. Barre, Mass., Aug. 12, 1789; attended common schs.; studied law; at least 1 son, Worthington Curtis. Moved to St. Albans, Vt.; admitted to bar, 1810, practiced in St. Albans; state's atty. for Franklin County, 1826-32; mem. Vt. Ho. of Reps., 1827-37, speaker, 1831-33; mem. U.S. Ho. of Reps. (Democrat) from Vt., 26th Congress, 1839-41; engaged in constrn. railroads. Died St. Albans, Nov. 26, 1858; buried Greenwood Cemetery.

SMITH, John Ambler, congressman, lawyer; b. Village View, nr. Dinwiddie Court House, Dinwiddie County, Va., Sept. 23, 1847; grad. law dept. Richmond Coll. (later U. Va.). Admitted to bar, 1867, practiced in Richmond, Va.; apptd. commr. in chancery for Richmond cts., 1868; Commonwealth atty. Charles City and New Kent counties; mem. Va. Senate, 1869; mem. U.S. Ho. of Reps. (Republican) from Va., 43d Congress, 1873-75; practiced in Washington, D.C.; mem. immigration commn. to London, Eng. Died Washington, Jan. 6, 1892; buried Glenwood Cemetery.

SMITH, John Armstrong, congressman, lawyer; b. Hillsboro, O., Sept. 23, 1814; grad. Miami U., Oxford, O., 1834; studied law. Admitted to bar, 1835, practiced in Hillsboro; mem. Ohio Ho. of Reps., 1841; mem. Ohio constl. convs., 1850, 73; mem. U.S. Ho. of Reps. (Republican) from Ohio, 41st-42d congresses, 1869-73. Died Hillsboro, Mar. 7, 1892; buried Hillsboro Cemetery.

SMITH, John Augustine, physician, coll. pres.; b. Westmoreland County, Va., Aug. 29, 1782; s. Rev. Thomas and Mary (Smith) S.; grad. Coll. William and Mary, 1800; studied St. Thomas Hosp., London, 1808-09; m. Letitia Lee, 1809, 9 children. Mem. 1st faculty Coll. Physicians and Surgeons, N.Y.C., lectr. on anatomy, 1807, prof. anatomy, surgery, 1808, prof. anatomy, surgery, physiology, 1811, 1825-31, pres. coll., 1831-43; pres. Coll. William and Mary, 1814-25, attempted unsuccessfully to move coll. to Richmond. Author: Prelections on Some of the More Important Subjects Connected with Moral and Physical Science, 1853. Editor: Medical and Physiological Jour., 1809; co-editor N.Y. Med. and Physical Jour., 1828. Died N.Y.C., Feb. 9, 1865.

SMITH, John Blair, clergyman, coll. pres.; b. Pequea, Pa., June 12, 1756; s. Rev. Robert and Elizabeth (Blair) S.; grad. Coll. of N.J. (now Princeton), 1773; m. Elizabeth Nash, 1779, 6 children. Tutor, Hampden-Sydney Acad. (rechartered as Hampden-Sydney Coll.), 1775-79, pres. 1779-89; an early supporter of movement for Am. independence, became capt. co. of Hampden-Sydney students in Va. Militia, circa 1778; ordained to ministry Presbyn. Ch. by Hanover (Va.) Presbytery, 1779, leader revival movement in Va., 1789-91; pastor 3d Presbyn. Ch. of Phila., 1791-95, 99; pres. Union Coll:, Schenectady, N.Y., 1795-99; pres. Presbyn. Gen. Assembly, 1798. Died Phila., Aug. 22, 1799.

SMITH, John Cotton, gov. Conn.; b. Sharon, Conn., Feb. 12, 1765; s. Rev. Cotton Mather and Temperance Worthington (Gale) S.; grad. Yale, 1783; m. Margaret Evertson, Oct. 29, 1786; 1 son, William Mather. Admitted to Conn. bar, 1786; mem. Conn. Ho. of Reps:, 1793, 96-1800, clk., 1799, speaker, 1800; ardent Federalist and Congregationalist; mem. U.S. Ho. of Reps. from Connecticut, 6th-9th congresses, November 17, 1800-August 1806 (resigned); member of Conn. Legislature, 1808-09; judge Conn. Supreme Ct., 1809; lt. gov. Conn., 1811, acting gov., 1812, gov., 1813-17, favored agrl. and merc. interests, refused to place state militia under fed. authority; approved Conn. representation in Hartford Conv. and defended this gathering; 1st pres. Conn. Bible Soc.; pres. Am. Bible Soc., 1831-45, Am. Bd. Fgn. Missions, 1826-41. Died Litchfield County, Conn., Dec. 7, 1845; buried Hillside Cemetery.

SMITH, John Cotton, clergyman, editor; b. Andover, Mass., Aug. 4, 1826; s. Thomas Mather and Mary (Woods) S.; grad. Phillips Acad., Andover, Mass.; grad. Bowdoin Coll., 1847; studied theology Kenyon Coll., Gambier, O., 1848; m. Harriet Appleton, Dec. 19, 1849, 6 children. Ordained priest Episcopal Ch. by bishop of Me., 1850; rector St. John's Ch., Bangor, Me., 1850-52; became asst. minister Trinity Ch., Boston, 1852; rector Ch. of the Ascension, N.Y.C., 1860-82; mem. fgn. com. of bd. of missions Episcopal Ch., circa 1860-80; became asso. editor The Protestant Churchman, 1867; advocate of tenement house reform, pioneered constrn. of model houses, N.Y.C.; exponent of unification of Am. Protestant Christianity; mem. Gen. Conv. of Episcopal Ch., 1880. Author: A Plea for Liberty in the Church, 1865; Limits of Legislation as to Doctrine and Ritual, 1874; Improvements of the Tenement House System of New York, 1879; The Church's Mission of Reconciliation, 1880. Died Jan. 9, 1882.

SMITH, John Eugene, army officer; b. Berne, Switzerland, Aug. 3, 1816; s. John Banler Smith; m. Aimee A. Massot, 1836. Came to U.S., settled in Phila., 1817; moved to Galena, Ill., 1836, established jewelry business; treas. Jo Daviess County, Ill., 1860; organized 45th Ill. Infantry, 1861; commd. col. 45th Ill. Inf., U.S. Army, 1861; served at Battle of Shiloh, 1862; commd. brig. gen. U.S. Volunteers, 1862; in command div. under Gen. Grant throughout Vicksburg campaign, 1863, led charge at Missionary Ridge, Tenn.; largely responsible (through swift deployment of his div.) for forcing Confederate Army to evacuate Savannah, Ga., 1864; brevetted maj. gen. U.S. Volunteers, 1865; in command Dist. of Western Tenn., 1865-66; commd. col. 27th Inf., U.S. Army, 1866; brevetted brig. gen., maj gen. U.S. Army (for gallant service at Vicksburg and Savannah), 1867. Died Chgo., Jan. 29, 1897; buried Galena, Ill.

SMITH, John Gregory, gov. Vt., railroad exec.; b. St. Albans, Vt., July 22, 1818; s. John and Maria (Curtis) S.; grad. U. Vt., 1830, LL.D. (hon.), 1871; studied law Yale, until 1841; m. Eliza Ann Brainerd, Dec. 27, 1843, 6 children. Admitted to Vt. bar, 1842; pres. bd. trustees V . Central R.R., 1858, extended line to Canadian border, 1863, persuaded Canadian capitalists to build connecting link to Montreal, 1868; mem. Vt. Senate, 1858-59; mem. lower house Vt. Legislature, 1860-62, speaker, 1862; gov. Vt. (Republican), 1863-64; pres. Central Vt. R.R. Co., 1873-91, receiver of Vt. Central R.R., line became a system with terminals at Ottawa and New London, and with independent freight lines on St. Lawrence and L.I. Sound; pres. N.P. Ry., 1866-72; chmn. Vt. delegation to Rep. Nat. Conv., 1872, 80, 84; lifelong mem. First Congregational Soc. of St. Albans; pres. Welden Nat. Bank, Peoples' Trust Co., Franklin County Creamery Assn. Died St. Albans, Nov. 6, 1891.

SMITH, John Hyatt, congressman, clergyman; b. Saratoga, N.Y., Apr. 10, 1824; studied theology. Clk., Detroit; bank clk., Albany, N.Y.; ordained to ministry; pastor in Poughkeepsie, N.Y., 1848, Cleve., 3 years, Buffalo, N.Y., 1855-60, Phila., 1860-66, Bklyn., 1866-80, also at later date; served in Va. with U.S. Christian Commn. during Civil War, 1862; chaplain 47th Regt., N.Y. State N.G., 1869; mem. U.S. Ho. of Reps. (Independent Republican, Democrat) from N.Y., 47th Congress, 1881-83; apptd. by Pres. Arthur a commr. to inspect Pacific R.R. Died Bklyn., Dec. 7, 1886; buried Greenwood Cemetery.

SMITH, John Jay, editor, librarian; b. Green Hill, Burlington County, N.J., June 16, 1798; s. John and Gulielma (Morris) S.: M. Rachel Collins Pearsall, Apr. 12, 1821, 7 children including Lloyd Pearsall. Publisher (with George Taylor) Pa. Gazette, 1827-29; librarian Library Co. of Phila., 1829-51, gathered large collection of autographs and manuscripts on history of N.J. and Pa.; editor (with Adam Waldie) Waldie's Select Circulating Library (weekly, republishing famous fgn. books), 1832; editor Mus. of Fgn. Literature, Science, and Art, 1835; treas. Phila. Mus.; founder Girard Life Ins., Annuity, and Trust Co., also Laurel Hill Cemetery; editor The North American Sylva (Francois Andre Michau), 1850-51; editor (assisted by John F. Watson) Am. Hist. and Literary Curiosities, 1847, 2d series issued, 1860; editor Smith's Weekly Volume, 1845-46, Letters of Dr. Richard Hill, 1854. Died Phila., Sept. 23, 1881.

SMITH, John Lawrence, chemist, med. scientist; b. Charleston, S:C., Dec. 17, 1818; s. Benjamin Smith; attended U. Va., 1835-37; M.D., Med. Coll. of S.C., 1840; m. Sarah Julia Guthrie, June 24, 1852. With Dr. S. D. Sinkler founded So. Jour. of Medicine and Pharmacy (later became Charleston Med. Jour. and Review), 1846; adviser on cotton culture to Turkish govt., circa 1847, investigated their mineral resources and discovered emery and coal deposits, 1847-50; these observations were useful in discovery of several emery deposits in U.S.; prof. chemistry U. Va., 1852; prof. med: chemistry, toxicology U. Louisville (Ky.), 1854-66; his collection of meteoric stones (one of finest in Am.) sold to Harvard; pres. Louisville Gas Works; founder, liberal benefactor Baptist Orphanage of Louisville; pres. A.A.A.S., 1872; mem. Nat. Acad. Sciences. Author: (collected papers) Mineralogy and Chemistry: Original Researches, 1873. Died Louisville, Ky:, Oct. 12, 1883; buried Cave Hill Cemetery, Louisville.

SMITH, John Rowson, painter; b. Boston, May 11, 1810; s. John Rubens and Elizabeth (Sanger) S.; m. Emma Louise Broughton, Jan. 5, 1841, at least 1 child. Became painter scenery for theaters, New Orleans, St. Louis and other cities, 1832, in N:Y.C., 1840's and 50's; experimented with painting panoramas; completed panorama of Mississippi River from Falls of St. Anthony to Gulf of Mexico, 1844, took it on financially successful tour of U.S., then abroad, 1848; produced Panorama of the Tour of Europe, circa 1853, The Siege of Sebastopol, 1854; Died Phila., Mar. 21, 1864; buried Laurel Hill Cemetery, Phila.

SMITH, John Rubens, painter, engraver; b. Covent Garden, London, Eng., Jan. 23, 1775; s. John Raphael and Hannah (Croome) S.; m. Elizabeth Pepperal Sanger, Apr. 14, 1809; son, John Rowson. Exhibited nearly 50 paintings at annual exhbns. of Royal Acad., 1796-1811; came to U.S. as early as 1809; painter series of topographical water colors of local landmarks, Boston, 1809-14; became tchr. art, N.Y.C., 1814, pupils include: Thomas Seir Cummings, Anthony DeRose, Frederick Styles Agate; career limited by violent temper; made mezzotints of portraits of Benjamin Lincoln and James Patterson. Author: The Juvenile Drawing-Book, 8th edit., 1847; A Key to the Art of Drawing the Human Figure, 1831. Died N.Y.C., Aug. 21, 1849.

SMITH, John Speed, congressman, lawyer; b. nr. Nicholasville, Jessamine County, Ky., July 1, 1792; attended pvt. sch., Mercer County; studied law; at least 1 son, Green Clay. Served as pvt. in Indian Campaign of 1811; admitted to bar, 1812, practiced in Richmond, Ky.; enlisted as pvt. in War of 1812; promoted maj.; a.d.c. to Gen. Harrison with rank of col.; mem. Ky. Ho. of Reps., 1819, 27, 30, 39, 41, 45, speaker, 1827; mem. U.S. Ho. of Reps. (Democrat, filled vacancy) from Ky., 17th Congress, Aug. 6, 1821-23; U.S. dist. atty. for Ky., 1828-32; mem. Ky. Senate, 1846-50. Died Richmond, June 6, 1854; buried Richmond Cemetery.

SMITH, John T., congressman; b. Phila.; attended common schs., Phila. Mem. U.S. Ho. of Reps. (Democrat) from Pa., 28th Congress, 1843-45.

SMITH, Jonathan Bayard, Continental congressman; b. Phila., Feb. 21, 1742; s. Samuel Smith; grad. Princeton, 1760; m. Susannah Bayard, at least 1 child, Samuel Harrison: Mem: Pa. Provincial Conf., 1774, sec. Pa. Provincial Conv., 1775, sec. Pa. Provincial Conf., 1776; helped overthrow old provincial govt., 1776; mem., sec. Com. of Safety, 1775-77; lt. col. of a bn. of "Associators" served in Brandywine campaign, 1777; mem. Continental Congress, 1777-78; mem. Bd. of War, 1778; prothonotary of Ct. Common Pleas for City and County of Phila., 1777-79, justice, 1778; auditor gen. Pa., circa 1794. Trustee U. Pa., also Princeton, 1779-1808; mem. Am. Philos. Soc. Died Phila., June 16, 1812:

SMITH, Joseph, naval officer; b. Hanover, Mass., Mar. 30, 1790; s. Albert and Anne Lentham (Eels) S.; m. Harriet Bryant, Mar. 1, 1818, 4 children including Joseph Bryant. Commd. in U.S. Navy, 1814; served in Battle of Lake Champlain; participated in engagements with Algerines in Barbary War, 1815; master commandant, 1827; capt., 1837, aided in fitting out the Wilkes exploring expdn.; chief Bur. Navy Yards and Docks, 1846-69; ranking naval officer on a naval bd. on iron-clad constrn., 1861, instrumental in bldg. iron-clad ship Monitor; rear adm. on ret. list, 1862; pres. retiring bd., 1870-71. Died Washington, D.C., Jan. 17, 1877.

SMITH, Joseph, Mormon prophet; b. Sharon, Windsor County, Vt., Dec. 23, 1805; s. Joseph and Lucy (Mack) S.; m. Emma Hale, Jan. 18, 1827, 8 children including Joseph III (contention that he advocated and practiced polygamy is shrouded in controversy). Received visions between 1820-27 revealing that he was selected to restore Ch. of Christ to earth; discovered "plates" of gold nr. Manchester (N.Y.) recording history of the true church, published this history as The Book of Mormon, 1830; founder Ch. of Jesus Christ of Latter-day Saints at Fayette, N.Y., 1830, relying for doctrine and orgn. on contemporary exptl. groups and cults; removed community to Kirtland, O., 1831, Jackson County, Mo. (because of bank failure), 1838, Commerce (renamed Nauvoo), Ill., 1839; community at Nauvoo grew rapidly attracting many immigrants and received large powers in local govt.; ruled community as civil, religious and mil. leader, with power based on his own personality; became candidate for Pres. U.S., 1844; arrested for dictatorial methods following riot of June 10, 1844. Shot by mob in Carthage, Ill., June 27, 1844.

SMITH, Joseph Mather, physician; b. New Rochelle, N.Y., Mar. 14, 1789; grad. Coll. Physicians and Surgeons, N.Y.C., 1815; m. Henrietta M. Beare, May 1831, 5 children. Licensed to practice medicine by Med. Soc. Westchester County, N.Y., 1812; practiced medicine, N.Y.C., 1815-66; prof. theory and practice of physic Coll. Physicians and Surgeons, 1826-55; prof. materia medica, 1855-66; pres. N.Y. Acad. Medicine, 1854; pres. Common Council Hygiene of Citizen's Assn. N.Y., 1864. Author: (works including) Elements of the Etiology and Philosophy of Epidemics, 1824. Died Apr. 22, 1866.

SMITH, Joseph Showalter, congressman, lawyer; b. Connellsville, Fayette County, Pa., June 20, 1824; attended common schs.; studied law. Moved to Oregon City, Ore., 1844, became rail splitter; moved to Salem, Ore., taught sch.; admitted to bar; moved to Olympia, Wash., 1853; speaker Wash. Territorial Ho. of Reps., 1856; apptd. U.S. atty. for Wash. Territory by Pres. Buchanan, 1857; returned to Salem, 1858, practiced for 12 years; mem. U.S. Ho. of Reps. (Democrat) from Ore., 41st Congress, 1869-71; moved to Portland, Ore., 1870, practiced law; unsuccessful Dem. candidate for gov. Ore., 1882. Died Portland, July 13, 1884; buried Riverview Cemetery.

SMITH, Josiah, congressman; b. Pembroke, Plymouth County, Mass., Feb. 26, 1738; grad. Harvard, 1774; studied law. Admitted to bar, practiced law; mem. Mass. Ho. of Reps., 1789-90, Mass. Senate, 1792-94, 97; treas. Mass., 1797; mem. U.S. Ho. of Reps. from Mass., 7th Congress, 1801-03. Died Pembroke, Apr. 4, 1803; buried Pembroke Cemetery.

SMITH, Julia Evelina (Mrs. Amos G. Parker), suffragette; b. Glastonbury, Conn., May 27, 1792; d. Zephaniah Hollister and Hannah Hadassah (Hickock) Smith (family of abolitionist background); m. Amos A. Parker, Apr. 9, 1879. Attended (with sister Abby Smith) suffrage meeting, Hartford, Conn., 1869, hearing on equal suffrage amendment before com. of U.S. Senate, 1878; student of Latin, Greek and Hebrew, made translation of Bible from the original, published 1876. Author: Abby Smith and Her Cows, with a Report of the Law Case Decided Contrary to Law, 1877. Died Hartford, Mar. 6, 1886.

SMITH, Junius, mcht., planter; b. Plymouth, (then part of Watertown), Conn., Oct. 2, 1780; s. Gen. David and Ruth (Hitchcock) S.; grad. Yale, 1802, LL.D. (hon:), 1840; studied Tapping Reeve's Law Sch., Litchfield, Conn., 1802-04; m. Sarah Allen, Apr. 9, 1812. Opened law office, New Haven, Conn., 1804, mem. New Haven bar, 1804-05; mcht., London, Eng., 1805-43; conceived idea of line of transatlantic steamers, 1832; organized (with Macgregor Laird) Brit. & Am. Steam Navigation Co., 1836; chartered little ship Sirius from Cork S.S. Co. (left Cork, Ireland for N.Y.C., 1838, marked beginning of regular transatlantic steamship service) launched (under Laird's supervision) "largest ship in world" the President, 1839, ship disappeared on return voyage from N.Y., 1841 (disaster led to close of Brit. & Am. Steam Navigation Co.); purchased plantation, Greenville, S.C., attempted to grow tea in U.S. Author: Letters upon Atlantic Steam Navigation, 1841; Essays on the Cultivation of the Tea Plant, in the United States of America, 1848. Died Astoria, N.Y., Jan. 22, 1853.

SMITH, Lloyd Pearsall, librarian, publisher, editor; b. Phila., Feb. 6, 1822; s. John Jay and Rachel (Pearsall) S.; grad. Haverford Coll., 1837; m. Hannah E. Jones, Oct. 13, 1844, 1 adopted child. Published Smith's Weekly Volume (edited by his father), 1845-46; published Medical Library; asst. librarian Library Co. of Phila., 1849-51, librarian, 1851-86; issued 3d volume of Catalogue of Books Belonging to the Library Company of Philadelphia, 1856; 1st editor Lippincott's Mag., 1868-69; one of original asso. editors Am: Library Jour. 1876. Died Phila., July 2, 1886.

SMITH, Marcus, (known as Mark Smith), comedian; b. New Orleans, Jan. 7, 1829; s. Solomon Franklin and Martha (Mathews) Smith S.; m. Elizabeth McKenney, 3 surviving children, Kate, Mark, Percival. Appeared with various stock companies, 1848-62; 1st appeared with company of Lester Wallack, 1862; joint mgr. (with Lewis Baker) N.Y. Theatre, 1866; stage mgr. for Edwin Booth, N.Y.C., 1869; played in One Hundred Years Old, 1872-73, toured U.S. in role. Died Paris, France, Aug. 11, 1874.

SMITH, Margaret Bayard, society leader; b. Feb. 20, 1778; d. John Bubenheim and Margaret (Hodge) Bayard; m. Samuel Harrison Smith, Sept. 29, 1800, 4 children. Leader in Washington society, circa 1801-40; contbr. to Godey's Lady's Book, So. Literary Messenger, Peter Parley's Annual; author novel A Winter in Washington; or, Memoirs of the Seymour Family, 2 vols., 1824; letters published under title The First Forty Years of Washington Society (important source book for Jefferson adminstrn.), 1906. Died June 7, 1844.

SMITH, Mark, see Smith, Marcus.

SMITH, Martin Luther, army officer; b. Danby, Tompkins County, N.Y., Sept. 9, 1819; s. Luther Smith; grad. U.S. Mil. Acad., 1842; m. Sarah Nisbet, 1846. Served as lt. topog. engrs. in Mexican War; commd. 1st lt. U.S. Army, 1853, capt., 1856; chief engr. Fernanda & Cedar Key R.R., 1856-61; maj. of engrs. Confederate Army, 1861; aided in planning fortifications commanded troops in defense of New Orleans and Vicksburg, 1862, 63; col. 21st La. Inf., 1862; commd. brig. gen., then maj. gen., 1862; chief engr. Army of Northern Va. and Hood's Army of Tenn., 1864, constructed field works used in their campaigns; chief engr. to Beauregard, 1864-65; in command Western theatre, strengthened defenses of Mobile, Ala., 1864-65. Died Savannah, Ga., July 29, 1866.

SMITH, Matthew Hale, clergyman, lawyer; b. Portland, Me., 1816; s. Dr. Elias Smith; m. Mary Adams, 7 children. Ordained to ministry Universalist Ch., 1823; converted to Calvinism, 1842; ordained as orthodox minister, Malden, Mass., 1850; began study of law, after 1850; became lectr., toured No. and Western parts of country, 1850-79; chaplain 12th N.Y. Regt. 1861-65. Died Bklyn., Nov. 7, 1879.

SMITH, Melancton, Continental congressman, merchant, lawyer; b. Jamaica, L.I., N.Y., May 7, 1744; s. Samuel and Elizabeth (Bayles) S.; at least 1 son, Melancton. Sheriff, Dutchess County (N.Y.), 1744, 77, 79; del. from Dutchess County in 1st N.Y. Provincial Congress, 1775; organized and capt. 1st company of Rangers of Dutchess County Minutemen; mem. commn. for inquiring into, detecting and defeating all conspiracies . . . against liberties of America, 1777; apptd. to commn. to settle disputes between army and contractors at West Point, N.Y., 1782; moved to N.Y.C., 1785, entered upon extensive merc. enterprises and law practice; mem. Continental Congress, 1785-88; anti-Federalist del. to Poughkeepsie Conv. of 1788 to consider ratification of U.S. Constn.; mem. N.Y. State Assembly, 1791; circuit judge N.Y., 1792. Died N.Y.C., July 29, 1798; buried Jamaica Cemetery.

SMITH, Meriwether, Continental congressman; b. "Bathurst," Essex County, Va., 1730; s. Col. Francis and Lucy (Meriwether) S.; m. Alice (Lee) Clarke, circa 1760; m. 2d, Elizabeth Daingerfield, Aug. 3, 1769; 4 children including George William. A signer Westmoreland Assn. (in opposition to Stamp Act) 1766; mem. Essex County Com., 1774; signer Williamsburg Assn. resolutions, 1776; mem. Va. Ho. of Burgesses, 1770, revolutionary convs., 1775, 76, Ho. of Dels., 1776-78, 81-82, 85-88; prepared (with Edmund Pendleton and Patrick Henry) draft of resolutions of independence, 1776; del. to Continental Congress, 1778-82, offered a scheme of finance to Congress, 1781 (not accepted); declined election to Annapolis Conv., 1786; mem. Va. Conv. which ratified U.S. Constn., 1788, opposed ratification. Died "Marigold," Essex County, Jan. 25, 1790.

SMITH, Morgan Lewis, army officer; b. Mexico, Oswego County, N.Y., Mar. 8, 1821; s. Cyrus and Laura (Wales) S.; m. Louise Genella, Dec. 18, 1866. Enlisted as pvt. U.S. Army, 1843; sgt., drill instr. recruit depot, Newport, Ky., 1845-50; organized 8th Mo. Volunteer Inf., commd. col., 1861; as brigade comdr. fought at Ft. Donelson, Tenn., also in expdn. up Tennessee River and in battles of Shiloh, Corinth praised for courage by Lew Wallace, Sherman, Grant; commd. brig. gen. U.S. Volunteers, 1862; took part in Sherman's campaign against Vicksburg as comdr. 2d div.; comdr. 2d div. XV Corps, 1863, fought at Battle of Missionary Ridge; temp. cmdr., Dist. Vicksburg, brought peace to city; U.S. consul gen., Honolulu, Hawaii, 1867-69; counsel in Washington, D.C. for collection claims of applicants for U.S. Govt. pensions. Died Jersey City, N.J., Dec. 28, 1874.

SMITH, Nathan, physician, surgeon, educator, founder med. schs.; b. Rehoboth, Mass., Sept. 30, 1762; s. John and Elizabeth (Ide) Hills S.; M.B., Harvard, 1790, M.D. (hon.), 1811; M.D. (hon.), Dartmouth, 1801; m. Elizabeth Chase, Jan. 1791; m. 2d, Sarah Hall Chase, Sept. 1794; 10 children including Nathan Ryno. Practiced medicine in Cornish, N.H., 1787-96; prompted establishment of professorship of medicine at Dartmouth, 1798, prof., 1798-1814; pres. Vt. State Med. Soc., 1811; prof. Yale, 1813-29, through his personal efforts Conn. Legislature appropriated $20,000 to Yale Med. Sch. and development of bot. garden; performed successful ovariotomy, 1821; wrote Practical Essay on Typhous Fever, 1824; edited American Medical Review, 1824-26. Died New Haven, Conn., Jan. 26, 1829.

SMITH, Nathan, senator; b. Woodbury, Conn., Jan. 8, 1770; s. Richard and Annis (Hurd) S.; read law with Judge Topping Reeve, Litchfield, Conn.; M.A. (hon.), Yale, 1808; 6 children. Admitted to Litchfield County (Conn.) bar, 1792; practiced in New Haven, Conn., 1792; del. to Hartford Conv., 1814; participant in fight for charter for Trinity Coll. in Hartford, Conn.; pros. atty. New Haven County (Conn.), 1817-35; del. to Conn. Constl. Conv., 1817, a framer of reformed Conn. constn. of 1818 separating church and state; U.S. atty. for Conn., 1828-29; mem. Conn. Ho. of Reps., 1833-35; mem. U.S. Senate (Whig) from Conn., 1833-Dec. 16, 1835. Died Washington, D.C., Dec. 6, 1835; buried New Haven, Conn.

SMITH, Nathan Ryno, surgeon, educator; b Cornish, N.H., May 21, 1797; s. Dr. Nathan and Sarah Hall (Chase) S.; A.B., Yale, 1817, M.D., 1823; postgrad. U. Pa. Med. Sch., 1825, 26; m. Juliette Octavia Penniman, 1824; 8 children including Alan Penniman. Established med. sch. at U. Vt., circa 1824, with aid of his father; prof. anatomy, physiology, 1824-36; tchr. anatomy, mem. 1st faculty Jefferson Med. Coll., 1826-27; with father and others edited Am. Med. Review, circa 1825-26; founder Phila. Monthly Jour. of Medicine and Surgery, 1827, editor, 1827-28; prof. anatomy U. Md., 1827, prof. surgery, 1829-38, 40-70, prof. emeritus, 1870-77; founder, editor Balt. Monthly Jour. Medicine and Surgery, 1830; published Surgical Anatomy of the Arteries, 1832; constructed the anterior splint; prof. surgery Transylvania U., Lexington, Ky., 1838-40. Died Balt., July 3, 1877.

SMITH, Nathaniel, congressman, jurist; b. Woodbury, Conn., Jan. 6, 1762; s. Richard and Annis (Hurd) S.; student in law office of Judge Topping Reeve; M.A. (hon.), Yale, 1795; m. Ruth Benedict, at least 1 child. Admitted to Vt. bar, 1787; began practice law, Woodbury, Conn., 1789; Woodbury rep. in Conn. Gen. Assembly, 1789-95; mem. U.S. Ho. of Reps. from Conn., 4th-5th congresses, 1795-99, voted for ratification of Jay Treaty with Gt. Britain; rep. Woodbury in Conn. Council, 1800-04; mem. Conn. Senate, 1800-05; asso. judge Superior Ct. Conn., 1806-19; mem. Hartford Conf., 1814. Died Woodbury, Conn., Mar. 9, 1822; buried Episcopal Ch. Cemetery, Woodbury.

SMITH, O'Brien, congressman; b. Ireland, circa 1756. Came to S.C. just after end of Revolutionary War, took oath of allegiance to Govt. of U.S., 1784; mem. S.C. Assembly, 1796, S.C. Senate, 1803; mem. U.S. Ho. of Reps. from S.C., 9th Congress, 1805-07. Died Apr. 27, 1811; buried in burial ground of Chapel of Ease, St. Bartholomew's Parish, Colleton County, S.C., nr. Jacksonboro, S.C.

SMITH, Oliver, philanthropist; b. Hatfield, Mass., Jan. 20, 1766; s. Samuel and Mary (Morton) S. Became wealthy through investments in farms and securities; a Jeffersonian, later a Nat. Republican; mem. Mass. Constl. Conv., 1820; presdl. elector, 1824; mem. Mass. Legislature, 1827-28; dir. of bank, Northampton, Mass.; established trust in his will to provide grants for poor young people and widows and found agrl. sch. at Northampton; bequeathed $10,000 to Am. Colonization Soc.; Smith's Agrl. Sch. and Northampton Sch. of Tech. established in accordance with will, 1907. Died Dec. 22, 1845.

SMITH, Oliver Hampton, senator, congressman; b. Smith's Island, nr. Trenton, N.J., Oct. 23, 1794; s. Thomas and Letitia S.; m. Mary Branfield, 1821, 3 children. Admitted to Ind. bar, 1820; mem. Ind. Ho. of Reps., 1822-24; pros. atty. 3d Judicial Dist., 1824-25; mem. U.S. Ho. of Reps. (Jacksonian Democrat) from Ind., 20th Congress, 1827-29; mem. U.S. Senate (Whig) from Ind., 1837-43; promoted Indpls. & Bellefontaine R.R., 1st pres. Author: Early Indiana Trials and Sketches, 1858. Died Indpls., Mar. 19, 1859; buried Crown Hill Cemetery, Indpls.

SMITH, Perry, senator; b. Woodbury, Conn., May 12, 1783; completed prep. studies; attended Litchfield Law Sch. Admitted to bar, practiced in New Milford, Litchfield County, Conn., 1807; mem. Conn. Ho. of Reps., 1822-23, 35-36; postmaster New Milford, 1829-37; judge Probate Ct., 1833-35; mem. U.S. Senate (Democrat) from Conn., 1837-43. Died New Milford, June 8, 1852; buried Center Cemetery.

SMITH, Persifor Frazer, army officer; b. Phila., Nov. 16, 1798; s. Jonathan and Mary Anne (Frazer) S.; A.B., Princeton, 1815; m. Frances Jeanette Bureau, Jan. 19, 1822; m. 2d, Anne Monica Millard) Armstrong, Apr. 18, 1854; at least 1 child. Adj. Gen. La., circa 1820; col. La. Volunteers in Seminole War, 1836-38; judge City of Lafayette (La.), 1838, later Parish of Jefferson; col. rifle regt. U.S. Army, 1846; brevetted brig. gen. for service at Monterey, 1846; made surprise attack 1847 which resulted in destruction of Valencia's army; distinguished at Churubusco and Contreras, 1847; brevetted maj. gen., 1848; mil. gov. Mexico City, 1848; brevetted maj. gen., 1849; in command of Pacific Div., 1848-50, then Department of Tex. and Cal., 1850-56, Western Dept., 1856; commd. brig. gen., 1856; assigned to command Dept. of Utah, 1858, died before reaching there. Died Ft. Leavenworth, Kan., May 17, 1858; buried Laurel Hill Cemetery, Phila.

SMITH, Peter, land owner; b. Tappan, N.Y., Nov. 15, 1768; s. Gerrit and Wyntje (Lent) S.; m. Elizabeth Livingston, Feb. 5, 1792, 6 children including Gerrit; m. 2d, Sarah Pogson, circa 1819. Owner stationery shop, N.Y.C., 1785-88; partner (with John Jacob Astor) in fur trade, N.Y., 1788-89; opened gen. store, Utica, N.Y., 1789, traded with Indians, engaged in land speculation; secured lease on large tract of Oneida Indian land, N.Y., 1794, built Town of Smithfield on tract; 1st judge in Madison County, N.Y.; acquired land holdings totalling close to 1,000,000 acres in various parts of N.Y.; ret. from bus. activities, turned interests over to son Gerrit, 1819. Died Schenectady, N.Y., Apr. 14, 1837.

SMITH, Richard, Continental Congressman, diarist; b. Burlington, N.J., Mar. 22, 1735; s. Richard and Abigail (Rapier or Raper) S.; m. Elizabeth Rodman, June 5, 1762, 5 children including Richard R. Admitted to N.J. bar, circa 1760; commd. clk. Burlington County (N.J.), 1762; propr. who received land grant Otego Patent of 6900 acres in N.Y., 1768; del. to Continental Congress, 1774-76; kept historically useful diary of Congress proceedings from Sept. 12, 1775-Oct. 1, 1775, Dec. 12, 1775-Mar. 30, 1776; signed Olive branch petition to King, 1775; mem. N.J. Council, 1776; treas. of N.J., 1776-77. Died nr. Natchez, Miss., Sept. 17, 1803; buried Natchez Cemetery.

SMITH, Richard Penn, editor, writer; b. Phila., Mar. 13, 1799; s. William Moore and Ann (Rudulph) S.; m. Elinor (Blodget) Lincoln, May 5, 1823; m. 2d, Isabella Stratton Knisell, 1836; 10 children including Horace Wemyss. Admitted to Phila. bar, 1821; purchaser Phila. Aurora, 1822, merged with Franklin Gazette, 1824, editor both papers, 1824-27 (sold 1827); author 20 plays (15 performed), 1825-35, best include The Deformed, 1830, Caius Marius, 1831; author novel The Forsaken, 1831; credited with authorship of Col. Crockett's Exploits and Adventures in Texas, 1836. Died Schuylkill, nr. Phila., Aug. 12, 1854.

SMITH, Richard Somers, army officer, coll. pres.; b. Phila., Oct. 30, 1813; grad. U.S. Mil. Acad., 1834; m. Ellen Clark, 6 children. Commd 1st lt. U.S. Army, 1846; instr., asst. prof. drawing U.S. Mil. Acad., 1840-55; quartermaster, 1846-51; prof. mathematics, engring., drawing Bklyn. Collegiate and Poly. Inst., 1856-59; commd. maj. 12th Inf., 1861; with Army of Potomac, 1862; pres. Girard Coll., Phila., 1863-67; prof. engring. Polytechnic Coll. of Pa., Phila., 1868-70; prof. mathematics U.S. Naval Acad., Annapolis, Md., 1870-77, prof drawing, 1873-77, Author: Manual of Topographical Drawing, 1853; Manual of Linear Perspective. 1857. Died Annapolis, Jan. 23, 1877.

SMITH, Robert, architect.; patriot; b. probably in Glasgow, Scotland, 1722; 3 children. Came to U.S.; mem. Carpenters Co., Phila.; built Nassau Hall, Princeton U., 1754, progenitor of a school of Am. college architecture; designed St. Peter's Ch., Phila., 1758; mem. Pa. Com. of Correspondence, 1774, originated plan to block Delaware River; Phila.'s most eminent architect; became mem. Am. Philos. Soc., 1768. Died Feb. 11, 1777.

SMITH, Robert, clergyman; b. Worstead, Norfolk, Eng., June 25, 1732; s. Stephen and Hannah (Press) S.; B.A., Gonville and Caius Coll., Cambridge (Eng.) U., 1754, fellow, 1755; m. Elizabeth Pagett, July 9, 1758; m. 2d, Sarah Shubrick, early 1774; m. 3d, Anna Maria (Tilghman) Goldsborough, after 1779; 3 children. Ordained deacon Protestant Episcopal Ch., 1756, priest, 1756; came to Charleston, S.C., 1757; rector St. Philip's Ch., Charleston, 1759-75, 83-1801; served as chaplain 1st S.C. Regt., also Continental Hosp., Charleston, 1776; chaplain-gen. So. dept. Continental Army, circa 1778; imprisoned by British, Charleston, 1780; later banished to Phila.; returned to Charleston. 1783; founded sch. (known as Coll. of Charleston after 1790) circa 1785, prin., 1790-98; instrumental in summoning S.C. conv. Protestant Episcopal Ch. which sent dels. to Gen. Conv., 1785; consecrated 1st Protestant Episcopal bishop S.C., 1795. Died Charleston, Oct. 28, 1801; buried St. Philip's Cemetery, Charleston.

SMITH, Robert, cabinet officer; b. Lancaster, Pa., Nov. 3, 1757; s. John and Mary (Buchanan) S.; grad. Coll. of N.J. (now Princeton), 1781; m. Margaret Smith, 8 children. Admitted to Balt. bar, circa 1784; mem. Md. Senate, 1793-95, Md. Ho. of Dels., 1796-1800; mem. Balt. City Council, 1798-1801; Republican; U.S. sec. of navy, 1802-05, maintained blockading squadron in Mediterranean during war against Barbary states; acting atty. gen., 1805; Jefferson's rep. in diplomatic negotiations with British concerning impressment of U.S. seamen, 1808; U.S. sec. state under Madison, 1809-11, resigned after criticism from Pres. Madison, 1811; received positions due in part to influence of brother Gen. Samuel Smith. Died Balt., Nov. 26, 1842.

SMITH, Robert, congressman, businessman; b. Peterborough, Hillsboro County, N.H., June 12, 1802; attended public schs., New Ipswich Acad.; studied law. Taught sch.; became mcht., 1822, manufactured textile goods, Northfield, N.H., 1823; admitted to bar, practiced law; moved to Ill., settled in Alton, 1832, became mcht.; elected capt. Ill. Militia, 1832; extensive land owner, in real estate business; mem. Ill. Ho. of Reps., 1836-40, elected enrolling and engrossing clk., 1840, 42; mem. U.S. Ho. of Reps. (Democrat) from Ill., 28th-30th, 35th congresses, 1843-49, 57-59; served as paymaster during Civil War; engaged in water-power devel. and railroad enterprises. Died Alton, Dec. 21, 1867; buried Alton City Cemetery.

SMITH, Robert Hardy, lawyer, Confederate legislator; b. Camden County, N.C., Mar. 21, 1813; s. Robert Hard and Elizabeth (Gregory) S.; m. Evelina Inge, Jan. 12, 1839; m. 2d, Emily Inge, Nov. 25, 1845; m. 3d, Helen Herndon, Apr. 9, 1850; 13 children. Admitted to Ala. bar, 1835; rep. from Sumter County in Ala. Legislature, 1849-51; a Whig leader in Ala.; del.-at-large, mem. Provisional confederate Congress, 1861, assisted com. which framed permanent constn. for Confederacy; organizer, col. 36th Ala. Inf., 1862. Author: An Address to the Citizens of Alabama on the Constitution and Laws of the Confederate States of America, 1861. Died Mobile, Ala., Mar. 13, 1878.

SMITH, Roswell, lawyer, publisher; b. Lebanon, Conn., Mar. 30, 1829; s. Asher Ladd and Wealthy (Pratt) S.; attended Brown U., 1848-50; m. Annie Ellsworth, 1852. Went to N.Y. to enter employ Paine & Burgess, publishers, 1843; practiced in Lafayette, Ind., 1851; partner Scribner & Co., 1870, published 1st issue Scribner's Monthly, became The Century Magazine, 1881; conceived The Century Dictionary and Cyclopedia, published under his direction, 1892; bd. dirs. Am. Tract Soc. Died N.Y.C., Apr. 19, 1892.

SMITH, Russell, painter; b. Glasgow, Scotland, Apr. 26, 1812; s. William Thompson and Margaret (Russell) S.; m. Mary Pricilla Wilson, 2 children, Xanthus, Mary Smith. Came to U.S., 1819; scenery painter, 1833-55; commd. to produce landscape scenery for Phila. Acad. Music, 1855-56; painted all scenery for Am. Acad. Music, Balt., also principal theatrical houses in Phila., Boston, Bklyn. Died Glenside, Pa., Nov. 8, 1896.

SMITH, Samuel, senator; b. Carlisle, Pa., July 27, 1752; s. John and Mary (Buchanan) S.; grad. Princeton; m. Margaret Spear, 1778, 8 children. Served as capt., maj., lt. col., organized co. of volunteers, 1775; participated in battles of Long Island and Monmouth; helped suppress the "Whiskey Rebellion", 1791; commd. brig. gen. militia, 1794; mem. U.S. Ho. of Reps. from Md., 3d-7th, 14th-17th congresses, 1793-1803, Jan. 31, 1816-Dec. 17, 1822; acting sec. navy U.S., 1801; mem. U.S. Senate from Md., 1803-15, Dec. 17, 1822-33, pres. pro tem., 1805-08; leader in opposing nomination of Madison 1808; author non-importation legislation of 1806; maj. gen., head forces which defended Balt. from the British during War of 1812; Federalist, became a Jeffersonian Republican; mayor Balt., 1835-38. Died Balt., Apr. 22, 1839; buried Old Westminster Burying Ground, Balt.

SMITH, Samuel, congressman, mfr.; b. Peterboro, N.H., Nov. 11, 1765; attended Phillips Exeter (N. H.) Acad., Philips Acad., Andover, Mass. Became mcht.; moderator town meetings, 1794-1811; mem. U.S. Ho. of Reps. (Federalist) from N.H., 13th Congress, 1813-15; in paper and cotton goods mfg., 1828. Died Peterboro, Apr. 25, 1842; buried Village Cemetery.

SMITH, Samuel, congressman. Asso. judge Erie County (Pa.), 1803-05; mem. U.S. Ho. of Reps. (filled vacancy) from Pa., 9th-11th congresses, Nov. 7, 1805-11.

SMITH, Samuel A., congressman; b. Harrow, Nockamixon Twp., Bucks County, Pa., 1795; attended common schs. Commd. Justice of peace for Rockhill-Milford Dist. before age of 21; register of wills Bucks County, 1824-29; brigade insp. of militia for Bucks and Montgomery County dist., resigned 1832; mem. U.S. Ho. of Reps. (Independent Democrat, filled vacancies) from Pa., 21st-22d congresses, Oct. 13, 1829-33; mem. Pa. Senate, 1841-43; apptd. asso. judge Bucks County Cts. by Gov. Porter, 1844-49; became mcht., Doylestown, Pa., later Point Pleasant, Pa.; mem., presiding officer many Dem. county convs. Died Point Pleasant, May 15, 1861; buried Presbyn. Churchyard, Doylestown.

SMITH, Samuel Axley, congressman; b. Monroe County, Tenn., June 26, 1822; studied law. Taught sch.; admitted to bar, 1845, practiced in Cleveland, Tenn.; dist. atty. gen., 1845-50; del. Nat. Democratic Conv., Balt., 1848; mem. U.S. Ho. of Reps. (Dem.) from Tenn., 33d-35th congresses, 1853-59; commr. Gen. Land Office, apptd. by Pres. Buchanan 1860; served in Confederate Army during Civil War, 1861. Died Ladd Springs, Polk County, Tenn., Nov. 25, 1863; buried Amos Ladd's Burial Ground.

SMITH, Samuel Francis, clergyman, editor, poet; b. Boston, Oct. 21, 1808; s. Samuel and Sarah (Bryant) S.; grad. Harvard, 1829; grad. Andover Theol. Sem., 1832; m. Mary Smith, Sept. 16, 1834, 6 children including Daniel Appleton White. Wrote "My Country 'tis of Thee" 1st published in Mason's The choir, 1832; wrote "The Morning Light is Breaking," ordained to ministry Baptist Ch., 1834; pastor at Waterville, Me., 1834-42, Newton Center, Mass., 1842-54; edited The Christian Review, 1842-48; editorial sec. Am. Bapt. Missionary Union, 1854; collected poetry Poems of Home and Country, published 1895. Died Boston, Nov. 16, 1895.

SMITH, Samuel Harrison, journalist, banker; b. 1772; s. Jonathan Bayard and Susannah (Bayard) S.; m. Margaret Bayard, Sept. 29, 1800, 4 children. Founder, The New World (Jeffersonian newspaper), Phila., 1796, The Universal Gazette, 1797; founder tri-weekly The Nat. Intellligencer and Washington Advertiser (Jeffersonian publ.), 1800, owner, 1800-10; publisher Jefferson's Manual of Parliamentary Practice, 1801, also exec. proclamations, public notices; received half of congressional printing; a commr. revenue, 1813; pres. Washington (D.C.) br. U.S. Bank, 1828-37. Died Washington, Nov. 1, 1845; buried Rock Creek Cemetery, Washington.

SMITH, Samuel Stanhope, clergyman, coll. pres.; b. Pequea, Lancaster County, Pa., Mar. 16, 1750; s. Rev. Robert and Elizabeth (Blair) S.; grad. Princeton, 1769; m. Ann Witherspoon, 9 children. Licensed to preach by Presbyn. Ch. in Western Va., 1773; founded Hampden-Sydney Acad. (later Coll.), pres. until 1779; prof. moral philosophy Princeton U., 1779-95, pres., 1795-1812, called to College 1st undergrad. tchr. chemistry and natural science in U.S., 1795. Author: Causes of the Variety of the Complexion and Figure of the Human Species, 1788; Oration on the Death of Washington, 1800; Sermons, 1801; Lectures on the Evidences of the Christian Religion, 1809; Love of Praise, 1810; Lectures . . . on the Subjects of Moral and Political Philosophy, 2 vols., 1812; A Continuation of Ramsay's History of the United States; The Principles of Natural and Revealed Religion. Died Balt., Aug. 21, 1819.

SMITH, Seba, (pseudonym Maj. Jack Downing), polit. satirist; b: Buckfield, Me., Sept. 14, 1792; s. Seba and Aphia (Stevens) S.; grad. Bowdoin Coll., 1818; m. Elizabeth Oakes Prince, Mar. 6, 1823, 5 children. Editor, Eastern Argus, Portland, Me., 1820-26; founded Portland Courier (1st daily newspaper in Me.), 1829; wrote "Downing letters" (a humorous satire of politics of

Jacksonian period), from 1830, published letters as book The Life and Writings of Major Jack Downing of Downingville, 1833; wrote articles for various periodicals from 1839; moved to N.Y.C., 1842; edited Emerson U.S. Magazine, 1854-59; established Great Republic, a monthly, 1859; political satire contained in My Thirty Years Out of the Senate, 1859. Died Patchogue, L.I., N.Y., July 29, 1868.

SMITH, Soloman Franklin (known as Sol Smith), comedian, theatre mgr.; b. Norwich, N.Y., Apr. 20, 1808; s. Levi and Hannah (Holland) S.; m. Martha Mathews, 1822; m. 2d, Elizabeth Pugsley, 1839; 7 surviving children including Marcus, Soloman Franklin. Started and edited Independent Press and Freedom's Advocate, Cincinnati, 1822; independent theatre trooping in Southeastern states, 1831-39; jr. partner in theatre mgmt. firm of Ludlow & Smith which controlled theatres in St. Louis, Mobile, New Orleans; practiced law, St. Louis, 1853-69; mem. state conv. that kept Mo. from secession, 1861. Author: Theatrical Management in the West and South, 1868. Died Feb. 14, 1869.

SMITH, Sophia, philanthropist; b. Hatfield, Mass., Aug. 27, 1796; d. Joseph and Lois (White) Smith. Heiress to fortune of brother, 1861; on suggestion of John Morton Greene, minister of Hatfield Congregational Ch., made will providing for library, acad. and instn. for deaf at Hatfield (all later established in accordance with will); urged by Greene to endow women's college, 1868, made provision in new will for coll. "with design to furnish for my own sex means and facilities for education equal to those of which are afforded now in our colleges to young men," changed location in last will (1870) from Hatfield to Northampton, Mass.; Smith Coll (based on "Plan for a Woman's College" prepared by Greene) opened under terms of her bequest, 1875. Died Hatfield, June 12, 1870.

SMITH, Thomas, Continental congressman; b. nr. Cruden, Aberdeenshire, Scotland, 1745; attended U. Edinburgh (Scotland); studied law. Came to Am., settled in Bedford, Pa., 1769; dep. surveyor, 1769; admitted to bar, practiced law, 1772; dep. register of wills and prothonotary, 1773; justice of peace, 1774; mem. Com. of Correspondence, 1775; served as dep. col. of militia in Revolutionary Army; del. Pa. Constl. Conv., 1776; mem. Pa. Ho. of Reps., 1776-80; mem. Continental Congress from Pa., 1780-82; judge Ct. Common Pleas, 1791, Pa. Supreme Ct., 1794-1809. Died Phila., Mar. 31, 1809; buried Christ Churchyard.

SMITH, Thomas, congressman; b. Pa. Lived in Tinicum Twp., Delaware County, Pa.; mem. Pa. Ho. of Reps., 1806-07; mem. U.S. Ho. of Reps. (Federalist) from Pa., 14th Congress, 1815-17; moved to Darby Twp. (later Darby Borough), 1815; justice of peace until 1846. Died Darby, Delaware County, Jan. 29, 1846; buried St. James's (Old Swedes) Cemetery, Paschall (now part of Phila.), Pa.

SMITH, Thomas, congressman; b. Fayette County, Pa., May 1, 1799. Moved to Rising Sun, Ind., 1818, learned tanner's trade; moved to Versailles, Ripley County, Ind., 1821, established tanyard; became col. in militia; mem. Ind. Ho. of Reps., 1829, 30, 33-36; mem. Ind. Senate, 1836-39; mem. U.S. Ho. of Reps. (Democrat) from Ind., 26th, 28th-29th congresses, 1838-41, 43-47; retired to pvt. life; del. Ind. Constl. Conv., 1850. Died Versailles, Apr. 12, 1876; buried Cliff Hill Cemetery.

SMITH, Thomas Adams, army officer; b. Essex County, Va., Aug. 12, 1781; s. Francis and Lucy (Wilkinson) S.; m. Cynthia Berry White, Sept. 17, 1807, 8 children including Lucy Anne Tucker. Commd. 2d lt. arty; U.S. Army, 1803, capt. rifles, 1808, lt., then col., col. of the regt. during War of 1812; engaged at battles of Plattsburg, Sacketts Harbor, and Burlington; promoted brig. gen., 1814; col., comdr. rifle regt., 1815; comdr.-in-chief Territories of Mo. and Ill: with hdqrs. at Bellefontaine, nr. St. Louis, 1815; receiver of public monies (apptd. by Pres. Monroe), Franklin, Mo., 1818-26; Ft. Smith (Ark.) named for him. Died June 25, 1844.

SMITH, Thomas Kilby, army officer, diplomat; b. Boston, Sept. 23, 1820; attended mil. acad., Cincinnati; studied law under Chief Justice Chase. Apptd. spl. agt. Post Office Dept., 1853; served to maj. gen. U.S. Army during Civil War, in charge of dept. of So. Ala. and Fla.; apptd. U.S. consul in Panama, 1866; later engaged in journalism in N.Y. Died N.Y.C., Dec. 14, 1887.

SMITH, Truman, senator; b. Roxbury, Conn., Nov. 27, 1791; s. Phineas and Deborah Ann (Judson) S.; grad. Yale, 1815; attended Litchfield Conn.) Law Sch.; m. Maria Cook; m. 2d, Mary A. Dickinson; 9 children. Admitted to Litchfield bar, 1818; mem. Conn. Ho. of Reps., 1831-32, 34; mem. U.S. Ho. of Reps. from Conn., 26th-27th, 29th-30th congresses, 1839-43, 45-49; presdl. elector on Whig ticket, 1844; 1st chmn. Whig Nat. Com., 1848, directed Taylor's campaign; mem. U.S. Senate from Conn., 1849; May 24, 1854; obtained land grant to assist in constrn. of Sault Sainte Marie canal; opened law office in N.Y.C., 1854-72; judge ct. of arbitration for trial of Brit. and Am. vessels suspected of engaging in slave trade, 1862-70; judge ct. of claims under 1862 treaty with Gt. Britain, N.Y. Died Stamford, Conn., May 3, 1884; buried Woodland Cemetery, Stamford.

SMITH, William, jurist; b. Newport-Pagnell, Buckinghamshire, Eng., Oct. 8, 1697; s. Thomas and Susanna (Odell) S.; grad. Yale, 1719, M.A., 1722; m. Mary Het, May 11, 1727; m. 2d, Elizabeth Scott Williams; 15 children including William, Joshua, Hett. Came to Am., 1715; admitted to N.Y. bar, 1724, to Gray's Inn, London, Eng., 1727; identified with radicals in polit. affairs; endeavored to curb N.Y. Gov.'s prerogative; asserted that both English and colonial cts. rested upon statutory authority in speech to Gen. Assembly of Colony of N.Y., 1734; defended Peter Zenger in his trial for seditious libel, 1735, disbarred for attacking judges' rights to appointments in this case; readmitted to practice law, 1737; counsel in many leading cases in Mayor's Ct. of N.Y.C.; atty. gen. N.Y., 1751; mem. N.Y. Provincial Council, 1753-67; mem. com. that formulated plan of union, Albany (N.Y.) Congress, 1754; asso. justice N.Y. Supreme Ct., 1763-69; an incorporator Princeton U.; founder, trustee N.Y. Soc. Library. Died N.Y.C., Nov. 22, 1769.

SMITH, William, clergyman, educator; b. Aberdeen, Scotland, Sept. 17, 1727; s. Thomas and Elizabeth (Duncan) S.; A.M., U. Aberdeen, 1747, D.D. hon.), 1759; D..D. (hon.) Oxford (Eng.) U., 1759; D.D. (hon.), U. Dublin (Ireland), 1763; m. Rebecca Moore, June 3, 1758, 5 children including Rebecca. Sailed for N.Y., 1751; ordained priest Anglican Ch., Dec. 23, 1753; tchr. rhetoric and logic Coll., Acad. and Charitable Sch. of Phila., 1754, provost, 1754-79, 89-91; Mason; charged with seditous libels and exonerated, 1758; rector Trinity Ch., Oxford, Pa., 1766-77; mem. Am. Philos. Soc., 1768; founder Kent Sch. (chartered as Washington Coll. 1782), 1779; rector Chester Parish, Kent County, Md., 1779. Author: Plain Truth; Addressed to the Inhabitants of America (expressing Loyalist views during Am. Revolution). Died Phila., May 14, 1803.

SMITH, William, Continental congressman, congressman; b. Donegal Twp., Lancaster County, Pa., Apr. 12, 1728. Moved to Balt., 1761; apptd. mem. Com. of Correspondence, 1774; mem. Com. of Observation, 1775; on com. apptd. by Congress to constitute naval board, 1777; mem. Continental Congress from Md., 1777, 78; on com. to organize defense of Balt. and to address and receive Gen. Washington, 1781; became mcht.; mem. U.S. Ho. of Reps. (Federalist) from Md., 1st Congress, 1789-91; 1st auditor U.S. Treasury, 1791; presdl. elector, 1796; mem. Md. Senate, 1801. Died Balt., Mar. 27, 1814; buried Old Westminster Graveyard.

SMITH, William, jurist, historian, Loyalist; b. N.Y.C., June 25, 1728; s. William and Mary (Het) S.; grad. Yale, 1745; m. Janet Livingston, Nov. 3, 1752, 11 children including William. Admitted to N.Y. bar, 1750; published (with William Livingston) 1st digest of colony statutes in force at time entitled Laws of New York from 1691 to 1751, Inclusive, 1752; published Laws of New York . . . 1752-62, 1762; chief contbn. The History of the Province of New York, from the First Discovery to the Year MDCC XXXII, published in London, 1757, reissued, 1814; became chief justice Province of N.Y:, 1763, chief justice state of N.Y., 1779, never actually served; proceeded to England on evacuation of N.Y., 1783; chief justice of Canada, 1789-93. Died Quebec, Can., Dec. 3, 1793.

SMITH, William, clergyman; b. Aberdeen, Scotland, 1754; s. Dr. William Smith; probably attended Aberdeen U.; m. Magdalen Milne, several children. Ordained in Scottish Non-juring Episcopal Ch.; pastor, various Episcopal chs. in Pa., Md., R.I. and Conn., 1785-90; rector Trinity Ch., Newport, R.I., 1790-97; an organizer Diocese of R.I.; opened grammar sch., N.Y.C., 1800; prin. Episcopal Acad., Cheshire, Conn., 1802-06. Author several books including Churchman's Choral Companion, 1809; Office of Institutions of Ministers (written for Cinn. clergy, adopted by Gen. Conv. of Episcopal Ch.). Died N.Y.C. Apr. 6, 1821.

SMITH, William, congressman; b. Chesterfield, Va.; completed prep. studies. Mem. Va. Ho. of Dels., 1782; mem. U.S. Ho. of Reps. from Va., 17th-19th congresses, 1821-27.

SMITH, William, senator; b. N.C., 1762; grad. Mt. Zion Collegiate Inst., Winnsborough, S.C., 1780; m. Margaret Duff, 1781, 1 child. Admitted to S.C. bar, 1784; mem. U.S. Ho. of Reps. (Democrat) from S.C., 5th Congress, 1797-99; mem. S.C. Senate, 1802-08, pres., 1806; circuit judge S..C, 1808-16; mem. U.S. Senate (Democrat) from S.C., 1816-23, 26-31, twice elected pres. pro tem, delivered his most important speech in Mo. debates, 1820, defended So. position in Union, championed So. rights; mem. S.C. Ho. of Reps., 1824-26; received the 7 electoral votes of Ga. for vice pres. U.S. 1829; mem. S.C. Senate, 1831; moved to La., then Ala., 1833; mem. lower house Ala. Legislature, 1836-40; Jeffersonian Democrat. Died Huntsville, Ala., June 26, 1840.

SMITH, William, gov. Va.; b. "Marengo," King George County, Va., Sept. 6, 1797; s. Col. Caleb and Mary (Waugh) S.; m. Elizabeth H. Bell, 1821. In law practice, Culpeper, Va., 1818; established a daily post service from Washington, D.C. to Milledgeville, Ga., 1834; mem. Va. Senate, 1836-41; mem. U.S. Ho. of Reps. from Va., 27th, 33d-36th congresses, 1841-43, 1853-61; presdl. elector, 1844; gov. Va., 1846-49, 64-65, signed the act accepting the retrocession to Va. of the part of D.C. south of Potomac River, 1847; commd. col. 49th Va. Inf., Confederate Army, 1861, brig. gen., 1862; mem. Confederate Congress, 1862; brevetted maj. gen., 1863; mem. Va. Ho. of Dels., 1877-79. Died "Monterosa" nr. Warrenton, May 18, 1887; buried Hollywood Cemetery, Richmond, Va.

SMITH, William Alexander, congressman, railroad exec.; b. Warren County, N.C., Jan. 9, 1828; attended common schs. Became farmer; mem. N.C. Constl. Conv., 1865; mem. N.C. Senate, 1870; pres. N.C. R.R., 1868, Yadkin River R.R.; mem. U.S. Ho. of Reps. (Republican) from N.C., 43d Congress, 1873-75. Died Richmond, Va., May 16, 1888; buried Hollywood Cemetery.

SMITH, William Andrew, clergyman, coll. pres., author; b. Fredericksburg, Va., Nov. 29, 1802; s. William and Mary (Porter) S.; m. Mahala Miller; m. 2d, Laura Brooking; m. 3d, Mrs. Eliza V. Williams; 4 children. Preacher, Methodist Episcopal Ch., 1825, del. to gen. confs., 1832-44, del. to Southern confs., until 1870; pres. Randolph-Macon Coll., Ashland, Va., 1846-66, prof. moral and intellectual philosophy; elected pres. Central Coll., Fayette, Mo., 1868. Died Richmond, Va., Mar. 1, 1870; buried Hollywood Cemetery, Richmond.

SMITH, William Ephraim, congressman, lawyer; b. Augusta, Ga., Mar. 14, 1829; had academic course; studied law. Admitted to bar under spl. act of Ga. Legislature, 1846, practiced in Albany, Ga.; also became planter; ordinary of Dougherty County, Ga., 1853; solicitor gen. of S.W. Circuit, 1858-60; enlisted as 1st lt. 4th Ga. Volunteer Infantry in Confederate Army during Civil War, elected capt., 1862; elected to Ho. of Reps. of 2d Confederate Congress, 1863; mem. U.S. Ho. of Reps. (Democrat) from Ga., 44th-46th congresses, 1875-81; pres. Ga. Dem. Conv., 1886; mem. Ga. Senate, 1886-88. Died Albany, Mar. 11, 1890; buried Oakview Cemetery.

SMITH, William Henry, actor; b. Montgomeryshire, Wales, Dec. 4, 1806; m. Sarah (Lapsley) Riddle; m. 2d, Lucy; 2 children. Arrived in U.S., 1827; actor and stage mgr., numerous theatres, 1827-43; actor Shakespearean roles with Junius B. Booth, N.Y.C., 1840; stage mgr., actor with stock company at Boston Mus., 1843-59, revised and presented "The Drunkard" (gt. popular success), 1844; stage mgr., actor Cal. Theater, San Francisco, circa 1866-72. Died Jan. 17, 1872.

SMITH, William Henry, journalist; b. Austerlitz, Columbia County, N.Y., Dec. 1, 1833; s. William Deforest Smith; m. Emma Reynolds, 1855, 1 child. Correspondent for Cincinnati newspapers, circa 1853; pvt. sec. to Ohio Gov. John Brough; sec. of state Ohio, 1864-66; editor Cincinnati Evening Chronicle, 1866-70; head Western Asso. Press, 1870; collector Port of Chgo., 1877; effected combination of N.Y. Asso. Press and Western Asso. Press, 1882, became gen. mgr. of joint orgn.; a founder Mergenthaler Linotype Co.; editor papers of Arthur St. Clair, published 1882. Died Lake Forest, Ill., July 27, 1896.

SMITH, William Loughton, congressman, diplomat; b. Charleston, S.C., circa 1758; s. Benjamin and Anne (Loughton) S.; m. Charlotte Izard, May 1, 1786; m. 2d, Charlotte Wrag, Dec. 19, 1805; 3 children. Admitted to S.C. bar, 1784; mem. privy council, 1784; mem. S.C. Ho. of Reps., 1784-88, 1808; mem. U.S. Ho. of Reps. from S.C., 1st-5th congresses, 1789-July 1797; minister to Portugal and Spain, 1797-1801; made unsuccessful attempt to reenter Congress, 1804; lt. S.C. Militia, 1808; pres. Santee Canal Co. Author: (pamphlet attacking Jefferson) The Politicks and Views of A Certain Party Displayed, 1792; other pamphlets.

Died Charleston, S.C., Dec. 19, 1812; buried St. Philips Ch.

SMITH, William Nathan Harrell, congressman, jurist; b. Murfreesboro, N.C., Sept. 24, 1812; s. William Lay and Ann (Harrell) S.; grad. Yale, 1834, attended Law Sch., 1836, LL.D. (hon.), 1881; LL.D. (hon.), Wake Forest Coll., 1874, U. N.C., 1875; m. Mary Olivia Wise, Jan. 14, 1839; 3 sons, James Murdock, William W., E. Chambers. Admitted to N.C. bar, circa 1836; Whig mem. N.C. Ho. of Commons, 1840, 58, 65-66; mem. N.C. Senate, 1848; solicitor of N.C., 1849-57; mem. U.S. Ho. of Reps. from N.C., 36th Congress, 1859-61; served in all 3 Confederate congresses, 1862-65; del. to Nat. Union Conv., 1866; leader in organizing conservative opposition to radical control of N.C.; del. to Democratic Nat. Conv., 1868; one of Gov. Holden's counsel in impeachment trial, 1871; chief justice N.C. Supreme Ct., 1878-89. Died Raleigh, N.C., Nov. 14, 1889; buried Oakwood Cemetery, Raleigh.

SMITH, William Russell, congressman, univ. pres.; b. Russellville, Ky., Mar. 27, 1815; s. Ezekiel and Elizabeth (Hampton) S.; attended U. Ala., 1831-34; m. Jane Binion, 1843; m. 2d, Mary Jane Murray, Jan. 3, 1847; m. 3d, Wilhelmine M. Easby, June 14, 1854; 3 children. Capt., Ala. Militia in campaign against Creek Indians, 1836; admitted to Ala. bar, circa 1835; founded and edited Whig newspaper the Mirror, Tuscaloosa, Ala., 1837-circa 1838; mayor Tuscaloosa, 1839; mem. Ala. Gen. Assembly as Whig, 1841-43, left party, 1843; brig. gen. Ala. Militia, 1845; circuit judge of Ala., 1850-51; mem. U.S. Ho. of Reps. from Ala., 32d-34th congresses, 1851-57; opposed secession in Ala. State Conv. of 1861; recruited and became col. 26th Ala. Regt., 1861; mem. Confederate Ho. of Reps., 1861-65; pres. U. Ala., 1869-71, Author: History and Debates of the Convention of Alabama, 1861; Key to Homer's Iliad, 1871; College Musing, or Twigs from Parnassus (vol. of poetry), 1833; best known poem: The Uses of Solitude, 1860. Died Washington, D.C., Feb. 26, 1896; buried Tuscaloosa.

SMITH, William Stephens, army officer, congressman; b. L.I., N.Y., Nov. 8, 1755; s. John and Margaret (Stephens) S.; grad. Princeton, 1774; m. Abigail Amelia Adams, June 12, 1786, 3 children. Aide-de-camp to Gen. Sullivan as maj. 1776; participated in Battle of White Plains; lt. col. in William R. Lee's Regt.; fought at battles of Monmouth and Newport, 1778; insp. and adjutant to a corps of light inf. under Gen. Lafayette, 1780-81; served in 22 engagements in Revolutionary War; aide to George Washington, 1781; charged with supervision of evacuation of N.Y.C. by British in accordance with treaty of peace, 1781; sec. legation, London, Eng., 1785-88; visited Prussia to study orgn. of Frederick the Great, circa 1786; sent on diplomatic mission to Spain and Portugal, circa 1787; was fed. marshal, supr. of the revenue, surveyor Port of N.Y., 1789-1800; commanded 12th Inf., 1798; mem. U.S. Ho. of Reps. (Federalist) from N.Y., 13th Congress, 1813-15, presented his credentials of election to 14th Congress, did not qualify and Westel Willoughby, Jr. successfully contested his election, Dec. 1815; a founder Soc. of Cincinnati in N.Y., pres., 1795-97. Died Lebanon, N.Y., June 10, 1816.

SMITH, Worthington, univ. pres.; b. Hadley, Mass., Oct. 11, 1795; grad. Williams Coll., 1816; studied theology at Andover, 1816-18; D.D. (hon.), U. Vt., 1845. Licensed to preach Vt., 1819; prin. Hopkins Acad., 1820-25; ordained to ministry, St. Albans Ch., Windsor, Vt., 1823; mem. bd. control Middlebury Coll., 1825-56; pres. U. Vt., 1849-55. Author: Sermon on Popular Instruction, 1846; Inaugural Address, 1849. Died Feb. 13, 1856.

SMITH, Worthington Curtis, congressman; b. St. Albans, Franklin County, Vt., Apr. 23, 1823; son of John Smith; grad. U. Vt., 1843; studied law. Engaged in iron trade; assisted in raising 1st Regt., Vt. Volunteer Infantry during Civil War; mem. Vt. Ho. of Reps., 1863; mem. Vt. Senate, 1864-65, elected pres. pro tem, 1865; mem. U.S. Ho. of Reps. (Republican) from Vt., 40th-42d congresses, 1867-73; pres. St. Albans Foundry Co. Died St. Albans, Jan. 2, 1894; buried Greenwood Cemetery.

SMITHERS, Nathaniel Barrett, congressman, lawyer; b. Dover, Del., Oct. 8, 1818; grad. Lafayette Coll., Pa., 1836; studied law. Admitted to bar, practiced in Dover, 1840; sec. state Del., 1863; mem. U.S. Ho. of Reps. (Republican, filled vacancy) from Del., 38th Congress, Dec. 7, 1863-65; del. Nat. Rep. Conv., Balt., 1864. Died Dover, Jan. 16, 1896; buried Old Methodist Cemetery.

SMITHSON, James, scientist; b. France, 1765; s. Hugh and Elizabeth Keate (Macie) S.; grad. Pembroke Coll., Oxford (Eng.) U., 1786; never married. Became mem. Royal Soc., 1787; devoted his life to study of chemistry and mineralogy; Smithsonite (carbonate of zinc) named for him; never visited U.S.; made his will, 1826, leaving his estate to a nephew, with the provision that if the nephew should die childless, the estate would go "to the United States of America, to found at Washington, under the name of the Smithsonian Institution, an Establishment for the increase and diffusion of knowledge among men." Died Genoa, Italy, June 26, 1829; buried Genoa, reinterred main entrance of Smithsonian Instn.

SMYTH, Alexander, congressman, army officer; b. on island of Rathlin, off Ireland, 1765; s. Rev. Adam Smyth; m. Nancy Binkley, Jan. 1791, 4 children. Came to Va., 1775; dep. clk. Botetourt County (Va.), 1785; licensed and admitted to Va. bar, 1789; practiced in Abingdon, Va., 1789; mem. Va. Ho. of Dels., 1792-96, 1801-02, 04-08, 16-17, 26-27; mem. Va. Senate, 1808-09; col. S.W. Va. Rifle Regt., 1808-11; ordered to Washington (D.C.) to prepare system of army discipline, 1811; insp. gen. U.S. Army with rank of brig. gen., 1812; in command of brigade of regulars ordered to Niagra for projected invasion of Canada, 1812, took command of Stephen Van Rensselaer's force at Buffalo, N.Y., failed to invade Canada because of lack of trained troops; mem. U.S. Ho. of Reps. from Va., 15th-18th, 20th-21st congresses, 1817-25, 1827-30. Died Washington, D.C., Apr. 17, 1830; buried Congressional Cemetery, Washington.

SMYTH, George Washington, congressman; b. N. C., May 16, 1803; attended college, Murfreesboro, Tenn. Moved to Tex. (then part Republic of Mexico), 1828, settled in municipality of Bevell, Zavalas Colony (now Jasper County); apptd. by Mexican Govt. as surveyor, later made commr. of titles; del. Gen. Consultation of Tex., San Felipe de Austin, 1835; mem. Tex. State Conv., signer Tex. Declaration of Independence, 1836, also signed Republic of Tex. Constn.; apptd. by Pres. Lamar of Tex. as commr. in charge of boundary line between Republic of Tex. and U.S.; became farmer; dep. Congress of Republic of Tex., 1845, assisted in framing Constn. State of Tex.; elected commr. Tex. Gen. Land Office, 1848; mem. U.S. Ho. of Reps. (Democrat) from Tex., 33d Congress, 1853-55; served in Confederate Army during Civil War; mem. Tex. Constl. Conv., 1866. Died Austin, Tex., Feb. 21, 1866; buried State Cemetery.

SMYTH, Thomas, clergyman, philanthropist; b. Belfast, Ireland, June 14, 1808; s. Samuel and Ann (Magee) S.; attended Belfast Coll., 1827-29, Highbury Coll., 1829-30, Princeton Theol. Sem., 1830-31; m. Margaret Adger, July 9, 1832, 10 children. Came to U.S., 1830; ordained to ministry Presbyn. Ch., 1831; pastor 2d Presbyn. Ch., Charleston, S.C., 1834-70; gave his library with endowment to Columbia (S.C.) Theol. Sem., (most extensive pvt. collection of theol. works in Am., now at Decatur, Ga.); endowed Smyth lectureship, at Columbia Theol. Sem. Author: Lectures on Apostolic Succession, 1840; Ecclesiastical Catechism, 1841; Policy, 1844; Ruling Elders, 1845; Rite of Confirmation, 1845; Complete Works of Rev. Thomas Smyth (edited by Rev. J. William Flinn, D.D. and Jean Adger Finn), 10 vols., 1908-12. Died Charleston, Aug. 20, 1873.

SMYTH, Timothy Clement, clergyman; b. Finlea, Clare, Ireland, Jan. 24, 1810; attended Trinity Coll., Dublin, Ireland, also Mt. Melleray. Joined Cistercian Order, 1838, ordained priest Roman Catholic Ch., 1841; came to U.S., founded New Melleray monastery, nr. Dubuque, Ia., 1849; apptd. titular bishop of Thanasis, coadjutor of Dubuque, 1857; named bishop of Dubuque, 1858; adminstr. of Chgo., 1858-59. Died Dubuque, Sept. 22, 1865.

SMYTH, William, educator, reformer; b. Pittston, Me., Feb. 2, 1797; s. Caleb and Abiah (Colburn) S.; grad. Bowdoin Coll., 1822, D.D. (hon.), 1863; attended Andover Theol. Sem., 1822-23; m. Harriet Porter Coffin, 1827, 9 children including Egbert, Newman. Instr. Greek, mathematics Bowdoin Coll., 1823-28, became prof. mathematics, 1828; cooperated with Underground Railroad; helped raise money required to build Mem. Hall in honor of Bowdoin men who fought in Civil War; introduced a system of grade schs. at Brunswick, Me. Author series of textbooks including Elements of Algebra, 1830, Elements of Analytic Geometry, 1830. Died Brunswick, Apr. 4, 1868.

SMYTH, William, congressman, lawyer; b. Eden, County Tyrone, Ireland, Jan. 3, 1824; came to U.S., 1838; attended U. Ia.; studied law. Admitted to bar, 1847, practiced in Marion, Ia.; pros. atty. Linn County, 1848-53; judge dist. ct. for 4th Jud. Dist. of Ia., 1853-57; chmn. commn. to codify and revise Ia. laws, 1858; col. 31st Regt., Ia. Volunteer Infantry in Union Army during Civil War for 2 years; mem. U.S. Ho. of Reps. (Republican) from Ia., 41st Congress, 1869-Sept. 30, 1870. Died Marion, Sept. 30, 1870; buried Oak Shade Cemetery.

SNAPP, Henry, congressman, lawyer; b. Livonia, Livingston County, N.Y., June 30, 1822; attended common schs., Rochester, N.Y., also Homer, Will County, Ill.; studied law; at least 1 son, Howard Malcolm. Admitted to bar, 1843, practiced in Joliet, Ill.; mem. Ill. Senate, 1869-71; mem. U.S. Ho. of Reps. (Republican, filled vacancy) from Ill., 42d Congress, 1871-73. Died Joliet, Nov. 26, 1895; buried Oakwood Cemetery.

SNEAD, Thomas Lowndes, army officer, Confederate congressman; b. Henrico County, Va., Jan. 10, 1828; s. Jesse and Jane (Johnson) S.; grad. Richmond Coll., 1846; grad. U. Va., 1848; m. Harriet Vairin Reel, Nov. 24, 1852, 2 surviving children. Admitted to Va. bar, 1850; mem. staff St. Louis Bulletin, 1860, 61; aide to Gov. Jackson of Mo., 1861; acting adjutant-gen. with rank of col. Mo. State Guard; one of Mo.'s 2 commrs. in mil. conv. with Confederate States, 1861; asst. adjutant gen. with rank of maj. Confederate Army, 1862, chief of staff to Gen. Sterling Price in S.W.; rep. from Mo. to Confederate Congress, 1864-65; mng. editor N.Y. Daily News, 1865-66; admitted to N.Y. bar, 1866. Author: The Fight for Missouri, 1886. Died Hotel Royal, N.Y.C., Oct. 17, 1890; buried Bellefontaine Cemetery, St. Louis.

SNEED, William Henry, congressman, lawyer; b. Davidson County, Tenn., Aug. 27, 1812; completed prep. studies; studied law. Admitted to bar, 1834, practiced in Murfreesboro, Tenn.; mem. Tenn. Senate, 1843-45; moved to Knoxville, Tenn., 1845, practiced law; mem. U.S. Ho. of Reps. (Am. Party) from Tenn., 34th Congress, 1855-57. Died Knoxville, Sept. 18, 1869; buried Old Gray Cemetery.

SNELL, George, architect; b. London, Eng., 1820; attended King's Coll.; studied with Brit. architect H. L. Elmes. Came to U.S., 1850; organized Snell & Gregerson, archtl. firm, Boston, 1860; designed old Music Hall, Studio Bldg., Hotel Oxford, warehouses on Atlantic Av. and State St. (all Boston, none still standing). Died 1893.

SNELLING, Henry Hunt, photographic journalist; b. Plattsburg, N.Y., Nov. 8, 1817; s. Col. Josiah and Abigail (Hunt) S.; m. Anna L. Putnam, 1837. Gen. sales mgr. for E. Anthony's mfrs. sales photog. supplies, 1843; established, edited Photog. Art Jour., 1851-circa 1857; invented enlarging camera, 1852; announced a color process, 1856; editor Cornwall (N.Y.) Reflector, 1879-87; published "Photographic Entertainments" in Wilson's Photog. Mag., 1889-90. Author: The History and Practise of the Art of Photography (1st bound vol. on photography pub. in Am.), 1849; A Dictionary of the Photographic Art, 1854. Died Meml. Home., St. Louis, June 24, 1897.

SNELLING, Josiah, army officer; b. Boston, 1782; m. Elizabeth Bell, Aug. 29, 1809; m. 2d, Abigail Hunt, 1812; at least 5 children including William Joseph, Henry Hunt. Commd. 1st lt. 4th, later 5th Inf. U.S. Army, 1808, capt., 1809; distinguished at Battle of Tippecanoe, 1811, Battle of Brownstone, 1812; maj., asst. insp. gen., then lt. col. 4th Rifles, col., insp. gen., 1813-14, lt. col. 6th Inf., 1814, col. 5th Inf., 1819; acted as mil. comdr. and constructing engr. during and after bldg. of Ft. St. Anthony (adjacent to cities of St. Paul and Mpls.), 1820-28, responsible for governing settlement, name changed to Ft. Snelling (in his honor) by War Dept., 1825. Died Washington, D.C., Aug. 20, 1828.

SNELLING, William Joseph, journalist, satirist; b. Boston, Dec. 26, 1804; s. Col. Josiah and Elizabeth (Bell) S.; attended U.S. Mil. Acad., 1818-20; married circa 1822; m. 2d, Lucy Jordan, Mar. 2, 1838; at least 3 children. Lived among Dakota Indians, circa 1820-28; wrote under pseudonym Solomon Bell, circa 1828; editor Boston Herald, 1847-48; much of his writing lost because of use of pseudonyms. Author: Tales of the Northwest, or Sketches of Indian Life and Character, 1830; Truth: A New Year's Gift for Scribblers (sensational satire on contemporary poets), 1831; The Rat-Trap; or Cogitations of a Convict in the House of Correction, 1837. Died Chelsea, Mass., Dec. 24, 1848.

SNETHEN, Nicholas, clergyman; b. Glen Cove, L.I., N.Y., Nov. 15, 1769; s. Barak and Ann (Weeks) S.; ed. by pvt. tutor; m. Susannah Worthington, 1804, at least 1 dau. Admitted as preacher to Methodist Circuit in New Eng., 1794; preacher, Charleston, S.C., 1799; ordained to ministry, 1800; preacher, Balt., 1801-05; farmer, Frederick, Md., 1806-09; preacher, Balt., also Georgetown, D.C., 1809-14, ret. from preaching, after 1814; advocated lay representation in confs. of Ch. at Methodist Conf., 1812; contbr. to reformist Wesleyan Repository (founded 1820); leader of reform element in Balt. Conv. of 1828 which seceded from Methodist Ch. (after Gen. Conf. of Ch. refused to consider proposals for change) and founded Methodist Protestant Ch.; moved to Sullivan County, Ind., 1829, resumed preaching; editor (with

Asa Shinn) Mutual Rights and Methodist Protestant, Balt., 1834; in charge of Meth. sem. of dissident Meth. Protestant Ch., 1836; made unsuccessful attempt to found coll., Lawrenceburg, Ind., 1827. Died while in process of starting coll. in Iowa City, Ia. Territory, May 30, 1845.

SNODGRASS, John Fryall, congressman; b. Berkeley County, Va. (now W.Va.), Mar. 2, 1804; completed prep. studies; studied law. Admitted to bar, 1843, practiced in Parkersburg, Va.; del. Va. Constl. Conv., 1850-51; mem. U.S. Ho. of Reps. (Democrat) from Va., 33d Congress, 1853-June 5, 1854. Died Parkersburg (now W.Va.), June 5, 1854.

SNOW, Eliza Roxey, poet, Mormon woman leader; b. Becket, Berkshire County, Mass., Jan. 21, 1804; d. Oliver and Rosetta L. (Pettibone) S.; m. Joseph Smith, June 29, 1842; m. 2d, Brigham Young, 1849. Became mem. Mormon Ch., 1835; moved with family to Kirkland, O., lived with family of Mormon prophet Joseph Smith. 1835; settled in Nauvoo, Ill., 1840; 1st sec. Relief Soc., 1842; arrived in Utah, 1847; mgr. women's work in Mormon Endowment House, 1855-66; pres. Women's Relief Soc., 1866-87; mem. Mormon missionary party which visited Palestine, 1872-73; writer Mormon hymns including "O My Father, Thou That Dwellist"; poet, put Mormon history into verse. Died Dec. 5, 1887.

SNOW, William W., congressman, businessman; b. Heath, Franklin County, Mass., Apr. 27, 1812; attended public schs. Learned wool-carding and cloth dressing trades; moved to Oneonta, Otsego County, N.Y., 1831, in wool-carding business, 1841, in tin and hardware business, 1842; also became farmer; mem. N.Y. State Assembly, 1844, 70; mem. U.S. Ho. of Reps. (Democrat) from N.Y., 32d Congress, 1851-53; supr. town of Oneonta, 1873, 74; N.Y. State excise commr., 1877; mem. village bd. trustees; became banker. Died Oneonta, Sept. 3, 1886; buried Riverside Cemetery.

SNOWDEN, James Ross, govt. ofcl., numismatist; b. Chester, Pa., Dec. 9, 1809; s. Rev. Nathaniel Randolph and Sarah (Gustine) S.; ed. Dickinson Coll.; m. Susan Patterson, Sept. 13, 1848, 5 children. Admitted to Pa. bar, 1829; dep. atty. gen. (dist. atty.) Venango County (Pa.), circa 1831; mem. Pa. Ho. of Reps., 1838-44, speaker, 1842-44; col. Pa. Militia, circa 1830; presided Pa. Mil. Conv., Harrisburg, 1845; treas. State of Pa., 1845-47, improved state loans; treas. U.S. Mint, also asst. treas. U.S., Phila., 1848-50; solicitor Pa. R.R. Co., 1850; dir. U.S. Mint, Phila., 1854-61 prothonotary Pa. Supreme Ct., 1861-73. Author: (pamphlet) A Measure Proposed to Secure a Safe Treasury and a Sound Currency, 1857; A Description of Ancient and Modern Coins in the Cabinet Collection at the Mint of the United States, 1860. Died Hulmeville, Pa., Mar. 21, 1878.

SNYDER, Adam Wilson, congressman; b. Connellsville, Fayette County, Pa., Oct. 6, 1799; attended common schs.; studied law. Moved to Cahokia, Ill., 1817; admitted to bar, 1820, practiced in Cahokia; apptd. pros. atty. for 1st Jud. Dist., 1822, resigned 1823; became farmer, 1824-32; mem. Ill. Senate, 1830, 32, 40-41 (resigned); served as capt. throughout Black Hawk War; moved to Belleville, Ill., 1833; mem. U.S. Ho. of Reps. (Van Buren Democrat) from Ill., 25th Congress, 1837-39; Dem. presdl. elector, 1840; nominated as candidate for gov. Ill., died before election. Died Belleville, May 14, 1842; buried Green Mount Cemetery, nr. Belleville.

SNYDER, John, congressman, businessman; b. Selinsgrove, Snyder County, Pa., Jan. 29, 1793; attended rural schs. Served as capt. Selinsgrove Rifle Volunteers, Pa. Militia in War of 1812; with Snyder Spring Oil Co. and paper mills; mem. U.S. Ho. of Reps. from Pa., 27th Congress, 1841-43. Died Selinsgrove, Aug. 15, 1850; buried New Lutheran Cemetery.

SNYDER, Oliver P., congressman, lawyer; b. Mo., Nov. 13, 1833; completed prep. studies; studied law. Moved to Ark., 1853; admitted to bar, practiced in Pine Bluff, Jefferson County, Ark.; mem. Ark. Ho. of Reps., 1864-65; del. Ark. Constl. Conv., 1867; Republican presdl. elector, 1868; mem. Ark. Senate, 1868-71; mem. com. to revise and rearrange statutes of Ark., 1868; mem. U.S. Ho. of Reps. (Rep.) from Ark., 42d-43d congresses, 1871-75; elected treas. Jefferson County, 1882. Died Pine Bluff, Nov. 22, 1882; buried Bellewood Cemetery.

SNYDER, Simon, gov. Pa.; b. Lancaster, Pa., Nov. 5, 1759; s. Anthony and Maria Knippenburg (Kraemer) S.; m. Elizabeth Michael; m. 2d, Catherine Antes, June 12, 1796; m. 3d, Mrs. Mary Slough Scott, Oct. 16, 1814. Justice of the peace, Selin's Grove, Pa., circa 1786, later judge Ct. of Common Pleas, Northumberland County, Pa.; mem. Pa. Constl. Conv., 1789-90; mem. Pa. Legislature, 1797-1807, speaker 3 terms; gov. Pa., 1808-17; 1st rep. of German farming class to be elected gov.; strong states rights Republican, opposed jud. and financial power in state govt.; mem. Pa. Senate, 1817. Died Selin's Grove, Nov. 9, 1819.

SOBOLEWSKI, J. Friedrich Edvard, conductor, composer; b. Konigsberg, E. Prussia, Oct. 1, 1808; m. Bertha Dorn; m. 3d, Bertha von Kliest; 13 children. Dir. music Konigsberg Theatre, 1830; cantor Altstadtische Kirche, 1835; condr. Philharmonische Gesellschaft, 1838, Musikalische Akademie, 1843; composer, condr. and producer operas, Imogen, 1832, Velleda, 1835, Salvator Rosa, 1848; dir. music Bremen Theatre, 1854-59; composer opera Komala, prod. under aegis of Franz Liszt at Weimar, 1858; came to Milw., 1859; composer opera Mohega, 1859; condr. Milw. Philharmonic Soc. in its only season, 1860; condr. St. Louis Philharmonic Soc., 1860-66; contbr. articles "The New School of Music" (1868), "Mendelssohn" (1873), to Jour. of Speculative Philosophy. Died May 17, 1872.

SOLGER, Reinhold Ernst Friedrich Karl, author; b. Stethin, Prussia, July 17, 1817; s. Friedrich Ludwig and Auguste (Jungnickel) S.; attended U. Halle (Germany), 1837-40; doctor's degree, U. Greifswald (Germany), 1842; m. Adele Bemere, Feb. 19, 1848, 4 children. Referendary, Potsdam, circa 1843; went as tutor to Liverpool, Eng., circa 1844; served as adj. and interpreter to revolutionary leader Gen. Mieroslawski during fighting at Baden, 1848; came to U.S., 1853, settled in Roxbury, Mass.; writer and lectr. on German history, delivered series of lectures Lowell Inst., 1857-59; became Am. citizen, 1859; apptd. asst. register U.S. Treasury for aid in attracting German vote to Republican Party, 1861-64. Author: Erinnerung (eulogistic poem, won prize in N.Y.), 1859; Anton in Amerika (novel, given award by Bellestristisches Journal of N.Y.), 1862. Died Jan. 11, 1866.

SOLLERS, Augustus Rhodes, congressman, lawyer; b. nr. Prince Frederick, Calvert County, Md., May 1, 1814; studied law. Admitted to bar, 1836, practiced law, Prince Frederick; mem. U.S. Ho. of Reps. (Whig) from Md., 27th, 33d congresses, 1841-43, 53-55; del. Md. Constl. Conv., 1851; Democratic presdl. elector, 1856. Died Prince Frederick, Nov. 26, 1862; buried St. Paul's Churchyard, nr. Prince Frederick.

SOMERVILLE, William Clark, author; b. Bloomsbury, Md., Mar. 25, 1790; s. William and Anna (Hebb) S. Joined Venezuelan Army, before 1817, served cause of S.Am. independence; toured Europe, 1817-18; wrote articles and books on politics, 1818-26; active Whig supporter of J. Q. Adams. Author: Letters from Paris on the Causes and Consequences of the French Revolution, 1822; Extracts from a Letter on the Mode of Choosing the President, 1825. Died Auxerre, France, Jan. 25, 1826; buried La Grange (estate of Gen. Lafayette), France.

SOMES, Daniel Eton, congressman; b. Meredith (now Laconia), N.H., May 20, 1815; had academic edn. Moved to Biddeford, Me., 1846, founded Eastern Journal (later known as Union and Journal); mfr. loom harnesses, reed twine and varnishes; mayor Biddeford, 1855-57; pres. City Bank of Biddeford, 1856-58; mem. U.S. Ho. of Reps. (Republican) from Me., 36th Congress, 1859-61; del. Washington (D. C.) Peace Conv., 1861; practiced patent law, Washington until 1888. Died Washington, Feb. 13, 1888; buried Rock Creek Cemetery.

SOPHOCLES, Evangelinus Apostolides, classicist; b. Tsangarada, Thessaly, nr. Mt. Pelion, circa 1805; s. Apostolides Sophocles; ed. in establishment belonging to monastary of St. Catherine at Mt. Sinai, Cairo, Egypt. Came to Mass., circa 1827; taught at Mt. Pleasant Classical Inst. (later Amherst Acad.), circa 1830-34; instr. mathematics, Hartford, Conn., 1834; tutor Greek, Harvard, 1842-59, asst. prof., 1859, became prof., 1860; a neo-Hellenist. Author: A Greek Grammar for the Uses of Learners, 1835; First Lessons in Greek, 1839, Greek Exercises (both textbooks), 1841; A Romaic Grammar (this publ. altered theory of Aeolic-Doric origin of Modern Greek and correctly traced it to the Byzantine), 1842; A Catalogue of Greek Verbs, 1844; History of the Greek Alphabet, 1848. Died Holworthy Hall, Boston, Dec. 17, 1883.

SORIN, Edward Frederick, clergyman, coll. pres.; b. Ahvelle, nr. Laval, France, Feb. 6, 1814; Ordained priest Roman Catholic Ch., 1838, entered Congregation of Holy Cross, 1840; came to U.S. to do missionary work in Ind., 1841; obtained charter from Ind. Gen. Assembly for U. Notre Dame at South Bend, St. Joseph County, 1844; pres., 1844-65, completed 1st coll. bldg., 1844, secured site of present motherhouse, adjacent to Notre Dame, 1854, moved sisters' community house and acad. there; acted as provincial superior in charge of mission posts in north-eastern Ill., northern Ind. and southern Mich.; published family mag., Ave Maria, 1865; superior gen. Congregation of Holy Cross, 1868, directed missionary activities in France, Can., Bengal and U.S.; active in deliberations of Plenary Council of Balt., 1883; honored with insignia of officer of Public Instrn. by French Govt., 1888. Died Oct. 31, 1893.

SOTHERN, Edward Askew, actor, comedian; b. Liverpool, Eng., Apr. 1, 1826; s. John Sothern; m. Frances Stewart, children—Lytton Edward, Eva Mary, George, Edward Hugh. Became profl. actor in Guernsey under name Douglas Stewart, 1849; came to Am., circa 1852; 1st engagement at Nat. Theatre, Boston, 1852; actor in Lester Wallack's N.Y. Co., 1854-58; played successful role in Our American Cousin, 1858, started own co. to produce his version in Am., 1858, at Haymarket in London, Eng., 1861; subsequently gained great popularity as low comedian; produced plays including Robehtson's David Garrick and a version of Henry Bryon's The Prompter's Box (called A Crushed Tragedian). Died London, Jan. 20, 1881; buried Southampton, Eng.

SOULE, Asa Titus, businessman; b. Duanesburg, N.Y., Aug. 2, 1824. Made fortune mfg. and merchandizing panacea known as Hop Bitters; co-owner Eureka Irrigating Canal Co.; built Soule irrigation canal and railroad from Dodge City to Montezuma; owner townsite of Ingalls; pres. Dodge City 1st Nat. Bank. Founder Soule Coll., Dodge City. Died Rochester, N.Y., Jan. 17, 1890.

SOULE, Joshua, clergyman; b. Bristol, Me., Aug. 1, 1781; s. Joshua and Mary (Cushman) S.; m. Sarah Allen, Sept. 18, 1803, 11 children. Admitted on trial to New Eng. Methodist Episcopal Conf., 1799, ordained elder, 1802; an early itinerant preacher in New Eng., 1803-16; presiding elder Me. Dist., 1804; 1st editor Methodist Mag., 1818; pastor Meth. Episcopal chs. in N.Y. and Balt. confs., 1820-24; bishop, assigned to Western and So. confs., 1824-44; writer new constn. for Meth. Episcopal Ch., 1808, provided for delegated and representative Gen. Conf.; sr. bishop So. br. Episcopal Methodism, 1846. Died Nashville, Tenn., Mar. 6, 1867; buried City Cemetery, reinterred Vanderbilt U., Nashville.

SOULE, Nathan, congressman; b. N.Y.: completed prep. studies. Mem. U.S. Ho. of Reps. from N.Y., 22d Congress, 1831-33; mem. N.Y. State Assembly, 1837.

SOULE, Pierre, senator, jurist, diplomat; b. Castillonen-Couserans in French Pyrenees, Aug. 28, 1801; s. Joseph and Jeanne (Lacroix) S.; attended College de l'Esquille, Toulouse until 1816; Bachelor's degree, U. Bordeaux, 1819; m. Armantine Mercier, 1828, 1 child. Practiced law in France, 1822; arrested for polit. activites, escaped and came to U.S., 1825; settled in New Orleans, admitted to La. bar; del. to conv. of 1844 for revising La. constn.; mem. La. Senate, 1846; mem. U.S. Senate from La., 1847-Apr. 11, 1853, leader of states rights wing of Southern Democracy in Senate; U.S. minister to Spain, 1853-55, sought acquisition of Cuba by purchase, by favor of Queen Mother, or as collateral for a royal loan; author (with James Buchanan and John Y. Mason) Ostend Manifesto, 1854, proposed acquisition of Cuba by purchase or force, resigned, 1855, a scapegoat for administration's change of policy in affair; arrested by fed. forces in New Orleans, 1862; during Civil War served on Beauregard's staff, commd. brig. gen. Died New Orleans, Mar. 26, 1870; buried St. Louis Cemetery Number 2.

SOUTHACK, Cyprian, cartographer, privateer; b. London, Eng., Mar. 25, 1662; s. Cyprian and Elizabeth Southack; m. Elizabeth, several children. Went to Boston, 1685; protected New Eng. coast from pirates and privateers from 1689; mem. Sir William Phips' unsuccessful expedition to N.S., 1690; published map of St. John River, 1697; made chart St. Lawrence River, 1710; a commr. to adjust boundaries of N.S., 1718; made several charts surveying N.E. coast of N.Am. in New England Coasting Pilot, 1720; presented copy of his Draught of New England, Newfoundland, Nova Scotia, and the River of Canada to King William III of Eng., 1694; published the Harbour of Casco Bay and Islands Adjacent, and Map of Canso Harbour, 1720; A New Chart of the British Empire in North America, 1746. Died Boston, Mar. 27, 1745; buried Granary Burying Ground.

SOUTHALL, James Cocke, editor; b. Charlottesville, Va., Apr. 2, 1828; s. Valentine Wood and Martha (Cocke) S.; M.A., U. Va., 1846; m. Eliza Sharp, Nov. 10, 1869, 2 children. Licensed to practice law, 1849; founder Charlottesville Review, circa 1860; purchaser Charlottesville Daily Chronicle, 1865, editor, 1865-68; chief editor Richmond (Va.) Enquirer, 1868-74; mem. Va. Constl. Conv., 1867; asst. to supt. public instn., 1874; purchaser (with Rev. William T. Richardson) Central Presbyn., 1880, editor, 1880-89. Author: The Recent Origin of Man, 1875; Man's Age in the World, 1878. Died Sept. 13, 1897.

SOUTHARD, Henry, congressman, farmer; b. Hempstead, L.I., N.Y., Oct. 7, 1747; attended common schs.; 2 sons, Isaac, Samuel Lewis. Worked on farm; served as pvt. and later as wagon master during Revolutionary War; became farmer; justice of peace, 1787-92; mem. N.J. Gen. Assembly, 1797-99, 1811; mem. U.S. Ho. of Reps. (Democrat) from N.J., 7th-11th, 14th-16th congresses, 1801-11, 15-21; retired from public life. Died Basking Ridge, Somerset County, N.J., May 22, 1842; buried Basking Ridge Cemetery.

SOUTHARD, Isaac, congressman; b. Basking Ridge, Somerset County, N.J., Aug. 30, 1783; s. Henry Southard; ed. at classical sch., Basking Ridge. In gen. merchandise business until 1814; apptd. dep. collector internal revenue Somerset County; apptd. maj. 2d Battalion, 2d Regt., Somerset Brigade, 1815, promoted lt. col., 1816, col., 1817; served as aide to Maj. Gen. Peter I. Stryker of Uniformed Militia, 3d Div. as late as 1829; dir. State bank at Morristown, N.J.; apptd. a lay judge Somerset Ct. Common Pleas, 1820; commd. justice of peace, 1820; moved to Sommerville, N.J.; clk. Somerset County, 1820-30; mem. U.S. Ho. of Reps. (Clay Democrat) from N.J., 22d Congress, 1831-33; apptd. master and examiner in chancery by Gov. Elias P. Seeley, 1833; col. N.J. Militia; treas. N.J., 1837-43 lived in Trenton, N.J. several years. Died Somerville, Sept. 18, 1850; buried Old Cemetery.

SOUTHARD, Lucien, composer; b. Sharon, Vt., Feb. 4, 1827; s. Alva Southard; attended Trinity Coll., Hartford Conn., 1844-46; studied music, Boston, circa 1847-50; married. Supr. of music Boston Public Schs., 1851-58; choir dir., music tchr., Norfolk, Va., 1858-61; organist North Congregational Ch.,, Hartford, Conn., 1858-61; commd. capt. calvary U.S. Army, 1862, served in Army of Potomac, 1862-65; returned to Boston, 1865, composed pieces for use in church; taught music, 1865-68; apptd. 1st dir. Peabody Inst., conservatory in Balt., 1868; active as choral dir. and composer, Boston, 1871-75. Composer (opera) Omano (presented in Boston), 1858; (compositions for ch. services) Ave Maria, Te Deum and Jubilate, Two Masses (1867), The Standard Singing School (1868). Compiler: (with Benjamin F. Baker) The Haydn Collection of Church Music, 1850; The Union Glee Book, 1852. Died Atlanta, Ga., Jan. 10, 1881.

SOUTHARD, Samuel Lewis, senator, gov. N.J., sec. navy; b. Basking Ridge, N.J., June 9, 1787; s. Henry and Sarah (Lewis) S.; grad. Princeton, 1804; LL.D. (hon.), U. Pa., 1832; m. Rebecca Harrow, June 1812. Admitted to Va. bar, 1809; prosecutor Hunterdon County (N.J.), 1814; mem. N.J. Assembly, 1815; asso. justice N.J. Supreme Ct., 1815-20; reported and edited 4 or 5 N.J. Reports, 1818-20; presdl. elector for Monroe, 1820; mem. U.S. Senate from N.J., Jan. 26, 1821-23, 33-42, mem. joint com. on Mo. question, pres. pro tempore, 1841, pres., 1841-42; U.S. sec. of navy, 1823-29, his recommendations included naval code, bldg. of 1st naval hosp. in 1828; served as sec. of treasury ad interim, 1825, sec. of war, 1828; atty. gen. N.Y. State, 1829-33; gov. N.J., 1832-33; mem. U.S. Senate from N.J., trustee Princeton, 1822-42. Died Fredericksburg, Va., June 26, 1842; buried Congressional Cemetery, Washington, D.C.

SOUTHERD, Lucien H., composer; b. Sharon, Vt., Feb. 4, 1827; studied music, Boston. Supr. pub. schs., Boston, 1851-58; served in Union Army during Civil War; condr. orch. of Peabody Conservatory, Balt., 1868-71; resided in Boston, 1871-75, Augusta, Ga., 1875-81; composed 2 operas, ch. music, glees and organ pieces; edited collections of sacred music. Died Augusta, Jan. 10, 1881.

SOUTHGATE, Horatio, clergyman; b. Portland, Me., July 5, 1812; s. Horatio and Abigail (McLellan) S.; grad. Bowdoin Coll., 1832, Andover Theol. Sem, 1835; m. Elizabeth Browne, Jan. 29, 1839; m. 2d, Sarah Elizabeth Hutchinson, Dec. 28, 1864; children—Richard, Henry, William, Hutchinson, Marianne, Charles, Horatio, Harriet, Clara, Edward, Octavia, Frederic, Hiram. Confirmed in Protestant Episcopal Ch., 1834, ordained deacon, 1835; sent to visit Turkey and Persia by fgn. com. of bd. of missions, 1836-38: ordained priest, 1839; missionary to Constantinople, 1840; consecrated as missionary bishop, 1844, involved in dispute with other missionaries from Am. Bd. Fgn. Missions; returned to Am:, 1849, resigned mission, 1850; rector St. Luke's Ch., Portland, Me., 1851, Ch. of Advent, Boston, 1852, involved in controversy with local bishop over high ch. ritual; obtained canon regulating relation of bishop and parishes from Gen. Conv., 1856: Author: Narrative of a Tour Through Armenia, Kurdistan, Persia and Mesopotamia (account of his travels), 1840; A Treatise on the Antiquity, Doctrine Ministry and Worship of the Angelican Church (written in Greek), 1849. Died Ravenswood, N.Y., Apr. 12, 1894.

SOUTHGATE, William Wright, congressman, lawyer; b. Newport, Campbell County, Ky., Nov. 27, 1800; grad. Transylvania Coll., Lexington, Ky.; studied law. Moved to Covington, Kenton County, Ky.; admitted to bar, 1821, practiced in Lexington; pros. atty., 1825-27; mem. Ky. Ho. of Reps., 1827, 32, 36; mem. U.S. Ho. of Reps. (Whig) from Ky., 25th Congress, 1837-39; Whig presdl. elector, 1840, 44. Died Covington, Dec. 26, 1849; buried Linden Grove Cemetery.

SOUTHWICK, Soloman, journalist; b. Newport, R.I., Dec. 25, 1773; s. Soloman and Ann (Gardner) S.; m. Jane Barber, Mar. 31, 1795, 9 children including Alfred. Partner anti-Federalist paper Albany (N.Y.) Register, circa 1795-1800; founded (with John Barber) circulating library of 400 volumes, 1799; an organizer Apprentices' Library; clk. N.Y. Assembly, 1803-07; clk. N.Y. State Senate, 1807; owner, editor Albany Register, 1808-17; state printer until 1814; lost influence in Republican Party, circa 1813; edited Christian Visitant, 1815-16, Plough Boy (1st agrl. periodical in Albany County), 1819-23, Nat. Democrat, 1823-26; delivered lectures on Bible, temperance and self improvement, 1831-37. Author: Five Lessons for Young Men, by a Man of Sixty, 1837; Died Albany, Nov. 18, 1839.

SOWER, Christopher, printer, publisher; b. Laasphe on the Lahn, Germany, 1693; m. Maria Christina before 1721, 1 son, Christopher. Came to U.S., 1724, settled in Germantown, Pa.; 1st German printer and publisher in Am.; published Eine Ernstliche Ermahnung, in Junge und Alte, 1738; began publishing almanac Zionitischer Weyrauchs Hügel oder Myrrhen Berg, 1739-58; 1st number of newspaper appeared Der Hoch-Deutsch Pensylvanische Geschicht-Schreiber; published edit. of Bible (most renowned of his publs.) 1743; his 1st English publication Extract from the Laws of William Penn, 1740; built paper mill, 1744. Died Germany, Sept. 25, 1758.

SOWER, Christopher, clergyman, printer; b. Laasphe, Westphalia, Germany, Sept. 26, 1721; s. Christopher and Maria (Christina) S.; m. Catharine Sharpnack, Apr. 21, 1751; 9 children including Peter, Christopher, Catharine. Came to U.S., 1724; leader of Dunken sect. German Baptist Brethren, circa 1753-84, ordained deacon, 1747, elder, 1748; inherited father's printing bus., 1758, published 2d (1763) and 3d (1776) editions of Sower or Germantown Bible; built paper mill on the Schuykill River, Pa., 1773; suspected of loyalist sympathies, 1778, arrested and his property confiscated; a founder Germantown Acad. Died Methatchen, Pa., Aug. 26, 1784.

SOWER, Christopher, Loyalist; b. Germantown, Pa:, Jan. 27, 1754; s. Christopher and Catherine (Sharpnack) S.; m. Hannah Knorr, Jan. 8, 1775, 6 children. Took charge of father's printing firm, Christopher Sower & Son, Germantown, 1774; pubished Loyalist newspaper Die Germantowner Zeitung, Germantown, 1774-77, pro-Brit. paper Der Pennsylvanische, Staats Courier, Phila., 1777; formed Loyalist Assns. in Pa. and N.Y. while accompanying Brit. forces in Phila. and N.Y.C., 1778-80; advocated loose imperial tie between Eng. and Am. colonies as basis of peace; went to Eng., 1781, received indemnification for confiscated family properties in Pa.; moved to New Brunsick, Can., 1785, served as postmaster, royal printer of province: Died while visiting brother's family, Balt., July 3, 1799.

SPAIGHT, Richard Dobbs, gov. N.C.; congressman; b. New Bern, N.C., Mar. 25, 1758; s. Richard and Margaret (Dobbs) S.; attended U. Glasgow; m. Mary Leach, 1795, at least 3 children. Served as aide-de-camp to Gen. Caswell, Continental Army, 1778; mem. N.C. Ho. of Commons, 1779, 81-83, 85-87, 92; speaker, 1787; mem. Continental Congress, 1782-85; del. Fed. Constl. Conv., 1787, voted for and signed U.S. Constn.; mem. N.C. Ratification Conv., 1788; gov. N.C., 1792-95, proclaimed neutrality in French Revolutionary Wars, detained French privateers in Wilmington, N.C.; presdl. elector, 1793; mem: U.S. Ho. of Reps. (Republican) from N.C., 5th-6th congresses, Dec. 10, 1798-1801; mem. N.C. Senate, 1801-02; Died (from wounds received in duel with John Stanley) New Bern, Sept. 6, 1802; buried "Clermont," Craven County, N.C.

SPAIGHT, Richard Dobbs, Jr., gov. N.C., congressman; b. New Bern, N.C., 1796; s. Richard Dobbs Spaight; attended New Bern Acad.; grad. U. N.C., 1815; studied law. Admitted to bar, 1818, practiced in New Bern; mem. N.C. Ho. of Commons, 1819-22; mem. U.S. Ho. of Reps. (Democrat) from N.C., 18th Congress, 1823-25; mem. N.C. Senate, 1825-26; gov. N.C., 1835-37; del. N.C. Dem. Conv., 1835; became farmer. Died New Bern, May 2, 1850; buried family sepulcher at Clermont, nr. New Bern.

SPALDING, Catherine, founder religious order; b. Charles County, Md., Dec. 23, 1793; d. Ralph Spalding. Joined Sisters of Charity of Nazareth, Bardstown, Ky., as charter mem:, 1813, elected 1st mother superior of order, 1813-19, 25-31 (four terms); founder St. Vincent's Acad., Union County, circa 1820; dir. Acad. of St. Catherine's, 1823; established Presentation Acad. (1st Catholic sch. in Louisville, Ky.) 1831; founded St. Vincent's Infirmary, Louisville, 1836; established Sch. of St. Frances, Owensboro, Ky., 1850. Died Louisville, Mar. 20, 1858.

SPALDING, Eliza Hart, pioneer; m. Henry H. Spalding, circa 1833; at least 1 child. Lived in Utica, N.Y. prior to marriage; worked with missionary husband, traveling west with him in Marcus Whitman party, 1836; she and Mrs. Whitman 1st white women to cross N. Am. continent; versatile with Indian langs. Died of scarlet fever, circa 1843.

SPALDING, Henry Harmon, missionary; b. circa 1803; entered Prattsburg (N.Y.) Acad., circa 1825; A.B., Western Res. Coll., Ohio; attended Lane Theol. Sem., Cin.; m. Eliza Hart, circa 1833; at least 1 child. Ordained to ministry Presbyn. Ch., 1835, apptd. to Osage Indian mission, western Mo.; went west with Marcus Whitman party, 1836; worked at Lapwai mission, Ida., until removed in 1842. Died of scarlet fever, circa 1843.

SPALDING, Lyman, physician, surgeon; b. Cornish, N.H., June 5, 1775; s. Dyer and Elizabeth (Parkhurst) S.; grad. at Charlestown, Mass., 1794; M.B., Harvard, 1797, M.D. (hon.); M.B., M.D. (hon.), Dartmouth; m. Elizabeth Coves, Oct. 9, 1802, 5 children. A founder Dartmouth Med. Sch., 1798, lectr. chemistry and materia medica, 1797-99; Portsmouth, N.H.; practiced medicine, Portsmouth, N.H., 1799-1812, also contract surgeon for U.S. Army troops in harbor; founded med. society which became Eastern Dist. br. of N.H. Med. Soc., 1802; lectured on chemistry and surgery at acad., Fairfield, N.Y., 1810-17 (became Coll. Physicians and Surgeons of Western Dist. N.Y., 1813), pres., 1813-17; practiced in N.Y.C., 1817-21; studied yellow fever, vaccination, hydrophobia; founded U.S. Pharmacopoeia; trustee N.Y.C., Coll. Author: Reflections on Fever, 1817. Died Portsmouth, Oct. 21, 1821.

SPALDING, Martin John, bishop; b. Rolling Fork, Ky., May 23, 1810; s. Richard and Henrietta (Hamilton) S.; grad. St. Mary's Coll., 1826; D.D., Urban Coll., Rome, Italy, 1830. Ordained priest Roman Catholic Ch., 1834; editor Catholic Advocate, 1835; rector St. Joseph's Coll., 1838-40; vicar gen. of Louisville (Ky.), 1844; became bishop coadjutator of Louisville with right of succession, became bishop, 1850; established schs. in diocese, an orphanage, a house for Magdalens, and a conf. of St. Vincent de Paul Soc., 1854, built chs., a cathedral, 1852; introduced Xaverian Brothers from Bruges into diocese, 1854; with Bishop Peter Paul Lefevre of Detroit encouraged creation of The Am. Coll. of Louvain, 1857; transfered to Balt. as archbishop, 1864, organized confs. of St. Vincent de Paul Soc., the Cath. Protectory under the Xaverian Bros.; took leading part in Vatican Council as mem. commns. of faith and postulate, 1870. Author: Miscellanea (series of essays), 1855; A History of the Protestant Reformation, 2 vols., 1860. Died Balt., Feb. 7, 1872; buried in Cathedral, Balt.

SPALDING, Rufus Paine, congressman, lawyer; b. West Tisbury, Mass., May 3, 1798; grad. Yale, 1817; studied law. Admitted to bar; moved to Little Rock, Ark., 1820, practiced law; moved to Warren, O., 1821 practiced until 1835; moved to Ravenna, O., practiced law; mem. Ohio Ho. of Reps., 1839-42, speaker 1 term; asso. judge Ohio Supreme Ct., 1849-52; practiced in Cleve.; mem. U.S. Ho. of Reps. (War Democrat) from Ohio, 38th-40th congresses, 1863-69. Died Cleve., Aug. 29, 1886; buried Lake View Cemetery.

SPALDING, Thomas, planter, congressman; b. Frederica, St. Simon's Island, Ga., Mar. 26, 1776; s. James and Margery (McIntosh) S.; m. Sarah Leake, Nov. 5, 1795, 16 children. Admitted to Ga. bar, 1795; mem. Ga. Constl. Conv., 1798; mem. Ga. Legislature from Glynn County, 1794; mem. Ga. Senate; Mem. U.S. Ho. of Reps. from Ga., 9th Congress, Dec. 24, 1805-06; sent to Bermuda to investigate claims of Am. citizens against Gt. Britain for destruction of property, 1815; rep. from Ga. on Ga.-Fla. Boundary Commn., 1826; mem. Milledgeville (Ga.) Anti-Tariff Conv., 1832; pres. Ga. Conv. (concerned with slavery and secession), 1850; supported Compromise of 1850; pioneer of sea island cotton in South; 1st to grow sugar cane and manufacture sugar in Ga.; wrote "A Sketch of the Life of General James Oglethrope" published in Collections of the Georgia Historical Society, Vol. I, 1840. Died Darien, Ga., Jan. 5, 1851; buried St. Andrews Cemetery of Christ Church, Frederica.

SPANGENBERG, Augustus Gottlieb, bishop Moravian Ch.; b. Klettenburg, Prussia, July 15, 1704; s. George and Elizabeth (Nesen) S.; M.A. in Theology, U. Jena (Germany), 1726; m. Mrs.

Eva (Ziegelbauer) Immig; m. 2d, Mrs. Mary (Jaehne) Miksch, Mar. 5, 1740; at least 2 children. Prof. religious edn. U. Halle (Germany), circa 1732-circa 34; responsible for establishment Moravian missions in Surinam and in Ga.; came to Am. 1735; aided in founding Bethlehem, Pa. settlement; founded group to seek financial support of Ch. of Eng. for Moravian missions, London, 1741; consecrated Moravian bishop, 1744, sailed for Am. to become overseer Bethlehem settlement; organized new settlement in N.C. on large tract, 1457-52; returned to Herrnhut, Germany, 1762; an authority on Moravian missions. Author: Lebendes Herrn Nichlaus Ludwig Grafen und Herrn Zingendorf, 3 vols., 1772-75; Idea Fidei Fratrum, 1779. Died Herrnhut, Sept. 18, 1792.

SPANGLER, David, congressman, lawyer; b. Sharpsburg, Washington County, Md., Dec. 2, 1796; attended pub. schs.; studied law. In blacksmith's trade; became mcht.; admitted to bar, 1824, practiced in Zanesville, O.; moved to Coshocton, O., 1832, practiced law; mem. U.S. Ho. of Reps. (Whig) from Ohio, 23d-24th congresses, 1833-37. Died Coshocton, Oct. 18, 1856; buried South Lawn Cemetery.

SPANGLER, Jacob, congressman; b. York, Pa., Nov. 28, 1767; attended York County Acad. Became surveyor; served as trumpeter in Capt. McClellan's Light Horse Co. of York, 1799; county commr., 1800, 14; postmaster York, 1795-1812; dep. surveyor York County, 1796-1815; mem. U.S. Ho. of Reps. (Federalist) from Pa., 15th Congress, 1817-Apr. 20, 1818 (resigned); surveyor gen. Pa., 1818-21, 30-36; comdr. Pa. Militia with title of gen.; clk. York County Ct. until 1830. Died York, June 17, 1843; buried Prospect Hill Cemetery.

SPARKS, Jared, clergyman, coll. pres., historian; b. Willington, Conn., May 10, 1789; probably s. Joseph and Eleanor (Orcutt) S.; grad. Harvard, 1815, LL.D. (hon.), 1843; Master's degree, Harvard Divinity Sch., 1819; m. Frances Anne Allen, Oct. 16, 1832; m. 2d, Mary Crowinshield Silsbee, May 21, 1839; 6 children. Became editor North Am. Review, 1819, purchased, edited, 1823-29; ordained to ministry Unitarian Ch., 1819, pastor First Independent Ch. (Unitarian), Balt., 1818-23; chaplain U.S. Congress, 1821; edited George Washington's writings for publication (edited out candid remarks, improved grammar), 1827-37; pioneer in purchasing and collecting manuscripts dealing with Am. history; mem. Mass. Bd. Edn., 1837-40; McLean prof. ancient and modern history Harvard (1st prof. non-eccles. history in U.S.), 1839-49, organized dept. history, pres., 1849-53, encouraged greater use of lectures in instrn., a return to compulsory courses, encouraged prestige of Harvard Obs. (then only research unit at Harvard.); discovered a copy of D'Anville's map marked by Franklin, 1841; made efforts to discover and publish Am. documents which are significant in providing materials for later historians; mem. Phi Beta Kappa. Author: The Life of John Ledyard, 1828; The Diplomatic Correspondence of the American Revolution, 12 vols., 1829-30; The Life of Gouverneur Morris, 3 vols., 1832; Writings of George Washington, 12 vols., 1834-37; The Library of American Biography, 1st series, 10 vols., 1834-38; The Works of Benjamin Franklin, 10 vols., 1834-38; Correspondence of the American Revolution, 4 vols., 1853. Died Cambridge, Mass., Mar. 14, 1866.

SPARKS, William Henry, lawyer, poet; b. St. Simon's Island, Ga., Jan. 16, 1800; studied law, Litchfield, Conn. Practiced law, Greensboro, Ga.; mem. Ga. Legislature; became sugar planter nr. Natchez, Miss., 1830; practiced law (with J. P. Benjamin), New Orleans, 1852-61; contbd. to So. mags.; wrote poems (most of which were never published) including Somebody's Darling, The Dying Year. Author: Memories of Fifty Years, 1870. Died Marietta, Ga., Jan. 13, 1882.

SPARROW, William, clergyman, ednl. adminstr.; b. Charlestown, Mass., Mar. 12, 1801; s. Samuel and Mary (Roe) S.; attended Columbia, 1819-circa 1821; D.D. (hon.), Kenyon Coll., 1838; m. Frances Greenleaf, Feb. 13, 1832, 10 children. Prof. langs. Miami U., Oxford, O., 1824-25; a founder theol. sem., Washington, O., 1825, served as prin., tchr., sem. became Kenyon Coll. and Gambier Theol. Sem., Gambier, O., v.p., adminstr., 1828-41; ordained deacon Episcopal Ch., 1826, priest, 1826; prof. Theol. Sem. in Va., Alexandria, 1841, dean, tchr. theology, until 1874; del. various Episcopal diocesan convs., leading figure in low ch. evang. work. Died Alexandria, Jan. 17, 1874.

SPAULDING, Elbridge Gerry, congressman; b. Cayuga, N.Y., Feb. 24, 1809; s. Edward and Mehitable (Goodrich) S.; m. Jane Antionette Rich, before 1841; m. 2d, Nancy Seldon Strong, Sept. 5, 1842; m. 3d, Mrs. Delia (Strong) Robinson, May 2, 1854. Began law practice, Buffalo, N.Y., circa 1835; brought Farmers' Mechanics' Bank of Batavia (N.Y.) to Buffalo, circa 1842; mayor of Buffalo, 1847, assemblyman, 1848; treas. N.Y. State, 1853; mem. U.S. Ho. of Reps. from N.Y., as Whig, 31st Congress, 1849-51, as Republican, 36th-37th congresses, 1859-63, introduced bill authorizing treasury notes payable on demand, 1861, resultant law provided for the issuance of the legal tender notes or greenbacks to the amount of $150,000,000, 1862; published a history of legal tender issue during war, 1869; known as father of the greenbacks. Died Buffalo, May 5. 1897; buried Forest Lawn Cemetery, Buffalo.

SPAULDING, Levi, missionary; b. Jaffrey, N.H., Aug. 22, 1791; s. Phineas and Elizabeth (Bailey) S.; grad. Dartmouth, 1815; grad. Andover Theol. Sem., 1818; m. Mary Christie, Dec. 10, 1818, 3 children. Ordained to ministry, Salem, Mass., 1818; sailed to Calcutta, (India) under auspices Am. Bd. Commrs. for Fgn. Missions, 1819; reached Jaffnapatem (Jaffra), Ceylon, 1820, settled at Uduvil, nr. Jaffra, 1820, permanent mission center, 1820-73; in charge of ch., edn., preaching among the villages of area; took charge Misson's Female Boarding Sch. at Manepay, 1825-28; conducted boys' prep. sch. at Tellippaliai. Translated Pilgrim's Progress; prepared a Tamil dictionary and revised and enlarged English-Tamil Dictionary, 1852; largely responsible for making Tamil Bible idiomatic, 1847-49; revised Tamil Old Testament, 1865-71. Died Uduvil, June 18, 1873.

SPEAR, Charles, clergyman; b. Boston, May 1, 1801; m. Mrs. Frances King, Dec. 22, 1829; m. 2d, Catharine Swan Brown, circa 1858. Became Universalist minister, Boston, 1839; a founder, sec. Soc. for Abolition of Capital Punishment, 1844; founder weekly paper The Hangman (title later changed to The Prisoner's Friend) propr., 1845-59; attended Congress of Friends of Universal Peace, London, Eng., 1851; hosp. chaplain, Washington, D.C., 1861-63. Author: Essays on the Punishment of Death, 1844; A Plea for Discharged Convicts, 1846. Died Washington, Apr. 13, 1863.

SPEAR, Samuel Thayer, clergyman; b. Ballston Spa, N.Y., Mar. 4, 1812; grad. Coll. Physicians and Surgeons, N.Y.C., 1833; studied theology, Troy, N.Y., 1833-35; D.D. (hon.), Union Coll., 1851. Ordained to ministry Presbyn. Ch.; pastor 2d Presbyn. Ch., Lansingburg, N.Y., 1835-43; pastor South Presbyn. Ch., Bklyn., 1843-70; pres. Bd. of Ch. Extension of new sch. br. Presbyn. Ch., in charge of collection of funds for building new chs., 1854-67; mem. staff The Independent, mag., 1871-91. Author: Family Power, 1846; Religion and the State, 1876; The Bible Heaven, 1886. Died N.Y.C., Mar. 31, 1891; buried N.Y.C.

SPEED, James, cabinet officer; b. "Farmington," Louisville, Ky., Mar. 11, 1812; s. John and Lucy (Fry) S.; grad. St. Joseph's Coll., Bardstown, Ky., 1828; studied law dept. Transylvania U.; m. Jane Cochran, 1841, 7 children. Practiced law, Louisville, 1833; mem. Ky. Legislature, 1841; tchr. law U. Louisville, 1856-58, 72-79; mem. Union Party Central Com. set up to merge Bell and Douglas forces; an uncompromising Union man in Ky. Senate, 1861-63; leading adviser of Lincoln on Ky. affairs until 1864; U.S. atty. gen., 1864-66, at first supported Lincoln's reconstrn. plans, became radical reconstructionist under Johnson, advocated Negro suffrage and opposed veto of Freedman's Bur. Bill, resigned after condemning Phila. Conv., 1866; chmn. So. Radical Conv., 1866; del. to Rep. Nat. Conv., 1872, 76; later abandoned radical views and supported Grover Cleveland, 1884. Died "The Poplars," Louisville, June 25, 1887; buried Cave Hill Cemetery, Louisville.

SPEED, Thomas, congressman; b. Charlotte County, Va., Oct. 25, 1768; taught by his father. Worked in Office Clk. of Gen. Ct.; became mcht., Danville, Bardstown, Ky., 1790; became farmer; clk. Bullitt and Nelson circuit cts.; served as maj. of Volunteers in War of 1812; mem. U.S. Ho. of Reps. from Ky., 15th Congress, 1817-19; contbr. articles to Nat. Intelligencer, Washington, D.C.; mem. Ky. Ho. of Reps., 1821-22, 40; became mem. Whig Party when it was organized. Died on his farm Cottage Grove, nr. Bardstown, Feb. 20, 1842; buried on his farm.

SPEER, Robert Milton, congressman; b. Cassville, Huntingdon County, Pa., Sept. 8, 1838; attended Cassville Acad.; studied law. Taught sch.; admitted to bar, 1859, practiced in Huntingdon, Pa.; elected asst. clk. Pa. Ho. of Reps., 1863; mem. U.S. Ho. of Reps. (Democrat) from Pa., 42d-43d congresses, 1871-75; del. Nat. Dem. Conv., 1872, 80; a propr. Huntingdon Monitor, 1876; Dem. presdl. elector, 1888. Died N.Y.C., Jan. 17, 1890; buried Riverview Cemetery, Huntingdon.

SPEER, Thomas Jefferson, congressman; b. Monroe County, Ga., Aug. 31, 1837; attended common schs. Became mcht., planter; elected justice of peace, 1861, 65; apptd. collector Confederate taxes for Pike County, 1863-65; elected justice Pike County Inferior Ct., 1865-68; del. Ga. Constl. Conv., 1867-68; mem. Ga. Senate, 1868-70; mem. U.S. Ho. of Reps. (Republican) from Ga., 42d Congress, 1871-Aug. 18, 1872. Died Barnesville, Lamar County, Ga., Aug. 18, 1872; buried Zebulon Street Cemetery.

SPEIGHT, Jesse, senator, congressman; b. Greene County, N.C., Sept. 22, 1795; attended country schs. Speaker N.C. Ho. of Commons, 1820; mem. N.C. Senate, 1823-27; mem. U.S. Ho. of Reps. from N.C., 21st-24th congresses, 1829-37; moved to Plymouth, Miss.; mem. Miss. Senate, 1841-44, pres.; mem. U.S. Senate (Democrat) from Miss., 1845-May 1, 1847. Died Columbus, Miss., May 1, 1847; buried Friendship Cemetery.

SPEIR, Samuel Fleet, physician; b. Bklyn., Apr. 9, 1838; s. Robert and Hannah (Fleet) S.; attended Bklyn. Poly. Inst.; grad. med. dept. N.Y.U., 1860; m. Frances S. Hegeman, 1869, 3 children. Attended European clinics, mainly in Paris, 1860-62; publicized plaster of Paris splint, later used by mil. authorities in battlefields of Civil War; given 2 boats by Sanitary Commn. to care for wounded of Army of Potomac, 1862; went to Europe for postgrad. study in ophthalmology and otology, 1865; leading figure in med. profession in Bklyn.; mem. surg. staff Bklyn. Eye and Ear Infirmary and Bklyn. Dispensary; physician curator and microscopist Bklyn. City Hosp.; demonstrator of anatomy L.I. Coll. Hosp., 1864-65; awarded Gold medal for paper "On the Pathology of Jaundice," by A.M.A., 1865; invented artery constrictor; mem. county and state med. socs., A.M.A., N.Y. Path. Soc.; fellow N.Y. Acad. Medicine. Author: The Use of the Microscope in the Differential Diagnosis of Morbid Growths, 1871. Died Bklyn., Dec. 19, 1895.

SPENCE, John Selby, senator, congressman; b. nr. Snow Hill, Worcester County, Md., Feb. 29, 1788; attended common schs.; grad. med. dept. U. Pa., 1809. Practiced medicine, Worcester County; mem. Md. Ho. of Dels.; mem. Md. Senate; mem. U.S. Ho. of Reps. (Democrat) from Md., 18th, 22d congresses, 1823-25, 31-33; mem. U.S. Senate (filled vacancy) from Md., Dec. 31, 1836-Oct. 24, 1840. Died nr. Berlin, Worcester County, Oct. 24, 1840; buried Episcopal Churchyard.

SPENCE, Thomas Ara, congressman, lawyer; b. nr. Accomac Court House, Accomac County, Va., Feb. 20, 1810; attended local acad.; grad. Yale, 1829; studied law. Admitted to bar, practiced in Snow Hill, Worcester County, Md.; mem. U.S. Ho. of Reps. (Whig) from Md., 28th Congress, 1843-45; became affiliated with Republican Party; owned large iron-ore properties, Worcester County; judge Worcester County and 12th Jud. Circuit, 1857-67; practiced in Salisbury, Wicomico County, Md.; asst. atty. gen. Post Office Dept., 1872-77. Died Washington, D.C., Nov. 10, 1877; buried Makamie Meml. Ch. Cemetery, Snow Hill.

SPENCER, Ambrose, congressman, jurist; b. Salisbury, Conn., Dec. 13, 1765; s. Philip and Abigail (Moore) S.; grad. Harvard. 1783; m. Laura Canfield, Feb. 18, 1784; m. 2d, Mary (Clinton) Norton, circa 1808; m. 3d, Catherine (Clinton) Norton, Sept. 1809; at least 8 children. including John Canfield. Admitted to N.Y. bar, 1788; clk. City of Hudson (N.Y.), 1786-93; mem. N.Y. State Assembly (Federalist) 1793-95, N.Y. State Senate, 1795-1804 (became Republican, also supporter of DeWitt Clinton, 1798); asst. atty. gen. Columbia and Dutchess counties (N.Y.), 1796; mem. N.Y. Council of Appointment, 1797-1821, with DeWitt Clinton began spoils system in N.Y.; atty. gen. N.Y. State 1802-04; judge N.Y. State Supreme Ct, 1804-23, chief justice, 1819-23; establised Albany (N.Y.) Republican (to oppose Clinton on issues of war and bank), circa 1812; dominant power in Democratic Party, 1812-16; lost power in N.Y. politics, after 1821; mayor Albany, 1824-25; mem. U.S. Ho. of Reps. from N.Y., 21st Congress, 1829-31; pres. Whig Conv., Balt. 1844 apptd by U.S. Ho. of Reps. to conduct impeachment proceedings against James H. Peck (U.S. judge for Dist. of Mo.) 1830. Died Lyons, N.Y., Mar. 13, 1848; buried Lyons Rural Cemetery.

SPENCER, Elihu, clergyman; b. East Haddam, Conn., Feb. 12, 1721; s. Isaac and Mary (Selden) S.; grad. Yale, 1746; D.D. (hon.), U. Pa., 1782; m. Joanna Eaton, Oct. 15, 1749 (or 50), 2 children. Ordained to ministry Presbyn. Ch., 1748; missionary to the Oneidas, 1748-49; pastor Presbyn. Ch., Elizabethtown, N.J., 1750-56, Jamaica, N.Y., 1756-58; trustee Princeton, 1752-84; pastor, Trenton, N.J., 1769-84; synod del. to Congregational and Presbyn. Council, 1770-75; visited (with Alexander McWhorter) the more isolated portions of the South 1775, informed people of move for independence, obtained support for Am. Revolution; chaplain hosps. in vicinity of Trenton, 1777-81. Died Trenton, Dec. 27, 1784; buried churchyard, Trenton.

SPENCER, Elijah, congressman, farmer; b. Columbia County, N.Y., 1775. Moved to Jerusalem (later Benton), N.Y., 1791, became farmer; supr.

Town of Benton, 1810-19, 26-28; mem. N.Y. State Assembly, 1819; mem. U.S. Ho. of Reps. (Democrat) from N.Y., 17th Congress, 1821-23; mem. N.Y. State Constl. Conv., 1846. Died Benton, Dec. 15, 1852; buried Lake View Cemetery, Penn Yan, N.Y.

SPENCER, George Eliphaz, senator; b. Champion, Jefferson County, N.Y., Nov. 1, 1836; attended Montreal (Can.) Coll.; studied law. Moved to Ia.; sec. Ia. Senate, 1856; admitted to bar, 1857; practiced law; entered U.S. Army as capt. during Civil War, brevetted brig. gen. for gallantry on field when he resigned, 1865; practiced in Decatur, Ala.; apptd. register in bankruptcy for Ala. 4th Dist., 1867; mem. U.S. Senate (Republican) from Ala., July 13, 1868-79; retired to his ranch in Nev. Died Washington, D.C., Feb. 19, 1893; buried Arlington (Va.) Nat. Cemetery.

SPENCER, Herbert, philosopher; b. Derby, Eng., Apr. 27, 1820; son of William G. Spencer. Engr., London & Birmingham R.R., 1837-46; an editor Economist, 1848-53; attempted to synthesize scientific knowledge of his day, especially concept of evolution, and systematically apply it to all fields of human endeavor; advocate of polit. laissez-faire, believed that struggle for existence in polit. sense would lead to survival of fittest, i.e., best form of govt.; his philosophy was widely accepted in Am. Author: Principles of Psychology, 1855; Synthetic Philosophy (including Principles of Biology, Principles of Sociology, Principles of Ethics), 10 vols., 1860-96. Died Dec. 8, 1903.

SPENCER, Ichabod Smith, clergyman; b. Rupert, Vt., Feb. 23, 1798; grad. Union Coll., 1822; D.D. (hon.), Hamilton Coll., 1840. Licensed to preach by Presbytery of Geneva (N.Y.), 1826; asso. pastor, Northampton, Mass., 1828-32; pastor 2d Presbyn. Ch., Bklyn., 1832-54; a founder Union Theol. Sem., N.Y.C., 1836, prof. Bibl. history, 1836-40. Author: Pastor's Sketches, 1850; (collected sermons published posthumously) Sacramental Discourses, 1861, Evidences of Divine Revelation, 1865. Died Bklyn., Nov. 23, 1854.

SPENCER, James Bradley, congressman; b. Salisbury, Conn., Apr. 26, 1781. Moved to Franklin County, N.Y., settled in Ft. Covington; raised company for War of 1812; served as capt. 29th U.S. Inf.; apptd. local magistrate, 1814; surrogate Franklin County, 1828-37; apptd. loan commr., 1829; mem. N.Y. State Assembly, 1831-32; Democratic presdl. elector, 1832; mem. U.S. Ho. of Reps. (Dem.) from N.Y., 25th Congress, 1837-39. Died Ft. Covington, Mar. 26, 1848; buried probably in Old Cemetery, nr. Ft. Covington.

SPENCER, Jesse Ames, clergyman, educator; b. Hyde Park, N.Y., June 17, 1816; s. Reuben and Mary (Ames) S.; attended Trinity Sch., 1833-34; grad. Columbia, 1837, S.T.D. (hon.), 1852; grad. Gen. Theol. Sem., 1840; S.T.D. (hon.), Trinity Coll., 1872; m. Sarah J.E. Loutrel, Sept. 4, 1840, at least 1 surviving child. Ordained deacon Episcopal Ch., 1840, priest, 1841; edited Greek and Latin textbooks for D. Appleton & Co., circa 1843-circa 1848; edited monthly mag. The Young Churchman's Miscellany, 1845-48; prof. Latin and Oriental langs. Burlington (N.J.) Coll., 1850-51; editor, sec. Episcopal Sunday Sch. Union of N.Y., 1851-57 rector St. Paul's Ch., Flatbush (Bklyn.), 1863-65; sec. Corp. of the Relief of Widows and Children of Clergymen in N.Y., circa 1865; prof. Greek, N.Y.U., 1869-79. Author: The Christian Instructed in the Ways of the Gospel and the Church, 1844; The East, 1850; History of the United States, 4 vols., 1858; Sketch if the History of the Protestant Episcopal Church in the United States, 1878; Papalism versus Catholic Truth and Light, 1896. Editor: The New Testament in Greek, 1847. Died N.Y.C., Sept. 2, 1898.

SPENCER, John Canfield, congressman, cabinet officer; b. Hudson, N.Y., Jan. 8, 1788; s. Ambrose and Laura (Canfield) S.; grad. Union Coll., Schenectady, N.Y., 1806; m. Elizabeth Scott Smith, May 20, 1809, 3 children including Philip. Admitted to N.Y. bar, 1809; judge adv. gen. in active service along frontier. 1813; postmaster Canandaigua (N.Y.), 1814; asst. atty. gen. and dist. atty. for 5 western counties of N.Y., 1815; mem. U.S. Ho. of Reps. from N.Y., 15th Congress, 1817-19; mem. N.Y. Gen. Assembly, 1820, 21, 22, 33, 38, speaker, 1820; mem. N.Y. State Senate, 1825-28; asso. with Anti-Masonic Party; spl. pros. officer to investigate abduction of William Morgan, 1839; U.S. sec. of war, 1841-43; U.S. sec. of treasjoined Whig Party during 1830's; sec. of state N.Y., 1839; U.S. sec. f war, 1841-43; U.S. sec. of treasury, 1843-44, resigned over opposition to annexation of Tex.; defended Dr. Eliphalet Nott (pres. Union Coll.) against charge of misappropriating Coll. funds. Author; a portrait of Free Masonry, 1832; editor Democracy in America (De Tocqueville), 1838, Died Albany, N.Y., May 18, 1855; buried Albany Rural Cemetery.

SPENCER, Joseph, Continental congressman, army officer; b. Haddam, Conn., Oct. 3, 1714; s. Isaac and Mary (Selden) S.; m. Martha Barainerd, Aug. 2, 1738; m. 2d, Hannah Brown Southmayd, 1756; 13 children. Dep., Conn. Assembly, 1750-66; probate judge, Haddam, 1753-89; commd. H. Conn. Militia, 1747, maj., 1757, lt. col., 1759, col., 1766; commd. brig. gen. Conn. Militia, Continental Army, 1775, resigned after Continental Congress promoted Israel Putnam over him, 1775, returned to service with Continental Army in Boston and N.Y. State, later in year; commd. maj. gen., 1776, served in Providence, R.I., 1777, attempted unsuccessful movement against enemy, investigated by spl. ct. of inquiry, cleared; resigned from Continental Army, 1778; mem. Continental Congress from Conn., 1779; mem. Conn. Council of Safety, 1780-81. Died East Haddam, Conn., Jan. 13, 1789; buried East Haddam.

SPENCER, Pitman Clemens, surgeon; b. Charlotte County, Va., July 28, 1793; s. Gideon and Catherine (Clements or Clemens) S.; M.D., U. Pa., 1818; studied surgery, anatomy in London (Eng.) and Paris (France), 1827-30. Performed 1st lithotomy, 1833; published 1st article, "Case of Uninary Calculus successfully treated by Lithotrity," in Am. Jour. Med. Sciences, 1833; pres. Petersburg (Va.) Med. Faculty, 1851; v.p. Med. Soc. Va., 1855. Author: Results of Fifteen Operations for Lithotomy, 1850. Died Petersburg, Jan. 15, 1860.

SPENCER, Platt Rogers, calligrapher; b. East Fishkill, N.Y., Nov. 7, 1800; s. Caleb and Jerusha (Covell) S.; m. Persis Duty, 1828, 6 sons, 5 daus. Engaged in farming and sch. teaching, Geneva, O., from circa 1818; became skilled in calligraphy at an early age, became travelling instr. of penmanship (urged higher standards) in schs. and acads., No. Ohio, 1820's, 30's; sec. Ashtabula County (O.) Hist. Soc., 1838-50; published 1st handwriting copy books, 1848, rapidly became popular all over U.S., published in many edits. (in later years by his sons); devoted attention to anti-slavery and temperance movements, from 1830's. Died Geneva, May 16, 1864; buried Geneva.

SPENCER, Richard, congressman, farmer; b. Spencer Hall, Talbot County, Md., Oct. 29, 1796; attended common schs.; studied law, Balt. Admitted to Talbot County bar, 1819; moved to his farm Solitude, nr. St. Michaels, Md., 1822, became farmer; mem. Md. Ho. of Dels., 1823-25, 33-34; helped establish Eastern Shore Whig, 1828, in control until 1834; mem. U.S. Ho. of Reps. (Democrat) from Md., 21st Congress, 1829-31; moved to Ga., 1837, became cotton planter; moved to Ala., 1852, settled at Cottage Hill, nr. Mobile. Died Cottage Hill, Sept. 3, 1868; probably buried on his estate Cottage Hill.

SPENCER, Thomas, physician; b. Great Barrington, Mass., 1793. Founder, Med. Inst. (now part of Hobart Coll.), Geneva, N.Y., 1835, prof. theory and practice of medicine, 1835-50; later taught at med. schs., Phila. and Chgo.; served as surgeon in U.S. Army during Mexican War; pres. N.Y. State Med. Assn. Author: Observations on Epidemic Diarrhea, Known as Cholera, 1832; Lectures on Vital Chemistry, or Animal Heat, 1845; The Atomic Theory of Life, 1853. Died Phila., May 30, 1857.

SPENCER, William Brinerd, congressman, lawyer; b. Home Plantation, Catahoula Parish, La., Feb. 5, 1835; grad. Centenary Coll., Jackson, La., 1855; grad. law dept. U. La., 1857. Admitted to bar, 1857, practiced in Harrisonburg, La.; served in Confederate Army with rank of capt. until 1863, captured, remained prisoner of war at Johnsons Island (O.) until close of Civil War; practiced in Vidalia, La., 1866; mem. U.S. Ho. of Reps. (Democrat, contested election) from La., 44th Congress, June 8, 1876-Jan. 8, 1877 (resigned); asso. justice La. Supreme Ct., 1877-80; practiced in New Orleans. Died Jalpa, Mexico, Feb. 12, 1882; buried Magnolia Cemetery, Baton Rouge, La.

SPIES, August, labor leader, anarchist; b. Germany, 1855; m. Nina Van Zandt, 1886. Engaged in furniture bus.; mem., also for a time employee Socialist Publishing Soc., led unemployed in demonstration at Haymarket Sq., Chgo., 1884; leader Central Labor Union; editor anarchist newspaper Arbeiter-Zeitung, 1880-1886; led demonstration for 8-hour day, Haymarket, May 1, 1886; active in demonstration against McCormick Harvester Works, which turned into riot marking culmination of worker-police hostilities, May 4, 1886; convicted (with 7 assos.) for murder of 11 people in bomb explosion during riot; hanged (with assos. Albert Parsons, George Engel, Adolph Fischer), Chgo., Nov. 11, 1887.

SPINK, Cyrus, congressman; b. Berkshire County, Mass., Mar. 24, 1793. Moved to Stark County, O., 1815; taught sch., Kendall, Stark County for several years; apptd. dep. surveyor Wayne County, 1815-16; county surveyor, 1816-21, also for time dist. surveyor; county auditor, 1820-21; mem. Ohio Ho. of Reps., 1821-22; with Register's Office, Wooster, O., 1822-24; apptd. register by Pres. Monroe, 1824, reapptd. by Pres. Adams, 1828-32; became mcht., Wooster; Whig presdl. elector, 1844; mem. Ohio Bd. Equalization, 1846; del. Nat. Whig Conv., Balt., 1852; apptd. by Gov. Chase as a dir. Ohio Penitentiary, 1856; mem. U.S. Ho. of Reps. (Republican) from Ohio, 36th Congress, Mar. 4-May 31, 1859. Died Wooster, May 31, 1859; buried Wooster Cemetery.

SPINK, Solomon Lewis, congressman; b. Whitehall, Washington County, N.Y., Mar. 20, 1831; grad. Castleton (Vt.) Sem.; studied law. Taught sch. several years; admitted to bar, 1856, practiced in Burlington, Ia.; moved to Paris, Ill., 1860; editor, publisher Prairie Beacon, Paris; mem. Ill. Ho. of Reps,, 1864; sec. N.D. Territory (apptd. by Pres. Lincoln), Yankton, Dakota, 1865-69; mem. U.S. Congress (Republican) from Dakota Territory, 41st Congress, 1869-71; practiced in Yankton, S.D. Died Yankton, Sept. 22, 1881; buried City Cemetery.

SPINNER, Francis Elias, treas. U.S., congressman; b. German Flats, N.Y., Jan. 21, 1802; s. John Peter and Mary (Brument) S.; attended schs. in Mohawk Valley, N.Y.; m. Caroline Caswell, June 22, 1826, 3 daus. Mcht., Herkimer, N.Y., circa 1820; served as maj. gen. N.Y. State Militia, 1830's; cashier, later pres. Mohawk Valley, Herkimer; active in Democratic Party; auditor Port of N.Y., 1845-49; mem. U.S. Ho. of Reps. from N.Y., 34th Congress (as anti-slave Democrat), 1855-57, 35th-36th congresses (as Republican), 1857-61; treas. U.S. (apptd. by Pres. Lincoln), 1861-75, responsible for 1st employment of women in Civil Service, resigned in personal dispute with Treasury Dept., 1875; lived in retirement, Jacksonville, Fla., 1875-90. Died Jacksonville, Dec. 31, 1890.

SPINOLA, Francis Barretto, congressman; b. Stony Brook, L.I., N.Y., Mar. 19, 1821; attended Quaker Hill Acad., Dutchess County, N.Y.; studied law. Admitted to bar, 1844, practiced in Bklyn.; elected alderman 2d Ward, Bklyn., 1846, 47, re-elected 1849, served 4 years; mem. N.Y. State Assembly, 1855; mem. N.Y. State Senate, 1858-61; del. Nat. Democratic Conv., Charleston, 1860; harbor commr.; apptd. brig. gen. Volunteers for "meritorious conduct in recruiting and organizing brigade of 4 regiments and accompanying them to the field" in Civil War, 1862, wounded twice, discharged, 1865; alternate del. Nat. Dem. Conv., Chgo., 1884; in insurance business and banking; mem. U.S. Ho. of Reps. (Dem.) from N.Y., 50th-52d congresses, 1887-Apr. 14, 1891. Died Washington, D.C., Apr. 14, 1891; buried Greenwood Cemetery, Bklyn.

SPOONER, Lysander, lawyer, reformer; b. Athol, Mass., Jan. 19, 1808; s. Asa and Dolly (Brown) S.; read law with John Davis, Worcester, Mass., 1833-35. Admitted to bar, 1835, practiced in Worcester; practiced in Ohio, circa 1837-43; moved to Boston, 1844, established Am. Letter Mail Co. carrying mail between N.Y.C. and Boston, later established service to Phila. and Balt., business liquidated after threat of govt. prosecution, 1845; known as strong abolitionist, wrote campaign material for anti-slavery Liberty Party, 1848; practiced law, wrote on banking and legal reform as well as anti-slavery subjects, Boston, 1844-87. Author: Essay on the Trial by Jury, 1853; A New Banking System, 1873; The Law of Intellectual Property, 1855. Died May 14, 1887.

SPOONER, Shearjashub, dentist, art promoter; b. Orwell, Vt., Dec. 3, 1809; M.D., Coll. Physicians and Surgeons, N.Y.C., 1835; m. Jane E. (Foot) Darrow, Nov. 26, 1836. Retired from practice of dentistry to devote himself to art and promotion of art appreciation in Am., 1842; went to Europe, 1842, purchased John Boydell's illustrations of Shakespeare; bought paintings Musee Francais and Musee Royal in Paris, returned them to France when govt. refused to remit heavy import duty. Author: Guide to Sound Teeth, or A Popular Treatise on the Teeth, 1836. Anecdotes of Painters, Engravers, Sculptors and Architects, and Curiosities of Art, 3 vols., 1850; The American Edition of Boydell's Illustrations of the Dramatic Works of Shakespeare, 1852. Died Plainfield, N.J., Mar. 14, 1859.

SPOTSWOOD, Alexander, colonial ofcl.; b. Tangier, Africa, 1676; s. Robert and Catherine (Mercer) Elliott Spotswood; m. Anne Butler Brayne, 1724, 4 children. Served as ensign English Army in War of Grand Alliance, 1693; served under Lord Cadogan, rose to rank lt. col., during War of Spanish Succession, 1703-13; apptd. lt. gov. Va., 1710-22, served under nominal gov. George Hamilton (Earl of Orkney), tried to regulate and stabilize fur trade and finance enlightened Indian policy by organizing Va. Indian Co. with hdqrs. at Ft. Christanna, 1714 (reforms not supported by council and Ho. of Burgesses because they thought he had usurped their power); tried to protect colony from

Iroquois raids by establishing settlements of friendly Indians powerful enough to resist attack; concluded treaty with Iroquois stipulating that they keep North of Potomac and West of Blue Ridge Mountains, 1722; after he was removed from office he retired to Germanna (colony Germans organized as part of scheme of frontier defense); bought or granted to himself (while gov.) over 70,000 acres of land in Va., most of which according to his instructions from the Brit. Govt. was not to be sold to anyone; removed from office because he had acquired such a large stock in lands of Va. that he was more on colonist side than that of Royal Govt. in London; title to his lands challenged and went to Eng. to adjust it, 1724; apptd. postmaster-gen. for Am. colonies, 1724, served until 1740; apptd. maj. gen. in charge of recruiting regt. of colonist that would serve under Lord Cathcart, 1740. Died in course of duties, Annapolis, Md., June 7, 1740.

SPOTTED TAIL, Indian chief; b. nr. Ft. Laramie, Wyo., 1833. Captured in fight nr. Ft. Laramie, 1854, interned 2 years; attended Ft. Laramie Council, June 1866, favored whites; a signer of treaty providing for Indian reservation on western part of present state of S.D. and for withdrawal of Indian opposition to railroad constrn., 1868; joined Red Cloud in unsuccessful effort to sell mineral rights to govt. when gold was discovered in Black Hills, 1874; helped bring about surrender of Crazy Horse, 1877; chief of Lower Brule, Sioux Indians; became head chief Oglalas and Sioux, 1880. Murdered in Wyo., Aug. 5, 1881.

SPRAGUE, Achsa W., spiritualist; b. Plymouth Notch, Vt., circa 1828; d. Charles and Betsy S.; Following sudden recovery of disease of the joints after being bedridden 6 years, attributed restoration of health to divine powers, 1854; trance medium, lectured all over U.S.; devoted reformer, outspoken on condemning slavery; writer large quantity of poetry, many produced while under "automatic control," guided by divine forces; afflicted with old ailment, 1861, survived only a year. Author: I Still Live, A Poem for the Times, 1862; The Poet and Other Poems, 1864. Died July 6, 1862.

SPRAGUE, Charles, banker, poet; b. Boston, Oct. 26, 1791; s. Samuel and Joana (Thayer) S.; m. Elizabeth Rand, May 8, 1814, 4 children including Charles James. Cashier, Globe Bank, Boston, 1824; delivered poem Curiosity at Harvard Phi Beta Kappa exercises, 1829; collected works 1st published, 1841, included poems, The Funeral, The Tomb of Emmeline, To My Cigar, The Winged Worshippers. Died Boston, Jan. 22, 1875.

SPRAGUE, John Titcomb, army officer; b. Newburyport, Mass., July 3, 1810. Apptd. 2d lt. Marine Corps, 1834, served in war against Seminole Indians, 1838-39; brevetted capt., 1839; served in Tex., commanded Dept. of Fla., 1846, brevetted maj. while serving in Tex., 1848; promoted maj. 1st U.S. Inf., 1861; stationed in Tex., arrested and paroled, 1861; commd. brig. gen. N.Y. State Militia, 1862-65, served as mustering and disbursing agt., adj. gen. of state, 1862-65; brevetted col. 7th U.S. Inf., 1865, served as mil. gov. Fla., 1865-66; retired from U.S. Army, 1870. Author: Origin, Progress, and Conclusion of the Florida War, circa 1845. Died N.Y.C., Sept. 6, 1878; buried N.Y.C.

SPRAGUE, Kate Chase, hostess; b. Cincinnati, Aug. 13, 1840; d. Salmon Portland and Eliza Ann (Smith) Chase; attended Heyl's Sem., Columbus, O., also Henrietta Haines' Sch., N.Y.C., 1847-56; m. William Sprague, Nov. 12, 1863 (div. 1882), 4 children. Ofcl. hostess for her father, gov. of Ohio, 1856-61; actively campaigned for father's nomination as Republican presdl. candidate, Chgo., 1860; became social leader in Washington (D.C.) while father served as U.S. sec. of treasury, 1861-64; engaged in polit. activities on her father's behalf, 1864, 68, knew of "Pomeroy Circular," 1864; entertained lavishly at home "Canchonet," nr. Washington, from 1868; divorced her husband (following public quarrel 1879), 1882; lived at father's home "Edgewood," Washington, from 1886, suffered financial difficulties until death. Died Washington, July 31, 1899.

SPRAGUE, Peleg, congressman; b. Rochester, Mass., Dec. 10, 1756; attended Harvard; grad. Dartmouth, 1783; studied law. Clk. in store, Littleton, Mass.; admitted to bar, 1785, practiced in Winchedon, Mass.; moved to Keene, N.H., 1787; selectman, 1789-91; solicitor Cheshire County, 1794; mem. N.H. Ho. of Reps., 1797; mem. U.S. Ho. of Reps. (filled vacancy) from N.H., 5th Congress, Dec. 15, 1797-99. Died Keene, Apr. 20, 1800; buried Washington Street Cemetery.

SPRAGUE, Peleg, senator, jurist; b. Duxbury, Mass., Apr. 27, 1793; s. Seth and Deborah (Sampson) S.; grad. Harvard, 1812, LL.D. (hon.), 1847; attended Litchfield (Conn.) Law Sch.; m. Sarah Deming, Aug. 1818, 4 children. Admitted to Litchfield bar, 1815; served in 1st Me. Legislature, 1820-22; corporatae mem. Me. Hist. Soc.; mem. U.S. Ho. of Reps. from Me. 19th-20th congresses, 1825-29; mem. U.S. Senate from Me., 1829-Jan. 1, 1835; Whig presdl. elector, 1840; U.S. dist. judge for Mass., 1841-65; delivered important opinion in maritime law regarding right of way of steam vessels meeting sailing ships, 1854; delivered charge construing broadly govt. authority to suppress rebellion in Civil War, 1863. Died Boston, Oct. 13, 1880; buried Mt. Auburn Cemetery, Cambridge, Mass.

SPRAGUE, William, textile mfr.; b. Cranston, R.I., June 5, 1773; s. William and Isabel (Waterman) S.; m. Anna Porter, 5 children. A pioneer cotton cloth mfr. in R.I., erected 42 loom cotton mill, Natick Falls, Kent County, R.I., 1821, began printing calicos known as indigo blues, 1824; candidate for gov. R.I. on Anti-Masonic ticket, 1832. Died Cranston. Mar. 28, 1836.

SPRAGUE, William, senator, gov. R.I., congressman; b. Cranston, R.I., Nov. 3, 1799; ed. in classical studies. Became mcht.; mem. R.I. Ho. of Reps., speaker, 1832-35; mem. U.S. Ho. of Reps. (Whig) from R.I., 24th Congress, 1835-37; gov. R.I., 1838-39; mem. U.S. Senate (filled vacancy) from R.I., Feb. 18, 1842-Jan. 17, 1844 (resigned); Whig presdl. elector, 1848; became cotton and paint mfr. Died Providence, R.I., Oct. 19, 1856; buried Swan Point Cemetery.

SPRAGUE, William, congressman, clergyman; b. Providence, R.I., Feb. 23, 1809; attended public schs.; studied theology. Moved to Mich., settled in Kalamazoo; ordained to ministry; presiding elder Kalamazoo dist. Methodist Episcopal Ch., 1844-48; mem. U.S. Ho. of Reps. (Whig) from Mich., 31st Congress, 1849-51; retired to his farm, nr. Oshtemo, Kalamazoo County, Mich. Died Kalamazoo, Sept. 19, 1868; buried Mountain Home Cemetery.

SPRAGUE, William Buell, clergyman; b. Hebron, Conn., Oct. 16, 1795; s. Benjamin and Sibyl (Post) S.; grad. Yale, 1815; attended Princeton Theol. Sem., until 1819; D.D. (hon.) Columbia, 1828; m. Charlotte Eaton, Sept. 5, 1820; m. 2d, Mary Lathrop, Aug. 2, 1824; m. 3d, Henrietta Burritt Lathrop, May 13, 1840; 10 children. Ordained to ministry Presbyn. Ch., 1819, installed as colleague of Rev. Joseph Lathrop, West Springfield, Mass., 1820-29; minister 2d Presbyn. Ch., Albany, N.Y., 1829-69, became one of best-known clergymen of era. Author: Memoirs of the Rev. John McDowell, D.D., 1864; Annals of the American Pulpit (his most valuable work), 9 vols., 1852. Died Flushing, L.I., N.Y., May 7, 1876.

SPRIGG, James Cresap, congressman, lawyer; b. Frostburg, Md., 1802; completed prep. studies; studied law. Moved to Shelbyville, Shelby County, Ky.; admitted to bar, practiced law; held several local offices; mem. Ky. Ho. of Reps., 1830-34, 37-40, 52; mem. U.S. Ho. of Reps. from Ky., 27th Congress, 1841-43. Died Shelbyville, Oct. 3, 1852; buried Grove Hill Cemetery.

SPRIGG, John Thomas, congressman, lawyer; b. Peterborough, Northamptonshire, Eng., Apr. 5, 1825; brought to U.S., 1836; attended Hamilton Coll.; grad. Union Coll., Schenectady, N.Y., 1848; studied law. Admitted to bar, 1848, practiced in Whitesboro, N.Y.; pros. atty. Oneida County, N.Y., 1853, treas., 1854; del. Democratic nat. convs., Balt., 1860, 72, Cincinnati, 1880; mayor Utica (N.Y.), 1868-80; mem. U.S. Ho. of Reps. (Dem.) from N.Y., 48th-49th congresses, 1883-87. Died Utica, Dec. 23, 1888; buried Whitesboro Cemetery.

SPRIGG, Michael Cresap, congressman, businessman; b. Frostburg, Md., July 1, 1791; completed prep. studies. Held number local offices; presdl. elector on Monroe ticket, 1820; mem. Md. Ho. of Dels., 1821, 23, 37, 40, 44; pres. Chesapeake & Ohio Canal Co., 1841-42; mem. U.S. Ho. of Reps. (Democrat) from Md., 20th-21st congresses, 1827-31. Died Cumberland, Allegany County, Md., Dec. 18, 1845; buried Rose Hill Cemetery.

SPRIGG, Richard, Jr., congressman; b. Prince Georges County, Md. Mem. Md. Ho. of Dels., 1792-93; mem. U.S. Ho. of Reps. (filled vacancy) from Md., 4th-5th, 7th congresses, May 5, 1796-99, 1801-Feb. 11, 1802 (resigned); apptd. asso. judge Md. Ct. Appeals, 1806.

SPRIGG, Thomas, congressman; b. Prince Georges County, Md., 1747. Served as ensign in Md. Battalion of Flying Camp in Revolutionary War, 1776; 1st register of wills Washington County, Md., 1777-80; apptd. lt. Washington County by gov. and Md. Council, 1779; mem. U.S. Ho. of Reps. from Md., 3d-4th congresses, 1793-97. Died Washington County, Md., Dec. 13, 1809.

SPRING, Gardiner, clergyman; b. Newburyport, Mass., Feb. 24, 1785; s. Samuel and Hannah (Hopkins) S.; grad. Yale, 1805; postgrad. Andover Theol. Sem., 1809; D.D. (hon.), Hamilton Coll., 1819, Lafayette Coll., 1853; m. Susan Barney, May 25, 1806; m. 2d, Abba Grosvenor Williams, Aug. 14, 1861; 15 children. Admitted to Conn. bar; 1808; pastor Brick Presbyn. Ch., N.Y.C., 1810-73; a founder Am. Bible Soc., 1816; Calvinist of liberal persuasion, protested strongly against exclusion of several synods from Presbyn. Ch., 1837; mem. Old Sch. Presbyn. Gen. Assembly, 1869, pleaded powerfully for reunion of New Sch. and Old Sch. branches of Presbyn. Ch. Author: Brick Church Memorial, 1861; Pulpit Ministration, 2 vols., 1864; Personal Reminiscences, 2 vols., 1866. Died N.Y.C., Aug. 18, 1873.

SPRING, Samuel, clergyman; b. Northbridge, Mass., Mar. 10, 1747; s. Col. John and Sarah (Read) S.; grad. Princeton, 1771, studied theology under John Witherspoon 1771-74; D.D. (hon.), Williams Coll., 1806; m. Hannah Hopkins, Nov. 4, 1779, 11 children including Gardiner. Served with Continental Army as chaplain Gen. Arnold's expdn. to Can., 1775-76; ordained to ministry Congregational Ch., 1777; pastor North (now Central) Congregational Ch., Newburyport, Mass., 1777-1819; known as leader extreme Calvinist group Ch.; a founder Mass. Missionary Soc., 1799, editor its publ. Mass. Missionary Mag. (established 1803); a founder Mass. Gen. Assn. (a union of conservative, moderate wing Conglists. to combat Unitarianism), 1803, secured endowment for sem. of strict Hopkinsian principles as Andover Theol. Sem., West Newbury, opened 1808 (represented both factions of Conglists.) founder Am. Bd. Commrs. for Fgn. Missions, 1810. Author: Christian Knowledge and Christian Confidence Inseparable (sermons), 1785; The Exemplary Pastor, 1791; Two Discourses on Christ's Self-existence, 1805. Died Newburyport, Mar. 4, 1819.

SPRINGER, Reuben Runyan, philanthropist; b. Frankfort, Ky., Nov. 16, 1800; s. Charles and Catherine (Runyan) S. Given partnership in grocery firm of Kilgour, Taylor & Co., circa 1832, ret., 1840; became stockholder, dir. Little Miami and Pitts., Ft. Wayne & Chgo. R.R.; leading patron of music and art in Cincinnati; donor to Catholic Ch., especially interested in edn. of young men for priesthood; chiefly responsible for providing Cincinnati with music hall and coll. music through donations of $200,000; an incoporator Cincinnati Museum Assn., 1881; bequeathed $20,000 to Art Sch. of Cincinnati. Died Cincinnati, Dec. 11, 1884.

SPROULL, Thomas, clergyman; b. nr. Lucesco, Westmoreland County, Pa., Sept. 15, 1803; s. Robert and Mary (Dunlap) S.; grad. Western U. Pa., 1829, LL.D. (hon.), 1886; D.D. (hon.), Westminister Coll., 1857; m. Madgeline Wallace, July 1, 1834, 12 children. Licensed to preach by Presbytery of Pitts., 1832; pastor Old School Ch., Allegheny (now North Pitts.), Pa., 1834-68, a staunch adherent old sch. wing of Presbyn. Ch.; prof. theology at theol. sem. ch., Allegheny, 1838-45, 56-74; moderator ch. synod, 1847; editor Christian Witness, circa 1837-38; editor Reformed Presbyn., 1855-63, Reformed Presbyn. and Covenanter, 1863-74. Author: Prelections on Theology, 1882. Died Allegheny, Mar. 21, 1892.

SPRUANCE, Presley, senator; b. Kent County, Del., Sept. 11, 1785. Became mfr. and mcht., Smyrna, Del.; del. Del. Constl. Conv., 1831; mem. Del. Senate, 1828, 40, 46, pres.; mem. U.S. Senate (Whig) from Del., 1847-53. Died Smyrna, Feb. 13, 1863; buried Presbyn. Cemetery.

SPURZHEIM, Johann Kaspar, phrenologist; b. nr. Trier, Germany, Dec. 31, 1776; studied medicine, Vienna, Austria. Student of Franz Joseph Gall (founder of what came to be phrenology), 1800-05, became Gall's asst., 1805; travelled from Vienna to France, Eng. and later Am. in effort to spread Gall's doctrines, 1813; 1st to coin term phrenology; gave names to some mental faculties and parts of skull which are still in use today; lived and worked in U.S., circa 1813-32; believed that skull had 37 "powers" corresponding to 37 "organs." Author: (with Gall) Anatomie et Physiologie du Système Nerveux en Genéral, et du Cerveau en Particulier, avec Observations sur la Possibilité de Reconnaitre Plusiers Dispositions Intellectuelles et Morales de l'Homme et des Animaux par la Configuration de Leurs Têtes, 2 vols., 1810-19; The Physiognomical System of Gall and Spurzheim, 1815. Died Boston, Nov. 10, 1832.

SQUANTO (nicknamed Tisquantum), Indian guide and interpreter. A Pawtuxet Indian, kidnapped by Capt. Thomas Hunt at Pawtuxet (Plymouth), Mass., circa 1610, sold into slavery at Malaga, Spain; escaped to Eng., lived in London with John Slany, treas. New Foundland Co., 1612-14; sent to Newfoundland by Slany, 1614-18, returned to Eng. with Capt. Thomas Dermer; served as Dermer's pilot to New Eng. coast, summer 1619, made his way to Pawtuxet and found he was sole survivor of his tribe; served as guide and interpreter to Edward Winslow in concluding treaty of Plymouth between Indian chief Massasoit and Pilgrims, 1621; hated by Indians for exploiting his friendship with English; served as guide and interpreter on Gov. William Bradford's expdn. around Cape Cod, contracted fever and died. Died Chatham Harbor, Mass., 1622.

SQUIBB, Edward Robinson, pharmacist, chemist, physician; b. Wilmington, Del., July 4, 1819; s. James R. and Catherine H. (Bonsal) S.; studied pharmacy under Warder Morris, Phila., 1837, under J. H. Sprague, Phila., 1837-42; M.D., Jefferson Med. Coll., 1845; m. Caroline F. Lownds, Oct. 7, 1852, 3 children. Commd. asst. surgeon U.S. Navy, 1847; med. officer in ships Perry, Erie, Cumberland, 1847-51; assigned to duty Bklyn. Naval Hosp., 1851; authorized by Navy Dept. to establish his own lab. for manufacture pharmaceuticals and chemicals, 1852; resigned U.S. Navy, 1853, became mfg. copartner in firm Thomas E. Jenkins & Co. (known as Louisville Chem. Works), Louisville, Ky.; established chem. and pharm. lab. under name Edward R. Squibb, M.D., Bklyn., 1858, severely injured when lab. burned, 1858, later rebuilt factory, admitted his 2 sons as co-partners, 1892, changed name to E. R. Squibb & Sons; contbr. many articles to Am. Journal of Pharmacy. Died Bklyn., Oct. 25, 1900.

SQUIER, Ephraim George, editor, diplomat; b. Bethlehem, N.Y., June 17, 1821; s. Joel and Catharine (Kilmer or Kulmer) S.; m. Miriam Florence Folline, 1858; m. 2d, Miriam F.F. Leslie, circa 1874. Founder, Poet's Magazine, Albany, N.Y., 1842, published only 2 issues; asso. N.Y. State Mechanic (organ for prison reform), 1842-43; editor Evening Jour. (Whig publ.), Hartford, Conn., 1844-45; publisher Scioto Gazette, Chillicothe, O., circa 1845; clk. Ohio Ho. of Reps., 1847, 48; interested in archaeology, examined native remains in N.Y., published Aboriginal Monuments of the State of New York (his chief work on subject) 1851; charge d'affaires to C. Am., 1849-51; sec. Honduras Interoceanic Ry. Co., 1853; editor publishing firm Frank Leslie, supervised Frank Leslie's Pictorial History of the American Civil War, 2 vols., 1861-62; U.S. commr. to Peru, 1863-65; consul gen. of Honduras, N.Y.C., 1868. Author: Tropical Fibres, and Their Economic Extraction, 1861; Honduras, 1870; Is Cotton King?, 1861. Died Bklyn., Apr. 17, 1888.

SQUIER, Miles Powell, clergyman; b. Cornwall, Vt., May 4, 1792; grad. Middlebury (Vt.) Coll., 1811, Andover Theol. Sem., 1814. Preacher, Congregational Ch., Oxford, Mass., 1814-15; missionary in Western N.Y., 1815-16; pastor 1st Presbyn. Ch., Buffalo, N.Y., 1816-24; financial agt. Auburn Theol. Sem., 1824-26; sec. of branch Am. Home Missionary Soc., Geneva, N.Y., 1826-34; mgr. of a lyceum, Geneva, 1831-41; prof. intellectual and moral philosophy, Beloit Coll., Wis., 1849-63. Author: The Problem Solved; or, Sin Not of God, 1855; Reason and the Bible, 1860. Died Geneva, June 22, 1866.

ST. ANGE, Louis De Bellerive, army officer, colonial gov.; b. Montreal, Que., Can., Oct. 3, 1698; s. Robert Groston and Marguerite Crevier (de Bellerive) de St. A. In command of one detachment with Etienne Vinyard on expdn. Westward to make alliance with Padouka Indians, 1724; apptd. to succeed Jean Baptiste Bissot at Ft. Orleans on Wabash River, with rank of capt., 1736-1764 conducted evacuation of Ft. Chartres as successor to Neyon de Villiers, the comdt., 1764, acting gov. Upper La., 1764-65; in command of St. Louis, 1765-70. Died St. Louis, Dec. 27, 1774.

ST. CLAIR, Arthur, pres. Continental Congress, army officer, territorial gov.; b. Thurso, Aithness County, Scotland, Apr. 3, 1737; s. William and Elizabeth (Balfour) St.C.; m. Phoebe Bayard, May 15, 1760, 7 children. commd. ensign Brit. Army, 1757, served with Gen. Jeffrey Amherst at capture of Louisburg, Can., 1758; resigned as lt., 1762; bought estate in Ligonier Valley, Western Pa., circa 1762, became largest resident property owner in Pa. West of mountains; apptd. colonial agt. in this frontier area by gov. Pa., 1771; justice Westmoreland County (Pa.) Ct., 1773; mem. Westmoreland County Com. Safety; sent as col. to take part in retreat of Continental Army from Can., 1775; commd. brig. gen., served with Washington in campaign and battles of Trenton, Princeton, 1776-77; as maj. gen. ordered to defense of Fort Ticonderoga, 1777, evacuated post, exonerated by ct. martial, 1778; mem. Pa., Council of Censors, 1783; del. from Pa. to Continental Congress, 1785-87, pres. 1787; 1st gov. Northwest Territory, 1787-1802; maj. gen. comdr. U.S. Army, defeated by Indians nr. Fort Wayne, 1791; ordered to erect chain mil. posts from Fort Washington, nr. mouth of Miami River, to rapids of Maumee River, work very poorly planned and executed; resigned commn., 1792; Federalist; objected to statehood for Northwest Territory as premature, sought to gerrymanader territory into smaller territories so as to postpone statehood indefinitely; denounced the Ohio enabling act of Congress as a nullity at Ohio Constl. Conv. of 1802; Died at home "Hermitage," nr. Ligonier, Pa., Aug. 31, 1818.

ST. DENIS, Louis Juchereau de, see de St. Denis, Louis Juchereau.

ST. HUSSON, Sieur de, see Daumont, Simon Francois.

St. JOHN, Charles, congressman, businessman; b. Mt. Hope, Orange County, N.Y., Oct. 8, 1818; attended common schs., Goshen, Newburgh (N.Y.) acads. In lumbering business on Delaware River; mcht., banker, Port Jervis, N.Y.; internal revenue collector during Civil War, later pres. Barrett Bridge Co.; mem. U.S. Ho. of Reps. (Republican) from N.Y., 42d-43d congresses, 1871-75; Rep. presdl. elector, 1880. Died Port Jervis, July 6, 1891; buried Laurel Grove Cemetery.

St. JOHN, Daniel Bennett, congressman, businessman; b. Sharon, Conn., Oct. 8, 1808. In real estate business, mcht., Monticello, N.Y., 1831; mem. N.Y. State Assembly, 1840; mem. U.S. Ho. of Reps. (Whig) from N.Y., 30th Congress, 1847-49; moved to Newburgh, N.Y.; del. Nat. Constl.-Union Conv., Balt., 1860; mem. N.Y. State Senate, 1875; del. Nat. Democratic Conv., St. Louis, 1876; chief registrar banking dept. State of N.Y. Died N.Y.C., Feb. 18, 1890; buried Woodlawn Cemetery, Newburgh.

St. JOHN, Henry, congressman, farmer; b. Washington County, Vt., July 16, 1783. Served during War of 1812; moved to Wooster, O., 1815, to Crawford County, O., 1828, to Seneca County, O., 1837; became farmer, miller, storekeeper, nr. Tiffin, O.; mem. U.S. Ho. of Reps. (Democrat) from Ohio, 28th-29th congresses, 1843-47; retired from public life. Died Tiffin, May 1869.

ST. JOHN, Isaac Munroe, army officer, engr.; b. Augusta, Ga., Nov. 19, 1827; s. Isaac Richards and Abigail Richardson (Munroe) St.J.; grad. Yale, 1845; m. Ella J. Carrington, Feb 28, 1865, 6 children. Asst. editor Balt. Patriot, circa 1847; mem. engring. staff B. & O. R.R., 1848-55; in charge of constrn. divs. Blue Ridge R.R. in Ga., 1855-60; enlisted for engring. duty in U.S. Army, 1861, transferred to Magruder's Army of Peninsula, became chief engr.; commd. capt. engrs., 1862, promoted to maj. 1862, chief of the nitre and mining bur., Richmond, Va.; lt. col. and col.; apptd. commissary gen. with rank brig. gen. Confederate States Army, 1865, organized an efficient system for collecting and storing supplies and for forwarding them to the armies; chief engr. Louisville, Cincinnati & Lexington R.R., 1866-69; city engr. Louisville (Ky.), 1869-71; made 1st topog. map of Louisville and planned city's 1st complete sewerage system; became cons. engr. C. & O. R.R., 1871; chief engr. Elizabeth, Lexington & Big Sandy R.R., 1873. Died "Greenbrier," White Sulphur Springs, W.Va., Apr. 7, 1880.

ST. JOHN, J. Hector, see de Crevecoeur, Michel-Guillaume Jean.

ST. LAUSSON, Simon Francois Daumont (Sieur de St. Lausson), colonial ofcl.; m. Marguerite Berin, 1 child. Owned land, served as agt. for supt. of New France (now Canada), 1663-68, 70-73; head French expdn. which took possession of lands around Lake Superior where copper had been discovered, 1670-71; land formally ceded to King Louis XIV by Indian chiefs of region in ceremony at Ste. Sault-Marie, 1671; served in Acadia, 1671-72. Died 1674.

ST. LEGER, Barry, army officer; b. Eng., 1737. Apptd. ensign 28th Regt. of Foot, Brit. Army, 1756; served in French and Indian War, at siege of Louisbourg, battles of Que. and Montreal; apptd. brigade maj., 1760, maj., 1762; led siege of Ft. Stanwix, defeated by Americans under Gen. Benedict Arnold, 1777; promoted col., 1780; led Brit. rangers in guerrilla warfare; started expdn. against Ticonderoga, 1781, withdrew upon learning of defeat of Cornwallis; comdt. Brit. forces in Can., 1784, ret., 1785. Died 1789.

St. MARTIN, Louis, congressman; b. St. Charles Parish, La., May 17, 1820; attended St. Mary's Coll., Mo., Jefferson Coll., La.; studied law in notarial office. Apptd. clk. New Orleans Post Office; elected mem. La. Ho. of Reps., 1840, 46-50; apptd. by Pres. Polk as register U.S. Land Office for Southeastern dist. La., 1846-49; mem. U.S. Ho. of Reps. (Democrat) from La., 32d, 49th congresses, 1851-53, 85-87; became mcht.; apptd. register of voters for New Orleans by La. gov., reapptd.; del. Nat. Dem. Convs., 1852, 68, 76, 80; Dem. presdl. elector, 1868, 76; with Office Public Accounts, New Orleans. Died New Orleans, Feb. 9, 1893; buried St. Vincent de Paul Cemetery.

St. VRAIN, Ceran De Hault De Lassus de, se[e] de St. Vrain, Ceran DeHault Delassus.

STACKHOUSE, Eli Thomas, congressman; b. Little Rock, Marion County, S.C., Mar. 27, 1824; attended common schs. Worked on father's farm taught sch. several years; became farmer; enlisted in Confederate Army, 1861, served throughout Civil War, commd. col. 8th Regt., S.C. Volunteers wounded in battles of Antietam, Gettysburg and Chickamauga; mem. S.C. Ho. of Reps., 1862-68; mem. 1st bd. trustees Clemson A. and M. Coll., 1887; 1st pres. S.C. Farmers' Alliance, 1888; mem. U.S. Ho. of Reps. (Democrat) from S.C., 52d Congress, 1891 June 14, 1892. Died Washington, D.C., June 14 1892; buried Little Rock Cemetery.

STAGER, Anson, telegraph pioneer, army officer b. Ontario County, N.Y., Apr. 20, 1825; m. Rebecca Sprague, Nov. 14, 1847, 3 children. Worked in office Rochester (N.Y.) Daily Advertiser owned by Henry O'Reilly, 1841, bookkeeper by 1845; studied telegraphy in spare time; apptd. telegraph operator at Lancaster (Pa.) office, 1847 (after O'Reilly had contracted with Samuel F. B. Morse to build telegraph from Phila. to Middle West circa 1845); mgr., Pitts. office, 1847; mgr. operating dept. of Pitts., Cincinnati & Louisville Telegraph Co., 1847-51; apptd. gen. supt. N.Y. & Mississippi Valley Printing Telegraph Co., 1852-56; gen supt. Western Union Telegraph Co., 1856-61, assigned to rearrange many telegraph lines and establish good relations with railroads, established hdqrs. at Cleve.; commd. capt. and asst. q.m. gen U.S. Army, 1861, placed in Washington (D.C.) as chief U.S. mil. telegraphs; promoted col., assigned as a.d.c. to Gen. Henry W. Halleck at War Dept., 1862; brevetted brig. gen. for meritorious services, 1865, discharged, 1866; became supt. Central div. Western Union Telegraph Co. with hdqrs at Cleve., later at Chgo., v.p. until 1881; pres. Western Edison Electric Light Co. from its formation until 1885. Died Chgo., Mar. 26, 1885.

STAGG, Charles, actor; m. Mary Stagg. With William Levinston built theater, Williamsburg, Va. (probably 1st theater in Am.), 1716; with Mary Stagg and company presented play for Alexander Spotswood (gov. Va.), Williamsburg, 1718; became leading actor pioneer Am. theater. Died Williamsburg, 1735.

STALLWORTH, James Adams, congressman; b. Evergreen, Conecuh County, Ala., Apr. 7, 1822; attended Old Field Piney Woods Schs.; studied law. Became planter; admitted to bar, 1848, practiced in Evergreen; mem. Ala. Ho. of Reps., 1845-48; solicitor Ala. 2d Jud. Circuit, 1850, 55; mem. U.S. Ho. of Reps. (Democrat) from Ala., 35th-36th congresses, 1857-Jan. 21, 1861 (withdrew). Died nr. Evergreen, Aug. 31, 1861; buried Evergreen Cemetery.

STANBERY, Henry, atty. gen.; b. N.Y.C., Feb. 20, 1803; s. Dr. Jonas and Ann Lucy (Seaman) S.; grad. Washington (now Washington and Jefferson) Coll., 1819; m. Frances E. Beecher, 1829; m. 2d, Cecelia Bond; 5 children. Admitted to bar, 1824; elected 1st atty. gen. Ohio, 1846, organized new dept. of justice; practiced in U.S. cts. and Ohio Supreme Ct.; influential mem. Ohio Constl. Conv. of 1850, contbd. to improvement organic laws of state; became atty. gen. U.S., 1866; resigned Mar. 1868 to serve as Pres. Johnson's chief counsel in impeachment proceeding, made opening and closing arguments with distinction; reapptd. atty. gen., 1868 (rejected by Senate); pres. Law Assn., Cincinnati. Died N.Y.C., June 26, 1881.

STANBERY, William, congressman, lawyer; b. Essex County, N.J., Aug. 10, 1788; had academic edn.; studied law, N.Y.C. Admitted to bar; moved to Ohio 1809, settled in Newark, Licking County, practiced law; mem. Ohio Senate, 1824-25; mem. U.S Ho. of Reps. (Jacksonian Democrat, filled vacancy) from Ohio, 20th-22d congresses, Oct. 9, 1827-33. Died Newark, Jan. 23, 1873; buried Cedar Hill Cemetery.

STANDIFER, James, congressman; b. Sequatchie Valley, nr. Dunlap, Tenn.; grad. U. Tenn. Mem. U.S. Ho. of Reps. (Whig) from Tenn., 18th, 21st-25th congresses, 1823-25, 29-Aug. 20, 1837. Died nr. Kingston, Tenn., Aug. 20, 1837; buried Baptist Cemetery, Kingston.

STANDIFORD, Elisha David, congressman; b. nr. Louisville, Ky., Dec. 28, 1831; attended St. Mary's Coll., nr. Lebanon, Ky.; grad. Ky. Sch. Medicine. Practiced medicine, Louisville, for a time, then became farmer, also engaged in business activities; mem. U.S. Ho. of Reps. (Democrat) from Ky., 43d Congress, 1873-75; pres. Louisville & Nashville R.R. Co., 1875-79; mem. Ky. Senate, 1868, 71; mem. U.S. Ho. became banker. Died Louisville, July 26, 1887; buried Cave Hill Cemetery.

STANDISH, Myles, Pilgrim father; b. Lancashire, Eng., circa 1584; s. John Standish; m. Rose Standish; m. 2d, Barbara Standish, 1624; 6 children. Hired to accompany Pilgrims, sailed from London, Eng. on ship Mayflower, 1620; a mem. of small party that made 1st landing at Plymouth, Dec. 1620; supervised building of fort; learned Indian langs. and became Pilgrims' intermediary with natives; chosen to return to Eng. on behalf of Pilgrims who claimed rights to land or property in New World, 1625-26; an undertaker who assumed debts of colony, 1627; atty. for Council for New Eng. to deliver their land to Pilgrims under new grant, 1630; treas. of colony for 6 years, asst. on Gov.'s Council for 29 years; founder (with John Alden) Duxbury (Mass.), 1631; no hist. basis for tale of John Alden's proposal to Priscilla on Standish's behalf. Died Duxbury, Oct. 3, 1656.

STANFORD, John, clergyman; b. Wandsworth, Surrey, Eng., Oct. 20, 1754; s. William and Mary S.; m. Sarah Ten Eyck, June 26, 1790, at least 4 children. Came to U.S., 1786; pastor 1st Bapt. Ch., Providence, R.I., 1788-89; founder ch., sch. and residence on Fair (now Fulton) St., N.Y.C., 1795, pastor, 1795-98; preacher in Bapt. chs. in N.Y., N.J., Pa. and Conn.; urged city ofcls. to separate young offenders from hardened criminals, responsible for founding House of Refuge, 1825. Author: The Aged Christian's Cabinet, 1829. Died Jan. 14, 1834.

STANFORD, (Amasa) Leland, railroad builder, senator, gov. Cal.; b. Watervliet, N.Y., Mar. 9, 1824; s. Josiah and Elizabeth (Phillips) S.; m. Jane Elizabeth Lathrop, Sept. 30, 1850; at least 1 son, Leland, Jr. Admitted to bar, 1847; practiced law, Port Washington, Wis., 1848-52; storeowner, Michigan Bluff, Cal., 1853; became active Republican Party, 1856, gov. Cal., 1861-63, kept state securely in Union, approved several measures to provide pub. capital for constrn. Central and Western Pacific railroads; pres. Central Pacific R.R., 1861-93, organized So. Pacific Co., 1884, pres., 1885-90 (company leased Central and So. Pacific lines, thereby retaining control of promoters eve: though a great deal of stock had been sold to public); an original asso. Central Pacific enterprise, contributed much of energy and foresight which made possible a transcontinental railroad, 1869, did not risk his own capital as much as that of the public in the promotion; used polit. influence to resist pub. regulation of railroads, defended practices of discrimination and consolidation common in railroads of the period; mem. U.S. Senate from Cal. (elected as Republican over candidate supported by Collis P. Huntington, which resulted in displacement of Stanford by Huntington as pres. So. Pacific Co., 1890, 1885-93, indicated little interest in important bills, little ability in dealing with legislative problems, mem. com. on naval affairs, circa 1885; founder Leland Stanford Junior U. in memory of his son (now known as Stanford U.), Palo Alto, Cal., 1885, opened, 1891. Died Palo Alto, June 21, 1893; buried Stanford U.

STANFORD, Richard, congressman; b. nr. Vienna, Md., Mar. 2, 1767; completed prep. studies. Moved to Hawfields, N.C., circa 1793, founded acad.; mem. U.S. Ho. of Reps. (Democrat) from N.C., 5th-14th congresses, 1797-Apr. 9, 1816. Died Georgetown, D.C. Apr. 9, 1816; buried Congressional Cemetery, Washington, D.C.

STANLEY, John Mix, painter; b. Canandaigua, N.Y., Jan. 17, 1814. Began painting Indians nr. Fort Snelling, 1838-39; traveled widely in West, painting Indians wherever he went, 1842-54; exhbtd. 83 canvases in Cincinnati and Louisville, Ky., 1846; returned to West, 1846; joined expdn. of Stephen Watts Kearny overland to Cal. from Santa Fe, exhibited pictures at New Haven and Hartford, Conn., also Washington, D.C., 1851; collection contained portraits from 43 different Indian tribes, left in Smithsonian Instn., 1852, all but 5 pictures destroyed by fire, 1865 (list of original collection available in catalogue); apptd. artist of expdn. sent by U.S. Govt. to explore a route for Pacific R.R. from St. Paul, Minn. to Puget Sound; 1853; organized Western Art Assn., most important work: The Trial of Red Jacket. Died Detroit, Apr. 10, 1872.

STANLY, Edward, congressman; b. New Bern, N.C., July 13, 1810; s. John and Miss (Frank) S.; m. Miss Jones, circa 1832; m. 2d, Cornelia Baldwin, circa 1860. Admitted to N.C. bar, 1832; mem. U.S. Ho. of Reps. (Whig) from N.C., 25th 27th, 31st-33d congresses, 1837-43, 48-53, became leader of his party; del. to Nat. Whig Conv., Balt., 1844; elected to N.C. Ho. of Commons, 1846, 48, 49, speaker, 1846; atty. gen. N.C., 1847; moved to Cal., 1853; apptd. mil. gov. of N.C. by Lincoln, 1862-63; opposed radical reconstruction policy and left Republican party, 1867. Died San Francisco, July 12, 1872; buried Mountain View Cemetery, Oakland, Cal.

STANLY, John, congressman, lawyer; b. New Bern, N.C., Apr. 9, 1774; attended Princeton; studied law; at least 1 son, Edward. Admitted to bar, 1799, practiced law; clk. and master in equity; mem. N.C. Ho. of Commons, 1798-99, 1812-15, 18-19, 23-26; mem. U.S. Ho. of Reps. from N.C., 7th, 11th congresses, 1801-03, 09-11. Died New Bern, Aug. 2, 1834; buried Episcopal Cemetery.

STANSBURY, Howard, army officer; b. N.Y.C., Feb. 8, 1806; s. Arthur Joseph and Susanna (Brown) S.; m. Helen Moody, Sept. 1, 1827, at least 2 children. Surveyor route of Mad River & Lake Eire R.R., 1832-35, lower part James River, Va., 1836, proposed railroad route from Milw. to Mississippi River, 1838; commd. lt. Topog. Engrs., U.S. Army, 1838, capt., 1840, surveyed harbor, Portsmouth, N.H.; in charge exploring expdn. to Gt. Salt Lake area, 1849; builder mil. roads in Minn., 1851-61; mustering officer for Columbus (O.) region, 1861; promoted maj., 1861, ret., 1861; re-entered service, became mustering and disbursing officer, Madison, Wis. Died Madison, Apr. 17, 1863.

STANSBURY, Joseph, alleged Loyalist, poet; b. London, Eng., Jan. 9, 1750; s. Samuel and Sarah (Porter) S.; m. Sarah Ogier, Apr. 2, 1765, 9 children. Came to Phila., 1767; an opponent of colonial independence, wrote songs about race kinship during Am. Revolution and incurred suspicion of his loyalty; arrested on suspicion of carrying on secret correspondence with enemy, circa 1780; carried Benedict Arnold's 1st proposals to Brit. hdqrs.; moved to N.Y.C., 1793, sec. United Ins. Co. for several years; poems collected in The Loyal Verses of Joseph Stansbury and Odell, published 1860. Died N.Y.C., Nov. 1809.

STANTON, Benjamin, congressman, lawyer; b. Mt. Pleasant, Jefferson County, O., June 4, 1809; had academic studies; studied law. Learned tailor's trade; admitted to bar, 1834, practiced in Bellefontaine, O.; mem. Ohio Senate, 1841, 43; del. Ohio Constl. Conv., 1850; mem. U.S. Ho. of Reps. (Whig) from Ohio, 32d, 34th-36th congresses, 1851-53, 55-61; lt. gov. Ohio, 1862; practiced law Martinsburg, W. Va., 1865-67, Wheeling, W.Va., from 1867. Died Wheeling, June 2, 1872; buried Greenwood Cemetery.

STANTON, Edwin McMasters, cabinet officer; b. Steubenville, O., Dec. 19, 1814; s. David and Lucy (Norman) S.; attended Kenyon Coll., Gambier, O.; m. Mary Ann Lamson, Dec. 31, 1836; m. 2d, Ellen M. Hutchison, June 25, 1856; 6 children. Admitted to Ohio bar, 1836; pros. atty. Harrison County (O.), 1837-39; leading counsel McCormick vs. Manny patent case; spl. counsel for Cal. in land fraud cases, 1858; U.S. atty. gen., Dec. 1860-Mar. 1861; adherent Democratic Party (but opposed to Southern control), until 1862, supported Wilmot Proviso, Dred Scott decision; strict constitutionalist and Unionist after 1860; U.S. sec. of war, 1862-68, instituted changes in orgn. of dept. to increase honesty and efficiency; received Congressional sanction for governmental control of railroads and telegraph; maintained close relations with joint Senate-House on conduct of war; reputation as adminstr. based on grasp of detail and quickness of decision; his dispatch of support to Rosecrans in Chattanooga (Sept. 1863) considered one of greatest adminstrn. achievements of war; frequently interferred in plans of field commanders, disliked because of dictatorial and arrogant manners; suppressed evidence tending to show defendent's innocence in trial of Mary Surratt before mil. court; approved Pres. Johnson's reconstrn. policies in cabinet (but evidence indicates that he connived with adminstrn. opposition in Congress); supported Mil. Reconstrn. Act of 1867; author of requirement that all Presdl. army orders be issued through War Dept., 1867; opposed Tenure of Office Act as unconstl.; resisted pressures to resign (although Pres. Johnson opposed his presence in cabinet after 1866), flatly refused Johnson's request for resignation, Aug. 1867; supported by Senate under Tenure of Office Act in this refusal, but resigned in May 1868 following acquittal of Pres. Johnson in impeachment trial; supported Grant in 1868 campaign; nominated to U.S. Supreme Ct. by Grant, 1869, confirmed, Dec. 1869, died before serving. Died Washington, D.C., Dec. 24, 1869; buried Washington.

STANTON, Frederick Perry, congressman; b. Alexandria, Va., Dec. 22, 1814; s. Richard and Harriet (Perry) S.; A.B., Columbian Coll. (now George Washington U.), 1833; m. Jane Lanphier, 9 children. Admitted to Memphis (Tenn.) bar; principal Elizabeth City (N.C.) Acad., 1833-35; contbd. polit. editorials to Memphis Gazette; mem. U.S. Ho. of Reps. from Tenn., 29th-33d congresses, 1845-55, chmn. com. on vaval affairs, 1849; sec. Kan. Territory (apptd. by Pres. Buchanan), 1857-58, acting gov. territory, twice during 1858, held pro-slavery position first, but advocated free-state status by 1858 removed from office for cooperation with Free-Soil elements 1861; practiced law, Washington, D.C., from 1862. Died Stanton, nr. Ocala, Fla., June 4, 1894; buried South Lake Weir (Fla.) Cemetery.

STANTON, Henry Brewster, lawyer, reformer, journalist; b. Griswold, Conn., June 27, 1805; s. Joseph and Susan (Brewster) S.; attended Lane Theol. Sem.; m. Elizabeth Cady, May 10, 1840, 7 children. Dep. clk. Monroe County (N.Y.), 1829-32; helped organize anti-slavery soc. in Cincinnati, 1834; agt. Am. Anti-Slavery Soc., also mem. exec. com.; wrote for abolitionist jours. including Liberator, also for religious publs., polit. papers including National Era, Washington, N.Y. American; tried to form strong polit. orgn. of abolitionists, 1837-40; admitted to Mass. bar, circa 1845; mem. N.Y. Senate from Seneca Falls, 1849-53; helped draft Free Soil platform, Buffalo, 1848; an organizer Republican Party in N.Y., 1855; connected with N.Y. Tribune after Civil War; with N.Y. Sun, 1869-87. Died N.Y.C., Jan. 14, 1887.

STANTON, Joseph, Jr., senator, congressman; b. Charlestown, R.I., July 19, 1739. Served in expdn. against Canada, 1759; mem. R.I. Ho. of Reps., 1768-74, 94-1800; served as col. in Revolutionary Army; del. R.I. Constl. Conv., 1790; mem. U.S. Senate (Democrat) from R.I., June 7, 1790-93; mem. U.S. Ho. of Reps. (Dem.) from R.I., 7th-9th congresses, 1801-07. Died Charlestown, 1807; buried family cemetery.

STANTON, Richard Henry, congressman, jurist; b. Alexandria, D.C., (now Va.) , Sept. 9, 1812; s. Richard and Harriet (Perry) S.; m. Asenath Throop, 1833, 9 children including Henry Thompson. Admitted to Maysville (y.) bar, 1835; edited Maysville Monitor, 1835-42; published Maysville Express; edited Maysville Bulletin; postmaster Maysville 1845-49; mem. U.S. Ho. of Reps. from Ky., 31st-33d congresses, 1849-55; chmn. com on pub. grounds and. bldgs.. during 2d term, instrumental in advancing constrn. and improvement of the Capitol; commonwealth's atty. for 10th Jud. Dist. of Ky., 1858-62; became judge circuit ct. for 14th Jud. Dist., Maysville, 1868; del. Democratic Nat. Conv., 1844, 52; presdl. elector for James Buchanan, 1856; mem. Union Conv. at Phila., 1866; attended N.Y. Cinv. which nominated Horatio Seymour for U.S. Pres., 1868. Author: Code of Practice in Civil and Criminal Cases for the State of Kentucky, 1859; The Revised Statutes of Kentucky , 2 vols., 1867. Died Maysville, Ky., Mar. 20, 1891; buried Maysville Cemetery.

STANWICK, John, congressman; b. 1740. A mcht.; published a volume of poetry; mem. U.S. Ho. of Reps. (Democrat) from Pa., 4th-5th congresses, 1795-98. Died Phila., Aug. 1, 1798; buried St. Peter's Churchyard.

STAPLES, Waller Redd, jurist, Confederate congressman; b. Stuart, Patrick County, Va., Feb. 24, 1826; s. Col. Abram Penn and Mary (Penn) S.; grad. Coll. William and Mary, 1846. Admitted to Va. bar, 1848; del. from Montgomery County to Va. Ho. Dels., 1853-54; Va. rep. to provisional Confederate Congress, Montgomery, Ala., 1861-62; mem. Confederate Ho. of Reps., 1862-65; justice Va. Supreme Ct. of Appeals, 1870-82, notable decisions included dissent in Coupon Case (Antoni vs. Wright, 63 Va. Reports, 833), 1878, which led to formation of Readjuster Party and to partial repudiation of a portion of state debt; counsel Richmond & Danville R.R., circa 1882-84; twice Democratic presdl. elector; refused Dem. nominations for gov. and senator; prepared Code of Va., 1884, published 1887. Died Patrick County Va., Aug. 20, 1897.

STAPLES, William Read, historian; b. Providence, R.I., Oct. 10, 1798; s. Samuel and Ruth (Read) S.; grad. Brown U., 1817; m. Rebecca Power, Nov. 1821 m. 2d, Evelina Eaton, Oct. 1826; 13 children. Admitted to R.I. bar, 1819; asso. justice Supreme Ct. R.I., 1835-54, chief justice, 1854-56; state auditor R.I., 1856; an incorporator R.I. Hist. Soc., 1822, librarian. Author: Annals of the Town of Providence, 1843; Rhode Island in the Continental Congress, 1870. Editor: The Documentary History of the Destruction of the Gospel, 1845. Died Providence, Oct. 19, 1868.

STARK, John, army officer; b. Londonderry, N.H., Aug. 28, 1728; s. Archibald and Eleanor (Nichols) S.; m. Elizabeth Page, Aug. 20, 1758. Leader exploring expdns.; served at Crown Point and Ticonderoga in French and Indian War, 1759; col. at Battle of Bunker Hill, 1775; resigned commn., 1777; promoted to brig. gen. Continental Army, 1777; captured Ft. Edward; in command No. Dept. twice; joined George Washington in Battle of Short Hills, Morristown, N.J., 1778; served with Gates in R.I., 1779; served in Battle of Springfield, 1780; brevetted maj. gen., 1783. Died Manchester, N.H., May 2, 1822.

STARKWEATHER, David Austin, congressman, diplomat; b. Preston, Conn., Jan. 21, 1802; had academic edn.; studied law. Admitted to bar, 1825, practiced in Mansfield, O.; moved to Canton, O., 1827, practiced law; judge higher ct., Stark County (O.), mem. Ohio Ho. of Reps., 1833-35, Ohio Senate, 1836-38; mem. U.S. Ho. of Reps. (Democrat) from Ohio, 26th, 29th congresses, 1839-41, 45-47; practiced in Cleve.; presdl. elector on Cass and Butler ticket, 1848; chmn. Nat. Dem. Conv., July 12, 1876; buried Lake View Cemetery.

STARKWEATHER, George Anson, congressman, lawyer; b. Preston, Conn., May 19, 1794; grad. Union Coll., Schenectady, N.Y., 1819; studied law. Admitted to bar, practiced in Cooperstown, N.Y.; mem. U.S. Ho. of Reps. (Democrat) from N.Y., 30th Congress, 1847-49; practiced in Milw., 1853-68. Died Cooperstown, Oct. 15, 1879; buried Lakewood Cemetery.

STARKWEATHER, Henry Howard, congressman; b. Preston, Conn., Apr. 29, 1826; attended common schs.; studied law. Admitted to bar, practiced in Norwich, Conn.; mem. Conn. Ho. of Reps., 1856; del. Republican nat. conv., Chgo., 1860, 68; postmaster Norwich, 1861-65; mem. U.S. Ho. of Reps. (Rep.) from Conn., 40th-44th congresses, 1867-Jan. 28, 1876. Died Washington, D.C., Jan. 28, 1876; buried Yantic Cemetery, Norwich.

STARR, Belle (Myra Belle Shirley Starr), outlaw; b. nr. Carthage, Mo., 1848; d. John and Eliza Shirley; m. Sam Starr (an Indian), 1880. Moved with family to Dallas, 1864, there became involved with Younger and James gangs; had child by Cole Younger; her outlaw exploits became legendary; after her marriage, home in Indian Terr. (Okla.) was hangout for desperadoes. Shot and killed by unknown gunman, Indian Terr., 1889.

STAUGHTON, William, clergyman, coll. pres.; b. Coventry, Warwickshire, Eng., Jan. 4, 1770; s. Sutton and Keziah S.; attended Bristol Baptist Coll.; m. Anna Peale, Aug. 27, 1829. Came to Charleston, S.C., 1793; became head of an acad. Bordentown, N.J., 1795; ordained to ministry Bapt. Ch., 1797; became pastor 1st Bapt. Ch., Phila., 1805, Sansom St. Bapt. Ch., Phila., 1811; an organizer Triennial Conv., 1814; became tutor Bapt. Edn. Soc., 1812; principal theol. dept. Triennial Conv.; a founder, 1st pres. Columbian Coll. (later George Washington U.), 1822-29, tchr. history and philosophy, editions of The Works of Virgil, 1813, Edward Wentenhall's published A Compendious System of Greek Grammar, 1813 Died Washington, D.C., Dec. 12, 1829.

STAUNTON, William, clergyman; b. Chester, Eng., Apr. 20, 1803. Came to U.S., 1818; ordained deacon Protestant Episcopal Ch., 1833, priest, 1834; rector St. James' Ch., Roxbury, Mass., 1835-37, St. Peter's Ch., Morristown, N.J., 1840-47; founder, rector St. Peter's Ch., Bklyn., 1848-51; rector Trinity Ch., Potsdam, N.Y., 1852-59; musical editor Johnson's Encyclopedia. Author: Dictionary of the Church. Died Sept. 20, 1889.

STAYTON, John William, jurist; b. Washington County, Ky., Dec. 24, 1830; s. Robert G. and Harriet (Pirtle) S.; LL.B., U. Louisville, 1856; m. Eliza Jane Weldon, 3 children. Moved to Tex., 1856; dist. atty. San Antonio County (Tex.), 1858-62; enlisted as pvt. Confederate Army, 1862, later commd. capt. cavalry; founder law firm with Samuel C. Lackey, 1866; mem. Tex. State Constl. Conv., 1875; asso. justice Tex. Supreme Ct., 1881-88, chief justice, 1888-94. Died Tyler, Tex., July 5, 1894.

STEARNS, Abel, pioneer; b. Lunenburg, Mass., Feb. 9, 1798; s. Levi and Elizabeth (Goodrich) S.; m. Maria Francisca Paula Arcadia Bandini, circa 1840. Became sindico (fiscal agt.) Los Angeles, 1836; active in revolution which expelled Gov. Manuel Micheltorena, 1844-45; mem. Cal. Constl. Conv., 1849; builder Arcadia Block (largest structure south of San Francisco), 1858; projected a found. to benefit new U. So. Cal. Died San Francisco, Aug. 23, 1871; buried Los Angeles.

STEARNS, Asahel, congressman, lawyer; b. Lunenburg, Mass., June 17, 1774; s. Hon. Josiah and Mary (Carey) S.; grad. Harvard, 1797; m. Frances Whitney, 1800, at least 2 children. Apptd. dist. atty. for Middlesex County (Mass.), 1813-15, 17-32; mem. U.S. Ho. of Reps. from Mass., 14th Congress, 1815-17; rep. in Mass. Gen. Ct., 1817-18; mem. Mass. Senate, 1830-31; prof. law Harvard Law Sch., 1817-29; a commr. to make 1st revision Mass. statutes, 1832. Author: A Summary of the Law and Practice of Real Actions (series of lectures which became pioneer Am. law book), 1824; The Revised Statutes of the Commonwealth of Massachusetts (result of commn.), 1836; compiler (with Lemuel Shaw) Private and Special Statutes of . . . Massachusetts, vols. 4, 5, 1823. Died Cambridge, Mass., Feb. 5, 1839.

STEARNS, Eben Sperry, univ. chancellor; b. Bedford Mass., Dec. 23, 1819; s. Rev. Samuel Horatio and Abigail (French) S.; B.A. (hon.), Harvard, 1841, M.A. (hon.), 1846; m. Ellen Kuhn, Aug. 27, 1854; m. 2d, Betty Irwin, 1880; at least 4 children. Prin. Newburyport (Mass.) Female High Sch., 1846-49, Albany (N.Y.) Female Acad., 1855-69; 1st pres. Robinson Female Acad., Exeter, N.H., 1869; 1st pres. State Normal Sch., Nashville, Tenn. (selected by Peabody Fund), 1875; chancellor U. Nashville, 1875-87, tried to raise ednl. standards throughout South. Died Nashville, Apr. 11, 1887.

STEARNS, George Luther, anti-slavery leader; b. Medford, Mass., Jan. 8, 1809; s. Luther and Mary (Hall) S.; m. Mary Train, Jan. 31, 1836; m. 2d, Mary L. Preston, Oct. 12, 1843. A leader in movement that put Charles Sumner in U.S. Senate, 1851; raised subscription to equip free state forces in Kan. with Sharpe's rifles, 1856, mad John Brown agt. to receive arms and ammunition for defense of Kan., 1857; maj., recruited many negro soldiers for Mass. regts. in Civil War, 1862-64; founder Right Way (paper supporting radical Republican policies), 1865. Died N.Y.C., Apr. 9, 1867; buried Mt. Auburn Cemetery, Cambridge, Mass.

STEARNS, John Newton, temperance reformer; b.New Ipswich, N.H., May 24, 1829; m. Matilda Loring, 1854. An original mem. Order Sons of Temperance, 1848; purchased Merry's Museum, (children's magazine), 1853; chosen publishing agt. of Nat. Temperance Soc., 1865; became editor Nat. Temperance Advocate, 1866; given highest office in Sons of Temperance, 1866; edited Nat. Temperance Almanac and Teetotaler's Year Book for 27 years; most worthy templar Supreme Council of Templars of Honor and Temperance of N. Am., 1876-78; edited Temperance Hymn-Book, 1869, The Temperance Speaker, 1869. Died Bklyn., Apr. 21, 1895.

STEARNS, Junius Brutus, artist; b. Arlington, Vt., July 2, 1810; attended N.A.D. Exhibited at N.A.D., 1838, elected asso., 1848, mem., 1849, sec., 1851-65; exhibited at Apollo Assn., 1838; went to Europe, 1849; painted portraits, also known for hist. subjects including series on George Washington. Died Bklyn., Sept. 17, 1885.

STEARNS, Oliver, clergyman, profl. sch. dean; b. Lunenburg, Mass., June 3, 1807; s. Maj. Thomas and Priscilla (Cushing) S.; grad. Harvard, 1826, A.M. and D.D. (hon.); grad. Harvard Divinity Sch., 1830; m. Mary Blood Sterling, May 14, 1832; m. 2d, Augusta Carey, July 2, 1872; 8 children. Ordained as pastor 2d Congregational Soc. (Unitarian), Northampton, Mass., 1839; pastor 3d Congl. Soc., Hingham, Mass., 1840-56, successful in reconciling Unitarianism with Transcendentalism; pres. Meadville (Pa.) Theol. Sch., 1856; apptd. Parkman prof. pulpit eloquence Harvard Divinity Sch., 1863, modernized Unitarian tradition of sch., taught systematic theology and ethics, dean, 1870-78. Author: The Gospel as Applied to the Fugitive Slave Law, 1851; also articles "Peace Through Conflict" (Monthly Religious Mag.), 1851, "The Aim and Hope of Jesus" (Christianity and Modern Thought), 1872. Died Cambridge, Mass., July 18, 1885.

STEARNS, Ozora Pierson, senator, jurist; b. De Kalb, St. Lawrence County, N.Y., Jan. 15, 1831; attended Oberlin Coll.; grad. U. Mich., 1858, grad. law dept., 1860. Admitted to bar, 1860, practiced law, Rochester, Minn.; elected pros. atty. Olmstead County, 1861; mayor Rochester, 1866-68; served as lt. 9th Regt., Minn. Volunteer Inf. in U.S. Army during Civil War, also col. 39th Regt., U.S. Colored Troops, until 1865; mem. U.S. Senate (Republican, filled vacancy) from Minn., Jan. 23-Mar. 3, 1871; moved to Duluth, Minn., 1872, practiced law; judge Minn. 11th Jud. Dist., 1874-95; regent U. Minn., 1890-95. Died Pacific Beach, Cal., June 2, 1896; remains cremated in Los Angeles, ashes interred Forest Hill Cemetery, Duluth.

STEARNS, Shubal, clergyman; b. Boston, Jan. 28, 1706; s. Shubal and Rebecca (Lairabee or Lariby) S.; m. Sarah Johnson, Mar. 27, 1727. Came under influence of Great Awakening, 1745, attached himself to New Lights (Separatists) and became preacher among them; ordained to ministry Baptist Ch. by Rev. Wait Palmer, 1751; preached in New Eng. area, 1751-53; with several married couples moved to Opequon Creek, 1753, then Cacapon, Va., finally settled in Sandy Creek, N.C., became pastor Baptist Ch., Sandy Creek, 1755-71; as preaching evangelist he greatly influenced growth of Bapt. faith in Carolinas, Ga., Va.; paved way for union of Regular and Separatist Bapts., producing blend of Calvinistic orthodoxy and evangelistic fervor. Died Nov. 20, 1771.

STEARNS, William Augustus, clergyman, coll. pres.; b. Bedford, Mass., Mar. 17, 1805; s. Rev. Samuel Horatio and Abigail (French) S.; grad. Harvard, 1827; attended Andover Theol. Sem.; m. Rebecca Frazar, Jan. 10, 1832; m. 2d, Olive Gilbert, Aug. 1857; 6 children including Frazar Augustus. Ordained to ministry Congregational Ch., 1831; pastor congregation, Cambridgeport, Mass., until 1854; pres. Amherst (Mass.) Coll., 1854-76, strengthened and enlarged curriculum; mem. Mass. Bd. Edn.; trustee Phillips Acad., Andover Theol. Sem.; influential in counsels of Am. Bd. Commrs. for Fgn. Missions. Author: Life of Rev. Samuel H. Stearns, 3d and enlarged edit., 1846. Died Amherst, June 8, 1876.

STEBBINS, Emma, sculptor; b. N.Y.C., Sept. 1, 1815; studied sculpture under Paul Akers, Rome, Italy, 1860's. Produced amateur portraits of assos. and friends, before 1857; lived and sculpted in Rome, 1857-70, became friends with Charlotte Cushman, Harriet Hosmer; completed statue Angel of the Waters (installed in Central Park, N.Y.C.); edited letters of actress Charlotte Cushman. Died N.Y.C., Oct. 25, 1882.

STEBBINS, Henry George, congressman; b. Ridgefield, Conn., Sept. 15, 1811; attended pvt. schs. Moved to N.Y., became banker; col. 12th Regt.; pres. Dramatic Fund Assn., Acad. of Music; mem. U.S. Ho. of Reps. (War Democrat) from N.Y., 38th Congress, 1863-Oct. 24, 1864 (resigned); became stock broker; pres. N.Y. Stock Exchange; apptd. pres. Central Park Commn.; chmn. Com. of Seventy. Died N.Y.C., Dec. 9, 1881; buried Greenwood Cemetery, Bklyn.

STEBBINS, Horatio, clergyman; b. South Wilbraham, Mass., Aug. 8, 1821; s. Calvin and Amelia (Adams) S.; grad. Harvard, 1848, attended Div. Sch., 1848-51; m. Mary Ann Fisher, June 3, 1851; m. 2d, Lucy Ward, Nov. 9, 1876; 5 children. Ordained to ministry Unitarian Ch., 1851, worked under Rev. Calvin Lincoln at Unitarian Ch., Fitchburg, Mass.; worked under Dr. Ichabod Nichols at First Ch., Portland, Me., 1855, became pastor after Nichols' death, 1859-64; accepted call to succeed Thomas Starr King as pastor Unitarian Ch., San Francisco, 1864; trustee Coll. of Cal., San Francisco, 1865, soon became pres. bd. trustees; supported establishment of state univ., partly responsible for liberal arts dept. in Agrl., Mining, and Mech. Arts Coll.; a friend and adviser of Leland Stanford, helped in establishing Stanford U., became a trustee; resigned pastorate and returned East, 1900. Died Cambridge, Mass., Apr. 8, 1902.

STEBBINS, Rufus Phineas, clergyman; b. Wilbraham, Mass., Mar. 3, 1810; s. Luther and Lucina (Stebbins) S.; grad. Amherst Coll., 1834; attended Harvard Divinty Sch., 3 years; D.D. (hon.), Harvard; m. Eliza Livermore, Sept. 11, 1837. Ordained pastor Congregational Ch., Leominster, Mass., 1837; 1st pres. Theol. Sch. of Meadville, Pa., 1844; pastor Meadville Unitarian Ch., 1844-49, pastor, Woburn, Mass., 1857-63; pres. Am. Unitarian Assn., 1863, sec., 1865; took charge Unitarian Ch., Ithaca, N.Y., 1871-78; organized Unitarian Ch., Newton Center, Mass., 1878-85; opposed the German higher criticism. Author: Academic Culture, 1851; Study of the Pentateuch, 1881; contbr. article to Christian Examiner, Christian Palladium, Christian Repository. Died Cambridge, Mass., Aug. 13, 1885.

STECK, George, piano mfr.; b. Cassel, Germany, July 19, 1829; at least 2 children. Came to U.S., 1853; founder George Steck & Co., piano makers, N.Y.C., 1857, specialized in designing scales for pianos; awarded 1st prize of merit for pianoforte at Grand Vienna Exhbn., 1873; ret. from bus., 1887; experimented in constructing piano which would stay permanently in tune, 1887-97. Died N.Y.C., Mar. 31, 1897.

STEDMAN, William, congressman, lawyer; b. Cambridge, Mass., Jan. 21, 1765; grad. Harvard, 1784; studied law. Admitted to bar, 1787, practiced in Lancaster, Charlestown, Worcester; apptd. justice of peace, 1790; clk. Town of Lancaster, 1795-1800; mem. Mass. Ho. of Reps., 1802; exec. chancellor Lancaster, 1803-07; mem. U.S. Ho. of Reps. (Federalist) from Mass., 8th-11th congresses, 1803-July 16, 1810 (resigned); clk. Worcester County Cts., 1810-16; moved to Newburyport, Essex County, Mass. Died Newburyport, Aug. 31, 1831; buried Old Hill Burying Ground.

STEEDMAN, Charles, naval officer; b. Parish of St. James, Santee, S.C., Sept: 20, 1811; s. Charles John and Mary (Blake) S.; m. Sarah Bishop, Feb. 7, 1843, 6 children. Commd. midshipman U.S. Navy, 1828, passed midshipman, 1834, advanced through grades to rear adm., 1871; served in naval operations on Gulf Coast during Mexican War; ordered to duty in Chesapeake Bay, 1861; commanded ship Bienville, participated in Port Royal expdn., 1861; served in ship Paul Jones, 1862, reduced batteries on St. John's Bluff, Fla.; commanded ship Ticonderoga in cruise against Confederate raiders, 1863; participated in attacks on Ft. Fisher (N.C.); in charge oston Navy Yard, 1869-72, South Pacific Squadron, 1872-73; ret., 1873. Died Nov. 13, 1890.

STEEDMAN, James Blair, army officer, state ofcl.; b. Northumberland County, Pa., July 29, 1817; s. Mellum and Margaret (Blair) S.; m. Miranda Stiles, 1838; m. 2d, Rose Barr; m. 3d, Margaret Gildea. Became mem. Ohio Legislature, 1847; del. to numerous Democratic convs.; commd. col. 14th Ohio Inf., 1861, brig. gen. U.S. Volunteers, 1862; commanded div. which came to rescue of George Henry Thomas at Battle of Chickamauga; maj. gen. volunteers, 1864, served at Battle of Nashville; resigned commn., 1866; collector internal revenue New Orleans, 1866-69; editor No. Ohio Democrat; mem. Ohio Senate; chief of police Toledo (O.). Died Toledo, Oct. 18, 1883.

STEELE, Frederick, army officer; b. Delhi, N.Y., Jan. 14, 1819; s. Nathaniel Steele; grad. U.S. Mil. Acad., July 1, 1843. Commd. 2d lt., 2d Inf., U.S. Army, 1843, served in Mexican War. Twice brevetted for gallant conduct; promoted 1st lt.. 1848; served as maj. 11th Inf., 1855-61, col. 8th Ia. Inf., 1861-62; commd. brig. gen., then maj. gen. U.S. Volunteers, 1862; served in Ark., Vicksburg and Mobile campaigns; in command Dept. of Columbia, 1865-68; commd. lt. col. U.S. Army, 1863, col., 1866. Died San Mateo, Cal., Jan. 12, 1868.

STEELE, George W., architect; b. Va., 1798; married, 1823, children—Mathew, George, John, Angelo. Became architect and builder, Huntsville, Ala., after 1833; operated brick kilns which furnished much of brick for his structures, also operated cotton mill, Huntsville, until 1835; highly successful in adapting Greek Revival style to domestic and public architecture; credited with design of many mansions in Huntsville, including his home "Oak Place," also with public bldgs. including First Nat. Bank Bldg., Madison County Court House. Died 1842.

STEELE, Joel Dorman, educator; b. Lima, N.Y., May 14, 1836; s. Rev. Allen and Sabra (Dorman) S.; grad. Genesee Coll. (now Syracuse U.), 1858; m. Esther Baker, July 7, 1859. Taught in dist. schs. to finance his coll. edn.; instr., then prin. Mexico (N.Y.) Acad., 1858-61; raised 81st N.Y. Volunteers, 1861, capt.; wounded at Battle of Seven Pines, 1862, forced out of war; prin. high school, Newark, N.J., 1863-66, Elmira Free Acad., 1866-72; did not use regular textbooks, substituted his own outlines which grew into his Fourteen Weeks series of texts (1st published 1867); at request of Alfred Cutler Barnes, his friend and publisher, devoted rest of life to writing textbooks, 1872-86. Author: Barnes Brief History Series (most famous: A Brief History of the United States for Schools, 1871). Died May 25, 1886.

STEELE, John, congressman; b. Salisbury, N.C., Nov. 1, 1764; s. William Gillespie and Elizabeth (Maxwell) Steel (or Steele); m. Mary Nesfield, Feb. 9, 1783, at least 3 children. Assessor, Town of Salisbury, 1784, town commr., 1787; mem. N.C. Ho. of Commins, 1788, 94, 95, 1806; 11-13-speaker, 1811; commr. to negotiate with Cherokee and Chickasaw Indians, 1788; Federalist mem. conv. to consider U.S. Constn., Hillsboro, N.C., 1788; del. Fayetteville (N.C.) Conv. which ratified U.S. Constn., 1789; mem. U.S. Ho. of Reps. from N.C., 1st, 2d congresses, 1789-93; maj. gen. N.C. Militia, 1794; comptroller U.S. Treasury (apptd.) by George Washington, 1796-1802; mem. commn. to determine boundary between N.C. and S.C., 1805, 14. Died Salisbury, Aug. 14, 1815.

STEELE, John Benedict, congressman; b. Delhi, N.Y., Mar. 28, 1814; attended Delaware Acad., Delhi; grad. in law Williams Coll. Admitted to Otsego County bar, 1839, practiced in Cooperstown, N.Y.; dist. atty. Otsego County, 1841-47; moved to Kingston, N.Y., 1847; elected spl. judge Ulster County, 1850; mem. U.S. Ho. of Reps. (Democrat) from N.Y., 37th-38th congresses, 1861-65. Accidentally killed in Rondout, nr. Kingston, Sept. 24, 1866; buried Wiltwyck Cemetery, Kingston.

STEELE, John Nevett, congressman; b. Weston, Dorchester County, Md., Feb. 22, 1796; completed prep. studies; studied law. Admitted to bar, 1819, practiced in Dorchester County, Md.; mem. Md. Ho. of Dels., 1822-24, 29-30; mem. U.S. Ho. of Reps. (Whig, filled vacancy) from Md., 23d-24th congresses, May 29, 1834-37; unsuccessful Whig candidate for gov. Md., 1838; became farmer. Died Cambridge, Md., Aug. 13, 1853; buried Christ Protestant Episcopal Ch. Cemetery.

STEELE, Walter Leak, congressman; b. Steeles Mill (later Littles Mills), nr. Rockingham, Richmond County, N.C., Apr. 18, 1823; attended Randolph-Macon Coll., Wake Forest Coll.; grad. U. N.C., 1844; studied law. Mem. N.C. Ho. of Commons, 1846, 48, 50, 54; trustee U. N.C., 1852-91; mem. N.C. Senate, 1852, 58; del. Democratic nat. convs., Charleston, Balt., 1860; sec. N.C. Conv. which passed ordinance of secession, 1861; admitted to bar, 1865, practiced in Rockingham; Dem. presdl. elector, 1876; mem. U.S. Ho. of Reps. (Dem.) from N.C., 45th-46th congresses, 1877-81; became cotton mfr., banker. Died Balt., Oct. 16, 1891; buried Leak Cemetery, nr. Rockingham.

STEELE, William Gaston, congressman; b. Somerville, Somerset County, N.J., Dec. 17, 1820; attended public schs., Somerville Acad. Became banker; mem. U.S. Ho. of Reps. (Democrat) from N.J., 37th-38th congresses, 1861-65; became broker. Died Somerville, Apr. 22, 1892; buried Somerville City Cemetery.

STEENDAM, Jacob, eulogist, poet; b. The Netherlands, 1616; m. Sara de Rosschou. Settled in New Netherland as mcht., 1652; contbr. to fund raised for defense of New Amsterdam against the Indians, 1653, 55; orphan master, 1655; became 1st poet of New Netherland, poems praised the advantages of the Dutch colony and sought support from mother country. Author: Den Distelvink (poems), 3 vols., 1649-50; "Complaint of New Amsterdam in New Netherland to Her Mother," 1659; T Lof van Nuw Nederland, 1661. Died 1672.

STEENROD, Lewis, congressman, lawyer; b. nr. Wheeling, Va. (now W.Va.), May 27, 1810; attended common schs.; studied law. Admitted to bar, 1835, practiced in Wheeling; mem. U.S. Ho. of Reps. (Democrat) from Va., 26th-28th congresses, 1839-45; mem. Va. Senate, 1853-56. Died nr. Wheeling, Oct. 3, 1862; buried Stone Ch. Cemetery, Elm Grove, W.Va.

STEENWYCK, Cornelis, mayor, mcht.; b. Holland; m. Margaretha de Rieiner, June 5, 1658, 7 children. Resident of New Amsterdam (now N.Y.C.), 1651, successful mcht.; became burgomaster New Amsterdam, 1662, commr. to negotiate with English over status of New Netherland, 1664; mem. New Netherland Gov.'s Adv. Council under English, circa 1670; mayor N.Y.C., 1668-70, 82-83, presided over ct. gen. sessions, 1682-83; prominent in govt. of colony when returned to Dutch control, 1670's, and later when restored to English control, 1680's; elder Dutch Reformed Ch.; one of wealthiest men in colony. Died 1684.

STEERS, George, naval architect; b. Washington, D.C., July 20, 1820; s. Henry Steer. never married; Built fast pilot schooner Mary Taylor (radically new design), 1849; managed boatyard Hathorn & Steers on Williamsburg side East River, N.Y.C., 1845-49; built (with brother James) many fast vessels including steamship Adriatic, warship Niagara (helped lay 1st transatlantic cable), 1849; built pleasure craft, most famous was the America, sailed in race around Isle of Wight, 1851, revolutionized yacht design in U.S. and fgn. countries. Died Great Neck, L.I. N.Y., Sept. 25, 1856.

STEINER, Lewis Henry, physician, librarian; b. Frederick, Md., May 4, 1827; s. Christian and Rebecca (Weltzheimer) S.; grad. Marshall Coll., Mercersburg, Pa., 1846; M.D., U. Pa., 1849; m. Sarah Smyth, Oct. 30, 1866, 6 children including Bernard Christian. Prof. chemistry, natural history Columbian Coll., Washington, D.C.; prof. chemistry, pharmacy Nat. Med. Coll., Washington, 1853-55; lectr. on chemistry, physics Coll. of St. James, Hagerstown, Md., 1854-59; lectr. on applied chemistry Md. Inst., 1855, 56; a reorganizer of Md. Coll. Pharmacy, 1856. prof. chemistry, 1856-61; asst. editor Am. Med. Monthly, N.Y.C., 1859-61; served with U.S. Sanitary Commn. in Civil War; chief of sanitation Army of Potomac, 1863-64; pres. Frederick County Sch. Bd., 1865, aided in providing sch. facilities for Negro children; mem. Md. Senate (Republican), 1871-83; polit. editor Frederick Examiner, 1873-84; librarian Enoch Pratt Free Library, Balt., 1886-92; mem. Potomac Synod of Reformed Ch.; mem. Md. Acad. Science, A.A.A.S., a founder Am. Acad. Medicine, 1876, pres., 1878. Author: translations from the German of a number of children's stories, including Adventures of Leo Rembrandt, 1869; Outlines of Chemical Analysis (Heinrich Will); collaborator (on hymn book) Cantate Domino, 1859. Died Feb. 18, 1892.

STEINWAY, Christian Friedrich Theodore, piano mfr.; b. Seesen, Germany, Nov. 6, 1825; s. Henry Engelhard and Juliane (Thiemer) S.; attended Jacobsohn Coll., Seesen; m. Johanna Luederman, Oct. 10, 1852. Partner piano mfg. firm, Germany, used scientific principles to build pianos to meet demand of masters, 1852-65; came to N.Y.C., 1865, took charge constrn. factory dept. Steinway & Sons, investigated, tested relative qualities of various woods, continued study of chemistry to determine best ingredients of glue, varnish, oils, experimented in metallurgy to find proper alloy for casting iron plates strong enough for heavy strain, remained in N.Y.C., 1865-70, asso. with Am. firm until 1889. Died Brunswick, Germany, Mar. 26, 1889.

STEINWAY, Henry Engelhard, (original name Steinweg legally changed 1864), piano mfr.; b. Wolfshagen, Duchy of Brunswick, North Germany, Feb. 15, 1797; m. Juliane Thiemer, Feb. 1825; children—Christian Friedrich Theodore, Doretta, Charles, Henry, Wilhelmina, William, Albert. Served in Napoleonic War, 1815; became organ maker, 1818; organist, village ch., Seesen, Germany, 1818-20; made his 1st piano, circa 1825; recipient Gold medal for piano manufacture Brunswick Fair, 1839; came to U.S., 1851; founder piano mfg. firm Steinway & Sons, 1853, gradually expanded bus. into various kinds of pianos, received numerous awards; built Steinway Hall, N.Y.C., 1867. Died N.Y.C., Feb. 7, 1871.

STEINWAY, William, piano mfr.; b. Seesen, Germany, Mar. 5, 1835; s. Henry Engelhard and Juliane (Thiemer) S.; ed. Jacobsohn Coll., Seesen; m. Johanna Roos, Apr. 23, 1861; m. 2d, Elizabeth Raupt, Aug. 16, 1880; 5 children. Came with family to U.S., 1851; apprentice in piano mfg. William Nunns & Co., 1851-53; joined father's firm, 1853, took over mgmt., 1865, pres. Steinway & Sons, Inc., 1876-96; influential in opening Steinway Hall, N.Y.C., 1867, London, Eng., 1876; subsidized various concert artists in Am.; conducted aggressive advt. campaign to sell pianos; established factory, Hamburg, Germany, 1880; 1st chmn. Rapid Transit Commn. which planned 1st subway in N.Y.C.; founder Town of Steinway (L.I., N.Y.). Died N.Y.C., Nov. 30, 1896.

STEPHENS, Abraham P., congressman; b. nr. New City, Rockland County, N.Y., Feb. 18, 1796. Justice of peace; mem. U.S. Ho. of Reps. (Democrat) from N.Y., 32d Congress, 1851-53. Died Nyack, Rockland County, Nov. 25, 1859; buried Oak Hill Cemetery.

STEPHENS, Alexander Hamilton, Confederate govt. ofcl., congressman; b. Wilkes County (later Taliaferro County), Ga., Feb. 11, 1812; s. Andrew and Margaret (Grier) S.; grad. U. Ga., 1832. Admitted to Ga. bar, 1834; elected to Ga. Legislature, 1836-40, 42; mem. U.S. Ho. of Reps. from Ga., 28th-35th congresses, 1843-59, opposed dispatch of troops to Rio Grande in 1846, Wilmot Proviso and Clayton Compromise, 1848, supported Compromise of 1850 while proclaiming right of secession of any state; always Whig by convenience, repudiated Whig nat. ticket, 1852, joined Democratic party soon after; friend of Stephen Douglas, supported Kan.-Neb. Act of 1854, had major role in securing its passage in Congress; defended slavery in many speeches in 1850's; following election of Lincoln in 1860 urged moderation and secession only as last resort; as del. from Ga. attended convention in Montgomery (Ala.) to frame constn. for Confederacy, elected v.p. of Confederacy by Provisional Congress, Feb. 9, 1861, became leader opposition to Davis government, against conscription, suspension of habeas corpus, and local mil. govts.; attempted peace negotiations with Lincoln, June 1863, met Lincoln and Seward near Fortress Monroe but unable to agree on peace terms, Feb. 3, 1865; elected to U.S. Senate, Jan. 1866, denied entrance; denied power of Fed. Govt. to enfranchise Negroes; purchased interest in newspaper The Southern Sun, 1871, opposing fusion of Liberal Republicans and Democrats in 1872; elected to United States House of Representatives from Ga., 43d-47th congresses, 1873-82; elected gov. of Ga., 1882; published A Constitutional View of the Late War Between the States, 1870, expounding doctrines of state sovereignty; wrote sch. history A Compendium of the History of The United States, 1872. Died Atlanta, Ga., Mar. 4, 1883.

STEPHENS, Ann Sophia, author, editor; b. Derby, Conn., 1813; d. John and Ann Winterbottam; m. Edward Stephens, 1831, 2 children. Established (with husband) Portland Mag. (literary monthly), 1834-36, contbd. a large part of its poems, sketches, literary content; edited The Portland Sketch Book, 1836; asso. editor N.Y. Ladies' Companion, 1837; an editor Graham's Mag., 1842; work published in numerous mags. during 1840's; asso. with what later became Peterson's Mag., 1843-86; undertook own mag. Mrs. Stephen's Illustrated New Monthly, 1856-58; published more than 25 books, also serials, poems, articles, 1854-80. Author: Fashion and Famine, 1854; The Rejected Wife, 1863. Died Newport, R.I., Aug. 20, 1886.

STEPHENS, John Lloyd, transp. exec.; b. Shrewsbury, N.J., Nov. 28, 1805; s. Benjamin and Clemence (Lloyd) S.; grad. Columbia, 1822; attended Litchfield (Conn.) Law Sch. Admitted to N.Y. State bar, 1825, retired from law practice to travel abroad, 1834; known as "the American traveler"; sent as Democrat on diplomatic mission to C.Am. by Van Buren, 1839, observed ancient civilizations which became basis of his writings on subject; dir. Ocean Steam Navigation Co.; active supporter Hudson River R.R.; promoter Panama R.R., elected v.p. co., 1849, became pres., circa 1851; mem. N.Y. Constl. Conv., 1846. Author: Incidents of Travel in Egypt, Arabia, Petraea and the Holy Land, 2 vols., 1837; Incidents of Travel in Greece, Turkey, Russia and Poland, 2 vols., 1838; Incidents of Travel in

Central America, Chiapas and Yucatan, 2 vols., 1841. Died N.Y.C., Oct. 12, 1852.

STEPHENS, Linton, legislator; b. nr. Crawfordville, Ga., July 1, 1823; s. Andrew Baskins and Matilda S. (Lindsey) S.; grad. Franklin Coll. (now part of U. Ga.), 1843; LL.B., U. Va., 1845; m. Emmeline (Thomas) Bell, Jan. 1852; m. 2d, Mary W. Salter, June 1867. Admitted to Ga. bar, 1846; mem. Ga. Legislature (Whig) from Taliaferro County, 1849-52, 63-64, opposed conscription and suspension of writ of habeas corpus, 1863, introduced resolutions justifying Confederacy and peace resolutions of 1864; mem. Ga. Senate from Hancock County, 1853-55, opposed Kan.-Neb. Bill; del. Democratic Nat. Conv., Cincinnati, 1856, helped write Ga. Dem. platform of 1857; del. So. Comml. Conv., 1858, advocated secession unless Kan. was admitted as slave state; apptd. judge Ga. Supreme Ct., 1859, resigned, 1860; mem. Ga. Conv. of 1861 which voted against secession; raised a company at beginning of Civil War; commd. lt. col. 15th Ga. Volunteers on duty in Va., 1861-62; col. Ga. Cavalry, 1863; made speech which vigorously opposed Southern support for Horace Greeley, Atlanta, Ga. 1872. Died July 14, 1872; buried Sparta, Ga; reinterred "Liberty Hall," nr. Crawfordville.

STEPHENS, Philander, congressman; b. nr. Montrose, Susquehanna County, Pa., 1788; had limited edn. Became farmer, mcht.; coroner, 1815; county commr., 1818; sheriff, 1821; mem. Pa. Ho. of Reps., 1824, 25; mem. U.S. Ho. of Reps. (Jacksonian Democrat) from Pa., 21st-22d congresses, 1829-33. Died probably Springville, Susquehanna County, July 8, 1842; buried Stephens Burying Ground, Dimock Twp., Susquehanna County.

STEPHENS, Uriah Smith, labor union ofcl.; b. nr. Cape May, N.J., Aug. 3, 1821; indentured to a tailor; studied econs. with J.L. Lenhardt, others. Taught sch. in N.J. for short time, then moved to Phila., 1845; began traveling through West Indies, C. Am., Mexico, 1853, spent 5 years in Cal., returned to Phila., active in influencing workers to move West; an abolitionist, supported Fremont in 1856, Lincoln in 1860; pres. nat. conv. workingmen opposed to Civil War, 1861; an organizer Garment Cutters' Assn. Phila., 1862; co-founder Noble Order Knights of Labor, 1869, resigned as grand master workman, 1879; advocated union policies of secret ritual, union of all trades, promotion of edn. and cooperation, boycott rather than strike; unsuccessful Greenback candidate for Congress from 5th Dist. Pa., 1878. Mason, Odd Fellow, K.P. Died Phila., Feb. 13, 1882.

STEPHENSON, Benjamin, congressman; b. Ky. Moved to Ill. Territory, 1809, settled in Randolph County; apptd. 1st sheriff Randolph County by Gov. Edwards, 1809; moved to Edwardsville, Ill., became mcht.; apptd. adjutant gen. Ill. Territory, 1813; served as col. in 2 campaigns during War of 1812; mem. U.S. Congress (Democrat) from Ill. Territory, 13th-14th congresses; receiver public moneys Land Office, Edwardsville, 1816-22; del. conv. to frame 1st Ill. Constn., 1818; pres. Bank of Edwardsville, 1819. Died Edwardsville, Oct. 10, 1822.

STEPHENSON, Benjamin Franklin, physician, assn. founder; b. Wayne County, Ill., Oct. 3, 1823; s. James and Margaret (Clinton) S.; grad. Rush Med. Coll., Chgo., 1850; m. Barbara B. Moore, Mar. 30, 1855, at least 3 children. Lectr. on gen., spl., surg. anatomy in med. dept. State U. of Ia., Keokuk, 1855-57; joined 14th Ill. Volunteers, 1861, regtl. surgeon, mustered out, 1864; a founder Grand Army of Republic (nat. assn. Union vets.), organized Post Number 1, Decatur, Ill., 1866, issued the call for a nat. conv. to meet at Indianapolis, Ind., 1866, became adjutant-gen.; monument erected in his honor, Washington, D.C., 1909. Died Aug. 30, 1871.

STEPHENSON, James, congressman; b. Gettysburg, Pa., Mar. 20, 1764. Moved to Martinsburg, Va. (now W.Va.); volunteer rifleman under Gen. St. Clair in Indian expdn., 1791; brigade insp.; mem. Va. Ho. of Dels., 1800-03, 06-07; mem. U.S. Ho. of Reps. (Federalist, filled vacancy) from Va., 8th, 11th, 17th-18th congresses, 1803-05, 09-11, Oct. 28, 1822-25. Died Martinsburg, Aug. 7, 1833.

STEPHENSON, John, mfr.; b. County Armagn, Ireland, July 4, 1809; s. James and Grace (Stuart) S.; attended Wesleyan Sem.; m. Julia A. Tiemann, 1833, 3 children. Opened shop for repair of all kinds vehicles, 1831, conceived, built 1st omnibus or horse-car made in N.Y.C.; employed to build horse-drawn car for new N.Y. & Harlem R.R. (1st car for 1st street railway in world), 1831; largest street-car builder in world, made horse cars, cable, electric, open cars; 1st patent granted, 1833; factory produced carriages and pontoons for U.S. Govt. during Civil War. Died New Rochelle, N.Y., July 31, 1893; buried Beechwood Cemetery, New Rochelle.

STERETT, Andrew, naval officer; b. Balt., Jan. 27, 1778; s. John and Deborah (Ridgley) S. Commd. lt. U.S. Navy, 1798; exec. officer frigate Constellation at capture of Insurgente; given command schooner Enterprise, 1800, captured L'amour de la Patrie in West Indies, 1800; commanded the Enterprise during Tripolitan War in Mediterranean, 1801, greatest exploit was capture of ship Tripoli due to superior maneuvering, 1801; received a commendation and a sword from U.S. Congress; promoted master comdt., placed in command of brig under constrn., Balt.; resigned to enter U.S. Mcht. Marine, 1805; U.S. destroyer named for him. Died Lima, Peru, Jan. 9, 1807.

STERETT, Samuel, congressman; b. Carlisle, Pa., 1758; grad. U. Pa. Held several local offices, Balt.; mem. independent mil. co. of Balt. mchts., 1777; apptd. pvt. sec. to pres. of Congress, 1782; mem. Md. Senate, 1789; mem. U.S. Ho. of Reps. (Anti-Federalist) from Md., 2d Congress, 1791-93; sec. Md. Soc. for Promoting Abolition of Slavery, 1791; mem. Balt. Com. of Safety, 1812; served as capt. independent company at Battle of North Point, 1814; wounded at Battle of Bladensburg; grand marshal at laying of found. stone of B. & O. R.R., 1828. Died Balt., July 12, 1833; buried burying ground Westminster Ch.

STERIGERE, John Benton, congressman; b. Upper Dublin Twp., nr. Ambler, Montgomery County, Pa., July 31, 1793; studied law. Worked on farm; taught at Puffs Ch. Sch.; apptd. justice of peace, 1818; mem. Pa. Ho. of Reps., 1821-24; admitted to bar, 1829, practiced in Norristown, Pa.; mem. U.S. Ho. of Reps. (Democrat) from Pa., 20th-21st congresses, 1827-31; del. Pa. Constl. Conv., 1838; mem. Pa. Senate, 1839, 43-46; del. Nat. Dem. Conv., Balt., 1852; retired from public life; editor Register; apptd. chmn. commn. to improve Town of Norristown by Pa. Assembly. Died Norristown, Oct. 13, 1852; buried Upper Dublin Lutheran Ch. Cemetery, Ambler.

STERLING, Ansel, congressman, jurist; b. Lyme, New London County, Conn., Feb. 3, 1782; attended common schs.; studied law. Admitted to bar, 1805, practiced in Salisbury, Conn.; moved to Sharon, Litchfield County, Conn., 1808, practiced law; mem. Conn. Ho. of Reps., 1815, 18-21, 25-26, 29, 35-37, clk., 1815, 18-20; mem. U.S. Ho. of Reps. from Conn., 17th-18th congresses, 1821-25; chief justice Litchfield County Ct. Common Pleas, 1838-40. Died Sharon, Nov. 6, 1853; buried Sharon Burying Ground.

STERLING, James, clergyman; b. Dowrass, Ireland, 1701; son of James Sterling; grad. Trinity Coll., Dublin, Ireland, 1720, M.A., 1733; married 3 times; m. 2d, Rebecca Holt, Sept. 19, 1743; m. 3d, Mary Smith, Sept. 7, 1749; at least 1 child, Rebecca. Became a playwright; ordained priest Anglican Ch., 1733; came to Am., 1737; rector All Hallows Parish, Anne Arundel County, Md., also St. Ann's, Annapolis, Md., 1737-40; rector St. Paul's, Kent County, Md., 1740-63; returned briefly to Gt. Britain, 1752; collector of customs Chester, Md., 1752-63. Author: (plays) Rival Generals, 1722, Parricide, 1736; (poetry) The Loves of Hero and Leander (translated from Musaeus), 1728, Poetical Works of Rev. James Sterling, 1734; An Epistle to the Hon. Arthur Dobbs, 1748. Died Nov. 10, 1763.

STERLING, John Whalen, educator; b. Blackwalnut, Wyoming County, Pa., July 17, 1816; s. Daniel and Rachel (Brooks) S.; grad. Princeton, 1840, attended Princeton Theol. Sem., 1841-44; m. Harriet Dean, Sept. 3, 1851, 8 children. Prin., Wilkes-Barre (Pa.) Acad., 1841; tutor Coll. of N.J. (now Princeton); taught at Carroll Coll., 1846; opened pvt. school, Waukesha, Wis., 1847; prof. mathematics, natural philosophy and astronomy U. Wis., 1849, also prin: preparatory dept., acting chancellor, 1859, chief adminstrv. officer and dean until 1865, vice chancellor, v.p., 1869-85, prof. emeritus, 1883; Sterling Hall (U. Wis.) named in his honor, 1921. Died Mar. 9, 1885.

STERLING, Micah, congressman, lawyer; b. Lyme, Conn., Nov. 5, 1784; grad. Yale, 1804; studied law Litchfield (Conn.) Law Sch. Admitted to bar, 1809, practiced in Adams, Jefferson County, N.Y.; moved to Watertown, N.Y., 1809, practiced law; held several local offices; treas. Village of Watertown, 1816; dir. Jefferson County Bank; mem. U.S. Ho. of Reps. (Federalist) from N.Y., 17th Congress, 1821-23; mem. N.Y. State Senate, 1836-39. Died Watertown, Apr. 11, 1844; buried Brookside Cemetery.

STETEFELDT, Carl August, metallurgist; b. Holzhausen, Gotha, Germany, Sept. 28, 1838; s. August Heinrich Christian and Friederika Christiane (Credner) S.; grad. U. Gottingen (Germany), 1862; m. Dec. 31, 1872. Came to U.S., 1863; asst. to Charles A. Joy (prof. chemistry Columbia), N.Y.C.; asst. to cons. firm Aedlberg & Raymond, 1864; partner (with John H. Bialt) assay office and cons. bus., Austin, Nev., 1865; builder 1st lead blast furnace in dist. of Eureka (Nev.); designer Stetefeldt furnace (a metall. advance in processing sulphide ores containing gold and silver by chlorination process); v.p. Am. Inst. Mining Engrs., contbr. to inst.'s Transactions. Author: The Lexivication of Silver-ores with Hyposulphite Solutions, 1888. Died Oakland, Cal., Mar. 17, 1896.

STETSON, Charles, congressman, lawyer; b. New Ipswich, Hillsborough County, N.H., Nov. 2, 1801; attended Hampden (Me.) Acad.; grad. Yale, 1823; studied law. Admitted to bar, practiced in Hampden, 1826; admitted to U.S. Supreme Ct. bar, 1828; held various local offices; moved to Bangor, Me., 1833; judge Bangor Municipal Ct., 1834-39; mem. Bangor Common Council, 1843-44; mem. Me. Exec. Council, 1845-48; mem. U.S. Ho. of Reps. Democrat) from Me., 31st Congress, 1849-51; became affiliated with Republican Party, 1860. Died Bangor, Mar. 27, 1863; buried Mt. Hope Cemetery.

STETSON, Charles Augustus, hotel mgr.; b. Newburyport, R.I., Apr. 1, 1810; s. Prince and Hepzibeth (Patch) S.; m. Lucy Ann Brown, Mar. 14, 1832, 8 children including Charles. Employed in various capacities, Tremont House, Boston, 1829-38; mgr. Astor House, N.Y.C., 1838-68; apptd. q.m. gen. N.Y. State Militia, 1851. Died Reading, Pa., Mar. 28, 1888.

STETSON, Lemuel, congressman, lawyer; b. Champlain, Clinton County, N.Y., Mar. 13, 1804; attended Plattsburg Acad.; studied law. Admitted to bar, 1824, practiced in Keeseville, Essex County, N.Y.; mem. N.Y. State Assembly, 1835, 36, 42, 46; dist. atty. Clinton County, 1838-43; mem. U.S. Ho. of Reps. (Democrat) from N.Y., 28th Congress, 1843-45; mem. N.Y. State Constl. Conv., 1846; moved to Plattsburg, N.Y., 1847; judge Clinton County, 1847-51; del. Nat. Dem. Conv., Balt., 1860. Died Plattsburg, May 17, 1868; buried Riverside Cemetery.

STEUBEN, Friedrich Wilhelm Ludolf Gerhard Augustin von, see Von Steuben, Friedrich Wilhelm Ludolf Gerhard Augustin.

STEVENS, Aaron Fletcher, congressman; b. Londonderry, Rockingham County, N.H., Aug. 9, 1819; attended Pinkerton Acad., Derry, N.H., Crosby's Nashua (N.H.) Literary Inst.; studied law. Machinist's apprentice, journeyman for several years; admitted to bar, practiced law, Nashua; mem. N.H. Ho. of Reps., 1845, 76-84; held several local offices; served as maj. 1st Regt., N.H. Volunteer Inf. in Union Army during Civil War, also col. 13th N.H. Volunteer Inf., brevetted brig. gen.; del. Nat. Whig Conv., Balt., 1852; pres. Nashua Common Council, 1853-54; solicitor Hillsborough County, N.H., 1856-61; solicitor Nashua, 1859-60, 65, 72, 75-77; mem. U.S. Ho. of Reps. (Republican) from N.H., 40th-41st congresses, 1867-71. Died Nashua, May 10, 1887; buried Nashua Cemetery.

STEVENS, Abel, clergyman, editor, historian; b. Phila., Jan. 17, 1815; s. Samuel and Mary (Hochenmeller) S.; attended Wesleyan U.; M.A., Brown U.; LL.D. (hon.), Ind. U., 1856; m. Marguerite Bartholomew, 1838; m. 2d, Amelia Dayton, Sept. 8, 1869; m. 3d, Frances C. Greenough, 1871; at least 6 children. Admitted on trial to New Eng. Conf. Meth. Episcopal Ch., 1834, ordained elder, 1838; served Church St. Ch. and Bennet St. Ch. in Boston, 1835-37; became minister Meth. Ch., Providence, R.I., 1838; editor Zion's Herald (a Meth. Jour.), Boston, 1840-52; editor new Meth. mag. called National Mag., 1852-56; editor Christian Advocate and Jour., N.Y.C., 1855; opposed expulsion of slaveholders from ch. and to further this view N.Y. leaders in the ch. established independent jour., The Methodist, 1860, asso. editor, 1871-74. Author: The History of the Religious Movement of the Eighteenth Century Called Methodism, 1858-61; The History of the Methodist Episcopal Church in the United States, 1864-67. Died San Jose, Cal., Sept. 11, 1897.

STEVENS, Alexander Hodgdon, surgeon, coll. pres.; b. N.Y.C., Sept. 4, 1789; s. Ebenezer and Lucretia (Ledyard) S.; A.B., Yale, 1807; M.D., U. Pa., 1811; LL.D. (hon.), U. State N.Y., 1849; m. Mary Jane Bayard, 1813; m. 2d, Catherine Morris, Apr. 1825; m. 3d, Phoebe Coles Lloyd, 1841; 4 children. Prof. surgery Queens Coll. (later Rutgers U.), 1815-26; prof. surgery Coll. Physicians and Surgeons, N.Y.C., 1826-38, trustee, 1820-37, pres., 1843-55; surgeon N.Y. Hosp.; a founder N.Y. Acad. Medicine, pres., 1851; pres. A.M.A., 1848; pres. Med. Soc. State N.Y., 1849-51. Died N.Y.C., Mar. 30, 1869.

STEVENS, Bradford Newcomb, congressman; b. Boscawen, Merrimack County, N.H., Jan. 3, 1813; attended schs., N.H., also Montreal, Can.; grad. Dartmouth, 1835. Taught sch., Hopkinsville, Ky., also N.Y.C. for 6 years; moved to Bureau County, Ill., 1846, became mcht., farmer; county surveyor; mayor Tiskilwa, Ill.; mem. U.S. Ho. of Reps. (Independent Democrat) from Ill., 42d Congress, 1871-

73. Died Tiskilwa, Nov. 10, 1885; buried Mt. Bloom Cemetery.

STEVENS, Charles Abbot, congressman, mfr.; b. North Andover (then part of Andover), Essex County, Mass., Aug. 9, 1816; attended Franklin Acad., North Andover. Mfr. flannels and broadcloths, Ware, Hampshire County, Mass., 1841; mem. Mass. Ho. of Reps., 1853; del. Republican nat. convs., Chgo., 1860, 68; mem. Mass. Gov.'s Council, 1867-70; mem. U.S. Ho. of Reps. (Rep., filled vacancy) from Mass., 43d Congress, Jan. 27-Mar. 3, 1875. Died N.Y.C., Apr. 7, 1892; buried Aspen Grove Cemetery, Ware.

STEVENS, Clement Hoffman, army officer; b. Norwich, Conn., Aug. 21, 1821; s. Clement W. and Sarah J. (Fayssoux) S.; m. Annie Bee, several children. Designed and built battery on Morris Island (1st armored fortification ever constructed); elected col. 24th S.C. Inf., 1862; contributed greatly to Confederate victory at Secessionville, 1862; participated in Vicksburg Campaign, 1863; promoted brig. gen., 1864, commanded a Ga. brigade during Atlanta campaign. Killed at Battle of Peach Tree Creek (Ga.), July 25, 1864.

STEVENS, Edwin Augustus, engr., inventor; b. Hoboken, N.J., July 28, 1795; s. John and Rachel (Cox) S.; m. Mary B. Picton, 1836; m. 2d, Martha Bayard Dod, Aug. 22, 1854; 9 children including Mary Picton Stevens Garnett. Invented, patented (with Robert L. Stevens) a plow, 1821; took charge Union Stage-Coach Line (operated between N.Y.C. and Phila.), 1825, purchased it with his brothers, 1827; mgr. Camden & Amboy R.R. Transp. Co. (1st railroad in N.J.), 1830-65; invented, patented (with brother Robert) "closed fire room" system of forced draft, 1842, 1st applied on Robert's steamboat North America; interested in naval vessels, applied to Navy Dept., received permission to build an armored vessel designed by Robert, 1842; The Stevens Battery was begun in 1852, never finished; founder Stevens Inst. Tech., Hoboken. Died Paris, France, Aug. 7, 1868.

STEVENS, Elisha (also spelled Stephens), pioneer; b. circa 1805; blacksmith by trade; possibly roustabout for Eells-Walker-Gray missionary party, 1838; led a party from Council Bluffs, Ia. to Cal., using direct route following Platte, Sweetwater, Humboldt (then Mary's) and Truckee rivers to Sutter's Fort, 1844; trapper in Santa Clara County mountains; lived for 23 years as hermit, raising poultry and keeping bees, on present site of Bakersfield, Cal. Died 1884.

STEVENS, Henry, bibliographer; b. Barnet, Vt., Aug. 24, 1819; s. Henry and Candace (Salter) S.; attended Middlebury Coll., 1839; B.A., Yale, 1843; attended Harvard Law Sch., 1844; m. Mary (Newton) Kuczynski, Feb. 25, 1854, at least 1 child. Clk., Treasury Dept., U.S. Senate, Washington, D.C., 1840; helped build up collections of John Carter Brown, Providence, R.I., James Lenox, N.Y.C., Smithsonian Instn., Library of Congress; early advocate of use of photography to supplement bibliography; moved to London, Eng., 1845; agt. Brit. Mus. for procuring North and South Am. books of all kinds; expert early editions English Bible and early voyages and travels to America; fellow Soc. Antiquarians, 1852; mem. Librarians' Assn., 1877. Author: American Bibliographer, 1854; Catalogue of a Library of Works Relating to America, 1854; Catalogue of American Books in the Library of the British Museum, 1857; Bibliotheca Historica, 1870; The Bibles in the Caxton Exhibition, 1878. Died South Hampstead, Eng., Feb. 28, 1886; buried Hampstead Cemetery, London, Eng.

STEVENS, Hestor Lockhart, congressman, lawyer; b. Lima, Livingston County, N.Y., Oct. 1, 1803; attended common schs.; studied law. Admitted to bar, practiced in Rochester, N.Y.; maj. gen. Western N.Y. Militia; moved to Pontiac, Mich.; mem. U.S. Ho. of Reps. (Democrat) from Mich., 33d Congress, 1853-55; practiced in Washington, D.C. Died Georgetown, D.C., May 7, 1864; buried Oak Hill Cemetery.

STEVENS, Hiram Sanford, congressman; b. Weston, Windsor County, Vt., Mar. 20, 1832. Became a farmer; enlisted in Company I, 1st U.S. Dragoons for service in N.M., 1851; participated in engagements against Apaches, 1852, 54; discharged at Ft. Thorn, N.M., 1856; moved to Tucson, Ariz., became gen. mcht., supplier forage for Army; elected to Ariz. Territorial Ho. of Reps., 1868; mem. Ariz. Territorial Council, 1871-73; assessor, supr. Pima County; treas. Tucson, 1871; mem. U.S. Congress (Democrat) from Ariz. Territory, 44th-45th congresses, 1875-79; resumed activities as mcht., also raised cattle. Died Tucson, Mar. 22, 1893; buried Old Tucson Cemetery; reinterred Evergreen Cemetery.

STEVENS, Isaac Ingalls, territorial gov., congressman, army officer; b. Andover, Mass., Mar. 25, 1818; s. Isaac and Hannah (Cummings) S.; grad. U.S. Mil. Acad., 1839; m. Margaret Hazard, Sept. 8, 1841, 5 children. Commd. 2d lt. of engrs. U.S. Army; engaged in constrn. or repair of fortification on New Eng. coast; commd. 1st lt., 1840; engr. adjutant on Scott's staff in Mexico during Mexican War; at Battle of Contreras, siege of Vera Cruz, battles of Cerro Gordo, Churubusco, and Chapultepec, brevetted capt. and maj.; reassigned to engring. duties in coastal fortifications after war, 1848-49; apptd. exec. asst. in U.S. Coast Survey, 1849-53; gov. Wash. Territory, circa 1853-57, helped pacify Indians; dir. of exploration for No. route of Pacific Ry. surveys, 1853, determined navigability of Missouri and Columbia rivers; made treaties with Indians, 1854-55; concluded lasting peace with Blackfoot Indians, 1855; elected territorial del. to U.S. Congress, 1857; del. to Democratic Nat. Conv., Charleston, 1860; at outbreak of Civil War became col. 79th Regt. of N.Y. Volunteers (The Highlanders); promoted to brig. gen., 1861, maj. gen., 1862. Author: Campaigns of the Rio Grande and Mexico, 1851; Report of Exploration for a Route for the Pacific Railroad, 1855. Killed in action at Battle of Chantilly, Sept. 1, 1862; buried Island Cemetery, Newport, R.I.

STEVENS, James, congressman, lawyer; b. in part of Stamford which is now New Canaan, Fairfield County, Conn., July 4, 1768; studied law. Admitted to bar, practiced in Stamford; mem. Conn. Ho. of Reps., 1804-05, 08-10, 14-15, 17-18; judge probate Stamford Dist., 1819; mem. U.S. Ho. of Reps. (Democrat) from Conn., 16th Congress, 1819-21; justice of peace Stamford, 1819-26; postmaster Stamford, 1822-29; judge Fairfield County Ct., 1823. Died Stamford, Apr. 4, 1835; buried St. John's and St. Andrew's Episcopal Cemetery.

STEVENS, John, Continental congressman; b. Perth Amboy, N.J., 1715. Mcht. and shipowner, in trade with West Indies and Madeira; large landowner and mine owner, Hunterdon, Union, Somerset counties (N.J.); mem. Gen. Colonial Assembly, 1751; active in raising troops and money for Crown Point in French and Indian War, 1755; helped build blockhouses at Drake's Ft., Normenach, Philipsburg; mem. def. com. to protect N.Y. and N.J. against Indian attacks; commr. to Indians, 1758; paymaster Col. Schuyler's Regt., the Old Blues, 1756-60; mem. com. of 4 who prevented issued of stamps under Stamp Act, N.Y.C., 1765; apptd. commr. to define boundary line between N.Y. and N.J., 1774; v.p. N.J. Council, 1770-82; pres. Council East Jersey Proprs., 1783; mem. Continental Congress from N.J., 1783-84; presided over N.J. Constl. Conv., 1787. Died Hoboken, N.J., May 10, 1792; buried Frame Meeting House Cemetery, Bethlehem Twp., Hunterdon County.

STEVENS, John, engr., inventor; b. N.Y.C., 1749; s. John and Elizabeth (Alexander) S.; grad. Columbia, 1768; m. Rachel Cox, Oct. 17, 1782, at least 7 children including John Cox, Robert Livingston, Edwin Augustus, Mary, Harriet. Studied law, 1768-71, apptd. an atty., N.Y.C., 1771; served from capt. to col., obtaining loans for Continental Army during Revolutionary War; loan commr. for Hunterdon County (N.J.); treas. N.J., 1776-79; surveyor gen. Eastern div. N.J., 1782-83; instrumental in framing 1st patent laws, 1790; became cons. engr. for Manhattan Co. (organized to furnish adequate water supply to N.Y.C.), circa 1800; became pres. Bergen Turnpike Co., 1802; received patent for multitubular boiler, 1803; his steamboat Little Juliana (operated by twin screw propellers) put into use on Hudson River, 1804; attempted to operate regular line of steamboats on Hudson between N.Y.C. and Albany and on other inland rivers, prevented by lawsuits; sent the Phoenix (1st sea-going steamboat in world) to Phila., 1809; built the Juliana, began regular ferry service, 1811; obtained 1st Am. railroad authorization from N.J. Assembly in 1815; authorized by Pa. Legislature to build Pa. R.R., 1823; designed, built exptl. locomotive on his estate in Hoboken, N.J. (1st Am.-made steam locomotive though never used for actual service), 1825; proposed a vehicular tunnel under the Hudson as well as an elevated railroad system for N.Y.C. Died Hoboken, Mar. 6, 1838.

STEVENS, John, artist; b. Utica, N.Y., 1819. Engaged in farming, Rochester, Minn., 1853; became house and sign painter, 1858; painted 1st version of his panorama of Sioux Massacre of 1862, 1863, painted other versions, 1868, 70, 74; exhibited in Middle West, 2 versions now at Minn. Hist. Soc. and Gilcrease Museum, Tulsa, Okla. Died 1879.

STEVENS, John Austin, banker; b. N.Y.C., Jan. 22, 1795; s. Ebenezer and Lucretia Ledyard (Sands) S.; grad. Yale, 1813; m. Abby Weld, 1824, at least 2 children including John Austin. Partner in his father's merc. firm, N.Y.C., 1818-39; 1st pres. Bank of Commerce, N.Y.C., 1839-66; pres. Asso. Banks of N.Y., Phila. and Boston; pres. Mchts. Exchange; sec. N.Y.C. C. of C. Died N.Y.C., Oct. 19, 1872.

STEVENS, John Leavitt, journalist, diplomat; b. Mt. Vernon, Me., Aug. 1, 1820; s. John and Charlotte (Lyford) S.; LL.D. (hon.), Tufts U., 1883; m. Mary Lowell Smith, May 10, 1845, 4 children. Became Universalist minister, 1845, (with James Gillespie Blaine) Kennebec Jour., Augusta, Me., 1855-69, became editor-in chief, 1857; mem. Me. Ho. of Reps., 1865-70; U.S. minister to Paraguay and Uruguay, 1870-74; U.S. minister resident to Sweden and Norway, 1877-83; U.S. minister to Hawaii, 1893, recognized Sanford Dole and Provisional Govt., 1893; accused of overstepping limits as diplomatic rep. in fgn. country (James Henderson Blount, spl. commr. of Pres. Cleveland, charged that he had entered into conspiracy with revolutionists, and had promised in advance the use of Am. forces to overthrow royal govt.); denied all complicity before Senate com., 1894. Author: Picturesque Hawaii, 1894. Died Augusta, Feb. 8, 1895.

STEVENS, Robert Livingston, engr., shipbuilder, inventor; b. Hoboken, N.J., Oct. 18, 1787; s. John and Rachel (Cox) S.; never married. Aided his father in building ferryboat Juliana, (inaugurating world's 1st steam-ferry system), 1811; leader in profession of naval architecture; designed, built at least 20 steamboats and ferries; introduced a forced-draft firing system under boilers, the split paddle wheel, "hog-framing" for boats, the present type of ferry slip; an organizer Camden & Amboy R.R. & Transp. Co., 1830, elected pres., chief engr.; designed the Trail and "hook-headed spike," circa 1830; began 1st steam railway service in N.J.; developed a percussion shell for naval use which could be fired from a cannon during War of 1812; interested in use of armor on ships of war; designed, built several craft including yacht Maria (fastest sailing vessel of her day), 1850. Died Hoboken, Apr. 20, 1856.

STEVENS, Robert Smith, congressman; b. Attica, Wyoming County, N.Y., Mar. 27, 1824; had academic course; studied law. Admitted to bar, 1846; moved to Kan., practiced law; became interested in real estate, devel. coal lands, mgmt. and building of railroads; mem. Kan. Ho. of Reps.; retired from business, 1880, returned to N.Y.; became farmer; mem. U.S. Ho. of Reps. (Democrat) from N.Y., 48th Congress, 1853-55; retired from public life because of ill health, became farmer. Died Attica, Feb. 23, 1893; buried Forest Hill Cemetery.

STEVENS, Thaddeus, congressman; b. Danville, Vt., Apr. 4, 1792; s. Joshua and Sally (Morrill) S.; grad. Dartmouth, 1814. Admitted to bar, Bel Air, Md., 1816; practiced law, Gettysburg, Pa., 1816-30, appeared in cases before Pa. Supreme Ct., defended many fuigtive slaves without charge; became partner (with James D. Paxton) in iron bus., Adams County, Pa., 1826; mem. Pa. Ho. of Reps., 1833-35, 37, 41; supported free sch. system of Phila. for whole State of Pa., 1834; instrumental in resolution to abolish slave trade in Washington, D.C., 1836-37; mem. U.S. Ho. of Reps. from Pa. (as Whig) 31st-32d congresses, 1849-53, (as Republican), 36th-40th congresses, 1859-68; del. Rep. nat. convs., 1856, 60, helped reform Rep. Party; chmn. Ho. Ways and Means Com., sponsored Internal Revenue Act, 1862, favored nation-wide paper currency; 1 of 2 mems. Ho. who did not vote for Crittenden Resolution which stipulated that Civil War was not fought to conquer South nor to destroy its instns., 1861; strongly supported Civil War effort; opposed Pres. Lincoln's Reconstrn. Plan, 10% Plan and seating of dels. from La. to U.S. Congress; secured passage of Civil Rights Bill of 1866 and Freedmen's Bur. Bill over Pres. Johnson's veto; advocated 14th Amendment (opposed by Johnson, became dominant issue in Congressional election 1866), supported by popular vote for amendment; initiated 15th Amendment, favored mil. control over South; charged that Pres. Johnson violated Tenure of Office Act in removing Sec. of War Edwin M. Stanton from office, began impeachment proceedings against Johnson, 1868. Died Aug. 11, 1868; buried Shreiner's Cemetery, Lancaster, Pa.

STEVENS, Thomas Holdup, naval officer; b. Charleston, S.C., Feb. 22, 1795; m. Elizabeth Sage, Nov. 1815, 6 children. A leader of detachment which captured 2 enemy guns, Niagara frontier, Nov. 27-28, 1812; made acting lt. U.S. Navy, 1813; commanded sloop Trippe in Battle of Lake Erie, recipient Silver medal awarded by Congress to officers in the action; 1st lt. of ship Niagara, 1814; duty on ships Alert and Constellation at Norfolk, 1818-20; commd. master comdt., 1825; served in ship Ontario, Mediterranean Squadron, 1829-31; in charge of Boston naval rendezvous, 1832-36; commd. capt., 1836, in command of Washington (D.C.) Navy Yard. Died Washington, Jan. 21, 1841; buried Arlington (Va.) Nat. Cemetery.

STEVENS, Thomas Holdup, naval officer; b. Middletown, Conn., May 27, 1819; s. Thomas Holdup and Elizabeth (Sage) S.; m. Anna Maria Christie, Nov. 2, 1844, 9 children inclucing Thomas H. Entered U.S. Navy as midshipman, 1836, passed midshipman, 1842; aide to Pres. Tyler; naval storekeeper, Honolulu, Hawaii, 1845-48; in Chilean ship Maria Helena wrecked on Christmas Island, 1848, remained there nearly 3 months before rescued; served with Colo. Home Squadron, 1858-60; commanded gunboat Ottawa in capture of Port Royal in Civil War, 1861; commanded monitor Patapsco around Charleston, Aug.-Sept. 1863; in charge of night attack on Ft. Sumter, Sept. 1863; in ship Winnebago in Battle of Mobile; sr. officer operating off Tex., 1865; commd. capt., 1866, lighthouse inspector, 1867-70; in command of ship Guerriere in European Squadron, 1870-71; commd. commodore, 1872, rear adm., 1879; on duty in Norfolk, Va., 1873-80; in command of Pacific Squadron, 1880-81; ret., 1881, Contbr. article Service under Du Pont to Times, Phila., 1886. Died Rockville, Md., May 15, 1896; buried Arlington (Va.) Nat. Cemetery.

STEVENS, Walter Husted, army officer; b. Penn Yan, N.Y., Aug. 24, 1827; s. Samuel Stephens; grad. U.S. Mil. Acad., 1848; married. Commd. in Corps Engrs., U.S. Army, 1848, promoted to 1st lt., 1855, resigned commn., 1861; apptd. capt. engrs. Confederate Army, 1861; promoted maj. at Battle of Bull Run, made chief engr. Army of No. Va., 1862; col. in charge of defenses of Richmond (Va.), circa 1862; commd. brig. gen., 1864, also chief engr. Lee's Army until its surrender, 1865; became supt., constructing engr. of a railroad between Vera Cruz (Mexico) and Mexico City, 1865, subsequently chief engr. Died Vera Cruz, Nov. 12, 1867.

STEVENS, William Bacon, clergyman, b. Bath, Me., July 13, 1815; s. William and Rebecca (Bacon) S.; attended Med. Coll. State of S.C.; M.D., Dartmouth, 1837; D.D. (hon.), U. Pa., 1848; LL.D. (hon.), Union Coll., 1862; m. Alethea Coppee; m. 2d, Anna Conyngham, 1869; 5 children. Physician and surgeon for orphan asylum and Central of Ga. R.R., Savannah; health officer Port of Savannah; founder Ga. Hist. Soc., 1839, 1st rec. sec., later librarian, edited 1st two volumes of its Collections 1840, 42; state historian of Ga., 1841; wrote editorials for Georgian, prin. Newspaper in Savannah; ordained deacon Episcopalian Ch.; apptd. missionary, Athens, Ga., 1843; rector Episcopal Ch., Athens, 1844, advanced to priesthood; prof. oratory and literature U. Ga., Athens, 1844; rector St. Andrews Ch., Phila., 1848; prof. liturgies and homiletics Phila. Div. Sch., 1861; asst. bishop Discese of Pa., 1862, bishop, 1865; in charge of Am. Episcopal churches in Europe, 1868-74; a founder Lehigh U., trustee, 1869-87. Author: A History of Georgia from Its First Discovery by Europeans to the Adoption of the Present Constitution, 2 vols., 1847, 59; The Past and Present of St. Andrews, 1858; Early History of the Church in Georgia, 1873. Died Phila., June 11, 1887.

STEVENSON, Andrew, congressman, diplomat; b. Culpeper County, Va., Jan. 21, 1784; s. James and Frances (Littlepage) S.; ed. Coll. William and Mary; studied law; m. Mary Page White; m. 2d, Sarah Coles, 1816; m. 3d, Mary Schaff, at least 1 son, John White. Admitted to Va. bar; mem. Va. Ho. of Dels.. 1809-16, 18-21, speaker, 1812-15; dir. Richmond br. Bank of U.S., 1817; mem. U.S. Ho. of Reps. from Va., 17th-23d congresses, 1821-June 2, 1834, speaker, 1827-34; sided with Union, played large part in preventing Va. from following S.C. in nullification crisis, 1832; chmn. Nat. Democratic Conv. (which nominated Van Buren for Pres. U.S.), Balt., 1835; U.S. minister to Gt. Britain (apptd. by Pres. Jackson 1834), 1836-41; elected pres. Va. Soc. Agr., 1845; became mem. bd., visitors U. Va., 1845, rector, 1856. Died "Blenheim," Albemarle County, Va., Jan. 25, 1857; buried "Enniscorthy," Albemarle County.

STEVENSON, Carter Littlepage, army officer; b. nr. Fredericksburg, Va., Sept. 21, 1817; s. Carter Littlepage and Jane (Herndon) S.; grad. U.S. Mil. Acad., 1838; m. Martha Griswold; Commd. 2d lt. 5th Inf., U.S. Army, 1838; fought in Mexican War; promoted to capt., 1836; served in Utah expdn., 1858; commd. lt. col. inf. Confederate Army, 1861, them col. 53d Va. Inf.; apptd. brig. gen., sent to West, 1862, commd. maj. gen., 1862; fought at battles of Champion's Hill and Big Black Ridge in Vicksburg campaign, at Battle of Missionary Ridge in Hardee's corps, also with Hood's corps in Atlanta Campaign; participated in campaign of the Carolinas, also at Battle of Bentonville; civil and mining engr. after Civil War. Died Caroline County, Va., Aug. 15, 1888.

STEVENSON, James, ethnologist, explorer; b. Maysville, Ky., Dec. 24, 1840; m. Matilda Coxe Evans, Apr. 18, 1872. Spent several winters among Blackfoot and Sioux Indians; participated in survey of Yellowstone region, 1871, leader in making it a nat. park; in charge of exploration of Snake and Columbia rivers in Ida. and Wyo. territories, 1872, prepared maps of region; in survey trip of 1872 climbed Great Teton (1st white man known to have reached ancient Indian altar on its summit); served as col. with 13th N.Y. Volunteers, Union Army, 1861-65; engaged in research among Pueblo Indians and the remains of their former settlements for Bur. Ethnology at its inception, 1879; outfitted, conducted expdns. investigating ancient ruins and the living Navaho, Zuni, Hopi, other Indian tribes; published 1st studies among the Navaho as "Ceremonial of Hasjelti Dailjis and Mythical Sand Painting of the Navajo Indians;" his ornithol. collections in U.S. Nat. Mus., Smithsonian Instn. Died N.Y.C., July 25, 1888.

STEVENSON, James S., congressman; b. York County, Pa., 1780; completed prep. studies; studied law. Admitted to bar, practiced law; mem. Pa. Ho. of Reps., 1822, 23; pres. Pa. Bd. Canal Commrs. until 1831; mem. U.S. Ho. of Reps. from Pa., 19th-20th congresses, 1825-29; became mfr., Pitts. Died Pitts., Oct. 16, 1831; buried First Presbyn. Cemetery.

STEVENSON, John White, senator, gov. Ky.; b. Richmond, Va., May 4, 1812; s. Andrew and Mary (White) S.; attended Hampden-Sydney Coll., 1828-29; grad. U. Va., 1832; m. Sibella Winston, 1842, 5 children. Admitted to bar, Vicksburg, Miss., circa 1833, began law practice; settled in Covington, Ky., 1841; County atty. Kenton County (Ky.); mem. Ky. Legislature from Kenton County, 1845, 46, 48; mem. Ky. Constl. Conv., Frankfort, 1849. del. Nat. Democratic Conv., 1848, 52, 56; Dem. presdl. elector, 1852, 56; mem. U.S. Ho. of Reps. from Ky., 35th-36th congresses, 1857-61; urged Republicans to accept Crittenden proposals, 1861; del. Union Conv., Phila., 1865, called for endorsement of Pres. Johnson's reconstrn. plans; elected lt. gov. Ky., 1867, gov., 1867-71, opposed "Regulators", aided devel. of pub. sch. system; mem. U.S. Senate from Ky., 1871-77, strict constructionist Jeffersonian-Jacksonian, opposed rivers and harbor appropriations bill of 1875; taught criminal law and contracts Cincinnati Law Sch., circa 1878; chmn. Nat. Dem. Conv., 1880; pres. Am. Bar Assn., 1884. Died Covington, Aug. 10, 1886; buried Spring Grove Cemetery, Cincinnati.

STEWARD, Ira, labor leader; b. New London, Conn., Mar. 10, 1831; m. Jane (Steward) Henning, 1880. Del. conv. Internat. Union of Machinists and Blacksmiths, Boston, 1863; secured passage of a resolution which for first time demanded 8 hour labor law; secured funds from own union and Boston Trades' Assembly for legislative lobbying; desired to use polit. means as well as econ. to improve low living standard of the masses; pres. Boston Eight-Hour League, Nat. Ten Hour League, 1883; helped establish Mass. Bur. Labor Statistics, (1st in country), 1869, bur. published pioneer work on the condition of women and child wage earners; an organizer Internat. Labor Union, (1st large-scale attempt in Am. to organize unskilled workers); planned a book entitled The Political Economy of Eight Hours (fragments of original manuscript in library of Wis. Hist. Soc.); insp. Boston Custom House, in early 1870's; wrote articles for leading newspapers supporting thesis that shorter hours would develop consumer spending and thus more jobs and higher wages; believed in ultimate triumph of socialism in U.S. industry. Died Plano, Ill., Mar. 13, 1883.

STEWARD, Joseph, artist; b. Upton, Mass., July 6, 1753; grad. Dartmouth, 1780; married, 1789. Ordained to ministry; became artist, 1793; opened portrait studio, Hartford, Conn., 1796; opened museum in State House, 1797; resumed preaching in later years. Died Apr. 22, 1822.

STEWARD, Lewis, congressman, mfr., farmer; b. nr. Hollisterville, Wayne County, Pa., Nov. 21, 1824; attended common schs.; studied law. Admitted to bar, never practiced law; became farmer and large landowner, mfr. harvesters, mowers, binders in Plano, Ill., later in West Pullman; unsuccessful Democratic candidate for gov. Ill., 1876; mem. U.N. Ho. of Reps. (Dem.) from Ill., 52d Congress, 1891-93. Died Plano, Aug. 27, 1896; buried Plano Cemetery.

STEWARDSON, John, architect; b. Phila., Mar. 21, 1858; s. Thomas and Margaret (Haines) S.; attended Harvard, 1878-79; studied architecture Atelier Pascal; entered Ecole des Beaux Arts, Paris, France, 1881. Entered office of T.P. Chandler, 1882-85; partner Walter Cope, 1886-96; as an architect primarily an artist, used Gothic style (especially English Gothic); his designs for U. Pa. reflected brickwork of St. John's Coll., Cambridge; designer choir screen St. Luke's Ch., Phila.; architect Bryn Mawr Coll., also Blair Hall at Princeton U.; fellow A.I.A.; a founder T-Square Club, pres., 1885-86, 91-92; Stewardson Fellowship (a travelling fellowship for U. Pa. Sch. of Architecture) established with fund collected by friends, 1897. Died Phila., Jan. 6, 1896.

STEWART, Alexander Turney, mcht.; b. Lisburn County Antrim, Ireland, Oct. 12, 1803; s. Alex ander and Margaret (Turney) S.; attended U. Bel fast (Ireland), Trinity Coll., Dublin, Ireland; m Cornelia Mitchell Clinch, Oct. 16, 1823. Opene dry goods shop in N.Y.C., 1823 developed into grea retail store A. T. Stewart & Co., expanded bus. 1846, 50; opened largest retail store in the world 1862; had controlling interests in numerous mill in New Eng., N.Y., N.J., mfg. textiles; owned Gran Union Hotel, a retail store at Saratoga Springs, N.Y. Metropolitan Hotel, Globe Theatre, Niblo's Garde (N.Y.C.); contbd. to charities; sent shipload of provisions to Ireland during famine of 1847; purchase Hempstead Plains on L.I. for which he built "model town" of Garden City; apptd. sec. treasury, 1869, but bus. holdings barred him from holding the office. Died N.Y.C., Apr. 10, 1876.

STEWART, Alvan, lawyer, abolitionist; b. South Granville, N.Y., Sept. 1, 1790; s. Uriel Stewart; attended U. Vt., 1809-12; m. Keziah Holt, 5 children. Admitted to Cherry Valley (N.Y.) bar; advocated protective tariff; joined newly organized Am. Anti-Slavery Soc., 1834; led in establishing abolitionist orgns. in N.Y.; issued call for anti-slavery conv. which assembled, Utica, N.Y., 1835; founder, pres. N.Y. State Anti-Slavery Soc., proposed at meeting of Am. Anti-Slavery Soc., 1838; that agts. of nat. soc. be excluded from all state auxiliaries (proposal adopted); believed in separate polit. anti-slavery action; called, presided at anti-slavery polit. conv., which organized Liberty Party and nominated him for gov. N.Y., Albany, 1840; eloquently challenged constitutionality of slavery before N.J. Supreme Ct. in test case arranged by local abolitionists, 1845. Author: (pamphlet) Common Sense, 1828; Prize Address for the New York City Temperance Society, 1835; Writings and Speeches of Alvan Stewart on Slavery, 1860. Died N.Y.C., May 1, 1849.

STEWART, Andrew, congressman; b. German Twp., Fayette County, Pa., June 11, 1791; s. Abraham and Mary (Oliphant) S.; studied law, Uniontown, Pa.; m. Elizabeth Shriver, 6 children. Admitted to Pa. bar, 1815; mem. Pa. Ho. of Reps., 1815-18; U.S. atty. for Western Dist. of Pa., 1818-20; mem. U.S. Ho. of Reps. from Pa., 17th-20th, 22d-23d, 28th-30th congresses, 1821-29, 31-35, 43-49, supported constrn. of Chesapeake and Ohio Canal, the Cumberland Road, advocated protective tariff (known as "Tariff Andy"); dir. Chesapeake and Ohio Canal Co.; Stewart Twp. (Fayette County, Pa.) named for him; affiliated with Republican Party in later life. Died Uniontown, July 16, 1872; buried Union Cemetery, Uniontown.

STEWART, Charles, Continental congressman; b. Gortlea, County Donegal, Ireland, 1729. Came to Am., 1750; became farmer; commd. lt. col. Hunterdon County (N.J.) Militia, 1771; active in pre-Revolutionary movements; commd. col. battalion of Minutemen, 1776; apptd. commissary gen. of issues by Continental Congress, 1777; mem. Continental Congress from N.J., 1784-85. Died Flemington, N.J., June 24, 1800; buried Old Stone Ch., Bethlehem Twp., Hunterdon County.

STEWART, Charles. naval officer; b. Phila., July 28, 1778; s. Charles and Sarah (Ford) S.; m. Delia Tudor, Nov. 25, 1813, 2 children. Commd. lt. U.S. Navy, 1798, in command schooner Experiment, 1800, command brig Siren, 1802; served in war with Tripoli and Tunis; commd. capt., 1806, supr. constrn. gunboats, N.Y., 1806-07; comdr. ship Constellation, 1812, ship Constitution, 1813, ship Franklin, 1816; commodore squadron in Pacific, 1824; naval commr., 1830-32; in charge Phila. Navy Yard, 1838-41, 46, 54-61; sr. commodore, 1856, rear adm., ret., 1862. Died Bordentown, N.J., Nov. 6, 1869.

STEWART, Charles, congressman, lawyer; b. Memphis, Tenn., May 30, 1826; attended common schs., Galveston, Tex.; studied law. Admitted to bar, 1854, practiced in Marlin, Falls County, Tex.; pros. atty. 13th Jud. Dist., 1856-60; del. to secession conv., 1861; enlisted in Confederate Army, served throughout Civil War, served with 10th Regt., Tex. Inf., later with Baylor's Cavalry; moved to Houston, Tex., 1866, practiced law; atty. Houston, 1874-76; mem. Tex. Senate, 1878-82; mem. U.S. Ho. of Reps. (Democrat) from Tex., 48th-52d congresses, 1883-93. Died Santa Rosa Hosp., San Antonio, Tex., Sept. 21, 1895; buried Glenwood Cemetery, Houston.

STEWART, David, senator, lawyer; b. Balt., Sept. 13, 1800; attended Princeton; grad. Union Coll., Schenectady, N.Y., 1819; studied law. Admitted to bar, circa 1821, practiced in Balt.; mem. U.S. Senate (Whig, filled vacancy) from Md., Dec. 6, 1849-Jan. 12, 1850. Died Balt., Jan. 5, 1858; buried Stewart vault, Old Westminster Burying Ground.

STEWART, Jacob Henry, congressman, physician; b. Clermont, Columbia County, N.Y., Jan. 15, 1829; grad. Phillips Acad., Peekskill, N.Y.; attended Yale; grad. U. Med. Coll. of N.Y.C., 1851. Practiced medicine, Peekskill; moved to St. Paul, Minn., 1855; med. officer Ramsey County, 1856; mem. Minn. Senate, 1858-59; served as surgeon in Union Army in Civil War, 1861; captured at 1st Battle of Bull Run, paroled, cared for wounded at Sudley Ch. Hosp.; surgeon gen. State of Minn., 1857-63; mayor St. Paul, 1864, 68, 72-74, postmaster, 1865-70; mem. U.S. Ho. of Reps. (Republican) from Minn., 45th Congress, 1877-79; surveyor gen. Minn., 1879-82. Died St. Paul, Aug. 25, 1884; buried Oakland Cemetery.

STEWART, James, congressman, mcht., farmer; b. Scotland, Nov. 11, 1775; had limited edn. Came to U.S., settled nr. Stewartsville, Richmond County, N.C., became mcht., farmer; mem. N.C. Ho. of Commons, 1798, 99; mem. N.C. Senate, 1802-04, 13-15; mem. U.S. Ho. of Reps. (filled vacancy) from N.C., 15th Congress, Jan. 5, 1818-19. Died nr. Laurinburg, N.C., Dec. 29, 1821; buried Old Stewartsville Cemetery, nr. Laurinburg.

STEWART, James Augustus, congressman, jurist; b. Tobacco Stick (now Madison), Dorchester County, Md., Nov. 24, 1808; attended local schs.; studied law, Balt. Admitted to bar, 1829, practiced in Cambridge, Dorchester County, also built ships and houses; mem. Md. Ho. of Dels., 1843-15; mem. U.S. Ho. of Reps. (Democrat) from Md., 34th 36th congresses, 1855-61; mem. Md. Ct. of Apbridge, Apr. 3, 1879; buried Christ Protestant Epispeals; chief justice Circuit Ct., 1867-79. Died Camcopal Ch. Cemetery.

STEWART, John, congressman; completed prep. studies. Mem. Pa. Ho. of Reps., 1789-96; mem. U.S. Ho. of Reps. (Democrat, filled vacancy) from Pa., 6th-8th congresses, Jan. 15, 1801-05. Died Elmwood, nr. York, Pa., 1820; buried on his estate nr. Elmwood.

STEWART, John, congressman, ship builder; b. Chatham, Conn., Feb. 10, 1795; completed prep. studies. Became shipbuilder, mcht., Middle Haddam, Conn.; mem. Conn. Ho. of Reps., 1830, 54; mem. Conn. Senate, 1832-37, 46; judge County Ct. of Middletown; mem. U.S. Ho. of Reps. (Democrat) from Conn., 28th Congress, 1843-45. Died Chatham, Sept. 16, 1860; buried Union Hill Cemetery, Middle Haddam, Chatham.

STEWART, John David, congressman; b. nr. Fayetteville, Fayette County, Ga., Aug. 2, 1833; attended Marshall Coll., Griffin, Ga.; studied law, theology. Taught sch., Griffin for 2 years; admitted to bar, 1856, practiced law, Griffin; probate judge Spalding County, 1858-60; lt. and capt. 13th Ga. Regt., during Civil War; mem. Ga. Ho. of Reps., 1865-67; ordained to ministry Baptist Ch., 1871; mayor Griffin, 1875-76; judge Superior Ct., 1879-86; mem. U.S. Ho. of Reps. (Democrat) from Ga., 50th-51st congresses, 1887-91. Died Griffin, Jan. 28, 1894, buried Oak Hill Cemetery.

STEWART, Philo Penfield, missionary, coll. ofcl., inventor; b. Sherman, Conn., July 6, 1798; s. Philo and Sarah (Penfield) S.; m. Eliza Capen, 1878. Apptd. asst. missionary among Choctaws at Mayhew, Miss. by Am. Bd. Commrs. for Fgn. Missions, 1821; with John J. Shipherd evolved a plan of combination community and sch. whereby students could defray all their expenses by working, 1832, founder Oberlin (O.) Coll. (opened 1833), treas., gen. mgr., 1833-36; patented Oberlin Stove, 1834, began mfg. stoves, Troy, N.Y.; proceeds of stove patents went to aid Oberlin Coll. Lived Troy, N.Y. Died Oberlin, Dec. 13, 1868.

STEWART, Robert Marcellus, gov. Mo., railroad exec.; b. Truxton, Cortland County, N.Y., Mar. 12, 1815; s. Charles and Elisabeth (Severance) S. Admitted to Ky. bar, 1838; del. Mo. Constl. Conv., 1845; mem. Mo. Senate, 1846-57; atty., lobbyist in Washington for a grant of fed. land for Hannibal & St. Joseph R.R., became pres. 1854; gov. Mo. (anti-Benton Democrat), 1857-61, favored generous policy towards railroads, preservation of Union; editor St. Joseph (Mo.) Jour., 1861-63. Died St. Joseph, Sept. 21, 1871.

STEWART, William, congressman, lawyer; b. Mercer, Pa., Sept. 10, 1810; grad. Jefferson Coll., Canonsburg, Pa.; studied law. Admitted to bar, practiced in Mercer; mem. Pa. Senate; mem. U.S. Ho. of Reps. (Republican) from Pa., 35th-36th congresses, 1857-61. Died Mercer, Oct. 17, 1876; buried Mercer Cemetery.

STEWART, Sir William Drummond, sportsman, pioneer; b. Scotland. Went to Ft. Vancouver, 1834, 37; explored Oregon trail; hired Balt. artist Alfred Jacob Miller to accompany him on some of travels in Northwest; gave lavish parties on trips.

STIEFFEL, Hermann, artist; b. Wiesbaden, Germany, 1826; joined U.S. Army, N.Y., 1857, served with Co. K, 5th Inf., in Kan. and Mont., 1857-82; painted watercolor landscapes of Western frontier and views of army posts, many now in collection of Smithsonian Instn.

STIEGEL, Henry William (Baron von Stiegel), glassmaker, ironmaster; b. Cologne, Germany, May 13, 1729; s. John Frederick and Dorothea Elizabeth Stiegel; m. Elizabeth Huber, Nov. 7, 1752; m. 2d, Elizabeth Holz, Oct. 4, 1758; 3 children. Arrived in Phila., 1750; bought and added to father-in-law's iron mfg. bus., 1758, named it Elizabeth Furnace, made six and ten plate stoves, kettles; purchased forge, Berks County, Pa., 1760; acquired 1/3d interest in 729 acres land in Lancaster County from Stedman bros., 1762, laid out town of Manheim, built, sold houses; brought skilled glassmakers from Eng., 1763-64, began erection of glass factory, Manheim, 1764; experimented in making bottles and window glass at Elizabeth Furnace; built 2d factory at Manheim, became Am. Flint Glass Mfg. Co. 1772, 1769 made Stiegel glassware at Manheim works; examples of work in Hunter Collection at Met. Mus. Art, N.Y.C., also Pa. Mus. Art; went bankrupt, by 1774; became country sch. master, music tchr., Brickerville and Schaefferstown, 1779; clk. at Reading Furnaces, Berks County. Died Charming Forge, Berks County, Jan. 10, 1785; buried in unmarked grave.

STILES, Ezra, clergyman, coll. pres.; b. North Haven, Conn., Nov. 29, 1727 (old style calendar); s. Isaac and Keziah (Taylor) S.; grad. Yale, 1746; D.D. (hon.), U. Edinburgh (Scotland), 1765; D.D. (hon.), Dartmouth, 1780; D.D. (hon.), Princeton, 1784, LL.D., 1784; m. Elizabeth Hubbard, Feb. 10, 1757; m. 2d, Mary (Cranston) Checkley, Oct. 17, 1782; 8 children including Ezra, Isaac, Ruth. Licensed to preach by New Haven Assn. Ministers, 1749; tutor Yale, 1749-55; engaged in some of 1st elec. experiments in New Eng. when Benjamin Franklin sent an elec. apparatus to Yale, 1749,; admitted to Conn. bar, 1783; ordained to ministry Congregational Ch., 1755; pastor Congregational Ch., Newport, R.I., 1755; elected mem. Am. Philos. Soc., 1768, also councilor, 1781; a founder R.I. Coll. (now Brown U.), 1763; pres. Yale, 1777, prof. eccles. history, 1778; 1st pres. soc. for abolition slavery formed in Conn., 1790. Author: History of Three of the Judges of King Charles I, 1794. Died New Haven, Conn., May 12, 1795.

STILES, John Dodson, congressman, lawyer; b. Town Hill, Luzerne County, Pa., Jan. 15, 1822; completed prep. studies; studied law. Admitted to bar, 1844, practiced in Allentown, Pa.; elected dist. atty. Lehigh County, Pa., 1853, served 3 years; del. Democratic nat. convs., Cincinnati, 1856, N.Y. C., 1868; del. Nat. Union Conv., Phila., 1866; mem. U.S. Ho. of Reps. (Democrat, filled vacancy) from Pa., 37th-38th, 41st congresses, June 3, 1862-65, 69-71. Died Allentown, Oct. 29, 1896; buried Fairview Cemetery.

STILES, William Henry, congressman, lawyer; b. Savannah, Ga., Jan. 1, 1808; studied law Yale. Admitted to bar, 1831, practiced in Savannah; solicitor gen. Eastern Dist. Ga., 1833-36; mem. U.S. Ho. of Reps. (Democrat) from Ga., 28th Congress, 1843-45; chargé d'affaires to Austria (apptd. by Pres. Polk), 1845-49; mem. Ga. Ho. of Reps., speaker, 1858; del.-at-large from Ga. to Comml. Congress, Montgomery, Ala., 1858; del. Dem. Nat. Conv., Balt., 1860; served as col. in Confederate Army during Civil War. Died Savannah, Dec. 20, 1865; buried Laurel Grove Cemetery.

STILLMAN, Samuel, clergyman; b. Phila., Feb. 27, 1737 (old style calendar); M.A. (hon.), Coll. of Phila., 1761; M.A. ad eundem (hon.), Harvard, 1761; M.A. (hon.), Brown U., 1769, D.D., hon.), 1788; m. Hannah Morgan, May 1759, 14 children. Ordained to ministry Baptist Ch., 1759; asst. pastor 2d Bapt. Ch., Boston, 1763; pastor First Bapt. Ch., Boston, 1765-1807; a founder Brown U., one of original trustees, 1764, fellow, 1765-1807; was Calvinistic and evangelical in ideas; gave addresses published as Select Sermons on Doctrinal and Practical Subjects, 1808. Died Boston, Mar. 12, 1807.

STILLWELL, Thomas Neel, congressman; b. Stillwell, O., Aug. 29, 1830; attended Oxford and College Hill colls.; studied law. Admitted to bar, 1852, practiced in Anderson, Ind.; mem. Ind. Ho. of Reps., 1856; served with U.S. Army during Civil War; mem. U.S. Ho. of Reps. (Republican) from Ind., 39th Congress, 1865-67; minister resident to Venezuela, 1867-68; pres. First Nat. Bank of Anderson until 1874. Died as result of gunshot wound, Anderson, Jan. 14, 1874; buried Maplewood Cemetery.

STILWELL, Silas Moore, lawyer, financial writer; b. N.Y.C., June 6, 1800; s. Stephen and Nancy (Moore) S.; m. Caroline Norsworthy, 4 children. Mem. Tenn. Legislature, 1822; admitted to Va. bar, 1824; mem. Va. Ho. Burgesses, mem. N.Y. Assembly (Republican), 1830-33, author Stilwell Act of 1831 which ended debt imprisonment; alderman N.Y.C., 1836; alleged to be author Free Banking Law of 1838; U.S. miarshall for So. Dist. N.Y., 1841, sent on spl. mission to the Hague, Netherlands by Pres. Tyler; his claim of authorship of Nat. Banking Act not recognized by historians of Am. banking; wrote articles of financial subjects pseudonym Jonathan Oldbuck for N.Y. Herald, 1861-72. Author: A System of Credit for a Republic, and the Plan of A Bank for the State of New York, 1838; Private History of the Origin and Purpose of the National Banking Law, 1879. Died N.Y.C., May 16, 1881.

STIMPSON, William, naturalist, conchologist; b. Roxbury, Mass., Feb. 14, 1832; s. Herbert H. and Mary (Brewster) S.; attended Boston Latin Sch., 1848; studied under Louis Agassiz; M.D., Columbia, 1860; m. Annie Gordon, July 28, 1864, 3 children. First naturalist to employ deep sea dredging in work; apptd. to North Pacific Exploring Expdn., 1852-56, began classification of immense amount of data gathered during those years, with hdqrs. in Smithsonian Instn., Washington, D.C., 1856; results published in Smithsonian Miscellaneous Collections, Vol. XLIX, 1907; became dir. Chgo. Acad. Sciences, 1865, gathered collections and great manuscripts from naturalists all over the world; became youngest mem. Nat. Acad. Sciences, 1868; never recovered from loss of bldg. and its treasures when Chgo. Acad. Sciences was destroyed by great Chgo. Fire of 1871. Author (written in Latin): A Revision and Synonymy of the Mestaceous Mollusks of New England, 1851; Notes on North American Crustacea, 1859. Died Ilchester, Md., May 26, 1872.

STITH, William, historian, coll. pres.; b. Va., 1707; s. Capt. John and Mary (Randolph) S.; B.A., Queens Coll., Oxford (Eng.) U., 1728, M.A., 1730; m. Judith Randolph, July 13, 1738, 3 children. Ordained to ministry, 1728; chaplain Va. Ho. of Burgesses, 1731; pastor Henrico County (Va.) Parish, 1736-52; master grammar sch. Coll. William and Mary, 1731, became pres. coll., 1752; served as minister York-Hampton Parish, York County, Va. Author: History of Virginia from the First Settlement to the Dissolution of the London Company, 1747; History of First Discovery and Settlement of Virginia (only a portion was finished), 1747. Died Williamsburg, Va., Sept. 19, 1755.

STIVERS, Moses Dunning, congressman; b. nr. Beemerville, Sussex County, N.J., Dec. 30, 1828; attended Mt. Retirement Sem., Wantage, Sussex County. Taught sch.; became mcht., Ridgebury, N.Y., Middletown, N.Y., 1855-64; clk. Orange County, 1864-67, resided in Goshen, N.Y.; returned to Middletown, became propr. Orange County Press, 1868; a propr., editor Middletown Daily Press; U.S. collector internal revenue for 11th Dist. N.Y. (apptd. by Pres. Grant), 1869-83; del. Republican Nat. Conv., Chgo., 1880; pres. N.Y. State Press Assn., 1887; trustee Middletown State Hosp. for Insane; became banker; mem. U.S. Ho. of Reps. (Rep.) from N.Y., 51st Congress, 1889-91. Died Middletown, Feb. 2, 1895; buried Hillside Cemetery.

STOBO, Robert, army officer; b. Glasgow, Scotland, 1727; s. William Stobo; attended U. Glasgow, circa 1742. Capt., Va. Militia, fought with George Washington at Fort Necessity, 1754, captured by French; tried for treason by French, 1755, sentenced to be executed (sentence never confirmed); escaped down St. Lawrence River, 1759; received thanks of Va. Ho. of Burgesses and gift of 1000 pounds, 1759; capt. Foot's 15th Regt.; his life served as model for character of Tismahago in Smollett's The Expedition of Humphry Clinker. Author: Memoirs of Major Robert Stobo of the Virginia Regiment, published posthumously, 1800. Died circa 1772.

STOCK, Joseph Whiting, artist; b. Springfield, Mass., Jan. 30, 1815. Worked in Springfield, travelled as far as New Bedford, Mass., New Haven, Conn., Warren, Bristol and Providence, R.I.; painted miniatures and portraits, landscapes, marine paintings; painted over 900 portraits, 1842-45. Died Springfield, June 28, 1855.

STOCKBRIDGE, Francis Brown, senator; b. Bath, Me., Apr. 9, 1826; attended common schs. Clk. wholesale house, Boston, 1843-47; moved to Chgo., opened lumber yard; moved to Saugatuck, Allegan County, Mich., 1851, became sawmill operator, also mcht.; entered lumber business, Kalamazoo, Mich., 1863; mem. Mich. Ho. of Reps., 1869, Mich. Senate, 1871; mem. U.S. Senate (Republican) from Mich., 1887-94. Died Chgo., Apr. 30, 1894; buried Mountain Home Cemetery, Kalamaz.

STOCKBRIDGE, Henry Smith, lawyer; b. North Hadley, Mass., Aug. 31, 1822; s. Jason and Abigail (Montague) S.; grad. Amherst Coll., 1845; studied law in office of Coleman Yellot; m. Fanny E. Montague, 1 son, Henry. Admitted to Md. bar, 1848; leader in proceedings of Murray Inst.; Unionist in Civil War; commr. of the draft and spl. dist. atty. War Dept., 1862; mem. Md. Legislature, 1864, chmn. com. on judiciary; judge Circuit Ct. for Baltimore County (Md.), 1865; v.p. Republican Nat. Conv., 1868; chmn. Md. Rep. Com., 1879-83; 1st v.p. Md. Hist. Soc.; trustee Howard U.; a founder Humphrey Moore Inst. Died Balt., Mar. 11, 1895.

STOCKDALE, Thomas Ringland, congressman; b. Greene County, Pa., Mar. 28, 1828; s. Willliam and Hannah (McQuaid) S.; grad. Jefferson (now Washington and Jefferson) Coll., 1856; law degree, U. Miss., 1858; m. Fannie Wicker, Feb. 13, 1867, at least 1 son, 1 dau. Moved to Miss., 1856; admitted to Miss. bar practiced law, Holmesville, Miss.; became pvt. Quitman Guards, Miss. Militia, 1861, rose to lt. col., served during Civil War; returned to practice law, 1865; mem. Democratic Nat. Conv., 1868; Dem. presdl. elector, 1872-84; mem. U.S. Ho. of Reps. (Democrat) from Miss., 51st-53d congresses, 1887-95; asso. judge Miss. Supreme Ct., 1896-97. Died Summit, Miss., Jan. 8, 1899; buried Woodlawn Cemetery.

STOCKTON, John Potter, senator; b. Princeton, N.J., Aug. 2, 1826; s. Commodore Robert Field and Harriet Maria (Potter) S.; grad. Coll. of N.J. (now Princeton), 1843; read law under Richard Stockton Field; m. Sarah Marks, 2 sons, 1 dau. Admitted to N.J. bar, 1850; a commr. to codify N.J. law; reporter N.J. Ct. of Chancery, 1852-58; minister resident to Papal States (apptd. through his father's influence with James Buchanan), 1857-61; returned to practice law, Trenton, 1861; mem. U.S. Senate (held contested seat, declared vacant) 1865-66, (as Democrat), 1869-75; atty. gen. N.J., 1877-97. Died Jan. 22, 1900; buried Princeton.

STOCKTON, Richard, Continental congressman; b. Princeton, N.J., Oct. 1, 1730; s. John and Abigail (Phillips) S.; grad. Coll. of N.J. (now Princeton), 1748; m. Annis Boudinot, 6 children including Richard, Julia (Stockton) Rush. Admitted to N.J. bar, 1754; trustee Coll. of N.J., circa 1765; mem. N.J. Exec. Council; became judge N.J. Supreme Ct., 1774; drafted and sent to Lord Dartmouth "a plan of self-govt. for Am., independent of Parliament, without renouncing allegiance to the Crown" 1774; elected to Continental Congress, 1776, mem. numerous coms.; visited No. Army with George Clymer, 1776; signer Declaration of Independence, 1776; chmn. of com. to inspect No. Army at Ticonderoga; taken prisoner by British, Nov. 30, 1776, released Dec. 29, 1776. Died Princeton, Feb. 28, 1781; buried Quaker Cemetery, Princeton.

STOCKTON, Richard, senator; b. Morven, Princeton, N.J., Apr. 17, 1764; s. Richard and Annis (Boudinot) S.; M.A., Princeton, 1783; m. Mary Field, 9 children including Robert Field. Admitted to N.J. bar, 1784; treas. Princeton, 1788, trustee, 1791-1828; argued before U.S. Supreme Ct., 1804, 05; presdl. elector, 1792-1801; mem. U.S. Senate (Federalist) from N.J., Nov. 12, 1796-99; unsuccessful Federalist candidate for gov. N.J., 1801, 02, 03, 04; mem. U.S. Ho. of Reps. from N.J., 13th Congress, 1813-15; opposed War of 1812; interested in devel. of steamboat, improvement of canals; mem. N.J. commn. to settle boundary dispute with N.Y., 1827. Died "Morven," Princeton, N.J., Mar. 7, 1828; buried Princeton Cemetery.

STOCKTON, Robert Field, naval officer, senator; b. Princeton, N.J., Aug. 20, 1795; s. Richard and Mary (Field) S.; attended Princeton, 1808; m. Harriet Maria Potter, 1823/24, 9 children including John Potter. Commd. midshipman U.S. Navy, 1811, lt., 1812; 1st lt. in ship Spitfire in War with Algiers, 1815; interested in Am. Colonization Soc., carried Dr. Eli Ayres (agt. for soc.) to West Coast of Africa and obtained by treaty new site for agency Cape Mesurado (later Liberia); employed in suppressing piracy in West Indies, 1822; had surveying duties, 1823-24, 27-28; invested in Del. & Raritan Canal, circa 1829, 1st pres.; invested in Camden & Amboy R.R.; owned racing horses; organized N.J. Colonization Soc., 1st pres.; commd. master comdt., 1830, capt., 1838; in command of Ohio as fleet capt. and capt., 1838; campaigned for Harrison in presdl. election, 1840; assisted in constrn. of steamer Princeton, 1st comdr., 1843-45; in command land operations in Cal., 1846; combined forces of navy and army, entered Los Angeles and claimed it for U.S.; organized civil and mil. govt. as gov. and comdr. in chief, resigned, 1850; mem. U.S. Senate (Democrat) from N.J., 1851-Jan. 10, 1853, introduced bill providing for abolition of flogging in navy and urged adequate harbor defenses; pres. Del. & Raritan Canal Co., 1853-66. del. to Peace Conf., Washington, D.C., 1861. Died Princeton, Oct. 7, 1866; buried Princeton Cemetery.

STOCKTON, Thomas Hewlings, clergyman; b. Mt. Holly, N.J., June 4, 1808; s. William Smith and Elizabeth (Hewlings) S.; attended Jefferson Med. Coll., 1827; m. Anna Roe McCurdy, 1828, 11 children. Ordained to ministry Methodist Protestant Ch., circa 1829; pastor in No. Md.; chaplain U.S. Ho. of Reps., 1833-36; pastor, Balt., active in anti-slavery controversy; apptd. editor Methodist Protestant, 1838, resigned almost immediately because forbidden to discuss slavery issue; preached to non-sectarian congregations Phila., 1838-47; organized independent non-sectarian congregations, Cincinnati, Balt. and Phila. from 1849; chaplain U.S. Senate, 1863; conducted services at dedication of Gettysburg Nat. Cemetery; considered one of greatest pulpit orators of his day. Author: Floating Flowers from a Hidden Brook (collected poems), 1844, Poems, 1862; Sermons for the People (collected addresses), 1854. Died Oct. 9, 1868.

STOCKWELL, Samuel B., artist; b. Boston; at least 1 dau. Actor, then scene painter Tremont Theatre, Boston, during 1830's; painted scenery, Charleston, S.C., 1841, Mobile, Ala., 1843, New Orleans, 1843, 46; worked with Henry Lewis on panorama of Mississippi River, partnership dissolved, completed separate version, 1848; exhibited panorama in St. Louis, New Orleans, Charleston, Boston; painted scenery, St. Louis, 1852-53. Died of yellow fever, Savannah, Ga., Sept. 23, 1854.

STODDARD, Amos, army officer, territorial gov.; b. Woodbury, Conn., Oct. 26, 1762; s. Anthony and Phebe (Reade) S.; never married. Enlisted in inf., 1779; asst. clk. Supreme Ct., Mass., 1784; commd. officer in suppression of Shay's Rebellion, 1787; admitted to Mass. bar, 1793; mem. Mass. Legislature, 1797; served with Mass. Militia, 1796-98; commd. capt. 2d Regt. Artillerists and Engrs., U.S. Army, 1798, maj., 1807; commd. 1st civil and mil. comdt. Upper La., 1803; agt. and commr. of France at transfer of Upper La. Territory from Spain to France to U.S., 1804; acting gov. La. Territory, 1804-12; defended Fort Meigs (O.) in War of 1812. Author: The Political Crisis, 1791. Died Fort Meigs, May 11, 1813.

STODDARD, David Tappan, missionary; b. Northampton, Mass., Dec. 2, 1818; s. Soloman and Sarah (Tappan) S.; attended Williams Coll., 1834; grad. Yale, 1838, studied theology at Yale, 1840-42; attended Andover Theol. Sem., 1839; m. Harriet Briggs, Feb. 14, 1843; m. 2d, Sophia Dance Hazen, Feb. 14, 1851. Tutor, Marshall and Middlebury Colls., 1838-39; theology tutor Yale, 1840-42; licensed to preach by Congregationalist Ch. Mass., 1842, ordained minister New Haven, Conn., 1843; missionary (under auspices Am. Bd. Commrs. for Fgn. Missions) among Nestorians, Persia, 1843-48, 51-57, headed school for boys Seir, Persia, preached among Nestorians; in charge of Dayspring and Journal of Missions, publs. of Am. Bd. Commrs. for Fgn. Missions, 1848. Translator: (with Rev. Justin Perkins) New Testament into modern Syriac. Author: Grammar of the Modern Syriac Language published in Jour. of Oriental Soc.) 1855-56. Died Seir, Jan. 22, 1857.

STODDARD, Ebenezer, congressman, lawyer; b. Union, Tolland County, Conn., May 6, 1785; attended Woodstock Acad., 1802-03; grad. Brown U., 1807; studied law. Admitted to bar, 1810, practiced in West Woodstock, Conn.; mem. U.S. Ho. of Reps. from Conn., 17-18th congresses, 1821-25; mem. Conn. Senate, 1825-27; lt. gov. Conn., 1833, 35-37. Died West Woodstock, Aug. 19, 1847; buried Bungay Cemetery.

STODDARD, John Fair, educator; b. Greenfield, N.Y., July 20, 1825; s. Phineas and Marilda (Fair) S.; grad. State Normal Coll., Albany, N.Y., 1847; A.M. (hon.), N.Y.U., 1853; m. Eliza Ann Platt, Oct. 18, 1865, 1 child. Headed Liberty Normal Inst., 1847-51, U. No. Pa., 1851-54, Lancaster County Normal Sch., 1855-57; purchased property of defunct U. No. Pa., opened it as tchrs. coll., 1857 (soon destroyed by fire); established Susquehanna County Normal Sch., Montrose, Pa., 1857; pres. Pa. State Tchrs. Assn., 1857; prin. Grammar Sch. Number 10, N.Y.C., 1859. Author: (textbook) The American Intellectual Arithmetic, 1849; also other widely used arithmetic textbooks (some with W.D. Henkle). Died Kearny, N.J., Aug. 6, 1873.

STODDARD, Joshua C., inventor; b. Pawlet, Vt., Aug. 26, 1814; s. Nathan Ashbel and Ruth (Judson) S.; m. Lucy Maria Hersey, Jan. 23, 1845, at least 2 children. Worked on father's farm for long period, interested primarily in bee culture, honey prodn.; inventor improvements and variants on horse-drawn hay rake, received 16 patents; his most famous invention was steam calliope, patented 1855; organized Am. Steam Music Co., Worcester, Mass., 1855, forced out of co. by 1860; many calliopes placed on side-wheelers, other river vessels of day; received no financial benefit from most of inventions; patented a fruit-paring machine, 1901. Died Springfield, Mass., Apr. 3, 1902.

STODDARD, Solomon, clergyman; b. Boston, Sept., 1643; s. Anthony and Mary (Downing) S.; grad. Harvard, 1662; m. Mrs. Esther (Warham) Mather, 12 children including John, Esther (Stoddard) Edwards. First librarian Harvard, 1667-74; pastor, Northampton, Mass., 1670-1729; ordained to ministry Congregational Ch., 1670; accepted Half-Way Covenant proposed by synod of 1662; introduced into his church practice of allowing Christians to take communion and enjoy other privileges of full membership even when uncertain of grade (practice called "Stoddardeanism"); advocated nat. ch. governed by a synod; urged sumptuary laws of 1676; promoted revivals in Northampton, 1679, 83, 1712, 18. Author: The Inexcusableness of Neglect in an Unconverted Condition, 1708. Died Northampton, Feb. 11, 1729.

STODDERT, Benjamin, sec. navy; b. Charles County, Md., 1751; s. Thomas and Sarah (Marshall) S.; m. Rebecca Lowndes, June 17, 1781. Served as capt. Pa. Regt., 1777, resigned, 1779; began career as mcht. in firm Forrest, Stoddert & Murdock, Georgetown, Md.; incorporator, later pres. Bank of Columbia, organized 1794; aided gov. in acquisition lands in D.C. at fair prices; 1st sec. navy, May 1798-1801, apptd. by Pres. John Adams; organized fleet of 50 ships during war scare with France, 1798-99, drew up bill for governing of Marine Corps, began constrn. naval hosp. at Newport, began work of locating docks and the establishment of navy yards. Died Bladensburg, Md., Dec. 17, 1813.

STODDERT, John Truman, congressman; b. Smith Point, Nanjemoy, Charles County, Md., Oct. 1, 1790; grad. Princeton, 1810; studied law. Admitted to bar, practiced law; served in War of 1812; mem. Md. Ho. of Dels., 1820; mem. U.S. Ho. of Reps. (Jackson Democrat) from Md., 23d Congress, 1833-35; became farmer. Died Wicomico House, West Hatton estate, Charles County, July 19, 1870; buried family burying ground on his estate.

STOEVER, Martin Luther, educator, editor; b. Germantown, Pa., Feb. 17, 1820; grad. Gettysburg Coll., 1838; Ph.D. (hon.), Hamilton Coll., 1856; LL.D. (hon.), Union Coll., 1869; m. Elizabeth McConaughy, June 14, 1850, 1 son, William Caspar. Tchr., Jefferson, Frederick County, Md., 1838-42; prin. Gettysburg Acad., 1842-51; prof. history Gettysburg Coll., 1844-56, prof. Latin, 1851-70, acting pres., 1850; sec. Gen. Synod of Evangelical Lutheran Ch. in U.S.; an editor Evangelical Review, 1857-61, editor, propr., 1862-70; wrote many biog. sketches of Lutheran clergy including Memoir of the Life and Times of Henry Melchior Muhlenberg, 1856, Memorial of Rev. Philip F. Mayer, 1858. Died Phila., July 22, 1870; buried Germantown.

STOKELY, Samuel, congressman, lawyer; b. Washington, Pa., Jan. 25, 1796; grad. Washington Coll. (now Washington and Jefferson Coll.), 1813; studied law. Admitted to bar, practiced in Steubenville, O., 1817; U.S. land receiver, 1827-28; mem. Ohio Senate, 1837-38; mem. U.S. Ho. of Reps. (Whig) from Ohio, 27th Congress, 1841-43. Died Steubenville, May 23, 1861; buried Union Cemetery.

STOKES, Montfort, senator, gov. N.C.; b. Lunenberg County, Va., Mar. 12, 1762; s. David and Sarah (Montfort) S.; m. Mary Irwin; m. 2d, Rachel Montgomery; children include Montfort S. Enlisted in Continental Navy, 1776, soon captured and imprisoned by British; clk. N.C. Senate, 1786-91; clk. Superior Court of Rowan County (N.C.), 1790; trustee U. N.C. 1805-38; Democratic presdl. elector, 1804, 12, 24, 28; served as maj. gen. N.C. Militia in War of 1812; mem. U.S. Senate from N.C., Dec. 4, 1816-23; pres. N.C. Constl. Conv., Raleigh, 1823; mem. N.C. Senate, 1826-29, N.C. Ho. of Commons, 1829-30; gov. N.C., 1830-32; a commr. to investigate conditions in present state of Okla., 1832; sub-agt. for Cherokee, Seneca and Shawnee Indians in Ark., 1836, agt., 1837-41. Died Ft. Gibson, Ark., Nov. 4, 1842; buried with mil. honors, Ft. Gibson Cemetery.

STOKES, William Brickly, congressman; b. Chatham County, N.C., Sept. 9, 1814; attended common schs.; studied law. Moved to Tenn., became farmer; mem. Tenn. Ho. of Reps., 1849-52; mem. Tenn. Senate, 1855-56; mem. U.S. Ho. of Reps. from Tenn. (as Whig) 36th, (as Republican) 39th-41st congresses, 1859-61, July 24, 1866-71; served as maj. Tenn. Volunteers in U.S. Army during Civil War, 1862, brevetted maj. gen., discharged, 1865; admitted to bar, 1867, practiced law, Alexandria,

Tenn.; supr. internal revenue for Tenn. Died Alexandria, Mar. 14, 1897; buried East View Cemetery.

STONE, Alfred Parish, congressman; b. Worthington, Mass., June 28, 1813; attended common schs. Moved to Columbus, O., 1832, became mcht.; mem. U.S. Ho. of Reps. (Democrat, filled vacancy) from Ohio, 28th Congress, Oct. 8, 1844-45; treas. Ohio, 1857-62; apptd. collector internal revenue for Columbus, 1862-65. Died Columbus, Aug. 2, 1865; buried Green Lawn Cemetery.

STONE, Amasa, railroad builder, philanthropist; b. Charlton, Mass., Apr. 27, 1818; s. Amasa and Esther (Boyden) S.; m. Julia Ann Gleason, Jan. 13, 1842, 3 children. With William Howe secured contract to build 1st railroad bridge over Connecticut River at Springfield, 1840; supt. New Haven, Hartford & Springfield R.R., 1844; with Stillman Witt and Frederick Harbach contracted to build Cleve., Columbus & Cincinnati R.R., 1849, supt., pres.; obtained contract to build Chgo. & Milw. R.R.; built Cleve., Painesville & Ashtabula R.R., pres., 1856-68, merged with Lake Shore R.R., 1869, mng. dir. of merged system; mng. dir. Lake Shore R.R., 1872-74; pres. of bank at Toledo, O.; dir. Western Union Telegraph Co.; pres. Mercer Iron & Coal Co.; prin. financial founder Western Res. U., Cleve. Died Cleve., May 11, 1883.

STONE, Barton Warren, evangelist; b. nr. Port Tobacco, Md., Dec. 24, 1772; s. John and Mary (Warren) S.; m. Elizabeth Campbell, July 2, 1801; m. 2d, Celia Bowen, Oct. 31, 1811; 11 children. Licensed to preach by Orange Presbytery, N.C., 1796, took churches at Cane Ridge and Concord, Bourbon County, Ky., circa 1798; withdrew (with four others) from Synod of Ky., formed Springfield Presbytery (group known only as Christians, later became closely allied with Disciples of Christ or Campbellites); founder, editor Christian Messenger, 1826; author many theol. tracts. Died Hannibal, Mo., Nov. 9, 1844; buried Cane Ridge, Ky.

STONE, Charles Pomeroy, army officer, engr.; b. Greenfield, Mass., Sept. 30, 1824; s. Dr. Alpheus Fletcher and Fanny Lincoln (Cushing) S.; grad. U.S. Mil. Acad., 1845; m. Maria Louisa Clary, 1853; m. 2d, Annie Granier Stone, 1863; 6 children. Served as 1st lt. U.S. Army in Mexican War, 1846; resigned commn., 1856; commd. col. D.C. Volunteers, 1861, col. 14th Inf., U.S. Army, 1861, brig. gen. U.S. Volunteers, 1861; unjustly blamed for death of ex-senator Baker (col. in command at Battle of Ball's Bluff 1861) arrested 1862, imprisoned in Ft. Lafayette, released, 1862; served at Ft. Hudson and in Red River campaign; mustered out of volunteer commn., commd. col. U.S. Army; assigned to Army of Potomac, resigned, 1864; eng., supt. Dover Mining Co., Goochland County, Va., 1865-69; served in Egyptian army, 1870-83, chief of staff, lt. gen.; chief engr. Fla. Ship Canal Co., 1883-84; constructing engr. for foundations of Statue of Liberty. Died N.Y.C., Jan. 24, 1887; buried West Point, N.Y.

STONE, David, senator, gov. N.C.; b. Hope (nr. Windsor), N.C., Feb. 17, 1770; s. Zedekiah and Elizabeth (Williamson) Hobson S.; grad. Princeton, 1788; m. Hannah Turner, Mar. 13, 1793; m. 2d, Sarah Dashiell, June 1817; 4 children. Admitted to N.C. bar, 1790; mem. N.C. Ho. of Commons from Bertie County, 1791-94, 1811-12; judge N.C. Superior Ct., 1794-98; mem. U.S. Ho. of Reps. from N.C., 6th Congress, 1799-1801, mem. 1st standing com. of ways and means, voted to repeal Sedition Act; mem. U.S. Senate from N.C., 1801-07, 1813-Dec. 24, 1814 (resigned); gov. N.C., 1808-10. Died Raleigh, Wake County, N.C., Oct. 7, 1818; buried nr. Raleigh.

STONE, David Marvin, editor, publisher; b. Oxford, Conn., Dec. 23, 1817; s. Noah and Rosalind (Marvin) S.; m. Delia Hall, Sept. 7, 1841, no children. Wrote correspondence for Dry Goods Reporter, N.Y.C., circa 1842, editor, 1849; writer with N.Y. Jour. of Commerce, 1849, managed paper, circa 1861, editor in chief, 1866-circa 1884, sole owner, 1884; edited a popular mag. Ladies' Wreath in 1850's; contributed weekly financial review to New York Observer and Hunt's Mchts. Mag.; wrote Sunday school novel Frank Forrest, 1850; pres. N.Y. Asso. Press, 1869-94. Died Bklyn., Apr. 2, 1895.

STONE, Eben Francis, congressman, lawyer; b. Newburyport, Essex County, Mass., Aug. 3, 1822; attended North Andover Acad.; grad. Harvard, 1843, Law Sch., 1846. Admitted to bar, 1847, practiced in Newbuyport; pres. Common Council, 1851; mem. Mass. Senate, 1857-58, 61; enlisted in U.S. Army during Civil War, commanded 48th Regt., Mass. Volunteer Militia; mayor Newburyport, 1867; mem. Mass. Ho. of Reps., 1867, 77-78, 80; mem. U.S. Ho. of Reps. (Republican) from Mass., 47th-49th congresses, 1881-87. Died Newburyport, Jan. 22, 1895; buried Oakhill Cemetery.

STONE, Ebenezer Whittier, army officer; b. Roxbury, Mass., June 1801. Served with U.S. Army, 1817-21; became officer Mass. Militia, 1822; mem. lower house Mass. Legislature, 1840-41, mem. mil. com.; adj. gen. Mass., 1851-60; organized light arty. battery Mass. Militia (1st battery of light arty. outside of U.S. Army), 1853; secured adoption of rifled musket in Mass. Militia, 1855; designed 1st rifled cannon for U.S. Army, 1859; chief ordnance officer Mass. Militia, 1861. Author: Digest of the Militia Laws of Massachusetts, 1851; Manual of Percussion Arms, 1857. Died Boston, Apr. 18, 1880.

STONE, George Washington, jurist; b. Bedford County, Va., Oct. 24, 1811; s. Micajah and Sarah (Leftwich) S.; m. Mary Gillespie, Dec. 16, 1834; m. 2d, Emily Moore, Sept. 4, 1849; m. 3d, Mrs. Mary (Harrison) Wright, Feb. 8, 1866; several children. Admitted to Ala. bar, 1834; judge Circuit Ct., Ala. Supreme Ct., 1856-65, 76-84, chief justice, 1884-94; helped restore law to ordered state during Reconstrn. era; aided in preparing Revised Penal Code, 1865; advocate of judicial reform. Died Montgomery, Ala., Mar. 11, 1894.

STONE, Horatio, sculptor; b. Jackson, Washington County, N.Y., Dec. 25, 1808; s. Reuben and Nancy (Fairchild) S.; studied sculpture, Washington, D.C., 1848. never married. Physician in N.Y.C., 1841-47; Contract surgeon U.S. Army, Civil War, 1862-65, stationed Washington, also Ft. Delaware, Del.; active organizer Washington Art Assn., pres. 1857 (assn. resulted in art commn. apptd. by Pres. Buchanan, 1859, also incorporation Nat. Gallery of Art, 1860); exhibited at N.A.D., N.Y.C., 1849, 69. Prin. works include 4 sculptures preserved in Capitol Bldg., Washington, D.C.: bust of Chief Justice Roger Taney, statues of Alexander Hamilton, 1864, Senator Edward Dickinson Baker of Ore., 1874, John Hancock, 1856. Author: Freedom (small vol. poems containing "Eleutheria" and "Day"), 1864. Died Carrara, Italy, Aug. 25, 1875.

STONE, James W., congressman; b. Taylorsville, Spencer County, Ky., 1813; attended common schs.; studied law. Admitted to bar, practiced law; held several local offices; mem. Ky. Ho. of Reps., 1837, 39; mem. U.S. Ho. of Reps. (Democrat) from Ky., 28th, 32d congresses, 1843-45, 51-53. Died Taylorsville, Oct. 13, 1854.

STONE, John Augustus, actor, dramatist; b. Concord, Mass., Dec. 15, 1800; s. Joshua and Sarah (Avery) S.; m. Mrs. Amelia (Greene) Legge, 1822, at least 2 children. Made debut in play Douglas at Washington Garden Theatre, Boston, 1824; author plays including: Restoration; or, The Diamond Cross (1st play), 1824; Metamora (most important play, produced Park Theatre 1829); The Knight of the Golden Fleece (prod. posthumously at Park Theatre 1834). Committed suicide (threw himself into Schuylkill River from Spruce St. Wharf, Phila.), May 29, 1834; buried Machpelah Cemetery, nr. Phila.

STONE, John Seely, clergyman; b. West Stockbridge, Mass., Oct. 7, 1795; s. Ezekiel and Mary (Seely) S.; grad. Union Coll., Schenectady, N.Y., 1823; attended Gen. Theol. Sem., N.Y.C.; m. Sophie Morrison Adams, May 2, 1826; m. 2d, Mary Kent, Sept. 5, 1839; at least 8 children including James Kent, Henry, Elizabeth. Involved in minor skirmish with British at Boston, 1814; ordained deacon Protestant Episcopal Ch., 1826, priest, 1827; tutor Greek and Latin, Hobart Coll., Hartford, Conn., 1825-27; rector St. Michael's Ch., Litchfield, Conn., All Saints Ch., Frederick, Md., 1828-29; rector Trinity Ch., New Haven, Conn., 1830-32, St. Paul's, Boston, 1832-41, Christ Ch., Bklyn., 1842-52, St. Paul's Ch., Brookline, Mass., 1852-62; prof. theology Phila. Divinity Sch., 1862-67. Author: Memoir of Life of Rt. Rev. Alexander Viets Griswold, 1844; The Mysteries Opened, 1844; The Divine Rest, 1867. Died Jan. 13, 1882.

STONE, Lucy, reformer, b. West Brookfield, Mass., Aug. 13, 1818; d. Francis and Hannah (Matthews) Stone; grad. Oberlin Coll., 1847; m. Henry Brown Blackwell, May 1, 1855, 1 dau., Alice Stone Blackwell. Tchr., Quaboag Sem., Warren, Mass., Wesleyan Acad., Wilbraham, Mass., Mt. Holyoke Female Sem.; became lectr. for Anti-Slavery Soc., 1848; headed 1st nat. woman's rights conv., Worcester, Mass., 1850, arranged for annual convs.; mem. exec. com. of newly-formed Am. Equal Rights Assn., 1866; pres. N.J. Woman Suffrage Assn., 1867; a founder New Eng. Suffrage Assn., 1868; a founder Am. Woman Suffrage Assn., concentrated on gaining suffrage by states; a founder and financial backer Woman's Journal (organ of women's rights), 1870-93, joint editor with husband, 1872-93; a leader Mass. Woman Suffrage Assn. (organized 1870). Died Boston, Oct. 18, 1893.

STONE, Michael Jenifer, congressman; b. Equality, nr. Port Tobacco, Charles County, Md., 1747; completed prep. studies. Mem. Md. Ho. of Dels., 1781-83; mem. Md. Conv. to ratify U.S. Constn., 1788; mem. U.S. Ho. of Reps. from Md., 1st Congress, 1789-91; apptd. judge Md. 1st Jud. Dist., 1791. Died Charles County, 1812; buried on his estate Equality.

STONE, Samuel, clergyman; b. Hertford, Eng., July 1602; s. John Stone; B.A., Emmanuel Coll., Cambridge (Eng.) U., 1623; married before 1640; m. 2d, Elizabeth Allen, 1641; at least 5 children. Took holy orders at Peterborough; curate at Stisted Essex, 1627-30; came to Newtown (now Cambridge), Mass. as colleague minister in place of John Cotton, 1633; selected site of Hartford, Conn., purchased in 1636, town probably named in honor of his birthplace; represented his church at New Eng. synods of 1637, 43, 46-48; served as chaplain in Pequot War of 1637; accompanied Gov. Winthrop of Conn. to England, 1661; believed in aristocratic essence of Congregationalism; involved in prolonged controversy with elders over ch. membership and baptism. Author: Confutation of the Antinomians; A Body of Divinity. Died Hartford, July 20, 1663.

STONE, Thomas, Continental congressman; b. "Poynton Manor," Charles County, Md., 1743; s. David and Elizabeth (Jenifer) S.; m. Margaret Brown, 1768, at least 3 children. Admitted to Md. bar, 1764; mem. Continental Congress, 1775, 79, 84, 85; mem. com. that framed Articles of Confederation; signed Declaration of Independence, 1776; mem. Md. Senate, 1776-87, opposed movement for paper currency; a Md. commr. negotiating with Va. over jurisdiction Chesapeake Bay; mem. Congress of Confederation, 1784-85; because of family illness declined election to Constl. Conv., Phila., 1787. Died Alexandria, Va., Oct. 5, 1787; buried "Garden" Cemetery, Havre de Venture, Charles County.

STONE, Thomas Treadwell, clergyman; b. Waterford, Me., Feb. 8, 1801; grad. Bowdoin Coll., 1820, D.D., 1855. Served Congregational Ch., Andover, Me., 1824-30; in charge of Congregational Ch., East Machias, Me., 1832-46; pastor 1st Unitarian Ch., Salem, Mass., 1846-52; 1st Congregational Ch., Bolton, Mass., 1852-60, 1st Eccles. Soc., Brooklyn, Conn., 1863-71; contbr. articles to many religious periodicals. Died Bolton, circa 1875.

STONE, Warren, physician; b. Saint Albans, Vt., Feb. 3, 1808; s. Peter and Jerusha (Stone) S.; M.D., Berkshire Med. Instn., Pittsfield, Mass., 1831; m. Malvina D. Johnson, 1843, at least 3 children including Warren. Asst. surgeon Charity Hosp., New Orleans, La., 1834, resident surgeon, 1835-39, vis. surgeon, 1839-72; cons. physician Hotel Dieu; founder (with Dr. William E. Kennedy) Maison de Sante (one of earliest pvt. hosps. in Am.), 1839; mem. staff Med. Coll. La. (now Tulane U.), 1834-72, prof., 1839-72; served as officer Confederate Army, Civil War, apptd. surgeon-gen. La.; 1st to resect part of a rib to secure permanent drainage in cases of empyema; made 1st successful cure for traumatic vertebral aneurism, 1850; responsible for 1st cure of an aneurism of 2d portion subclavian artery; made 1st use silver wire for ligation of the external iliac. Contbr. articles to New Orleans Med. and Surg. Jour., co-editor, 1857-59. Died New Orleans, Dec. 6, 1872.

STONE, William, colonial gov.; b. Northamptonshire, Eng., 1605; m. Virlinda Cotton, 7 children. Came to Va. before 1628; justice Accomac County (Va.), 1633; sheriff of Northampton, 1 term; gov. Md., 1648, Toleration Act of 1649 (which required oath to England) passed under his administration, 1649; opposed by Puritan parliamentary commn. from Eng., 1652-54, forced by them to resign, 1654; under orders from Lord Baltimore gathered small force and met Puritans in Battle of the Severn, 1655, defeated, wounded and captured, sentenced to death by council of war but saved by friends among the Puritans; mem. Gov. Josias Fendall's Council, 1657. Died on estate, Charles County, Md., circa 1660.

STONE, William, congressman; b. Sevier County, Tenn. (then N.C.), Jan. 26, 1791; completed prep. studies. Held several local offices; served as capt. in Creek War, commd. brig. gen. for gallantry at Battle of Horseshoe; served with Gen. Jackson in Battle of New Orleans; presented cane by Congress for bravery at Battle of Tippecanoe; mem. U.S. Ho. of Reps. (filled vacancy) from Tenn., 25th Congress, Sept. 14, 1837-39. Died Delphi (later Davis), Sequatchie County, Tenn., Feb. 18, 1853; buried family burying ground at Delphi.

STONE, William Leete, journalist, historian; b. New Paltz, N.Y., Apr. 20, 1792; s. Rev. William and Tamson (Graves) S.; m. Susannah Wayland, Jan. 31, 1817; 1 adopted son, William Henry. Owned the Federalist Herkimer American, 1813-14; bought

Northern Whig, 1814; edited 2 literary periodicals Lounger and Spirit of the Forum; purchased Albany Daily Advertiser, 1816, merged it with Albany Gazette; editor Mirror, Hartford, Conn., 1818; a propr. N.Y. Comml. Advertiser, 1821-44; Federalist, adherent of Gov. Clinton; one of 1st to espouse publicly cause of Greek independence; dir. Instn. for Deaf and Dumb; supt. common schs. of N.Y.C., 1843-44; Mason; helped found N.Y. State Hist. Agy., 1838, result of interest in early history of region; wrote social satire Ups and Downs in the Life of a Distressed Gentleman, 1836; wrote history of Iroquois beginning with Life of Joseph Brant Thayendanegea, 1838. Author: Letters on Masonry and Anti-Masonry, 1832. Died Saratoga Springs, N.Y., Aug. 15, 1844.

STONE, William Oliver, portrait painter; b. Derby, Conn., Sept. 26, 1830; s. Frederick William and Ellen S.; married, 1 dau., Louise (Stone) Ingalls. Opened studio, N.Y.C., 1854; mem: and exhibitor N.A.D., 1859-75; exhibited portraits at Royal Acad. exhbns., London, Eng.; portraits include: Gorden Bennett, Mrs. Hoey, Miss Rawle (shown at Met. Mus., N.Y.C.), Thomas Jefferson Bryant (now owned by N.Y. Hist. Soc.), Cyrus W. Field, William W. Corcoran, Bishop William I. Kip of Cal. Died Newport, R.I., Sept. 15, 1875.

STONEMAN, George, army officer, gov. Cal.; b. Busti, N.Y., Aug. 8, 1822; s. George and Catherine (Cheney) S.; grad. U.S. Mil. Acad., 1846; m. Mary Oliver Hardisty, circa 1865, 4 children. Brevetted 2d lt. 1st Dragoons (now 1st cavalry); q.m. "Mormon Battalion," a part of Gen. Kearney's expdn. to Cal., 1846, served in Southwest until 1855; capt. 25th U.S. Cavalry; maj. 4th Cavalry, 1861, on Gen. McClellan's staff; brig. gen. volunteers, cavalry officer Army of Potomac; in command 1st div. III Corps, Peninsular Campaign of 1862; maj. gen. U.S. Volunteers, 1862; commd. col. U.S. Army, served in battles of Fredericksburg, then Chancellorsville, 1863; chief Cavalry Bur., Washington, D.C., 1863; served in cavalry corps Army of the Ohio, 1864, with Sherman in march through Ga., captured Aug. 1864, exchanged, Oct. 1864; brevetted brig. gen. and maj. gen. U.S. Army, 1865; commanded in Petersburg and Richmond, 1865-69; col. 21st Inf., 1866, commanded Dept. of Ariz., 1869-71; gov. Cal. (Democrat), 1883-87; ry. commr., 1879, opposed influence of Pacific rys. in state affairs; restored to army list as col., ret., by spl. act of Congress, 1891. Died Buffalo, N.Y., Sept. 5, 1894; buried Lakewood, Chaletauqua Lake, N.Y.

STORER, Bellamy, congressman, lawyer; b. Portland, Me., Mar. 26, 1796; attended Bowdoin Coll., 1809; studied law, Boston. Admitted to Portland bar, 1817, practiced in Cincinnati, 1817; mem. U.S. Ho. of Reps. (Whig) from Ohio, 24th Congress, 1835-37; Whig presdl. elector, 1844; prof. Cincinnati Law Sch., 1855-74; judge Cincinnati Superior Ct., 1854-72, resigned. Died Cincinnati, June 1, 1875; buried Spring Grove Cemetery.

STORER, Clement, senator, congressman; b. Kennebunk, Me., Sept. 20, 1760; completed prep. studies; studied medicine, Portsmouth, N.H., also Europe. Practiced medicine, Portsmouth; served from capt. to maj. gen. of militia; mem. N.H. Ho. of Reps., 1810-12, speaker 1 year; mem. U.S. Ho. of Reps. from N.H., 10th Congress, 1807-09; mem. U.S. Senate (filled vacancy) from N.H., June 27, 1817-19; high sheriff Rockingham County, 1818-24. Died Portsmouth, N.H., Nov. 21, 1830; buried North Cemetery.

STORER, David Humphreys, obstetrician, naturalist; b. Portland, Me., Mar. 26, 1804; s. Woodbury and Margaret (Boyd) S.; grad. Bowdoin, 1822; grad. Harvard Med. Sch.,1825; m. Abby Jane Brewer, 5 children including Horatio Robinson, Francis Humphreys. Joined Boston Soc. Natural History, 1830; lectured Harvard Med. Sch., prof. obstetrics and med. jurisprudence, 1854-68, dean, 1854-68; through his efforts over 10,000 volumes of med. works collected for Boston Public Library; collected coins; apptd. to com. for natural history survey of Mass.; mem. staff Mass. Gen. Hosp., 1849-58; founder Obstet. Soc. of Boston; gave discourse An Address on Medical Jurisprudence: Its Claims to Greater Regard from the Student and the Physician before Mass. Med. Soc., 1851; collected and described Mollusca of Mass.; issued translation of L. C. Kiener's work on shells General Species and Iconography of Recent Shells, Comprising the Massena Museum, the Collection of Lamarck, the Collection of the Museum of Natural History and the Recent Discoveries of Travelers, 1837; expanded volume into A History of Fishes in Massachusetts, 1867; other writings include: Report on the Ichthyology and Herpetology of Massachusetts, 1839; Synopsis of the Fishes of North America, 1846. Died Boston, Sept. 10, 1891.

STOREY, Wilbur Fisk, journalist; b. Salisbury, Vt., Dec. 19, 1819; s. Jesse and Elizabeth (Pierce) S.; m. Maria Isham, 1847; m. 2d, Mrs. Harriet Dodge, 1870; m. 3d, Eureka Bissell Pearson, Dec. 2, 1874. Learned printing trade, Middlebury Free Press, 1831-36; compositor N.Y. Jour. of Commerce, 1836-38; moved to Ind., 1838; published 2 short-lived papers, La Porte Herald, Mishawaka Toscin; later owned a drug store, read law, published Patriot (all Jackson, Mich.); postmaster Jackson, 1845-49; del. Mich. Constl. Conv., 1850; apptd. state prison insp., 1850; publisher Detroit Free Press, 1853-61; became owner Daily Chgo. Times, 1861, changed name to Chgo. Times, built new plant after Chgo. Fire, 1871, continued active interest in paper until 1878. Died Oct. 27, 1884.

STORROW, James Jackson, lawyer; b. Boston, July 29, 1837; s. Charles and Lydia (Jackson) S.; A.B., Harvard, 1857, studied Harvard Law Sch., 1 year; m. Annie Perry, Aug. 28, 1861; m. 2d, Ann Dexter; 3 children including James Jackson. Admitted to bar, 1860; specialist in patent law, gained fame in legal circles in Lawrence vs. Pana copyright case of 1869; counsel (with Chauncey Smith) Bell Telephone Co. in patent litigation, 1878-96; went to Caracas to help in Venezuela boundary question, 1896, went again in 1897 to submit protocol for arbitration treaty agreed upon by Britain and Venezuela, instrumental in persuading British to submit dispute to arbitration. Died Washington, D.C., Apr. 15, 1897; buried Newport, R.I.

STORRS, Henry Randolph, congressman, lawyer; b. Middletown, Conn., Sept. 3, 1787; grad. Yale, 1804; studied law. Admitted to bar, 1807, practiced law, Champion, N.Y., later practiced in Whitesboro, Utica, N.Y.; mem. U.S. Ho. of Reps. (Federalist) from N.Y., 15th-16th, 18th-21st congresses, 1817-21, 23-31, a mgr. apptd. by House to conduct impeachment proceedings against James H. Peck (U.S. judge for Mo. Dist.), 1830; presiding judge Oneida County Ct. Common Pleas, 1825-29; moved to N.Y.C. practiced law. Died New Haven, Conn., July 29, 1837; buried Grove Street Cemetery.

STORRS, Richard Salter, clergyman, editor; b. Longmeadow, Mass., Feb. 6, 1787; s. Richard Salter and Sarah (Williston) S.; attended Yale, 1802; grad. Williams Coll., 1807; grad. Andover Theol. Sem., 1810; m. Sarah Woodhull, Apr. 2, 1812; m. 2d, Harriet Moore, Sept. 16, 1819, m. 3d, Anne Stebbins, Oct. 18, 1835. In charge of Clinton Acad., circa 1803; licensed by Suffolk Presbytery, circa 1808; missionary work in Ga. as agent Am. Edn. Soc., circa 1809; ordained and installed as pastor First Congregational Ch., Braintree, Mass., 1811, pastor, 1811-73; promoter Sunday Schs., temperance socs.; sec. Am. Tract Soc., 1820-25; dir. Am. Edn. Soc., 1821-30; officer of Mass. Missionary Soc.; editorial writer Recorder (later Boston Recorder), 1816-24; editor The Congregationalist, 1850-56. Author: American Slavery and the Means of its Removal, 1844. Died Braintree, Aug. 11, 1873.

STORRS, William Lucius, congressman, jurist; b. Middletown, Conn., Mar. 25, 1795; grad. Yale, 1814; studied law. Admitted to Whitestown (N.Y.) bar, 1817, returned to Conn., 1817, practiced in Middletown; mem. Conn. Ho. of Reps., 1827-29, 34, speaker, 1834; mem. U.S. Ho. of Reps. from Conn., 21st-22d, (Whig) 26th congresses, 1829-33, 39-June 1840 (resigned); apptd. asso. judge Conn. Supreme Ct., 1840, chief justice, 1856-61; prof. law Wesleyan U., Middletown, 1841-46, Yale, 1846, 47. Died Hartford, Conn., June 25, 1861; buried Old North Cemetery.

STORY, Isaac, writer; b. Marblehead, Mass., Aug. 7, 1774; s. Rev. Isaac and Rebecca (Bradstreet) S.; grad. Harvard, 1793, studied law; never married. Edited Castine (Me.) Jour.; wrote children's poems (signed "The Stranger") including Liberty, 1795, All the World's a Stage; wrote essays (signed "The Traveler") published in Columbian Centinel of Boston; best-known for his verses (signed "Peter Quince") written originally for Newburyport Polit. Gazette. Author: An Eulogy on the Glorious Virtues of the Illustrious Gen. George Washington, 1800; A Parnassian Shop, Opened in the Pindaric Stile, by Peter Quince, Esquire, 1801. Died Marblehead, July 19, 1803.

STORY, Joseph, asso. justice U.S. Supreme Ct.; b. Marblehead, Mass., Sept. 18, 1779; s. Dr. Elisha Story. Admitted to Essex County (Mass.) bar, 1801; mem. Mass. Legislature, 1805-08, 11, speaker, 1811; chmn. com. which urged creation of ct. of chancery in Mass., 1808; mem. U.S. Ho. of Reps. (Republican) from Mass., 11th Congress, May 23, 1808-09, resigned partly as result of disagreement with his party over Embargo Act (which he opposed); asso. justice U.S. Supreme Ct. (youngest ever apptd.), 1811-45; an early decision reversed custom of circuit cts. of allowing appeals from dist. ct. in jury cases at common law; instrumental in extension of admiralty jurisdiction claimed by fed. cts. after War of 1812 (De Lovio vs. Boit one of most famous admiralty cases of the period); delivered key opinion in case of Martin vs. Hunter's Lessee, 1816, held that appellate jurisdiction of U.S. Supreme Ct. could b exercised over state cts.; delivered opinion in Vida vs. Phila. which held the will of Stephen Girar valid in its exclusion of clergyman from coll. pro vided for in will, 1844; noted for dissenting opin ion in Charles River Bridge case, 1837, affirme principle of sanctity of contracts; pres. Mchts. Bank of Salem (Mass.), 1815-53; v.p. Salen Savs. Bank 1818-30; overseer Harvard, 1819 mem. corp., 1825, apptd. prof. law, 1829, enlarge law library; author Crimes Act of 1825 (introduce by Daniel Webster); published commentarie (a result of his teaching methods at Harvar 1832-45, began with Bailments, 1832, ende with Promissory Notes, 1845); other publs. include: A Selection of Pleadings in Civil Actions 1805, Public and General Statutes Passed by th Congress of the United States, 1789-1827, published 1828; known internationally for treatises On the Constitution, The Conflict of Laws. Died Cambridge, Mass., Sept. 10, 1845; buried Mt. Auburn Cemetery.

STORY, William Wetmore, lawyer, sculptor; b. Salem, Mass., Feb. 12, 1819; s. Joseph and Sarah Waldo (Wetmore) S.; A.B., Harvard, 1838, LL.B., 1840; D.C.L. (hon.), Oxford (Eng.) U., U. Bologna (Italy); m. Emelyn Eldredge, Oct. 31, 1843; children—Thomas Waldo, Julian Russel, Joseph, Madame Edith Story Peruzzi. Admitted to bar, circa 1840, practiced with firm Hillard and Sumner; U.S. commr. in bankruptcy; commr.U.S. cts. in Mass., Me., Pa.; reporter U.S. Circuit Ct., Dist. of Mass.; sculptor, from 1847; lived in Rome, Italy, from 1856; exhibited sculpture, London, 1862; (became leading figure Anglo-Am. sculpturer); U.S. commr. fine arts World's Fair, Paris, France, 1879; decorated by Italy, France. Prin. works include: Cleopatra (described in Hawthorne's Marble Faun), Libyan Spy (now in Nat. Gallery Art, Washington, D.C.), Saul, 1863, Medea, 1864 (at centennial Expn., Phila., now Met. Mus., N.Y.C.), Salome, 1870, Jerusalem in Her Desolation, 1873 (now in Pa. Acad. Fine Arts, Phila.), Alcestis, 1874, statue Judge Joseph Story (his father). Author: (legal textbooks) A Treatise on the Law of Contracts Not Under Seal, 1844, A Treatise on the Law of Sales of Personal Property, 1847; (collections essays) Robadi Roma, 1862, The Graffiti d'Italia, 1868, Vallambrosa, 1881, Excursions in Arts and Letters, 1891; (treatise) The Proportions of the Human Figure, 1866. Contbr. poems, essays Boston Miscellany and Pioneer. Died Vallombrosa, Rome, Italy, Oct. 7, 1895; buried Protestant Cemetery, Rome.

STOUGHTON, Edwin Wallace, lawyer, diplomat; b. Springfield, Conn., May 1, 1818; s. Thomas D. and Susan (Bradley) S.; m. Mary Fiske, Mar. 3, 1855, no children. Admitted to N.Y. bar, 1840; practiced law, specializing in patent suits, noteworthy cases include Charles Goodyear patent cases, Woodworth planing machine cases; appeared for U.S. and N.J. in U.S. vs. Callicott (14, 710 Federal Cases); mem. commn. to report on controversial Hayes-Tilden election of 1876 in La.; wrote article "The Electoral Commission Bubble Exploded" in N. Am. Review, 1877; U.S. ambassador to Russia, 1877-79; contributed $15,000 to Dartmouth to found museum of anatomy. Died N.Y.C., Jan. 7, 1882.

STOUGHTON, William, colonial ofcl.; b. England, Sept. 30, 1631; s. Israel Stoughton; grad. Harvard, 1650; M.A., New Coll., Oxford (Eng.) U., 1653. Curate Rumboldswyke, Sussex, Eng., 1659; assistant of Mass. Bay Co., 1671-86; commr. United Colonies, 1674-76, 80-86; represented Mass. before King in controversy over Mason claims, 1676-79; deputy from Mass. Colony to Eng., 1677-79; dep. pres. temporary govt., 1686; lt. gov. Mass., 1692-1701, acting gov., 1694-99, 1700-01; chief justice Superior Ct. of oyer and terminer which tried Salem witchcraft cases, 1692. Died Dorchester, Mass., July 7, 1701.

STOUGHTON, William Lewis, congressman, lawyer; b. Bangor, N.Y., Mar. 20, 1827; attended Kirkland, Painesville, Madison (O.) acads.; studied law, Ohio, Ind., Mich., 1849-51. Admitted to bar, practiced law, Sturgis, Mich., 1851; pros. atty., 1855-59; del. Republican Nat. Conv., Chgo., 1860; apptd. by Pres. Lincoln as U.S. dist. atty. for Mich. dist., 1861, resigned few months later; served as col. and brig. gen. U.S. Army, during Civil War, brevetted maj. gen., resigned because of ill health, 1864; mem. Mich. Constl. Conv., 1867; atty. gen. Mich., 1867-68; mem. U.S. Ho. of Reps. (Rep.) from Mich., 41st-42d congresses, 1869-73. Died Sturgis, June 6, 1888; buried Oak Lawn Cemetery.

STOUT, Byron Gray, congressman; b. Richmond, Ontario County, N.Y., Jan. 12, 1829; grad. U. Mich., 1851; studied law. Supt., prin. Pontiac (Mich.) High Sch., 1853-54; mem. Mich. Ho. of Reps., 1855, 57, speaker, 1857; mem. Mich. Senate, 1860, pres. pro tem; mem. Union Conv. of Conservatives, Phila., 1866; del. Democratic nat. convs., 1868, 80, 88; in pvt. banking before 1869; mem.

U.S. Ho. of Reps. (Dem.) from Mich., 52d Congress, 1891-93; pres. Oakland County Bank, 1893-96. Died Pontiac, June 19, 1896; buried Oak Hill Cemetery.

STOUT, Lansing, congressman, lawyer; b. Watertown, Jefferson County, N.Y., Mar. 27, 1828; attended public schs.; studied law. Admitted to bar; moved to Placer County, Cal., 1852, practiced law; mem. Cal. Assembly, 1855; moved to Portland, Ore., 1857, practiced law; judge Multonomah County (Ore.) Ct., 1858; mem. U.S. Ho. of Reps. (Democrat) from Ore., 36th Congress, 1859-61; instrumental in securing daily overland mail between Portland and Sacramento, Cal., also payment of Ore. and Wash. Territory Indian war debt; mem. Ore. Senate, 1868-71. Died Portland, Mar. 4, 1871; buried Riverview Cemetery.

STOVER, John Hubler, congressman; b. Aaronsburg, Center County, Pa., Apr. 24, 1833; completed prep. studies Bellefonte (Pa.) Acad.; studied law. Admitted to bar, 1857, practiced law, Bellefonte; held several local offices; dist. atty. Center County, 1860-62; enlisted in U.S. Army as pvt. during Civil War, 1861, commd. capt., maj; commd. col. 184th Regt., Pa. Volunteer Inf.; after war moved to Versailles, Morgan County, Mo., practiced law; dist. atty. Morgan County, 1866-68; mem. U.S. Ho. of Reps. (Republican, filled vacancy) from Mo., 40th Congress, Dec. 7, 1868-69; in real estate business, mining activities, Versailles; del. Centennial Expn., Phila., 1876. Died Aurora Springs, Mo., Oct. 27, 1889; buried City Cemetery, Versailles.

STOW, Baron, clergyman; b. Croydon, N.H., June 16, 1801; s. Peter and Deborah (Nettleton) S.; grad. Columbian Coll., 1825; m. Elizabeth Skinner, Sept. 7, 1826. Did editorial work on Columbian Star Jour. of the Triennial Conv., 1826-27; ordained to ministry Baptist Ch., Portsmouth, N.H., 1827; pastor 2d Bapt. Ch., Boston, 1832-48; pastor Rowe St. Bapt. Ch., Boston, 1848-67; actively associated with fgn. missions enterprise; one of leaders in its reorgn. by No. Baptists, 1845; one of compilers Psalmist (hymnal), 1849. Author: History of the Baptist Mission to India, 1835; Daily Manna, 1842; First Things, 1859; Christian Brotherhood, 1859. Died Boston, Dec. 27, 1869.

STOW, Silas, congressman; b. Middlefield, Middlesex County, Conn., Dec. 21, 1773; attended common schs.; studied law. Moved to Lowville, Lewis County, N.Y., became farmer; land agt. for Nicholas Low; moved to Oneida County, 1797; apptd. judge Oneida County, 1801; returned to Lewis County; mem. U.S. Ho. of Reps. (Federalist) from N.Y., 12th Congress, 1811-13; sheriff Lewis County, 1814-15, judge, 1815-23. Died Lowville, Jan. 19, 1827; buried East State Street Burying Ground.

STOWE, Calvin Ellis, educator; b. Natick, Mass., Apr. 26, 1802; s. Samuel and Hepzibah (Biglow) S.; grad. Bowdoin Coll., 1824; grad. Andover Theol. Sem., 1829; m. Eliza Tyler, 1832; m. 2d, Harriet Beecher, Jan. 6, 1836; 7 children. Prof. Greek, Dartmouth, 1831; prof. Bibl. lit. Lane Theol. Sem., Cincinnati, 1833; prin. founder Coll. of Tchrs., Cincinnati, 1833; commr. to investigate pub. sch. systems of Europe; prof. religion Bowdoin Coll., 1850; prof. sacred lit. Andover Theol. Sem., 1852-64; visited Europe with wife, 1853, 56, 59. Author: Introduction to the Criticism and Interpretation of the Bible, 1835; Report on Elementary Instruction in Europe, 1837, reprinted by legislatures of Mass., Pa., Mich., other states in Common Schools and Teachers' Seminaries, 1839. Died Aug. 22, 1886.

STOWE, Harriet Elizabeth Beecher, author, humanitarian; b. Litchfield, Conn., June 14, 1811; d. Lyman and Roxana (Foote) Beecher; m. Calvin Ellis Stowe, Jan. 6, 1836, 7 children. Wrote composition "Can the Immortality of the Soul be Proved by the Light of Nature," 1822; became ardent abolitionist during residence in Cincinnati, 1833-50; wrote sketches including "Prize Tale, A New England Sketch" for Western Monthly Mag., 1834, which appeared as "Uncle Tim" in The Mayflower; published serial in National Era as Uncle Tom's Cabin, or Life Among the Lowly, published in 2 vols. by John P. Jewett, 1852, book became important factor in solidifying sentiment in North against slavery making issue a moral one (a significant factor in causing Civil War); Uncle Tom's Cabin was one of most popular plays produced on Am. stage; Southern Literary Messenger declared book a "criminal prostitution of the high functions of the imagination;" abolitionists their only partisans; reply to criticism resulted in A Key to Uncle Tom's Cabin, 1853; 1st Am. writer to take the Negro seriously and to conceive a novel with black man as hero. Author: (2d anti-slavery novel) Dred, A Tale of the Great Dismal Swamp, 1856; The Minister's Wooing, 1859; The Pearls of Orr's Island, 1862; Old Town Folks, 1869; (article pub. Atlantic Monthly) "The True Story of Lady Byron's Life," 1869; (elaboration of article) Lady Byron Vindicated, 1870; Sam Lawson's Oldtown Fireside Stories, 1872; Poganuc People, 1878; Principles of Domestic Science, 1870; The New Housekeeper's Manual, 1873; Religious Poems, 1867. Died Hartford, Conn., July 1, 1896.

STOWER, John G., congressman; b. Madison, N.Y.; completed prep. studies. Mem. U.S. Ho. of Reps. (Jacksonian Democrat) from N.Y., 20th Congress, 1827-29; mem. N.Y. State Senate, 1833-34.

STRACHEY, William, colonial ofcl.; b. Eng.; flourished 1606-18; son of John Strachey. Arrived in Jamestown (Va.), 1610; sec. and recorder under Lord De La Warr in Va., 1610-11; editor 1st written code of laws for Va. settlement, in London, Eng., 1611. Author: The Historie of Travaile into Virginia Britannia . . . Togither with the Manners and Customes of the People (valuable 1st hand account of life in Jamestown colony), 1849.

STRADER, Peter Wilson, congressman, businessman; b. Shawnee, Warren County, N.J., Nov. 6, 1818; attended common schs. Worked in printing office for 3 years; moved to Cincinnati, 1835, connected (as clk. and engr.) with steamboat interests on Ohio and Mississippi rivers, 1835-48; gen. ticket agt. Litle Miami R.R., 1848-67; mem. U.S. Ho. of Reps. (Democrat) from Ohio, 41st Congress, 1869-71; moved to Ashtabula, O., 1876. Died Ashtabula, Feb. 25, 1881; buried Spring Grove Cemetery, Cincinnati.

STRAIN, Isaac G., naval officer, explorer; b. Roxbury, Pa., Mar. 4, 1821; s. Robert and Eliza (Geddes) S.; attended naval sch., Phila., 1842-43. Became midshipman U.S. Navy, 1837; served in W.I. and S.Am., 1837-42; on leave of absence, 1843-44, led expdn. partially financed by Acad. Natural Scis. of Phila. to Brazil; served in frigate Constitution in East Indies, 1844; served in ship Ohio during Mexican War, 1848; crossed S.Am. from Valparaiso to Buenos Aires, 1848-49; served to Mexican boundary commn. of Dept. of Interior, 1850; led exploration of Isthmus of Darien to evaluate route for possible canal, 1853; joined Lt. O. H. Berryman's expdn. in ship Arctic to investigate possibility of laying submarine cable between U.S. and Gt. Britain, 1856. Author: Cordillera and Pampa, Mountain and Plain, 1853; A Paper on the History and Prospects of Interoceanic Communication by the American Isthmus, 1856. Died May 14, 1857.

STRAKOSCH, Maurice (Moritz), pianist, impresario; b. Gross-Seelovitz, Moravia, 1825; studied music Vienna, Austria. Made concert tours as pianist; lived in N.Y.C. as tchr. and concert pianist, 1848-60; became impresario, 1856; mgr. Adelina Patti; gave 1st season of Italian opera in N.Y.C., 1857, took co. to Chgo., 1859; returned to Europe, 1860. Author: Souvenirs d'un Impresario, 1887; Ten Commandments of Music for the Perfection of the Voice, published posthumously, 1896. Died Paris, France, Oct. 9, 1887.

STRANAHAN, James Samuel Thomas, congressman; b. Peterboro, N.Y., Apr. 25, 1808; s. Samuel and Lynda (Josselyn) S.; m. Marianmne Fitch, May 4, 1837; m. 2d, Clara Cornelia Harrison, after circa 1886; 3 children. Assemblyman, Albany (N.Y.), 1838; railroad contractor, Newark, N.J., 1840; one of 1st contractors to take railroad stock in payment for constrn. work; moved to Bklyn., 1844, worked for harbor and dock improvements; mem. U.S. Ho. of Reps. (Whig) from N.Y., 34th Congress, 1855-57; mem. Metropolitan Police Commn., N.Y.C., 1857; pres. Bklyn. Park Bd., 1860-82; urged adoption of plans for East River and Bklyn. bridges; supported Greater N.Y. consolidation plan involving the loss of Bklyn's. identity. Died Saratoga, N.Y., Sept. 3, 1898; buried Greenwood Cemetery, Bklyn.

STRANG, James Jesse, leader religious sect; b. Scipio, N.Y., Mar. 21, 1813; s. Clement and Abigail (James) S.; m. Mary Perce, 1836, also 4 polygamous wives. Admitted to N.Y. bar, 1836; postmaster Ellington (N.Y.), 1838-43; owner and editor Randolph Herald, 2 years; became a Mormon, 1843; a prophetic successor to Joseph Smith at Voree, Wis., 1844; founder City of St. James in Beaver Island, Mich., 1849; crowned king of New Zion, 1850, ruled community as virtual dictator; mem. Mich. Legislature (Democrat), 1852-54; acquitted of charges of robbing mails and counterfeiting, 1851; announced revelation proclaiming sanctity of plural marriage, 1850; shot by Alexander Wentworth, June 16, 1856; refused to name a successor and church expired. Author: The Book of the Law of the Lord, 1856. Died Mich., July 9, 1856.

STRANGE, Robert, senator; b. Manchester, Va., Sept. 20, 1796; attended Washington Coll. (now Washington and Lee U.); grad. Hampden-Sydney Coll.; studied law. Admitted to N.C. bar, practiced law in Fayetteville, N.C.; mem. N.C. Ho. of Commons, 1821-23, 26; judge Superior Ct. of N.C., 1827-36; mem. U.S. Senate (Democrat, filled vacancy) from N.C., Dec. 5, 1836-Nov. 16, 1840 (resigned); became solicitor 5th Jud. Dist. of N.C.; became a writer. Died Fayetteville, Feb. 19, 1854; buried family burial ground at "Myrtle Hill," nr. Fayetteville.

STRATTON, Charles Creighton, congressman; b. Swedesboro, N.J., Mar. 6, 1796; grad. Rutgers Coll., 1814. Became a farmer; mem. N.J. Gen. Assembly, 1821, 23, 29; mem. U.S. Ho. of Reps. (Whig) from N.J., 25th, 27th congresses, 1837-39, 41-43; mem. N.J. Constl. Conv., 1844; gov. N.J., 1845-48; resided in Europe, 1857-58. Died Swedesboro, Mar. 30, 1859; buried Episcopal Cemetery.

STRATTON, Charles Sherwood (known as Gen. Tom Thumb), midget; b. Bridgeport, Conn., Jan. 4, 1838; s. Sherwood Edwards and Cynthia (Thompson) S.; m. Mercy Lavinia Warren Bumpus, Feb. 10, 1863, 1 child. Exhibited at (P. T.) Barnum's Museum, N.Y.C., when he was 4 years old, weighing 16 pounds and measuring 2 feet tall; reached mature growth of 40 inches in height and 70 pounds in weight; went to Eng., received by Queen Victoria at Buckingham Palace, 1844; received 3 times at French Ct., Belgian Ct.; excellent businessman, accumulated fortune in early years in trips to Europe and tours of U.S.; monument to his memory in Bridgeport, Conn. Died on his estate, Middleboro, Mass., July 15, 1883.

STRATTON, John, congressman, lawyer; b. nr. Eastville, Va., Aug. 19, 1769; studied law. Admitted to Va. bar, practiced law; mem. Va. Ho. of Dels., 1779-92; mem. U.S. Ho. of Reps. from Va., 7th Congress, 1801-03. Died Norfolk, Va., May 10, 1804; buried St. Paul's Ch. Cemetery.

STRATTON, Nathan Taylor, congressman; b. nr. Swedesboro, N.J., Mar. 17, 1813; attended common schs. Moved to Mullica Hill, N.J., 1829, became clk. in store, partner of employer, 1835; owned a business, 1840-86; mem. N.J. Assembly, 1843-44; justice of peace, 1844-47, also in real estate bus., farming; held several local offices; mem. U.S. Ho. of Reps. (Democrat) from N.J., 32d-33d congresses, 1851-55; elected mem. Harrison Twp. com., 1865; served as N.J. tax commr.; trustee state reform sch. for boys, Jamesburg, N.J., 1865-87; del. Union Nat. Conv. of Conservatives, Phila., 1866. Died Mullica Hill, Mar. 9, 1887; buried Baptist Cemetery.

STRAUB, Christian Markle, congressman; b. Milton, Pa., 1804; studied law. Admitted to the bar; prothonotary of Schuylkill County, 1845, sheriff, 1849; mem. U.S. Ho. of Reps. (Democrat) from Pa., 33d Congress, 1853-55; mem. Pa. Senate, 1856-58. Died Washington, D.C.; buried Pottsville, Pa.

STRAWBRIDGE, James Dale, congressman, physician; b. Liberty Twp., Mountour County, Pa., Apr. 7, 1824; grad. Princeton, 1844; grad. med. dept. U. Pa., 1847. Practiced medicine at Danville, Pa.; served as brigade surgeon of Volunteers in Civil War, imprisoned in Libby Prison, 3 months; mem. U.S. Ho. of Reps. (Republican) from Pa., 43d Congress, 1873-75. Died Danville, July 19, 1890; buried Fairview Cemetery.

STRAWBRIDGE, Robert, clergyman; b. Drumsna, Carrick-on-Shannon, County Leitram, Ireland; s. Robert Strawbridge; 6 children. Came to Md., between 1759 and 1766; probable founder 1st Methodist soc. in Am., small soc. formed in log cabin ch. at Sam's Creek, Md., continued for about 16 years; made preaching tours in Eastern Md. and neighboring states; cooperated with Wesley's missionaries and conformed with English forms of Methodist procedure, 1769; apptd. to Balt. Circuit (Meth.), 1773; withdrew from Meth. Conf. over issue of administration of sacraments by laymen, circa 1775. Died nr. Towson, Md., Aug. 1781; buried Mt. Olivet Cemetery, Balt.

STRAWN, Jacob, cattleman; b. Somerset County, Pa., May 30, 1800; s. Isaiah and Rachel (Reed) S.; m. Matilda Green, 1819; m. 2d, Phoebe Gates, 1832; 13 children. Began farming in Central Ohio, 1819; bought 400 acres nr. Jacksonville, Ill., 1828, extended holdings to 20,000 acres; became largest cattle dealer in Midwest; introduced method for fattening cattle by corn feeding to Ill.; virtually controlled St. Louis livestock market for a time. Died Jacksonville, Aug. 23, 1865; buried Diamond Grove Cemetery, Jacksonville.

STREET, Alfred Billings, lawyer, poet, librarian, author; b. Poughkeepsie, N.Y., Dec. 18, 1811; s. Randall Sanford and Cornelia (Billings) S.; m. Elizabeth Weed, Nov. 3, 1841, 1 child. Admitted to N.Y. bar; published poems A Winter Scene and A Day in March in N.Y. Evening Post, 1826; editor literary mag. Northern Light, Albany, N.Y., 1843-

44; dir. N.Y. State Library, 1848-62, law librarian until 1868; noted as poet of nature, work typified by accurate description and directness; best known works are The Burning of Schenectady, 1842, and Frontenac (historical poem of 7,000 lines), 1849; other poems include Nature, 1840, Our State, 1849, Woods and Waters, 1860, Burgoyne, 1877, In Memorium: President Lincoln Dead, 1870; other works include The Poems of Alfred B. Street, 1845; The Council of Revision of State of New York: Its History, 1859; A Collection of Poems, 1866. Died Albany, June 2, 1881.

STREET, Augustus Russell, philanthropist; b. New Haven, Conn., Nov. 5, 1791; s. Titus and Amaryllis (Atwater) S.; grad. Yale, 1812; studied law with Judge Charles Chauncey; m. Caroline Leffingwell, Oct. 29, 1815, 7 children. Treas., New Haven Tontine Co., 1827; made contbns. to Yale for devel. of modern langs. and arts, established Titus Street Professorship of Ecclesiastical History and scholarship in theol. dept., 1855, donated bldg. for sch. of fine arts partially endowed Yale Sch. Fine Arts (founded 1866), one of 1st art schs. in country connected with a coll., co-educational (1st admission of women to Yale); mem. Phi Beta Kappa, Linonian Soc. Died New Haven, June 12, 1866; buried Grove Street Cemetery, New Haven.

STREET, Joseph Montfort, editor; b. Lunenburg County, Va., Dec. 18, 1782; s. Anthony Waddy and Mary (Stokes) S.; m. Eliza Maria Posey, Oct. 9, 1809, 14 children. Became publisher (with John Wood) Western World, Frankfort, Ky., 1806, began investigations in his Federalist paper leading to grand jury proceedings against Aaron Burr, proved Benjamin Sebastian guilty of accepting Spanish pensions; his journalistic attacks on public figures brought him much hatred, frequent challenges to duel; lost expensive libel suit, which caused him to move to Shawneetown, Ill., 1812; became brig. gen. local militia; apptd. Indian agt. to Winnebago Indians at Prairie du Chien, 1827, later at Rock Island, actively attempted to champion Indian rights, with little success. Died May 5, 1840.

STREET, Randall S., congressman, lawyer; b. Catskill, N.Y., 1780; studied law. Admitted to the bar, began practice law in Poughkeepsie, N.Y.; dist. atty. for 2d jud. dist., 1810-11, 13-15; lt. col. N.Y. Militia, War of 1812; mem. U.S. Ho. of Reps. (Democrat) from N.Y., 16th Congress, 1819-21; moved to Monticello, N.Y., circa 1825, continued practice law. Died Monticello, Nov. 21, 1841; buried Poughkeepsie.

STREET, Robert, artist; b. Germantown, Pa., Jan. 17, 1796; married 3 times, 6 children, including Claude L., Rubens C., Theophilus. Began exhibiting in Phila., 1815; held exhbn. in Washington, D.C., painted portrait of Andrew Jackson, 1824; held exhbn. of his own paintings and old masters at Artists' Fund Hall, Phila., 1840.

STRICKLAND, Randolph, congressman, lawyer; b. Dansville, N.Y., Feb. 4, 1823; studied law. Moved to Mich., 1844, taught sch.; admitted to Mich. bar, 1849, began practice law in De Witt, then in St. Johns (both Clinton County, Mich.); elected pros. atty. Clinton County, 1852, 54, 56, 58, 62; mem. Mich. Senate, 1861-62; provost marshal Sixth Congressional Dist., 1863-65; del. Republican Nat. convs., 1856, 68; mem. U.S. Ho. of Reps. (Republican) from Mich., 41st Congress, 1869-71. Died Battle Creek, Mich., May 5, 1880; buried DeWitt Cemetery.

STRICKLAND, William, architect, engr.; b. Phila., circa 1787; s. John Strickland. Designed Masonic Temple (his 1st major bldg.), Phila. (so-called Gothic), 1810, also Custom House (1st in U.S.), Phila., 1819, Bank of U.S., 1824, Mchts. Exchange, Phila., 1834, New Chestnut St. Theatre, Phila., U.S. Mint, 1829; leading architect in Greek revival mode in Am. architecture; reconnaissance engr. Chesapeake and Del. Canal, 1824, engr. Pa. State Canal; designed, built Delaware Breakwater, begun 1829; made survey for a railroad between Wilmington, Del. and Susquehanna River, 1835; became mem. Am. Philos. Soc., 1820; engraved a number of plates for Port Folio and Architecture Mag., dealing chiefly with scenes and episodes of War of 1812. Author: Tomb of Washington at Mount Vernon (report), 1840. Died Nashville, Tenn., Apr. 6, 1854; buried beneath Tenn. Capitol, Nashville.

STRINGHAM, Silas Horton, naval officer; b. Middletown, N.Y., Nov. 7, 1797; s. Daniel and Abigail (Horton) S.; m. Henrietta Hicks, 1819, 4 children. Commd. midshipman U.S. Navy, 1809; served in War of 1812, then in 2d war with Algiers pirates; served on patrol duty off African coast to suppress slave trade, 1820-22; exec. officer on brig. Hornet in West Indies, 1822-24; commanded ship-of-the-line Ohio in Mexican War, 1847; commanded Mediterranean Squadron, 1853-55; apptd. to head Ft. Sumter relief fleet which never took place; in command of successful naval expdn. against Hatteras, Va.; commanded Atlantic Blockade Squadron in Civil War, 1861, asked to be relieved of assignment, 1861; rear adm., 1862, in command of Boston Navy Yard, 1862-64. Died Bklyn., Feb. 7, 1876.

STROHM, John, congressman; b. Little Britain (later Fulton) Twp., nr. Centerville, Pa., Oct. 16, 1793; attended public schs. Taught sch. several years; moved to Providence, Pa.; mem. Pa. Ho. of Reps., 1831-33; mem. Pa. Senate, 1834-42, speaker, 1842; mem. U.S. Ho. of Reps. (Whig) from Pa., 29th-30th congresses, 1845-49; surveyor and justice of the peace Providence Twp., several years; del. Whig Nat. Conv., Balt., 1852; del. state conv., 1869. Died Lancaster, Pa., Sept. 12, 1884; buried Mennonite Cemetery.

STRONG, Caleb, gov. Mass., congressman; b. Northampton, Mass., Jan. 9, 1745; s. Caleb and Phoebe (Lyman) S.; grad. with highest honors, Harvard, 1764, LL.D. (hon.), 1801; m. Sara Hooker, Nov. 20, 1777, 9 children. Admitted to the bar, 1772; selectman of Northampton, 1772; del. to Mass. Constl. Conv., 1779; mem. Mass. Ho. of Reps., 1776-78, Mass. Senate, 1780-88; rep. from Mass. to U.S. Constl. Conv., 1787; mem. U.S. Senate from Mass., 1789-June 1, 1796, active in framing Judiciary Act, reported Hamilton's plan for a nat. bank, 1791; gov. Mass., 1800-07, 12-16; refused to cooperate with nat. govt. in supplying troops for fed. use from Mass. Militia, 1812; approved Hartford Conv., 1814. Died Northampton, Nov. 7, 1819; buried Bridge St. Cemetery, Northampton.

STRONG, Charles Lyman, mining engr.; b. Stockbridge, Vt., Aug. 15, 1826; s. David Ellsworth and Harriet (Fay) S.; m. Harriett Williams Russell, Feb. 26, 1863, at least 4 children. Went to San Francisco as agt. Wells & Co. of N.Y. to establish bank, 1850; partner firm Le Count & Strong, booksellers, publishers of The Pioneer (literary periodical in Cal.), 1852; 1st supt. Gould & Curry Mine (part of Comstock Lode), Virginia City, Nev., 1860, built plant for reduction of ore, successful as dir. mining operations, fought encroachments on company mining properties; retired to San Gabriel Valley, Cal., 1864; interested in various mining ventures in Cal. and Nev. Committed suicide, Feb. 9, 1883.

STRONG, George Crockett, army officer; b. Stockbridge, Vt., Oct. 16, 1832; grad. U.S. Mil. Acad., 1857. Asst. ordnance officer Watervliet Arsenal, 1859-61, chief ordnance officer, 1861; commd. maj., asst. adj. gen. U.S. Volunteers, 1861; served at Battle of Bull Run; chief of staff for Gen. Benjamin F. Butler, 1862; promoted brig. gen. U.S. Volunteers, 1862; led 2 expdns. into Miss., 1862; promoted capt. ordnance U.S. Army, 1863; 1st to reach enemy positions in Battle of Morris Island, 1863; mortally wounded in defense of Battery Wagner, July 18, 1863. Died N.Y.C., July 30, 1863.

STRONG, James, congressman; b. Windham, Conn., 1783; grad. U. Vt., 1806. Moved to Hudson, N.Y.; mem. U.S. Ho. of Reps. (Federalist) from N.Y., 16th, 18th-21st congresses, 1819-21, 23-31. Died Chester, N.J., Aug. 8, 1847.

STRONG, James, Bibl. scholar, educator; b. N.Y.C., Aug. 14, 1822; s. Thomas and Maria (Peers) S.; grad. (valedictorian) Wesleyan U., Middletown, Conn., 1844, S.T.D. (hon.), 1856, LL.D., 1881; m. Marcia Ann Dustin, July 18, 1845, 6 children including Emma. Tchr., Greek and Latin, Troy (Vt.) Conf. Acad., 1844-66; pres. Flushing R.R. Co. (N.Y.), 1852-54; pres. corp. Village of Flushing, 1855; prof. Bibl. lit. Troy U., 1858-63; acting pres.; prof. exegetical theology Drew Theol. Sem., Madison, N.J., 1868-93; del. Gen. Conf. Methodist Episcopal Ch., 1872. Author: A New Harmony and Exposition of the Gospels, 1852; Harmony in Greek, 1854; Theological Compend, 1859; The Exhaustive Concordance of the Bible, 1890; The Doctrine of a Future Life, 1891; Sketches of Jewish Life in the First Century, 1891. Died Round Lake, N.Y., Aug. 7, 1894; buried Flushing.

STRONG, James Hooker, naval officer; b. Canandaigua, N.Y., Apr. 26, 1814; s. Elisha Beebe and Dolly (Hooker) S.; attended Polytechnic Sch., Chittenango, N.Y.; m. Maria Louisa Von Cowenhoven, 1844, 2 children. Commd. midshipman U.S. Navy, 1829, participated in expdn. which apprehended pirate Vernet in Falkland Islands, 1832; comdr. ship Mohawk, 1861, steamer Flag in South Atlantic Blockading Squadron, 1862; in command ships Monogahela, Owasco and Virginia, 1863, convoyed expdn. of 9,000 men to mouth of Rio Grande, capturing Brownsville, Corpus Christi and Arkansas Pass; won surrender of ram Tennessee at Battle of Mobile, 1864; commd. capt., 1865; insp. Bklyn. Navy Yard, 1866-67; commanded steam-sloop Canandaigua in European Squadron, 1868-69; promoted commodore, 1870; house insp., 1871-73; in command South Atlantic Station, 1874; commd. rear adm., 1873, ret., 1876. Died Columbia, S.C., Nov. 28, 1882.

STRONG, Jedediah, Continental congressman, lawyer; b. Litchfield, Conn., Nov. 7, 1738; grad. Yale, 1761; studied law. Admitted to the bar, 1764, began practice law in Litchfield; mem. Conn. Ho. of Reps., 1771-1801; town clk., 1773-89; mem. com. of inspection, 1774-75; commissary of supplies for Continental Army, 1775; declined election to Continental Congress, 1779; clk. Conn. Ho. of Reps., 1779-88; asso. judge Litchfield County Ct., 1780-91; mem. Continental Congress from Conn., 1782-84; del. Conn. Conv. to ratify U.S. Constn., 1788; mem. Gov.'s Council, 1789-90. Died Litchfield, Aug. 21, 1802; buried West Burying Ground.

STRONG, Julius Levi, congressman, lawyer; b. Bolton, Conn., Nov. 8, 1828; attended Wesleyan U., Middletown, Conn., Union Coll., Schenectady, N.Y., Nat. Law Sch., Balston Spa, N.Y. Mem. Conn. Ho. of Reps., 1852, 55, Conn. Senate, 1853; admitted to the bar, 1853, began practice law in Hartford, Conn.; pros. atty., 1864-65; pres. of common council; mem. U.S. Ho. of Reps. (Republican) from Conn., 41st-42d congresses, 1869-72. Died Hartford, Sept. 7, 1872; buried Cedar Hill Cemetery.

STRONG, Moses McCure, surveyor, legislator; b. Rutland, Vt., May 20, 1810; s. Moses and Lucy Maria (Smith) S.; attended Middlebury Coll., 1825-28; grad. Dartmouth, 1829; attended Litchfield (Conn.) Law Sch., 1830-33; m. Caroline Frances Green, July 31, 1832, 4 children. Admitted to Conn. bar, 1831; practiced law, Rutland, Vt., 1831-36; dep. surveyor gen. Vt.; moved to Wis., 1836, opened law and land office, Mineral Point, 1836; U.S. surveyor to survey West of Mississippi River, 1837; U.S. atty. for Territory of Wis., 1838-41; mem. Territorial Council, 1842-46; del. Wis. Constl. Conv., 1846; mem. Wis. Assembly, 1850, 57; active in railroad speculation and promotion, 1850's. Died July 20, 1894.

STRONG, Selah Brewster, congressman, lawyer; b. Brookhaven, N.Y., May 1, 1792; grad. Yale, 1811; studied law. Admitted to the bar, 1814, began practice law, N.Y.C.; commd. ensign and q.m. Tenth Regt., Third Brigade, N.Y.C. and N.Y. County troops, in War of 1812, promoted lt., then capt., 1815; master in chancery, 1817; moved to Brookhaven, 1820; dist. atty. Suffolk County, 1821-47; apptd. judge advocate 1st Div., N.Y. State Inf., 1825; mem. U.S. Ho. of Reps. (Democrat) from N.Y., 28th Congress, 1843-45; judge of supreme ct. for 2d Jud. Dist., 1847-60; mem. N.Y. State Constl. Conv., 1867. Died on estate "St. George's Manor," Setauket, L.I., N.Y., Nov. 29, 1872; buried on estate.

STRONG, Solomon, congressman, lawyer; b. Amherst, Mass., Mar. 2, 1780; grad. Williams Coll., 1798; studied law. Admitted to the bar, Northampton, Mass., 1800, began practice of law; mem. Mass. Senate, 1812-13, 43-44; judge Circuit Ct. of Common Pleas, 1818; judge Ct. of Common Pleas, 1821-42; mem. U.S. Ho. of Reps. (Federalist) from Mass., 14th-15th congresses, 1815-19. Died Leominster, Mass., Sept. 16, 1850; buried Evergreen Cemetery.

STRONG, Stephen, congressman, lawyer; b. Lebanon, Conn., Oct. 11, 1791; attended Hamilton Coll., Clinton, N.Y.; studied law. Admitted to N.Y. bar, 1822, began practice law; dist. atty. Tioga County, 1836-38, 44-47; judge of Tioga County, 1838-43, 55-59; mem. U.S. Ho. of Reps. (Democrat) from N.Y., 29th Congress, 1845-47; moved to Watertown, N.Y., 1861, practiced law. Died Watertown, Apr. 15, 1866.

STRONG, Theodore, mathematician; b. South Hadley, Mass., July 26, 1790; s. Joseph and Sophia (Woodbridge) S.; grad. Yale, 1812; m. Lucy Dix, Sept. 23, 1818, 2 sons, 5 daus. Tutor mathematics Hamilton Coll., Clinton, N.Y., 1812-16, prof. mathematics and natural sci., 1816-27; prof. mathematics Rutgers Coll., 1827-61, prof. emeritus, 1861-69; fellow Am. Acad. Arts and Scis., 1832, Am. Philos. Soc., 1844; an incorporator Nat. Acad. Scis., 1863. Author: Treatise on Elementary and Higher Algebra, 1859; Treatise on Differential and Integral Calculus, 1869; contbr. to Gill's Math. Miscellany; Sillman's Am. Journal of Sci.; Runkle's Math. Monthly. Died Feb. 1, 1869.

STRONG, Theron Rudd, congressman, lawyer; b. Salisbury, Conn., Nov. 7, 1802; studied law Litchfield (Conn.) Law Sch. Admitted to the bar, 1821, began practice law, Palmyra, N.Y.; master and examiner in chancery for several years, held several local offices; dist. atty. Wayne County, N.Y., 1835-39; mem. U.S. Ho. of Reps. (Democrat) from N.Y., 26th Congress, 1839-41; mem. N.Y. State Assembly, 1842; asso. justice Supreme Ct. of N.Y., 1851-59; judge Ct. of Appeals, 1859; practiced law, Rochester, N.Y., from 1860, N.Y.C., 1867-73. Died May 14, 1873; buried Mt. Hope Cemetery, Rochester.

STRONG, William, congressman; b. Lebanon, Conn., 1763; self-educated. Moved to Hartford, Vt. with parents, 1764; became a land surveyor; mem. Vt. Ho. of Reps., 1798-99, 1801-02, 1815-18; sheriff Windsor County, 1802-10; mem. U.S. Ho. of Reps. (Democrat) from Vt., 12th-13th, 16th congresses, 1811-15, 19-21; judge supreme ct., Windsor County, 1819-21; mem. council of censors, 1834. Died Hartford, Jan. 28, 1840; buried Quechee Cemetery.

STRONG, William, asso. justice U.S. Supreme Ct.; b. Somers, Conn., May 6, 1808; s. William Lighthouse and Harriet (Deming) S.; B.A., Yale, 1828, M.A., 1831, attended Yale Law Sch.; m. Priscilla Lee Mallery, Nov. 28, 1836; m. 2d, Rachel (Davies) Bull, Nov. 22, 1849. Admitted to Phila. bar, 1832; mem. U.S. Ho. of Reps. (Democrat), from Pa., 30th-31st congresses, 1847-51; mem. Pa. Supreme Ct., 1857-68; asso. justice U.S. Supreme Ct., 1870-80, involved in controversy over Legal Tender Act, 1862, wrote majority opinion in Knox vs. Lee (1871), also opinions in Bigelow vs. Forrest (concerned with Confiscation Act), Tenn. vs. Davis (concerned with power of fed. courts within states); mem. Electoral Commn., 1877; taught law George Washington U.; v.p. Am. Bible Soc., 1871-95; pres. Am. Sunday Sch. Union, 1883-95. Died Lake Minnewassa, N.Y., Aug. 19, 1895; buried Charles Evans Cemetery, Reading, Pa.

STROTHER, David Hunter (pen name Porte Crayon), writer, illustrator; b. Martinsburg, W.Va., Sept. 26, 1816; s. Col. John and Elizabeth (Hunter) S.; attended Jefferson Coll., Canonsburg, Pa.; studied art in Phila., Italy, France, 1840-43; m. Anne Wolfe, 1849; m. 2d, Mary Hunter; 3 children including Emily (Strother) Walker. Illustrated 1851 edition of Swallow Barn; did drawings for The Blackwater Chronicle, 1853; contbd. to Harper's New Monthly Mag., 1853; did series of articles, entitled "North Carolina Illustrated" for Harper's, 1857, "A Winter in the South," 1857-58, "A Summer in New England," 1860-61; served in Topog. Corps as asst. adjutant gen. and mem. staffs of Gens. McClellan, Banks, Pope, and Hunter; became col. 3d W.Va. Cavalry; resigned, 1864; brevetted brig. gen., 1865; contributed series of articles "Personal Recollections of the War by a Virginian" to Harper's, 1866-68; U.S. consul gen. in Mexico City, 1879. Author: Virginia Illustrated, by Porte Crayon (collected sketches) 1857. Died Jefferson County, W.Va., Mar. 8, 1888.

STROTHER, George French, congressman, lawyer; b. Stevensburg, Va., 1783; attended Coll. William and Mary; studied law; at least 1 son, James French. Admitted to bar, began practice law, Culpeper, Va.; mem. Va. Ho. of Dels., 1806-09; mem. U.S. Ho. of Reps. (Democrat) from Va., 15th-16th congresses, 1817-20 (resigned); receiver public moneys, St. Louis, Mo. Died St. Louis, Nov. 28, 1840; buried Christ Ch. Cemetery, reinterred Bellefontaine Cemetery, 1860.

STROTHER, James French, congressman, lawyer; b. Culpeper, Va., Sept. 4, 1811; s. George French; attended St. Louis U.; studied law. Admitted to the bar, began practice law, Washington, Va.; mem. Va. Ho. of Dels., 1840-51, speaker, 1851; del. Va. Constl. Conv., 1850; mem. U.S. Ho. of Reps. (Whig) from Va., 32d Congress, 1851-53. Died nr. Culpeper, Sept. 20, 1860; buried Masonic Cemetery.

STROUSE, Myer, congressman, lawyer; b. Oberstrau, Germany, Dec. 16, 1825; studied law. Came to U.S., 1832; settled in Pottsville, Pa.; editor North American Farmer, Phila., 1848-52; admitted to bar, 1855, began practice law, Pottsville; mem. U.S. Ho. of Reps. (Democrat) from Pa., 38th-39th congresses, 1863-67; atty. for Molly Maguires (secret orgn. in mining regions Pa.), 1876-77. Died Pottsville, Feb. 11, 1878; buried Odd Fellows Cemetery.

STRUBBERG, Friedrich Armand, novelist; b. Cassel, Germany, Mar. 18, 1806; s. Heinrich Friedrich and Frederique (Marville) S.; M.D., Med. Sch., Louisville, Ky.; m. Antoinette Sattler, June 5, 1866. Came to U.S., 1839; fled from N.Y.C. after killing a man in duel, 1841, settled on Tex. frontier; physician and colonial dir. Mainzer Adelsverein to aid and guide German immigrants to Tex., 1843; practiced medicine in Ark., 1850-54; returned to Germany, 1854; became novelist, works described frontier life and experiences of German immigrants in U.S. Author over 50 fiction works, the best-known including: Amerikanische Jagd-und Reiseabent euer aus meinem Leben in den Westlichen Indianergebieten (pen name Armand, 17, edits.), 1858. Alte und neve Heimath, 1859, Carl Scharnhors (12 edits.), 1863. Died Gelnhausen, Hesse, Germany, Apr. 3, 1889.

STRUDWICK, Edmund Charles Fox, physician; b. Hillsboro, N.C., Mar. 25, 1802; s. William Francis and Martha (Shepperd) S.; M.D., U. Pa., 1824; m. Ann E. Nash, 1827, 5 children. Physician, Phila. Almshouse, 1824-26; began practice of medicine, Hillsboro, 1826; leading lithotomist in N.C.; dir. N.C. R.R.; supported Confederacy; 1st pres. N.C. Med. Soc. Died Nov. 30, 1879.

STRUDWICK, William Francis, congressman; b. nr. Wilmington, N.C. Farmer; del. N.C. Conv., 1789; mem. N.C. Senate, 1792-97; held several local offices; mem. U.S. Ho. of Reps. (Federalist, filled vacancy) from N.C., 4th Congress, Nov. 28, 1796-97; mem. N.C. Ho. of Reps., 1801-03. Died N.C., 1812; buried on estate at "Hawfields," Orange County, N.C.

STRUVE, Gustav, journalist; b. Munich, Germany, Oct. 11, 1805; s. Johann Gustav and Friederike (von Hockstetter) von S.; attended Karlsruhe; studied law Gottingen and Heidelberg (Germany) univs.; 1824-26; m. Amalie Dusar, 1845; m. 2d, Frau von Centener; 3 children. Sec. Oldenburg legation, Frankfort, circa 1826; judge, Jinver; lawyer, Mannheim; founded publ. Zeitschrift fur Phrenologie, 1843; editor polit. jour. Das Mannheimer Tageblatt, 1845; founder, owner Deutsher Tuschaver (favored agitation for German Republic which culminated in Revolution of 1848), 1846-48; a leader in calling mass meeting, Offenburg, Baden, 1848; mem. Vorparlament; led armed revolt, 1848, exiled; came to Am., 1851; editor socialist publ. Die Sociale Republik, 1858, 59; worked for cooperation of labor groups, N.Y.C., Phila.; served from pvt. to capt. 8th German Vol. Regt., U.S. Army, 1861-62; returned to Germany, 1863. Author: Weltgeschichte (written in U.S., presented view that progress in Am. due to absence tyrannical restrictions), 1852-60; (autobiographical) Diesserts und Jenseits des Oceans, 1863. Died Vienna, Austria, Aug. 21, 1870.

STUART, Alexander Hugh Holmes, congressman, sec. interior; b. Staunton, Va., Apr. 2, 1807; s. Archibald and Eleanor (Briscoe) S.; grad. U. Va., 1828; m. Frances Baldwin, Aug. 1, 1833, 9 children. Admitted to Va. bar, 1828; a leader Young Men's Nat. Conv., Washington, D.C., 1832; mem. Va. Ho. of Dels. (Whig), 1836-39, 73-76; mem. U.S. Ho. of Reps. from Va., 27th Congress, 1841-43; Whig presdl. elector, 1844, 48; U.S. sec. of interior under Fillmore, 1850-53; mem. Va. Senate, 1857-61, chmn. legislative com. which drew up report on John Brown's raid; mem. Va. Secession Conv., 1861, opposed secession; mem. com. which secured changes in Underwood Constn. to avoid carpet bag rule, 1870; rector U. Va., 1876-82, 84-86; trustee Peabody Edn. Fund, 1871-89. Died Staunton, Va., Feb. 13, 1891; buried Thornrose Cemetery, Staunton.

STUART, Andrew, congressman; b. nr. Pitts., Aug. 3, 1823; self-educated. Worked in newspaper office; moved to Steubenville, O., 1850; editor Am. Union, 1850-57; mem. U.S. Ho. of Reps. (Democrat) from Ohio, 33d Congress, 1853-55; in shipping bus. on Gulf of Mexico, also in transp. of mail, supplies from Leavenworth, Kan. to Santa Fe, N.M.; lived in Washington, D.C., 1869-72. Died Apr. 30, 1872; buried Union Cemetery, Steubenville.

STUART, Archibald, legislator, jurist; b. Staunton, Va., Mar. 19, 1757; s. Alexander and Mary (Patterson) S.; m. Eleanor Briscoe, May 1791, 1 son, Alexander Hugh Holmes. Represented Botetourt County in Va. Ho. Dels., 1783-89; leader in ratification of U.S. Constn., 1788; mem. Va.-Ky. Boundary Commn., 1795; mem. Va. Senate, 1800, leader in passage of Va. Resolutions; judge Gen. Ct. of Va., 1800-32; leader conservative br. Jeffersonian Democrats in Va.; supported John Quincy Adams in 1828. Died Staunton, July 11, 1832.

STUART, Archibald, congressman, lawyer; b. Lynchburg, Va., Dec. 2, 1795; studied law. Served as officer, War of 1812; admitted to bar, practiced law in Lynchburg; mem. Va. Ho. of Dels., 1830-31; del. Va. convs., 1829, 30, 50, 51; mem. U.S. Ho. of Reps. (Whig) from Va., 25th Congress, 1837-39; mem. Va. Senate, 1852-54. Died at his home "Laurel Hill," Patrick County, Va., Sept. 20, 1855; buried family cemetery at Laurel Hill.

STUART, Charles, abolitionist, author; b. Jamaica, B.W.I., 1783. Served as lt. B.W.I. Co., 1801-14, ret. on pension with rank of capt., 1814; traveled at own expense through B.W.I. lecturing against slavery, 1828, also wrote pamplets on subject; successfully opposed 1831 campaign of Am. Colonization Soc.; lectr. for Am. Anti-Slavery Soc. in Ohio, Vt., N.Y., 1834-38; visited W.I. to study freed men, 1838-40; agt. Am. Anti-Slavery Soc. at World Anti-Slavery Conv., 1842. Author: Is Slavery Defensible from Scripture, 1831; A Memoir of Graham Sharp, 1836. Died Lake Simcoe, Can., 1865.

STUART, Charles Beebe, engr.; b. Chittenango Springs, N.Y., June 4, 1814; s. Henry Y. and Deborah S.; m. Sarah Breese, July 2, 1836; m. 2d, Frances Welles, Apr. 17, 1841; 3 children. Chief engr. N.Y. & Erie R.R., 1840; chief engr. of a railroad line between Batavia and Rochester, N.Y., 1842; surveyor of Rochester; dir. Am. and Canadian bridge cos., 1847; contracted with Charles Ellet, Jr. for constrn. of railroad and carriage bridge over Niagara River; engr. and surveyor N.Y. State, 1849; in charge of Bklyn. drydocks for U.S. Govt., 1849; engr.-in-chief U.S. Navy, 1850-53; wrote specifications for Cal. floating drydocks; pres. Ia. Land Co., circa 1856, participated in laying out Clinton (Ia.); cons. engr. for projected railroad in Tex., 1860; raised Col. Stuart's Independent Regt., N.Y. Inf., 1861; served with Army of Potomac on fortification constrn. Author: Lives and Works of Civil and Military Engineers of America, 1871. Died Geneva, N.Y., Jan. 4, 1881.

STUART, Charles Edward, senator, congressman, lawyer; b. nr. Waterloo, N.Y., Nov. 25, 1810; studied law. Admitted to the bar, 1832, began practice law, Waterloo; moved to Kalamazoo, Mich., 1835; mem. Mich. Ho. of Reps., 1842; mem. U.S. Ho. of Reps. (Democrat, filled vacancy) from Mich., 30th, 32d congresses, Dec. 6, 1847-49, 51-53; mem. U.S. Senate from Mich., 1853-59; del. Democratic nat. convs., Charleston, S.C. and Balt., 1860, Nat. Conv. of Conservatives, Phila., 1866; organizer, col. 13th Regt., Mich. Vol. Inf. during Civil War, resigned commn. because of poor health. Died Kalamazoo, May 19, 1887; buried Mountain Home Cemetery.

STUART, David, congressman; lawyer; b. Bklyn., Mar. 12, 1816; studied law. Admitted to the bar, began practice law in Detroit; mem. U.S. Ho. of Reps. (Democrat) from Mich., 33d Congress, 1853-55; moved to Chgo.; commn. lt. col. 42d Regt., Ill. Vol. Inf., U.S. Army, 1861, col. 55th Regt., Ill. Vol. Inf., 1861, apptd. brig. gen. Volunteers, 1862 (nomination declined by U.S. Senate, 1863), resigned from army, 1863; resumed practice law, Detroit. Died Detroit, Sept. 12, 1868; buried Elmwood Cemetery.

STUART, Gilbert (Charles), painter; b. North Kingston (now Narraganset), R.I., Dec. 3, 1755; s. Gilbert and Elizabeth (Anthony) S.; studied under Benjamin West, London, Eng., 1776; m. Charlotte Coates, May 10, 1786, 12 children including Charles, Jane, Ann (Stuart) Stebbens, Agnes, Emma. Arrived London, 1775; contbd. 1 portrait Royal Acad. exhbn., 1777, three, 1779, two, 1781, four, 1782, exhibited at acad. for last time, 1785; brought to public attention by Portrait of a Gentleman Skating; mem. Exhbn. of Incorporated Soc. Artists, 1783; lived Dublin, Ireland, 1787-93, N.Y.C., 1793; worked in Phila., 1794-96 (painted George Washington from life 3 times; period also important for series of women's portraits) lived in Boston, 1805-28; talented musician, conversationalist; often left portraits unfinished. Best known portraits: Gibbs-Channing portraits (in Met. Mus. Art, N.Y.C.), John Adams, John Quincy Adams, Thomas Jefferson, James Madison, Joseph Story, Judge Stephen Jones. Chosen for Hall of Fame, 1910. Died Boston, July 9, 1828; buried Central Burying Grounds, Boston Common.

STUART, Isaac William (pseudonym: Scaova), orator; b. New Haven, Conn., June 13, 1809; s. Rev. Moses and Abigail (Clark) S.; grad. Yale, 1828; m. Caroline Bulkeley, Nov. 1834, 3 children. Prof. Greek, Latin at S.C. Coll., Columbia, circa 1830-40; mem. Conn. Ho. of Reps., 1844, Conn. Senate, 1845, 46; known as orator concerned with politics, history. Author: Hartford in the Olden Time, 1853; (under pseudonym Scaeva) Life of Captain Nathan Hale, the Martyr-Spy of the American Revolution, 1856. Died Conn., Oct. 2, 1861.

STUART, James Ewell Brown (Jeb Stuart), army officer; b. "Laurel Hill" plantation, Patrick County, Va., Feb. 6, 1833; s. Archibald and Elizabeth (Pannill) S.; attended Emory and Henry Coll., 1848-50; grad. U.S. Mil. Acad., 1854; m. Flora Cooke, Nov. 14, 1855, 3 children. Commd. 2d lt. U.S. Army, 1854, 1st lt., 1855, capt., 1861; patented device for attaching cavalry sabre to belt, 1859; resigned to become lt. col. Va. Inf. and capt. cavalry Confederate Army, 1861; promoted brig. gen. for role in 1st Battle of Manassas, 1861; fought with well-organized cavalry outpost in engagement at Dranesville, Va., Dec. 1861; covered army retreat to Chickahominy during Peninsular campaign, 1862; executed reconnaissance mission to McClellan's right (exemplary in method, results), June 1862; led rash attack from Evelington Heights, during Seven Days campaign, July 1862; raided Pope's hdqrs. at 2d Battle of Manassas, Aug. 1862 (praised by Lee); made highly successful raid into Pa. (riding around Fed. troops), Sept. 1862; conducted skillful arty. attack from Confederate right at Battle of Fredericksburg; informed Lee of Hooker's movements at beginning of Chancellorsville campaign, became key intelligence source to Lee; played disputed role in Gettysburg campaign (because of failure to join main body Confederate Army until 2d day of battle); his cavalry activity declined in 1864 due to lack of supplies, but he managed to successfully block movement of Gen. Sheridan's forces toward Richmond,

Va., May 9, 1864. Equestrian statue erected in his honor, Richmond, 1907. Died of wounds received in action, Richmond, Va., May 12, 1864; buried Hollywood Cemetery, Richmond.

STUART, John, army officer, supt. Indian affairs; b. Scotland, 1700; m. Miss Fenwick before 1759, at least 1 son, Lt. Gen. Sir John. Came to U.S., circa 1748; capt. S.C. Provincial Militia 1757; supt. Indian affairs for So. dist. S.C, 1762, responsible to secs. of state in Eng. following proclamation of 1763; in Floridas, 1764, named mem. East Fla. governing council by Gov. James Grant; gained imperial status (responsible to King, rather than secs. of state) for his dept., 1765; became refugee in Floridas, arrest ordered by S.C. Assembly on charge of attempting to incite Catawba and Cherokee Indians in Brit. interest, 1775; organized 3 cos. of refugees to further Brit. interest in South, 1778. Died Pensacola, Fla., Mar. 25, 1779.

STUART, John Todd, congressman; b. Lexington, Ky., Nov. 10, 1807; s. Robert and Hannah (Todd) S.; ed. Centre Coll., Danville, Ky., 1826; m. Mary Nash. Licensed as atty., 1827; served in Black Hawk War, elected maj.; Whig leader in Sangamon region; mem. Ill. Legislature, 1832-36, 38-40, mem. com. on territories; mem. firm Stuart and (Abraham) Lincoln, 1837-41; mem. U.S. Ho. of Reps. from Ill., as Whig, 26th-27th congresses, 1839-43, as Democrat, 38th Congress, 1863-65, opposed emancipation policy of Pres. Lincoln; mem. Ill. Senate, 1848-52; active in Springfield (Ill.) City Ry. Co.; founder Bettie Stuart Inst. (sch. for girls). Died Springfield, Nov. 23, 1885; buried Oak Ridge Cemetery, Springfield.

STUART, Moses, clergyman, educator; b. Wilton, Conn., Mar. 26, 1780; s. Isaac and Olive (Morehouse) S.; grad. at head of class, Yale, 1801; m. Abigail Clark, 1806, 9 children including Isaac William. Admitted to Danbury (Conn.) bar, 1802; tutor Yale, 1802; licensed to preach, 1803; ordained to ministry Congregational Ch., 1806; became pastor First Ch. of Christ (Congl.), New Haven, Conn.; prof. sacred literature Andover (Mass.) Theol. Sem., 1810-48; one of 1st Am. theologians to teach Hebrew; wrote short Hebrew grammar in 1821; translated from German A Greek Grammar of the New Testament (Georg Benedikt Winer), 1825, Hebrew Grammar of Gesenius as Edited by Roediger, 1846; 1st Am. theologian to become favorably known abroad. Author: Elements of Interpretation, Translated from the Latin of J.A. Ernesti, 1822; Critical History and Defence of the Old Testament Canon, 1845; almost 40 books, brochures. Died Andover, Jan. 4, 1852.

STUART, Philip, congressman, army officer; b. nr. Fredericksburg, Va., 1760; prep. edn. Moved to Md.; served in Continental Army as lt. 3d Continental Dragoons, wounded at Eutaw Springs, 1781, transferred to Baylor's Dragoons, 1782, lt. Second Artillerists and Engrs., 1798-1800; served in War of 1812; mem. U.S. Ho. of Reps. (Federalist) from Md., 12th-15th congresses, 1811-19. Died Washington, D.C., Aug. 14, 1830; buried Congressional Cemetery.

STUART, Robert, fur trader; b. Perthshire, Scotland, Feb. 19, 1785; s. John and Mary (Buchanan) S.; m. Elizabeth Emma Sullivan, July 21, 1813, 2 sons including David, 3 daus. Arrived in Montreal, Can., 1807, joined his uncle David Stuart, agt. of N.W. Fur Co.; became partner J. J. Astor's Pacific Fur Co., 1810; traveled widely from Astoria, N.Y.C., St. Louis, 1812-20; head of Am. Fur Co. for upper Gt. Lakes, stationed Mackinac Island, Lake Mich., 1820-34; moved office to Detroit, 1834, also invested in real estate, Detroit; treas. State of Mich., 1840-41; moved to Chgo., 1845, became sec. Ill.-Mich. Canal Corp. Died Oct. 29, 1848.

STUART, Robert Leighton, mcht., philanthropist; b. N.Y.C., July 21, 1806; s. Kimloch and Agnes S.; m. Mary McCrea. Formed partnership (with brother Alexander) in candy bus. as R.L. and A. Stuart, 1828-56, firm engaged in refining, marketing sugar, began use of steam as new method in sugar-refining process, 1832; donated well over $1,000,000 to Presbyn. Hosp., Princeton Theol. Sem., Princeton Coll., 1852-79. Died N.Y.C., Dec. 12, 1882.

STURGEON, Daniel, senator, physician; b. Mount Pleasant, Pa., Oct. 27, 1789; grad. Jefferson Coll. (now Washington and Jefferson Coll.), also Jefferson Med. Coll., Phila. Began practice medicine, Uniontown, Pa., 1813; apptd. county coroner; mem. Pa. Ho. of Reps., 1818-24; mem. Pa. Senate, 1825-30, pres., 1828-30; auditor gen. of Pa., 1830-36, treas. State of Pa., 1838-39; mem. U.S. Senate (Democrat, filled vacancy, then reelected) from Pa., Jan. 14, 1840-51; treas. U.S. Mint, Phila. (apptd. by Pres. Franklin Pierce), 1853-58; engaged in banking. Died Uniontown, July 3, 1878; buried Oak Grove Cemetery.

STURGES, Jonathan, congressman; b. Fairfield, Conn., Aug. 23, 1740; grad. Yale, 1759; at least 1 son, Lewis Burr. Admitted to bar, 1772, began practice law in Fairfield; mem. Conn. Ho. of Reps., 1772, 73-84, 86; justice of peace, 1773; mem. Continental Congress from Conn., 1774-87; judge probate ct. for dist. of Fairfield, 1775; mem. U.S. Ho. of Reps. from Conn., 1st-2d congresses, 1789-93; asso. justice Conn. Supreme Ct., 1793-1805; Federalist presdl. elector, 1796, 1804. Died Fairfield, Oct. 4, 1819; buried Old Burying Ground.

STURGES, Lewis Burr, congressman; b. Fairfield, Conn., Mar. 15, 1763; son of Jonathan Sturges; grad. Yale, 1782. Became a mcht., New Haven, Conn.; returned to Fairfield, 1786; clk. of probate ct., Dist. of Fairfield, 1787-91; mem. Conn. Ho. of Reps., 1794-1803; mem. U.S. Ho. of Reps. (Federalist, filled vacancy) from Conn., 9th-14th congresses, Sept. 16, 1805-17; moved to Norwalk, O. Died Norwalk, Mar. 30, 1844; buried St. Paul's Episcopal Churchyard.

STURGIS, John Hubbard, architect; b. Manila, P.I., 1834; son of Russell Sturgis; ed. in Eng. Came to Boston, 1850's; became asso. with Gridley Bryant, architect, Boston, 1850's, later partner, until early 1870's; organizer (with Charles Brigham) and head of Sturgis & Brigham, archtl. firm, Boston, early 1870's-88; designer (with Brigham) 1st 2 sects. Mus. of Fine Arts in Copley Sq. (utilized terra cotta as exterior decorative feature), Ch. of Advent (incorporated brick and stone in interior finish), also comml. bldgs., pvt. homes (all Boston); v.p. Boston Soc. Architects; returned to Eng., 1886. Died London, Eng., Feb. 13, 1888.

STURGIS, Samuel Davis, army officer; b. Shippensburg, Pa., June 11, 1822; s. James and Mary (Brandenburg) S.; grad. U.S. Mil. Acad., 1846; m. Jerusha Wilcox, 1 son, Samuel Davis. Joined 2d Dragoons; fought in Mexican War; served as 1st lt., 1st Dragoons in West, 1853; capt. with 1st (now 4th) Cavalry, 1855; mem. Utah expdn., 1858; maj., 1861, fought at Wilson's Creek; brig. gen. U.S. Volunteers, 1861; in charge of dist. of Kan.; served at 2d Battle of Bull Run, Battle of Antietam; mustered out of volunteer service, 1865; lt. col. 6th Cavalry, col. 7th Cavalry, 1869. Author: The Other Side as Viewed by Generals Grant, Sherman, and Other Distinguished Officers, Being a Defence of His Campaign into N.E. Mississippi in Year 1864, 1882. Died St. Paul, Minn., Sept. 28, 1889.

STURGIS, William, mcht.; b. Barnstable, Mass., Feb. 25, 1782; s. William and Hannah (Mills) S.; m. Elizabeth Marston Davis, 1810, 1 son, 5 daus. Deckhand on voyage to Northwest, 1797; master of ship Caroline, 1801, later of ship Atahualpa; partner (with John Bryant) in mcht. firm, Boston, 1810-63, controlled about half of entire U.S.-China trade, 1810-40; mem. Mass. Ho. of Reps., 1834-46; pres. Boston Marine Soc.; mem. Mass. Hist. Soc.; gave $10,000 to observatory, Cambridge, Mass.; erected monument to Dr. Johann Gaspar Spurzheim, Mt. Auburn Cemetery, Cambridge. Author: (pamphlet) The Oregon Question, 1845; contbr. article Examination of the Russian Claims to the Northwest Coast of America, published N.Am. Review, Oct. 1822. Died Boston, Oct. 21, 1863.

STURTEVANT, Benjamin Franklin, inventor, mfr.; b. Martins Stream, Me., Jan. 18, 1833; s. Seth and Hulda (Besse) S.; m. Phoebe Chamberlaine, 1852, 2 children. Inventor shoe pegging machine, 1857-59, obtained 5 patents for improvements, retained no rights; inventor pegwood lathe, 1860-63, retained only patent rights to shoe pegs; founder pegwood factory, Conway, N.H. (with proceeds of sale of patents); patentee rotary exhaust fan, 1867, built factory for manufacture (largest of kind in world), Jamaica Plains, Mass., 1878; liberal contbr. to ednl. instns. including Colby U., Vt. Acad. Died Jamaica Plains, Apr. 17, 1890.

STURTEVANT, Edward Lewis, agrl. scientist; b. Boston, Jan. 23, 1842; s. Lewis W. and Mary (Leggett) S.; grad. Bowdoin Coll., 1863; grad. Harvard Med. Sch., 1866; m. Mary Mann, Mar. 9, 1864; m. 2d, Hattie Mann, Oct. 22, 1883; 5 children including Grace. Commd. lt., Co. G, 24th Me. Volunteers, 1861, later capt.; with brother purchased and began devel. of Waushakum Farm, South Framingham, Mass., 1867; conducted numerous agrl. expts., particularly interested in physiology of milk and milk secretion (gained acceptance for his research); editor or co-editor Scientific Farmer, 1876-79; erected 1st lysimeter in Am. at Waushakum Farm; studied history of edible plants; 1st dir. N.Y. Agrl. Expt. Station at Geneva, 1882; leader movement for expt. stas. Author: (with brother Joseph) The Dairy Cow: A Monograph on the Ayrshire Breed, 1875; North American Ayrshire Register, 4 vols., 1875-80; Sturtevant's Notes on Edible Plants (edited by U. P. Hedrick), 1919. Died South Framingham, July 30, 1898.

STURTEVANT, Julian Monson, clergyman, coll. pres.; b. Warren, Conn., July 26, 1805; s. Warren and Lucy (Tanner) S.; grad. Yale, 1826, studied theology; m. Elizabeth Fayerweather, Aug. 31, 1829; m. 2d, Hannah Fayerweather, Mar. 3, 1841; 10 children. Ordained to ministry Congregational Ch., Woodbury, Conn., 1829; became 1st instr. Ill. Coll., Jacksonville, 1830, prof. mathematics, natural philosophy, astronomy, 1831-44, pres., prof. mental science, science of govt., 1844-76, kept. coll. free from narrow sectarian control; delivered opening sermon at 1st Nat. Council of Congl. Chs., Boston, 1865; radical abolitionist; sent to Eng. during Civil War to win more sympathetic support for No. cause; occasional contbr. to New Englander, the Congregational Review, the Princeton Review. Author: Economics, or the Science of Wealth, 1827. Died Jacksonville, Feb. 11, 1886.

STUYVESANT, Petrus (called Peter by English), colonial ofcl.; b. Friesland Province, Netherlands, 1592; s. Rev. Balthazar and Margaretta (Hardenstein) S.; academic edn.; m. Judith Bayard, at least 2 children, Balthazar Lazarus, Nicholas William. Supercargo, Dutch West India Co., Brazil, 1635; gov. Dutch possession, Curacao, Leeward Islands 1643; lost a leg while leading expdn. against island St. Martin, 1644; dir. gen. New Netherlands colony, 1646; church warden, 1647, reconstructed ch. at Ft. Amsterdam, N.Y.; a strict adherent Dutch Reformed Ch., instituted restrictions on alcohol, enforced Sunday observance, proclaimed ordinance restricting freedom of worship, 1656; promoted better relations with English, ousted Swedish from Del.; created 9-man bd. to plan welfare measures, 1647; his rule often harsh and people demanded independent municipal control, 1649, granted, 1653; became large landowner, following grant of 1650, erected mansion nr East River (now N.Y.C.), circa 1659; surrendered New Netherlands to English at his home, 1664, retired from govt. Died N.Y.C., Feb. 1672; buried beneath chapel on his farm (now St. Mark's Episcopal Ch., N.Y.C.).

SUBLETTE, William Lewis, fur trader; b. Lincoln County, Ky., circa 1799; s. Philip and Isabel (Whitley) S.; m. Frances Hereford, Mar. 21, 1844. Constable, St. Charles, Mo., 1818-20; joined Ashley's expdn. to Rocky Mountains, circa 1820; took part in Arikara Indian campaign in N.D., 1823; established firm (with Jedediah S. Smith and David E. Jackson) to transport people across Rocky Mountains; took trips over Rocky Mountains, 1823-30; led expdn. to Santa Fe, N.M., 1831; became partner (with Robert Campbell) to collect furs on Platte and Missouri rivers, 1832; fur trader in area around St. Louis, 1832-42; apptd. col. on staff lov. Thomas Reynolds of Mo., 1841. Died Pitts., July 23, 1845; buried St. Louis.

SULLIVAN, George, congressman; b. Durham, N. H., Aug. 29, 1771; s. Gen. John and Lydia (Worcester) S.; grad. Harvard, 1790; studied law; m. Clarissa Lamson, Aug. 6, 1799; m. 2d Philippa Call, Jan. 14, 1838; 10 children. Admitted to N.H. bar; mem. N.H. Legislature (Federalist) from Exeter, 1805; atty. gen. N.H., 1805-06, 16-35; mem. U.S. Ho. of Reps. (Federalist) from N.H., 12th Congress, 1811-13, opposed War of 1812; mem. N.H. Ho. of Reps., 1813-14, N.H. Senate, 1814-15; represented N.H. in Dartmouth Coll. Case. Died Exeter, N.H., Apr. 14, 1838; buried Old Cemetery Exeter.

SULLIVAN, James, gov. Mass., mem. Continental Congress; b. Berwick, Mass. (now Me.), Apr. 24, 1744; s. John and Margaret (Browne) S.; m. Mehitable Odiorne, Feb. 22, 1768; m. 2d, Martha Langdon, Dec. 31, 1786; at least 6 children including William. Mem. Provincial Congress of Mass Com. of Safety, 1774-75; mem. Mass. Gen. Ct., 1775-76; justice Mass. Supreme Ct., 1776-82, mem. to reorganize laws, 1780; del. from Mass. to Continental Congress, 1782; mem. Mass. Exec. Council, 1787; judge of probate for Suffolk County, Mass., 1788; atty. gen. of Mass., 1790-96; agt. at Halifax conf. to settle disputed Me. boundary, 1796; gov. Mass. (Democratic-Republican), 1807-08; wrote pamphlets against Federalist Party; mem. Am. Acad. Arts and Scis.; a founder Mass. Hist. Soc., pres. for number of years, contbr. to its early Collections. Author: The History of the District of Maine, 1795; The History of Land Titles in Massachusetts, 1801; A Dissertation upon the United States of America, 1801. Died Boston, Dec. 10, 1808; buried Central Boston Common Cemetery.

SULLIVAN, John, army officer, Continental congressman, gov. N.H.; b. Somersworth, N.H., Feb. 17, 1740; s. John and Margery (Browne) S. Del. to Continental Congress, 1774, 75, 80-81; apptd. brig. gen. by 2d Continental Congress, 1775; served in siege of Boston, 1775; commd. maj. gen. with command on L.I., 1776; served at Valley Forge, 1777-78; completely routed combined Indian and Loyalist forces at Elmira, N.Y., 1779; resigned commn., 1779; mem. N.H. Constl. Conv., 1782; atty. gen. N.H., 1782-86; speaker

N.H. assembly, 1785, 88; gov. N.H., 1786, 87, 89, suppressed paper-money riots; chmn. N.H. Conv. which ratified U.S. Constn., 1788; U.S. dist. judge for N.H., 1789-95. Died Durham, N.H., Jan. 23, 1795; buried in Sullivan family cemetery, Durham.

SULLIVAN, Peter John, diplomat; b. Cork, Ireland, Mar. 15, 1821; brought to U.S., 1823; attended U. Pa. Served in Mexican War; stenographer U. S. Senate; admitted to Ohio bar, 1848; served as brig. gen. U.S. Volunteers during Civil War; U.S. minister to Colombia, 1865-69. Died Cincinnati, Mar. 2, 1883.

SULLIVAN, William, writer, govt. ofcl.; b. Biddeford, Me., Nov. 1774; s. James and Mehitable (Odiorne) S.; grad. Harvard, 1792, LL.D. (hon.), 1826; m. Sarah Webb, May 19, 1802; at least 1 child. Admitted to Mass. bar, 1795; mem. Mass. Gen. Ct., 1804-30; del. Federalist Conv., N.Y.C., 1812, Mass. Constl. Conv., 1830; engaged in writing about polit. instns. of U.S., after 1830. Author: The Political Class Book, 1831; The Moral Class Book, 1831; The Historical Class Book, 1833; Familiar Letters on Public Characters and Public Events from the Peace of 1783 to the Peace of 1815, 1834. Died Sept. 3, 1839.

SULLIVANT, William Starling, botanist; b. Columbus, O., Jan. 15, 1803; s. Lucas and Sarah (Starling) S.; studied Ohio U.; grad. Yale, 1823; LL.D. (hon.), Kenyon Coll., 1864; m. Jane Marshall, Apr. 7, 1824; m. 2d, Elisa Griscom Wheeler, Nov. 29, 1834; m. 3d, Caroline Sutton, Sept. 1, 1851; 13 children including Thomas Starling. Compiler, A Catalogue of Plants, Native and Naturalized, in the Vicinity of Columbus, Ohio, 1840; contbr. 2 important sects. to 2d edit. Gray's Manual, 1856, republished separately as The Musci and Hepaticae of the Unites States East of the Mississippi River, 1856; greatest work: Icones Muscorum, 1864 (supplement 1874); distinguished as America's foremost bryologist; commemorated by genus Sullivantia which he discovered in Ohio; mem. Am. Acad. Arts and Scis., 1845. Died Columbus, Apr. 30, 1873

SULLY, Alfred, army officer; b. Phila., 1821; s. Thomas Sully; grad. U.S. Mil. Acad., 1841. Served in Seminole War, war with Mexico, 1846-47; distinguished himself in battles of Fair Oaks and Malvern Hill during Civil War; made brig.-gen., Volunteers, 1862; comdr. Dept. Dakota, 1863, led Sully Expdn., 1864; brevetted maj. gen. Volunteers, brig.-gen. U.S. Army; col. 10th Inf., 1872. Died Ft. Vancouver, Wash., Apr. 17, 1879.

SULLY, Thomas, painter; b. Horncastle, Lincolnshire, Eng., June 8, 1783; s. Matthew and Sarah (Chester) S.; studied painting under Belzons; m. Sarah (Annis) Sully, June 27, 1805, 9 children. Came to Am., 1792, settled in Charleston, S.C.; joined Pa. Academicians, served on com. for mgmt. schs. of acad.; hon. mem. Garrick Club; produced approximately 2600 works; recognized as leading portrait painter in Am., after circa 1827. Portraits include: Washington Irving, Frances Anne Kemble, Charles King (1809), Queen Victoria (1838, portrait belongs to Soc. of Sons of St. George in Phila.), Thomas Jefferson, Rembrandt Peale, Lafayette, Charles Carroll, Dr. Benjamin Rush, Gen. Jackson; other works include Washington Crossing the Delaware, circa 1818 (now in Boston Mus. Art), The Capture of Major Andre. Died Phila., Nov. 5, 1872; buried Laurel Hill Cemetery, Phila.

SUMMERFIELD, Charles, see Arrington, Alfred W.

SUMMERS, George William, congressman; b. Fairfax County, Va., Mar. 4, 1804; s. Col. George and Ann (Radcliffe) S.; grad. Ohio U., Athens, 1826; m. Amacella Laidley, Feb. 14, 1833, 5 children. Admitted to Va. bar, 1827; mem. Va. Ho. of Dels. from Kanawha, 1830, 31, 34, 35; opposed slavery and urged that public land receipts pay for emancipation, 1831-32; mem. U.S. Ho. of Reps. (Whig) from Va., 27th-28th congresses, 1841-45; represented Western interests in Va. Constl. Conv., 1850; judge 18th Jud. Circuit of Va., 1852-58; del. Peace Conf., Washington, D.C., 1861; del. to Richmond Conv. (which passed Va. Ordinance of Secession), spoke for cause of the Union, 1861. Died Charleston, Va. (now W.Va.), Sept. 19, 1868; buried Walnut Grove Cemetery, Putnam County, W.Va.

SUMMERS, Thomas Osmond, clergyman, editor; b. Corfe Castle, Dorsetshire, Eng., Oct. 11, 1812; s. James and Sarah S.; m. N. B. Sexton, 1844; 1 child, Came to .US., 1830; admitted to Balt. Conf., Methodist Ch., 1835, stationed in Balt., 1836-39, ordained elder, 1839; Meth. preacher, West River, Md., 1839-40; took part in missionary work in Houston and Galveston, Tex., 1840-44; mem. Ala. Conf., 1844; del. Gen. Conv. which organized Meth. Episcopal Ch. South, Louisville, Ky., 1845; sec. Gen. Conf., 1845-82; asst. editor So. Christian Advocate, 1846-50; editor Sunday Sch. Visitor, 1851-56, Quarterly Review of Meth. Episcopal Ch. South, 1858-61, 79-82, Christian Advocate, Nashville, Tenn., 1868-78; prof. systematic theology Vanderbilt U., Nashville, 1875-82. Died Nashville, May 6, 1882.

SUMNER, Charles, senator; b. Boston, Jan. 6, 1811; s. Charles Pinckney and Relief (Jacob) S.; A. B., Harvard, 1830, grad. Harvard Law Sch. 1833, LL.D. (hon.); m. Mrs. A. M. Hooper, October 27, 1866. Admitted to Mass. bar, 1834; lectr. Harvard Law Sch., 1835-37; toured Europe gaining acquaintance with leaders in polit. life, 1837-40; gained reputation as orator, 1840's; a founder Free-Soil Party, 1848; mem. U.S. Senate from Mass., 1851-74; became anti-slavery leader in Senate, delivered several notable speeches opposing fugitive slave laws, Kan.-Neb. Act; an organizer Republican Party in Mass.; castigated many prominent Democratic senators in Crime of Kan. speech, 1856 (resulted in caning on Senate floor by Representative Preston Brooks of S.C.; injuries suffered in attack resulted in 3 year absence from Senate); returned to Senate floor, 1859, delivered Barbarism of Slavery speech condemning slavery on moral, econ. and social grounds; opposed Washington (D.C.) Peace Conf. (held Feb. 1861); chmn. Senate fgn. relations com., 1861-71, urged release of Mason and Slidell in Trent Affair, 1861; announced his doctrine that Confederate states had forfeited rights under U.S. Constn., 1862; opposed Pres. Lincoln's reconstrn. policies during Civil War; determined to secure civil equality for Negroes in South; his belief in Congressional (rather than exec.) jurisdiction over Reconstrn. policies led to break with Pres. Johnson; strongly supported movement to impeach Johnson; deprived of chairmanship of fgn. relations com., primarily for his role in opposing annexation of Santo Domingo, 1871. Author: The Works of Charles Sumner, 15 vols., published 1870-83. Died Washington, D.C., Mar. 11, 1874; buried Mt. Auburn Cemetery, Cambridge, Mass.

SUMNER, Edwin Vose, army officer; b. Boston, Jan. 30, 1797; s. Elisha and Nancy (Vose) S.; m. Hannah W. Forster, Mar. 31, 1822, at least 3 children including Brig. Gen. Edwin Vose, Jr., Maj. Gen. Samuel Storrow, 1 dau. Commd. 2d lt., 2d Inf., U.S. Army, 1819, promoted 1st lt., 1823, capt., 1833; served with 1st U.S. Dragoons, mainly on frontier duty; commd. maj. 2d Dragoons, 1846, assigned to army under Gen. Winfield Scott in Mexico, 1846; placed in command of 3d Cavalry by Scott; wounded at Cerro Gordo; brevetted for Mexican War service; promoted lt. col. 1st Dragoons, 1848; mil. comdr., acting gov. N.M., 1852; promoted col. 1st Cavalry, 1855; left Ft. Leavenworth for Ft. Laramie, 1855, turned back after marching 400 miles, claimed that further marching would sacrifice horses; charges preferred against him for this action by commanding officer Gen. Harney (War Dept. backed Sumner); commanded Ft. Leavenworth, 1856-57, attempted to keep order between warring pro-slavery and Free Soil factions in Kan.; became comdr. Dept. of West, hdqrs. St. Louis, 1857; promoted brig. gen., 1861; commanded II Corps in Peninsular campaign at S. Mountain and Antietam; apptd. maj. gen. U.S. Volunteers, 1862; relieved from duty at his own request. Died Mar. 21, 1863.

SUMNER, Increase, gov. Mass., jurist; b. Roxbury, Mass.; Nov. 27, 1746; s. Increase and Sarah (Sharp) S.; grad. Harvard, 1767; m. Elizabeth Hyslop, Sept. 30, 1779. Admitted to Mass. bar, 1770; rep. in Mass. Gen. Ct., 1776-79; mem. Mass. Senate, 1780-82; mem. Mass. Constl. Conv., 1779-80; elected to Continental Congress, 1782 (never took seat); apptd. asso. justice Supreme Jud. Ct. of Mass., 1782; mem. Mass. Conv. which ratified U.S. Constn. 1788; gov. Mass., 1797, 98, 99, had popular adminstrn., worked to increase munitions. Died Roxbury, Mass., June 7, 1799; buried Granary Burial Ground, Boston.

SUMNER, Jethro, army officer; b. Nansemond County, Va., circa 1733; s. Jethro and Margaret (Sullivan) S.; m. Mary Hurst, circa 1764; 1 dau., Jacky Sullivan (Sumner) Blount. Served as lt. Va. Militia, 1755-61; commanded Ft. Bedford during French and Indian War; justice of the peace Warren County (N.C.), 1768, sheriff, 1772-77; Warren County rep. N.C. Revolutionary Provisional Congress, 1775, which elected him maj. Minutemen; col. third bn. N.C. Regt., Continental Army, 1776; commd. brig. gen. Continental Army, led brigade to S.C., participated in battle of Stone Ferry, 1779, also recruited in N.C.; assisted in defense of N.C. against Cornwallis' invasion, 1780; in charge of N.C. Militia, 1781-83. Died Warren County, between Mar. 15-19, 1785.

SUMTER, Thomas, senator, congressman; b. Hanover County, Va., Aug. 14, 1734; coll. edn. Became a surveyor; moved to S.C., circa 1760, settled on plantation, nr. Stateburg; served as lt. col. 6th Continental Regt., Continental Army; became brig. gen. S.C. Militia, 1780; mem. S.C. Senate, 1781-82; elected to privy council, 1782; del. to S.C. Conv. which ratified U.S. Constn. (which he opposed); mem. U.S. Ho. of Reps. (Democrat) from S.C., 1st-2d, 5th-7th congresses, 1789-93, 1797-Dec. 15, 1801 (resigned); mem. U.S. Senate (Democrat, filled vacancy) from S.C., Dec. 15, 1801-Dec. 16, 1810 (resigned); elected del. State Rights and Free Trade Conv., Charleston, S.C., 1832 (did not serve). Died on his plantation "South Mount," nr. Stateburg, June 1, 1832; buried pvt. burial ground on estate.

SUMTER, Thomas DeLage, congressman; b. Germantown, Pa., Nov. 14, 1809; grad. U.S. Mil. Acad., 1835. Served from 1st lt. to col. U.S. Army, 1835-41, served in war against Seminole Indians; moved to Stateburg, S.C.; mem. U.S. Ho. of Reps. (Democrat) from S.C., 26th-27th congresses, 1839-43; tchr., surveyor, farmer; agt. S.C. R.R. Co. Died on plantation "South Mount," nr. Stateburg, July 2, 1874; buried on estate.

SUNDERLAND, LeRoy, abolitionist, author; b. Exeter, R.I., Apr. 22, 1804; married, at least 1 child. Admitted to New Eng. Conf., Methodist Episcopal Ch., 1826, withdrew from active ministry, 1833; editor Zion's Watchman, N.Y.C., 1836; withdrew from Meth. Episcopal Ch. because of opposition of ch. leaders, 1842; invented faith called "Panthetism", later became leading exponent of atheism. Author: Appeal (against slavery), 1834; Panthetism . . . An Essay Toward a Correct Theory of Mind, 1847; Book of Psychology, 1853; Book of Human, 1853; The Trace, and How Introduced, 1860; Ideaology, 1885. Died Quincy, Mass., May 15, 1885.

SURRAT, Mary Eugenia Jenkins, alleged conspirator; b. Waterloo, Md., 1817; ed. Catholic Female Sem., Alexandria, Va.; m. John H. Surrat, 1835 (died 1862); children—Isaac, Anne E., John H. Settled nr. Glensboro, Md., after marriage; moved to Prince George's County, Md., opened a tavern on her farm, later a post office, location henceforth known as Surrattsville; moved to Washington, D.C., 1864, began renting rooms; arrested by police as conspirator 2 days after assassination of Pres. Lincoln because her son John was a friend of John Wilkes Booth; executed after a 6 week trial; probably did not have any knowledge about the abduction planned by Booth, or the actual assassination. Executed Washington, July 9, 1865.

SURRATT, John H., conspirator; probably born in Md., 1844; son of Mary E. Surratt; studied for Roman Catholic priesthood St. Charles Coll., until 1862. Became Confederate dispatch rider, 1862; made acquaintance of John Wilkes Booth, Dec. 1864, agreed on plot to kidnap Pres. Lincoln (which came to nothing), 1865; went to Can., did not take part in actual assassination of Lincoln; kept in hiding by a Catholic priest; later went to Europe, was captured, escaped, then recaptured, brought to Am., 1866; on trial for 2 months, June-Aug. 1867, but govt. unable to convict him of role in Lincoln murder; kept in jail until June 1868.

SUTHERLAND, Joel Barlow, congressman, jurist, coll. pres.; b. Clonmel, N.J., Feb. 26, 1792; s. Daniel and Jane S.; grad. U. Pa. Med. Sch., 1812; m. Mary Read, Apr. 13, 1815. Served from asst. surgeon Jr. Artillerists of Phila. to lt. col. of rifles Pa. Militia during War of 1812; mem. Pa. Assembly (insurgent Democratic-Republican), 1813-16; admitted to Pa. bar, 1819; mem. lower house Pa. Legislature, 1821-25, speaker, 1825; mem. Pa. Senate, 1816-17, 26; mem. U.S. Ho. of Reps. from Pa., 20th-24th congresses, 1827-37, chmn. com. on commerce, 1831-37; dep. county pros. atty., Phila., 1830, 32, 33; asso. judge Ct. of Common Pleas, 1833-34; a founder, trustee Jefferson Med. Coll., later pres.; 1st pres. Soc. of War of 1812. Author: Manual of Legislative Practice and Order of Business in Deliberate Bodies, 1827; Congressional Manual, 1839. Died Phila., Nov. 15, 1861; buried Old Pine St. Presbyn. Ch. Cemetery, Phila.

SUTHERLAND, Josiah, congressman, lawyer; b. nr. Stissing, Dutchess County, N.Y., June 12, 1804; grad. Union Coll., Schenectady, N.Y., 1824; studied law in Waterford and Hudson. Admitted to the bar, 1828, began practice law, Johnstown, N.Y.; dist. atty. Columbia County, 1832-43; moved to Hudson, N.Y., 1838, continued practice law; mem. U.S. Ho. of Reps. (Democrat) from N.Y., 32d Congress, 1851-53; moved to N.Y.C., 1857, practiced law; asso. justice N.Y. Supreme Ct., 1857-71; mem., presiding judge Ct. of Gen. Sessions, 1872-78. Died N.Y.C., May 25, 1887; buried Woodlawn Cemetery.

SUTRO, Adolph Heinrich Joseph, mayor San Francisco, mining engr.; b. Aix-la-Chapelle, Prussia, Apr. 29, 1830; m. Leah Harris, 1856, 6 children. Came to Am., 1850; went to San Francisco, 1851; went to Nev., 1860, established quartz-reducing mill at East Dayton; originated scheme for driving a tunnel 10 feet high, 12 feet wide and some 3 miles long with lateral branches, nr. Comstock, Nev.; formed Sutro Tunnel Co., chartered by Nev. Legislature, 1865; granted (with assos.) right of way through public lands penetrated by tunnel by U.S.

Congress, 1866 (tunnel completed, 1878); invested tunnel profits in real estate in San Francisco City and County; mayor of San Francisco (Populist), 1894-96; left library of over 200,000 rare volumes, half destroyed in fire, 1906, remainder now in San Francisco Public Library. Died San Francisco, Aug. 8, 1898.

SUTTER, John Augustus (originally Johann Augustus Suter), pioneer; b. Kandern, Baden, Feb. 1803; s. Johann Jakob and Christine (Stoberin) Suter; m. Anna Dübeld (or Dubelt), 1826, 4 children including John A. Sailed for Am., 1834; accompanied trading party to Santa Fe., N.M., 1835, 36; accompanied Eells-Walker missionary party to Ore., 1838; presented plan for establishing a colony on Northern frontier to Mexican gov. of Monterey (Cal.), 1839; began settlement called Neuva Helvetia on South bank of American River at its junction with Sacramento River, land cleared and irrigated, orchards planted with great success; Mexican citizen granted 11 sq. leagues of land, 1841; Gov. Micheltorena gave 22 leagues, 1845; known as General Sutter during 1840's; his fort was a center for opposition to Mexican rule; Gen. Frémont was suspicious of his attitudes, seized his fort, 1846; gold discovered on his property, Jan. 24, 1848, during subsequent gold rush his workmen deserted, his sheep and cattle were stolen, and squatters took his land; del. to conv. which drafted Cal. State Constn., 1849; bankrupted, 1852; given pension of $250 a month by State of Cal.; although U.S. Supreme Ct. validated his claim to 11 leagues of land granted in 1841, he could not afford litigation. Died Mades' Hotel, Washington, D.C., June 18, 1880.

SVININ, Pavel Petrovitch, artist; b. Russia, 1787/88; studied at Acad. Fine Arts of St. Petersburg (Russia). Entered service of Fgn. Office; came to Am. as sec. to Russian consul-gen. with hdqrs. at Phila., 1811; travelled extensively from Me. to Va., 1811-13, made over 50 watercolors of Am. scenes (now owned by Met. Museum of Art, N.Y.C.); returned to Russia, 1813; published A Picturesque Voyage in North America; editor patriotic mag., 1818-30. Died St. Petersburg, Apr. 21, 1839.

SWAIN, David Lowry, gov. N.C., coll. pres.; b. Asheville, Buncombe County, N.C., Jan. 4, 1801; s. George and Caroline (Lane) Lowey Swain; grad. U. N.C., 1821; m. Eleanor White, Jan. 12, 1823. Admitted to N.C. bar, 1822; solicitor of a dist. Eastern N.C., 1829; judge N.C. Superior Ct. 1830, also mem. N.C. Bd. Internal Improvements; gov. N.C. (youngest in history of state up to that time), 1832-35; mem. N.C. Constl. Conv., 1835; pres. U. N.C., 1835-68, taught constl. and internat. law, history and moral science; established N.C. Hist. Soc.; founded U. N.C. Mag. 1853; commr. of N.C. Legislature to govt. Confederate States Am., Montgomery, Ala. 1861; a Unionist Whig before secession; adviser to gov. N.C throughout Civil War; spl. commr. to meet Gen. Sherman to arrange surrender of Raleigh (N.C.), 1865; adviser to Pres. Johnson on Reconstrn., 1865-68; Supported tax reform, public edn., internal improvements while in polit. office. Died N.C., Aug. 27, 1868.

SWAIN, James, journalist; b. N.Y.C., July 30, 1820; s. Joseph and Jerusha (Everts) S.; m. Relief Davis, 1842, children include son Chellis. Began newspaper work on Horace Greeley's The Log Cabin, 1840; ran private printing business; published The Life and Speeches of Henry Clay, 1843; published Hudson River Chronicle and small paper at Sing Sing, 1844-49; asst. N.Y. Tribune; independent printer; city editor N.Y. Times, 1852, corr. at Albany, N.Y., Washington corr., 1860; railroad commr. State of N.Y.,, 1855-57; established Free State Advocate, 1856; founded Albany Statesman, 1857; introduced correspondent system; apptd. 2d, later 1st lt. N.Y. Militia, 1861; organized 11th N.Y. Cavalry; commd. lt. col., 1862; saw no fighting, dismissed from command, 1864, dismissal revoked, 1866; apptd. engr.-in-chief to Gov. Reuben S. Fenton of N.Y., 1865; conceived triple-decked rapid transit system of N.Y.C.; received charter for Met. Transit Co., 1872, scheme failed; weigher N.Y. Customs House, 1867-71 reporter N.Y. Tribune, 1872, clk. of a com. N.Y. Assembly; editor Hudson River Chronicle, 1876-95. Died May 27, 1895.

SWAINSON, William, ornithologist; b. England. Swainson's hawk named in his honor, 1838, also Swainson's warbler and Swainson's thrush. Emigrated to and died in New Zealand.

SWAN, James, revolutionary patriot, financier; b. Fifeshire, Scotland, 1754; m. Hepzibah Clarke, circa 1776, 4 children. Came to Boston, 1765; mem. Sons' of Liberty; participated in Boston Tea Party; aide-de-camp to Gen. Joseph Warren at battle of Bunker Hill; attained rank of maj., later col.; sec. to Mass. Bd. of War, 1777; mem. Mass. Legislature as adj. gen. of commonwealth, 1778; went to France, 1787; gained control of remainder of U.S. debt. to France, 1787, apptd. agt. French Republic; as both agt. France and as broker he profited from having Am. debt obligations from France accepted in payment for supplies furnished or to be furnished the French marine; put in debtor's prison in Paris, 1800. Author: A Dissuasion to Great Britain and the Colonies, from the Slave Trade to Africa, 1773. Died in debtor's prison, Paris, July 31, 1830.

SWAN, John, Continental congressman; b. Pasquotank County, N.C., 1760; attended Coll. William and Mary, circa 1780. Apptd. del. Continental Congress (filled vacancy) from N.C., 1788; farmer in N.C.; urged adoption of proposed U.S. Constn. by N.C. Died 1793; buried on plantation "The Elms," Pasquotank County.

SWAN, Joseph Rockwell, jurist; b. Westernville, N.Y., Dec. 28, 1802; s. Jonathan and Sarah (Rockwell) S.; ed., Aurora, N.Y.; m. Hannah Andrews, 1833, at least 5 children. Admitted to bar, Columbus, O.; pros. atty. Franklin County (O.) 1830-35; judge Ct. Common Pleas, Franklin County, 1834-45, mem. Ohio Constl. Conv., 1850; judge Ohio Supreme Ct., 1854-59; an abolitionist; reputation founded on his opinion in that the state could not interfere with fed. ct.; (in case Ex parte Bushnell), 1859; pres. Columbus & Xenia R.R.; became known as legal writer. Author: Commentaries on Pleading under Ohio Code, with Precedents of Petitions, 1861; 4 gen. revisions Ohio Statutes, 1841, 54, 60, 68; A Treatise on the Law Relating to the Powers and Duties of Justices of the Peace . . . in the State of Ohio; Swan's Pleadings and Practice. Died Columbus, Dec. 18, 1884.

SWAN, Samuel, congressman, physician; b. nr. Scotch Plains, N.J., 1771; studied medicine. Practiced medicine, Boundbrook, N.J., 1800-06, Somerville, N.J., 1806-09; sheriff Somerset County, 1804-06, county clk., 1809-20; mem. U.S. Ho. of Reps. from N.J., 17th-21st congresses, 1821-31; mem. Whig Party. Died Boundbrook, Aug. 24, 1844; buried De Groot vault in Presbyn. Cemetery.

SWAN, Timothy, composer; b. Worcester, Mass., July 23, 1758; s. William and Lavina (Keyes) S.; m. Mary Gay, Apr. 10, 1784; 14 children. Apprenticed to Mr. Barnes (a Loyalist), 1772-75; lived in Groton (Mass.) with brother, 1775-82; published book Select Harmony (containing six tunes he composed), 1783, music very popular at the time; composed song China, 1st sung in public, 1794; published The Songsters' Assistant, 1800, New England Harmony, 1801, The Songsters' Museum, 1803. Died Northfield, Mass., July 23, 1842.

SWANN, Thomas, gov. Md., congressman; b. Alexandria, Va., Feb. 3, 1809; s. Thomas and Jane (Byrd) Page S.; attended U. Va., 1826-27; studied law; m. Elizabeth Gilmor Sherlock, 1834; m. 2d, Josephine (Ward) Thomson, June 1878; at least 1 child. Sec. of commn. sent to Naples, Italy, to negotiate settlement of spoilation claims, 1833; pres. B.& O. R.R. Co., 1848-53, Northwestern Va. R.R. (now Grayton-Parkersburg Line of B.& O.), 1853-56; mayor Balt. (Am. Party), 1856-58, replaced volunteer fire cos. by a municipal fire dept., installed police and fire alarms, telegraph system, street ry.; elected gov. Md. (Unionist), 1864; mem. U.S. Ho. of Reps. (Democrat) from Md., 41st-45th congresses, 1869-79. Died "Morven Park" nr. Leesburg, Va., July 24, 1883; buried Greenmount Cemetery, Balt.

SWART, Peter, congressman, lawyer; b. Schoharie, N.Y., July 5, 1752; studied law. Admitted to the bar, began practice law, Schoharie; judge Schoharie County Ct. of Common Pleas, 1795; mem. N.Y. State Assembly, 1798-99; mem. U.S. Ho. of Reps., 10th Congress, 1807-09; sheriff Schoharie County, 1810, 13; mem. N.Y. State Senate, 1817-20; resumed practice law, Schoharie. Died Schoharie, Nov. 3, 1829; buried Old Stone Fort Cemetery.

SWARTWOUT, Samuel, army officer, mcht., speculator; b. Poughkeepsie, N.Y., Nov. 17, 1783; s. Abraham and Maria (North) S.; m. Alice Ann Cooper, 1814, 2 children. Asso. with Aaron Burr, 1804-06; delivered famous cipher letter from Burr to Gen. James Wilkinson (used as evidence of Burr's treason), 1806, arrested in New Orleans and sent to Washington (D.C.) for trial as accomplice in Burr's schemes, 1807, tried and acquitted, important witness against Burr, preceded Burr to Eng. to prepare for his favorable reception; involved in scheme to open up trade with Mississippi Valley through Mobile and Pensacola in violation of Jefferson's embargo; served as capt. in War of 1812; asso. with Andrew Jackson from 1814, worked for Jackson's nomination and election to Presidency, his services recognized by his appointment as collector Port of N.Y., 1829-38; later investigations revealed he had used over million dollars in public funds for land and railroad speculations. Died N.Y. C., Nov. 21, 1856.

SWAYNE, Noah Haynes, asso. justice U.S. Supreme Ct.; b. Frederick County, Va., Dec. 7, 1804; s. Joshua and Rebecca (Smith) S.; LL.D. (hon.), Dartmouth, 1863, Marietta Coll., 1863, Yale, 1865; m. Sarah Wagner, 1832, at least 1 child, Wagner. Admitted to Va. bar, 1823; pros. atty. Coshocton County (O.), 1826; mem. Ohio Legislature (Jeffersonian Democrat), 1829; U.S. atty. Dist of Ohio, 1830-39; leading mem. Ohio bar; mem. state fund commn. managing Ohio debt; mem. commn. to settle Ohio-Mich. boundary dispute; mem. commn. to study need for state instn. for care of blind; asso. justice U.S. Supreme Ct., 1862-81, became known as exponent of nationalist position, exemplified in approval of income tax; most noteworthy opinions given in cases Gelpcke vs. City of Dubuque (68 U.S., 175) and Springer vs. U.S. (102 U.S., 586). Died N.Y.C., June 8, 1884; buried Oak Hill Cemetery, Washington, D.C.

SWEARINGEN, Henry, congressman; b. Panhandle of Va., circa 1792. Moved to area nr. Steubenville, O.; sheriff Jefferson County (O.), 1824-28, 30-32; mem. U.S. Ho. of Reps. (Democrat, filled vacancy) from Ohio, 25th-26th congresses, Dec. 3, 1838-41. Died on board ship while on his way home from Cal.; buried at sea.

SWEENEY, Thomas William, army officer; b. County Cork, Ireland, Dec. 25, 1820; s. William and Honora (Sweeny) S.; m. Eleanor Swain Clark; m. 2d, Eugenia Octavia Reagan at least 4 children. Came to U.S., 1832; served as 2d lt. 1st N.Y. Volunteers in Mexican War, 1846, served from Vera Cruz to capture of Churubusco; commd. capt., 1848; participated in operations against the Yuma Indians of the Southwest, or the Sioux of Neb. region, 1848-61; ordered to U.S. arsenal, St. Louis, 1861; commd. brig. gen. of Three Months' Mo. Volunteers, 1861; mustered out of Mo. Volunteers, commd. col. 52d Ill. Regt., 1862, aided in capture Ft. Donelson; served in battles of Corinth, 1862, Kenesaw Mountain, 1864, Atlanta, 1864; commd. brig. gen. U.S. Volunteers, 1862, maj. 16th Inf., 1863, honorably discharged, 1865; leader unsuccessful Fenian raid on Can., 1866; sec. war of "Irish Republic" circa 1865; retired from U.S. Army with rank brig. gen., 1870. Died Astoria, L.I., N.Y., Apr. 10, 1892.

SWEENEY, William Northcut, congressman, lawyer; b. Liberty, Ky., May 5, 1832; attended Bethany (W.Va.) Coll.; studied law. Admitted to the bar, 1853, began practice law in Liberty; moved to Owensboro, Ky., 1853; pros. atty. Daviess County (Ky.), 1854-58; Democratic presdl. elector, 1860; mem. U.S. Ho. of Reps. (Democrat) from Ky., 41st Congress, 1869-71. Died Owensboro, Apr. 21, 1895; buried Elmwood Cemetery.

SWEENY, George, congressman, lawyer; b. nr. Gettysburg, Pa., Feb. 22, 1796; grad. Dickinson Coll.; studied law. Admitted to bar, began practice law, Gettysburg, 1820; moved to Bucyrus, O., 1830; pros. atty. Crawford County, O., 1838, 56; mem. U.S. Ho. of Reps. from Ohio, 26th-27th congresses, 1839-43; practiced law, Geneseo, Ill., 1853-56; returned to Bucyrus, 1856; ret. from practice law, engaged in lit., scientific pursuits. Died Bucyrus, Oct. 10, 1877; buried Oakwood Cemetery.

SWEETSER, Charles, congressman, lawyer; b. Dummerston, Vt., Jan. 22, 1808; studied law. Moved with family to Delaware, O., 1817, worked in store; admitted to Ohio bar, 1832, began practice law, Delaware; mem. U.S. Ho. of Reps. (Democrat) from Ohio, 31st-32d congresses, 1849-53. Died Delaware, Apr. 14, 1864; buried Oak Grove Cemetery.

SWIFT, Benjamin, senator, congressman; b. Amenia, N.Y., Apr. 3, 1781; studied law. Moved with father to Bennington, Vt., 1786; admitted to the bar, 1806, began practice law, Bennington; moved to Manchester, then to St. Albans (Vt.), 1809, practiced law, also farmer, banker; mem. Vt. Ho. of Reps., 1813, 25-26; mem. U.S. Ho. of Reps. (Federalist) from Vt., 20th-21st congresses, 1827-31; mem. U.S. Senate from Vt., 1833-39. Died St. Albans, Nov. 11, 1847; buried Old Cemetery, S. Main St.

SWIFT, John Franklin, lawyer, diplomat; b. Bowling Green, Ky., Feb. 28, 1829; m. Miss Wood. Admitted to Cal. bar, 1857; Cal. Assembly, 1863, 73, 77; leader anti-monopoly movement; register U.S. Land Office, San Francisco, 1865-66; won suits brought against San Francisco by Spring Valley Water Co., wrote provisions in Cal. Constn. which gave county bds. suprs. authority to control water rates; mem. commn. to negotiate modifications Burlingame Treaty with China, 1880; aided U.S. atty. gen. in obtaining decision before U.S. Supreme Ct. sustaining constitutionality of Chinese Exclusion Act, 1888; del.-at-large Republican Nat. Conv., 1888; apptd. U.S. minister to Japan, 1889; regent U. Cal., 1872-88. Author: Going to Jericho, 1868; Robert Greathouse, 1870. Died Tokyo, Japan, Mar. 10, 1891; buried Lone Mountain Cemetery, San Francisco.

SWIFT, Joseph Gardner, army officer, engr.; b. Nantucket, Mass., Dec. 31, 1783; s. Dr. Foster and Deborah (Delano) S.; grad. U.S. Mil. Acad. (1st graduating class), 1802; m. Louisa Walker, June 6, 1805, 1 son. Served as cadet in corps of artillerists and engrs., Newport, R.I., 1800, trans. to U.S. Mil. Acad., 1801; commd. 1st. lt. Engr. Corps, U.S. Army, 1805, capt., 1806, maj., 1808, lt. col., 1812, became col. and chief engr., 1812; served with Gen. Wilkinson during abortive invasion of Can., 1813, brevetted brig. gen., 1814; charge constrn. of fortifications N.Y.C., 1814; supt. U.S. Mil. Acad., 1816-18; resigned commn., 1818; surveyor Port of N.Y., 1818-26; chief engr. various railroads including Balt. & Susquehanna, New Orleans & Lake Pontchartrain, 1826; civil engr. in U.S. Govt. service, in charge harbor improvement on Gt. Lakes, 1829-45; 1st Am. engr. trained wholly in U.S. Died Geneva, N.Y., July 23, 1865.

SWIFT, William Henry, army officer, engr.; b. Taunton, Mass., Nov. 6, 1800; s. Dr. Foster and Deborah (Delano) S.; grad. U.S. Mil. Acad.; m. Mary Stuart, 1825; m. 2d, Hannah Howard, 1844; Commd. 2d lt. arty. U.S. Army, 1st lt., 1824; worked on coastal improvements on surveys for Chesapeake and Ohio Canal for a projected canal across Fla. peninsula; brevetted capt., 1832, also asst. topog. engr.; commd. capt., 1838; prin. asst. in Topog. Bur., Washington, D.C., 1843-49; responsible for constrn. of 1st skeleton iron tower lighthouse in U.S., Black Rock Harbor, Conn., resigned Commn., 1849; became pres. Phila., Wilmington & Balt. R.R., also Mass. Western R.R.; pres. bd. trustees Ill. & Mich. Canal, 1845-71; published report on Chesapeake & Ohio Canal, 1846. Died N.Y.C., Apr. 7, 1879.

SWIFT, Zephaniah, congressman, jurist; b. Wareham, Mass., Feb. 27, 1759; s. Roland and Mary (Dexter) S.; B.A., Yale, 1778, M.A., 1781; m. Jerusha Watrous before 1792; m. 2d, Lucretia Webb, Mar. 14, 1795; 8 children including Mary A. Admitted to Conn. bar; mem. Conn. Gen. Assembly, 1787-93, clk. lower house for 4 sessions, speaker, 1792; mem. U.S. Ho. of Reps. from Conn., 3d-4th congresses, 1793-97; sec. to Oliver Ellsworth on mission to France, 1800; mem. council Conn. Gen. Assembly, circa 1801; vigorous opponent of slavery; judge Conn. Supreme Ct., 1801-10, chief justice, 1806-19; supported Hartford Conv., 1814; mem. Conn. Ho. of Reps., 1820-22. Author: Oration of Domestic Slavery, 1791; System of the Laws of Connecticut, 1795-96. Died Warren, O., Sept. 27, 1823; buried Oakwood Cemetery, Warren.

SWINBURNE, John, congressman, physician; b. Deer River, N.Y., May 30, 1820; grad. Albany Med. Coll., 1847. Began practice medicine, 1847; apptd. chief med. officer on staff Gen. John F. Rathbone, 1861, placed in charge of depot for recruits, Albany; served as surgeon Volunteers with rank of med. supt. of N.Y. wounded troops, 1862; taken prisoner of war, 1862; apptd. health officer port of N.Y. by gov. of N.Y., 1864; in charge of Am. Ambulance Corps during siege of Paris by Prussians, 1870-71; elected mayor Albany, 1882; mem. U.S. Ho. of Reps. (Republican) from N.Y., 49th Congress, 1885-87. Died Albany, Mar. 28, 1889; buried Albany Rural Cemetery.

SWING, David, clergyman; b. Cincinnati, Aug. 23, 1830; s. David and Karenda (Gayley) S.; grad. Miami U., Oxford, O., 1852; m. Elizabeth Porter, 2 children. Prof. Latin and Greek, Miami U., 1853-66; pastor Westminster Presbyn. Ch., Chgo., 1866-75; gave sermons which began to attract attention and were published in Chgo. Tribune and Inter Ocean, after 1871; charged with heresey by Prof. Francis L. Patton, 1874, but charge was not substantiated; citizens interested in giving him a platform from which to preach established Central Music Hall, 1880. Author compilations of sermons including: Sermons, 1874, 84, 95; Truths for Today, 1876; Motives of Life, 1876. Died Chgo., Oct. 3, 1894.

SWINTON, William, journalist; b. Salton, Scotland, Apr. 23, 1833; s. William and Jane (Currie) S.; attended Amherst Coll; m. Catherine Linton, May 4, 1853, 5 children. Came to U.S., 1846. prof. langs. Edgeworth Sem., Greenborough, N.C., 1853; taught in Mt. Washington Collegiate Inst., N.Y.C., 1855-58; with N.Y. Times, 1858, became Times spl. corr. with armies in the field, an order was issued depriving him of privileges as a corr. and forbidding him to remain with army because of his unsavory means of obtaining information, 1864; prof. English U. Cal., 1869-74. Author: Campaigns of the Army of the Potomac, 1866; The Twelve Decisive Battles of the War, 1867; also sch. textbooks. Died Bklyn., Oct. 24, 1892.

SWISSHELM, Jane Grey Cannon, journalist, reformer; b. Pitts., Dec. 6, 1815; d. Thomas and Mary (Scott) Cannon; m. James Swisshelm, Nov. 18, 1836, 1 child. Took charge of sem. at Butler, Pa., 1840; wrote articles on abolition and property rights of women; established Pitts. Saturday Visiter (a weekly advocating abolition, temperence, woman's suffrage), 1847; attacked Daniel Webster's pvt. life in jour., 1850; published St. Cloud Democrat (a Republican paper), 1858-63; contbr. to N.Y. Tribune; clerical work in govt. office, Washington, D.C., during Civil War; began The Reconstructionist, a radical paper attacking the Pres. (Andrew Johnson), dismissed from govt. service, 1866. Author: Half a Century (autobiography), 1880. Died Swissvale, (Pa.), July 22, 1884.

SWOOPE, Jacob, congressman; b. Phila.; attended common schs. Moved to Staunton, Va., 1789, became a mcht.; held several local offices; elected 1st mayor of Staunton under new charter, 1801, reelected, 1804; mem. U.S. Ho. of Reps. (Federalist) from Va., 11th Congress, 1809-11; mem. Va. Constl. Conv., 1812; Federalist presdl. elector, 1812. Died Staunton, 1832; buried Trinity Episcopal Churchyard.

SWOPE, Samuel Franklin, congressman, lawyer; b. Bourbon County, Ky., Mar. 1, 1809; attended Georgetown (Ky.) Coll.; studied law. Admitted to bar, 1830, began practice law in Georgetown; moved to Falmouth, Ky., 1832, practiced law; mem. Ky. Ho. of Reps., 1837-39, 41; mem. Ky. Senate, 1844-48; mem. U.S. Ho. of Reps. (Am. Party) from Ky., 34th Congress, 1855-57; became affiliated with Republican Party, 1856. Died Falmouth, Apr. 19, 1865; buried Riverside Cemetery.

SYKES, George, congressman; b. nr. Sykesville, N.J., Sept. 20, 1802; pvt. edn. Became a surveyor and conveyancer; mem. U.S. Ho. of Reps. (Democrat) from N.J., 28th Congress, 1843-45, (filled vacancy) 29th Congress, Nov. 4, 1845-47; mem. Council of Properties of West Jersey; mem. N.J. Assembly, 1877-79. Died nr. Columbia, N.J., Feb. 25, 1880; buried Upper Springfield Cemetery, nr. Wrightstown, N.J.

SYKES, George (nickname Tardy George), army officer; b. Dover, Del., Oct. 9, 1822; s. William Sykes; attended U.S. Mil. Acad., 1842; m. Elizabeth Goldsborough. Commd. 2d lt., 3d Infantry, took part in Seminole War, 1842; 1st lt. in war with Mexico from Vera Cruz to Mexico City, 1846; brevetted capt. for gallant conduct at Battle of Cerro Gordo, 1855; maj. in Civil War, served in 1st Battle of Bull Run, 1861; commd. brig. gen. U.S. Volunteers, Sept. 1861; at Malvern Hill, 1862; commanded V Corps in Gettysburg campaign, brevetted brig. gen. U.S. Army; went to Kan., 1864; mustered out of U.S. volunteers as maj. gen., reverted to rank lt. col. 5th Inf., U.S. Army, 1866; col. 20th Inf., Ft. Brown, Tex., 1868. Died Ft. Brown, Feb. 8, 1880; buried West Point, N.Y.

SYKES, James, Continental congressman, lawyer; b. 1725; studied law. Admitted to bar, began practice law; lt. Capt. Caesar Rodney's Co. of Dover Militia, 1756; mem. council of safety, 1776; mem. Del. Constl. Conv., New Castle, 1776, 90; mem. Continental Congress from Del., 1777-78; clk. of the peace, 1777-92; prothonotary of Kent County, 1777-93; mem. Del. Council, 1780; mem. Del. Legislature which ratified U.S. Constn., 1787; presdl. elector, 1792, voted for Washington and Adams; judge High Ct. of Errors and Appeals of Del. Died Dover, Del., Apr. 4, 1792; buried Christ Ch. Burial Ground.

SYLVESTER, James Joseph, mathematician, educator; b. London, Eng., Sept. 3, 1814; s. Abraham Joseph; grad. St. John's Coll., Cambridge (Eng.) U., 1831 (barred from degree by Jewish faith, but awarded B.A. and M.A. after Test Act of 1872); B.A., M.A., U. Dublin (Ireland), 1841; never married. Prof. natural philosophy U. Coll., London, 1837-41; prof. mathematics U. Va., 1841-42; returned to London in 1844, did actuarial work, 1844-56; called to the bar, Eng., 1850; prof. mathematics Johns Hopkins U., Balt., 1876-83; a leader in advancing math. research in U.S.; 1st editor Am. Jour. Mathematics, 1878-84; Savilian prof. geometry Oxford (Eng.) U., 1883-97. Author: The Collected Mathematical Papers of James Joseph Sylvester, 4 vols., 1904-12 (edited by H.F. Baker); The Laws of Verse, 1870; translations of Horace, German poets. Died Oxford, Mar. 15, 1897.

SYLVIS, William H., reformer, labor leader; b. Armagh, Indiana County, Pa., Nov. 26, 1828; s. Nicholas and Maria (Mott) S.; m. Amelia A. Thomas, Apr. 11, 1852; m. 2d, Florrie Hunter, 1866; 5 children. Joined, apptd. recording sec. of an iron molders' union, 1857; organizer 1st conv. of Iron-Moulders Internat. Union, Phila., 1859, elected treas., 1860; became Union Democrat, 1860; prominent in nat. conv. of workingmen opposed to war, 1861; elected pres. Moulders' Union at conv., Pitts., 1863, reorganized union (weakened during Civil War); urged establishment of coop. foundries and formation of nat. trades assembly, 1864; leader in Labor Congress, Balt., 1866; pres. 1st meeting of Nat. Labor Union, 1868; led some of early struggles of Am. trade unions; edited Iron-Moulders Internat. Jour., circa 1866; joint propr. Workingman's Advocate (organ of Nat. Labor Union), 1869. Died July 27, 1869.

SYMES, George Gifford, congressman, lawyer; b. Ashtabula County, O., Apr. 28, 1840; studied law. Admitted to bar, practiced law; enlisted as pvt. Co. B, 2d Regt., Wis. Volunteers, U.S. Army, 1861, wounded in 1st Battle of Rull Run, adjutant 25th Regt., Wis. Inf.; served in Sioux Indian (1862), Vicksburg (1863), Atlanta (1864) campaigns, wounded at Battle of Atlanta, 1864, commd. col. 44th Regt., Wis. Volunteers, 1864, commanded post at Paducah, Ky., 1865; began practice law, Paducah, 1865; asso. justice Mont. Territory Supreme Ct., 1869-71; practiced law, Helena, Mont.; moved to Denver, Colo., 1874; mem. U.S. Ho. of Reps. (Republican) from Colo., 49th-50th congresses, 1885-89. Died Denver, Nov. 3, 1893; buried Fairmount Cemetery.

SYMMES, John Cleves, Continental congressman, pioneer, jurist; b. Southold, L.I., N.Y., July 21, 1742; s. Rev. Timothy and Mary (Cleves) S.; m. Anna Tuttle; m. 2d, Mrs. Mary Halsey; m. 3d, Susanna Livingston; at least 2 children. Chmn. Sussex County (N.J.) Com. of Corr., 1774; col. N.J. Militia, 1775; aso. justice N.J. Supreme Ct., 1777, 83; mem. Continenal Congress from N.J., 1785, 86; received grant of 1 million acres "The Miami Purchase" in Ohio between Miami and Little Miami rivers, 1788; became judge Northwest Territory, 1788; founded settlement at North Bend (O.), 1789; founded colony around present Cincinnati (a significant mil. and trading outpost in West). Died Cincinnati, Feb. 26, 1814.

SYMS, Benjamin, planter, philanthropist; b. probably Eng., circa 1591. Came to Am. before 1625, settled in Jamestown, Va., before 1630; probably 1st inhabitant of any N. Am. colony to bequeath property for establishment of free sch.; wrote will leaving 200-acre farm in Elizabeth County, Va. and other property to provide free sch. to children of Elizabeth City and Kiquotan parishes, 1934/35. Died circa 1642.

SYNG, Philip, silversmith; b. Cork, Ireland, Sept. 29, 1703; s. Philip and Abigail (Murdock) S.; m. Elizabeth Warner, Feb. 5, 1729/30; 21 children including Philip. Came to Annapolis, Md., 1714; opened shop in Phila., circa 1720; most famous silver work was inkstand made for Pa. Assembly, 1752 (used at signing both Declaration of Independence and U.S. Constn.; mem. Benjamin Franklin's Junto and one of few serious experimenters with Franklin in electricity in 1740's; invented a machine which aided in generation of electricity, by 1747; mem. Am. Philos. Soc., treas., 1769-71; a grantee charter for Phila. Library Co. a founding trustee Coll. and Acad. of Phila. (later part U. Pa.); warden Phila., 1753, treas., 1759-69; mem. Pa. Provincial Commn. of Appeals, 1765; signer Non-Importation Agreement, 1765. Died Phila., May 8, 1789.

T

TABER, Stephen, congressman, businessman; b. Dover, N.Y., Mar. 7, 1821; s. of Thomas Taber 2d; prep. edn. Became a farmer in Queens County, N.Y.; mem. N.Y. State Assembly, 1860-61; mem. U.S. Ho. of Reps. (Democrat) from N.Y., 39th-40th congresses, 1865-69; an organizer L.I. North Shore Transp. Co., 1861, pres. several years; dir. L.I. R.R. Co.; 1st pres. Roslyn Savs. Bank, 1876. Died N.Y.C., Apr. 23, 1886; buried Roslyn (N.Y.) Cemetery.

TABER, Thomas, 2d, congressman; b. Dover, N.Y., May 19, 1785; attended common schs.; at least 1 son, Stephen. Became a farmer; mem. N.Y. State Assembly, 1826; mem. U.S. Ho. of Reps. (Democrat, filled vacancy) from N.Y., 20th Congress, Nov. 5, 1828-29. Died Roslyn, L.I., N.Y., Mar. 21, 1862; buried Friends Cemetery, Westbury, L.I., N.Y.

TABOR, Horace Austin Warner, senator, businessman; b. Holland, Vt., Nov. 26, 1830; s. Cornelius Dunham and Sarah (Farrin) T.; m. Augusta Pierce, Jan. 31, 1857; m. 2d Elizabeth (McCourt) Doe, Mar. 1, 1883. Stone cutter, Vt., 1847-55; joined group of Free-Soil Immigrants bound for Kan., 1855; mem. Kan. Legislature, 1856-57; joined Pike's Peak gold rush, 1859; went to headwaters of Arkansas River, 1860, mined gold, also set up gen. store, Leadville, Colo.; outfitted August Rische, also George F. Hook, (men who discovered silver in worked-out gold mines), Denver, Colo., received 1/3 of their findings; lt. gov. Colo., 1879-83; mem. U.S. Senate (Republican) from Colo., Jan. 27-Mar. 3, 1883; bankrupted by crash of 1893, also repeal of Sherman Act; postmaster, Denver, 1898-99. Died Denver, Apr. 10, 1899; buried Mt. Calvary Cemetery, Denver.

TAFFE, John, congressman, lawyer; b. Indianapolis, Ind., Jan. 30, 1827; studied law. Admitted to bar in Indpls.; moved to Neb., 1856; mem. Neb.

Territory Ho. of Reps., 1858-59; mem., pres. territorial council, 1860-61; served as maj. 2d Regt., Neb. Volunteer Cav., U.S. Army, Civil War; mem. U.S. Ho. of Reps. (Republican) from Neb., 40th-42d congresses, 1867-73; receiver of pub. land office, North Platte, Neb. Died North Platte, Mar. 14, 1884; buried Prospect Hill Cemetery, Omaha, Neb.

TAFT, Alphonso, cabinet officer, diplomat, judge; b. Townshend, Vt., Nov. 5, 1810; s. Peter Rawson and Sylvia (Howard) T.; grad. Yale, 1833, LL.D. (hon.), 1867; m. Fanny Phelps, Aug. 29, 1841; m. 2d, Louisa Torrey, Dec. 26, 1853; 10 children including William Howard, Henry Waters, Horace Dutton, Fanny Louise, Charles Phelps, Peter Rawson. Admitted to Conn. bar, 1838; settled as lawyer in Cincinnati, circa 1840; judge Superior Ct. of Cincinnati, 1865-72; apptd. U.S. sec. of war by Grant, 1876, atty. gen., 1876-77; assisted in drafting bill which created commn. to settle Hayes-Tilden election; U.S. minister to Austria-Hungary, 1882; ambassador to Russia, 1884-85; trustee Yale. Died San Diego, Cal., May 21, 1891.

TAGGART, Samuel, congressman, clergyman; b. Londonderry, N.H., Mar. 24, 1754; grad. Dartmouth, 1774; studied theology. Licensed to preach, 1776; ordained to ministry Presbyn. Ch., 1777, became pastor ch., Colrain, Mass.; traveled as missionary Western N.Y.; mem. U.S. Ho. of Reps. (Federalist) from Mass., 8th-14th congresses, 1803-17; resigned as pastor Colrain Presbyn. Ch., 1818. Died on his farm, Colrain, Apr. 25, 1825; buried Chandler Hill Cemetery.

TAGLIABUE, Giuseppe, inventor, instrument maker; b. Como, Italy, Aug. 10, 1812; s. Caesar Tagliabue; m. 2d, Adelaide Arniboldi; 6 children. Began mfg. thermometers, N.Y..C, 1829; became one of most prominent and successful instrument makers of U.S., 1831-78; produced variety of new hydrometers; hydrometer for proving of whiskey officially adopted by U.S. Revenue Bur.; perfected and patented several instruments including mercurial barometers and apparatus for testing iron and coal, 1859-71; known for precision of instruments. Died Mt. Vernon, N.Y., May 7, 1873.

TAIT, Charles, senator; b. Louisa County, Va., Feb. 1, 1768; s. James and Rebecca (Hudson) T.; attended Wilkes Acad., Washington, Ga., 1786-87, Cokesbury Coll., Abingdon, Md., 1788; m. Mrs. Anne Lucas Simpson, Jan. 3, 1790; m. 2d, Mrs. Sarah Williamson Griffin, 1822; at least 1 child. Admitted to Elberton (Ga.) bar, 1795; began law practice, Lexington, Ga., 1798; judge Superior Ct. for Western dist. Ga., 1803-09; mem. U.S. Senate from Ga., Nov. 27, 1809-19, chmn. com. on Naval affairs which secured appropriations for U.S. Navy, 1814-18; aided in formation of Ala. as separate territory and in obtaining its admission to U.S.; 1st U.S. judge Ala. dist., 1820-26; publicized Claiborne beds (Eocene deposits); mem. Am. Philos. Soc., 1827; corr. mem. Acad. Natural Scis. of Phila., 1832. Died Wilcox County, Ala., Oct. 7, 1835; buried Dry Forks Cemetery, Wilcox County.

TALBOT, Isham, senator, lawyer; b. nr. Talbot, Va., 1773; studied law. Admitted to the Ky. bar, began practice law, Versailles, Ky.; moved to Frankfort, Ky., practiced law; mem. Ky. Senate, 1812-15; mem. U.S. Senate from Ky. (filled vacancies), Jan. 3, 1815-19, Oct. 19, 1820-25. Died nr. Frankfort, Sept. 25, 1837; buried State Cemetery, Franfort.

TALBOT, John, clergyman; b. Wymondham, Eng., 1645; s. Thomas and Jane (Mede) T.; B.A., Cambridge (Eng.), U. 1634, M.A., 1671; m. dau. of Sir Arthur Jenny, 1668; m. 2d, Mrs. Anne Herbert, circa 1725; Fellow of Peterhouse, Cambridge, Eng., 1664-68; rector, Icklingham, Suffolk, Eng., 1673-89, Fretherne, Gloucestershire, Eng., 1695-1701; sailed from Eng. for Boston (Mass.) as chaplain aboard the Centurion, 1702; chosen missionary for Soc. of Propogation of Gospel in Fgn. Parts, 1702; rector St. Mary's Ch., Burlington, N.J., 1704-06; returned to Eng. to secure support for the Soc., 1706-08; accused of omitting certain prayers of the liturgy by Gov. Robert Hunter of Jersey; visited Eng., 1720-23; removed from Soc. at insistence of Rev. John Urmiston who claimed that he was acting in the capacity of a bishop. Died Burlington, Nov. 29, 1727; buried St. Mary's Ch., Burlington.

TALBOT, Silas, naval officer, congressman; b. Dighton, Bristil County, Mass., Jan. 11, 1751; s. Benjamin and Rebecca (Allen) T.; m. Miss Richmond, 1772; m. 2d, Miss Morris; m. 3d, Mrs. Pintard; at least 4 children. Mcht., Providence, R.I., circa 1772; apptd. capt. R.I. Regt., 1775; commd. capt. Continental Navy, 1775-79, maj., lt. col., 1777-78, captured by British and held prisoner, 1779-81; mem. N.Y. Assembly, 1792-93; mem. U.S. Ho. of Reps. from N.Y., 3d Congress, 1793-95; commd. capt. U.S. Navy, 1794, supt. constn. of frigate President, N.Y.C.; comdr. Santo Domingo naval station, cruised in West Indies in command ship Constitution. Died N.Y.C., June 30, 1813; buried Trinity Churchyard, N.Y.C.

TALBOTT, Albert Gallatin, congressman; b. nr. Paris, Ky., Apr. 4, 1808; attended Forrest Hill Acad., Jessamine County, Ky.; studied law, did not practice. Became a farmer and gen. trader, 1831; moved to Mercer County, Ky., 1838, in real estate bus., 1838-46; moved to Danville, Ky., 1846; del. Ky. Constl. Conv., 1849; mem. Ky. Ho. of Reps., 1850, 83; mem. U.S. Ho. of Reps. (Democrat) from Ky., 34th-35th congresses, 1855-59; resumed real estate bus.; mem. Ky. Senate, 1869-73; moved nr. Chestnut Hill, Pa., became a farmer, stock raiser. Died Phila., Sept. 9, 1887; buried Bellevue Cemetery, Danville, Ky.

TALCOTT, Andrew, army officer, engr.; b. Glastonbury, Conn., Apr. 20, 1797; s. George and Abigail (Goodrich) T.; grad. U.S. Mil. Acad., 1818; m. Catherine Thompson, Apr. 1826; m. 2d, Harriet Randolph Hackley, Apr. 11, 1832; 11 children. Brevetted 2d lt. U.S. Army, 1818; 1st lt. Engr. Corps, 1820, capt., 1830; engr., aide-de-camp to Gen. Henry Atkinson in establishment of posts on Upper Missouri and Yellowstone rivers, 1820-21; chief engr. Ft. Delaware, Del., 1824-25; supt. constrn. canal through Dismal Swamp in Va., 1826-28; supervised constrn. Ft. Monroe, Ft. Calhoun, Hampton Roads, Va., 1828-34; astronomer for determining boundaries between Ohio and Mich., 1828-35; chief engr. in charge of Western div. N.Y. & Erie R.R., 1836-37; supt. improvement of delta of Mississippi River, 1837-39; chief engr. Richmond & Danville R.R., 1848-55; astronomer, surveyor for making the northern boundary of Ia., 1852-53; chief engr. Ohio & Miss. R.R. from Cincinnati and St. Louis, 1856-57; located, constructed railroad from Vera Cruz to Mexico City, 1857-60, 61-67; mgr. Sonora Exploring & Mining Co., chief engr. State of Va., 1860-61; elected chief engr. Va., 1861; devised method of determining terrestrial latitudes through the observation of stars near the zenith; mem. Am. Philos. Soc. Died Richmond, Va., Apr. 22, 1883.

TALCOTT, Joseph, colonial gov.; b. Hartford, Conn., Nov. 1669; s. Lt. Col. John and Helena (Wakeman) T.; m. Abigail Clark, 1693; m. 2d, Eunice (Howell) Wakeman, June 26, 1706; 9 children. Chosen selectman of Hartford, 1692; justice of peace for Hartford County (Conn.), 1705; dep. from Hartford to Conn. Gen. Assembly, 1708, speaker lower house, 1710; maj. 1st Regt., Conn. Militia, 1710-24; mem. upper chamber Conn. Gen. Assembly, 1711-23; judge county ct., ct. of probate Hartford County, 1714; judge Conn. Superior Ct., 1721; dep. gov. Conn., 1723, gov., 1724-41. Died Hartford, Nov. 11, 1741.

TALIAFERRO, Benjamin, congressman; b. in Va., 1750; prep. edn. Served as lt., rifle corps commanded by Gen. Morgan, Continental Army, promoted capt., captured by British at Charleston, 1780; settled in Ga., 1785; mem., pres. Ga. Senate; del. Ga. Constl. Conv., 1798; mem. U.S. Ho. of Reps. from Ga., 6th-7th congresses, 1799-1802 (resigned); judge of superior ct.; trustee Ga. U. Died Wilkes County, Ga., Sept. 3, 1821.

TALIAFERRO, John, congressman, lawyer; b. nr. Fredericksburg, Va., 1768; studied law. Admitted to the bar, began practice law, Fredericksburg; mem. U.S. Ho. of Reps. from Va., (Democrat) 7th Congress, 1801-03, (contested election) 12th Congress, Nov. 29, 1811-13, (filled vacancy) 18th-21st congresses, Mar. 24, 1824-31, (Whig) 24th-27th congresses, 1835-43; Democratic presdl. elector, 1804, 20; librarian U.S. Treasury Dept., 1850-52. Died at residence "Hagley," nr. Fredericksburg, Aug. 12, 1852; buried at "Hagley."

TALIAFERRO, Lawrence, Indian agt.; b. Whitehall, King George County, Va., Feb. 28, 1794; s. James Garnett and Wilhelmina (Wishart) T.; m. Eliza Dillon, summer 1828, 1 child. Commd. 1st lt. U.S. Army, circa 1814; Indian agt., Ft. Snelling, Minn., 1819, in charge of both Sioux and Chippewa Indians, 1819-27, in charge of Sioux, 1827-39, endeavored to keep peace between hostile tribes, often successful, became friend of Indians, his efforts on tribes' behalf resulted in enmity of traders and Am. Fur Co., resigned as agt., 1839; served in q.m. dept. U.S. Army, 1857-63. Died Bedford, Pa., Jan. 22, 1871.

TALIAFERRO, William Booth, army officer; b. Belleville, Gloucester County, Va., Dec. 28, 1822; s. Warner and Frances (Booth) T.; grad. Coll. William and Mary, 1841; studied law Harvard; m. Sally Lyons, 8 children. Capt. 11th U.S. Infantry in Mexico; discharged with rank of maj., 1848; mem. Va. Ho. of Dels., 1850-53; col. Confederate Army, 1861, brig. gen., 1862, led brigade under Jackson throughout Valley campaign; defended Battery Wagner on Morris Island during assault on Charleston Harbor, S.C., July 18, 1863; safeguarded garrison of Savannah in escaping from Sherman, 1864; maj. gen., 1865; mem. Va. Legislature, 1874-79; judge Gloucester County (Va.) Ct., 1891-97; mem. bd. visitors Coll. William and Mary. Died Dunham Massie, Va., Feb. 27, 1898; buried cemetery of Ware Ch., Gloucester County.

TALLEYRAND-PÉRIGORD, Charles Maurice de, diplomat; b. Paris, France, Feb. 13, 1754; studied for priesthood at College d'Harcourt and Reims; m. Mrs. Grand, 1803. Gen. agt. to clergy, 1780; bishop of Autun, 1789; dep. from Autun to Estates-General, 1789; became mem. Nat. Assembly, after the storming of Bastille; a founder Soc. of Friends of Constn. (forerunner of Jacobin Club); founder Club des Feuillants, 1789; pres. Nat. Assembly, 1790; excommunicated from ch. by Papal brief for forming a constl. clergy, 1792; lived in exile in U.S., 1794-95; minister of fgn. affairs, 1797-99; recognized potential of Bonaparte; negotiated treaties of Luneville, Amiens; instigated murder of Duc d'Enghien, 1803; opposed La. Purchase, 1803; grand chamberlain of French Empire, 1804; negotiated Peace of Presburg, 1805; created prince of Benevento, 1806; concluded Peace of Tilsit, 1807; joined Royalist Party, circa 1808, sought to overthrow Napoleon; headed provisional govt. after unsuccessful Russian expdn., procured Napoleon's abdication, Apr. 1, 1814; re-established Louis XVIII on throne; resigned rather than sign 2d Peace of Paris, 1815; participated very little in politics, 1815-30; advised Louis Philippe to accept French throne, 1830; ambassador to Eng., 1830-35; helped constitute Quadruple Alliance, 1834. Died Paris, May 17, 1838.

TALLIAFERO, Richard, architect. Practiced architecture in Va. during Pre-Revolutionary period, known as 1 of ablest designers of his time; only recorded work is mansion now known as George Wythe house (served as Gen. Washington's hdqrs. 1781) Williamsburg, Va. Died 1755.

TALLMADGE, Benjamin, army officer, congressman; b. Brookhaven, N.Y., Feb. 25, 1754; s. Benjamin and Susannah (Smith) T.; grad. Yale, 1773; m. Mary Floyd, Mar. 18, 1784; m. 2d Maria Hallett, May 3, 1808; 7 children including Frederick Augustus. Supt., Wetherfield (Conn.) High Sch., 1773-76; apptd. lt. adj. Conn. Militia, 1776, capt., 1776, maj., 1777, brevetted lt. col., 1873; fought in battles of Brandywine, L.I., Monmouth; captured Ft. George, L.I., N.Y., 1780; officer in charge of taking custody of Maj. John Andre; mem. U.S. Ho. of Reps. (Federalist) from Conn., 7th-14th congresses, 1801-17; mem. Soc. of Cincinnati. Died Litchfield, Conn., Mar. 7, 1835; buried East Cemetery, Litchfield.

TALLMADGE, Frederick Augustus, congressman, lawyer; b. Litchfield, Conn., Aug. 29, 1792; s. of Benjamin Tallmadge; grad. Yale, 1811; studied law Litchfield Law Sch. Admitted to the bar, 1811, began practice law, N.Y.C., 1813; served as capt., War of 1812; mem. bd. aldermen N.Y.C., 1834, common council, 1836; mem. N.Y. State Senate, 1837-40, pres. pro tem., 1840; recorder City of N.Y., 1841-46, 48-51; mem. U.S. Ho. of Reps. (Whig) from N.Y., 30th Congress, 1847-49; supt. met. police, N.Y.C., 1857-62; clk. N.Y. Ct. of Appeals, 1862-65; practiced law, N.Y.C., 1865-69; returned to Litchfield, 1869. Died Litchfield, Sept. 17, 1869; buried East Cemetery.

TALLMADGE, James, Jr., congressman; b. Stanford, N.Y., Jan. 20, 1778; s. Col. James and Ann (Southerland) T.; grad. R.I. Coll. (now Brown U.), 1798; m. Laura Tallmadge, Jan. 21, 1810; 2 children including Mary (Tallmadge) Van Rensselaer. Sec. to Gov. Clinton of N.Y., 1798-1800; began practice of law, Poughkeepsie, N.Y., circa 1800; Democrat; commd. brig. gen. N.Y. Militia, 1813, commanded defense of N.Y.C., circa 1814; mem. U.S. Ho. of Reps. from N.Y., 15th Congress, June 6, 1817-19, introduced Tallmadge Amendment to bill regarding admission of Mo. to statehood designed to prohibit further introduction of slaves into Mo., 1819 (bill defeated in Ho. of Reps.), del. N.Y. Constl. Conv., 1821, 46; mem. N.Y. State Legislature, 1824; lt. gov. N.Y., 1824-26; a founder N.Y. U., pres. council, 1834-46; founder Am. Inst. of City of N.Y. (for promotion of useful arts), pres., 1837-53; while in Europe obtained removal of some quarantine restrictions which hampered U.S. trade with No. Europe, 1838. Died N.Y.C., Sept. 29, 1853; buried Marble Cemetery, N.Y.C.

TALLMADGE, Nathaniel Pitcher, senator, territorial gov.; b. Chatham, N.Y., Feb. 8, 1795; grad. Union Coll., Schenectady, N.Y., 1815; studied law. Admitted to N.Y. bar, 1818, began practice law in Poughkeepsie, N.Y.; mem. N.Y. State Assembly, 1828, N.Y. State Senate, 1830-33; mem. U.S. Senate (Democrat) from N.Y., 1833-44 (resigned); apptd. by Pres. Tyler as gov. Wis. Territory, 1844, removed from office, 1845; wrote religious tracts. Died Battle Creek, Mich., Nov. 2, 1864; buried Rienzi Cemetery, Fond du Lac, Wis.

TALLMAN, Peleg, congressman; b. Tiverton, R.I., July 24, 1764; attended pub. schs. Served in Revolutionary War on privateer Trumbull, lost an arm in naval engagement, 1780, captured, imprisoned in Eng. and Ireland, 1781-83; became a mcht. in Bath, Me. (part of Mass. until 1820); mem. U.S. Ho. of Reps. (Democrat) from Mass., 12th Congress, 1811-13; overseer Bowdoin Coll., Brunswick, Me., 1802-40; mem. Me. Senate, 1821-22. Died Bath, Mar. 12, 1840; buried Maple Grove Cemetery, reinterred Forest Hills Cemetery, Roxbury, Mass.

TALMAGE, John Van Nest, missionary; b. Somerville, N.Y., Aug. 18, 1819; s. David and Catharine (Van Nest) T.; grad. Rutgers U., 1842, D.D. (hon.), 1867; grad. New Brunswick Theol. Sem., 1845; m. Abby F. Woodruff, Jan. 15, 1850; m. 2d, Mary Van Deventer, Nov. 1864; 4 children. Ordained to ministry Dutch Reformed Ch., 1846, sailed for Amoy (China) as missionary, 1847; contbd. to growth of Chinese church; developed Romanized form of writing vernacular to enable illiterate Christians to read Bible and other religious literature quickly, including primer, 1852, reader, 1853, portions of New Testament; finished dictionary in Amoy dialect, circa 1890. Author: History and Ecclesiastical Relations of the Churches of the Presbyterian Order at Amoy, China, 1863. Died N.J., Aug. 19, 1892.

TALON, Pierre, explorer; b. Quebec, Can., 1676. Went with parents to La., 1684, moved to Mexico City after Spaniards occupied La.; became mem. of viceroy's retinue, Mexico City; later joined Spanish marines; when his ship was captured, enrolled in French marines; described Southern part of Am. for French authorities, Brest, France; possibly crossed Mississippi River before LaSalle's discovery. Died in France.

TAMARON, Pedro, clergyman; b. LaGuardia, Toledo, Spain; doctor's degree U. Santa Rosa, Caracas. Came to Am. as youth; domestic chaplain of Bishop of Caracas, Venezuela; prof. canonical law U. Santa Rosa, curate cathedral, prof. divinity and pecentor; made bishop of Durango, 1758, personally visited all provinces of his diocese as far North as N.M., 1758-68. Author: Description of the Bishopric of Durango; or, Diary of the Holy Visit of the Whole Diocese, Dedicated to the King . . . Carlos III (in archives of diocese of Durango) (diary of his episcopal tour; of historic value for information about life in provinces). Died Pueblo of Bamoa, Sinaloa, Dec. 21, 1768.

TAMMANY, Indian chief; b. along Delaware River, Buck County, Pa. Chief of Lenni-Lenape (or Delaware) Indians; attended council between Pa. settlers and Indians, 1694, spoke in favor of friendship with settlers; few records exist of his activities; had become a symbol of Am. resistance to Brit. tyranny by advent of Revolutionary War; became symbol of democracy vs. aristocracy after Am. Revolution; name adopted by Soc. of Tammany of N.Y.C. (founded by William Mooney), 1786.

TANEY, Roger Brooke, chief justice U.S. Supreme Ct.; b. Calvert County, Md., Mar. 17, 1777; s. Michael and Monica (Brooke) T.; grad. Dickinson Coll., 1795, LL.D. (honorary); m. Anne P.C. Kay, Jan. 7, 1806, several children. Admitted to Md. bar, 1799; mem. Md. Legislature, 1799-1800; leader of dissenting Federalist faction "Coodies" supporting war, 1812; mem. Md. Senate, 1816-21, dominating Md. Federalist party; moved to Balt. where recognized as eminent lawyer, 1823; chmn. Md. com. for Jackson's candidacy, 1828; atty. gen. of Md., 1827-31, U.S. atty. gen., 1831-33; acting sec. of war, 1831; advised Pres. Jackson on Bank of U.S. controversy, aided him in framing veto message to bank recharter bill, suggested that Jackson remove deposits from Bank of U.S.; sec. treasury, 1833-1834 (appointment rejected by Senate), set up system of depositories for government funds, 1833-34; nominated for asso. justice U.S. Supreme Ct., 1835 (rejected by Senate), renominated later in 1835, confirmed by Senate as chief justice U.S. Supreme Ct., 1836; held in Charles River Bridge vs. Warren Bridge that rights granted by charter were to be construed narrowly; in State of R.I. vs. State of Mass. denied jurisdiction of Supreme Ct. in suits between states to determine boundary lines; in Dred Scott case argued that Negroes could not possess rights of citizenship entitling him to bring suit in a federal court, and that Scott was not free because of residence in territory made free by act of Congress since Congress never possessed power to exclude slavery from territories; decision subjected to fierce attack of abolitionist opinion; Taney's own view held that slavery was a necessary evil as long as Negro remained in U.S.; other notable opinions include Ex Parte Merryman in which he defended right of civilians in wartime; believed that federal government erred in its use of force to compel Southern adherence to Union, therefore often in contention with government during Civil War. Died Washington, D.C., Oct. 12, 1864.

TANNEBERGER, David, organ builder; b. Berthelsdorf, Saxony, Mar. 21, 1728; s. Johann and Judith (Nitschmann) T.; m. Anna Rosina Kerner, June 15, 1749; m. 2d, Anna Marie (Fisher) Hall, 1800; 5 children. Came to Am., 1749, settled in Bethlehem, Pa.; learned organ building craft from John Gottlob Klemm, 1757; constructed organs, Bethlehem, 1760-65, Lititz, Pa., 1765-1804; made organs for Morovian, Reformed, Lutheran, Roman Catholic chs., in places as far away as Albany (N.Y.); name also spelled Tanneberg, Tannenberg. Died York, Pa., Mar. 19, 1804; buried York.

TANNEHILL, Adamson, congressman; b. Frederick County, Md., May 23, 1750; attended pub. schs. Served as capt. of riflemen Continental Army, Revolutionary War; became a farmer, nr. Pitts.; held several local offices; served as brig. gen. Pa. Volunteers, U.S. Army, 1812; mem. U.S. Ho. of Reps. (Democrat) from Pa., 13th Congress, 1813-15. Died nr. Pitts., Dec. 23, 1820; buried churchyard 1st Presbyn. Ch., reinterred Allegheny Cemetery, Pitts., 1849.

TANNER, Adolphus Hitchcock, congressman, lawyer; b. Granville, N.Y., May 23, 1833; studied law. Admitted to the bar, 1854, began practice law, Whitehall, N.Y.; capt. U.S. Army, 1862, commd. lt. col. 123d Regt., N.Y. Volunteer Inf., served until end of Civil War; mem. U.S. Ho. of Reps. (Republican) from N.Y., 41st Congress, 1869-71. Died Whitehall, Jan. 14, 1882; buried Evergreen Cemetery, Salem, N.Y.

TANNER, Benjamin, engraver; b. N.Y.C., Mar. 25, 1775; m. Mary Bioren, Sept. 6, 1806. Apprenticed to engraver Peter C. Verger, N.Y.C., 1790-96; moved to Phila., set up own engraving shop, 1799-1811; worked with brother Henry Schenck Tanner in map engraving, Phila., 1811-17; established bank note engraving bus. with Francis Kearny and Cornelius Tiebout, 1817-18, organized gen. engraving co. with same partners, 1818-24; he (or his brother) devised way in which check blank could be engraved so that it could not be altered without detection, 1828; engaged mainly in engraving check and note blanks under trade name "Stereograph," 1835-45; went to Balt. to receive treatment for abcess on brain, 1845; engravings include: Perry's Victory, Capture of the Macedonian, Surrender of Cornwallis. Died Balt., Nov. 14, 1848.

TANNER, Henry Schenck, cartographer; b. N.Y. C., 1786. Partner in mapmaking with brother Benjamin Tanner, Francis Kearny and Cornelius Tiebout, 1811-17; engraved 3 maps in A New and Elegant General Atlas Containing Maps of Each of the United States (John Melesh), 1812; drew most of the maps in A Military and Topographical Atlas of the United States (John Melesh), 1813; published An American Atlas; Containing Maps of the Several States of the North American Union, Projected and Drawn from Documents Found in the Public Offices of the United States . . . And Other Original and Authentic Information (his greatest work), 1818-23; published a map entitled United States of America, 1829; published a guide book The American Traveler, 1834; The Central Traveler, 1840; A Description of the Canals and Railroads of the U.S., 1840. Died N.Y.C., 1858.

TAPPAN, Arthur, philanthropist, abolitionist, silk mcht.; b. Northampton, Mass., May 22, 1786; s. Benjamin and Sarah (Homes) T.; m. Frances Antill, Sept. 8, 1810, 8 children. Established firm Tappan & Sewall, Portland, Me., 1807; started firm Arthur Tappan & Co., wholesale silk business, N.Y., 1826; founded N.Y. Journal of Commerce, 1827; with brother aided in erecting building for Charles Grandison Finney, N.Y.C.; contributed to establishment Kenyon Coll., (Gambier, O.), Auburn Theol. Sem., Lane Theol. Sem. (Cincinnati), a founder Oberlin Coll., 1835; an organizer Emancipator, N.Y., 1833; an organizer, 1st pres. N.Y.C. Anti-Slavery Soc., 1833, Am. Anti-Slavery Soc., 1833; founder, pres. Am. and Fgn. Antislavery Soc.; founded Am. and Fgn. Anti-Slavery Reporter; a founder Am. Missionary Assn., mem. exec. com., 1846-65. Died New Haven, Conn., July 23, 1865.

TAPPAN, Benjamin, senator; b. Northampton, Mass., May 25, 1773; s. Benjamin and Sarah (Homes) T.; m. Nancy Wright, Mar. 20, 1801; m. 2d, Betsy (Lord) Frazer, 1823; 2 children, Benjamin, Eli Todd. Admitted to Conn. bar; became 1st settler of Portage County (O.), 1799; mem. Ohio Senate, 1803-05; aide-de-camp to Gen. William Wadsworth in War of 1812; pres., judge 5th Circuit Ct. of Common Pleas, Ohio, 1816-23, decisions for 1816-19 published as Cases Decided in the Courts of Common Pleas in the Fifth Circuit of . . . Ohio, 1818-19 (the 1st law reports in the state); Ohio canal commr., circa 1823; Democratic presdl. elector, supporter of Jackson, 1832; fed. dist. judge, 1826-33, presiding judge Dist. of Ohio, 1833-39; mem. U.S. Senate from Ohio, 1839-56; opposed to Bank of U.S.; supported Fremont for Pres., 1856. Died Steubenville, O., Apr. 12, 1857; buried Union Cemetery, Steubenville.

TAPPAN, Eli Todd, coll. pres.; b. Steubenville, O., Apr. 30, 1824; s. Benjamin and Betsy (Lord) T.; attended St. Mary's Coll., Balt., 1842, A.M. (hon.), 1860; LL.D. (hon.), Williams Coll., 1873, Washington and Jefferson Coll., 1874; m. Lydia L. McDowell, Feb. 4, 1851, 2 children including Mary (Tappan) Wright. Admitted to bar, 1846; founded weekly Ohio Press, Columbus, 1846, editor, 1846-48; mayor Steubenville, 1852; pres. Ohio Tchrs. Assn., 1856; supt. Ohio Pub. Schs., 1858-59; prof. mathematics Ohio U., 1859-60, 65-68; tchr. mathematics Mt. Auburn Young Ladies' Inst., 1860-65; pres. Kenyon Coll., Gambier, O., 1869-75, prof. mathematics and polit. economy, 1875; charter mem. council N.E.A., treas., 1880-81, pres., 1883; commr. common schools of Ohio, 1887-88. Author: Treatise on Plane and Solid Geometry, 1864; also a history of sch. legislation in Ohio. Died Columbus, O., Oct. 23, 1888.

TAPPAN, Henry Philip, clergyman, univ. pres.; b. Rhinebeck on the Hudson, N.Y., Apr. 18, 1805; s. Peter and Ann (De Witt) T.; B.A., Union Coll., Schenectady, N.Y., 1825, D.D. (hon.), 1845; grad. Auburn Theol. Sem., 1827; LL.D. (hon.), Columbia, 1853; m. Julia Livingston, Apr. 17, 1828, 5 children. Ordained to ministry Congregational Ch., Pittsfield, Mass., 1828; prof. moral and intellectual philosophy U. City of N.Y. (now N.Y.U.), 1832-38, head pvt. sem. for young ladies, Leroy Pl., Bleecker Street, N.Y.C., 1837; 1st pres. U. Mich., 1852-63; responsible for founding astronomical observatory at Detroit. Author: A Review of Edward's Inquiry into the Freedom of the Will, 1839; Elements of Logic, 1844; University Education, 1851. Died Vevay, Switzerland, Nov. 15, 1881; buried on slopes of Vevey facing Lake Geneva, Switzerland.

TAPPAN, Lewis, mcht., abolitionist; b. Northampton, Mass., May 23, 1788; s. Benjamin and Sarah (Homes) T.; m. Susanna Aspinwall, Sept. 7, 1813; m. 2d, Mrs. Sarah J. Davis, 1854. Wrote pamphlets upholding Evang. convictions against Unitarianism, circa 1828; partner (with brother Arthur), credit mgr. Arthur Tappan & Co., silk jobbers, N.Y.C., 1828-circa 37; took over N.Y. Jour. of Commerce from Arthur, 1828, sold it, 1831; under firm name Lewis Tappan & Co. established "The Mercantile Agy." (1st comml. credit-rating agy. in Am.), 1841-49; a founder N.Y. Anti-Slavery Soc.; a founder Am. Anti-Slavery Soc., 1833, withdrew, 1840 because of Garrison's effort to include other reform issues in movement; mem. com. which undertook freeing Amistad captives; founder, 1st treas. Am. and Fgn. Anti-Slavery Soc., 1840, resigned office (held more radical views on slave emancipation than soc.), 1855; attended internat.anti-slavery conv., London, Eng., 1843; a founder, treas., pres. Am. Missionary Soc., 1846; took office in new orgn., Abolition Soc., 1855. Author: Is It Right to Be Rich?, 1869; The Life of Arthur Tappan, 1870. Died Bklyn., June 21, 1873.

TAPPAN, Mason Weare, congressman, lawyer; b. Newport, N.H., Oct. 20, 1817; attended Hopkinton and Meriden acads.; studied law. Admitted to the bar, 1841, began practice law, Bradford, N.H.; mem. N.H. Ho. of Reps., 1853-55, 60-61; mem. U.S. Ho. of Reps. (Republican) from N.H., 34th-36th congresses, 1855-61; served as col. 1st Regt., N.H. Volunteer Inf., U.S. Army, Civil War; atty. gen. State of N.H., 1876-86. Died Bradford, Oct. 25, 1886; buried Pleasant Hill Cemetery.

TAPPAN, William Bingham, poet; b. Beverly, Mass., Oct. 29, 1794. Taught sch., Phila.; agt. Am. Sunday Sch. Union, 1822-49; licensed to preach, 1840. Author: Poetry of the Heart, 1845; Gems, 1846; Sacred and Miscellaneous Poems, 1846; Poetry of Life, 1847; The Sunday School, 1848; Late and Early Poems, 1849. Died West Needham, Mass., June 18, 1849.

TARBELL, Joseph, naval officer; b. Mass., circa 1780; m. Eliza Cassin, 1808, 2 children. Apptd. midshipman U.S. Navy, 1798, lt., 1800; master Washington (D.C.) Navy Yard, 1806; mem. ct. which tried Capt. James Barron after Chesapeake-Leopard affair, 1808; promoted master-comdr., 1808; comdr. ship Siren, 1810-11, enforced embargo, Charleston, S.C., suppressed slave trade at New Orleans; commanded ship Constellation, later gunboat flotilla, Norfolk, Va., during War of 1812; commd. capt., 1813. Died Washington, D.C., Nov. 25, 1815.

TARBOX, Increase Niles, author, clergyman; b. East Windsor, Conn., Feb. 11, 1815; s. Thomas and Lucy (Porter) T.; A.B., Yale,, 1839, grad. Divinity Sch., 1844, D.D. (hon.); D.D., (hon.), Ia. Coll., 1869; m. Delia (or Adelia) Waters, June 4, 1845, 4 children. Ordained to ministry Congregational Ch., 1844; pastor Congregational Ch., Farmington, Mass., 1844-51; founder, an original editor Congregationalist, 1849-51; sec. Am. Edn. Soc. (reorganized as Am. Coll. and Edn. Soc., 1874), 1851; edited Sir Walter Raleigh and His

Colony in America, 1884, Life of Israel Putnam . . . . Major General in the Continental Army, 1876; historiographer New Eng. Historic Geneal. Soc., 1881-88, wrote numerous brief memoirs of mems. of soc, which appeared in New England Historical and Genealogical Register. Author: Winnie and Walter Stories, 4 vols., Boston, 1860; When I Was a Boy, 1862; Nineveh, or the Buried City, 1864; The Curse or the Position Occupied in History by the Race of Ham, 1865; Tyre and Alexandria the Chief Commercial Cities of Scripture Times, 1865; Missionary Patriots: James H. and Edward M. Schneider, 1867; Uncle George's Stories, 1868; Life of Israel Putnam (Old Pul), Major-General in the Continental Army, 1876; Sir Walter Raleigh and His Colony in America, 1884; Songs and Hymns for Common Life, 1885; Diary of Thomas Robbins, D.D., 2 vols., 1886-87. Died West Newton, Mass., May 3, 1888; buried Framingham, Mass.

TARBOX, John Kemble, congressman, lawyer; b. Methuen nr. Lawrence, Mass., May 6, 1838; studied law. In newspaper work; admitted to the bar, 1860, practiced law; served as 1st lt. 8th Regt., Mass. Volunteer Inf., U.S. Army, Civil War; mem. Mass. Ho. of Reps., 1868, 70-71; mem. Mass. Senate, 1872; mayor of Lawrence, 1873-74; mem. U.S. Ho. of Reps. (Democrat) from Mass., 44th Congress, 1875-77; city solicitor Lawrence, 1882-83; ins. commr. State of Mass., 1884-87. Died Boston, May 28, 1887; buried Bellevue Cemetery, Lawrence.

TARR, Christian, congressman; b. Balt., May 25, 1765. Became a farmer in Westmoreland County, Pa., 1794; mfr. pottery, Fayette County, Pa.; mem. U.S. Ho. of Reps. from Pa., 15th-16th congresses, 1817-21; mem. Pa. Ho. of Reps., 1821-22; supt. U.S. Govt. rd. built from Cumberland, Md. to Wheeling, Va. (now W.Va.), 1827-29. Died Washington Twp., Fayette County, Feb. 24, 1833; buried Methodist Graveyard, Brownsville, Pa.

TATE, Magnus, congressman, lawyer; b. Berkeley County, Va. (now W.Va.), 1760; studied law. Admitted to the bar, practiced law; farmer; apptd. justice Berkeley County Ct., 1798; sheriff Berkeley County, 1819-20; mem. Va. Ho. of Dels., 1797, 1803, 09-10; mem. U.S. Ho. of Reps. (Federalist) from Va., 14th Congress, 1815-17. Died nr. Martinsburg, Va. (now W.Va.), Mar. 30, 1823.

TATHAM, William, civil engr., geographer; b. Hutton-in-the-Forest, Cumberland, Eng., Apr. 13, 1752; s. Rev. Sandford and Miss (Marsden) T. Clk., Watauga Assn., drafted petition of inhabitants on Western waters for incorporation into govt. of N.C., 1776; with Col. John Todd prepared History of the Western Country, 1780; clk. Va. Council of State, circa 1783; admitted to N.C. bar, 1784; del. N.C. Gen. Assembly, 1787; lt. col. N.C. Militia, circa 1787; contbr. to various publs. engring. and agrl. subjects, London, circa 1796-1805; supt. constrn. Wapping Docks on Thames River, London, 1801; surveyed coast from Cape Fear to Cape Hatteras, 1805-circa 1810; 1st to define functions of nat. library for U.S.; draftsman, geographer Dept. of State, Washington, circa 1810-circa 1815. Author: Memorial on the Civil and Military Government of the Tennessee Colony, 1790; Remarks on Inland Canals, 1798; Political Economy of Inland Navigation, Irrigation, and Drainage, 1799. Died Richmond, Va., Feb. 22, 1819.

TATOM, Absalom, congressman; b. N.C., 1742. Served as sgt. Greenville (N.C.) Militia, 1763; commd. 1st lt. First N.C. Continental Regt., 1775, promoted capt., 1776, resigned from Continental Army, 1776; enlisted as asst. q.m. and keeper of the arsenal N.C. service at Hillsborough, 1778; contractor for Hillsborough, 1778; maj. of detachment N.C. Light Horse, 1779; clk. Randolph County Ct., 1779; dist. auditor Hillsborough, 1781; a commr. apptd. by Congress to survey lands granted to Continental soldiers in western territory (later Tenn.), 1782; pvt. sec. to Gov. Thomas Burke, 1782; state tobacco agt., 1782; elected surveyor of N.C. by Continental Congress, 1785; commr. to sign N.C. paper money, 1785; del. Constl. Conv., 1788; mem. U.S. Ho. of Reps. (Republican) from N.C., 4th Congress, 1795-June 1, 1796 (resigned); mem. N.C. House of Commons, 1797-1802. Died Raleigh, N.C., Dec. 20, 1802; buried Old City Cemetery.

TATTNALL, Edward Fenwick, congressman; b. Savannah, Ga., 1788; ed. in Eng. Held several local offices; solicitor gen., 1816-17; mem. Ga. Ho. of Reps., 1818-19; mem. U.S. Ho. of Reps. from Ga., 17th-20th congresses, 1821-27 (resigned before 20th Congress convened); 1st capt. of Savannah Volunteer Guards. Died Savannah, Nov. 21, 1832; buried Bonaventure Cemetery.

TATTNALL, Josiah, senator, gov. Ga., b. Bonaventure, nr. Savannah, Ga., 1764; attended Eaton Coll., Eng. Served under Gen. Anthony Wayne in Continental Army, 1782; col. regt. Ga. Militia (organized to protect state against Indians), 1793, promoted brig. gen., 1801; mem. Ga. Ho. of Reps., 1795-96; mem. U.S. Senate (filled vacancy) from Ga., Feb. 20, 1796-99; gov. State of Ga., 1801-02 (resigned). Died Nassau, New Providence, B.W.I., June 6, 1803; buried Bonaventure Cemetery, Savannah.

TATTNALL, Josiah, naval officer; b. "Bonaventure" nr. Savannah, Ga., Nov. 9, 1795; s. Josiah and Harriet (Fenwick) T.; m. Harriette Fenwick Jackson, Sept. 6, 1821, at least 3 children. Apptd. midshipman U.S. Navy, 1812, took part in War of 1812; engaged against Algierian pirates, 1815; promoted lt., 1818; served in Mediterranean and Caribbean against West Indian pirates, 1823-31; comdt. Boston Navy Yard, 1838-40; served in African Squadron, 1843-44; promoted capt., 1850; served in Pacific Squadron, 1854-55, comdr. East India Squadron, 1857-60; commd. sr. flag officer Ga. Navy, 1861; engaged in coastal defense for Confederate Navy; burned iron-clad Merrimac to prevent her capture when Norfolk (Va.) Naval Yard was captured by Union Navy; in charge of Ga. Naval Defenses, 1863-65; resided in Halifax, N.S., Can., 1866-70; insp. Port of Savannah, 1870-71. Died June 14, 1871.

TAUL, Micah, congressman, lawyer; b. Bladensburg, Md., May 14, 1785; studied law. Admitted to bar, 1801, began practice law in Monticello, Ky.; clk. Wayne County Cts., 1801; served as col. Wayne County Volunteers, War of 1812; mem. U.S. Ho. of Reps. (Democrat) from Ky., 14th Congress, 1815-17; moved to Winchester, Tenn., 1826, practiced law; moved to Mardisville, Ala., 1846, farmed. Died Mardisville, May 27, 1850; buried on his plantation, Mardisville.

TAULBEE, William Preston, congressman, clergyman, lawyer; b. nr. Mount Sterling, Ky., Oct. 22, 1851; studied law. Ordained to ministry Methodist Episcopal Ch., admitted to Ky. conf. M.E. Ch. South; elected clk. Magoffin County Ct., 1878, 82; admitted to the bar, 1881; mem. U.S. Ho. of Reps. (Democrat) from Ky., 49th-50th congresses, 1885-89. Shot by Charles E. Kincaid in Capitol Bldg., Washington, D.C., Feb. 28, 1890, died from wounds, Mar. 11, 1890; buried family burying ground, nr. Mt. Sterling.

TAYLER, Lewis, educator; b. Northumberland, N.Y., Mar. 27, 1802; s. Samuel and Sarah (Van Valkenburg) T.; grad. Union Coll., Albany, N.Y., 1820; m. Jane Keziah, 1833. Admitted to bar, Saratoga, N.Y., 1825, began practice of law, Ft. Miller, N.Y.; prin. Waterford (N.Y.) Acad., 1833-35, Ogdensburg (N.Y.) Acad., 1835-37; prof. Greek, U. City N.Y., 1838-50; prof. Bibl. literature and Oriental langs. (Syriac, Coptic, Arabic, Chaldean), Union Coll., from 1850; mem. Am. bd. of Com. for Revision of Old Testament. Author: The Six Days of Creation, 1855; The Bible and Science, 1856; The Divine Human in the Scriptures, 1860. Died Albany, May 11, 1877.

TAYLOR, Alexander Wilson, congressman, lawyer; b. Indiana, Pa., Mar. 22, 1815; attended Jefferson Coll., Canonsburg, Pa.; grad. law sch. at Carlisle, Pa. Admitted to the bar, 1841, began practice law in Indiana; clk. of ct. Indiana County, 1845-48; mem. Pa. Ho. of Reps., 1859-60; mem. U.S. Ho. of Reps. (Republican) from Pa., 43d Congress, 1873-75. Died Indiana, Pa., May 7, 1893; buried Greenwood Cemetery.

TAYLOR, Bayard, traveler, translator; b. Kennett Square, Chester County, Pa., Jan. 11, 1825; s. Joseph Taylor and Rebecca (Bauerway) T.; m. Mary Agnew, Oct. 24, 1850; m. 2d, Marie Hansen, Oct. 27, 1857; at least 1 child. Published Ximena (1st volume of verse), 1844; commd. by N.Y. Tribune to take trip to Europe sending back letters from place to place, 1844-46; bought and soon sold Gazette (renamed Pioneer), Phoenixville, Pa., 1846-47; contbr. weekly article to Literary World, 1847-48; mgr., literary dept. N.Y. Tribune, 1848, on commn. for Tribune made trip to Cal., 1849-59, corr. at Washington, D.C. during Civil War; sec. of legation under Simon Cameron at St. Petersburg (Leningrad), 1862; translated in original meters Goethe's Faust, 2 vols., 1870-71; non-resident prof. German literature Cornell U., 1870-77; U.S. minister to Germany, 1878. Author: Travels in Greece and Rome, N.Y., 1859; Travels in Arabia, 1872; Egypt and Iceland, 1874; (novels) Hannah Thurston, 1863; The Story of Kennett, 1866; (poetry) Poems, 1865; The Poets Journal, Boston, 1867; Ballad of Abraham Lincoln, 1869. Died Berlin, Germany, Dec. 19, 1878; buried Hicksite Cemetery, Longwood, Pa.

TAYLOR, Benjamin Franklin, journalist, poet; b. Lowville, N.Y., July 19, 1819; grad. Hamilton Literary and Theol. Inst., 1838; m. Mary Elizabeth Bromley, Sept. 2, 1839; m. 2d, Lucy E. Leaming, June 7, 1852; at least 2 children. Lived in Mich., 1838-41; tchr. pub. schs., Springville and Norwich (N.Y.), 1841-45; moved to Chgo., 1845; literary editor Chgo. Daily Jour., 1845-65; free lance writer, poet, Laporte, Ind., 1865-87. Author: The World on Wheels (a travel book) 1874; Old Time Pictures and Sheanes of Rhyme, 1874; Songs of Yesterday, 1875; Dulce Domum, 1884; Complete Poetical Works, 1886. Died Cleve., Feb. 24, 1887; buried University Cemetery, Hamilton, N.Y.

TAYLOR, Caleb Newbold, congressman, banker; b. nr. Newportville, Pa., July 27, 1813; prep. edn. Became a farmer; del. Pa. Whig Conv., Harrisburg, 1832; presdl. elector; del. numerous state convs.; del. Republican Nat. Conv., Chgo., 1860; mem. U.S. Ho. of Reps. (Republican) from Pa., 40th Congress, 1867-69, (contested election) 41st Congress, Ap. 13, 1870-71; pres. Farmers' Nat. Bank of Bucks County, Bristol, Pa., 1875-87. Died at his home "Sunbury Farm," nr. Newportville, Nov. 15, 1887; buried Friends Burying Ground, Bristol, Pa.

TAYLOR, Charles Fayette, orthopedic surgeon; b. Williston, Vt., Apr. 25, 1827; s. Brimage and Miriam (Taplin) T.; attended lectures N.Y. Med. Coll., 1855; M.D., U. Vt., 1856; m. Mary Salina Skinner, Mar. 7, 1854, 4 children including Henry Ling. Began practice of medicine, N.Y.C., 1857; became interested in phys. therapy, invented braces and orthopedic devices to treat bone and joint lesions; devised cure for Pott's disease (an infection of spinal vertebrae), 1857-63. Author: Mechanical Treatment of Angular Curvature or Pott's Disease of the Spine, 1863; Mechanical Treatment of Diseases of the Hip, 1873. Died Los Angeles, Jan. 25, 1899.

TAYLOR, Charlotte De Bernier Scarbrough, entomologist, writer; b. Savannah, Ga., 1806; d. William and Julia (Bernard) Scarborough; ed. Madam Benzes' Sch., N.Y.C.; m. James Taylor, Apr. 27, 1829; 3 children. Published her most important articles in Harper's New Monthly Mag., during 1850's, showing her clear understanding of agrl. significance of entomology, called attention to econ. necessity for systematic destruction of wheat parasites, Dec. 1859, predicted revival of silk-raising industry in U.S., May 1860, published study on anatomy and natural history of spiders, Sept. 1860; wrote Microscopic Views of the Insect World for N.Y. Am. Agriculturist, 1858-59, 60; other works include Homestead, 1859, The Unwelcome Guest of Insects, The Soundings. Died Isle of Man, Nov. 26, 1861.

TAYLOR, Creed, judge, educator; b. Cumberland County, Va., 1766; d. Samuel and Sophia Taylor; m. Sally Woodson, 1797, 5 adopted children. Mem. Va. Ho. of Dels., 1788; mem. Va. Senate, 1798-1805, speaker last 2 terms; judge Va. Gen. Ct., 1805; helped John Randolph of Roanoke enter politics in Va. chancellor Va. Superior Ct. of Chancery for Richmond dist., 1806-31, Lynchburg dist. added to his jurisdiction, 1813; a founder Town of Farmville (Va.); a commr. to choose site for U. Va.; conducted law school Needham, Va., circa 1810-20; Anti-Federalist in election of 1800; presdl. elector, presided when electors met to vote in Richmond, 1800. Died Jan. 17, 1836.

TAYLOR, Edward, clergyman, poet; b. Leicestershire, Eng., 1645; A.B., Harvard, 1671, M.A. (hon.), 1720; m. Elizabeth Fitch, Nov. 5, 1674; m. 2d, Ruth Wyllys, June 21, 1692; 13 children including Kezia. Arrived in Boston, 1668; pastor church at Westfield, Mass., 1671-1729; ordained, 1679; wrote poem Gods Determinations, probably before 1690; wrote Sacramental Meditations (brief stanzaic voluntaries undertaken about 5 times a year from 1682-1725 as private reflections upon Bible texts chosen from communion services); poems collected in Poetical Works (1st edition edited by T. H. Johnson), 1939. Died Westfield, Mass., June 24, 1729.

TAYLOR, Edward Thompson, clergyman; b. Richmond, Va., Dec. 25, 1793; an orphan, parents names unknown; m. Deborah Millett, Oct. 12, 1819, 6 children. Licensed to preach, Boston, after 1839; admitted to New Eng. Conf. Meth. Episcopal Ch., 1843; chaplain to Seamen's Bethel (Meth. group to further moral and religious welfare of sailors), Boston, 1830-71; considered one of great preachers of day, friend of Ralph Waldo Emerson; sailed as chaplain on ship Macedonia with supplies for starving Irish, circa 1846. Died Boston, Apr. 5, 1871.

TAYLOR, George, Continental congressman; b. No. Ireland, 1716; m. Mrs. Anne Taylor Savage, 1742; m. 2d, Naomi Smith; 7 children. Arrived in Pa., circa 1736; justice of peace Dearham, Northhampton County, Pa., 1757, 61, 63, 64-72; mem. Pa. Provincial Assembly, 1764-67, 75; judge circuir ct., 1770; mem. Com. of Safety, 1775-76; Pa. del. to Continental Congress, 1776, 77; signer Declaration of Independence, Aug. 2, 1776; elected from Northhampton to 1st Supreme Exec. Council of Pa., 1777; ironmaster. Died Easton, Pa., Feb. 23, 1781; buried St. John's Lutheran Ch. Cemetery, Easton.

TAYLOR, George, congressman, lawyer; b. Wheeling, Va. (now W.Va.), Oct. 19, 1820; studied medicine and law. Admitted to the bar, practiced law in Ind.; moved to Ala., 1844, to Bklyn., 1848, practiced law; held several local offices; mem. U.S. Ho.

of Reps. (Democrat) from N.Y., 35th Congress, 1857-59; practiced law in Washington, D.C. Died Washington, Jan. 18, 1894; buried Rock Creek Cemetery.

TAYLOR, James Barnett, clergyman; b. Barton-upon-Humber, Eng., Mar. 19, 1804; s. George and Chrisanna (Barnett) T.; m. Mary Scott Williams, Oct. 30, 1828, 6 children including George. Came to U.S., 1805; licensed to preach, 1824, missionary in Va., 1826; ordained to ministry Baptist Ch., 1826; pastor 2d Bapt. Ch., Richmond, Va.; founded Va. Bapt. Edn. Soc. (resulted in Richmond Coll.), 1830; did editorial work for Religious Herald; elected moderator Gen. Assn., Va., 1836; chaplain U. Va., 1839-40; pastor 3d Ch. (Grace Ch.), Richmond, 1840; attended conv. at Charleston which formed So. Bapt. Conv., 1845; corr. sec. Fgn. Mission Bd., sec., 1846. Author: Lives of Virginia Baptist Ministers, 1837; Memoir of Luther Rice, 1840. Died Richmond, Dec. 22, 1871.

TAYLOR, James Earl, illustrator; b. Cincinnati, Dec. 12, 1839; grad. U. Notre Dame, 1845. Painted panorama of Revolutionary War, 1847; joined Union Army, 1861; artist-correspondent for Leslie's Mag., 1863-83; went West to portray Indians and frontier life on Gt. Plains, after Civil War; worked as independent illustrator and watercolorist, 1883-1901. Died N.Y.C., June 22, 1901.

TAYLOR, James Wickes, diplomat; b. Starkey, N.Y., Nov. 6, 1819; s. James and Maria (Wickes) T.; grad. Hamilton Coll., 1838; m. Chloe Sweeting Langford, 1845, 4 children. Founded Cincinnati Morning Signal, 1846; mem. 2d Ohio Constl. Conv., 1850-51; sec. commn. to revise judicial code Ohio, 1851-52; head of Ohio State Library, 1854-56; began practice law, St. Paul, Minn. Territory, 1856; spl. agt. U.S. Treasury Dept. to investigate U.S.-Canadian trade, 1859-69; agt. Lake Superior & Miss. R.R., 1869; spl. agt. U.S. State Dept. charged with investigating Red River Rebellion in Can., 1869; Am. consul at Winnipeg, Can., 1870-93, prevented Fenian attack on Manitoba from U.S., 1871. Author: Victim of Intrigue, 1847; History of the State of Ohio, 1854; Manual of the Ohio School System, 1857. Died Apr. 28, 1893; buried Utica, N.Y.

TAYLOR, John, frontier preacher; b. Fauquier County, Va., 1752; s. Lazarus and Anna (Bradford) T.; m. Elizabeth Kavanaugh, 1782. Preached, organized Baptist churches among scattered settlements on Shenandoah, Potomac, Monongahela and Green Brier rivers (one of best examples of farmer-preachers responsible for founding Bapt. chs. in Western Va., N.C., Ky., and Tenn.); published pamphlet called Thoughts on Missions, 1820, attacked missionary socs. for their mercenary objects; related story of his pastoral activities in A History of Ten Baptist Churches, 1823. Died Franklin County, Ky., Apr. 12, 1835.

TAYLOR, John, (known as John Taylor of Caroline), senator, polit. writer; b. Caroline County, Va., May 17, 1753; s. James and Ann (Pollard) T.; grad. Coll. William and Mary, 1770; m. Lucy Penn, 1783, 8 children. Admitted to Va. bar, 1774; served with Continental Army; lt. col. Va. Militia, 1781; mem. Va. Ho. of Dels, 1779-85, 96-1800; mem. U.S. Senate from Va., 1792-94, 1803, 22-24; introduced "Va. Resolutions" asserting right of states to interpose authority in case of overextension of fed. powers, 1798; opposed War of 1812 as expansion of powers of central govt.; defended old agrarian order, one of 1st to present well developed states' rights view; opposed permanent debt; held that Congress had no legitimate right to interfere with instn. of slavery established by law; published Inquiry into the Principles and Policy of the United States Government, 1814, refuting John Adams' defense of constn. and ideas of natural aristocracy; wrote Construction Construed and Constitutions Vindicated, 1820, argued unlimited right of states to tax within borders; wrote Tyranny Unmasked (attack on protective tariff as sectional device), 1820; described his agricultural theories in The Arator. Died Caroline County, Aug. 20, 1824; buried Cadd, nr. Port Royal, Caroline County.

TAYLOR, John, senator, gov. S.C., congressman; b. nr. Granby, S.C., May 4, 1770; grad. Princeton, 1790; studied law. Admitted to bar, 1793, began practice law in Columbia, S.C., also a planter; mem. S.C. Ho. of Reps. 1796-1802, 04-05; circuit ct. solicitor, 1805-06; served as 1st intendent of Columbia, 1806-07; mem. U.S. Ho. of Reps. (Democrat) from S.C., 10th-11th congresses, 1807-Dec. 30, 1810; mem. U.S. Senate from S.C. (filled vacancy then elected to full term), Dec. 31, 1810-Nov. 1816 (resigned); mem. S.C. Senate, 1818-26; gov. S.C., 1826-28; trustee S.C. Coll. (now U. S.C.) at Columbia; dir. Columbia Theol. Sem. Died Camden, S.C., Apr. 16, 1832; buried family burying ground, Columbia.

TAYLOR, John, congressman. presdl. elector on Jefferson and Clinton ticket, 1805; mem. U.S. Ho. of Reps. from S.C., 14th Congress, 1815-17; unsuccessful candidate for reelection to Congress, 1816, 20.

TAYLOR, John, religious leader; b. Milnthorpe, Westmoreland County, Eng., Nov. 1, 1808; s. James and Agnes (Taylor) T.; m. Leonora Cannon, 1833, had 7 more wives (plural marriage), 34 children. Baptized a Mormon, 1836; "ordained" in ch. by Brigham Young, 1838; introduced Mormonism into Scotland, Ireland; at Nauvoo, Ill., 1842-46, edited Times and Seasons (the Mormon periodical), owned and published Nauvoo Neighbor (Mormon newspaper); prominent ofcl. in Nauvoo govt.; established Mormon newspaper, N.Y.C., 1854; mem. Utah Territorial Legislature, 1857-76, speaker lower house, 5 sessions; probate judge Utah County, 1868-70; elected territorial supt. schs., 1877; directed affairs of ch. as acting pres., 1877-80; officially installed as 3d pres. Utah Br., Mormon Ch., 1880; forced into exile to escape arrest by U.S. govt. for polygomy, 1884, managed ch. affairs from his retreat, 1884-87. Died Kaysville, Utah, July 25, 1887.

TAYLOR, John James, congressman, lawyer, businessman; b. Leominster, Mass., Apr. 27, 1808; attended Groton Acad.; grad. Harvard, 1829; studied law. Tchr. for short period; admitted to bar, 1834, practiced law, Greene, N.Y., then Owego, N.Y., 1834; dist. atty. Tioga County, N.Y., 1838-43; mem. village bd. of trustees, 1839, 43, 48; 1st chief engr. of fire dept., 1844; mem. N.Y. State Constl. Conv., 1846; mem. U.S. Ho. of Reps. (Democrat) from N.Y., 33d Congress, 1853-55; declined appointment as commr. to settle northwestern boundary of U.S.; unsuccessful candidate for lt. gov. N.Y. State, 1858; pres. Village of Owego, 1859; banker; v.p., later pres. So. Central Ry. Co., later the Auburn div. of Lehigh Valley R.R. Co. Died Owego, July 1, 1892; buried Evergreen Cemetery.

TAYLOR, John Lampkin, congressman, lawyer; b. Stafford County, nr. Fredericksburg, Va., Mar. 7, 1805; studied law, Washington, D.C. Admitted to the bar, 1828, began practice law, Chillicothe, O., 1829; served as maj. gen. Ohio Militia; mem. U.S. Ho. of Reps. (Whig) from Ohio, 30th-33d congresses, 1847-55; clk. in Interior Dept., Washington, 1870. Died Washington, Sept. 6, 1870; buried family burying ground on Taylor estate "Mansfield," nr. Louisa, Va.

TAYLOR, John Louis, jurist; b. London, Eng., Mar. 1, 1769; attended Coll. William and Mary; m. Julia Rowan; m. 2d, Jane Gaston, 1797; 3 children. Came to U.S.; admitted to N.C. bar, 1788; mem. N.C. Ho. of Commons from Fayetteville, 1792, 94-95; Federalist presdl. elector, 1792; elected judge N.C. Superior Ct., 1798, chief justice, 1811; judge N.C. Supreme Ct., 1818-19, chief justice, 1819-29, his opinions found in 1-12 North Carolina Reports; issued Cases Determined in the Superior Courts, 1802, A Revisal of the Laws. . ., 1827; grand master Masonic order in N.C., 1802-05, 14-17; benefactor U. N.C., trustee, 1793-1818. Died Raleigh, N.C., Jan. 29, 1829.

TAYLOR, John W., congressman; b. Charlton, N.Y., Mar. 26, 1784; s. John and Chloe (Cox) T.; attended Union Coll., Schenectady, N.Y.; m. Jane Hodge, July 10, 1806, 8 children. Admitted to N.Y. bar, 1807; mem. N.Y. Assembly, 1811-12; mem. U.S. Ho. of Reps. from N.Y., 13th-22d congresses, 1813-33, submitted proposal prohibiting the introduction of slavery into territories North of 36° 30' parallel, delivered many of earliest anti-slavery speeches heard in Congress, speaker, 1820-21, 25-27; mem. N.Y. Senate, 1840-42. Died Cleve., Sept. 18, 1854; buried Ballston Spa, Saratoga County, N.Y.

TAYLOR, Jonathan, congressman, lawyer; b. nr. Mansfield, Conn., 1796; studied law. Admitted to the bar, began practice law, Newark, O.; apptd. commr. to settle boundary dispute between Ohio and Mich.; brig. gen. Ohio Militia; mem. Ohio Ho. of Reps., 1831-33; mem. Ohio Senate, 1833-36; mem. U.S. Ho. of Reps. (Democrat) from Ohio, 26th Congress, 1839-41. Died Newark, Apr. 1848; buried Old Cemetery, reinterred Cedar Hill Cemetery.

TAYLOR, Joseph Wright, physician, philanthropist; b. Upper Freehold Twp., N.J., Mar. 1, 1810; s. Edward and Sarah T.; M.D., U. Pa., 1830; never married. Sailed on mcht. vessel as a surgeon, 1830-33; purchasing agt. for his brother's tanning bus., Cincinnati, 1833-48; went on European tour, 1849-50; lived in Burlington, N.J., 1850-61; supported abolitionist, temperance and peace movements; a mgr. Haverford (Pa.) Coll., 1854-80; founder Bryn Mawr Coll., purchased land and supervised bldg. of coll. Died Jan. 18, 1880.

TAYLOR, Marshall William, clergyman, editor; b. Lexington, Ky., July 1, 1846; s. Samuel Boyd and Nancy Ann (Williams) T.; D.D. (hon.), Central Tenn. Coll.; m. Kate Heston, 2 children. Served with Army of the Cumberland, 1862-65; taught sch., Breckenridge County, Ky., 1866; licensed as Methodist Episcopal preacher, 1869, admitted on trial to Lexington Conf., 1872, ordained deacon, 1874, elder, 1876; published Ky. Methodist, 1872-75; pastor, Litchfield (Conn.) Circuit; placed in charge of Coke Chapel, Indianapolis, Ind., 1875, sent to Union M.E. Ch., Cincinnati, 1877; became presiding elder Ohio dist., 1878, presiding elder Louisville Dist., 1883; sr. ministerial del. to Gen. Conf. of 1884; in 1884 declined the bishopric of West Africa; elected editor of Southwestern Christian Advocate. Author: The Famous Negro Missionary Evangelist, 1886. Died Louisville, Ky., Sept. 11, 1887.

TAYLOR, Miles, congressman; b. Saratoga Springs, N.Y., July 16, 1805; studied medicine, law. Admitted to the bar, began practice law, Donaldsonville, La.; moved to New Orleans, circa 1847; held several local offices; apptd. by gov. as mem. com. to revise Civil Code, Code of Procedure, and Statutes of La.; mem. U.S. Ho. of Reps. (Democrat) from La., 34th-36th congresses, 1855-Feb. 5, 1861 (resigned); chmn. Douglas Nat. Exec. Com., 1869; leader of sugar growers in La. for many years. Died Saratoga Springs, N.Y., Sept. 23, 1873; buried family plantation "Front Scattery," nr. Belle Alliance, La.

TAYLOR, Moses, business exec.; b. N.Y.C., Jan. 11, 1806; s. Jacob B. and Mary (Cooper) T.; m. Catherine Wilson, 1832, 5 children. Became factor in handling output Cuban sugar planters, 1832; became pres. City Bank, 1855; purchased stock in Delaware, Lackawanna & Western R.R. at 5 dollars a share and obtained controlling interest of railroad, 1857; treas. 1st Atlantic cable venture; chmn. bankers' com. which took 1st fed. loan in 1861; chief interest besides railroad was Lackawanna Coal & Iron Co. Died N.Y.C., May 23, 1882.

TAYLOR, Nathaniel Green, congressman, lawyer; b. Happy Valley, Tenn., Dec. 29, 1819; attended Washington Coll., nr. Jonesboro, Tenn.; grad. Princeton, 1840; studied law; at least 2 sons, Alfred Alexander, Robert Love. Admitted to the bar, 1841, began practice law in Elizabethton, Tenn.; Whig presdl. elector, 1852; mem. U.S. Ho. of Reps. (Whig, filled vacancy) from Tenn., 33d, 39th congresses, Mar. 30, 1854-55, July 24, 1866-67; presdl. elector Constl. Union ticket, 1860; mem. relief assn. formed for aid of War sufferers in east Tenn., lectr. on their behalf in East; commr. of Indian affairs, 1867-69; ret. to farming and preaching. Died Happy Valley, Apr. 1, 1887; buried old Taylor pvt. cemetery.

TAYLOR, Nathaniel William, clergyman, educator; b. New Milford, Conn., June 23, 1786; s. Nathaniel and Anne (Northrop) T.; grad. Yale, 1807; D.D. (hon.), Union Coll., 1823; m. Rebecca Maria Hine, Oct. 15, 1810, at least 1 child. Studied theology with Timothy Dwight, New Haven, Conn., circa 1808; ordained to ministry Congl. Ch., 1812; minister First Ch. of Christ, New Haven, 1812-22; Dwight prof. didactic theology Yale Div. Sch., 1822-58, his theology upheld principle of freedom of will and split Congl. chs. into "Taylorites" and "Tylerites" (who upheld traditional doctrine of free will as an illusion); contbd. articles chiefly to Christian Spectator, Spirit of the Pilgrims; Nathanel W. Taylor Lectureship established by his dau. at Yale Divinity Sch., 1902. Author: Lectures on the Moral Government of God, 1859. Died New Haven, Mar. 10, 1858.

TAYLOR, Nelson, congressman, lawyer; b. South Norwalk, Conn., June 8, 1821; grad. law dept. Harvard, 1860. Served as capt. First Regt., N.Y. Volunteer Inf., U.S. Army, 1846-48, sent to Cal. before outbreak of Mexican War, 1846; remained in Cal., engaged in bus., Stockton; mem. Cal. Senate, 1850-56; elected sheriff San Joaquin County, 1855; moved to N.Y.C.; admitted to bar, practiced law; commd. col. 72d Regt., N.Y. Volunteer Inf., U.S. Army, 1861, in command of troops at Harlem during draft riots in N.Y.C.; brig. gen. Volunteers, 1862, resigned, 1863; resumed practice law, N.Y.C.; mem. U.S. Ho. of Reps. (Dem.) from N.Y., 39th Congress, 1865-67; moved to South Norwalk, 1869, practiced law; city atty., several terms. Died South Norwalk, Jan. 16, 1894; buried Riverside Cemetery.

TAYLOR, Raynor, musician, composer; b. England, circa 1747. Music dir. Sadler's Wells Theatre, London, Eng., 1765; came to U.S., 1792; organist St. Anne's Ch., Annapolis, Md., St. Peter's Ch., Phila.; founder Mus. Fund Soc., Phila. 1820; known for his parodies and burlesques; gave concert of own works, 1796; wrote scores for ballad-operas, composed for piano; presented one-act The Gray Mare's the Best Horse (one of earliest operettas), 1793; wrote 2 songs "The Merry Piping Lad," "The Wand'ring Village Maid" (now in Yale Library). Died Aug. 17, 1825.

TAYLOR, Richard, army officer; b. "Springfield," nr. Louisville, Ky., Jan. 27, 1826; s. Gen. Zachary and Margaret (Mackall) T.; attended Harvard; grad. Yale, 1845; m. Louise Marie Myrthe, Feb. 1851, 5 children. Chmn. com. on fed. relations La. Senate, 1865-61, chmn. com. mil. and naval affairs; col. La. 9th Inf., 1861, apptd. brig. gen. in Valley campaign under Stonewall Jackson, 1861; promoted maj. gen., 1862, assigned command Dist. of West La., at Pleasant Hill and Mansfield (Sabine Crossroads), 1864; promoted lt. gen., 1864, assigned to Dept. East La., Miss., Ala.; surrendered the last Confederate army East of Mississippi River, 1865; trustee Peabody Edn. Fund. Author: Destruction and Reconstruction (his reminiscences), 1879. Died N.Y.C., Apr. 12, 1879.

TAYLOR, Richard Cowling, geologist; b. Suffolk, Eng., Jan. 18, 1789; s. Samuel Taylor; apprenticed to a land surveyor, Gloucestershire, Eng., 1805-11; studied with William Smith in Am.; m. Emily Ervington, 1820, at least 4 children. Surveyed in various parts of Eng., 1811-13; engaged in ordnance survey of Eng., 1826-27; sailed to U.S., 1830; engaged in survey of Blossburg (Pa.) coal region; explored many mineral deposits, went as far as copper mines in Cuba and gold fields in Panama; expert on stratification of deposits. Author: Index Monasticus, or the Abbeys and Other Monasteries. . . Formerly Established in the Diocese of Norwich and the Ancient Kingdom of East Anglia, 1820; On the Geology of East Norfolk, 1827; Statistics of Coal, 1848. Died Phila., Oct. 27, 1851.

TAYLOR, Robert, congressman; b. Orange Court House, Va., Apr. 29, 1763; studied law. Admitted to bar, 1783, began practice law, Orange Court House; held several local offices; mem. Va. Senate, 1804-15, pres. pro tem; mem. U.S. Ho. of Reps. from Va., 19th Congress, 1825-27; ret. from polit. life, managed plantation. Died on his estate "Meadow Farm," Orange County, Va., July 3, 1845; buried in family burying ground on estate.

TAYLOR, Samuel Harvey, educator; b. Londonberry, N.H., Oct. 3, 1807; s. Capt. James and Persis (Hemphill) T.; grad. Dartmouth Coll., 1832, Andover Theol. Sem., 1837; m. Caroline Persis Parker, Dec. 8, 1837, at least 3 sons. Prin., Philips Acad., Andover, Mass., 1837-71, also taught several subjects each semester, as well as Sunday Bible Sch. Author 5 textbooks on classics including Guide for Writing Latin, 1843; Grammar of Greek Language, 1844; Method of Classical Study, 1861. Died Andover, Mass., Jan. 29, 1871.

TAYLOR, Waller, senator; b. Lunenburg County, Va., before 1786; studied law. Admitted to the bar, practiced law in Va.; mem. Va. Ho. of Dels., 1800-02; moved to Vincennes, Ind., 1804, practiced law; apptd. chancellor of Ind. Territory, 1807; apptd. maj. territorial militia, 1807; served as aide-de-camp to Gen. William H. Harrison, War of 1821, promoted adj. gen., 1814; mem. U.S. Senate (Democrat) from Ind., Dec. 11, 1816-25. Died while visiting Lunenburg County, Aug. 26, 1826; buried family burying ground, nr. Lunenburg.

TAYLOR, William, congressman, physician; b. Suffield, Conn., Oct. 12, 1791; studied medicine. Practiced medicine in N.Y. State; mem. U.S. Ho. of Reps. (Democrat) from N.Y., 23d-25th congresses, 1833-39; mem. N.Y. State Assembly, 1841-42; del. N.Y. Constl. Conv., 1846. Died Manlius, N.Y., Sept. 16, 1865; buried Christ Ch. Cemetery.

TAYLOR, William Mackergo, clergyman; b. Kilmarnock, Scotland, Oct 23, 1829; s. Peter and Isobel (Mackergo) T.; grad. U. Glasgow (Scotland), 1849; LL.D., Coll. of N.J. (now Princeton), 1883; m. Jessie Steedman, Oct. 4, 1853, 9 children. Trained for ministry Divinity Hall, United Presbyn. Ch., Edinburgh, Scotland, 1849-52; came to U.S., 1871; installed pastor Broadway Tabernacle, N.Y.C., 1872-92, pastor emeritus, 1892; editor-in-chief The Christian at Work, 1876-80; corporate mem. Am. Bd. Commrs. for Fgn. Missions, 1872-95; pres. Am. Missionary Assn.; pres. Congl. Ch. Bldg. Soc., 1885-95. Author: David King of Israel, 1875; Elijah the Prophet, 1876; The Ministry of the Word, 1876. Died N.Y.C., Feb. 8, 1895.

TAYLOR, William Penn, congressman; b. Fredericksburg, Va. Held several local offices; mem. U.S. Ho. of Reps. (Whig) from Va., 23d Congress, 1833-35. Died "Hayfield," nr. Fredericksburg; buried family graveyard at "Hayfield."

TAYLOR, William Rogers, naval officer; b. Newport, R.I., Nov. 7, 1811; s. William Vigneron and Abby (White) T.; m. Caroline Silliman, Apr. 30, 1840, at least 2 children. Apptd. midshipman U.S. Navy, 1828; aboard Hudson in Brazil station, 1829-32; made lt., 1840; during Mexican War took part in the St. Mary's attack on Tampico, 1846; promoted comdr., 1855; promoted capt. and assigned to steam sloop Housatonic on the Charleston blockade, 1862; was Adm. Dahlgren's fleet capt. during offensive against Morris Island, 1863; commanded ship Juniata during 1st attacks on Fort Fisher, 1864; promoted commodore, 1866, rear adm., 1871; commanded Northern squadron of Pacific Fleet, 1869-71; pres. Naval examining bd., 1871-72; had command South Atlantic sta., 1872-73; pres. bd. to revise navy regulations, 1866-67. Died Washington, D.C., Apr. 14, 1884; buried Congressional Cemetery, Washington.

TAYLOR, William Vigneron, naval officer; b. Newport, R.I., Apr. 11, 1780; s. James and Mary (Vigneron) T.; m. Abby White, Dec. 31, 1810, 7 children including William Rogers and Oliver Hazard Perry. Joined navy at Newport, War of 1812; warranted sailing-master, 1813; in command flagship Lawrence in Battle of Lake Erie, 1813; received thanks of Congress and a sword, 1814; sailed on ship Java to the Mediterranean, 1815; Mediterranean cruise aboard the Ontario, 1824-26; service in Brazil station, 1829-30; had command sloops Erie, Warren, Concord, Columbus in Gulf of Mexico in late 1830's; made capt., 1841; during Mexican War (1847) took warship Ohio around Cape Horn for operations on the Mexican west coast until end of war, 1848; placed on reserved list, 1855. Died Newport, R.I., Feb. 11, 1858; buried Island Cemetery, R.I.

TAYLOR, Zachary, 12th Pres. U.S., army officer; b. Montebello, Va., Nov. 24, 1784; s. Richard and Mary (Strother) T.; m. Margaret Mackall Smith, June 18, 1810, 6 children including Ann Mackall, Sarah Knox, Mary Elizabeth, Richard Taylor. Commd. 1st lt. 7th Inf., U.S. Army, 1808; served as capt., Ft. Knox, Ky., 1810; defended Ft. Harrison against Indian attack, 1812, brevetted maj.; in command of Ft. Knox, 1814-15; commd. lt. col. 4th Inf., New Orleans, 1819; built Ft. Jessup on La. frontier, 1822; Indian supt. at Ft. Snelling, 1829-32; col. in charge of 1st Regt., Ft. Crawford, 1832; led troops in Black Hawk War, 1838, brevetted brig. gen., received nickname "Old Rough and Ready;" in command of army in Tex., 1845; ordered to march to Rio Grande, 1846, victorious at battles of Palo Alto (defeated force 3 times his own) and Resaca de la Palma, 1846; brevetted maj. gen., 1846; captured at Monterey, Mexico, 1846; defeated Mexicans at Battle of Buena Vista, 1847; Whig; in "Allison" letters, 1848, stated his polit. views: that executive should be coordinate branch of govt., veto used sparingly, Wilmot Proviso was insignificant and that he would be "untrammeled by party schemes"; Whig candidate for U.S. Pres., elected Nov. 1848; gave inaugural address, Mar. 5, 1849, promised honesty and capability as qualifications for office holding, encouragement of commerce and mfg., agr., conciliation of sectional controversies; gave spl. messages, Jan. 21, 23, 1850, urged unconditional admission of Cal., statehood for N.M.; most notable achievement in foreign affairs was Clayton-Bulwer Treaty of 1850; encountered opposition to admission of Cal. which led to Compromise of 1850; determined to reorganize cabinet because of "Galphin Claim" scandal (involving Sec. War Crawford), shortly before his death. Died Washington, D.C., July 9, 1850.

TAZEWELL, Henry, senator; b. Brunswick County, Va., Nov. 15, 1753; s. Littleton and Mary (Gray) T.; grad. Coll. William and Mary, 1772; m. Dorothy Waller, Jan. 1774, at least 1 child, Littleton Waller. Brunswick rep. Va. Ho. of Burgesses, 1775-78; elected to Va. Supreme Ct., 1785-93; Williamsburg rep. Va. Gen. Assembly, 1778-85; served on reorganized gen. ct., 1788, chief justice Va. Supreme Ct., 1789; apptd. judge Va. High Ct. of Appeals, 1793; one of revisors of law, 1792; mem. U.S. Senate (Anti-Federalist) from Va., Dec. 29, 1794-99, elected pres. pro tem., 1795, re-elected, 1796. Died Phila., Jan. 24, 1799; buried Christ Ch. Yard, Phila.

TAZEWELL, Littleton Waller, senator, gov. Va.; b. Williamsburg, James City County, Va., Dec. 17, 1774; s. Henry and Dorothy (Waller) T.; grad. Coll. William and Mary, 1792; m. Anne Nirison, 1802, several children. Obtained law license, 1796; mem. Va. Ho. Dels. from James City County, 1796-1800, 16; mem. U.S. Ho. of Reps. from Va., 6th Congress, Nov. 26, 1800-01; took part in case of the Santissima Trinidad (7, Wheaton, 283); mem. Va. Gen. Assembly, 1804-06, 16-17; spokesman for City of Richmond in its defiance of Brit. fleet after attack on the Chesapeake by the Leopard, 1807; opposed Embargo of 1807, the Non-Intercourse Act, the War of 1812 (favored declaration of war against both Gt. Britain and France); apptd. by Monroe as one of commrs. under 11th article of 1819 treaty with Spain, 1820; mem. U.S. Senate from Va., Dec. 1824-July 16, 1832, mem., later chmn. fgn. affairs com., author of report against Panama mission, pres. pro tem., 1832; mem. Va. Constl. Conv., 1829-30, also mem. com. of 7 to draft new Va. constn.; declined posts in Jackson's cabinet, critical of Jackson's position on S.C. nullification, 1832; gov. Va., 1834-36, refused to forward instrns. to Va. senators regarding expunging resolutions; Jeffersonian Democrat; extreme individualist, highly regarded by John Marshall, William Wirt. Died on Eastern shores of Va., May 6, 1860; buried Elmwood Cemetery, Norfolk, Va.

TEACH, Edward (or Thatch), pirate; b. Bristol, Eng.; married a N.C. girl. Engaged as privateersman by English in War of Spanish Succession, 1701-14, turned pirate after peace was signed; in command of a sloop, 1717, accompanied by another ship commanded by Benjamin Hornigold; captured a French Guinea ship, refitted and renamed ship Queen Anne's Revenge; failed to sail to Bahamas to receive ofcl. pardon being granted to all former privateersmen turned pirate, 1717; sailed in W.I. and along Carolina and Va. coasts; robbed Charleston (S.C.) of a medicine chest; his ship was wrecked at Topsail Inlet, off N.C. coast, June 10, 1718; escaped with his crew on his other 2 ships; journeyed to Bath, capital of N.C. Province, surrendered to King's order; according to tradition, formed secret privateering partnership with Gov. Charles Eden of N.C. and Tobias Knight (sec. to gov.); preyed upon N.C. planters and local sailing vessels; when planters appealed to Col. Alexander Spottswood (lt. gov. Va.) for aid, sloops Pearl and Lyme were sent to Ocracoke Island (Teach's hideout), 1718; in ensuing battle, all officers of Lyme were slain. Killed in hand-to-hand combat with Robert Maynard (1st lt. of Pearl), Ocracoke Island, N.C., Nov. 22, 1718.

TEALL, Francis Augustus, editor; b. Fort Ann, N.Y., Aug. 16, 1822; s. Horace Valentine and Sarah (Buyss) T.; A.M. (hon.), U. Rochester, 1875; m. Orcelia Shaw, circa 1850, 4 children. Learned printer's trade; went to N.Y.C., 1841; staff mem. Am. Review (a Whig jour.), 1844-53; editor Long Islander, Huntington, 1853-57; contracted to take charge of proofs for Am. Cyclopedia (published by D. Appelton & Co.), 1857; supervised proofs of Century Dictionary, 1882. Author: Errors in Use of English, 1852. Died Bloomfield, N.J., Nov. 16, 1894.

TECUMSEH (also known as Tikamthi or Tecumtha), Indian chief; b. Great Springs, nr. Old Chillicothe (now Oldtown), O., Mar. 1768; s. Puckshinwa. Chief, Sewanee Indians; attempted to stop flow of Westward emigration and preserve Indian lands intact; believed that consent of tribes involved was necessary to render any cession of land legal, based claims on Treaty of Greeneville of 1795; planned to combine all tribes into confederacy to prevent land cessions and strengthen Indian character against temptations offered by white settlers; relied on British mil. aid during period when Gov. W. H. Harrison negotiated numerous cession treaties, 1803-11; his brother (the Prophet) was manuevered into Battle of Tippecanoe durin his absence, 1811, idea of confederacy was destroyed with the subsequent Indian defeat; participated in fighting on Brit. side with rank of brig. gen. during War of 1812. Killed at Battle of Thames while leading an Indian force, Oct. 5, 1813.

TEDYUSKUNG, (also known as Honest John and War Trumpet), Indian chief; b. nr. Trenton, N.J., 1700; s. Old Captain Harris; m. Elizabeth. Lived in Wyoming Valley (Pa.) region, circa 1740; became mem. Indian Christian settlement of Gnadenhuetten on Mahoning River, baptized there; took name of Gideon; became a Delaware Indian chief, 1754; asserted Delaware independence of Iroquois Indians; largely responsible for British success at Ft. Duquesne, also for ultimate failure of French arms; effectiveness as leader impaired by alcoholic habits; his house in Wyoming Valley set on fire, probably by some Iroquois for revenge. Died Wyoming Valley, Apr. 19, 1763.

TEESE, Frederick Halstead, congressman, lawyer; grad. Princeton, 1843; studied law. Admitted to bar, 1846, began practice law in Newark, N.J.; mem. N.J. House of Assembly, 1860-61, speaker 1861; presiding judge Ct. of Common Pleas of Essex County, N.J., 1864-72; mem. U.S. Ho. of Reps. (Democrat) from N.J., 44th Congress, 1875-77. Died N.Y.C., Jan. 7, 1894; buried Mt. Pleasant Cemetery, Newark.

TEFFT, Benjamin Franklin, clergyman, coll. pres.; b. Utica, N.Y., Aug. 20, 1813; grad. Wesleyan U., 1835, A.M., 1838; D.D. (hon.), Ohio Wesleyan U.; LL.D., Madison U., 1852; m. Sarah Ann Dunn, July 26, 1835, 8 children. Taught at Me. Wesleyan Sem., 1835-39; pastor Methodist Episcopal Ch., Bangor, Me., 1839-41, Odeon Ch., Boston, 1842-43; prof. Greek and Hebrew, Ind. Asbury U., 1843-46; editor Ladies' Repository, 1846-52; 1st pres. Genesee Coll., 1851-53; pastor, Bangor, 1856-60; served as chaplain 1st Me. Cavalry, 1861-62; U.S. consul at Stockholm, also acting minister to Sweden, 1862-64; became pastor Central Meth. Episcopal Ch., Portland, 1866; editor The Northern Border, Bangor, 1873-78. Author: Hungary and Kossuth, 1851; Memorials of Prison Life, 1854; Our Political Parties, 1880. Died Bangor, Sept. 16, 1885.

TEFFT, Thomas A., architect; b. R.I., Aug. 3, 1826; grad. Brown U., 1851. Designed Sch. for Young Ladies, Providence, 1840's; drew plans for old R.R. Depot, Providence, R.I. (built under supervision of firm Tallman & Bucklin, Providence), 1848; designed several eccles. bldgs. including Central Congregational Ch. (no longer standing), Central Bapt. Ch. (later remodeled as Meml. Hall) (both Providence), South Bapt. Ch., Hartford, Conn., Bapt. chs., Wakefield and South Kingston, R.I., St. Paul's old wooden Ch., Wickford, R.I.; designed Bank of N.Am. Bldg., Providence, 1856, also several residences; went to Europe, 1856; charter mem. A.I.A., 1857. Died Rome, Italy, Dec. 12, 1859.

TELFAIR, Edward, gov. Ga., Continental congressman; b. "Town Head", Scotland, circa 1735; m. Sally Gibbons, May 18, 1774, 6 children. Came to Va., circa 1758; joined "Liberty Boys" as a prominent rebel, 1774-76; organized donations for the Boston sufferers, 1774; attended first 3 Ga. provincial congresses; mem. original Ga. Council of Safety, 1775-76; del. to Provincial Congress at Savannah, Ga., 1776; asst. comdr. up-country militia; was listed in a group described as dangerous to the liberties of Am. by British, 1776; his name was in the lists attainted for high treason by restored Brit. authority in Savannah, 1780, 81; mem. Continental Congress, 1777-79, 80-83, ratified and signed Articles of Confederation, declined to serve again, 1785; Indian commr. to treat with the Creeks and Cherokees, 1783; to Ga. Legislature, 1785; elected gov. Ga., 1786; mem. Ga. Conv. which ratified U.S. Constn., 1788; mem. Ga. Legislature from Richmond County, 1789; became 1st gov. under new Ga. Constn. of 1789-93, reckless with state lands, involved in conflict with U.S. Govt. over Indian affairs. Died Savannah, Sept. 17, 1807; buried Bonaventure Cemetery, Savannah.

TELFAIR, Thomas, congressman; b. Savannah, Ga., Mar. 2, 1780; son of Edward Telfair; grad. Princeton, 1805; studied law. Admitted to Ga. bar, began practice law in Savannah; mem. U.S. Ho. of Reps. (Democrat) from Ga., 13th-14th congresses, 1813-17. Died Savannah, Feb. 18, 1818; buried Bonaventure Cemetery.

TELLER, Isaac, congressman; b. Matteawan, Dutchess County, N.Y., Feb. 7, 1799; prep. edn. Held several local offices; mem. U.S. Ho. of Reps. (Democrat, filled vacancy) from N.Y., 33d Congress, Nov. 7, 1854-55; farmer. Died Matteawan (now Beacon), N.Y., Apr. 30, 1868; buried Rural Cemetery, Fishkill, N.Y.

TEMPLE, Henry John (3rd viscount Palmerston), Brit. prime minister; b. Broadlands, nr. Romsey Hunts, Eng., Oct. 20, 1784; attended U. Cambridge (Eng.); married widow of 5th earl Cowper, 1839. Mem. English Ho. of Commons, 1807-65; sec. of war, 1809-28; sec. of fgn. affairs, 1830-41, 46-51, antagonized America by his grandiose actions and disregard for Am. fgn. policy; led attack against Webster-Ashburton Treaty in Ho. of Commons, 1841-46; sec. of state, 1853-55; prime minister, 1855-65, strongly enforced English neutrality, recognized North's blockade of South, vigorously protested violation of neutral shipping rights which occurred with "Trent Affair" (2 Southern agts. enroute to Europe were taken from Brit. ship in internat. waters), demanded release of agts., which resulted in war scare in both Eng. and Am. until Pres. Lincoln ordered agts. released; refused to recognize Confederacy as a belligerent, thus became more popular in Am. Died Brocket Hall, Eng., Oct. 18, 1865; buried Westminster Abbey.

TEMPLE, William, congressman; b. Queen Anne County, Md., Feb. 28, 1814; prep. edn. Moved to Smyrna, Del., became a mcht.; speaker Del. Ho. of Reps., 1844; mem. Del. Senate, 1845-54; acting gov. Del., 1846-47; mem. U.S. Ho. of Reps. (Democrat) from Del., 38th Congress, 1863. Died Smyrna, May 28, 1863; buried Episcopal Cemetery.

TEMPLE, William Grenville, naval officer; b. Rutland, Vt., Mar. 23, 1824; s. Robert and Charlotte Eloise (Green) T.; grad. U.S. Naval Acad., 1846; m. Catlyna Totten, Oct. 7, 1851. Commd. midshipman U.S. Navy, 1840; made 1st cruise on ship Constellation around the world, 1840-44; passed midshipman, 1846; took part in chief naval operations during Mexican War, 1847, capture of Alvarado, occupation of Tuxpan and Tabasco; served on Mediterranean cruise, 1852-55; promoted master, 1854; flag lt. Pacific Squadron, 1859-61; served in U.S. coast survey; commanded steamer Flambeau during Civil War, 1861, ship Pembina on Mobile Blockade, 1862-63; commd. lt. comdr., 1862; fleet capt. Eastern Gulf squadron, 1862-64; commanded side-wheeler Pontoosue, 1864-65, participated in both attacks on Fort Fisher, 1864-65; promoted comdr., 1865, capt., 1870, commodore, 1878; rear adm., 1884; ordnance duty, Portsmouth, N.H., 1866-69; chief of staff European Squadron, 1871-73; capt. N.Y. Navy Yard, 1875-77; mem. Navy Retiring Bd., 1879-84; ret., 1884. Died Washington, D.C., June 28, 1894; buried Congressional Cemetery, Washington.

TEN BROECK, Abraham, army officer, jurist; b. Albany, N.Y., May 13, 1734; s. Dirck and Grietja (Cuyler) Ten B.; m. Elizabeth Van Rensselaer, Nov. 1, 1763, 5 children. Mem. Colonial Assembly of N.Y., 1761-65; dep. N.Y. Provincial Congress, 1775-77; mem. N.Y. Constl. Conv. of 1777; served as brig. gen. N.Y. Militia during Am. Revolution; had key role in Battle of Bemis Heights which resulted in forced retreat of Gen. Burgoyne, 1777; resigned commn., 1781; 1st judge Ct. of Common Pleas of Albany County (N..Y.), 1781-94; mayor Albany, 1779-83, 96-99; mem. N.Y. State Senate, 1780-83; pres., dir. Albany Bank. Died Albany, Jan. 19, 1810.

TEN BROECK, Richard, horseman; b. Albany, N.Y., May 1812; s. Richard Ten Broeck; attended U.S. Mil. Acad., 1829-30; m. 2d, Mrs. H. D. Newcomb. Began horse racing career in South, 1830; became partner of William R. Johnson in racing on So. tracks, 1847; purchased colt called Lexington, 1853, horse set record for a 4 mile race; raced his horses in Eng., 1856-66, won almost $200,000 in purses and matches. Died Menlo Park, Cal., Aug. 1, 1892.

TENE-ANG POTE (Kicking Bird), Kiowa Indian chief. Accepted reservation in what is now Okla., 1865; prevented tribe from going to war when Tex. Govt. refused to release 2 Kiowa chiefs as fed. govt. had promised, 1873; his efforts resulted in refusal of two-thirds of Kiowas to follow Lone Wolf to war. Died May 3, 1875.

TEN EYCK, Egbert, congressman, lawyer; b. Schodack, N.Y., Apr. 18, 1779; grad. Williams Coll., 1799; studied law. Admitted to bar, 1807, began practice law in Watertown, N.Y.; mem. N.Y. State Assembly, 1812-13, speaker; supr. of Jefferson County, 1816; trustee Village of Watertown, 1816; an incorporator Jefferson County Nat. Bank; 1st sec. Jefferson County Agrl. Soc., 1817; pres. Village of Watertown, 1820; del. N.Y. Constl. Conv., 1822; mem. U.S. Ho. of Reps. from N.Y., 18th Congress, 1823-25, (election contested) 19th Congress, Mar. 4-Dec. 15, 1825; judge Jefferson County Cts., 9 years. Died Watertown, Apr. 11, 1844; buried Brookside Cemetery.

TEN EYCK, John Conover, senator; b. Freehold, N.J., Mar. 12, 1814; studied law. Admitted to the bar, 1835, began practice law, Burlington, N.J.; pros. atty. Burlington County, 1839-49; del. N.J. Constl. Conv., 1844; mem. U.S. Senate (Republican) from N.J., 1859-65; del. Rep. Nat. Conv., Chgo., 1860; apptd. mem. commn. to revise N.J. Constn., 1875, sometime pres. commn. Died Mt. Holly, N.J., Aug. 24, 1879; buried St. Andrew's Cemetery.

TENNENT, Gilbert, clergyman; b. County Armagh, Ireland, Feb. 5, 1703; s. William and Catharine (Kennedy) T.; A.M. (hon.), Yale, 1725; m. 2d, Cornelia De Peyster Clarkson, 1741; m. 3d, Sarah Spofford; at least 3 children. Came to Am., circa 1717; licensed to preach by Phila. Presbytery, 1725; assisted father in newly established "Log College"; accepted call to New Brunswick, N.J., 1726, ordained by Phila. Presbytery; became supporter Whitefield's Evangelistic Crusade; leader in New Brunswick organized conflict with Phila. Synod, 1728; sermons and pamphlets stressed need for conversion experience among clergy, expressed in "Nottingham Sermon," 1740; trustee Coll. of N.J. (now Princeton). Author: Irenicum Ecclesiasticum, or a Humble Impartial Essay upon the Peace of Jerusalem, 1749. Died Phila., July 23, 1764; buried Abington, Pa.

TENNENT, John, physician; b. Eng., circa 1700; m. Dorothy Paul, 1730; m. 2d, Mrs. Hanger, Nov. 8, 1741. Came to Am., 1725; developed treatment for pleurisy using rattlesnake root, 1735; returned to Eng., 1739, met with little success in securing recognition for rattlesnake root medicine (which he claimed would cure pleurisy, gout, rheumatism, dropsy, nervous disorders). Author: Essay on the Pleurisy, 1736; Detection of a Conspiracy . . . The Singular Case of John Tennent, published by him in London (defense of his career), 1743; Every Man His Own Doctor, advocated use of medicines grown in Am., 2d edit., 1724. Died circa 1760.

TENNENT, William, clergyman; b. Ireland, 1673; grad. U. Edinburgh (Scotland), 1695; m. Catharine Kennedy, May 15, 1702, 5 children including Gilbert. Ordained deacon Ch. of Ireland, 1704, priest, 1706; came to Phila., between 1716-18; admitted to Presbyn. ministry by Phila. Synod, 1718; served at ch., Bedford, Pa., 1720-26, pastor, Neshaming, Pa., 1726-46, also took charge of a congregation at Deep Run, 1726-38; erected "Log College" (the beginning of Princeton Theol. Sem.) to prepare Presbyn. ministers, 1736; Phila. Synod rejected this tng. as insufficient, 1738 (ignored by those who had received it); trained many ministers to a evangelistic approach and through support of the "new side" contbd. to schism in Presbyn. Ch., 1741. Died Nashaminy, May 6, 1746.

TENNENT, William, clergyman; b. County Armagh, Ireland, June 3, 1705; s. William and Catherine (Kennedy) T.; studied theology under Gilbert Tennent (his brother); m. Catherine Noble, Aug. 23, 1738, at least 3 children. Almost buried alive (due to an apparent cessation of bodily activity), sometime before 1730, claimed certain supernatural experiences during this suspension; licensed to preach by Presbyn. Ch., 1731; pastor Presbyn. Ch., Freehold, N.J., 1732-77. Died Freehold, Mar. 8, 1777; buried Presbyn. Ch., Freehold.

TENNEY, Samuel, congressman, physician; b. Byfield, Mass., Nov. 27, 1748; attended Dummer Acad.; grad. Harvard, 1772; studied medicine. Taught sch., Andover, Mass.; began practice medicine, Exeter, N. H.; surgeon in Revolutionary War; del. N.H. Constl. Conv., 1788; judge of probate Rockingham County, 1793-1800; mem. U.S. Ho. of Reps. from N.H. (filled vacancy), 6th-9th congresses, Dec. 8, 1800-07; pursued literary, hist., sci. studies. Died Exeter, Feb. 6, 1816; buried Old Cemetery.

TENNEY, Sarah Brownson, author; b. Chelsea, Mass., 1839; dau. of Orestes Brownson; m. William J. Tenney, 1873. Wrote literary criticism for her father's Review. Author: (novels) Marian Elwood, 1863, At Anchor; Heremore Brandon; also a life of Prince Demetrius Gallitzen, 1873. Died Elizabeth, N.J., Oct. 30, 1876.

TENNEY, Tabitha Gilman, novelist, compiler; b. Exeter, N.H., Apr. 7, 1762; d. Samuel and Lydia (Robinson) Gilman; m. Samuel Tenney, Sept. 6, 1788. Wrote novel Female Quixotism: Exhibited in the Romantic Opinions and Extravagant Adventures of Dorcasina Sheldon (satire on prevailing literary tastes, a warning to young women to dispense with the affectations of foolish romanticism) 1801; edited The Pleasing Instructor (anthology of selections from poets and classical writers). Died Exeter, May 2, 1837.

TENNEY, William Jewett, editor; b. Newport, R.I., 1811; s. Caleb and Ruth (Channing) T.; grad. Yale, 1832; m. Elizabeth M. Benton, 1839; m. 2d Sarah Brownson. Worked at Retreat for Insane, Hartford, Conn., 1835; journalist N.Y.C. mags. including N.Y. Jour. of Commerce, Evening Post, Mining Mag., 1840-53; reader, editor D. Appleton & Co., 1853-83, edited Appleton's Annual Cyclopaedia. Author: Military and Naval History of the Rebellion in the United States, 1865; A Grammatical Analyzer, 1866; Rise and Fall of the Confederate Government, 1881. Died Newark, N.J., Sept. 20, 1883.

TENSKWATAWA, (original name Lalawethika), Indian prophet and chief; b. Old Chillicothe (now Oldtown), Ohio, in March 1768; son of Pucksinwa; brother of Tecumseh. Announced himself to be a prophet, assumed name of Tenskwatawa, circa 1805; usually referred to by Whites as the Prophet (sometimes called Elskwatawa); used mystic rites, preached doctrine of primitivism, necessity for Indians of giving up alcohol and of becoming self supporting again; forbade intermarriage with Whites; urged common possession of all property; lost standing following defeat in Battle of Tippecanoe, 1811. Died Thames, Can., Oct. 5, 1813.

TERESA, MOTHER (Alice Lalor), nun; b. Ireland, 1766. Came to Am., 1795; served in Phila. during yellow fever epidemic, 1797-98; went to Georgetown, D.C. with 2 widows, Mrs. McDermott and Mrs Sharpe, 1799; lived with The Poor Clares (group of nuns); founder (with group and help of Rev. Leonard Neale) 1st Visitation Order of Nuns in U.S., 1816, mother superior, 1816-19; founded houses in Mobile, Ala., 1832, St. Louis, Mo., 1833, Balt., 1837. Died Balt., Sept. 9, 1846.

TERRELL, James C., congressman, lawyer; b. Franklin County, Ga., Nov. 7, 1806; studied law. Admitted to Ga. bar by an act of legislature, practiced law, Carnesville, Ga.; mem. Ga. Ho. of Reps., 1830-34; mem. U.S. Ho. of Reps. (Union Democrat) from Ga., 24th Congress, Mar. 4-July 8, 1835 (resigned due to ill health). Died Carnesville, Dec. 1, 1835.

TERRELL, William, congressman, physician; b. Fairfax County, Va., 1778; grad. med. dept. U. Pa. Began practice of medicine, Sparta, Ga.; mem. Ga. Ho. of Reps., 1810-13; held various local offices; mem. U.S. Ho. of Reps. (Democrat) from Ga., 15th-16th congresses, 1817-21. Died Sparta, July 4, 1855; buried Sparta Cemetery.

TERRY, Alfred Howe, army officer; b. Hartford, Conn., Nov. 10, 1827; s. Alfred and Clarissa (Howe) T.; attended Yale Law Sch. Admitted to Conn. bar, 1849; commd. col. Conn. Militia, 1861; served in 1st Battle of Bull Run; organized 7th Conn. Volunteers, 1861, commd. col.; promoted brig. gen. U.S. Volunteers, 1862; in command forces on Hilton Head, 1862; assigned to Army of the James, 1863; participated in operations against Richmond and Petersburg, 1864; brevetted maj. gen. U.S. Volunteers, 1864; took Ft.

Fisher, N.C., 1865, as result commd. brig. gen. U.S. Army, 1865; commd. maj. gen. volunteers, 1865; assumed command Dept. of Dakota, 1866, head Dept. Dakota during exploration of Black Hills and Sioux War, 1874; commd. maj. gen. U.S. Army, 1866 (only general on army list not a U.S. Mil. Acad. graduate); in command Div. of Mo. with hdqrs. at Chgo., 1886; ret. for disability, 1888; mem. Indian Commn. created by U.S. Congress, 1867; mem. bd. of army officers to review court martial and sentence of Gen. Fitz John Porter. Died New Haven, Conn., Dec. 16, 1890.

TERRY, David Smith, jurist, army officer, political leader; b. Todd County, Ky., Mar. 8, 1823; s. Joseph R. and Sarah (Smith) T.; m. Cornelia Runnels, 1852; m. 2d, Sarah Althea Hill, Jan. 7, 1886. Volunteer in war for Texan independence, 1836; served as lt. in company Tex. Rangers Mexican War; practiced law in Stockton, Cal.; elected asso. justice Cal. Supreme Ct., 1855, chief justice, 1857-59; sent to San Francisco to aid in organizing resistance to Vigilantes, 1856; joined Confederate Army, 1863; returned to Cal., resumed practice of law, Stockton, 1869; elected to Cal. Constl. Conv., 1878. Killed in assault by a circuit judge, Stockton, Aug. 14, 1889.

TERRY, Eli, inventor, clock mfr.; b. East Windsor, Conn., Apr. 13, 1772; s. Samuel and Huldah (Burnham) T.; m. Eunice Warner, Mar. 12, 1795; m. 2d, Harriet Ann (Pond) Peck, Oct. 1840; 11 children. Worked for numerous clockmakers in Conn., 1786-92; made his 1st clock, 1792; built 1st clock factory in Am., manufactured 10 to 20 clocks at a time by means of water power, 1800; established (with Seth Thomas and Silas Hoadley) firm Terry, Thomas & Hoadley, 1807; established his own business at Plymouth Hollow, 1810; devised "Pillarcroll top case" clock, 1814; patented about 10 improvements in clocks. Died Plymouth, Conn., Feb. 26, 1852.

TERRY, John Orville. poet; b. Orient, N.Y., Aug. 13, 1796; studied medicine, never practiced. Made several voyages to S.Am.; settled on farm, N.Y. Author: The Poems of J.O.T., 1850. Died Greenport, N.Y., Apr. 7, 1869.

TERRY, Nathaniel, congressman, businessman, lawyer; b. Enfield, Conn., Jan. 30, 1768; attended Dartmouth; grad. Yale, 1786; studied law. Admitted to the bar, 1790, began practice law in Enfield; moved to Hartford, Conn., 1796; comdr. Gov.'s Foot Guard of Hartford, 1802-13; judge Hartford County Ct., 1807-09 (resigned); mem. Conn. Ho. of Reps., 1804-15; mem. U.S. Ho. of Reps. from Conn., 15th Congress, 1817-19; mem. Conn. Constl. Conv., 1818; pres. Hartford Fire Ins. Co., 1810-35; pres. Hartford Bank, 1819-28; mayor Hartford, 1824-31; served as gen. Conn. Militia. Died New Haven, Conn., June 14, 1844; buried Old North (Spring Grove) Cemetery, Hartford.

TERRY, William, congressman, lawyer; b. Amherst County, Va., Aug. 14, 1824; grad. U. Va., 1848; studied law. Taught sch.; admitted to Va. bar, 1851, began practice law, Wytheville, Va.; in newspaper work; served as lt. 4th Regt., Va. Inf., Confederate Army, promoted maj., 1862, col., 1864, was last comdr. of "Stonewall Jackson" brigade; resumed practice law, Wytheville; mem. U.S. Ho. of Reps. (Conservative) from Va., 42d, 44th congresses, 1871-73, 75-77; del. Democratic Nat. Conv., Cincinnati, 1880. Drowned while trying to ford creek nr. Wytheville, Sept. 5, 1888; buried East End Cemetery, Wytheville.

TEST, John, congressman, lawyer; b. Salem, N.J., Nov. 12, 1771; studied law. Operator Fayette Chance Furnace in Pa., several years; moved to Cincinnati, then to Brookville, Ind., operated grist mill; admitted to Ind. bar, began practice law in Brookville; held several local offices; judge 3d Dist. Circuit, 1816-19; mem. U.S. Ho. of Reps. (Clay Democrat) from Ind., 18th-19th, (as Whig) 21st congresses, 1823-27, 29-31; presiding judge Ind. Circuit Ct.; moved to Mobile, Ala., practiced law. Died nr. Cambridge City, Ind., Oct. 9, 1849; buried Cambridge City.

TESTUT, Charles, journalist, poet; b. France, circa 1818. Assisted at founding French newspaper L'indicateur, 1839; bought Le Chronique, circa 1843; went to Mobile (Ala.), launched bilingual paper Ala. Courrier, 1850; organized newspapers La Semaine de la Nouvelle Orleans, 1852, L'Equite, 1871, La Semaine Litteraire, 1876; wrote Les Echos (1st book of verses), 1849; wrote Fleurs d'Ete, 1851; wrote shirt criticisms of local writers under title Portraits Litteraires, 1850. Died July 1, 1892.

TEVIS, Lloyd, businessman; b. Shelbyville, Ky., Mar. 20, 1824; s. Samuel and Sarah (Greathouse) T.; read law with father; m. Susan G. Sanders, Apr. 20, 1854, 5 children. Salesman wholesale dry goods store, Louisville, Ky., 1844, became assignee of that co. when it failed; dir. Bank of Ky., before 1849; went to Cal. during Gold Rush, 1849; established law partnership with Ben Ali Haggin, Sacramento, Cal., 1850; moved profitable law and investment bus. to San Francisco, 1853; a prin. owner Cal. Steam Navigation Co.; negotiated purchase of State Telegraph Co. by Western Union; engaged in many comml. interests in Cal.; pres. joint co. of Wells, Fargo and Co. and Pacific Express Co., 1872-92; owned shares of many silver and gold mines; owned shares of Anaconda copper properties in Mont. Died San Francisco, July 24, 1899.

THACHER, George, congressman, jurist; b. Apr. 12, 1754; s. Peter and Anner (Lewis) T.; grad. Harvard Coll., 1776; studied law with Shearjashub Bourne; m. Sarah Savage, July 21, 1784, 10 children. Admitted to Mass. bar, 1778; del. Continental Congress from Mass., 1787; mem. U.S. Ho. of Reps. (Federalist) from Me. dist. of Mass., 1st-6th congresses, 1789-1801, favored assumption of state debts, Sedition Act; asso. judge Mass. Supreme Ct., 1801-24; a founder 2d Ch., Biddeford, Me.; del. Me. Constl. Conv., 1819. Died Biddeford, Apr. 6, 1824; buried Woodlawn Cemetery, Biddeford.

THACHER, James, physician, army officer; b. Barnstable, Mass., Feb. 14, 1754; s. John and Content (Norton) T.; M.D. (hon.), Harvard, 1810; m. Susannah Hayward, Apr. 28, 1785, 6 children. Served with 1st Va. Regt., 1778-79; took part in ill-fated Penobscot Expdn.; acted as surgeon to select corps of light infantry, 1781; at siege of Yorktown and surrender of Lord Cornwallis; retired from army, 1783; began practice medicine and surgery, 1784; kept diary during the American Revolutionary War published under title A Military Journal, 1823, 2d edit., 1826, reprinted as Military Journal, 1854; wrote The American Medical Biography (1st publ. of its kind), 1828; mem. Am. Acad. Arts and Scis., Mass. Med. Soc. Author: Observations on Hydrophobia, 1812: American Modern Practice, 1817. Died Plymouth, Mass., May 23, 1844.

THACHER, Peter, clergyman; b. Salem, Mass., July 18, 1651; s. Thomas and Eliza (Partridge) T.; grad. Harvard, 1671; m. Theodora Oxenbridge, Nov. 21, 1677; m. 2d, Susannah Bailey, Dec. 25, 1699; m. 3d, Elizabeth (Thacher) Gee, 1727; 10 children. Tutor, Harvard, 1671-74; fellow, 1674-76; pastor, Barnstable, Mass., 1676-80; ordained to ministry Congregational Ch., Milton, Mass., 1681, pastor, 1680-1727; missionary among Indians; Calvinist. Author: Unbelief Detected and Condemned, 1708; The Alsufficient Physician, 1711. Died Dec. 17, 1727.

THACHER, Peter, clergyman; b. Milton, Mass., Mar. 21, 1752; s. Oxenbridge and Sarah (Kent) T.; grad. Harvard, 1769; m. Elizabeth (Haukes) Poole, Oct. 8, 1770, 10 children. Ordained and installed as pastor Congregatonal Ch., Malden, Mass., 1770-84; made speech An Oration Delivered at Watertown . . . To Commemorate the Bloody Massacre at Boston Perpetrated Mar. 5, 1770, 1776, as result of this address Provincial Congress gave him recruiting powers for sea-coast defense of Mass.; chaplain Mass. Gen. Ct., 1776-1802; credited with authorship of Malden resolutions to Mass. Gen. Ct. rep.; Malden del. to Mass. Constl. Conv., 1780; installed as pastor Brattle Street Ch., Boston, 1785; mem. Am. Acad. Arts and Scis.; founder Mass. Hist. Soc., 1790. Author: A Narrative of the Battle of Bunker Hill. Died Savannah, Ga., Dec. 16, 1802.

THACHER, Samuel Cooper, theologian; b. Boston, Dec. 14, 1785; s. Peter and Elizabeth (Hawkes) T.; grad. Harvard, 1804. Tchr. Latin, Public Latin Sch., Boston, 1805-06; traveled in Europe with an ill friend Rev. Jospeh Stevens Buckminister, 1806-07; librarian Harvard, 1808-11; pastor New South Ch., Boston, 1811-15; contracted tuberculosis, lived in Eng. trying to find a cure, 1815-18. Died Moulins, France, Jan. 2, 1818.

THACHER, Thomas Anthony, classicist, coll. adminstr.; b. Hartford, Conn., Jan. 11, 1815; s. Peter and Anne (Parts) T.; grad. Yale, 1835; Studied in Germany, 1843-45; LL.D. (hon.), Western Res. U., 1869; m. Elizabeth Day, Sept. 16, 1846; m. 2d, Elizabeth Sherman, Aug. 1, 1860; at least 9 children. Apptd. tutor, Yale, 1838, asst. prof. Latin and Greek, 1842, prof. Latin, 1851; mem. Mass. Bd. Edn.; mem. com. for building Yale Art Sch.; one of 1st advocates of grad. instrn. in non-technical fields; edited Cicero's De Officiis, 1850, published (with Karl Zumpt) A Latin Grammar for the Use of Schools, 1871; an editor Webster's Dictionary of the English Language, 1847-64. Died New Haven, Conn., Apr. 7, 1886.

THATCH, Edward, see Teach, Edward.

THATCHER, Benjamin Bussey, author, lawyer; b. Warren, Knox County, Me., Oct. 8, 1809; s. Samuel and Sarah (Brown) T.; grad. Bowdoin Coll., 1826; studied law in Boston. Admitted to Mass. bar, circa 1827; practiced law, 1827-40, chiefly interested in writing; went to Eng. for reasons of health, 1836; works include: Memoir of Phillis Wheatley, 1834; Memoir of S. Osgood Wright, 1834; Traits of the Tea Party, 1835; The Boston Book, 1837. Died July 14, 1840.

THATCHER, Henry Knox, naval officer; b. Thomaston, Me., May 26, 1806; s. Ebenezer and Lucy Flucker (Knox) T.; attended U.S. Mil. Acad.; m. Susan C. Croswell, Dec. 26, 1831, 1 adopted child. Apptd. midshipman U.S. Navy, 1823; served in ship United States, 1824-27; made cruise in west Indies as acting master in Erie, 1831; commd. lt., 1833; commanded storeship Relief of Brazil Squadron, 1851-52; exec. officer Naval Asylum, Phila., 1854-55; comdr., 1855; commanded Decatur in Pacific, 1857-59; exec. officer Boston Navy Yard, 1861; in command corvette Constellation for special duty in Mediterranean, Nov. 1861; commodore, 1862; assigned in Colorado of North Atlantic Squadron, 1863; commanded 1st div. of Adm. Porter's fleet and served with distinction at attack on Ft. Fisher, N.C., Dec. 1864-Jan. 1865; apptd. acting rear adm., ordered to take command of West Gulf blockading squadron, 1865; commanded North Pacific Squadron, 1866-68; promoted rear adm., 1866, ret. 1868. Died Boston, Apr. 5, 1880.

THATCHER, Samuel, congressman, lawyer; b. Cambridge, Mass., July 1, 1776; grad. Harvard, 1793; studied law. Admitted to bar, 1797, began practice law in New Gloucester, Mass. (now Me.); moved to Warren, Mass., 1800; mem. Mass. Ho. of Reps., 1801-11; mem. U.S. Ho. of Reps. (Democrat, filled vacancy) from Mass., 7th-8th congresses, Dec. 6, 1802-05; sheriff Lincoln County (Me.), 1814-21; mem. Me. Ho. of Reps., 1824; moved to Bangor, Me., 1860. Died Bangor, July 18, 1872; buried Mt. Hope Cemetery.

THAW, William, businessman, philanthropist; b. Pitts., Oct. 12, 1818; s. John and Elizabeth (Thomas) T.; attended Western U. of Pa. (now U. Pitts.); m. Eliza Blair, 1841; m. 2d, Mary Copley, 1867; at least 10 children. With firm McKee, Clarke & Co., 1835; in partnership with Thomas Clarke, 1840; owner Pa. & Ohio Canal Line, receiving and forwarding mdse. by river and canal, 1840-55; owned interests in over 150 steamboats operating on various lines including Pitts. & Cincinnati Packet Line, 1840-59; joined firm Leech & Co., freight agts. of Pa. R.R., 1856; with Thomas Clarke formed Clarke & Co. to undertake freight business West of Pitts., 1857; promoted extension of Pa. R.R. to St. Louis; elected v.p. Pa. Co., 1871; organized 1st system of direct freight transp. over different lines; dir. Pa. R.R., 1881-89; v.p. Chgo., St. Louis & Pitts. R.R. Co., 1884; benefactor Western U. Pa.; supported Samuel Pierpont Langley in his work at Allegheny Observatory; gave financial aid to John A. Brashear. Died Aug. 17, 1889.

THAXTER, Celia Laighton, poet; b. Portsmouth, N.H., June 29, 1835; d. Thomas B. and Eliza (Rymes) Laighton; m. Levi Lincoln Thaxter, Sept. 30, 1851, 3 children. Lived with family on White Island, off coast of N.H.; came to mainland of N.H., 1848; moved to Newtonville, Mass., began to write poems; works include: Poems, 1872; Among the Isles of Shoals, 1873; Driftweed, 1879; Poems for Children, 1884; Idyls and Pastorals, 1886; An Island Garden, 1894. Died Appledore Island off N. H., Aug. 26, 1894.

THAYENDANEGEA, see BRANT, Joseph.

THAYER, Alexander Wheelock, biographer, diplomat; b. South Natick, Mass., Oct. 22, 1817; s. Dr. Alexander and Susanna (Bigelow) T.; grad. Harvard, 1843, LL.B., 1848. Employed at Harvard Coll. library; mem. staff N.Y. Tribune, 1852; contbr. to Dwight's Journal of Music, Boston; completed 1st volume of biography on Beethoven, 1856, 2d vol., 1872, 3d vol., 1879 (last vol. unfinished), the 3 volumes covered all but last 10 years of Beethoven's life, considered standard work on subject; revision appeared as The Life of Ludwig van Beethoven, 1921; edited Signor Masoni and Other Papers of the Late L. Brown, Berlin, 1862; had post in legation at Vienna, Austria, 1862; U.S. consul at Trieste, 1864-82. Author: The Hebrews and the Red Sea, Andover, Mass., 1883. Died Trieste, July 15, 1897.

THAYER, Andrew Jackson, congressman, lawyer; b. Lima, N.Y., Nov. 27, 1818; studied law. Admitted to the bar, 1849, began practice law in Lima; moved to area nr. Corvallis, Ore., 1853, practiced law, farmed; U.S. atty. for dist. of Ore., 1859; mem. U.S. Ho. of Reps. (Democrat, election contested) from Ore., 37th Congress, Mar. 4-July 30, 1861; atty. for 2d Dist. Ore., 1862-64; circuit judge 2d Jud. Dist. of Ore., 1870-73. Died Corvallis, Apr. 28, 1873; buried Crystal Lake Cemetery.

THAYER, Eli, congressman; b. Mendon, Mass., June 11, 1819; s. Cushman and Miranda (Pond)

T.; grad. Brown U., 1845; m. Caroline M. Capron, Aug. 6, 1845, 7 children. Prin., Worcester (Mass.) Manual Labor High Sch., 1847-49; supervised constrn. Oread Collegiate Inst., Worcester, 1848-52; mem. Worcester Sch. Bd., 1852; alderman Worcester, 1852-53; mem. Mass. Ho. of Reps., 1853-54; secured charter, organized New Eng. Emigrant Aid Co. (sent anti-slavery settlers into Kan.); mem. U.S. Ho. of Reps. (Republican) from Mass., 35th-36th congresses, 1857-61; del. from Ore. to Nat. Rep. Conv., 1860; agt. U.S. Treasury, 1861-62; land agt. in N.Y. for Western railroad interests, 1864-70; spent later years of life in railroad bus. Died Worcester, Apr. 15, 1899; buried Hope Cemetery, Worcester.

THAYER, Gideon French, educator; b. Watertown, Mass., Sept. 21, 1793; s. Zephion and Susannah (Bond) T.; m. Nancy Pierce, Aug. 27, 1821, 4 children. Established pvt. sch. with gymnastic equipment, Boston, 1820, stressed importance of well-balanced program mental, moral and phys. instruction; founder Chauncy-Hall Sch., 1828; a founder 1st high sch., in Quincy, Mass., 1825, also alyceum for cultural activities and interests; a founder Am. Inst. Instrn., pres., 1848-52; a founder Am. Assn. for Advancement of Edn., Mass. Tchrs. Assn.; an editor Mass. Teacher, 1848; mem. Boston Common Council, 1839, 44-48; pres. Quincy Fire and Marine Ins. Co. (later Prescott Ins. Co.), 1856-60. Died Keene, N.H., Mar. 27, 1864.

THAYER, John, missionary; b. Boston, May 15, 1758; s. Cornelius and Sarah (Plaisted) T.; A.B. (hon.), Yale, 1779. Licensed as Congregational minister, circa 1778; served as chaplain under John Hancock at Castle William, 1780-81; entered Roman Catholic Ch., 1783, ordained priest, 1787; held services, prepared to build church, Alexandria, Va., 1793; abolitionist; went to assist Stephen Theodore Badin as Ky. missionary, 1799; went to Limerick (Ireland) as missionary, 1803; left legacy which enabled several postulants to go to Three Rivers, Que., Can., 1817, and on completion of their novitiate, to establish house in Boston, 1819 (nucleus of Ursuline Convent, Charlestown, Mass.). Author: The Conversion of John Thayer . . . Written by Himself, 1787. Died Limerick, Ireland, Feb. 17, 1815.

THAYER, Nathaniel, financier, philanthropist; b. Lancaster, Mass., Sept. 11, 1808; s. Rev. Nathaniel and Sarah (Toppan) T.; m. Cornelia Van Rensselaer, June 10, 1846, 7 children. Associated with banking firm of brother, circa 1840, mng. dir., 1857; became prominent in Am. investment banking; built one of largest fortunes of any New Englander of that time; overseer Harvard, 1866, mem. bd. fellows, 1868-75, directed financial mgmt. of coll., underwrote Agassiz expdn. to Brazil, 1865, built students' dining hall, herbarium for dept. of botany, dormitory Thayer Hall (named for him). Died Boston, Mar. 7, 1883; buried Mt. Auburn Cemetery, Cambridge, Mass.

THAYER, Samuel J. F., architect; b. Boston, 1842. Began career as architect, later 1860's, designed many types of public bldgs. in New Eng. Prin. works include: Town Hall, Brookline, Mass.; City Hall, Providence, R.I., 1878; library at Dartmouth, 1885, also other bldgs. on campus; Farragut House (hotel), Rye N.H.; Nevins Meml. Hall and Library, Methuen, Mass. Died Mar. 1, 1893.

THAYER, Sylvanus, mil. engr., educator; b. Braintree, Mass., June 9, 1785; s. Nathaniel and Dorcas (Faxon) T.; attended Dartmouth, 1807, LL.. (hon.), 1846; grad. U.S. Mil. Acad., 1808; LL.D. (hon.), St. John's Coll., Kenyon Coll., 1846, Harvard, 1857. Commd. 2d lt. Corps Engrs., U.S. Army, 1808; served on Canadian frontier and Norfolk (Va.) during War of 1812; commd. capt., 1813; brevetted maj., 1815; apptd. supt. U.S. Mil. Acad., West Point, N.Y., 1817-33; commd. maj., 1828, col., 1833; engr. in charge constrn. of fortifications at Boston Harbor and improvement of harbors on New Eng. coast, 1833-63; profl. duty in Europe, 1843-46; brevetted brig. gen., 1862; retired from army, 1863; established and endowed Thayer Sch. Engring., Dartmouth Coll., 1867. Author: Papers on Practical Engineering, 1844. died South Braintree, Sept. 7, 1872; buried West Point.

THAYER, Thomas Baldwin, clergyman, editor, author; b. Boston, Sept. 10, 1812; s. Benjamin and Catherine (Davis) T.; m. Sarah Harris, Mar. 1853, 1 child. Ordained by Universalists, Boston, 1832; pastor First Universalist Soc., Lowell, Mass., 1833-45, 51-59; established and edited (assisted by Rev. Abel C. Thomas) The Star of Bethlehem, 1841-42; assisted in publishing Lowell Offering, circa 1844; edited The Golden Rule and Odd Fellows' Family Companion (fraternal publ.); pastor Shawmut Avenue Universalist Ch., Boston, 1859-67; contbr. to Univeralist Quarterly, editor, 1858-64, 64-71. Author: (with Rev. Abel C. Thomas) Lowell Tracts; Christianity against Infidelity, 1836; The Bible Class Assistant, or Scriptural Guide for Sunday Schools, 1840. Died Roxbury, Mass., Feb. 12, 1886.

THAYER, Whitney Eugene, organist; b. Mendon, Mass., Dec. 11, 1838; s. Perry and Charlotte (Taft) T.; studied music in Germany, 1865; m. Elizabeth Davis Eaton, Oct. 8, 1862, 5 children. Made concert tour of Europe, 1866, played organ at Westminster Abbey, also St. Paul's, London, Eng.; returned to Boston, 1866; played organ successively at Arlington Street Ch., Hollis Street Ch., Old First Unitarian Ch., Harvard Ch. in Brookline (all Mass.), 1866-81; started long series of concerts in Boston, 1868 (1st free organ concerts in U.S.); organized 1st school for organists in U.S., 1875; organist Fifth Avenue Presbyn. Ch., N.Y.C., 1881-86; edited Organists Journal and Review, also Choir Journal and Review, 1870-81. Author: The Art of Organ Playing Complete in Five Parts, 1874; Vest Pocket Harmony Book, 1883. Committed suicide, Burlington, Vt., June 27, 1889.

THAYER, William Makepeace, clergyman, editor, author; b. Franklin, Mass., Feb. 23, 1820; s. Davis and Betsey (McKepiece) T.; A.B., Brown U., 1843; m. Rebecca W. Richards, Oct. 19, 1845, 5 children. Licensed to preach by Mendon conf. of Congregational orthodox churches, 1844; began preaching at Edgartown, Martha's Vineyard, Mass.; pastor Congl. Ch., Ashland, Mass., 1849-57; editor The Home Monthly, 1858-62; editor the Nation, 1864-68, Mother's Assistant, 1868-72; mem. Mass. Gen. Ct., 1857-58, 63-64; sec. Mass. State Temperance Alliance, 1860-76; wrote many biographies for children including: Life at the Fireside; the Poor Boy and Merchant Prince . . . the Life of . . . Amos Lawrence, 1857; Unfinished Autobiography of William M. Thayer (printed by his son). Died Franklin, Mass., Apr. 7, 1898.

THEAKER, Thomas Clarke, congressman, patent lawyer; b. York County, Pa., Feb. 1, 1812; attended common schs. Moved to Bridgeport, O., 1830, became a machinist, wheelwright; mem. U.S. Ho. of Reps. (Republican) from Ohio, 36th Congress, 1859-61; mem. bd. commrs. to investigate Patent Office, 1864, later mem. bd. examiners in chief; commr. of patents U.S. Govt., 1865-68; practiced patent law, Washington, D.C. Died Oakland, Md., July 16, 1883; buried Weeks Cemetery, nr. Bridgeport.

THÉBAUD, Augustus J., clergyman, educator; b. Nantes, France, Nov. 20, 1807; studied theology Grand Sem., Nantes. Ordained priest Roman Catholic Ch. before 1835; "vicare" St. Clement's Ch., Nantes; joined Soc. of Jesus, 1837; arrived in N.Y.C., 1838; taught chemistry St. Mary's Coll., Marion County, Ky., 1838-46, rector, 1846; rector St. John's Coll., Fordham, N.Y., 1846-52; pastor St. Joseph's Ch., Troy, N.Y., 1852-60; rector, prof. Fordham Coll., 1860-63, 74-75; pastor at Troy, 1863-69, 73-74; prof. St. Mary's, Montreal, Que., Can., 1870-73; tchr., pastor St. Francis Xavier's Coll. and Ch., N.Y.C., 1875-85. Author: The Irish Race in the Past and Present, 1873; Gentilism, 1876; The Church and the Moral World, 1881. Died Fordham, Dec. 17, 1885; buried Fordham Coll. Cemetery.

THEUS, Jeremiah, artist; b. Switzerland, circa 1719; m. Elizabeth Catherine Schaumlöffel, Jan. 26, 1742; m. 2d, Mrs. Eva Rosanna Hilt. Came with parents to Orangeburg County, S.C., 1739; established as painter in S.C. by 1740; painted many portraits of important people in area, left many portraits unsigned (now lost). Died Mar. 18, 1774.

THIBODEAUX, Bannon Goforth, congressman, lawyer; b. nr. Thibodeaux, La., Dec. 22, 1812; studied law, Hagerstown, Md. Admitted to La. bar, began practice law in Lafourche and Terrebonne parishes, La.; mem. La. constl. convs., 1845, 52; held several local offices; mem. U.S. Ho. of Reps. from La., 29th-30th congresses, 1845-49; resumed activities as lawyer, also sugar planter, mfr. Died Terrebonne Parish, Mar. 5, 1866; buried Halfway Cemetery, nr. Houma, La.

THIERRY, Camille, poet; b. New Orleans, Oct. 1814; son of a Frenchman from Bordeaux (France) and his octoroon mistress. Left fortune by his father, squandered it in Paris, France; began to write poetry under agency of Lafitte, Dufilho & Co., 1855; became a hermit when his agents went bankrupt, died in poverty. Author: Idées, 1843; Les Vagabondes, 1874. Died Bordeaux, Apr. 1875.

THOMAS, Amos Russell, homoeopathic physican, educator; b. Watertown, N.Y., Oct. 3, 1826; s. Azariah and Sarah (Avery) T.; grad. Syracuse Med. Coll., Feb. 1854; attended Pa. Med. U.; m. Elizabeth M. Bacon, Sept. 26, 1847, 2 children. Prof. anatomy Pa. Med. U., 1856-66; lectr. artistic anatomy Phila. Acad. Fine Arts, 1856-70; surgeon during Civil War, Washington, D.C.; prof. anatomy Hahnemann Med. Coll. of Phila., 1867-95, dean, 1874-95; editor Am. Jour. Homoeopathic Materia Medica, 1871-76; pres. Homoeopathic Med. Soc. of Pa., 1887. Author: A Practical Guide for Making Post-Mortem Examinations and for the Study of Morbid Anatomy, 1873; History of Anatomy, 1893. Died Phila., Oct. 31, 1895.

THOMAS, Benjamin Franklin, congressman, lawyer; b. Boston, Feb. 12, 1813; attended Lancaster Acad.; grad. Brown U., 1830; studied law, Cambridge, Mass. Admitted to the bar, 1833, began practice law, Worcester, Mass.; held several local offices; mem. Mass. Ho. of Reps., 1842; commr. of bankruptcy, 1842; judge of probate, 1844-48; Whig presdl. elector, 1848; judge Mass. Supreme Ct., 1853-59; practiced law in Boston; mem. U.S. Ho. of Reps. (Conservative Unionist, filled vacancy) from Mass., 37th Congress, June 11, 1861-63; nominated by gov. as chief justice Mass. Supreme Ct., 1868, nomination not confirmed by council. Died Beverly Farms, Mass., Sept. 27, 1878; buried Forrest Hill Cemetery, Boston.

THOMAS, Charles Randolph, congressman; b. Beaufort, N.C., Feb. 7, 1827; grad. U. N.C., 1849; studied law. Admitted to the bar, 1850, began practice law, Beaufort; moved to New Bern, N.C., practiced law; mem. N.C. Constl. Conv., 1861; sec. of state N.C., 1864; apptd. by gov. as pres. Atlantic & N.C. R.R., 1867; judge superior ct., 1868-70; mem. U.S. Ho. of Reps. (Republican) from N.C., 42d-43d congresses, 1871-75. Died New Bern, Feb. 18, 1891; buried Cedar Grove Cemetery.

THOMAS, Christopher Yancy, congressman, lawyer; b. Pittsylvania County, Va., Mar. 24, 1818; grad. pvt. acad., 1838; studied law. Admitted to bar, 1844, began practice law in Martinsville, Va.; mem. Va. Senate, 1860-64; mem. commn. to settle boundary line between Va. and N.C.; treas. Henry County; pros. atty. Henry County; mem. Va. Constl. Conv., 1868; mem. Va. Ho. of Dels., 1869; mem. U.S. Ho. of Reps. (Republican, contested election) from Va., 43d Congress, Mar. 5, 1874-75. Died Martinsville, Feb. 11, 1879; buried family cemetery Leatherwood, Henry County, Va.

THOMAS, Cornelia Frances, see Jefferson, Cornelia Burke.

THOMAS David, army officer, congressman; b. Pelham, Mass., June 11, 1762; s. David and Elizabeth (Harper) T.; m. Jeannette Turner, 1784. Took part in expdns. of Mass. Militia for relief of R.I., 1777; re-entered Mass. Militia, 1781, served with 3d, 5th regts.; mem. N.Y. Assembly (Anti-Federalist), 1793, 98, 99; served in N.Y. Militia, rose to maj. gen. in comand 3d div.; mem. U.S. Ho. of Reps. from N.Y., 7th-10th congresses, 1801-May 1, 1808; treas. State of N.Y., 1808-10; agt. for Bank of Am., 1811. Died Providence, R.I., Nov. 27, 1831.

THOMAS, David, iron mfr.; b. Glamorganshire, South Wales, Nov. 3, 1794; s. David and Jane Thomas; m. Elizabeth Hopkins, 5 children. Gen. supt. Yniscedwyn Iron Works, 1817; went to Scotland to observe hotblast methods being employed, circa 1836, returned with permission to use this process, work started immediately on constrn. furnace, blown, 1837; hired by Lehigh Coal & Navigation Co. of Pa. to construct and operate similar furnaces on Lehigh River, circa 1838; arrived in Allentown, Pa., 1839; organized Lehigh Crane Iron Co. (1st furnace produced good foundry anthracite iron, 1840, 1st anthracite-iron mfg. facility to be permanently successful from both engring. and comml. standpoint, included higher and larger furnaces, better and more powerful blast machinery); organized (with several others) Thomas Iron Co., Hokendauqua, Pa., 1854; pres. Catasaugua & Fogelsville R.R., 1st pres. Am. Inst. Mining Engrs. Died Catasauqua, Pa., June 20, 1882.

THOMAS, E. A., jurist; b. Cayuga County, N.Y., Apr. 27, 1838. Practiced law; mayor Auburn (N.Y.); served as capt. U.S. Army during Civil War; asso. justice Supreme Ct. of Wyo. Territory, 1873-77; compiled 1st volume Wyo. Supreme Ct. Reports. Died Norristown, Pa., Sept. 2, 1890.

THOMAS, Ebenezer Smith, journalist; b. West Cambridge, Mass., 1775; apprenticed as printer to Isaiah Thomas, Worcester, Mass. Operated bookstore, also published City Gazette, Charleston, S.C., 1810-16; mem. Md. Legislature, 1818-19; publisher Daily Advertiser, 1829-35, Evening Post, 1835-39 (both Cincinnati). Author: Reminiscences, 4 vols., 1840. Died Cincinnati, Oct. 22, 1845.

THOMAS, Francis, gov. Md., congressman; b. "Montevue," Frederick County, Pa., Feb. 3, 1799; s. John and Eleanor (McGill) T.; m. Sally Mc Dowell, June 8, 1841; Admitted to Md. bar, 1820; became a leading lawyer in Western Md.; mem. Md. Assembly (Democrat), 1822, 27, 29, speaker; mem. U.S. Ho. of Reps. from Md., 22d-26th congresses, 1831-41, chmn. judiciary cim., supported Andrew Jackson; pres. Chesapeake & Ohio Canal Co., 1839-40; gov. Md., 1841-44, saved state from repudiation of its debts; mem. Md. Constl. Conv., 1850-51; opposed over-representation of small slaveholding counties of Eastern Md.; enlisted a volunteer regt. of 3,000 during Civil War; mem. U.S. Ho. of Reps. (Unionist), 37th-40th congress, 1861-69; internal revenue collector for Md., 1870; U.S. minister to Peru, 1872-75. Died Frankville, Md., Jan. 22, 1876; buried Rose Hill Cemetery, Cumberland, Md.

THOMAS, Frederick William, journalist, author: b. Providence, R.I., Oct. 25, 1806; s. Ebenezer Smith and Ann (Fonerden) T. Admitted to Md. bar, 1828; practiced law, Balt.; assisted father in editing Comml. Daily Advertiser, Cincinnati, 1831; editor Cincinnati Democratic Intelligencer; clk. U. S. Treasury Dept., Washington, D.C., circa 1841-46, collected library for Treasury Dept.; prof. rhetoric and English literature U. Ala., 1847-48; entered ministry Methodist Episcopal Ch., Cincinnati, 1850; literary editor Richmond (Va.) Enquirer, 1860; staff mem. Columbia South Carolinian; published 1st novel Clinton Bradshaw or the Adventures of a Lawyer, 2 vols., 1835 (published anonymously); other works include: East and West, 1836; An Autobiography of William Russell (novel), 1852. Died Washington, Aug. 27, 1866.

THOMAS, George, colonial gov.; b. Antiqua, B. W.I., circa 1695; s. Col. George and Sarah (Winthrop) T.; m. Elizabeth King, Apr. 18, 1717, 5 children. Dep. gov. of Pa. and Lower Counties (now Del.), 1737-47; involved in quarrel with Pa. Colonial Assembly over financial and mil. affairs in Pa., concluded treaties with Iroquois confederacy at Phila., 1742, at Lancaster, Pa., 1744; gov. Leeward Islands, 1753-66; created baronet, 1766, ret. to Eng. Died London, Eng., Dec. 31, 1774; buried Willingdon, Sussex, Eng.

THOMAS, George Henry, army officer; b. Southampton County, Va., July 31, 1816; s. John and Elizabeth (Rochelle) T.; grad. U.S. Mil. Acad., 1840; m. Frances Lucretia Kellogg, Nov. 17, 1852. Commd. 2d lt. 3d Arty., U.S. Army during Fla. War; brevetted 1st lt. for gallantry in action against Indians; served in several Southern garrisons; commd. 1st lt., 1844; served throughout Taylor's Mexican campaign; brevetted capt. and maj. for gallantry at battles of Monterey and Buena Vista; instr. arty. and cavalry U.S. Mil. Acad., 1851-54; commd. lt. col., 1861, col., 1861; commanded brigade in Shenandoah Valley; commd. brig. gen. U.S. Volunteers, 1861; assumed command 1st Div., Army of Ohio, 1861; won victory at Mill Springs, 1862; promoted maj. gen. volunteers, comdr. right wing of Halleck's army, 1862; commanded XIV Army Corps at Stone's River, 1862-63, became known as "the Rock of Chickamauga" as result of Battle of Chickamauga, 1863; promoted brig. gen. U.S. Army, 1863; Sherman's Atlanta campaign began, 1864, Thomas' Army of Cumberland participated in every offensive move; received surrender of Atlanta; ordered to Nashville, Tenn., 1864; defeated Hood near Nashville, 1864; promoted maj. gen. U.S. Army, 1865; received thanks of U.S. Congress, 1865; name sent by Pres. Johnson to Senate for promotion to rank of maj. gen. U.S. Army, and for brevets of lt. gen. and gen., 1868, declined ranks; assumed command Mil. Div. of Pacific, San Francisco, 1869. Died San Francisco, Mar. 28, 1870.

THOMAS, Griffith, architect; b. Isle of Wight, 1820; son of Thomas Thomas; ed. in Eng. Came to N.Y.C., 1838, entered his father's archtl. firm; designed many brown-stone residences, particularly on Fifth Av., N.Y.C. Prin. works include: U.S. Mortgage Co. Bldg. on Wall St., Greenwich Savs. Bank on 6th Av., N.Y. Life Ins. Bldg., Grand Opera House on 8th Av., Mt. Sinai Hosp., Fifth Av. Hotel, St. James, Nicholas hotels, Kemp Bldg., Singer Machine Co. Bldg., Duncan Bldg., Potter Bldg., Arnold Constable Store, Lord & Taylor's store (1st of iron comml. bldgs.), Dr. Spring's Brick Ch. on Fifth Av., Bapt. chs., Madison Av., 23d St. (all N.Y. C.). Died Jan. 11, 1878.

THOMAS, Isaac, congressman, lawyer; b. Sevierville, Tenn., Nov. 4, 1784; studied law. Admitted to bar, 1808, began practice law in Winchester, Tenn.; mem. U.S. Ho. of Reps. (Democrat) from Tenn., 14th Congress, 1815-17; moved to Alexandria, La., 1819, practiced law, became one of the largest landowners and slaveholders in La.; 1st man to introduce cultivation sugar cane Central La.; also mcht., operator sawmills, steamboats; served as brig. gen. La. Militia; mem. La. Senate, 1823-27; moved to Cal., 1849, returned to Alexandria. Died Alexandria, Feb. 2, 1859; buried Flint lot, Rapides Cemetery, Pineville, La.

THOMAS, Isaiah, publisher; b. Boston, Jan. 30, 1750; s. Moses and Fidelity (Grant) T.; A.M. (hon.), Dartmouth, 1814; LL.D. (hon.), Allegheny Coll., 1818; m. Mary Dill, Dec. 25, 1769; m. 2d, Mary Fowle Thomas, May 26, 1779; m. 3d, Rebecca Armstrong, Aug. 10, 1819; at least 2 children, Mary Anne, Isaiah. Learned printing trade at early age; printer Halifax (N.S., Can.) Gazette, 1766; employed with S.C. and Am. Gen. Gazette, Charleston; returned to Boston, founded (with Zechariah Fowle) Mass. Spy, 1770, became sole owner; driven from Boston by Brit. occupation, 1775, published Mass. Spy in various towns in Mass. during Revolutionary War (moved from town to town according to fortunes of war); became leading publisher in Am. after Revolution; published textbooks, almanacs, dictionaries, also mags. including Royal Am. Mag., 1774-75, Mass. Mag., 1789-96; founder, incorporator Am. Antiquarian Soc., 1812, became 1st pres.; postmaster Town of Worcester (Mass.), 1775-1801; noted for philanthropies. Author: The History of Printing in America, 2 vols., 1810. Died Worcester, Apr. 4, 1831.

THOMAS, James Houston, congressman, lawyer; b. Iredell County, N.C., Sept. 22, 1808; grad. Jackson Coll., Columbia, Tenn., 1830; studied law. Admitted to the bar, 1831, began practice law, Columbia, Tenn.; atty. gen. State of Tenn., 1836-42; mem. U.S. Ho. of Reps. (Democrat) from Tenn., 30th-31st, 36th congresses, 1847-51, 59-61. Died nr. Fayetteville, Tenn., Aug. 4, 1876; buried St. John's Cemetery, Ashwood, Tenn.

THOMAS, Jesse Burgess, senator; b. Shepherdstown, Va. (now W.Va.), 1777; s. Jesse and Sabina (Symmes) T.; studied law; m. Rebecca (Mackenzie) Hamtranck, Dec. 2, 1806. Clk., Mason County (Ky.), 1799-1803; elected to lower br. Ind. Territorial Legislature, 1805, speaker 3 years; apptd. capt. Dearborn County (Ind.) Militia, 1805; elected Ind. territorial del. to U.S. Ho. of Reps., 1808, worked for div. of Ind. Territory; U.S. judge for Ill. Territory (apptd. by Pres. Madison), circa 1809-18; pres. 1st Ill. Constl. Conv., 1818; mem. U.S. Senate from Ill., Dec. 3, 1818-29, introduced amendment prohibiting slavery North of line 36° 30', (embodied in Mo. Compromise); moved to Mt. Vernon, O., 1829; del. Whig Nat. Conv., 1839, nominated William H. Harrison for U.S. Pres.; set up 1st wool-carding machine in Ill., 1817. Died Mt. Vernon, May 3, 1853; buried Mound View Cemetery.

THOMAS, John, army officer; b. Marshfield, Mass., Nov. 9, 1724; s. John and Lydia (Waterman) T.; m. Hannah Thomas, 1761, 3 children. Commd. lt. and surgeon's mate, 1755, empowered to enlist volunteers in province; served in N.S. and in expdn. dispatched to Can. under Amherst, 1759-60; apptd. by Gov. Hutchinson as justice of peace, Kingston, Mass., 1770; commd. lt. gen. Mass. Militia, 1775; commd. brig. gen. by Continental Congress, 1775; in command at Roxbury (important post in Am. siege lines) winter 1775-76; seized and fortified strategic site of Dorchester (Mass.), 1776, as result British were forced to evacuate Boston; promoted maj. gen. and ordered North, 1776; summoned council of war at Quebec, Can., 1776, unanimously decided to retreat and fell back to Sorel. Died of smallpox, June 2, 1776; buried Chambly, Que.

THOMAS, John Chew, congressman, lawyer; b. Perryville, Md., Oct. 15, 1764; grad. U. Pa., 1783; studied law. Admitted to bar in Phila., 1787, did not engage in active practice law; mem. U.S. Ho. of Reps. (Federalist) from Md., 6th Congress, 1799-1801; moved to Pa. Died nr. Leiperville, Pa., May 10, 1836; buried Friends Cemetery, nr. Chester, Pa.

THOMAS, John Jacobs, pomologist, writer; b. Ledyard, N.Y., Jan. 8, 1810; s. David and Hannah (Jacobs) T. Owned nurseries successively at Palmyra, Macedon and Union Springs, N.Y.; became asst. editor Genesee Farmer, 1838; an editor New Genesee Farmer and Gardener's Jour., 1840-41; asso. editor Country Gentleman, 1853-94; organized Am. Pomol. Congress, 1855; classified fruits according to various characteristics; wrote The American Fruit Culturist (became textbook in horticulture), 1849, Farm Implements and Machinery, 1854; editor 9 volumes entitled Rural Affairs, 1869-81. Died Feb. 22, 1895.

THOMAS, John Lewis, Jr., congressman, lawyer; b. Balt., May 20, 1835; studied law. Admitted to the bar, 1856, began practice law, Cumberland, Md.; city counselor Cumberland, 1856-57; moved to Balt., 1857, practiced law; city solicitor of Balt., 1860-62; del. Md. Constl. Conv., 1863; state's atty., 1863-65; mem. U.S. Ho. of Reps. (Republican, filled vacancy) from Md., 39th Congress, Dec. 4, 1865-67; collector Port of Balt., 1869-73, 77-82. Died Balt., Oct. 15, 1893; buried Greenmount Cemetery.

THOMAS, Joseph, lexiocgrapher; b. Ledyard, N. Y., Sept. 23, 1811; s. David and Hannah (Jacobs) T.; A.B., Rensselaer Poly Inst., 1830; attended Yale, 1832; M.D., U. Pa., 1837; never married. Taught Latin and Greek, Haverford Coll., 1833-34; asso. with J. B. Lippincott and Co., Phila., 1854-71, edited series of reference books A New and Complete Gazetteer of the United States, 1844, Lippincott's Pronouncing Gazetteer: A Complete Geographical Dictionary of the World, 1855, A Comprehensive Medical Dictionary, 1864; founder (with Edward Parrish) of Swarthmore Coll., 1866, gave 1st series of lectures in English literature, 1874-75, prof. English, 1874-87. Died Dec. 24, 1891.

THOMAS, Lorenzo, army officer; b. New Castle, Del., Oct. 1804; s. Evan and Elizabeth (Sherer) T.; grad. U.S. Mil. Acad., 1823. Commd. maj. 4th Inf., U.S. Army, 1848; quartermaster in Seminole War, 1836-37; adjutant-gen., Washington, D.C., 1838; brevetted maj. 1846-53; joined volunteer div. of Maj. Gen. William O. Butler as chief of staff in Mexican War; designated chief of staff to Lt. Gen. Winfield Scott, 1853; promoted to col. in charge adjutant's office, 1861; made adjutant-gen., given rank brig. gen., 1861-63; organized Negro regts. in Mississippi Valley, 1863-65; brevetted maj. gen., 1865; after adjutant-gen. resumed full charge of bureaus, 1868; sec. ad interim for Johnson, 1868; arrested for violation of Tenure of Office Act, 1868, immediately admitted to bail and discharged; ret. 1869. Died Washington, D.C., Mar. 2, 1875.

THOMAS, Philemon, congressman; b. Orange County, Va., Feb. 9, 1763; attended common schs. Served in Revolutionary War; moved to Mason County, Ky.; del. conv. which framed Ky. Constn.; mem. Ky. Ho. of Reps., 1796-99; mem. Ky. Senate, 1800-03; moved to La., 1806; mem. La. Ho. of Reps.; leader of an uprising against Spanish authorities who controlled Miss. and La., comdr. forces which captured Spanish fort at Bston Rouge, 1810; served in War of 1812; maj. gen. La. Militia, 1814-15; mem. U.S. Ho. of Reps. (Democrat) from La., 22d-23d congresses, 1831-35. Died Baton Rouge, Nov. 18, 1847; buried Old Am. Graveyard, reinterred Nat. Cemetery, Baton Rouge.

THOMAS, Philip Evan, railroad pioneer; b. Mt. Radnor, Montgomery County, Md., Nov. 11, 1776; s. Evan and Rachel (Hopkins) T.; m. Elizabeth George, Apr. 20, 1801, 7 children. Hardware mcht., Balt., 1800; pres. Mechanics' Bank, Balt. by 1827; Md. commr. reviving project of Chesapeake and Ohio Canal, 1826-27; leading promoter B. & O. R.R. (incorporated 1827; 2d railroad charter in U.S. to carry passengers), pres., dir., 1827-36; pres. Mech. Fire Co.; 1st pres. Md. Bible Soc.; mem. Soc. of Friends. Died Yonkers, N.Y., Sept. 1, 1861.

THOMAS, Philip Francis, gov. Md., sec. of treasury; b. Easton, Talbot County, Md., Sept. 12, 1810; s. Tristan and Maria (Francis) T.; grad. Dickinson Coll., 1830; m. Sarah Maria Kerr, Feb. 5, 1835; m. 2d, Clintonia (Wright) May, Jan. 29, 1876; 13 children. Admitted to Md. bar, 1831; del. Md. Constl. Conv., 1836; mem. Md. Ho. of Dels., 1838, circa 1840-43, 43-45, 63, 78, 83; mem. U.S. Ho. of Reps. from Md, 26th, 44th congresses, 1839-41, 75-77; judge Land Office Ct. Eastern Shore, 1841; gov. Md. (Democrat), 1848-51; practiced law, St. Louis, circa 1850-57; comptroller U.S. Treasury, 1851-53; collector Port of Balt., 1853-60; U.S. commr. of patents, 1860; U.S. sec. of treasury, 1860-61; elected mem. U.S. Senate from Md. for term 1867-68, denied seat on charge of disloyalty; mem. Md. Assembly, 1878, 84; del. to Md. Democratic Conv., 1883. Died Balt., Oct. 2, 1890; buried Spring Hill Cemetery, Easton.

THOMAS, Richard, congressman; b. West Whiteland, Pa., Dec. 30, 1744; ed. by pvt. tchrs. Served as col. 1st Regt., Chester County Volunteers, Continental Army, Revolutionary War; mem. U.S. Ho. of Reps. (Federalist) from Pa., 4th-6th congresses, 1795-1801; farmer. Died Phila., Jan. 19, 1832; buried Friends Western Burial Ground.

THOMAS, Robert Bailey, editor, publisher; b. Grafton, Mass., Apr. 24, 1766; s. William and Azabah (Goodale) T.; self educated; attended mathematics school run by Osgood Carleton, almanacmaker, Boston, 1790-92; m. Hannah Beamon, Nov. 17, 1803. Started The Farmer's Almanack . . . for the Year of Our Lord 1793, 1792-1846, afterwards called The Farmer's Almanack, later The Old Farmer's Almanack, had wide range of topics including patriotic, geographic and epigrammatic materials; memoir of his life appeared in Almanack, 1833-37, 39. Died West Boylston, Mass., May 19, 1846.

THOMAS, Seth, pioneer clock mfr.; b. Wolcott, Conn., Aug. 19, 1785; s. James and Martha (Barnes) T.; m. Philena Tuttler, Apr. 20, 1808; m. 2d, Laura Andrews, Apr. 14, 1811; 6 children, including Seth. Manufactured clocks in partnerships with Eli Terry and Silas Hoadley, 1807-12; purchased mfg. rights to Terry's clock, 1814, built highly successful business, incorporated as Seth Thomas Clock Co., 1853; the factory portion of Plymouth (Conn.) became new town called Thomaston in his honor. Died Plymouth, Jan. 29, 1859.

THOMASSON, William Poindexter, congressman, lawyer; b. New Castle, Ky., Oct. 8, 1797; studied law. Served in Capt. Duncan's Co., War of 1812; admitted to the bar, began practice law in Corydon, Ind., before age 21; mem. Ind. Ho. of Reps., 1818-20; pros. atty. Corydon, 1818; moved to Louisville, Ky., 1841; mem. U.S. Ho. of Reps. (Whig) from Ky., 28th-29th congresses, 1843-47; moved to Chgo., practiced law; served with 71st Regt., N.Y. Volunteer Inf., U.S. Army, Civil War. Died nr. LaGrange, Ky., Dec. 29, 1882; buried Cave Hill Cemetery, Louisville.

THOMES, William Henry, author; b. Portland, Me., May 5, 1824; s. Job and Mary (Lewis) T.; attended pub. schs. Boston; married, 1847; m. 2d, Frances Allen, 1850. Shipped on Admittance in the Cal. hide-trade, 1842, left Cal., 1846; printer, reporter Boston Daily News, 1847; sailed for Hawaiian Islands, 1851, visited Guam, P.I., China, gold mines in Victoria, returning to U.S. by way of Cape of Good Hope, 1855; reporter Boston Herald, circa 1857-60; partner Elliot and Thomes, publishers of American Union weekly, 1860; partner successively of Elliott, Thomes and Talbot, then Thomes and Talbot, publishers Flag of Our Union, Ballou's Monthly. Author: The Gold Hunters' Adventures; or Life in Australia, 1866, The Bushrangers (sequel), 1866; A Whaleman's Adventures, 1871; The Gold-Hunters in Europe, 1872. Died Boston, Mar. 6, 1895.

THOMPSON, Alfred Wordsworth, painter; b. Balt., May 26, 1840. Opened studio in Balt., 1861, drew many war pictures; went to Paris, 1861, studied art, worked at Ecole des Beaux Arts, 1864-65; returned to U.S., opened studio, 1868; one of 1st mems. Soc. Am. Artists, 1877; elected as mem. N.A.D., 1875, regularly sent pictures to Nat. Acad. exhibits; exhibited On the Sands, East Hampton at Centennial Exhbn., Phila., 1876; best known works include Annapolis in 1776 (Albright Art Gallery, Buffalo, N.Y.), The Parting Guests (N.Y. Hist. Soc.). Died Summit, N.J., Aug. 28, 1896.

THOMPSON, Benjamin (Count Rumford), physicist, philanthropist; b. Woburn, Mass., Mar. 26, 1753; s. Benjamin and Ruth (Simonds) T.; m. Sarah (Walker) Rolfe, Nov. 1772; m. 2d, Madame Lavoisier (Marie Anne Pierrette), Oct. 24, 1805; at least 1 child, Sarah. Commd. maj. 2d N.H. Provincial Regt., 1773; applied for commn. in Washington's army but was refused, 1775; left for London, 1775; apptd. to secretaryship Province of Ga.; elected fellow Royal Soc., 1779; under-sec. state Northern Dept., 1780; commd. lt. col. Brit. Army for service in Am., circa 1781; engaged in acton nr. Charleston, S.C., 1782; served as commdr. regt. on L.I., until 1783; knighted, 1784; in service of Bavaria, 1784-95, col. of cavalry and gen. aide-de-camp, 1784; maj. gen., head war dept. of Bavaria, 1788; elected to academies of Berlin, Munich, Mannheim; elector of Bavaria gave him title Count Rumford, 1791; returned to Eng., 1795; published 1st volume Essays, Political, Economical, and Philosophical, 1796, 3d edit., 2 vols., 1798, 5th edit., 3 vols., 1880, 4th vol. added, 1802; installed non-smoking, more efficient fireplaces in 150 homes in London; established Rumford prize and medal for discovery or improvement on heat or light, 1796; presented $5,000 to Am. Acad. Arts and Sciences (became fgn. hon. mem., 1789), for most important discovery in same fields, 1796; head council of regency, prevented French and Austrian armies from entering neutral city of Munich, 1796; head dept. gen. police of Bavaria; Royal Instn. incorporated as outcome of Rumford's proposals, 1800; elected fgn. asso. Inst. of France, 1803; developed calorimeter and photometer; improved lamps and illumination. Died Auteuil, nr. Paris, France, Aug. 21, 1814.

THOMPSON, Benjamin, congressman; b. Charlestown, Mass., Aug. 5, 1798; attended pub. schs. Became a mcht.; mem. Mass. Ho. of Reps., 1830-31, 33-36; mem. Mass. Senate, 1841; mem. U.S. Ho. of Reps. (Whig) from Mass. 29th, 32d congresses, 1845-47, 51-52. Died Charlestown, Sept. 24, 1852; buried Congressional Cemetery, Washington, D.C.

THOMPSON, Cephas Giovanni, painter; b. Middleboro, Mass., Aug. 3, 1809; s. Cephas and Olive (Leonard) T.; m. Mary Gouveneur Ogden, Dec. 1843, 3 children. Conducted studio, N.Y.C., 1837-52, 59; mem. clique of William Cullen Bryant; painted portraits, copied old masters, Rome, Italy, 1852-59; works remembered for historic importance; elected asso. N.A.D., several portraits acquired by N.Y. Hist. Soc. Died N.Y.C., Jan. 5, 1888; buried Church of the New Jerusalem, N.Y.C.

THOMPSON, Charles Oliver, engr., educator; b. East Windsor Hill, Conn., Sept. 25, 1836; s. Rev. William and Eliza (Butler) T.; B.A., Dartmouth, 1858, Ph.D. (hon.), 1870; m. Maria Goodrich, May 14, 1862, 3 children. Prin., Peacham Acad., circa 1858-64, Cotting High Sch., Arlington, Mass., 1864-68, Worcester County Free Inst. of Indsl. Science (later Worcester Poly. Inst.), 1868; made European trip, 1868, resulted in innovations in Am. tech. edn. such as mech. arts course equipped with workshop; one of 1st to introduce shop practice in engring. teaching; organizer, 1st pres. Rose Poly. Inst., Terre Haute, Ind., 1883-85; mem. A.A.A.S. Author: Hints Toward a Profession of Teaching, 1867; Manual Training in the Public School. Died Terre Haute, Mar. 17, 1885.

THOMPSON, Charles Perkins, congressman, lawyer; b. Braintree, Mass., July 30, 1827; attended Hollis Inst. of Braintree, Amherst (Mass.) Coll.; studied law. Admitted to bar, 1854, began practice law in Gloucester, Mass., 1857; mem. Mass. Ho. of Reps., 1871-72; del. Democratic Nat. Conv., Balt., 1872; mem. U.S. Ho. of Reps. (Democrat) from Mass., 44th Congress, 1875-77; city solicitor Gloucester, 1874-75, 77, 79; unsuccessful Democratic candidate for gov. Mass., 1880, 81; judge Superior Ct. of Mass., 1885-94. Died Gloucester, Jan. 19, 1894; buried Oak Grove Cemetery.

THOMPSON, Daniel Pierce, state legislator, author; b. Charlestown, Mass., Oct. 1, 1795; s. Daniel and Rebecca (Praker) T.; grad. Middlebury Coll., 1820; m. Eunice Knight Robinson, Aug. 31, 1831, 6 children. Admitted to Va. bar, 1823; practiced in Montpelier, Vt.; judge probate for Washington County (Vt.), 1837-40, 41-42; mem. Vt. Supreme Ct., 1843-45; Vt. sec. state, 1853-55; complied The Laws of Vermont . . . Including the Year 1834, 1835; a founder Vt. Hist. Soc.; prominent in Liberty Party, 1849-56, later Republican Party; edited Green Mountain Freeman (weekly anti-slavery paper); described Vt.'s early history in novels, including The Green Mountain Boys (best known), 1839; Locke Amsden, 1847; Tales of the Green Mountains, 1852. Died Montpelier, June 6, 1868.

THOMPSON, David, explorer, geographer, fur trader; b. London, Eng., Apr. 30, 1770; s. David and Ann (Thompson) T.; attended Oxford (Eng.) U.; m. Charlotte Small, June 1799, 13 children. Came to Am., circa 1784; apprenticed to Hudson's Bay Co.; with Hudson's Bay Co. and N.W. Co. making records of all travels for 25 years, served in Western Can., 1789-1812; discovered new route to Lake Athabasca; discovered Turtle Lake, claimed source of Mississippi River, Apr. 27, 1798; marked crossing 49, by Red River; surveyed No. source of Mississippi River and course of St. Louis River to Lake Superior, 1798; discovered Columbia River, 1807, surveyed Columbia River from source to mouth, 1811; in charge Brit. Commn. to mark boundary of U.S. and Can. from St. Lawrence River West to Lake of the Woods, 1816-26. David Thompson's Narrative of his Explorations in Western America published in vol. XII of Champlain Soc. Publications, 1916. Died Longueil, Montreal, Que., Can., Feb. 10, 1857; buried Mt. Royal Cemetery, Montreal.

THOMPSON, Egbert, naval officer; b. N.Y.C., June 6, 1822; s. Egbert and Catherine (Dibble) T.; m. Emily B. Thompson, at least 1 dau. Served with Wilkes Exploring Expdn. in Antarctic, 1838-42; passed midshipman, 1843; in brig Somers; exec. in schooner Bonita during Mexican War; joined Adm. Foote's Miss. flotilla, 1862; commanded gunboat Pittsburg in attack on Ft. Donelson, 1862; ran heavy batteries at Island Number 10 in Mississippi River to aid Polk's army below; commanded ships Commodore, McDonough, later Cimarron on blockade duty, 1864-65; commd. capt., 1867; commanded Dacotah, 1866-67, Canandaigua, 1871-72. Died Washington, D.C., Jan. 5, 1881.

TMOMPSON, George Western, congressman, lawyer; b. St. Clairsville, O., May 14, 1806; grad. Jefferson (now Washington and Jefferson) Coll., Pa., 1824; studied law, Richmond, Va. Admitted to bar, 1826, began practice law, St. Clairsville, 1828; moved to western Va., 1837; apptd. dep. postmaster at Wheeling, 1838; apptd. to commn. to settle jurisdiction of Ohio River between Va. and Ohio; U.S. atty. for western dist. Va., 1848-50; mem. U.S. Ho. of Reps. (Democrat) from Va., 32d Congress, 1851-July 30, 1852 (resigned); judge circuit ct. of Va., 1852-61 (removed from office on refusal to take oath of office to support what he considered unconstl. action to set up present state of W.Va.); ret. from practice law. Died on estate, Wheeling, W.Va., Feb. 24, 1888; buried Elm Grove Cemetery, Wheeling.

THOMPSON, Hedge, congressman, physician; b. Salem, N.J., Jan. 28, 1780; grad. med. dept. U. Pa., 1802. Began practice medicine, Salem; mem. N.J. Gen. Assembly, 1805; mem. N.J. Council, 1819; apptd. asso. justice Salem County, N.J., 1815, 24; collector for Salem County, 1826-28; mem. U.S. Ho. of Reps. from N.J., 20th Congress, 1827-28. Died Salem, July 23, 1828; buried St. John's P.E. Churchyard.

THOMPSON, Jacob, congressman, cabinet officer; b. Leasburg, N.C., May 15, 1810; s. Nicholas and Lucretia (Van Hook) T.; grad. U. N.C., 1831; m. Catherine Jones. Admitted to N.C. bar, 1834; practiced law in Pantotoc, Miss.; mem. U.S. Ho. of Reps. from Miss., 26th-31st congresses, 1839-51; played important part in Nat. Democratic convs., 1854, 56; U.S. sec. of interior, 1857-61, reorganized dept. to increase efficiency; served with Confederate Army until 1863, chief insp. of army under Pemberton; elected to Miss. Legislature, 1863; sent to Can. as Confederate secret agt., 1864, cooperated with "Sons of Liberty," sought to free Confederate soldiers imprisoned nr. Gt. Lakes; took part in plans to burn No. cities including N.Y.C.; charged with complicity in Lincoln's assasination; lived in Can. and Europe until 1868; returned to Oxford, Miss., 1868. Died Memphis, Tenn., Mar. 24, 1885; buried Elmwood Cemetery, Memphis.

THOMPSON, James, congressman, jurist; b. Middlesex, Pa., Oct. 1, 1806; learned printer's trade; studied law. Admitted to bar, 1829, began practice law in Erie, Pa.; mem. Pa. Ho. of Reps., 1832-34, 55, speaker, 1834; Democratic presdl. elector, 1836; del. Pa. Constl. Conv., 1838; presiding judge 6th Jud. Dist. Ct., 1838-44; mem. U.S. Ho. of Reps. (Democrat) from Pa., 29th-31st congresses, 1845-51; asso. justice Supreme Ct. of Pa., 1857-66, chief justice, 1866-72; resumed practice law. Died Phila., Jan. 28, 1874; buried Woodlands Cemetery.

THOMPSON, Jeremiah, mcht., ship owner; b. Rawdon, Yorkshire, Eng., Dec. 9, 1784; s. William Thompson. Came to N.Y., 1801; began business on own account and also joint owner of mcht. ship Pacific (1815), Amity (1816), Courier (1817) added to line of packets employed in regular sailings to Liverpool, Eng.; organized 1st line of Am. packets to make scheduled sailings from Am. to Liverpool, Eng., 1818, doubled fleet to provide bi-monthly service, called "Old Line of Packets," 1822; an organizer packet lines from N.Y. to Belfast and Greenock, also Phila. to Liverpool; owner largest ship holdings in U.S., most extensive cotton dealer in world by 1827; became insolvent, 1828, but participated in formation Union line of packets for steerage passengers only, 1828; founded emigrant packet office, 1831, led to formation of Black Star line of packets and Guion line of steamships. Died N.Y.C., Nov. 10, 1835.

THOMPSON, Jerome B., painter; b. Middleboro, Mass., Jan. 30, 1814; s. Cephas and Olive (Leonard) T.; studied painting in Eng., 1852; m. Maria Louisa Colden, Mar. 23, 1839; m. 2d, Marie May Tupper, Apr. 19, 1876; 1 child. Established himself as sign and ornamental painter, Barnstable, Mass.; Daniel Webster sat for him; established farm, Mineola, L.I., N.Y., 1853, gained reputation as gardener; paintings include: The Old Oaken Bucket; Coming Through the Rye; Home, Sweet Home. Died Glen Gardens N.J., May 1, 1886.

THOMPSON, Joel, congressman, lawyer; b. Stanford, N.Y., Oct. 3, 1760; studied law. Admitted to bar, practiced law in Duanesburg and Sherburne, N. Y.; served in Continental Army, 1779-80; mem. N. Y. State Assembly, 1798, 1803-04; asst. justice Chenango County Ct. of Common Pleas, 1799-1807, judge of Chenango County, 1807-14; mem. U.S. Ho. of Reps. (Federalist) from N.Y., 13th Congress, 1813-15; resumed practice law, Sherburne. Died Bklyn., Feb. 8, 1843; buried Greenwood Cemetery.

THOMPSON, John, congressman, jurist; b. Litchfield, Conn., Mar. 20, 1749; attended common schs. Apptd. justice Still Water Twp., N.Y., 1788; mem. N.Y. State Assembly, 1788-89; mem. U.S. Ho. of Reps. (Democrat) from N.Y., 6th, 10th, 11th congresses, 1799-1801, 07-11; del. N.Y. Constl. Conv., 1801; apptd. by gov. as 1st judge of Saratoga County, N.Y., 1791-1809. Died Stillwater, N.Y., 1823; buried Stillwater.

THOMPSON, John, banker, publisher; b. Portridgefield, Mass., Nov. 2, 1802; s. Amherst and Sarah (Clarke) T.; attended Harley Acad., Mass.; m. Electra Ferris, 1829, at least 3 children. Opened brokerage office on Wall Street, N.Y.C., 1833; began periodical pub. Thompson's Bank Note and Comml. Reporter which gave facts on notes of So. and Western banks, 1842; received charter for 1st Nat. Bank, N.Y.C., 1863, pres., 1863-77; founder (with sons) Chase Nat. Bank, 1877, pres., 1884. Died N.Y.C., Apr. 19, 1891.

THOMPSON, John, congressman, lawyer; b. Rhinebeck, N.Y., July 4, 1809; grad. Union Coll., Schenectady, N.Y.; grad. Yale; studied law. Admitted to the bar, began practice law, Poughkeepsie, N.Y.; mem. U.S. Ho. of Reps. (Republican) from N.Y., 35th Congress, 1857-59. Died New Hamburg, N.Y., June 1, 1890. buried Poughkeepsie Rural Cemetery, Poughkeepsie.

THOMPSON, John Burton, senator, congressman, lawyer; b. nr. Harrodsburg, Ky., Dec. 14, 1810; studied law. Admitted to the bar, practiced law, Harrodsburg; commonwealth atty.; mem. Ky. Senate, 1829-33; mem. Ky. Ho. of Reps., 1835, 37;

mem. U.S. Ho. of Reps. (Whig) from Ky., (filled vacancy) 26th-27th, 30th-31st congresses, Dec. 7, 1840-43, 47-51; lt. gov. State of Ky., 1852; mem. U.S. Senate from Ky., 1853-59. Died Harrodsburg, Jan. 7, 1874; buried Spring Hill Cemetery.

THOMPSON, John Reuben, editor, poet, journalist; b. Richmond, Va., Oct. 23, 1823; s. John and Sarah (Dyckman) T.; attended U. Va., 1840-42, LL.B., 1845; Owner, Literary Messenger, 1847-53, editor, 1853-60, published works of leading Southern writers, 1859, printed travel sketches by Derby and Jackson with title Across the Atlantic, 1856; editor weekly publ. So. Field and Fireside, 1860-61; asst. sec. Commonwealth of Va., 1861-64, helped edit Richmond Record and Illustrated News; chief writer Index (organ of Confederate opinion in Eng.), 1864-65; prepared "Memoirs of the Confederate War for Independence" for Blackwood's Edinburgh Magazine, 1865-66, published in 2 vols., 1866; went to U.S., 1866; Am. corr. for London Standard; apptd. by William Cullen Bryant to lit. editorship New York Evening Post, 1867-73. Collected poetical works published as Poems (edited by John S. Patton), 1920. Died N.Y.C., Apr. 30, 1873; buried Hollywood Cemetery, Richmond, Va.

THOMPSON, Joseph Parrish, clergyman, editor, author; b. Phila., Aug. 7, 1819; s. Isaac and Mary Anne (Hanson) T.; grad. Yale, 1838; D.D. (hon.), Harvard, 1856; LL.D. (hon.), U. N.Y., 1868; m. Lucy Olivia Bartlett, May 5, 1841; m. 2d, Elizabeth Coit Gilman, Oct. 25, 1853, 6 children including William Gilman, John Hanson. Ordained to ministry Congregational Ch., 1840; pastor Chapel Street Ch., Oct. 28, 1840-45, Broadway Tabernacle, N.Y., 1845-71; a leader home missionary movement, 1852; promoter Albany Conglist. Conf.; helped Leonard Bacon found New Englander, circa 1844; mem. editorial bd. Independent, 1848-62; retired and moved to Berlin, Germany, 1871; lectured in Eng., Scotland, Germany, Switzerland, France, Italy. Author: The College as a Religious Institution, 1859; Man in Genesis and Geology, 1869; Church and State in the United States, 1873; The United States as a Nation, 1877. Died Berlin, Sept. 20, 1879; buried Jerusalem Church, Berlin.

THOMPSON, Launt, sculptor; b. Abbeyleix, Ireland, Feb. 8, 1833; A.M. (hon.), Yale; m. Maria L. Potter, Sept. 1869. Came to U.S., 1847; studio in N.Y.C., 1857-75; made productions in relief, portrait busts and statues; asso. N.A.D., 1859, full mem. 1862; exhibited at Paris Expn., 1867; had studio in Italy, 1875-81; executed statue Abraham Pierson erected on Yale campus,, 1874, bronze figure of Gen. Winfield Scott at Old Soldiers' Home, Washington, D.C.; best-known medallions include Morning Glory, John H. Dix; busts include William C. Bryant, James Gordon Bennett the elder, Edwin Booth; statues include Ambrose E. Burnside, Providence, R.I., John Sedgwick, West Point, N.Y., Napoleon I, Milford, Pa. Died Middletown, N.Y., Sept. 26, 1894.

THOMPSON, Martin E., architect; b. circa 1786. Commd. to design 2d Bank of U.S. on Wall Street, N.Y.C., 1822-23, later U.S. Assay office, then facade of South front of Am. wing of Met. Mus. of Art; designed Merchants' Exchange, completed 1827; in partnership with Ithiel Town, 1827-28, their office known as Architectural Room, contained Town's extensive library of architectural books and engravings; built Church of the Ascension, 1828, tower and spire of St. Mark's Ch. in Bowery; a founder N.A.D., 1826; designer Columbia Grammar Sch., begun 1829; submitted design for Ohio State Capitol at Columbus, 1839; street commr. of N.Y.C., 1847-50; made plans for enlarging N.Y.C. City Hall, circa 1840's. Died N.Y.C., July 24, 1877.

THOMPSON, Philip, congressman, lawyer; b. on Shawnee Run, nr. Harrodsburg, Ky., Aug. 20, 1789; studied law. Served as lt., War of 1812; held several local offices; admitted to the bar, began practice law, Hartford Ky.; moved to Owensboro, Ky.; mem. Ky. Ho. of Reps.; mem. U.S. Ho. of Reps. from Ky., 18th Congress, 1823-25. Died Owensboro, Nov. 25, 1836; buried Moseley burying ground on Fifth St., reinterred Rural Hill (later Elmwood) Cemetery, 1856.

THOMPSON, Philip Rootes, congressman, lawyer; b. nr. Fredericksburg, Va., Mar. 26, 1766; grad. Coll. of William and Mary; studied law. Admitted to bar, began practice law in Fairfax, Va.; mem. Va. Ho. of Dels., 1793-97; mem. U.S. Ho. of Reps. (Democrat) from Va., 7th-9th congresses, 1801-07. Died Kanawha County, Va. (now W.Va.), July 27, 1837; buried Coals Mouth (now St. Albans), W.Va.

THOMPSON, Robert Augustine, congressman, lawyer; b. nr. Culpeper Court House, Va., Feb. 14, 1805; attended U. Va.; studied law; at least 1 son, Thomas Larkin. Admitted to the bar, 1826, began practice law, Charleston, Va. (now W.Va.); mem. Va. Senate, 1839-46; Democratic presdl. elector, 1844; mem. U.S. Ho. of Reps. (Democrat) from Va., 30th Congress, 1847-49; del. Democratic Nat. Conv., Balt., 1852; mem. bd. visitors U. Va., 1852; moved to San Francisco, Cal., 1853; apptd. mem. commn. to settle pvt. land claims in Cal., 1853; apptd. reporter Cal. Supreme Ct., 1870; mem. justices' ct. of San Francisco, 1870-76. Died San Francisco, Aug. 31, 1876; buried Laurel Hill Cemetery.

THOMPSON, Samuel Rankin, scientist, coll. dean; b. South Shenango, Pa., Apr. 17, 1833; s. William and Mary (Latta) T.; B.A., Westminster Coll., New Wilmington, Pa., 1863, M.A., 1881; m. Lucy Gilmour, 1859, 1 dau. Began teaching in Clarion County, Pa.; taught sch. in Neb., 1848-56 (except 1854-55); supt. Crawford County (Pa.) Schs., 1860-65; prof. natural scis., vice prin. State Normal Sch., Ellenboro, Pa., 1865-67; prin. Pottsville (Pa.) High Sch., 1868; organized state normal sch. at Marshall Coll., Huntington, W. Va., 1869-71; became prof. agr. U. Neb., 1871, 1st dean Coll. of Agr., 1872-75; prin. Neb State Normal Sch., Peru, 1876-77, prof. agr. and didactics, 1882-84; returned to Westminster Coll. as prof. physics, 1884-96. Died New Wilmington, Oct. 28, 1896.

THOMPSON, Smith, asso. justice U.S. Supreme Ct., sec. navy; b. Amenia, N.Y., Jan 17, 1768; s. Ezra and Rachel (Smith) T.; grad. Coll. of N.J. (Princeton), 1788; m. Sarah Livingston, 1744; m. 2d, Eliza Livingston, 1836. Admitted to N.Y. bar, 1792; mem. N.Y. State Legislature, 1800; mem. N.Y. Constl. Conv., 1801; asso. justice N.Y. Supreme Ct., 1802-14, chief justice, 1814-18; U.S. sec. of navy, 1819-23; became asso. justice U.S. Supreme Ct., 1824, opposed nationalism of John Marshall, voted to overrule Marshall in Ogden vs. Saunders (12 Wheaton, 214), wrote strong concurring opinion upholding validity of state bankruptcy law, 1827, spoke for Court in Kendall vs. U.S. (12 Peters, 524), upheld right of fed. courts to require cabinet officer by mandamus to perform ministerial duty, 1838; regent U. State of N.Y., 1813. Died Poughkeepsie, N.Y., Dec. 18, 1843.

THOMPSON, Thomas Larkin, diplomat, journalist; b. Charleston, Va. (now W. Va.), May 31, 1838; s. Robert Augustine and Mary (Slaughter) T.; m. Marian Satterlee, 1859, 5 children. Worked on San Francisco Herald, 1856-58; established, edited Petaluma (Cal.) Weekly Jour. and Sonoma County Advertiser, 1855-56; published Sonoma Democrat, Santa Rosa, Cal., 1860-68, became owner, 1871; publisher weekly Solano Democrat, 1860-68; published Vallejo (Cal.) Daily Independent, 1868-73; del. Democratic nat. convs., Cincinnati, 1880, Chgo., 1892; sec. state Cal., 1882-86; mem. U.S. Ho. of Reps. (Democrat) from Cal., 50th Congress, 1887-89; commr. from Cal. to Columbian Exposition, Chgo., 1893; U.S. minister to Brazil (apptd. by Pres. Cleveland), 1893-97, remained impartial to Brazilian Revolt in 1893, cooperated with U.S. naval officers to protect and continue Am. commerce without interruption, negotiated and signed extradition treaty for U.S. with Brazil (ratified 1903). Died Santa Rosa, Cal., Feb. 1, 1898; buried Rural Cemetery, Santa Rosa.

THOMPSON, Thomas Weston, senator, congressman, lawyer; b. Boston, Mar. 15, 1766; attended Dummer Acad.; grad. Harvard, 1786; studied law. Admitted to the bar, 1791, practiced law, Salisbury, N.H., 1791-1810; postmaster Salisbury, 1798-1803; trustee Dartmouth, 1801-21; moved to Concord, N. H., 1810, practiced law; mem. N.H. Ho. of Reps., 1807-08, 13-14, speaker, 1813-14; mem. U.S. Ho. of Reps. from N.H., 9th Congress, 1805-07; treas. State of N.H., 1809-11; mem. U.S. Senate (filled vacancy) from N.H., June 24, 1814-17. Died Concord, Oct. 1, 1821; buried Old North Cemetery.

THOMPSON, Waddy, diplomat, congressman; b. Pickensville, S.C., Sept. 8, 1798; s. Waddy and Eliza (Blackburn) T.; grad. S.C. Coll. (now U. of S.C.), 1814; m. Emmala Butler, circa 1820; m. 2d, Cornelia Jones, 1851; at least 1 child. Admitted to S.C. bar, 1819; mem. S.C. Legislature, 1826-30; chosen solicitor for Western Dist. by S.C. Legislature, 1830; became ardent nullifier; brig. gen. S.C. Militia organized against fed. interference, circa 1832-42; mem. U.S. Ho. of Reps. (Whig) from S.C., 24th-26th congresses, Sept. 10, 1835-41; U.S. minister to Mexico, 1842-44, obtained release of 300 prisoners (mostly U.S. citizens) captured in Tex.-Mexico war; opposed Mexican War; practiced law, Greenville, S.C., until 1867; moved to Fla., 1867. Died Tallahassee, Fla., Nov. 23, 1868; buried Madison, Fla.

THOMPSON, Wiley, congressman, Indian agt.; b. Amelia County, Va., Sept. 23, 1781; s. Isham and Elizabeth (Williams) T.; m. Mrs. Ellington. Commr., Elbert County (Ga.) Acad., 1808; maj. gen. 4th Div., Ga. Militia, 1817-24; mem. Ga. Senate, 1817-19; mem. commn. to determine boundary of Ga. and East Fla., 1819; mem. U.S. Ho. of Reps. from Ga., 17th-22d congresses, 1821-33; del. to Ga. Constl. Conv., 1833; apptd. agt. Seminole Indians in Fla., circa 1833, ordered end to sale of liquor and ammunition to Indians and slaves, 1834; supt. of emigration of Seminole tribe to So. Fla., 1834; removed Osceola and 4 other intransigent chiefs from council, 1835. Killed by hostile Indians nr. Ft. King, Fla., Dec. 28, 1835; buried Elberton, Ga.

THOMPSON, William, army officer; b. Ireland, 1736. Came to Am., 1756; settled in Carlisle, Pa., became surveyor and justice of peace; served as capt. during French and Indian War, participated in John Armstrong's expdn. against Kittanning; elected mem. Com. of Correspondence for Cumberland County (Pa.), 1774; mem. Pa. Com. of Safety, 1775; in command of a battalion of riflemen raised in Southeastern counties of Pa., 1775; served in 2d Pa. Regt. (1st body of men to reach Boston from South); repulsed attack on Lechmere Point, 1775; commd. brig. gen. Continental Army, 1776, ordered to Can. in charge of detachment of 2,000 men; attempted to attack Three Rivers, 1776, failed because of treachery, made prisoner, exchanged, 1780. Died Carlisle, Sept. 3, 1781; buried Carlisle.

THOMPSON, William, congressman, army officer, editor; b. Fayette County, Pa., Nov. 10, 1813; attended common schs. Moved to Mt. Pleasant, Ia.; mem. Ia. Territorial Ho. of Reps., 1843; sec. Ia. Constl. Conv., 1846; mem. U.S. Ho. of Reps. (Democrat) from Ia., 30th-31st congresses, 1847-June 29, 1850 (when seat was declared vacant); commd. capt. 1st Ia. Volunteer Cav., U.S. Army, 1861, promoted maj., 1863, col., 1864, brevetted brig. gen. of Volunteers for gallant services, 1865, honorably mustered out, 1866, recommd. capt. 7th Cav., U.S. Army, 1866, brevetted maj., 1867 for gallant services at Prairie Grove, Ark., lt. col. for gallant services in action at Bayou Metoe, Ark., 1867, ret., 1875; became editor Ia. State Gazette. Died Tacoma, Wash., Oct. 6, 1897; buried Tacoma Cemetery.

THOMPSON, William Tappan, editor, humorist; b. Ravenna, O., Aug. 31, 1812; s. David and Catherine (Kerney) T.; m. Carolina A. Carrie, July 12, 1837, several children. Apptd. asst. to James D. Wescott (sec. Territory of Fla.), 1830; asso. with Augustus Baldwin Longstreet in editing States Rights Sentinel, Augusta, Ga., 1835; edited Family Companion and Ladies' Mirror, 1838-43; author humorous articles published as Major Jones' Courtship, 1843; editor weekly Miscellany, Madison, Ga., 1843-45; a partner of Park Benjamin in weekly publ. Western Continent, Balt., 1845, sole publisher, 1845-50; founder, editor Savannah Morning News, 1850-82; del. Nat. Democratic Conv., 1868; mem. Ga. Constl. Conv., 1877. Author: Major Jones' Sketches of Travel, 1848; The Slave Holder Abroad (vol. fictional propaganda of excerpts from Brit. newspapers showing higher crime rate in Eng. than in South), 1860. Died Savannah, Ga., Mar. 24, 1882.

THOMPSON, Zadock, historian, naturalist, mathematician; b. Bridgewater, Vt., May 23, 1796; s Capt. Barnabas and Sarah (Fuller) T.; grad. U. Vt., 1823; m. Phebe Boyce, Sept. 2, 1824, 2 children. Published an almanac, 1819; gazeteer of Vt., 1824; tutor U. Vt., 1825-33, prof. chemistry and natural history, 1851; wrote The Youths' Assistant in Practical Arithmetick (his only lucrative venture), 1825; edited mag. Iris, 1828, also Green Mountain Repository, 1832; taught in Can., 1833-37; ordained deacon Protestant Episcopal Ch., 1835; tchr. Vt. Episcopal Inst., Burlington, 1837; state naturalist Vt., 1853. Author: History of the State of Vermont, from Its Earliest Settlement to the Close of The Year 1832, 1833; Geography and History of Lower Canada, 1835; Natural, Civil, and Statistical History of Vermont (most important work), 1841-43; Geography and Geology of Vermont, 1848. Died Burlington, Jan. 9, 1856.

THOMSON, Alexander, congressman, lawyer, educator; b. Franklin County, Pa., Jan. 12, 1788; apprenticed to a sickle maker; studied law. Admitted to the bar, 1816, began practice law, Chambersburg, Pa.; held several local offices; mem. Pa. Ho. of Reps.; mem. U.S. Ho. of Reps. from Pa. (filled vacancy), 18th-19th congresses, Dec. 6, 1824-May 1, 1826 (resigned); mayor City of Lancaster (Pa.); pres. judge 16th Jud. Dist. of Pa., 1827-41; prof., law sch. Marshall Coll., Lancaster. Died Chambersburg, Aug. 2, 1848; buried Falling Spring Presbyn. Cemetery.

THOMSON, Charles, sec. Continental Congress; b. County Derry, Ireland, Nov. 29, 1729; s. John Thomson; LL.D., Princeton, 1822; m. Ruth Mather; m. 2d, Hannah Harrison, Sept. 1, 1774. Came to Am. 1739; tutor Phila. Acad., 1750; master Latin sch. in what became William Penn Charter Sch., 1757-60; became mcht., Phila., 1760; active in Pa. politics during years before Am. Revolution; one of key mems. Sons of Liberty who persuaded Pa. to support Mass. position; sec. Continental Congress, 1774-89; notified George Washington of his election as U.S. Pres.; published translations of Septuagint and the New Testament under title The Holy Bible Containing the Old and New

Covenant, 4 vols., 1808; Synopsis of the Four Evangelists, 1815; Critical Annotations on Gilbert Wakefield's Works. Died Lower Merion, Pa., Aug. 16, 1824.

THOMSON, Edward, clergyman, coll. pres.; b. Portsea, Portsmouth, Eng., Oct. 12, 1810; s. Benjamin and Eliza (Moore) T.; grad. U. Pa., 1829; M.D., Cincinnati Med. Coll., 1836; m. Maria Louisa Bartley, July 4, 1837; m. 2d, Annie E. Howe, May 9, 1866. Came to U.S., 1818; admitted to med. practice, 1829; joined Methodist Episcopal Ch., 1831, licensed to preach, admitted on trial to Ohio Conf., 1832; pres. Norwalk Sem., 1838; 1st pres. Ohio Wesleyan U., 1842-60; editor Ladies' Repository, Cincinnati, 1844-46, Christian Advocate and Journal (chief Methodist organ in U.S.), 1860; rep. of N. Ohio Meth. Conf. in Gen. Conf., 1840-64; elected bishop, 1864, sent to visit Meth. missions in Orient. Author: Our Oriental Missions, 2 vols., 1870; Evidences of Revealed Religion, 1872. Died Wheeling, W. Va., Mar. 22, 1870.

THOMSON, Frank, railroad exec.; b. Chambersburg, Pa., July 5, 1841; s. Alexander and Jane (Graham) T.; m. Mary Elizabeth Clarke, June 5, 1866, 3 children. Started career with Pa. R.R. as apprentice in machine shop, Altoona, Pa.; asst. to Thomas Scott, pres. Pa. R.R. (who had been apptd. asst. sec. of war in charge of mil. railroads), 1861-64; supt. eastern division Phila. & Erie R.R., 1864-73; supt. motive power Pa. R.R., 1873-74, gen. mgr. eastern dist., 1874-82, 2d v.p., 1882-88, 1st v.p., 1888-97, pres., 1897-99; made various innovations in rail transp., including track inspection system, block signal system. Died Merion, Pa., June 5, 1899.

THOMSON, John, orator, political writer; b. Va., Nov. 3, 1776; s. Dr. John and Anne T.; attended Coll. William and Mary, circa 1790-92; studied law, Petersburg, Va., 1792-circa 1794. Practiced law in Petersburg, 1795; published views in press under classical signatures of Cassius, Grachus, Curtius; his writing widely copied by Republican papers; attacked Jay's treaty in speech before people of Petersburg, 1795; publicly attacked Marshall views on Alien and Sedition Acts, 1798. Died Petersburg, Jan. 25, 1799.

THOMSON, John, congressman, physician; born in Ireland, Nov. 20, 1780; came to Am., 1787; studied medicine. Moved to New Lisbon, O., 1806, began practice medicine; mem. Ohio Ho. of Reps., 1816; mem. Ohio Senate, 1814-15, 17-20; mem. U.S. Ho. of Reps. (Democrat) from Ohio, 19th, 21st-24th congresses, 1825-27, 29-37. Died New Lisbon (now Lisbon), O., Dec. 2, 1852; buried New Lisbon Cemetery.

THOMSON, John Edgar, railraod exec.; b. Springfield Twp., Pa., Feb. 10, 1808; s. John and Sarah (Levis) T.; m. Lavinia Frances Smith, 1 adopted dau. Chief asst. in charge engring. div. Camden & Amboy R.R., 1830; chief engr. Ga. R.R., 1832-47, chartered to build line from Augusta to Atlanta; apptd. chief engr. Pa. R.R. to build line from Harrisburg to Pitts., completed 1854, pres., 1852-74, consolidated Western lines into Pitts., Ft. Wayne & Chgo. Ry., by 1856, formally leased by Pa. R.R., 1869, acquired part interest in Southern Ry. Security Co., gained access to So. routes, 1873; mem. Phila. Park Commn.; estate left in trust to educate and maintain daughters of railroad men killed in discharge of their duties (known as St. John's Orphanage). Died Phila., May 27, 1874.

THOMSON, John Renshaw, senator, businessman; b. Phila., Sept. 25, 1800; attended Coll. of N.J. (now Princeton). Became a mcht.; went to China, 1817, became a mcht. in Canton; U.S. consul at Canton, 1823-25; returned to U.S., lived in Princeton, N.J.; dir., sec. Del. & Raritan Canal Co.; pres., later treas. Phila. & Trenton R.R. Co.; mem. N.J. Constl. Conv., 1844; unsuccessful Democratic candidate for gov. of N.J., 1844; mem. U.S. Senate (Democrat, filled vacancy) from N.J., 1853-62. Died Princeton, Sept. 12, 1862; buried Princeton Cemetery.

THOMSON, Mark, congressman; b. Norriton Twp., nr. Norristown, Pa., 1739. Became a miller; justice of peace Sussex County, N.J., 1773; mem. provincial conv., 1774, Provincial Congress, 1775; commd. lt. col. 1st Regt., Sussex County Militia, 1775; lt. col. Col. Charles Stewart's Battalion of Minutemen, 1776, col. 1st Regt., Sussex County Militia, 1776, col. Battalion of Detached N.J. Militia, 1776; mem. N. J. Gen. Assembly, 1779; mem. state council, 1786-88; apptd. lt. col. and a.d.c. on staff Gov. Richard Howell of N.J., 1793; mem. U.S. Ho. of Reps. (Federalist) from N.J., 4th-5th congresses, 1795-99. Died Marksboro, Sussex (later Warren) County, N.J., Dec. 14, 1803; buried Presbyn. Ch. Cemetery.

THOMSON, Mortimer Neal, humorist; b. Riga, Monroe County, N.Y., Sept. 2, 1831; s. Edwin and Sophia (Thomson) T.; attended U. Mich., 1849-50 (expelled); m. Anna H. Van Cleve, Oct. 24, 1857; m. 2d, Grace Eldridge, July 1861; 2 children. Wrote series of humorous letters appearing in Detroit Daily Advertiser, N.Y. Tribune, Spirit of the Times (N.Y.), 1854-55, published under name "Doesticks: What He Says," 1855; joined staff N.Y. Tribune, 1855, wrote police-court sketches The History and Records of the Elephant Club, 1856; wrote poem Nothing to Say (parody of William Allen Butler's Nothing to Wear, 1857; wrote Pluri-bus-tap, a Song That's-by-no-Author (mock heroic and parody of Longfellow's Hiawatha), 1856; edited N.Y. Picayune, humorous weekly of day, 1858; dramatic critic for N.Y. Tribune, circa 1860, staff reporter; asso. editor Mpls. Tribune, circa 1870; N.Y. editor Frank Leslie's Illustrated Weekly, 1873-75. Died June 25, 1875

THOMSON, Samuel, physician; b. Alstead, N.H., Feb. 9, 1769; s. John and Hannah (Cobb) T.; m. Susan Allen, July 7, 1790, 8 children. Began farming, experimented with herb cures, eventually devoted full time to med. practice, circa 1790; his use of medical roots "Thomsonian System" involved him in many law suits, once charged with murder; believed that all ills were based on cold and treated with heat producers; treatment consisted of labelia herb followed by Cayenne pepper and vapor bath, patented, 1813, revised, 1823; short-lived journals advocating system were Botanic Sentinel, 1835-40, Thomsonian Recorder (later called Botanic-Medical Recorder), lasted until 1852. Author: A Brief Sketch of the Causes and Treatment of Disease, 1821; Materia Medica and Family Physician; New Guide to Health: or Botanic Family Physician, 1822. Died Boston, Oct. 4, 1843.

THOMSON, Samuel Harrison, clergyman, educator; b. Nicholas County, Ky., Aug. 26, 1813; grad. Hanover (Ind.) Coll., 1837. Sch. tchr., Ind., 1837-44; prof. mathematics Hanover Coll., 1844-74, acting pres. of coll. several times; ordained to Gospel ministry, 1857; moved to Cal., 1877. Died Pasadena, Cal., Sept. 2, 1882; buried Pasadena.

THOMSON, William, army officer; b. Pa., Jan. 16, 1727; s. Moses and Jane Thomson; m. Eugenia Russell, Aug. 14, 1755, 12 children. Worked on his father's plantation, S.C., also traded with Indians; served as maj. S.C. Militia during Cherokee War (for which Assembly voted him bonus and land); indigo planter, justice of peace, enquirer and collector of taxes, at various times; mem. Ga. Legislature; served as col. Orangeburg Militia; a commr. to relocate N.C.-S.C. border, 1772; mem. 1st Ga. Provincial Assembly; lt.-col.-comdt. Continental Army, blocked British attempt to land on Sullivan's Island at entrance to Charleston harbor, 1776; received Congressional thanks for this action; promoted col. Continental Army, 1776, resigned, 1778; imprisoned for having broken parole to British following capture of Charlestown, 1781; mem. S.C. Conv. to ratify U.S. Constn., 1788. Died Nov. 2, 1796.

THOMSON, William McClure, clergyman, missionary, author; b. Spring Dale, O., Dec. 31, 1806; s. Rev. John Thompson; grad. Miami U., Oxford, O., 1828; attended Princeton Theol. Sem., 1824-31; m. Eliza Nelson Hanna, June 6, 1832; m. 2d, Mrs. Maria Abbot, Aug. 3, 1835; 3 children. Ordained by Presbytery of Cincinnati, 1831; sailed for Syria, 1832; in Beirut, Lebanon, 1833-34, Jerusalem, 1834, imprisoned as spy; opened boys' boarding sch., Beirut, 1835; moved to station he had helped establish at Ubeih, Lebanon, 1843; helped Maronite Christians escape to Beirut in Druses-Christian War, 1846; went to Syria, managed post at Hasbeiyeh, 1850-57; went to Beirut as missionary, 1859; adviser to Lord Dufferin (rep. of allied powers in reorgn. govt. of Lebanon), 1860; returned to Am., 1876. Author: The Land and the Book, 3 vols., 1880-85 (became best seller). Died Denver, Apr. 8, 1894.

THORBURN, Grant (pen name Lawrie Todd), seed mcht., author; b. Dalkeith, Scotland, Feb. 18, 1773; s. James and Elizabeth (Fairley) T.; m. Rebecca Sickles, June 1797; m. 2d, Hannah Wortemby, 1801; m. 3d, Maria, June 12, 1853; several children. First important seedsman in Am.; founder bus. that functioned more than a century; published The Gentleman and Gardener's Kalendar for the Middle States of North America (1st seed catalogue in Am.), 1812; wrote articles for newspapers and mags. under pen name Lawrie Todd, published as Sketches from the Note-book of Lawrie Todd, 1847; other writings include: Forty Years' Residence in America, 1834; Flowers from the Garden of Lawrie Todd, 1852; Life and Writings of Grant Thorburn, 1852. Died New Haven, Conn., Jan. 21, 1863.

THOREAU, Henry David, writer; b. Concord, Mass., July 12, 1817; s. John and Cynthia (Dunbar) T.; grad. Harvard, 1837. Opened pvt. sch. with brother John, 1838; gave 1st of nearly annual lectures to Concord Lyceum, 1838; lived at home of Ralph Waldo Emerson, 1841-43, 47-49; edited The Dial during Emerson's absence, 1843; tutor in home of William Emerson on S.I., N.Y., 1843-44; resided at Walden Pond, arrested for failure to pay poll tax, 1845; wrote journals which formed basis of Walden; lived in family home in Concord, 1849-62; published Walden (his only organized work), 1854; his life at Walden Pond was an experiment designed to prove that a meaningful existence was possible apart from industrialism and materialism of New Eng.; set his own conscience above laws of govt. thus incurring charge of anarchism; philosophy of his essay on civil disobedience (classic statement of individualism in conflict with State) present in Walden; descriptions of nature contained in this and other works established him as naturalist (though not as a scientist); though not a reformer, deeply concerned with problem of slavery, spoke vigorously in defense of John Brown, 1859; Thoreau was part of extremely close-knit family and participated in pencil mfg. conducted in family home; his influence on later Am. literature has been ascribed to his pithy and forceful style which employed vivid imagery; mem. Transcendentalist Club (including Amos Bronson Alcott, J.F. Clarke, Margaret Fuller, F.H. Hodge); distrusted group action and relied upon his own definitions of morality believing in human perfectibility; his skill in writing made him foremost interpreter of Am. flora and fauna; wrote A Week on the Concord and Merrimac Rivers (notable for literary criticism and nature studies), 1849; from his journals describing trips to Me., Cape Cod, and Can., 1848-53, there were published posthumously: Excursions, 1863; The Maine Woods, 1864; Cape Cod, 1865; A Yankee in Canada, 1866; Letters to Various Persons, edited by R.W. Emerson, 1865; Early Spring in Massachussets, 1881, Summer, 1884, Winter, 1888, Autumn, 1892, selections from journals edited by H.G.O. Blake; Poems of Nature, edited by Salt and Sanborn, 1895; Walden edition of Writings of Henry David Thoreau, 20 vols., 1906, contains all journals except Apr. 1843-July 1845. Died Concord, Mass., May 6, 1862; buried New Burying Ground, Concord, reinterred Sleepy Hollow Cemetery.

THORFINN (Thorfinn Karlsefni), explorer; b. Iceland, circa 980; m. Gudrid (widow of Eric the Red's son Thorstein); at least 1 son, Snorri (1st white child born in N. Am.). Arrived with about 80 persons in 2 ships to colonize N.W. coast of Greenland, autumn 1003; instead spent winter on estate of Eric the Red in Brattahlid; set out with 130 persons in 3 ships, spring 1004, landed at Baffin Island, naming it Helluland (Land of Flat Stones), then proceeded to wooded area farther south, naming it Markland (Forest Land) (these names used earlier by Leif Ericsson, but not necessarily for same areas); spent 1st winter in area still farther south which he believed to be Vinland, visited there by friendly natives; spent 2d winter in another location, successfully withstood native attack; after 3d winter, disbanded colony (with most individuals sailing for Greenland); spent another winter in Greenland, then returned to Iceland.

THORNBURGH, Jacob Montgomery, congressman, lawyer; b. New Market, Tenn., July 3, 1837; studied law. Admitted to the bar, 1861, began practice law in Jefferson County, Tenn.; served from pvt. to lt. col., 4th Regt., Tenn. Volunteer Cav., U.S. Army, 1861-63; resumed practice law, Jefferson County; moved to Knoxville, Tenn., 1867; apptd. atty. gen. 3d Jud. Circuit of Tenn., 1866, elected, 1868, 70; U.S. commr. at Internat. Expn., Vienna, Austria, 1872; mem. U.S. Ho. of Reps. (Republican) from Tenn., 43d-45th congresses, 1873-79; del. Republican nat. convs., 1872, 76, 80. Died Knoxville, Sept. 19, 1890; buried Old Gray Cemetery.

THORNDIKE, Israel, shipper, state legislator; b. Beverly, Mass., Apr. 30, 1755; s. Andrew and Anne (Morgan) T.; attended pub. schs.; m. Anna Dodge, 12 children. Commd. comdr. schooner Warren, 1776; comdr. privateer Resource; became active partner shipping firm Brown and Thorndike, sole mgr. after Brown's retirement, 1800, involved in extensive trade with China and Orient originating in Salem, Mass., later expanded from Boston; mem. Mass. Legislature, 1788-1814; mem. Mass. constl. convs., 1788, 1820; gave library of Prof. Ebeling of Hamburg, Germany to Harvard, 1818. Died Boston, May 8, 1832; buried Mt. Auburn Cemetery, Cambridge, Mass.

THORNE, Charles Robert, actor, mgr.; b. N.Y. C., 1814; m. Maria Ann Mestayer, Dec. 1830; m. 2d, Mrs. James Stark; 5 children including Charles Robert, Edwin. Began acting career, 1829; propr. Chatham Theatre, N.Y., 1831; led wandering actor's life (with wife), 1831-35; appeared as Glaucus in The Last Days of Pompeii at Bowery Theatre, 1835; ran Chatham Theatre, 1840-43; actor and mgr., various cities on East Coast, 1843-49; acted in San Francisco, 1849; traveled around world, sometime after 1853; unsuccessful mgr. Niblo's Theatre, N.Y.C., 1874. Died Dec. 13, 1893.

THORNE, Charles Robert, actor; b. N.Y.C., June 11, 1840; s. Charles Robert and Maria (Mestayer) T.; attended St. John (later Fordham) Coll., 1854-57; m. Miss Calder, 1859. Acted with father in San Francisco, 1854; became mem. Jefferson's Co. at Laura Keene's Theatre, N.Y.C., 1857; leading man Boston Theatre, 1866-69; mem. Union Sq. Theatre Co., N.Y.C., 1871-82; last performance was in The Corsican Brothers, N.Y.C., 1883. Died N.Y.C., Feb. 10, 1883.

THORNTON, Jessy Quinn, pioneer; born August 24, 1810; studied law, London, England, 3 years; married Mrs. Nancy M. Logue, February 8, 1838. Admitted to bar, 1833, practiced law, Palmyra, Missouri, 1835; began editing paper, Palmyra, 1836; lived in Quincy, Illinois, 1841-46; went to Oregon, 1846; appointed judge Oregon Territorial Supreme Ct., 1847; delegated to lobby in Washington (D.C.) for immediate admission of Ore. as organized U.S. territory, 1847-48 (Congressional acceptance of 49th parallel made his mission successful, 1848); apptd. Indian sub-agt. in Ore.; mem. Ore. Legislature from Benton County, 1864-65. Author: Oregon and California in 1848; contbr. articles Transactions of Ore. Pioneer Assn. Died Salem, Ore., Feb. 5, 1888; buried Methodist Churchyard, Salem.

THORNTON, John Wingate, historian; b. Saco, Me., Aug. 12, 1818; s. James and Eliza (Goukin) T.; grad. Harvard Law Sch., 1840; m. Elizabeth Wallace Bowles; children—Henry, Thornton, Elizabeth, Agnes. Began practice of law in Boston, 1840; a founder New Eng. Historic Geneal. Soc., 1844, The Prince Soc., 1858; discovered Trelawny papers concerning fishing station at Richmond Island for the Me. Hist. Soc., 1872; v.p. Am. Statis. Assn. Author: The First Records of Anglo-American Colonization, 1859; The Historical Relation of New England to the English Commonwealth, 1874; numerous fugitive papers. Died Scarboro, Me., June 6, 1878.

THORNTON, Matthew, Continental congressman; b. Ireland, circa 1714; s. James and Elizabeth (Jenkins) T.; grad. Dartmouth, 1797; m. Hannah Jack, 1760, 5 children. Came to Am., 1718; began practice medicine, Londonderry, N.H., circa 1740; col. militia under Royal Govt.; mem. N.H. Assembly from Londonderry, 1758, 60, 61; pres. N.H. Provincial Congress, 1775, also chmn. com. of safety; speaker N.H. Gen. Assembly, 1776; col. N.H. Militia during Revolutionary War; mem. N.H. Council, pres. Constl. Conv. of N.H., circa 1776-77; asso. justice Superior Ct. of N.H., 1776-82; mem. Continental Congress, 1776-78; signer Declaration of Independence, 1776; mem. N.H. Senate, 1784-86; mem. N.H. Gen. Assembly, 1783; state councilor, 1785; chief justice N.H. Ct. of Common Pleas. Died Newburyport, Mass., June 24, 1803; buried Merrimack, N.H.

THORNTON, William, architect, inventor, pub. ofcl.; b. Jost van Dyke, Virgin Islands, May 20, 1759; s. William and Dorcas Downing (Zeagens) T.; attended U. Edinburgh (Scotland), 1781-84; M.D., Aberdeen (Scotland) U., 1784; m. Anna Maria Brodeau, Oct. 13, 1790. Arrived in N.Y.C., 1787, became U.S. citizen in Del., 1788; earned prize for design of Library Co. of Phila., 1789; asso. with John Fitch in experimenting with paddle-driven steamboats, 1778-90, advanced much of cost; won competition for design of Nat. Capitol, Washington, D.C., 1792, received post as commr. City of Washington, 1794-1802, supervised constrn. Capitol until replaced by Latrobe, 1803; North Wing constructed in accordance with Thornton's ideas, constrn. of South Wing conformed with it, 1800; his idea of great central rotunda also adhered to by later architects of bldg.; supervised constrn. of George Washington's 2 houses in Washington, D.C., 1798-99; built the Octagon for John Tayloe, 1798-1800 (standing in 1935 and had become hdqrs. A.I.A.); made sketches for 2 bldgs. at U. Va., one of which (Pavillion VII) was built; clk. in charge patents State Dept., 1802-28, saved Patent Office from destruction during capture of Washington by British, 1814. Died Washington, Mar. 28, 1828; buried Congressional Cemetery, Washington.

THORNWELL, James Henley, clergyman, coll. pres.; b. Marlboro Dist., S.C., Dec. 9, 1812; s. James and Martha (Terrel) T.; grad. S.C. Coll., 1831; attended Andover (Mass.) Theol. Sem., 1834; D.D. (hon.), Hampden-Sydney Coll., Jefferson Coll., Centre Coll.; m. Nancy White Witherspoon, Dec. 3, 1835. Joined Presbyn. Ch., 1832; licensed to preach by Harmony Presbytery, Synod of S.C., 1834; pastor several churches, Lancaster Dist., S.C., circa 1834-37; prof. metaphysics S.C. Coll., 1837-40, chaplain, prof. sacred literature, 1841-51, pres., 1851-53; prof. didactic and palemic theology Presbyn. Theol. Sem., Columbia, S.C., 1847; founded Southern Presbyn. Review, Columbia, 1847; induced Synod of S.C. to endorse political secession, 1861; leading organizer Presbyn. Ch. in Confederate States Am.; Works collected in The Collected Writings of J.H. Thornwell (edited by J.B. Adger and J.L. Girardeau) 4 vols., 1871-73. Died Charlotte, N.C., Aug. 1, 1862.

THORP, John, machinist, inventor; b. Rehoboth, Mass., 1784; s. Reubin and Hannah (Bucklin) T.; m. Eliza A. Williams, Aug. 18, 1817. Received 1st patent for hand water loom, 1812, renewed, 1843, 2d patent for power loom, 1816; received 3 patents for improvements in spinning and twisting cotton (called "ring spinning;" basic method of continuous spinning still used), 1828; patent for netting machine, 1828; received 4 patents including narrow fabric loom (possibly 1st gang loom operated by power), 1829; established as machine builder, Providence, R.I., later North Wrenthan, Mass., 1830's. Died Nov. 15, 1848.

THORPE, Thomas Bangs, artist, author; b. Westfield, Mass., Mar. 1, 1815; s. Rev. Thomas Thorpe; attended Wesleyan U., Middletown, Conn., 1833-35; married. Had studio in Baton Rouge, La., 1835-53; painted full length portrait of Pres. Taylor (considered his masterpiece), purchased by Va. Legislature and Ho. of Reps.; published "Big Bear of Arkansas" (his most important story), 1841; stories collected under titles Mysteries of the Backwoods, 1846, The Hive of the Bee-Hunter, 1854; edited Whig newspapers in La., 1843-50, including New Orleans Comml. Times, New Orleans Daily Tropic; co-propr., co-editor N.Y. Spirit of the Times, 1860; staff officer to Gen. B.F. Butler with rank col. U.S. Volunteers, 1862; surveyor Port of New Orleans, 1862-63; surveyor of N.Y.C., 1865-69; chief warehouse dept. of N.Y. Custom House, 1869-78. Author: Our Army on the Rio Grande, 1846, Our Army at Monterey (earliest descriptions of battles of Mexican War), 1847; Scenes in Arkansaw, 1859. Died Sept. 20, 1878.

THORVALDSSON, Eric, see Eric the Red.

THRASHER, John Sidney, journalist, adventurer; b. Portland, Me., 1817; ed. in U.S.; m. Mrs. Rebecca Mary Menard, 1859. Moved with parents to Cuba, 1832/33; clk. merc. firm, 1844-47; revolutionary agitator, propagandist assisting Narciso Lopez and others, 1848-51; an editor anti-Spanish newspaper El Faro Industrial de la Habana, 1850-51; imprisoned by Spanish authorities, 1851, freed, 1852, moved to New Orleans to aid John A. Quitman and Cuban Revolutionaries, decleared for Cuban annexation to U.S.; became corr. in Mexico and S.Am. for N.Y. Herald, 1855; connected with So. Asso. Press, Atlanta, during Civil War; editor or contbr. to Beacon of Cuba, De Bow's Review, Picayune of New Orleans, several other periodicals. Died Galveston, Tex., Nov. 10, 1879; buried Magnolia Cemetery, Galveston.

THROCKMORTON, James Webb, gov. Tex., congressman, lawyer, physician; b. Sparta, Tenn., Feb. 1, 1825; studied medicine in Princeton, Ky.; studied law. Practiced medicine in Collin County, Tex.; served as surgeon, Mexican War; admitted to the bar, began practice law, McKinney, Tex.; mem. Tex. Ho. of Reps., 1851-56; candidate as Whig presdl. elector, 1852; mem. Tex. Senate, 1856-61, 65; mem. Tex. Secession Conv., 1861; served as capt. and maj. Confederate Army, 1861-63; brig. gen. Tex. Militia, 1864, comdr. on northwest border of Tex.; del. and presiding officer reconstrn. conv. under Pres. Johnson's proclamation, 1866; elected, inaugurated gov. of Tex., 1866, removed by order of Gen. Sheridan, 1867; resumed practice law, Collin County; mem. U.S. Ho. of Reps. (Democrat) from Tex., 44th-45th, 48th-49th congresses, 1875-79, 83-87; Democratic presdl. elector, 1880; del. Dem. Nat. Conv., Chgo., 1892. Died McKinney, Tex., Apr. 21, 1894; buried Pecan Grove Cemetery.

THROOP, Enos Thompson, gov. N.Y., jurist, congressman; b. Johnstown, N.Y., Aug. 21, 1784; s. George Bliss and Abiah (Thompston) T.; m. Evelina Vredenburgh, July 14, 1814, 3 children. Admitted to N.Y. bar, 1806; apptd. county clk., Auburn, N.Y., 1811; mem. U.S. Ho. of Reps. from N.Y., 14th Congress, 1815-June 4, 1816; circuit judge, N.Y., 1823-27; lt. gov., N.Y., 1829, acting gov., 1829-31, gov., 1831-33, established 1st state insane asylum; apptd. naval officer Port of N.Y. by Pres. Jackson 1833-38; apptd. charge d'affaires Kingdom of Two Sicilies, 1838-42. Died Auburn, Nov. 1, 1874; buried St. Peter's Churchyard, Auburn.

THROOP, Montgomery Hunt, lawyer; b. Auburn, N.Y., Jan. 26, 1827; s. George B. and Francis (Hunt) T.; attended Hobart Coll.; read law with uncle (Ward Hunt); m. Charlotte Williams Gridley, June 22, 1854, 2 sons. Accompanied uncle (Enox Thompson Throop) on diplomatic missions to Geneva and Naples; admitted to N.Y. bar, 1848; practiced in partnership with uncle, Utica, N.Y., 1848-56; with Roscoe Conkling, 1856-62; moved to N.Y.C., practiced law, 1864-80; mem. N.Y. Codification Commn., 1870-77. Author: The Future: A Political Essay, 1864; Treatise on Validity of Verbal Agreements, 1870; Revised Statues of State of New York, 1882; Treatise on the Law Relating to Public Officers and Sureties in Official Bonds, 1892. Died Albany, N.Y., Sept. 11, 1892.

THRUSTON, Buckner, senator, jurist; b. Petsoe Parish, Gloucester County, Va., Feb. 9, 1764; grad. Coll. William and Mary, 1783; studied law. Moved to Lexington, Fayette County, Va. (now Ky.), 1788; admitted to bar, began practice law; mem. Va. Assembly, 1789; elected 1st clk. of 1st Ky. Senate, 1792; apptd. a commr. to settle boundary dispute between Ky. and Va.; dist. judge of Ky., 1791, judge of circuit ct., 1802-03; declined appointment as U.S. judge ct. of Territory of Orleans, 1804; mem. U.S. Senate (Democrat) from Ky., 1805-Dec. 18, 1809 (resigned); judge U.S. Circuit Ct. for D.C., 1809-45. Died Washington, D.C., Aug. 30, 1845; buried Congressional Cemetery.

THUMB, Gen. Tom, see Stratton, Charles Sherwood.

THURBER, Charles, inventor, mfr., educator; b. East Brookfield, Mass., Jan. 2, 1803; s. Rev. Laban and Abigail (Thayer) T.; A.B., A.M., Brown U., 1827; m. Lucinda Allen, 1827; m. 2d, Caroline Esty. 1852; 2 daus. Tchr., Milford, (Mass.) Acad., 1827-31; prin. Latin Grammar Sch., Worcester, Mass., 1831-39; in partnership with brother-in-law Ethan Allen to manufacture firearms, Worcester, 1836-56; granted patent for hand printing machine which preceded typewriter, 1843; received 2d patent for a "mechinical chirographer" (a writing machine), 1845; county commr. in Mass., 1842-44; mem. Mass. Senate, 1852-53; trustee Brown U., 1853-86; ret. from bus., 1856. Died Nashua, N.H., Nov. 7, 1886.

THURBER, George, botanist, horticulturist, author, editor; b. Providence, R.I., Sept. 2, 1821; s. Jacob and Alice Ann (Martin) T.; attended Union Classical and Engring. Sch., Providence; M.D., N.Y. Med. Coll., 1859. Partner in a pharmacy, stimulated his interest in chemistry; lectured on chemistry with Franklin Soc., Providence; botanist, q.m., commissary on survey of boundary between U.S. and Mexico, 1850; with U.S. Assay Office, N.Y.C., 1853-56; lectr. botany Coll. of Pharmacy, N.Y., 1856-61, 65-66; lectr. Cooper Union; prof. botany and horticulture Mich. State Agrl. Coll. (later Mich. State Coll.), 1859-63; editor Agriculturist, N.Y.C., 1863-85; specialized in study of Am. grasses; pres. Torrey Bot. Club, 1873-80; life mem. Am. Pomol. Soc.; became corr. mem. Royal Hort. Soc. of London, 1886. Author: American Weeds and Useful Plants (a revision of William Darlington's Agricultural Botany, published 1847), 1859. Died Passaic, N.J., Apr. 2, 1890.

THURMAN, Allen Granberry, senator; b. Lynchburg, Va., Nov. 13, 1813; s. Pleasant and Mary Granberry (Allen) T.; m. Mary Dun, Nov. 14, 1844, several children. Admitted to Ohio bar, 1835; practiced in state and fed. cts.; mem. U.S. Ho. of Reps. (Democrat) from Ohio, 29th Congress, 1845-47; asso. justice Ohio Supreme Ct., 1851-54, chief justice, 1854-56; a "Peace Democrat" opposed extra-const. measures of Lincoln adminstrn.; mem. U.S. Senate from Ohio, 1869-81, became Dem. leader, adhered to strict Jeffersonian constructionist tradition, chmn. judiciary com., also pres. pro tem., 1879; author Thurman Act compelling Pacific railroad corps. to fulfill obligations to govt.; mem. Electoral Commn., 1877, voted to seat Tilden; apptd. by Pres. Garfield U.S. rep. to Internat. Monetary Conf., Paris, 1881; presdl. candidate in Dem. convs. 1876, 80, 84. Died Columbus, O., Dec. 12, 1895; buried Green Lawn Cemetery, Columbus.

THURMAN, John Richardson, congressman; b. N.Y.C., Oct. 6, 1814; grad. Columbia, 1835. Became a farmer, nr. Chestertown, Warren County, N.Y.; held several local offices; mem. U.S. Ho. of Reps. (Whig) 31st Congress, 1849-51. Died Friends Lake, Warren County, N.Y., July 24, 1854; buried family cemetery; reinterred Oakwood Cemetery, Troy, N.Y.

THURSTON, Benjamin Babock, congressman, mcht.; b. Hopkinton, R.I., June 29, 1804; attended common schs. Became a mcht.; mem. R.I. Ho. of Reps., 1831-37; Democratic presdl. elector, 1836; lt. gov. State of R.I., 1838; mem. U.S. Ho. of Reps. (Democrat) from R.I., 30th, 32d-34th congresses, 1847-48, 51-57; moved to New London, Conn.; mem. bd. aldermen New London, 1862-63; mem. Conn. Ho. of Reps., 1869-70; became a mcht. Died New London, May 17, 1886; buried Cedar Grove Cemetery.

THURSTON, Robert Lawton, mfr. steam engines; b. Portsmouth, R.I., Dec. 13, 1800; s. Peleg and Ruth (Lawton) T.; m. Eliza Stratton, 1827; m. 2d, Harriet Taylor, Jan. 5, 1839; 3 children including Robert Henry. Built with John Babcock, Sr.) an exptl. steam engine and "safety tubular boiler" of Babcock's invention, 1821, placed them in small boat designed for use at Slade's Ferry, nr. Fall River, Mass.; completed 2 steamboats, The Babcock, the Rushlight for the Providence-N.Y.C. run, 1826, 28; became partner (with John Babcock, Jr.) Providence Steam Engine Co. (R.I.) (1st co. of its kind in New Eng., 3d in U.S.), 1830, disaster forced reorgn. as Thurston, Green and Co., 1845, purchased and incorporated the "drop cut off" for steam engines, became 1st mfrs. in Am. to build a standard form of expansion steam engine, 1846; retired, 1863. Died Providence, Jan. 13, 1874.

THURSTON, Samuel Royal, congressman, lawyer; b. Monmouth, Me., Apr. 15, 1816; attended Wesleyan Sem., Readfield, Me., also Dartmouth; grad. Bowdoin Coll., 1843; studied law. Admitted to the bar, 1844, began practice law in Brunswick, Me.; moved to Burlington, Ia., 1845, practiced law; editor Ia. Gazette; moved to Oregon City, Ore., 1849, practiced law; mem. U.S. Congress (Democrat) from Ore. Territory, 31st Congress, 1849-51. Died at sea (on way to Washington, D.C.), Apr. 9, 1851; buried Acapulco, Mexico; reinterred Odd Fellows Cemetery, Salem, Ore.

TIBBATTS, John Wooleston, congressman, lawyer; b. Lexington, Ky., June 12, 1802; studied law. Admitted to the bar, 1826, began practice law in Newport, Ky.; held several local offices; mem. U.S. ho. of Reps. (Democrat) from Ky., 28th-29th congresses, 1843-47; served as col., Mexican War; resumed practice law in Newport. Died Newport, July 5, 1852; buried Evergreen Cemetery.

TIBBITS, George, congressman, businessman; b. Warwick, R.I., Jan. 14, 1763; classical edn. Entered bus., Lansingburg, N.Y., 1784; moved to Troy, N.Y., 1797, became a mcht.; mem. N.Y. State Assembly, 1800; mem. U.S. Ho. of Reps. (Federalist) from N.Y., 8th Congress, 1803-05; mem. N.Y. Senate, 1815-18; mem. commn. on state prisons which rendered a favorable report on the Auburn Prison system, 1824; mem. commn. in charge of constrn. Sing Sing Prison; mayor City of Troy, N.Y., 1830-36. Died Troy, July 19, 1849; buried Oakwood Cemetery.

TICHENOR, Isaac, senator, gov. Vt.; b. Newark, N.J., Feb. 8, 1754; grad. Coll. of N.J. (now Princeton), 1775; read law, Schenectady, N.Y.; m. Elizabeth. Served with Continental Army, 1776; mem. Vt. Legislature, 1781-85, speaker, 1783-84; Vt. agt. to Continental Congress, 1782-89; apptd. commr. for N.Y.-Vt. boundary dispute, 1790; judge Vt. Supreme Ct., 1791-96; mem. U.S. Senate (Federalist) from Vt., 1796-97, 1815-21; gov. Vt., 1797-1807, 1808-09. Died Dec. 11, 1838; buried Village Cemetery, Old Bennington, Vt.

TICHENOR, Isaac Taylor, clergyman, coll. pres.; b. Spencer County, Ky., Nov. 11, 1825; s. James and Margaret (Bennett) T.; m. Monomia Cook, Dec. 16, 1853; m. 2d, Emily C. Boykin, Apr. 1861; m. 3d, Lulah Boykin, Oct. 1865; m. 4th, Mrs. Eppie Reynolds McGraw; at least 4 children. Prin., Taylorsville (Ky.) Acad.; became agt. Am. India Mission Assn., 1847; ordained to ministry Baptist Ch., 1848; pastor, Columbus, Ky., 1848-50; pastor 1st Bapt. Ch., Montgomery, Ala., 1852-68; served as chaplain Confederate Army during part of Civil War; pastor 1st Bapt. Ch., Memphis, Tenn., 1871-72; pres. State Agrl. and Mech. Coll., Auburn, Ala., 1872-82; sec. home missionary bd. So. Bapt. Ch., 1882-99. Died Atlanta, Ga., Dec. 2, 1902.

TICKNOR, Elisha, educator, mcht.; b. Lebanon, Conn., Mar. 25, 1757; s. Col. Elisha and Ruth (Knowles) T.; grad. Dartmouth, 1783; m. Elizabeth Billings, May 23, 1790, 1 son, George. Apptd. master Moor's Charity Schs., Hanover, N.H., 1783-85; opened private sch., Boston, 1785-88; apptd. prin. South Writing Sch., Boston, 1788-94; began bus. as grocer, 1795; organized Mass. Mut. Fire Ins. Co., 1798; suggested establishment of free primary schs. for children unable to read, 1805; founded (with James Savage) Provident Instn. for Savs. (one of 1st in U.S.), 1816; elected selectman of Boston, 1815. Died Boston, June 22, 1821.

TICKNOR, Francis Orray, physician, poet; born Fortville, Jones County, Ga., Nov. 12, 1822; s. Dr. Orray and Harriet (Coolidge) T.; M.D., Phila. Coll. Medicine, 1843; m. Rosalie Nelson, Jan. 18, 1847, 8 children. Practiced medicine, Shell Creek, Muscogee County, Ga., 1843; wrote on martial and chivalrous theme; noted for prosody and compactness of style; best known poems include The Virginians of the Valley, Loyal, Little Griffen; credited with authorship of The Barefooted Boys. Died Columbus, Ga., Dec. 18, 1874.

TICKNOR, George, historian, educator; b. Boston, Aug. 1, 1791; s. Elisha and Elizabeth (Billings) T.; grad. Dartmouth, 1807, LL.D. (hon.), 1858; attended U. Göttingen (Germany), 1815-17; LL.D. (hon.), Harvard, 1850, Brown U., 1850; m. Anna Eliot, Sept. 18, 1821, 4 children. Admitted to Mass. bar, 1813; prof. French and Spanish, Harvard, 1819-33, apptd. mem. bd. visitors U.S. Mil. Acad., 1826; published History of Spanish Literature (1st extensive survey of Spanish letters), 3 vols., 1849; a founder Boston Pub. Library, 1852, donated many books during his lifetime, bequeathed it his collection of Spanish literature. Died Boston, Jan. 26, 1871.

TICKNOR, William Davis, publisher; b. Lebanon, N.H., Aug. 6, 1810; s. William and Betsey (Ellis) T.; m. Emeline Staniford Holt, Dec. 25, 1832; 7 children. Founded Allen and Ticknor, publishers, 1832-33, later Ticknor and Fields; published Atlantic Monthly, also works of leading authors including Tennyson, Browning, Hawthorne, and Emerson; among 1st to give English authors full payment for copyrights; active mem. Baptist Ch.; close friend of Nathaniel Hawthorne. Died Phila., Apr. 10, 1864.

TIEBOUT, Cornelius, engraver; b. N.Y.C., 1777; s. Tunis and Elizabeth (Lamb) T.; m. Esther Young, Apr. 20, 1799, 3 children. Engraved maps, portraits and subject plates for N.Y. Mag. and John Brown's Self-Interpreting Bible during apprenticeship, circa 1790; made plates of Rembrandt Peale's Thomas Jfferson and Barralet's View of the Water Works at Centre Square; made plate reproducing Sir Joshua Reynolds' Hope; joined Benjamin Tanner and Francis Kearny in exploiting Henry S. Tanner's patent for engraving ornaments on bank notes to make them difficult to counterfeit; in business until 1822; represented in exhibition of One Hundred Notable Engravers at N.Y. Public Library, 1928. Died Ky., 1832.

TIFFANY, Alexander Ralston, jurist; b. Niagara, Can., Oct. 16, 1796; son of Sylvester Tiffany. Admitted to bar, began practice of law, Palmyra, N.Y., circa 1820; 1st judge Wayne County (N.Y.) Ct., 1823-circa 1830; moved to Palmyra, Mich., 1832; pros. atty. Lenawee County (Mich.), 1834-36; probate judge Lenawee County, 1836-44, county judge, 1846-50; mem. Mich. Constl. Conv., 1850; mem. Mich. Legislature, 1855. Author: Tiffany's Justice Guide, 1855; Tiffany's Criminal Law, 1860. Died Palmyra, Mich., Jan. 14, 1868; buried Palmyra.

TIFFIN, Edward, senator, gov. Ohio; b. Carlisle, Eng., June 19, 1766; s. Henry and Mary (Parker) T.; attended Jefferson Med. Coll., Phila.; m. Mary Worthington, 1789; m. 2d, Mary Porter, Apr. 16, 1809; 5 children. Came to Am., 1784; began practice of medicine, Charles Town, Va. (now Jefferson City, W.Va.); ordained Methodist lay preacher, 1792; moved to Chillicothe, O., 1798; apptd. prothonotary of Ohio Territorial Ct. of Common Pleas, 1798; mem., speaker Ohio Territorial Legislature, 1799-1800; pres. Ohio Constl. Conv., 1802; 1st gov. Ohio, 1803-07; held that English common-law crimes should not be recognized by Ohio cts. (thus all crimes in Ohio are statutory); made vigorous attempts to capture Aaron Burr's flotilla, 1805-06, destroyed Burr-Blennerhasset expdn.; mem. U.S. Senate from Ohio, 1807-09; mem., speaker Ohio Ho. of Reps., 1809-10, 10-11; land office commr., 1812-14; surveyor-gen. of N.W. Territory, 1814-29. Died Chillicothe, O., Aug. 9, 1829; buried Grand View Cemetery, Chillicothe.

TIFT, Nelson, congressman, businessman; b. Groton, Conn., July 23, 1810; attended village sch. Moved to Key West, Fla., 1826, to Charleston, S. C., 1830, became a mcht.; became a mcht. in Augusta, Ga., 1835, at Hawkinsville, Ga., 1836, Albany, Ga., 1836; founder Augusta Guards, 1835; founder City of Albany, 1836; justice of peace; del. from Baker County to Ga. conv. to reduce membership of state legislature, 1839; elected to Baker County Inferior Ct., 1840-41, 49; elected col. Baker County Militia, 1840; mem. Ga. Ho. of Reps., 1841, 47, 51-52; founder, editor, publisher Albany Patriot, 1845-58; served as capt. Confederate States Navy Supply Dept., Civil War; mem. U.S. Ho. of Reps. (Democrat) from Ga., 40th Congress, July 25, 1868-69; owner large plantation, operator lumber, flour, corn-meal mills; a promoter of the bldg. of several railroads, pres. of some; del. Ga. Constl. Conv., 1877. Died Albany, Nov. 21, 1891; buried Oakview Cemetery.

TILDEN, Daniel Rose, congressman, lawyer; b. Lebanon, Conn., Nov. 5, 1804; studied law. Admitted to the Ohio bar, 1836, began practice law in Ravenna, O.; pros. atty. Portage County, O., 1838-41; mem. U.S. Ho. of Reps. (Whig) from Ohio, 28th-29th congresses, 1843-47; del. Whig nat. convs., 1848-52; moved to Cleve., O., 1852; probate judge Cuyahoga County, 1855-88. Died Cleve., Mar. 4, 1890; remains cremated at Buffalo, N.Y., ashes deposited in Buffalo Cemetery.

TILDEN, Samuel Jones, corp. lawyer, gov. N.Y., candidate for U.S. Pres.; b. New Lebanon, N.Y., Feb. 9, 1814; s. Elam and Polly Younglove (Jones) T.; attended Yale, 1834, LL.D. (hon.), 1875; grad. Law Sch., Univ. City N.Y. (now N.Y.U.) 1841. Democratic partisan, wrote article defending Pres. Jackson's veto of U.S. Bank Bill, 1833; wrote polit. tracts and articles during 1830's; admitted to N.Y. bar, 1841; corp. counsel N.Y.C., 1843; established, published N.Y. Morning News, 1844; leader Dem. faction known as Barnburners, 1845; served in N.Y. State Legislature, 1846, 72; mem. N.Y. Constl. Conv., 1846; specialized in refinancing, reorgn. of railroads; built one of Am.'s largest personal fortunes; advised Democrats to offer "loyal opposition" to Lincoln adminstrn.; opposed original decision to go to war, 1861; chmn. N.Y. State Dem. Com., 1866-74; del. from N.Y.C. to N.Y. State Constl Conv., 1867; leader in destruction of Tweed Ring, N.Y.C., 1868-72; founder Bar Assn. City N.Y.; responsible for reforming N.Y. judiciary; Dem. gov. N.Y., 1875-76, reduced state taxes, reduced expenditures after discovery and elimination of frauds, broke up Canal Ring (bi-partisan group accumulating wealth through control of expenditures for repairing, extending state canal system); Dem. candidate for U.S. Pres., received more votes than Republican candidate Rutherford B. Hayes, Tilden was assured of 184 electoral votes, Hayes 163, Rep. mgrs. claimed doubtful states Ore., La., S.C., Fla., and their 22 electoral votes; U.S. Congress created Electoral Commn. to examine and report of returns from doubeful states, commn. declared by party line votes that Hayes carried all doubtful states; Tilden accepted result to avoid possible civil disturbance, but maintained he was wrongfully deprived of U.S. Presidency; bequeathed bulk of estate ($6,000,000) to be administered by Tilden Trust to establish free library for N.Y.C. Died Greystone, nr. Yonkers, N.Y., Aug. 4, 1886.

TILESTON, Thomas, printer, mcht., shipowner; b. Boston, Aug. 13, 1793; s. Lemuel and Mary (Minns) T.; m. Mary Porter, Apr. 11, 1820, 9 children. Editor, Merrimack Intelligencer, Haverhill, Mass., circa 1813, supervised printing of revised Am. edition King James version of Bible, 1814, bought interest in firm; went to N.Y.C., 1818; in partnership with Paul Spofford, sold Haverhill manufactured goods, later entered shipping bus., traded with ports of West Indies, S.Am., and South; Spofford and Tileston became agts. for line of packets to Boston, 1822, built 2 packets for Havana trade, also bought other ships, built ship Southerner for N.Y.-Charleston run, 1846, Northerner, 1847, later added many other ships; founder, dir. Atlantic Ins. Co., 1829; purchased sailing ships of Collin's Line, 1850; pres. Phoenix Bank, 1840-64; organizer, chmn. N.Y. Clearing House, 9 years. Died N.Y.C., Feb. 29, 1864.

TILGHMAN, Edward, lawyer; b. Wyl, Md., Feb. 22, 1751; s. Edward and Elizabeth (Chew) T.; grad. Coll., Acad. and Charitable Sch. of Phila. (now U. Pa.), 1767; m. Elizabeth Chew, May 26, 1774, 4 children including Mary Anna. Admitted to Middle Temple, London, Eng., 1772; admitted to Phila. bar, 1774; enlisted as pvt. during Revolutionary War, rose to brigade maj.; leading lawyer, Phila., known for trial practice and procedure, expert in field of contingent remainders and executory devices. Died Nov. 1, 1815.

TILGHMAN, Matthew, Continental congressman; b. Queen Anne County, Md., Feb. 17, 1718; s. Richard and Anna Maria (Lloyd) T. (adopted by cousin Matthew Tilghman Ward 1737); m. Anna Lloyd, Apr. 6, 1741, 5 children including Anna Maria. Apptd. asso. justice Talbot County (Md.) Ct., 1741, justice of the quorum, 1749-69; mem. Md. Assembly, 1751-58, 60-61, 68-75, speaker, 1773-74; mem. com. to draft remonstrance to king against Townshend Acts, 1768; signed Non-Importation Agreement of 1769; presided over Md. convs. which formed Assn. of Freemen of Md., 1774-76; chmn. Talbot County Com. of Correspondence; pres. Council of Safety, 1775; head of every Md. delegation to Continental Congress, 1774-77, declared in favor of independence, recommended a session of Md. Conv. to remove restrictions to independence; pres. 1st Md. Constl. Conv., Annapolis, 1776; mem. Md. Senate, 1776-83, sometimes pres. Died Queen Anne's County, Md., May 4, 1790; buried family cemetery.

TILGHMAN, Richard Albert, chemist; b. Phila., May 24, 1824; s. Benjamin and Anna Maria (McMurtrie) T.; B.A., U. Pa., 1841; studied chemistry under James C. Booth, Phila.; m. Susan Price Toland, 1860, 5 children. Wrote and delivered paper On the Decomposing Power of Water at High Temperatures (1st systematic study of hydration) before Am. Philos. Soc., 1847; developed process of hydrolysis for extracting acid from animal fat; produced caustic soda through hydrolysis; developed processes for mfg. potassium dichromate, paper pulp, and for producing gas from coal; sold discoveries to various industries in U.S. and Eng.; developed sand-blast process for forming articles made of hard, brittle materials; dir. George Richards & Co., Ltd., mfrs. machine tools, also Tilghman Sand Blast Co., nr. Manchester, Eng. Died Mar. 24, 1899.

TILGHMAN, Tench, army officer; b. "Fausley," Talbot County, Md., Dec. 25, 1744; s. James and Anna (Francis) T.; grad. Coll., Acad. and Charitable Sch. of Phila. (now U. Pa.), 1761; m. Anna Maria Tilghman (cousin), June 9, 1783, 2 children. Mcht., Phila., 1761-75; sec. and treas. to commrs. of Continental Congress Six Nations, 1775; capt. of an independent company which joined Flying Camp, 1776; a.d.c. and personal mil. sec. to Gen. Washington, 1776-81; comr lt. col. Continental Army for service to Gen. Washington; selected for honor of carrying message of Cornwallis' surrender to Continental Congress,

1781. Died Balt., Apr. 18, 1786; buried St. Paul's Churchyard, Balt.

TILGHMAN, William, jurist; b. Fausley, Talbot County, Md., Aug. 12, 1756; s. James and Anna (Francis) T.; grad. Coll., Acad. and Charitable Sch. of Phila. (now U. Pa.), 1772; m. Margaret Elizabeth Allen, July 1, 1794, 1 child. Admitted to Md. bar, 1783; practiced law; mem. Md. Assembly, 1788-91; delegate to Md. Conv. for ratification U.S. Constn.; mem. Md. Senate, 1791-93; admitted to Phila. bar, 1794; chief judge 3d U.S. Circuit Ct. of Pa., 1801-02; apptd. as pres. judge Ct. of Common Pleas for Phila. dist. and surrounding areas, 1805, also judge Pa. High Ct. of Errors and Appeals; chief justice Pa. Supreme Ct., 1806-27 (his court prepared for Legislature report of English statutes in force in Pa.); his chief contribution: incorporation of principles of scientific equity with law of Pa.; pres. Am. Philos. Soc., 1824-27; trustee U. Pa., 1802-27. Died Phila., Apr. 29, 1827.

TILLINGHAST, Joseph Leonard, congressman, lawyer; b. Taunton, Mass., 1791; studied law. Publisher Providence (R.I.) Gazette, 1809; admitted to the bar, 1811, began practice law in Providence; mem. R.I. Ho. of Reps., 1826-33, speaker, 1829-32; mem. U.S. Ho. of Reps. (Whig) from R.I., 25th-27th congresses, 1837-43; trustee Brown U., 1833-44. Died Providence, Dec. 30, 1844; buried North Burial Ground.

TILLINGHAST, Thomas, congressman, jurist; b. East Greenwich, R.I., Aug. 21, 1742; prep. edn. Mem. R.I. Ho. of Reps., 1772-73, 78-80; held several offices under Revolutionary authorities; judge Ct. of Common Pleas, 1779; mem. council of war; asso. justice R.I. Supreme Ct., 1780-97; mem. U.S. Ho. of Reps. from R.I. (filled vacancy), 5th, 7th congresses, Nov. 13, 1797-99, 1801-03. Died East Greenwich, R.I., Aug. 26, 1821.

TILLMAN, Lewis, congressman; b. nr. Shelbyville, Tenn., Aug. 18, 1816; attended common schs.; Served as pvt., Seminole War; became a farmer; clk. Bedford County Circuit Cit., 1852-60; col. Tenn. Militia before Civil War; editor of a newspaper in Shelbyville; clk., also master of the chancery ct., 1865-69; mem. U.S. Ho. of Reps. (Republican) from Tenn., 41st Congress, 1869-71. Died Shelbyville, May 3, 1886; buried Willow Mount Cemetery.

TILLOTSON, Thomas, physician, state ofcl.; b. in Md., 1750; studied medicine. Practiced medicine; served as 1st lt. Md. Militia, 1776; apptd. by Congress as physician and surgeon gen. No. Dept., Continental Army, 1780 until close of Revolutionary War; began practice medicine in N.Y.; mem. N.Y. State Assembly from Red Hook, Dutchess County, 1788-90; mem. N.Y. Senate, 1791-99; mem. council of appointment, 1791; elected to U.S. Ho. of Reps. from N.Y., 7th Congress (did not qualify, or take seat, resigned Aug. 10, 1801); sec. State of N.Y., 1801-06, 07-08. Died Rhinebeck, N.Y., May 5, 1832; buried in vault at rear of Rhinebeck Reformed Dutch Ch.

TILTON, James, congressman; b. Kent County, Del., June 1, 1745; M.B., Coll. of Phila. (now U. Pa.), 1768, M.D., 1771. Served as surgeon Del. Regt., Continental Army, 1776; in charge of mil. hosps. at Princeton, Trenton (N.J.), New Windsor (Md.), 1777-80 (to improve san. conditions built "hosp. huts" for each 6 patients); promoted sr. hosp. physician, surgeon, 1780; operated hosp. at Williamsburg, Va. during Yorktown campaign; mem. Continental Congress, also Del. Ho. of Reps., 1783-85; govt. commr. loans, Del., 1785-1801; physician and surgeon-gen. U.S. Army, 1813-15, made tour inspection along No. frontier instituting widespread san. reforms. Author: Economical Observations on Military Hospitals: and the Prevention and Cure of Diseases Incident to an Army, 1813; Regulations for the Medical Department, 1814. Died nr. Wilmington, Del., May 14, 1822; buried Wilmington and Brandywine Cemetery.

TILTON, John Rollin, landscape painter; b. Loudon, N.H., June 8, 1828; s. Daniel Tilton; m. Caroline Tilton, 2 children. Lived in Italy, 1852-88, had studio in Barberini Palace, Rome; exhibited painting Palace of Thebes at Royal Acad., London, 1873, Lagoons of Venice and Komombo at Centennial Exhbn., Phila., 1876; exhibited at N.A.D., N.Y.C., also Boston Athenaeum; other works include Venetian Fishing Boats, Rome from Mt. Aventine (now in Corcoran Gallery, Washington, D.C.). Died Rome, Mar. 22, 1888.

TIMBERLAKE, Henry, army officer; b. Hanover County, Va., 1730; s. Francis and Sarah (Austin) T. Joined Patriot Blues against French and Indians under George Washington, 1756; apptd. to regt. of William Byrd III in campaign against French at Ft. Duquesne, 1758; placed in command Ft. Necessity, Pa., 1759; made 22 day voyage (with Thomas Sumpter) to Cherokee Indian villages, 1761-62, remained 3 months; accompanied a Cherokee chief and 2 warriors on visit to England, 1762; commd. lt. for services; conducted another group of Cherokee warriors overseas, 1764. Author: Memoirs of Lieutenant Henry Timberlake, London (valuable source for ethnologists), 1765. Died London, Eng., Sept. 30, 1765.

TIMM, Henry Christian, musician; b. Hamburg, Germany, July 11, 1811; studied music under Albert C. Methfessel and Jacob Schmitt. Came to U.S., 1835; made Am. debut as condr. Park Theatre, N.Y.C., 1835; appeared in various orchestras, N.Y.C., also Balt., several years; organist All Souls' Ch., N.Y.C., 18 years; mem. Philharmonic Soc. of N.Y.C., asst. dir., 1844-46, v.p., 1846-47, pres., 1848-63, appeared often as piano soloist. Died Hoboken, N.J., Sept. 5, 1892.

TIMON, John, clergyman; b. Conewaga, Pa., Feb. 12, 1797; s. James and Margaret (Leddy) T.; studied theology at Lazarist sem. The Barrens, St. Louis, Mo., circa 1823. Went on missionary circuits through Mo., circa 1823; ordained priest Congregation of the Mission (Vincentians or Lazarists), 1825; assigned to missions of S.W. with center at Cape Girardeau, Mo., circa 1828; apptd. visitor gen. of Vincentians, 1835, built permanent foundation at Cape Girardeau; visited Europe to petition for missionaries, 1837; apptd. prefect-apostolic of Tex., circa 1840; a founder 1st conf. of Soc. of St. Vincent de Paul of St. Louis, 1844; became bishop diocese of Buffalo, N.Y., 1847; founded many charitable instns., hosp. under Sisters of Charity, Providence Lunatic Asylum, home for mutes, Magdalen asylum, 1st Am. Catholic instn. for unmarried mothers, Niagara Sem. under the Lazarists, 1848; dedicated Cathedral of St. Joseph for which he made collections in Europe and in Mexico, 1855; published Missions in Western New York and Church History of the Diocese of Buffalo, 1862. Died Buffalo, Apr. 16, 1867.

TIMOTHY, Lewis, printer; m. Elizabeth Timothy, 6 children including Peter. Came to Am., 1731, settled in Phila.; did editorial work on Benjamin Franklin's Philadelphische Zeitung (1st German lang. paper in Am.), 1732; librarian Phila. Library Soc., 1732; journeyman printer for Benjamin Franklin, 1733, in partnership with Franklin in printing business, Charleston, S.C., 1733; revived South Carolina Gazette, 1734, also printed ofcl. govt. documents; printed his most important work The Laws of the Province of South Carolina (compiled by Nicholas Trott, LL.D.), 2 vols., 1736; printed only 18 other pieces. Died Dec. 1738.

TIMROD, Henry, poet; b. Charleston, S.C., Dec. 8, 1828; s. William Henry and Thyrza (Prince) T.; attended Franklin Coll. (now U. Ga.), 1847-49; m. Kate Goodwin, Feb. 16, 1864, 1 child. Tchr., tutor on a S.C. plantation; wrote verses for So. Literary Messenger, other periodicals; a founder Russell's Mag., 1857, contbr. numerous works; published small collection of poems, 1860; wrote Ethnogenesis, 1861, also war poems which stirred South and earned him title of laureate of the Confederacy, poems included A Cry to Arms, Carolina, Carmen Triumphale, Charleston; enlisted in Co. B, 30th S.C. Regt., 1862; joined Confederate Army of West as correspondent of Charleston Mercury, 1862; partial propr., asso. editor South Carolinian, Columbia, S.C., 1864 until burning of Columbia, 1865; completed Magnolia Cemetery Ode, 1866; known as one of ablest So. poets of century; poems edited by Hayne as The Poems of Henry Timrod, 1873; meml. edit. of all his works published, 1898. Died Columbia, Oct. 6, 1867.

TINGEY, Thomas, naval officer; b. London, Eng., Sept. 11, 1750; m. Margaret Murdoch, Mar. 30, 1779; m. 2d, Ann Bladen Dulany, Dec. 9, 1812; m. 3d, Ann Evelina Craven, May 19, 1817; 3 children. Commanded brig Lady Clausen sailing from St. Croix, V.I. to Europe, 1778; served in Am. mcht. marine, after 1781; commd. capt. U.S. Navy, 1798; commanded 3 vessels in the Windward Passage, 1798-99, rejected demand of Brit. frigate Surprise to have his crew examined for presence of Brit. seamen; sr. officer in W.I., 1799; organizer, comdt. Washington (D.C.) Navy Yard, 1800, 04-14; supt., 1800-03, financial agt., 1803-04, naval agt., 1804-14, burned navy yard when British invaded, 1814. Died Washington, Feb. 23, 1829; buried Congressional Cemetery, Washington.

TIPTON, John, army officer, state legislator; b. Baltimore County, Md., Aug. 15, 1730; s. Jonathan and Elizabeth T.; m. Mary Butler, circa 1753; m. 2d, Martha (Denton) Moore, July 22, 1779; 15 children. A founder Woodstock, Dunmore County (later Shenandoah County), Va.; justice of peace Beckford Parish (Va.); an organizer, signer Independence Resolutions, Woodstock, 1774; mem. Dunmore County Com. of Safety and Correspondence, also recruiting officer; mem. Va. Ho. of Burgesses, 1774-81; rep. to Va. Conv., Williamsburg, 1776; commd. lt. col. Va. Militia; high sheriff of Shenandoah County during Revolutionary War; elected to N.C. Assembly in opposition to John Sevier (gov. State of Franklin), 1785; served as col. Washington County (N.C.) Militia; both Sevier and Tipton's factions maintained cts. and militias, raiding parties from both sides carried off ct. records and ofcl. papers, civil war lasted 3 years, Tipton was victorious after a battle at his home nr. Jonesboro, Tenn., 1788; rep. from Washington County in 1st Tenn. Assembly, 1793, 94-95; trustee Washington Coll., 1795; helped draft Tenn. Constn., 1796; mem. Tenn. Senate. Died Sinking Creek, N.C., Aug. 1813.

TIPTON, John, senator, army officer; b. Sevier County, Tenn., Aug. 14, 1786; s. Joshua and Jennett (Shields) T.; m. Jennett Shields (his cousin), 1818, 3 children; m. 2d, Matilda Spencer, 1825, 3 children. Served with "Yellow Jackets" of U.S. Army in Tippecanoe campaign, 1809; promoted brig. gen. Ind. Militia, 1811; justice of peace Ind. Territory, 1810; commanded troop of rangers Ind. Militia on Ohio River frontier; elected maj. gen. 2d Div., Ind. Militia, 1822; sheriff Harrison City, Ind. Territory, 1815-19; mem. Ind. Assembly, 1819-23; surveyor Ind.-Ill. boundary, 1821; U.S. Indian agt. for Ft. Wayne dist. Northern Ind., 1823, negotiated important treaties, 1826, 28, 36; land speculator; mem. U.S. Senate from Ind., Jan. 3, 1832-39; a Jacksonian Democrat; wrote journal published in Indpls. News, Apr. 17, May 5, 1879. Died Logansport, Ind., Apr. 5, 1839; buried Mt. Hope Cemetery.

TISQUANTUM, see Squanto.

TITUS, Obadiah, congressman, lawyer; b. in what is now Millbrook, N.Y., Jan. 20, 1789; studied law. Admitted to the bar, began practice law in Washington, Dutchess County, N.Y.; served as capt. Inf., War of 1812; elected county judge; elected sheriff Dutchess County, 1828; mem. U.S. Ho. of Reps. (Democrat) from N.Y., 25th Congress, 1837-39. Died Washington, N.Y., Sept. 2, 1854; buried Nine Partners (Friends) Burial Ground, Millbrook.

TIYANOGA, see Hendrick.

TOBEY, Edward Silas, mcht.; b. Kingston, Mass., Apr. 5, 1813; s. Silas and Betsey (Fuller) T.; m. Hannah Brown Sprague, Apr. 5, 1841, 10 children. Partner, Phineas and Seth Sprague, shipping firm, Boston, 1833-66; officer S.S. Co. which became Fall River Line; treas. U.S. Ins. Co.; treas. Russell Mills, cotton-duck factory, Plymouth, Mass.; mem. com. on defense of Boston Harbor, 1861; mem. adv. com. on financial policy of U.S. Govt.; pres. Boston Bd. of Trade, 1861-63; pres. Boston YMCA; made speeches on public questions which were later published; trustee Bradford Acad., 1863-75, Dartmouth, 1863-70; founder Mass. Inst. Tech.; mem. Mass. Senate, 1866; mem. Bd. Commrs. of Indian Affairs, 1869; postmaster of Boston, 1875-86. Died Brookline, Mass., Mar. 29, 1891.

TOCQUEVILLE, Alexis Henri Maurice Clérel de, see de Tocqueville.

TOD, David, gov. Ohio, coal and iron exec.; b. nr. Youngstown, O., Feb. 21, 1805; s. George and Sarah (Isaacs) T.; m. Maria Smith, June 4, 1832, 7 children. Admitted to Ohio bar, 1827; postmaster of Warren (O.), 1830-38; mem. Ohio Senate, 1838-40; U.S. minister to Brazil, 1847-51, failed to stop African slave trade to Brazil; founder Youngstown's iron industry; promoter Cleve. and Mahoning Valley R.R., pres., 1858-68; del. to Democratic Nat. Conv., 1860; gov. Ohio (Unionist), 1861, defeated for renomination; declined appointment as U.S. sec. of treasury, 1864; Republican presdl. elector, 1868. Died Ohio, Nov. 13, 1868.

TOD, George, jurist; b. Suffield, Conn., Dec. 11, 1773; s. David and Rachel (Kent) T.; grad. Yale, 1795; attended Litchfield (Conn.) Law Sch.; m. Sarah Isaacs, Sept. 18, 1797, at least 5 children including David. Apptd. pros. atty. Trumbull County in N.W. Territory, Georgetown, O. 1800; mem. Ohio Senate (in opposition to extreme Republicans), 1804-06; judge Ohio Supreme Ct., 1807-10; mem. Ohio Senate,, 1810-12; served as maj. 19th Inf. in No. Ohio, lt. col. 17th Inf., U.S. Army, in War of 1812; presiding judge 3d Dist., Circuit Ct. of Appeals in Ohio, 1816-29. Died Youngstown, O., Apr. 11, 1841.

TOD, John, congressman; b. Suffield, Conn., Nov. 1779; s. David and Rachel (Kent) T.; m. Mary R. Hanna, 1817, 3 children. Clk. Bradford County (Pa.) commn., 1806-07; mem. Pa. Ho. of Reps., 1810-13, twice speaker; mem. Pa. Senate, 1814-16, pres. part of term; mem. U.S. Ho. of Reps. (Democrat) from Pa., 17th-18th congresses, 1821-24, mem. com. on mil. affairs, chmn. house com. on manufactures which urged higher duties, expanded protective list, 1823-24; pres. judge 16th Jud. Circuit of Pa., 1824; asso. justice Pa.

Supreme Ct., 1827. Died Bedford, Pa., Mar. 27, 1830.

TODD, Charles Stewart, lawyer, diplomat; b. Danville, Ky., Jan. 22, 1791; s. Thomas and Elizabeth (Harris) T.; grad. Coll. William and Mary, 1809; attended Litchfield (Conn.) Law Sch.; m. Letitia Shelby, June 16, 1816, 12 children. Admitted to Ky. bar, 1811; served as volunteer acting q.m. in left wing of Northwestern Army in War of 1812, commd. col. and insp. gen., 1815; sec. of state Ky., 1816; Franklin County rep. in Ky. Legislature, 1817-18; apptd. by Pres. Monroe as diplomatic agt. in Colombia (S.Am.), 1820; commr. to Presbyn. Gen. Assembly, 1837; campaigned for William Henry Harrison for U.S. Pres., 1840, collaborated with Benjamin Drake in writing campaign biography of Harrison; published Cincinnati Republican; apptd. by Pres. Tyler as U.S. minister to Russia, 1841; a commr. to negotiate with Indian tribes on Mexican border, 1850; editor Louisville Indsl. and Comml. Gazette. Died Baton Rouge, La., May 17, 1871.

TODD, Eli, physician; b. New Haven, Conn., July 22, 1769; s. Michael and Mary (Rowe) T.; grad. Yale, 1787; studied medicine; m. Rhoda Hill, Aug. 9, 1796; m. 2d, Catherine Hill, Nov. 1828. Treated epidemic of "spotted fever", Farmington, Conn., 1808; practiced medicine in Hartford, Conn., 1820; mem. Conn. Med. Soc., v.p., 1823, pres., 1827-28; investigated conditions in insane asylums and became interested in treatment of mentally ill, 1812; a founder Soc. for Relief of Insane, 1822; a founder Conn. Retreat for Insane, Hartford, 1824, 1st supt., 1824-33, used trained personnel, recognized alcoholism as a mental disease. Author med. articles. Died Hartford, Nov. 17, 1833.

TODD, John, clergyman; b. Rutland, Vt., Oct. 9, 1800; s. Dr. Timothy and Phoebe (Buel) T.; grad. Yale, 1822; attended Andover Theol. Sem.; D.D. (hon.), Williams Coll., 1845; m. Mary Skinner Brace, Mar. 11, 1827, 9 children. Ordained to ministry Congregational Ch., 1827; pastor, Groton, Mass., 1827-33, Edwards Ch., Northampton, Mass., 1833-36, Congregational Ch., Phila., 1836-42; published sermon Principles and Results of Congregationalism, 1837; pastor 1st Congl. Ch., Pittsfield, Mass., 1842-73; a founder Mt. Holyoke Sem.; trustee Williams Coll. Author: Lectures to Children, 1834 (translated into 5 langs.); The Student's Manual, 1835; Died Pittsfield, Aug. 24, 1873.

TODD, John Blair Smith, congressman; army officer; b. Lexington, Ky., Apr. 4, 1814; grad. U.S. Mil. Acad., 1837; studied law. Commd. 2d lt. Sixth Inf., U.S. Army, 1837, 1st lt., 1837, capt., 1843, served in Fla. War, 1837-42, also in war with Mexico, resigned, 1856; became an Indian trader, settled in Ft. Randall, Dakota; admitted to bar, 1861, began practice of law, Yankton, Dakota; served as brig. gen. Volunteers, Union Army, 1861, 62; mem. U.S. Congress (Democrat) from Dakota Territory, 37th Congress, Dec. 9, 1861-63, (contested election) 38th Congress, June 17, 1864-65; mcht., lawyer in Dakota; speaker Territorial Ho. of Reps., 1866-67. Died Yankton County, Dakota (now S.D.), Jan. 5, 1872; buried Yankton Cemetery.

TODD, Lawrie, see Thorburn, Grant.

TODD, Lemuel, congressman, lawyer; b. Carlisle, Pa., July 29, 1817; grad. Dickinson Coll., Carlisle, 1839; studied law. Admitted to Pa. bar, 1841, began practice law, Carlisle; mem. U.S. Ho. of Reps. from Pa., 34th, (as Republican) 43d congresses, 1855-57, 73-75; served as maj., 1st Regt., Pa. Volunteer Res. Corps, U.S. Army, Civil War; insp. gen. of Pa. on gov.'s staff. Died Carlisle, May 12, 1891; buried Ashland Cemetery.

TODD, Sereno Edwards, agriculturist, editor; b. Tompkins County, N.Y., June 3, 1820; s. Josiah and Lucretia (Ingersoll) T.; m. Rhoda Peck, June 19, 1844; m. 2d, Dora Amanda Peterson, Mar. 19, 1887; 2 children including Prof. David Peck. Contbr. to Country Gentleman, 1860; agrl. adviser to Gov. Alonzo B. Cornell of N.Y.; asso. editor Am. Agriculturist, 1865; in charge of agrl. dept. of N.Y. Times, 1866; editor home dept. of N.Y. Observer; editorial writer Hearth and Home; agrl. editor N.Y. Tribune; edited Practical Farmer; patented power ditching machine, 1872. Author: The Young Farmer's Manual, vol. 1, 1860, vol. 2, 1867; The American Wheat Culturist, 1868. Died Orange, N.J., Dec. 26, 1898.

TODD, Thomas, asso. justice U.S. Supreme Ct.; b. King and Queen County, Va., Jan. 23, 1765; s. Richard and Elizabeth (Richards) T.; m. Elizabeth Harris, 1788; m. 2d, Lucy Payne, 1811; 8 children including Col. Charles Stewart. Served in Am. Revolution; admitted to Ky. bar, 1786; clk. U.S. Ct. for Ky. dist., circa 1787-92; clk. Ky. Ct. of Appeals, 1792-1801, became judge, 1801; clk. Ky. Ho. of Reps., 1792; became chief justice Ky. Supreme Ct., 1806, wrote many decisions establishing basis for land law of Ky.; asso. justice U.S. Supreme Ct., 1807-26, served on Western circuit. Died Frankfort, Ky., Feb. 7, 1826.

TOEBBE, Augustus Marie, clergyman; b. Meppen, Hanover, Germany, Jan. 15, 1829; attended Mt. St. Mary of the West Sem., Cincinnati. Ordained priest Roman Catholic Ch., 1854; pastor in Cincinnati; theologian at 1st Plenary Council of Balt., 1852; apptd. bishop of Covington (Ky.), 1870. Died Covington, May 2, 1884.

TOLAND, Hugh Huger, surgeon, coll. pres.; b. Guilder's Creek, S.C., Apr. 16, 1806; s. John and Mary (Boyd) T.; grad. (1st in class) Transylvania U., Lexington, Ky., 1828; m. Mary Goodwin, 1833; m. 2d, Mary Avery, 1844; m. 3d, Mrs. Mary B. (Morrison) Gridley, 1860; 3 children. Performed successful operations for relief of clubfoot and strabimus (using lithotomy forceps), Columbia, S.C., 1833; went to Cal., 1852; chief surgeon Marine Hosp., San Francisco, 1853; staff mem. county hosp.; founder Toland Med. Coll., San Francisco, 1864, pres., prof. surgery, 1864-80, gave all facilities of sch. to U. Cal., 1873; wrote 71 articles, many published in Pacific Medical and Surgical Jour.; wrote textbook on surgery; noted for work on bladder stones, plastic surgery. Died S.C., Feb. 27, 1880.

TOLMIE, William Fraser, physician; med. officer Hudson Bay Co.; Tolmie's warbler named in his honor (also known as MacGillivray's warbler).

TOME, Jacob, mcht., banker, philanthropist; b. Manheim Twp., Pa., Aug. 13, 1810; s. Christian and Christiana (Badger) T.; m. Carolyn M. Webb, Dec. 6, 1841; m. 2d, Eva S. Nesbitt, Oct. 1, 1884. Partner of David Rinehart, lumber mcht., Port Deposit, Md., 1835; partner firm John and Thomas E. Bond, 1855; organized steamship co. for Balt.-Fredericksburg (Md.) run, 1849; established Cecil Bank, Port Deposit, 1850, owner banks at Elkton, Hagerstown, Md., Fredricksburg, Va.; mem. Md. Senate, 1863-64, chmn. finance com.; incorporated, 1889, opened Jacob Tome Inst. (later called Tome Sch. for Boys), Port Deposit, 1894; benefactor, trustee Dickinson Coll., Carlisle, Pa.; builder Tome Meml. Meth. Episcopal Ch., Port Deposit. Died Mar. 16, 1898.

TOMLINSON, Gideon, senator, gov. of Conn., congressman; b. Stratford, Conn., Dec. 31, 1780; grad. Yale, 1802; studied law. Admitted to the bar, began practice law, Fairfield, Conn., 1807; clk. Conn. Ho. of Reps., 1817, mem. and speaker, 1818; mem. U.S. Ho. of Reps. (Democrat) from Conn., 16th-19th congresses, 1819-27; gov. Conn., 1827-31; mem. U.S. Senate from Conn., 1831-37; trustee Trinity Coll., 1832-36. Died Fairfield, Oct. 8, 1854; buried Old Congregational Cemetery.

TOMLINSON, Thomas Ash, congressman, lawyer; b. N.Y.C., Mar. 1802; studied law. Admitted to the bar, began practice law in Keeseville, Essex County, N.Y., 1823; mill owner, land dealer; served as col. N.Y. Militia; mem. N.Y. State Assembly, 1835-36; mem. U.S. Ho. of Reps. (Whig) from N.Y., 27th Congress, 1841-43; practiced law, also in real estate bus. Died Keeseville, June 18, 1872; buried Evergreen Cemetery.

TOMOCHICHI, Indian chief; b. Apalachicola, nr. Columbus, Ga. (now Ala.), 1650; m. Scenawki. Chief of Creek Indians, established home at Yamacraw on Savannah River, nr. what is now Savannah, Ga., 1721; signed peace treaty with 1st Ga. colonists under James E. Oglethorpe, 1733; persuaded other Creek tribes to sign treaties with English; taken to Eng. by Oglethorpe, 1734, received by King George II and Archbishop of Canterbury. Died nr. Savannah, Oct. 5, 1739; buried Percival Square (now Court House Square), Savannah.

TOMPKINS, Caleb, congressman; b. nr. Scarsdale, N.Y., Dec. 22, 1759. Mem. N.Y. State Assembly, 1804-06; judge Ct. of Common Pleas also county Westchester County (N.Y.) Ct., 1807-11, 20-24; mem. U.S. Ho. of Reps. from N.Y., 15th-16th congresses, 1817-21. Died Scarsdale, Jan. 1, 1846; buried First Presbyn. Ch. Cemetery, White Plains, N.Y.

TOMPKINS, Christopher, congressman, lawyer; b. Green County, Ky., Mar. 24, 1780; studied law. Admitted to the bar, began practice law, Glasgow, Ky.; mem. Ky. Ho. of Reps., 1805, 35-36; mem. U.S. Ho. of Reps. from Ky., 22d-23d congresses, 1831-35; Whig presdl. elector, 1837. Died Glasgow, Aug. 9, 1858; buried family burying ground, Glasgow.

TOMPKINS, Cydnor Bailey, congressman; b. nr. St. Clairsville, O., Nov. 8, 1810; grad. Ohio U., 1835; studied law; at least 1 son, Emmett. Admitted to Ohio bar, 1837, began practice law, McConnelsville, O.; recorder of McConnelsville, 1840; pros. atty. Morgan County (O.), 1848-51; street commr. McConnelsville, 1850; mem. Republican State Conv., 1855; mem. U.S. Ho. of Reps. (Republican) from Ohio, 35th-36th congresses, 1857-61. Died McConnelsville, July 23, 1862; buried McConnelsville Cemetery.

TOMPKINS, Daniel D., vice pres. U.S., gov. N.Y.; b. Scarsdale, N.Y., June 21, 1774; s. Jonathan G. and Sarah (Hyatt) T.; grad. Columbia, 1795; m. Hannah Minthorne, 1797, 7 children. Admitted to bar, 1797; mem. N.Y. Constl. Conv., 1801; mem. N.Y. Assembly, 1803; elected to U.S. Ho. of Reps. 9th Congress, 1804, resigned before taking seat to become asso. justice N.Y. Supreme Ct., 1804-07; gov. N.Y., 1807, 10, 13, prevented establishment Bank of N. Am.; instrumental in passage of law to extinguish slavery in N.Y. State, 1817 (became effective 1827); served as comdr.-in-chief N.Y. Militia, War of 1812; commanded 3d Mil. Dist., including So. N.Y., Eastern N.J., 1814, used personal credit to pay and maintain troops (later accused of irregularities in wartime financial conduct, cleared, compensated for expenditures by Congress); vice. pres. U.S., 1817-25; pres. N.Y. Constl. Conv., 1821; a founder N.Y. Hist. Soc. Died Staten Island, N.Y., June 11, 1825; buried St. Mark's Churchyard, N.Y.C.

TOMPKINS, Patrick Watson, congressman, lawyer; b. in Ky., 1804; studied law. Admitted to the bar, began practice law in Vicksburg, Miss.; judge of the circuit ct.; mem. U.S. Ho. of Reps. (Whig) from Miss., 30th Congress, 1847-49; moved to Cal. during gold rush, 1849. Died San Francisco, Cal., May 8, 1853; buried Yerba Buena Cemetery.

TOMPSON, Benjamin, educator; b. Quincy, Mass., July 14, 1642; s. William and Abigail Tompson; grad. Harvard, 1662; m. Susanna Kirtland, 1667, 9 children. Master of free sch. (now Boston Latin Sch.), 1667-71; tchr., Charlestown, Mass., 1671-74, Braintree, Mass., 1679-99, 1704-10, Roxbury, Mass., 1699-1704; also practiced medicine, wrote poetry. Author: New England Crisis, 1676; New England's Tears for Her Present Miseries, 1676; A Funeral Tribute to Gov. John Winthrop, 1676; A Narrative of the Troubles with the Indians, 1677; The Grammarians Funeral, 1708; A Neighbour's Tears on Mrs. Rebekah Sewall, 1710. Died Apr. 10, 1714.

TONER, Joseph Meredith, physician; b. Pitts., Apr. 30, 1825; s. Meredith and Ann (Layton) T.; attended Western U. Pa., Pitts., Mt. St. Mary's Coll., Emmitsburg, Md.; attended Jefferson Med. Coll., 1849-50, M.D., 1853; M.D., Vt. Med. Coll., Woodstock, 1850; never married. Began practice of medicine, Washington, D.C., 1855; a founder St. Joseph's Orphan Asylum, physician; physician St. Vincent's Female Orphan Asylum, St. Ann's Infant Asylum; pres. A.M.A., 1873, Am. Pub. Health Assn., 1874; donated 27,000 volumes to Library of Congress, 1882; made subject index for all Am. med. jours. up to 1870; began library for A.M.A., 1868, later removed to Newberry Library, Chgo.; a founder Columbia Hist. Soc., 1894; Author: Internal Instinct, 1864; The Medical Men of the Revolution, 1876; Address on Medical Biography, 1876; Editor: Washington's Rules of Civility and Decent Behavior, 1888; Journal of Colonel George Washington . . . in 1754, published 1893. Died Cresson, Pa., July 30, 1896; buried family plot, Derry, Pa.

TONTY, Henry de, see de Tonty, Henry.

TOOMBS, Robert Augustus, senator, Confederate ofcl.; b. Wilkes County, Ga., July 2, 1810; s. Robert and Catherine (Huling) T.; attended U. Ga.; grad. Union Coll., Schenectady, N.Y., 1828; m. Julia DuBose, 1830, 3 children. Admitted to bar, 1830; active in Whig Party; mem. Ga. Legislature, 1837-41, 42-43; mem. U.S. Ho. of Reps. from Ga., 29th-32d congresses, 1845-53, did not appear as spokesman for So. interests until 1850 crisis when he threatened secession, but urged support of Compromise of 1850 after passage; mem. U.S. Senate from Ga., 1853-Feb. 4, 1861 (elected Constl. Union Party candidate and Breckinridge supporter, 1858); advocated secession when Crittenden Compromise did not pass in Congress, 1861; Ga. del. to Confederate Provisional Congress, Montgomery, Ala., 1861; sec. of state Confederate States Am., 1861, resigned because of dissatisfaction with leadership of Jefferson Davis; commd. brig. gen. Confederate Army, 1861, served in Va. theater, effectiveness as mil. leader impaired by continued polit. activity; resigned commn. after failure to obtain promotion after Battle of Antietam, 1862; retired to home in Washington, Ga., became a vehement critic of Confederate govt. and conduct of the war; lived in London, Eng., 1865-67; returned to Ga., leading opponent of Radical Reconstrn., urged solution of So. problems through Democratic Party; mem. Ga. Conv. of 1877, repudiated Carpetbag govt. debts and limited Negro suffrage. Died Washington, Ga., Dec. 15, 1885; buried Rest Haven Cemetery, Washington.

TOPLIFF, Samuel, news dealer; b. Boston, Apr. 25, 1789; s. Samuel and Mindwell (Bird) T.; m. Jane Sisson Blackstock, Dec. 2, 1829, 8 children. In charge of books Marine and Gen. Newsroom, 1811-14, became owner, 1814, changed name to Mchts.' Reading Room, co-owner (with brother Benjamin), 1824-42; built business into largest, most efficient newsroom in U.S., sold news from correspondents to papers in Boston, N.Y.C. and Phila.; mem. Boston City Council, 1844-49, alderman, 1855. Died Boston, Dec. 11, 1864.

TOPPAN, Charles, engraver; b. Newburyport, Mass., Feb. 10, 1796. Employed by Murray, Draper, Fairman & Co., other banknote engraving firms, Phila., until 1835; partner Draper, Toppan, Longacre & Co., 1835-39, Draper, Toppan & Co., 1840-44, Toppan, Carpenter & Co., 1845-50, 56-61, Toppan, Carpenter, Casilear & Co., 1851-55, all Phila.; moved to N.Y.C., circa 1855; a founder Am. Bank Note Co., N.Y.C., 1858, 1st pres., 1858-60. Died Florence, Italy, Nov. 20, 1874.

TORBERT, Alfred Thomas Archimedes, army officer, diplomat; b. Georgetown, Del., July 1, 1833; s. Jonathan R. and Catherine (Milby) T.; grad. U.S. Mil. Acad., 1855; m. Mary E. Curry, Jan. 17, 1866. Apptd. brevet 2d lt. inf. U.S. Army, 1855; served on frontier, 1856-61; promoted 2d lt., 1856, 1st lt., 1861; commd. col. 1st N.J. Volunteers, 1861; commd. capt. U.S. Army, 1861; participated in siege of Yorktown, battles of West Point, Gaine's Mills; commanded a brigade of VI Corps; brevetted brig. gen. U.S. Volunteers, 1862; assigned command 1st Cavalry div. Army of Potomac, 1864; defeated Confederate Army at battles of Hanovertown, Matadequin Creek, Cold Harbor; apptd. chief of cavalry of middle mil. div. Army of Shenandoah, 1864; brevetted maj. gen. U.S. Army, 1865; U.S. minister to Salvador, 1869-71; consul gen. Havana, Cuba, 1871-73, Paris, France, 1873-78; resigned to enter bus. enterprise in Mexico, 1878. Drowned off coast of Fla., Aug. 29, 1880.

TORRENCE, Joseph Thatcher, iron mfr., ry. developer; b. Mercer County, Pa., Mar. 15, 1843; s. James and Rebecca Torrence; m. Elizabeth Norton, Sept. 11, 1872, 1 child. Chief salesman Reis, Brown, and Berger, iron mfrs., New Castle, Pa., 1863-68; engr. for constrn. of iron works for Joliet Iron and Steel Co. (Ill.), 1870-74; cons. engr. Green Bay and Bangor Furnace Co., Chgo., 1874-circa 1880; an organizer Joseph H. Brown Iron & Steel Co., Chgo.; organizer Chgo. & Calumet Terminal Ry. Co., 1886 (firm began system of belt lines now surrounding Chgo.); purchased land on which East Chicago was developed, 1886; an organizer Chgo. Elevated Terminal Ry. Co., 1890; commd. col. Ill. Nat. Guard, 1874, promoted brig. gen., 1876; civil and mil. dictator of Chgo. and Cook County during railroad strikes of 1877, resigned 1881. Died Chgo., Oct. 31, 1896.

TORREY, Charles Turner, abolitionist; b. Scituate, Mass., Nov. 21, 1813; s. Charles Turner and Hannah (Turner) T.; A.B., Yale, 1833; attended Andover Theol. Sem., 1834; studied theology under Rev. Jacob Ide, West Midway, Mass., m. Mary Ide, Mar. 29, 1837. Licensed to preach by Mendon Assn., 1836; ordained to ministry Congregational Ch., Providence, R.I., 1837; pastor Richmond Street Congregational Ch., Providence, 1837, Harvard Street Congregational Ch., Salem, Mass., 1838-39; left ministry because abolitionist activities interferred with pastoral duties; organized conservative abolitionists against Garrison's leadership, 1838; editor Mass. Abolitionist (founded by conservatives), 1838; an organizer Mass. Abolitionist Soc., apptd. soc.'s agt., resigned soon after; freelance correspondent in Washington, D.C., 1841; while reporting "Convention of Slaveholders" at Annapolis (Md.), Jan. 1842, identified as abolitionist, arrested, freed 5 days later; notoriety gained him position as editor unsuccessful publs. Tocsin of Liberty and Albany Patriot; moved to Balt., engaged in business, helped escaping slaves from Va. and Md.; arrested, sentenced (in widely publicized trial) to 6 years in Md. State Penitentiary. Author: Home, or the Pilgrims Faith Reviewed, 1846. Died Balt., May 9, 1846; buried Boston.

TORREY, John, botanist, chemist, educator; b. N.Y.C., Aug. 15, 1796; s. Capt. William and Margaret (Nichols) T.; M.D., Coll. Physicians and Surgeons, N.Y.C., 1818; A.M. (hon.), Yale, 1823; LL.D. (hon.), Amherst Coll., 1845; m. Eliza Shaw, Apr. 20, 1824, at least 4 children. Catalogued plants growing near N.Y.C., 1817; gave spl. attention to plants of Northeastern U.S.; as result of govt. sponsored expedition (1820), reported on plants collected by David Bates Douglass near source of Mississippi River, 1820; apptd. prof. chemistry, mineralogy and geology U.S. Mil. Acad., 1824-27; prof. chemistry Coll. Physicians and Surgeons, 1827-55, prof. emeritus until 1873; prof. chemistry and natural history Coll. of N.J. (now Princeton), 1830-54; worked with Asa Gray on Flora of North America, 1838-43; apptd. N.Y. State botanist, 1836; wrote reports of exploring expdns. of Frémont, Marcy and others, circa 1836-58; elected fgn. mem. Linnean Soc. of London, 1839; mem. Am. Acad. Arts and Scis., 1841; U.S. assayer, 1853-73; Torrey's Peak (Colo.) named for him; plants named in his honor include Torreya Taxifolia, Torreya Californica, Torreya Nucifera, Torreya Grandis. Author: Flora of Northern and Middle Sections of the United States, 1823; A Compendium of the Flora of the Northern and Middle States, 1826; Flora of the State of New York, 2 vols., 1843. Died N.Y.C., Mar. 10, 1873.

TORREY, Joseph, coll. pres.; b. Rowley, Mass., Feb. 2, 1797; grad. Dartmouth, 1816, Andover Theol. Sem., 1819; D.D. (hon.), Harvard, 1850. Missionary, Congregational Ch., 1819-24; pastor Congregational Ch., Royalton, Vt., 1824-27; prof. Greek and Latin, U. Vt., Burlington, 1827-42, prof. moral philosophy, 1842-62, acting pres., 1862-66. Author: A Theory of Art, 1874. Translator: General History of the Christian Religion and Church (Neander), 5 vols., 1847-54. Died probably Burlington, Nov. 26, 1867.

TOTTEN, George Muirson, civil engr.; b. New Haven, Conn., May 28, 1809; s. Gilbert and Mary (Rice) T.; grad. Norwich (Vt.) Mil. Acad., 1827; m. Harriet Seely, July 12, 1835, at least 2 children. Asst. engr. on Farmington Canal, 1827, on Juniata Canal, Pa., 1828-31, on Delaware and Raritan Canal, N.J., 1831-35; assisted in constrn. railroad from Reading to Port Clinton, Pa., 1835, also railroads in Va., Pa., N.C.; with Pa. Sunbury and Danville R.R., 1837-40, Gaston & Raleigh R.R. (N.C.), 1840-43; received 1st S.Am. commn. as chief engr. to build Canal del Dique, Columbia, 1843; joined Panama R.R. as engr.-in-chief, 1850, remained on Isthmus of Panama, 25 years; engr. on railroads in Venezuela; cons. engr. on 1st Panama Canal project, circa 1879-83; mem. Am. Philos. Soc., 1851. Died N.Y.C,. May 17, 1884.

TOTTEN, Joseph Gilbert, army officer, engr.; b. New Haven, Conn., Aug. 23, 1788; s. Peter and Grace (Mansfield) T.; grad. U.S. Mil. Acad., 1805; A.M. (hon.), Brown U., 1829; m. Catlyna Pearson, 1816, 7 children. Commd. 2d lt. engrs. U.S. Army, 1805, 1st. lt., 1810, capt., 1812; asst. engr. harbor defenses N.Y.C., 1808, spl. supr. Ft. Clinton, Castle Garden, N.Y.; asst. in defenses of New Haven, New London (Conn.), Sag Harbor; chief engr. U.S. Army on Niagara frontier, 1812; brevetted maj., 1813, lt. col., 1814; engaged in coastal fortifications, 1815-38; promoted maj., 1818, lt. col., 1828, col., 1838; chief engr. U.S. Army, insp. U.S. Mil. Acad., 1838-64; served with Gen. Winfield Scott as chief engr. and mem. so-called Little Cabinet; originated successful plan of operations at Battle of Veracruz during Mexican War; brevetted brig. gen., 1847; mem. Lighthouse Bd., 1851-58, 60-64; instrumental in putting into use system of lighting by Fresnel lenses; commd. brig. gen. U.S. Army, 1863; supr. defensive works around Washington, D.C.; mem. bd. to regulate and fix heavy ordnance, 1861-62; brevetted maj. gen. by U.S. Congress, 1864; published Essays on Hydraulic and Common Mortars and on Lime-Burning, 1838; corporator Nat. Acad. Scis., 1863; studied conchology, 2 shells (gemma and succinca tottenii) named for him; Ft. Totten (N.Y.C. Harbor) named for him. Died Washington, D.C., Apr. 22, 1864.

TOTTEN, Silas, coll. pres.; b. Schoharie County, N.Y., Mar. 26, 1804; grad. Union Coll., 1830, D.D. (hon.), 1838. Ordained to ministry Protestant Episcopal Ch., 1833; prof. natural philosophy and mathematics Washington Coll. (became Trinity Coll. 1845), Hartford, Conn., 1833-37, pres., 1837-43; prof. English literature Coll. William and Mary, 1848-59; chancellor U. Ia., 1859-64; rector Episcopal Ch., Decatur, Ill., 1864-66. Author: New Introduction to Algebra, 1836; The Analogy of Truth, 1848. Died Lexington, Ky., Oct. 7, 1873; buried Lexington.

TOUCEY, Isaac, senator, gov. Conn., cabinet sec.; b. Newtown, Conn., Nov. 5, 1796; s. Zalmon and Phebe (Booth) T.; m. Catherine Nichols, Oct. 28, 1827. Admitted to Conn. bar, 1818; states atty. for Hartford County (Conn.), 1822-35, 42-44; mem. U.S. Ho. of Reps. from Conn., 24th, 25th congresses, 1835-39; gov. Conn. (Democrat, chosen by Legislature), 1846; U.S. atty. gen. under Polk, 1848-49; acting U.S. sec. of state; mem. Conn. Senate, 1850, Conn. Ho. of Reps., 1852; mem. U.S. Senate from Conn., 1852-57, supported Kan.-Neb. bill, 1854; U.S. sec. of navy under Buchanan, 1857-61, supervised naval expdn. to Paraguay, 1858; accused of being Southern sympathizer, but supported Union cause in Civil War. Died Hartford, Conn., July 30, 1869; buried Cedar Hill Cemetery, Hartford.

TOULMIN, Harry, coll. pres., jurist; b. Tauton, Somersetshire, Eng., Apr. 7, 1766; s. Rev. Joshua and Jane (Smith) T.; m. twice, several children. Came to U.S., 1792; 1st pres. Transylvania U., 1794-96; sec. Commonwealth of Ky., 1796-1804; apptd. judge Superior Ct. for Eastern District of Miss. Territory, 1805-19, made great efforts to impose order on chaotic situation in West Fla. region, restrained Mobile Soc.'s attempts to occupy West Fla., 1810; mem. Ala. Constl. Conv., 1819. Author: Revision of Criminal Law of Commonwealth of Kentucky, 1804-06; The Magistrates' Assistant, 1807; edited The Statutes of the Mississippi Territory, 1807; compiled A Digest of the Territorial Laws of Alabama, 1823. Died Washington County, Ala., Nov. 11, 1823.

TOURJÉE, Eben, musician; b. Warwick, R.I., June 1, 1834; s. Ebenezer and Angelina (Ball) T.; studied at East Greenwich Sem., circa 1848-49; took academic subjects at East Greenwich Sem.; m. Abbie I. Tuell, Oct. 1855; m. 2d, Sarah Lee, Oct. 1871; 4 children. Opened school which exemplified for 1st time in New Eng. conservatory system of teaching, Fall River, Mass.; pvt. tchr., organist, Newport, R.I.; became music dir. East Greenwich Sem., 1861; musical organizer of enlistment rallies during Civil War; studied in Germany, circa 1863; reorganized Musical Inst. of Providence (later Providence Conservatory of Music), 1864; founded New Eng. Conservatory of Music, Boston, circa 1867. Died Boston, Apr. 12, 1891.

TOUSEY, Sinclair, news agy. exec.; b. New Haven, Conn., July 18, 1815; s. Zerah and Nerissa (Crane) T.; m. Mary Ann Goddard; m. 2d, Amanda Fay; 4 children. Reputed to have established penny daily newspaper Daily Times, Louisville, Ky. (1st of its kind west of Alleghenies), 1836; farmer in N.Y. State, 1840-53; entered firm Ross, Jones, Tousey, wholesale news agts. and booksellers, N.Y.C., 1853, became sole propr., 1860; ardent Republican, strong opponent of slavery, from 1856; served with 14th N.Y. Regt. Volunteer Engrs., 1861-63; formed Am. News Co. from various mergers, 1864, pres. co., 1864-87; chmn. exec. com. Prison Assn. Author: Life in Union Army (verse), 1864. Died N.Y.C., June 16, 1887.

TOUSSAINT L'OUVERTURE, Pierre François Dominique, Haitian liberator; b. nr. Cape François, 1743. Born a slave; served with Negro army during Insurrection of the Blacks, 1791; gen. of brigade, 1795; commanding gen. of French troops in Santo Domingo, 1797; assumed dictatorship after signing treaty which resulted in evacuation of Santo Domingo by British, 1801; framed constn. which made him pres. of Haiti for life; overthrown by French, 1803, taken prisoner and sent to France. Died Fort de Joux, nr. Besancon, France, Apr. 27, 1803.

TOWER, John, shipowner, mfr.; b. Phila., Sept. 10, 1758; m. Susan Leake. Apprentice ship-carpenter, Phila.; became owner several ships (from which he derived title Capt.); constructed 1st mill in Manayunk, Pa.; served at Battle of Trenton, Revolutionary War; engaged in mfg., Germantown, Pa., 1812. Died Manayunk, Apr. 25, 1831.

TOWLE, George Makepeace, journalist, author; b. Washington, D.C., Aug. 27, 1841; s. Nathaniel Carter and Eunice (Makepeace) T.; grad. Yale, 1861; LL.B., Harvard, 1863; m. Nellie Lane, Sept. 16, 1866, no children. Admitted to Suffolk County (Mass.) bar, 1862; asso. editor Boston Post, 1865; U.S. consul at Nantes, France, 1866-68; comml. agt. in Bradford, Eng., 1868-70; contbd. to Charles Dickens' All the Year Round on Am. affairs; correspondent for London Athenaeum in Boston, 1870; mng. editor Boston Comml. Bulletin, 1870-71; fgn. editor Boston Post, 1871-76; contbr. to most Boston newspapers; mem. Mass. Senate (Republican), 1890, 91. Author: American Society, 1870; A Brief History of Montenegro, 1877; Pizarro, 1879; Marco Polo, 1880; Raleigh, His Exploits and Voyages. copyright, 1881; translated Dr. Ox and Other Stories by Jules Verne. Died Brookline, Mass., Aug. 9, 1893; buried Mt. Auburn Cemetery, Cambridge, Mass.

TOWLER, John, educator, diplomat, tech. writer; b. Rathmell, Eng., June 20, 1811; s. George Towler of Sheepwash; attended Cambridge (Eng.) U.; M.D., Geneva (now Hobart) Med. Coll., 1855; m. 2d, Caroline Lili Kaiser, 4 children. Pvt. tchr. English, Karlsruhe, Germany; translated Schiller's poetry, also German war songs into English verse, circa 1841; came to Am., 1850; prof. modern langs., mathematics, natural philosophy Hobart Coll., Geneva, N.Y., 1852-68, prof. civil engring., chemistry, mathematics, modern langs., 1868-82; dean, also prof. toxicology and med. jurisprudence Geneva Med. Coll., 1853-72; contbr. monthly articles to Phila. Photographer, 1868-72; one of 1st to use sodium biochromate for photog. use; U.S. consul at Trinidad, 1882-86; ret. to writing, Orange, N.J., 1886. Author books on photography including: The Silver Sunbeam (most important work), 1864, The Porcelain Picture, 1865, Dry Plate Photography; or the Tannin Process, 1865, The Negative and the Print; or the Photographer's Guide, 1866, The

Magic Photograph, 1866; Guide to a Course of Quantitative Chemical Analysis, 1871. Died West Orange, N.J., Apr. 2, 1889.

TOWN, Ithiel, architect; b. Thompson, Conn., Oct. 3, 1784; s. Archelaus and Martha (Johnson) T.; never married; 1 dau. Designed Center Ch., New Haven, Conn. (1st work), circa 1812; commd. to design, build Trinity Ch., New Haven, 1814; designer numerous public bldgs. including a hosp., city custom house Wall St., N.Y.C., state capitols, Indpls., Ind., New Haven, Conn., Raleigh, N.C.; partner of Martin E. Thompson, 1827-28, exhibited many of their designs at N.A.D.; designer Cathedral of St. John the Divine, N.Y.C.; granted patent for a truss bridge, 1820, became famous as bridge builder; assembled one of finest collections relating to architecture and the fine arts then extant; wrote on mathematics and the bldg. of sch. houses; published a plan for establishing sch. of fine arts in N.Y.C., 1835. Died New Haven, June 13, 1844; buried Grove St. Cemetery, New Haven.

TOWNE, Benjamin, printer, journalist; b. Lincolnshire, Eng. Journeyman printer, Phila., 1766; partner Pa. Chronicle and Universal Advertiser, 1766-70; started own print shop, 1774, published Pa. Evening Post (1st evening newspaper in Phila.), 1774-84, paper had loyalist leanings during British occupation of Phila., 1775; cited for high treason by Supreme Exec. Council Pa. but charges were dropped after he changed his paper to pro-patriot sentiments. Died Phila., July 8, 1793.

TOWNE, John Henry, engineer, philanthropist; b. Pitts., Feb. 20, 1818; s. John and Sarah (Robinson) T.; m. Maria R. Tevis, 1843, 3 children including Henry Robinson. Received engineering tng. with firm Merrick & Agnew, Phila., jr. partner, 1836-49; engaged in private engrng. projects after 1849, particularly building gas works; v.p. North Pa. R.R. Co., 1856-58; became partner I.P. Morris and Co., 1861 (company owned Port Richmond Iron Works); produced engines for Monitor, Monadnock and other vessels during Civil War; built engines for federal mint and blowing machinery for manufacture anthracite iron; company's reputation based on its ability to construct large and heavy machinery; dir. Phila. and Reading R.R. Co., 1862-64; benefactor U. Pa. Hosp., Pa. Acad. Fine Arts, Acad. Natural Sciences of Phila.; trustee U. Pa. to which he bequeathed residuary estate, Towne Scientific Sch. created in his memory. Died Paris, France, Apr. 6, 1875.

TOWNER, Zealous Bates, army officer, engr.; b. Cohasset, Mass., Jan. 12, 1819; s. Nichols and Ann (Bates) T.; grad. U.S. Mil. Acad., 1841. Engaged in mil. constrn. duty U.S. Army, 1841-46; served in Mexican War, 1847-48; brevetted maj. for gallantry, 1847; in charge of San Francisco defenses, 1855-58; commanded Ft. Barrancas (Fla.), 1861; brevetted lt. col. U.S. Army, commd. brig. gen. U.S. Volunteers for defense of ft. against Confederate Army; served in battles of Cedar Mountain and 2d Bull Run, severely wounded, out of field service for 1 year; brevetted col. and brig. gen. U.S. Army, 1862; supt. U.S. Mil. Acad., 1864; in charge of field defense, Nashville, Tenn., 1864; insp. gen. fortifications Dept. of Miss.; brevetted maj. gen. U.S. Volunteers and maj. gen. U.S. Army, 1865; ret., 1883. Died Cohasset, Mar. 20, 1900.

TOWNS, George Washington Bonaparte, gov. Ga., congressman; b. Wilkes County, Ga., May 4, 1801; s. John Hardwick and Margaret (George) T.; studied law, Montgomery Ala.; m. Miss Campbell; m. 2d, Mary Jones; 7 children. Admitted to Ala. bar, 1824; mem. lower house Ga. Legislature, 1829-30; mem. Ga. Senate, 1832-34; leader in obtaining resolution asking S.C. to retrace steps at Ga. Nullification Conv., 1832; mem. U.S. Ho. of Reps. from Ga. (Union Democrat), 24th-25th congresses, Mar. 4, 1835-Sept. 1, 1836, 26th Congress, 1837-39, 30th Congress, Jan. 27, 1846-Mar. 3, 1847; gov. Ga., 1847-51; promoted pub. schs., railroads; known as Fire-eater. Died Macon, Ga., July 15, 1854; buried Rose Hill Cemetery, Macon.

TOWNSEND, Amos, congressman, businessman; b. Brownsville, Pa., 1821; attended common schs., Pitts. Clk. in store, Pitts.; moved to Mansfield, O., 1839, became a mcht.; served as U.S. marshal during Kan. troubles; moved to Cleveland, O., 1858, became a wholesale grocer; mem. Cleve. City Council, 1866-76, pres. 7 years; mem. Ohio Constl. Conv., 1873; mem. U.S. Ho. of Reps. (Republican) from Ohio, 45th-47th congresses, 1877-83; mem. of a wholesale food-packing firm. Died St. Augustine, Fla., Mar. 17, 1895; buried Lake View Cemetery, Cleveland.

TOWNSEND, Charles Haskell, naturalist; b. Pa.; named and described the bird Townsend's shearwater, 1890.

TOWNSEND, Edward Davis, army officer; b. Boston, Aug. 22, 1817; s. David S. and Eliza (Gerry) T.; attended Harvard 1 year; grad. U.S. Mil. Acad., 1837; m. Ann Wainwright, May 9, 1848, 5 children. Commd. 2d lt. 2d Arty., U.S. Army, 1837; served in Seminole War; served on Pacific Coast and Washington, D.C., 1846-61; adj. gen. to Winfield Scott, 1860; sr. asst. Adj. General's Dept., 1861; adj. gen. U.S. Army, 1862-65; brevetted maj. gen., 1865; adj. gen. (apptd. by Pres. Grant), 1869-80; collected all war papers, later published as War of the Rebellion: Official Records; ret 1880; mem. Soc. of Cincinnati. Died Washington, D.C., May 10, 1893.

TOWNSEND, George, congressman; b. Lattingtown, Queens County, N.Y., 1769. Farmer; mem. U.S. Ho. of Reps. (Democrat) from N.Y., 14th-15th congresses, 1815-19. Died Lattingtown, Aug. 17, 1844.

TOWNSEND, John Kirk, ornithologist; b. Phila., Aug. 10, 1809; s. Charles and Priscilla (Kirk) T.; m. Charlotte Holmes, 1 child. Joined overland expdn. to Ore., 1835, to H.I., 1835; surgeon Ft. Vancouver, 1835-36; assembled valuable collection of birds and mammals; new birds from Ore. country described by him in Jour. of Acad. of Natural Scis. of Phila.; conceived idea of preparing work on birds of U.S., published one part of Ornithology of the United States of North America, 1840; Townsend's Bunting is named for him; birds from his collection were painted for last volume of Audubon's Birds of America, 1844, his mammals described and painted by Audubon and John Bachman in Viviparous Quadrupeds of North America; secured and mounted birds for Nat. Inst., Washington, D.C., 1842; studied dentistry, Phils., 1845; elected mem. Acad. Natural Sciences of Phila., 1833, life mem. 1850. Author: Narrative to a Journey Across the Rocky Mountains to the Columbia River, 1839. Died Washington, D.C., Feb. 6, 1851.

TOWNSEND, Mira Sharpless, writer, philanthropist; b. Phila., Sept. 26, 1798; d. Jesse and Joanna (Townsend) Sharpless; m. Samuel Townsend, Jan. 23, 1828, 6 children. Contbr. poems to contemporary newspapers, mags., including semi-monthly Advocate and Family Guardian; promoted public meeting of women to consider abolition of capital punishment, 1847; successfully petitioned Pa. Legislature for $3000 appropriation for Rosine Assn. (home for rehab. of women of ill repute), treas., mem. bd. mgrs., until 1859; v.p. Female Guardian Soc. of N.Y.; founder (with sister Eliza Parker) Temporary Home (for unemployed women), sec., mem. bd. mgrs.; aided in bringing House of Good Shepherd to Phila.; active in anti-slavery and prohibition movements; Author: Reports and Realities from the Sketch Book of a Manager (privately printed), 1855. Died Phila., Nov. 20, 1859; buried Fair Hill Cemetery, Phila.

TOWNSEND, Robert, naval officer; b. Albany, N.Y., Oct. 21, 1819; s. Isaiah and Hannah (Townsend) T.; grad. Union Coll., 1835; attended naval sch., Phila., 1835; m. Harriet Monroe, 1850, 3 children. Apptd. midshipman U.S. Navy, 1837; served in Mediterranean on brig Ohio, 1838-40; served in brig Porpoise, 1846, participated in expdn. against Tampico and capture of Mexican schooner Ormigo; served in seige and occupation of Vera Cruz and San Juan d'Ulua; resigned, 1851; reentered U.S. Navy, assigned to ship Harriet Lane of Potomac flotilla, 1861, later in ship Miami on blockade duty off N.C.; transferred to ship Mississippi, 1863; commanded steamer Essex in capture of Port Hudson; participated in Red River Expdn.; commd. capt., 1866, sent to Chinese Coast, 1866, Died ship off Chin-Kiang-Lu, China, Aug. 15, 1866.

TOWNSEND, Washington, congressman, lawyer; b. West Chester, Pa., Jan. 20, 1813; attended West Chester Acad.; studied law. Bank teller, 1828-44; admitted to Pa. bar, 1844, began practice law in West Chester; pros. atty. Chester County, 1848; dep. atty. under Attys. Gen. Darragh and Cooper; cashier Bank of Chester County, 1849-57, pres. bank, 1879-94; del. Whig Nat. Conv., Balt., 1852; del. Republican Nat. Conv., Chgo., 1860; mem. U.S. Ho. of Reps. (Republican) from Pa., 41st-44th congresses, 1869-77. Died West Chester, Mar. 18, 1894; buried Oakland Cemetery, nr. West Chester.

TOWNSHEND, Charles, Brit. govt. ofcl.; b. Aug. 29, 1725; s. Charles (3d viscount) and Audrey (Harrison) T.; attended U. Leyden (Holland); m. Caroline, dau. of Duke of Argyll, widow of Francis, Lord Dalkeith, Aug. 1755. Became mem. Parliament, 1747; Brit. sec. of war, 1761-62; became pres. Bd. of Trade which shared in control of N.Am. colonies, 1763; became virtual head of English govt. after resignation of William Pitt; proposed a land tax (which was defeated), decided to make up loss in revenues by taxing Am. colonies; secured passage of Townshend Act providing for suspension of N.Y. Assembly, duties on exports to colonies (including paper, glass, white and red lead, painters colors, tea), creation of Bd. of Custom Commrs. to enforce revenue laws. Died shortly after passage of act London, Eng., Sept. 4, 1767.

TOWNSHEND, Norton Strange, congressman, physician, educator; b. Clay-Coaton, Northamptonshire, Eng., Dec. 25, 1815; came to Am., 1830; grad. Univ. Physicians and Surgeons, N.Y.C., 1840; studied medicine in hosps., London, Paris, Edinburgh, Dublin, 1840. Tchr. in dist. sch., before 1840; del. World's Antislavery Conv., London, Eng., 1840; began practice medicine, Avon, O., 1841; moved to Elyria, O.; mem. Ohio Ho. of Reps., 1848-49; del. Ohio Constl. Conv., 1850; mem. U.S. Ho. of Reps. (Democrat) from Ohio, 32d Congress, 1851-53; mem. Ohio Senate, 1854-55; served as med. insp., lt. col. U.S. Army, 1863-65; became a farmer, nr. Avon; dir. Ohio Bd. Agr., 1858-69, 86-89; prof. Iowa Agrl. Coll., 1869; one of 1st trustees Ohio Agrl. and Mech. Coll., 1870-73, resigned to become prof. agr. at new Ohio State Coll., 1873-92, prof. emeritus, 1892-95. Died Columbus, O., July 13, 1895; buried Protestant Cemetery, Avon Center, O.

TOWNSHEND, Richard Wellington, congressman, lawyer; b. nr. Upper Marlboro, Prince Georges County, Md., Apr. 30, 1840; attended pub. and pvt. schs.; studied law. Served as page U.S. Ho. of Reps. as a boy; moved to Cairo, Ill., 1858; sch. tchr., Fayette County, Ill.; admitted to Ill. bar, 1862, began practice law in McLeansboro, Ill.; clk. circuit ct. Hamilton County, 1863-68; pros. atty. 12th Jud. Dist. of Ill., 1868-72; mem. Ill. Democratic Central Com., 1864-65, 74, 75; del. Dem. Nat. Conv., Balt., 1872; moved to Shawneetown, Ill., 1873, practiced law; mem. U.S. Ho. of Reps. (Democrat) from Ill., 45th-51st congresses, 1877-89. Died Washington, D.C., Mar. 9, 1889; buried Rock Creek Cemetery.

TRACY, Albert Haller, congressman, lawyer; b. Norwich, Conn., June 17, 1793; studied medicine and law. Moved to N.Y. State, 1811; admitted to N.Y. bar, began practice law, Buffalo, N.Y., 1815; mem. U.S. Ho. of Reps. (Democrat) from N.Y., 16th-18th congresses, 1819-25; mem. N.Y. State Senate, 1830-37; refused cabinet positions offered by Pres. John Q. Adams and Pres. Tyler. Died Buffalo, Sept. 19, 1859.

TRACY, Andrew, congessman, lawyer; b. Hartford, Vt., Dec. 15, 1797; attended Royalton and Randolph accads., Dartmouth Coll.; studied law. Admitted to Vt. bar, 1826, practiced law in Quechee, Vt., 1826-38; moved to Woodstock, Vt., 1838, practiced law; mem. Vt. Ho. of Reps., 1833-37, 43-45, speaker; mem. Vt. Senate, 1839; mem. U.S. Ho. of Reps. (Whig) from Vt., 1853-55. Died Woodstock, Oct. 28, 1868; buried Old Cemetery on River St.

TRACY, Henry Wells, congressman, mcht.; b. Ulster Twp., Bradford County, Pa., Sept. 24, 1807; attended Angelica Sem., Allegany County, N.Y.; studied law. Became a mcht., also road contractor, Standing Stone, Pa., Havre de Grace, Md., Towanda, Pa.; del. Republican Nat. Conv., Chgo., 1860; mem. Pa. Ho. of Reps., 1861-62; mem. U.S. Ho. of Reps. (Independent Republican) from Pa., 38th Congress, 1863-65; collector Port of Phila., 1866. Died Standing Stone, Apr. 11, 1886; buried Brick Church Cemetery, Wysox, Pa.

TRACY, Joseph, clergyman, editor; b. Hartford, Vt., Nov. 3, 1793; s. Joseph and Ruth (Carter) T.; grad. Dartmouth, 1814; studied law and theology; m. Elizabeth Washburn, June 9, 1819; m. 2d, Sarah C. Prince, June 3, 1845. Taught sch., Albany, N.Y., Royalton, Vt.; ordained to ministry Congregational Ch., 1821; assumed double pastorate of Post Mills and West Fairlee, Vt., 1821; editor Vt. Chronicle, 1829, Boston Recorder, 1834, editor New York Observer, 1835-74; sec. Mass. Colonization Soc., 1842; chosen sec. bd. trustees Donations of Edn. in Liberia, 1851; wrote annual reports of Mass. and Am. colonization societies; Author: History of American Missions to the Heathen, 1840; Colonization and Missions, 1844. Died Beverly, Mass., Mar. 24, 1834.

TRACY, Nathaniel, mcht.; b. Newbury (now Newburyport), Mass., Aug. 11, 1751; s. Capt. Patrick and Helen (Gookin) T.; grad. Harvard Coll., 1769, M.A., 1772; m. Mary Lee, Feb. 28, 1775, 11 children. Began bus. as shipowner, 1769; outfitted fleet of privateers, 1775, sent out 24 cruisers and captured 120 British vessels, 1775-83; rendered valuable service in capturing ammunition and supplies bound for British Army during Am. Revolution; by 1783 only one of his vessels remained, the others were captured or destroyed; contributed large sums of money and supplies to Continental Congress to finance Am. Revolution; dep. to Mass. Gen. Ct., 1781-82; charter mem. Am. Acad. Arts and Scis. Died Newbury, Sept. 20, 1796.

TRACY, Phineas Lyman, congressman, lawyer; b. Norwich, Conn., Dec. 25, 1786; grad. Yale, 1806; studied law. Taught Sch., 2 years; admitted to N.Y.

State bar, 1811, began practice law in Madison, N.Y.; moved to Batavia, N.Y., circa 1815, continued practice law; mem. U.S. Ho. of Reps. (Whig, filled vacancy) from N.Y., 20th-22d congresses, Nov. 5, 1827-33; Whig presdl. elector, 1840; presiding judge Genesee County Ct., 1841-46. Died Batavia, Dec. 22, 1876; buried Batavia Cemetery.

TRACY, Uri, congressman, clergyman; b. Norwich, Conn., Feb. 8, 1764; grad. Yale, 1789. Ordained to ministry Presbyn. Ch., became missionary to Indians; moved to Oxford, N.Y., 1791; 1st prin. Oxford Acad., 1794; 1st sheriff Chenango County, N.Y., 1798-1801; county clk., 1801-15; mem. N.Y. State Assembly, 1803; 1st postmaster, Oxford, 1802-05; mem. U.S. Ho. of Reps. (Democrat) from N.Y., 9th, 11th-12th congresses, 1805-07, 09-13; apptd. 1st judge Chenango County, 1819-23. Died Oxford, July 24, 1838; buried Riverview Cemetery.

TRACY, Uriah, senator; b. Norwich, Conn., Feb. 2, 1735; s. Eliphalet and Lucy (or Sarah) (Manning) T.; grad. Yale, 1778; m. Susan (or Susannah) Bull, 5 children. Admitted to Conn. bar, 1781; states atty. for Litchfield County (Conn.), 1794-99; mem. Conn. Ho. of Reps., 1788-93 speaker, 1793; served as maj. gen. Conn. Militia; mem. U.S. Ho. of Reps. from Conn., 3d, 4th congresses, 1793-Oct. 1796; mem. U.S. Senate from Conn., Oct. 1796-July 1807, pres. pro tem., 1800, known as agile politician, respected by Federalist colleagues. Author: (brochure) Reflections on Monroe's View of the Conduct of the Executive, circa 1798. Died Washington, D.C., July 19, 1807; buried Congressional Burying Ground, Washington.

TRAIN, Charles Russell, congressman, lawyer; b. Framingham, Mass., Oct. 18, 1817; grad. Brown U., 1837; studied law Harvard. Admitted to Mass. bar, began practice law, Framingham, 1841; mem. Mass. Ho. of Reps., 1847, 48, 68-71; dist. atty., 1848-54; declined appointment as asso. justice U.S. Supreme Ct., 1852; del. Mass. Constl. Conv., 1853; del. Rep. Nat. Conv., Phila., 1856, Balt., 1864; mem. gov.'s council, 1857-58; mem. U.S. Ho. of Reps. (Republican) from Mass., 36th, 37th congresses, 1859-63, a mgr. apptd. by Ho. of Reps. to conduct impeachment proceedings against West H. Humphreys, U.S. judge for several dists. of Tenn., 1862; served as volunteer a.d.c. to Gen. McClellan during Civil War; moved to Boston; atty. gen. State of Mass., 1871-78; resumed practice law. Died Conway, N.H., July, 28, 1885; buried Edgell Grove Cemetery, Framingham.

TRAIN, Enoch, mcht., shipowner; b. Weston, Mass., May 2, 1801; s. Enoch and Hannah (Ewing) T.; m. Adeline Dutton, 1 dau., Adeline Dutton (Train) Whitney; m. 2d, Almira Cheever, Jan. 1836. Established line of sailing packets (known as Warren Line), between Boston and Liverpool (Eng.), 1844, line owned or chartered at least 24 different ships including several clipper ships built by McKay; during Irish famine began bringing immigrants to Boston, 1846, advertised for passengers in Europe, did $1,000,000 a year business in sending remittances from immigrants in Am. to their old homes; philanthropic activities included development of Fenway Court. Died Saugus, Mass., Sept. 8, 1869; buried Mt. Auburn Cemetery, Cambridge, Mass.

TRAJETTA, Philip, musician, b. Venice, Italy, circa 1776; s. Tommaso Michele Francesco Trajetta. Pvt. music instr. in Italy; left Italy for polit. reasons circa 1798; settled in Boston, 1799; tchr. music, N.Y.C., 1816-18; theatrical mgr. in So. cities, circa 1819-25; lived quietly in Va. mountains, 1825, visited by James Madison and James Monroe; established The Am. Conservatorio, Phila., 1829. Composer: (cantata) The Christian's Joy; (opera) The Venetian Maskers, (oratorios) Jerusalem in Affection; 1828, Daughter of Zion, 1829. Author: An Introduction to the Art and Science of Music, 1829; Rudiments of the Art of Singing, 2 vols., 1841-43. Died Jan. 9, 1854.

TRAPIER, Paul, Continental congressman; b. Prince George's Parish, Winyah, nr. Georgetown, S. C., 1749; ed. in Eng., attended Eton Coll., 1763-65; admitted pensioner St. John's Coll., Cambridge U., 1766; admitted to Middle Temple, London, 1767. Mem. Provincial Congress, also com. of safety for Georgetown; mem. S.C. Gen. Assembly, 1776; justice of peace, 1776; served as capt. Georgetown Arty., Continental Army, Revolutionary War; mem. Continental Congress from S.C., 1777-78. Died nr. Georgetown, July 8, 1778; buried churchyard of Prince George, Winyah, S.C.

TRAUTWINE, John Cresson, engr.; b. Phila., Mar. 30, 1810; s. William and Sarah (Wilkinson) T.; m. Eliza Ritter, circa 1838, at least 2 children. Civil engr. assisting in erection public buildings including U.S. Mint; asst. engr. Phila., Wilmington & Balt. R.R., 1835; chief engr. Hiwassee R.R., 1836; worked on constrn. of Canal del Dique, New Granada (now Columbia), S.A., 1844-49; went to Isthmus of Panama to make surveys for Panama R.R., 1849-51; in Panama to seek inter-oceanic canal route (reported no possibility of canal), 1852; surveyed Lackawanna & Lanesboro R.R., 1856; surveyed route for interoceanic railway in Honduras, 1857; planned system of docks for Montreal, 1858; planned harbor for Big Glace Bay, N.S., Can., 1864; consultant on various engring. problems. Author: Engineers' Pocket Book, 1871. Died Phila., Sept. 14, 1883.

TRAVIS, William Barret, army officer; b. nr. Red Banks, S.C., Aug. 9, 1809; s. Mark and Jemima (Stallworth) T.; m. Rosanna Cato, Oct. 26, 1828, 2 children. Admitted to Ala. bar, 1829; opened law office in San Felipe, Tex., Oct. 1832; apptd. sec. of ayuntamiento (Spanish colonial municipal governing council); leader of war party in local politics, which insisted on preservation of rights of Am. colonists; raised a volunteer co., captured and disarmed garrison at fort at Anahuac, 1835; commanded a scouting co., fall 1835; maj. of arty., Dec. 1835; lt. col. cavalry, circa 1836; joint commander (with James Bowie) of Alamo, San Antonio, Tex., Feb. 13-23, 1836; sole commander, Feb. 23-Mar. 6, when entire garrison of 188 Texans was destroyed by Mexican Army under Gen Antonio Santa Anna. Killed in Battle of Alamo, Mar. 6, 1836.

TREADWELL, Daniel, inventor, educator; b. Ipswich, Mass., Oct. 10, 1791; s. Capt. Jabez and Elizabeth (Dodge) T.; studied medicine with Dr. John Ware, 10 years; A.M. (hon.), Harvard, 1829; m. Adeline Lincoln, Oct. 6, 1831, no children. Silversmith, circa 1807-11; built a screw-making machine, circa 1812, put into operation, Saugus, Mass., circa 1813; elected fellow Am. Acad. Arts and Scis., 1823, recording sec., 1833-39, v.p., 1852-63; an editor Boston Jour. of Philosophy and Arts, 1823-26; invented a means of printing on both sides of a paper without shifting the sheet; superintended constrn. water system for Boston, 1825; mem. 2 commns. to investigate practicability of a water supply for Boston, 1825, 37; patented 1st power press in U.S., 1826, 1st used in newspaper work by Boston Daily Advertiser, 1829; received 4 patents on a machine for spinning hemp, 1831-35; Runford prof. on the applications of science Harvard, 1834-45; organized the Steel Cannon Co. to manufacture for U.S. Govt., 1842. Author: The Relation of Science to the Useful Arts, 1855. Died Cambridge, Mass., Feb. 27, 1872.

TREADWELL, John, gov. of Conn., Continental congressman; b. Farmington, Conn., Nov. 23, 1745; grad. Yale, 1767; studied law. Admitted to the bar, began practice law in Farmington; mem. Conn. Ho. of Reps., 1776-85; clk. ct. of probate, 1777-84; mem. gov.'s council, 1785; mem. Continental Congress from Conn., 1785-86; mem. Conn. Council, 1786-97; judge ct. of common pleas; del. Conn. Conv. which ratified U.S. Constn., 1788; judge of probate and the supreme ct. of errors, 1789-1809; lt. gov. State of Conn., 1798-1809, gov., 1809-11; del. Conn. Constl. Conv., 1818. Died Farmington, Aug. 18, 1823; buried Old Cemetery.

TREAT, Robert, colonial gov.; b. Pitminster, Eng., circa 1622; s. Richard and Alice (Gaylard) T.; m. Jane Tapp, 1647; m. 2d, Elizabeth Bryan, Oct. 24, 1705; 8 children. Settled in Wethersfield, Conn., by 1639; dep. from Milford to Gen. Ct. of Colony of New Haven, 1644-58; mem. Conn. Gov.'s Council, 1653-59, asst. to gov., 1657-65; lt. chief mil. officer, Milford, Conn., 1654; magistrate, 1659-64; dep. from Milford to Conn. Gen. Assembly, 1663-65; moved to N.J., circa 1666; dep. from Newark to Assembly of East Jersey, 1667-72; magistrate, recorder, Newark; returned to Milford, 1672; assistant of Conn. from Milford, 1673; capt. Milford Train Band, 1661, commnd. maj., circa 1673; apptd. comdr.-in-chief Conn. Militia, 1675; participated in defeat of Indians, Hadley, Mass., 1675; dep. gov. Conn. (for war against Narragansett Indians), 1676-83, gov., 1683-98, dep. gov., 1698-1708; resisted Sir Edmund Andros' attempts at authority over Conn., until 1687, retained validity of Conn. charter (govt. restored under charter on overthrow of Andros, 1689). Died Milford, July 12, 1710.

TREAT, Samuel, jurist; b. Portsmouth, N.H., Dec. 17, 1815; s. Samuel Lancton and Lydia (Sheldon) T.; A.B., Harvard, 1837; m. Caroline Bryan, Aug. 21, 1841, 1 child. Admitted to Mo. bar, 1841, practiced law in St. Louis; sec. Democratic Nat. Conv., 1848; judge St. Louis Ct. of Common Pleas, 1849-57; U.S. dist. judge for Eastern Mo., 1857-87; an expert in admiralty law; a founder, dir. Washington U., St. Louis, 1853, founder Washington U. Law Sch., 1867, prof. admiralty law, 1867-87. Died Rochester, N.Y., Aug. 31, 1902.

TREAT, Samuel Hubbel, jurist; b. Plainfield, N.Y., June 21, 1811; s. Samuel and Elsie (Tracy) T.; m. Ann Bennett, 1837. Admitted to N.Y. bar, 1834; judge Circuit Ct., Springfield, Ill., 1839-41; justice Supreme Ct. of Ill., 1841-55, chief justice, 1848-55; apptd. by Pres. Pierce as U.S. judge So. Dist. Ill., 1855-87; collected one of finest libraries in Ill.; helped compile and annotate The Statutes of Illinois, 2 vols., 1858; Democrat. Died Springfield, Mar. 27, 1887.

TREDWAY, William Marshall, congressman, lawyer; b. nr. Farmville, Va., Aug. 24, 1807; grad. Hampden-Sydney Coll., 1827; studied law. Admitted to the bar, 1830, began practice law in Danville, Va.; mem. U.S. Ho. of Reps. (Democrat) from Va., 29th Congress, 1845-47; del. Va. Democratic Conv., 1850; mem. Va. Secession Conv., 1861; judge Circuit Ct. of Va., 1870-79; resumed practice law, Chatham, Va. Died Chatham, May 1, 1891; buried Chatham Cemetery.

TREDWELL, Thomas, congressman, lawyer; b. Smithtown, L.I, N.Y., Feb. 6, 1743; grad. Princeton, 1764; studied law. Admitted to N.Y. bar, began practice law, Plattsburg, N.Y.; del. Provincial Congress of N.Y., 1774-75; del. N.Y. constl. convs., 1776, 77, 1801; mem. N.Y. State Assembly, 1777-83; judge ct. of probate, 1778-87; mem. N.Y. State Senate, 1786-89, 1803-07; surrogate of Suffolk County, 1787-91; del. State Conv. which ratified U.S. Constn., 1788; mem. U.S. Ho. of Reps. from N.Y., (filled vacancy), 2d-3d congresses, May 1791-95; surrogate of Clinton County, N.Y., 1807-31. Died Plattsburg, N.Y., Dec. 30, 1831; buried pvt. burial ground, Beekmantown, nr. Plattsburg.

TREMAIN, Lyman, congressman, lawyer; b. Durham, N.Y., June 14, 1819; attended Kinderhook Acad.; studied law. Admitted to N.Y. bar, 1840, began practice law in Durham; elected supr. of Durham, 1842; apptd. dist. atty., 1844; elected surrogate and county judge Greene County, 1846; moved to Albany, N.Y., 1853, practiced law; atty. gen. (Democrat) State of N.Y., 1858-60; mem. N.Y. State Assembly, 1866-68, speaker, 1867; mem. U.S. Ho. of Reps. (Republican) from N.Y., 43d Congress, 1873-75. Died N.Y.C., Nov. 30, 1878; buried Rural Cemetery, Albany.

TRENCHARD, Edward C., engraver; b. Salem, N.J., circa 1777; married Miss Sands, 1814. A founder Columbianium, 1794; engraver, Boston, 1796-98; entered U.S. Navy as midshipman, 1800, served in War of 1812, rose to capt. Died Bklyn., Nov. 3, 1824.

TRENCHARD, Stephen Decatur, naval officer; b. Bklyn., July 10, 1818; s. Capt. Edward and Eliza (Sands) T.; entered Kenyon Coll., Gambier, O., 1829; m. Ann O'Conner Barclay, Dec. 1, 1848, 1 son, Edward. Entered U.S. Navy as midshipman, 1834, passed midshipman, 1840; served in Mediterranean, 1840-44; assigned to coast survey, 1844; joined Commodore Perry's Squadron off Vera Cruz, took part in expdn. against Tabasco, 1847; commd. lt., 1847; in command ship Vixen, 1856, rescued Brit. vessel Adieu off Gloucester, Mass., presented sword by Queen Victoria as reward; commanded ship Keystone State during Civil War, helped save Cumberland from capture, 1861; commanded brig Rhode Island with orders to transport supplies to blockading squadrons, 1861; on blockade duty, 1862; joined Adm. Porter's fleet at Hampton Roads, 1864, participated in both attacks on Fort Fisher; commd. comdr., 1862, capt., 1866; exec. officer N.Y. Navy Yard, 1865-69; made mem. Bd. Naval Examiners, 1872; lighthouse insp., 1873-75; promoted rear adm., 1875; commanded North Atlantic Squadron, 1876-78; ret., 1880. Died N.Y.C., Nov. 15, 1883.

TRENHOLM, George Alfred, cotton broker, Confederate ofcl.; b. Charleston, S.C., Feb. 25, 1807; s. William and Irene (de Greffin) T.; m. Anna Helen Holmes, Apr. 3, 1828, 13 children including Anna Helen Morgan, William Lee. Partner, John Fraser & Co., shippers of sea-island cotton, became sr. partner, prin. owner, 1853; rep. from St. Philip's and St. Michael's (Charleston) parishes to Gen. Assembly of S.C., 1852-56; outfitted (at own expense) a flotilla of 12 small boats for defense of Charleston; Liverpool (Eng.) br. of Fraser, Trenholm & Co. acted as financial reps. of Confederacy; over 60 of his ships ran blockade to Eng., exchanged cotton for war materials; mem. S.C. Ho. of Reps. during part of Civil War; sec. of treasury (succeeding Christoper Memminger) Confederate States Am., 1864, resigned, 1865; imprisoned, released, 1865, his company became bankrupt, 1867, reorganized; elected to Gen. Assembly of S.C. (Democrat), 1874. Died Charleston, Dec. 9, 1876; buried Magnolia Cemetery, Charleston.

TRENT, William, Indian trader; b. Phila., Feb. 13, 1715; s. William and Mary (Coddington) T.; m. Sarah Wilkins, 1752, 6 children. Apptd. capt. Pa. Militia, 1746; partner George Croghan in Indian trade along Ohio River, 1749-54; attended councils with Indians, 1752, 57, 59; agt. for Va. in charge of expdn. transporting gifts to Miami Indians, 1752; began constrn. fort on Ohio River, 1754 (post captured by French, completed, named Fort Duquesne); mem. expdn. to recapture fort, 1758; mem. Simon, Trent, Levy & Franks, traders, 1760-63; bought large tract of land on Ohio River from Six Nations, 1768 (later became most of Indiana); merged tract with Vandalia project, 1769, unsuccessful in attempts to obtain royal, later Congressional, confirmation of grant. Died Phila., 1787.

TRESCOT, William Henry, historian, diplomat; b. Charleston, S.C., Nov. 10, 1822; s. Henry and Sarah (McCrady) T.; grad. Coll. of Charleston, 1841; m. Eliza Cuthbert, 1848, at least 5 children. Admitted to S.C. bar, 1843; apptd. sec. legation in London, Eng., 1852-57; asst. U.S. sec. state, June-Dec. 1860; had important part in negotiations over Charleston forts; in Civil War, mem. staffs Gov. Andrew Magarth and Gen. Roswell S. Ripley, as a mem. Exec. Council of S.C.; rep. Anderson Dist. in S.C. Legislature, 1862-66; a counselor for U.S. before Halifax Fishery Commn., 1877; went to China to arrange for modification of Burlingame Treaty regarding Chinese immigration, 1880; concluded treaty with Colombia for the regulation of Am. rights in Isthmus of Panama, 1881; apptd. to negotiate a comml. treaty with Mexico, 1882 (never put in operation); del. to Pan-Am. Conf., 1889. Author: The Position and Course of the South (summary of social and econ. view), 1850; Diplomatic History of the Administrations of Washington and Adams, 1857. Died Pendleton, S.C., May 4, 1898.

TREVELLICK, Richard F., labor leader; b. St. Mary's (a Scilly Island, off coast of Eng.), May 1830; married, 5 children. Came to U.S., 1857; pres. of a ship carpenters' and caulkers' union, New Orleans, won fight for 9 hour day; pres. Detroit Trades Assembly, 1864; del. Louisville Conv. which organized Internat. Indsl. Assembly of N.Am., 1864; pres. Internat. Union of Ship Carpenters and Caulkers, 1865; del. congress of Nat. Labor Union, 1867; pres., 1869, 71, 72; led one of 1st successful labor lobbies, obtained an act of Congress establishing 8 hour day for fed. workmen, mechanics and laborers; led fight against the blacklist; a founder Greenback Party, del. conv., 1876; temporary chmn. conv. which formed Nat. Greenback Labor Party, Toledo, O., 1878; toured the West, 1867-68, spoke to labor groups, organized 47 unions; a founder 200 local unions, 3 state orgns., 1870. Died Detroit, Feb. 15, 1895.

TREZVANT, James, congressman, lawyer; b. Sussex County, Va.; studied law. Admitted to bar, began practice law, Jerusalem, Va.; atty. gen. State of Va.; del. Va. Constl. Conv., 1820; mem. Va. Ho. of Dels.; mem. U.S. Ho. of Reps. from Va., 19th-21st congresses, 1825-31. Died Southampton County, Va., Sept. 2, 1841.

TRIGG, Abram, congressman, lawyer; b. nr. Old Liberty (now Bedford), Va., 1750; studied law. Admitted to bar, began practice law, Montgomery County, Va.; lived on his estate "Buchanan's Bottom," on New River; held various local offices including clk. and judge, Montgomery County; served as lt. col. of militia, Continental Army, 1782, later gen. Va. Militia; del. Va. Conv. which ratified U.S. Constn., 1788; mem. U.S. Ho. of Reps. from Va., 5th-10th congresses, 1797-1809. Died and buried on family estate.

TRIGG, John Johns, congressman; b. nr. Old Liberty (now Bedford), Va., 1748; liberal edn. Became a farmer; raised a co. of militia in Bedford County, Va., 1775; commd. capt. Continental Army, 1778, promoted maj., 1781, served under Gen. George Washington at siege of Yorktown; mem. Va. Conv. which ratified U.S. Constn., 1788; lt. col. Va. Militia, 1791, maj. 2d Battalion, 10th Regt., Va. Militia, 1793; justice of peace, Bedford County; mem. Va. Ho. of Dels., 1784-92; mem. U.S. Ho. of Reps. from Va., 5th-8th congresses, 1797-1804. Died Old Liberty, Bedford County, Va., May 17, 1804; buried on his estate.

TRIMBLE, Allen, gov. Ohio, agriculturist; b. Augusta County, Va., Nov. 24, 1783; s. James and Jan. (Allen) T., m. Margaret McDowell, Jan. 1806; m. 2d, Rachael Woodrow, Jan. 10, 1811; at least 5 children. Clk., Ct. of Common Pleas, Highland County, O., 1809-16; col. of an expdn. against the Indians of Upper Wabash and Eel rivers for the relief of the garrison at Ft. Wayne during War of 1812; mem. Ohio Ho. of Reps., 1816-17; mem. Ohio Senate, 1817-25, speaker 7 years; acting gov. Ohio, 1821-22; one of 1st canal fund commrs., 1824-25; gov. Ohio, 1826-30, was authorized by legislature to select ½ million acres of land for canals; a founder Ohio Bd. of Agr., pres., 1846-48; adherent of Nat. Republican Party, later Whig Party. Died Hillsboro, O., Feb. 3, 1870.

TRIMBLE, Carey Allen, congressman, physician; b. Hillsboro, O., Sept. 13, 1813; grad. Ohio U., Athens, O., 1833; grad. Cincinnati Med. Coll., 1836. Taught sch., 4 years; practiced medicine, Chillicothe, O.; mem. U.S. Ho. of Reps. (Republican) from Ohio, 36th-37th congresses, 1859-63; moved to Columbus, O. Died Columbus, May 4, 1887; buried Grand View Cemetery, Chillicothe.

TRIMBLE, David, congressman, lawyer; b. Frederick County, Va., June 1782; grad. Coll. William and Mary, 1799; studied law. Admitted to the bar, began practice law, Mt. Sterling, Ky.; served in War of 1812 as brigade q.m. 1st Brigade, Ky. Mounted Militia, later as pvt. Battalion of Ky. Mounted Inf. Volunteers commanded by Maj. Dudley; mem. U.S. Ho. of Reps. (Democrat) from Ky., 15th-19th congresses, 1817-27. Died Trimble's Furnace, Greenup County, Ky., Oct. 20, 1842.

TRIMBLE, Isaac Ridgeway, army officer, engr.; b. Culpeper County, Va., May 15, 1802; s. John Trimble; grad. U.S. Mil. Acad., 1822; m. Maria Presstman; m. 2d, Ann Presstman; 2 children. Served with U.S. Army, until 1832; asst. engr. Boston & Providence R.R., 1832-35; successively chief engr. Balt. Susquehanna R.R., Phila., Wilmington & Balt. R.R., Phila. & Balt. Central, 1835-59; gen. supt. Balt. & Potomac R.R., 1859-61; burned bridges to obstruct movement of Union troops to Washington, D.C., 1861; col. of engrs. in Va., 1861; commd. brig. gen. Confederate Army, 1861; constructed defences of Norfolk, Va.; constructed batteries on Potomac to prevent passage of U.S. vessels, 1861; commanded a brigade in Army of No. Va., 1862; took part in Stonewall Jackson's operations in Shenandoah Valley, 1862; participated in Seven Days' battles, nr. Richmond, 1862; captured Union depot of supplies at Manassas Station, 1862; as maj. gen. led division at Battle of Chancellorsville, 1863; had command of troops in Shenandoah Valley, June 1863, campaigned as far north as Carlisle, Pa.; assigned command of a division of Hill's Corps at Battle of Gettysburg, 1863, lost leg on 3d day of battle; prisoner, 1863-65. Died Balt., Jan. 2, 1888.

TRIMBLE, John, congressman, lawyer; b. Roane County, Tenn., Feb. 7, 1812; attended U. Nashville; studied law. Admitted to Tenn. bar, began practice law, Nashville, Tenn.; atty. gen. State of Tenn., 1836-42; mem. Tenn. Ho. of Reps., 1843-44; mem. Tenn. Senate, 1845-46, 59, 61, 65-67; U.S. atty., 1862-64; mem. U.S. Ho. of Reps. (Republican) from Tenn., 40th Congress, 1867-69. Died Nashville, Feb. 23, 1884.

TRIMBLE, Robert, asso. justice U.S. Supreme Ct.; b. Augusta County, Va., 1777; s. William Trimble; ed. Ky. Acad., Woodford County, circa 1797; m., circa 1801. Began practice of law, Paris, Ky., 1800, admitted to Ky. bar, 1803; mem. Ky. Legislature, 1802; judge Ky. Ct. Appeals, 1807-09; U.S. dist. atty for Ky., 1813-17, U.S. dist. judge, 1817-26; asso. justice U.S. Supreme Ct., 1826-28, affirmed fed. supremacy over state laws; Trimble County (Ky.) named for him. Died Paris, Ky., Aug. 25, 1828.

TRIMBLE, William Allen, senator, lawyer, army officer; b. Woodford, Ky., Apr. 4, 1786; grad. Transylvania Coll., Lexington, Ky.; studied law. Admitted to the bar, 1811, began practice law, Highland County, O.; adjutant in campaign against Pottawatomie Indians, 1812; maj. Ohio Volunteers, 1812, taken prisoner at capture of Detroit; maj. 26th U.S. Inf., 1813, brevetted lt. col. for gallantry at Ft. Erie where he was severely wounded, 1814; lt. col. 1st U.S. Inf., 1814, transferred to 8th U.S. Inf., 1815-19; mem. U.S. Senate from Ohio, 1819-21. Died Washington, D.C., Dec. 13, 1821; buried Congressional Cemetery.

TRIPLETT, Philip, congressman; b. Madison County, Ky., Dec. 24, 1799; studied law in Owensboro, Ky. Admitted to Ky. bar, began practice law in Owensboro, 1824; mem. Ky. Ho. of Reps., 1824; Whig presdl. elector, 1836, 44; mem. U.S. Ho. of Reps. (Whig) from Ky., 26th-27th congresses, 1839-43; del. Ky. Constl. Conv., 1849. Died Owensboro, Mar. 30, 1852; buried Elwood Cemetery.

TRIPPE, John, naval officer; b. Dorchester County, Md., 1785; s. William and Mary (Noel) T.; never married. Entered U.S. Navy as midshipman, 1799; served on extended voyages on ships United States, the Experiment, 1799-1801; acting lt. on ship Vixen, served with distinction in Mediterranean during Tripolitan War, 1803-04; service on Mediterranean Sea, 1806; duty in Charleston, S.C., to enforce embargo legislation, 1808; sent on a trade mission to Holland on board Enterprise, 1809; U.S. sloop-of-war and a destroyer named after him. Died Havana, Cuba, July 9, 1810.

TRIST, Nicholas Philip, diplomat, lawyer; b. Charlottesville, Va., June 2, 1800; s. Hore Browse and Mary (Brown) T.; attended U.S. Mil. Acad.; studied law; m. Virginia Randolph. Clk., U.S. Dept. State circa 1827, chief clk., 1845; pvt. sec. to Pres. Jackson, 1829; U.S. consul to Havana, Cuba, 1833-41, spl. agt. to negotiate a treaty of peace in Mexico, 1847, recalled, but negotiated a peace treaty to prevent collapse of Mexican govt.; drew up the Treaty of Guadalupe Hidalgo in accordance with his original liberal instructions, 1848; postmaster of Alexandria (Va.), 1870. Died Alexandria, Feb. 11, 1874.

TROOST, Gerard, mineralogist; b. Bois-le-Duc, Holland, Mar. 15, 1776; s. Everhard Joseph and Anna Cornelia (van Haeck) T.; M.D., U. Leyden; Master in Pharmacy, U. Amsterdam, 1801; pupil of René Haüy in mineralogy, crystallography; m. Margaret Tage, Jan. 14, 1811; m. 2d, Mrs. O'Reilly; 2 children. Collected minerals for Cabinet of King of Holland, 1807-09; apptd. mem. Dutch scientific commn. to Java, 1809; corr. mem. Museum of Natural History of France, Paris; arrived in Phila., 1810; established a pharm. and chem. lab., Phila., 1812-17; prof. mineralogy Phila. Museum, 1821; prof. pharm. and gen. chemistry Phila. Coll. Pharmacy, 1821-22; prof. mineralogy, chemistry U. Nashville (Tenn.), 1828-50; state geologist Tenn., 1831-50; his meteorite collection now at Yale; mem. Am. Philos. Soc., Geol. Soc. Pa.; did important research on fossil crinoids in Tenn., results published, 1909. Died Nashville, Aug. 14, 1850.

TROTT, Benjamin, artist; b. Boston, circa 1770. Set up as a painter, N.Y.C., 1791; copied minatures from portraits by Gilbert Stuart; exhibited Pa. Acad., 1812; painted in Charleston, S.C., 1819-20, Phila., 1820-23, Newark, N.J., 1823-29, N.Y.C., 1829-32, Boston, 1833-39, moved to Balt., 1839; minatures include portraits of Nicholas Biddle, Robert Morris, Charles Wilkins, Sally Waln; work known for excellent use of colors and broad stroke. Died circa 1841.

TROTT, Nicholas, jurist; b. Eng., Jan. 30, 1663; s. Nicholas Trott; m. Jane Cooke; m. 2d, Sarah (Cooke) Rhett, Mar. 15, 1728; at least 1 child, Mary. Atty. gen. in Bermuda, 1696-97; atty. gen., naval officer for So. part of Province of Carolina (now S.C.), 1698-1700; speaker Carolina Commons Ho. of Assembly, 1700; chief justice of Carolina, 1703-29; mem. Gov.'s Council of Carolina. Author: Clavis Linguae Sanctae, 1719; The Laws of the British Plantations in America, Relating to the Church and the Clergy, Religion and Learning, 1721; The Laws of the Province of South Carolina, 2 vols., 1736. Died Feb. 1, 1740.

TROTTER, James Fisher, senator, jurist, educator; b. Brunswick County, Va., Nov. 5, 1802; studied law. Admitted to the bar, 1820, began practice law, Hamilton, Miss., 1823; mem. Miss. Ho. of Reps., 1827-29; mem. Miss. Senate, 1829-33; judge Circuit Ct. of Miss., 1833; mem. U.S. Senate (Democrat, filled vacancy) from Miss., Jan. 22-July 10, 1838 (resigned); judge Supreme Ct. of Miss., 1839-42, resigned; moved to Holly Springs, Miss., resumed practice law, 1840; vice chancellor No. Dist. of Miss., 1855-57; prof. law U. Miss., 1860-62; apptd. circuit judge, 1866. Died Holly Springs, Mar. 9, 1866; buried Hill Crest Cemetery.

TROTTER, Newbold Hough, painter; b. Phila., 1827; studied with W.T. van Starkenborg, cattle painter, The Hague, Holland; specialized in painting animal pictures, Boston and Phila. Died Atlantic City, 1898.

TROTTI, Samuel Wilds, congressman, lawyer; b. Barnwell, S.C., July 18, 1810; grad. S.C. Coll. (now U.S.C.), 1832; studied law. Admitted to the bar, practiced law; served in Seminole War; mem. S.C. Ho. of Reps.; mem. U.S. Ho. of Reps. (filled vacancy) from S.C., 27th Congress, Dec. 17, 1842-43. Died Buckhead, Fairfield Dist. (now County), S.C., June 24, 1856.

TROUP, George Michael, senator, gov. Ga.; b. McIntosh's Bluff, Ala., Sept. 8, 1780; s. George and Catherine (McIntosh) T.; grad. Coll. of N.J. (now Princeton), 1797; m. Anne McCormick, Oct. 30, 1803; m. 2d, Anne Carter, Nov. 8, 1809; 6 children. Admitted to Ga. bar, 1799; mem. Ga. Ho. of Reps. from Chatham County, 1803-05; mem. U.S. Ho. of Reps. from Ga., 10th-13th congresses, 1807-15, supported Jefferson Embargo, opposed rechartering of U.S. Bank; mem. U.S. Senate from Ga., Nov. 13, 1816-Sept. 23, 1818, 29-33, supported S.C. nullification, proposed secession if fed. tariff and bank policies were not reversed; gov. Ga., 1823-27, advocated state programs for schs., canals, railroads, secured cession of all Creek Indian lands; attended States-Rights Conv., Milledgeville, Ga., 1832; favored annexation of Tex., 1844, opposed Compromise of 1850. Died "Rosemont," Montgomery County, Ala., Apr. 26, 1856; buried "Rosemont."

TROUP, Robert, army officer, jurist; b. N.Y.C., 1757; probably s. Robert and Elinor (Bisset) T.; grad. King's Coll. (now Columbia), studied law, circa 1780-83. Served as lt. Continental Army during Am. Revolution, a.d.c. to Brig. Gen. Timothy Woodhull; promoted lt. col., 1777, on staff of Gen. Horatio Gates; present at Battle of Stillwater and at surrender of Burgoyne, 1777; sec. bd. war, 1778; mem. N.Y. State Assembly; supported adoption of U.S. Constn., 1787-88; involved in land speculation in Western N.Y., 1794-1832; judge U.S. Dist. Ct. N.Y., 1796; gave financial aid to the founding of Hobart Coll.; agt. for Pulteney estate, 1801-31. Died N.Y.C., Jan. 14, 1832.

TROUT, Michael Carver, congressman, businessman; b. Hickory Twp., Mercer County, Pa., Sept. 30, 1810; limited edn. Employed as hatter, 3 years, then became carpenter and contractor; pres. Hickory Twp. Sch. Bd. 20 years; elected burgess of Sharon, 1841; recorder Mercer County, Pa., 1842-45; prothonotary, 1846-51; mem. U.S. Ho. of Reps. (Democrat) from Pa., 33d Congress, 1853-55; engaged in iron mfg., banking, coal mining. Died Hickory Twp., June 25, 1873; buried Morefield Cemetery, Hickory Twp., nr. Sharon, Pa.

TROW, John Fowler, printer, bookseller, publisher; b. Andover, Mass., Jan. 30, 1810; s. Lt. John and Martha (Swan) T.; m. Catharine Swift, Aug. 12, 1834, 5 children. Went to N.Y.C., 1833; formed partnership with John T. West, printer, 1834-37; asso. with Jonathan Leavitt, 1844-49, carried on bookshop as well as printing establishment; founded firm John F. Trow & Co., printers and publishers, 1866; officer Trow City Directory Co., 1873-86, Trow's Printing and Bookbinding Co., 1877-86; published Trow's N.Y.C. Directory, 1st issued 1852-53; began printing and publishing Wilson's Bus. Directory of N.Y.C., 1847-84; credited with being among 1st to introduce electrotyping into printing business; published N.Y. Citizen and Am. Republican (daily paper), 1844-45. Died Orange, N.J., Aug. 8, 1886.

TROWBRIDGE, Edmund, jurist; b. Cambridge, Mass., 1709; s. Thomas and Mary (Goffe) T.; grad. Harvard, 1728; m. Martha Remington, Mar. 15, 1737/38. Prominent mem. Mass. bar, 1730's-60's; atty. gen. Mass., 1749-67; gained reputation for fairness in Boston Massacre trial, 1771; expert in real property; author tract on mortgages, one of few known colonial studies in pvt. law; Loyalist at outset of Am. Revolution, became and remained neutral. Died Cambridge, Apr. 2, 1793.

TROWBRIDGE, Rowland Ebenezer, congressman; b. Horseheads, Chemung County, N.Y., June 18, 1821; grad. Kenyon Coll., Gambier, O., 1841. Became a farmer, Oakland County, Mich.; mem. Mich. Senate, 1856-60; mem. U.S. Ho. of Reps. (Republican) from Mich., 37th, 39th-40th congresses, 1861-63, 65-69; commr. of Indian affairs, 1880-81. Died Birmingham, Mich., Apr. 20, 1881; buried Greenwood Cemetery.

TROWBRIDGE, William Pettit, engineer, scientist, educator; b. Troy, N.Y., May 25, 1828; s. Stephen Van Rensselaer and Elizabeth (Conkling) T.; grad. U.S. Mil. Acad., 1848; A.M. (hon.), Rochester U., 1856, Yale, 1870; Ph.D. (hon.), Princeton, 1879; LL.D. (hon.), Trinity Coll., 1883, U. Mich., 1887; m. Lucy Parkman, Apr. 21, 1857, 6 surviving children. Asst. prof. chemistry U.S. Mil. Acad., 1847-48; commd. 2d lt. Corps Topog. Engrs., U.S. Army, 1848; served on Atlantic coastal survey, 1849; commd. 1st lt., 1854; prof. mathematics U. Mich., 1856-57; asst. supr. Coast Survey; selected to install self-registering instrument of permanent magnetic observatory established at Key West, 1860; executed hydrographic survey of Narragansett Bay, 1860, established navy yard; in charge of army engr. agy. for supplying materials for fortifications and for constructing engring. equipage for armies in field, N.Y.C., 1861; superintending engr. of constrn. at fort, Willets Point, N.Y., 1861; v.p., gen. mgr. Novelty Iron Works, N.Y.C., 1865-71; prof. dynamic engring. Yale, 1871-77; prof. engring. Columbia, 1877-92; mem. New Haven (Conn.) Board Harbor Commrs.; councilor N.Y. Acad. Sciences, 1878-84, v.p., 1885-89; prominent mem. A.A.A.S.; mem. Nat. Acad. Sciences. Died New Haven, Aug. 12, 1892.

TROYE, Edward, painter; b. nr. Geneva, Switzerland, 1808; s. Jean Baptiste de Troy; m. Cornelia Ann Vander Graff, July 1839, at least 1 child. Came to U.S., 1830; did best work between 1835-74; painted for plantation owners before Civil War; chief patrons were F. Keene Richards, Georgetown, Ky. and Alexander family of Lexington; went with Richards to Arabia and Holy Land, 1850's, painted horses, Damascus cattle, Dead Sea, bazaar of Damascus; most notable paintings include those of race horses Am. Eclipse, Sir Henry, Boston, Lexington, Glencoe, Revenue, Bertrand, Richard Singleton, Reality, Black Maria, Leviathan, Wagner, Ophelia; best known for painting of Gen. Winfield Scott; chief collections in Am. owned by Jockey Club, N.Y.C., Alexander family, Ky., Yale. Author: The Race Horses of America, 1867. Died Georgetown, Ky., July 25, 1874.

TRUMBO, Andrew, congressman, lawyer; b. Montgomery (now Bath) County, Ky., Sept. 15, 1797; studied law. Employed in county clk.'s office; admitted to Ky. bar, began practice law, Owingsville, Ky., 1824; clk. of Bath County, 1830; commonwealth atty. for Bath County, 1830; mem. U.S. Ho. of Reps. (Whig) from Ky., 29th Congress, 1845-47; Democratic presdl. elector, 1848; moved to Franklin County, Ky. Died Frankfort, Ky., Aug. 21, 1871; buried City Cemetery, Owingsville.

TRUMBULL, Benjamin, clergyman, historian; b. Hebron, Conn., Dec. 19, 1735; s. Benjamin and Mary (Brown) Trumble; grad. Yale, 1759; m. Martha Phelps, Dec. 4, 1760, 7 children. Licensed to preach by Windham Assn. of Ministers, 1760; pastor Congregational Ch., North Haven, Conn., 1760-1820; chaplain Gen. Wadsworth's brigade in Revolutionary War, June-Dec. 1776; capt. company of 60 volunteers, North Haven. Author: A Plea, in Vindication of the Connecticut Title to the Conquested Lands, Lying West of New York, 1774; An Appeal to the Public . . . with Respect to the Unlawfulness of Divorces, 1788; A Complete History of Connecticut . . . to the Year 1764, 2 vols., 1818; A General History of the United States of America . . . 1492-1792 (projected 3 vol. work, had completed only 1st vol. by time of death). Died Feb. 2, 1820.

TRUMBULL, James Hammond, historian, philologist; b. Dec. 20, 1821; s. Gurdon and Sarah Ann (Swan) T.; attended Yale, 1838-40; m. Sarah A. Robinson, 1855, at least one child, Annie Eliot. Asst. sec. of state, Conn., 1847-58; Conn. librarian and registrar, 1847; Republican sec. of state of Conn., 1861-66; trustee, librarian Watkinson Library of Reference, Hartford, Conn., full time librarian after 1866, librarian emeritus, 1890; transcribed, edited The Public Records of the Colony of Connecticut, Prior to the Union with New Haven Colony, May, 1665, published 1850, The True-Blue Laws of Connecticut and New Haven and the False-Blue Laws Invented by the Rev. Samuel Peters, His Defenders and Apologists, 1877; edited The Memorial History of Hartford County, Connecticut, 1633-1884, 2 vols., 1886; translated John Eliot's Catechism for Indians and edited Roger Williams A Key into the Language of America, 1865; contbd. 7 papers on language of Indians to Transactions of Am. Philol. Assn., 1869, 76; lectr. on Indian langs. Yale; bibliographical works include Catalogue of the American Library of the Late Mr. George Brinley of Hartford, Conn., 5 vols., 1879-97. Died Hartford, Aug. 5, 1897.

TRUMBULL, John, poet, jurist; b. Westbury, Conn., Apr. 24, 1750; s. John and Sarah (Whitman) T.; grad. Yale, 1767, M.A. (Berkeley fellow), 1770; studied law under John Adams; m. Sarah Hubbard, Nov. 21, 1776, 4 children. Published series of Addisonian essays in Boston Chronicle, 1769-70; gave valedictory oration An Essay on the Uses and Advantages of the Fine Arts, Yale, 1770, tutor, 1772-73; published series of 38 essays (under pen name The Correspondent) in Conn. Journal, 1770-73; admitted to Conn. bar, 1773; wrote An Elegy on the Times (his 1st poem reflecting on nat. affairs), 1774; literary leader of Hartford Wits, 1780's-90's; contbd. to anthology The Echo (1st published in Am. Mercury, 1807); states atty. for Hartford County, 1789; mem. Conn. Legislature, 1792-1800; judge Conn. Supreme Ct., 1801-19, Supreme Ct. of Errors, 1808-19. Author: Epithalamium (poem), 1769; The Progress of Dullness (satire on contemporary ednl. methods), 1772-73; M'Fingal (comic epic, reprinted 30 times to 1840), 1784; The Poetical Works of John Trumbull, 2 vol., 1820. Died Detroit, May 11, 1831.

TRUMBULL, John, painter; b. Lebanon, Conn., June 6, 1756; s. Gov. Jonathan and Faith (Robinson) T.; grad. Harvard, 1773; studied under Benjamin West, London, Eng., 1780, 82-83, 84-85; m. Sarah (Hope) Harvey, Oct. 1, 1800. Served as adjutant to Gen. Joseph Spencer of 1st Conn. Regt. in Revolutionary War; 2d a.d.c. to Gen. Washington, 1775; maj. of brigade, 1775, in action at Dorchester Heights; dep. adjutant-gen. with rank of col. under Gen. Horatio Gates, Crown Point, Ticonderoga and Pa., 1776; began painting hist. and Revolutionary War subjects as West's pupil; 1st paintings include Battle of Bunker's Hill, Death of General Montgomery in Attack of Quebec, 1786, Declaration of Independence, The Surrender of Lord Cornwallis at Yorktown, Death of General Mercer at Battle of Princeton, Captured Hessians at Trenton, Sortie Made by the Garrison of Gibralter; went to Paris, 1787, 89; painted Washington before the Battle of Princeton, 1792; pvt. sec. to John Jay, envoy extraordinary to Gt. Britain, 1793; engaged in diplomatic and business speculation, 1793-1804; painted portraits of Timothy Dwight and Stephen Van Rensselaer; went to Europe, 1808-15; commd. by Congress to paint 4 pictures in Rotunda of Capitol, 1817, painted Surrender of General Burgoyne at Saratoga, Resignation of Washington, Surrender of Cornwallis of Yorktown, Declaration of Independence; pres. Am. Acad. Fine Arts, 1817; designed and contbd. collection to Trumbull Gallery, Yale (earliest art museum connected with an ednl. instn. in Am.); planned series of dormitory bldgs. for Yale, 1792; designed Congregational ch. in Lebanon, 1804, Barclay Street quarters of Am. Acad., 1831, Author: Autobiography, Letters, and Reminiscences of John Trumbull, 1756-1841, published 1841. Died N.Y.C., Nov. 10, 1843; buried under Trumbull Gallery, reinterred New Yale Gallery of Fine Arts, 1928.

TRUMBULL, Jonathan, gov. Conn.; b. Lebanon, Conn., Oct. 12, 1710; s. Joseph and Hannah (Higley) Trumble; grad. Harvard, 1727; LL.D. (hon.), Yale, U. Edinburgh (Scotland); m. Faith Robinson, Dec. 9, 1735, 6 children including John, Jonathan, Joseph. Licensed to preach by Windham Assn., entered father's merc. bus., 1731; outstanding figure in Conn. commerce by 1760's, went bankrupt, 1766; mem. Conn. Gen. Assembly, 1733, speaker, 1739; mem. Conn. Council, 1740-50, 1754; dep. gov., chief justice of Conn., 1766-69; judge Windham County Ct. (Conn.), 1746, Windham Probate Ct., 1747; gov. Conn., 1769-84; active supporter of Continental Army, supplied armies with food, clothing and munitions; encouraged Conn. industry in frequent contact with George Washington during Am. Revolution; called "Brother Jonathan" by Washington which became Am. symbol (later supplanted by Uncle Sam); mem. Am. Acad. Arts and Scis. Died Aug. 17, 1785.

TRUMBULL, Jonathan, senator, gov. Conn.; b. Lebanon, Conn., Mar. 26, 1740; s. Jonathan and Faith (Robinson) T.; grad. Harvard, 1759, M.A., 1762; m. Eunice Backus, Mar. 1767, 5 children including John. Selectman of Lebanon, 1770-75; represented Lebanon in Conn. Legislature, 1774, 75, 79, 80, 88, speaker, 1788; paymaster forces of N.Y. dept. Continental Army, 1775-78; 1st U.S. comptroller of treasury, 1778-79; sec. to George Washington, 1781-83; mem. U.S. Ho. of Reps. (Federalist) from Conn., 1st-3d congresses, 1789-95, speaker, 1791-93; mem. U.S. Senate from Conn., 1795-96; dep. gov. Conn., 1796, gov., 1797-1809; leader Federalist Party in Conn. Died Aug. 7, 1809; buried Old Cemetery, Lebanon.

TRUMBULL, Joseph, Army officer; b. Lebanon, Conn., Mar. 11, 1737; s. Jonathan and Faith (Robinson) T.; grad. Harvard, 1756; m. Amelia Dyer, Mar. 1777. With father's merchant firm, 1756-67; mem. Gen. Assembly of Conn., 1767-73; mem. Conn. Com. of Correspondence 1773; (mem. Continental Congress from Conn., 1774-75; commissary-gen. Conn. troops, 1775; commissary-gen. Continental Army with rank of col., 1775-77; mem. board of war, 1777-78. Died Lebanon, July 23, 1778; buried Old Cemetery, Lebanon.

TRUMBULL, Joseph, gov. of Conn., congressman; b. Lebanon, Conn., Dec. 7, 1782; grad. Yale, 1801; studied law. Admitted to the bar at Windham County, 1803, began practice law, Hartford, Conn.; pres. Hartford Bank, 1828-39; later pres. Providence, Hartford & Fishkill R.R. Co.; mem. Conn. Ho. of Reps., 1832, 48, 51; mem. U.S. Ho. of Reps. (Whig, filled vacancy) from Conn., 23d, 26th-27th congresses, Dec. 1, 1834-35, 39-43; gov. State of Conn., 1849, 50. Died Hartford, Aug. 4, 1861; buried Old North Cemetery.

TRUMBULL, Lyman, senator, jurist; b. Colchester, Conn., Oct. 12, 1813; s. Benjamin and Elizabeth (Mather) T.; m. Julia Jayne, June 21, 1843, at least 3 children; m. 2d, Mary Ingraham, Nov. 3, 1877. Admitted to Ga. bar, 1836; practiced in Belleville, Ill.; mem. Ill. Legislature (Democrat), 1840-41; Ill. sec. state, 1841-43; justice Ill. Supreme Ct., 1848-54; mem. U.S. Senate (Republican) from Ill. 1855-73, chmn. judiciary com., 1864, introduced resolution which became basis of 13th Amendment of Constitution; voted against impeachment of Pres. Johnson; became Liberal Republican, 1872, Democrat, 1876; counsel for Tilden side in disputed election, 1876; drafted platform for Chgo. Populists, 1894. Died Chgo., June 25, 1896; buried Oakwood Cemetery, Chgo.

TRUTEAU, Jean Baptiste, Indian trader, explorer, schoolmaster; b. Montreal, Que., Can., Dec. 11, 1748; s. Joseph and Catherine (Menard) T.; m. Madeleine (LeRoy) Bellhomme, May 1, 1781. Schoolmaster, Village of St. Louis, 1774-1827; engaged in Mo. Trading Co., 1794-97, in charge of exploration expdn.; began jour. (which became valuable contbn. to knowledge of Upper Missouri River and its Indian tribes), 1794-95; gave money to aid Spain in war. Died nr. St. Louis, circa Jan. 30, 1827; buried Carondelet, Mo.

TRUXTUN, Thomas, naval officer; b. Hempstead, L.I., N.Y., Feb. 17, 1755; s. Thomas and Sarah (Axtell) T.; m. Mary Fundran, May 27, 1775, 13 children. Went to sea at age 12, ship comdr. in mcht. service by age 20; served during Am. Revolution as lt. in privateer Congress, also commanded ships Independence and Mars, captured many prizes, 1777, served in or commanded other privateers; commd. capt. U.S. Navy; took 1st ship (the Canton) from Phila. to China, 1786; commanded frigate Constellation, won 2 important naval engagements during naval war with France, 1798-1800; received Gold medal from U.S. Congress; commd. to lead squadron against Tripoli, 1801, withdrew because his flagship was not given a capt. (withdrawal taken by hostile adminstrn. as resignation); refused offer naval command in Aaron Burr's western scheme, 1806; sheriff Phila., 1816-19. Died Phila., May 5, 1822; buried Christ Churchyard, Phila.

TRUXTUN, William Talbot, naval officer; b. Phila., Mar. 11, 1824; s. William and Isabelle (Martin) T. m. Annie Scott, Oct. 15, 1856; m. 2d, Mary Walke, Sept. 2, 1875; 8 children including William. Served in ships Dolphin and Falmouth in Home Squadron, 1841, later in brig Truxton on African coast; passed midshipman, 1847; on Brazilian station, 1847-48; served in Dolphin, 1853; exec. sailing sloop-of-war Dale in North Atlantic Blockading Squadron, 1861; lt. comdr., 1862; commanded the Chocura, 1862-63, Tacony until close of war; in action with batteries at Plymouth, N.C., attacks on Ft. Fisher, 1864, 65; supt. naval coal shipments, 1866-67; in command of Jamestown in North Pacific Squadron, 1868-70, Brooklyn in North and South Atlantic, 1873-75; comdr. Boston and Norfolk (Va.) navy yards, 1876-80; commodore, 1882; in command of Norfolk Navy Yard, 1885-86. Died Norfolk, Feb. 25, 1887.

TRYON, George Washington, conchologist; b. Phila., May 20, 1838; s. Edward K. and Adeline (Savidt) T.) Manufactured and sold firearms and hunting equipment; mem. Acad. Natural Scis. of Phila., 1859, largely responsible for erection of new bldg., an organizer conchological sect., 1866, donated his private collection over 10,000 species, curator, 1869-76, conservator conchological sect., 1875-88; wrote paper "On the Mollusca of Harper's Ferry, Virginia," 1861; wrote more than 70 papers on land, freshwater and marine mollusks; edited, published Am. Jour. of Conchology, 1865-72; wrote Manual of Conchology, Structural and Systematic, with Illustrations of the Species (chief work), 1st vol., 1879, 3 vols. published 1888, continued by Dr. Henry A. Pilsbry; wrote comic opera Amy Cassonet or the Elopement, 1875; went to Europe, 1874, 77; wrote accounted of earlier trip The Amateur Abroad, 1875; published Structural and Systematic Conchology, 3 vols., 1882-84. Died Feb. 5, 1888.

TRYON, William, colonial gov.; b. Norbury Park, Surrey, Eng., 1729; s. Charles and Lady Mary (Shirley) T.; m. Margaret Wake, 1757. Commd. lt. 1st Regt., Foot Guards, Brit. Army, 1751, capt. with army rank of lt. col., 1753; lt. gov. N.C. Colony, 1764, gov., 1765; broke up Regulator Movement (settlers demanding reform of currency, taxation and adminstrn.) in Battle of Alamance, 1771; responsible for establishing N.C. provincial capital at New Bern and erected "Tryon's Palace" as exec. residence; transferred to N.Y. as gov., 1771; commd. col. army, 1772; commanded a force of Loyalists, 1777; maj. gen., 1778; col. 70th Foot Guards; led raids upon Conn. for purpose of destroying supplies and diverting some supplies from support of Washington's army to home defense; returned to Eng., 1780; lt. gen., 1782, col. 29th Foot Regt., 1783. Died London, Eng., Jan. 27, 1788; buried in family tomb, Twickenham, Eng.

TUCK, Amos, congressman; b. Parsonsfield, Me., Aug. 2, 1810; s. John and Betsey (Towle) T.; grad. Dartmouth, 1835; m. Sarah Ann Nudd; m. 2d, Mrs. Catharine (Townsend) Shepard, Oct. 10, 1847; at least 8 children, including Edward. Admitted to N.H. bar, 1838; served term in N.H. Legislature, 1842; mem. U.S. Ho. of Reps. from N.H., 30th-32d congresses, 1847-53; v.p. Republican Nat. Conv., 1856, mem. platform com., 1860; attended Peace Conf., Washington, D.C., 1861; naval officer for Boston and Charlestown (Mass.) dist., 1861-65; trustee Phillips Exeter Acad., 1853-79, Dartmouth, 1857-66; Amos Tuck Sch. Adminstrn. and Finance established at Dartmouth by Edward Tuck, 1900. Died Exeter, N.H., Dec. 11, 1879.

TUCKER, (Nathaniel) Beverley, jurist, educator; b. Matoax, Chesterfield County, Va., Sept. 6, 1784; s. St. George and Frances (Bland) Randolph T.; grad. Coll. William and Mary, 1801; m. Mary Coalter; m. 2d, Eliza Taylor, Apr. 13, 1830; m. 3d, Lucy Anne Smith. Served as lt. U.S. Navy during War of 1812, promoted to staff appointment; an organizer Jefferson County (Mo.); judge circuit cts. Mo. Territory, later Mo. State; prof. law Coll. William and Mary, circa 1833-51; contbd. ideas to devel. of Pres. Tyler's exchequer plan; del. from Va. to Nashville Conv. of 1850. Author: George Balcombe (published anonymously), 1836; The Partisan Leader, 2 vols., 1836; Gertrude (serial in So. Lit. Messenger), 1844-45; A Discourse on the Importance of the Study of Political Science as a Branch of Academic Education n the United States, 1840; The Principles of Pleading, 1846. Died Winchester, Va., Aug. 26, 1851.

TUCKER, Ebenezer, congressman; b. Tuckers Beach, N.J., Nov. 15, 1758; attended common schs. Served in Revolutionary War under Gen. George Washington at Battle of L.I. other engagements; judge of ct. of common pleas, justice ct. of quarter sessions, judge orphans' ct. of Burlington County, 1820-25; moved to what is now Tuckerton, N.J. (named after him), became a mcht., shipbuilder; postmaster of Tuckerton, 1806-25, 31-45; mem. U.S. Ho. of Reps. from N.J., 19th-20th congresses, 1825-29; 1st collector of revenue Port of Tuckerton. Died Tuckerton, Sept. 5, 1845; buried Old Methodist Cemetery.

TUCKER, George, polit. economist, congressman; b. Bermuda, Aug. 20, 1775; s. Daniel and Elizabeth (Tucker) T.; grad. Coll. William and Mary, 1797; m. Maria Ball Carter, 1801; m. 2d, Mary (Byrd) Farley, after 1823; m. 3d, Louisa (Bowdoin) Thompson, before 1859; 5 children. Mem. Va. Legislature, 1815; mem. U.S. Ho. of Reps. from Va., 16th-18th congresses, 1819-25; prof. moral philosophy U. Va., 1825-45, 1st chmn. faculty, 1825, mem. Am. Philos. Soc. Author: Essays of Subjects of Taste, Morals, and National Policy, by a Citizen of Virginia, 1822; The Valley of Shenandoah, 2 vols., 1824; The Life of Thomas Jefferson, 2 vols., 1837; The Laws of Wages, Profits, and Rent Investigated, 1837; The Theory of Money and Banks Investigated, 1839; The History of the United States, 4 vols., 1856-57; Political Economy for the People, 1859; Essays, Moral, and Metaphysical, 1860; Speech of Mr. Tucker, of Virginia, on the Restriction of Slavery in Missouri . . . February 25, 1820, published 1820. Died Sherwood, Va., Apr. 10, 1861; buried U. Va. Cemetery, Albemarle County, Va.

TUCKER, Henry Holcombe, clergyman, coll. pres.; b. Warren County, Ga., May 10, 1819; s. Germain and Frances (Holcombe) T.; attended U. Pa., 1834-circa 1836; A.B., Columbian Coll. (now George Washington U.), 1838; m. Mary West, 1848; m. 2d, Sarah Stevens, circa 1853; 2 children. Admitted to Ga. bar, 1846; licensed to preach, circa 1849; held position with So. Female Coll., Lagrange, Ga.; ordained to ministry Baptist Ch., 1851; prof. Richmond (Va.) Female Inst.; pastor ch., Alexandria, Va., circa 1853-56; prof. belle-lettres, metaphysics Mercer U., Penfield, Ga. (now at Macon, Ga.), 1856-62, pres., 1866-71; organized Ga. Relief and Hosp. Assn. (for care sick and wounded soldiers); editor Christian Index, 1866; went to Europe, 1871; assisted in establishing Bapt. Ch., Rome, Italy; preached for Am. Ch., Paris, 1871; chancellor U. Ga., 1874-78; propr., editor Christian Index, 1878-89. Author: The Gospel of Enoch, 1869; The Old Theology Restated in Sermons, 1884. Died Atlanta, Ga., Sept. 9, 1889.

TUCKER, Henry St. George, jurist; b. Matoax, Chesterfield County, Va., Dec. 29, 1780; s. St. George and Frances Bland (Randolph) T.; grad. Coll. William and Mary, 1799; m. Anne Hunter, Sept. 23, 1806, at least 2 children, John Randolph, Nathaniel Beverley. Mem. Va. Ho. of Dels., 1807-08; served as volunteer in War of 1812; mem. U.S. Ho. of Reps. from Va., 14th-15th congresses, 1815-19; mem. Va. Senate, 1819-23; judge superior cts. of chancery for Winchester (Va.) and Clarksburg (Va.) dists., 1824; pres. Va. Supreme Ct. of Appeals, 1831-41; became prof. law U. Va., 1841, chmn. faculty, 1842, upon his motion honor system was adopted by U. Va. Died Winchester, Aug. 28, 1848.

TUCKER, John Randolph, naval officer; b. Alexandria, Va., Jan. 31, 1812; s. John and Susan (Douglas) T.; m. Virginia Webb, June 7, 1838, 3 children. Commd. midshipman U.S. Navy, 1826, passed midshipman, 1833, lt., 1837; known to sailors as handsome Jack; served as 1st exec. officer, then capt. on ship Stromboli during Mexican War; commissioned comdr., 1855, resigned commn., 1861; commd. comdr. Confederate States Navy, 1861; in charge of naval defenses of James River; commanded steamer Yorktown (converted into cruiser Patrick Henry), until 1862; participated in Battle of Hampton Roads, 1862; had command of ironclad ram Chicora, 1862; commanded Charleston Squadron; capt. Provisional Navy of Confederate States, 1863; served in Battle of Sailor's Creek, 1865; imprisoned at Fort Warren, 1865, released upon taking oath of allegiance to U.S.; commd. rear adm. Peruvian Navy; commanded fleets of Peru and Chile in war with Spain, 1869; head hydrographical commn. to survey upper waters of Amazon River, 1869. Died Petersburg, Va., June 12, 1883.

TUCKER, John Randolph, coll. dean, congressman; b. Winchester, Va., Dec. 24, 1823; s. Henry St. George and Anne Evelina (Hunter) T.; received law degree U. Va., 1843; LL.D. (hon.), Yale, 1887; m. Laura Powell, Oct. 5, 1848; 1 son, Henry St. George. Practiced law, Winchester, Va., 1845-57; Democratic elector, 1852, 56; atty. gen. Va., 1857-65; prof. law Washington and Lee U., 1870-74, 1887-97, prof. constl. and internat. law, 1889-93, dean Law Sch., 1893-97; mem. U.S. Ho. of Reps. from Va., 44th-49th congresses, 1875-87; pres. Am. Bar Assn., 1892-93; lawyer for Jefferson Davis in his trial for treason, also in case concerning Fla. electoral vote of 1876. Author: The Constitution of the United States, 2 vols., 1899; public addresses The Southern Church Justified in its Support of the South, 1863; The History of the Federal Convention of 1787, published 1887. Died Feb. 13, 1897.

TUCKER, Luther, agrl. journalist; b. Brandon, Vt., May 7, 1802; s. Stephen and Olive (Green) T.; m. Naomi Sparhawk, Nov. 19, 1827; m. 2d, Mary Sparhawk, Oct. 4, 1833; m. 3d, Margaret (Smith) Burr, June 1, 1846; 8 children including Luther H., Gilbert Mulligan. Partner of printer Henry C. Sleight of Jamaica, L.I., 1825; established Rochester (N.Y.) Daily Advertiser under firm name Luther Tucker & Co., 1827; established, owned weekly Genesee Farmer, 1831-39; publisher Monthly Genesee Farmer and Horticulturist, 1836-39; purchased Albany Cultivator, 1839, merged it with Genesee Farmer; mem. N.Y. State Agrl. Soc.; established Horticulturist, 1846, sold 1852; began weekly edit. of Cultivator called the Country Gentleman, called Cultivator and Country Gentleman, 1866. Compiler: (with Willis Gaylord) American Husbandry, 1840. Died Albany, N.Y., Jan. 26, 1873; buried Albany Rural Cemetery.

TUCKER, Nathaniel Beverley, Confederate agt.; b. Winchester, Va., June 8, 1820; s. Henry St. George and Anne (Hunter) T.; attended U. Va.; m. Jane Ellis, Jan. 21, 1841, 8 children. Editor, Washington (D.C.) Sentinel, 1853-56; U.S. consul at Liverpool, Eng., 1857 joined Confederate Army, entered into contract to provide supplies for army; sent to Can. on mission to arrange for exchange of cotton for bacon, also to make some secret diplomatic representations to Northern men of influence, 1864; included in "wanted" list of Union Govt. during war, accused of complicity in plot to murder Lincoln, charges dropped. Died July 4, 1890.

TUCKER, St. George, army officer, jurist; b. Port Royal, Bermuda, July 10, 1752; s. Henry and Anne (Butterfield) T.; grad. Coll. William and Mary, 1772; m. Frances (Bland) Randolph, Sept. 23, 1778; m. 2d, Lelia (Skipwith) Carter, Oct. 8, 1791; at least 2 children, Nathaniel Beverley, Henry St. George. Admitted to Va. bar; served as col. Chesterfield County (Va.) Militia, lt. col. Va. Cavalry, during Revolutionary War; served at Battle of Guilford Court House, took part in siege of Yorktown; commr. Annapolis Conv., 1786; judge of Gen. Ct. of Va., 1788-1800; prof. law Coll. William and Mary, 1800-03; judge Supreme Ct. of Appeals of Va., 1803-11; judge U.S. Dist. Ct. for Va., 1813-28; his opinion in Kamper vs. Hawkins (1 Va. Reports, 20) held that state constn. was sovereign act of people, opinion in Turpin vs. Locket (6 Call Reports, 113) sustained constitutionality of 1802 act for relief of poor. Author: Dissertation on Slavery: with a Proposal for its Gradual Abolition in Virginia (pamphlet), 1796, reprinted, 1861; published annotated edition of Blackstone's Commentaries, 5 vols., 1803; Liberty, a Poem on the Independence of America, 1788, The Probationary Odes of Jonathan Pindar, 2 parts, 1796. Died Nelson County, Va., Nov. 10, 1827.

TUCKER, Samuel, naval officer; b. Marblehead, Mass., Nov. 1, 1747; s. Andrew and Mary (Belcher) T.; m. Mary Gatchell, Dec. 21, 1768. Commanded ship Young Phoenix, 1775; capt. ship Franklin, preyed on Brit. vessels, 1776; transferred to ship Hancock; commd. capt. Continental Navy, 1777; commanded frigate Boston; sailed for France, 1778; carried John Adams to his post as commr. to France, 1778; continued attacks on Brit. commerce, 1778-80; commanded several vessels trading with West Indian and European ports, 1783-85; mem. Mass. Legislature, 1814-18; elected to Me. Ho. of Reps., 2 terms. Died Bremen, Me., Mar. 10, 1833.

TUCKER, Starling, congressman; b. Halifax County, N.C., 1770 limited edn. Moved to Mountain Shoals (now Enroe), S.C.; held several local offices; mem. S.C. Ho. of Reps.; mem. U.S. Ho. of Reps. from S.C., 15th-21st congresses, 1817-31. Died Mountain Shoals, Jan. 3, 1834; buried pvt. burial ground on family estate nr. Enroe.

TUCKER, Thomas Tudor, treas. U.S., congressman, physician; b. Port Royal, Bermuda, June 25, 1745; studied medicine U. Edinburgh (Scotland). Moved to S.C., practiced medicine; served as surgeon, Revolutionary War; mem. Continental Congress from S.C., 1787, 88; mem. U.S. Ho. of Reps. (Federalist) from S.C., 1st-2d congresses, 1789-93; treas. U.S. (apptd. by Pres. Jefferson), 1801-28. Died Washington, D.C., May 2, 1828.

TUCKER, Tilghman Mayfield, gov. Miss., congressman; b. nr. Lime Stone Springs, N.C., Feb. 5, 1802; studied law. Farmer; moved to Hamilton, Miss.; admitted to bar, began practice law in Columbus, Miss.; mem. Miss. Ho. of Reps., 1831-35; mem. Miss. Senate, 1838-41; gov. Miss., 1841-43; mem. U.S. Ho. of Reps. (Democrat) from Miss., 28th Congress, 1843-45; ret. to his plantation "Cottonwood" in La. Died at home of father, nr. Bexar, Ala., Apr. 3, 1859.

TUCKERMAN, Edward, botanist, educator; b. Boston, Dec. 7, 1817; s. Edward and Sophia (May) T.; B.A., Union Coll., 1837, M.A., 1843; grad. Harvard Law Sch., 1839, B.A., Harvard, 1847, grad. Harvard Div. Sch., 1852; m. Sarah Eliza Sigourney Cushing, May 17, 1854. Curator coll. museum Union Coll., 1842-43; lectr. in history Amherst (Mass.) Coll., 1854-58, prof. botany, 1858-86; contbd. articles to N.Y. Churchman on biog., hist. and theol. topics; in 1842 described Oakesia (a new genus of flowering plants from New Eng.); authority in field of Am. lichenology; 1st to explore mountains of New Eng. for lichens; mem. Nat. Acad. Scis., 1868. Author: Enumeratio Methodica Caricum Quarundam, issued privately, 1843; Enumeration of North American Lichens, 1845, also supplement, "Synopsis of the Lichens of New England, the Other Northern States, and British America;" Lichens of California, Oregon, and the Rocky Mountains, 1866; General Lichenum: An Arrangement of North American Lichens (probably his greatest work) 1872; Catalogue of Plants Growing without Cultivation within Thirty Miles of Amherst College, issued privately, 1875; A Synopsis of North American Lichens, Part I, 1882. Died Amherst, Mar. 15, 1886.

TUCKERMAN, Frederick Goddard, poet; b. Boston, Feb. 4, 1821; s. Edward and Sophia (May) T.; attended Harvard, 1838, grad. Harvard Law Sch., 1842; m. Hannah Lucinda Jones, June 17, 1847, 3 children including Frederick. Admitted to Mass. bar, 1844; authority on flora of Greenfield (Mass.); contbr. poems to Living Age, Putnam's, Atlantic Monthly mags., also privately printed in vol. entitled Poems, 1860; works collected in The Sonnets of Frederick Goddard Tuckerman (edited by Witter Bynner), 1931. Died Greenfield, May 9, 1873.

TUCKERMAN, Henry Theodore, critic, essayist, poet; b. Boston, Apr. 20, 1813; s. Henry Harris and Ruth (Keating) T.; attended Harvard, 2 years, M.A. (hon.), 1850; never married. Travelled chiefly in Italy, 1833-34, his various trips often basis for his books; decorated by King of Italy "in recognition of his labors on behalf of Italian exiles in U.S.;" wrote travel romances Isabel, or Sicily, A Pilgrimage, 1839, A Month in England, 1853; other works include: Characteristics of Literature, 1849, 51; Artist-Life, or Sketches of American Painters, 1847; The Life of Silas Talbot, 1850; Poems, 1851; Mental Portraits, 1853; Essays, Biographical and Critical, 1857; America and her Commentators: with a Critical Sketch of Travel in the United States, 1864; Book of the Artists: American Artist Life, 1867; The Life of John Pendleton Kennedy, 1871. Died N.Y.C., Dec. 17, 1871; buried Mt. Auburn Cemetery, Cambridge, Mass.

TUCKERMAN, Joseph, clergyman; b. Boston, Jan. 18, 1778; s. Edward and Elizabeth (Harris) T.; grad. Harvard, 1798; m. Abigail Parkman, July 5, 1803; m. 2d, Sarah Cary, Nov. 3, 1808; 10 children. Ordained to ministry Unitarian Ch., 1801; became original mem. Anthology Soc. (publishers Monthly Anthology and Boston Review), 1805; started Boston Soc. for Religious and Moral Improvement of Seamen (1st of its kind in Am.), 1812; began Ministry at Large (actually a city mission for poor), Boston, 1826, described his work there in The Principles and Results of the Ministry at Large in Boston, 1838; established missions, London and Liverpool, Eng., 1833-34; a soc. of women who called themselves Tuckerman's Sewing Circle sewed and sold what they made for the Poor's Purse, as late as 1888. Died Havana, Cuba, Apr. 20, 1840.

TUCKERMAN, Samuel Parkman, musician; b. Boston, Feb. 11, 1819; studied music with Carl Zeuner, Boston; Mus.D., 1853. Organist, choirmaster St. Paul's Ch., Boston, 1840; gave lectures on early cathedral music and ch. music; resided in Eng., 1856-64, in Switzerland, many years. Editor: The Episcopal Harp, The National Lyre, Cathedral Chants, 1858, Trinity Collection of Church Music, 1864; composed much ch. music. Died Newport, R.I., June 30, 1880.

TUCKEY, William, organist, choirmaster, composer; b. Somersetshire, Eng., 1708; married, several children. Parish clk. Trinity Ch., N.Y.C., 1753-56; conducted performance in N.Y.C. of overture and 16 numbers from Handel's Messiah (1st Am. rendering), 1770; gave concerts of secular music, earliest of which was announced in Post Boy as, "Concert of Vocal and Instrumental Musick," 1755; composed Anthem Taken Out of the 97th Psalm (called Liverpool; only extant work). Died Phila., Sept. 14, 1781; buried Christ Ch. Burial Grounds, Phila.

TUDOR, Frederic, ice mcht.; b. Boston, Sept. 4, 1783; s. Col. William and Delia (Jarvis) T.; m. Euphemia Fenno, Jan. 2, 1834, 6 children. Sent (with brother) cargo of ice to Martinique, 1804, vessel arrived in Saint-Pierre, 1806; established bus. in Havana, Cuba and Charleston, S.C., New Orleans by 1821; learned how to ship ice with least possible loss, devised structure which kept ice in warm climates, succeeded in making use of ice accepted in cities; sent 1st cargo to Calcutta, India, 1833; increased shipping from 130 tons in 1806 to 146,000 tons in 1856; designed new type of hull for sailing vessels; developed graphite mine Sturbridge, Mass.; created Maolis Gardens (probably 1st amusement park in U.S.), Nahant, Mass. Known as ice king. Died Boston, Feb. 6, 1864.

TUDOR, William, writer, diplomat; b. Boston, Jan. 28, 1779; s. Col. William and Delia (Jarvis) T.; grad. Harvard, 1796. Developed (with brother) trade in ice, 1804; mem. Mass. Legislature; founder, 1st editor N.Am. Review, 1815-17; mem. Anthology Soc., 1805, contbr. to its mag. Monthly Anthology and Boston Review; a founder Boston Athenaeum, suggested plan for purchase of land on Bunker Hill, Charlestown, Mass.; mem. Mass. Hist. Soc., 1816; critic of contemporary manners in Letters on the Eastern States, 1820; published The Life of James Otis, of Massachusetts, 1823; U.S. consul at Lima, Peru, 1823; chargé d'affaires, Rio de Janeiro, Brazil, 1827-30. Died Rio de Janeiro, Mar. 9, 1830.

TUFTS, Charles, b. Medford (now part of Somerville), Mass., July 17, 1781; s. Daniel and Abigail (Tufts) T.; m. Hannah Robinson, Apr. 8, 1821. Offered land for a theol. sem. proposed at Mass. Conv. of Universalists, 1840, affair became identified with attempts to bolster up the Clinton Liberal Inst., 1845, and so resulted in project for a Universalist coll., 1847; offered approximately 20 acres of land on Medford-Somerville line; charter for incorporation obtained for Tufts Coll., 1852; deeded other properties to coll. under various conditions (one of which was that its name could never be changed), 1856, 64, eventually gave more than 100 acres of land; trustee Tufts Coll., 1856-76. Died Dec. 24, 1876.

TUFTS, Cotton, physician; b. Medford, Mass., May 30, 1732; s. Simon and Abigail (Smith) T.; A.M., Harvard, 1749, M.D. (hon.), 1785; m. Lucy Quincy, Dec. 2, 1765; m. 2d, Mrs. Susanna Warner, Oct. 22, 1789; 1 son, Cotton. Began practice of medicine, Weymouth, Mass., 1752, became leading practitioner there; planned Mass. Med. Soc., 1765, an organizer, 1781, pres., 1787; charter mem. Am. Acad. Arts and Scis.; rep. from Weymouth in meetings against Stamp Act; trustee Derby Acad., Hingham, Mass.; pres. Soc. for Reformation of Morals; deacon of ch. Died Dec. 8, 1815.

TUFTS, John, clergyman; b. Medford, Mass., May 5, 1689; s. Capt. Peter and Mercy (Cotton) T.; grad. Harvard, 1708; m. Sarah Bradstreet, Nov. 9, 1714, 4 children. Ordained Congregational minister 2d Ch. of Christ, West Newbury, Mass., 1714; Author: A Very Plain and Easy Introduction to the Art of Singing Psalm Tunes, Contrived in Such Manner, As That the Learner May Attain the Skill of Singing Them with the Grestest Ease and Speed Imaginable (established type of hymn of psalm singing and method of printing music which is still used in many backcountry So. chs., had heavy influence on ch. music of U.S. for over a century), 1714 15; Anti-Ministerial Objections Considered, 1725; A Humble Call to Archippus, Or the Pastor Exhorted, To Take Heed That He Fulfill his Ministry, 1729 Died Amesbury, Mass., Aug. 17, 1752.

TUIGG, John, clergyman; b. Donaghmore, Cork, Ireland, Feb. 19, 1821; studied in Dublin, Ireland, also at St. Michael's, Pitts. Ordained priest Roman Catholic Ch., Pitts., 1850; founded several parishes, Pitts.; apptd. vicar of eastern area Diocese of Pitts., 1869; bishop of Pitts., 1876-89, also adminstr. Allegheny City see, 1877-89 (absorbed into Diocese of Pitts., 1889). Died Altoona, Pa., Dec. 7, 1889

TULANE, Paul, mcht., philanthropist; b. Princeton, N.J., May 10, 1801; s. Louis Tulane; never married. Built up retail and wholesale trade in dry goods and clothes, formed firms Paul Tulane & Co., New Orleans, also Tulane, Baldwin & Co. of N.Y.C.; gave gifts which made possible establishment of U. La., New Orleans, 1834, became Tulane U. of La., 1884, gave sch. all his New Orleans real estate. Died Princeton, Mar. 27, 1887.

TULLY, Pleasant Britton, congressman, lawyer; b. Henderson County, Tenn., Mar. 21, 1829; studied law. Moved to Ark., 1838, to Cal., 1853; became a miner; resided in Gilroy, Cal., after 1857; admitted to bar, practiced law; del.-at-large Cal. Constl. Conv., 1879; mem. U.S. Ho. of Reps. (Democrat) from Cal., 48th Congress, 1883-85. Died Gilroy, Mar. 24, 1897; buried Masonic Cemetery.

TULLY, William, physician, coll. pres.; b. Saybrook Point, Conn., Nov. 18, 1785; s. Col. William and Eunice (Tully) T.; grad. Yale, 1806, A.M. (hon.), 1807, M.D. (hon.), 1819; attended Med. Sch., Dartmouth; m. Mary Potter, Jan. 5, 1813; 11 children. Licensed to practice medicine by Conn. Med. Soc., 1810; began practice in Enfield, Conn., 1811; pres., prof. theory and practice and med. jurisprudence Vt. Acad. Medicine, Castleton, 1824-30, prof. materia medica and therapeutics, 1830-35; prof. materia medica and therapeutics Yale, 1829-42; made 1st half-ounce of quinine sulfate from chona bark produced in U.S. Author: Catalogue of the Phenogamous Plants and the Ferns Growing without Cultivation, Within Five Miles of Yale College, 1831; Materia Medica, or, Pharmacology and Therapeutics, 2 vols., 1857-58; also articles "On the Ergot of Rye" in Am. Jour. Sci., 1820, "Scutellaria Laterifolia" in Middlesex Gazette, 1820, "An Essay, Pharmacological and Therapeutical, on Sanguinaria-Canadensis" in Am. Med. Recorder, 1828. Died Springfield, Conn., Feb. 28, 1859; buried Grove St. Cemetery, New Haven, Conn.

TUOMEY, Michael, geologist; b. Cork, Ireland, Sept. 29, 1808; grad. Rensselaer Poly. Inst., 1835. Came to U.S. at early age; became a farmer; tchr., also civil engr., Somerset County, Md., 1835-40; state geologist Md., 1845-48; prof. mineralogy, geology and agr. U. Ala., 1847-54; state geologist Ala., 1848-57; mem. A.A.A.S., Boston Soc. Natural History. Editor (with Francis S. Holmes) Fossils of South Carolina, 1855-57. Died Tuscaloosa, Ala., Mar. 30, 1857.

TUPPER, Benjamin, army officer, pioneer; b. Stoughton, Mass., Mar. 11, 1738; s. Thomas and Remember (Perry) T.; m. Huldah White, Nov. 18, 1762, 7 children, including Rowena (Tupper) Sargent. Served to sgt. during French and Indian Wars, 1756; commd. lt. Western Mass. Militia, 1774; participated in siege of Boston, destruction of Brit. light house on Castle Island, 1775; commd. lt. col., 1776; col. Mass. Militia in Battle of L.I., Saratoga campaign, Battle of Monmouth; retired with brevet rank brig. gen., 1783; mem. Mass. Legislature, circa 1783; one of Continental officers to sign Newburgh Petition of 1783, seeking creation of new territory in the N.W.; rep. from Mass. on corps of state surveyors sent West by U.S. Congress; conducted preliminary surveying, 1785; aided movement which led to formation of Ohio Co.; accompanied original settlers to Marietta, O., 1788; judge Ct. Common Pleas and Quarter Sessions (1st civil ct. in Ohio Territory), 1788-92. Died June 7, 1792.

TURNBULL, Andrew, physician, colonizer; b. circa 1718; m. Maria Gracia Dura Bin, 7 children, including Robert James. Granted 20,000 acres of land (now Ponce de Leon, Fla.), by mandamus, 1766; returned to Eng., 1767; brought about 1400 immigrants to Am., 1768; mem., sec. Fla. Provincial Council; supported Am. Revolution, as a result lost his land in Fla.; practiced medicine, Charleston, S.C., circa 1781-92. Died Mar. 13, 1792.

TURNBULL, Robert, clergyman; b. Whiteburn, Scotland, Sept. 10, 1809; grad. U. Glasgow (Scotland), circa 1831. Came to U.S., 1833, became pastor Baptist Ch., Danbury, Conn.; pastor, Detroit, 1835-37, Hartford, Conn., 1837-39, 45-77, Boston, 1839-45; asso. editor Christian Review. Author: Olympia Morata, 1842; Theophany, 1851; Christ in History, 1856. Translator: Vital Christianity (A.R. Vinet), 1846. Editor: Discussions on Philosophy (Sir William Hamilton), 1855. Died Hartford, Nov. 20, 1877; buried Hartford.

TURNBULL, Robert James, polit. writer; b. New Smyrna, Fla., Jan. 1775; s. Andrew and Maria Gracia (Dura Bin) T.; m. Claudia Gervais, Jan. 10, 1797; m. 2d, Valeria Lightwood; m. 3d, Anna McCall. Admitted to S.C. bar, 1794; practiced law, Charleston, S.C., 1794-1810; mem. Columbia (S.C.) Free Trade Conv., attended similar conv., Charleston, 1832; chief spokesman of nullification and radical states rights in S.C., 1827-33. Author: A Visit to the Philadelphia Prison, 1796; The Crisis: or Essays of the usurpations of the Federal Government (his most important work, defined doctrine of nullification), 1827; The Tribunal of Dernier Ressort, 1830; Address (of S.C. Nullification Conv.), 1833. Died June 15, 1833.

TURNBULL, William, army officer, engr.; b. Phila., 1800; s. William and Mary (Nisbet) T.; grad. U.S. Mil. Acad., 1819; m. Jane Graham Ramsay, 1826, 10 children, including Charles N. Commd. 2d lt. on topog. duty Corps Arty., U.S. Army, 1819-31, 1st lt., 1823; capt. Topog. Engrs. on survey of railroad route in Miss., 1831-32; assigned to constrn. of Potomac Aqueduct across Potomac River at Georgetown, D.C., 1832-43 (one of 1st important Am. engrng. works); published Report on the Construction of the Piers of the Aqueduct of the Alexandria Canal across the Potomac River at Georgetown, District of Columbia, 1836, 2d report, 1838; chief topog. engr. on staff of Gen. Winfield Scott, participated in operations from siege of Vera Cruz to capture of Mexico City; brevetted lt. col. for services in battles of Contreras, Churubusco, col.

for Battle of Chapultepec; superintending engr. of constrn. custom house, New Orleans, 1848-49; surveyed Whales Back Rock, Portsmouth, N.H. (for a lighthouse site), examined practicability of bridging Susquehanna River at Havre de Grace, 1850-52; mem. bd. to examine feasibility of additional canal around the Falls of the Ohio, 1853-56; engaged in lighthouse constrn., Oswego, N.Y., 1853-55. Died Dec. 9, 1857.

TURNER, Asa, clergyman, educator; b. Templeton, Mass., June 11, 1799; s. Asa and Abigail (Baldwin) T.; grad. Yale, 1827, attended Divinity Sch., 1827-circa 1830; m. Martha Bull, Aug. 31, 1830. Ordained by New Haven West Assn., 1830; one of group of 7 theol. students known as Yale Bund who went to Ill. to establish a sem., 1829; a founder Ill. Coll., Jacksonville, 1829, trustee, 1829-44, went East to solicit funds, 1832; established a Presbyn. Ch., Quincy, Ill., 1830, adopted Congregational form of govt. (1st of this denomination in Ill.), 1833; chief organizer Ia. Assn. (formed by Yale Bund), 1837; established 1st Congregational Ch. West of Mississippi River, Denmark, Ia., 1838, pastor, 1838-68; missionary agt. for Ia. representing Am. Home Missionary Soc., 1839-68; missionary agt. for Ia. representing Am. Home Missionary Soc., 1839-68; explored No. Ia.; obtained charter from Ia. Territorial Assembly for Denmark Acad. (later Ia. Coll.), Davenport, Ia., 1843, trustee, 1843-85. Died Oskaloosa, Ia., Dec. 13, 1885.

TURNER, Benjamin Sterling, congressman; b. nr. Weldon, N.C., Mar. 17, 1825; a Negro raised as a slave, no early edn., later self-educated. Moved to Ala., 1830, became a mcht.; elected tax collector Dallas County, Ala., 1867; councilman City of Selma, Ala., 1869; mem. U.S. Ho. of Reps. (Republican) from Ala., 42d Congress, 1871-73; del. Republican Nat. Conv., Chgo., 1880; farmer in Ala. Died Selma, Mar. 21, 1894; buried Live Oak Cemetery.

TURNER, Charles, Jr., congressman; b. Duxbury, Mass., June 20, 1760; attended common schs., Duxbury and Scituate, Mass. Commd. adjutant Mass. Militia, 1787, promoted maj., 1790, lt. col. commandant, 1798-1812; apptd. 1st postmaster of Scituate, 1800; justice of peace; mem. Mass. Ho. of Reps., 1803, 05-08, 17, 19, 23; mem. U.S. Ho. of Reps. (War Democrat, contested election) from Mass., 11th-12th congresses, June 28, 1809-13; mem. Mass. Senate, 1816; apptd. steward Marine Hosp. at Chelsea, Mass.; del. Mass. Constl. Conv., 1820; became a farmer. Died Scituate, May 16, 1839; buried in burial ground of First Parish of Norwell (formerly Scituate).

TURNER, Daniel, naval officer; b. probably Richmond, S.I., N.Y., 1794; m. Catharine Bryan, May 23, 1837, at least 1 dau. Apptd. midshipman U.S. Navy, 1808; served in Constitution, 1809-11; ordered to take command of gunboats at Norwich, Conn., 1812; commd. lt., 1813; given command of Caledonia, participated in defeat of British at Battle of Lake Erie, victory over British, 1813, received silver medal from Congress, sword from N.Y.; commanded Scorpion, 1814, participated in capture of several Brit. vessels on Lake Huron, burning of the fort and barracks at St. Joseph, and attack on Mackinac; captured by enemy while in Scorpion; with frigate Java, 1815-17, cruiser Nonesuch, 1819-24; master comdt., 1825; cruised in West Indies, 1827-30, comdr. ship Erie; commd. capt., 1835; commanded Constitution in Pacific Squadron, 1838-41; commanded Brazil Squadron, 1843-46; comdt. Portsmouth Navy Yard, 1846-49. Died Phila., Feb. 4. 1850.

TURNER, Daniel, congressman; b. nr. Warrenton, N.C., Sept. 21, 1796; son of James Turner; grad. U.S. Mil. Acad., 1814; student Coll. William and Mary, 2 years sometime after 1815. Commd. 2d lt. Arty., U.S. Army, 1814; served as acting asst. engr., War of 1812; resigned commn., 1815; moved to N.C.; mem. N.C. House of Commons, 1819-23; mem. U.S. Ho. of Reps. (Democrat) from N.C., 20th Congress, 1827-29; prin. Warrenton Female Sem.; superintending engr. of constrn. of pub. works at Mare Island (Cal.) Navy Yard, 1854-60. Died Mare Island, July 21, 1860; buried Mare Island Naval Cemetery.

TURNER, Edward, jurist; b. Fairfax County, Va., Nov. 25, 1778; s. Lewis Ellzey and Theodosia (Payne) T.; ed. Transylvania U.; m. Mary West, Sept. 5, 1802; m. 2d, Eliza Baker, Dec. 27, 1812; at least 2 children. Aide-de-camp, pvt. sec. to gov. Miss., 1801; clk. lower house Territorial Legislature of Miss., 1801; clk. Jefferson County (Miss.) Ct., 1802; register land office Washington, Miss., 1803-04; practiced law in Jefferson County, 1804-10; mem. Miss. Legislature, 1811-13, 15, chosen to prepare a digest of the territorial laws, published as Statutes of the Mississippi Territory . . . Digested by Authority of the General Assembly, 1816; city magistrate Natchez, Miss., 1813, pres. bd. selectmen. Died Natchez, May 23, 1860.

TURNER, James, senator, gov. N.C.; b. Southampton County, Va., Dec. 20, 1766; attended common schs.; at least 1 son, Daniel. Engaged in planting, Warren County, N.C.; served as pvt. N.C. Volunteers during Revolutionary War; mem. N.C. Ho. of Commons, 1797-1800, N.C. Senate, 1801-02; gov. N.C., 1802-05; mem. U.S. Senate (Democrat) from N.C., 1805-Nov. 21, 1816 (resigned). Died on plantation "Bloomsbury," nr. Warrenton, N.C., Jan. 15, 1824; buried Bloomsbury Cemetery.

TURNER, James, congressman, farmer; b. nr. Bel Air, Md., Nov. 7, 1783; attended Classic Acad. of Madonna (Md.). Served as capt. militia in War of 1812; established 1st large dairy farm at Parkton, Balt. County, Md., 1811; collector of state and county taxes, 1817; justice of peace, 1824; mem. Md. Ho. of Dels., 1824-33, 37-38; mem. U.S. Ho. of Reps. (Democrat) from Md., 23d-24th congresses, 1833-37; mem. Md. Senate, 1855-59. Died Mar. 28, 1861; buried Bethel Cemetery, nr. Madonna.

TURNER, John Wesley, army officer; b. nr. Saratoga, N.Y., July 19, 1833; grad. U.S. Mil. Acad., 1855; m. Blanche Soulard, Sept. 18, 1869, several children. Commd. lt. U.S. Army, 1855, capt., 1861; chief commissary under Gen. David Hunter, 1861-62, under Gen. Benjamin F. Butler, New Orleans, 1862; chief commissary and later chief of staff Dept. of the South, 1863; took part in attack on Ft. Sumter, S.C., 1863; brevetted maj. U.S. Army, commd. brig. gen. U.S. Volunteers, 1863; commanded a div. under Gen. Butler in Va., 1864; brevetted lt. col. U.S. Army and maj. gen. Volunteers; chief of staff Army of the James, 1864-65; brevetted col., then brig. gen. and maj. gen. U.S. Army, 1865; commanded dist. of Henrico (including city of Richmond, Va.), 1865-66; resigned from army, 1871; pres. Bogey Lead Mining Co., St. Louis, 1872-77; commr. streets St. Louis, 1877-88; pres. St. Joseph Gas & Mfg. Co., St. Louis 1888-97; dir. Am. Exchange Bank, St. Louis, 1893-99, St. Louis Savs. & Safe Deposit Co. Died St. Louis, Apr. 8, 1899.

TURNER, Jonathan Baldwin, educator; b. Templeton, Mass., Dec. 7, 1805; s. Asa and Abagail (Baldwin) T.; grad. (in absentia) Yale, 1833; m. Rodolphia S. Kibbe, Oct. 22, 1835, 7 children. Instr., Latin and Greek, Ill. Coll., Jacksonville, 1833-34, prof. rhetoric and belles-lettres, 1834-47; an organizer Ill. Tchrs. Assn., 1836; editor Statesman (an anti-slavery organ), Jacksonville; 1st pres. Ill. Natural History Soc.; a founder indsl. sch. which became U. Ill. Author: Mormonism in All Ages, 1842; The Three Great Races of Men, 1861; Universal Law and Its Opposites, 1892. Died Jacksonville, Jan. 10, 1899.

TURNER, Josiah, editor; b. Hillsboro, N.C., Dec. 27, 1821; s. Josiah and Eliza (Evans) T.; ed. U. N.C.; m. Sophia Devereux, 1856, 4 sons, 1 dau. Admitted to N.C. bar, circa 1845; mem. N.C. Ho. of Reps., 1852-56; mem. N.C. Senate, 1858-61, 1st opposed secession; resigned N.C. Senate seat to become capt. N.C. Militia; mem. Confederate Congress from N.C., 1863-65, opposed Davis administration; elected to U.S. Ho. of Reps. from N.C., 1865, denied seat; pres. N.C. R.R., 1866-68; elected to N.C. Senate, 1868, denied seat; bought Raleigh (N.C.) Sentinel, 1868, through paper became known as rabid opponent of congressional reconstrn. in N.C.; declined nomination for U.S. Ho. of Reps., 1872; sold paper because of debt, 1876; mem. N.C. Ho. of Reps., 1879, expelled because of disorderly behavior; defeated for U.S. Ho. of Reps., 1884. Died Hillsboro, N.C., Oct. 26, 1901.

TURNER, Nat, insurrectionist; b. Southampton County, Va., Oct. 2, 1800; m. Nancy. Became slave of Joseph Travis, 1830; a preacher, became leader among Negroes; believed himself chosen through divine inspiration to lead the Negro from slavery; an eclipse of sun convinced him the time was near, 1831, enlisted 4 other slaves, uprising abandoned; after a new sign, they decided on Aug. 21, 1831 as the day of deliverance; with 7 others he attacked Travis family, murdered all; killed 51 white persons in the neighborhood; hid in dugout for 6 weeks, discovered, tried, convicted and sentenced to death; as a result of his insurrection almost every So. state enacted new laws which increased severity of slave codes, meant end to manumission socs. flourishing in South (South was never again free from fear of a successful slave uprising). Hung at Jerusalem, Va., Nov. 11, 1831.

TURNER, Oscar, congressman, lawyer; b. New Orleans, Feb. 3, 1825; grad. law dept. Transylvania U., Lexington, Ky., 1847. Commonwealth atty., 1851-55, admitted to bar, practiced law until 1861; mem. Ky. Senate, 1867-71; mem. U.S. Ho. of Reps. Independent (Democrat) from Ky., 46th-48th congresses, 1879-85; resumed practice of law. Died Louisville, Ky., Jan. 22, 1896; buried Cave Hill Cemetery.

TURNER, Samuel Hulbeart, clergyman, educator; b. Phila., Jan. 23, 1790; s. Rev. Joseph and Elizabeth (Mason) T.; grad. U. Pa., 1807; m. Mary Beach, May 23, 1826, at least 3 children. Ordained deacon Protestant Espicopal Ch., 1811, priest, 1814; pastor, Chestertown, Md., 1814-17; went to Phila., 1817; supt. theol. students in Pa. Diocese, 1818; prof. historic theology Gen. Theol. Sem., N.Y.C., 1818-22, prof. Bibl. learning and interpretation, 1822-61; prof. Hebrew lang. and lit. Columbia, 1830-61. Author: A Companion to the Book of Genesis, 1841; Autobiography of Rev. Samuel H. Turner, D.D., published posthumously, 1863. Died N.Y.C., Dec. 21, 1861.

TURNER, Thomas Johnston, congressman, lawyer; b. Trumbull County, O., Apr. 5, 1815; studied law. Admitted to bar, 1840; began practice of law, Freeport, Ill.; judge Stephenson County Probate Ct., 1842; postmaster Freeport, 1844; state dist. atty., 1845; founder Prairie Democrat, (1st weekly newspaper in Stephenson County); mem. U.S. Ho. of Reps. (Democrat) from Ill., 30th Congress, 1847-49; mem. Ill. Ho. of Reps., 1854, speaker; 1st mayor Freeport, 1855; del. Washington (D.C.) Peace Conv., 1861; served as col. 15th Regt., Ill. Volunteer Inf. during Civil War, 1861-62; practiced law, Chgo., from 1871. Died Hot Springs, Ark., Apr. 4, 1874; buried City Cemetery, Freeport.

TURNEY, Hopkins Lacy, senator, congressman; b. Dixon Springs, Smith County, Tenn., Oct. 3, 1797; apprenticed to a tailor; studied law. Served in Seminole War, 1818; admitted to bar, practiced law, Jasper, Tenn., then Winchester, Tenn.; mem. Tenn. Ho. of Reps., 1828-38; mem. U.S. Ho. of Reps. (Democrat) from Tenn., 25th-27th congresses, 1837-43; mem. U.S. Senate from Tenn., 1845-51. Died Winchester, Aug. 1, 1857; buried Winchester Cemetery.

TURNEY, Jacob, congressman, lawyer; b. Greensburg, Pa., Feb. 18, 1825; attended Greensburg Acad.; apprenticed to a printer; studied law. Admitted to bar, 1849, began practice of law, Greensburg; dist. atty. for Westmoreland County, 1850-55; Democratic presdl. elector, 1856; mem. Pa. Senate, 1858-60, pres., 1859; mem. U.S. Ho. of Reps. (Democrat) from Pa., 44th-45th congresses, 1875-79. Died Greensburg, Oct. 4, 1891; buried St. Clair Cemetery.

TURRELL, Jane, poet; b. Boston, Mar. 8, 1709; d. Benjamin and Jane (Clark) Colman; m. Ebenezer Turrell, Aug. 22, 1726, 4 children. Began writing poetry at age of 11; later kept a religious diary, wrote poetic eulogies on Sir Richard Blackmore and Edmund Waller; works published posthumously under title Memoirs of the Life and Death of the Pious and Ingenious Mrs. Jane Turrell 1735. Died Apr. 6, 1735.

TURRILL, Joel, congressman, lawyer; b. Shoreham, Vt., Feb. 22, 1794; grad. Middlebury Coll., 1816; studied law, Newburgh, N.Y. Admitted to bar, 1819, began practice of law, Oswego, N.Y.; justice of peace; county judge, 1828-33; mem. N.Y. State Assembly, 1831; mem. U.S. Ho. of Reps. (Jackson Democrat) from N.Y., 23d-24th congresses, 1833-37; dist. atty. for Oswego County, 1838-40; surrogate Oswego County, 1843; U.S. consul to Sandwich Islands, 1845-50. Died Oswego, Dec. 28, 1859; buried Riverside Cemetery.

TUTHILL, Joseph Hasbrouck, congressman, businessman; b. Blooming Grove, Orange County, N.Y., Feb. 25, 1811; attended common and pvt. schs. Moved to Ulster County, N.Y., 1824, engaged in business and agriculture; became businessman, N.Y. C., 1828, Ulsterville, N.Y., 1832, Ellenville, N.Y., 1834; mem. Ulster County Bd. of Suprs., 1842-43, 61-62, 65-70; clk. Ulster County, 1843-47; pres. Ellenville Glass Works; mem. U.S. Ho. of Reps. (Democrat) from N.Y., 42d Congress, 1871-73. Died Ellenville, July 27, 1877; buried Fantinekill Cemetery, nr. Ellenville.

TUTHILL, Selah, congressman; b. Blooming Grove, Orange County, N.Y., Oct. 26, 1771; attended public and pvt. schs. Mem. N.Y. State Assembly from Ulster County, 1805, from Orange County, 1820; mem. U.S. Ho. of Reps. from N.Y., 17th Congress, 1821. Died Goshen, N.Y., Sept. 7, 1821; buried Riverside Cemetery, Marlboro, N.Y.

TUTTLE, Charles Wesley, astronomer, lawyer; b. Newfield, Mass., Nov. 1, 1829; s. Moses and Mary (Merrow) T.; attended Harvard Law Sch., 1854, A. M. (hon.), 1854; Ph.D. (hon.), Dartmouth, 1880; m. Mary Louisa Park, Jan. 31, 1872. Asst., Harvard Observatory, 1850; made his most important contbn. to astronomy by explaining Saturn's "dusky" ring, 1850; discovered a comet, 1853; computed cometary orbits and ephemirides; participated in eclipse expdn. to summit of Mt. Washington, 1854; admitted to Mass. bar, 1856; practiced, Boston, 1856; admitted to practice in U.S. circuit cts., 1858, U.S. Supreme Ct., 1861; took testimony for use before Ct. of Ala. Claims, 1874; made hist. and antiquarian studies of Me. and N.H. Author: Captain John Mason (edited by J. W. Dean), published posthumously, 1887; also numerous articles published in New Eng. Hist. and Geneal. Register, Proceedings of Mass. Hist. Soc., Notes and Queries. Died July 17, 1881.

TUTTLE, Herbert, journalist, educator; b. Bennington, Vt., Nov. 29, 1846; s. Charles J. and Evaline (Boynton) T.; grad. U. Vt., 1869; m. Mary Thompson, July 6, 1875. With Boston Daily Advertiser as Washington corr., spl. corr. in Paris, France, 1871; Berlin corr. London (Eng.) Daily News, 1873-79; reported proceedings of Ct. of Ala. Claims, Geneva, Switzerland, for N.Y. Tribune, 1872; lectr. internat. law U. Mich., 1880-81, lectr. Cornell U., 1881-83, asso. prof., 1883-87, prof. internat. law and history of polit. instns., 1887-90, prof. modern European history, 1890; an original mem. Am. Hist. Assn. Author: German Political Leaders, 1876; 1st volume of History of Prussia, 1884 (of 5 vols. planned he lived to complete the introduction, two vols. on Frederick, published 1888, part of 3d, published 1896. Died June 21, 1894.

TUTWILER, Henry, educator; b. Harrisonburg, Va., Nov. 16, 1807; s. Henry and Margaret (Lorchbaugh) T.; grad. U. Va., 1829, postgrad. in law, 1830; m. Julia Ashe, Dec. 24,, 1835, 11 children including Julia Strudwick. Prof. ancient langs. U. Ala., 1831-37; prof. at various small Ala. colls., 1837-47; opened Greene Springs Sch. for Boys (called "Rugby of the South"), nr. village of Havana in Hale (then part of Greene) County, Ala., 1847, head sch., 1847-84; twice declined appointment as pres. U. Ala. Died Green Springs, Ala., Sept. 22, 1884.

TWEED, William Marcy, congressman, polit. leader; b. N.Y.C., Apr. 3, 1823; s. Richard and Eliza Tweed; m. Mary Jane Skaden, 1844, 8 children. Volunteer fireman, N.Y.C., organized new engine Americus Number 6, 1848, head of tiger painted on engine became symbol of Tweed's polit. orgn., Tammany Hall; elected to Common Council, N.Y.C. (known as "Forty Thieves"), alderman, 1852-55; mem. U.S. Ho. of Reps. from N.Y., 33d Congress, 1853-55; joined Peter B. Sweeny and Richard B. Connolly in faction of Tammany Hall, considered one of most powerful men in orgn. by 1859; mem. bd. suprs. intended to check corruption at elections which itself became agency for graft, 1856; sch. commr., 1856-57; mem. bd. suprs. New York County, 1858; apptd. chmn. gen. com. Tammany Hall; practiced law, 1860; dep. street commr., 1861-70; bought controlling interest in a printing concern (which all railroads, ferries and ins. cos. patronized if they wished franchises); 1864, thereafter did all city's printing; organized marble co. and bought quarry in Mass. from which stone for new county courthouse was used; assisted in launching Bklyn. Bridge project, 1866; secured polit. control of State, 1868; mem. N.Y. State Senate, 1867-71; made grand sachem of Tammany, 1868; aided Jay Gould and James Fisk in plundering of Erie R.R.; became dir. banks, gas and street railroad cos. through control of issuance of franchises and control of law enforcement; commr. Dept. Public Works, N.Y.C., 1870; Harper's Weekly with Thomas Nast as cartoonist began campaign against Tweed, 1870; gained approval of new city charter, 1870; discontented ofcls. turned over to N.Y. Times proof of public works swindling by Tammany ring, 1871, evidence published; injunction obtained against further taxation or payment of money to city contractors; arrested on criminal action, 1871, convicted and sentenced to 12 years in prison, fined $12,750, 1873, sentence reduced to year and $250 fine, released Jan. 1875; arrested on civil action brought by state to recover $6,000,000 of Tammany ring's graft, Jan. 1875, sent to prison, escaped, Dec. 1875, fled to Spain; identified by Spanish ofcls. through Nast cartoons, arrested, 1876; amount which his ring stole from city has been estimated at from $30,000,000 to $200,000,000. Died Ludlow Street Jail, N.Y.C., Apr. 12, 1878; buried Greenwood Cemetery, Bklyn.

TWEEDY, John Hubbard, congressman; b. Danbury, Fairfield County, Conn., Nov. 9, 1814; grad. Yale, 1834, Yale Law Sch., 1836. Admitted to bar, 1836, began practice of law, Milw.; commr., receiver of canal lands, 1839-41; mem. Wis. Territorial Council, 1842; del. Wis. Constl. Conv., 1846; mem. U.S. Congress (Whig) from Wis. Territory, 30th Congress, 1847-May 29, 1848; unsuccessful Whig candidate for gov. Wis., 1848; mem. Wis. Assembly, 1853; a railroad developer, dir. Milw. & Miss. R.R., also Milw. & Watertown R.R. Died Milw., Nov. 12, 1891; buried Wooster Cemetery, Danbury.

TWEEDY, Samuel, congressman; b. Nine Partners, Dutchess County, N.Y., Mar. 8, 1776. Moved to Danbury, Conn.; mem. Conn. Ho. of Reps., 1818, 20, 24, Conn. Senate, 1826-28; held many local offices; mem. U.S. Ho. of Reps. (Whig) from Conn., 23d Congress, 1833-35. Died Danbury, July 1, 1868; buried Wooster Cemetery.

TWICHELL, Ginery, congressman, businessman; b. Athol, Mass., Aug. 26, 1811; attended common schs. Became interested in stage coach business at age 19, became owner of several stage lines, contracted for carrying mails; engaged in railroading, 1848; became pres. Boston & Worcester Ry., 1857; del. Republican Nat. Conv., 1864; mem. U.S. Ho. of Reps. (Rep.) from Mass., 40th-42d congresses, 1867-73; pres. A., T. & S.F. Ry., 1870-74, Boston, Barre & Gardner R.R. Co., 1873-78. Died Brookline, Mass., July 23, 1883; buried Rural Cemetery, Worcester, Mass.

TWIGGS, David Emanuel, army officer; b. Richmond County, Ga., 1790; s. Gen. John and Ruth (Emanuel) T.; m. Elizabeth Hunter; m. 2d, Mrs. Hunt; 2 children. Commd. capt., inf. U.S. Army, 1812; served in War of 1812; commd. maj., 1814, commn. withdrawn at end of War, commd. maj. 1st U.S. Inf., 1825, lt. col. 4th U.S. Inf., 1831, col. 2d U.S. Dragoons, 1836; served in Mexican War; commd. brig. gen. U.S. Army, 1846, brevetted maj. gen. for bravery, 1846; recipient sword for services in Mexican War by vote of U.S. Congress, 1847; mil. gov. Veracruz (Mexico), 1847-48; in command Dept. of Tex., U.S. Army, 1861; a Southern sympathizer, surrendered his command to Confederacy, dismissed from U.S. Army; commd. maj. gen. Confederate Army, assigned to command Dist. of La., too old for active service. Died Augusta, Ga., Sept. 15, 1862; buried Twiggs Cemetery, nr. Augusta.

TWINING, Alexander Catlin, engr., astronomer, inventor; b. New Haven, Conn., July 5, 1801; s. Stephen and Almira (Catlin) T.; B.A., Yale, 1820, M. A., 1822; attended Andover Theol. Sem., 1823; studied civil engring. U.S. Mil. Acad., 1833; m. Harriet Kinsley, Mar. 2, 1829, at least 6 children. Tutor, Yale, 1823-24; observed star shower of Nov. 1833; formulated theory of cosmic origin of meteors (that shooting stars are bodies coming into air from external space); railroad engr. for Hartford & New Haven R.R. Co., 1834-39; prof. mathematics and natural philosophy Middlebury (Vt.) Coll., 1839-49; inventor method of mfg. ice (one of earliest applications of absorption process for mfg. ice on comml. scale), patented 1853. Died New Haven, Nov. 22, 1884.

TWITCHELL, Amos, surgeon; b. Dublin, N.H., Apr. 11, 1781; s. Samuel and Alice (Willson) T.; A.B., Dartmouth, 1802, A.M., B.M., 1805, M.D., 1811; studied medicine under Nathan Smith; m. Elizabeth Goodhue, 1815. Leading surgeon in Northern New Eng.; one of 1st in U.S. to perform extensive amputations for malignant disease, operations for stones in bladder and ovarian tumors, tracheotomy, trephining of long bones for suppuration; performed 1st tying off of carotid artery in U.S., 1807; overseer Dartmouth, 1816; pres. N.H. Med. Soc., 1829-30; mem. A.M.A., Coll. Physicians of Phila., Nat. Instn. for Promotion of Science, 1841. Died Keene, N.H., May 26, 1850.

TYLER, Asher, congressman, businessman; b. Bridgewater, Oneida County, N.Y., May 10, 1798; grad. Hamilton Coll., Clinton, N.Y., 1817; studied law. Admitted to bar, began practice of law, Ellicottville, N.Y., 1836; became agt. Deveraux Land Co.; held several local offices; mem. U.S. Ho. of Reps. (Whig) from N.Y., 28th Congress, 1843-45; engaged in railroading, Elmira, N.Y., 1846; an incorporator Elmira Rolling Mill Co. Died Elmira, Aug. 1, 1875; buried Woodlawn Cemetery.

TYLER, Bennet, clergyman, coll. pres.; b. Middlebury, Conn., July 10, 1783; s. James and Anne (Humgerford) T.; grad. Yale, 1804; m. Esther Stone, Nov. 12, 1807; 12 children. Ordained to ministry Congregational Ch., 1807; minister, South Britain, Conn., 1807-22; pres. Dartmouth, 1822-28; pastor 2d Ch., Portland, Me., 1828-34; a founder Theol. Inst. Conn., 1834 (an instn. designed to school young ministers in old school Calvinist thought as opposed to New Divinity being taught by Dr. Nathaniel W. Taylor and his followers), pres., prof. Christian Theology, 1834-57. Author: Letters on the Origin and Progress of the New Haven Theology, 1837; Preview of President Day's Treatise on the Will, 1838; A Treatise on the Sufferings of Christ, 1845. Died May 14, 1858.

TYLER, Daniel, army officer, industrialist; b. Brooklyn, Conn., Jan. 7, 1799; s. Daniel and Sarah (Edwards) Chaplin T.; grad. U.S. Mil Acad., 1819; attended Arty. Sch., Metz, France, 1828; m. Emily Lee, May 23, 1832, at least 5 children, including Alfred. Went to France to study French mil. system, 1828; translated many French books on arty.; U.S. Army, 1819, supt. insps. of contract arms, 1832, resigned, 1834; pres. Norwich & Worcester R.R., Morris Canal & Banking Co., during 1840's; completed constrn. railroad from Macon to Atlanta (Ga.), 1844-45; comdr. 1st Conn. Regt., U.S. Volunteers, during Civil War, commd. brig. gen., 1861; participated in battles of Bull Run, Corinth, 1862; in command at battles of Md. Heights, also Harpers Ferry, 1863; organized (with Samuel Noble) Woodstock Iron Co. (after examining iron deposits in Eastern Ala.), 1872; pres. Mobile & Montgomery R.R. Died N.Y.C., Nov. 30, 1882; buried Anniston, Ala.

TYLER, John, gov. Va., jurist; b. York County, Va., Feb. 28, 1747; s. John and Anne (Contesse) T.; attended Coll. William and Mary; m. Mary Armistead, 1776, at least 2 children, including John. Mem. Charles City County (Va.) Com. of Safety, 1774; a judge High Ct. of Admiralty of Va., 1776; mem. Va. Ho. of Dels. from Charles City County, 1777-88, speaker, 1781-84, presented a resolution calling a fed. conv. which was to meet at Annapolis, Md.. 1786; mem. Va. Council of State, 1780-81; v.p. Va. Conv. of 1788, opposed adoption of U.S. Constn.; gov. Va., 1808-11; judge U.S. Circuit Ct. Va., 1811-13. Died "Greenway," Charles City County, Jan. 6, 1813.

TYLER, John, 10th Pres. U.S.; b. Greenway, Charles City County, Va., Mar. 29, 1790; s. Judge John and Mary (Armistead) T.; grad. Coll. William and Mary, 1807; m. Letitia Christian, Mar. 20, 1813; m. 2d, Julia Gardiner, June 26, 1844; 14 children including Robert. Admitted to bar, Charles City County, 1809; served as capt. co. of Richmond volunteers in War of 1812; mem. Va. Ho. of Dels., 1811-16, 23, 38; mem. Va. Exec. Council, 1815-16; mem. U.S. Ho. of Reps. (Democrat) from Va., 15th-16th congresses, 1817-21, mem. com. to report on Bank of U.S.; identified with William H. Crawford faction in election of 1824; gov. Va., 1825-26; mem. U.S. Senate from Va., 1827-36, opposed Pres. Andrew Jackson on constl. issues, resigned seat rather than support expunging censure of Jackson, 1836; vice pres. U.S., 1841, became 10th Pres. U.S. (upon death of William Henry Harrison), 1841-45, remained loyal to anti-nationalist views in bank question that created crisis between Pres. and Whig party, 1841, opposed measure to allow a Nat. Bank to establish branches in states without their previous consent, originated and recommended to Congress plan known as exchequer system for govt. funds, (Clay rejected this); reorganized navy; established depot for nautical charts and instruments (later became Nat. Observatory); ended Seminole War; upheld power of Pres. over cabinet (resulted in cabinet's resignation); negotiated the first trade treaty with China; enforced Monroe Doctrine in case of Tex. and Hawaiian Islands; greatest achievements: negotiation of Webster-Ashburn Treaty, 1842; annexation of Tex., 1845; chmn. Washington (D.C.) Peace Conv., Feb. 1861; mem. Va. Secession Conv. 1861, remained loyal to Va. when it seceded; mem. Provisional Congress of Confederacy, 1861; elected to Confederate Ho. of Reps., died before serving. Died Va., Jan. 18, 1862; buried Hollywood Cemetery, Richmond, Va.

TYLER, Ransom Hubert, jurist; b. Franklin County, Mass., Nov. 18, 1815; s. Peter and Eunice T.; A.M. (hon.), Hamilton Coll., 1853; m. Nancy Caldwell; m. 2d, Mary Douglas; at least 1 child. Admitted to N.Y. bar, 1840; master of chancery N.Y. State, 1844-46; dist. atty. N.Y., 3 years; judge Oswego County (N.Y.), 1852-55, 64-67; editor Oswego County Gazette, 1856; bank pres.; served to brig. gen. N.Y. Militia. Author: The Bible and Social Reform, or, the Scriptures as a Means of Civilization, 1860; American Ecclesiastical Law (his 1st legal textbook) , 1866; Commentaries on the Law of Infants, Marriage and Divorce, and the Respecting Statutory Policy of the Several States in Respect to Husband and Wife 1868, 2d edit., 1882; A Treatise on the Law of Boundaries and Fences, 1874; A Treatise on the Remedy by Ejectment and the Law of Adverse Enjoyment in the United States, 1870, 74, 76, A Treatise on the Law of Fixtures, 1877. Died Fulton, N.Y., Nov. 21, 1881.

TYLER, Robert, Confederate ofcl.; b. Charles City County, Va., Sept. 9, 1816; s. John (10th Pres. U.S.) and Letitia (Christain) T.; grad. Coll. William and Mary, 1835, postgrad. in law; m. Elizabeth Cooper, Sept. 12, 1839. Admitted to Va. bar; pvt. sec. to his father when he became Pres. U.S., 1841; pres. Irish Repeal Assn., 1844; solicitor to sheriff of Phila., 1847; prothonotary to Phila. Supreme Ct.; recruited in a Phila. regt. during Mexican War; an early advocate of a Pacific ry., 1854; chmn. Pa. Democratic Exec. Com., 1858; became register Confederate Treasury, 1861; editor Montgomery (Ala.) Mail and Advertiser, 1867; chmn. Ala. Dem. Central Com. Author poems: Ahasuerus, 1842; Death: or Medorus' Dream, 1843. Died Montgomery, Dec. 3, 1877.

TYLER, Robert Ogden, army officer; b. Hunter, Md., Dec. 22, 1831; s. Frederick and Sophia (Sharp) T.; grad. U.S. Mil. Acad., 1853. Commd. 2d lt. 3d Arty., U.S. Army, 1853, 1st lt., 1856;

mem. garrison at Ft. Columbus Recruiting Sta. (N.Y.) during Civil War; capt. Q.M. Dept., 1861; served at open supply depot, Alexandria, Va.; commd. col. 1st Conn. Heavy Arty.; participated in battles of Gaines Mill and Malvern Hill, 1862; commd. brig. gen. U.S. Volunteers, 1862; commanded arty, res. of 130 guns during Gettysburg campaign, helped to stop Pickett's charge; his arty. served as inf. throughout Wilderness campaign, 1864; participated in battles of Spotsylvania, Cold Harbor, 1864; brevetted maj. gen., 1865; mustered out of volunteer service, 1866; commd. lt. col. Q.M. Dept., U.S. Army; kept diary published posthumously as Memoirs of Brevet Major General Robert Ogden Tyler, 1878. Died Boston, Dec. 1, 1874; buried Hartford, Conn.

TYLER, Royall, playwright, jurist; b. Boston, July 18, 1757; s. Royall and Mary (Steele) T.; m. Mary Palmer, 1794, at least 1 child, Rev. Thomas P. grad. Harvard, 1776, B.A. (hon.), Yale, 1776; Commd. Maj. Independent Co. of Boston, Continental Army, aide to Gen. Sullivan, 1778; commd. maj., participated in attack on Newport, R.I., 1778; admitted to Mass. bar, 1780; joined staff of Gen. Benjamin Lincoln, assisted in suppression of Shay's Rebellion, 1787; went to N.Y.C., 1787; author play, The Contrast (1st comedy written by native Am. and produced by a profl. co.), produced by Am. Co., 1787; author May Day in Town; or, New York in an Uproar, performed at John St. Theatre, 1787; wrote play The Georgia Spec; or, Land in the Moon, 1st played in Boston, 1797; wrote farce The Farm House; or The Female Duelists; wrote 3 sacred dramas: The Origin of the Feast of Purim, or The Destinies of Haman and Mordecai; Joseph and His Brethren; The Judgement of Solomon; entered into lit. partnership with Joseph Dennie under name Colon and Spondee (Tyler as Spondee), wrote satirical verse and prose, pieces in Eagle; or Dartmouth Centinel, later in The New Hampshire Jour., or The Farmers Weekly Museum; author novel The Algerine Captive, 1797; series of letters Yankey in London, 1809; state's atty. for Windham County (Vt.), 1794-1801; asst. judge Vt. Supreme Ct., 1801-07, chief justice, 1807-13; trustee U. Vt., 1802-13, prof. jurisprudence 1811-14. Died Brattleboro, Vt., Aug. 26, 1826.

TYLER, Samuel, lawyer, writer; b. Prince George's County, Md., Oct. 22, 1809; s. Grafton and Anne (Plummer) T.; attended Middlebury (Vt.) Coll., 1826-28; m. Catherine Bayly, Apr. 16, 1833, 4 children. Admitted to Md. bar, 1831; apptd. by Md. Legislature a commr. to simplify practice and pleading in Md. cts.; wrote A Treatise on the Maryland Simplified Preliminary Procedure and Pleading, 1857; published articles on logic and metaphysics in Princeton Review, collected under titles A Discourse of the Baconian Philosophy, 1844, The Progress of Philosophy in the Past and in the Future, 1858; prof. law Columbian (now George Washington) U., 1867-77; published Am. edit. Treatise on the Principles of Pleading (H.J. Stephen), 1871, Memoir of Roger Brooke Taney, LL.D., 1872, Commentary on the Law of Partnership, 1877, Died Georgetown, D.C., Dec. 15, 1877; buried Oak Hill Cemetery, Washington, D.C.

TYLER, William, clergyman; b. Derby, Vt., June 5, 1806; s. Noah and Abigail (Barber) T.; educated privately by Bishop Benedict J. Fenwick. Ordained priest Roman Catholic Ch., 1829; petitioned Rome at 5th Provincial Council of Balt. bishops to erect new See at Hartford (Conn.) with Tyler as bishop, 1844, became bishop of Hartford, 1844; crusaded against intemperance at Cathedral of Sts. Peter and Paul, Providence, R.I. Died June 18, 1849.

TYLER, William Seymour, educator; b. Hartford, Pa., Sept. 2, 1810; s. Joab and Nabby (Seymour) T.; attended Hamilton Coll., 1827; grad. Amherst Coll., 1830; attended Andover Theol. Sem., 1832, 34; m. Amelia Whiting, Sept. 4, 1839, 4 children. Prof., Latin and Greek, Amherst Coll., 1836-92, Williston prof. Greek, 1847-92, prof. emeritus, 1893-97; ordained to ministry Congregational Ch., North Amherst, Mass., 1859; chiefly responsible for framing constn. and policy of Williston Sem., pres. bd. trustees; trustee Mt. Holyoke Sem. (now Coll.), 1862-97, Smith Coll., 1877-97, served as pres. both bds. trustees; founder Amherst chpt. Phi Beta Kappa. Author: History of Amherst College During its First Half Century, 1873. Died Nov. 9, 1897.

TYNDALE, Hector, mcht., army officer; b. Phila., Mar. 24, 1821; s. Robinson and Sarah (Thorne) T.; m. Julia Nowlen, Aug. 1842. Became partner (with Edward P. Mitchell) in glass importing bus., 1845; mem. 1st Republican Com. in Phila.; commd. maj. 28th Regt., Pa. Volunteers, 1861, served in 43 engagements during Civil War; commanded forces nr. Harper's Ferry, 1861; commd. lt. col., then brig. gen., 1862, served with Gen. Nathaniel Bank's Corps in Shenandoah Valley campaign in Battle of Chantilly and 2d Battle of Bull Run; served at battles of Antietam, Missionary Ridge; resigned, 1864, brevetted maj. gen., 1865; trustee of fund which provided univ. scholarships in physics, including Hector Tyndale scholarship at U. Pa. Died Phila., Mar. 19, 1880.

TYNG, Edward, naval officer; b. Boston, 1683; s. Col. Edward and Miss (Clarke) T.; m. Elizabeth (Southack) Parnel, Jan. 8, 1725; m. 2d, Ann Waldo, Jan. 27, 1731; 7 children. Capt. of south and north batteries and fortifications, Boston, 1740; comdr. vessel Prince of Orange, 1740, cruised after Spanish privateers, chiefly off New Eng. coast, 1741-43; commodore of provincial fleet during King George's War, 1744, captured French privateer commanded by Capt. Delabroitz; in command of frigate Massachusetts, 1745; sr. officer Mass. Navy, participated in taking of the Vigilante, capture of Louisbourg and destruction of St. Ann. Died Boston, Sept. 8, 1755.

TYNG, Stephen Higginson, clergyman; b. Newburyport, Mass., Mar. 1, 1800; s. Dudley Atkins and Sarah (Higginson) T.; grad. Harvard, 1817; m. Anne Griswold, Aug. 5, 1821; m. 2d, Susan Mitchell, July 1833; 9 children. Ordained as deacon Episcopal Ch., 1821, priest, 1824; pastor St. John's Ch., Georgetown, D.C., 1821-23, Queen Ann's Parish, Prince Georges County, Md., 1823-29, St. Paul's Ch., Phila., Ch. of Epiphany, Phila., 1834-45, St. George's Ch., N.Y.C., 1845-78; one of 1st to recognize importance of Sunday schs. and city missions; editor Episcopal Recorder, Phila., Protestant Churchman, N.Y. Author: Lectures on the Law and the Gospel, 3d edit., 1844; The Israel of God, 1849; Fellowship with Christ, 1854; The Captive Orphan; Esther, Queen of Persia, 1860; The Spencers, a Story of Home Influence, 1869. Died Irvington-on-Hudson, N.Y., Sept. 3, 1885.

TYSON, Jacob, congressman, lawyer; b. Staten Island, N.Y., Oct. 8, 1773; attended common schs.; studied law. Admitted to bar, practiced law. Supr., Town of Castletown, 1811-21; judge Richmond County, 1822-40; mem. U.S. Ho. of Reps. from N.Y., 18th Congress, 1823-25; mem. N.Y. Senate, 1828. Died Staten Island, July 16, 1848; buried Reformed Protestant Dutch Ch. Cemetery, Port Richmond, S.I.

TYSON, Job Roberts, congressman; b. Phila., Feb. 8, 1803; s. Joseph and Ann (Trump) T.; self-educated; LL.D. (hon.), Dickinson Coll., 1851; m. Eleanor Cope, Oct. 4, 1832. Tchr., Hamburg, Pa.; admitted to Pa. bar, 1827; vice provost Phila. Law Acad., 1833-58; solicitor Pa. R.R., 1847-55; mem. Pa. Ho. of Reps.; dir. Phila. Public Schs.; mem. Select Council of Phila., 1846-49; mem. U.S. Ho. of Reps. (Whig) from Pa., 34th Congress, 1855-57; mem. Soc. for Alleviating Miseries of Public Prisons, drafted report against capital punishment; mgr. Apprentices Library, Phila.; trustee Girard Coll., Pa. Female Coll.; became mem. Am. Philos. Soc., 1836; early mem. Hist. Soc. Pa., officer, 1829-48; mem. joint com. of philos. and hist. societies instrumental in petitioning Pa. Legislature to provide for printing Pa. archives, 1836. Author: Essay on the Penal Laws of Pennsylvania, 1827; The Lottery System of the United States, 1833; Discourse . . . on the Colonial History of the Eastern and Some of the Southern States, 1842; Social and Intellectual State of the Colony of Pennsylvania Prior to 1743, 1843; Discourse on the 200th Anniversary of the Birth of William Penn, 1844; Letters on the Resources and Hall, Montgomery County, Pa., June 27, 1858; Commerce of Philadelphia, 1852. Died Woodlawn buried South Laurel Hill Cemetery, Phila.

U

UDREE, Daniel, congressman, mcht.; b. Phila., Aug. 5, 1751; attended common schs. Became a mcht., Berks County, Pa.; mem. Pa. Ho. of Reps., 1799-1805; mem. U.S. Ho. of Reps. (Democrat, filled vacancies) from Pa., 13th, 16th, 17th-18th congresses, Oct. 12, 1813-15, Dec. 26, 1820-21, Dec. 10, 1822-25. Died Reading, Pa., July 15, 1828; buried Oley (Pa.) Cemetery.

ULLOA, Antonio, see de Ulloa, Antonio.

ULLOA, Francisco de, explorer; flourished circa 1539. A capt. under Hernando Cortés in Mexico; sent by Cortés (against orders of the viceroy) to explore Gulf of Cal., 1939, sailed to head of gulf and proved Lower Cal. to be a peninsula; may have been forced to return to New Spain when supplies ran out, 1540 and killed there by a soldier; according to other authorities, disappeared with 1 of his ships.

UNCAS, Indian chief; b. 1588; s. Oweneco and Meekunump; married twice, at least 3 children. Rebelled against Sassacus (chief sachem of Pequot Indians), defeated and banished, circa 1630; allowed to return, rebelled again causing split in Pequot tribe; followers of Uncas became known as Mohegans; joined English settlers of Mass., Conn. and Narragansett Indians in war against Pequots, 1637; signed peace treaty with English and Narragansetts, Hartford, Conn., 1638; at war with Narragansetts, 1643-45; made unprovoked war on Massasoit, 1661; forced by English to give up captives, stolen goods; forced to surrender arms to English at Boston to prevent him from participating in King Philip's War, 1675. Died 1683.

UNCLE Sam, see Wilson, Samuel.

UNDERHILL, John, colonial ofcl.; b. circa 1597; s. John and Honor (Pawley) U.; m. Helena de Hooch, Dec. 12, 1628; m. 2d, Elizabeth Feake, after 1658; at least 8 children. Went to Boston to help organize militia of Mass. Bay Colony, 1630, capt. militia, 1630; chosen one of 1st selectmen of Boston, 1634; went to Eng. in effort to enlarge mil. stores, 1634-35; in service of Saybrook Plantation in destroying Pequot Indians, 1637; disenfranchised by Massachusetts Bay Colony because he aided Antinomians (religious sect), 1637, reinstated, 1640; representative in New Haven Court from Stamford (Connecticut), 1643; employed by Dutch to fight Indians, circa 1643; member Council for New Amsterdam in L.I.; denounced Stuyvesant's govt.; secured commn. as privateer at Providence, R.I., 1653, seized Dutch West Indies Co.'s property at Hartford, Conn., 1653, precipitated 10 year dispute with Hartford Govt.; helped English conquer New Amsterdam; 1664/65; mem. Hempstead Conv., 1664/65; surveyor of customs for L.I., 1665; high constable and undersheriff of North Riding, Yorkshire, L.I. Died Killingworth, Oyster Bay, L.I., N.Y., Sept. 21, 1672.

UNDERHILL, Walter, congressman; b. N.Y.C., Sept. 12, 1795. Trustee of house of refuge; treas. N.Y.C., several years; mem. bd. mgrs. Soc. for Reformation of Juvenile Delinquents in N.Y.C., 1845-66, treas., 1857-66; mem. U.S. Ho. of Reps. (Whig) from N.Y., 31st Congress, 1849-51; pres. Mechanics & Traders' Ins. Co., N.Y.C., 1853-66. Died Whitestone, L.I., N.Y., Aug. 17, 1866; buried Woodlawn Cemetery, N.Y.C.

UNDERWOOD, Francis Henry, author, diplomat; b. Enfield, Mass., Jan. 12, 1825; s. Roswell and Phoebe (Hall) U.; attended Amherst Coll., 1843; LL.D. (hon.), U. Glasgow (Scotland); m. Louisa Maria Wood, May 18, 1848; m. 2d, Frances Findlay, circa 1893; 5 children. Admitted to Ky. bar, 1847; clk. Mass. Senate, 1852; literary editor Phillips Sampson & Co., publishing house, Boston; a founder Atlantic Monthly, asst. editor, 1857-59; clk. Superior Criminal Ct., Boston, 1859-66; original mem., 2d pres. Papyrus Club; mem. Boston Sch. Com., 10 years; wrote manuals of English and Am. literature; wrote volume short stories Lord of Himself, 1874; U.S. consul at Glasgow, 1886-88, Leith, Scotland, 1892-94; other writings include: Cloud-Pictures, 1872; Man Proposes, 1885; Quabbin, the Story of a Small Town, 1893; Doctor Gray's Quest, 1895. Died Edinburgh, Scotland, Aug. 7, 1894.

UNDERWOOD, John Curtiss, jurist; b. Litchfield, N.Y., Mar. 14, 1809; s. John and Mary (Curtiss) U.; grad. Hamilton Coll., 1832; m. Maria Jackson, Oct. 24, 1839, 3 children. A founder Alpha Delta Phi frat.; Freesoiler; del. Republican nat. convs., 1856, 60; nominated U.S. consul, Callao, Peru, 1861; 5th U.S. auditor of treasury, 1861-64; judge U.S. Dist. Ct. for Va., 1864, most noted in connection with case of Jefferson Davis, 1866; del., pres. Va. Constl. Conv., Richmond, 1867, drew up what came to be known as Underwood Constn. Died Washington, D.C., Dec. 7, 1873.

UNDERWOOD, John William Henderson, congressman, jurist; b. Ellenton, Ga., Nov. 20, 1816; studied law. Admitted to bar, 1835, began practice of law, Clarksville, Ga.; solicitor gen. Western Jud. Circuit of Ga., 1843-47; del. Ga. Constl. Conv., 1850; del. Ga. Democratic Conv., 1857; mem. Ga. Ho. of Reps., 1857-59, served as speaker; mem. U.S. Ho. of Reps. (Democrat) from Ga., 36th Congress, 1859-Jan. 23, 1861 (withdrew); served as brigade insp. Confederate Army during Civil War; resumed practice of law, Rome, Ga.; judge Superior Ct. of Ga., 1867-69, 73-82; del. Dem. Nat. Conv., N.Y.C., 1868; apptd. mem. 1st U.S. Tariff Commn. by Pres. Arthur, 1884. Died Rome, July 18, 1888; buried Myrtle Hill Cemetery.

UNDERWOOD, Joseph Rogers, senator; b. Goochland County, Va., Oct. 24, 1791; s. Thomas William Underwood; grad. Transylvania Coll., Lexington, Ky., 1811. Enlisted in 13th Ky. Regt. during War of 1812, imprisoned at Ft. Wayne after defeat of his co., 1813; mem. Ky. Ho. of Reps., 1816-20, 46-47, 60-63, speaker, 1846, 61, mem. U.S. Ho. of Reps. (Whig) from Ky., 24th-27th congresses, 1835-43; mem. U.S. Senate (Whig) from Va., 1847-53; del. Democratic Nat. Conv., 1864; concluded his career in pvt. law practice. Died Bowling Green, Ky., Aug. 23, 1876.

UNDERWOOD, Warner Lewis, congressman, lawyer; b. Goochland County, Va., Aug. 7, 1808; grad. U. Va. at Charlottesville, 1829; studied law. Admitted to bar, began practice of law, Bowling Green, Ky., 1830; moved to Tex., 1834; atty. gen. Eastern Dist. Tex.; returned to Bowling Green, 1840; mem. Ky. Ho. of Reps., 1848, Ky. Senate, 1949-53; mem. U.S. Ho. of Reps. (Am. Party) from Ky., 34th-35th congresses, 1855-59; U.S. consul to Glasgow, Scotland, 1862-64; practiced law, San Francisco, circa 1865, Ky., 1866-72. Died nr. Bowling Green, Mar. 12, 1872; buried Fairview Cemetery, Bowling Green.

UPCHURCH, John Jordan, labor leader; b. Franklin County, N.C., Mar. 26, 1820; s. Ambrose and Elizabeth (Hill) U.; m. Angelina Greene, June 1, 1841, 15 children. Opened hotel with John Zeigenfuss, Raleigh, N.C., 1st temperance house south of Mason Dixon Line; moved to Pa., 1846, master mechanic Mine Hill & Schuylkill Haven R.R., 1851-65, operated road in interest of govt. during strike, 1864; joined League of Friendship, Supreme, Mechanical Order of Sun (secret workers' order), Meadville, Pa., 1863; responsible for section or Order reorganized as Jefferson Lodge Number 1 of Ancient Order of United Workmen, 1868, became model for fraternal movement characteristic of the period in Am.; named past supreme master workman, 1873; founder mutual benefit system; worked as master mechanic for various r.r.s until circa 1881. Author: The Life, Labors, and Travels of Father J. J. Upchurch (autobiography), 1887. Died Steelville, Mo., Jan. 18, 1887; buried Bellefontaine Cemetery, St. Louis.

UPDEGRAFF, David Brainard, clergyman, editor; b. Mt. Pleasant, O., Aug. 23, 1830; s. David and Rebecca (Taylor) U.; attended Haverford Coll., 1851-52; m. Rebecca B. Price, Sept. 23, 1852; m. 2d, Eliza Mitchell, Sept. 4, 1866; 8 children. Began Quaker meetings in his home, 1869; leader popular summer gatherings at Mountain Lake Park, Garret County, Md., Pitman Grove, N.J., and great interdenominational camp meetings in East and West; exponent of religious thought called Pentecostal Christianity; advocated introduction of singing and pastoral leadership into Quakerism; edited periodical Friends' Expositor, 1887-93. Author: Old Corn (volume of sermons and addresses), 1892. Died Mt. Pleasant, May 23, 1894.

UPDIKE, Daniel, state ofcl.; b. North Kingstown, R.I., circa 1693; s. Ludowick and Catherine (Newton) U.; m. Sarah Arnold, Dec. 20, 1716; m. 2d, Antis Jenkins, Dec. 22, 1722; m. 3d, Mary (Godfrey) Wanton, Mar. 14, 1745. Admitted to R.I. bar; atty. gen. of R.I., 1722-32, 43-57, conducted trial of 36 pirates captured by English vessel off L.I. (N.Y.) coast, 1723; a commr. to determine boundary line between Conn. and R.I., 1724; represented R.I. in boundary debate with Mass., 1740; atty. gen. Kings County (R.I.), 1741-43; charter mem. local soc. for promotion of knowledge and science (beginning of Redwood Library), Newport, R.I., 1730. Died May 15, 1757.

UPHAM, Charles Wentworth, clergyman, congressman; b. St. John's, N.B., Can., May 4, 1802; grad. Harvard, 1817; attended Cambridge Divinity Sch.; m. Ann Susan Holmes, Mar. 29, 1826, 14 children. Apothecary's apprentice, Salem, Mass.; ordained to ministry Unitarian Ch., 1824; asso. pastor 1st Ch. (Unitarian), of Salem, 1832-44; mem. Mass. Ho. of Reps., 1840-49, 59-61, Mass. Senate, 1857-58; mayor Salem, 1852; del. Mass. Constl. Conv., 1853; mem. U.S. Ho. of Reps. (Whig) from Mass., 33d. Congress, 1853-55; devoted energies to investigation of Salem witch trials, after 1860. Author: Salem Witchcraft, 2 vols., 1867. Died June 15, 1875; buried Harmony Grove Cemetery, Salem.

UPHAM, George Baxter, congressman, lawyer; b. Brookfield, Mass., Dec. 27, 1768; attended Phillips Exeter Acad.; grad. Harvard, 1789; studied law. Admitted to bar, 1792, began practice of law, Claremont, N.H.; solicitor of Cheshire County, 1796-1804; mem. U.S. Ho. of Reps. from N.H., 7th Congress, 1801-03; mem. N.C. Ho. of Reps., 1804-13, 15, speaker, 1809, 15; mem. N.H. Senate, 1814; also a banker. Died Claremont, N.H., Feb. 10, 1848; buried Pleasant Street Cemetery.

UPHAM, Jabez, congressman, lawyer; b. Brookfield, Mass., Aug. 23, 1764; grad. Harvard, 1785; studied law. Admitted to bar, began practice of law, Sturbridge, Mass.; continued practice of law, Claremont, N.H., then in Brookfield; mem. Mass. Ho. of Reps., 1804-06, 11; mem. U.S. Ho. of Reps. from Mass., 10th-11th congresses, 1807-10 (resigned). Died Brookfield, Nov. 8, 1811; buried New Cemetery, West Brookfield, Mass.

UPHAM, Nathaniel, congressman; b. Deerfield, N.H., June 9, 1774; attended Phillips Exeter Acad., Exeter, N.H., 1793. Became mcht., Gilmanton, 1794, Deerfield, 1796, Portsmouth, 1801, Rochester, 1802; mem. N.H. Ho. of Reps., 1807-90; gov.'s counselor, 1811-12; mem. U.S. Ho. of Reps. (Democrat) from N.H., 15th-17th congresses, 1817-23, Died Rochester, N.H., July 10, 1829; buried Old Rochester Cemetery.

UPHAM, Thomas Cogswell, educator, author; b. Deerfield, N.H., Jan. 30, 1799; s. Nathaniel and Judith (Cogswell) U.; grad. Dartmouth, 1818; grad. Andover Theol. Sem., 1821; m. Phebe Lord, May 18, 1825, several adopted children. Asso. pastor Congregational Ch., Rochester, N.H., 1823-24; prof. mental and moral philosophy Bowdoin Coll., 1824-67; patron of colonization of Negroes; supported temperance movement; published translation of Jahn's Biblical Archaeology, 1823; wrote Outlines of Imperfect and Disordered Mental Action, (one of early original contbns. to psychology), 1834; wrote essay published in Prize Essays on a Congress of Nations, 1840; wrote religious classic Principles of the Interior or Hidden Life, 1843; wrote verse American Cottage Life, 1851; other works include: A Philosophical and Practical Treatise on the Will, 1834; Letters Aesthetic, Social and Moral, Written from Europe, Egypt, and Palestine, 1855. Died N.Y.C., Apr. 2, 1872.

UPHAM, William, senator; b. Leicester, Mass., Aug. 5, 1792; attended Montpelier (Vt.) Acad.; studied law. Admitted to bar, 1811, began practice of law, Montpelier, 1812; mem. Vt. Ho. of Reps., 1827-28, 30; states atty. Washington County, 1829; mem. U.S. Senate (Whig) from Vt., 1843-53. Died Washington, D.C., Jan. 14, 1853; buried Congressional Cemetery.

UPJOHN, Richard, architect; b. Shaftesbury, Dorsetshire, Eng., Jan. 22, 1802; s. James and Elizabeth (Mitchell) U.; m. Elizabeth Parry, Nov. 14, 1826, 5 children including Richard Mitchell. Began as apprentice to cabinetmaker; established his own business in Shaftesbury in 1824; came to U.S., 1829; draftsman, New Bedford, Mass., 1830-34; architect for Alexander Parris, Boston, 1834-38; designed St. John's Ch., Bangor, Me., 1837; moved to N.Y.C., 1839, practiced as architect; archtl. works include: Trinity Ch., N.Y.C., 1839, New Trinity Church in New York City, N.Y., 1846; Trinity Bldg., N.Y.C., 1852, Italian villa (house for Edward King, Newport, R.I.), 1850, Corn Exchange Bank Bldg., N.Y.C., Ch. of the Pilgrims, Bklyn., also the Grace Church, in Newark, New Jersey; Trinity Chapel, N.Y.C., 1853; a founder A.I.A., 1857, pres., 1857-76; hon. mem. Royal Inst. Brit. Architects, Inst. Portuguese Architects. Died Garrison, N.Y., Aug. 17, 1878.

UPSHUR, Abel Parker, cabinet officer; b. Northampton County, Va., June 17, 1790; s. Littleton and Ann (Parker) U.; attended Princeton, Yale; m. Elizabeth Dennis; m. 2d, Elizabeth Upshur (cousin); 1 child. Practiced law, Richmond, Va., circa 1810; mem. Va. Ho. of Dels., 1812-13, 25-27; mem. Va. Constl. Conv., advocated preservation of aristocratic state govt., took position against doctrines of natural rights, 1829-30; justice Va. Supreme Ct., 1826-41; apptd. U.S. sec. of navy by Pres. Tyler, 1843, U.S. sec. of state by Tyler, 1843, urged annexation of Tex.; identified with extreme states' rights group of Southern apologists, opposed doctrine of majority rule. Killed in ship on Potomac River nr. Washington, D.C., Feb. 28, 1844.

UPSON, Charles, congressman, lawyer; b. Southington, Conn., Mar. 19, 1821; attended Yale Law Sch., 1844. Taught sch., Farmington. Conn., 1840-42, Constantine, Mich., 1846-47; dep. clk. St. Joseph County, 1847; admitted to bar, 1847, began practice of law, Kalamazoo, Mich.; county clk., 1848-49; pros. atty., 1852-54; mem. Mich. Senate, 1855-56, 80; continued practice of law, Coldwater, Mich., 1856; mem. Mich. Bd. R.R. Commrs., 1857; atty. gen. Mich., 1861-62; mem. U.S. Ho. of Reps. (Republican) from Mich., 38th-40th congresses, 1863-69; judge 15th Circuit Ct., 1869-72; mem. commn. to revise Mich. Constn., 1873; mayor City of Coldwater, 1877. Died Coldwater, Sept. 5, 1885; buried Oak Grove Cemetery.

UPTON, Charles Horace, congressman, diplomat; b. Salem, Mass., Aug. 23, 1812; grad. Bowdoin Coll., Brunswick, Me., 1834. Engaged in agrl. and literary pursuits, Falls Church, Va., 1836; held several local offices; mem. U.S. Ho. of Reps. (Republican) from Va., 37th Congress, May 23, 1861-Feb. 27, 1862; U.S. consul to Switzerland (apptd. by Pres. Lincoln), 1863-77. Died Geneva, Switzerland, June 17, 1877; buried Congressional Cemetery, Washington, D.C.

UPTON, Emory, army officer; b. Batavia, N.Y., Aug. 27, 1839; s. Daniel and Electra (Randall) U.; attended Oberlin Coll., 1855-56; grad. U.S. Mil. Acad., 1861; m. Emily Norwood Martin, Feb. 19, 1868. Commd. 2d lt. 4th Arty., U.S. Army, 1861, 1st lt., 5th Arty., 1861, also served in inf., cavalry, often cited for bravery; commd. brig. gen., 1864; brevetted maj. gen. U.S. Army during Civil War; mem. bd. to consider system mil. tactics U.S. Mil. Acad., 1867, comdt. of cadets, instr. arty., cavalry and inf. tactics, 1870-75; went on world trip to study foreign army orgns., 1875-77; wrote plan for Chinese Mil. Acad., 1876; supt. theoretical instrn. arty. sch. Ft. Monroe, Va., 1878-81; commanded 4th Arty. and Presidio of San Francisco; commited suicide because of an incurable disease. Author: A New System of Military Tactics, Double and Single Ranks, Adapted to Am. Topography and Improved Firearms, 1867; The Armies of Asia and Europe, 1878; The Military Policy of the U.S., published posthumously, 1904. Died Presidio of San Francisco, Mar. 15, 1881; buried Ft. Hill Cemetery, Auburn, N.Y.

UPTON, George Bruce, mcht., state legislator; b. Eastport, Me., Oct. 11, 1804; s. Daniel Putnam and Hannah (Bruce) U.; m. Ann Hussey, May 2, 1826, 8 children. Confidential clk. Baker & Barrett, dry goods firm, Nantucket Island, 1821, formed partnership with Barrett, 1825; mem. Mass. Legislature, 1837, 41; mem. Mass. Senate from Nantucket and Dukes County, 1839, 40, 43; del. to Whig Nat. Conv., 1844; agt. for a print works, Manchester, N.H., 1845; moved to Boston, 1846; treas. Mich. Central R.R., 1846-54; del. to Mass. Constl. Conv., 1853; promoted Sailors' Snug Harbor, Quincy, Mass. Died Boston, July 1, 1874.

UPTON, Robert, actor, theatrical co. mgr.; b. Eng. Sent to Am. by London producer William Hallam "to obtain permission to perform, erect a building and settle everything against our arrival," 1750: joined Murray-Kean company, Nassau Street Theater, N.Y.C., 1751; organized own company; mgr. New Co. of Comedians which gave 1st Am. prodn. of Othello, Nassau Street Theater; managed prodns. of Lethe, The Provok'd Husband, The Fair Penitent at Nassau Street Theater, 1752.

URSO, Camilla, violinist; b. Nantes, France, June 13, 1842; d. Salvator and Emilie (Girouard) U.; studied under Lambert-Joseph Massart in Paris (France) Conservatory; m. Frédéric Luères, 1862. Gave her 1st recital, Nantes, 1849; came to Am., 1852, gave concerts in Am., 1852-55; again went on concert tours in Am., Europe, Australia, S. Africa, 1862-95; moved to N.Y.C., 1895, taught violin, 1895-1902. Died N.Y.C., Jan. 20, 1902.

USHER, John Palmer, sec. of interior; b. Brookfield, N.Y., Jan. 9, 1816; s. Dr. Nathaniel and Lucy (Palmer) U.; studied law under Henry Bennett, New Berlin, N.Y.; m. Margaret Patterson, Jan. 26, 1844, 4 children. Admitted to N.Y. bar, 1839; moved to Ind., 1840; served in lower house Ind. Legislature, 1850-51; atty. gen. Ind., 1861; asst. U.S. sec. interior, 1861-63, sec. of interior, 1863-65; recommended a tax on profit of gold and silver mines and larger Indian reservations in his first report; went to Kan., 1865; chief counsel Union Pacific R.R., 1865-89. Died Phila., Apr. 13, 1889.

USHER, Noble Luke, frontier theater mgr.; b. Ky. Recruited theatrical company (from John Bernard's Co., Albany, N.Y.) for his theaters in Frankfort, Lexington and Louisville (Ky.), 1814; instrumental in bringing drama to Ky. and then to Far West. Died 1815.

V

VAIL, Aaron, diplomat; b. Lorient, France, Oct. 24, 1796; s. Aaron and Elizabeth (Dubois) V. Came to U.S., 1815; sec. U.S. legation, London, 1831-32, 1836, chargé d'affaires, 1832-36; apptd. spl. agt. to Can. to investigate suspicions that Am. participants in Canadian Rebellion of 1837 were being denied trial and held arbitrarily, 1838, found these suspicions groundless; chief clk. Dept. of State, 1838-40; U.S. chargé d'affaires, Madrid, Spain, 1840-42. Died Paris, France, Nov. 4, 1878.

VAIL, Alfred Lewis, mfr.; b. Morristown, N.J., Sept. 25, 1807; s. Stephen and Bethiah (Young) V.; grad. U. City N.Y., 1836; m. Jane Elizabeth Cummings, July 23, 1839; m. 2d Amanda Eno, Dec. 17, 1855; 3 children. Bought an interest in Samuel F. B. Morse's telegraph, 1837, agreed to manufacture complete set of telegraphic instruments and to finance U.S. and fgn. patents; made 1st public exhbn. of telegraph, N.Y.C., 1838; demonstrated telegraph before Franklin Inst., Phila., also U.S. Congress, 1838; Phila. rep. Speedwell Iron Works of Morristown, 1839-43; became Morse's chief asst. after Congress provided funds for exptl. telegraph line between Washington, D.C. and Balt., 1843; received test message "What hath God wrought!" at Balt., 1844; supt. telegraph lines at Phila., 1844-48. Author: The American Electro Magnetic Telegraph, 1845. Died Morristown, Jan. 18, 1859.

VAIL, George, congressman, diplomat; b. Morristown, N.J., July 21, 1809; attended Morris Acad., Morristown. Became mfr. of telegraph instruments; mem. N.J. Gen. Assembly, 1843-44; apptd. by gov. N.J. to represent state at World's Fair, London, Eng., 1851; mem. U.S. Ho. of Reps. (Democrat) from N.J., 33d-34th congresses, 1853-57; consul to Glasgow, Scotland (apptd. by Pres. Buchanan) 1858-

61; engaged in literary pursuits, Morristown, after 1861; mem. ct. of pardons; judge N.J. Ct. of Errors and Appeals, 1865-71. Died Morristown, May 23, 1875; buried 1st Presbyn. Ch. Cemetery.

VAIL, Henry, congressman, mcht.; b. nr. Milbrook, Dutchess County, N.Y., 1782. Engaged in retail business, 1806-15, wholesale business, 1815-32; mem. U.S. Ho. of Reps. (Democrat) from N.Y., 25th Congress, 1837-39. Died Troy, N.Y., June 25, 1853; buried Oakwood Cemetery.

VAIL, Stephen Montfort, clergyman, diplomat, educator; b. Union Vale, Dutchess County, N.Y., Jan. 15, 1816; s. James and Anna (Montfort) V.; grad. Bowdoin Coll., 1838; grad. Union Theol. Sem., N.Y.C., 1842; m. Louisa Cushman, Sept. 1842, at least 6 children. Ordained deacon Methodist Episcopal Ch., 1844, elder, 1846; pastor, Fishkill, N.Y., 1842-44, Sharon, Conn., 1844-46, Pine Plains, N.Y., 1846-47; prin. Pennington (N.J.) Sem., 1847-49; prof. Hebrew, Methodist Gen. Bibl. Inst., Concord, N.H., 1849-69; U.S. consul at Ludwigshafen, Bavaria, 1869-74. Author: Ministerial Education in the Methodist Episcopal Church, 1853; sermons The Church and the Slave Power, 1860, The Bible Against Slavery, 1864. Died Jersey City, N.J., Nov. 26, 1880.

VAIL, Thomas Hubbard, clergyman; b. Richmond, Va., Oct. 21, 1812; grad. Washington (now Trinity) Coll., 1831; D.D. (hon.), Brown U., 1858. Ordained priest Episcopal Ch., 1837; rector Christ's Ch., Cambridge, Mass., 1837-39, St. John's Ch., Essex, Conn., 1839-44, Christ Ch., Westerly, R.I., 1844-57, St. Thomas' Ch., Taunton, Mass., 1857-63, Trinity Ch., Muscatine, 1863-64; bishop of Kan., 1864-89. Author: The Comprehensive Church (his prin. work), 1841. Died Bryn Mawr, Pa., Oct. 6, 1889.

VAILLANT DE GUESLIS, Francois, missionary; b. Orléans, France, July 20, 1646. Joined Soc. of Jesus, 1665, sent to Can., 1670, ordained priest Roman Catholic Ch., 1675; missionary among Mohawk Indians, 1679-84; worked in Que., 1685-92, 96-1702; superior, Montreal, 1692-96; ambassador to Gov. Thomas Dongan of N.Y., 1688; missionary to Seneca Indians, 1702-05; served in Montreal, 1709-15; returned to France. Died Moulins, France, Sept. 24, 1718.

VALENTINE, David Thomas, hist. compiler; b. East Chester, N.Y., Sept. 15, 1801; s. Daniel and Miriam (Fisher) V.; m. Martha Carnell, June 24, 1821; m. 2d, Caroline Spicer; 5 children. Mem. Nat. Guard, circa 1818-26; clk. Marine Ct., N.Y.C., 1826-30; dep. clk. of Common Council, N.Y.C., 1830, clk. of council and chief legislative dept., 1842-68; mem. New Eng. Historic and Geneal. Soc., 1855; wrote Manual of the Corporation of City of New York, 1841, added a volume annually until 1867; other compilations include: Ordinances of the Mayor, Aldermen, and Commonalty, 1859; A Compilation of the Laws of the State of New York, Relating Particularly to the City of New York, 1862; Compilation of Existing Ferry Leases and Railroad Grants Made by the Corporation of the City of New York, 1866. Died Feb. 25, 1869.

VALK, William Weightman, congressman, physician; b. Charleston, S.C., Oct. 12, 1806; grad. U. S. C. at Columbia, 1830; studied medicine. Began practice of medicine, Bridgeport, Conn.; served as asst. surgeon in U.S. frigate Constellation; went to Cal. during Gold Rush, circa 1849; then practiced medicine, Flushing, L.I., N.Y.; mem. U.S. Ho. of Reps. (Am. Party candidate) from N.Y., 34th Congress, 1855-57; served as surgeon 2d Regt., Md. Volunteer Inf. during Civil War; clk. U.S. Pension Office, Washington, D.C., 1867-79. Died Washington, Sept. 20, 1879; buried Flushing Cemetery.

VALLANDIGHAM, Clement Laird, congressman; b. New Lisbon, O., July 29, 1820; s. Rev. Clement and Rebecca (Laird) V.; attended Jefferson Coll., Cannonsburg, Pa., 1837-40; m. Louisa A. McMahon, Aug. 27, 1846, 2 children. Admitted to Ohio bar, 1842; mem. Ohio Legislature, 1845-46; editor Dayton (O.) Empire, 1847-49; del. Nat. Democratic Conv., 1856, 68; mem. U.S. Ho. of Reps. from Ohio, 35th-37th congresses, May 25, 1858-63, offered series resolutions in 37th Congress in which he argued against use of war in preserving Union; sec. Nat. Dem. Conv., 1860; arrested in Dayton, 1863, tried for treason, convicted but released by Pres. Lincoln; worked for peace orgn. in Northern cities, 1863-64. Died Lebanon, O., June 17, 1871; buried Woodland Cemetery, Dayton.

VALLEJO, Mariano Guadalupe, army officer; b. Monterey, Cal., July 7, 1808; s. Ignacio and Maria Antonia (Lugo) V.; m. Maria Francisca Felipa Benicia Carrillo, Mar. 6, 1832, 13 to 17 children. Ensign in company at Presidio (now San Francisco), 1827; served against Estanislao Indian Rebellion, 1829; dep. to territorial congress, 1830; comdt. new garrison at Sonoma (Cal.), organized frontier defenses and controlled Indians; adminstr. of Solano mission; supported nephew Juan Bautista Alvarado in rebellion that led to proclamation "free state of California," 1836; comdr. of state forces, 1838; lived in Sonoma as semi-independent chief with Indian allies and Mexican troops devoted to his cause, 1836-46; powerful agent in securing submission of Cal. to U.S.; mem. Cal. Constl. Conv. of 1849; mem. 1st Cal. Senate. Died Sonoma, Jan. 18, 1890.

VAN AERNAM, Henry, congressman, physician; b. Marcellus, Onondaga County, N.Y., Mar. 11, 1819 attended Geneva, Willoughby med. colls. Practiced medicine; mem. N.Y. State Assembly, 1858; served as surgeon 154th Regt., N.Y. Volunteer Inf. during Civil War, 1862-64; mem. U.S. Ho. of Reps .(Republican) from N.Y., 39th-40th, 46th-47th congresses, 1865-69, 79-83; commr. of pensions, 1869-71; resumed practice of medicine, Franklinville, N.Y. Died Franklinville, June 1, 1894; buried Mt. Prospect Cemetery.

VAN ALEN, James Isaac, congressman; b. Kinderhook, N.Y., 1776; attended common schs. City clk. Kinderhook, 1797-1801; mem. N.Y. state constl. convs., 1801, 03; justice of peace, 1801-04; mem. N.Y. State Assembly, 1804; surrogate Columbia County, 1804-08, 15-22; mem. U.S. Ho. of Reps. (Federalist) from N.Y., 10th Congress, 1807-09. Died Newburgh, N.Y., Dec. 23, 1870; buried Kinderhook Cemetery.

VAN ALEN, John Evert, congressman; b. Kinderhook, N.Y., 1749. Engaged in farming, De Freestville, 1778; surveyed Town of Greenbush, 1790, ran gen. store, Greenbush; a civil engr. and surveyor; asst. ct. justice Rensselaer County, 1791; mem. U.S. Ho. of Reps. from N.Y., 3d-5th congresses, 1793-99; mem. N.Y. State Assembly, 1800-01. Died Mar. 1807.

Van BEUREN, Johannes, physician; b. Amsterdam, Holland, circa 1680; student of Dutch physcian Hermannus Boerhaave; m. Maria Meyer, June 15, 1707, 15 children including Beekman, John. Came to N.Y., 1702; practiced medicine in N.Y., 1702-55; 1st med. dir. almshouse Publick Workhouse and House of Correction, 1736-55 (now Bellevue Hosp.). Died N.Y.C., July 27, 1755.

VAN BUREN, John, congressman, lawyer; b. Kingston, N.Y., May 13, 1799; grad. Union Coll., Schenectady, N.Y., 1818; studied law. Admitted to bar, began practice of law, Kingston; mem. N.Y. State Assembly, 1831; judge Ulster County, 1836-41; mem. U.S. Ho. of Reps. (Democrat) from N.Y., 27th Congress, 1841-43; dist. atty. Ulster County, 1846-50. Died Kingston, Jan. 16, 1855; buried Old Houghtaling Cemetery.

VAN BUREN, John, lawyer; b. Kinderhook, N.Y., Feb. 10, 1810; s. Martin and Hannah (Hoes) Van B.; grad. Yale; m. Elizabeth Vanderpoel, June 22, 1841, 1 dau., Anna. Admitted to Albany (N.Y.) bar, 1831; attache Am. legation, London, Eng., 1831, nicknamed "Prince John" and "Young Fox" by Am. press; mem. "Albany Regency," 1834; law examiner, Albany, also law partner of James McKnown, 1837-45; atty. gen. (Democrat) N.Y., 1845, prosecuted anti-rent cases; atty. in famous Edwin Forrest divorce suit; lobbyist N.Y. Legislature, denounced Fugitive Slave Law; del. to nearly all Dem. state convs., 1836-48; wrote pamphlet "The Syracuse Convention," 1847; an organizer "Barnburners," splinter party of Dem. Party, N.Y., 1843-48; supported compromise measures of 1850. Died in ship Scotia enroute to N.Y.C., Oct. 13, 1866; buried Albany.

VAN BUREN, Martin, 8th Pres. U.S.; b. Kinderhook, N.Y., Dec. 5, 1782; s. Abraham and Maria Hoes (Van Alen) Van B.; studied law under Francis Silvester, later William Van Ness; m. Hannah Hoes, Feb. 21, 1807, children—Abraham, John, Martin, Smith Thompson. Del. to congressional caucus, Troy, N.Y., 1800; admitted to N.Y.C. bar, 1803; surrogate Columbia County (N.Y.), 1808-13; mem. N.Y. State Senate, 1813-20; regent U. State of N.Y., 1815; atty. gen. N.Y. State, 1816-19; requested N.Y. State Constl. Conv., held 1821, chmn. com. on appointments, attempted to change judiciary appointments; head group of politicians nicknamed Albany Regency which controlled N.Y. State during most of 1820's, 30's; mem. U.S. Senate from N.Y., 1821-Dec. 20, 1828, chmn. judiciary com.; resigned to become gov. N.Y., Jan. 1,-Mar. 12, 1829; resigned to become U.S. sec. state, 1829-31; chief adviser to Pres. Jackson, wrote Maysville Road veto, settled disputes with Gt. Britain over trade, secured French agreement to pay damages done to Americans during Napoleonic Wars, investigated chance to buy Tex. from Mexico; resigned as sec. state in successful attempt to oust J.C. Calhoun's supporters from cabinet; apptd. U.S. minister to Gt. Britain, 1831, appointment rejected by deciding vote of Vice Pres. Calhoun, 1832; vice pres. U.S. under Pres. Jackson, 1833-37; supported war on Bank of U.S., supported Jackson against nullifiers led by Calhoun; nominated for Pres. U.S. by Nat. Democratic Conv., Balt., 1836; 8th Pres. U.S., 1837-41, opposed abolition of slavery in D.C., kept Americans out of Canadian revolt against Gt. Britain, 1837, refused to annex Tex.; term ruined by Depression of 1837, backed independent Treasury bill in attempt to end depression; defeated as Dem. candidate for Pres. by William Henry Harrison, 1840; leading Dem. candidate for nomination in 1844, unacceptable because of his refusal to annex Tex. (felt this would lead to war); Free-Soil Party candidate for Pres., 1848, ran on platform which forbade further extension of slavery through war with Mexico or annexation of Tex. as slave state; Free-Soil party later joined Republicans, supported Lincoln, 1860. Called "the Red Fox of Kinderhook" or "the Little Magician." Author: Inquiry into the Origin and Cause of Political Parties in the United States, 1867; Autobiography of Martin Van Buren, 1920 (both works published posthumously). Died Kinderhook, N.Y., July 24, 1862; buried Kinderhook Cemetery.

Van BUREN, William Holme, physician; b. Phila., Apr. 4, 1819; s. Abraham and Sarah (Holme) Van Beuren; attended Yale, 1838-40; M.D., U. Pa., 1840; m. Louisa Mott, Nov. 8, 1842, 3 children. Asst. surgeon in U.S. Army, 1840-45, served in Fla. and Canadian frontier; mem. surg. staff Bellevue Hosp., N.Y.C.; prof. genito-urinary organs and venereal diseases Med. Dept., U. City of N.Y., 1851-52, prof. anatomy, 1852-66; prof. surgery Bellevue Hosp. Med. Coll., 1866-83; vis. surgeon N.Y. Hosp., 1852-65, pres. med. bd., 1876; mem. cons. staff Bellevue, Women's, Presbyn. and other hosps.; v.p. N.Y. Acad. Medicine, 1859; mem. standing exec. com. of U.S. Sanitary Commn. during Civil War. Author: Contributions to Practical Surgery, 1865; Lectures upon Diseases of the Rectum, 1870; translated (with C. E. Isaacs) Bernard and Huettes' Illustrated Manual of Operative Surgery and Surgical Anatomy, 1852, C. B. Morel's Compendium of Human Histology, 1861. Died N.Y.C., Mar. 25, 1883.

VANCE, Joseph, congressman, gov. Ohio; b. Catfish (now Washington), Pa., Mar. 21, 1786. Moved to Urbana, O., 1805, engaged in agriculture; served as capt. of rifle co., 1811-12; served from maj. to maj. gen. Ohio Militia during War of 1812; mem. Ohio Ho. of Reps., 1812-13, 15-16, 18-19; del. Ohio Constl. Convs., 1820, 51; a mcht., Urbana and Perrysburg, O.; laid out City of Findlay (O.); mem. U.S. Ho. of Reps. from Ohio (as Democrat), 17th-23d congresses, 1821-35, (as Whig), 28th-29th congresses, 1843-47; gov. Ohio, 1836-38; del. Whig Nat Conv., Phila., 1848. Died nr. Urbana, Aug. 24, 1852 buried Oak Dale Cemetery.

VANCE, Robert Brank, congressman, physician; b. nr. Asheville, N.C., 1793; attended Newton Acad., Asheville, med. sch. of Dr. Charles Harris, Cabarrus County, N.C. Began practice of medicine, Asheville, 1818; held several local offices; mem. U.S. Ho. of Reps. (Democrat) from N.C., 18th Congress, 1823-25. Mortally wounded in duel with Samuel P. Carson (his opponent for election to 20th Congress), nr. Saluda Gap, N.C., 1827; buried family burial ground on Reems Creek, nr. Asheville.

VANCE, Zebulon Baird, senator, gov. N.C.; b. Buncombe County, N.C., May 13, 1830; s. David and Mira (Baird) V.; attended Washington (Tenn.) Coll., 1843-44; studied law U. N.C., 1851-52; m. Harriet Newell Espy, Aug. 3, 1853; m. 2d, Mrs. Florence Steele Martin, June 1880; 4 children. Admitted to the bar, Asheville, N.C., 1852; pros. atty. Asheville, 1852; admitted to practice Superior Ct., N.C., 1853; mem. N.C. Ho. of Commons, 1854; mem. U.S. Ho. of Reps. from N.C., 35th-36th congresses, Dec. 7, 1858-61, elected to 37th Congress, N.C. secession prevented taking seat; organized, became capt. of company "Rough and Ready Guards" in Asheville, 1861; col. 26th N.C. Regt. in New Bern campaign, Seven Day's battle nr. Richmond, 1861; gov. N.C., 1862-66, committed his adminstrn. to vigorous war policy; surrendered to Gen. Schofield, Greensboro, N.C., 1865, arrested by orders of Pres. Johnson, May 13, 1865, released, July 6, 1865; elected to U.S. Senate, 1870, denied seat by Senate; gov. N.C., 1877-79; mem. U.S. Senate from N.C., 1879-94, minority leader on finance com., last speech in Senate in opposition to repeal of Sherman Silver Act; delivered his most popular lecture "The Scattered Nation" (dealing with history of Jews) in most U.S. cities. Author: The Duties of Defeat, 1866; The Last Days of the Civil War in North Carolina, 1885. Died Washington, D.C., Apr. 14, 1894; buried Riverside Cemetery, Asheville, N.C.

Van CORTLANDT, Oloff Stevenszen, mcht., colonial ofcl.; b. Wijk, nr. Utrecht, Holland, 1600; adopted surname Van Cortlandt, 1643; m. Anneken Loockermans, Feb. 26, 1642, 7 children including Stephanus, Jacobus, Maria (Van Cortlandt) Van Rensselaer. Arrived in New Amsterdam (now N.Y. C.), 1638; commr. of cargoes, 1640; began purchase of real estate, New Amsterdam, 1641; ran a store, 1643; one of Eight Men, 1645, presided over Nine Men, 1650; city treas., New Amsterdam, 1657,

59, 60, 61, 64, burgomaster (mayor), 1655-60, 62-63; commr. to determine New Amsterdam-Conn. boundary, 1663; became deacon Reformed Ch., circa 1646, elder circa 1670; chosen to negotiate with English, 1664; alderman, N.Y.C., 1665, 67, 70, 72, dep. mayor 1667; Van Cortlandt Park (N.Y.C.) named after him. Died N.Y.C., Apr. 5, 1684.

Van CORTLANDT, Philip, congressman, army officer; b. N.Y.C., Aug. 21, 1749; s. Pierre and Joanna (Livingston) Van C.; grad. King's Coll. (now Columbia), 1768; never married. Mem. Provincial Conv. at the Exchange in N.Y.C., 1775; one of Westchester County's reps. in 1st N.Y. Provincial Congress, 1775; lt. col. 4th N.Y. Regt., 1775, col. 2d N.Y. Regt. at Valley Forge; mem. ct. martial which heard charges preferred by Pa. authorities against Benedict Arnold, 1778; ordered to join Continental forces on lower Hudson in time to take active part in campaign against Cornwallis which culminated in his surrender, 1781; distinguished at Battle of Yorktown under Gen. Lafayette, brevetted brig. gen., 1783; del. to Poughkeepsie Conv., 1788, voted to ratify U.S. Constn.; supr., sch. commr., road master Town of Cortlandt (N.Y.); mem. N.Y. State Assembly, 1788, 90; mem. N.Y. Senate, 1791-93; mem. U.S. Ho. of Reps. from N.Y., 3d-10th congresses, 1793-1809; accompanied Gen. Lafayette on his tour through U.S. in 1831; charter mem. Soc. of Cincinnati. Died Croton, N.Y., Nov. 1, 1831; buried Hillside Cemetery, Peekskill, N.Y.

Van CORTLANDT, Pierre, state ofcl.; b. N.Y.C., Jan. 10, 1721; s. Philip and Catharine (De Peyster) Van C.; m. Joanna Livingston, May 28, 1748; several children including Philip. Served in provincial militia during French and Indian Wars; mem. N.Y. Assembly, 1768; col. 3d Regt., Westchester Militia, 1775; mem. 2d, 3d, 4th N.Y. provincial congresses; leader in Com. of Safety, 1776; pres. Council of Safety, 1777; presided over 1st N.Y. Constl. Conv.; 1st lt. gov. N.Y. State, 1777-95; mem. bd. regents U. State of N.Y., 1784-95; donated land and subscribed to bldg. fund for local Methodist meeting house. Died Manor House, Croton, N.Y., May 1, 1814; buried family cemetery on estate, Croton.

VAN CORTLANDT, Pierre, Jr., congressman, banker; b. Van Cortlandt Manor, Croton, N.Y., Aug. 29, 1762; grad. Queen's Coll. (now Rutgers), New Brunswick, N.J., 1783; studied law in office of Alexander Hamilton. Admitted to bar, practiced law for a time, then retired to manage his estate, Westchester County; presdl. elector on Jefferson ticket, 1800, on Harrison ticket, 1840; mem. N.Y. State Assembly, 1811-12; mem. U.S. Ho. of Reps. (Democrat) from N.Y., 12th Congress, 1811-13; founder, pres. Westchester County Bank, Peekskill, N.Y., 1833-48. Died Peekskill, July 13, 1848; buried Hillside Cemetery.

Van CORTLANDT, Stephanus, colonial ofcl.; b. New Amsterdam (now N.Y.C.), May 7, 1643; s. Oloff Stevenszen and Anneken (or Annetje) (Loockermans) Van C.; m. Gertrude Schuyler, Sept. 10, 1671, at least 1 child, Philip. Commd. ensign, Kings County Militia, 1668, rose to rank of col.; mem. Gov.'s Council, 1674; 1st native-born mayor of N.Y. C., 1677, 86, 87; one of 42 councilors of Dominion of New Eng. under Sir Edmund Andros; presided at intervals over Mayor's Ct., N.Y.C., after 1677; judge Ct. of Oyer and Terminer of Kings County; became asso. justice N.Y. Supreme Ct., 1691, chief justice, 1700; chancellor of N.Y. Colonial Ct. of Chancery; adviser on Indian relations; accompanied gov. of N.Y. to Albany conf. with sachems of Five Nations, 1693; commr. of customs and collector of revenues, 1698-1700; used ofcl. position to secure large grants of land, Croton, N.Y.; mcht. throughout his life. Died N.Y.C., Nov. 25, 1700.

VANCOUVER, George, naval officer; b. Eng., 1758; never married. Entered Brit. Navy, 1771; accompanied Capt. James Cook on his 2d and 3d voyages, 1772-74, 76-80; assigned to exploring project in ship Discovery, Jan. 1790 (project abandoned because of Nootka Sound controversy); given command of ship Courageux; promoted comdr., Dec. 1790, placed in charge of ship Discovery and sent to N.W. coast of Am. to regain territory taken over by Spanish, also to survey coast North to latitude 30° and to search for Northwest passage; set sail, Apr. 1791, went by way of Cape of Good Hope to Australia, then to New Zealand (which he explored), Tahiti and Hawaii; sighted West coast of Am., Apr. 18, 1792; carefully surveyed coast North to latitude 52° 18′; discovered Gulf of Georgia, circumnavigated Vancouver Island (named for him); visited Hawaiian Islands again, Feb.-Mar. 1793, then returned for further explorations of Am. coast; surveyed coast North to 56° latitude and South to 35°N, Apr. 1793; returned to Hawaiian Islands, accepted their submission to Gt. Britain (annexation never ratified); then surveyed Am. coast North of San Francisco, also So. part of Lower Cal. and Galapagos Islands; returned to Eng., Oct. 1795. Died Petersham, Surrey, Eng., May 10, 1798.

Van CURLER, Arent, colonist; b. Nykerk, Netherlands, 1620; s. Hendrik or Joachin Van Curler; m. Anthonia Slachboom, 1644. Went to New Netherland, 1638, asst. to commissary of Rensselaerswyck, later sec. and bookkeeper; commis (Dutch colonial title), full rep. authority in govt. and trade with some judicial powers in charge of welfare of tenant farmers, also had responsibilities related to breed of horses and cattle, care of growing fur trade, fostered export trade along Atlantic coast; procured license to purchase Indian land Schonowe on Mohawk (now Schenectady, N.Y.), 1661; took part in treaty which terminated 1st Esopus War, 1660; headed movement to supply Mohawk country with provisions, 1666; commr. to M. de Courcelles, French gov. of Can., 1666. meml. tablet dedicated in Schenectady, 1909. Drowned in Perou Bay (later Corlaer's Bay), Lake Champlain, July 1667.

VAN DAM, Rip, mcht., colonial ofcl.; b. Ft. Orange (Albany), N.Y., circa 1660; s. Claas Ripse and Maria (Bords) van D.; m. Sara van der Spiegel, Sept. 1684, at least 6 children. Mcht., ship capt., ship builder, N.Y.C.; mem. bd. aldermen N.Y.C., 1693-96; mem. Council of N.Y., 1702-36, pres., 1731-36, became exec. head Province of N.Y. upon death of Gov. John Montgomerie, 1731-36. Died N.Y.C., June 10, 1749.

VAN DEN BROEK, Theodore J., missionary; b. Amsterdam, Holland, Nov. 5, 1783. Ordained priest Roman Catholic Ch. in Germany, 1808, joined Dominican Order, 1817; came to U.S., 1832, served as missionary in Balt., Cincinnati, Ky.; missionary to Menominee and Winnebago Indians, Wis., 1836-47, 48-51; returned to Holland to obtain immigrants, 1847-48. Died Little Chute, Wis., Nov. 5, 1851.

VANDENHOFF, George, actor, lawyer; b. Liverpool, Eng., Feb. 18, 1820; s. John Vandenhoff; studied law Stonyhurst Coll.; m. Mary MaKeath, Aug. 20, 1855. Solicitor to the trustees of Liverpool Docks; made stage debut in 1839 as Leon in Beaumont and Fletcher's Rule A Wife and Have A Wife, at Covent Garden, London; Am. debut at Park Theatre in N.Y.C. as Hamlet, followed with Macbeth; played Cariolanus and Hotspur in Boston; toured New Orleans, La., Richmond, Va., Balt., Phila., Boston, 1843; taught elocution and gave many public readings of Shakespeare, Sheridan and the Poets, 1843-53; leading man Chestnut St. Theatre, Phila., 1843; staged English version of Sophocles' Antigone at Palmo's Opera House, N.Y.C., 1845; went to Eng., 1853, returned to U.S., circa 1854; admitted to N.Y. bar, 1858; made last appearance in play Jane Shore, 1874. Author: Leaves from an Actor's Note Book, 1860; The Art of Elocution, 1861; Life (poem), 1861. Died Brighton, Eng., June 16, 1885.

Van DEPOELE, Charles Joseph, scientist, inventor; b. Lichtervelde, Belgium, Apr. 27, 1846; s. Peter John and Maria (Algoed) Van D.; attended Imperial Lyceum, Lille, France; m. Ada Van Hoogstraten, Nov. 23, 1870, 7 children including Romaine Adeline. Came to U.S., settled in Detroit, 1869; became mfr. ch. furniture; exhibited arc lights, 1870; demonstrated feasibility of electric transp. by both overhead and underground conductors, 1874; worked on vibratory regulation for arc lights, demonstrated improved lights publicly, 1879; formed Van Depoele Electric Light Co., Inc. as Van Depoele Electric Light Co. of Chgo., 1881, Van Depoele Electric Mfg. Co., 1884; made 1st practical demonstration in world of a spring pressed under-running trolley at Chgo. Inter-State Indsl. Expn., 1883; successful with both the underground and overhead circuits in Toronto, Ont., Can., 1884, 85; overhead system in operation in South Bend, Ind., 1885, adopted in Minneapolis, Minn., Montgomery, Ala., 1885-86; eight lines installed in U.S., Can., 1886; sold electric railway patents to Thomson-Houston Electric Co., Lynn, Mass., 1888; sold Van Depoele Electric Mfg. Co., 1889; made 444 patent applications, granted 249 in his name including; little "Giant" generator, 1880, 1st patent on electric rys., 1883, 1st on overhead conductor, 1885, patent for carbon contract brushes in electric motors, 1888, coal mining machine, 1891; experimented with electric refrigeration, 1886; made photographs in color, 1889-90. Died Lynn, Mar. 18, 1892; buried St. Mary's Cemetery, Lynn.

VANDERBILT, Cornelius, transp. promoter; b. Port Richmond, S.I., N.Y., May 27, 1794; s. Cornelius and Phebe (Hand) Vander Bilt; m. Sophia Johnson, Dec. 19, 1813; m. 2d, Frank Armstrong Crawford, Aug. 21, 1869; 13 children including George, Cornelius Jeremiah, William Henry. Bought small sailing vessel, 1810, began freight and passenger ferrying business between S.I. and N.Y.C.; received contract from U.S. Govt. for provisioning forts around N.Y. harbor during War of 1812; built schooner for service on L.I. Sound, 1814; sold all his sailing vessels, worked as captain for Thomas Gibbons, owner of ferry between New Brunswick, N.J. and N.Y.C., 1818-29; operated (with wife) hotel, New Brunswick, 1818-29; entered steamboat bus. on his own, 1829, shipping service on Hudson, forced Daniel Drew (his competitor) out of business by price war, 1834; became known as Commodore Vanderbilt, circa 1845, started line of his own via Nicaragua through San Juan River to Lake Nicaragua, 1850; sold Am. Atlantic & Pacific Ship Canal Company (line to California), 1858; had controlling interest in N.Y. & Harlem R.R. stock, 1862-63, induced city council to give him permission to extend line to the Battery, combined with Hudson River R.R., buying control; got control of N.Y. Central R.R., 1867; sought control of Erie Ry., 1868, Drew, Jay Gould and James Fisk, Jr. who were in control out-manoeuvered him, putting 50,000 shares of fradulent stock into market; bought control of Lake Shore & Mich. Southern Ry., Mich. Central R.R. and Can. Southern Ry., 1873; created one of great Am. transp. systems; with panic of 1873 at its worst he announced that N.Y. Central was paying its dividends as usual and sublet contracts for buildings of Grand Central Terminal in N.Y.C.; fortune estimated at $100,000,-000; contributed $1,000,000 to Central (renamed Vanderbilt) U., Nashville, Tenn., regarded as founder; contributed $50,000 to Ch. of the Strangers, N.Y.C. Died N.Y.C. Jan. 4, 1877.

VANDERBILT, William Henry, financier, railroad opeator; b. New Brunswick, N.J., May 8, 1821; s. Cornelius and Sophia (Johnson) V.; m. Maria Louisa Kissam, 1840, children—Cornelius, William Kissam, Frederick W., George W., Mrs. Elliot F. Shepherd, Mrs. William D. Sloane, Mrs. W. Seward Webb, Mrs. H. McK. Twombly. Clk., Drew, Robinson & Co., banking house, 1839; received S.I. R.R., 1857; v.p. N.Y. & Harlem R.R., 1864; influenced father to buy control of Lake Shore & Mich. Southern R.R., 1873, became pres. affiliated corps.; bought control of C. & N.-W. R.R., large interest in Cleve., Columbus, Cincinnati & Indpls. R.R.; improved operations of all his railroad holdings; distributed $100,000 among his workers in appreciation for their loyalty in not joining railroad strike of 1877; shareholder, dir. Western Union Telegraph Co., resigned, 1881; resigned all railroad presidencies, 1883; contributed $450,000 to Vanderbilt U.; contributed gifts to St. Bartholomew's Episcopal Ch., YMCA, Met. Mus. of Art, Little Moravian Ch., S.I., Coll. Phys. and Surg., N.Y.C.; paid expense of transporting ancient obelisk given by Khedive of Egypt to N.Y., 1880. Died N.Y.C., Dec. 8, 1885.

VANDERBURGH, William Henry, fur trader; b. Vincennes, Ind., circa 1798; s. Henry and Frances (Cornoyer) V.; attended U.S. Mil. Acad., 1813. Fur trader with Mo. Fur Co.; capt. Mo. Fur Co.'s volunteers in Leavenworth Expdn. to upper Missouri, 1823, participated in demonstration against villages of Arikara Indians; Aug. 10; became partner in Am. Fur Co.; penetrated to heart of Rocky Mountains, 1829-30; aided Am. Fur. Co. in gaining monopoly of fur trade. Ambushed and killed by Blackfoot warriors, Jefferson River, Mo., Oct. 14, 1832; buried Mo.

van der DONCK, Adriaen, colonist, lawyer; b. Breda, North Brabant, Holland, May 7, 1620; s. Cornelius and Agatha (van Bergen) van der D.; studied law U. Leyden (Holland), 1638, finished legal course receiving degree Supremus in jure, 1653; m. Mary Doughty, 1645. Came to Am.; officer of justice of Rensselaerswyck, New Netherland, 1641-44, served as sheriff or officer of justice in charge of collection of debts due the patroon from tenants; successfully negotiated a treaty between Dutch and the Mohawk Indians, 1645, for this service was given permission to establish colony Colen Donck at Nepperhaen on left bank of Hudson River (now Yonkers, N.Y., from the name "Jonker" by which he was known); sec. Bd. of 9 Men under Peter Stuyvesant, 1649; wrote Remonstrance (setting forth the people's grievances), sent to The Hague to present it to the States-Gen.; admitted to practice as an advocate before Supreme Ct. of The Netherlands; wrote account of New Netherland published as Beschrijvinge van Nieuvv Nederlant, 1655; returned to Am., 1653, only lawyer in Am., could not plead cases because he would have had unfair advantage. Died Manhattan Island, 1655.

VANDERGRIFT, Jacob Jay, river capt., oil investor; b. Allegheny, Pa., Apr. 10, 1827; s. William and Sophia (Sarver) V.; m. Henrietta Morrow, Dec. 29, 1853, 4 daus., 5 sons; m. 2d, Frances G. Anshutz Hartley, Dec. 4, 1883. Cabin boy on Allegheny River boats Bridgewater and Pinta; capt. boat Hail Columbia on Wabash River, 1850's; owned shares in boats Red Fox and Conestoga, 1858; began speculating in oil before Civil War; shipped, dealt and profited in oil, Oil City, Pa., during Civil War; founded Vandergrift, Forman & Co., 1868, expanded into laying of pipelines (these interests consolidated as United Pipe Lines, 1877, then merged into Nat. Transit Co., 1884); established Imperial Refinery, 1872; asso. with laying of 1st important natural gas line; invested in banks, gas cos., iron, steel, real estate; endowed an orphan home, aided chs. and hosps., late in life. Died Pitts., Dec. 26, 1899; buried Allegheny Cemetery, Pitts.

van der KEMP, Francis Adrian, polit. writer; b. Kampen, Overyssel, Netherlands, May 4, 1752; s. John and Anna (Leyclekker) van der K.; attended Groningen U., 1770-73; Bapt. Sem., Amsterdam; m. Reinira Engelberta Johanna Vos, May 20, 1782, 3 children. Admitted as candidate for ministry, 1775, installed as pastor at Leyden, 1776; author (often anonymous) polit. works which got him in trouble with Dutch authorities, 1776-87; interested in and supported Am. Revolution; came to Am. after being banished from the Netherlands, 1787; experimented with agr., nr. Kingston, N.Y.; justice of peace; organizer Soc. of Agr. and Natural History; translator 24 manuscript vols. of Dutch Colonial Records. Died Olden Barneveld (now Barnevelde), N.Y., Sept. 7, 1829.

VANDERLYN, John, painter; b. Kingston, N.Y., Oct. 15, 1775; s. Nicholas and Sarah (Tappen) V.; never married. Aaron Burr became his 1st patron; worked in Thomas Barrow's print shop, 1792-94; studied for 3 years, 1st lessons in drawing under Archibald Robertson, sent by Aaron Burr to study under Gilbert Stuart, Phila., then supplied by Burr with means for five years' stay in Paris, 1796-1801; returned to Am., 1801; painted 2 pictures of Niagara Falls, 1802; returned to Europe, 1803, in Paris, 1803-05, 08-15, Rome, 1805-07; at Paris Salon received gold medal at behest of Napoleon, 1808; painted Ariadne (now in Pa. Acad. of Fine Arts), 1st painting of nude to be exhibited in Am., caused a scandal, 1812; returned to N.Y.C., 1815; painted portraits of James Monroe, James Madison, Andrew Jackson, Zachary Taylor (now in Corcoran Gallery of Art, Washington, D.C.), John C. Calhoun, Burr, George Clinton, Robert R. Livingston; painted portraits of John A. Sidell, Francis L. Waddell, and a self-portrait (all in Met. Mus. Art, N.Y.C.); commd. by U.S. Ho. of Reps. to make full-length copy of Gilbert Stuart's Washington, 1832; one of 4 painters invited to undertake painting in the Rotunda of Capitol, 1837, executed The Landing of Columbus; for 12 years his large panoramas of Paris, Versailles, Athens, Mexico were exhibited in N.Y. Rotunda built for this purpose in City Hall Park, N.Y.C. Died Kingston, N.Y., Sept. 23, 1852.

VANDERPOEL, Aaron, congressman, lawyer; b. Kinderhook, N.Y., Feb. 5, 1799; studied law. Admitted to bar, 1820, began practice of law, Kinderhook; mem. N.Y. State Assembly, 1826-30; mem. U.S. Ho. of Reps. (Democrat) from N.Y., 23d-24th, 26th congresses, 1833-37, 39-41; settled in N.Y.C.; judge Superior Ct., 1842-50. Died N.Y.C., July 18, 1870; buried Woodlawn Cemetery.

VANDERVEER, Abraham, congressman; b. Kings County, N.Y., 1781; attended common schs. Clk., Kings County, 1816-21, 22-37; 1st treas. Bklyn. Savs. Bank; mem. U.S. Ho. of Reps. (Democrat) from N.Y., 25th Congress, 1837-39. Died Bklyn., July 21, 1839; buried Reformed Dutch Cemetery.

VANDER WEE, John Baptist, clergyman; b. Antwerp, Belgium, Feb. 20, 1824. Joined Congregation of Bros. of St. Francis Xavier, 1845; undertook various religious duties, Eng., 1848-72; came to U.S., 1872; strengthened or founded Mt. St. Joseph's Coll. and Provincial House, Balt., St. Xavier's Coll., Louisville, Ky., St. John's Prep. Sch., Danvers, Mass also coll. novitiate, Old Point Comfort, Va.; served or taught at Lowell, Lawrence, Somerville and Worcester (all Mass.), Norfolk and Portsmouth (Va.), also Wheeling, W. Va. Died Feb. 24, 1900; buried Bonnie Brae Cemetery, Balt.

Van de VELDE, James Oliver, clergyman, coll. pres.; b. Teromnde, Belgium, Apr. 3, 1795; studied theology Coll. at Mechlin, Belgium, Georgetown Coll., Washington, D.C. Came to U.S., 1817; entered Soc. of Jesus; taught at Georgetown Coll.; ordained priest Roman Catholic Ch., 1827; chaplain Visitation Convent, attended missions, Montgomery County, Md., 1827-circa 31; prof. St. Louis U., 1831, v.p., 1833, pres., 1840-43; rep. of Vice-province of Mo. in congregation of procurators of Soc. of Jesus, Rome, Italy, 1841; vice provincial of Mo., 1843-48, erected several chs.; province rep. at 6th Council of Balt., 1846; became bishop of Chgo., 1849; petitioned to resign, petition refused by Rome; transferred to Diocese of Natchez (Miss.), 1853, founded two schs. and a coll. Died Natchez, Nov. 13, 1855.

VANDEVER, William, congressman; b. Balt., Mar. 31, 1817; attended common schs.; studied law. Moved to Ill., 1839, to Ia., 1851; admitted to bar, 1852, began practice of law, Dubuque, Ia.; mem. U.S. Ho. of Reps. (Republican) from Ia., 36th-37th congresses, 1859-61; mem. Washington (D.C.) Peace Conv., 1861; served as col. 9th Regt., Ia. Volunteer Inf., during Civil War; promoted brig. gen. U.S. Volunteers, 1862, brevetted maj. gen., 1865; resumed practice law, Dubuque, Ia.; U.S. Indian insp. (apptd. by Pres. Grant), 1873-77; moved to San Buenaventura, Cal., 1884; mem. U.S. Ho. of Reps. (Rep.) from Cal., 50th-51st congresses, 1887-91. Died Ventura, Cal., July 23, 1893; buried Ventura Cemetery.

Van DORN, Earl, army officer; b. Port Gibson, Miss., Sept. 17, 1820; s. Peter Aaron and Sophia Ponelson (Caffery) Van D.; grad. U.S. Mil. Acad., 1842; m. Caroline Godbold, 1843. Served in Mexican War; commd. 1st lt., 1847, took part in Seminole War in Fla., 1848-50; capt. 2d Cavalry, U.S. Army, 1855-61, served in Tex. and Indian Territory, promoted maj., 1860; resigned from army, 1861; commd. brig. gen. Miss. Militia, 1861, maj. gen., 1861; col. of cavalry Confederate Army, assigned to duty in Tex.; promoted brig. gen., 1861, maj. gen., 1861; comdr. Trans-Mississippi dist., 1862; raided Union depots at Holly Springs, Miss., captured garrison. Killed at Battle of Spring Hill (Tenn.), May 8, 1863.

Van DYCK, Cornelius Van Alen, Arabic scholar, med. missionary; b. Kinderhook, N.Y., Aug. 13, 1818; s. Henry L. and Catherine (Van Alen) Van D.; grad. Jefferson Med. Coll., Phila., 1839; m. Julia Abbott, Dec. 23, 1842, at least 4 children including W. T. Van Dyck. Missionary, Am. Bd. Commrs. for Fgn. Missions, Syria, 1840, Beirut, 1841; studied Arabic; moved to 'Abeih in the Lebanon with Dr. William Thompson, June 1843, conducted high school for boys; prepared Arabic textbooks on geography, navigation, natural history, algebra, geometry, plane and spherical trigonometry; ordained by the mission, 1846; transferred to Sidon, headquarters for extensive medical practice and preaching tours, 1849-57; completed translation of Bible into Arabic (begun by Eli Smith, 1848), 1865; returned to U.S., 1865; tchr. Hebrew, Union Theol. Sem., 1865-67; returned to Beirut, 1867, editor journal al-Nashrah; prof. pathology in med. dept. Syrian Protestant Coll., prof. astronomy dept. arts and scis., dir. astron. and meteorol. observatory; had medical practice; wrote Arabic texts on pathology, chemistry, internal medicine, phys. diagnosis and astronomy; resigned professorship, 1883; practiced in Hosp. of St. George, Beirut, 1883-93; had important part in modern renaissance of Arabic literature. Died Beirut, Nov. 13, 1895.

VAN DYKE, Henry Jackson, clergyman; b. Abington, Montgomery County, Pa., Mar. 2, 1822; grad. U. Pa., 1843, Princeton Theol. Sem., 1845; D.D. (hon.), U. Mo., 1860; m. Henrietta Ashmead, 1845, 6 children. Pastor, 2d Ch. (Presbyn.), Bridgeton, N.J., 1845-52; pastor 1st Ch., Bklyn., 1853-91; mem. com. of dels. to So. Presbyn. Assembly, Louisville, Ky., from 1870. Author: (sermons) Moses, the Servant of the Lord; How Old Art Thou?; The Commandment of Promise; Giving Thanks for All Things; The Lord's Prayer (1872). Died Bklyn., May 25, 1891.

VAN DYKE, John, congressman, jurist; b. Lamington, N.J., Apr. 3, 1807; studied law. Admitted to bar, 1836, began practice of law, New Brunswick, N.J.; pros. atty. Middlesex County, 1841; mayor New Brunswick, 1846-47; pres. Bank of N.J. at New Brunswick; mem. U.S. Ho. of Reps. (Whig) from N.J., 30th-31st congresses, 1847-51; del. Republican Nat. Conv., Phila., 1856; judge N.J. Supreme Ct., 1859-66; moved to Wabasha, Minn., 1868; mem. Minn. Senate, 1872-73; judge 3d Jud. Dist. Minn., 1873-78. Died Wabasha, Dec. 24, 1878; buried Riverview Cemetery.

VAN DYKE, Nicholas, pres. Del., Continental congressman; b. New Castle, Del., Sept. 25, 1738; s. Nicholas and Lytie (Dirks) Van D.; m. Elizabeth Nixon; m. 2d, Charlotte Standly; at least 1 son, Nicholas. Admitted to Pa. Supreme Ct. bar, 1765; mem. Del. Provincial Com. of Correspondence; mem. Del. com. to solicit funds for relief of people of Boston, 1774; mem. New Castle Council of Safety, 1776; participated in formulating rules for Del. Constl. Conv., 1776, mem. com. charged with provisioning state's troops, assisted in preparing declaration of rights, wrote preliminary draft of Del. Constn.; apptd. judge Ct. Admiralty, 1777; mem. Continental Congress, 1777-82; signer Articles of Confederation; pres. State of Del., 1783-86; mem. Del. Council, 1786. Died New Castle County, Del., Feb. 19, 1789; buried Immanuel Churchyard, New Castle.

Van DYKE, Nicholas, senator; b. New Castle, Del., Dec. 20, 1769; s. Nicholas and Elizabeth (Nixon) Van D.; grad. Coll. of N.J. (now Princeton), 1788; m. Mary Johns, at least 1 child, Dorcas Montgomery. Admitted to Del. bar, 1792; mem. Del. Ho. of Reps., 1799; atty. gen. Del., 1801-06; mem. U.S. Ho. of Reps. (Federalist) from Del., 10th-11th congresses, Oct. 6, 1807-11; mem. Del. Senate, 1815-17; mem. U.S. Senate (Federalist) from Del., 1817-26. Died New Castle, Del., May 21, 1826; buried on farm at St. Georges Hundred, reinterred Immanuel Churchyard, New Castle.

VANE, Sir Henry, colonial gov.; b. Debden, Essex, Eng., 1613; s. Sir Henry and Frances (Darcy) V.; attended Magdalen Hall at Oxford; m. Frances Wray, July 1, 1640, 13 children. Went to Mass. in ship Abigail, 1635, arrived in Boston, Oct. 1635; admitted as mem. ch. 1635, admitted as freeman of colony, 1636; chosen to serve on commn. for mil. discipline, 1636; one of 3 arbiters to whom citizens of Boston had to submit their cases before they could proceed to law; gov. Mass., 1636; took side of Mrs. Anne Hutchison in theol. dispute, thus destroyed his career in America; unsuccessful candidate for gov. Mass., 1637, returned to Eng., 1637; joint treasurer of navy, 1639; knighted by Charles I, 1640; elected to both Short and Long Parliaments, 1640, instrumental in securing condemnation of Strafford and Laude; helped Roger Williams secure R.I. charter which bore Vane's signature as one of commrs. for plantations, 1644; instrumental in having rescinded the commn. granted to William Coddington, 1652; leading counciler of England; following Restoration he was exempted from act of indemnity; tried for treason, after 2 years in prison, found guilty. Executed on Tower Hill, London, Eng., June 14, 1662.

VAN GAASBECK, Peter, congressman, mcht.; b. Ulster County, N.Y., Sept. 27, 1754; attended grammar schs. Became a mcht., Kingston, N.Y.; served as capt. and maj. Ulster County Militia during Revolutionary War; mem. U.S. Ho. of Reps. (Anti-Federalist) from N.Y., 3d Congress, 1793-95. Died Kingston, 1797; buried 1st Reformed Dutch Churchyard.

Van HAGEN, Peter Albrecht, composer; b. Holland; married; children include Peter. Came to Am.; became music tchr., Charleston, S.C., 1774, N.Y.C., 1789; gave concerts with wife and son; moved to Boston, 1796; composer Federal Overture, 1797, Funeral Dirge for George Washington, 1800, also much theatrical music.

VAN HORN, Burt, congressman; b. Newfane, N.Y., Oct. 28, 1823; attended Yates Acad., also Hamilton Coll. (now Colgate U.), Hamilton, N.Y. Engaged in Agriculture, Niagara County, later became cloth mfr.; mem. N.Y. State Assembly, 1858-60; mem. U.S. Ho. of Reps. (Republican) from N.Y., 37th, 39th-40th congresses, 1861-63, 65-69; resumed farming, also engaged in loan business; collector internal revenue, Rochester, N.Y., 1877-82. Died Lockport, N.Y., Apr. 1, 1896; buried Glenwood Cemetery.

VAN HORNE, Archibald, congressman. Apptd. adjutant 14th Regt., Md. Militia, 1798, commd. capt., 1802; mem. Md. Ho. of Dels., 1801-03, 05, 14-16, speaker, 1805; mem. U.S. Ho. of Reps. from Md., 10th-11th congresses, 1807-11; mem. Md. Senate, 1816-17. Died Prince Georges County, Md., 1817.

VAN HORNE, Espy, congressman; b. Lycoming County, Pa., 1795; mem. U.S. Ho. of Reps. (Democrat) from Pa., 19th-20th congresses, 1825-29. Died Williamsport, Pa., Aug. 25, 1829.

VAN HORNE, Isaac, congressman; b. Tollbury Twp., Bucks County, Pa., Jan. 13, 1754; apprenticed as carpenter and cabinetmaker. Became ensign of militia co., 1775; apptd. ensign Continental Army by Com. of Safety, assigned to Col. Samuel McGaw's Regt., Jan. 1776; held prisoner, Nov. 1776-78, exchanged; served from 1st lt. to capt. until end of Revolutionary War; justice of peace Tollbury Twp., several years; coroner Bucks County, 4 years; mem. Pa. Ho. of Reps., 1796-97; mem. U.S. Ho. of Reps. (Democrat) from Pa., 7th-8th congresses, 1801-05; moved to Zanesville, O., 1805; receiver of land office, Zanesville, 1805-26. Died Zanesville, Feb. 2, 1834; buried Woodlawn Cemetery.

VAN HOUTEN, Isaac B., congressman; b. Clarkstown (now New City), Rockland County, N.Y., June 4, 1776; attended common schs. Engaged in milling and agriculture; mem. N.Y. State Assembly, 1833-35; mem. U.S. Ho. of Reps. (Democrat) from N.Y., 23d Congress, 1833-35. Died Clarkstown, Aug. 16, 1850; buried family burying ground on his estate nr. Clarkstown.

Van ILPENDAM, Jan Jansen, colonial ofcl.; b. Holland, circa 1595; m. Judick Hame, 1616; m. 2d, Catalyntje van Strassel. Supercargo on ship Rensselaerwyck, 1636, arrived in Manhattan, 1637; commissary, Ft. Nassau, 1637; protested to Peter Minuit for settling area of South River (now part of N.J.) for Queen of Sweden, 1638, made similar protest to Peter Ridder, 1640; expelled English (Delaware Co.) from Schuylkill, 1641; a commr. in Swedish ct. of inquiry ordered by Gov. Printz to examine English who continued trade on Varkens kill, 1643; accused of fraud in trading matters by New Amsterdam, summoned to appear at Manhattan, 1645, case investigated by Cornelis vander Hoykens; ordered to be sent to Amsterdam (Holland) for further inquiry, 1646. Died 1647.

VAN LENNEP, Henry John, missionary, educator; b. Smyrna, Asiatic Turkey, Mar. 18, 1815; s. Richard and Adele Marie (de Heidenstam)

Van L.; grad. Amherst Coll., 1837; attended Andover Theol. Sem., 1837-38; m. Emma L. Bliss, Nov. 3, 1839; m. 2d, Mary Elizabeth Hawes, Sept. 4, 1843; m. 3d, Emily Ann Bird, Apr. 18, 1850; children include William Bird, E.J. Van L. Came to U.S., 1830; ordained to ministry Congregational Ch., Amherst, 1839; missionary Am. Bd. Commrs. for Fgn. Missions, sailed for Turkey, 1839; visited U.S., 1843; returned to Turkey, 1844, conducted a mission, Constantinople (now Instanbul), 1844-54, taught in Sem. (later Robert Coll.), Bebek, Turkey; returned to U.S., 1849; established mission station and theol. sem., Tokat, Turkey, 1854; returned permanently to U.S., 1869; taught natural sci., Greek and modern langs. Ingham U., LeRoy, N.Y., 1869-72. Author: Oriental Album, 1862; Travels in Little-Known Parts of Asia Minor, 2 vols., 1870; Bible Lands, Their Modern Customs and Manners Illustrative of Scripture, 1875. Died Great Barrington, Mass., Jan. 11, 1889.

VANMETER, John Inskeep, congressman, lawyer; b. nr. Moorefield, Hardy County, Va. (now W.Va.), Feb. 1798; attended Coll. William and Mary, Williamsburg, Va.; grad. Princeton, 1821; attended Judge Gould's law sch., Litchfield, Conn. Admitted to bar, Va., 1822, began practice of law, Moorefield; mem. Va. Ho. of Dels., 1826; moved to Pike County, O., 1826, engaged in agriculture; mem. Ohio Ho. of Reps., 1836, Ohio Senate, 1838; mem. U.S. Ho. of Reps. (Whig) from Ohio, 28th Congress, 1843-45; moved to Chillicothe, O., 1855; became mem. Democratic Party, 1856. Died Chillicothe, Aug. 3, 1875; buried Grand View Cemetery.

VAN NESS, John Peter, congressman, mayor Washington; b. Ghent, Columbia County, N.Y., 1770; attended Columbia; studied law. Admitted to bar, never practiced law; Democratic presdl. elector, 1800; mem. U.S. Ho. of Reps. (Democrat, filled vacancy) from N.Y., 7th Congress, Oct. 6, 1801-Jan. 17, 1803; apptd. maj. militia in D.C. by Pres. Jefferson; pres. second council, 1803; promoted lt. col. commandant 1st legion of militia, 1805, brig. gen., 1811, maj. gen., 1813; alderman City of Washington (D.C.), 1829, mayor, 1830-34; 2d v.p. Washington Nat. Monument Soc., 1833; pres. commrs. Washington Canal, 1834; pres. branch bank of U.S., Washington; 1st pres. Nat. Met. Bank, 1814-46. Died Washington, D.C., Mar. 7, 1846; buried mausoleum at Oak Hill Cemetery.

Van NESS, William Peter, jurist; b. Claverack (now Ghent) N.Y., circa 1778; s. Peter and Elbertie (Hogeboom) Van N.; grad. Columbia, 1797; studied law in office of Edward Livingston. Began practice law, N.Y.C., 1800; became protege of Aron Burr; defended Burr's polit. actions in Peter Irving's Morning Chronicle; wrote pamphlet An Examination of the Various Charges Exhibited against Aaron Burr, signed Aristides, 1803; Burr's second in duel with Alexander Hamilton duel, 1804, indicted by coroner's jury as accesory in murder of Hamilton; fled to Kinderhook, N.Y.; became asso. with Martin Van Buren as dir. Bank of Hudson; judge U.S. Ct. for So. Dist. N.Y., 1812-26; codified (with John Woodworth, at request of N.Y. Legislature) laws for public information in Laws of the State of New York, 1813. Author: Reports of Two Cases in the Prize Court for the New York District, 1814; A Concise Narrative of General Jackson's First Invasion of Florida, 1826. Died Sept. 6, 1826.

Van NEST, Abraham Rynier, clergyman; b. N.Y.C., Feb. 16, 1823; s. George and Phoebe (Van Nest) Van N.; grad. Rutgers Coll., 1841, D.D. (hon.), 1860; grad. New Brunswick Theol. Sem., 1847; D.D. (hon.), U. Pa., 1860; Pastor, 21st Street Reformed Ch., N.Y.C., 1848-62; went to Europe, 1862; in charge of Am. Chapel, Paris, France, 1863-64, Am. Chapel, Rome, Italy, 1864-65; founder Am. Union Ch. which drew people of diverse religious beliefs, Florence, Italy, 1866-75; pres. evangelization com. of Free Ch. of Italy, 1875; founder Am. Union Ch., Geneva, Switzerland, 1875; returned to U.S., 1878; pastor 3d Reformed Ch. of Phila., 1878-83; pres. Gen. Synod Reformed Ch. in U.S., 1879; trustee Rutgers Coll., 1878-92. Author: Memoir of Rev. George W. Bethune, D.D., 1867; editor Lectures on Pastoral Theology by James Spencer Cannon, 1853; Expository Sermons on the Heidelberg Catechism by George W. Bethune, 2 vols., 1864. Died N.Y.C., June 1, 1892.

VAN NORSTRAND, David; publisher; b. N.Y.C. Dec. 5, 1811; s. Jacob and Harriet (Rhodes) Van N.; m. Miss Lewis; m. 2d, Sarah A. Nichols; no children. Opened bookstore at Broadway & John St., N.Y.C., 1848, customers included U.S. Mil. Acad. and other instns.; published and issued trade editions; took over publication of The Rebellion Record edited by Frank Moore) from George Palmer Putnam, 1864, issued volumes VII-XI, 1864-68; installed own printing plant, founded publishing house Van Norstrand Co., specializing tech. and mil. works, 1869; established Van Norstrand's Eclectic Engring. Mag.; credited with furthering scientific investigation in U.S. by importation of fgn. treatises; encouraged Am. tech. men. to write by publishing their writings; sponsored Handbook for Active Service (Egbert L. Viele), 1861, Infantry Tactics (Brig. Gen. Silas Casey), 1862, Life of Napoleon (Henry Jomini; translated from French by Gen. H. W. Halleck), 2 vols., 1864; mem. Union League Club, St. Nicholas Soc.; a founder Holland Soc. of N.Y. Died N.Y.C., June 14, 1886.

Van OSDEL, John Mills, architect; b. Balt., July 31, 1811; s. James H. Van Osdel; m. Caroline Gailer, 1831; m. 2d, Martha McClellan, 1846; 4 adopted children. Started in bus. for himself, 1829 employed by William Ogden to plan and erect large mansion in Chgo. (Ogden House, Ontario and Rush sts.), 1837; asso. editor Am. Mechanic, circa 1840; opened archtl. office (after bldg. contractors of Chgo. promised their support), 1844; constructed 600 bldgs., 1844; during gt. fire of 1871 dug large pit in which he buried his plans and records; prin. works include 2d Presbyn. Ch. (in Gothic style), 1851; Palmer House, Tremont House, Oriental and Kendal bldgs., McCormick and Reaper blocks (all designed by 1872); Peter Schuttler Residence, Chgo., Joel D. Matteson Residence, Springfield, Ill., John Woodin Quincy Residence; trustee Ill. Indsl. U. (later U. Ill.); honored as Chgo.'s 1st architect. Author: Inland Architect and Builder (recollections), 1883. Died Dec. 21, 1891.

Van QUICKENBORNE, Charles Felix, clergyman, educator; b. Peteghem, East Flanders, Jan. 21, 1788; ed. Sem. at Ghent. Ordained priest Roman Catholic Ch., 1812; curate, St. Genoix, nr. Courtrai, Belgium; entered Jesuit novitiate at Rumbeke, 1815, assigned to Md. Mission of Soc. of Jesus, 1817; tchr. scriptures Georgetown Coll.; condr. religious services, Alexandria, Va.; master of novices, Whitemarsh, Md., built stone chapel there; named superior to conduct Jesuit band of priests, novices and lay brotrers to Mo., 1823; founder St. Louis Coll., 1828, incorporated into St. Louis U., 1832; missionary to Osage Indians, 1827, later to Potawatomi, Kickapoo and other Western tribes; founder 1st Jesuit mission with resident priest among Kickapoo tribesmen, 1836; founder St. Mary's Mission among Potawatomi Indians nr. what is now Leavenworth, Mo.; wrote accounts of missions to his superiors, published in Annales de la Propagation de la Foi, 1826-36. Died missionary parish, Portage des Sioux, Aug. 17, 1837.

van RAALTE, Albertus Christiaan, pioneer; b. Wanneperveen, nr. Zwartsluis, Netherlands, Oct. 17, 1811; s. Rev. Albertus and Christina (Harking) van R.; studied medicine, then theology U. Leylen (Holland); m. Christiana Johanna De Moen, Mar. 11, 1836, 7 children. Minister of new Gereformeerde Ch. (formed by seceders from Hervormde Ch.), 1834-44, went to Arnhem (Belgium) to assist in training candidates for ministry in newly formed denomination (br. of Dutch Reformed Ch.), 1844; decided to come to Northern U.S., 1845, arrived in N.Y.C., Nov. 1846, in Detroit, Dec. 1846; arrived with wife and several men in Western Mich., Feb. 9, 1847, named their settlement Holland; served as both preacher and physician; a founder Hope Coll., also theol. sem. at Holland; founder De Hope (religious periodical in Dutch lang.). Died Nov. 7, 1876.

Van RENSSELAER, Cortland, clergyman; b. Albany, N.Y., May 26, 1808; s. Stephen and Cornelia (Paterson) Van R.; grad. Yale, 1827; attended Princeton Theol. Sem., also Union Sem., Hampden-Sydney, Va.; m. Catharine Cogswell, Sept. 13, 1836, 7 children. Admitted to N.Y. bar, 1830; ordained to ministry by Presbytery of Hanover, N.J., 1835; founder, pastor ch., Burlington, N.J., 1836-40; apptd. to solicit funds for Princeton Theol. Sem., 1843; corr. sec., chief exec. officer Presbyn. Bd. Edn., 1846-60; founder, editor Presbyn. Mag., 1851-59; published ann. vol. of articles on edn. under title The Home, The School, and the Church, 1850-60; moderator Gen. Assembly of Old Sch. Presbyn. Ch., 1857. Author: Essays and Discourses (published posthumously), 1861. Died Burlington, N.J., July 25, 1860; buried, Albany, N.Y.

VAN RENSSELAER, Henry Bell, congressman, army officer; b. Manor House, Albany, N.Y., May 14, 1810; son of Stephen Van R.; grad. U.S. Mil. Acad., 1831. Commd. brevet 2d lt. 5th Regt., U.S. Inf., 1831, resigned, 1832; engaged in agriculture, nr. Ogdensburg, N.Y.; mem. U.S. Ho. of Reps. (Whig) from N.Y., 27th Congress, 1841-43; interested in mining enterprises; commd. brig. gen. U.S. Army, chief of staff under Gen. Winfield Scott, at beginning of Civil War; served as insp. gen., with rank of col., 1862-64. Died Cincinnati, Mar. 23, 1864; buried Grace Episcopal Churchyard, Jamaica, L.I., N.Y.

VAN RENSSELAER, Jeremiah, congressman; b. N.Y., Aug. 27, 1738; grad. Princeton, 1758; at least 1 son, Solomon Van Vechten. Mem. Albany (N.Y.) Com. of Safety; mem. U.S. Ho. of Reps. from N.Y., 1st Congress, 1789-91; mem. N.Y. State Assembly, 1789; mem. 1st bd. dirs. Bank of Albany, 1791, pres. bank, 1798-1806; Democratic presdl. elector, 1800; lt. gov. N.Y., 1801-04; curator Evang. Lutheran Sem., Albany, 1804. Died Albany, Feb. 19, 1810; buried Dutch Reformed Cemetery.

VAN RENSSELAER, Killian Killian, congressman, lawyer; b. Greenbush, Rensselaer County, N. Y., June 9, 1763; attended Yale; studied law. Admitted to bar, 1784, began practice of law, Claverack, N.Y.; pvt. sec. to Gen. Philip Schuyler; mem. U.S. Ho. of Reps. (Democrat) from N.Y., 7th-11th congresses, 1801-11. Died Albany, N.Y., June 18, 1845; buried pvt. cemetery, Greenbush.

Van RENSSELAER, Nicholas, clergyman; b. Amsterdam, Holland, Sept. 25, 1636; s. Kiliaen and Anna (van Wely) van R.; V.D.M. (minister of God's word), U. Leyden (Holland), 1670; m. Alida Schuyler, Feb. 10, 1675, no children. Received in Classis of Amsterdam, 1662; chaplain to Dutch embassy at London, 1662-70; licensed to preach to Dutch congregation at Westminster, Eng., 1665; ordained deacon Ch. of Eng., 1665; lectr. St. Margaret's Sch., Lothbury, Eng., 1665-70; arrived N.Y. C., 1675; apptd. minister Ch. of Holland congregation, Albany, N.Y., 1675, not recognized by congregation because of ties with Ch. of Eng.; installed as pastor after affirming faith in doctrines of Ch. of Holland, 1675; charged with leading immoral life, removed from pastorate, 1677. Died 1678.

VAN RENSSELAER, Solomon Van Vechten, congressman; b. Rensselaer County, N.Y., Aug. 6, 1774; s. Henry Kiliain and Alida (Bradt) Van R.; m. Harriet Van Rensselaer (cousin), Jan. 17, 1797, several children. Served as cornet in U.S. Cavalry, 1792, capt. under Gen. Anthony Wayne in Indian campaigns, 1794; commd. maj. U.S. Army, 1799, discharged, 1800; adj. gen. N.Y., 1801-11, 13-21; became aide-de-camp to Maj. Gen. Stephen Van Rensselaer at beginning of War of 1812, served in attack on Queenston, Ont., Can., 1812, wounded; mem. U.S. Ho. of Reps. (Federalist) from N.Y., 16th-1t7h congresses, 1819-22; postmaster Albany (N.Y.), 1822-39, 41-43; del. from N.Y. to opening of Erie Canal, 1825. Died Albany, Apr. 23, 1852; buried Albany Rural Cemetery.

Van RENSSELAER, Stephen, congressman; b. N.Y.C., Nov. 1, 1764; s. Stephen and Catherine (Livingston) Van R.; attended Coll. of N.J. (now Princeton); grad. Harvard, 1782; m. Margaret Schulyer, June 6, 1783, 3 children including Henry Bell; m. 2d, Cornelia Paterson, May 17, 1802, 9 children. Mem. N.Y. Assembly (Federalist), 1789-90, 98, 1818; mem. N.Y. Senate (Federalist), 1791-96; lt. gov. N.Y., 1795-1801; commd. maj. N.Y. Militia, 1801, led unsuccessful attack on Queenston, Ont., Can., 1812; bd. regents U. N.Y., 1819-39; 1st pres. N.Y. Bd. of Agr., 1820; mem. U.S. Ho. of Reps. from N.Y., 17th-20th congresses, 1822-29; established sch. (became Rensselaer Inst. 1826, later Rensselaer Poly. Inst.), 1824; pres. Albany Lyceum of Natural History, Albany Inst. Died Albany, Jan. 26, 1839; buried Albany Rural Cemetery.

VAN SANT, Joshua, congressman, mayor Balt.; b. Millington, Kent County, Md., Dec. 31, 1803; attended common schs., Phila. Moved to Balt., engaged in hat mfg., 1817-35; del. Md. Constl. Conv., 1836; postmaster Balt., 1839-41; mem. Md. Ho. of Dels., 1845; commr. finances Balt., 1846-55; trustee city and county almshouse, 1847-53, 61; commr. public schs., 1852-54, pres., 1854; mem. U.S. Ho. of Reps. (Democrat) from Md., 33d Congress, 1853-55; Democratic presdl. elector, 1860; del. Md. Constl. Conv., 1867; dir. Md. State Penitentiary, 1867-69, pres. 2 years; mem. bd. trustees McDonough Ednl. Fund and Inst., 1867-71, pres., 1871; pres. bd. Bay View Asylum, 1868-70; mayor Balt., 1871-75; apptd. city comptroller Balt., 1876-81, later elected to same office, served until 1884. Died Balt., Apr. 8, 1884; buried Greenmount Cemetery.

Van SANTVOORD, George, lawyer; b. Belleville, N.J., Dec. 8, 1819; s. Staats Van Santvoord; grad. Union Coll., Schenectady, N.Y., 1841; m. Elizabeth Van Schaack, 1 son, Seymour. Admitted to N.Y. bar, 1844; practiced law, Lafayette, Ind., 1844-46, Kinderhook, N.Y., 1846-51; partner of David L. Seymour, Troy, N.Y., 1852-59, of Benjamin Hall, Troy, 1859-63; mem. N.Y. Assembly from Columbia County, 1852, from Rensselaer County, 1856; dist. atty. Rensselaer County, 1860-63. Author: Indiana Justice, 1845; A Treatise on the Principles of Pleading in Civil Actions under the New York Code of Procedure, 1852; The Study of Law as a Science, 1856; Sketches of the Lives and Judicial Services of the Chief Justices of the U.S., 1859. Died East Albany, N.Y., Mar. 6, 1863.

Van SCHAACK, Henry Cruger, antiquarian; b. Kinderhook, N.Y., Apr. 2, 1802; s. Peter and Elizabeth (Van Alen) Van S.; m. Adaline Ives, 1827, 14 children. Admitted to N.Y. bar, 1823; practiced law, Manlius, N.Y., 1827-87; began collection of documents, 1823, collected papers of Henry Van

Schaack, Henry Cruger Van Schaack, John Frey, Matthew Vischer, John Jay, letters and documents of colonial govs., army officers, Am. patriots, autographs of all U.S. presidents, v.p.'s, cabinet mems., writers U.S. Constn., signers Declaration of Independence. Author: The Life of Peter Van Schaack, 1842; A History of Manlius Village, 1873; An Old Kinderhook Mansion, 1878; Memoirs of the Life of Henry Van Schaack (published posthumously), 1892. Died Dec. 16, 1887.

Van SCHAACK, Peter, revolutionary leader, lawyer; b. Kinderhook, N.Y., Mar. 1747; s. Cornelius and Lydia (Van Dyck) Van S.; grad. King's Coll. (now Columbia), 1766; m. Elizabeth Cruger, 1765, 10 children. Admitted to N.Y. bar, 1769; apptd. to revise statues of Colony of N.Y., 1773; mem. N.Y. Com. of 51 (com. to correspond with other colonies) and N.Y. Com. of 60 (com. to enforce non-importation of manufactured goods from Gt. Britain), 1774; mem. N.Y. Com. of 100, 1775, also N.Y. Com. of Safety; refused to take up arms against Gt. Britain, 1776; refused to pledge allegiance to State of N.Y., 1777, on parole until 1778, banished from colonies, 1778; in Eng., 1778-85; citizenship restored, 1784, returned to Kinderhook, 1785, readmitted to N.Y. bar, 1786; practiced, taught law privately, 1786-1832. Author: Conductor Generalis, 1786. Died Kinderhook, Sept. 17, 1832.

Van SCHAICK, Gosen, army officer; b. Albany, N.Y., Sept. 16, 1736; s. Sybrant and Alida (Roseboom) Van S.; m. Maria Ten Broeck, Nov. 15, 1770, 6 children. Served as capt. N.Y. Militia, French and Indian War; served in campaign against Fort Frontenac, 1758; commd. lt. col. 2d Regt., N.Y. Provincials, 1760; lt. col. 1st N.Y. Regt., 1760-62; commd. col. 1st N.Y. Regt., Continental Army, 1776, served in battles of Ticonderoga and Monmouth; led expdn. against Onondaga Indians, 1779; brevetted brig gen., 1783, ret. 1783. Died Albany, July 4, 1789.

Van SICKLE, Selah, artist; b. Cayuga, N.Y., June 8, 1812; married, 1834. Moved to Nauvoo, Ill., 1845, painted portrait of Brigham Young; moved to St. Joseph County, Mich., 1846; painted portrait now in La Porte (Ind.) Hist. Museum, 1849; moved to Delaware County, O., 1851; painted panorama of life of Christ; engaged in farming, Ohio, Mich., Ia., 1857-80.

VAN SWEARINGEN, Thomas, congressman; b. nr. Shepherdstown, Jefferson County, Va. (now W.Va.), May 5, 1784; attended common schs. Mem. Va. Ho. of Dels., 1814-16; mem. U.S. Ho. of Reps. from Va., 16th-17th congresses, 1819-22. Died Shepherdstown, Aug. 19, 1822; buried Elmwood Cemetery.

VAN TRUMP, Philadelph, congressman, lawyer; b. Lancaster, O., Nov. 15, 1810; learned printing trade; studied law. Became editor Gazette and Enquirer, Lancaster; admitted to bar, began practice of law, Lancaster, 1838; del. Whig Nat. Conv., Balt., 1852; unsuccessful Am. Party candidate for gov. Ohio, 1856; pres. Ohio Bell and Everett Conv., 1860; judge Ct. of Common Pleas, 1862-67; mem. U.S. Ho of Reps. (Democrat) from Ohio, 40th-42d congresses, 1867-73; pres. Ohio Democratic Conv., 1869. Died Lancaster, July 31, 1874; buried Elmwood Cemetery.

Van TWILLER, Wouter, colonial gov.; b. Gelderland (now part of Netherlands), 1580; s. Rijckert and Maria (Van Rennsselaer) Van T.; m. Maria Momma. Clk. for Dutch East India Co., circa 1630-33; gov. New Netherland, 1633-37, promoted agriculture in colony; started settlement on L.I., 1636; purchased for own use Pagganck (now Governor's) Island, also 2 islands on East River (now Ward's and Blackwell's islands), 1637; mgr. patroonship of Kiliaen Van Rensselaer, circa 1640-56. Died 1656.

VANUXEM, Lardner, geologist; b. Phila., July 23, 1792; s. Jame and Rebecca (Clarke) V.; grad. École des Mines, Paris, France, 1819; m. Elizabeth Newbold, 1830. Prof. chemistry and mineralogy S.C. Coll. (now U. S.C.), 1819-27, made geol. surveys of N.C., S.C.; made geol. surveys of N.Y., Ohio, Ky., Tenn., Va., 1827-30; bought farm nr. Bristol, Pa., 1830; assigned to 3d and 4th dists. for geol. surveys of N.Y., 1836-42; mem. group which established 1st uniform geol. nomenclature; founder Assn. Am. Geologists and Naturalists (now A.A.A.S.), 1840. Died Bristol, Jan. 25, 1848.

VAN VALKENBURGH, Robert Bruce, congressman, diplomat; b. Prattsburg, Steuben County, N. Y., Sept. 4, 1821; attended Franklin Acad., Prattsburg; studied law. Admitted to bar, began practice of law, Bath, N.Y.; mem. N.Y. State Assembly, 1852, 57-58; in command of recruiting depot, Elmira, N.Y., organized 17 regts. for Civil War; mem. U.S. Ho. of Reps. (Republican) from N.Y., 37th-38th congresses, 1861-65; served as col. 107th Regt., N.Y. Volunteer Inf., commanded regt. at Battle of Antietam; acting commr. Indian affairs, 1865; minister resident to Japan, 1866-69; settled in Fla.; asso. justice Fla. Supreme Ct., 1874-88. Died Suwanee Springs, nr. Live Oak, Fla., Aug. 1, 1888; buried Old St. Nicholas Cemetery, nr. Jacksonville, Fla.

Van VECHTEN, Abraham, lawyer; b. Catskill, N. Y., Dec. 5, 1762; s. Teunis and Judijke (Ten Broeck) Van V.; attended King's Coll. (now Columbia); m. Catharine Pieterse, May, 1784, 15 children. Admitted to N.Y. bar, 1785, practiced law, Albany, N.Y.; dist. atty. 5th Dist. N.Y., 1796-98; mem. N.Y. State Senate, 1798-1805; recorder of Albany, 1798-1805; mem. N.Y. Assembly from Albany County, 1805-09, 11-13; atty. gen. N.Y., 1809-11, 13-15; mem. N.Y. Constl. Conv. from Albany County, 1821; argued against right of N.Y. State to grant monopoly on navigation of state's waterways in case of Gibbons vs. Ogden before N.Y. Supreme Ct., 1824. Died Jan. 6, 1837.

VAN VORHES, Nelson Holmes, congressman; b. Washington County, Pa., Jan. 23, 1822; apprenticed to printer, 6 years. Editor, propr. Athens (O.) Messenger, 1844-61; mem. Ohio Ho. of Reps., 1850-72, speaker, 4 years; del. Republican Nat. Conv., Chgo., 1860; served from pvt. to col. U.S. Army, during Civil War; mem. U.S. Ho. of Reps. (Republican) from Ohio, 44th-45th congresses, 1875-79. Died Athens, Dec. 4, 1882; buried West Union Street Cemetery.

VAN WINKLE, Peter Godwin, senator; b. N.Y.C. Sept. 7, 1808; s. Peter and Phoebe (Godwin) Van W.; m. Juliette Rathbun, 1831, several children. Admitted to Va. bar, 1835; began practice law, Parkersburg, Va. (now W.Va.); pres. town bd. if trustees, 1844-50; mem. Va. Constl. Conv., 1850; treas. Northwestern Va. R.R. Co., 1852; mem. Wheeling Reorgn. Conv. which resulted in formation of W.Va., 1861; mem. adv. bd. of 1st gov., Francis H. Pierpont; influential mem. 1st W.Va. Legislature, 1861-63; mem. U.S. Senate (Unionist) from W. Va., 1863-69. Died Parkersburg, Apr. 15, 1872; buried View Cemetery, Parkersburg.

Van WYCK, Charles Henry, senator, congressman; b. Poughkeepsie, N.Y., May 10, 1824; s. Dr. Theodorus C. and Elizabeth (Mason) Van W.; grad. with highest honors Rutgers, 1843; m. Kate Brodhead, Sept. 15, 1869, at least 1 dau. Admitted to bar, 1847; dist. atty. Sullivan County (N.Y.), 1850-56; mem. U.S. Ho. of Reps. (Republican) from N.Y., 36th-37th, 40th-41st congresses, 1859-63, 67-71; commanded 56th N.Y. Volunteers in Civil War, 1861-65, promoted brig. gen., 1865; moved to Nebraska City, Neb., 1874; attended Neb. Constl. Conv., 1875; mem. Neb. Senate, 1877-81; mem. U.S. Senate (Rep.) from Neb., 1881-87; active in Farmer's Alliance, Populist movements; unsuccessful Populist candidate for Neb. Senate, 1894. Died Washington, D.C., Oct. 24, 1895; buried Milford (Pa.) Cemetery.

VAN WYCK, William William, congressman; b. nr. Fishkill, Dutchess County, N.Y., Aug. 9, 1777; attended Fishkill Acad. Engaged in agriculture; mem. U.S. Ho. of Reps. (Democrat) from N.Y., 17th-18th congresses, 1821-25; moved to Sudley, Va., engaged in planting. Died Fishkill, Aug. 27, 1840; buried Dutch Reformed Churchyard.

VAN ZANDT, Charles Collins, gov. R.I.; b. Newport, R.I., Aug. 10, 1830; s. Edward and Lydia (Collins) Van Z.; grad. Trinity Coll., Hartford, Conn., 1851; studied law under Hon. Thomas C. Perkins, Hartford; m. Arayelia Greene, Feb. 12, 1863. Admitted to R.I. bar, 1853; city solicitor Newport, 1855-60; mem. R.I. Ho. of Reps., 1858-73, R.I. Senate, 1873-74; chmn. R.I. Republican Conv. that nominated Grant, 1868; lt. gov. R.I., 1873-75, gov., 1877-80. Died June 4, 1894.

VARDILL, John, clergyman, spy; b. N.Y.C., 1749; s. Thomas and Hannah (Tiebout) V.; grad. King's Coll. (now Columbia), 1766, M.A., 1769; M.A. (hon.), Oxford (Eng.) U., 1774; married, 1 child. Asst. prof. anatomy King's Coll., 1766-73, apptd. fellow and prof. natural law, 1773; wrote articles opposing Non-Importation Agreement; ordained deacon and priest Ch. of Eng., London, 1774; elected asst. minister Trinity Ch., N.Y.C., also Regius prof. divinity King's Coll., 1774, but never returned to Am.; spied on Americans and Am. sympathizers in Eng., 1775-81, stole entire correspondence between Am. commrs. and French Ct., Mar.-Oct. 1777 (verified suspicions that France would intervene on side of Americans). Died Jan. 16, 1811.

VARELA Y MORALES, Felix Francisco Jose María de la Concepcion, clergyman; b. Havana, Cuba, Nov. 20, 1788; s. Francisco Varela and Josepha de Morales; grad. Coll. and Sem. of San Carlos, Havana. Ordained priest Roman Catholic Ch., 1811; prof. philosophy, tchr. physics, chemistry Coll. and Sem. of San Carlos, 1811-22; del. to the Cortes, Madrid, Spain, 1822, formulated plan of provincial govt. which would have abolished slavery and made the colony more autonomous; came to U.S., 1823; founder, editor newspaper El Habanero, Phila., 1824-26; asst. St. Peter's Ch., N.Y.C., 1825; pastor Christ Ch., N.Y.C., 1825-35; pastor Ch. of Transfiguration, 1835-51; editor Cath. Expositor and Literary Mag., 1841-44; vicar gen. of N.Y., 1839-53. Author: Las Lecciones de Filosofia, 4 vols., 1818-20; Observaciones sobre la Constitucion Politica de la Monarquia Española, 1821; Miscelanea Filosófica, 1827. Died St. Augustine, Fla., Feb. 18, 1853; buried St. Augustine.

VARICK, James, clergyman; b. Newburgh, N.Y., circa 1750; married, 3 sons, 4 daus. Helped establish separate services for fellow Negro mems. Methodist Episcopal Ch. of N.Y.C., 1796; organized (with his congregation) African Methodist Episcopal Zion Ch., 1799, dedicated their own meeting house, 1800, became preacher (with Abraham Thompson) after declaring independence from Methodist Episcopal Ch., 1820; dist. chmn. of Conf. held in connection with chs. of Phila., New Haven (Conn.) and L.I. (N.Y.); elected elder, 1822; bishop African Methodist Episcopal Zion Ch., 1822-28. Died 1828.

VARICK, Richard, army officer, mayor N.Y.C.; b. N.J., Mar. 25, 1753; s. Johannes and Jane (Dey) V.; m. Cornelia Hoffman Roosevelt, May 8, 1786, no children. Became capt. 1st N.Y. Regt., 1775, mil. sec. to Gen. Philip John Schuyler; promoted lt. col., later dep. mustermaster-gen. No. Dept., Continental Army; became aide to Benedict Arnold, West Point, 1780; recording sec. to arrange, classify and copy all corr. and records of Continental Army (apptd. by Gen. Washington), 1781-83; recorder of N.Y.C., 1784-86; in charge (with Samuel Jones) of codification N.Y. Statutes, 1786; speaker N.Y. Assembly, 1787-88; atty. gen. N.Y., 1788-89; mayor N.Y.C., 1790-1801; pres. N.Y. Soc. of Cincinnati, 1806-31; an appraiser Erie Canal, 1817; a founder Am. Bible Soc., pres., 1828, 31. Died July 30, 1831.

VARNUM, James Mitchell, army officer, Continental congressman; b. Dracut, Mass., Dec. 17, 1748; s. Maj. Samuel and Hannah (Mitchell) V.; attended Harvard; grad. with honors R.I. Coll. (now Brown U.), 1769; read law in office of Oliver Arnold, R.I.; m. Martha Child, Feb. 8, 1770, no children. Taught sch.; admitted to R.I. bar, 1771; commd. col. Kentish Guards, 1774; col. 1st Regt., R.I. Inf. (later 9th Continental Inf.), 1775; served in seige of Boston, battles of Long Island and White Plains; commd. brig. gen. R.I. Militia, 1776, also brig. gen. Continental Army (confirmed by Gen. Washington); wintered at Valley Forge with Washington, 1777-78; comdr. R.I. Dept., 1779; resigned to revive law practice, 1779; served as maj. gen. R.I. Militia, 1779-88; served irregularly as mem. Continental Congress, 1780-87; early mem. Soc. of Cincinnati; dir. Ohio Co. of Assos.; apptd. U.S. judge for N.W. Territory, 1788-89, assisted in drawing up territorial law. Died Jan. 10, 1789; buried Mound Cemetery, R.I.

VARNUM, John, congressman; b. Dracut, Middlesex County, Mass., June 25, 1778; grad. Harvard, 1798; studied law. Admitted to bar, began practice of law, Haverhill, Mass., 1802; mem. Mass. Senate (Federalist), 1811; moved to Lowell, Mass.; mem. U.S. Ho. of Reps. from Mass., 19th-21st congresses, 1825-31; later moved to Niles, Mich. Died Niles, July 23, 1836; buried Silverbrook Cemetery.

VARNUM, Joseph Bradley, senator; b. Dracut, Mass., Jan. 29, 1750; s. Samuel and Hannah (Mitchell) V.; m. Molly Butler, Jan. 26, 1773, 12 children. Served as capt. Dracut Militia, 1770-74; present at Battle of Lexington; served as capt. Dracut Minute-men, 1776-87, served against Burgoyne, 1777, fought in R.I., 1778; mem. lower house Mass. Legislature, 1780-85, Mass. Senate, 1786-88, 95, 1817-21; served in suppression of Shays' Rebellion, 1786; mem. Mass. Conv. to ratify U.S. Constn., 1788; mem. U.S. Ho .of Reps. from Mass., 4th-12th congresses, 1795-1811, speaker, 10th-11th congresses (charged with corrupt election in 1794); mem. U.S. Senate from Mass., 1811-17, only New Eng. supporter of War Hawks (to bring on War of 1812), pres. pro tem, 1813; del. Mass. Constl. Conv., 1820; mem. Mass. Peace Soc. (later Am. Peace Soc.). Author: An Address Delivered to the Third Division of Massachusetts Militia . . . , 1800. Died Dracut, Sept. 11, 1821; buried Varnum Cemetery, Dracut.

VASEY, George, botanist; b. Scarborough, Yorkshire, Eng., Feb. 28, 1822; brought to N.Y., 1823; attended Oneida (N.Y.) Inst., Berkshire Med. Inst., Pittsfield, Mass.; m. Miss Scott, 1846; m. 2d, Mrs. (Barber) Cameron, 1867; at least 6 children. Practiced medicine, Dexter, N.Y., 1846-48, Elgin and Ringwood, Ill., 1848-66; collected, classified and studied prairie flora; organizer, 1st pres. Ill. Natural History Soc., 1866; accompanied Maj. John Wesley Powell on Colo. bot. expdn., 1868; curator natural history mus. Ill. State Normal U., 1869; became co-editor Am. Entomologist and Botanist, 1870; botanist U.S. Dept. of Agr., 1872, also in charge U.S. Nat. Herbarium. Author: Catalogue of the Forest Trees of the United States Which Usually Attain a Height of Sixteen Feet or More, 1870; Agricultural

Grasses of the United States, 1884; Grasses of the Southwest, 1890-91; Grasses of the Pacific Slope, 1892-93. Died Washington, D.C., Mar. 4, 1893.

VASSALL, John, land speculator; b. Stepney, Middlesex County, Eng., 1625; s. William and Anne (King) V.; m. Anne Lewis, at least 2 children, Samuel, Leonard. Came to Roxbury, Mass., 1635, then moved to Scituate; mem. Scituate Militia, 1643, promoted lt., 1652; procured (with aid of brother Henry in London) land for colonial settlement in area of Cape Fear (now N.C.); began colonial enterprise, 1664; apptd. surveyor gen., 1664; moved (because of failure of colony) to Jamaica, B.W.I., 1672; maintained his connection with N. Am. colonies by nature of his large land holdings and trading activities. Died Jamaica, July 1688.

VASSAR, Matthew, brewer; b. East Tuddingham, Eng., Apr. 29, 1792; s. James and Anne (Bennett) V.; m. Catherine Valentine, Mar. 7, 1813, no children. Brought to Am., family settled in Dutchess County, N.Y., 1796; farm laborer and store clk., 1805-08; returned to family brewery, Poughkeepsie, N.Y., 1808; founded own brewing firm, 1811, also speculated in Mich. lands and whaling; travelled in Europe, 1845; constructed bldg. for Vassar Coll., 1861-65, opened, supported and quickly proved the worth of a women's coll. on par with contemporary men's instns., 1865, gave over $800,000 to coll. during lifetime; wrote autobiography, published posthumously, 1916. Died June 23, 1868.

VATTEMARE, Nicolas Marie Alexandre, ventriloquist; b. Paris, France, Nov. 8, 1796; married, at least 2 sons including Hippolyte. Began to practice ventriloquism, Germany, 1814; appeared as ventriloquist, London, Eng., 1822; presented shows in U.S. and Can., 1839-41; sent meml. to Congress suggesting system of exchange between museums and libraries of various countries, 1840; returned (with many items for exchange) to France, 1841; expanded internat. exchange procedures, 1841-47; returned to U.S., 1847; managed his appointment as Congressional agt. to enlarge exchange mechanisms; must be credited with idea of exchanges, though his system as devised was unsuccessful even in his own lifetime; enthusiastic supporter of public libraries; asso. with founding of Boston Public Library; named chevalier Legion d'Honneur. Author: Album Cosmopolite, 1837; Report on the Subject of International Exchanges, 1848. Died Paris, Apr. 7, 1864.

VAUDREUIL-CAVAGNAL, Pierre de Rigaud (Marquis de Vaudreuil), colonial gov.; b. Can., 1704; s. Philippe Rigaud (Marquis de Vaudreuil) and Louise Elizabeth (de Joybert) de Vaudreuil; married, no children. Served as maj. French Colonial Army, 1726, participated in Sieur de Lignery expdn. against Fox Indians in Wis., 1728; decorated Croix de St. Louis, 1730; gov. Trois Rivières, New France, 1733-43; gov. La., 1743-53; gov. New France, 1755-60, his incapabilities substantially contbd. to French loss of New France; countermanded Gen. Montcalm's orders at Plains of Abraham, 1759 (important factor in French defeat); took charge after Montcalm's death, surrendered Montreal, 1760; returned to Paris, France, imprisoned, 1760; acquitted of dishonesty in subsequent trial, 1761, but not of culpability. Died Paris, Aug. 4, 1778.

VAUGHAN, Benjamin, polit. economist; b. Jamaica, Apr. 30, 1751; s. Samuel and Sarah (Hallowell) V.; ed. Cambridge (Eng.) U.; read law Inner Temple, London, Eng.; studied medicine, Edinburgh, Scotland; hon. degrees Harvard, 1807, Bowdoin Coll., 1812; m. Sarah Manning, June 30, 1781, 3 sons, 4 daus. Propagandized for independence during Am. Revolution; joined father-in-law's mcht. firm; unofcl. mem. Brit. commn. which concluded Treaty of Paris, 1782; supported free trade, French Revolution; became mem. Parliament from Calne, 1792; escaped to France when he feared investigation of French Revolution supporters; imprisoned in France, 1794, soon released to Switzerland; came to Am., settled in Hallowell, Me., 1796; maintained wide correspondence with Am. polit. figures; founder Me. Hist. Soc.; mem. many lit. and sci. socs.; owned largest individually-owned library in New Eng. (divided after his death among Harvard, Bowdoin Coll. and Augusta Insane Hosp.). Author: Letters on the Subject of the Concert of Princes and the Dismemberment of Poland and France, 1793. Editor: Political, Miscellaneous and Philosophical Pieces . . . written by Benjamin Franklin, 1779. Died Dec. 8, 1835.

VAUGHAN, Charles, mcht., real estate promoter; b. London, Eng., June 30, 1759; s. Samuel and Sarah (Hallowell) V.; m. Frances Western Apthorp, 1790, at least 2 sons, 2 daus. Raised on father's plantation, Jamaica; moved to New Eng., 1785; partly successful developer of town sites on Kennebec River in Me.; went to Eng. to attempt to publicize his speculative ventures, 1790-91; mcht. in Boston, 1791-96, went bankrupt, 1798; incorporator Boston Library Soc., Mass. Soc. for Promoting Agr., Mass. Soc. for Aid of Immigrants, Hallowell Acad. Died May 15, 1839.

VAUGHAN, Daniel, educator, mathematician; b. Glenomara, Ireland, 1818; s. John Vaughan. Came to U.S., 1840; tutor to Col. Stamp, Bourbon County, Ky., 1842; prof. Greek coll. in Bardstown, Ky., 1845-50; moved to Cincinnati, 1850; lectr. chemistry Eclectic Med. Inst., 1850; mem. A.A.A.S., 1851; lectured widely on astronomy and other scientific topics; prof. chemistry Cincinnati Coll. Medicine and surgery, 1860-72; contributed frequently to Proceedings of A.A.A.S. Author: Destiny of the Solar System, 1854. Died Apr. 6, 1879.

VAUGHAN, William Wirt, congressman, lawyer; b. LaGuardo (now Martha), Tenn., July 2, 1831; grad. Cumberland U., Lebanon, Tenn.; studied law. Admitted to bar, began practice of law, Brownsville, Tenn.; mem. U.S. Ho. of Reps. (Democrat) from Tenn., 42d Congress, 1871-73; a builder branch of C.& O. Ry. from Brownsville to Newbern, became pres. of system. Died Crockett Mills, Tenn. (while campaigning for election to 46th Congress), Aug. 19, 1878; buried Oakwood Cemetery, Brownsville.

VAUX, Calvert, landscape architect; b. London, Eng., Dec. 20, 1824; s. Calvert Bowyer and Emily (Brickwood) V.; m. Mary Swan McEntee, May 4, 1854, 4 children including Mrs. G.L. Hendrickson, Architect to assist Jackson Downing, Newburgh, N.Y., 1850-52, assisted in design grounds about U.S. Capitol and Smithsonian Instn., Washington, D.C.; collaborator with Frederick Law Olmsted to submit design for Central Park, N.Y.C., 1857, design accepted; collaborator with Olmsted in design of Prospect Park (Bklyn.), Morningside Park, Riverside Park (N.Y.C.), South Park (Chgo.); landscape architect to N.Y.C. Dept. Pub. Parks; 1888-95; an architect for 1st bldgs. for Mus. of Art, Mus. of Natural History (both N.Y.C.). Author: Villas and Cottages: a Series of Designs Prepared for Execution in the United States, 1857, revised, 1864, reprinted, 1867. Died Graves-end Bay nr. N.Y.C., Nov. 19, 1895.

VAUX, Richard, penologist, congressman; b. Phila., Dec. 19, 1816; s. Roberts and Margaret (Wistar) V.; m. Mary Waln, Mar. 12, 1840, 1 son, 4 daus. Admitted to Phila. bar, 1837; sec. legation ad interim, London, Eng., circa 1837, later pvt. sec. to minister to Eng.; returned to Phila., 1839; del. Pa. Democratic Conv., 1840; insp. Eastern Penitentiary, mem. gov. bd., 1839-92, pres. 1852-92; mem. bd. controllers Phila. Public Schs.; recorder Phila., 1841-47, had no decisions reversed on appeal; mayor Phila., 1856; bd. dirs. Girard Coll., 1859, pres. bd., 1862-65, instrumental in introducing vocational and tech. tng. into coll. curriculum; mem. U.S. Ho. of Reps. from Pa., 51st Congress, May 20, 1890-91; grand master Pa. Grand Lodge Masons; pres. Phila. Club, 1888-94; mem. Hist. Soc. Pa., Am. Philos. Soc.; initiated wearing of gowns by Phila. judiciary. Author: Brief Sketch of the Origin and History of State Penitentiary for Eastern District of Pennsylvania, at Philadelphia, 1872; Short Talks on Crime-Cause and Convict Punishment, 1882. Died Mar. 22, 1895.

VAUX, Roberts, philanthropist; b. Phila., Jan. 21, 1786; s. Richard and Ann (Roberts) V.; m. Margaret Wistar, Nov. 30, 1814, 2 children including Richard. Mcht., Phila., 1807-14, ret., 1814; mem. Phila. Common Council, 1814-16; pres. Bd. Controllers of Public Schs. Phila., 1818-31; officer Phila. Soc. for Alleviating Miseries of Public Prisons; mem. commn. which planned Phila. Eastern Penitentiary, 1821; a founder ho. of refuge for juvenile delinquents, 1826; mgr. Pa. Hosp.; pres. Pa. State Temperance Soc.; v.p. U.S. Temperance Conv.; a founder Frankford Asylum for Insane, Phila. Saving Fund Soc., Phila. Hose Co., Apprentices' Library Co.; active Acad. Natural Scis., Linneaen Soc., Franklin Inst., Athenaeum, Hist. Soc. Pa.; justice Ct. of Common Pleas, 1835. Author: Memoirs of the Life of Anthony Benezet, 1817; Notices of the Original, and Successive, Efforts to Improve the Discipline of the Prison at Philadelphia: with a Few Observations on the Penitentiary System, 1826. Died Jan. 7, 1836.

VEAZEY, Thomas Ward, gov. Md.; b. Cecil County, Md., Jan. 31, 1774; son of Edward Veazey; grad. Washington Coll., Chestertown, Md., 1795; m. Sarah Worrell, Nov. 18, 1794; m. 2d, Mary Veazey; m. 3d, Mary Wallace, Sept. 24, 1812; at least 11 children. Settled on family plantation "Cherry Grove," Cecil County; presdl. elector, 1808, 12; mem. Md. Ho. of Dels., 1811-12; served as lt. col. Md. Militia in 2d war with Eng., 1812-14; mem. Gov.'s Council, 1833-35; gov. Md. (Whig), 1836-38. Died "Cherry Grove," July 1, 1842.

VENABLE, Abraham Bedford, senator, congressman; b. nr. Prince Edward Court House (now Worsham), Va., Nov. 20, 1758; attended Hampden-Sydney (Va.) Coll.; grad. Princeton, 1780; studied law. Engaged in planting, Prince Edward County, Va.; admitted to bar, 1784, began practice of law, Prince Edward Court House; mem. U.S. Ho. of Reps. from Va., 2d-5th congresses, 1791-99; mem. U.S. Senate (filled vacancy) from Va., Dec. 7, 1803-June 7, 1804 (resigned); became pres. of 1st nat. bank organized in Va., 1804. Died in theater fire, Richmond, Va., Dec. 26, 1811; ashes buried (with those of other fire victims) under stone in front of altar in Monumental Ch., Richmond.

VENABLE, Abraham Watkins, congressman, lawyer; b. Springfield, Prince Edward County, Va., Oct. 17, 1799; grad. Hampden-Sydney (Va.) Coll., 1816; studied medicine, 2 years; grad. Princeton, 1819; studied law. Admitted to bar, 1821, began practice of law, Prince Edward and Mecklenburg counties, Va.; moved to N.C., 1829; Democratic presdl. elector, 1832, 36, 60; mem. U.S. Ho. of Reps. (Democrat) from N.C., 30th-32d congresses, 1847-53; del. from N.C. to Provisional Confederate Congress, 1861; mem. Confederate Ho. of Reps., 1862-64. Died Oxford, N.C., Feb. 24, 1876; buried Shiloh Presbyn. Churchyard, Granville County, N.C.

VERBECK, Guido Herman Fridolin, missionary; b. Zeist, Netherlands, Jan. 23, 1830; s. Carl and Ann (Kellerman) Verbeek; attended Polytechnic Inst. of Utrecht; attended Presbyn. Theol. Sem., Auburn, N.Y., 1855-59; D.D. (hon.), Rutgers U., 1875; m. Maria Manion, Apr. 18, 1859, at least 7 children including William. Came to U.S., 1862 settled in Wis., then Bklyn.; ordained to ministry Dutch Reformed Ch., 1859-98, sent as missionary to Nagasaki, Japan, 1859, baptized 1st two converts, 1866; established a small sch. teaching English by means of Bible; head of sch. which laid foundations for Imperial U., Yedo (now Tokyo), Japan, 1869; Iwakura mission sent to Am. and Europe partly as result of his suggestion, 1871-73; translated or supervised translation for Japanese Govt. of Code Napoleon, the consts. of many Western states, numerous Western laws, legal documents, treatises on law; decorated by Emperor of Japan; preached, taught in theol. sch. which later became part of the Meiji Gauin; lectr. at govt. sch. for nobles; helped prepare a hymn book, other religious literature; assisted in translating Bible into Japanese. Died Tokyo, Mar. 10, 1898.

VERENDRYE, Sieur de la, see La Verendrye, Pierre Gaultier de Varennes.

VERGENNES, comte de, see Gravier, Charles.

VERHAEGEN, Peter Joseph, clergyman, coll. pres.; b. Haecht, Flanders, June 21, 1800. Came to Phila., 1821; entered novitiate of Jesuits at Whitemarsh, Md., 1821; ordained priest at Sem. of Barrens in Perry County, Mo., 1825; rector acad. at St. Louis, 1829, obtained act incorporating it as St. Louis U., 1832, prof. dogmatic and moral theology; superior of Indian missions (described in article "The Indian Missions of the United States under the Care of the Missouri Province of the Society of Jesus"), 1836-44; pres. St. Joseph's Coll., Bardstown, Ky., 1874-50; pastor, St. Charles, Mo., 1850-68. Died July 21, 1868.

VERNON, Samuel, silversmith; b. Narragansett, R.I., Dec. 6, 1683; s. Daniel and Ann Hutchinson (Dyre) V.; m. Elizabeth Fleet, Apr. 10, 1707, 8 children including William. Silversmith in R.I., work represented in collections in Victoria and Albert Museum, London, Eng.; signed work with mark of heart containing initials in Roman capitals over a fleur-de-lis; engraved plates for 1st indented bills of credit of 1st bank established by Colony of R.I. and Providence Plantations, 1715; asst. in R.I. Gen. Ct., 1729-37; judge Superior Ct. of Judicature. Died Dec. 5, 1737.

VERNON, William, mcht.; b. Newport, R.I., Jan. 17, 1719; s. Samuel and Elizabeth (Fleet) V.; m. Judith Harwood, 3 children, Samuel, William H., Philip. Partner with brother in firm Samuel and William Vernon, Newport, 1744-73, active in slave, rum and molasses trade, firm engaged in privateering in King George's War, owned privateer Duke of Marlborough; apptd. (with others) by R.I. Assembly to petition King about cod fisheries, 1773; mem. local com. of correspondence, 1774; mem. com. apptd. to gather information on Brit. depredations, 1775; chmn. Eastern Navy Bd. in charge of 4 Eastern states under direction of Marine Com., 1777; 2d pres. Redwood Library, Newport; benefactor Coll. of N.J. (now Princeton). Died Newport, Dec. 22, 1806.

VEROT, Jean Marcel Pierre Auguste, clergyman; b. Le Puy, France, May 23, 1805; ed. St. Sulpice, Paris, France. Ordained priest Roman Catholic Ch., 1828; came to U.S., 1830; tchr., St. Mary's Coll. and Sem., Balt., 1830-54; pastor, Ellicott's Mills, Md., Sykesville, Pa., Clarksville and Doughoregan Manor, 1854-58; vicar-apostolic of Fla., 1858-61, virtually a missionary, established schs., improved chs., encouraged nuns and priests to emigrate to area; transferred to Savannah, Ga. (retained control of Fla.), 1861; begged throughout the North following Civil War; opposed papal infallibility at Vatican Council, 1870. Died June 10, 1876.

VERPLANCK, Daniel Crommelin, congressman, lawyer; b. N.Y.C., Mar. 19, 1762; grad. Columbia, 1788; studied law. Admitted to bar, began practice of law, N.Y.C., 1789; also a banker; mem. U.S. Ho. of Reps. (Federalist, filled vacancy) from N.Y., 8th-10th congresses, Oct. 17, 1803-09; judge Dutchess County Ct. of Common Pleas, 1828-30. Died at his home "Mt. Gulian," nr. Fishkill, N.Y., Mar. 29, 1834; buried Trinity Ch. Cemetery, Fishkill.

VERPLANCK, Gulian Crommelin, congressman; b. N.Y.C., Aug. 6, 1786; s. Daniel C. and Elizabeth (Johnson) V.; grad. Columbia, 1801; read law under Josiah O. Hoffman; m. Mary Elizabeth Fenno, Oct. 2, 1811, 2 sons including Julian Crommelin. Admitted to N.Y. bar, 1807; involved in Columbia commencement riot, 1811, fined by presiding judge De Witt Clinton, became and remained polemical enemy of Clinton; travelled in Europe, 1815-17; co-founder (with Charles King) N.Y. American, 1817; mem. N.Y. State Assembly, 1820-22; prof. Gen. Theol. Sem. of Episcopal Ch., N.Y.C., 1821-24; mem. U.S. Ho. of Reps. (Democrat) from N.Y., 19th-22d congresses, 1825-33, chmn. ways and means com., 1831-33, chiefly instrumental in obtaining law to improve authors' copyrights, 1831; mem. bd. regents U. State N.Y., 1826-70, vice-chancellor, 1858-70; editor Talisman, 1828; mem. N.Y. Senate, 1838-41; pres. Bd. Commrs. of Emigration, 1848-70. Author: A Fable for Statesmen and Politicians, 1815; The State Triumvirate, a Political Tale, and the Epistles of Brevet Major Pindar Puff, 1819; Essays on the Nature and Uses of the Various Evidences of Revealed Religion, 1824; Discourses and Addresses on Subjects of American History, Arts, and Literature, 1833; Shakespeare's Plays: with His Life, 1847. Died N.Y.C., Mar. 18, 1870; buried Trinity Churchyard, Fishkill, Dutchess County, N.Y.

VERRAZANO, Giovanni da, explorer; b. Val di Greve, Italy, circa 1480. Entered naval service of Francis I of France, became well known privateer, especially against Spanish treasure ships; sent by Francis on exploratory trip to New World, 1524; perhaps author of letter which describes N.Y. harbor, Hudson River and New Eng. coast. May have been killed by Indians on a trip to West Indies, 1526; or may have been captured off coast of Cadiz, 1527 and executed as pirate (under name Juan Florin) at Puerto del Pico, Spain, Nov. 1527.

VERREE, John Paul, congressman, mfr.; b. "Verree Mills," Pennypack Creek, nr. what is now Fox Chase Station, Phila., Mar. 9, 1817. Became iron mfr., later dealer in edged tools, iron and steel; mem. Phila. Select Council, 1851-57, pres., 1853-57; mem. U.S. Ho. of Reps. (Republican) from Pa., 36th-37th congresses, 1859-63; pres. of life ins. co.; pres. Phila. Union League, 1875-76. Died "Verree Mills," June 27, 1889; buried Cedar Hill Cemetery, Frankford (now part of Phila.).

VERY, Jones, poet; b. Salem, Mass., Aug. 28, 1813; s. Jones and Lydia (Very) V.; grad. Harvard, 1836. Asst., Fisk Latin Sch. of Henry Kemble Oliver, 1832; freshmen Greek tutor Harvard; overcome by religious ecstasy, began writing religious verse, 1837; spent month in McLean Asylum, 1838; championed by Emerson, other transcendalists; wrote sonnets published in Western Messenger, 1839; published book Essays and Poems, 1839; licensed to preach by Cambridge Assn., 1843; held temporary pastorates in Eastport, Me., North Beverly, Mass. Died a self-proclaimed "failure," Salem, May 8, 1880.

VESEY, Denmark, insurrectionist; b. Africa, 1767. Slave belonging to slave dealer Capt. Vesey, 1780-1800; purchased freedom with part of $1500 lottery prize won in 1800; opened carpenter shop, Charleston, S.C.; admitted to Second Presbyn. Ch., Charleston, 1817; joined African Methodist congregation; planned slave uprising intended to take over city, 1818-22, conspiracy collapsed when a slave betrayed plot; court of 2 magistrates and 5 freeholders convened as judge and jury to try suspects, Vesey and 35 compatriots hanged, 34 sent out of state, 61 acquitted, 4 whites fined for their part in plot. Died Charleston, July 2, 1822.

VESEY, William, clergyman; b. Braintree, Mass., Aug. 10, 1674; s. William and Mary V.; grad. Harvard, 1693; M.A. (hon.), Merton Coll., Oxford, Eng., 1697; m. Mary Reade, 1698. Ordained priest Anglican Ch. by Bishop of London, 1697; pastor Trinity Ch., N.Y.C., 1697-1746, went to England to lay case before Bishop of London as result of disagreements about church policy, 1714, exonerated; became bishop's commissary in N.Y. and N.J., 1714-46; cooperated with Soc. for Propogation of Gospel in Fgn. Parts in providing missionaries and teachers for poor; established charity school in connection with Trinity; Vesey and Rector streets (N.Y.C.) named for him. Died N.Y.C., July 11, 1746.

VESPUCCI, Amerigo, navigator; b. Florence, Italy, Mar. 9, 1451; son of Nastogio Vespucci. Employed by comml. house of Medici, for a time; accompanied Alonso de Ojeda on expdn., 1499-1500, separated from Ojeda, and he alone discovered and explored mouth of Amazon River, then sailed along coast of No. South America; entered service of Portugal, 1501; made voyage on which he discovered mouth of Rio De La Plata, explored 6,000 miles of S.Am. coastline, 1501-02; on this trip calculated new method of determining longitude, also calculated earth's equatorial circumference (only 50 miles short of correct figure); also proved that S.Am. was separate continent, not part of Asia; name America (in his honor) was 1st applied to New World by Martin Waldseemüller in Cosmographiae introductio, 1507. Died of malaria, Seville, Spain, Feb. 22, 1512.

VETCH, Samuel, trader, army officer; b. Edinburgh, Scotland, Dec. 9, 1668; s. William and Marion (Fairly) Veitch; ed. Coll. Utrecht (Holland); m. Margaret Livingston, Dec. 20, 1700. Capt. in a Scottish regt.; mem. William Paterson's Trading Co., 1698; mem. Darien (C.Am.), Colonial Council; went to N.Y.C., 1699; Indian trader, Albany, N.Y., with bus. including illegal trade overland with French at Montreal; trader in Boston, circa 1702, engaged in maritime commerce with Acadia and Can., contrary to Brit. trade laws; went to Que. to negotiate truce with gov. Can. and arrange prisoner exchange, 1705; tried by Mass. Gen. Ct. and fined, 1706, carried case to Eng. where Privy Council ruled that Mass. Gen. Ct. (being legislative body) had no power to try cases, and ordered retrial by Suffolk County Ct.; proposed plan for conquering French in America via Lake Champlain and St. Lawrence River; conquered Nova Scotia, became mil. gov., 1710-14; took part in unsuccessful expdn. against Can., 1711, fled to Eng., 1714; civil gov. N.S., 1715-17. Died in Debtor's Prison, London, Eng., Apr. 30, 1732.

VETHAKE, Henry, economist, coll. pres.; b. Essequibo County, Brit. Guiana, 1792; grad. Columbia, 1808; m. 1836. Came to U.S., 1796; tchr. mathematics and geography Columbia, 1810-13; prof. mathematics and natural history philosophy Queens Coll. (now Rutgers U.), 1813-17; taught at Princeton, 1817-21, Dickinson Coll., 1821-29; prof. moral philosophy Coll. of N.J., 1829-32; prof. U. of City of N.Y., 1832-35; pres. Washington Coll., Lexington, Va., 1835-36, prof. intellectual and moral philosophy; prof. mathematics and philosophy U. Pa., 1836-55, prof. philosophy, 1855-59, vice provost, 1845-55, provost, 1855-59; prof. mathematics Poly. Coll. Phila., 1859-66; mem. Am. Philos. Soc. Author: Introductory Lecture on the Political Economy, 1831; The Principles of Political Economy, 1838, 44; edited and published McCulloch's A Dictionary, Practical, Theoretical and Historical, of Commerce and Commercial Navigation, 1840; contbr. to Encyclopedia Americana, Supplementary Vol., 1848. Died Phila. Dec. 16, 1866.

VIBBARD, Chauncey, railroad exec., congressman; b. Galway, N.Y., Nov. 11, 1811; s. Timothy and Abigail (Nash) V.; m. Mary Vedder, at least 3 children. Chief clk. Utica & Schenectady R.R., 1836, gen. supr., stockholder, 1849, drew up 1st railroad timetable followed in N.Y., increased comfort of passenger travel, urged consolidation of roads between Albany and Buffalo, resulted N.Y. Central R.R., 1853, gen. supt. consol. line, 1853-65; mem. U.S. Ho. of Reps. (Democrat) from N.Y., 27th Congress, 1861-63; dir., supt. mil. railroads, 1862; partner Vibbard & Foote, dealers railroad supplies; Dem. presdl. elector, 1864; an owner Day Line (steamboats) between N.Y.C. and Albany; 1st pres. Family Fund Ins. Co., 1864-67; an original stockholder in N.Y.C.'s 1st elevated railway; dir. Central br. Union Pacific R.R.; interested in devel. of Southern (U.S.) railroads, also enterprises in S. Am. and Central Am. Died Macon, Ga., June 5, 1891; buried Riverside Cemetery, Macon.

VICK, James, nurseryman, publisher; b. Chichester, Eng., Nov. 23, 1818; s. James and Elizabeth (Prime) V.; m. Mary Elizabeth Seelye, July 5, 1842, 7 children. Came to U.S., 1833; worked on Knickerbocker Mag.; moved to Rochester, N.Y., 1837; owned paper Workingman's Advocate; published Frederick Douglass' paper North Star; began to import seed from abroad, 1848; under signature of "Young Digger" contributed articles to Genesee Farmer, an editor, 1850; purchased mag. Horticulturist, publisher, 1853-55; editor Rural New Yorker, 1857-62; abandoned literary work for seed business by 1862; wrote Floral Guide (annual catalogue), reached 200,000 copies; founder, editor Vick's Monthly Mag., 1878, later Vick's Illustrated Monthly Mag.; made advances in cross breeding of garden flowers, among his creations white double phlox, fringed petunia, white gladiolus, "sunrise" amaranthus, Japanese cockscomb; his name commemorated in Vick Park and Portsmouth Terrace (named after his birthplace), Rochester; sec. Am. Pomological Soc., 1862-64; corr. mem. Royal Hort. Soc.; supt. Sunday sch., 25 years. Died Rochester, N.Y., May 16, 1882; buried Mt. Hope Cemetery, Rochester.

VICKERS, George, senator, lawyer; b. Chestertown, Kent County, Md., Nov. 19, 1801; studied law. Admitted to bar, 1832, began practice of law, Chestertown; del. Whig Nat. Conv., Balt., 1852; served as maj. gen. Md. Militia, 1861; Democratic presdl. elector, 1864; v.p. Union Nat. Conv. of Conservatives, Phila., 1866; mem. Md. Senate, 1866-67; mem. U.S. Senate (Democrat, filled vacancy) from Md., Mar. 7, 1868-73. Died Chestertown, Oct. 8, 1879; buried Chester Cemetery.

VICTOR, Frances Fuller, historian; b. Rome Twp., N.Y., May 23, 1826; d. Adonijah and Lucy (Williams) Fuller; m. Jackson Barritt, 1853; m. 2d, Henry Clay Victor, 1862. Family moved to Ohio, 1839; wrote a vol. of verse with her sister called Poems of Sentiment and Imagination, with Dramatic and Descriptive Pieces, 1851; moved to San Francisco, 1863, Portland, Ore., 1865, wrote books on this region including The River of the West, 1870, All Over Oregon and Washington, 1872; asst. to Henry Hubert Bancroft in preparation of History of the Northwest Coast, 2 vols., 1884, History of Oregon, 2 vols., 1886-88, History of Washington, Idaho, and Montana, 1890, History of Nevada, Colorado and Wyoming, 1890; author: The Early Indian Wars of Oregon, 1894; Poems, 1900. Died Portland, Nov. 14, 1902.

VICTOR, Metta Victoria Fuller, author; b. Erie, Pa., Mar. 2, 1831; d. Henry and Lucy (Williams) Fuller; attended sem., Wooster, O., 1830-circa 1841; m. Orville J. Victor, 1854. Wrote her 1st story at age 13, was writing fiction professionally by 1846; contbr. (under pseudonym Singing Sybil) to N.Y. Home Journal, Saturday Evening Post, Saturday Evening Bulletin, from 1846; popular writer of serials and novels (some published anonymously), from 1850's. Author: The Senator's Son, 1853; Too True, 1860; Figure Eight, 1869; The Gold Hunters, 1874; Dead Letter, 1874; Bad Boy's Diary, 1880; The Rasher Family, 1884. Died Hohokus, N.J., June 26, 1886.

VIDAL, Michel, congressman, diplomat; b. Carcassonne, Languedoc, France, Oct. 1, 1824; attended coll. Came to Republic of Tex. during adminstrn. of Pres. Anson Jones; moved to La. when Tex. was annexed to U.S.; engaged in literary and scientific activities; asso. editor of several Am. and French papers, U.S. and Can.; moved to Opelousas, La., 1867; founder, editor St. Landry Progress; editor N.Y. Courier des États-Unis, New Orleans Picayune; apptd. registrar for City of New Orleans, at end of Civil War; del. La. Constl. Conv., 1867, 68; mem. U.S. Ho. of Reps. (Republican) from La., 40th Congress, July 18, 1868-69; apptd. U.S. commr. under conv. concluded with Peru, 1868; U.S. consul at Tripoli (apptd. by Pres. Grant), 1870-76.

VIEL, (Francois) Etienne Bernard Alexandre, clergyman, educator; b. New Orleans, Oct. 31, 1736; s. Dr. Bernard Alexandre and Marie (Macarthy) V.; grad. Royal Acad. of Juilly (France), circa 1756. Joined Oratorians (1st native born Louisianian to take holy orders); sent as instr. to Soissons, then to Mans; tchr. humanities and rhetoric at Royal Acad., grand prefet, 1778; returned to La., 1792; parish priest of Attakapas (La.), 1792-1812; went to France to aid in reestablishment of his order, 1812, tchr. at Royal Acad. Translator: Fenelon's Telemaque (from French into rhymed Latin version), 1797; Le Voyage de la Grande Chartreuse, 1787. Died Royal Acad., Juilly, Dec. 16, 1821.

VIELE, Aernout Cornelissen, trader; b. New Amsterdam (now N.Y.C.), May 27, 1640; probably son of Cornelis Volkertszen and Maria (du Trieux) V.; m. Gerritje Gerritse Vermeulen, 1663, at least 2 children including Aernout. Joined in petition to forbid white men trading within Indian Country; spl. envoy to Iroquois Indians at conf. between 5 Nations and Md. commrs., Albany, N.Y., 1682; led large party of advance agts. of N.Y. trade into Ottawa country north of Gt. Lakes; captured by French, taken to Quebec (Can.); lived with Onondaga Indians, 1688-90, which led to Iroquoiqs allegiance to colonists rather than French; made effort to protect N.Y. border; enrolled as fusilier, 1691; held large land grants in central N.Y. and along Hudson River. Died N.Y.C., 1704.

VIGO, Joseph Maria Francesco, (known as Francis Vigo), army officer, fur trader; b. Mondoni, Piedmont, Italy, Dec. 3, 1747; s. Matheo and Maria Magdalena (Iugalibus) V.; m. Elizabeth Shannon, before 1783. Engaged in New Orleans-St. Louis fur trade; reached post at St. Louis, ultimately formed secret partnership with Fernando de Leyba (Spanish gov. of St. Louis); twice journeyed to Kaskaskia from St. Louis to give assistance to George Rogers Clark during Revolutionary War; executor under will of Gov. de Leyba, 1780; Vigo County (Ind.) named for him. Died Vincennes, Ind., Mar. 22, 1836; buried Protestant Cemetery, Vincennes.

VILLAGRÁ, Gaspar Perez de, see Perez de Villagrá, Gaspar.

VILLARD, Henry (Ferdinand Heinrich Gustav Hilgard), journalist, railroad exec.; b. Speyer, Bavaria, Apr. 10, 1835; s. Gustav Leonhard and Katherina Antonia Elisabeth (Pfeiffer) Hilgard; attended univs. Munich, Wurstburg; m. Helen Frances Garrison, Jan. 3, 1866, at least 3 children. Came to U.S., 1853, took name Villard; travelled to Cincinnati, Chgo., and to relatives in Belleville, Ill.; read law, sold books, edited a small paper, 1855-56; spl. correspondent for Staats Zeitung of N.Y., 1858, covered Lincoln-Douglas senatorial debates, became friend of Lincoln; reporter for Cincinnati Comml., 1859-60, went to Pike's Peak gold region as reporter; covered Campaign of 1860 for Comml., also for St. Louis Daily Mo. Democrat and N.Y. Herald; corr. for N.Y. Herald and N.Y. Tribune during Civil War, 1861-63; Washington corr. Chgo. Daily Tribune, 1864-65; free lance writer, 1865-68; sec. Am. Social Sci. Assn., 1868-71; traveled in Germany, 1871-73; went to Ore. to represent com. for protection of bondholders of Ore. & Cal. R.R., 1874; became pres. Ore. & Cal. R.R. and Ore. S.S. Co., 1876; gained control of N.P. R.R., 1880-81, became dir., 1888; in Germany, 1884-86; saved Ore. & Transcontinental R.R. with German capital, 1887; financed Edison Gen. Electric Co., 1889. Died Dobbs Ferry, N.Y., Nov. 12, 1900.

VILLERE, Jacques Philippe, gov. La.; b. Parish St. John the Baptist, La., Apr. 28, 1761; s. Joseph Roy and Louise Marguerite (de la Chaise) V.; m. Jeanne Henriette Fazende, 1784. Served as lt. of arty. in Santo Domingo; leading sugar planter New Orleans; commd. maj. gen. La. Militia, 1815; mem. La. Constl. Conv. (framed 1st constitution for State of La.), 1812; gov. La., 1816-20 (1st Creole to hold that position); advanced opinion that yellow fever was not due directly to climate, observed that La. prisoners segregated from city did not become victims; during his administration state debt paid off and $40,000 surplus accumulated. Died on his plantation outside New Orleans, Mar. 7, 1830.

VIMEUR, Jean Baptiste Donatien de (comte de Rochambeau), army officer; b. Vendôme, France, July 1, 1725; s. Joseph Charles (comte de Rochambeau) and Claire (Begon) de Vimeur; attended Collège de Vendôme; m. Jeanne d'Acosta, Dec. 1749. Served in War of Austrian Succession, Seven Years War; promoted brig. gen., 1761, became insp. cavalry; apptd. gov. Villefrancheen-Roussillon, 1776; came to Am. as comdr. French troops in Am. Revolution, sailed from Brest to Newport, R.I., with 6,000 men, 1780; joined Continental Army under Washington at White Plains, N.Y., 1781; beseiged Cornwallis at Yorktown, aided in gaining his surrender, Oct. 1781; returned to France, 1783; became comdr. of important mil. dist. with hdqrs. at Calais, France; active mem. Soc. of Cincinnati; mem. 2d Assembly of Notables; made comdr. dist. of Alsace (France); placed in charge of No. Mil. Dept., 1790; created marshal of France, 1791; honored by Napoleon; mem. Legion of Honor. Author: Memoirs, published Paris, 1809, in English, 1838. Died Alsace, May 10, 1807; buried Thoré, France.

VINCENNES, sieur de, see Bissot, Jean Baptiste.

VINCENNES, sieur de, see Bissot, François Marie.

VINCENT, Mary Ann Farlow, actress; b. Portsmouth, Eng., Sept. 18, 1818; d. John Farlow; m. James R. Vincent, Aug. 1835; m. 2d, John Wilson, 1854. Made theatrical debut as chambermaid in The Review, or the Wags of Windsor, in Cowes, Isle of Wight, 1835; played Volante in The Honeymoon; after marriage known on stage as Mrs. J.R. Vincent; came to Am. with husband, 1846; played Miss Biffin in Popping the Question, 1846; appeared at theatre of Boston Museum as mem. stock co., 1852-87; played Nancy Sikes in Oliver Twist, Mrs. Malaprop in The Rivals, Mrs. Candour in School for Scandal, Maria in Twelfth Night, Goneril in King Lear, Queen Gertrude in Hamlet, Mrs. Hardcastle in She Stoops to Conquer, Mrs. Pontifex in Naval Engagements; Vincent Meml. Hosp. (Boston) founded in her memory, 1891; Vincent Club (of young society women) named for her. Died Boston, Sept. 4, 1887; interred Mt. Auburn Cemetery, Cambridge, Mass.

VINING, John, senator, congressman; b. Dover, Kent County, Del., Dec. 23, 1758; studied law. Admitted to bar, 1782, began practice of law, New Castle County; mem. Continental Congress from Del., 1784-86; mem. Md. Ho. of Reps., 1787-88; mem. U.S. Ho. of Reps. from Del., 1st-2d congresses, 1789-93; mem. Del. Senate, 1793; mem. U.S. Senate from Del., 1793-Jan. 19, 1798 (resigned). Died Dover, Feb. 1802; buried Episcopal Cemetery.

VINTON, Alexander Hamilton, clergyman; b. Providence, R.I., May 2, 1807; s. David and Mary (Atwell) V.; attended Brown U., 3 years; M.D., Yale, 1828; attended Gen. Theol. Sem., N.Y.C.; m. Eleanor Stockbridge Thompson, Oct. 15, 1835, 6 children. Practiced medicine, Pomfret, Conn., 1828-32; turned to ministry, 1834, ordained deacon Protestant Episcopal Ch., 1835, priest, 1836, in charge ch., Portland, Me.; rector Grace Ch., Providence, 1836-42, St. Paul's Ch., Boston, 1842-58, Holy Trinity, Phila., 1858-61, St. Mark's, N.Y.C., 1861-69, Emmanuel Ch., Boston, 1869-77; mem. Mass. Bd. Edn., 1851; lectr. Cambridge (Mass.) Divinity Sch., 1877; a signer Muhlenberg Meml.; pres. 1st Am. Ch. Congress, 1870. Died Phila., Apr. 26, 1881.

VINTON, Francis, clergyman; b. Providence, R.I., Aug. 29, 1809; s. David and Mary (Atwell) V.; grad. U.S. Mil. Acad., 1830; studied law at Harvard; attended Gen. Theol. Sem., N.Y.C.; S.T.D. (hon.), Columbia, 1848; D.C.L. (hon.), Coll. William and Mary, 1869; m. Maria Whipple, Oct. 8, 1838; m. 2d, Elizabeth Mason Perry, Nov. 3, 1841; 7 children. Commd. 2d lt. U.S. Army, 1830, stationed in garrison at Fort Independence, Mass., 1830-32; on topog. and engring. duty, 1832-33; admitted to N.H. bar, 1834; saw active service in Creek War, 1836; resigned from army, 1836; ordained deacon Protestant Episcopal Ch., 1838, priest, 1839, had 1st parish at Wakefield, R.I., then to St. Stephen's, Providence; rector Trinity Ch., Newport, R.I., 1841-44, Emmanuel Ch., Bklyn., 1844-45; asst. minister Trinity Parish, N.Y.C., 1855-59, Trinity Ch., N.Y.C., 1859; 1st prof. eccles. polity and canon law Gen. Theol. Sem., 1869-72. Author: Evidences of Christianity, 1855; Orations of the Annals of Rhode Island and Providence Plantations, 1863; A Manual Commentary of General Canon Law and the Constitution of the Protestant Episcopal Church in the United States, 1871. Died Bklyn., Sept. 29, 1872.

VINTON, Francis Laurens, army officer, engr.; b. Fort Preble, Me., June 1, 1835; s. John Rogers and Lucretia (Parker) V.; grad. U.S. Mil. Acad., 1856; attended Ecole des Mines, France, 1856-60. Instr. mech. drawing Cooper Union, N.Y.C., 1860; led expdn. to explore mineral resources of Honduras, 1861; commd. capt. 16th U.S. Inf., 1861, raised 43d N.Y. Volunteers, commd. col, 1861 served in various battles Va. peninsular campaign, 1862, commanded brigade in VI Corps, Army of the Potomac, 1862, wounded in Battle of Fredericksburg, 1862; commd brig. gen. U.S. Volunteers, 1863, resigned commn., 1863; prof. civil, mining engring. Sch. Mines, Columbia, 1864-77; cons. mining engr., Denver, Colo., 1877-79; Colo. corr. Engring. and Mining Jour. of N.Y. Died Leadville, Colo., Oct. 6, 1879.

VINTON, Frederic, librarian; b. Boston, Oct. 9, 1817; s. Josiah and Betsey S. (Giles) V.; grad. Amherst Coll., 1837; attended Andover Theol. Sem., Yale, 1840-42; m. Phoebe Clisby, Sept. 13, 1843; m. Mary Curry, June 1, 1857; 6 children. In charge of ch. at St. Louis, 1843-45; in 1851 engaged by brother to catalogue his large pvt. library (now in library of Princeton U.); asst. librarian Boston Pub. Library, 1856-65, aided Edward Capen in preparation of printed catalogues, issued 1858, 61, 65; largely responsible for classification of Bates Hall collection; 1st asst. librarian Library of Congress, 1865-72, engaged in preparation of Catalogue of the Library of Congress: Index of Subjects, 1869, and annual volumes of Alphabetical Catalogue, 1867-72; 1st full-time librarian of Princeton (N.J.) U., 1873, classified and arranged volumes of Chancellor Green Library Bldg.; prepared Subject-Catalogue of Library of the College of New Jersey at Princeton, 1884; one of founders A.L.A., 1876; contbd. articles to Princeton Review. Died Princeton, Jan. 1, 1890.

VINTON, John Adams, clergyman, genealogist; b. Boston, Feb. 5, 1801; grad. Dartmouth, 1828, Andover Theol. Sem., 1831. Ordained to ministry Congregational Ch., 1832; pastor, missionary in No. New Eng.; chaplain of almshouse, Monson, Mass., 1859-60; devoted himself primarily to genealogical studies. Author: The Vinton Memorial, 1858; The Giles Memorial, 1864; The Sampson Family in America, 1864; The Symmes Memorial, 1873; The Upton Memorial, 1874; The Richardson Memorial, 1876. Died Winchester, Mass., Nov. 13, 1877.

VINTON, Samuel Finley, congressman; b. South Hadley, Mass., Sept. 25, 1792; s. Abiathia and Sarah (Day) V.; grad. Williams Coll., 1814; studied law under Stephen Titus Hosner; m. Romaine Madeline Bureau, 1824, 2 children including Sarah Madeleine (Vinton) Dahlgren. Admitted to Conn. bar, 1816; moved to Ohio, 1816; mem. U.S. Ho. of Reps. (Whig) from Ohio, 18th-24th congresses, 1842-51, mem. coms. pub. lands, roads, canals and the judiciary, chmn. com. ways and means during Mexican War, 1846-48; Whig presdl. elector, 1840; pres. Cleve. and Toledo R.R., 1853-54; a commr. to appraise the emancipated slaves from D.C., 1862. Died Washington, D.C., May 11, 1862; buried Pine St. Cemetery, Gallipolis, O.

VIZCAINO, Sebastian, mcht., explorer; b. Huelva, Spain, circa 1550; s. Antonio Vizcaino; married before 1589, 1 child. Went to Mexico, 1585; intrested in China trade; orgaziner, comdr. of company for exploration of Gulf of Cal., 1593; sailed from Acapulco with 3 ships, 230 men, 1596; explored outer coast of Cal. as far as Cape Mendocino, 1602, hoped to find supposed Strait of Anian, discovered Monterey Bay, made maps of coast (1st scientific exploration of West Coast, did much to disprove myth of the Northwest passage) 1602; recommended establishing port at Monterey, pleaded case before Council of Indies, in Spain, received royal decree, establishing port under his command, 1607, plan later abandoned; in command of expdn. to discover islands Rica de Oro and Rica de Plata, 1611, established nonexistence of the islands, made unsuccessful attempt to promote relations with Japan, returned to Mexico, 1614; enlisted a force in New Spanish provence of Avalos to defend coast against Dutch attack, 1615. Died Madrid, Spain, 1628.

VOLK, Leonard Wells, sculptor; b. Wellstown (later Wells), N.Y., Nov. 7, 1828; s. Garret and Elizabeth (Gesner) V.; m. Emily Barlow, Apr. 22, 1852, 2 children. Went to St. Louis, 1848; early works include: marble copy of Voel T. Hart's bust of Henry Clay, a portrait of Father Theobald Mathew, 1850; commd. by Archbishop Kenrick of St. Louis to execute high-relief portraits for a mausoleum; given funds to study in Rome by Stephen A. Douglas, 1855; returned to U.S., 1857; opened studio in Chgo., became leader in art movement there; organized 1st art exhbn., Chgo., 1859; a founder Chgo. Acad. of Design, 1867; made close studies of Lincoln and Douglas, executed Douglas monument at Chgo., a marble statue and bust of Lincoln, 1860, statues of Lincoln and Douglas in Ill. State Capitol, Springfield, 1876; executed statuary for soldiers monument, Girard, Pa. (1st of its kind in country), soldiers monument, Rock Island, Ill.; executed a bronze statue of Gen. James Shields for Statuary Hall, Washington, D.C., 1893, a statue of Lincoln at Rochester, N.Y.; did studies of his contemporaries, including David Davis and Zachariah Chandler. Author: History of the Douglas Monument at Chicago, 1880. Died Osceola, Wis., Aug. 19, 1895.

Von der LAURITZ, Robert Eberhard Schmidt, sculptor; b. Riga, Russia, Nov. 4, 1806; had classical and mil. edn.; studied sculpture with uncle and under Albert Thorvaldsen, Rome, Italy for 4 years. Came to N.Y.C., friendless, deaf, unable to speak English, 1828; became journeyman for John Frazee in marble business, N.Y.C., later partner, 1831; trained Thomas Crawford; named mem. N.A. D. for bas-relief Venus and Cupid, 1833. Prin. woks include: meml. portrait statue of Charlotte Canda, 1845, N.Y. Firemen's Monument (both Greenwood Cemetery, Bklyn.), monument for dead patriots in Bivouac of Dead, State Cemetery, Frankfurt, Ky.; statue of Casimir Pulaski, Savannah, Ga., 1854. Died N.Y.C., Dec. 13, 1870.

Von EGLOFFSTEIN, Frederick W., army officer; b. Aldorf, Bavaria, May 18, 1824. Served in army; came to U.S. (N.Y.), engaged engraver Samuel Sartain to work with him on new engraving process involving photography and glass screens covered wtih an opaque varnish; served as col. N.Y. Volunteers during Civil War; wounded in N.C., ret. as brig. gen. Died N.Y.C., 1885.

von FERSEN, Count, see Axel, Hans.

Von KOCHERTHAL, Josua, clergyman; b. Bretten, Germany, circa 1669; m. Sybilla Charlotte, 5 children. Leader Palatine emigration to Province of N.Y., arrived, 1708, settled at Newburgh, N.Y.; returned to N.Y. with 10 shiploads of Palatines, 1719; settled at Newtown in West Camp area. Died Columbia County, N.Y., Dec. 27, 1719; buried Saugerties, Ulster County, N.Y.

Von PHUL, Anna Maria, painter; b. Phila., 1786; moved with family to Lexington, Ky., 1800; encouraged in her painting by portraitist Matthew Harris Jouett; visited St. Louis, 1818, 20, settled there, 1821; some of her watercolor portraits of St. Louis residents now in collection Mo. Hist. Soc. Died Edwardsville, Ill., 1823.

von SCHWEINITZ, Lewis David, clergyman, botanist; b. Bethlehem, Pa., Feb. 13, 1780; s. Baron Hans Christian Alexander and Anna Dorothea Elizabeth (de Watteville) von S.; entered Moravian Theol. Sem., Niesky, Silesia, Germany, 1798; m. Louisa Amelia Ledoux, 4 children including Edmund Alexander de Schweinitz. Tchr., Moravian Theol. Sem., Niesky, 1800-07; pastor, Gnadenberg, Germany, 1807-14, Gnadou, Saxony, 1807-12; gen. agt. Moravian Ch., Salem, N.C., 1812-21, adminstr. No. province, 1821-34; 1st to describe fungi in N.C. and Pa.; discovered over 1,000 new species; wrote Fungi of Lusatia, 1805, Fungi of North Caroline, 1818, a pamphlet describing 76 Hepaticae, 1821, a monograph on genus Viola, naming 5 new species which he submitted to Am. Jour. of Science, 1821, Narrative of an Expedition to the Source of St. Peter's River, 1824; published his greatest work A

Synopsis of North American Fungi, 1831, contained description of 3,098 species belonging to 246 genera (of which he discovered 1,203 species and 7 genera) Schweinitzia Ororata (North Atlantic plant) named in his honor. Died Bethlehem, Feb. 8, 1834; buried Moravian Cemetery, Bethlehem.

Von STEUBEN, Friedrich Wilhelm Ludolf Gerhard Augustin (Baron von Steuben), army officer; b. Magdeburg, Prussia, Germany, Sept. 17, 1730; s. Wilhelm Augustin and Maria Dorothea (von Jagow) von S. Served as staff officer with rank of capt. under Frederick the Great in Seven Years War; recommended as mil. expert to Am. govt. by Benjamin Franklin and French ofcls.; arrived at Portsmouth, N.H., 1777; directed by Continental Congress to serve under George Washington at Valley Forge; acting insp. gen. Continental Army, highly successful in drilling the army, apptd. insp. gen. with rank of maj. gen., 1778; fought with distinction at Battle of Monmouth; wrote drill manual Regulations for the Order and Discipline of the Troops of the United States (invaluable for tng. Am. volunteers, immediately adopted by Continental Army), winter 1778-79; Gen. Washington's rep. with Continental Congress in efforts to reorganize army, winter 1779-80; in command in Va. under Gen. Greene, 1780-81; commanded a div. at Battle of Yorktown, 1781; served as Washington's aide in mil. planning, helped prepare plan for future defense of U.S., demobilization of Continental Army, spring 1783; honorably discharged, 1784; became Am. citizen by act of Pa. Legislature, 1783, by act of N.Y. Legislature, 1786; prominent founder Soc. of Cincinnati, pres. N.Y. br.; pres. German Soc.; elected a regent Univ. State N.Y., 1787. Died Utica, N.Y., Nov. 28, 1794.

von STIEGEL, Baron, see Stiegel, Henry William.

VOORHEES, Daniel Wolsey, senator; b. Butler County, O., Sept. 26, 1827; s. Stephen and Rachel (Elliot) V.; grad. Ind. Asbury (now DePauw) U., 1849; m. Anna Hardesty, July 18, 1850, 4 children. Admitted to Ind. bar, 1851; practicing atty. for Circuit Ct. of Ind., 1853; U.S. dist. atty. for Ind., 1858-61; mem. U.S. Ho. of Reps. (Democrat) from Ind., 37th-39th, 41st-42d congresses, 1861-Feb. 26, 1866, 69-73; mem. U.S. Senate (Dem.) from Ind., 1877-97, chmn. com. on finance, fought for repeal of Sherman Silver Purchase Act during the extra session, 1893, nominal mgr. for Wilson Tariff Bill, 1894; sobriquet of "Tall Sycamore of the Wabash"; best known achievements in the field of law include his defense of John E. Cook (one of John Brown's assos. in the Harper's Ferry tragedy) and his def. of Mary Harris for murder; influential in building of Library of Congress. Died Washington, D.C., Apr. 9, 1897; buried Terre Haute, Ind.

VOORHEES, Philip Falkerson, naval officer; b. New Brunswick, N.J., 1792; m. Anne Randall, May 12, 1835, 2 children. Apptd. midshipman U.S. Navy, 1809; in War of 1812 participated in capture ship Macedonian by brig United States and of Epervier by the Peacock; awarded silver medal by Congress; on Mediterranean cruise in vessel North Carolina, 1825-27; with rank of capt. sailed for Mediterranean commanding frigate Congress, 1842; joined Brazil squadron under Commodore Daniel Turner, 1843; assisted in rescuing H.M.S. Gorgon stranded in the Rio de la Plata, 1844; court-martialed for his action against Argentine squadron, 1845, sentenced to reprimand and suspension for 3 years, also court-martialed on series of charges, chiefly disobedience to Commodore Turner, found guilty on two specifications, suspended for 18 months, dismissed from service by ct., Aug. 1845, Pres. Polk lessened his sentence to suspension for 5 years, removed suspension, 1847; commanded East India squadron, 1849; placed by naval retiring bd. on res. list with furlough pay, 1855, appealed and received leave pay; petitioned unsuccessfully to return to active duty. Died Annapolis, Md., Feb. 23, 1862.

VOORHIS, Charles Henry, congressman, lawyer; b. Spring Valley, Bergen County, N.J., Mar. 13, 1833; grad. Rutgers Coll., New Brunswick, N.J., 1853; studied law. Admitted to bar, 1856, began practice of law Jersey City, N.J.; del. Republican Nat. Conv., Balt., 1864; presiding judge Bergen County, 1868-69; an organizer Hackensack (N..J) Improvement Commn., 1869; an organizer Hackensack Acad.; organizer, 1st pres. Hackensack Water Co., 1873; interested in banking; mem. U.S. Ho. of Reps. (Rep.) from N.J., 46th Congress, 1879-81. Died Jersey City, Apr. 15, 1896; buried N.Y. Cemetery, Hackensack.

VOSE, Roger, congressman; b. Milton, Norfolk County, Mass., Feb. 24, 1763; grad. Harvard, 1790; studied law. Admitted to bar, 1793, began practice of law Walpole, N.H.; mem. N.H. Senate, 1809-10, 12; mem. U.S. Ho. of Reps. (Federalist) from N.H., 13th-14th congresses, 1813-17; mem. N.H. Ho. of Reps., 1818; chief justice Ct. of Common Pleas, 1818-20, Ct. of Sessions, 1820-25. Died Walpole, Oct. 26, 1841; buried Village Cemetery.

VROOM, Peter Dumont, gov. N.J.; b. Hillsboro Twp., N.J., Dec. 12, 1791; s. Col. Peter Dumont and Elsie (Bogert) V.; grad. Columbia Coll., 1808, LL.D. (hon.); LL.D. (hon.) Princeton; m. Ann V.D. Dumont, May 21, 1817; m. 2d, Maria Wall, Nov. 4, 1840; 2 children, Peter Dumont, Garret D.W. Admitted to N.J. bar as atty., 1813, as counselor, 1816, as sergeant-at-law, 1828; practiced in Schooleys Mountain, 1813, Hackettstown, 1814-16, Fleming, 1817-21, Somerville, 1821-circa 1841; mem. N.J. Assembly, 1826, 27, 29; elected to combined office of gov. and chancellor N.J., 1829-32, 33-36; a commr. to adjust land reserve claims in Miss. under treaty with Choctaw Indians, 1837; mem. U.S. Ho. of Reps. from N.J., 26th Congress, 1839-41; del. Constl. Conv., 1844; framed statutes (with Henry Woodhull Green, William Lewis Dayton, Stacy G. Potts) to comply with new constn., 1848; Democratic presdl. elector, 1852-68; minister to Prussia, 1853-57; reporter N.J. Supreme Ct., 1862-72; mem. Washington (D.C.) Peace Conf., 1861; a commr. N.J. sinking fund, 1864-73; v.p. Am. Colonization Soc., Am Bible Soc.; ruling elder Reformed Dutch Ch., Somerville, N.J. Author: Reports of the Supreme Court of New Jersey, 6 vols., 1866-73. Died Trenton, N.J., Nov. 18, 1873; buried 1st Reformed Dutch Ch., Somerville.

W

WABASHA (also spelled Wapasha), Indian chief; probably b. nr. Winona, Minn., circa 1773; s. 1st Chief Wabasha. Chief, Mdewakanton Sioux; held conf. with Zebulon M. Pike on the Mississippi River, 1805; apparently favored Americans in War of 1812; British suspected him and tried Rolette his son-in-law) by ct. martial for collusion with the Americans; took part in great council at Prairie du Chien (Wis.) between reps. of U.S. Govt. and tribes of Central North, 1825; supported Americans in Sauk War of 1832. Died circa 1855.

WACHSMUTH, Charles, paleontologist; b. Hanover, Germany, Sept. 13, 1829; s. Christian Wachsmuth; m. Bernandina Lorenz, 1855. Came to N.Y.C. as agt. merc. house in Hamburg, 1852; went to Burlington, Ia., 1854; gathered large collection of rare crinoids and established spl. library on the subject which attracted attention of scientists; Louis Agassiz purchased the material for Mus. of Comparative Zoology, Cambridge, Mass., 1873; went with Agassiz to Cambridge, worked with him, until 1873; engaged in study of N.Am. crinoids (with Frank Springer), after 1873. Author: (with Springer) North American Crinoidea Camerata (monograph) 1897. Died Burlington, Feb. 7, 1896; buried Aspen Grove Cemetery, Burlington.

WADDEL, James, clergyman; b. Newry, Ireland, July 1739; s. Thomas Waddel; attended "Log College" of Samuel Finley, Nottingham, Pa.; D.D. (hon.), Dickinson Coll., 1792; m. Mary Gordon, 1768, 10 children. Came to Am. with family, 1739; tutor at "Log Coll."; licensed to preach by Presbytery of Hanover, Va., 1761; served congregations in Northumberland and Lancaster counties (Va.), 1762; accepted call from Tinkling Spring congregation in Augusta County, 1776-77; went to Shenandoah Valley, 1778; established group of chs. in Orange, Louisa, Albemarle counties, Va. Died Gordonsville, Va., Sept. 17, 1805.

WADDEL, Moses, clergyman, coll. pres.; b. Rowan (now Iredell County), N.C., July 29, 1770; s. William and Sarah (Morrow) W.; grad. Hampden-Sydney Coll., 1791; studied theology under Va. clergymen; D.D. (hon.), S.C. Coll., 1807; m. Catherine Calhoun, 1795; m. 2d, Elizabeth Woodson Pleasants, 1800; at least 1 child, John Newton. Licensed to preach, 1792; established sch., Appling, Ga.; opened sch., Willington, S.C., 1804, most distinguished pupils were John C. Calhoun, William H. Crawford, Hugh S. Legaré, George McDuffie, A. B. Longstreet, James L. Petigru; pres. Franklin Coll. (now part of U. Ga.), 1819-29. Author: Memoirs of the Life of Miss Caroline Elizabeth Smelt, 1818. Died Athens, Ga, July 21, 1840.

WADDELL, Hugh, army officer; b. Lisburn, County Down, Ireland, 1734; s. Hugh and Isabella (Brown) W.; m. Mary Haynes, 1762, 3 children. Served as lt. with regt. of James Innes to help drive French from Ohio, 1754; clk. Gov.'s Council of N.C., 1754-55; on frontier duty in Western Carolina, 1755; as Va. commr. negotiated offensive-defensive alliance with Cherokee and Catawba Indian tribes, 1756; maj. in command 3 cos. to aid expdn. of John Forbes against Fort Duquesne, 1758; col. in command 2 cos. with authority to summon the militia of the frontier counties and cooperate with S.C. or Va., 1759; defended Ft. Dobbs against Indian attack, 1760; foremost soldier of N.C. before Am. Revolution; justice of the peace in Rowan and Bladen (N. C.); rep. N.C. Colonial Assembly from Rowan, 1757, 58, 59, 60, from Bladen, 1762, 66, 67, 71; a leader of colonists against Gen. William Tryon's attempt to enforce Stamp Act, 1765; took part in suppression of Regulator movement in N.C., 1771. Died Bladen County, N.C., Apr. 9, 1773.

WADDELL, James Iredell, naval officer; b. Pittsboro, N.C., July 13, 1824; s. Francis Nash and Elizabeth Davis (Moore) W.; m. Ann Iglehart, 1848. Apptd. midshipman U.S. Navy, 1841; served on ship Somers off Vera Cruz during Mexican War; passed midshipman, 1847, lt., 1855; taught navigation U.S. Naval Acad., 1846-48; secretly entered Confederate lines by way of Balt., 1862; commd. lt. Confederate States Navy, 1862-63; took command of Sea King in 1864 and transformed her into Confederate vessel Shenandoah; on cruise from Melbourne (Australia) in command of Shenandoah destroyed over 30 U.S. whalers in Bering Sea, 1865, landed at Liverpool, Eng.; capt. Pacific Mail Co., 1875; commanded Md. State Flotilla for policing oyster beds, circa 1883-86. Died Annapolis, Md., Mar. 15, 1886.

WADDELL, John Newton, clergyman, educator; b. Willington, S.C., Apr. 2, 1812; s. Moses and Elizabeth (Pleasants) W.; grad. Franklin Coll. (now part of U. Ga.), 1829; m. Martha Robertson, Nov. 27, 1832; m. 2d, Mary Werden, Aug. 24, 1854; m. 3d, Harriet (Godden) Snedecor, Jan. 31, 1866; 8 children. Established Montrose (Miss.) Acad., 1842, charter mem. bd. trustees; ordained to ministry Presbyn. Ch., 1843; a founder U. Miss., Oxford, taught ancient langs. U. Miss., 1848-57; pastor Presbyn. Ch., Oxford, 1848-57; taught ancient langs., 1857-60, Presbyn. Synodical Coll., LaGrange, Tenn., pres., 1860-62; received ofcl. orders to discontinue duties minister when U.S. Army occupied LaGrange, 1862; chaplain Confederate Army; a leader in orgn. of 1st Gen. Assembly of So. Presbyn. Ch., Augusta, Ga., clk., 1861-65, moderator, 1868; chancellor U. Miss., 1865-74; sec. edn. So. Presbyn. Ch., Memphis, Tenn., 1874-79; chancellor Southwestern Presbyn. U., Clarksville, Tenn., 1879-88. Author: Historical Discourse . . . on the . . . University of Mississippi, 1873. Died Birmingham, Ala., Jan. 9, 1895.

WADE, Benjamin Franklin, senator; b. Feeding Hills, Mass., Oct. 27, 1800; s. James and Mary (Upham) W.; m. Caroline M. Rosekrans, May 19, 1841; children—James F., Henry P. Moved to Ohio with family, 1821; admitted to Ohio bar, 1828; in law partnerships with Joshua R. Giddings, 1831, Rufus P. Ranney, 1838; pros. atty. Ashtabula County (O.), 1835-37; mem. Ohio Senate, 1837-38, 41; pres. judge 3d Ohio Jud. Circuit, 1847-51; mem. U.S. Senate from Ohio, 1851-69, pres. pro tem, 1867, mem. com. of 13 who voted against Crittenden proposals, 1860, demanded swift and decisive mil. action at outbreak Civil War, set up Com. on Conduct of War (with senators Zacariah Chandler and J.W. Grimes), 1861; issued Wade-Davis Manifesto (condemned Lincoln's "executive usurpation" as outrage on legislative authority, insisted that in matters of reconstrn. Congress was supreme), 1864; endorsed Pomeroy circular designed to replace Lincoln with Salmon P. Chase; del. to Southern Loyalists Conv., Phila., 1866; urged impeachment of Pres. Johnson, 1867 (as pres. pro tem of Senate would have succeeded to presidency in event of Johnson's removal); voted for Johnson's conviction; defeated for re-election to U.S. Senate, 1868; gen. counsel for N.P. Ry., 1869; a govt. dir. U.P. Ry.; mem. commn. of investigation which visited Santo Domingo and recommended its annexation, 1871; chmn. Ohio delegation Rep. Nat. Conv., Cincinnati, 1876. Died Jefferson, O., Mar. 2, 1878; buried Oakdale Cemetery.

WADE, Edward, congressman, lawyer; b. West Springfield, Mass., Nov. 22, 1802; studied law. Admitted to bar, 1827, began practice of law, Jefferson, Ashtabula County, O.; justice of peace Ashtabula County, 1831; moved to Unionville, 1832; pros. atty. Ashtabula County, 1833; moved to Cleve., O., 1837; mem. U.S. Ho. of Reps. from Ohio (as Free-Soiler), 33d Congress, 1853-55, (as Republican), 34th-36th congresses, 1855-61. Died East Cleveland, O., Aug. 13, 1866; buried Woodland Cemetery, Cleve.

WADE, Jeptha Homer, financier; b. Romulus, Seneca County, N.Y., Aug. 11, 1811; s. Jeptha and Sarah (Allen) W.; m. Rebecca Eacer, Oct. 15, 1832; m. 2d, Susan Fleming, Sept. 5, 1837. Studied painting with Randall Palmer; learned of invention of daguerrotype, purchased a camera to widen his artistic field; contracted to build a telegraph wire from Detroit to Jackson (Mich.), and other lines (came to be known as Wade Lines) from Detroit to Milw., Detroit to Buffalo by way of Cleve., from Cleve. to Cincinnati and St. Louis, lines of Wade and Royal E. House were consolidated with Wade as gen. agt., 1854; most of Western lines were combined in Western Union Telegraph Co., 1856, became gen. agt.; organized Cal. State Telegraph Co., Pacific Telegraph Co. (1st pres.) to connect St. Louis with San Francisco; completed line to Salt Lake City from the West, 1861; mng. dir. Western Union, pres., 1866-67; organizer Citizens Savs. & Loan Assn., Cleve., 1867, pres.; pres. Nat. Bank of Commerce; dir. most railroads entering Cleveland; sinking-fund commr., mem. pub. park commn., dir. workhouse bd. (all Cleve.); mem. Nat. Garfield Monument Assn.; gave Wade Park to City of Cleve., 1882; donated land which became part of site of Western Res. U. Died Cleve., Aug. 9, 1890.

WADHAMS, Edgar Philip, clergyman; b. Lewis, N.Y., May 17, 1817; attended Middletown Coll., Conn., also Gen. Theol. Sem., N.Y., St. Mary's Sem., Balt. Ordained deacon Episcopalian Ch.; convert to Roman Catholic Ch., 1846, ordained priest, Albany, N.Y., 1850; became rector of Albany cathedral, vicar gen. Diocese of Albany; apptd. 1st bishop Diocese of Ogdensburg (N.Y.), 1872; attended 3d Plenary Council of Balt., 1884. Died Ogdensburg, Dec. 5, 1891.

WADLEIGH, Bainbridge, senator, lawyer; b. Bradford, Merrimack County, N.H., Jan. 4, 1831; attended Kimball Union Acad., Plainfield, N.H.; studied law. Admitted to bar, 1850, began practice of law, Milford, N.H.; town moderator, 6 terms; mem. N.H. Ho. of Reps., 1855-56, 59-60, 69-72; mem. U.S. Senate (Republican) from N.H., 1873-79; resumed practice of law, Boston. Died Boston, Jan. 24, 1891; buried West Street Cemetery, Milford.

WADSWORTH, Daniel, artist; b. 1771; married. Mcht., Hartford, Conn.; founder Wadsworth Athenaeum Gallery, Hartford, 1844; made sketches on trip to Que., Can., 1819, some were engraved to illustrate published account of his trip; made watercolor views of his mansion "Monte Video" nr. Hartford (now in Conn. Hist. Soc.). Died 1848.

WADSWORTH, James, Continental congressman; b. Durham, Middlesex County, Conn., July 8, 1730; grad. Yale, 1748; studied law. Admitted to bar; town clk., 1756-86; justice of peace, 1762; apptd. judge New Haven County Ct., 1773, presiding judge, 1778; mem. Com. of Safety; served as col. and brig. gen. Conn. Militia during Revolutionary War, promoted 2d maj. gen., 1777; mem. Continental Congress from Conn., 1783-86; mem. Conn. Exec. Council, 1785-89; comptroller Conn., 1786-87; mem. Conn. Conv. to ratify U.S. Constn., 1788, opposed U.S. Constn. and refused to take oath of allegiance. Died Durham, Sept. 22, 1817; buried Old Cemetery.

WADSWORTH, James, ednl. pioneer; b. Durham, Conn., Apr. 20, 1768; s. John Noyes and Esther (Parsons) W.; grad. Yale, 1787; m. Naomi Wolcott, Oct. 1, 1804, at least 4 children including James Samuel. Acquired property on bank of Genesee River (now twps. of Geneseo and Avon), N.Y.; aided in devel. Genesee County; went to Europe (with cooperation of Robert Morris, Aaron Burr, De Witt Clinton and others) to interest fgn. capitalists in Am. investments, 1796-98; urged establishment of county academies; instrumental in securing the enactment of legislation authorizing sending the publ. Lectures on School-Keeping to each sch. dist.; responsible for establishment of sch. dist. library system in N.Y. State; built and endowed a pub. library for Geneseo (N.Y.). Died Geneseo, June 7, 1844.

WADSWORTH, Jeremiah, army officer, congressman; b. Hartford, Conn., July 12, 1743; s. Rev. Daniel and Abigail (Talcott) W.; hon. degrees from Yale and Dartmouth; m. Mehitable Russell, Sept. 29, 1767, 3 children. Engaged in mcht. service, 1761-71; commissary gen. to Col. Joseph Trumbull of Revolutionary forces raised in Conn., 1775; dep. commissary gen. of purchases Continental Army, 1777, commissary-gen., 1778-79; at request of Gen. Rochambeau also commissary to French troops in America to end of war; went to Paris to submit report of his transactions, 1783; mem. Continental Congress from Conn., 1787-88; mem. Conn. Conv. to consider ratification of U.S. Constn., 1788; mem. U.S. Ho. of Reps. (Federalist) from Conn., 1st-3d congresses, 1789-95; mem. Conn. Legislature, 1795; mem. Conn. Exec. Council, 1795-1801; founder Bank of N.Am. in Phila. and Hartford Bank Conn.); dir. U.S. Bank; pres. Bank of N.Y.; a promoter Hartford Mfg. Co., established 1788; established 1st insurance partnership in Conn., 1794; introduced fine breeds of cattle from abroad, engaged in experiments to improve agriculture. Died Hartford, Conn., Apr. 30, 1804; buried Ancient Burying Ground, Hartford.

WADSWORTH, Peleg, army officer, congressman; b. Duxbury, Mass., May 6, 1748; s. Peleg and Lusanna (Sampson) W.; grad. Harvard, 1769; m. Elizabeth Bartlett, June 18, 1772, 11 children including Henry, Zilpah (Wadsworth) Longfellow. Capt. of a co. of minute men, 1774; mem. Com. Correspondence of Plymouth County (Mass.); a.d.c. to Artemas Ward, 1776; served under Washington in L.I., N.Y., 1776; served under Sullivan in R.I., 1778; adj. gen. Mass. Militia, 1778, brig. gen., 1779; rep. from Duxbury in Mass. Legislature, 1777-78; 2d in command of expdn. to expel British from Ft. George, Castine, Me., 1779; commanded Eastern Dept. of Mass. with hdqrs. at Thomaston, Me., 1780; raided by party of British, held captive, until 1781; land agt., 1784; mem. Mass. Senate, 1792; selectman of Falmouth (now Portland), Me.; mem. U.S. Ho. of Reps. (Federalist) from Mass., 3d-9th congresses, 1793-1807. Died "Wadsworth Hall" Hiram, Me., Nov. 12, 1829; buried family graveyard at "Wadsworth Hall."

WADSWORTH, William Henry, congressman, lawyer; b. Maysville, Mason County, Ky., July 4, 1821; grad. Augusta Coll., Ky., 1841; studied law. Admitted to bar, 1844, began practice of law, Maysville; mem. Ky. Senate, 1853-56; Constl. Union presdl. elector, also pres. Ky. electoral coll., 1860; mem. U.S. Ho. of Reps. (Unionist) from Ky., 37th-38th congresses, 1861-65, (as Republican), 49th Congress, 1885-87; served as col., aide to Gen. Nelson at Battle of Ivy Mountain, during Civil War; declined appointment by Pres. Grant as minister to Austria; apptd. U.S. commr. to Mexico by Pres. Grant, 1869. Died Maysville, Apr. 2, 1893; buried Maysville Cemetery.

WAGENER, David Douglas, congressman, businessman; b. Easton, Pa., Oct. 11, 1792; attended common schs. Served as capt. Easton Union Guards, 1816-29; engaged in merc. pursuits; mem. U.S. Ho. of Reps. (Democrat) from Pa., 23d-26th congresses, 1833-41; founder Easton Bank, 1852, pres., 1852-60. Died Easton, Oct. 1, 1860; buried Easton Cemetery.

WAGGAMAN, George Augustus, senator; b. "Fairview," nr. Cambridge, Dorchester County, Md., 1790 studied law. Admitted to bar, Caroline County, Md., 1811; served under Gen. Jackson at New Orleans in War of 1812; began practice of law, Baton Rouge, La., 1813; atty. gen. 3d Dist. of La., 1813; judge 3d Jud. Circuit Ct., 1818; asst. judge New Orleans Criminal Ct., 1819; a sugar cane planter; sec. State of La., 1830-32; mem. U.S. Senate (Nat.-Republican, filled vacancy) from La., Nov. 15, 1831-35. Died of injuries received in a duel, New Orleans, Mar. 22, 1843; buried Girod Cemetery.

WAGNER, Daniel, artist; b. Leyden, Mass., Apr. 14, 1802. Practiced portrait and miniature painting in collaboration with his sister Maria Louisa, Chenango Valely, N.Y., during 1830's; maintained studio, Albany, 1842-60, N.Y.C., 1862-68, Norwich, N.Y., after 1868; exhibited at N.A.D., Centennial Exhbn., Phila.; works include portraits of Erastus Corning, Martin Van Buren, Silas Wright, Millard Fillmore, Daniel Webster. Died Norwich, Jan. 21, 1888.

WAGNER, Peter Joseph, congressman, lawyer; b. Wagners Hollow, Palatine, Montgomery County, N.Y., Aug. 14, 1795; attended Fairfield Acad., 1810-11; grad. Union Coll., Schenectady, N.Y., 1816; studied law. Admitted to bar, 1819, began practice of law, Ft. Plain, N.Y.; also engaged in agriculture, banking; mem. U.S. Ho. of Reps. (Whig) from N.Y., 26th Congress, 1839-41. Died Ft. Plain, Sept. 13, 1884; buried Ft. Plain Cemetery.

WAGNER, Webster, mfr.; b. Palatine Bridge, N. Y., Oct. 2, 1817; s. John and Elizabeth (Strayer) W.; m. Susan Davis, 5 children. Station mgr., freight agt. N.Y. Central R.R., Palatine Bridge, 1843-circa 1858; designed a sleeping car; with financial help of Commodore Vanderbilt completed 4 sleeping-cars put into operation on N.Y. Central R.R., 1858; organized N.Y. Central Sleeping Car Co. at Palatine Bridge to manufacture cars for exclusive use on N.Y. Central R.R., (reoganized as Wagner Palace Car Co. mfg. sleeping and drawing-room cars, 1865); contracted with George M. Pullman to make Pullman's newly patented folding upper berth and hinged back and seat cushions for the lower berth with understanding that Wagner Co. would use them only on N.Y. Central R.R., 1870; received contract to run cars over Mich. Central R.R. (made connection for Vanderbilt lines between N.Y.C. and Chgo.), 1875, as a result of this breach of contract Pullman Co. brought an infringement suit against Wagner's co. for $1,000,000 (suit still in process at his death); mem. N.Y. Assembly from Montgomery County, 1870; mem. N.Y. Senate from 18th Dist., 1871-72; del. to Republican Nat. Conv., Chgo., 1880. Died in train collision at Spuyten Duyvil, N.Y., Jan. 13, 1882.

WAGNER, William, naturalist, philanthropist; b. Phila., Jan. 15, 1796; s. John and Mary Ritz (Baker) W.; grad. Phila. Acad., 1808; m. Caroline Say, Jan. 1, 1824; m. 2d, Louisa Binney, Mar. 1841. Asst. supercargo in Stephen Girard's ship Helvetius to Far East, 1816-18, during voyage gathered a large collection of minerals, shells, plants, and organic remains which became basis of Wagner Free Inst. of Science; arranged museum for his collection at his home; obtained permission to use part of Commrs. Hall in Dist. of Spring Garden (dist. absorbed into Phila. 1854), 1847, received permission from city govt. for continued use of bldgs., established Wagner Free Inst. of Science, granted charter by Pa. Legislature, 1855, empowered to confer degrees; read paper before Acad. Natural Sci., Phila., published in Journal 1839; name applied to several fossil specimens (which he described for 1st time). Died Phila., Jan. 17, 1885; buried in tomb in Wagner Free Inst. of Science.

WAILES, Benjamin Leonard Covington, naturalist, planter; b. Columbia County, Ga., Aug. 1, 1797; s. Levin and Eleanor (Davis) W.; attended Jefferson Coll., Washington, Miss. Territory; m. Rebecca Covington, Mar. 30, 1820, 10 children. Surveyor and clk., land offices in Miss. Territory, 1814-20; asst. to Choctaw agt., attended treaty confs. of 1818 and 1820 with Choctaws; register of land office, Washington, Miss., 1826-35; managed small plantation at Washington, 2 others in Warren County; collected specimans of soil, rocks, fossils, shells, plant and animal life; helped build collections at Jefferson Coll., U. Miss. and at Miss. capitol; supplied information and specimans of natural history of region to other scientists and Smithsonian Instn.; asst. prof. agriculture and geol. scis. U. Miss.; performed field work for projected survey of Miss.; founder, 1st pres. Miss. Hist. Soc.; trustee Jefferson Coll., 40 years, pres. bd. at time of death; mem. Miss. Legislature, 1825, 26. Author: Report on the Agriculture and Geology of Mississippi, 1854. Died Nov. 16, 1862.

WAINWRIGHT, Jonathan Mayhew, naval officer; b. N.Y.C., July 21, 1821; s. Jonathan Mayhew and Amelia (Phelps) W.; m. Maria Page, Dec. 1844, 4 children including Marie, Jonathan Mayhew. Commd. midshipman U.S. Navy, serving on sloop Porpoise, 1837; in ship John Adams on E. Indies cruise, 1838-40; passed midshipman, 1843; on ship Columbia, E. Indies cruise, 1845-46; commd. lt., 1850, served on ship San Jacinto in Mediterranean, 1851-53; spl. service on ship Merrimack, 1858-59; lt. on ship Minnesota in Atlantic Blockading Squadron, 1861; in command Harriet Lane, flagship of W. Gulf Blockading Squadron, 1862, seized Confederate vessel Joanna Ward; participated on ship Harriet Ward in capture of Galveston, Tex., Oct., 1862. Killed during Confederate attack on Galveston, Jan. 1, 1863; buried Trinity Ch. Cemetery, N.Y.C.

WAINWRIGHT, Richard, naval officer; b. Charlestown, Mass., Jan. 5, 1817; s. Robert Dewar and Maria (Auchmuty) W.; m. Sally Bache, Mar 1, 1849, at least 4 children including Richard. Commd. midshipman U.S. Navy, 1831; cruised in Mediterranean, 1833-36; passed midshipman, 1837, commd. lt. 1841; served on ship Vincennes in Home Squadron, 1842-45; with ship Columbia in Brazil Squadron, 1846-47; with Coast Survey, 1848-56; on brig Merrimac of Pacific Squadron, 1857-60; served ordnance duty at Washington (D.C.) Navy Yard, 1860-61; promoted comdr., 1861; commanded the Hartford (flagship of Flag Officer David Farragut), 1861-62. Died on board Hartford, Donaldsville, La., Aug. 10, 1862.

WAIT, Robert T.P., architect; born 1846. Partner (with Amos P. Cutting) in Wait & Cutting, Reading, Mass. Prin. works of firm include: state armories and county court houses, Eastern Mass.; Registry of Deeds Bldg., Dedham, Mass.; Lincoln and Hamilton Grammar Sch., Wakefield. Died Mar. 21, 1898.

WAIT, Samuel, coll. pres.; b. White Creek, Washington County, N.Y., Dec. 19, 1789; s. Joseph and Martha Wait; theol. student at Phila.; grad. Columbian Coll. (now George Washington U.), 182 A.M., Waterville Coll., 1825; D.D. (hon.), Wake Forest U., 1849; m. Sarah Merriam, June 17, 1818, 1 child. Joined Baptist Ch., 1809; pastor Sharon, Mass., 1816; ordained to ministry, 181 tutor Columbian Coll., 1822-26; pastor, New Bern, N.C., 1827; an organizer N.C. Bapt. Conv., 1830 also gen. agt., toured N.C. as part of duties, 1830-32; prin. Wake Forest (N.C.) Manual Labour Inst. (established 1834), 1834-38, became Wake Forest Coll., 1838, pres., 1838-46, pres. bd. trustees, 1846-67; wrote Origin and Early History of Wake Forest College, between 1850-60, published in Wake Forest Student; pres. Oxford Female Coll., 1851-56; Died Wake Forest, N.C., July 28, 1867.

WAIT, William, lawyer; b. Ephratah, N.Y., Feb. 2, 1821; s. William and Polly (Vail) W.; m. Margaret Stewart, 1850; m. 2d, Caroline Van Alen, 1858; 5 children: Admitted to N.Y. bar, 1846; pros. atty. Fulton County (N.Y.), 1848. Author: The Law and Practice in Civil Actions, 1865; Digest of New York Reports, 5 vols., 1869-77; The Code of Civil Procedure of the State of New York, 1870 (published 5 times, 1871-77); A Table of Cases Affirmed, Reversed, or Cited, for State of New York, 1872; The Practice at Law, in Equity, and in Special Proceedings in All the Courts of Record in the State of New York, 7 vols., 1872-80; A Treatise upon Some of the General Principles of the Law . . . Including . . . Actions and Defenses, 7 vols., 1877-79; published Commentaries on the

Laws of England (Herbert Broom), 1875. Died Johnstown, N.Y., Dec. 29, 1880.

WAITE, Morrison Remick, chief justice U.S. Supreme Ct.; b. Lyme, Conn., Nov. 29, 1816; s. Henry Matson and Maria (Selden) W.; attended Yale, 1837; LL.D. (hon.), Kenyon Coll., 1874, Ohio U., 1879; m. Amelia Warner, Sept. 21, 1840, 5 children. Admitted to Ohio bar, 1839; argued 31 cases before Ohio Supreme Ct., 1851-61; mem. Ohio Legislature, 1849-50; leader of Union cause in Civil War, adviser of gov. of Ohio, 1863; served as one of Am. counsel in Geneva Arbitration, 1871; pres. Ohio Constl. Conv., 1873; chief justice U.S. Supreme Ct., 1874-88, wrote opinions in Tappan vs. Merchants Nat. Bank (86 U.S., 490), McCready vs. Va. (U.S., 391), U.S. vs. Reese (92 U.S., 214), Minor vs. Happersett (88 U.S., 162), held that suffrage was not privilege of U.S. citizenship and that 14th Amendment did not add to privileges and immunities of citizens; Munn vs. Ill. (94 U.S., 113) upheld state power to regulate grain elevator charges; gave opinions in cases Stone vs. Farmers' Loan and Trust Co., Reynolds vs. U.S. (98 U.S., 145); Wildenhus's Case (120 U.S., 1), U.S. vs. Rauscher (119 U.S., 407); trustee Peabody Ednl. Fund, 1874-88; mem. corp. Yale, 1882-88; vestryman Protestant Episcopal Ch. Died Washington, D.C., Mar. 23, 1888.

WAKEFIELD, Cyrus, mfr.; b. Roxbury, N.H., Feb. 14, 1811; s. James and Hannah (Hemingway) W.; m. Eliza Bancroft, Oct. 31, 1841. Engaged in grocery bus., Boston, 1834-44; manufactured chairs partially made from rattan-cane, 1844-54; manufactured cane in U.S. (necessitated by Opium War), continued to make furniture from it, 1856-73. Died Wakefield, Mass., Oct. 26, 1873.

WAKELEY, Joseph Burton, clergyman; b. Danbury, Conn., Feb. 18, 1809; s. James and Rebecca (Cooke) W.; m. Jane McCord, July 1831. Learned hatter's trade, Danbury, went into business for himself; joined N.Y. Conf., Methodist Episcopal Church on trial, 1833, ordained deacon, 1835, elder, 1837; pastor in churches, N.Y., including Trenton, Newark, Jersey City, Poughkeepsie, Yonkers; presiding elder Poughkeepsie dist., 1866-68, Newbury dist., 1868-72. Author: The Heroes of Methodism, 1856; Lost Chapters Recovered from the Early History of American Methodism, 1858; The Bold Frontier Preacher: A Portraiture of Rev. William Cravens, of Virginia, 1869; The American Temperance Cyclopaedia of History, Biography, Anecdote and Illustration, 1875. Died N.Y.C., Apr. 27, 1875.

WAKEMAN, Abram, congressman, lawyer; b. Greenfield Hill, Conn., May 31, 1824; grad. Herkimer Acad., N.Y.; studied law, Little Falls, N.Y. Admitted to bar, began practice of law, N.Y.C., 1847; mem. N.Y. State Assembly, 1850-51; mem. U.S. Ho. of Reps. (Whig, supported by Am. Party) from N.Y., 34th Congress, 1855-57; del. Republican Nat. Conv., Phila., 1856; raised 81st Pa. Volunteers at beginning of Civil War; postmaster N.Y.C., 1862-64; surveyor Port of N.Y.C. Died N.Y.C., June 29, 1889; buried Greenwood Cemetery, Bklyn.

WAKEMAN, Seth, congressman, lawyer; b. Franklin, Vt., Jan. 15, 1811; attended common schs.; studied law, Batavia, N.Y. Admitted to bar, began practice of law; dist. atty. Genesee County, 1850-56; mem. N.Y. State Assembly, 1856-57; mem. N.Y. Constl. Conv., 1867-68; mem. U.S. Ho. of Reps. (Republican) from N.Y., 42d Congress, 1871-73. Died Batavia, Jan. 4, 1880; buried Elmwood Cemetery.

WALBRIDGE, David Safford, congressman, businessman; b. Bennington, Vt., July 30, 1802; attended common schs. Engaged in business and agriculture, Geneseo, N.Y., 1820-26, Jamestown, 1826-42; engaged in merc. pursuits, Kalamazoo, Mich., 1842, also became large landowner, stock raiser; mem. Mich. Ho. of Reps., 1848, Mich. Senate, 2 terms; permanent chmn. 1st Mich. Republican Conv., Jackson, 1854; mem. U.S. Ho. of Reps. (Rep.) from Mich., 34th-35th congresses, 1855-59; apptd. postmaster Kalamazoo by Pres. Johnson. Died Kalamazoo, June 15, 1868; buried Mountain Home Cemetery.

WALBRIDGE, Henry Sanford, congressman, lawyer; b. Norwich, Conn., Apr. 8, 1801; attended sch. Bennington, Vt.; studied law. Admitted to bar, began practice of law, Ithaca, N.Y.; clk. bd. suprs. Tompkins County, 1824; mem. N.Y. State Assembly, 1829, 46; pres. council Village of Ithaca, 1829, 42; mem. U.S. Ho. of Reps. (Whig) from N.Y., 32d Congress, 1851-53; trustee Ithaca Acad., 1858-68; judge, surrogate Tompkins County, 1859-68; moved to Leonia, N.J., 1868, practiced law, N.Y.C. Killed in railroad accident, Bergen Tunnel, nr. Hoboken, N.J., Jan. 27, 1869; buried Ithaca City Cemetery.

WALBRIDGE, Hiram, congressman; b. Ithaca, N.Y., Feb. 2, 1821; attended Ohio U. at Athens; studied law. Admitted to bar, 1842, began practice of law, Toledo, O.; apptd. brig. gen. militia, 1843; moved to Buffalo, N.Y., engaged in business; mem. bd. aldermen; moved to N.Y.C., 1847; mem. U.S. Ho. of Reps. (Democrat) from N.Y., 33d Congress, 1853-55; pres. Internat. Comml. Conv., Detroit, 1865; del. So. Loyalist Conv., Phila., 1866. Died N.Y.C., Dec. 6, 1870; buried Glenwood Cemetery, Washington, D.C.

WALCOT, Charles Melton, actor, dramatist; b. London, Eng., circa 1816; m. Miss Powell, circa 1838, at least 1 son, Charles Melton. Came to U.S., 1837; treas. Charleston Theatre, 1837; played Wormwood in The Lottery Ticket at Military Garden, N.Y., 1842; 1st to play Don César de Bazan in Am., 1844; wrote The Imp of the Elements, or The Lake of the Dismal Swamp, 1844, Don Giovanni in Gotham, The Don not Done, or Giovanni from Texas, Old Friends and New Faces, The Marriage of Figaro, 1844; played Sir Harcourt Courtly in Dion Boucicault's London Assurance at Arch Street Theatre, Phila., 1847; adapted plays The Course of True Love, 1839, The Haunted Man, 1848. Died Phila., May 15, 1868.

WALCUTT, William, artist; b. Columbus, O., 1819. Began career as portrait painter, Columbus, circa 1840; studied sculpture in London (Eng.) and Paris (France), 1852-55; opened studio, N.Y.C., 1855; worked on monument to Oliver Hazard Perry, Cleve., 1859-60. Died 1882 or 1895.

WALDEN, Hiram, congressman, mfr.; b. Pawlet, Vt., Aug. 21, 1800; attended dist. schs. Moved to Berne, N.Y., 1818, Waldenville, N.Y., 1821; manufactured axes; served as maj. gen. militia; mem. N.Y. State Assembly, 1836; a supr. Town of Wright, 1842; mem. U.S. Ho. of Reps. (Democrat) from N.Y., 31st Congress, 1849-51; returned to mfg., also worked in customhouse, N.Y.C. Died Waldenville, July 21, 1880; buried Pine Grove Cemetery, Berne.

WALDEN, Madison Miner, congressman; b. nr. Scioto, Brush Creek, O., Oct. 6, 1836; attended Denmark Acad., Ia., also Wesleyan Coll., Mt. Pleasant, Ia.; grad. Wesleyan U., Delaware, O., 1859. Served as capt. 6th Regt., Ia. Volunteer Inf., also 8th Regt., Ia. Volunteer Cavalry, during Civil War, 1861-65; taught sch.; publisher Centerville (Ia.) Citizen, 1865-74; mem. Ia. Ho. of Reps., 1866-67, Ia. Senate, 1868-69; lt. gov. Ia., 1870; mem. U.S. Ho. of Reps. (Republican) from Ia., 1871-73; engaged in agriculture, coal mining, Centerville; apptd. chief clk. in office of Solicitor of Treasury, Washington, D.C., 1889. Died Washington, July 24, 1891; buried Oakland Cemetery, Centerville.

WALDERNE, Richard, colonial legislator; b. Alchester, Eng., Jan. 1615; s. William and Catharine (Raven) Walderne; m. 1st wife before 1640; m. 2d, Anne Scammon: Came to New Eng., 1640; rep. from N.H. (then part of Mass.) to Gen. Ct. at Boston, 1654-74, 77; delegated to deal with so-called Quaker menace, Dover, N.H., 1662; maj. Norfolk County (Mass.) Militia; mem. N.H., President's Council, 1680, acting pres., 1681; large landowner, sued by Robert Mason (who was attempting to validate his hereditary land claims), judgement made against Walderne. Tortured and killed by Indians on raid because of his previous cruel treatment of them, June 1689.

WALDO, David, physician, trader; b. Clarksburg, Va. (now W.Va.), Apr. 30, 1802; s. Jedediah and Polly (Porter) W.; studied medicine Transylvania U., Lexington, Ky.; m. Elizabeth Norris, Mar. 2, 1849, 5 children. Moved to Gasconade County, Mo., 1820; practiced medicine, Gasconade County, later Taos, Mexico (now N.M:); became Santa Fe trader, 1827; became Mason (3°), Mo. Lodge 1, 1829; became citizen Mexico, 1830; served in municipal govt. Taos; served as capt. Company A of Mo. in Mexican War; translated documents captured from Mexicans by Am. troops during war; returned to Independence, Mo., 1848; contbd. land to Bent Lodge 204 of Masonic Order, Taos, 1860; head of teamster co. to carry mail and provisions to U.S. Army in far West; became a banker. Died Independence, May 20, 1878.

WALDO, Loren Pinckney, congressman, lawyer; b. Canterbury, Conn., Feb. 2, 1802; attended common schs.; studied law. Became a sch. tchr. and farmer; moved to Tolland, Conn., 1823; admitted to bar, 1825, began practice of law, Somers; supt. of schs., postmaster Somers, 1829-30; returned to Tolland, 1830; mem. Conn. Ho. of Reps., 1832-34, 39, 47-48, clk., 1833; states atty., 1837-49; judge of probate for Tolland Dist., 1842-43; mem. com. to revise statutes, 1847, 64; mem. U.S. Ho. of Reps. (Democrat) from Conn., 32d Congress, 1849-51; commr. sch. fund of Conn.; commr. of pensions under Pres. Pierce, 1853-56; resumed practice of law, Hartford, Conn. Died Hartford, Sept. 8, 1881; buried Cedar Hill Cemetery.

WALDO, Samuel, mcht., land speculator; b. Boston, Dec. 1695; s. Jonathan and Hannah (Mason) W.; m. Lucy Wainwright; children include Samuel, Lucy, Hannah, Francis, Sarah, Ralph. Mcht., engaged in importing bus., Boston; land speculator, turned attention to lands on coast of Me. between Muscongus and Penobscot rivers, 1729; became chief propr. Muscongus grant (henceforth called Waldo patent), after 1731, started to settle region and produce lime and iron; served as brig. gen. in command Mass. Colonial Army in Louisburg campaign of 1745; renewed his land schemes, 1750's, advertised abroad (chiefly in Scotland, Ireland and Germany) for settlers; Waldoboro, Waldo County, Brigadier's Island, Mt. Waldo (all in Me.) named for him. Died Bangor, Me., May 23, 1759; reinterred King's Chapel Burial Ground, Boston.

WALDO, Samuel Lovett, artist; b. Windham, Conn., Apr. 6, 1783; s. Zacheus and Esther (Stevens) W.; m. Josephine Wood, Apr. 8, 1808; m. 2d, Deliverance Mapes, May 8, 1826. Took studio at Hartford, Conn., 1803; had success in Charleston, S.C., circa, 1803; went to England with letters of introduction to Benjamin West and John Singleton Copley, 1806; returned to U.S., 1809, settled in N.Y.C.; engaged in partnership with William Jewett, after 1820; a founder N.A.D., 1826, asso., 1847; it is probable that he painted heads and hands while his assistant painted backgrounds and costumes; painted portrait of G. W. Parke Custis (now in Corcoran Gallery, Washington, D.C.); painted sketch from life of Gen. Andrew Jackson, 1817, Old Pat, the Independent Beggar (a self-portrait and portrait of his 2d wife); represented in Met. Museum of Art, N.Y.C.; painted portraits of Mrs. William Steel (in City Art Museum, St. Louis), Peter Remsen (in N.Y. Hist. Soc.), Pres. James Madison, John Trumbull. Died N.Y.C., Feb. 16, 1861.

WALDO, Samuel Putnam, author; b. Pomfret, Charles V. Riley) Am. Entomologist, 1868; state nam) W.; studied law, East Windsor, Conn. Practiced law, East Windsor, 1805-16; wrote out Capt. Archibald Robbins' oral narrative of his shipwreck and slavery, 1817, published as Journal Comprising an Account of the Loss of the Brig Commerce . . . by Archibald Robbins; established Rural Magazine and Farmers' Monthly Museum, 1819; wrote "A Brief Sketch on the Indictment, Trial and Conviction of Stephen and Jesse Boorn for the Murder of Russell Colvin," 1820; other works include: The Tour of James Monroe, President of the United States, through the Northern and Eastern States in 1817, published 1818; Memoirs of Andrew Jackson, Major General . . . and Commander in Chief of the Division of the South, 1818, 5 editions; Life and Character of Stephen Decatur, 1821. Died Hartford, Conn., Feb. 23, 1826.

WALDRON, Henry, congressman, businessman; b. Albany, N.Y., Oct. 11, 1819; attended Albany Acad.; grad. Rutgers Coll., New Brunswick, N.J., 1836. Became civil engr. in railroad work, Mich., 1837; settled in Hillsdale, Mich., 1839; mem. Mich. Legislature, 1843; built 1st warehouse on Mich. So. R.R., 1843, mem. bd. dirs., 1846-48; a promoter, 1st pres. Detroit, Hillsdale & Southwestern R.R.; pres. 2d Nat. Bank of Hillsdale, until 1876; Whig presdl. elector, 1848; mem. U.S. Ho. of Reps. (Republican) from Mich., 34th-36th, 42d-44th congresses, 1855-61, 71-77; pres. 1st Nat. Bank of Hillsdale, 1876-80. Died Hillsdale, Sept. 13, 1880; buried Oak Grove Cemetery.

WALDSEEMÜLLER, Martin, cartographer; b. Freiburg, Germany, circa 1470; studied theology U. Freiburg. Became interested in cartography and geography as a youth; published map of world, Universalis cosmographia (contains 1st mention of name America, shows S.Am. as island) and Cosmographiae introductio (contains explanation of use of name America, suggests this name for New World), 1507 (a 1st edit. now in N.Y. Public Library); published Latin translation of 4 voyages of Amerigo Vespucci; produced Carta itineraria Europae (1st printed wall map of Europe), 1511; helped prepare 1513 edit. of Ptolemy's Geography (considered 1st modern atlas); apptd. canon of St. Dié, Lorraine, France, 1514; produced Carta marina navigatoria, 1516; often signed his maps with Greek spelling of his name, Illacomilus. Died St. Dié, circa 1522.

WALES, George Edward, congressman, lawyer; b. Westminster, Vt., May 13, 1792; attended common schs.; studied law, Westminster and Woodstock, Vt. Admitted to bar, 1812, began practice of law, Hartford, Vt.; treas. White River Bridge Co., 1818; mem. Vt. Ho. of Reps., 1822-24, speaker; mem. U.S. Ho. of Reps. from Vt., 19th-20th congresses, 1825-29; town clk. Hartford, 1840-60; judge of probate for Hartford Dist., 1847-50. Died Hartford, Jan. 8, 1860; buried Hartford Cemetery.

WALES, James Albert, cartoonist; b. Clyde, O., Aug. 30, 1852; s. William Washington and Martha (Dimm) W.; m. Claudia Cooper, Mar. 25, 1878, children. Worked for engraving firm Bogart & Stillman, Cincinnati; drew polit. cartoons on presidential campaign of 1872 for Cleveland Leader; went to N.Y.C., 1873, cartoonist for Wild Oats and Frank Leslie's Illustrated Newspaper; went to London, 1875, drew for Judy, Illustrated Sporting and

Dramatic News, London Illustrated News; joined staff English edition of Puck, 1877, started series of full-page polit. portraits under general title "Puck's Pantheon," did front and back covers and double page spreads for Puck on social and polit. subjects, including those on Chinese question, also "A Suggestion for the Next St. Paddy's Day Parade," 1879, "The Irish Idea of a Christian Burial," 1879; took prominent part in the Judge, 1881; returned to Puck, 1885; one of foremost Am. cartoonists. Died N.Y.C., Dec. 6, 1836; buried Clyde, O.

WALES, John, senator, lawyer; b. New Haven, Conn., July 31, 1783; grad. Yale, 1801; studied law. Admitted to bar, 1801, practiced law, New Haven, then Phila., later in Balt.; became pres. Nat. Bank of Wilmington and Brandywine, Wilmington, Del., 1815; sec. State of Del., 1845-49; mem. U.S. Senate (filled vacancy) from Del., Feb. 3, 1849-51; a founder Del. Coll., Newark. Died Wilmington, Dec. 3, 1863; buried Wilmington and Brandywine Cemetery.

WALES, Leonard Eugene, judge; b. Wilmington, Del., Nov. 26, 1823; s. John and Ann (Patten) W.; grad. Yale, 1845; studied law; never married. Admitted to Del. bar, 1848; editorial work on Del. State Journal, (Whig party organ); clk. U.S. circuit and dist. cts. for Del., 1849-64; city solicitor Wilmington, 1853-54; a founder Del. Republican Party, 1856; 2d lt. Company E, 1st Del. Volunteers, 1861; mem. Del. Board of Enrollment (administered national draft law), 1863; asso. justice Del. Superior Ct. for New Castle County, 1864; pres. Hist. Soc. Del., many years; founder West End Reading Room, Wilmington, Ferris Reform Sch.; U.S. dist. judge for Del., 1884-97, for N.J., 1886-89. Died Wilmington, Feb. 8, 1897.

WALKE, Henry, naval officer; b. "The Ferry," Princess Anne County, Va., Dec. 24, 1808; m. Sara J. Aim; m. 2d, Jane Ellen Burges; m. 3d, Julia Reed; at least 4 children. Commd. midshipman U.S. Navy, 1827; served in Natchez, 1827, in Ontario, 1829; commd. lt., 1839, sailed around world in ship Boston, 1840-43; exec. of brig Vesuvius against Vera Cruz, Alvarado, Tuspan and Tabasco in Mexican War; with Commodore Foote's Flotilla on Upper Mississippi River, 1861-63; in Carondelet in attack on Ft. Henry (Tennessee River), 1862; in attack on Ft. Donelson (Cumberland River), carried on alone 6-hour bombardment; most celebrated exploit was running of batteries at Island Number 10 (one of most famous events of Civil War); capt. in command ironclad Lafayette, 1862; served under Porter in passing of Vicksburg batteries and 5-hour action at Grand Gulf, 1863; commanded Sacramento, 1863-65; commd. commodore, 1866; commanded Mound City Naval Station, 1868-69; commd. rear adm., 1870-71; ret. to Bklyn., 1871. Author: Naval Scenes and Reminiscences of the Civil War, 1877. Died Bklyn., Mar. 8, 1896.

WALKER, Alexander, journalist; b. Fredericksburg, Va., Oct. 13, 1818; s. Alexander Walker; attended U. Va., 1836-37, 38-39; m. Mary McFarlane, 1842, at least 2 children. Practiced law, New Orleans, 1840; a mgr. Jeffersonian (chief Democratic organ of La.), New Orleans; judge City Ct., New Orleans, 1846-50; connected with New Orleans Daily Delta, 1846-48, Delta office published his City Digest, 1852; wrote unsigned account of yellow fever epidemic in New Orleans which appeared in Harpers Mag., 1853; edited Cincinnati Enquirer (leading Dem. paper in West); 1855-57; published Jackson and New Orleans, 1856; returned to New Orleans and Daily Delta, 1858; mem. La. Secession Conv., 1861; compiled (with Henry J. Labatt) The Bankrupt Law, 1867; edited New Orleans Times, 1867; helped establish Herald, 1872, merged with Daily Picayune, 1874; contbd. series of articles on Gen. Butler in New Orleans to Times-Democrat, 1884. Died Ft. Smith, Ark., Jan. 24, 1893.

WALKER, Amasa, congressman, economist; b. Woodstock, Conn., May 4, 1799; s. Walter and Priscilla (Carpenter) W.; m. Emeline Carleton, July 6, 1826; m. 2d, Hannah Ambrose, June 23, 1834; 3 children including Francis Amasa. Owner store, West Brookfield, Mass., 1820-23; agt. Methuen Mfg. Co., 1823-25; went to Boston, 1825, establish boot and shoe store with Charles G. Carlton; a founder, 1st sec. Boston Lyceum, 1829; wrote series of articles published in Boston Daily Advertiser and Patroit under signature South Market Street, urging building of railroad to connect Boston and Albany, 1837; mem. com. to visit Albany to convince citizens to build their end of railroad, 1837; pres. Boston Temperance Union, 1839; a founder Oberlin (O.) Coll., lectr. on polit. economy, 1842-49; v.p. Internat. Peace Congress, London, Eng., 1844, Paris Congress of 1849; mem. Mass. Ho. of Reps., 1849, Mass. Senate, 1850; sec. of state Mass., 1851-52; chmn. com. on suffrage in Mass. Constl. Conv., 1853; examiner in polit. economy Harvard, 1853-60; lectr. Amherst Coll., 1860-69; mem. Mass. Ho. of Reps., 1860, assisted in revising Mass. banking laws; mem. U.S. Ho. of Reps. (Republican) from Mass., 37th Congress, Dec. 1, 1862-63. Author: The Nature and Use of Money and Mixed Currency, 1857; The Science of Wealth: A Manual of Political Economy, 1866. Died North Brookfield, Mass., Oct. 29, 1875; buried Maple Street Cemetery, North Brookfield.

WALKER, Benjamin, congressman; b. London, Eng., 1753; attended Blue-Coat Sch. Came to U.S., settled in N.Y.C.; served as aide-de-camp to Gen. von Steuben, also mem. Gen. Washington's staff, during Revolutionary War; naval officer of customs Port of N.Y., 1791-98; moved to Ft. Schuyler (now Utica), N.Y., 1797; agt. of landed estate of Earl of Bath; mem. U.S. Ho. of Reps. (Democrat) from N. Y., 7th Congress, 1801-03. Died Utica, Jan. 13, 1818; buried Old Village Burying Ground; reinterred Forest Hill Cemetery, 1875.

WALKER, Charles Christopher Brainerd, congressman, businessman; b. Drewsville, nr. Keene, N.H., June 27, 1824. Moved to Corning, N.Y., 1848; postmaster Corning, 1856-60; engaged in contracting, hardware and lumber businesses; served as brigade q.m. with rank of capt. N.Y. State Militia during Civil War; del. Democratic nat. convs., Charleston, 1860, Balt., 1872; mem. U.S. Ho. of Reps. (Democrat) from N.Y., 44th Congress, 1875-77; mem. bd. control N.Y. Agrl. Expt. Sta. 1885-88. Died Corning, Jan. 26. 1888; buried Palmyra (N.Y.) Cemetery.

WALKER, David, abolitionist; b. Wilmington, N.C., Sept. 28, 1785; m. Miss Eliza, 1828, 1 child, Edwin G. Born free man; established 2d hand clothing business on Brattle Street, Boston before 1827; wrote pamphlet Walker's Appeal in Four Articles Together with a Preamble to the Colored Citizens of the World, but in particular and Very Expressly to Those of the United States of America, (appeal to violence in effort to get slaves to rise against owners) 1829; circulation of this pamphlet became capital offense in Ga.; price put on Walker's head in South. Died June 28, 1830.

WALKER, David, congressman; b. Brunswick County, Va.; attended public and pvt. schs. Served as pvt. under Gen. Lafayette, during Revolutionary War; present at surrender of Cornwallis at Yorktown; moved to Logan County, Ky.; clk. county and circuit cts.; mem. Ky. Ho. of Reps., 1793-96; served as maj. on staff Gov. Shelby of Ky. in Battle of Thames, during War of 1812; mem. U.S. Ho. of Reps. from Ky., 15th-16th congresses, 1817-20. Died Washington, D.C., Mar. 1, 1820; buried Congressional Cemetery, Washington.

WALKER, David, jurist; b. Todd County, Ky., Feb. 19, 1806; s. Jacob Wythe and Nancy (Hawkins) W.; m. Jane Lewis Washington, 1833, 8 children. Admitted to Ky. bar, 1829; pros. atty. of Fayetteville (Ark.), 1833-35; mem. Ark. Constl. Conv., 1836; mem. Ark. Senate (Whig), 1840; asso. justice Ark. Supreme Ct., 1848-66, 74-78, chief justice, 1866-67; pres. Ark. Secession Conv., 1861, actively supported Union cause; went to Boston in effort to secure railroad for No. Ark., 1870; del. Centennial Expn., Phila., 1876. Died Fayetteville, Sept. 30, 1879.

WALKER, David Shelby, jurist, gov. Fla.; b. Russellville, Ky., May 2, 1815; s. David and Mary (Barbour) W.; studied law with brother, George Walker; 1837-circa 1840; m. Philiclea Alston, May 22, 1842; m. 2d, Elizabeth Duncan; 5 children. Admitted to Fla. bar, circa 1840; mem. 1st Fla. Senate from 7th dist., 1845; mayor City of Tallahassee (Fla.), 1848; mem. Fla. Ho. of Reps. from Leon County, 1848-49; register of public lands, ex-officio supt. schs., 1850-59; asso. justice Fla. Supreme Ct., 1859-65; gov. Fla., 1865-67; judge 2d Jud. Circuit Ct., 1879-91. Died Tallahassee, July 20, 1891; buried Episcopal Cemetery, Tallahassee.

WALKER, Edward Dwight, editor; b. New Haven, Conn., 1858; grad. Williams Coll., 1876. Mem. editorial staff Harper & Bros. Co., 1876-78; editor Cosmopolitan Mag., 1878-90. Author: Reincarnation. Drowned while fishing in Roanoke River, N.C., 1890.

WALKER, Felix, congressman; b. Hampshire County, Va. (now W.Va.), July 19, 1753; attended country schs., nr. Columbia, S.C. also Burke County, N.C. Became clk. to a mcht., Charleston, S.C., 1769, also engaged in farming; founded (with Daniel Boone, others) Boonsboro, Ky., 1775; clk. Ct. of Washington Dist. (now mostly in Tenn.), 1775-76, Washington County Ct., 1777-78; served in Revolutionary and Indian wars; served as lt. Capt. Richardson's Co. in rifle regt. from Mecklenburg County; also capt. co. of light dragoons on Nolachucky River; clk. Rutherford County (N.C.) Ct., 1779-87; mem. N.C. Ho. of Commons, 1792, 99-1802, 06; resumed farming, also trader and land speculator, Haywood County, N.C.; mem. U.S. Ho. of Reps. (Democrat) from N.C., 15th-17th congresses, 1817-23; became farmer and trader, Miss., circa 1824. Died Clinton, Miss., 1828; probably buried in pvt. cemetery.

WALKER, Francis, congressman; b. "Castle Hill," nr. Cobham, Albemarle County, Va., June 22, 1764; magistrate Albemarle County; served as col. 88th Regt., Va. Militia; mem. Va. Ho. of Dels., 1788-91, 97-1801; mem. U.S. Ho. of Reps. from Va., 3d Congress, 1793-95. Died "Castle Hill," Mar. 1806; buried family cemetery at "Castle Hill."

WALKER, Francis Amasa, economist, coll. pres.; b. Boston, July 2, 1840; s. Amasa and Hannah (Ambrose) W.; A.B., Amherst Coll., 1860, A.M. (hon.), 1863, Ph.D. (hon.), 1875, LL.D. (hon.), 1881; studied law, 1860-61; A.M. (hon., Yale, 1873, LL.D. (hon.), 1881; Ph.D. (hon., U. Halle (Germany), 1894; LL.D. (hon.), Harvard, 1883, Columbia, 1887, St. Andrews Coll., 1888, U. Dublin (Ireland), 1892, U. Edinburgh (Scotland), 1896; m. Exene Stoughton, 1865, 7 children. Fought in Civil War, 1861-65, rose from pvt. to brig. gen.; taught Latin and Greek, Williston Sem., Easthampton, N.Y., 1865-68; spl. dep. of revenue under David Wells, then chief Bur. of Statistics, 1869; supt. 9th U.S. Census, 1870, 10th Census, 1879-81; prof. polit. economy and history Sheffield Scientific Sch. at Yale, 1873-81; pres. Mass. Inst. Tech., 1881-97; advocate of internat. bimetallism; del. to Internat. Monetary Conf., 1878; trustee Amherst Coll., 1879-89, Boston Public Library, 1895; mem. Nat. Acad. Sciences, 1878, v.p., 1891-97; pres. Am. Econ. Assn., 1885-92, Am. Statis. Assn., 1882-97. Author: Commerce and Navigation of the United States, 2 vols., 1868-69; Statistical Atlas of the United States, 1874; Money, 1878; Land and its Rent, Political Economy, 1883; International Bimetallism, 1896. Died Boston, Jan. 5, 1897.

WALKER, Freeman, senator; b. Charles City, Va., Oct. 25, 1780; attended common schs.; studied law. Admitted to bar, 1802, began practice of law, Augusta, Ga.; mem. Ga. Ho. of Reps., 1807-11; mayor Augusta, 1818-19, 23; mem. U.S. Senate (Democrat, filled vacancy) from Ga., Nov. 8, 1819-Aug. 6, 1821 (resigned). Died Augusta, Sept. 23, 1827; buried Spring Hill Cemetery.

WALKER, George, senator, lawyer; b. Culpeper County, Va., 1763; attended common schs.; studied law. Served under gens. Green and Morgan during Revolutionary War, 1780-81; admitted to bar, began practice of law, Nicholasville, Ky., 1799; a commr. Ky. River Co., 1801; mem. Ky. Senate, 1810-14; mem. U.S. Senate (filled vacancy) from Ky.,Aug. 30-Dec. 16, 1814. Died Nicholasville, 1819; buried on his estate nr. Nicholasville.

WALKER, Gilbert Carlton, gov. Va., congressman; b. South Gibson, Susquehanna County, Pa., Aug. 1, 1833; grad. Hamilton Coll., 1854; m. Olive Evans, 1857. Practiced law, Oswego, N.Y., 1855-59, Chgo., 1859-64; went to Norfolk, Va., 1865, organizer, pres. Exchange Nat. Bank; gov. Va., 1869-74; mem. U.S. Ho. of Reps. from Va., 44th-45th congresses, 1875-79; pres. N.Y. Underground R.R. Co. Died N.Y.C., May 11, 1885; buried Spring Forest Cemetery, Binghamton, N.Y.

WALKER, Isaac Pigeon, senator, lawyer; b. nr. Wheeling, Va. (now W.Va.), Nov. 2, 1815; attended common schs., Ill.; studied law. Employed as clk. in store; admitted to bar, 1834, began practice of law, Springfield; mem. Ill. Ho. of Reps., 1 term; Democratic presdl. elector, 1840; moved to Milw., 1841, continued practice of law; mem. spl. session 5th Legislative Assembly, 1847; mem. Wis. Territorial Legislature, 1847-48; mem. U.S. Senate (Democrat) from State of Wis., June 8, 1848-55; engaged in agriculture, Waukesha County; returned to Milw. Died Milw., Mar. 29, 1872; buried Forest Home Cemetery.

WALKER, James, clergyman, coll. pres.; b. Woburn (now Burlington), Mass., Aug. 16, 1794; s. James and Lucy (Johnson) W.; grad. Harvard, 1814, S.T.D. (hon.), 1835, LL.D. (hon.), 1860; studied divinity Cambridge (Eng.) U.; LL.D. (hon.), Yale, 1853; m. Catherine Bartlett, Dec. 21, 1829, no children. Licensed to preach, 1817; ordained to ministry Congregational Ch., 1818; leader among liberals in controversy between Trinitarians and Unitarians; organizer Am. Unitarian Assn., 1825; contbr. to Am. Unitarian Tracts and The Christian Examiner, editor, 1831-39; Alford prof. natural religion, moral philosophy and civil polity Harvard, 1839-53, pres., 1853-60; wrote pamphlet Philosophy of Man's Spiritual Nature in Regard to the Foundations of Faith published in Am. Unitarian Tracts; edited Dugald Stewart's Philosophy of the Active and Moral Powers, 1849; edited Thomas Reid's Essays on the Intellectual Powers of Man, 1850; published Sermons Preached in the Chapel of Harvard College, 1861; contributed his library and $15,000 to Harvard; mem. Mass. Hist. Soc.; fellow Am. Acad. Arts and Scis. Died Cambridge, Mass., Dec. 23, 1874.

WALKER, James, artist; b. Eng., June 3, 1819. Brought to Am. as child; went to New Orleans, later to Mexico City at outbreak of Mexican War, escaped from city, joined Am. forces as interpreter, present at capture of city and its occupation; returned to N.Y.C., 1848, established studio; visited S.Am.; painted Battle of Chapultepec for U.S. Capitol, Washington, D.C., 1857-62; painted numerous other hist. works, primarily concerned with battles of Civil War; went to Cal., 1884. Died Watsonville, Cal., Aug. 29, 1889.

WALKER, James Barr, clergyman, editor; b. Phila., July 29, 1805; s. James and Margaret (Barr) W.; grad. Western Res. Coll., 1831, D.D. (hon.); m. Rebecca Randall, June 6, 1833; m. 2d, Mary (Myrtle) Weamer, Apr. 3, 1876; 13 children. Bought half-interest in Western Courier, Ravenna, O.; practiced law; agt. for Am. Bible Soc.; conducted religious paper at Hudson, 1833-35; ordained to ministry Presbyn. Ch., 1837; pastor Presbyn. Ch., Akron, O., 1837-39; editor religious papers The Watchman of the Valley, Cincinnati, 1840-42, The Herald of the Prairies, Chgo., 1846-50; pastor Congregational Ch., Mansfield, O., 1842-46, 50-57, Sandusky, O., 1857-63; lectr. Chgo. Theol. Sem., 1859-65; went to Mich., 1865; mem. Mich. Senate, 1865; prof. intellectual and moral philosophy and belles-lettres Wheaton (Ill.) Coll., 1870; pastor Congregational Ch., Wheaton, 1871. Author: The Philosophy of the Plan of Salvation, (used as textbook in U.S., translated into several fgn. langs.), 1841; Philosophy of Skepticism and Ultraism, 1857. Died Wheaton, Mar. 6, 1887.

WALKER, James Peter, congressman; b. nr. Memphis, Tenn., Mar. 14, 1851; attended boys' coll., Durhamville, Tenn. Employed as clk. in country store, in early youth; moved to Dunkin County, Mo., 1867, engaged in agriculture; moved to Point Pleasant, 1871, entered transp. bus. on Mississippi River; became dry-goods mcht., Dexter, Mo., 1876, grain mcht., 1882; del. Democratic Nat. Conv., Cincinnati, 1880; mem. U.S. Ho. of Reps. (Democrat) from Mo., 50th-51st congresses, 1887-90. Died Dexter, July 19, 1890; buried Dexter Cemetery.

WALKER, John, senator, lawyer; b. "Castle Hill," nr. Cobham, Albemarle County, Va., February 13, 1774; grad. Coll. William and Mary, Williamsburg, Va., 1764; studied law. Became a planter, "Belvoir," Albemarle County; commd. (with father) to make spl. terms to retain friendship of Indians at Ft. Pitt (Pa.) during Revolutionary war; served as col., extra aide to Gen. Washington, 1777; admitted to bar, practiced law; mem. U.S. Senate (filled vacancy) from Va., Mar. 31-Nov. 9, 1790; resumed agrl. activities. Died nr. Madison Mills, Orange County, Va., Dec. 2, 1809; buried family cemetery "Belvoir."

WALKER, John Williams, senator, lawyer; b. Amelia County, Va., Aug. 12, 1783; grad. Princeton, 1806; studied law; at least 1 son, Percy. Admitted to bar, 1810, began pactice of law, Huntsville, Ala.; speaker Territorial Ho. of Reps., 1817; pres. Ala. Constl. Conv., 1819; mem. U.S. Senate (Democrat) from Ala., Dec. 14, 1819-Dec. 12, 1822 (resigned). Died Huntsville, Apr. 23, 1823; buried Maple Hill Cemetery.

WALKER, Jonathan Hoge, jurist; b. Hogestown, Pa., July 20, 1754; s. William and Elizabeth (Hoge) W.; grad. Dickinson Coll., 1787; m. Lucretia Duncan, circa 1788, 2 children including Robert J. Admitted to Northumberland County (Pa.) bar, 1790; president judge 3th Pa. Dist., 1806-18; U.S. judge for Western Pa. dist., 1818-24. Died Natchez, Miss., Jan. 1824.

WALKER, Joseph Reddeford, trapper, trader; b. Va., Dec. 13, 1798. Accompanied group of trappers into N.M., 1820, was quickly expelled; trapper and trader, operating from Independence, Mo., 1820-32; sheriff Jackson County (Mo.), for short time; trapper, trader and guide in Rocky and Sierra mountains, 1832-47; may have been 1st white man to cross Sierra Mountains from East, 1883; believed to have been discoverer Yosemite Valley; lived with Shoshone Indians; mem. Fremont's 2d expdn., guide on 3d Cal. expdn.; lived in Jackson County, 1847-49; an early "Forty-niner," 1849; operated out of Cal. gold mines, 1849-61. Died Oct. 27, 1876.

WALKER, Leroy Pope, Confederate ofcl.; b. Huntsville, Ala., Feb. 7, 1817; s. John Williams and Maria (Pope) W.; attended U. Ala., 1835-38; studied law U. Va.; m. Miss Hopkins; m. 2d, Eliza Pickett, July 1850. Admitted to Miss. bar, 1837; practiced in Miss.; solicitor State of Ala.; mem. Ala. Ho. of Reps. from Lawrence County, 1843, from Lauderdale County, 1847-50, speaker, 1847-50; judge Ala. Circuit Ct., 1850-53; presdl. elector at large, 1848, 52, 56, 76, 84; chmn. Ala. delegation to Democratic Nat. Conv., Charleston, S.C., 1860; del. to Richmond Conv.; spl. commr. to Tenn. to plead for her secession; sec. war in 1st cabinet of Confederate States Am., 1861, resigned; commd. brig. gen. Confederate Army, 1861, served in Dept. of Ala. and West Fla., 1861-62; judge of a mil. ct., 1863-65; pres. Ala. Constl. Conv. of 1875. Died Huntsville, Aug. 22, 1884.

WALKER, Mary (Mrs. Elkanah Walker), diarist; b. 1811; m. Elkanah Walker, Mar. 1838; son, Cyrus Hamlin (born on Ore. Trail). Accompanied her missionary husband to Ore. mission of Am. Bd. Missions (Presbyn.-Conglist.); made westward trip with party including Mr. and Mrs. William H. Gray, 1838; kept diary (original still extant), part of which, covering travels from lower Platte River to Columbia River, was pub. in Frontier, Mar. 1931.

WALKER, Percy, congressman; b. Huntsville, Ala., Dec. 1812; son of John Williams Walker; grad. med. dept. U. Pa. at Phila., 1835; studied law. Began practice of medicine, Mobile, Ala.; served in campaign against Creek Indians; admitted to bar, practiced law, Mobile; states atty. 6th Jud. Dist.; mem. Ala. Ho. of Reps., 1839, 47, 53; mem. U.S. Ho. of Reps. (Am. Party candidate) from Ala., 34th Congress, 1855-57. Died Mobile, Dec. 31, 1880; buried Magnolia Cemetery.

WALKER, Pinkney Houston, jurist; b. Adair County, Ky., June 18, 1815; s. Joseph G. and Martha (Scott) W.; m. Susan McCrosky, June 2, 1840; 9 children. Admitted to the bar, 1839; circuit judge Ill., 1853-58; justice Ill. Supreme Ct., 1858-85, chief justice, 1864-67, 74-75; important opinions include Carroll vs. East St. Louis, 1873, Starkweather vs. Am. Bible Soc., 1874, Rugles vs. People, 1878; wrote approximately 3,000 opinions (said to be largest number written by a U.S. judge). Died Springfield, Ill., Feb. 7, 1885.

WALKER, Reuben Lindsay, army officer, civil engr.; b. Logan, Va., May 29, 1827; s. Meriwether Lewis and Maria (Lindsay) W.; grad. Va. Mil. Inst., 1845; m. Maria Eskridge, 1848; m. 2d, Sally Elam, 1857; 8 children. Commd. capt. in Confederate Army in Civil War, 1861; maj. chief arty., A.P. Hill's div., 1862, connected with Hill's command throughout war, promoted col., chief of arty. when Hill became comdr. III Army Corps; brig. gen. arty., 1865; supt. Marine and Selma R.R., 1872-74; employed by Richmond & Danville R.R., 1876-77; supt. Richmond (Va.) street railways; constrn. engr. Richmond & Alleghany R.R.; superintended building of women's dept. Va. State Penitentiary; supt. constrn. Tex. State Capitol, 1884. Died on his farm at fork of Rivanna and James rivers, Va. June 7, 1890.

WALKER, Robert James, senator, lawyer; b. Northumberland, Pa., July 23, 1801; grad. U. Pa. at Phila., 1819; studied law. Admitted to bar, 1821, began practice of law, Pitts., 1822; chmn. Pa. Democratic Conv., 1823; moved to Natchez, Miss., 1826; mem. U.S. Senate (Democrat) from Miss., 1835-45 (resigned); U.S. sec. of treasury under Pres. James Polk, 1845-49; declined mission to China, 1853; gov. Kan., Apr.-Dec. 1857; U.S. financial agt. to Europe, 1863-64; practiced law, Washington, D.C. Died Washington, Nov. 11, 1869; buried Oak Hill Cemetery.

WALKER, Robert John, senator, sec. of treasury; b. Northumberland Pa., July 23, 1801; s. Jonathan Hoge and Lucretia (Duncan) W.; grad. U. Pa., 1819; m. Mary Bache, Apr. 4, 1825, 8 children. Admitted to Pitts. bar, 1821; nominated Andrew Jackson for U.S. Pres. Pa. Democratic Conv., 1824; moved to Natchez, Miss., 1826; mem. U.S. Senate from Miss., 1835-45, conspicuous in debates connected with surplus revenues and "American system," credited with passage of permanent preemption law of 1841, introduced and put through Senate resolution calling for recognition of independence of Tex., 1837, leader Tex. annexationists, drafted compromise resolutions which finally broke deadlock in Senate over annexation, 1845; head of Dem. Campaign Com., Washington, D.C., 1844; circulated pamphlet The South in Danger (characterized Whigs as antislavery), 1844; U.S. Sec. of treasury under Pres. James K. Polk, 1845-49, established independent treasury system, advocated free trade in report on state of finances, 1845, largely responsible for framing Tariff Bill of 1846 (lowered most tariffs), carried out financing of Mexican War, established warehouse system for handling imports; mainly responsible for creation of Dept. of Interior, 1849; gov. Kan. Territory, Apr.-Dec. 1857, resigned when Lecompton Constn. rejected; Unionist in Civil War; propr. (with F. P. Stanton) and contbr. to Continental Monthly, 1862-64; U.S. financial agt. to Europe, 1863, 64; concerned with peace parleys at Montreal, Que., Can., 1864-65. Died Washington, Nov. 11, 1869; buried Oak Hill Cemetery, Washington.

WALKER, Sears Cook, mathematician, astronomer; b. Wilmington, Mass., Mar. 23, 1805; s. Benjamin and Susanna (Cook) W.; grad. Harvard, 1825. Became actuary Pa. Co. for Ins. on Lives and Granting Annuities, 1836; founded one of 1st astron. observatories in connection with Phila. High Sch., 1837; prepared parallactic tables which reduced time required to compute phases of occultation, 1834; mem. staff U.S. Naval Observatory, Washington, D.C., 1845, discovered that planet Neptune was identical with star seen twice by Lalande in 1795, which had been referred to as star Number 26266, 1847; in charge of computations of geog. longitude in U.S. Coast Survey, 1847-53; originated telegraphing of transits of stars; developed registry of time observations known as Am. method. Published articles on astron. subjects. Died Cincinnati, Jan. 30, 1853.

WALKER, Thomas, army officer, explorer; b. King and Queen County, Va., Jan. 25, 1715; s. Thomas and Susanna (Peachy) W.; studied medicine under his uncle Dr. George Gilmer, Williamsburg, Va.; m. Mildred (Thornton) Meriwether, 1741; m. 2d, Elizabeth Thornton after 1778; 12 children including Francis, John. Became chief agt. Loyal Land Co., 1749; mem. Va. Ho. of Burgesses, 1752; dep. surveyor Augusta County (Va.), 1752; commissary gen. to Va. Militia, 1755; mem. Va. Ho. of Burgesses from Hampshire County, 1756-61, from Albemarle County, 1761; commr. to sell lots in Charlottesville, 1763; a signer Non-Importation Agreement, 1769; mem. Va. Com. of Safety, 1776; mem. Va. Exec. Council, 1776; mem. Va. Council, 1779; on committee to vindicate Va.'s claim to Western land. Died "Castle Hill," Albemarle County, Va., Nov. 9, 1794.

WALKER, Timothy, clergyman; b. Woburn, Mass., July 27, 1705; s. Capt. Samuel and Judith (Howard) W.; grad. Harvard, 1725; m. Sarah Burbeen, Nov. 12, 1730; 5 children including Sarah (Walker) Rolfe Thompson. Ordained minister Congregational Ch., 1730; pastor 1st parish to be established in Penacook (later Rumford, now Concord), N.H., 1739-82; went to Eng. as agt. for Rumford proprietors (when the Crown made settlement putting twp. into N.H., thus threatening Mass. pioneers with dispossession), gained favorable decision from Crown, 1753-55. Author: Diaries of Rev. Timothy Walker, edited by J. B. Walker, published 1889. Died Concord, N.H., Sept. 1, 1782.

WALKER, Timothy, lawyer, b. Wilmington, Mass., Dec. 1, 1802; s. Benjamin and Susanna (Cook) W.; grad. (1st scholar) Harvard, 1826, postgrad. in law 1829-30; studied in law office Storer & Fox, 1830; m. Ella Wood, Mar. 11, 1840, 5 children. Contbr. North Am. Review; lectr. on natural sci.; admitted to Ohio bar, 1831; teacher and organizer (with Judge John C. Wright) pvt. law sch., 1833 (later became part of U. Cincinnati 1896); judge Ct. Common Pleas, Hamilton County (O.), 1842-43; founder, editor Western Law Jour., 1843; apptd. to draw up rules of practice for circuit and dist. cts. Southern Dist. Author: Elements of Geometry, 1829; Introduction to American Law, 1837. Died Cincinnati, Jan. 15, 1856.

WALKER, William, adventurer; b. Nashville, Tenn., May 8, 1824; s. James and Mary (Norvell) W.; grad. U. Nashville, 1838; M.D., U. Pa., 1843; studied law. Admitted to New Orleans bar; an editor and propr. New Orleans Daily Crescent, 1848; went to Cal. as part of gold rush, 1850; interested in colonizing Mexican states of Sonora and Lower Cal. with Am. settlers, 1853, did not receive permission of Mexico; organized armed expdn., 1853, landed at La Paz, proclaimed Lower Cal. an independent republic with himself as pres.; annexed State of Sonora, 1854; forced out of Mexico by Mexican attacks; retreated northward into U.S., surrendered to Am. force at border, 1854; brought to trial for violating neutrality laws, acquitted; fitted out expdn. of emigrants to Nicaragua to fight in revolution there, 1855; with help of Accessory Transit Co. (Am. transp. concern operating between Atlantic ports and San Francisco by way of Nicaragua) captured Granada, brought revolution to end; new regime recognized by U.S., 1856, inaugurated pres.; opposition to his plans headed by Cornelius Vanderbilt who wanted control of Accessory Transit Co.; cut off from U.S. reinforcements, besieged by allied forces from Honduras, El Salvador, Guatemala and Costa Rica; surrendered to Comdr. Charles Henry Davis of U.S. Navy, 1857; sailed from Mobile to Nicaragua, 1857; landed at Gray Town, arrested by Commodore Hiram Paulding of U.S. Navy, sent back to U.S.; landed in Honduras, evaded Am. and Brit. naval forces stationed on coast of Nicaragua to prevent his landing there; arrested and turned over to Honduran authorities, condemned to death by court martial. Author: The War in Nicaragua, 1860. Executed by firing squad, Trujillo, Honduras, Sept. 12, 1860.

WALKER, William Adams, congressman; b. N.H., June 5, 1805; attended Northampton Law Sch. Admitted to bar, never practiced law; moved to N.C., 1832; prin. of public sch., N.Y.C.; county supt. common schs., 1843-47; mem. bd. aldermen, 1846; commr. of jurors; mem. U.S. Ho. of Reps. (Democrat) from N.Y., 33d Congress, 1853-55. Died

Irvington, West Chester County, Dec. 18, 1861; buried Sleepy Hollow Cemetery, Tarrytown, N.Y.

WALKER, William Henry Talbot, army officer; b. Augusta, Ga., Nov. 26, 1816; s. Freeman and Mary Washington (Creswell) W.; grad. U.S. Mil. Acad., 1837; m. Mary Townsend, 4 children. Commd. 2d lt. 6th Inf., U.S. Army, 1837; served in Fla. Indian War, brevetted 1st lt. for gallant conduct at Battle of Okeechobee; resigned from army, 1838, reappointed, 1840, rejoined his regt. and served through Fla. war; commd. capt., 1845; participated in all battles of Mexican War, brevetted maj. for heroic conduct at Contreras, 1847, lt. col. for gallantry at Molino del Rey, 1847; presented with sword of honor by State of Ga., 1849; in recruiting service, 1847-52, dep. gov. of mil. asylum, East Pascagoula, Miss., 1852-54; comdt. of cadets, instr. mil. tactics U.S. Mil. Acad., 1854-56; commd. maj., 1855; resigned from U.S. Army, 1860, entered Confederate service; commd. maj. gen. Ga. Volunteers, 1861, brig. gen. Confederate Army, 1861; brigade comdr. in Northern Va.; resigned commn., 1861; maj. gen. Ga. Militia, Nov. 1861; reentered Confederate service as brig. gen., 1863, promoted maj. gen., 1864; in command reserves at Battle of Chickamauga; with Army of Tenn. during campaign in Northern Ga. Killed in action, July 22, 1864; buried family burial ground, Summerville (now part of Augusta), Ga.

WALKER, William Johnson, physician, financier, philanthropist; b. Charlestown, Mass., Mar. 5, 1790; s. Maj. Timothy and Abigail (Johnson) W.; grad. Harvard, 1810, M.D., 1813; studied abroad under Laennec, Corvisart, Sir Astley Cooper; m. Eliza Hurd, Apr. 16, 1816. Returned to Charlestown, 1816; physician, surgeon to Mass. State Prison; cons. physician Mass. Gen. Hosp., 1816; orator before Mass. Med. Soc., 1845, presented An Essay on the Treatment of Compound and Complicated Fractures, 1845; offered Harvard approximately $130,000 for reforming Med. Sch., gift refused because he demanded new faculty acceptable to himself; willed gifts to Amherst Coll., Tufts U., Mass. Inst. Tech., Boston Soc. Natural History; endowed professorships in mathematics at Amherst and Tufts, 1861; contbns. to ednl. instns. total over $1,000,000. Died Newport, R.I., Apr. 2, 1865.

WALL, Garret Dorset, senator, lawyer; b. Middletown, N.J., Mar. 10, 1783; studied law; at least 1 son, James Walter. Licensed as atty., 1804, as counselor, 1807, practiced law, Burlington, N.J.; commanded volunteer regt. from Trenton in War of 1812; clk. N.J. Supreme Ct., 1812-17; q.m. gen. N. J., 1815-37; mem. N.J. Gen. Assembly, 1827; U.S. dist. atty. N.J., 1829; elected gov. N.J., 1829, declined to serve; mem. U.S. Senate (Democrat) from N.J., 1835-41; judge N.J. Ct. of Errors and Appeals, 1848-50. Died Burlington, Nov. 22, 1850; buried St. Mary's Churchyard.

WALL, James Walter, senator, lawyer; b. Trenton, N.J., May 26, 1820; son of Garret Dorset Wall; grad. Princeton, 1838; studied law. Admitted to bar, 1841, began practice of law, Trenton; commr. in bankruptcy; moved to Burlington, N.J., 1847; mayor Burlington, 1850; mem. U.S. Senate (Democrat, filled vacancy) from N.J., Jan. 14-Mar. 3, 1863; resumed practice of law, Burlington, also engaged in writing. Died Elizabeth, N.J., June 9, 1872; buired St. Mary's Protestant Episcopal Churchyard, Burlington.

WALL, William, congressman, businessman; b. Phila., Mar. 20, 1800. Became rope mfr.; moved to Kings County, L.I., N.Y., 1822; trustee, commr. of highways, supr., mem. bd. of finance, commr. of waterworks of Williamsburg (now part of N.Y.C.); mayor Williamsburg, 1853; an incorporator Williamsburg Savs. Bank, pres. for number of years; a founder Williamsburg City Bank (later 1st Nat. Bank), Williamsburg Dispensary; mem. U.S. Ho. of Reps. (Republican) from N.Y., 37th Congress, 1861-63; del. Loyalist Conv., Phila., 1866. Died Bklyn., Apr. 20, 1872; buried Greenwood Cemetery.

WALL, William Guy, artist; b. Dublin, Ireland, 1792; married. Came to Am., 1818, settled in N.Y.C.; painted views of Hudson River and N.Y.C. (became well known), some of which were engraved and published in Hudson River Portfolio, 1820; a founder N.A.D., exhibitor; exhibited Pa. Acad., Apollo Assn.; moved to Newport, R.I., circa 1828, to New Haven, Conn., circa 1834, Bklyn., circa 1836; returned to Ireland, settled in Dublin; painted pictorial backgrounds for silhouettist Hubard; exhibited in Dublin, London, Eng., several Am. galleries, circa 1840-60; returned to Am., settled in Newburgh, N.Y., 1856-62; returned to Dublin.

WALLACE, Alexander Stuart, congressman, planter; b. nr. York, S.C., Dec. 30, 1810. Became a planter, nr. York; mem. S.C. Ho. of Reps., 1854-58; mem. U..S Ho. of Reps. (Republican, contested election) from S.C., 41st-44th congresses, May 27, 1870-77. Died nr. York, June 27, 1893; buried Rose Hill Cemetery, York.

WALLACE, Daniel, congressman, lawyer; b. nr. Laurens, S.C., May 9, 1801; studied law. Moved to Union County, S.C., 1833; served as maj. gen. state militia; admitted to bar, practiced law, Union and Jonesville, S.C.; also engaged in agriculture; mem. S.C. Ho. of Reps., 1844-48; mem. U.S. Ho. of Reps. (Whig, filled vacancy) from S.C., 30th-32d congresses, June 12, 1848-53. Died Jonesville, May 18, 1859; buried Old Presbyn. Cemetery, Union.

WALLACE, David, gov. Ind., congressman; b. nr. Lewistown, Mufflin County, Pa., Apr. 4, 1799; s. Andrew and Eleanor (Jones) W.; grad. U.S. Mil. Acad., 1821; m. Esther Test; m. 2d, Zerelda Sanders; 7 children including Gen. Lewis. Tchr. mathematics U.S. Mil. Acad., 1821-22, resigned commn., 1822; admitted to Ind. bar, 1824; mem. Ind. Ho. of Reps., 1828-30; lt. gov. Ind., 1831-37, 6th gov., 1837-40; mem. U.S. Ho. of Reps. from Ind., 27th Congress, 1841-43,, mem. ways and means com., 1841-42; mem. Ind. Constl. Conv., 1850; judge Ind. Ct. Common Pleas, 1856-59. Died Indpls., Sept. 4, 1859; buried Crown Hill Cemetery.

WALLACE, Horace Binney, author, critic; b. Phila., Feb. 26, 1817; s. John Bradford and Susan (Binney) W.; attended U. Pa., 1830-32, med. student, 1838; A.B., Coll of N.J. (now Princeton), 1835. Admitted to Phila. bar, 1840. Author: Stanley, or The Recollections of a Man of the World, 2 vols., 1838; credited with authorship of Napoleon and the Marshals of the Empire (also attributed to Rufus W. Griswold), 2 vols., 1848; wrote pamphlet "The Military and Civil Life of George Washington," 1849; wrote extensive critical commentaries on works by John William Smith, Frederick Thomas White and Owen Davies Tudor; 2 lit. miscellanies, Art Scenery and Philosophy in Europe (1855) and literary Criticisms and Other Papers (1856) published posthumously. Died Paris, France, Dec. 16, 1852 (presumably a suicide); buried Montmarte, Paris, reinterred St. Peter's Churchyard, Phila.

WALLACE, James M., congressman; b. Lancaster (now Dauphin) County, Pa., 1750; attended sch. in Phila. Served with various cos. in Revolutionary War, maj. battalion of Associators at end of war; commanded co. of rangers in defense of frontier, 1779; commd. maj. Dauphin County Militia, 1796; a commr. Dauphin County, 1799-1801; mem. Pa. Ho. of Reps., 1806-10; mem. U.S. Ho. of Reps. (filled vacancy) from Pa., 14th-16th congresses, Oct. 10, 1815-21; retired to his farm. Died nr. Hummelstown, Pa., Dec. 17, 1823; buried Old Derry Church Graveyard, Derry (now Hershey), Pa.

WALLACE, John William, legal scholar; b. Phila., Feb. 17, 1815; s. John Bradford and Susan (Binney) W.; grad. U. Pa., 1833; m. Dorothea Willing, June 15, 1853, 1 child. Admitted to the bar, 1836; librarian Law Assn. Phila., 1841-60, treas., 1841-63; contbd. American Notes to 3d volume of Cases Chiefly Relating to the Criminal and Presentment Law Reserved for Consideration; published anonymously The Reporters, Chronologically Arranged. . ., 1844; standing master in chancery of Pa. Supreme Ct., 1844; wrote reports Cases in the Circuit Court of the United States for the Third Circuit covering years 1842-62, appeared 1849, others, 1854, 71; reporter U.S. Supreme Ct., 1863-75; published 23 volumes of Wallace's Reports covering period 1863-74; mem. Hist. Soc. Pa., 1844, pres., 1868-84. Author: The Want of Uniformity of the Commercial Law between the Different States of Our Union, 1851. Died Phila., Jan. 12, 1884.

WALLACE, John Winfield, congressman, physician; b. nr. Beaver Falls, Pa., Dec. 20, 1818; attended Darlington (Pa.) Acad.; grad. Jefferson Med. Coll., Phila., 1846. Began practice of medicine, Darlington; moved to New Castle, Pa., 1850; held several local offices; mem. U.S. Ho. of Reps. (Republican) from Pa., 37th, 44th congresses, 1861-63, 75-77; served as paymaster in U.S. Army, during Civil War; Republican presdl. elector, 1872, 88. Died New Castle, June 24, 1889; buried Grandview Cemetery, nr. Beaver Falls.

WALLACE, Jonathan Hasson, congressman, lawyer; b. Columbiana County, O., Oct. 31, 1824; grad. Washington (Pa.) Coll. (now Washington and Jefferson U.), 1844; studied law. Admitted to bar, began practice of law, New Lisbon, O.; pros. atty. Columbiana County, 1851, 53; mem. U.S. Ho. of Reps. (Democrat, contested election) from Ohio, 48th Congress, May 27, 1884-85; judge Ct. of Common Pleas, 1885-86. Died Lisbon, O., Oct. 28, 1892; buried Lisbon Cemetery.

WALLACE, Nathaniel Dick, congressman, businessman; b. Columbia, Tenn., Oct. 27, 1845; grad. Trinity Coll., Dublin, Ireland, 1865. Entered commn. business, New Orleans, 1878; pres. New Orleans Produce Exchange, twice; also engaged in mfg.; mem. U.S. Ho. of Reps. (Democrat, filled vacancy) from La., 49th Congress, Dec. 9, 1886-87; pres. Consumers Ice Co., New Orleans, 1886-94. Died Kenilworth, nr. Asheville, N.C., July 16, 1894; buried Metairie Cemetery, New Orleans.

WALLACE, William Alexander Anderson, frontiersman; b. Lexington, Va., Apr. 3, 1817; s. Andrew and Jane (Blair) W.; never married. Went to Tex., 1837; joined a Ranger band under John Coffee Hays, 1840; sgt. in R. A. Gillespie's Mounted Rangers, 1845-46 (unit became part of Tex. Mounted Rifle Volunteers, 1846); served to 1st lt. during Mexican War; apptd. by gov. of Tex. to raise a co. of volunteers for Indian fighting, 1850; engaged in frontier duty against Indians in Tex., during Civil War. Died Devine, Tex., Jan. 7, 1899; buried State Cemetery, Austin, Tex.

WALLACE, William Andrew, senator, lawyer; b. Huntingdon, Pa., Nov. 28, 1827; attended schs., Clearfield, Pa.; studied law. Admitted to bar, circa 1847, began practice of law, Clearfield; taught sch., Clearfield; del. Pa. Democratic Conv., 1861; mem. Pa. Senate, 1863-75, 82-87, speaker, 1871; del. Dem. nat. convs., 1864, 72, 76, 80, 84, 92, chmn. Pa. delegation, 1872, 76; chmn. Pa. Dem. Central Com., 1865-68; mem. commn. to suggest amendments to Pa. Constn., 1874; mem. U.S. Senate, 1875-81; interested in developing coal fields, Clearfield region; also pres. Beech Creek R.R. Died N.Y.C., May 22, 1896; buried Hillcrest Cemetery, Clearfield.

WALLACE, William Henson, congressman, lawyer; b. Troy, O., July 19, 1811; attended common schs., Ind.; studied law. Admitted to bar, practiced law; moved to Ia., 1837; served as col. Ia. troops; apptd. receiver public money, Fairfield, Ia.; moved to Wash. Territory, 1853; mem. Territorial Council, 1855-56, served as pres.; mem. U.S. Congress (Republican) from Wash. Territory, 37th Congress, 1861-63, from Ida. Territory, 38th Congress, Feb. 1, 1864-65; apptd. 1st gov. Ida. Territory, 1863. Died Steilacoom, Pierce County, Wash., Feb. 7, 1879; buried Ft. Steilacoom Cemetery.

WALLACE, William Ross, poet; b. Lexington or Paris, Ky., 1819; studied law Hanover (Ind.) Coll., 1833-35; married twice; m. 2d, Miss Riker, Oct. 1856; 3 children. Published 1st poem, The Battle of Tippecanoe, Cincinnati, 1837; practiced law, N.Y.C., 1841-48; contbr. to Harper's Mag., Harper's Weekly, Godey's Lady's Book, N.Y. Ledger, Celtic Monthly. Author: (poetical romance) Alban the Pirate, 1848; (collection of lyrics, odes, love songs) Meditations in America, and Other Poems, 1851; wrote patriotic songs including The Sword of Bunker Hill, Keep Step with the Music of the Union, 1861, The Liberty Bell, 1862; authored lines "And the hand that rocks the cradle . . . Is the hand that rules the world." Died N.Y.C., May 3, 1881.

WALLACK, Henry John, actor; b. London, Eng., 1790; s. William H. and Elizabeth (Field Granger) W.; m. Fanny Jones; m. 2d Miss Turpin, circa 1834; children—James William, Julia, Fanny. Made Am. debut in Balt., 1819, 1st N.Y. appearance at Anthony St. Theatre, 1821; during long Am. contract played roles including Brutus, Octavian, Rob Roy, Coriolanus, Capt. Bertram (in Eternal Discord), Gambia (in opera The Slave); leading man of Chatham Garden Theatre, 1824-28; returned to Eng., 1828-32, 34-36, summer 1840; appeared opposite Edwin Forrest in various parts, 1839; played Sir Peter Teazle in play The School for Scandal, Broadway Theatre, 1847; played roles ranging from Rolla in Pizarro, Fagin in Oliver Twist, Anthony Absolute in The Rivals to Shakespearean plays. Died N.Y.C., Aug. 30, 1870.

WALLACK, James William, actor, theatrical mgr.; b. London, Eng., Aug. 24, 1795; s. William H. and Elizabeth (Field) Granger Wallack; attended Academic Theatre, Leicester Square, London; m. Susan Johnstone, 1817, at least 2 children, John Lester, Charles. With Company of Drury Lane Theatre, London, Royal Hibernian Theatre, Dublin, Ireland; made Am. debut as Macbeth at Park Street Theatre, N.Y.C., 1818; toured Am.; played Don César de Bazan, Capt. Bertram in Fraternal Discord, Massaroni in The Brigand, Don Felix in The Wonder; played season in England, 1820, returned to Am.; played Hamlet, Rolla, Macbeth, Richard III, and Romeo in N.Y.C.; appeared at Arch Street Theater, Phila., 1828; mgr. National Theatre, N.Y.C., 1837; managed Niblo's Garden, 1839; appeared at Park Street Theatre, 1844; owner, mgr. Brougham's Lyceum, N.Y.C., 1852-61; with son Lester opened New Wallack's Theatre at Broadway and 13th St., N.Y.C., 1861; made frequent appearances in Eng. throughout career. Died N.Y.C., Dec. 25, 1864.

WALLACK, James William, actor; b. London, Eng., Feb. 24, 1818; s. Henry John and Fanny (Jones) W.; m. Mrs. Ann Waring Sefton, 2 children. Came to U.S. 1819; joined father (then stage mgr. Convent Gardens), London, 1835; played Fag in The Rivals, 1837; played Othello at Haymarket, London, 1851, Macbeth in Phila., 1852; toured Am.; then mgr., London, also Paris, France, 1853, 55; played Leon de Bourbon in The Man in the Iron Mask; joined stock co. of his cousin at Lester Wallack Theatre, N.Y., 1865; played Fagin in Oliver Twist, 1867, Johnson in The Lancanshire Lass, Mathias in The Bells, 1872-73. Died on train nr. Aiken, S.C., May 24, 1873.

WALLACK, John Johnstone Lester (stage name Lester Wallack), actor, dramatist; b. N.Y.C., Jan. 1, 1820; s. James William and Susan (Johnstone) W.; m. Emily Millais, 1848, 4 children. Made 1st profl. appearance as Angelo in Tortesa the Usurer, billed as Allan Field; billed as John Lester, circa 1841; stage mgr., actor at Theatre Royal, Southampton, Eng., 1844; played Benedick and Mercutio at Queen's Theatre, Manchester, Eng., 1845; returned to U.S., 1847, made 1st appearance at Broadway Theatre as Sir Charles Coldstream in Used Up, N.Y.C.; played Captain Absolute, Mercutio; Sir Frederick Blount in Bulwer-Lytton's Money and Osric in Hamlet; played Don César de Bazan at Chatham Theatre, 1848; played Cassio to Edwin Forrest's Othello at The Broadway, 1848; played Edmond Dantes in The Count of Monte Cristo, 1848; presented his plays The Three Guardsmen and The Four Musketeers, or Ten Years After, 1849; entered Burton's company at Chambers Street Theatre, N.Y.C., 1850; stage mgr. at Brougham's Lyceum, 1852; appeared in own plays Two to One, 1854, First Impressions, 1856, The Veteran; mgr. Wallack's Theatre at Broadway and 13th St., 1861, appeared there for 1st time as Lester Wallack; played Elliot Grey in his own play Rosedale, 1863, Hugh Chalcote in Ours, Henry Beauclerc in Diplomacy, 1878, Prosper Couramont in A Scrap of Paper, 1879. Author: Memories of Fifty Years, 1889. Died Stamford, Conn., Sept. 6, 1888.

WALLER, Emma, actress; b. Eng., 1820; m. Daniel Wilmarth Waller, 1849, at least 1 son. Came to Am. with husband after minor career on English stage, 1851; acted with husband in Australia, 1853; made debut at Drury Lane Theater, London, Eng., as Pauline in The Lady of Lyons; returned to U.S., 1857; made Am. debut as Ophelia at Walnut Street Theatre, Phila., also played Lady Macbeth in Phila.; made N.Y.C. debut as Marina in the Duchess of Malfi, 1858; other famous characterizations include Queen Margaret in Richard III, Queen Katherine in Henry VIII; also famous as female impersonator of Shakespearean male roles, especially Iago and Hamlet. Died N.Y.C., Feb. 28, 1899.

WALLER, John Lightfoot, clergyman, editor; b. Woodford County, Ky., Nov. 23, 1809; s. Edmund and Elizabeth (Lightfoot) W.; m. Amanda Beatty, Aug. 1834. Taught school, Jessamine County, Ky., 1828-34; joined Glen's Creek Baptist Ch., 1833; wrote pamphlet Letters to a Reformer, Alias Campbellite, 1835; editor bi-weekly Baptist Banner, Shelbyville, Ky., 1835, only Baptist paper in Ky., known as Baptist Banner and Western Pioneer, 1841; ordained to ministry Baptist Ch., Louisville, Ky., 1840; gen. agt. Gen. Assn. of Ky. Baptists, 1841-43; helped establish Sunday schools, Bible, missionary and benevolent socs. as gen. agt. Gen. Assn. Ky. Bapts.; founded Western Baptist Review (later called Christian Repository), 1845; del. to Ky. Constl. Conv., 1849; pres. Bible Revision Assn., 1852-54. Died Louisville, Oct. 10, 1854; buried Frankfort, Ky.

WALLEY, Samuel Hurd, congressman, lawyer; b. Boston, Aug. 31, 1805; attended Phillips Acad., Andover, Mass.; attended Yale, 1822; grad. Harvard, 1826; studied law. Admitted to Suffolk bar, 1831, practiced law, Boston and Roxbury; also a banker; treas. Vt. Central R.R.; promoter, 1st treas. Wis. Central R.R.; mem. Mass. Ho. of Reps,, 1836, 40-46, speaker, 1844-46; corporate mem. Am. Bd. Commrs. Fgn. Missions, 1848-67; mem. U.S. Ho. of Reps. (Whig) from Mass., 33d Congress, 1853-55; unsuccessful Whig candidate for gov. Mass., 1855; pres. Revere Nat. Bank. Died Nantasket Beach, Plymouth County, Mass., Aug. 27, 1877; buried Mt. Auburn Cemetery, Cambridge, Mass.

WALLING, Ansel Tracy, congressman, lawyer; b. Otsego County, N.Y., Jan. 10, 1824; attended acad., Erie County, Pa.; studied medicine, practiced briefly; studied law. Moved to Ohio, 1843, became a journalist; clk. Ohio Legislature, 1851-52; admitted to bar, 1852, practiced law; editor Daily Times, Keokuk, Ia., 1855-58; del. Democratic Nat. Conv., Cincinnati, 1856; resumed practice of law, Circleville, O., 1861; mem. Ohio Senate, 1865; mem. Ohio Ho. of Reps., 1867, speaker pro tem; mem. U.S. Ho. of Reps. (Democrat) from Ohio, 44th Congress, 1875-77. Died Circleville, June 22, 1896; buried Forest Cemetery.

WALLIS, Severn Teackle, lawyer; b. Balt., Sept. 8, 1816; s. Philip and Elizabeth (Teackle) W.; grad. St. Mary's Coll., Balt., 1832. Admitted to Md. bar, 1837; a founder Md. Hist. Soc., 1844, pres., 1892-94; corresponding mem. Royal Acad. of History, Madrid, Spain, 1844; fellow Royal Soc. of No. Antiquities, Copenhagen, Denmark, 1846; made 1st visit to Spain, 1847, 2d visit, 1849; commd. by U.S. Govt. to report upon public land titles in Fla., 1849; joined polit. reform movement, Balt., 1858, mem. com. which drew up series of reform bills (adopted by Legislature 1860), 1859; del. to spl. assembly, Frederick, Md., 1861, chmn. com. on fed. relations of Ho. of Dels.; leader of Md. bar, almost 50 years; provost U. Md., 20 years; an original trustee Peabody Inst., pres. bd., until 1894; pres. Civil Service Reform Assn. of Md., Reform League of Balt. Author: Writings of Severn Teackle Wallis, published in 4 vol. Meml. Edition, 1896. Died Apr. 11, 1894.

WALN, Nicholas, lawyer, clergyman; b. Fair Hill, Pa., Sept. 19, 1742; s. Nicholas and Mary (Shoemaker) W.; m. Sarah Richardson, May 22, 1771, 7 children. Admitted to Pa. bar, 1762; mem. Soc. of Friends, 1772-1813; visited Quaker meetings and families in Eng., 1783-85, Ireland, 1795; traveled to most of the centers of Quaker life and thought in Am.; clk. meeting of ministers and elders dealing with "Free Quakers" for supporting Revolutionary War with arms, 1777-89; apptd. chief ofcl. Phila. Yearly Meeting, 1789; a character in Hugh Wynne (novel by Dr. S. Weir Mitchell) based on his life. Died Sept. 29, 1813.

WALN, Robert, textile mfr., congressman; b. Phila., Feb. 22, 1765; s. Robert and Rebecca (Coffin) W.; m. Phebe Lewis, Oct. 10, 1787; 9 children including Robert. Mem. Pa. Legislature, 1794-98; mem. U.S. Ho. of Reps. from Pa., 5th-6th congresses, 1798-1801; v.p. Phila. C. of C., 1809; dir. Phila. Ins. Co., 1804-13; constructed cotton textile mills, Trenton, N.J., during War of 1812; supporter of high tariff acts of 1816, 24, 28; 1st pres. Merc. Library, 1821-24; trustee U. Pa., 1829; mem. Phila. Common Council, 1794, 96, Select Council, 1807, 09, 11. Author: Seven Letters to Elias Hicks, 1825; An Examination of the Boston Report, 1828. Died Jan. 24, 1836.

WALN, Robert, author; b. Phila., Oct. 20, 1794; s. Robert and Phebe (Lewis) W. Lived entire life on family estate Waln-Grove, Pa., except for visit to China, 1819-20; wrote The Hermit in America on a Visit to Philadelphia . . . Edited by Peter Atall (a satire on manners of wealthy Phila. society), Esq., 1819; other works include: Sisyphi Opus, or Touches of the Times, 1820, American Bards, 1820, Account of the Asylum for the Insane Established by the Society of Friends, near Frankford, in the Vicinity of Philadelphia (published posthumously), 1825; editor Biography of the Signers to the Declaration of Independence, vols. 3, 4, 1823-24. Died Providence, R.I., July 4, 1825.

WALSH, Benjamin Dann, entomologist; b. Clapton, London, Eng., Sept. 21, 1808; s. Benjamin Walsh; B.A., Trinity Coll., Cambridge (Eng.) U., 1831, M.A. (hon.), 1834; m. Rebecca Finn, 1837. Came to U.S., 1838; pioneer in demonstrating that Am. farmers aided multiplication of insects by improper planting of crops, also pioneered introduction of fgn. parasites and natural enemies of imported insect pests; founder and editor (with Charles V. Riley) Am. Entomologist, 1868; state entomologist Ill., published his only ofcl. report in Transactions of the Ill. State Hort. Soc., 1867. Author: The Comedies of Aristophanes, Translated into Corresponding English Metres, published in Blackwood's Mag., 1837; contbr. agrl. articles to Proceedings of Boston Soc. of Natural History, also Transactions of Am. Entomol. Soc. Died Rock Island, Ill., Nov. 18, 1869.

WALSH, Michael, editor, congressman; b. nr. Cork, Ireland, circa 1815; s. Michael Welsh; m. Catherine Riley (or Wiley), at least 2 children. Reporter and Washington (D.C.) corr. for Aurora, N.Y.C., 1839-43; started organized polit. opposition to Tammany control of N.Y.C. Democratic orgn., 1840; founder paper The Subterranean, N.Y.C., 1843, merged with George Henry Evans' Working Man's Advocate, 1844, revived as Subterranean, 1844-46; mem. N.Y. State Assembly, 1846, 47, 52; mem. U.S. Ho. of Reps. from N.Y., 33d Congress, 1853-55. Died N.Y.C., Mar. 17, 1859.

WALSH, Robert, journalist; b. Balt., Aug. 30, 1784; s. Robert and Elizabeth (Steel) W.; attended Georgetown Coll.; B.A., M.A., St. Mary's Sem.; m. Anna Moylan, May 8, 1810; m. 2d, Mrs. Stocker; 12 children. Contbd. article on mil. conscription to Edinburgh Rev., 1809; editor Am. Register, 1809-10; practiced law briefly; wrote brochure "A Letter on the Genius and Dispositions of the French Government," 1810; founder 1st Am. quarterly Am. Review of History and Politics; mem. Am. Philos. Soc., 1812; founder, editor 2d Am. Register, 1817-18; founder (with William Fry) Nat. Gazette and Literary Register, 1820-35; editor Museum of Fgn. Literature and Science, 1822-23; established Am. Quarterly Review, 1827-37; prof. English, U. Pa., 1818-28, trustee, 1828-33; mgr. Rumford's Mil. Acad., Mt. Airy, Pa.; moved permanently to Paris, France, 1837, founded what was probably 1st Am. salon; U.S. consul-gen. in Paris, 1844-51. Author: Essay on the Future State of Europe and Correspondence Respecting Russia Between Robert Goodloe Harper, Esq. and Robert Walsh, 1813; An Appeal from the Judgments of Great Britain Respecting the United States of America, 1819; biog. sketches Ency. Americana, 1829-33; editor The Works of the British Poets. Died Paris, Feb. 7, 1859; buried Versailles, France.

WALSH, Thomas W., architect; b. Kilkenny, Ireland, Feb. 15, 1826; son of William Walsh; studied architecture in office of William Dean Butler, Dublin, Ireland. Came to Am., settled in St. Louis; practiced architecture, St. Louis, 1850-90. Prin. works include: O'Fallon Poly. Sch. (later known as Wabash Bldg.), Lindel Hotel, old Four Courts Bldg., St. John's Catholic Ch., Federal Bldg. Died Mar. 1890.

WALSH, Thomas Yates, congressman, lawyer; b. Balt., 1809; attended St. Mary's Coll., Balt., 1821-24; studied law. Admitted to bar, 1832, began practice of law, Balt.; mem. Balt. City Council, 1847-48; mem. U.S. Ho. of Reps. (Whig) from Md., 32d Congress, 1851-53. Died Balt., Jan. 20, 1865; buried St. Paul's Protestant Episcopal Cemetery.

WALSH, William, congressman, lawyer; b. nr. Tullamore, County Kings, Ireland, May 11, 1828; came to U.S., 1842; grad. Mt. St. Mary's Coll., Emmitsburg, Md.; studied law. Admitted to bar, Va., 1850, began practice of law, Cumberland, Md., 1852; Democratic presdl. elector, 1860, 72; mem. Md. Constl. Conv., 1867; mem. U.S. Ho. of Reps. (Democrat) from Md., 44th-45th congresses, 1875-79. Died Cumberland, May 17, 1892; buried St. Patrick's Cemetery.

WALTER, Albert G., surgeon; b. Germany, June 21, 1811; M.D., Konigsberg U.; postgrad. in Berlin; m. Frances Anne Butler, 1846, 1 son, 1 dau. Practiced medicine, Pitts., 1837-76; an early Am. pioneer in orthopedic surgery; skilled oculist; famed as accident surgeon; performed 1st japarotomy for relief of ruptured bladder, 1859; early practitioner of antisepsis; 1st pres. Humane Soc. Pitts. Author: Conservative Surgery in its General and Successful Adaptation in Cases of Severe Traumatic Injuries of the Limbs, 1867. Died Pitts., Oct. 14, 1876.

WALTER, Thomas, botanist; b. Hampshire, Eng., circa 1740; m. Anne Lesesne, Mar. 26, 1769; m. 2d, Ann Peyre, Mar. 20, 1777, 2 daus.; m. 3d, Dorothy Cooper, after 1780, 1 dau. Collected herbarium, presented to Linnean Soc. of London, 1849, acquired by Brit. Mus. Natural History, 1863; tried to introduce (with John Fraser) a native Carolina grass, Agrostis perennans, into gen. cultivation in Eng. Author: Flora Caroliniana (sole record of work, describing approximately 1,000 species of flowering plants representing 435 genera, from specimins collected with Fraser in S.C.). Died Jan. 17, 1789; buried in small bot. garden on plantation on bank of Santee River, S.C.

WALTER, Thomas Ustick, architect; b. Phila., Sept. 4, 1804; s. Joseph Saunders and Deborah (Wood) W.; m. Mary Ann E. Hancocks; m. 2d, Amanda Gardiner; 12 children including Joseph S. Master bricklayer, 1825; began pvt. practice architecture and engring., 1830; built (in castellated manner) Phila. County Prison, 1830; designed Girard Coll., 1833; studied practical arrangements of English and Continental schs., in Europe, 1838; constructed breakwater, La Guaira, Venezuela, 1843-45; in charge of extension of U.S. Capitol Bldg., Washington, D.C., 1851-65, added the wings and dome, projected center extension; completed U.S. Treasury Bldg., built St. Elizabeth's Hosp., also extensions of Old Post Office and Land Office (all Washington); other works include: Preston Retreat, Wills Eye Hosp., also residences, Phila.; court houses, Reading and West Chester (Pa.); Hibernian Hall, Charleston, S.C., also chs. and banks, West Chester, Balt., Richmond (Va.); an organizer Am. Inst. Architects, 1857, pres., 1876-87. Author: A Guide to Workers in Metals and Stone, 1846; (with J. Jay Smith) Two Hundred Designs for Cottages and Villas, 1846. Died Oct. 30, 1887.

WALTER, William Henry, organist; b. Newark, N.J., July 1, 1825; Mus.D. (hon.), 1864. Became organist Ch. of Epiphany, N.Y.C., 1842; organist 4 other chs., N.Y.C.; became organist Columbian Coll. Chapel, Washington, D.C., 1856; composed anthems, psalms, services. Died N.Y.C., after 1870.

WALTERS, William Thompson, businessman; b. Liverpool, Pa., May 23, 1820; s. Henry and Jane (Thompson) W.; m. Ellen Harper, 1845, at least 1 son, Henry. Employed by Burd Patterson at Pioneer Furnace, Pottsville, Pa.; entered produce comm. bus., Balt., 1841, traded principally with Pa.; controlling dir. Balt. & Susquehanna R.R. (became No. Central R.R.); partner (with Charles Harvey) in fgn. and domestic liquor trade, 1847-83; invested in steamship line between Balt. and Savannah; purchased and organized many small So. railroads; made agreement with No. rds. for carrying perishable produce from Carolinas and Va. to Phila., N.Y.C. and Boston; incorporated Atlantic Improvement & Constrn. Co., holding co., Conn., 1889, changed name to Atlantic Coast Line Co., 1893; art collector, purchased pictures by Corot, Millet, Gerôme and Delacroix; attended Paris expns., 1867, 78, 89, Vienna Expn., 1873; trustee Corcoran Gallery, Washington, D.C.; chmn. art gallery com. Peabody Inst., Balt. Died Nov. 22, 1894.

WALTHALL, Edward Cary, army officer, senator; b. Richmond, Va., Apr. 4, 1831; s. Barrett White and Sally (Wilkinson) W.; m. Sophie Bridges, 1856; m. 2d, Mary Lecky Jones, 1859; 1 adopted dau. Dep. clk. Circuit Ct. of Miss.; admitted to Miss. bar, 1852; dist. atty. 10th Jud. Dist. Miss., 1856-61; elected 1st lt. Yalobusha Rifles (volunteer co.), Confederate Army, 1861; commd. col. 29th Miss. Inf., 1862, in command at Battle of Corinth; promoted brig. gen., 1863; served in battles of Chickamaugua, Lookout Mountain and Missionary Ridge, in fighting around Atlanta; in command inf. of rear-guard cooperating with Gen. Nathan Forrest's cavalry in retreat from Nashville; commd. maj. gen., 1864; a leader in overthrow of Carpet-bag govt. in Miss.; del. to all Nat. Democratic convs., except one, 1868-84; mem. U.S. Senate from Miss., 1885-Jan. 24, 1894, 1895-98, chmn. com. on mil. affairs, mem. coms. on public lands and Mississippi River improvement. Died Washington, D.C., Apr. 21, 1898; buried Holly Springs, Miss.

WALTHER, Carl Ferdinand Wilhelm, clergyman; b. Langenschursdorf, nr. Waldenburg, Saxony (now Germany), Oct. 25, 1811; s. Gottlob and Johanna (Zschenderlein) W.; grad. U. Leipzig (Saxony), 1833; m. Christiane Bunger, Sept. 21, 1841, 6 children. Ordained pastor Lutheran Ch., Braunsdorf, Germany, 1837; came to U.S., 1839; pastor, Dresden and Johannesburg, Mo., 1839-41; founder Concordia Theol. Sem. (originally opened 1839, moved to St. Louis 1850, became largest Protestant theol. sem. in U.S.), prof. theology, 1850-87; pastor Trinity Ch., St. Louis, 1841-87; began publishing religious jour. Der Lutheraner (exponent of strict confessional Lutheranism), 1844; an organizer German Synod of Mo., Ohio and Other States (known as Mo. Synod), Chgo., 1847, pres., 1847-50, 64-78; established periodical Lehre and Wehre, 1855; 1st pres. Synodical Conf. (loose confedn. of Mo. and other midwestern synods), 1872. Author: Die Stimme unserer Kirche in der Frage von Kirche und Amt, 1852; Die evangelisch-lutherische Kirche die wahre sichbare Kirche Gottes auf Erden, 1867; Lutherische Brosamen, 1876. Died St. Louis, May 7, 1887; buried Concordia Cemetery, St. Louis.

WALTON, Eliakim Persons, congressman, journalist; b. Montpelier, Vt., Feb. 17, 1812; attended common schs.; apprenticed to printer; studied law. Engaged in journalism; editor Walton's Vt. Register; organizer, 1st pres. Editors and Publishers' Assn.; owner The Watchman, 1853-68; mem. Vt. Ho. of Reps., 1853; mem. U.S. Ho. of Reps. (Republican) from Vt., 35th-37th congresses, 1857-63; del. Rep. Nat. Conv., Balt., 1864; mem. Vt. Constl. Conv., 1870; mem. Vt. Senate, 1875, 77; trustee U. Vt., also state agrl. coll., 1875-87; pres. Vt. Hist. Soc., 1876-90. Died Montpelier, Dec. 19, 1890; buried Green Mount Cemetery.

WALTON, George, senator, gov. Ga.; b. Farmville, Va., 1741; s. Robert and Sally (or Mary) (Hughes) W.; m. Dorothy Camber, 1775, 2 children. Admitted to Ga. bar, 1774; mem. Com. on Resolutions, Com. of Correspondence; mem. group that called and organized Ga. Provincial Congress, Liberty Pole, 1775; sec., also mem. coms. of intelligence, helped draw up articles of association; wrote addresses to people and to King; pres. Ga. Council of Safety; del. Continental Congress, 1776-77, 80-81, mem. coms. on Western lands, treasury bd., Indian affairs, mem. exec. com. in charge fed. affairs in Phila.; signer Declaration of Independence; with George Taylor represented govt. and negotiated treaty with Six Nations, Easton, Pa., 1777; commd. col. 1st Regt., Ga. Militia, 1778, captured by British at siege of Savannah, 1778, exchanged, 1779; gov. Ga., 1779-80, 89-90; disqualified from holding any office in state patriot legislature by Loyalist Assembly of 1781, but immediately apptd. commr. of Augusta (Ga.) and authorized to lay out City of Washington (Ga.); commd. by Confederation to negotiate treaty with Cherokee Indians in Tenn., 1783; chief justice Ga., 1783-89, 93; commr. to locate boundary line between Ga. and S.C., 1786; mem. Ga. Constl. Conv. of 1788; presdl. elector, 1789; judge Superior Ct. Ga., 1790-92, 93-95, 99-1804; mem. U.S. Senate from Ga., 1795. Feb. 20, 1796; a founder, trustee Richmond Acad.; mem. com. to locate Franklin Coll.; trustee U. Ga.; judge Ga. Middle Circuit, 1799-1804. Died College Hill, Ga., Feb. 2, 1840; buried Augusta.

WALTON, Matthew, congressman. Mem. convs. held in Danville, 1785, 87; mem. 1st Ky. Constl. Conv., 1792; mem. Ky. Ho. of Reps., 1792, 95, 1808; Democratic presdl. elector, 1809; mem. U.S. Ho. of Reps. from Ky., 8th-9th congresses, 1803-07. Died Springfield, Ky., Jan. 18, 1819; buried Springfield Cemetery.

WALWORTH, Mansfield Tracy, author; b. Albany, N.Y., Dec. 3, 1830; son of Reuben Hyde Walworth; grad. Union Coll., 1849; attended Harvard Law Sch.; at least 1 son. Practiced law, Albany, for a short time; contbd. stories and articles to Home Jour., Met. Mag. Author: (novels) The Mission of Death, 1853; Lulu, 1860; Hotspur, 1861; Stormcliff, 1865; Warwick, 1868; Delaplaine, 1872; Beverley, 1873. Died N.Y.C., June 3, 1873.

WALWORTH, Reuben Hyde, congressman, jurist; b. Bozrah, Conn., Oct. 26, 1788; s. Benjamin and Apphia (Hyde) W.; m. Maria Ketchum Averill, Jan. 6, 1812; m. 2d, Sarah Ellen (Smith) Hardin, Apr. 16, 1851; 7 children including Clarence A. Admitted to N.Y. bar, 1809; master in chancery, also justice of peace Clinton County (N.Y.) 1812; served as adj. gen. N.Y. Militia in War of 1812, distinguished in land battles at Plattsburgh, N.Y.; mem. U.S. Ho. of Reps. (Democrat) from N.Y., 17th Congress, 1821-23; circuit judge N.Y. Supreme Ct., 1823-28; chancellor N.Y., 1828-48 (abolition of Ct. of Chancery under N.Y. Const. of 1846 has been attributed in large part to desire of bar to retire him to pvt. life); del. to Peace Conv., Washington, D.C., 1861; active Presbyn.; incorporator Am. Bd. Fgn. Missions; v.p. Am. Bible Soc., Am. Tract Soc.; pres. Am. Temperance Union. Author: Hyde Genealogy (extensive genealogy of mother's family), 2 vols., 1864. Died Nov. 28, 1867.

WANTON, Joseph, gov. R.I.; b. R.I., Aug. 15, 1705; s. William and Ruth (Bryant) W.; m. Mary Winthrop, Aug. 21, 1729, 8 children including Joseph, William. Admitted a freeman R.I. Colony, 1728; dep. collector customs Newport (R.I.), 1738-48; partner in gen. merchandising firm Joseph & William Wanton, exporters fish, cheese, lumber, pork, mutton and loaf sugar, 1759-80; gov. R.I., 1769-75; remained loyal to Eng. during Am. Revolution. Died July 19, 1780.

WARBOURG, Eugene, sculptor; b. of free Negro parents, New Orleans. Maintained studio, New Orleans, circa 1840-52, executed busts and cemetery sculpture; executed Ganymede offering a Cup of Nectar to Jupiter, raffled in New Orleans, 1850; went to Europe, 1852, patronized by Duchess of Sutherland, received commn. to execute series of bas-reliefs based on Uncle Tom's Cabin; visited France and Belgium, settled in Rome, Italy. Died Rome, Jan. 12, 1859.

WARD, Aaron, congressman, lawyer; b. Sing Sing (now Ossining), N.Y., July 5, 1790; attended Mt. Pleasant Acad.; studied law. Served from lt. to capt. 29th Inf., during War of 1812; admitted to bar, began practice of law, Sing Sing; dist. atty. Westchester County; served as col., brig. gen., maj. gen. N.Y. Militia; mem. U.S. Ho. of Reps. (Democrat) from N.Y., 19th-20th, 22d-24th, 27th congresses, 1825-29, 31-37, 41-43; del. N.Y. State Constl. Conv., 1846; trustee Mt. Pleasant Acad. Died at son-in-law's home, Georgetown, D.C., Mar. 2, 1867; buried Dale Cemetery, Ossining.

WARD, Artemas, army officer, congressman; b. Shrewsbury, Mass., Nov. 26, 1727; s. Nahum and Martha (How) W.; grad. Harvard, 1748; m Sarah Trowbridge, 8 children. Established gen. store, Shrewsbury, 1750, held various town offices including assessor, clk., selectman, moderator, treas.; commd. col. 3d Regt., Mass. Militia, 1758; justice Worcester County Ct. of Common Pleas, 1762, chief justice, 1775; mem. Mass. Gen. Ct. from Shrewsbury for many years; mem. convs. held in Worchester County to champion colonial rights; mem. 1st and 2d Mass. provincial congresses; commd. gen., comdr.-in-chief Mass. Militia, 1775, directed siege of Boston; commd. maj. gen., 2d-in-command Continental Army by Continental Congress, 1775, resigned commn., 1776; mem. Mass. Exec. Council, 1777-80, Continental Congress, 1780-81; mem. Mass. Legislature, 1782-87; mem. U.S. Ho. of Reps. (Federalist) from Mass., 1st-2d congresses, 1791-95; homestead now property of Harvard, maintained as meml. Died Oct. 28, 1800; buried Mountain View Cemetery, Shrewsbury.

WARD, Artemas, Jr., congressman, jurist; b. Shrewsbury, Mass., Jan. 9, 1762; son of Artemas Ward; grad. Harvard, 1783; studied law. Admitted to bar, 1783, began practice of law, Weston; mem. Mass. Ho. of Reps., 1796-1800, 1811; moved to Charlestown, 1800; mem. bd. overseers Harvard, 1810-44; mem. U.S. Ho. of Reps. (Federalist) from Mass., 13th-14th congresses, 1813-17; mem. Mass. Senate, 1818-19; mem. Mass. Constl. Conv., 1820; chief justice Ct. of Common Pleas, 1820-39. Died Boston, Oct. 7, 1847.

WARD, Artemus, see Browne, Charles Farrar.

WARD, Cyrenus Osborne, editor, labor leader; b. N.Y. State, Oct. 28, 1831; s. Justus and Silence (Rolph) W.; m. Stella Owen, Oct. 25, 1857. Family moved to Ill., 1848, engaged in various bus. enterprises up to outbreak of Civil War; machinist Bklyn. Navy Yard, 1864; became interested in labor problems, wrote articles for N.Y. Sun, N.Y. Tribune; established own printing office, published 1st book A Labor Catechism of Political Economy, 1878; editor newspaper Voice of the People; apptd. translator, librarian U.S. Bur. of Labor, circa 1885. Author: A History of the Ancient Working People, 2 vols., 1887-1900; The Equilibration of Human Aptitudes and Powers of Adaptation, 1895. Died Yuma, Ariz., Mar. 19, 1902.

WARD, Elijah, congressman, lawyer; b. Sing Sing (now Ossining), N.Y., Sept. 16, 1816; attended law dept. N.Y. U. Admitted to bar, 1843, began practice of law, N.Y.C.; judge adv. gen. N.Y., 1853-55; del. Democratic Nat. Conv., Cincinnati, 1856; mem. U.S. Ho. of Reps. (Democrat) from N.Y., 35th, 37th-38th, 44th congresses, 1857-59, 61-65, 75-77. Died Roslyn, N.Y., Feb. 7, 1882; buried Woodlawn Cemetery, N.Y.C.

WARD, Frederick Townsend, adventurer; b. Salem, Mass., Nov. 29, 1831; s. Frederick Gamaliel and Elizabeth (Spencer) W.; attended Norwich (Vt.) U., 1846-48; m. Chang Mei. Travelled throughout world on sea voyages and comml. ventures, 1848-60, also in mil. service in Tehuantepec, Mexico, and with French in Crimea; appeared in Shanghai, China, 1859, organized troops to aid Chinese govt. in supressing Taiping Rebellion; arrested by British, who opposed his plans for using Chinese Army with fgn. officers to put down rebels, 1861, escaped, became brig. gen. in command "Ever Victorious Army"; cited for bravery in capture of Tsingpu, 1861. Killed in attack on rebel forces at Tzeki, China, Sept. 21, 1862; buried Sungkiang, China.

WARD, Henry Dana, reformer, clergyman; b. Shrewsbury, Mass., Jan. 13, 1797; s. Thomas Walter and Elizabeth (Denny) W.; B.A., Harvard, 1816, M.A., 1819; m. Abigail Porter Jones; m. 2d, Charlotte Galbraith; 4 children including Henry Galbraith, Artemas. Active in Anti-Masonic movement; published Free Masonry: Its Pretentions Exposed in Faithful Extracts of its Standard Authors; with A Review of Town's Speculative Masonry . . . by a Master Mason, 1838; published monthly mag., Anti-Masonic Review and Magazine, 1828; an organizer Anti-Masonic Party in Vt., 1829; interested in Adventist movement, chmn. Gen. Conf. of Christians Expecting the Advent of the Lord Jesus Christ, Boston, 1840, published The First Report of the Gen. Conf. of Christians . . ., 1841; ordained to ministry Protestant Episcopal Ch. by bishop of R.I., 1844; rector of parish, Kanawha County, Va. (now W. Va.), 1844-circa 1847; established girls' sch., N.Y.C., 1848; rector St. Jude's Ch., N.Y.C., 1850-circa 1852; taught in N.Y.C. or Flushing, L.I., N.Y., until 1868. Author: The Gospel of the Kingdom. 1870; The History of the Cross, 1871; The Faith of Abraham and of Christ, 1872. Died Phila., Feb. 29, 1884; buried Shrewsbury.

WARD, Jacob C., artist; b. Bloomfield, N.J., 1809; s. Caleb Ward. Began career as artist, N.Y. C., circa 1829; exhibited at Nat., Am. acads., Apollo Assn., Am. Art-Union, 1829-52; painted view of scene of Hamilton-Burr duel at Weehawken, N.J., 1830, engraved by his father; joined his brother Charles in Chile, 1845, took daguerreotypes, sketched scenery in Chile, Bolivia, Peru, Panama; returned to N.J., 1847/48. Died Bloomfield, 1891.

WARD, James Edward, shipowner; b. N.Y.C., Feb. 25, 1836; s. James Otis and Martha (Dame) W.; m. Harriet A. Morrill, Oct. 1, 1857, 3 children. Owner, James E. Ward & Co.,, chandlery bus., 1856, chartered steamers for Cuban trade; owner Ward Line (incorporated as N.Y. & Cuba Mail S.S. Co. 1881), instituted direct passenger and mail service to Havana, 1877, expanded to become heaviest-tonnage Am. line in fgn. service, chmn. bd., 1881-94; strong supporter of Am. Shipping and Indsl. League. Died Gt. Neck, L.I., N.Y., Ju. 23, 1894.

WARD, James Harmon, naval officer; b. Hartford, Conn., Sept. 25, 1806; s. James and Ruth (Butler) W.; grad. Am. Literary, Scientific and Mil. Acad., Norwich, Vt.; studied science Trinity Coll., Hartford, 1828; m. Sarah Whittemore, Apr. 11, 1833, 3 children. Commd. midshipman U.S. Navy, 1823, served on ship Constitution in Mediterranean, 1824-28; became a recognized authority on ordnance and naval tactics; exec. officer U.S. Naval Acad., Annapolis, Md., 1845-47, head dept. of ordnance and gunnery; in command ship Cumberland, 1847; stationed at Bklyn. Navy Yard, at start of Civil War; commanded small fleet called Potomac Flotilla, 1861, silenced Confederate batteries at Aquia Creek, Va., 1861. Author: An Elementary Course of Instruction on Ordnance and Gunnery (adopted as U.S. Naval Acad. textbook), 1845; A Manual of Naval Tactics, 1859; Steam for the Million, 1860. Killed while leading attack on batteries at Matthias Point, Va., June 27, 1861; buried Hartford.

WARD, James Warner, librarian; b. Newark, N.J., June 5, 1816; s. William and Sara (Warner) W.; m. Roxanna Wyman Blake, 1835; m. 2d, Catherine Lea, June 29, 1848; 2 children. Opened sch., Columbus, O., 1834; prof. gen. lit. and botany Ohio Female Coll., 1851-54; editor Hort. Review and Bot. Mag., Cincinnati, circa 1855; clk., dep. auditor Customs House, N.Y..C, 1859-74; librarian Grosvenor Library, Buffalo, N.Y., 1874-95; an early mem. Am. Library Assn., 1876; actively interested in music., art, astronomy, botany and microscopy; wrote Woman (poem), 1852; mem. serveral micros. socs., Torrey Bot. Club. Author: Home Made Verses and Stories in Rhyme (signed Yorick), 1857; Higher Water (parody on Hiawatha), 1868; editor Niagara River and Falls from Lake Erie to Lake Ontario (A. W. Sangster), 1886. Died Buffalo, June 28, 1897.

WARD, Jonathan, congressman; b. Eastchester, N.Y., Sept. 21, 1768. Assessor, Eastchester, 1791; sheriff Westchester County, 1802-06; mem. N.Y. Senate, 1807; mem. council of appointment, 1809; mem. U.S. Ho. of Reps. (Democrat) from N.Y., 14th Congress, 1815-17; mem. N.Y. Constl. Conv., 1821; surrogate Westchester County, 1828-40. Died Eastchester, Sept. 28, 1842.

WARD, Joseph, clergyman, coll. pres.; b. Perry Centre, N.Y., May 5, 1838; s Dr. Jabez and Aurilla (Tufts) W.; grad. Brown U., 1865; attended Andover Theol. Sem., 1865-68; m. Sarah Wood, Aug. 12, 1868, at least 5 children. Missionary, Yankton (then capital Dakota Territory), S.D.; ordained to ministry Congregational Ch., Yankton, 1869; a founder Congregational Assn. of Dakota; opened pvt. sch., Yankton (became Yankton Acad. 1872); founder Yankton Coll. (1st coll. in Upper Miss. Valley), 1881, pres., prof. mental and moral philosophy, 1882-89; largely responsible for Edn. Law of S.C., also for establishing Dakota Hosp. for Insane, 1879; a founder Citizens Constl. Assn. Died Dec. 11, 1889.,

WARD, Marcus Lawrence, gov N.J., congressman; b. Newark, N.J., Nov. 9, 1812; s. Moses and Fanny (Brown) W.; m. Susan Morris, June 30, 1840, 8 children including Marcus L. Partner in firm M. Ward & Son, Newark; dir. Nat. State Bank, Newark, 1846; chmn. exec. com. N.J. Hist. Soc.; a founder Newark Library Assn., N.J. Art Union; del. Republican Conv., Chgo., 1860; established free pension bureau (to secure soldiers' pay and transmit it to their families); founder Ward U.S. Hosp. (soldiers' hosp.), Newark; del. Rep. Conv., Balt., 1864, presdl. elector; mem. Rep. Nat. Com., 1864-68; gov. N J., 1865-69; mem. U.S. Ho. of Reps. from N.J., 43d Congress, 1873-75. Died Newark, Apr. 25, 1884; buried Mt. Pleasant Cemetery, Newark.

WARD, Matthias, senator; b. Elbert County, Ga., Oct. 13, 1805; attended coll., Huntsville, Ala.; studied law. Taught sch., 2 years; moved to Republic of Tex., 1836, became a trader; mem. Congress of Republic of Tex., several years; mem. Tex. State Senate; del. Democratic nat. convs., 1852, 56; pres. Tex. Dem. Conv., Austin, 1856; mem. U.S. Senate (Democrat, filled vacancy) from Tex., Sept. 27, 1858-Dec. 5, 1859. Died Warm Springs, N.C., Oct. 5, 1861; buried Old City Cemetery, Nashville, Tenn.

WARD, Nancy, Indian leader (called "Beloved Woman" or "Pretty Woman" by Indians); b. circa 1740. A Cherokee Indian, enjoyed right to sit in council, and to revoke by her single will any tribal sentence of punishment or death; introduced Negro slavery and use of cattle among Cherokee Indians; helped white frontiersmen; supplied Americans with beef cattle from her own large herd during Am. Revolution.

WARD, Nathaniel, clergyman; b. Haverhill, Eng., circa 1578; s. John and Susan Ward; A.B., Emmanuel Coll., Cambridge (Eng.) U., 1599, A.M., 1603. Became Puritan clergyman after meeting David Pareus, 1618; curate St James's, Picadilly, London. Eng., 1626-28; rector Stondon Massey, Eng., 1628-31; came to Mass. Bay Colony, 1634; asisted in preparing 1st legal code of Mass., 1638; minister, Shenfield, Eng., 1648-52. Author: The Simple Cobler of Aggawam in America (under pseudonym Theodore de la Guard), 1647; A Religious Retreat Sounded to a Religious Army, 1647; Discolliminium, 1650. Died Eng., Oct. 1652.

WARD, Richard, colonial gov.; b. Newport, R I., Apr. 15, 1689; s. Thomas and Amy (Smith) W.; m. Mary Tillinghast, Nov. 2, 1709, 14 children including Samuel, Thomas, Henry. Mem. R.I. Assembly, 1714; dep. gov. Colony of R.I., 1740, gov. 1740-43; mem. Council of War of R.I. Assembly, proclamation of council's creation caused rise in enlistments at beginning of French and Indian War, 1741; present at siege of Louisbourg, 1745. Died Aug. 21, 1763.

WARD, Samuel, colonial gov ; b. Newport, R.I., May 27, 1725; s. Richard and Mary (Tillinghast) W.; m. Anne Ray, 1745, 11 children. Dep. to R.I. justice R.I., 1761, 62; signed charter R.I. Coll. (now Brown U.), 1765, an original trustee; held indignation meeting at his home over punishment of Boston after Boston Tea Party; del. to 1st and 2d Continental congresses, 1774-76; proposed and helped secure appointment of George Washington as comdr.-in-chief Continental Army. Died Phila., Mar. 26, 1776; buried Old Cemetery, Newport.

WARD, Samuel, army officer, mcht.; b. Westerly, R I., Nov. 17, 1756; s. Gov. Samuel and Ann (Ray) W.; grad. R.I. Coll. (now Brown U.), 1771; m. Phoebe Greene, Mar. 8, 1778, 10 children including Samuel. Commd. capt. 1st R.I. Regt., Continental Army, 1775, taken prisoner at siege of Quebec, 1775, released, 1776; commd. maj., 1777, wintered at Valley Forge, 1777-78; lt. col., 1779, ret., 1781; founded firm Samuel Ward & Brother, N.Y.C.; one of 1st Americans to visit Far East; mem. Soc. of Cincinnati, 1784; del. Annapolis Conv., 1786; pres. N.Y. Marine Ins. Co., 1806-08; a rep. from R.I. to Hartford Conv., 1814. Died N.Y.C., Aug. 10, 1832.

WARD, Samuel, banker; b. Warwick, R.I., May 1, 1786; s. Samuel and Phebe (Greene) W ; m. Julia Rush Cutler, Oct. 1812, 7 children including Samuel, Louise Ward Crawford, Julia Ward Howe. Head of banking firm Prime, Ward & King, N.Y.C., after 1808; obtained loan of approximately 5 million dollars from Bank of Eng. to make it possible for N.Y. banks to resume specie payments (May 1838) after panic of 1837; a founder Bank of Commerce, N.Y.C , 1839, became pres.; contbd. to missions and ednl. instns. of Protestant Episcopal Ch.; a founder, 1st treas. Univ. City N.Y., (now N.Y.U.), 1830; 1st pres. N.Y.C. Temperance Soc., 1831; helped finance Stuyvesant Inst., 1836. Died Nov. 27, 1839.

WARD, Samuel, lobbyist, author; b. N.Y.C., Jan. 25, 1814; s. Samuel and Julia (Cutler) W.; B.A., Columbia, 1831; m. Emily Astor, 1837; m. 2d, Medora Grymes, 1884; 3 children including Margaret. Mem. banking house Prince, Ward and King, N.Y.C., 1834-39; located in Cal., 1849-59, conducted a ferry and a billiard parlor, studied Cal. Indian dialects; employed as a lobbyist by financiers interested in nat. legislation, Washington, 1864-77. Author: Lyrical Recreations (volume of verse), 1865; Days with Longfellow (written as one of his close friends) for N.Am. Review, 1882; revised 1st Am. edition of An Elementary Treatise on Algebra (J. R. Young), 1832; reviewed works of John Locke, Leonard Euler for the Am. Quarterly Review, 1832, 33. Died Pegli, Italy, May 19, 1884.

WARD, Samuel Ringgold, abolitionist; b. Eastern Shore of Md., Oct. 17, 1817; m. Miss Reynolds. Tchr., Negro schs., N.Y.C., until 1839; agt. Am. Anti-Slavery Soc., 1839; transferred to service with N.Y. State Anti-Slavery Soc.; licensed to preach by N.Y. Congregational (Gen.) Assn., 1839; pastor South Butler, N.Y., 1841-43, Cortland, N.Y., 1846-51; travelling speaker for Liberty Party, frequently advertised during tours as "the black Daniel Webster"; agt. Anti-Slavery Soc. of Can., 1851-66, went to Eng. to secure financial aid, 1853; speaker at meetings of British and Fgn. Anti-Slavery Soc., 1853, 54; pastor of small Baptist group, Kingston, Jamaica, B.W.I., circa 1855. Author: Autobiography of a Fugitive Negro, 1855; Reflections Upon the Gordon Rebellion, 1866. Died St. George Parish, Jamaica, 1866.

WARD, Thomas, congressman; b. Newark, N.J., circa 1759; studied law. Admitted to bar, began practice of law, Newark; served from capt. to maj. during Whisky Insurrection, 1794; sheriff Essex County (N.J.), 1797; elected a judge Essex County Ct., 1804, reelected, 1809; mem. legislative council, 1808-09; mem. U.S. Ho. of Reps. (Democrat) from N.J., 13th-14th congresses, 1813-17; served as sr. officer N.J. Cavalry. Died Newark, Mar. 4, 1842; buried First Presbyn. Churchyard.

WARD, Thomas (pseudonym: Flaccus), author; b. Newark, N.J., June 8, 1807; s. Thomas Ward; attended Coll. of N.J. (now Princeton), 1823; M.D., Rutgers Med. Coll., N.Y.C.; married; at least 1 child Kate (Ward) Woolsey. Author: A Month of Freedom, an American Poem (pub. anonymously), 1837; Passaic, a Group of Poems Touching that River: with Other Musings by Flaccus, 1842; pamphlet) War Lyrics, 1865; (word and music—operettas) Flora, or the Gipsy's Frolic, 1858; The Fair Truant, 1869. Editor: The Road Made Plain to Fortune for the Million, 1860. Contbr. (under pseudonym Flaccus) series of verse tales to Knickerbocker Mag. Died Apr. 13, 1873.

WARD, Thomas Bayless, congressman, lawyer; b. Marysville, O., Apr. 27, 1835; attended Wabash Coll., Crawfordsville, Ind.; grad. Miami U., Oxford, O., 1855; studied law. Clk., City of Lafayette (Ind.), 1855-56; admitted to bar, 1857, began practice of law, Lafayette; city atty., 1859-60; mayor Lafayette, 1861-65; judge Tippecanoe County (Ind.) Superior Ct., 1875-80; mem. U.S. Ho. of Reps. (Democrat) from Ind., 48th-49th congresses, 1883-87. Died Lafayette, Jan. 1, 1892; buried Springvale Cemetery.

WARD, Thomas Wren, mcht.; b. Salem, Mass., Nov. 20, 1786; s. William and Martha (Procter) W.; m. Lydia Gray, Nov. 13, 1810, 8 children including Samuel G., John G. Partner, import and export firm Ropes & Ward, Boston; resident Am. agt. Baring Bros. & Co., London, Eng., 1830-53, retained Daniel Webster as counsel for firm; visited Pres. Polk in an effort to maintain peaceful relations between Gt. Britain and U.S., 1845; treas. Boston Athenaeum, 1828-36, Harvard, 1830-42; bequeathed portions of $650,000 estate to Boston Athenaeum, Harvard, Am. Peace Soc. and Boston Missionary Soc. Died Mar. 4, 1858.

WARD, William, congressman, lawyer; b. Phila., Jan. 1, 1827; attended Girard Coll., Phila.; learned printing in office of Delaware County Republican, Chester, Pa.; studied law. Admitted to bar, 1859, began practice of law, Chester; also entered land business, banking; mem. Chester City Council, also city solicitor; mem. U.S. Ho. of Reps. (Republican) from Pa., 45th-47th congresses, 1877-83. Died Chester, Feb. 27, 1895; buried Rural Cemetery.

WARD, William Thomas, congressman, lawyer; b. Amelia County, Va., Aug. 9, 1808; attended St. Mary's Coll., nr. Lebanon, Ky.; studied law. Admitted to bar, began practice of law, Greensburg, Ky.; served as maj. 4th Ky. Volunteers in Mexican War, 1847-48; mem. Ky. Ho. of Reps., 1850; mem. U.S. Ho. of Reps. (Whig) from Ky., 32d Congress, 1851-53; commd. brig. gen., 1861, served throughout Civil War, brevetted maj. gen., 1865. Died Louisville, Ky., Oct. 12, 1878; buried Cave Hill Cemetery.

WARDE, Mary Francis Xavier, nun; b. Mountrath, Queen's County, Ireland, 1810. Joined Sisters of Mercy, 1828; apptd. superior of Carlow convent, 1837; founded convent of Naas, 1839, of Weyford, 1840; came to U.S., established convent in Pitts., 1843, Chgo., 1846, Loretto, Pa., 1848, Providence, R.I., 1850, also other convents and schs. throughout U.S. Died Manchester, N.H., Sept. 17, 1884.

WARDEN, David Ballie, diplomat, author; b. Bally Castle, County Down, Ireland, 1772; s. Robert and Elizabeth (Ballie or Baillie) W.; A.M., U. Glasgow (Scotland), 1797. Licensed to preach by Presbytery of Bangor, Scotland, 1797; col. and confidential agt. of United Irishmen; came to U.S., 1799; prin. Columbia Acad., Kinderhook, N.Y.; prin. tutor Kingston Acad., Ulster County, N.Y., 1801-04; naturalized, 1804; went to Paris as pvt. sec. to Gen. John Armstrong, designated consul pro tem, 1808, consul at Paris and agt. for prize cases, 1810-14; mem. Am. Philos. Soc., Lyceum of Natural History, N.Y.C. Author: Chorographical and Statistical Description of the District of Columbia, 1816; A Statistical, Political and Historical Account of the United States of America, 3 vols., 1819; Bibliotheca America Septentirionalis, 1820; Bibliotheca Americana, 1831. Died France, Oct. 9, 1845.

WARDEN, Robert Bruce, jurist; b. Bardstown, Ky., Jan. 18, 1824; s. Robert Bruce Augustine and Catherine E. (Lewis) W.; attended Starling Med. Coll., Columbus, O., circa 1853; m. Catharine Eliza Kerdolff, Oct. 15, 1843, 3 children, also 1 adopted son, Charles J. Admitted to Ohio bar, 1845; judge Hamilton (O.) County Ct. of Common Pleas, 1851; reporter Ohio Supreme Ct., 1853-55, judge, 1855; practiced law, Washington, D.C., circa 1877-88; mem. D.C. Bd. of Health, 1877. Author: A Familiar Forensic View of Man and Law, 1860; An Account of the Private Life and Public Services of Salmon Portland Chase, 1874; A Voter's Version of the Life and Character of Stephen Arnold Douglas, 1860; A System of American Authorities, 1870; An Essay on the Law of Art, 1878; Law for All, 1878. Died Dec. 3, 1883.

WARDER, John Aston, physician, horticulturist, forester; b. Phila., Jan. 19, 1812; s. Jeremiah and Ann (Aston) W.; grad. Jefferson Med. Coll., 1836; m. Elizabeth Haines, 1836, at least 4 children. Practiced medicine, Cincinnati, 1837-55; mem. Western Acad. Natural Scis., Cincinnati Soc. Natural History; pres. Ohio Hort. Soc. many years; sec., v.p. Am. Pomol. Soc.; edited Western Horticultural Review, 1850-53; 1st described Catalpa Speciosa; contbd. articles on systematic pomology and fruit culture to publs. including Am. Jour. of Horticulture; an author "Report of the Flax and Hemp Commission;" edited Vineyard Culture (DuBreuil), 1867; mem. Ohio Bd. Agr., 1871-76; pres. Am. Forestry Assn., 1875-82; an organizer Am. Forestry Congress; did much to foster landscape gardening and beautification of parks and cemeteries. Author: Hedges and Evergreens: A Complete Manual for the Cultivation, Pruning, and Management of All Plants Suitable for American Hedging, 1858; American Pomology: Apples, 1867; Report of the Commissioner (ofcl. report on forests and forestry), vol. 1, 1876. Died July 14, 1883.

WARDWELL, Daniel, congressman, lawyer; b. Bristol, R.I., May 28, 1791; grad. Brown U., Providence, R.I., 1811; studied law. Admitted to bar, began practice of law, Rome, N.Y.; moved to Mannsville, N.Y., 1814; judge Jefferson County (N.Y.) Ct. of Common Pleas; mem. N.Y. State Assembly, 1825-28; mem. U.S. Ho. of Reps. (Republican) from N.Y., 22d-24th congresses, 1831-37; resumed practice of law, Rome. Died Rome, Mar. 27, 1878; buried Maplewood Cemetery, Mannsville.

WARE, Ashur, editor, jurist; b. Sherborn, Mass., Feb. 10, 1782; s. Joseph and Grace (Coolidge) W.; grad. Harvard, 1804; m. Sarah Morgridge, June 20, 1831, 4 children. Tutor in Greek, Harvard, 1807-11, prof. Greek, 1811-15; co-editor newspaper Yankee, Boston; editor Eastern Argus, Portland, Me., 1817-20; sec. of state Me., 1820; judge U.S. Dist. Ct. for Me., 1822-66, opinions collected and published, 1839, 49; contbr. several articles to Bouvier's Law Dictionary; trustee Bowdoin Coll., 1811-44; pres. Androscoggin & Kennebec R.R. Co.; 1st pres. Casco Bank, 1825; an incorporator Me. Hist. Soc. Died Sept. 10, 1873.

WARE, Edmund Asa, educator; b. North Wrentham, Mass., Dec. 22, 1837; s. Asa Blake and Catharine (Slocum) W.; grad. Yale, 1869, 4 children including Edward Twichell. Tchr., Norwich Acad., 1863-65; an organizer schs. of Nashville (Tenn.), 1865; supt. schs. (under auspices Am. Missionary Assn.) for Atlanta (Ga.) dist., 1866-67; licensed to preach by Congregational Ch., Atlanta, 1866; apptd. supt. edn. for Ga. by Freedman's Bureau, 1867; a founder, 1st pres. Atlanta U. (admitted both White and Negroes), 1867-85. Died Sept. 25, 1885.

WARE, Henry, clergyman; b. Sherborn, Mass., Apr. 1, 1764; s. John and Martha (Prentice) W.; grad. Harvard, 1785; m. Mary Clark, Mar. 31, 1789; m. 2d, Mary (Otis) Lincoln, Feb. 9, 1807; m. 3d, Elizabeth Bowes, Sept. 18, 1807; 19 children including Henry, John, William. In charge of town sch., Cambridge, Mass., 1785-87; ordained to ministry Unitarian Ch., 1787; pastor 1st Parish Ch., Hingham, Mass., 1787-1805; Hollis prof. divinity Harvard, 1805-40, prof. systematic theology and evidences of Christianity, 1816-45, acting pres., 1810, 28-29. Author: Letters Addressed to Trinitarians and Calvinists Occasioned by Dr. Leonard Woods' Letters to Unitarians, 1820; Answer . . . in a Second Series of Letters Addressed to Trinitarians and Calvinists, 1822; A Postscript to the Second Series of Letters, 1823; An Enquiry into the Foundation, Evidences, and Truths of Religion (lectures), 1842; also funeral sermons published on deaths of George Washington and John Adams. Died July 12, 1845.

WARE, Henry, Jr., clergyman; b. Hingham, Mass., Apr. 21, 1794; s. Henry and Mary (Clark) W.; grad. Harvard, 1812; m. Elizabeth Watson Waterhouse, Oct. 1817; m. 2d, Mary Lovell Pickard, June 11, 1827; 9 children including William Robert, John Fothergill Waterhouse. Tchr., Phillips Acad., Exeter, N.H., 1812-14; ordained minister Unitarian Ch.,, 1817; pastor Second Ch., Boston, 1817-30; editor Christian Disciple, 1819-23; a founder Am. Unitarian Assn.; 1st prof. pulpit eloquence and pastoral care Harvard Divinity Sch., 1828-42; an organizer, pres. Cambridge Anti-Slavery Soc. Author: A Poem Pronounced . . . at the Celebration of Peace, 1815; Hints on Extemporaneous Preaching, 1824; (poem) The Vision of Liberty (delivered at annual Phi Beta Kappa meeting, Harvard 1824); On the Formation of the Christian Character, 1831; The Life of the Saviour, 1833; The Works of Henry Ware, Jr., D.D. (edited by Chandler Robbins), 4 vols., 1846-47. Contbr. articles signed Artinius to Christian Register, 1821. Died Framingham, Mass., Sept. 22, 1843; buried Mt. Auburn Cemetery, Cambridge, Mass.

WARE, John, physician, educator; b. Hingham; Mass., Dec. 19, 1795; s. Rev. Henry and Mary (Clark) W.; grad. Harvard, 1813, M.D., 1816; m. Helen Lincoln, Apr. 22, 1822; m. 2d, Mary Green Chandler, Feb. 25, 1862; 8 children including Maj. Robert. Began practice medicine, Boston, 1814; an editor Boston Jour. of Philosophy and the Arts, 1823-26; co-editor Boston Med. and Surg. Jour., 1828; Hersey prof. theory and practice of physic Harvard Med. Sch., 1836-64; a founder Boston Soc. Med. Improvement, 1839; pres. Mass. Med. Soc., 1848-52. Author: (novel) Charles Ashton, 1823; (essay) Remarks on the History and Treatment of Delerium Tremens, 1831; Memoir of the Life of Henry Ware, Jr. (chief literary effort), 1846; Discourses on Medical Education and on the Medical Profession, 1847; Hints to Young Men, 1850; On Hemoptysis as a Symptom, 1860; Philosophy of Natural History, 1860. Editor: Philosophy of Natural History (William Snellie), 1824; Natural Theology (William Paley), 1829. Died Apr. 29, 1864.

WARE, John Fothergill Waterhouse, clergyman; b. Boston, Aug. 31, 1818; s. Henry and Elizabeth (Waterhouse) W.; grad. Harvard, 1838, Harvard Divinity Sch., 1842; m. Caroline Parsons Rice, May 27, 1844; m. 2d, Helen Rice, Oct. 10, 1849; 4 children. Pastor, Unitarian ch., Fall River, Mass., 1843-46, Cambridgeport, Mass., 1846-64; served Union cause during Civil War by lecturing in various parts of country, preparing tracts and visiting soldiers in camp; minister First Independent Soc. of Balt., 1864-67; pastor of new religious group, Ch. of the Saviour, Balt., 1867-72; interested in welfare of freedmen, established schs. for Negro children; organized a church, Swampscott, Mass., circa 1870; pastor Arlington Street Ch., Boston, 1872-81. Author: The Silent Pastor, or Consolations for the Sick, 1848; Home Life: What It Is and What It Needs, 1864; (sermons) Wrestling and Waiting, published posthumously, 1882. Died Milton, Mass., Feb. 26, 1881.

WARE, Nathaniel A., territorial ofcl.; b. Mass. or S.C., 1780 or 89; m. Sarah (Percy) Ellis, after 1815; children—Catherine Ann (Ware) Warfield, Eleanor Percy (Ware) Lee. Served as maj. Miss. Militia; land speculator; sec. Miss. Territory, 1815-17, acting gov., 1815-16; advocated diversification of crops in South and growth of industry as means of raising standard of living; supported scientific farming and protective tariffs. Author: Notes on Political Economy as Applicable to the United States (signed "A Southern Planter"), 1844. Died of yellow fever, Galveston, Tex., 1854.

WARE, Nicholas, senator, lawyer; b. Caroline County, Va., 1769; studied medicine for a time; studied law, Augusta, Ga., also Litchfield (Conn.) Law Sch. Admitted to bar, began practice of law, Augusta; mem. Ga. Ho. of Reps., 1808-11, 14-15; mayor Augusta, 1819-21; mem. U.S. Senate (filled vacancy) from Ga., Nov. 10, 1821-24. Died N.Y.C., Sept. 7, 1824; buried under Grace Church annex.

WARE, William, clergyman; b. Hingham, Mass., Aug. 3, 1797; s. Henry and Mary (Clark) W.; grad. Harvard, 1816; m. Mary Waterhouse, June 10, 1823, 7 children. Taught sch., Hingham, later, Cambridge, Mass.; ordained to ministry Unitarian Ch., 1821; pastor 1st Unitarian Ch. established in N.Y.C., 1821-36; pastor, Waltham, Mass., 1837-38, West Cambridge, Mass., 1844-45; editor, publisher Christian Examiner, 1839-44; editor Am. Unitarian Biography, 2 vols., 1850-51. Author: Letters of Lucius M. Piso from Palmyra, to His Friend Marcus Curtius at Rome, 1837; Zenobia: or, The Fall of Palmyra: An Historical Romance; Probus: or, Rome in the Third Century (published later under title Aurelian: or, Rome in the Third Century), 1838; Julian: or, Scenes in Judea, 1841; Sketches of European Capitals (lectures), 1851; Lectures on the Works and Genius of Washington Auston, 1852. Died Cambridge, Feb. 19, 1852.

WARFIELD, Catherine Ann Ware, poet, novelist; b. Natchez, Miss., June 6, 1816; d. Nathaniel A. and Sarah (Percy) Ellis Ware; m. Robert Elisha Warfield, 1833. Lived most of her adult life on husband's estate nr. Louisville, Ky.; one of 1st important female novelists from South; wrote poetry (with Sister), including The Wife of Leon, and Other Poems, by Two Sisters of the West, 1844, The Indian Chamber, and Other Poems, 1846; published poetry showing Confederate sympathies in Emily V. Mason's Southern Poems of the War, 1867; novels include: The Household of Bouverie, 1860, The Romance of the Green Seal, 1866, Miriam Monfort, 1873, A Double Wedding, 1875, Lady Ernestine, 1876, The Cardinal's Daughter, 1877. Died May 21, 1877.

WARFIELD, Henry Ridgely, congressman; b. Anne Arundel County, Md., Sept. 14, 1774. Held several local offices; settled in Frederick, Md.; mem. U.S. Ho. of Reps. (Federalist) from Md., 16th-18th congresses, 1819-25. Died Frederick, Mar. 18, 1839.

WARING, George Edwin, agriculturist, san. engr.; b. Poundridge, N.Y., July 4, 1833; s. George Edwin and Sarah (Burger) W.; m. Euphemia Blunt, Feb. 22, 1855; m. 2d, Virginia Clark, Dec. 27, 1865; m. 3d, Mrs. Louise E. Yates, July 20, 1898; at least 1 dau. Lectr. on scientific agr. to farmers in Me. and Vt., 1854-55; managed Horace Greeley's farm, Chappaqua, N.Y., 1855-57; drainage engr. Central Park N.Y.C., 1857-61; maj. Garibaldi Guards, U.S. Army 1861, raised 6 cos.; commd. col. 4th Mo. Cavalry U.S. Volunteers, 1862; installed system of sewers Memphis, Tenn., 1878; spl. agt. for 10th Census 1879; street cleaning commr. of N.Y.C., 1895-98 went to Havana to report to U.S. Govt. steps necessary to rid Havana of yellow fever, 1898, contracted disease. Author: The Elements of Agriculture, 1854 The Handybook of Husbandry: A Guide for Farmers, Young and Old, 1870; The Sanitary Drainage of Houses and Towns, 1876; The Sewerage of Memphis, London, 1881; Street Cleaning and the Disposal of a City's Wastes, 1897. Died of yellow fever, N.Y.C., Oct. 29, 1898.

WARNER, Hiram, congressman, jurist; b. Williamsburg, Mass., Oct. 29, 1802; s. Obadiah and Jane (Coffin) W.; m. Sarah Abercrombie Staples, 1827, 1 dau. Sch. tchr., Sparta, also Blountsville (Ga.); admitted to Ga. bar, 1824; mem. Ga. Legislature from Crawford County, 1828-31; judge Ga. Superior Ct., 1833-40; asso. justice Ga. Supreme Ct., 1846-53, chief justice, 1867-80; mem. U.S. Ho. of Reps. (Democrat) from Ga., 34th Congress, 1855-57; mem. Ga. Secession Conv., 1860, opposed secession; judge Coweta Circuit Ct., 1865-67. Died Atlanta, Ga., June 30, 1881; buried Town Cemetery, Greenville, Ga.

WARNER, James Cartwright, industrialist; b. Gallatin, Tenn., Aug. 20, 1830; s. Jacob L. and Elizabeth (Cartwright) W.; m. Mary Williams, Nov. 3, 1852, 8 children. Established hardware business, Chattanooga, Tenn., 1852; mayor Chattanooga, 1 term; mem. Tenn. Gen. Assembly, 1861; sec. Tenn. Coal, R.R. Co., 1868-74; spent 25 years in developing mineral resources of South; purchased Rising Fawn iron property in Ga.; pres. Tenn. Coal, Iron & R.R. Co., 1874-98; noted for his revival and modernization of charcoal iron industry in Middle Tenn.; organized Warner Iron Co. composed of Nashville (Tenn.) capitalists, 1880, pres., 1880-89; 50-ton hotblast Warner Furnace set new precedent in charcoal iron industry by its efficient operation; built charcoal by-product plant. Died July 21, 1895.

WARNER, Jonathan Trumbull, pioneer; b. Hadlyme, Conn., Nov. 20, 1807; s. Selden and Dorothy (Selden) W.; m. Anita Gale, 1837, several children. Clk. trading expdn. to N.M., 1831; joined trading expdn. to Cal., arrived in Los Angeles, 1831; trapped and hunted, 1831-33; opened store in Los Angeles, 1836; changed name to Juan José, circa 1837; delivered lecture which urged retention of Ore. with acquisition of Cal. and suggested practicability of transcontinental railway, Rochester, N.Y., 1840, later published in England and U.S.; became Mexican citizen, 1843; mem. Cal. Senate from San Diego County, 1850; published weekly newspaper Southern Vineyard, 1858; mem. Cal. Assembly, 1860; provost marshal of Los Angeles. Author: The Warn and the Cold Ages of the Earth in the Northern Latitudes, (pamphlet), 1884; Reminiscences of Early California from 1831 to 1846; co-author An Historical Sketch of Los Angeles County, 1876. Died Los Angeles, Apr. 22, 1895.

WARNER, Olin Levi, sculptor; b. Suffield, Conn., Apr. 9, 1844; s. Levi and Sarah B. (Warner) W.; attended, Ecole des Beaux Arts, Paris, France, 1869-72; m. Sylvia Martinach, 1886, at least 2 children. Joined French Fgn. Legion, circa 1870; returned to U.S., 1872; exhibited medallion of Edwin Forrest, 1876; sculptures include: J. Alden Weir, 1880, Maud Morgan, 1881; William C. Brownell; John Insley Blair at Met. Mus., N.Y.C.; Twilight, 1879; Dancing Nymph, 1881; Cupid and Psyche, 1882; did portrait studies of heads Indian chiefs Joseph, Vincent, Seltice, also Lot and Moses; completed granite drinking fountain, 1890, placed in Union Square, N.Y., moved to Central Park; executed standing figure Gen. Charles Devens, 1894, souvenir half-dollar, 1893, statue of Hendrik Hudson; designed and modelled 2 great bronze doors for Library of Congress, Washington, D.C. (themes were Oral Tradition and Writing); mem. N.A.D., Soc. Am. Artists, Nat. Sculpture Soc., Archtl. League of N.Y. Died Aug. 14, 1896.

WARNER, Samuel Larkin, congressman, lawyer; b. Wethersfield, Conn., June 14, 1828; attended Wilbraham (Mass.) Acad., law dept. Yale; grad. law dept. Harvard, 1854. Admitted to bar, Boston, 1854, began practice of law, Portland, Conn., 1855; mem. Conn. Ho. of Reps., 1858; moved to Middletown, Conn., 1860, mayor, 1862-66; del. Republican Nat. Conv., Balt., 1864, served as a conv. sec.; mem. U.S. Ho. of Reps. (Republican) from Conn., 39th Congress, 1865-67; del.-at-large to Rep. nat. convs., 1888, 92. Died Middletown, Feb. 6, 1893; buried Indian Hill Cemetery.

WARNER, Seth, army officer; b. Roxbury, Conn., Apr. 25, 1795; s. Dr. Benjamin and Silence (Hurd) W.; m. Hester Hurd, 1765, 3 children. Leader (with Ethan Allen and others) people of

Vt. in resisting attempts of N.Y. to control Colony of Vt.; outlawed by N.Y. Gen. Assembly, 1772; aided Ethan Allen and Benedict Arnold in capture of Ticonderoga, 1775, Crown Point, 1775; obtained authorization of Continental Congress (with Allen) for creation of regt. called Green Mountain Boys, elected lt. col., commandant, 1775; brought up rear forces during Am. retreat from Can. and collected reinforcements in Vt., 1776; arrived with regt. during latter part of Battle of Bennington, responsible for Am. victory, 1777; promoted brig. gen. by Vt. Assembly, 1778. Died Roxbury, Dec. 26, 1784.

WARNER, Susan Bogert (pseudonym Elizabeth Wetherell), author; b. N.Y.C., July 11, 1819; d. Henry Whiting and Anna (Bartlett) Warner. Lived on Constitution Island (N.Y.), 1837-85; wrote novels primarily of a religious nature, also stories for children; works include: The Wide, Wide World (under pseudonym; ranks with Uncle Tom's Cabin as one of most popular novels written in Am. in 19th century), 1850; Queechy, 1852; The Old Helmet, 1863; Melbourne House, 1864; Daisy, 1868; Diana, 1877; My Desire, 1879; Nobody, 1882; Stephen, M.D., 1883. Died Highland Falls, N.Y., Mar. 17, 1885.

WARRELL, James, artist; b. circa 1780; married. Came to Am., 1792. Made debut as actor, Phila., 1794; opened dancing sch., Richmond, Va., circa 1799; turned to painting after leg injury, 1808; painted stage scenery, drop curtains; painted portraits and hist. subjects, Richmond and Petersburg, Va.; opened (with his brother-in-law) Richmond's 1st museum, 1817, closed, 1836; worked in New Orleans, 1825, 26-27, N.Y.C., 1829-31. Died before 1854.

WARREN, Cornelius, congressman, lawyer; b. Phillipstown, N.Y., Mar. 15, 1790; studied law. Admitted to bar, practiced law; apptd. judge Ct. of Common Pleas, 1841; mem. U.S. Ho. of Reps. (Whig) from N.Y., 30th Congress, 1847-49. Died Cold Spring, N.Y., July 28, 1849; buried Old Cemetery.

WARREN, Cyrus Moors, chemist, mfr.; b. Fox Hill, West Dedham, Mass., Jan. 15, 1824; s. Jesse and Betsey (Jackson) W.; B.S., Lawrence Scientific Sch., 1855; studied chemistry, Paris, France and Heidelberg, Germany; m. Lydia Ross, Sept. 12, 1849, 7 children. Partner (with brother Samuel) tarred roofing mfg. co., Cincinnati, 1847; established laboratory, Boston, 1863, developed improved process of fractional condensation, studied complex mixture of hydrocarbons in Pa. petroleum, invented process of purifying Trinidad asphalt; founder, pres., treas. Warren Chem. Mfg. Co., Boston, Warren-Scharf Asphalt Paving Co., N.Y.C.; prof. organic chemistry Mass. Inst. Tech., 1866-68; left bequests for promotion of science to Harvard and Am. Acad. Arts and Scis. Contbr. 13 papers to publs. including Poggendorff's Annalender Physik, Am. Jour. of Sci., Proceedings and Memoirs of Am. Acad. Arts and Scis. Died Manchester, Vt., Aug. 13, 1891.

WARREN, Edward Allen, congressman, lawyer; b. nr. Eutaw, Ala., May 2, 1818; studied law. Admitted to bar, 1843, began practice of law, Clinton, Miss.; mem. Miss. Ho. of Reps., 1845-46; moved to Camden, Ark., 1847; mem. Ark. Ho. of Reps., 1848-49, speaker, 1849; judge Circuit Ct., 6th Dist. Ark.; mem. U.S. Ho. of Reps. (Democrat) from Ark., 33d, 35th congresses, 1853-55, 57-59. Died Prescott, Ark., July 2, 1875; buried Moscow Cemetery, nr. Prescott.

WARREN, Gouverneur Kemble, army officer, engr.; b. Cold Spring, N.Y., Jan. 8, 1830; s. Sylvanus Warren; grad. U.S. Mil. Acad., 1850; m. Emily Forbes Chase, June 17, 1863, 2 children. Brevetted 2d lt. Corps Topog. Engrs., 1850, commd. 2d lt., 1854, 1st lt., 1856; engaged in making map and reconnaissances of Dakota Territory, 1856-59; asst. prof mathematics U.S. Mil. Acad., 1859-61; lt. col. 5th N.Y. Volunteers, 1861; col. of a regt. of engrs. U.S. Army, 1861, capt., 1861; brevetted lt. col. for service in Battle of Gaine's Mill, 1862; brig. gen. U.S. Volunteers, 1862; chief topographic engr. Army of Potomac, 1863; brevetted col. U.S. Army for services in Battle of Gettysburg; commd. maj., 1864, brevetted maj. gen., 1865; resigned volunteer commn. 1865, re-entered Corps Engrs., U.S. Army; superintending engr. of surveys and improvements of upper Mississippi River; commd. lt. col. Corps Engrs., 1879; mem. Am. Philos. Soc., Nat. Acad. Sciences. Author: An Account of the Operations of the Fifth Army Corps, 1866; Report on Bridging the Mississippi River between St. Paul, Minnesota and St. Louis, Missouri, 1878. Died Newport, R.I., Aug. 8, 1882.

WARREN, Henry Clarke, orientalist; b. Cambridge, Mass., Nov. 18, 1854; s. Samuel Dennis and Susan Cornelia (Clarke) W.; B.A., Harvard, 1879; postgrad. Johns Hopkins, 1879-84. Learned Greek and Latin; chiefly interest in Sanskrit and Pali, 1st Am. scholar to gain distinction in Pali, originated Harvard Oriental Series, 1891; founder Warren Paper Co. Author: Buddhism in Translations (most important work), 1896; translation of Buddhaghosa's Visuddhimagga (died before completing) Died Cambridge, Jan. 3, 1899.

WARREN, Israel Perkins, clergyman, editor; b. Woodbridge, Conn., Apr. 8, 1814; s. Isaac and Leonora (Perkins) W.; grad. Yale, 1838, attended Yale Divinity Sch., 1839-41; m. Jane Stanley Stow, Aug. 25, 1841; m. 2d, Sarah (Linden) Cushman, Jan. 2, 1882; m. 3d, Juliet Stanley, Oct. 6, 1886; 3 children. Minister, Congregational Ch., Granby, Conn., 1841-45; ordained to ministry Congregational Ch., 1842; pastor Mt. Carmel Ch., Hamden, Conn., 1846-51, Plymouth, Conn., 1851-56; asso. sec. Am. Seamen's Friend Soc., 1856; editor Sailor's Mag., N.Y.; sec., editor of publs. Am. Tract Soc. of Boston, 1859-circa 1870; editor Christian Mirror, 1875, purchased it and reestablished it in Portland, Me., editor, publisher, 1876-92. Author: Sadduceeism, 1860, revised edit., 1867; A Vision, 1861; A Chapter from the Book of Nature, 1863; The Cup Bearer, 1865; The Three Judges, 1873; Parousia, a Critical Study of the Scripture Doctrines of Christ's Second Coming, 1879, enlarged edit., 1884; The Book of Revelation, 1886. Died Portland, Oct. 9, 1892.

WARREN, James, legislator; b. Plymouth, Mass., Sept. 28, 1726; s. James and Penelope (Winslow) W.; grad. Harvard, 1745; m. Mercy Otis, Nov. 14, 1754; 5 children. Sheriff of Plymouth County, 1757-75; mem. Mass. Ho. of Reps., 1766-78, 80, 87, speaker circa 1778, 87; paymaster gen. Continental Army, 1776; served on Navy Bd. for Eastern dept., 1776-81; maj. gen. Provincial Militia, 1776; mem. Mass. Gov.'s Council, 1792-94; presdl. elector Mass., 1804. Died Plymouth, Nov. 28, 1808.

WARREN, John, surgeon; b. Roxbury, Mass., July 27, 1753; s. Joseph and Mary (Stevens) W.; grad. Harvard, 1771, M.D. (hon.), 1786; m. Abigail Collins, Nov. 4, 1777, 17 children including John Collins, Edward. Surgeon, Col. Pickering's Regt.; Mass. Militia, 1773; took active part in Boston Tea Party, 1773; sr. surgeon hosp. at Cambridge, Mass., 1775; went to N.Y., surgeon gen. hosp. on L.I., 1776; established hosp. for innoculation when smallpox prevalent, Boston, 1778; gave pvt. course of anatomical lectures at mil. hosp., Boston, 1780-81; an organizer Boston Med. Soc., 1780; established 1st school of medicine connected with Harvard, 1782, became prof. anatomy and surgery, 1783; pioneer in abdominal operations, amputation at shoulder joint; prominent in dealing with yellow fever epidemic, Boston, 1798; grand master Mass. Lodges Free and Accepted Masons, 1783-84; a founder, pres. Mass. Humane Soc.; mem. Agrl. Soc., Am. Acad. Arts and Scis. Author: A View of the Mercurial Practice in Febrile Diseases, 1813. Died Boston, Apr. 4, 1815.

WARREN, John Collins, surgeon, educator; b. Boston, Aug. 1, 1778; s. John and Abigail (Collins) W.; grad. (valedictorian) Harvard, 1797, M.D. (hon.) 1819; studied medicine under his father in Europe, 1799-1802; m. Susan Powell, Nov. 17, 1803; m. 2d, Anne Winthrop, Oct. 1843; 6 children. Pres., Hasty Pudding Club, Harvard; partner in father's med. office, 1802; an original mem. Anthology Club; helped prepare Pharmacopeia for Mass. Med. Soc., 1808; adjunct prof. anatomy and surgery Harvard Med. Sch., 1809-15, full prof., 1815-47, prof. emeritus, 1847, dean, 1816-19; surgeon Mass. Gen. Hosp., 1821; a founder New Eng. Jour. of Medicine and Surgery, 1821; 1st surgeon in U.S. to operate for strangulated hernia; connected with 1st demonstration of ether anesthesia, 1846; active in temperance reform, 1827-56; pres. Mass. Temperance Soc., 1827-56; contributed $10,000 in his will to temperance cause; active mem. Mass. Agr. Soc.; pres. Boston Soc. Natural History; left many paleontol. and geol. specimens to Harvard Med. Sch., formed Warren Museum. Author: A Comparative View of the Sensorial and Nervous Systems in Men and Animals, 1822; Surgical Observations on Tumours with Cases and Operation, 1837; Physical Education and the Preservation of Health, 1845; Etherization; with Surgical Remarks, 1848; The Mastodon Giganteus of North America, 1852, 55; The Preservation of Health, 1854. Died Boston, May 4, 1856.

WARREN, Joseph, physician, patriot; b. Roxbury, Mass., June 11, 1741; s. Joseph and Mary (Stevens) W.; grad. Harvard, 1759; studied medicine under his uncle Dr. James Lloyd; m. Elizabeth Hooton, Sept. 6, 1764, 4 children. Became Free Mason, 1761, made provincial grand master, 1769; practiced medicine in Boston; Whig; active in polit. clubs of his day; mem. com. apptd. by town meeting after Boston Massacre to inform Gov. Hutchinson to remove Brit. troops; mem. Com. of Safety; one of 3 men chosen to draw up report A State of the Rights of Colonists, 1772; leader in organizing opposition to Regulating Act, drafted "Suffolk Resolves;" made his celebrated 2d oration in commemoration of Boston Massacre, 1775; sent William Dawes and Paul Revere to Lexington to inform John Hancock and Samuel Adams of their danger, Apr. 1775; pres. pro tem Mass. Provincial Congress, mem. Com. of Safety, head com. to organize army in Mass., 1775; commd. maj. gen., June 1775. Shot by Brit. soldier in Battle of Bunker Hill, Charlestown, Mass., June 17, 1775.

WARREN, Joseph Mabbett, congressman, businessman; b. Troy, N.Y., Jan. 28, 1813; attended Rensselaer Poly. Inst., Troy; grad. Washington (now Trinity) Coll., Hartford, Conn., 1834. In wholesale grocery business, then engaged in whole-hardware business, 1840; dir. Bank of Troy, pres., 1853-65; dir. United Nat. Bank of Troy; trustee Rensselaer Poly. Inst.; mayor Troy, 1852; commr. Troy Water Works, 1855-67; mem. U.S. Ho. of Reps. (Democrat) from N.Y., 42d Congress, 1871-73. Died Sept. 9, 1896; buried Warren Chapel, Oakwood Cemetery.

WARREN, Josiah, philosopher, inventor; b. Boston, circa 1798. Orchestra leader, tchr. of music, Cincinnati, circa 1818; granted patent for lard-burning lamp, 1821; established lamp factory, Cincinnati; resident, participant in Robert Owen's community, New Harmony, Ind., 1825-27; formulated theory having basic principle of "sovereignty of the individual" and "cost the limit of price"; invented speed press, 1830, not patended; started jour. The Peaceful Revolutionist, 1833; made own press type molds and stereotype plates; invented and perfected cylinder press self-inking and fed from continuous roll of paper, 1837-40; established 3 towns based on concept of mutualism, eliminating any hierarchy in community (1st: Village of Equity, Ohio, 1834, 2d: Utopia, 1846, 3d and most famous: Modern Times, L.I., N.Y., 1850-62); at various times operated "equity stores" in which he neither received profit nor loss; founder of philos. anarchism in Am. Author: Equitable Commerce, 1846; Written Music Remodeled, and Invested with the Simplicity of an Exact Science, 1860; True Civilization an Immediate Necessity, 1863; True Civilization: a Subject of Vital and Serious Interest to all People, 1875. Died Charlestown, Mass., Apr. 14, 1874; interred Mt. Auburn Cemetery, Cambridge, Mass.

WARREN, Lott, congressman, lawyer; b. Burke County, nr. Augusta, Ga., Oct. 30, 1797; attended common schs.; studied law. Served as 2d lt. Volunteers in expdn. against Seminole Indians, 1818; admitted to bar, 1821, began practice of law, Dublin, Ga.; ordained to ministry Baptist Ch.; served as maj. Ga. Militia; mem. Ga. Ho. of Reps., 1824, 31, Ga. Senate, 1830; solicitor gen., judge So. Circuit of Ga., 1831-34; mem. U.S. Ho. of Reps. (Whig) from Ga., 26th-27th congresses, 1839-43; moved to Albany, Ga., 1842; judge Ga. Superior Ct., 1843-52. Died Albany, June 17, 1861; buried Riverside Cemetery.

WARREN, Mercy Otis, author; b. Barnstable, Mass., Setp. 25, 1728; d. James and Mary (Allyne) Otis; m. James Warren, Nov. 14, 1754, 5 children. Maintained extensive correspondence with John Adams, James Winthrop, Thomas Jefferson, and Elbridge Gerry, others. Author: The Adulateur (polit. satire), 1773, The Group (polit. satire), 1775; The Sack of Rome, 1778; The Ladies of Castile, 1778; Poems Dramatic and Miscellaneous, 1790; History of the Rise, Progress and Termination of the American Revolution, 3 vols., 1805. Died Plymouth, Mass., Oct. 19, 1814.

WARREN, Sir Peter, naval officer; b. Warrenstown, County Meath, Ireland, Mar. 10, 1703; m. Susannah De Lancey, July 1731, 6 children including Anne (Warren) Fitzroy, Susannah (Warren) Skinner, Charlotte (Warren) Abingdon. Entered Brit. Navy as midshipman, 1715; served in West Indies and off N.Am. coast in ship Rose, 1718; served in N.Y. Harbor as capt., comdr. H.M.S. Solebay, 1730; purchased tract of 14,000 acres in Mohawk Valley, N.Y., 1736, established Warren Farm (now Greenwich Village, N.Y.C.); commanded gunboats Squirrel, 1735-42, Launceton, 1742-45, Superbe, promoted to rear adm. of Blue fleet, 1745; took part in capture of Louisbourg, 1745; gov. of Louisbourg and Cape Breton Island, 1745; mem. Gov.'s Council of N.Y.; led Brit. naval force to victory over French off Cape Finistere, 1747; knighted with Cross of Bath, 1747; vice adm. of White fleet, 1747, Red fleet, 1748; Warren Street (N.Y.C.) named for him. Died Dublin, Ireland, July 29, 1752; buried church at Knockmark, nr. Warrenstown, Ireland.

WARREN, Russell, architect, engr.; b. Tiverton, R.I., Aug. 5, 1783; s. Gamaliel and Ruth (Jenckes) W.; m. Sarah Gladding, Mar. 10, 1805; m. 2d, Lydia Gladding, 1817; no children. Served as maj. Bristol (R.I.) Militia; diversified archtl. achievements included churches, banks, public bldgs., residences; constructed bridge over Great Pedee River, S.C.; most notable works are Athenaeum and Arcade, Providence, R.I., Unitarian Ch., Free Public Library, Bedford, Mass.; architect stone mansion of John Avery Parker (most significant work), 1834; leader Greek revival movement in U.S. Died Providence, Nov. 16,, 1860.

WARREN, William, actor, theatrical mgr.; b. Bath, Eng., May 10, 1767; s. Philip Warren; m. 2d, Ann Brunton Merry, Aug. 15, 1806; m. 3d, Esther Fortune, 1809; 6 children, Hester Warren Proctor, Anna Warren Marble, Emma Warren Price Hanchett, Mary Ann Warren Rice, William, Henry. Made stage debut as Young Norval in play Douglas, 1784; came to U.S., 1796; played Friar Lawrence in Romeo and Juliet, Bundle in The Waterman, Phila., 1796; actor, mgr., Balt. and Phila.; best known as comedian especially in roles of old men such as Falstaff and Sir Toby Belch; retired from mgmt., 1829, acted only occasionally; made farewell stage appearance as Sir Robert Bramble in The Poor Gentleman, 1831. Died Balt., Oct. 10, 1832.

WARREN, William, actor; b. Phila., Nov. 17, 1812; s. William and Esther (Fortune) W.; never married. Made 1st appearance as Young Norval in play Douglas, 1832; played Sir Lucius O'Trigger in The Rivals, Boston, 1846; played Billy Lackaday in Sweethearts and Wives, also Gregory Grizzle in My Young Wife and Old Umbrella, Boston, 1847; a comedian; played nearly 600 roles in 14,000 performances extending from Shakespearean comedy characters to such 18th century comedy characters to such 18th century comedy roles as Bob Acres, Sir Peter Teazle, Tony Lumpkin; made last stage appearance as Old Eccles in Caste, 1883; acted in only one theater (Boston Museum) and with one stock company except for one season (1864-65), a few appearances in N.Y.C. and one in England. Author: Life and Memoirs of William Warren, 1889. Died Boston, Sept. 21, 1888; buried Mt. Auburn Cemetery, Cambridge, Mass.

WARREN, William Wirt, congressman, lawyer; b. Brighton (now part of Boston), Feb. 27, 1834; grad. Harvard, 1856; studied law. Admitted to bar, began practice of law, 1857; assessor of internal revenue 7th Mass. Dist., 1865; del. Democratic Nat. Conv., N.Y.C., 1868; mem. Mass. Senate, 1870; mem. U.S. Ho. of Reps. (Democrat) from Mass., 44th Congress, 1875-77. Died Boston, May 2, 1880; buried Evergreen Cemetery.

WARRINGTON, Lewis, naval officer; b. Williamsburg, Va., Nov. 3, 1782; attended Coll. William and Mary; m. Margaret Cary King, Mar. 3, 1817. Apptd. midshipman U.S. Navy, 1800; cruised West Indies in Chesapeake; participated in war with Barbary corsairs in ships President, Vixen and Enterprise, 1802-07; promoted lt., 1805; attached to Siren, 1809; 1st lt . in Congress during War of 1812; commd. master comdt., 1813; took command of sloop-of-war Peacock, 1813; forced Brit. brig Epervier to surrender, 1814; awarded gold medal by Congress, sword by State of Va., took many prizes during War of 1812; commanded the Macedonian, 1816, Java, 1819-20, Guerriere of Mediterranean Squadron, 1820-21; commr. of Navy bd. charged with adminstrn. of naval materiel, 1826-30, 40-42; chief Bur. Yards and Docks, 1842-46; U.S. sec. of navy ad interim, 1844; chief Bureau of Ordnance, 1846-51. Died Washington, D.C., Oct. 12, 1851.

WARWICK, John George, congressman, businessman; b. County Tyrone, Province of Ulster, Ireland, Dec. 23, 1830; attended common schs., Ireland. Came to U.S., circa 1850; became bookkeeper in dry-goods firm, Navarre, O.; clk. in dry-goods store, Massillon, O.; later engaged in flour milling, coal mining, agriculture, railroad constrn.; lt. gov. Ohio, 1884-86; mem. U.S. Ho. of Reps. (Democrat) from Ohio, 52d Congress, 1891-92. Died Washington, D. C., Aug. 14, 1892; buried Protestant Cemetery, Massillon.

WASHAKIE, Indian chief; b. probably Mont., circa 1804. Became chief of Eastern Shoshone Indians, circa 1842; friendly toward whites (paper signed by many emigrants to the West attested to his friendly acts); often employed by Am. Fur Co. and Hudson's Bay Co.; unable to prevent some of his tribe from warring on whites, 1862; gave up his Green River Valley land in Mont. in exchange for reservation in Wind River region, Wyo., 1868; aided Gen. Crook against Sioux Indians in Sioux War, 1876; Fort Washakie (Wyo.) named for him. Died Fort Washakie, Feb. 15, 1900; buried (accorded full mil. funeral) Fort Washakie.

WASHBURN, Cadwallader Colden, industrialist, gov. Wis., congressman; b. Livermore, Me., Apr. 22, 1818; s. Israel and Martha (Benjamin) W.; m. Jeanette Garr, Jan. 1, 1849, at least 2 children. Surveyor, Rock Island County (Ill.), 1840; admitted to Wis. bar, 1842, opened law office at Mineral Point; formed partnership with Cyrus Woodman and speculating, 1844-55, carried on operations alone, 1855; a founder Mineral Pt. Bank, 1852; mem. U.S. Ho. of Reps. (Republican) from Wis., 34th-36th, 40th-41st congresses, 1855-61, 1867-71; an organizer Mpls. Mill Co., 1856; participated in Washington (D.C.) Peace Conf., 1861; raised 2d Wis. Volunteer Cavalry, served as col.; commd. maj. gen. U.S. Volunteers during Civil War, 1862; gov. Wis., 1872-74; devoted later years to operation and expansion of vast indsl. enterprises; one of nation's foremost mfrs. of flour; organized Washburn Crosby & Co., 1877; a projector and builder of Minn. & St. Louis R.R.; pres. Wis. Hist. Soc.; philanthropies include Washburn Observatory at U. Wis.; Pub. Library, La Crosse, Wis., an orphan asylum in Minn. Died Eureka Springs, Ark., May 15, 1882; buried Grove Cemetery, La Crosse.

WASHBURN, Charles Ames, diplomat; b. Livermore, Me., Mar. 16, 1822; grad. Bowdoin Coll., 1848. Editor Alta Cal. (newspaper), 1853-58, Daily Times, 1858-60 (both San Francisco); presdl. elector for Cal., 1860; U.S. commr. to Paraguay, 1861 63, U.S. minister, 1863-68, escaped from Paraguay in U.S.S. Wasp when Americans were accused of giving aid to Brazil during Brazilian-Paraguayan War, 1868; inventor typograph. Author: Philip Thaxter (novel), 1861; Gomery of Montgomery (novel), 1865; Political Evolution, 1877; From Poverty to Competence, 1877; History of Paraguay, 2 vols., 1879. Died N.Y.C., Jan. 26, 1889; buried Livermore.

WASHBURN, Edward Abiel, clergyman; b. Boston, Apr. 16, 1819; s. Abiel and Paulina (Tucker) W.; grad. Harvard, 1838; attended Andover Theol. Sem. and Yale Divinity Sch.; D.D. (hon.), Trinity Coll., 1861; m. Frances Lindsey, June 16, 1853, 1 dau. Licensed to preach by Worcester Assn. of Congregational Minister, 1842; deacon Episcopal Trinity Ch., Boston, 1844, priest, 1845; rector St. Paul's Ch., Newburyport, Mass., 1845-51; made world trip, 1851-53; rector St. Johns Ch., Hartford, Conn., 1853-62; also lectr. on eccles. policy Berkeley Div. Sch., Middletown, Conn.; rector St. Mark's Ch., Phila., 1862-65, Calvary Ch., N.Y.C., 1865-81; a founder The Living Church, periodical of liberal churchmen; interested in work of Evangelical Alliance, presented papers at its sessions, 1873, 79; mem. Am. New Testament Company of Revisors of Bible. Author: The Social Law of God (sermons), 1875, Sermons, 1882; Epochs in Church History and Other Essays, 1883; Voices from a Busy Life (poems), 1883; The Beatitudes and Other Sermons, 1884. Died N.Y.C., Feb. 2, 1881.

WASHBURN, Emory, gov. Mass.; b. Leicester, Mass., Feb. 14, 1800; s. Joseph and Ruth (Davis) W.; attended Dartmouth, 2 years; grad. Williams Coll., 1817, LL.D. (hon.), 1854; attended Harvard Law Sch., 1819-29, LL.D. (hon.), 1854; m. Marianne Giles, Nov. 2, 1830, 3 children. Admitted to Mass. bar, 1821; mem. Mass. Ho. of Reps. from Leicester, 1826-28, from Worcester, 1838, from Cambridge, 1876; mem. Mass. Senate, 1841-42; judge Mass. Ct. Common Pleas, 1844-47; gov. Mass., 1854 55; lectr. Harvard Law Sch., 1855, prof. law, 1856-76; v.p. Mass. Hist. Soc., 1874-78; mem. Am. Antiquarian Soc.; mem. Mass. B.E., Internat. Code Commn. Author: Sketches of the Judicial History of Mass. from 1630-1775, 1840; History of Leicester, 1860; A Treatise on the Am. Law of Real Property, 1860-62; A Treatise on Am. Law of Easements and Servitudes, 1863. Died Cambridge, Mar. 18, 1877.

WASHBURN, Henry Dana, congressman; b. Windsor, Vt., Mar. 28, 1832; attended common schs.; grad. N.Y. State and Nat. Law Schs. A tanner, currier and sch. tchr., in youth; admitted to bar, 1853, began practice of law, Newport, Ind.; county auditor, 1854-61; commd. lt. col. 18th Regt., Ind. Volunteer Inf., 1861, promoted col., 1862; brevetted brig. gen. Volunteers, 1864, maj. gen., 1865; mem. U.S. Ho. of Reps. (Republican, contested election) from Ind., 39th-40th congresses, Feb. 23, 1866-69; surveyor gen. Mont., 1869-71, headed expdn. to find headwaters of Yellowstone River, 1870, discovered Yellowstone Park; Mt. Washburn (Mont.) named for him. Died Clinton, Ind., Jan. 26, 1871; buried Riverside Cemetery.

WASHBURN, Ichabod, mfr., philanthropist; b. Kingston, Mass., Aug. 11, 1798; s. Ichabod and Sylvia (Bradford) W.; m. Ann Brown, Oct. 6, 1823; m. 2d, Elizabeth Cheever, 1859; at least 1 dau. Entered partnership with W.H. Howard to manufacture lead pipe and machinery used in prodn. of woolen goods, 1821; partner Washburn & Goddard, mfrs. machinery for carding and spinning wool, 1823-24; devised wire drawblock; manufactured wire, Worcester, Mass., 1834-68, firm name I. Washburn & Moen after 1859; made steel piano wire, 1850; introduced galvanized iron telegraph wire; developed 1st continuous method of tempering and hardening metal, 1856; benefactor Lincoln (now Washburn) Coll. (Kan.); trustee, benefactor Worcester County Free Inst. of Indsl. Sci. Died Worcester, Dec. 30, 1868.

WASHBURN, Israel, gov. Me., congressman; b. Livermore, Me., June 6, 1813; s. Israel and Martha (Benjamin) W.; m. Mary Webster, Oct. 24, 1841; m. 2d, Rebina Brown, Jan. 1876; 4 children. Admitted to Me. bar, 1834; mem. Me. Ho. of Reps., 1842-43; mem. U.S. Ho. of Reps. from Me., 32d-36th congresses, 1851-61; founder Republican Party in Me.; gov. Me., 1861-62; collector of customs Port of Portland (Me.), 1863-77; pres. Rumford Falls & Buckfield R.R., 1878-83; frequent contbr. to Universalist Quarterly; pres. bd. trustees Tufts Coll., 1852-83. Author: Notes, Historical, Descriptive, and Personal, of Livermore . . . Maine, 1874. Died Phila., May 12, 1883; buried Bangor, Me.

WASHBURN, Peter Thacher, gov. Vt.; b. Lynn, Mass., Sept. 7, 1814; s. Reuben and Hannah (Thacher) W.; grad. Dartmouth, 1835; studied law under Senator Upham of Vt.; m. Almira E. Ferris; m. 2d, Almira P. Hopkins; 3 children. Admitted to Vt. bar, 1838; practiced law, Ludlow, Vt., 1838-44; reporter decisions Vt. Supreme Ct., 1844-52; mem. Vt. Ho. of Reps., 1853-54; del. Republican Nat. Conv., 1860; in command of Woodstock Light Inf., 1861 (joined 1st Vt. Regt.), chosen adjutant and insp. gen. Vt.; gov. Vt., 1869-70. Died Woodstock, Vt., Feb. 7, 1870.

WASHBURN, William Barrett, senator, congressman; b. Winchendon, Mass., Jan. 31, 1820; attended Westminster, Hancock acads.; grad. Yale, 1844. A clk. in Orange, 1844-47; engaged in mfg., Erving, Mass., 1847-57; mem. Mass. Senate, 1850, Mass. Ho. of Reps. 1853-55; became a banker, Greenfield, Mass., 1858; mem. U.S. Ho. of Reps. (Republican) from Mass., 38th-42d congresses, 1863-Dec. 5, 1871 (resigned); mem. U.S. Senate (filled vacancy) from Mass., Apr. 17, 1874-75; pres. Greenfield Nat. Bank; trustee Smith Coll.; dir. Conn. River R.R.; alumnus trustee Yale, 1872-81; mem. bd. overseers Amherst (Mass.) Coll. Died Springfield, Mass., Oct. 5, 1887; buried Green River Cemetery, Greenfield.

WASHBURNE, Elihu Benjamin, diplomat, congressman; b. Livermore, Me., Sept. 23, 1816; s. Israel and Martha (Benjamin) Washburn; attended Harvard Law Sch., 1839-40; m. Adele Gratiot, July 31, 1845, 7 children. Admitted to Mass. bar, 1840; settled in Galena, Ill., 1840; nominated Henry Clay for U.S. Pres., Whig Nat. Conv., Balt., 1844; mem. U.S. Ho of Reps from Ill., 33d-41st congresses, 1853-69, chmn.. com. on commerce and on appropriations for 2 years, proposed Grant's name as brig. gen. U.S Volunteers, sponsored bills by which Grant was made lt. gen.,. then gen.; U.S. sec. of state under Grant, Mar. 5-16, 1869; U.S. minister to France, 1869-77, only ofcl. rep. of fgn. govt. to remain in Paris throughout seige and Commune; pres. Chgo. Hist. Soc., 1884-87; edited papers of Gov. Ninian Edwards, 1884. Author: Recollections of a Minister to France, 1869-1877, published 1887. Died Chgo., Oct. 22, 1887; buried Greenwood Cemetery, Galena, Ill.

WASHINGTON, Bushrod, asso. justice U.S. Supreme Ct.; b. Westmoreland County, Va., June 5, 1762; s. John Augustine and Hannah (Bushrod) W.; grad. Coll. William and Mary, 1778; m. Julia Ann Blackburn, 1785, no children. Served as pvt. during Revolutionary War; admitted to Va. bar; mem. Va. Ho. of Dels., 1787; mem. Va. Conv. to ratify U.S. Constn., 1787; asso. justice U.S. Supreme Ct., 1798-1829, rendered majority opinion in such cases as Marine Ins. Co. vs. Tucker (3 Cranch, 357), 1806, Eliason vs. Henshaw (4 Wheaton, 225), 1819, Dartmouth Coll. vs. Woodward (4 Wheaton, 518), 1819, Green vs. Biddle (8 Wheaton, 213), 1823, Thornton vs. Wynn (12 Wheaton, 183), 1827, Ogden vs. Saunders (12 Wheaton, 213), 1827, Buckner vs. Finley (2 Peters, 586), 1829, U.S. vs. Bright (24 Fed. Cas., 1232); 1st pres. Am. Colonization Soc., 1816; an executor of his uncle George Washington's will, inherited "Mt. Vernon." Died Phila., Nov. 26, 1829; buried "Mt. Vernon," Va.

WASHINGTON, George, 1st Pres. U.S.; b. Bridges Creek, Westmoreland County, Va., Feb. 22, 1732; s. Augustine and Mary (Ball) W.; ed. privately; m. Mrs. Martha (Dandridge) Custis, Jan. 6, 1759, 2 stepchildren. Aided in survey of Shenandoah Valley, Va., 1748; apptd. county surveyor Culpeper County (Va.), 1749; inherited estate "Mt. Vernon" from half-brother Lawrence, 1752; apptd. by Gov. Robert Dinwiddie dist. adj. for S. Va., 1752; apptd. by Dinwiddie to carry ultimatum to French to leave English lands in Ohio country, 1753, received unconciliatory reply, also instructed to strengthen ties with the Six Nations, his report to Dinwiddie printed as Journal of Major George Washington . . . , 1754; commd. lt. col. Va. Militia, 1754; recommended establishment of post on site of present Pitts., found French entrenched there; erected Ft. Necessity, Great Meadow, Pa.; surprised and defeated French force, May 27, obtained generous terms in parley with French after 10-hour battle, July 3, 1754; served in unsuccessful expdn. under Gen. Braddock against Ft. Duquesne, 1755; apptd. col. and comdr.-in-chief of all Va. forces, 1755, responsible for defending 300 miles of mountainous frontier with about 300 men, 1755-58; accompanied British under Gen. Forbes who occupied Ft. Duquesne, 1758; resigned and became gentleman farmer, Mt. Vernon, 1759; contbr. to instns. Including Washington Coll., Md., Liberty Hall (later Washington and Lee Coll.), Lexington, Va.; urged establishment of nat. univ. in nation's capitol and provided endowment for it in his will; mem. Va. Ho. of Burgesses, 1759-74; justice of Fairfax County (Va.); a leader colonial opposition to Brit. policies in Am.; acted as chmn. meeting in Alexandria which adopted Fairfax Resolutions, July 18, 1774; mem. Continental Congress from Va., 1774-75, mem. com. for drafting army regulations and planning defense of N.Y.C.; elected comdr.-in-chief Continental Army, June 15, 1775, took command at Cambridge, Mass., July 3, 1775; forced Brit. evacuation of Boston, May 17, 1776; defeated at Battle of L.I., 1776; made Christmas night crossing of Delaware River; crushed Hessians at Battle of Trenton, Dec. 26, 1776, dislocated entire line of Brit. posts along Delaware River; won Battle of Princeton, forced Brit. retirement to Brunswick, N.J.; sought Congress' full co-operation in developing regular Continental Army, but still was forced to rely on militia to swell his ranks; defeated at Battle of Brandywine, Sept. 11, 1777; lost Battle of Germantown, Oct. 3-4, 1777; endured hardships with Continental Army at Valley Forge, winter 1777-78, but Army emerged better trained; heartened by French alliance, 1778; overtook British at Monmouth (N.J.), held field while British retired to N.Y.C., June 28, 1778; pursued siege of Yorktown (Va.) with aid of French under de Grasse and Rochambeau, Oct. 19, 1781; held army together until British evacuated N.Y.C., Apr. 19, 1783; bade his officers farewell at Fraunces Tavern, N.Y.C., Dec. 4, 1783; resigned commn., Dec. 23, 1783; retired to "Mt. Vernon," 1783; held meeting at Mt. Vernon on navigation rights on Potomac River, 1785 (indirectly led to U.S. Constl. Conv.); pres. U.S. Constl. Conv., Phila., 1787; unanimously elected 1st Pres. U.S. under new constn., 1788, took oath of office on balcony of U.S. Bldg. N.Y.C. (site of Washington statue at old Sub-Treasury Bldg.), Apr. 30, 1789; unopposed for re-election, 1792; stated Am.'s position regarding French Revolutionary War in Proclamation of Neutrality (issued 1793); strong nationalist; demonstrated power of U.S. Govt. by crushing Indians and suppressing Whiskey Rebellion, firmly fixed govtl. credit through Alexander Hamilton's policies, desired size of U.S. to internat. importance; strongly backed Pinckney Treaty with Spain and Jay Treaty with Gt. Britain (1795) though neither was completely satisfactory; during his adminstrn. certain fundamental patterns of Am. politics developed including: formation of polit. parties (which he opposed), establishment of basic functions and rights of different branches of govt. (such as method of treaty ratification, presdl. consent for use of exec. documents in Congress), even patterns of patronage (such as having each major sect. of country represented in cabinet); made farewell address, Sept. 1796; served as lt. gen. and cmdr.-in-chief U.S. Army (being raised in expectation of war with France), 1798-99. Died "Mt. Vernon," Dec. 14, 1799; buried "Mt. Vernon."

WASHINGTON, George Corbin, congressman, planter; b. "Haywood Farms," nr. Oak Grove, Va., Aug. 20, 1789; attended Harvard; studied law. Engaged in agriculture on Md. plantation, resided in Georgetown, D.C.; mem. U.S. Ho. of Reps. from Md., 20th-22d, 24th congresses, 1827-33, 35-37; pres. Chesapeake & Ohio Canal Co.; apptd. by Pres. Tyler commr. to adjust and settle claims with Cherokee Indians, 1844. Died Georgetown, July 17, 1854; buried Oak Hill Cemetery.

WASHINGTON, John Macrae, army officer; b. Windsor Forest, Stafford County, Va., Oct. 1797; s. Baily and Euphan (Wallace) W.; grad. U.S. Mil. Acad., 1817; m. Fanny Macrae, 3 children. Commd. 3d lt. of arty., 1817, 2d lt. and battalion q.m. of arty., 1818, 1st lt., 1810, sent to Fla. frontier; served at Savannah Harbor, 1821-22, Ft. Moultrie, 1822-24, Augusta, Ga., 1824; instr. mathematics at arty. sch., Ft. Monroe, Va., 1824-26, ordnance officer, 1828-33; brevetted capt., 1830, commd. capt., 1832; fought against Seminoles in Fla., 1833-38; aided Gen. Winfield Scott in transporting Cherokee Nation to Okla., 1838-39; detailed to assist Scott in peacefully quelling Canadian border disturbances, 1840-42; served at Battle of Buena Vista in Mexican War, 1847, positioned at critical pass of La Angostura, largely responsible for maintaining Am. position and securing Am. victory; promoted maj., 1847, brevetted lt. col., 1847; civil and mil. gov. of N.M., 1848-49; served at Ft. Constitution, N.H., 1850-52. Drowned at sea nr. mouth of Delaware River, Dec. 24, 1853.

WASHINGTON, Martha Dandridge Custis, 1st lady; b. New Kent County, Va., June 2, 1732; m. Daniel Parke Custis, 1749 (dec. 1757); children—Martha (died at age 17), Col. John Parke (died 1781), also 2 children who died in infancy; m. 2d, George Washington, Jan. 6, 1759 (dec. Dec. 14, 1799). Characterized as "the prettiest and richest widow in Virginia" after Custis' death; lived at Mt. Vernon (Va.) after her marriage to Washington; managed his plantations in his absence, visited him at Valley Forge, Newburgh, other camps; a gracious hostess at ofcl. functions at the Washington mansion, N.Y.C., during her husband's term of office. Died 1802; buried Mt. Vernon.

WASHINGTON, William Henry, congressman, lawyer; b. nr. Goldsboro, N.C., Feb. 7, 1813; studied law. Admitted to bar, 1835, began practice of law, New Bern, N.C.; mem. U.S. Ho. of Reps. (Whig) from N.C., 27th Congress, 1841-43; mem. N.C. Ho. of Commons, 1843, 46, N.C. Senate, 1848, 50, 52. Died New Bern, Aug. 12, 1860; buried Cedar Grove Cemetery.

WATERHOUSE, Benjamin, physician; b. Newport, R.I., Mar. 4, 1754; s. Timothy and Hannah (Proud) W.; apprenticed to Dr. John Halliburton, surgeon, 1770; med. student at Edinburgh, 1775; grad. U. Leyden, 1780; attended med. dept. of Harvard, 1783; m. Elizabeth Oliver, June 1, 1788; m. 2d, Louisa Lee, Sept. 19, 1819; 6 children. Prof. theory and practice of physic, med. dept. of Harvard, 1783-1812 (forced to resign); pioneer Am. vaccinator; received from England vaccine for small pox in form of infected threads, immediately used it on his son, 1800; vaccinated others with cowpox with good results; sent vaccine to Pres. Jefferson (who had about 200 persons vaccinated with it), 1802; wrote many newspaper articles on vaccination; lectured on natural history, mineralogy and botany at R.I. Coll. (now Brown U.), 1784-86, at Cambridge, Mass., from 1788; drew up plans for Humane Soc. of Commonwealth of Mass., 1785; med. supt. of all mil. posts in New Eng., 1813-20; editor John B. Wyeth's Oregon (published to deter Western emigrations), 1833. Author: A Synopsis of a Course of Lectures, on the Theory and Practice of Medicine, 1786; A Prospect of Exterminating the Small Pox (his 1st report on smallpox), 1800. Cautions to Young Persons Concerning Health . . . Shewing the Evil Tendency of the Use of Tobacco . . . with Observations on the Use of Ardent and Vinous Spirits, 1805; The Botanist, 1811; A Circular Letter, from Dr. Benjamin Waterhouse, to the Surgeons of the Different Post, 1817. Died at home, Cambridge, Oct. 2, 1846; buried Mt. Auburn Cemetery, Cambridge.

WATERHOUSE, Sylvester, educator; b. Barrington, N.H., Sept. 15, 1830; s. Samuel and Dolla (Kingman) W.; grad. with honors Harvard, 1853, LL.B., 1857; never married. Lost an eye and a leg in youth; acting prof. Latin, Antioch Coll., Yellow Springs, O., 1856-57, instr. Greek, 1857-64, prof. Greek, 1864-68; Collier prof. Greek, Washington U., St. Louis, 1868-1901; U.S. commr. to Paris Expn., 1878; Mo. commr. to Am. Expn., London, Eng., 1887; sec. St. Louis Bd. Trade; wrote numerous pamphlets on Mississippi River devel., also agrl. diversification, essays on St. Louis history, mining resources of Mo.; gave bulk of estate to various colls. Died St. Louis, Feb. 12, 1902; cremated, ashes placed in Pine Hill Cemetery, Dover, N.H.

WATERMAN, Lewis Edson, inventor, mfr.; b. Decatur, N.Y., Nov. 20, 1837; s. Elisha and Amanda (Perry) W.; m. Sarah Ann Roberts, June 29, 1858; m. 2d, Sarah Ellen Varney, Oct. 3, 1872; at least 3 children. Moved to Ill., 1853; engaged in various jobs as tchr., lockseller, carpenter; began selling life insurance, 1862; Boston rep. Aetna Life Ins. Co., 1864-70; perfected type of fountain pen, 1st patent issued, 1884 (his improvement over other types was in ink-feeding device); organized, operated Ideal Pen Co., 1884-87, reorganized and incorporated as L. E. Waterman Co., 1887, pres., mgr., 1887-1901, continued to improve pen throughout these years. Died Bklyn., May 1, 1901; buried Forest Hill Cemetery, Boston.

WATERMAN, Robert H., sea capt.; b. Hudson, N.Y., Mar. 4, 1808; s. Thaddeus and Eliza (Coffin) W.; m. Cordelia Sterling, 1846. First mate packet-ship Britannia sailing between N.Y.C. and Liverpool, 1829; in command of ship South America, 1833-37; sent to China with ship Natchez, 1842, made 1st 2 voyages homeward from Canton to N.Y.C. in 92 days and 94 days respectively (very close to record); made voyage from Macao to N.Y.C. in 78 days (established new world's record); established records which still stand as best and 2d best runs for sailing vessels between China and any North Atlantic port, 77 days from Macao to N.Y.C., 1848, 74 days and 14 hours from Hong Kong to N.Y., 1849; agreed to take command clipper Challenge (then largest clipper ship afloat), 1851, took her from N.Y. to San Francisco, tried for murder of some crew members, 1851, exonerated (charges came about because of near mutiny during voyage of Challenge); hull insp. for U.S. Govt., San Francisco, 1851-70; prin. founder Fairfield (Cal.) (donated land); bred fine strains of poultry and cattle; considered one of great sea capts. of U.S. Died San Francisco, Aug. 9, 1884; reinterred Bridgeport, Conn.

WATERMAN, Thomas Whitney, lawyer, editor; b. Binghamton, N.Y., June 28, 1821; s. Thomas Glasby and Pamela Whitney) W.; attended Yale, 1838-41; m. Miss Andrews, 1850, at least 2 children. Admitted to N.Y. bar, 1848; edited Am. edition of Compendium of the Law and Practice of Vendors and Purchasers of Real Estate (Joseph Henry Dart), 1851; edited 4th edit. of Treatise on the Principles and Practice of the Action of Ejectment (John Adams), 1854; edited 2d edit. of A Treatise on the Law of New Trials in Cases Civil and Criminal (David Graham), 1855; published Am. edit. of Reports of Cases Decided in the High Court of Chancery (John Tamlyn(, 1865. Author: Treatise on the Civil Jurisdiction of Justices of the Peace, 1849, The American Chancery Digest, 1851; A Treatise on the Law of Set-Off, Recoupment and Counter Claim, 1869; A Digest of Decisions on Criminal Cases, 1877; A Practical Treatise on the Laws Relating to the Specific Performance of Contracts, 1881; A Treatise on the Law of Corporations, 2 vols., 1888. Died Binghamton, N.Y., Dec. 7, 1898.

WATERS, Daniel, naval officer; b. Charlestown, Mass., June 20, 1731; s. Adam and Rachel (Draper) W.; m. Agnes Smith, July 1759; m. 2d, Mary (Wilcox) Mortimer, June 8, 1779; m. 3d, Sarah Sigourney, July 29, 1802; 1 dau. Mem. Malden (Mass.) Minutemen, fought against British, 1776; requested by Malden Com. of Safety to prepare cannon of town; in command schooner Lee, 1776, captured 2 enemy vessels; commd. capt. Continental Navy, 1777; served on West Indies cruise in Continental sloop General Gates, 1779; commanded Mass. ship General Putnam; his most famous exploit occurred in privateer Thorn, 1779, defeated 2 enemy privateers of about equal armament but more heavily manned; captured the Sparlin, 1780; in privateer Friendship, 1781. Died Malden, Mar. 26, 1816.

WATIE, Stand, Indian leader, army officer; b. at what is now Rome, Ga., Dec. 12, 1806; s. David and Susannah Vowatie or Uweti; m. Sarah C. Bell, 1843, 5 children. With brother published newspaper Cherokee Phoenix; co-signed treaty of New Echota, 1835; became leader minority or treaty party of Cherokee Indians; raised Cherokee co. of home guards, 1861, capt.; raised 1st Cherokee regt. of volunteers known as Cherokee Mounted Rifles, 1861; made col. by Confederate Govt.; served in battles of Wilson's Creek and Pea Ridge; commd. brig gen., 1864; one of last Confederate officers to surrender, 1865; went to Washington (D.C.) as member of So. delegation of Cherokee, circa 1865. Died Sept. 9, 1871.

WATKINS, Albert Galiton, congressman, lawyer; b. nr. Jefferson City, Tenn., May 5, 1818; grad. Holston Coll., Tenn.; studied law. Admitted to bar, began practice of law, Panther Springs, Tenn., 1839; mem. Tenn. Ho. of Reps., 1845; Whig presdl. elector, 1848; mem. U.S. Ho. of Reps. (Whig) from Tenn., 31st-32d congresses, 1849-53, (Democrat), 34th-35th congresses, 1855-59. Died Mooresburg, Tenn., Nov. 9, 1895; buried Westview Cemetery, Jefferson City.

WATKINS, George Claiborne, jurist; b. Shelbyville, Ky., Nov. 25, 1815; s. Maj. Isaac and Maria (Toncre) W.; attended Tapping Reeve's Law Sch., Litchfield, Conn.; m. Mary Crease, 1841; m. 2d, Mrs. Sophia (Fulton) Curran; 8 children. Partner (with Chester Ashley) in law firm, Little Rock, Ark., 1837; atty. gen. of Ark., 1843; chief justice Ark. Supreme Ct., 1852-54, made most important decision in Merrick vs. Avery, 1854; supporter of Confederacy; mem. mil. ct. attending troops under Gen. T.H. Holmes, Confederate Army, 1862. Died St. Louis, Dec. 7, 1872.

WATMOUGH, John Goddard, congressman; b. Wilmington, Del., Dec. 6, 1793; grad. Princeton; postgrad. U. Pa. at Phila. Served with 4th Co., 4th Detachment, Pa. Militia, 1813; commd. 2d lt. U.S. Army, 1813, brevetted 1st lt., 1814; mem. U.S. Ho. of Reps. from Pa., 22d-23d congresses, 1831-35; high sheriff Phila., 1835-36; surveyor Port of Phila., 1841-45. Died Phila., Nov. 27, 1861; buried Christ Ch. Cemetery.

WATSON, Cooper Kinderdine, congressman, lawyer; b. Jefferson County, Ky., June 18, 1810; studied law. Admitted to bar, began practice of law, Delaware, O.; moved to Marion, O., then to Tiffin, O.; mem. U.S. Ho. of Reps. (Free-Soiler) from Ohio, 34th Congress, 1855-57; moved to Sandusky, O.; mem. Ohio Constl. Conv., 1871; judge Ct .of Common Pleas, 1876-80. Died Sandusky, May 20, 1880; buried Greenlawn Cemetery, Tiffin.

WATSON, Elkanah, businessman, agriculturist; b. Plymouth, Mass., Jan. 22, 1758; s. Elkanah and Patience (Marston) W.; m. Rachel Smith, Mar. 3, 1789, 5 children. Employed by Brown family, R.I. mchts., 1773-79, went to S.C. to invest funds for his employers, 1777; partner (with M. Cossoul) in mcht. firm, 1779-84; embarked for France to carry money and dispatches to Benjamin Franklin, 1779; made spl. study of inland waterways of Holland; organized Bank of Albany (N.Y.); promoted 2 canal cos., also stage line from Albany to Schenectady, N.Y.; lobbied successfully for charter which authorized a company to build canal around Niagara Falls; secured charter for N.Y. State Bank; staged cattle show which preceded incorporation of Berkshire Agrl. Soc. (which sponsored 1st county fair in U.S., 1810). Author: A Tour of Holland. . ., 1790; History of Agricultural Societies on the Modern Berkshire System, 1820; History of the Rise and Progress, and Existing Condition of the Western Canals in the State of New York, 1820; Men and Times of the Revolution; or Memoirs of Elkanah Watson, published 1856. Died Port Kent, Essex County, N.Y., Dec. 5, 1842.

WATSON, Henry Clay, journalist, author; b. Balt., 1831. Mem. editorial staffs N.Am. and U.S. Gazette, Phila. Evening Journal; editor Sacramento (Cal.) Daily Union, 1861, was art critic, book reviewer, news editor, polit. writer; wrote hist. stories for young people. Author: Camp-Fires of the Revolution; or the War of Independence, 1850; The Old Bell of Independence; or Philadelphia in 1776, 1851; Nights in a Block-House, or Sketches of Border Life, 1852; The Yankee Tea-Party, or Boston in 1773, 1852; Lives of the Presidents of the United States, 1853; Heroic Women in History, 1853; Thrilling Adventures of Hunters in the Old World and the New, 1853; The Camp-Fires of Napoleon, copyright 1854; The Ladies' Glee-Book, 1854; The Masonic Musical Manual, 1855. Died Sacramento, June 24, 1867; buried City Cemetery, Sacramento.

WATSON, Henry Cood, editor, music critic; b. London, Eng., Nov. 4, 1818; s. John Watson. Studied music, Eng., circa 1833; wrote poetry and other literary works; came to N.Y., 1841, became music critic for paper New World; founded mag. Musical Chronicle (later known as Am. Musical Times), 1843; a founder short-lived Broadway Journal, 1845; editor Frank Leslie's Illustrated Newspaper, 1855; founder, editor Watson's Weekly Art Journal (became Am. Art Journal 1868), 1864-70; music critic N.Y. Tribune, 1863-67; composer many published songs and pieces; lectr. at Vocal Inst.; an organizer Mendelssohn Concert at Castle Garden, Am. Mus. Fund Assn., also Vocal Soc. (later became Mendelssohn Union); a founder Philharmonic Soc. of N.Y., 1842. Author: A Familiar Chat about Musical Instruments, 1852; libretto for Wallace's opera Lurline. Died N.Y.C., Dec. 2, 1875.

WATSON, James, senator; b. Woodbury, Conn., Apr. 6, 1750; grad. Yale, 1776; studied law. Commd. lt. in Conn. regt., 1776, capt., 1777; admitted to bar, practiced law; apptd. by assembly as purchasing commissary for Conn. Line, 1780; moved to N.Y.C., 1786, engaged in merc. activities; mem. N.Y. Assembly, 1791, 94-96, speaker, 1794; regent N.Y. U., 1795-1806; mem. N.Y. State Senate, 1796-98; mem. U.S. Senate (Democrat, filled vacancy) from N.Y., Aug. 17, 1798-Mar. 19, 1800 (resigned); U.S. naval officer at N.Y.C. (apptd. by Pres. Adams); mem. Soc. of Cincinnati; organizer, 1st pres. New Eng. Soc. in N.Y.C., 1805-06. Died N.Y.C., May 15, 1806.

WATSON, James Craig, astronomer; b. Fingal, Ont., Can., Jan. 28, 1838; s. William and Rebecca (Bacon) W.; grad. U. Mich., 1857; Ph.D. (hon.), U. Leipsig (Germany), Yale; LL.D. (hon.), Columbia; m. Annette Waite, May 1860, no children. Came to U.S., 1850; mastered theoretical and practical astronomy studying under Francis Brunnow; while still a student, ground, polished and mounted 4" achromatic objective; published 15 astron. papers before age 21; prof. astronomy in charge of observatory U. Mich., 1859, prof. physics, 1860-63, prof. astronomy, dir. observatory, 1863-79; discovered asteroid Eurynome (1st of his 22 astron. discoveries), 1863; participated in eclipse expdns. to Ia., 1869, Sicily, 1870, Wyo., 1878; in charge of expdn. to observe transit of Venus in China, 1874; dir. Washburn Observatory, U. Wis., Madison, 1879-80; mem. Nat. Acad. of Scis., 1868, Royal Acad. of Scis. in Italy, Am. Philos. Soc.; recipient Lalande prize French Acad. of Scis., 1870; named knight comdr. of Imperial Order of Medjidich of Turkey and Egypt, 1875; contbr. papers to Am. Journal of Sci., Gould's Astron. Journal, Brunnow's Astron. Notices and Astronomische Nachrichten. Author: Popular Treatise on Comets, 1861; Theoretical Astronomy (became textbook in U.S., Germany, France, Eng.), 1868; Tables for the Calculation of Simple or Compound Interest, 1878. Died Madison, Wis., Nov. 22, 1880.

WATSON, John Fanning, banker, historian; b. Batsto, N.J., June 13, 1779; s. William and Lucy (Fanning) W.; m. Phebe Crowell, 1812, 7 children. Clk., U.S. War Dept., 1798-1804; commissary of provisions for army posts in La., circa 1805; opened book store, entered publishing bus., Phila., 1809; cashier Bank of Germantown (Pa.), 1814-47; a founder Hist. Soc. Pa., 1824; led movements for proper marking of graves of hist. personages; treas., sec. Phila., Germantown & Norristown R.R., 1847. Author: Select Reviews of Literature and Spirit of the Foreign Magazines, 1809; Annals of Philadelphia, 1830; Historic Tales of Olden Time Concerning the Early Settlement and Advancement of New York City and State, 1832; Historic Tales of Olden Time Concerning the Early Settlement and Progress of Philadelphia and Pennsylvania, 1833; Annals and Occurrences of New York City and State, 1846. Died Germantown, Pa., Dec. 23, 1860.

WATSON, John William Clark, Confederate senator; b. Albemarle County, Va., Feb. 27, 1808; s. John and Elizabeth (Finch) W.; B.L., U. Va., 1830; m. Catherine Davis, Sept. 8, 1831, 8 children. Practiced law, Abingden, Va., 1830-45; moved to Miss., 1845; Whig mem. Miss. State Conv., 1851, concurred in action of that body denying right of secession, but accepted various offices in Confederate Govt.; mem. Confederate Senate, 1864-65; received 33 votes for pres. U.S. at Miss. Republican ("Black and Tan") Conv., 1868; active in overthrow of radical Rep. govt. of Miss., 1875; judge Miss. Circuit Ct., 1876-82; represented Miss. before U.S. Supreme Ct. in railroad commn. cases, 1885; elder Presbyn. Ch., more than 40 years; a pioneer prohibitionist in Miss. Died Holly Springs, Miss., Sept. 24, 1890.

WATSON, Lewis Findlay, congressman, businessman; b. Crawford County, Pa., Apr. 14, 1819; attended common schs.; studied law, Warren Acad., 1839-40. A mcht., Titusville, 1832-35, Warren, Pa., 1835-37, 40-60; engaged in lumber and petroleum prodn., 1860-75; organizer, 1st pres. Conewango Valley R.R. Co., 1861; 1st pres. Warren Savs. Bank, 1870; mem. U.S. Ho. of Reps. (Republican) from Pa., 45th, 47th, 51st congresses, 1877-79, 81-83, 89-90. Died Washington, D.C., Aug. 25, 1890; buried Oakland Cemetery, Warren.

WATSON, Sereno, botanist; b. East Windsor Hill, Conn., Dec. 1. 1826; s. Henry and Julia (Reed) W.; grad. Yale, 1847, began study of chemistry and mineralogy Sheffield Scientific Sch., 1866; Ph.D. (hon.), Ia. Coll., 1878; never married. Permitted to join Clarence King exploration party in Cal. as volunteer aid, 1867, commissioned to collect plants and secure data regarding them; asst. Gray Herbarium, Cambridge, Mass., 1873, curator, 1874-92, revised Gray's Manual of Botany, 1889. Author: Botany, 1871; Botany of California, 1st vol., 1876, 2d vol., 1880; Bibliographical Index to North American Botany, 1878; Manual of the Mosses of North America, 1884. Died Cambridge, Mass., Mar. 9, 1892; buried Harvard Lot at Mt. Auburn Cemetery, Cambridge.

WATTERSON, Harvey Magee, editor, congressman, b. Beech Grove, Tenn., Nov. 23, 1811; s. William S. Watterson; attended Cumberland Coll., Princeton, Ky.; m. Talitha Black, 1830, 1 son, Henry. Established and edited a paper, Shelbyville, Tenn.; admitted to Tenn. bar; mem. lower house Tenn. Legislature, 1831-39; mem. U.S. Ho. of Reps. (Democrat) from Tenn., 26th-27th congresses, 1839-43; mem. diplomatic mission to Buenos Aires, Argentina, 1841; presiding officer Tenn. Senate, 1845-47; propr. Nashville (Tenn.) Daily Union, 1849, editor, 1850-51; editor Washington Union, 1851-55; mem. Tenn. Secession Conv., opposed secession; mem. com. to investigate conditions in the states "lately in rebellion", 1866; mem. editorial staff Courier Jour., Louisville, Ky., 1891. Presbyn. Died Louisville, Oct. 1, 1891; buried Cave Hill Cemetery, Louisville.

WATTERSTON, George, librarian; b. on shipboard, N.Y. Harbor, Oct. 23, 1783; s. David Watterston; m. Maria Shanley, Oct. 26, 1811, 8 children. Practiced law, Hagerstown, Md.; editor Washington (D.C.) City Gazette, 1813; librarian of Congress, 1815-29; held several municipal offices, Washington; on staff Nat. Journal, Washington, 1829, editor, 1830; started movement to build Washington Monument, 1833; sec. Washington Nat. Monument Soc., 1834-54. Author: The Lawyer, or Man as he Ought Not To Be, 1808. Died Washington, Feb. 4, 1854; buried Congressional Cemetery, Washington.

WATTS, Frederick, agriculturist, govt. ofcl.; b. Carlisle, Pa., May 9, 1801; s. David and Julian (Miller) W.; attended Dickinson Coll.; m. Eliza Cranston, Sept. 1827; m. 2d, Henrietta Edge, Mar. 1835; 9 children. Practiced law, Carlisle; sec. bd. control Dickinson Coll., 1824-28, mem. bd., 1828-33, 41-44; reported cases of Western dist. Pa. Supreme Ct., 1829-45; pres. Cumberland Valley R.R. Co., 1845-71; judge 9th Pa. Jud. Dist., 1849-52; experimented with farm bldgs. and equipment, breeds of livestock, encouraged agrl. fairs; pres. Pa. State Agrl. Soc., Cumberland County Agrl. Soc.; successful in putting through Legislature a charter for Farmers' High Sch. which developed into Pa. State Coll., 1854, 1st pres. bd. trustees; U.S. commr. of agr., 1871, div. of microscopy established during his term, started what later became forestry div. of Dept. Agr. Died Carlisle, Aug. 17, 1889; buried Carlisle.

WATTS, John, congressman; b. N.Y.C., Aug. 27, 1749; studied law. Last recorder of N.Y. under the Crown; mem. N.Y. State Assembly, 1791-93; speaker, 1792-93; mem. commn. to build Newgate Prison, N.Y.C., 1796-99; mem. U.S. Ho. of Reps. from N.Y., 3d Congress, 1793-95; judge Westchester County, 1802-07; established and endowed Leake and Watts Orphan House. Died N.Y.C., Sept. 3, 1836; buried in vault Trinity Churchyard.

WATTS, John Sebrie, congressman, lawyer; b. Boone County, Ky., Jan. 19, 1816; grad. Ind. U. at Bloomington; studied law. Admitted to bar, practiced law; mem. Ind. Ho. of Reps., 1846-47; asso. justice U.S. Ct. in N.M. Territory, 1851-54; mem. U.S. Congress (Republican) from N.M. Territory, 37th Congress, 1861-63; del. Rep. Nat. Conv., Balt., 1864; active in equipping troops for U.S. Army during Civil War; chief justice N.M. Supreme Ct., 1868; resumed practice of law, Santa Fe, then returned to Bloomington. Died Bloomington, June 11, 1876; buried Rose Hill Cemetery.

WATTS, Thomas Hill, gov. Ala., Confederate atty. gen.; b. Ala. Territory, Jan. 3, 1819; s. John Hughes and Prudence (Hill) W.; grad. U. Va., 1839; m. Eliza Allen, Jan. 10, 1842; m. 2nd, Ellen (Noyes) Jackson, Sept. 1875; 10 children. Admitted to Ala. bar, 1840; mem. Ala. Legislature from Butler County, 1842, 44, 45, from Montgomery County, 1849; mem. Ala. Senate, 1853; leader Union forces in Ala. in campaign of 1860; mem. Ala. Secession Conv. of 1861; organizer col. 17th Ala. Regt., 1861; honorably discharged to become atty. gen. Confederacy, 1862; 16th gov. Ala., 1863-65; sent to Northern prison, 1865, received pardon from Pres. Johnson, 1868; resumed law practice, Montgomery, Ala., circa 1868. Died Montgomery, Sept. 16, 1892.

WAUGH, Alfred S., artist, writer; b. Ireland. Came to U.S., circa 1833; modelled several busts, Raleigh, N.C., 1838; went to Mo. with John B. Tisdale, 1845, worked at Jefferson City, Independence, Lexington; made trip to Santa Fe., N.M., 1846, painted portraits and miniatures, Boonville, Mo., 1847; moved to St. Louis, 1848; executed numerous busts and portraits; wrote several articles on artistic subjects for Western Jour.; lectr. on artistic subjects; wrote autobiography Travels in Search of the Elephant (only part of which is extant). Died St. Louis, Mar. 18, 1856.

WAUGH, Beverly, clergyman; b. Fairfax County, Va., Oct. 25, 1789; s. Capt. James and Henrietta (Turley) W.; m. Catharine B. Bushby, Apr. 21, 1812. Mgr. store, Middleburg, Va., 1807; admitted to Balt. Conf., Methodist Episcopal Ch., 1809, ordained deacon, 1811, elder, 1813; del. Gen. Conf., 1816, 20, 28, 36; prin. book agt. of Meth. Episcopal Ch., 1832; became bishop, 1836, presided over Troy Conf., Pawlet, Vt., 1836, sr. bishop, 1852; tried unsuccessfully to prevent church from splitting over the slavery issue. Died Balt., Feb. 9, 1858; buried Mt. Olivet Cemetery, Balt.

WAUGH, Samuel Bell, artist; b. Mercer, Pa., 1814; m. Mary Eliza Young, children include Frederick Judd, Ida. Spent 8 years in Italy, before 1841; worked primarily in Phila., also in N.Y.C., 1844-45, Bordentown, N.J., 1853, painted Italian panorama 1st exhibited in Phila., 1849; painted 2d series entitled Italia, exhibited, 1854-58; elected asso. N.A.D., 1845, hon. profl. mem., 1847. Died Janesville, Wis., 1855.

WAYLAND, Francis, clergyman, coll. pres.; b. N.Y.C., Mar. 11, 1796; s. Francis and Sarah (Moore) W.; grad. Union Coll., 1813, D.D., (hon.), 1828; D.D. (hon.), Harvard, 1829, LL.D. (hon.), 1852; attended Andover Theol. Sem., 1816; m. Lucy Lane Lincoln, Nov. 21, 1825; m. 2d, Mrs. Hepsy S. Howard Sage, Aug. 1, 1838; 3 children including Francis, H. L. Tutor, Union Coll., 1817-21, prof. mathematics and natural philosophy, 1826; called to First Baptist Ch., Boston, 1821; his sermons The Moral Dignity of the Missionary Enterprise (1823) and The Duties of An American Citizen (1825) became famous in their time; pres. Brown U., 1827-55, during his adminstrn. curriculum augmented, faculty enlarged, library endowed, new buildings added; wrote textbooks in moral philosophy, intellectual philosophy and polit. economy; instrumental in devising school system for Providence, R.I.; 1st pres. Am. Inst Instrn., 1830; pastor First Baptist Ch., Providence, for a time, after 1855; trustee Butler Hosp.; mem. state prison bd.; outlined plan for nat. univ., 1838. Author: Elements of Moral Science, 1835; Elements of Political Economy, 1837; The Limitations of Human Responsibility, 1838; Thoughts on the Present Collegiate System in the United States, 1842; The Duty of Obedience to the Civil Magistrate, 1847; Report on the Condition of the University, 1850; A Memoir of the Life and Labors of the Rev. Adoniram Judson, D.D., 1853; The Elements of Intellectual Philosophy, 1854; Sermons to the Churches, 1858; Letters on the Ministry of the Gospel, 1863. Died Providence, Sept. 30, 1865.

WAYMAN, Alexander Walker, clergyman; b. Caroline County, Md., Sept. 1821; s. Francis and Matilda Wayman; 1st wife died 1860; m. 2d, Harriet

Ann Elizabeth Wayman. Converted to Methodist Episcopal Ch., circa 1836; joined African Meth. Episcopal Ch., Phila., 1840, licensed as exhorter; asst. on Princeton (N.J.) circuit, 1842, taught at small primary school, New Brunswick, N.J.; admitted on trial at Phila. Conf., 1843, ordained deacon, 1845, elder., 1847; transferred to Balt. Conf., 1848; pastor chs., Washington, D.C. and Balt., 1848-64 (except for 2 years); organized Ebenezer Ch., Georgetown, D.C., St. Paul's, South Washington, Allen Chapel, Good Hope, Md.; mem. all gen. confs., 1848-64, served as asst. sec.; prepared and published (with 2 others;) new edit. of Discipline, 1860; elected bishop, 1864, organized Va., Ga. and Fla. confs., supervised dist. which included Ind., Ill., Mo. and Cal., 1872; made several journeys to Pacific Coast; chaplain at unveiling of Lincoln Meml., Springfield, Ill., 1874. Author: My Recollections of African Methodist Episcopal Ministers, 1881; Cyclopaedia of African Methodism, 1882. Died Balt., Nov. 30, 1895.

WAYMOUTH, George, navigator, explorer; b. Devonshire, Eng.; flourished, 1601-12. Employed by East India Co. to find N.W. Passage, sailed, 1602, turned back because of mutiny (Waymouth cleared of blame); comdr. ship Archangel on voyage of exploration of Va. (probably part of English Catholic attempt at colonization in Am.); took 5 captured Indians back to Eng.; wrote Errors and Defects in the Usual Building of Ships, circa 1605; took part in siege of Julich (Germany), 1610; wrote manuscript "A Journall Relation of the Service at the Takeing in of the Towne and Castle of Gulicke. . . ."

WAYNE, Anthony, army officer; b. Waynesboro, Pa., Jan. 1, 1745; s. Isaac and Elizabeth (Iddings) W.; m. Mary Penrose, Mar. 25, 1766, 2 children. Chmn. com. of Chester County (Pa.) to frame resolutions of protest against British, 1774; mem. Pa. Provincial Assembly from Chester County, 1775; col. of a Chester County regt., sent with Pa. brigade to reinforce Canadian expn., 1776; brig. gen. Continental Army, joined Washington at Morristown, N.J., 1777, took command Pa. troops; served in battles of Brandywine and Germantown, 1777; with Washington at Valley Forge, winter 1777-78; served in Battle of Monmouth, 1778; received medal from Congress for taking over 500 Brit. prisoners and munitions at Stony Point, 1779; sent to oppose British, Loyalists and hostile Indians in Ga., 1781; negotiated treaties of submission with Creek and Cherokee Indians, winter 1782-83; retired from active service as brevet maj. gen., 1783; mem. Pa. Gen. Assembly from Chester County, 1784, 85; mem. U.S. Ho. of Reps. from Ga., 2d Congress, 1791-92; maj. gen. in command U.S. Legion, 1791; defeated Indians at Fallen Timbers on Maumee River nr. what is now Toledo, O. Died Presque Isle (now Erie), Pa., Dec. 15, 1796.

WAYNE, Isaac, congressman, lawyer; b. nr. Paoli, Chester County, Pa., 1772; grad. Dickinson Coll., Carlisle, Pa.; studied law. Admitted to Chester County bar, 1795; mem. Pa. Ho. of Reps., 1799-1801, 06; mem. Pa. Senate, 1810; raised, equipped and served as capt. troop of Pa. Horse, during War of 1812, then commd. col. 2d Regt., Pa. Volunteer Inf.; unsuccessful Federalist candidate for gov. Pa., 1814; mem. U.S. Ho. of Reps. from Pa., 18th Congress, 1823-25; engaged in agriculture. Died Chester County, Oct. 25, 1852; buried St. David's Episcopal Ch. Cemetery, Radnor, Pa.

WAYNE, James Moore, asso. justice U.S. Supreme Ct.; b. Savannah, Ga., 1790; s. Richard and Elizabeth (Clifford) W.; grad. Coll. of N.J. (now Princeton), 1808, LL.B. (hon.), 1849; read law under Judge Chauncey, New Haven, Conn.; m. Mary Campbell, circa 1810, 3 children. Practiced law in Savannah, 1810; officer in Ga. Hussars during War of 1812; mem. Ga. Ho. of Reps., 1815-16; mayor Savannah, 1815-16; judge Superior Ct. Ga., 1824-29; mem. U.S. Ho. of Reps. (Democrat) from Ga., 21st-23d congresses, 1829-35, chmn. com. fgn. relations; asso. justice U.S. Supreme Ct. U.S., 1835-67. Died Washington, D.C., July 5, 1867; buried Laurel Grove Cemetery, Savannah, Ga.

WEAKLEY, Robert, congressman; b. Halifax County, Va., July 20, 1764; attended schs., Princeton, N.J. Served with Continental Army until close of Revolutionary War; engaged in agriculture in section of N.C. which later became Tenn.; mem. N.C. Conv. that ratified U.S. Constn., 1789; mem. 1st State Ho. of Reps., 1796; mem. U.S. Ho. of Reps. from Tenn., 11th Congress, 1809-11; apptd. U.S. commr. to treat with Chickasaw Indians, 1819; mem. Tenn. Constl. Conv., 1834. Died nr. Nashville, Tenn., Feb. 4, 1845; buried family vault at "Lockland," on his estate, Nashville suburbs.

WEARE, Meshech, pres. N.H.; b. Hampton Falls, N.H., Jan. 16, 1713; s. Nathaniel and Mary (Waite) W.; grad. Harvard, 1735, studied law; m. Elizabeth Shaw, July 20, 1738; m. 2d, Mehitable Wainwright, Dec. 11, 1746; 10 children. Mem. N.H. Legislature from Hampton, 1745-55, served intermittently, 1755-75, speaker, 3 years, clk., 8 years; justice N.H. Superior Ct., 1747-75; mem. Albany Congress, 1754; served as col. N.H. Militia; pres. N.H. Council, 1776-84; chmn. N.H. Com. of Safety; chief justice N.H., 1776-82; pres. N.H., 1784-85. Died Hampton Falls, Jan. 14, 1786.

WEATHERFORD, William (Indian name Red Eagle), Indian chief; b. nr. Montgomery, Ala., circa 1780; m. Mary Moniac (dec. 1804); m. 2d, Sapoth Thlanie; m. 3d, Mary Stiggins, 1817. Chief, Creek Indians; led followers in battle during Creek War, circa 1813; responsible for massacre at Ft. Mims (Ga.) in which 500 were put to death; a leader Creek Indians in Battle at Horseshoe Bend (Ala.), 1814. Died Mar. 9, 1824.

WEAVER, Archibald Jerard, congressman, lawyer; b. Dundaff, Susquehanna County, Pa., Apr. 15, 1844; grad. Wyoming Sem., Kingston, Pa.; grad. law dept., Harvard, 1869. Mem. faculty Wyoming Sem., 1864-67; admitted to bar, Boston, 1869; began practice of law, Falls City, Neb., 1869; mem. Neb. constl. convs., 1871- 75; dist. atty. 1st Dist. Neb., 1872; judge 1st Jud. Dist. Neb., 1875-83; mem. U.S. Ho. of Reps. (Republican) from Neb., 48th-49th congresses, 1883-87. Died Falls City, Apr. 18, 1887; buried Steele Cemetery.

WEAVER, Philip cotton mfr.; b. North Scituate, R.I., 1791; s. John and Ruth (Wilbur) W.; m. Miriam Keene, at least 4 children. Worked for Dudley Cotton Mfg. Co. (Mass.), 1812; arrested for non-payment of debts, S.C., 1819; established Weaver & Co., Spartonville, S.C., (one of 1st cotton mills in area), 1819, worked mill until 1826. Killed by a runaway horse, Attica, Ind., 1861.

WEBB, Daniel, army officer; b. Eng., circa 1700. Became ensign 1st Foot Guards, Brit. Army, 1721, capt. lt. with rank of capt., 1722; served with 4th Horse Corps, 1732-52, commd. capt., 1732, maj., 1742, lt. col., 1745, led squadron at battles of Dettingen and Fontenay, 1742; commd. col. 48th Foot Guards; came to Am., 1755, held temporary commn. as comdr. in chief, 1756, temporary maj. gen., sent up Mohawk River to defend against French attack, retreated instead, 1757; recalled to Eng., 1757; q.m. gen., 1758, served in Germany; commd. maj. gen., 1759, lt. gen., 1761. Died Nov. 11, 1773.

WEBB, George James, musician, composer; b. Wiltshire, Eng., June 24, 1803; s. James Millett and Isabel Ann (Archer) W.; studied music at home, also Falmouth, Eng.; m. Caroline (Haven) Merriam, 6 children. Came to Boston, 1830; organist Old South Ch., Boston, 1830; in charge of secular music for Boston Acad. Music, 1830, organized its orchestra; helped found Normal Musical Convs. for training of music tchrs., Boston; co-editor (with Lowell Mason) of various song and hymn collections; edited Scripture Worship, 1834, Massachusetts Collection of Psalmody, 1840, The American Glee Book, 1841; principally known for his hymn "Webb," originally written as secular tune beginning "Tis dawn, the lark is singing," became converted to "Stand up, stand up for Jesus." Died Orange, N.J., Oct. 7, 1887.

WEBB, James Watson, journalist, diplomat; b. Claverack, N.Y., Feb. 8, 1802; s. Gen. Samuel Blachley and Catharine (Hogeboom) W.; m. Helen Lispenard Stewart, July 1, 1823; m. 2d, Laura Virginia Cram, Nov. 9, 1849; 13 children including Alexander Stewart. Commd. 2d lt. U.S. Army, 1819; volunteered to carry news of meditated Indian attack on Ft. Snelling (Minn.) to Ft. Armstrong on Mississippi River, 1822; promoted 1st lt., 1827; resigned commn., 1827; acquired Morning Courier, N.Y.C., 1827, merged it with New York Enquirer, 1829, editor, propr., 1829-61; apptd. U.S. charge d'affaires to Austria, 1849, Senate refused to ratify appointment; U.S. minister to Brazil, 1861-69, instrumental in obtaining promise of French withdrawal from Mexico, 1865. Author: To the Officers of the Army, 1827; Slavery and Its Tendencies, written 1856; A Letter . . . to J. Bramley-Moore, Esq., M.P.; A National Currency, 1875; Reminiscences of General Samuel B. Webb, 1882. Died N.Y.C., June 7, 1884.

WEBB, Thomas, missionary; b. Eng., circa 1724; married twice, 2 children, Gilbert, Charles. Commd. q.m. Brit. Army, 1754, lt., 1755; sent to Am. during French and Indian War, 1758, lost an eye at Quebec; converted to Methodism under influence of John Wesley, 1764; returned to Am. as barrackmaster of Albany, circa 1766; assisted Philip Embury in establishing Methodism in Am.; preached in L.I., also Burlington, Vt., and Phila.; raised money to build Wesley Chapel (completed 1768); went to Eng., 1772-73, made strong appeals for Am. Methodism, urged ch. to send more ministers; worked in colonies as missionary with Thomas Rankin and George Shadford (both admired his preaching), 1773-circa 1775. Died Bristol, Eng., Dec. 10, 1796; buried Portland Street Chapel, Bristol.

WEBB, Thomas Smith, fraternal ofcl.; b. Boston, Oct. 30, 1771; s. Samuel and Margaret (Smith) W.; m. Mrs. Martha Hopkins, autumn 1797; m. 2d, her sister, 1809; 9 children. Received 1st 3 Masonic degrees, Keene, N.H., known as founder Am. system of chpt. and encampment of Masonry, presiding officer conv. which formed gen. grand chpt. Royal Arch Masons, Boston, 1797; established paperstaining factory, Albany, N.Y., 1793; a founder Psalonian Soc. (orgn. concerned with knowledge and practice of sacred music), 1809; a founder Handel-Haydn Soc. of Boston, 1815, 1st pres., 1815-circa 1817. Died July 6, 1819; buried Providence, R.I.

WEBBER, Charles Wilkins, author, journalist, explorer; b. Russellville, Ky., May 29, 1819; s. Dr. Augustine and Agnes Maria (Tannehill) W.; attended Princeton Theol. Sem., 1843-44; m. 1849. Served with Tex. Rangers, 1838; wrote articles on Tex. adventure for New World, N.Y.C.; wrote for Lit. World, Democratic Review, Sunday Dispatch, Graham's Mag.; editor, joint propr. Am. Review (later Am. Whig Review), 2 years; organized expdn. to Colorado and Gila rivers which failed, 1849; reported to have obtained charter from N.Y. Legislature to form camel co., circa 1855; went to Central Am., 1855. Author: Old Hicks the Guide, or Adventures . . . in Search of a Gold Mine, 1848; The Gold Mines of the Gila, 1849; The Hunter-Naturalist, 1851; The Texan Virago . . . and Other Tales, 1852; The Wild Girl of Nebraska, 1852; Spiritual Vampirism, 1853; "Sam," or the History of Mystery, 1855; History and Revolutionary Incidents of the Early Incidents of the Early Settlers of the United States, 1859; A Letter to the Country and Whig Party with Regard to the Conduct of the "American Whig Review" (pamphlet), 1847. Died Rivas, Nicaragua, Apr. 1856.

WEBBER, Samuel, coll. pres.; b. Byfield, Mass., 1759; grad. Harvard, 1784, S.T.D. (hon.), 1806. Ordained to ministry Congregational Ch., 1785; tutor Harvard, 1787-89, Hollis prof. mathematics and natural philosophy, 1789-1804, pres. coll., 1806-10; a commr. to settle boundary between U.S. and Brit. provinces; v.p. Am. Acad. Arts and Scis. of Boston; mem. Am. Philos. Soc. Author: A System of Mathematics. Died Cambridge, Mass., July 17, 1810.

WEBER, Albert, piano mfr.; b. Bavaria, July 8, 1828. Came to N.Y.C., 1844; gave music lessons in evenings and played organ in chs. on Sundays; founded Weber Piano Co., 1851, opened warerooms on Fifth Ave. at 16th St., N.Y.C., 1860; credited with originating term baby grand. Died June 25, 1879.

WEBSTER, Daniel, senator, sec. state; b. Salisbury, N.H., Jan. 18, 1782; s. Ebenezer and Abigail (Eastman) W.; grad. Dartmouth, 1801; m. Grace Fletcher, May 29, 1808; m. 2d, Caroline LeRoy, Dec. 12, 1829; at least 3 children, Fletcher, Edward, Julia (Webster) Appleton. Admitted to Mass. bar, 1805; practiced in Portsmouth, N.H., 1807-16; mem. U.S. Ho. of Reps. (Federalist) from N.H., 13th-14th congresses, 1813-17, from Mass., 18th-20th congresses,1823-29 ; opposed War of 1812 as mem. com. on fgn. relations, defended merc. interests of New Eng., opposed high tariffs, chmn. jud. com., 1823-27; reentered full-time practice of law, 1817; achieved reputation leading lawyer in Dartmouth Coll. case, 1819, legal fame also enhanced as counsel for Bank of U.S. in McCulloch vs. Md., 1819; presdl. elector, 1820; mem. Mass. Constl. Conv., 1820-21; mem. Mass. Ho. of Reps., 1822; built reputation as orator in speeches commemorating landing of Pilgrims, 1820, and Battle of Bunker Hill, 1825; mem. U.S. Senate from Mass., 1827-Feb. 22, 1841, 1845-July 22, 1850; advocated high tariffs to protect New Eng. textile industry, gave speech "Reply to Hayne" which earned him reputation as great orator, 1830; became known as "defender of constitution" for his role in opposing nullification in crisis of 1832-33, opposed Compromise Tariff of 1833, attacked annexation of Tex. in 1845, opposed extension of slavery but believed in right of Southern states to regulate own institutions including slavery, supported Compromise of 1850 in his famous "Seventh of March" speech, defending view that preservation of union transcended anti-slavery in importance, stand on this issue severely criticized by his constituents in Mass.; nominated for U.S. Pres. by Mass. Whigs, 1836; received electoral support only in New Eng.; U.S. sec. state (apptd. by Pres. Harrison), 1841-43, 50-52, negotiated Webster-Ashburton Treaty of 1842 settling Me. boundary dispute; wrote "Hulsemann letter" regarding Am. attitude toward Hungarian revolt; aspired to Whig nomination for U.S. Pres., 1852. Died Marshfield, Mass., Oct. 24, 1852.

WEBSTER, Edwin Hanson, congressman, lawyer; b. nr. Churchville, Harford County, Md., Mar. 31, 1829; attended Churchville, New London acads.; grad. Dickinson Coll., Carlisle, Pa., 1847; studied law. Admitted to bar, 1851, began practice of law, Bel Air, Md.; mem. Md. Senate, 1855-59; Am. Party presdl. elector, 1856; served as col. 7th Regt., Md. Volunteer Inf., during Civil War, 1862-63; mem. U.S. Ho. of Reps. (Republican) from Md., 36th-39th congresses, 1859-July 1865 (resigned); collector of customs Port of Balt., 1865-69, 82-86; also engaged in banking, 1882-93. Died Bel Air, Apr. 24, 1893; buried Calvary Cemetery, nr. Churchville.

WEBSTER, John White, educator; b. Boston, May 20, 1793; s. Redford and Hannah (White) W.; M.A., Harvard, 1811, M.D., 1815; studied medicine, in London, Eng.; m. Harriet Fredrica Hickling, May 16, 1818, 4 daus. Mem. staff Guy's Hosp., London, 1815 tchr. chemistry Harvard, 1824-27, Erving prof. chemistry and mineralogy, 1827-49; asso. editor Boston Journal of Philosophy and the Arts, 1824-26; editor A Manual of Chemistry, 1826. became involved in financial difficulties with Dr. George Parkman from whom he had borrowed money, 1849; after Parkman was reported missing for over a week, human remains were found in vault beneath Webster's lab.; arrested, attempted suicide; his trial famous for judge's charge to jury on meaning of circumstantial evidence; his plea of innocence rejected by gov. Author: A Description of the Island of St. Michael, 1821. Hanged for murder, Boston, Aug. 30, 1850.

WEBSTER, Joseph Dana, engr., army officer; b. Hampton, N.H., Aug. 25, 1811; s. Josiah and Elizabeth (Wright) W.; grad. Dartmouth, 1832; m. Miss Wright, 1844, at least 3 children. Entered govt. service as civil engr., 1835; commd. 2d lt. Topog. Engrs., U.S. Army, 1838, 1st lt., 1849, capt., 1853; resigned, 1854; engaged in mfg. farming implements, Chgo.; mem. Chgo. Sewerage Commn., 1855; maj., paymaster in U.S. Volunteers, 1861; commd. col. 1st Ill. Light Arty.; chief of staff under U. S. Grant, in charge of all mil. rys. in Grant's area; commd. brig. gen. U.S. Volunteers, 1862 chief of staff under Gen. William T. Sherman at Battle of Nashville; brevetted maj. gen. volunteers 1865; resigned commn., 1865; assessor internal revenue, 1869-72; asst. treasurer U.S., 1872-75; collector internal revenue, 1875-76. Died Chgo., Mar. 12, 1876.

WEBSTER, Noah, lexicographer; b. West Hartford, Conn., Oct. 16, 1758; s. Noah and Mercy (Steele) W.; B.A., Yale, 1778; m. Rebecca Greenleaf, Oct. 26, 1789, 8 children. Admitted to Hartford (Conn.) bar, 1781; taught sch., Goshen, N.Y., prepared 1st part of speller, 1782, grammar, 1784, reader, 1785; agitated for uniform copyright law, 1782-89, became staunch Federalist, advocated strong central govt.; carried on correspondence with Benjamin Franklin on spelling reform; gradually came to propagate traditional spelling; editor Am. Mag. N.Y.C., 1787-88; practiced law, Hartford, 1788-93; launched daily pro-Federalist newspaper Minerva (became Comml. Advertiser, 1797), also semiweekly Herald, N.Y.C. (became Spectator, 1797), 1793-98; ret. on income from sch. books, 1803; represented Hampshire County in Mass. Legislature, 1815, 19; a founder Amherst Coll., 1819-21. Author: A Grammatical Institute of the English Language, 1782; The American Spelling Book (contributed to standardization spelling in U.S.); An American Selection of Lessons in Reading and Speaking (contained patriotic pieces on Am. history and geography); Sketches of American Policy, pamphlet which expressed Federalist views), 1785; Dissertations on the English Language, 1789; The Prompter (essays) 1791; Aristides Letter to Hamilton, 1800; A Compendious Dictionary of the English Language (1st work of lexicography) 1806; Philosophical and Practical Grammar of the English Language (important contribution to lexicography), 1807; An American Dictionary of the English Language (greatest work, recorded words on basis of their popular usage), 1828; Authorized Version of the English Bible, 1833 (a revision). Died New Haven, Conn., May 28, 1843.

WEBSTER, Pelatiah, polit. economist; b. Lebanon, Conn., Nov. 24, 1726; s. Pelatiah and Joanna (Crowfoot Smith) W.; grad. Yale, 1746; m. Mrs. Ruth Kellogg, Sept. 1750; m. 2d, Rebecca Hunt, Oct. 8, 1785; 5 children. Preached in Greenwich, Mass., 1749; ordained pastor, 1749; became mcht., Phila., 1755; taught at Germantown (Pa.) Acad.; taken prisoner by British, 1777; opposed issue of paper currency; advocated a nat. govt. with complete powers. Author: Remarks on the Address of Sixteen Members of the Assembly of Pennsylvania to their Constituents dated September 29, 1787, published 1787; The Weakness of Brutus Exposed: or, Some Remarks in Vindication of the Constitution Proposed by the Late Federal Convention against the Objections and Gloomy Fears of That Writer, 1787; A Dissertation on the Political Union and Constitution of the Thirteen United States of North America, 1783; Political Essays on the Nature and Operation of Money Public Finances and Other Subjects; Published During the American War, 1791 (in favor support of war by taxation rather than by loans and free trade policy). Died Sept. 2, 1795.

WEBSTER, Taylor, congressman, businessman; b. Pa., Oct. 1, 1800; attended Miami U., Oxford, O. Editor and publisher Western Telegraph, Hamilton, O., 1828-36; clk. Ohio Ho. of Reps., 1829, speaker, 1830; mem. U.S. Ho. of Reps. (Jackson Democrat) from Ohio, 23d-25th congresses, 1833-39; clk. of ct. Butler County (O.), 1842-46; moved to New Orleans, 1863, employed in clerical position. Died New Orleans, Apr. 27, 1876; buried Lafayette Cemetery Number 1.

WEED, Thurlow, journalist, polit. leader; b. Greene County, N.Y., Nov. 15, 1797; s. Joel and Mary (Ellis) W.; m. Catherine Ostrander, Apr. 26, 1818, 4 children. Printer's apprentice as youth; a Clinton supporter, worked on various N.Y. newspapers, 1817-21; became asso. with Rochester Telegraph, 1821, owner, 1825; did much to unite Adams and Clay factions in N.Y.; became involved in anti-Masonic movement, 1826, published Anti-Masonic Enquirer; supported John Quincy Adams on nat. level; mem. N.Y. State Assembly, 1829; publisher Albany Evening Journal, 1830-60; emerged as state leader of Whig Party, led swing to Whigs and helped create new party on state level because of opposition to Jackson and Van Buren; a friend of William Seward, supported him for U.S. Senate; joined Republican Party with Seward, main supporter of Seward's unsuccessful attempt as Republican presdl. nominee, 1860; only nominal supporter of Lincoln, 1864; gradually lost polit. control in N.Y. as radical Republicans gained upper hand; became editor N.Y. Comml. Advertiser, 1867. Author: Letters from Europe and West Indies, 1866; The Silver Dollar of the United States and Its Relation to Bimetalism, 1889. Died N.Y.C., Nov. 22, 1882.

WEEKS, John Wingate, congressman; b. Greenland, N.H., Mar. 31, 1781; attended common schs.; learned carpenter's trade. Recruiter, capt. of company, 11th Regt., U.S. Infantry, during War of 1812, promoted maj.; resided in Coos County, N.H., after war, held several local offices; mem. U.S. Ho. of Reps. from N.H., 21st-22d congresses, 1829-33. Died Lancaster, N.H., Apr. 3, 1853; buried Old Cemetery.

WEEKS, Joseph, congressman; b. Warwick, Mass., Feb. 13, 1773; attended common schs. Moved to Richmond, N.H., engaged in agriculture; town clk. Richmond, 1802-22; mem. N.H. Ho. of Reps., 1807-09, 12-13, 21-26, 30, 32-34; asso. judge Ct. of Common Pleas, 1823, 27; mem. U.S. Ho. of Reps. (Democrat) from N.H., 24th-25th congresses, 1835-39. Died Winchester, N.H., Aug. 4, 1845.

WEEKS, Joseph Dame, tech. journalist, statistician; b. Lowell, Mass., Dec. 3, 1840; s. Jonathan and Mary (Dame) W.; grad. Wesleyan U., 1869; m. Mattie J. Fowler, Feb. 28, 1871. Served with U.S. Christian Commn., 1863-65; editor Am. Manufacturer, 1872-76 (consolidated with Iron World in Pitts., 1874), obtained control, continued as editor, 1886-96; instrumental in fixing iron prices; responsible for 1st wage scale offered to Amalgamated Assn. Iron and Steel Workers; conducted experiments that led to 1st use of gas in puddling furnace; made survey iron ores of James River Valley, Va.; pres. Am. Assn. Mining Engrs., 1895; spl. agt. for Census of 1880; wrote volume on wages in mfg. industries with supplementary reports on trade soc. strikes and lockouts for Census of 1890; prepared articles on mining petroleum gas and manganese and manufacture refined petroleum coke and gas; employed by dept. mineral resources U.S. Geol. Survey, 1885-95; judge awards dept. mines and mining World's Columbian Expn., 1893; chmn. Pa. Tax Conf. Commn., 1896. Author: History of the Knights of Pythias, 1871; Report on the Practical Operation of Arbitration and Conciliation . . . in England, 1879; Industrial Conciliation and Arbitration in New York, Ohio and Pennsylvania, 1881; Labor Differences and Their Settlement, 1886. Died Pitts., Dec. 26, 1896.

WEEKS, Robert Kelley, poet; b. N.Y.C., Sept. 21, 1840; grad. Yale, 1862; studied law Columbia. Admitted to N.Y. bar, 1864; gave up practice law to write poetry. Author: (vols. of verse) Poems, 1866; Episodes and Lyric Pieces, 1876. Died N.Y.C., Apr. 13, 1876.

WEEMS, John Crompton, congressman; b. Waterloo, Calvert County, Md., 1778; attended St. John's Coll., Annapolis, Md. Became a planter; mem. U.S. Ho. of Reps. (Democrat, filled vacancy) from Md., 19th-20th congresses, Feb. 1, 1826-29. Died on his plantation "Loch Eden," Anne Arundel County, Md., Jan. 20, 1862; buried pvt. cemetery on estate.

WEEMS, Mason Locke, clergyman, book agt.; b. Anne Arundel County, Md., Oct. 11, 1759; s. David and Esther (Hill) W.; m. Frances Ewell, July 2, 1795, 10 children. Ordained deacon, then priest Anglican Ch., 1784 (1 of 1st two candidates to be ordained for Am. service); served as Anglican priest in Md., 1784-92; book agt. for Mathew Carey, 1794-1825, traveled over most of Eastern and Southern U.S. Author: The Life and Memorable Actions of George Washington (his best known work, in which he invented story of George Washington and the cherry tree), 5 edits., from 1800; Life of General Francis Marion, 1809; God's Revenge Against Murder, 1807; The Drunkard's Looking Glass, 1812; God's Revenge Against Duelling, 1820; Bad Wife's Looking Glass, 1823. Died Beaufort, S.C., May 23, 1825; buried "Bel Air," nr. Dumfries, Va.

WEIDENMANN, Jacob, landscape architect; b. Winterthur, Canton Zurich, Switzerland, Aug. 22, 1829; s. Jacob and Elise (Gubbler) W.; attended Akademie der Bildenden Künste, Munich, Germany; m. Anna Marguerite Svácher, at least 3 children. Came to U.S., 1861; supt. parks Hartford (Conn.), 1861-63; a designer Cedar Hill Cemetery, Hartford; designed (with F. L. Olmsted) several important works including grounds of Schuylkill Reservoir, Phila., Congress Spring Park, Saratoga, Capitol grounds, Des Moines, Ia., state hosp. grounds, St. Lawrence, N.Y.; pioneer in movement for cemetery in which enclosures were discarded and monuments restricted. Author: Beautifying Country Homes; A Handbook of Landscape Gardening, 1870; Modern Cemeteries, 1888. Died Feb. 6, 1893.

WEIGHTMAN, Richard Hanson, congressman; b. Washington, D.C., Dec. 28, 1816; grad. U. Va. at Charlottesville, 1834; attended U.S. Mil. Acad., 1835-37; studied law. Admitted to D.C. bar, 1841, did not practice law; moved to St. Louis; elected capt. Clark's Battalion, Mo. Volunteer Light Arty., 1846, served with distinction at Battle of Sacramento, during Mexican War, 1847; served as additional paymaster Volunteers, New Orleans, 1848-49; edited newspaper, Santa Fe, N.M., 1851; apptd. agt. for Indians in N.M., 1851; mem. U.S. Congress (Democrat) from N.M. Territory, 32d Congress, 1851-53; resumed newspaper work in Kan., then in Independence, Mo.; commd. col. 1st Regt. Cavalry, 8th Div., Mo. State Guard, Confederate States Army, 1861, promoted to command of 1st Brigade, 8th Div., June 1861, served at Battle of Carthage (Mo.), July 1861. Killed while commanding 1st Brigade at Wilson Creek, Mo., Aug. 10, 1861; buried battlefield nr. Springfield, Mo.

WEIR, Robert Walter, painter, educator; b. New Rochelle, N.Y., June 18, 1803; s. Robert Walter and Mary (Brinkley) W.; m. Louise Ferguson, 1829; m. 2d, Susan Bayard, 1845; 16 children including John Ferguson, Julian Alden. Employed in cotton factory, later in merc. house; turned entire attention to painting, 1821; painted Paul Preaching at Athens; went to Italy, 1824, illustrated much of Dante's Inferno; completed Christ and Nicodemus, Angel Relieving Peter, Florence, Italy; opened studio, N.Y.C., 1827; elected mem. N.A.D., 1829; instr. drawing U.S. Mil. Acad., 1834, prof., 1846-76; worked on The Embarkation of the Pilgrims for rotunda of Capitol, Washington, D.C., 1836-40; designed, erected stone ch., Highland Falls, nr. West Point, N.Y.; made illustrations The Drawing Book in Am. Juvenile Keepsake, 1835, also for George P. Morris's The Deserted Bride, 1853; painted portraits Red Jacket, General Winfield Scott, (both in Met. Mus. Art, N.Y.C.) Governor Throop, Mayor Lee (in N.Y. City Hall); painted The Boat Club, Church of the Holy Innocents, Highland Falls; designed altarpiece Ch. of the Holy Cross, Troy, N.Y.; did stained glass windows for Trinity Chapel, also Calvary Ch., N.Y.C. Died N.Y.C., May 1, 1889.

WEISER, Johann Conrad, Indian agt.; b. nr. Herrenberg, Wurttemberg, Germany, Nov. 2, 1696; s. Johann Conrad and Anna Magdalena (Jebele) W.; m. Anna Eve Feck, Nov. 22, 1720, 15 children including Peter. Came to Am., 1710; learned Mohawk Lang., Indian customs, 1713-14; served as interpreter, nr. Schoharie, N.Y., 1719-29; arranged for confs. at Phila. which resulted in winning Iroquois to interest of Penns, 1731, 36; averted war between Iroquois and Va., 1743; won over Western tribes (with George Croghan) at treaty of Logstown, 1748 (helped to extend Pa. Indian trade to the Mississippi); mostly devoted energies to religious activities, 1735-40 41, chief elder German Reformed Ch. by 1735, also mem. cloister under name Brother Enoch, 1735; consecrated priest, 1740; interested in Moravian missions to Indians (made trip to Onondaga to aid them); justice of the peace Lancaster County (Pa.), 1741; ranger for No. Lancaster County, 1742; joined Lutheran Ch., 1747; justice of the peace Berks County, 1752, 1st president judge, 1752-60; led expdn. on frontier, French and Indian War; commd. col. Berks County Regt. Died Womelsdorf, Pa., July 13, 1760.

WEISS, John, clergyman; b. Boston, June 28, 1818; s. John and Mary (Galloupe) W.; grad. Harvard, 1837, Harvard Divinity Sch., 1840; attended U. Heidelberg, 1842-43; m. Sarah Fiske Jennison, Apr. 9, 1844, at least 5 children. Pastor Unitarian Ch., Watertown, Mass., at intervals 1843-69; pastor 1st Congregational Soc. New Bedford, Mass., 1847-59; contbr. articles, reviews, poems to Christian Examiner, the Atlantic Monthly, Old and New, the Galaxy; a founder Free Religious Assn., 1867; opposed Negro slavery; helped introduce German lit. to Am. Author: Life and Correspondence of Theodore Parker, 1863; American Religion, 1871; Wit, Humor and Shakespeare: Twelve

Essays, 1876. Translator: The Aesthetic Letters, Essays, Philosophical Letters of Schiller (with introduction), 1845; Goethe's West-Easterly Divan (with introduction, notes), 1877. Died Boston, Mar. 9, 1879.

WEITZEL, Godfrey, army officer, engr.; b. Cincinnati, Nov. 1, 1835; s. Louis and Susan Weitzel; grad. U.S. Mil. Acad., 1855; m. 2d, Louisa Bogen, circa 1864; at least 1 child. Brevetted 2d lt. engrs. U.S. Army, 1855, commd. 2d lt., 1856, 1st lt., 1860; served in fortification of New Orleans, 1855-59; asst. prof. engring. U.S. Mil. Acad., 1859-61; with an engr. co. on expdn. to Ft. Pickens (Fla.) to save it for Union, 1861; chief engr. fortifications of Cincinnati, 1861; chief engr. under Gen. Benjamin Butler in expdn. against New Orleans, 1862; asst. mil. comdr. New Orleans; commd. brig. gen. U.S. Volunteers, 1862; capt. Engr. Corps, U.S. Army, 1863, brevetted maj. and lt. col. for gallantry at battles of Thibodeaux and Port Hudson; chief engr. Second Div., XVIII Army Corps, 1864; brevetted maj. gen. volunteers; brevetted col. regular army for gallantry at capture of Fort Harrison (Va.); maj. gen. volunteers, 1864; brevetted brig. general, major general, U.S. Army for service in final operations against Richmond (Va.), 1865; commanded Rio Grande Dist., 1865; mustered out of U.S. Volunteers, 1866, returned to duty with Corps Engrs., promoted maj., 1866; asso. with constrn. of ship canals at falls of Ohio River, and Sault Sainte Marie (Mich.), lighthouse at Stannard's Rock in Lake Superior; commd. lt. col., 1882. Died Phila., Mar. 19, 1884.

WELBY, Amelia Ball Coppuck (pseudonym Amelia), poet; b. St. Michaels, Md., Feb. 3, 1819; d. William and Mary (Shield) Coppuck; m. George Welby, 1 child. Moved with family to Louisville, Ky., 1833; began contbg. poetry signed "Amelia" to George D. Prentice's Louisville Daily Jour., circa 1837; best known poems: "The Rainbow," "The Bereaved," "I Know Thee Not"; poetry praised by Edgar Allan Poe; collected edition of Poems by "Amelia" published 1845. Died Louisville, May 3, 1852; buried Cave Hill Cemetery, Louisville.

WELCH, Adonijah Strong, senator, coll. pres.; b. East Hampton, Conn., Apr. 12, 1821; s. Bliss and Elizabeth (Strong) W.; B.A., U. Mich., 1846, M.A., 1852; m. Eunice P. Buckingham (dec. 1866); m. 2d, Mary (Beaumont) Dudley, 1868; 3 children. Admitted to Mich. bar, 1847; prin. union sch., Jonesville, Mich., 1847-49; 1st prin. Mich. State Normal Sch., Ypsilanti, 1852-65; conducted numerous tchrs. insts., 1852-53; an organizer, 1st pres. Mich. Tchrs. Assn.; trustee Mich. Agrl. Coll.; engaged in business in Fla., 1865-68; mem. U.S. Senate from Fla., 1868-69; 1st pres. Ia. State Agrl. Coll., Ames, 1869-84, taught history, psychology at coll., 1884-89; defended indsl. edn., supported women's rights to obtain coll. edn.; sent by U.S. commr. of agr. to report on agrl. schs. in Germany, Belgium, Eng., 1883. Author: Analysis of the English Sentence, 1855; Report on the Organization and Management of Seven Agricultural Schools in Germany, Belgium and England, 1885; The Teachers' Psychology, 1889. Died Pasadena, Cal., Mar. 14, 1889; buried Ames.

WELCH, Ashbel, civil engr.; b. Nelson, Madison County, N.Y., Dec. 4, 1809; s. Ashbel and Margaret (Dorrance) W.; m. Mary Hannah Seabrook, Oct. 25, 1834, at least 4 children. Became asso. with Del. & Raritan Canal, Trenton, N.J., 1830, chief engr., in charge of all engring. work, 1835, designed and built wooden lock, Bordentown, N.J., 1847; builder Belvidere Del. R.R.; a designer steamship Princeton; examined coal and iron properties in Va.; designer and builder Chesapeake & Del. Canal, 1853; v.p. Camden & Amboy R.R., 1862, presented plan for telegraphic safety signals, 1865; pres. United Cos. of N.J., in charge all adminstrv. matters,, 1867-71; active in improvement of railroad rolling stock; mem. Am. Soc. C.E., v.p., 1880, pres., 1882. Died Lambertville, N.J., Sept. 25, 1882.

WELCH, Frank, congressman, mcht.; b. Bunker Hill, Charlestown, Mass., Feb. 10, 1835; grad. Boston High Sch. Became a civil engr.; engaged in merc. activities, Decatur, Neb. Territory, 1857; mem. Territorial Council, 1864; mem. Neb. Territorial Ho. of Reps., 1865-66, presiding officer, 1865; register land office, West Point, Neb., 1871-76; mem. U.S. Ho. of Reps. (Republican) from Neb., 45th Congress, 1877-78. Died Neligh, Neb., Sept. 4, 1878; buried Forest Hills Cemetery, Jamaica Plain, Mass.

WELCH, John, congressman, jurist; b. Harrison County, O., Oct. 28, 1805; s. Thomas and Martha (Daugherty) W.; grad. Franklin Coll., 1828; m. Martha Starr, 1830, 4 children. Admitted to Ohio bar, 1833; practiced in Athens, O.; pros. atty. Athens County (O.), 1841-43; mem. Ohio Senate, 1845-47; mem. U.S. Ho. of Reps. (Whig) from Ohio, 32d Congress, 1851-53; del. Whig Nat. Conv., 1852; mem. Electoral College, 1856; judge common pleas, 1862-65; judge Ohio Supreme Court 1865-78, chief justice, 1877, gave opinion on McIntire Administrators et al vs. The City of Lanesville (17 Ohio State Reports 352). Author: Mathematical Curiosities, 1883; An Index-Digest to the Reports of Cases Decided in the Courts of Ohio, 1887. Died Athens, Aug. 5, 1891; buried West Union Street Cemetery, Athens.

WELCH, Philip Henry, humorist, journalist; b. Angelica, N.Y., Mar. 1, 1849; s. Joseph B. and Mary (Collins) W.; m Margaret Hamilton, 4 children. Wrote column "The Present Hour" for Rochester (N.Y.) Post-Express, 1882; conducted column "Accidentally Overheard" in Phila. Call, 1883; contbr. to Puck, Life, Judge, Epoch, Times, Drake's Mag., Harper's Bazaar; mem. staff N.Y. Sun, 1884-89; Welch Meml. Fund raised to provide for edn. of children. Author: The Tailor-Made Girl, 1888; Said in Fun, 1889; Died at home in Bklyn., Feb. 24, 1889; buried Angelica, N.Y.

WELCH, William Wickham, physician, congressman; b. Norfold, Conn., Dec. 10, 1818; s. Benjamin and Elizabeth (Loveland) W.; M.D., Yale Med. Sch., 1839; m. Emeline Collin, Nov. 7, 1845; m. 2d, Emily Sedgwick, May 2, 1866; 2 children including William Henry. Practiced medicine, Norfolk; interested in treatment of hydrophobia and venomous reptile bites; mem. Conn. Ho. of Reps., 1848-50, 69, 81, Conn. Senate, 1851-52; mem. U.S. Ho. of Reps. (Am. Party) from Conn., 34th Congress, 1855-57; pres. Norfolk Leather Co.; an incorporator Conn.-Western R.R., Norfolk Savs. Bank. Died Norfolk, July 30, 1892; buried Norfolk Cemetery.

WELD, Theodore Dwight, abolitionist; b. Hampton, Conn., Nov. 23, 1803; s. Rev. Ludovicus and Elizabeth (Clark) W.; entered Oneida Inst., Whitesboro, N.Y., circa 1825; m. Angelina Grimké, May 14, 1838, 5 children. Active in temperance, anti-slavery movements; urged Arthur and Lewis Tappan to found theol. seminary in West, commd. to find site for sem., 1831, preached emancipation; took over publicity, initiated new and successful pamphlet campaign for Am. Anti-Slavery Soc.; lobbied in Washington (D.C.) to break Whig party on slavery issue, 1841-43; considered greatest of abolitionists. Author: "Wythe," The Power of Congress over Slavery in the District of Columbia, 1st edit., 1836; The Bible Against Slavery, 1st edit., 1837; J. A. Thorne and J. H. Kimball—Emancipation in the West Indies, 1st edit., 1837; American Slavery As It Is, 1st edit., 1839; Slavery and the Internal Slave Trade in the United States, 1831. Died Hyde Park, Mass., Feb. 3, 1895.

WELD, Thomas, clergyman; b. Sudbury, Suffolk, Eng., 1595; s. Edmond and Amy Weld; B.A., Trinity Coll., Cambridge (Eng.) U., 1614, M.A., 1618; m. Margaret Dereskye; m. 2d, Judith; m. 3d, Margaret; 4 children. Ordained deacon and priest Ch. of Eng., Peterborough, Eng., 1618; arrived in Boston, 1632; 1st pastor ch. at Roxbury, Mass., 1632; participated in trial of Anne Hutchinson, 1636; overseer Harvard, 1638, secured 1st scholarship fund; helped prepare The Whole Booke of Psalmes (1st book printed in English Am.), 1640; edited and wrote part of New England's First Fruits, pub. London, 1643; agt. of Bay Colony in Eng., 1641-45, accused of misappropriation of funds, vindicated, 1654; rector Wanlip, Leicester, 1646; rector St. Mary's Ch., Gateshead, Durham, Eng., 1649, thereafter remained in Eng. Author: A Short Story of the Rise, Reign, and Ruine of the Antinomians, 1844; A Brief Narration of the Practices of the Churches in New England, 1645. Name also spelled Welde. Died London, Mar. 12, 1661.

WELLBORN, Marshall Johnson, congressman; b. nr. Eatonton, Ga., May 29, 1808; attended U. Ga. at Athens; studied law. Admitted to bar, 1826, began practice of law, Columbus, Ga.; held several local offices; mem. Ga. Ho. of Reps., 1833-34; judge Ga. Superior Ct., 1838-42; mem. U.S. Ho. of Reps. (Democrat) from Ga., 31st Congress, 1849-51; ordained to ministry Baptist Ch., 1864, minister, Columbus, 1864-74. Died Columbus, Oct. 16, 1874; buried Oakland Cemetery, Atlanta, Ga.

WELLER, John B., senator, gov. Cal.; b. Montgomery, Hamilton County, O., Feb. 22, 1812; attended Miami U., Oxford, O., 1825-29; m. Miss Ryan; m. 2d, Miss Bryan; m. 3d, Susan McDowell Taylor; m. 4, Lizzie Brocklebank Stanton. Admitted to Ohio bar, 1832; pros. atty. Butler County (O.), 1833-36; mem. U.S. Ho. of Reps. (Democrat) from Ohio, 26th-28th congresses, 1839-45; served as col. U.S. Volunteers, Mexican War; chmn. commn. to determine boundary between U.S. and Mexico under Treaty of Guadalupe Hidalgo, 1849; opened law office, San Francisco, 1850; mem. U.S. Senate (Union Democrat) from Cal., 1851-57; gov. Cal., 1858-60; U.S. minister to Mexico, 1860-61; practiced law, New Orleans, 1867-75. Died New Orleans, Aug. 17, 1875.

WELLES, Charles F., businessman; b. Bradford County, Pa., circa 1812; 7 children. Established country store, Bradford, 1835, later started branch stores along North Branch Canal; railway constructor, 1850-55; built sects. of N.Y. & Erie R.R., Buffalo & State Line R.R., Del., Lackawanna & Western R.R.; constructed Brunswick & Fla. R.R., 1856, pres., 1856-58; organized North Branch Canal Co. (shipped coal west to Chgo.), 1859. Died Oct. 9, 1872.

WELLES, Gideon, sec. of navy; b. Glastenbury (now Glastonbury), Conn., July 1, 1802; s. Samuel and Ann (Hale) W.; attended Am. Lit., Scientific and Mil. Acad. (now Norwich U.), 1823-25; m. Mary Jane Hale, June 16, 1835, 9 children. Part-owner, editor Hartford (Conn.) Times, 1826-36; mem. lower house Conn. Legislature, 1827-35; author Conn. incorporation law which became model for other states; comptroller pub. accounts State of Conn., 1835, 42, 43; postmaster Hartford, 1836-41; chief Bur. Provisions and Clothing, USN, 1846-49; left Democratic Party, circa 1854; established Republican paper Hartford Evening Press, 1856; head Conn. delegation to Rep. Nat. Conv., Chgo., 1860; U.S. sec. of navy, 1861-69 (saw need of ironclads for U.S. Navy, urged enlistment of Negroes, enforced blockade of Confederate coast, supported Reconstruction program of Johnson); returned to Dem. party, 1868, became a liberal Republican, 1872; retired, 1869. Author: Diary of Gideon Welles, 3 vols., 1911 (an important look at Civil War Am.); contbr. articles to various publs. Died Hartford, Conn., Feb. 11, 1878.

WELLES, Noah, clergyman; b. Colchester, Conn., Sept. 25, 1718; s. Noah and Sarah (Wyatt) W.; grad. Yale, 1741, fellow, 1774-76; D.D. (hon.), Princeton, 1774; m. Abigail Woolsey, Sept. 17, 1751, 13 children. Tutor, Yale, 1745-46; pastor Congregational Ch., Stamford, Conn., 1746-76. Author: Patriotism Described and Recommended (sermon), 1764; The Real Advantages Which Ministers and People May Enjoy Especially in the Colonies by Conforming to the Church of England, Truthfully Considered and Impartially Represented in a Letter to a Young Gentleman, 1762; The Divine Right of Presbyterian Ordination Asserted, and the Ministerial Authority Claimed and Exercised in the Established Churches of New England, Vindicated and Proved, 1763. Died Stamford, Dec. 31, 1776.

WELLING, James Clarke, coll. pres.; b. Trenton, N.J., July 14, 1825; s. William and Jane (Hill) W.; grad. Coll. of N.J. (now Princeton), 1844; m. Genevieve H. Garnett, 1850; m. 2d, Clementine Dixon, 1882; 3 children, Asso. prin. N.Y. Collegiate Sch., 1848; lit. editor Daily Nat. Intelligencer, Washington, D.C., 1850-56, asso. editor, 1856-65; clk. U.S. Ct. of Claims, Washington, D.C., circa 1866; pres. St. John's Coll., Annapolis, Md., 1867-70; prof. rhetoric and English lit. Coll. of N.J., 1870; pres. Columbian Coll. (now George Washington U.), Washington, 1871-94, also tchr. philosophy of history and internat. law; pres. Cosmos Club, Washington, 1880, Washington Philos. Soc., 1884, Anthrop. Soc. of Washington, 1891-92; regent Smithsonian Instn., 1884-94; pres. bd. trustees Corcoran Art Gallery, 1881-94. Died Hartford, Conn., Sept. 4, 1894.

WELLINGTON, Arthur Mellen, civil engr., editor; b. Waltham, Mass., Dec. 20, 1847; s. Oliver Hastings and Charlotte (Kent) W.; m. Agnes Bates, 1878. Surveyor Bklyn. Park Dept., circa 1867; joined Buffalo, N.Y. & Phila. R.R., 1870, became prin. asst. engr.; locating engr. Mich. Central R.R., 1873; engr. in charge of Toledo, Can. So. & Detroit R.R.; prin. asst. engr. N.Y., Pa. & Ohio R.R., 1878; engr. in charge of location, surveys Mexican Nat. Ry., 1881-84, later asst. gen. mgr.; part owner, an editor Engring. News, 1887; mem. bd. engrs. Nicaragua Canal, 1890; adviser to Mass. Legislature on street rys. in Boston. Author: Methods for the Computation from Diagrams of Preliminary and Final Estimates o Railway Earthwork, 1874; The Economic Theory of the Location of Railways, 1877. Died May 16, 1895.

WELLONS, William Brock, clergyman; b. Littleton, Sussex County, Va., Nov. 9, 1821; s. Hartwell and Mary W. Wellons; m. Mrs. Sarah L. Beasley, Apr. 12, 1850. Sch. tchr., 1840-45; admitted as licentiate to Eastern Va. Conf., 1845, ordained minister Christian Connection, 1846; pastor, New Bern, N.C.; del. Quadrennial Christian Conv., Cincinnati, 1854, southern mem. Com. of 3 to consider question of slavery; pres. Gen. Conv. of Christian Ch. South (organized after Gen. Conv. split over slavery issue), 1856; editor-in-chief Christian Sun, 1855-61, publisher and editor, 1865-77; editor Army and Navy Messenger, circa 1861; condr. sch. for young women, Suffolk, Va.; a founder Holy Neck Female Sem., Nansemond County, Va., 1853; prin. Suffolk Collegiate

Inst., 1872-77; active in Va. temperance movement. Died Suffolk, Feb. 16, 1877.

WELLS, Alfred, congressman; b. Dagsboro, Sussex County, Del., May 27, 1814; studied law. Admitted to bar, 1837, began practice of law, Ithaca, N.Y.; an owner Ithaca Journal and Advertiser, 1839-53; dist. atty. Tompkins County (N.Y.), 1845-47; judge Tompkins County Ct., 1847-51; del. Anti-Neb. convs., Saratoga and Auburn, 1854; mem. U.S. Ho. of Reps. (Republican) from N.Y., 36th Congress, 1859-61; U.S. assessor of internal revenue, Ithaca, 1862-67. Died Ithaca, July 18, 1867; buried City Cemetery.

WELLS, David Ames, economist; b. Springfield, Mass., June 17, 1828; s. James and Rebecca (Ames) W.; grad. Williams Coll., 1847, Lawrence Scientific Sch., Harvard, 1851; m. Mary Sanford Dwight, May 9, 1860; m. a second time; 2 children. Published (with George Bliss) The Annual of Scientific Discovery, Cambridge, Mass., 1850-66; chmn. Nat. Revenue Commn., 1865; spl. commr. revenue (post created for him), 1866-70; leading advocate of free trade policies, from 1868; mem. Cobden Club; leading advocate of abolition of tariff; chmn. N.Y. State Tax Commn., 1870; a receiver Ala. & Chattanooga R.R.; mem. bd. arbitration Asso. Rys.; del. Democratic nat. convs., several times; strong advocate laissez faire, opposed depreciated monetary standards. Author: The Science of Common Things, 1857; Wells's Principle and Applications of Chemistry, 1858; Wells's First Principles of Geology, 1861; Wells's Natural Philosophy, 1863; Our Burden and Our Strength (pamphlet which became prominent as 1st econ. work in which he reassured fgn. investors, people of the North by showing dynamic character of No. economy), 1864; The Reports of the Special Commissioners of the Revenue, 1866-69; The Relation of the Government to the Telegraph, 1873; True Story of the Leaden Statuary, 1874; Robinson Crusoe's Money, 1876; The Silver Question, 1877; Why We Trade and How We Trade, 1878; A Primer of Tariff Reform, 1884; The Theory and Practice of Taxation, 1900. Died Norwich, Conn., Nov. 5, 1898.

WELLS, Erastus, congressman, street railway builder; b. Sacketts Harbor, N.Y., Dec. 2, 1823; s. Otis and Mary (Symonds) W.; m. Isabella Bowman Henry, 1850; m. 2d, Eleanor (Warfield) Bell, 1879; 5 children including Rolla. Induced prominent business man to finance omnibus (said to be 1st conveyance of its kind West of Mississippi River), St. Louis, 1844; founder, head Mo. Ry. Co., 1859-83; pres. Laclede Gas Light Co., St. Louis, 1880-83; mem. legislative body of St. Louis, 1848, alderman or councilman, 1855-69; mem. U.S. Ho. of Reps. (Democrat) from Mo., 41-44th, 46th congresses, 1869-77, 79-81, worked for appropriations for various tribes in Indian Territory, sponsored bills for marine hosps. and other govt. bldgs. Died St. Louis, Oct. 2, 1893; buried Bellefontaine Cemetery, St. Louis.

WELLS, Henry, express. co. exec.; b. Thetford, Vt., Dec. 12, 1805; s. Shipley Wells; m. Sarah Daggett; m. 2d, Mary Prentice, 1861. Agt. at Albany (N.Y.) for Harnden's Express between N.Y.C. and Albany, 1841; founder Livingston, Wells & Pomeroy Co. operating between Albany and Buffalo, N.Y., 1843; founder Wells & Co., express line between Buffalo and Detroit, with William G. Fargo as messenger, 1844; pres. Am. Express Co. (merger of above cos. due to competition on route between Albany and Buffalo), 1850-68; organizer (with assos.) Wells Fargo & Co., express line to Cal., N.Y.C., 1852, took over Pony Express during last month of its operation; pres. First Nat. Bank, Aurora, N.Y.; 1st pres. Cayuga Lake R.R.; founder Wells Sem. (now Wells Coll.). Author: The American Express in its Relation to . . . Buffalo, 1864; Sketch of the Rise, Progress and Present Conduct of the Express System, 1864. Died Glasgow, Scotland, Dec. 10, 1878; buried Aurora.

WELLS, Horace, dentist, anesthetist; b. Hartford, Vt., Jan. 21, 1815; s. Horace and Betsy (Heath) W.; m. Elizabeth Wales, July 4, 1838, 1 child. Opened dentistry office, Hartford, Conn., 1836; became interested in narcotic effects of nitrous oxide inhalation, circa 1840; suggested its use as means of deadening pain in tooth extraction; had tooth extracted without pain, 1844; claimed to have used ether in extractions, and believed it might be used in major operations (also wrongly believed nitrous oxide superior to ether); 1st printed statement of his claims to discovery of anesthesia appeared in Hartford Courant, 1846, taught dentistry to William T.G. Morton. Author: An Essay on Teeth; Comprising a Brief Description of Their Formation, Diseases and Proper Treatment, 1838; A History of the Discovery of the Application of Nitrous Oxide Gas, Ether, and Other Vapors, to Surgical Operations, 1847. Committed suicide largely because of discouragements in profl. life, Jan. 24, 1848.

WELLS, James Madison, gov. La.; b. "New Hope" nr. Alexandria, La., Jan. 8, 1808; s. Samuel Levi and Mary Elizabeth (Calvit) W.; read law under Charles Hammond, Ohio; m. Mary Ann Scott, May 13, 1833, 14 children. Owned extensive plantations in Rapides Parish, La; opposed secession, had considerable property confiscated and destroyed by Confederate Govt. during Civil War; lt. gov. La. under Lincoln Reconstrn. program, 1864-65; gov. La., 1865-67, removed from office by Gen. Sheridan (mil. comdr. of New Orleans); mem. La. Election Commn., 1876. Died Feb. 28, 1899.

WELLS, John, lawyer; b. Cherry Valley, Otsego County, N.Y., circa 1770; s. Capt. Robert Wells; grad. Coll. of N.J. (now Princeton), 1788; m. Eliza Lawrence, 1796; m. 2d, Sabina Huger, 1815; 5 children. Admitted to N.Y. bar as atty., 1791, as counselor, 1795; revised for publication papers known as The Federalist (final revision done by Alexander Hamilton), 1802; counselor for Gibbons in Gibbons vs. Ogden before N.Y. Supreme Ct., also appeared in Griswold vs. Waddington. Died Sept. 7, 1823.

WELLS, John, congressman, lawyer; b. Johnstown, N.Y., July 1, 1817; attended Johnstown, Acad.; grad. Union Coll., Schenectady, N.Y., 1835; studied law. Admitted to bar, 1839, began practice of law Palmyra, N.Y.; judge Fulton County (N.Y.), 1847-51; mem. U.S. Ho. of Reps. (Whig) from N.Y., 32d Congress, 1851-53; resumed practice of law, Johnstown, also engaged in literary activities. Died Johnstown, May 30, 1877; buried Johnstown Cemetery.

WELLS, John Sullivan, senator, lawyer; b. Durham, N.H., Oct. 18, 1803; attended Pembroke (N.H.) Acad.; studied law. Admitted to bar, 1828; practiced law, Guildhall, Vt., 1828-35, Lancaster, N.H., 1836-46; solicitor Coos County, 1838-47; moved to Exeter, N.H.; mem. N.H. Ho. of Reps., 1839-41, speaker, 1841; atty. gen. N.H., 1847; pres. N.H. Senate, 1851-52; mem. U.S. Senate (filled vacancy) from N.H., Jan. 16-Mar. 3, 1855. Died Exeter, Aug. 1, 1860.

WELLS, Robert William, jurist; b. Winchester, Va., Nov. 29, 1795; s. Richard Wells; m. Harriet Amanda Rector, Jan. 30, 1830; m. 2d, Eliza Covington, June 1840; 6 children. Engaged in surveying, 1819; began practice law, St. Charles, Mo., 1820; designed Gt. Seal of Mo., 1822; mem. Mo. Gen. Assembly from St. Charles County, 1824; atty. gen. Mo., 1826-36; U.S. dist. judge Mo., 1836-37; U.S. judge Western Dist., 1857-64; mem. 1st bd. curators U. Mo.; mem. Democratic Central Com., 1840; pres. Osage River Improvement Conv. of 1843; urged Mo. Gen. Assembly to construct state's 1st lunatic asylum, 1845; charter mem. Mo. Fruit Growers' Assn., 1859; pres. Emancipation Conv., Mo., 1862, Mo. Radical Emancipation Conv., 1863, Union Conv., Phila., 1863. Author: Observations on the Pleadings and Practice of the Courts of Justice of Missouri and a Radical Change Therein Recommended, 1847; Law of the State of Missouri Regulating Pleading and Practice of the Courts of Justice, 1849. Died Bowling Green, Ky., Sept. 22, 1864; buried Jefferson City, Mo.

WELLS, Samuel Roberts, phrenologist; b. West Hartford, Conn., Apr. 4, 1820; s. Russell Wells; studied phrenology under Lorenzo and Orson Fowler; m. Charlotte Fowler, Oct. 13, 1844. Mem. publishing firm O.S. & L.N. Fowler (became Fowler & Wells 1844), sole propr., circa 1846; advocate of physiognomy as means of reading and guiding human character; taught utility of shorthand; advocated improved agrl. methods including proper soil cultivation, crop rotation, irrigation, draining, subsoiling, proper fencing and selection of implements; a founder (with his wife) inst. of phrenology, managed famous phrenological cabinet, N.Y. C., 1850-62. Died N.Y.C., Apr. 13, 1875.

WELLS, William Charles, physician; b. Charleston, S.C., May 24, 1757; s. Robert and Mary Wells; M.D., U. Edinburgh, 1780; never married. Fled to Eng. at outbreak of Am. Revolution; surgeon with Scotting regt. in mercenary service with Dutch in Europe, 1779; returned to Am., 1781; returned to Eng., 1784, practiced medicine, London, 1794-1817; licentiate Royal Coll. of Physicians, 1788; mem. Royal Soc., 1793; a pioneer in recognizing principle of natural selection; claimed to have been 1st to experiment with use of belladonna for the eyes; wrote essay on single vision with two eyes, also essay on nature and quality of dew. Died London, Sept. 18, 1817; buried parish ch. St. Brides', London.

WELLS, William Harvey, educator; b. Tolland, Conn., Feb. 27, 1812; s. Harvey and Rhoda (Chapman) W.; attended Tchrs. Sem., Andover, Mass., 1834; m. Hannah Smith, July 23, 1840; m. 2d, Tabitha Ordway, May 8, 1843; m. 3d, Lydia Graves, July 30, 1849; 11 children. Prin. grammar sch., East Hartford, Conn., 1835; taught English, mathematics Tchrs. Sem., Andover, 1836-47; active lectr. on tchr. tng.; pres. Essex County (Mass.) Tchrs. Assn., 1848-49; founder Mass. Tchrs. Assn., pres. 1851-53; one of 1st editors Mass. Tchr.; supt. pub. schs., Chgo., 1854-56; mem. Ill. Bd. Edn., 1857, an organizer state normal sch. in Ill., 1857, trustee, 1857-69, introduced a graded sch. system, 1861; pres. Ill. Tchrs. Assn., 1860. Author: Graded Course of Instruction, 1861; The Graded School, 1862; Historical Authorship of English Grammar, 1878; A Shorter Course in English Grammar and Composition, 1880. Died Jan. 21, 1885.

WELLS, William Hill, senator, lawyer; b. Burlington, N.J., Jan. 7, 1769; studied law. Became a mcht., Dagsboro and Millsboro, Del.; admitted to bar, practiced law, Georgetown, Del.; moved to Dover, Del.; mem. Del. Gen. Assembly, 1794-98; mem. U.S. Senate (filled vacancies) from Del., Jan. 17, 1799-Nov. 6, 1804 (resigned), May 28, 1813-17; active in oil business in Pa.; Town of Wellsboro (Pa.) named in his honor. Died nr. Dagsboro, Mar. 11, 1829; buried Prince Georges Churchyard, nr. Dagsboro.

WELLS, William Vincent, author; b. Boston, Jan. 2, 1826; s. Samuel Adams Wells; ed. common schs.; married. Officer, U.S. Mcht. Marine; mem. Boston and Cal. Joint Stock Mining and Trading Co.; 1st mate in ship Edward Everett, Boston, 1849; mem. editorial staff Comml. Advertiser, San Francisco, 1853; agt. Honduras Mining and Trading Co., 1854; consul to Honduras, 1855-74; asso. with Alta Cal., also Daily Times, 1850's; participated in Frazer River Gold Rush, 1858; cashier, impost clk. U.S. Naval Office, San Francisco, during Civil War; held appointment under Emperor Maximilian of Mexico, 1865; clk. to mayor San Francisco, 1869-74; admitted to state asylum for insane, Napa, Cal., 1876. Author: Explorations and Adventures in Honduras, 1857; Life and Public Services of Samuel Adams (his grandfather), 1865; compiler: Walker's Expedition to Nicaragua, 1856; contbr. articles to Harper's, Overland Monthly. Died in asylum, Napa, June 1, 1876.

WELSH, John, mcht., diplomat, philanthropist; b. Phila., Nov. 9, 1805; s. John and Jemima (Maris) W.; m. Rebecca B. Miller, Apr. 30, 1829; m. 2d, Mary Lowber, Feb. 6, 1838. Joined brothers in family West India trade, 1854; mem. Phila. Select Council, 1855-57; mem., chmn. Phila. Sinking Fund Commn., 1867-71; mem. Fairmount Park Commn., 1867-86; vestryman St. Peter's Protestant Episcopal Ch.; pres. N. Pa. R.R.; mgr. finances Centennial Exhbn. of 1876, Phila. (most outstanding achievement); trustee U. Pa., established John Welsh Centennial Professorship of History and English Lit.; U.S. minister London, Eng., 1877-79. Died Apr. 10, 1886.

WEMYSS, Francis Courtney, actor, mgr.; b. London, Eng., May 13, 1797; m. Miss Strembeck, Apr. 10, 1823, several children. Came to U.S., 1822; made Am. debut as Vapid in play The Dramatist, Chestnut Street Theatre, Phila., 1822; made N.Y.C. debut as Marplot, Chatham Garden, 1824; stage mgr. Chestnut Street Theatre, 1827, lessee, 1829-33; opened and managed new theatre in Pitts., 1833; mgr. American (formerly Walnut Street) Theatre, Phila., 1834; stage mgr. Nat. Theatre, N.Y.C., 1841; played Belmour in play Is He Jealous?, 1841; made last appearance as stage mgr. for benefit performance to raise money to buy Mt. Vernon as nat. shrine, 1858. Author: Twenty-Six Years of the Life of an Actor and Manager, 2 vols., 1847; Chronology of American Stage from 1752 to 1852, published 1852; editor 16 vols. of Acting American Theatre. Died N.Y.C., Jan. 5, 1859.

WENDOVER, Peter Hercules, congressman; b. N. Y.C., Aug. 1, 1768; received liberal edn. Held several local offices; mem. Volunteer Fire Dept., N.Y.C., 1796; del. N.Y. state constl. convs., 1801, 21; mem. N.Y. State Assembly, 1804; mem. U.S. Ho. of Reps. (Democrat) from N.Y., 14th-16th congresses, 1815-21; sheriff N.Y. County, 1822-25. Died N.Y.C., Sept. 24, 1834; buried Dutch Reformed Ch. Cemetery.

WENTWORTH, Benning, colonial gov.; b. Portsmouth, N.H., July 24, 1696; s. Lt. Gov. John and Sarah (Hunking) W.; grad. Harvard, 1715; m. Abigail Ruck, Dec. 31, 1719; m. 2d, Martha Hilton, Mar. 15, 1760; 3 children. Mem. N.H. Assembly; mem. N.H. Gov.'s Council, 1734, endeavored to make N.H. independent of Mass.; 1st royal gov. Province of N.H., 1741-67, made extensive land grants (N.H. Grants) in area claimed by both N.H. and N.Y., 1761, caused long dispute finally settled by creation of Vt.; promoter of Anglican Ch. Died Little Harbor, N.H., Oct. 14, 1770; buried Wentworth tomb Queen's Chapel Graveyard, St. John's Ch., Portsmouth.

WENTWORTH, John, colonial gov.; b. Portsmouth, N.H., Aug. 20, 1737; s. Mark Hunking and Elizabeth (Rindge) w.; grad. Harvard, 1755; m. Frances Wentworth Atkinson, 1 child. Went to Eng. as rep. of his father's business, 1763, also negotiated for N.H. for repeal of Stamp Act; capt. gen. N.H. Militia, 1766; surveyor gen. His Majesty's Wood in Am., also royal gov. N.H., 1766-75, instrumental in dividing N.H. into 5 counties; granted charter for Dartmouth Coll., 1769, mem. original bd. trustees; Loyalist, sailed from Boston at outbreak of Revolution, 1775; lt. gov. Nova Scotia, 1792-1808; created baronet, 1795. Died Halifax, N.S., Apr. 8, 1820.

WENTWORTH, John, Jr., Continental congressman, lawyer; b. Salmon Falls, Strafford County, N.H., July 17, 1745; grad. Harvard, 1768; studied law. Admitted to bar, began practice of law, Dover, N.H., 1771; register of probate Strafford County, 1773-87; apptd. mem. Com of Correspondence 1774; mem. N.H. Ho. of Reps., 1776-80; apptd. mem. N.H. Com. of Safety, 1777, moderator, 1777-86; mem. Continental Congress from N.H., 1778-79; a signer Articles of Confedn.; mem. N.H. Council, 1780-84, N.H. Senate, 1784-86. Died Dover, Jan. 10, 1787; buried Pine Hill Cemetery.

WENTWORTH, John, editor, congressman; b. Sandwich, N.H., Mar. 5, 1815; s. Paul and Lydia (Cogswell) W.; grad. Dartmouth, 1836; m. Roxanna Loomis, Nov. 13, 1844, 5 children. Went to Chgo., 1836; editor weekly Chgo. Democrat, 1836, owner, 1839; 1st ofcl. printer for Chgo., 1839; started Daily Democrat, 1840; admitted to Ill. bar, 1841; mem. U.S. Ho. of Reps. from Ill., 28th-31st, 33d, 39th congresses, 1843-51, 53-55, 65-67; mayor of Chgo. (on Republican Fusion ticket), 1857-63, instituted 1st paid fire dept. in Chgo.; owned more Chgo. real estate than any other man; mem. Ill .Bd. Edn., 1861-64, 68-72; del. Ill. Constl. Conv., 1861; contributed $10,000 to Dartmouth; pres. Dartmouth Alumni Assn., 1883. Author: Wentworth Genealogy, 1878. Died Chgo., Oct. 16, 1888; buried Rosehill Cemetery, Chgo.

WENTWORTH, Paul, secret agt. Ambitious to obtain a position from Brit. govt. to gain polit. prestige; became colonial agt. of N.H., London, Eng., 1770's; an important mem. Brit. secret service during Revolutionary War; most noteworthy exploit: attempt to halt negotiations between France and Am., Dec. 1777-Jan. 1778; became mem. Parliament, 1780; retired to his plantation, Surinam (Dutch Guiana). Died at plantation, Dec. 1793.

WENTWORTH, Tappan, congressman, lawyer; b. Dover, N.H., Feb. 24, 1802; studied law. Admitted to bar, 1826, began practice of law, York County, Me.; continued practice of law, Lowell, Mass.,1833; mem. Common Council, 1836-41; mem. Mass. Ho. of Reps., 1851, 59-60, 63-64, Mass. Senate, 1848-49, 65-66; mem. U.S.Ho. of Reps. (Whig) from Mass., 33d Congress, 1853-55. Died Lowell, June 12, 1875; buried Lowell Cemetery.

WENTWORTH, William Pitt, architect; b. Vt., 1839; studied architecture, N.Y.C. Practiced architecture, Boston, over 30 years. Prin. works include: Flower Meml. Ch., Watertown, N.Y.; State Hosp. for Insane, Medfield, Mass. Died Apr. 12, 1896.

WERDEN, Reed, naval officer; b. Delaware County, Pa., Feb. 28, 1818; s. Col. William Werden. Commd. midshipman U.S. Navy, 1834; served with Brazil and Mediterranean Squadrons; on world cruise on ship Boston, 1840-43; commd. lt., 1847, in sloop Germantown in Mexican War; served in Minnesota at capture of Hatteras Inlet during Civil War, 1861; commanded some vessels in Albemarle Sound until 1862; comdr. in Conemaugh, 1862; fleet capt. of East Gulf Squadron, 1864, commanded Powhatan; blockaded Confederate ship Stonewall at Havana until surrender, 1865; commd. capt., 1866, commodore, 1871, rear adm., 1875; stationed at Mare Island (Cal.) Navy Yard, 1868-71; head New London (Conn.) Naval Station, 1872-74; commanded South Pacific Squadron, 1875-76; ret., 1877. Died Newport, R.I., July 11, 1886.

WERNWAG, Lewis, bridge builder, civil engr.; b. Riedlingen, Wurttemberg, Germany, Dec. 4, 1769; children include Lewis, William. Came to Am., 1786; built 29 bridges during career, including bridge across Neshaminy Creek (his 1st bridge), 1810, drawbridge across Frankford Creek, Bridgeburg, Pa., 1811, bridge across Schuylkill River at Upper Ferry, later Fairmount sect. (Colossus of Fairmount, 340 feet span, largest in Am. at time), 1812; built bridge across Delaware River near New Hope, Pa. (6 arch spans of 175 feet, 2 wagon ways, 2 footways), 1813; planned Fairmount waterworks and dam, Phila.; moved to Conowingo Md., built bridge over Susquehanna River and sawmill for preparing his timber; built railroad bridge for B. & O. R.R., 1830. Died Harpers Ferry, Va. (now W.Va.), Aug. 12, 1843.

WERTMÜLLER, Adolph Ulrich, artist; b. Stockholm, Sweden, Feb. 18, 1751. Maintained studio, Paris, France, 1783-88, Bordeaux, France, 1788-94; came to Am., 1794, worked in Phila., 1794-96; returned to Sweden, 1796; settled permanently in Am. on farm "Claymont," Newcastle County, Del., 1800; best known works include Danae, Ariadne; painted portrait of George Washington. Died "Claymont," Oct. 5, 1811.

WEST, Benjamin, publisher; b. Rehoboth, Mass., Mar. 1730; s. John West; M.A. (hon.), Brown U., 1770, LL.D. (hon.), 1792; M.A. (hon.), Harvard, 1770; M.A. (hon.), Dartmouth, 1782; m. Elizabeth Smith, June 7, 1753, 8 children. Patriot, engaged in mfg. clothes for troops throughout Revolutionary War, Providence, R.I.; tchr. Protestant Episcopal Acad., Phila., 1787-88; prof. mathematics and astronomy R.I. Coll., 1786-98; produced 1st scientific publication An Almanack for the year of our Lord Christ, 1763 . . . (became The New-England Almanack or Lady's and Gentleman's Diary), issued annually at Providence, 1765-68 (except for publication in Boston, 1769); revived name Isaac Bickerstaff (originated by Dean Swift, 1707) and issued Bickerstaff's Boston Almanac for the Year of Our Lord, 1768, continued annually through issue 1779, 83-93, 1st illustrated almanac in Mass.; prepared The North-American Calendar: or Rhode Island Almanac, 1781-87, and the Rhode Island Almanac, 1804-06; collaborated in preparations for observation of transit of Venus in 1769, wrote a pamphlet An Account of the Observation of Venus upon the Sun the Third Day of June 1769; prof. mathematics and nautral philosophy Brown U., 1798-99; postmaster of Providence, 1802-13; elected fellow Am. Acad. Arts and Scis., 1781. Died Providence, Aug. 26, 1813.

WEST, Benjamin, painter; b. Springfield, Pa., Oct. 10, 1738; s. John and Sarah (Pearson) W.; attended Coll. of Phila., 1756; m. Elizabeth Shewell, Sept. 2, 1764, 2 children. Commd. to paint portrait of Mrs. Ross of Lancaster, Pa. (his 1st commn.), 1753; lived in England, 1763-1820; mem. Incorporated Soc. of Artists, (forerunner Royal Acad. of Arts), 1765; charter mem. Royal Acad. Arts, 1768; apptd. hist. painter to King George III, did many portraits of royal family; exhibited painting Death of Wolfe in Royal Acad., 1771; pres. Royal Acad. (succeeding Sir Joshua Reynolds), 1792-1820 — (except for 1 year); most famous paintings include: Angelica and Medoro (circa 1762), The Parting of Hector and Andromache (circa 1764), The Departure of Regulus from Rome (1769), Christ Healing the Sick (1801), Christ Rejected (circa 1815), Death on the Pale Horse (1817); trained many Am. painters including Gilbert Stuart and Thomas Sully. Died London, Eng., Mar. 11, 1820; buried St. Paul's Cathedral.

WEST, Francis, colonial gov. Va.; b. Wherwell, Hampshire, Eng., Oct. 28, 1586; s. Thomas (2d baron de la Warr) and Anne (Knollys) W,; m. Mrs. Margaret Blayney; m. 2d, Temperance (Flowerdieu) Yeardley; m. 3d, Jane Davye; at least 1 child, Francis. Came to Va., 1608; a grantee of 2d charter, 1609; mem. group which quarrelled with Capt. John Smith, deposed him in favor George Percy, Sept. 1609; comdr. at Jamestown, Va., 1612; master of ordinance, 1617; commd. adm. of New Eng., 1622; gov. Va., 1627-29; mem. gov.'s council 1631-33. Died Jamestown, 1634.

WEST, George, paper mfr., congressman; b. Bradninch, Eng., Feb. 17, 1823; s. George and Jane W.; m. Louisa Rose, 1844, 2 children. Apprenticed to paper mfr. in Eng.; came to Am., 1849; engaged in paper mfg., N.Y.C., owned 9 mills by 1878 (largest paper mfr. in U.S.), sold interests for over $1,000,000 to Union Bag and Paper Co., 1899; mem. N.Y. State Ho. of Reps., 1872-76; mem. U.S. Ho. of Reps. (Republican) from N.Y., 47th, 49th-50th congresses, 1881-83, 85-89. Died Ballston Spa., N.Y., Sept. 20, 1901; buried Ballston Spa Cemetery.

WEST, Henry Sergeant, physician, missionary; b. Binghamton, N.Y., Jan. 21, 1827; s. Dr. Silas and Lucy C. (Sergeant) W.; attended Yale, 1844-45; M.D., Coll. Physicians and Surgeons, N.Y.C., 1850; m. Charlotte Youts, Sept. 20, 1858. Practiced medicine, Binghamton; went to Turkey under auspices of Am. Bd. Commrs. for Fgn. Missions, 1859, maintained mission, Sivas, Turkey, 1859-76. performed med. services, trained Am. and Turkish doctors. Died Sivas, Apr. 1, 1876.

WEST, Joseph, colonial gov. S.C.; b. England; married. Agent and storekeeper for the propr., dep. for Duke of Albemarle, placed in command of 3 vessels to Carolina, 1669; settled at Albemarle Point; elected colonial gov. S.C. by Council, 1671, directed colony, 1671-72, 74-82, 84-85, made regulations respecting militia, roads, status of servants and slaves; moved location of govt. from Albemarle Point to what was called New Charles Town, circa 1680 (name changed to Charlestown, 1682, became Charleston, 1783). Died N.Y., 1692.

WEST, Samuel, clergyman; b. Yarmouth, Mass., Feb. 21, 1731; s. Dr. Sackfield and Ruth (Jenkins) W.; grad. Harvard, 1754; m. Experience Howland, Mar. 7, 1768; m. 2d, Mrs. Lovisa (Hathway) Jenne, Jan. 1790; 6 children. Ordained to ministry Congregational Ch.; pastor church Dartmouth (later New Bedford), Mass., 1761-1803; served as chaplain Continental Army in Revolutionary War; noted for deciphering treasonable code letter for George Washington (letter written by Dr. Benjamin Church, intended for Brit. admiral at Newport, R.I.); mem. com. to frame Mass. Constn.; mem. Mass. Conv. for adoption U.S. Constn.; took Arminian side in theol. argument with Calvinists. Died Tiverton, R.I., Sept. 24, 1807.

WEST, Thomas, (baron de la Warr), colonial gov.; b. Wherwell, Eng., July 9, 1577; s. Thomas (baron de la Warr) and Anne (Knollys) W.; attended Queen's Coll., Oxford (Eng.) U., 1592, M.A. (hon.), 1605; m. Celia Shirley, Nov. 25, 1596, 7 children including Jane, Henry. Mem. Parliament, 1597; served with army in Ireland, 1599; created knight, 1599; inherited father's title, 1602, became mem. Privy Council; grantee of 2d charter of Va. Co. of London; mem. council of Va. Co., 1609; apptd. 1st gov. and capt. gen. of Va., 1610; arrived in Jamestown (Va.) in time to stop colonists from leaving for lack of supplies, 1610; supervised constrn. of 3 forts at Jamestown, 1610; sailed for West Indies for health, 1611, returned to Eng. after being blown off course; sailed for Va. again, 1618. Author: The Relation of the Right Honorable the Lord De-la Warr, Lord Governour and Captaine General of the Colonie planted in Virginia, 1611. Died (probably from poison) Tereceira, Azores Islands, June 7, 1618.

WEST, William Edward, painter; b. Lexington, Ky., Dec. 10, 1788; son of Edward West; studied painting under Thomas Sulley, Phila. Started career as portrait painter in Natchez, Miss.; went to Europe, 1822; became noted for portrait of Lord Byron; traveled and painted in France, Eng., Italy; returned to Am., 1840. Paintings include: portraits of G. H. Cahert, Thomas Swann; The Confessional (now in N.Y. Hist. Soc.). Died Nashville, Tenn., Nov. 2, 1857.

WESTBROOK, John, congressman; b. Sussex County, N.J., Jan. 9, 1789; attended pvt. schs. Engaged in lumbering and agriculture, Pike County, Pa.; col. Pa. Militia, 1812; sheriff Pike County, 1817; mem. Pa. Ho. of Reps., 1833; mem. U.S. Ho. of Reps. (Democrat) from Pa., 27th Congress, 1841-43. Died nr. Dingmans Ferry, Pa., Oct. 8, 1852; buried Laurel Hill Cemetery, Milford, Pa.

WESTBROOK, Theodoric Romeyn, congressman, jurist; b. Fishkill, Dutchess County, N.Y., Nov. 20, 1821; grad. Rutgers Coll., 1838; studied law. Admitted to bar, 1843, began practice of law, Kingston, Ulster County, N.Y.; mem. U.S. Ho. of Reps. (Democrat) from N.Y., 33d Congress, 1853-55; justice N.Y. Supreme Ct., 1873-85. Died while holding ct., Troy, N.Y., Oct. 6, 1885; buried Wiltwyck Cemetery, Kingston.

WESTCOTT, Edward Noyes, banker, author; b. Syracuse, N.Y., Sept. 27, 1846; s. Amos and Clara (Babcock) W.; m. Jane Dows, June 1874, at least 3 children. Teller, First Nat. Bank, later cashier Wilkinson & Co., bankers, Syracuse, circa 1870; organized firm Westcott & Abbott, bankers and brokers, 1880; sec. to Syracuse Water Commn. until 1895. Author: David Harum, A Story of American Life, published 1898, (later dramatized, then film); (short story) The Teller, published 1901; composed words and music of several songs. Died Syracuse, Mar. 31, 1898.

WESTCOTT, James Diament, Jr., senator, lawyer; b. Alexandria, Va., May 10, 1802; studied law. Admitted to bar, 1824, began practice of law; clk. Consular Bur., Washington, D.C.; sec. Fla. Territory, 1830-34; U.S. atty. for Middle Dist. Fla., 1834-36; mem. Fla. Territorial Ho. of Reps., 1832; del. Fla. Constl. Conv., 1838, 39; mem. U.S. Senate from Fla., July 1, 1846-49; practiced law, N.Y.C., 1850-62; moved to Canada, 1862. Died Montreal, Can., Jan. 19, 1880; buried City Cemetery, Tallahassee, Fla.

WESTCOTT, Thompson, journalist, author; b. Phila., June 5, 1820; s. Charles and Hannah (Davis) W.; studied law with his' uncle Henry M. Phillips, Phila. Admitted to Phila. bar, 1841; wrote humorous stories (signed Joe Miller, Jr.) for St. Louis Reveille, Evening Mirror, N.Y., Knickerbocker or N.Y. Monthly Mag. law reporter for Phila. Public Ledger, 1846-51; became editor Sunday Dispatch, 1848; editorial writer for Phila. Inquirer, 1863-69; wrote for Phila. Commercial List; edited Old Franklin Almanac, 1860-72, Public Ledger Almanac, 1870-circa 1887; mem. editorial staff Phila. Record; began doing hist. writing with series of articles for Sunday-Dispatch titled "History of Philadelphia: from the Time of the First Settlements on the Delaware to the Consolidation of the City and Districts in 1854." Author: Life of John Fitch, Inventor of Steamboat, 1857; Chronicles of Great Rebellion, 1867; Official Guide Book of Philadelphia, 1875, 76, also sections in History of Philadelphia (J. T. Sharf and Thompson Wescott), 3 vols., 1884. Died Phila., May 8, 1888.

WESTERLO, Rensselaer, congressman, lawyer, b. Albany, N.Y. Apr. 29, 1776; grad. Columbia, 1795; studied law. Admitted to bar, practiced law; mem. U.S. Ho. of Reps. (Federalist) from N.Y., 15th Congress, 1817-19. Died Albany, Apr. 18, 1851; buried Albany Rural Cemetery.

WESTERN, (Pauline) Lucille, actress; b. New Orleans, Jan. 8, 1843; d. George and Jane Western; m. James Harrison Meade, 1859. Dancer, Nat. Theatre, Boston, 1849; actress, dancer in theatres of New Eng. circuit, N.Y.C., appeared in The Three Fast Men, also The Female Robinson Crusoes; specialized in acting of emotional roles; played dual roles of Lady Isabel and Madame Vine in East Lynne, played roles Camille, Lucretia Borgia, Leah the Forsaken, Cynthia in Flowers of the Forest, Peg Woffington in Masks and Faces, Mrs. Haller in The Strange; one of most popular impersonations was Nancy in Oliver Twist. Died Bklyn., Jan. 11, 1877.

WESTERVELT, Jacob Aaron, shipbuilder, mayor N.Y.C.; b. Tenafly, N.J., June 20, 1800; s. Aaron and Vroutie (Westervelt) W.; m. Eliza M. Thompson, Apr. 25, 1825, 8 children including Daniel, Aaron. Built 2 schooners with slave labor, Charleston, S.C., 1820; built 71 vessels in N.Y. (mostly in Carlear's Hook), 1822-35, including transatlantic packets Montano (1822), Paris (1823), Edward Bonafee (1824), Philadelphia (1832); reputed to have built 247 vessels of all descriptions including at least 91 ships and 36 steamers, 1821-68, including packets Baltimore (1836), Oneida (1841); 1st important steamships were 1700 ton Washington and West Point (both 1847); produced clipper ships N.B. Palmer, Eureka, Hornet, Golden Gate (all 1851), Golden City, Contest (both 1852), Golden State, Resolute Kathay (both 1853); contracted to build U.S. steam frigate Brooklyn, 1854; built hulls for several gunboats during Civil War; mayor N.Y.C. (Democrat) 1852-54; supt. docks N.Y.C., 1870, pres. dock commrs. N.Y.C., 1873-79; pres. Soc. Mechanics and Tradesman. Died Feb. 21, 1879.

WESTON, Thomas, mcht., colonist; b. 1575; at least 1 child, Elizabeth. Secured patent from Va. Co., 1620, underwrote Pilgrim expdn. to Am.; purchased Mayflower for group of 67 pilgrims, including Miles Standish, John Alden; fitted out vessel Fortune, 1621, came with 35 new colonists to Plymouth colony with no supplies, arrived in Plymouth, 1623; engaged in controversial trading enterprises on Mass. coast, 1623-24; settled in Va., 1624; mem. Va. Ho. of Burgesses, 1628; moved to Md., received grant of 1200 acres, 1642; mem. Md. Assembly. Died Bristol, Eng., 1644.

WESTON, William, civil engr.; b. nr. Oxford, Eng., circa 1752. Engr. of stone bridge across Trent River at Gainsborough, Eng., 1790, also turnpike rd.; contracted with Schuylkill & Susquehanna Navigation Co., Pa. to engr. its canal, served 2 years; arrived in U.S., early 1793; examined and reported on locks under constrn. at Gt. Falls of the Potomac, 1795; engr. for Western Island Lock Navigation Co., N.Y., 1796, 97; pioneer in design and constrn. of locks and canals; sources of future water for N.Y.C., 1799; designer piers for Permanent Bridge across the Schuylkill River in Phila., also deep coffer dam in connection with bridge; returned to Eng., 1800. Author: An Historial Account of the Rise, Progress and Present State of the Canal Navigation in Pennsylvania, 1795. Died London, Eng., Aug. 29, 1833.

WETHERED, John, congressman, mfr.; b. nr. Wetheredville, Baltimore County, Md., May 9, 1809. Held several local offices; manufactured woolen goods, Wetheredville; mem. U.S. Ho. of Reps. (Democrat) from Md., 28th Congress, 1843-45; del. Md. Constl. Conv., 1867; retired to estate "Ashland," nr. Catonsville, Md., 1868. Died "Ashland," Feb. 15, 1888; buried Greenmount Cemetery, Balt.

WETHERELL, Elizabeth, see Warner, Susan Bogert.

WETHERILL, Charles Mayer, chemist; b. Phila., Nov. 4, 1825; s. Charles and Margaretta (Mayer) W.; grad. U. Pa., 1845; M.A., Ph.D., U. Giessen, 1848; M.D. (hon.), N.Y. Med. Coll., 1853; m. Mary Benbridge, Aug. 12, 1856. Conducted chem. lab. for pvt. instrn. and analysis, Phila., 1848-53; elected to Am. Philos. Soc., 1851; published treatise The Manufacture of Vinegar, 1860; apptd. chemist U.S. Dept. Agr., 1862; published Report on the Chemical Analysis of Grapes (1st scientific bulletin issued by Dept. of Agr.), 1862; chemist Smithsonian Instn., Washington, 1863-66, conducted investigation of ventilation of new House and Senate chambers in U.S. Capitol extensions; prof. chemistry Lehigh U., Bethlehem, Pa., 1866-71. Author: Syllabus of Lectures on Chemical Physics, 1867; Lecture Notes on Chemistry, 1868. Died Bethlehem, Mar. 5, 1871.

WETHERILL, Samuel, mfr., founder religious soc.; b. nr. Burlington, N.J., Apr. 12, 1736; s. Christopher and Mary (Stockton) W.; m. Sarah Yarnall, Apr. 5, 1762, at least one child, Samuel. Became mfr., leader in movement to make colonies industrially free of Eng.; mem. United Co. of Pa. for Establishment of Am. Mfg., 1775; mem. band of Quakers to take allegiance oath to colonies; defended right of Am. colonists to armed resistance to Britain and consequently deprived of membership in Soc. of Friends, 1777; formed soc. called Free or Fighting Quakers; established chem. firm for weaving and mfr. of dye stuffs (with son Samuel), 1785; began prodn. of white lead (1st manufactured in U.S.), 1790, erected white lead factory, 1804; v.p. yellow fever com. Phila., 1793; mem. Phila. City Council, 1802-03. Author: A Confutation of the Doctrines of Antinomianism, 1790; The Divinity of Jesus Christ Proved, 1792; An Apology for the Religious Society, Called Free Quakers. Died Phila., Sept. 24, 1816.

WETHERILL, Samuel, inventor, zinc co. exec., army officer; b. Phila., May 27, 1821; s. John Price and Maria Kane (Lawrence) W.; grad. U. Pa., 1845; m. Sarah Maria Chatton, Jan. 1, 1844; m. 2d, Thyrza A. James, Oct. 19, 1870; 10 children. Joined firm Wetherill & Brother, 1845, operated white lead and chem. works; employed by N.J. Zinc Co., 1850; inventor process for deriving white oxide of zinc direct from the ore, 1852; founder Lehigh Zinc Co., 1853; developer process for manufacture of metallic zinc and rolled zinc sheets, 1857; commd. capt. 11th Pa. Cavalry, 1861, maj., 1861, honorably discharged, 1864; brevetted lt. col., 1865. Died Oxford, Md., June 24, 1890.

WETZEL, Lewis, Indian fighter; probably b. Lancaster County, Pa., 1764; s. John and Mary (Bannett) W. Fought in 1st siege Wheeling, Va., 1777; served in several expdns. against Indians in Ohio, notably against Indian village on site of present town of Coshocton (O.), 1781; employed as scout; waylaid and killed a prominent Indian during negotiations with Ohio tribes at Ft. Harmar, escaped trial and punishment for this murder; Wetzel County, Va. (now W.Va.), named for him. Died circa 1808, nr. Natchez, Tenn.

WHALEY, Kellian Van Rensalear, congressman; b. Onondaga County, nr. Utica, N.Y., May 6, 1821; attended public schs., Ohio. Engaged in lumbering business, Ceredo, Va., 1842; mem. U.S. Ho. of Reps. (Republican) from Va., 37th Congress, 1861-63, from W.Va., 38th-39th congresses, Dec. 7, 1863-67; recruited several regts. for U.S. Army during Civil War; del. Rep. Nat. Conv., Balt., 1864; collector of customs, Brazos de Santiago, Tex., 1868. Died Point Pleasant, W. Va., May 20, 1876; buried Lone Oak Cemetery.

WHALLEY, Edward, army officer; b. Nottinghamshire, Eng., circa 1620; s. Richard and Frances (Cromwell) W.; m. Judith Duffell, m. 2d, Mary Middleton; at least 1 child. Entered Brit. Army during English Civil War, commd. maj., 1643, lt. col., 1644, col., 1645; in charge of imprisoned King Charles I, had to answer to Parliament for Charles' escape; mem. High Ct. of Justice apptd. to try King, signer death warrant; participated in battles of Dunbar and Worcester; commissary gen. under Oliver Cromwell; one of officers who presented army petition to Parliament, 1652; commd. maj. gen., 1655; apptd. to Cromwell's Ho. of Lords, 1657; a supporter of Richard Cromwell, warrant issued for his arrest by Council of State, 1660, fled to Boston, 1660; eluded arrest by Mass. authorities when he was exempted from Act of Indemnity. Died Hadley, Mass., circa 1674.

WHALLON, Reuben, congressman, businessman; b. Bedminster, Somerset County, N.J., Dec. 7, 1776; attended common schs. Moved to Argyle, N.Y.; justice of peace Twp. of Argyle, 1806-11; moved to Essex, N.Y., 1814, became landowner, farmer, mill owner, mcht., ironmaster; served as capt. and maj. N.Y. State Militia, 1803-14; mem. N.Y. State Assembly, 1808-09, 11; supr. Town of Essex, 1818-19, 27-28; 1st judge Essex County Ct. of Common Pleas, 1831-38; mem. U.S. Ho. of Reps. (Jackson Democrat) from N.Y., 23d Congress, 1833-35. Died Whallons Bay, Essex, N.Y., Apr. 15, 1843; buried Whallons Bay Cemetery.

WHARTON, Charles Henry, clergyman; b. St. Mary's County, Md., June 5, 1748; s. Jesse and Anne (Bradford) W.; attended Jesuit Coll., St. Omer, France, 1760-62; m. Mary Weems, June 2, 1798; m. 2d, Ann Kinsly; no children. Ordained priest Jesuit order, 1772; chaplain to Roman Catholics, Worcester, Eng., 1773-77; left Roman Cath. Ch., 1783; rector Immanuel Ch. (Episcopal), New Castle, Del., 1785; dep. to 1st gen. conv. called to prepare constn. for Episcopal Ch., 1785; rector Swedish Church, Wilmington, Del., 1791-92, St. Mary's Ch., Burlington, N.J., 1798-1833; pres. Columbia Coll., N.Y. for short time 1801; an editor Quarterly Theol. Mag. and Religious Repository, 1813-17; elected to Am. Philos. Soc., 1786. Author: A Letter to the Roman Catholics of the City of Worcester from the Late Chaplain of that Society . . . Stating the Motives which Induced Him To Relinquish their Communion, and Become a Member of the Protestant Church, 1784; A Short and Candid Inquiry into the Proofs of Christ's Divinity; in which Dr. Priestly's History of Opinions Concerning Christ is Occasionally Considered, 1791. Died July 23, 1833.

WHARTON, Francis, lawyer, clergyman; b. Phila., Mar. 7, 1820; s. Thomas Isaac and Arabella (Griffith) W.; grad. Yale, 1839; m. Sidney Paul, Nov. 4, 1852; m. 2d, Helen Elizabeth Ashhurst, Dec. 27, 1860. Admitted to Pa. bar, 1843; studied and wrote in area criminal law; editor Episcopal Reader, 1854 also lay preacher for Episcopal Ch.; toured Mo. Valley in wagon while distributing Bibles and religious readings, 1856; prof. history and literature Kenyon Coll., Gambier, O., 1856-63; ordained priest Episcopal Ch., 1862; prof. Episcopal Theol. Sem., Cambridge, Mass., 1871-81; examiner claims, chief of legal div. Dept. of State, 1885-89. Author: A Treatise on the Criminal Law of the United States, 1846; A Treatise on the Law of Homicide in the United States, 1855; Treatise on the Conflict of Laws, 1872; A Digest of the International Law of the United States, 3 vols., 1886; The Revolutionary Diplomatic Correspondence of the United States, 6 vols., 1889. Died Washington, D.C., Feb. 21, 1889; buried Rock Creek Cemetery, Washington.

WHARTON, Jesse, senator, congressman; b. Covesville, Albemarle County, Va., July 29, 1782; studied law. Admitted to bar, began practice of law, Albemarle County; moved to Tenn.; mem. U.S. Ho. of Reps. from Tenn., 10th Congress, 1807-09; mem. U.S. Senate (filled vacancy) from Tenn., Mar. 17, 1814-Oct. 10, 1815; mem. bd. visitors U.S. Mil. Acad., 1832. Died Nashville, Tenn., July 22, 1833; buried Mt. Olivet Cemetery.

WHARTON, Richard, mcht., promoter; b. Eng.; m. Bethia Tiping; m. 2d, Sarah Higginson; m. 3d, Martha Wintrap; 7 children. Came to Am., circa 1659; seized Dutch vessel involved in trade with New Eng. during 2d Dutch War, involuntarily involving New Eng. in comml. warfare with Dutch, lost privilege as atty.; influential in establishment of Dominion New Eng., 1686; mcht., importer, owned vessels and wharves; sought and received monopoly of salt prodn. from Gen. Ct. Mass., later applied for royal monopoly grant; largest scheme was organizing co. for developing mines in New Eng.; bought Penebscot Purchase in Me. (a tract of about 500,000 acres). Died May 14, 1689.

WHARTON, Robert, mayor Phila., mcht., sportsman; b. Southwark, Phila., Jan 12, 1757; s. Joseph and Hannah (Owens) Ogden W.; m. Salome Chancellor, Dec. 17, 1789, 2 children. Wholesale grocer and flour mcht., Phila.; mem. Phila. Common Council, 1792-95; apptd. alderman Phila., 1796; suppressed riot of mcht. men who were striking for higher wages; mayor Phila., 1798-99, 1806-07, 10, 14-18, 20-24, killed 2 mutinying convicts while in charge of Walnut Street Jail, asked grand jury to investigate incident, grand jury held he was upholding law; mem. Gloucester (N.J.) Fox Hunting Club, pres., 1812-18; mem. Schuylkill Fishing Co., 1790-1828; joined 1st Troop, Phila. City Cavalry, 1798, promoted capt., col., 1810; commd. brig. gen. 1st Brigade, Pa. Militia, 1811. Died Phila., Mar. 7, 1834.

WHARTON, Samuel, land speculator, Continental congressman; b. Phila., May 3, 1732; s. Joseph and Hannah (Carpenter) W.; m. Sarah Lewis, before 1775, 6 children. Asso. firm Baynton and Wharton (became Baynton, Wharton & Morgan 1763); granted large land tract (now in W. Va., known as "Indiana Grant"), ceded to him by the Six Nations at Ft. Stanwix, 1768; while in Eng. to secure confirmation of grant, some correspondence with Benjamin Franklin was discovered; forced to flee with Franklin to France; returned to Phila., 1780; an organizer Grand Ohio Co. (generally known as Wadpole Co.); mem. Continental Congress from Del., 1782, 83; justice of peace Southwark (Pa.) dist., 1784-86, judge Ct. of Common Pleas, 1790-91. Died Phila., Mar. 1800.

WHARTON, Thomas, mcht., chief exec. Pa.; b. Chester County, Pa., 1735; s. John and Mary (Dobbins) W.; m. Susannah Kearney, Nov. 4, 1762; m. 2d, Elizabeth Fishbourne, Dec. 7, 1774; 8 children. Partner, Stocken & Wharton Exporters; del. Pa. Provincial Conv., 1774; mem. Pa. Provincial Com. Safety, 1775; pres. Pa. Council Safety, 1776; councillor Phila., 1777; pres. Supreme Exec. Council Pa., 1777-78; comdr. in chief forces of Pa. Died Lancaster, Pa., May 22, 1778; buried with full mil. honors Trinity Lutheran Ch., Lancaster.

WHARTON, Thomas Isaac, lawyer; b. Phila., May 17, 1791; s. Isaac and Margaret (Rawle) W.; grad.

U. Pa., 1807; studied law under his uncle, William Rawle; m. Arabella Griffith, Sept. 11, 1817, 4 children. Served in War of 1812; became successful lawyer, Phila.; mem. Tuesday Club; contbr. to various mags.; editor Analectic Mag., for a time; elected mem. Am. Philos. Soc., 1830; an organizer Pa. Hist. Soc.; trustee U. Pa., 1837-56. Author: Reports of Cases . . . in the Supreme Court of Pennsylvania, 1836; A Letter to Robert Toland and Isaac Elliot, Esqs., on the Subject of the Right and Power of the City of Philadelphia to Subscribe for Stock in the Pennsylvania Railroad (proved to be main legal found. of Pa. R.R.), 1846. Died Phila., Apr. 7, 1856.

WHARTON, Thomas Kelah, artist; b. Hull, Eng., Apr. 17, 1814. Came to Am., 1830, settled in Ohio; entered office of architect Martin E. Thompson, N.Y.C., 1832; exhibited landscapes at N.A.D., 1834-35; drew and lithographed a view of Reading (Pa.), 1838; drew 2 pencil views of Natchez (Miss.), circa 1850 (now in Stokes Collection at N.Y. Pub. Library). Died New Orleans, 1862.

WHARTON, William H., army officer, diplomatic agt.; b. Albemarle County, Va., 1802; s. John Austin and Judith (Harris) W.; m. Sarah Ann Groce, Dec. 5, 1827; 1 son, John Austin. Planter, Eastern Tex., 1827; pres. Tex. Constl. Conv., 1833; judge advocate, col. Army of Texans organized at Gonzales, 1835, resigned, 1835; sent to U.S. for aid to Tex. Revolution, 1835; minister to U.S. (apptd. by Sam Houston), to negotiate recognition and eventual annexation of Tex. to U.S., 1836; mem. Tex. Senate, 1838-39; Wharton County (Tex.) named in his honor. Died Houston, Tex., Mar. 14, 1839; buried Eagle Island Plantation, Tex.

WHATCOAT, Richard, clergyman; b. Quinton, Eng., Feb. 23, 1736; s. Charles and Mary Whatcoat. Apprenticed to mcht., Birmingham, Eng., 1749-57; converted from Anglican Ch. to Methodist Ch., by 1761, became class leader, then steward, exhorter; itinerant preacher Methodist Ch., Eng., Ireland and Wales, 1769-84; ordained deacon by John Wesley, selected to go to Am., 1784; an organizer Meth. Episcopal Ch. in N.Y.; itinerant preacher over most of Eastern U.S., 1785-1800; ordained bishop, 1800. Died Dover, Del., July 5, 1806.

WHEATLEY, Phillis, poet; b. Senegal, Africa, 1753; received liberal edn.; m. Dr. John Peters (free Negro), 1778, 3 children. Kidnapped on slave ship to Boston, circa 1761; personal servant for wife of John Wheatley who educated her, wrote 1st verses entitled To the University of Cambridge in New England, circa 1766, To the King's Most Excellent Majesty, 1768, On the Death of Rev. Dr. Sewell, 1769, An Elegiac Poem on the Death of a Celebrated Divine . . . George Whitefield, 1770, Poems on Various Subjects, Religious and Moral, 1773; went to London for health and returned to Boston, 1773; freed before her marriage, 1778; died in poverty at age 30. Author: Memoir and Poems of Phillis Wheatley, 1834; The Letters of Phillis Wheatley, the Negro-Slave Poet of Boston, appeared 1864; Poems. London, 1773; Elegy Sacred to the Memory of Dr. Samuel Cooper, 1784. Died Boston, Dec. 5, 1784.

WHEATLEY, William, actor, theatrical mgr.; b. N.Y.C., Dec. 5, 1816; s. Frederick and Sarah (Ross) W.; m. 2d. Elizabeth A. Beckett; married 3 times, at least 1 child. Began career as Albert in J. S. Knowles's William Tell, Park Theatre, N.Y.C., 1826; gained nat. reputation for part of Tom Thumb, N.Y. C.; appeared at Bowery Theatre as "walking gentleman," 1833; wrote and produced tragedy Sassacus, or Indian Wife, 1836; mgr. Nat. Theatre, N.Y.C., circa 1838; most characteristic roles include Doricourt in The Belle's Stratagem, Capt. Murphy Maguire in The Serious Family; directed Washington (D. C.) Theatre, 1852; mgr. (with John Drew) Arch Street Theatre, Phila., 1853-56, sole manager, 1856-58; opened Chestnut Street Theatre, Phila., 1863; operated Niblo's Garden, N.Y.C., 1862-68, produced The Duke's Motto, Bel DeMonio, The Connie Soogah, Arrahna-Pogue, The Black Crook, also directed and starred in many plays. Died N.Y.C., Nov. 3, 1876.

WHEATON, Henry, lawyer, diplomat; b. Providence, R.I., Nov. 17, 1785; s. Seth and Abigail (Wheaton) W.; grad. R.I. Coll: (now Brown U.), 1802, LL.D. (hon.), 1819; LL.D. (hon.), Hamilton Coll., 1843, Harvard, 1845; m. Catherine Wheaton (cousin), 1811, at least 3 children. Admitted to R.I. bar, 1806; editor Nat. Advocate, 1812-15; div. judge adv. U.S. Army, 1814-15; apptd. justice Marine Ct.; N.Y.C., 1815-19; reporter U.S. Supreme Ct., 1816-27; mem. N.Y. State Constl. Conv, 1821; elected to N.Y. Assembly, 1823; U.S. charge d'affaires to Denmark under Pres. John Quincy Adams, 1827-34; charge d'affaires at Berlin at request of Prussia, 1835-37; E.E. and M.P. to Prussia, 1837-46; returned to U.S., 1847; most distinguished as expounder and historian of internat. law; elected mem. Scandinavian and Icelandic lit. socs., 1830; fgn. mem. Prussian Royal Acad. of Scis.; elected to Acad. Moral and Polit. Scis. in French Inst., 1842; contbr. to N. Am. Review and Am. Quarterly, 1810-27; lectr. internat. law Harvard, 1847. Author: A Digest of the Law of Maritime Captures and Prizes, 1815; A Digest of the Decisions of the Supreme Court of the United States, 1821; Some Accounts of the Life, Writings and Speeches of William Pinkney, 1826; History of the Northmen, 1831; Elements of International Law (most famous work), 1836; History of the Law of Nations in Europe and America, from the Earliest Times to the Treaty of Washington, 1842, 1845. Died Dorchester, Mass., Mar. 11, 1848; buried Providence.

WHEATON, Horace, congressman, businessman; b. New Milford, Litchfield County, Conn., Feb. 24, 1803; grad. Pompey (N.Y.) Acad. Engaged in merc. activities; mem. N.Y. State Assembly, 1834; a commr. to build railroad between Syracuse and Utica; postmaster Pompey, 1840-42; supr. Pompey, also city treas.; mem. U.S. Ho. of Reps. (Democrat) from N.Y., 28th-29th congresses, 1843-47; moved to Syracuse, N.Y., 1846; mayor Syracuse, 1851-53, city treas., 1857-58; engaged in hardware, saddlery and merc. pursuits. Died Syracuse, June 23, 1882; buried Oakwood Cemetery.

WHEATON, Laban, congressman, jurist; b. Mansfield, Mass., Mar. 13, 1754; attended Wrentham (Mass.) Acad.; grad. Harvard, 1774; studied theology, Woodstock, Conn.; also studied law. Admitted to bar, 1788, began practice of law, Milton, Mass.; judge Bristol County (Mass.) Ct.; mem. Mass. Ho. of Reps., 1803-08, 25; mem. U.S. Ho. of Reps. (Federalist) from Mass., 11th-14th congresses, 1809-17; chief justice Bristol County Ct. of Common Pleas, 1810-19, Ct. of Sessions, 1819-46. Died Norton, Mass., Mar. 23, 1846; buried Norton Cemetery.

WHEATON, Nathaniel Sheldon, coll. pres., clergyman; b. Washington, Conn., Aug. 20, 1792; s. Sylvester and Marcy (Sperry) W.; grad. Yale, 1814. Ordained deacon Episcopal Ch., 1817, priest, 1818; rector Christ Ch., Hartford, Conn., 1821-31; an original mem. bd. trustees Washington (now Trinity) Coll., Hartford, 1823, pres. coll., 1831-37; rector Christ Ch., New Orleans, 1837-44, contracted yellow fever during epidemic there; spent last years in Marbledale, Conn. Author: The Providence of God Displayed in the Rise and Fall of Nations, 1828; A Journal of a Residence of Several Months in London, 1830. Died Mar. 18, 1862.

WHEDON, Daniel Denison, clergyman, author; b. Onondaga, N.Y., Mar. 20, 1808; s. Daniel and Clarissa (Root) W.; grad. Hamilton Coll., 1828; D.D. (hon.), Emory and Henry Coll.; LL.D. (hon.), Wesleyan U., 1856; m. Eliza Ann Searles, July 15, 1840, 5 children. Joined Methodist Ch.; apptd. tchr. Greek and mental philosophy Oneida Conf. Sem., Cazenovia, N.Y., 1830-31; tutor Hamilton Coll., 1831; prof. ancient langs. and literature Wesleyan Coll., Middletown, Conn., 1833-43; ordained deacon and elder Methodist Episcopal Ch., 1843; pastor Meth. Ch., Pittsfield, Mass., 1843, Rensselaerville, N.Y., 1845; prof. logic and philosophy of history U. Mich., 1845-52; opened sch., Ravenswood, L.I., N.Y.; editor Methodist Quarterly Review, 1856-84. Author: The Freedom of the Will . . . , 1864; Commentary on Matthew and Mark, 1860, Commentary on the New Testament, 5 vols., 1866-75, Commentary on the Old Testament, 7 vols. Died Atlantic City, N.J., June 8, 1885.

WHEELER, Ezra, congressman, lawyer; b. Chenango County, N.Y., Dec. 23, 1820; grad. Union Coll., Schenectady, N.Y., 1842; studied law. Admitted to bar, began practice of law, Berlin, Green Lake County, Wis.; mem. Wis. Assembly, 1853; judge Green Lake County, 1854-62; mem. U.S. Ho. of Reps. (Democrat) from Wis., 38th Congress, 1863-65; moved to Pueblo, Colo., 1870; register land office, Pueblo, 1871. Died Pueblo, Sept. 19, 1871; buried Oakwood Cemetery, Berlin.

WHEELER, Grattan Henry, congressman; b. nr. Providence, R.I., Aug. 25, 1783; attended public, prep. schs. Moved to Steuben County, N.Y., circa 1800; engaged in farming and lumber business, nr. Wheeler, N.Y.; mem. N.Y. State Assembly, 1822, 24, 26; mem. N.Y. Senate, 1826-30; mem. U.S. Ho. of Reps. from N.Y., 22d Congress, 1831-33; Whig presdl. elector, 1840. Died Wheeler, Mar. 11, 1852; buried pvt. cemetery on Wheeler homestead.

WHEELER, Harrison H., congressman; b. Farmers Creek, Lapeer County, Mich., Mar. 22, 1829; attended common schs.; studied law. A sch. tchr., until 1861; joined U.S. Army as pvt. 10th Regt., Mich. Volunteer Inf., at beginning of Civil War, 1861, promoted 2d lt., 1862, 1st lt., 1863, capt., 1865; wounded at Buzzards Roost Gap, Kenesaw Mountain and Jonesboro, Ga.; settled in Bay City, Mich., circa 1865; clk. Bay County, 1866; admitted to bar, 1868, began practice of law, Bay City; mem. Mich. Senate, 1870, 72; moved to Ludington, Mich., 1873; circuit judge, 1874-78; postmaster, 1878-82; mem. U.S. Ho. of Reps. (Democrat) from Mich., 52d Congress, 1891-93; U.S. pension agt. at Detroit, 1894-96. Died while on a visit, Farmers Creek, nr. Lapeer, Mich., July 28, 1896; buried Lakeview Cemetery, Ludington.

WHEELER, John Hill, diplomat, lawyer; b. Murfreesboro, N.C., Aug. 2, 1806; s. John and Elizabeth (Jordan) W.; grad. Columbian Coll. (now George Washington U.), 1826; A.M., U. N.C., 1828; m. Mary Elizabeth Brown, Apr. 19, 1830; m. 2d, Ellen Oldmixon Sully, Nov. 8, 1838; 5 children. Licensed to practice law, 1827; mem. N.C. Ho. of Commons from Hertford County, 1827-30; supt. Charlotte (N.C.) branch of U.S. Mint, 1837-41; treas. of N.C., 1842-44; mem. N.C. Ho. of Commons, 1852; U.S. minister to Nicaragua, 1854-57; sec. bd. commrs. under treaty with France to adjudicate spoliative claims against France under Berling and Milan decrees, 1831; edited The Narrative of Colonel David Fanning, 1861. Author: Indexes to Documents Relating to North Carolina; Historical Sketches of North Carolina, 1851; The Legislative Manual and Political Register of the State of North Carolina, published 1874; Reminiscences and Memoirs of North Carolina, published 1884. Died Washington, D.C., Dec. 7, 1882.

WHEELER, Nathaniel, inventor, mfr.; b. Watertown, Conn., Sept. 7, 1820; s. David and Sarah (De Forest) W.; m. Huldah Bradley, Nov. 7, 1842; m. 2d, Mary E. Crissey, Aug. 3, 1858; at least 14 children. Engaged in carriage building in father's shop, 1841-46; formed partnership Warren, Wheeler and Woodruff, mfrs. metalware, Watertown, 1848; assumed control mfg. Allen B. Wilson's sewing machine, engaged Wilson to superintend factory, 1850, reorganized co. under name Wheeler and Wilson Mfg. Co., 1851-53, moved factory to Bridgeport, Conn., 1856, served as pres. until 1893; invented, patented wood-filling compound, 1876-78, ventilating system for houses and railroad cars, 1883; dir. N.Y., N.H. & H. R.R.; served in Conn. Legislature, 1866, 68, 70, 72-74. Died Bridgeport, Conn., Dec. 31, 1893.

WHEELER, Royall Tyler, jurist; b. Vt., 1810; s. John and Hannah (Thurston) W.; m. Emily Walker, 1839, 3 sons, 1 dau. Following admission to bar, 1837, moved to Fayetteville, Ark.; became law partner of Williams S. Oldham; moved to Tex., 1839, practiced law in partnership with K. L. Anderson (v.p. Republic of Tex.); apptd. judge Tex. 5th Dist., 1844; strong advocate of U.S. annexation of Tex.; judge Tex. Supreme Ct., 1845-64, chief justice, 1858-64; became mentally ill due to shock of Civil War. Committed suicide, Washington County, Tex., Apr. 1864.

WHEELER, William Adolphus, lexicographer, bibliographer; b. Leicester, Mass., Nov. 14, 1833; s. Amos Dean and Louisa (Warren) W.; A.B., Bowdoin Coll., 1853, A.M., 1856; m. Olive Winsor Frazar, July 13, 1856, at least 6 children. Asst. of Joseph Emerson Worcester in preparing his quarto Dictionary of the English Language, 1860; mem. editorial staff Merriam Co., supervised new unabridged quarto edit. Webster Dictionary, also new edits. of Nat., Academic and smaller dictionaries, 1864; asst. supt. Boston Public Library, 1868-74; published edit. of Mother Goose's Melodies, 1869; edited Brief Biographical Dictionary, 1866, Dickens Dictionary, 1873. Author: A Manual of English Pronunciation and Spelling, 1861; An Explanatory and Pronouncing Dictionary of the Noted Names of Fiction, 1865; Who Wrote It?, 1881; Familiar Allusions, 1882. Died Boston, Oct. 28, 1874.

WHEELER, William Alman, vice pres. U.S.; b. Malone, N.Y., June 30, 1819; s. Alman and Eliza (Woodworth) W.; attended U. Vt.; m. Mary King, Sept. 17, 1845. Admitted to N.Y. bar, 1845; trustee for mortgage holders of No. Ry., 1853-66; dist. atty. Franklin County (N.Y.), 1846-49; mem. N.Y. Assembly, 1850-51; mem., pres. pro tem N.Y. Senate, 1858-60; mem. U.S. Ho. of Reps. (Republican) from N.Y., 37th, 41st-45th congresses, 1861-63, 69-77; pres. N.Y. State Constl. Conv., 1867-68; vice pres. U.S. under Rutherford Hayes, 1877-81. Died Malone, June 4, 1887; buried Morningside Cemetery, Malone.

WHEELOCK, Eleazar, clergyman, coll. pres.; b. Windham, Conn., Apr. 22, 1711; s. Ralph and Ruth (Huntington) W.; grad. Yale, 1733; D.D., U. Edinburgh (Scotland), 1767; m. Mrs. Sarah (Davenport) Maltby, Apr. 29, 1735; m. 2d, Mary Brinsmead, Nov. 21, 1747; 11 children Including John (eldest son). Licensed to preach, Congregational Ch., 1734; pastor 2d (or North) Soc., Lebanon, Conn., 1735; envisaged plan to educate and convert Indians after having privately educated Samson Occoman (a Mohegan Indian), 1743; conducted Moor's Charity Sch., 1754-68 which had

127 Indians by 1765, sch. closed as result of governmental disapproval and poor results among grads.; obtained charter for Dartmouth Coll. from Gov. John Wentworth of N.H., 1769, started sch. with funds raised in Eng., served as pres. Dartmouth Coll. and Moor's Charity Sch., Hanover, N.H., 1770-79; published several sermons and "Narrative of the Indian School at Lebanon," 1762-75. Died Hanover, Apr. 24, 1779.

WHEELOCK, John, coll. pres.; b. Lebanon, Conn., Jan. 28, 1754; s. Eleazar and Mary (Brinsmead) W.; attended Yale, 3 years; grad. Dartmouth, 1771, D.D., 1789; m. Maria Suhm, 1786, 1 dau., Maria. Served as lt. col. of a N.Y. inf. co. during Am. Revolution; pres. Dartmouth, Hanover, N.H., 1779-1817, revived father's Indian edn. program, 1800, founded Dartmouth Med. Sch., 1798; engaged in dispute with trustees, 1806-17, became polit. issue and resulted in 2 parallel sets of administrns., in court action, rights of trustees under original charter were upheld; case tried in N.H. cts., then by U.S. Supreme Ct. (Trustees of Dartmouth College vs. Woodward, 4 Wheaton, 518), and won for Coll. by Daniel Webster, 1818. Author: Sketches of the History of Dartmouth, 1816. Died Hanover, Apr. 4, 1817.

WHEELWRIGHT, John, clergyman; b. Saleby, Eng., circa 1592; s. Robert Wheelwright; B.A., Sidney Coll., Cambridge, Eng., 1614, M.A., 1618; m. Marie Storre, Nov. 8, 1621; m. 2d, Mary Hutchinson, before 1636; at least 5 children. Ordained priest Anglican Ch., 1619; vicar of Bilsby, 1622-33; arrived (with family) in Boston 1636; banished from Mass. colony because of stand he took in Antinomian controversy, 1637, supported Anne Hutchinson (his sister-in-law); bought land from Indians in N.H., 1638; permitted to return to Mass. colony (after reversal of court decision), 1644; rector of church, Hampton, N.H., 1646-55; lived in Eng., 1655-62; pastor church, Salisbury, N.H., 1662-79. Died Salisbury, Nov. 15, 1679.

WHEELWRIGHT, William, entrepreneur; b. Newburyport, Mass., Mar. 16, 1798; s. Ebenezer and Anna (Coombs) W.; m. Martha Gerrish Bartlet, 1829, 3 children. U.S. consul at Guayaquil, Ecuador, 1824-29; obtained charter for Pacific Steam Navigation Co. to run from Panama to Cal., 1840; built 1st railroad in S. Am., 1848-52; built 1st S. Am. telegraph line in Chile, 1850; conceived idea of trans-Andean railroad running across S. Am. from Caldera, Chile to Rosario on the Parana, Argentina (approximately 1000 miles long); opened Grand Central Argentine Ry. from Rosario to Cordoba, 1870 (completed 1910); help create Port of La Plata. Author: Statements and Documents Relative to the Establishment of Steam Navigation in the Pacific, 1838; Observations on the Isthmus of Panama, 1844. Died Eng., Sept. 26, 1873.

WHELAN, James, clergyman; b. Kilkenny, Ireland, 1822; came to U.S.; studied at St. Rose Convent, Springfield, Ky., St. Joseph's Priory, Somerset, Joined Dominican Order, 1839, ordained priest Roman Catholic Ch., Somerset, 1846; became tchr. St. Joseph's Priory, then sub-prior, 1848-50, pres., 1851-54; provincial of Dominicans in U.S., 1854-58; appt. titular bishop of Marcopolis, coadjutor of Nashville (Tenn.), 1859, bishop, 1860-64 (resigned); apptd. titular bishop of Diocletianapolis, 1864. Died Zanesville, O., Feb. 18, 1878.

WHELAN, Richard Vincent, clergyman; b. Balt., Jan. 28, 1809; attended Mt. St. Mary's Coll., Emmitsburg, Md., also St. Sulpice, Paris, France. Ordained priest Roman Catholic Ch., 1831; parish priest, Richmond, Va., 1831-40; consecrated bishop of Richmond, 1841; founder St. Vincent's Sem. and Coll., Richmond, 1841, pres. until instn. closed, 1846; 1st bishop Wheeling (W.Va.), 1850; built cathedral, diocesan sem., St. Vincent's Coll.; attended 1st, 2d plenary councils of Balt., also Vatican Council of 1869-70. Died Balt., July 7, 1874.

WHIPPLE, Abraham, naval officer; b. Providence, R.I., Sept. 26, 1733; m. Sarah Hopkins, Aug. 2, 1761, 3 children. Commanded privateer Gamecock against French, 1759-60; commd. capt. Continental Navy, 1775; commodore of several vesesls, captured, brought to port 8 East Indiamen with cargoes worth over $1,000,000; participated in naval defense of Charleston, S.C., 1779; farmer in Ohio, after Revolutionary War. Died Marietta, O., May 27, 1819.

WHIPPLE, Amiel Weeks, topog. engr., army officer; b. Greenwich, Mass., 1816; s. David and Abigail (Pepper) W.; grad. U.S. Mil. Acad., 1841; m. Eleanor Sherburne, Sept. 12, 1843. Mem. survey team established to settle Northeastern boundary of U.S., 1844-49; surveyed boundary between Mexico an U.S., 1849-53; surveyed route for railroad line to Pacific Ocean, 1853-56; supervised operation designed to open Gt. Lakes for large craft, 1856-61; chief topog. engr. at Battle of Bull Run, 1860; commd. maj. U.S. Army, 1861; promoted brig. gen. U.S. Volunteers, 1862; wounded 2d day of fighting at Battle of Chancellorsville, 1863; promoted maj. gen. U.S. Volunteers before his death. Died Washington, D.C., May 7, 1863.

WHIPPLE, Edwin Percy, author, lectr.; b. Gloucester, Mass., Mar. 8, 1819; s. Matthew and Lydia (Gardiner) W.; m. Charlotte B. Hastings, June 21, 1847, 1 son, 1 dau. Worked for Salem Bank and wrote for local newspaper, 1834-37; joined Boston brokerage house Dana, Fenno & Henshaw, 1837; supt. Mchts. Exchange, Boston, 1840's-60; contbr. to periodicals, wrote essays, books and lectured. Author: Essays and Reviews, 1848-49; Lectures on Subjects Connected with Literature and Life, 1850; Character and Characteristic Man, 1866; Literature of the Age of Elizabeth, 1869. Died Boston, June 16, 1886.

WHIPPLE, Squire, civil engr., inventor; b. Hardwick, Mass., Sept. 16, 1804; s. James and Electa (Johnson) W.; A.B., Union Coll., 1830; m. Anna Case, 1837. Resident engr. div. N.Y. & Erie R.R., 1836-37; invented lock for weighing boats, 1840; invented truss of trapezoidal form used in bridges, 1846, used truss design in 1st long railroad bridge span on Rensselaer & Saratoga line, 1853; built drawbridge with left span over Erie Canal, Utica N.Y., 1872 hon. mem. Am. Soc. Civil Engrs. Author: A Work on Bridge Building (his chief contbn. to bridge engring.), 1847; The Doctrine of Central Forces, 1866. Died Albany, N.Y., Mar. 15, 1888.

WHIPPLE, Thomas, Jr., congressman, physician; b. Lebanon, Grafton County, N.H., 1787; studied medicine, Haverhill and Hanover, N.H.; grad. Dartmouth, 1814. Began practice of medicine Wentworth, N.H.; mem. N.H. Ho. of Reps., 1818-20; mem. U.S. Ho. of Reps. from N.H., 17th-20th congresses, 1821-29. Died Wentworth, Jan. 23, 1835.

WHIPPLE, William, Continental congressman; b. Kittery, Me., Jan. 14, 1730; s. William and Mary (Cutt) W.; m. Catharine Moffatt, no children. Mcht. and mariner engaged in slave trade 1752-60, later freed his own slaves; mem. N.H. Provincial Congress, 1775; del. to Continental Congress, 1775, 76, 78, signer Declaration of Independence, 1776; mem. council N.H. Com. of Safety, 1776; commd. brig. gen. H.H. Militia; mem. N.H. Assembly, 1780-84; asso. justice N.H. Superior Ct., 1782-85; judge N.H. Supreme Ct., 1782-85; financial receiver state of N.H., 1782-84; justice of peace and quorum, N.H., 1784. Died Portsmouth, N.H., Nov. 28, 1785; buried North Cemetery, Portsmouth.

WHISTLER, George Washington, civil engr., army officer; b. Fort Wayne, Ind., May 19, 1800; s. John and Ann (Bishop) W.; grad. U.S. Mil. Acad., 1819; m. Mary Roberdeau Swift; m. 2d, Anna Mathilda McNeill, Nov. 3, 1831; 8 children including Deborah Dleano (Dasha), George William, James Abbott McNeill (painter Whistler's Mother), William Gibbs McNeill. Commd. 2d lt. arty. U.S. Army, assigned to topog. duty, 1819-21; asst. drawing tchr. U.S. Mil. Acad., 1821-22; surveyed internat. boundary between Lake Superior and Lake of the Woods; served in cabinet of U.S. Pres. as commr. to make surveys, plans, estimates, 1826-28, assigned to locate Balt. and Susquehanna R.R., then Paterson and Hudson R.R., circa 1829; resigned from U.S. Army as 1st lt., 1833; supr. Providence & Stonington R.R., 1837; cons. engr. Western R.R. of Mass., chief engr., 1840-42; began work in Russia, 1842, supr. constrn. of fortifications and docks at Cronstadt, ran bridge over Neva River (both in Russia). Decorated Order of St. Anne by Emperor of Russia, 1847. Died St. Petersburg, Russia, Apr. 7, 1848; buried Stonington, Conn.

WHITAKER, Alexander, clergyman; b. Cambridge, Eng., 1585; s. William and Elizabeth (Culverwell) W.; B.A., Cambridge (Eng.) U., 1604/05, M.A., 1608. Ordained to ministry Ch. of Eng., 1608; went to Jamestown, Va., 1611; minister of 2 new settlements Henricopolis and Bermuda Hundreds; published sermon News from Virginia, 1613; instructed Pocahontas in principles of Christian faith, baptized her, Apr. 5, 1613. Died Henrico County, Va., Mar. 1616/17.

WHITAKER, Daniel Kimball, editor, lawyer, journalist; b. Sharon, Mass., Apr. 13, 1801; s. Rev. Jonathan and Mary (Kimball) W.; B.A., Harvard, 1820, M.A., 1823; m. 2d, Mary Furman Miller; 4 children. Practiced law, Charleston, S.C.,circa 1833; organized, edited several periodicals including So. Literary Jour. and Mag. of Arts, Charleston, 1835-37, Whitaker's Mag., 1841-61, So. Quarterly Review, New Orleans, 1842-47, New Orleans Monthly Review, 1874-76; held govtl. position during Buchanan's adminstrn., 1857-61; employed by Post Office Dept., Confederate Govt.; frequent contbr. to Nat. Intelligencer, Washington, D.C., Charleston Courier, New Orleans Times, contbd. his best work to So. Quarterly Review; sec. local acad. of sciences, New Orleans; joined St. Patrick's Catholic Ch., New Orleans, 1878. Died Houston, Tex., Mar. 24, 1881; buried New Orleans.

WHITAKER, Nathaniel, clergyman; b. Huntington, L.I., N.Y., Nov. 1730; s. Jonathan and Elizabeth (Jervis) W.; grad. Princeton, 1752; studied for ministry in Presbyn. faith; D.D. (hon.), St. Andrew's U., London, Eng., 1767; m. Sarah Smith, 5 children. Licensed to preach by N.Y. Presbytery, circa 1752; minister Presbyn. ch., Woodbridge, N.J., 1755-60, Sixth Parish, Norwich, Conn., 1760-65; traveled to Eng. with Rev. Samson Occom for purpose collecting funds for educating Am. Indians, 1765-67, obtained 12,000 pounds; minister Third Ch., Salem, Mass., 1769-84, Presbyn. ch., Skowhegan, Me., 1785-90. Died Hampton, Va., Jan. 26, 1795.

WHITCHER, Frances Miriam Berry, (penname: Frank), author, caricaturist; b. Whitesboro, N.Y., Nov. 1, 1814; d. Lewis and Elizabeth (Wells) Berry; m. Rev. Benjamin W. Whitcher, Jan. 6, 1847, 1 child. Used pen name Frank in Joseph C. Neal's Saturday Gazette and Lady's Literary Museum, 1846; wrote series "Aunt Magwire's Experience" for Godey's Lady's Book; wrote several hymns and devotional poems; wrote primarily satires based on people of Elmira (N.Y.) where she lived. Author: The Widow Spriggins; The Widow Bedott's Table-Talk; The Widow Bedott Papers, 1856; Widow Spriggins, Mary Elmer, and Other Sketches, 1867 (last 2 vols. of prose writings collected posthumously). Died Whitesboro, N.Y., Jan. 4, 1852.

WHITCHER, Mary (Mrs. Benjamin Whitcher); converted (with husband) to Shaker sect, 1782; turned their 100-acre ancestral farm nr. Canterbury, N.H. into Canterbury Shaker Community, 1792, serving as trustee community, 1792-97. Author: (cookbook) Shaker Housekeeper. Died 1797.

WHITCOMB, James, senator, gov. Ind.; b. nr. Windsor, Vt., Dec. 1, 1795; s. John and Lydia (Parmenter) W.; grad. Transylvania U., 1819; m. Martha Ann Renwick Hurst, Mar. 24, 1846, 1 dau. Admitted to Fayette County (Ky.) bar, 1822; pros. atty. Bloomington (Ind.), 1826-29; mem. Ind. Senate, 1830-31, 32-36; commr. Gen. Land Office under Pres. Jackson, 1836-41; gov. Ind., 1843-49; mem. U.S. Senate (Democrat) from Ind., 1849-52; bequeathed his extensive library to Ind. Asbury (now DePauw) U.; v.p. Am. Bible Soc., 1852. Author: Facts for the People, (treatise which opposed protective tariffs), 1843. Died N.Y.C., Oct. 4, 1852; buried Crown Hill Cemetery, Indpls.

WHITE, Albert Smith, senator; b. Orange County, N.Y., Oct. 24, 1803; s. Nathan H. and Frances (Howell) W.; grad. Union Coll., Schenectady, N.Y., 1822; m. Miss Randolph, at least 4 children. Admitted to N.Y. bar, 1825, later to Ind. bar; asst. clk. Ind. Ho. of Reps., 1830-31, clk., 1831-35; Whig presdl. elector, 1836; mem. U.S. Ho. of Reps. from Ind. as Whig, 25th Congress, 1837-39, as Republican, 37th Congress, 1861-63; mem. U.S. Senate from Ind., 1839-45, chmn. com. on Indian affairs; practiced law, 1845-60; pres. Lafayette and Indpls. R.R.; apptd. by Lincoln as a commr. to adjust claims of Minn. and Dakota citizens as result of Sioux Indian massacre (Aug. 1862) on Minn. frontier, 1863; judge U.S. Dist. Ct. of Ind., 1864. Died nr. Stockwell, Ind., Sept. 24, 1864; buried Greenbush Cemetery, Lafayette, Ind.

WHITE, Alexander, congressman; b. Frederick County, Va., circa 1738; s. Robert and Margaret (Hoge) W.; attended Edinburgh (Scotland) U.; studied Inner Temple, London, Eng., 1762, Gray's Inn, London, 1763; m. Elizabeth Wood; m. 2d, Sarah Hite. Mem. Va. Ho. of Burgesses from Hampshire County, 1772; mem. Va. Assembly, 1782-86, 88; dominant leader of Federalists in Northwestern Va., 1788; del. Va. Conv. to ratify U.S. Constn., 1788; mem. U.S. Ho. of Reps. from Va., 1st-2d congresses, 1789-93; mem. commn. to lay out new capital, Washington, D.C., 1795-1802; mem. Va. Assembly, 1799-1801. Died Frederick County, Sept. 19, 1804; buried "Woodville," nr. Winchester, Va.

WHITE, Alexander, pioneer mcht., art collector; b. Elgin, Morayshire, Scotland, Mar. 30, 1814; s. David and Margaret (Gowe) W.; m. Ann Reid, Dec. 12, 1837, 8 children. Came to U.S., 1836; opened store for paints and oils, Chgo., 1837; invested surplus capital in Chgo. real estate, 1857-67; made 3 European trips to buy notable paintings (chiefly by European contemporaries), 1857, 66, 70, supplemented by works of Am. artists bought in U.S.; had 1st private art gallery in Chgo.; sold art collection at N.Y. auction in order to rebuild after Chgo. fire, 1871; closely associated with Chgo. improvements and pub. instns. Died Lake Forest, Ill., Mar. 18, 1872.

WHITE, Alexander, congressman, lawyer; b. Franklin, Williamson County, Tenn., Oct. 16, 1816; attended U. Tenn. at Knoxville; studied law. Served in Seminole War, 1836; admitted to bar, 1838, began practice of law, Talladega, Ala.; mem. U.S. Ho. of Reps. from Ala. (as Union Whig), 32d Congress, 1851-53, (as Republican), 43d Congress, 1873-75; del. Ala. Constl. Conv., 1865; mem. Ala. Ho. of Reps., 1872; asso. justice U.S. Ct. for Utah Territory, 1875; moved to Dallas, Tex., 1876, resumed practice of law. Died Dallas, Dec. 13, 1893; buried Greenwood Cemetery.

WHITE, Allison, congressman, lawyer; b. Pine Twp., nr. Jersey Shore, Pa., Dec. 21, 1816; grad. Allegheny Coll., Meadville, Pa.; studied law. Admitted to bar, began practice of law, Lock Haven, Pa.; mem. U.S. Ho. of Reps. (Democrat) from Pa., 35th Congress, 1857-59; engaged in lumber and coal bus., Phila. Died Phila., Apr. 5, 1886; buried Highland Cemetery, Lock Haven.

WHITE, Andrew, missionary; b. London, Eng., 1579; attended St. Alban's Coll., France, St. Hermenegild's Coll., Seville, Spain. Ordained to priesthood Roman Catholic Ch., 1605; joined Soc. of Jesus, 1609; missionary to Suffolk and Devon, Eng., 1625-28, Hampshire, Eng., 1629-33; sailed for Am., 1633, arrived in Md., 1634; worked among colonists and Indians for whom he compiled grammar, dictionary and catechism in their native tongue, 1634-44; shipped to London (Eng.) in irons on charge treason against England, 1644, sentenced to banishment; served in Hampshire as secret missionary until 1656. Died London, Dec. 27, 1656.

WHITE, Bartow, congressman, physician; b. Yorktown, Westchester County, N.Y., Nov. 7, 1776; son of Dr. Ebenezer White; studied medicine with his father. Began practice of medicine, Fishkill, N.Y., 1800; mem. U.S. Ho. of Reps. from N.Y., 19th Congress, 1825-27; Whig presdl. elector, 1840. Died Fishkill, Dec. 12, 1862; buried Dutch Reformed Ch. Cemetery.

WHITE, Benjamin, congressman; b. Goshen (now Vienna), Me., May 13, 1790; attended common schs., Farmington Acad. Taught sch. for several years; helped raise troops, Augusta, Me., during War of 1812, also served with troops stationed at Castine and Eastport, Me.; taught sch., Montville, Me., until 1821; entered sawmill business and farming, 1821; town selectman; mem. Me. Ho. of Reps., 1829, 41-42; mem. U.S. Ho. of Reps. (Democrat) from Me., 28th Congress, 1843-45. Died Montville, June 7, 1860; buried Halldale Cemetery, North Montville, Me.

WHITE, Campbell Patrick, congressman, businessman; b. Ireland, Nov. 30, 1787. Came to U.S., 1816, became a mcht., N.Y.C.; mem. U.S. Ho. of Reps. (Jackson Democrat) from N.Y., 21st-24th congresses, 1829-35 (resigned before convening of 24th Congress); apptd. q.m. gen. N.Y. Militia, 1831; del. N.Y. State Constl. Conv., 1845. Died N.Y.C., Feb. 12, 1859; buried St. Paul's Cemetery.

WHITE, Canvass, civil engr.; b. Whitesboro, N.Y., Sept. 8, 1790; s. Hugh and Tryphena (Lawrence) W.; m. Louisa Loomis, 1821, 3 children. Shipped as supercargo on mcht. vessel for Russia, 1811; returned, 1814, served as enlisted man during War of 1812; made extended trip to examine canal constrn. in Gt. Britain, 1817; patented waterproof cement, 1820; worked on Eastern sect. Erie Canal, 1816-25, supr. Glens Falls feeder; chief engr. Union Canal of Pa., 1825; cons. engr. Schuylkill Navigation Co., locks at Windsor (on Connecticut River), Farmington Canal; chief engr. Delaware & Raritan Canal (N.J.), Lehigh (Pa.) Canal. Died St. Augustine, Fla., Dec. 18, 1834.

WHITE, Charles Ignatius, clergyman, editor; b. Balt., Feb. 1, 1807; s. John and Nancy (Coombs) W.; attended Mt. St. Mary's Coll., Emmitsburg, Md.; studied theology St. Sulpice, Paris, France; S.T.D., St. Mary's Sem., Balt. 1848. Ordained priest Roman Catholic Ch., 1830; curate at Fells Point, Md., 1830-33; asst., rector Cathedral of Balt., 1833-43; editor, founder Religious Cabinet, 1842-48; prof. moral theology St. Mary's Sem., 1843-45; pastor St. Vincent de Paul's Ch., Balt., 1845-49, church at Pikesville, Md., 1849-57; founder, editor Catholic Mirror, archdiocesian newspaper of Balt., 1849-55; editor Metropolitan Mag. 1853; rector St. Matthew's Ch., Washington, D.C., 1857-78; a founder St. Anne's Infant Asylum and St. Matthew's Inst., Washington. Died Apr. 1, 1878.

WHITE, David, congressman, lawyer; b. 1785; studied law. Admitted to bar, began practice of law, New Castle, Ky.; mem. Ky. Ho. of Reps., 1826; mem. U.S. Ho. of Reps. from Ky., 18th Congress, 1823-25. Died Franklin County, Ky., Oct. 19, 1834.

WHITE, Edward Brickell, architect; born 1806. Became well-known architect in S.C., mid-19th century. Works include: Centenary Methodist Ch., 1842; Ch. of the Huguenots (Gothic Revival design), 1845; Grace Episcopl Ch., 1847; addition of wings to old Citadel; probably designed St. John's Lutheran, Trinity Episcopal chs. (all Charleston, S.C.). Died 1882.

WHITE, Edward Douglass, congressman; b. Maury County, Tenn., Mar. 1795; s. James and Mary (Wilcox) W.; grad. U. Nashville (Tenn.), 1845; studied law office of Alexander Porter; m. Catherine Ringgold, 5 children. Practiced law, Donaldsonville, Tenn. before 1825; asso. judge New Orleans City Ct., 1825-28; mem. U.S. Ho. of Reps. from La., 21st-23d, 26th-27th congresses, 1829-34, 1839-43, opposed Pres. Andrew Jackson in Congress; gov. La., 1835-39; practiced law, Thibodaux, La., 1843-47. Died New Orleans, Apr. 18, 1847; buried St. Joseph's Catholic Cemetery, Thibodaux.

WHITE EYES, Indian chief. Became chief sachem of Delaware tribe of Indians who lived in Ohio, 1776; led his tribe's peaceful acceptance of White man; led people to neutrality in Dunmore's War, 1774, resulted in complete defeat of Shawnee Indians; committed his tribe to Am. cause at Treaty of Ft. Pitt, 1775; deceived into signing treaty of alliance with Am. confedn., 1778; led Gen. Lachlin McIntosh's troops in unsuccessful attempt to capture Detroit from British, 1778. Murdered by Am. soldiers in this attack, 1778.

WHITE, Francis, congressman; b. nr. Winchester, Va.; attended common schs., Winchester. Engaged in farming; mem. Va. Ho. of Dels., 1794, 1809-13, 1818; mem. U.S. Ho. of Reps. from Va., 13th Congress, 1813-15; mem. Va. Senate, 1823-24; apptd. sheriff of Hampshire County, Va. (now W. Va.), 1823. Died Hampshire County, Nov. 1826.

WHITE, George, clergyman, historian; b. Charleston, S.C., Mar. 12, 1802; m. Elizabeth Millen, 8 children. Licensed to preach in Methodist Ch., 1820; lived in Savannah, Ga., 1823-49, established acad. for boys; in charge of publically-owned Chatham Acad., Savannah, 1826-27; clergyman Protestant Episcopal Ch., Savannah, 1833-39, engaged in missionary work along Ga. coast; helped organize Ga. Hist. Soc., 1839; resided in Marietta, Ga., 1849-54; missionary to La Grange and West Point, Ga., 1854-56; rector Trinity Ch., Florence, Ala., 1856-58, Calvary Ch., Memphis, Tenn., 1858-85. Author: Statistics of the State of Georgia, 1849; An Accurate Account of the Yazoo Travel Compiled from Offical Documents, 1852; Historical Collectons of Georgia, 1854. Died Apr. 30, 1887.

WHITE, George Leonard, musician, educator; b. Cadiz, N.Y., Sept. 20, 1838; s. William B. and Nancy (Leonard) W.; m. Laura Amelia Cravath, Aug. 11, 1867; m. 2d, Susan Gilbert, Apr. 12, 1876; 3 children. Choir leader in Ohio, 1858; joined "Squirrel Hunters" to defend Cincinnati at battles of Chancellorsville and Gettysburg early in Civil War; with Freedmen's Bur., Nashville, Tenn., 1865-67; instr. vocal music Fisk U., Nashville, 1867, subsequently trustee, treas., led student concert tour to raise money for Fisk, 1871; took larger choir to World Peace Jubilee, Boston, 1872; sailed for England to tour Gt. Britain, 1873; raised more than $90,000 for Fisk U.; taught music State Normal Sch., Fredonia, N.Y., 1885, Biddle (later Johnson C. Smith) U., N.C., 1886-87; connected with Sage Coll., Cornell U., 1893-95. Died Ithaca, N.Y., Nov. 8, 1895.

WHITE, George W., artist; b. Oxford, O., Nov. 8, 1826. Travelled with minstrel show, several years; worked as painter, Cincinnati, 1847-57; painted 2 views of Powers' statue The Greek Slave (1st successful work), 1848; moved to Hamilton, Ohio, 1857. Died Hamilton, 1890.

WHITE, Henry, mcht., Loyalist; b. Md., Mar. 28, 1732; m. Eva Van Cortlandt, May 13, 1761. Developed larger merc. holdings, N.Y.C., 1758-69; mem. N.Y. City Council, 1769-76; gov. King's Coll. (now Columbia); a founder Marine Soc. of N.Y.; joined with N.Y. mchts. in opposing Stamp and Townshend acts, 1766; a founder, pres. N.Y.C. C. of C., 1772-73; a consignee of East India Co., 1773; went to Eng., 1775, returned when British occupied N.Y.C., 1776; property in N.Y.C. confiscated under the Act of Attainder, 1779; lived in London, Eng., 1779-86. Died London, Dec. 23, 1786.

WHITE, Henry, clergyman; b. Durham, N.Y., June 19, 1800; grad. Union Coll., 1824; studied theology Princeton Sem. Licensed to preach by Columbia Presbytery, 1826; agt. for Am. Bible Soc. in South, 1826-28; pastor Allen Street Ch., N.Y.C., 1828-50; a founder Union Theol. Sem., prof. systematic theology, 1836-50. Died N.Y.C., Aug. 25, 1850.

WHITE, Hugh, congressman; b. Whitestown, N.Y., Dec. 25, 1798; grad. Hamilton Coll., Clinton, N.Y., 1823; studied law. Became businessman, Chittenango, N.Y., 1825, later in Roundout, N.Y.; involved in bldg. Mich. So. & No. Ind. R.R.; moved to Cohoes, N.Y., 1830; interested in devel. of water power from Mohawk River; organizer Rosendale Cement Works; mem. U.S. Ho. of Reps. (Republican) from N.Y., 29th-31st congresses, 1845-51. Died Waterford, N.Y., Oct. 6, 1870; buried Albany Rural Cemetery.

WHITE, Hugh Lawson, senator; b. Iredell County, N.C., Oct. 30, 1773; s. James and Mary (Lawson) W.; studied law in Lancaster, Pa. under James Hopkins, 1795; m. Elizabeth Moore Carrick, 1798; m. 2d, Mrs. Ann E. Peyton, Nov. 30, 1832; 12 children. Pvt. sec. to Gov. William Blount of Tenn., 1793-94; participated in expdn. against Cherokee Indians under Gen. John Sevier, killed Chief Kingfisher; judge Superior Ct. of Tenn., 1801-07; mem. Tenn. Senate, 1807-09; 17-25; dist. atty. for Eastern Tenn., 1808-09; judge Tenn. Supreme Ct., 1809-15; pres. Tenn. State Bank, 1812-27; mem. U.S. Senate from Tenn. Oct. 28, 1825-40; pres. pro tem., 1832-33; received electoral votes of Ga. and Tenn. for Pres. U.S., 1836. Died Knoxville, Tenn., Apr. 10, 1840; buried First Presbyn. Ch. Cemetery, Knoxville.

WHITE, James, army officer, pioneer, legislator; b. Rowan County, N.C., 1747; s. Moses and Mary (McConnell) W.; m. Mary Lawson, Apr. 14, 1770, 7 children, including Hugh Lawson. Served as capt. N.C. Militia, 1779-81; began an exploration on French, Broad, Holston rivers, 1783; settled present site of Knoxville, Tenn., 1786; mem. N.C. Ho. of Commons from Hawkins County, 1789; justice of peace, 1790; maj. N.C., Militia, 1790; mem. Tenn. Constl. Conv., 1796; commd. brig. gen. Tenn. Militia, circa 1798; elected to Tenn. Senate from Knox County, 1796, presiding officer, 1801, 03; donor site for Blount Coll. (now U. Tenn.), trustee, 1794. Died Knoxville, Aug. 14, 1821; buried 1st Presbyn. Ch., Knoxville.

WHITE, James, Continental congressman; b. Phila., June 16, 1749; attended a Jesuit coll., St. Omer, France; studied medicine U. Pa.; studied law; children include Edward Douglass. Moved to Davidson County, N.C.; mem. N.C. Gen. Assembly, 1785; mem. Continental Congress from N.C., 1786-88; supt. Indian affairs for So. Dist., 1786; mem. 1st Territorial Legislature from Davidson County, 1794; del. U.S. Congress from Territory South of Ohio River (now Tenn.), 1794-96; moved to La., 1799; apptd. judge Attakapas (La.), Dist. 1804; later judge St. Martin Parish (La.). Died Attakapas, Oct. 1809.

WHITE, James Bain, congressman; b. Stirlinghsire, Scotland, June 26, 1835; attended common schs. Came to U.S., 1854, settled in Ft. Wayne, Ind.; engaged as calico printer and tailor; served as capt. Co. I, 13th Regt., Ind. Volunteers during Civil War, 1862; wounded in Battle of Shiloh; elected mem. Ft. Wayne Common Council, 1874; operated a dept. store; engaged in wheel mfg., banking; mem. U.S. Ho. of Reps. (Republican) from Ind., 50th Congress, 1887-89; del. Rep. Nat. Conv., Mpls., 1892; commr. World's Columbian Expn., Chgo., 1893. Died Ft. Wayne, Oct. 9, 1897; buried Linwood Cemetery, Ft. Wayne.

WHITE, John, colonial gov., painter; b. Eng.; flourished 1585-93 (as an artist); at least 1 child, Ellinor (White) Dare (mother of Virginia Dare). Commd. by Sir Walter Raleigh to go to Roanoke Island, N.C. to paint pictures which would stimulate interest of Europeans in New World, 1585, sent by Raleigh as gov. Roanoke Colony; fought in war with Spain (1589-90) which delayed his return to colony of Roanoke until 1591 when he found colony had disappeared. Probably died in Eng.

WHITE, John, clergyman, colonizer; b. Stanton, Oxfordshire, Eng., 1575; grad. Oxford (Eng.) U. Rector, Holy Trinity Ch., Dorchester, Eng., 1606-48; formed joint stock assn. called Dorchester Adventurers to establish colony in Mass., 1623; purchased Cape Ann, sent 14 colonists there, 1623 (these colonists later established Naumkeag now Salem, Mass.); sent 140 Puritans to Am., 1630 (founded Mattapan, now Dorchester, Mass.). Died Dorchester, Eng., Aug. 1, 1648.

WHITE, John, congressman; b. nr. Cumberland Gap (now Middlesboro), Ky., Feb. 14, 1802; studied law. Admitted to Ky. bar, began practice in Richmond; mem. Ky. Ho. of Reps., 1832; mem. U.S. Ho. of Reps. (Whig) from Ky., 24th-28th congresses, 1835-45, speaker, 1841-43; judge 19th Ky. Jud. Dist., 1845. Died Richmond, Sept. 22, 1845; buried State Cemetery, Frankfort, Ky.

WHITE, John Blake, artist, dramatist; b. Eutaw Springs, S.C., Sept. 2, 1781; s. Blake Leay and Elizabeth (Bourquin) W.; m. Elizabeth Allston, Mar. 28, 1805; m. 2d, Ann Rachel O'Driscoll, Oct. 2, 1819; 11 children including Edward Brickell. Admitted to S.C. bar, 1808; painted several hist. pictures and portraits, 1804-40, including Battle of Ft. Moultrie (now in Capitol, Washington, D.C.), 2 pictures engraved for 10 and 5 dollar banknotes issued by S.C., 1861; most important portraits include: John C. Calhoun, Charles C. Pinckney, Gov. Henry Middleton; received gold medal from S.C.

Inst. for best hist. paintings, 1840, also from Apollo Assn., N.Y.C.; founded Literary Lyceum of S.C.; author plays produced mainly in Charleston, including Toscari, or the Venetian Exile, 1806, Modern Honor, 1812. Died Charleston, Aug. 24, 1859.

WHITE, John DeHaven, dentist; b. New Holland, Pa., Aug. 19, 1815; s. John and Sarah (DeHaven) W.; studied medicine and dentistry, 1836, grad. Jefferson Med. Coll., 1844; m. Mary Elizabeth Meredith, 1836, 11 children. Carpenter's apprentice, 1833-36; practiced dentistry, Phila., 1837-93; an organizer Pa. Assn. Dental Surgeons, 1845, pres., 1857; mem. Am. Soc. Dental Surgeons, 1850; an organizer Phila. Coll. Dental Surgery, 1852, prof. anatomy and physiology, 1854-56; editor-in-chief Dental News Letter, 1853-59; an editor Dental Cosmos, 1859-65; v.p. Am. Dental Conv., 1861. Author: Mary Blaine and Hazel Dell and Miscellaneous Poems, (volume of poetry) 1870. Died Masonic Home, Phila., Dec. 25, 1895.

WHITE, Joseph Livingston, congressman; b. Cherry Valley, N.Y.; studied law, Utica, N.Y. Admitted to the bar; began practice of law, Madison, Ind.; mem. U.S. Ho. of Reps. (Whig) from Ind., 27th Congress, 1841-43; moved to N.Y.C., practiced law; Whig presdl. elector, 1844; shot while on a bus. trip to Nicaragua, Jan. 5, 1861. Died Corinto, Nicaragua, Jan. 12, 1861; buried Corinto.

WHITE, Joseph M., congressman; b. Franklin County, Ky., May 10, 1781; studied law. Admitted to the bar, practiced law; moved to Pensacola, Fla., 1821; a commr. for ascertaining claim to Territory of Fla., 1822; del. U.S. Congress from Fla. Territory, 1825-37. Author: New Collection of Laws, Charters, etc., of Great Britain, France, and Spain Relating to Cessions of Lands with the Laws of Mexico, 2 vols., 1839. Died St. Louis, Oct. 19, 1839.

WHITE, Joseph Worthington, congressman; b. Cambridge, O., Oct. 2, 1822; attended Cambridge Acad.; studied law. Admitted to Ohio bar, 1844, began practice in Cambridge; pros. atty. Guernsey County (O.), 1845-47; mayor of Cambridge; del. Democratic Nat. Conv., Balt., 1860; mem. U.S. Ho. of Reps. (Dem.) from Ohio, 38th Congress, 1863-65; Died Cambridge, Aug. 6, 1892; buried South Cemetery, Cambridge.

WHITE, Leonard, congressman; b. Haverhill, Mass., May 3, 1767; grad. Harvard, 1787. Mem. Mass. Ho. of Reps., 1809; held local offices; mem. U.S. Ho. of Reps. (Democrat) from Mass., 12th Congress, 1811-13; town clk. Haverhill; cashier Merrimack Bank of Haverhill, 1814-36; Died Haverhill, Oct. 10, 1849; buried Pentucket Cemetery, Haverhill.

WHITE, Phillips, Continental congressman; b. Haverhill, Mass., Oct. 28, 1729; attended Harvard. Served at Lake George during French and Indian War, 1755; moved to N.H.; mem. N.H. Ho. of Reps., 1775-82, speaker, 1775, 82; probate judge Rockingham County (N.H.), 1776-90; mem. Continental Congress from N.H., 1782-83; mem. N.H. Council, 1792-94. Died South Hampton, N.H., June 24, 1811; buried Old Cemetery, South Hampton.

WHITE, Phineas, congressman; b. South Hadley, Mass., Oct. 30, 1770; grad. Dartmouth, 1797; studied law. Admitted to the bar, 1800, began practice in Pomfret, Vt.; register of probate for Windsor County (Vt.), 1800-09; county atty., 1813; judge of Windham County (Vt.), 1814, 15, 17, 20; judge of probate for Westminster (Vt.) Dist., 1814-15; mem. Vt. Constl. convs., 1814-36; mem. Vt. Ho. of Reps., 1815-20; mem. U.S. Ho. of Reps. (Democrat) from Vt., 17th Congress, 1821-23; mem. Vt. Senate, 1836-37; trustee Middlebury Coll. Died Putney, Vt., July 6, 1847; buried Maple Grove Cemetery, Putney.

WHITE, Richard Grant, critic, author; b. N.Y.C., May 23, 1821; s. Richard Mansfield and Ann Eliza (Tousey) W.; grad. U. City of N.Y., 1839; m. Alexina Black Mease, Oct. 16, 1850, at least 2 children, Richard, Stanford. Admitted to N.Y. bar, 1845; helped edit Yankee Doodle (short-lived humorous paper), 1846; began writing for American Mag., 1853; musical critic with James Watson Webb's Morning Courier and New York Enquirer until 1859; with N.Y. World, 1860; chief clk. Marine Bur. of N.Y. Custom House, 1861-78; contbr. to periodicals Putnam's Mag., Galaxy, Atlantic Monthly; works include: Handbook of Christian Art, 1853; The Works of William Shakespeare, 12 vols., 1857-66; The New Gospel of Peace, 4 vols., 1863-66; Words and Their Uses Every-day English, 1880; England Without and Within, 1881; Studies in Shakespeare, 1886. Died N.Y.C., Apr. 8, 1885.

WHITE, Samuel, senator; b. Maspillion Hundred, Kent County, Del., Dec. 1770; s. Thomas and Margaret (Nutter) W.; attended Cokesbury Coll., Hartford County, Md.; never married. Admitted to Del. bar, 1793; commd. capt. and raised a company, 1799; practiced in Dover, Del.; presdl. elector, 1800; mem. U.S. Senate (Federalist) from Del., Feb. 28, 1801-09, opposed Apportionment Bill of 1802, La. Purchase and adoption of 12th Constl. Amendment; adj. gen. Del. Militia, 1807. Died Wilmington, Del., Nov. 4, 1809; buried Old Swedes Churchyard, Wilmington.

WHITE, Samuel Stockton, dentist; b. Hulmeville, Bucks County, Pa., June 19, 1822; s. William Rose and Mary (Stockton) W.; m. Sarah Jane Carey, Mar. 31, 1846, 7 children. Began practice of dentistry, 1843; began mfg. artificial teeth with firm Jones and White, Phila., circa 1845, branches established, N.Y.C., 1846, Boston, 1850, Chgo., 1858, largest co. in world for prodn. of porcelain teeth, for 75 years, also manufactured instruments, appliances, supplies for dentists, introduced new improved dental chairs, engines, appliances, instruments, materials for dental offices and laboratories; mem. Pa. Assn. Dental Surgeons; mem. exec. com. Am. Dental Conv., 1868. Died Paris, France, Dec. 30, 1879.

WHITE, Thomas Willis, printer, publisher; b. Williamsburg, Va., Mar. 28, 1788; s. Thomas and Sarah (Davis) W.; m. Dec. 12, 1809, several daus., at least 1 son. Apprenticed to printers of Virginia Federalist, Rind and Stuart, 1799, moved with paper to Washington, D.C., 1800-07; worked for 2 Richmond (Va.) papers (one owned by uncle A. Davis, other by Samuel Pleasants), 1808-08; compositor Norfolk Gazette and Publick Ledger, 1808-10; compositor, Phila., 1810-12, Boston, 1812-17; moved permanently to Richmond, 1817; founder editor, publisher So. Lit. Messenger, 1834. Died Richmond, Jan. 19, 1843; buried 1st Presbyn. Ch., Richmond.

WHITE, William, clergyman; b. Phila., Apr. 4, 1748; s. Col. Thomas and Esther (Hewlings) W.; grad. Coll. of Phila., 1765, D.D. (hon.), 1783; m. Mary Harrison, Feb. 1773, 8 children. Ordained deacon Protestant Episcopal Ch., London, 1770, priest, 1772; asst. minister Christ Ch., Phila., 1772-79, rector, 1779-1836; chaplain of Congress; an organizer Protestant Episcopal Ch. in U.S., adopted 1785, revised, 1789; 1st Protestant Episcopal bishop of diocese of Pa., 1787-1836; active in promotion of Sunday Sch. Author: Christian Baptism, 1808; Lectures on the Catechism, 1813; Comparative Views of the Controversy between the Calvinists and the Arminians, 2 vols., 1817; Memoirs of the Protestant Episcopal Church in the United States of America, 1820; Commentary on Clerical Duties, 1833. Died Phila., July 17, 1836; buried Christ Church, Phila.

WHITE, William Nathaniel, horticulturist, editor; b. Longridge, Conn., Nov. 28, 1819; s. Anson and Anna (Fitch) W.; grad. Hamilton Coll., N.Y., 1847; m. Rebecca Benedict, Aug. 28, 1848, 9 children. Moved to Terminus (now Atlanta), Ga. for health reasons, 1847, taught 30 pupils there; mgr. bookstore owned by W. C. Richards, Athens, Ga., 1848, owner, operator, 1849-67; became expert in horticulture and pomology; wrote for Atlanta Luminary Horticulturist, Gardener's Monthly; asst. editor newspaper Southern Cultivator, 1862, assumed full control, 1863, maintained paper throughout Civil War; mem. 9th Regt., Ga. State Guards, 1863-64. Author: Gardening for the South, 1856. Died July 14, 1867.

WHITEFIELD, Edwin, artist; b. 1816. Came to U.S., circa 1840; painted views of Hudson Valley estates, 1841-42; worked in N.Y.C., 1844; illustrated American Wild Flowers in Their Native Haunts (Emma C. Embury), 1845; published series of views under title North American Scenery, 1847; made several trips to Minn. to promote his real estate interests, 1856-59; painted several watercolor landscapes now in Minn. Hist. Soc.; lived in Boston and Reading, Mass., during 1880's, published The Homes of Our Forefathers (showed early New Eng. houses), 3 vols.; planned trip to Eng. to promote English settlement in Minn. Died 1892.

WHITEFIELD, George, evangelist; b. Gloucester, Eng., Dec. 28, 1715; s. Thomas and Elizabeth (Edwards) W.; grad. Oxford (Eng.) U., 1736; A.M. (hon.), Coll. of N.J. (now Princeton), 1754; m. Elizabeth (Burnell) James, Nov. 14, 1741, 1 child. Ordained deacon Anglican Ch., 1736, priest, 1739; preached extensively in Eng. before 1737, drew great crowds of people; came to Savannah; Ga., 1737; preached in Savannah and area; returned to Eng. to raise funds for orphanage in Ga., 1738; found most English churches were closed to him due to opposition, preached in open air; returned to Am., 1739, became interant preacher from Ga. to Mass.; when he was refused a pulpit in Phila., Benjamin Franklin led group to build non-denominational ch. for him; received 500 acres from Ga. colony to build Bethesda Orphanage, supported by colonial funds; preached all along New Eng. coast, 1740-41, produced "Great Awakening" in Christianity; engaged in bitter controversy with John Wesley over Calvinistic principles, in Eng., 1741-44; preached with great success in New Eng., 1744-48; became domestic chaplain to Countess of Huntingdon (Eng.), 1748; made 4 more visits to Am. 1751-52, 54-55, 63-64, 69-70; his Am. trips resulted in numerous conversions to Calvinism and weakening of established ch. in South; published number of sermons, pamphlets and letters. Author: The Nature and Necessity of Our New Birth in Christ Jesus in Order to Salvation, 1737; A Journal of A Voyage from London to Savannah in Georgia, 1738; Short Account of God's Dealing with the Reverend Mr. Whitefield, 1746; The Two First Parts of His Life, with His Journals Revised, Corrected and Abridged, 1756. Died Newburyport, Mass., Sept. 30, 1770; buried First (South) Presbyn. Ch., Newburyport.

WHITEHEAD, William Adee, historian; b. Newark, N.J., Feb. 19, 1810; s. William and Abby (Coe) W.; m. Margaret Elizabeth Parker, Aug. 11, 1834, at least 2 sons, 1 dau. Surveyed boundary lines of Key West Island (partly owned by brother John), 1828; returned to N.J.; made trip to Havana, Cuba, 1829; apptd. collector Port of Key West, 1831; later became maj. of militia, organized 1st church, established newspaper; in various businesses, N.Y.C., 1838-48; began keeping daily weather reports, 1843; a founder N.J. Hist. Soc., 1845, corr. sec., 1845-84; sec. N.H. R.R. & Transp. Co., 1848, 59-71; mem. Newark Bd. Edn., 1861-71; trustee N.J. State Normal Sch., 1862-84; concerned solely with history and literary work, 1879-84. Author: East Jersey under the Proprietary Governments, 1846; The Papers of Lewis Morris, Governor of New Jersey, 1852; Documents Relating to the Colonial History of the State of New Jersey, 8 vols., 1880-85; contbr. over 600 articles to various newspapers. Died Aug. 8, 1884.

WHITEHILL, James, congressman; b. Strasburg, Pa., Jan. 31, 1762; s. John Whitehill; studied law. Admitted to Pa. bar, began practice in Strasburg; asso. judge Lancaster County (Pa.) Ct., 1811-13, 20-22; served as maj. gen. Pa. Militia during War of 1812; mem. U.S. Ho. of Reps. from Pa., 13th Congress, 1813-Sept. 1, 1814 (resigned); engaged in merc. bus., Strasburg; burgess of Strasburg, 1816. Died Strasburg, Feb. 26, 1822; buried Presbyn. Ch. Cemetery, Leacock, Pa.

WHITEHILL, John, congressman; b. Salisbury Twp., Lancaster County, Pa., Dec. 11, 1729; studied law; children include James. Admitted to Pa. bar, began practice in Lancaster County; apptd. justice of peace, justice Lancaster County Orphans' Ct., 1777; mem. Pa. Ho. of Reps., 1780-82, 93; mem. Pa. Council of Censors, 1783; del. Pa. Supreme Exec. Council, 1784; mem. Pa. Conv. which ratified U.S. Constn., 1785; asso. judge Lancaster County, 1791; mem. U.S. Ho. of Reps. from Pa., 8th-9th congresses, 1803-07. Died Salisbury Twp., Sept. 16, 1815; buried Pequea Presbyn. Ch. Cemetery, Salisbury Twp.

WHITEHILL, Robert, congressman; b. Lancaster County, Pa., July 21, 1738; s. James and Rachel (Cresswell) W.; m. Eleanor Reed, 1765. Mem. Pa. Conv. that approved Declaration of Independence, 1776; mem. Pa. Assembly, 1776-78, 84-87, 97-1801; mem. Pa. Council of Safety, 1777; mem. Pa. Supreme Exec. Council, 1779-81; mem. Pa. Conv. to ratify U.S. Constn., 1787; del. to Pa. Constl. Conv., 1790; mem. Pa. Senate, 1801-05, speaker, 1804; mem. U.S. Ho. of Reps. from Pa., 9th-13th congresses, 1805-13. Died Cumberland County, Pa., Apr. 7, 1813; buried Silver Spring Presbyn. Ch. Cemetery, Hampden Twp., Pa.

WHITEHOUSE, John Osborne, congressman; b. Rochester, N.H., July 19, 1817; ed. common schs. Moved to N.Y.C., 1835, retail clk., until 1839; moved to Bklyn., 1839, engaged as mcht. and shoe mfr.; moved to Poughkeepsie, N.Y., 1860, engaged as shoe mfr.; mem. U.S. Ho. of Reps. (Liberal Democrat) from N.Y., 43d-44th congresses, 1873-77; engaged in banking, railroad promotion; owner Daily News, Poughkeepsie, 1872-80. Died Poughkeepsie, Aug. 24, 1881; buried Greenwood Cemetery, Bklyn.

WHITELEY, Richard Henry, congressman; b. County Kildare, Ireland, Dec. 22, 1830; ed. privately; studied law. Came to U.S., 1836; engaged in mfg., Ga.; admitted to Ga. bar, 1860, began practice in Bainbridge; opposed secession; entered Confederate Army after adoption of secession ordinance, served to maj. during Civil War; mem. Ga. Constl. Conv., 1867; mem. U.S. Ho. of Reps. (Republican) from Ga., 41st-43d congresses, Dec. 22, 1870-75; resumed law practice, Boulder, Colo., 1877. Died Boulder, Sept. 26, 1890; buried Masonic Cemetery, Boulder.

WHITELEY, William Gustavus, congressman; b. nr. Newark, Del., Aug. 7, 1819; grad. Princeton, 1838; studied law. Admitted to Del. bar, 1841, began practice in Wilmington; prothonotary of New Castle County (Del.), 1852-56, 62-67; mem. U.S. Ho. of Reps. (Democrat) from Del., 35th-36th congresses, 1857-61; mayor of Wilmington, 1875-78; mem. commn. to settle fishery disputes between N.J. and Del., 1877; census enumerator for Del.,

1880; asso. judge Superior Ct. of Del., 1884-86. Died Wilmington, Apr. 23, 1886; buried Bridgeton (N.J.) Cemetery.

WHITESIDE, Jenkin, senator; b. Lancaster, Pa., 1772; studied law. Admitted to Pa. bar; moved to Tenn., began practice of law, Knoxville; a commr. of Knoxville, 1801-02; mem. U.S. Senate from Tenn., Apr. 11, 1809-Oct. 8, 1811. Died Nashville, Tenn., Sept. 25, 1822; buried (probably) Old Cemetery, Nashville.

WHITESIDE John, congressman; b. nr. Lancaster, Pa., 1773; attended Chestnut Level Acad. Employed on father's farm; engaged in hotel bus. operated a distillery; justice of peace; mem. Pa. Ho. of Reps., 1810-11, 25; mem. U.S. Ho. of Reps. (Democrat) from Pa., 14th-15th congresses, 1815-19; resumed hotel bus., Lancaster; register of wills. Died Lancaster, July 28, 1830; buried Lancaster Cemetery.

WHITFIELD, Henry, clergyman; b. London, Eng., 1597; s. Thomas and Mildred (Manning) W.; B.D., U. Cambridge (Eng.) 1631; m. Dorothy Sheaffe, 1618. Arrived in New Haven, Conn., 1639; founded (with 5 assos.) Town of Menunkatuck (Conn.), built up town, 1639-49; joined Soc. for Propogation of Gospel in New Eng., 1649; returned to Eng., 1650; pastor church, Winchester, Eng., 1650-57. Author: The Light Appearing More and More to the Perfect Day, 1651; Strength out of Weakness, 1652. Died Winchester, circa 1657.

WHITFIELD, James, clergyman; b. Liverpool, Eng., Nov. 3, 1770; attended Sulpician sem., Lyons, France. Ordained priest Roman Catholic Ch., 1809; came to U.S., served as pastor in Balt. (working especially among Negro population); apptd. titular bishop of Apollonia, coadjutor of Balt., 1828; consecrated archbishop of Balt., 1828; opened 1st, 2d provincial councils of Balt., 1829, 33. Died Balt., Oct. 19, 1834.

WHITFIELD, John Wilkins, congressman; b. Franklin, Tenn., Mar. 11, 1818; attended local schs. Served in Mexican War, 1846; Indian agt. to Pottawatomies, 1853, to Arkansas Indians, 1855-56; del. U.S. Congress from Territory of Kan., 1855-56, 56-57; register land office, Doniphan, Kan., 1857-61; commd. capt. 27th Tex. Cavalry, 1861, promoted maj., 1862; engaged in battles of Pea Ridge and Iuka, 1862; promoted col.; served in cavalry battle nr. Spring Hill, 1863; received several citations for bravery; commd. brig. gen., 1863; settled in Lavaca County, Tex., 1865; engaged in farming and stock raising; mem. Tex. Ho. of Reps. Died nr. Hallettsville, Tex., Oct. 27, 1879; buried Hallettsville Cemetery.

WHITING, Henry, army officer; b. Lancaster, Mass., Nov. 28, 1788; son of John Whiting. Joined U.S. Army, 1808, commd. 2d lt., 1809, 1st lt., 1811; served on staff of Gen. J. P. Boyd during War of 1812, participated in capture of Ft. George in Upper Canada, 1813; promoted capt., 1817; served with 1st Arty., 1821-35, Q.M. Corps, from 1835; chief q.m. army under Gen. Taylor during Mexican War, 1846-47; brevetted brig. gen. for conduct at Buena Vista, 1847. Author: Life of Zebulon Pike; contbr. to N.Am. Review. Editor: George Washington's Revolutionary Orders, 1846. Died St. Louis, Sept. 16, 1851; buried St. Louis.

WHITING, Richard Henry, congressman; b. West Hartford, Conn., Jan. 17, 1826; attended common schs. Moved to Altona, Ill., 1850, to Galesburg, Ill., 1860, built gas works; served as paymaster U.S. Volunteers during Civil War, 1862-66; assessor internal revenue for 5th Ill. Dist., 1870-73, collector internal revenue, 1873-75; mem. U.S. Ho. of Reps. (Republican) from Ill., 44th Congress, 1875-77; del. Rep. Nat. Conv., Chgo., 1884. Died N.Y.C., May 24, 1888; buried Springdale Cemetery, Peoria, Ill.

WHITING, Samuel, clergyman; b. Boston, Lincolnshire, Eng., Nov. 20, 1597; grad. Cambridge (Eng.) U., 1616; married twice; m. 2d, dau of Oliver St. John; at least 2 children. Ofcl. minister Ch. of Eng. for Lynn and Skirbeck (Eng.), 1616-36; fled Eng. to escape prosecution by Archbishop Laud, came to Am., 1636; 1st minister Congregational Ch., of Lynn, Mass., 1636-79. Author: Oratio (in Latin), 1649; Last Judgment, 1664; Abraham Interceding, 1666. Died Lynn, Dec. 11, 1679.

WHITING, William, lawyer; b. Concord, Mass., Mar. 3, 1813; s. William and Hannah (Conant) W.; A.B., Harvard, 1833, LL.B., 1838; LL.D: (hon.), Colby U., 1872; m. Lydia Cushing Russell, Oct. 28, 1840; children—Rose Standish, William St. John, William Russell, Harold. Admitted to Mass. bar, 1838; expert in patent law; pres. New Eng. Hist. and Geneal. Soc., 1853-58; spl. counselor U.S. War Dept., 1862, solicitor, 1863-65; presdl. elector, 1868; elected to U.S. Ho. of Reps. (Republican) from Mass., 1872, died before taking seat. Author: (book) War Powers Under the Constitution of the United States, 1864; (pamphlet) Military Arrests in Time of War, 1869. Died Roxbury, Mass., June 29, 1873; buried Sleepy Hollow Cemetery, Concord.

WHITING, William Henry Chase, army officer; b. Biloxi, Miss., Mar. 22, 1824; s. Levi and Mary Whiting; grad. Georgetown Coll., Washington, D.C. 1840; grad. U.S. Mil. Acad., 1845; m. Kate D. Walker. Apptd. 2d lt. U.S. Corps Engrs., 1845; supervised constrn. river and harbor improvements in North, also fortifications in Cal., 1845-61; worked on constrn. projects on Cape Fear River, N.C.:, 1856-57; resigned from U.S. Army to join Confederate Army, 1861; planned defenses for Charleston (S.C.) harbor and Morris Island; commanded division which later joined Gen. Thomas J. Jackson's army in Shenandoah Valley, Va., 1862; mil. comdr. of Wilmington, N.C., 1862-64; apptd. maj. gen. Confedrate States Army, 1863; sent to take command at Petersburg, Va:, 1864; mortally wounded in defense of Ft. Fisher, N.C., 1865. Died Ft. Columbus, Governor's Island, N.Y., Mar. 10, 1865.

WHITLOCK, Eliza Kemble, actress; b. Eng., 1762. Brought to Am. by Thomas Wignell, 1793; appeared with Wignell's co., Chestnut Street Theatre, Phila., 1794; appeared at John Street Theatre, N.Y.C., 1797, (with husband) at Chestnut Street Theatre, 1801; appeared at Park Theatre, N.Y.C., 1803. Died 1836.

WHITMAN, Ezekiel, congressman; b. Bridgewater, Mass., Mar. 9, 1776; s. Josiah and Sa. (Sturtevant) W.; A:B., R.I. Coll. (now Brown U.), 1795; m. Hannah Mitchell, Oct. 31, 1799, 3 children. Admitted to bar, Plymouth County, Mass., 1799; mem. U.S. Ho. of Reps. from Mass., 11th Congress, 1809-11; mem. Mass. Exec. Council, 1815-16; mem. Brunswick Conv. which considered separation of Me. from Mass., 1816; mem. U.S. Ho. of Reps. from Me., 15th-17th congresses, 1817-21; mem. conv. which formed Me. Constn., 1819; judge Ct. of Common Pleas, Me., 1822-41; chief justice Me. Supreme Ct., 1841-48. Author: Memoir of John Whitman and His Descendants, 1832. Died East Bridgewater, Mass., Aug. 1, 1866; buried Portland, Me.

WHITMAN, Lemuel, congressman; b. Farmington, Conn., June 8, 1780; grad. Yale, 1800; grad. Litchfield (Conn.) Law Sch. Taught in a sem., Bermuda, 1801; admitted to Conn. bar, began practice in Farmington; apptd. judge superior ct., 1818; asso. judge Hartford County (Conn.) Ct., 1819-21, chief judge, 1821-23; mem. com. to prepare revision of statutes of State of Conn., 1821; mem. Conn. Senate, 1822; mem. U.S. Ho. of Reps. (Democrat) from Conn., 18th Congress, 1823-25; mem. Conn. Ho. of Reps., 1831-32. Died Farmington, Nov. 13, 1841.

WHITMAN, Marcus, physician, missionary; b. Rushville, N.Y., Sept. 4, 1802; s. Beza and Alice (Green) W.; M.D., Coll. Physicians and Surgeons of Western Dist. N.Y., 1832; m. Narcissa Prentiss, Feb. 1836; 1 dau. (1837-39). Practiced medicine; became missionary for joint Presbyn.-Congregational Bd., 1835; traveled west with missionary party including Henry and Eliza Spalding, 1836; party established 2 missions, at present sites of Lewiston, Ida., and Walla Walla, Wash. (then Waiilatpu, Ore.); pioneered portions of Ore. Trail from Ft. Boise, Ida. to Waiilatpu, 1836; taught Indians methods of farming by irrigation, value of domesticated cattle, better housing; disputes among Whitman and other missionaries led bd. to close one of missions; made 6-month cross-continental ride, 1842-43, to N.Y.C., Boston, and Washington, D.C. to convince the bd. of value of the missions, also to stimulate govt. and pvt. interest in Ore.; returned to Ore. with an emigrant party, 1843; killed with wife and 12 others in Cayuse Indian uprising, 1847. Died Ore., Nov. 29, 1847.

WHITMAN, Narcissa Prentiss, pioneer; b. 1808; d. Judge Prentiss; m. Marcus Whitman, Feb. 18, 1836; 1 dau. (1837-39). Traveled to Ore. with husband and party including Henry H. and Eliza Spalding, 1836; she and Mrs. Spalding 1st white women to cross N. Am. continent; worked with husband at Presbyn. mission, Waiilatpu, Ore. (nr. present site Walla Walla, Wash.), where they were killed in Cayuse Indian raid, 1847. Died Nov. 29, 1847

WHITMAN, Sarah Helen Power, poet; b. Providence, R.I., Jan. 19, 1803; d. Nicholas and Anna (Marsh) Power; m. John Winslow Whitman, July 10, 1828. Published 1st poem entitled Retrospection in Ladies' Mag., 1829; contbr. articles on spiritualism to N.Y. Tribune, 1851; 1st book of verse Hours of Life and Other Poems, published 1853; engaged to Edgar Allen Poe, 1848, subject of his 2d poem To Helen; Poe's Annabel Lee was a message to her; published book Edgar Poe and His Critics, 1860; a collection The Last Letters of Edgar Allen Poe to Sarah Helen Whitman, published 1909. Died Providence, June 27, 1878; buried North Burial Ground, Providence.

WHITMAN Walter (Walt), poet; b. West Hills, Huntington, L.I., N.Y., May 31, 1819; s. Walter and Louisa (Van Velsor) W.; schooling ended in his 11th or 13th year. Held various jobs such as office boy, printer's devil, sch. tchr., typesetter and journalist, 1830-46; worked for L.I. Democrat, 1839-40; associated with at least 10 newspapers and mags. including Aurora and Tattler, 1841-48; edited Bklyn. Eagle, 1846-48; went to New Orleans and wrote for Crescent, 1848; editor Freeman, Bklyn., 1848-49, helped father build houses, Blkyn., 1851-54; published Leaves of Grass, 1855, became somewhat more known but book unfavorably received by critics, constantly enlarged and revised in editions of 1856, 60, 67, 71, 76, 81, 82, 88-89, and last edition of 1891-92; editor Times, Bklyn., 1857-59; wrote articles on Bklyn. history for Standard, 1861-62; served as hosp. nurse, Washington, D.C., 1862-64; clk. Dept. of Interior, 1865, Office of Atty. Gen., 1865-73; wrote When Lilacs Last in the Dooryard Bloom'd as meml. tribute to Lincoln, 1865, printed as supplement to his Drum Taps; suffered paralytic stroke, 1873, forced into semi-retirement, friends helped him out financially, continued to write and lecture; wrote poems Two Rivulets, 1876 November Boughs, 1888. Good Bye My Fancy, 1891, Specimen Days and Collect, 1882-83, all from Civil War experiences; fame gradually grew in America, poetry well received in Europe, by 1868; also contributed valuable criticisms of other poets such as Poe, Longfellow and Whittier, other works include: Drum Taps, 1865; Memoranda During the War, 1875; Passage to India, 1871; Democratic Vistas, 1871; The Death of Abraham Lincoln; Sands at Seventy, 1888; As Strong as a Bird on Pinions Free, 1872. Died Camden, N.J., Mar. 26, 1892.

WHITMER, David, religious leader; b. Harrisburg, Pa., Jan. 7, 1805; s. Peter and Mary (Musselman) W.; m. Julia A. Jolly, 1830. Met by Joseph Smith, Mormon leader who claimed to have divine authority to reestablish Ch. of Christ, 1828; with Smith when he formally organized Mormon sect, 1830, followed him to Jefferson County, Mo., 1830; left for Clay County, Mo., 1833; pres. High Council of Zion established to watch over Mo. Mormons, 1834; excommunicated from Church (as result of many disagreements with Smith 1836-38), 1838; resided in Richmond, Mo., 1838-88; made unsuccessful attempts to organize Ch. of Christ (a Mormon sect), 1847, 67, Author: An Address to All Believers in Christ by a Witness to the Divine Authenticity to the Book of Mormon, 1887. Died Richmond, Ray County, Mo., Jan. 25, 1888.

WHITMORE, Elias, congressman; b. Pembroke, N.H., Mar. 2, 1772. Settled in Windsor, N.Y.; engaged in merc. bus.; mem. U.S. Ho. of Reps. (Democrat) from N.Y., 19th Congress, 1825-27. Died Windsor, Dec. 26, 1853; buried Village Cemetery, Windsor.

WHITMORE, George Washington, congressman; b. McMinn County, Tenn., Aug. 26, 1824; attended pub. schs.; studied law. Admitted to Tex. bar, 1848, practiced in Tyler; mem. Tex. Ho. of Reps., 1852-53, 58; dist. atty. 9th Tex. Jud. Dist., 1866; apptd. register in bankruptcy, 1867; mem. U.S. Ho. of Reps. (Republican) from Tex., 41st Congress, Mar. 30, 1870-71. Died Tyler, Oct. 14, 1876; buried Oakwood Cemetery, Tyler.

WHITNEY, Asa, inventor, mfr.; b. Townsend, Mass., Dec. 1, 1791; s. Asa and Mary (Wallis) W.; m. Clarinda Williams, Aug. 22, 1816, at least 5 children. Small scale mfr. of axles for horse-erecting machinery on inclined planes, Albany and Schenectady, N.Y., also bldg. railroad cars for Mohawk and Hudson R.R., 1830-39; canal commr. N.Y. State, 1838-42; obtained patent for locomotive steam engine, 1840, 2 patents for cast-iron car wheel with corrugated center web, and for method of manufacturing same, 1847; organized (with 3 sons) Asa Whitney & Sons, Phila., 1847; received patent for improved process of annealing and cooling cast iron wheels, 848; pres. Reading R.R., 1860-61; bequeathed $50,000 to U. Pa. to establish chair of dynamic engring., $12,500 to Franklin Inst., $20,000 to Old Men's Home, Died Phila., June 4, 1874.

WHITNEY, Asa, mcht., railroad pioneer, b. North Groton, Conn., Mar. 14, 1797; s. Shubail and Sarah (Mitchell) W.; m. Herminie Antoinette Pillet; m. 2d, Sarah Jay Munro, Nov. 3, 1835; m. 3d, Catherine (Moore) Campbell, Oct. 6, 1852. Departed for China as agt. for N.Y. firms and on own account, 1840, remained 15 months, accumulated great wealth; presented plan to U.S. Congress for transcontinental railroad as means for promoting trade with China, 1844; sought to interest English govt. in building railroad across Can., 1851. Author pamphlets: "A Project for a Railroad to the Pacific," 1849, "A Plan for a Direct Communication between the Great Centres of Populations of Europe and Asia, 1851." Died Washington, D.C., Sept. 17, 1877.

WHITNEY, Eli, inventor; b. Westboro, Mass., Dec. 8, 1765; s. Eli and Elizabeth (Fay) W.; grad. Yale, 1792; m. Henrietta Frances Edwards, Jan. 6, 1817, 3 children. Made and repaired violins, manufactured nails in father's shop, 1780-82; designed cotton gin on Mrs. Nathaneal Greene's plantation in Ga., with which one operator could clean 50 pounds of cotton daily, 1793; in partnership with Phineas

Miller to patent and manufacture cotton gins, 1793; received patent for cotton gin, 1794, failed to benefit because of infringements and long litigation; U.S. exports in 1795 were 40 times greater than before invention of cotton gin; received U.S. Govt. contract for 10,000 muskets to be delivered in 2 years, 1798; devised system of manufacturing interchangeable gun parts; purchased mill site for factory for firearms prodn., nr. New Haven, Conn., site now known as Whitneyville; built 1st successful milling machine. Died New Haven, Jan. 8, 1825.

WHITNEY, Josiah Dwight, geologist; b. Northampton, Mass., Nov. 23, 1819; s. Josiah Dwight and Sarah (Williston) W.; grad. Yale, 1839; m. Louisa (Goodard) Howe, June 1854, 1 dau. Read law, 1841; travelled and studied in France, Germany, Italy, 1842-45; worked survey of mineral lands of Northern peninsula of Mich., 1847-49; independent cons. expert in mining, 1849-54; Ia. State chemist and prof. mineralogy Ia. State U., 1855-58; mem. Ill. State Survey; geologist of Cal., 1860-74, began survey of state; promoted Cal. Acad. Science; commr. Yosemite; mem. Am. Philos. Soc., Nat. Acad. Sciences; apptd. to Harvard faculty, 1865, opened Harvard Sch. Mines, 1868, Sturgis-Hooper prof. geology, 1875-96; returned briefly to Cal. to continue survey; elected to Geol. Soc. London. Author: Metallic Wealth of the United States, 1854; The Auriferous Gravela of the Sierra Nevada of California, 1880; Climatic Changes of Later Geological Times, 1882; Names and Places, 1888. Died Lake Sunapee, N.H., Aug. 19, 1896.

WHITNEY, Thomas Richard, congressman; b. N.Y.C., May 2, 1807. Engaged in journalism; mem. N.Y. State Assembly, 1854-55; mem. U.S. Ho. of Reps. (Am. Party rep.) from N.Y., 34th Congress, 1855-57. Died N.Y.C., Apr. 12, 1858; buried Greenwood Cemetery, Bklyn.

WHITNEY, William Dwight, Sanskrit scholar; b. Northampton, Mass., Feb. 9, 1827; s. Josiah Dwight and Sarah (Williston) W.; grad. Williams Coll., 1845, LL.D. (hon.), 1861; attended Yale, 1849-50, Univs. Berlin and Tübingen (Germany), 1850-53; Ph.D., U. Breslau, 1861; LL.D. (hon.), Coll. William and Mary, 1869, Harvard, 1876, Columbia, 1886; J.U.D., St. Andrews Coll., 1874; m. Elizabeth Wooster Baldwin, Aug. 27, 1856, 3 sons, 3 daus. including Marian P. Clk. in father's bank, 1846-49; joined brother Josiah on Lake Superior Survey, 1849; mem. Am. Oriental Soc., 1850-94, librarian, 1855-73, editor publications, 1857-84, pres., 1884-92; prof. Sanskrit, Yale, 1854-94, Harvard, 1869-70; a founder, pres. Am. Philol. Assn., 1869. Author: Language and the Study of Language, 1867; Oriental and Linguistic Studies, 2 vols., 1873-74; The Life and Growth of Language, 1875; Sanskrit Grammar, 1879; The Roots, Verbforms, and Primary Derivations of the Sanskrit Language, 1885; translator (with R. Roth): Atharva Veda Sankita, 1856; Tāttirīya-Prāticākhya, 1871; editor-in-chief The Century Dictionary: An Encyclopedic Lexicon of the English Language, 6 vols., 1889-91. Died New Haven, Conn., June 7, 1894.

WHITTELSEY, Abigail Goodrich, editor; b. Ridgefield, Conn., Nov. 29, 1788; d. Rev. Samuel and Elizabeth (Ely) Goodrich; m. Rev. Samuel Whittelsey, Nov. 10, 1808, 7 children. Taught sch. in rural Conn.; lived in New Preston, Conn., 1808-18; moved to Hartford, Conn., 1818; matron Am. Sch. for Deaf, 1818-24; dir. (with husband) Ontario Female Sem., Canandaigua, N.Y., 1824-27; conducted another sem., Utica, N.Y., 1827-33; began editing Mother's Mag., Utica, moved mag. to N.Y.C., 1834, continued publ., 1834-46, 48-49; issued new periodical Mrs. Whittelsey's Mag. for Mothers, 1850-52. Died Colchester, Conn., July 16, 1858; buried Maple Cemetery, Berlin, Conn.

WHITTEMORE, Amos, inventor, mfr.; b. Cambridge, Mass., Apr. 19, 1759; s. Thomas and Anna (Cutter) W.; m. Helen Weston, June 18, 1781, at least 12 children. After public sch. edn. apprenticed to gunsmith; mfr. brushes for carding cotton and wool, 1795, supt. mech. equipment in 3 factories; received patents for machine which cut nails, loom for weaving duck, form of mech. ship's log, 1796; patented machine which eliminated all hand labor in making cotton and wool cards, 1797, attempted unsuccessfully to introduce new machine into England, 1799-1800; in partnership (with brother William and Robert Williams) to make card-making machines and cards themselves, 1800-12; renewed patent, 1808, sold patent rights and machinery to a N.Y.C. co., 1812, ret. Died West Cambridge (now Arlington), Mass., Mar. 27, 1828.

WHITTEMORE, Benjamin Franklin, congressman; b. Malden, Mass., May 18, 1824; attended pub. schs., Worcester, Mass.; studied theology. Engaged in merc. bus., until 1859; ordained to ministry Methodist Ch., 1859; served as chaplain 53d Regt., Mass., Volunteers, later with 30th Regt., Vet. Volunteers; settled in Darlington, S.C., after Civil War; del. S.C. Constl. Conv., 1867; founder New Era, Darlington; mem. S.C. Senate, 1868, 77, del. Republican Nat. Conv., Chgo., 1868; mem. U.S. Ho. of Reps. (Rep.) from S.C., 40th-41st congresses, July 18, 1868-Feb. 24, 1870 (resigned pending investigations of some of his appointments to U.S. mil. and naval acads.); returned to Mass., settled in Woburn, became publisher. Died Montvale, Mass., Jan. 25, 1894; buried Salem St. Cemetery, Woburn.

WHITTEMORE, Thomas, clergyman, editor, author, financier; b. Boston, Jan. 1, 1800; s. Joseph and Comfort (Quiner) W.; D.D. (hon.), Tufts Coll., 1858; m. Lovice Corbett, Sept. 17, 1821, at least 1 son. Ordained to ministry Universalist Ch., Milford, Mass., 1821; pastor, Cambridge, Mass., 1822-28; purchased (with Russell Steeter) semi-monthly Universalist Mag., 1828, issued it weekly under title Trumpet and Universalist Mag., sole owner and editor until 1861; composed and compiled hymn books; elected to Mass. Legislature, 1830; lectured on temperance, 1833-45; dir. bank, Cambridge, 1840, later pres.; pres. Vt. and Mass. R.R., 1849. Author: The Modern History of Universalism, 1830; Notes and Illustrations of the Parables of the New Testament, 1832; Songs of Zion, 1837; Commentaries on Revelation and Daniel, 1838; The Early Days of Thomas Whittemore, an Autobiography, 1839; The Gospel Harmonist, 1841; Conference Hymns, 1842-43; The Sunday School Choir, 1844; Life of Walter Balfour, 1853. Died Cambridge, Mar. 21, 1861.

WHITTHORNE, Washington Curran, senator, congressman; b. nr. Farmington, Tenn., Apr. 19, 1825; grad. U. Tenn., 1843; studied law. Admitted to Tenn. bar, 1845; auditor's clk., held other govtl. positions, 1845-48; began practice of law, Columbia, Tenn., 1848; mem. Tenn. Senate, 1855-58, mem. Tenn. Ho. of Reps., 1859, speaker, 1859; presdl. elector, 1860; asst. adj. gen. Provisional Army of Tenn., 1861; adj. gen. State of Tenn., Confederate Army, 1861-65; mem. U.S. Ho. of Reps. (Democrat) from Tenn., 42d-47th, 50th-51st congresses, 1871-83, 87-91; mem. U.S. Senate (Dem.) from Tenn., Apr. 16, 1886-87. Died Columbia, Sept. 21, 1891; buried Rose Hill Cemetery, Columbia.

WHITTIER, John Greenleaf, poet, abolitionist; b. Haverhill, Mass., Dec. 17, 1807; s. John and Abigail (Hussey) W. Published "The Exile's Departure," 1826; editor Am. Manufacturer, Boston, 1829, New Eng. Weekly Review, 1830-32; published Legends of New England in Prose and Verse (1st book), 1831; edited The Literary Remains of John G. C. Brainard, With a Sketch of His Life, 1832; wrote 15 poems on subjects connected with abolition, circa 1833-63; del. anti-slavery conv., Phila., 1833, signed its declaration; mem. Mass. Legislature from Haverhill, 1835; editor Pa. Freeman, 1838-40; Middlesex Standard, 1844-45; among 1st to suggest formation Republican Party; frequent contbr. Atlantic Monthly. Works include: Moll Pitcher, 1832; Lays of My Home and Other Poems, 1843; Voices of Freedom (anti-slavery poems), 1846; Old Portraits and Modern Sketches, 1850; Songs of Labor, 1850; The Chapel of the Hermits, 1853; Literary Recreations and Miscellanies, 1854; The Panorama and other Poems (contains "Maud Muller," "Barefoot Boy"), 1856; Home Ballads, Poems and Lyrics (contains "Skipper Ireson's Ride," "Telling the Bees"), 1860; In War Time and Other Poems (contains "Barbara Frietchie"), 1864; Snow-Bound (considered greatest work), 1866; The Tent on the Beach, 1867; Among the Hills, 1869; Miriam and Other Poems, 1871; Hazel-Blossoms, 1875; The Vision of Echard, 1878; Saint Gregory's Guest, 1886; At Sundown, 1890. Died Hampton Falls, Mass., Sept. 7, 1892; buried Amesbury, Mass.

WHITTINGHAM, William Rollinson, clergyman; b. N.Y.C., Dec. 2, 1805; s. Richard and Mary Ann (Rollinson) W.; grad. Gen. Theol; Sem., N.Y.C., 1821 (made fellow of Coll.); S.T.D., Columbia, 1827; m. Hannah Harrison, Apr. 15, 1830, 3 children. Collaborated in translating and editing An Introduction to the Old Testament, 1827; ordained deacon Protestant Episcopal Ch., 1827, priest, 1829; rector St. Mark's Ch., Orange, N.J., 1829-30, St. Luke's Ch., N.Y., 1831-36; prof. eccles. history Gen. Theol. Sem., 1836-40; elected bishop of Md., consecrated in St. Paul's Ch:, Balt., 1840; bequeathed his library of 17,000 volumes to Diocese of Md. (became nucleus of Md. Diocesan Library); a founder St. James' Coll., Hagerstown, Md., 1842; a founder Ch. Home and Infirmary, Balt.; represented Am. ch. in Congress of Cologne, 1872. Author: The Pursuit of Knowledge, 1837; The Godly Quietness of the Church, 1842; The Body of Christ, 1843; The Work of the Ministry in a Day of Rebuke, 1846; Gifts and Their Right Estimate, 1855; The Work of Christ by His Ministry, 1856; Fifteen Sermons, 1880. Died Orange, N.J., Oct. 17, 1879.

WHITTLESEY, Elisha, congressman; b. Washington, Conn., Oct. 19, 1783; attended common schs., Danbury, Conn.; studied law, Danbury. Admitted to Fairfield County (Conn.) bar, practiced in Danbury and Fairfield County, later in New Milford, Conn., 1805; moved to Canfield, O., 1806, practiced law, taught sch.; pros. atty. Mahoning County (O.); mil. and pvt. sec. to Gen. William Henry Harrison, also brigade maj. Army of N.W., during War of 1812; mem. Ohio Ho. of Reps., 1820-21; mem. U.S. Ho. of Reps. from Ohio, 18th-25th congresses, Mar. 18, 1821-Dec. 18, 1843 (resigned); resumed practice of law, Canfield; a founder Whig Party; apptd. gen. agt. Washington Monument Assn., 1847; 1st comptroller U.S. Treasury (apptd. by Pres. Taylor, reapptd. by Pres. Lincoln), 1849-57, 61-63. Died Washington, D.C., Jan. 7, 1863; buried Canfield Village Cemetery.

WHITTLESEY, Frederick, congressman; b. New Preston, Conn., June 12, 1799; grad. Yale, 1818; studied law. Admitted to N.Y. bar, 1821, began practice in Cooperstown, 1822; moved to Rochester, N.Y., 1822; treas. Monroe County (N.Y.), 1829-30; mem. U.S. Ho. of Reps. (Whig) from N.Y., 22d-23d congresses, 1831-35; city atty. Rochester, 1838; vice chancellor 8th Jud. Dist. of N.Y., 1839-47; justice N.Y. Supreme Ct., 1847-48; prof. law Genesee (N.Y.) Coll., 1850-51. Died Rochester, N.Y., Sept. 19, 1851; buried Mt. Hope Cemetery, Rochester.

WHITTLESEY, Thomas Tucker, congressman; b. Danbury, Conn., Dec. 8, 1798; grad. Yale, 1817; attended Litchfield (Conn.) Law Sch. Admitted to Conn. bar, 1818, began practice in Danbury; judge of probate; mem. U.S. Ho. of Reps. (Democrat) from Conn., 24th-25th congresses, Apr. 29, 1836-39; moved to Pheasant Branch, nr. Madison, Wis., 1846, practiced law, engaged in farming; mem. Wis. Senate, 1853-54. Died Pheasant Branch, Aug. 20, 1868; buried Forest Hill Cemetery, Madison.

WHITTLESEY, William Augustus, congressman; b. Danbury, Conn., July 14, 1796; grad. Yale, 1816; studied law. Taught sch.; moved to Canfield, O., 1818; admitted to Ohio bar, 1821, began practice in Canfield; moved to Marietta, O., 1821; auditor Washington County (O.), 1825-27; mem. Ohio Ho. of Reps., 1839-40; mem. U.S. Ho. of Reps. (Democrat) from Ohio, 31st Congress, 1849-51; mayor of Marietta, 1856, 60, 62. Died Bklyn., Nov. 6, 1866; buried Mound Cemetery, Marietta.

WICK, William Watson, congressman; b. Canonsburg, Pa., Feb. 23, 1796; studied medicine, Cincinnati, until 1818, later studied law. Taught sch., Cincinnati; admitted to Ind. bar, 1819, began practice in Connersville, Ind., 1820; clk. Ind. Ho. of Reps., 1820; asst. clk. Ind. Senate, 1821; pres. judge 5th Ind. Jud. Circuit, 1822-25, 34-37, 50-53; sec. of state Ind., 1825-29; pros. atty. 5th Ind. Jud. Circuit 1829-31; mem. U.S. Ho. of Reps. (Democrat) from Ind., 26th, 29th-30th congresses, 1839-41, 1845-49; resumed law practice, Indpls.; postmaster of Indpls., 1853-57; adj. gen. Ind. Militia; moved to Franklin, 1857, practiced law. Died Franklin, May 19, 1868; buried Greenlawn Cemetery, Franklin.

WICKERSHAM, James Pyle, educator; b. Newlin Twp., Pa., Mar. 5, 1825; s. Caleb and Abigail Swayne (Pyle) W.; m. Emerine Isaac Taylor, Dec. 24, 1847, at least 4 children. Headmaster of acad., Marietta, Pa., 1845; an organizer Lancaster County Ednl. Assn., 1851, Pa. State Tchrs. Assn., 1852, Nat. Tchrs. Assn. (later N.E.A.), served as pres. all 3 orgns.; 1st supt. schs. Lancaster County (Pa.), 1854; established institute at Millersville (Pa.) Acad., 1855; urged establishment of state normal sch. system, assisted in framing normal sch. law, 1857; served as col. 47th Regt., Pa. Volunteer Emergency Militia, 1863; supt. Pa. common schs., 1866-81; a founder Soldiers' Orphans Sch., 1864; editor, part owner Pa. Sch. Journal, 1870-81; awarded medal at Paris Expn. for his exhibit of state school reports, laws and other documents; mgr., pres. Inquirer Printing and Publishing Co., Lancaster, Pa., 1873; apptd. U.S. chargé d'affaires to Denmark, May 1882, minister resident and consul general, July-Aug. 1882 (resigned). Author: School Economy, 1864; Methods of Instruction, 1865; A History of Education in Pennsylvania, 1886. Died Lancaster, Mar. 25, 1891.

WICKES, Eliphalet, congressman; b. Huntington, L.I., N.Y., Apr. 1, 1769; studied law. Employed as express rider during Am. Revolution, at storming of Stony Point, 1779, carried news to Gen. Gates at Providence, R.I.; admitted to N.Y. bar, began practice in Jamaica, L.I.; mem. U.S. Ho. of Reps. from N.Y., 9th Congress, 1805-07; 1st postmaster of Jamaica, 1797-1806, 07-35; master in chancery. Died Troy, N.Y., June 7, 1850; buried Oakwood Cemetery, Troy.

WICKES, Lambert, naval officer; b. Eastern Neck Island, Md., 1735; s. Samuel Wickes. Went to sea; master mcht. ships from Phila. and Chesapeake Bay ports, 1769; part owner of vessel, 1774; refused to carry East India tea from London, 1774; given command of armed ship Reprisal, 1776; carried William Bingham to Martinique, 1776, captured 3 prizes and H. M. S. Shark; transported Benjamin Franklin to France (becoming 1st Continental warship to enter European waters), 1776; raided English Channel and upturned 5 Brit. ships, 1777; commanded flotilla of 3 ships, 1777, took 18 Brit. prizes off Britain, 1777. Drowned when ship floundered off Newfoundland banks while returning to colonies (all drowned except cook) Oct. 1, 1777.

WICKES, Stephen, physician; b. Jamaica, L.I., N.Y., Mar. 7, 1813; s. Van Wyck and Eliza (Herriman) W.; grad. Union Coll., Schenectady, N.Y., 1831; attended Rensselaer Poly. Inst., Troy, N.Y.; studied medicine under Dr. Thomas W. Blatchford; M.D., U. Pa., 1834; m. Mary Whitney Heyer, Feb. 24, 1836; m. 2d, Lydia Matilda Wickes, Apr. 1, 1841; at least 3 daus. Practiced medicine, N.Y.C., went to Troy until 1852, Orange, N.J., 1852-89; chmn. standing com. N.J. Med. Soc., 1860-83, editor Transactions, 1862-82, pres., 1883; mem. med. staff Meml. Hosp., Orange, 1873; retired from practice, 1883; trustee Rensselaer Poly. Inst.; mem. N.J. Hist. Soc. Author: The History of Medicine in New Jersey, and of its Medical Men, from the Settlement of the Province to A.D. 1880, 1879; The History of the Newark Mountains, 1888. Died July 8, 1889.

WICKHAM, John, lawyer; b. Southold, L.I., N.Y., June 6, 1763; s. John and Hannah (Fanning) W.; attended mil. sch., Arras, France; studied law, Williamsburg, Va.; m. Mary Smith Fanning Dec. 24, 1791; m. 2d, Elizabeth Selden McClurg; many children, at least 2 sons. Moved to Richmond, Va., 1790; counsel (opposing lawyer was John Marshall) for Brit. creditor in Ware vs. Hylton, 1793, successfully contended that Treaty of 1783 made states responsible for debts incurred befor Am. Revolution; successfully defended Aaron Burr in his treason trial, 1807. Died Jan. 22, 1839.

WICKLIFFE, Charles Anderson, gov. Ky., congressman; b. Springfield, Ky., June 8, 1788; s. Charles and Lydia (Hardin) W.; m. Margaret Cripps, 1813, 8 children including Robert C. Admitted to Ky. bar, 1809; mem. Ky. Ho. of Reps. from Nelson County, 1812-13, 20-21, 33-36; enlisted in M.H. Wickliffe's co. of Ky. Cavalry, 1813, aide-de-camp to Gen. Caldwell; commonwealth atty. for Nelson County, 1816; mem. U.S. Ho. of Reps. from Ky., 18th-22d congresses, 1823-33; lt. gov. Ky., 1836-39, became gov. after death of James Clark, 1839-40; U.S. postmaster gen., 1841-45; apptd. (by Pres. Polk) agt. to France and Eng. to discourage designs on Tex., 1845; mem. Ky. Constl. Conv., 1849; mem. com. apptd. to revise statutes of Ky., 1850; mem. Washington (D.C.) Peace Conf., Border State Conf., 1861; mem. U.S. Ho. of Reps. (Union Whig) from Ky., 37th Congress, 1861-63; del. Nat. Democratic Conv., 1864. Died Ilchester, Md., Oct. 31, 1869; buried Bardstown (Ky.) Cemetery.

WICKLIFFE, Robert Charles, gov. La.; b. Bardstown, Ky., Jan. 6, 1819; s. Charles A. and Margaret (Cripps) W.; grad. Centre Coll., Danville, Ky., 1840; m. Anna Dawson, Feb. 1843; m. 2d, Annie (Davis) Anderson, 1870; 4 children. Mem. La. Senate from West Felician Parish, 1851-53, pres., 1853; Democratic gov. La., 1856-60; elected to 40th U.S. Congress, 1866, denied admission; elector-at-large on Tilden ticket, chmn. La. delegation Dem. Nat. Conv., 1876. Died Shelbyville, Ky., Apr. 18, 1895.

WIDGERY, William, congressman; probably b. Devonshire, Eng., circa 1753; attended common schs.; studied law. Came to Am. with parents, settled in Phila.; engaged in shipbldg.; served at lt. on a privateer during Revolutionary War; admitted to the bar, began practice in Portland, Mass. (now Me.), circa 1790; mem. Mass. Ho. of Reps., 1787-93, 95-97; del. Mass. Constl. Conv., 1788; mem. Mass. Senate, 1794, Mass. Exec. Council, 1806-07; mem. U.S. Ho. of Reps. (Democrat) from Mass., 12th Congress, 1811-13; judge ct. of common pleas, 1813-21. Died Portland, July 31, 1822; buried Eastern Cemetery, Portland.

WIGFALL, Louis Tresevant, senator, Confederate senator; b. Edgefield, S.C., Apr. 21, 1816; s. Levi Durand and Eliza (Thompson) W.; grad. S.C. Coll. (now U. S.C.), 1837; m. Charlotte Maria Cross, 1844, 5 children. Admitted to Va. bar, 1839; mem. Tex. Ho. of Reps., 1849-50, Tex. Senate, 1857-59; mem. U.S. Senate from Tex., 1859-61; an author of Southern Address (urging secession and orgn. of Confederacy), signed Dec. 14, 1860; apptd. col. 21st Tex. Inf., Confederate States Army, 1861, promoted brig. gen., 1861; represented Tex. in Confederate Senate, 1862-65, leader congressional opposition to Pres. Jefferson Davis, favored separation of chief exec. and chief mil. powers (resulted in appointment of Robert E. Lee as gen.-in-chief Confederate armies). Died Galveston, Tex., Feb. 18, 1874; buried Episcopal Cemetery, Galveston.

WIGGINTON, Peter Dinwiddie, congressman; b. Springfield, Ill., Sept. 6, 1839; attended U. Wis.; studied law. Admitted to Wis. bar, 1859, practiced law; editor Dodgeville (Wis.) Advocate; moved to Snelling, Cal., 1862, practiced law; dist. atty. Merced County (Cal.), 1864-68; mem. U.S. Ho. of Reps. (Democrat) from Cal., 44th, 49th congresses, 1875-77, Feb. 7, 1878-79 (successfully contested election); resumed practice of law, San Francisco, 1880; Am. Party nominee for vice pres. U.S., 1888. Died Oakland, Cal., July 7, 1890; buried Mountain View Cemetery, Oakland.

WIGGLESWORTH, Edward, educator, theologian; b. Cambridge, Mass., Feb. 7, 1732; s. Edward and Rebecca (Coolidge) W.; grad. Harvard, 1749; m. Margaret Hill, Oct. 1765; m. 2d, Dorothy Sparhawk, Jan. 6, 1778; m. 3d, Sarah Wigglesworth, Oct. 20, 1785; 5 children. Tutor, Harvard, 1764, Hollis prof. divinity, 1765, fellow of coll., 1779, acting pres., 1780. Author: Calculations on American Population, 1775; The Authority of Tradition Considered (lecture), 1778; The Hope of Immortality (funeral sermon on John Winthrop), 1779. Died Cambridge, June 17, 1794.

WIGGLESWORTH, Edward, dermatologist; b. Boston, Dec. 30, 1840; s. Edward and Henrietta May (Goddard) W.; grad. Harvard, 1861, M.D., 1865; studied dermatology in Europe, 1865-70; m. Mrs. Sarah (Willard) Frothingham, Apr. 4, 1882, 3 children. Served with Union Army during Civil War; founded and maintained Boston Dispensary for Skin Diseases, 1872-77; head dept. of skin diseases Boston City Hosp.; instr. dermatology Harvard Med. Sch.; pres. Am. Dermatol. Assn., 1885; active in introducing law to require registration of physicians in Mass.; founded Boston Med. Register. Died Boston, Jan. 23, 1896.

WIGGLESWORTH, Michael, clergyman; b. Yorkshire, Eng., Oct. 18, 1631; s. Edward and Esther Wigglesworth; B.A., Harvard, 1651; m. Mary Reyner, May 18, 1655; m. 2d, Martha Mudge, 1679; m. 3d, Sybil (Sparhawk) Avery, June 23, 1691; 8 children including Edward. Came to Mass. Bay Colony, 1638; tutor Harvard, 1652-54, fellow, 1652-54, 97-1705; ordained to ministry Puritan Ch., Malden, Mass., circa 1656; preached Election sermon, 1686, Arty. Election sermon, 1696. Author: The Day of Doom (long poem, ran through many edits.), 1662; Meat out of the Eater or Meditations Concerning the Necessity, End, and Usefulness of Afflications Unto God's Children (edificatory verse), 1669. Died May 27, 1705.

WIGHT, Orlando Williams, physician, author; b. Centerville, Alleghany County, N.Y., Feb. 19, 1824; s. Thomas and Caroline (Van Buren) W.; attended Rochester Collegiate Inst.; studied theology, N.Y.C.; M.D., L.I. Coll. Hosp. Instr. langs. and mathematics Aurora Acad., 1845-47; ordained to ministry Universalist Ch., 1847; minister, Newark, N.J., 1847-53; practiced medicine, Oconomowoc, Wis., then Milw., 1857-74; surgeon gen. of Wis., 1874-78; health officer Milw., 1878-80, Detroit, 1882-88. Author: The Philosophy of Sir William Hamilton, 1853; Life of Abelard and Héloise, 1853; Maxims of Public Health, 1884; A Winding Journey Around the World, 1888. Editor: Standard French Classics, 14 vols., 1859 and following. Died Detroit, Oct. 19, 1888.

WIGNELL, Thomas, comedian, theatrical dir.; b. circa 1753; s. J. Wignell; m. Ann Brunton Merry, Jan. 1, 1803. Came to Am. to join acting co., 1744, left for Jamaica with fellow actors after Continental Congress recommended closing public amusements, 1774; acted in Jamaica, 1774-84; gave 1st performance in Am., N.Y.C., 1785; became popular comedian in roles including Joseph Surface in The School for Scandal; became theatrical dir. in partnership with Alexander Reinagle, 1791, opened Chestnut Theatre, Phila., also built theatre in Balt., 1794, opened 1st theatre in Washington, D.C., 1800; brought actors and actresses from Eng.; considered best comic actor of time. Died Feb. 21, 1803.

WIKOFF, Henry, author, adventurer; b. circa 1813; said to be s. Henry Wikoff (his diary suggests he was son of S.P. Wetherill); attended Yale almost 3 years; grad. Union Coll., 1832. Inherited fortune; admitted to Pa. bar, 1834; made grand tour of Europe, 1834-40; attache U.S. legation in London, 1836; decorated by Queen of Spain; editor Democratic Review, 1849; agt. Brit. Fgn. Office, 1850; planned to marry Jane C. Gamble in London, 1851, she went to Genoa, he planned to abduct her, arrested, prosecuted and imprisoned for 15 months, Author: Napoleon Louis Bonaparte, First President of France, 1849; My Courtship and its Consequences, 1855 (best known book); The Adventures of a Roving Diplomatist, 1857; Secession, and its Causes, in a Letter to Viscount Palmerston (pamphlet on question Am. slavery), 1861; The Reminiscences of an Idler (most important lit. work), 1880. Died of paralysis, Brighton, Eng., May 2, 1884.

WILBER, David, congressman; b. nr. Quaker Street, Schenectady County, N.Y., Oct. 5, 1820; attended common schs., Milford, N.Y. Engaged in lumber and hop businesses, farming; mem. bd. suprs. Otsego County (N.Y.), 1858-59, 62, 65, 66; dir. Albany & Susquehanna R.R., 2d Nat. Bank of Cooperstown (N.Y.); pres. Wilbert Nat. Bank of Oneonta (N.Y.), 1874-90; mem. U.S. Ho. of Reps. (Republican) from N.Y., 43d, 46th, 50th-51st congresses, 1873-75, 79-81, 87-90; del. Rep. nat. conv., Chgo., 1880, 88; moved to Oneonta, N.Y., 1886. Died Oneonta, Apr. 1, 1890; buried Glenwood Cemetery, Oneonta.

WILBOUR, Isaac, congressman; b. Little Compton, R.I., Apr. 25, 1763; studied law. Admitted to R.I. bar, 1793, practiced law; engaged in farming; held local offices, 1793-1800; mem. R.I. Ho. of Reps., 1805-06, speaker, 1806; lt. gov R.I., 1806-07, 10-11, acting gov., 1806; mem. U.S. Ho. of Reps. (Federalist) from R.I., 10th Congress, 1807-09; declined appointment to fill vacancy in U.S. Senate, 1807; asso. justice R.I. Supreme Ct., 1818, chief justice, 1819-27. Died Little Compton, Oct. 4, 1837; buried Seaconnet Cemetery, Little Compton.

WILBUR, Hervey, clergyman; b. Cummington, Hampshire County, Mass., July 20, 1786; studied Congregational Sem., Mass.; A.M. (hon.), Dartmouth, 1812; m. Ann Toppan, 6 children. Pastor, Congregational Ch., Wendell, Mass., 1817-23; later prin. several seminaries for young girls. Author: A Discourse on the Religious Education of Youth, 1814; A Reference Bible, 1828; Elements of Astronomy, 1828; Lexicon of Useful Knowledge, 1830; A Reference Testament for Bible Classes (1 of 1st Bible class textbooks), 1831. Died Newburyport, Mass., Jan. 5, 1852.

WILBUR, Hervey Backus, educator; b. Wendell, Franklin County, Mass., Aug. 18, 1820; s. Hervey and Ann (Tappan) W.; attended Dartmouth, 1834-36; B.A., Amherst Coll., 1838, M.A., 1841; grad. Berkshire Med. Instn., Pittsfield, Mass., 1843; m. Harriet Holden, May 12, 1847, at least 2 sons; m. 2d, Emily Petheram, Aug. 13, 1874; at least 2 sons. Took a group of mentally defective children into his home, Barre, Mass., 1848, organized in charge of Inst. for Idiots (1st school for this class of unfortunates in U.S.), became N.Y. State Asylum for Idiots, 1854; became authority on care of insane; a founder Syracuse (N.Y.) U.; lectr. on mental diseases; pres. Nat. Assn. for Protection Insane and Prevention of Insanity. Author: Aphasia (pamphlet), 1867; Report on Management of Insane in Great Britain, 1876. Died Syracuse, May 1, 1883.

WILBUR, John, clergyman; b. Hopkinton, R.I., June 17, 1774; s. Thomas and Mary (Hoxie) W.; m. Lydia Collins, Oct. 17, 1793. Taught in R.I. public schs.; minister Soc. of Friends, 1812; on preaching tour in Gt. Britain and Ireland, 1831-33; strong opponent of evang. movement sweeping Quakers; vainly sought to return Quakers to old principles of "Inner Light," 1834-43; his attacks on Joseph John Gurney (evang. preacher) led to his expulsion from membership, 1843; Soc. of Friends split into "Wilburites" and larger "Gurneyites," 1845; made 2d trip to Eng., 1853-54. Author: Letters to a Friend on Some of the Primitive Doctrines of Christianity, 1832. Died Hopkinton, May 1, 1856.

WILBUR, Samuel, mcht., colonist; b. Eng., circa 1585; m. Ann; m. 2d, Elizabeth Lechford; at least 4 children. Came to Am., circa 1633, settled in Boston; a purchaser of Boston Common, 1634; banished for his part in Antinomian controversy, 1637; went to R.I.; a purchaser Aquidneck Island (now island of R.I.) from Narragansett Indians; a signer Portsmouth Compact which organized govt. of Colony of R.I.; returned to Mass., 1645, found colony of brink of war with Narragansetts, apptd. a messenger to return Indians' peace presents, succeeded in preventing war. Died Boston, July 29, 1656.

WILCOX, Cadmus Marcellus, army officer; b. Wayne County, N.C., May 29, 1824; s. Reuben and Sarah (Garland) W.; grad. U.S. Mil. Acad., 1846. Brevetted 2d lt. 4th U.S. Inf., 1846; promoted 2d lt., 7th Inf., 1847, trans. to Gen. Scott's army; served at Vera Cruz, Cerro Gordo; aide to Gen. John A. Quitman in advance on Mexico City; groomsman to Ulysses S. Grant at his wedding, 1848; commd. 1st lt., 1851; asst. instr. inf. tactics U.S. Mil. Acad,. 1852-57; commd. capt., 1860; commd. col. 9th Ala. Inf., Confederate Army, after resigning from U.S. Army, 1861; served throughout war with Lees army; commd. brig. gen., 1861, maj. gen., 1864; chief railroad div. Gen. Land Office under Pres. Cleveland, 1886-90. Author: Rifles and Rifle Practice, 1859; History of the Mexican War, pub. posthumously, 1892. Died Dec. 2, 1890.

WILCOX, Jeduthun, congressman; b. Middletown, Conn., Nov. 18, 1768; studied law; children include Leonard. Admitted to N.H. bar, 1802, began practice in Orford; mem. N.H. Ho. of Reps., 1809-11; mem. U.S. Ho. of Reps. (Federalist) from N.H., 13th-14th congresses, 1813-17. Died Orford, July 18, 1838; buried Orford Cemetery.

WILCOX, John A., congressman; b. Greene County, N.C., Apr. 18, 1819; attended common schs., Tenn. Settled in Aberdeen, Miss.; sec. Miss. Senate; served as lt., adj. and lt. col. during Mexican War; mem. U.S. Ho. of Reps. (Union Whig) from Miss., 32d Congress, 1851-53; moved to Tex., 1853; mem. Confederate Congress. Died Richmond, Va., Feb. 7, 1864; buried Hollywood Cemetery, Richmond.

WILCOX, Leonard, senator; b. Hanover, N.H., Jan. 29, 1799; s. Jeduthun Wilcox; grad. Dartmouth, 1817; studied law. Admitted to N.H. bar, 1820, began practice in Orford; mem. N.H. Ho. of Reps., 1828-34; judge N.H. Superior Ct., 1838-40, 48-50; bank commr., 1838-42; mem. U.S. Senate (Democrat) from N.H., Mar. 1, 1842-43; judge N.H. Ct. of Common Pleas, 1847-48. Died Orford, June 18, 1850; buried West Congregational Churchyard, Orford.

WILCOX, Stephen, inventor, engr., mfr.; b. Westerly, R.I., Feb. 12, 1830; s. Stephen and Sophia (Vose) W.; m. Harriet Hoxie, 1865. Inventor, also patentee (with partner D.M. Stillman) safety water-tube boiler with inclined tubes, 1856; patentee steam generator based on principle of earlier boiler (designed with George Herman Babcock), 1867; founder firm Babcock, Wilcox and Co., 1867, pres., 1867-93; secured total of 47 patents. Died Bklyn., Nov. 27, 1893.

WILD, John Caspar, artist; b. Zurich, Switzerland, circa 1804. Came to U.S., circa 1830; worked in Phila., and Cincinnati; partner with J. B. Chevalier, Phila., 1838, engraved set of 20 views of Phila. and vicinity after drawings by Wild; moved to St. Louis, 1839, to Davenport, Ia., 1845; published Views of St. Louis, 1840, The Valley of the Mississippi Illustrated in a Series of Views, 1841; made numerous paintings and lithographs of towns in Ill., Ia. and Minn. Died Davenport, Aug. 1846.

WILDE, Richard Henry, congressman, author; b. Dublin, Ireland, Sept. 24, 1789; s. Richard and Mary (Newitt) W.; m. Mrs. Caroline Buckle, 1819, at least 2 sons including William Cumming. Came to U.S., 1797; family moved to Augusta, Ga., 1803; admitted to Ga. bar, 1809; atty. gen. of Ga., 1811-13; mem. U.S. Ho. of Reps. (Democrat) from Ga., 14th, 18th, 20th-23d congresses, 1815-17, 25, 27-350 lived in Europe 1835-40; returned to New Orleans, 1843; prof. constl. law U. La. (now Tulane U.), 1847. Author: Conjectures and Researches Concerning the Love, Madness, and Imprisonment of Torquato Tasso, 2 vols., 1842; wrote poem My Life is Like a Summer Rose, 1819. Died New Orleans, Sept. 10, 1847; buried City Cemetery, Augusta.

WILDER, Abel Carter, congressman; b. Mendon, Mass., Mar. 18, 1828. Engaged in merc. bus., Mendon, later in Rochester, N.Y.; moved to Leavenworth, Kan., 1857, engaged in merc. bus.; del. Osawatomie Conv., 1859; chmn. Republican Nat. Conv., Chgo., 1860; served as capt. Kan. Brigade during Civil War, 1 year; mem. U.S. Ho. of Reps. (Rep.) from Kan., 38th Congress, 1863-65; del. Rep. nat. convs., 1864, 68, 72; returned to Rochester, 1865, published Morning and Evening Express, 1865-68; mayor of Rochester, 1872-73. Died San Francisco, Dec. 22, 1875; buried Mt. Hope Cemetery, Rochester.

WILDER, Marshall Pinckney, mcht., agriculturist; b. Rindge, N.H., Sept. 22, 1798; s. Samuel Locke and Anna (Sherwine) W.; m. Tryphosa Jewett, Dec. 31, 1870; m. 2d, Abigail Baker, Aug. 19, 1833; m. 3d, Julia Baker, Sept. 3, 1855; 14 children. Postmaster, Rindge, circa 1819, also taught vocal music; rep. Mass. Legislature, 1839; mem. Mass. Exec. Council, 1849; pres. Mass. Senate, 1850; capt. Ancient and Honorable Arty. Co., 1856; a founder Constl. Union Party of 1860; founder Mass. Inst. Tech., v.p., 1865-70, trustee, 1870-86; became mem. New Eng. Historic Geneal. Soc. 1850, pres., 1868-86; Mason (33° mem. supreme council); planted nursery, Boston, 1832, began hort. expts.; developed "Wilder Rose"; pres. Mass. Hort. Soc., 1840-48; called a conv. of fruit growers, N.Y.C. which resulted in Am. Pomol. Soc., pres., 1848-86; instigated Mass. Central Bd. Agr. (composed of several socs.), 1851, pres.; pres. U.S. Agrl. Soc., 1852-58; prin. founder Mass. Agrl. Coll.; mem. U.S. Commn. to Paris Universal Expn., 1867; contbr. articles to agrl. jours. including Horticulturist, New Eng. Farmer, Country Gentleman, Genessee Farmer. Died Dec. 16, 1886.

WILDER, Sampson Vryling Stoddard, mcht.; b. Boston, May 20, 1780; s. Levi and Sarah (Stoddard) W.; m. Electa Barrell, June 15, 1814. Apprentice in mcht. firm, Gardner, Mass.; European agt. for various mcht. houses, N.Y.C. and Boston, 1803-23; pres. Am. Tract Soc., 1825-42; held banking interests, N.Y., Phila.; wrote number of religious tracts. Died Northampton, Mass., Apr. 2, 1865.

WILDMAN, Zalmon, congressman; b. Danbury, Conn., Feb. 16, 1775. Engaged in hat mfg.; established 1st hat stores in Charleston (S.C.) and Savannah (Ga.), 1802; 1st pres. Danbury Nat. Bank, 1824-26; mem. Conn. Ho. of Reps., 1818-19; postmaster of Danbury, 1805-35; mem. U.S. Ho. of Reps. (Democrat) from Conn., 24th Congress, 1835. Died Washington, D.C., Dec. 10, 1835; buried Wooster Cemetery, Danbury.

WILDRICK, Isaac, congressman; b. Marksboro, N.J., Mar. 3, 1803; attended common schs. Engaged in farming, nr. Blairstown, N.J.; constable, 1827-32, coroner, 1829-31, justice of peace, 1834-39, judge, 1839, sheriff, 1839-41; dir. county poorhouse, 1842-48; mem. freeholder, 1845-48, 56-59; mem. U.S. Ho. of Reps. (Democrat) from N.J., 31st-32d congresses, 1849-53; resumed farming; mem. N.J. Assembly, 1882-85. Died Blairstown, Mar. 22, 1892; buried Presbyn. Cemetery, Marksboro, N.J.

WILEY, Calvin Henderson, clergyman, educator; b. Guilford County, N.C., Feb. 3, 1819; s. David L. and Anne (Woodburn) W.; grad. U. N.C., 1840; m. Mittie Towles, Feb. 25, 1862, 7 children. Edited Oxford (S.C.) Mercury, 1841-43; mem. N.C. Legislature, 1850-52; supt. common schs. of N.C., 1853-65; established Common Sch. Jour., 1856; gen. agt. Am. Bible Soc., 1869; licensed to preach by Presbyn. Ch., 1855, ordained, 1866; believed in universal free edn. Author: Alamance; or, the Great and Final Experiment, 1847; Roanoke; or Where Is Utopia? (novel), 1849; The North Carolina Reader (standard school text), 1851. Died Winston, N.C., Jan. 11, 1887.

WILEY, David, clergyman; b. circa 1768; grad. Coll. of N.J. (now Princeton), 1788, M.A., 1801; many children. Tutor, Hampden-Sydney Coll., 1788-90; licensed to preach at Cedar Spring and Spring Creek (Pa.) chs., by New Castle (Pa.); Presbytery, 1793; ordained to ministry by Presbytery of Carlisle (Pa.), 1794; pastor, Sinking Spring, Pa., 1793-94, Spring Creek, 1794-99; prin., librarian Columbian Acad., Georgetown, D.C.; mayor Georgetown, 1811-12; sec. Columbian Agrl. Soc. for Promotion of Rural and Domestic Economy, 1811-13; editor Agrl. Museum (probably 1st agrl. jour. in U.S.). Died N.C., 1813.

WILEY, Ephraim Emerson, clergyman, coll. pres.; b. Malden, Mass., Oct. 6, 1814; s. Ephraim and Rebecca (Emerson) W.; grad. Wesleyan U., 1837; m. Elizabeth H. Hammond, Feb. 18, 1839; m. 2d, Elizabeth J. Reeves, Oct. 1870; 9 children. Prof. ancient langs. and lit. Emory and Henry Coll., 1838-52, pres., 1852-79, treas., financial agt., 1886-93; ordained to ministry Methodist Ch., 1843; pres. Martha Washington Coll., Abingdon, Va., 1881-86; adherent of So. Meth. Ch. after schism of 1844; del. Ecumenical Methodist Confs., 1881-91; slaveholder, advocate of So. rights. Died Mar. 13, 1893.

WILEY, Isaac William, clergyman; b. Lewistown, Pa., Mar. 29, 1825; grad. med. dept. U. City N.Y. (now N.Y. U.), 1844; D.D. (hon.), Wesleyan U, 1864; LL.D. (hon.), Ohio Wesleyan U., 1879. Licensed to preach Methodist Episcopal Ch., 1843; practiced medicine, Western Pa., 1846-50; med. missionary, Foochow, China, 1850-54; pastor in N.J., 1854-58; prin. Pennington (N.J.) Sem., 1858-63; editor Ladies Repository, Cincinnati, 1864; elected bishop, 1872. Author: The Fallen Missionaries of Fuh-Chauh, 1858; Religion in the Family. Died Foochow, Nov. 1884.

WILEY, James Sullivan, congressman; b. Mercer, Me., Jan. 22, 1808; grad. Colby Coll., 1836; studied law. Instr., Foxcroft Acad., Dover, Me.; admitted to Piscataquis County (Me.) bar, 1839, began practice in Dover; mem. U.S. Ho. of Reps. (Democrat) from Me., 30th Congress, 1847-49; moved to Fryeburg, Me., 1889, practiced law. Died Fryeburg, Dec. 21, 1891; buried Smart Hill Cemetery, Fryeburg.

WILKES, Charles, naval officer; b. N.Y.C., Apr. 3, 1798; s. John De Ponthieu and Mary (Seton) W.; m. Jane Jeffrey Renwick, Apr. 16, 1826; m. 2d, Mary H. (Lynch) Bolton, Oct. 3, 1854; 4 children. Apptd. midshipman U.S. Navy, 1818; 1st cruised Mediterranean in ship Guerriere, later in Pacific in ship Franklin; engaged in surveying Narragansett Bay, 1832-33; in charge of Depot of Charts and Instruments, Washington, D.C., 1833; commanded Porpoise, engaged in survey St. George's Bank and Savannah River, 1837-38; on expdn. to explore coast of Antarctic continent, islands of Pacific Ocean, Am. N.W. coast, 1838-42; awarded Founder's medal Royal Geog. Soc. of London, 1847; tried by court martial and sentenced to public reprimand for illegal punishment of his men, 1842; commd. comdr., 1843, capt., 1855; overhauled Brit. mail steamer Trent in Bahama Channel, 1861, took from vessel Confederate commrs. James M. Mason and John Slidell, brought them to Boston, viewed as hero, congratulated by Sec. of Navy Gideon Welles, thanked by U.S. Ho. of Reps., event was actually act of war on Eng., case disallowed and Mason and Slidell sent on to Eng.; in command James River flotilla, 1862; transferred to Potomac flotilla; made acting rear adm., 1862; placed on ret. list as captain, 1862, commodore, 1863; court martialed, guilty of disobedience, disrespect, insubordination, conduct unbecoming an officer, sentenced to reprimand and suspended from duty 3 years, 1864; commd. rear adm. (ret.), 1866. Author: Narrative of the United States Exploring Expedition, 5 vols., 1844; Western America, 1849; Theory of the Zodiacal Light, 1857; On the Circulation of Oceans, 1859. Died Feb. 8, 1877.

WILKES, George, journalist; b. N.Y., 1817; s. George and Helen Wilkes; married twice. Editor, Flash, Whip, Subterranean (newspaper); started Nat. Police Gazette, 1845-57; publisher paper Spirit of the Times, 1856-85; introduced parimutual system of betting to Am.; active in Republican politics, promotion of prize fights, after Civil War; received Grand Cross, Order of St. Stanislas from Russian czar for advocating railroad through Russian territory to India and China, 1870; lived later life in London, Eng., Paris, France. Author: Europe in a Hurry, circa 1853; Shakespeare from an American Point of View, 1877, 3d edit., 1882. Died N.Y.C., Sept. 23, 1885.

WILKESON, Samuel, mayor Buffalo; b. Carlisle, Pa., June 1, 1781; s. John and Mary (Robinson) W.; m. Jane Oram, before 1802; m. 2d, Sarah St. John; m. 3d, Mary Peters; 6 children. Moved to Lake Erie nr. Westfield, N.Y., 1809; built keel boats and engaged in lake and river trade; served with Pa. Militia in unsuccessful defense of Buffalo (N.Y.) against British, 1814; constructed harbor at mouth of Buffalo Creek for Western terminus of Erie Canal, 1820; 1st judge Erie County (N.Y.) Ct. of Common Pleas, 1821; mem. N.Y. Senate, 1824; mayor Buffalo, 1836; mem. Am. Colonization Soc. Author: (series of articles on own experiences) American Pioneer of Cincinnati, 1842-43. Died Kingston, Tenn., July 7, 1848.

WILKIE, Franc Bangs, journalist; b. West Charlton, N.Y., July 2, 1832; s. John and Elizabeth (Penny) W.; attended Union Coll., Schenectady, N.Y., 1855-56; m. Ellen Morse, 1857, at least 2 children. Held variety of jobs in youth; moved to Davenport, Ia., 1856; began Davenport Daily Evening News, 1856-57; city editor Dubuque (Ia.) Daily Herald, 1858-61; war corr. with Western armies, 1861-63; asst. editor Chgo. Times, 1863-88; a founder, 1st pres. Chgo. Press Club, 1880; independent journalist, 1881-83; worked for Chicago Globe and Chgo. Herald, 1888-90. Author: Davenport, Past and Present, 1859; Sketches Beyond the Sea, 1879; Pen and Powder, 1888; Personal Reminiscences of Thirty Years of Journalism, 1891. Died Norwood Park, Ill., Apr. 12, 1892; buried Elgin, Ill.

WILKIN, James Whitney, congressman; b. Wallkill, N.Y., 1762; grad. Coll. of N.J. (now Princeton), 1785; studied law; children include Samuel Jones. Admitted to N.Y. bar, 1788, began practice in Goshen; mem. N.Y. State Assembly, 1800, 08-09, speaker, 1809; served to maj. gen. N.Y. Militia; mem. N.Y. State Senate, 1801-04, 11-14; mem. Council of Appointment, 1801, 11, 13; mem. U.S. Ho. of Reps. (Democrat) from N.Y., 14th-15th congresses, June 7, 1815-19; unsuccessful candidate for U.S. Senate, 1815; clk. Orange County (N.Y.), 1819-21, treas., several years. Died Goshen, Feb. 23, 1845; buried Slate Hill Cemetery, Goshen.

WILKIN, Samuel Jones, congressman; b. Goshen, N.Y., Dec. 17, 1793; s. James Whitney Wilkin; grad. Princeton, 1812; studied law. Admitted to N.Y. bar, 1815, began practice in Goshen; mem. N.Y. State Assembly, 1824-25; mem. U.S. Ho. of Reps. (Democrat) from N.Y., 22d Congress, 1831-33; unsuccessful Whig candidate for lt. gov. N.Y., 1844; mem. N.Y. State Senate, 1848-49; canal appraiser, 1850. Died Goshen, Mar. 11, 1866; buried Slate Hill Cemetery, Goshen.

WILKINS, Ross, jurist; b. Pitts., Feb. 19, 1799; s. John and Catherine (Stevenson) W.; grad. Dickinson Coll., Carlisle, Pa., 1816; m. Maria Duncan, May 13, 1823, 7 children. Admitted to Pa. bar, by 1820; practiced law, Pitts., 1823-32; territorial judge, Mich., 1832-37; mem. Mich. Constl. Conv., 1835; mem. bd. regents U. Mich., 1837-42; recorder Detroit, 1837; U.S. judge Eastern Dist., Mich., 1837-70; opinions published in Federal Cases, Reports of Admiralty Cases . . . 1842 to 1857 (J.S. Newberry 1857), United States Admiralty and Revenue Cases (R.B. Brown, 1876). Died May 17, 1872.

WILKINS, William, senator, sec. of war, diplomat; b. Carlisle, Pa., Dec. 10, 1779; s. John and Catherine (Rowan) W.; grad. Dickinson Coll., Carlisle, 1802; m. Catherine Holmes, 1815; m. 2d, Mathilda Dallas, Oct. 1, 1818; 7 children.

Admitted to Allegheny County (Pa.) bar, 1801; pres. Bank of Pitts., 1814-19; pres. Monongahela Bridge Co.; pres. Greensburg and Pitts. Turnpike Co.; pres. Pitts. Common Council, 1816-19; mem. Pa. Legislature (Federalist), 1819; presiding judge 5th Jud. Dist. of Pa., 1821-24; judge U.S. Dist. Ct. for Western Pa., 1824-31; mem. U.S. Senate (Democrat) from Pa., 1831-34, resigned to become U.S. minister to Russia, 1834-35; mem. U.S. Ho. of Reps. (Dem.) from Pa., 28th Congress, 1843-Feb. 14, 1844; sec. of war under Tyler, 1844-45; mem. Pa. Senate, 1855-57; maj. gen. Pa. Home Guard, 1862; Wilkins Av. (Pitts.), Wilkins Twp. and borough of Wilkinsburg in Allegheny County (Pa.) named for him. Died Homewood, nr. Pitts., June 23, 1865; buried Homewood Cemetery, Wilkensburg.

WILKINSON, David, inventor, mfr.; b. Smithfield, R.I., Jan. 5, 1771; s. Oziel and Lydia (Smith) W.; m. Martha Sayles, 4 children. Obtained patent for machine for cutting screw threads which incorporated slide rest, 1798; established iron manufactory (with brother) known as David Wilkinson & Co., Pawtucket, R.I., circa 1800; perfected mill to bore cannon by water power (cannon revolved around the boring tool). Died Caledonia Springs, Ont:, Can., Feb. 3, 1852; buried Pawtucket.

WILKINSON, James, army officer, gov. La.; b. Calvert County, Md., 1757; s. Joseph Wilkinson; m. Ann Biddle; m. 2d, Celestine Laveau (Trudeau), Mar. 5, 1810; at least 3 children including 2 daus., 1 son, James B. Commd. capt. Continental Army, 1776; with Benedict Arnold in retreat from Montreal to Albany, 1776; a.d.c. to Gen Gates in battles of Trenton and Princeton, 1776; served as lt. col. under George Washington, 1777; brevetted brig. gen. by Continental Congress, 1777; sec. bd. of war, 1778; involved in Conway cabal (intrigue in Continental Congress to remove George Washington as comdr.-in-chief of armed forces), forced to resign commn., 1778 brig. gen. Pa. Militia, 1783; elected to Pa. Assembly, 1783; involved in trading venture in Ky., 1784; took oath of allegiance to Spanish monarch to aid his own financial position; mem. Ky. Conv., 1788; led a force of volunteers against Indians, 1791; commd. lt. col. U.S. Army, 1791; brig. gen. under Gen. Wayne, 1792; took over Detroit from British, 1796; became ranking officer U.S. Army at death of Gen. Anthony Wayne, 1796; shared (with Gov. William C. C. Claiborne) honor of taking possession of La. Purchase, 1803; gov. La., 1805-06; chief witness against Aaron Burr at his trial for conspiracy with Spain, narrowly escaped indictment by grand jury, acquitted, stood 2d ct. martial trial, 1811, again acquitted; commd. maj. gen., 1813; commanded Am. forces on Canadian front, made a fiasco of campaign against Montreal, stood 3d ct. martial trial, circa 1814, acquitted; received honorable discharge, 1815; tried to collect claims for Mexico's creditors, also indirectly represented Am. Bible Soc. in Mexico, 1821. Author: Memoirs of my Own Times, 3 vols., 1816. Died Dec. 28, 1825; buried Ch. of Archangel San Miguel, Mexico City, Mexico.

WILKINSON, Jemima, religious leader; b. Cumberland, R.I., Nov. 29, 1752; d. Jeremiah and Elizabeth Amey (Whipple) Wilkinson. Following an illness (circa 1774) believed she was possessed by a spirit from God; took name of Public Universal Friend, preached at revival meetings in R.I. and Conn.; established chs., New Milford, Conn., also South Kingston and East Greenwich, R.I., 1777-82; founded colony of Jerusalem (following hostility of public to her disparagement of instn. of marriage), nr. Seneca Lake, N.Y., 1790. Author: The Universal Friend's Advice to Those of the Same Religious Society, Recommended To Be Read in Their Public Meetings for Divine Worship, 1784. Died July 1, 1819.

WILKINSON, Jeremiah, mfr., inventor; b. Cumberland, R.I., July 6, 1741; s. Jeremiah and Elizabeth Amey (Whipple) W.; m. Hope Mosier; m. 2d, Elizabeth Southwick; at least 6 children. Worked as blacksmith, silversmith, during youth; began mfg. hand cards for carding wool, circa 1772; developed machine for shaping iron wire used in wool cards; invented mill for grinding cornstalks; manufactured pins and needles; farmed in Cumberland Valley, throughout life. Died Jan. 29, 1831.

WILKINSON, John, naval officer; b. Norfolk, Va., Nov. 6, 1821; s. Jesse Wilkinson. Commd. midshipman U.S. Navy, 1837. ordered to South Atlantic in ship Independence; assigned to sloop Boston, 1840; passed midshipman, 1843; promoted lt, 1850; in command steamer Corwin collecting data for charts of waters on Fla. coast including Bahamas, 1859-61; resigned to enter Confederate Navy, 1861; ordered to ship Louisiana, 1861, as ranking officer ordered her destroyed when capture was certain, 1862; captured and exchanged, 1862; served spl. duty in England, purchased and commanded blockade-runner Giraffe (which he rechristened (Robert E: Lee), successful over Naussau to Wilmington (N.C.) route; assumed leadership in unsuccessful expdn. to capture Johnson's Island in Lake Erie and release Confederate prisoners, 1863; in command of ship Chickamauga; ended services with command blockade-runner Chameleon; engaged in business in Nova Scotia after Civil War. Author: Narrative of a Blockade-Runner, 1877. Died Annapolis, Md., Dec. 29, 1891.

WILKINSON, Morton Smith, senator, congressman; b. Skaneateles, N.Y., Jan. 22, 1819; attended common schs.; studied law. Engaged in railroading in Ill., 1837-39; returned to Skaneateles, 1840; admitted to the bar, 1842; began practice of law, Eaton Rapids, Mich., 1843; moved to Stillwater, Minn., 1847; mem. 1st Minn. Territorial Legislature, 1849; register of deeds Ramsey County (Minn.), 1851-53; moved to Mankato, Minn., 1858; mem. bd. commrs. to prepare code of laws for Territory of Minn., 1858; mem. U.S. Senate (Republican) from Minn., 1859-65; del. Rep. Nat. Conv., Balt., 1864; mem. U.S. Ho. of Reps. (Rep.) from Minn., 41st congress, 1869-71; moved to Wells, Minn.; mem. Minn. Senate, 1874-77; pros. atty. Faribault County, 1880-84. Died Wells, Feb. 4, 1894; buried Glenwood Cemetery, Mankato.

WILLARD, Charles Wesley, congressman; b. Lyndon, Vt., June 18, 1827; grad. Dartmouth, 1851; studied law. Admitted to Vt. bar, began practice in Montpelier, 1853; sec. of state Vt., 1855-56; mem. Vt. Senate, 1860-61; became editor and publisher Montpelier Freeman, 1861; mem. U.S. Ho. of Reps. (Republican) from Vt., 41st-43d congresses, 1869-75; resumed law practice, Montpelier; mem. commn. to revise laws of Vt., 1879-80. Died Montpelier, June 8, 1880; buried Green Mount Cemetery, Montpelier.

WILLARD, Emma Hart, educator; b. Berlin, Conn., Feb. 23, 1787; d. Capt. Samuel and Lydia (Hinsdale) Hart; attended dist. sch. and Berlin Acad.; m: John Willard, Aug. 10, 1809, 1 son, John Hart; m. 2d, Dr. Christian Yates, Sept. 17, 1838. In charge of Female Acad., Middlebury, Vt., 1807-09; opened Middlebury Female Sem. in own home, 1814; established Waterford Acad., chartered by N.Y. Legislature, 1819; founded Troy (N.Y.) Female Sem., 1821; wrote poem Rocked in the Cradle of the Deep; 1st woman to take public stand for higher edn. of women. Author: An Address to the Public: Particularly to the Members of the Legislature of New York, Proposing a Plan for Improving Female Education, 1819; The Fulfillment of a Promise (poems), 1831; Advancement of Female Education: or A Series of Addresses, in Favor of Establishing at Athens in Greece, A Female Seminary, 1833; A Treatise on the Motive Powers which Produce the Circulation of the Blood, 1846; Last Leaves of American History, 1849; Late American History, 1856. Died Apr. 15, 1870.

WILLARD, Frances Elizabeth Caroline, reformer; b. Churchville, N.Y., Sept. 28, 1839; d. Josiah Flint and Mary Thompson (Hill) Willard; grad. Northwestern Female Coll., 1859. Tchr. in country school, nr. Evanston, Ill., 1860; taught at Pitts: Female Coll., 1863-64, Genesee Wesleyan Sem., Lima, N.Y., 1866-67; pres. Evanston Coll. for Ladies, 1871-74; pres. Chgo. Woman's Christian Temperance Union, 1874; sec. Ill. Woman's Christian Temperance Union; pres. Nat. Woman's Christian Temperance Union, 1879; an organizer Prohibition Party, 1882; pres. Nat. Council of Women, 1882, World Woman's Christian Temperance Union, 1891; statue erected in her honor in Capitol, Washington, D.C., 1905. Author: Woman and Temperance, 1883; Glimpses of Fifty Years, 1889. Editor: A Woman of the Century, 1893. Died N.Y.C., Feb. 18, 1898.

WILLARD, John, jurist; b. New Haven County, Conn., May 20, 1792; grad. Middlebury (Vt.) Coll., 1813; studied law in Vt.; LL.D. (hon.) Dartmouth, 1850. Practiced law, Salem, Washington County, N.Y., 1817-36; judge, vice-chancellor 4th Circuit Ct. of N.Y., 1836-46; justice N.Y. Supreme Ct., 1846-55; mem. U.S. commn. investigating old land titles of Cal., 1856; mem. judiciary com. N.Y. Senate, 1861-62. Author: Equity Jurisprudence, 1855; Law of Executors, Administrators and Guardians, 1859; Law of Real Estate, 1861. Died Saratoga, N.Y., Aug. 31, 1862.

WILLARD, Joseph, univ. pres:; b. Biddeford, Me., Dec: 29, 1738; s. Rev. Samuel and Abigail (Wright) W.; grad. Harvard, 1765; m. Mary Sheafe, Mar. 7, 1774, 13 children including Sidney, Joseph. Greek tutor Harvard, 1766-72; ordained to ministry Congregational Ch., Beverly, Mass., 1772; minister Congl. Ch., Beverly, 1772-81; a founder Am. Acad: Arts and Scis., 1780, became sec., later v.p.; pres. Harvard, 1781-1804, founded Harvard Med: Sch.; mem. Royal Soc. Gottingen (Germany), Med. Soc. of London (Eng.). Died New Bedford, Mass., Sept. 25, 1804.

WILLARD, Joseph, lawyer; b. Cambridge, Mass., Mar. 14, 1798; s. Joseph and Mary (Sheafe) W:; grad. Harvard, 1816, LL.B., 1820; m. Susanna Hickling Lewis, Feb. 24, 1830, 1 son, Sidney. Mem. Mass. Legislature, 1828-29; librarian Mass. Hist. Soc., 1833-35, rec. sec., 1835-37, corr. sec., 1857-64; apptd. master in chancery, 1839; clk. Ct. of Common Pleas, Suffolk County, Mass., 1841-65; an incorporator New Eng. Historic Geneal. Soc., 1845. Author: Willard Memoir, or Life and Times of Major Simon Willard, 1858. Died Boston, May 12, 1865.

WILLARD, Samuel, clergyman; b. Concord, Mass., Feb. 10, 1640; s. Simon and Mary (Sharpe) W.; M.A., Harvard, 1659; m. Abigail Sherman, Aug. 8, 1664; m. 2d, Eunice Tyng, July 29, 1679; 18 children. Called to pulpit, Groton, Mass., 1663; ordained as Puritan minister, 1664; installed as colleague pastor Old South Ch., Boston, 1678; fellow Harvard, 1692, v.p., directed affairs of coll., 1700-07. Author: (lectures) Compleat Body of Divinity, 1726 (largest volume ever to come from colonial presses). Died Sept. 12, 1707.

WILLARD, Samuel, clergyman, educator; b. Petersham, Mass., Apr. 18, 1775; s: William and Katherine (Wilder) W.; grad. Harvard, 1803; m. Susan Barker, May 30, 1808. Taught at Phillips Exeter (N.H.) Acad., 1804; tutor Bowdoin Coll., 1804-05; licensed to preach by Cambridge Assn., 1805; ordained to ministry Unitarian Ch., 1807; pastor Deerfield (Mass.) Ch., 1807-29, 36-39. Author: The Franklin Primer, 2d edit., 1802; Deerfield Collection of Sacred Music (hymns for service), 1814; Regular Hymns, on a Great Variety of Evangelical Subjects, 1824; The General Class-Book, 1828; Rhetoric, or the Principles of Elocution 1830; Sacred Music and Poetry Reconciles (collection of 518 hymns), 1830; An Introduction to the Latin Language, 1835; History of the Rise, Progress and Consummation of the Rupture, Which now Divided the Congregational Clergy and Churches of Massachusetts, 1858. Died Oct. 8, 1859.

WILLARD, Sidney, educator, editor, mayor; b. Beverly, Mass., Sept. 19, 1780; s. Joseph and Mary (Sheafe) W.; grad. Harvard, 1798; m. Elizabeth Ann Andrews, Dec. 28, 1815; m. 2d, Hannah Staniford, Jan. 26, 1819; 4 children. Taught dist. sch., Waltham, Mass., 1798-99; librarian Harvard, 1800-05, tchr., Burlington, Vt., 1806-30; Hancock prof. Hebrew and Oriental Langs., 1806-30, prof. Latin, 1827-31; mem. Anthology Soc., 1807, thereafter helped edit Monthly Anthology; contbr. to Gen. Repository and Review; established Am. Monthly Review, 1831, 1st appeared, 1832; mem. Mass. Gen. Ct., 1833, 37, 43, Mass. Senate, 1834, 35, 39, 40, Mass Council, 1837, 38; selectman Cambridge (Mass.), mem: com. which drafted petition for city charter, 1846, mayor, 1848-50. Author: A Hebrew Grammar, Compiled from some of the Best Authorities, 1817; Memories of Youth and Manhood, 2 vols., 1855. Died Dec. 6, 1856.

WILLARD, Simon, colonist; b. Eng., 1605; s. Richard and Margery (Willard) W.; m. Mary Sharpe; m. 2d, Elizabeth Dunster; m. 3d, Mary Dunster; 17 children including Samuel. Came to Mass., 1634; a founder (with Peter Bulkeley and others) Town of Concord (Mass.), 1635, served as local magistrate, commanded militia; represented Concord in Mass. Gen. Ct., 1636-54 (except 1643, 47, 48); apptd. chief of com. to carry on and regulate fur trade, 1641; sgt.-maj. Middlesex Regt., 1653; formed (with 3 others) fur trade on Merrimac River (purchased rights for 25 pounds), 1657; expert on Indian matters, extensively employed by Gen. Ct. in Indian affairs; comdr. colonial forces in Indian fighting, circa 1675, headed expdn. to relieve Brookfield, Mass. when attacked by Indians during King Phillip's War, 1675. Died May 5, 1676.

WILLARD, Simon, clockmaker; b. Grafton, Mass:, Apr. 3, 1753; s. Benjamin and Sarah (Brooks) W.; m. Hannah Willard (his cousin), Nov. 29, 1776; m. 2d, Mary (Bird) Leeds, Jan. 23, 1788; 11 children. Apprenticed to clockmaker, Grafton, 1765, made 1st grandfather clock (better than his master's), 1766; established clock factory, Roxbury, Mass., circa 1777-78; patented Willard Patent Timepiece (came to be known as banjo clock), 1802; patented alarm clock, 1819; ret., 1839. Died Aug. 30, 1848.

WILLARD, Solomon, sculptor, architect; b. Petersham, Mass., June 26, 1783; s. William and Katherine (Wilder) W.; never married. Went to Boston to work as carpenter, 1804; built spiral stairs in Exchange Coffee House, Boston, 1808; executed colossal eagle on old Boston Customs House (his 1st sculpture), 1809; began carving figureheads for ships, 1813; made models for Unitarian Ch., Balt., scale models of Pantheon, Parthenon for Boston Athenaeum; invented (not patented) hot-air heating device used in many churches; architect for Doric U.S. Branch Bank,

Boston, 1824; later archtl. works include: Suffolk County Ct. House, Boston, 1825, Norfolk County Ct. House, Dedham, 1826; Boston Ct. House, 1832; apptd. architect Bunker Hill Monument, 1825 (famous chiefly for this); Author: Plans and Section of the Obelisk on Bunker's Hill, with the Details of Experiments Made in Quarrying the Granite, 1843. Died Quincy, Mass., Feb. 27, 1861.

WILLARD, Sylvester David, physician; b. Wilton, Fairfield County, Conn., June 19, 1825; grad. Albany (N.Y.) Med. Coll., 1848. Practiced medicine, Albany, 1848-65; sec. N.Y. Med. Soc., 1857-65; editor of its Transactions, 1858-59; served as surgeon U.S. Army, 1862-65; surgeon-gen. N.Y., 1865; insane asylum (N.Y. State) named in his honor. Author: Memoirs of Physicians of Dr. T. Spencer, 1858. Died Albany, Apr. 2, 1865.

WILLETT, Marinus, army officer, mayor N.Y.C.; b. Jamaica, L.I., N.Y., July 31, 1740; s. Edward and Aletta (Clowes) W.; attended Kings Coll. (now Columbia); m. Mary Dearsee, Apr. 2, 1760; m. 2d Mrs. Susannah Vardill, Oct. 3, 1793; m. 3d Margaret Bancker, circa 1799; at least 5 children. A wealthy mcht., N.Y.C.; served as 2d lt. Oliver De Lancey's N.Y. Regt.; leader Sons of Liberty, early supporter of Am. Revolution; helped seize arms from N.Y.C. arsenal, 1775; became 1st lt., 1st N.Y. Regt., 1775-76, lt. col. 3d N.Y. Regt., 1776; voted sword by Congress after courageous defense of Ft. Stanwix, 1777; joined Gen. Washington's army, 1778; sheriff City and County of N.Y., 1784-88, 92-96; concluded Creek Indian treaty, 1790; mayor N.Y.C., 1807-11. Died Cedar Grove, N.Y., Aug. 22, 1830.

WILLEY, Calvin, senator; b. East Haddam, Conn., Sept. 15, 1776; attended common schs.; studied law. Admitted to Conn. bar, 1798, began practice in Chatham; moved to Stafford, Conn., 1800; mem. Conn. Ho. of Reps., 1805-06; postmaster of Stafford Springs (Conn.), 1806-08; moved to Tolland County, Conn., 1808; mem. Conn. Ho. of Reps., 1810, 12, 20-21; postmaster of Tolland, 1812-16; probate judge Stafford dist., 1818-25; mem. Conn. Senate, 1823-24; presdl. elector, 1824; mem. U.S. Senate (Democrat) from Conn., 1825-31. Died Stafford, Aug. 23, 1858; buried Skungamaug Cemetery, Tolland.

WILLIAM III, King of England (Prince of Orange); b. The Hague, Netherlands, Nov. 4, 1650; son of William II of Nassau and Henrietta Mary Stuart; m. Mary (dau. of James II of Eng.), Nov. 1677, no children. Proclaimed King of Eng. (though his claim to throne was doubtful), Feb. 13, 1689; allied himself with Whig Party in return for Whig support of his religious wars in Europe; involved Eng. in War of League of Augsburg (called King William's War in Am., limited to Indian raids on the frontier), 1688-97. Died Kensington, Eng., Mar. 8, 1702.

WILLIAMS, Alfred Mason, journalist; b. Taunton, Mass., Oct. 23, 1840; s. Lloyd and Prudence (Padelford) W.; attended Brown U., circa 1858-60; m. Cora Leonard, 1870. Volunteered for service with U.S. Army, 1861, served in Gen. Banks' campaign, La., 1862; became mem. staff Taunton Daily Gazette, 1863, city editor, 1865-68; mem. lower house Mass. Legislature, 1868-69; chief editorial writer Providence (R.I.) Journal, 1870-84, editor, 1884-91. Author: The Poets and Poetry of Ireland; Sam Houston and the War of Independence in Texas, 1893; Studies in Folk Song and Popular Poetry, 1894. Died St. Kitts, W.I., Mar. 9, 1896.

WILLIAMS, Alpheus Starkey, army officer, congressman; b. Saybrook, Conn., Sept. 20, 1810; s. Ezra and Hepzibah (Starkey) W.; grad. Yale, 1831, attended Yale Law Sch. 3 years; m. Jane Hereford (Lained) Pierson, Jan. 1838; m. 2d, Martha Ann (Conant) Tellman, Sept. 17, 1873; 7 children. Probate judge, Detroit, 1840-44; published Detroit Daily Advertiser, 1844-47; served as lt. col. 1st Mich. U.S. Volunteers, Mexican War, 1847-48; postmaster, Detroit, 1849-53; pres. Mich. Oil Co., 1853-61; apptd. brig. gen. Mich. Militia, in charge of camp instrn. Ft. Wayne, Detroit, 1861; commd. brig. gen. U.S. Volunteers, 1861; in charge of mil. dist in Ark. until 1866; minister resident to Republic of Salvador, 1866-69; mem. U.S. Ho. of Reps. (Democrat) from Mich., 44th-45th congresses, 1875-78, chmn. com. on D.C. Died Washington, D.C., Dec. 21, 1878.

WILLIAMS, Archibald Hunter Arrington, congressman; b. nr. Louisburg, N.C., Oct. 22, 1842; attended Emory and Henry Coll. Enlisted as pvt. Confederate Army, during Civil War, served with Army of No. Va., 4 years, rose to capt. of his co.; wounded in Battle of Gettysburg; engaged in farming and retail trade, Oxford, N.C.; pres., Oxford & Henderson R.R.; mem. N.C. Ho. of Reps., 1883-85; mem. U.S. Ho. of Reps. (Democrat) from N.C., 52d Congress, 1891-93. Died Chase City, Va., Sept. 5, 1895; buried Elmwood Cemetery, Oxford.

WILLIAMS, Barney (real name Bernard Flaherty), actor; b. Cork, Ireland, July 20, 1823; s. Michael Flaherty; m. Mrs. Maria (Pray) Mestayer, 1849, at least 1 child. Assumed name Williams for stage; first appeared in plays in N.Y.C., 1836; played Jack in Jack Robinson and His Monkey in circus at Vauxhall Gardens, N.Y., 1843; appeared in The Irish Lion and The Happy Man, 1848; toured country with wife in Born to Good Luck, other plays with Irish leading roles, 1849; made London (Eng.) debut at Adelphi Theatre in play Rory O'Mare, 1855; managed old Wallack's Theatre (called the Broadway), 1867-69; made last appearance in The Connie Soogah and The Fairy Circle at Booth's Theatre, Christmas night, 1875. Died Murray Hill, N.Y., Apr. 25, 1876.

WILLIAMS, Benjamin, congressman; b. nr. Smithfield, N.C., Jan. 1, 1751; attended country schs. Engaged in farming; mem. N.C. Provincial Congress, 1774-75; served as 2d lt. Continental Army during Revolutionary War, promoted capt., 1776, promoted col. for gallantry at Guilford (N.C.), 1781; mem. N.C. Ho. of Commons, 1779, 85, 89; mem. N.C. Senate, 1781, 84, 86, 88; mem. U.S. Ho. of Reps. from N.C., 3d Congress, 1793-95; gov. N.C., 1799-1802, 07-08. Died Moore County, N.C., July 20, 1814; buried nr. Carbonton, N.C.

WILLIAMS, Catharine Read Arnold, author; b. Providence, R.I., Dec. 31, 1787; d. Capt. Alfred and Amey R. Arnold; m. Horatio N. Williams, Sept. 28, 1824 (div. 1826); 1 dau., Amey R., 1 adopted son, Lewis Cass DeWolf. Became sch. tchr., Providence, 1826, then turned to writing to support herself; published volume of poems (1st work), 1828. Author: Tales, National and Revolutionary, 1830; Aristocracy, or the Holbey Family, 1832; Biography of Revolutionary Heroes, 1839; The Neutral French, or the Exiles of Nova Scotia, 1841; Annals of the Aristocracy, 2 vols., 1843-45. Died Providence, Oct. 11, 1872.

WILLIAMS, Charles Grandison, congressman; b. Royalton, N.Y., Oct. 18, 1829; studied law, Rochester, N.Y. Moved to Wis., 1856, settled in Janesville; admitted to Wis. bar, began practice in Janesville; Republican presdl. elector, 1868; mem. Wis. Senate, 1869-72, pres. pro tem; mem. U.S. Ho. of Reps. (Republican) from Wis., 43d-47th congresses, 1873-83; resumed law practice. Died Watertown, S.D., Mar. 30, 1892; buried Oak Hill Cemetery, Janesville.

WILLIAMS, Christopher Harris, congressman; b. nr. Hillsboro, N.C., Dec. 18, 1798; attended U. N. C.; studied law. Admitted to N.C. bar, circa 1820, practiced law; mem. U.S. Ho. of Reps. (Whig) from N.C., 25th-27th, 31st-32d congresses, 1837-43, 49-53; resumed law practice, Lexington, Tenn. Died Lexington, Nov. 27, 1857; buried Lexington Cemetery.

WILLIAMS, David Rogerson, congressman, mfr.; b. Robbin's Neck, S.C., Mar. 8, 1776; s. David and Anne (Rogerson) W.; attended R.I. Coll. (now Brown U.); m. Sarah Power, Aug. 14, 1796; m. 2d, Elizabeth Witherspoon, 1809. Published City Gazette and Weekly Carolina Gazette, Charleston, S.C., 1801-04; mem. U.S. Ho. of Reps. (Democrat) from S.C., 9th-10th, 12th congresses, 1805-09, 11-13; apptd. brig. U.S. Army by Pres. Madison, served on Northern frontier in War of 1812, 1813, resigned, 1814; mem. N.C. Senate, 1824-27; erected mill for manufacture cotton yarns N.C.; owned hat and shoe factory; manufactured cottonseed oil; introduced mules into Southern agr. Died Nov. 17, 1830.

WILLIAMS, Edwin, journalist, author; b. Norwich, Conn., Sept. 25, 1797; s. Joseph and Abigail (Coit) W.; m. Grace Caroline Clarke, Aug. 24, 1834, at least 2 children. A founder and original mem. Am. Inst. of City of N.Y., chartered 1829, recording sec., trustee, 1830-37; contbr. to N.Y. Herald; mem. N.Y. Hist. Soc., Mechanics' Inst., St. David's Benevolent Soc. Author: The New York Annual Register, 1830-45; The Book of the Constitution, 1833; A Political History of Ireland, 1843; The Wheat Trade of the United States and Europe, 1846; The Presidents of the United States, 1849; The Twelve Stars of the Republic, 1850; The Napoleon Dynasty, 1852. Died N.Y.C., Oct. 21, 1854; buried Norwich.

WILLIAMS, Eleazar, missionary; b. Caughnawaga, Can., circa 1789; s. Thomas and Mary Ann (Kenewatsenri) W.; m. Madeleine Jourdain, Mar. 3, 1823; 3 children. Served as scout for Am. forces on No. border N.Y. in War of 1812; became missionary Episcopal Ch. to Oneida Indians, after the war, established chapel on their reservation, translated Episcopal Prayer Book into Iroquois lang; interested in founding an Indian empire; led group of Oneida Indians to Green Bay (in what is now Wis.), 1822, settled on Fox River by agreement with Indians in that area; started sch. at Green Bay, preached for many years (although replaced as Episcopal missionary and schoolmaster); made 1st claim to be Dauphin of France, circa 1839, received nat. attention through article he wrote for U.S. Mag. and Democratic Review; preacher to St. Regis Indians, Hogansburg, N.Y., 1850-58. Author: Good News to the Iroquois Nation, 1813; Prayers for families and for Particular Persons, Selected from the Book of Common Prayer, 1816. Died Hogansburg, Aug. 28, 1858.

WILLIAMS, Elisha, clergyman; b. Hatfield, Mass., Aug. 24, 1694; s. Rev. William and Elizabeth (Cotton) W.; grad. Harvard, 1711; studied theology under his father; m. Eunice Chester, Feb. 23, 1714; m. 2d, Elizabeth Scott, Jan. 29, 1751; 6 children. Preached in Wethersfield, Conn., then in Nova Scotia; returned to Wethersfield; tchr. at Yale, 1716-19, rector, 1726-39; mem. Gen. Assembly from Wethersfield, 1717-22, 40-49; ordained to ministry Congregational Ch., 1722, pastor at Newington Parish, until 1726; judge Conn. Superior Ct., 1740-43; made trip to Eng., 1749-51; del. Albany Congress, 1754. Died Wethersfield, July 24, 1755.

WILLIAMS, Elisha, state polit. leader; b. Pomfret, Conn., Aug. 29, 1773; s. Ebenezer and Jerusha (Porter) W.; m: Lucia Grosvenor, 1795, 5 children. Admitted to N.Y. bar, 1793; mem. N.Y. Assembly from Columbia County, 1800, 12-15; del. N.Y. Constl. Conv., 1821; pres. Bank of Columbia, Hudson, N.Y., several years; founder Town of Waterloo (Seneca County, N.Y.), 1815; a leader N.Y. State Federalist Party, controlled Central N.Y. for many years; devised plan to make Houston a sea port during War of 1812; acquired great wealth. Died June 29, 1833.

WILLIAMS, Elkanah, ophtalmologist; b. Lawrence County, Ind., Dec. 19, 1822; s. Isaac and Amelia (Gibson) W.; grad. Ind. Asbury U. (now DePauw U.), 1847; M.D., U. Louisville, 1850; m. Sarah L. Farmer, Dec. 1847; m. 2d, Sarah B. McGrew, Apr. 7, 1857. Practiced medicine, Cincinnati, 1855, specialized in diseases of eye and ear (one of 1st in country to limit his practice to this specialty); established charity eye clinic similar to European instns. in connection with Miami Med. Coll., 1855; prof. ophthalmology and aural surgery Miami Med. Coll. (1st chair devoted to this specialty in U.S) 1865-68; one of 1st in Am. to make use of ophthalmoscope; published article "The Ophthalmoscope" in London Med. Times and Gazette, 1854; co-editor Cincinnati Lancet and Observer, 1867-73; mem. Am. Ophthal. Soc., pres., 1876; mem. Am. Otological Soc.; hon. mem. Ophthal. Soc. of Gt. Britain, 1884; mem. staff Cincinnati Hosp., 1862-73; asst. surgeon U.S. Marine Hosp., Cincinnati, during Civil War. Died Oct. 5, 1888.

WILLIAMS, Ephraim, army officer, philanthropist; b. Newton, Mass., Nov. 7, 1714; s. Ephraim and Elizabeth (Jackson) W. Represented Stockbridge in Mass. Gen. Ct., before 1745; commd. Capt., circa 1745, maj., 1753, col. of a regt., 1755; left bequest to establish free sch. chartered as Williams Coll., Williamstown, Mass., 1793. Killed in battle at Lake George, Sept. 8, 1755.

WILLIAMS, George Huntington, mineralogist, petrologist, educator; b. Utica, N.Y., Jan. 28, 1856; s. Robert Stanton and Abigail (Doolittle) W.; B.A., Amherst Coll., 1878; Ph.D., U. Heidelburg (Germany), 1882; m. Mary Clifton Wood, Sept. 15, 1886, 3 children. Asso. in mineralogy Johns Hopkins, 1883-85, asso. prof. mineralogy, 1885-89, asso. prof. inorganic geology, 1889-91, prof. inorganic geology, 1891-94. Author: The Gabbros and Associated Hornblende Rocks Occurring in the Neighborhood of Baltimore, Md. (Bulletin 28 of U.S. Geol. Survey), 1886; Elements of Crystallography (textbook), 1899; The Greenstone Schist Areas of the Menominee and Marquette Regions of Michigan (most valuable publication; Bull. 62 of U.S. Geol. Survey), 1890. Died July 12, 1894.

WILLIAMS, George Washington, clergyman, diplomat, state legislator; b. Bedford Spring, Pa., Oct. 16, 1849; s. Thomas and Nellie (Rouse) W.; grad. Newton Theol. Instn., Newton Center, Mass., 1874. Enlisted as pvt. 6th Mass. Regt. 1862; sailed for Tex., 1865, col., comdr. troops to capture munitions sold to Mexico; ordained to ministry Baptist Ch., 1874; pastor 12th Street Bapt. Ch., Boston, 1875, Union Bapt. Ch., Cincinnati 1876-79; contr. articles signed "Aristides" to Cincinnati Comml.; admitted to Ohio bar, 1877; mem. Ohio Legislature, 1879-81; U.S. minister to Haiti, 885-86; del. to World Conf. of Fgn. Missions, London, 1886; became employee of Belgian govt. in Congo, 1890. Author: History of the Negro Race in America, 1833; A History of the Negro Troops in the War of the Rebellion, 1888; Report upon the Congo State and Country to the President of the Republic of the United States, 1890; An Open Letter to . . . Leopold II, 1890. Died Blackpool, Eng., Aug. 4, 1891.

WILLIAMS, Henry, congressman; b. Taunton, Mass., Nov. 30, 1805; studied law. Admitted to Mass. bar, 1829, began practice in Taunton; mem. Mass. Ho. of Reps., 1834, Mass. Senate, 1836-37; mem. U.S. Ho. of Reps. (Democrat) from Mass., 26th, 28th congresses, 1839-41, 43-45. Died Taunton, May 8, 1887; buried Mt. Pleasant Cemetery, Taunton.

WILLIAMS, Henry Willard, ophthalmologist; b. Boston, Dec. 11, 1821; s. Willard and Elizabeth (Osgood) W.; grad. Harvard Med. Sch., 1849; m. Elizabeth Dewe, 1848; m. 2d, Elizabeth Adeline Law, 1860; 6 children. Organized voluntary class of Harvard students for ophthalmology lectures, 1850; lectr. ophthalmology Harvard Med. Sch., 1866-71, 1st prof. ophthalmology, 1871-95; ophthal. surgeon Boston City Hosp., 1864-91; a founder Am. Ophthal. Soc., 1864, pres., 1868-75; wrote article on cataract operation for Boston Med. and Surg. Jour., 1850; pres. Mass. Med. Soc., 1880-82. Author: A Practical Guide to the Study of the Diseases of the Eye, 1862; Our Eyes, and How To Take Care of Them, 1871; The Diagnosis and Treatment of the Diseases of the Eye, 1881. Died Boston, June 13, 1895.

WILLIAMS, Hezekiah, congressman; b. nr. Woodstock, Vt., July 28, 1798; grad. Dartmouth, 1820; studied law. Admitted to Me. bar, began practice in Castine, 1825; register of probate for Hancock County (Me.), 1824-38; selectman of Castine, 1833-35, 43-44, trustee sch. fund, 1834, mem. sch. com., 1840; mem. Me. Senate, 1839-41; mem. U.S. Ho. of Reps. (Democrat) from Me., 29th-30th congresses, 1845-49; resumed law practice. Died Castine, Oct. 23, 1856; buried Castine Cemetery.

WILLIAMS, Isaac, Jr., congressman; b. Goshen, Conn., Apr. 5, 1777; s. Isaac Williams. Moved to Otsego County, N.Y., 1793; apptd. undersheriff of Otsego County, 1810, sheriff, 1811-13; mem. U.S. Ho. of Reps. (Democrat; contested election) from N.Y., 13th, 15th, 18th congresses, Dec. 20, 1813-15, 17-19, 23-25; unsuccessful candidate for sheriff, 1828. Died Cooperstown, N.Y., Nov. 9, 1860; buried Warren Cemetery, Otsego, N.Y.

WILLIAMS, Israel, Loyalist; b. Hatfield, Mass. Nov. 30, 1709; s. Rev. William and Christian (Stoddard) W.; grad. Harvard, 1727; m. Sarah Chester, 1731, 7 or 8 children. Selectman, Hatfield, 1732-63; 2d in command of Hampshire County Regt., Mass. Militia, 1744, apptd. col., 1748; responsible for defense of Western Mass. throughout French and Indian War; justice of peace, clk. Hampshire County Ct.; judge Hampshire County Ct. Common Pleas, 1758-74; mem. Mass. Legislature from Hatfield, intermittently, 1733-73; mem. Mass. Gov.'s Council, 1761-67; executor under will of Ephraim Williams, instrumental in founding "free school" (became Williams Coll.); considered Loyalist in Western Mass. during early years of Revolution, imprisoned for Loyalism, 1777, deprived of citizenship until 1780. Died Hatfield, Jan. 10, 1788.

WILLIAMS, James, journalist, diplomatic agt.; b. Grainger County, Tenn., July 1, 1796; s. Ethelred and Mary (Copeland) W.; m. Lucy Jane Graham, 2 children. Founded Knoxville (Tenn.) Post, 1841, editor; elected to Tenn. Ho. of Reps., 1843; founder Deaf and Dumb Asylum, Knoxville; published essays under pseudonym "Old Line Whig;" U.S. minister to Turkey (apptd. by Pres. Buchanan), 1858-60; traveled through Syria, Egypt and Palestine on behalf Am. missionaries; Confederate propagandist and minister at large in Europe, 1860; contbr. articles to Times, Standard, Index which helped swing middle and upper class of England to So. side. Author: Letters on Slavery from the Old World, 1861; The Rise and Fall of the Model Republic, 1863. Died Gratz, Austria, Apr. 10, 1869; buried Gratz.

WILLIAMS, James Douglas, gov. Ind.; b. Pickaway County, O., Jan. 16, 1808; s. George Williams; m. Nancy Huffman, Feb. 17, 1831, 7 children. Owned grist mill, saw mill, packing plant, Wheaton, Ind.; justice of peace, Wheaton, 1839-43; mem. Ind. Ho. of Reps., 5 terms between 1843-69, Ind. Senate, 3 terms between 1858-73; mem. Ind. Bd. Agr., 1855-75, pres., 1871-75; mem. U.S. Ho, of Reps. (Democrat) from Ind., 44th Congress, 1875-77, chmn. com. on accounts; Dem. gov. Ind., 1877-80. Died Indpls., Nov. 20, 1880; buried Walnut Grove Cemetery, nr. Monroe City, Knox County, Ind.

WILLIAMS, James Wray, congressman; b. Md., Oct. 8, 1792. Mem. Md. Ho. of Dels., speaker, 1830; mem. U.S. Ho. of Reps. (Democrat) from Md., 27th Congress, 1841-42. Died Prieshford farm, Deer Creek, Md., Dec. 2, 1842; buried Prieshford farm.

WILLIAMS, Jared, congressman; b. Montgomery County, Md., Mar. 4, 1766. Engaged in farming; mem. Va. Ho. of Dels., 1812-17; mem. U.S. Ho. of Reps. (Jacksonian Democrat) from Va., 16th-18th congresses, 1819-25; Dem. presdl. elector, 1828. Died nr. Newton, Va., Jan. 2, 1831.

WILLIAMS, Jared Warner, senator, gov. N.H.; b. West Woodstock, Conn., Dec. 22, 1796; grad. Brown U., 1818; attended Litchfield (Conn.) Law Sch. Admitted to N.H. bar, 1822, began practice in Lancaster; mem. N.H. Ho. of Reps., 1830-31, N.H. Senate, 1832-34; mem. U.S. Ho. of Reps. (Democrat) from N.H., 25th-26th congresses, 1837-41; gov. N. H., 1847-49; mem. U.S. Senate from N.H., Nov. 29, 1853-July 15, 1854. Died Lancaster, Sept. 29, 1864; buried Summer St. Cemetery, Lancaster.

WILLIAMS, Jesse Lynch, civil engr.; b. Westfield, N.C., May 6, 1807; s. Jesse and Sarah (Terrell) W.; m. Susan Creighton, Nov. 15, 1831. Held minor position in 1st survey of Miami & Erie Canal in Ohio (Cincinnati to Maumee Bay), 1828; mem. bd. engrs. using reservoirs rather than longfeeders from distant streams to supply summit level of canal with water; chief engr. Wabash Erie Canal, 1832; surveyed all other canals of Ind., 1835; engr.-in-chief all canal routes in Ind., 1836, all railroads and turnpikes, 1837; chief engr. Wabash & Erie Canal, 1847-76, Ft. Wayne Chgo. R.R., 1854-56; U.S. dir. U.P. Ry., 1864-69; apptd. receiver Grand Rapids & Ind. R.R., 1869; apptd. chief engr. in charge of completion of Cincinnati, Richmond & Ft. Wayne R.R., 1871; an original dir. Presbyn. Theol. Sem. of N.W. (later McCormick Theol. Sem.). Died Oct. 9, 1886.

WILLIAMS, John, clergyman; b. Roxbury, Mass., Dec. 10, 1664; s. Deacon Samuel and Theoda (Park) W.; B.A., Harvard, 1683; m. Eunice Mather, July 21, 1687; m. 2d, Abigail (Allen) Bissell, Sept. 16, 1707; 13 children. Ordained 1st pastor Congregational Ch., Deerfield, Mass., 1688; held captive by raiding band of Indians and French, 1704-06; returned to post, Deerfield, 1707; chaplain expdn. against Port Royal, 1711; commr. to Can. to obtain return of English prisoners, 1713-14. Author: (with Cotton Mather's help) The Redeemed Captive Returning to Zion, 1707. Died Deerfield. June 12, 1729.

WILLIAMS, John, Continental congressman; b. Hanover County, Va., Mar. 14, 1731; studied law, Admitted to N.C. bar, began practice in Williamsboro; a founder U. N.C.; dep. atty. gen., 1768; del. N.C. Provincial Congress, 1775; mem. N.C. Ho. of Commons, 1777-78, served as speaker; mem. Continental congress from N.C., 1778-79; judge N.C. Supreme Ct., 1779-99. Died Montpelier, N.C., Oct. 10, 1799; buried family cemetery, Montpelier.

WILLIAMS, John, congressman; b. Barnstable, Eng., Sept. 1752; studied medicine and surgery St. Thomas Hosp., London, Eng. Served as surgeon's mate on an English man of war, 1 year; came to Am., 1773, settled in New Perth (now Salem), N. Y., practiced medicine; mem. N.Y. Provincial Congress, 1775-77; apptd. surgeon N.Y. State Militia, 1775, col. Charlotte County (N.Y.) Regt., 1776; mem. N.Y. State Senate, 1777-78, N.Y. State Assembly, 1781-82; apptd. mem. 1st bd. regents N.Y. U., 1784; commd. brig. gen., 1786; del. N.Y. Conv. to ratify U.S. Constn., 1788; mem. Council of Appointment, 1789; mem. U.S. Ho. of Reps. from N.Y., 4th-5th congresses, 1795-99; owner extensive land holdings; promoter, dir. co. organized to build Erie Canal; judge county ct. Died Salem, July 22, 1806; buried Salem Cemetery.

WILLIAMS, John, satirist, critic; b. London, Eng., Apr. 28, 1761. Better known as Anthony Pasquin; came to U.S., 1797/98; editor, publisher weekly Columbian Gazette, N.Y.C., 1799; editor Boston Democrat, 1804; wrote "Hamiltoniad" (anti-federalist poem) under pseudonym, preface dated 1804. Author: A Life of Alexander Hamilton, 1804; Dramatic Censor, 1812. Died Bklyn., Oct. 12, 1818.

WILLIAMS, John, senator; b. Surry County, N.C., Jan. 29, 1778; s. Joseph and Rebecca (Lanier) W.; m. Melinda White; children—Joseph Lanier, Margaret (Williams) Pearson, Col. John. Admitted to Knoxville (Tenn.) bar, 1803; served as capt. 6th Inf., U.S. Army, 1779-1800, col. Tenn. Volunteers, 1812-14, col. 39th U.S. Inf., 1814; mem. U.S. Senate from Tenn., 1815 (apptd. to fill vacancy), 1817-23, chmn. com. mil. affairs; U.S. charge d'affaires (apptd. by Pres. Adams) to Fedn. of Central Am., 1825; elected to Tenn. Senate, 1827. Died Knoxville, Aug. 10, 1837.

WILLIAMS, John, congressman; b. Utica, N.Y., Jan. 7, 1807. Moved to Rochester, N.Y., 1824, engaged in merc. bus., flour mfg.; alderman Rochester, 1844, mayor, 1853; mem. U.S. Ho. of Reps. (Democrat) from N.Y., 34th Congress, 1855-57; engaged in milling bus., 1858-70; served as maj. gen. 7th Div., N.Y. Nat. Guard; exise commr. and mgr. house of refuge, 1870; city treas. Rochester, 1871-75. Died Rochester, Mar. 26, 1875; buried Mt. Hope Cemetery, Rochester.

WILLIAMS, John, clergyman, coll. pres.; b. Old Deerfield, Mass., Aug. 30, 1817; s. Ephriam and Emily (Trowbridge) W.; attended Harvard, 1831-33; grad. Washington (now Trinity) Coll., 1835. Read for Episcopal orders, 1835-38; tutor Washington Coll., 1837-40; ordained deacon Protestant Episcopal Ch., Middletown, Conn., 1838, priest, 1841; traveled in Europe, 1840-41; rector St. George's Ch., Schenectady, N.Y., 1842-48; pres. Trinity Coll., Hartford, Conn., 1848-53, Hobart prof. history and literature, lectr. history, 1853-92, vice chancellor, 1853-65, chancellor, 1865; apptd. bishop coadjutor Diocese of Conn., 1851, bishop, 1865; chartered Berkeley Divinity Sch., Middletown, 1854, dean, prof. theology, 1854-99. Author: Ancient Hymns of Holy Church, 1845; Thoughts on Gospel Miracles, 1848; The Seabury Centenary, 1885. Died Middletown, Feb. 7, 1899.

WILLIAMS, John Fletcher, sec., librarian Minn. Hist. Soc.; b. Cincinnati, Sept. 25, 1834; s. Samuel and Margaret (Trautner) W.; attended Ohio Wesleyan U.; m. Catherine Roberts, July 1865, several children. Journalist, St. Paul, Minn., 1855-70; sec., librarian Minn. Hist. Soc., 1867-93, supplied material for authorized survey of source of Mississippi River; commr. from Minn. to Centennial Exhbn., Phila., 1876; mem. Ind. Order Odd Fellows. Died Rochester, Minn., Apr. 28, 1895.

WILLIAMS, John Foster, naval officer; b. Boston, Oct. 12, 1743; m. Hannah Homer, Oct. 6, 1774. Commd. capt. Mass. state sloop Republic, 1776; transferred to ship Massachusetts, 1776; made 2 cruises in Mass. state brig. Hazard, captured several prizes, 1778-79; forced Brit. brig Active (18 guns) to surrender off St. Thomas, W. I., 1779; commanded Protector (largest ship in Mass. navy); communicated an invention to distill fresh water from salt water with appropriate drawings to Boston Marine Soc., 1792; surveyed Nantasket Harbor, reported results to U.S. Govt., 1803; commanded U.S. revenue cutter Massachusetts, 1790-1814. Died June 24, 1814; buried Granary Buring Ground, Boston.

WILLIAMS, John Insco, artist; b. Oldtown, O., 1813; married, 2 daus. Became profl. portrait painter, circa 1832; itinerant portraitist in Ind., 3 years; settled in Cincinnati, circa 1840; completed panorama of Bibl. history, 1849, exhibited very successfully in Cincinnati, Dayton (O.), Balt., Washington (D.C.), Boston, destroyed by fire in Independence Hall, Phila., 1851; exhibited 2d version of panorama, 1856-71. Died Dayton, 1873.

WILLIAMS, John McKeown Snow, congressman; b. Richmond, Va., Aug. 13, 1818; attended pub. schs., Boston. Engaged in merc. bus. and shipping; mem. Mass. Ho. of Reps., 1856, Mass. Senate, 1858; Republican presdl. elector, 1868; mem. U.S. Ho. of Reps. (Rep.) from Mass., 43d Congress, 1873-75. Died Cambridge, Mass., Mar. 19, 1886; buried Mt. Auburn Cemetery, Cambridge.

WILLIAMS, Jonathan, army officer; b. Boston, May 26, 1750; s. Jonathan and Grace (Harris) W.; m. Marianne Alexander, Sept. 12, 1779. Joined Benjamin Franklin (his uncle), Paris, France, 1776; agt. of Continental Congress at Nantes to inspect arms and other supplies being shipped from that port; engaged in various business ventures in Europe, 1785; asso. judge Phila. Ct. of Common Pleas, 1796; insp. fortifications 1st supt. U.S. Mil. Acad. with rank of maj. U.S. Army, (apptd. by Thomas Jefferson) 1801-03, resigned, 1803, accepted reappointment with rank of lt. col. engrs. with complete authority over all cadets, 1805; resigned commn., 1812; a founder Mil. Philos. Soc. (to promote mil. science and history); mem. Am. Philos. Soc. Author: Theromometrical Navigation, 1799; The Elements of Fortification (translated from French), 1801; Manoeuvres of Horse Artillery (translation of work by Tadeuz Kosciuszko), 1808. Died May 16, 1815.

WILLIAMS, Joseph Lanier, congressman; b. nr. Knoxville, Tenn., Oct. 23, 1810; s. John Williams; attended U. East Tenn., U.S. Mil. Acad.; studied law. Admitted to Tenn. bar, began practice in Knoxville; mem. U.S. Ho. of Reps. (Whig) from Tenn., 25th-27th congresses, 1837-43; practiced law, Washington, D.C.; apptd. judge U.S. Dist. Ct. for Dakota Territory by Pres. Lincoln. Died Knoxville, Dec. 14, 1865; buried Old Gray Cemetery, Knoxville.

WILLIAMS, Lemuel, congressman; b. Taunton, Mass., June 18, 1747; grad. Harvard, 1765; studied law. Admitted to Mass. bar, practiced in Bristol and Worcester counties; town clk. of New Bedford (Mass.), 1792-1800; mem. U.S. Ho. of Reps. from Mass., 6th-8th congresses, 1799-1805; mem. Mass. Ho. of Reps., 1806. Died Acushnet, Mass., Nov. 8, 1828; buried Acushnet Cemetery.

WILLIAMS, Lewis, congressman; b. Surry County, N.C., Feb. 1, 1786; grad. U. N.C., 1808. Mem. N.C.

Ho. of Comons, 1813-14; mem. U.S. Ho. of Reps. from N.C., 14th-27th congresses, 1815-42, known as "father of the house." Died Washington, D.C., Feb. 23, 1842; buried Panther Creek Cemetery, Surry County.

WILLIAMS, Marmaduke, congressman; b. Caswell County, N.C., Apr. 6, 1772; studied law. Admitted to N.C. bar, practiced law; mem. N.C. Senate, 1802; mem. U.S. Ho. of Reps. (Democrat) from N.C., 8th-10th congresses, 1803-09; moved to Huntsville, Ala., 1810, to Tuscaloosa, Ala., 1818; del. Ala. Constl. Conv., 1819; returned to N.C.; unsuccessful candidate for gov. N.C., 1819; mem. N.C. Ho. of Commons, 1821-29; judge Tuscaloosa County Ct., 1832-42. Died Tuscaloosa, Oct. 29, 1850; buried Greenwood Cemetery, Tuscaloosa.

WILLIAMS, Nathan, congressman; b. Williamstown, Mass., Dec. 19, 1773; attended common schs., Burlington, Vt.; studied law, Troy, N.Y. Admitted to N.Y. bar, 1795, began practice in Utica; a founder, librarian Utica Pub. Library; pres. corp. Village of Utica; pres. Manhattan Bank; dist. atty. for 6th N.Y. Dist., 1801-13; mem. U.S. Ho. of Reps. (Democrat) from N.Y., 9th Congress, 1805-07; served in War of 1812; mem. N.Y. State Assembly, 1816-18, 19; regent Univ. State N.Y., 1817-24; dist. atty. Oneida County (N.Y.), 1818-21; del. N.Y. Constl. Conv., 1821; judge circuit ct., 1823-33; apptd. clk. N.Y. State Supreme Ct., 1834. Died Geneva, N.Y., Sept. 25, 1835; buried "Burying Ground," Utica, reinterred Forest Hill Cemetery, Utica.

WILLIAMS, Nathaniel, schoolmaster, physician; b. Boston, Aug. 25, 1675; s. Deacon Nathaniel and Mary Oliver (Shrimpton) W.; grad. Harvard, 1693; m. Anne Bradstreet, 8 children including Ann (Williams) Nayes, Mary (Williams) Smebert. Ordained in Colledge Hall at Cambridge to preach to non-conformist church at Barbadoes, 1698; assisted Ezekiel Cheever in Boston Latin Sch. 1703, master, 1708-1733; advocate of inoculation against smallpox. Author: The Method of Practice in the Small Pox . . . Taken from a Manuscript of the Late Dr. Nathanael Williams (edited and published by Thomas Prince), 1752. Died Jan. 10, 1737/38.

WILLIAMS, Otho Holland, army officer; b. Prince Georges County, Md., Mar. 1747; s. Joseph and Prudence (Holland) W; m. Mary Smith, 1786, 4 sons. Apptd. 1st lt. in company raised in Md., 1775; participated in siege of Boston, promoted capt.; commd. maj. Continental Army, 1776; wounded and taken prisoner, 1776; 1st paroled in N.Y.C., then thrown into provost's jail charged with secretly communicating mil. information to George Washington, exchanged, 1778; apptd. col. 6th Md. Regt., 1776; took part in battles of Monmouth and Camden; promoted brig. gen., 1782; naval officer of Balt. dist., 1783-89; founded town of Williamsport (Md.), 1787; collector Port of Balt., 1789-93. Died Miller's Town, Va., July 15, 1794; buried Riverview Cemetery, Williamsport.

WILLIAMS, Reuel, senator; b. Hallowell (now Augusta), Me., June 2, 1783; s. Seth and Zilpha (Ingraham) W.; m. Sarah Lowell Cony, Nov. 1807, 9 children. Admitted to Me. bar, 1802; law practice included adminstrn. of "Kennebec Purchase" and Bowdoin Coll. timberlands; mem. Me. Ho. of Reps., 1822-26, 29-32, Me. Senate, 1827-28; mem. commn. to divide public lands between Me. and Mass., 1825; commr. public bldgs. Me., 1831; mem. N.E. Boundary Commn., 1836; mem. U.S. Senate (Democrat) from Me., 1837-43; mem. commn. for defense in No. states, 1861; responsible for moving Me. capitol from Augusta to Portland, 1827; contbd. $10,000 toward state insane asylum, Augusta; worked for improvement of Kennebec River navigation; supported Me. in boundary dispute with New Brunswick (Can.), reopened question leading to so-called Aroostook or Madawaska "war" and Webster-Ashburton Treaty, 1842; chief promoter, 1st pres. 72-mile Kennebec & Portland Ry. (now part of Me. Central R.R.); trustee Bowdoin Coll., 1822-60. Died Augusta, July 25, 1862.

WILLIAMS, Robert, clergyman; b. Eng., circa 1745; married, 1774. Came to Am., 1769; mem. Irish Methodist Conf., 1766-69; began work Wesley Chapel, N.Y.C.; active around N.Y. and Md., 1769-71; preached in Norfolk, Va., 1772, Petersburg, Va., 1773; organized Brunswick circuit which extended South from Petersburg into N.C., 1774; pioneer of Am. Methodism, 1st traveling Meth. preacher to come to Am., preached 1st Meth. sermon and formed 1st Meth. soc. in N.C. Died between Portsmouth and Suffolk, Va., Sept 26, 1775.

WILLIAMS, Robert, territorial gov., congressman; b. Prince Edward County, Va., July 12, 1773; studied law, N.C. Admitted to N.C. bar, began practice in what is now Rockingham County; mem.N.C. Senate, 1792-95; mem. U.S. Ho. of Reps. from N.C., 5th-7th congresses, 1797-1803; mem. commn. apptd. by Pres. Jefferson to determine rights of land claims West of Pearl River in Miss. Territory, 1803-07; Gov. Miss. Territory, 1805-09; practiced law, Miss. and N.C., also engaged in planting; adj. gen. N.C.; moved to Ouachita, La. Died Ouachita, Jan. 25, 1836; buried nr. Monroe, La.

WILLIAMS, Roger, clergyman, pres. R.I.; b. London, Eng., circa 1603; s. James and Alice (Pemberton) W.; B.A., Pembroke Coll., Cambridge, 1627; m. Mary Barnard, Dec. 15, 1629. Ordained to ministry Ch. of Eng., circa 1628; chaplain to Sir William Masham, Essex, Eng.; at conference of founders of Puritan colony in Am., 1629; came to Am., 1630; called to serve in Puritan Church in Boston upon arriving at Mass. Bay Colony, 1631, declined to serve; indulged in severe criticism of Puritans for enforcing religious precepts with powers of civil govt., became opponent of regime; rulers of colony refused to allow him to become tchr. in Ch. at Salem (Mass.) where he had been invited, 1631; received tolerantly at Plymouth Colony, 1631-33; assumed pastorate Congregation 1633, attacked Puritan expropriation of Indian lands; tried by Gen. Ct. of Mass. Bay colony and found guilty of spreading "dangerous opinions," 1635, banished from colony; tried to organize Salem congregation into separate colony, 1635, pursued by Puritan Leaders and forced to flee from Mass., winter 1635-36; with group of followers founded settlement in R.I. (Providence), 1636, came to be known for democratic instns. including separation of ch. and state, town govt. and religious toleration; played vital role in making peace with Indians during Pequot War, 1637; became "Seeker" in religious affairs identifying with no sect and accepting only fundamentals of Christianity, 1639; went to England, 1643, following establishment New Eng. Confedn., received patent for governing Narragansett Bay area; went to England again, 1652, following Coddington's attempts to take over govt. of colony, received commn. revoking latter's authority as gov.; pres. R.I. Colony, 1654-57. Author: The Bloody Tenet of Persecution (most famous work), 1644; The Bloody Tenet Yet More Bloody (written in reply to John Cotton), 1652. Died 1683.

WILLIAMS, Samuel May, pioneer, banker; b. Providence, R.I., Oct. 4, 1795; s. Howell and Dorethea (Wheat) W.; m. Sarah Scott, Mar. 18, 1828, 8 children. Pvt. sec. to Stephen F. Austin at new settlement San Felipe de Autsin (Tex.), 1824; made extensive land speculations in Tex. after 1834; resigned connections with Austin colony, organized merc. partnership with Thomas F. McKinney, Quintana, Tex., before Tex. Revolution; opened similar business, Galveston, Tex., 1837, involved in a number of promotion enterprises, opened the Comml. & Agrl. Bank, Galveston (1st chartered bank in Tex.), 1847, did extensive business in state, 1847-57, established br., Brownsville, Tex.; law suits filed against Comml. & Agrl. Bank to annul charter, bank closed after his death. Died Galveston, Sept. 13, 1858.

WILLIAMS, Samuel Wells, missionary, diplomat; b. Utica, N.Y., Sept. 22, 1812; s. William and Sophia (Wells) W.; attended Rensselaer Poly. Inst., Troy, N.Y., 1831-32; m. Sarah Walworth, Nov. 25, 1847, 5 children. Printer for Am. Bd. Commrs. for Fgn. Missions; sailed for China, 1833; moved his press to Macoa, 1835; assisted with Chinese Repository; prepared (with Elijah Bridgeman) A Chinese Chrestomathy in the Canton Dialect, 1841; edited A Chinese Commercial Guide, 2d edit., 1844; in U.S., 1845-48; interpreter on Commodore Perry's visit to Japan, 1853; sec., interpreter Am. legation to China, 1856-76; in charge of legation at Peking, 1863; helped Sweden obtain treaty with China, 1870; prof. Chinese lang. and literature Yale, 1877-84; pres. Am. Bible Soc., Am. Oriental Soc. Author: Easy Lessons in Chinese, 1842; An English and Chinese Vocabulary in the Court Dialect, 1844; Chinese Topography, 1844; The Middle Kingdom, 2 vols., 1848; A Tonic Dictionary of the Chinese Language in the Canton Dialect, 1856; Syllabic Dictionary to the Chinese Language, 1874. Died Feb. 16, 1884.

WILLIAMS, Sherrod, congressman; b. Pulaski County, Ky., 1804; studied law. Learned brickmaker's trade, Monticello, Ky.; admitted to Ky. bar, practiced law; mem. Ky. Ho. of Reps., 1829-34, 46; mem. U.S. Ho. of Reps. (Whig) from Ky., 24th-26th congresses, 1835-41. Died in one of the Southern states.

WILLIAMS, Stephen West, medical historian; b. Deerfield, Mass., Mar. 27, 1790; s. William Stoddard and Mary (Hoyt) W.; A.M. (hon.), Williams Coll., 1829, M.D. (hon.), 1842; M.D. (hon.), Berkshire Med. Instn., 1824; m. Harriet Godhue, Oct. 20, 1818. 4 children including Helen (Williams) Huntington. Explored hills of Western Mass. collecting herbarium of imdigenous medical plants; lectr. medical jurisprudence Berkshire Med. Instn., 1823-31; faculty Willoughby (O.) U., 1838-53; lectr. Dartmouth Med. Sch., 1838-41; added notes to A Compendium of Medical Practice (James Bedingfield), 1823; wrote papers for N.Y. Hist. Soc., similar assns.; contbr. biographies to American Medical Biography, published 1845. Author: Floral Calendar Kept at Deerfield, Mass., 1819; (lecture) A Catechism of Medical Jurisprudence, 1835. Died Laona, Ill., July 6, 1855.

WILLIAMS, Thomas, congressman; b. Greensburg, Pa., Aug. 28, 1806; grad. Dickinson Coll., Carlisle, Pa., 1825; studied law. Admitted to Pa. bar, 1828, began practice in Greensburg; moved to Pitts., 1832, practiced law; mem. Pa. Senate, 1838-41; mem. U.S. Ho. of Reps. (Republican) from Pa., 38th-40th congresses, 1863-69, a mgr. apptd. to conduct impeachment of Andrew Johnson, 1868. Died Allegheny City, Pa., June 6, 1872; buried Allegheny Cemetery, Pitts.

WILLIAMS, Thomas Hickman, senator; b. Williamson County, Tenn., Jan. 20, 1801; attended common schs. Moved to Miss., settled in Pontotoc County, engaged in planting; mem. U.S. Senate (Democrat) from Miss., Nov. 12, 1838-39; a founder U. Miss., sec., treas., 1845-51; known as "father of the state univ." Died on family estate nr. Pontotoc, Miss., May 3, 1851; buried family estate.

WILLIAMS, Thomas Hill, senator; b. N.C., 1780; studied law. Admitted to Miss. bar, practiced law; register land office for Territory of Miss., 1805; apptd. sec. Miss. Territory, 1805, 07, acting gov., 1806, 09; collector of customs Port of New Orleans, 1810; del. Miss. Constl. Conv.; mem. U.S. Senate (Democrat) from Miss., Dec. 10, 1817-29; moved to Tenn. Died Robertston County, Tenn., 1840.

WILLIAMS, Thomas Scott, jurist; b. Wethersfield, Conn., June 26, 1777; s. Ezekiel and Prudence (Stoddard) W.; grad. Yale, 1794; attended Litchfield (Conn.) Law Sch.; m. Delia Ellsworth, Jan. 7, 1812; m. 2d, Martha Coit, Nov. 1, 1842; no children. Admitted to Conn. bar, 1799; practiced law in Mansfield, Conn.; mem. Conn. Gen. Assembly, 1813, 15, 16, clk. of house, 1815, 16; mem. U.S. Ho. of Reps. from Conn., 15th Congress, 1817-19; mem. Conn. Legislature, 1819, 25, 27-29; mayor of Hartford (Conn.), 1831-35; apptd. asso. justice, 1834-47; pres. Am. Asylum for Deaf and Dumb, 1840-67; v.p. Conn. Retreat for Insane, Am. Bd. Commrs. for Fgn. Missions; pres. Am. Tract Soc., 1848-67; Sunday Sch. tchr. 1st Ch. of Hartford, 1834-61, deacon, 1836-67, liberal contbr. to Yale, also to charity; his judical opinions appear in 7-8 Connecticut Reports. Author: Chief Justice Williams on the Maine Law, Its Expediency and Constitutionality (pamphlet), circa 1851; The Tract Society and Slavery (address), 1859. Died Dec. 15, 1861.

WILLIAMS, Thomas Wheeler, businessman, congressman; b. Stonington, Conn., Sept. 28, 1789; attended pub. schs. Clk., N.Y.C.; engaged in bus. mission to Norway, Sweden and Russia; engaged in shipping bus., 8 years; moved to New London, Conn., 1818; became leader in whaling bus.; mem. U.S. Ho. of Reps. (Whig) from Conn., 26th-27th congresses, 1839-43; mem. Conn. Ho. of Reps., 1846-47; Whig presdl. elector, 1848; became pres. New London, Willimantic, and Palmer R.R. (later New London Northern R.R.), 1847. Died New London, Dec. 31, 1874; buried Cedar Grove Cemetery, New London.

WILLIAMS, William, Continental Congressman; b. Lebanon, Conn., Apr. 8, 1731; s. Solomon and Mary (Porter) W.; grad. Harvard, 1751; m. Mary Trumbull, Feb. 14, 1771, 3 children: Participated in operations at Lake George under Ephraim Williams during French and Indian War, 1755; helped Gov. Jonathan Trumbull compose state papers; contbd. promissory note which defrayed cost of sending Conn. troops to aid in capture of Ticonderoga, 1775; offered own specie for needed army supplies, 1779; placed his home at disposal of officers when French regt. quartered in Lebanon, 1780-81; selectman of Lebanon, 1760-80, town clk., 1752-96; mem. lower house Conn. Legislature, 1757-76, 81-84; mem. coms. to consider Stamp Act. Conn.'s claim to Susquehannah lands, case of Mich. Indians; represented Conn. at confs. of dels. from New Eng.; mem. Continental Congress, 1776-78, 83-84, signer Declaration of Independence 1776, mem. bd. war, 1777; mem. Conn. Gov.'s Council, 1784-1803; helped frame Articles of Confederation; del. to Conn. Conv. to ratify U.S. Constn., 1788; judge Windham County Cts., 1776-1805; judge of probate for Windham dist., 1775-1809. Died Lebanon, Aug. 2, 1811; buried Lebanon.

WILLIAMS, William, printer, publisher; b. Framingham, Mass., Oct. 12, 1787; s. Thomas and Susanna (Dana) W.; m. Sophia Wells, Nov. 5, 1811; m. 2d, Catherine Huntington, Mar. 26, 1833; 14 children including Samuel Wells. Partner printing firm Seward & Williams, Utica, N.Y.,

1807; partner Seward book store, 1814; published Utica directory (1st book bearing his name alone as printer), 1817; had largest book store west of Albany, N.Y., 1820; printed almanacs, directories and books, 1807-38; served on staff Gen. Oliver Collins during War of 1812, raised co. of volunteers, Utica, 1813; brigade insp. 13th N.Y. Inf., 1816; editor newspapers Patriot and Patrol, Utica, supported Federalists; strong supporter of De Witt Clinton in the early 1820's; he was active in raising Utica company; brig. insp. 13th N.Y. Inf., 1816. Lived in Tonawanda, N.Y., as result of financial difficulties, after 1836. Died Utica, June 10, 1850.

WILLIAMS, William, artist; b. Westmoreland County, Pa., Dec. 6, 1796. Businessman, Westmoreland County; went to Ia., 1850, established provisions store at Ft. Dodge; made drawing of Ft. Dodge, 1852; bought mil. bldgs., laid out town of Ft. Dodge, 1854, 1st mayor, 1869-71. Died Ft. Dodge, Feb. 26, 1874.

WILLIAMS, William, congressman; b. Bolton, Conn., Sept. 6, 1815; ed. common schs. Bank clk., Windham, Conn.; moved to Sandusky, O., 1838, to Buffalo, N.Y., 1839, engaged in banking; mgr. and pres. of a railroad; mem. N.Y. State Assembly, 1866-67; mem. U.S. Ho. of Reps. (Democrat) from N.Y., 42d Congress, 1871-73. Died Buffalo, Sept. 10, 1876; buried Forest Lawn Cemetery, Buffalo.

WILLIAMS, William, congressman; b. nr. Carlisle, Pa., May 11, 1821; attended commons schs.; studied law. Admitted to the bar, 1845, began practice in Warsaw, Ind.; treas. Kosciusko County (Ind.), 1852; unsuccessful candidate for lt. gov. Ind., 1853; mgr. Bank of Warsaw, several years; dir. Ft. Wayne & Chgo. Ry., 1854-56, Michigan City Prison, 1859-62; served with Union Army as commandant Camp Allen, Ft. Wayne, Ind., during Civil War, 1862, later paymaster U.S. Volunteers, Louisville, Ky., until 1865; mem. U.S. Ho. of Reps. (Republican) from Ind., 40th-44th congresses, 1867-75; resumed practice of law, Warsaw; chargé d'affaires to Paraguay and Uruguay (apptd. by Pres. Arthur), 1882-85. Died Warsaw, Apr. 22, 1896; buried Oakwood Cemetery, Warsaw.

WILLIAMS, William R., clergyman; b. N.Y.C., Oct. 14, 1804; s. Rev. John and Gainar (Roberts) W.; grad. Columbia Coll., 1822; m. Mary S. Bowen, Apr. 1847, 2 sons. Ordained to ministry Baptist Ch., circa 1832; pastor Amity Street Baptist Ch., N.Y.C., 1832-85; gained public attention by address The Conservative Principle in Our Literature, 1844; pres. N.Y. Bapt. Union for Ministerial Edn., 1850-51; founded Rochester (N.Y.) Theol. Sem.; trustee Columbia Coll., 1838-48; mem. N.Y. Hist. Soc., Am. Tract Soc., Am. Bible Soc. Author: (collection of essays) Miscellanies, 1850; Religious Progress, 1850; Lectures on the Lord's Prayer, 1851; Lectures on Baptist History, 1877; Eras and Character of History, 1882. Died Apr. 1, 1885.

WILLIAMS, William Sherley, mountain man; b. Ky.; s. Joseph and Sarah (Musick) W. Itinerant Methodist minister, wandered West; mem. Joseph C. Brown's party which surveyed much of Santa Fe Trail, 1825-26; obtained passport to trap in N.M., 1826; lived with Hopi Indians, 1827, attempted to convert them to Christianity; fur trapper in Northern Colo., 1832, later in Tex.; mem. William Walker's Cal. expdn., 1833-34; lived among Ute Indians, 1835-40, learned lang. in Mo., 1841; guide to various parties to West Coast and N.M., 1841-48; guide to Frémont's 4th expdn., 1848. Killed by Indians (probably Utes), Mar. 1849.

WILLIAMSON, Andrew, army officer; b. Scotland, circa 1730; m. Eliza Tyler, 4 children. Established as planter on Hard Labor Creek, Savannah, by 1765; commd. lt. S.C. Militia, 1760, promoted maj., 1775; served in "Snow Campaign," 1775; led 2d Cherokee expdn., 1776, ambushed at Essenecca; promoted col.; signed treaty which took large land cession from Indians, 1777; brig. gen. in command S.C. Militia in Robert Howe's Fla. expdn., 1778, shared blame for failure; sent troops home when it became obvious that British would take Charleston, S.C., 1779, accused of treason after fall of that city but not proved. Died St. Paul's Parish, nr. Charleston, Mar. 21, 1786.

WILLIAMSON, Charles, land promoter; b. Bulgray, Scotland, July 12, 1757; s. Alexander and Christian (Robertson) W.; m. Abigail Newell, 1782, 4 children. Commd. ensign 25th Regt. of Foot, 1775; captured by Continental Navy enroute to Am.; land promoter, rep. of Brit. syndicate of speculators, Western N.Y., 1791; built hotel, Geneva, N.Y., laid out turnpikes, built bridges, provided post riders in effort to encourage immigration to Western N.Y.; became Am. citizen, circa 1792; mem. N.Y. Assembly, 1796-1800; returned to Eng., 1803, resumed Brit. citizenship, advised Brit. Govt. on Am. affairs. Died Havana, Cuba, Sept. 4, 1808.

WILLIAMSON, Hugh, congressman, scientist; b. West Nottingham, Pa., Dec. 5, 1735; s. John W. and Mary (Davison) W.; grad. Coll. of Phila. (now U. Pa.), 1757; studied medicine in Edinburgh, London, Utrecht, 1764; M.D., U. of Utrecht (Holland); hon. degree U. Leyden; m. Maria Apthorpe, Jan. 1789, 2 sons. Prof. mathematics Coll. of Phila.; became mem. Am. Philos. Soc., 1768; commd. to study orbits of Venus and Mercury, 1769; published An Essay on Comets; carried 1st news of Boston Tea Party to Eng.; authored The Plea of the Colonies (anonymous letter to Lord Mansfield), 1775; sailed for U.S., 1776; began merc. bus. in Charleston, S.C., moved to Edenton, N.C., traded with French W.I.; as physician to Gov. Caswell of N.C. sent to New Bern to inoculate troops against smallpox; surgeon-gen. N.C. troops; at Battle of Camden; mem. N.C. Ho. of Commons, 1782, 85; mem. Continental Congress, 1782-85, 87-89; apptd. to Annapolis Conv., 1786; del. U.S. Constl. Conv., 1787, worked for ratification by publishing Remarks on the New Plan of Government in a N.C. newspaper; del. Fayetteville Conv., 1789; agt. to settle N.C. accounts with fed. govt., 1788; mem. U.S. Ho. of Reps. from N.C., 1st-2d congresses, 1789-93; mem. Holland Soc. of Science, Soc. of Arts and Sci. of Utrecht; founder Lit. and Philos. Soc. of N.Y.; prominent mem. N.Y. Hist. Soc.; original trustee U. N.C.; trustee Coll. of Phys. and Surg., U. State of N.Y. Author: Historical Papers Published by the Trinity College Historical Society (pamphlet); Letters of Sylvius (published anonymously; opposed paper currency, advocated excise instead of land or poll tax); Of the Fascination of Serpents; Conjectures Respecting the Native Climate of Pestilence; Observations on Navigable Canals; Observations on the Climate in Different Parts of America (1811); The History of North Carolina, 2 vols., 1812. Died May 22, 1819.

WILLIAMSON, Isaac Halstead, gov. N.J.; b. Elizabethtown, N.J., Sept. 27, 1767; s. Gen. Mathias and Susannah (Halsted) W.; m. Anne Crossdale Jouet, Aug. 6, 1808, 2 sons including Benjamin. Admitted to N.J. bar, 1791; prosecutor for Morris County (N. J.); mem. N.J. State Assembly (Democrat), 1815; gov. and chancellor N.J., 1817-29, revived alternative office of chancellor, made exhaustive study of English court of chancery, drew up set 58 rules for N.J., 1822; aided repeal statute forbidding citing of English precedent made after 1776 in N.J. court of law or equity; mem. N.J. Legislature, 1831-32; mayor of Elizabeth (N.J.), 1830-33; became chief justice of N.J., 1832; instrumental in separating offices of gov. and chancellor so court would not be dependant on fortunes of frequent elections, 1844. Died Elizabeth, July 10, 1844.

WILLIAMSON, William Durkee, congressman, state ofcl.; b. Canterbury, Conn., July 31, 1779; s. George and Mary (Foster) W.; entered Williams Coll., 1800; grad. Brown U., 1804; m. Jemima Rice, June 10, 1806; m. 2d, Susan White, June 3, 1823; m. 3d, Clarissa (Emerson) Wiggin, Jan. 27, 1825; 5 children. Practiced law, Bangor, Me., 1807; atty. gen. for Hancock County, Me., 1808-09, 11-16; mem. Mass. Senate, 1816-19, chmn. com. on Eastern lands; postmaster, Bangor, 1809-20; 1st mem. Me. Senate from Penobscot County, 1820; acting gov. Me., 1821; mem. U.S. Ho. of Reps. from Me., 17th Congress, 1821-23; judge probate for Penobscot County, 1824-40; commr. to examine banks of Me., 1834, 39; chmn. commn. of Me. State Prison, 1840; pres. People's Bank, Bangor. Author: History of the State of Maine, 2 vols., 1832. Died Bangor, May 27, 1846.

WILLIE, Asa Hoxie, congressman, jurist; b. Washington, Ga., Oct. 11, 1829; s. James and Caroline (Hoxie) W.; read law with his brother, Brenham, Tex.; m. Bettie Johnson, Oct. 20, 1859, 10 children. Admitted to Tex. bar, 1849; began practice law with his brother, Brenham; dist. atty., 1852-56; moved to Austin, Tex., 1852-56; practiced law with his brother-in-law, Marshall, Tex., 1858-66; served under Generals John Gregg, Pemberton, Johnson, Bragg, Hardee in Confederate Army, during Civil War; headed cotton export operations from San Antonio, 1865; judge Tex. Supreme Ct., 1866-68, 82-88; mem. U.S. Ho. of Reps. (Democrat) from Tex., 43d Congress, 1873-75; city atty. Galveston (Tex.), 1875-76. Died Galveston, Mar. 16, 1899; buried Episcopal Cemetery, Galveston.

WILLING, Thomas, banker, Continental congressman, mayor Phila.; b. Phila., Dec. 30, 1731; s. Charles and Anne (Shippen) W.; m. Anne McCall, June 9, 1763, 13 children including Anne (Willing) Bingham: Entered father's counting house, 1749, became partner, 1751, controlled bus., 1754; formed partnership Willing, Morris & Co., merc. firm, Phila., 1754; asst. sec. to Pa. delegation at Albany Congress, 1754; elected to Common Council of Phila., 1757; a Pa. commr. for trade with Western Indians, 1758-65; trustee Acad. and Charitable Sch. of Province of Pa. (now U. Pa.), 1760-91; a commr. to supervise surveying of Pa.-Md. boundary line; apptd. judge Orphans' Ct. of Phila., 1761; elected mayor of Phila., 1763; elected to Pa. Provincial Assembly, 1764-67; justice Pa. Provincial Supreme Ct., 1767-77; signer Non-Importation Agreement directed against Stamp Act, 1765; championed colonial rights, 1774-76; pres. 1st Provincial Congress of Pa.; mem. 2d Continental Congress, 1775; pres. Bank of N.Am., 1781; apptd. by Pres. Washington as commr. to receive subscriptions to 1st Bank of U.S., pres., 1791-97. Died Phila., Jan. 19, 1821.

WILLIS, Albert Shelby, diplomat, congressman; b. Shelbyville, Ky., Jan. 22, 1843; s. Dr. Shelby and Harriet (Button) W.; grad. Louisville Law Sch., 1863; m. Florence Dulaney, Nov. 20, 1878, at least 1 child. Partner (with J.L. Clemmans) in law firm, Louisville, Ky., 1864; Democratic presdl. elector from Louisville dist., 1872; atty. Jefferson County, Ky., 1874-77; mem. U.S. Ho. of Reps. (Dem.) from Ky., 45th-50th congresses, 1877-87, chmn. com. on rivers and harbors, 1883-87; E.E. and M.P. to Hawaii (apptd. by Pres. Cleveland), 1893-97; founder, pres. Sun Life Ins. Co. Died Honolulu, Hawaii, Jan. 6, 1897.

WILLIS, Benjamin Albertson, congressman; b. Roslyn, L.I., N.Y., Mar. 24, 1840; grad. Union Coll., Schenectady, N.Y., 1861; studied law. Admitted to N.Y. bar, 1862, began practice in N.Y.C.; enlisted in Union Army during Civil War, 1862, served as capt. 119th N.Y. Volunteers, later col. 12th Regt., N.Y. Volunteers, discharged, 1864; mem. N.Y. State Assembly, 1872-78; mem. U.S. Ho. of Reps. (Democrat) from N.Y., 44th-45th congresses, 1875-79; engaged in law practice, real estate bus. Died N.Y.C., Oct. 14, 1886; buried Friends Cemetery, Westbury, L.I., reinterred Woodlawn Cemetery, Westbury.

WILLIS, Francis, congressman; b. Frederick County, Va., Jan. 5, 1745. Served as capt. and col. during Revolutionary War, 1877-78; moved to Wilkes County, Ga., 1784; mem. U.S. Ho. of Reps. from Ga., 2d Congress, 1791-93; moved to Maury County, Tenn. Died Jan. 25, 1829.

WILLIS, Nathaniel, journalist; b. Boston, June 6, 1780; s. Nathaniel and Lucy (Douglas) W.; m. Hannah Parker, July 21, 1803; m. 2d, Susan (Capen) Douglas, Mar. 21, 1844; 9 children including Nathaniel Parker, Sarah Payson, Julia Dean, Richard Storrs. Established paper Eastern Argus in opposition to Federal Party, Portland, Me., 1803, sued for libel, sentenced to prison, forced to sell, 1809; moved to Boston, 1812; published Recorder (later Boston Recorder, 1st religious newspaper in world), 1816-40, originated Youth's Companion as dept. for children in Recorder, produced it in separate covers, 1827-57. Died May 26, 1870.

WILLIS, Nathaniel Parker, journalist, poet; b. Portland, Me., Jan. 20, 1806; s. Nathaniel and Hannah (Parker) W.; grad. Yale, 1827; m. 2d, Cornelia Grinnell, Oct. 1, 1846; 3 daus., 2 sons including Grinnell, Bailey. Published 1st verses in father's Boston Recorder under signatures "Roy" or "Cassius;" established Am. Monthly Mag., Boston, 1829-31; fgn. corr. N.Y. Mirror; made attaché by Am. minister in Paris; contbd. under name "Philip Slingsby" to Met. Monthly, Court Mag., New Monthly; returned to Am., 1836; joined George P. Morris as partner, editor weekly New Mirror 1840, became daily Evening Mirror; joined Morris in Nat. Press, renamed Home Jour., 1846, Washington corr., 1861. Author: Sketches (paraphrases of Bibl. themes), 1827; Fugitive Poetry, 1829; Melanie and Other Poems, 1835; Inklings of Adventure (collection of Slingsby papers) 3 vols., 1836; Biana Visconti, 1839, Tortesa, or the Usurer Matched, 1839 (both plays); Rural Letters, 1849; Health Trip to the Tropics, 1853; Paul Fane (novel), 1857; Fun Jottings (last two short stories). 1853. Died "Idlewild" on Hudson River, N.Y., Jan. 20, 1867; buried Mt. Auburn Cemetery, Cambridge, Mass.

WILLIS, William, state legislator, local historian; b. Haverhill, Mass., Aug. 31, 1794; s. Benjamin and Mary (McKinstry) W.; grad. Harvard, 1813; m. Julia Whitman, Sept. 1, 1823, 8 children including Pauline. Admitted to Suffolk (Mass.) bar, 1819; practiced law in partnership with Prentiss Mellen, Portland, Me., 1820; mem. Me. Senate; mayor of Portland; presdl. elector; bank commr.; chmn. Me. Bd. Railroad Commrs. dir., v.p. Me. Central R.R.; mem. "Portland Wits;" sec., treas., pres. Me. Hist. Soc., editor 1st 6 volumes of its Collections, 1831-59. Author (chief works): The History of Portland, 1831-33; A History of the Laws, the Courts, and the Lawyers of Maine, 1863. Died Feb. 17, 1870.

WILLISTON, Samuel, philanthropist; b. Easthampton, Mass., June 17, 1795; s. Payson and Sarah (Birdseye) W.; m. Emily Graves, May 27, 1822, 4 children. Partner (with Joseph and Joel Hayden) in button mfg., Haydenville, Mass., 1822, partnership dissolved, 1847; pres., or asso. with numerous banks, railroads, gas and water power companies, Easthampton, Northampton and Holyoke (Mass.); mem. lower house Mass. Legislature, 1841; mem. Mass. Senate, 1842-43; contbd. over $1,000,000 to various religions and charitable enterprises during his lifetime; founder Williston Sem., Easthampton, 1841, pres. bd. trustees 33 years; trustee Amherst Coll., 1841-74; an original trustee Mt. Holyoke Female Sem., Mass. State Reform Sch.; corporate mem. Am. Bd. Commrs. for Fgn. Missions. Died Easthampton, July 18, 1874.

WILLISTON, Seth, clergyman; b. Suffield, Conn., Apr. 4, 1770; s. Consider and Rhoda (King) W.; grad. Dartmouth, 1791; m. Dibyl (Stoddard) Dudley, May 1804, 1 son. Licensed to preach by Tolland County Assn. of Congregational Ch., 1794; ordained by North Assn. of Hartford County, Conn., 1797; organized First Congregational Ch., Lisle, N.Y., 1797, pastor, 1797-1810; also did home missionary work; missionary (apptd. by Conn. Gen. Assn.,, later organized as Conn. Missionary Soc.), in central N.Y., 1798-1801; pastor, Lisle, also continued missionary activities, organized at least 9 churches, 1801-10; removed to Durham, N.Y., 1810-28. Author: Harmony of Divine Truth, 1836. Died Guilford Center, N.Y., Mar. 2, 1851.

WILLITS, Edwin, congressman, coll. pres.; b. Otto, N.Y., Apr. 24, 1830; grad. U. Mich., 1855. Settled in Monroe, Mich., 1856; editor Monroe Comml., 1856-61; admitted to Mich. bar, 1857, began practice in Monroe; pros. atty. Monroe County, 1860-62; mem. Mich. Bd. Edn., 1860-72; postmaster of Monroe (apptd. by Pres. Lincoln), 1863-66; mem. commn. to revise Mich. Constn., 1873; mem. U.S. Ho. of Reps. (Republican) from Mich., 45th-47th congresses, 1877-83; prin. Mich. State Normal Sch., Ypsilanti, 1883-85; pres. Mich. Agrl. Coll., 1885-89; 1st asst. U.S. sec. of agr., 1889-93; practiced law, Washington, D.C. Died Washington, Oct. 22, 1896; buried Woodlawn Cemetery, Monroe.

WILLOUGHBY, Westel, Jr., physician, congressman, coll. pres.; b. Goshen, Conn., Nov. 20, 1769; studied medicine. Practiced medicine, Newport, N. Y.; judge Herkimer County (N.Y.) Ct. of Common Pleas, 1805-21; pres. Herkimer County Med. Soc., 1806-16, 18-36; mem. N.Y. State Assembly, 1808-09; pres. Coll. Physicians and Surgeons for Western Dist. N.Y., 1812-44; mem. med. staff N.Y. Militia, served in War of 1812; mem. U.S. Ho. of Reps. (Democrat; contested election) from N.Y., 14th Congress, Dec. 13, 1815-17; founder Town of Willoughby (O.). Willoughby Coll. (now part of Syracuse U.). Died Newport, Oct. 3, 1844; buried 1st Baptist Church Cemetery, Newport.

WILLSON, Forceythe, journalist; b. Little Genesee, N.Y., Apr. 10, 1837; son of Hiram Willson; attended Harvard, 1855-56; m. Elizabeth Smith, 1863. Mem. staff Louisville (Ky.) Journal, circa 1857-64, strong supporter of Union cause during Civil War, contbd. many pro-Unionist editorials to paper; contbd. numerous poems to Journal, 1857-64, including The Old Sergeant (best known poem), 1863; published volume of collected verse, Cambridge, Mass., 1864. Died Alfred, N.Y., Feb. 2, 1867.

WILMER, James Jones, clergyman; b. Eastern Shore, Md., Jan. 26, 1750; s. Simon and Mary (Price) W.; attended Christ Ch., Oxford (Eng.) U.; m. Sarah Magee, May 21, 1783; m. 2d, Mrs. Letitia Day, 1803. Ordained and licensed to ministry Anglican Ch. in Eng., 1773; rector successively of 4 parishes in Kent and Hartford counties, Md., 1779-89; sec. conv. of Anglican clergyman of Eastern Shore, Chestertown, Md., 1780; led group which founded 1st new ch. soc. in Am. (Swedenborgianism), Balt.; became minister Ch. of New Jerusalem, 1792; reinstated as clergyman Episcopal Ch., 1799, pastor of charges in Del., Md., Va.; a chaplain of Congress, 1809-13; served as chaplain U.S. Army, 1813. Author: (pamphlet) Memoirs by James Wilmer, 1792; (books) Consolation, being a Replication to Thomas Paine, 1794; The American Nepos, 1805. Died Detroit, Mich., Apr. 14, 1814.

WILMER, Joseph Pere Bell, clergyman; b. Feb. 11, 1812; s. Rev. Simon and Rebecca (Frisby) W.; grad. Theol. Sem., Alexandria, Va., 1834; m. Helen Skipwith, Mar. 29, 1842, 4 sons, 2 daus. Ordained deacon Episcopal Ch., 1834; in charge of St. Anne's Parish, Albemarle County, Va., 1834-37, chaplain U. Va., 1837-38; ordained priest, 1838; chaplain U.S. Navy, 1839-44; in charge of Hungar's Parish, Northampton County, Va., 1842-43, St. James-Northam Parish, Goochland County, Va., 1844; rector St. Mark's Ch., Phila., 1849-circa 1861; went to Eng. to purchase Bibles for soldiers, 1863; consecrated Episcopal bishop of La., 1866. Author: A Defense of Louisiana (polit. pamphlet), 1868. Died New Orleans, Dec. 2, 1878.

WILMER, Richard Hooker, clergyman; b. Alexandria, Va., Mar. 15, 1816; s. Rev. William Holland and Marion Hannah (Cox) W.; grad. Yale, 1836, Theol. Sem., Va., 1839; m. Margaret Brown, Oct. 6, 1840, 3 children. Ordained deacon Episcopal Ch., 1839, priest, 1840; pastor rural parishes, Va., 1840-59; dep. Gen. Conv. of Episcopal Ch., 1859; bishop Diocese of Ala. and La., 1860-1900. Author: The Recent Past from a Southern Standpoint, 1887. Died June 14, 1900; buried Magnolia Cemetery, Mobile, Ala.

WILMER, William Holland, clergyman, coll. pres.; b. Kent County, Md., Oct. 29, 1782; s. Simon and Ann (Ringgold) W.; attended Washington Coll:, Kent County; m. Harriet Ringgold; m. 2d, Marian Cox, Jan. 23, 1812; m. 3d, Anne Bruce Fitzhugh; 8 children including Richard Hooker, George T. Ordained to ministry Episcopal Ch., 1808; in charge of Chester Parish, Chestertown, Md., 1808-12; rector St. Paul's Ch., Alexandria, D.C. (now Va.), 1812-13; called (with William Meade) conv. of Episcopal Ch. in Va., 1813, pres. standing com., apptd. dep. from diocese to every meeting of Gen. Conv. Protestant Episcopal Ch., 1814-27, pres. House of Clerical and Lay Deputies, 4 times, leader revival of ch. in Va.; rector St. John's Ch., Washington, D.C., 1813-14; pres. D.C. br. Soc. for Edn. of Pious Young Men for Ministry of Protestant Episcopal Ch. (now called Protestant Episcopal Edn. Soc.), 1818, established, edited Theol. Repertory, ofcl. mag. of orgn., 1819-26, established unsuccessful theol. professorship at Coll. of William and Mary, 1821, also unsuccessful in attempt to establish theol. sch. in Md. with Wilmer as pres., 1822; a founder Theol. Sem. Va., Alexandria, 1823; pres. Coll. William and Mary, also rector Bruton Parish, Williamsburg, Va., 1826. Author: The Episcopal Manual, 1815; The Alexandria Controversy, 1817. Died July 24, 1827.

WILMOT, David, senator, congressman; b. Bethany, Pa., Jan. 20, 1814; s. Randall and Mary (Grant) W.; read law with George W. Woodward, Wilkes Barre, Pa., 1832; m. Ann Morgan, Nov. 28, 1836, 3 children. Admitted to bar, 1834; practiced law, Towanda, Pa., 1834-44; del. Pa. Democratic Conv., 1844; mem. U.S. Ho. of Reps. (Democrat) from Pa., 29th-31st congresses, 1845-51; author Wilmot Proviso (anti-slavery amendment to Pres. Polk's request for $2,000,000 slush fund to conclude speedy end to Mexican War, failed to pass Senate), 1846; became a leading Free-soiler, 1848; judge 13th Pa. Jud. Dist., 1851-61; a founder Republican Party; 1st Rep. gubernatorial candidate in Pa. (unsuccessful), 1857; mem. U.S. Senate from Pa. (filled vacancy caused by Cameron's appointment to Lincoln's cabinet), 1861-63; judge U.S. Ct. of Claims, 1862-68. Died Towanda, Mar. 16, 1868; buried Riverside Cemetery, Towanda.

WILSHIRE, William Wallace congressman; b. Shawneetown, Ill., Sept. 8, 1830; ed. country schs.; studied law. Gold miner, Cal., 1852-55; returned to Port Byron, Ill., 1855, engaged in coal mining, merc. bus.; admitted to Ill. bar, 1859; served as maj. 126th Regt., Ill. Volunteer Inf., Union Army, during Civil War, 1862-64; settled in Little Rock, Ark., began practice of law; apptd. solicitor gen. State of Ark., 1867; chief justice Ark. Supreme Ct., 1868-71; mem. U.S. Ho. of Reps. from Ark., as Republican, 43d Congress, 1873-June 16, 1874 (lost seat as result of contested election), as Conservative, 44th Congress, 1875-77; practiced law, Washington, D.C. Died Washington, Aug. 19, 1888; buried Mt. Holly Cemetery, Little Rock.

WILSON, Alexander, congressman; b. Va. Mem. Va. Ho. of Dels., 1803-04; mem. U.S. Ho. of Reps. from Va., 8th-10th congresses, Dec. 4, 1804-09.

WILSON, Alexander, poet, ornithologist; b. Seed Hills of Paisley, Scotland, July 6, 1766; s. Alexander and Mary (McNab) W. Published volume Poems, 1790; came to Am., 1794; took over sch. at Gray's Ferry on Schuylkill River, Phila., 1802; asst. editor Abraham Ree's Cyclopaedia; wrote verse The Foresters, 1805; visited ornithological wilderness West of Alleghanies, 1810. Author: American Ornithology, 9 vols., 1808-14; also work published posthumously as Poems; Chiefly in the Scottish Dialect, by Alexander Wilson, Author of American Ornithology, with an Account of His Life and Writings, 1816. Died Aug. 23, 1813; buried Graveyard, Old Swedes Ch., Phila.

WILSON, Allen Benjamin, inventor; b. Willet, N.Y., Oct. 18, 1824; s. Benjamin and Frances (Wilson) W.; m. Harriet Brooks, 1850, at least 1 child. Journeyman cabinet maker in East and Middle West; conceived idea of sewing machine about same time as Elias Howe, 1847, prepared full-sized drawings; began constrn. 1st machine, 1849, secured U.S. Patent (a year after Howe's), 1850, sold all interests; designed rotary hook and bobbin to substitute for double-pointed shuttle, patented 1851; began mfg. sewing machines as partner Wheeler, Wilson & Co.; contrived stationary bobbin; patented four-motion feed (used on later sewing machines), 1854. Died Woodmont, Conn., Apr. 29, 1888, buried Waterbury, Conn.

WILSON, Bird, jurist, clergyman; b. Carlisle, Pa:, Jan. 8, 1777; s. James and Rachel (Bird) W.; grad. Coll. of Phila. (now U. Pa.), 1792. Admitted to Pa. bar, 1797; apptd. pres. judge Ct. Common Pleas, 7th Circuit, 1802; a founder St. John's Ch., Norristown, Pa., served as warden, dep. to diocesan conv.; resigned to study for ministry, 1817; ordained deacon Episcopal Ch., 1819, priest, circa 1820; became prof. systematic divinity Gen. Theol. Sem., 1821, dean of sem., 1844-45, presided over trial of several tractarian students accused of Catholic sympathies, ret. as prof. emeritus, 1850. sec. House of Bishops, 1829-41; conducted services with Prof. S.H. Turner which resulted in formation of St. Peter's Ch., 1827; Author: Memoir of the Life of the Rt. Rev. William White, 1839. Editor: The Works of the Honorable James Wilson, 3 vols., 1804; an Am. edit. of A New Abridgment of the Law (Matthew Bacon), 7 vols., 1811. Died Apr. 14, 1859.

WILSON, Edgar Campbell, congressman; b. Morgantown, Va. (now W. Va.), Oct. 18, 1800; s. Thomas Wilson; studied law; children include Eugene McLanahan. Admitted to Va. bar, 1832, began practice in Morgantown; mem. U.S. Ho. of Reps. (Whig) from Va., 23d Congress, 1833-35; apptd. pros. atty. Marion County (Va.) Circuit Ct., 1842. Died Morgantown, Apr. 24, 1860; buried Oak Grove Cemetery, Morgantown.

WILSON, Ephraim King, congressman; b. nr. Snow Hill, Md., Sept. 15, 1771; grad. Coll. of N.J. (now Princeton), 1790; studied law; children include Ephraim King. Admitted to Md. bar, 1792, began practice in Snow Hill; Democratic presdl. elector, 1804; mem. U.S. Ho. of Reps. (Dem.) from Md., 20th-21st congresses, 1827-31. Died Snow Hill, Jan. 2, 1834; buried Makemie Presbyn. Churchyard, Snow Hill.

WILSON, Ephraim King, senator, congressman; b. Snow Hill, Md., Dec. 22, 1821; s. Ephraim King Wilson; grad. Jefferson Coll., Canonsburg, Pa., 1840; studied law. Taught sch., 6 years; admitted to Md. bar, 1848, began practice in Snow Hill; mem. Md. Ho. of Dels., 1847; Democratic presdl. elector, 1852; ret. from law practice because of ill health, 1867; examiner 2nd treas. Worcester County (Mo.) Sch. Bd., 1868; mem. U.S. Ho. of Reps. (Dem.) from Md., 43d Congress, 1873-75; judge 1st Md. Jud. Circuit, 1878-84; mem. U.S. Senate (Dem.) from Md., 1885-91. Died Washington, D.C., Feb. 24, 1891; buried Makemie Presbyn. Churchyard, Snow Hill.

WILSON, Eugene McLanahan, congressman; b. Morgantown, Va. (now W. Va.), Dec. 25, 1833; s. Edgar Campbell Wilson; grad. Jefferson Coll., Canonsburg, Pa., 1852; studied law. Admitted to the bar, 1855, began practice in Winona, Minn.; U.S. dist. atty. for Minn., 1857-61; practiced law, Mpls.; served as capt. Co. A, 1st Minn. Mounted Rangers, Union Army, during Civil War; mem. U.S. Ho. of Reps. (Democrat) from Minn., 41st Congress, 1869-71; elected mayor of Mpls., 1872, 74; del. Dem. Nat. Conv., St. Louis, 1876; mem. Minn. Senate, 1878-79; unsuccessful candidate for gov. Minn., 1888. Died Nassau, New Providence Island, B.W.I., Apr. 10, 1890; buried Lakewood Cemetery, Mpls.

WILSON, George Francis, mfr., inventor; b. Uxbridge, Mass., Dec. 7, 1818; s. Benjamin and Mercy (Wilson) W.; m. Clarissa Bartlett, 1844, at least 5 children. Founded and conducted Chgo. Acad., 1844-48; went to Providence, R.I., 1848; partner (with Eben N. Hirsford) in George F. Wilson and Co., chem. mfrs., 1855, name changed to Rumford Chem. Co.; invented process of steel manufacture, a turning paper-pulp boiler, improvements in illuminating apparatus for lighthouses; mem. R.I. Ho. of Reps., 1860-62; mem. Providence Sch. Com., Providence Town Council; bequeathed $100,000 to Brown U., $50,000 to Dartmouth for scientific purposes. Died Jan. 19, 1883.

WILSON, Grenville Dean, musician; b. Plymouth, Conn., Jan. 26, 1833; studied with A.W. Johnson, Boston. Published some compositions before age of 10; taught music, Lenox, Mass., N.Y.C., Saratoga and Lasell Sem.; took charge of music dept. Rockland Inst., Nyack, N.Y., 1871; organized Nyack Symphonic Soc., 1877, Nyack Choral Soc., 1880. Died Nyack, Sept. 20, 1897.

WILSON, Henry, congressman; b. Dauphin, Pa., 1778; studied law, Harrisburg, Pa. Admitted to Pa. bar, 1812, began practice in Allentown; prothonotary and clk. Lehigh County (Pa.) Cts., 1815-21; mem. U.S. Ho. of Reps. (Democrat) from Pa., 18th-19th congresses, 1823-26. Died Allentown, Aug. 14, 1826; buried Union Cemetery, Allentown.

WILSON, Henry, vice pres. U.S.; b. Farmington, N.H., Feb: 16, 1812; s. Winthrop and Abigail (Witham) Colbath (name legally changed from Jeremiah Jones Colbath, 1832); m. Harriet Malvina Howe, Oct. 28, 1840, 1 son, Henry Hamilton. Engaged as shoemaker, Natick, Mass.; active in Natick Debating Soc.; mem. Mass. Ho. of Reps., 1840-52; protested against extension of slavery in Concord Conv., 1845; chosen (with John Greenleaf Whittier) to present petition of Mass. citizens against annexation of Tex.; Mass. del. to Whig Nat. Conv., Phila., 1848; editor Boston Republican (organ of Free Soil Party), 1848-51; pres. Mass. Senate, 1851-52; chmn. Free Soil Nat. Conv., 1852; mem. U.S. Senate from Mass., Jan. 1855-73, chmn. com. on mil. affairs, responsible for passage of legislation necessary to enlist and support army during Civil War; active participant Lincoln's election campaign; served with Mass. Militia, 9 years, rose to brig. gen.; vice pres. U.S. under Grant, 1873-75. Author: History of the Antislavery Measures of the Thirty-Seventh and Thirty-eighth United States Congresses, 1864; History of the Reconstruction Measures of the Thirty-ninth and Fortieth Congresses, 1868; History of the Rise and Fall of the Slave Power in America, 3 vols., 1872-77. Died Washington, D.C., Nov. 22, 1875; buried Old Dell Park Cemetery, Natick.

WILSON, Henry Parke Custis, gynecologist; b. Workington, Md., Mar. 5, 1827; s. Henry Parke Custis and Susan E. (Savage) W.; B.A., Coll. of N.J. (now Princeton), 1848; studied medicine U. Va.; grad. U. Md., 1851; m. Alicia Griffith, 1858, 5 children. Surgeon in charge Balt. City Almshouse Infirmary, 1857-58; cons. surgeon St. Agnes Hosp., 1879, Johns Hopkins Hosp., 1889; with William T. Howard founded Hosp. for Women of Md., 1882; 1st physician in Md. to remove uterine appendages by abdominal section, 2d in Md. to perform successful ovariotomy, 1866, 2d in world to remove ultrauterine tumor filling whole pelvis by marcellation; devised instruments for gynecol. surgery; pres. Med and Chirurg. Faculty of Md., 1880-81; founder Balt. Obstet. and Gynecol. Soc., also Am. Gynecol. Soc., 1880-81; mem. Brit. Gynecol. Assn.; hon. fellow Edinburgh (Scotland) Obstet. Soc. Died Balt., Dec. 27, 1897.

WILSON, Isaac, congressman; b. Middlebury, Vt., June 25, 1780; Served as capt. of cavalry during War of 1812; moved to Genesee County, N.Y.; mem. N.Y. State Assembly, 1816-17; N.Y. State Senate, 1818-21; judge Genesee County Ct., 1821-23, 30-36; mem. U.S. Ho. of Reps. from N.Y., 18th Congress, 1823-Jan. 7, 1823 (lost seat as result of contested election); moved to Batavia, Ill.; postmaster of Batavia, 1841-46. Died Batavia, Oct. 25, 1848; buried East Batavia Cemetery.

WILSON, James, asso. justice U.S. Supreme Ct.; b. Carskerdo, Scotland, Sept. 14, 1742; s. William and Aleson (Londale) W.; attended U. St. Andrews, 1757-59, U. Glasgow, 1759-63, U. Edinburgh, 1763-65 (all Scotland); M.A. (hon.), Coll. of Phila., 1776; m. Rachel Bird, Nov. 5, 1771; m. 2d, Hannah Gray, Sept. 19, 1793; 7 children including son Bird. Came to Am., 1765; admitted to bar, 1767; head Com. of Correspondence, Carlisle, Pa., 1774, elected to 1st Pa. Provincial Conf., Phila.; proponent of loose imperial ties between Eng. and Am. colonies; elected col. 4th Bn., Cumberland County Associators, 1775; mem. Continental Congress from Pa., 1775-76, 82-83, 85-87, mem. coms. to secure friendship of Western Indians, voted for independence, mem. bd. of war with quasi-jud. duties as chmn. standing com. on appeals; signer Declaration of Independence; one of 1st to urge relinquishment Western claims of states, to advocate revenue and taxation powers for Congress; tried to strengthen fed. govt.; del. U.S. Constl. Conv., 1787; dominated Pa. Conv. to ratify U.S. Constn., 1788; asso. justice U.S. Supreme Ct., 1789-98, gave majority opinion in Chisholm vs. Georgia, 1793; became 1st prof. law U. Pa., 1790; commd. to make digest of laws of Pa. Died Edenton, N.C., Aug. 21, 1798; buried Christ Churchyard, Phila.

WILSON, James, congressman; b. Peterboro, N.H., Aug. 16, 1766; attended Phillips Acad., Andover, Mass.; grad. Harvard, 1789; studied law; children include James. Admitted to N.H. bar, 1792, began practice in Peterboro; mem. N.H. Ho. of Reps., 1803-09, 12-14; member U.S. Ho. of Reps. (Federalist) from N.H., 11th Congress, 1809-11; moved to Keene, N.H., 1815, practiced law. Died Keene, Jan. 4, 1839; buried Woodland Cemetery, Keene.

WILSON, James, congressman; b. Millerstown (now Fairfield), Pa., Apr. 28, 1779; attended common schs. Learned cabinet-maker's trade; engaged in merc. and real estate businesses; justice of peace, 1811-22, 30-59; mem. U.S. Ho. of Reps. (Democrat) from Pa., 18th-20th congresses, 1823-29. Died Gettysburg, Pa., July 19, 1868; buried Evergreen Cemetery, Gettysburg.

WILSON, James, congressman; b. Peterboro, N.H., Mar. 18, 1797; s. James Wilson; grad. Middlebury Coll., 1820; studied law. Served from capt. to maj. gen.; N.H. Militia, 1820-40; admitted to N.H. bar, 1823, began practice in Keene; mem. N.H. Ho. of Reps., 1825-37, 40, 46, 71-72, speaker, 1828; unsuccessful candidate for gov. N.H., 1835, 38; del. Whig Nat. Conv., Harrisburg, Pa., 1840; surveyor gen. public lands Wis. and Ia. territories, 1841-45; mem. U.S. Ho. of Reps. (Whig) from N.H., 30-31st congresses, 1847-Sept. 9, 1850 (resigned); apptd. commr. to settle pvt. land claims in Cal., 1851-53; settled in San Francisco; returned to Keene, 1867; declined brig. gen's commn. in U.S. Army offered by Pres. Lincoln during Civil War. Died Keene, May 29, 1881; buried Woodland Cemetery, Keene.

WILSON, James, congressman; b. Crawfordsville, Ind., Apr. 9, 1825; grad. Wabash Coll., Crawfordsville, 1842; studied law; children include John Lockwood. Admitted to Ind. bar, 1848, began practice in Crawfordsville; served in Mexican War, 1846-47; served as capt. U.S. Volunteers, 1862-65, discharged as brevet lt. col., 1865; mem. U.S. Ho. of Reps. (Republican) from Ind., 35th-36th congresses, 1857-61; U.S. minister to Venzuela, 1866-67. Died Caracas, Venezuela, Aug. 8, 1867; buried Oak Hill Cemetery, Crawfordsville.

WILSON, James Falconer, senator, congressman; b. Newark, O., Oct. 19, 1828; s. David S. and Kitty Ann (Bramble) W.; m. Mary Jewett, May 25, 1852, 2 sons, 1 dau. Popularly called "Jefferson Jim"; admitted to bar, 1851; del. to Ia. Constl. Conv., 1857; apptd. to Des Moines River Improvement Commn., 1857; mem. Ia. Ho. of Reps., 1857-59; mem. Ia. Senate, 1859-61, helped revise Ia. code, 1860, pres. pro tem, 1861; mem. U.S. Ho. of Reps. (Republican) from Ia., 37th-40th congresses, 1861-69, chmn. judiciary com. to forward abolition and Union program, trial mgr. impeachment proceedings against Pres. Andrew Johnson, 1868; mem: com. to formulate articles (recognized as more moderate element of radical wing); govt. dir. U.P. R.R., 1874-82; mem. U.S. Senate (Rep.) from Ia., 1883-95; a framer original Interstate Commerce Act of 1887, secured passage Original Package Act, 1890. Died Fairfield, Ia., Apr. 22, 1895; buried Evergreen Cemetery, Fairfield.

WILSON, James Jefferson, senator; b. Essex County, N.J., 1775; attended common schs. Editor and publisher True American, Trenton, N.J., 1801-24; clk. N.J. Gen. Assembly, 1804; judge adv. and capt. Hunterdon Brigade, N.J. Militia, 1806, capt. 3d Regt., 1814; surrogate Hunterdon County, 1808; mem. N.J. Gen. Assembly, 1809-11; brig. gen. and adj. gen. of N.J., 1810-12, 14; capt. Maj. Isaac Andruss' detachment, N.J. Militia, 1814; mem. U.S. Senate (Democrat) from N.J., 1815-Jan. 8, 1821; brig. gen. and q.m. gen., of N.J., 1821-24; postmaster of Trenton, 1821-24. Died Trenton, July 28, 1824; buried 1st Baptist Ch. Cemetery, Trenton.

WILSON, James Knox, architect; b. 1828. Practiced architecture, Cincinnati, 20 years; designed several business blocks, other structures; mem. A. I.A., an organizer, 1st pres. Cincinnati chpt., 1870; ret. because of ill health, 1890, moved to Denver. Died Denver, Oct. 13, 1894.

WILSON, John, clergyman, writer; b. Windsor, Eng., circa 1591; s. William and Isabel (Woodhall) W.; B.A. (fellow), King's Coll., Cambridge (Eng.) U., 1608, M.A., 1613; admitted to Inner Temple, 1610; m. Elizabeth Mansfield, May 1615, at least 3 children, Elizabeth, Mary, John. Lectr., Sudbury, Suffolk, Eng., 1618-30; came to Am., 1630; tchr. First Ch., Boston, 1630, 35-67; went to Eng., 1631, 34-35; one of 1st to work for conversion of Indians in Mass. Author: A Song, or, Story, for the Lasting Remembrance of Divers Famous Works (long children's poem), 1626, reissued in Boston as A Song of Deliverance, 1680; 8 anagrams in verse in Thomas Shepard's The Church-Membership of Children, 1663; A Discourse on the Last Judgement, 1664; preface to The Summe of Certain Sermons (Richard Mather), 1652, preface to The Cause of God (John Higginson), 1663; A Seasonable Watchword unto Christians (sermon), 1677; credited with authorship of Some Helps to Faith, 1625, The Day Breaking of the Gospell with the Indians, 1647. Died Aug. 7, 1667.

WILSON, John, congressman; b. Wilson's Ferry (now Pelzer), S.C., Aug. 11, 1773; attended common schs. Engaged in farming, nr. Golden Grove, S.C.; operated public ferry across Saluda River at Pelzer; mem. U.S. Ho. of Reps. from S.C., 17th-19th congresses, 1821-27. Died on his plantation nr. Golden Grove, Aug. 13, 1828; buried family cemetery on his plantation (now part of Pelzer).

WILSON, John, congressman; b. Peterboro, N.H., Jan. 10, 1777; grad. Harvard, 1799; studied law. Admitted to N.H. bar, 1802; began practice in Belfast, Mass. (now Me.); served as capt. Mass. Militia; mem. U.S. Ho. of Reps. (Federalist) from Mass., 13th, 15th congresses, 1813-15, 17-19. Died Belfast, Aug. 9, 1848; buried Grove Cemetery, Belfast.

WILSON, John Leighton, missionary; b. Salem, S.C., Mar. 25, 1809; s. William and Jane E. (James) W.; grad. Union Coll., Schenectady, 1829; grad. Columbia Sem., 1831; m. Jane Bayard, May 21, 1834. Ordained to ministry Presbyn. Ch. at Harmony, S.C., 1833; contbr. to Missionary Herald; missionary in Cape Palmas and Gabun, West Africa, 1834-52; treated sick, founded schs., chs.; compiled grammars, dictionaries, translated gospels, tracts into Grebo and Mpongwee; returned to Am., 1852; sec. Bd. Fgn. Missions at Gen. Assembly, 1853; editor mag. Home and Fgn. Record, 1853-61; chaplain Confederate Army; mem. Assembly of the Presbyn. Ch. in the Confederate States of Am. (later Presbyn. Ch. in U.S.), 1861, in charge of its fgn. missions, 1863-72; editor The Missionary, 1866-circa 1886; wrote for So. Presbyn. Review. Author: Notice of the External Characters and Habits of Troglodytes Gorilla, a New Species of Orang from the Gaboon River, 1847; Western Africa, Its History, Conditions and Prospects, 1856. Died Salem, July 13, 1886.

WILSON, John Thomas, congressman; b. Bell, O., Apr. 16, 1811. Engaged in merc. bus., farming; served from 1st lt. to capt. Co. E, 70th Regt., Ohio Volunteer Inf., 1861-62; mem. Ohio Senate, 1863-66; mem. U.S. Ho. of Reps. (Republican) from Ohio, 40th-42d congresses, 1867-73; engaged in handling loans and mortgages. Died Tranquillity, Adams County, O., Oct. 6, 1891; buried Tranquillity Cemetery.

WILSON, Joseph, carver; b. Marblehead, Mass., Nov. 2, 1779; at least 2 children, Albert, James Warner. Worked in Chester, N.Y., 1796-98, Newburyport, Mass., 1798-57; carved several portrait statues and animal figures for Timothy Dexter's house, Newbury, Mass., including figures of Washington, Adams, Jefferson, Dexter, Napoleon, Lord Nelson, Adam and Eve, Fame, a traveling preacher. Died Newburyport, Mar. 25, 1857.

WILSON, Joseph Gardner, congressman; b. Acworth, N.H., Dec. 13, 1826; grad. Marietta (O.) Coll., 1846, Cincinnati Law Sch., 1852. Prof., Farmer's Coll., nr. Cincinnati, 1849; traveled in New Eng., 1850; admitted to Ohio bar, 1852; moved to Ore. Territory, 1852, began practice of law in Salem; clk. Ore. Territorial Legislature, 1853; 1st sec. Willamette Wollen Co., 1854; pros. atty. Marion County (Ore.), 1860-62; asso. judge Ore. Supreme Ct., 1864-66, 68-70; mem. U.S. Ho. of Reps. (Republican) from Ore., 43d Congress, 1873. Died Marietta, July 2, 1873; buried Pioneer Cemetery, The Dalles, Ore.

WILSON, Joshua Lacy, clergyman; b. Bedford County, Va., Sept. 22, 1774; s. Henry Wright and Agnes (Lacy) W.; m. Sarah B. Mackay, Oct. 22, 1801, 8 children including Samuel Ramsay. Licensed to preach by Presbytery of Transylvania (Ky.), 1802, ordained minister Presbyn. Ch., 1804; pastor chs., Bardstown and Big Spring, Ky., 1804-08, First Presbyn. Ch. of Cincinnati, 1808-46; a founder Cincinnati Coll:, 1819, became prof. moral philosophy and logic; 1st chmn. bd. trustees Lane Theol. Sem., Cincinnati, 1828-30; fostered Sunday schs., Bible socs. and libraries, attacked theaters, dancing and Masonic order; published pamphlet "Episcopal Methodism; or Dragonism Exhibited," 1811; founded papers The Pandect, 1828, The Standard, 1831; opposed New Eng. theology and operation of "Plan of Union"; published Four Propositions against the Claims of the American Home Missionary Society, 1831; helped prepare "Western Meml.," 1834; signer "Act and Testimony," 1835; mem. Old Sch. Conv., 1837, moderator Old Sch. Gen. Assembly, 1839. Died Cincinnati, Aug. 14, 1846.

WILSON, Matthew, artist; b. London, Eng., July 17, 1814. Came to U.S., 1832, settled in Phila.; went to Paris, France, 1835; settled in Bklyn., exhibited at N.A.D., became asso., 1843; worked in New Orleans, Balt., Ohio, Boston, Hartford; returned to Bklyn., 1863; painted portraits of prominent men in Washington, D.C., during Civil War, including portrait of Lincoln, 1865. Died Bklyn., Feb. 23, 1892.

WILSON, Nathan, congressman; b. nr. Greenwich, Mass., Dec. 23, 1759; attended sch., Greenwich. Moved to New Perth (now Salem) N.Y.; enlisted as pvt. 16th Regt., Albany County (N.Y.) Militia; apptd. adj. Washington County Regt., N.Y. Militia, 1791; town collector, 1801-02, sheriff of Washington County, 1802-06; mem. U.S. Ho. of Reps. (Democrat) from N.Y., 10th Congress, June 3, 1808-09; justice of peace, 1808-16; engaged in farming. Died nr. Salem, July 25, 1834; buried Evergreen Cemetery, Salem.

WILSON, Peter, educator, legislator; b. Ordiquhill, Scotland, Nov. 23, 1746; grad. U. Aberdeen (Scotland); M.A. (hon.) Brown U., 1786; LL.D. (hon.) Union Coll., 1798; m. 2d, Catherine Duryea; 5 daus., 2 sons. Came to Am., 1763; prin. Hackensack (N.J.) Acad.; Bergen County rep. N.J. Assembly, 1777-81, 87; selected to revise and codify N.J. laws, 1783; prof. Greek and Latin, Columbia, 1789-92; prin. Erasmus Hall Acad., Flatbush, L.I., N.Y., 1792-97, titular head acad., 1797-1805; prof. Greek and Latin, Grecian and Roman antiquities Columbia, 1797-1820. Author: Introduction to Greek Prosody . . . . . . with an Appendix on the Metres of Horace, Adapted to the Use of Beginners, 1811; Rules of Latin Prosody for the Use of Schools, 1810. Died Barbadoes, N.J., Aug. 1, 1825.

WILSON, Robert, senator; b. nr. Staunton, Va., Nov. 1803. Moved to Howard County, Mo., 1820, taught sch.; probate judge of Howard County, 1825; clk. circuit and county cts., 1829-40; apptd. brig. gen. Mo. Militia, 1837, served in "Mormon War;" admitted to Mo. bar, began practice, 1840; moved to Huntsville, Mo.; mem. Mo. Ho. of Reps., 1844; moved to Andrew County, Mo., 1852; mem. Mo. Senate, 1854; del. Mo. Secession Conv. (Unionist) 1861, elected v.p., later pres.; mem. U.S. Senate (Unionist) from Mo., Jan. 17,1862-63; engaged in farming. Died Marshall, Mo., May 10, 1870; buried Mt. Mora Cemetery, St. Joseph, Mo.

WILSON, Samuel (called Uncle Sam), meat packer; b. Menotomy (now Arlington), Mass., Sept. 13, 1766; s. Edward and Lucy (Francis) W.; m. Betsey Mann, Jan. 3, 1797, 4 children. Enlisted as service-boy in Continental Army, 1780; moved to Troy, N.Y., 1789; engaged at various times in brickmaking, farming, distilling; operated a gen. store; started (with brother Ebenezer) a meat packing company; meat insp. for U.S. Army during War of 1812; packed meat which bore mark E A U S (stood for Elbert Anderson and United States), jokingly referred to as meaning "Uncle Sam" (nickname of Samuel Wilson), name spread, soldiers stationed in upper N.Y. State reportedly would eat only Uncle Sam's meat, term became popular characterization of U.S., replaced Brother Jonathan in cartoons and plays as symbol of U.S. Died Troy, July 31, 1854; buried Oakwood Cemetery, Troy.

WILSON, Samuel Mountford, lawyer; b. Steubenville, O., Aug. 12, 1823; s. Peter and Frances (Stokeley) W.; m. Emily Scott, July 5, 1848, 4 children including Russell. Admitted to Ohio bar, 1844; partner with Col. Joseph P. Hoge in law practice, Galena, Ill., then San Francisco, until 1864; mem. Cal. Constl. Com., 1878-79, also chmn. judiciary bd., refused to sign finished constn.; mem. bd. freeholders which drafted new municipal charter for San Francisco, 1879; delivered oration at laying of cornerstone Cal. State Capitol, Sacramento, 1861; delivered eulogy on Samuel Fuller, 1886; leading Cal. lawyer, especially in civil cases, wills; appeared in nearly all the important Cal. land cases of his time; founded firm Wilson & Wilson, 1874. Died San Francisco, June 4, 1892.

WILSON, Samuel Ramsay, clergyman; b. Cincinnati, June 4, 1818; s. Jc ua Lacy and Sarah (Mackay) W.; attended Mian.. U., Oxford, O., D.D. (hon.), 1856; A.B., Hanove. (Ind.) Coll., 1836, A.M. (hon.), 1843; grad. Princeton Theol. Sem., 1840; m. Nancy Johnston, Mar. 25, 1841, 5 children; m. 2d, Mary Bell, Jan. 29, 1852, 7 children; m. 3d, Annie Steele, Jan. 11, 1876, 2 children. Licensed by Presbytery of New Brunswick, N.J., 1840; served at First Presbyn. Ch., Cincinnati, 1840-61; ordained to ministry, 1842; So. sympathizer in Civil War; minister Grand St. Presbyn. Ch., N.Y.C., 1861-63, Mulberry Presbyn. Ch., Shelby County, Ky., 1863-65, 1st Presbyn. Ch., Louisville, Ky., 1865-79, 2d Presbyn. Ch., Madison, Ind., 1880-83. Author: The Causes and Remedies of Impending National Calamities, 1860; A Pan-Presbyterian Letter . . . to Presbyterians both in North and South, 1875; editor Hymns of the Church, 1872. Died Louisville, Mar. 3, 1886.

WILSON, Samuel Thomas, clergyman; b. London, Eng., 1761; ed. Dominican coll., Holy Cross, Bornhem, Belgium; studied theology Coll. St. Thomas of Aquin, Louvain, Belgium. Took solem vows, 1785; ordained priest Order of Friar Preachers (Dominicans), 1786; tchr., Holy Cross, Bornhem, 1786-94; vicar-provincial of community during French Revolution; came to U.S., arriving in Md., 1805; missionary, Cartwright's Creek, nr. Springfield, Ky., 1805, also conducted grammar sch. for boys; named provincial, 1807; founder Ch. of St. Rose, also Coll. of St. Thomas Aquin, nr. Springfield; founded 1st Am. convent of Sisters of 3d Order of St. Dominic, 1822. Died Cartwright's Creek, May 23, 1824.

WILSON, Stephen Fowler, congressman; b. Columbia, Pa., Sept. 4, 1821; studied law. Admitted to Pa. bar, practiced law; held local offices; mem. Pa. Senate, 1863-65; del. Republican Nat. Conv., Balt., 1864; mem. U.S. Ho. of Reps. (Republican) from Pa., 39th-40th congresses, 1865-69; additional judge 4th Pa. Jud. Dist., 1871-81; apptd. asso. justice N.M. Territorial Supreme Ct., 1884; pres. judge 4th Pa. Jud. Dist., 1887-89; resumed law practice, Wellsboro, Pa. Died Wellsboro, Mar. 30, 1897; buried Wellsboro Cemetery.

WILSON, Theodore Delavan, naval engr. b. Bklyn., May 11, 1840; s. Charles and Ann Elizabeth (Cock) w.; m. Sarah Stults, before 1867, 4 children. Entered U.S. Navy as ship's carpenter, 1861, served in ship Cambridge, N. Atlantic Squadron, until 1863; asst. naval constructor Pensacola (Fla.) Navy Yard, then Phila., 1866; instr. in ship constrn. U.S. Naval Acad., 1869-73; invented bolt extractor, 1880; promoted naval constructor, 1873; mem. 1st Naval Adv. Bd. to formulate plans for new steel navy, 1881; chief bur. of constrn. and repair, 1882-93; supervised constrn. of 45 ships; 1st Am. mem. Brit. Instn. Naval Architects; 1st v.p. Soc. Naval Architects; 1st v.p. Soc. Naval Architects and Marine Engrs., 1893, contbr. article "The Steel Ships of United States Navy" to its Transactions, 1893. Author: An Outline of Shipbuilding, Theoretical and Practical (published as textbook at U.S. Naval Acad.), 1873; (pamphlet) The Center of Gravity of the U.S. Steamer Shawmut, 1874. Died Boston, June 29, 1896.

WILSON, Thomas, congressman; b. Staunton, Va., Sept. 11, 1765; studied law, Staunton; children include Edgar Campbell. Admitted to Va. bar, 1789, began practice in Morgantown, Va. (now W.Va.); mem. Va. Senate, 1792-95, 1800-04; mem. Va. Ho. of Dels., 1799-1800, 16-17; mem. U.S. Ho. of Reps. (Federalist) from Va., 12th Congress, 1811-13. Died Morgantown, Jan. 24, 1826; buried Oak Grove Cemetery, Morgantown.

WILSON, Thomas, congressman; b. nr. Sunbury, Pa., 1772; attended common schs. Contracted for supplying Western forts of U.S. from Niagara to New Orleans; engaged in shipbldg., Erie, Pa., 1805; built comml. vessels for Gt. Lakes; burgess of Erie, 1807, town clk., 1808; treas. Erie County, 1809-12, county commr., 1811; justice of peace; mem. U.S. Ho. of Reps. (Democrat) from Pa., 13th-14th congresses, May 4, 1813-17; mem. Pa. Ho. of Reps., 1817-20; prothonotary and clk. of ct. Erie County, 1819-24. Died Erie, Oct. 4, 1824.

WILSON, William, congressman; b. New Boston, N.H., Mar. 19, 1773; grad. Dartmouth, 1797; studied law, Johnstown, N.Y. Admitted to N.Y. bar; moved to Chillicothe, O., circa 1805, practiced law; chief judge Ct. of Common Pleas, Newark, O., 1808-23; mem. U.S. Ho. of Reps. from Ohio, 18th-20th congresses, 1823-27. Died Newark, June 6, 1827; buried Old Cemetery, reinterred Cedar Hill Cemetery, Newark, 1853.

WILSON, William, jurist; b. Loudoun County, Va., Apr. 27, 1794; m. Mary S. Davidson, Apr. 1820, 10 children. Practiced law, White County, Ill., 1817; asso. justice Ill. Supreme Ct., 1819-24, chief justice, 1824-48, rendered important decision in Field vs. The State of Illinois ex rel McClernand (denied gov. the power to remove sec. of state apptd. by gov's predecessor on ground that Ill. Constn. did not expressly place any limitations upon duration of term of office), 1839. Died White County, Apr. 29, 1857.

WILSON, William, congressman. Mem. U.S. Ho. of Reps. from Pa., 14th-15th congresses, 1815-19.

WILSON, William, publisher, poet; b. Crieff, Scotland, Dec. 25, 1801; m. Jane M'Kenzie; m. 2d, Jane Sibbald; 4 children. Editor, Dundee Literary Olio, before 1833; came to Am., 1833; partner (with Paraclete Potter) in bindery and book store, Poughkeepsie, N.Y., 1834, became sole owner, added publishing bus., 1841; a founder St. Paul's Ch., Poughkeepsie, 1836; contbr. poetry to N.Y. Post, Albion, Knickerbocker Mag., Chgo. Record; best known poems: "The Mitherless Wean," "Work Is Prayer". Posthumous edits. of Poems published 1869, 75, 81. Died Poughkeepsie, Aug. 25, 1860.

WILSON, William Lyne, congressman, U.S. postmaster-gen., coll. pres.; b. Middleway, Va. (now W.Va.), May 3, 1843; s. Benjamin and Mary Whiting (Lyne) W.; grad. Columbian Coll. (now George Washington U.), 1860, LL.B., 1867; attended U. Va., 1860-61; m. Nannine Huntington, Aug. 6, 1868; 6 children. Enlisted in 12th Va. Cavalry during Civil War, 1861; served in Shenandoah Valley, 1861-63; later fought with J. E. B. Stuart and was with Lee at Appomattox; asst. prof. ancient langs. Columbian Coll., 1865-71; law partner with cousin George W. Baylor, 1871-82; pres. W.Va. U., 1882; mem. U.S. Ho. of Reps. (Democrat) from W.Va., 48th-53d congresses, 1883-95, continually fought for downward revision of tariff; permanent chmn. Nat. Dem. Conv., 1892; U.S. postmaster gen. under Pres. Cleveland, 1895-97, began rural free delivery and enlarged classified list of civil service; pres. Washington and Lee U., Lexington, Va., 1896-1900. Died Lexington, Oct. 17, 1900; buried Edgehill Cemetery, Charles Town, W.Va.

WILTZ, Louis Alfred, gov. La.; b. New Orleans, Oct. 22, 1843; s. J. B. Theophile and Louise Irene (Villaneuva) E.; m. Michael Bienvenu, 1862, 7 children. Served as capt. Confederate Army, captured, exchanged, then became provost marshal; accountant, commn. house, New Orleans, 1865-71; became a banker, 1873; mem. parish and state central coms. Democratic Party; mem. La. Legislature, 1868, 74, speaker, 1875; mem. New Orleans Common Council, also sch. bd., 1868; pres. bd. aldermen New Orleans, then mayor, 1872-74; lt. gov. La., 1876; pres. La. Constl. Conv., 1879; gov. La., 1880-81. Author: The Great Mississippi Flood of 1874 . . . A Circular . . . to the Mayors of American Cities and Towns and to the Philanthropic throughout the Republic, 1874. Died New Orleans, Oct. 16, 1881.

WIMAR, Carl (baptized Karl Ferdinand), painter; b. Siegburg, Germany, Feb. 19, 1828; s. Ludwig Gottfried and Elizabete (Schmitz) W.; studied art under Joseph Fay and Emanuel Leutze, Dusseldorf, Germany, 5 years circa 1852; m. Anna von Senden, Mar. 7, 1861, 1 dau., Winona. Came to United States and settled in St. Louis, 1843; made three trips aboard American Fur Company steamboats to trading posts on upper Missouri and Yellowstone rivers to paint Indians; painted 4 hist. panels in St. Louis Courthouse; prin. works include: "The Capture of Daniel Boone's Daughter," "The Captive Charger," "Attack on an Emigrant Train" (awarded 1st prize St. Louis Fair 1869). Died St. Louis, Nov. 28, 1862.

WIMMER, Boniface, clergyman; b. Thalmassing, Bavaria, Jan. 14, 1809; attended U. Munich (Germany), 1827-29. Ordained priest Roman Catholic Ch., Regensburg, Bavaria, 1831; made solemn vows as Benedictine at Monastery of Metten under name Boniface, 1833; came to Am., 1846; invested 18 companions with religious habit, founding 1st Benedictine Order in U.S., 1846; founded coll. and sem., St. Vincent, Pa., 1848; apptd. 1st abbot St. Vincent Abbey, 1855; founded priory (now St. John Abbey and U.), Minn., 1856, St. Benedict Abbey and Coll. of Atchison, Kan., 1857; established Benedictine monasteries, Carrolltown, Pa., 1848, St. Marys Pa., 1851, Johnstown, Pa., 1859, Chgo., 1861, Richmond, Va., 1867, Pitts., 1868; founder Am. Cassinese Congregation, 1866, pres., 1870, attended Vatican Council, Rome, Italy; founder monastery, Belmont (N.C.) Abbey and Coll.; sent missionaries to Ala. to pave way for St. Bernard Abbey and Coll., Cullman; founded agrl. sch. for Negroes, Skidway Island, nr. Savannah, Ga.; apptd. archabbot, 1883. Died St. Vincent, Westmoreland County, Pa., Dec. 8, 1887.

WINANS, Edwin Baruch, gov. Mich., congressman; b. Avon, N.Y., May 16, 1826; attended Albion Coll., Mich. Engaged in mining, nr. Placerville, Cal., 1850; worked in Cal., until 1857; returned to Mich., 1858, settled in Hamburg, engaged in farming; mem. Mich. Ho. of Reps., 1861-65; del. Mich. Constl. Conv., 1867; probate judge of Livingston County, 1877-81; mem. U.S. Ho. of Reps. (Democrat) from Mich., 48th-49th congresses, 1883-87; resumed farming, Livingston County; gov. Mich., 1891-93. Died Hamburg, July 4, 1894; buried Hamburg Cemetery.

WINANS, James January, congressman; b. Maysville, Ky., June 7, 1818; attended U. Lexington (Ky.); studied law. Admitted to Ky. bar, 1841, began practice in Ind.; moved to Xenia, O., 1843, practiced law; clk. Greene County (Ohio) Cts., 1845-51; mem. Ohio Senate, 1857, Ohio Ho. of Reps., 1863; judge Ct. of Common Pleas, 1864-71; mem. U.S. Ho. of Reps. (Republican) from Ohio, 41st Congress, 1869-71. Died Xenia, Apr. 28, 1879; buried Woodlawn Cemetery, Xenia.

WINANS, Ross, railroad engr.; b. Sussex County, N.J., Oct. 17, 1796; s. William and Mary Winans; m. Julia De Kay, Jan. 22, 1820; m. 2d, Elizabeth K. West, 1854; 5 children including Julia, Thomas De Kay, William L. Sold horses to B. & O. R.R., Balt., 1828; invented model "rail wagon" with friction wheel; engr. B. & O. R.R., assisted Peter Cooper with Tom Thumb engine, 1829-30; mem. firm Gillingham & Winans, 1834-59, took charge of improving railroad machinery, B. & O. R.R. shops, Mt. Clare, Md.; planned 1st 8-wheel passenger car; credited with mounting car on 2 four-wheeled trucks; constructed locomotive Mud-Digger (used until 1844), 1842; retired from locomotive building, 1860; mem. Md. Legislature, 1861; Southern sympathizer in Civil War, twice arrested and paroled, 1861. Died Balt., Apr. 11, 1877.

WINANS, Thomas DeKay, engr., inventor; b. Vernon, N.J., Dec. 6, 1820; s. Ross and Julia (De Kay) W.; m. Celeste Revillon, Aug. 23, 1847, 4 children. Engr. with Harrison, Winans & Eastwick (firm organized to handle Russian railroad constrn. venture), went to Russia to take charge of mech. dept. of railroad from St. Petersburg to Moscow, 1843, contracted to equip railroad with locomotives and other rolling stock in 5 years, established shops at Alexandrovsky; returned to U.S. (left brother in charge in Russia), 1851, recalled to Russia for new constrn. contract, 1866; business interests taken over by Russian Govt. with payment of large bonus, 1868; dir. B. & O. R.R.; established soup station opposite his home during Civil War; devised (with his father) cigar-shaped hull for trans-Atlantic steamers, 1859; invented device which made organ as easy of touch as piano, invented glass feeding vessels for fish (adopted by Md. Fish Commn.); used undulation of waves to pump water of a spring to reservoir at top of his villa, Newport, R.I. Died Newport, June 10, 1878.

WINANS, William, clergyman; b. Chestnut Ridge, Allegheny County, Pa., Nov. 3, 1788; m. Martha DuBose, 1815. Class leader and exhorter in Methodist Ch., 1807; admitted on trial into Western Conf., Methodist Episcopal Ch., 1808; preached on circuits in Ky. and Ind., 1808-10; volunteered for pioneer work in Mississippi Valley, 1810; ordained deacon, 1812, assigned to New Orleans, 1813; returned to Miss., ordained an elder, mem. Tenn. Conf., 1814; clergyman, Miss., 1820-57; trustee Elizabeth Female Acad.; trustee Centenary Coll., travelling agt., 1845, 49; erected 1st Meth. Ch., New Orleans; supt. Choctaw Indian mission of Miss. Conf., 1824; attended every Gen. Conf. of Meth. Episcopal Ch., 1824-44, sponsored resolution condemning abolitionism adopted by Gen. Conf. of 1836, mem. com. that drafted Plan of Separation for the division of the Ch., Gen. Conf. of 1844; del. to conv. that organized Meth. Episcopal Ch., South, Louisville, Ky., 1845, attended confs., 1846, 50, 54. Author: (sermons) A Series of Discourses on Fundamental Religious Subjects, 1855. Died Amite County, Miss., Aug. 31, 1857.

WINCHELL, Alexander, educator, geologist; b. Town of Northeast, Dutchess County, N.Y., Dec. 31, 1824; s. Horace and Caroline (McAllister) W.; grad. Wesleyan U., Middletown, Conn., 1847, LL.D. (hon.), 1867; m. Julia F. Lines, Dec. 5, 1849, 6 children. Sch. tchr., South Lee, Mass., 1841-42, Pennington (N.J.) Male Sem., N.J., 1847-49; prof. natural history Amenia Sem., N.Y., 1849; in charge of acad., Newbern, Ala., 1850; opened Mesopotamia Female Sem., Eutaw, Ala., 1851; pres. Masonic U., Selma, Ala., 1853; prof. physics and engring. U. Mich., Ann Arbor, 1853-55, prof. geology, zoology and botany, 1855-73, prof. geology and paleontology, 1879-91; directed state geol. survey Mich., 1859-61, 69-71, located salt beds of Saginaw Valley; chancellor Syracuse (N.Y.) U., 1872-74; prof. geology and zoology Vanderbilt U., 1875-78; chmn. com. to organize Geol. Soc. of Am., pres., 1891. Author: Sketches of Creation, 1870; Preadamites, 1880; World Life, 1883; (textbook) Geological Studies, 1886; also published bibliography of over 250 titles. Died Ann Arbor, Mich., Feb. 19, 1891.

WINCHESTER, Elhanan, clergyman; b. Brookline, Mass., Sept. 30, 1751; s. Elhanan and Sarah Winchester; m. Alice Rogers, Jan. 18, 1770; m. 2d, Sarah Peck, 1776; m. 3d, Sarah Luke, 1778; m. 4th, Mary Morgan, 1781; m. 5th, Maria Knowles; 1 child. Preacher, Rehoboth, Mass., 1771, started revival resulting in establishment of Baptist Ch. in Rehoboth; ordained to ministry Bapt. Ch., pastor Welch Neck, S.C., 1774-80; Bapt. Ch., Phila., 1780-87, lost position due to unorthodox beliefs in universal restoration; preached in chapel Parliament Ct., London, Eng., 1787, returned to Am., 1794. Author: A New Book of Poems on Several Occasions, 1773; The Faces of Moses Unveiled by the Gospel, or, Evangelical Truths, Discovered by Law, 1787; The Universal Restoration: Exhibited in a Series of Dialogues Between a Minister and His Friend, 1788; The Three Woe Trumpets, 1793; Ten Letters Addressed to Mr. Paine; Being an Answer to His First Part of the Age of Reason, 1795; A Plain Political Catechism, 1796. Died Hartford, Conn., Apr. 18, 1797.

WINCHESTER, James, army officer; b. Carroll County, Md., Feb. 6, 1752; s. William and Lydia (Richards) W.; m. Susan Black, 1803, 14 children including Marcus. Served with Md. Battalion of Flying Camp, Am. Revolution, 1776, wounded and captured, Staten Island, 1777, exchanged, 1778; captured again, Charleston, S.C., 1780; promoted capt., 1780, served at Yorktown, 1781; moved to Middle Tenn., 1785; mem. N.C. Conv. to ratify U.S. Constn., 1788; capt., col., brig. gen. of Mero dist., Tenn. Militia, famous for Indian campaigns; speaker Tenn. Senate, 1796; commd. brig. gen. U.S. Army, in command Army of N.W., War of 1812; commr. to run Chickasaw Boundary Line between Tenn. and Miss., 1819; a founder Memphis (Tenn.). Died July 26, 1826; buried "Cragfont," nr. Memphis.

WINCHESTER, Oliver Fisher, arms mfr.; b. Boston, Nov. 30, 1810; s. Samuel and Hannah (Bates) W.; m. Jane Ellen Hope, Feb. 20, 1834, 2 children. Engaged in constrn. work, Balt., 1830-37; started import business (with John M. Davies), N.Y.C., 1847; patented new method for mfg. shirts, began production, 1848; became stockholder Volcanic Repeating Arms Co. (reorganized as Winchester Repeating Arms Co., 1865), New Haven, Conn., then prin. owner, 1856, pres., 1857-80, started producing new repeating rifle, 1860, established factory, Bridgeport, Conn., circa 1865; produced new Winchester rifle (purchased Nelson King's patent for loading magazine through gate of frame, incorporated this with Tyler Henry's rifle design), 1866; councilman New Haven, 1863; presdl. elector-at-large for Lincoln, 1864; lt. gov. Conn., 1866; contbd. $100,000 to Yale, also gifts to scientific depts., theol. sch. Died New Haven, Dec. 11, 1880.

WINDER, John Henry, army officer; b. Rewston, Md., Feb. 21, 1800; s. William H. and Gertrude (Polk) W.; grad. U.S. Mil. Acad., 1820; m. Elizabeth Shepard, 1823; m. 2d, Mrs. Catherine Cox Eagle. Instr. tactics U.S. Mil. Acad., 1823; assigned to duty in Me. and Fla., 1827-45; brevetted maj., then lt. col. for conduct in Mexican War; commd. maj. arty. U.S. Army, 1860, resigned, 1861; commd. brig. gen. Confederate Army, 1861, provost marshal and comdr. Northern prisons, Richmond, Va.; in charge of mil. prison, Danville, Va., then all prisons in Ga. and Ala., 1864; commissary gen. all Confederate mil. prisons east of the Mississippi, 1864-65. Died Florence, S.C., Feb. 8, 1865.

WINDER, Levin, gov. Md.; b. Somerset County, Md., Sept. 4, 1757; s. William and Esther (Gillis) W.; m. Mary Sloss, 3 children. Commd. 1st lt. Continental Army, 1776; capt. 4th Regt., Md. Militia, 1776; commd. maj., 1777, lt. col., 1781, ret., 1783; mem. Md. Ho. of Dels. (Federalist) from Somerset County, 1806-09, speaker, 1809; gov. Md., 1812-15; mem. Md. Senate, 1816. Died Balt., July 1, 1819.

WINDER, William Henry, army officer, lawyer; b. Somerset County, Md., Feb. 18, 1775; s. John Winder; m. Gertrude Polk, 1799; 1 son, John Henry. Apptd. lt. col. 14th Inf., U.S. Army, 1812; promoted col., serving on No. frontier, 1812; commd. brig. gen., 1813, captured in Battle of Stony Creek, released on parole; in command at Battle of Bladensburg (Va.), 1814, court martialed for ordering retreat resulting in abandonment of Washington (D.C.) to enemy, honorably acquitted; discharged from U.S. Army, 1815; practiced law, Balt., 1815-24. Died Balt., May 24, 1824.

WINDOM, William, senator; b. Belmont County, O., May 10, 1827; s. Jezekiah and Mercy (Spencer) W.; m. Ellen P. Hatch, Aug. 20, 1856, 3 children including Ellen H., Florence B. Admitted to Ohio bar, 1850; public prosecutor (Whig) for Knox County, O., 1852-55; settled in Winona, Minn. Territory, 1855; mem. law firm Sargent, Wilson & Windom; supporter and friend of Lincoln; mem. U.S. Ho. of Reps. from Minn., 36th-40th congresses, 1869-79, mem. com. of 33, chmn. com. on Indian affairs for 2 terms, head spl. com. to visit Indian tribes, 1865, mem. com. to investigate conduct of Indian commr., 1867; mem. U.S. Senate, 1870-81, 81-83, voted for Bland-Allison Act of 1878, chmn. spl. com. on transp. routes to seaboard; U.S. sec. of treasury, 1881, 89-91, advocated internat. bimetalism. Died Delmonico's Restaurant, N.Y.C., Jan. 29, 1891; buried Rock Creek Cemetery, Washington, D.C.

WINEBRENNER, John, clergyman; b. Walkerville, Frederick County, Md., Mar. 25, 1797; s. Phillip and Eve (Barrick) W.; attended Dickinson Coll., Carlisle, Pa.; studied theology under Samuel Helffenstein, Phila., 3 years; m. Charlotte Reutter, Oct. 10, 1822; m. 2d, Mary Mitchell, Nov. 2, 1837; at least 6 children. Ordained minister German Reformed Ch., Hagerstown, Md., 1820; pastor ch., Harrisburg, Pa., also 4 affiliated rural chs., itinerant preacher, Pa. and Md., 1822-30; dropped from German Reformed Synod, 1828; rebaptized, 1830; organized (with friends). Gen. Eldership of Ch. of God. (name changed to Gen. Eldership of Chs. of God in N. Am. 1845), 1830; editor, publisher Gospel Publisher, 1835-40, Church Advocate, 1846-47. Author: Brief Views of the Church of God, 1840; A Treatise on Regeneration, 1844; Doctrinal and Practical Sermons, 1860. Editor: A Testament and Gazetteer, 1836; The Seraphina, 1853; Church Hymn-Book, 1859. Died Harrisburg, Sept. 12, 1860; buried Harrisburg Cemetery.

WINES, Enoch Cobb, clergyman, penologist, coll. pres.; b. Hanover, N.J., Feb. 17, 1806; s. William and Eleanor (Baldwin) W.; grad. Middlebury (Vt.) Coll., 1827; m. Emma Stansbury, June 14, 1832, 7 sons including Frederick Howard. Schoolmaster on frigate Constellation, 1829; operated sch. for boys, Edgehill, N.J., 1832-circa 1838; tchr. People's Coll., Phila., 1839-circa 1843; editor Am. Jour. Edn., circa 1845; ordained to ministry Congregational Ch., 1849, pastor, Cornwall, Vt., East Hampton, L.I., N.Y., 1849-53, Washington, Pa., 1853-59; prof. classics Washington (Pa.) Coll., 1853-59; pres. City Coll. of St. Louis, 1859-61; sec. Prison Assn. of N.Y., 1862-79; visited prisons in all No. states, 1865; issued report which recommended establishment of non-partisan bd. of commrs. independent of polit. control to plan permanent program of prison reform, also a system of graded prisons and parole system, 1867; instrumental in drawing up program of Cincinnati Congress of prison reformers (became basis of prison reform movement in following generation), 1870; sec. Nat. Prison Assn., 1870-77; toured European prisons (as commr. created by Congress), 1871; instrumental in summoning 1st Internat. Penitentiary Congress, London, 1872. Author: The State of Prisons and Child Saving Institutions in the Civilized World, 1880. Died Cambridge, Mass., Dec. 10, 1879.

WINFIELD, Charles Henry, congressman; b. Crawford, N.Y., Apr. 22, 1822; studied law. Admitted to N.Y. bar, 1846, began practice in Goshen; dist. atty. for Orange County (N.Y.), 1850-56; mem. U.S. Ho. of Reps. (Democrat) from N.Y., 38th-39th congresses, 1863-67. Died Walden, N.Y., June 10, 1888; buried Wallkill Valley Cemetery, Walden.

WING, Austin Eli, congressman; b. Conway, Mass., Feb. 3, 1792; attended Athens (O.) Coll.; grad. Williams Coll., 1814. Moved to Detroit; mem. U.S. Ho. of Reps. (Whig) from Mich., 19th-20th, 22d congresses, 1825-29, 31-33; moved to Monroe, Mich.; mem. Mich. Ho. of Reps., 1842; mem. bd. regents U. Mich., 1845-50; U.S. marshal for Mich., 1846-49. Died Cleve., Aug. 27, 1849; buried Woodlawn Cemetery, Monroe.

WINGATE, Joseph Ferdinand, congressman; b. Haverhill, Mass. (now Me.), June 29, 1786. Engaged in merc. bus., Bath, Me.; mem. Mass. Ho. of Reps., 1818-19; collector of customs Port of Bath, 1820-24; mem. U.S. Ho. of Reps. (Democrat) from Me., 20th-21st congresses, 1827-31; moved to Windsor, Me. Died South Windsor, Me.; buried Rest Haven Cemetery, South Windsor.

WINGATE, Paine, senator, clergyman; b. Amesbury, Mass., May 14, 1739; s. Rev. Paine and Mary (Balch) W.; grad. Harvard, 1759; m. Eunice Pickering, May 23, 1765, 5 children. Ordained minister Congregational Ch., 1763; pastor, Hampton Falls, N.H., 1763-76; moved to Stratham, N.H., 1776; refused to sign "Association Test," 1776; del. to N.H. Constl. Conv., 1781; mem. N.H. Legislature, 1783; mem. Continental Congress, 1787-88; mem. U.S. Senate from N.H., 1789-93; mem. U.S. Ho. of Reps. from N.H., 3d Congress, 1793-95; mem. N.H. Legislature, 1795; judge N.H. Superior Ct., 1798-1809. Died Stratham, Mar. 7, 1838.

WINGFIELD, Edward Maria, adventurer; b. Eng., flourished 1586-1613; s. Thomas and Mrs. (Kerrye or Kaye) Wingfield. Became interested in establishing Va. Colony, headed list of those granted charter, 1606, sailed for Va., 1606, arrived within Va. capes, 1607; elected 1st pres. Va. Colony by Council, 1607, removed from office, sent home, imprisoned, charged with improper distbn. of supplies, defended himself with "A Discourse of Virginia," acquitted; active in reorgn. accompanying granting of 2d charter, 1609, named a grantee; an investor London Co.

WINKLER, Edwin Theodore, clergyman, editor; b. Savannah, Ga., Nov. 13, 1823; s. Shadrach and Jane (Wetzer) W.; grad. Brown U., 1843; attended Newton Theol. Instn., 1843-45; married. Ordained minister Baptist Ch., 1846; editor Christian Index, Bapt. paper of Ga., 1846-47; pastor, Albany, Ga., 1847-49, Gillisonville, S.C., 1849-52; exec. sec. So. Bapt. Publishing Soc., 1852-54; editor So. Baptist, 1853; pastor 1st Bapt. Ch. in Charleston, 1854-61; served as chaplain Confederate Army, Civil War; in charge of Citadel Square Bapt. Ch., Charleston, 1865-72; pastor, Marion, Ala., 1872-74; editor Ala. Baptist, 1874-83; pres. Home Missionary Bd. of So. Bapt. Conv., 10 years; prepared Notes and Questions for Oral Instruction of Colored People, 1857. Author: The Spirit of Missions, 1853; The Sacred Lute, 1855; Rome, Past, Present and Future, 1877; Commentary on the Epistle of James, 1888. Died Marion, Nov. 10, 1883.

WINLOCK, Joseph, educator, astronomer; b. Shelby County, Ky., Feb. 6, 1826; s. Fielding and Nancy (Peyton) W.; grad. Shelby Coll., 1845; A.M. (hon.), Harvard, 1868; m. Mary Isabella Lane, Dec. 10, 1856, 6 children. Prof. mathematics and astronomy Shelby Coll., Shelbyville, Ky., 1845-52; mem. staff Am. Ephermeris and Nautical Almanac, Cambridge, Mass., 1852-57, supt., 1858-59, circa 1862-66; prof. mathematics U..S Naval Observatory, 1857; head dept. mathematics U.S. Naval Acad., 1859; Phillips prof. astronomy, also dir. observatory Harvard, 1866-75; 1st astronomer to obtain photograph of corona during solar eclipse, also 1st to adapt to photographic purposes telescope of long focus, fixed horizontally and used without eye piece; corporate mem. Nat. Acad. Scis.; mem. Am. Acad. Arts and Scis. Died Cambridge, June 11, 1875.

WINN, Richard, army officer, congressman; b. Fauquier County, Va., 1750; s. Minor and Margaret (O'Conner) W.; m. Pricilla McKinley, several children. Commd. 1st lt. 3d S.C. Regt., Continental Army, 1775; made justice of peace S.C., 1775; fought in Battle of Ft. Moultrie, 1776; as capt. in command defended Ft. McIntosh, Ga., 1777; took part in defense of Charleston, 1780; joined Thomas

Sumter's guerrillas as maj., 1780; rep. to Jacksonborough Assembly, 1782; commd. brig. gen. S.C. Militia, 1783, maj. gen., 1800; surveyed Camden Dist., S.C., 1783; gave 100 acres to Mt. Zion Soc. (youth edn.), 1785; mem. S.C. Legislature; commr. to buy (later sell) lands for new state capital at Columbia, 1786; supt. Indian affairs for Creek Nation, 1788; mem. U.S. Ho. of Reps. (Democrat) from S.C., 3d-4th, 7th-12th congresses, 1793-97, Jan. 24, 1803-13; moved to Tenn., 1813, became planter and mcht. Died Duck River, Tenn., Dec. 19, 1818; buried Winnsboro, S.C.

WINNEMUCCA, Sarah (Indian name: Tocmetone), educator; b. Humbolt Lake, Nev., circa 1844; d. Winnemucca; m. Lt. Hopkins, Jan. 9, 1882. Woman of Shoshonean tribe of Paviotsos (commonly called Paiute Indians); became interpreter on reservation, 1868; taught Indian sch., Malheur reservation, Ore., 1876; guide, messenger and interpreter for Gen. O. O. Howard during Bannock War of 1878; went to Washington, D.C. to intercede for her people, who had been arbitrarily removed to Yakima reservation, 1879-80; interpreter, Malheur Agy., 1880; tchr. Indian sch., Vancouver Barracks, Wash., 1881; lectured in Boston, 1881; condr. sch., Lovelock, Nev., 1883-86. Author: Life Among the Paiutes: Their Wrongs and Claims, 1883. Died Monida, Mont., Oct. 16, 1891.

WINSER, Henry Jacob, journalist; b. Bermuda Islands, Nov. 23, 1823; s. Francis and Louisa (Till) W.; m. Edith Cox, 1866. Came to U.S., 1840, became mem. staff of printing firm owned by his half-brother, John, N.Y.C.; became proofreader N.Y. Times, 1851, later mem. city staff; served as 1st lt. 1st Regt., N.Y.C. Fire Zouaves, 1861; correspondent for N.W. Times during Civil War, accompanied expdn. to Port Royal, S.C., 1861; wrote 1st description of bombardment of New Orleans published in the North, 1862; covered battle at Cold Harbor, 1864; head of city dept. N.Y. Times, 1867-69; U.S. consul to Sonneberg, Germany, 1869-81; in charge of information bur. N.P R.R., 1881-83; free lance journalist N.Y.C., 1883-96. Died N.Y.C., 1896.

WINSLOW, Edward, colonial gov.; b. Droitwich, Eng., Oct. 18, 1595; s. Edward and Magdalene Ollyver (or Oliver) W.; m. Elizabeth Barker, May 16, 1618; m. 2d, Susanna Fuller White, May 12, 1621. Joined John Robinson's Separatist congregation, Leyden, Netherlands, 1617; sailed for Am. on English ship Speedwell, 1620, transferred to Mayflower, landed Dec. 21, 1620; chosen envoy to Indian chieftain Massasoit, spring 1621, made 1st treaty with Indians; sent 4 narratives of explorations and dealings with Indians to Eng., 1622, published as A Relation or Journal of the Beginning and Proceedings of the English Plantation settled at Plimoth in New England (1st published book written about Am. by an American), 1622; went to Eng. as 1 of 5 assts. to negotiate with mchts.; became 1 of colony's undertakers (assumed colony's debts in return for trading privileges), 1627; established trading posts in Me., later on Connecticut River; agt. for Plymouth Colony, 1629, assisted in securing grant of land from Council of New Eng., 1630; defended colonists against charges of Christopher Gardener and Ferdinando Gorges before Privy Council, 1633; assistant of Plymouth Colony, 1624-46, gov., 1633, 36, 44; an organizer New Eng. Confedn.; instrumental in reorganizing colonial and local govt., 1636, also in drafting new code of laws; resisted encroachments of Mass., R.I. and Conn. on Plymouth's trading posts; returned to Eng. to defend Mass. Bay Co. against Samuel Gorton's charges of religious intolerance, 1646-55; a founder Soc. for Propagation of Gospel in New Eng., 1649; apptd. by Oliver Cromwell chmn. of Joint English-Dutch commn. to settle Brit. naval damages in neutral Denmark, 1654; apptd. chief of 3 commrs. (with Adm. Venables, Sir William Penn) to capture Spanish West Indies, 1654. Author: Good News from New England or a True Relation of Things Very Remarkable at the Plantation of Plymouth in New England . . . (narrative of years 1621-23, 1st history of Plymouth Colony), 1624; Hypocrisie Unmasked by the True Relation of the Proceedings of the Governor and Company of the Massachusetts against Samuel Gorton, 1646; New England's Salamander Discovered by an Irreligious and Scornfull Pamphlet, 1647; The Glorious Progress of the Gospel among the Indians in New England, 1649. Died at sea, May 8, 1655; buried at sea.

WINSLOW, Edward, silversmith, colonial govt. ofcl; b. Boston, Nov. 1, 1669; s. Edward and Elizabeth (Hutchinson) W.; m. Hannah Moody; m. 2d, Elizabeth Pemberton; m. 3d, Susanna (Furman) Lyman. Apptd. constable, Boston, 1699, tithingman, 1703, surveyor, 1705, overseer of poor, 1711-12, selectman, 1714; apptd. capt. Suffolk County Arty. Co., 1714; justice Inferior Ct. of Common Pleas, Suffolk County; silversmith, work among most valuable in Am., examples exhibited in Met. Mus., N.Y.C. Died Boston, Dec. 1, 1753.

WINSLOW, Hubbard, clergyman, educator; b. Williston, Vt., Oct. 30, 1799; s. Nathaniel and Joanna (Kellogg) W.; attended Middlebury Coll.; grad. Yale, 1825; attended Yale Divinity Sch., Andover Theol. Sem., 1826-27; D.D. (hon.), Hamilton Coll., 1857; m. Susan Ward Cutler, May 21, 1829, 4 children including William Copley. Ordained pastor 1st Congregational Ch., Dover, N.H., 1828-32; pastor Bowdoin Street Ch., Boston, 1832-44; an editor Religious Mag., 1837-40; established and conducted Mt. Vernon Sch. for Young Ladies, Boston, 1844-53; pastor 1st Presbyn. Ch., Geneva, N.Y., 1857-59, 50th Street Presbyn. Ch. Bklyn., 1837-40. Author: The Young Man's Aid to Knowledge, Virtue and Happiness, 1837; The Appropriate Sphere of Woman, 1837; Are You a Christian, 2d edit., 1839; The Christian Doctrine, 1844; Elements of Intellectual Philosophy, 1850; Elements of Moral Philosophy, 1858. Died Williston, Aug. 13, 1864.

WINSLOW, John, army officer; b. Marshfield, Mass., May 10, 1703; s. Isaac and Sarah (Wensley) W.; m. Mary Little, 1725; m. 2d, Bethiah (Barker) Johnson; children—Pelham, Isaac. Apptd. capt. co. of Mass. Militia by Mass. Council, 1740, served in West Indian expdn.; entered Brit. Army, 1741, served at Cartagena; returned to Mass. for reinforcements; served in Phillip's Regt. Brit. Inf. in Nova Scotia, 1744-51; commd. maj. gen. Mass. Militia, served on Kennebec River, 1754; built Ft. Western as trading post for proprietors of Plymouth Colony, also Ft. Halifax; apptd. lt. col., commandant both New Eng. battalions, 1755; commanded provincial army raised in New Eng. and N.Y. in capture of Crown Point, 1775; mem. Mass. Gen. Ct. from Marshfield, 1757-58, 61-65; instrumental in surveying and supervising Kennebec River devel.; commr. on St. Croix Boundary, 1762; Town of Winslow (formerly Ft. Halifax, Kennebec County, Me.) named for him, 1771. Died Hingham, Mass., Apr. 17, 1774.

WINSLOW, John Ancrum, naval officer; b. Wilmington, N.C., Nov. 19, 1811; s. Edward and Sara (Ancrum) W.; m. Catherine Winslow, Oct. 18, 1837, at least 3 children. Commd. midshipman U.S. Navy, 1827; decorated with sword-knot and pair of epaulettes Queen Victoria (of Eng.) for action in fire in hold of Cunard steamer in Boston Harbor, 1841; lost 1st command, schooner Morris, in gale while blockading Mexico, 1846; promoted comdr., 1855; served on Mississippi River. 1862; commd. capt., 1862, patrolled from Azores to English Channel in command ship Kearsage, 1863-64; defeated Confederate sloop Alabama commanded by Raphael Semmes, 1864; commanded Gulf Squadron, 1866-67; commd. rear adm., 1870, in command of Pacific fleet, 1870-72. Died Boston Highlands, Mass., Sept. 29, 1873.

WINSLOW, John Flack, iron industry exec.; b. Bennington, Vt., Nov. 10, 1810; s. Richard and Mary Corning (Seymour) W.; LL.D. (hon.), U. Vt., 1888; m. Nancy Beach Jackson, Sept. 12. 1832; m. 2d, Harriet Wicks, Sept. 5, 1867; 2 children. Became mgr. Boston agy. N.J. Iron Co., 1832; owner pig iron producing plants, Bergen and Sussex counties, N.J., 1833; partner with Erastus Corning, 1837-67; controlled Albany and Rensselaer iron works; built (with John H. Griswold and C. S. Bushnell) Capt. John Ericsson's turret ship Monitor for U.S. Govt., 1861; delegated Alexander L. Holley to purchase Am. rights to Bessemer steel process in Eng., 1863; designed, built Bessemer steel plant (1st of kind in U.S.) Troy, N.Y., operating by 1865; pres. Rensselaer Poly. Inst., 1865-68; dir. several banks; pres. co. constructing bridge over Hudson River. Died Poughkeepsie, N.Y., Mar. 10, 1892.

WINSLOW, Josiah, gov. Plymouth Colony; b. Marshfield, Mass., circa 1629; s. Edward and Susanna (Fuller) W.; attended Harvard; m. Penelope Pelham, circa 1657, 2 children including Isaac. Commanded militia, Marshfield, 1652; dep. to Gen. Ct., 1653, 57; asst. gov. Mass., 1657-73; Plymouth commr. for United Colonies, 1658-72; succeeded Myles Standish as comdr.-in-chief Plymouth Colony, 1659; captured Indian chief Alexander (son and successor of Massasoit), thus ending danger of Indian uprising, 1662; a signer Articles of Confederation of New Eng. Colonies, 1672; gov. New Plymouth (1st native-born gov. in Am.), 1673-80; established 1st public sch. in Plymouth, 1674; signed declaration of war and issued statement denying any legitimate grievance to Indians because Pilgrims had honestly bought their land, at beginning of Indian uprisings, 1675; comdr.-in-chief of forces of United Colonies (1st native-born comdr. Am. Army), 1675-76; won decisive battle against Narragansett Indians, 1675. Died Marshfield, Dec. 18, 1680.

WINSLOW, Kate Reignolds, actress; b. Eng., 1814; m. Harry Farren, Dec. 1857; m. 2d, Irving Winslow. Came to U.S., 1828; made debut as Virginia in Forrest's Virginius, N.Y. Theatre, N.Y.C.; became mem. William E. Barton's acting co.; leading lady in Laura Keene's stock co.; appeared at Princess Theatre, London, 1868. Author: Yesterdays with Actors, 1887.

WINSLOW Miron, missionary; b. Williston, Vt., Dec. 11, 1789; s. Nathaniel and Joanna (Kellog) W.; grad. Middlebury Coll., 1815, D.D. (hon.), 1864; B.D., Andover Theol. Sem., 1818; A.M. (hon.), Yale; LL.D. (hon.), Harvard, 1858; m. Harriet Wadsworth Lathrop, Jan. 11, 1819; m. 2d, Catherine Waterbury, Apr. 23, 1835; m. 3d, Anna Spiers, Sept. 2, 1838; m. 4th, Mrs. Mary W. Billings) White, Mar. 12, 1845; m. 5th, Ellen Augusta Reed, May 20, 1857; 10 children. Licensed to preach by Londonberry Presbytery, East Bedford, Mass., 1818, ordained as missionary, Salem, Mass.; sailed for India, 1819; preacher, educator, translator working among Tamils, Oodooville, Ceylon, 1819-33; made visits to Am., 1833-35, 1856-57; missionary, Madras, 1836-64, chosen by Madras Bible Soc. to serve on com. for revising Tamil Bible. Author: A Sketch of Missions, 1819; A Memoir of Mrs. Harriet Wadsworth Winslow, Combining a Sketch of the Ceylon Mission, 1835; Comprehensive Tamil and English Dictionary of High and Low Tamil, 1862; Reports of the Madras Mission; Hints on Missions to India, 1856. Died Capetown, S. Africa, Oct. 22, 1864; buried Capetown.

WINSLOW, Warren, congressman; b. Fayetteville, N.C., Jan. 1, 1810; grad. U. N.C., 1827; studied law. Admitted to N.C. bar, practiced in Fayetteville; mem. N.C. Senate, served as speaker; acting gov. N.C., 1854; mem. U.S. Ho. of Reps. (Democrat) from N.C., 34th-36th congresses, 1855-61. Died Fayetteville, Aug. 16, 1862; buried Cross Creek Cemetery, Fayetteville.

WINSOR, Justin, librarian, historian; b. Boston, Jan. 2, 1831; s. Nathaniel and Ann Thomas (Howland) W.; attended Harvard, 1849-53, received degree, 1868 (as of class of 1853); LL.D. (hon.), U. Mich., 1887, Williams Coll., 1893; m. Caroline T. Barcker, Dec. 18, 1855, 1 child, Trustee Boston Pub. Library, 1866-68, supt., 1868-77; librarian Harvard, 1877-97; attended 1st Internat. Conf. of Librarians, London, Eng.; a founder Library Journal, 1876; a founder Am. Library Assn., 1876, pres., 1876-85, 97; Author: A History of the Town of Duxbury, 1849; The Reader's Handbook of the American Revolution. 1879; The Memorial History of Boston, 4 vols., 1880-81; Narrative and Critical History of America (most important work), 8 vols., 1884-89; Christopher Columbus, 1891; Cartier to Frontenac, 1894; The Mississippi Basin, 1895; The Westward Movement, 1897. Died Cambridge, Mass., Oct. 22, 1897.

WINSTON, John Anthony, gov. Ala., planter; b. Madison County, Ala., Sept. 4, 1812; s. William and Mary (Baker) W.; attended Cumberland Coll. (now U. Nashville, Tenn.); m. Mary Agnes Walker, 1832; m. 2d, Mary W. Logwood, 1842. Owner large plantations in Ala., Miss., Tex., Ark.; owner cotton commn. house, Mobile, Ala., 1845-71; mem. Ala. Ho. of Reps., 1840, 42; mem. Ala. Senate, 1843-53, pres., 1845-49; leader So.-Rights Democrats; gov. Ala. (1st native-born Alabaman to hold office) 1853-57; del. Dem. Conv., Balt., 1848; del. Charleston Conv., 1860; Ala. commr. to State of La.; commd. col. 8th Ala. Inf., Confederate Army, served in Peninsular Campaign; del. to Ala. Constl. Conv., 1865; elected to U.S. Senate for term 1867-73, but denied seat for refusal to take oath of allegiance. Died Mobile, Dec. 21, 1871.

WINSTON, Joseph, congressman; b. Louisa County, Va., June 17, 1746; s. Samuel Winston; 3 children. Mem. Hillsboro (N.C.) Conv., 1775, took steps to organize provincial govt.; commd. maj. N.C. Militia, 1775; mem. expdn. against Scotch Loyalists assembled at Cross Creek, 1776; ranger of Surry County, N.S., fought against Cherokee Indians, 1776; mem. N.C. Ho. of Commons, 1777; commr. to treat with Cherokees; served at Battle of King's Mountain, 1780; mem. N.C. Senate, 1790, 91, 1802, 07, 12; mem. U.S. Ho. of Reps. from N.C., 3d, 8th-9th congresses, 1793-95, 1803-07; presdl. elector voting for Jefferson and Burr, 1800; trustee U. N.C., 1807-13; promoted lt. col. Stokes County (N.C.) Militia; Winston (now Winston-Salem) N.C. named for him. Died Germantown, N.C., Apr. 21, 1815; buried Guilford Battle Ground, nr. Greensboro, N.C.

WINTER, Elisha I., congressman; b. N.Y.C., July 15, 1781. Engaged in mining ore, Clinton County, N.Y., circa 1806; mem. U.S. Ho. of Reps. (Federalist) from N.Y., 13th Congress, 1813-15; engaged in planting, nr. Lexington, Ky.; instrumental in bldg. Lexington & Ohio R.R. (1st railroad in the area), became pres. Died Lexington, June 30, 1849; buried Lexington Cemetery.

WINTER, George, artist; b. Portsea, Eng., June 10, 1810. attended N.A.D., 3 years; came to Am., 1830; settled in N.Y.C.; moved to Cincinnati, circa 1835, to Logansport, Ind., 1836, to Lafayette, Ind., 1851; painted portraits of many early Ind. settlers and Indians, also landscapes; work published in The

Journals and Indian Paintings of George Winter 1837-1839, 1948. Died Lafayette, Feb. 1, 1876.

WINTHROP, James, jurist; b. Cambridge, Mass., Mar. 28, 1752; s. Prof. John and Rebecca (Townsend) W.; grad. Harvard, 1769. Librarian, Harvard, 1770-77; served with Continental forces at Battle of Bunker Hill, 1775; postmaster Cambridge, 1776; register of probate for Middlesex County (Mass.) 1772-87; an original mem. Am. Acad. Arts and Scis.; served with Mass. Militia against Capt. Daniel Shays' rebels, 1789; judge Ct. of Common Pleas, Middlesex, 1791; surveyor for proposed Cape Cod canal, 1791; promoter West Boston Bridge, Middlesex Canal; founder Mass. Hist. Soc.; overseer Allegheny Coll., bequeathed his large, valuable library to Coll.; contbr. articles to Literary Miscellany. Died Cambridge, Sept. 26, 1821.

WINTHROP, John, colonial gov.; b. Edwardstone, Suffolk, Eng., Jan. 23, 1588; s. Adam and Anne (Browne) W.; attended Trinity Coll., Cambridge (Eng.), U., 1602-04; m. Mary Forth, Apr. 16, 1605; m. 2d, Thomassine Clopton, Dec. 1615; m. 3d, Margaret Tyndal, Apr. 1618; 7 children including John. Admitted to practice Gray's Inn, London, Eng., 1613; apptd. an atty. for court of wards and liveries, 1626; admitted to Inner Temple, 1628; became associated with Puritans who received merc. charter (conferring complete governing powers on gov. and Gen. Ct.) and land grant for settlement in Am. from Charles I. 1629; chosen gov. Mass. Bay Colony, 1629, reelected, 1631, 32, 33, 37-40, 42-44, 46-49; deferred to wishes of clergy respecting matters of discipline, accepted violations of original charter to create more democratic govt.; presided at trial of Anne Hutchinson during Antinomian controversy, 1637, ordered her banished; declined to run for reelection in 1640 to avoid establishing tradition of life tenure in governorship; sided with magistrates (who represented the wealthy) in their claim to sit separately from deputies (who represented more democratic elements), 1644; severely criticized for giving arms and ships to French from Acadia without consulting Gen. Ct., 1643; head Mass. delegation to form New Eng. Confederation, 1st pres. of Confederation, 1645; unjustly accused of improper action in regard to militia officer's appointment in 1645. Died Mar. 26, 1649.

WINTHROP, John, colonial gov.; b. Groton, Suffolk, Eng., Feb. 23, 1606; s. John and Mary (Forth) W.; attended Trinity Coll., Dublin; studied law in London; m. Martha Jones, Feb. 8, 1631; m. 2d, Elizabeth Reade, Oct. 6, 1635; 2 children. Admitted to Inner Temple, London, Eng., 1625; arrived in New Eng., 1631; elected assistant Mass. Gen. Ct., 1631; a founder Ipswich (Mass.), 1633; in Eng., 1634-35, received appointment as gov. Conn. settlements, became gov. Conn., 1636; returned to Mass., established residence at Salem, 1639; went to Eng. to gain capital for promotion of foundry venture, 1641; built furnaces at Lynn and Braintree, Mass., 1644; magistrate of Pequot (later New London), Conn., 1648; moved to Conn. permanently, 1649; made freeman of Conn., 1650; elected assistant Conn. Gen. Ct., 1651; gov. Conn., 1657-58, 59-76, dep. gov., 1658-59; more successful mission to Eng. to secure new and more liberal charter for Conn., 1661-63; became mem. Royal Soc., 1663 (1st Am. member). Died Boston, Apr. 5, 1676.

WINTHROP, John (called Fitz-John Winthrop), gov. Conn., army officer; b. Ipswich, Mass., Mar. 14, 1639; s. John and Elizabeth (Reade) Winthrop II; attended Harvard, 2 years; m. Elizabeth Tongue, 1 dau. Had commn. in Parliamentary Army in England, served in mil. campaign in Scotland; returned to New London, Conn., 1663; dep. to Conn. Gen. Assembly, 1671, 78; apptd. chief mil. officer for New London County, 1672; comdr. Conn. troops in fight against Dutch on L.I., N.Y. (Dutch forced to retreat to New Amsterdam), 1673; fought in King Phillip's War, 1675-76; apptd. to Mass. Gov.'s Council by Joseph Dudley, 1686, also an assistant of Gov. Andros; apptd. maj. gen. and comdr. united force of colonists in unsuccessful invasion of Canada during King William's war, 1690, freed of blame for failure by Conn. Gen. Assembly; gov. Conn., 1698-1707. Died Boston, Nov. 27, 1707.

WINTHROP, John, astronomer; b. Boston, Dec. 19, 1714; s. Adam and Anne (Wainwright) W.; A.B., Harvard, 1732, LL.D. (1st hon. LL.D. given by Harvard), 1773; LL.D. (hon.), U. Edinburgh (Scotland), 1771; m. Rebecca Townesend, July 1, 1746; m. 2d, Hannah (Fayerweather) Tolman, Mar. 24, 1756; several children including James. Hollis prof. mathematics and natural philosophy Harvard, 1738-79; did research in astronomy, published results in Philos. Transactions of the Royal Soc.; made series of sun-spot observations, Apr. 19-22, 1739 (1st set observations sun-spots in Mass. Colony); made study of transit of Mercury over sun, 1740, also reported transits, 1743, 69; established 1st lab. of exptl. physics in Am. at Harvard, 1746, demonstrated laws of mechanics, light, heat, movement of celestial bodies according to Newtonian system, introduced into math. curriculum elements of fluxions (now known as differential and integral calculs), 1751; reported on earthquake that shook New England, 1755; delivered lecture on return of Halley's Comet of 1682, 1759 (1st predicted return of a comet); made preparations for transits of Venus, 1761, 69, dir. 1st astron. expdn. sent by Harvard, to St. John's, (Newfoundland) for 1761 transit; elected fellow Royal Soc., 1766; mem. Am. Philos. Soc., 1769; a founder Am. Acad. Arts and Scis., 1769; 1st astronomer in Am. Author: Relation of a Voyage from Boston to Newfoundland for the Observation of the Transit of Venus, 1761; Two Lectures on the Parallax and Distance of the Sun, 1769. Died Cambridge, Mass., May 3, 1779; buried King's Chapel Burying ground, Boston.

WINTHROP, Robert Charles, senator, congressman; b. Boston, May 12, 1809; s. Lt. Gov. Thomas Lindall and Elizabeth (Temple) W.; grad. Harvard, 1828; m. Eliza Blanchard, Mar. 12, 1832; m. 2d, Laura (Derby) Welles, Oct. 15, 1859; m. 3d, Adele Granger, Nov. 15, 1865; 4 children. Admitted to Mass. bar, 1831; mem. Mass. Gen. Ct., 1832-40; mem. Mass. Ho. of Reps., 1835-40, speaker, 1838-40; mem. U.S. Ho. of Reps. (Whig) from Mass., 26th-31st Congresses, Nov. 1840-July 1850; mem. U.S. Senate from Mass., 1850-51, defeated for reelection by Charles Sumner; Whig. presdl. elector, 1852; refused to join Republican Party in 1850's, supported Whig candidate for Pres., 1856, Gen. McClellan, 1864; conservative toward prosecution of Civil War; delivered before joint session of Congress address celebrating 100th anniversary of Cornwallis' surrender at Yorktown, 1881; chmn. bd. Peabody Ednl. Fund; mem. Mass. Hist. Soc., 1839-94. Died Boston, Nov. 16, 1894; buried Mt. Auburn Cemetery, Cambridge, Mass.

WINTHROP, Theodore, author; b. New Haven, Conn., Sept. 28, 1828; s. Francis Beyard and Elizabeth (Woolsey) W.; grad. Yale, 1848. Traveled throughout nation in youth; employee Pacific Mail S.S. Co., N.Y.C., 1851; ticket seller Panama R.R., 1853; admitted to N.Y. bar, 1855; enlisted in 7th Regt., N.Y. Militia, 1861. Author: Mr. Waddy's Return (1st novel), published 1904; A Companion to the Heart of the Andes, 1859; Cecil Dreeme, pub. 1861; Canoe and the Saddle, 1863. Killed while leading charge on Great Bethel, Va., June 10, 1861.

WIRT, William, U.S. atty. gen.; b. Bladensburg, Md., Nov. 8, 1772; s. Jacob and Henrietta Wirt; studied law under William P. Hunt; m. Mildred Gilmer, May 28, 1795; m. 2d, Elizabeth (Gamble) Washington, Sept. 7, 1802; 12 children. Admitted to Va. bar, circa 1790; elected clk. Va. Ho. of Dels., 1800, mem., 1808; served as counsel for James Thomson Callender in famous trial under Alien and Sedition Acts, 1800; elected by Va. Legislature as presiding judge of chancery dist., 1802; a prosecutor in case against Aaron Burr, 1806; argued his 1st case before Supreme Ct., 1816; U.S. atty. for Richmond dist., 1816-17; atty. gen. U.S., 1817-29, established precedent of preserving all ofcl. records of office, participated in cases of Gibbons vs. Ogden (1824), Dartmouth Coll. vs. Md., 1819. Author: (series of essays) The Old Bachelor, 1810-13; Life and Character of Patrick Henry, 1817. Died Washington, D.C., Feb. 18, 1834; buried Arlington (Va.) Nat. Cemetery.

WIRZ, Henry, army officer; b. Switzerland. Confederate supt. of Andersonville (Ga.) Mil. Prison, where conditions were extremely unfavorable, resulting in death of many Union prisoners; after Civil War, was charged with having conspired with Jefferson Davis to deliberately murder some of prisoners; found guilty of charges at mil. trial, Aug. 1865; subsequent research has shown that many of accusations against Wirz were unfounded. Hanged Nov. 10, 1865.

WISE, Aaron, clergyman; b. Erlau, Hungary, May 2, 1844; s. Rabbi Joseph Hirsch and Rachel (Rosenfeld) Weisz; Rabbi, Jewish Sem. of Eisenstadt (Hungary), 1867; attended univs. Berlin, Leipzig (Germany); Ph.D., U. Halle (Germany); m. Sabine de Fischer Farkashazy, 1870; at least 6 children including Stephen Samuel. Edited a weekly Judeo-German newspaper in support of Orthodox Jewry, circa 1871; came to U.S., 1874, became rabbi Congregation Beth Elohim, Bklyn.; rabbi Temple Rodeph Sholom, (orthodox congregation, became conservative-reformed under his leadership), N.Y.C., 1875-96, founded temple sisterhood, 1891 (sisterhood later founded Aaron Wise Indsl. Sch. in his memory); mem. Soc. German Oriental Scholars; a founder Jewish Theol. Sem. of N.Y., 1886. Died N.Y.C., Mar. 30, 1896.

WISE, Daniel, clergyman, author; b. Portsmouth, Hampshire, Eng., Jan. 10, 1813; s. Daniel and Mary Wise; attended classical sch. of which ofcls. of Christ Ch., Oxford, Eng. were patrons; m. Sarah Ann Hill, Aug. 1836, 2 children. Apprenticed to grocer in early years; came to U.S., 1833; preacher Methodist ch., Lisbon, N.H., 1834, Quincy, Mass., 1837; editor Sunday Sch. Messenger, 1838-44, Ladies Pearl, 1840-43; ordained elder Methodist Episcopal Ch., 1843; pastor, Nantucket and Fall River, Mass., also Providence, R.I., 1845-56; editor Zion's Herald, 1852; corr. sec. Sunday Sch. Union, 1856-72; editor Methodist Review, 1887-88. Author: novels for children under pseudonyms Lawrence Lancewood and Francis Forrester, including: The Young Lady's Counsellor, 1852; Stephen and his Trumpet 1873; Uncrowned Kings, 1875. Died Englewood, N.J., Dec. 19, 1898.

WISE, Henry Alexander, gov. Va., army officer; b. Drummondtown, Va., Dec. 3, 1806; s. Maj. John and Sarah Corbin (Cropper) W.; grad. Washington (Pa.) Coll., 1825; attended law sch., Winchester, Va.; m. Ann Jennings, Oct. 8, 1828; m. 2d, Sarah Sergant, Nov. 1840; m. 3d, Mary Lyons, 1853; 5 children including John Sergeant, Richard Alsop. Admitted to bar, Nashville, Tenn., 1828; practiced law, Nashville, 1828-30, Accomac County, Va., from 1830; supporter of Jackson, 1828, joined Whigs in Bank of U.S. controversy, 1832; mem. U.S. Ho. of Reps. from Va., 23d-28th congresses, 1833-Feb. 12, 1844; influential in nomination of Tyler as Whig candidate for vice pres. U.S., 1840; apptd. U.S. minister to France, rejected by Senate, 1843; U.S. minister to Brazil, 1844-47; Democratic presdl. elector, Va., 1848, 52; mem. Va. Constl. Conv., 1850-51; del. to Nat. Dem. Conv., 1852, worked for nomination of Franklin Pierce; gov. Va., 1856-60, sponsored internal improvement schemes, quelled John Brown's raid, 1859, destroyed influence of Know-Nothing Party in Va.; del. to Va. Secession Conv., 1861, opposed secession ordinance, but later was strong supporter of Confederacy; commd. brig. gen. Confederate Army, 1861, raised regt., served in Western Va. and Roanoke Island, N.C. Author: Seven Decades of the Union, 1872. Died Richmond, Va., Sept. 12, 1876; buried Hollywood Cemetery, Richmond.

WISE, Henry Augustus, naval officer, author; b. N.Y. Naval Shipyard, Bklyn., May 24, 1819; s. Capt. George Stewart and Catherine (Stansberry) W.; m. Charlotte Everett, Aug. 20, 1850, 4 children. Apptd. midshipman U.S. Navy, 1834, passed midshipman, 1840, promoted master, 1846, commd. lt., 1847; served as lt. in razee (cut-down sailing ship-of-line) Independent during Mexican War; mem. U.S.-Japanese Commn., Japan, 1860; promoted comdr., 1862; a naval ordnance expert, had secretly investigated Krupp weapon manufacture; asst. in bur. of ordnance, 1862, acting chief, 1864, chief, 1866, resigned because of ill health, 1868 Author: Los Gringos, or an Inside View of Mexico and California, with Wanderings in Peru, Chile and Polynesia (war experiences), 1849; Tales for the Marines, 1855; Scampavias from Gibel-Tarek to Stamboul, 1857; (stories for children) The Story of the Gray African Parrot, 1860; Captain Brand of the Centipede, 1864. Died Naples, Italy, Apr. 2, 1869.

WISE, Isaac Mayer, clergyman, coll. pres.; b. Steingrub, Bohemia, Mar. 29, 1819; s. Leo and Regina Weis; attended U. Prague, U. Vienna; m. Therese Bloch, May 26, 1844, 10 children; m. 2d, Selma Boudi, Apr. 25, 1876, 4 children. Became rabbi, 1842; rabbi, Radnitz, Bohemia, 1843; came to N.Y.C., 1846; rabbi, Albany, N.Y., 1846-54, Bene Yeshurun congregation, Cincinnati, 1854-1900; published Israelite, Cincinnati, 1854; pres. Hebrew Union Coll., 1875-1900; pres. Central Conf. Am. Rabbis, 1889-1900. Author: History of the Israelitish Nation from Abraham to the Present Time, 1854; The Cosmic God, 1876; History of the Hebrews' Second Commonwealth, 1880; Pronaos to Holy Writ, 1891. Died Cincinnati, Mar. 26, 1900.

WISE, John, clergyman; b. Roxbury, Mass., Aug. 1652; s. Joseph and Mary (Thompson) W.; grad. Harvard, 1673; m. Abigail Gardner, Dec. 5, 1678, 7 children. Preached at Branford, Conn., 1675-76, Hatfield, Mass., 1677-78; minister Congregational Ch., Ipswich, Mass., 1680-1725, ordained, 1683; led townspeople of Ipswich in resistance to province tax imposed by Gov. Edmund Andros, 1687; found guilty of opposing govt. attempt to impose new tax in court, deprived of ministerial function, Oct. 1687 (decision reversed by Andros, Nov. 1687); apptd. (by Mass. Gen. Ct.) chaplain Mass. expdn. against Quebec (Can.), 1690. Died Apr. 8, 1725.

WISE, John, balloonist; b. Lancaster, Pa., Feb. 24, 1808; married, 1 child. Developed intense desire to study aerostatics as a youth; apprenticed to cabinet maker, 1831-35; made his 1st ascent in balloon, Phila., 1835; made one of 1st proposals to use balloons in tactical warfare during Mexican War; set distance record for balloon trip, traveling 804 miles from St. Louis to Henderson

(N.Y.), 1859; failed in attempted balloon trip to Europe, landed in Canaan Conn., 1873; credited with inventing rip panel (safety device). Author: A System of Aeronautics, 1850; Through the Air, 1873. Drowned while ballooning over Lake Michigan, Sept. 29, 1879, body never recovered.

WISLIZENUS, Frederick Adolph, physician; b. Königsee, Germany, May 21, 1810; attended U. Jena and Tübingen; m. Lucy Crane, July 23, 1850, 1 child. Fled to Switzerland to escape polit. unrest in Germany, 1833; came to U.S., 1835; became country physician, Mascontah, St. Clair County, Ill.; practiced medicine, St. Louis, 1839-44; joined Albert Speyer's trading caravan (carrying arms to Mexican Army) bound for Santa Fé, 1846, pursued but not overtaken by Gen. Stephen Watts Kearney's Army; practiced medicine, St. Louis, during cholera epidemic, 1848-49; went to Europe, 1850-51; founder Mo. Hist. Soc., Acad. of Science St. Louis. Author: Memoir of a Tour to Northern Mexico, 1848. Died St. Louis, Sept. 22, 1889.

WISNER, Henry, Continental congressman; b. Goshen, N.Y., circa 1720; s. Hendrick and Mary (Shaw) W.; m. Sarah (or Mary) Norton, circa 1739; m. 2d, Sarah Waters, Apr. 1769; 5 children. Asst. justice N.Y. Ct. of Common Pleas; mem. N.Y. Colonial Assembly from Orange County, 1759-69; mem. 1st, 2d continental congresses, 1774-77, signed non-importation agreement; mem. N.Y. Provincial Congress, 1775-77, mem. com. which drafted 1st N.Y. State Constn.; mem. N.Y. Senate, 1777-82; operated powdermill, Ulster County, N.Y., during Am. Revolution, constructed 2 other powdermills, Orange County; assisted Continental Army by supplying powder and improving roads; helped plan 1st chain of defenses on Hudson River, 1776; mem. com. of eight (apptd. by N.Y. Provincial Conv.) to confer with Gen. Putnam concerning new defenses on Hudson, 1778, resulted in West Point fortifications; established acad., Goshen, N.Y., 1784; mem. 1st bd. regents Univ. State N.Y., 1784-87; mem. N.Y. Constl. Conv., 1788, voted against adoption of U.S. Constn. because distrustful of delegating so much power to fed. govt. Died Mar. 4, 1790; buried Old Wallkill Cemetery, Phillipsburg, N.Y.

WISSLER, Jacques, engraver; b. Strasbourg, France, 1803. Trained as lithographer and engraver, Paris, France; came to Am., 1849; with firm Dreser & Wissler, N.Y.C., 1860; went to Richmond, Va., 1861; engraved plates for paper currency and bonds for Confederate States Am.; moved to Macon, Miss., after Civil War, later to Camden, N.J.; successful portrait artist. Died Camden, Nov. 25, 1887.

WISTAR, Caspar, glass mfr.; b. Wald-Hilsbach, Baden, Feb. 3, 1696; s. Johannes Caspar and Anna Catharina (Wüster) W.; m. Catharine Jansen, May 25, 1726, 3 sons, 4 daus. Arrived in Phila., 1717; began mfg. brass buttons; joined Soc. of Friends, 1725; turned to making window and bottle glass; bought pine-wooded acres, Salem County, West Jersey, 1738; hired 4 experienced glass-blowers from Belgium; began one of colonies earliest glass firms, 1740, managed works, supplied materials, sold wares while retained 2/3 of profits and giving 1/3 share to workers; imported another group of German, Belgian and Italian blowers, 1748, factory prospered and Wistar technique became famous; son Richard ran works after his death. Died Mar. 21, 1752.

WISTAR, Caspar, physician; b. Phila., Sept. 13, 1761; s. Richard and Sarah (Wyatt) W.; B.M., U. State of Pa., 1782; M.D., Edinburgh U., 1786; m. Isabella Marshall, May 15, 1788; m. 2d, Elizabeth Mifflin, Nov. 28, 1798; 3 children. Served 2 terms as pres. Royal Med. Soc. (student orgn.) at Edinburgh, also assisted in founding natural history soc.; elected jr. fellow Coll. Physicians of Phila. (organized 1787), 1787; prof. chemistry med. sch. Coll. of Phila., 1789; adjunct prof. anatomy, surgery and midwifery at new U. Pa., 1792, prof. anatomy and midwifery, 1808, prof. anatomy, 1810-18; mem. staffs Phila. Dispersary, Pa. Hosp., 1793-1810; elected mem. Am. Philos. Soc., 1787, curator, 1793, v.p., 1795, pres., 1815-18; served in yellow fever epidemic, 1793; founded soc. for promotion of vaccination, 1809; plant Wistaria named for him; his family gave his anatomical collection to U. Pa. for museum. Author: System of Anatomy (1st Am. textbook on subject), 2 vols., 1811; Eulogium on Doctor William Shippen, 1818. Died Phila., Jan. 22, 1818.

WISTER, Sally, diarist; b. Phila., July 20, 1761; d. Daniel and Lowry (Jones) Wister; ed. informally; never married. Began a journal at age 16; continued diary while her family was living nr. Phila., 1777-78; journal survives as hist. document and account of Quaker girl during Am. Revolution. Died Germantown, Pa., Apr. 21, 1804.

WITHERELL, James, congressman; b. Mansfield, Mass., June 16, 1759; studied medicine. Served as mem. 11th Mass. Regt. during Revolutionary War, 1775-83; licensed to practice medicine, 1788; moved to Hampton, Vt., 1788, to Fair Haven, Vt., 1789, practiced medicine; mem. Vt. Ho. of Reps., 1798-1802; asso. judge Rutland County (Vt.), 1801-03, judge, 1803-06; mem. Vt. Exec. Council, 1802-06; mem. U.S. Ho. of Reps. (Democrat) from Vt., 10th Congress, 1807-May 1, 1808; U.S. judge for Mich. Territory, 1808-28, sec., 1828-30; commanded troops at Detroit in absence of Gen. Hull, taken prisoner, exchanged. Died Detroit, Jan. 9, 1838; buried Russell St. Cemetery, reinterred Elmwood Cemetery, Detroit.

WITHERS, Frederick Clarke, architect; b. Somersetshire, Eng., Feb. 4, 1828; s. John Alexander and Maria (Jewell) W.; studied architecture under Thomas Henry Wyatt, London, Eng.; m. Emily A. de Wint, 1856, 3 children; m. 2d, Beulah Alice Higbee, Aug. 4, 1864, 8 children. Came to U.S., 1853; practiced architecture, Newburgh, N.Y.; designed 1st Presbyn. Ch., Newburgh, 1857, St. Michael's Ch., Germantown, Pa., 1858; partner Vaux and Olmstead, N.Y.C., 1864-71; aided in archtl. design of Central Park, N.Y.C.; designed Columbia Inst. for Deaf and Dumb, Washington, D.C., 1867. Author: Church Architecture: Plans, Elevations, and Views of Twenty-One Churches and Two School Houses, 1873. Died Yonkers, N.Y., Jan. 7, 1901.

WITHERSPOON, John, clergyman, coll. pres.; b. Gifford, Haddingtonshire, Scotland, Feb. 5, 1723; s. Rev. James and Anne (Walker) W.; M.A.,U. Edinburgh (Scotland), 1739, divinity degree, 1743; D.D. (hon.), U. St. Andrews, 1764; m. Elizabeth Montgomery, Sept. 2, 1748; m. 2d, Ann Dill, May 30, 1791; 12 children. Licensed to preach by Haddington (Scotland) Presbytery, 1743; ordained to ministry Presbyn. Ch., 1745, became minister at Beith, Ayrshire; pastor, Paisley, 1757-68; prolific writer on controversial religious subjects, 1745- 68, took conservative position; moderator Synod of Glasgow and Ayr, 1758; became pres. Coll. of N.J. (now Princeton), 1768-94, expanded coll., introduced study of French, philosophy; became a leader of Presbyn. Ch. in Am.; mem. N.J. Com. of Correspondence from Somerset County, 1775; mem. N.J. Provincial Congress, 1776; mem. Continental Congress from N.J., 1776-82, signed Declaration of Independence, mem. bd. of war, secret com. on conduct of war (1778), state council (1780), drafted instrns. to Am. peace commrs., 1781; opposed printing of paper money and bond issues without retirement provisions; mem. N.J Ho. of Reps., 1783, 89; mem. N.J. Conv. which ratified U.S. Constn., 1787; planned reorgn. of Presbyn. Ch., 1785-89, responsible for introducing new catechisms, credo and order of worship; moderator 1st Presbyn. Nat. Gen. Assembly, 1789. Author: Ecclesiastical Characteristics (attack on humanist influences in Presbyn. Ch.), 1753; collected writings published in 9 vols., Edinburgh, 1815. Died nr. Princeton, N.J., Nov. 15, 1794; buried President's Lot, Witherspoon Street Cemetery, Princeton.

WITHERSPOON, Robert, congressman; b. nr. Kingstree, S.C., Jan. 29, 1767; attended commonity schs. Elected treas. State of S.C., 1800; mem. S.C. Ho. of Reps., 1806-08; mem. U.S. Ho. of Reps. (Democrat) from S.C., 11th Congress, 1809-11; owner large planting interests in Sumter County, S.C.; opposed Nullification Act, 1832. Died nr. Mayesville, S.C., Oct. 11, 1837; buried Salem Brick Ch. Cemetery, Mayesville.

WITHINGTON, Leonard, clergyman; b. Dorchester, Mass., Aug. 9, 1789; grad. Yale, 1814; attended Andover Theol. Sem., 1814-16; D.D. (hon.), Bowdoin Coll., 1850. Ordained to ministry Congregational Ch., 1816; pastor 1st Congregational Ch., Newbury, Mass., 1816-58, sr. asso. pastor, 1858-85. Author: The Puritan (under pseudonym Jonathan Oldberg), 2 vols., 1836; Solomon's Song, Translated and Explained, in Three Parts, 1861. Died Newbury, Apr. 22, 1885.

WITT, John Henry, artist; b. Dublin, Ind., May 18, 1840; studied art, Cincinnati. Maintained studio, Columbus, O., 1862-79, painted portraits of several early Ohio govs. and prominent citizens; moved to N.Y.C., 1879; elected asso. N.A.D., 1885. Died N.Y.C., Sept. 13, 1901.

WITTE, William Henry, congressman; b. Columbia, N.J., Oct. 4, 1817; attended common schs., Springtown, Pa. Moved to Phila., 1840, engaged in merc. and real estate businesses; mem. U.S. Ho. of Reps. (Democrat) from Pa., 33d Congress, 1853-55; engaged in newspaper work, real estate bus. Died Phila., Nov. 24, 1876; buried Durham (Pa.) Cemetery.

WOFFORD, William Tatum, army officer; b. Habersham County, Ga., June 28, 1823; s. William Holingsworth and Nancy (Tatum) W.; m. Julia A. Dwight, 1859; m. 2d, Margaret Langdon, 1878; 6 children. Studied law in Athens, Ga.; admitted to Ga. bar; capt. volunteer cavalry under Gen. Winfield Scott in Mexican War, 1848; mem. Ga. Legislature, 1849-53, clk. lower house, 1853-54; edited (with John W. Burke) Athens Banner, 1852, later established Cassville (Ga.) Standard; del. to So. Comml. Conv., Knoxville, Tenn., 1857, Montgomery, Ala., 1858; mem. Ga. conv., 1861, voted against secession; commd. col. 18th Ga. Regt. at beginning of Civil War; served briefly in N.C., then transferred to Gen. John Hood's brigade, served around Richmond, Va.; led brigade at battles of 2d Manassas, South Mountain and Sharpsburg; served under Gen. Thomas Cobb, promoted brig. gen. after Cobb's death, 1863; after battles of Chancellorsville and Gettysburg sent to East Tenn. with Gen. James Longstreet; transferred back to Richmond after Knoxville; wounded at Spotsylvania and the Wilderness; in command of Dept. of Northern Ga., 1865, defended area with 7,000 troops, finally surrendered to Gen. H. M. Judah at Resaca, Ga., 1865; elected to Congress, 1865, refused seat by radical Republicans; an organizer Cartersville & Van Wert R.R., Atlanta & Blue Ridge R.R.; trustee Cherokee Baptist Coll., Cassville, Cassville Female Coll.; contbd. land and money to Wofford Acad.; mem. Ga. Constl. Conv., 1877. Died nr. Cass Station, Ga., May 22, 1884; buried Cassville Cemetery.

WOLCOTT, Oliver, gov. Conn., sec. treasury; b. Litchfield, Conn., Jan. 11, 1760; s. Oliver and Laura (Collins) W.; grad. Yale, 1778, LL.D. (hon.); attended Litchfield (Conn.) Law Sch.; LL.D. (hon.), Princeton, Brown Coll.; m. Elizabeth Stoughton, June 1, 1785, 7 children. Served in quartermaster's corps in charge army stores and ordnance, Litchfield, 1776; commr. to settle Conn. claims against U.S., 1784; Conn. comptroller pub. accounts, reorganized finances of Conn., 1788-89; auditor U.S. Treasury, 1789-91, comptroller, 1791, initiated plan for creation branch banks of Bank of U.S.; U.S. sec. of treasury (apptd. by Washington), 1795-1800, followed Hamiltonian financial program, remained in office under Pres. John Adams, resigned as result of Adams-Hamilton break, 1800; apptd. by Adams judge U.S. Circuit Ct. for 2d dist., 1801, service ended when Congress repealed act which created circuit court on which he served, 1802; partner in N.Y.C. trading firm, 1803-05; in trading business for self, 1805-15; elected to bd. dirs. Bank of U.S. 1810; a founder Bank of Am., chartered by N.Y., 1812, pres. until 1814 when removed for political reasons; supported War of 1812 as "War Federalist"; elected gov. Conn. on Toleration ticket, 1817-27; presided over Conn. Constl. Conv. which separated church and state, 1818, disestablished Congregational Ch., granted religious toleration, created stronger executive and independent judiciary; urged aid to agr., banking regulations, pub. schs., labor laws, defeated for reelection by Republican factional machine in state, 1827. Died N.Y.C., June 1, 1833; buried Litchfield.

WOLCOTT, Roger, colonial gov.; b. Windsor, Conn., Jan. 4, 1679; s. Simon and Martha (Pitkin) W.; m. Sarah Drake, Dec. 3, 1702, 15 children including Oliver, Roger. Owner clothing business, 1699; selectman Windsor, 1707; dep. Conn. Assembly, 1709, clk. lower house, 1710-11; became justice of peace, South Windsor, Conn., 1710; assistant Conn. Gen. Ct., 1714-17, 20-41; judge Hartford County (Conn.) Ct., 1721; commd. capt. Conn. Militia, 1722; judge Superior Ct., Hartford (Conn.) Dist., 1732-41; chief justice Conn. Supreme Ct., 1741; commd. col. 1st Regt., Conn. Militia, 1739; dep. gov. Conn., 1741-50, served on many coms. dealing with frontier affairs; gov. Conn., 1750-54. Author: (poetry) Poetical Meditations, Being the Improvement of Some Vacant Hours, 1725. Died Windsor, May 17, 1767.

WOLF, George, gov. Pa., congressman; b. Allen Twp., Northampton County, Pa., Aug. 12, 1777; s. George and Mary Wolf; studied law; m. Mary Erb, June 5, 1798, 9 children. Admitted to Pa. bar, 1798; postmaster Easton (Pa.), 1802-03; clk. Orphans' Ct. of Northampton County, 1803-09; mem. Pa. Ho. of Reps., 1814; mem. U.S. Ho. of Reps. from Pa., 18th-21st congresses. Dec. 9, 1824-29; gov. Pa., 1829-35, recommended that Pa. Legislature appoint commn. to revise statute law of state, 1830, secured passage of free public sch. act, 1834; 1st U.S. comptroller of treasury, 1836-38; collector of customs Port of Phila., 1838-40. Died Phila., Mar. 11, 1840; buried Harrisburg (Pa.) Cemetery.

WOLF, William Penn, congressman; b. Harrisburg, O., Dec. 1, 1833; attended Holbrook Sem.; studied law. Admitted to Ia. bar, 1859, began practice in Tipton; supt. pub. schs.; mem. Ia. Ho. of Reps., 1862-64, 81-85, speaker, 1884; served as capt. Co. I, 46th Regt., Ia. Volunteer Inf., Union Army, during Civil War, wounded, 1864; apptd. asst. assessor internal revenue, 1865; mem. Ia. Senate, 1867-69; mem. U.S. Ho. of Reps. (Republican) from Ia., 41st Congress, Dec. 6, 1870-71; judge 18th

Ia. Jud. Dist., 1894-96. Died Tipton, Sept. 19, 1896; buried Masonic Cemetery, Tipton.

WOLFE, Catharine Lorillard, philanthropist, art patron; b. N.Y.C., Mar. 1828; d. John David and Dorothea Ann (Lorillard) Wolfe. Gave away more than $4,000,000, 1872-87; built many chs. and schs. in South and West; contbd. building funds to Grace Ch., N.Y., St. Luke's Hosp., Italian mission on Mulberry St.; contbd. to Union Coll.; assembled gallery collection of paintings, 1873-87, bequeathed entire collection with endowment to Met. Mus. Art; underwrote Babylonian archaeological expdn., 1884; known as benefactor especially of Episcopal Ch. Died N.Y.C., Apr. 4, 1887.

WOLFE, James, army officer; b. Westerham, Kent, Eng., Jan. 2, 1727; s. Edward and Henrietta (Thompson) W. Commd. 2d lt. 44th Foot Inf., Brit. Army, 1741, served in European Wars, promoted maj., 1749; placed in command of Brit. regt. under Gen. Jeffrey Amherst in attack on Louisburg (Can.), 1758; maj.-gen., 1759, led attack on Quebec (held by French under Gen. Montcalm); made surprise attack by climbing poorly guarded path up high cliffs between river and city; defeated Montcalm's troops on Plains of Abraham in front of city, Sept. 12-13. Died in battle, Sept. 13, 1759; buried St. Albege, Greenwich, Eng.

WOLFE, John David, mcht., philanthropist; b. N.Y.C., July 24, 1792; s. David and Catherine (Forbes) W.; m. Dorothea Ann Lorillard, 1 dau., Catherine Lorillard. Very successful in hardware bus., N.Y.C.; made large investments in Manhattan real estate under firm name Wolfe & Bishop; vestryman Trinity Ch., sr. warden Grace Ch.; founded Episcopal High Sch. for Girls, also Wolfe Hall, Denver, Colo.; supported Episcopal diocesan sch. for girls, Topeka, Kan.; provided bldg. for theol. sem. at Kenyon Coll., Gambier, O.; expanded home for crippled and destitute children and home for aged and destitute nr. St. Johnsland, L.I., N.Y.; erected bldg. for Sheltering Arms charity, N.Y.C.; played important role in establishing Home for Incurables of St. Luke's Hosp., N.Y.; pres. Am. Museum Natural History, Working Women's Protective Union. Author: Mission Service (translated it into 4 langs., also printed it). Died N.Y.C., May 17, 1872.

WOLFE, Simeon Kalfius, congressman; b. nr. Georgetown, Ind., Feb. 14, 1824; grad. law dept. U. Ind., 1850. Admitted to Ind. bar, 1851, began practice in Corydon; Democratic presdl. elector, 1856; editor and publisher Corydon Democrat, 1857-65; mem. Ind. Senate, 1860-64; del. Dem. nat. convs., Charleston (S.C.) and Balt., 1860; moved to New Albany, Ind., 1870, practiced law; mem. U.S. Ho. of Reps. (Democrat) from Ind., 43d Congress, 1873-75; judge Foyd and Clark Circuit Ct., Ind., 1880-84. Died New Albany, Nov. 18, 1888; buried Fairview Cemetery, New Albany.

WOLFF, George Dering, editor; b. Martinsburg, W.Va., Aug. 25, 1822; attended Marshall Coll. Admitted to bar; became a minister of German Reformed Ch.; convert to Roman Catholic Ch., 1871; editor Balt. Catholic Mirror, 1872, Phila. Catholic Standard, 1873-94; a founder Am. Catholic Quarterly Review, 1876, mem. staff, 1876-94. Died Norristown, Pa., Jan. 29, 1894.

WOLFORD, Frank Lane, congressman; b. nr. Columbia, Ky., Sept. 2, 1817; attended common schs.; studied law. Admitted to Ky. bar, began practice in Liberty; mem. Ky. Ho. of Reps., 1847, 48, 65, 66; served as col. 1st Ky. Volunteer Cavalry during Civil War, 1861-64; Democratic presdl. elector, 1864, 68; adj. gen. State of Ky., 1867-68; mem. U.S. Ho. of Reps. (Democrat) from Ky., 48th-49th congresses, 1883-87; practiced law, Columbia. Died Columbia, Aug. 2, 1895; buried Columbia Cemetery.

WOLFSKILL, William, trapper, pioneer; b. Richmond, Ky., Mar. 20, 1798; m. Magdalena Lugo, Jan. 1841, 4 children. Mem. 1st expdn. of Americans known to have entered So. Utah, 1824; became Mexican citizen, 1830; leader expdn. which pioneered new route to Western portion of Spanish Trail to Cal., 1830; built schooner Refugia (one of 1st ships built on Pacific coast), 1831; settled in Los Angeles as carpenter, 1832; planted vineyard near settlement, 1836; planted one of 1st orange groves in territory, 1841; chosen councilman of a village in Sacramento Valley, 1844. Died at his ranch, Oct. 3, 1866.

WOLLENHAUPT, Hermann Adolf, musician; b. Schkeuditz, nr. Leipzig, Germany, Sept. 27, 1827; studied with J. Knorr and M. Hauptmann, Leipzig. Came to N.Y.C., 1845; played with N.Y. Philharmonic Soc.; gained reputation as concert pianist and tchr.; made concert tour in Europe, 1855; composed numerous piano pieces. Died N.Y.C., Sept. 18, 1863.

WOLLENWEBER, Ludwig August, journalist; b. Ixheim, Germany, Dec. 5, 1807. Learned printing trade at early age; wrote for Deutsche Tribune, Hamburg, Germany, 1832 (journal was suppressed); came to U.S., 1834; founder, editor Democrat, Phila., 1835-53; pursued literary interests, Reading, Pa., 1853-88; 1 of earliest authors to write in Pa. Dutch dialect. Author works including: Gila, das Indianermadchen oder die Wiedergefundenen deutschen Kinder unter den Indianern; Aus Berks County Schweister Zeit. Died Reading, 1888.

WOOD, Abiel, congressman; b. Wiscasset, Mass. (now Me.), July 22, 1772; attended common schs. Engaged in merc. bus.; mem. Mass. Ho. of Reps., 1807-11, 16; Federalist presdl. elector, 1812; mem. U.S. Ho. of Reps. (Federalist) from Mass., 13th Congress, 1813-15; del. Me. Constl. Conv., 1819; mem. Me. State Council, 1820-21; resumed merc. bus., engaged in shipping; bank commr. for Me., until 1834. Died Belfast, Me., Oct. 26, 1834; buried Woodlawn Cemetery, Wiscasset.

WOOD, Abraham, army officer, colonial ofcl. Mem. Va. Ho. of Burgesses for Henrico County, 1644-46, for Charles City County, 1654, 56; mem. expdn. to Occoneechee Islands, 1650; mem. Va. Gov.'s Council, 1658-80; apptd. mem. spl. commn. of oyer and terminer for Va. following Bacon's Rebellion, 1676; capt. militia at Ft. Henry, 1646; commd. maj. gen.; maintained a fort and garrison at Ft. Henry, 1646; Col. Charles City and Henrico Regt., 1656; sent 1st party to cross Appalachian Mountains, 1671; sent group which reached what is now Tenn., 1673. Died 1680.

WOOD, Amos Eastman, congressman; b. Ellisburg, N.Y., Jan. 2, 1810; attended common schs. Moved to Sandusky County, O., 1833, engaged in farming; mem. Ohio Ho. of Reps., 1840-42, Ohio Senate, 1845; mem. U.S. Ho. of Reps. (Democrat) from Ohio, 31st Congress, Dec. 3, 1849-50. Died Fort Wayne, Ind., Nov. 19, 1850; buried Woodville (O.) Cemetery.

WOOD, Benjamin, congressman; b. Shelbyville, Ky., Oct. 13, 1820; attended pub. schs., N.Y.C. Entered shipping bus. purchased Daily News, N.Y.C., 1860, editor, publisher, 1860-1900; chmn. Democratic Editors, 1860; mem. U.S. Ho. of Reps. (Dem.) from N.Y., 37th-38th, 47th congresses, 1861-65, 81-83; mem. N.Y. State Senate, 1866-67. Died N.Y.C., Feb. 21, 1900; buried Calvary Cemetery, Long Island City, N.Y.

WOOD, Bradford Ripley, congressman, diplomat; b. Westport, Conn., Sept. 3, 1800; grad. Union Coll., Schenectady, N.Y., 1824; attended Litchfield (Conn.) Law Sch. Admitted to N.Y. bar, 1827, began practice in Albany; apptd. solicitor N.Y. State Ct. of Chancery, 1827, chancellor, 1830; mem. Albany County Bd. Suprs., 1844; mem. U.S. Ho. of Reps. (Democrat) from N.Y., 29th Congress, 1845-47; trustee Union Coll., 1848-72; pres. Young Men's Temperance Soc., 1851; trustee Williams Coll., Albany Law Sch.; v.p. Albany Med. Coll.; a founder Republican Party in N.Y. State, 1856; v.p. Am. Home Missionary Soc.; founder 1st Congregational Ch., Albany; U.S. minister to Denmark, 1861-65. Died Albany, Sept. 26, 1889; buried Albany Rural Cemetery.

WOOD, De Volson, educator, inventor; b. Smyrna, N.Y., June 1, 1832; s. Julius and Amanda (Billings) W.; grad. Rensselaer Poly. Inst., Troy, N.Y., 1857; m. Cordera E. Crane, 1859; m. 2d, Frances Hartson, 1868; 7 children. Prof. civil engring. U. Mich., 1857-72; prof. mathematics and mechanics Stevens Inst., Hoboken, N.J., 1872-85, prof. engring., 1885-97; invented an air compressor, steam rock drill; mem. Am. Soc. C.E., Soc. Mech. Engrs., A.A.A.S. Died Hoboken, June 27, 1897.

WOOD, Fernando, congressman, mayor N.Y.C.; b. Phila., June 14, 1812; s. Benjamin and Rebecca (Lehman) W.; m. Miss Taylor, 1832; m. 2d, Ann Dole Richardson, Apr. 23, 1841; m. 3d, Alice Fenner Mills, Dec. 2, 1860; 16 children. Leader young men's group of Tammany Hall, N.Y.C., 1838-40; mem. U.S. Ho. of Reps. (Democrat) from N.Y., 27th Congress, 1841-43; dispatch agt. for U.S. State Dept., N.Y.C., 1844-47; a leader Tammany Hall (Democratic Party orgn.), by 1850; elected mayor N.Y.C., 1854, 56, failed in renomintion because of patronage disputes with other politicians in his party, 1857; involved in conflict with state legislature dominated by Republicans because of corruption of his adminstrn.; a financial supporter of Stephen A. Douglas in latter's senatorial campaign against Lincoln, 1858; organized polit. soc. "Mozart Hall", elected mayor N.Y.C., 1859, adminstrn. known for establishment of Central Park and promotion of municipal univ. for young ladies; mem. U.S. Ho. of Reps. from N.Y., 38th, 40th-46th congresses 1863-65, 67-81, opposed Lincoln adminstrn.'s conduct of Civil War; an organizer "Peace Democrats," 1863, attacked radical reconstrn. plans for South after end of Civil War, defended principles of sound currency and lower tariffs, responsible for bill refunding nat. debt, 1880, served as majority floor leader of Dems., chmn. ways and means com., after 1877. Died Hot Springs, Ark., Feb. 13, 1881; buried Trinity Cemetery, N.Y.C.

WOOD, George, lawyer; b. Chesterfield, N.J., Jan. 1789; grad. Coll. of N.J. (now Princeton), 1808; studied law, LL.D. (hon.), Hamilton Coll., 1842, Union Coll., 1845; married, 4 children. Admitted to N.J. bar, 1812; often appeared before U.S. Supreme Ct.; presented arguments in cases involving charity bequests that influenced N.J. legal development; represented Presbyn., Dutch, Methodist Episcopal chs. in cases involving property; moved to N.Y.C., 1831; atty. for N.Y.C. in boundary cases; considered for appointment to U.S. Supreme Ct., 1841. Died N.Y.C., Mar. 17, 1860.

WOOD, George, author; b. Newburyport, Mass., 1799. Clk. in war dept., 1819-22; with treasury dept., 1822-40; contbr. to Knickerbocker Mag., 1846-47. Author: Peter Schlemihl in America, 1848; Modern Pilgrims, Showing the Improvements in Travel with the Newest Methods of Reaching the Celestial City. Died Saratoga, N.Y., Aug. 24, 1870.

WOOD, George Bacon, physician, educator; b. Greenwich, Cumberland County, N.J., Mar. 12, 1797; s. Richard and Elizabeth (Bacon) W.; A.B., U. Pa., 1815, M.D., 1818; m. Caroline Hahn, Apr. 2, 1823. A founder U. Pa. Coll. Pharmacy, 1821; prof. chemistry Phila. Coll. Pharmacy, 1822-31; prof. materia medica U. Pa., 1831-35, prof. theory and practice of medicine, 1850-60, prof. emeritus, 1860; trustee, 1863-79; attending physician Pa. Hosp., 1835-59, pres. bd. mgrs., 1874-79; pres. Coll. Physicians of Phila., 1848-79, A.M.A., 1855-56, Am. Philos. Soc., 1859-79; chmn. nat. com. for revision U.S. pharmacopeia, 1850-60; left funds for establishment of bot. garden, conservatory and other gifts to U. Pa.; donated funds to establish Peter Hahn ward at U. Pa. Hosp.; contributed $500 annually to Coll. Physicians of Phila. on condition that library be open daily, 1866-79. Author: The Dispensatory of the United States, 1833; History of University of Pennsylvania, 1834; Treatise on the Practice of Medicine, 1847; Materia Medica, 1856. Died Phila., Mar. 30, 1879.

WOOD, James, clergyman, coll. pres.; b. Greenfield, N.Y., July 12, 1799; s. Jonathan and Susanna W.; grad. Union Coll., 1822, Princeton Theol. Sem., 1825; m. Janetta Pruyn, Oct. 3, 1826. Ordained by Presbytery, Albany, N.Y., 1826; agt. Presbyn. Bd. Edn., 1834-39, agt., corr. sec., 1851-54; involved in Presbyn. Ch. controversy, 1837, sided with conservative wing; prof. theology in what is now Presbyn. Theol. Sem., Chgo., 1839-51; pres. Hanover Coll., 1859-65; moderator Old Sch. Presbyn. Ch., 1864; pres. Van Rensselear Inst., Hightstown, N.J., 1866-67. Author: Facts and Observations Concerning the Organization and State of the Churches in the Three Synods of Western N.Y. and the Synod of Western Reserve, 1837. Died Hightstown, N.J., Apr. 7, 1867.

WOOD, James Frederick, clergyman; b. Phila., Apr. 27, 1813; s. James Wood; attended Irish Coll., Rome, 1837, Coll. of Propaganda. Clk., Franklin Bank, Cincinnati, 1827-33, teller, 1833, cashier, 1836; converted and baptized in Roman Catholic Ch. 1836, ordained priest, 1844; asst. priest at cathedral, Cincinnati, 1844; rector St. Patrick's Ch., Cincinnati, 1854; apptd. titular bishop of Antigonia and coadjutor to Bishop J. N. Newman of Phila.; consecrated coadjutor to bishop of Phila., 1857, financial adminstr. of diocese, became head diocese, 1860; founded Cath. home for Destitute Girls and House of Good Shepherd, introduced Little Sister of Poor into diocese, established Sister Servants of Immaculate Heart, trebled number of parochial schs.; succeeded in having new diocese of Harrisburg and Scranton created out of diocese of Phila., 1867; asst. at pontifical throne, 1862; attended rites commemorating martydom of Sts. Peter and Paul, 1867; sent large contbns. to Rome; apptd. archbishop to newly elevated Met. See of Phila., 1875. Died Phila., June 20, 1883; buried Phila.

WOOD, James Rushmore, surgeon; b. Mamaroneck, L.I., N.Y., Sept. 14, 1816; s. Elkanah and Mary (Rushmore) W.; grad. Vt. Acad. Medicine, Castleton, 1834; m. Emma Rowe, 1853. Instr. anatomy Vt. Acad. Medicine, 1834; practiced medicine, N.Y.C., 1837; a founder Bellevue Hosp., N.Y.C., 1847, mem. bd.; an organizer Bellevue Hosp. Med. Coll., 1856, prof. operative surgery and surg. pathology, 1886, created 1st hosp. ambulance service in U.S., 1869; opened 1st tng. sch. for nurses in U.S. at Bellevue, 1873; pioneer in cure of aneurism by pressure; perfected bisector for rapid operation for vesical calculus; wrote paper "Early History of the Operation of Ligature of the Primitive Carotid Artery"; established one of largest collections of post-mortem and pathological material in world; twice pres. N.Y. Path. Soc.; mem. N.Y. Acad. Medicine, N.Y. State, Mass. med. socs., mem. A.M.A., N.Y. Surg. Soc., Med. Jour. Assn. Died N.Y.C., May 4, 1882.

WOOD, Jethro, inventor; b. Dartmouth, Mass. (or White Creek, N.Y.), Mar. 16, 1774; s. John and Dinah (Hussey or Starbuck) W.; m. Sylvia Howland, Jan. 1, 1793. Owned farm, Poplar Creek, Cayuga County, N.Y., 1800-34; obtained 1st patent for cast-iron plow, 1814; patented the Wood plow, featuring good balance, strength and interchangeable parts, 1819 (design and constrn. principles copied throughout North). Died Scipio, N.Y., Sept. 18, 1834.

WOOD, John, author, cartographer; b. Scotland, 1775. Travelled in Switzerland, 1789; came to N.Y. C., 1800; tutor to Aaron Burr's daughter Theodosia; as pamphleteer supported Burr's polit. activities in such writings as "A Letter to Alexander Addison, Esq. . . . in Answer to His Rise and Progress of Revolution," 1801; after writing attack on Adams' adminstrn., Burr felt it so vicious that he sought to buy out edition, 1802, publication under title "The Suppressed History" led to separation of Burr and Wood; had short assn. with Frankfort (Ky.) Western World, 1806, opened publicity on activities of James Wilkinson and other Spanish agts.; settled in Richmond, Va., circa 1808; contracted with state of Va. to make accurate chart of each county and gen. map of state, 1819, work nearly finished by 1822. Author: A General View of the History of Switzerland, 1799; A Full Statement of the Trial and Acquittal of Aaron Burr, 1807. Died May 15, 1822.

WOOD, John, gov. Ill.; b. Moravia, N.Y., Dec. 20, 1798. Settled in Adams County, Ill., 1819; built 1st log cabin on site of Quincy, Ill.; mem. upper house 17th, 18th Ill. Gen. Assemblies; elected lt. gov. Ill., 1859, served out term of dec. gov., 1860-61; apptd. commr. from Ill. to Peace Conf., Washington, 1861; apptd. q.m.-gen. of Ill., 1862; made col. 100th, 37th Ill. Volunteers, 1864. Died Quincy, Ill., June 11, 1880.

WOOD, John Jacob, congressman; b. Clarkstown (now New City), N.Y., Feb. 16, 1784. Town clk. Clarkstown, 1809-12, insp. schs., 1815, 23, 29-31, 35-37; mem. U.S. Ho. of Reps. (Jacksonian Democrat) from N.Y., 20th Congress, 1827-29; surrogate of Rockland County (N.Y.), 1837; del. N.Y. State Constl. Conv., 1846. Died New City, May 20, 1874; buried Old Wood Burying Ground, New City.

WOOD, John M., congressman; b. Minisink, N.Y., Nov. 17, 1813; attended common schs. Engaged in railroad constrn., N.J.; moved to Portland, Me., 1846; a contractor in constrn. of Atlantic & St. Lawrence R.R.; engaged in banking; mem. Me. Ho. of Reps., 1852-53; owner and publisher Portland Daily Advertiser, 1853-57; mem. U.S. Ho. of Reps. (Republican) from Me., 34th-35th congresses, 1855-59; contractor for bldg. Air Line R.R. between Woonsocket and New Haven (Conn.). Died Boston, Dec. 24, 1864; buried Greenwood Cemetery, Bklyn.

WOOD, Joseph, Continental congressman; b. Pa., 1712. Moved to Sunbury, Ga., circa 1774; served as maj., lt. col., and col. 2d Pa. Battalion (became 3d Pa. Regt.) during Am. Revolution, on duty in Can., 1776; returned to Ga., engaged in planting; mem. Ga. Council of Safety; mem. Continental Congress from Ga., 1777-79. Died nr. Sunbury, Sept. 1791.

WOOD, Joseph, portrait painter; b. Clarkstown, N.Y., 1778. Ran away from farm to N.Y.C. at age 15; worked at various jobs, occasionally played violin; apprentice to silversmith for short period; in miniaturist partnership with John Wesley Jarvis, 1804-09; continued to paint, N.Y.C., 1809-12; artist, Phila., 1813-27, Washington, D.C., 1827-32; prolific and at times prosperous painter, died in poverty. Died Washington, 1832.

WOOD, Reuben, gov. Ohio, diplomat; b. Middletown, Rutland County, Vt., circa 1792; s. Nathaniel Wood; studied law with Gen. Jonas Clark, Middletown; m. Mary Rice, 1816, 2 children. Lived with uncle in Can. until War of 1812, forced to flee; engaged in brief mil. service after war; moved to Cleve., 1818, set up law practice; mem. Ohio Senate, 1825-30; pres. judge Ohio Ct. of Common Pleas, 1830-33; judge Ohio Supreme Ct., 1833-47; Democratic gov. Ohio, 1850-53, criticized Fugitive Slave Law, opposed nullification and secession; Am. consul at Valparaiso, Chile, 1853-55; resumed law practice in Ohio; supported James Buchanan in party split of 1860, chmn. Ohio Dem. Conv. supporting John C. Breckinridge against Stephen Douglas. Died Oct. 1, 1864.

WOOD, Richard D., mcht., mfr.; b. Greenwich, N.J., Mar. 29, 1799. In Salem, N.J., 1821-23; joined Phila. firm Wood, Abbott and Wood, mchts., 1823, one of 1st to introduce bleaching and dyeing of cotton on large scale basis; responsible for advancement of Town of Millville (N.J.) by bldg. Millville and Glassboro R.R.; began mfg. cast-iron gas and water pipes under firm R.D. Wood & Co., 1851; erected factories at May's Landing, N.J., 1867, also constructed dam on Maurice River, Millville; one of largest owners Cambria Iron Works, Johnstown, Pa.; dir. numerous railroads, corps., public instns. Died Apr. 1, 1869.

WOOD, Samuel, book publisher; b. Oyster Bay, L.I., N.Y., July 17, 1760; s. Samuel and Freelove (Wright) W.; m. Mary Searing, Aug. 8, 1782, 13 children including Samuel S., John, William. Born William, changed name to Samuel after father's early death; joined Soc. of Friends in early life; taught sch., Manhasset, L.I., Clinton, Hibernia Hills, New Rochelle, N.Y., 1787-1803; opened second-hand book store in N.Y.C., 1804; wrote, published and edited children's books, circa 1806-circa 1815; went into partnership with sons Samuel S. and John under name Samuel Wood and Sons, 1815, later opened branch in Balt., admitted son William to firm, 1817, firm became largest publisher of med. books in Am.; a founder Soc. for Prevention of Pauperism, 1817, grew into House of Refuge; ret., 1836, firm continued by sons as Samuel S. and William Wood until 1861, as William Wood's until 1863, as William Wood and Co., 1863-1932; a founder N.Y. Inst. for Blind, 1831; trustee Public Sch. Soc. of N.Y., 20 years. Author: The Young Child's A B C, or First Book, Printed by J. C. Totten, for Samuel Wood, 1806; Devout Meditations, 1807; The Animal Economy, 1808; Poetic Tales for Children, 1814. Died N.Y.C., May 5, 1844; buried Prospect Park, Bklyn.

WOOD, Samuel Newitt, state legislator; b. Mt. Gilead, O., Dec. 30, 1825. Founded Kan. Tribune, Lawrence, 1855; elected mem. Kan. Senate, 1859, speaker Kan. Ho. of Reps., 1877; active Farmers' Alliance; mem. Greenback or Nat. party; an original stockholder Sante Fe R.R. Killed by James Brennan, Hugoton, Kan., June 23, 1891.

WOOD, Sarah Sayward Barrell Keating, author; b. York, Me., Oct. 1, 1759; d. Nathaniel and Sarah (Sayward) Barrell; m. Richard Keating, Nov. 23, 1778; m. 2d, Gen. Abiel Wood, Oct. 28, 1804; 3 children including Capt. Richard Keating. Anonymous contbr. to Mass. Mag.; 1st novelist in State of Me. Author: Julia and the Illuminated Baron, 1800; Dorval: or the Speculator; Amelia, or the Influence of Virtue, an Old Man's Story, 1802; Ferdinand and Elmira: A Russian Story; Tales of the Night (contains stories Storms and Sunshine; or the House on the Hill, The Hermitage), 1827. Died Kennebunk, Me., Jan. 6, 1855.

WOOD, Silas, congressman; b. West Hills, N.Y., Sept. 14, 1769; grad. Coll. of N.J. (now Princeton), 1789; studied law. Tchr., Coll. of N.J., 5 years; admitted to N.Y. bar, began practice in Huntington; apptd. dist. atty. Suffolk County (N.Y.), 1818, 21; mem. U.S. Ho. of Reps. (Democrat) from N.Y., 16th-20th congresses, 1819-29. Died Huntington, Mar. 2, 1847; buried Old Public Cemetery, Huntington.

WOOD, Thomas, surgeon; b. Smithfield, O., Aug. 22, 1813; s. Nathan and Margaret W.; M.D., U. Pa., 1839; studied medicine abroad, 1844; m. Emily A. Miller, Mar. 14, 1843; m. 2d, Elizabeth J. Reiff, 1855; m. 3d, Carrie C. Fels, July 27, 1876; at least 2 children. Apptd. to Friends' Asylum for Insane, nr. Phila., 1839; returned to Smithfield and established practice, 1842; prof. anatomy and physiology Ohio Coll. Dental Surgery, 1845; instr. anatomy Med. Coll. of Ohio, 1853; owner, co-editor Western Lancet, Cincinnati, 1853-57; mem. A.M.A., Cincinnati Acad. Medicine; chief surgeon Cincinnati, Hamilton and Dayton R.R. Author: A Compendium of Anatomy, Designed to Accompany the Anatomical Chart. Died Nov. 21, 1880.

WOOD, Walter Abbott, congressman, inventor, mfr.; b. Mason, N.H., Oct. 23, 1815; s. Aaron and Rebecca (Wright) W.; m. Bessie A. Parsons, 1842; m. 2d, Elizabeth Warren Nichols, Sept. 2, 1868; 4 children. Partner with John White in mfg. plows, Hoosick Falls, N.Y., 1840's; with J. R. Parsons founded firm Wood and Parsons to build mowing and reaping machines, 1852, firm reorganized under name Walter A. Wood Mowing & Reaping Co., 1865, became pres.; received over 40 patents for improvements on machines; began to market products in Europe, 1856, later exhibited at fairs and expositions in U.S. and abroad; won over 1,000 prizes in exhibits all over world; decorated chevalier Legion of Honor following exhbn. of machines at Paris Expn. of 1867; decorated Imperial Order of Franz Joseph, Vienna, 1873; mem. U.S. Ho. of Reps. (Republican) from N.Y., 46th-47th congresses, 1879-83. Died Hoosick Falls, N.Y., Jan. 15, 1892; buried Maple Grove Cemetery, Hoosick Falls.

WOOD, William, author; b. England. Came to Mass., 1629; made freeman, Lynn, Mass., 1631; left New Eng., 1633; nothing known positively of either early or later life. Author: (sole work) New England's Prospects (account of New Eng. for period 1629-33), 1634.

WOOD, William Burke, actor, mgr.; b. Montreal, Que., Can., May 26, 1779; s. Thomizen (English) Wood; m. Juliana Westray, Jan. 30, 1804. In poor health and financial condition in earliest years; began acting with Thomas Wignell's troupe, Annapolis, Md., 1798, became asst. acting mgr., 1803, mgr. of co. (with William Warren), 1803-09, partner (with Warren), 1809-25; mgr. Chestnut Theatre, Phila., 1825-26, remained as actor, 1826-28; mgr. Arch Street Theatre, Phila., 1828; with Walnut Street Theatre, Phila., 1829-46. Author: Personal Recollections of the Stage, 1855. Died Sept. 23, 1861.

WOODBRIDGE, Frederick Enoch, congressman; b. Vergennes, Vt., Aug. 29, 1818; grad. U. Vt., 1840; studied law. Admitted to Vt. bar, 1843, began practice in Vergennes; mem. Vt. Ho. of Reps., 1849, 57, 58; mayor of Vergennes, 5 years; auditor State of Vt., 1850-52; pros. atty., 1854-58; engaged in railroad constrn.; mem. Vt. Senate, 1860-61, pres. pro tem, 1861; mem. U.S. Ho. of Reps. (Republican) from Vt., 38th-40th congresses, 1863-69. Died Vergennes, Apr. 25, 1888; buried Prospect Cemetery, Vergennes.

WOODBRIDGE, John, clergyman, banker; b. Stanton, Wellshire, Eng., 1613; s. John and Sarah (Parker) W.; attended Oxford (Eng.) U.; m. Mercy Dudley, 1639, 12 children. Came to New Eng., 1634, settled in Newbury, Mass.; 1st town clk. of Newbury, 1636-38, selectman, 1636; dep. to Mass. Gen. Ct., 1637-38, 40-41; schoolmaster in Boston, 1643-45; 1st pastor church at Andover, Mass., 1645-47; went to England, 1647, held various pastorates, 1648-63; returned to New Eng., circa 1664, joined uncle in pastorate at Newbury; proposed bank of deposit and issue with land and commodities as collateral, 1667-68; dismissed from his ministry, 1670; Newbury's commr. for small causes, 1677-79, 81, 90; elected assistant in Mass. Gen. Ct., 1683-84. Died Newbury, Mar. 17, 1695.

WOODBRIDGE, William, senator, gov. Mich.; b. Norwich, Conn., Aug. 20, 1780; s. Dudley and Lucy (Backus) W.; attended Litchfield (Conn.) Law Sch., 1797-80; m. Juliana Trumbull, June 29, 1806, 4 children. Admitted to Ohio bar, 1806; mem. Ohio Assembly, 1807; pros. atty. New London (now Washington) County (O.), 1808-14; sec. Mich Territory (apptd. by Pres. Madison), 1814-28; mem. U.S. Ho. of Reps. from Mich. Territory, 16th Congress, 1819-Aug. 9, 1820; territorial judge Mich., 1828-32; del. Mich. Constl. Conv., 1835; mem. Mich. State Senate, 1837-39; gov. Mich. (Whig), 1840-41; mem. U.S. Senate from Mich., 1841-47. Died Detroit, Oct. 20, 1861; buried Elmwood Cemetery, Detroit.

WOODBRIDGE, William Channing, educator; b. Medford, Mass., Dec. 18, 1794; s. Rev. William and Ann (or Nancy) (Channing) W.; A.B., Yale, 1811; attended Princeton Theol. Sem.; m. Lucy Ann Reed, Nov. 27, 1832. Prin. acad., Burlington, N.J., 1812; instr. asylum for deaf and dumb, Hartford, Conn., 1817-20; licensed to preach in Congregational chs. of Hartford area, 1819; lived in Europe, 1820; studied ednl. systems of Switzerland and Germany; early Am. adherent of Pestalozzian ednl. system; owner, editor The Annals of Education and Instruction, 1831-38. Author: Rudiments of Geography, on a New Plan, Designed To Assist the Memory by Comparison and Classification (new approach to teaching geography), 1821; Universal Geography, Ancient and Modern, 1824. Died Boston, Nov. 9, 1845.

WOODBURY, Daniel Phineas, army officer, engr.; b. New London, N.H., Dec. 16, 1812; s. Daniel and Rhapisma (Messenger) W.; attended Dartmouth; grad. U.S. Mil. Acad., 1836; m. Catherine Rachel Childs, Dec. 12, 1845, 4 children. Commd. 2d lt., 3d Arty., U.S. Army, 1836; transferred to Corps Engrs., commd. 1st lt., 1838; supervised constrn. of Ft. Kearny on Missouri River and Ft. Laramie (Wyo.), 1847-50; supervised constrn. Ft. Jefferson, Tortugas, W.I., also Ft. Taylor, Key West, Fla.; commd. capt., 1853; helped plan defenses of Washington, D.C., 1861; promoted maj. C.E., 1861; commd. lt. col. U.S. Volunteers, 1861, brig. gen., 1862; constructed seige works before Yorktown during Peninsular campaign, 1862; worked on defenses of Washington, 1862; in command of dist. including Tortugas and Key West, 1863. Author: (treatises) Sustaining Walls, 1845. Died Key West, Aug. 15, 1864.

WOODBURY, Isaac Baker, composer; b. Beverly, Mass., Oct. 23, 1819; s. Isaac and Nancy (Baker) W.; studied music, Boston, London, Paris; 6 children. Tchr. music Bay State Glee Club, Boston, 1839-45; organized, conducted N.H. and Vt. Musical Assn., Bellows Falls, Vt.; dir. music Rutgers Street Ch., N.Y., circa 1848-51; edited Am. Monthly Musical Review, circa 1849, Boston Musical Edn. Soc.'s Collections, 1842. Author: Self-Instructor in Musical Composition and Thorough Bass, . . . with a Translation of Schneider's . . . Arranging for the Work on Full Orchestra and Military Band (educational treatise), originally issued 1844. Died Charleston, S.C., Oct. 26, 1858.

WOODBURY, Levi, asso. justice U.S. Supreme Ct., senator; b. Francestown, N.H., Dec. 22, 1789;

s. Peter and Mary (Woodbury) W.; grad. Dartmouth, 1809, LL.D. (hon.), 1823; LL.D. (hon.), Wesleyan U., 1843; m. Elizabeth Williams Clapp, June 1819, 5 children. Admitted to N.H. bar, 1812; clk. N.H. Senate, 1816; asso. justice N.H. Superior Ct., 1817-23; gov. N.H., 1823-24; speaker, N.H. Ho. of Reps., 1825; mem. U.S. Senate (Democrat) from N.H., Mar. 16, 1825-31, 1841-Nov. 20, 1845; U.S. sec. of navy, 1831-34; U.S. sec. of treasury (apptd. by Pres. Jackson), 1834-41, opposed Bank of U.S., aided Jackson in establishing independent treasury system, advocated hard money; backed Polk for U.S. Pres., 1844; asso. justice U.S. Supreme Ct., 1845-51; regarded as strong possibility for Democratic nominee for Pres. U.S. in 1852 election. Died Portsmouth, N.H., Sept. 4, 1851; buried Harmony Grove Cemetery, Portsmouth.

WOODCOCK, David, congressman; b. Williamstown, Mass., 1785; attended pub. schs.; studied law. Admitted to Mass. bar, practiced law; moved to Ithaca, N.Y.; commd. postmaster of Ithaca, 1808; apptd. master of ct. of chancery, 1808; mem. N.Y. State Assembly, 1814-15; apptd. dist. atty. Tompkins County (N.Y.), 1817, surrogate, 1817; asst. atty. gen. State of N.Y., 1817; pres. Cayuga Steamboat Co., 1819; mem. U.S. Ho. of Reps. (Democrat) from N.Y., 17th, 20th congresses, 1821-23, 27-29; pres. and trustee Village of Ithaca, 1823, 24, 26; mem. prominent in Anti-Masonic Crusade and State Conv., Utica, N.Y., 1827. Died Ithaca, Sept. 18, 1835; buried City Cemetery, Ithaca.

WOODFORD, William, army officer; b. Caroline County, Va., Oct. 6, 1734; s. Maj. William and Anne (Cocke) W.; m. Mary Thornton, June 26, 1762, 2 children. Justice of peace Caroline County, circa 1756-63; elected mem. Com. of Correspondence of Caroline County, 1774; sat as alternate to Edmund Pendleton in Va. Conv., 1775; col. 3d Va. Regt., Continental Army, 1775; defeated Brit. force of 300, 1775; apptd. by Continental Congress as col. 2d Va. Regt., 1776; commd. brig. gen., 1777; fought at battles of Brandywine, Germantown, Monmouth; relieved Charleston (S.C.) at Washington's order, 1779; besieged the British with 700 troops, 1780, taken prisoner when Clinton took city, taken to N.Y.C., 1780; Woodford County (Ky.) named for him. Died N.Y.C., Nov. 13, 1780; buried Old Trinity Church Yard, N.Y.C.

WOODHOUSE, James, chemist, physician; b. Phila., Nov. 17, 1770; s. William and Anne (Martin) W.; B.A., U. State of Pa. (now U. Pa.), 1789, M.A., 1790, M.D., 1792; never married. Founder, Chem. Soc. of Phila., 1792; prof. chemistry U. Pa., 1795; experimented with prodn. of white starch and indsl. purification of camphor, 1804; undertook expts. on nitrous oxide gas, confirming its anaesthetic properties, 1806; proved superiority of anthracite over lituminous coal for indsl. use, 1808; known for work in chemistry of plants and in develop. of chem. analysis. Author: Observations on the Combinations of Acids, Bitters and Astringents, 1793; The Young Chemist's Pocket Companion (1st manual of chem. expts. for students), 1797; Experiments and Observations in the Vegetation of Plants, 1802; edited Parkinson's Chemical Pocket Book. Phila., 1802. Died Phila., June 4, 1809.

WOODHOUSE, Samuel W., physician, ornithologist; asst. surgeon Med. Corps, U.S. Army; participated Pacific Railroad surveys; Woodhouse's jay named in his honor.

WOODHULL, Nathaniel, colonial legislator, army officer; b. Mastic, L.I., N.Y., Dec. 30, 1722; s. Nathaniel and Sarah (Smith) W.; m. Ruth Floyd, 1761, 1 child. Commd. maj. N.Y. Militia, 1758, col. 3d Regt., N.Y. Provincals, 1760; mem. N.Y. Colonial Assembly, 1768-75; represented Suffolk County in conv. which chose N.Y. dels. to 1st Continental Congress; apptd. brig. gen., 1775; mem. N.Y. Provincial Congress from Suffolk County, pres., 1775; assigned to remove supplies from L.I. (N.Y.) after Brit. landings, 1776; captured by British nr. Jamaica, N.Y. Died as result of ill treatment, New Utrecht, L.I., Sept. 20, 1776; buried Mastic.

WOODMAN, John, reformer; b. Ancocas (now Rancocas), N.J., Oct. 19, 1720; s. Samuel and Elizabeth (Burr) W.; m. Sarah Ellis, Oct. 18, 1749. Tailor by trade; itinerant Quaker preacher, 1743-72, inveighed against slavery, spoke in all colonies and in England, opposed conscription, active in Indian conversions, best known as pioneer advocate of abolition of slavery; preached to Indians in Wyoming region, 1763; went to Eng., 1772, established reputation as abolitionist thinker; published writings on slavery based on visits to slave trading centers in U.S. and extensive travel in South. Author: Some Considerations on the Keeping of Negroes, 1754; A Plea for the Poor, 1763; Serious Consideration, with Some of His Dying Expressions, 1773; Journal, 1774. Died York, Eng., Oct. 7, 1772.

WOODRUFF, George Catlin, congressman; b. Litchfield, Conn., Dec. 1, 1805; grad. Yale, 1825; studied law. Admitted to Conn. bar, 1827, began practice in Litchfield; postmaster of Litchfield, 1832-42, 42-46; mem. Conn. State Ho. of Reps., 1851, 66, 74; mem. U.S. Ho. of Reps. (Democrat) from Conn., 37th Congress, 1861-63. Died Litchfield, Nov. 21, 1885; buried East Cemetery, Litchfield.

WOODRUFF, John, congressman; b. West Hartford, Conn., Feb. 12, 1826. Moved to Catskill, N.Y., 1835, returned to Conn., 1841, settled in Bristol; worked in clock factory, Bristol; moved to New Haven, Conn., 1845; mem. New Haven Common Council, 1848, served several terms; mem. Conn. Gen. Assembly, 1852; mem. U.S. Ho. of Reps. (Am. Party rep.) from Conn., 34th, 36th congresses, 1855-57, 59-61; collector of internal revenue for 2d Dist. Conn., 1862-68. Died New Haven, May 20, 1868; buried Evergreen Cemetery, New Haven.

WOODRUFF, Theodore Tuttle, inventor, mfr.; b. Burrville, N.Y., Apr. 8, 1811; s. Simeon and Roxanna (Tuttle) W.; 1 child. Master car-builder for Terre Haute and Alton R.R., Alton, Ill., in 1840's; received 2 patents for sleeping-cars on trains, 1856; successfully demonstrated sleeping-car coach to Pa. R.R.; with brother began T. T. Woodruff and Co., small scale mfrs. of sleeping cars, Phila., 1858; received 2 additional patents for improvements of his car seat and couch, 1859-60; established Norris Iron Co., Norristown, Pa., circa 1870; received patents for process and apparatus for mfg. indigo, 1872, coffee hulling machine, 1872; ended bus. career in bankruptcy, 1875; received patents for later inventions, including steam plow, improved surveyor's compass, screw propellers to be used at side of vessel. Died Gloucester, N.J., May 2, 1892; buried Watertown, N.Y.

WOODRUFF, Thomas M., congressman; b. N.J., May 3, 1804. Mem. U.S. Ho. of Reps. (Democrat) from N.J., 29th Congress, 1845-47; employed as cabinetmaker, later engaged in furniture bus., N.Y.C. Died N.Y.C., Mar. 28, 1855; buried 1st Presbyn. Ch. Cemetery, Newark, N.J.

WOODRUFF, Wilford, clergyman; b. Farmington (now Avon), Hartford County, Conn., Mar. 1, 1807; s. Aphek and Beulah (Thompson) W.; m. Phebe Carter, Apr. 13, 1837; also 4 polygamous wives, 33 children. Converted to Mormonism, 1833; moved to Kirtland, O., 1834; Mormon missionary in Ark. and Tenn., 1834-36; one of missionaries who began Mormon activities in Me. and other parts of New Eng., 1837; ordained apostle by Brigham Young, 1839; chaplain Nauvoo (Ill.) Legion (Mormon mil. orgn.), bus. mgr. ofcl. Mormon publ. Times and Seasons; one of 1st group of Mormons to enter valley of Great Salt Lake, 1847; devoted career to founding and strengthening Mormon communities in Utah; asst. historian Mormon Ch., 1856, historian and recorder, 1875; stimulated scientific agr. and encouraged irrigation; pres. quorum of "Twelve Apostles" of Mormon Ch. (2d ofcl. in hierarchy), 1880; became pres. Mormon Ch., 1889. Died Salt Lake City, Utah, Sept. 2, 1898.

WOODRUFF, William Edward, journalist; b. Bellport, Suffolk County, N.Y., Dec. 24, 1795; s. Nathaniel and Hannah (Clark) W.; m. Jane Eliza Mills, Nov. 14, 1827, 8 children. Apprenticed as printer L.I. (N.Y.) Star, 1808-15; founder, editor and publisher Ark. Gazette (only newspaper published in Ark. Territory until 1830, ardently Democratic editorial policy), Arkansas Post, Ark., 1819-53; founder, editor and publisher Ark. Democrat, 1846-53; ret. to pvt. life, 1853. Died Little Rock, Ark., June 19, 1885.

WOODS, Alva, coll. pres.; b. Shoreham, Vt., Aug. 13, 1794; s. Abel and Mary (Smith) W.; grad. Harvard, 1817; attended Andover Theol. Sem., 1817-21; m. Almira Marshall, Dec. 10, 1823, 2 children. Ordained to ministry Baptist Ch., 1821; prof. mathematics, natural philosophy Columbian Coll. (now George Washington U.), Washington, D.C.; prof. mathematics and natural history Brown U., 1824, trustee 1843-59, pres. Transylvania U., Lexington, Ky., 1828-31; 1st pres. U. Ala., Tuscaloosa, 1831-37, resigned because of friction over his anti-slavery views; trustee Newton Theol. Instn., Newton Center, Mass., after 1853. Author: Literary and Theological Addresses, 1868. Died Providence, R.I., Sept. 6, 1887.

WOODS, Charles Robert, army officer; b. Newark, O., Feb. 19, 1827; s. Ezekiel S. and Sarah Judith (Burnham) W.; grad. U.S. Mil. Acad., 1852; m. Cecilia Impey, 1860. Commd. 2d lt., 1st Inf., U.S. Army, 1852; served in Indian warfare in 1850's; col. 76th Ohio Inf. Volunteers, 1861; participated in capture of Ft. Donelson, 1862, served at Battle of Shiloh; brig. gen. U.S. Volunteers, 1863; commanded expdns. on Mississippi River to destroy Confederate supply depots, 1863; participated in Atlanta campaign and "march to sea," 1864; with Sherman on march through Carolinas; brevetted maj. gen. volunteers, 1865; discharged from volunteer service, 1866, commd. col. infantry in regular army; served in West in Indian warfare, led expdn. against Indians in Kan., 1870; ret., 1874. Died Feb. 26, 1885.

WOODS, Henry, congressman; b. Bedford, Pa., 1764; attended subscription schs. of Bedford County; studied law. Participated in pre-Revolutionary affairs; admitted to Pa. bar, 1792, began practice in Bedford; mem. U.S. Ho. of Reps. from Pa., 6th-7th congresses, 1799-1803; engaged as land speculator. Died Bedford, 1826.

WOODS, John, congressman; b. Bedford, Pa., 1761; studied law. Admitted to the bar in Washington County, 1783, Westmoreland and Fayette counties, 1784, Allegheny County, 1788, Bedford County, 1791 (all Pa.), practiced law; presdl. elector, 1796; assisted in laying out City of Pitts., 1784; mem. Pa. Senate, 1797; mem. U.S. Ho. of Reps. (Federalist) from Pa., 14th Congress, 1815-17, never attended because of illness. Died Brunswick County, Va., Dec. 16, 1816.

WOODS, John, congressman; b. Johnstown, Pa., Oct. 18, 1794; attended common schs., Ohio; studied law. Served in War of 1812; operated sch., Springborough, O., 2 years; admitted to Ohio bar, 1819, began practice in Hamilton; pros. atty. Butler County (O.), 1820-25; mem. U.S. Ho. of Reps. (Whig) from Ohio, 19th-20th congresses, 1825-29; became editor and publisher Hamilton Intelligencer, 1829; auditor State of Ohio, 1845-51; pres. Cincinnati, Hamilton & Indpls. R.R. Died Hamilton, July 30, 1855; buried Greenwood Cemetery, Hamilton.

WOODS, Leonard, clergyman, educator; b. Princeton, Mass., June 19, 1774; s. Samuel Underwood and Abigail (Whitney) W.; grad. Harvard, 1796; m. Abigail Wheeler, Oct. 8, 1799; m. 2d widow of Dr. Ansel Ives; 8 children including Leonard. Ordained pastor, Newbury (now West Newbury), Mass., 1798; became mediator between Hopkinsians (extreme Calvinists) and Old Calvinists; contbr. to Hopkinsian Massachusetts Missionary Mag., 1803, Old Calvinist Panoplist, 1805, his efforts led to consolidation of the 2 publications; responsible for union of Hopkinsian Mass. Missionary Soc. (1799) and Old Calvinist Mass. Gen. Assn. (1803); 1st prof. theology Andover (Mass.) Theol. Sem., 1808-46; participated in "Wood'n Ware Controversy," 1820-22; a founder Am. Bd. Commrs. for Fgn. Missions, 1810, mem. governing com., 1819-44; a founder Am. Tract Soc., 1814. Author: Letters to Nathaniel W. Taylor, (pamphlets), 1830; History of Andover Theological Seminary, published posthumously, 1885. Died Andover, Aug. 24, 1854.

WOODS, Leonard, clergyman, coll. pres.; b. Newbury, Mass., Nov. 24, 1807; s. Leonard and Abigail (Wheeler) W.; attended Dartmouth; grad. Union Coll., Schenectady, N.Y., 1827; attended Andover (Mass.) Theol. Sem., 1830; D.D. (hon.), Harvard, 1846; LL.D. (hon.) Bowdoin Coll., 1866; never married. Abbot resident at Andover Theol. Sem., 1830-32; licensed to preach by Londonderry Presbytery in Conn., 1830; ordained by 3d Presbytery of N.Y., 1833; editor Literary and Theol. Review, N.Y.C., 1833-36; prof. Bibl. lit. Bangor (Me.) Theol. Sem., 1836; pres. Bowdoin Coll., 1839-66, replaced formal discipline system with honor system, largely responsible for planning and erection of King Chapel, resigned partly because of unpopularity of his lack of support for No. prosecution of Civil War, 1867. Translator: Lectures on Christian Theology (G. C. Knapp), 2 vols., 1831-33. Died Boston, Dec. 24, 1878.

WOODS, William, congressman; b. Washington County, N.Y., 1790; studied law, Bath, N.Y. Admitted to N.Y. bar, practiced in Bath; mem. N.Y. State Assembly, 1823-25; mem. U.S. Ho. of Reps. (Democrat) from N.Y., 18th Congress, Nov. 3, 1823-25; surrogate of Steuben County (N.Y.), 1827-35. Died Bath, Aug. 7, 1837; buried Grove Cemetery, Bath.

WOODS, William Allen, jurist; b. nr. Farmington, Tenn., May 16, 1837; s. Allen Newton and Mrs. (Ewing) W.; grad. Wabash Coll., Crawfordsville, Ind., 1859; m. Mata A. Newton, Dec. 6, 1870, 1 son, 1 dau. Tchr., Marion, Ind., 1860; admitted to Ind. bar, 1861; mem. Ind. Legislature, 1867-69; judge 34th Jud. Circuit, Ind., 1873-80; judge Ind. Supreme Ct., 1880-82, U.S. Dist. Ct., Ind., 1882-92. Died Indpls., June 20, 1901.

WOODS, William Burnham, jurist; b. Newark, O., Aug. 3, 1824; s. Ezekiel S. and Sarah Judith (Burnham) W.; attended Western Res. Coll.; grad. Yale, 1845; read law with S .D. King, Newark, O.; m. Anne E. Warner, June 21, 1855, 1 son, 1 dau. Admitted to bar, 1847; partner in law firm (with S. D. King), 1847-61; mayor Newark, 1856; mem. (Democrat) Ohio Gen. Assembly, 1857, 59; commd. lt. col. 76th Ohio Inf., 1862, left in service as brevet maj. gen., 1866; settled in Ala.; chancellor Middle Chancery Div. of Ala., 1868; judge 5th U.S. Circuit Ct. (apptd. by Pres. Grant), 1869-80; justice U.S. Supreme Ct., 1880-87. Author: Wood's Reports, 4 vols., 1875-83. Died Washington, D.C., May 14, 1887.

WOODSIDE, John Archibald, artist; b. Phila., 1781; children include Abraham, John A. Sign painter, Phila., 1805-52; mem. Artists' Fund Soc.; exhibited at Pa. Acad., 1817-36. Died 1852.

WOODSON, Samuel Hughes, congressman; b. nr. Charlottesville, Va., Sept. 15, 1777; studied law; children include Samuel Hughes. Admitted to Ky. bar, 1802, began practice in Nicholasville; 1st clk. Jessamine County (Ky.) Circuit Ct., 1803-19; mem. U.S. Ho. of Reps. from Ky., 17th Congress, 1821-23; mem. Ky. Ho. of Reps., 1825-26. Died "Chaumiere," Jessamine County, July 28, 1827; buried Crocket Burying Ground, Jessamine County.

WOODSON, Samuel Hughes, congressman; b. nr. Nicholasville, Ky., Oct. 24, 1815; s. Samuel Hughes Woodson; grad. Centre Coll., Danville, Ky., law dept. of Transylvania U., Lexington, Ky. Admitted to the bar, 1838, began practice in Independence, Mo., 1840; mem. Mo. Ho. of Reps., 1853-54; del. Mo. Constl. Conv., 1855; mem. U.S. Ho. of Reps. (Am. Party rep.) from Mo., 35th-36th congresses, 1857-61; joined Democratic Party; judge 24th Mo. Jud. Circuit, 1875-81. Died Independence, Jan. 23, 1881; buried Woodlawn Cemetery, Independence.

WOODWARD, Augustus Brevoort, jurist; b. N.Y.C., 1774; s. John and Ann (Silvester) W.; grad. Columbia, 1793; never married. Born Elias Brevoort, changed name to Augustus; took active part in obtaining incorporation of City of Washington (D.C.), elected mem. council; moved to Georgetown, D.C., 1797, practiced law, active in civic affairs; apptd. judge Territory of Mich. by Pres. Jefferson, 1805; compiled early The Laws of Michigan (known as Woodward Code), 1806; remained in Detroit after its surrender to British in 1812; judge U.S. ct. for Fla. dist. (apptd. by Pres. Monroe), 1824-27. Author: Considerations on the Executive Government of the United States of America, 1809; System of Universal Science, 1816; collected and published series of articles as Presidency of United States, 1825. Died June 12, 1827.

WOODWARD, George Washington, congressman; b. Bethany, Pa., Mar. 26, 1809; attended Geneva (N.Y.) Sem. (now Hobart Coll.), Wilkes-Barre (Pa.) Acad.; studied law. Admitted to Pa. bar, 1830, began practice in Wilkes-Barre; del. Pa. constl. convs., 1837; pres. judge 4th Pa. Jud. Dist., 1841-51; unsuccessful candidate for U.S. Senate, 1845; apptd. justice U.S. Supreme Ct. by Pres. Polk, 1845, appointment not confirmed by Senate; asso. judge Pa. Supreme Ct., 1852-63, chief justice, 1863-67; unsuccessful Democratic Candidate for gov. Pa., 1863; mem. U.S. Ho. of Reps. (Dem.) from Pa., 40th-41st congresses, Nov. 21, 1867-71; del. Dem. Nat. Conv., N.Y.C., 1868; moved to Phila., 1871, practiced law; traveled in Europe, 1874-75. Died Rome, Italy, May 10, 1875; buried Hollenback Cemetery, Wilkes-Barre.

WOODWARD, Henry, explorer; b. perhaps Barbados, circa 1646; m. Margaret Woodward; m. 2d, Mrs. Mary Browne. Joined Carolina settlement nr. Cape Fear, 1664; went to Port Royal in Carolinas on exploration trip, 1666, abducted by Spanish, escaped from Spaniards with pirate Robert Searles when Searles raided St. Augustine, Fla., 1668; 1st English settler in S.C., served proprs. as interpreter and Indian agt.; apptd. by Earl of Shaftesbury as agt. in opening interior Indian trade, 1674, apptd. dep. 1677; made alliance with Westo Indians, 1674; aided expansion of trading frontier of Carolina westward to towns of Lower Creeks on middle Chattahoochee; went to England, received commn. to explore interior beyond Savannah River, 1682; laid foundation for English alliance with Lower Creeks. Died circa 1686.

WOODWARD, Joseph Addison, congressman; b. Winnsboro, S.C., Apr. 11, 1806; grad. U. S.C.; studied law. Admitted to S.C. bar, practiced law; mem. S.C. Ho. of Reps., 1837-43; mem. U.S. Ho. of Reps. (Democrat) from S.C., 28th-32d congresses, 1843-53; moved to Ala., practiced law. Died Talladega, Ala., Aug. 3, 1885; buried Oak Hill Cemetery, Talladega.

WOODWARD, Joseph Janvier, physician; b. Phila., Oct. 30, 1833; s. Joseph Janvier and Elizabeth Graham (Cox) W.; M.D., U. Pa., 1853; married twice; m. 2d, Blanche Wendell; at least 1 son, Janvier. Began practice of medicine, Phila.; became asst. surgeon Med. Corps, U.S. Army, 1861, served at 1st Battle of Bull Run; transferred to Surgeon Gen.'s Hdqrs., Washington, D.C., with duties of planning hosp. constrn., performing surgery, keeping med. records, 1862-65; asst. to curator Army Med. Museum; in charge of med. part of Medical and Surgical History of the War of the Rebellion, 1870-88; promoted maj. U.S. Army, 1876; mem. Nat. Acad. Scis., A.A.A.S., Washington Philos. Soc.; pres A.M.A., 1881. Author various works including: Official Record of the Post-Mortem Examination of the Body of Pres. James A. Garfield, 1881. Died Wawa, Pa., Aug. 17, 1884.

WOODWARD, Samuel Bayard, physician; b. Torrington, Conn., Jan. 10, 1787; s. Dr. Samuel and Polly (Griswald) W.; M.D. (hon.), Yale; m. Maria Porter, 1815, 11 children. Began practice of medicine, 1808; a founder Conn. Retreat for Insane, Hartford, 1824; resident physician Conn. State Prison, 1827-32; med. examiner Yale Med. Sch.; mem. Conn. Senate (Democrat), 1830; supt. Lunatic Asylum, Worcester, Mass., 1832-46; founder, 1st pres. Assn. Med. Supts. of Am. Instns. for Insane (now Am. Psychiat. Assn.); helped many states draw up laws regarding feeble minded. Died Northampton, Mass., Jan. 3, 1850.

WOODWARD, William, congressman. Mem. U.S. Ho. of Reps. from S.C., 14th Congress, 1815-17.

WOODWORTH, James Hutchinson, congressman; b. Greenwich, N.Y., Dec. 4, 1804. Taught sch., Fabius, N.Y.; engaged in merc. bus., 1823, insp. common schs., 1826; moved to Erie, Pa., 1827, justice of peace, 1829-32; moved to Chgo., 1833, engaged in dry-goods bus.; mem. Ill. Senate, 1839-42, Ill. Ho. of Reps., 1842-47; owner and mgr. Chgo. Hydraulic Flouring Mills, 10 years; mem. Chgo. City Council, 1845-48; mayor of Chgo., 1848-50; mem. U.S. Ho. of Reps. (Republican) from Ill., 34th Congress, 1855-57; apptd. mem. bd. auditors on war claims; pres. Mchts. and Mechanics' Bank of Chgo., Treasury Bank of Chgo.; a founder U. Chgo. Died Highland Park, Ill., Mar. 26, 1869; buried Oakland Cemetery, Chgo.

WOODWORTH, Laurin Dewey, congressman; b. Windham, O., Sept. 10, 1837; attended Hiram (O.) Coll., Ohio State U.; studied law Union Law Coll., Cleve. Admitted to Ohio bar, 1859, began practice in Ravenna; mem. Portage County (O.) Bd. Sch. Examiners; served as maj. 104th Ohio Volunteer Inf. during Civil War, 1862; moved to Youngstown, O., 1864, resumed practice of law; elected to Ohio Senate, 1867, 69, pres. pro tem; mem. U.S. Ho. of Reps. (Republican) from Ohio, 43d-44th congresses, 1873-77. Died Youngstown, Mar. 13, 1897; buried Windham Cemetery.

WOODWORTH, Samuel, journalist, author; b. Scituate, Mass., Jan. 13, 1784; s. Benjamin and Abigail (Bryant) W.; m. Lydia Reeder, Sept. 23, 1810, many children. Edited juvenile paper Fly, Boston, 1805-06; started Belles-Lettres Repository, weekly periodical, New Haven, Conn., 1808; printer, N.Y.C., 1809; published War (weekly account of War of 1812), 1812-14; editor newspaper Republican Chronicle, 1817; published Ladies' Literary Cabinet, 1819-20; published mag. Woodworth's Literary Casket, 1821; editor N.Y. Mirror, 1823-24; published 2 Swedenborgian mags. Halcyon Luminary, 1812-13, New Jerusalem Missionary, 1823-24; wrote novel The Champions of Freedom, 1816; wrote plays The Deed of Gift, 1822, La Fayette, 1824, The Forest Rose (most successful), 1825, The Widow's Son, 1825; best known poems include The Bucket (became song The Old Oaken Bucket), The Hunters of Kentucky. Died N.Y.C., Dec. 9, 1842.

WOODWORTH, William W., congressman; b. New London, Conn., Mar. 16, 1807. Supr. of Hyde Park (N.Y.), 1838, 41, 43; apptd. judge Dutchess County (N.Y.), 1838, reapptd., 1843; mem. U.S. Ho. of Reps. (Democrat) from N.Y., 29th Congress, 1845-47; owned bus. interests in Cuba; formed a stock co. of Hudson River State Co., Clinton, N.Y.; contracted to build a sect. of Hudson River R.R.; moved to Yonkers, N.Y., 1849, engaged in real estate bus., banking; pres. of Yonkers, 1857-58, apptd. receiver of taxes, 1870. Died Yonkers, Feb. 13, 1873; buried Oakland Cemetery, Yonkers.

WOOL, John Ellis, army officer; b. Newburgh, N.Y., Feb. 29, 1784; m. Sarah Moulton, Sept. 27, 1810. Raised co. of volunteers during War of 1812, Troy, N.Y.; commd. capt. 13th Inf., U.S. Army, 1812; promoted to maj. 29th Inf., 1813; brevetted lt. col. for gallant conduct in Battle of Plattsburg, 1814; col. and insp. gen. U.S. Army, 1816-circa 1841; brevetted brig. gen., 1826; personally assisted Gen. Winfield Scott in moving of Cherokee Indian nation to West, 1836; commd. brig. gen. U.S. Army, 1841; prepared and mustered 12,000 volunteers in 6 weeks at opening of Mexican War, 1846; 2d in command at. Battle of Buena Vista for which he was brevetted maj. gen., 1846; commanded Eastern Mil. Div., 1848-53, Dept. of Pacific, 1854-57; commd. maj. gen. U.S. Army in command Middle Mil. Dept. and Dept. of East, 1862-63; ret. from active service, 1863. Died Troy, Nov. 10, 1869.

WOOLF, Benjamin Edward, musician, journalist; b. London, Eng., Feb. 16, 1836; s. Edward and Sarah (Michaels) W.; m. Josephine Orton, Apr. 15, 1867. Mem. orch. of Boston Museum, 1859; became music critic Boston Globe, 1870; mem. editorial staff Saturday Evening Gazette, Boston, 1871-92, became publisher-editor, 1892; music critic Boston Herald. Composer: (operetta) Pounce and Co., or Capital vs. Labor, 1882. Died Feb. 7, 1901.

WOOLLETT, William L., architect; b. nr. Maidstone, Kent, Eng., 1815; at least one son, William M. Came to U.S., circa 1834, practiced architecture in Albany (N.Y.) area; fellow A.I.A.; lived in Londonville, N.Y., during last years of life. Prin. works include: Delavam House (hotel), Albany Savs. Bank, 1st Congregational Ch., many pvt. homes (all Albany); Jermain Meml. Ch., West Troy, N.Y. Died Apr. 2, 1874.

WOOLLETT, William M., architect; b. Albany, N.Y., July 6, 1850; son of William L. Woollett; attended Mass. Inst. Tech., circa 1870; at least 4 children including William Lee. Took charge of his father's archtl. office, Albany, 1874, designed numerous residences, other bldgs., in Albany area. Prin. works include: Fort Bldg., Calvary Baptist Ch. (both completed after his death, Albany). Author: Villas and Cottages (collection of his designs), Old Homes Made New. Died Londonville, N.Y., Oct. 17, 1880.

WOOLMAN, John, religious leader; b. Ancocas, West Jersey (now N.J.), Oct. 19, 1720; s. Samuel and Elizabeth (Burr) W.; m. Sarah Ellis, Oct. 18, 1749. A leading Quaker, traveled throughout Am. visiting Friends' meetings from Mass. to N.C., 1743-71; advocated abolition of slavery; influenced (through his writings and travels) the Phila. Yearly Meeting to forbid its mems. to own slaves, 1776; his asceticism grew stronger as he became older; curtailed, then virtually abandoned his flourishing tailor shop in Mt. Holly, N.J.; died of smallpox on walking trip (had given up riding horses as a vanity) to English Quakers. Author: Some Considerations on the Keeping of Negroes, 1754; A Plea for the Poor, 1763; Journal of John Woolman (most famous work), posthumously published 1774. Died York, Eng., Oct. 7, 1772; buried York.

WOOLSEY, Melancthon Taylor, naval officer; b. N.Y., June 5, 1780; s. Col. Melancthon Lloyd and Alida (Livingston) W.; m. Susan Cornelia Tredwell, Nov. 3, 1817, 7 children. Apptd. midshipman U.S. Navy, 1800; participated in Barbary War, 1800-05; promoted lt., 1804; began tour of duty on Gt. Lakes, 1808, built ship Oneida on Lake Ontario; defeated superior Brit. force at Sackett's Harbor, Lake Ontario during War of 1812; participated in attack on Kingston and in combined army-navy siege of York (Ont.), 1813; commd. master comdt. in command of Sylph, 1813; on convoy duty from Oswego to Sackett's Harbor, 1814; commd. capt., 1816; commanded Constellation, 1825; on duty patrolling West Indies against pirates, 1825-26; in command of Pensacola Navy Yard, 1826-30; in command of Brazil squadron with rank of commodore, 1833-34. Died Utica, N.Y., May 19, 1838.

WOOLSEY, Theodore Dwight, coll. pres.; b. N.Y.C., Oct. 31, 1801; s. William Walton and Elizabeth (Dwight) W.; grad. Yale, 1820; attended Princeton Theol. Sem., 1821-23; studied Arabic, Paris, France, 1827; m. Elizabeth Salisbury, Sept. 5, 1833; m. 2d, Sarah Sears Prichard, Sept. 6, 1854; 13 children including Theodore Salisbury. Tutor at Yale, 1823-25, became prof. Greek, 1831, pres. coll., 1846-71; instructed in history, polit. sci., internat. law; Woolsey Hall at Yale named in his honor. Author: Alcestis of Euripides, 1834; Introduction to the Study of International Law, Designed as an Aid in Teaching and in Historical Studies, 1860; Communism and Socialism, 1880; The Religion of the Past and of the Future, 1871. Died New Haven, Conn., July 1, 1889.

WOOLSON, Constance Fenimore, author; b. Claremont, N.H., Mar. 1840; d. Charles Jarvis and Hannah (Pomeroy) Woolson; grad. Madame Chegary's Sch., N.Y.C., 1858. Published poem Two Women, 1862; contbr. to Harper's, Lippincott's, Galaxy, Atlantic Monthly; lived in Europe, from 1879; used Fla. and Carolinas settings in many stories describing reconstrn. era in So. history. Author: The Old Stone House (under pseudonym Anne March), 1873; Castle Nowhere: Lake Country Sketches (9 tales), 1875; Rodman the Keeper: Southern Sketches, 1880; Anne (1st novel) 1883; East Angels, 1886; Horace Chase, 1894. Died Venice, Italy, Jan. 24, 1894; buried Protestant Cemetery, Rome, Italy.

WOOMER, Ephraim Milton, congressman; b. Jonestown, Pa., Jan. 14, 1844; attended common schs. Enlisted in Co. A, 93d Regt., Pa. Volunteer Inf., during Civil War, 1861, promoted sgt., wounded at Battle of Salem Heights, lost leg at Battle of Wilderness, 1864; discharged from hosp., 1865; taught sch., until 1869; engaged in merc. bus.; clk. Lebanon County (Pa.) Orphans Ct., 1869-72; cashier People's Bank of Lebanon (Pa.); mem. council Borough of Lebanon, 1884-86; pres. select council City of Lebanon, 1886-90; del. Republican Nat. Conv., Chgo., 1888; mem. U.S. Ho. of Reps. (Rep.) from Pa,, 53d-54th congresses, 1893-97; engaged in banking. Died Lebanon, Nov. 29, 1897; buried Mt. Lebanon Cemetery.

WOOSTER, Charles Whiting, naval officer; b. New Haven, Conn., 1780; s. Thomas and Lydia (Sheldon) W.; m. Frances Stebbens, 1 child. Commanded ship Fair American, 1801; commanded privateer Saratoga, during War of 1812, captured 22 Brit. vessels including Rachel in Battle of La Guayra (Venezuela); commd. capt. of battalion of ships to protect N.Y. Harbor, 1814; commd. in Chilean Army in war of independence, 1817; commd. rear-adm. Chilean Navy; returned to U.S., 1835. Died San Francisco, 1848.

WOOSTER, David, army officer; b. Stratford, Conn., Mar. 2, 1711; grad. Yale, 1738; m. Mary Clap, Mar. 1746, 4 children. Apptd. lt. Conn. Colony, 1741; apptd. capt. of sloop Defense, to protect coast, 1742; served as capt. Conn. Militia, 1745; organizer Hiram Lodge (1 of earliest Free Mason lodges in Conn.), 1750; served as col. Conn. regt., Seven Years War, 1756-63; mem. Conn. Assembly from New Haven, 1757; apptd. by Conn. Assembly maj. gen. of 6 regts. and col. 1st Regt., 1775; in command of Continental Army before Quebec, Can., 1775; recalled by Continental Congress on charge of incompetence, 1776, acquitted of charge, retained rank of brig. gen. but was not given a command. Died May 2, 1777.

WOOTTON, Richens Lacy, trapper, pioneer; b. Mecklenburg County, Va., May 6, 1816; m. Dolores Le Fevre, circa 1850, 3 children. Engaged in trading and trapping, 1836-40; owned ranch, Pueblo, Colo., 1841; in Battle of Sacramento, 1847; engaged in bus. at Taos, N.M., 1847; guide for Col. Edward Newby in latter's Navajo campaign, 1848; participated in driving 9,000 sheep to Cal., 1852; in partnership with George C. McBride built toll road of 27 miles from Trinidad (Colo.) across Raton Pass to Canadian River, 1865, opened, 1866, built residence and inn at entrance to road, lived there until 1891. Died Trinidad, Aug. 21, 1893.

WORCESTER, Joseph Emerson, lexicographer; b. Bedford, N.H., Aug. 24, 1784; s. Jesse and Sarah (Parker) W.; grad. Yale, 1811; LL.D. (hon.), Brown U., 1847, Dartmouth, 1856; m. Amy Elizabeth McKean, June 29, 1841. Taught at Salem, Mass., 1811-16 (Nathaniel Hawthorne one of his students) published a Geographical Dictionary or Universal Gazetteer, Ancient and Modern, 1817, A Gazetteer of the United States, 1819, Johnson's English Dictionary . . . with Walker's Pronouncing Dictionary, Combined (contained his permanent contbn. to lexicography, "compromise vowel," new sound attributed to letter "a"), 1828; editor American Almanac and Repository of Useful Language, 1831-42; accused by Noah Webster of plagiarism, 1830, resulted in "War of Dictionaries," which continued until 1860's published pamphlet concerning controversy, A Gross Literary Fraud Exposed, 1853; published A Dictionary of the English Language (most important work), 1860; mem. Mass. Hist. Soc., Am. Acad., Oriental Soc., Royal Geog. Soc. London (Eng.). Died Cambridge, Mass., Oct. 27, 1865.

WORCESTER, Noah, clergyman; b. Nov. 25, 1758; s. Noah and Lydia (Taylor) W.; m. Hannah Huntington, May 1789. Served as fifer Continental Army at battles of Bunker Hill (1776), Bennington (1777); town clk., justice of peace, mem. N.H. Legislature, 1782-87; ordained to ministry Congregational Ch., Thornton, N.H., 1787; missionary for N.H. Missionary Soc. in No. part of N.H.; became 1st editor Christian Disciple (periodical), 1813. Author: Bible News of the Father, Son, and Holy Spirit, in a Series of Letters, 1810; A Solemn Review of the Custom of War, 1814; The Atoning Sacrifice, a Display of Love, Not of Wrath, 1829. Died Brighton, Mass., Oct. 31, 1837; buried Mt. Auburn Cemetery, Cambridge, Mass.

WORCESTER, Samuel, clergyman; b. Hollis, N.H., Nov. 1, 1770; s. Noah and Lydia (Taylor) W.; grad. Dartmouth, 1795; m. Zervia Fox, Oct. 20, 1797, 11 children. Ordained to ministry Congregational Ch., Fitchburg, Mass., 1797; an organizer Mass. Missionary Soc., 1799; a founder Mass. Missionary Mag., 1803; pastor Tabernacle Ch., Salem, Mass., 1803-15; a founder Am. Bd. Commrs. for Fgn. Missions, 1810. Author: American Unitarianism; or a Brief History of the Progress and Present State of the Unitarian Churches in America, 1815; Sermons on Various Subjects, published posthumously, 1823. Died while visiting missionary stations in South, at Brainerd, Tenn., June 7, 1821; buried Harmony Grove Cemetery, Salem.

WORCESTER, Samuel Austin, missionary; b. Mass., Jan. 19, 1798; s. Rev. Leonard and Elizabeth (Hopkins) W.; grad. U. Vt., 1819, Andover Theol. Sem., 1823; m. Ann Orr, July 19, 1825; m. 2d, Erminia Nash, Apr. 3, 1841; 1 dau., Anna Eliza. Ordained to ministry Congregational Ch., Boston, 1825; missionary, Bainard Mission, Cherokee Country of Eastern Tenn., 1825; translated portions of Bible from Greek to Cherokee, New Echota, Ga., 1827; a founder newspaper Cherokee Phoenix, circa 1827; sentenced to 4 years in prison for violating Ga. statute forbidding white persons to live among Indians without obtaining license, 1831, appealed case to U.S. Supreme Ct., 1832 (ct. held Ga. act unconstl.), not released until Jan. 1833; established Park Hill Mission for Cherokee Indians in Okla.; established 1st printing press in Indian Territory; printed Cherokee almanac, 1838-61; organized Cherokee Bible Soc., 1841. Died Cherokee Mission, Okla., Apr. 20, 1859; buried Worcester Cemetery, Okla.

WORCESTER, Samuel Thomas, congressman; b. Hollis, N.H., Aug. 30, 1804; grad. Harvard, 1830; studied law. Admitted to the bar, 1835, began practice in Norwalk, O.; mem. Ohio Senate, 1849-50; judge Ct. of Common Pleas, 1859-60; mem. U.S. Ho. of Reps. (Republican) from Ohio, 37th Congress, July 4, 1861-63. Died Nashua, N.H., Dec. 6, 1882; buried South Cemetery, Hollis.

WORCESTER, Thomas, clergyman; b. Hollis, N.H., Nov. 22, 1768. Pastor, Salisbury, N.H., 1791-1823. Author, A Call for Scripture Evidence, 1811; The True God but One Person, 1819. Died Dec. 24, 1831.

WORD, Thomas Jefferson, congressman; b. Surry County, N.C. Mem. N.C. Ho. of Commons, 1832; moved to Pontotoc, Miss.; mem. U..S Ho. of Reps. (Whig; filled vacancy after election was set aside when he contested it) from Miss., 25th Congress, May 30, 1838-39.

WORDEN, John Lorimer, naval officer; b. Westchester County, N.Y., Mar. 12, 1818; s. Ananias and Harriet (Graham) W.; m. Olivia Taffey, 4 children. Apptd. midshipman U.S. Navy, 1834, commd., 1840; served at Naval Observatory, 1844-46, 50-52; fought in storeship Southampton during Mexican War; captured at Pensacola, Fla., 1861, exchanged; apptd. comdr. in Monitor, 1862, wounded in Monitor-Merrimac fight; commd. capt., 1863; served in South Atlantic Blockade Squadron at battles of Ft. McAllister and Charleston; commd. commodore, 1868, rear adm., 1872; supt. U.S. Naval Acad., 1869-74; commanded European Squadron, 1875-77; pres. Navy Retiring Bd., 1878-86; ret., 1886. Died Washington, D.C., Oct. 18, 1897; buried Pawling, N.Y.

WORK, Henry Clay, song-writer; b. Middleton, Conn., Oct. 1, 1832; s. Alanson and Aurelia Work; 3 children. Became a printer, Chgo., 1854; met 1st success as a song-writer with song We're Coming, Sister Mary; wrote several Civil War songs including Kingdom Coming, 1861, Babylon is Fallen, 1863, Wake Nicodemus, 1864, Marching through Georgia, 1865; wrote famous temperance song Come Home, Father, 1864, poem The Upshot Family, 1868; published Grandfather's Clock after Civil War; wrote at least 73 songs, according to family records. Died Hartford, Conn., June 8, 1884; buried Spring Grove Cemetery, Hartford.

WORMAN, Ludwig, congressman; b. Tinicum Twp., Pa., 1761. Learned tanning bus.; moved to Earl Twp., Pa., 1784, established tannery; mem. U.S. Ho. of Reps. (Federalist) from Pa., 17th Congress, 1821-22. Died Earl Twp., Oct. 17, 1822; buried Earl Twp. Cemetery.

WORMLEY, James, hotel owner, caterer; b. Jan. 16, 1819; son of Pere Leigh Wormley; m. Anna Thompson, 1841, 4 children. Became a hack-driver at his father's livery station, Washington, D.C., later secured most of hack trade of Washington's 2 major hotels (The National, Willard's); went to Cal. during Gold Rush, 1849; opened Wormley's Hotel, Washington, before Civil War, became famous as caterer. Died Boston, Oct. 18, 1884.

WORMLEY, Theodore George, physician, toxicologist, educator; b. Wormleysburg, Pa., Apr. 1, 1826; s. David and Isabella (Foster) W.; attended Dickinson Coll., Carlisle, Pa., 1842-45, Ph.D. (hon.), 1870; M.D., Phila. Coll. Medicine, 1849; LL.D. (hon.), Marietta Coll., 1870; Ph.D. (hon.) Pa. Coll., 1877; m. Ann Eliza Gill. Prof. toxicology Capitol U., Columbus, O., 1852-73, Starling Med. Coll., 1852-77; gas commr. for State of Ohio, 1867-75; chemist Ohio Geog. Survey, 1869-74; editor Ohio Med. and Surg. Jour., 1862-64; delivered address on toxicology before Internat. Med. Congress, Phila., 1876; prof. chemistry and toxicology med. dept. U. Pa., 1877-97. Author: The Micro-Chemistry of Poisons, 1867. Died Phila., Jan. 3, 1897.

WORTENDYKE, Jacob Reynier, congressman; b. Chestnut Ridge, N.J., Nov 27, 1818; grad Rutgers Coll., 1839; studied law. Taught sch., 10 years; admitted to N.J. bar, 1853, began practice in Jersey City; mem. U.S. Ho. of Reps. (Democrat) from N.J., 35th Congress, 1857-59; pres. water bd. Jersey City, 1860-68; trustee Rutgers Coll., 1862-68; pres. Riparian Commn. of N.J., 1865-68; del. Dem. Nat. Conv., N.Y.C., 1868. Died Jersey City, Nov. 7, 1868; buried Dutch Reformed Ch. Cemetery, Park Ridge, N.J.

WORTH, Jonathan, gov. N.C.; b. Guilford County, N.C., Nov. 18, 1802; s. Dr. David and Eunice (Gardner) W.; attended Caldwell Inst., Greensboro, N.C.; m. Martitia Daniel, Oct. 20, 1824, 8 children. Began practice of law, Asheboro, N.C., 1824; mem. N.C. Ho. of Commons, 1830-32, led in drawing up protest against nullification, 1831; clk. of cts. Randolph County, N.C., 1840's; mem. N.C. Ho. of Reps., 1858-60, N.C. Senate, 1860-62, opposed secession movement; treas. State of N.C., 1862-65; gov. N.C., 1865-68, cooperated with Johnson adminstrn., removed from office following enactment of mil. reconstrn. Died Raleigh N.C., Sept. 5, 1869.

WORTH, William Jenkins, army officer; b. Hudson, N.Y., Mar. 1, 1794; s. Thomas Worth; m. Margaret Stafford, Sept. 18, 1818, 4 children. Apptd. 1st lt. 23d Inf., U.S. Army, 1813; served with Gen. Winfield Scott as a.d.c., 1818; brevetted capt. and maj.; comdt. U.S. Mil. Acad., 1820-28; brevetted lt. col., 1824; col. 8th Inf., 1838; brevetted brig. gen. by Pres. Polk for service in Seminole War of 1838, 1845; served in Mexican War, 1846, 1st to plant flag on Rio Grande; brevetted maj. gen., 1846, presented with sword by resolution of Congress, 1847; participated with distinction in engagements from Vera Cruz to Mexico City; involved him in dispute with Gen. Scott due to his ambition and tactlessness, 1847; in command of Dept. of Tex., 1848. Died May 7, 1849.

WORTHEN, Amos Henry, geologist; b. Bradford, Vt., Oct. 31, 1813; s. Thomas and Susannah (Adams) W.; m. Sarah B. Kimball, Jan. 14, 1834, 7 children. Moved to Warsaw, Ill., 1836, entered dry-goods bus.; moved to Boston, 1842; ret. from business, became geologist assisting in Ill. Geol. Survey, 1844; became geologist Ia. Geol. Survey, 1855; apptd. state geologist Ill., 1858; described over 1600 species of fossils; particularly interested in classification of lower Carboniferous strata; mem. Am. Philos. Soc., Nat. Acad. Scis. Author: Geological Survey of Illinois, 8 vols., 1866-90. Died Warsaw, May 6, 1888.

WORTHINGTON, Henry Rossiter, engr., inventor; b. N.Y.C., Dec. 17, 1817; s. Asa and Frances (Meadwocraft) W.; m. Laura I. Newton, Sept. 24, 1839, 4 children. Worked on problems of city water supply as hydraulic engr., N.Y.C., circa 1838; placed exptl. steam canal boat in operation, 1840; invented automatic feeding pump, patented, 1840; received patent for improvement in propelling of canal boats, 1844; 1st to build direct steam pump, 1845-55; built pump manufacturing plant in N.Y.C., 1859; developed duplex steam feed pump which was adopted widely in waterworks, 1859, also invented pump engine using no flywheel, and various machine tools; pres. Nason Mfg. Co., N.Y.; founder Am. Soc. M.E. Died Tarrytown, N.Y., Dec. 17, 1880.

WORTHINGTON, John, lawyer; b. Springfield, Mass., Nov. 24, 1719; s. John and Mary (Pratt) W.; grad. Yale, 1740; m. Hannah Hopkins, Jan. 10, 1759; m. 2d, Mary Stoddard, Dec. 7, 1768. Practiced law, Springfield, 1744; king's attorney in Western Mass. in 1750's; took active part in raising troops in French and Indian Wars; col. Hampshire regts., circa 1754-75; active in land speculation; Town of Worthington (Mass.) named for him, 1768; polit. leader of Springfield, mem. bd. selectmen and moderator of town meetings; represented Springfield at Mass. Gen. Ct., 1747-74; attended Albany Congress, 1754; mem. Mass. Gov.'s Council, 1767-69; lost popularity when he opposed independence, later changed views; served as commn. to settle Mass.-Conn. boundary, 1791. Died Springfield, Apr. 25, 1800.

WORTHINGTON, John Tolley Hood, congressman; b. "Shewan" nr. Balt., Nov. 1, 1788. Engaged in farming; mem. U.S. Ho. of Reps. (Democrat) from Md., 22d, 25th-26th congresses, 1831-33, 37-41; resumed farming. Died "Shewan," Apr. 27, 1849; buried pvt. cemetery "Shewan," reinterred St. John's Episcopal Churchyard, Worthington Valley, Md.

WORTHINGTON, Thomas, senator, gov. Ohio; b. Charles Town, Va. (now W.Va.), July 16, 1773; s. Robert and Margaret (Matthews) W.; m. Eleanor Van Swearingen, Dec. 13, 1796, many children. Went to Chillicothe (O.) as surveyor, 1796, purchased Va. mil. land warrants; mem. Ohio Territorial Ho. of Reps., 1799-1803; apptd. register public lands in charge of sales, Chillicothe, 1800; mem. 1st Ohio Constl. Conv., 1802; leader in "Chillicothe Junto" which achieved supremacy of Republicans in Ohio; mem. Ohio Gen. Assembly, 1803, 07-08; mem. U.S. Senate (Federalist) from Ohio, 1803-07, Dec. 15, 1810-Dec. 1, 1814 (resigned); gov. Ohio, 1814-18, a founder state library, branch Bank of U.S., Chillicothe; mem. Ohio Ho. of Reps., 1821-23, 24-25; canal commr. Ohio, 1818-27. Died N.Y.C., June 20, 1827; buried Grandview Cemetery, Chillicothe.

WORTHINGTON, Thomas Contee, congressman; b. nr. Annapolis, Md., Nov. 25, 1782; studied law. Served as capt. during War of 1812; admitted to Md. bar, 1817, began practice in Annapolis; moved to Frederick, Md., 1818, practiced law; mem. Md. Ho. of Reps., 1818; brig. gen. 9th Brigade, Md. Militia, 1818-47; mem. U.S. Ho. of Reps. (Democrat) from Md., 19th Congress, 1825-27; mem.

Md. Exec. Council, 1830. Died Frederick, Apr. 12, 1847; buried Mt. Olivet Cemetery, Frederick.

WRAGG, William, colonial ofcl.; b. S.C., 1714; s. Samuel and Marie (DuBose) W.; admitted to Middle Temple, London, Eng., 1725; m. Mary Wood; m. 2d, Henrietta Wragg, Feb. 5, 1769; 2 children. Admitted to bar, Eng., 1733; returned to S.C., circa 1734; mem. S.C. Gov.'s Council, 1753, 69; justice of peace, S.C., 1756; mem. S.C. Assembly, 1763-68; refused to sign Articles of Non-Importation, 1769; a leading landowner and man of affairs in S.C., by 1776; a supporter of royal authority in colonies; banished for Loyalist attitudes, 1777, sailed in ship Commerce for Amsterdam, Holland. Died in shipwreck off coast of Holland, Sept. 2, 1777.

WRAXALL, Peter, army officer, colonial ofcl.; b. England; m. Elizabeth Stillwell, Dec. 9, 1756. Came to N.Y., 1746; commanded a co. of L.I. Militia raised for expdn. against Can.; in Eng., 1747-52, received king's appointment to offices of sec. and agt. for Indian affairs in N.Y., also town clk., clk. Ct. of Common Pleas in County and City of Albany (N.Y.), 1750; chosen sec. to Albany Congress, 1754; capt. N.Y. forces at Battle of Lake George, 1755; aide to Sir William Johnson during Crown Point expdn., 1755; highly successful in reducing influence of French among Six Nations of Indian tribes during French and Indian wars. Died N.Y.C. July 10, 1759.

WRIGHT, Ashley Bascom, congressman; b. Hinsdale, Mass., May 25, 1841; attended Lincoln Acad., Hinsdale. Moved to North Adams, Mass., 1861; chief dep. collector internal revenue for 10th Mass. Dist., 1861-65; engaged in merc. bus.; selectman North Adams; commr. Berkshire County (Mass.), 1884-87, chmn., 1 year; mem. Mass. Exec. Council, 1890-91; mem. U.S. Ho. of Reps. (Republican) from Mass., 53d-55th congresses, 1893-97. Died North Adams, Aug. 14, 1897; buried Hinsdale Cemetery.

WRIGHT, Augustus Romaldus, congressman; b. Wrightsboro, Ga., June 16, 1813; attended Franklin Coll., U. Ga.; attended Litchfield (Conn.) Law Sch. Admitted to Ga. bar, 1835, began practice in Crawfordville; moved to Cassville, Ga., 1836; judge Superior Cts. of Cherokee Circuit, 1842-49; moved to Rome, Ga., 1855, practiced law; mem. U.S. Ho. of Reps. (Democrat) from Ga., 35th Congress, 1857-59; del. Ga., Confederate secession convs. (opposed secession); declined provisional governorship of Ga. offered by Pres. Lincoln; mem. Confederate Congress; organized Wright's Legion, 38th Ga. Inf. during Civil War; mem. Ga. Constl. Conv., 1877. Died "Glenwood" nr. Rome, Mar. 31, 1891; buried Myrtle Hill Cemetery, nr. Rome.

WRIGHT, Benjamin, canal engr.; b. Wethersfield, Conn., Oct. 10, 1770; s. Ebenezer and Grace (Butler) W.; m. Philomela Waterman, Sept. 27, 1798, 9 children including Benjamin H. Land surveyor Oneida and Oswego counties (N.Y.), 1792-96; active in promoting canal bldg. to facilitate transport of farm produce, 1792; elected to N.Y. State Legislature, circa 1797; reported on canal route from Rome on Mohawk to Waterford on Hudson for state canal commission, 1811; apptd. county judge, 1813; in charge of bldg. middle sect. of Erie Canal, 1816, later in charge of constrn. Eastern sect., chief engr., until 1827; cons. engr. on several canal projects; chief engr. Chesapeake & Ohio Canal, 1828-31, St. Lawrence Canal, 1833; street commr. N.Y.C., 1833; made surveys for road from Havana to interior of Cuba, 1835-36. Died N.Y.C., Aug. 24, 1842.

WRIGHT, Charles, botanist; b. Wethersfield, Conn., Oct. 29, 1811; s. James and Mary (Goodrich) W.; grad. Yale, 1835; never married. Taught sch., Miss., also East Tex., 1835-44; tchr. Rutersville (Tex.) Coll., 1845; accompanied battalion of U.S. troops from San Antonio to El Paso, Tex., summer 1849, collected plants and sent many specimens to Asa Gray at Harvard; botanist on U.S.-Mexican boundary survey, 1851-52; became botanist of N. Pacific Exploring and Surveying Expdn., 1852; made collections of plants at Cape of Good Hope, Hong Kong, Loo Choo Islands, Japan, 1853-56; conducted bot. explorations of Cuba, 1856-67; curator herbarium, Cambridge, Mass., 1868. Died Wethersfield, Aug. 11, 1885.

WRIGHT, Charles Barstow, railroad exec.; b. Bradford, Pa., Jan. 8, 1822; s. Rufus and Elizabeth Wright; m. 2d, Susan Townsend; 4 children. Commd. to investigate land holdings of group of Eastern capitalists nr. Chgo., 1843; co-founder bank, Erie, Pa., 1855; active in bldg. Phila. and Erie R.R.; formed syndicate to construct railroad to Oil City, Pa.; dir. N.P. Ry., 1870, v.p., 1873, pres., 1874-79, resigned, guided railroad through several financial crises, chmn. finance com., 1880-93, enabled company to build link between East and West portions of road, ret. from co., 1893; philanthropies included founding of Annie Wright Sem. for Young Ladies, Tacoma, Wash. Died Phila., Mar. 24, 1898.

WRIGHT, Charles Cushing, medallist; b. Damariscotta, Me., May 1, 1796; m. Lavinia Dorothy Simons; at least 1 son, Charles Washington. Worked for silversmith, Utica, N.Y., circa 1817; worked in Albany (N.Y.) and N.Y.C., later in Savannah (Ga.), Charleston (S.C.); moved to N.Y.C., 1823; best known as medallist; engraver with firms, Durand & Wright, 1826-27, Bale & Wright, 1829-33, Wright & Prentiss, 1835-38, all N.Y.C.; a founder N.A.D., also exhibitor; exhibited at Am. Art-Union. Died N.Y.C., June 7, 1854.

WRIGHT, Chauncey, philosopher; b. Northampton, Mass., Sept. 20, 1830; s. Ansel and Elizabeth Baleyn (or Bullen) W.; grad. Harvard, 1852; never married. A computer for American Ephemeris and Nautical Almanac, 1852; recording sec. Am. Acad. Arts and Scis., 1863-70; published 1st of series of philos. Essays in N. Am. Review, 1864; delivered course on principles of psychology at Harvard, 1870, instr. math. physics, 1874-75; naturalist, predecessor of William James and others in his instrumentalist concepts; one of first to introduce Brit. methods of empiricism in Am.; wrote article "Evolution of Self-Consciousness." Died Cambridge, Mass., Sept. 12, 1875.

WRIGHT, Daniel Boone, congressman; b. nr. Mt. Pleasant, Tenn., Feb. 17, 1812; grad. Cumberland U., Lebanon, Tenn., 1837; studied law. Admitted to the bar, 1840, began practice in Ashland, Miss.; moved to Salem (later Hudsonville), Miss., 1850, practiced law, engaged in farming; mem. U.S. Ho. of Reps. (Democrat) from Miss., 33d-34th congresses, 1853-57; apptd. lt. col. 34th Regt., Miss. Inf., Confederate Army during Civil War; wounded at Battle of Perryville, 1862, captured and sent to Camp Chase, O., exchanged, 1863; resigned commn., 1863; apptd. col. of cavalry, 1864; judge mil. cts. Gen. N. B. Forrest's Cavalry Div.; captured, 1865, surrendered at La Grange, Tenn., later paroled. Died Ashland, Miss., Dec. 27, 1887; buried McDonald Cemetery, nr. Ashland.

WRIGHT, Edwin Ruthvin Vincent, gov. N.J., congressman; b. Hoboken, N.J., Jan. 2, 1812; studied law. Engaged in journalism, 1835; editor Jersey Blue, Hoboken, 1836; admitted to N.J. bar, 1839, began practice in Jersey City; moved to Hudson City, N.J., practiced law; mem. N.J. Council, 1846; dist. atty. for Hudson County (N.J.), 1851-55; mayor of Hudson, 1855; mem. U.S. Ho. of Reps. (Democrat) from N.J., 39th Congress, 1865-67; elected gov. N.J., 1869. Died Jersey City, Jan. 21, 1871; buried Hoboken Cemetery, New Durham, N.J.

WRIGHT, Elizur, reformer, actuary, journalist; b. South Canaan, Conn., Feb. 12, 1804; s. Elizur Wright; grad. Yale, 1826; m. Susan Clark, Sept. 13, 1829, 18 children. Prof. mathematics Western Res. Coll., Hudson, O., 1829-33; became interested in abolition movement, 1832, apptd. sec. N.Y. Anti-Slavery Soc., 1833, corr. sec. Am. Anti-Slavery Soc., 1833; edited Quarterly Anti-Slavery Mag., 1835-37, Mass. Abolitionist, 1839; began newspaper Weekly Chronotype, Boston, 1846, opposed life ins. firms as well as slavery and tariff, sold paper to Free Soil Party paper Weekly Commonwealth, 1850, continued as editor until dismissed, 1852; began lobbying in Mass. Legislature for law to require all life ins. cos. operating in Mass. to maintain adequate reserves, 1853, law passed, 1858; apptd. Mass. commr. of ins., 1858-66, obtained passage of non-forfeiture law by which cos. were forbidden to appropriate reserves for their own use, 1861, instrumental in passage of legislation which compelled ins. cos. to pay policy holders cash value of lapsed policies, 1880; published his findings of fraud, theft, perjury and bribery in ins. co. practice especially in N.Y. Author Life Insurance Valuation Tables, 1853; Politics and Mysteries of Life Insurance, 1873. Died Medford, Mass., Nov. 21, 1885.

WRIGHT, Frances (Fanny), reformer; b. Dundee, Scotland, Sept. 6, 1795; d. James Wright; m. William Phiquepal D'Arusmont, July 22, 1831. Came to N.Y., 1818; wrote, published and produced play Altorf, N.Y.C., 1819; went to Eng., 1820; returned to Am., 1824, settled in Nashoba, Tenn., to experiment in emancipation of slaves; editor (with Robert Dale Owen) New Harmony Gazette, 1828; attacked religion, edn. and legal obligation of marriage in lectures; editor and publisher Free Inquirer, N.Y.C. 1829; went to Europe, 1830-35; lectured throughout U.S. on birth control, emancipation of women and slaves, 1835-50. Author: Views of Society and Manners in America, 1821; A Few Days in Athens, 1822; Course of Popular Lectures, 1829. Died Dec. 13, 1852.

WRIGHT, George Frederick, artist; b. Washington, Conn., Dec. 19, 1828; studied at N.A.D., circa 1848, also in Baden and Rome, circa 1857-60. Became profl. portrait painter, Wallingford, Conn.; custodian Wadsworth Athenaeum Gallery, Hartford, Conn.; went to Springfield (Ill.) to paint Abraham Lincoln, 1860; painted 2d portrait of Lincoln at Washington (D.C.), 1860; worked in Hartford and in South. Died Hartford, 1881.

WRIGHT, George Grover, senator, jurist; b. Bloomington, Ind., Mar. 24, 1820; s. John and Rachel (Seaman) W.; grad. Ind. U., 1839; studied law, Rockville, Ind.; m. Hannah Dibble, Oct. 19, 1843, 7 children. Admitted to Ia. bar, 1840; practiced in Keosauqua, Ia. Territory; pros. atty. Van Buren County (Ia.), 1846-48; mem. Ia. Senate, 1849-51; justice Ia. Supreme Ct., 1854-70, wrote many important opinions dealing with prohibition contracts and law of libel; pres. Ia. Agri. Soc., 1860-65; a founder Coll. of Law, U. Ia., 1865; prof. law dept. Ia. State u., 1865-71; lectr. on profl. ethics,1881-96. mem. U.S. Senate (Republican) from Ia., 1871 opposed liquor trade in territories, urged expansion of paper currency; pres.; Am. Bar Assn., 1887-88. Died Des Moines, Ia., Jan. 11, 1896; buried Woodland Cemetery, Des Moines.

WRIGHT, George Washington; congressman; b. Concord, Mass., June 4, 1816; attended pub. schs. Employed in bus. dept. Boston Courier, 1835; engaged in merc. bus., Boston; moved to San Francisco, 1849, engaged in merc. bus., banking, mining; a founder banking house Palmer, Cook & Co., San Francisco; mem. U.S. Ho. of Reps. (Independent) from Cal., 31st Congress, Sept. 11, 1850-51; joined Republican Party, supported John C. Frémont for U.S. Pres., 1856; moved to Washington, D.C.; built steam revenue vessel Commodore Perry, Buffalo N.Y., during Civil War; returned to Washington, served as atty. for Choctaw Indians; declined appointment as U.S. sec. of interior under Pres. Johnson; engaged in pvt. scientific work; ret., moved to Dorchester, Mass., 1880. Died Dorchester, Apr. 7, 1885; buried Sleepy Hollow Cemetery, Concord, Mass.

WRIGHT, Hendrick Bradley, congressman; b. Plymouth, Pa., Apr. 24, 1808; grad. Dickinson Coll., Carlisle, Pa., 1829; studied law. Admitted to Pa. bar, 1831, began practice in Wilkes-Barre; apptd. dist. atty. for Luzerne County, 1834; mem. Pa. Ho. of Reps., 1841-43, speaker, 1843; del. Democratic Nat. Conv., Balt., 1844, served as temporary and permanent chmn.; del. Dem. nat. convs., Balt., 1848, 52, 60, Cincinnati, 1856, N.Y.C., 1868, St. Louis, 1876; mem. U.S. Ho. of Reps. (Democrat) from Pa., 33d, 37th, 45th-46th congresses, 1853-55, July 4, 1861-63, 77-81. Died Wilkes-Barre, Sept. 2, 1881; buried Hollenback Cemetery, Wilkes-Barre.

WRIGHT, Henry Clarke, reformer; b. Sharon, Litchfield County, Conn., Aug. 29, 1797. Licensed to preach, 1823; settled in West Millbury, Mass., 1833; mem. New Eng. Anti-Slavery Soc., 1835. Author: Man-Killing by Individuals and Nations Wrong, 1841; A Kiss for a Blow, 1843; Human Life Illustrated, 1849; The Living Present and the Dead Past, 1865. Died Pawtucket, R.I., Aug. 16, 1870.

WRIGHT, Henry Harry, baseball player; b. Sheffield, Eng., Jan. 10, 1835; s. Samuel and Ann (Tone) W.; m. Mary Fraser, Sept. 10, 1868; m. 2d, Miss Mulford; m. 3d, 1st wife's sister; 8 children. Came to U.S., 1836; previously cricket player, began to play baseball with Knickerbocker Club team, N.Y.C., 1856; went to Cincinnati as instr. for Union Cricket Club, 1866; organized, captained Cincinnati Baseball Club, 1866; pitcher 2 seasons, later played center field; organized, captained, managed Cincinnati Red Stockings (1st profl. baseball team in U.S.), 1869-71, toured U.S. with team, 1869, 70, disbanded, 1871; toured England with baseball team, 1874; mgr. Boston team of Nat. League of Profl. Baseball Clubs, 1876-81 Providence team, 1882-83, Phila. team, 1884-93; apptd. chief of umpires of Nat. League, 1893-95. Died Atlantic City, N.J., Oct. 3, 1895; buried Bklyn.

WRIGHT, Horatio Governeur, army officer, engr.; b. Clinton, Conn., Mar. 5, 1820; s. Edward Wright; grad. U.S. Mil. Acad., 1841; m. Louise M. Bradford, Aug. 11, 1842, 2 children. Commd. 2d lt. Corps Engrs., U.S. Army, 1841, capt., 1855; asst. to chief engr., Washington, D.C., 1861, built defenses for Capitol; fought in Battle of Bull Run; chief engr. Port Royal expdn.; commd. brig. gen. U.S. Volunteers, 1861, maj. gen., 1864; chief engr. Dept. of Ohio, U.S. Army, 1862; fought in battles of Gettysburg, Mine Run, Wilderness; commanded VI Corps, U.S. Army, his troops were first to pierce Petersburg (Va.) defenses; commanded Dept. of Tex., 1865-66; returned to various constrn. assignments after Civil War; promoted brig. gen. U.S. Army, chief engrs., 1879; ret., 1884. Died Washington, July 2, 1899; buried Arlington (Va.) Nat. Cemetery.

WRIGHT, James Lendrew, labor leader; b. County Tyrone, Ireland, Apr. 6, 1816. Settled in Phila., 1827; owner clothing store, Frankford, Pa., 1847; mgr. large clothing store, Phila., 1854; joined Tailor's Benevolent Soc. of Phila., 1837; an organizer (with Uriah Smith Stephens) Garment Cutters' Assn., 1862, pres. 4 years; a founder, treas. Phila. Trades' Assembly, 1863; a founder (with Stephens, 5 others) Order of Knights of Labor, 1869, leading functionary for 20 years; chmn. pro tem Pitts. conv. which attempted to set up nat. labor orgns., 1876; attended Harrisburg Conv. of United Workingmen, 1877; Greenback-Labor candidate for state sec. of internal affairs Pa., 1878; leader Knights of Labor, 1879. Died Germantown, Pa., Aug. 3, 1893.

WRIGHT, John Crafts, congressman; b. Wethersfield, Conn., Aug. 17, 1783; studied law, Litchfield, Conn. Learned printer's trade; moved to Troy, N.Y., editory Troy Gazette; admitted to the bar, began practice in Steubenville, O., 1809; U.S. dist. atty., 1817; mem. U.S. Ho. of Reps. (Democrat) from Ohio, 18th-20th congresses, 1823-29; judge Ohio Supreme Ct., 1831-35; moved to Cincinnati, 1835, engaged in journalism; published Cincinnati Gazette, 13 years; dir. Cincinnati, Hamilton Dayton Ry. Co.; del., hon. pres. Washington (D.C.) Peace Conv., 1861. Died Washington, Feb. 13, 1861; buried Spring Grove Cemetery, Cincinnati.

WRIGHT, John Stephen, editor; b. Sheffield, Mass., July 16, 1815; s. John and Huldah (Dewey) W.; m. Catherine B. Turner, Sept. 1, 1846. Took census of Chgo., 1833; published 1 of earliest lithograph maps of Chgo., 1834; began real-estate bus., Chgo., 1834; built at personal expense 1st public sch. bldg. erected in Chgo., 1835; sec., gen. mgr. Union Agr. Soc., 1839; began publishing Union Agriculturist, 1839, merged with Western Prairie Farmer, 1841, changed name to Prarie Farmer, 1843, owner-editor, 1843-57; contbd. articles on Western products and advantages of Ill. and Chgo. to N.Y. Comml. Advertiser, 1845, also contbd. articles to N.Y. Evening Post, Am. R.R. Jour.; wrote series of articles advocating constrn. of railroads in West, 1847; worked for land grant to build railroad from Chgo. to Gulf of Mexico, 1848; interested in self-raking reaper invented by Jearum Atkins, manufactured Atkins Automaton, 1852-59; formed a land co., 1859. Author: Chicago, Past, Present and Future, 1868; Illinois to Massachusetts, Greeting!, 1866. Died Chgo., Sept. 26, 1874.

WRIGHT, Jonathan Jasper, jurist; b. Luzerne County, Pa., Feb. 11, 1840; attended Lancasterian U., Ithaca, N.Y. Mem. Am. Missionary Soc., sent to organize schools for Negroes in S.C., 1865; 1st Negro admitted to Pa. bar, 1866; legal adviser to refugees and freedmen, S.C., 1866-68; mem. S.C. Constl. Conv., 1868; mem. S.C. Senate from Beaufort, 1868; asso. justice S.C. Supreme Ct., 1870-77. Died Charleston, S.C., Feb. 18, 1885.

WRIGHT, Joseph, portrait painter; b. Bordentown, N.J., July 16, 1756; s. Joseph and Patience (Lovell) W.; studied painting with John Trumbull, under Benjamin West; m. Miss Vandervoort, 1787, 3 children. Settled in London, 1772; exhibited at Royal Acad., by 1780; painted portrait of Prince of Wales, 1782, later of George IV; painted portraits of fashionable ladies, under patronage of Benjamin Franklin, Paris, 1782; sailed for Am., 1782; painted Gen. and Mrs. George Washington, Phila., 1783, another Washington portrait, 1784; established himself in N.Y., 1787; apptd. by Washington 1st draftsman and die-sinker U.S. Mint, 1792, 1st U.S. coins and medals attributed to him; made dies for George Washington medal (after Houdon bust, medal voted by Congress to Maj. Henry Lee); painted portraits of Madison and family; his portrait of John Jay (1786) now in collections of N.Y. Hist. Soc. Died Phila., 1793.

WRIGHT, Joseph Albert, senator, gov. Ind., diplomat; b. Washington, Pa., Apr. 17, 1810; s. John and Rachel (Seaman) W.; attended Ind. State Sem. (now Ind. U.), Bloomington; m. Louisa Cook, 1831. Admitted to Ind. bar, 1829; mem. Ind. Ho. of Reps., 1833, 36, Ind. Senate, 1840; mem. U.S. Ho. of Reps. (Democrat) from Ind., attempted to raise standard of living of farmers; U.S. minister to Prussia (apptd. by Pres. Buchanan), 1857-61, 65-67, arranged for exchange of German and Am. seeds; mem. U.S. Senate from Ind., Feb. 24, 1862-Jan. 14, 1863; U.S. commr. to Hamburg (Germany) Exhbn., 1863. Died Berlin, Germany, May 11, 1867; buried N.Y.C.

WRIGHT, Joseph Jefferson Burr, physician, army officer; b. Wilkes-Barre, Pa., Apr. 27, 1801; A.B., Washington (Pa.) Coll., 1821; attended U. Pa. Sch. of Medicine, 1825-26; m. Eliza Jones; 3 children including Joseph P. Served as asst. surgeon U.S. Army, 1833-40, in Seminole War, 1840-41, 43; with 8th Inf. in occupation of Tex., 1846; served in battles of Palo Alto and Resaca de la Palma during Mexican War; in charge of hosp., Matamoras; wrote report on cholera epidemic published in So. Med. Reports, 1849; on field duty with troops in Kan., 1857, Utah expdn., 1858; served as med. dir. Dept. of Ohio on Gen. George B. McClellan's staff, Civil War; in battles of Rich Mountain, Carrick's Ford (W.Va.); surgeon Cavalry Recruiting Depot, Carlisle, Pa., 1862-76; brevetted col., 1864; promoted brig. gen., 1865; contbd. case reports to surg. vol. Medical and Surgical History of War of Rebellion, 6 vols., 1870-88. Died Carlisle, May 14, 1878.

WRIGHT, Myron Benjamin, congressman; b. Forest Lake, Pa., June 12, 1847; attended common schs. Taught sch.; clk. 1st Nat. Bank of Susquehanna (Pa.), 1865-66, elected asst. cashier, 1867, cashier, 1869; engaged in varous bus. enterprises; mem. U.S. Ho. of Reps. (Republican) from Pa., 51st-53d congresses, 1889-94. Died Trenton, Can., Nov. 13, 1894; buried Grand St. Cemetery, Susquehanna.

WRIGHT, Patience Lovell, sculptor; b. Bordentown, N.J., 1725; m. Joseph Wright, Mar. 20, 1748, 3 children including Phoebe, Joseph. Modeller in wax, went to London, Eng., 1772, opened exhbn. room on Cockspur Street; modeled bas-relief of Benjamin Franklin, busts of King George III, Queen Charlotte, Lord Chatham; called "The Promethean Modeller" in article in London Mag., 1775; believed to have sent Brit. mil. plans to Benjamin Franklin during Am. Revolution. Died London, Mar. 23, 1786.

WRIGHT, Robert, senator, gov. Md.; b. "Marborough," nr. Chestertown, Queen Annes County, Md. Nov. 20, 1752; s. Solomon and Mary (Tidmarsh) W.; attended Washington Coll., Chestertown; m. Sarah De Courcy; m. 2d, Miss Ringgold; 2 children. Admitted to Md. bar, 1773; served with Md. Minute Men against Loyalists, Eastern shore Va., 1776; capt. Md. Militia, 1779-84; mem. Md. Ho. of Dels. from Queen Annes County, 1776, 84, from Kent County, 1786; mem. Md. Senate, 1787; mem. U.S. Senate (Jeffersonian Democrat) from Md., 1801-06; gov. Md., 1806-09; clk. Queen Annes County, 1810; mem. U.S. Ho. of Reps. from Md., 11th-14th congresses, 1810-17 (mem. com. on judiciary, 14th Congress), 1821-23 (mem. com. on fgn. affairs); judge Dist. Ct. for lower Eastern shore Md., 1822-26. Died "Blakeford," Queen Annes County, Sept. 7, 1826; buried Cheston-on-Wye, Queen Annes County.

WRIGHT, Robert William, editor, satirist; b. Ludlow, Vt., Feb. 22, 1816; s. Stephen and Zibiah (Richardson) W.; grad. Yale, 1842; m. Laurine Louise Luke, Aug. 13, 1844; m. 2d, Sarah Louise Martyn, Oct. 14, 1852; 8 children. Admitted to Mass. bar, 1845; practiced law, Waukesha, Wis., 1845-55; successively editor various newspapers including Waterbury (Conn.) Jour., Hartford (Conn.) Daily Post, N.Y. Daily News, N.Y.C., 1856-77; asserted he had been 1st to record Comet of 1861. Author: Practical Legal Reforms, 1852; Ecclesiastical Councils Viewed from Celestial and Satanic Stand-Points (under pseudonym Quevedo Redivivus, Jr.), 1867; Life; Its True Genesis (best known work, anti-Darwinian study), 1880. Died Cleve., O., Jan. 9, 1885.

WRIGHT, Rufus, painter; b. 1832; student N.A.D., N.Y.C.; painted portraits of Civil War period statesmen; also known for genre subjects.

WRIGHT, Samuel Gardiner, congressman; born Wrightstown, N.J., Nov. 18, 1781. Engaged in merc. bus., Phila.; owned country place, nr. Imlaystown, N.J.; owner several iron furnaces in N.J. and Del. mem. U.S. Ho. of Reps. (Whig) from N.J., 29th Congress, 1845. Died nr. Imlaystown, July 30, 1845; buried East Branch Cemetery, nr. Imlaystown.

WRIGHT Silas, Jr., senator, gov. N.Y.; b. Amherst, Mass., May 24, 1795; s. Silas and Eleanor (Goodale) W.; grad. Middlebury (Vt.) Coll., 1815; studied law under Roger Skinner, Sandy Hill, N.Y.; m. Clarissa Moody, Sept. 11, 1833. Admitted to N.Y. bar, 1819, began practice law, Canton, N.Y.; mem. N.Y. State Senate, 1823-27, chmn. com. on canals; known as mem. "Albany Regency"; commd. brig. gen. N.Y. Militia, 1827; mem. U.S. Ho. of Reps. (Democrat) from N.Y., 20th Congress, 1827-Feb. 16, 1829, mem. com. on manufactures; comptroller State of N.Y., 1829-33; ardent supporter of Andrew Jackson, 1832; mem. U.S. Senate from N.Y., Jan. 1, 1833-Dec. 1, 1844, supported Martin Van Buren's policies, chmn. finance com., 1836-41, worked for tariff reduction and ind. treasury system; gov. N.Y., 1845-47, not re-elected because role in anti-rent riots alienated "Hunkers." Died Canton, Aug. 27, 1847; buried Old Canton Cemetery.

WRIGHT, Turbutt, Continental congressman; b. "White Marsh" nr. Chester Mills (now Centerville), Md., Feb. 5, 1741, engaged in farming; mem. Md. Gen. Assembly, 1773-74; a signer Assn. of Freemen of Md., 1775; mem. Md. Constl. Conv., 1776; apptd. mem. Council of Safety, 1777; commd. justice of Queen Annes County (Md.), 1779, register of wills, 1779-80; mem. Continental Congress from Md., 1781-82; subscribed to fund for establishment of Washington Coll., Chestertown, Md. Died "White Marsh" 1783; buried "White Marsh."

WRIGHT, William, journalist; b. Ohio, May 9, 1829; m., 1 child. Went to Ia., circa 1847, began to write for Graham's Mag. (a Phila. publ.); went West, 1857; wrote sketches signed Dan De Quille (thereafter generally known by that name); became city editor Daily Territorial Enterprise, Virginia City, Nev., 1861, close friend of Mark Twain who worked on same newspaper. Author: History of the Big Bonanza, 1877. Died West Lafayette, Ia., Mar. 16, 1898.

WRIGHT, William Bull, physician, poet; b. Orange County, N.Y., Sept. 20, 1840; grad. Coll. of N.J. (now Princeton), 1859; grad. N.Y. Coll. Surgeons and Physicians. Tchr. in Buffalo, 1859-62; served with 5th N.Y. Arty., 1862-65, brevetted maj., 1865; practiced medicine, Orange County, N.Y., 1871-78. Author: (collections of poems) Highland Rambles, 1868; The Brook and Other Poems, 1873. Died Atlanta, Ga., Mar. 29, 1880.

WURTS, John, congressman; b. Flanders, N.J., Aug. 13, 1792; grad. Princeton, 1813; studied law. Admitted to Pa. bar, 1816, began practice in Phila.; mem. Pa. Ho. of Reps. 1817, Pa. Senate, 1820; mem. U.S. Ho. of Reps. (Nat.-Republican) from Pa., 19th Congress, 1825-27; U.S. dist. atty., 1827-31; mem. Phila. City Council; pres. Del. Hudson Canal Co., 1831-58; went abroad for health reasons, 1859. Died Rome, Italy, Apr. 23, 1861; buried family cemetery, Pleasant Mills, N.J.

WÜRTTEMBERG, Friedrich Paul Wilhelm (Duke of Württemberg, Prince Paul), natural scientist; b. Germany, 1797; mil. edn. Abandoned mil. career to devote life to natural scis., 1817; made 1st of 5 trips to Am., traveling up Missouri River as guest of Am. Fur Co., 1822-24; pub. jour. of trip, Stuttgart, 1835; settled in Mergentheim, assembled charts, tables and sketches of his journeys; traveled in Am., circa 1850-58, made last trip, 1857-58. Died 1860.

WYANT, Alexander Helwig, landscape painter; b. Evans Creek, O., Jan. 11, 1836; s. Daniel and Hannah Wyant; studied art (with financial assistance of Nicholas Longworth) N.Y.C.; studied under Hans Gude in Germany, 1865, m. Arabella Locke, 1880, 1 child. Elected to Nat. Acad. of Design for picture The Upper Susquehanna, 1869; joined govt. expdn. to Ark., 1873, became ill, paralyzed on right side, had to paint with left hand; prin. works include Mohawk Valley, 1866, An Old Clearing, 1881 (both in Met. Mus., N.Y.C.); In the Still Forest, 1881 (now in Worcester Mus.). Died N.Y.C., Nov. 29, 1892.

WYATT, Sir Francis, colonial gov.; b. Boxley Abbey, Eng., 1588; s. George and Jane (Finch) W.; m. Margaret Sundys, 1618. Heir to family seat at Boxley Abbey; created knight, 1603; invested in Va. Co., London, Eng., 1620; gov. Va., 1620-26, 39-41, supported representative govt. in Va. Died Boxley Abbey, Aug. 1644; buried Boxley Abbey.

WYETH, John, editor; b. Cambridge, Mass., Mar. 31, 1770; s. Ebenezer and Mary (Winship) W.; m. Louisa Weiss, June 6, 1793; m. 2d, Lydia Allen, May 2, 1826; 13 children. Printer's apprentice in youth; supt. large printing establishment, Santo Domingo, 1791; co-owner (with John W. Allen) Harrisburg (Pa.) Advertiser, 1792-1827, editorially supported Federalist Party; 1st postmaster Harrisburg, 1793; established printing bus. and bookstore, circa 1798; a founder Harrisburg Acad. for Boys, 1809. Died Jan. 23, 1858.

WYETH, Nathaniel Jarvis, trader, explorer; b. Jan. 29, 1802; s. Jacob and Elizabeth (Jarvis) W.; m. Elizabeth Jarvis Stone, Jan. 29, 1824. Mgr. ice co. owned by Frederick Tudor, 1824; established important ice trade to West Indies; failed in attempt to exploit Columbia River and surrounding region for furs and fish; built Ft. William at mouth of Willamette River, Ore.; convoyed party of Jason Lee (who established mission leading to 1st Am. settlement of Ore.), 1834. Died Aug. 31, 1856.

WYLIE, Andrew, clergyman, coll. pres.; b. Washington, Pa., Apr. 12, 1789; s. Adam Wylie; grad. Jefferson Coll., Cannonsburg, Pa., 1810; D.D. (hon.) Union Coll., 1825; m. Margaret Ritchie, May 1813. Ordained to ministry Presbyn. Ch., 1812; pastor in Ohio, 1812, Miller's Run, Pa., 1813-16; prin., Jefferson Coll., 1814; became pres. Washington Coll., 1816; 1st pres. Indiana Coll. (now Ind. U.), Bloomington, 1828-51; ordained priest Episcopal Ch., 1842. Author: English Grammar, 1822; Uses of History, 1831; Eulogy of General Lafayette, 1834; Latin and Roman Classics, 1838. Died Bloomington, Nov. 11, 1851.

WYLIE, Robert, artist; b. Douglas, Isle of Man, 1839; attended École des Beaux-Arts, Paris, France, 1864; studied under Antoine-Louis Barye. Exhibited painting Reading the Letter from the Bridegroom, Paris Salon, 1869; exhibited Baz-Walen, demandeur en mariage dans la Basse-Bretagne, 1870, L'Accueil de l'Orphelin, Bretagne, 1873, Le Conteur de Légendes, 1878 (all at various salons); important works include Mendicants, Breton Group, Death of a Vendeau Chief, A Fortune-Teller of Brittany, 1872. Died France, Feb. 1877.

WYLIE, Samuel Brown, educator, clergyman; b. Moylarg, Ireland, May 21, 1773; s. Adam and Margaret (Brown) W.; grad. U. Glasgow (Scotland), 1797; D.D. (hon.), Dickinson Coll., 1816: m. Margaret Watson, Apr. 5, 1802, 7 children Fought for Irish independence, left Ireland, 1797, arrived in Phila., 1797; became instr. grammar sch. U. Pa., 1797; licensed to preach by Reformed Presbyn. Ch., 1799, ordained, 1800; del. to Presbyn. Chs. of Ireland and Scotland, 1802; prof. Presbyn. Sem., Phila., 1810-17; prof. Latin and Greek, U. Pa., 1828, vice provost, 1836-45; mem. Am. Philos. Soc., 1806. Author: The Two Sons of Oil, 1803; Memoir of Alexander McLeod, D.D., 1855. Died Oct. 13, 1852.

WYLLYS, George, colonial ofcl.; b. Hartford, Conn., Apr. 24, 1710; s. Hezekiah and Elizabeth (Hobart) W.; grad. Yale, 1729; m. Mary Woodbridge, 6 children. Sec. pro tem Colony of Conn., 1730-34, sec., 1734-96; town clk. Hartford, 1732-96; commd. capt. Conn. Militia, 1738, served as lt. col. in French and Indian War, 1757; unsympathetic with policy of separation from Eng., 1775-76. Died Hartford, Oct. 6, 1796.

WYMAN, Jefferies, physician, educator; b. Chelmsford, Mass., Aug. 11, 1814; s. Dr. Rufus and Ann (Morrill) W.; grad. Harvard, 1833; M.D., Mass. Gen. Hosp., 1837; m. Adeline Wheelwright, Dec. 19, 1850; m. 2d, Annie Williams Whitney, 1861; 3 children. Lectr., Lowell Inst., 1840; prof. anatomy and physiology, med. sch. Hampden Sydney Coll., Richmond, Va., 1843; prof. anatomy Harvard, 1847, curator dept. archeology, and ethnology, 1866; asso. (with brother Morrill Wyman, others) pvt. med. sch., Cambridge, Mass., 1857-66; first to scientifically explain structure of gorilla; pres. A.A.A.S., 1857, Boston Soc., 1856-70. Died White Mountains, Conn., Sept. 4, 1874.

WYMAN, Morrill, physician; b. Chelmsford, Mass., July 25, 1812; s. Rufus and Ann (Morrill) W.; grad. Harvard, 1833, M.D., 1837; m. Elizabeth Aspinwall Pulsifer, Aug. 14, 1839, 2 children including Morrill. Practiced medicine, Cambridge, Mass.; performed 2 successful operations in treatment of pleurisy (1st in U.S.) 1850; adjunct Hersey prof. theory and practice of medicine Harvard Med. Sch., 1853-56; organized (with 3 others) pvt. med. sch., Cambridge, 1857; U.S. insp. hosps. during Civil War; overseer Harvard, 1875-87; founder Cambridge Hosp., 1886. Author: A Practical Treatise on Ventilation, 1846; Autumnal Catarrh (Hay Fever), 1872. Died Jan. 30, 1903.

WYMAN, Robert Harris, naval officer; b. Portsmouth, N.H., July 12, 1822; s. Thomas White and Sarah (Harris) W.; studied Phila. Naval Sch., 1842; m. Emily Madeline Dallas, Sept. 27, 1847, 3 children. Apptd. midshipman U.S. Navy, 1837, assigned to steamer Independence, 1838; sailed in ship John Adams (commanded by his father) to East Indies, 1838-40; served under Commodore David Conner in Home Squadron in Mexican War; commanded expdn. up Rappahannock River, destroying Confederate property, 1862; took part in capture of Port Royal, S.C.; commanded gunboat Sonoma, 1863, captured Confederate ships Britannia and Lizzi; in charge of Hydrographic Office, Washington, D.C., 1871; commd. rear adm., 1878, in command of N.Am. Squadron. Author: Coasts of Chile, Bolivia and Peru, 1876; Navigation of Coasts and Islands in Mediterranean Sea, 1872. Died Washington, Dec. 2, 1882.

WYMAN, Seth, burglar; b. Goffstown, N.H., Mar. 4, 1784; s. Seth and Sarah (Atwood) W.; m. Welthy (Loomis) Chandler, Dec. 18, 1808, 6 children. Indulged in theft from youth (1st confession of guilt not obtained until circa 1804); committed twice to Amherst County (Mass.) Jail; convicted of larceny, Augusta, Mass. (now Me.), 1817, sentenced to Mass. State Prison, Charlestown, for 3 years, pardoned, 1818; served 3 years in N.H. State Prison for stealing cloth, Concord, 1820-23. Author: The Life and Adventures of Seth Wyman, Embodying the Principal Events of a Life Spent in Robbery, Theft, Gambling . . . , 1843. Died Goffstown, Apr. 2, 1843.

WYNKOOP, Henry, congressman; b. Northampton Twp., Pa., Mar. 2, 1737. Mem. Pa. Assembly, 1760-61; asso. justice Bucks County (Pa.) Cts., 1764-77, pres. judge, 1777-89; mem. com. of observation, 1774; del. Pa. provincial confs., 1774, 75; maj. Bucks County Asso. Battalions; mem. Gen. Com. of Safety, 1776-77; mem. Continental Congress from Pa., 1779-83; justice Pa. High Ct. Errors and Appeals, 1783-89; mem. U.S. Ho. of Reps. from Pa., 1st Congress, 1789-91; asso. justice Bucks County, until 1816. Died Bucks County, Mar. 25, 1816; buried Low Dutch Reformed Ch. Graveyard, Richboro, Pa.

WYNNS, Thomas, congressman; b. nr. Barfields, N.C., 1764; ed. in England. Captured at sea on ship Fair American, 1780, taken to London; returned to N.C., engaged in planting, Hertford County; an original trustee U. N.C.; mem. N.C. Ho. of Commons, 1787; del. N.C. Conv. to ratify U.S. Constn., 1788-89; mem. N.C. Senate, 1790-1802, 07-17; Federalist presdl. elector, 1800, 08; mem. U.S. Ho. of Reps. (Federalist) from N.C., 7th-9th congresses, Dec. 7, 1802-07; mem. N.C. Exec. Council, 1818-24; served as brig. gen. N.C. Militia. Died nr. Winton, N.C., June 3, 1825; buried Maneys Cemetery, nr. Maneys Ferry, N.C.

WYTHE, George, jurist; b. Elizabeth City County, Va., 1726; s. Thomas and Margaret (Walker) W.; attended Coll. William and Mary; studied law under Stephen Dewey, Prince George County, Va.; m. Ann Lewis, Dec. 1747; m. 2d, Elizabeth Taliaferro, 1755; 1 child. Admitted to Va. bar, 1746; practiced law (with John Lewis) Spotsylvania County, Va.; atty. gen. Va. Colony (in absence of Peyton Randolph), 1754; mem. Va. Ho. of Burgesses, 1754-55, 58-68, clk., 1769-75; mayor Williamsburg (Va.), 1768; mem. Continental Congress, 1775-76; signed Declaration of Independence, 1776; revised laws of Va. (with Edmund Pendleton and Thomas Jefferson), 1779; speaker Va. Ho. of Dels., 1777; judge Va. High Ct. of Chancery, 1778; prof. law and police (1st chair of law in Am.), Coll. William and Mary, 1779, also mem. bd. visitors; ex-officio mem. Va. Supreme Ct. Appeals, delivered opinion in Commonwealth vs. Caton, 1782; mem. Va. Conv. to ratify U.S. Constn., 1788; founded small law sch., 1790; emancipated his Negro servants in his will; poisoned (along with a servant) by grand-nephew George Wythe Sweeney to gain his inheritance; lived long enough to disinherit grandnephew. Author: Decisions of Cases in Virginia, 1795. Died Richmond, Va., June 8, 1806; buried St. John's Churchyard, Richmond.

X

XÁNTUS, János, ornithologist; b. Csokonya, Hungary, Oct. 5, 1825. Admitted to bar, Pest, Hungary, 1857; served in Hungarian War of Independence, 1848, captured by Austrians, 1849, escaped, 1850; came to U.S., 1851; topographer on Pacific R.R. expdn., 1852; mem. U.S. survey expdn. to find most feasible railroad route from Mississippi River to Pacific Ocean, 1855-57, collected bird specimens for Smithsonian Instn., discovered several new species; mem. U.S. expdn. to make meteorol. observation of Paciifc Ocean, 1861, credited with discovering 89 islands and sand banks; his descriptions of newly-discovered Am. birds published in Vols. X-XII of Proceedings of Acad. of Natural Scis. Phila., 1859-61; apptd. U.S. consul to Manzanillo, Mexico, 1861; resumed permanent residence in Hungary, 1864; keeper of ethnographical div. Nat. Museum, Budapest, Hungary, until 1894. Author: Levelei Ejszakameukából (account of his travels), 1858; Utazás Kalifornia déli Részeibeu (dealt with So. Cal.). Died Budapest, Dec. 13, 1894.

Y

YALE, Elihu, colonial gov.; b. Boston, Apr. 5, 1649; s. David and Ursula Yale; m. Catherine Hynmers, Nov. 4, 1680, 3 daus. Apptd. clk. East India Co., 1671, became factor and bookkeeper, Madras, India; pres., gov. Ft. St. George, Madras, 1687-92, built Ft. St. David, Cuddalore, Madras, did much to consolidate Brit. civil power in India, also acquired large personal fortune; high sheriff Denbighshire, Eng., 1704; a well known philanthropist; donated books to Collegiate Sch. (now Yale) Saybrook, Conn., 1714; asked by Cotton Mather for further aid when new coll. bldg. was erected, New Haven, Conn., 1718, sent books and goods valued at 800 pounds, Yale U. named for him. 1718. Died Eng., July 8, 1721.

YALE, Linus, lock mfr.; b. Salisbury, N.Y., Apr. 4, 1821; s. Linus and Chlotilda (Hopson) Y.; m. Catherine Brooks, Sept. 14, 1844, 3 children. Entered lock mfg. bus., Shelburne Falls, Mass., 1851; introduced Monitor Bank Lock (1st combination bank lock), 1862, became consultant on bank locks; invented Cylinder Lock based on pin-tumbler mechanism (later adopted generally throughout U.S.); patented pin-tumbler lock, 1861, 65; partner (with Henry R. Towne) Yale Lock Mfg. Co., Stamford, Conn., 1868. Died N.Y.C., Dec. 25, 1868.

YANCEY, Bartlett, congressman; b. nr. Yanceyville, N.C., Feb. 19, 1785; attended U. N.C., 1804-06; studied law. Admitted to N.C. bar, 1807, practiced law; mem. U.S. Ho. of Reps. from N.C., 13th-14th congresses, 1813-17; mem. N.C. Senate, presiding officer, 1817-27; declined appointment by Pres. John Quincy Adams as U.S. minister to Peru, 1826; declined appointment as judge N.C. Supreme Ct. Died nr. Yanceyville, Aug. 30, 1828; buried family cemetery, nr. Yanceyville.

YANCEY, Joel, congressman; b. Albemarle County, Va., Oct. 21, 1773. Mem. Ky. Ho. of Reps., 1809-11, Ky. Senate, 1816-20, 24-27; mem. U.S. Ho. of Reps. (Democrat) from Ky., 20th-21st congresses, 1827-31, unsuccessful candidate for reelection, 1830. Died Barren County, Ky., Apr. 1838; buried Barren County.

YANCEY, William Lowndes, congressman, secessionist; b. Warren County, Ga., Aug. 10, 1814; s. Benjamin Cudworth and Caroline (Bird) Y.; attended Williams Coll., 1830-33; m. Sarah Caroline Earle, Aug. 13, 1835, 5 children. Unionist editor of Greenville (S.C.) Mountaineer; moved to Dallas County, Ala., 1837; became owner Wetumpka Coml. Advertiser, 1839, also owner Wetumpka Argus; practiced law, Ala.; became mem. lower ho. Ala. Legislature, 1841, upper ho., 1843, advocated white population as basis of representation; mem. U.S. Ho. of Reps. from Ala., 28th-29th congresses, 1844-Sept. 1, 1846 (resigned); wrote Ala. Platform for Democratic Party Conv., Balt., 1848 (designed to uphold states rights vs. fed. govt.; rejected); a leader in forming So. right assns. (which transcended party lines, exerted pressure on candidates of each party) in all parts of South; founded League of United Southerners, 1858; as a leading lawyer and orator commanded attention of Southerners in hundreds of speeches stressing that South could not remain in Union if its constl. rights were violated; organized Constl. Dem. Party, nominating Breckenridge for Pres. U.S. (following withdrawal of So. dels. from Nat. Dem. Conv.), 1860; personally wrote out ordinance of secession of Ala. Conv. of 1861; Confederate commr. to Eng. and France, 1861-62; mem. Confederate Senate, 1862-63. Died Montgomery, Ala., July 27, 1863; buried Oakwood Cemetery, Montgomery.

YANDELL, David Wendel, physician; b. Murfreesboro, Tenn., Sept. 4, 1826; s. Lunsford Pitts and Susan Juliet (Wendel) Y.; attended Centre Coll., Danbury, Ky.; M.D., U. Louisville (Ky.), 1846; m. Frances Jane Crutcher, 1851, 4 children. Mem. staffs hosps., London (Eng.), Dublin (Ireland), Paris (France), wrote 2 series of letters for publ.; apptd. instr. anatomy U. Louisville, 1848, later prof. clin. medicine, prof. medicine, 1867-68, apptd. prof. clin. surgery, 1869; founder Stokes Dispensary, circa 1853, established classes in clin. medicine; served as med. officer on staff Gen. Albert Sidney Johnston, Dept. of West, Confederate Army, 1861-65; v.p. A.M.A., 1865, pres., 1871; established (with Theopilus Parrun) Am. Practitioner, 1870, merged with Med. News, 1886, editor, 1870-98; pres. Am. Surg. Assn., 1889; fellow Phila. Coll. Medicine; surgeon gen. Ky. Militia, 1887. Died Louisville, May 2, 1898.

YANDELL, Lunsford Pitts, physician, paleontologist; b. nr. Hartsville, Tenn., July 4, 1805; s. Dr. Wilson and Elizabeth (Pitts) Y.; studied medicine under his father; attended Transylvania U., Lexington, Ky., 1822-23; grad. U. Md., Balt., 1825; m. Susan Juliet Wendal, Oct. 1825; m. 2d, Eliza Bland, Aug. 1861; 4 children. Practiced medicine, Murfreesboro, Tenn., 1826; moved to Nashville, Tenn., 1830; prof. chemistry and pharmacy Transylvania U., 1831-37; edited Transylvania Jour. of Medicine and Asso. Scis., Lexington, 1832-36; an organizer Louisville (Ky.) Med. Inst., 1837, prof. chemistry and materia medica, 1837-59, prof. physiology, after 1849; co-editor Western Jour. of Medicine and Surgery, 1840-55; taught in med. sch. Memphis, Tenn. until Civil War; joined Confederate Army as hosp. surgeon, 1861; entered ministry Presbyn. Ch., 1862, ordained pastor, Dancyville, Tenn., 1864, resigned, 1867; returned to med. practice, Louisville, 1867-78. Author: (with Dr. B. F. Shumard) Contributions to the Geology of Kentucky, 1847; author many articles in various periodicals concerned with medicine, geology, local history, education, and religion. Died Louisville, Feb. 4, 1878.

YATES, Abraham (also known as Abraham Yates, Jr.), Continental congressman; b. Albany, N.Y., Aug. 1724; s. Christoffel and Catelynte (Winne) Y.; m. Antje De Ridder, 4 children. Mem. Albany Common Council, 1754-73; sheriff Albany County, 1755-59; associator, mem., chmn. Albany Com. of Corr., 1774-76; mem. all N.Y. provincial congresses and convs. of 1775-77, pres. pro tem, 1775, 76; chmn. com. of conv. which drafted 1st N.Y. State Constn.; mem. Council of Appointment, 1777; mem. 1st, 2d N.Y. councils of safety, 1777-78; mem. N.Y. State Senate, 1778-90; receiver of Albany, 1778, 79; ardent anti-federalist, 1780's; wrote frequently (under name Rough Hewer and Rough Hewer, Jr.) in defense of sovereignty of his state and in opposition to congressional aggrandizement; 1st postmaster Albany, 1783; mem. Continental Congress (anti-federalist), 1787-88; mayor Albany, 1790-96; presdl. elector, 1792. Died Albany. June 30, 1796; buried Albany Rural Cemetery.

YATES, John Barentse, congressman; b. Schenectady, N.Y., Feb. 1, 1784; grad. Union Coll., Schenectady, 1802; studied law. Admitted to N.Y. bar, 1805, began practice in Schenectady; served on No. frontier during War of 1812, later apptd. a.d.c. to Gov. Daniel D. Tompkins; mem. U.S. Ho. of Reps. (Democrat) from N.Y., 14th Congress, 1815-17; aided in constrn. of Welland Canal; founder Yates Poly. Inst., 1825; moved to Chittenango, N.Y., 1816; judge Madison County (N.Y.), 1835-36; mem. N.Y. State Assembly, 1836. Died Chittenango, July 10, 1836; buried Walnut Grove Cemetery, nr. Chittenango.

YATES, John Van Ness, state ofcl.; b. Albany, N.Y., Dec. 18, 1779; s. Robert and Jannetje (Van Ness) Y.; m. Eliza Ross Cunningham, June 7, 1806, several children. Practiced law, Albany, N.Y.; mem. com. named by Albany Common Council to request N.Y. Legislature to locate construct 1st state capitol in Albany, 1797; apptd. capt. light inf. co. Albany Regt., N.Y. Militia, 1806; master in chancery, N.Y., 1808; recorder City of Albany, 1808-09; mem. N.Y. Ho. of Reps., 1819; sec. of state N.Y., 1818-26. Author: Select Cases Adjudged in the Courts of the State of New York, 1811; Collection of Pleadings and Practical Precedents with Notes Thereon, 1837. Died Albany, Jan. 10, 1839.

YATES, Matthew Tyson, missionary; b. Wake County, N.C., Jan. 8, 1819; s. William and Delilah Yates; grad. Wake Forest Coll., 1846; m. Eliza E. Moring, Sept. 27, 1846. Ordained to ministry Bapt. Ch., 1846; apptd. to mission in China by Fgn. Mission Bd. of So. Baptist Conv.; arrived in Shanghai (China), 1847; built substantial church largely from own funds (because of lack of support after 1861); founded Bapt. missions and opened number of out-stations in cities of Kiangsu Province; U.S. vice consul and interpreter in Shanghai, 1873; Author: Ancestral Worship and Fung Shuy, 1867; The Tai Ping Rebellion, 1876; translated New Testament into Shanghai vernacular. Died Shanghai, Mar. 17, 1888.

YATES, Peter Waldron, Continental congressman; b. Albany, N.Y., Aug. 23 1747; studied law. Admitted to N.Y. bar, began practice in Albany; mem. Com. of Correspondence, 1775, reelected but declined to serve; regent U. State of N.Y., 1784; mem. N.Y. State Assembly, 1784-85; mem. Continental Congress from N.Y., 1785-87; resumed law practice. Died Caughnawaga, N.Y., Mar. 9, 1826.

YATES, Richard, senator, gov. Ill.; b. Warsaw, Ky., Jan. 18, 1815; s. Henry and Millicent (Yates) Y.; grad. Ill. Coll., Jacksonville, 1835; studied law Transylvania U., Lexington, Ky.; m. Catherine Geers, July 11, 1839, at least 5 children including Richard. Admitted to Ill. bar, 1837; practiced in Jacksonville; mem. Ill. Legislature, 1842-46, 48-50; mem. U.S. Ho. of Reps. (Whig) from Ill., 32d-33d congresses, 1851-55, opposed Kan.-Neb. Bill; del. to Republican nat. convs. which nominated Abraham Lincoln, 1860, Ulysses S. Grant, 1868; gov. Ill., 1861-65, gave Grant his 1st Civil War commn. as col. 21st Regt., Ill. Volunteers, 1861, fought Democratic majority in state legislature opposing conduct of war; mem. U.S. Senate from Ill., 1865-71, favored vindictive measures against South. Died St. Louis, Nov. 27, 1873; buried Jacksonville.

YATES, Robert, jurist; b. Schenectady, N.Y., Jan. 27, 1738; s. Joseph and Maria (Dunbar) Y.; studied law with William Livingston; m. Jannetje Van Ness, Mar. 5, 1765, 6 children including John Van Ness. Admitted to N.Y. bar, 1760; mem. bd. aldermen N.Y.C., 1771-75; radical Whig mem. Albany (N.Y.) Com. of Safety; mem. 4 N.Y. provincial congresses and convs. from Albany County, 1775-78; assigned to secret com. to obstruct channel of Hudson River, 1776-77; mem. com. of 13 which drafted 1st N.Y. Constn.; justice N.Y. Supreme Ct., 1777-90, chief justice, 1790-98; apptd. mem. commn. which settled N.Y.-Vt. boundary dispute, 1780, Mass.-N.Y. boundary dispute, 1786; leader Antifederalists, circa 1780-85; apptd. to represent N.Y. at U.S. Constl. Conv., Phila., 1787; attacked U.S. Constn. in series of letters (signed Brutus, later signed Sydney) in N.Y Journal, 1787, 88; commr. for settling title to lands in Onondaga County (N.Y.), 1800; collected papers published as Political Papers Addressed to the Advocates for a Congressional Revue, 1786, Secret Proceedings and Debates of the Convention Assembled . . . for the Purpose of forming the Constitution of the United States, 1821. Died Albany, Sept. 9, 1801.

YEAGER, Joseph, engraver, publisher, railroad exec.; b. circa 1792. Engraved books for William Charles, Phila., 1809-24; signed engravings include: The Great Bend of the Susquehanna River in Susquehanna County, Pennsylvania, Symptoms of Restiveness, The Death of Addison; engraved title page of Life of Washington (John Marshall), circa 1822; did unsigned work for other publishers; entered partnership with William H. Morgan (a carver and gilder), published toy books, stock included about 60 titles; pres. Harrisburg & Lancaster R.R. Co.; 1848; mem. bd. controllers 4th Sch. Sect. of Phila. Died Phila., June 9, 1859; buried Laurel Hill Cemetery, Phila.

YEAMANS, Sir John, colonial gov.; b. Bristol, Eng., circa 1611; s. John Yeamans; m. Mrs. Berringer, 8 children including Maj. William. Advanced through grades to col. Royalist Army; emigrated to Barbados, West Indies, 1650; created baronet, 1665; commd. gov. Carolina, 1665, established colony at Cape Fear (now in S.C.), abandoned colony, 1667, returned to Barbados; apptd. William Sayle gov. when 2d expdn. was attempted by Joseph West; built house in Carolina, introduced 1st Negro slaves to Carolina, 1671; claimed and received governorship, 1672; founded permanent settlement on Ashley Point, 1672, laid out site for Charles Town (now Charleston, S.C.); his commn. revoked by proprs. because of lack of interest in colony, 1674. Died probably in Carolina (now S.C.), circa Aug. 1675.

YEARDLEY, Sir George, colonial gov.; b. circa 1587; s. Ralph and Rhoda (Marston) Y.; m. Temperance Flowerdieu, children—Argall, Francis, Elizabeth. Sailed for Va. with Sir Thomas Gates, 1609, shipwrecked in Bermuda, did not arrive until 1610; acting gov. Va., 1616-17, gov., 1618-21, 26-27; summoned and presided over 1st rep. assembly in Am. colonies, Jamestown, Va., 1619; mem. Va. Colonial Council; returned to Eng. with petitions for needs of colonists, 1625. Died Jamestown, Nov. 10, 1627.

YEARDON, Richard, editor, state legislator; b. Charleston, S.C., Oct. 23, 1802; s. Richard Adams and Mary (You) Y.; grad. S.C. Coll., 1820; m. Mary Videau Marion, Dec. 23, 1829, 1 child. Admitted to S.C. bar, 1824; wrote articles supporting Unionist policy during nullification controversy for City Gazette, Charleston, 1831; editor Charleston Daily Courier, 1832-44; ardent Whig, opponent of John C. Calhoun; mem. S.C. Ho. of Reps., 1856-60, 62-64; supported conservative policies of Jefferson Davis during Civil War; originated ordinance establishing Charleston High Sch. Died Apr. 25, 1870.

YEATES, Jasper, jurist; b. Phila., Apr. 17, 1745; s. John and Elizabeth (Sidebottom) Y.; grad. Coll. of Phila. (now U. Pa.), 1761; m. Sarah Burd, Dec. 30, 1767, at least 4 children. Admitted to Pa. bar, 1765; chmn. Lancaster County (Pa.) Com. of Correspondence, 1775; favored reconciliation with Eng. until outbreak of Am. Revolution; mem. commn. apptd. by Continental Congress to negotiate treaty with Indians at Ft. Pitt, circa 1776; mem. Pa. Constl. Conv., 1787; asso. justice Pa. Supreme Ct., 1791-1817; mem. commn. apptd. by Pres. Washington to treat with inhabitants of Western Pa. who participated in Whiskey Rebellion, 1794. Died Lancaster, Pa., Mar. 14, 1817; buried Churchyard of St. James Episcopal Ch., Lancaster.

YEATES, Jesse Johnson, congressman; b. nr. Murfreesboro, N.C., May 29, 1829; attended Emory and Henry Coll.; studied law. Admitted to N.C. bar, 1855, began practice in Murfreesboro; pros. atty. Hertford County (N.C.), 1855-60; mem. N.C. Ho. of Commons, 1860-62; solicitor 1st N.C. Jud. Dist., 1860-66; served as capt. and maj. 31st N.C. Inf., Confederate Army during Civil War; mem. N.C. Gov's Council; del. N.C. Democratic Conv., 1871; mem. N.C. Constl. Conv., 1871; mem. U.S. Ho. of Reps. (Democrat) from N.C., 44th-45th, 46th congresses, 1875-79, Jan. 29-Mar. 3, 1881; resumed law practice, Washington, D.C. Died Washington, Sept. 5, 1892; buried Glenwood Cemetery, Washington.

YELL, Archibald, gov. Ark., congressman; b. N.C., Aug. 1797; studied law; m. 2d, Nancy; m. 3d, Marie; 5 children. Served in Creek campaign and War of 1812 under Gen. Andrew Jackson; participated in Battle of New Orleans; served in Seminole War in Fla.; admitted to Tenn. bar; mem. Tenn. Legislature from Bedford County; in charge of U.S. Land Office, Little Rock, Ark., 1831; territorial judge Ark. (apptd. by Pres. Jackson), 1832-35; mem. U.S. Ho. of Reps. from Ark., 24th-25th, 29th congresses, Aug. 1, 1836-39, 1845-July 1, 1846; gov. Ark., 1840-44; served as col. 1st Regt., Ark. Volunteer Cavalry during Mexican War. Killed at Battle of Buena Vista (Mexico), Feb. 23, 1847; buried Fayetteville (Ark.) Cemetery.

YEOMANS, John William, clergyman, coll. pres.; b. Hinsdale, Mass., Jan. 7, 1800; grad. Williams Coll., 1824; attended Andover Theol. Sem., 1824-26; m. Laetitia Synder, 1828, 5 children. Tutor, Williams Coll., 1826-27; gathered a congregation in North Adams (Mass.) which became its 1st Congregational Ch., pastor, 1828-32; ordained to ministry Presbyn. Ch., 1828; pastor 1st Congregational Ch., Pittsfield, Mass., 1832-34, 1st Presbyn. Ch., Trenton, N.J., 1834-41; pres. Lafayette Coll., Easton, Pa., 1841-44; pastor Mahoning Presbyn. Ch., Danville, Pa., 1845-63; chosen moderator Gen. Assembly of Old Sch. Presbyn. Ch., 1860; contbr. articles to Bibl. Repertory and Princeton Review. Died June 22, 1863.

YERGER, William, lawyer; b. Lebanon, Tenn., Nov. 22, 1816; s. Edwin Michael and Margaret (Shall) Y.; grad. U. Nashville, 1833; m. Malvina Hogan Rucks, May 23, 1837, 12 children including Mrs. Florence Yerger Guilbert. Admitted to Tenn. bar; asso. justice Miss. Supreme Ct., 1851-53; mem. Miss. Legislature, circa 1861-65; one of 2 reps. sent to Pres. Andrew Johnson to discuss terms of Miss. reentry to Union; mem. Miss. Constl. Conv., 1865. Died June 7, 1872.

YOAKUM, Henderson, army officer; b. Powell's Valley, Tenn., Sept. 6, 1810; s. George and Cally (Maddy) Y.; grad. U.S. Mil. Acad., 1832; m. Eveline Conner, Feb. 13, 1833. Brevetted 2d lt., 3d Arty., U.S. Army, 1832; commd. capt. Murphreesboro Sentinels, co. of Tenn. Mounted Militia, circa 1833; served as col. regt. Tenn. Inf. in Cherokee War, 1838; mem. Tenn. Senate, 1839-45; admitted to Republic of Tex. bar, 1845; served with regt. of Tex. Mounted Rifles during Mexican War, 1845-46, 1st lt. at Battle of Monterey; county in West Tex. named in his honor, 1876. Author: History of Texas from Its First Settlement in 1685 to Its Annexation to the United States in 1846 (1st history of Tex.), 1855. Died Houston, Tex., Nov. 30, 1856.

YOCUM, Seth Hartman, congressman; b. Catawissa Pa., Aug. 2, 1834; attended rural schs.; grad. Dickinson Coll., Carlisle, Pa., 1860; studied law. Learned printer's trade, Phila., 1850; taught sch.; enlisted as pvt. Union Army during Civil War, promoted 1st lt. 5th Pa. Cavalry; admitted to Schuylkill County (Pa.) bar, 1865, began practice in Ashland, Pa.; moved to Bellefonte, Pa., 1873, practiced law; dist. atty. Center County (Pa.), 1875-79; mem. U.S. Ho. of Reps. (Republican) from Pa., 46th Congress, 1879-81; moved to Johnson City, Tenn., engaged in tanning bus.; mayor of Johnson City, 1885; moved to Pasadena, Cal., engaged in orange growing. Died Santa Monica, Cal., Apr. 19, 1895; buried Mountain View Cemetery, Pasadena.

YORKE, Thomas Jones, congressman, railroad exec.; b. Hancocks Bridge, N.J., Mar. 25, 1801; attended Salem Acad. Served as scout for U.S. Army during War of 1812; engaged in merc. bus., Salem; county collector Salem County, (N.J.), 1830; judge Salem County Ct. of Common Pleas, 1833, 34, 45-54; served as presiding judge; mem. N.J. Gen. Assembly, 1835; mem. U.S. Ho. of Reps. (Whig) from N.J., 25th, 27th congresses, 1837-39, 41-43; dir. West Jersey R.R. Co., sec. and treas., 1853, pres., 1866-75; pres. Cape May & Millville R.R. Co.; dir. Swedesborough R.R. Co., Salem R.R. Co., Camden & Phila. Ferry Co., West Jersey Marl & Transp. Co. Died Salem, Apr. 4, 1882; buried St. John's Episcopal Cemetery, Salem.

YOST, Jacob Senewell, congressman; b. Pottsgrove Twp., Pa., July 29, 1801; attended 4th Street Acad., Phila. Engaged in farming; publisher and editor La Fayette (Pa.) Aurora; mem. Pa. Ho. of Reps., 1836-39; mem. U.S. Ho. of Reps. (Democrat) from Pa., 28th-29th congresses, 1843-47; resumed farming, nr. Pottstown, Pa.; U.S. marshal for Eastern Pa., Phila., 1857-60. Died Pottstown, Mar. 7, 1872; buried Edgewood Cemetery, Pottstown.

YOU, Dominique, buccaneer; b. St. Jean d'Angely, France, circa 1772. Known as Capt. Dominique, joined Jean Laffite's pirate colony at Barataria, 1810, became a leader under Laffite, engaged in raids on many Spanish vessels in Gulf of Mexico; mem. Am. forces protecting New Orleans against British, 1815; served as officer in Andrew Jackson's arty. in battles of Jan. 1, 8 and 21, 1815; pardoned by Pres. Madison for earlier career, settled in New Orleans, 1817; active in plot to bring Napoleon to New Orleans from imprisonment on St. Helena, circa 1820. Died Nov. 14, 1830; buried St. Louis Cathedral, New Orleans.

YOUMANS, Edward Livingston, scientist, author; b. Caeymans, N.Y., Jan. 3, 1821; s. Vincent and Catherine (Scofield) Y.; M.D., U. Vt., circa 1851; m. Catherine (Newton) Lee, 1861. More than half blind most of life, aided by his sister, Eliza Ann; popular lectr. on science, 1851-68; became disciple of Herbert Spencer after reading his Principles of Psychology, 1856; called apostle of evolution; established Popular Science Monthly (later Scientific Monthly), N.Y.C., 1872. Author: A Class-book of Chemistry (became standard text), 1851; Hand-Book of Household Science, 1857. Editor: The Culture Demanded by Modern Life, 1867, Correlation and Conservation of Forces, 1864 (both collections of papers); The International Scientific Series, introduced with publ. of Forms of

Water (Tyndall), 1872. Died N.Y.C., Jan. 18, 1887.

YOUMANS, William Jay, physician, editor; b. Milton, N.Y., Oct. 14, 1838; s. Vincent and Catherine (Scofield) Y.; student Yale, 1860-61; M.D., N.Y.U., 1865; studied under Thomas Huxley, London, Eng.; m. Celia Greene, Aug. 2, 1866, 4 children. Began practice of medicine, Winona, Minn.; edited Thomas Huxley's The Elements of Physiology and Hygiene: A Textbook for Educational Institutions, 1868; editor (with brother) Popular Science Monthly, N.Y.C., circa, 1872, sole editor, 1887-90; contbr. to Popular Science Monthly, Appleton's Annual Cyclopedia. Died Mt. Vernon, N.Y., Apr. 10, 1901.

YOUNG, Aaron, botanist, diplomat; b. Wiscasset, Me., Dec. 19, 1819; s. Aaron and Mary (Colburn) Y.; attended Bowdoin Coll., 1840-41, Jefferson Med. Coll., Phila., 1842-43. Asst. to Prof. Parker Cleaveland in natural history dept. Bowdoin Coll., 1840-41; sec. Bangor Natural History Soc., 1840's; state botanist Me., 1847-49, explored Mt. Kathadin and Castine Bay, published report on 1st surveys of Mt. Katahdin in Me. Farmer, Mar.-May, 1848; practiced medicine specializing in ear surgery, Auburn, Lewiston and Portland (Me.); founded, wrote and printed 3 small weekly newspapers, Farmer and Mechanic, Pansophist, Touchstone (all Farmington, Me.), 1852-54; published Franklin Journal of Aural Surgery and Rational Medicine, Farmington; Am. counsul to Rio Grande do Sul, Brazil, 1863-73; mem. Mass. Med. Soc., circa 1875. Author: A Flora of Maine, 1848. Died Jan. 13, 1898.

YOUNG, Alexander, clergyman, author; b. Boston, Sept. 22, 1800; s. Alexander and Mary (Loring) Y.; grad. Harvard, 1820, Harvard Divinity Sch., 1824; m. Caroline James, Nov. 1, 1826, 12 children. Ordained to ministry Unitarian Ch., 1825; pastor New South Ch., Church Green, Boston, 1824-54; bd. overseers Harvard Coll., 1837-53; corr. sec. Mass. Hist. Soc., 1837-53; a friend of Henry Wadsworth Longfellow; author of works still used as source material and for critical content, including: The Library of the Old English Prose Writers, 9 vols., 1831-34; Chronicles of the Pilgrim Fathers of the Colony of Plymouth from 1602-1625, 1841; Chronicles of First Planters of the Colony of Massachusetts Bay from 1623-36, 1846. Died Boston, Mar. 16, 1854.

YOUNG, Alfred, clergyman; b. Bristol, Eng., Jan. 21, 1831; s. Thomas and Sarah Agnes (Stubbs) Y.; grad. Coll. of N.J. (now Princeton), 1848, Med. Sch., U. City N.Y. (now N.Y. U.), 1853; attended St. Sulpice, Paris, France. Converted from Protestant Episcopal to Roman Catholic Ch., 1850, ordained priest, 1856; instr. in classics Seton Hall Coll., South Orange, N.J., also pastor Village of Princeton (N.J.), 1857-61; pastor St. John's Ch., Trenton, N.J., circa 1862; joined Soc. of St. Paul, 1862, did missionary work throughout U.S., debated with John Jay, Robert Ingersoll; founded Paulist Choir to foster restoration of Gregorian Chant, 1873. Author: The Complete Sodality Manual and Hymn Book, 1863; Catholic and Protestant Countries Compared, 1895. Died Apr. 4, 1900.

YOUNG, Ammi Burnham, architect; b. Lebanon, N.H., June 19, 1798; s. Capt. Samuel and Rebecca (Burnham) Y.; A.M. (hon.), U. Vt., circa 1838, Dartmouth, 1841; married 3 times; m. Polly Hough, Jan. 11, 1823, 1 dau., Helen L.; m. 2d, Hannah Green Ticknor. Architect for Congregational Ch., Norwich, Vt.; designed Thornton and Wentworth halls (1828-29), Reed Hall (1839) at Dartmouth; apptd. architect for Vt. State Capitol, Montpelier, 1832; built Boston Customs H[illegible] 1836-47; supervising architect U.S. Treasury Dept., circa 1852-62, designed numerous customs houses, ct. houses, post offices, marine hosps. (in classic, modified "Italian," Greek Revival styles), 1850's; architect south front of Treasury Bldg. (on Robert Mills' original plans), 1860. Prin. works include: Bromfield Street Meth. Episcopal Ch., Boston; court houses, Worcester, Mass. (1844), Lowell, Mass.; customs houses, Norfolk, Va. (1853-59), Galveston, Tex. (1856-58), appraiser's stores, St. Louis (1852-59), San Francisco; Indpls. Ct. House and Post Office (1856-61), New Haven (Conn.) Customs House and Post Office (1855-60). Author: General Descriptions and Specifications of the Alterations . . . In the Present Custom House Building in . . . New York . . ., 1862. Died Mar. 13, 1874.

YOUNG, Augustus, congressman; b. Arlington, Vt., Mar. 20, 1784; studied law. Admitted to Vt. bar 1810, began practice in Stowe; moved to Craftsbury, Vt., 1812; mem. Vt. Ho. of Reps., 1821-24, 26, 28-30, 32; state's atty. for Orleans County (Vt. 1824-28, judge of probate, 1830-31; mem. Vt. Senate, 1836-38; mem. U.S. Ho. of Reps. (Whig) from Vt., 27th Congress, 1841-43; moved to St. Albans, Vt., 1847; asst. judge Franklin County (Vt.) Ct., 1851-54. Died St. Albans, June 17, 1857; buried Greenwood Cemetery, St. Albans.

YOUNG Brigham, religious leader; b. Whitingham, Vt., June 1, 1801; s. John and Abigail (Howe) Y.; m. Miriam Angeline Works, Oct. 8, 1824; m. 2d, Mary Ann Angell, Feb. 18, 1834; also 17 to 25 polygamous wives; 56 children. Joined Methodist Ch. (in search of religion that permitted literal interpretation of Bible), 1823; studied Book of Mormon, circa 1828-32; baptized into Ch. of Jesus Christ of Latter Day Saints, Mendon, N.Y., 1832; led band of converts to Kirtland, O., 1833; became Mormon missionary, traveled throughout Eastern U.S.; went with Joseph Smith to oppose persecutions in Jackson County, Mo.; apptd. 3d in seniority to newly organized Quorum of Twelve Apostles, 1835, sr. mem., 1838; directed Mormon removal to Nauvoo, Ill.; missionary in Eng., 1839-41; became leading fiscal officer Mormon Ch., Nauvoo, 1841; made campaign tour in support of Smith's candidacy for Pres. U.S., 1844; after Smith's assassination and burning of Mormon homes in Nauvoo, directed and superintended (with aid of fgn. missions and U.S. Govt.) Mormon migration to Great Salt Lake, Utah (originally planned to march to Cal.); elected pres. Mormon Ch. while at winter quarters in Neb., 1847; organized and directed settlement at Salt Lake with authority of a mil. comdr. (thought in terms of a religious totalitarian state); built chain of outposts against Indians, started irrigation system; proclaimed and practiced polygamy; 1st gov. Territory of Utah, 1849-57 (resigned only when Pres. Buchanan sent army of Gen. Albert Sidney Johnson to remove him); indicted for polygamy, 1871, not convicted. Died Salt Lake City, Utah, Aug. 29, 1877.

YOUNG, Bryan Rust, congressman; b. nr. Bardstown, Ky., Jan. 14, 1800; grad. U. Louisville (Ky.); studied medicine. Practiced medicine, Nelson County, Ky.; mem. Ky. Ho. of Reps., 1839-61-63, 65-67; mem. U.S. Ho. of Reps. (Democrat) from Ky., 29th Congress, 1845-47; Dem. presdl. elector, 1848. Died Elizabethtown, Ky., May 14, 1882; buried Elizabethtown Cemetery.

YOUNG, David, almanac-maker, poet; b. Pine Brook, N.J., Jan. 27, 1781; s. Amos and Sarah (Mott) Y.; m. Mary Atkins, May 28, 1808. Taught sch., Elizabeth Town, N.J., also Turkey (now New Providence), N.J., 1801-circa 1814; appeared as almanac-maker under name of Philom in Citizens and Farmers' Almanac (published by Jacob Mann, Morristown, N.J.), 1814-32; also appeared in Farmers' Almanac, Hutchins' Improved Almanac, Family Christian Almanac, Methodist Almanac; worked longest with Mann's Farmers' Almanac (pub. by Benjamin Olds, Newark, N.J.). Author: The Contrast (blank verse poem in 2 parts), 1804; The Perusal, or the Book of Nature Unfolded, 1818. Died Feb. 13, 1852; buried Pine Brook Cemetery, N.J.

YOUNG, Ebenezer, congressman; b. Killingly, Conn. Dec. 25, 1783; grad. Yale, 1806; studied law. Admitted to Conn. bar, began practice in Westfield (now Danielson); engaged in cloth mfg., East Killingly, Conn.; mem. Conn. Ho. of Reps. (Federalist), 1810, 11, 16, 26-28, speaker, 1827-28; mem. Conn. Senate, 1823-25; mem. U.S. Ho. of Reps from Conn., 21st-23d congresses, 1829-35. Died West Killingly, Conn., Aug. 18, 1851; buried Westfield Cemetery, Danielson.

YOUNG, Ewing, trapper, colonizer; b. Eastern Tenn.; 1 illegitimate son by Mexican woman, Joaquin (recognized as his heir by Ore. Territorial Supreme Ct. 1855). Probably mem. William Becknell's expdn. which opened Santa Fe Trail, 1821; under name "Joaquin Joon" led co. to Gila River (N.M.-Ariz.) where group successfully battled band of Pima and Maricopa Indians, Aug. 1826; led co. which included Kit Carson across Mohave Desert into Cal., trapped on San Joaquin River, 1829; organized (with David Waldo, David E. Jackson) expdns. to Cal., arrived Los Angeles, Mar. 1832; led expdn. over greater parts of Cal., and to Colorado River at Yuma, Oct. 1832, returned to Los Angeles, summer 1834; became promoter (with Jackson Kelley) Ore. colonization movement, arrived at Ft. Vancover, Oct. 1834; thought to be a horse thief by Dr. John McLoughlin (local head Hudson's Bay Co.), settled on farm on the Chehalem (Ore.), was ostracized by community until 1837 when he was exonerated of thievery charges; rapidly became leader of community; made initial efforts to free community from control of Hudson's Bay Co. Died Ore., Feb. 15, 1841.

YOUNG, John, gov. N.Y., congressman; b. Chelsea, Vt., June 12, 1802; s. Thomas and Mary (Gale) Y.; m. Ellen Harris, 1833, at least 3 children. Admitted to N.Y. Supreme Ct. bar, 1829; mem. N.Y. State Legislature, 1833, 44, 45; mem. U.S. Ho. of Reps. (Whig) from N.Y., 24th, 27th congresses, Nov. 9, 1836-37, 41-43; leader Whig Party in N.Y.; leader in pushing through bill calling for revision of N.Y. Constn.; gov. N.Y., 1847-49; asst. treas. of U.S., N.Y.C., 1849-52. Died N.Y.C., Apr. 23, 1852; buried Temple Hill Cemetery, Geneseo, N.Y.

YOUNG, John Clarke, coll. pres., clergyman; b. Greencastle, Pa., Aug. 12, 1803; s. Rev. John and Mary (Clarke) Y.; attended Columbia; grad. Dickinson Coll., Carlisle, Pa., 1823, Princeton Theol. Sem., 1827; m. Frances Breckinridge, Nov. 3, 1829; m. 2d, Cornelia Crittenden, 1839; 10 children including Dr. William, Sarah Lee, Eugenia. Tutor, Coll. of N.J. (now Princeton); pastor McChord (now 2d) Presbyn. Ch., Lexington, Ky., 1828; pres. Centre Coll., Danville, Ky., 1830-57; became pastor Presbyn. Ch., Danville, 1834; organized 2d Presbyn. Ch. for students at Centre Coll., 1852; moderator Synod of Ky., 2 times; opposed abolitionists, but favored gradual emancipation; moderator Gen. Assembly of Presbyn. Ch., 1853. Author: (sermons) An Address to the Presbyterians of Kentucky, Proposing a Plan for the Instruction and Emancipation of their Slaves, 1836; Scriptural Duties of Masters, 1846; The Efficacy of Prayer, 1858. Died Danville, June 23, 1857.

YOUNG, John Richardson, physician; b. Elizabeth Town, Md., 1782; s. Dr. Samuel and Ann (Richardson) Y.; grad. Coll. of N.J. (now Princeton), 1799; M.D., U. Pa. at Phila., 1803. Practiced medicine with his father, 1803-04. Author: An Experimental Inquiry into the Principles of Nutrition and the Digestive Process (written as a student, published in his inaugural thesis for med. degree; shows that gastric juice is itself acid and that acidity is not result of fermentation; work later influenced William Beaumont's studies in digestion), 1803. Died Hagerstown, Md., June 8, 1804.

YOUNG, John Russell, journalist, diplomat; b. Tyrone County, Ireland, Nov. 20, 1840; s. George and Rebecca (Rankin) Y.; m. Rose Fitzpatrick; m. 2d, Julia Coleman; m. 3d, May Dow Davids; at least 2 children. Came with family to Am., circa 1841, settled at Downington, Pa.; asst. proofreader for William Young, publisher and printer, Phila., 1855; became copy boy for Phila. Press, 1857, accompanied John W. Forney (editor of Press) to Washington, D.C., 1861; became famous as result of being 1st to report facts of Battle of Bull Run; became mng. editor of Forney's 2 daily newspapers, Phila., 1862; a founder Union League of Phila., 1862; went to N.Y.C. at request of Jay Cook, 1865, became writer for Horace Greeley's N.Y. Tribune, became mng. editor, 1866; sent abroad by Sec. of Treasury George S. Boutwell, 1866, by Sec. of State Hamilton Fish, 1871; mem. editorial staff N.Y. Herald, 1872, worked for his paper in London, Eng., for next few years; accompanied Ulysses S. Grant on trip around world, 1877; U.S. minister to China under Pres. Chester Arthur, 1882-85, mediated between France and China in dispute over Annam and Tong King; resumed editorial position on N.Y. Herald, 1885; librarian of Congress, 1897-99. Author: Around the World with General Grant, 2 vols., 1879; Men and Memories, 2 vols., 1901. Died Washington, D.C., Jan. 17, 1899.

YOUNG, Josue Maria, clergyman; b. Shapleigh, Me., Oct. 29, 1808; s. Jonathan and Mehetable (Moody) Young; studied for priesthood at Mt. St. Mary's Sem., Emmitsburg, Md. Apprenticed in shop of Eastern Argus, Portland, Me.; publisher Me. Democrat, Saco; joined Roman Catholic Ch. (as result of assn. with John Crease, 1828); worked as printer in Ky. and Ohio, after 1830; with Catholic Telegraph, Cincinnati, also taught sch.; ordained priest Roman Catholic Ch., 1838; became diocesan missionary, also taught at St. Xavier's Acad., Cincinnati; pastor St. Mary's Church, Lancaster, O.; consecrated bishop for see of Erie, Pa. at St. Peter's Cathedral, Cincinnati; promoted an acad. and hosp. (of St. Joseph nuns), Erie, also acads. at Corsica and Meadville, Pa. Died Erie, Sept. 18, 1866.

YOUNG, Pierce Manning Butler, diplomat, congressman; b. Spartanburg, S.C., Nov. 15, 1836; s. Robert Maxwell and Elizabeth Caroline (Jones) Y.; grad. Ga. Mil. Acad. at Marietta, 1856; attended U.S. Mil. Acad., 1857. Joined Confederate Army, 1861, commd. 2d lt. of arty., stationed Pensacola, Fla., 1861; promoted 1st lt., aide-de-camp to Gen. W. H. T. Walker; apptd. adj. T. R. R Cobb's legion; promoted maj. for gallantry, 1862; commd. lt. col., 1862, commanded cavalry of legion under Wade Hampton; promoted col., served at Fleetwood or Brandy Station and Gettysburg; promoted brig. gen., 1863; in command of Hampton's Brigade, 1864; promoted maj. gen., 1864; mem. U.S. Ho. of Reps. (Democrat) from Ga., 40th, 41st-43d congresses, July 25, 1868-69, Dec. 22, 1870-75, opposed radical measures against South; del. Dem. nat. convs., Balt., 1872, St. Louis, 1876, Cincinnati, 1880; apptd. commr. to Paris Exposition, 1878; U.S. consul gen. to St. Petersburg (now Leningrad), Russia, 1885-87; U.S. minister to Guatemala and Honduras, 1893-96, developed friendship and comml. relations with Central Am. states. Died Presbyn. Hosp., N.Y.C., July 6, 1898; buried Oak Hill Cemetery, Catersville, Ga.

YOUNG, Richard Montgomery, senator; b. Fayette County, Ky., Feb. 20, 1798; attended Forest Hill Acad., Jesamine County, Ky.; studied law. Admitted to Ky. bar, 1816; served with Ky. Militia; moved to Ill., 1817, began practice of law, Jonesboro; apptd. capt. Ill. Militia; mem. Ill. Ho. of Reps.,

1820-22; circuit judge 5th Ill. Circuit, 1825-37; mem. U.S. Senate (Democrat) from Ill., 1837-43; mem. mission to Eng. to negotiate loan for State of Ill., 1839; asso. justice Ill. Supreme Ct., 1843-47; commr. Gen. Land Office (apptd. by Pres. Polk), 1847-49; clk. U.S. Ho. of Reps., 1850-51; resumed law practice, Washington, D.C. Died Washington, Nov. 28, 1861; buried Congressional Cemetery, Washington.

YOUNG, Thomas, physician; b. New Windsor, N.Y., Mar. 2, 1732; s. John and Mary (Crawford) Y.; m. Mary Winegar, 6 children. Began study of medicine, Amenia, N.Y., 1753, was especially successful in treating smallpox; moved to Albany, N.Y., 1764; actively opposed operation of Stamp Act; moved to Boston, 1766; delivered 1st of annual orations in commemoration of Boston Massacre, 1771; member Boston Com. of Correspondence (most active mem. after Samuel Adams); moved to Phila. to avoid a Brit. plot to kidnap him, 1774; sec. Whig Soc., Phila.; framed Pa. Constn. (with small group of leaders including Benjamin Franklin), 1776; supported movement to make N.H. Grants territory the new State or Vermont (name which he suggested), tried to influence U.S. Congress in the cause of Vt. statehood (Congress voted censure for his activity). Author: (with Ethan Allen) Reason, The Only Oracle of Man, or A Compendious System of Natural Religion, 1784. Contracted fever while practicing as sr. surgeon in a Continental hosp. in Phila., died the next day, June 24, 1777.

YOUNG, Thomas Lowry, congressman; b. Killyleagh, County Down, Ireland, Dec. 14, 1832; grad. Cincinnati Law Sch. Came to U.S., 1847; enlisted as musician U.S. Army, rose to 1st sgt. Co. A, 3d Arty., 1848-58; settled in Cincinnati, instr. Ohio State Reform Sch.; served as capt. Benton Cadets, Mo. Volunteers during Civil War, 1861; commd. maj. 118th Regt., Ohio Volunteer Inf., 1862, lt. col., 1863; col., 1864; brevetted brig. gen. U.S. Volunteers for meritorious service in Battle of Resaca (Ga.), 1865; resigned, 1865; admitted to Ohio bar, 1865, began practice in Cincinnati; asst. city auditor Cincinnati, 1865; mem. Ohio Ho. of Reps., 1866-68; elected recorder of Hamilton County (O.), 1867; apptd. supr. internal revenue, 1868; del. Republican Nat. Conv., Chgo., 1868; mem. Ohio Senate, 1871-73; lt. gov. Ohio, 1875; acting gov., 1877; mem. U.S. Ho. of Reps. (Rep.) from Ohio, 46th-47th congresses, 1879-83; mem. bd. pub. affairs Cincinnati, 1886-88. Died Cincinnati, July 20, 1888; buried Spring Grove Cemetery, Cincinnati.

YOUNG, William Singleton, congressman; b. nr. Bardstown, Ky., Apr. 10, 1790; studied medicine with Dr. Bemiss, Bloomfield, Ky.; grad. U. Louisville (Ky.). Began practice of medicine, Bloomfield; moved to Elizabethtown, Ky., 1814; mem. U.S. Ho. of Reps. (Democrat from Ky., 19th-20th congresses, 1825-27. Died Elizabethtown, Sept. 20, 1827; buried Elizabethtown Cemetery.

YOUNGS, John, colonial ofcl.; b. Southwold, Eng., Apr. 1623; s. Rev. John and Joan (Herrington) Y.; m. Mary Gardner, circa 1653; m. 2d, Mrs. Hannah (Wines) Tooker, 1691; 5 children. Came to Am., 1637, moved (with family) to L.I., 1640; ran bark between L.I. and English colonies for a time; attempted unsuccessfully to get English colonists to drive Dutch out of New Amsterdam; mem. Conn. colonial legislature from Southold, 1660; urged union of L.I. and Conn. (which angered Dutch ofcls.), 1662; served in English-Dutch War in which New Amsterdam was conquered by English, 1663-64; mem. Conn. Gov.'s Council, 1664; mem. of assembly which formed Yorkshire under laws of Duke of York, 1665; led Southold and other L.I. towns to go under Conn. control for a time after Dutch retook N.Y., 1673; sheriff Yorkshire, 1680-83; mem. 1st N.Y. Assembly, 1683; mem. commn. to determine N.Y.-Conn. border, 1683; lt. col. Suffolk Militia, 1686, col., 1689; mem. N.Y. Gov's Council, 1686-98. Died Apr. 12, 1698.

YOUNT, George Concepcíon, trapper, pioneer; b. Dowden Creek, Burke County, N.C.. May 4, 1794; s. Jacob Yount; m. Eliza Cambridge Wilds, 1818; m. 2d, Mrs. Gashwiler, 1855; 2 children. Moved to Cape Girardeau, Missouri, 1804; helped defend Cape Girardeau against Indians during War of 1812; engaged in cattle-raising, lost fortune through embezzlement by a neighbor; went on expdn. to Santa Fe, 1825, became interested in trapping; made several other expdns. to Southwest for trapping purposes, 1827, 28-29, on latter expdn. Yount's Peak named for him at mouth of Yellowstone River; joined expdn. to Cal., 1830; joined Roman Catholic Ch., 1825, added Concepcíon to his name; became Mexican citizen, 1835; built ranch called Caymus Rancho, Cal., 1836, sent for family, 1841 (however wife had remarried). Died Oct. 5, 1865.

YULEE, David Levy, senator; b. St. Thomas, W.I., June 12, 1810; s. Moses Elias Levy; studied law, St. Augustine, Fla.; m. Miss Wickliffe, 1846, 1 son, several daus. Became overseer of 1 of his father's plantations, Fla.; admitted to Fla. bar, 1836; del. Fla. Constl. Conv., 1838; mem. U.S. Ho. of Reps. from Fla., 27th-28th congresses, 1841-45; mem. U.S. Senate from Fla., July 1, 1845-51, Mar. 21, 1855-Jan. 21, 1861, chmn. com. of naval affairs; a leader of Southern movement, also mem. caucus com. which prepared Address to Southern People; supported Cal. as a free state; advocated secession, 1850; owner Atlantic and Gulf R.R. (incorporated 1853); supported Stephen Douglas for U.S. Pres., 1860; mem. Confederate Congress during Civil War; imprisoned at Pulaski, Fla., released by Gen. U.S. Grant. Died N.Y.C., Oct. 10, 1886; buried New York Avenue Presbyn. Ch., N.Y.

YUSUF KARAMANLI, pasha of Tripoli; b. Tripoli; s. Ali Karamanli. Forced older brother Hamet from throne, circa 1795; signed treaty with U.S. which provided for $40,000 and $12,000 annually in return for not attacking Am. shipping, 1796; demanded U.S. brig Sophia as present, 1799; angered because of supposed slights to his dignity, accused U.S. of giving more money to Tunis and Algiers than to him; declared war on U.S., 1801; U.S. blockaded Port of Tripoli, 1803; Yusuf increased his demands for money, and imprisoned Americans in the city; proposed peace in return for $200,000 and property claims, 1805; reached agreement whereby prisoners were exchanged, force that had captured Derna under William Eaton was removed, family of Hamet was restored to him, and Yusuf was to receive $60,000; made depredations against Am. shipping during War of 1812; Stephen Decatur destroyed ships, blockaded Port of Tripoli, and forced Yusuf to pay $25,000 indemnity and release some captives he held as slaves (treaty marked end of Tripoli pirate trouble), 1816.

Z

ZACHOS, John Celivergas, clergyman, educator; b. Constantinople, Turkey, Dec. 20, 1820; s. Nicholas and Euphrosyne Zachos; grad. Kenyon Coll., 1840; attended Miami U. Med. Sch.; m. Harriet Tomkins Canfield, July 26, 1849, 6 children. Came to U.S., 1830; asso. prin. Cooper Female Sem., Dayton, O., 1851-54; co-editor Ohio Journal of Edn., 1852-53; prin. grammar sch. Antioch Coll., Yellow Springs, O., 1854-57; served as asst. surgeon U.S. Army stationed Parris Island, Port Royal, S.C., at outbreak of Civil War; ordained to ministry Unitarian Ch., West Newton, Mass., 1865; pastor Unitarian Ch., Meadville, Pa., also prof. rhetoric Meadville Theol. Sch., 1866-67; taught literature and oratory Cooper Union, N.Y.C., 1871-98; patented printing machine for English texts, 1876; demonstrated with series of tests that Negroes could be educated by instruction, early 1860's. Author: New American Speaker, 1851; Phonic Primer and Rearer, 1864; Phonic Test, 1865. Died N.Y.C., Mar. 20, 1898; buried Boston.

ZALVIDEA, Jose Maria de, missionary; b. Bilbao, Vizcaya, Spain, Mar. 2, 1780. Joined Franciscan Order, 1798; sent to Coll. of San Fernando, Mexico, 1804, to Cal., 1805; missionary to Indians of Cal., 1805-46. Died Mission San Luis Rey, Cal., 1846.

ZAMORANO, Austin Juan Vincente, colonial ofcl., printer; b. St. Augustine, Fla., May 5, 1798; s. Gonzalo and Francisca (Sales del Corral) Zamorano y Gonzalez; m. Maria Luisa Argriello, 7 children. Served as cadet in Mexican War of Independence, 1821; exec. sec. Cal., 1825-36, maintained mil. govt. after Cal. Gov. Jose M. Echeandia was wounded in Popular revolt, 1831-33; 1st printer in Cal., printed works including Reglamento Provincal para el Gobierno Interior, 1834, Manifesto a la Republica Mejicana (Jose Figueroa, most important work pub. in Cal. before Am. occupation), 1835; returned to Mexico, 1838; mil. comdr. Lower Cal., 1839-40; named adj. insp. Cal. Territory, 1842. Died San Diego, Cal., Sept. 16, 1842.

ZANE, Ebenezer, pioneer; b. Hardy County, W.Va., Oct. 7, 1747; m. Elizabeth McCulloch, 13 children. Claimed (with his brothers) land at mouth of Wheeling Creek in Ohio, 1769; served as col. Va. Militia in Dunmore's War; helped repel siege of Ft. Henry, 1777, 82, during Revolutionary War; obtained permission from Congress to build road from Wheeling to Limestone, Ky., also received grants of mile-square plots of land where road crossed Muskingum, Hocking and Scioto rivers, 1796 (town of Zanesville founded on 1st plot, 1799, town of Lancaster on 2d plot, 1800). Died Nov. 19, 1812; buried family plot, Martin's Ferry, O.

ZEILIN, Jacob, marine officer; b. Phila., July 16, 1806; s. Jacob Zeilin; attended U.S. Mil. Acad.; m. Virginia Freeman, Oct. 23, 1845, 3 children including William F. Commd. 2d lt. U.S. Marine Corps, 1831; served in ship Erie off Brazil, 1835-37; promoted 1st lt., 1836; served aboard Congress in Mexican War, served in landings in Cal. and Mexico; brevetted maj., 1847, promoted capt., 1847; marine officer of E. India Squadron under Matthew Perry, served on ships Mississippi and Susquehanna; wounded at 1st Battle of Bull Run; promoted col., 1864; commandant of Marine Corps, 1864-76; promoted brig. gen., 1867, ret., 1876. Died Nov. 18, 1880; buried Laurel Hill Cemetery, Phila.

ZEISBERGER, David, missionary; b. Apr. 11, 1721; s. David and Rosina Zeisberger; m. Susan Lecron, June 4, 1781. Joined Moravian colony in Pa., circa 1740; helped arrange treaty allying Six Nations, 1745-63; lived with Delaware Indians, 1763; established Christian Indian settlement at Schonebrunn in Tuscarawas Valley, 1771, built 1st ch. and sch. west of Ohio River; helped establish settlements at New Salem, O., Fairfield, Can., 1786-98. Died Nov. 17, 1808.

ZENGER, John Peter, printer; b. Germany, 1697; m. Mary White, July 28, 1719; m. 2d, Anna Maulin, Sept. 11, 1722; 6 children including John. Came to N.Y., 1710; apprenticed to William Bradford (a well known printer), 1711-19; became freeman of N.Y., 1723; established printing shop, 1726; founded N.Y. Weekly Journal, 1733, maintained editorial policy which was outspokenly critical of the govt., imprisoned and tried for libel, 1734-35, acquitted; public printer N.Y., 1737, N.J., 1738; published Arithmetica (1st arithmetic text pub. in N. Am.), 1730. Author: A Brief Narrative of the Case and Tryal of John Peter Zenger, 1736. Died July 28, 1746.

ZENTMAYER, Joseph, inventor; b. Mannheim, Germany, Mar. 27, 1826; m. Catherine Bluim, 1849. Forced to leave Germany for polit. reasons due to his part in revolution of 1848; instrument maker, Phila., 1853-87; invented photog. lens for microscope, 1865; awarded Elliott Cresson gold medal for his scientific inventions, 1874; received gold medal for his improvements of microscope at Centennial Expn., Phila., 1876, Paris Exhbn., 1878. Died Phila., Mar. 28, 1888.

ZEUNER, Charles, composer, organist; b. Eisleban, Saxony (now Germany), Sept. 20, 1795; received musical edn. in Germany, probably under Johann Nepomuk Hummel and Michael B. Fischer of Erfurt (nr. Frankfurt). Came to U.S., circa 1824; elected organist to Handel and Haydn Soc., Boston, 1830, pres., 1838-39 (resigned because of quarrel with bd. trustees); soloist with organ concertos of his own composition, also ch. organist, pres. Musical Profl. Soc., Boston, 1830-34; became organist St. Andrew's, also Arch Street Presbyn. Ch., Phila., circa 1840; his musical library now in Library of Congress. Composer: The Feast of Tabernacles (oratorio in 2 parts with words by Rev. Henry Ware, Jr. of Cambridge, Mass., presented for 1st time by Boston Acad. of Music, at Odeon, Mass., 1837), written circa 1832. Author: Church Music: consisting of New England and Original Anthems, Motets, and Chants, 1831; The American Harp, 1832; Lyra Sacra, 1832; The Ancient Lyre, 1833. Died Camden, N.J., Nov. 7, 1857.

ZIEGLER, David, army officer; b. Heidlberg, Palatinate (now part of Germany), Aug. 16, or July 13, 1748; s. Johann Heinrich and Louise Fredericka (Kern) Z.; m. Lucy Sheffield, Feb. 22, 1789. Served with Russian Army against Turks on lower Danube and Crimea, promoted to rank of commissioned officer, 1768; came to U.S., settled in Carlisle, Pa., circa 1774; served as lt. Pa. battalion of riflemen led by William Thompson in siege of Boston, 1775; fought at L.I., Brandywine, Germantown, Paoli, Monmouth; commd. capt. Pa. Militia, 1778; commissary gen. Dept. of Pa. with hdqrs. at Waynesboro, 1779-80; mem. regt. which joined Lafayette in Va., 1781, attached to Gen. Nathanael Greene's Army, S.C., 1782; opened grocery store, Carlisle, 1783; commd. capt. in Josiah Harmer's expdns. against Indians, 1784, stationed at fts. Mackintosh (Beaver, Pa.), Harmer (Marietta, O.), Washington (Cincinnati); maj. 1st Inf., sent to Marietta, 1790, resigned from Army, 1792; pres. Cincinnati City Council (with duties of chief magistrate), 1802-04; 1st marshal Ohio Dist., 1803; adj. gen. Ohio, 1807; apptd. surveyor Port of Cincinnati, 1807. Died Sept. 24, 1811.

ZINZENDORF, Nicholaus Ludwig, clergyman; b. Dresden, Saxony (now Germany), May 26, 1700; s. George Ludwig, Count von Zinzendorf und Pottendorf and Carlotta Justina von Gersdorf; m. Miss Reuss, at least 1 dau., Benigna. Desired to visit Pa. after reading letters of Augustus Gottlieb Spangenberg and George Whitefield; arrived in N.Y.C., 1741, proceeded to Phila.; attempted to unite all Protestant sects under name of Congregation of God in the Spirit, called for union synod to be held at Germantown, 1742, held similar convs. at Swamp, Oley and Phila. (all Pa.); did missionary work in Lehigh Valley, Pa.; assisted in establishing Moravian congregation at Bethlehem, Nazareth, Phila., Lancaster and York (Pa.); his dream of unity never realized among people preferring separatism; returned permanently to Saxony, 1743. Died Herrnhert, Saxony, May 9, 1760.

ZOLLICOFFER, Felix Kirk, editor, congressman, army officer; b. Maury County, Tenn., May 19, 1812; s. John Jacob and Martha (Kirk) Z.; attended Jackson Coll., Columbia, Tenn.; m. Louisa

Gordon, Sept. 24, 1835, 11 children. Editor, part-owner Columbia Observer, Huntsville, Ala., 1834; an editor Southern Agriculturist, also Huntsville Mercury; state printer Tenn., 1835, 37; served as lt. U.S. Volunteers, Seminole War, 1836; apptd. editor Nashville (Tenn.) Republican Banner, Whig Party organ, 1843; adj. gen., comptroller Tenn., 1845-49; mem. Tenn. Senate, 1849-52; del. Whig Nat. Conv., Balt., 1852; mem. U.S. Ho. of Reps. (Whig) from Tenn., 33d-35th congresses, 1853-59; mem. Peace Conf., Washington, D.C., 1861; served as brig. gen. Confederate Army, in command of East Tenn. during Civil War; one of Tenn. gens. whose figures are carved in Stone Mountain, Atlanta, Ga. Died nr. Mill Springs, Ky., Jan. 19, 1862; buried Old City Cemetery, Nashville.

ZUBLY, John Joachim, Continental congressman, clergyman; b. St. Gall, Switzerland, Aug. 27, 1724; s. David Zubly; A.M. (hon.), Coll. of N.J. (now Princeton), 1770, D.D. (hon.), 1774; m. Ann Tobler, Nov. 12, 1746, 2 children. Ordained to ministry Presbyn. Ch. at German Ch., London, Eng., 1744; became 1st pastor Presbyn. (later Independent Presbyn.) Ch., Savannah, Ga., 1760; del. Ga. Provincial Congress, 1775; mem. 1st Continental Congress from Ga., 1775-77, opposed complete break with Eng.; accused of having given information to Sir James Wright (royal gov. N.Y.), banished from Ga., had half of his property confiscated, 1777-79; lived in S.C. until royal govt. was restored in Ga., 1779, then returned to Savannah, resumed ministerial duties until death. Author: The Stamp Act Repealed, 1766; An Humble Inquiry, 1769; Great Britain's Right to Tax Her Colonies, 1774; The Law of Liberty (sermon), 1775. Died Savannah, July 23, 1781; buried Colonial Park, Savannah.

ZUNDEL, John, organist; b. Erslingen, Germany, 1815. Came to U.S., became organist and music tchr., Bklyn.; organist Plymouth Ch., also St. George's Ch., N.Y.C. Author: Instruction Book for the Melodeon, 1853; The Amateur Organist, 1854; The Modern Melodeon Instructor, The Modern Organ School, 1860. Died Cannstadt, Germany, July 1882.

ADDENDUM

SUPPLEMENTAL BIOGRAPHIES

CONSISTING OF: (1) LISTINGS RESEARCHED TOO LATE FOR INCLUSION IN THE MAIN BIOGRAPHICAL SECTION; (2) SKETCHES OF INDIVIDUALS CONSIDERED TO BE OF REQUISITE REFERENCE INTEREST FOR INCLUSION, BUT WHO WERE NOT LISTED IN VOLUMES I, II, OR III OF WHO WAS WHO AND WHO DIED SUBSEQUENT TO 1905, THE TERMINAL DATE FOR LISTING IN THE MAIN SECTION; AND (3) ADDITIONAL DATA ON INDIVIDUALS SKETCHED IN OTHER VOLUMES OF WHO WAS WHO, WITH REFERENCES TO THE VOLUME NUMBER.

ADAMS, Henry, author: (novels) Democracy (written anonymously), 1880, Esther (under pseudonym); The Education of Henry Adams privately printed, 1907, posthumously published, 1918. (see sketch page 7, Who Was Who in America, Vol. I)

ADLER, Alfred, psychologist; b. Vienna, Austria, Feb. 7, 1870; s. Leopold and Pauline Adler; M.D., Vienna U., 1895; LL.D.; m. Raissa Epstein, 1898; 1 son, 3 daus. Worked in Vienna Gen. Hosp. and Polyclinic, 1895-97; gen. med. practitioner, nerve specialist, Vienna, 1897-1927; organized (with others) Child Guidance Centres to prevent neurosis and delinquency in childhood, at 30 schs. in Vienna, from 1912; founded Jour. Individual Psychology, 1914; attached to Austrian Army, Vienna, also Cracow, 1914-18; lectr. Pedagocical Inst. City of Vienna, 1924; lectr. Columbia U., N.Y.C., 1927, later at Med. Centre, N.Y.C.; clin. dir. Mariahilfer Ambulatorium, Vienna, 1928; became vis. prof. med. psychology, cons. psychologist L.I. Coll. Medicine, 1932; founded Jour. Individual Psychology in U.S.A., 1935. Author: Individual Psychology; Practice and Theory of Individual Psychology, 1920, transl., 1927; The Science of Living, 1929; Education of Children, 1930; The Pattern of Life, 1930; What Life Should Mean to You, 1931; Social Interest: a Challenge to Mankind, 1937; Understanding Human Nature, transl. 1946; Problem Child, transl. 1963; The Education of the Individual; also numerous books in German on Individual psychology, edn., religion, homosexuality. Founder sci. of individual psychology. Died May 28, 1937.

AGEE, James, author; b. Knoxville, Tenn.; attended St. Andrews Sch.; grad. Harvard, 1932. Recipient Poetry Prize, editor Advocate, both at Harvard; employed by Fortune mag., 1936, Time mag., 1939-43; wrote text for Let Us Now Praise Famous Men (photographs by Walker Evans), published 1941; film critic The Nation, 1943-48; wrote screen plays for movies, including The Quiet One, The African Queen; wrote film biography Mr. Lincoln (presented on television show Omnibus); author Permit Me Voyage (collection of poetry), 1934, The Morning Watch, 1951, A Death in the Family (Pulitzer Prize winner, 1958), published posthumously. Died May 16, 1955.

AGUINALDO, Emilio, Filipino leader; b. Cavite Province, P.I., Mar. 22, 1869; s. Carlos Aguinaldo; m. Hilaria del Rosario, 1896 (dec. 1930), 6 children; m. 2d, Maria Agoncillo, 1930 (dec. 1963). Became leader Filipino revolt against Spain, 1896, was exiled to Hong Kong by peace treaty that ended hostilities; fought with U.S. forces during Spanish-Am. War; organized and assumed presidency of Philippine Republic with capital at Malolos, 1898 (Republic not recognized by U.S. peace treaty); fought against U.S. occupying forces until captured by Brig. Gen. Frederick Funston, 1901, then swore allegiance to U.S.; defeated by Manuel Quezon in presdl. election, 1935; wore black bow tie as symbol of mourning for Philippine Republic until Philippines was granted independence from U.S., 1946; accused of cooperating with Japanese in Philippines during World War II, taken into custody, 1945, but never tried. Died Veterans Meml. Hosp., Manila, P.I., Feb. 6, 1964.

ALBANI, Emma, (real name Emma Lajeunesse), soprano; b. Chambly, Que., Can., Nov. 1, 1852; studied under Gilbert Benoist, Paris, France, under Francesco Lamperti, Milan, Italy; m. Ernest Gye, 1878. Moved with family to Albany, N.Y.; made debut as Amina in La Somnambula, Messina, Italy, 1870; soon became world-famous operatic soprano; made 1st Am. tour, 1874-75; royal court singer to German emperor, for a time; recipient Order of Merit from both Germany and Denmark, Victoria Badge from Gt. Britain; named dame comdr. Order Brit. Empire, 1925. Best roles include: Elsa in Lohengrin, Lucia de Lammermoor, Martha, Manon Lescaut. Died London, Eng., Apr. 3, 1930.

ALPHONSA, Mother (Rose Hawthorne), religious superior; b. Lenox, Mass., May 20, 1851; d. Nathaniel and Sophia (Peabody) Hawthorne; m. George Parsons Lathrop, circa 1871 (dec. 1898). Became interested in victims of incurable cancer, 1896, opened small home; devoted life to helping cancer victims after husband's death; founded sisterhood known as Servants of Relief for Incurable Cancer, took name of Sister Alphonsa; became superior, circa 1899; founded Rosary Hill Home, Hawthorne, N.Y., 1901, St. Rose's, N.Y.C., 1912. Author: Along the Shore (verse), 1888; Memories of Hawthorne, 1897; A Story of Courage, 1894. Died July 9, 1926.

ALTMAN, Benjamin, mcht., philanthropist; b. N.Y.C., July 12, 1840; worked in drygoods stores, Newark, N.J., and N.Y.C., 1860-65; operated store, N.Y.C., 1865-76; owner, operator dept. store at 6th and 19th streets, N.Y.C., 1876-1906, Fifth Avenue, 1906-13; left art pieces worth 20 million dollars to N.Y. Met. Museum. Died N.Y.C., Oct. 7, 1913.

AMATEIS, Louis, sculptor; b. Turin, Spain, Dec. 13, 1855; s. Gen. Paolo and Carolina A.; studied sculpture, Paris, France, 1878; grad. Inst. Tech., Turin, 1880; m. Dora Ballin, Feb. 24, 1889. Recipient gold medal from Royal Acad. Fine Arts, Turin, 1879; came to Am., 1883; with archtl. firm McKim, Mead & White, N.Y.C., 1883-93; prof. fine arts dept. architecture Columbian (now George Washington) U., 1893-1913; best known for a pair of bronze doors made for U.S. Capitol, never hung due to necessary structural changes; mem. Nat. Art Soc. Died Mar. 16, 1913.

AMES, James Barr, legal educator; b. Boston, June 22, 1846; s. Samuel T. and Mary H. (Barr) A.; grad. Harvard, 1870, Harvard Law Sch., 1873; m. Sarah Russell, June 29, 1880, at least 2 children. Asst. prof. law Harvard, 1873-77, prof. law, 1877-1910; a founder Harvard Law Review, 1887; author works on legal subjects including Lectures on Legal History and Miscellaneous Legal Essays, published posthumously, 1913. Died Jan. 8, 1910.

ANAGNOS, Michael, educator; b. Epirus, Turkey, Nov. 7, 1837; grad. U. Athens (Greece), 1859; m. Julia Romana Howe, Dec. 1870. Became a journalist, circa 1859; became acquainted with Dr. Samuel Gridley Howe, dir. Perkins Instn. and Mass. Sch. for Blind, when Howe visited Greece, 1867; came to Am. as Howe's asst., became dir. of instn. when Howe died, 1867; improved sch. by securing permanent printing fund and establishing kindergarten section. Author: Education of the Blind, 1882; Through Education to Independence, 1900; also juvenile books. Died 1906.

ANDERSON, Mary, actress; b. Cal., 1859. Made debut as Juliet, Louisville, Ky., 1875; toured New Orleans, San Francisco, Washington, D.C., Boston, 1876; praised by Longfellow; made 1st appearance in N.Y.C. in The Lady from Lyons, Fifth Avenue Theatre, 1877; travelled to London, Eng., 1883, well received at Lyceum Theatre; made last profl. performance in A Winter's Tale, Washington, 1889; boasted she had never played secondary role. Died 1940.

ANSON, Adrian Constantine, baseball mgr.; b. Marshalltown, Ia., Apr. 17, 1852. Player-mgr. with Chgo. Nat. League team, 1879-97; mgr. N.Y. Giants, 1898; 1st Nat. League player to achieve .400 batting average (1879, 87); won Nat. League batting championship 4 times during career; had lifetime batting average of .339; as mgr. of Colts, led team to 5 pennants (1880, 81, 82, 85, 86); introduced new batting technique; elected to Baseball Hall of Fame, 1939. Died Apr. 14, 1922.

ANTROBUS, John, artist; b. Warwickshire, Eng., circa 1837; m. Jeannie Watts, after 1865. Came to U.S., before 1855; advertised as a portrait painter, Montgomery, Ala., 1855; poet and genre painter, New Orleans, circa 1860; left New Orleans to paint scenes of plantation life, 1860; commd. lt. Delhi Southrons at outbreak of Civil War, 1861; lived in Chgo. and Washington (D.C.) after Civil War; settled in Detroit, circa 1875, became leading local portrait and landscape painter; frequent contbr. to local newspapers. Died Detroit, Oct. 18, 1907.

ASHMORE, William, missionary; b. Putnam, O., Dec. 25, 1824; grad. Granville Coll. (now Denison U.), 1845; grad. Western Bapt. Theol. Inst., Covington, Ky., 1848; m. Martha Ann Sanderson; m. 2d, Eliza Dunlevy; m. 3d, Charlotte A. Brown. Missionary to China for Baptist Ch., 1849-58; returned to Am. for health reasons, 1858-61; in charge of mission, Swatow, China, hdqrs. S. China Mission, 1861-76, 1890-1903; established schs. in 1870's which became Bibl. Tng. Sch. for Men, 1892 (later renamed Ashmore Sem.); home sec. Am. Bapt. Missionary, 1889-90; lived in Wollaston, Mass., 1903-09, wrote for Journal and Messenger. Died Apr. 21, 1909.

AVERY, John, congressman, physician; b. Watertown, Jefferson County, N.Y., Feb. 29, 1824; studied medicine Grass Lake Acad., Jackson, Mich.; grad. Cleve. Med. Coll., 1850. Practiced medicine, Ionia, Mich., 1850-52, Otsego, Mich., 1852, Greenville, Mich., 1868; asst. surgeon and surgeon 21st Regt., Mich. Volunteer Inf. during Civil War; served in Army of Cumberland in Ky. and Tenn.; with Sherman on his march to the sea; mem. Mich. Ho. of Reps., 1869-70; apptd. mem. Mich. Bd. Health, 1880, 86; mem. U.S. Ho. of Reps. (Republican) from Mich., 53d-54th congresses, 1893-97. Died Greenville, Jan. 21, 1914; buried Forest Home Cemetery.

B

BAKER, George Holbrook, artist, lithographer, publisher; b. Boston or East Medway, Mass., Mar. 9, 1827; studied at N.A.D., 1848. Joined Gold Rush to Cal., arrived in San Francisco, 1849; publisher and lithographer, Sacramento, Cal., 1852-62, made many sketches of mining camps; moved to San Francisco, 1862. Died San Francisco, Jan. 1906.

BARR, Charles, yacht capt.; b. Gourock, Scotland, July 11, 1864. Sailed cutter Clara to U.S. (with brother John), 1884, entered races; naturalized, 1889; commanded yachts Shona, Minerva, Wasp, Colonia; commanded Columbia in race with Brit. yachts Shamrock I, 1899, Shamrock II, 1901; commanded Reliance winning race with Shamrock III, 1903; won 19 out of 22 races in Brit. and German waters with yacht Ingomar; won German Emperor's Cup in race across the ocean comdg. Atlantic, 1905; in charge of August Belmont's 70 foot yacht Mineola and Cornelius Vanderbilt's Rainbow, 1905-09. Died New London, Conn., Jan. 24, 1911.

BARTÓK, Béla, pianist, composer; b. Nagyszentmiklós, Hungary, Mar. 25, 1881; studied music with Laszlo Erkel, Pressburg, Hungary, 1893-99; grad. Royal Acad. Music, Budapest, Hungary, 1903; hon. degree, Columbia, 1940; married twice; m. 2d, Ditta Pasztory; 1 son, Peter. Finished 2d in Anton Rubinstein Internat. Piano Competition, 1905; prof. piano Royal Acad. Music, Budapest, 1905-40; his ardent Hungarian nationalism shows in his 1st performed work, Kossuth Symphony, 1903; studied folk-music (which came to have a heavy influence on his work), 1905-45, became expert in Hungarian, Rumanian, Turkish, Serbian, Bulgarian, Arabic folk-music, published many volumes on his researches; wrote ednl. edits. of piano music of Bach, Mozart, Chopin, others; used folk-music as basis for ednl. piano pieces designed to train beginners in modern music (For Children, 1908-09); composed Mikrokosmos for more advanced piano tng., 1935; founder New Hungarian Music Soc., 1911; toured Europe and Am. as concert pianist and composer, 1927-28, 39; forced to flee Hungary because of his anti-Nazi activities, which included forbidding the playing or sales of his music in Germany; research fellow Columbia U., N.Y.C., 1940-45; his Hungarian citizenship and awards were restored to him at end of World War II; elected hon. mem. Hungarian Parliament, 1945. Works include: 6 string quartets; (opera) Duke Bluebeard's Castle, 1911; (nine plays) The Wooden Prince, 1915, The Miraculous Mandarin, 1919; Cantata Profana, 1930; Music for Strings, Percussion and Celesta, 1936; Contrasts, 1938; Divertimento for Strings, 1939; Concerto for Orchestra, 1943; 3 piano concertos. Died N.Y.C., Sept. 26, 1945.

BATES, George Handy, state legislator; b. Dover, Del., Nov. 19, 1845; s. Judge Daniel Moore Bates; attended U. Pa., 1862-64, Harvard Law Sch.; m. Elizabeth B. Russell, May 26, 1870. Admitted to Del. bar, 1869, practiced in Wilmington, 1869-70, 89-1916; dep. atty. gen. Del., 1870-74; del. nat. Dem. convs., 1880, 84, 88; mem. Del. Legislature, 1882-83, speaker of house, 1883; mem. bd. park commrs. City of Wilmington, 1883-94; spl. agt. to investigate affairs in Samoa, 1886-89; moved to Phila., 1896. Died Phila., Oct. 31, 1916.

BAYLOR, Frances Courtenay, author; b. Fort Smith, Ark., Jan. 20, 1848; d. James L. and Sophie (Dawson) Baylor; m. George Sherman Barnum, 1896. Works include: Petruchio Tamed; Behind the Blue Ridge, 1887; Juan and Juanita, 1888; Claudia Hyde, 1894; Miss Nina Barrow, 1897. Died Winchester, Va., Oct. 19, 1920.

BECK, Martin, theatrical mgr. Worked with B. F. Keith and E. F. Albee, 1906; responsible for bldg. Orpheum circuit (extending from San Francisco up and down Pacific Coast and eastward to Chgo., comprising 17 theaters by 1905) into most powerful Western circuit; built Palace Theatre, Broadway and 47th St. (became symbol big-time vaudeville), N.Y.C., 1913.

BEIDERBECKE, Leon Bix, jazz cornetist, pianist, composer; b. Davenport, Ia., Mar. 10, 1903; s. Bismarck Biederbecke; student Lake Forest Acad., 1 year; largely self-taught musically, influenced by Freddie Keppard, Fate Marable, Original Dixieland Jazz Band, New Orleans Rhythm Kings, Oliver, Armstrong, Noone, Emmet Hardy, and classical composers MacDowell, Eastwood Lane, Debussy, Ravel, Stravinsky, Holst. Star of Wolverines (jazz band), 1923, played at Roseland, N.Y.C.; with Charlie Straight at Rendezvous, Chgo., 1925, also sat in with Joe (King) Oliver, Louis Armstrong, Jimmie Noone; with Frankie Trumbauer, Arcadia Ballroom, St. Louis, 1926; played intermittently with Jean Goldkette, 1925-27, Paul Whiteman, 1927-29. Contbd. to Chgo. jazz style via Frank Teschemacher, Jimmy McPartland, Bud Freeman, others, and ultimately to modern "cool" jazz via Trumbauer, and indirectly, Lester Young and Miles Davis; compositions include: Davenport Blues, In A Mist, ad lib solo for Singing' the Blues; inspired novel Young Man with a Horn (Dorothy Baker). Died L.I., N.Y., Aug. 7, 1931; buried Davenport, Ia.

BELLAMY, Francis, clergyman, editor; b. Mt. Morris, N.Y., May 18, 1855; s. David Bellamy; grad. Rome (N.Y.) Free Acad., 1872, U. Rochester, 1876, Rochester Theol. Sem. Ordained to ministry Baptist Ch., 1879; pastor 1st Bapt. Ch., Little Falls, N.Y., 3 years, later held 2 pastorates in Boston; joined staff Youth's Companion Mag., Boston, 1891; chmn. exec. com. which proposed and publicized Nat. Pub. Schs. Celebration of Columbus Day, 1892; wrote Pledge of Allegiance to the Flag, pub. in Youth's Companion, Sept. 8, 1892 (dispute as to whether he or fellow staff mem. James Upham wrote pledge was decided in Bellamy's favor by U.S. Flag Assn. com. of 3 scholars 1939). Died Tampa, Aug. 28, 1931; buried in family plot, Rome, N.Y.

BERGSON, Henri (Lewis), died Paris, France, Jan. 4, 1941. (see sketch page 59, Who Was Who in America, Vol. II)

BERKMAN, Alexander, anarchist; b. Vilna, Russia, Nov. 21, 1870. Came to U.S., 1887; became involved with Jewish labor groups, N.Y.C.; attempted to assassinate Henry C. Frick, gen. mgr. Carnegie Steel Co., during Homestead steel strike, July 23, 1892; convicted and sentenced to 22 years imprisonment, Western Penitentiary (Pa.), released after serving 14 years, May 1906; editor Blast, San Francisco; convicted for obstructing operation of selective service law, 1917; served 2 years in Atlanta Penitentiary, released Oct. 1919; deported to Russia, 1919, to Sweden, 1922; lived in Germany, circa 1922-30, France, 1930-36. Author: Prison Memoirs of an Anarchist, 1912; The Bolshevik Myth, 1925. Committed suicide, Nice, France, June 28, 1936.

BETTENDORF, William Peter, inventor, mfr.; b. Mendota, Ill., July 1, 1857; s. Michael and Catherine (Reck) B.; m. Mary Wortman, 1879; m. 2d, Mrs. Elizabeth Staby, 1908. Worked for Peru Plow Co. (Ill.), 1872-75, supt. shops, 1882-86; worked for Moline Plow Co. (Ill.), 1875-82; invented power lift sulky plow, 1878, Bettendorf metal wheel, 1880; manufactured wheels, Davenport, Ia., 1886-1910; concentrated on substituting steel for wood in mfg. railroad cars; other inventions include cast steel side frame truck, Bettendorf integral journal-box. Died June 3, 1910.

BIERCE, Ambrose Gwinett, journalist; b. Meigs County, O., June 24, 1842; s. Marcus Aurelius and Laura (Sherwood) B.; m. Mary Day, Dec. 25, 1871. Served with 9th Ind. Inf., U.S. Army, during Civil War, 1861-66; employed by U.S. Mint, San Francisco, 1866-68; contbr. articles to Argonaut, 1866-68, 76-89; contbr. to News Letter, 1866-68, editor, 1868-71; mem. editorial staff Fun, 1871-75; wrote for Wasp, 1876-87, Examiner, San Francisco, 1887-96; corr. N.Y. American, Washington, D.C., 1896-1909; published Devil's Dictionary, 1906; went to Mexico to support revolutionary groups, 1913; published Collected Works, 1909-12. Disappeared in Mexico, circa 1914.

BIGELOW, Daniel Folger, artist; b. Peru, N.Y., July 22, 1823; moved to Chgo., 1858, gained reputation as landscape painter, became asso. of G.P.A. Healy and group of artists who founded Chgo. Acad. Design. Died Chgo., July 1910.

BISHOP, Charles Reed, banker; b. Glens Falls, N.Y., Jan. 25, 1822; s. Samuel and Maria (Reed) B.; m. Bernice Pauahi Paki, June 4,1859. Went to Hawaii, 1846; clk. Am. consulate, Honolulu, collector of customs, Honolulu, 1849-53; founder, owner Bishop & Co., bank, Honolulu, 1858-95; minister of fgn. affairs Hawaii, 1873-74; trustee Oahu Coll., Honolulu, 20 years; came to Cal., 1894; dir., v.p. Bank of Cal., San Francisco. Died June 7, 1915.

BIXBY, Horace Ezra, river pilot; b. Genesco, N.Y., May 8, 1826; s. Sylvanus and Hannah (Barnes) B.; m. Susan Weibling, 1860; m. 2d, Mary Sheble, 1868. Began career as steamboat pilot on Mississippi River, 1846, became well-known for his exceptional knowledge of uncharted river and its tributaries; engaged in Missouri River trade, 1850's; trained Samuel Clemens (Mark Twain) as pilot, 1857, took Clemens as co-pilot on Mississippi voyages until circa 1860; served as pilot gunboat Benton during Civil War, later chief of Union River Service; capt. comml. vessel running to Ft. Benton, Mont., 1866-68; partner in Anchor Line of steamers between St. Louis and New Orleans, circa 1869-90; capt. City of Baton Rouge; capt. govt. boats on Mississippi River, 1890's, active as pilot until death. Died Maplewood, Mo., Aug. 1, 1912.

BLY, Nelly, see Seaman, Elizabeth Cochrane.

BOLDEN, Charles (Buddy), jazz musician; b. New Orleans, 1868; barber by trade, also published a tabloid; leader and cornetist in world's 1st (identified) great jazz band, before 1895 (Bunk Johnson mem. band 1895-99); said to have played in as many as 6-7 bands in course of 1 evening; suffered mental breakdown during parade performance, 1906; last known job was in funeral with Allen Brass Band, 1907; committed to E. La. State Hosp., 1907, remained there until death. Influenced Joseph (King) Oliver, Louis Armstrong; spltys. included: Make Me a Pallet on the Floor; Bucket's Got a Hole in It; Funky Butt, Funky Butt, Take it Away. Died New Orleans, Nov. 4, 1931.

BONFILS, Frederick Gilmer, editor, publisher; b. Lincoln County, Mo., Dec. 31, 1860; s. Eugene Napoleon and Henrietta B. (Lewis) B.; attended U.S. Mil. Acad., 1878-81; m. Belle Barton, 1882, children—Helen, May. Co-editor, publisher (with Harry Heye Tammen) Denver (Colo.) Post, 1895-1933; seriously wounded when shot by W. W. Anderson (as result of feud with Gov. Charles S. Thomas of Colo.), 1900; brought Teapot Dome Scandal to nat. attention, 1922-24; carried on feud with Rocky Mountain News which reached temporary peace, 1928. Died Denver, Feb. 2, 1933; buried Fairmount Cemetery, Denver.

BORDEN, Lizzie Andrew, alleged murderess; b. Fall River, Mass., July 19, 1860; d. Andrew J. and Sarah (Morse) B. Tried for murder of her father and step-mother (Abby Durfee Gray), June 1893; maintained that she had been in barn on evening of Aug. 4, 1892, upon returning to house, found her father's body (head bashed in by axe) and her step-mother's body in another room; no murder weapon was ever found; a friend testified she had discovered Lizzie burning a dress in kitchen stove shortly after the murder; acquitted, though strong suspicions of her guilt still exist. Died June 1, 1927.

BOUCHER, Horace Edward, shipmodeler, architect; b. Italy, Apr. 24, 1873; s. Henry and Sarah Ann (Rodgers) B.; m. Zelia A. Schumacher, Mar. 2, 1897, no children. Ship draftsman N.Y. Navy Yard, circa 1890; built model ships for U.S. Navy, Washington, D.C.; in charge of naval display La. Purchase Expn., St. Louis, 1904, Lewis and Clark Centennial Expn., Portland, Ore., 1905; began ship modeling shop, N.Y.C., circa 1905 (later became H. E. Boucher Mfg. Corp.); built hist. display of 175 model vessels from Bonhomme Richard to submarines; made models of ships Flying Cloud, Santa Maria, Constitution, Constellation; expanded business to include models of bldgs. and bridges; mem. model com. N.Y. Yacht Club, 1923-35. Died Apr. 27, 1935.

BOYLE, Ferdinand Thomas Lee, artist; b. Ringwood, Eng., 1820; studied under Henry Inman. Came to Am. as child; lived in New Rochelle, N.Y., 1843, N.Y.C., 1844-55; became asso. N.A.D., 1849; moved to St. Louis, 1855; a founder Western Acad. Art; returned to N.Y.C., 1866; prof. art Bklyn. Inst.; head art dept. Adelphi Coll.; works include portraits of Lincoln, Grant, Archbishop Bailey of N. J., Charles Dickens. Died Bklyn., Dec. 2, 1906.

BRADY, James Buchanan (Diamond Jim), financier; b. N.Y.C., 1856. Started as hotel bell-boy, N.Y.C., later was employed by N.Y.C. R.R.; advanced from salesman for ry. supply firm to officer of several corps. related to railroad industry; became celebrated figure in Broadway nightlife, a lavish spender with wide circle of friends; gained his nickname by practice of wearing diamonds, other precious stones (value later estimated at $2 million). Established James Buchanan Brady Urol. Inst. at Johns Hopkins, Balt. Died Atlantic City, Apr. 13, 1917.

BRASHEAR, John Alfred, lense mfg. co. exec.; b. Brownsville, Pa., Nov. 24, 1840; s. Basil Brown Brashear; attended Duff's Merc. Coll., Pitts., 1855; m. Phoebe Stewart, Sept. 24, 1862. Pattern maker, Brownville, 1856-61, Pitts., 1861-81; founded lense making firm, Pitts., 1881; produced astron. lenses and precision instruments of internat. renown, form 1880's; perfected technique of making plane surfaces; produced plates from which Rowland Diffraction Gratings were made; invented method for silvering mirrors; trustee Western U. Pa. (now U. Pitts.), 25 years, acting chancellor, 3 years; chmn. Allegheny Observatory Com.; helped plan Carnegie Inst. Tech., Frick Ednl. Commn. Died Pitts., Apr. 8, 1920; buried Pitts.

BRECHT, Bertolt Eugen Friedrich, playwright, poet; b. Augsburg, Germany, 1898; studied science and philosophy at univs. Munich, Berlin (Germany); m. Helen Weigel. Came to prominence in Germany with play Drums in the Night (Kleist Drama prize winner), produced 1922; began collaboration with composer Kurt Weill, 1927, produced works including The Rise and Fall of the City of Mahagonny, The Three-Penny Opera (most famous work, 1928); fled Germany when Hitler came to power, unsuccessfully sought polit. asylum in Denmark, Sweden and Finland; came to Am., lived in Hollywood, Cal., 1941-48; called before Un-American Activities Com., U.S. Ho. of Reps., 1946, denied membership in Communist Party; accepted East German govt.'s offer of a theatre, 1948; recipient Stalin Peace prize, 1954. Other works include: Private Life of the Master Race, Mother Courage, The Good Woman of Setzuan, Galileo, The Caucasian Chalk Circle; also poetry. Died Berlin, Aug. 14, 1956.

BROKMEYER, Henry C., politician, philosopher; b. nr. Minden, Prussia, Aug. 12, 1828; s. Frederick William Brockmeyer; m. Elizabeth Robertson (dec. 1864); m. 2d, Julia Keinlen, Jan. 1867; several children. Emigrated to N.Y. at age 16, worked as bootblack, learned trades of currier, tanner, shoemaker; traveled, mostly on foot, to Ohio and Ind., then settled and worked in Memphis for 2 years; entered prep. dept. Georgetown Coll., was dismissed as result to theol. dispute with coll. pres.; then studied philosophy with Wayland at Brown U., Providence; returned West, settled and studied philosophy in abandoned cabin, Warren County, Mo., 1954-56; moved to St. Louis, 1956, worked as iron-molder, studied and instructed William Torrey Harris and others in German philosophy; resumed solitary life until illness forced his return to St. Louis; served with Mo. Militia in Civil War, imprisoned for organizing a regt.; elected as War Democrat to Mo. Legislature, 1962-64, opposed disenfranchisement of So. sympathizers; elected alderman of St. Louis, 1966, Mo. senator, 1870; mem. Mo. Constl. Conv., 1887; became lt. gov. Mo., 1876; organized St. Louis Philos. Soc., 1866, gained large following as leader of St. Louis Movement in philosophy; propagated German Idealism with emphasis on Hegel, envisaged St. Louis as future Athens of Am.; later became lawyer for Gould railroads; received largest popular vote in Mo. to that time as elector-at-large, 1884; took several western trips. Contrb. articles to Jour. Speculative Philosophy; wrote some poetry; translated Hegel's Larger Logic (never published). Died July 26, 1906.

C

CABRINI, Saint Frances Xavier, founder religious community; b. Sant'Angelo Lodigiano, Lombardy, Italy, July 15, 1850; d. Augustino and Stella (Oldini) Cabrini. Taught sch., Vidardo, Italy, 1872-74; supr. of orphanage, Codogno, Italy, 1874; founder Inst. of Missionary Sisters of Sacred Heart, 1877; established orphanages and schs., Milan, Grumello, Borghetto, Rome (Italy); came to U.S., 1889; established orphanage and novitiate, N.Y.C.; became naturalized citizen U.S., 1909; founded country schs. and orphanages, Bklyn., Denver, Los Angeles, New Orleans, Seattle, Phila., Scranton (Pa.), Newark and Arlington (N.J.); organized convents and schs., Panama, Peru, Buenos Aires (1895), Paris (1898), Madrid (1899), London (1901); founder Columbus Hosp., N.Y.C., 1892, Columbus Hosp., Seattle, Washington, 1916; pronounced venerable by Roman Catholic Ch., 1933, beatified, 1937, canonized (1st Am. citizen to be canonized), 1946. Died Columbus Hosp., Chgo., Dec. 22, 1917; buried Community Cemetery, West Park, N.Y.

CARVER, George Washington, developed over 300 uses for peanuts, over 100 uses for sweet potatoes, in his efforts to make his soil-enrichment plans for So. agr. financially feasible. (see sketch page 106, Who Was Who in America, Vol. II)

CHANEY, Lon, actor; b. Colorado Springs, Colo., Apr. 1, 1883; s. Frank H. and Emma Chaney; m. Hazel Hastings. Made 1st appearance in The Little Tycoon; comedian in Chgo., went with vaudeville troop to Cal.; became mem. Ferris Hartmann Opera Co.; his 1st motion picture success was in Hell Morgan's Girl, 1917; portrayed "the Frog" in The Miracle Man, 1919; played strong character parts in The Hunchback of Notre Dame, 1923, The Phantom of the Opera, 1925, Tell It to the Marines, 1926, Mr. Wu, 1927; appeared in The Unholy Three (his only talking picture), 1930; called "man of a thousand faces" because of unique effects he achieved with make-up. Died Aug. 26, 1930.

CHISOLM, Alexander Robert, army officer, financier; b. Beaufort, S.C., Nov. 19, 1834; s. Edward N. and Mary (Hazzard) C.; attended Columbia, 1851; m. Helen (Schieffelin) Graham, Apr. 7, 1875. Commd. lt. col. S.C. Militia, 1861; served on Gen. Beauregard's staff during Civil War; fought at battles of Bull Run, Shiloh, Charleston; moved to N.Y.C., 1869, founded A. R. Chisolm & Co., stock brokerage; founded Mining Record, 1877 (named changed to Financial and Mining Record), co-editor, 1882-90. Died N.Y.C., Mar. 10, 1910.

COBB, Tyrus Raymond, baseball player; b. Bank County, Ga., Dec. 18, 1886. Played with Augusta (Ga.) team, South Atlantic League, 1902-05; center fielder Detroit Tigers, 1905-20, player-mgr., 1921-26; with Phila. Athletics, 1927-28; ret. from baseball, 1928; held records for most runs scored, most hits, most stolen bases in lifetime, most times at bat, most years leading league in batting; held record lifetime batting average of .367; elected to Baseball Hall of Fame, 1936. Died Atlanta, Ga., July 17, 1961; buried Atlanta.

COMPTON, Arthur H(olly), physicist, univ. chancellor; b. Wooster, O., Sept. 10, 1892; s. Elias and Otelia Catherine (Augspurger) C.; B.S., Coll. Wooster, 1913, ScD., 1927; M.A., Princeton, 1914, Ph.D. (Porter Ogden Jacobus fellow), 1916, Sc.D., 1934; postgrad. Cambridge (Eng.) U., 1919-20; Sc.D., Ohio State U., 1929, Yale, 1929, Brown U., 1935, Harvard, 1936, U. San Marcos, 1941, U. Arequipa, 1941, Lehigh U., 1946; LL.D., Washington U., 1928, U. Cal., 1930; M.A. Oxford U., 1934; L.H.D., U. Tampa, 1941, Jewish Theol. Sem. Am., 1942; m. Betty Charity McCloskey, June 28, 1916; children—Arthur Alan, John Joseph. Instr. physics U. Minn., 1916-17; research engr. Westinghouse Lamp Co., 1917-19, also civilian asso. U.S. Signal Corps, developing airplane instruments, 1917-18; nat. research fellow physics Cavendish Lab., Cambridge, 1919-20; prof. physics, head dept. Washington U., 1920-23; prof. physics U. Chgo., 1923-29, Charles H. Swift distinguished service prof., 1929-45, chmn. dept. physics, dean div. phys. scis., 1940-45, dir. Metall. Atomic Project, 1942-45; chancellor Washington U., St. Louis, 1945-53, prof. natural history, 1953-61. Chmn. com. on X-rays and radioactivity NRC, 1922-25; Guggenheim fellow, spl. lectr. Punjab U., Lahore, India, 1926-27; mem. Solvay Internat. Congress Physics, 1927; Eastman vis. prof. Oxford U., fellow Balliol Coll., 1934-35; research asso. Carnegie Instn., 1931-41; Walker-Ames vis. prof. U. Wash., 1940; mem. Nat. Cancer Adv. Bd., 1937-44; v.p. Chgo. Tumor Inst., 1937-45; pres. Am. Assn. Sci. Workers, 1939-40; active Com. for Econ. Devel., 1946, UN AEC, 1946; mem. civilian adv. com. to sec. navy, 1946; mem. Presdl. Commn. on Higher Edn., 1946; U.S. del. UNESCO, Paris, 1946. Gen. chmn. Laymens Missionary Movement, 1937-41; co-chmn. Nat. Conf. Christians and Jews, from 1938. Chmn. bd. trustees Coll. Wooster, from 1940; regent Smithsonian Instn., from 1938. Recipient Rumford Gold medal Am. Acad. Arts and Scis., 1927; Nobel prize for physics, 1927; Gold medal Radiol. Soc. N.Am., 1928; Matteucci Gold medal Italian Acad. Scis., 1930; Hughes medal Royal Soc. London, 1940; Franklin medal Franklin Inst., 1940; St. Louis Distinguished Service award, 1946; Medal for Merit, U.S. Govt., 1946. Fellow Am. Phys. Soc. (v.p. 1933, pres. 1934), A.A.A.S. (v.p. sect. B, 1927, pres. 1942), Western Soc. Engrs. (hon., Washington award 1945); mem. Am. Philos. Soc. (Franklin medal 1946), Nat. Acad. Scis. (chmn. physics sect. 1938-41), Phi Beta Kappa, Sigma XI, Alpha Tau Omega, Gamma Alpha; fgn. mem. Reale Accademia dei Lincei, Rome, Prussian Acad. Scis., Berlin, Royal Akademie, Amsterdam, Royal Soc. Scis., Upsala, Brazilian Acad. Scis., Peruvian Acad. Scis.; hon. mem. Royal Soc. New Zealand, Deutsche Akad. der Naturforscher, Indian Acad. Scis., Akad. der Wissenchaften in Vienna, Chinese Phys. Soc. Presbyn. Clubs: University, Tavern, Noonday, St. Louis Country (St. Louis); Cosmos (Washington). Author: (monograph) Secondary Radiations Produced by X-rays, 1922; X-rays and Electrons, 1926; The Freedom of Man, 1935; with S.K. Allison) X-rays in Theory and Experiment, 1935; Human Meaning of Science, 1940, also numerous sci. articles; co-author: On Going to College, 1938. Discoverer change in wave-length of X-rays when scattered; total reflection of X-rays; (with C.H. Hagenow) complete polarization of X-rays; (with R.L. Doan) X-ray spectra from ruled gratings; elec. character of cosmic ray; directed world cosmic ray survey, 1931-34; directed work resulting in 1st atomic chain reaction. Home: 6510 Ellenwood Av. Office: Washington Univ., St. Louis. Died Mar. 15, 1962.

COQUELIN, Benoit Constant, actor; b. France, 1841. Toured Am., 1888, opened engagement in N.Y.C. with Les Precieuses Ridicules (Moliere); made short tour of U.S., 1894; made 3d visit to U.S., 1900, performed with Sarah Bernhardt in Cyrano de Bergerac (role created for him in Paris 1897) and L'Aiglon. Died 1909.

CORBETT, James John (Gentleman Jim), pugilist; b. San Francisco, Sept. 1, 1866; s. Patrick and Katherine (McDonald) C.; m. Olive Lake, June 8, 1886; m. 2d, Jessie Taylor, Aug. 15, 1895; no children. Began boxing (as mem. Olympic Club), 1884; defeated Joe Choynski in 28th round of bout which began May 30, 1889 and ended week later on barge in San Francisco Bay (after being stopped by police); defeated Jake Kilrain, New Orleans, Feb. 1890, Dominick McCaffrey, Bklyn., Apr. 1890; fought Peter Jackson to draw after 61 rounds; fought John L. Sullivan in exhbn. match of 4 1-minute rounds; defeated Sullivan in 21 rounds, Sept. 1892; defeated Charlie Mitchell (English champion) and Peter Courtney, 1894; knocked-out by body blow from Robert Fitzsimmons, Mar. 17, 1897; toured country in play Gentleman Jack; beaten by Jim Jefferies in 23 rounds, 1900, again defeated by Jefferies, 1903; ret. from ring, appeared in drama and vaudeville. Author: The Roar of the Crowd, 1925. Died Bayside, Queens, L.I., N.Y., Feb. 18, 1933.

CRAM, Ralph Adams, designed Cathedral of St. John the Divine, N.Y.C., Calvary Episcopal Ch., Pitts., Rice Inst., Houston, Tex., The Chapel at U.S. Mil. Acad. (see sketch page 132, Who Was Who in America, Vol. II)

CROSS, Henry H., artist; b. Flemingville, N.Y., Nov. 23, 1837; studied in France, 1853-55. Worked with traveling circus; painted portraits of Indians; settled in Chgo., 1860; made several painting trips into Indian country; collection of works at Walker Art Gallery, Mpls. Died Chgo., Apr. 2, 1918.

CUMMINGS, Henry Johnson Brodhead, congressman; b. Newton, Sussex County, N.J., May 21, 1831; attended public schs., Muncy, Pa.; studied law. Editor newspaper, Schuylkill County, Pa., 1850; admitted to bar, Williamsport, Pa., 1855; moved to Winterset, Ia., 1856; pros. atty. Madison County (Ia.), 1856-58; served as capt. Co. F., 4th Regt., Ia. Volunteer Inf., 1861-62, as col. 39th Regt., 1862-64; became propr., editor Winterset Madisonian, 1869; mem. U.S. Ho. of Reps. (Republican) from Ia., 45th Congress, 1877-79. Died Winterset, Apr. 16, 1909; buried Winterset Cemetery.

CUTLER, James Gould, inventor, mayor; b. Albany, N.Y., Apr. 24, 1848; s. John Nathan and Mary E. (Gould) C.; m. Anna K. Abbey, Sept. 27, 1871. Draftsman, Rochester, N.Y., 1872; invented mail chutes for office bldgs. known as letter box connection, patented 1883; formed (with brother) Cutler Mfg. Co. to build and install letter chute, 1884; mem. White Charter Commn. of N.Y. State, 1895; cons. architect N.Y. State Capitol, 1897; commr. pub. safety Rochester, mayor, 1903-07. Died Apr. 21, 1927.

D

DAFT, Leo, elec. engr.; b. Birmingham, Eng., Nov. 13, 1843; s. Thomas B. and Emma Matilda (Sturges) D.; m. Katherine Anna Flansburgh, Mar. 11, 1871, at least 4 children. Came to U.S., 1866; owner, operator photographic studio, Troy, N.Y., 1871-79; with N.Y. Electric Light Co. (later Daft Electric Co.); experimented with electric railroad, built electric locomotive for Saratoga & Mt. McGregor R.R., 1883; installed Balt. Union Passenger Ry. (1st comml. electric railroad in U.S.), 1885; mem. Am. Inst. E.E., A.A.A.S., Electro-Chem. Soc. Died Mar. 28, 1922.

DAHLE, Herman Bjorn, mcht., congressman; b. Perry, Dane County, Wis., Mar. 30, 1855; grad. U. Wis. at Madison, 1877. Became a mcht., Mt. Vernon, Wis., 1877, Mt. Horeb, Wis., 1887, also became a banker, 1890; mem. U.S. Ho. of Reps. (Republican) from Wis., 56th-57th congresses, 1899-1903. Died Mt. Horeb, Apr. 25, 1920; buried Lutheran Cemetery.

DANNREUTHER, Gustav, musician; b. Cincinnati, O., July 21, 1853; s. Abraham and Sophie (Fishbacher) D.; studied violin, Cincinnati and Berlin, Germany, 1871-74; m. Nellie M. Taylor, 1882. Taught violin, gave public performances, London, Eng., 1874-77; returned to U.S.; mem. Mendelssohn Quintet Club, Boston, until 1880; mem. Boston Symphony Orch., 1881; condr. Buffalo Philharmonic Soc., 1882-84; formed Beethoven String Quartet, 1884, renamed Dannreuther Quartet, 1894; instr. music Vassar Coll., 1907. Died Dec. 19, 1923.

DAVENPORT, Ira Erastus, medium; b. Buffalo, N.Y., Sept. 17, 1839; s. Ira and Virtue (Honeysett) D.; m. Augusta Green, Feb. 1862; m. 2d, Louise Toulet, 1866. Considered (with brother William Henry Harrison Davenport) to possess supernatural powers; sounds came from musical instruments near them when both were tied with ropes and placed in darkened room; method of tieing brothers came to be known as Davenport Ties; went to N.Y.C., 1855, exposed as fraud and returned home; devised act which required him and his brother to be tied hand and foot to opposite ends of a cabinet, musical instruments played, bells rang, spirit hand appeared when doors of cabinet were closed, became popular with this exhibition; went to Europe, 1864-68; toured U.S., 1868-74; ret. to farm in Mayville, N.Y., after brother's death, circa 1877. Died Mayville, July 8, 1911.

De BARDELEBEN, Henry Fairchild, industrialist; b. N.Y. State, July 22, 1841; s. Henry and Jennie (Fairchild) De B.; m. Ellen Pratt, Feb. 4, 1863; m. 2d, Miss McCroffin; at least 2 sons, Henry Charles. Became ward of Ala. industrialist Daniel Pratt, 1856; served with Prattville Dragoons, Confederate Army, participated in battles of Pensacola, Shiloh; mgr. Red Mountain Iron & Coal Co., 1872; inherited Daniel Pratt's fortune, 1873; investor Eureka Coal Co., nr. Birmingham, Ala., 1877, became Pratt Coal & Coke Co., 1878; went to Mexico for health reasons, 1881-82; formed De Bardeleben Coal & Iron Co., 1886; organized Pinchard & De Bardeleben Land Co., merged with Tenn. Coal & Iron Co., 1891, v.p., 1891-93, lost entire fortune in attempt to take over control of co., 1893. Died Dec. 6, 1910.

De FOREST, John William, army officer, author; b. Humphreysville (now Seymour), Conn., May 31,

1826; s. John H. and Dotha (Woodward) DeF.; A.M. (hon.), Amherst Coll., 1859; m. Harriet Silliman Shepard, June 5, 1856. Travelled extensively and related his experience in books; in Europe at outbreak of Civil War, immediately returned to Am. and recruited company (Company I, 12th Conn. Volunteers), New Haven, Conn.; acted as insp. gen. 1st Div., XIX Corps, U.S. Army, also aide on corps staff; brevetted maj. U.S. Volunteers, 1865; wrote descriptions of battle scenes for Harper's Monthly during Civil War; commd. capt. Vet. Res. Corps of Company I, 14th Regt., after Civil War; dist. comdr. Freedman's Bur. with hdqrs. at Greenville, S.C.; mustered out of service, 1868; spent most of rest of life at New Haven. Author: History of the Indians of Connecticut, 1851; Oriental Acquaintance, 1856; European Acquaintance, 1858; Miss Ravnel's Conversion from Secession to Loyalty (novel), 1867. Died July 17, 1906.

DEGAS, Hilaire Germain Edgar, artist; b. Paris, France, July 19, 1834; enrolled in École des Beaux Arts, Paris, 1855; studied in studio of Louis Lamottre. First exhibited at Paris Salon, 1865; served with arty. during Franco-Prussian War, 1870-71; visited U.S., stayed with relatives in New Orleans, 1872; painted New Orleans Cotton Office (study of figures absorbed in occupational movement), 1873; participated in 1st Impressionist exhbn. with Monet, Manet, others, 1874; executed many paintings of ballet dancers. Died Paris, Sept. 26, 1917.

de HAAS, Jacob Judah Aaron, Zionist leader; b. London, Eng., Aug. 13, 1872; s. Aaron and Anna (Haarbleek) De H.; m. Lillian E. Eisenberg, Mar. 1, 1905; children—Florence, Aaron. Asso. editor Jewish World, London, 1892-1900; asst. to Theodor Herzl (Zionist advocate), 1896-1904; sec. Am. Zionist Fedn., 1901-05; came to U.S., 1902; editor The Maccabaean, N.Y.C., 1902-05; editor Jewish Advocate, Boston, 1908-18; exec. sec. Provisional Com. for Zionist Affairs, 1916. Author: The Great Betrayal, 1930; History of Palestine, 1934. Died N.Y.C., Mar. 21, 1937; buried Shearith Israel, Spanish and Portuguese Synagogue Cemetery, N.Y.C.

DELANO, Jane Arminda, nurse; b. Townsend, N.Y., Mar. 12, 1862; d. George and Mary Ann (Wright) Delano; grad. Bellevue Hosp. Sch. Nursing, N.Y.C., 1886. Supt. nurses of a hosp., Jacksonville, Fla., 1887, U. Pa. Hosp. Sch. Nursing, 1891-96; dir. girls' dept. House of Refuge, Randall's Island, N.Y., 1900-02; dir. Bellevue Hosp. Sch. Nursing, 1902-06; chmn. nat. com. A.R.C., 1909; supt. Nurse Corps, U.S. Army, 1909, made Red Cross Nursing Service the reserve of Army Nurse Corps; pres. bd. dirs. Am. Jour. Nursing; pres. Am. Nurses' Assn., 1909-12; in charge of selection and assignment of all mil. nursing units, 1916; dir. Dept. of Nursing (World War I orgn.), 1918; went to France, 1919. Author: American Red Cross Textbook on Elementary Hygiene and Home Care of the Sick, 1913. Died Savenay Hosp. Center, France, Apr. 15, 1919.

DELIUS, Frederick, composer; b. Bradford, Eng., Jan. 29, 1862; attended Conservatory of Leipzig. Came to Am., 1884; supt. orange plantation in Fla.; later taught music, Danville, Va., then became organist in N.Y.C.; returned to Europe to study; settled at Grez-sur-Loing, France, 1899, did most of his composing there. Compositions include: A Village Romeo and Juliet (opera), 1901; Margot la Rouge, 1902; Appalachia, 1902; Florida; A Mass of Life (choral); Brigg Fair; Fennimore and Gerda, 1910; In a Summer Garden; Summer Night on the River; On Hearing the First Cuckoo in Spring. Died Grez-sur-Loing, June 10, 1934; buried Limpsfield, Eng.

DEMUTH, Charles, painter; b. Lancaster, Pa., 1883; studied drawing, painting under Thomas Anshutz and William Chase, Pa. Acad. Fine Arts, from 1903. Went to Europe, 1907, 11, 12, 13; influenced by Neo-Impressionism and Cubism while in Paris; upon return to Am., won acclaim for series of line and wash illustrations of works of Henry James, Poe and Zola; known for vaudeville and circus series; best known for still-lifes, particularly flower studies; paintings reveal freshness of perception, are characterized by sense of detachment. Represented in permanent collections Phillips Meml. Gallery, Washington, D.C., Barnes Found., Merion, Pa., Fogg Art Mus., Cambridge, Mass., Cleve. Mus. Art, Columbus (O.) Gallery Fine Arts, Art Inst. Chgo., Gallery Living Art, Whitney Mus. Am. Art, Met. Mus. Art (all N.Y.C.). Died Lancaster, Pa., Oct. 23, 1935.

DEVOY, John, rebel, journalist; b. Kill, County Kildare, Ireland, Sept. 3, 1842; s. Elizabeth (Dunne) Devoy. Joined Irish Republican Brotherhood, 1861; mem. French Fgn. Legion, Algeria, 1861-62; organized Fenians in Brit. Army; aided escape of James Stephens from Dublin (Ireland) Jail; arrested for treason, 1866, sentenced to 15 years, released 1871; came to Am., 1871; reporter, telegraph editor, in charge of fgn. news N.Y. Herald, N.Y.C., 1871-79; organized rescue of Irish prisoners from Australia, 1875-76; founder, editor Irish Nation, N.Y.C., 1881-85, Gaelic American, N.Y.C., 1903-28; gave financial support to Dublin Easter Week Rebellion of 1916. Author: Recollections of an Irish Rebel. Died Sept. 29, 1928.

DIXON, William (Billy), frontiersman; b. Ohio County, Va. (now W.Va.), Sept. 25, 1850; m. Olive King, Oct. 18, 1894. Driver in govt. mule trains, Colo. and Okla., 1865-69; became buffalo hunter, 1869; took part in Battle of Adobe Walls (28 whites withstood attack of about 700 Comanche Indians), in what is now Hutchinson County, Tex., 1874; scout for U.S. Calvary, 1874-83; received (with 4 companions) Congressional medal of honor for surviving attack of over 125 Indians; homesteaded on claim in Hutchinson County, 1883, later sheriff Adobe Walls (Tex.); established homestead served as postmaster, land commr., justice of peace, in what is now Cimarron County, Okla., 1906. Died Mar. 9, 1913.

DORGAN, Thomas Aloysius, cartoonist, sportswriter; b. San Francisco, Apr. 29, 1877; s. Thomas and Anna (Tobin) D.; employed by art dept. Bulletin, San Francisco, 1891, became comic artist, before 1902; wrote syndicated sports column using signature Tad, circa 1900-circa 1920; became authority on boxing, attended every championship fight, circa 1900-circa 1920; polit. cartoonist N.Y. Jour., N.Y.C., 1902-05; took over cartoon characters Judge Rumhauser and Silk Hat Harry, circa 1907; coined numerous slang expressions including "Yes, We have no bananas," "23, skidoo," "Officer, call a cop," "Let him up, he's all cut," "The first hundred years are the hardest," coined expressions "apple-sauce" for flattery, "chin-music" for idle chatter, "skimmer" for hat, "dogs" for shoes, "nickle-nurser" for a stingy person; best known simile "Am busy as a one-armed paper-hanger with the hives." Died Great Neck, L.I., N.Y., May 2, 1929.

DRESSER, Paul, songwriter; b. Terre Haute, Ind., Apr. 21, 1857; s. John Paul and Sarah (Schnab) Dreiser; bro. of novelist Theodore Dreiser; m. May Howard. Left home to join medicine show, 1873; changed name to Dresser; joined stock co. billed as Sensational Comique; wrote 1st song, Wide Wings, circa 1875; joined Billy Rice Minstrels, 1884; formed Howley, Haviland and Dresser, song publishers, 1901. Songs include: The Letter that Never Came, 1886; The Blue and the Gray, 1890; On the Banks of the Wabash, Far Away (ofcl. song of Ind.), 1899; Just Tell Them that You Saw Me; My Gal Sal, 1903. Author: Paul Dresser Songster. Died Bklyn., Jan. 30, 1906.

DUFFY, Francis Patrick, clergyman; b. Cobourg, Ont., Can., May 2, 1871; s. Patrick and Mary (Ready) D.; grad. St. Michael's Coll., Toronto, Can., 1893; M.D., St. Francis Xavier's Coll., N.Y.C., S.T.B., Catholic U., Washington, D.C., 1898. Entered St. Joseph's Sem., Troy, N.Y., 1894; ordained priest Roman Catholic Ch., 1896; became U.S. citizen, 1902; prof. philosophy and moral theology St. Joseph's Sem., Dunwoodie, until 1912; pastor Our Savior parish, Bronx, N.Y., 1912; served as chaplain Fighting 69th Regt., N.Y. N.G., accompanied regt. to Mexican border, 1916; became chaplain 165th Regt., AEF, at outbreak World War I, went to Europe with regt., 1917; earned nicknames "Iron Man" and "Front Line" Duffy during war; decorated D.S.C., D.S.M., Cross of Legion of Honor, Croix de Guerre with palm, badge of Canadian War Vets; returned to N.Y. after war; pres. Cath. Summer Sch., Cliff Haven; pastor Holy Cross parish, N.Y.C., 1920-32. Author: Father Duffy's Story, a Tale of Humor and Heroism, of Life and Death with the Fighting Sixty-Ninth, 1919. Died June 26, 1932.

DUNCAN, Isadora, dancer; b. San Francisco, May 27, 1878; d. Joseph Charles and Dora (Gray) Duncan; m. Sergei Yessenin, May 1922. Developed new mode of dancing interpretive of poetry, music and art, free from discipline and limitations of ballet, at age 15; danced with Augustin Daly's co., N.Y.C., 1895; went to London, Eng., where her dancing style met wide approval, 1897; toured Europe with family, 1898-1900; founded sch. of dance nr. Berlin, Germany, 1904, moved sch. to Paris, France, 1913; toured U.S., 1906; attempted to establish sch. in Athens, 1920, failed because of polit. difficulties; opened sch. in Moscow, 1921, had no role in its mgmt.; known for her dancing of Marche Slave (Tschaikowsky), Marche Funebre (Chopin). Author: (autobiography) My Life, 1927. Died Nice, France, Sept. 14, 1927; buried Paris.

DURHAM, Caleb Wheeler, inventor; b. Tunkhannock, Pa., Feb. 6, 1848; s. Alpha and Elizabeth (Riggs) D.; attended Williston Acad. (Mass.), 1866; studied civil engring. U. Mich. at Ann Arbor, 1867-69; m. Clarissa Safford Welles, May 28, 1873. Served with 42d Regt., Pa. Militia, 1861-62, with 195th Pa. Volunteers, 1862-64; with Phila. & Reading R.R., 1864-66; employed engring. depts. several railroads including N.Y.C. R.R., 1869-73; became civil engr. specializing in sanitation, Chgo., 1873; invented hot-air heater, 1875, manufactured heater for brief period; devised spl. fittings for drainage pipes, 1880; devised house drainage method later known as Durham System; established Durham House Drainage Co., Chgo., 1881; built drainage system for entire town of Pullman (Ill.); moved business to Peekskill, N.Y., 1883; designed installations for Carnegie Hall, N.Y.C., also Capitol Bldg., Washington, D.C.; mem. Engrs. Club N.Y. Died Peekskill, Mar. 28, 1910; buried Peekskill.

DURYEA, Charles Edgar, automobile inventor, mfr.; b. nr. Canton, Ill., Dec. 15, 1861; s. George Washington and Louisa Melvina (Turner) D.; m. Rachel Steer, 1884; children—Rhea Edna, Grace Louise, Merle Junius. Owner bicycle bus., Peoria, Ill.; invented 1st Am. car, 1893, improved car (used 4 cycle water-cooled motor, clutch and gear transmission, pneumatic tires) by 1905; his car won over an imported fgn. model in Chgo. Times Herald race, 1895; pres. Am. Motor League; co-owner Duryea Motor Wagon Co., Springfield, Ill., until 1898; owner Duryea Power Co., Reading, Pa., circa 1900-14. Author: The Handbook of the Automobile, 1906. Died Phila., Sept. 28, 1938; buried Ivy Hill Cemetery, Phila.

DUSE, Eleonora, actress; b. Italy, 1859. Made U.S. debut as Camille, N.Y.C., 1893; returned to U.S. to star in plays written for her by Gabriele d'Annunzio including La Gioconda, Francesca da Rimini, La Città Morta, 1903; became famous for her acting in Ibsen's plays including Ghosts and The Lady from the Sea; made final visit to U.S. appearing 8 times at Met. Opera House, N.Y.C., 1923, then began tour which ended in her death. Died Pitts., Apr. 1924.

DYAS, Ada, actress; b. England, 1843. Made debut with company of John Augustin Daly as Anne Sylvester in play Man and Wife, Fifth Avenue Theatre, N.Y.C., 1874, later performed in Foline, The Fast Family, Divorce; because of disagreement with Augustin Daly over his policy of billing no "stars," joined company of Lester Wallack. Died 1908.

E

EARP, Wyatt Berry Stapp, marshall; b. Monmouth, Ill., Mar. 19, 1848; s. Nicholas and Virginia (Cooksey) E.; married, 1868; m. 2d, Josephine Sarah Marcus, circa 1897; no children. Moved with family to Cal., 1864; drove stagecoach between San Bernardino and Los Angeles, 1865; drove coaches to Ariz. and Utah, 1865-67, later worked as buffalo hunter, horse handler for railroads; hunter for U.S. Govt. surveyors in Kan., Okla., Tex., 1870-71; independent buffalo hunter, 1871-73; earned reputation for bravery and skill with firearms; marshall of Ellsworth, Kan., 1873; dep. marshall Wichita, Kan., 1874-76, Dodge City, Kan., 1876, 77-79; dep. sheriff Cochise County (Ariz.) at Tombstone, 1879-82, marshall, 1882; led brothers Virgil and Morgan and Doc Holliday against Ike Clanton's band in battle of O.K. Corral, Tombstone, 1881; after retirement from law enforcement, lived off real estate, oil, mining investments and gambling. Died Los Angeles, Jan. 13, 1929.

ELLIS, John Washington, banker, mcht.; b. Williamsburg, O., July 15, 1817; s. Benjamin and Sallie (Tweed) E.; attended Kenyon Coll.; m. Caroline Lindley, 1845. Mcht. in Cincinnati, 1840-70; a founder Young Men's Merc. Library Assn., Cincinnati, pres., 1843; organized Ellis & McAlpin (became a leading merc. firm), Cincinnati, 1847; pres. Cincinnati, Hamilton & Dayton R.R.; a founder, pres. 1st Nat. Bank of Cincinnati, 1863-69; head of Winslow, Lanier & Co., N.Y.C., 1870-83; negotiated $40,000,000 loan for N.P. Ry., 1881; mediated agreement between Erie R.R. and Atlantic & Gt. Western R.R.; helped purchase Panama R.R. for Panama Canal Co.; pres. 3d Nat. Bank of N.Y.C., 1876. Died N.Y.C., Dec. 28, 1910.

F

FERRIER, Kathleen, singer; b. Higher Walton, Lancashire, Eng.; d. William and Alice (Murray) Ferrier; studied voice with Dr. J. E. Hutchinson, Newcastle-on-tyne, 1940-42, with Roy Henderson, London, Eng., 1942. Pianist and accompanist in Eng., 1927-36; entered singing contest as part of a bet, 1938, won contest and decided to study voice; made London debut as soloist in Handel's Messiah, 1943; made N.Y.C. debut, 1948; toured U.S., Can., Eng.; especially noted for her singing of English folk-music, works of Mahler, Bach and Handel. Died Oct. 8, 1953.

FORD, Ford Madox, b. Merton, Eng., 1873; changed name from Ford Madox Hueffer, 1919; aided Joseph Conrad in learning English, collaborated with Conrad in writing The Inheritors, 1901, Romance, 1903; founded The English Review, 1908, editor, 1908-11; founded Transatlantic Review, 1924, gave 1st publication to writers including James Joyce,

Ernest Hemingway. (See sketch page 193, Who Was Who in America, Vol. II.)

FOSTER, Thomas Jefferson, journalist; b. Pottsville, Pa., Jan. 1, 1843; s. Thomas and Amanda (Ruch) F.; attended Eastman Bus. Coll., Poughkeepsie, N.Y., 1864-65; m. Fanny C. Miller, 1869; m. 2d, Blandina Harrington; children—Joel, Jeremiah, Amanda, Mary, Emma, Thomas Jefferson. Founder (with Henry C. Boyer) Weekly Herald, Shenandoah, Pa., 1870, Evening Herald, 1875; published Mining Herald; established Colliery Engr., Scranton, Pa., 1888; opened Colliery Engr. Sch. of Mines (1st of Internat. Correspondence Schs.), 1891. Died Oct. 14, 1936.

FRASCH, Herman, chem. engr., inventor; b. Würtemberg, Germany, Dec. 25, 1851; son of Johannes Frasch; m. Romalda Berks; m. 2d, Elizabeth Blee. Came to U.S., 1868, worked for Phila. Coll. of Pharmacy; moved to Cleve., 1877, opened chem. lab. to study petroleum refining; organized Empire Oil Co., London, Ont., Can., 1885; developed Frasch process for desulfurization of crude petroleum oil; received 21 U.S. patents for refining of petroleum, 1887-94, sold patents to Standard Oil Co.; received patent for mining of sulfur by means of superheated water, 1891; organizer, pres. Union Sulfur Co., 1892; recipient Perkin Gold medal in chemistry, 1912. Died Paris, France, May 1, 1914.

FREUD, Sigmund, psychoanalyst; b. Freiberg, Moravia, May 6, 1856; M.D., U. Vienna (Austria), 1881; m. Martha Bernays, 1886, 6 children including Anna. Studied psychol. aspects of hysteria under Jean Charcot, Paris, France, 1885-86; collaborated with Josef Breur on use of hypnosis to cure hysteria by having patient recall origin and express emotions attendent with hysteria; replaced hypnosis with free association which permitted study of phenomena of resistance and transference; studied his own unconscious mental processes by applying his psychol. knowledge to himself, 1897; a founder (with Eugen Bleuler and C. G. Jung) Jahrbuch für psychoanalytische und pyschopathologische Forschungen, 1908; gave series of lectures (with Jung) at Clark U., Worcester, Mass., 1909; formed Internat. Psychoanalytical Assn., 1910; recipient Goethe prize, 1930; elected mem. Royal Soc., 1936; moved to London after annexation of Austria by Nazi Germany, 1938; his discovery of the role of the subconscious in conscious activity has had widespread ramifications in nearly all areas of human endeavor. Author: On the Psychological Mechanism of Hysterical Phenomena, 1893; Studient Über Hysteria, 1895; The Interpretation of Dreams, 1900; The Psychopathology of Everyday Life, 1904; Totem and Taboo, 1913; The Ego and the Id, 1923; Moses and Monotheism, 1939. Died London, Eng., Sept. 23, 1939.

FULTON, Weston Miller, Sr., inventor; b. Stewart, Ala., Aug. 3, 1871; s. William Frierson II and Mary Brown (Hudson) F.; student Howard Coll., Birmingham, 1887-89; B.S. with highest honors, U. Miss., 1892; postgrad. in engring., Tulane U., 1896-98; M.S., U. Tenn., 1902; m. Barbara S. Murrian, Aug. 17, 1910; children—Weston Miller, Jr. (dec.), Barbara Alexander (Mrs. Fenton Gentry), Robert William, Jean Hudson (Mrs. James Talley III), Mary Helen (Mrs. C.J. Hartley). With U.S. Weather Bur., Vicksburg, Miss., 1892-98, Knoxville, Tenn., 1898-1903; inventor Sylphon (a seamless metal bellows now used in radiators, refrigerators, atomic plants, diesel, automobile and airplane engines; used in anti submarine depth bombs World War I), 1904; organizer (to produce the Sylphon) The Fulton Co. (later became Fulton Sylphon Co., now Fulton Sylphon div. Robertshaw Fulton Controls Corp.), Knoxville, 1904, prin. owner, 1904-28; pres., owner W. J. Savage Co., 1930-36, Tenn.-Odin Ins. Co. (name now So. Fire & Casualty Ins. Co.), 1935-46, Royal Mfg. Co., 1940-45 (all Knoxville). Prof. meteorology U. Tenn., 1898-1903. Recipient Modern Pioneer award N.A.M., 1940; certificate of appreciation Pres. Roosevelt, 1945. A separate sect. U.S. Patent Office set aside to house his 125 patents which include the sylphon and other thermostatic devices. Died Knoxville, May 16, 1946; buried Highland Meml. Cemetery, Knoxville, Tenn.

G

GARVEY, Marcus Moziah, reformer; b. St. Ann's Bay, Jamaica, Aug. 17, 1887; s. Marcus Moziah and Sarah Jane (Richards) G.; m. Amy Ashwood, 1919; m. 2d, Amy Jacques, 1922, children—Marcus Jacques, Julius Winston. Moved to Kingston, Jamaica, 1904; co-leader of unsuccessful printers strike, Kingston, 1907; in London, Eng., 1912-14; organized Universal Negro Improvement and Conservation Assn. and African Communities League (known as U.N.I.A.), Jamaica, 1914; came to N.Y.C., 1916, established branch of U.N.I.A., 1917; publisher Negro World, N.Y.C., circa 1917; organized Black Star Line, Negro steamship co. which traded among Negro areas, 1919, convicted of mail fraud when line failed, 1923, served 2 years (of 5 year sentence), 1925-27; organized Negro Factories Corp.; organized unsuccessful Black Cross Navigation and Trading Co., 1924; advocated Back to Africa movement; deported to Jamaica, 1927; went to London, 1934, published Black Man, London. Died London, June 10, 1940; buried St. Mary's Cemetery, Kensal Green, London.

GERONIMO (Indian name Goyathlay), Indian warrior; b. Ariz., June 1829; s. Taklishim and Juana. Joined Chiricahua Apaches as a youth, took part in raids led by Cochise and Mangas Coloradas; led party of warriors on raid when Apaches were moved to San Carlos Reservation, Ariz., 1876; led other raids, 1880, 82-83, captured each time and returned to reservation; made most infamous raid, May 1885-Mar. 1886, captured in Mexico by Gen. George Crook of U.S. Cavalry; escaped, later recaptured by detachment of army under Gen. Nelson A. Miles on Bavispe River, Mexico; imprisoned at Ft. Pickens, Fla., then at Mt. Vernon, Ala., finally at Ft. Sill, Okla.; became farmer on reservation; joined Dutch Reformed Ch., 1903; appeared in inaugural procession of Pres. Theodore Roosevelt, 1905; dictated his memoirs, 1906. Died Ft. Sill, Feb. 17, 1909.

GILLESPIE, Mabel, labor leader; b. St. Paul, Minn., Mar. 4, 1867; d. James and Ida (Scott) Gillespie; attended Radcliffe Coll., 1898-1900; never married. Sec., Boston Asso. Charities; became mem. Women's Trade Union League, Boston, 1903, exec. sec., 1909-23; active in textile workers' strike, 1903-04; exec. sec. Child Labor Com. and Consumers' League, Buffalo, N.Y., 1904-09; active in organizing women of various professions; mem. Mass. Minimum Wage Commn. (1st in U.S.); 1st woman elected to exec. com. Mass. branch AFL, became v.p., 1918; mgr. dressmaking shop, Boston; a founder Trade Union Coll., Boston, 1919; mem. adminstrv. com. Bryn Mawr Summer Sch. for Women Workers, 1921-23. Died Boston, Sept. 24, 1923.

GILMORE, Joseph Henry, clergyman, educator; b. Boston, Apr. 29, 1834; s. Joseph Albree and Ann (Whipple) G.; grad. Phillips Andover Acad., 1854, Brown U., 1858, Newton Theol. Inst., 1861; m. Mary Parkhurst, May 10, 1861; m. 2d, Lucy Brown, Sept. 21, 1865. Preacher in Phila., 1861; minister Baptist Ch. in Fisherville, N.H., 1862-64; pvt. sec. to father and editor Concord (N.H.) Daily Monitor, 1861-65; minister Bapt. Ch., Rochester, N.Y., 1865,67; tchr. Hebrew, Rochester Theol. Sem., 1867-68; prof. English, U. Rochester, 1868-1908. Author: The Art of Expression, 1875; Outlines of Logic, 1876; He Leadeth Me and Other Religious Poems, 1877; English Literature, 1880. Died July 23, 1918.

GLIDDEN, Joseph Farwell, farmer, inventor, mfr.; b. Charleston, N.H., Jan. 18, 1813; s. David and Polly (Hurd) G.; attended sem., Lima, N.Y.; m. Clarissa Foster, 1837; m. 2d, Lucinda Warne, 1851; at least 1 child. Worked his way West from N.H. as thresher, 1842-44; purchased land in De Kalb County (Ill.), a cattle ranch in Tex.; sheriff of De Kalb County, 1852-53; patented improvement on barb wire fences, 1874; organized (with Isaac L. Ellwood) Barb Wire Fence Co., De Kalb County, 1875; sold his half interest to Washburn & Moen Mfg. Co., 1876, lived on royalties. Died Oct. 9, 1906.

GOLDMAN, Emma, anarchist; b. Kovno, Lithuania, June 27, 1869; d. Araham and Taube Goldman; m. Jacob Kershner, Feb. 1887; m. 2d, James Colton. Came to Rochester, N.Y., 1885; moved to N.Y.C., 1889, became acquainted with Alexander Berkman; convicted of inciting riot among unemployed workers, N.Y.C., Oct. 1893, imprisoned in Blackwell's Island prison until Aug. 1894; toured Europe, 1895, 99; worked as nurse, 1900; founder, editor Mother Earth, anarchist journal, 1906-17; early advocate of birth control, 1916; convicted of obstructing selective service law, 1917, served 2 year sentence in Mo. State Prison, Jefferson City; deported to Russia, 1919, to Riga, Latvia, 1921; in Eng., 1924-26; lived in St. Tropez, France, circa 1931; visited U.S., 1934; went to Spain as advocate of anti-Franco movement during Spanish Civil War; made lecture tour of Canada, 1940. Died Toronto, Can., May 14, 1940; buried Waldheim Cemetery, Chgo.

GOODNIGHT, Charles, rancher; b. Macoupin County, Ill., Mar. 5, 1836; m. Mary Ann Dyer, 1871; m. 2d, Corinne Goodnight, Mar. 5, 1927; 1 child. Became rancher, Palo Pinto County, Tex., 1857; mem. Frontier Regt., Tex. Rangers in action against Indians, 1861-66; established 1st Tex. cattle ranch on Pecos River, southern N.M., 1866; established ranch on Apishapa River, Colo., 1868, on Arkansas River, Colo., 1870; laid out Goodnight Cattle Trail from Belknap, Tex. to Ft. Sumner, N.M., (1866), Goodnight-Loving Trail from N.M. to Wyo., New Goodnight Trail from Alamogordo, N.M. to Granada, Colo. (1875); established ranch Palo Duro Canyon in Tex. Panhandle, 1876; laid out trail from Panhandle to Dodge City, Kan., 1877; became owner (with John George Adair) JA Ranch, 1877 (eventually covered over 1 million acres); crossed buffalo with Polled Angus cattle to produce 1st herd of cattalo; organized 1st Panhandle stockmen's assn. to fight rustlers and outlaws, 1880. Died Dec. 12, 1929.

GORDON, Laura De Force, lawyer, journalist; b. Erie County, Pa., Aug. 17, 1838; d. Abram and Katy (Allen) De Force; m. Charles H. Gordon, 1862 (div. 1880). Joined (with husband) wagon train to White Plains, Nev., 1865, became 1st white woman in that city; moved to Mokelumne, Cal., 1870; edited woman's column in Narrow Gauge, Stockton, Cal., 1873; published Stockton Weekly Leader, 1873, Daily Leader, 1874-75; lobbied in Cal. Legislature for passage of bill to allow women to practice law in Cal., 1878; one of 1st 2 women admitted to Cal. bar, 1879, to practice before U.S. Supreme Ct. bar, to be enrolled in a Cal. state univ. Died San Joaquin County, Cal., Apr. 6, 1907.

GRANT, George Barnard, inventor, mech. engr.; b. Gardiner, Me., Dec. 21, 1849; s. Peter and Vesta (Capen) G.; B.S., Harvard, 1873; never married. Obtained patents for calculating machine, 1872, 73; exhibited his calculator "Grant's Difference Engine" at Phila. Centennial Expn., 1876; opened gear-cutting machine shop, Charleston, Mass., 1873; established Grant Gear Works, Inc., Boston. Author: Chart and Tables for Bevel Gears, 1885; A Handbook on the Teeth of Gears. . .with Odontographs, 1885. Died Pasadena, Cal., Aug. 16, 1917.

GRASS, John, Indian chief; b. 1837. Chief of Blackfoot Sioux Indians; received warrior name Charging Bear for bravery in battle with Crow Indians, 1854; advocated peace with white man, realizing that war would ruin his people, 1870's; chief justice Ct. of Indian Offenses at Ft. Yates, circa 1880-1918; Indian commr. at council to cede lands in S.D. to U.S. Govt., 1888, broke off original negotiations, later accepted treaty with more favorable terms for his people. Died May 10, 1918.

GRIFFES, Charles Tomlinson, composer, educator; b. Elmira, N.Y., Sept. 17, 1884; s. Wilbur G. and Clara (Tomlinson) G.; studied piano with Mary S. Broughton, Elmira Acad.; studied piano with E. Jedliczka and G. Galston, theory with Klatte and Loewengrad, composition with P. Rüfer and E. Humperdinck (all Berlin, Germany). Taught privately in Berlin until 1907; returned to N.Y., became music master Hackley Sch. for Boys, Tarrytown, also taught privately until death. Wrote for orch., chamber groups, piano and voice; work displays 3 periods: early Germanic, middle Impressionistic and Oriental, late exptl.; works include: Four Roman Sketches, Opus 7, Three Songs, Opus 10, The Pleasure Dome of Kubla Khan; Two Sketches Based on Indian Themes; his Sonata (piano composition of late period) was influential in devel. of modern Am. mus. idiom. Died N.Y., Apr. 8, 1920.

GRIFFITH, David (Lewelyn) Wark, film dir.; b. Oldham County, Ky., Jan. 22, 1875. Bit player with Mefert stock co., 1897-99; played lead in Rescued From the Eagle's Nest, 1907; dir. Biograph Studios, 1908-13; produced 1st 4 reel Am. film Judith of Bethulia, 1913; introduced flashback, long shot, fade-in, close-up, fade-out; made film Birth of a Nation (a turning point in history of film as artistic medium), 1915, film's sympathetic treatment of Ku Klux Klan led to controversy; released movie Intolerance, 1916; formed United Artists Corp. with Charles Chaplin, Douglas Fairbanks, Mary Pickford, 1919; made films Way Down East, 1920, Orphans of the Stars, 1922; 1st to use night photography in films. Died Hollywood, Cal., July 23, 1948.

GROSSET, Alexander, publisher; b. Windsor Mills, Que., Can., Jan. 17, 1870; s. Alexander Shaw and Janet (Finlay) G.; m. Alice Carey, Feb. 27, 1893; m. 2d, Frances Sparks Hood, June 17, 1915; children—Alexander Donald, Alexandra, Janet, Barbara. Came to N.Y.C., 1890; with John W. Lovell's U.S. Book Co., circa 1890-98; took control (with George T. Dunlap) Am. Publisher's Corp., 1898, changed name to Grosset & Dunlap, 1900, pres., 1900-34; his firm attained prominence by publishing Barrack-Room Ballads (Rudyard Kipling), The Christian (Hall Crane), The Choir Invisible (James Lane Allen); introduced low-priced, hardbound books to public with The Damnation of Theron Ware (Harold Frederic); added line of children's books including The Rover Boys, Tom Swift, The Bobbsey Twins; later published Zane Grey's novels; a founder Nat. Assn. Book Publishers, 1920. Died Oct. 27, 1934.

GUNN, James Newton, indsl. engr.; b. Springfield, O., 1867; s. Rev. James and Mary (Johnson) G.; m. Mabel Scott, 3 daus. With Library Bur. of Boston, circa 1892-1901, developed use of comml. card indices, patented tab index card and vertical file; early worker in field of indsl. and prodn. engring.; organized Gunn, Richards & Co., Bus. Consultants, 1901; cons. for Campbell's Soup Co., Pa. Steel Corp., Studebaker Corp., 1901-11; pres. U.S. Tire Co., also asst. to pres. U.S. Rubber Co., 1915-23; an organizer Harvard Grad. Sch. of Bus. Adminstrn.; represented Rubber Assn. on War Industries Bd., 1917-18; pres. Lincoln Hwy. Assn. Died Nov. 26, 1927.

H

HAAS, Jacob Judah Aaron de, see de Haas, Jacob Judah Aaron.

HAISH, Jacob, inventor, mfr.; b. Baden, Germany, Mar. 9, 1826; s. Christian and Christina (Layman) H.; m. Sophia Brown, May 24, 1847. Came to U.S. with parents, 1836; worked on farm, Pierce, Ill., 1849-51; applied for patent for his improvements in barbed wire, 1873, found that a similar patent had been applied for by J. F. Gilden; patented "S" barbed wire, 1875; his patents purchased by Washburn & Moen Mfg. Co. (which soon controlled prodn. of barbed wire in U.S.), 1876; fought ultimately unsuccessful ct. battle to retain sole right to manufacture barbed wire, 1876-92; founder Barb City Bank, DeKalb, Ill. Died Feb. 19, 1926.

HAMILTON, William Thomas, trapper, scout; b. Eng., Dec. 6, 1822; married, 1850. Came to U.S., 1825; mem. trapping party going to Northwest, 1842-45; served in Rogue River War, 1855, Modor War, 1856; traded with Blackfoot, Crow, other Indians in Walla Walla (Wash.) area to determine and report on their activities to Col. George Wright, 1857; sheriff Missoula County, 1861; marshal for Crow Indians, 1873; scout for Gen. George Crook in Sioux War, 1876-77. Author: My Sixty Years on the Plains, 1905; My Experiences in Montana (unpublished). Died May 24, 1908.

HAMMOND, James Bartlett, inventor, mfr.; b. Boston, Apr. 23, 1829; s. Thomas and Harriet (Trow) H.; grad. U. Vt., 1861, Union Theol. Sem., 1865; never married. Reported Henry Ward Beecher's sermons for Boston Daily Traveller, 1861; with N.Y. Tribune, 1862-63, started working on devel. of typewriter, circa 1871, patented typewriter, 1880; his machine won Elliott Cresson Gold medal when publicly demonstrated at New Orleans Centennial Expn., 1884; pres. Hammond Co., typewriter mfg. firm, N.Y., 1884-1909; left his large fortune to Met. Mus. Art, N.Y.C. Died St. Augustine, Fla., Jan. 27, 1913.

HARLOW, Jean (real name Harlean Carpenter), actress; b. Kansas City, Mo., Mar. 3, 1911; d. Mont Clair and Jean (Harlow) Carpenter; m. Charles Fremont McGrew, Sept. 21, 1927; m. 2d, Paul Bern, July 1932; m. 3d, Harold Rosson, Sept. 1933. Moved to Beverly Hills, Cal., before 1928; registered with Central Casting Bur., began playing bit parts; played leading role in Hell's Angels, 1930; created fad of "platinum blonde"; appeared in The Secret Six, 1931, Public Enemy, 1931, Beast of the City, 1932, Red-Headed Women, 1932; began playing comedy roles with Dinner at Eight, Hold Your Man, Bombshell, 1933; her last film, Saratoga, released after her death at age 26. Died of uremic poisoning, Los Angeles, June 7, 1937; buried Forest Meml. Park, Glendale, Cal.

HARRINGTON, Mark Walrod, astronomer, coll. pres.; b. Sycamore, Ill., Aug. 18, 1848; s. James and Charlotte (Walrod) H.; attended Northwestern U., 1864-66; grad. U. Mich., 1868, A.M. (hon.), 1870, LL.D. (hon.), 1894; attended U. Leipzig (Germany), 1876-77. Taught mathematics and geology U. Mich., 1868-71, 71-76, prof. astronomy, 1879-91; worked for U.S. Coastal Survey in Alaska, 1870-71; taught mathematics and astronomy at Fgn. Office Cadet Sch., Peking, China, 1877-78; prof. astronomy U. La., 1878-79; founder, editor Am. Meteorol. Jour., 1884-92; 1st civilian head U.S. Weather Bur., 1891-95; pres. U. Wash., 1895-97; mem. Imperial Anthrop. Soc. Moscow, Linnean Soc. of London, Austrian Meteorol. Soc.; corr. mem. Scottish Geog. Soc. discovered irregular periodic change of light in star Vesta, trifid character of Gt. Hercules nebula. Author: About the Weather, 1899; also many scientific papers. Died Oct. 9, 1926.

HARTFORD, George Huntington, food chain exec.; b. Augusta, Me., 1833; married; children—George L., John. Worked briefly in St. Louis, 1859; opened store selling tea he imported himself by clipper ship-load from China, hence could sell at relatively low price, N.Y.C., 1859 (beginning of Gt. Atlantic & Pacific Tea Co.); employed promotional techniques including large, illuminated signs, elaborate interior decoration, brass band, nat. mag. advt.; added coffee to mdse. line; made use of transcontinental ry. to supply his A & P stores; bus. continued by his sons. Died 1917.

HASBROUCK, Lydia Sayer, reformer; b. Warwick, N.Y., Dec. 20, 1827; d. Benjamin and Rebecca (Forshee) Sayer; grad. Central Coll., Elmira, N.Y.; M.D., Hygeia-Therapeutic Coll., N.Y.C., 1855; m. John W. Hasbrouck, July 27, 1856, 3 children. Became advocate of movement for dress-reform as safeguard to health; adopted Bloomer costume, circa 1849, wore it for rest of life; also advocated temperance, women's suffrage; del. World's Temperance Conv., 1853; practiced medicine, Washington, D.C., 1955-56; co-editor (with husband) Sybil, dress-reform paper, Middletown, N.Y., 1856-64; pres. Nat. Dress Reform Assn., 1864-65; co-editor Whig Press, Middletown, 1864-68; mem. Middletown Sch. Bd., 1880-81; published (with husband) Liberal Sentinel, women's suffrage paper, Middletown, 1881-1909. Died "Sybil Ridge," nr. Middletown, Aug. 24, 1910.

HASKELL, Ella Louise Knowles, lawyer; b. Northwood Ridge, N.H., July 31, 1860; d. David and Louisa (Bigelow) Knowles; grad. Bates Coll., Lewiston, Me., 1884; studied law under Henry E. Burnham, Manchester, N.H.; married Henri J. Haskell, May 23, 1895, no children. First woman admitted to Mont. bar, 1889; practiced law, Helena, Mont.; dep. atty. gen. Mont., 1892-96; del. Populist Nat. Conv., 1896, nat. committeewoman for Mont., 1896-1900; later practiced law, also invested in mining property, Butte, Mont.; mem. exec. com. Internat. Mining Congress; advocate of equal rights for women in all fields. Died Jan. 27, 1911.

HAUK, Minnie, opera singer; b. N.Y.C., Nov. 16, 1852; studied under Curto in New Orleans, circa 1865; m. Baron Ernst von Hesse-Wartegg, 1881. Moved to N.Y.C., 1866; made debut as Amina in Sonnambula, Bklyn. Acad. Music, 1866; studied under Moritz Strakosch, 1867, played Juliette in 1st Am. prodn. of Gounod's Roméo et Juliette; appeared in Am. premiere of Carmen, also Manon; made London debut, 1868; toured Europe, sang in Paris, Moscow, Berlin; prima donna assoluta of Komische Oper, Vienna, Austria; toured U.S. and Can., 1883-84, gave concert in White House; ret., 1895. Died Feb. 6, 1929.

HAWTHORNE, Rose, see Alphonsa, Mother.

HAYWOOD, William Dudley (Big Bill), labor leader; b. Salt Lake City, Utah, Feb. 4, 1869; s. William Haywood; m. Jane Minor, 1889; m. 2d, in Russia, 1927. Employed as miner, cowhand; homesteader; became mem. Western Fedn. Miners, 1896, del. nat. conv., 1898, mem. exec. bd., 1899, sec.-treas., 1900; organized miners' activities during conflict with Colo. mine owners, 1901-05; chmn. conv. which founded I.W.W., 1905; arrested in Denver for alleged conspiracy in 1905 assassination of former Ida. Gov. Frank R. Steunenberg, Feb. 1906; his transportation to jail in Ida. prompted sympathizers to contend he had been kidnapped; nominated by Socialist party for gov. Colo. while in prison, polled 16,000 votes; defended by Clarence Darrow and acquitted in trial ending July 1907; a leader in mill workers' strike, Lawrence, Mass., 1912; expelled from nat. exec. bd. Socialist party for alleged advocacy of violence, 1912; became nat. sec.-treas. Indsl. Workers World; helped lead textile workers' strike, Paterson, N.J., 1913; convicted of sedition, 1918; fled U.S., 1921; active in revolutionary socialist movements. Author: (with Frank Bohn) Industrial Socialism, 1911; Bill Haywood's Book (autobiography), 1929. Died Moscow, Russia, May 18, 1928.

HILL, Joe (Joel Hägglund), labor union leader, songwriter; b. Sweden, Oct. 7, 1879; came to U.S., 1902, changed name to Joseph Hillstrom. Various jobs, 1902-12; joined San Pedro (Cal.) local Indsl. Workers of World, 1910; while working as dockwalloper in San Pedro, wrote 1st song, Casey Jones—the Union Scab, to help S. Pacific Line strikers, 1911; made many contbns. to The Little Red Song Book; supported increased female membership in Indsl. Workers World; suggested Workers Moratorium League of N.Y. (later realized in IWW Unemployed League); convicted of murder of grocer in Salt Lake City, 1914; executed by firing squad (despite internat. defense movement on his behalf, and 2 pleas from Pres. Wilson to Utah Gov. William Spry to reconsider case), 1915; his funeral procession in Chgo. had estimated 30,000 marchers. Author: The Letters of Joe Hill (edited by Philip S. Foner), pub. 1965. Died Nov. 19, 1915.

HIRES, Charles Elmer, soft drink mfr.; b. nr. Roadstown, N.J., Aug. 19, 1851; s. John Dare and Mary (Williams) H.; m. Clara Kate Smith, 1875; children—Linda Smith John Edgar, Harrison Streeter, Charles Elmer, Clara Sheppard; m. 2d, Emma Waln, 1911. Worked in drug store, Bridgeton, N.J., 1863-67; moved to Phila., 1867; became propr. pharmacy, Phila., 1869; experimented with sarsaparilla root, developed drink which he named Hires Root Beer, 1875, sold drink at Centennial Expn., Phila., 1876; at 1st sold root beer as a package of dried roots and herbs to be brewed at home, later sold it in form of concentrated extract; organized Charles E. Hires Co., 1890; pioneer in processing of condensed milk (taken over by Nestlé Co. 1918). Died Haverford, Pa., July 31, 1937; buried Westminster Cemetery, nr. Cynwyd, Pa.

HOHFELD, Wesley Newcomb, lawyer, educator; b. Oakland, Cal., Aug. 8, 1879; s. Edward and Rosalie (Hillebrand) H.; grad. U. Cal., 1901; grad. cum laude Harvard Law Sch., 1904; never married. With Morrison, Cope & Brobeck, law firm, San Francisco, 1904; prof. law Stanford U., 1905-14, Yale, 1914-18; developed Hohfeld system of legal analysis, which more precisely defined legal terminology. Died Alameda, Cal., Oct. 21, 1918.

HOLLAND, John Philip, inventor; b. Liscanor, County Clare, Ireland, Feb. 29, 1840; s. John and Mary (Scanlon) H.; m. Margaret Foley, Jan. 17, 1887, 4 children. Taught sch., Ireland, 1858-72; came to U.S., 1873, taught sch., Paterson, N.J.; offered design of submarine to U.S. Navy, 1875 (offer rejected); constructed his 1st submarine with financial backing of revolutionary Fenian Soc. (sank on 1st trial, 1878; launched Fenian Ram, 1881 (proved impractical); contracted to build submarine Plunger for U.S. Navy, 1895, but his designs were radically altered; launched his own submarine the Holland, 1898 (1st submarine equipped to move underwater by electric power and on surface by gasoline engine; 1 of 1st designed to dive by inclining its axis); sold Holland, with 6 sister ships, to U.S. Navy, 1900; also built submarines for Russia, Japan, Gt. Britain; invented repirator for escape from disabled submarines, 1904. Died Newark, N.J., Aug. 12, 1914.

HOLLERITH, Herman, inventor, mfr.; b. Buffalo, N.Y., Feb. 29, 1860; s. George and Franciska (Brunn) H.; grad. Columbia U. Sch. of Mines, 1879; m. Lucia Beverly Talcott, Sept. 15, 1890; children—Lucia, Nannie, Virginia, Herman, Richard, Charles. Asst. to statistician William Petit, Columbia, 1880; instr. mech. engring. Mass. Inst. Tech., 1882; went to St. Louis, 1883; with Patent Office, Washington, D.C., 1884-90; invented tabulating machine which worked on principle of punched holes in non-conducing material (counting took place as electric current passed through holes); his tabulating machine used for Census of 1890; read paper concerning his invention before Berne session Internat. Statis. Inst., 1895; founded Tabulating Machine Co., N.Y., 1896, merged with 2 other cos. to become Computing-Tabulating-Recording Co., 1911, later became IBM. Died Washington, Nov. 17, 1929.

HOLLIDAY, William Helmus, mfr., state legislator; b. Hamilton County, O., May 21, 1843; s. Eli and Annetta (Bogart) H.; m. Emily Coykendall, May 5, 1869, children—Catherine, Guy, Albert, Lois, Elizabeth, Ruth, Margaret; m. 2d, Sarah East, Feb. 20, 1897, children—Mary, Helen. Worked in sawmill in what is now Albany County, Wyo., 1867-70; lumber mfr., nr. Sherman, Wyo., 1870-73; pres. W. H. Holliday Co. (1 of largest mfg. and merchandising firms in Wyo.); mem. Wyo. Ho. of Reps., 1873-75; mem. Wyo. Territorial Council, 1875, 77, 84, 88; mem. delegation to Washington, D.C. which secured Wyo. statehood, 1890; mem. Wyo. Senate, 1892-96, 1908-16; pres. Carnegie Library Assn. Died 1916.

HORNSBY, Rogers, baseball player; b. Winters, Tex., Apr. 27, 1896. Began profl. baseball career as shortstop with St. Louis Cardinals, 1915, changed to 2d base, 1920; batting champion Nat. League, 1920-25, 28, batted .424 (still a modern maj. league record), 1924; player-mgr. St. Louis Cardinals, 1925-26, led team to winning World Series, 1926; traded to N.Y. Giants, 1927; player-mgr. Boston Braves, 1928; played for Chgo. Cubs, 1930-32; played briefly for St. Louis Cardinals, 1933; mgr. St. Louis Browns, 1933-37; maintained .358 lifetime batting average, 1915-33; won most valuable player award, 1925, 28; elected to Nat. Baseball Hall of Fame, 1942. Died Jan. 6, 1963.

HUBERT, Conrad, inventor; b. Minsk, Russia, 1855; married, 1914. Owned distillery in Russia; came to U.S. to escape Russian persecution of Jews, 1890; invented elec. device for lighting gas, 1898; later invented electric time alarm; invented electric battery and small electric lamp (forming basis for modern flashlight); founder, pres. Am. Ever Ready Co., flashlight mfg. firm, N.Y.C., circa 1903-14, sold out to Nat. Carbon Co., 1914; founder, chmn. bd. Yale Electric Corp., 1914-28. Died Cannes, France, Mar. 14, 1928; buried N.Y.C.

HUFFMAN, Laton Alton, photographer; b. Castalia, Ia., Oct. 31, 1854; s. Perrin Cuppy and Chastina (Baird) H.; learned photography from his father; married, at least 1 dau., Ruth. Opened studio, Postville, Ia., 1875; traveled and photographed western frontier, Indians, Rocky Mountains, 1875-1919; army post photographer Ft. Keogh, Mont., 1878; commr. Custer County (Mont.), 1886; mem. Mont. Ho. of Reps., 1893; advocate of conservation; served as hunting guide; left large collection of photographs of Old West. Died Billings, Mont., Dec. 28, 1931.

HUGGINS, Miller James, baseball player; b. Cincinnati, Apr. 19, 1879; s. James Thomas and Sarah (Reid) H.; grad. U. Cincinnati, 1902; never married. Capt. baseball team U. Cincinnati; played 2d base for St. Paul, Minn. (Am. Assn.), 1900-03, Cincinnati Reds (Nat. League), 1904-08, St. Louis Cardinals (Nat. League), 1909-13; mgr. St. Louis Cardinals, 1913-17, N.Y. Yankees (Am. League), 1918-29; led Yankees to 1st 6 pennants and 1st 3 world championships. Died N.Y.C., Sept. 25, 1929; buried Cincinnati.

HUNTER, Thomas, educator; b. Ardglass, Ireland, Oct. 19, 1831; s. John and Mary (Norris) H.; m. Annie McBride, 1854, 4 children. Came to U.S., 1850; tchr. 13th Street Sch. (later P.S. No. 35), N.Y.C., 1850-57, prin., 1857-69; founded first evening high sch. in N.Y.C., 1866; founder, pres. N.Y.C. Normal and High Sch., 1869-1906 (name changed to Normal Coll. of City of N.Y., 1870, to Hunter Coll. of City of N.Y., 1914). Died N.Y.C., Oct. 14, 1915.

HUSSERL, Edmond, philosopher; b. Prossnitz, Moravia, Apr. 18, 1859; ed. Gymnasium of Olmütz; studied astronomy, math., physics, philosophy at univs. Leipzig, Berlin, Vienna; Dr. Math.; studied under Franz Brentano, Vienna, 1884-86. Privatdozent, teaching philosophy, Halle, 1887-1901; prof. philosophy, Gottingen, 1906-16, Freiburg im Breisgau, 1916-28, ret., 1928. Founder phenomenological movement, dealing with consciousness in relation to objects and the structure of experience; exercised great influence on existential and other philosophy and psychology. Author: Cartesian Meditations; Ideas; Ideas: General Introduction to Pure Phenomenology; Phenomenology and the Crisis of Philosophy; Phenomenology of Internal Time-consciousness. Died Freiburg, Breisgau, Germany, Apr. 27, 1938.

J

JAMES, Henry, moved permanently to Europe, 1875, settled in London, Eng., 1876, visited Am. only occasionally thereafter; became naturalized Brit. citizen, 1914. (See sketch page 628, Who Was Who in America, Vol. I.)

JOHNSON, Byron, baseball exec.; b. Norwalk, O., Jan. 6, 1865; grad. Marietta (O.) 1887. Sports writer, Cincinnati Gazette, 1887-circa 1893; organized Western Baseball League, 1893, pres., 1894-1901; organized Am. League, 1900, pres., 1901-27, controlled many of clubs through ownership of stock, resigned due to friction with baseball commr. Judge Landis over Speaker-Cobb case, 1926; organized 1st World Series contest between Am. and Nat. Leagues, 1903; mem. commn. to run major league baseball, 1903-20, engaged in disagreements with other commrs. Died St. Louis, Mar. 28, 1921; buried St. Louis.

JOHNSON, Jonathan Eastman, artist; b. Lovell, Me., July 29, 1824; s. Phillip and Mary Johnson; studied in art studio of Leutze, Düsseldorf, 1849-51, studied The Hague, 1853-57. Worked for Bufford's lithograph shop, Boston, 1840-41; did crayon portraits, 1841-45; opened art studio, N.Y.C., 1858; became mem. Nat. Acad. Art, 1860. Works include: Old Kentucky Home, The Husking Bee, Two Men, Family Group (1871), also many portraits of famous Americans. Died Apr. 5, 1906.

JOHNSON, Justin, aircraft co. exec.; b. Minneapolis, Minn., Oct. 19, 1903; student U. Minn., 1922-25; m. 2d, Mary Lane, Apr. 15, 1948. Studied music in youth and coll.; moved to Cal., 1925; mem. Casa Del Mar Orch., Santa Monica, Cal., 1925-27; appeared in motion pictures, also helped write mus. score for pictures including Seventh Heaven (1927), Street Angel, 1927-29; taught music, Cal., 1929-31; film work, night club performer, 1931-37; mem. Ted Lewis Band, Los Angeles, 1937-40; led own orch., performed at Biltmore Hotel, Santa Barbara, Cal., 1940-42; served with Signal Corps, AUS, 1942-45, ETO; did mus. work, Hollywood, Cal., worked on pictures including Humoresque, The Jolson Story, 1946-47; gardener-caretaker Los Angeles City Civil Service, 1947; with Cal. Dept. of Employment, 1947-51; with personnel dept., also community relations and pub. affairs supr. Hughes Aircraft Co., Culver City, Cal., 1951-62; part-time lectr. social science dept. Long Beach (Cal.) Coll., also Los Angeles State Coll. Grad. Sch. Counselor Tng. Mem. Pres.'s Com. on Employment of Physically Handicapped, 1953-62; chmn. Cal. Gov.'s Com. on Employment of Handicapped, 1956-60; pres. Los Angeles Coordinating Council on Employment of Handicapped; bd. dirs. Pres.'s People to People Program; gov. Goodwill Industries. Mem. Westchester (dir.), Culver City (pres. 1958-60) chambers commerce, Nat. Rehab. Assn., Am. Legion, Disabled Am. Vets. Died Washington, D.C., May 9, 1962; buried Forest Lawn Cemetery, Hollywood Hills, Cal.

JOHNSON, Walter Perry, baseball player; b. Humboldt, Kan., Nov. 6, 1887. Played with Weiser (Ida.) Baseball Team, 1904-06; pitcher for Washington Senators, Am. League, 1907-27, became team mgr., 1928; set records for number of games completed (531), strikeouts (3947), shutouts (113), consecutive scoreless innings (56 in 1913); recipient Am. League's Most Valuable Player award, 1924; elected to Baseball Hall of Fame, 1936. Died Washington, D.C., Dec. 10, 1946.

JONES, Mary Harris (Mother Jones), labor leader; b. Cork, Ireland, May 1, 1830; dau. of Richard Harris; married, 1861, 4 children (all died of yellow fever 1867). Lost all her possessions in Chgo. Fire, 1871; attended meetings of Knights of Labor; participated in many major labor battles, including Pitts. labor riots, 1877; in Chgo. at time of Haymarket tragedy, 1886; in Birmingham during Am. Ry. Union strike, 1894; organizer for United Mine Workers, 1900, 02, led marches of strikers' wives armed with mops and brooms; led march of children working in textile mills from Kensington, Pa. to Oyster Bay to bring evils of child labor to attention of Pres. Theodore Roosevelt, 1902; led strike in Colo. coal mines which was called off by union pres. (leading to her defection from United Mine Workers), 1903; participated in strike of machinists of So. Pacific R.R.; attempted to secure release of Mexican revolutionaries imprisoned in U.S., 1910; organizer for United Mine Workers in W.Va., 1911-13; delivered speeches around the country, 1914, testified before Com. on Mines and Mining of U.S. Ho. of Reps., protested to Pres. Woodrow Wilson against mine conditions and Ludlow Massacre; participated in garment and street-car strikes in N.Y.C., 1915-16, in steel strike, 1919; spoke before Pan-Am. Fedn. of Labor, Mexico City, 1921. Died Nov. 30, 1930; buried United Mine Workers Cemetery, Mt. Olive, Ill.

JOY, Agnes Elisabeth Winona Leclercq, see SALM-SALM, Princess.

K

KEARNEY, Denis, labor leader; b. County Cork, Ireland, Feb. 1, 1847; m. Mary Ann Leary, 1870; 4 children. Came to Am.; settled in San Francisco, established draying bus., 1868; naturalized, 1876; active in Draymen's and Teamsters' union, San Francisco, during 1870's; opposed power of bus. interests in Cal., but did not advocate violence; a founder Workingmen's Party of Cal. (sometimes known as Kearney movement), 1877, pres., 1877-80, party platform protested against monopolies, unemployment, state taxation policies; del. Cal. Constl. Conv., 1878; supported James B. Weaver for U.S. Pres., 1880. Died Alameda, Cal., Apr. 24, 1907; buried Alameda.

KELLEY, Oliver Hudson, founder agrl. orgn.; b. Boston, Jan. 7, 1826; s. William Robinson and Nancy (Hancock) K.; m. Lucy Earle, 1849; m. 2d, Temperance Baldwin Lane, 1852; 4 children. Became farmer, Sherburne County, Minn., 1849; encouraged immigration to Minn.; clk. U.S. Bur. of Agr., Washington, D.C., 1864-66; founded Nat. Grange of Patrons of Husbandry, 1867, sec., 1867-78, traveled throughout Midwest organizing local granges, 1868; began speculating in land in Fla., 1875; founded Town of Carrabelle (Fla.), circa 1876. Author: Origin and Progress of the Order of the Patrons of Husbandry, 1875. Died Washington, D.C., Jan. 20, 1913; buried Rock Creek Cemetery, Washington.

KELLY, Luther Sage (Yellowstone Kelly), scout; b. Geneva, N.Y., July 27, 1849; s. Luther and Jeannette (Sage) K.; m. Alice May Morrison, 1885. Served as pvt. U.S. Army, in the West, 1865-68; became hunter and trapper, Wyo., Mont., Dakotas; later served as dispatch bearer U.S. Army; guide to Gen. George A. Forsyth's expdn. to upper Missouri River and Yellowstone area, 1873; chief army scout for Gen. Nelson A. Miles in campaigns against Sioux and Cheyenne Indians, 1876-78; regular army scout in Colo., 1880; later served as clk. War Dept., Chgo., also Pension Bur., Washington, D.C.; guide to Capt. Edwin Glenn's exploring expdn. to Alaska, 1898, to Harriman expdn., 1899; capt. U.S. Volunteers in Philippines, 1900; treas. Province of Surigao (Philippines), 1903-04; Indian agt., San Carlos Reservation, Ariz., 1904-08; operated fruit ranch, Paradise, Cal., 1915-28. Author: Yellowstone Kelly: The Memoirs of Luther S. Kelly, 1926. Died Paradise, Dec. 17, 1928; buried Kelly Mountain, Billings, Mont.

KING, Samuel Archer, balloonist; b. Tinicum, Pa., Apr. 9, 1828; son of Isaac B. King; m. Margaret Roberts, 2 children. Made 1st ascent in balloon, 1851; made career of ascending in balloons at fairs and celebrations; believed it possible to cross Atlantic ocean in balloon, but never made trip; made several ascents for experimenters of U.S. Signal Service. Died Phila., Nov. 3, 1914.

KRANS, Olaf, artist; b. Selja, Sweden, Nov. 2, 1838. Came to Am. with parents, 1850, settled in Bishop Hill, Ill. (a Swedish religious colony); served in Civil War; changed name from Olson to Krans; moved to Galesburg, Ill, became house, sign and decorative painter; moved to Galva, Ill., 1867; painted scenes of pioneer life at Bishop Hill (now in Colony Ch., Bishop Hill). Died Altoona, Ill., Jan. 1916.

KREHBIEL, Christian, clergyman, colonizer; b. Weierhof, Germany, Oct. 18, 1832; s. Johannes and Katharine (Krehbiel) K.; m. Susanna A. Ruth, 1858, 16 children. Came to U.S., 1850; farmer, Summerfield, Ill., 1860-79; elected minister Mennonite Ch., 1864; began encouraging Mennonite emigration to Kan., 1872, attracted settlers from eastern Europe, Russia and U.S.; immigrants settled in large numbers in Central Kan., introduced Turkey-red hard winter wheat (made Kan. leading wheat producing state in U.S.); pres. Mennonite Bd. of Guardians, 1872; founder Mennonite Fgn. Mission Bd., 1872, pres., 1872-96; farmed nr. Halstead, Kan., 1879-1909; a founder Mennonite Acad., Halstead (now Bethel Coll., Newton, Kan.), circa 1881; supt. Indian mission sch., Halstead, 1886-96; founded Mennonite Charity, orgn. which owned Halstead Hosp., 1908. Died nr. Halstead, Apr. 30, 1909.

KURZ, Louis, lithographer; b. Austria, 1833. Came to Am., 1848; moved to Chgo., 1852, began career as scene painter; began lithographic work, Milw., circa 1850, asso. with Henry Seifert; served with Union Army during Civil War; returned to Chgo.; founder Chgo. Lithographic Co., 1863, propr., 1863-71; head Am. Oleograph Co., Milw., during 1870's; partners of Alexander Allison in chromo-lithographic firm, Chgo., 1880-99; best known for series of views for Chicago Illustrated (Jevne and Almini), 1866. Died Chgo., Mar. 21, 1921.

L

LANGE, Dorothea, photographer; student N.Y. Tng. Sch. for Tchrs., also photographer Clarence H. White of Columbia; m. Paul Schuster Taylor, Dec. 6, 1935. Worked from rented chicken-coop darkroom on Palisades early in career, eventually acquired own studio in San Francisco; handled many govtl. and other assignments, specializing in photographs of humans in their social and phys. environment. First exhbn., 1934; retrospective exhibit of 200 prints, Mus. Modern Art, N.Y.C., 1966. Author: (with husband) An American Exodus, 1939. Died Oct. 11, 1965.

LARRÍNAGA, Tulio, govt. ofcl.; b. Trujillo Alto, Puerto Rico, Jan. 15, 1847; attended Rensselaer Poly. Inst., Troy, N.Y., 1865-68; m. Bertha Goyro Saint Victor, June 22, 1879, 5 children. Worked on constrn. Grand Central Sta., N.Y.C.; apptd. architect City of San Juan, P.R.; built 1st railroad in P.R., 1880; engr. for Provincial Deputation, 1880-89; sub-sec. public works, 1898; del. Puerto Rican Legislature, 1902-04; pres. commr. for P.R. in U.S., 1905-11; an Am. rep. at 3d Pan-Am. Congress, Brazil, 1906; apptd. by Pres. Wilson mem. Exec. Council of P.R., 1915. Died Santurce, P.R., Apr. 28, 1917.

LEOPOLD, Aldo, conservationist, ecologist, forester; a founder profession of wildlife mgmt. Author: Sand County Almanac, pub. posthumously, 1949, Round River, 1953. (see sketch page 319, Who Was Who in America, Vol. II)

LILIUOKALANI, Queen of Hawaiian Islands; b. Honolulu, Hawaii, Sept. 2, 1838. Ascended Hawaiian throne, 1891; opposed Constn. of 1887, aroused popular hostility by refusal to recognize principle of selection of cabinet from assembly majority; planned to hold conv. to abrogate constn. and write new one, 1892 (plan rejected by nat. legislature); dismissed legislature, attempted to restore Constn. of 1864, in Jan. 1893; met resistance from elements desiring annexation to U.S. in order to achieve polit. and econ. stability; deposed by Com. of Safety in Honolulu (which set up provisional Republic of Hawaii), Jan. 16, 1893; failed to secure restoration of throne though supported by Pres. Cleveland, 1893-94; made another unsuccessful attempt to regain throne, 1895; wrote song Aloha Oe. Died Honolulu, Nov. 11, 1917; buried Honolulu.

LOW, Juliette Gordon, founder youth orgn.; b. Savannah, Ga., Oct. 31, 1860; d. Gen. William W. and Eleanor (Kinzie) G.; m. William Low, Dec. 21, 1886. Became interested in scouting movement through friendship with Robert Baden-Powell (founder Boy Scouts) and his sister (founder Girl Guides); organized group of Girl Guides in Scotland, 1911; organized 1st troop of Girl Guides in U.S. at Savannah, 1912, group changed name to Girl Scouts, 1913, established nat. hdqrs. in N.Y.C.; given title of founder by Nat. Conv. of Girl Scouts, her birthday designated as Scouts Founder's Day; by time of her death, membership in orgn. numbered over 140,000; officer Savannah Art Club. Died Savannah, Jan. 17, 1927.

M

MacDONALD, James Wilson Alexander, artist; b. Steubenville, O., Aug. 25, 1824. Worked for publishing firm, St. Louis; began sculpting, 1845; became known for marble bust of Senator Benton; moved to N.Y.C. after Civil War, practiced successfully as portrait sculptor; painted some portraits and landscapes. Died Yonkers, N.Y., Aug. 14, 1908.

MAHLER, Gustav, composer, condr.; b. Kalischt, Bohemia, July 1, 1860; ed. Conservatory and Univs. Prague, Vienna; studied with Bruckner; m. Alma Maria Schindler, Mar. 10, 1902; children-Maria Ann (dec. 1907), Anna J. Condr., Prague, 1885, Leipzig, 1886-88; dir. Royal Opera House, Budapest, 1888-91; condr. Hamburg Opera, 1891-97; artistic dir. Vienna Opera, 1897-1907; condr. Met. Opera, N.Y.C., 1907, N.Y. Philharmonic, N.Y.C., 1908-11. Compositions include: Das Klagende Lied (cantata), 1880; Songs of a Wayfarer, 1884; Youth's Magic Horn (lieder), 1888; ten symphonies, 1888-1910 (10th posthumously edited for concert performance); Five Songs from Ruckert, 1902; Kindertotenlieder, 1902; Das Lied von der Erde, 1908. Died Vienna, May 18, 1911; buried Grinzing, Vienna.

MARSCHALL, Nicola, artist; b. Germany, Mar. 16, 1829; studied art, Munich, Germany, and Italy, 1857-59. Came to Am., 1849, settled in Mobile, Ala.; taught painting, music and modern langs. Marion (Ala.) Sem.; designed Confederate flag and uniform for Confederate Army, 1861; served in Confederate Army; moved to Louisville, Ky., 1873. Died Louisville, Feb. 24, 1917.

MASTERSON, William Barclay (Bat Masterson), peace officer, sports writer; b. Iroquois County, Ill., Nov. 24, 1853; s. Thomas and Catherine (McGurk) M.; m. Emma Walters, Nov. 21, 1891. Joined party of buffalo hunters setting out from Ft. Dodge, 1872; distinguished himself in battle with Indians at Adobe Walls, 1874; dep. marshal Dodge City, spring 1876; joined in Deadwood gold rush, 1876; sheriff Ford County (Kan.), 1877-79, killed 2 gunmen who had shot his brother Edward (then acting marshal Dodge City), 1878; lived in Tombstone, 1 of most lawless towns in West, 1880-81, often assisted fed. marshal Wyatt Earp; earned his living in West mainly by gambling; moved to N.Y.C., 1902; sports writer N.Y. Morning Telegraph, 1903-21; fed. dep. marshal (apptd. by Pres. Roosevelt), 1905-07. Died N.Y.C., Oct. 25, 1921; buried Woodlawn Cemetery, N.Y.C.

MATHEWSON, Christopher, baseball player; b. Factoryville, Pa., Aug. 12 ,1880; s. Gilbert B. and Minerva (Capwell) M.; attended Bucknell Coll., Lewisburg, Pa.; m. Jane Stoughton, 1 son, Christopher. Played baseball, football while in coll.; pitcher N.Y. Giants, 1900-16, sometimes outfielder, 1st baseman; pitched no-hit, no-run game against St. Louis, 1901; pitched 3 shutouts against Phila. Athletics in World Series, 1905; made his best won-lost record (37-11), 1908; mgr. Cincinnati Reds, 1916-18; served as capt., gas and flame div. U.S. Army, 1918-19; coach for N.Y. Giants, 1919-20, forced to resign because of pulmonary tuberculosis; pres. Boston Braves, 1923-25. Died Saranac, N.Y., Oct. 7, 1925; buried Lewisburg.

McCOY, Elijah, inventor; b. Can., Mar. 27, 1843; s. George and Mildred (Goins) McC. Patented steam-engine lubricator, 1872; obtained 6 patents for lubricators, also patent for ironing table, 1872-76; received 44 patents (36 of them for lubricating devices), 1882-1926; developed means for lubricating machinery by means of oil drops from cup, which removed need for stopping machinery for lubrication (thus increased productivity); patented steam dome for locomotives, 1885; organized Elijah McCoy Mfg. Co., Detroit, circa 1920. Died Eloise, Mich., Oct. 10, 1929; buried Detroit.

McGRAW, John Joseph, baseball player, mgr.; b. Truxton, N.Y., Apr. 7, 1873; s. John and Ellen (Comerfort) McG.; attended St. Bonaventure's Coll., Allegany, N.Y.; m. Blanche Sindall, 1902, no children. Mem. Olean (N.Y.) baseball club of Oil and Iron League, 1890; infielder Wellsville (N.Y.) baseball club of Western N.Y. League, 1890; shortstop Cedar Rapids (Ia.) baseball club of Ill.-Ia. League, circa 1891; 3d baseman, Balt. Orioles, 1891-99; an organizer Am. League, 1900; mgr. St. Louis club, 1900-02; mgr. N.Y. Giants, Nat. League, 1902-32, won 106 games in 1904, beat Phila. in World Series, 1905; team won 10 pennants, 3 World Series under his mgmt.; elected to Baseball Hall of fame, 1937. Author: My Thirty Years in Baseball, 1923. Died New Rochelle, N.Y., Feb. 25, 1934; buried Balt.

McMURRICH, James Playfair, anatomist; b. Toronto, Can., Oct. 16, 1859; s. John and Janet (Dickson) McM.; grad. Upper Can. Coll., 1879; M.A., U. Toronto, 1881; Ph.D., Johns Hopkins, 1885; m. Katie Moodie Vickers, 1882, children—James Ronald, Kathleen Isabel. Taught biology Ont. Agrl. Coll., 1882-84; instr. mammalian anatomy Johns Hopkins, 1884-86; prof. biology Haverford (Pa.) Coll., 1886-89; asst. prof. animal morphology Clark U., 1889-92; prof. biology U. Cincinnati, 1892-94; prof. anatomy U. Mich., 1894-1907; prof. anatomy U. Toronto, 1907-30, dean sch. grad. studies, 1922-30. Author: A Text-book of Invertebrate Morphology, 1894; The Development of the Human Body, 1902; Leonardo da Vinci, the Anatomist, 1930. Died Toronto, Feb. 9, 1939; buried Mt. Pleasant Cemetery, Toronto.

McPHERSON, Aimee Semple, m. Robert Semple; m. 2d, Harold McPherson; 1 son, Rolf. (See sketch page 365, Who Was Who in America, Vol. II.)

McTAMMANY, John, inventor; b. nr. Glasgow, Scotland, June 26, 1845; s. John and Agnes (McLean) McT. Came to U.S., 1862; served with 115th Ohio Volunteer Inf., 1863-65, critically wounded nr. Chattanooga; while convalescing at Nashville, repaired music box, which gave him idea for an instrument operated by depressions; developed player-piano, 1866; built 3 models of player-piano, also 2 machines to prepare perforated sheets, 1866-76; gave public exhbn. of piano, St. Louis, 1876; prevented by circumstances from getting patent on his invention within prescribed time limit; declared to be original inventor of player-piano, after long and costly litigation against competitors, 1880; received 3 patents on invention, 1881; patented 1st voting machine, which pneumatically registered votes using perforated roll (1st machine ever used in an election), 1892. Died Stamford, Conn., Mar. 26, 1915; buried Westlawn Cemetery, Canton, O.

MEANS, Gaston Bullock, detective, swindler; b. Blackwelder's Spring, N.C., July 11, 1879; attended U. N.C., 1898-1901; m. Julie Patterson, 1914, 1 son, William. Salesman, Cannon Mills, Concord, N.C 1904-14; espionage agt. for Capt. Karl Boy-Ed (attached to German embassy, Washington, D.C.) to discover Allied purchasing and shipping information, 1914; mem. William J. Burns Internat. Detective Agy., 1914-18; assigned to protect Mrs. Maude King, persuaded her to let him manage her financial affairs, gambled away her money in 3 years, 1914-17; acquitted of her murder when she was found dead (after having gone target shooting with him), 1917; became spl. agt. FBI, 1921; suspended for forging a will, 1922; convicted of withdrawing liquor from govt. warehouses, also of extorting $65,000 from stock promoters, 1925, served 2 years in Fed. Penitentiary, Atlanta, Ga., 1926-28; extorted $104,-000 from Mrs. Evelyn Walsh McLean for his supposed discovery of Charles A. Lindbergh's child, 1932; convicted of grand larceny, sentenced to 15 years. Author: The Strange Death of President Harding, 1930. Died Med. Center for Fed. Prisoners, Springfield, Mo., Dec. 12, 1938; buried Concord, N.C.

MENDELSOHN, Erich, architect; b. Allenstein, East Prussia, Mar. 21, 1887; s. David and Esther (Jaruslawsky) M.; M.A., U. Munich, 1911; m. Louise Maas, Oct. 5, 1915; 1 dau., Esther (Mrs. Peter Joseph). Came to U.S., 1941, naturalized, 1946. Mem. German Expressionist movement, active in expressionist theatre; friend and asso. Kandinsky, Marc, Klee, Ball; opened archtl. office, Berlin, 1918, working largely on factory and dept. store design; visited Israel in connection with Ruthenberg electrification project, won 1st prize for Haifa bus. center designs, 1923; visited U.S., 1924; emigrated to Holland when Hitler came to power, 1933, then worked in London; lived in Israel, 1937-41; came to U.S.; lectured at Columbia, Yale, Harvard, U. Mich.; cons. U.S. War Dept., Washington, 1942-44; moved to San Francisco, 1945; exhibited one-man shows Berlin, 1919, 28, N.Y.C., 1929, 41, London, 1931, Milan, 1932, Chgo., San Francisco, 1941. Served with C.E., German Army, World War I. Guggenheim fellow, N.Y.C., 1943. Fellow Royal Inst. Brit. Architects, Mexican Inst. Architects; mem. A.I.A., Acad. Arts Berlin; hon. mem. Internat. League Modern Architecture Tokyo, Arts Club London. Leading exponent of expressionism in architecture (bldgs. imaginative, yet functional); a major influence on Am. design; prin. works include: Einstein Tower (astrophysics lab.), Potsdam, 1920; Univ. Med. Center, Mt. Scopus, Israel; (with sculptor Ivan Mestrovic) meml. to 6,000,000 Jews killed in World War II, N.Y.C., 1947. Author: America—Architect's Picture Book, 1926; Russia, Europe, America—an Architectural Cross-section, 1928; The Creative Spirit of the World Crisis, 1930; New House, New World, 1931. Died Sept. 15, 1953.

MICHEL, Virgil George, clergyman; b. St. Paul Minn., June 26, 1890; s. Fred and Mary (Griebler) M.; Ph.B., St. John's U., 1912, M.A., 1913; Ph.D., Catholic U. of Am., Washington, D.C., 1918; studied philosophy under Joseph Gredt, Internat. Benedictine Coll. of St. Anselin, Rome, 1924, U. Louvain, 1924-25. Ordained priest Order of St. Benedict, Roman Catholic Ch., 1916; instr. religion, English and philosophy St. John's U., 1918-24; editor Orate Fratres, 1925-30; organizer Am. Liturgical Movement, 1925-30. Died Collegeville, Minn., Nov. 26, 1938; buried cemetery St. John's Abbey, Collegeville.

MORAN, Thomas, painter; b. Bolton, Lancashire, Eng., 1837. Came to U.S., 1844; apprenticed to wood engraver, Phila., 1855; went to Europe to study art and paint, 1862; mem. expdns. of U.S. Geol. Survey to Yellowstone region, 1871, made sketches from which he painted huge canvas, The Grand Canyon of the Yellowstone. Died Santa Barbara, Cal., 1926.

MORSE, Charles Wyman, speculator; b. Bath, Me., Oct. 21, 1856; s. Benjamin and Anna (Rodbird) M.; grad. Bowdoin Coll., 1877; m. Hattie Hussey, Apr. 14, 1884, 4 children; m. 2d, Clemence (Cowles) Dodge, 1901. Engaged in shipping bus. while in coll., 1873-77; formed C. W. Morse & Co., ice and lumber shipping firm; moved to Wall St., N.Y.C., 1897, organized Consol. Ice Co., merged with other cos. to form Am. Ice Co., 1899; manipulated stock through Ice Securities Corp. (holding co.), made over $12,000,000 before irregularities and corruption ended his co.'s control of ice market; formed Consol. S.S. Co., 1905, had near monopoly of shipping along Atlantic coast by 1907, came to be called "Adm. of the Atlantic Coast"; gained partial control (with F. A. Heinze and E. R. Thomas) of 12 N.Y. banks including Bank of N.Am., Merc. Nat. Bank; investigated and indicted (with assos.) as result of panic of 1907, imprisoned Atlanta (Ga.) Penitentiary, 1910-12; retained H. M. Daughtery (later atty. gen. under Harding) for fee of $5,000 to help secure his release from prison; pardoned by Pres. Taft on report that he was dying (actually had drunk mixture of chemicals and soapsuds calculated to produce grave symptoms); his Hudson Navigation Co. was sued for unfair competition, 1915; proposed orgn. of a transoceanic shipping co., 1916; contracted by Shipping Bd. to build 36 ships during World War I, borrowed capital to build ships from Emergency Fleet Corp.; indicted for conspiracy to defraud govt. when an investigation after the war revealed that he had used much of borrowed money to build shipyards instead of ships; also indicted for using mails to defraud prospective U.S. steamship investors; U.S. Govt. was awarded $11,500,000 from his Va. Shipbuilding Co., 1925; placed under guardianship of probate ct. of Bath, 1926. Died Bath, Jan. 12, 1933.

MORTON, Ferdinand Joseph La Menthe (Jelly Roll), jazz musician; b. Gulfport, La., Sept. 20, 1885. Began on guitar, 1892, on piano, 1895; started playing piano in Storeyville quarter, New Orleans, 1902, later performed in Memphis, St. Louis, Kansas City, working only part-time as profl. musician; spent much of time in Cal., 1917-22; made 1st record (series of solos), Richmond, Ind., 1923-24; achieved fame with long series of Victor rec. sessions, made mostly in N.Y.C. and Chgo., under name of Morton's Red Hot Peppers, featuring Kid Ory, Johnny and Baby Dodds, Omer Simeon, others, 1926-30; his ostentation was legendary during period of greatest success, late 1920's, but his fame and prosperity ended in 1930's; ran night club, Washington, circa 1937; made record series, N.Y.C., 1939-40, then moved to Cal. Winner Record Changer All-Time Star Poll, 1951. The most documented jazz musician; his claims for his contbns. to jazz are much disputed; composer works including: King Porter Stomp; Milenburg Joys; Wolverine Blues; The Pearls; Shoe Shiner's Drag; Wild Man Blues; Kansas City Stomps. Died Los Angeles, July 10, 1941.

MOST, Johann Joseph, anarchist; b. Augsburg, Germany, Feb. 5, 1846; son of Josef Most. Underwent surgery which left his face disfigured for life, 1853; joined Internat. Workingmen's Assn., Zurich, 1864; edited socialist papers, Vienna, Chemnitz and Berlin, 1868-78; imprisoned in Austria and Germany, expelled from both countries because of his socialist activities; founded Die Freiheit, London, 1878; expelled from German Socialist Party because of his anarchist views, 1880; imprisoned for his article supporting assassination of Alexander II, 1881-82; came to N.Y.C., 1882, began publication of Freiheit; became leader of extreme anarchists in U.S.; wrote the principles adopted by Pitts. conv. (became guide for Am. anarchists), 1883; imprisoned 1 year on Blackwell's Island for inciting violence, 1886, again imprisoned for 1 year for writing pamphlet on methods of revolution and destruction, 1887; ridiculed Alexander Berkman's attempted assassination of Frick, 1892, by this action lost support of younger, more extreme anarchists; sentenced to 1 year on Blackwell's Island after assassination of McKinley, 1901. Died Cincinnati, Mar. 17, 1906.

MOZEE, Phoebe Anne Oakley (Annie Oakley), markswoman; b. Darke County, O., Aug. 13, 1860; d. Jake and Susanne Mozee; m. Frank E. Butler, June 22, 1876. Began shooting small game at age 9; paid off mortgage on family farm by selling game in Cincinnati; began vaudeville career by defeating Frank Butler in shooting contest, Cincinnati, 1875; toured (with husband) with Sells Bros. Circus; star performer Buffalo Bill Cody's Wild West Show, 1885-1902; held world record for shooting glass balls, once hit 4772 out of 5000 in one day; shot cigarette from mouth of Crown Prince of Germany (later William II); severely injured in train wreck, 1901, continued to set records for 20 years. Died Greenville, O., Nov. 3, 1926; buried Brock, O.

MULDOON, William, wrestler; b. Caneada, N.Y., May 25, 1852; s. Patrick and Maria (Donohue) M.; married twice. Mem. police force, N.Y.C., 1876-82; organized Police Athletic Assn.; defeated Edwin Bibby, 1878; wrestled 8-hour draw match with Clarence Whistler; wrestled draw match with Evan "Strangler" Lewis; played part of wrestler Charles in As You Like It, 1882-83; toured Japan with wrestling troupe; introduced Graeco-Roman wrestling in U.S.; ret. from wrestling, 1908; trained John L. Sullivan for fight with Kilrain, 1889; developed health resort on his estate, Westchester County, N.Y.; invented "medicine ball"; chmn. N.Y. State Boxing Commn., 1921-23; initiated (with Gene Tunney) Tunney-Muldoon Trophy as emblem of world's heavyweight boxing championship, 1928; known as The Solid Man, The Iron Duke, The Old Roman. Died June 3, 1933.

MURPHY, Michael Charles, athletic coach; b. Westboro, Mass., Feb. 28, 1861; m. Nora Long. Established athletic tng. camp nr. Westboro, 1885; athletic trainer at Yale, 1887-89; with Detroit Athletic Club, 1886-92; track coach, football trainer Yale, 1892-96, 1900-05; coach U. Pa., 1896-1900, 05-13; track coach N.Y. Athletic Club during summer vacations; coached Am. Olympic Team at London, 1908, at Stockholm, 1912; chosen to coach Am. team at 1916 Olympics (called off because of war); introduced crouching start in sprinting; improved techniques of jumping, pole vaulting, hurdling. Author: Athletic Training, published 1914. Died June 4, 1913.

N

NAST, Thomas, artist; drew 1st cartoon using donkey as Dem. Party label, 1st using elephant as Rep. Party label, 1874. (see sketch, page 888, Who Was Who in America, Vol. I)

NATION, Carry Amelia Moore, temperance leader; b. Garrard County, Ky., Nov. 25, 1846; d. George and Mary (Campbell) Moore; m. Dr. Charles Gloyd, Nov. 21, 1867; m. 2d, David Nation, 1877; 1 dau., Charlien. Experienced conversion in revival meeting at 10 years of age; became temperance advocate because of her husband's drinking; taught sch., Holden, Mo., 1867-71; lived in numerous small towns with her 2d husband, 1877-88, engaged mainly in clerking in hotels; had many mystical experiences during this period; engaged in anti-liquor activities by smashing saloons and liquor stocks with a hatchet, from 1890, gained an internat. reputation; her mind later became somewhat unbalanced. Died in relative obscurity, Leavenworth, Kan., June 9, 1911; buried Belton, Mo.

NOBLE, Thomas Satterwhite, artist; b. Lexington, Ky., May 29, 1835; studied in Paris, France. Served as capt. Confederate Army during Civil War; opened studio, N.Y.C., after Civil War, became known as hist. painter; prin. and prof. art Sch. of Design, McMicken U., Cincinnati, 1869-1904; elected asso. N.A.D., 1867. Died N.Y.C., Apr. 27, 1907.

NOONAN, James Patrick, labor leader; b. St. Louis, Dec. 15, 1878; s. Thomas P. and Bridget (Kemmey) N.; m. Inez Mitchell, June 26, 1901. Served as pvt. in Spanish-Am. War, 1898-99; became electric lineman, St. Louis, 1899; mem. Internat. Brotherhood of Elec. Workers, 1901-29, pres. local union, 1903, pres. Mo.-Ill. Dist. Council, 1903, v.p. internat. union, 1904-17, acting pres., 1917-19, pres., 1919-29; v.p. bldg. trades dept. AFL, 1922, mem. exec. council, 1924; only rep. of Am. labor at World Power Conf., London, 1924; mem. Pres.'s Conf. on Unemployment, 1921-24. Died Washington, D.C., Dec. 4, 1929; buried St. Louis.

NUNÓ, Jaime, composer, condr.; b. San Juan de las Abedesos, Spain, Sept. 8, 1824; studied music, Barcelona; married, 2 children. Bandmaster, Spanish Army, 1851, sent to Cuba to establish mil. bands, 1851; gen. band insp. of Mexican Army, 1853; a dir. Nat. Conservatory of Music, Mexico City, 1854; fled to U.S. after overthrow of Santa Anna, 1855; orch. condr. for Sigismund Thalberg on tour in U.S., 1856; conducted French and Italian Opera, Havana; directed opera in Cuba, U.S., Mexico, 1863-69; singing tchr., Buffalo, N.Y., 1869-78; organist, choirmaster, Rochester, N.Y., 1878-82. Composer, Himno Nacional Mejicano, officially adopted as nat. anthem of Mexico, 1854, given its inaugural performance, 1859. Died Bayside, L.I., N.Y., July 17, 1908.

O

OAKLEY, Annie, see Mozee, Phoebe Anne Oakley.

OBERHOLTZER, Sara Louisa Vickers, editor, civic worker; b. Chester County, Pa., May 20, 1841; d. Paxson and Ann (Lewis) Vickers; m. John Oberholtzer, Jan. 1, 1862, 2 sons. Organized Anti-Tobacco Soc., 1881, Longport Agassiz Microscopical Soc., 1884; pres. Pa. Women's Press Assn., 1903-05; advocate of sch. savs. banks, edited School Savings (published as Thrift Tidings 1907-23); by time of her death, 15,598 schs. participated in savs. program. Author: Violet Lee, 1873; Come for Arbutus, 1882; Hope's Heart; Bells, 1884. Died Phila., Feb. 2, 1930.

OCKERSON, John Augustus, engr.; b. Skane, Sweden, Mar. 4, 1848; s. Jans and Rose (Datler) Akerson; grad. U. Ill., 1873; m. Helen Chapin, Nov. 3, 1875; m. 2d, Clara Shackelford, June 4, 1890. Came to U.S., 1850; served with 132d Ill. Inf., 1864, 1st Minn. Heavy Arty., 1865; asst. engr. on fed. Great Lakes survey, 1873-78; prin. asst. engr. in charge of surveys and phys. examinations on Mississippi River Commn., 1879-88, 90-98; mem. Mississippi River Commn., 1898-1924; engineered constrn. of levees to control flood waters on Colorado River, 1910, received Presdl. Commendation for this project; U.S. del. Internat. Congress on Navigation, 1900, 05, 08, 12; pres. Am. Soc. C.E., 1912. Author: Dredges and Dredging of the Mississippi River, 1898. Died St. Louis, Mar. 22, 1924.

O'LEARY, Daniel, pedestrian; b. Clonakilty, County Cork, Ireland, probably June 29, 1846. Came to U.S., 1866; walked 100 miles in 23 hours, 17 minutes at West Side Rink, Chgo., 1874; walked 500 miles in 5 days, 21 hours, beginning Apr., 1875; defeated John Ennis by walking 100 miles in 18 hours, 53 minutes, 40 seconds, Oct. 16, 1875; beat Edward P. Weston by walking 501½ miles in 5 days, 23 hours, Nov. 15-20, 1875; established O'Leary Belt as trophy for long-distance walking championship; beaten by Weston in 2,500 mile walk, 1896; walked a mile every hour for 1,000 hours, 1907. Died Los Angeles, May 29, 1933.

OLIVER, Joseph (King Oliver), jazz musician; b. New Orleans, circa 1885. Butler to white family, New Orleans, circa 1902-11; mem. various marching bands, New Orleans, 1900-18; also appeared as cornetist various New Orleans cabarets by 1910, acquired nickname King during this period; 1st cornetist with 2 jazz bands in Chgo., 1918-21; also formed own band composed of New Orleans musicians, Chgo., 1920; toured Cal. with King Oliver's Jazz Band, 1921-22; formed King Oliver's Creole Jazz Band (including Louis Armstrong, Johnny Dodds), Chgo., 1922; 1 of 1st Negro musicians to make recordings; largely responsible for introducing Negro music in jazz fashion to wide audience; influenced by his playing style the devel. of jazz; wrote 49 compositions; his band gradually broke up; finally ruined professionally and financially by ill health and the depression, spent last years in poverty in New Orleans. Died New Orleans, Apr. 8, 1938; buried Woodlawn Cemetery, N.Y.C.

OSTROMISLENSKY, Iwan Iwanowich, chemist; b. Moscow, Russia, Sept. 8, 1880; s. Iwan and Olga (Iowanowa) O.; attended U. Moscow, 1896-99; Ph.D., U. Zurich (Switzerland), 1902, M.D., 1906; grad. Karlsruhe Polytechnicum, Germany, 1907; m. Olga; children—Tatiana, George. Asst. prof. chemistry Polytechnicum of Moscow, Moscow U., Sch. Dentistry of Moscow, 1907-12; researcher, pvt. chem. lab., Moscow, 1911-16; dir. chemotherapeutic dept. Scientific Inst., Moscow, 1916; prof. chemistry U. Nizhni-Novgorod, 1917; went to Riga, Latvia; mem. research staff United Rubber Co., N.Y.C., 1922-25; developed many improvements in synthetic rubber mfg.; established Ostro Research Labs. (became Hopkinson Labs.), N.Y.C., 1925; became U.S. citizen, circa 1930. Died N.Y.C., Jan. 16, 1939; cremated Mt. Olivet Cemetery, Fresh Pond, L.I., N.Y.

P

PAINTER, William, engr., inventor; b. Montgomery County, Md., Nov. 20, 1838; s. Dr. Edward and Louisa (Gilpin) P.; m. Harriet Deacon, Sept. 9, 1861, 3 children. Apprentice, patent leather factory, Wilmington, Del., 1855-59; patented a fare box, 1858, railroad car seat and couch, 1858, kerosene lamp, 1863, wire-retaining rubber stopper which could be removed with 1 hand, 1885; founder Triumph Bottle Stopper Co., Balt., 1885; patented bottle seal, 1885, organized Bottle Seal Co. for its manufacture; patented a metal bottle cap (of type still used), 1892; sec., gen. mgr. Crown Cork and Seal Co., 1892-1903. Died July 15, 1906.

PALMER, A(lexander) Mitchell, as atty. gen. received notoriety during "Red Scare"; investigated by various Congressional coms. for his conduct while alien property custodian (charges dismissed), credited with writing most of platform at Nat. Democratic Conv., 1932. (see sketch page 930, Who Was Who in America, Vol. I)

PALMER, Daniel David, founder chiropractic; b. nr. Toronto, Can., Mar. 7, 1845; 1 son, Bartlett Joshua. Practiced magnetic healing, Burlington, Ia., 1883-95; made 1st attempt at spinal adjustment, Davenport, Ia., 1895; founded Palmer Sch. of Chiropractic, 1898; opened Portland Coll. of Chiropractic, Portland, Ore., 1903; arrested and imprisoned for practicing medicine without license, 1906. Author: The Science of Chiropractic, 1906; Textbook of the Science, Art and Philosophy of Chiropractic, 1910; The Chiropractor, 1914. Died Los Angeles, Oct. 20, 1913.

PARKER, Charles Christopher (Bird, Yardbird), jazz saxophonist; b. Kansas City, Kan., Aug. 29, 1920; m. 4 times, 1 son. Began playing alto sax at age 11, played baritone horn in sch. band, left sch. at age 15; played with various groups in N.Y.C., 1939-45; became closely asso. with Dizzy Gillespie, performing at Minton's Playhouse and other clubs, where they developed style known as bebop (later bop), early 1940's; appeared with Gillespie at Billie Berg's in Cal., 1945; suffered nervous breakdown after rec. session, July, 1946, spent next 6 months in Camarillo State Hosp.; then made recordings in Los Angeles before returning East and performing with various groups of sidemen; attended Paris Jazz Festival, 1949, traveled to Scandanavia, 1950; made last appearance at Birdland (named for him), Mar., 1955. Recipient New Star award Esquire Poll, 1946; won Down Beat Poll, 1948-53, Down Beat Critics' Poll, 1953-54; named to Down Beat Hall of Fame, 1955, as Greatest Ever in Ency. of Jazz Poll, 1956. His influential style advanced art of improvisation and rhythm, replacing diatonic with chromatic runs. Best known works include: Now's the Time, Yardbird Suite, Relaxin' at Camarillo. Died N.Y.C., Mar. 12, 1955.

PARSONS, Charles, artist; b. Rowland's Castle, Hampshire, Eng., May 8, 1821. Brought to Am., grew up in N.Y.C.; became employee Endicott & Co., N.Y.C., asso. with firm, until 1861; executed many lithographs for Currier & Ives; head art dept. Harper & Bros., N.Y.C., 1861-89; elected asso. N.A.D., 1862; mem. Am. Watercolor Soc. Died Bklyn., Nov. 9, 1910.

POLLOCK, Jackson, artist; b. Cody, Wyo., Jan. 28, 1912. First Am. exponent of Tachismor action painting; developed his style from surrealism to abstract and "first drip" paintings; works include: One, Number 32, Echo. Died in automobile accident, Aug. 12, 1956.

PRICE, Samuel Woodson, artist; b. Nicholasville, Ky., Aug. 5, 1828. Painted portraits in Ky. and Tenn. until 1861; served as col. Union Army during Civil War, wounded at Battle of Kennesaw Mountain, brevetted brig. gen., 1865; painted portraits, Washington, D.C., after Civil War; postmaster of Lexington (Ky.), 1869-76; painted portraits and figure paintings until he went blind, 1881. Author: Old Masters of the Bluegrass (biographical accounts of Ky. painters dictated after he went blind), 1902. Died St. Louis, Jan. 22, 1918.

PRICE, William Cecil, proslavery leader; b. Russell County, Va., Apr. 1, 1818; s. Crabtree and Linny (Cecil) P.; m. Sarah J. Kimbrough, June 1842; 7 children; m. 2d, Lydia C. Dow, Aug. 1860, 3 children. Admitted to Mo. bar, 1838; judge Green County (Mo.), 1842-45; worked for repeal of Mo. Compromise, advocated proslavery policy for state; led campaign against Thomas H. Benton's anti-slavery convictions, 1844-50; mem. Mo. Senate, 1854-57; treas. U.S., 1860-61; served with Confederate Army, 1861, taken prisoner, held in Alton, Ill., until Sept. 1862; lived in Springfield, Mo., 1870-1907, loaned money to Easterners. Died Chgo., Aug. 6, 1907.

PURNELL, Benjamin, religious leader; b. Mayville, Ky., Mar. 27, 1861; m. Angelina Brown, 1877; 1 child; m. 2d, Mary Stollard, 1880. Became mem. Seventh Angelic Messengers, 1892, proclaimed himself the Seventh Messenger, 1895, expelled from Messengers; itinerant evangelist, 1895-1902; established House of David, Benton Harbor, Mich., declared himself Seventh Messenger and younger brother of Christ; preached that Millennium was to begin, 1906, forbade all sexual relations, even among the married; predicted that he would rise on 3d day after his death. Author: The Rolling Ball of Fire, 3 vols., 1915-25; The Little Book in the Hand of the Angel, 1927; The Key of the House of David, 1927. Died Dec. 16, 1927.

Q

QUANAH, Indian chief; b. No. Tex.; s. Peta Nocone and Cynthia Ann Parker (a White captive), married 3 wives, including Too-nicey. Organized band of Comanche Indians, 1866, became chief, 1867; refused to accept Medicine Lodge Treaty of 1867 which required Comanches, Kiowas, Kiowa Apaches, So. Cheyennes and Arapahos to settle on reservation in Indian Territory; led series of raids terrorizing frontier; in continual warfare with white settlers, 1867-75; defeated by Ranald S. Mackenzie and Nelson A. Miles, 1875; after defeat took up ways of white man, initiated bldg. projects, agrl. improvements; grew wealthy as result of leasing surplus lands to stockmen; rode with Geronimo in Pres.

Theodore Roosevelt's inaugural procession. Died Indian Territory, Feb. 23, 1911.

R

RAINEY, Ma (Gertrude Malissa Nix Pridgett), singer; b. Columbus, Ga., Apr. 26, 1886; m. William (Pa) Rainey. Started singing in cabarets, circa 1900; played Negro vaudeville circuits, many years; began recording series for Paramount, accompanied by Lovie Smith's Serenaders, 1923; her simple, direct blues style achieved peak popularity, 1923-29; her accompanists included Tommy Ladnier, Joe Smith, Louis Armstrong; her best known protégée was Bessie Smith; ret. from music, 1933, settled in Rome, Ga., where she owned 2 theaters. Records include: Shave 'Em Dry, Jelly Bean Blues, Countin' the Blues, See See Rider. Died Columbus, Ga., Dec. 22, 1939.

RANSOM, Caroline L. Ormes, artist; b. Newark, O., 1838; grad. Oberlin Coll.; studied art, N.Y.C. and Munich, Germany. Taught at Oberlin Coll.; maintained studios, Sandusky, O., 1858-60, later in Cleve. and N.Y.C.; settled in Washington, D.C.; a founder D.A.R., Classical Club of Washington; painted several portraits which are now in U.S. Capitol. Died Washington, Feb. 12, 1910.

RED CLOUD, Indian chief; b. Blue Creek, Neb., 1822; s. Lone Mann and Walks As She Thinks. Born into Oglala Tribe of Teton Sioux Indians; became known as great warrior; head of an Indian band; chief Oglala tribe, main spokesman of allied Sioux and Cheyenne Indians, 1866; walked out of Ft. Laramie council talks because of Whites' attitude, 1866; leader Sioux and Cheyenne warfare which succeeded in temporarily closing Bozeman trail to settlers; advocated peace with U.S. Govt., after 1868; visited Washington (D.C.) and N.Y.C., 1870; constant critic of corrupt Indian agts.; opposed Sioux's desire for war, 1876; sent letter to Pres. Garfield demanding removal of Indian agt. V. T. McGillycuddy, 1881, deposed as tribal chief by McGillycuddy. Died Pine Ridge Indian Agy., S.D., Dec. 10, 1909.

REID, James L., corn breeder; b. Red Oak, O., Dec. 26, 1844; s. Robert Drake and Anne (Moore) R.; m. Marietta Jenks, Apr. 1870. Corn farmer, Boynton Center, Ill., 1865-80, developed new type of corn (Reid's Yellow Dent) by crossing a late maturing Ohio variety with type known as Little Yellow; unsuccessfully farmed (according to Ill. methods) in Osage County, Kan., 1880-88; farmed at Boynton Center, 1888-1910; his breed of corn introduced at World's Columbian Expn., 1892; established mail-order firm to handle seed-corn orders, East Lynn, Vermillion County, Ill., 1902; attended Nat. Corn Expn., Omaha, Neb., 1908. Died June 1, 1910.

RICKARD, George Lewis (Tex Rickard), prize fight promoter; b. Kansas City, Mo., Jan. 2, 1871; m. Edith Mae Rickard; m. 2d, Maxine Hodges; 1 child. Moved with family to Sherman, Tex., 1875; operated gambling bus., Yukon, Alaska, 1890's, made $500,000 which he squandered buying worthless land; turned to fight promoting, 1906, brought Gans-Nelson fight to Sherman (receipts went to $62,000); promoted Jeffries-Johnson fight, 1910; lost several fortunes in beef market of Central and South America, 1910-16; promoted Willard-Moran bout in N.Y., 1916; sponsored Willard-Dempsey fight, 1919; promoted highly successful Dempsey-Carpentier bout in arena he constructed in Boyle's Acres, Jersey City, N.J., 1921; acquired Madison Square Garden; promoted Dempsey-Firpo fight, 1923, Dempsey-Tunney bout, 1926; Dempsey-Sharkey match, 1927, very lucrative Dempsey-Tunney fight, 1927. Died Miami Beach, Fla., Jan. 6, 1929.

RINGLING, Charles, circus propr.; b. McGregor, Ia., 1863; s. August and Marie Salome (Julian) Rüngeling; m. Edith Conway, 2 children including Robert E. With his 4 brothers, Otto (1858-1911), Albert C. (1852-1916), Alfred T. (1861-1919) and John (1866-1936) started a small circus, Baraboo, Wis., early 1880's; acquired 1st elephant, 1888; placed show on 18 railroad cars, 1890; acquired Forepaugh-Sells Circus, 1906, Barnum & Bailey Circus, 1907, merged all circuses into 1 show, 1919; organized Charles Ringling Co. for devel. of Fla. land holding, especially in area around Sarasota; helped establish Sarasota as winter resort; pres. Ringling Bank and Trust Co., Sarasota. Died Sarasota, Dec. 3, 1926.

ROBINSON, William, inventor, engr.; b. Coal Island, County Tyrone, Ulster, Ireland, Nov. 22, 1840; grad. Wesleyan U., 1865; Ph.D., Boston U. Brought to U.S., 1844; prin. high sch., Ansonia, Conn., 1865-66; worked in Pa. oil fields, 1866-67; prin. Spring Valley Acad., N.Y., 1867-69; in oil bus., Pa., 1869-72; exhibited model of automatic railroad signal system, 1870; patented closed track circuit system of automatic electric signalling for railroads in U.S. and France, 1872; organized Robinson Electric Ry. Signal Co., St. Petersburg, Pa., 1872; organized firm in Boston area, 1875-82; other inventions include bond wire system of connecting adjacent rails electrically, wireless electric ry. signal system; developed use of fiber for insulated railjoints. Author: History of Automatic Electric and Electrically Controlled Fluid Pressure Signal Systems for Railroads, 1906. Died Bklyn., Jan. 2, 1921; buried Bklyn.

ROCKWELL, Kiffin Yates, aviator; b. Newport, Tenn., Sept. 20, 1892; attended Va. Mil. Inst., U.S. Naval Acad., Washington and Lee U. Went to Pacific coast, 1912, ran advt. agy., San Francisco, for a time; enlisted in French Fgn. Legion to aid France in World War I, 1914; transferred to 1st Fgn. Regt., 1915, served in Battle of La Targette, wounded during attack; became pilot in Escadrille Lafayette, 1916, became 1st American to shoot down an enemy plane; fought 70 battles, July-Aug. 1916; decorated Medaille Militaire, Cross of chevalier Legion of Honor. Killed over Thann, Alsace, Sept. 23, 1916.

ROGERS, Harriet Burbank, educator; b. North Billerica, Mass., Apr. 12, 1834; d. Calvin and Ann (Faulkner) Rogers. Tutored a deaf girl, using accepted method of finger spelling and signs, 1864-66; opened small pvt. sch. for deaf children, Chelmsford, Mass., 1866-67; prin. Clarke Inst. for Deaf Mutes, (1st sch. for deaf children in U.S.), 1867-82; learned new methods from Alexander Graham Bell, who worked for a time in the sch.; pioneered oral teaching of mutes; lived in Colo. for health reasons, 1884-86; returned to Billerica, 1886, but unable to assume burden of teaching. Died Dec. 12, 1919.

ROOSEVELT, Franklin Delano, as Pres. U.S. attempted to revive nat. economy by series of "pump priming" measures including NRA, A.A.A., Pub. Works Adminstrn. (NRA, A.A.A. later declared unconstl. by U.S. Supreme Ct.); also set up TVA, SEC: failed in attempt to reorganize U.S. Supreme Ct, 1937; initiated Good Neighbor Policy regarding Latin Am.; drafted Atlantic Charter with Winston Churchill, 1941; took part in various war-time confs. including Que., Teheran, Yalta; firm supporter of UN. (see sketch page 457, Who Was Who in America, Vol. II.)

ROOSEVELT, Theodore, during his adminstrn. U.S. Dept. of Commerce and Labor was organized, 1903; noted for formulation of Roosevelt Corollary to Monroe Doctrine, which stated that U.S. had direct interest in affairs of Latin Am.; his actions helped prepare way for constrn. Panama Canal, 1905; formulated (with Sec. of State John Hay) "Dollar Diplomacy" policy in Caribbean area; instituted Gentleman's Agreement with Japan to exclude Japanese immigration to U.S. because of anger of people in Cal. over their arrival, 1907. (See sketch page 1055, Who Was Who in America, Vol. I)

ROSS, Edmund Gibson, senator, journalist; b. Ashland, O., Dec. 7, 1826; s. Sylvester F. and Cynthia (Rice) R.; m. Fanny M. Lathrop, 1848, 5 children. Worked as apprentice, later journeyman printer; joined Republican Party, 1856, led party of free state settlers to Kan.; owner, publisher (with his brother) Kan. Tribune, Topeka, 1857-59; owner, publisher Kan. State Record, 1859-62; mem. Free State Wyandotte Constl. Conv., 1859; promoter, dir. Santa Fe R.R.; suggested name Atchison, Topeka and Santa Fe R.R.; served as capt. 11th Kan. Volunteer Regt., 1862, promoted maj., 1864; editor Lawrence (Kan.) Tribune, 1865-66; mem. U. S. Senate (Republican) from Kan., 1866-71, entered Senate as staunch radical, later changed his views, voted against conviction of Pres. Johnson at impeachment trial; left Republican Party, 1872; publisher various newspapers in Kan., 1871-82; unsuccessful Democratic candidate for gov. Kan., 1880; del. Dem. Nat. Conv., St. Louis, 1876; gov. N.M. Territory (apptd. by Pres. Cleveland), 1885-89; admitted to N.M. bar, 1889; sec. Bur. of Immigration, 1894-96. Died Albuquerque, N.M., May 8, 1907; buried Fairview Cemetery, Albuquerque.

ROTHAFEL, Samuel Lionel, theatre mgr.; b. Stillwater, Minn., July 9, 1881; s. Gustave and Cecelia S. Rothapfel; m. Rosa Freedman, Jan. 31, 1909; children—Beta, Arthur. Served as pvt. U.S. Marines, 1902-05; mgr. Lyric Theatre, Mpls., Minn., 1912; later mgr. Regent Theatre, N.Y.C.; introduced well-known orchestras, world-famous singers and precision dancing by "Rockettes" to complement motion pictures; mng. dir. Strand, Rialto, Rivoli, Capital theatres, N.Y.C.; mgr. Roxy Theatre (built especially for him), 1927-31; mem. Radio Keith-Orpheum syndicate to develop theatres for Rockefeller Center, N.Y.C., 1931; mgr. Radio City Music Hall, 1932-33. Died N.Y.C., Jan. 13, 1936; buried Linden Hills Cemetery, Bklyn.

S

SACKVILLE-WEST, Lionel (2d baron Sackville), diplomat; b. Eng., 1827. Asst. to earl of Aberdeen (fgn. minister), 1845-46; held diplomatic posts in Lisbon, Naples, Berlin, Madrid, Buenos Aires, 1846-68; E.E. and M.P. to France, 1868-72; English ambassador to U.S., 1881-88; implied in a letter that the reelection of Grover Cleveland would be to the British interest, incident publicized by Republican candidate Benjamin Harrison, 1888; recalled to Eng. at request of Pres. Cleveland, 1888. Died 1908.

SAFFIN, William, labor union ofcl.; pres. Moulders' Internat. Union. 1873.

SALM-SALM, Princess (Agnes Elisabeth Winona Leclercq Joy), adventuress; born Vt. or Que., Can., Dec. 25, 1840; d. William and Julia (Willard) Joy; m. Felix Constantin Alexander Johann Nepomuit (Prince Salm-Salm), Aug. 20, 1862; m. 2d, Charles Heneage, 1876. Spent most of childhood in Que.; went to Washington, D.C. at start of Civil War, there met and married Prince Salm-Salm, a German soldier of fortune who was attempting to get commn. in U.S. Army; aided in getting her husband apptd. col. 8th N.Y. Volunteers; accompanied husband in field, became an acquaintance of many notable Union figures; accompanied husband to Mexico when he entered service under Emperor Maximilian, 1866; decorated Grand Cordon of Order of San Carlos by Maximilian; attempted to use bribery to effect release of Maximilian after his capture, also pleaded for mercy for him before Jaurez; later served as nurse, did army relief work for German Army during Franco-Prussian War, 1870; pensioned by Austrian emperor; decorated Prussian Medal of Honor; resided in Germany, visited Am. in effort to get support for Boers in S. Africa during Boer War, 1899-1900 elected mem. N.J. chpt. D.A.R., 1900; subject of an hist. painting by Manuel Ocaranza, 1873, also subject in several novels; a figure in Franz Werfel's play Juarez and Maximilian. Author: Zehn Jahre Aus Meinem Leben, 1875, translated into English as Ten Years of My Life, 2 vols., 1876. Died Karlsruhe, Germany, Dec. 21, 1912.

SCHLESINGER, Benjamin, labor leader; b. Kouno, Lithuania, Dec. 25, 1876; son of Judith Schlesinger; m. Rae Schanhouse, 3 children. Came to U.S., 1891, became sewing machine operator, Chgo., became involved in labor relations; mgr. Jewish Daily Forward; sec. Chgo. Cloth Makers' Union, treas. Internat. Cloth Makers' Union of Am.; pres. Internat. Ladies' Garment Workers' Union, 1903-04, 14-23, 31; gen. mgr. N.Y. Cloth Makers' Union, 1904-07; bus. mgr. Jewish Daily Forward, 1907-12, mgr., 1923-31. Died Colorado Springs, Colo., June 6, 1932.

SCHULTZ, Henry, economist; b. Szarkowszczyzna, Poland, Sept. 4, 1893; s. Sam and Rebecca (Kissin) S.; grad. Coll. City N.Y., 1916; postgrad. London Sch. Econs. and Polit. Sci., also Galton Lab. Eugenic Research of U. London (Eng.), 1919; Ph.D., Columbia, 1925; m. Bertha Alice Greenstein, 1920, children—Ruth, Jean. Came to U.S., 1907; statis. researcher Bur. of Census, Tariff Commn., 1920-26; prof. econs. U. Chgo., 1926-38; wrote The Theory and Measurement of Demand, 1938, dealt with statis. Measurement of demand, written in 3 sects. (1) explanation of theory of demand in math. lang., (2) quantitative methods for measuring demand, (3) studies of demand for agrl. goods in U.S. Died nr. San Diego, Cal., Nov. 26, 1938; buried New Mt. Carmel Cemetery, Queens County, N.Y.C.

SEAMAN, Elizabeth Cochrane (Nelly Bly), journalist; b. Cochrane's Mills, Armstrong County, Pa., May 5, 1867; ed. at home by father, then attended boarding sch., Indiana, Pa., 1880-81; m. Robert L. Seaman, 1895 (dec. 1904). Moved with family to Pitts., circa 1881, began writing stories and sketches; wrote angry letter in response to article What Girls Are Good For, In Pitts. Dispatch; her letter went unpublished, but go her job on Dispatch staff; wrote series of articles on working girls' conditions in Pitts., later became society editor in charge drama and art depts.; pseudonym Nelly Bly given her by Dispatch mng. editor G.A. Madden, who took it from Stephen Foster song; toured Mexico (with her mother) for Dispatch 1887, wrote series of articles later collected in Six Months in Mexico, 1888; joined staff of World, N.Y.C., 1888, feigned insanity to get committed to Blackwell's Island, wrote exposé of instn. upon release, later pub. as Ten Days in a Mad-House; made unaccompanied world tour, 1889-90; during which she interviewed Jules Verne at Amiens, France; wrote Nelly Bly's Book: Around the World in Seventy-two Days, 1890; managed husband's business after his death, but lost all her money in litigation proceedings; returned to journalism on staff N.Y. Jour. until death. Died N.Y.C., Jan. 27, 1922.

SENNETT, Mack (Michael Sinnott), movie producer, dir.; b. Danville, Que., Can., 1884; began working for D.W. Griffith at Biograph Co., 1909; founded Keytsone Co., 1912 (bankrupt 1933); became 3d producer Triangle Corp., with Griffith and Thomas Ince, 1916; famous for 1-2 reel slapstick comedies with fantastic chases and custard pie throwing scenes; his Keystone Kops and Mack Sennett Bathing Beauties were especially popular; his stars included Charlie Chaplin, Harold Lloyd, Buster Keaton, Ben Turpin, Roscoe (Fatty) Arbuckle, Mabel Normand, Marie Dressler, Gloria Swanson; later asso. producer 20th Century Fox. Films include: Hypnotized; Bride's Relations; Broadway Blues; Old Barn; Whirls and Girls; Mickey; Molly 'O; Extra Girl. Author: (autobiography) King of Comedy, 1954. Died Woodland Hills, Cal., Nov. 5, 1960.

SILVERMAN, Sime, journalist; b. Cortland, N.Y., May 18, 1873; s. George and Rachel (Ganz) S.; m. Hattie Freeman, Mar. 1, 1898, at least 1 son. Theatre critic N.Y. Morning Telegraph; founder Variety, weekly theatrical trade paper, 1905, editor, publisher, 1905-33; maintained editorial policy of not yielding to external pressures, used theatrical jargon; 1 of earliest to review movies and radio; bought and published N.Y. Clipper, 1924; willed 49 percent of Variety to his 225 employees, remainder to wife and son. Died Los Angeles, Sept. 22, 1933.

SIMS, Charles N., clergyman, univ. chancellor; b. Fairfield, Ind., May 18, 1835; s. John and Irene (Allen) S.; grad. Indiana Asbury (now De Pauw) U., Greencastle, 1859; m. Eliza A. Foster, Aug. 12, 1858. Urged by John P. Durbin to prepare for ministry; admitted on trial to Northwest Ind. Conf. of Methodist Episcopal Ch., 1857, ordained to ministry, 1859; pres. Valparaiso (Ind.) Coll., 1860-61; in charge of chs. in Ind. and Ill., 1862-70; pastor Methodist chs., Balt., also Newark, N.J., Bklyn., 1870-80; chancellor Syracuse U., 1881-93, instrumental in increasing univ.'s endowment and bldg. program; apptd. by N.Y. Legislature a commr. to investigate conditions of Onondaga Indians, 1882; pastor Meridian Street Ch., Indpls., 1893-98, 1st Ch., Syracuse, N.Y., 1898-1904. Died Liberty, Ind., Mar. 27, 1908.

SLOAN, James Forman (Tod Sloan), jockey; b. nr. Kokomo, Ind., Aug. 10, 1874; m. Julia Sanderson, 1907; m. 2d, Elizabeth Malone, 1920; 1 dau. Became a profl. jockey with his brother Cassius; worked for horse trainer John S. Campbell; developed riding style (lying near neck and shoulders of horse) that cut down considerably on wind resistance; rode in Eng., 1897, won 21 races with his unorthodox position; principle rider for William C. Whitney stables; selected to ride horses of King Edward VII in Eng.; denied license by Jockey Club in Eng., 1901, led to his being banned by all racing orgns.; introduced practice of forcing pace from beginning, rather than waiting to win. Author: Tod Sloan by Himself, 1915. Died Los Angeles, Dec. 21, 1933.

SLOCUM, Joshua, mariner; b. Wilmot Twp., N.S., Can., Feb. 20, 1844; s. John and Sarah (Southern) S.; m. Virginia A. Walker, Jan. 1871; m. 2d, Henrietta M. Elliott, Feb. 1886; 4 children. Shipmaster in Pacific trade, 1869-86; commanded ship Northern Light, 1874-86; began trading on S. Am. coast, 1886; shipwrecked off Brazil, 1887; built 25-foot canoe The Liberdade, in which he and his wife sailed to N.Y.; built 1-man ship The Spray in which he made 1st solitary voyage around world, sailing from Boston, 1895, returning to Newport, R.I., 1898; earned expenses by lecturing and displaying boat enroute; sailed in The Spray again, Nov. 1909, never seen again. Author: Voyage of the Liberdade, 1890; Sailing Alone Around the World, 1900. Died circa 1910.

SMALLS, Robert, congressman; b. Beaufort, S.C., Apr. 5, 1839; s. Robert and Lydia Smalls; m. Hannah, 1856; m. 2d, Annie Wigg, Apr. 9, 1890; at least 2 children. A slave, impressed by Confederacy into service as crewman in steamer The Planter in Charleston harbor, 1861; became nationally famous when he guided The Planter past Charleston forts into U.S. Squadron blockading the harbor, May 1862; became pilot U.S. Navy; capt., comdr. The Planter, 1863-66; del. S.C. Constl. Conv., 1868; mem. S.C. Ho. of Reps., 1868-70, S.C. Senate, 1870-74; mem. U.S. Congress (Republican) from S.C., 44th-45th, 47th-49th congresses, 1875-79, July 19, 1882-83, 84-87; supported bill to provide equal service for all races in interstate travel; opposed civil service reform, attempted to have compensation of $30,000 voted to him for his capture of The Planter; served to maj. gen. S.C. Militia, 1865-77; port collector, Beaufort, 1889-93, 97-1913; convicted of accepting $5,000 bribe, 1877, sentenced to 3 years in prison, but pardoned by Gov. Simpson; del. S.C. Constl. Conv., 1895. Died Beaufort, Feb. 22, 1915; buried Tabernacle Bapt. Ch. Cemetery, Beaufort.

SMITH, Bessie, blues singer; b. Chattanooga, Tenn., Apr. 15, 1894; d. William and Laura Smith; m. John Gee, June 7, 1923. Made 1st profl. appearance, Chattanooga, 1903; singer in tent shows and carnivals, toured South and Midwest, early 1920's; made 1st recording, Gulf Coast Blues, 1923; made over 80 recordings, which sold about 6,000,000 copies, 1924-27; known as Empress of the Blues, considered best blues singer of her time. Fatally injured in automobile accident nr. Clarksdale, Miss., Sept. 26, 1937; buried Mt. Lawn Cemetery, Phila.

SMITH, Robert Sidney, cartoonist; b. Bloomington, Ill., Feb. 13, 1877; s. Thomas H. and Frances A. (Shafer) S.; m. Gertrude C. Craddock; children—Gladys, Robert Sidney; m. 2d, Mrs. Kathryn Imogen Eulette. Artist, Indpls. (Ind.) News; later with Indpls. Press, Phila. Inquirer, Pitts. Post, Pitts. Press, Indpls. Sentinel, Toledo (O.) News Bee; mem. staff Chgo. Daily Tribune, drew series Light Occupations, The Bunk of a Busy Brain, Self-Made Heroes; began Andy Gump comic strip, 1917; credited with adding continuity to comic strips by continuing situations day after day; signed contract with Chgo. Tribune Syndicate for The Gumps series, 1922 (1st $1,000,000 contract for comic strip artist). Author: Book of the Gumps, 1918; Andy Gump, His Life Story, 1924. Died nr. Harvard, Ill., Oct. 20, 1935.

SMOHALLA, Indian chief, religious leader; b. circa 1815. Became chief of Wanapum branch Nez Percés Indians; also noted as medicine man; fought against Whites in Yakima War, 1855-56; believed to have been killed in fight with neighboring tribe, left for dead, but rescued by some white men; rather than immediately returning to his people, wandered throughout Cal., Ariz., Mexico and Utah; then returned home and was thought by his people to have returned from the dead; founded Dreamer religion which claimed that Indians were only true people on earth and would eventually control whole earth; very influential during Nez Percé War of 1877. Died 1907.

ST. JOHN, John Price, gov. Kan.; b. Brookville, Franklin County, Ind., Feb. 25, 1833; s. Samuel and Sophia (Snell) St. John; m. Mary Jane Brewer, 1852; m. 2d, Susan J. Parker, Mar. 28, 1861; at least 2 children. Admitted to Ill. bar, 1860; served to lt. col. 43d Ill. Regt. during Civil War; practiced law, Independence, Mo., 1866-69; mem. Kan. Senate, 1873-74; gov. Kan. (Prohibitionist), 1878-82, secured adoption of constl. prohibition of liquor in Kan., 1882; unsuccessful Nat. Prohibition Party candidate for Pres. U.S., 1884 (supported by many Republicans, which led to election of 1st Democrat since Civil War). Died Olathe, Kan., Aug. 31, 1916.

STANLEY, Francis Edgar, inventor, mfr.; b. Kingfield, Me., June 1, 1849; s. Solomon and Apphia (French) S.; grad. Farmington State Normal and Tng. Sch., 1871; m. Augusta Walker, Jan. 1, 1870, 3 children. Lived in Lewiston, Me., 1874-83, became a leading portrait photographer; organizer (with his brother Freelan) Stanley Dry Plate Co., 1883, sold firm to Eastman Kodak Co., 1905; produced 1st successful steam-operated automobile in New Eng., 1897; began quantity constrn. of car, 1898, but sold patent rights and business to J. B. Walker; repurchased patents (with his brother), organized Stanley Motor Carriage Co. (which produced famous Stanley Steamer), 1902, pres., 1902-12. Author: Theories Worth Having, published 1919. Died July 31, 1918.

STERN, Joseph William, music publisher; b. N.Y.C., Jan. 11, 1870; s. Charles and Theresa (Katz) S.; m. Leona Lewis, 1899. Produced (with E. B. Marks) song The Little Lost Child, 1894; formed (with Marks) Joseph W. Stern & Co., 1894, firm published songs including A Hot Time In the Old Town, Sweet Rosie O'Grady; ret. from song publishing bus., 1920. Died Brightwaters, L.I., N.Y., Mar. 31, 1934.

STEUER, Max David, lawyer; b. Homino, Austria (now Czechoslovakia), Sept. 1870; s. Aaron and Dinah (Goodman) S.; attended Coll. City N.Y., 1886-89; LL.B., Columbia, 1893; m. Bertha Popkin, 1897, children—Aron, Ethel, Constance. Came to U.S., 1876; admitted to N.Y. bar, 1893, U.S. Supreme Ct. bar, 1904; became known for his jury trials; successfully defended actor Raymond Hitchcock, (1908), owners in Triangle clothing factory case (1911), George L. (Tex) Rickard on morals charge, Charles E. Mitchell (pres. Nat. City Bank of (N.Y.C.) for income tax evasion, Atty. Gen. Harry M. Daugherty for conspiracy to defraud govt. Died Jackson, N.H., Aug. 21, 1940.

STONE, William Alexis, gov. Pa., congressman, lawyer; b. nr. Wellsboro, Tioga County, Pa., Apr. 18, 1846; attended Pa. Normal Sch., Mansfield; studied law, Wellsboro, Pa. Served in Civil War as 2d lt. Company A, 187th Regt., Pa. Volunteer Inf.; became lt. col. Pa. Nat. Guard after war; admitted to bar, 1870, practiced in Wellsboro and Pitts.; dist. atty. Tioga County, 1874-76, resigned, moved to Pitts.; U.S. atty. for Western Dist. Pa., 1880-86; mem. U.S. Ho. of Reps. (Republican) from Pa., 52d-55th congresses, 1891-Nov. 9, 1898 (resigned); gov. Pa., 1899-1903; prothonotary Eastern Dist. Pa., 1916-20. Died Phila., Mar. 1, 1920; buried Wellsboro Cemetery.

STUART, James Reeve, artist; b. Beaufort, S.C., 1834; attended U. Va., Harvard, Royal Acad., Munich, Germany. Worked in Savannah (Ga.), Memphis (Tenn.), St. Louis, after Civil War; settled in Madison, Wis., 1872; best known as portrait painter (35 portraits now in Wis. State Hist. Museum); taught at Milw. Coll., U. Wis. Died Madison, 1915.

SULLIVAN, Harry Stack, psychiatrist; b. Norwich, N.Y., Feb. 21, 1892; s. Timothy J. and Ella M. (Stack) S. Graduated Chicago College of Medicine and Surgery 1917 and became industrial surgeon; mil. service World War I as 1st lt., jr. mem. Board of Examiners for Medical Corps; assist. med. officer, 8th Dist. Hdqtrs. of Rehabilitation Div., Federal Board for Vocational Ed.; U.S. Veterans liaison officer; on staff St. Elizabeth's Hosp., Washington, D.C.; Dir. of Clinical Rsch. Sheppard and Enoch Pratt Hosp., Baltimore, Md.; primarily concerned with schizophrenia, psychological rehabilitation, place for psychiatry among social sciences; promoted est. of standing committee on relations of psychiatry and social sciences, American Psychiatric Assoc.; assoc. prof. of psychiatry, U. of Md. Med. Sch.; entered private practice in N.Y.C. 1931; Pres. William Alanson White Psychiatric Found.; co-ed. Psychiatry: J. of Biology and Pathology of Interpersonal Relations; 1940 consultant in psychiatry to Selective Service System; med. advisor, personnel sect., War Dept. General Staff; publications in American J. of Psychiatry, Psychoanalytic Review. Died Jan. 15, 1949.

SULLIVAN, John L(awrence), pugilist; b. Boston, Oct. 15, 1858; s. Michael Sullivan; m. Annie Bates, 1883; m. 2d, Kate Harkins, 1908. Gave boxing exhbns. in variety show, offered 25 dollars to anyone who could last 1 round with him, 1877-78; won bare knuckles championship of world, knocked out Paddy Ryan in 9th round, Mississippi City, Miss., 1882; retained title, defeated all comers (with exception of draw with Charlie Mitchell, Chantilly, France, 1888), 1882-93; won his last victory over Jake Kilrain in 75 rounds, Richburg, Miss., 1889; lost championship to James J. Corbett in 21st round (using gloves), 1892; appeared in vaudeville, operated bar to pay his debts, N.Y.C.; reformed, became temperance lectr., 1905; lived on farm, West Abington, Mass., 1912-18. Died Feb. 2, 1918.

SWEENY, Peter Barr, city govt. ofcl.; b. N.Y.C., Oct. 9, 1825; s. James and Mary (Barr) S.; attended Columbia; studied law with James T. Brady; m. Sara Potherty, 1 son. Admitted to N.Y. bar; active on Tammany Gen. Com., 1852; lobbied for N.Y.C. stage-coach franchises against streetcars, 1854; elected dist. atty., 1857, resigned because of his inability to speak in public; controlled Tammany Hall (with William M. Tweed), from 1863; chamberlain N.Y.C., 1866, turned over $200,000 of public fund interest to City Treasury, 1867; commr. of parks N.Y.C., 1869; elected (with Tweed) to bd. dirs. Erie R.R. by stock manipulation involving James Fisk, 1869; held meeting in his Albany (N.Y.) hotel room, 1869, at which it was decided that 50% for graft would be added to all city and county bills (graft divided into equal shares for Sweeny, Tweed, Comptroller R. B. Connolly, Mayor Hall and bribery of other politicians); resigned his offices when Tweed Ring was broken up, 1871, fled to Can., then to France. Died Lake Mahopac, N.Y., Aug. 30, 1911.

T

TAMMEN, Harry Heye, journalist; b. Balt., Mar. 6, 1856; s. Heye Heinrich and Caroline Henriette (Piepenbrinker) T.; m. Agnes Reid. Moved to Denver, Colo., 1880; co-owner, co-editor Denver Post, 1895-1924, raised daily circulation from 4,000 to 150,000, initiated many bizarre journalistic stunts including red headlines; seriously wounded when shot by W. W. Anderson because of feud with Gov. Charles S. Thomas of Colo., 1900; carried on feud with Rocky Mountain News, Denver; involved in Sells-Floto circus trial; reached nat. prominence because of part in Teapot Dome scandal, 1922-24. Died Denver, July 19, 1924.

TEILHARD de CHARDIN, Pierre, philosopher, paleontologist; b. Auvergne, France, May 1, 1881; s. Emmanuel T. de C.; student religion Jesuit sch., Villefranche, later in Sussex, Eng.; student geology in Paris; Sc.D., U. Paris, 1922. Taught sci., Cairo, Egypt; ordained priest Soc. of Jesus, Roman Cath. Ch., 1912; worked under Marcellin Boule, Inst. Human Paleontology, Mus. Natural History, Paris; prof. geology Catholic Inst. Paris; made several sci. expdns. to Far East, taking part in discovery skull of Peking man; named dir. Lab. Advanced Studies in Geology and Paleontology, Paris, 1938; in China during World War II; returned to Paris, 1946, was forbidden by superiors to publish philosophy or put forward his candidature for professorship in Coll. de France; elected Membre de l'Institut; moved to U.S.

1951, conducted anthrop. projects for Wenner-Gren Found., N.Y.C. Dir. research Centre National de la Recherche Scientifique. Served as stretcher bearer, World War I. Named officer Legion of Honor. Corr. mem. Acad. des Sciences. Contbd. to Western understanding of paleontology and geology of Far East; his philosophy (pub. posthumously) fuses sci. and religion in analyzing the evolution, phenomenon and future of man. Author books including: Building the Earth; Phenomenon of Man, 1959; Divine Milieu, 1960; Letters from a Traveller, 1962; Future of Man, 1964; Hymn of the Universe, 1965; Making of a Mind, 1965. Died after a stroke, N.Y.C., Apr. 10, 1955.*

TESCHEMACHER, Frank, jazz musician; b. Kansas City, Mo., Mar. 14, 1906; ed. pub. schs., Chgo.; influenced by New Orleans Rhythm Kings, Joe (King) Oliver, Johnny Dodds, Jimmy Noone, Bix Beiderbecke and Wolverines, classicist Holst. Formed (with Jimmy McPartland, Bud Freeman, others) Austin High Gang of jazzmen, Chgo.; played clarinet and saxophone with them in their Blue Friars band, 1924-25; later played with Husk O'Hare's Wolverines, Midway Gardens Orch. (with Muggsy Spanier) and McKenzie and Condon's Chicagoans; asso. with Red Nichols and others in N.Y.C., then, as interest in jazz waned, with comml. bands; pioneer in Chgo. style jazz, distinguished by hard, driving beat, shuffle, rhythm, flareup, explosion and instrumental solos. Killed in automobile accident, Chgo., Feb. 29, 1932.

THALBERG, Irving Grant, motion picture producer; b. Bklyn., May 30, 1899; s. William and Henrietta (Heymann) T.; m. Norma Shearer, Sept. 29, 1927, children—Irving, Katharine. Sec. to Carl Leammle (pres. Universal Pictures Corp.); went to Cal., 1919; became mgr. Metro and Goldwyn studios, later v.p. Metro-Goldwyn-Mayer; brought Greta Garbo and John Gilbert together on screen; developed multiple-star system with Grand Hotel, 1932; best known prodns. include: The Barretts of Wimpole Street, Mutiny on the Bounty, Romeo and Juliet, The Good Earth. Died Santa Monica, Cal., Sept. 14, 1936; buried Forest Lawn Meml. Park, Glendale, Cal.

THOMAS, Dylan Marlais, poet; b. Carmarthenshire, Wales, Oct. 27, 1914; ed. Swansea Grammar Sch.; m. Caitlin Macnamara, 1936; children—Llewellyn, Colm, Aeron. Became newspaper reporter at age 17, worked for a time as journalist and at various odd jobs; gained immediate fame with publ. of 1st vol. of poetry, 1934; wrote scripts for documentary films, short stories, scripts for BBC; made poetry-reading tours of U.S., 1950, 52, 53; wrote in intense and personalized idiom, utilizing images based on Welsh folklore, Christian legend and Freudian symbols; influenced by James Joyce, Gerard Manley Hopkins. Recipient Oscar Blumenthal prize Poetry mag., Chgo., 1938. Author: Eighteen Poems, 1934; Twenty-five Poems, 1936; The Map of Love, 1939; Portrait of the Artist as a Young Dog, 1940; The World I Breathe (U.S. 1940); Deaths and Entrances, 1946; In Country Sleep (U.S. 1952); Collected Poems, 1953; (motion picture script) The Doctor and the Devils, 1953; (prose) Quite Early One Morning, 1954; (radio scripts) A Child's Christmas in Wales, 1954, Under Milk Wood, 1954; Adventures in the Skin Trade, and Other Stories, 1955. Died N.Y.C., Nov. 9, 1953; buried Laugharne, Wales.☆

THORPE, James Francis, athlete; b. nr. Prague, Okla., May 28, 1888; s. Hiram and Charlotte (View) T.; attended Carlisle (Pa.) Indian Sch., 1907-12; m. Iva Miller, 1913; m. 2d, Frieda Kirkpatrick, 1926; m. 3d, Patricia Askew, 1945. Mem. Carlisle football team, 1908-12, played left halfback, led team victory over Harvard, Army, U. Pa., U. Minn., 1911-12; voted All American player, 1908, 11, 12; participated in Olympic games, Stockholm, Sweden, 1912, won 4 1st places in Pentathlon, 4 in Decathlon; returned medals at request of Amateur Athletic Union (because of his participation in profl. baseball, 1909-10), 1913; played baseball with N.Y. Giants, 1913, 14, 17-19, Boston Braves, 1919; player-mgr. Canton (O.) Bulldogs profl. football team, 1915-22, 27; played football with N.Y. Giants, 1925, Chgo. Cardinals, 1929; supr. recreation Chgo. Parks, during 1930's; voted greatest football player of 1st half of 20th Century, 1932. Author: (with T. F. Collison) Jim Thorpe's History of the Olympics, 1932. Died Mar. 28, 1953.

TILDEN, William Tatem (Big Bill Tilden), tennis player; b. Germantown, Pa., 1893. British singles champion, 1920-21, 30; U.S. tennis champion, 1920-25, 29 (only man to win Am. championship 6 consecutive years); won several other nat. tennis titles; turned professional, 1931, won pro singles championship, 1931, 35; won pro doubles championship (with Vincent Richards) at age 52, 1945; engaged as journalist, film actor; editor, publisher Racquet Mag. Author: The Art of Lawn Tennis, 1920; The Phantom Drive, 1924; Glory's Net (novel). Died Hollywood, Cal., June 5, 1953.

TILGHMAN, William Matthew, peace officer; b. Ft. Dodge, Ia., July 4, 1854; s. William Matthew and Amanda (Shepherd) T.; m. Flora Kendal, 1878, 4 children; m. 2d, Zoe Stratton, July 15, 1903, 3 children. Became buffalo hunter, 1870; settled in Ft. Dodge (Kan.) region, 1871, acquired reputation as hunter and skilled gun handler; dep. sheriff Ford County, under Bat Masterson, 1877; participated in settlers' race that marked opening of Okla., 1889; dep. U.S. marshall in Okla., 1891-1910; mem. Okla. Senate, 1910-11; police chief Oklahoma City, 1911-13; adviser in making of movie The Passing of the Oklahoma Outlaws, 1915; marshal Cromwell, Okla., 1924. Shot in the street, Cromwell, Nov. 1, 1924; buried Oklahoma City.

TILYOU, George Cornelius, amusement park owner; b. N.Y.C., Feb. 3, 1862; s. Peter and Ellen (Mahoney) T.; m. Mary O'Donnell, 1893, 3 sons, 2 daus. Set up souvenir stand nr. his father's hotel on Coney Island, 1876; later laid out Coney Island's famous Bowery, built Tilyou's Surf Theatre; built Steeplechase Park, 1897; patented and perfected many amusement rides and devices including Electric Seat, Funny Stairway, Barrel of Love; helped remove John Y. McKane (polit. boss of Coney Island); operated amusement parks in Atlantic City, Rockaway Beach (N.Y.), St. Louis, San Francisco. Died Nov. 30, 1914.

TIMKEN, Henry, inventor, mfr.; b. nr. Bremen, Germany, Aug. 16, 1831; son of Jacob Timken; m. Fredericka Heinzelmann, 1855, 5 children. Came to U.S., 1841; apprentice and journeyman wagon maker, 1847-55; owner-operator carriage factory, St. Louis, 1855-60, 65-87, 94-97; prospected for gold nr. Pike's Peak, 1860; served as capt. 13th Regt., Mo. Militia, 1861-64; patented carriage spring (Timken Spring), 1877, tapered roller bearing, 1898; organized Timken Roller Bearing Axle Co., Canton, O.; pres. Carriage Builders' Nat. Assn., 1896-97. Died San Diego, Cal., Mar. 16, 1909.

TOLLER, Ernst, German expressionist dramatist, poet; b. Samotschin, German Poland, Dec. 1, 1893; ed. Bomberg gymnasium, circa 1906-13, univs. Heidelberg, Munich, Grenoble; m. Lili Christiane Grantoff. Enlisted in Germann Army at outbreak World War I, sent on sick leave after 13 months at front, finally discharged; an organizer Students' League foi Peace, Heidelberg, winter 1917; ordered arrested, fled to Munich where he met Kurt Eisner; arrested and imprisoned for organizing strike of munition workers; released by November Revolution, 1918, elected pres. Bavarian Soviet Republic; sentenced to death when revolution was suppressed by Social Democratic govt., 1919, but soldiers refused to fire at him, and sentence was commuted to life imprisonment; wrote his 1st vol. poetry and 1st plays while imprisoned in Fortress of Niederschöenfeld; released in 1924, traveled to USSR, gave lecture tour in U.S.; resided in Munich until Nazis burned his books, confiscated his property and exiled him, 1933; came to N.Y., spent remaining years of life lecturing in Europe and Am., pleading cause of individual freedom, liberty and brotherhood. Author works including: (plays) Transfiguration, 1919, Man and the Masses, 1920, The Machine-Wreckers, 1922, Brokenbrow, 1924, Pastor Hall, 1939; (autobiography) I Was a German, 1933; Look through the Bars, 1935. Committed suicide, N.Y.C., May 22, 1939.

TRAVIS, Walter John, golfer; b. Victoria, Australia, Jan. 10, 1862; s. John Walter and Susan (Eyelet) T.; attended Trinity Coll., Melbourne, Australia; m. Anne A. Bent, Jan. 8, 1890, 1 son, 1 dau. Came to U.S., 1885; became mgr. N.Y. office McLean Bros. & Rigg, 1885; won the 1st golf tournament he ever played, Meadowbrook, L.I., N.Y., 1897; won Amateur Championship of U.S., 1900 01, 02; especially noted for his accurate putting skill; won Brit. Amateur Championship on Sandwich course (1st American ever to do so), 1904; editor, publisher The American Golfer, 1908. Author: Practical Golf, 1901. Died Denver, Colo., July 31, 1927; buried Manchester, Vt.

TRUMBAUER, Horace, architect; b. Phila., Dec. 28, 1868; s. Josiah Blyler and Mary Malvina (Fabel) T.; m. Sarah Thompson Williams, Apr. 25, 1902. Draftsman, George W. and W. D. Hewitt, archtl. firm; designed Gray Towers, Glenside, Pa., 1894, Widener Library at Harvard, 1914; head of his own archtl. firm, which designed skyscraper for N.Y. Evening Post, 1925; drew plans for Duke U. campus, Durham, N.C., circa 1925. Died Phila., Sept. 18, 1938; buried West Laurel Hill Cemetery, Phila.

TUBMAN, Harriet, abolitionist; b. Dorchester County, Md., circa 1820. Escaped from slavery, 1849; helped over 300 slaves escape via Underground Railroad; nurse and spy for U.S. forces in S.C. during Civil War. Died 1913.

TUCKER, Benjamin Ricketson, journalist, anarchist; b. South Dartmouth, Mass., Apr. 17, 1854; s. Abner Ricketson and Caroline A. (Cummings) T.; attended Mass. Inst. Tech., 1870-73; m. Pearl Johnson, 1 child, Oriole. Went to France, circa 1874; translated What Is Property? (Pierre Joseph Proudhon), 1876; published Radical Review, 1877; mem. staff Boston Globe, 1878; published Liberty, Boston, 1881-92, N.Y., 1892-1908; editor Engring. Mag., N.Y.C., 1892. Died Monaco, June 22, 1939; buried Pont Ste. Dévote, Monaco.

TURPIN, Ben, comedian; b. New Orleans, Sept. 1869; s. Ernest and Sarah (Buckley) T.; m. Carrie Lemieux, circa 1907; m. 2d, Babette Dietz. Went to N.Y., circa 1876; roamed country as hobo working on odd jobs, 1886-91; became vaudeville comedian, Chgo., 1891; portrayed character Happy Hooligan on vaudeville circuit, 1897-1914; motion picture comedian Keystone Studio, Edendale, Cal., 1916-25, worked under Mack Sennett; starred in Shriek of Araby, 1923. Died Santa Monica, Cal., July 1, 1940; buried Forest Lawn Meml. Park, Glendale, Cal.

TUTHILL, William Burnet, architect; b. N.Y.C., Feb. 11, 1855; s. George and Jane (Price) T.; grad. Coll. City N.Y., 1875; m. Henrietta Corwin, 1881, 1 dau., 1 son. With R. M. Hunt, architect, 1875-77; pvt. practice architecture, 1877-1929; sec. Oratorio Soc. of N.Y., 1881-1917; founder Soc. for Publ. of Am. Music, 1919. Prin. works include: Harlem YMCA, 1888; (with Adler and Sullivan) Carnegie Hall (his greatest success, 1 of most acoustically perfect auditoriums in world), 1891; Princeton (N.J.) Inn., 1893. Author: Practical Lessons in Architectural Drawing, 1881; The City Residence, Its Design and Construction, 1890. Died Aug. 25, 1929.

U

UNDERWOOD, John Thomas, typewriter mfr.; b. London, Eng., Apr. 12, 1857; s. John and Elizabeth Grant (Maire) U.; m. Grace Brainard, Apr. 24, 1901, 1 dau., Gladys Evelyn. Came to N.J., 1873; with father started firm John Underwood & Co., moved business to Bklyn., 1883; began marketing Underwood typewriters (based on model invented by Franz X. Wagner), 1897; organized Underwood Typewriter Mfg. Co., 1898, merged both cos. into Underwood Typewriter Co., 1903, later merged to form Underwood Elliot Fisher Co., 1927. Died Wianno, Mass., July 2, 1937; buried Greenwood Cemetery, Bklyn.

V

VILLA, Francisco (Pancho) (original name Doroteo Arango); Mexican revolutionary; b. San Juan del Río Durango, Mexico, June 5, 1878. Killed a man for molesting his sister and fled to mountains at age 16, spent next 15 years as rustler, bandit and occasional laborer; organized band and joined Madero's revolt against Diaz, 1910; captured by Huerta, 1912, but escaped from prison to U.S., Nov. 1912; joined Venustiano Carranza against Huerta after Madero's assassination; defeated Huerta, then contended for power with Carranza, 1914-15; driven from Mexico City by Obregón, 1915; possibly responsible for execution of 16 U.S. citizens in Santa Isabel following U.S. recognition of Carranza's govt., also perhaps responsible for bandit raid on Columbus, N.M.; hunted by expdn. under Pershing (expdn. unsuccessful because of Garranza's resistance and Villa's great popularity among people of Chihuahua); continued legendary bandit activities until overthrow of Carranza's regime, 1920, then made peace with Huerta's govt.; ret. to ranch in Durango granted him by govt., lived there until his assassination. Died Parral Chihuahua, July 20, 1923.

VOUGHT, Chance Milton, aircraft designer, mfr.; b. N.Y.C., Feb. 26, 1890; s. George and Annie (Colley) V.; attended N.Y.U., U. Pa.; m. Ena Lewis, Dec. 4, 1920, 2 children. Learned how to fly from Wright Bros., 1910; cons. engr. for Aero Club of Ill., 1912; editor Aero and Hydro mag., 1914; designed trainer used by British in World War I, 1914; chief engr. Wright Co., Dayton, O., 1916, built Vought-Wright Model V mil. biplane; organized (with financing by B. B. Lewis) Lewis & Vought Corp., 1917; produced Vought VE-7, 1919; merged with Pratt & Whitney and Boeing airplane cos. to from United Aircraft & Transport Corp., 1929. Died Southampton, L.I., N.Y., July 25, 1930.

W

WAGNER, John Henry, baseball player; b. Mansfield, Pa., Feb. 24, 1874. Called the Flying Dutchman; played with Paterson (N.J.) team in Atlantic League, 1896-97; played with Louisville (Ky.) Colonels, 1897-99; shortstop with Pitts. Pirates, Nat. League, 1900-17, coach, 1933-52, won 8 league batting championships, 1900-11; established league records for doubles and triples; held lifetime batting average of .329, fielding average of .945; elected to Baseball Hall of Fame, 1936. Died Carnegie, Pa., Dec. 6, 1955; buried Carnegie.

WARD, Aaron Montgomery, mcht.; b. Chatham, N.J., Feb. 17, 1843; s. Sylvester and Julia (Green) W.; m. Elizabeth Cobb, Feb. 22, 1872, 1 adopted dau., Marjorie. Worked in gen. store, St. Joseph, Mich., 1862-65, rose to $100 monthly salary; with Field, Palmer & Leiter, Chgo., 1865-67; traveling salesman Walter M. Smith & Co.; conceived idea of mail order house which would lessen discrepancy between low prices for farm goods and high prices for retail; opened dry goods store and mail order house, Chgo., 1872; issued 1st catalogue (only 1 sheet), 1872, catalogue expanded to 150 pages by 1876; his firm had annual sales of $1,000,000 by 1888; built Ward Tower, Chgo., 1900; had customers all over the world, and annual sales totalling $40,000,000, by 1913. Died Highland Park, Ill., Dec. 7, 1913.

WARD, Lester Frank, geologist, sociologist. Prof. sociology Brown U., from 1906. Pres. Institut Internat. de Sociologie, 1903. Developer theory of intellectual and social evolution called "telesis"; believed that planned social democracy could evolve into "sociocracy." Writings include Glimpses of the Cosmos, pub. 1913-18. Died Washington, D.C., Apr. 18, 1913. (see sketch page 1298, Who Was Who in America, Vol. I)

WEST, Nathanael (Nathan Wallenstein Weinstein), novelist; b. N.Y.C., Oct. 17, 1902; Ph.B., Brown U., 1924; m. Eileen McKenney. Worked as hotel mgr. Sutton Pl., N.Y.C.; asso. William Carlos Williams in editing Contact mag.; motion picture scriptwriter, Hollywood, Cal., 1935-40, adapted some of own work for screen, collaborated on several screenplays, including Five Came Back (RKO); gained popularity after World War II for his satirical, semi-surrealistic novels, noted for their precision of lang. and often humorous comments on life in N.Y. and Hollywood. Author: The Dream Life of Balso Snell, 1931; Miss Lonelyhearts, 1933 (adapted for Broadway play 1957); A Cool Million, 1934; The Day of the Locust, 1939. Killed (with wife) in automobile accident, nr. El Centro, Cal., Dec. 22, 1940.

WHIFFEN, Mrs. Thomas, actress; b. 1845; m. Thomas Whiffen. Made Am. debut with Galten Opera Co., Wood's Museum, N.Y.C., 1868; made 1st dramatic performances in Hazel Kirke, Esmeralda, The Private Secretary, The Rajah, May Blossom at Square Madison Theatre, N.Y.C.; appeared with Daniel Frohman's company in plays Bladion, The Wife, Sweet Lavender, The Charity Ball, The Amazons, The Benefit of the Doubt, An Ideal Husband, The Princess and the Butterfly, Trelawney of the Wells, John Ingerfield at Lyceum, N.Y.C., 1887-1900; joined Charles Frohman's Empire Stock Co. at Empire Theater, N.Y.C., 1900; appeared with Margaret Anglin in Zira, 1905; played in The Great Divide at the Hudson, N.Y.C., 1905-07; performed in The Brass Bottle, Electricity, Cousin Kate, The Indiscretion of Youth, Just Suppose, Trelawney of the Wells, N.Y.C., 1910-27; considered character actress of excellent ability. Died 1936.

WHITE, Ellen Gould Harmon, religious leader; b. Gorham, Me., Nov. 26, 1827; d. Robert and Eunice (Gould) Harmon; m. Rev. James White, Aug. 30, 1846. Converted by William Miller to Seventh-day Adventist Ch., 1840's; expected coming of Christ on Oct. 22, 1844, rapidly declined in health when expectation was not fulfilled; while praying had a vision she had been transported to heaven, Dec. 1844; an organizer (with her husband) Gen. Conf. of Adventist Chs., 1863; a founder Western Health Reform Inst., Battle Creek, Mich., 1866, Battle Creek Coll. (1st Seventh-day Adventist sch.), 1874; an organizer So. Publishing Assn., 1901; a founder Coll. of Med. Evangelists, Loma Linda, Cal., 1909. Author: Life Sketches. . .of Elder James White and His Wife, Mrs. Ellen G. White, 1880; Life Sketches of Ellen G. White, 1915. Died St. Helena, Cal., July 16, 1915.

WHITE, Harry Dexter, b. Boston, Oct. 29, 1892; B.A., Stanford, 1924, M.A., 1925. Served as lt. Inf., U.S. Army, World War I; prof. econs. Lawrence Coll., Appleton, Wis. (see sketch page 571, Who Was Who in America, Vol. II)

WHITE, Pearl, actress; b. Greenridge, Mo., Mar. 4, 1889; d. Edward Gilman and Lizzie G. (House) White; m. Victor C. Sutherland, Oct. 12, 1907; m. 2d, Wallace McCutcheon, circa 1919. Motion picture actress with Powers Film Co., N.Y.C., 1910; slapstick comedienne Crystal Films, N.Y.C., 1912-14; starred in The Perils of Pauline, for Pathé Frères, Jersey City, N.Y., 1914; starred in serials The Exploits of Elaine, The Iron Claw, Pearl of the Army, The Fatal Ring, The Black Secret; went to France, 1922. Died Paris, France, Aug. 4, 1938; buried Passy Cemetery, France.

WHITEHEAD, Wilbur Cherrier, bridge expert; b. Cleve., O., May 22, 1866; m. Parthenia. Pres., Simplex Automobile Co.; rep. of Am. corps. in Europe, became expert golfer, billiards and card player; 1st to develop systematic bidding system for bridge, assigning set point values for all cards and defining proper connotation of each bid; chmn. card com. Knickerbocker Whist Club; founder, 1st pres. Cavendish Club; conducted series of radio bridge games with M.C. Work, 1925-29; co-editor Auction Bridge and Mah Jong Mag., 1925-29; donated Whitehead trophy for women's nat. contract pair championship, 1930; chmn. Vanderbilt Cup com., 1931. Author: Whitehead's Conventions of Auction Bridge, 1914; Auction Bridge Standards, 1921. Died June 27, 1931.

WIDENER, Joseph Early, b. Phila., Aug. 19, 1872; son of P. A. B. Widener. Presented art collection (valued from $25,000,000 to $50,000,000) to Nat. Gallery Art, Washington, D.C., 1942. (see sketch page 575, Who Was Who in America, Vol. II).

WILLARD, Archibald M., artist; b. Bedford, O., Aug. 1836. Carriage painter; went to N.Y.C. to study art, 1873; best known for The Spirit of '76 (painted at least 4 versions). Died Cleve., Oct. 11, 1918.

WILSON, Charles, labor union ofcl.; early leader Brotherhood Locomotion Engrs., circa 1866.

WILSON, Woodrow, revived presdl. custom of addressing Congress in person, 1913 (had been dropped by Jefferson 1801); his presdl. term noted for series of reforms called The New Freedom; Fed. Res. System instituted, 1913; Clayton Anti-Trust Act passed, 1914; 17th, 18th, 19th amendments added to U.S. Constn., 1913, 19, 20; punitive expdn. under Gen. John Pershing against Villa in Mexico took place, 1916; attempted to maintain neutrality after outbreak of World War I, finally asked for declaration of war against Germany, Apr. 2, 1917 (passed by Congress Apr. 6, 1917); outlined famous Fourteen Points for European peace, Jan. 8, 1918; helped secure adoption of establishment of League of Nations, unsuccessful in attempts to get U.S. to join league. (see sketch page 1364, Who Was Who in America, Vol. I)

WINDRIM, John Torrey, architect; b. Phila., 1866; son of James H. Windrim; studied architecture under his father. Practiced architecture, Phila., until 1934; became mem. A.I.A., 1901, fellow, 1926. Prin. works include: Lankerman Hosp. Research Inst., Evans Dental Inst. and Grad. Sch. Medicine bldg. at U. Pa., Presbyn. Hosp., Jefferson Hosp., Lincoln Liberty Bldg., N. Am. Office Bldg., Commonwealth Trust Co. Bldg., Franklin Inst. Mus. (all Phila.); Barton Research Lab. on Franklin Inst. Campus, Swarthmore (Pa.); Western State Penitentiary, Bellefonte, Pa.; State Mus., Harrisburg, Pa. Died Phila., June 7, 1934.

WOODHULL, Victoria Claflin, reformer; b. Homer, O., Sept. 23, 1838; d. Reuben and Roxanna (Hummel) Claflin; m. Dr. Canning Woodhull, 1853; m. 2d, John Martin, Oct. 31, 1883; 2 children. Claimed to experience visions, 1841, claimed that Demosthenes appeared before her, 1848; moved around Ohio giving spiritualistic exhbns.; went to N.Y. with her sister, Tennessee, 1868; opened stock brokerage office (supported by Cornelius Vanderbilt), N.Y.; founder Woodhull and Claflin's Weekly, advocating equal rights for women, free love, single moral standard, 1870; appeared before Ho. Judiciary Com. to advocate women's suffrage, 1871; unsuccessful Equal Rights Party candidate for Pres. U.S., 1872; arrested for publishing article alleging immoral behavior of clergyman Henry Ward Beecher, 1872; began publication of Humanitarian, 1892. Author: Origin, Tendencies and Principles of Government, 1871; The Human Body; the Temple of God, 1890; Humanitarian Money, 1892; Died June 10, 1927.

WOOLSEY, John Munro, made famous decision lifting ban on distbn. in Am. of novel Ulysses (James Joyce), Dec. 6, 1933. (see sketch page 592, Who Was Who in America, Vol. II)

WOVOKA, religious leader; b. nr. Esmeralda County, Nev., circa 1856; son of Tavibo. Developed philosophy of Ghost Dance, through mystical experience asso. with either an illness or an eclipse of sun, 1889; believed he was messenger from Heaven to tell Indians to live righteously, love all men, live in peace and pray for day of reunion of all Indians; originally predicted coming of state of reunion and eternal happiness for 1891, forced toward end of year to change his teaching to envision a better life in indefinite future. Died Oct. 1932.

Y

YOUNG, Denton True, baseball player; b. Gilmore, O., Mar. 28, 1867; s. McKenzie Young. Played with profl. baseball team, Canton, O., 1890; pitcher for Cleve. Indians, Nat. League, 1890-98, 1909-11; with St. Louis Cardinals, Nat. League, 1899-1900; pitcher for Boston Red Sox, Am. League, 1901-08; with Boston Braves, Nat. League, 1911; achieved lifetime record of 511 victories against 313 losses; pitched 3 no-hitters, 1897, 1904, 08; won 35 games, lost 10, for .778 season, 1895; maintained win-loss record of over .700 for 5 seasons, over .600 for 11 seasons; elected to Baseball Hall of Fame, 1937. Died Nov. 4, 1955.

YOUNGER, Thomas Coleman (Cole Younger), desperado; b. Jackson County, Mo., Jan. 15, 1844; s. Col. Henry and Busheba (Fristoe) Y. Served as Confederate guerilla under Quantrill and Anderson during Civil War; capt. Gen. Joseph O. Shelby's Iron Brigade; mem. Jesse James' gang, participated in attempted bank robbery in which 2 civilians were killed, Northfield, Minn., Sept. 7, 1876; captured, along with 2 of his brothers (3 other gang members killed), sentenced to life imprisonment, Nov. 1876; paroled by Minn. Bd. of Pardon, July 1901. Died Mar. 21, 1916.

Z

ZAHARIAS, Babe Didrikson, athlete; b. Port Arthur Tex., June 26, 1912; d. Ole and Hanna Marie (Olson) Didrikson; m. George Zaharias. Competed in Olympic Games, Los Angeles, 1932, broke 4 world records for women, including Javelin, 80 meter hurdle, high jump; won Women's Nat. Track and Field Championship, 1932; suspended by Am. Athletic Union for using her name in an advt. campaign, 1932, became profl. athlete; played as only girl on Babe Didrikson's All-American Basketball Game; played on Bearded House of David's baseball team; entered several golf tournaments, 1944-46, won all women's amateur golf honors, by 1948; voted greatest woman athlete of 20th Century by Asso. Press, 1949. Died Galveston, Tex., Sept. 27, 1956.

NOTES

NOTES

NOTES

NOTES

NOTES

NOTES

NOTES

NOTES

NOTES

NOTES

NOTES

NOTES

NOTES

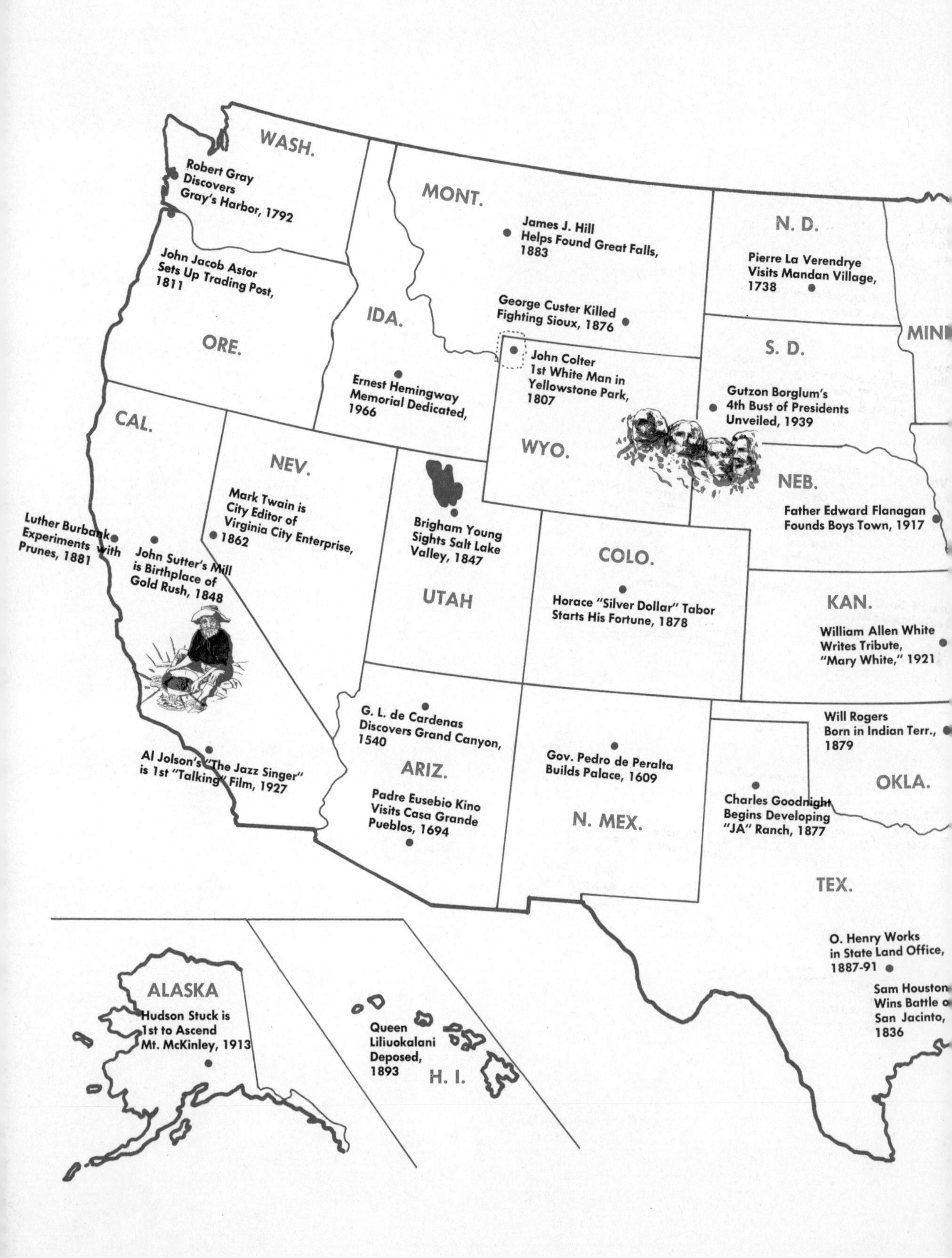
WASH.
Robert Gray Discovers Gray's Harbor, 1792
John Jacob Astor Sets Up Trading Post, 1811
ORE.
MONT.
James J. Hill Helps Found Great Falls, 1883
N. D.
Pierre La Verendrye Visits Mandan Village, 1738
George Custer Killed Fighting Sioux, 1876
IDA.
John Colter 1st White Man in Yellowstone Park, 1807
S. D.
MINN
Ernest Hemingway Memorial Dedicated, 1966
Gutzon Borglum's 4th Bust of Presidents Unveiled, 1939
CAL.
WYO.
NEV.
NEB.
Mark Twain is City Editor of Virginia City Enterprise, 1862
Brigham Young Sights Salt Lake Valley, 1847
Father Edward Flanagan Founds Boys Town, 1917
Luther Burbank Experiments with Prunes, 1881
John Sutter's Mill is Birthplace of Gold Rush, 1848
COLO.
UTAH
Horace "Silver Dollar" Tabor Starts His Fortune, 1878
KAN.
William Allen White Writes Tribute, "Mary White," 1921
G. L. de Cardenas Discovers Grand Canyon, 1540
Will Rogers Born in Indian Terr., 1879
Gov. Pedro de Peralta Builds Palace, 1609
Al Jolson's "The Jazz Singer" is 1st "Talking" Film, 1927
ARIZ.
OKLA.
Padre Eusebio Kino Visits Casa Grande Pueblos, 1694
Charles Goodnight Begins Developing "JA" Ranch, 1877
N. MEX.
TEX.
O. Henry Works in State Land Office, 1887-91
ALASKA
Hudson Stuck is 1st to Ascend Mt. McKinley, 1913
Sam Houston Wins Battle of San Jacinto, 1836
Queen Liliuokalani Deposed, 1893
H. I.